The *American Heritage*® Student Dictionary

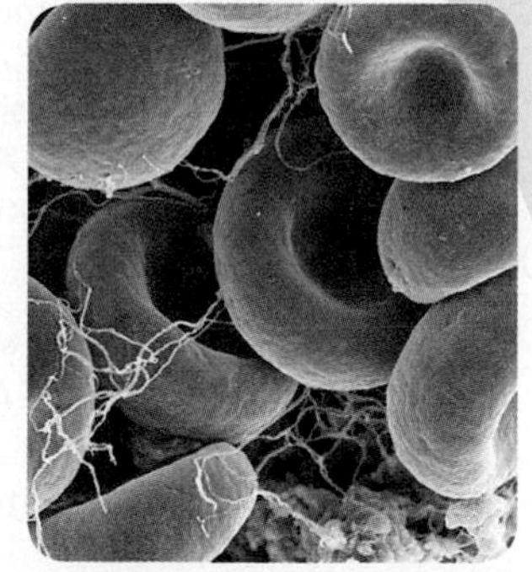

Houghton Mifflin Harcourt
Boston | New York

ISBN-13: 978-1-328-78734-7

Visit our websites: hmhco.com *and* ahdictionary.com

Library of Congress Cataloging-in-Publication Data

The American Heritage student dictionary. -- [New ed.]
p. cm.
ISBN 978-0-547-65958-9
1. English language--Dictionaries, Juvenile. [1. English language--Dictionaries.] I. Title: Student dictionary.
PE1628.5.A45 2012
423--dc23

2011051462

Manufactured in the United States of America

1 2 3 4 5 6 7 8 9 10 - DOW - 25 24 23 22 21 20 19 18

4500712090

Table of Contents

Editorial and Production Staff

Senior Vice President, Publisher, General Interest Group
Bruce Nichols

Executive Editor
Steven R. Kleinedler

Senior Editors
Peter Chipman
Louise E. Robbins

Contributing Editors
Katherine M. Isaacs
Elizabeth Kassab
Joseph P. Pickett
Catherine T. Pratt
David R. Pritchard
Susan I. Spitz
Patrick Taylor

Associate Editor
Emily A. Snyder

Proofreaders
Nicholas A. Durlacher
Diane Fredrick
Robert Knippen
Deborah M. Posner

Technology and Database Production Specialist
Christopher J. Granniss

Senior Art and Production Editor
Margaret Anne Miles

Editorial and Production Coordinator
Sarah Iani

Print Production Director
Donna Baxter McCarthy

Lead Print Production Coordinator
Diane Varone

Text Design
Miro Design, Inc.

Pre-Press Development
Chakra Communications, Inc.

The staff wishes to acknowledge Christopher Leonesio for his invaluable guidance in the preparation of this new edition.

Introduction

In today's digital world, you can easily use a cell phone or a computer to find information about almost any subject. Never before in human history has access to knowledge been so readily available to so many people.

What, then, is the purpose of the dictionary in front of you? What advantages does it offer?

For one thing, the information on the Internet is sometimes not accurate, and it's hard to verify. Because dictionaries are researched and written by experts, their content has an accuracy and clarity that many websites lack. Dictionary editors spend all day paying close attention to how real people use language and crafting definitions that reflect that usage. This dictionary is not intended to replace your online quest for information. Instead, it complements and enhances your search. Sometimes you're online and you need to know a simple definition or the spelling of a word quickly, and you can easily find the answer without hassle. You get the information you need and you move on. But sometimes you need to know more; you need to know exactly how a word is used, how it differs from related words, how it is pronounced, and how it might be used in a sentence.

This brings us to the question, Why should you use this particular dictionary?

Just open to any page and you will see that this book is more than a simple reference tool. You can surf a dictionary much as you surf the web. When you look up a word in the *American Heritage Student Dictionary*, chances are your eye will stop on a nearby word, an interesting note, or an arresting photograph or chart, and suddenly you are lost in print, learning about things that you didn't expect to learn when you opened the book. This accidental discovery of knowledge is much like what happens when you surf the web, but it's a very different experience.

The editors have made this dictionary with those factors in mind. We hope that when you look up a word you will find yourself getting temporarily lost in a world of words. You'll learn, for example, about words that are spelled almost the same—perhaps they were words you might easily confuse. In an earlier paragraph, I used the word *complement*. Did you confuse it with *compliment*? Did you know there was a difference? Go to page 203, and not only will you see that there's a difference, you'll also be able to read a Usage Note that explains that difference. And perhaps while you're on that page you'll encounter the word *complaisance* (not to be confused with *complacence*), which you may have been unfamiliar with. You'll see a Word Building Note at the word *compose* that talks about the usefulness of the root *pos*—which leads you to information about *expose, oppose,* and *impose*. And so you go in turn to one of those words and get caught up in the page again. In looking up one word, you're bolstering your vocabulary by learning about others.

In addition to the Usage Notes and Word Building Notes, you'll find fascinating Word History Notes, Science Notes, and Biography Notes. Notes titled "Writers Choose Their Words" show how words are used in context by skillful writers like J.K. Rowling and Lois Lowry. On every page, beautiful photographs and careful drawings help you understand the meanings of words through pictures. And look for the full-page charts on the development of the alphabet, the periodic table of the elements, geologic time periods, and much more.

Language is always changing, and to keep up with those changes, we have prepared this brand-new edition of the dictionary. The editorial staff has reviewed every single entry. We've made tens of thousands of changes. We've added thousands of new words and meanings. Every edit has been made with you, the reader, in mind, to make your experience as richly rewarding and satisfying as possible, in the hope that you will return to your dictionary again and again.

Steven R. Kleinedler
Executive Editor

Elements of the Dictionary

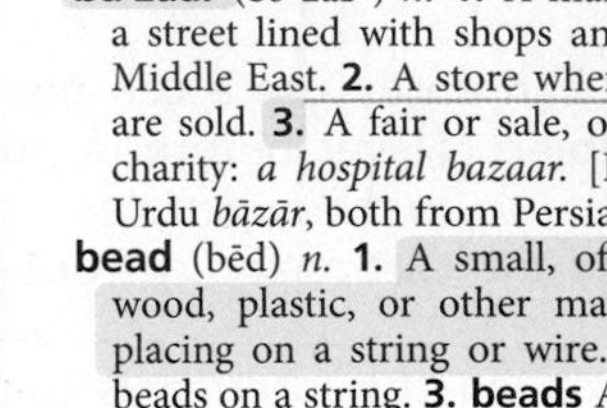

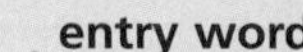

ba·zaar (bə-**zär′**) *n.* **1.** A market, usually consisting of a street lined with shops and stalls, especially in the Middle East. **2.** A store where various kinds of things are sold. **3.** A fair or sale, often to raise money for a charity: *a hospital bazaar.* [From Italian *bazarro* and Urdu *bāzār*, both from Persian *bāzār*.]

beadwork

bead (bĕd) *n.* **1.** A small, often round piece of glass, wood, plastic, or other material that is pierced for placing on a string or wire. **2. beads** A necklace of beads on a string. **3. beads** A rosary. **4.** A small round object, such as a drop of moisture: *beads of sweat on one's forehead.* **5.** A small knob of metal located at the muzzle of a rifle or pistol and used in taking aim. ❖ *tr. & intr.v.* **bead·ed, bead·ing, beads** To furnish with or collect into beads: *bead the collar around a sweater; water beading on the soda can.* [From Old English *gebed*, prayer.]

bead·work (**bĕd′**wûrk′) *n.* Decorative work in beads.

beak (bēk) *n.* **1.** A bird's bill, especially a strong curved one such as that of a hawk or a finch. **2.** A similar, often horny, part in other animals, such as turtles and octopuses. **3.** A projecting part that resembles a bird's beak. [From Middle English *bek*, from Latin *beccus*, of Celtic origin.] **—beaked** (bēkt) *adj.*

be·gin (bĭ-**gĭn′**) *v.* **be·gan** (bĭ-**găn′**), **be·gun** (bĭ-**gŭn′**), **be·gin·ning, be·gins** ❖ *—intr.* **1.** To do or undergo the first part of an action; start: *When I clean my room, I begin with my desk. The rain began around noon.* **2.** To come into being; originate: *Education begins at home.* **3.** To have as a first element or part: *The movie begins with a car chase.* **4.** To have as a first position, stage, or job: *The restaurant began as an ice-cream shop. The principal began as a math teacher.* ❖ *—tr.* **1.** To take the first step in doing (something); start: *She began the project last month. When did you begin taking photos? We began to eat lunch.* **2.** To say as the first in a series of remarks: *"I bought some plane tickets," he began.* **3.** To bring into being; originate: *The owner's grandfather began the newspaper many years ago.* **4.** To come first in: *The letter A begins the alphabet.* [From Old English *beginnan*.]

beak
top to bottom: black skimmer, pileated woodpecker, and American goldfinch

SYNONYMS begin, start, commence, launch, initiate These verbs mean to take the initial step in doing something. **Begin** and **start** are the most general words: *My teacher began the class after everyone arrived. I had just started to eat dinner when the lights went out.* **Commence** is a more formal word, and it often indicates that what is beginning is serious or important: *Our meetings always commence with a call to order.* **Launch** suggests beginning something with energy and expectation: *She looked for a job that could launch her career as a journalist.* **Initiate** applies to taking the first steps in a process or procedure: *My mother initiated a lawsuit against the driver who hit her car.* **ANTONYM end**

ber·ke·li·um (bər-**kē′**lē-əm *or* **bûrk′**lē-əm) *n. Symbol* **Bk** A radioactive element that has been artificially produced by scientists. The half-life of its longest-lived isotope is about 1,380 years. Atomic number 97. See **Periodic Table.** [After *Berkeley*, California.]

Be·thune (bə-**tho͞on′**), **Mary McLeod** 1875–1955. American educator and reformer. In 1935 she founded the National Council of Negro Women, serving as its president until 1949.

bet·ter (**bĕt′**ər) *adj.* Comparative of **good. 1.** Greater in excellence or higher in quality than another of the same kind: *Which of the twins is the better skater?* **2.** More useful, suitable, or desirable: *I know a better way to go.* **3.** Larger; greater: *It took the better part of an hour to get there.* **4.** Healthier than before: *Many days passed before I began to feel better.* ❖ *adv.* Comparative of **well**². **1.** In a more excellent way: *He sings better than his father.*

entry word
sense number
definition
part-of-speech label
pronunciation
etymology
inflected forms
illustrative example
synonym paragraph
symbol
table cross-reference
biographical entry
cross-reference

guidewords

idioms

homophones

abbreviation entry

run-on form

homograph

usage label

geographical entry

variant

status label

2. To a greater extent or larger degree: *I like fish better when it's broiled.* **3.** More: *The play was first performed better than 20 years ago.* ❖ *n.* **1.** The superior of two: *Both are good, but which is the better?* **2.** A superior: *I leave the delicate work to my betters.* ❖ *v.* **bet·tered, bet·ter·ing, bet·ters** ❖ *—tr.* **1.** To make better; improve: *The purpose of education is to better ourselves.* **2.** To surpass or exceed: *The old record stood until another athlete bettered it.* ❖ *—intr.* To become better: *Conditions bettered with time.* ◆ **better off** In a better condition: *With vaccines, people are better off than they were years ago.* **for the better** Resulting in or aiming at an improvement. **had better** Ought to; must: *We had better leave before dark.* [From Old English *betera.*] —SEE NOTE.

❑ *These sound alike:* **better, bettor** (one who bets).

BeV *abbr.* An abbreviation of billion electron volts.

bi·cy·cle (bī′sĭk′əl *or* bī′sĭ-kəl) *n.* A vehicle consisting of a light metal frame mounted on two wheels one behind the other and having a seat for the rider, who steers the front wheel by handlebars and pushes pedals that drive the rear wheel. ❖ *intr.v.* **bi·cy·cled, bi·cy·cling, bi·cy·cles** To ride on a bicycle: *bicycle down to the store.* **—bi′cy·cler, bi′cy·clist** *n.*

big·heart·ed (bĭg′här′tĭd) *adj.* Generous; kind. **—big′heart′ed·ly** *adv.* **—big′heart′ed·ness** *n.*

bill[2] (bĭl) *n.* **1.** The horny, projecting structure that extends forward from the head of a bird and has an upper and a lower part. Birds that eat different kinds of food have bills of different sizes and shapes. **2.** The visor of a cap. [From Old English *bile.*]

bi·o·eth·ics (bī′ō-ĕth′ĭks) *n. (used with a singular verb)* The study of the ethical and moral questions raised by new biological and medical research, as in the fields of genetic engineering and cloning.

birth·day (bûrth′dā′) *n.* **1.** The day of a person's birth. **2.** The anniversary of that day.

Bish·kek (bĭsh′kĕk *or* bēsh′kĕk) Formerly **Frun·ze** (fro͞on′zə). The capital of Kyrgyzstan, in the north-central part of the country.

blue·ish (blo͞o′ĭsh) *adj.* Variant of **bluish.**

book·case (bo͝ok′kās′) *n.* A piece of furniture with shelves for holding books.

brain stem or **brain·stem** (brān′stĕm′) *n.* The part of the brain connecting the spinal cord to the forebrain.

bran·dish (brăn′dĭsh) *tr.v.* **bran·dished, bran·dish·ing, bran·dish·es** To wave or exhibit in a dramatic or threatening way: *brandish one's fist in defiance.*

breath·er (brē′*th*ər) *n. Informal* A short rest period.

breeze (brēz) *n.* **1.** A light current of air; a gentle wind. **2.** *Informal* Something that is easy to do. ❖ *intr.v.* **breezed, breez·ing, breez·es** *Informal* To make rapid progress without effort: *We breezed through the homework.*

breth·ren (brĕ*th*′rən) *n.* A plural of **brother** (sense 3).

brief·case (brēf′kās′) *n.* A flat rectangular case for carrying books or papers.

brush (brŭsh) *n.* **1.** An implement consisting of bristles, hairs, or wire fastened to a handle, used especially for scrubbing, applying paint, or grooming the hair. **2.** An application of a brush: *give one's hair a good brush.* **3.** A sweeping movement or light touch: *the brush of a branch against my coat.* **4.** A brief encounter with something undesirable or dangerous: *a brush with the law.* **5.** Dense vegetation consisting of shrubs or small trees: *The explorers hacked a trail through the brush.* **6.** Broken or cut branches; brushwood: *Pile the brush at the curb.* **7.** A sliding connection completing a circuit between a fixed and a moving conductor, as in a motor or generator. ❖ *v.* **brushed, brush·ing, brush·es** ❖ *—tr.* **1.** To clean, polish, or groom with a brush: *brush shoes until they shine.* **2.** To apply with a

Mary McLeod Bethune
photographed in 1949

USAGE NOTE

better In writing, the phrase *had better,* meaning "must, ought to," is correct only as long as the *had* or (*'d,* the contraction of *had*), is present. You can say *You had better do it* or *You'd better do it* but not *You better do it.*

WRITERS CHOOSE THEIR WORDS

"Allow me!" shouted Lockhart. He **brandished** his wand at the snake and there was a loud bang; the snake, instead of vanishing, flew ten feet into the air and fell back to the floor with a loud smack.

—J.K. Rowling
Harry Potter and the Chamber of Secrets

Guide to Using the Dictionary

This guide is designed to help you find and understand the information contained in this dictionary.

Guidewords

This dictionary has just one alphabetical list. It presents entries, including single words, phrases, hyphenated compounds, abbreviations, proper names, prefixes, and suffixes. To help you find the word you want to look up, we have put a pair of boldface guidewords at the top of each page in this book:

chasm | check

The guideword to the left of the line represents the first boldface entry on that page. The guideword to the right of the line represents the last boldface entry on that page. Thus, the entry words **chasm** and **check** and all entries that fall between them are listed on the page that has these guidewords.

The Entry Word

The word or phrase you look up in the dictionary is called an *entry word* or an *entry,* or sometimes a *main entry.* The entry words are printed in boldface a little to the left of the rest of the column. They are listed in alphabetical order. Words that begin with the same letter are put into the alphabetical order using their second letter, or, if the first two letters are the same, the third letter, and so on, as is shown in the list below:

beagle
beak
beaker
beam
bean
beanstalk

Some entries consist of more than one word. These may be written as phrases, such as *water buffalo* and *water mill,* or as hyphenated compounds, such as *heavy-duty* and *low-pressure.* Such phrases and compounds are listed in alphabetical order as if they were written as one word.

Superscript Numbers

Some words have identical spellings but different meanings and histories. These words, called *homographs,* are entered separately. Each has a superscript, or raised, number printed after the entry word:

sole[1] (sōl) *n.* **1.** The bottom surface of the foot. **2.** The bottom surface of a shoe or boot, often excluding the heel.
sole[2] (sōl) *adj.* **1.** Being the only one; single; only: *Her sole purpose in coming is to see you.* **2.** Belonging or relating exclusively to one person or group: *She took sole command of the ship.*
sole[3] (sōl) *n., pl.* **sole** or **soles** Any of various flatfishes used as food.

Syllabification

Entry words of more than one syllable are divided into syllables by centered dots:

clas·si·cal (klăs′ĭ-kəl) *adj.*

Inflected and derived forms are also divided into syllables:

clas·si·fy (klăs′ə-fī′) *tr.v.* **clas·si·fied, clas·si·fy·ing, clas·si·fies** **1.** To arrange in classes or assign to a class; sort; categorize: *A librarian classifies books according to subject matter.* **2.** To designate (information) as available only to authorized people. **—clas′si·fi′a·ble** *adj.* **—clas′si·fi′er** *n.*

At entries that consist of two or more words, centered dots are omitted for words that are divided into syllables at other entries in the dictionary:

Con·es·to·ga wagon (kŏn′ĭ-stō′gə) *n.*

Thus, the word *wagon,* which is a separate entry, has no centered dots at the entry for *Conestoga wagon.*

The syllabification of an entry word reflects the traditional practices of printers and editors in breaking words at the end of a line. Pronunciations are divided into syllables according to the way a word is pronounced. Therefore, the syllabification of an entry word does not always match that of its pronunciation:

ac·count·a·ble (ə-koun′tə-bəl) *adj.*

Variants

Some words have two or more different spellings. The variant spelling or spellings are shown in boldface after the entry word. The word *or* indicates that both spellings are used with equal frequency:

ad·vis·er or **ad·vi·sor** (ăd-vī′zər) *n.*

The word *also* joining an entry word and variant form indicates that the variant form is used less frequently than the main entry word:

a·moe·ba also **a·me·ba** (ə-mē′bə) *n.*

Variants that do not fall within three entries from their main entry word in alphabetical order are entered at their own alphabetical places:

a·me·ba (ə-mē′bə) *n.* Variant of **amoeba.** **—a·me′bic** (ə-mē′bĭk) *adj.*

British variants. A number of variants consist of spellings preferred in England and other parts of the United Kingdom. These variants, such as *defence* and *colour,* have the label *Chiefly British.* They are entered at their own alphabetical places but are not given as variants at the entries to which they refer:

> **de·fence** (dĭ-fĕns′) *n. Chiefly British* Variant of **defense.**

Parts of Speech

The following italicized labels indicate the various parts of speech:

adj.	adjective
adv.	adverb
conj.	conjunction
def.art.	definite article
indef.art.	indefinite article
interj.	interjection
n.	noun
prep.	preposition
pron.	pronoun
v.	verb

Plurals are indicated by the label *pl.* The label *pl.n.* appears at entries for words, such as *clothes* and *cattle,* that are only used in the plural.

These italicized labels are used for the traditional classification of verbs:

tr.	transitive
intr.	intransitive
aux.	auxiliary

A transitive verb is a verb that requires a direct object to complete its meaning. *Enforce* and *foster* are examples of transitive verbs. An intransitive verb never takes an object; verbs such as *rejoice* and *tremble* are intransitive. Many verbs, of course, can be transitive or intransitive depending on how they are used. An auxiliary verb, such as *have* or *may,* is used with another verb to indicate tense, mood, or voice.

Certain entries do not carry part-of-speech labels. They include contractions (*I'll*), symbols (*He,* the symbol for *helium*), trademarks (*Band-Aid*), abbreviations (*Blvd.*), prefixes (*anti–*), suffixes (*–ment*), biographical entries (*George Washington*), and geographical entries (*Atlanta*).

Parts of Speech in Combined Entries

Many words can be used as more than one part of speech. For example, *paint* can be both a verb (as in *to paint a wall*) and a noun (as in *a gallon of paint*). In such cases, the different parts of speech are defined in a single entry called a *combined entry.* In an entry of this kind, each part of speech receives its own part-of-speech label. Each part of speech that follows the first part of speech is preceded by the ❖ symbol.

If a piece of information, such as a pronunciation or a status label, appears before the first part of speech in an entry, that piece of information applies to all parts of speech in that entry. Labels and pronunciations appearing after a part of speech apply to that part of speech only. Some entries, such as *rebel,* have a different syllabification and pronunciation for each part of speech:

> **re·bel** (rĭ-bĕl′) *intr.v.* **re·belled, re·bel·ling, re·bels 1.** To refuse loyalty to and oppose by force an established government or a ruling authority. **2.** To resist or defy an authority or a generally accepted convention: *rebelled against wearing a tie in summer.* ❖ *n.* **reb·el** (rĕb′əl) **1.** A person who rebels or is in rebellion.

Inflected Forms

An inflected form of a word differs from the main entry form by the addition of a suffix or by a change in the normal spelling of the main entry. Thus, the verb *walk* forms its past tense *walked* by the addition of the suffix *–ed,* and *swim* forms its past tense *swam* by changing its spelling.

In this dictionary, inflected forms are given in full. They appear in boldface, are divided into syllables, and have pronunciations when necessary. An inflected form immediately follows the part-of-speech label or the number of the definition to which it applies.

Principal parts of verbs. The principal parts of verbs are entered in this order: *past tense, past participle, present participle,* and *third person singular present tense:*

> **fly**[1] (flī) *v.* **flew** (flo͞o), **flown** (flōn), **fly·ing, flies** (flīz)

When the past tense and the past participle are identical, one form represents both. For example, *walked* is the past tense and past participle of the verb *walk:*

> **walk** (wôk) *v.* **walked, walk·ing, walks**

Comparison of adjectives and adverbs. Adjectives and adverbs that form the comparative and superlative degrees by adding *–er* and *–est* show these forms in full immediately after the part-of-speech label:

> **high** (hī) *adj.* **high·er, high·est 1a.** Being a relatively great distance above a certain level, as above sea level or the surface of the earth: *These high mountains are over 15,000 feet.* **b.** Extending a specified distance upward: *The cabinet is four feet high. . . .* ❖ *adv.* **higher, highest** At, in, or to a high position, level, or degree: *Hawks fly high in the sky. A general ranks high above a private.*

Irregular comparative and superlative forms are also given in full:

> **good** (go͝od) *adj.* **bet·ter** (bĕt′ər), **best** (bĕst)

Plural forms of nouns. Regular plurals formed by adding the suffixes *–s* or *–es* to a noun are not normally shown in this dictionary, but irregular plurals are always shown following the label *pl.*:

mouse (mous) *n., pl.* **mice** (mīs)

When a noun has a regular and an irregular plural form, both forms appear, with the most common form shown first:

cer·e·brum (sĕr′ə-brəm *or* sə-rē′brəm) *n., pl.* **cer·e·brums** or **cer·e·bra** (sĕr′ə-brə *or* sə-rē′brə)

Regular plurals are also shown when spelling might be a problem:

po·ta·to (pə-tā′tō) *n., pl.* **po·ta·toes**

Sometimes inflected forms apply only to certain senses of a word. In such cases, the inflected form appears in boldface after the sense number or letter to which it applies:

fly[1] (flī) *v.* **flew** (flo͞o), **flown** (flōn), **fly·ing, flies** (flīz) *—intr.* . . . **7.** *past tense and past participle* **flied** In baseball, to hit a fly ball.

From this example you can see that the verb *fly* usually has the past tense *flew* and the past participle *flown,* but when used in baseball, it has *flied* as its past tense and past participle.

Separate Entries for Inflected Forms

Irregular inflected forms involving a change in spelling of the main form of a word are entered separately when they fall more than two entries away from the main entry form. Thus, *flew,* the past tense of *fly,* and *men,* the plural of *man,* both have their own entries:

flew (flo͞o) *v.* Past tense of **fly**[1].
❑ *These sound alike:* **flew, flu** (influenza), **flue** (pipe).

men (mĕn) *n.* Plural of **man.**

The dictionary does not normally give separate entries for inflected forms of words ending in *–y,* such as *berry, happy,* and *carry,* because forms such as *berries, happiest,* and *carried* entail a regular, easily recognized change in spelling. However, this dictionary does enter inflected forms of words having only one syllable ending in *–y,* because the change in spelling affects the base form of the word:

dri·est (drī′ĭst) *adj.* A superlative of **dry.**

spied (spīd) *v.* Past tense and past participle of **spy.**

Labels

This dictionary uses labels to identify words and meanings whose use is limited in some way—to a particular style of expression, for example, or to a geographical region. When a label applies to all parts of an entry, it appears before the first part of speech:

snitch (snĭch) *Slang v.* **snitched, snitch·ing, snitch·es** ❖ *—intr.* To tell on someone; turn informer: *snitched on his brother.* ❖ *—tr.* To steal (something of little value): *snitched candy from the store.* ❖ *n.* **1.** A thief. **2.** An informer. **—snitch′er** *n.*

Thus the positioning of the label *Slang* in the preceding example means that both the noun and verb senses of the word are slang.

A label may apply only to a single part of speech, in which case it follows the part-of-speech label. Sometimes a label applies only to a single definition or subdefinition, in which case it follows the sense number or letter to which it applies:

hot (hŏt) *adj.* **hot·ter, hot·test** . . . **7.** *Informal* Most recent; new or fresh: *a hot piece of news.*

In this entry, the label *Informal* applies only to sense 7.

Status Labels

Status labels indicate that an entry word or a definition is limited to a particular level or style of usage. All words and definitions not restricted by such a label should be regarded as appropriate for use in all contexts.

Nonstandard. This, the most restrictive label in the dictionary, applies to forms and usages that educated speakers and writers consider unacceptable:

ir·re·gard·less (ĭr′ĭ-gärd′lĭs) *adv. Nonstandard* Regardless.

Slang. This label indicates a style of language that uses extravagant, often humorous expressions as a means of making an effect. Some forms of slang occur in most educated speech but not in formal discourse. An example of a word labeled *Slang* follows:

rin·ky-dink (rĭng′kē-dĭngk′) *Slang adj.* **1.** Old-fashioned; worn-out. **2.** Unimportant. **3.** Of cheap or poor quality.

Informal. Words that people use commonly in conversation and in informal writing but not in formal writing are identified by the label *Informal.* Informal words are ones you might use in conversation with a friend but should avoid using in a report for one of your classes:

fish·y (fĭsh′ē) *adj.* **fish·i·er, fish·i·est 1.** Tasting, resembling, or smelling of fish. **2.** Cold or expressionless: *a fishy stare.* **3.** *Informal* Inspiring doubt or suspicion: *something fishy about that excuse.* **—fish′i·ness** *n.*

Offensive. This label is reserved for words and expressions that are viewed as hurtful to the people they refer to.

Temporal Label

The temporal label *Archaic* signals words or senses that were once common but are now rare:

fain (fān) *Archaic adv.* Willingly or gladly. ❖ *adj.* Willing or glad.

English-Language Labels

These labels identify entries or senses whose use is restricted to specific areas of the English-speaking world:

lor·ry (lôr′ē) *n., pl.* **lor·ries** *Chiefly British* A motor truck.

bairn (bârn) *n. Scots* A child.

bon·net (bŏn′ĭt) *n.* . . . **3.** *Chiefly British* The hood of an automobile.

Cross-References

A cross-reference is a word referring you to another word. It signals that more information can be found at another entry. A cross-reference is helpful in avoiding the repetition of information at two entries, and it serves to indicate where further discussion of a word occurs.

The word referred to in a cross-reference appears in boldface and is preceded by a short phrase:

bade (băd *or* bād) *v.* A past tense of **bid.**

This cross-reference tells you that *bade* is a past tense of the word *bid.* This indicates that more information about the entry can be found at *bid.*

If a cross-reference refers to only one sense of a word that has more than one sense, then the cross-reference will show that sense number:

tzar (zär *or* tsär) *n.* Variant of **czar** (sense 1).

This cross-reference tells you that *tzar* is a variant spelling of *czar,* but that it refers only to the use that is defined at the first sense.

Some cross-references refer to tables. The word or words in boldface tell you at which entry word the table can be found:

Mes·o·zo·ic (mĕz′ə-**zō′**ĭk *or* mĕs′ə-**zō′**ĭk) *n.* The era of geologic time from about 251 to 65 million years ago. The Mesozoic Era was characterized by the development of flowering plants and by the appearance and extinction of dinosaurs. See table at **geologic time.** **—Mes′o·zo′ic** *adj.*

Other cross-references refer you to a note that appears at another entry:

huge (hyo͞oj) *adj.* **hug·er, hug·est** Of great size, extent, or quantity: *a huge tree; a huge difference.* See Synonyms at **large.**

pro·scribe (prō-**skrīb′**) *tr.v.* **pro·scribed, pro·scrib·ing, pro·scribes 1.** To forbid; prohibit. **2.** To banish; outlaw: *The queen proscribed the rebels.* —SEE NOTE AT **prescribe.**

These cross-references tell you that there is more information about the word in a note at another entry.

Order of Senses

Entries having more than one sense are arranged with the central meanings first. The central meaning of a word will most often be the meaning you are seeking. In addition, senses and subsenses that are related in meaning are grouped together. For example, in the entry for *nice* shown below, the commonly sought meaning "Good; pleasant; agreeable" appears first, and the less common sense "Able to notice small differences" comes as sense 6b:

nice (nīs) *adj.* **nic·er, nic·est 1.** Good; pleasant; agreeable: *The seaside hotel was a nice place to stay.* **2.** Having a pleasant appearance; attractive: *a nice dress.* **3.** Courteous and polite; considerate: *It's nice of you to help.* **4.** Morally upright; respectable. **5.** Done with skill and delicacy: *a nice bit of work.* **6a.** Requiring the ability to notice small differences: *a nice distinction.* **b.** Able to notice small differences: *a nice ear for music.* **7.** Used as an intensive with *and: The weather at the beach was nice and warm.*

Division of senses. Letters that appear in boldface before senses indicate that two or more subsenses are closely related in meaning:

prin·ci·pal (prĭn′sə-pəl) *adj.* First or foremost in rank or importance; chief: *the principal character in the story.* ❖ *n.* **1.** A person who holds a leading position, especially the head of a school. **2.** A main participant, as in a business deal. **3a.** A sum of money originally invested, as opposed to the interest paid or accruing on it. **b.** A sum of money owed as a debt, on which interest is calculated.

When an entry has more than one part of speech, the definitions are numbered in separate sequence beginning with each new part of speech:

dream (drēm) *n.* **1.** A series of mental images, ideas, and emotions occurring during sleep. **2.** A daydream. **3.** A state of abstraction; a trance: *wandering about in a dream.* **4.** A hope or aspiration: *dreams of world peace.* **5.** Something especially gratifying, excellent, or useful: *The new car runs like a dream.* ❖ *v.* **dreamed** or **dreamt** (drĕmt), **dream·ing, dreams** ❖ *—intr.* **1.** To have a dream while sleeping. **2.** To daydream: *dreaming of far-off places.* **3.** To consider as feasible or practical: *I wouldn't even dream of going.* ❖ *—tr.* **1.** To have a dream about (something) during sleep: *Did it storm last night, or did I dream it?* **2.** To conceive of; imagine: *We never dreamed it might snow so hard.* ◆ **dream up** To invent; concoct: *dreamed up a plan to get rich quick.*

Usage phrases. Some noun entries have added information that tells you whether the word takes a singular or plural verb or whether it can take either a singular or a plural verb. This information appears as a usage phrase in italics before the sense or part of speech that it applies to:

ge·net·ics (jə-**nĕt′**ĭks) *n.* **1.** *(used with a singular verb)* The branch of biology that deals with genes, especially their inheritance and expression and their distribution among different individuals and organisms. **2.** *(used with a plural verb)* The genetic makeup of an individual or group.

In the entry *genetics* above, the usage phrase tells you that sense 1 takes a singular verb only and sense 2 takes a plural verb only.

Forms That Apply to Specific Senses

Information such as an inflected form that applies only to a particular sense or subsense is shown after the number or letter of that sense or subsense:

broth·er (**brŭth′**ər) *n.* **1a.** A boy or man having the same mother and father as someone else. **b.** A boy or man having one parent in common with someone else; a half brother. **c.** A stepbrother. **2a.** A boy or man who shares common ancestors, a common allegiance to a country, or a common purpose with another or others. **b.** A fellow male member of a group, such as a profession, fraternity, or labor union. **3.** *plural* **broth·ers** or **breth·ren** (**brĕth′**rən) **a.** A member of a men's Christian religious order who is not a priest. **b.** A fellow male member of a Christian church.

In this entry, the plural form *brethren* applies only to the third sense of brother. For all of the other senses, the only common plural is *brothers.*

Some nouns have senses in which they are usually used in the plural. In these cases, the boldface plural form of the noun appears just before the definition to show you that it is used in the plural:

jack (jăk) *n.* . . . **5a. jacks** *(used with a singular or plural verb)* A game in which each player in turn bounces and catches a small ball while picking up small six-pointed metal pieces with the same hand.

In this entry, the sense of *jack* that refers to the game occurs only in the plural form *jacks.*

The same style is used for any change in the form of a word as it shifts from one sense to another:

Af·ghan (ăf′găn′) *adj.* Relating to Afghanistan or the Afghans. ❖ *n.* **1.** A native or inhabitant of Afghanistan. **2. afghan** A colorful wool blanket or shawl knitted or crocheted in squares, circles, or other designs.

Here the boldface lowercase form of the word appears just before the definition it applies to, telling you that in this sense the word only occurs in the lowercase form *afghan.*

Illustrative Examples of Definitions

In addition to giving clear definitions of words, this dictionary also gives you thousands of examples showing how a word is used in context. You will find that these examples are especially useful for illustrating figurative senses of a word, transitive and intransitive verbs, and multiple senses of very common words:

a·round (ə-**round′**) *adv.* **1.** On all sides or in all directions: *We drove around looking for a parking place.* **2.** In a circle or circular motion: *The skater spun around twice.* **3.** In or toward the opposite direction: *The horse turned around and ran toward the barn.* **4.** From one place to another; here and there: *wander around.* **5.** In or near one's current location: *He waited around all day.* **6.** To a specific place or area: *when you come around again.* **7.** Approximately; about: *Around 20 rafts floated down the Rio Grande.*

Idioms

An *idiom* is a group of words whose meaning as a group cannot be understood from the meanings of the individual words in the group. In this dictionary, idioms are defined at the entry for the first important word in the phrase. For example, *walk on air* is defined at *walk.*

In this dictionary, idioms appear at the very end of the definitions of an entry in alphabetical order, following the ◆ symbol. Each idiom is shown in boldface.Verbs form many idioms with adverbs or prepositions, as this example shows:

take (tāk) . . . ◆ **take advantage of 1.** To put to good use; avail oneself of: *take advantage of the sale.* **2.** To use unfairly and selfishly; exploit: *They took advantage of our friendship just to get a ride to the movies.* **take after** To resemble in appearance, temperament, or character: *He takes after his grandfather.* **take apart** To divide into parts; disassemble: *We had to take the chair apart to refinish it.* **take back** To retract (something stated or written): *I took back my promise when I saw I had been cheated.* **take care** To be careful: *Take care when you cross the street.* **take care of** To assume responsibility for the maintenance, support, or treatment of: *I'm taking care of the puppy now.* **take effect 1.** To become operative, as under law or regulation: *The new rules are to take effect today.* **2.** To produce a desired effect: *The antibiotic finally took effect.* **take for 1.** To regard as: *Many take him for a genius.* **2.** To consider mistakenly: *The teacher took me for my sister.* **take for granted 1.** To assume to be true, real, or forthcoming: *took it for granted that he would pass the test.* **2.** To underestimate the value of: *volunteers who felt they were being taken for granted.* **take hold 1.** To seize, as by grasping. **2.** To become established: *The new shrubs took hold on the hill.* **take in 1.** To receive (an amount of money) for a business or activity: *We took in $5,000 in donations.* **2.** To grant admittance to; receive as a guest or employee. **3.** To reduce in size; make smaller or shorter: *He had to take in the slacks before he could wear them.* **4.** To understand: *We took in the lecture despite its complexity.* **5.** To look at thoroughly; view: *We took in the scenery.* **6.** To deceive: *I was taken in by a swindler.* **take into account** To consider: *Taking into account how little time he had to recover, he played well.* **take off 1.** To remove, as clothing: *took off our coats in the hallway.* **2.** To go off; leave: *She took off early from practice.* **3.** To rise in flight: *A flock of geese took off from the pond.* **4.** To spend (time) away from work. **take offense** To become angered, resentful, or displeased: *I took offense at his comment.* **take on 1.** To undertake or begin to handle: *took on some extra duties while a coworker was out.* **2.** To hire; engage: *take on an assistant.* **3.** To oppose in competition: *offered to take on any opponent.* **take (one's) time** To act slowly or at one's leisure. **take out 1.** To extract; remove: *had to have two teeth taken out.* **2.** *Informal* To escort, as a date. **3.** To express (a pent-up emotion): *took out his anger on the recruits.* **take over** To assume the control or management of (a company, for example). **take place** To happen; occur: *When did the event take place?* **take sick (**or **take ill)** To become sick. **take sides** To associate with and support a particular faction, group, cause, or person. **take to 1.** To go to, as for safety: *took to the hills.* **2.** To become fond of or attached to: *The new kitten really took to me.* **take up 1.** To absorb: *roots taking up water.* **2.** To develop an interest in or engage in: *decided to take up stamp collecting.* **3.** To use up or occupy: *The job took up all of her time. The bed takes up half the room.* **take up with** *Informal* To begin to associate with; consort with.

This dictionary lists only nonliteral or unusual senses of idioms. Thus in the example below, *back out,* meaning "to retire or withdraw from something," is defined in that sense, but not in the sense "to leave a parking space in reverse." You should be able to figure out this latter meaning of the phrase by the meanings of the two words themselves, and therefore we do not define it:

> **back** (băk) . . . ◆ **back away** To withdraw from a position; retreat: *He backed slowly away from the skunk.* **back down** To withdraw from a stand that one has taken: *There was an argument because neither side was willing to back down.* **back off** To retreat or fall back, as from something dangerous or risky: *The senator backed off from his support of the unpopular bill.* **back out** To withdraw from something one has agreed to: *They accepted the invitation but backed out at the last minute.* **back to back** In a series, without interruption: *broadcast six episodes of the sitcom back to back.* **back up 1.** To make a copy of (a computer program or file). **2.** To accumulate: *Traffic backed up at the intersection.* **behind (one's) back** When one is not present: *Don't talk about me behind my back.*

Etymology

Many entries in this dictionary have etymologies that show how a word was spelled in earlier forms of English and, in many cases, what language or languages it came from. The etymology appears in brackets near the end of the entry:

> **school**[1] (sko͞ol) *n.* **1.** An institution for teaching and learning. **2.** A division of an educational institution, especially one for special study within a university: *a law school.* **3.** The student body of an educational institution. **4.** The building or group of buildings housing an educational institution. **5.** The instruction given at a school: *School ends early today.* **6.** The process of being educated formally: *What are your plans when you finish school?* **7.** A group of people, especially artists or writers, whose thought, work, or style shows common influences or underlying beliefs. ❖ *tr.v.* **schooled, school·ing, schools** To instruct or train: *schooling him in manners.* See Synonyms at **teach.** [From Old English *scōl,* from Latin *schola,* from Greek *skholē.*]

The etymology of a word shows its history—the story of how it became an English word. The etymologies in this dictionary show if the first use of a word in English was in Old English or Middle English. In those earlier forms of English, most words were spelled in a variety of ways. In some cases, scholars studying Old English and Middle English have determined which spelling is the most common, and in other cases, they have chosen a particular spelling to stand as the head word in dictionaries of Old English and Middle English. If that form is different from the Modern English spelling of the word, we show that form.

For example, the word for "school" in Old English was *scōl.* Since *scōl* means the same thing as the Modern English word *school,* a definition isn't shown within the etymology.

If an earlier form of a word had a different meaning, the meaning of the term in that language is shown:

> **deer** (dîr) *n., pl.* **deer** Any of various hoofed mammals, such as the elk or white-tailed deer, that chew their cud and have antlers, usually only in the male. [From Old English *dēor,* beast.]

This etymology tells you that the word *deer* originated in Old English but meant "beast," that is, any animal. This tells you that word's meaning has since narrowed to refer only to certain kinds of beasts.

Most words have come into English from other languages, and this information is given next in the etymology. Thus, in the example of *school*[1] presented above, the speakers of Old English got their word from the Latin word *schola,* which itself came from a Greek word, *skholē.* So our modern word *school*[1] ultimately goes back to ancient Greek but shows the influence of Latin as well.

Words that come from compound words in other languages can best be understood by breaking down the compound into its parts. In the etymologies in this dictionary, a colon is used to introduce these parts, as in the following example:

> **con·tain** (kən-tān′) *tr.v.* **con·tained, con·tain·ing, con·tains 1.** To have within; hold: *This bottle contains drinking water. The document contains important information.* **2.** To consist of; comprise; include: *A gallon contains four quarts.* **3.** To hold back; restrain: *I could scarcely contain my laughter.* **4.** To halt the spread or development of: *a method of containing disease.* [From Middle English *conteinen,* from Latin *continēre* : *com-,* together + *tenēre,* to hold.] **—con·tain′a·ble** *adj.* —SEE NOTE AT **tenacious.**

Here you can see that our word *contain* goes back to the Latin compound *continēre.* This compound has two parts: the prefix *com-,* meaning "together," and the verb *tenēre,* meaning "to hold." So from an analysis of its history the word *contain* means basically "to hold together."

Of course, not all Modern English words arose from Middle English or Old English. There are many other sources for the development of a word, including coming directly from other languages (*chocolate*), arising from preexisting roots (*telephone*), or coming from proper names (*einsteinium*). You will find examples of these throughout the dictionary.

Run-On Forms

This dictionary includes many additional words formed from an entry word by the addition of a suffix. These words are located at the end of an entry. They are obviously related to the main entry word and have the same essential meaning, but they have different endings and different parts of speech. Run-on entries appear in boldface followed by a part-of-speech label. Syllabification and stress are indicated on run-on words that have more than one syllable, and pronunciations are given where needed:

> **re·gret·ful** (rĭ-grĕt′fəl) *adj.* Full of regret; sorrowful or sorry. **—re·gret′ful·ly** *adv.* **—re·gret′ful·ness** *n.*

When two or more run-on forms have the same part of speech, they are separated by a comma and have a single part-of-speech label:

> **rap·id** (răp′ĭd) *adj.* **rap·id·er, rap·id·est** Fast; swift: *rapid progress; walking with rapid strides.* See Synonyms at **fast**[1]. ❖ *n.* often **rapids** An extremely fast-moving part of a river, caused by a steep descent in the riverbed: *went over the rapids in a kayak.* **—ra·pid′i·ty** (rə-pĭd′ĭ-tē), **rap′id·ness** *n.* **—rap′id·ly** *adv.*

Homophones

Some words, such as *cent, scent,* and *sent,* sound the same but are unrelated and have different spellings and meanings. These words are called *homophones.* To help you keep track of these words, the dictionary provides a list of words that sound alike at the end of each entry for a homophone. The homophones are listed in alphabetical order with the main entry word first, preceded by the phrase *These sound alike.* Each homophone following the main entry in the list is followed by a word or phrase enclosed in parentheses that identifies its meaning. Proper nouns and foreign words are not entered as homophones.

> **row**[1] (rō) *n.* **1.** A series of persons or things placed next to each other, usually in a straight line: *a row of poplar trees.* **2.** A succession without a break or gap in time: *won the title for three years in a row.* **3.** A line of adjacent seats, as in a theater. **4.** A continuous line of buildings along a street. [From Old English *rāw.*]
>
> ❑ *These sound alike:* **row**[1] (series), **rho** (Greek letter), **roe** (fish eggs), **row**[2] (use oars).

Synonym Paragraphs

This dictionary has 100 Synonym Paragraphs that list and describe words that have similar meanings. Each paragraph follows the entry for the central word of each synonym group. The paragraphs are introduced by the heading *Synonyms,* and the synonyms themselves appear in boldface. A list of antonyms, or words with meanings opposite those of the synonyms, appears when applicable in boldface at the end of the paragraph.

There are two kinds of Synonym Paragraphs. The first gives a central meaning shared by the synonyms in the list, and illustrative examples for each word:

> SYNONYMS **authentic, genuine, real, true** These adjectives mean not counterfeit or copied. *An expert assured us that the chair is an authentic antique from the 1700s. The recipe calls for genuine Italian olive oil, but the store sells only American brands. The bouquets were made with silk flowers instead of real ones. A true friend would be more understanding.*

The second kind explains the varying shades of meaning that distinguish the synonyms and shows how these words are used in context:

> SYNONYMS **break, crack, fracture, splinter, shatter** These verbs mean to cause to separate into parts or pieces. **Break** is the most general: *He accidentally broke the glass while cleaning it.* **Crack** means to break, often with a sharp snapping sound, without dividing into parts: *A small pebble cracked our windshield while we were driving.* **Fracture** applies to a break or crack in a rigid body: *She fractured her hip in the accident.* **Splinter** means to split into long, thin, sharp pieces: *Lightning struck the tree and splintered it.* **Shatter** means to break into many loose scattered pieces: *She dropped the vase and shattered it.*

Every word that is discussed in a Synonym Paragraph has at its own entry a cross-reference to the entry that has the Synonym Paragraph. Thus, the entry for *headstrong* has a cross-reference to the synonym list presented at *obstinate:*

> **val·iant** (văl′yənt) *adj.* Possessing or exhibiting valor; brave: *a valiant knight; a valiant effort.* See Synonyms at **brave.**

Marginal Notes

In the margins of this dictionary you will find a variety of notes providing more information about individual words. These notes describe how words are and should be used, where words come from, and how their meanings can be deciphered from an understanding of their parts. Some notes supply additional information about certain entries—information that is too extensive to be included in a definition. The words *See Note* at the end of an entry direct you to a note in the margin discussing that entry.

Usage Notes. Some words are easily confused with others or present difficulties in how they should be used. These entries have Usage Notes that offer explanations and advice on how to avoid usage problems. Here is a typical Usage Note:

> USAGE NOTE
>
> **affect**[1] The words **affect** and **effect** look and sound similar. Their meanings, however, are very different. The verb *affect* means "to influence": *That decision will affect my whole life.* The verb *effect* means "to make happen": *We effected some helpful changes.* The noun *effect* can mean "a result" or "an influence," but only the verb *affect* means "to influence."

When a word is discussed in a Usage Note in the margin next to an entry elsewhere in the book, it has a cross-reference to that entry. Thus, at *effect* you are directed to the note at *affect*[1], where *effect* is also discussed:

> **ef·fect** (ĭ-fĕkt′) *n.* **1.** Something brought about by a cause or agent; a result: *The effect of advertising should be an increase in sales.* . . .—SEE NOTE AT **affect**[1].

Word Histories. In addition to etymologies, this dictionary also provides informative paragraphs that tell the story of many words that have an interesting past. Some notes explain how a word has moved from one language to another before coming into English. Others explain how words that are spelled differently in fact have a common origin. Still others explain the processes by which words change or develop new meanings. An example of a Word History Note can be found at the entry *gleam:*

WORD HISTORY

gleam Many English words having to do with the notion of "shining" begin with gl: **glare, gleam, glimmer, glint, glisten, glitter, glossy,** and **glow** are some examples. The *gl* comes from a common root that they share, meaning "shining" or "yellow." This root is also at the source of the word **gold,** "the shining or yellow metal," and of some words suggestive of quick motion, such as **glide** and **glimpse.**

Word Building Notes. Word Building Notes help you understand how word parts are joined together to make longer, more complex words. There are two kinds of Word Building Notes—Affix Notes and Word Root Notes. Affix Notes show how prefixes and suffixes are attached to words to make new words. These notes often describe the history of the affix, which in many cases goes back to Latin or Greek:

WORD BUILDING

trans– The prefix **trans–** comes from the Latin prefix *trāns–,* from the Latin preposition *trāns,* "across, beyond, through." Many of the most common English words beginning with *trans–* are derived from Latin words or elements, such as *transfer, transfuse, translate, transmit, transpire,* and *transport.* Another large group of words has *trans–* in combination with English adjectives, as in *transatlantic, transcontinental, transoceanic, transpacific,* and *transpolar,* with the meaning "across" or "through" a particular geographic element.

Word Root Notes describe how Greek and Latin roots form the heart of many words that have different but related meanings:

WORD BUILDING

compose The word root *pos–* in English comes from the French verb *poser,* "to put." **Compose** therefore literally means "to put together" (using the prefix *com–,* "with, together"); **expose** means "to put out" (*ex–,* "out, out of"); **propose** is literally "to put forward" (*prō,* "forward, in front"); **oppose** is literally "to put against" (*op–,* a form of *ob–,* "toward, against"). The French verb *poser* comes ultimately from the Latin verb *pōnere,* whose present participle was *pōnēns* or *pōnent-.* This is where the English nouns that contain *–ponent* and correspond to verbs containing *–pose* come from: **component, exponent, proponent,** and **opponent.**

Writers Choose Their Words. Masterful writers don't just have original ideas and large vocabularies. They pick and choose their words with care, crafting sentences in which the words work together to communicate an idea or describe a scene. To show how famous authors have used language for maximum effect, many pages of this dictionary include a "Writers Choose Their Words" feature in the margin, where we present a quotation from a well-known book that highlights a skillful use of a particular word:

WRITERS CHOOSE THEIR WORDS

Claudia, who had eaten cereal and drunk pineapple juice, scolded him about the need to eat properly. Breakfast food for breakfast, and lunch food for lunch. Jamie **countered** with complaints about Claudia's narrow-mindedness.

—E.L. Konigsburg
From the Mixed-up Files of Mrs. Basil E. Frankweiler

Other Notes. Biographical Notes tell a story in greater detail about the accomplishments of important people, such as Thomas Jefferson or Sacagawea, identified at certain entries.

Geographical Notes tell how the 50 states of the United States came to have the names they do.

Science Notes supply background information about terms used in science, such as *blood type* or *greenhouse effect.*

Capitalization, Punctuation, and Style Guide

This section of the dictionary sets forth the basic points of style used in written and printed American English. Shown here are rules for the correct use of capital letters, punctuation marks, numbers, and italics or underlining. Each rule is illustrated with an example phrase or sentence. If you want to know more about any of the points discussed in the guide, consult your grammar or composition textbook or one of the many style manuals available for writers and researchers.

Capitalization

Rules for Capitalization

- **Capitalize the names of geographical entities, such as cities, states, and countries, and geographical features, such as rivers, mountains, and lakes:**

Boston	Arctic Circle
Middle East	Connecticut River
Minnesota	Western Hemisphere
Gulf Coast	Lake Geneva
Brazil	South Pole
the South	Blue Ridge Mountains
Mountain States	Fertile Crescent
the Midwest	Pacific Ocean

But do not capitalize directions:

We live ten miles west of Philadelphia.

- **Capitalize titles or their abbreviations when used with a person's name:**

Governor Warner
President Bush
Dr. Lin

- **Capitalize words showing a familial relationship when used with a person's name:**

Uncle Bob
Grandmother Burrows

but

her uncle, Robert Smith
my grandmother, Dora Burrows

- **Capitalize words derived from proper names:**

We ate at a Hungarian restaurant.
She is French.

- **Capitalize the names of nationalities, languages, religions, and tribes:**

Canadian	Maori
Spanish	Bantu
Old English	Roman Catholic Church

- **Capitalize the names of days, months, holidays, and holy days:**

Monday	Passover
January	Ramadan
Labor Day	Easter

- **Capitalize the names of specific school subjects when followed by a number:**

History I	Geography 101

- **Capitalize the names of councils, congresses, organizations and their members, and historical periods and events:**

the Free and Accepted Masons	the Potsdam Conference
a Mason	the Battle of Bull Run
the Republican Party	the Harlem Renaissance
the House of Representatives	the Middle Ages

- **Capitalize the names of streets, highways, buildings, bridges, and monuments:**

Fifth Avenue	Vietnam Veterans Memorial
Route 9	the Pentagon
Golden Gate Bridge	

- **Capitalize the first word and all words, except conjunctions and prepositions of four letters or fewer and articles, in the titles of documents and literary, dramatic, artistic, and musical works:**

the novel *To Kill a Mockingbird*
the play *A Raisin in the Sun*
the short story "The Necklace"
Bartok's *Concerto for Orchestra*
an article titled "The Exports of Italy"
Robert Frost's poem "The Road Not Taken"
Picasso's *Guernica*

- **Capitalize the first word of each main topic and subtopic in an outline:**

I. Types of libraries
  A. Large public library
  B. Bookmobile
  C. School library
II. Library services

- **Capitalize the first word in the greeting and closing of a letter:**

Dear Marcia,	Your friend,
Dear Ms. Olsen:	Sincerely yours,

- **Capitalize the first word of a direct quotation that is a complete sentence:**

The candidate said, "Actions speak louder than words."
Who said "I think, therefore I am"?

Punctuation

End Marks

■ **A *period* (.) ends a declarative or imperative sentence. A *question mark* (?) follows an interrogative sentence. An *exclamation point* (!) is used after an exclamatory sentence and after an interjection that expresses strong feeling.**

The scissors are on my desk. (declarative)
Look up the spelling of that word. (imperative)
How is the word spelled? (interrogative)
This is your best poem so far! (exclamatory)
Wow! We've just won the essay prize. (interjection)

Apostrophe

■ **To form the possessive of a singular noun, add an apostrophe and s:**

sister-in-law's family's Agnes's

■ **To form the possessive of a plural noun that does not end in s, add an apostrophe and s:**

women's mice's sisters-in-law's

■ **To form the possessive of a plural noun that ends in s, add an apostrophe only:**

sisters' families' Joneses'

■ **Use an apostrophe and s to form the plural of single letters, numerals, symbols, and words that are used to stand for words:**

s's i's 2's *'s
Fill in the questionnaire with *yes*'s and *no*'s.

but

We bought two TVs.
Our house was built in the 1920s.

Colon

■ **Use a colon to separate the hour from the minute:**

7:30 pm 8:15 am

■ **Use a colon after the greeting in a business letter:**

Dear Ms. Trimby: Dear Sir or Madam:

■ **Use a colon before a list introduced by words such as *the following* or *these*:**

Call the following: Hester, Wanda, Daryl, and Carl.

But do not use a colon after a verb or a preposition:

Next year I am taking English, history, and math.
He arrived with a suitcase, a coat, and an umbrella.

Comma

■ **Use commas to separate words in a series:**

Cheryl asked if we had any apples, peaches, or grapes.

■ **Use commas between two or more adjectives that come before a noun unless the adjectives are used together to express a single idea:**

He had a solid, heavy gait.

but

The bird had shiny yellow feathers on its head.

■ **Use a comma to separate the independent clauses in a compound sentence:**

Some students were at lunch, but others were studying.

■ **Use commas after words, phrases, and subordinate clauses that come at the beginning of sentences:**

No, you cannot avoid the deadline.
Following the applause, the speaker continued.
When you are in doubt, ask for advice.

■ **Use commas to separate interrupters such as *of course, however,* and *by the way* from the rest of the sentence:**

Chris, of course, was late for the bus again.
The driver, however, had forgotten the directions.

■ **Use commas to set off an appositive from the rest of the sentence when the appositive is not necessary to the meaning of the sentence:**

Texas, the Lone Star State, borders Mexico.
(The appositive is extra, not needed for meaning.)

but

The writer Charles Dickens created complex plots.
(The appositive is necessary to the meaning.)

■ **Use commas to set off a nonessential phrase or clause—one that adds optional information not necessary to the meaning of the sentence. If a phrase or clause is essential, do not use commas:**

Emily Dickinson, who was born in 1830, was a poet.
(The clause is not necessary to the meaning.)
The man who read the poem is my father.
(The clause is necessary to the meaning.)

■ **Use a comma to set off a word in direct address:**

Thank you, Joe, for your help.
How was your trip, Mom?

- **Use a comma to separate the month and day from the year. Use a comma to separate the year from the rest of the sentence. Do not use commas if a specific day is not included:**

  January 12, 2011, was the date of the banquet.

but

  Halley's Comet appeared last in April 1986.

- **Use a comma after an interjection that expresses emotion:**

  Oh, I didn't see you there!

- **Use a comma to set off short quotations and sayings:**

  Jo told him, "Come tomorrow for dinner."
  "I don't know if I can," he said, "but maybe I will."

- **Use a comma between the names of a city and a state in an address. If the address is within a sentence, also use a comma after the name of the state. Do not use a comma before the Zip Code:**

  Does Chicago, Illinois, have the world's tallest building?
  My grandparents live at 10 Palm Court, Lima, OH 45807-3212.

- **Use a comma after the greeting in a personal letter and after the closing in all letters:**

  Dear Deena,
  Sincerely yours,

Semicolon

- **Use a semicolon to connect independent clauses that are closely related in thought or have commas within them:**

  There were five movie tickets left; Ed needed six.
  He bought nuts, dates, and figs; we ate them all.

- **Use a semicolon to join two independent clauses when the second clause begins with an adverb such as *however, therefore,* or *consequently*:**

  It was growing dark; however, there were no clouds.

Hyphens, Dashes, and Parentheses

- **Use a hyphen to join the parts of compound numbers, to join two or more words that work together as one adjective before a noun, or to divide a word at the end of a line:**

  thirty-two long-range plans

  Raphael is known as one of Italy's many magnif-icent painters.

- **Use a dash to show a sudden change of thought:**

  The sky grew dark—it might mean snow.

- **Use parentheses to enclose unnecessary information:**

  Gina was reelected (once more) as treasurer.

Quotation Marks

- **Use quotation marks to set off titles of short stories, articles, songs, poems, and book chapters:**

  "The Party" (short story) "If" (poem)
  "Crewelwork" (article) "Saxon Art" (chapter)
  "America" (song)

- **Use quotation marks to enclose direct quotations:**

  "What was Berlin like during the war?" she asked.
  Eleanor Roosevelt said, "We must do the things we think we cannot do."

Numbers

- **Spell out numbers *zero* through *ten* and *first* through *tenth* and numbers at the beginning of a sentence. Use numerals for numbers greater than *ten* or *tenth*:**

  My team has 25 players.
  Two hundred people were in the audience.
  There are 147 apartments in my building.
  It happened in the tenth century BC.
  He came in 14th out of 200.

Italics

- **Titles of books, magazines, newspapers, long musical works, poems, plays, works of art, movies, and TV series are italicized:**

  In a Pickle (book) *As You Like It* (play)
  Miami Herald (newspaper) *Mona Lisa* (painting)
  Requiem (musical work) *Nature* (TV series)

- **Use italics to indicate a word, number, or letter used as such:**

  The word *straight* has two *t*'s.
  A *6* looks like an inverted *9*.

- **Use italics to distinguish the scientific names of genera and species of living things:**

  Homo sapiens (human being)
  Phaseolus vulgaris (string bean)

- **Use italics to set off the names of ships, planes, and often spacecraft:**

  USS *Kitty Hawk*
  Spirit of St. Louis
  Voyager II

- **In handwritten or typewritten documents, italics are indicated by underlining:**

  Melville's Moby Dick
  the movie The Wizard of Oz

Pronunciation

Pronunciations appear in parentheses after boldface entry words. If an entry word has a variant and they have the same pronunciation, the pronunciation follows the variant. If the variant does not have the same pronunciation, pronunciations follow the forms to which they apply. If a word has more than one pronunciation, the first pronunciation is usually more common than the other, but often they are equally common. Pronunciations are shown within an entry where necessary. A short form of the Pronunciation Key below appears in the margin of every other page throughout the dictionary.

Stress. Stress is the relative degree of emphasis with which a word's syllables are spoken. An unmarked syllable has the weakest stress in the word. The strongest, or primary, stress is indicated with a bold mark (**ʹ**). A lighter mark (ʹ) indicates a secondary level of stress. Words of one syllable have no stress mark, because there is no other stress level to which the syllable is compared.

Pronunciation Symbols. The pronunciation symbols used in this dictionary are shown below. To the right of the symbols are words that show how the symbols are pronounced. The letters whose sound corresponds to the symbols are shown in boldface. The symbol (ə) is called *schwa.* It represents a vowel with the weakest level of stress in a word. The schwa sound varies slightly according to the vowel it represents or the sounds around it:

a·bun·dant (ə-**bŭnʹ**dənt)
mo·ment (**moʹ**mənt)
grate·ful (**grātʹ**fəl)
civ·il (**sĭvʹ**əl)
pro·pose (prə-**pōzʹ**)

In English, the consonants *l* and *n* can be complete syllables. Examples of words with syllabic *l* and *n* are **needle** (**nēdʹ**l) and **sudden** (**sŭdʹ**n).

Foreign Symbols. Some foreign words use sounds that are not found in English. The (œ) sound is made by rounding the lips as though you were going to make the (ō) sound, but instead you make an (ā) sound. The (ü) sound is made by rounding the lips as though you were going to make the (o͞o) sound, but instead you make an (ē) sound. The (KH) sound is like a (k), but the air is forced through continuously, not stopped as with a (k). The (N) sound shows that the vowel before it is nasalized—that is, air escapes through the nose (and the mouth) when you say it.

Pronunciation Key

ă	**p**a**t**	ĭ	**p**i**t**	ôr	**c**o**re**	*th*	**th**is
ā	**p**ay	ī	**p**ie, **b**y	oi	**n**oi**se**	ŭ	**c**u**t**
âr	**c**a**re**	îr	**d**ea**r**, **d**ee**r**, **p**ie**r**	o͝o	**t**oo**k**	ûr	**u**rge, **t**e**rm**, **f**i**rm**, **w**o**rd**, **h**ea**rd**
ä	**f**a**th**er	j	**j**u**dge**	o͝or	**l**u**re**	v	**v**al**v**e
b	**b**i**b**	k	**k**ic**k**, **c**at, pi**que**	o͞o	**b**oo**t**	w	**w**i**th**
ch	**ch**ur**ch**	l	**l**id, need**l**e	ou	**ou**t	y	**y**es
d	**d**ee**d**, mi**ll**ed	m	**m**u**m**	p	**p**o**p**	z	**z**ebra, **x**ylem
ĕ	**p**e**t**	n	**n**o, su**dd**en	r	**r**oa**r**	zh	vi**s**ion, plea**s**ure, gara**ge**
ē	**b**ee	ng	thi**ng**	s	**s**au**c**e	ə	**a**bout, it**e**m, ed**i**ble, gall**o**p, circ**u**s
f	**f**i**f**e, **ph**ase, rou**gh**	ŏ	**p**o**t**	sh	**sh**ip, di**sh**	ər	butt**er**
g	**g**a**g**	ō	**t**oe	t	**t**igh**t**, stoppe**d**		
h	**h**at	ô	**c**au**ght**, **p**aw	th	**th**in		

a[1] or **A** (ā) *n., pl.* **a's** or **A's** also **as** or **As** **1.** The first letter of the English alphabet: *There are three a's in "alfalfa."* **2. A** The best or highest grade: *get an A on a report; grade A eggs.* **3. A** In music, the sixth tone in the scale of C major. **4. A** One of the four types of blood in the ABO system. ♦ **from A to Z** Completely; thoroughly: *The school board considered the teachers' complaints from A to Z.*

a[2] (ə; ā *when stressed*) *indef.art.* **1.** One: *I didn't say a single word.* **2.** The same: *Birds of a feather flock together.* **3.** Any: *A cat will always eat fish.* **4.** An example of a kind of: *Water is a liquid.*

a[3] (ə) *prep.* In each; for each; per: *once a month; ten dollars a trip.*

A *abbr.* An abbreviation of: **1.** ampere. **2.** area.

a–[1] or **an–** *pref.* A prefix that means without or not: *amoral; atypical.* —SEE NOTE.

a–[2] *pref.* A prefix that means: **1.** On or in: *abed; aboard.* **2.** In the direction of: *astern.* **3.** In a particular condition: *afire.*

Aa·chen (ä′kən) A city of western Germany near the Belgian and Dutch borders. Charlemagne may have been born here in 742.

aard·vark (ärd′värk′) *n.* A burrowing mammal of sub-Saharan Africa having long claws and a long, sticky tongue used for feeding on ants and termites. [From obsolete Afrikaans, earth pig : Afrikaans *aarde*, earth + *vark*, pig.]

Aar·on (âr′ən) In the Bible, the elder brother of Moses who helped lead the Hebrews out of Egypt.

Aaron, Henry Louis Known as "Hank." Born 1934. American baseball player who retired (1976) with a total of 755 home runs.

AAVE *abbr.* An abbreviation of African American Vernacular English.

AB[1] (ā′bē′) *n.* One of the four types of blood in the ABO system.

AB[2] *abbr.* An abbreviation of Alberta.

ab·a·ca (ăb′ə-kä′ *or* ä′bə-kä′) *n.* A plant resembling the banana that is native to the Philippines and yields a fiber used to make cordage, fabric, and paper.

a·back (ə-băk′) *adv.* By surprise: *I was taken aback by his angry words.*

ab·a·cus (ăb′ə-kəs) *n., pl.* **ab·a·cus·es** or **ab·a·ci** (ăb′ə-sī′) A computing device consisting of a frame holding parallel rods with sliding beads. [Ultimately from Greek *abax*, board strewn with dust for drawing geometrical diagrams, probably of Semitic origin, akin to Hebrew *'ābāq*, dust.]

a·baft (ə-băft′) *prep.* Toward the stern from: *The cargo hatch is abaft the mainmast.* ❖ *adv.* Toward a ship's stern: *It was fast sailing with the wind abaft.*

ab·a·lo·ne (ăb′ə-lō′nē) *n.* Any of various edible mollusks that have a large shallow shell lined with mother-of-pearl.

a·ban·don (ə-băn′dən) *tr.v.* **a·ban·doned, a·ban·don·ing, a·ban·dons** **1.** To withdraw one's support or help from: *abandon a friend in trouble.* **2.** To leave and not intend to return; desert: *abandon a sinking ship.* **3.** To give up completely; stop trying to accomplish: *They abandoned the attempt to climb the peak.* See Synonyms at **yield. 4.** To yield (oneself) to an impulse or emotion: *Don't abandon yourself to despair.* ❖ *n.* Great enthusiasm or lack of restraint: *skied down the hill with abandon.* [From Old French *abandoner*, from *abandon*, security given for a loan, pawn : *a*, at, in + *bandon*, power, control.] **—a·ban′don·ment** *n.*

a·ban·doned (ə-băn′dənd) *adj.* **1.** Deserted or given up; forsaken: *During the snowstorm the highway was littered with abandoned cars.* **2.** Recklessly unrestrained: *an abandoned life.*

a·base (ə-bās′) *tr.v.* **a·based, a·bas·ing, a·bas·es** To lower in rank, dignity, or reputation; humble or degrade: *abased himself by lying.* **—a·base′ment** *n.*

a·bash (ə-băsh′) *tr.v.* **a·bashed, a·bash·ing, a·bash·es** To make ashamed or uneasy; embarrass: *The teacher was abashed by her careless mistake.*

a·bate (ə-bāt′) *v.* **a·bat·ed, a·bat·ing, a·bates** *—tr.* To reduce in amount, degree, or intensity: *The horse galloped around the curve without abating his speed. —intr.* To become less in degree or intensity: *After several hours of heavy wind and rain, the storm abated.* **—a·bate′·ment** *n.*

a·bay·a (ə-bī′ə) *n.* A loose robe worn by Muslim women, especially in Arabic-speaking regions, covering the body from head to toe or the neck down and often worn with a headscarf and veil. [From Arabic *'abā'a*.]

ab·bess (ăb′ĭs) *n.* A nun who is the head of a convent.

ab·bey (ăb′ē) *n., pl.* **ab·beys** **1.** A monastery or convent. **2.** A church that is or was once part of a monastery or convent.

ab·bot (ăb′ət) *n.* A monk who is the head of a monastery.

abbr. *abbr.* An abbreviation of abbreviation.

ab·bre·vi·ate (ə-brē′vē-āt′) *tr.v.* **ab·bre·vi·at·ed, ab·bre·vi·at·ing, ab·bre·vi·ates** **1.** To reduce (a word or group of words) to a shorter form by leaving out some of the letters: *abbreviate "hour" to "hr."* **2.** To shorten: *abbreviate a long explanation.* [From Late Latin *abbreviāre* : Latin *ad-*, to + *breviāre*, to shorten (from *brevis*, short).]

ab·bre·vi·a·tion (ə-brē′vē-ā′shən) *n.* **1.** The act or process of abbreviating; abridgement: *His abbreviation of the story left out many details.* **2.** A shortened form of a word or group of words, such as *Mr.* for *Mister* or *USA* for *United States of America.*

ABCs also **ABC's** (ā′bē-sēz′) *pl.n.* **1.** The alphabet. **2.** The basic facts of a subject: *After learning the ABCs of arithmetic, most students are ready for algebra.*

ab·di·cate (ăb′dĭ-kāt′) *v.* **ab·di·cat·ed, ab·di·cat·ing, ab·di·cates** *—tr.* To give up (power or responsibility): *abdicate the throne. —intr.* To give up power or responsibility formally: *The king abdicated to allow his son to take over.* **—ab′di·ca′tion** *n.* **—ab′di·ca′tor** *n.*

WORD BUILDING

a–[1] The basic meaning of the prefix a– is "without." For example, *achromatic* means "without color." Before vowels and sometimes *h*, a– becomes *an–*: *anaerobic.* Many of the words beginning with this prefix are used in science or medicine, such as *aphasia, anoxia,* and *aseptic.*

aardvark

abacus

Ralph Abernathy

WORD BUILDING

–able The suffix **–able,** which forms adjectives, comes from the Latin suffix *–ābilis,* meaning "capable or worthy of." Thus a *likable* person is one who is capable of or worthy of being liked. The suffix *–ible* is closely related to *–able* and has the same meaning, as in *flexible.* Since they sound exactly alike, it is important to consult your dictionary when spelling words that end in this suffix.

ă	pat	ôr	core
ā	pay	oi	boy
âr	care	ou	out
ä	father	ŏŏ	took
ĕ	pet	ŏŏr	lure
ē	be	ōō	boot
ĭ	pit	ŭ	cut
ī	bite	ûr	urge
îr	pier	th	thin
ŏ	pot	*th*	this
ō	toe	zh	vision
ô	paw	ə	about

ab·do·men (ăb′də-mən) *n.* **1a.** In humans and other mammals, the front or lower part of the body from below the chest to about where the legs join, containing the stomach, intestines, and other organs. **b.** The corresponding part of other vertebrates. **2.** The last part of the body of an arthropod: *A bee's stinger is in its abdomen.* [From Latin *abdōmen,* belly.]

ab·dom·i·nal (ăb-**dŏm′**ə-nəl) *adj.* Relating to or in the abdomen: *abdominal muscles.* ❖ *n.* An abdominal muscle: *exercises that strengthen the abdominals.* **—ab·dom′i·nal·ly** *adv.*

ab·duct (ăb-**dŭkt′**) *tr.v.* **ab·duct·ed, ab·duct·ing, ab·ducts** To carry away by force; kidnap. **—ab·duct·ee′** *n.* **—ab·duc′tor** *n.*

a·beam (ə-**bēm′**) *adv.* At right angles to the keel of a ship.

a·bed (ə-**bĕd′**) *adv.* In bed: *She lay abed with a cold.*

A·bel (**ā′**bəl) In the Bible, the son of Adam and Eve who was killed by his elder brother, Cain.

Ab·e·na·ki (ä′bə-**nä′**kē *or* ăb′ə-**năk′**ē) *n., pl.* **Abenaki** or **Ab·e·na·kis 1.** A member of any of various Native American peoples of northern New England and southeast Canada. **2.** Either of the Algonquian languages of the Abenaki.

Ab·er·deen (ăb′ər-**dēn′**) A city of northeast Scotland on the North Sea. It is known as "the Granite City" because stone from local quarries is used in many of its buildings.

Ab·er·nath·y (**ăb′**ər-năth′ē), **Ralph David** 1926–1990. American civil rights leader who advocated nonviolence and worked closely with Martin Luther King, Jr.

ab·er·rant (**ăb′**ər-ənt *or* ă-**bĕr′**ənt) *adj.* Differing from what is normal or typical: *aberrant behavior.*

ab·er·ra·tion (ăb′ə-**rā′**shən) *n.* **1.** A departure or a differing from what is normal or typical: *Wearing a tie to work is an aberration for him.* **2.** A mental disorder or lapse. **3.** A deviation in the normal structure or number of chromosomes in an organism. **4.** The failure of a lens, mirror, or telescope to bring rays of light coming from a source, such as a star, to a single focus, causing a distorted or blurred image. **5.** The apparent change in the position of a celestial object caused by the motion of Earth during the time it takes for light from the object to reach an observer on Earth.

a·bet (ə-**bĕt′**) *tr.v.* **a·bet·ted, a·bet·ting, a·bets** To encourage or help: *They have abetted our efforts to build a new gym.* **—a·bet′ment** *n.*

a·bet·tor or **a·bet·ter** (ə-**bĕt′**ər) *n.* A person who encourages or helps someone else.

a·bey·ance (ə-**bā′**əns) *n.* A state or condition of being put off to a later time; a postponement or temporary suspension: *Let's hold the plan in abeyance until we know more about the details.*

ab·hor (ăb-**hôr′**) *tr.v.* **ab·horred, ab·hor·ring, ab·hors** To feel disgust or hatred for; regard with horror or loathing: *I abhor getting into needless arguments.* **—ab·hor′rer** *n.*

ab·hor·rence (ăb-**hôr′**əns) *n.* **1.** A feeling of disgust or hatred: *an abhorrence of prejudice.* **2.** Something regarded with disgust or loathing: *Cheating in any form is an abhorrence.*

ab·hor·rent (ăb-**hôr′**ənt) *adj.* Causing disgust or loathing; hateful; horrible: *an abhorrent crime.*

a·bide (ə-**bīd′**) *v.* **a·bode** (ə-**bōd′**) or **a·bid·ed, a·bid·ing, a·bides** *—tr.* To put up with; bear; tolerate: *Most gardeners can't abide weeds.* *—intr.* To continue in existence; endure: *Generations come and go, but the earth abides.* ◆ **abide by** To act in agreement with; comply with: *We abided by the terms of the agreement.* [From Old English *ābīdan,* to remain.] **—a·bid′er** *n.*

a·bid·ing (ə-**bī′**dĭng) *adj.* Continuing or lasting for a long time: *The doctor had an abiding faith in good nutrition.*

Ab·i·djan (ăb′ĭ-**jän′**) The largest city and former capital of Côte d'Ivoire, in the southeast of the country on an enclosed lagoon of the Gulf of Guinea.

Ab·i·lene (**ăb′**ə-lēn′) A city of west-central Texas west-southwest of Fort Worth. Abilene was founded in 1881 with the coming of the railroad.

a·bil·i·ty (ə-**bĭl′**ĭ-tē) *n., pl.* **a·bil·i·ties 1.** The power to do something: *Monkeys don't have the ability to speak.* **2.** Skill or talent: *a violinist of great musical ability.* **3.** The quality of being suited to a specified treatment: *a metal with the ability to be hammered into thin sheets.*

–ability or **–ibility** *suff.* A suffix that means ability, preference, or appropriateness for some action or condition: *acceptability; accessibility.*

a·bi·ot·ic (ā′bī-**ŏt′**ĭk) *adj.* Nonliving: *The abiotic factors of the environment include light, temperature, and atmospheric gases.*

ab·ject (**ăb′**jĕkt′) *adj.* **1.** Deserving contempt; base: *an abject coward.* **2.** Miserable; wretched: *Medieval serfs lived in abject poverty.* **—ab′ject′ly** *adv.* **—ab·ject′ness** *n.* —SEE NOTE AT **inject.**

ab·jure (ăb-**jŏŏr′**) *tr.v.* **ab·jured, ab·jur·ing, ab·jures** To vow to give up; renounce; repudiate: *New citizens abjure allegiance to their former country.* **—ab′ju·ra′tion** *n.* **—ab·jur′er** *n.*

ab·la·tion (ă-**blā′**shən) *n.* **1.** The wearing away or destruction of the outer or forward surface of an object, such as a meteorite or spacecraft, as it moves very rapidly through the atmosphere. **2.** The process by which snow and ice are removed from a glacier or other mass of ice through melting or sublimation.

a·blaze (ə-**blāz′**) *adj.* **1.** On fire; in flames; blazing: *The barn was ablaze.* **2.** Brightly shining: *During the celebration the sky was ablaze with fireworks.* **—a·blaze′** *adv.*

a·ble (**ā′**bəl) *adj.* **a·bler, a·blest 1.** Having the power, ability, or means to do something: *We were not able to fix the leak. He is able to work part-time after school.* **2.** Having considerable skill or ability; capable or talented: *Most cats are very able hunters.* [From Latin *habilis,* adaptable, fit, from *habēre,* to have, handle.] **—a′bly** *adv.*

–able or **–ible** *suff.* A suffix that means: **1.** Capable of or likely to be affected by a certain action: *breakable; washable.* **2.** Worthy of a certain action: *honorable.* **3.** Inclined to a certain action: *variable.* —SEE NOTE.

a·ble-bod·ied (**ā′**bəl-**bŏd′**ēd) *adj.* Physically strong and healthy.

able seaman *n.* An experienced seaman certified to perform all routine duties at sea.

a·bloom (ə-**blōōm′**) *adj.* In bloom; flowering.

ab·lu·tion (ə-**blōō′**shən) *n.* A washing of the body, especially as part of a religious ceremony.

ab·ne·gate (**ăb′**nĭ-gāt′) *tr.v.* **ab·ne·gat·ed, ab·ne·gat·ing, ab·ne·gates** To renounce or give up: *abnegated his citizenship.*

ab·ne·ga·tion (ăb′nĭ-**gā′**shən) *n.* A giving up of one's rights, interests, or desires.

ab·nor·mal (ăb-**nôr′**məl) *adj.* Differing from what is normal, usual, or expected; not standard or ordinary: *flooding caused by an abnormal amount of rain.* **—ab·nor′mal·ly** *adv.*

ab·nor·mal·i·ty (ăb′nôr-**măl′**ĭ-tē) *n., pl.* **ab·nor·mal·i·ties 1.** The condition of not being normal. **2.** Something that is not normal: *I wear glasses because of abnormalities in my eyes.*

a·board (ə-**bôrd′**) *adv.* On, onto, or in a ship, train, or other passenger vehicle. ❖ *prep.* On, onto, or in: *life aboard ship.*

a·bode (ə-**bōd′**) *v.* A past tense and a past participle of **abide.** ❖ *n.* The place where one lives; a home. [From Middle English *abod,* home, from *abiden,* to wait; abide, from Old English *ābīdan.*]

a·bol·ish (ə-bŏl′ĭsh) *tr.v.* **a·bol·ished, a·bol·ish·ing, a·bol·ish·es** To put an end to; do away with: *Let's abolish the regulation that forbids eating in the study hall.*

ab·o·li·tion (ăb′ə-**lĭsh′**ən) *n.* **1.** The act or state of abolishing: *Many people favor an abolition of smoking.* **2.** often **Abolition** The abolishing of slavery in the United States.

ab·o·li·tion·ist (ăb′ə-**lĭsh′**ə-nĭst) *n.* **1.** A person who favors abolishing a custom, law, or practice. **2.** often **Abolitionist** A person favoring the abolition of slavery.

A-bomb (**ā′**bŏm′) *n.* An atomic bomb.

a·bom·i·na·ble (ə-**bŏm′**ə-nə-bəl) *adj.* **1.** Causing disgust or hatred; detestable; horrible: *an abominable crime.* **2.** Thoroughly unpleasant or disagreeable: *The cold, windy day was abominable weather for a hike.* [From Middle English, from Latin *abōminārī*, to abhor.] **—a·bom′i·na·bly** *adv.*

abominable snowman *n.* A hairy humanlike animal purported to inhabit the snows of the high Himalaya Mountains.

a·bom·i·nate (ə-**bŏm′**ə-nāt′) *tr.v.* **a·bom·i·nat·ed, a·bom·i·nat·ing, a·bom·i·nates** To detest; abhor: *He abominates most modern architecture.*

a·bom·i·na·tion (ə-bŏm′ə-**nā′**shən) *n.* **1.** A feeling of hatred or disgust: *an abomination of cruelty.* **2.** Something that causes hatred or disgust: *Many of these ugly concrete buildings are abominations.*

ab·o·rig·i·nal (ăb′ə-**rĭj′**ə-nəl) *adj.* **1.** Having existed in a region from the earliest times; native: *an aboriginal species.* **2a.** Relating to aborigines: *an aboriginal language.* **b.** often **Aboriginal** Relating to the peoples native to Australia.

ab·o·rig·i·ne (ăb′ə-**rĭj′**ə-nē) *n.* **1.** A member of a group of people who are the first known to have lived in a region. **2.** often **Aborigine** A member of any of the peoples native to Australia. [From Latin *aborīginēs*, original inhabitants : *ab*, from + *orīgō*, beginning.]

a·bort (ə-**bôrt′**) *v.* **a·bort·ed, a·bort·ing, a·borts** —*intr.* **1.** To miscarry. **2.** To end something, such as a rocket launch, before it is completed. —*tr.* **1.** To cause the abortion of (an embryo or fetus). **2.** To end before completion: *Heavy fog forced the pilot to abort the landing.*

a·bor·tion (ə-**bôr′**shən) *n.* **1.** The termination of a pregnancy, either deliberately or spontaneously. **2.** The ending of something before it is completed: *the abortion of the secret mission.*

a·bor·tive (ə-**bôr′**tĭv) *adj.* **1.** Not successful; fruitless: *an abortive revolution.* **2.** Partially or imperfectly developed: *an abortive organ.* **3.** Causing or meant to cause abortion: *an abortive drug.* **—a·bor′tive·ly** *adv.*

ABO system (ā′bē-**ō′**) *n.* A system for classifying human blood that uses four groups, A, B, AB, and O, to determine compatibility for transfusion.

a·bound (ə-**bound′**) *intr.v.* **a·bound·ed, a·bound·ing, a·bounds 1.** To be present in large numbers; be plentiful: *Books abound on the library shelves.* **2.** To be full; teem: *The forest abounds in wildlife.*

a·bout (ə-**bout′**) *adv.* **1.** Approximately; roughly: *The river is about 600 yards wide.* **2.** Almost; nearly: *The new highway is just about completed.* **3.** To or in a reverse direction: *Instantly the shark turned about.* **4.** In no particular direction: *We wandered about all afternoon.* **5.** To and fro: *Great waves tossed the ship about.* **6.** Everywhere; all around: *looking about for a hiding place.* **7.** In the area or vicinity; near: *people standing about, waiting for the store to open.* **8a.** On the point of. Followed by the infinitive with *to: We are just about to go.* **b.** *Informal* Anywhere near intending: *I'm not about to do anything he asks.* ❖ *prep.* **1a.** On all sides of; all around: *Thick fog is all about our boat.* **b.** Over different parts of; around: *a bear lumbering about the woods.* **2.** Near; close to: *The thief is still about the premises.* **3.** Concerning; having to do with; relating to: *stories about animals; the need to be careful about handling broken glass.* ❖ *adj.* Moving here and there; astir: *The patient is up and about.* [From Old English *onbūtan* : *on*, in + *būtan*, outside.]

a·bout-face (ə-**bout′fās′**) *n.* **1.** The act of turning the body to face in the opposite direction, especially in a military drill. **2.** A change to an opposite attitude or opinion: *The candidate's abrupt about-face on that issue startled everyone.* ❖ *intr.v.* **a·bout-faced, a·bout-fac·ing, a·bout-fac·es** To do an about-face.

a·bove (ə-**bŭv′**) *adv.* **1.** In or to a higher place; overhead: *Clouds floated above.* **2.** In an earlier part of a book, article, or other written piece: *in remarks quoted above.* ❖ *prep.* **1.** Over or higher than: *seagulls hovering just above the waves; a tree that rises above the others.* **2a.** Higher in rank, degree, or number than: *The president is above all military officers.* **b.** Too honorable to undertake: *He is above telling a lie.* **3.** Farther on than; beyond: *The road is closed above the bridge.* **4.** Beyond the level or reach of: *The noise was audible above the music.* **5.** North of: *Utah is above Arizona.* ❖ *adj.* Appearing or stated earlier: *the above figures.* ❖ *n.* **1.** An earlier part of a book, article, or other written piece. **2.** The people or things already referred to in a text: *All of the above are correct answers.* ◆ **above all** More than anything else: *truth above all.* [From Old English *abūfan* : *a-*, on + *būfan*, above.]

a·bove·board (ə-**bŭv′**bôrd′) *adv. & adj.* Without deceit or trickery; open; honest: *All dealings of government should be aboveboard.* [Originally a gambling term referring to the fact that when gamblers' hands were above the board or gaming table, they could not engage in trickery, such as changing cards, below the table.]

ab·ra·ca·dab·ra (ăb′rə-kə-**dăb′**rə) *n.* A word used as a magical incantation or charm.

a·brade (ə-**brād′**) *tr.v.* **a·brad·ed, a·brad·ing, a·brades** To wear down, rub away, or scrape by friction: *Flowing water abrades rocks in a stream.*

A·bra·ham (**ā′**brə-hăm′) In the Bible, the first patriarch of the Hebrew people. He was the husband of Sarah and the father of Isaac and Ishmael.

a·bra·sion (ə-**brā′**zhən) *n.* **1.** The act or process of scraping off or rubbing away by means of friction. **2.** A scraped area on the skin.

a·bra·sive (ə-**brā′**sĭv *or* ə-**brā′**zĭv) *adj.* **1.** Causing a rubbing away or wearing off: *Sand is an abrasive substance.* **2.** Harsh and rough in manner: *an abrasive personality.* ❖ *n.* A substance used in rubbing, grinding, or polishing. **—a·bra′sive·ly** *adv.* **—a·bra′sive·ness** *n.*

a·breast (ə-**brĕst′**) *adv.* **1.** Side by side in a line: *The band marched up the street four abreast.* **2.** Up to date: *keeping abreast of the latest news.*

a·bridge (ə-**brĭj′**) *tr.v.* **a·bridged, a·bridg·ing, a·bridg·es 1.** To reduce the length of; condense: *abridge a long novel by leaving out some chapters.* **2.** To limit; curtail: *The law was ruled unconstitutional because it abridged the rights of citizens.* [From Middle English *abregen*, from Old French *abregier*, from Late Latin *abbreviāre*, to shorten.]

a·bridg·ment also **a·bridge·ment** (ə-**brĭj′**mənt) *n.* **1.** The act of abridging or the condition of being abridged: *an abridgment of freedom.* **2.** An abridged version of something, such as a book or article.

a·broad (ə-**brôd′**) *adv. & adj.* **1.** Out of one's country; in or to foreign places: *traveling abroad.* **2.** Broadly or widely: *The wind scattered seeds abroad.* **3.** In circulation: *With rumors abroad, soon the whole town was in an uproar.*

ab·ro·gate (**ăb′**rə-gāt′) *tr.v.* **ab·ro·gat·ed, ab·ro·gat·ing, ab·ro·gates** To abolish (a law or privileges, for example); annul: *War abrogated the treaty between the neighboring countries.* **—ab′ro·ga′tion** *n.*

a·brupt (ə-**brŭpt′**) *adj.* **1.** Unexpected; sudden: *an abrupt*

WRITERS CHOOSE THEIR WORDS

Wednesday morning I take the bus wearing an **abomination** of an outfit that I pick out of the bag. It's a dress with a million polka dots of bright pink, red, green, and blue, with a red handkerchief over my hair.

—Lizabeth Zindel
The Secret Rites of Social Butterflies

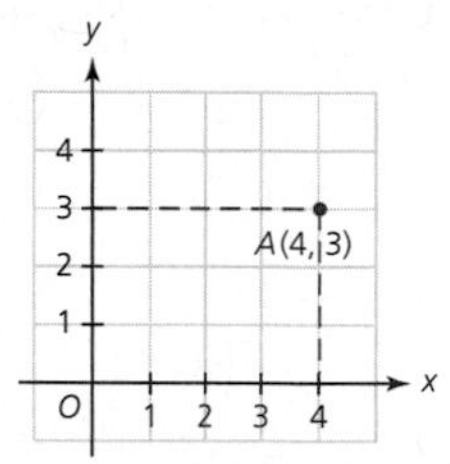

abscissa
The coordinates for *A* are (4,3); the abscissa is 4 and the ordinate is 3.

change in temperature. **2.** Short and brief so as to suggest rudeness or displeasure; brusque: *an abrupt answer made in anger.* **3.** Very steep: *The path ends in an abrupt descent to the water.* [From Latin *abruptus*, past participle of *abrumpere*, to break off : *ab-*, away + *rumpere*, to break.] **—a·brupt′ly** *adv.* **—a·brupt′ness** *n.*

ab·scess (ăb′sĕs′) *n.* A mass of pus formed at one place in the body and surrounded by inflamed tissue.

ab·scessed (ăb′sĕst′) *adj.* Having an abscess: *an abscessed tooth.*

ab·scis·sa (ăb-sĭs′ə) *n., pl.* **ab·scis·sas** or **ab·scis·sae** (ăb-sĭs′ē) The distance of a point from the y-axis on a graph. It is measured parallel to the x-axis in the Cartesian coordinate system.

ab·scond (ăb-skŏnd′) *intr.v.* **ab·scond·ed, ab·scond·ing, ab·sconds** To leave quickly and secretly and hide oneself, especially to avoid arrest: *The cashier absconded with the money.*

ab·sence (ăb′səns) *n.* **1.** The state of being away: *Soccer practice was canceled because of the coach's absence.* **2.** The period during which one is away: *an absence of four days.* **3.** A lack: *Rumors spread in the absence of reliable information.*

ab·sent (ăb′sənt) *adj.* **1.** Not present; not on hand: *Two students are absent today.* **2.** Lacking; missing: *Scales are absent in eels.* **3.** Not paying attention; absorbed in thought: *The dazed boy had an absent look on his face.* ❖ *tr.v.* (ăb-sĕnt′) **ab·sent·ed, ab·sent·ing, ab·sents** To keep (oneself) away: *I absented myself from work because of illness.* [From Middle English, from Latin *abesse*, to be away : *ab-*, away + *esse*, to be.]

ab·sen·tee (ăb′sən-tē′) *n.* A person who is absent. ❖ *adj.* **1.** Absent. **2.** Living somewhere else: *an absentee landlord.*

absentee ballot *n.* A ballot that is submitted before an election by a voter who is unable to go to the polls.

ab·sen·tee·ism (ăb′sən-tē′ĭz′əm) *n.* Habitual failure to appear, especially for work or other regular duty.

ab·sent·ly (ăb′sənt-lē) *adv.* As if lost in thought: *stared absently out the window.*

ab·sent-mind·ed (ăb′sənt-mīn′dĭd) *adj.* Tending to be lost in thought and to forget what one is doing; forgetful or preoccupied. **—ab′sent-mind′ed·ly** *adv.* **—ab′-sent-mind′ed·ness** *n.*

absent without leave *adj.* In the military, absent from one's post or duty without official permission.

ab·sinthe (ăb′sĭnth) *n.* A strong green alcoholic liquor flavored with wormwood and anise.

ab·so·lute (ăb′sə-lo͞ot′ *or* ăb′sə-**lo͞ot′**) *adj.* **1.** Complete; total: *absolute silence.* **2.** Not limited in any way: *absolute monarchy; absolute freedom.* **3.** Being fully so; utter: *an absolute mess.* **4.** Not to be doubted; positive: *absolute proof.* [From Middle English, from Latin *absolūtus*, unrestricted, past participle of *absolvere*, to absolve : *ab-*, away + *solvere*, to loosen.] **—ab′so·lute′ness** *n.*

ab·so·lute·ly (ăb′sə-lo͞ot′lē *or* ăb′sə-**lo͞ot′**lē) *adv.* Completely; perfectly: *I am absolutely certain. Stand absolutely still.*

absolute pitch *n.* **1.** The precise pitch of a tone as established by its frequency. **2.** The ability to identify any pitch heard or produce any pitch referred to by name; perfect pitch.

absolute temperature *n.* Temperature measured relative to absolute zero.

absolute value *n.* The value of a number without regard to its sign. For example, +3 and −3 each have the absolute value of 3.

absolute zero *n.* The lowest possible temperature of matter, at which all molecules stop moving, and equal to −459.67°F or −273.15°C.

ab·so·lu·tion (ăb′sə-**lo͞o′**shən) *n.* The formal forgiveness of a sin by a priest.

ab·so·lut·ism (ăb′sə-lo͞o′tĭz′əm) *n.* A form of government in which the ruler has unlimited power.

ab·solve (əb-**zŏlv′** *or* əb-**sŏlv′**) *tr.v.* **ab·solved, ab·solv·ing, ab·solves 1.** To clear of blame of guilt: *Evidence absolved the suspect of being involved in the crime.* **2.** To grant formal forgiveness to (someone) for sins committed. **3.** To release, as from a promise, duty, or obligation: *Paying off the loan absolved her of any obligation to the bank.* [From Middle English *absolven*, from Latin *absolvere*.] **—ab·solv′a·ble** *adj.*

ab·sorb (əb-**zôrb′**) *tr.v.* **ab·sorbed, ab·sorb·ing, ab·sorbs 1.** To take in; soak up: *A paper towel absorbed the water.* **2.** To take in and make a part of something: *Plants absorb energy from the sun. New York absorbed many immigrants.* **3.** To take in without transmitting or reflecting: *Thick curtains absorb sound.* **4.** To receive or withstand with little effect or reaction: *The car bumper absorbed the force of the collision.* **5.** To occupy the full attention of: *Homework completely absorbed her thoughts.* **6.** To learn; acquire: *We had trouble absorbing the new material in math.* **7.** To take up completely: *My job after school absorbs all of my time.* **8.** To assume the burden of: *Many businesses absorb the extra costs of mailing.* [From Latin *absorbēre*, to swallow up : *ab-*, away + *sorbēre*, to suck.] **—ab·sorb′er** *n.*

ab·sorbed (əb-**zôrbd′**) *adj.* Completely interested: *The absorbed look on their faces indicated they enjoyed hearing the story.*

ab·sor·bent (ăd-**zôr′**bənt) *adj.* Capable of absorbing: *absorbent cotton.*

ab·sorb·ing (əb-**zôr′**bĭng) *adj.* Extremely interesting: *an absorbing novel.*

ab·sorp·tion (əb-**zôrp′**shən) *n.* The act or process of absorbing or the condition of being absorbed: *absorption through the skin; absorption of new graduates in the job market.*

absorption spectrum *n.* A spectrum produced when light or other radiation passes through a gas or liquid that absorbs only certain wavelengths, resulting in a distinctive pattern of light and dark bands that indicates what chemical element or compound is present.

ab·stain (ăb-**stān′**) *intr.v.* **ab·stained, ab·stain·ing, ab·stains 1.** To keep from doing something by one's own choice; refrain: *He abstains from eating meat.* **2.** To refrain from voting: *Two councilors voted in favor of the measure and three councilors abstained.* **—ab·stain′er** *n.*

ab·ste·mi·ous (ăb-**stē′**mē-əs) *adj.* Eating and drinking in moderation. **—ab·ste′mi·ous·ly** *adv.*

ab·sten·tion (ăb-**stĕn′**shən) *n.* **1.** The practice of abstaining: *Abstention from candy helps prevent cavities.* **2.** A vote that is deliberately withheld, as in a meeting or legislature: *one vote for, two against, and four abstentions.*

ab·sti·nence (**ăb′**stə-nəns) *n.* The act or practice of refraining from indulging an appetite or desire. **—ab′sti·nent** *adj.*

ab·stract (ăb-**străkt′** *or* **ăb′**străkt′) *adj.* **1.** Thought of apart from any particular object or thing. For example, *softness* is an abstract quality. **2.** Difficult to understand: *Your complicated explanation is too abstract for me.* **3.** In art, concerned with designs or shapes that do not realistically represent any person or thing: *an abstract painting full of strange shapes.* ❖ *n.* (**ăb′**străkt′) A brief summary of the main points of a text: *a short abstract of a speech.* ❖ *tr.v.* (ăb-**străkt′**) **ab·stract·ed, ab·stract·ing, ab·stracts 1.** To take away; remove. **2.** To consider (an idea, for example) as separate from particular examples or objects: *abstract a law of nature from a laboratory experiment.* **3.** To make a summary of: *It was not easy to abstract his article.* ◆ **in the abstract** In theory but not necessarily in practice: *In the abstract, canoeing is relaxing, but we found it to be hard work.* [From Middle English, from Latin *abstrahere*, to draw away :

ă	pat	ôr	core
ā	pay	oi	boy
âr	care	ou	out
ä	father	o͝o	took
ĕ	pet	o͝or	lure
ē	be	o͞o	boot
ĭ	pit	ŭ	cut
ī	bite	ûr	urge
îr	pier	th	thin
ŏ	pot	*th*	this
ō	toe	zh	vision
ô	paw	ə	about

abs-, ab-, away + *trahere*, to draw.] **—ab·stract′ly** *adv.* **—ab·stract′ness** *n.*

ab·stract·ed (ăb-străk′tĭd) *adj.* Lost or deep in thought; absent-minded. **—ab·stract′ed·ly** *adv.*

ab·strac·tion (ăb-străk′shən) *n.* **1.** The act or process of considering something, such as a quality, apart from particular instances or things. **2.** An idea or quality that is thought of apart from any particular instance or thing: *Truth and beauty are abstractions.* **3.** Absent-mindedness: *In his abstraction, he didn't say "hello."* **4.** An abstract work of art.

ab·struse (ăb-stro͞os′) *adj.* Hard to understand: *abstruse theories of atomic interaction.* **—ab·struse′ly** *adv.* **—ab·struse′ness** *n.*

ab·surd (əb-sûrd′ *or* əb-zûrd′) *adj.* Plainly untrue or contrary to common sense; ridiculous: *It would be absurd to walk backward all the time.* **—ab·surd′ly** *adv.* **—ab·surd′ness** *n.*

ab·surd·i·ty (əb-sûr′dĭ-tē *or* əb-zûr′dĭ-tē) *n.* **1.** The state of being absurd; foolishness. **2.** An absurd action, thing, or idea.

A·bu Dha·bi (ä′bo͞o dä′bē) The capital of the United Arab Emirates, in eastern Arabia on the Persian Gulf. Abu Dhabi has enormous oil revenues.

A·bu·ja (ä-bo͞o′jä) The capital of Nigeria, in the central part of the country northeast of Lagos.

a·bun·dance (ə-bŭn′dəns) *n.* **1.** A great amount or quantity; a plentiful supply: *The heavy spring rains gave us an abundance of water for the summer.* **2.** The condition of being in rich supply: *We found berries in abundance growing by the roadside.*

a·bun·dant (ə-bŭn′dənt) *adj.* **1.** Existing in great supply; very plentiful: *Abundant rainfall swelled the rivers.* **2.** Rich; abounding: *a forest abundant in oak trees.* [From Middle English *aboundant*, from Latin *abundāre*, to overflow.] **—a·bun′dant·ly** *adv.*

a·buse (ə-byo͞oz′) *tr.v.* **a·bused, a·bus·ing, a·bus·es 1.** To use improperly; misuse: *abuse a special privilege.* **2.** To hurt or injure by treating badly; mistreat: *abused his eyesight by reading in poor light.* **3.** To subject to unwanted or improper sexual activity. **4.** To attack or injure with words; revile: *The candidates abused each other in sharp debate.* ❖ *n.* (ə-byo͞os′) **1a.** Improper use; misuse: *drug abuse.* **b.** Rough treatment: *The truck received a lot of abuse when we moved the furniture.* **2a.** Treatment so harsh or severe as to cause injury to the body or mind: *physical abuse; psychological abuse.* **b.** Unwanted and inappropriate sexual activity, especially when forced on one person by another. **3.** A corrupt practice or evil custom: *Punishing his employees without reason was an abuse of power.* **4.** Insulting language: *Baseball umpires take a lot of abuse from the crowd.* [From Middle English *abusen*, from Latin *abūtī* : *ab-*, away + *ūtī*, to use.] **—a·bus′er** *n.*

a·bu·sive (ə-byo͞o′sĭv) *adj.* **1.** Using coarse and insulting language: *abusive remarks.* **2.** Causing physical or psychological harm to another person. **—a·bu′sive·ly** *adv.* **—a·bu′sive·ness** *n.*

a·but (ə-bŭt′) *v.* **a·but·ted, a·but·ting, a·buts** *—intr.* To touch at one end or side; lie adjacent: *Our fence abuts on our neighbor's property.* *—tr.* To border on; be next to: *The garage abuts the house.*

a·but·ment (ə-bŭt′mənt) *n.* **1.** A support for the end of a bridge, arch, or beam. **2.** The point where a support joins the thing it is supporting.

a·buzz (ə-bŭz′) *adj.* **1.** Filled with a buzzing sound. **2.** Filled with activity or talk.

a·bys·mal (ə-bĭz′məl) *adj.* **1.** Too deep to be measured; bottomless: *abysmal despair; abysmal ignorance.* **2.** Very bad: *an abysmal performance.* **—a·bys′mal·ly** *adv.*

a·byss (ə-bĭs′) *n.* A very deep and large hole; a seemingly bottomless space: *The scientists sent a probe into the abyss of the volcano.* [From Middle English *abissus*, from Greek *abussos*, bottomless : *a-*, without + *bussos*, bottom.]

Ab·ys·sin·i·a (ăb′ĭ-sĭn′ē-ə) A name historically used for Ethiopia until the mid-1900s.

Ac The symbol for the element **actinium.**

AC *abbr.* An abbreviation of: **1.** also **A/C** air conditioning. **2.** alternating current. **3.** area code.

a·ca·cia (ə-kā′shə) *n.* Any of various often spiny trees or shrubs of warm climates, having feathery leaves and clusters of small usually yellow flowers.

acacia

ac·a·dem·ic (ăk′ə-dĕm′ĭk) *adj.* **1.** Relating to a school or college: *an academic degree.* **2.** Relating to studies that involve reading and abstract thinking instead of practical or technical skills: *History and languages are academic studies.* **3.** Having no practical purpose or value: *Your point is purely academic and won't make any difference in the end.* **—ac′a·dem′i·cal·ly** *adv.*

ac·a·de·mi·cian (ăk′ə-də-mĭsh′ən *or* ə-kăd′ə-mĭsh′ən) *n.* A member of an academy or a society for promoting literature, art, science, and other studies.

a·cad·e·my (ə-kăd′ə-mē) *n., pl.* **a·cad·e·mies 1.** A school for a special field of study: *a naval academy.* **2.** A private high school. **3.** A society of scholars, scientists, or artists. [From Middle English *Achadomie*, the school where Plato taught, from Greek *Akadēmeia*.]

A·ca·di·a (ə-kā′dē-ə) A region and former French colony of eastern Canada, chiefly in Nova Scotia but also including Prince Edward Island and the coastal area from the St. Lawrence River south into Maine. During the French and Indian War many Acadians migrated or were deported to southern territories, including Louisiana, where their descendants came to be known as Cajuns.

A·ca·di·an (ə-kā′dē-ən) *adj.* Relating to Acadia or its people, language, or culture. ❖ *n.* **1.** One of the French settlers of Acadia. **2.** A descendant of these settlers.

a·can·thus (ə-kăn′thəs) *n., pl.* **a·can·thus·es** or **a·can·thi** (ə-kăn′thī′) **1.** Any of various plants of the Mediterranean region with large spiny leaves and showy spikes of white or purplish flowers. **2.** A design in the form of acanthus leaves, such as the carving on the capital of a Corinthian column.

acanthus
acanthus pattern on a Corinthian column

a cap·pel·la (ä′ kə-pĕl′ə) *adv.* In music, without instrumental accompaniment: *a duet sung a cappella.*

Ac·a·pul·co (ăk′ə-po͞ol′kō *or* ä′kä-po͞ol′kō) A city of southern Mexico on the Pacific Ocean. It is a popular resort.

ac·cede (ăk-sēd′) *intr.v.* **ac·ced·ed, ac·ced·ing, ac·cedes 1.** To consent; agree; yield: *I acceded to her request and went in spite of my cold.* **2.** To come or succeed to a public office or position: *The young princess acceded to the throne.*

ac·cel·er·an·do (ä-chĕl′ə-rän′dō) *adv. & adj.* In music, gradually becoming faster.

ac·cel·er·ate (ăk-sĕl′ə-rāt′) *v.* **ac·cel·er·at·ed, ac·cel·er·at·ing, ac·cel·er·ates** *—tr.* **1.** To cause to go faster; speed up: *accelerate one's pace to a run.* **2.** In physics, to change the speed or direction of (a moving body): *Gravity accelerates a falling object at 32 feet per second per second near the earth's surface.* **3.** To cause to happen earlier; hasten: *Eating a lot of candy may accelerate tooth decay.* *—intr.* To move, act, or occur at a faster pace: *The car accelerated on the downhill slope. Erosion of the soil accelerated after the brush fire.* [From Latin *accelerāre* : *ad-*, intensive prefix + *celerāre*, to quicken.]

ac·cel·er·a·tion (ăk-sĕl′ə-rā′shən) *n.* **1.** The act or process of accelerating. **2.** The rate of change in the speed or direction of a moving body with respect to time. —SEE NOTE AT **force.**

ac·cel·er·a·tor (ăk-sĕl′ə-rā′tər) *n.* **1.** A device that controls the speed of a machine, especially the pedal that increases the flow of fuel to the motor of an automobile or truck. **2.** A substance that increases the rate of a chemical reaction. **3.** A particle accelerator.

ac·cel·er·om·e·ter (ăk-sĕl′ə-**rŏm′**ĭ-tər) *n.* An instrument that measures acceleration, especially of an aircraft.

ac·cent (**ăk′**sĕnt′) *n.* **1.** The stress or force with which a speaker utters one or more syllables of a word compared with the other syllables of the word. In the word *butter,* the accent is on the first syllable. **2.** An accent mark. **3.** A style of speech or pronunciation that is typical of a certain region or country: *She speaks with a French accent.* **4a.** Emphasis given to a musical note, as by making it louder or lengthening its duration. **b.** A mark in musical notation indicating such emphasis. **5.** Rhythmical stress given to a word or syllable in a line of poetry. **6.** A special feature or distinguishing quality; an emphasis: *a cooking show with an accent on hot spices.* ❖ *tr.v.* (**ăk′**sĕnt′ *or* ăk-**sĕnt′**) **ac·cent·ed, ac·cent·ing, ac·cents 1.** To stress in speech or in music: *accent the first syllable of a word; accent every third note.* **2.** To place an accent mark over. **3.** To give emphasis or prominence to; accentuate: *Her speech accented the accomplishments made over the last decade.* [From Middle English, from Latin *accentus,* accentuation : *ad-,* to + *cantus,* song.]

accent mark *n.* **1.** A mark showing that a syllable in a word is accented or stressed when the word is pronounced. **2.** In certain foreign languages, and in English words borrowed from such languages, a mark placed over a letter to indicate a certain feature of pronunciation. For example, in the word *exposé* the final *e* is pronounced like the *a* in *state.* **3.** A mark indicating rhythmical stress in a line of poetry.

ac·cen·tu·ate (ăk-**sĕn′**cho͞o-āt′) *tr.v.* **ac·cen·tu·at·ed, ac·cen·tu·at·ing, ac·cen·tu·ates 1.** To give prominence to; stress or emphasize: *A red background accentuates the letters of a stop sign.* **2.** To pronounce with a stress or accent. **3.** To mark with an accent mark. **—ac·cen′tu·a′tion** *n.*

ac·cept (ăk-**sĕpt′**) *v.* **ac·cept·ed, ac·cept·ing, ac·cepts** *—tr.* **1.** To receive (something offered), especially with approval: *accept a birthday gift.* **2.** To admit to a group: *They accepted me as a new member of the club.* **3.** To regard as proper or right: *Both sides accepted the judge's ruling.* **4.** To regard as correct or true; believe in: *We accepted your explanation of what happened.* **5.** To put up with; endure: *You can accept the situation or do something to change it.* **6.** To say "yes" to; answer affirmatively: *I accept your invitation.* **7.** To take up; assume: *You must accept responsibility for your own actions.* *—intr.* To receive something offered. [From Middle English *accepten,* from Latin *accipere* : *ad-,* to + *capere,* to take.]

ac·cept·a·ble (ăk-**sĕp′**tə-bəl) *adj.* **1.** Adequate to satisfy a need, requirement, or standard; satisfactory: *acceptable behavior.* **2.** Satisfactory but not superior: *Her work in chemistry is acceptable, but she could do better.* **—ac·cept′a·bil′i·ty** *n.* **—ac·cept′a·bly** *adv.*

ac·cep·tance (ăk-**sĕp′**təns) *n.* **1.** The act of taking something offered: *the acceptance of a new job.* **2.** The act of admitting to a group or organization: *acceptance of new members into the club.* **3.** A notification that someone or something has been accepted: *received an acceptance from her first-choice college.* **4.** Favorable reception; approval: *Acceptance of seat belts among the public has greatly reduced injuries in car accidents.* **5.** Belief in something as true; agreement: *Acceptance of the theory has been slow.*

ac·cept·ed (ăk-**sĕp′**tĭd) *adj.* Widely used or recognized: *an accepted treatment for pneumonia.*

ac·cess (**ăk′**sĕs) *n.* **1.** The right to enter, reach, or use: *We have access to secret information.* **2.** A way of approaching or reaching: *The only access to the pond is by a dirt road.* ❖ *tr.v.* **ac·cessed, ac·cess·ing, ac·cess·es** To obtain access to: *accessed her bank account online.* [From Middle English *acces,* from Latin *accēdere,* to arrive : *ad-,* to + *cēdere,* to come.]

access card *n.* A plastic card that can be swiped or held near a sensor to make electronic transactions or to gain entry to a restricted area.

access code *n.* A code that allows a person access to something, such as a computer network.

ac·ces·si·ble (ăk-**sĕs′**ə-bəl) *adj.* **1.** Easy to reach or approach: *The lake is accessible from the highway.* **2.** Easy to obtain: *The information is accessible on our computer.* **3.** Easy to understand or appreciate: *an accessible artwork.* **—ac·ces′si·bil′i·ty** *n.* **—ac·ces′si·bly** *adv.*

ac·ces·sion (ăk-**sĕsh′**ən) *n.* **1.** The act of coming to power or high office: *the king's accession to the throne.* **2.** An increase; an addition: *The museum has been improved by the accession of new fossils.* **3.** Something added: *The library's latest accession is a new encyclopedia.*

ac·ces·so·ry (ăk-**sĕs′**ə-rē) *n., pl.* **ac·ces·so·ries 1.** Something that is beyond what is needed but adds to the usefulness or appearance of something else: *a car full of accessories including a DVD player; a red scarf worn as an accessory with a black coat.* **2.** A person who is not present at the time a crime is committed but who aids a criminal either before or after a crime is committed. ❖ *adj.* Helping or adding to something more important: *The camera does not include accessory items like a flash.* [From Middle English *accessorie,* from Medieval Latin *accessor,* helper.]

ac·ci·dent (**ăk′**sĭ-dənt) *n.* **1.** An unexpected and undesirable event, especially one resulting in damage or harm; a mishap: *an automobile accident.* **2.** Something that happens without being planned or known in advance: *Our meeting was a lucky accident.* **3.** Chance or coincidence: *She ran into an old friend by accident.* [From Middle English, from Latin *accidere,* to happen : *ad-,* to + *cadere,* to fall.]

ac·ci·den·tal (ăk′sĭ-**dĕn′**tl) *adj.* Happening without being expected or intended: *the accidental discovery of gold in a river.* ❖ *n.* In music, a sharp, flat, or natural that is not in the key signature. **—ac′ci·den′tal·ly, ac′ci·dent′ly** *adv.*

ac·ci·dent-prone (**ăk′**sĭ-dənt-prōn′) *adj.* Tending to have accidents.

ac·claim (ə-**klām′**) *tr.v.* **ac·claimed, ac·claim·ing, ac·claims** To praise or approve publicly and enthusiastically: *The new movie has been acclaimed by all the critics.* ❖ *n.* Enthusiastic praise or approval. [From Latin *acclāmāre* : *ad-,* to + *clāmāre,* to shout.]

ac·cla·ma·tion (ăk′lə-**mā′**shən) *n.* **1.** Enthusiastic praise or applause; acclaim. **2.** An enthusiastic voice vote of approval taken without making an actual count.

❑ *These sound alike:* **acclamation, acclimation** (adaptation).

ac·cli·mate (**ăk′**lə-māt′) *tr. & intr.v.* **ac·cli·mat·ed, ac·cli·mat·ing, ac·cli·mates** To adapt or become adapted to new environmental conditions or surroundings: *acclimating the fish to the tank; has acclimated to the new routine.*

ac·cli·ma·tion (ăk′lə-**mā′**shən) *n.* The process of acclimating or the condition of being acclimated.

❑ *These sound alike:* **acclimation, acclamation** (acclaim).

ac·cli·ma·tize (ə-**klī′**mə-tīz′) *tr. & intr.v.* **ac·cli·ma·tized, ac·cli·ma·tiz·ing, ac·cli·ma·tiz·es** To acclimate. **—ac·cli′ma·ti·za′tion** (ə-klī′mə-tĭ-**zā′**shən) *n.*

ac·co·lade (**ăk′**ə-lād′ *or* **ăk′**ə-läd′) *n.* **1.** An expression of approval or praise: *That movie received the Academy Award and other accolades.* **2.** A ceremonial giving of knighthood, marked by a tap on the shoulder with the flat of a sword. [From Old French *acoler,* to embrace.]

ac·com·mo·date (ə-**kŏm′**ə-dāt′) *tr.v.* **ac·com·mo·dat·**

WRITERS CHOOSE THEIR WORDS

The sun streamed in from the windows behind him, and shadows lay over his face and **accentuated** the lines of his cheeks and jaw.

—Chaim Potok
The Chosen

WRITERS CHOOSE THEIR WORDS

Everyone in the room rose to applaud him. He seemed taken aback by the **accolade** and hastily gestured for us to resume our seats.

—Joan Manley
She Flew No Flags

ă	pat	ôr	core
ā	pay	oi	boy
âr	care	ou	out
ä	father	o͝o	took
ĕ	pet	o͝or	lure
ē	be	o͞o	boot
ĭ	pit	ŭ	cut
ī	bite	ûr	urge
îr	pier	th	thin
ŏ	pot	*th*	this
ō	toe	zh	vision
ô	paw	ə	about

ed, ac·com·mo·dat·ing, ac·com·mo·dates 1. To have enough space for: *an airport built to accommodate the largest planes.* **2.** To provide lodging or living space for: *accommodate guests at a hotel.* **3.** To take into consideration or make adjustments for; allow for: *a plan that accommodates the interests of teenagers.* **4.** To do (someone) a favor; oblige; help: *The clerk promised to accommodate us in our request.*

ac·com·mo·dat·ing (ə-**kŏm′**ə-dā′tĭng) *adj.* Inclined or ready to give assistance; helpful and obliging: *a clerk with an agreeable and accommodating manner.* **—ac·com′mo·dat′ing·ly** *adv.*

ac·com·mo·da·tion (ə-kŏm′ə-**dā′**shən) *n.* **1.** The act of accommodating or the state of being accommodated; adjustment: *His accommodation to suburban life was a painful experience.* **2. accommodations** A furnished room or other space provided for lodging: *We found the accommodations a bit cramped.* **3.** Adjustment by the lens of the eye in focusing on objects at differing distances.

ac·com·pa·ni·ment (ə-**kŭm′**pə-nē-mənt *or* ə-**kŭmp′**nē-mənt) *n.* **1.** Something that goes along with or supplements something else: *Crackers are a good accompaniment to soup.* **2.** A musical part played as support or embellishment, especially for a soloist.

ac·com·pa·nist (ə-**kŭm′**pə-nĭst *or* ə-**kŭmp′**nĭst) *n.* A performer who plays or sings a musical accompaniment.

ac·com·pa·ny (ə-**kŭm′**pə-nē) *tr.v.* **ac·com·pa·nied, ac·com·pa·ny·ing, ac·com·pa·nies 1.** To go along with: *The dog accompanied him through the woods.* **2.** To occur or happen in connection with: *Heat accompanies fire.* **3.** To provide with an addition; supplement: *The teacher accompanied the lesson with slides.* **4.** To play a musical accompaniment for: *A guitarist accompanied the singer on the song.*

SYNONYMS accompany, conduct, escort, chaperone These verbs mean to be with or to go with another or others. *Accompany* suggests going on an equal basis: *My friends accompanied me to the mall. Conduct* refers to the guidance of others: *The usher conducted the patrons to their seats in the theater. Escort* stresses that protective guidance: *The bodyguards escorted the candidate through the crowd. Chaperone* specifies the supervision by adults of young people: *The teachers will chaperone students during the field trip to the zoo.*

---

ac·com·plice (ə-**kŏm′**plĭs) *n.* A person who helps another do something wrong or illegal.

ac·com·plish (ə-**kŏm′**plĭsh) *tr.v.* **ac·com·plished, ac·com·plish·ing, ac·com·plish·es** To carry out; achieve; complete: *We accomplished our goal of building a greenhouse.* [From Middle English *accomplisshen*, from Old French *acomplir* : *a-*, to + *complir*, complete (from Latin *complēre*, to fill out).]

ac·com·plished (ə-**kŏm′**plĭsht) *adj.* Skilled because of practice or study; expert: *an accomplished musician.* See Synonyms at **proficient.**

ac·com·plish·ment (ə-**kŏm′**plĭsh-mənt) *n.* **1.** The act of carrying out; completion: *the accomplishment of a task.* **2.** Something accomplished; an achievement: *The first walk on the moon was a huge accomplishment in technology.* **3.** A skill acquired through training and practice: *Singing and painting are among the actor's many accomplishments.*

ac·cord (ə-**kôrd′**) *v.* **ac·cord·ed, ac·cord·ing, ac·cords** *—tr.* To give; grant: *Citizens are accorded certain rights by our Constitution. —intr.* To be in agreement or harmony: *Your ideas accord with mine.* ❖ *n.* **1.** Agreement; harmony: *His ideas are in accord with mine.* **2.** A formal act of agreement; settlement between conflicting parties: *The strikers and the employers reached an accord.* ◆ **of (one's) own accord** or **on (one's) own accord** By one's own choice or wish; voluntarily: *The children returned of their own accord.* [From Middle English *accorden*, from Medieval Latin *accordāre*, to bring into agreement, ultimately from Latin *cor*, heart.]

ac·cor·dance (ə-**kôr′**dns) *n.* Agreement; keeping: *Play the game in accordance with the rules.*

ac·cord·ing·ly (ə-**kôr′**dĭng-lē) *adv.* **1.** In keeping with what is known, stated, or expected: *Learn the rules and act accordingly.* **2.** Therefore; consequently: *The student was sick; accordingly, the teacher called the parents.*

ac·cord·ing to (ə-**kôr′**dĭng) *prep.* **1.** As stated or indicated by; on the authority of: *According to the weather report, it will rain tomorrow.* **2.** In keeping with; in agreement with: *Proceed according to instructions.* **3.** As determined by: *a list arranged according to the first letter of each word.* **4.** In proportion to: *Salt is added according to the amount of water used.*

ac·cor·di·on (ə-**kôr′**dē-ən) *n.* A portable wind instrument with a small keyboard and metal reeds that sound when air is forced past them by means of a pleated bellows. ❖ *adj.* Having folds like the bellows of an accordion: *a skirt with accordion pleats.* [From German *Akkordion*, from Old French *acorder*, to be in harmony, from Medieval Latin *accordāre*, to bring into agreement.]

accordion

ac·cost (ə-**kôst′**) *tr.v.* **ac·cost·ed, ac·cost·ing, ac·costs** To come up to and speak to, often in an aggressive or insistent way: *A stranger accosted me and asked me for money.*

ac·count (ə-**kount′**) *n.* **1.** A written or spoken description of events; a narrative: *The explorers gave an exciting account of their adventures.* **2a.** A reason given for an action or event: *Give an account for your strange behavior.* **b.** A basis or ground: *You do not have to worry on that account.* **3.** A record or written statement of business dealings or money received or spent: *A bookkeeper kept the company's accounts.* **4.** A business arrangement, as with a bank or store, in which money is kept, exchanged, or owed: *a savings account in the local bank; a charge account at the drugstore.* **5.** A customer or client of a company or store: *an advertising agency with several accounts that are big manufacturing companies.* **6.** A formal arrangement granting access to a computer system or online service, usually protected by a password. **7.** Importance; standing; worth: *Most gossip is of little account.* ❖ *tr.v.* **ac·count·ed, ac·count·ing, ac·counts** To believe to be; consider; regard: *The judge was accounted fair and wise.* ◆ **account for 1.** To give the reason for; explain: *How do you account for your absence from practice?* **2.** To be the reason for: *Bad weather accounted for the delay in their arrival.* **on account** On credit: *I bought this coat on account.* **on account of** Because of: *We were late on account of the traffic jam. Don't stay home on account of me.* **on no account** Under no circumstances: *On no account should you touch live wires.* **on (someone's) account** For someone's benefit: *Don't worry on my account.* [From Middle English, from Latin *computāre*, to sum up.]

ac·count·a·ble (ə-**koun′**tə-bəl) *adj.* Expected or required to answer for one's actions; responsible: *Senators are accountable to the people who elect them.* **—ac·count′a·bil′i·ty** *n.*

ac·coun·tant (ə-**koun′**tənt) *n.* A person who keeps or inspects financial records, as of a business, government agency, or person.

ac·count·ing (ə-**koun′**tĭng) *n.* The occupation or methods of keeping financial records, as of a business or government agency.

ac·cou·tre or **ac·cou·ter** (ə-**ko͞o′**tər) *tr.v.* **ac·cou·tred, ac·cou·tring, ac·cou·tres** or **ac·cou·tered, ac·cou·ter·ing, ac·cou·ters** To equip with clothing and equipment, especially for a particular purpose: *The explorers were accoutred for outdoor living.*

ac·cou·tre·ments or **ac·cou·ter·ments** (ə-ko͞o′trə-mənts *or* ə-ko͞o′tər-mənts) *pl.n.* **1.** Articles of clothing or equipment: *boots, breeches, and other accoutrements of riding.* **2.** A soldier's equipment, including bedding and a backpack, but not including clothing and weapons.

Ac·cra (ăk′rə *or* ə-krä′) The capital of Ghana, in the southeast part of the country on the Gulf of Guinea. Accra has been an important economic center since the completion of the railroad in 1923.

ac·cred·it (ə-krĕd′ĭt) *tr.v.* **ac·cred·it·ed, ac·cred·it·ing, ac·cred·its 1.** To regard as the work of; ascribe or attribute: *The discovery of radium is accredited to Marie Curie.* **2.** To approve or record as having met certain standards: *This high school has been accredited by the state.* **3.** To give official standing to (an ambassador, envoy, or other representative).

ac·cred·i·ta·tion (ə-krĕd′ĭ-tā′shən) *n.* Official approval of a school, hospital, or agency for having met certain standards.

ac·cre·tion (ə-krē′shən) *n.* **1.** The process of increasing in size as a result of being added to or growing: *stalactites formed by the slow accretion of minerals.* **2.** Something added that produces such an increase: *thick accretions of rust on the pipes.*

ac·cru·al (ə-kro͞o′əl) *n.* **1.** The process of accruing; increase: *Education leads to an accrual of knowledge.* **2.** Something that has accrued.

ac·crue (ə-kro͞o′) *intr.v.* **ac·crued, ac·cru·ing, ac·crues 1.** To come to someone as a gain or addition: *Interest accrues in my savings account.* **2.** To increase or come about as a result of growth: *Our knowledge of disease has accrued from scientific research.* [From Middle English *acreuen*, from Latin *accrēscere*, to grow : *ad-*, to + *crēscere*, to arise.]

ac·cu·mu·late (ə-kyo͞om′yə-lāt′) *v.* **ac·cu·mu·lat·ed, ac·cu·mu·lat·ing, ac·cu·mu·lates** —*tr.* To gather together; pile up; collect: *By working hard and spending little he accumulated a great deal of money.* See Synonyms at **gather.** —*intr.* To become larger in amount or number: *During the storm deep piles of snow accumulated on the sidewalk.* [From Latin *accumulāre*, from *cumulus*, heap.]

ac·cu·mu·la·tion (ə-kyo͞om′yə-lā′shən) *n.* **1.** The collection or amassing of something: *a collection of seashells created by accumulation over many years.* **2.** An accumulated amount or mass of something: *the weekly accumulation of rubbish.*

ac·cu·ra·cy (ăk′yər-ə-sē) *n.* **1.** Freedom from error or mistake; correctness: *check the results for accuracy.* **2.** Exactness; precision: *a clock having great accuracy.*

ac·cu·rate (ăk′yər-ĭt) *adj.* **1.** Free from errors or mistakes; correct: *accurate answers.* **2.** Exact; precise: *an accurate description; an accurate method of measurement.* **3.** Working carefully and making few or no mistakes; meticulous: *an accurate proofreader.* [From Latin *accūrāre*, to do with care.] **—ac′cu·rate·ly** *adv.* **—ac′cu·rate·ness** *n.*

ac·curs·ed (ə-kûr′sĭd *or* ə-kûrst′) also **ac·curst** (ə-kûrst′) *adj.* **1.** Under a curse; damned. **2.** Hateful or detestable: *the accursed trade in ivory.* **—ac·curs′ed·ly** *adv.* **—ac·curs′ed·ness** *n.*

ac·cu·sa·tion (ăk′yo͞o-zā′shən) *n.* **1.** A statement or formal declaration that a person is guilty of wrongdoing: *The lawyer presented a written accusation against the suspected criminal.* **2.** The act of accusing or the state of being accused of wrongdoing: *False accusation is a serious offense.*

ac·cu·sa·tive (ə-kyo͞o′zə-tĭv) *adj.* Relating to the grammatical case in languages like Latin that indicates the direct object of a verb or the object of a preposition. ❖ *n.* The accusative case.

ac·cuse (ə-kyo͞oz′) *tr.v.* **ac·cused, ac·cus·ing, ac·cus·es 1.** To make a declaration charging (someone) with wrongdoing: *The lawyers accused them of polluting the river.* **2.** To find at fault; blame: *She accused her little brother of messing up her room.* [From Middle English *acusen*, from Latin *accūsāre*.] **—ac·cus′er** *n.*

ac·cused (ə-kyo͞ozd′) *n., pl.* **accused** The defendant in a criminal case: *The accused was put on trial for theft.*

ac·cus·tom (ə-kŭs′təm) *tr.v.* **ac·cus·tomed, ac·cus·tom·ing, ac·cus·toms** To make familiar with; get (someone) used to: *Growing up in Florida had accustomed her to hot weather.*

ac·cus·tomed (ə-kŭs′təmd) *adj.* Usual; habitual; familiar: *The researcher presented his discovery with his accustomed modesty.* ◆ **accustomed to** Used to; in the habit of: *Farmers are accustomed to working long days.*

ace (ās) *n.* **1.** A playing card with one figure of its suit in the center. **2.** A person who can do something very well or is an expert in some field: *That senior is our school team's pitching ace.* **3.** In tennis, a point scored when one's opponent fails to return a serve. **4.** A fighter pilot who has destroyed a number of enemy planes. ❖ *tr.v.* **aced, ac·ing, ac·es 1.** To serve an ace against (an opposing player) in tennis. **2.** *Slang* To perform extremely well on: *aced the test; aced my interview.* ◆ **ace in the hole** A hidden advantage or resource kept in reserve until needed. [From Middle English *as*, side of a die with one dot, from Latin, unit of weight, small copper coin.]

a·cel·lu·lar (ā-sĕl′yə-lər) *adj.* Not made up of cells or not containing cells: *acellular vaccines.*

a·cer·bic (ə-sûr′bĭk) *adj.* Sour or bitter, as in taste, character, or tone: *acerbic insults.* **—a·cer′bi·cal·ly** *adv.*

ac·e·tate (ăs′ĭ-tāt′) *n.* **1.** A salt or ester of acetic acid: *lead acetate.* **2.** Cellulose acetate or a product derived from it, such as a fabric or fiber.

a·ce·tic acid (ə-sē′tĭk) *n.* A clear, pungent, colorless organic acid that occurs naturally in vinegar and is also produced commercially from ethyl alcohol and from wood. It is used as a solvent, in making rubber and plastics, and in photographic chemicals.

ac·e·tone (ăs′ĭ-tōn′) *n.* A colorless, strong-smelling liquid that vaporizes very easily, burns very readily, and is widely used as a solvent.

a·ce·tyl·cho·line (ə-sēt′l-kō′lēn′) *n.* A chemical compound that acts as a neurotransmitter in the central and autonomic nervous systems and activates muscles in the peripheral nervous system.

a·cet·y·lene (ə-sĕt′l-ēn′ *or* ə-sĕt′l-ən) *n.* A colorless, very flammable gas that is composed of carbon and hydrogen, is used in torches to cut through metal, and can be burned to produce light.

a·ce·tyl·sal·i·cyl·ic acid (ə-sēt′l-săl′ĭ-sĭl′ĭk) *n.* Aspirin.

ache (āk) *intr.v.* **ached, ach·ing, aches 1.** To hurt with or feel a dull steady pain: *My tooth aches. I ache all over.* **2.** To feel sadness or sympathy: *My heart aches for the student who didn't get the award.* **3.** To want very much; long; yearn: *I am aching to get home.* ❖ *n.* **1.** A dull, steady pain: *Growing pains often appear as aches in the legs.* **2.** A feeling of sadness or longing. [From Old English *acan*.]

a·chieve (ə-chēv′) *tr.v.* **a·chieved, a·chiev·ing, a·chieves 1.** To gain with effort or despite difficulty: *achieve fame as a singer.* See Synonyms at **reach. 2.** To succeed in accomplishing; bring about: *achieved a reduction in air pollution.* [From Middle English *acheven*, from Old French *(venir) a chef*, (to come) to a head.] **—a·chiev′er** *n.*

a·chieve·ment (ə-chēv′mənt) *n.* **1.** The act or process of attaining or accomplishing something: *The achievement of voting rights for women was the main focus of her life.*

ace
four aces from a deck of playing cards

acorn squash

ă	pat	ôr	core
ā	pay	oi	boy
âr	care	ou	out
ä	father	o͝o	took
ĕ	pet	o͝or	lure
ē	be	o͞o	boot
ĭ	pit	ŭ	cut
ī	bite	ûr	urge
îr	pier	th	thin
ŏ	pot	*th*	this
ō	toe	zh	vision
ô	paw	ə	about

2. Something that has been achieved, especially as an outstanding accomplishment: *The development of the computer is a great achievement in technology.*

achievement test *n.* A test to measure how much a person has learned, especially at a particular grade level.

A·chil·les (ə-**kĭl′**ēz) *n.* In Greek mythology, a Greek hero of the Trojan War who was killed by an arrow shot into his heel, the only part of his body in which he could be wounded.

A·chil·les′ heel (ə-**kĭl′**ēz) *n.* A point of weakness or a vulnerable place: *Poor defense is the Achilles' heel of their team.*

Achilles tendon *n.* A strong tendon at the back of the leg connecting the calf muscles with the bone of the heel.

ach·ro·mat·ic (ăk′rə-**măt′**ĭk) *adj.* **1.** Refracting white light without breaking it up into the colors of the spectrum: *an achromatic telescope.* **2.** Lacking color; colorless.

achromatic lens *n.* A combination of lenses that forms an image in which the various colors of the spectrum that compose white light meet at a single focus.

ach·y (**ā′**kē) *adj.* **ach·i·er, ach·i·est** Filled with aches; having an ache: *Flu is usually accompanied by an achy feeling.*

ac·id (**ăs′**ĭd) *n.* Any of a class of substances that release hydrogen ions when dissolved in water and can react with a base to form salts. Acids turn blue litmus paper red and have a pH of less than 7. ❖ *adj.* **1.** Relating to or containing an acid: *an acid solution.* **2.** Having a sour taste: *the acid taste of lemons.* **3.** Sharp and biting; scornful or sarcastic: *an acid remark.* [From Latin *acidus*, sour.] —**ac′id·ly** *adv.* —**ac′id·ness** *n.*

a·cid·ic (ə-**sĭd′**ĭk) *adj.* **1.** Relating to or containing an acid: *an acidic solution.* **2.** Tending to form an acid.

a·cid·i·fy (ə-**sĭd′**ə-fī′) *tr. & intr.v.* **a·cid·i·fied, a·cid·i·fy·ing, a·cid·i·fies** To make or become acid.

a·cid·i·ty (ə-**sĭd′**ĭ-tē) *n.* The condition, quality, or degree of being acid: *The acidity of some soils is very high.*

acid rain *n.* Rain or other precipitation containing a high amount of acidity from polluting substances that form acid in water vapor. Acid rain is usually composed of a solution of sulfuric or nitric acid.

acid test *n.* A situation that provides a decisive test.

ac·knowl·edge (ăk-**nŏl′**ĭj) *tr.v.* **ac·knowl·edged, ac·knowl·edg·ing, ac·knowl·edg·es 1.** To admit the existence or truth of: *acknowledge one's mistakes.* **2.** To recognize the standing or authority of: *The teacher was acknowledged as an authority on butterflies.* **3a.** To express thanks for: *acknowledge a favor.* **b.** To recognize and reply to: *acknowledge the cheers of the crowd.* **4.** To state that one has received: *The college acknowledged my application with a postcard.* [From Middle English *aknowlechen*, probably blend of *knowlechen*, to acknowledge, and *aknouen*, to recognize (both from Old English *cnāwan*, to know).]

ac·knowl·edg·ment or **ac·knowl·edge·ment** (ăk-**nŏl′**ĭj-mənt) *n.* **1.** Something done or given in answer to or recognition of another's gift, favor, or message: *send an acknowledgment of an invitation.* **2.** The act of admitting the existence or truth of something; recognition: *His smile was acknowledgment that I had passed the test.*

ACL *abbr.* An abbreviation of anterior cruciate ligament.

ac·me (**ăk′**mē) *n.* The highest point, as of achievement or development: *the acme of perfection.*

ac·ne (**ăk′**nē) *n.* A condition in which the oil glands of the skin become clogged and infected, often causing pimples to form, especially on the face.

ac·o·lyte (**ăk′**ə-līt′) *n.* **1.** A person who assists the priest in performing religious ceremonies. **2.** An assistant, attendant, or follower.

A·con·ca·gua (ăk′ən-**kä′**gwə *or* ä′kən-**kä′**gwə) A mountain, 22,841 feet (6,962 meters) high, in the Andes of western Argentina near the Chilean border. It is the highest peak of the Western Hemisphere.

ac·o·nite (**ăk′**ə-nīt′) *n.* **1.** Any of various poisonous plants having blue, purple, or yellowish flowers shaped somewhat like a hood. **2.** The dried leaves and roots of some of these plants, formerly used medicinally.

a·corn (**ā′**kôrn′) *n.* The fruit of an oak, consisting of a thick-walled nut set in a woody base. [From Old English *æcern*.]

acorn squash *n.* A type of squash that is shaped somewhat like an acorn and has orange flesh and a hard, usually green rind.

a·cous·tic (ə-**ko͞o′**stĭk) *adj.* **1.** also **a·cous·ti·cal** (ə-**ko͞o′**stĭ-kəl) **a.** Relating to sound, the sense of hearing, or the science of sound: *the acoustic quality of a concert hall.* **b.** Designed to absorb or direct sound: *an acoustic ceiling.* **2.** Relating to a musical instrument that does not have electronic components for producing or enhancing sound: *an acoustic guitar.* —**a·cous′ti·cal·ly** *adv.*

a·cous·tics (ə-**ko͞o′**stĭks) *n.* **1.** *(used with a singular verb)* The scientific study of sound and its transmission. **2.** *(used with a plural verb)* The structural features of a room or building that determine how well sounds can be heard in it: *The acoustics of the concert hall were improved by lowering its ceiling.*

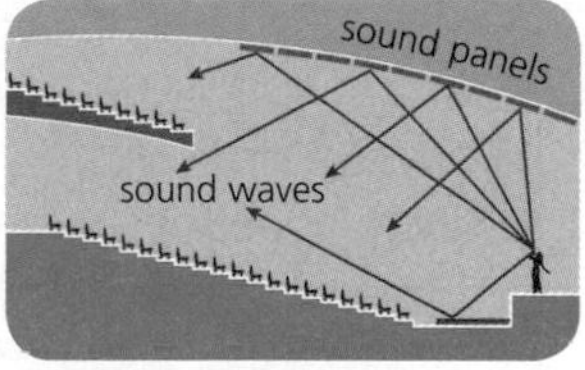

acoustics
Sound waves from a stage are deflected by sound panels and distributed throughout an auditorium.

ac·quaint (ə-**kwānt′**) *tr.v.* **ac·quaint·ed, ac·quaint·ing, ac·quaints 1.** To inform: *Acquaint us with your plans as soon as possible.* **2.** To make familiar: *Let me acquaint myself with the facts of the case.* [From Middle English *aqueinten*, from Medieval Latin *accognitāre*, to make known to.]

ac·quain·tance (ə-**kwān′**təns) *n.* **1.** Knowledge gained from experience; familiarity: *I have an acquaintance with Chinese painting.* **2.** A person whom one knows but who is not a close friend: *We have many acquaintances in town.* ◆ **make (someone's) acquaintance** To meet someone for the first time. —**ac·quain′tance·ship′** *n.*

ac·quaint·ed (ə-**kwān′**tĭd) *adj.* **1.** Known to one or each other: *We've been acquainted for years.* **2.** Informed; familiar: *I am not acquainted with her novels.*

ac·qui·esce (ăk′wē-**ĕs′**) *intr.v.* **ac·qui·esced, ac·qui·esc·ing, ac·qui·esc·es** To agree or yield without protest; consent quietly: *acquiesce to a demand; acquiesce in a decision.*

WRITERS CHOOSE THEIR WORDS

"I may be forced to **acquiesce** in these recent developments," responded his lordship, "but I can hardly be expected to make merry over them. I think that with your permission I will now wish you all a very good-night."

—Arthur Conan Doyle
"The Adventure of the Noble Bachelor"

ac·qui·es·cence (ăk′wē-**ĕs′**əns) *n.* Submission without protest; quiet agreement.

ac·qui·es·cent (ăk′wē-**ĕs′**ənt) *adj.* Agreeing or submitting without protest. —**ac′qui·es′cent·ly** *adv.*

ac·quire (ə-**kwīr′**) *tr.v.* **ac·quired, ac·quir·ing, ac·quires 1.** To get as the result of planning or endeavor; acquire: *acquire a bicycle; acquire new skills.* **2.** To come to have: *acquired a dislike of cats after being bitten several times.* [From Latin *acquīrere* : *ad-*, to + *quaerere*, to seek, get.] —**ac·quir′a·ble** *adj.*

ac·quired immunity (ə-**kwīrd′**) *n.* Immunity to a disease that develops from the presence of antibodies in the blood, as after an attack of the disease or vaccination against it.

ac·quire·ment (ə-**kwīr′**mənt) *n.* **1.** The act or process of acquiring: *the acquirement of property by inheritance.* **2.** A skill or an ability gained by effort or experience; an attainment: *a talented student of many acquirements.*

ac·qui·si·tion (ăk′wĭ-**zĭsh′**ən) *n.* **1.** The act or process of acquiring: *The museum's acquisition of a large art collection took many years.* **2.** Something acquired, especially as an addition to a collection or one's possessions: *the museum's newest acquisitions to its art collection.*

ac·quis·i·tive (ə-**kwĭz′**ĭ-tĭv) *adj.* **1.** Eager to acquire things, especially possessions: *an acquisitive collector of books.* **2.** Tending to acquire information: *the acquisitive mind of a scientist.* —**ac·quis′i·tive·ly** *adv.* —**ac·quis′i·tive·ness** *n.*

Acropolis
Athens, Greece

Washing
Ashore
Volumes of water
Ebb and flow on
Sandy beaches

acrostic

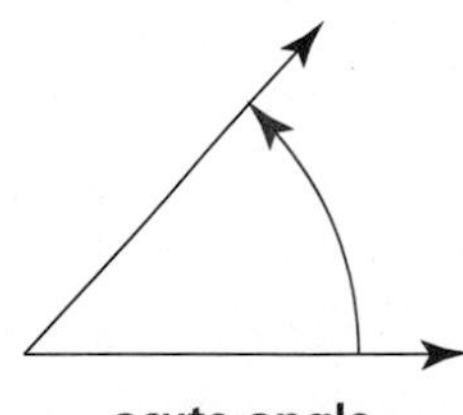

acute angle

ă	pat	ôr	core
ā	pay	oi	boy
âr	care	ou	out
ä	father	o͝o	took
ĕ	pet	o͝or	lure
ē	be	o͞o	boot
ĭ	pit	ŭ	cut
ī	bite	ûr	urge
îr	pier	th	thin
ŏ	pot	*th*	this
ō	toe	zh	vision
ô	paw	ə	about

ac·quit (ə-**kwĭt′**) *tr.v.* **ac·quit·ted, ac·quit·ting, ac·quits 1.** To free or clear from a formal accusation of wrongdoing: *A jury acquitted the suspect of the crime.* **2.** To conduct (oneself); behave: *The firefighters acquitted themselves bravely.* **—ac·quit′ter** *n.*

ac·quit·tal (ə-**kwĭt′**l) *n.* The freeing of a person from an accusation of wrongdoing by the judgment of a court: *The jury's vote of not guilty resulted in the defendant's acquittal.*

a·cre (**ā′**kər) *n.* **1.** A unit of area used in measuring land, equal to 43,560 square feet or about 4,047 square meters. **2. acres** Property in the form of land. [From Old English *æcer.*]

a·cre·age (**ā′**kər-ĭj *or* **ā′**krĭj) *n.* Land area measured in acres: *a national park of vast acreage.*

a·cre-foot (**ā′**kər-**fo͝ot′**) *n.* The volume of water that will cover an area of one acre to a depth of one foot; 43,560 cubic feet or about 1,235 cubic meters of water.

ac·rid (**ăk′**rĭd) *adj.* **1.** Harsh or bitter to the sense of taste or smell: *Acrid smoke from the blazing chemical plant filled the air.* **2.** Sharp or biting in tone or manner; nasty: *acrid comments of discontent.* [From Latin *ācer*, sharp.] **—ac′rid·ly** *adv.* **—ac′rid·ness** *n.*

ac·ri·mo·ni·ous (ăk′rə-**mō′**nē-əs) *adj.* Bitter or stinging in language or tone: *acrimonious exchanges among the candidates.* **—ac′ri·mo′ni·ous·ly** *adv.* **—ac′ri·mo′ni·ous·ness** *n.*

ac·ri·mo·ny (**ăk′**rə-mō′nē) *n.* Bitterness or ill-natured sharpness in manner or language: *sudden outbursts of acrimony between jealous partners.*

ac·ro·bat (**ăk′**rə-băt′) *n.* A person who performs athletic feats requiring great agility and balance, such as swinging on a trapeze or walking a tightrope. [From Greek *akrobatēs*, one who walks on tiptoe, acrobat : *akros*, topmost, outermost + *bainein*, to walk.]

ac·ro·bat·ic (ăk′rə-**băt′**ĭk) *adj.* Relating to or suggestive of an acrobat or acrobatics: *an acrobatic dive into the pool.* **—ac′ro·bat′i·cal·ly** *adv.*

ac·ro·bat·ics (ăk′rə-**băt′**ĭks) *n.* **1.** *(used with a singular or plural verb)* The art or performance of an acrobat. **2.** *(used with a plural verb)* A display of great skill and agility: *the singer's vocal acrobatics.*

ac·ro·nym (**ăk′**rə-nĭm′) *n.* A word formed from the first letters or parts of a series of words, such as *radar*, from *ra*dio *d*etection *a*nd *r*anging, and *OPEC*, from *O*rganization of *P*etroleum *E*xporting *C*ountries. [From Greek *akros*, topmost, outermost + Greek *onuma*, name.]

a·crop·o·lis (ə-**krŏp′**ə-lĭs) *n.* **1.** The high, fortified part of an ancient Greek city. **2. Acropolis** The hill in Athens on which the Parthenon stands.

a·cross (ə-**krôs′**) *prep.* **1.** On, at, or from the other side of: *a house across the road.* **2.** From one side of to the other: *a bridge across a river.* **3.** So as to cross; over; through: *draw lines across the paper.* ❖ *adv.* **1.** From one side to the other: *The bridge swayed as they drove across.* **2.** On or to the opposite side: *He sat across from me at the table.* **3.** In a way that is understandable: *put our ideas across to the listeners.* [From Middle English *acrois*, from Anglo-Norman *an croiz*, crosswise : *en, an*, in + *croiz*, cross.]

a·cros·tic (ə-**krô′**stĭk) *n.* A poem or series of lines in which certain letters, usually the first in each line, spell out a name, phrase, or message.

a·cryl·ic (ə-**krĭl′**ĭk) *n.* **1.** An acrylic resin. **2.** A paint made with acrylic resin. **3.** Any of a number of artificial fibers derived from acrylic acid and used in making certain long-wearing fabrics.

acrylic acid *n.* A colorless strong-smelling liquid that is used to form acrylic resins and is soluble in alcohol and water.

acrylic resin *n.* Any of a number of tough, clear plastics derived from acrylic acid and used in making paints and automobile parts.

act (ăkt) *n.* **1.** The process of doing something: *Police caught the robber in the act of stealing.* **2.** Something done; a deed: *an act of bravery.* **3.** A law, especially one enacted by a legislative body: *an act of Congress.* **4a.** One of the main divisions of a play or other dramatic work: *a play in three acts.* **b.** A performance for an audience, often forming part of a longer show: *a comedian's act.* **5.** An insincere pretense; a false show: *His buying you flowers was just an act to look good in front of others.* ❖ *v.* **act·ed, act·ing, acts** *—intr.* **1.** To behave; conduct oneself: *She acts like a born leader.* **2.** To perform in a dramatic presentation: *act in a play.* **3.** To put on a false show; pretend: *He tried to look brave, but he was only acting.* **4.** To appear or seem to be: *The dog acted ferocious.* **5.** To do something; perform an action: *By acting quickly, we prevented the fire from spreading.* **6.** To serve or function: *One of the older students acted as teacher. The heart acts like a pump.* *—tr.* **1.** To play the part of; perform as: *She acted Juliet in the play.* **2.** To behave like: *act the fool.* **3.** To behave as suitable for: *Act your age.* ◆ **act on** or **act upon** To do something as a result of: *I finally acted on my doctor's advice and gave up chocolate.* **act out** To perform in or as if in a play; dramatize: *act out a story.* **act up 1.** To misbehave: *The children were acting up all day, and their mother was upset.* **2.** To work improperly: *The car's motor was acting up.* **3.** To become painful or troublesome again: *His back is acting up.* [From Middle English, from Latin *agere*, to do.] **—act′a·ble** *adj.*

ACTH (ā′sē′tē′**āch′**) *n.* A hormone secreted by a lobe of the pituitary gland. It stimulates the adrenal glands to produce cortisone and related hormones.

act·ing (**ăk′**tĭng) *adj.* Serving temporarily or in place of another person: *the acting principal.* ❖ *n.* The occupation or performance of an actor or actress.

ac·tin·ic radiation (ăk-**tĭn′**ĭk) *n.* A form of radiation, such as ultraviolet rays or x-rays, that can cause chemical changes in an object that it strikes.

ac·ti·nide (**ăk′**tə-nīd′) *n.* Any of a series of chemically similar, radioactive metallic elements with atomic numbers ranging from 89 to 103. See **Periodic Table.**

ac·ti·nism (**ăk′**tə-nĭz′əm) *n.* The action or property in radiant energy that produces chemical changes, as the effects of actinic radiation on photographic film.

ac·tin·i·um (ăk-**tĭn′**ē-əm) *n. Symbol* **Ac** A highly radioactive metallic element somewhat like radium, found in uranium ore and used as a source of alpha rays. Atomic number 89. See **Periodic Table.**

ac·tion (**ăk′**shən) *n.* **1.** The process or fact of doing something: *firefighters springing into action; an emergency requiring immediate action.* **2.** A thing done; a deed: *take responsibility for one's actions.* **3.** The series of events in a play or story: *The action of the play takes place in a castle.* **4.** A series of fast-moving, exciting, or dangerous events: *a movie with lots of action.* **5.** A physical change, as in position, mass, or energy, that an object or system undergoes: *the action of a sail in the wind.* **6a.** The way in which something works or acts, often upon a larger system: *the action of the liver in digestion.* **b.** The effect of this: *the corrosive action of acid on metal.* **7.** A lawsuit. **8.** Battle; combat: *send the troops into action.* **9.** The operating parts of a mechanism: *the action of a piano.*

action verb *n.* A verb that expresses action. Action verbs are either transitive, as *activate* (*Electricity activates the fan's motor*) or intransitive, as *sleep* (*We all slept soundly*).

ac·ti·vate (**ăk′**tə-vāt′) *tr.v.* **ac·ti·vat·ed, ac·ti·vat·ing, ac·ti·vates 1.** To make active; set in operation or motion: *The motor is activated by a battery.* **2.** To start or accelerate a chemical reaction in, as by heating. **3.** To make (a substance) radioactive. **—ac′ti·va′tion** *n.*

ac·tive (**ăk′**tĭv) *adj.* **1.** Moving or tending to move about; engaging in physical action: *Nurses are more active than office workers.* **2.** Performing or capable of performing an action or process; functioning; working: *an active volcano.* **3a.** Taking part or involving participation in activities: *had an active role in organizing the parade.* **b.** Currently in use or effect: *has an active membership in the club.* **4.** Full of energy; busy: *an active and useful life; an active mind.* **5.** Causing an action or change; effective: *active ingredients in the detergent.* **6.** In grammar, relating to the active voice. ❖ *n.* **1.** The active voice in grammar. **2.** A verb form in the active voice. **—ac′tive·ly** *adv.* **—ac′tive·ness** *n.* —SEE NOTE AT **verb.**

active duty *n.* Military service with full pay and regular duty.

active transport *n.* The movement of ions or molecules across a cell membrane from an area of lower concentration to one of higher concentration using energy supplied by ATP. Active transport helps regulate a cell's metabolic activities, including food absorption and the secretion of hormones and enzymes.

active voice *n.* In grammar, a form of a verb that shows that the subject is performing or causing the action expressed by the verb. In the sentence *John bought the book, bought* is in the active voice.

ac·tiv·ism (ăk′tə-vĭz′əm) *n.* The use of direct action, as in a demonstration or strike, to support or oppose a cause. **—ac′tiv·ist** *n.*

ac·tiv·i·ty (ăk-tĭv′ĭ-tē) *n., pl.* **ac·tiv·i·ties 1.** The condition or process of being active: *mental or physical activity.* **2.** A particular kind of action or behavior: *the nesting activities of birds.* **3.** A planned or organized thing to do, as in a school subject or social group: *Outside activities usually make school more fun.* **4.** Vigorous movement or action; liveliness: *The department store was a scene of great activity.*

ac·tor (ăk′tər) *n.* **1.** A person who acts a part in a play, motion picture, or television program. **2.** A person or group that takes part in or accomplishes something: *England, France, and Spain were actors in the colonizing of North America.*

ac·tress (ăk′trĭs) *n.* A woman who is an actor.

Acts of the Apostles (ăkts) *pl.n. (used with a singular verb)* A book of the New Testament giving a history of the early Christian Church.

ac·tu·al (ăk′cho͞o-əl) *adj.* Existing or happening in fact; real: *Actual sales greatly exceeded estimated sales.*

ac·tu·al·i·ty (ăk′cho͞o-ăl′ĭ-tē) *n., pl.* **ac·tu·al·i·ties** Real existence or circumstance; reality; fact: *In 1969, the human dream of walking on the moon became an actuality.*

ac·tu·al·ly (ăk′cho͞o-ə-lē) *adv.* In fact; really: *That tree is actually a fir, not a pine.*

ac·tu·ar·y (ăk′cho͞o-ĕr′ē) *n., pl.* **ac·tu·ar·ies** A person who estimates risks and calculates rates and premiums for an insurance company. **—ac′tu·ar′i·al** *adj.*

ac·tu·ate (ăk′cho͞o-āt′) *tr.v.* **ac·tu·at·ed, ac·tu·at·ing, ac·tu·ates 1.** To put into action or motion: *Stepping on a pedal actuates the brake.* **2.** To move to action; motivate: *His remarks actuated a heated discussion.* **—ac′tu·a′tion** *n.* **—ac′tu·a′tor** *n.*

a·cu·i·ty (ə-kyo͞o′ĭ-tē) *n.* Keenness of mind or perception: *The doctor diagnosed the patient's problem with great acuity.*

ac·u·men (ăk′yə-mən *or* ə-kyo͞o′mən) *n.* Quickness and wisdom in making judgments; keen insight: *The owner's business acumen permitted the store to grow rapidly.*

ac·u·punc·ture (ăk′yo͝o-pŭngk′chər) *n.* A practice originating in traditional Chinese medicine, in which thin needles are inserted into the body at specific points in order to relieve pain, treat a disease, or anesthetize parts of the body during surgery. [From Latin *acus,* needle + English *puncture.*]

a·cute (ə-kyo͞ot′) *adj.* **1.** Keen; perceptive: *an acute sense of hearing; an acute awareness of one's surroundings.* **2.** Sharp and intense: *A toothache can cause acute pain.* **3.** Developing suddenly and having a short but severe course: *acute appendicitis.* **4.** Very serious; critical: *an acute lack of funds.* **5.** Having an acute angle: *an acute triangle.* [From Middle English, from Latin *acuere,* to sharpen.] **—a·cute′ly** *adv.* **—a·cute′ness** *n.*

acute accent *n.* **1.** A mark (´) placed above a vowel to indicate that the vowel is pronounced differently than it would be without the mark, as in the word *cliché.* **2.** A mark (´) indicating metrical stress in poetry.

acute angle *n.* An angle whose measure is between 0° and 90°.

ad (ăd) *n.* An advertisement.
❑ *These sound alike:* **ad, add** (combine to form a sum).

AD or **AD** *abbr.* An abbreviation of anno Domini (in the year of the Lord; that is, after the birth of Jesus). —SEE NOTE AT **Common Era.**

ad– *pref.* A prefix that means toward or to: *adsorb.*

ad·age (ăd′ĭj) *n.* A short proverb or saying generally considered to be wise and true; for example, "Haste makes waste" is an adage.

a·da·gio (ə-dä′jō *or* ə-dä′jē-ō′) *adv. & adj.* In music, in a slow tempo. ❖ *n.* A slow musical passage, movement, or work.

Ad·am (ăd′əm) In the Bible, the first man and the husband of Eve.

ad·a·mant (ăd′ə-mənt) *adj.* Firm and unyielding; not giving in easily: *Our parents were adamant and showed no sign of yielding in their decision.* [From Middle English, from Greek *adamās,* unconquerable, hard steel, diamond.] **—ad′a·mant·ly** *adv.*

ad·a·man·tine (ăd′ə-măn′tēn′ *or* ăd′ə-măn′tīn′ *or* ăd′ə-măn′tĭn) *adj.* **1.** Having a hardness like that of a diamond: *an adamantine rock.* **2.** Unyielding; hard: *the tyrant's adamantine will.*

Ad·ams (ăd′əmz), **Abigail Smith** 1744–1818. First lady of the United States (1797–1801) as the wife of John Adams. Her many letters provide a vivid picture of life in colonial Massachusetts.

Adams, John 1735–1826. The first vice president (1789–1797) and second president (1797–1801) of the United States. He helped draft the Declaration of Independence and the US Constitution.

Adams, John Quincy 1767–1848. The sixth president of the United States (1825–1829). After his presidency he served in the House of Representatives (1831–1848), where he strongly opposed slavery.

Adams, Samuel 1722–1803. American Revolutionary leader who incited Bostonians to rebel against Great Britain. He was a member of the First and Second Continental Congresses and signed the Declaration of Independence.

Ad·am's apple (ăd′əmz) *n.* The lump at the front of the throat where a part of the larynx projects forward, most noticeably in men. [From French *pomme d'Adam,* Adam's apple, partial translation (influenced by the European belief that the forbidden fruit eaten by Adam and Eve in the Garden of Eden was an apple and the fact that the Adam's apple is most noticeable in men) of Medieval Latin *pōmum grānātum,* pomegranate, Adam's apple, translation of Arabic *rummāna,* pomegranate, Adam's apple.]

a·dapt (ə-dăpt′) *v.* **a·dapt·ed, a·dapt·ing, a·dapts** *—tr.* **1.** To make fit or suitable for a new use or situation: *adapted the novel into a movie.* **2.** To cause to be able to survive and reproduce under certain conditions. Used in the passive: *a species that is adapted to a specific environment.* *—intr.* **1.** To change in order to meet the requirements of new circumstances or conditions: *The music business had to adapt to digital technology.* **2.** To become able to survive and reproduce under certain conditions: *Hawks have adapted to living in cities.* [From

WORD BUILDING

ad– The prefix **ad–** comes from the Latin prefix *ad–,* meaning "to, toward, on top of." In Latin, when this prefix was followed by *c, f, g, l, n, p, r, s,* or *t,* it became *ac–, af–, ag–, al–, an–, ap–, ar–, as–,* or *at–,* respectively. Thus Latin *ad–* is easy to see in English words such as *adhere, admit,* and *adverse,* but it is not so obvious in words such as *affix, apply,* and *attend.*

Abigail Adams
c. 1766 pastel portrait by Benjamin Blythe (1740?–1787?)

John Adams

John Quincy Adams
1847 portrait by George Peter Alexander Healy (1813–1894)

Jane Addams

ă	pat	ôr	core
ā	pay	oi	boy
âr	care	ou	out
ä	father	ŏŏ	took
ĕ	pet	ŏŏr	lure
ē	be	ōō	boot
ĭ	pit	ŭ	cut
ī	bite	ûr	urge
îr	pier	th	thin
ŏ	pot	*th*	this
ō	toe	zh	vision
ô	paw	ə	about

Middle English *adapten,* from Latin *adaptāre* : *ad-,* to + *aptāre,* to fit.]

SYNONYMS adapt, adjust, conform These verbs mean to change in order to suit one's circumstances: *After her family moved to a new state, she was quick to adapt to her new school. It took him a couple of days to get adjusted to the heat when he vacationed in southern Florida. I revised my essay so that it conformed to the guidelines my teacher established.*

a·dapt·a·ble (ə-**dăp′**tə-bəl) *adj.* Able to change or be adjusted to fit in with new or different uses or situations: *an adaptable schedule that is easy to rearrange; an adaptable person.* **—a·dapt′a·bil′i·ty** *n.*

ad·ap·ta·tion (ăd′ăp-**tā′**shən) *n.* **1.** The act or process of adapting; change or adjustment to meet new conditions: *The friendly student's adaptation to a new school was easy and quick. The water wheel permitted adaptation of water power for the driving of early machinery.* **2.** Something that is produced by being adapted: *The movie was an adaptation of a story written by Charles Dickens.* **3a.** Change or adjustment in structure or habits by which a species becomes better able to function in its environment. Adaptation occurs during evolution through the action of natural selection. **b.** A structure or habit that results from this process: *The fur on the feet of polar bears is an adaptation to a cold climate.*

a·dapt·er also **a·dap·tor** (ə-**dăp′**tər) *n.* **1.** A device for putting together different parts of an apparatus that otherwise would not fit together. **2.** A device for putting a machine or a piece of equipment to a different use.

a·dap·tive (ə-**dăp′**tĭv) *adj.* **1.** Relating to or resulting from adaptation: *adaptive learning; large ears as an adaptive trait.* **2.** Tending to adapt easily: *an adaptive good nature.*

add (ăd) *v.* **add·ed, add·ing, adds** *—tr.* **1.** To combine (two or more numbers) to form a sum: *If one adds 6 and 8 the total is 14.* **2.** To join or unite so as to increase, change, or improve something: *add a suffix to a word; add an annex to a building.* **3.** To say or write as something extra; say further: *Give directions and add a word of caution. —intr.* **1.** To find a sum in arithmetic: *Most store clerks can add in their heads.* **2.** To cause an increase or addition: *He adds to his savings each week.* ◆ **add up** To be reasonable; make sense: *What she said did not add up.* **add up to** To amount to: *A group of friends and some music add up to a good time.* [From Middle English *adden,* from Latin *addere.*]

❑ *These sound alike:* **add, ad** (advertisement).

ADD *abbr.* An abbreviation of attention deficit disorder.

Ad·dams (**ăd′**əmz), **Jane** 1860–1935. American social reformer and pacifist who founded Hull House (1889), a care and education center for the poor of Chicago.

ad·dax (**ăd′**ăks′) *n.* A large grayish-white antelope of northern Africa, having long spirally twisted horns.

ad·dend (**ăd′**ĕnd′ *or* ə-**dĕnd′**) *n.* A number or quantity to be added to another number. For example, in 9 + 2 = 11, the numbers 9 and 2 are addends.

ad·den·dum (ə-**dĕn′**dəm) *n., pl.* **ad·den·da** (ə-**dĕn′**də) **1.** An appendix to a book or document. **2.** Something to be added; an addition.

ad·der (**ăd′**ər) *n.* **1.** Any of several venomous snakes, especially a viper of Eurasia or Africa. **2.** Any of several nonvenomous snakes of North America, such as a hognose snake. [From Middle English *addre,* from the phrase *an addre,* an adder, misinterpretation of earlier Middle English *a naddre,* an adder, from Old English *nædre,* adder.] —SEE NOTE AT **apron.**

ad·dict (**ăd′**ĭkt) *n.* **1.** A person who has an addiction, as to drugs or gambling. **2.** A person who is deeply involved in or very enthusiastic about something: *a baseball addict.* [From Latin *addīcere,* to assign, hand over, enslave : *ad-,* to + *dīcere,* to adjudge.]

ad·dict·ed (ə-**dĭk′**tĭd) *adj.* **1.** Having a medically or psychologically significant addiction. **2.** Disposed or devoted, as by habit or interest: *addicted to gossiping on the phone; addicted to a radio program.*

ad·dic·tion (ə-**dĭk′**shən) *n.* **1.** A condition involving use of a substance (such as a drug or alcohol) or engagement in a behavior (such as gambling) in which a person has strong cravings, cannot stop or limit the activity, continues the activity despite harmful consequences, and experiences anxiety or discomfort when stopping the activity. **2.** The condition of being habitually occupied with or involved in something: *an addiction to watching soap operas.*

ad·dic·tive (ə-**dĭk′**tĭv) *adj.* Causing addiction: *an addictive substance.*

Ad·dis Ab·a·ba (**ăd′**ĭs **ăb′**ə-bə *or* **ä′**dĭs **ä′**bə-bä′) The capital of Ethiopia, in the center of the country on a plateau more than 8,000 feet (2,440 meters) above sea level.

ad·di·tion (ə-**dĭsh′**ən) *n.* **1.** The act, process, or operation of adding two or more numbers. **2.** The act or process of adding something extra to a thing: *the addition of seasoning to food.* **3.** An added thing, part, or person: *My new baby brother is an addition to our family.* ◆ **in addition** Also; as well: *We ate at a restaurant and saw a movie in addition.* **in addition to** Along with; besides: *In addition to riding her bike, she played her guitar this morning.* —SEE NOTE AT **together.**

ad·di·tion·al (ə-**dĭsh′**ə-nəl) *adj.* Added; extra; more: *The instructions are incomplete and we need additional information to finish the project.* **—ad·di′tion·al·ly** *adv.*

ad·di·tive (**ăd′**ĭ-tĭv) *n.* A substance added in small amounts to something in order to improve its performance or quality, preserve its usefulness, or make it more effective: *a food additive to prevent spoiling.* ❖ *adj.* **1.** Marked by or involving addition. **2.** Being any of the primary colors of light that can be mixed to produce light of any hue.

ad·dle (**ăd′**l) *tr.v.* **ad·dled, ad·dling, ad·dles** To confuse; befuddle: *Lack of sleep addled his mind.*

add-on (**ăd′**ŏn′) *n.* **1.** One thing that is added to complete or improve another thing. **2.** An item of computer hardware or software that increases the capabilities of another item of hardware or software. **3.** An additional amount or charge: *the add-ons increased the price by $50.*

ad·dress (ə-**drĕs′**) *tr.v.* **ad·dressed, ad·dress·ing, ad·dress·es 1.** To speak to: *The librarian addressed the student softly.* **2.** To give a speech to: *The president will address the nation on TV.* **3.** To direct to a particular person, group, or place: *The teacher's remarks were addressed to the new students.* **4.** To call (someone one is speaking to) by a particular name or term: *Address the judge as "Your Honor."* **5.** To put a destination on (a piece of mail) to show where it should go: *address an envelope.* **6.** To direct the efforts or attention of (oneself): *The committee addressed itself to plans for a new town hall.* **7.** To begin to deal with: *We must address this problem.* ❖ *n.* **1.** (*also* **ăd′**rĕs′) The place where a person lives or where a business is located: *your home address.* **2.** (*also* **ăd′**rĕs′) **a.** The information on a piece of mail, indicating where it is to be delivered. **b.** A name or a series of characters that designates an email account or a specific site on the Internet or another computer network. **3.** A formal speech: *the president's inaugural address.* **4.** A way of speaking or behaving: *a woman of polite address.* [From Middle English *adressen,* to direct, from Old French *adrecier,* from Latin *ad-,* to + *dirīgere,* to direct.]

ad·dress·ee (ăd′rĕ-**sē′** *or* ə-drĕs′**ē′**) *n.* The person to whom a letter or package is addressed.

ad·duce (ə-**dōōs′**) *tr.v.* **ad·duced, ad·duc·ing, ad·duc·es** To offer as a reason; give as an example or means of proof: *The defendant was unable to adduce evidence to support his innocence.*

A·den (ăd′n *or* ād′n) A city of southern Yemen on the **Gulf of Aden,** an inlet of the Arabian Sea. It has been one of the chief ports of southern Arabia since ancient times.

ad·e·nine (ăd′n-ēn′ *or* ăd′n-ĭn) *n.* A base that is a component of DNA and RNA.

ad·e·noi·dal (ăd′n-oid′l) *adj.* Relating to the adenoids.

ad·e·noids (ăd′n-oidz) *pl.n.* A mass of tissue located at the back of the nose in the upper part of the throat in children. Adenoids are part of the immune system, but if they become infected and swollen they can obstruct normal breathing and make speech difficult.

a·dept (ə-dĕpt′) *adj.* Very skillful and effective; proficient: *Tailors are adept at sewing. The inventor was an adept mechanic.* See Synonyms at **proficient.** ❖ *n.* (ăd′-ĕpt′) A highly skilled person; an expert. [From Latin *adeptus*, past participle of Latin *adipīscī*, to attain : *ad-*, to + *apīscī*, to grasp.] **—a·dept′ly** *adv.* **—a·dept′ness** *n.*

ad·e·qua·cy (ăd′ĭ-kwə-sē) *n.* The condition of being adequate; sufficiency.

ad·e·quate (ăd′ĭ-kwĭt) *adj.* Sufficient to satisfy a requirement or meet a need: *adequate supplies to meet our needs.* [From Latin *adaequāre*, to equalize : *ad-*, to + *aequāre*, to make equal (from *aequus*, equal).] **—ad′e·quate·ly** *adv.* **—ad′e·quate·ness** *n.*

ADHD *abbr.* An abbreviation of attention deficit hyperactivity disorder.

ad·here (ăd-hîr′) *intr.v.* **ad·hered, ad·her·ing, ad·heres 1.** To stick or hold fast: *The wallpaper adheres to the wall.* **2.** To remain devoted; support: *adhere to one's religious beliefs.* **3.** To carry out something without changes: *They adhered to the original plan.* [From Latin *adhaerēre* : *ad-*, to + *haerēre*, to stick.]

ad·her·ence (ăd-hîr′əns) *n.* **1.** The process or condition of adhering or sticking fast: *the gum's annoying adherence to my shoe.* **2.** Faithful attachment or support: *adherence to one's principles.*

ad·her·ent (ăd-hîr′ənt) *n.* A loyal supporter or faithful follower: *Adherents of conservatism oppose most increases in government spending.* ❖ *adj.* Sticking or holding fast; clinging.

ad·he·sion (ăd-hē′zhən) *n.* The process or condition of sticking fast or adhering: *the adhesion of glue to wood.*

ad·he·sive (ăd-hē′sĭv *or* ăd-hē′zĭv) *adj.* **1.** Tending to hold fast to another material; sticky. **2.** Coated with glue or another sticky substance: *an adhesive label.* ❖ *n.* An adhesive substance, such as paste or glue. **—ad·he′sive·ness** *n.*

ad hoc (ăd hŏk′ *or* ăd hōk′) *adv. & adj.* For a specific and often unexpected purpose: *called an ad hoc meeting to deal with the emergency.*

ad·i·a·bat·ic (ăd′ē-ə-băt′ĭk *or* ā′dī-ə-băt′ĭk) *adj.* Occurring without gain or loss of heat: *The passage of sound through air is generally adiabatic.* **—ad′i·a·bat′i·cal·ly** *adv.*

a·dieu (ə-dyo͞o′ *or* ə-do͞o′) *interj.* An expression used to say goodbye; farewell. ❖ *n., pl.* **a·dieus** or **a·dieux** (ə-dyo͞oz′ *or* ə-do͞oz′) A farewell: *say one's adieus upon leaving.* [From Middle English, from Old French *a dieu*, (I commend you) to God : *a*, to + *dieu*, God.]

❑ *These sound alike:* **adieu, ado** (fuss).

ad in·fi·ni·tum (ăd ĭn′fə-nī′təm) *adv.* Without limit; forever; endlessly: *talk on ad infinitum.*

ad·i·os (ä′dē-ōs′) *interj.* An expression used to say goodbye; farewell. [From Spanish *adiós* : *a*, to + *Dios*, god.]

ad·i·pose (ăd′ə-pōs′) *adj.* Relating to or consisting of animal fat: *adipose tissue.*

Ad·i·ron·dack Mountains (ăd′ə-rŏn′dăk′) A group of mountains in northeast New York between the St. Lawrence River valley in the north and the Mohawk River valley in the south. The range rises to 5,344 feet (1,629 meters).

adj. *abbr.* An abbreviation of adjective.

ad·ja·cent (ə-jā′sənt) *adj.* **1.** Next to; adjoining: *I can hear all the noise from the room adjacent to mine.* **2.** Lying near or close; nearby; neighboring: *the city and adjacent farmlands.* **—ad·ja′cent·ly** *adv.*

adjacent
adjacent houses

adjacent angle *n.* Either of a pair of angles that have a vertex and a side in common.

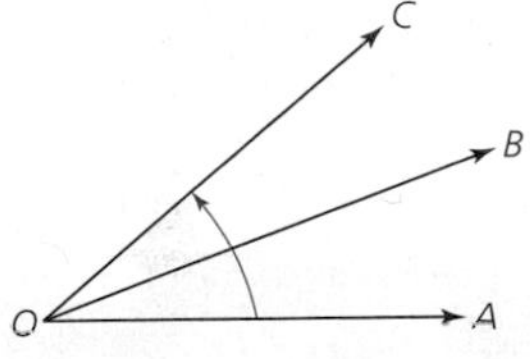

adjacent angle
The common vertex is *O*; angle *AOB* is adjacent to angle *BOC*.

ad·jec·ti·val (ăj′ĭk-tī′vəl) *adj.* Relating to or functioning as an adjective: *an adjectival phrase.* **—ad′jec·ti′val·ly** *adv.*

ad·jec·tive (ăj′ĭk-tĭv) *n.* **1.** The part of speech that modifies a noun by describing it or limiting or adding to its meaning. **2.** A word belonging to this part of speech. For example, in the sentence *The young boy is very tall, young* and *tall* are adjectives. —SEE NOTE.

ad·join (ə-join′) *v.* **ad·joined, ad·join·ing, ad·joins** —*tr.* To be next to or connected with; share a boundary with: *The bath adjoins the bedroom.* —*intr.* To be side by side or connected: *These rooms adjoin.*

ad·join·ing (ə-joi′nĭng) *adj.* Next to or connected with; alongside: *a bedroom and adjoining bath; a row of adjoining houses.*

ad·journ (ə-jûrn′) *v.* **ad·journed, ad·journ·ing, ad·journs** —*tr.* To bring (a meeting or session) to a close, putting off further business until later: *The judge adjourned the trial for the holidays.* —*intr.* **1.** To stop proceedings until a later time; break up: *The court adjourned for the weekend.* **2.** To move to a less formal setting: *The dinner guests adjourned to the living room.* [From Middle English *ajournen*, from Old French *ajourner* : *a-*, to + *jour*, day (from Late Latin *diurnum*, from Latin *diurnus*, daily, from *diēs*, day).]

ad·journ·ment (ə-jûrn′mənt) *n.* **1.** The act of adjourning or the state of being adjourned. **2.** The time during which a legislature or a court is not in session.

ad·judge (ə-jŭj′) *tr.v.* **ad·judged, ad·judg·ing, ad·judg·es 1.** To determine, rule, or declare by law: *The accused thief was adjudged guilty.* **2.** To award by law: *The injured motorist was adjudged damages for medical costs.*

ad·ju·di·cate (ə-jo͞o′dĭ-kāt′) *tr.v.* **ad·ju·di·cat·ed, ad·ju·di·cat·ing, ad·ju·di·cates 1.** To hear and settle (a legal case). **2.** To study and settle (a dispute): *The mediator adjudicated the workers' complaints.* **—ad·ju′di·ca′tion** *n.*

ad·junct (ăj′ŭngkt′) *n.* A separate, less important thing added to something: *The card shop is an adjunct of the bookstore.*

ad·ju·ra·tion (ăj′ə-rā′shən) *n.* An earnest appeal: *a judge's adjuration to a witness to tell the whole truth.*

ad·jure (ə-jo͝or′) *tr.v.* **ad·jured, ad·jur·ing, ad·jures 1.** To command solemnly. **2.** To ask or entreat earnestly: *I adjure you on your honor to keep my secret.*

ad·just (ə-jŭst′) *v.* **ad·just·ed, ad·just·ing, ad·justs** —*tr.* **1.** To bring the parts of (a mechanism, for example) into a more effective arrangement: *The mechanic adjusted the carburetor on my car.* **2.** To change, set, or regulate in order to improve or make suitable: *I adjusted the height of the microphone so the speaker could be heard.* See Synonyms at **adapt. 3.** To change or adapt to suit new circumstances or conditions: *Some wild animals do not adjust themselves to living in a cage.* **4.** To decide how much is to be paid on (an insurance claim). —*intr.* To change oneself or one's behavior to suit new circumstances or conditions: *We can adjust to living in a smaller apartment.* [From Middle English *ajusten*, from Old French *ajoster* : from Latin *ad-*, to + Latin *iūxtā*, near.] **—ad·just′er** *n.*

ad·just·a·ble (ə-jŭs′tə-bəl) *adj.* Capable of being adjusted: *an adjustable wrench; an adjustable lens of a telescope.*

USAGE

adjectives Words that modify nouns are called **adjectives.** If an adjective precedes a noun, it is called an *attributive adjective*. In the phrase *a blue coat, blue* is an attributive adjective. If an adjective follows a noun and a linking verb, such as *be, grow,* or *seem,* the adjective is called a *predicate adjective,* as in the sentence *The sky grew dark.*

ad·just·ment (ə-**jŭst′**mənt) *n.* **1.** The act of adjusting or the state of being adjusted: *Winter weather requires an adjustment to colder temperature.* **2.** The state of being adjusted: *valves in proper adjustment.* **3.** A means by which a device can be adjusted: *Our TV set has several adjustments to regulate the color of the picture.* **4.** A settlement of a claim or debt.

ad·ju·tant (**ăj′**ə-tənt) *n.* **1.** An army officer who acts as an assistant to a commanding officer. **2.** A helper or assistant.

ad-lib (ăd′**lĭb′**) *v.* **ad-libbed, ad-lib·bing, ad-libs** —*tr.* To make up (words, music, or actions) while performing: *ad-lib a joke.* —*intr.* To make up words, music, or actions while performing: *The actor forgot his lines and ad-libbed.* ❖ *n.* (**ăd′**lĭb′) A line, speech, action, or passage of music made up on the spot. ❖ *adj.* (**ăd′**lĭb′) Made up on the spot; improvised: *an ad-lib remark.* [Short for Latin *ad libitum*, at pleasure.]

ad·min·is·ter (ăd-**mĭn′**ĭ-stər) *v.* **ad·min·is·tered, ad·min·is·ter·ing, ad·min·is·ters** —*tr.* **1.** To direct the affairs of; manage: *The mayor administers the city government.* **2.** To give formally or officially: *administer an oath of office.* **3.** To give as a remedy: *administer a sedative.* **4a.** To deal out; dispense: *A judge administers justice.* **b.** To give and supervise: *administer a test.* **5.** To manage (property), as under a will. —*intr.* To be helpful; contribute: *The Red Cross administered to the needs of the flood victims.* [From Middle English *administren*, from Latin *administrāre* : *ad-*, to + *minister*, servant.]

adobe

ad·min·is·tra·tion (ăd-mĭn′ĭ-**strā′**shən) *n.* **1.** The act or process of administering: *the administration of justice; the administration of a vaccine.* **2.** The management of a government or large institution. **3.** The people who manage an institution or direct an organization: *Our school administration is made up of the principal and a staff of teachers.* **4.** often **Administration** The executive branch of a government. **5.** The time that a chief executive is in office or that a government is in power: *Many civil rights laws were enacted during the Johnson administration.*

ad·min·is·tra·tive (ăd-**mĭn′**ĭ-strā′tĭv) *adj.* Relating to government or management: *a manager with administrative ability; the president and other administrative officers of the government.* **—ad·min′is·tra′tive·ly** *adv.*

ad·min·is·tra·tor (ăd-**mĭn′**ĭ-strā′tər) *n.* **1.** A person in charge of directing or managing affairs; an executive. **2.** A person appointed by a court to manage the property left by a dead person: *Our family's lawyer is the administrator of my grandfather's estate.*

ad·mi·ra·ble (**ăd′**mər-ə-bəl) *adj.* Worthy of admiration; excellent: *Honesty is an admirable quality.* **—ad′mi·ra·ble·ness** *n.* **—ad′mi·ra·bly** *adv.*

ad·mi·ral (**ăd′**mər-əl) *n.* **1.** The commanding officer of a navy or fleet of ships. **2a.** A rank in the US Navy or Coast Guard that is above vice-admiral and below Admiral of the Fleet. **b.** An officer in the US Navy or Coast Guard ranking above a captain, including admiral, vice admiral, and rear admiral. **3.** Any of various brightly colored butterflies. [From Middle English *amiral*, from Arabic *ʾamīr al-* . . ., commander of the . . . (in phrases like *ʾamīr al-baḥr*, commander of the sea).]

Admiral of the Fleet *n.* The highest-ranking officer in the US Navy.

ad·mi·ral·ty (**ăd′**mər-əl-tē) *n., pl.* **ad·mi·ral·ties 1.** The body of law or the court that deals with matters involving ships and the sea. **2. Admiralty** The former department of the British government that was in charge of naval affairs.

ad·mi·ra·tion (ăd′mə-**rā′**shən) *n.* **1.** A feeling of pleasure, wonder, or approval: *The tourists gazed at the Grand Canyon in admiration.* **2.** An object of great wonder or respect: *The ballerina was the admiration of younger dancers.*

ad·mire (ăd-**mīr′**) *tr.v.* **ad·mired, ad·mir·ing, ad·mires 1.** To look at with wonder, pleasure, and delight: *admire a beautiful picture.* **2.** To have a high opinion of; feel great respect for: *People admire her ability as a musician.* [From Latin *admīrārī*, to wonder at : *ad-*, at + *mīrārī*, to wonder.] **—ad·mir′ing·ly** *adv.*

ad·mis·si·ble (ăd-**mĭs′**ə-bəl) *adj.* Accepted or permitted; allowable: *Admissible evidence in court must be based on fact.* **—ad·mis′si·bil′i·ty** *n.* **—ad·mis′si·bly** *adv.*

ad·mis·sion (ăd-**mĭsh′**ən) *n.* **1.** The act of accepting or allowing to enter: *Congress must approve the admission of new states to the Union.* **2.** The right to enter or be accepted: *Admission to public school is open to all children.* **3.** A price charged or paid to enter a place: *The spectators paid an admission of two dollars each.* **4.** An acknowledgment of the truth; a confession: *an admission of guilt.*

ad·mit (ăd-**mĭt′**) *v.* **ad·mit·ted, ad·mit·ting, ad·mits** —*tr.* **1.** To acknowledge or confess to be true or real: *I must admit that you are right. Never admit defeat.* **2a.** To allow or permit to enter: *This pass will admit one person free.* **b.** To accept and take in as a new member, student, or patient: *The hospital admitted the accident victim.* **3.** To have room for: *The harbor is large enough to admit many ships at once.* —*intr.* **1.** To allow the possibility: *That problem admits of no solution.* **2.** To allow access: *The screen door admits to the porch.* [From Middle English *admitten*, from Latin *admittere* : *ad-*, to + *mittere*, to send.]

ad·mit·tance (ăd-**mĭt′**ns) *n.* **1.** Permission or right to enter: *The sign said "no admittance."* **2.** The act of admitting: *gained admittance with a key.*

ad·mit·ted·ly (ăd-**mĭt′**ĭd-lē) *adv.* By general admission; without denial: *Admittedly, I am an optimist, but I think things will get better.*

ad·mix·ture (ăd-**mĭks′**chər) *n.* **1.** The act of mixing. **2.** Something formed by mixing; a combination, mixture, or blend: *An admixture of flour and water makes paste.* **3.** Something added in mixing.

ad·mon·ish (ăd-**mŏn′**ĭsh) *tr.v.* **ad·mon·ished, ad·mon·ish·ing, ad·mon·ish·es 1.** To advise, warn, urge, or caution: *She admonished us to be careful on the ice.* **2.** To criticize for a fault in a kind but serious way: *The uncle admonished the twins for their lateness.* **—ad·mon′ish·ment** *n.*

ad·mo·ni·tion (ăd′mə-**nĭsh′**ən) *n.* A gentle criticism or friendly warning: *Remember the doctor's admonition to keep the bandage dry.*

ad·mon·i·to·ry (ăd-**mŏn′**ĭ-tôr′ē) *adj.* Given or expressing a warning; urging caution: *an admonitory word of advice.*

a·do (ə-**dōō′**) *n.* Fuss; bother: *They said their goodbyes and set off quickly without further ado.*

❑ *These sound alike:* **ado, adieu** (farewell).

a·do·be (ə-**dō′**bē) *n.* **1.** A building material consisting of clay mixed with straw or dung, fashioned into sun-dried bricks or used as mortar or plaster. **2.** Clay or soil from which such material is made. **3.** A building made with such material. [From Spanish, from Arabic *aṭ-ṭūba*, the brick, ultimately from Egyptian.]

ad·o·les·cence (ăd′l-**ĕs′**əns) *n.* **1.** The period of growth and physical development that leads from childhood to adulthood. **2.** A period of change and development to maturity: *the adolescence of the computer industry.*

ad·o·les·cent (ăd′l-**ĕs′**ənt) *adj.* Relating to or going through adolescence: *an adolescent youngster.* ❖ *n.* A boy or girl, especially a teenager, in the stage of growth and development between childhood and adulthood. [From Middle English, from Latin *adolēscere*, to grow up.]

A·don·is (ə-**dŏn′**ĭs) *n.* **1.** In Greek mythology, a young

ă	pat	ôr	core
ā	pay	oi	boy
âr	care	ou	out
ä	father	ŏŏ	took
ĕ	pet	ŏŏr	lure
ē	be	ōō	boot
ĭ	pit	ŭ	cut
ī	bite	ûr	urge
îr	pier	th	thin
ŏ	pot	*th*	this
ō	toe	zh	vision
ô	paw	ə	about

man loved by the goddess Aphrodite for his beauty. **2.** often **adonis** A very handsome and often vain young man.

a·dopt (ə-dŏpt′) *tr.v.* **a·dopt·ed, a·dopt·ing, a·dopts 1.** To take (a new member) into one's family through legal means and treat as one's own: *Our neighbors adopted a baby girl.* **2.** To take and make one's own: *Samuel Clemens adopted the name Mark Twain.* **3a.** To accept and use or follow: *adopt a suggestion; adopt new methods.* **b.** To pass by vote or approve officially: *The legislature adopted the proposed law.* **4.** To put on; assume: *Some people adopt a confident air to hide their uneasiness.* **5.** To take on; acquire: *English has adopted the Italian word "concerto" and many other foreign words.* [From Middle English *adopten*, from Latin *adoptāre* : *ad*-, to + *optāre*, to choose.] **—a·dopt′a·ble** *adj.* —SEE NOTE.

a·dop·tion (ə-dŏp′shən) *n.* **1.** The act of adopting: *the couple's adoption of a child; the city's adoption of a new zoning law.* **2.** The condition of being adopted: *the child's adoption by his stepfather; the new law's adoption by the city council.*

a·dop·tive (ə-dŏp′tĭv) *adj.* Related by adoption: *the baby's adoptive mother.* —SEE NOTE AT **adopt.**

a·dor·a·ble (ə-dôr′ə-bəl) *adj.* **1.** Delightful; lovable; charming: *an adorable puppy.* **2.** Worthy of adoration. **—a·dor′a·ble·ness** *n.* **—a·dor′a·bly** *adv.*

ad·o·ra·tion (ăd′ə-rā′shən) *n.* **1.** The act of worship. **2.** Great and devoted love: *Many famous screen actors have enjoyed the adoration of millions of fans.*

a·dore (ə-dôr′) *tr.v.* **a·dored, a·dor·ing, a·dores 1.** To love deeply and devotedly; idolize: *The girl adored her mother.* **2.** To like very much: *Audiences everywhere adore the circus.* **3.** To worship as God or a god. [From Middle English *adouren*, worship, from Latin *adōrāre*, to pray to : *ad*-, to + *ōrāre*, to pray.] **—a·dor′er** *n.* **—a·dor′ing·ly** *adv.*

a·dorn (ə-dôrn′) *tr.v.* **a·dorned, a·dorn·ing, a·dorns** To decorate with something beautiful or ornamental: *The table was adorned with flowers.* **—a·dorn′er** *n.*

a·dorn·ment (ə-dôrn′mənt) *n.* **1.** The act of adorning; decoration: *jewelry worn for personal adornment.* **2.** Something that adorns or beautifies; an ornament or a decoration: *They wore no jewels or other adornments.*

ADP (ā′dē′pē′) *n.* An organic compound, having the formula $C_{10}H_{15}N_5O_{10}P_2$, that is converted to ATP for the storage of energy during cell metabolism. [From the chemical name *a(denosine) d(i)p(hosphate).*]

ad·re·nal (ə-drē′nəl) *adj.* Relating to or derived from the adrenal glands: *adrenal disorders.* ❖ *n.* An adrenal gland.

adrenal gland *n.* Either of two endocrine glands, one located above each kidney, that produce epinephrine and certain other hormones.

a·dren·a·line (ə-drĕn′ə-lĭn) *n.* Epinephrine.

A·dri·at·ic Sea (ā′drē-ăt′ĭk) An arm of the Mediterranean Sea between Italy and the Balkan Peninsula.

a·drift (ə-drĭft′) *adv. & adj.* **1.** Drifting or floating without direction: *The raft was adrift for weeks in the middle of the sea.* **2.** Without direction or purpose: *The editorial department was adrift until a new supervisor was hired.*

a·droit (ə-droit′) *adj.* Skillful or clever at doing or handling something difficult: *The aide gave an adroit answer to a complicated question.* **—a·droit′ly** *adv.* **—a·droit′ness** *n.*

ad·sorb (ăd-zôrb′) *tr.v.* **ad·sorbed, ad·sorb·ing, ad·sorbs** To take up and hold (a gas, liquid, or dissolved substance) in a thin layer of molecules on the surface of a solid substance: *A dye is adsorbed in a tightly held layer on the surface of cloth fiber.* **—ad·sorp′tion** (ăd-zôrp′shən) *n.*

ad·u·late (ăj′ə-lāt′) *tr.v.* **ad·u·lat·ed, ad·u·lat·ing, ad·u·lates** To praise or admire too much.

ad·u·la·tion (ăj′ə-lā′shən) *n.* Excessive praise or admiration: *The leader sought respect, not adulation.*

ad·u·la·to·ry (ăj′ə-lə-tôr′e) *adj.* Praising or admiring too much: *an adulatory biography that avoided mention of the president's mistakes.*

a·dult (ə-dŭlt′ *or* ăd′ŭlt) *n.* **1.** A person of legal age, usually over 18 or 21 years old, typically having the right to vote, enter into legal contracts, and fulfill certain duties. **2.** An animal or plant that is fully grown and developed. ❖ *adj.* **1.** Fully developed; mature: *an adult cat and her kittens.* **2.** Intended or suitable for mature people: *adult education.* [From Latin *adultus*, from *adolēscere*, to grow up.]

a·dul·ter·ant (ə-dŭl′tər-ənt) *n.* A substance used to adulterate something.

a·dul·ter·ate (ə-dŭl′tə-rāt′) *tr.v.* **a·dul·ter·at·ed, a·dul·ter·at·ing, a·dul·ter·ates** To reduce the quality of (something) by adding impure, inferior, or improper substances: *adulterate milk with water.* [From Latin *adulterāre*, to pollute : *ad*-, to + *alterāre*, to alter.] **—a·dul′ter·a′tion** *n.*

a·dul·ter·er (ə-dŭl′tər-ər) *n.* A person who commits adultery.

a·dul·ter·ess (ə-dŭl′trĭs *or* ə-dŭl′tər-ĭs) *n.* A woman who commits adultery.

a·dul·ter·ous (ə-dŭl′tər-əs) *adj.* Relating to or guilty of adultery. **—a·dul′ter·ous·ly** *adv.*

a·dul·ter·y (ə-dŭl′tə-rē *or* ə-dŭl′trē) *n.* Voluntary sexual intercourse between a married person and someone who is not the person's spouse. [From Middle English *adulterie*, from Latin *adulter*, adulterer, from *adulterāre*, to adulterate, make impure, commit adultery with.]

a·dult·hood (ə-dŭlt′ho͝od′) *n.* The time or condition of being fully grown and developed; maturity.

adv. *abbr.* An abbreviation of adverb.

ad·vance (ăd-văns′) *v.* **ad·vanced, ad·vanc·ing, ad·vanc·es** *—tr.* **1.** To move (something) forward, onward, or ahead: *In checkers players advance their pieces one square at a time.* **2.** To put forward; propose or offer: *advance a theory.* **3.** To aid the growth or progress of; promote: *Scientific research advances knowledge.* **4.** To raise in rank or position: *advance a soldier from private to sergeant.* **5a.** To move ahead to a later time: *Advance your watch one hour in the spring.* **b.** To move from a later to an earlier time: *advance a deadline from June to May.* **6.** To lend or pay (money) ahead of time: *The company advanced him a week's pay.* *—intr.* **1.** To move forward, onward, or ahead: *A cat advanced toward the bird.* **2.** To make progress; improve or grow: *We are advancing in our studies.* **3.** To rise in rank or position: *The police officer advanced from sergeant to lieutenant.* ❖ *n.* **1.** Forward or onward movement: *the rapid advance of fire through the forest.* **2.** A forward step; an improvement or development: *recent advances in science.* **3.** A loan or payment made ahead of time: *Can you get an advance on your allowance?* **4. advances** Approaches or efforts made to win someone's friendship or favor: *advances to make up after a quarrel.* ❖ *adj.* **1.** Made or given ahead of time: *advance warning.* **2.** Going before: *the advance guard.* ◆ **in advance** Ahead of time; beforehand: *Make your travel plans in advance.* **in advance of** In front of; ahead of: *She skied in advance of us, showing us the way.* [From Middle English *avauncen*, from Latin *abante*, in front.]

ad·vanced (ăd-vănst′) *adj.* **1.** Highly developed or complex; beyond in progress: *an advanced technology.* **2.** At a level higher than others: *an advanced student; advanced courses.* **3.** Far along in course or time: *illness in its advanced stages; advanced age.*

ad·vance·ment (ăd-văns′mənt) *n.* **1.** The act of advancing or the condition of being advanced. **2.** A forward step; an improvement or development: *new advance-*

USAGE

adopt The two words **adopted** and **adoptive** are similar in appearance, but they refer to different situations. Someone who is *adopted* has been taken into a family by legal means and raised as the child of that family. The word *adoptive* means "adopting" or "having adopted" and refers to the family who has adopted a child.

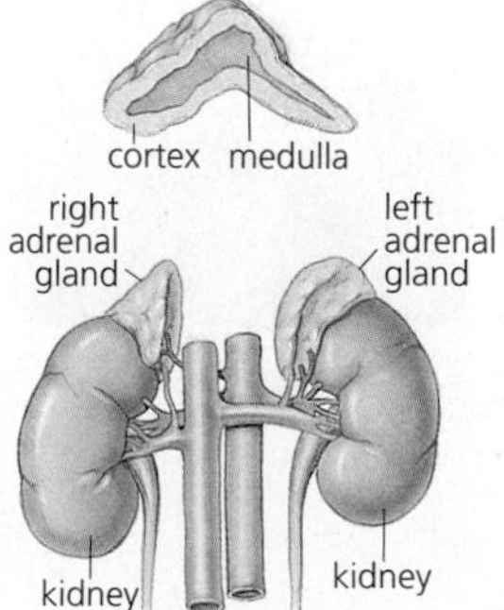

adrenal gland
top: cross section of a right adrenal gland
bottom: placement of adrenal glands relative to kidneys

ments in science. **3.** A promotion: *an advancement to a managerial position.*

ad·van·tage (ăd-**văn′**tĭj) *n.* **1.** A beneficial factor or feature: *Museums and libraries are some of the advantages of city life.* **2.** Benefit or profit: *She learned from her mistake, turning it to her advantage.* **3.** A favorable or preferred position: *Their early start gave them the advantage.* ◆ **to advantage** To good effect; favorably: *The summer job let him display his talents to advantage.* [From Middle English *avantage*, from Old French *avant*, before, from Latin *abante*, in front.]

ad·van·ta·geous (ăd′vən-**tā′**jəs) *adj.* Providing an advantage: *an advantageous location.* **—ad′van·ta′geous·ly** *adv.* **—ad′van·ta′geous·ness** *n.*

ad·vent (**ăd′**vĕnt′) *n.* **1.** The coming of a new person or thing: *before the advent of the airplane.* **2. Advent** The birth or coming of Jesus. **3. Advent** The period including the four Sundays before Christmas, observed by many Christians as a time of prayer and penitence. [From Old English, from Latin *adventus*, arrival, from *advenīre*, to come to : *ad-*, toward + *venīre*, to come.]

Ad·vent·ist (**ăd′**vĕn′tĭst *or* ăd-**vĕn′**tĭst) *n.* A member of a Christian denomination that believes Jesus's Second Coming and the end of the world are near. **—Ad′vent′·ism** *n.*

ad·ven·ti·tious (ăd′vĕn-**tĭsh′**əs) *adj.* **1.** Acquired or happening by chance: *an adventitious occurrence.* **2.** In zoology and botany, appearing in an unusual place or in an irregular manner: *a plant with adventitious shoots.*

ad·ven·ture (ăd-**vĕn′**chər) *n.* **1.** A bold, dangerous, or risky undertaking: *They set out on a daring adventure in the wilderness.* **2.** An unusual, exciting, or memorable experience: *Going to the art museum is always an adventure.* **3.** Excitement, danger, or discovery arising from bold action or new experience: *in search of adventure.* ❖ *v.* **ad·ven·tured, ad·ven·tur·ing, ad·ven·tures** *—intr.* To go in search of new or exciting experiences. *—tr.* To venture; risk. [From Middle English *aventure*, from Latin *advenīre*, to arrive.]

ad·ven·tur·er (ăd-**vĕn′**chər-ər) *n.* **1.** A person who seeks or has adventures. **2.** A person who seeks wealth in dangerous undertakings or by less than honest means: *The prospector was an old adventurer.*

ad·ven·ture·some (ăd-**vĕn′**chər-səm) *adj.* Bold; daring; adventurous.

ad·ven·tur·ous (ăd-**vĕn′**chər-əs) *adj.* **1.** Fond of adventure; seeking new experience; willing to take risks: *adventurous youths hiking in the wilderness.* **2.** Full of adventure or risk: *the pioneer's adventurous journey.* **—ad·ven′tur·ous·ly** *adv.* **—ad·ven′tur·ous·ness** *n.*

ad·verb (**ăd′**vûrb) *n.* **1.** The part of speech that modifies a verb, adjective, or other adverb. **2.** A word belonging to this part of speech. For example, in the sentences *They left early, The peacock is very pretty,* and *The dog ran very fast,* the words *early, very,* and *fast* are adverbs.

ad·ver·bi·al (ăd-**vûr′**bē-əl) *adj.* **1.** Used as an adverb: *an adverbial phrase.* **2.** Relating to an adverb: *an adverbial form.* **—ad·ver′bi·al·ly** *adv.*

ad·ver·sar·y (**ăd′**vər-sĕr′ē) *n., pl.* **ad·ver·sar·ies** An opponent or enemy: *The lawyers for the two sides were adversaries.*

ad·verse (ăd-**vûrs′** *or* **ăd′**vûrs′) *adj.* **1.** Not favorable; hostile: *adverse criticism; an adverse decision.* **2.** In an opposite direction: *Adverse currents pushed against the boat.* [From Middle English, from Latin *adversus*, past participle of *advertere*, to turn toward : *ad-*, toward + *vertere*, to turn.] **—ad·verse′ly** *adv.* **—ad·verse′ness** *n.*

ad·ver·si·ty (ăd-**vûr′**sĭ-tē) *n., pl.* **ad·ver·si·ties** Great misfortune; hardship.

ad·ver·tise (**ăd′**vər-tīz′) *v.* **ad·ver·tised, ad·ver·tis·ing, ad·ver·tis·es** *—tr.* **1.** To call public attention to (a product or business), especially in hope of increasing sales: *Manufacturers advertise their products.* **2.** To make known; call attention to: *Mistakes in arithmetic advertised the student's carelessness. —intr.* To give public notice of something, as something wanted or offered for sale: *The building's owner advertised in the newspaper for a tenant.* [From Middle English *advertisen*, from Old French *advertir*, to notice.] **—ad′ver·tis′er** *n.*

ad·ver·tise·ment (**ăd′**vər-tīz′mənt) *n.* A public notice, as in a newspaper or on television, designed to call attention to a product, meeting, or event.

ad·ver·tis·ing (**ăd′**vər-tī′zĭng) *n.* **1.** The activity of attracting public attention to a product or business. **2.** The business of preparing and distributing advertisements: *Many people are employed in advertising.* **3.** Advertisements considered as a group: *How much advertising does the magazine have?*

ad·vice (ăd-**vīs′**) *n.* Opinion about how to solve a problem; guidance: *The pupil sought advice from the teacher.*

ad·vis·a·ble (ăd-**vī′**zə-bəl) *adj.* Worth recommending or suggesting; wise; sensible: *Driving fast in the rain is not advisable.* **—ad·vis′a·bil′i·ty** *n.* **—ad·vis′a·bly** *adv.*

ad·vise (ăd-**vīz′**) *tr.v.* **ad·vised, ad·vis·ing, ad·vis·es 1.** To give advice to: *The doctor advised the patient to get some rest.* **2.** To recommend: *Our mechanic advised a complete overhaul of the car's motor.* **3.** To inform; notify: *The radio advised us of the coming storm.* [From Middle English *avisen*, from Old French *avis*, advice.]

ad·vised (ăd-**vīzd′**) *adj.* **1.** Thought out; considered: *a poorly advised decision.* **2.** Informed; notified: *Police kept motorists advised of all new developments in road conditions.*

ad·vis·ed·ly (ăd-**vī′**zĭd-lē) *adv.* With careful consideration; deliberately.

ad·vise·ment (ăd-**vīz′**mənt) *n.* Careful consideration: *Your request will be taken under advisement.*

ad·vis·er or **ad·vi·sor** (ăd-**vī′**zər) *n.* **1.** A person who offers advice, especially officially or professionally: *The local doctor served as the school's health adviser.* **2.** A teacher who advises students in selecting courses and planning careers.

ad·vi·so·ry (ăd-**vī′**zə-rē) *adj.* **1.** Having the power to advise: *an advisory committee.* **2.** Relating to or containing advice: *an advisory report.* ❖ *n., pl.* **ad·vi·so·ries** A report giving information and especially a warning: *a weather advisory.*

ad·vo·ca·cy (**ăd′**və-kə-sē) *n.* Active support, as of an idea, cause, or policy.

ad·vo·cate (**ăd′**və-kāt′) *tr.v.* **ad·vo·cat·ed, ad·vo·cat·ing, ad·vo·cates** To be or speak in favor of; recommend; urge: *advocate changes in the law controlling air pollution.* ❖ *n.* (**ăd′**və-kĭt) **1.** A person who supports or speaks in favor of a cause: *an advocate of animal rights.* **2.** A lawyer. [From Middle English *advocat*, lawyer, from Latin *advocāre*, to summon for counsel : *ad-*, toward + *vocāre*, to call.] **—ad′vo·ca′tion** *n.* **—ad′vo·ca′tor** *n.*

adze or **adz** (ădz) *n.* A tool used for shaping wood and resembling an axe but having a slightly curved blade that is roughly parallel to the ground when the shaft is positioned vertically. [From Old English *adesa.*]

Ae·ge·an Sea (ĭ-**jē′**ən) An arm of the Mediterranean Sea off southeast Europe between Greece and Turkey. Most of the **Aegean Islands** belong to Greece.

ae·gis (**ē′**jĭs) *n.* **1.** Protection or care: *an expanse of land under the aegis of the state.* **2.** Sponsorship or patronage: *a conference under the aegis of the United Nations.* [From Greek *aigis*, shield covered with goatskin, from *aix*, goat.]

Ae·ne·as (ĭ-**nē′**əs) *n.* In Greek and Roman mythology, the Trojan warrior and son of Aphrodite who escaped during the fall of Troy and wandered for seven years before settling in Italy.

WRITERS CHOOSE THEIR WORDS

I saw no need to tell him about my letter to my brother. Abraham has always told me that the less you let an **adversary** know about you, the better off you'll be.

—Ann Rinaldi
A Ride into Morning: The Story of Tempe Wick

aerialist

ă	pat	ôr	core
ā	pay	oi	boy
âr	care	ou	out
ä	father	o͝o	took
ĕ	pet	o͝or	lure
ē	be	o͞o	boot
ĭ	pit	ŭ	cut
ī	bite	ûr	urge
îr	pier	th	thin
ŏ	pot	*th*	this
ō	toe	zh	vision
ô	paw	ə	about

Ae·ne·id (ĭ-nē′ĭd) *n.* An ancient Latin epic poem written by Virgil, relating the adventures of Aeneas and his followers after the fall of Troy.

Ae·o·lus (ē′ə-ləs) *n.* In Greek mythology, the god of the winds.

ae·on (ē′ŏn′ *or* ē′ən) *n.* Variant of **eon.**

aer– *pref.* Variant of **aero–.**

aer·ate (âr′āt) *tr.v.* **aer·at·ed, aer·at·ing, aer·ates 1.** To expose to the circulation of the air: *Open the windows and aerate the room.* **2.** To supply with oxygen: *The lungs aerate the blood.* **3.** To supply or charge (a liquid) with air or another gas, such as carbon dioxide. **—aer·a′tion** *n.* **—aer′a′tor** *n.*

aer·i·al (âr′ē-əl) *adj.* **1.** In, relating to, or caused by air: *aerial currents.* **2.** For, by, or relating to aircraft: *aerial reconnaissance.* **3.** High; lofty. **4.** Growing in air without underground support: *aerial roots.* ❖ *n.* An antenna for receiving or transmitting radio or television signals. **—aer′i·al·ly** *adv.*

aer·i·al·ist (âr′ē-ə-lĭst) *n.* An acrobat who performs in the air, as on a tightrope or trapeze.

aer·ie or **aer·y** also **ey·rie** (âr′ē *or* îr′ē) *n., pl.* **aer·ies** also **ey·ries 1.** The nest of an eagle or other bird of prey, built on a cliff or other high place. **2.** A house or stronghold built on a height.
❑ *These sound alike:* **aerie, airy** (breezy).

aero– or **aer–** *pref.* A prefix that means: **1.** Air or atmosphere: *aerodynamics; aeroplane.* **2.** Gas: *aerosol.* **3.** Aviation: *aeronautics.* [From Greek *āēr,* air.]

aer·o·bat·ic (âr′ə-băt′ĭk) *adj.* Relating to spectacular maneuvers, such as rolls and loops, performed by an airplane or by groups of airplanes flying together.

aer·obe (âr′ōb′) *n.* An organism that requires oxygen to live.

aer·o·bic (â-rō′bĭk) *adj.* **1.** Needing or using oxygen to live: *aerobic bacteria.* **2.** Relating to exercise that is intended to improve the body's ability to use oxygen: *aerobic dancing.*

aer·o·bics (â-rō′bĭks) *n. (used with a singular or plural verb)* Physical exercise intended to improve the body's use of oxygen. Aerobics often involves calisthenics, dance routines, and other activities that raise the heart rate.

aer·o·drome (âr′ə-drōm′) *n. Chiefly British* An airport or airfield.

aer·o·dy·nam·ic (âr′ō-dī-năm′ĭk) *adj.* **1.** Relating to aerodynamics. **2.** Designed to reduce wind drag: *a car with an aerodynamic shape.* **—aer′o·dy·nam′i·cal·ly** *adv.*

aer·o·dy·nam·ics (âr′ō-dī-năm′ĭks) *n. (used with a singular verb)* **1.** The scientific study of the motions of and forces associated with air and other gases, especially as they interact with objects moving through them. **2.** The interaction of a moving object with the atmosphere: *the aerodynamics of a new car design.*

aer·o·nau·tic (âr′ə-nô′tĭk) also **aer·o·nau·ti·cal** (âr′ə-nô′tĭ-kəl) *adj.* Relating to aeronautics. **—aer′o·nau′ti·cal·ly** *adv.*

aer·o·nau·tics (âr′ə-nô′tĭks) *n. (used with a singular verb)* **1.** The design and construction of aircraft. **2.** The theory and practice of flying aircraft.

aer·o·plane (âr′ə-plān′) *n. Chiefly British* Variant of **airplane.**

aer·o·sol (âr′ə-sôl′) *n.* **1.** A substance consisting of very fine particles of a liquid or solid suspended in a gas: *Mist and fog are aerosols.* **2.** A substance, such as paint, insecticide, or hair spray, packaged under pressure for use in this form. **3.** An aerosol can.

aerosol can *n.* A can containing a liquid, such as paint or a deodorant, packaged under pressure with a gas to be released as a spray.

aer·o·space (âr′ō-spās′) *adj.* **1.** Relating to Earth's atmosphere and the space beyond. **2.** Relating to the science and technology of flight.

aer·y (âr′ē *or* îr′ē) *n.* Variant of **aerie.**

Ae·sir (ā′sîr′ *or* ā′zîr′) *pl.n.* The gods of Norse mythology.

Ae·sop (ē′səp *or* ē′sŏp′) Sixth century BC. Greek storyteller who is traditionally considered the author of *Aesop's Fables,* including "The Tortoise and the Hare."

aes·thet·ic (ĕs-thĕt′ĭk) *adj.* **1.** Relating to aesthetics. **2.** Relating to beauty or good taste: *a room with a strong aesthetic quality.* ❖ *n.* An underlying set of principles that influences style or taste: *the building's stark Modernist aesthetic.*

aes·thet·ics (ĕs-thĕt′ĭks) *n. (used with a singular verb)* The study of the nature and forms of beauty, as in art.

Aet·na (ĕt′nə), **Mount** See Mount **Etna.**

AF *abbr.* An abbreviation of: **1.** air force. **2.** audio frequency.

AFAIK *abbr.* An abbreviation of as far as I know.

a·far (ə-fär′) *adv.* Far away; far off: *saw the bird afar off.* ◆ **from afar** From a long distance: *a star shining afar.*

AFB *abbr.* An abbreviation of air force base.

af·fa·ble (ăf′ə-bəl) *adj.* Easy to speak to; pleasant; friendly. **—af′fa·bil′i·ty** *n.* **—af′fa·bly** *adv.*

af·fair (ə-fâr′) *n.* **1.** An occurrence, action, event, or procedure: *Building a skyscraper is a long and costly affair.* **2.** A matter of concern: *Their argument was a private affair.* **3. affairs** Matters of business interest or public concern: *affairs of state.* **4.** A social gathering: *The ball was a glittering affair.* **5.** A brief romantic relationship between two people. [From Middle English *afer,* from Old French *a faire,* to do, (needing) to be done : *a,* to + *faire,* to do.]

af·fect[1] (ə-fĕkt′) *tr.v.* **af·fect·ed, af·fect·ing, af·fects 1.** To have an influence on; bring about a change in: *The drought has affected the fruit crop.* **2.** To touch or move the emotions of: *The movie affected us deeply.* **3.** To attack or infect: *Arthritis affects many older people.* [From Middle English *affecten,* from Latin *affectāre,* to try to achieve, strive after, from *afficere,* to have an effect on.] —SEE NOTE.

af·fect[2] (ə-fĕkt′) *tr.v.* **af·fect·ed, af·fect·ing, af·fects** To put on a false show of; pretend to have: *He affected indifference, though he was hurt by the remark.* [From Middle English *affecten,* from Old French *affecten,* from Latin *affectāre,* to strive after, feign, from *afficere,* to have an effect on.]

af·fec·ta·tion (ăf′ĕk-tā′shən) *n.* A way of behaving that is not natural but is adopted to impress others: *Everyone thought his British accent was an affectation.*

af·fect·ed[1] (ə-fĕk′tĭd) *adj.* **1.** Acted upon, influenced, or changed: *the affected business in this recession.* **2.** Acted upon in an injurious way, as by disease or malfunction: *rubbed ointment on the affected area.*

af·fect·ed[2] (ə-fĕk′tĭd) *adj.* Speaking or behaving in an artificial way to make an impression: *an affected tone of voice.* **—af·fect′ed·ly** *adv.* **—af·fect′ed·ness** *n.*

af·fect·ing (ə-fĕk′tĭng) *adj.* Touching the emotions; moving: *an affecting tale of woe.*

af·fec·tion (ə-fĕk′shən) *n.* A fond or tender feeling toward someone or something; fondness.

af·fec·tion·ate (ə-fĕk′shə-nĭt) *adj.* Having or showing affection; tender; loving. **—af·fec′tion·ate·ly** *adv.*

af·fer·ent (ăf′ər-ənt) *adj.* Directed or leading toward a central organ or part of an organism: *an afferent nerve.*

af·fi·ance (ə-fī′əns) *tr.v.* **af·fi·anced, af·fi·anc·ing, af·fi·anc·es** To promise to marry: *The lovers were affianced to each other.*

af·fi·da·vit (ăf′ĭ-dā′vĭt) *n.* A written declaration made under oath before a notary public or other authorized officer. [From Latin *affidāvit,* he has pledged.]

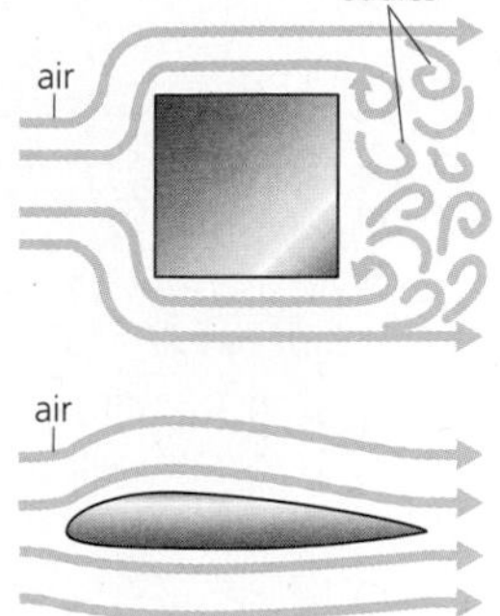

aerodynamics
top: high drag on a less aerodynamic shape
bottom: low drag on a more aerodynamic shape

WRITERS CHOOSE THEIR WORDS

He was **affable,** courteous, and cooperative, remaining calm when besieged by newsmen and doing his best to fulfill their requests.

—Walter Farley
The Black Stallion and the Girl

USAGE

affect[1] The words **affect** and **effect** look and sound similar. Their meanings, however, are very different. The verb *affect* means "to influence": *That decision will affect my whole life.* The verb *effect* means "to make happen": *We effected some helpful changes.* The noun *effect* can mean "a result" or "an influence," but only the verb *affect* means "to influence."

af·fil·i·ate (ə-fĭl′ē-āt′) *v.* **af·fil·i·at·ed, af·fil·i·at·ing, af·fil·i·ates** —*tr.* To adopt or accept as a member, subordinate associate, or branch: *The local unit of the Red Cross is affiliated with the national organization.* —*intr.* To become connected or associated: *The two unions voted to affiliate.* ❖ *n.* (ə-fĭl′ē-ĭt *or* ə-fĭl′ē-āt′) A person or organization associated or joined with a larger or more important body: *Our company has affiliates in Europe as well as the United States.* [From Medieval Latin *affiliāre*, to adopt : Latin *ad-*, to + Latin *fīlius*, son.]

af·fin·i·ty (ə-fĭn′ĭ-tē) *n., pl.* **af·fin·i·ties 1.** A natural attraction; a liking: *Our dog has an affinity for young children.* **2.** A similarity based on relationship: *The twins have a closer affinity than most members of their family.* **3.** An attraction or force between particles or chemicals that causes them to combine. [From Middle English *affinitee*, relationship by marriage, from Latin *affīnitās*, from *affīnis*, related by marriage.]

af·firm (ə-fûrm′) *tr.v.* **af·firmed, af·firm·ing, af·firms 1.** To declare positively; say firmly: *She affirmed her intention to run for the Senate seat.* **2.** To give approval or validity to; confirm: *The appeals court affirmed the lower court's ruling.*

af·fir·ma·tion (ăf′ər-mā′shən) *n.* **1.** The act of affirming; assertion. **2.** Something declared to be true.

af·fir·ma·tive (ə-fûr′mə-tĭv) *adj.* Affirming that something is true, as with the answer "yes": *an affirmative response.* ❖ *n.* **1.** A word or statement of agreement or assent. **2.** The side in a debate that supports the proposition in question. ◆ **in the affirmative** Expressing agreement; saying "yes." —**af·fir′ma·tive·ly** *adv.*

affirmative action *n.* A policy or program that actively attempts to correct past discrimination by improving the opportunities for members of underrepresented groups in employment and education.

A-frame

af·fix (ə-fĭks′) *tr.v.* **af·fixed, af·fix·ing, af·fix·es 1.** To fasten to something; attach: *affix a label to a package.* **2.** To add at the end; append: *I affixed my name to the letter.* ❖ *n.* (ăf′ĭks′) A word element, usually one or more syllables in length, that is added at the beginning or the end of a word or word part to change its meaning or make another word; a prefix or suffix.

af·flict (ə-flĭkt′) *tr.v.* **af·flict·ed, af·flict·ing, af·flicts** To cause distress to; cause to suffer: *Humans are afflicted with many diseases.* [From Middle English *afflighten*, from Latin *afflīgere*, to knock down.]

af·flic·tion (ə-flĭk′shən) *n.* **1.** A condition of pain or distress. **2.** A cause of pain or suffering: *Scurvy used to be a common affliction among sailors.*

af·flu·ence (ăf′lo͞o-əns *or* ə-flo͞o′əns) *n.* A plentiful supply of goods or money; wealth.

af·flu·ent (ăf′lo͞o-ənt *or* ə-flo͞o′ənt) *adj.* Having plenty of money, property, or possessions; wealthy. —**af′flu·ent·ly** *adv.*

af·ford (ə-fôrd′) *tr.v.* **af·ford·ed, af·ford·ing, af·fords 1.** To be able to pay for: *By saving we can afford a new computer.* **2.** To be able to give or spare: *I am too busy to afford the time just now.* **3.** To be able to do without harming oneself: *Anyone can afford to be kind.* **4.** To give or furnish; provide: *This window affords a view of the mountains.* [From Middle English *aforthen*, from Old English *geforthian*, to carry out.]

af·fray (ə-frā′) *n.* A noisy quarrel or brawl.

af·fright (ə-frīt′) *tr.v.* **af·fright·ed, af·fright·ing, af·frights** To frighten; terrify.

af·front (ə-frŭnt′) *tr.v.* **af·front·ed, af·front·ing, af·fronts** To insult intentionally or openly. ❖ *n.* An intentional insult or offense.

Af·ghan (ăf′găn′) *adj.* Relating to Afghanistan or the Afghans. ❖ *n.* **1.** A native or inhabitant of Afghanistan. **2. afghan** A colorful wool blanket or shawl knitted or crocheted in squares, circles, or other designs. **3.** A large, slender dog of a breed having long thick hair, a pointed snout, and drooping ears.

af·ghan·i (ăf-găn′ē *or* ăf-gä′nē) *n.* The basic monetary unit of Afghanistan.

Afghani *adj.* Relating to Afghanistan; Afghan. ❖ *n., pl.* **Af·ghan·is** A native or inhabitant of Afghanistan; an Afghan.

Af·ghan·i·stan (ăf-găn′ĭ-stăn′) A landlocked, mostly mountainous country of southwest-central Asia east of Iran. US forces invaded in 2001 as a response to the 9/11 attacks. Kabul is the capital.

a·fi·cio·na·do (ə-fĭsh′ē-ə-nä′dō) *n., pl.* **a·fi·cio·na·dos** An enthusiastic admirer; a devotee.

a·field (ə-fēld′) *adv.* **1a.** Away from one's usual environment; to or at a distance: *The children wandered far afield in search of butterflies.* **b.** Off or away from the subject: *The witness's remarks went farther afield.* **2.** In or on the field: *The geologist preferred working afield to reading papers in the office.*

a·fire (ə-fīr′) *adv. & adj.* On fire; burning: *The room was afire.*

a·flame (ə-flām′) *adv. & adj.* **1.** In flames: *The house is aflame.* **2.** Intensely excited: *aflame with curiosity.*

AFL-CIO *abbr.* An abbreviation of American Federation of Labor and Congress of Industrial Organizations.

a·float (ə-flōt′) *adv. & adj.* **1.** In a floating condition: *The raft was afloat on the lake.* **2.** On a boat or ship; at sea. **3.** In circulation: *Talk of a change in managers is afloat.* **4.** Free of difficulty, especially financial difficulty: *couldn't keep the business afloat.*

a·flut·ter (ə-flŭt′ər) *adj.* **1.** Fluttering: *The flags were aflutter.* **2.** Nervously excited.

a·foot (ə-fo͝ot′) *adv. & adj.* **1.** On foot; walking: *They traveled afoot.* **2.** In the process of happening; astir: *Something strange is afoot.*

a·fore (ə-fôr′) *adv. & prep.* A dialectal variant of **before.**

a·fore·men·tioned (ə-fôr′mĕn′shənd) *adj.* Mentioned before.

a·fore·said (ə-fôr′sĕd′) *adj.* Spoken of earlier.

a·fore·thought (ə-fôr′thôt′) *adj.* Planned beforehand; premeditated: *with malice aforethought.*

a·foul of (ə-foul′) *prep.* **1.** In entanglement with: *The anchor fell afoul of the fishing lines.* **2.** In trouble with: *ran afoul of the law.*

Afr. *abbr.* An abbreviation of: **1.** Africa. **2.** African.

a·fraid (ə-frād′) *adj.* **1.** Filled with fear; fearful: *afraid of the dark.* **2.** Reluctant; hesitant: *not afraid of work.* **3.** Feeling concern or regret: *I'm afraid you don't understand.* [From Middle English *affraied*, from Old French *esfraier*, to disturb.]

A-frame (ā′frām′) *n.* A house built on a frame shaped like the letter A.

a·fresh (ə-frĕsh′) *adv.* Anew; again: *We must start afresh.*

Af·ri·ca (ăf′rĭ-kə) The second-largest continent, connected to Asia by the Isthmus of Suez and lying between the Mediterranean Sea and the Atlantic and Indian Oceans.

Af·ri·can (ăf′rĭ-kən) *adj.* Relating to Africa or its peoples, languages, or cultures. ❖ *n.* **1.** A native or inhabitant of Africa. **2.** A person of African ancestry.

Af·ri·ca·na (ăf′rĭ-kä′nə *or* ăf′rĭ-kā′nə) *n.* *(used with a plural verb)* Things that are examples of the history or culture of African peoples: *a room decorated with Africana such as weavings and masks.*

African American or **Af·ri·can-A·mer·i·can** (ăf′rĭ-kən-ə-mĕr′ĭ-kən) *n.* A black American of African ancestry. —**Af′ri·can-A·mer′i·can** *adj.*

African American Vernacular English *n.* Any of the nonstandard varieties of English spoken by African Americans.

African elephant *n.* Either of two elephants native to sub-Saharan Africa, having larger ears than the Asian

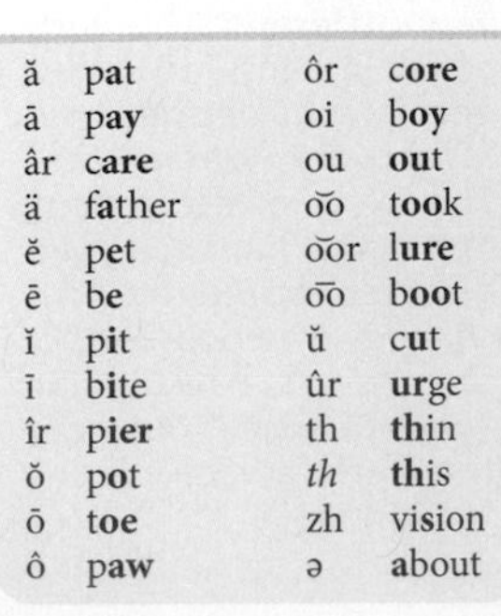

ă	pat	ôr	core
ā	pay	oi	boy
âr	care	ou	out
ä	father	o͝o	took
ĕ	pet	o͝or	lure
ē	be	o͞o	boot
ĭ	pit	ŭ	cut
ī	bite	ûr	urge
îr	pier	th	thin
ŏ	pot	*th*	this
ō	toe	zh	vision
ô	paw	ə	about

elephant. Both males and females usually have tusks.

African violet *n.* A popular houseplant, originally from Africa, with usually purplish flowers and velvety leaves.

Af·ri·kaans (ăf′rĭ-**käns′** *or* ăf′rĭ-**känz′**) *n.* A language that developed from 17th-century Dutch and is an official language of South Africa.

Af·ri·ka·ner (ăf′rĭ-**kä′**nər) *n.* An Afrikaans-speaking South African of European and especially Dutch ancestry.

Af·ro (**ăf′**rō) *n., pl.* **Af·ros** A hairstyle in which the hair is rounded, thick, and tightly curled. ❖ *adj.* African in style or origin.

Af·ro-A·mer·i·can (ăf′rō-ə-**mĕr′**ĭ-kən) *n.* An African American. **—Af′ro-A·mer′i·can** *adj.*

Af·ro-A·si·at·ic (af′rō-ā′zhē-**ăt′**ĭk) *n.* A family of languages spoken in northern Africa and southwest Asia, including the Semitic and ancient Egyptian languages. **—Af′ro-A′si·at′ic** *adj.*

Af·ro·cen·tric (ăf′rō-**sĕn′**trĭk) *adj.* Centered or focused on Africa or African peoples: *an Afrocentric history textbook.*

aft (ăft) *adv. & adj.* Toward or near the stern of a ship or aircraft: *going aft; the aft cabin.* [From Middle English *afte*, back, from Old English *æftan*, behind.]

af·ter (**ăf′**tər) *prep.* **1.** Behind in place or order: *Z comes after Y.* **2.** In pursuit of: *running after the fire engine.* **3.** About; concerning: *I asked after you.* **4.** At a later time than: *They arrived after dinner.* **5.** Past the hour of: *five minutes after three.* **6.** Suiting the nature or desires of: *a writer after my own heart.* **7.** With the same name as; in honor of: *named after his grandfather.* ❖ *adv.* **1.** At a later time: *We left shortly after.* **2.** Behind; in the rear: *First came the tractor and then the wagon came rumbling after.* ❖ *adj.* **1.** Later; following: *in after years.* **2.** Nearer a ship's stern: *the after quarter.* ❖ *conj.* Following the time that: *We can eat after we get home.* ◆ **after all** In spite of everything; nevertheless. [From Old English *æfter.*]

af·ter·birth (**ăf′**tər-bûrth′) *n.* The placenta and fetal membranes expelled from the uterus following birth.

af·ter·burn·er (**ăf′**tər-bûr′nər) *n.* A device in a jet engine that increases its power by injecting extra fuel into the hot exhaust gases.

af·ter·deck (**ăf′**tər-dĕk′) *n.* The part of a ship's deck near or toward the stern.

af·ter·ef·fect (**ăf′**tər-ĭ-fĕkt′) *n.* An effect that follows its cause after some delay, especially a delayed bodily or mental response to something: *The driver's nervousness was an aftereffect of the accident.*

af·ter·glow (**ăf′**tər-glō′) *n.* **1.** Light that remains after its source has disappeared, as the atmospheric glow that remains for a short time after sunset. **2.** A comfortable feeling after a pleasant experience.

af·ter·im·age (**ăf′**tər-ĭm′ĭj) *n.* An image that persists after the original source is no longer active: *the afterimage one sees after the flash of a camera.*

af·ter·life (**ăf′**tər-līf′) *n.* A life or existence believed to follow death.

af·ter·math (**ăf′**tər-măth′) *n.* **1.** A consequence or result, especially of a disaster or misfortune: *the aftermath of a hurricane.* **2.** A new growth or crop in the same season, especially of grass after mowing. [From *after* + obsolete *math*, a mowing (from Old English *mǣth*).]

af·ter·noon (ăf′tər-**no͞on′**) *n.* The part of day from noon until dinnertime or sunset.

af·ter·school (**ăf′**tər-**sko͞ol′**) *adj.* Relating to or being a program providing care for children following school classes.

af·ter·shock (**ăf′**tər-shŏk′) *n.* A less powerful quake coming after an earthquake.

af·ter·taste (**ăf′**tər-tāst′) *n.* **1.** A taste that remains in the mouth after the substance that caused it is no longer there. **2.** A feeling that lingers after an event: *an experience that left an unpleasant aftertaste.*

af·ter·thought (**ăf′**tər-thôt′) *n.* An idea that occurs to a person after something, such as an event or decision, has passed.

af·ter·ward (**ăf′**tər-wərd) also **af·ter·wards** (**ăf′**tər-wərdz) *adv.* At a later time; subsequently.

Ag The symbol for the element **silver.**

a·gain (ə-**gĕn′**) *adv.* **1.** Once more; anew: *If you don't win, try again.* **2.** To a previous place or position: *They left home but went back again.* **3.** As previously stated: *Again, I'm no expert.* **4.** On the other hand: *They might go, and again they might not.* **5.** In addition to a particular amount: *a new job paying half as much again as the old one.* ◆ **again and again** Often; repeatedly. [From Old English *ongeagn*, in the opposite direction, back.]

a·gainst (ə-**gĕnst′**) *prep.* **1.** In a direction or course opposite to: *sailing against the wind.* **2.** So as to come into contact with: *waves washing against the shore.* **3.** In hostile opposition or resistance to: *struggling against prejudice.* **4.** Contrary to: *against my better judgment.* **5.** In competition with: *raced against the record holder.* **6.** In contrast to: *dark colors against a light background.* **7.** As a defense or safeguard from: *wearing gloves against the cold.* **8.** To the account or debt of: *drew a check against my bank balance.* [From Middle English *againes*, from Old English *ongeagn*, in the opposite direction, back.]

a·gal (ə-**gäl′**) *n.* A band or series of cords used to hold a keffiyeh in place on the head. [From Arabic *'iqāl*, cord for hobbling a camel, agal.]

Ag·a·mem·non (ăg′ə-**mĕm′**nŏn′) *n.* In Greek mythology, the king of Mycenae and leader of the Greeks in the Trojan War.

A·ga·na (ə-**gä′**nyə) The capital of Guam, on the western coast of the island.

a·gape (ə-**gāp′**) *adv. & adj.* In a state of wonder or surprise: *The magician's dazzling tricks set the audience agape.*

a·gar (ā′gär′ *or* **ä′**gär′) also **a·gar-a·gar** (ā′gär-**ā′**gär′ *or* ä′gär-**ä′**gär′) *n.* A gelatinous material obtained from certain algae, used as a base on which bacteria are grown and as a thickener and stabilizer in food products.

Ag·as·siz (**ăg′**ə-sē), **(Jean) Louis (Rodolphe)** 1807–1873. Swiss-born American naturalist who introduced the idea of the Ice Age. He is also noted for his study of fossil fish.

ag·ate (**ăg′**ĭt) *n.* **1.** A type of quartz found in various colors that are arranged in bands or in cloudy patterns. **2.** A marble used in games that is made of this quartz or of glass.

a·ga·ve (ə-**gä′**vē) *n.* Any of numerous plants of hot dry regions of the Americas, having a tall flower stalk and tough, usually spiny leaves that were formerly an important source of fiber used for making rope or sacks.

age (āj) *n.* **1.** The length of time during which a person or thing has existed; a lifetime or lifespan: *Elephants are known for their great age.* **2.** One of the stages of life: *the age of adolescence.* **3.** The time in life when a person is allowed to assume adult rights and responsibilities, usually at 18 or 21 years: *Children are under age.* **4.** The state of being old; old age. **5.** often **Age** A distinctive period of history: *the Iron Age.* **6.** **ages** A long time: *It took ages to clean up after dinner.* ❖ *v.* **aged, ag·ing, ag·es** —*tr.* **1.** To cause to grow old: *The crisis seemed to age the president.* **2.** To allow to mature or become flavorful: *They aged the wine in oak casks.* —*intr.* **1.** To become or look old: *The flimsy house aged poorly through the years.* **2.** To develop a certain quality of ripeness; become mature: *cheeses aging at room temperature.* ◆ **come of age** To reach maturity or adulthood. [From Middle English, from Old French, from Latin *aetās.*]

–age *suff.* A suffix that means: **1a.** Collection; mass: *leaf-*

African violet

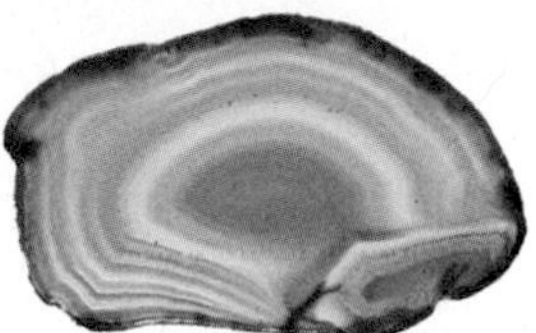

agate

agave

age. **b.** Amount: *mileage.* **2.** Condition; state: *patronage.* **3.** Charge or fee: *postage.* **4.** Residence or place: *orphanage.* **5.** Act or result: *breakage; spoilage.*

ag·ed (ā′jĭd) *adj.* **1.** Old; elderly. **2.** (ājd) Having reached the age of: *a child aged five.* **3.** (ājd) Ripe; mature: *aged cheese.* ❖ *n.* Elderly people considered as a group: *Many of the aged continue to exercise.*

age·ing (ā′jĭng) *n. Chiefly British* Variant of **aging.**

age·ism (ā′jĭz′əm) *n.* Discrimination based on age, especially against elderly people, as in regard to employment and housing.

age·less (āj′lĭs) *adj.* **1.** Experienced or old and still active and vibrant: *an ageless movie star.* **2.** Existing forever or for a very long time: *ageless stories of daring and adventure.* **—age′less·ly** *adv.*

a·gen·cy (ā′jən-sē) *n., pl.* **a·gen·cies 1.** The process of acting on behalf of someone else: *Through the producer's agency, another show was added to the schedule.* **2.** A business with agents who negotiate deals for clients: *a real estate agency.* **3.** A governmental department of administration or regulation: *the agency that administers the recycling program.*

a·gen·da (ə-jĕn′də) *n., pl.* **a·gen·das** A list of things to be considered or done, as a program of business at a meeting.

a·gent (ā′jənt) *n.* **1.** A person with the power or authority to act for another: *a ticket agent; a publicity agent.* **2.** A representative of a government or a governmental department: *an FBI agent.* **3a.** A substance that has a chemical or biological effect. **b.** An organism or other factor that causes disease, such as a bacterium or virus. **4.** A means by which something is done or caused: *Wind and rain are agents of erosion.* [From Middle English, from Latin *agere*, to do.]

age-old (āj′ōld′) *adj.* Very old; ancient: *an age-old story.*

ag·glom·er·ate (ə-glŏm′ə-rāt′) *tr. & intr.v.* **ag·glom·er·at·ed, ag·glom·er·at·ing, ag·glom·er·ates** To make or form into a rounded mass: *Heat and pressure have agglomerated much of the earth's rock.* ❖ *adj.* (ə-**glŏm′**-ər-ĭt) Gathered and shaped into a rounded mass. ❖ *n.* (ə-**glŏm′**ər-ĭt) **1.** A mass of things jumbled together. **2.** A volcanic rock consisting of rounded and angular fragments fused together.

ag·glom·er·a·tion (ə-glŏm′ə-**rā′**shən) *n.* **1.** The act or process of massing things together: *the continual agglomeration of rocks at the foot of the cliff.* **2.** A jumbled mass.

ag·glu·ti·nate (ə-glo͞ot′n-āt′) *v.* **ag·glu·ti·nat·ed, ag·glu·ti·nat·ing, ag·glu·ti·nates** *—tr.* To cause (cells or particles) to clump together. *—intr.* To undergo agglutination.

ag·glu·ti·na·tion (ə-glo͞ot′n-**ā′**shən) *n.* **1.** The clumping together of cells or particles, especially bacteria or red blood cells, usually in the presence of a specific antibody or other substance. **2.** The clumped mass formed in this way.

ag·gran·dize (ə-**grăn′**dīz′ *or* **ăg′**rən-dīz′) *tr.v.* **ag·gran·dized, ag·gran·diz·ing, ag·gran·diz·es** To make greater, as in power or influence. **—ag·gran′dize·ment** (ə-**grăn′**dĭz-mənt) *n.* **—ag·gran′diz′er** *n.*

ag·gra·vate (ăg′rə-vāt′) *tr.v.* **ag·gra·vat·ed, ag·gra·vat·ing, ag·gra·vates 1.** To make worse: *aggravate an injury.* **2.** To annoy or provoke: *Our constant noise aggravated the neighbors.* [From Middle English *aggravate*, weighed down, from Latin *aggravāre*, to weigh down : *ad-*, to + *gravāre*, to burden (from *gravis*, heavy).] **—ag′gra·vat′ing·ly** *adv.* **—ag′gra·va′tor** *n.*

ag·gra·va·tion (ăg′rə-**vā′**shən) *n.* **1.** The act or process of aggravating. **2.** Irritation; annoyance.

ag·gre·gate (**ăg′**rĭ-gĭt) *adj.* Gathered into or considered together as a whole; total. ❖ *n.* **1.** A total or whole; a gross amount. **2.** The mineral materials, such as sand and stone, used to make concrete. ❖ *tr.v.* (**ăg′**rĭ-gāt′) **ag·gre·gat·ed, ag·gre·gat·ing, ag·gre·gates 1.** To gather into a mass, sum, or whole. **2.** To amount to; total. ◆ **in the aggregate** Taken as a whole; considered collectively. [From Middle English *aggregat*, from Latin *aggregāre*, to add to : *ad-*, to + *gregāre*, to collect (from *grex*, flock).] **—ag′gre·gate·ly** *adv.* **—ag′gre·gate·ness** *n.*

ag·gre·ga·tion (ăg′rĭ-**gā′**shən) *n.* **1.** The collecting of separate things into one mass or whole. **2.** The group or mass collected.

ag·gres·sion (ə-**grĕsh′**ən) *n.* **1.** Hostile or violent action or behavior: *I was frightened by the dog's aggression and left the package outside the gate.* **2.** The practice of taking hostile actions or making military attacks. **3.** Behavior that is disagreeably assertive or overbearing: *The politician showed displeasure with the reporter's aggression.* [From Latin *aggressiō*, an attack, from *aggredī*, to approach, assault : *ad-*, to + *gradī*, to step.]

ag·gres·sive (ə-**grĕs′**ĭv) *adj.* **1.** Characterized by aggression: *aggressive behavior.* **2.** Given to aggression: *an aggressive person.* **3.** Vigorous; energetic: *an aggressive campaign to promote physical fitness.* **—ag·gres′sive·ly** *adv.* **—ag·gres′sive·ness** *n.*

ag·gres·sor (ə-**grĕs′**ər) *n.* **1.** A person or animal that behaves with aggression. **2.** A country that makes military attacks against another.

ag·grieved (ə-**grēvd′**) *adj.* Feeling that one has been treated wrongly; offended: *The aggrieved worker wrote a letter of complaint to her boss.*

a·ghast (ə-**găst′**) *adj.* Shocked or horrified, as by something terrible. [From Middle English *agast*, from Old English *gāst*, ghost.]

ag·ile (**ăj′**əl *or* **ăj′**īl′) *adj.* **1.** Able to move quickly and easily; nimble: *an agile mountain climber.* **2.** Mentally quick or alert: *an agile mind.* [From Latin *agilis*, from *agere*, to drive, do.] **—ag′ile·ly** *adv.* **—ag′ile·ness** *n.*

a·gil·i·ty (ə-**jĭl′**ĭ-tē) *n.* The quality or condition of being agile; nimbleness.

ag·i·tate (**ăj′**ĭ-tāt′) *v.* **ag·i·tat·ed, ag·i·tat·ing, ag·i·tates** *—tr.* **1.** To shake or stir up violently: *The storm agitated the sea.* **2.** To disturb; upset: *Our quarrel agitated everyone present.* *—intr.* To stir up public interest in a cause: *agitate for civil rights.* [From Latin *agitāre*, to agitate.] **—ag′i·tat′ed·ly** *adv.*

ag·i·ta·tion (ăj′ĭ-**tā′**shən) *n.* **1.** The act of agitating. **2.** Great emotional disturbance or excitement. **3.** Energetic action to arouse public interest in a cause.

ag·i·ta·tor (**ăj′**ĭ-tā′tər) *n.* **1.** A person who is active in stirring up interest in a cause. **2.** A mechanism that stirs or shakes, as in a washing machine.

a·gleam (ə-**glēm′**) *adv. & adj.* Shining: *a lantern agleam in the window.*

a·glit·ter (ə-**glĭt′**ər) *adv. & adj.* Glittering; sparkling: *eyes aglitter with excitement.*

a·glow (ə-**glō′**) *adv. & adj.* Glowing: *a sky aglow with stars.*

ag·nos·tic (ăg-**nŏs′**tĭk) *n.* One who believes that it is impossible to know whether there is a God. ❖ *adj.* Relating to or being an agnostic. **—ag·nos′ti·cal·ly** *adv.*

ag·nos·ti·cism (ăg-**nŏs′**tĭ-sĭz′əm) *n.* The belief that it is impossible to know whether or not a God exists.

Ag·nus De·i (ăg′nəs **dē′**ī′ *or* **än′**yo͞os dā′ē) *n.* **1.** In Christianity, the Lamb of God; Jesus. **2.** A prayer to Jesus that is part of the Roman Catholic Mass and begins with the words "Agnus Dei." **3.** A musical composition for this prayer.

a·go (ə-**gō′**) *adv. & adj.* **1.** Gone by; past: *two years ago.* **2.** In the past: *They lived there long ago.*

a·gog (ə-**gŏg′**) *adv. & adj.* Full of eager anticipation; greatly excited.

ag·o·nist (**ăg′**ə-nĭst) *n.* **1.** A drug or other chemical that can combine with a receptor on a cell to produce a physiologic reaction typical of a naturally occurring

ă	pat	ôr	core
ā	pay	oi	boy
âr	care	ou	out
ä	father	o͝o	took
ĕ	pet	o͝or	lure
ē	be	o͞o	boot
ĭ	pit	ŭ	cut
ī	bite	ûr	urge
îr	pier	th	thin
ŏ	pot	*th*	this
ō	toe	zh	vision
ô	paw	ə	about

substance. **2.** A contracting muscle that is resisted or counteracted by another muscle, the antagonist. **3.** A person involved in a struggle or competition. [From Late Latin *agōnista*, contender.]

ag·o·nize (ăg′ə-nīz′) *intr.v.* **ag·o·nized, ag·o·niz·ing, ag·o·niz·es** To suffer mental anguish or worry about something: *agonize over a decision.*

ag·o·niz·ing (ăg′ə-nī′zĭng) *adj.* Causing great pain or anguish: *an agonizing decision.* **—ag′o·niz′ing·ly** *adv.*

ag·o·ny (ăg′ə-nē) *n., pl.* **ag·o·nies** Intense and prolonged pain or suffering.

ag·o·ra (ăg′ər-ə) *n., pl.* **ag·o·rae** (ăg′ə-rē′) or **ag·o·ras** The marketplace of an ancient Greek city, used as a meeting place.

a·gor·a·pho·bi·a (ə-gôr′ə-fō′bē-ə *or* ăg′ər-ə-fō′bē-ə) *n.* Fear of or anxiety caused by being in open or public places. **—a·gor′a·phobe′** *n.* **—a·gor′a·pho′bic** *adj.*

a·gou·ti (ə-go͞o′tē) *n., pl.* **a·gou·tis** Any of several brownish burrowing rodents of tropical America, which resemble a rabbit with short ears or a guinea pig with long legs.

a·grar·i·an (ə-grâr′ē-ən) *adj.* **1.** Relating to or concerning farmland or its ownership: *agrarian countries.* **2.** Relating to farming or farmers; agricultural.

a·gree (ə-grē′) *v.* **a·greed, a·gree·ing, a·grees** *—intr.* **1.** To have or share the same opinion; concur: *I agree with you.* **2.** To consent: *A smart investor would never agree to such a crazy scheme.* **3.** To be in harmony or accord: *The two versions of the story do not agree.* **4.** To come to an understanding or settlement: *The jury could not agree on a verdict.* **5.** To be suitable, pleasing, or healthful: *Hot peppers do not agree with me.* **6.** In grammar, to correspond in number, gender, case, or person: *In this sentence the verb agrees with the subject.* *—tr.* To grant or concede: *My parents agreed that we should go.* [From Middle English *agreen*, from Old French *agreer* : Latin *ad-*, to + Latin *grātus*, pleasing.]

a·gree·a·ble (ə-grē′ə-bəl) *adj.* **1.** Pleasing; pleasant: *an agreeable smell.* **2.** Willing to agree or consent: *The teacher was agreeable to the suggestion.* **—a·gree′a·ble·ness** *n.* **—a·gree′a·bly** *adv.*

a·gree·ment (ə-grē′mənt) *n.* **1.** Harmony of opinion: *The neighboring countries were in agreement and signed a treaty.* **2.** An arrangement or understanding between two parties: *an agreement between states over water rights.* **3.** In grammar, correspondence between words in gender, number, case, or person.

ag·ri·busi·ness (ăg′rə-bĭz′nĭs) *n.* The business of producing, processing, and distributing agricultural products in large quantities.

ag·ri·cul·tur·al (ăg′rĭ-kŭl′chər-əl) *adj.* Relating to agriculture. **—ag′ri·cul′tur·al·ly** *adv.*

ag·ri·cul·ture (ăg′rĭ-kŭl′chər) *n.* The science, art, and business of cultivating the soil, producing crops, and raising livestock; farming. [From Middle English, from Latin *agrīcultūra* : *ager*, field + *cultūra*, cultivation.]

ag·ri·cul·tur·ist (ăg′rĭ-kŭl′chər-ĭst) *n.* A farmer or other expert in farming.

a·gron·o·my (ə-grŏn′ə-mē) *n.* The study of soil and the improvement of crop production; scientific farming. **—a·gron′o·mist** *n.*

a·ground (ə-ground′) *adv. & adj.* Stranded in shallow water or on a reef or shoal: *During the storm the ship ran aground near shore.*

a·gue (ā′gyo͞o) *n.* A disease, such as malaria, characterized by periods of chills and fever.

ah (ä) *interj.* An expression used to show surprise, delight, pity, or other emotions.

a·ha (ä-hä′) *interj.* An expression used to show sudden, pleased recognition or understanding: *Aha! Just as I thought, the cat was hiding behind the couch!*

a·head (ə-hĕd′) *adv.* **1.** At or to the front: *Let's move ahead to the front of the bus.* **2.** In advance: *To get tickets, you have to phone ahead.* **3.** For the future: *plan ahead.* **4.** Forward or onward: *The train moved ahead.* **5.** In or into a more advantageous position: *wanted to get ahead in life.* ◆ **be ahead** To be winning or in a superior position: *Our team is ahead by two goals.*

ahead of *prep.* **1.** In front of: *the path ahead of us.* **2.** At an earlier time than: *She arrived ahead of us.* **3.** More successful than: *Your class is ahead of ours in mathematics.*

a·hem (ə-hĕm′) *interj.* An expression used to attract attention or to express doubt or warning.

a·hold (ə-hōld′) *n.* Hold; grip: *I took ahold of Billy's hand as we crossed the street.*

a·hoy (ə-hoi′) *interj.* An expression used to hail a ship or to attract someone's attention.

AI *abbr.* An abbreviation of artificial intelligence.

aid (ād) *v.* **aid·ed, aid·ing, aids** *—tr.* To provide help or assistance to: *aid a friend in distress.* *—intr.* To provide help or assistance: *Many people aided in the effort to clean up the playground.* ❖ *n.* **1.** An act or thing that provides help or assistance: *The spy was caught giving aid to the enemy. The government sent aid to the flooded region.* **2.** An assistant or helper. **3.** A device that helps or is helpful: *a hearing aid; visual aids used in teaching.* [From Middle English *aiden*, from Latin *adiūtāre*.] **—aid′er** *n.*

❑ *These sound alike:* **aid, aide** (helper).

aide (ād) *n.* **1.** An assistant or helper: *a nurse's aide.* **2.** An aide-de-camp.

❑ *These sound alike:* **aide, aid** (help).

aide-de-camp (ād′dĭ-kămp′) *n., pl.* **aides-de-camp** A military officer acting as secretary and assistant to a general.

AIDS (ādz) *n.* A severe disease caused by HIV, in which the immune system is attacked and weakened, making the body susceptible to other infections and to certain kinds of cancer. [From *a(cquired) i(mmune) d(eficiency) s(yndrome).*]

aground

ai·grette or **ai·gret** (ā-grĕt′ *or* ā′grĕt′) *n.* **1.** A tuft of upright plumes or feathers, especially those from an egret's tail. **2.** An arrangement of jewels that resembles these feathers.

ai·ki·do (ī-kē′dō *or* ī′kē-dō′) *n.* A Japanese method of self-defense in which one uses sudden holds and twisting movements to throw one's opponent to the ground. [From Japanese *aikidō* : *ai-*, meeting, mutual + *ki*, spirit + *dō*, way, art.]

ail (āl) *v.* **ailed, ail·ing, ails** *—intr.* To be ill: *Their grandmother has been ailing for months.* *—tr.* To cause pain; make ill: *A fever is a sure sign that something is ailing you.* [From Old English *eglian*, from *egle*, troublesome.]

❑ *These sound alike:* **ail, ale** (strong beer).

ai·lan·thus (ā-lăn′thəs) *n.* The tree of heaven.

ai·le·ron (ā′lə-rŏn′) *n.* A small flap on the back edge of an airplane wing that can be moved up or down to control the plane's rolling and banking movements.

aileron

ail·ment (āl′mənt) *n.* A mild illness or disease: *a heart ailment.*

aim (ām) *v.* **aimed, aim·ing, aims** *—tr.* **1.** To cause (a weapon, a device, or stream of energy) to be turned toward someone or something; point: *aimed the telescope at the moon; aimed the flashlight down the stairs.* **2.** To propel toward a point: *aimed the snowball at the window.* **3.** To form or direct (something) with a particular goal or group in mind: *aimed her campaign speeches at improving health care; aimed his criticism at the movie's director.* *—intr.* **1.** To point an object such as a weapon: *She aimed carefully at the target.* **2.** To determine a course: *aim for a better education.* **3.** To propose; intend: *aim to solve a problem.* ❖ *n.* **1a.** The act of pointing something toward a target: *take careful aim.* **b.**

The ability of a person to hit a target: *The hunter's aim was perfect.* **2.** Purpose; goal: *My aim is to be a writer.* [From Middle English *aimen*, from Old French *esmer*, from Latin *aestimāre*, to estimate.]

aim·less (ām′lĭs) *adj.* Without direction or purpose: *We spent an aimless afternoon strolling in the park.* —**aim′less·ly** *adv.* —**aim′less·ness** *n.*

ain't (ānt) *Nonstandard* Contraction of *am not, is not, are not, has not,* or *have not.* —SEE NOTE AT **nonstandard.**

Ai·nu (ī′no͞o) *n., pl.* **Ainu** or **Ai·nus 1.** A member of a native people of Japan now living on its northernmost islands and on islands in the possession of Russia. **2.** The language of the Ainu.

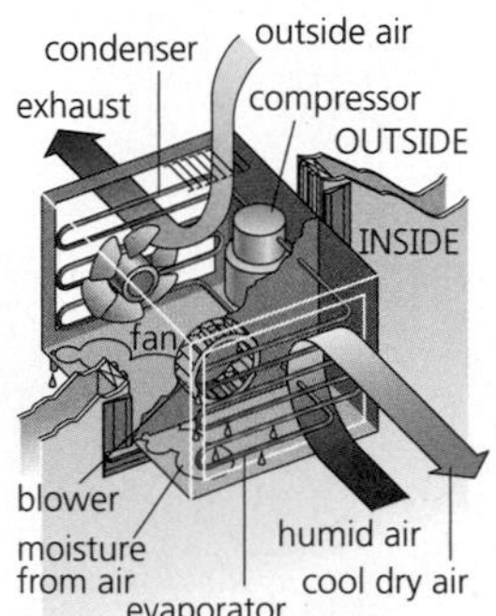

air conditioner
window-style unit

air (âr) *n.* **1.** The colorless, odorless, tasteless mixture of gases that surrounds the earth. Air contains about 78 percent nitrogen and 21 percent oxygen, with the remaining part being made up of argon, carbon dioxide, neon, helium, and other gases. **2.** The sky: *a photograph taken from the air.* **3.** Transportation by aircraft: *travel by air; ship goods by air.* **4.** The appearance or manner of a person or thing: *The judge has a very dignified air.* **5. airs** An affected, unnatural way of acting, intended to impress people: *putting on airs by speaking with an accent.* **6.** A melody or tune. ❖ *v.* **aired, air·ing, airs** —*tr.* **1.** To expose to the air so as to dry, cool, or freshen: *air a blanket.* **2.** To express publicly: *air one's grievances.* **3.** To broadcast: *networks that aired the inauguration.* —*intr.* **1.** To become fresh or cool by exposure to the air: *give the room a chance to air out.* **2.** To be broadcast: *a show that airs during prime time.* ◆ **in the air** Noticeable; all about: *rumors in the air.* **off the air** Not being broadcast. **on the air** Being broadcast. **up in the air** Not yet decided; uncertain. [Partly from Middle English *eir* (ultimately from Greek *āēr*, mist, atmosphere), with some senses partly from French *air*, nature, quality (from Latin *ager*, field, and Latin *ārea*, open space), and from French *air*, tune (from Italian *aria*, tune, aria).]

❑ *These sound alike:* **air, e'er** (ever), **ere** (before), **heir** (inheritor).

Airedale

airbag (âr′băg′) *n.* A safety device in an automobile, consisting of a bag that inflates in a collision to prevent injury to the driver or passengers.

air base *n.* A base for military aircraft.

air bladder *n.* **1.** A swim bladder of a fish. **2.** An air-filled sac in certain aquatic organisms, such as kelp, that helps maintain buoyancy.

air·borne (âr′bôrn′) *adj.* **1.** Carried or transported by air: *airborne troops.* **2.** In flight; flying: *Drinks are served shortly after the plane is airborne.*

air brake *n.* A type of brake, often used on large trucks or trains, that is operated by the power of compressed air.

air·brush (âr′brŭsh′) *n.* A small spray gun used to apply paints, inks, or dyes to a surface, as in painting or drawing. ❖ *tr.v.* **air·brushed, air·brush·ing, air·brush·es 1.** To spray with an airbrush. **2.** To alter (an image or part of an image) in order to conceal an unwanted feature.

air-con·di·tion (âr′kən-dĭsh′ən) *tr.v.* **air-con·di·tioned, air-con·di·tion·ing, air-con·di·tions 1.** To cool or ventilate (an enclosed space) by means of an air conditioner or air conditioners. **2.** To subject to or provide with air conditioning.

air-con·di·tioned (âr′kən-dĭsh′ənd) *adj.* Having air conditioning: *an air-conditioned theater.*

air conditioner *n.* A device that uses refrigerating coils to cool the air and reduce the humidity in a room or other enclosed space.

air conditioning *n.* A system of one or more air conditioners.

air-cooled (âr′ko͞old′) *adj.* Cooled by having air blown on it: *an air-cooled engine.*

air·craft (âr′krăft′) *n., pl.* **aircraft** A machine or device, such as an airplane, helicopter, glider, or dirigible, that is capable of flying.

aircraft carrier *n.* A large naval vessel having a long flat deck acting as a runway on which airplanes can take off and land.

air·drop (âr′drŏp′) *n.* A delivery, as of supplies or troops, by parachute from aircraft in flight. ❖ *tr. & intr.v.* **air·dropped, air·drop·ping, air·drops** To drop or be dropped from an aircraft in flight.

Aire·dale (âr′dāl′) *n.* A large terrier of a breed developed in England, having a wiry tan and black coat.

air·fare (âr′fâr′) *n.* Fare for travel by aircraft.

air·field (âr′fēld′) *n.* An area of fields and runways where aircraft take off and land.

air·flow (âr′flō′) *n.* A flow of air, especially the air currents caused by the motion of an aircraft, automobile, or similar object.

air·foil (âr′foil′) *n.* A part, such as an airplane wing, propeller blade, or rudder, that interacts with a flow of air to provide stability, rotation, lift, or thrust.

air force or **Air Force** *n.* The branch of a country's armed forces that is in charge of fighting war by using aircraft.

air·glow (âr′glō′) *n.* A faint glow visible in the sky at night, caused by chemical reactions in the upper atmosphere.

air gun *n.* A gun that is discharged by compressed air.

airhead (âr′hĕd′) *n. Slang* A silly or unintelligent person.

air hole *n.* A hole that allows for the passage of air: *I put air holes in the box so the gerbil can breathe.*

air·i·ly (âr′ə-lē) *adv.* In a carefree, light-hearted, or unconcerned manner: *He airily told me that he didn't care what I thought.*

air·i·ness (âr′ē-nĭs) *n.* The state or quality of being airy.

air·ing (âr′ĭng) *n.* **1.** Exposure to the air as for drying, cooling, or freshening. **2.** Public expression or discussion: *an airing of unpopular views.* **3.** A broadcast.

air lane *n.* A regular route of travel for aircraft.

air·less (âr′lĭs) *adj.* **1.** Having no air: *The moon is airless.* **2.** Lacking fresh air; stuffy: *a cramped and airless room.*

air letter *n.* A sheet of paper for writing a letter that can be folded to form an envelope and has an imprinted airmail stamp.

air·lift (âr′lĭft′) *n.* A system of transporting troops, civilian passengers, or supplies by aircraft, especially when surface routes are blocked. ❖ *tr.v.* **air·lift·ed, air·lift·ing, air·lifts** To transport in an airlift.

air·line (âr′līn′) *n.* A company that transports passengers and freight by air.

air·lin·er (âr′lī′nər) *n.* A large commercial passenger plane.

air·lock (âr′lŏk′) *n.* **1.** An airtight chamber in which air pressure can be regulated to allow passage between two areas of unequal pressure. **2.** A bubble or pocket of air in a pipe that stops the flow of fluid.

air·mail (âr′māl′) *n.* **1.** The system of transporting mail by aircraft. **2.** Mail transported by aircraft. ❖ *tr.v.* **air·mailed, air·mail·ing, air·mails** To send (a letter, for example) by aircraft: *airmailed a package to Japan.* ❖ *adj.* Relating to airmail: *an airmail letter.*

air·man (âr′mən) *n.* **1.** A pilot or other crew member of an aircraft. **2.** An enlisted person of the lowest rank in the US Air Force.

air mass *n.* A large body of air that has approximately the same temperature and humidity throughout.

air mattress *n.* An inflatable mattress.

air mile *n.* A unit of distance in air navigation equivalent to a nautical mile, about 6,076 feet (1,852 meters).

air piracy *n.* The hijacking of aircraft in flight.

air·plane (âr′plān′) *n.* Any of various aircraft, usually

ă	pat	ôr	core
ā	pay	oi	boy
âr	care	ou	out
ä	father	o͝o	took
ĕ	pet	o͝or	lure
ē	be	o͞o	boot
ĭ	pit	ŭ	cut
ī	bite	ûr	urge
îr	pier	th	thin
ŏ	pot	*th*	this
ō	toe	zh	vision
ô	paw	ə	about

driven by jet engines or propellors, that are held aloft by the lift generated as air flows past their wings.

air plant *n.* An epiphyte.

air pocket *n.* **1.** An isolated space containing trapped air, as in bread dough or a collapsed mine shaft. **2.** A downward current of air that makes an aircraft lose altitude suddenly.

air pollution *n.* Contamination of the atmosphere, as by the discharge of harmful industrial gases, automobile exhaust, or smoke.

air·port (âr′pôrt′) *n.* A level area for aircraft to take off and land, equipped with a control tower, hangars, refueling equipment, and accommodations for passengers and cargo.

air·pow·er or **air power** (âr′pou′ər) *n.* The military power of a nation for carrying on war in the air.

air pressure *n.* The force that is exerted by air per unit of area of a surface.

air pump *n.* A pump for compressing, removing, or forcing a flow of air.

air raid *n.* An attack by military aircraft, usually armed with bombs or rockets.

air rifle *n.* A rifle that uses compressed air or gas to shoot pellets.

air rights *pl.n.* The rights to use airspace, especially above an existing structure, such as a building or road.

air sac *n.* An air-filled space in the body, especially an alveolus of a lung or one of the spaces in a bird's body connecting the lungs and bone cavities.

air shaft *n.* A passage for letting fresh air into a tunnel, building, or other structure.

air·ship (âr′shĭp′) *n.* A self-propelled aircraft that is lighter than air; a dirigible.

air·sick (âr′sĭk′) *adj.* Having airsickness: *an airsick passenger.*

air·sick·ness (âr′sĭk′nĭs) *n.* Nausea and discomfort caused by the motions of an aircraft during flight.

air·space or **air space** (âr′spās′) *n.* The space in the atmosphere above a particular section of the earth.

air speed *n.* The speed of an aircraft relative to the air it is traveling through.

air·strip (âr′strĭp′) *n.* An aircraft runway without airport facilities.

air·tight (âr′tīt′) *adj.* **1.** Allowing no air or other gas to pass in or out: *an airtight seal.* **2.** Having no weak points; sound: *an airtight excuse.*

air·time (âr′tīm′) *n.* Time during a radio or television broadcast: *a news program giving more airtime to international events.*

air-to-air (âr′tə-âr′) *adj.* Passing between aircraft while flying: *air-to-air missiles; air-to-air radio communications.*

air·waves (âr′wāvz′) *pl.n.* Radio waves as used for broadcasting radio or television signals.

air·way (âr′wā′) *n.* **1.** A passage through which air circulates, as in ventilating a mine. **2.** The system of passages by which air enters and exits the lungs. **3.** often **airways** An airline.

air·wor·thy (âr′wûr′*thē*) *adj.* **air·wor·thi·er, air·wor·thi·est** In fit condition for flight: *an airworthy plane.* —**air′wor′thi·ness** *n.*

air·y (âr′ē) *adj.* **air·i·er, air·i·est 1.** Allowing air in; open to the air: *an airy porch.* **2.** Extensive in area or height; spacious: *the mansion's airy entryway.* **3.** Light; delicate: *airy silk.* **4.** Impractical or unrealistic: *airy schemes.*
❑ *These sound alike:* **airy, aerie** (nest).

aisle (īl) *n.* **1.** A passageway between rows of seats, as in an airplane or a theater. **2.** A similar passageway, as between counters in a department store. **3.** A part of a church divided from the nave, transept, or choir by a row of columns. [From Middle English *ele* (later influenced in spelling by *isle*, island, since a church aisle can be considered separated from the nave like an island from the mainland), from Latin *āla*, wing, wing of a building.]
❑ *These sound alike:* **aisle, I'll** (I will), **isle** (island).

a·jar (ə-jär′) *adv. & adj.* Partially open: *Leave the door ajar.* [From Middle English *on char* : *on*, on + *char*, turn (from Old English *cierr*).]

A·jax (ā′jăks′) *n.* In Greek mythology, a Greek hero of great strength and courage who fought against Troy.

AK *abbr.* An abbreviation of Alaska.

a·kim·bo (ə-kĭm′bō) *adv. & adj.* With the hands on the hips and the elbows bent outward: *stood akimbo before beginning the exercises.* [From Middle English *in kenebowe*, perhaps meaning "in (a shape like) jar handles" : *kene*, perhaps akin to *canne*, can, jar + *bowe*, bow, arch.]

akimbo

a·kin (ə-kĭn′) *adj.* **1.** Related by blood. **2.** Derived from the same origin: *The word "maternal" is akin to the word "mother."* **3.** Having a similar quality or character: *a feeling akin to sadness.*

Al The symbol for the element **aluminum.**

AL *abbr.* An abbreviation of Alabama.

–al¹ *suff.* A suffix that means relating to or characterized by: *adjectival; postal.*

–al² *suff.* A suffix that means action or process: *denial; arrival.*

Al·a·bam·a (ăl′ə-băm′ə) A state of the southeast United States west of Georgia. It was admitted as the 22nd state in 1819. Montgomery is the capital and Birmingham the largest city. —SEE NOTE.

GEOGRAPHY

Alabama The state of **Alabama** is named for a Native American people who inhabited the region when European explorers arrived. The name is sometimes translated "people who clear away thickets." The French first gave the name to the Alabama River and the state later took its name from the river.

al·a·bas·ter (ăl′ə-băs′tər) *n.* Any of various smooth, translucent minerals that are white, tinted, or banded and consist mainly of salts of calcium.

à la carte also **a la carte** (ä′ lə **kärt′** *or* ăl′ə **kärt′**) *adv. & adj.* With a separate price for each item on the menu: *Meals in many restaurants are à la carte.*

a·lack (ə-lăk′) *interj.* An expression used to show sorrow, regret, or alarm.

a·lac·ri·ty (ə-lăk′rĭ-tē) *n.* Speed and willingness in acting or responding: *The messenger carried out the assignment with alacrity.*

A·lad·din (ə-lăd′n) *n.* In the *Arabian Nights*, a boy who acquires a magic lamp with which he can summon a genie to fulfill any desire.

al·a·me·da (ăl′ə-**mē′**də *or* ăl′ə-**mā′**də) *n.* A shaded public walk lined with trees.

Al·a·mo (ăl′ə-mō′) A church built after 1744 as part of a mission in San Antonio, Texas. During the Texas Revolution against Mexican rule it was besieged from February 23 to March 6, 1836, by the Mexican army, who killed all the members of the Texas post.

à la mode (ä′ lə **mōd′** *or* ăl′ə **mōd′**) *adj.* **1.** According to the prevailing style or fashion. **2.** Served with ice cream: *apple pie à la mode.*

al·a·nine (ăl′ə-nēn′) *n.* A nonessential amino acid that is found in many proteins.

a·larm (ə-lärm′) *n.* **1.** Sudden fear caused by a sense of danger: *There is no cause for alarm.* **2.** A warning of approaching danger: *Rumors that the boiler broke were only a false alarm.* **3.** A device sounded to warn people of danger: *a fire alarm; a burglar alarm.* **4.** An alarm clock. ❖ *tr.v.* **a·larmed, a·larm·ing, a·larms 1.** To fill with alarm; frighten: *The loud noise alarmed us.* See Synonyms at **frighten. 2.** To warn of approaching danger. [From Middle English, from Old Italian *all'arme*, to arms.]

alarm clock *n.* A clock that can be set to wake someone up or alert attention at a particular time, as by sounding a bell or buzzer.

a·larm·ing (ə-lär′mĭng) *adj.* Causing great fear or anxi-

GEOGRAPHY

Alaska The state of Alaska gets its name from an Aleut word meaning "the mainland." The Aleut live mostly on the Aleutian Islands, and their word for "mainland" refers to the Alaska Peninsula, the narrow part of the mainland that juts out toward the islands. Before 1867, when it was purchased from Russia by the United States, the territory was known as "Russian America."

WORD HISTORY

albatross The word **albatross** sometimes means "something that is a sign of failure or is an obstacle to success," as in *The project started out well enough but has turned into an albatross.* How did this meaning get attached to the name of a sea bird? By a poem! The poem is *The Rime of the Ancient Mariner* by Samuel Taylor Coleridge. In the poem an old sailor tells the tale of how he shot an albatross with an arrow, and soon afterwards the wind died and the ship he was on stalled out at sea. The crew members thought shooting the albatross brought bad luck, and they blamed the ancient mariner, hanging the dead bird around his neck in punishment.

ă	pat	ôr	core
ā	pay	oi	boy
âr	care	ou	out
ä	father	o͝o	took
ĕ	pet	o͝or	lure
ē	be	o͞o	boot
ĭ	pit	ŭ	cut
ī	bite	ûr	urge
îr	pier	th	thin
ŏ	pot	*th*	this
ō	toe	zh	vision
ô	paw	ə	about

ety: *The wind is increasing at an alarming rate.* **—a·larm′ing·ly** *adv.*

a·larm·ist (ə-lär′mĭst) *n.* A person who frightens others needlessly or for little reason.

a·la·rum (ə-lär′əm *or* ə-lăr′əm) *n.* A warning or alarm, especially a call to arms.

a·las (ə-lăs′) *interj.* An expression used to show sorrow, regret, or grief.

A·las·ka (ə-lăs′kə) A state of the United States in extreme northwest North America, separated from the other mainland states by Canada. Purchased from Russia in 1867, Alaska was admitted as the 49th state in 1959. Juneau is the capital and Anchorage the largest city. **—A·las′kan** *adj. & n.* —SEE NOTE.

Alaska Native *n.* A member of any of the peoples that are native to Alaska, including Native American, Eskimo, and Aleut peoples.

Alaskan malamute *n.* A malamute.

Alaska Standard Time *n.* Standard time in the ninth time zone west of Greenwich, England, used throughout most of Alaska.

alb (ălb) *n.* A long white linen robe worn by a priest or minister during church services.

al·ba·core (ăl′bə-kôr′) *n., pl.* **albacore** or **al·ba·cores** A large tuna that is an important source of canned fish.

Al·ba·ni·a (ăl-bā′nē-ə) A country of southeast Europe on the Adriatic Sea northwest of Greece. Tiranë is the capital.

Al·ba·ni·an (ăl-bā′nē-ən) *adj.* Relating to Albania or its people, language, or culture. ❖ *n.* **1.** A native or inhabitant of Albania. **2.** The Indo-European language of Albania.

Al·ba·ny (ôl′bə-nē) The capital (since 1797) of New York, in the eastern part of the state on the west bank of the Hudson River.

al·ba·tross (ăl′bə-trôs′) *n., pl.* **albatross** or **al·ba·tross·es 1.** Any of several large, web-footed seabirds with a hooked beak and very long wings. **2.** Something that prevents one from accomplishing something or is impossible to bring to completion: *the albatross of high debt.* [Alteration of obsolete English *alcatras*, frigatebird, from Arabic *al-ġaṭṭās*, the grebe. Sense 2, from the poem "The Rime of the Ancient Mariner" by Samuel Taylor Coleridge, in which a sailor who brought bad luck on his ship by killing an albatross is made to wear its corpse around his neck.] —SEE NOTE.

al·be·do (ăl-bē′dō) *n., pl.* **al·be·dos** The fraction of light, expressed as a decimal, that is reflected by a surface such as a planet or a snow-covered area. An object with high albedo is bright; one with low albedo is dark.

al·be·it (ôl-bē′ĭt *or* ăl-bē′ĭt) *conj.* Even though; although: *They proposed an imaginative, albeit somewhat impractical, idea.*

Al·ber·ta (ăl-bûr′tə) A province of western Canada between British Columbia and Saskatchewan. It joined the Canadian confederation in 1905. Edmonton is the capital and Calgary the largest city.

al·bi·nism (ăl′bə-nĭz′əm) *n.* Any of several inherited conditions in which a person or animal has little or none of the pigment melanin, resulting in lack of pigmentation in the eyes, skin, and hair. Humans with albinism usually have vision problems.

al·bi·no (ăl-bī′nō) *n., pl.* **al·bi·nos** An individual with albinism. [From Portuguese, from Latin *albus*, white.]

Al·bi·on (ăl′bē-ən) A poetic name for England or Great Britain.

al·bum (ăl′bəm) *n.* **1.** A book with blank pages on which to mount such things as photographs or stamps or to collect autographs. **2.** A collection of personal photographs or other images that are arranged for private viewing, as in book or on a computer. **3.** A set of musical recordings that are issued together, usually by a single artist. [From Latin *album*, blank tablet, from *albus*, white.]

al·bu·men (ăl-byo͞o′mən) *n.* **1.** The white of an egg, consisting mostly of albumin dissolved in water. **2.** Albumin.

al·bu·min (ăl-byo͞o′mĭn) *n.* Any of several simple proteins that dissolve in water and are found especially in egg white, blood, and milk.

Al·bu·quer·que (ăl′bə-kûr′kē) The largest city of New Mexico, in the central part of the state on the upper Rio Grande southwest of Santa Fe. It was founded in 1706.

al·che·mist (ăl′kə-mĭst) *n.* A person who practices alchemy.

al·che·my (ăl′kə-mē) *n.* A medieval system of chemistry that had among its aims the changing of common metals into gold and the preparation of a potion that gives eternal youth. —SEE NOTE AT **alkali.**

al·co·hol (ăl′kə-hôl′) *n.* **1.** Any of a large number of flammable organic compounds that contain the radical OH, especially ethanol, the form that occurs in wines and liquors. **2.** Alcoholic beverages in general. [From early modern scientific Latin *alcohol*, distilled substance, from Medieval Latin, fine metallic powder, from Arabic *al-kuḥl*, the powder of antimony (used as eye shadow).]

al·co·hol·ic (ăl′kə-**hô′**lĭk) *adj.* **1.** Relating to or containing alcohol, especially ethanol: *an alcoholic beverage.* **2.** Having alcoholism. ❖ *n.* A person who has alcoholism.

al·co·hol·ism (ăl′kə-hô-lĭz′əm) *n.* A disorder involving a persistent pattern of alcohol use that causes harm, anxiety, or discomfort. It typically involves cravings for alcohol, inability to control how much one drinks, withdrawal symptoms in its absence, and the need to drink greater quantities to feel the same effects. It often results in impaired social functioning and significant damage to physical health.

Al·cott (ôl′kət *or* ôl′kŏt), **Louisa May** 1832–1888. American writer who is best known for her largely autobiographical novel *Little Women* (1868).

al·cove (ăl′kōv′) *n.* A small room opening on a larger one without being separated from it by a wall or door. [From Arabic *al-qubba*, the vault.] —SEE NOTE AT **alkali.**

Al·deb·a·ran (ăl-dĕb′ər-ən) *n.* A binary star in the constellation Taurus. It is one of the brightest stars.

al·der (ôl′dər) *n.* Any of various shrubs or small trees of cool damp places, having toothed leaves and woody, conelike catkins.

al·der·man (ôl′dər-mən) *n.* A member of the governing body of a city or town.

ale (āl) *n.* A beer that has been fermented at a relatively warm temperature.

❑ *These sound alike:* **ale, ail** (be ill).

a·lee (ə-lē′) *adv.* Away from the wind; leeward.

a·lert (ə-lûrt′) *adj.* **1.** Watchful; attentive; vigilant: *A good driver must remain constantly alert.* **2.** Mentally quick; perceptive; intelligent: *an alert child.* ❖ *n.* **1.** A warning signal against danger or attack. **2.** The period during which one must obey this signal. ❖ *tr.v.* **a·lert·ed, a·lert·ing, a·lerts 1.** To warn of approaching danger. **2.** To make aware of: *alert the public to the need for pollution control.* ◆ **on the alert** Watchful and prepared: *The police are on the alert to stop theft.* [From Italian *all'erta*, on the lookout.] **—a·lert′ly** *adv.* **—a·lert′ness** *n.*

A·leut (ə-lo͞ot′ *or* ăl′ē-o͞ot′) *n., pl.* **Aleut** or **A·leuts 1.** A member of a Native American people inhabiting the Aleutian Islands. **2.** Either of two languages, related to Eskimo, spoken by the Aleut. **—A·leu′tian** (ə-lo͞o′shən) *adj.*

Aleutian Islands A chain of rugged volcanic islands of southwest Alaska curving about 1,150 miles (1,850 kilometers) west from the Alaska Peninsula and separating the Bering Sea from the Pacific Ocean.

ale·wife (āl′wīf′) *n., pl.* **ale·wives** (āl′wīvz′) A fish of

North American Atlantic waters that swims up rivers to spawn.

Al·ex·an·der (ăl′ĭg-**zăn′**dər) Known as "Alexander the Great." 356–323 BC. King of Macedonia (336–323) and conqueror of Asia Minor, Syria, Egypt, Babylonia, and Persia.

Al·ex·an·dri·a (ăl′ĭg-**zăn′**drē-ə) **1.** A city of northern Egypt on the Mediterranean Sea at the western tip of the Nile Delta. It was founded by Alexander the Great in 332 BC. It was famous for its libraries and its lighthouse, one of the Seven Wonders of the World. **2.** A city of northern Virginia on the Potomac River opposite Washington, DC. George Washington helped lay out the streets in 1749.

Al·ex·an·dri·an (ăl′ĭg-**zăn′**drē-ən) *adj.* **1.** Relating to Alexandria. **2.** Relating to Alexander the Great.

al·fal·fa (ăl-**făl′**fə) *n.* A plant having compound leaves with three leaflets and clusters of purplish flowers, grown as feed for cattle and other livestock. [From Spanish, from Arabic *al-fasfaṣa*, from Persian *aspist*, clover.]

Al·fred (**ăl′**frĭd) Known as "Alfred the Great." 849–899. King of the West Saxons (871–899) who defeated the Danes and helped unite England.

al·fres·co (ăl-**frĕs′**kō) *adv. & adj.* In the fresh air; outdoors: *dining alfresco.*

al·ga (**ăl′**gə) *n., pl.* **al·gae** (**ăl′**jē) Any of various green, red, or brown organisms that lack true roots, stems, and leaves, are usually found in water, and range from single cells to large spreading seaweeds. Algae make their own food through photosynthesis, and many of them are classified as belonging to the kingdom of protists. **—al′gal** (**ăl′**gəl) *adj.*

al·ge·bra (**ăl′**jə-brə) *n.* A branch of mathematics that deals with the relations and properties of quantities by the use of letters and other symbols to represent unknown numbers, especially in equations, in order to solve problems. [From Arabic *al-jabr*, the bone-setting, the restoring.] **—al′ge·bra′ic** (ăl′jə-**brā′**ĭk) *adj.* —SEE NOTE AT **alkali.**

Al·ge·ri·a (ăl-**jîr′**ē-ə) A country of northwest Africa on the Mediterranean Sea west of Tunisia and Libya. Algiers is the capital.

Al·giers (ăl-**jîrz′**) The capital of Algeria, in the northern part of the country on the Mediterranean Sea.

Al·gon·qui·an (ăl-**gŏng′**kwē-ən *or* ăl-**gŏng′**kē-ən) *n., pl.* **Algonquian** or **Al·gon·qui·ans 1.** A family of Native American languages spoken over a large area of North America, including Ojibwa, Cree, and Blackfoot. **2.** A member of a people traditionally speaking an Algonquian language. **—Al·gon′qui·an** *adj.*

Al·gon·quin (ăl-**gŏng′**kwĭn *or* ăl-**gŏng′**kĭn) *n., pl.* **Algonquin** or **Al·gon·quins 1a.** A member of a Native American people living along the Ottawa River in Canada. **b.** The Algonquian language of this people. **2a.** A member of an Algonquian people. **b.** An Algonquian language. [From Canadian French, from a word meaning "they are our relatives" in an Algonquian language of eastern Canada.] **—Al·gon′quin** *adj.*

al·go·rithm (**ăl′**gə-rĭth′əm) *n.* A mathematical rule or process for computing a desired result: *an algorithm used in a computer program.*

Al·ham·bra (ăl-**hăm′**brə *or* äl-**äm′**brä) A citadel and palace on a hill overlooking Granada, Spain. Built by Moorish kings in the 1100s and 1200s, the Alhambra is the finest example of Moorish architecture in Spain.

A·li (ä-**lē′**) 600?–661. Muslim caliph (656–661) whose reign was marked by the division of Islam into Sunni and Shiite branches.

Ali, Muhammad Originally **Cassius Marcellus Clay** (klā) 1942–2016. American prizefighter who won the world heavyweight title in 1964, 1974, and 1978.

a·li·as (**ā′**lē-əs) *n.* An assumed name used to conceal a person's real identity. ❖ *adv.* Otherwise named: *William Blake, alias James Flynn.*

A·li Ba·ba (ä′lē **bä′**bə *or* ăl′ē **bä′**bə) *n.* In the *Arabian Nights*, a poor woodcutter who gains entrance to the treasure cave of the forty thieves by saying "Open Sesame!"

al·i·bi (**ăl′**ə-bī′) *n., pl.* **al·i·bis 1.** A claim that one was elsewhere when a crime or other wrongdoing was committed. **2.** Someone who can personally confirm such a claim. **3.** *Informal* An excuse: *No more of your alibis!*

a·li·en (**ā′**lē-ən) *adj.* **1.** Belonging to or coming from another country; foreign: *alien residents.* **2.** Unfamiliar or strange: *Having lived in the city, he found the suburb an alien place.* **3.** Inconsistent or opposed; contradictory: *an idea wholly alien to my philosophy.* ❖ *n.* **1.** A person living in one country while remaining a citizen of another. **2.** A being from outer space: *In the movie, Earth is invaded by aliens.* **3.** A species that is living or growing in a region to which it is not native: *starlings and other aliens that were introduced to North America.* [From Latin *aliēnus*, belonging to another, from *alius*, other.]

al·ien·ate (**āl′**yə-nāt′) *tr.v.* **al·ien·at·ed, al·ien·at·ing, al·ien·ates 1.** To lose the friendship or support of; estrange: *A barking dog tends to alienate the neighbors.* **2.** To cause to become emotionally withdrawn or isolated: *Treating people as if they were just numbers in a computer will only alienate them.* **—al′ien·a′tor** *n.*

al·ien·a·tion (āl′yə-**nā′**shən) *n.* The act of alienating or the condition of being alienated: *After two weeks of alienation, they made up and became friends again.*

a·light[1] (ə-**līt′**) *intr.v.* **a·light·ed** or **a·lit** (ə-**lĭt′**), **a·light·ing, a·lights 1.** To come down and settle, as after flight: *A bird alighted on the branch.* **2.** To get off; dismount: *Passengers alighted from a train.* [From Middle English *alighten*, from Old English *ālīhtan* : *ā-*, intensive prefix + *līhtan*, to lighten, make less heavy.]

a·light[2] (ə-**līt′**) *adj.* **1.** On fire; burning: *The discarded match was still alight.* **2.** Lighted; lit up: *The sky was alight with millions of stars.* [From Middle English, past participle of *alighten*, to set on fire, from Old English *ālīhtan*, to light up : *ā-*, intensive prefix + *līhtan*, to shine.]

a·lign (ə-**līn′**) *v.* **a·ligned, a·lign·ing, a·ligns** —*tr.* **1.** To arrange in a straight line: *The chairs were aligned in two rows.* **2.** To ally (oneself) with one side, as of an argument or cause: *The allies usually align themselves behind the same position in foreign policy.* **3.** To adjust (a device, mechanism, or some of its parts) in order to produce a proper relationship or condition: *The mechanic aligned the wheels of my car.* —*intr.* To fall into line: *The soldiers aligned.*

a·lign·ment (ə-**līn′**mənt) *n.* **1.** Arrangement or position in a straight line: *perfect alignment of the teeth.* **2.** The process of aligning a device or the condition of being aligned: *A mechanic must perform a wheel alignment on the car. The wheels are out of alignment.* **3.** An arrangement or positioning of players on a sports team: *Once we got a lead, the coach used a new defensive alignment.* **4.** The act of allying or the state of being allied: *the administration's policy of alignment with other democratic nations.*

a·like (ə-**līk′**) *adj.* **1.** Having close resemblance; similar: *Mother and daughter are very much alike.* **2.** Exactly or nearly exactly the same: *Parts for plumbing must be alike to fit.* ❖ *adv.* In the same way or manner or to the same degree: *We must try to treat everyone alike.*

al·i·men·ta·ry (ăl′ə-**mĕn′**tə-rē *or* ăl′ə-**mĕn′**trē) *adj.* Relating to food, nutrition, or digestion.

alimentary canal *n.* The digestive tract.

al·i·mo·ny (**ăl′**ə-mō′nē) *n., pl.* **al·i·mo·nies** An amount of money that a court orders a divorced person to pay

Louisa May Alcott

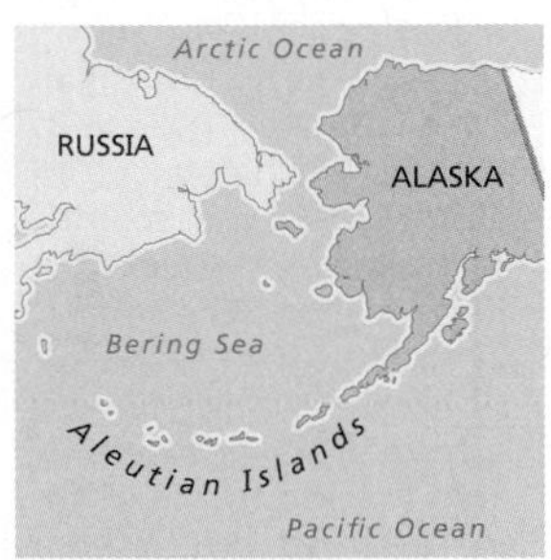

Aleutian Islands

Muhammad Ali
photographed in 2005

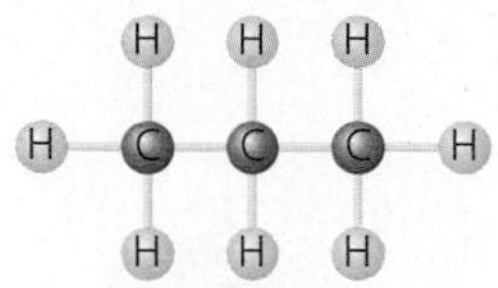

aliphatic
the straight chain of carbon atoms of a propane molecule

WORD HISTORY

alkali Many English words that begin with *al–* are borrowed from Arabic, where *al–* means "the." Many of these words concern chemistry and mathematics, to which Arab scientists made important contributions in the early Middle Ages. Thus **alkali** is from *al-qily*, "the ashes, the lye." **Alchemy** is from *al-kīmiyā'*, "the science of chemistry." **Algebra** is from *al-jabr*, "the setting of broken bones, the restoring"—that is, moving a term from one side of an equation to the other in order to put it in a form that is easier to solve. And **alcove** comes from *al-qubba*, "the vault."

ă	pat	ôr	core
ā	pay	oi	boy
âr	care	ou	out
ä	father	o͝o	took
ĕ	pet	o͝or	lure
ē	be	o͞o	boot
ĭ	pit	ŭ	cut
ī	bite	ûr	urge
îr	pier	th	thin
ŏ	pot	*th*	this
ō	toe	zh	vision
ô	paw	ə	about

as support to a former spouse. [From Latin *alimōnia*, sustenance, from *alere*, to nourish.]

al·i·phat·ic (ăl′ə-**făt′**ĭk) *adj.* Relating to organic chemical compounds in which the carbon atoms are linked together in straight chains rather than in rings.

a·lit (ə-**lĭt′**) *v.* A past tense and a past participle of **alight**[1].

A·li·to (ə-**lē′**tō), **Samuel Anthony, Jr.** Born 1950. American jurist who was appointed an associate justice of the US Supreme Court in 2006.

a·live (ə-**līv′**) *adj.* **1.** Having life; living: *The snake looked dead, but when it started to move we realized it was alive.* **2.** In existence or operation; active: *She kept her hopes alive despite the bad news.* **3.** Full of life; animated; alert: *The audience came alive when the president took the stage.* ◆ **alive to** Aware of; sensitive to: *He is usually alive to the moods of others.* **—a·live′ness** *n.*

al·ka·li (**ăl′**kə-lī′) *n., pl.* **al·ka·lis** or **al·ka·lies 1.** A strong base or hydroxide, such as ammonia or lye, that is soluble in water, neutralizes acids, and forms salts with them. Alkalis turn red litmus paper blue. **2.** A salt or mixture of salts that neutralizes acids and is found in arid soils. [From Middle English, from Arabic *al-qily*, the ashes, potash, lye.] —SEE NOTE.

alkali metal *n.* Any of a group of soft white metals that melt at low temperature, have a low density, and are highly reactive. They include lithium, sodium, potassium, rubidium, cesium, and francium. See table at **Periodic Table.**

al·ka·line (**ăl′**kə-lĭn *or* **ăl′**kə-līn′) *adj.* **1.** Relating to or containing an alkali. **2.** Having a pH greater than 7; basic.

al·ka·line-earth metal (**ăl′**kə-lĭn-**ûrth′** *or* **ăl′**kə-līn′-**ûrth′**) *n.* Any of a group of metallic elements that includes beryllium, magnesium, calcium, strontium, barium, and radium. See table at **Periodic Table.**

al·ka·lin·i·ty (ăl′kə-**lĭn′**ĭ-tē) *n.* The alkali concentration or alkaline quality of a substance.

al·ka·lize (**ăl′**kə-līz′) *tr. & intr.v.* **al·ka·lized, al·ka·liz·ing, al·ka·liz·es** To make or become alkaline or an alkali.

al·ka·loid (**ăl′**kə-loid′) *n.* Any of a class of alkaline organic compounds that contain nitrogen, including nicotine, quinine, and morphine. Many of these compounds are derived from plants.

all (ôl) *adj.* **1.** The total number of: *All cows eat grass. All the windows are open.* **2.** The whole of: *We spent all day in the museum.* **3.** The utmost possible: *In all seriousness, I think you should apply for the job.* **4.** Every: *He enjoys all manner of cooking.* **5.** Any: *proven beyond all doubt.* ❖ *n.* Everything one has: *The winning team gave their all.* ❖ *pron.* **1.** The whole amount: *All of the flowers grew.* **2.** Each and every one: *All aboard the ship were saved.* ❖ *adv.* **1.** Wholly; entirely: *The instructions are all wrong.* **2.** Each; apiece: *a score of five all.* ◆ **all along** From the beginning; throughout: *They saw through my disguise all along.* **all but** Nearly; almost: *The patient all but fainted.* **all in all** Everything being taken into account: *All in all, she's a good athlete.* **all of** *Informal* Not more than: *I was gone for all of an hour.* **all that** *Informal* To the degree expected: *It's not all that hard.* **all the same** Nevertheless; anyway: *It was hard, but I managed all the same.* **at all 1.** In any way: *I couldn't sleep at all.* **2.** To any extent; whatever: *not at all sorry.* **in all** Altogether: *The two buses held 100 passengers in all.*

❑ *These sound alike:* **all, awl** (pointed tool).

Al·lah (**ä′**lə) *n.* God, especially in Islam.

all-A·mer·i·can (ôl′ə-**mĕr′**ĭ-kən) *adj.* **1.** Typical of the people of the United States or their ideals: *an all-American hero.* **2.** In sports, chosen as the best amateur in the United States at a particular position or event: *an all-American fullback.* **3.** Composed entirely of American elements or materials: *The orchestra played an all-American program.* ❖ *n.* An all-American athlete.

al·lan·to·is (ə-**lăn′**tō-ĭs) *n., pl.* **al·lan·to·i·des** (ăl′ən-**tō′**-ĭ-dēz′) A membranous sac that develops from the lower end of the digestive tract in the embryos of mammals, birds, and reptiles. In most mammals it becomes part of the placenta and the umbilical cord.

all-a·round (ôl′ə-**round′**) also **all-round** (**ôl′round′**) *adj.* **1.** Comprehensive in extent: *an all-around education.* **2.** Able to do many or all things well: *an all-around athlete.*

al·lay (ə-**lā′**) *tr.v.* **al·layed, al·lay·ing, al·lays 1.** To set to rest; calm: *allay one's fears.* **2.** To lessen; reduce: *allay pain.* **—al·lay′er** *n.*

all clear *n.* A signal, usually by siren, that an air raid, threat of a tornado, or other danger is over.

al·le·ga·tion (ăl′ĭ-**gā′**shən) *n.* An assertion that someone has done something wrong, often made without proof.

al·lege (ə-**lĕj′**) *tr.v.* **al·leged, al·leg·ing, al·leg·es** To declare to be true, usually without offering proof: *The indictment alleges that the mayor took bribes.* **—al·lege′a·ble** *adj.* **—al·leg′er** *n.*

al·leged (ə-**lĕjd′** *or* ə-**lĕj′**ĭd) *adj.* Stated to be as described but without proof; supposed: *The alleged thief turned out to be innocent.* **—al·leg′ed·ly** (ə-**lĕj′**ĭd-lē) *adv.*

Al·le·ghe·ny Mountains (ăl′ĭ-**gā′**nē) also **Al·le·ghe·nies** (ăl′ĭ-**gā′**nēz) A range of the Appalachian Mountains extending about 500 miles (800 kilometers) from northern Pennsylvania to southwest Virginia and rising to approximately 4,860 feet (1,480 meters) in northeast West Virginia. The range sits on the eastern edge of the **Allegheny Plateau.**

Allegheny River A river rising in north-central Pennsylvania and flowing about 325 miles (523 kilometers) northwest and then southwest, finally joining the Monongahela River at Pittsburgh to form the Ohio River.

al·le·giance (ə-**lē′**jəns) *n.* Loyalty or devotion, as to one's country, a ruler, or a cause: *pledge allegiance to the United States.*

al·le·gor·i·cal (ăl′ĭ-**gôr′**ĭ-kəl) *adj.* Relating to or containing allegory: *In the allegorical tale, the owl represents wisdom.* **—al′le·gor′i·cal·ly** *adv.*

al·le·go·ry (**ăl′**ĭ-gôr′ē) *n., pl.* **al·le·go·ries** A story, play, or picture in which characters or events stand for ideas or principles.

al·le·gret·to (ä′lĭ-**grĕt′**ō) *adv. & adj.* In music, in a manner slightly slower than allegro.

al·le·gro (ə-**lĕg′**rō *or* ə-**lā′**grō) *adv. & adj.* In music, in a quick lively manner.

al·lele (ə-**lēl′**) *n.* Any of the versions in which a particular gene exists.

al·le·lu·ia (ăl′ə-**lo͞o′**yə) *interj.* Hallelujah.

Al·len (**ăl′**ən), **Ethan** 1738–1789. American Revolutionary soldier whose troops, the Green Mountain Boys, helped capture Fort Ticonderoga from the British (1775).

Allen wrench *n.* An L-shaped wrench with a six-sided end, used to turn screws that have a six-sided hole.

al·ler·gen (**ăl′**ər-jən) *n.* A substance, such as pollen, that causes an allergy.

al·ler·gen·ic (ăl′ər-**jĕn′**ĭk) *adj.* Causing an allergic reaction. **—al′ler·gen′i·cal·ly** *adv.*

al·ler·gic (ə-**lûr′**jĭk) *adj.* **1.** Relating to or caused by an allergy: *an allergic reaction.* **2.** Having an allergy: *allergic to fish.* **3.** *Informal* Having a dislike; averse: *allergic to hard work.*

al·ler·gist (**ăl′**ər-jĭst) *n.* A physician who specializes in the diagnosis and treatment of allergies.

al·ler·gy (**ăl′**ər-jē) *n., pl.* **al·ler·gies** A condition in which exposure to a substance, such as pollen, latex, animal dander, or certain foods or drugs, causes a reaction by the immune system that may include sneezing, itching, rash, and difficulty breathing or swallowing. [From German *Allergie* : Greek *allos*, other + Greek *ergon*, action.]

al·le·vi·ate (ə-lē′vē-āt′) *tr.v.* **al·le·vi·at·ed, al·le·vi·at·ing, al·le·vi·ates** To make more bearable; relieve; lessen: *Medicine will alleviate the pain.* [From Late Latin *alleviāre*, to lighten : Latin *ad-*, to + Latin *levis*, light.] **—al·le′vi·a′tion** *n.* **—al·le′vi·a′tor** *n.* —SEE NOTE AT **leaven.**

al·ley (ăl′ē) *n., pl.* **al·leys 1.** A narrow street or passageway between or behind buildings. **2.** A path between flowerbeds or trees in a garden or park. **3.** A bowling alley. ◆ **up (one's) alley** *Informal* Suitable to one's interests or abilities. [From Middle English *alei*, from Old French *alee*, from *aler*, to walk, from Latin *ambulāre*.]

alley cat *n.* A homeless or stray cat in an urban area.

al·ley·way (ăl′ē-wā′) *n.* A narrow passage between buildings.

All Fools' Day *n.* April Fools' Day.

All·hal·lows (ôl′hăl′ōz) *n.* All Saints' Day.

al·li·ance (ə-lī′əns) *n.* **1.** A formal agreement or union between nations, organizations, or individuals: *Britain and France sealed their alliance with a treaty.* **2.** A connection based on marriage, friendship, or common interest: *a strong alliance between cousins.*

al·lied (ə-līd′ *or* ăl′īd′) *adj.* **1.** Joined together in an alliance: *the allied countries of Europe.* **2.** Similar; related: *Biology and medicine are allied sciences.* **3. Allied** Relating to allied countries, especially the countries that fought against Germany and its allies in World War I and World War II.

al·li·ga·tor (ăl′ĭ-gā′tər) *n.* **1.** Either of two large reptiles having tough skin, sharp teeth, and powerful jaws, and living in lakes, rivers, or other wet areas. An alligator's snout is broader and shorter than a crocodile's. **2.** Leather made from the hide of an alligator. [Alteration of Spanish *el lagarto*, the lizard, from Latin *lacertus*.]

alligator pear *n.* An avocado.

all-im·por·tant (ôl′ĭm-pôr′tnt) *adj.* Very important; vital; crucial: *all-important efforts to keep the peace.*

al·lit·er·a·tion (ə-lĭt′ə-rā′shən) *n.* The repetition of the same sounds, usually consonants, especially at the beginning of words, as in *large luscious lemons.*

al·lit·er·a·tive (ə-lĭt′ə-rā′tĭv *or* ə-lĭt′ər-ə-tĭv) *adj.* Showing or characterized by alliteration: *an alliterative phrase.*

all-night (ôl′nīt′) *adj.* **1.** Continuing all night: *an all-night radio program.* **2.** Open all night: *an all-night diner.*

al·lo·cate (ăl′ə-kāt′) *tr.v.* **al·lo·cat·ed, al·lo·cat·ing, al·lo·cates** To set aside for a particular purpose: *allocate part of one's allowance for going to the movies.* **—al′lo·ca′tion** *n.*

al·lot (ə-lŏt′) *tr.v.* **al·lot·ted, al·lot·ting, al·lots 1.** To distribute or parcel out: *The profits of the business were allotted equally to each partner.* **2.** To assign a portion for a particular purpose; allocate: *We allotted 20 minutes for each speaker in the discussion.* **—al·lot′ter** *n.*

al·lot·ment (ə-lŏt′mənt) *n.* **1.** The act of allotting. **2.** Something allotted: *The soldiers' allotment of coffee was reduced during the winter.*

al·lo·trope (ăl′ə-trōp′) *n.* Any of the different structural forms that a chemical element may have. Charcoal, graphite, and diamond are allotropes of carbon.

al·lo·trop·ic (ăl′ə-trŏp′ĭk *or* ăl′ə-trō′pĭk) *adj.* Relating to or having allotropes.

al·lot·ro·py (ə-lŏt′rə-pē) *n.* The existence of different forms of the same chemical element, each form having a different structure of atoms.

all out *adv.* With every possible effort; vigorously: *studied all out and got an A in the course.*

all-out (ôl′out′) *adj.* Using all available resources; vigorous: *an all-out effort.*

all over *adv.* **1.** Over the whole area or extent: *a cloth embroidered all over with roses.* **2.** Everywhere: *searched all over for the keys.* **3.** In every respect; utterly: *Carefree and fun-loving—that's him all over.*

al·low (ə-lou′) *tr.v.* **al·lowed, al·low·ing, al·lows 1.** To accept (an activity) as proper or right; not prevent or prohibit: *Is eating ever allowed in the library?* **2.** To accept the activity of (someone) as proper or right: *Please allow me to finish.* **3.** To let (someone) have (something): *We allowed ourselves a treat.* **4.** To accept the presence of; let in: *We do not allow the dog upstairs.* **5.** To make provision for; assign: *The schedule allows time for a break before the second speaker.* **6.** To admit; concede; grant: *I'll allow that some mistakes have been made.* **7.** To give as a discount or in exchange: *The store allowed me $20 on my old hockey equipment.* ◆ **allow for** To take into consideration and make a provision for: *Our plans allow for changes in the weather.*

al·low·a·ble (ə-lou′ə-bəl) *adj.* Capable of being allowed; permissible. **—al·low′a·bly** *adv.*

al·low·ance (ə-lou′əns) *n.* **1.** The act of allowing. **2.** An amount, as of money or food, given at regular intervals or for a specific purpose: *a weekly allowance of $10; a travel allowance.* **3.** A price reduction given in exchange for used merchandise: *an allowance of $500 on one's old car.*

al·loy (ăl′oi′ *or* ə-loi′) *n.* **1.** A metal made by mixing and fusing two or more metals, or a metal and a nonmetal, to obtain desirable qualities such as hardness, lightness, and strength: *Pewter is an alloy of copper, antimony, and lead.* **2.** A combination or mixture: *an alloy of sadness and relief.* ❖ *tr.v.* (ə-loi′ *or* ăl′oi′) **al·loyed, al·loy·ing, al·loys 1.** To combine (metals) to form an alloy. **2.** To combine; mix: *My excitement was alloyed with doubts.* [From French *aloi*, from Old French *aleir*, to combine, from Latin *alligāre*, to bind together : *ad-*, to + *ligāre*, to bind.]

all-pur·pose (ôl′pûr′pəs) *adj.* Useful in many ways: *an all-purpose thread.*

all right *adj.* **1.** Satisfactory; in good condition: *The tires are old but all right.* **2.** Acceptable; allowable: *Going to the zoo is all right with me.* **3.** Correct: *These figures are perfectly all right.* **4.** Average; mediocre: *This work is all right, but it could be better.* **5.** Not injured; safe: *Are you all right?* ❖ *adv.* **1.** In a satisfactory way: *The motor was running all right.* **2.** Very well; yes: *All right, I'll go.* **3.** Without a doubt: *That's him, all right!*

all-round (ôl′round′) *adj.* Variant of **all-around.**

All Saints' Day *n.* November 1, observed by Christians as a feast in honor of all the saints.

All Souls' Day *n.* November 2, observed by Roman Catholics as a day of prayer for the souls in purgatory.

all·spice (ôl′spīs′) *n.* **1.** The fragrant strong-flavored berries of a tropical American tree, dried and used as a spice. **2.** The tree that bears such berries.

all-star (ôl′stär′) *adj.* Made up entirely of star performers: *an all-star cast.* ❖ *n.* A person chosen for an all-star team, cast, or other group.

all-time (ôl′tīm′) *adj.* Unsurpassed until now; of all time: *set an all-time attendance record.*

al·lude (ə-lo͞od′) *intr.v.* **al·lud·ed, al·lud·ing, al·ludes** To refer to something indirectly; mention something casually or in passing: *It is considered impolite to allude to how much money a person has.* [From Latin *allūdere*, to play with : *ad-*, to + *lūdere*, to play (from *lūdus*, game).]

al·lure (ə-lo͝or′) *tr.v.* **al·lured, al·lur·ing, al·lures** To attract; entice: *I was allured to the movie by the ads.* ❖ *n.* Strong attraction; fascination: *the allure of sailing.*

al·lu·sion (ə-lo͞o′zhən) *n.* **1.** The act of alluding; indirect reference. **2.** An instance of indirect reference: *allusions to Greek mythology in the poems.*

WRITERS CHOOSE THEIR WORDS

The judge came in and sat down, then took up a stack of papers from his desk. "I've read all the statements, the police and the eyewitness reports, and someone is definitely not telling the truth. So, I'll give you both one last chance to do the right thing. First, the store manager's **allegation** of theft. Anyone willing to own up to that?"

—Matt Christopher *Baseball Turnaround*

allegory
The Peaceable Kingdom, c. 1833, by Edward Hicks (1780–1849)

WRITERS CHOOSE THEIR WORDS

The Mole knew well that it is quite against animal-etiquette to dwell on possible trouble ahead, or even to **allude** to it; so he dropped the subject.

—Kenneth Grahame *The Wind in the Willows*

alluvial fan

aloe

alpaca

ă	pat	ôr	core
ā	pay	oi	boy
âr	care	ou	out
ä	father	o͝o	took
ĕ	pet	o͝or	lure
ē	be	o͞o	boot
ĭ	pit	ŭ	cut
ī	bite	ûr	urge
îr	pier	th	thin
ŏ	pot	*th*	this
ō	toe	zh	vision
ô	paw	ə	about

al·lu·sive (ə-lo͞o′sĭv) *adj.* Containing or making allusions; suggestive. **—al·lu′sive·ly** *adv.*

al·lu·vi·al (ə-lo͞o′vē-əl) *adj.* Relating to or found in alluvium: *rich alluvial deposits at the mouth of the river.*

alluvial fan *n.* A fan-shaped mass of alluvium deposited at the mouth of a ravine or where a tributary stream joins the main stream.

al·lu·vi·um (ə-lo͞o′vē-əm) *n., pl.* **al·lu·vi·ums** or **al·lu·vi·a** (ə-lo͞o′vē-ə) Sand, silt, mud, or other matter deposited by flowing water, as in a riverbed, river delta, or flood plain.

al·ly (ə-lī′ *or* ăl′ī) *tr.v.* **al·lied, al·ly·ing, al·lies** To join or unite for a specific purpose: *The United States allied itself with the Soviet Union during World War II.* ❖ *n.* (ăl′ī *or* ə-lī′) *pl.* **al·lies 1.** A person or country that is allied to another. **2. Allies a.** The nations, including Russia, France, Great Britain, and the United States, that were allied against the Central Powers during World War I. **b.** The nations, including Great Britain, the Soviet Union, and the United States, that were allied against the Axis during World War II. [From Middle English *allien*, from Old French *alier*, from Latin *alligāre* : *ad-*, to + *ligāre*, to bind.]

al·ma ma·ter or **Al·ma Ma·ter** (ăl′mə mä′tər *or* äl′mə mä′tər) *n.* **1.** The school, college, or university that a person has attended. **2.** The song or anthem of a school, college, or university. [From Latin *alma*, nourishing + Latin *māter*, mother.]

al·ma·nac (ôl′mə-năk′ *or* ăl′mə-năk′) *n.* **1.** A book published once a year containing calendars with weather forecasts, astronomical information, tide tables, and other related information. **2.** A book published once a year containing lists, charts, and other information, especially in many different fields. [From Medieval Latin *almanach*, from medieval scientific Arabic *al-manāḫ*, the calendar, astronomical almanac.]

al·might·y (ôl-mī′tē) *adj.* All-powerful; omnipotent: *almighty God.* ❖ *n.* **Almighty** God. **—al·might′i·ly** *adv.*

al·mond (ä′mənd *or* äl′mənd *or* ăm′ənd) *n.* **1.** An oval edible nut having a soft light-brown shell. **2.** The tree, native to the Mediterranean region, that bears such nuts.

al·mo·ner (ăl′mə-nər *or* ä′mə-nər) *n.* A person who gives out alms, as for a king or monastery.

al·most (ôl′mōst′ *or* ôl-mōst′) *adv.* Slightly short of; not quite: *was almost asleep when the doorbell rang.*

alms (ämz) *pl.n.* Money or goods given to the poor as charity. [From Middle English *almes*, from Old English *ælmesse*, from Greek *eleēmosunē*, pity, charity, from *eleēmōn*, pitiful, from *eleos*, pity.]

alms·house (ämz′hous′) *n.* A home for the poor, especially one that is maintained by private charity.

al·ni·co (ăl′nĭ-kō′) *n.* Any of several alloys of iron, aluminum, nickel, cobalt and sometimes copper, niobium, or tantalum, used to make strong permanent magnets.

al·oe (ăl′ō) *n.* Any of various tropical plants, chiefly of Africa, having thick spiny-toothed leaves and red or yellow flowers. [From Middle English, from Old English *aluwe*, from Greek *aloē*.]

aloe ver·a (vĕr′ə *or* vîr′ə) *n.* **1.** An aloe native to the Mediterranean region. **2.** The juice or gel obtained from the leaves of this plant, widely used in cosmetics and medicinal preparations, especially for use on the skin.

a·loft (ə-lôft′) *adv.* **1.** In or into a high place; high or higher up: *Jet planes fly thousands of feet aloft.* **2.** In or toward a ship's upper rigging.

a·lo·ha (ə-lō′hə *or* ä-lō′hä′) *interj.* An expression used as a greeting or farewell. It is the Hawaiian word for "love." —SEE NOTE AT **ukulele.**

a·lone (ə-lōn′) *adj.* **1.** Apart from the company of anyone else: *Once her friends left and she was alone in the studio, she was able to practice without interruption.* **2.** Being without anyone or anything else; only: *The teacher alone knows when the quiz will be given.* ❖ *adv.* **1.** Without others: *She likes to travel alone.* **2.** Without aid or help: *I can lift the rock alone.* ◆ **leave well enough alone** or **let well enough alone** To be satisfied with things as they are and not try to change them. **—a·lone′ness** *n.*

SYNONYMS **alone, solitary, lonesome, lonely** These adjectives describe being apart from others. **Alone** means lacking a companion but not necessarily feeling unhappy about it: *I walked alone on the beach while my brother went surfing.* **Solitary** often means being physically apart from others by choice: *A solitary diner sat at the table in the corner.* **Lonesome** means wishing for a companion: *After her best friend moved to another state, she felt lonesome.* **Lonely** often means sad at being by oneself: *She felt lonely while all her friends were away on vacation.*

---

a·long (ə-lông′) *prep.* **1.** Over the length of: *walked along the path.* **2.** On a line or course close to; beside: *trees growing along the river.* **3.** In accordance with: *Congress was split along party lines.* ❖ *adv.* **1.** Forward; onward: *The train moved along, crossing the plains.* **2.** As company: *Bring your friend along.* **3.** As an associate piece; together: *packed her binoculars along with her hiking boots.* **4.** On one's person; in hand: *He took a camera along.* —SEE NOTE AT **together.**

a·long·side (ə-lông′sīd′) *adv.* At or near the side; to the side: *stood with a bodyguard alongside; drove up alongside.* ❖ *prep.* By the side of; side by side with: *The boat is alongside the dock.*

a·loof (ə-lo͞of′) *adj.* Distant, reserved, or indifferent in manner: *an aloof manner.* ❖ *adv.* At a distance but within view; apart; withdrawn: *The new student stood aloof from the others.* **—a·loof′ly** *adv.* **—a·loof′ness** *n.*

a·loud (ə-loud′) *adv.* **1.** With the voice: *Read the story aloud.* **2.** In a loud tone; loudly: *If we speak aloud, it will awaken the baby.*

alp (ălp) *n.* A high mountain.

al·pac·a (ăl-păk′ə) *n., pl.* **alpaca** or **al·pac·as 1.** A South American mammal related to the llama, having long silky wool. **2.** Cloth made from the wool of this mammal. **3.** A fabric that is similar to alpaca. [From Spanish, from Aymara and Quechua *allpaqa*.]

al·pen·horn (ăl′pən-hôrn′) *n.* A curved wooden horn traditionally used by herders in the Alps to call cows to pasture.

al·pen·stock (ăl′pən-stŏk′) *n.* A long staff with an iron point formerly used by mountain climbers.

al·pha (ăl′fə) *n.* **1.** The first letter of the Greek alphabet, written Α, α. In English it is represented as *A, a.* **2.** The first one; the beginning.

alpha and omega *n.* **1.** The first and the last. **2.** The most important part of something.

al·pha·bet (ăl′fə-bĕt′) *n.* **1.** The letters of a language, arranged in the order fixed by custom. **2.** A system of characters or symbols representing sounds or things. See table. [From Greek *alphabētos* : *alpha*, alpha + *bēta*, beta.]

al·pha·bet·i·cal (ăl′fə-bĕt′ĭ-kəl) also **al·pha·bet·ic** (ăl′fə-bĕt′ĭk) *adj.* **1.** Arranged in the order of the alphabet: *The dictionary lists words in alphabetical order.* **2.** Based on or using an alphabet: *an alphabetic writing system.* **—al′pha·bet′i·cal·ly** *adv.*

al·pha·bet·ize (ăl′fə-bĭ-tīz′) *tr.v.* **al·pha·bet·ized, al·pha·bet·iz·ing, al·pha·bet·iz·es** To arrange in alphabetical order. **—al′pha·bet′i·za′tion** (ăl′fə-bĕt′ĭ-zā′shən) *n.* **—al′pha·bet·iz′er** *n.*

al·pha·nu·mer·ic (ăl′fə-no͞o-mĕr′ĭk) *adj.* Consisting of or using letters, numbers, punctuation marks, and other conventional symbols: *an alphanumeric computer code.*

alpha particle *n.* A positively charged particle that con-

Development of the Alphabet

The Roman alphabet has its ultimate roots in Egypt. Before around 1750 BC, the Canaanites, a Semitic people of Palestine and Syria who also lived in Egypt, developed an alphabet based on Egyptian hieroglyphs. They used an Egyptian sign to represent the first consonant of the Canaanite word for the thing depicted by the sign. For example, the Canaanite word for "house" began with the sound (b), so they used the sign for "house" to represent (b). The alphabet contained only consonants and could be written in virtually any direction. The Phoenicians brought a modified version of the alphabet to the Greeks through trade. Some of the letters represented non-Greek sounds that the Greeks probably did not perceive accurately. The Greeks took these letters to represent other sounds.

In Italy, a western variant of the Greek alphabet was adopted by the Etruscans. Our modern letters derive from the Romans, who adapted the Etruscan script for monumental inscriptions and wrote from left to right. Because Etruscan writing did not distinguish between the sounds of *c* and *g*, the Romans created the new letter *G* by adding a stroke to *C*. *Y* and *Z* were added to represent the sounds (ü) and (z) in words borrowed from Greek. The English alphabet reached its total of 26 letters only after medieval scribes added *w* (originally written *uu*) and Renaissance printers separated the pairs *i/j* and *u/v* into four different letters. During the Middle Ages, the Roman capitals evolved into uncials and Italic cursive script, which gave rise to many modern printed and handwritten letters.

PROTO-CANAANITE	PHOENICIAN	EARLY GREEK	ETRUSCAN	CLASSICAL ROMAN	UNCIAL	ITALIC CURSIVE	MODERN Printed	MODERN Script
c. 1750 BC	c. 1000 BC	c. 800 BC	c. 500 BC		AD 300–700	1400		
				A	A	a	A a	Aa
				B	B	b	B b	Bb
				C	C	c	C c	Cc
				D	D	d	D d	Dd
				E	E	e	E e	Ee
				F	F	f	F f	Ff
				G	G	g	G g	Gg
				H	h	h	H h	Hh
				I	I	i	I i	Ii
					J	j	J j	Jj
				K	K	k	K k	Kk
				L	L	l	L l	Ll
				M	M	m	M m	Mm
				N	N	n	N n	Nn
			⊞ X					
				O	O	o	O o	Oo
				P	P	p	P p	Pp
				Q	Q	q	Q q	Qq
				R	R	r	R r	Rr
				S	S	s	S s	Ss
				T	T	t	T t	Tt
						u	U u	Uu
				V	U	v	V v	Vv
						w	W w	Ww
				X	X	x	X x	Xx
				Y	Y	y	Y y	Yy
				Z	Z	z	Z z	Zz

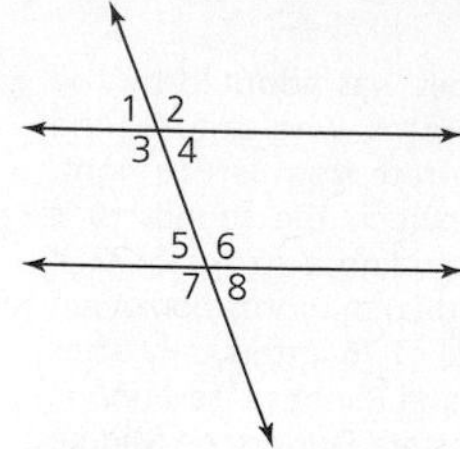

alternate angles
Angles 3 and 6 are alternate interior angles, as are angles 4 and 5. Angles 1 and 8 are alternate exterior angles, as are angles 2 and 7.

altocumulus

USAGE

altogether The word **altogether** and the phrase *all together* sound alike, but their meanings differ. *Altogether* means "completely": *I was altogether amazed by her actions. All together* means "with everybody or everything together or acting at the same time": *My friends and I went all together. All together* can be used only if you can rephrase the sentence and separate *all* and *together* by other words: *The books lay all together in a heap. All the books lay together in a heap.*

ă	pat	ôr	core
ā	pay	oi	boy
âr	care	ou	out
ä	father	o͝o	took
ĕ	pet	o͝or	lure
ē	be	o͞o	boot
ĭ	pit	ŭ	cut
ī	bite	ûr	urge
îr	pier	th	thin
ŏ	pot	*th*	this
ō	toe	zh	vision
ô	paw	ə	about

sists of two protons and two neutrons bound together. It is identical with the nucleus of a helium atom.

alpha ray *n.* A narrow stream of alpha particles.

al·pine (ăl**′**pīn′) *adj.* **1.** Relating to, living on, or growing in high mountains: *Edelweiss is an alpine plant.* **2. Alpine** Relating to the Alps.

Alps (ălps) A mountain system of south-central Europe, about 500 miles (800 kilometers) long and 100 miles (160 kilometers) wide, curving in an arc from the Mediterranean Sea through Italy, France, Switzerland, Germany, and Austria and into the northwest part of the Balkan Peninsula. The highest peak is Mont Blanc, 15,774 feet (4,808 meters), on the French-Italian border.

al-Qae·da (ăl-kī**′**də *or* ăl-kā**′**də) *n.* An international organization that tries to advance Islamic fundamentalism and disrupt the economies and influence of Western nations through attacks and bombings. [From Arabic *al-qā'ida* : *al-*, the + *qā'ida*, base.]

al·read·y (ôl-rĕd**′**ē) *adv.* **1.** By this time: *They are late and should be here already.* **2.** So soon: *Are you leaving already?*

al·right (ôl-rīt**′**) *adv. Nonstandard* All right.

Al·sace-Lor·raine (ăl′săs′lô-rān**′**) A region of northeast France that was annexed by Germany in 1871 and returned to France in 1919.

Al·sa·tian (ăl-sā**′**shən) *adj.* Relating to Alsace or to its inhabitants or culture. ❖ *n.* **1.** A native or inhabitant of Alsace. **2.** *Chiefly British* A German shepherd.

al·so (ôl**′**sō) *adv.* **1.** In addition; besides: *The label lists the ingredients and also gives nutritional information.* **2.** Likewise: *If you will stay, I will also.* ❖ *conj.* And in addition: *Many students studied French and math, also music and drawing.* [From Old English *ealswā*, entirely so.] —SEE NOTE AT **not.**

al·so-ran (ôl**′**sō-răn′) *n.* **1.** A horse that does not come in first, second, or third in a race. **2.** A person or thing that is defeated in a race, election, or other competition; a loser.

alt. *abbr.* An abbreviation of: **1.** alternate. **2.** altitude.

al·tar (ôl**′**tər) *n.* An elevated structure, often in the form of a table, before which religious ceremonies are conducted or upon which sacrifices are offered. [From Middle English *auter*, from Old English *altar*, from Latin *altāre*.]

❑ *These sound alike:* **altar, alter** (change).

altar boy *n.* A boy who is an altar server.

altar girl *n.* A girl who is an altar server.

al·tar·piece (ôl**′**tər-pēs′) *n.* A painting, carving, or similar work of art behind and above an altar in a church.

altar server *n.* An attendant who helps a priest in performing a Christian religious service.

al·ter (ôl**′**tər) *v.* **al·tered, al·ter·ing, al·ters** —*tr.* **1.** To change or make different; modify: *We altered our plans for the weekend.* **2.** To adjust (a garment) for a better fit: *You will have to have this jacket altered.* —*intr.* To change or become different: *Since their trip abroad, their whole outlook has altered.* [From Middle English *alteren*, from Medieval Latin *alterāre*, from Latin *alter*, other.] —**al′ter·a·ble** *adj.* —**al′ter·a·bly** *adv.*

❑ *These sound alike:* **alter, altar** (table for worship).

al·ter·a·tion (ôl′tə-rā**′**shən) *n.* **1.** The act or process of changing or altering: *Alteration of the school took several months.* **2.** A change: *many alterations to a suit.*

al·ter·ca·tion (ôl′tər-kā**′**shən) *n.* A noisy angry quarrel.

alter ego *n.* **1.** Another side of oneself; a second personality. **2.** An intimate friend or constant companion.

al·ter·nate (ôl**′**tər-nāt′) *v.* **al·ter·nat·ed, al·ter·nat·ing, al·ter·nates** —*intr.* **1a.** To occur in a repeating pattern or succession: *Showers alternated with sunshine.* **b.** To act or proceed by turns: *We alternated at the computer.* **2.** To pass back and forth from one state, action, or place to another: *alternate between hope and despair.* **3.** To reverse direction of flow at regular intervals: *measured how frequently the current alternates.* —*tr.* To do, perform, or use in turns: *We alternated shoveling and raking the topsoil.* ❖ *adj.* (ôl**′**tər-nĭt) **1.** Occurring in turns; succeeding each other: *alternate periods of rain and drought.* **2.** Every other; every second: *She works on alternate days of the week.* **3.** In place of another: *an alternate route.* ❖ *n.* (ôl**′**tər-nĭt) A person acting in place of another. [From Latin *alternāre*, from *alternus*, by turns, from *alter*, other.]

al·ter·nate angles (ôl**′**tər-nĭt) *pl.n.* Two angles, both interior or both exterior but not adjacent, formed on opposite sides of a line that crosses two other lines. If the two lines are parallel, the alternate angles are equal.

al·ter·nate·ly (ôl**′**tər-nĭt-lē) *adv.* In alternate order; in turn: *The crowd alternately booed and cheered.*

al·ter·nat·ing current (ôl**′**tər-nā′tĭng) *n.* An electric current that reverses its direction of flow at regular intervals. —SEE NOTE AT **current.**

al·ter·na·tion (ôl′tər-nā**′**shən) *n.* Regular and repeated change between two or more things: *the alternation of the seasons.*

al·ter·na·tive (ôl-tûr**′**nə-tĭv) *n.* **1.** One of two or more possibilities from which to choose: *We had two alternatives: to continue driving or wait for the storm to pass.* **2.** A choice between two or more possibilities: *The alternative is between hard work or failure.* See Synonyms at **choice. 3.** A remaining choice: *I have no alternative but to go without you.* ❖ *adj.* **1.** Relating to or allowing a choice between two or more possibilities: *The highway is closed. Seek alternative routes.* **2.** Existing outside traditional or established institutions or systems: *sources of alternative energy.* —**al·ter′na·tive·ly** *adv.*

alternative medicine *n.* Any of various health care practices, such as acupuncture and herbal medicine, that follow different methods from those used in conventional medicine.

al·ter·na·tor (ôl**′**tər-nā′tər) *n.* An electric generator that makes alternating current, especially one powered by a car's engine and used to keep the battery charged.

al·though (ôl-*th*ō**′**) *conj.* **1.** Regardless of the fact that; even though: *Although the trunk is big, it won't hold all the luggage.* **2.** But; however: *He says he has a dog, although I've never seen it.*

al·tim·e·ter (ăl-tĭm**′**ĭ-tər) *n.* An instrument that measures the height at which an object, such as an aircraft, is located.

al·ti·pla·no (äl′tĭ-plä**′**nō) *n., pl.* **al·ti·pla·nos** A high mountain plateau, as in certain parts of the Andes Mountains.

al·ti·tude (ăl**′**tĭ-to͞od′) *n.* **1.** The height of a thing above a reference level, usually above sea level or the earth's surface. **2.** In astronomy, the angle between a line aimed at the horizon and a line aimed at a celestial object: *a star at an altitude of 18°.* **3.** The perpendicular distance from the base of a geometric figure, such as a triangle, to the opposite vertex, side, or surface. [From Middle English, from Latin *altitūdō*, from *altus*, high.]

Alt key (ôlt) *n.* A key on a computer keyboard that is pressed along with another key to perform an alternate operation.

al·to (ăl**′**tō) *n., pl.* **al·tos 1.** A low female singing voice; a contralto. **2.** A countertenor. **3.** The range between soprano and tenor. **4.** A singer whose voice lies within this range. **5.** An instrument whose sound falls within this range. **6.** A part written in this range.

al·to·cu·mu·lus (ăl′tō-kyo͞o**′**myə-ləs) *n.* A round, fleecy white or gray cloud formation.

al·to·geth·er (ôl′tə-gĕ*th***′**ər) *adv.* **1.** Completely: *Soon the noise faded away altogether.* **2.** With all included or counted: *Altogether, there are 36 teachers in the school.* **3.**

On the whole; with everything considered: *Altogether it was a successful field trip.* —SEE NOTE.

al·to·strat·us (ăl′tō-**străt′**əs *or* ăl′tō-**strā′**təs) *n.* A cloud formation that extends in bluish or gray sheets or layers.

al·tri·cial (ăl-**trĭsh′**əl) *adj.* Hatched or born with the eyes closed and requiring care from a parent or parents. The young of dogs, cats, and most birds are altricial. [From Latin *altor*, nourisher, from *alere*, to nourish.]

al·tru·ism (**ăl′**tro͞o-ĭz′əm) *n.* Unselfish concern for the welfare of others. **—al′tru·ist** *n.*

al·tru·is·tic (ăl′tro͞o-**ĭs′**tĭk) *adj.* Showing concern for the welfare of others: *After the earthquake some altruistic doctors treated patients without charge.* **—al′tru·is′ti·cal·ly** *adv.*

al·um (**ăl′**əm) *n.* Any of various crystalline salts in which a metal such as aluminum or chromium is combined with another metal such as potassium or sodium, used in dyeing and sometimes in medicine to stop bleeding from a small cut.

a·lu·mi·na (ə-**lo͞o′**mə-nə) *n.* Any of several forms of aluminum oxide, Al_2O_3, such as bauxite or corundum, that occur naturally and are used in aluminum production and in ceramics and electrical insulation.

al·u·min·i·um (ăl′yə-**mĭn′**ē-əm) *n. Chiefly British* Variant of **aluminum.**

a·lu·mi·num (ə-**lo͞o′**mə-nəm) *n. Symbol* **Al** A lightweight, silvery-white metallic element that is easily shaped and conducts electricity well. It is used to make a wide variety of products from soda cans to airplane components. Atomic number 13. See **Periodic Table.** [From *alumin(a)* + *-(i)um*, chemical element suffix.]

a·lum·na (ə-**lŭm′**nə) *n., pl.* **a·lum·nae** (ə-**lŭm′**nē′) A woman who has graduated from a certain school, college, or university.

a·lum·nus (ə-**lŭm′**nəs) *n., pl.* **a·lum·ni** (ə-**lŭm′**nī′) A man who has graduated from a certain school, college, or university. [From Latin, pupil, from *alere*, to nourish.]

al·ve·o·lus (ăl-**vē′**ə-ləs) *n., pl.* **al·ve·o·li** (ăl-**vē′**ə-lī′) **1.** Any of numerous tiny air-filled sacs in the lungs where the exchange of oxygen and carbon dioxide takes place. Oxygen enters the blood and carbon dioxide leaves the blood through capillaries that surround the alveoli. **2.** A small bodily pit or cavity, such as a tooth socket in the jawbone. **—al·ve′o·lar** (ăl-**vē′**ə-lər) *adj.*

al·ways (**ôl′**wāz *or* **ôl′**wĭz) *adv.* **1.** On every occasion; without exception: *I always leave at six o'clock.* **2.** For all time; forever: *They will always be friends.* **3.** At any time; in any event: *If the bus is late, we can always walk.* [From Middle English *alweis*, from Old English *ealne weg*.]

Alz·hei·mer's disease (**älts′**hī-mərz) *n.* A disease of the brain that primarily affects elderly people and is characterized by the ongoing loss of memory and other mental abilities. It is associated with the development of abnormal tissues and protein deposits in the cerebral cortex. [After Alois *Alzheimer* (1864–1915), German neurologist.]

am (ăm) *v.* First person singular present tense of **be.**

Am The symbol for the element **americium.**

AM *abbr.* An abbreviation of: **1.** amplitude modulation. **2.** or **AM** ante meridiem (before noon).

Am. *abbr.* An abbreviation of: **1.** America. **2.** American.

a·mal·gam (ə-**măl′**gəm) *n.* **1.** An alloy of mercury with other metals: *The amalgam used in silvering mirrors contains mercury and tin.* **2.** A combination or mixture: *The play was an amalgam of satire and farce.*

a·mal·ga·mate (ə-**măl′**gə-māt′) *v.* **a·mal·ga·mat·ed, a·mal·ga·mat·ing, a·mal·ga·mates** *—tr.* **1.** To unite to make a unified whole; merge: *The company amalgamated several of its shops under one manager.* **2.** To alloy (a metal) with mercury. *—intr.* **1.** To be combined; consolidate: *Many different peoples amalgamated to form the United States.* **2.** To blend with another metal. **—a·mal′ga·ma′tor** *n.*

a·mal·ga·ma·tion (ə-măl′gə-**mā′**shən) *n.* **1.** The process of amalgamating. **2.** A consolidation or merger, as of businesses.

am·a·ni·ta (ăm′ə-**nē′**tə *or* ăm′ə-**nī′**tə) *n.* Any of various mushrooms with white spores and usually a ring around the stalk, many of which are very poisonous.

amanita

am·a·ranth (**ăm′**ə-rănth′) *n.* Any of various annual plants having dense green or reddish clusters of tiny flowers and including weeds, garden plants, and species grown for their edible leaves and seeds.

am·a·ryl·lis (ăm′ə-**rĭl′**ĭs) *n.* Any of several plants of tropical America having large, funnel-shaped flowers that are red, pink, or white.

amaryllis

a·mass (ə-**măs′**) *tr.v.* **a·massed, a·mass·ing, a·mass·es** To accumulate in large quantity: *amass wealth; amass knowledge.* **—a·mass′a·ble** *adj.*

am·a·teur (**ăm′**ə-tûr′ *or* **ăm′**ə-cho͝or′) *n.* **1.** A person who engages in art, science, or sport for enjoyment rather than as a profession or for money. **2.** A person who lacks the skill of a professional: *The fact that the window was not level showed that it was the work of an amateur.* ❖ *adj.* **1.** Relating to or done by an amateur: *an amateur gymnast.* **2.** Made up of amateurs: *an amateur orchestra.* **3.** Not skillful; amateurish: *an amateur performance.* [From Latin *amātor*, lover.]

am·a·teur·ish (ăm′ə-**tûr′**ĭsh *or* ăm′ə-**cho͝or′**ĭsh) *adj.* Done or performed as one would expect of an amateur rather than a professional. **—am′a·teur′ish·ly** *adv.*

am·a·to·ry (**ăm′**ə-tôr′ē) *adj.* Relating to or expressive of love: *an amatory look.*

a·maze (ə-**māz′**) *tr.v.* **a·mazed, a·maz·ing, a·maz·es** To fill with surprise or wonder; astonish: *The size of the skyscrapers amazed the tourists.* See Synonyms at **surprise.** **—a·maz′ed·ly** (ə-**mā′**zĭd-lē) *adv.*

a·maze·ment (ə-**māz′**mənt) *n.* Great surprise; astonishment.

a·maz·ing (ə-**mā′**zĭng) *adj.* Causing great surprise or amazement; astonishing: *The patient has made an amazing recovery from such serious injuries.* **—a·maz′ing·ly** *adv.*

Am·a·zon (**ăm′**ə-zŏn′ *or* **ăm′**ə-zən) *n.* A member of a legendary nation of women warriors believed in ancient times to have lived in Scythia.

Am·a·zo·ni·an (ăm′ə-**zō′**nē-ən) *adj.* **1.** Relating to the Amazon River or the region it drains. **2a.** Relating to the Amazon warriors. **b.** often **amazonian** Resembling an Amazon; vigorous or aggressive.

Amazon River The second-longest river in the world and the one with the greatest volume of water, flowing about 4,100 miles (6,600 kilometers) from Peru across northern Brazil to the Atlantic Ocean.

am·bas·sa·dor (ăm-**băs′**ə-dər *or* ăm-**băs′**ə-dôr′) *n.* **1.** A diplomatic official of the highest rank who represents a government in another country. **2.** A messenger or representative: *a goodwill ambassador.*

am·ber (**ăm′**bər) *n.* A hard, translucent, usually brownish-yellow substance that is the fossilized resin of ancient trees and frequently contains fossil insects. Amber is often used to make jewelry. ❖ *adj.* Made of amber: *an amber necklace.* [From Middle English *ambre*, from Arabic *'anbar*, ambergris, amber.]

amber

am·ber·gris (**ăm′**bər-grĭs′ *or* **ăm′**bər-grēs′) *n.* A waxy substance formed in the intestines of sperm whales that was formerly used in making perfume.

am·bi·ance also **am·bi·ence** (**ăm′**bē-əns) *n.* The special atmosphere or mood created by a particular environment: *the exotic ambiance of Paris streets.*

am·bi·dex·trous (ăm′bĭ-**dĕk′**strəs) *adj.* Able to use both hands equally well. [From Latin : *ambi-*, on both sides + *dexter*, right-handed.] **—am′bi·dex′trous·ly** *adv.*

am·bi·ent (ăm′bē-ənt) *adj.* Surrounding; encircling: *It was hard to hear each other in the restaurant because of all the ambient noise.*

am·bi·gu·i·ty (ăm′bĭ-gyo͞o′ĭ-tē) *n., pl.* **am·bi·gu·i·ties 1.** The condition of having two or more possible meanings. **2.** Something that is ambiguous: *There were several ambiguities in their conflicting statements.*

am·big·u·ous (ăm-bĭg′yo͞o-əs) *adj.* Having more than one interpretation; unclear: *A number of ambiguous sentences made the report hard to understand.* **—am·big′u·ous·ly** *adv.*

SYNONYMS **ambiguous, equivocal, vague** These adjectives mean lacking a clear meaning. **Ambiguous** means having two or more possible meanings: *Because the instructions were ambiguous, I made a mistake assembling the model airplane.* Something **equivocal** is unclear or misleading, often as a result of a person making it hard to know what his or her true thoughts or feelings are: *Because of her equivocal response, I wasn't sure if I should stay or leave.* What is **vague** is expressed in indefinite form or reflects imprecision of thought: *I only have a vague idea of what this movie is about.*

---

am·bi·tion (ăm-bĭsh′ən) *n.* **1.** A strong desire to achieve something: *The student's ambition was to become a great scientist.* **2.** Desire to achieve or do something, especially something requiring work or energy: *With so little ambition he was not likely to find a good job.* [From Middle English *ambicioun*, from Latin *ambitiō*, from *ambīre*, to go around (for votes).]

am·bi·tious (ăm-bĭsh′əs) *adj.* **1.** Full of ambition; eager to succeed: *The ambitious new worker learned very quickly.* **2.** Full of desire; eager: *The new doctor was ambitious for success.* **3.** Requiring great effort; challenging: *ambitious goals; an ambitious schedule.* **—am·bi′tious·ly** *adv.* **—am·bi′tious·ness** *n.*

am·biv·a·lence (ăm-bĭv′ə-ləns) *n.* The existence of two conflicting feelings at the same time: *His hesitation to join the band was evidence of his ambivalence.*

am·biv·a·lent (ăm-bĭv′ə-lənt) *adj.* Having or showing conflicting feelings about someone or something: *She was ambivalent about taking the job on the night shift.* **—am·biv′a·lent·ly** *adv.*

am·ble (ăm′bəl) *intr.v.* **am·bled, am·bling, am·bles** To walk or move along at a slow leisurely pace: *We ambled aimlessly down the street.* ❖ *n.* A slow leisurely walk: *They took an amble through the park after dinner.* **—am′bler** *n.*

am·bro·sia (ăm-brō′zhə) *n.* **1.** In Greek mythology, the food of the gods, thought to give immortality. **2.** Something highly pleasing to one's taste or smell. **3.** A dessert containing primarily oranges and flaked coconut. [From Greek *ambrosiā*, from *ambrotos*, immortal.] **—am·bro′sial** *adj.*

am·bu·lance (ăm′byə-ləns) *n.* A specially equipped vehicle used to transport sick and injured people.

am·bu·la·to·ry (ăm′byə-lə-tôr′ē) *adj.* **1.** Relating to walking or the ability to walk. **2.** Able to walk; not confined to one's bed: *an ambulatory patient.*

am·bus·cade (ăm′bə-skād′ *or* ăm′bə-skād′) *n.* An ambush. ❖ *tr.v.* **am·bus·cad·ed, am·bus·cad·ing, am·bus·cades** To ambush. **—am′bus·cad′er** *n.*

am·bush (ăm′bo͝osh) *n.* **1.** A sudden attack made from a concealed position: *The soldiers at the rear of the column fell victims to an ambush.* **2.** The hiding place used for such an attack: *The tiger crouches in ambush.* ❖ *tr.v.* **am·bushed, am·bush·ing, am·bush·es** To attack from a concealed position: *The soldiers hid among the rocks to ambush the pursuing forces.* [From Middle English *embushen*, to position in concealment; hide, from Old French *embuschier*.]

a·me·ba (ə-mē′bə) *n.* Variant of **amoeba. —a·me′bic** (ə-mē′bĭk) *adj.*

am·e·bi·a·sis also **am·oe·bi·a·sis** (ăm′ə-bī′ə-sĭs) *n.* Infection of the intestines with a certain kind of ameba that is transmitted by contaminated food or water and causes diarrhea, cramps, and nausea.

amebic dysentery *n.* Amebiasis.

a·me·lio·rate (ə-mēl′yə-rāt′) *tr. & intr.v.* **a·me·lio·rat·ed, a·me·lio·rat·ing, a·me·lio·rates** To make or become better; improve: *Lower taxes will ameliorate the conditions for hiring new workers.* **—a·me′lio·ra′tion** *n.* **—a·me′lio·ra′tor** *n.*

a·men (ā-mĕn′ *or* ä-mĕn′) *interj.* An expression used at the end of a prayer or a statement to express approval. [From Old English, from Late Latin *āmēn*, from Hebrew *'āmēn*, certainly.]

A·men (ä′mən) *n.* Variant of **Amun.**

a·me·na·ble (ə-mē′nə-bəl *or* ə-mĕn′ə-bəl) *adj.* **1.** Willing to consent: *I am amenable to your suggestion.* **2.** Responsible to an authority; accountable: *We are all amenable to the law.* **3.** Susceptible or open, as to testing or criticism: *a question that is amenable to scientific investigation.* **—a·me′na·bil′i·ty** *n.* **—a·me′na·bly** *adv.*

a·mend (ə-mĕnd′) *tr.v.* **a·mend·ed, a·mend·ing, a·mends 1.** To change for the better; improve: *I amended my earlier proposal to make it clearer.* **2.** To change or add to (a legislative motion, law, or constitution).

a·mend·ment (ə-mĕnd′mənt) *n.* **1.** The act of changing for the better; improvement: *Some treaties have provisions for amendment.* **2.** A legally adopted change or addition to a law or body of laws: *Giving voting rights to women was accomplished in an amendment to the Constitution.*

a·mends (ə-mĕndz′) *pl.n.* *(used with a singular or plural verb)* Something given or done to make up for an injury or insult: *By offering to pay for the repairs, they hoped to make amends for the damage.* [From Middle English *amendes*, from Old French, plural of *amende*, reparation.]

a·men·i·ty (ə-mĕn′ĭ-tē *or* ə-mē′nĭ-tē) *n., pl.* **a·men·i·ties 1.** The quality of being pleasant and agreeable: *the amenity of vacationing on the lake.* **2.** Something that provides or increases physical comfort; a convenience: *an apartment with all the amenities of modern living.* **3. amenities** Polite social behavior; social courtesies.

Amer. *abbr.* An abbreviation of: **1.** America. **2.** American.

A·mer·i·ca (ə-mĕr′ĭ-kə) **1.** The United States. **2.** also **the A·mer·i·cas** (ə-mĕr′ĭ-kəz) The landmasses and islands of North America, Central America, and South America.

A·mer·i·can (ə-mĕr′ĭ-kən) *adj.* **1.** Relating to the United States of America or its people, language, or culture: *American literature.* **2.** Relating to North or South America, the West Indies, or the Western Hemisphere: *American geology.* ❖ *n.* A native or inhabitant of the United States or of the Americas.

A·mer·i·ca·na (ə-mĕr′ə-kä′nə *or* ə-mĕr′ə-kăn′ə) *n.* *(used with a plural verb)* Things that are examples of American history, folklore, or geography.

American cheese *n.* A smooth mild white or yellow cheddar cheese.

American English *n.* English as used in the United States.

American Indian *n.* A member of any of the peoples native to the Americas except the Eskimo, Aleut, and Inuit. **—American Indian** *adj.* —SEE NOTE AT **Native American.**

A·mer·i·can·ism (ə-mĕr′ĭ-kə-nĭz′əm) *n.* **1.** A word or phrase originating in or peculiar to American English. **2.** A custom, trait, or tradition originating in the United States. **3.** Allegiance to the United States and its customs and institutions.

ă	pat	ôr	core
ā	pay	oi	boy
âr	care	ou	out
ä	father	o͝o	took
ĕ	pet	o͝or	lure
ē	be	o͞o	boot
ĭ	pit	ŭ	cut
ī	bite	ûr	urge
îr	pier	th	thin
ŏ	pot	*th*	this
ō	toe	zh	vision
ô	paw	ə	about

A·mer·i·can·ize (ə-mĕr′ĭ-kə-nīz′) *tr. & intr.v.* **A·mer·i·can·ized, A·mer·i·can·iz·ing, A·mer·i·can·iz·es** To make or become American in manner, customs, or speech. —**A·mer′i·can·i·za′tion** (ə-mĕr′ĭ-kə-nĭ-**zā′**-shən) *n.*

American Revolution *n.* The war between the American colonies and Great Britain (1775–1783), leading to the formation of the independent United States.

American Sa·mo·a (sə-**mō′**ə) A US territory in the southern Pacific Ocean northeast of Fiji made up of the eastern Samoan islands. Pago Pago is the capital.

American Sign Language *n.* The sign language used predominantly by deaf and hearing-impaired people in the United States and Canada.

American Spanish *n.* The Spanish language as used in the Western Hemisphere.

A·mer·i·cas (ə-**mĕr′**ĭ-kəz), **the** See **America** (sense 2).

am·er·i·ci·um (ăm′ə-**rĭsh′**ē-əm) *n. Symbol* **Am** A white, metallic, radioactive element that is artifically produced by scientists. Some of its isotopes are used as radiation sources in research, radiography, and smoke alarms. Atomic number 95. See **Periodic Table.**

Am·er·in·di·an (ăm′ə-**rĭn′**dē-ən) also **Am·er·ind** (**ăm′**-ə-rĭnd′) *n.* An American Indian. —**Am′er·in′di·an** *adj.*

am·e·thyst (**ăm′**ə-thĭst) *n.* **1.** A purple or violet form of transparent quartz used as a gemstone. **2.** A purple or violet color. [From Middle English *amatist*, from Greek *amethustos*, not drunk, amethyst (because it was believed to be a remedy for drunkenness) : *a-*, not + *methuein*, to be drunk.]

Am·har·ic (ăm-**hăr′**ĭk *or* äm-**hä′**rĭk) *n.* A Semitic language that is the official language of Ethiopia.

a·mi·a·ble (**ā′**mē-ə-bəl) *adj.* Friendly; good-natured: *an amiable laugh.* —**a′mi·a·bil′i·ty, a′mi·a·ble·ness** *n.* —**a′mi·a·bly** *adv.*

am·i·ca·ble (**ăm′**ĭ-kə-bəl) *adj.* Characterized by friendliness and goodwill: *an amicable discussion.* —**am′i·ca·bil′i·ty** *n.* —**am′i·ca·bly** *adv.*

a·mid (ə-**mĭd′**) also **a·midst** (ə-**mĭdst′**) *prep.* Surrounded by; in the middle of: *The swimmer's head appeared amid the waves.*

a·mid·ships (ə-**mĭd′**shĭps′) also **a·mid·ship** (ə-**mĭd′**-shĭp′) *adv.* In or toward the middle part of a ship: *The cabin passengers lived amidships.*

a·midst (ə-**mĭdst′**) *prep.* Variant of **amid.**

a·mi·go (ə-**mē′**gō) *n., pl.* **a·mi·gos** A friend. [From Spanish, from Latin *amīcus.*]

a·mine (ə-**mēn′** *or* **ăm′**ēn) *n.* Any of a group of organic compounds formed from ammonia (NH_3) by substituting organic radicals for one or more of the ammonia's hydrogens.

a·mi·no acid (ə-**mē′**nō *or* **ăm′**ə-nō′) *n.* Any of a large number of organic compounds that contain carbon, oxygen, hydrogen, and nitrogen, 20 of which are the basic components that join together in different combinations to make proteins. Humans and other animals can make some amino acids but must obtain others from food.

a·mir (ə-**mîr′** *or* ā-**mîr′**) *n.* Variant of **emir.**

A·mish (**ä′**mĭsh *or* **ăm′**ĭsh) *n.* **1.** An Anabaptist sect whose followers practice simple living. Most of the Amish live in Ohio, Pennsylvania, and Indiana. **2.** The followers of this religion considered as a group. ❖ *adj.* Relating to this religion or its followers.

a·miss (ə-**mĭs′**) *adj.* Faulty or incorrect: *Something is amiss when the train is this late.* ❖ *adv.* In an improper or defective way: *Your work is going amiss.*

am·i·ty (**ăm′**ĭ-tē) *n., pl.* **am·i·ties** A state of friendship, as between nations.

Am·man (ä-**män′** *or* **ä′**män) The capital of Jordan, in the northwest part of the country. The site has been inhabited since prehistoric times.

am·me·ter (**ăm′**mē′tər) *n.* An instrument that measures the amount of electric current in amperes.

am·mo·nia (ə-**mōn′**yə) *n.* **1.** A colorless gas, with a strongly irritating odor, that is composed of nitrogen and hydrogen and has the formula NH_3. It is used to manufacture fertilizers, explosives, and plastics. **2.** A solution of ammonia in water; ammonium hydroxide.

ammonia water *n.* Ammonium hydroxide.

am·mon·ite (**ăm′**ə-nīt′) *n.* A fossil shell of an extinct mollusk related to the octopuses and squids. Ammonite shells were coiled and had many internal chambers.

am·mo·ni·um (ə-**mō′**nē-əm) *n.* An ion, with the formula NH_4, that consists of four hydrogen atoms bound to a single nitrogen atom and that has a single positive charge. Its compounds are similar to those of alkali metals.

ammonium chloride *n.* A white crystalline salt that consists of an ammonium ion and a chloride ion bound together. It is used in dry cells, in soldering, and in metal finishing.

ammonium hydroxide *n.* A solution of ammonia in water, often used as a general cleanser.

ammonium nitrate *n.* A colorless crystalline salt composed of ammonium ions and nitrate ions bound together. It is used in fertilizers and explosives.

am·mu·ni·tion (ăm′yə-**nĭsh′**ən) *n.* **1.** Projectiles, such as bullets, shells, and shot, that can be fired from guns. **2.** Explosive objects, such as bombs or rockets, that are used as weapons. **3.** Something that is used to attack or defend an argument or point of view: *The senator's improper conduct gave opponents ammunition during the election campaign.*

am·ne·sia (ăm-**nē′**zhə) *n.* A partial or total loss of memory, usually caused by shock, brain injury, or illness. [From Greek *amnēsiā*, forgetfulness : *a-*, not + *mimnēskein*, to remember.]

am·nes·ty (**ăm′**nĭ-stē) *n., pl.* **am·nes·ties** A general pardon granted by a government: *The town government granted amnesty to people who failed to get licenses for their pets.* [From Latin *amnēstia*, from Greek *amnēstos*, not remembered : *a-*, not + *mimnēskein*, to remember.]

am·ni·on (**ăm′**nē-ən *or* **ăm′**nē-ŏn′) *n., pl.* **am·ni·ons** or **am·ni·a** (**ăm′**nē-ə) A tough thin membrane forming a sac that contains a watery liquid in which the embryo or fetus of a reptile, bird, or mammal is suspended. —**am′ni·ot′ic** (ăm′nē-**ŏt′**ĭk) *adj.*

a·moe·ba also **a·me·ba** (ə-**mē′**bə) *n.* A one-celled organism that can change shape. Amoebas are protozoans, and some of them cause disease in humans. [From Greek *amoibē*, change.] —**a·moe′bic, a·me′bic** (ə-**mē′**bĭk) *adj.*

am·oe·bi·a·sis (ăm′ə-**bī′**ə-sĭs) *n.* Variant of **amebiasis.**

amoebic dysentery *n.* Amebiasis.

a·mok (ə-**mŏk′**) also **a·muck** (ə-**mŭk′** *or* ə-**mŏk′**) *adv.* Into a state of uncontrolled or destructive activity: *When school ended, the kids ran amok.* [From Malay *amok.*]

A·mon (**ä′**mən) *n.* Variant of **Amun.**

a·mong (ə-**mŭng′**) also **a·mongst** (ə-**mŭngst′**) *prep.* **1.** In the midst of; surrounded by: *an oak among the pines.* **2.** In the company of: *among friends.* **3.** In the number or class of: *I count myself among the lucky ones.* **4.** By many or all of: *a custom popular among the Greeks.* **5.** With portions to each of: *The soda was shared among them.* **6.** With or against one another: *The dogs were fighting among themselves.* —SEE NOTE AT **between.**

a·mor·al (ā-**môr′**əl) *adj.* **1.** Not subject to moral distinctions or judgments; neither moral nor immoral: *Nature is amoral.* **2.** Not caring about right and wrong. —**a′mo·ral′i·ty** (ā′mô-**răl′**ĭ-tē) *n.* —**a·mor′al·ly** *adv.*

am·o·rous (**ăm′**ər-əs) *adj.* **1.** Full of or strongly disposed

ammonite

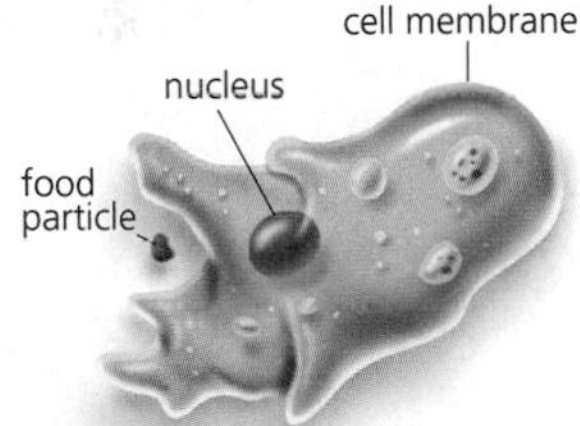

amoeba

WRITERS CHOOSE THEIR WORDS

Mrs. Bell had a stern look that [Gavin] associated with his worst childhood misdeeds. "I was relieved to discover that the robot running **amok** was not a member of staff," she said testily. "Imagine my embarrassment instead when I had to admit that it was our family robot." "Running **amok**?" said Fleur. "I don't believe it," said Gavin, but he couldn't suppress a fear that perhaps all robots had a tendency to frightening, erratic behavior.

—Helen Fox
Eager

to romantic love: *an amorous young knight.* **2.** Relating to or expressing romantic love or sexual desire: *an amorous look.* [From Middle English, from Latin *amor*, love.] **—am′or·ous·ly** *adv.*

a·mor·phous (ə-**môr′**fəs) *adj.* **1.** Lacking definite form or shape: *an amorphous mass of mud and rock.* **2.** Not made of crystals: *Glass is an amorphous substance.* **—a·mor′phous·ly** *adv.*

am·or·tize (ăm′ər-tīz′ *or* ə-**môr′**tīz′) *tr.v.* **am·or·tized, am·or·tiz·ing, am·or·tiz·es** To pay back (a debt) in regular equal installments, often including both principal and interest. **—am′or·ti·za′tion** (ăm′ər-tĭ-**zā′**shən) *n.*

amphitheater
Roman amphitheater, Nîmes, France

A·mos[1] (**ā′**məs) A Hebrew prophet of the eighth century BC.

A·mos[2] (**ā′**məs) *n.* A book of the Bible in which Amos denounces greed and social injustice.

a·mount (ə-**mount′**) *n.* **1.** The total of two or more quantities: *The amount of your bill is $8.72.* **2.** A number; a sum. **3.** Quantity: *a meager amount of rainfall.* ❖ *intr.v.* **a·mount·ed, a·mount·ing, a·mounts 1.** To add up in number or quantity: *Total sales for the day amounted to $655.* **2.** To add up in significance or effect: *Our effort to convince them didn't amount to much.* **3.** To be equivalent: *In some cases, disobeying orders amounts to treason.* [From Middle English *amounten*, to ascend, from Old French *amonter*, from Latin *ad montem*, to the hill.]

a·mour (ə-**mo͝or′**) *n.* A love affair, especially an illicit one.

amp (ămp) *n. Informal* **1.** An ampere. **2.** An amplifier, especially one used to amplify music.

am·per·age (**ăm′**pər-ĭj *or* **ăm′**pîr′ĭj) *n.* The strength of an electric current expressed in amperes.

am·pere (**ăm′**pîr′) *n.* A unit used to measure the amount of an electric current, equal to a flow of one coulomb of charge passing a given point per second. See table at **measurement.** [After André Marie *Ampère* (1775–1836), French physicist.]

Roald Amundsen

am·per·sand (**ăm′**pər-sănd′) *n.* The character or sign (&) representing *and.*

am·phet·a·mine (ăm-**fĕt′**ə-mēn′ *or* ăm-**fĕt′**ə-mĭn) *n.* Any of a group of drugs that stimulate the nervous system, causing heightened alertness and a faster heartbeat and metabolism. Amphetamines are highly addictive.

am·phib·i·an (ăm-**fĭb′**ē-ən) *n.* **1.** Any of various cold-blooded vertebrate animals, including the frogs, salamanders, and caecilians, having skin that is usually smooth and moist. Most amphibians live in the water and breathe with gills in early life but develop lungs and breathe air as adults. **2.** An aircraft that is capable of taking off from and landing on either land or water. **3.** A vehicle that is capable of traveling both on land and in water. [From Greek *amphibios*, amphibious : *amphi-*, both + *bios*, life.]

am·phib·i·ous (ăm-**fĭb′**ē-əs) *adj.* **1.** Able to live both on land and in water. **2.** Capable of traveling both on land and in water: *an amphibious vehicle.* **3.** Launched from the sea with navy, air, and land forces against an enemy on land: *an amphibious operation.* **—am·phib′i·ous·ly** *adv.* **—am·phib′i·ous·ness** *n.*

am·phi·bole (**ăm′**fə-bōl′) *n.* Any of a large group of minerals composed of a silicate joined to various metals, such as calcium, magnesium, iron, or sodium.

am·phi·the·a·ter (**ăm′**fə-thē′ə-tər) *n.* **1.** An oval or round structure having tiers of seats rising gradually outward from a central open space or arena. **2.** A level area surrounded by ground that slopes upward.

am·pho·ra (**ăm′**fər-ə) *n., pl.* **am·pho·rae** (**ăm′**fə-rē′) or **am·pho·ras** A tall earthenware jar with two handles, used by the ancient Greeks and Romans to store wine or oil.

am·ple (**ăm′**pəl) *adj.* **am·pler, am·plest 1.** Of large or great size, amount, extent, or capacity: *a rich nation with ample food for all.* **2.** Fully sufficient to meet a need or purpose: *had ample time to prepare for the test.* [From Middle English, from Latin *amplus.*] **—am′ple·ness** *n.*

am·pli·fi·ca·tion (ăm′plə-fĭ-**kā′**shən) *n.* **1a.** The act or result of amplifying, enlarging, or extending. **b.** An increase in the magnitude or strength of an electric current, a force, or another physical quantity. **2.** An expansion of a statement or idea: *The report is an amplification of the committee's views.*

am·pli·fi·er (**ăm′**plə-fī′ər) *n.* A device, especially an electronic device, that produces amplification of an electric signal.

am·pli·fy (**ăm′**plə-fī′) *tr.v.* **am·pli·fied, am·pli·fy·ing, am·pli·fies 1.** To produce amplification of: *A public-address system amplifies a speaker's voice.* **2.** To add to (something spoken or written); expand; make complete: *amplify earlier remarks.*

am·pli·tude (**ăm′**plĭ-to͞od′) *n.* **1.** Greatness of size; extent. **2.** Abundance; fullness. **3.** One half the full extent of a vibration, oscillation, or wave. For example, the distance between the position of rest and the highest swing of a pendulum is its amplitude; thus a pendulum swinging through an angle of 90 degrees has an amplitude of 45 degrees. **4.** The peak strength of an alternating electric current in a given cycle.

amplitude modulation *n.* A system of radio transmission in which the amplitude of the carrier wave is adjusted so that it is proportional to the sound or other information that is to be transmitted.

am·ply (**ăm′**plē) *adv.* More than sufficiently; generously, liberally: *The library was amply supplied with books, magazines, and computers.*

am·pu·tate (**ăm′**pyo͝o-tāt′) *tr.v.* **am·pu·tat·ed, am·pu·tat·ing, am·pu·tates** To cut off (a projecting body part), especially by surgery. [From Latin *amputāre*, to cut around : *am-*, *ambi-*, around + *putāre*, to cut.] **—am′pu·ta′tion** *n.* **—am′pu·ta′tor** *n.*

am·pu·tee (ăm′pyo͝o-**tē′**) *n.* A person who has had one or more limbs removed by amputation.

Am·ster·dam (**ăm′**stər-dăm′) The constitutional capital and largest city of the Netherlands, in the western part of the country. It is linked to the North Sea by a ship canal.

amt. *abbr.* An abbreviation of amount.

a·muck (ə-**mŭk′**) *adv.* Variant of **amok.**

am·u·let (**ăm′**yə-lĭt) *n.* An object worn, especially around the neck, as a charm against evil or injury.

A·mun also **A·men** or **A·mon** (**ä′**mən) *n.* In Egyptian mythology, the god of life and reproduction, sometimes represented as a man with the head of a ram. [From Egyptian *jmn.*]

A·mund·sen (**ä′**mənd-sən *or* **ä′**mo͝on-sən), **Roald** 1872–1928. Norwegian explorer who in 1911 became the first person to reach the South Pole.

A·mur River (ä-**mo͝or′**) also **Hei·longjiang** (**hā′**lông′-**jyäng′**) A river of northeast Asia flowing about 2,730 miles (4,400 kilometers) mainly along the border between China and Russia.

a·muse (ə-**myo͞oz′**) *tr.v.* **a·mused, a·mus·ing, a·mus·es 1.** To hold the attention of or occupy in an agreeable fashion: *The new game amused the neighborhood kids for hours.* **2.** To cause to laugh or smile by giving pleasure: *amused the crowd with jokes.* [From Old French *amuser*, to astonish : *a-*, to + *muser*, to stare stupidly.] **—a·mus′a·ble** *adj.*

a·muse·ment (ə-**myo͞oz′**mənt) *n.* **1.** The state of being pleasantly entertained: *They were too overcome with amusement to say a word.* **2.** Something that amuses or entertains: *charades, blindman's bluff, and similar amusements.*

amusement park *n.* A commercially operated park that

ă	pat	ôr	core
ā	pay	oi	boy
âr	care	ou	out
ä	father	o͝o	took
ĕ	pet	o͝or	lure
ē	be	o͞o	boot
ĭ	pit	ŭ	cut
ī	bite	ûr	urge
îr	pier	th	thin
ŏ	pot	*th*	this
ō	toe	zh	vision
ô	paw	ə	about

offers rides, games, and other forms of entertainment.

a·mus·ing (ə-myo͞o′zĭng) *adj.* Pleasantly entertaining or comical: *an amusing trick.* **—a·mus′ing·ly** *adv.*

a·myg·da·la (ə-mĭg′də-lə) *n., pl.* **a·myg·da·lae** (ə-mĭg′-də-lē) Either of two small, almond-shaped masses of gray matter, located in the temporal lobes of the brain, that are involved in the processing and display of emotion. [From Greek *amugdalē*, almond.]

am·y·lase (ăm′ə-lās′ *or* ăm′ə-lāz′) *n.* Any of various enzymes that are present in saliva, in pancreatic juice, and in plants and other organisms and that convert starches to sugars, as in digestion.

an (ən; ăn *when stressed*) *indef.art.* The form of *a* that is used before words beginning with a vowel sound: *an elephant; an hour; an umbrella.*

an– *pref.* Variant of **a–**[1].

–an *suff.* A suffix that means: **1.** Born in or being a citizen of: *American; Mexican.* **2.** Belonging to, associated with, or expert in: *Unitarian; librarian.* **3.** Relating to or resembling: *Herculean; Shakespearean.*

An·a·bap·tist (ăn′ə-băp′tĭst) *n.* A member of a Protestant religious movement viewing baptism as an external sign of faith and advocating the separation of church and state. **—An′a·bap′tist** *adj.*

anabolic steroid *n.* Any of a group of steroid hormones that promote the storage of protein and the growth of tissue, sometimes used by athletes to increase muscle size and strength. Prolonged use of anabolic steroids can cause various medical problems, including stunted growth, high blood pressure, and liver disease.

a·nab·o·lism (ə-năb′ə-lĭz′əm) *n.* The phase of metabolism in which complex molecules, such as proteins and fats, are formed from simpler ones. **—an′a·bol′ic** (ăn′-ə-bŏl′ĭk) *adj.*

a·nach·ro·nism (ə-năk′rə-nĭz′əm) *n.* **1.** The representation of something in a time other than its proper or historical time, as in a story. **2.** Something that is out of its proper time: *Cavalry is an anachronism in modern warfare.* [From Late Greek *anakhronismos* : Greek *ana-*, back + Greek *khronos*, time.]

a·nach·ro·nis·tic (ə-năk′rə-nĭs′tĭk) *adj.* Out of proper time; misplaced chronologically: *One anachronistic detail in the play is having General Washington get a message by telegraph.* **—a·nach′ro·nis′ti·cal·ly** *adv.*

an·a·con·da (ăn′ə-kŏn′də) *n.* Any of several large nonvenomous tropical American snakes that coil around and suffocate their prey. [From Sinhalese *heṇakaⁿdayā*, a kind of snake.]

an·aer·obe (ăn′ə-rōb′ *or* ăn-âr′ōb′) *n.* An organism that can live where there is no free oxygen.

an·aer·o·bic (ăn′ə-rō′bĭk) *adj.* Living or growing where there is no free oxygen: *anaerobic bacteria.*

an·a·gram (ăn′ə-grăm′) *n.* **1.** A word or phrase formed by changing the order of the letters of another word or phrase. **2. anagrams** A game in which players form words from a group of randomly picked letters.

a·nal (ā′nəl) *adj.* Relating to or near the anus. **—a′nal·ly** *adv.*

an·al·ge·si·a (ăn′əl-jē′zē-ə) *n.* A condition of reduced sensitivity to pain, often produced by a drug, without loss of consciousness.

an·al·ge·sic (ăn′əl-jē′zĭk *or* ăn′əl-jē′sĭk) *n.* A drug that produces analgesia; a painkiller: *Aspirin is a common analgesic.* ❖ *adj.* Relating to or causing analgesia.

an·a·log also **an·a·logue** (ăn′ə-lôg′) *n.* **1.** Something that bears an analogy to something else. **2.** An organ in a plant or animal that is similar in function to one in another kind of plant or animal. ❖ *adj.* **1.** Relating to analog computers. **2.** Relating to or using continuously varying physical quantities to encode a signal or represent changes in data. For example, the continuous motion of a phonograph needle produces an analog audio signal, and the level of a mercury thermometer is an analog representation of temperature.

a·nal·o·gous (ə-năl′ə-gəs) *adj.* Similar or parallel in certain ways: *The relation between addition and subtraction is analogous to that between multiplication and division.* **—a·nal′o·gous·ly** *adv.* **—a·nal′o·gous·ness** *n.*

a·nal·o·gy (ə-năl′ə-jē) *n., pl.* **a·nal·o·gies 1.** A similarity in some respects between things that are otherwise unlike: *sees an analogy between viral infection and the spread of ideas.* **2.** An explanation of something by comparing it with something similar: *The author uses the analogy of a beehive when describing the city.* [From Middle English *analogie*, from Greek *analogos*, proportionate.]

a·nal·y·sis (ə-năl′ĭ-sĭs) *n., pl.* **a·nal·y·ses** (ə-năl′ĭ-sēz′) **1.** The separation of something into its parts in order to determine its nature: *An analysis of the theory shows it is based on faulty evidence.* **2a.** The separation of a substance into its parts, usually by chemical means, for the study and identification of each component. **b.** A written report of the information obtained in this way. **3.** Psychoanalysis. [From Greek *analusis*, a dissolving : *ana-*, throughout + *lūein*, to loosen.]

an·a·lyst (ăn′ə-lĭst) *n.* **1.** A person who performs an analysis. **2.** A psychoanalyst.

an·a·lyt·ic (ăn′ə-lĭt′ĭk) or **an·a·lyt·i·cal** (ăn′ə-lĭt′ĭ-kəl) *adj.* Relating to analysis: *analytical chemistry.* **—an′a·lyt′i·cal·ly** *adv.*

analytic geometry *n.* The use of algebra to solve problems in geometry. In analytic geometry, geometric figures are represented by algebraic equations and plotted using coordinates.

an·a·lyze (ăn′ə-līz′) *tr.v.* **an·a·lyzed, an·a·lyz·ing, an·a·lyz·es 1.** To separate into parts in order to determine what something is or how it works: *They analyzed the ore and found gold in it.* **2.** To examine in detail: *analyze past expenses to make a budget for next year.* **3.** To psychoanalyze. **—an′a·lyz′a·ble** *adj.* **—an′a·ly·za′tion** (ăn′ə-lĭ-zā′shən) *n.* **—an′a·lyz′er** *n.*

an·a·pest (ăn′ə-pĕst′) *n.* In poetry, a metrical foot consisting of two unstressed syllables followed by one stressed syllable, as in *seventeen.*

an·a·phase (ăn′ə-fāz′) *n.* The stage of mitosis and meiosis during which the chromosomes separate into two groups that move to opposite sides of the cell.

anaconda

an·ar·chic (ăn-är′kĭk) or **an·ar·chi·cal** (ăn-är′kĭ-kəl) *adj.* **1.** Relating to or promoting anarchy. **2.** Lacking order or control; lawless: *the anarchic society of America's wild frontier.* **—an·ar′chi·cal·ly** *adv.*

an·ar·chism (ăn′ər-kĭz′əm) *n.* **1.** The theory or doctrine that all forms of government are oppressive and undesirable and should be abolished. **2.** Rejection of all forms of coercive organization or authority.

an·ar·chist (ăn′ər-kĭst) *n.* A person who advocates or supports anarchism.

an·ar·chy (ăn′ər-kē) *n., pl.* **an·ar·chies 1.** Absence of any governmental authority. **2.** Disorder and confusion resulting from lack of authority: *For several days after the hurricane the region was in a state of anarchy.* [From Greek *anarkhos*, without a ruler : *an-*, without + *arkhos*, ruler.]

A·na·sa·zi (ä′nə-sä′zē) *n., pl.* **Anasazi** or **A·na·sa·zis** A term sometimes used for the Native American people considered the ancestors of the Pueblo peoples. Their culture first developed around AD 100. [From Navajo *anaa' bizází*, enemy's ancestors.]

a·nath·e·ma (ə-năth′ə-mə) *n., pl.* **a·nath·e·mas 1.** A formal ban, curse, or excommunication imposed by a church. **2.** A strong denunciation or condemnation. **3.** A person or thing that is intensely disliked: *The idea of working sloppily on an experiment was anathema to her.*

a·nath·e·ma·tize (ə-năth′ə-mə-tīz′) *tr.v.* **a·nath·e·ma·**

anemometer

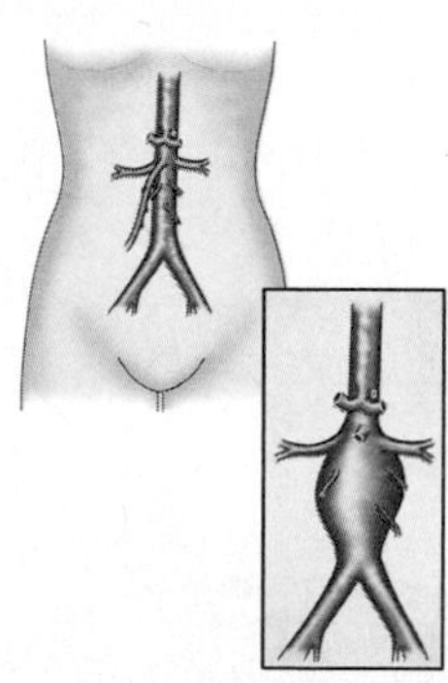

aneurysm
left: normal abdominal aorta
right: aneurysm of the abdominal aorta

ă	pat	ôr	core
ā	pay	oi	boy
âr	care	ou	out
ä	father	o͝o	took
ĕ	pet	o͝or	lure
ē	be	o͞o	boot
ĭ	pit	ŭ	cut
ī	bite	ûr	urge
îr	pier	th	thin
ŏ	pot	*th*	this
ō	toe	zh	vision
ô	paw	ə	about

tized, a·nath·e·ma·tiz·ing, a·nath·e·ma·tiz·es To proclaim an anathema on; denounce; curse. **—a·nath′-e·ma·ti·za′tion** (ə-năth′ə-mə-tĭ-**zā′**shən) *n.*

An·a·to·li·a (ăn′ə-**tō′**lē-ə) The Asian part of Turkey, covering a peninsula between the Mediterranean Sea and the Black Sea.

an·a·tom·i·cal (ăn′ə-**tŏm′**ĭ-kəl) also **an·a·tom·ic** (ăn′ə-**tŏm′**ĭk) *adj.* **1.** Relating to anatomy or dissection: *anatomical illustrations.* **2.** Relating to the structure of an organism as opposed to its functioning: *an anatomical abnormality.* **—an′a·tom′i·cal·ly** *adv.*

a·nat·o·my (ə-**năt′**ə-mē) *n., pl.* **a·nat·o·mies 1.** The structure of an organism or any of its parts: *Bones and muscles are part of the human anatomy.* **2.** The scientific study of the shape and structure of living things: *a professor of anatomy.* **3.** The human body: *the rugged anatomy of an athlete.* [From Middle English *anatomie,* from Greek *anatomē,* dissection : *ana-,* up, apart + *tomē,* a cutting.]

–ance *suff.* A suffix that means: **1.** State or condition: *resemblance.* **2.** Action: *compliance.*

an·ces·tor (**ăn′**sĕs′tər) *n.* **1.** A person from whom one is descended, especially if of a generation earlier than a grandparent: *His ancestors came to America from China.* **2.** A forerunner; a predecessor: *The harpsichord is an ancestor of the piano.* **3.** An organism or a type of organism, either known or supposed to exist, from which later organisms evolved: *The ancestors of whales were mammals that lived on land millions of years ago.* [From Middle English *auncestre,* from Latin *antecessor,* predecessor : *ante-,* before + *cēdere,* to go.]

an·ces·tral (ăn-**sĕs′**trəl) *adj.* Relating to or evolved from an ancestor or ancestors: *an ancestral trait.* **—an·ces′tral·ly** *adv.*

an·ces·try (**ăn′**sĕs′trē) *n., pl.* **an·ces·tries 1.** A line of descent; lineage. **2.** Ancestors considered as a group: *descended from noble ancestry.*

an·chor (**ăng′**kər) *n.* **1.** A heavy object attached to a boat or ship by a cable and dropped overboard to keep the vessel in place, either by its weight or by catching on the bottom. **2.** A rigid point of support, as for securing a rope or cable. **3.** Something that helps one feel secure: *Listening to music has been my anchor in tough times.* **4.** An anchorman or anchorwoman. ❖ *v.* **an·chored, an·chor·ing, an·chors** *—tr.* **1.** To secure with a fastener or similar device. **2.** To act as an anchorman or anchorwoman on (a news broadcast) or in (a relay race). *—intr.* To drop anchor or be held by an anchor: *The ship anchored off the coast.* [From Old English *ancor,* from Latin *ancora,* from Greek *ankura.*]

an·chor·age (**ăng′**kər-ĭj) *n.* **1.** A place where ships can anchor: *a safe anchorage in the harbor.* **2.** The action of anchoring or the condition of being held by an anchor.

An·chor·age (**ăng′**kər-ĭj) The largest city of Alaska, in the southern part of the state south-southwest of Fairbanks. It was founded in 1915.

an·cho·rite (**ăng′**kə-rīt′) *n.* A person who for religious reasons has withdrawn from society to live alone; a hermit.

an·chor·man (**ăng′**kər-măn′) *n.* **1.** A man who reads the news or introduces the reporters' stories on a newscast. **2.** A man who is the last member of a relay team in a race.

an·chor·per·son (**ăng′**kər-pûr′sən) *n.* An anchorman or anchorwoman.

an·chor·wom·an (**ăng′**kər-wo͝om′ən) *n.* **1.** A woman who reads the news or introduces the reporters' stories on a newscast. **2.** A woman who is the last member of a relay team in a race.

an·cho·vy (**ăn′**chō′vē *or* ăn-**chō′**vē) *n., pl.* **anchovy** or **an·cho·vies** Any of various small ocean fishes that are often salted and preserved. [From Spanish *anchova,* probably ultimately from Greek *aphuē.*]

an·cient (**ān′**shənt) *adj.* **1.** Very old; aged: *the ancient sequoias of the California forests.* **2.** Relating to times long past, especially the historical period before the fall of Rome in AD 476. ❖ *n.* **1.** A very old person. **2. ancients** The Greeks or Romans of ancient times. [From Middle English *auncien,* from Old French : Latin *ante,* before + Latin *-ānus,* adjective and noun suffix.] **—an′cient·ly** *adv.*

an·cil·lar·y (**ăn′**sə-lĕr′ē) *adj.* Serving as help or support but not of first importance: *an ancillary pump.*

–ancy *suff.* A suffix that means condition or quality: *buoyancy.*

and (ənd *or* ən; ănd *when stressed*) *conj.* **1.** Together with or along with; as well as: *The weather is clear and crisp.* **2.** Added to; plus: *Two and two makes four.* **3.** As a result: *Go, and you will enjoy yourself.* **4.** *Informal* To: *Try and find it.* —SEE NOTE AT **both.**

An·da·lu·sia (ăn′də-**lo͞o′**zhə) A region of southern Spain on the Mediterranean Sea, the Strait of Gibraltar, and the Atlantic Ocean.

an·dan·te (än-**dän′**tā) *adv. & adj.* In music, moderately slow. [From Italian, from present participle of *andare,* to walk.]

An·der·sen (**ăn′**dər-sən), **Hans Christian** 1805–1875. Danish writer of fairy tales, including "The Princess and the Pea" and "The Ugly Duckling."

An·der·son (**ăn′**dər-sən), **Marian** 1897–1993. American contralto who was the first African-American singer to perform at New York City's Metropolitan Opera (1955).

An·des (**ăn′**dēz) A mountain system of western South America extending more than 5,000 miles (8,000 kilometers) Venezuela to Tierra del Fuego parallel to the Pacific Coast. The Andes rise at many points to more than 21,000 feet (6,400 meters).

and·i·ron (**ănd′**ī′ərn) *n.* One of a pair of metal supports for holding up logs in a fireplace.

and/or (**ănd′ôr′**) *conj.* Used to indicate that either *and* or *or* may be used to connect words, phrases, or clauses, as in the sentence *Thin the paint with turpentine and/or linseed oil.*

An·dor·ra (ăn-**dôr′**ə) A tiny country of southwest Europe between France and Spain in the eastern Pyrenees. Andorra la Vella is the capital.

An·drew (**ăn′**dro͞o), Saint. Died about AD 60. One of the 12 Apostles.

An·dro·cles (**ăn′**drə-klēz′) *n.* In Roman legend, a slave spared in the arena by a lion that remembered him as the man who had once pulled a thorn from its paw.

an·dro·gen (**ăn′**drə-jən) *n.* A hormone, such as testosterone, that controls the development and maintenance of physical characteristics in males. **—an′dro·gen′ic** (ăn′drə-**jĕn′**ĭk) *adj.*

an·droid (**ăn′**droid′) *n.* A robot or automaton that moves, especially one that resembles a human.

An·drom·a·che (ăn-**drŏm′**ə-kē) *n.* In Greek mythology, the brave and faithful wife of Hector, captured by the Greeks at the fall of Troy.

An·drom·e·da (ăn-**drŏm′**ĭ-də) *n.* **1.** In Greek mythology, a princess who was offered as a sacrifice to a sea monster and married Perseus after he killed the monster. **2.** A constellation in the Northern Hemisphere, traditionally pictured as representing Andromeda.

an·ec·dote (**ăn′**ĭk-dōt′) *n.* A short account of an interesting or humorous event. [From Greek *anekdotos,* unpublished : *an-,* not + *ek-,* out + *dotos,* given.] **—an′ec·dot′al** *adj.* **—an′ec·dot′al·ly** *adv.*

a·ne·mi·a (ə-**nē′**mē-ə) *n.* A condition in which the blood cannot carry enough oxygen to the body tissues. It can be caused by lack of hemoglobin, too few red blood cells, or poorly formed red blood cells. [From Greek *anaimiā* : *an-*, without + *haima*, blood.]

a·ne·mic (ə-**nē′**mĭk) *adj.* **1.** Relating to or suffering from anemia. **2.** Lacking vitality; weak: *an anemic economic recovery.*

an·e·mom·e·ter (ăn′ə-**mŏm′**ĭ-tər) *n.* An instrument for measuring wind speed.

a·nem·o·ne (ə-**nĕm′**ə-nē) *n.* **1.** Any of various plants having lobed leaves and cup-shaped white, purple, or red flowers. **2.** A sea anemone.

an·er·oid barometer (**ăn′**ə-roid′) *n.* A barometer that measures changes in atmospheric pressure by means of the bulging and contraction of a thin metal disk covering a chamber in which there is a partial vacuum.

an·es·the·sia (ăn′ĭs-**thē′**zhə) *n.* **1.** Loss of sensation to pain or touch, usually produced by the administration of drugs, especially before surgery, or by an injury to a nerve. **2.** A drug that causes such loss of sensation.

an·es·the·si·ol·o·gy (ăn′ĭs-thē′zē-**ŏl′**ə-jē) *n.* The medical study of anesthetics, their effects, and their use. **—an′es·the′si·ol′o·gist** *n.*

an·es·thet·ic (ăn′ĭs-**thĕt′**ĭk) *adj.* **1.** Relating to or causing anesthesia. **2.** Lacking sensation or feeling; insensitive. ❖ *n.* A drug that causes anesthesia.

a·nes·the·tist (ə-**nĕs′**thĭ-tĭst) *n.* A person specially trained to administer anesthetics.

a·nes·the·tize (ə-**nĕs′**thĭ-tīz′) *tr.v.* **a·nes·the·tized, a·nes·the·tiz·ing, a·nes·the·tiz·es** To put into a condition of anesthesia, especially by means of a drug: *They anesthetized the injured dog in preparation for surgery.* **—a·nes′the·ti·za′tion** (ə-nĕs′thĭ-tĭ-**zā′**shən) *n.*

an·eu·rysm (**ăn′**yə-rĭz′əm) *n.* A swelling in a weakened part of a blood vessel or in the wall of the heart, caused by disease or injury.

a·new (ə-**nōō′**) *adv.* Over again: *ready to start anew.*

an·gel (**ān′**jəl) *n.* **1.** In Judaism, Christianity, and Islam, one of the immortal beings serving as attendants or messengers of God. **2.** A guardian spirit: *felt that an angel was with him during the ordeal.* **3.** A kind, lovable, or virtuous person. [From Middle English *aungel*, from Greek *angelos*, messenger.]

An·ge·le·no (ăn′jə-**lē′**nō) *n., pl.* **An·ge·le·nos** A native or inhabitant of Los Angeles, California.

an·gel·fish (**ān′**jəl-fĭsh′) *n.* Any of several brightly colored tropical fishes having a flattened body and often long extensions on the fins.

angel food cake *n.* A light sponge cake.

angel hair *n.* Pasta in long, extremely thin strands.

an·gel·ic (ăn-**jĕl′**ĭk) also **angelical** (ăn-**jĕl′**ĭ-kəl) *adj.* **1.** Relating to angels. **2.** Resembling an angel, as in goodness, kindness, or purity.

An·ge·lou (**ăn′**jə-lōō′), **Maya** Originally Marguerite Johnson. 1928–2014. American writer known for her autobiographical novels, including *I Know Why the Caged Bird Sings* (1970).

An·ge·lus also **an·ge·lus** (**ăn′**jə-ləs) *n.* **1.** In some Christian churches, a devotional prayer at morning, noon, and sunset in celebration of the Annunciation. **2.** A bell rung as a call to recite this prayer.

an·ger (**ăng′**gər) *n.* A feeling of great displeasure or hostility toward someone or something: *surprise and then anger at being cheated.* ❖ *tr. & intr.v.* **an·gered, an·ger·ing, an·gers** To make or become angry: *I was angered by his rudeness. She angers slowly.* [From Middle English, from Old Norse *angr*, sorrow.]

SYNONYMS **anger, rage, fury, indignation** These nouns refer to different degrees of strong displeasure. **Anger** is the most general: *He wasn't shouting, but we could sense his anger at the mix-up.* **Rage** and **fury** mean strong and often destructive anger: *They'll go into a rage when they learn who wrecked their car. In her fury at being teased, she threw her sister's books down the stairs.* **Indignation** is anger at something wrongful, unjust, or evil: *The ugly incident aroused the whole town's indignation.*

---

an·gi·na (ăn-**jī′**nə *or* **ăn′**jə-nə) *n.* Angina pectoris.

angina pec·to·ris (**pĕk′**tər-ĭs) *n.* A severe tightening and pain in the chest, often extending into the left shoulder and arm. It generally results from an insufficient supply of blood to the heart muscle, usually because of coronary artery disease.

an·gi·o·gen·e·sis (ăn′jē-ō-**jĕn′**ĭ-sĭs) *n.* The formation of new blood vessels.

an·gi·o·sperm (**ăn′**jē-ə-spûrm′) *n.* Any of a large group of plants that have flowers and produce seeds that are enclosed in an ovary; a flowering plant.

an·gle[1] (**ăng′**gəl) *intr.v.* **an·gled, an·gling, an·gles 1.** To fish with a hook and line. **2.** To try to get something by using schemes or tricks: *By posing as a reporter, the tourist angled for a chance to meet the celebrity.* [From Middle English *anglen*, from *angel*, fishhook, from Old English.]

an·gle[2] (**ăng′**gəl) *n.* **1.** A geometric figure formed by two lines that begin at a common point or by two planes that begin at a common line. **2.** The distance between such lines or planes, often measured in degrees. **3.** A projecting corner, as of a building: *The angle of the building blocked our view.* **4.** The place, position, or direction from which an object is presented to view; point of view: *a building that looks impressive from any angle.* **5.** A particular part or phase, as of a problem; an aspect: *studying every angle of the question.* ❖ *v.* **an·gled, an·gling, an·gles** *—tr.* To move or hit at an angle: *angling the camera for a clearer view.* *—intr.* To turn or continue along at an angle: *The road angles sharply at the river.* [From Middle English, from Latin *angulus*.]

Angle *n.* A member of a Germanic people who settled in England in the fifth century AD and together with the Jutes and Saxons formed the Anglo-Saxon peoples.

angle iron *n.* A length of iron or steel bent into a right angle to be used as a support.

angle of incidence *n.* The angle formed by a ray or wave, as of light or sound, striking a surface and a line perpendicular to the surface at the point of impact.

angle of reflection *n.* The angle formed by a ray or wave, as of light or sound, reflected from a surface and a line perpendicular to the surface at the point of reflection.

angle of refraction *n.* The angle formed by the path of a refracted ray or wave and a line drawn perpendicular to the refracting surface at the point where the refraction occurred.

an·gler (**ăng′**glər) *n.* **1.** A person who fishes with a hook and line. **2.** An anglerfish.

an·gler·fish (**ăng′**glər-fĭsh′) *n.* Any of various ocean fishes having on the top of the head a slender projection with a fleshy tip that dangles in front of the large mouth and acts as a lure to attract smaller fish.

an·gle·worm (**ăng′**gəl-wûrm′) *n.* A worm, especially an earthworm, that is used as bait in fishing.

An·gli·can (**ăng′**glĭ-kən) *adj.* Relating to the Anglican Church. ❖ *n.* A member of the Anglican Church.

Anglican Church *n.* The Church of England and those churches in other nations that are formally affiliated with it.

An·gli·can·ism (**ăng′**glĭ-kə-nĭz′əm) *n.* The beliefs, practices, and form of organization of the Anglican Church.

An·gli·cize (**ăng′**glĭ-sīz′) *tr.v.* **An·gli·cized, An·gli·ciz·ing, An·gli·ciz·es 1.** To adapt (a foreign word) to use in English, especially by changing its spelling or pronunciation: *The Greek name Odysseus, or Ulixes in Latin, was Anglicized as Ulysses.* **2.** To make English or similar

angelfish

Maya Angelou
photographed in 2001

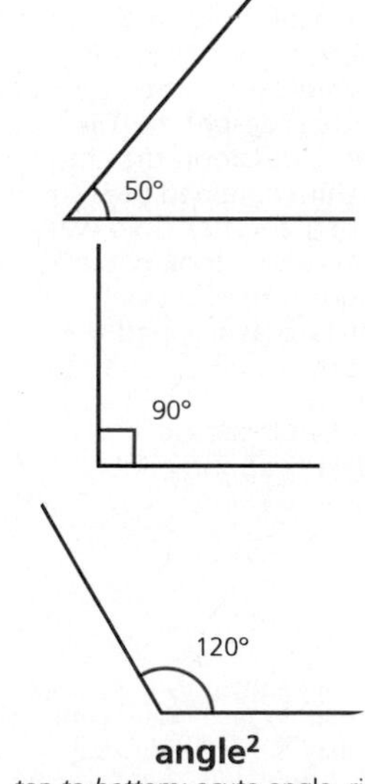

angle[2]
top to bottom: acute angle, right angle, and obtuse angle

Angora rabbit

WRITERS CHOOSE THEIR WORDS

The audience watched spellbound, almost unable to bear it, as Julia, still searching, became uncertain, then bewildered ... then afraid ... then desperate. Till she understood that the unthinkable had happened and her child was lost—and a look of such **anguish** spread over her face as stopped the heart.

—Eva Ibbotson
The Dragonfly Pool

ă	pat	ôr	core
ā	pay	oi	boy
âr	care	ou	out
ä	father	o͝o	took
ĕ	pet	o͝or	lure
ē	be	o͞o	boot
ĭ	pit	ŭ	cut
ī	bite	ûr	urge
îr	pier	th	thin
ŏ	pot	*th*	this
ō	toe	zh	vision
ô	paw	ə	about

to English in form, idiom, style, or character: *Some immigrants Anglicize their names when they move to the United States.*

an·gling (ăng′glĭng) *n.* The act or sport of fishing with a hook and line.

An·glo (ăng′glō) *n., pl.* **An·glos 1.** *Informal* An Anglo-American. **2.** An English-speaking person, especially a white North American who is not of Hispanic or French ancestry.

Anglo– *pref.* A prefix that means English: *Anglo-Saxon; Anglo-American.*

An·glo-A·mer·i·can (ăng′glō-ə-**mĕr′**ĭ-kən) *n.* An American, especially an inhabitant of the United States, who is of English ancestry. ❖ *adj.* **1.** Relating to or involving England and America, especially the United States. **2.** Relating to Anglo-Americans.

An·glo·cen·tric (ăng′glō-**sĕn′**trĭk) *adj.* Centered or focused on England or the English: *an Anglocentric view of history.*

An·glo-French (ăng′glō-**frĕnch′**) *adj.* Relating to or involving England and France, or their peoples. ❖ *n.* The dialect of Old French spoken by the Anglo-Normans or by English people after the Norman language fell out of use in England.

An·glo-Nor·man (ăng′glō-**nôr′**mən) *n.* **1.** One of the Normans who lived in England after the Norman Conquest of England in 1066 or a descendant of these settlers. **2.** The dialect of Old French, derived chiefly from Norman French, that was used by the Anglo-Normans. **—An′glo-Nor′man** *adj.*

An·glo·phone also **an·glo·phone** (ăn′glə-fōn′) *n.* A person who speaks English, especially one in a country or region where at least one other language besides English is spoken. **—An′glo·phone′** *adj.*

An·glo-Sax·on (ăng′glō-**săk′**sən) *n.* **1.** A member of one of the Germanic peoples, the Angles, the Saxons, and the Jutes, who settled in Britain in the fifth and sixth centuries. **2.** Any of the descendants of these people, who dominated England until the Norman Conquest in 1066. **3.** Old English. **4.** A person of English ancestry. **—An′glo-Sax′on** *adj.*

An·go·la (ăng-**gō′**lə) A country of southwest Africa on the Atlantic Ocean. Luanda is the capital.

An·go·ra (ăng-**gôr′**ə) *n.* **1.** An Angora cat, Angora goat, or Angora rabbit. **2. angora** Yarn or fabric made from the hair of an Angora goat or rabbit.

Angora cat *n.* A domestic cat having long silky hair.

Angora goat *n.* A domestic goat having long silky hair.

Angora rabbit *n.* A domestic rabbit having long, soft, usually white hair.

an·gry (ăng′grē) *adj.* **an·gri·er, an·gri·est 1.** Feeling or showing anger: *an angry customer; an angry expression.* **2.** Seeming to threaten: *angry dark storm clouds.* **3.** Inflamed: *an angry wound.* **—an′gri·ly** *adv.* **—an′gri·ness** *n.*

angst (ăngkst) *n.* A feeling of anxiety or apprehension. [From German.]

ang·strom (ăng′strəm) *n.* A unit of length equal to one hundred-millionth (10^{-8}) of a centimeter. It is used mainly in measuring wavelengths of light and shorter electromagnetic radiation. [After Anders Jonas *Ångström* (1814–1874), Swedish physicist.]

An·guil·la (ăng-**gwĭl′**ə) An island of the British West Indies in the northern Leeward Islands.

an·guish (ăng′gwĭsh) *n.* Severe pain or suffering of mind or body; torment: *They were in anguish until their lost puppy was found.* [From Middle English *angwisshe*, from Latin *angustiae*, distress.]

an·guished (ăng′gwĭsht) *adj.* Feeling, expressing, or caused by anguish: *the anguished faces of people whose homes were destroyed by the hurricane.*

an·gu·lar (ăng′gyə-lər) *adj.* **1.** Having, forming, or consisting of an angle or angles: *an angular point.* **2.** Measured by an angle: *angular distance.* **3.** Bony and lean: *an angular face.* **4.** Lacking grace or smoothness: *an angular gait.* **—an′gu·lar·ly** *adv.*

an·gu·lar·i·ty (ăng′gyə-**lăr′**ĭ-tē) *n., pl.* **an·gu·lar·i·ties** The condition or quality of being angular.

angular momentum *n.* A quantity that measures the motion of a body that is moving in a circle. The angular momentum depends on the mass and velocity of the body, and on the radius of the circle that it is moving along.

An·gus (ăng′gəs) *n.* A breed of hornless beef cattle that originated in Scotland and are usually black but also occur in a red variety.

an·hy·dride (ăn-**hī′**drīd′) *n.* A chemical compound formed from another by the removal of water.

an·hy·drous (ăn-**hī′**drəs) *adj.* Lacking water, especially water of crystallization: *Many crystals, like diamond and quartz, are anhydrous.*

an·i·line also **an·i·lin** (**ăn′**ə-lĭn) *n.* A colorless, oily, poisonous liquid derived from benzene and used in making dyes, rubber, drugs, and varnishes. ❖ *adj.* Derived from aniline.

an·i·mad·ver·sion (ăn′ə-măd-**vûr′**zhən) *n.* Hostile criticism or a remark that directs criticism or blame.

an·i·mal (**ăn′**ə-məl) *n.* **1.** Any of a kingdom of many-celled organisms that cannot make their own food and are usually able to move around during at least part of their life cycle. Some animals, such as sponges, corals, and insects, do not have a backbone, and some, such as fishes, birds, amphibians, reptiles, and mammals, do have a backbone. **2.** An animal organism other than a human: *Some animals got into the tent and ate our food.* **3.** A person who behaves in a coarse or cruel way. ❖ *adj.* **1.** Relating to, characteristic of, or derived from an animal or animals, especially when not human: *animal behavior; animal fat.* **2.** Relating to the physical as distinct from the rational or spiritual nature of people: *following his animal instincts.* [From Middle English, from Latin, from *anima*, spirit, soul.]

animal cracker *n.* A small cookie in the shape of an animal.

animal husbandry *n.* The care and breeding of domestic animals such as cattle, sheep, and hogs.

animal rights *pl.n.* The idea that animals are entitled to some of the same legal protections given to people and should not be killed, hurt, or held captive by humans.

an·i·mate (**ăn′**ə-māt′) *tr.v.* **an·i·mat·ed, an·i·mat·ing, an·i·mates 1.** To give life to; cause to come alive: *the belief that the soul animates the body.* **2.** To give interest or vitality to; enliven: *The party was animated by the dance music.* **3.** To inspire or motivate: *an explorer who is animated by curiosity.* **4.** To make or depict using animation: *Many children's stories have been animated by movie companies.* ❖ *adj.* (**ăn′**ə-mĭt) **1.** Living: *Babies quickly learn the difference between animate and inanimate objects.* **2.** Belonging to the class of nouns that stand for living things: *The word "dog" is animate; the word "car" is inanimate.* **—an′i·ma·cy** (**ăn′**ə-mə-sē) *n.*

an·i·mat·ed (**ăn′**ə-mā′tĭd) *adj.* **1.** Lively: *The band leader's personality was energetic and animated.* **2.** Made or depicted using animation: *an animated film.* **—an′i·mat′ed·ly** *adv.*

animated cartoon *n.* A cartoon produced using the techniques of animation.

an·i·ma·tion (ăn′ə-**mā′**shən) *n.* **1.** Liveliness; vitality. **2.** The art or process of making movies or videos that create the illusion of motion by rapidly displaying a series of drawings, objects, or computer graphics with slight changes from one to the next, rather than a series of photographs. **3.** A movie or video created through animation.

a·ni·ma·to (ä′nē-mä′tō) *adv. & adj.* In music, in an animated or lively manner.

an·i·ma·tor (ăn′ə-mā′tər) *n.* An artist or technician who works at making animation.

an·i·me (ăn′ə-mā′) *n.* A style of animation originating in Japan.

an·i·mism (ăn′ə-mĭz′əm) *n.* The belief in individual spirits that exist in natural objects or forces, such as trees, waterfalls, stones, winds, and tides. **—an′i·mist′** *n.*

an·i·mos·i·ty (ăn′ə-mŏs′ĭ-tē) *n.* Hatred or hostility: *There was much animosity between the two nations even before war broke out.*

an·i·mus (ăn′ə-məs) *n.* **1.** A feeling of animosity; hatred: *animus among bitter rivals.* **2.** An intention or a purpose; a motive behind an action.

an·i·on (ăn′ī′ən) *n.* An ion that has a negative charge and moves toward the positive electrode in electrolysis.

an·ise (ăn′ĭs) *n.* A plant related to parsley, having small licorice-flavored seeds used for flavoring.

anise seed or **an·i·seed** (ăn′ĭ-sēd′) *n.* The seed of the anise plant.

An·jou (ăn′jo͞o′ *or* äN-**zho͞o′**) A historical region and former province of northwest France in the Loire River valley. It became part of the kingdom of France in the 1480s.

An·ka·ra (ăng′kər-ə *or* äng′kər-ə) The capital of Turkey, in the west-central part of the country southeast of Istanbul. Ankara replaced Istanbul as the capital in 1923.

ankh (ăngk) *n.* A cross shaped like a T with a loop at the top, used as a symbol of life in ancient Egypt. [From Egyptian *ʿnḫ*, life.]

an·kle (ăng′kəl) *n.* **1.** The joint formed by the tibia and fibula of the lower leg and the talus of the foot. The ankle connects the foot with the leg. **2.** The slender part of the leg just above this joint. [From Middle English *ancle*, partly from Old English *anclēow* and partly of Scandinavian origin.]

an·kle·bone (ăng′kəl-bōn′) *n.* The main bone of the ankle; the talus.

an·klet (ăng′klĭt) *n.* **1.** A bracelet or chain worn around the ankle. **2.** A sock that reaches just above the ankle.

an·nals (ăn′əlz) *pl.n.* **1.** A record of events written in the order of their occurrence, year by year. **2.** A descriptive account or record; a history: *the annals of the American Revolution.*

An·nap·o·lis (ə-năp′ə-lĭs) The capital of Maryland, in the central part of the state on an inlet of Chesapeake Bay south-southeast of Baltimore. It was settled in 1649.

Anne (ăn) 1665–1714. Queen of Great Britain and Ireland (1702–1714) who was the first English ruler to reign over a unified England and Scotland (1707).

an·neal (ə-nēl′) *tr.v.* **an·nealed, an·neal·ing, an·neals** To treat (glass or a metal) by heating and slow cooling in order to toughen and reduce brittleness: *anneal hammered copper.*

an·ne·lid (ăn′ə-lĭd) *n.* Any of a group of worms and wormlike invertebrate animals, including the earthworms and leeches, having a long, soft, segmented body.

an·nex (ə-nĕks′ *or* ăn′ĕks′) *tr.v.* **an·nexed, an·nex·ing, an·nex·es 1.** To add or join to, especially to a larger or more significant thing: *The new gym is to be annexed to the school.* **2.** To add (territory) to an existing country or other area: *The city is trying to annex two of the suburbs.* ❖ *n.* (ăn′ĕks′) An extra building that is added to another bigger building and used for some related purpose: *the library annex of the school.* [From Middle English *annexen*, from Old French *annexer*, from Latin *annectere*, to connect.] **—an′nex·a′tion** (ăn′ĭk-sā′shən) *n.*

an·ni·hi·late (ə-nī′ə-lāt′) *tr.v.* **an·ni·hi·lat·ed, an·ni·hi·lat·ing, an·ni·hi·lates 1.** To destroy completely; wipe out. **2.** To defeat decisively; vanquish: *annihilated the opposition in the tournament.* [From Late Latin *annihilāre* : Latin *ad-*, to + Latin *nihil*, nothing.] **—an·ni′hi·la′tion** *n.*

an·ni·ver·sa·ry (ăn′ə-vûr′sə-rē) *n., pl.* **an·ni·ver·sa·ries 1.** The yearly returning of the date of an event that happened in an earlier year: *a wedding anniversary.* **2.** A date that follows a certain event by a specified amount of time: *his six-month anniversary of becoming a vegetarian.* [From Middle English *anniversarie*, from Latin *anniversārius*, returning yearly : *annus*, year + *vertere*, to turn.]

an·no Dom·i·ni (ăn′ō dŏm′ə-nī′ *or* ăn′ō dŏm′ə-nē′) *adv.* In a specified year since the birth of Jesus. Used chiefly in abbreviated form: *AD 500.* [From Latin *annō Dominī*, in the year of the Lord.]

an·no·tate (ăn′ō-tāt′) *tr.v.* **an·no·tat·ed, an·no·tat·ing, an·no·tates** To furnish (a written work) with explanatory notes: *Many textbooks are annotated with notes in the margin.* **—an′no·ta′tor** *n.*

an·no·ta·tion (ăn′ō-tā′shən) *n.* **1.** The act or process of annotating. **2.** An explanatory note: *an annotation in the margin.*

an·nounce (ə-nouns′) *v.* **an·nounced, an·nounc·ing, an·nounc·es** —*tr.* **1.** To bring to public notice; give formal notice of: *The principal announced a change in our schedule.* **2.** To make known the presence or arrival of: *The doorman announced us by telephone.* **3.** To serve as an announcer of: *announced hockey games on television.* —*intr.* To serve as an announcer on radio or television. [From Middle English *announcen*, from Latin *annūntiāre*, to report to, from *nūntius*, message.]

an·nounce·ment (ə-nouns′mənt) *n.* **1.** The act of announcing. **2.** A public declaration to make known something that has happened or that will happen; an official statement: *made an announcement concerning the policy changes.* **3.** A printed or published notice: *Read this announcement.*

ankh

an·nounc·er (ə-noun′sər) *n.* A person who announces, especially a person who introduces a show, makes comments, or reads news on radio or television.

an·noy (ə-noi′) *tr.v.* **an·noyed, an·noy·ing, an·noys** To cause (someone) to feel irritated or angry: *The children's screaming annoyed the neighbors.* [From Middle English *anoien*, from Old French *anoier*, from Latin *in odiō*, odious.]

an·noy·ance (ə-noi′əns) *n.* **1.** Irritation or displeasure: *Much to my annoyance, the bus was late.* **2.** Something causing trouble or irritation; a nuisance: *Heartburn is a relatively minor annoyance.*

an·noy·ing (ə-noi′ĭng) *adj.* Troublesome or irritating: *an annoying habit.* **—an·noy′ing·ly** *adv.* **—an·noy′ing·ness** *n.*

an·nu·al (ăn′yo͞o-əl) *adj.* **1.** Happening every year; yearly: *an annual medical examination.* **2.** Relating to or determined by a year's time: *What is the annual income of a nurse?* **3.** Living and growing only for one year or season: *annual plants.* ❖ *n.* **1.** A periodical published yearly; a yearbook. **2.** A plant that completes its entire life cycle in a single growing season. [From Middle English *annuel*, from Late Latin *annuālis*, from Latin *annus*, year.] **—an′nu·al·ly** *adv.*

annual ring

annual ring *n.* A growth ring in a woody plant that forms during a full year's growth.

an·nu·i·ty (ə-no͞o′ĭ-tē) *n., pl.* **an·nu·i·ties 1a.** An amount of money paid at regular intervals. **b.** A sequence of such payments. **2.** A contract or agreement by which one receives fixed payments on an investment for a lifetime or for a specified number of years. [From Middle English *annuite*, from Medieval Latin *annuitās*, from Latin *annuus*, yearly, from *annus*, year.]

an·nul (ə-nŭl′) *tr.v.* **an·nulled, an·nul·ling, an·nuls** To

annular eclipse
photographed from a satellite, January 4, 2011

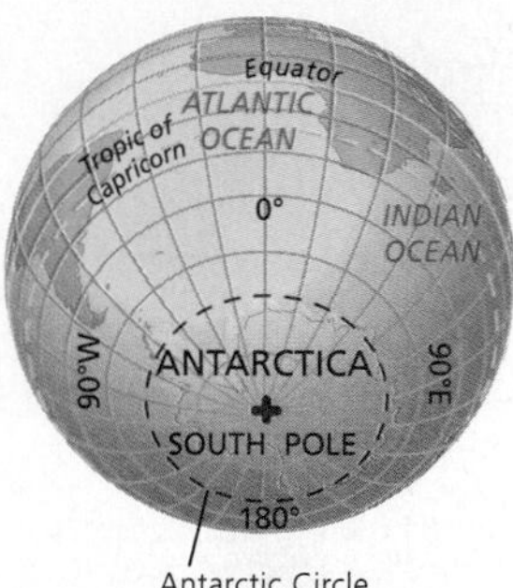

Antarctic Circle

anteater
giant anteater

ă	pat	ôr	core
ā	pay	oi	boy
âr	care	ou	out
ä	father	ŏŏ	took
ĕ	pet	ŏŏr	lure
ē	be	ōō	boot
ĭ	pit	ŭ	cut
ī	bite	ûr	urge
îr	pier	th	thin
ŏ	pot	*th*	this
ō	toe	zh	vision
ô	paw	ə	about

make or declare void; nullify; cancel: *The court annulled their marriage.*

an·nu·lar (ăn′yə-lər) *adj.* Forming or shaped like a ring. **—an′nu·lar′i·ty** (ăn′yə-lăr′ĭ-tē) *n.* **—an′nu·lar·ly** *adv.*

annular eclipse *n.* A solar eclipse in which the moon blocks all of the sun except for a bright ring around the edge of the sun.

an·nul·ment (ə-nŭl′mənt) *n.* **1.** The act of annulling. **2.** A legal declaration stating that a marriage was never valid.

an·nun·ci·a·tion (ə-nŭn′sē-ā′shən) *n.* **1.** The act of announcing: *The annunciation of the new policy stirred up controversy.* **2. Annunciation** In the New Testament, the angel Gabriel's announcement to the Virgin Mary that she was to become the mother of Jesus. **3.** The Christian feast on March 25 celebrating this event.

an·ode (ăn′ōd′) *n.* **1.** The positively charged electrode of an electrolytic cell or electron tube. **2.** The negatively charged electrode of a voltaic cell, such as a battery.

an·o·dyne (ăn′ə-dīn′) *adj.* **1.** Able to soothe or eliminate pain. **2.** Relaxing: *The anodyne effects of the drug cured his insomnia.* ❖ *n.* **1.** A medicine that relieves pain. **2.** Something that soothes or comforts.

a·noint (ə-noint′) *tr.v.* **a·noint·ed, a·noint·ing, a·noints 1.** To apply oil, ointment, or a similar substance to: *anoint the burn with salve.* **2.** To put oil on in a religious ceremony as a means of making pure or holy: *anoint a king.* **—a·noint′ment** *n.*

a·nom·a·lous (ə-nŏm′ə-ləs) *adj.* Differing from what is normal or common; abnormal.

a·nom·a·ly (ə-nŏm′ə-lē) *n., pl.* **a·nom·a·lies** Something that is unusual, irregular, or abnormal: *Flooding is an anomaly in desert regions of Africa.* [From Greek *anōmalos*, uneven.]

a·non (ə-nŏn′) *adv.* **1.** At another time; later. **2.** In a short time; soon.

anon. *abbr.* An abbreviation of anonymous.

an·o·nym·i·ty (ăn′ə-nĭm′ĭ-tē) *n., pl.* **an·o·nym·i·ties** The condition of being anonymous: *The donor made a large contribution on the condition of anonymity.*

a·non·y·mous (ə-nŏn′ə-məs) *adj.* **1.** Nameless or unnamed: *The prize was awarded by a panel of anonymous judges.* **2.** Having an unknown source: *The anonymous letter was sent without a return address.* [From Greek *anōnumos*, nameless : *an-*, without + *onuma*, name.] **—a·non′y·mous·ly** *adv.*

an·o·rak (ăn′ə-răk′) *n.* A heavy jacket with a hood; a parka.

an·o·rex·i·a (ăn′ə-rĕk′sē-ə) *n.* **1.** Loss of appetite, especially as a result of illness. **2.** Anorexia nervosa. [From Greek *anorexiā* : *an-*, without + *orexis*, appetite.]

anorexia ner·vo·sa (nûr-vō′sə) *n.* An eating disorder usually occurring in young women that is marked by an intense fear of becoming obese, a persistent unwillingness to eat, and severe weight loss.

an·o·rex·ic (ăn′ə-rĕk′sĭk) *adj.* Affected with anorexia nervosa.

an·oth·er (ə-nŭ*th*′ər) *adj.* **1.** Additional; one more: *another cup of coffee.* **2.** Different: *These baseball players have been another team since they got a new coach.* **3.** Some other: *We'll discuss this at another time.* ❖ *pron.* **1.** An additional one: *I had a drink of water and then another.* **2.** Something or someone different: *A baby is one thing to take care of; a 6-year-old is another.* **3.** One of a group of things: *for one reason or another.*

an·ox·i·a (ăn-ŏk′sē-ə) *n.* A lack of oxygen in body tissue, caused by poor blood supply or insufficient levels of oxygen in the blood.

an·swer (ăn′sər) *n.* **1.** A series of words spoken or written in reaction to a question, request, or other prompting: *I wrote weeks ago but never got an answer.* **2.** An act that serves as a reply or response: *Their answer was to ignore me.* **3a.** A solution or result, as to a problem: *We all got the right answer to that problem.* **b.** The correct solution or response: *Our teacher read the answers to the quiz.* ❖ *v.* **an·swered, an·swer·ing, an·swers** *—intr.* **1.** To speak or write as a reaction to a question or other prompting: *He couldn't take the call but answered with a text message.* **2.** To act in reaction or as a response: *She answered with a wink.* **3.** To be liable or accountable: *You will have to answer for this mess.* **4.** To match or correspond: *a car answering to this description.* *—tr.* **1.** To produce an answer to: *answer a letter.* **2.** To respond correctly to: *I can't answer the question.* **3.** To fulfill the demands of: *A good rest answered the weary traveler's needs.* **4.** To match or correspond to: *That dog answers the description of the one you're looking for.* [From Old English *andswaru*.]

SYNONYMS **answer, respond, reply, retort** These verbs refer to different kinds of reactions. **Answer, respond,** and **reply** mean to speak, write, or act in response to something: *Please answer my question. She responded to the reporter's comment with a smirk. The visiting team scored three runs and the home team replied with two of their own.* **Retort** means to answer verbally in a quick, sharp, or witty way: *"My shoes may not be new, but at least they're clean!" he retorted.*

---

an·swer·a·ble (ăn′sər-ə-bəl) *adj.* **1.** Responsible; accountable; liable: *You are answerable for the money in the account.* **2.** Capable of being answered or proved wrong: *scientific questions not wholly answerable.* **—an′swer·a·ble·ness** *n.*

an·swer·ing machine (ăn′sər-ĭng) *n.* A device that answers a telephone and records messages from callers.

ant (ănt) *n.* Any of numerous insects that live in highly organized colonies and build nests underground or in trees. Most ants are wingless; only the males and fertile females have wings. [From Old English *ǣmete*.]
❑ *These sound alike:* **ant, aunt** (sister of one's parent).

ant. *abbr.* An abbreviation of antonym.

Ant. *abbr.* An abbreviation of Antarctica.

ant– *pref.* Variant of **anti–.**

–ant *suff.* A suffix that means: **1.** Performing a certain action or being in a certain state: *defiant; flippant.* **2.** A person or thing that performs or causes a certain action: *coolant; deodorant.*

ant·ac·id (ănt-ăs′ĭd) *n.* A substance that neutralizes acids or counteracts acidity, especially one used to neutralize excess stomach acid.

an·tag·o·nism (ăn-tăg′ə-nĭz′əm) *n.* **1.** Unfriendly feeling; hostility: *antagonism among rival factions.* **2.** Opposition, as between conflicting principles or forces.

an·tag·o·nist (ăn-tăg′ə-nĭst) *n.* **1.** A person who opposes and actively competes with another; an adversary. **2.** Either of a pair of drugs or other substances that neutralize each other in the body: *An antitoxin is the antagonist of a toxin.* **3.** A muscle that counteracts the action of another muscle, the agonist.

an·tag·o·nis·tic (ăn-tăg′ə-nĭs′tĭk) *adj.* **1.** Opposed; contending: *antagonistic points of view.* **2.** Unfriendly; hostile: *an antagonistic attitude.* **—an·tag′o·nis′ti·cal·ly** *adv.*

an·tag·o·nize (ăn-tăg′ə-nīz′) *tr.v.* **an·tag·o·nized, an·tag·o·niz·ing, an·tag·o·niz·es** To cause (someone) to become angry or hostile; provoke bad feeling in: *They antagonized me by making fun of my suggestion.*

An·ta·na·na·ri·vo (ăn′tə-năn′ə-rē′vō *or* än′tə-nä′nə-rē′vō) The capital of Madagascar, in the east-central part of the country. It was founded in the 1600s.

Ant·arc·tic (ănt-ärk′tĭk) *adj.* Relating to the regions surrounding the South Pole: *the Antarctic climate.* ❖ *n.* Antarctica and its surrounding waters.

Ant·arc·ti·ca (ănt-**ärk′**tĭ-kə *or* ănt-**är′**tĭ-kə) The third-smallest continent, lying chiefly within the Antarctic Circle and surrounding the South Pole. About 95 percent of Antarctica is covered by a thick layer of solid ice.

Antarctic Circle The parallel of latitude approximately 66 degrees 33 minutes south. It forms the boundary between the South Temperate Zone and South Frigid Zone.

Antarctic Ocean See **Southern Ocean.**

an·te (**ăn′**tē) *n.* In poker, a bet that each player must make to begin or stay in the game. ❖ *v.* **an·ted** or **an·teed, an·te·ing, an·tes** —*tr.* **1.** To put (one's stake) into the pool in poker. **2.** To pay (money or a fee): *After lunch we anted up the bill.* —*intr.* **1.** To put one's stake into the pool in poker: *The players anted before the cards were dealt.* **2.** To pay for something: *anted for the tickets.*

ante– *pref.* A prefix that means: **1.** Prior to; earlier: *antedate; antediluvian.* **2.** In front of: *anteroom.*

ant·eat·er (**ănt′**ē′tər) *n.* **1.** Any of several tropical American mammals that lack teeth and feed on ants and termites. **2.** Any of several other animals that feed on ants, such as the aardvark.

an·te·bel·lum (ăn′tē-**bĕl′**əm) *adj.* Belonging to the period prior to the Civil War: *an antebellum mansion.*

an·te·ce·dent (ăn′tĭ-**sēd′**nt) *adj.* Going before; preceding; prior. ❖ *n.* **1.** A person or thing that precedes another. **2.** An occurrence or event prior to another. **3. antecedents** A person's ancestors: *I do not know my antecedents beyond my grandparents.* **4.** The word, phrase, or clause to which a pronoun refers. In the sentence *The teacher asked the children where they were going* the phrase *the children* is the antecedent of *they.* **—an′te·ce′dent·ly** *adv.*

an·te·cham·ber (**ăn′**tē-chām′bər) *n.* A waiting room at the entrance to a larger room.

an·te·date (**ăn′**tĭ-dāt′) *tr.v.* **an·te·dat·ed, an·te·dat·ing, an·te·dates 1.** To be of an earlier date than: *This novel antedates the writer's poetry.* **2.** To give (something) a date earlier than the actual date; date back: *Management antedated the union's contract to the first of the year.*

an·te·di·lu·vi·an (ăn′tĭ-də-**lo͞o′**vē-ən) *adj.* **1.** Believed to belong to the period before the flood described in Genesis. **2.** Very old; antiquated: *The horse and buggy is an antediluvian way of travel.*

an·te·lope (**ăn′**tl-ōp′) *n., pl.* **antelope** or **an·te·lopes 1.** Any of various swift-running mammals of Africa and Asia, having unbranched horns. **2.** The pronghorn of western North America. [From Middle English *antelope,* a heraldic beast, from Late Greek *antholops.*]

an·te me·rid·i·em (ăn′tē mə-**rĭd′**ē-əm) *adv. & adj.* Before noon. It is normally used in its abbreviated form to show time, as in 7:45 AM. [From Latin *ante,* before + Latin *merīdiem,* accusative of *merīdiēs,* noon.]

an·ten·na (ăn-**tĕn′**ə) *n.* **1.** *pl.* **an·ten·nae** (ăn-**tĕn′**ē) One of a pair of long, slender, segmented structures on the head of an insect, a centipede, or a crustacean such as a lobster or shrimp. Most antennae are organs of touch, but some are sensitive to odors and other stimuli. **2.** *pl.* **an·ten·nas** A metallic device for sending and receiving electromagnetic waves, such as radio or television signals. [From Latin *antenna,* sail yard.]

an·te·pe·nult (ăn′tē-**pē′**nŭlt′ *or* ăn′tē-pĭ-**nŭlt′**) *n.* The third syllable from the end of a word, as *te* in *antepenult.*

an·te·pe·nul·ti·mate (ăn′tē-pĭ-**nŭl′**tə-mĭt) *adj.* Coming third from the last in a series.

an·te·ri·or (ăn-**tîr′**ē-ər) *adj.* **1.** Placed in front; located forward: *a small anterior room leading to the main hall.* **2a.** In, relating to, or near the side of the human body on which the abdomen is found. **b.** In, relating to, or near the head of a nonhuman animal. **3.** Prior in time; earlier.

an·te·room (**ăn′**tē-ro͝om′ *or* **ăn′**tē-ro͞om′) *n.* An antechamber.

an·them (**ăn′**thəm) *n.* **1.** A song of praise or loyalty: *a national anthem.* **2.** A piece of music having words from a sacred text. **3.** A popular song, especially a rock song felt to sum up the attitudes or feelings associated with a period or social group. [From Old English *antefn,* from Late Greek *antiphōnos,* sounding in answer.]

an·ther (**ăn′**thər) *n.* The pollen-bearing part at the tip of the stamen of a flower.

ant·hill (**ănt′**hĭl′) *n.* A mound of earth or sand formed by ants in digging or building a nest.

an·thol·o·gy (ăn-**thŏl′**ə-jē) *n., pl.* **an·thol·o·gies** A collection of writings, such as poems or stories, by various authors.

An·tho·ny (**ăn′**thə-nē), **Susan Brownell** 1820–1906. American reformer and suffragist whose work led to laws that gave married women legal rights over their children, property, and wages. In 1869 she helped found the National Woman Suffrage Association. —SEE NOTE.

an·thra·cite (**ăn′**thrə-sīt′) *n.* A hard shiny coal that has a high carbon content. It burns with a clean flame without smoke.

an·thrax (**ăn′**thrăks′) *n.* An infectious, usually fatal disease of mammals, especially cattle and sheep, caused by a bacterium. It can spread to people, causing symptoms ranging from blistering of the skin to potentially fatal infection of the lungs.

an·thro·poid (**ăn′**thrə-poid′) *adj.* **1.** Belonging to the group of primates that consists of the monkeys and the apes, including humans. **2.** Resembling a nonhuman ape; apelike: *We caught a glimpse of an anthropoid figure in the vegetation.* ❖ *n.* An ape or apelike animal. [From Greek *anthrōpos,* person + English *-oid,* -like.]

an·thro·pol·o·gy (ăn′thrə-**pŏl′**ə-jē) *n.* The scientific study of the origin, the behavior, and the physical, social, and cultural development of humans. **—an′thro·po·log′i·cal** (ăn′thrə-pə-**lŏj′**ĭ-kəl) *adj.* **—an′thro·pol′o·gist** *n.*

anti– or **ant–** *pref.* A prefix that means: **1.** Opposite: *antihero.* **2.** Opposing: *anti-Semitism.* **3.** Counteracting or destroying: *antibiotic; antiaircraft.*

an·ti·air·craft (ăn′tē-**âr′**krăft′) *adj.* Designed for defense, especially from a position on the ground, against attack by aircraft: *antiaircraft missiles.*

an·ti·bal·lis·tic missile (ăn′tĭ-bə-**lĭs′**tĭk) *n.* A missile designed to intercept and destroy a ballistic missile in flight.

an·ti·bi·ot·ic (ăn′tĭ-bī-**ŏt′**ĭk) *n.* A substance, such as penicillin, that is capable of destroying or weakening certain microorganisms, especially disease-causing bacteria. Most antibiotics are obtained from other bacteria or from fungi, but some are made synthetically. ❖ *adj.* Relating to antibiotics: *an antibiotic drug.*

an·ti·bod·y (**ăn′**tĭ-bŏd′ē) *n.* Any of numerous proteins that are produced by a certain kind of white blood cell when an antigen, such as a bacterium or virus, is present. The antibody either destroys the antigen or causes other elements of the immune system to destroy it.

an·tic (**ăn′**tĭk) *n.* A playful, foolish, or funny act: *The clown's antics amused us.* [From Italian *antico,* ancient, old-fashioned, from Latin *antīquus,* former, old.]

an·ti·christ (**ăn′**tĭ-krīst′) *n.* **1. Antichrist** In some branches of Christianity, the great enemy who is expected to set himself up against Christ in the last days before the end of the world. **2.** An enemy of Christ.

an·tic·i·pate (ăn-**tĭs′**ə-pāt′) *tr.v.* **an·tic·i·pat·ed, an·tic·i·pat·ing, an·tic·i·pates 1.** To consider as a probable occurrence; expect: *We hadn't anticipated such a crowd at the zoo.* **2.** To think of (a future event) with pleasure; look forward to: *We anticipated a pleasant vacation in Canada.* **3.** To deal with beforehand: *Store owners anticipated the storm by boarding up their windows.* [From Latin *anticipāre,* to take before : *ante-,* before + *capere,* to take.] **—an·tic′i·pa′tor** *n.*

BIOGRAPHY

Susan B. Anthony

At the beginning of the 1800s, women were not equal to men under the law. When a woman married, for instance, she was forced to give up her property and wages to her husband, and husbands had sole rights over any children. Susan B. **Anthony,** teamed with friend and fellow reformer Elizabeth Cady Stanton, wanted to set right these inequalities and allow women freedom and respect. The two women worked for new legislation by writing articles, lecturing, and organizing conventions for women's rights, and they lobbied for laws that would protect the property, wages, and guardianship rights of married women. They also worked hard to try to secure women's legal right to vote. At the time of her death, Anthony was recognized as the unofficial leader of the women's suffrage movement. Anthony and Stanton's efforts helped to secure women's voting rights, clearing the path for the passage of the 19th Amendment in 1920.

Susan B. Anthony

an·tic·i·pa·tion (ăn-tĭs′ə-pā′shən) *n.* **1.** The act of expecting or foreseeing something, especially with eagerness or happiness: *She looked forward to vacation with great anticipation.* **2.** Action taken in order to prevent or counteract something: *The town's anticipation of big crowds made the street fair a success.*

an·ti·cler·i·cal (ăn′tē-klĕr′ĭ-kəl) *adj.* Opposed to the influence of the church or the clergy in public life.

an·ti·cli·mac·tic (ăn′tē-klī-măk′tĭk) *adj.* Relating to or being an anticlimax. **—an′ti·cli·mac′ti·cal·ly** *adv.*

an·ti·cli·max (ăn′tē-klī′măks′) *n.* **1.** A decline or letdown viewed as a disappointing contrast to what has gone before: *The rest of the story was an anticlimax to the scene in the courtroom.* **2.** A less important or trivial event that follows a series of significant ones: *Rain showers were an anticlimax after the full force of the hurricane.*

an·ti·cline (ăn′tĭ-klīn′) *n.* A fold of rock layers that slope downward on both sides from a crest. **—an′ti·cli′nal** (ăn′tē-klī′nəl) *adj.*

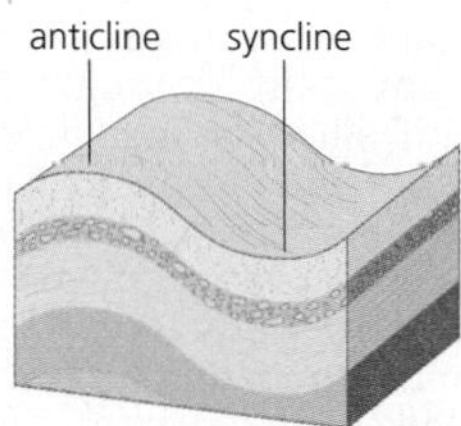

anticline

an·ti·co·ag·u·lant (ăn′tē-kō-ăg′yə-lənt) *n.* A substance that prevents or slows the clotting of blood.

an·ti·cy·clone (ăn′tē-sī′klōn′) *n.* A system of winds that spiral outward around a region of high atmospheric pressure, circling clockwise in the Northern Hemisphere and counterclockwise in the Southern Hemisphere.

an·ti·de·pres·sant (ăn′tē-dĭ-prĕs′ənt) *n.* A drug that is used to treat depression. **—an′ti·de·pres′sant** *adj.*

an·ti·do·tal (ăn′tē-dōt′l) *adj.* Relating to or serving as an antidote.

an·ti·dote (ăn′tĭ-dōt′) *n.* **1.** A substance that counteracts the effects of poison. **2.** Something that relieves or counteracts something: *Baking soda is often used as an antidote to indigestion.* [From Middle English *antidot*, from Greek *antidoton* : *anti-*, against + *didonai*, to give.]

An·tie·tam (ăn-tē′təm) A creek of north-central Maryland emptying into the Potomac River. The Civil War Battle of Antietam (or Sharpsburg) was fought along its banks on September 17, 1862.

an·ti·freeze (ăn′tĭ-frēz′) *n.* A substance added to a liquid, such as water, to lower its freezing point.

an·ti·gen (ăn′tĭ-jən) *n.* A substance that stimulates the production of an antibody when introduced into the body. Antigens include toxins, bacterial cells, and foreign blood cells. —SEE NOTE AT **blood type.**

An·tig·o·ne (ăn-tĭg′ə-nē) *n.* In Greek mythology, the daughter of Oedipus and Jocasta who performed funeral rites over her brother's body in defiance of her uncle, the king of Thebes.

an·ti·grav·i·ty (ăn′tē-grăv′ĭ-tē) *n.* A supposed physical force that would counteract gravity.

An·ti·gua and Bar·bu·da (ăn-tē′gə ănd bär-bo͞o′də) A country in the northern Leeward Islands of the Caribbean Sea, made up of three small islands. St. John's is the capital.

an·ti·he·ro (ăn′tē-hîr′ō) *n., pl.* **an·ti·he·roes** A main character in a novel, play, or other work who lacks traditional heroic qualities, such as courage.

an·ti·her·o·ine (ăn′tē-hĕr′ō-ĭn) *n.* An antihero who is a woman or girl.

an·ti·his·ta·mine (ăn′tē-hĭs′tə-mēn′ *or* ăn′tē-hĭs′tə-mĭn) *n.* Any of various drugs that relieve symptoms of allergies or colds by interfering with the action of histamine in the body.

an·ti·knock (ăn′tĭ-nŏk′) *n.* A substance added to gasoline to reduce pounding or clanking in an engine.

An·til·les (ăn-tĭl′ēz) The islands of the West Indies except for the Bahamas, separating the Caribbean Sea from the Atlantic Ocean and divided into the **Greater Antilles** to the north and the **Lesser Antilles** to the east.

an·ti·lock brakes (ăn′tē-lŏk′ *or* ăn′tĭ-lŏk′) *pl.n.* A braking system in a motor vehicle in which electronic sensors detect when the wheels have suddenly slowed down and a computer chip repeatedly decreases and increases brake pressure in order to prevent the wheels from locking and the vehicle from skidding.

an·ti·log (ăn′tē-lôg′) *n.* An antilogarithm.

an·ti·log·a·rithm (ăn′tē-lô′gə-rĭth′əm) *n.* The number whose logarithm is a given number. For example, the logarithm of 1,000 (or 10^3) is 3, so the antilogarithm of 3 is 1,000.

an·ti·ma·cas·sar (ăn′tĭ-mə-kăs′ər) *n.* A small cover placed on the back or arms of a chair or sofa to protect from dirt or damage or as a decoration.

an·ti·mat·ter (ăn′tĭ-măt′ər) *n.* A form of matter that is identical to ordinary matter except that it is made of positrons, antiprotons, and antineutrons.

an·ti·mis·sile (ăn′tē-mĭs′əl) *adj.* Designed to destroy a missile in flight: *an antimissile system.*

an·ti·mo·ny (ăn′tə-mō′nē) *n. Symbol* **Sb** A metallic element, the most common form of which is a hard, extremely brittle, blue-white crystal. It is used in a wide variety of alloys, especially with lead in car batteries. Atomic number 51. See **Periodic Table.** [From Middle English *antimonie*, from Medieval Latin *antimōnium*.]

an·ti·neu·tri·no (ăn′tē-no͞o-trē′nō) *n., pl.* **an·ti·neu·tri·nos** The antiparticle of the neutrino.

an·ti·neu·tron (ăn′tē-no͞o′trŏn′) *n.* The antiparticle of the neutron.

an·ti·nu·cle·ar (ăn′tē-no͞o′klē-ər) *adj.* Opposing the production or use of nuclear power or nuclear weaponry.

an·ti·ox·i·dant (ăn′tē-ŏk′sĭ-dənt *or* ăn′tī-ŏk′sĭ-dənt) *n.* A substance that inhibits oxidation, especially one (such as vitamin E or vitamin C) that protects cells from damage due to oxidation.

an·ti·par·ti·cle (ăn′tē-pär′tĭ-kəl) *n.* A particle of antimatter that corresponds to a particle of matter, such as an electron or proton, but has different electrical or magnetic properties. Positrons, antiprotons and antineutrons are examples of antiparticles.

an·ti·pas·to (än′tē-päs′tō) *n., pl.* **an·ti·pas·tos** or **an·ti·pas·ti** (än′tē-päs′tē) An appetizer usually consisting of an assortment of foods, such as smoked meats, cheese, and vegetables.

an·tip·a·thy (ăn-tĭp′ə-thē) *n., pl.* **an·tip·a·thies 1.** A feeling of dislike or opposition: *Some people always express antipathy to new ideas.* **2.** Incompatibility: *the antipathy between emotion and logic.*

an·ti·per·spi·rant (ăn′tē-pûr′spər-ənt) *n.* A preparation applied to the skin to reduce or prevent perspiration.

an·tip·o·dal (ăn-tĭp′ə-dəl) *adj.* Relating to or situated on opposite sides of the earth.

an·tip·o·des (ăn-tĭp′ə-dēz′) *pl.n.* Two places on directly opposite sides of the earth: *The North Pole and the South Pole are antipodes.*

an·ti·pov·er·ty (ăn′tē-pŏv′ər-tē) *adj.* Created or intended to reduce poverty: *antipoverty programs.*

an·ti·pro·ton (ăn′tē-prō′tŏn′) *n.* The antiparticle of the proton.

an·ti·psy·chot·ic (ăn′tē-sī-kŏt′ĭk *or* ăn′tī-sī-kŏt′ĭk) *adj.* Counteracting or diminishing the symptoms of psychotic disorders, such as schizophrenia. ❖ *n.* An antipsychotic drug.

an·ti·quar·i·an (ăn′tĭ-kwâr′ē-ən) *n.* A person who studies, collects, sells, or buys relics and ancient works of art. ❖ *adj.* Relating to antiquarians or the study of antiquities.

an·ti·quar·y (ăn′tĭ-kwĕr′ē) *n., pl.* **an·ti·quar·ies** An antiquarian.

an·ti·quate (ăn′tĭ-kwāt′) *tr.v.* **an·ti·quat·ed, an·ti·quat·ing, an·ti·quates** To make obsolete or old-fashioned.

an·ti·quat·ed (ăn′tĭ-kwā′tĭd) *adj.* Too old to be useful, suitable, or fashionable.

ă	pat	ôr	core
ā	pay	oi	boy
âr	care	ou	out
ä	father	o͝o	took
ĕ	pet	o͝or	lure
ē	be	o͞o	boot
ĭ	pit	ŭ	cut
ī	bite	ûr	urge
îr	pier	th	thin
ŏ	pot	*th*	this
ō	toe	zh	vision
ô	paw	ə	about

an·tique (ăn-**tēk′**) *adj.* **1.** Belonging to, made in, or typical of an earlier period: *antique furniture.* **2.** Relating to or belonging to ancient times, especially those of ancient Greece or Rome: *the antique legend of the founding of Rome.* **3.** Very old; old-fashioned: *an antique style of writing.* ❖ *n.* Something having special value because of its age, especially a work of art or handicraft that is over 100 years old: *The writing table was a treasured antique.* ❖ *tr.v.* **an·tiqued, an·tiqu·ing, an·tiques** To give the appearance of an antique to: *That chair has been antiqued.* [From Latin *antīquus.*] —**an·tique′ly** *adv.*

an·tiq·ui·ty (ăn-**tĭk′**wĭ-tē) *n., pl.* **an·tiq·ui·ties 1.** Ancient times, especially the times before the Middle Ages: *The pyramids of ancient Egypt belong to antiquity.* **2.** The people of ancient times, especially the writers of those times: *an invention unknown to antiquity.* **3.** The quality of being old: *a carving of great antiquity.* **4.** Something, such as a relic, that dates from ancient times: *That museum has a collection of many antiquities from ancient Greece.*

an·ti-Sem·i·tism (ăn′tē-**sĕm′**ĭ-tĭz′əm) *n.* Prejudice against or hostility toward Jews. —**an′ti-Se·mit′ic** (ăn′tē-sə-**mĭt′**ĭk) *adj.*

an·ti·sep·tic (ăn′tĭ-**sĕp′**tĭk) *adj.* **1.** Preventing infection, fermentation, or rot by stopping the growth and activity of microorganisms. **2.** Free of microorganisms that cause infection; aseptic. ❖ *n.* An antiseptic substance or agent, such as alcohol or boric acid. [From Greek *anti-*, against + Greek *sēptikos*, putrefying.] —**an′ti·sep′ti·cal·ly** *adv.*

an·ti·slav·er·y (ăn′tē-**slā′**və-rē) *adj.* Opposed to or against slavery.

an·ti·so·cial (ăn′tē-**sō′**shəl) *adj.* **1.** Avoiding the society or company of others; not sociable: *an antisocial recluse.* **2.** Hostile to or violating accepted rules of behavior: *Criminal acts are examples of antisocial behavior.* —**an′ti·so′cial·ly** *adv.*

an·ti·ter·ror·ist (ăn′tē-**tĕr′**ər-ĭst) *adj.* Designed to combat terrorists or terrorism: *antiterrorist experts.*

an·tith·e·sis (ăn-**tĭth′**ĭ-sĭs) *n., pl.* **an·tith·e·ses** (ăn-**tĭth′**ĭ-sēz′) **1.** Direct contrast; opposition: *Your behavior stands in antithesis to your beliefs.* **2.** The direct or exact opposite: *Hope is the antithesis of despair.* **3.** In speech or writing, the placing together of sharply opposed ideas.

an·ti·tox·in (ăn′tē-**tŏk′**sĭn) *n.* **1.** An antibody formed in response to and capable of acting against a biological toxin, such as one produced by bacteria. **2.** A serum containing antibodies, obtained from the blood of a human or other animal that has had a particular disease or was immunized against infection from the disease. The antitoxin is used to provide immunity against that disease.

an·ti·trust (ăn′tē-**trŭst′**) *adj.* Opposing or regulating trusts or similar business monopolies, especially in order to promote competition: *antitrust laws that prevent unfair business practices.*

an·ti·ven·in (ăn′tē-**vĕn′**ĭn) *n.* **1.** An antitoxin that counteracts the venom of a snake, scorpion, or other venomous animal. **2.** A human or animal serum containing such an antitoxin.

an·ti·war (ăn′tē-**wôr′**) *adj.* Opposing war: *an antiwar demonstration.*

ant·ler (**ănt′**lər) *n.* One of a pair of bony growths on the head of a deer, moose, elk, or other related animal, usually having several branches. Antlers are shed and grown again every year and are usually found only on males. [From Middle English *aunteler*, from Old French *antoillier* : Latin *ante-*, in front + Latin *oculāris*, of the eye.]

ant lion *n.* Any of various insects whose larvae have large jaws and dig conical pits in the sand to trap ants and other insects for food.

an·to·nym (**ăn′**tə-nĭm′) *n.* A word having a meaning opposite to that of another word; for example, *thick* is an antonym of *thin.*

ant·sy (**ănt′**sē) *adj.* **ant·si·er, ant·si·est** *Slang* Uneasy; anxious; restless.

Ant·werp (**ăn′**twərp) A city of northern Belgium north of Brussels. It is one of Europe's busiest ports.

A·nu·bis (ə-**nōō′**bĭs) *n.* In Egyptian mythology, a jackal-headed god who conducted the dead to the underworld.

a·nus (**ā′**nəs) *n., pl.* **a·nus·es** The opening at the lower end of the digestive tract through which solid waste is excreted. [From Latin *ānus*, ring.]

an·vil (**ăn′**vĭl) *n.* **1.** A heavy block of iron or steel, with a smooth flat top on which metals are shaped by hammering. **2.** The incus. [From Old English *onfilti.*]

anx·i·e·ty (ăng-**zī′**ĭ-tē) *n., pl.* **anx·i·e·ties 1.** A feeling of uneasiness and distress, especially about something in the future; worry: *The settlers were filled with anxiety about food supplies in the coming winter.* **2.** Eagerness or earnestness, often marked by uneasiness: *the pianist's anxiety to play well.*

anx·ious (**ăngk′**shəs *or* **ăng′**shəs) *adj.* **1.** Having a feeling of uneasiness; worried: *They were anxious about the upcoming exam.* **2.** Marked by uneasiness or worry: *anxious moments.* **3.** Eagerly desirous or earnest: *We were anxious for the bike race to begin.* [From Latin *ānxius*, from *angere*, to torment.] —**anx′ious·ly** *adv.* —**anx′ious·ness** *n.*

an·y (**ĕn′**ē) *adj.* **1.** One or some; no matter which: *Take any book you want. Do you have any information on Chinese cooking?* **2.** No matter how many or how few; some: *Are there any oranges left?* **3.** Every: *Any dog likes meat.* ❖ *pron. (used with a singular or plural verb)* Any person or thing or any persons or things; anybody or anything: *We haven't any left. Any of the teachers can help you.* ❖ *adv.* At all: *The patient doesn't feel any better.* [From Old English *ǣnig.*]

an·y·bod·y (**ĕn′**ē-bŏd′ē *or* **ĕn′**ē-bŭd′ē) *pron.* **1.** Any person; anyone. **2.** A person of importance: *Everybody who is anybody came to the party.*

an·y·how (**ĕn′**ē-hou′) *adv.* **1.** Anyway: *The twins were sick, but they didn't want to go anyhow.* **2.** Nonetheless: *You may know these words, but study them anyhow.*

an·y·more (ĕn′ē-**môr′**) *adv.* **1.** Any longer; at the present: *Do they make this style anymore?* **2.** From now on: *We promised not to shout in the library anymore.*

an·y·one (**ĕn′**ē-wŭn′) *pron.* Any person; anybody.

an·y·place (**ĕn′**ē-plās′) *adv.* Anywhere: *I can go anyplace I like.*

an·y·thing (**ĕn′**ē-thĭng′) *pron.* Any object, occurrence, or matter whatever. ❖ *adv.* To any degree or extent; at all: *Is your bike anything like mine?* ◆ **anything but** By no means; not at all: *This room is anything but warm.*

an·y·time (**ĕn′**ē-tīm′) *adv.* At any time: *Anytime we come inside we should wipe our feet.*

an·y·way (**ĕn′**ē-wā′) *adv.* **1.** In any case; at least: *I don't know if the book is lost or stolen; anyway, it's gone.* **2.** In any manner whatever: *Get the job done anyway you can.* **3.** Just the same; nevertheless; anyhow: *The ball was slippery, but the fielder caught it anyway.*

an·y·ways (**ĕn′**ē-wāz′) *adv. Nonstandard* In any case.

an·y·where (**ĕn′**ē-wâr′) *adv.* **1.** To, in, or at any place: *They travel anywhere they want to.* **2.** At all: *We aren't anywhere near finished.* **3.** Used to indicate the limits of a range of values: *A wolf's color can be anywhere from white to black.*

ao dai (**ou′** dī *or* **ô′** dī) *n., pl.* **ao dais** A traditional garment worn by Vietnamese women, consisting of a sleeved blouse that extends to the knees and is slit on the sides up to the hips. It is worn over loose-fitting pants.

A-OK (ā′ō-**kā′**) *adj. Informal* Perfectly all right: *It's A-OK with me if you want to leave.*

antler
white-tailed deer

anvil

ao dai

A-one (ā′wŭn′) *adj. Informal* First-class; excellent.

a·or·ta (ā-ôr′tə) *n., pl.* **a·or·tas** also **a·or·tae** (ā-ôr′tē) The main artery of the body, starting at the left ventricle of the heart and extending into the abdomen, where it branches into smaller arteries that carry blood to all the organs of the body except the lungs.

a·pace (ə-pās′) *adv.* At a rapid pace; swiftly: *The building of the new hospital is proceeding apace.*

A·pach·e (ə-păch′ē) *n., pl.* **Apache** or **A·pach·es 1.** A member of a Native American people of the southwestern United States. **2.** Any of the Athabascan languages of the Apache.

a·part (ə-pärt′) *adv.* **1.** Away from another in time or position: *two trees about ten feet apart.* **2.** In or into separate pieces; to pieces: *The wagon fell apart as it crashed into the rocks.* **3.** One from another: *Can you tell the puppies apart?* **4.** Aside or in reserve: *set money apart for a vacation.* **5.** Being excepted or excluded from consideration; aside: *Joking apart, I think you're crazy.* ❖ *adj.* Set apart; isolated: *Unusually strong winds made this storm one apart from the others.* **—a·part′ness** *n.*

apart from *prep.* Other than; not counting: *Apart from a few showers, we had fine weather on our vacation.*

a·part·heid (ə-pärt′hīt′ *or* ə-pärt′hāt′) *n.* An official policy of segregation formerly practiced in South Africa, involving legal and economic discrimination against nonwhites. [From Afrikaans : Dutch *apart*, separate + Dutch *-heid*, -hood.]

WRITERS CHOOSE THEIR WORDS

Right on cue, Leon performed a curtsy, brief but with such **aplomb** as to be fitting for an audience with the queen.

—Dr. Cuthbert Soup
A Whole Nother Story

a·part·ment (ə-pärt′mənt) *n.* A room or group of rooms to live in.

apartment building *n.* A building divided into apartments.

apartment house *n.* An apartment building.

ap·a·thet·ic (ăp′ə-thĕt′ĭk) *adj.* Feeling or showing little or no interest; uninterested; indifferent: *Adults who are apathetic about politics should not complain about poor government.* **—ap′a·thet′i·cal·ly** *adv.*

ap·a·thy (ăp′ə-thē) *n.* Lack of feeling or interest; indifference: *Apathy among our friends made it difficult to organize the skiing trip.* [From Greek *apathēs*, without feeling : *a-*, without + *pathos*, feeling.]

a·pat·o·sau·rus (ə-păt′ə-sôr′əs) *n.* A very large plant-eating dinosaur of the Jurassic Period, having a long neck and tail and a relatively small head. [From Greek *apatē*, untruth + Greek *sauros*, lizard.] —SEE NOTE AT **brontosaurus.**

ape (āp) *n.* Any of several large tailless primates. The apes include the gibbons, orangutans, gorillas, chimpanzees, bonobos, and humans. ❖ *tr.v.* **aped, ap·ing, apes** To imitate the actions of; mimic: *Everyone laughed when Brian started aping the teacher.* [From Old English *apa.*] **—ap′er** *n.*

Ap·en·nines (ăp′ə-nīnz′) A mountain system extending about 745 miles (1,200 kilometers) from northwest Italy to the southern tip of the mainland. The Apennines rise to 9,554 feet (2,912 meters).

a·pé·ri·tif (ä-pĕr′ĭ-tēf′) *n.* An alcoholic drink taken before a meal to stimulate the appetite.

ap·er·ture (ăp′ər-chər) *n.* **1.** A hole or an opening: *an aperture in the wall.* **2.** The diameter of the opening through which light can pass into a camera, telescope, or other optical instrument. [From Middle English, from Latin *apertūra*, from *aperīre*, to open.]

a·pex (ā′pĕks) *n., pl.* **a·pex·es** or **a·pi·ces** (ā′pĭ-sēz′ *or* ăp′ĭ-sēz′) **1.** The highest point of a geometric figure or of a structure: *the apex of a pyramid.* **2.** The highest level of a hierarchy: *working at the apex of a corporation.* **3.** The period of greatest achievement: *The runner won many victories at the apex of her great career.* [From Latin.]

a·pha·sia (ə-fā′zhə) *n.* The loss of some or all of the ability to speak, express ideas, or understand language, resulting from damage to the brain from injury or disease. **—a·pha′sic** (ə-fā′zĭk *or* ə-fā′sĭk) *adj. & n.*

a·phe·li·on (ə-fē′lē-ən) *n., pl.* **a·phe·li·a** (ə-fē′lē-ə) The point on the orbit of a celestial object that is farthest from the sun. [From New Latin *aphēlium* : Greek *apo-*, away + Greek *hēlios*, sun.]

a·phid (ā′fĭd *or* ăf′ĭd) *n.* Any of various small, soft-bodied insects that feed by sucking sap from plants.

aph·o·rism (ăf′ə-rĭz′əm) *n.* A short saying expressing a general truth; for example, "The only way to have a friend is to be one" is an aphorism.

aph·ro·di·si·ac (ăf′rə-dē′zē-ăk′ *or* ăf′rə-dĭz′ē-ăk′) *n.* A drug or food that stimulates sexual desire. ❖ *adj.* Sexually stimulating.

Aph·ro·di·te (ăf′rə-dī′tē) *n.* In Greek mythology, the goddess of love and beauty, identified with the Roman Venus.

API *abbr.* An abbreviation of Asian and Pacific Islander.

A·pi·a (ə-pē′ə *or* ä′pē-ä′) The capital of Samoa, in the southern Pacific Ocean.

a·pi·a·rist (ā′pē-ə-rĭst) *n.* A beekeeper.

a·pi·ar·y (ā′pē-ĕr′ē) *n., pl.* **a·pi·ar·ies** A place where bees and beehives are kept, especially a place where bees are raised for their honey.

a·pi·ces (ā′pĭ-sēz′ *or* ăp′ĭ-sēz′) *n.* A plural of **apex.**

a·piece (ə-pēs′) *adv.* To or for each one; each: *Give them an apple apiece.*

ap·ish (ā′pĭsh) *adj.* **1.** Resembling an ape. **2.** Foolishly imitative. **3.** Silly, ridiculous: *an apish grin.* **—ap′ish·ly** *adv.*

a·plen·ty (ə-plĕn′tē) *adj.* In abundance: *We'll have water aplenty when the floods come.*

a·plomb (ə-plŏm′ *or* ə-plŭm′) *n.* Self-confidence; poise; assurance: *Our teacher handled the situation with aplomb.*

ap·ne·a (ăp′nē-ə) *n.* Temporary absence of breathing.

APO *abbr.* An abbreviation of Army Post Office.

a·poc·a·lypse (ə-pŏk′ə-lĭps′) *n.* **1. Apocalypse** The book of Revelation. **2.** The end of the world. **3.** A prophecy or revelation, especially about the end of the world.

a·poc·a·lyp·tic (ə-pŏk′ə-lĭp′tĭk) *adj.* **1.** Relating to or predicting the end of the world, especially as described in the Bible or another religious text. **2.** Relating to or predicting widespread destruction or the collapse of civilization: *an apocalyptic novel.*

A·poc·ry·pha (ə-pŏk′rə-fə) *n. (used with a singular or plural verb)* **1.** Those books of the Old Testament that are accepted as canonical by Roman Catholic and Orthodox Christians but not by Protestants because they are not part of the Hebrew Scriptures. **2.** Various early Christian writings excluded from the New Testament.

a·poc·ry·phal (ə-pŏk′rə-fəl) *adj.* **1.** Of doubtful origin; false: *Folk legend is full of apocryphal stories of animals coming to the aid of humans in distress.* **2.** Relating to the Apocrypha. **—a·poc′ry·phal·ly** *adv.*

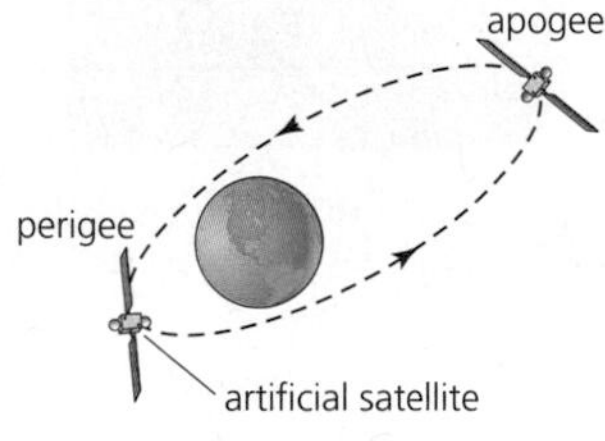

apogee

ap·o·gee (ăp′ə-jē) *n.* **1.** The point in an orbit around Earth where a satellite is farthest from Earth. **2.** The highest point; apex. [From Greek *apogaios*, far from the earth : *apo-*, away + *gaia*, earth.]

A·pol·lo (ə-pŏl′ō) *n.* In Greek and Roman mythology, the god of prophecy, music, medicine, and poetry, sometimes identified with the sun.

a·pol·o·get·ic (ə-pŏl′ə-jĕt′ĭk) *adj.* Expressing or making an apology: *The student's excuse was offered with an apologetic smile.* **—a·pol′o·get′i·cal·ly** *adv.*

a·pol·o·gist (ə-pŏl′ə-jĭst) *n.* A person who argues in defense or justification of an idea or cause, especially one that is controversial: *an apologist for imperialism.*

a·pol·o·gize (ə-pŏl′ə-jīz′) *intr.v.* **a·pol·o·gized, a·pol·o·giz·ing, a·pol·o·giz·es** To make an apology; say one is sorry: *Did he apologize for being late?*

a·pol·o·gy (ə-pŏl′ə-jē) *n., pl.* **a·pol·o·gies 1.** A state-

ă	pat	ôr	core
ā	pay	oi	boy
âr	care	ou	out
ä	father	o͝o	took
ĕ	pet	o͝or	lure
ē	be	o͞o	boot
ĭ	pit	ŭ	cut
ī	bite	ûr	urge
îr	pier	th	thin
ŏ	pot	*th*	this
ō	toe	zh	vision
ô	paw	ə	about

ment expressing regret for an offense or fault: *make an apology for being late.* **2.** A defense or justification, as of an idea or cause: *Her letter to the editor is an apology for animal rights.* **3.** An inferior substitute: *That short note was a poor apology for a letter.* [From Greek *apologiā* : *apo-*, away + *logos*, speech.]

ap·o·plec·tic (ăp′ə-plĕk′tĭk) *adj.* **1.** Extremely angry; furious. **2.** Relating to or resembling apoplexy. **—ap′o·plec′ti·cal·ly** *adv.*

ap·o·plex·y (ăp′ə-plĕk′sē) *n.* A condition in which a blood vessel in the brain breaks or becomes blocked, often resulting in paralysis, unconsciousness, or death; a stroke.

a·pos·ta·sy (ə-pŏs′tə-sē) *n., pl.* **a·pos·ta·sies** A giving up of a particular religious faith, political party, or cause.

a·pos·tate (ə-pŏs′tāt′ *or* ə-pŏs′tĭt) *n.* A person who has abandoned a particular religious faith, political party, or cause.

a·pos·tle (ə-pŏs′əl) *n.* **1.** often **Apostle** One of the twelve original disciples of Jesus. **2.** A missionary of the early Christian Church: *St. Patrick, the apostle of Ireland.* **3.** A person who leads or strongly supports a cause or movement: *an apostle of government reform.*

A·pos·tles' Creed (ə-pŏs′əlz) *n.* A Christian creed traditionally thought to have been written by the 12 Apostles.

ap·os·tol·ic (ăp′ə-stŏl′ĭk) *adj.* **1.** Relating to the 12 Apostles, their teaching, or their practices. **2.** In the Roman Catholic Church, relating to the pope as successor to Saint Peter: *apostolic authority.*

a·pos·tro·phe (ə-pŏs′trə-fē) *n.* A mark (') used to indicate the omission of a letter or letters from a word or phrase, as in *aren't*, or to show the possessive case, as in *Tom's hat*, or certain plurals, such as those of single letters, as in *A's*. [From Greek *apostrophos* : *apo-*, away + *strephein*, to turn.]

a·poth·e·car·ies' measure (ə-pŏth′ĭ-kĕr′ēz) *n.* A system of liquid volume measure used in pharmacy, now largely replaced by the metric system.

apothecaries' weight *n.* A system of weights used in pharmacy based on an ounce equal to 480 grains and a pound equal to 12 ounces, now largely replaced by the metric system.

a·poth·e·car·y (ə-pŏth′ĭ-kĕr′ē) *n., pl.* **a·poth·e·car·ies** A person who prepares or sells medicines; a pharmacist. [From Middle English *apotecarie*, from Late Latin *apothēcārius*, clerk, from Greek *apothēkē*, storehouse.]

ap·o·thegm (ăp′ə-thĕm′) *n.* A short and witty instructive saying; a maxim.

a·poth·e·o·sis (ə-pŏth′ē-ō′sĭs) *n., pl.* **a·poth·e·o·ses** (ə-pŏth′ē-ō′sēz′) **1.** The elevation to divine rank or status; deification: *the apotheosis of a Roman emperor.* **2.** A glorified ideal or example: *The dancer was considered the apotheosis of grace.*

app (ăp) *n.* A computer application.

Ap·pa·la·chi·a (ăp′ə-lā′chē-ə *or* ăp′ə-lăch′ē-ə) A rural region of the United States in the central and southern Appalachian Mountains. **—Ap′pa·la′chi·an** *adj.*

Appalachian Mountains also **Ap·pa·la·chi·ans** (ăp′-ə-lā′chē-ənz *or* ăp′ə-lăch′ē-ənz) A mountain system of eastern North America extending about 1,600 miles (2,575 kilometers) southwest from southeast Canada to central Alabama. The Appalachians rise to 6,684 feet (2,037 meters).

ap·pall (ə-pôl′) *tr.v.* **ap·palled, ap·pall·ing, ap·palls** To fill with horror and amazement; shock: *My mother was appalled when she saw the mess we made in the backyard.*

ap·pall·ing (ə-pô′lĭng) *adj.* Causing horrified disapproval or dismay: *the appalling working conditions of miners in the last century.* **—ap·pall′ing·ly** *adv.*

Ap·pa·loo·sa (ăp′ə-lo͞o′sə) *n.* Any of a breed of spotted horse originally bred in northwest North America.

ap·pa·rat·us (ăp′ə-răt′əs *or* ăp′ə-rā′təs) *n., pl.* **appa·ratus** or **ap·pa·rat·us·es 1.** A device, mechanism, or structure for a particular purpose: *an apparatus designed to measure oxygen consumption.* **2.** The means by which some function or task is performed: *Congress has a complicated apparatus for making laws.*

ap·par·el (ə-păr′əl) *n.* Clothing; attire: *a store that sells children's apparel.* ❖ *tr.v.* **ap·par·eled, ap·par·el·ing, ap·par·els** or **ap·par·elled, ap·par·el·ling, ap·par·els** To dress or clothe: *The queen was appareled in velvet robes.*

ap·par·ent (ə-pâr′ənt) *adj.* **1.** Readily understood or seen; obvious: *for no apparent reason.* **2.** Appearing as such but not necessarily so; seeming: *an apparent advantage.* **—ap·par′ent·ly** *adv.* **—ap·par′ent·ness** *n.*

ap·pa·ri·tion (ăp′ə-rĭsh′ən) *n.* **1.** A ghost; a specter. **2.** An eerie sight.

ap·peal (ə-pēl′) *n.* **1a.** An urgent or earnest request: *an appeal for help.* **b.** A request of a person to decide something in one's favor: *I wanted to go and made an appeal to my parents.* **2.** The power of attracting or of arousing interest: *The waterfront has great appeal for tourists.* **3a.** A higher court's review of the correctness of a decision by a lower court. **b.** A case so reviewed: *The judge will hear the appeal on Friday.* **c.** A request for a new hearing: *grant an appeal.* ❖ *v.* **ap·pealed, ap·peal·ing, ap·peals** *—intr.* **1.** To make an urgent or earnest request: *I appeal to you to help us.* **2.** To be attractive or interesting: *That fine automobile appealed to the buyer.* **3.** To make or apply for a legal appeal: *If the judge decides against us, we will appeal.* *—tr.* To make or apply for a legal appeal of: *appealed the decision to a higher court.* [From Middle English *apel*, from Latin *appellāre*, to entreat.]

ap·peal·ing (ə-pē′lĭng) *adj.* Attractive or interesting: *appealing clothes.*

ap·pear (ə-pîr′) *intr.v.* **ap·peared, ap·pear·ing, ap·pears 1a.** To come into view: *A ship appeared on the horizon.* **b.** To be shown or included: *Their logo appears on all of their products.* **2.** To seem or look: *The child appears unhappy.* **3.** To present oneself formally before a court of law: *The criminal appeared before the judge.* **4.** To come before the public: *The violinist has appeared in two concerts.* [From Middle English *aperen*, from Latin *appārēre* : *ad-*, to + *pārēre*, to show.]

ap·pear·ance (ə-pîr′əns) *n.* **1.** The act of appearing; a coming into sight: *the sudden appearance of storm clouds on the horizon.* **2.** The act of coming into public view: *nine years since the pianist's last personal appearance.* **3.** The way something or someone looks or appears: *A neat appearance helps to make a good impression.* **4.** A semblance or false show: *The frightened soldier was only keeping up an appearance of bravery.* ◆ **by all appearances** or **to all appearances** From what one can tell from external circumstances: *By all appearances the famous author was a quiet person living in a small town.*

ap·pease (ə-pēz′) *tr.v.* **ap·peased, ap·peas·ing, ap·peas·es 1a.** To calm the anger of (someone), especially by yielding to their demands. **b.** To calm, soothe, or quiet (someone): *The babysitter appeased the startled baby with a bottle.* **2.** To satisfy; relieve: *A tall glass of water appeased his thirst.* [From Middle English *appesen*, from Old French *apesier* : Latin *ad-*, to + Latin *pāx*, peace.] **—ap·peas′er** *n.*

ap·pease·ment (ə-pēz′mənt) *n.* **1.** An act of appeasing or a condition of being appeased. **2.** A policy of attempting to avoid war by meeting the demands of a threatening nation.

ap·pel·lant (ə-pĕl′ənt) *n.* A person who appeals a court decision.

ap·pel·late (ə-pĕl′ĭt) *adj.* Having the legal power to hear appeals and to reverse previous court decisions: *an appellate court.*

ap·pel·la·tion (ăp′ə-lā′shən) *n.* A name or title: *The tele-*

Appaloosa

phone company was known by the appellation "Ma Bell."

ap·pend (ə-pĕnd′) *tr.v.* **ap·pend·ed, ap·pend·ing, ap·pends** To attach; add: *The editor appended an index to the history book.*

ap·pend·age (ə-pĕn′dĭj) *n.* A part, such as an arm, leg, tail, or antenna, that hangs or projects from the body of an organism: *the feathery appendages of a barnacle.*

ap·pen·dec·to·my (ăp′ən-dĕk′tə-mē) *n., pl.* **ap·pen·dec·to·mies** The removal of the appendix by surgery.

ap·pen·di·ci·tis (ə-pĕn′dĭ-sī′tĭs) *n.* Inflammation of the appendix.

ap·pen·dix (ə-pĕn′dĭks) *n., pl.* **ap·pen·dix·es** or **ap·pen·di·ces** (ə-pĕn′dĭ-sēz′) **1.** A section at the end of a book containing additional material, tables, or other information relating to the subject of the book. **2.** The tubular projection attached to the large intestine near where it joins the small intestine. [From Latin, from *appendere*, to hang upon.]

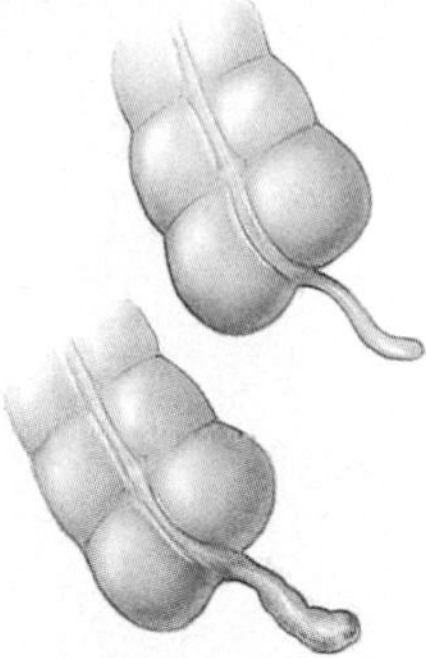

appendix
top: healthy appendix
bottom: inflamed appendix

ap·per·tain (ăp′ər-tān′) *intr.v.* **ap·per·tained, ap·per·tain·ing, ap·per·tains** To belong as a function or part; have relation; pertain: *the policies of government that appertain to economic reform.*

ap·pe·tite (ăp′ĭ-tīt′) *n.* **1.** The desire for food or drink. **2.** A strong desire for something: *an appetite for learning.* [From Middle English *apetit*, from Latin *appetītus*, strong desire, from *appetere*, to strive after.]

ap·pe·tiz·er (ăp′ĭ-tī′zər) *n.* A food or drink taken before a meal to stimulate the appetite.

ap·pe·tiz·ing (ăp′ĭ-tī′zĭng) *adj.* Stimulating or appealing to the appetite; tasty: *an appetizing meal.* **—ap′pe·tiz′ing·ly** *adv.*

ap·plaud (ə-plôd′) *v.* **ap·plaud·ed, ap·plaud·ing, ap·plauds** *—intr.* To express approval, especially by clapping the hands: *The audience applauded for ten minutes.* *—tr.* **1.** To express approval of, especially by clapping: *applauded the actors.* **2.** To praise; approve: *My parents applauded my decision to study Chinese.* [From Middle English *applauden*, from Latin *applaudere* : *ad-*, to, for + *plaudere*, to clap.] **—ap·plaud′a·ble** *adj.* **—ap·plaud′er** *n.* —SEE NOTE AT **explode.**

Appomattox Court House
Early 20th-century depiction of Lee's surrender to Grant at the village of Appomattox Court House, Virginia, by Jean Leon Gerome Ferris (1863–1930)

ap·plause (ə-plôz′) *n.* **1.** Praise or approval expressed by the clapping of hands: *The guitarist's performance was cheered with loud applause.* **2.** Public approval: *The vaccine for polio received applause from doctors everywhere.*

ap·ple (ăp′əl) *n.* **1.** A firm, rounded, edible fruit having thin red, yellow, or green skin. **2.** The tree that bears such fruit. ◆ **apple of (one's) eye** A person or thing that is especially liked or loved: *Her grandson is the apple of her eye.*

apple butter *n.* A dark-brown spread made of stewed apples and spices.

ap·ple·jack (ăp′əl-jăk′) *n.* A strong alcoholic drink made by concentrating fermented cider.

ap·ple·sauce (ăp′əl-sôs′) *n.* Apples stewed to a pulp and sometimes sweetened and spiced.

ap·pli·ance (ə-plī′əns) *n.* A device, especially an electrical one such as a toaster or washing machine, that performs a specific function for household use.

ap·pli·ca·ble (ăp′lĭ-kə-bəl *or* ə-plĭk′ə-bəl) *adj.* Capable of being applied; appropriate: *The new rule is not applicable in your case.* **—ap′pli·ca·bly** *adv.* **—ap′pli·ca·bil′i·ty** *n.*

ap·pli·cant (ăp′lĭ-kənt) *n.* A person who applies for something: *an applicant for a job.*

ap·pli·ca·tion (ăp′lĭ-kā′shən) *n.* **1.** The act of applying: *Careless application of paint left several bare spots on the wall.* **2.** Something that is applied, such as a medicine or a cosmetic: *a thick application of salve on a burn.* **3.** A method of applying or using; a specific use: *the application of science to industry.* **4.** A computer program designed for a specific task. **5.** The capacity of being usable; relevance: *Geometry has practical application to flying an airplane.* **6.** Careful work and attention; diligence: *Their application was rewarded by good grades in school.* **7a.** A request, as for a job or admittance to a school. **b.** The form or document upon which such a request is made.

ap·pli·ca·tor (ăp′lĭ-kā′tər) *n.* An instrument for applying something, such as medicine or glue.

ap·plied (ə-plīd′) *adj.* Put into practice; used in a particular way: *The new yacht was designed using applied physics.*

ap·pli·qué (ăp′lĭ-kā′) *n.* A decoration, design, or trimming made by attaching pieces of one material to the surface of another. ❖ *tr.v.* **ap·pli·quéd, ap·pli·qué·ing, ap·pli·qués** To put on or apply as appliqué: *appliqué a monogram on a coat.*

ap·ply (ə-plī′) *v.* **ap·plied, ap·ply·ing, ap·plies** *—tr.* **1.** To put on: *apply a little bit of glue to the paper.* **2.** To put to or adapt for a special use: *The international charity applied all its money to medical supplies.* **3.** To put into action: *apply the brakes.* **4.** To use (a special word or phrase) in referring to someone or something: Underground Railroad *was the name applied to the system that helped fugitive slaves escape.* **5.** To direct the attention or energy of (oneself) to an activity or pursuit: *The students applied themselves to their homework.* *—intr.* **1.** To be pertinent or relevant: *This rule for quiet in the library does not apply during a fire drill.* **2.** To request employment, acceptance, or admission: *Several people applied for the same job. Many high-school students applied to college.* [From Middle English *applien*, from Old French *aplier*, from Latin *applicāre*, to affix : *ad-*, to + *plicāre*, to fold.] **—ap·pli′er** *n.*

ap·point (ə-point′) *tr.v.* **ap·point·ed, ap·point·ing, ap·points 1.** To select or designate for an office, position, or duty: *appoint a new police chief.* **2.** To decide on or set by authority: *appointed three o'clock for the next meeting.* **3.** To furnish; equip: *The playroom was appointed with sturdy furniture.* [From Middle English *appointen*, from Old French *a point*, to the point.] **—ap·point′er** *n.*

ap·point·ee (ə-poin′tē′ *or* ăp′oin-tē′) *n.* A person who is appointed to an office, position, or duty.

ap·poin·tive (ə-poin′tĭv) *adj.* Relating to or filled by appointment: *an appointive office.*

ap·point·ment (ə-point′mənt) *n.* **1a.** The act of appointing someone to an office or position: *The appointment of a school principal is an important decision.* **b.** The office or position to which a person has been appointed: *Our principal accepted the appointment as superintendent.* **2.** An arrangement for a meeting at a particular time or place: *I called the dentist to change the time of my appointment.* **3. appointments** Furnishings, fittings, or equipment: *tables, chairs, lamps, and other appointments of the room.*

Ap·po·mat·tox Court House (ăp′ə-măt′əks) A village of south-central Virginia west of Richmond. Confederate general Robert E. Lee surrendered to Union general Ulysses S. Grant here on April 9, 1865, effectively ending the Civil War.

ap·por·tion (ə-pôr′shən) *tr.v.* **ap·por·tioned, ap·por·tion·ing, ap·por·tions** To divide and assign according to some plan or proportion; allot: *apportion money for several departments.*

ap·por·tion·ment (ə-pôr′shən-mənt) *n.* The act of apportioning or the condition of being apportioned: *the apportionment of taxes to pay for expenses of running the town government.*

ap·po·site (ăp′ə-zĭt) *adj.* Appropriate or relevant.

ap·po·si·tion (ăp′ə-zĭsh′ən) *n.* **1a.** In grammar, a construction in which a noun or noun phrase is placed with another noun as a further explanation or description. **b.** The relationship between such nouns or noun phrases. For example, *Rufus* and *the scientist* are in apposition in the sentence *Rufus, the scientist, made another discovery.*

ă pat	ôr core		
ā pay	oi boy		
âr care	ou out		
ä father	ŏŏ took		
ĕ pet	ŏŏr lure		
ē be	ōō boot		
ĭ pit	ŭ cut		
ī bite	ûr urge		
îr pier	th thin		
ŏ pot	*th* this		
ō toe	zh vision		
ô paw	ə about		

2. The act of placing side by side or next to each other. **—ap′po·si′tion·al** *adj.* **—ap′po·si′tion·al·ly** *adv.*

ap·pos·i·tive (ə-**pŏz′**ĭ-tĭv) *adj.* Relating to or being in apposition: *an appositive phrase.* ❖ *n.* A noun or phrase that is in apposition with another noun. In the sentence *My friend the chemist works in a laboratory,* the appositive is *the chemist.*

ap·prais·al (ə-**prā′**zəl) *n.* **1.** The act or an instance of appraising. **2.** An official or expert estimate of something, as for quality or worth.

ap·praise (ə-**prāz′**) *tr.v.* **ap·praised, ap·prais·ing, ap·prais·es 1.** To estimate the price or value of: *The jeweler appraised the customer's ring at $500.* **2.** To make a careful judgment about; assess: *The captain appraised the condition of the scuba gear and found it was excellent.* [From Middle English *appreisen,* from Late Latin *appretiāre* : Latin *ad-,* to + Latin *pretium,* price.] **—ap·prais′er** *n.*

ap·pre·cia·ble (ə-**prē′**shə-bəl) *adj.* Capable of being noticed or measured; noticeable: *an appreciable difference in the newly painted house.* **—ap·pre′cia·bly** *adv.*

ap·pre·ci·ate (ə-**prē′**shē-āt′) *v.* **ap·pre·ci·at·ed, ap·pre·ci·at·ing, ap·pre·ci·ates** *—tr.* **1.** To recognize the worth, quality, or importance of; value highly: *The citizens of the new democracy appreciate their freedoms.* **2.** To be aware of or sensitive to; realize: *I appreciate the difficulty of your situation.* **3.** To be thankful for: *The neighbors appreciated our help.* *—intr.* To rise in price or value: *The value of the painting has appreciated over the last ten years.* [From Late Latin *appretiāre,* to appraise.] **—ap·pre′ci·a′tor** *n.*

SYNONYMS appreciate, value, prize, treasure, cherish These verbs mean to have a favorable opinion of someone or something. **Appreciate** means to judge highly in comparison with something else: *That awful restaurant taught me to appreciate home cooking.* **Value** means to have a high opinion of something's importance or worth: *A true democracy values the free exchange of ideas.* **Prize** often suggests feeling pride in owning something: *He prized the movie star's autograph so highly that he is making a frame for it.* **Treasure** and **cherish** both mean to feel fondness when caring about something: *She treasures that quilt—it has been in her family for generations. A solid friendship is something to cherish.*

---

ap·pre·ci·a·tion (ə-prē′shē-**ā′**shən) *n.* **1.** Recognition of the worth, quality, or importance of something: *Your appreciation of her accomplishments has meant a lot to her.* **2.** Gratitude; gratefulness: *They expressed their appreciation with a gift.* **3.** Awareness of artistic values; understanding and enjoyment: *showing a great appreciation of music and sculpture.* **4.** A rise in value or price: *Appreciation of land has made some farmers wealthy.*

ap·pre·cia·tive (ə-**prē′**shə-tĭv *or* ə-**prē′**shē-ā′tĭv) *adj.* Showing or feeling appreciation: *applause of an appreciative audience.* **—ap·pre′cia·tive·ly** *adv.*

ap·pre·hend (ăp′rĭ-**hĕnd′**) *tr.v.* **ap·pre·hend·ed, ap·pre·hend·ing, ap·pre·hends 1.** To take into custody; arrest: *Police officers apprehended the suspect.* **2.** To grasp mentally; understand: *Researchers finally apprehended the true nature of the phenomenon.* [From Middle English *apprehenden,* from Latin *apprehendere,* to seize : *ad-,* to + *prehendere,* to grasp.] **—ap′pre·hend′er** *n.*

ap·pre·hen·sion (ăp′rĭ-**hĕn′**shən) *n.* **1.** Fear or dread of what may happen; anxiety about the future: *The fall in prices caused apprehension among the investors.* **2.** The act of capturing; an arrest: *apprehension of a criminal.* **3.** The ability to understand; understanding.

ap·pre·hen·sive (ăp′rĭ-**hĕn′**sĭv) *adj.* Anxious or fearful; uneasy: *apprehensive about the future.* **—ap′pre·hen′sive·ly** *adv.*

ap·pren·tice (ə-**prĕn′**tĭs) *n.* A person who works for another without pay or at low wages in return for instruction in a craft or trade. ❖ *v.* **ap·pren·ticed, ap·pren·tic·ing, ap·pren·tic·es** *—tr.* To engage (someone) as an apprentice: *In earlier times many children were apprenticed to craftsmen.* *—intr.* To work as an apprentice: *She apprenticed at the ceramics studio.* [From Middle English *apprentis,* from Latin *apprehendere,* to seize.]

ap·pren·tice·ship (ə-**prĕn′**tĭs-shĭp′) *n.* **1.** The condition of being an apprentice. **2.** The period during which one is an apprentice: *She learned many skills during her long apprenticeship in the potter's studio.*

ap·prise (ə-**prīz′**) *tr.v.* **ap·prised, ap·pris·ing, ap·pris·es** To cause to know; inform: *Please apprise your teacher of the principal's message.*

ap·proach (ə-**prōch′**) *v.* **ap·proached, ap·proach·ing, ap·proach·es** *—intr.* To come near or nearer in place or time: *As spring approached, our work neared completion.* *—tr.* **1.** To come near or nearer to (someone or something) in place or time: *The speaker approached the microphone. Our doctor is approaching retirement.* **2.** To come close to in quality, appearance, or other characteristics; approximate: *What could approach the beauty of this lake?* **3.** To begin to deal with or work on: *We approach the task with eagerness.* **4.** To make a proposal to; make overtures to: *I approached the owner for a job.* ❖ *n.* **1a.** The act of approaching: *The captain had to be cautious in his approach to the dock. Many birds fly south at the approach of winter.* **b.** The steps taken prior to a maneuver in a sport, such as the steps of a bowler before delivering the ball. **2.** A way or method of dealing or working with someone or something: *a new approach to the problem.* **3.** A way of reaching a place; an access: *the approach to the bridge.* [From Middle English *approchen,* from Late Latin *appropiāre* : Latin *ad-,* to + Latin *propius,* nearer.] **—ap·proach′er** *n.*

ap·proach·a·ble (ə-**prō′**chə-bəl) *adj.* **1.** Capable of being reached; accessible: *a small town approachable only through a mountain pass.* **2.** Easy to talk to; friendly: *an approachable person.* **—ap·proach′a·bil′i·ty** *n.*

ap·pro·ba·tion (ăp′rə-**bā′**shən) *n.* **1.** The act of approving, especially officially; approval: *The bill to protect the marsh received the approbation of all.* **2.** Praise; commendation: *not a murmur of approbation or blame.*

ap·pro·pri·ate (ə-**prō′**prē-ĭt) *adj.* Suitable for a particular person, condition, occasion, or place; proper: *What are the appropriate clothes for this occasion?* ❖ *tr.v.* (ə-**prō′**prē-āt′) **ap·pro·pri·at·ed, ap·pro·pri·at·ing, ap·pro·pri·ates 1.** To set apart for a particular use: *Congress appropriated money for education.* **2.** To take possession of exclusively for oneself, often without permission: *Another spectator appropriated my seat when I got up for a drink of water.* [From Late Latin *appropriāre,* to make one's own : Latin *ad-,* to + Latin *proprius,* own.] **—ap·pro′pri·ate·ly** *adv.* **—ap·pro′pri·ate·ness** *n.* **—ap·pro′pri·a′tor** *n.*

ap·pro·pri·a·tion (ə-prō′prē-**ā′**shən) *n.* **1.** The act of appropriating to oneself or to a specific use. **2.** Public funds set aside for a specific purpose: *Congressional appropriations for disaster relief.*

ap·prov·al (ə-**prōō′**vəl) *n.* **1.** Favorable regard: *The voters expressed their approval by voting for our mayor again.* **2.** An official consent or sanction: *The article was published with the approval of the editors.* ◆ **on approval** For examination or trial by a customer without the obligation to buy: *We bought our new car on approval.*

ap·prove (ə-**prōōv′**) *v.* **ap·proved, ap·prov·ing, ap·proves** *—tr.* **1.** To confirm or consent to officially; sanction; ratify: *The Senate approved the treaty.* **2.** To regard favorably; consider right or good: *The country approved the president's decision to fund more medical*

WRITERS CHOOSE THEIR WORDS

Frances was **apprehensive** during the train journey to Cambridge. Never having spent so long with Gabriel on his own before, she feared that he might become bored by her company during the weekend, or she by his.

—Ruth Elwin Harris
Frances' Story

WORD HISTORY

apron Sometimes the ear can play tricks on the speakers of a language. Things can be heard in more than one way, and misinterpreted, and the language can change as a result. This is what happened with the words **apron, adder,** and **umpire,** all of which once started with the letter *n.* Some people misheard "a napron" as if it were "an apron" and began writing it that way, moving the *n* to the article *a* as if the word began with a vowel. They did the same with the word *naeddre,* which meant "snake" and became our *adder.* The *nounpere* was literally a "non-equal," someone whose judgments were more important than the judgments of others. That *nounpere* is now calling balls and strikes behind home plate as an umpire.

apron

ă	pat	ôr	core
ā	pay	oi	boy
âr	care	ou	out
ä	father	o͝o	took
ĕ	pet	o͝or	lure
ē	be	o͞o	boot
ĭ	pit	ŭ	cut
ī	bite	ûr	urge
îr	pier	th	thin
ŏ	pot	*th*	this
ō	toe	zh	vision
ô	paw	ə	about

research. —*intr.* To feel, voice, or demonstrate approval: *The neighbors did not approve of our playing football in the street.* [From Middle English *appreven,* to show to be true, from Latin *approbāre* : *ad-,* to + *probāre,* to test (from *probus,* good).]

ap·prov·ing·ly (ə-pro͞o**′**vĭng-lē) *adv.* In a manner that expresses approval: *Our teacher nodded approvingly.*

approx. *abbr.* An abbreviation of: **1.** approximate. **2.** approximately.

ap·prox·i·mate (ə-**prŏk′**sə-mĭt) *adj.* Almost exact or accurate: *the approximate height of the building.* ❖ *v.* (ə-**prŏk′**sə-māt′) **ap·prox·i·mat·ed, ap·prox·i·mat·ing, ap·prox·i·mates** —*tr.* To come close to; be nearly the same as: *The temperatures of the Mediterranean Sea approximate those of Caribbean waters.* —*intr.* To come near or close in degree, nature, or other characteristic. **—ap·prox′i·mate·ly** *adv.*

ap·prox·i·ma·tion (ə-prŏk′sə-**mā′**shən) *n.* Something that is almost but not quite exact, correct, or true: *This table contains metric approximations of measures in yards, feet, and inches.*

ap·pur·te·nance (ə-**pûr′**tn-əns) *n.* **1.** Something added to another, more important thing; an accessory: *The TV set is an appurtenance of modern living.* **2. appurtenances** Equipment, such as clothing or tools, used for a specific purpose; gear: *a tent, cooking utensils, and other appurtenances of camping.* **3.** In law, a right, privilege, or property that belongs with a principal property and goes along with it in case of sale or inheritance.

a·pri·cot (**ăp′**rĭ-kŏt′ *or* **ā′**prĭ-kŏt′) *n.* **1.** A yellow-orange fruit that is similar to a peach but smaller. Apricots are often eaten dried. **2.** The tree that bears such fruit. [Ultimately from Arabic *al-barqūq,* the plum, from Latin *praecoquus,* ripe early : *prae-,* before + *coquere,* to cook, ripen.]

A·pril (**ā′**prəl) *n.* The fourth month of the year in the Gregorian calendar, having 30 days. [From Middle English, from Latin *aprīlis.*]

April Fools' Day *n.* April 1, traditionally celebrated as a day for playing practical jokes.

a·pron (**ā′**prən) *n.* **1.** A garment, usually tied in the back, worn over the front of the body to protect the clothes. **2.** The paved strip in front of an airport hangar or terminal. **3.** The part of the stage in a theater that is in front of the curtain. [From Middle English, from *an apron,* alteration of *a napron,* from Old French *naperon,* from Latin *mappa,* napkin.] —SEE NOTE.

ap·ro·pos (ăp′rə-**pō′**) *adj.* Relevant or fitting: *The teacher's explanation was apropos to the story we read.* ❖ *adv.* At an appropriate time. ❖ *prep.* Concerning; regarding: *Apropos our appointment, I'm afraid I can't make it.*

apropos of *prep.* With regard to: *The candidate told a funny story apropos of politics.*

apse (ăps) *n.* A semicircular, usually domed projection of a building, especially the end of a church in which the altar is located.

apt (ăpt) *adj.* **1.** Exactly suitable; appropriate: *The alert student gave an apt reply.* **2.** Having a tendency; inclined: *Most people are apt to accept the advice of an expert.* **3.** Quick to learn: *an apt student with high grades.* [From Middle English, from Latin *aptus,* past participle of *apere,* to fasten.] **—apt′ly** *adv.* **—apt′ness** *n.*

apt. *abbr.* An abbreviation of apartment.

ap·ti·tude (**ăp′**tĭ-to͞od′) *n.* **1.** A natural ability or talent: *She has a remarkable aptitude for mathematics.* **2.** Quickness in learning and understanding: *a student with high grades showing unusual aptitude.*

aptitude test *n.* A test used to measure a person's ability to learn some particular skill or acquire information.

A·qa·ba (ä′kə-bə *or* **ăk′**ə-bə), **Gulf of** An arm of the Red Sea between the Sinai Peninsula and northwest Saudi Arabia.

aq·ua (**ăk′**wə *or* **ä′**kwə) *n., pl.* **aq·uae** (**ăk′**wē *or* **ä′**kwī′) or **aq·uas 1.** Water. **2.** A light bluish green.

aq·ua·cul·ture (**ăk′**wə-kŭl′chər *or* **ä′**kwə-kŭl′chər) *n.* The cultivation of marine or freshwater organisms, especially food fish or shellfish such as salmon or oysters, under controlled conditions.

aq·ua·ma·rine (ăk′wə-mə-**rēn′** *or* ä′kwə-mə-**rēn′**) *n.* **1.** A transparent blue-green variety of beryl, used as a gemstone. **2.** A pale blue to light greenish blue.

aq·ua·plane (**ăk′**wə-plān′ *or* **ä′**kwə-plān′) *n.* A board on which a person stands and rides while it is towed over the water by a motorboat. ❖ *tr.v.* **aq·ua·planed, aq·ua·plan·ing, aq·ua·planes** To ride on an aquaplane. **—aq′ua·plan′er** *n.*

aqua re·gi·a (**rē′**jē-ə *or* **rē′**jə) *n.* A fuming corrosive mixture of nitric acid and hydrochloric acid, used for testing metals and dissolving gold and platinum.

a·quar·i·um (ə-**kwâr′**ē-əm) *n., pl.* **a·quar·i·ums** or **a·quar·i·a** (ə-**kwâr′**ē-ə) **1.** A tank or other container, such as a glass bowl, filled with water for keeping and displaying fishes or other animals and plants. **2.** A place where fishes and other sea animals are displayed to the public.

A·quar·i·us (ə-**kwâr′**ē-əs) *n.* **1.** A constellation in the Southern Hemisphere near Pisces, traditionally pictured as a man carrying a container of water. **2.** The eleventh sign of the zodiac in astrology.

a·quat·ic (ə-**kwăt′**ĭk *or* ə-**kwŏt′**ĭk) *adj.* **1.** Consisting of, relating to, or being in water: *an aquatic environment.* **2.** Living or growing in or on the water: *aquatic insects; aquatic plants.* **3.** Taking place in or on the water: *diving and other aquatic sports.*

aq·ue·duct (**ăk′**wĭ-dŭkt′) *n.* **1.** A large pipe or channel that carries water from a distant source. **2.** A structure that supports such a pipe or channel across low ground or a river. [From Latin *aquaeductus* : *aquae,* of water + *ductus,* a leading.]

a·que·ous (**ā′**kwē-əs *or* **ăk′**wē-əs) *adj.* Relating to, resembling, or containing water: *an aqueous solution of salt and water.*

aqueous humor *n.* A clear fluid that fills the space between the cornea and lens of the eye.

aq·ui·fer (**ăk′**wə-fər) *n.* An underground layer of sand, gravel, or porous rock that holds water.

aq·ui·line (**ăk′**wə-līn′ *or* **ăk′**wə-lĭn) *adj.* **1.** Curved or hooked like an eagle's beak: *an aquiline nose.* **2.** Relating to or resembling an eagle. [From Latin *aquilīnus,* from *aquila,* eagle.]

A·qui·nas (ə-**kwī′**nəs), Saint. **Thomas** 1225–1274. Italian friar, theologian, and philosopher.

Ar The symbol for the element **argon.**

AR *abbr.* An abbreviation of Arkansas.

-ar *suff.* A suffix that means relating to or resembling: *angular; linear.*

Ar·ab (**ăr′**əb) *n.* **1.** A member of a Semitic people inhabiting Arabia. **2.** A member of an Arabic-speaking people. **—Ar′ab** *adj.*

ar·a·besque (ăr′ə-**bĕsk′**) *n.* **1.** A ballet position in which the dancer stands on one leg with the other leg extending straight back. **2.** An intricate or interwoven pattern or design: *walls adorned with an arabesque of flowers and leaves.*

A·ra·bi·a (ə-**rā′**bē-ə) also **A·ra·bi·an Peninsula** (ə-**rā′**bē-ən) A peninsula of southwest Asia between the Red Sea and the Persian Gulf. It includes the countries of Saudi Arabia, Yemen, Oman, the United Arab Emirates, Qatar, Bahrain, and Kuwait.

Arabian horse *n.* Any of a breed of swift horse native to Arabia.

Arabian Nights *n.* A collection of ancient folk tales derived partly from Persian and Indian sources, originally written in Arabic in the ninth century.

Arabian Sea The northwest part of the Indian Ocean between Arabia and western India. It is an important trade route between India and the West.

Ar·a·bic (ăr′ə-bĭk) *adj.* Relating to Arabia, the Arabs, or their language or culture. ❖ *n.* A Semitic language consisting of many dialects that is spoken in many countries in southwestern Asia and northern Africa.

Arabic numeral *n.* One of the numerical symbols 1, 2, 3, 4, 5, 6, 7, 8, 9, or 0. They originated in India but are called Arabic numerals because Europeans first learned about them from Arabic written sources.

ar·a·ble (ăr′ə-bəl) *adj.* Fit for cultivation: *arable land.*

a·rach·nid (ə-răk′nĭd) *n.* Any of a large group of invertebrate animals that resemble insects but have eight rather than six legs, no wings or antennae, and a body divided into two rather than three parts. Spiders, scorpions, ticks, and mites are arachnids.

Ar·a·fat (ăr′ə-făt′), **Yasir** also **Yasser** 1929–2004. Leader of the Palestine Liberation Organization who in 1996 was elected president of the Palestinian Authority, the newly formed Palestinian self-rule government.

Ar·a·gon (ăr′ə-gŏn′) A region and former kingdom of northeast Spain. It was united with Castile in 1479 to form the core of modern Spain.

Ar·al Sea (ăr′əl) An inland sea between southern Kazakhstan and northwest Uzbekistan east of the Caspian Sea. The diversion of water from its major sources has greatly reduced the size of the Aral Sea.

Ar·a·ma·ic (ăr′ə-mā′ĭk) *n.* The Semitic language originally of the ancient Syrians, used in modern form in certain countries of southwest Asia.

A·rap·a·ho (ə-răp′ə-hō′) *n., pl.* **Arapaho** or **A·rap·a·hos 1.** A member of a Native American people living in Oklahoma and Wyoming. **2.** The Algonquian language of the Arapaho.

Ar·a·rat (ăr′ə-răt′), **Mount** A mountain peak of extreme eastern Turkey near the Iranian border rising to about 16,850 feet (5,136 meters). It is the traditional resting place of Noah's ark.

Ar·au·ca·ni·an (ăr′ô-kā′nē-ən) *n.* **1.** A family of languages spoken by native peoples of south-central Chile and western Argentina. **2.** A member of a people speaking an Araucanian language. **—Ar′au·ca′ni·an** *adj.*

Ar·a·wak (ăr′ə-wäk′) *n., pl.* **Arawak** or **Ar·a·waks 1.** A member of an American Indian people formerly living in the West Indies and now living chiefly in northeast South America. **2.** The Arawakan language of the Arawak.

Ar·a·wa·kan (ăr′ə-wä′kən) *n., pl.* **Arawakan** or **Ar·a·wa·kans 1.** A member of a widespread group of native peoples living in northern South America and formerly in most of the Greater Antilles. **2.** A family of languages spoken by these peoples. **—Ar′a·wa′kan** *adj.*

ar·bi·ter (är′bĭ-tər) *n.* **1.** A person chosen to judge a dispute; an arbitrator. **2.** A person or thing having the power to ordain or judge at will: *Celebrities often act as unofficial arbiters of fashion.*

ar·bi·trar·y (är′bĭ-trĕr′ē) *adj.* **1.** Based on a whim, impulse, or chance, not on reason or law: *Drawing numbers out of a hat was an arbitrary way to select the captain of the team.* **2.** Not limited by law; despotic: *The dictator's arbitrary government jailed many of his political opponents.* **—ar′bi·trar′i·ly** (är′bĭ-trâr′ə-lē) *adv.* **—ar′bi·trar′i·ness** *n.*

ar·bi·trate (är′bĭ-trāt′) *v.* **ar·bi·trat·ed, ar·bi·trat·ing, ar·bi·trates** *—tr.* **1.** To decide as an arbitrator: *arbitrate the boundary dispute between the two neighbors.* **2.** To submit to judgment by arbitration: *Management and labor agreed to arbitrate their differences.* *—intr.* To serve as an arbitrator: *Even strong nations must allow others to arbitrate between them.*

ar·bi·tra·tion (är′bĭ-trā′shən) *n.* The process of referring the issues in a dispute to an impartial person or group for judgment or settlement: *Many disputes between labor and management are settled by arbitration.*

ar·bi·tra·tor (är′bĭ-trā′tər) *n.* **1.** A person chosen to settle a dispute or controversy. **2.** A person having the ability or power to make authoritative decisions; an arbiter.

ar·bor (är′bər) *n.* A shady resting place in a garden or park, often made of latticework on which vines or other climbing plants grow: *a grape arbor; a rose arbor.* [From Middle English *herber*, from Old French *erbier*, garden, from *erbe*, herb.]

Arbor Day *n.* A day observed in many areas by planting trees, often occurring in the spring.

ar·bo·re·al (är-bôr′ē-əl) *adj.* **1.** Living in trees: *arboreal marsupials.* **2.** Relating to or resembling a tree. [From Latin *arbor*, tree.] **—ar·bo′re·al·ly** *adv.*

ar·bo·re·tum (är′bə-rē′təm) *n.* A place where trees and other plants are cultivated for scientific, educational, and ornamental purposes.

ar·bor·vi·tae (är′bər-vī′tē) *n.* Any of several evergreen trees or shrubs having scalelike leaves and small cones, often planted in hedges.

ar·bu·tus (är-byo͞o′təs) *n.* **1.** A low-growing eastern North American shrub having evergreen leaves and clusters of fragrant pink or white flowers. **2.** Any of various evergreen trees or shrubs of Europe and western North America, having flaky bark and small red fruit.

arc (ärk) *n.* **1.** Something shaped like a curve or arch: *the arc of a rainbow.* **2.** A segment of a circle. **3.** A stream of brilliant light or sparks produced when an electric current jumps across the gap between two electrodes separated by a gas. **4.** A progression of events in a story or narration, especially one that leads to a climax and settles in a conclusion. ❖ *intr.v.* **arced** (ärkt), **arc·ing** (är′kĭng), **arcs 1.** To form an arc. **2.** To take or follow a curved path: *The diver arced into the water.* [From Middle English *ark*, path of a heavenly body, from Latin *arcus*, bow.]

❑ *These sound alike:* **arc, ark** (ship).

ar·cade (är-kad′) *n.* **1.** A series of arches supported by columns or pillars. **2.** A roofed passageway, especially one with shops on either side. **3.** A commercial establishment where customers pay to play mechanical or electronic games.

Ar·ca·di·a (är-kā′dē-ə) A region of ancient Greece in the Peloponnesus. According to legend, its relatively isolated inhabitants lived a simple, pastoral life.

arch¹ (ärch) *n.* **1a.** A usually curved structure forming the upper edge of an open space and supporting the weight above it, as in a bridge or doorway. **b.** A structure, such as a monument, shaped like an upside-down U. **2.** A curved shape or object having the ends lower than the middle: *the arch of leaves overhanging the lane.* **3.** Any of various arch-shaped structures of the body: *the arch of the foot.* ❖ *v.* **arched, arch·ing, arch·es** *—tr.* **1.** To cause to form an arch or a similar curve: *The cat arched its back.* **2.** To provide or build with an arch: *The entrance to the store was arched.* *—intr.* To extend in an arch: *The bridge arched across the river.* [From Middle English, from Latin *arcus*.]

arch² (ärch) *adj.* **1.** Chief; principal: *our arch rivals.* **2.** Teasing, ironic, or sardonic: *an arch reply.* [From *arch-*, chief, from Greek *arkhi-*.] **—arch′ly** *adv.* **—arch′ness** *n.*

arch– *pref.* A prefix that means principal or chief: *archdiocese; archenemy.*

ar·chae·bac·te·ri·um (är′kē-băk-tîr′ē-əm) *n., pl.* **ar·chae·bac·te·ri·a** (är′kē-băk-tîr′ē-ə) An archaeon.

ar·chae·ol·o·gy or **ar·che·ol·o·gy** (är′kē-ŏl′ə-jē) *n.* The study of the remains of past human life and culture, such as graves, tools, and pottery. **—ar′chae·o·log′i·cal** (är′-

WRITERS CHOOSE THEIR WORDS

She began to describe this year's group [of children] and its variety of personalities, though she singled no one out by name. She mentioned that there was one who had singular skills at caretaking, another who loved newchildren, one with unusual scientific **aptitude,** and a fourth for whom physical labor was an obvious pleasure.

—Lois Lowry
The Giver

aqueduct
Pont du Gard, near Nîmes, France

arabesque

arch¹

SCIENCE

archaeon When the single-celled organisms now known as **archaea** were first described in the 1970s, they were named archaebacteria. "Bacteria" because they looked a lot like bacteria, and "archae" (ancient) because scientists thought their ancestors were the first life forms on Earth. But new research brought a name change. It's true that archaea have no nucleus, like bacteria; however, their cell walls are made of different chemicals, and their genes are quite different, too. They are as different from bacteria as bacteria are from us. And it turns out that archaea may have evolved from ancient bacteria rather than vice versa. Today they inhabit some of the most inhospitable places on the earth: boiling hot springs, super salty seas, ice-cold oceans, and the stomachs of cows.

archaeopteryx
fossilized skeleton

ă	pat	ôr	core
ā	pay	oi	boy
âr	care	ou	out
ä	father	o͝o	took
ĕ	pet	o͝or	lure
ē	be	o͞o	boot
ĭ	pit	ŭ	cut
ī	bite	ûr	urge
îr	pier	th	thin
ŏ	pot	*th*	this
ō	toe	zh	vision
ô	paw	ə	about

kē-ə-**lŏj′**ĭ-kəl) *adj.* **—ar′chae·o·log′i·cal·ly** *adv.* **—ar′chae·ol′o·gist** *n.*

ar·chae·on (är**′**kē-ŏn′) *n., pl.* **ar·chae·a** (**är′**kē-ə) Any of a group of one-celled organisms that are similar to bacteria in some ways, as in lacking a nucleus, but are different from them genetically and biochemically. Archaea usually live in extreme environments, such as very hot or salty ones. —SEE NOTE.

ar·chae·op·ter·yx (är′kē-**ŏp′**tər-ĭks) *n.* A small extinct vertebrate having feathered wings with claws, a long snout with teeth, and a feathered bony tail. It is thought to have been one of the earliest birds. [From Greek *arkhaios*, ancient + Greek *pterux*, wing.]

ar·cha·ic (är-**kā′**ĭk) *adj.* **1.** Not current; antiquated: *archaic laws to regulate horse-drawn traffic.* **2.** Relating to or characteristic of an early period of human culture or of evolutionary history: *archaic Greek art; archaic fishes from the Ordovician Period.* **3.** Relating to words that were once common but are now rare and used chiefly to suggest an earlier style: Methinks *is an archaic word meaning "It seems to me."* [From Greek *arkhaios*, ancient, from *arkhē*, beginning.] **—ar·cha′i·cal·ly** *adv.*

ar·cha·ism (**är′**kē-ĭz′əm *or* **är′**kā-ĭz′əm) *n.* An archaic word or expression.

arch·an·gel (**ärk′**ān′jəl) *n.* An angel of high rank.

arch·bish·op (ärch-**bĭsh′**əp) *n.* A bishop of the highest rank, heading an archdiocese or church province.

arch·dea·con (ärch-**dē′**kən) *n.* A church official, especially of the Anglican Church, in charge of business and other affairs in a diocese.

arch·di·o·cese (ärch-**dī′**ə-sĭs *or* ärch-**dī′**ə-sēs′) *n.* The area under an archbishop's jurisdiction.

arch·duch·ess (ärch-**dŭch′**ĭs) *n.* **1.** The wife or widow of an archduke. **2.** A princess of the former Austrian royal family.

arch·duke (ärch-**do͞ok′**) *n.* A prince of the former Austrian royal family.

arched (ärcht) *adj.* **1.** Provided, made, or covered with an arch: *an arched bridge.* **2.** Forming a curve like that of an arch: *the arched dome of the night sky.*

arch·en·e·my (ärch-**ĕn′**ə-mē) *n.* A chief or most important enemy: *France was the archenemy of Britain in Colonial America.*

ar·che·o·log·i·cal (är′kē-ə-**lŏj′**ĭ-kəl) *adj.* Variant of **archaeological.**

ar·che·ol·o·gist (är′kē-**ŏl′**ə-jĭst) *n.* Variant of **archaeologist.**

ar·che·ol·o·gy (är′kē-**ŏl′**ə-jē) *n.* Variant of **archaeology.**

arch·er (**är′**chər) *n.* A person who shoots with a bow and arrow.

arch·er·y (**är′**chə-rē) *n.* The sport or skill of shooting with a bow and arrow.

ar·che·type (**är′**kĭ-tīp′) *n.* An original model or form after which other, similar things are patterned: *The Wright brothers' first plane served as the archetype for later airplanes.*

Ar·chi·me·des (är′kə-**mē′**dēz) 287?–212 BC. Greek mathematician, engineer, and physicist. He made many mathematical discoveries, including formulas for the area and volume of various geometric figures.

ar·chi·pel·a·go (är′kə-**pĕl′**ə-gō′) *n., pl.* **ar·chi·pel·a·goes** or **ar·chi·pel·a·gos 1.** A large group of islands. **2.** A sea in which there is a large group of islands.

ar·chi·tect (**är′**kĭ-tĕkt′) *n.* **1.** A person who designs and directs the construction of buildings and other large structures. **2.** A person who plans, organizes, or designs something: *The delegates to the Constitutional Convention were the architects of the Constitution.* [From Greek *arkhitektōn* : *arkhi-*, principal, chief + *tektōn*, builder.]

ar·chi·tec·tur·al (är′kĭ-**tĕk′**chər-əl) *adj.* Relating to architecture. **—ar′chi·tec′tur·al·ly** *adv.*

ar·chi·tec·ture (**är′**kĭ-tĕk′chər) *n.* **1.** The art and occupation of designing and directing the construction of buildings and other large structures, such as bridges. **2.** A style of building: *Many government buildings in Washington DC are patterned on classical architecture.* **3.** Buildings and other large structures: *the stately architecture of the New York City skyline.* **4.** The orderly arrangement of parts; structure: *the architecture of a story.*

ar·chi·trave (**är′**kĭ-trāv′) *n.* The bottom part of an entablature in classical architecture.

ar·chive (**är′**kīv′) *n.* **1.** often **archives** A place or collection containing records and documents of historical interest: *We went to the film archives to research silent movies.* **2.** A long-term storage area of computer memory for backup copies of computer files, or for inactive computer files. **—ar·chi′val** *adj.*

arch·way (**ärch′**wā′) *n.* **1.** A passageway under an arch. **2.** An arch that covers or encloses an entrance or passageway.

–archy *suff.* A suffix that means a kind of rule or government: *oligarchy.*

arc lamp *n.* A lamp in which an electric current crosses between electrodes separated by a gas and generates an arc that produces light.

arc·tic (**ärk′**tĭk *or* **är′**tĭk) *adj.* Extremely cold; frigid: *arctic weather.* [From Middle English *artik*, northern, from Greek *arktikos*, from *arktos*, bear, the northern constellation Ursa Major.]

Arctic A region between the North Pole and the northern timberlines of North America and Eurasia. **—Arctic** *adj.*

Arctic Archipelago A group of more than 36,000 islands of northern Canada in the Arctic Ocean between North America and Greenland.

Arctic Circle The parallel of latitude approximately 66 degrees 33 minutes north. It forms the boundary between the North Temperate Zone and North Frigid Zone.

Arctic Ocean The waters surrounding the North Pole between North America and Eurasia. The smallest ocean in the world, it is covered by ice through much of the year.

Arc·tu·rus (ärk-**to͝or′**əs) *n.* The brightest star in the northern sky other than the sun. It is in the constellation Boötes.

ar·dent (**är′**dnt) *adj.* **1.** Expressing or full of warmth of passion, desire, or other emotion; passionate: *an ardent wish for his recovery.* **2.** Strongly enthusiastic; extremely devoted; eager: *an ardent defender of the free press.* [From Middle English *ardaunt*, from Latin *ārdēre*, to burn.] **—ar′dent·ly** *adv.*

ar·dor (**är′**dər) *n.* Great warmth or intensity of passion, desire, or other emotion: *the driving ardor of a reformer.*

ar·du·ous (**är′**jo͞o-əs) *adj.* Demanding great effort; difficult: *arduous training; an arduous task.* **—ar′du·ous·ly** *adv.* **—ar′du·ous·ness** *n.*

are (är) *v.* **1.** Second person singular present tense of **be. 2.** First, second, and third person plural present tense of **be.** [From Old English *aron, earon.*]

ar·e·a (**âr′**ē-ə) *n.* **1a.** A section or region, as of land: *an industrial area full of factories; the Los Angeles area including its suburbs.* **b.** A part or section, as of a building: *The cafeteria is an eating area for employees.* **2.** The extent of a surface or plane figure as measured in square units: *The area of a rectangle is the product of the length and the width.* **3.** A range, as of activity or study: *the area of medical research.* **—ar′e·al** *adj.*

area code *n.* A three-digit number used before a seven-digit telephone number. Area codes were originally assigned to specific geographical areas.

ar·e·a·way (**âr′**ē-ə-wā′) *n.* **1.** A small sunken area allowing access or light and air to basement doors or windows. **2.** A passageway between buildings.

a·re·na (ə-**rē′**nə) *n.* **1.** An enclosed area or building for presenting athletic contests and other events for large audiences. **2.** The space in the center of an ancient Roman amphitheater where athletic contests and other spectacles were held. **3.** An area of conflict or activity: *The new candidate stepped into the political arena.* [From Latin *arēna*, sand, a sand-strewn place of combat in an amphitheater.]

aren't (ärnt *or* **är′**ənt) **1.** Contraction of *are not: They aren't there.* **2.** Contraction of *am not.* Used in questions: *I'm properly dressed for school, aren't I?*

Ar·es (**âr′**ēz) *n.* In Greek mythology, the god of war, identified with the Roman Mars.

Ar·gen·ti·na (är′jən-**tē′**nə) A country of southeast South America extending from Bolivia to southern Tierra del Fuego, an island it shares with Chile. Buenos Aires is the capital.

ar·gi·nine (**är′**jə-nēn′) *n.* An essential amino acid that is found in plant and animal protein.

Ar·go (**är′**gō′) *n.* In Greek mythology, Jason's ship in his search for the Golden Fleece.

ar·gon (**är′**gŏn′) *n. Symbol* **Ar** A colorless, odorless, chemically inert gaseous element that makes up about one percent of the atmosphere and is used in electric light bulbs and fluorescent tubes. Atomic number 18. See **Periodic Table.**

Ar·go·naut (**är′**gə-nôt′) *n.* In Greek mythology, any of the men who sailed with Jason on the *Argo* in search of the Golden Fleece.

ar·go·sy (**är′**gə-sē) *n., pl.* **ar·go·sies 1.** A big sailing merchant ship. **2.** A fleet of such ships. [From Italian *ragusea*, vessel of Ragusa (Dubrovnik, in southern Croatia).]

ar·got (**är′**gō *or* **är′**gət) *n.* The jargon or slang of a particular class or group of people, often used to conceal meaning from outsiders.

ar·gue (**är′**gyo͞o) *v.* **ar·gued, ar·gu·ing, ar·gues** —*tr.* **1.** To give reasons for or against (something, such as an opinion or proposal); debate: *The lawyer argued the case in court.* **2.** To prove or attempt to prove by reasoning; maintain: *I argued that the vacant lot should be turned into a park.* **3.** To give evidence of; indicate: *Her vocabulary argues that she has read a lot.* **4.** To persuade or influence, as by presenting reasons: *He would not let us argue him into leaving early.* —*intr.* **1.** To put forth reasons for or against something: *argue against building a new airport.* **2.** To engage in a quarrel; dispute: *The twins seldom argued with each other.* [From Middle English *arguen*, from Old French *arguer*, from Latin *arguere*, to make clear.] **—ar′gu·a·ble** *adj.* **—ar′gu·a·bly** *adv.* **—ar′gu·er** *n.*

ar·gu·ment (**är′**gyə-mənt) *n.* **1.** A quarrel or dispute: *an argument over who goes first.* **2.** A discussion of differing points of view; a debate: *a scientific argument.* **3.** A series of statements logically connected in support of a position: *tried to formulate an argument for tax reform.*

ar·gu·men·ta·tive (är′gyə-**mĕn′**tə-tĭv) *adj.* **1.** Given to arguing: *an argumentative person.* **2.** Containing or full of arguments: *an argumentative paper.* **—ar′gu·men′ta·tive·ly** *adv.*

Ar·gus (**är′**gəs) *n.* In Greek mythology, a giant with one hundred eyes.

ar·gyle also **ar·gyll** (**är′**gīl′) *n.* **1.** A knitting pattern made up of diamond shapes in contrasting colors. **2.** A sock knit in such a pattern. [After Clan Campbell of *Argyle*, Argyll, a former county of western Scotland, originally from the pattern of their tartan.]

a·ri·a (**ä′**rē-ə) *n.* A melodic piece written for a solo singer accompanied by instruments, as in an opera, cantata, or oratorio. [From Italian *aria*, air, tune, aria, from Latin *āēr*, air, atmosphere, from Greek.]

Ar·i·ad·ne (ăr′ē-**ăd′**nē) *n.* In Greek mythology, the daughter of King Minos and Pasiphaë who helped Theseus escape from the Minotaur's labyrinth.

a·ri·a·ry (ä′rē-**ä′**rē) *n., pl.* **a·ri·a·ries** The basic monetary unit of Madagascar.

ar·id (**ăr′**ĭd) *adj.* **1.** Having little or no rainfall; dry: *an arid desert; an arid wasteland.* **2.** Lifeless; dull: *an arid lecture.* **—a·rid′i·ty** (ə-**rĭd′**ĭ-tē), **ar′id·ness** *n.* **—ar′id·ly** *adv.*

Ar·ies (**âr′**ēz) *n.* **1.** A constellation in the Northern Hemisphere, traditionally pictured as a ram. **2.** The first sign of the zodiac in astrology. [From Latin *ariēs*, ram.]

a·right (ə-**rīt′**) *adv.* Properly; correctly.

A·rik·a·ra (ə-**rĭk′**ər-ə) *n., pl.* **Arikara** or **A·rik·a·ras 1.** A member of a Native American people of North Dakota. **2.** The Caddoan language of the Arikara.

a·rise (ə-**rīz′**) *intr.v.* **a·rose** (ə-**rōz′**), **a·ris·en** (ə-**rĭz′**ən), **a·ris·ing, a·ris·es 1.** To get up: *He arose from his chair to greet me.* **2.** To awaken and get up: *She arose at dawn.* **3.** To ascend; move upward: *Mist arose from the lake.* **4.** To come into being; appear: *Take advantage of opportunities as they arise.* **5.** To result; proceed: *The breakdown arose from some temporary defect.*

ar·is·toc·ra·cy (ăr′ĭ-**stŏk′**rə-sē) *n., pl.* **ar·is·toc·ra·cies 1a.** A social class based on inherited wealth, status, and sometimes titles. **b.** A government controlled by such a class. **2.** A group considered superior to others: *the aristocracy of local landowners.* [From Greek *aristokratiā* : *aristos*, best + *-kratiā*, government.]

a·ris·to·crat (ə-**rĭs′**tə-krăt′ *or* **ăr′**ĭs-tə-krăt′) *n.* **1.** A member of a ruling class or of the nobility. **2.** A person who favors government by the aristocracy.

a·ris·to·crat·ic (ə-rĭs′tə-**krăt′**ĭk *or* ăr′ĭs-tə-**krăt′**ĭk) *adj.* **1.** Relating to or characteristic of the aristocracy: *aristocratic manners.* **2.** Having an aristocracy as a form of government: *aristocratic city-states of ancient Greece.* **—a·ris′to·crat′i·cal·ly** *adv.*

Ar·is·to·te·li·an (ăr′ĭ-stə-**tē′**lē-ən *or* ə-rĭs′tə-**tē′**lē-ən) *adj.* Relating to the Greek philosopher Aristotle or his philosophy. ❖ *n.* **1.** A follower of Aristotle or his teachings. **2.** A person who is guided by experience or tends to be scientific in methods or thought. **—Ar′is·to·te′li·an·ism** *n.*

Ar·is·tot·le (**ăr′**ĭ-stŏt′l) 384–322 BC. Greek philosopher and scientist whose works on logic, the natural sciences, politics, and poetry profoundly influenced Western thought. His systematic approach to scientific study later evolved into the basic scientific method in the Western world.

a·rith·me·tic (ə-**rĭth′**mĭ-tĭk) *n.* **1.** The study of numbers and their properties under the operations of addition, subtraction, multiplication, and division. **2.** Calculation using these operations: *I added up the bill, but my arithmetic was wrong.* ❖ *adj.* **ar·ith·met·ic** (ăr′ĭth-**mĕt′**ĭk) or **ar·ith·met·i·cal** (ăr′ĭth-**mĕt′**ĭ-kəl) Relating to arithmetic; according to the rules of arithmetic: *arithmetic computations.* [From Middle English *arsmetike*, from Greek *arithmētikē (tekhnē)*, (art) of counting, from *arithmos*, number.] **—ar′ith·met′i·cal·ly** *adv.*

a·rith·me·ti·cian (ə-rĭth′mə-**tĭsh′**ən) *n.* A person who specializes in the study of arithmetic.

ar·ith·met·ic mean (ăr′ĭth-**mĕt′**ĭk) *n.* An average of a set of quantities obtained by adding all the quantities and dividing the result by the number of quantities in the set.

ar·ith·met·ic progression (ăr′ĭth-**mĕt′**ĭk) *n.* A sequence of numbers such as 1, 3, 5, 7, 9 . . . or 14, 9, 4, −1 . . . in which the difference between any successive pair of numbers is the same.

Ar·i·zo·na (ăr′ĭ-**zō′**nə) A state of the southwest United States west of New Mexico on the Mexican border. It

WRITERS CHOOSE THEIR WORDS

"You know, Dad," Courtney said. "If I'm going to be home-schooled for a couple of months, I'm not going to be able to sit on that hard chair down here, in front of that **archaic** old bucket of bolts you call a computer. I think we're going to have to—" Courtney stopped short when she saw that her father had lifted up a cardboard box from behind the couch that, by the look of the markings on it, contained a brand-new laptop.

—D.J. MacHale
The Quillan Games

archery

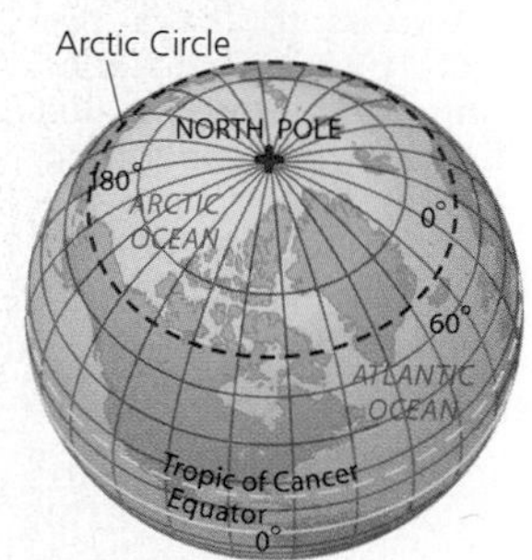

Arctic Circle

10 ft.

5 ft.

area

To calculate the area of a rectangle, multiply the length by the width. The area of this rectangle is 50 square feet.

GEOGRAPHY

Arizona The name **Arizona** comes to us through Spanish from a Native American word meaning "place of the small spring." What is now Arizona used to be part of Mexico, and in fact the spring referred to in the name is still in Mexico to this day. The name of the area around the spring spread to a region to the north that gradually became part of the United States: most of it was handed over by Mexico in 1848 after Mexico lost the Mexican-American War, and the rest of it was sold to the United States in 1853.

GEOGRAPHY

Arkansas The name **Arkansas** comes from *akansea,* the Illinois name for the Quapaw. The Quapaw were a Native American people living along the Arkansas River. The final *s* was added to the name by French explorers to make the word plural when referring to this group. But final *s* is not pronounced in French, and since the word came into English by way of French, the *s* is silent for us as well.

ă	pat	ôr	core
ā	pay	oi	boy
âr	care	ou	out
ä	father	o͝o	took
ĕ	pet	o͝or	lure
ē	be	o͞o	boot
ĭ	pit	ŭ	cut
ī	bite	ûr	urge
îr	pier	th	thin
ŏ	pot	*th*	this
ō	toe	zh	vision
ô	paw	ə	about

was admitted as the 48th state in 1912. Phoenix is the capital. —SEE NOTE.

ark (ärk) *n.* **1.** In the Bible, the ship built by Noah for survival during the Flood. **2.** The Ark of the Covenant. **3.** A cabinet in a synagogue in which the scrolls of the Torah are kept; the Holy Ark. [From Old English *arc,* from Latin *arca,* chest.]
❑ *These sound alike:* **ark, arc** (part of a curve).

Ar·kan·sas (är**′**kən-sô′) A state of the south-central United States north of Louisiana and bordered on the east by the Mississippi River. It was admitted as the 25th state in 1836. Little Rock is the capital. —SEE NOTE.

Ar·kan·sas River (är**′**kən-sô′ *or* är-**kăn′**zəs) A river of the south-central United States rising in central Colorado and flowing about 1,450 miles (2,350 kilometers) to the Mississippi River in southeast Arkansas. It was an important trade and travel route in the 1800s.

Ark of the Covenant *n.* In the Bible, the chest containing the Ten Commandments on stone tablets, carried by the Hebrews during their wanderings in the desert.

Ar·ling·ton (är**′**lĭng-tən) A county and city of northern Virginia across the Potomac River from Washington, DC. It is the site of **Arlington National Cemetery,** where American war dead and other prominent figures are buried.

arm¹ (ärm) *n.* **1a.** Either of the upper limbs of the human body, connecting the hand and wrist to the shoulder. **b.** A part similar to a human arm, such as the forelimb of an animal or a long part projecting from a central support in a machine. **2.** A relatively narrow extension sticking out from a large mass: *an arm of the sea.* **3.** Something designed to cover or support a human arm: *the arm of a shirt; the arm of a chair.* **4.** A division or branch of an organization: *the investigative arm of the Justice Department.* **5.** The skill of throwing or pitching a ball well: *The shortstop has a good arm.* ◆ **an arm and a leg** An excessively high price: *charged me an arm and a leg for the antiques.* **at arm's length 1.** With the arm extended straight out from the body: *The art dealer held the picture at arm's length and looked at it.* **2.** At a distance; not on friendly or intimate terms: *A shy person often keeps acquaintances at an arm's length.* **with open arms** In a very friendly manner: *welcomed friends with open arms.* [From Old English *earm.*]

arm² (ärm) *n.* **1.** A weapon, especially a firearm: *the troops stacked the arms and made camp.* **2. arms** Warfare or military power: *The besieged city could not be taken by force of arms.* **3. arms** A design or emblem used as an identifying mark, as by a family or nation. ❖ *v.* **armed, arm·ing, arms** —*tr.* **1.** To equip with weapons or other means of defense: *The governor of the young colony armed civilians during the emergency.* **2.** To equip or provide with something necessary or useful: *Many people do not arm themselves with the facts before getting into an argument.* **3.** To make ready; prepare: *arm the mechanism of a trap.* —*intr.* To prepare for war, as by amassing weapons and training soldiers: *As the countries armed, the leaders reached a settlement.* ◆ **up in arms** Very upset; angry: *The whole neighborhood was up in arms when the mayor closed the fire station.* [From Middle English *armes,* weapons, from Latin *arma.*]

ar·ma·da (är-mä**′**də *or* är-**mā′**də) *n.* A big fleet of warships. [From Spanish, from Medieval Latin *armāta.*]

ar·ma·dil·lo (är′mə-**dĭl′**ō) *n., pl.* **ar·ma·dil·los** Any of various burrowing mammals of southern North America and Central and South America, having an armorlike covering of jointed bony plates. [From Spanish, diminutive of *armado,* armored, from Latin *armāre,* to arm, from *arma,* arms.] —SEE NOTE.

Ar·ma·ged·don (är′mə-**gĕd′**n) *n.* **1.** In the Bible, the prophesied place where armies will gather for battle at the end of the world. **2.** A decisive or catastrophic conflict.

ar·ma·ment (är**′**mə-mənt) *n.* **1.** The weapons and supplies of war with which a military unit is equipped. **2.** often **armaments** All the military forces and war equipment of a country. **3.** Preparation for war: *Armament is a function of national security in time of war.*

ar·ma·ture (är**′**mə-chər) *n.* **1a.** A rotating part of an electric motor or generator, consisting of wire wound around an iron core. **b.** A piece of soft iron connecting the poles of a magnet. **c.** The part of an electromagnetic device, such as a relay, buzzer, or loudspeaker, that moves or vibrates. **2.** A framework, especially one used as a support for clay sculpture. **3.** A part or organ on an animal or plant that helps to protect it from attack or injury. A porcupine's quills are its armature.

arm·band (**ärm′**bănd′) *n.* A piece of cloth worn around the upper arm, often as a sign of mourning or protest.

arm·chair (**ärm′**châr′) *n.* A chair with supports on the sides for one's arms. ❖ *adj.* Remote from the field of action: *an armchair detective.*

armed¹ (ärmd) *adj.* **1.** Having arms: *an armed chair.* **2.** Having arms of a certain number or kind: *an eight-armed squid.*

armed² (ärmd) *adj.* **1.** Furnished with a weapon or weapons: *an armed police escort.* **2.** Using a weapon or weapons: *an armed attack.*

armed forces *pl.n.* The organizations and people involved in waging wars and defending a country from physical attack, including the army, navy, and air force.

Ar·me·ni·a (är-**mē′**nē-ə) A country of western Asia east of Turkey and north of Iran. It was formerly a kingdom that extended into northeast Turkey and northwest Iran. Armenia was part of the USSR from 1922 to 1991. Yerevan is the capital.

Ar·me·ni·an (är-**mē′**nē-ən) *adj.* Relating to Armenia or its people, language, or culture. ❖ *n.* **1.** A native or inhabitant of Armenia. **2.** The Indo-European language of the Armenians.

arm·ful (**ärm′**fo͝ol′) *n.* As much as one or both arms can hold: *an armful of flowers.*

arm·hole (**ärm′**hōl′) *n.* An opening in a garment for an arm.

ar·mi·stice (**är′**mĭ-stĭs) *n.* A temporary stop of fighting by mutual agreement; a truce. [From New Latin *armistitium* : Latin *arma,* arms + Latin *-stitium,* a stopping.]

Armistice Day *n.* Veterans Day as observed before 1954 to commemorate the the armistice that ended World War I in 1918.

arm·let (**ärm′**lĭt) *n.* **1.** A band worn on the arm for ornament or identification. **2.** A small arm, as of the sea.

arm·load (**ärm′**lōd′) *n.* The amount that can be carried in one arm or both arms: *an armload of firewood.*

arm·lock (**ärm′**lŏk′) *n.* A hold in wrestling or martial arts in which the opponent's arm is held so that it cannot be moved.

ar·moire (ärm-**wär′** *or* **ärm′**wär) *n.* A large, often highly decorated cabinet or wardrobe.

ar·mor (**är′**mər) *n.* **1.** A covering worn to protect the body in battle. **2.** A protective covering, such as the bony plates covering an armadillo or the metal plates on tanks or warships. **3.** The armored vehicles of an army. ❖ *tr.v.* **ar·mored, ar·mor·ing, ar·mors** To cover or protect with armor: *armor a warship.*

ar·mored (**är′**mərd) *adj.* **1.** Covered with or having armor: *tanks and other armored vehicles.* **2.** Equipped with armored vehicles: *an armored division of the Marines.*

ar·mor·er (**är′**mər-ər) *n.* **1.** A person or business that makes or repairs weapons. **2.** An enlisted person in charge of maintenance and repair of the small arms of a military unit.

armor plate *n.* A specially made hard steel plate designed to withstand enemy fire and protect warships, military aircraft, and armored vehicles.

ar·mor·y (är′mə-rē) *n., pl.* **ar·mor·ies 1.** A storehouse for weapons; an arsenal. **2.** A building that serves as the headquarters of a military reserve force. **3.** A weapons factory.

ar·mour (är′mər) *n. & v. Chiefly British* Variant of **armor.**

arm·pit (ärm′pĭt′) *n.* The hollow place under the arm at the shoulder.

arm·rest (ärm′rĕst′) *n.* A support for the arm, as on a chair or couch.

Arm·strong (ärm′strông′), **Louis** Known as "Satchmo." 1901–1971. American jazz trumpeter and popular singer who greatly influenced the development of jazz.

Armstrong, Neil Alden 1930–2012. American astronaut who as commander of Apollo 11 became the first person to walk on the moon (July 20, 1969).

ar·my (är′mē) *n., pl.* **ar·mies 1.** A large body of people organized and trained for warfare on land. **2.** often **Army a.** The entire military land forces of a country. **b.** The largest unit in a country's army, consisting of two or more corps: *the Ninth Army of the US Army.* **3.** A large group of people or things, especially when organized for a specific purpose: *an army of construction workers who built the bridge; a banquet with an army of waiters.* [From Middle English *armee*, from Latin *armāta*, from *armāre*, to arm.]

ar·ni·ca (är′nĭ-kə) *n.* **1.** Any of various plants having yellow flowers that resemble daisies. **2.** A medical preparation made from these flowers, used to treat sprains and bruises.

Ar·nold (är′nəld), **Benedict** 1741–1801. American Revolutionary general and traitor who unsuccessfully tried to surrender West Point to the British for 20,000 pounds (1780).

a·ro·ma (ə-rō′mə) *n., pl.* **a·ro·mas 1.** A quality that can be perceived by the sense of smell: *the aroma of fried onions.* See Synonyms at **smell. 2.** A pleasant characteristic smell, as of a plant or food: *the aroma of roses.* [From Middle English *aromat*, aromatic substance, from Old French, from Latin *arōmata*, aromatic herbs, from Greek.]

ar·o·mat·ic (ăr′ə-măt′ĭk) *adj.* **1.** Having an aroma; fragrant: *the aromatic scent of roses.* **2.** Relating to organic chemical compounds containing at least one benzene ring or similar ring-shaped component. **—ar′o·mat′i·cal·ly** *adv.*

a·rose (ə-rōz′) *v.* Past tense of **arise.**

a·round (ə-round′) *adv.* **1.** On all sides or in all directions: *We drove around looking for a parking place.* **2.** In a circle or circular motion: *The skater spun around twice.* **3.** In or toward the opposite direction: *The horse turned around and ran toward the barn.* **4.** From one place to another; here and there: *wander around.* **5.** In or near one's current location: *He waited around all day.* **6.** To a specific place or area: *when you come around again.* **7.** Approximately; about: *Around 20 rafts floated down the Rio Grande.* ❖ *adj.* In circumference: *a pond two miles around.* ❖ *prep.* **1.** On all sides of: *There are trees around the field.* **2.** So as to encircle or enclose: *He wore a belt around his waist.* **3.** All about; throughout: *The reporter looked around the room.* **4.** On or to the farther side of: *the house around the corner.* **5.** Close by; near: *She lives right around here.* **6.** So as to pass or avoid: *How can we get around the problem?* **7.** Approximately at: *I woke up around seven.* ◆ **have been around** *Informal* To have gained practical knowledge from having experienced many different things: *Don't let his simple manner fool you—this guy's been around.*

a·rous·al (ə-rou′zəl) *n.* The act of arousing or the condition of being aroused.

a·rouse (ə-rouz′) *tr.v.* **a·roused, a·rous·ing, a·rous·es 1.** To give rise to (a feeling, for example); stir up: *a story that aroused our interest.* **2.** To cause (someone) to be active, attentive, or excited: *a speech that aroused the crowd.* **3.** To awaken from sleep: *The baby's crying aroused me from my nap.* **—a·rous′a·ble** *adj.* **—a·rous′er** *n.*

ar·peg·gi·o (är-pĕj′ē-ō *or* är-pĕj′ō) *n., pl.* **ar·peg·gi·os 1.** The playing of the tones of a chord in succession rather than all at once. **2.** A chord played or sung in this way.

ar·que·bus (är′kə-bəs *or* är′kwə-bəs) *n.* Variant of **harquebus.**

ar·raign (ə-rān′) *tr.v.* **ar·raigned, ar·raign·ing, ar·raigns** To summon before a court of law to answer a charge or indictment: *The suspect was arraigned on charges of fraud.* **—ar·raign′er** *n.* **—ar·raign′ment** *n.*

ar·range (ə-rānj′) *v.* **ar·ranged, ar·rang·ing, ar·rang·es** —*tr.* **1.** To put in a specific order or relation: *Arrange these words alphabetically.* **2.** To plan or prepare for or bring about by planning: *How long did it take to arrange your trip?* **3.** To come to an agreement concerning; settle: *Have your friends arranged the date of the party?* **4.** To rework (a musical composition) for different voices or instruments or in a different style: *He arranged the piano piece for orchestra.* —*intr.* **1.** To cause something to happen by planning or to make plans for something to happen: *We arranged for a cab to pick us up at the airport.* **2.** To come to an agreement: *The company arranged with the union to grant more holidays.* [From Middle English *arengen*, to draw up in lines of battle, from Old French *arengier*, from *reng*, line, row.]

ar·range·ment (ə-rānj′mənt) *n.* **1.** The act of arranging: *The arrangement of a time and place for the meeting was quite difficult.* **2.** The manner or style in which things are arranged: *The arrangement of ideas in the essay was clear and logical.* **3.** A collection or set of things that have been arranged: *a flower arrangement.* **4.** An agreement: *We have an arrangement about who cooks dinner and who washes the dishes.* **5.** often **arrangements** A plan or preparation: *Make arrangements for a vacation.* **6.** A version of a musical composition that differs from the original in style or use of instruments: *a jazz arrangement of a popular tune.*

ar·rant (ăr′ənt) *adj.* Thoroughgoing; out-and-out: *an arrant coward.* **—ar′rant·ly** *adv.*

ar·ray (ə-rā′) *tr.v.* **ar·rayed, ar·ray·ing, ar·rays 1.** To put in an orderly arrangement, as troops. **2.** To dress, especially in fine clothes; adorn: *The dancers were arrayed in red velvet.* ❖ *n.* **1.** An orderly arrangement: *an array of data.* **2.** An impressively large number or group: *The cast for the play is a formidable array of talent.* **3.** Clothing or finery: *The princess was clad in rich array.* **—ar·ray′er** *n.*

ar·rears (ə-rîrz′) *pl.n.* **1.** An unpaid or overdue debt: *You have arrears of $23.00.* **2.** The state of being behind in fulfilling payments or an obligation: *After this is paid they will no longer be in arrears.*

ar·rest (ə-rĕst′) *tr.v.* **ar·rest·ed, ar·rest·ing, ar·rests 1.** To seize and hold under authority of law: *The police arrested the thief.* **2.** To stop the progress of; check: *The antibiotic arrested the spread of the infection.* **3.** To capture and hold; engage: *The exciting chapter arrested the reader's attention.* ❖ *n.* The act of arresting or the state of being arrested. [From Middle English *aresten*, from Old French *arester* : Latin *ad-*, to + Latin *restāre*, to stand still.]

ar·rest·ing (ə-rĕs′tĭng) *adj.* Capturing and holding the attention; striking: *the actor's arresting performance.* **—ar·rest′ing·ly** *adv.*

ar·rhyth·mi·a (ə-rĭ*th*′mē-ə) *n.* Irregularity in the force or rhythm of the heartbeat.

ar·ri·val (ə-rī′vəl) *n.* **1.** The act of arriving: *the arrival of*

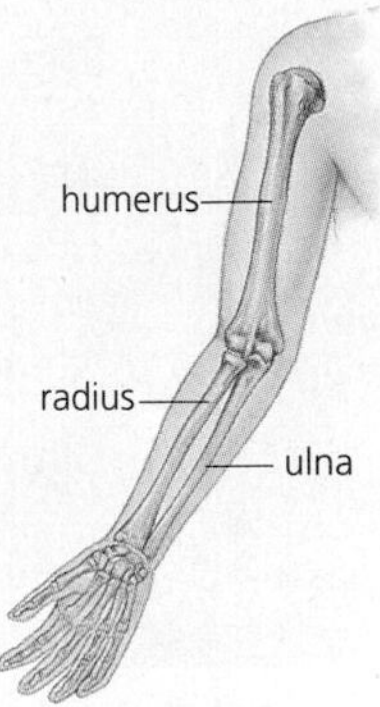

arm[1]

WORD HISTORY

armadillo The Spanish word **armadillo** literally means "a little armored animal." It comes from the adjective *armado*, "armed, armored," and the suffix *–illo*, which forms *diminutives*, words that express youngness, smallness, or affection. English has a number of diminutive suffixes: *–let*, as in *booklet*, *–ette*, as in *kitchenette*, and *–ling*, as in *duckling* and *darling*. (The last of these comes from the adjective *dear* plus the suffix *–ling.)*

Neil Armstrong
photographed in 1969

art deco
spire of the Chrysler Building, New York City

Chester Arthur
c. 1881 portrait by Ole P.H. Balling (1823–1906)

ă	pat	ôr	core
ā	pay	oi	boy
âr	care	ou	out
ä	father	o͝o	took
ĕ	pet	o͝or	lure
ē	be	o͞o	boot
ĭ	pit	ŭ	cut
ī	bite	ûr	urge
îr	pier	th	thin
ŏ	pot	*th*	this
ō	toe	zh	vision
ô	paw	ə	about

the passengers at the airport. **2.** The attainment of a goal or objective: *The principal's arrival at a decision came after much thought.* **3.** A person or thing that has arrived: *the newest arrivals at the video store.*

ar·rive (ə-rīv′) *intr.v.* **ar·rived, ar·riv·ing, ar·rives 1.** To reach a destination; come to a place: *They arrived in the city on time.* **2.** To come; take place: *Spring arrived early this year.* **3.** To achieve success or fame: *She has finally arrived as an artist.* ◆ **arrive at** To reach through effort or a process: *The jury arrived at a decision.* [From Middle English *ariven*, from Old French *ariver* : Latin *ad-*, to + Latin *rīpa*, shore.]

ar·ro·gance (ăr′ə-gəns) *n.* The quality or condition of being arrogant.

ar·ro·gant (ăr′ə-gənt) *adj.* **1.** Having or displaying excessive pride in oneself or an excessive sense of self-importance: *a conceited, arrogant person.* **2.** Marked by or arising from a feeling or assumption of one's superiority over others: *an arrogant refusal to listen to others.* **—ar′ro·gant·ly** *adv.*

SYNONYMS arrogant, haughty, disdainful These adjectives mean having an inflated ego and disdain for people or things that one considers to be inferior. A person who is **arrogant** is overbearingly proud and demands excessive power or consideration: *The arrogant professor was unpopular with both students and colleagues.* **Haughty** suggests an attitude of superiority, as by reason of high status: *The haughty family treated the waiter very rudely.* **Disdainful** emphasizes scorn or contempt: *My music teacher is disdainful of popular music.*

---

ar·ro·gate (ăr′ə-gāt′) *tr.v.* **ar·ro·gat·ed, ar·ro·gat·ing, ar·ro·gates** To take, claim, or assume for oneself without right: *The president cannot arrogate the power of Congress to declare war.* **—ar′ro·ga′tion** *n.*

ar·row (ăr′ō) *n.* **1.** A straight thin shaft with a pointed head at one end and feathers at the other, meant to be shot from a bow. **2.** Something similar in shape, as a sign or mark used to indicate direction. [From Old English *earh.*]

ar·row·head (ăr′ō-hĕd′) *n.* The pointed tip of an arrow, typically a wedge-shaped stone or fitted metal cap.

ar·row·root (ăr′ō-ro͞ot′ *or* ăr′ō-ro͝ot′) *n.* **1.** An edible, easily digested starch made from the rhizomes of a tropical American plant. **2.** The plant that has such rhizomes, having long leaves and small white flowers.

ar·roy·o (ə-roi′ō) *n., pl.* **ar·roy·os 1.** A small stream. **2.** A dry gulch in the southwest United States, formed by a stream. [From Spanish, from Latin *arrugia*, mine.]

ar·se·nal (är′sə-nəl) *n.* **1.** A building for the storage, manufacture, or repair of arms or ammunition. **2.** A stock of weapons.

ar·se·nic (är′sə-nĭk) *n.* **1.** *Symbol* **As** A brittle, gray metallic element that occurs chiefly in combination with other elements. Arsenic forms poisonous compounds with oxygen and is used to make insecticides, weed killers, and various alloys. Atomic number 33. See **Periodic Table. 2.** A highly poisonous compound containing arsenic and having the form of a white, odorless, tasteless powder, used to make insecticides, rat poisons, and weed killers. [From Middle English *arsenik*, from Greek *arsenikon*, a yellowish pigment, ultimately from ancient Iranian.]

ar·son (är′sən) *n.* The crime of intentionally setting fire to a building or other property. **—ar′son·ist** *n.*

art[1] (ärt) *n.* **1a.** The creation or production of something that is considered beautiful, as in painting, sculpture, poetry, or music. **b.** The study of these activities, especially the study of drawing, painting, and other visual arts: *I took art in school.* **c.** A work or works resulting from these activities, as a painting or a piece of sculpture: *an exhibit of modern art.* **2.** A practical skill: *the art of sewing; the art of negotiation.* **3. arts** The liberal arts; the humanities: *a college of arts and sciences.* [From Latin *ars.*]

art[2] (ärt) *v. Archaic* Second person singular present tense of **be.**

art. *abbr.* An abbreviation of article.

art dec·o also **Art Dec·o** (dĕk′ō) *n.* A style of decoration that originated in the 1920s, using geometrical patterns, bold colors, and plastic and glass.

Ar·te·mis (är′tə-mĭs) *n.* In Greek mythology, the goddess of the moon and the hunt, identified with the Roman Diana.

ar·te·ri·al (är-tîr′ē-əl) *adj.* **1.** Relating to or contained in the arteries of the body: *arterial blood.* **2.** Serving as a main route of transportation: *This highway is the arterial route through town.* **—ar·te′ri·al·ly** *adv.*

ar·te·ri·ole (är-tîr′ē-ōl′) *n.* Any of the smaller branches of an artery, especially one that ends in capillaries.

ar·te·ri·o·scle·ro·sis (är-tîr′ē-ō-sklə-rō′sĭs) *n.* Hardening and thickening of the walls of the arteries, which can interfere with the circulation of the blood.

ar·ter·y (är′tə-rē) *n., pl.* **ar·ter·ies 1.** Any of a branching system of blood vessels that carry blood away from the heart to various parts of the body. **2.** A major route of transportation into which local routes flow. [From Middle English *arterie*, from Greek *artēriā*, windpipe, artery (from the earlier belief that arteries carried air like the windpipe).]

ar·te·sian well (är-tē′zhən) *n.* A deep well that passes through hard impermeable rock and reaches water that is under enough pressure to rise to the surface without being pumped.

art form *n.* A type of creative activity or created work that is regarded as art: *art forms such as painting, poetry, and ballet.*

art·ful (ärt′fəl) *adj.* **1.** Showing art or skill; skillful: *an artful cook.* **2.** Crafty; cunning: *an artful peddler.* **—art′ful·ly** *adv.* **—art′ful·ness** *n.*

ar·thri·tis (är-thrī′tĭs) *n.* Inflammation and stiffness of a joint or joints in the body.

ar·thro·pod (är′thrə-pŏd′) *n.* Any of numerous invertebrate animals having a segmented body, jointed legs or wings, and an external skeleton. Insects, crustaceans, spiders, and centipedes are all arthropods.

ar·thro·scope (är′thrə-skōp′) *n.* An instrument that is used to examine the interior parts of a joint and is inserted through a small incision.

ar·thros·co·py (är-thrŏs′kə-pē) *n., pl.* **ar·thros·co·pies** A surgical procedure that involves examination of the interior of a joint, such as the knee, with an arthroscope and often includes diagnosis and repair of joint problems. **—ar′thro·scop′ic** (är′thrə-skŏp′ĭk) *adj.*

Ar·thur (är′thər) *n.* A legendary king of sixth-century Britain who gathered his knights at the Round Table and held court at Camelot. **—Ar·thu′ri·an** (är-tho͝or′ē-ən) *adj.*

Arthur, Chester Alan 1829–1886. The 21st president of the United States (1881–1885). He supported legislation to regulate the appointments of federal officials.

ar·ti·choke (är′tĭ-chōk′) *n.* **1.** The immature flower head of a plant related to the thistles, cooked and eaten as a vegetable. **2.** The plant that bears such a flower head. [From Old Spanish *alcarchofa*, from Arabic *al-ḫaršuf*, the artichoke.]

ar·ti·cle (är′tĭ-kəl) *n.* **1.** A written piece that forms an independent part of a publication; a report; an essay: *read an article about sports in the newspaper.* **2.** A section or item of a written document: *an article of the Constitution.* **3.** An individual thing; an item: *A bed is an article of furniture.* **4.** In grammar, the part of speech used to introduce nouns and to indicate whether the noun is definite and specific or indefinite and nonspecific. In English, the definite article is *the,* and the indefinite articles are *a* and *an.* [From Middle English, from Latin *articulus*, part, diminutive of *artus*, joint.]

ar·tic·u·late (är-tĭk′yə-lĭt) *adj.* **1.** Spoken clearly and distinctly: *a radio announcer's articulate speech.* **2.** Using or characterized by clear and effective language: *Teachers and lawyers must be articulate people.* **3.** Consisting of sections connected by joints: *The antennae of insects are articulate.* ❖ *v.* (är-tĭk′yə-lāt′) **ar·tic·u·lat·ed, ar·tic·u·lat·ing, ar·tic·u·lates** *—tr.* **1.** To utter (a speech sound or sounds) distinctly; enunciate: *Children begin to articulate words around age two.* **2.** To put (a feeling, for example) into words, especially clearly and effectively; express: *Our leader articulated the sentiments of the group.* **3.** To connect (body parts) by a joint or joints. *—intr.* **1.** To speak clearly and distinctly. **2.** To be jointed; form a joint: *the bones that articulate in the shoulder.* **—ar·tic′u·late·ly** *adv.* **—ar·tic′u·la′tor** *n.*

ar·tic·u·la·tion (är-tĭk′yə-lā′shən) *n.* **1.** The act or process of speaking or expressing oneself, especially clearly and effectively: *Good articulation is essential for a radio broadcaster.* **2.** The manner in which things, such as the parts of a building, are joined together. **3.** A joint between rigid body segments, such as bones.

ar·ti·fact (är′tə-făkt′) *n.* An object produced by human handiwork, especially one of archaeological or historical interest.

ar·ti·fice (är′tə-fĭs) *n.* **1.** A clever device or stratagem; a ruse. **2.** Deception; trickery.

ar·tif·i·cer (är-tĭf′ĭ-sər) *n.* A skilled worker; a person who practices a craft.

ar·ti·fi·cial (är′tə-fĭsh′əl) *adj.* **1.** Made by humans, especially in imitation of something natural: *an artificial sweetener; artificial flowers.* **2.** Not genuine or natural; affected: *an artificial display of tears and distress.* [From Middle English, from Latin *artificium*, craftsmanship, from *artifex*, craftsperson.] **—ar′ti·fi′ci·al′i·ty** (är′tə-fĭsh′ē-ăl′ĭ-tē) *n.* **—ar′ti·fi′cial·ly** *adv.*

artificial intelligence *n.* **1.** The ability of a computer or other machine to perform tasks normally thought to require intelligence, such as solving problems, recognizing specific human faces, or responding to spoken commands. **2.** The branch of computer science concerned with the development of machines having this ability.

artificial language *n.* An invented language developed for a specific purpose, such as computer programming.

artificial respiration *n.* Any of several methods for forcing air rhythmically in and out of the lungs, used to revive a living person who has stopped breathing.

artificial selection *n.* The process by which humans choose individual plants or animals with certain genetically based characteristics for breeding, so that those characteristics will become more common in future generations.

ar·til·ler·y (är-tĭl′ə-rē) *n., pl.* **ar·til·ler·ies 1.** Large mounted guns, such as cannons, that are operated by crews. **2.** The branch of an army that specializes in the use of such guns.

ar·til·ler·y·man (är-tĭl′ə-rē-mən) *n.* A soldier in the artillery.

ar·ti·san (är′tĭ-zən) *n.* A person who is skilled in making a product by hand. [From Italian *artigiano*, from Latin *artītus*, skilled in the arts.]

art·ist (är′tĭst) *n.* **1.** A person who produces works of art, especially in the fine arts such as painting or sculpture. **2.** A person who works in one of the performing arts, such as dancing or acting. **3.** A person who shows skill and creativity in an occupation or pastime: *That surgeon is a real artist.*

ar·tis·tic (är-tĭs′tĭk) *adj.* **1.** Relating to art or artists: *acclaimed by all artistic circles.* **2.** Sensitive to beauty: *an artistic temperament.* **3.** Showing imagination and skill: *an artistic flower arrangement.* **—ar·tis′ti·cal·ly** *adv.*

art·ist·ry (är′tĭ-strē) *n.* **1.** Artistic quality or workmanship: *the subtle artistry of a poem.* **2.** Artistic ability: *a painter of superb artistry.*

art·less (ärt′lĭs) *adj.* **1.** Free from deceit; guileless: *an artless child.* **2.** Not artificial; natural: *the artless beauty of a sunset.* **—art′less·ly** *adv.* **—art′less·ness** *n.*

art nou·veau often **Art Nou·veau** (är′ no͞o-vō′ *or* ärt′ no͞o-vō′) *n.* A style of decoration and architecture that originated in the 1890s, using curved lines and flower shapes.

art·work (ärt′wûrk′) *n.* **1a.** A work of art. **b.** Works of art considered as a group: *The archaeologists saved the artwork on the walls of the cave.* **2.** The illustrations and decorative parts of a book or other publication as distinct from the text.

art·y (är′tē) *adj.* **art·i·er, art·i·est** *Informal* **1.** Artistic in an elaborate or showy manner: *an arty movie.* **2.** Relating to artists or the fine arts.

A·ru·ba (ə-ro͞o′bə) An island and territory of the Netherlands in the Lesser Antilles north of the Venezuela coast. Oranjestad is the capital.

ar·um (âr′əm) *n.* Any of various plants having tiny flowers clustered on a fleshy spike and leaves that are often shaped like arrowheads.

–ary *suff.* A suffix that means: **1.** Relating to: *legendary.* **2.** One that relates to or is connected with: *boundary.*

Ar·y·an (âr′ē-ən) *n.* **1.** An Indo-Iranian. **2.** A member of a people speaking Proto-Indo-European or one of the Indo-European languages derived from it. In this sense, the word is not in technical use. **3.** In Nazi ideology, a non-Jewish Caucasian person, especially one of Nordic type. Nazis regarded Aryans as forming a master race. [From Sanskrit *ārya-*, the early Indic peoples' name for themselves.] **—Ar′y·an** *adj.*

as (ăz; əz *when unstressed*) *adv.* **1.** Equally: *You won't easily find someone as nice.* **2.** For instance: *large cats, as tigers and lions.* ❖ *conj.* **1.** To the same degree or quantity that; equally with: *sweet as sugar.* **2.** In the same way that: *When in Rome, do as the Romans do.* **3.** At the same time that; while: *They smiled as their eyes met.* **4.** Since; because: *I wanted to stay home, as I was ill.* **5.** Though: *Nice as it is, I don't want it.* **6.** In accordance with which; a fact that: *The sun is hot, as everyone knows.* ❖ *pron.* That; who; which: *I got the same grade as you did. We brought such things as were necessary.* ❖ *prep.* **1.** The same as; like: *They treated the old car as an honored relic of the past.* **2.** In the role or function of: *The diplomat was acting as a peacemaker.* ◆ **as is** *Informal* Just the way it is; without changes: *If you leave the bottle on the shelf as is, it will tip and fall.* **as it were** In a manner of speaking: *The hikers were explorers, as it were, until it began to rain.* **as much** All that; the same: *I might have guessed as much.*

As The symbol for the element **arsenic.**

As. *abbr.* An abbreviation of Asia.

as·a·fet·i·da (ăs′ə-fĕt′ĭ-də) *n.* A brownish resin with a strong odor, obtained from various Asian plants and used in cooking and in medicinal preparations. [From Middle English : Medieval Latin *asa*, gum + Latin *foetidus*, stinking.]

ASAP *abbr.* An abbreviation of as soon as possible.

as·bes·tos (ăs-bĕs′təs *or* ăz-bĕs′təs) *n.* Any of several fibrous mineral forms of magnesium silicate that are resistant to heat, flames, and chemical action. Some forms have been shown to contribute to certain lung diseases. For this reason, asbestos is no longer used in making insulation, fireproofing material, and brake linings. [From Middle English *abestus*, from Greek *asbestos*, unquenchable.]

as·cend (ə-sĕnd′) *v.* **as·cend·ed, as·cend·ing, as·cends** *—intr.* **1.** To go or move upward; rise: *The balloon as-*

artichoke

art nouveau

ash[2]

Arthur Ashe
photographed at Wimbledon in 1975

cended rapidly. **2.** To slope upward: *The trail ascends up the mountain.* **3.** To move to a higher rank or level: *The prince ascended to the throne and so became king.* —*tr.* **1.** To climb to or toward the top of: *The climbers ascended the mountain.* **2.** To slope upward toward or along: *The road ascends the ridge.* **3.** To come to occupy: *The queen ascended the throne upon the death of her father.* [From Middle English *ascenden,* from Latin *ascendere* : *ad-,* to + *scandere,* to climb.]

as·cen·dan·cy also **as·cen·den·cy** (ə-sĕn′dən-sē) *n.* Dominance in position or power: *Britain lost ascendancy in the United States after the Revolution.*

as·cen·dant also **as·cen·dent** (ə-sĕn′dənt) *adj.* Coming into a position of power or influence: *Rome was the ascendant power in Europe before the Middle Ages.* ◆ **in the ascendant** Rising in power or influence.

as·cend·ing (ə-sĕn′dĭng) *adj.* Moving, going, or growing upward: *in ascending order of importance; a tree with ascending branches.*

as·cen·sion (ə-sĕn′shən) *n.* **1.** The act or process of ascending. **2. Ascension** In Christian theology, the rising of Jesus into heaven 40 days after his resurrection.

Ascension Day *n.* The 40th day after Easter, on which the Christian feast of the Ascension of Jesus is observed.

as·cent (ə-sĕnt′) *n.* **1.** The act or process of rising or going upward: *the rocket's ascent through the atmosphere.* **2.** The act or process of rising from a lower level, degree, or status; development: *the industrialist's ascent to the upper class.* **3.** An upward slope: *the steep ascent to the mountain pasture.*

❑ *These sound alike:* **ascent, assent** (agreement).

as·cer·tain (ăs′ər-tān′) *tr.v.* **as·cer·tained, as·cer·tain·ing, as·cer·tains** To discover with certainty: *ascertain the truth.* —**as′cer·tain′a·ble** *adj.* —**as′cer·tain′a·bly** *adv.* —**as′cer·tain′ment** *n.*

as·cet·ic (ə-sĕt′ĭk) *n.* A person who renounces comforts and pleasures in order to practice rigid self-denial, often as an act of religious devotion. ❖ *adj.* Relating to or characteristic of an ascetic; self-denying; austere: *Most hermits lead an ascetic life.* —**as·cet′i·cal·ly** *adv.*

as·cet·i·cism (ə-sĕt′ĭ-sĭz′əm) *n.* Ascetic practice or discipline.

ASCII (ăs′kē) *n.* A standardized computer code for assigning binary numbers to letters, numbers, and symbols.

As·cle·pi·us (ə-sklē′pē-əs) *n.* In Greek mythology, the god of medicine.

a·scor·bic acid (ə-skôr′bĭk) *n.* Vitamin C.

as·cot (ăs′kət *or* ăs′kŏt′) *n.* A broad neck scarf that is knotted so that one end lies flat on top of the other. [After the racetrack near *Ascot,* England.]

as·cribe (ə-skrīb′) *tr.v.* **as·cribed, as·crib·ing, as·cribes** To think of (something) as belonging to or coming from a specific cause, origin, or source; attribute: *The farmers ascribed their poor harvest to drought. Most scholars ascribe the poem to Chaucer.* —**as·crib′a·ble** *adj.*

as·crip·tion (ə-skrĭp′shən) *n.* The act of ascribing something: *the ascription of the poem to Shakespeare.*

a·sep·tic (ə-sĕp′tĭk *or* ā-sĕp′tĭk) *adj.* Free from microorganisms that can cause infection: *aseptic surgical methods.* —**a·sep′ti·cal·ly** *adv.*

a·sex·u·al (ā-sĕk′shōō-əl) *adj.* Not involving reproductive organs or the union of reproductive cells: *asexual reproduction.* —**a·sex′u·al·ly** *adv.*

as for *prep.* With regard to; concerning: *As for me, I'll stay.*

As·gard (ăs′gärd′ *or* äz′gärd′) *n.* In Norse mythology, the heavenly dwelling place of the gods.

ash[1] (ăsh) *n.* **1.** The grayish-white powdery residue left when something is burned. **2.** The fine particles of solid matter thrown out of a volcano in an eruption. **3. ashes** The remains of a body after it has been cremated. [From Old English *æsce.*]

ash[2] (ăsh) *n.* **1.** Any of various trees having compound leaves, winged seeds, and strong tough wood. **2.** The wood of such a tree, used for making furniture, tool handles, and sporting goods such as baseball bats. [From Old English *æsc.*]

a·shamed (ə-shāmd′) *adj.* **1.** Feeling shame or guilt: *You should be ashamed for losing your temper.* **2.** Reluctant through fear of shame or embarrassment: *Don't be ashamed to ask for help.* —**a·sham′ed·ly** (ə-shā′mĭd-lē) *adv.*

A·shan·ti (ə-shăn′tē *or* ə-shän′tē) *n., pl.* **Ashanti** or **Ashan·tis 1.** A member of a people of Ghana. **2.** The Twi language of this people.

Ashe (ăsh), **Arthur Robert, Jr.** 1943–1993. American tennis player who was the first African-American player to win the US Open singles championship (1968) and the Wimbledon singles title (1975).

ash·en (ăsh′ən) *adj.* **1.** Resembling ashes: *an ashen sky.* **2.** Whitish-gray in complexion: *knew something was wrong when she saw his ashen face.*

Ash·ga·bat (ăsh′gä-bät′) also **Ash·kha·bad** (ăsh′gä-băd′ *or* ăsh′gä-bät′) The capital of Turkmenistan, in the south-central part of the country near the Iranian border. It was founded as a fortress in 1881.

a·shore (ə-shôr′) *adv.* **1.** To or onto the shore: *go ashore.* **2.** On land: *The sailors spent the day ashore.*

ash·tray (ăsh′trā′) *n.* A small receptacle for tobacco ashes.

Ash Wednesday *n.* The first day of Lent, when many Christians receive a mark of ashes on the forehead as a sign of penitence and mortality.

ash·y (ăsh′ē) *adj.* **ash·i·er, ash·i·est 1.** Relating to, resembling, or containing ashes: *ashy soil where the fire pit had been.* **2.** Having the color of ashes: *a bird with ashy feathers.*

A·sia (ā′zhə) The world's largest continent, lying between Europe and Africa to the west and the Pacific Ocean to the east. It is separated from Europe by the Ural Mountains.

Asia Minor A peninsula of western Asia between the Black Sea and the Mediterranean Sea, occupying the Asian part of Turkey.

A·sian (ā′zhən) *adj.* Relating to Asia or its peoples, languages, or cultures. ❖ *n.* **1.** A native or inhabitant of Asia. **2.** A person of Asian ancestry.

Asian American *n.* A US citizen or resident of Asian ancestry. —**A′sian-A·mer′i·can** *adj.*

Asian elephant *n.* An elephant native to South and Southeast Asia, having smaller ears than the African elephants. The females usually do not have tusks.

A·si·at·ic (ā′zhē-ăt′ĭk) *adj.* Asian: *an Asiatic plant.*

a·side (ə-sīd′) *adv.* **1.** To or toward one side: *step aside; draw the curtain aside.* **2.** Apart: *a day set aside for relaxation.* **3.** In reserve: *money put aside for a vacation.* **4.** Out of one's thoughts or mind: *put one's fears aside.* **5.** Being excepted or excluded from consideration: *Joking aside, can you swim 15 miles?* ❖ *n.* A remark spoken by a character in a play that the other actors on stage are not supposed to hear.

aside from *prep.* Apart from; except for: *Aside from a miracle, nothing can save their team from losing.*

as if *conj.* **1.** In the same way that it would be if: *She ran as if she would never tire.* **2.** That: *It seemed as if the day lasted forever.*

As·i·mov (ăz′ĭ-môv′), **Isaac** 1920–1992. Russian-born American scientist and writer whose works include popular explanations of scientific principles and volumes of science fiction, including *The Foundation Trilogy* (1951–1953).

as·i·nine (ăs′ə-nīn′) *adj.* Stupid or silly: *an asinine remark.* —**as′i·nine′ly** *adv.*

ă	pat	ôr	core
ā	pay	oi	boy
âr	care	ou	out
ä	father	ŏŏ	took
ĕ	pet	ŏŏr	lure
ē	be	ōō	boot
ĭ	pit	ŭ	cut
ī	bite	ûr	urge
îr	pier	th	thin
ŏ	pot	*th*	this
ō	toe	zh	vision
ô	paw	ə	about

ask (ăsk) *v.* **asked, ask·ing, asks** —*tr.* **1.** To put a question to: *When we realized that we didn't know the answer, we asked the teacher.* **2.** To seek an answer to: *asked a question.* **3.** To seek information about: *asked directions.* **4a.** To make a request of: *My sister asked me for help.* **b.** To make a request for. Often used with an infinitive or clause: *She asked to go along on the trip. He asked that he be allowed to stay out late.* **5.** To charge: *They are asking 20 dollars for this book.* **6.** To expect or demand: *Riding in a car all day is asking a great deal of a small child.* **7.** To invite: *Why don't we ask them to dinner?* —*intr.* **1.** To make inquiries: *We asked about the train schedule.* **2.** To make a request: *I asked for help.* [From Old English *ācsian, āscian.*] —SEE NOTE AT **pretty.**

SYNONYMS ask, inquire, question, examine, quiz
These verbs all mean to seek information. **Ask** is the most general: *We stopped at the corner and asked for directions to the stadium.* **Question** often means to ask a series of questions: *The lawyer questioned the witness in great detail about the robbery.* **Inquire** often suggests a polite or formal request: *The chairman inquired how to best secure the information.* **Examine** often means to question in order to test someone's knowledge: *All of their real-estate agents have been examined and licensed by the state board.* **Quiz** means to question students in a brief test: *The teacher will quiz us tomorrow on state capitals.*
ANTONYM answer

---

a·skance (ə-**skăns′**) *adv.* **1.** With a sidelong glance. **2.** With distrust or disapproval: *The reporter looked askance at such rumors.*

a·skew (ə-**skyo͞o′**) *adv. & adj.* Out of line; crooked; awry: *Wind knocked the sign askew.*

ASL *abbr.* An abbreviation of American Sign Language.

a·slant (ə-**slănt′**) *adv. & adj.* At a slant: *trees standing aslant on the hill.*

a·sleep (ə-**slēp′**) *adj.* **1.** Sleeping: *You must have been asleep when the phone rang.* **2.** Numb: *My foot is asleep.* ❖ *adv.* Into a sleep: *The campers fell asleep quickly after their long hike.*

as long as *conj.* **1.** During the time that: *I'll stay as long as you need me.* **2.** Because of the fact that; since: *As long as you're offering, I accept.* **3.** On the condition that: *I'll go on the camping trip as long as you lend me a tent.*

As·ma·ra (ăz-**mä′**rə) The capital of Eritrea, in the western part of the country.

a·so·cial (ā-**sō′**shəl) *adj.* **1.** Avoiding the company of others; not sociable. **2.** Unable or unwilling to conform to normal standards of social behavior; antisocial.

as of *prep.* From or at the time of: *As of last week I have $150 in my savings account.*

asp (ăsp) *n.* Any of several venomous snakes of Africa and Eurasia, especially a small cobra of northern Africa and southwest Asia.

as·par·a·gine (ə-**spăr′**ə-jēn′) *n.* A nonessential amino acid that is found in many proteins and some plants.

as·par·a·gus (ə-**spăr′**ə-gəs) *n.* **1.** The young tender stalks of a plant with feathery leaves. The stalks are cooked and eaten as a vegetable. **2.** The plant that has such stalks. [From New Latin *asparagus*, from Greek *asparagos.*]

as·par·tame (**ăs′**pər-tām′ *or* ə-**spär′**tām′) *n.* An artificial sweetener, about 200 times as sweet as sugar, containing four calories per gram.

as·par·tic acid (ə-**spär′**tĭk) *n.* A nonessential amino acid that is found in certain plants.

ASPCA *abbr.* An abbreviation for American Society for the Prevention of Cruelty to Animals.

as·pect (**ăs′**pĕkt) *n.* **1.** A way in which something can be considered: *From every aspect, the explorers were in a desperate situation.* **2.** A characteristic or feature of something: *This song has some interesting aspects.* **3.** The appearance or look of something: *the barren aspect of the desert.* **4.** A position facing or commanding a given direction; exposure: *a bright sunny room with a southern aspect.* **5.** A property of verbs that conveys the completion, duration, or repetition of the verb's action or state. [From Middle English, from Latin *aspectus*, a view : *ad-*, at + *specere*, to look.]

as·pen (**ăs′**pən) *n.* Any of various poplar trees having leaves that flutter readily in the wind because of their flattened leafstalks.

as·per·i·ty (ă-**spĕr′**ĭ-tē) *n.* Harshness of manner; irritability: *a note of asperity in one's voice.*

as·per·sion (ə-**spûr′**zhən *or* ə-**spûr′**shən) *n.* A damaging or slanderous report or remark: *The comment cast aspersions on my motives.*

as·phalt (**ăs′**fôlt′) *n.* **1.** A thick, sticky, dark-brown material consisting of petroleum tars and used in paving, roofing, and waterproofing. Asphalt is obtained in the refining of petroleum or is found in natural deposits. **2.** This material mixed with crushed stone gravel or sand, used for paving or roofing. ❖ *tr.v.* **as·phalt·ed, as·phalt·ing, as·phalts** To pave or coat with asphalt. [From Middle English *aspalt*, from Greek *asphaltos.*]

as·pho·del (**ăs′**fə-dĕl′) *n.* **1.** Any of several plants of the Mediterranean region having white or yellow flowers. **2.** Any of several other plants.

as·phyx·i·a (ăs-**fĭk′**sē-ə) *n.* Death or loss of consciousness caused by a lack of oxygen.

as·phyx·i·ate (ăs-**fĭk′**sē-āt′) *intr. & tr.v.* **as·phyx·i·at·ed, as·phyx·i·at·ing, as·phyx·i·ates** To undergo or cause to undergo asphyxia; suffocate: *Without air the bugs in the jar will asphyxiate. The thick smoke nearly asphyxiated us.* **—as·phyx′i·a′tion** *n.*

as·pic (**ăs′**pĭk) *n.* A jelly made from gelatin and chilled meat juices or vegetable juices and served as a garnish or as a molded dish.

as·pi·rant (**ăs′**pər-ənt *or* ə-**spīr′**ənt) *n.* A person who desires or strives for a particular position or honor: *an aspirant to high position and power.*

as·pi·rate (**ăs′**pə-rāt′) *tr.v.* **as·pi·rat·ed, as·pi·rat·ing, as·pi·rates 1.** To remove (a liquid or gas) from a body cavity by suction, usually by using an aspirator: *aspirate fluid from the lungs.* **2.** To pronounce (a vowel or word) with a puff of breath, as in *help.* ❖ *n.* (**ăs′**pər-ĭt) **1.** The sound of the letter *h* as in *help.* **2.** The puff of air accompanying or following certain speech sounds, as that accompanying *p* in *peach.*

as·pi·ra·tion (ăs′pə-**rā′**shən) *n.* **1a.** A strong desire, as for the realization of an ambition or ideal: *the student's aspiration to become a doctor.* **b.** An object of such desire; an ambitious goal: *To become a surgeon was my friend's aspiration.* **2.** The process of removing a liquid or gas from a body cavity by suction. **3.** The pronunciation of certain speech sounds with a puff of breath, especially at the beginning of a word, as *h* in *hurry.*

as·pi·ra·tor (**ăs′**pə-rā′tər) *n.* A suction pump, especially a small one used to draw fluids from body cavities.

as·pire (ə-**spīr′**) *intr.v.* **as·pired, as·pir·ing, as·pires** To have a great ambition; desire strongly: *aspire to become a good musician; aspire to great knowledge.* [From Middle English *aspiren*, from Latin *aspīrāre*, to desire : *ad-*, toward + *spīrāre*, to breathe.] **—as·pir′er** *n.*

as·pi·rin (**ăs′**pər-ĭn *or* **ăs′**prĭn) *n.* **1.** A white crystalline compound derived from salicylic acid and used as a drug to relieve fever and pain; acetylsalicylic acid. **2.** A tablet of aspirin.

ass (ăs) *n., pl.* **ass·es** (**ăs′**ĭz) **1.** Any of several hoofed mammals, such as the donkey, that resemble horses but have a smaller build and longer ears. **2.** A foolish or stupid person.

as·sail (ə-**sāl′**) *tr.v.* **as·sailed, as·sail·ing, as·sails** To

asparagus

aspen

WRITERS CHOOSE THEIR WORDS

After tea Mrs. Allan played and sang and she got Lauretta and me to sing, too. Mrs. Allan says I have a good voice and she says I must sing in the Sunday-school choir after this. You can't think how I was thrilled at the mere thought. I've longed so to sing in the Sunday-school choir, as Diana does, but I feared it was an honour I could never **aspire** to.

—L.M. Montgomery
Anne of Green Gables

attack physically or with words: *The candidate for mayor assailed her opponents with strong criticism.* —**as·sail′a·ble** *adj.* —**as·sail′er** *n.*

as·sail·ant (ə-sā′lənt) *n.* A person who assails someone; an attacker.

as·sas·sin (ə-săs′ĭn) *n.* A person who kills someone by surprise attack, especially one who kills a public official or other prominent figure for political reasons. [From Medieval Latin *assassinus*, from Arabic *ḥaššāš*, hashish user.]

as·sas·si·nate (ə-săs′ə-nāt′) *tr.v.* **as·sas·si·nat·ed, as·sas·si·nat·ing, as·sas·si·nates** To murder (a public figure) by surprise attack, usually for political reasons. —**as·sas′si·na′tion** *n.* —**as·sas′si·na′tor** *n.*

as·sault (ə-sôlt′) *n.* **1.** A violent physical or military attack: *The tanks made an assault upon the town.* **2.** An unlawful attempt or threat to injure another physically. **3.** A rigorous or energetic effort to accomplish something difficult: *an assault on poverty.* **4.** An act of expressing strong criticism; a denunciation: *a blogger's assaults on corrupt politicians.* ❖ *tr.v.* **as·sault·ed, as·sault·ing, as·saults 1.** To attack violently: *The troops assaulted the fort.* **2.** To attack verbally; criticize or denounce. [From Middle English *assaut*, from Latin *assultus*, from *assilīre*, to jump on.] —**as·sault′er** *n.*

assault and battery *n.* A criminal act involving both a threat of violence and actual physical contact with the victim.

assault weapon *n.* Any of various automatic or semiautomatic firearms with detachable magazines, designed for individual use.

as·say (ăs′ā′ *or* ă-sā′) *n.* **1.** A chemical analysis of something, especially an ore or drug. **2.** A specimen or sample subjected to an assay. ❖ *v.* (ă-sā′ *or* ăs′ā′) **as·sayed, as·say·ing, as·says** —*tr.* **1.** To analyze (an ore or alloy) to find out the quantity of gold, silver, or other metal in it. **2.** To test and evaluate; assess: *We assayed the chances of success and decided to make the film.* **3.** To attempt; try: *In spite of the dangers she still assayed the difficult journey.* —*intr.* To be shown by an assay to contain some ingredient: *The ore assayed at 1 percent uranium.* —**as·say′er** *n.*

as·sem·blage (ə-sĕm′blĭj) *n.* **1.** A collection of people or things: *The mayor spoke before a large assemblage in the town square.* **2.** The act of gathering or fitting together.

as·sem·ble (ə-sĕm′bəl) *v.* **as·sem·bled, as·sem·bling, as·sem·bles** —*tr.* **1.** To bring together as a group: *The teachers assembled their classes in the auditorium.* **2.** To perform the assembly of; put together: *The mechanic assembled the engine.* —*intr.* To come together; gather; congregate: *A group of friends assembled at the corner.* See Synonyms at **gather.** [From Middle English *assemblen*, from Old French *assembler* : Latin *ad-*, to + Latin *simul*, together.] —**as·sem′bler** *n.*

as·sem·bly (ə-sĕm′blē) *n., pl.* **as·sem·blies 1.** A group of people gathered together for a common purpose. **2. Assembly** The lower house of the legislature in certain US states. **3a.** The process of putting together a number of parts to make up a complete unit: *The assembly of a new car usually takes less than a day.* **b.** A set of parts that work together as a unit; an apparatus: *the steering assembly of a truck.*

assembly line *n.* An arrangement in which articles are assembled in successive stages, passing from worker to worker or machine to machine, often on some kind of conveyor.

as·sem·bly·man (ə-sĕm′blē-mən) *n.* A man who is a member of a legislative assembly.

as·sem·bly·wom·an (ə-sĕm′blē-wo͝om′ən) *n.* A woman who is a member of a legislative assembly.

as·sent (ə-sĕnt′) *intr.v.* **as·sent·ed, as·sent·ing, as·sents** To express agreement: *Everyone's parents assented to the class trip.* ❖ *n.* Agreement, as to a proposal, especially in a formal or impersonal manner: *The prime minister desired the king's assent.*

❑ *These sound alike:* **assent, ascent** (rising).

as·sert (ə-sûrt′) *tr.v.* **as·sert·ed, as·sert·ing, as·serts 1.** To state or declare positively; claim: *By opposing the bill, the senators asserted their independence from business leaders.* **2.** To insist upon recognition of; defend or maintain: *The lawyer asserted the defendant's right to a fair trial.* ◆ **assert (oneself)** To express oneself boldly or forcefully. —**as·sert′er, as·ser′tor** *n.*

as·ser·tion (ə-sûr′shən) *n.* **1.** The act of asserting. **2.** A statement or claim, especially one for which no proof is offered: *His assertions of innocence were found to be true.*

as·ser·tive (ə-sûr′tĭv) *adj.* Self-confident, especially in putting forward one's opinions: *She was assertive in her request for a raise.* —**as·ser′tive·ly** *adv.* —**as·ser′tive·ness** *n.*

as·sess (ə-sĕs′) *tr.v.* **as·sessed, as·sess·ing, as·sess·es 1.** To determine the significance, importance, or value of; estimate; evaluate: *Our teacher has special skills in assessing problems of learning.* **2.** To estimate the value of (property) for taxation: *The apartment building was assessed at several million dollars.* **3a.** To set the amount of (a tax, fine, or other payment): *assess a tax for road repairs.* **b.** To charge (a person) with a tax, fine, or other special payment: *Each member of the team will be assessed five dollars for new equipment.* **4.** In sports, to charge a player, coach, or team with (a foul or penalty). [From Middle English, from Latin *assidēre*, to sit by as an assistant judge : *ad-*, next to + *sedēre*, to sit.] —**as·sess′a·ble** *adj.*

as·sess·ment (ə-sĕs′mənt) *n.* **1.** The act of assessing. **2.** An amount assessed: *Property owners paid an assessment for street repairs.*

as·ses·sor (ə-sĕs′ər) *n.* An official whose job it is to assess the tax value of property.

as·set (ăs′ĕt′) *n.* **1.** A valuable quality or possession: *An agreeable personality is a great asset.* **2. assets** All the property owned by a person or business that has monetary value and may be applied directly or indirectly to the payment of debts. [From Anglo-Norman *asez*, enough, ultimately from Latin *satis*.]

as·sev·er·ate (ə-sĕv′ə-rāt′) *tr.v.* **as·sev·er·at·ed, as·sev·er·at·ing, as·sev·er·ates** To declare seriously or positively; affirm.

as·sid·u·ous (ə-sĭj′o͞o-əs) *adj.* Diligent; industrious: *an assiduous worker.* —**as·sid′u·ous·ly** *adv.* —**as·sid′u·ous·ness** *n.*

as·sign (ə-sīn′) *tr.v.* **as·signed, as·sign·ing, as·signs 1.** To select for a duty or office; appoint: *Which firefighters are assigned to the industrial area of the city?* **2.** To set apart for a purpose or place into a category; designate: *assign a day for the test; assign rocks to mineral groups.* **3.** To give out as a task; allot: *The teacher assigned homework to all of us.* **4.** To think of (something) as having a certain cause or origin; attribute: *The coach assigned blame for the loss to a lack of good defense.* [From Middle English *assignen*, from Latin *assignāre* : *ad-*, to + *signāre*, to mark (from *signum*, sign).] —**as·sign′a·ble** *adj.* —**as·sign′er** *n.* —SEE NOTE AT **sign.**

as·sign·ment (ə-sīn′mənt) *n.* **1.** The act of assigning something: *The work was divided among us by assignment.* **2.** Something assigned, especially a task or job: *What's the math assignment for tomorrow?* See Synonyms at **task. 3.** A position or post of duty to which one is assigned: *The journalist will take an assignment outside the United States.*

as·sim·i·late (ə-sĭm′ə-lāt′) *v.* **as·sim·i·lat·ed, as·sim·i·lat·ing, as·sim·i·lates** —*tr.* **1.** To take in and use (food or nutrients) in living tissue; absorb: *The body assimi-*

ă	pat	ôr	core
ā	pay	oi	boy
âr	care	ou	out
ä	father	o͝o	took
ĕ	pet	o͝or	lure
ē	be	o͞o	boot
ĭ	pit	ŭ	cut
ī	bite	ûr	urge
îr	pier	th	thin
ŏ	pot	*th*	this
ō	toe	zh	vision
ô	paw	ə	about

lates protein. **2.** To make part of one's knowledge; incorporate into one's understanding: *immigrants assimilating the culture of their new home.* **3.** To take into the cultural or social tradition of a group: *The United States has assimilated immigrants of many nationalities.* **4.** To alter (a speech sound) by assimilation. *—intr.* **1.** To be taken into the mind: *technological changes that are difficult to assimilate.* **2.** To be taken into a group: *immigrants assimilating into the broader culture.* [From Middle English *assimilaten*, from Latin *assimilāre*, to make similar to : *ad-*, to + *similis*, like.] **—as·sim′i·la′tor** *n.*

as·sim·i·la·tion (ə-sĭm′ə-lā′shən) *n.* **1.** The act or process of assimilating: *the assimilation of new technology.* **2.** In biology, the process by which nutrients are taken in and converted into living tissue, as by absorption and digestion. **3.** In linguistics, the process by which a sound becomes similar or identical to a nearby sound. For example, the prefix *in–* becomes *im–* in *impossible* by assimilation.

As·sin·i·boin (ə-sĭn′ə-boin′) *n., pl.* **Assiniboin** or **As·sin·i·boins 1.** A member of a Native American people of northeast Montana, Alberta, and Saskatchewan. **2.** The Siouan language of the Assiniboin.

as·sist (ə-sĭst′) *v.* **as·sist·ed, as·sist·ing, as·sists** *—tr.* To give help or support to; aid: *Our friends assisted us in repairing the roof.* *—intr.* To give help or support: *We're having trouble with the computer. Could you assist?* ❖ *n.* **1.** An act of giving help; aid: *give someone a quick assist.* **2a.** In baseball, an act of fielding or throwing the ball that enables a teammate to put a runner out. **b.** A pass that enables a teammate to score, as in basketball or hockey. [From Middle English *assisten*, from Latin *assistere* : *ad-*, next to + *sistere*, to stand.] **—as·sist′er** *n.*

as·sis·tance (ə-sĭs′təns) *n.* Help; aid: *The government provided financial assistance to farmers.*

as·sis·tant (ə-sĭs′tənt) *n.* A person who assists; a helper: *the president's special assistant.* ❖ *adj.* Acting under the authority of another person: *an assistant curator.*

as·sist·ed living (ə-sĭs′tĭd) *n.* A living arrangement in which people with special needs reside in a facility that provides help with everyday tasks.

as·siz·es (ə-sī′zĭz) *pl.n.* A court session formerly held periodically in each of the counties of England and Wales.

assn. *abbr.* An abbreviation of association.

assoc. *abbr.* An abbreviation of: **1.** associate. **2.** association.

as·so·ci·ate (ə-sō′sē-āt′ *or* ə-sō′shē-āt′) *v.* **as·so·ci·at·ed, as·so·ci·at·ing, as·so·ci·ates** *—tr.* **1.** To bring together in one's mind or imagination; connect: *We associate pumpkins with the harvest and with fall.* **2.** To connect or involve with a cause, group, or partner: *Which theater was Shakespeare associated with?* *—intr.* **1.** To keep company: *How long have you been associating with those people?* **2.** To join in or form a union or association: *the right for workers to associate in a union.* ❖ *n.* (ə-sō′sē-ĭt *or* ə-sō′shē-ĭt) **1.** A partner or colleague: *my business associate.* **2.** A companion; a comrade. **3.** A member who has only partial status: *an associate of the museum society.* ❖ *adj.* (ə-sō′sē-ĭt *or* ə-sō′shē-ĭt) **1.** Joined with another and having equal or nearly equal status; sharing in responsibility or authority: *an associate judge.* **2.** Having only partial status: *an associate member of a club.* [From Middle English *associat*, associated, from Latin *associāre* : *ad-*, to + *socius*, companion.] **—as·so′ci·a′tor** (ə-sō′sē-ā′tər *or* ə-sō′shē-ā′tər) *n.*

as·so·ci·ate's degree (ə-sō′sē-ĭts′ *or* ə-sō′shē-ĭts′) *n.* A degree given by a college to a person who has completed a two-year program or its equivalent.

as·so·ci·a·tion (ə-sō′sē-ā′shən *or* ə-sō′-shē-ā′shən) *n.* **1.** A group of people joined together for a common purpose or interest: *a trade association; a teachers' association.* **2.** A partnership or friendship: *a close association with old schoolmates.* **3a.** An idea or thought triggered by another idea or thought or by a feeling or sensation: *What associations does the word* whale *bring to your mind?* **b.** A correlation or causal connection: *There is a clear association of exercise with improved health.* **4.** The act of associating: *The author made a striking new association of ideas.*

association football *n. Chiefly British* Soccer.

as·so·ci·a·tive (ə-sō′shə-tĭv *or* ə-sō′sē-ā′tĭv *or* ə-sō′shē-ā′tĭv) *adj.* **1.** Characterized by, resulting from, or causing association. **2.** In mathematics, of or relating to the associative property. **—as·so′ci·a′tive·ly** *adv.*

associative property *n.* In mathematics, a principle stating that different groupings of numbers being added or multiplied will not change their sum or product, as long as the order of the numbers remains the same. For example, $2 + (3 + 4)$ will give the same sum as $(2 + 3) + 4$, and $(2 \times 3) \times 5$ will give the same product as $2 \times (3 \times 5)$.

as·so·nance (ăs′ə-nəns) *n.* **1.** Similarity in sound, especially the repetition in poetry of the same vowel sounds. **2.** A partial rhyme in which the stressed vowel sounds are the same but the consonants are different, as in *tent* and *sense.*

as·sort (ə-sôrt′) *tr.v.* **as·sort·ed, as·sort·ing, as·sorts** To separate into groups according to kinds; classify: *assort books by author.* **—as·sort′er** *n.*

as·sort·ed (ə-sôr′tĭd) *adj.* Consisting of various kinds: *shirts of assorted sizes; assorted screws.*

as·sort·ment (ə-sôrt′mənt) *n.* A collection of various kinds; a variety: *people with an unusual assortment of skills; an assortment of vegetables.*

asst. *abbr.* An abbreviation of assistant.

as·suage (ə-swāj′) *tr.v.* **as·suaged, as·suag·ing, as·suag·es 1.** To make less burdensome or painful: *Maybe your kind words will assuage their sorrow.* **2.** To satisfy; appease: *assuage one's thirst.* **3.** To pacify; calm: *Our apologies assuaged their anger.* **—as·suage′ment** *n.*

as·sume (ə-so͞om′) *tr.v.* **as·sumed, as·sum·ing, as·sumes 1.** To take for granted; suppose: *Let's assume that our guests will come on time.* **2.** To take upon oneself; undertake: *We assume responsibility for keeping the playground clean.* **3.** To undertake the duties of: *The new governor assumes office in January.* **4.** To take over; seize: *She assumed control of the project during the crisis.* **5.** To take on; put on: *assume a disguise.* **6.** To feign; pretend: *always assuming an air of indifference.* [From Middle English *assumen*, from Latin *assūmere* : *ad-*, to + *sūmere*, to take.] **—as·sum′a·ble** *adj.* **—as·sum′a·bly** *adv.* **—as·sum′er** *n.*

as·sumed (ə-so͞omd′) *adj.* **1.** Fictitious; adopted: *an assumed name.* **2.** Taken for granted; supposed: *an assumed increase in funding.*

as·sum·ing (ə-so͞o′mĭng) *conj.* On the assumption that: *Assuming the snowboard is for sale, would you buy it?*

as·sump·tion (ə-sŭmp′shən) *n.* **1.** An idea or statement accepted as true without proof: *Let's start with the assumption that all people have equal rights under the law.* **2.** The act of taking on a task or responsibility: *the new governor's assumption of office.* **3. Assumption** August 15, observed as a holiday in some branches of Christianity to commemorate the taking up of the Virgin Mary into heaven after her death.

as·sur·ance (ə-sho͝or′əns) *n.* **1.** A statement or indication that inspires confidence; a guarantee or pledge: *The debtor gave the bank solemn assurance that the debt would be paid.* **2.** Confidence; certainty: *We had no assurance that the car was in good condition.* **3.** Self-confidence: *The veteran actor played the part with complete assurance.*

as·sure (ə-sho͝or′) *tr.v.* **as·sured, as·sur·ing, as·sures 1.** To declare positively: *I can assure you that the train will be on time.* **2.** To cause to feel sure; convince: *She*

USAGE

assure The words **assure, ensure,** and **insure** all mean "to make secure or certain," but *assure* and *insure* have more specific meanings as well. Of the three, only *assure* means "to cause to feel sure," and it is the only one that can have a person for its direct object: *The duke assured the queen of his loyalty.* By contrast, *ensure* and *insure* never have a person for their direct object: *By changing his diet, he ensured (or insured) his good health.* Only *insure* can be used to mean "to guarantee people or property against risk," as in *We insured the car.*

aster

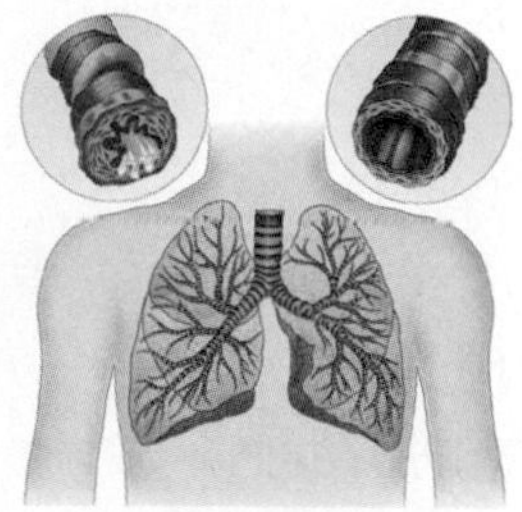

asthma
left: inflamed bronchial tube with contracted muscles and mucus discharge
right: normal bronchial tube

astride

ă	pat	ôr	core
ā	pay	oi	boy
âr	care	ou	out
ä	father	o͝o	took
ĕ	pet	o͝or	lure
ē	be	o͞o	boot
ĭ	pit	ŭ	cut
ī	bite	ûr	urge
îr	pier	th	thin
ŏ	pot	*th*	this
ō	toe	zh	vision
ô	paw	ə	about

assured me of her good intentions. **3.** To make certain; ensure: *The bank lent us the money to assure the success of the business.* **4.** To give confidence to; reassure: *The doctor assured me that I would recover quickly.* —SEE NOTE.

as·sured (ə-**sho͝ord′**) *adj.* **1.** Confident: *an assured manner.* **2.** Certain; guaranteed: *an assured success.* **—as·sur′ed·ly** (ə-**sho͝or′**ĭd-lē) *adv.*

As·syr·i·a (ə-**sîr′**ē-ə) An ancient empire of western Asia in the upper valley of the Tigris River. Between the ninth and seventh centuries BC, the empire included all of Mesopotamia and extended westward to the Mediterranean Sea. **—As·syr′i·an** *adj. & n.*

AST *abbr.* An abbreviation of: **1.** Alaska Standard Time. **2.** Atlantic Standard Time.

A·sta·na (ə-**stä′**nə) The capital of Kazakhstan, in the north-central part of the country. It was founded as a fortress in 1824.

As·tar·te (ə-**stär′**tē) *n.* In ancient Phoenician, Syrian, and Canaanite mythology, the goddess of love and war.

as·ta·tine (**ăs′**tə-tēn′ *or* **ăs′**tə-tĭn) *n. Symbol* **At** A highly unstable, radioactive nonmetallic element that is the heaviest element of the halogen group. The most stable of its many isotopes has a half-life of about eight hours. Atomic number 85. See **Periodic Table.**

as·ter (**ăs′**tər) *n.* Any of various plants having white, purplish, or pink flowers resembling daisies. [From Greek *astēr*, star, type of daisy.]

as·ter·isk (**ăs′**tə-rĭsk′) *n.* A symbol (*) used in printed and written matter to indicate an omission or reference to a footnote, for example. [From Middle English, from Greek *asteriskos*, diminutive of *astēr*, star.]

a·stern (ə-**stûrn′**) *adv. & adj.* **1.** Behind a ship or boat. **2.** At or toward the rear of a ship or boat. **3.** With the stern foremost; backward.

as·ter·oid (**ăs′**tə-roid′) *n.* Any of numerous small, often irregularly shaped bodies that orbit the sun, chiefly in the region between Mars and Jupiter. They range from the size of a speck of dust to several hundred miles in diameter. [From Greek *asteroeidēs*, starlike.]

asteroid belt *n.* The region of the solar system between the orbits of Mars and Jupiter, where most of the asteroids are found.

asth·ma (**ăz′**mə *or* **ăs′**mə) *n.* A chronic disease that is often caused by an allergy and is marked by narrowing of the breathing passages. It results in attacks of wheezing, coughing, difficulty in breathing, and tightness of the chest. [From Middle English *asma*, from Greek *asthma.*]

asth·mat·ic (ăz-**măt′**ĭk *or* ăs-**măt′**ĭk) *adj.* **1.** Relating to asthma. **2.** Having asthma: *an asthmatic child.* ❖ *n.* A person with asthma.

as though *conj.* As if: *They looked as though they were enjoying themselves.*

a·stig·ma·tism (ə-**stĭg′**mə-tĭz′əm) *n.* A defect of the eye in which the curvature of the cornea or lens is uneven. This unevenness prevents rays of light from being focused at a single point on the retina, resulting in indistinct or imperfect images. **—as′tig·mat′ic** (ăs′tĭg-**măt′**ĭk) *adj.*

a·stir (ə-**stûr′**) *adj.* **1.** In motion; moving about: *The miners' camp was astir after the news of the gold discovery.* **2.** Having gotten out of bed; up.

as to *prep.* **1.** With regard to: *There is much controversy as to nuclear energy.* **2.** According to: *The fabrics were arranged as to color.*

a·ston·ish (ə-**stŏn′**ĭsh) *tr.v.* **a·ston·ished, a·ston·ish·ing, a·ston·ish·es** To fill with wonder; amaze; surprise: *The results of the experiment astonished the researchers.* See Synonyms at **surprise.** [From Middle English *astonen*, from Old French *estoner* : Latin *ex-*, out + Latin *tonāre*, to thunder.]

a·ston·ish·ing (ə-**stŏn′**ĭ-shĭng) *adj.* Greatly surprising; amazing: *an astonishing discovery.* **—a·ston′ish·ing·ly** *adv.*

a·ston·ish·ment (ə-**stŏn′**ĭsh-mənt) *n.* Great surprise; amazement: *our astonishment at seeing a shooting star.*

a·stound (ə-**stound′**) *tr.v.* **a·stound·ed, a·stound·ing, a·stounds** To astonish and bewilder: *The price of the fancy car astounded me.* See Synonyms at **surprise.** [From Middle English *astoned*, past participle of *astonen*, to astonish.]

a·stound·ing (ə-**stoun′**dĭng) *adj.* Surprising; amazing: *an astounding success.* **—a·stound′ing·ly** *adv.*

a·strad·dle (ə-**străd′**l) *prep.* Astride; astride of: *astraddle a horse.*

as·tral (**ăs′**trəl) *adj.* Relating to, coming from, or resembling the stars.

a·stray (ə-**strā′**) *adv.* Away from the proper goal or path: *led astray by bad advice.*

a·stride (ə-**strīd′**) *adv.* **1.** With the legs on each side: *riding astride on a horse.* **2.** With the legs wide apart. ❖ *prep.* With a leg on each side of; bestriding: *The cowboy sat astride the horse's back.* ◆ **astride of** Astride: *She stood astride of the fallen tree.*

as·trin·gent (ə-**strĭn′**jənt) *adj.* Having the property of drawing together or contracting tissues. ❖ *n.* A substance that draws together or contracts body tissues. Astringents can be applied to the skin cosmetically or can be used medicinally to check the flow of blood or other secretions.

astro– *pref.* A prefix that means: **1.** Star: *astrophysics.* **2.** Celestial object or objects: *astrometry.* **3.** Outer space: *astronaut.*

as·tro·labe (**ăs′**trə-lāb′) *n.* A medieval instrument formerly used to determine the altitude of the sun and other celestial objects.

as·trol·o·gy (ə-**strŏl′**ə-jē) *n.* The study of the positions of the stars and planets in the belief that they influence the course of human affairs and natural occurrences on earth. **—as·tro·log′i·cal** (ăs′trə-**lŏj′**ĭ-kəl) *adj.* **—as′tro·log′i·cal·ly** *adv.* **—as·trol′o·ger** *n.*

as·trom·e·try (ə-**strŏm′**ĭ-trē) *n.* The scientific measurement of the positions and motions of celestial objects.

as·tro·naut (**ăs′**trə-nôt′) *n.* A person trained to serve as a member of the crew of a spacecraft. [From Greek *astron*, star + Greek *nautēs*, sailor.]

as·tro·nau·tics (ăs′trə-**nô′**tĭks) *n. (used with a singular or plural verb)* The science and technology of space flight. **—as′tro·nau′tic, as′tro·nau′ti·cal** *adj.*

as·tron·o·mer (ə-**strŏn′**ə-mər) *n.* A scientist who specializes in astronomy.

as·tro·nom·i·cal (ăs′trə-**nŏm′**ĭ-kəl) also **as·tro·nom·ic** (ăs′trə-**nŏm′**ĭk) *adj.* **1.** Relating to astronomy. **2.** Too large to be easily imagined; immense: *The budget for running the federal government is astronomical.* **—as′tro·nom′i·cal·ly** *adv.*

astronomical unit *n.* A unit of length equal to the mean distance from Earth to the sun, about 93 million miles (150 million kilometers), used to measure distances within the solar system.

astronomical year *n.* A solar year.

as·tron·o·my (ə-**strŏn′**ə-mē) *n.* The science that deals with the study of the universe and the objects in it, including stars, planets, and nebulae. Astronomy studies the size, composition, and energy of the universe and the relative motion and positions of the objects in it. [From Middle English *astronomie*, from Greek *astronomiā* : *astron*, star + *-nomiā*, field of study.]

as·tro·phys·ics (ăs′trō-**fĭz′**ĭks) *n. (used with a singular verb)* The branch of astronomy that deals with the physical processes, such as energy generation and transmission, that occur in stars, galaxies, and interstellar space. **—as′tro·phys′i·cal** *adj.*

As·tro·Turf (ăs′trō-tûrf′) A trademark for an artificial ground covering that resembles grass.

as·tute (ə-sto͞ot′) *adj.* Having or showing keen judgment; shrewd: *The reporter was an astute observer. Before advising us the carpenter made an astute appraisal of the blueprints.* **—as·tute′ly** *adv.* **—as·tute′ness** *n.*

A·sun·ción (ä-so͞on′syōn′) The capital of Paraguay, in the southern part of the country near the Argentinian border. It is Paraguay's chief port.

a·sun·der (ə-sŭn′dər) *adv.* **1.** Into separate parts or groups: *A tornado tore the house asunder.* **2.** Apart from each other in position or direction: *The curtains were drawn asunder.*

as well as *conj.* And in addition: *warm as well as sunny.* ❖ *prep.* In addition to: *The principal, as well as the teachers, was present at the meeting.*

a·sy·lum (ə-sī′ləm) *n.* **1.** Protection and immunity from extradition granted to a political refugee from another country. **2.** Shelter or protection, especially from physical danger: *We sought asylum from the storm in an old shed.* **3.** An institution for the care of chronically ill patients, especially those with severe mental disorders.

a·sym·met·ric (ā′sĭ-mĕt′rĭk) also **a·sym·met·ri·cal** (ā′-sĭ-mĕt′rĭkəl) *adj.* Not symmetrical; lacking symmetry. **—a′sym·met′ri·cal·ly** *adv.*

a·sym·me·try (ā-sĭm′ĭ-trē) *n.* Lack of symmetry or balance.

a·symp·to·mat·ic (ā′sĭmp-tə-măt′ĭk) *adj.* Causing or showing no disease symptoms: *an asymptomatic infection.*

as·ymp·tote (ăs′ĭm-tōt′) *n.* A line whose distance to a given curve gets closer and closer to zero. The curve may come closer and closer without ever touching the asymptote, or it may cross back and forth over the asymptote like ripples that get smaller and smaller without completely flattening out.

at (ăt; ət *when unstressed*) *prep.* **1.** In or near the position or location of: *at home; at the center of the room.* **2.** To or toward the direction or goal of: *look at us; jump at the chance.* **3.** Present during; attending: *at the dance.* **4.** On, near, or by the time or age of: *at noon.* **5.** In the state or condition of: *He's at peace with himself.* **6.** In the activity or field of: *skilled at playing chess; good at math.* **7.** In the rate, extent, or amount of: *at 40 miles per hour; at two dollars a gallon.* **8.** Because of: *rejoice at victory.* **9a.** Dependent upon: *at your mercy.* **b.** According to: *at the judge's discretion.* **10.** Through; by way of: *Come in at the side entrance.*

At The symbol for the element **astatine.**

at·a·vism (ăt′ə-vĭz′əm) *n.* The reappearance of a characteristic in an organism after several generations of absence.

at·a·vis·tic (ăt′ə-vĭs′tĭk) *adj.* Reappearing after an absence of several generations; being an atavism.

ate (āt) *v.* Past tense of **eat.**
❑ *These sound alike:* **ate, eight** (number).

-ate¹ *suff.* A suffix that means: **1.** Characterized by: *Latinate.* **2.** Resembling: *palmate.* **3.** One that is characterized by: *laminate.* **4.** Rank; office: *rabbinate.* **5.** To act upon in a specified manner: *insulate.*

-ate² *suff.* A suffix that means a salt or an ester of a specified acid whose name ends in *-ic*: *acetate.*

a tem·po (ä tĕm′pō) *adv. & adj.* In music, returning to the original tempo.

Ath·a·bas·can or **Ath·a·bas·kan** (ăth′ə-băs′kən) *n.* A group of languages of Native American people of the western United States and Canada and parts of Alaska. Apache and Navajo are two important Athabascan languages. **—Ath′a·bas′can** *adj.*

a·the·ism (ā′thē-ĭz′əm) *n.* Disbelief in or denial of the existence of God or gods. **—a′the·ist** *n.* **—a′the·is′tic** *adj.*

A·the·na (ə-thē′nə) *n.* In Greek mythology, the goddess of wisdom and the arts, identified with the Roman Minerva.

Ath·ens (ăth′ənz) The capital of Greece, in the eastern part of the country near an arm of the Aegean Sea. It was at the height of its cultural achievements and imperial power in the fifth century BC. Athens became the capital of modern Greece in 1834.

ath·er·o·scle·ro·sis (ăth′ə-rō-sklə-rō′sĭs) *n.* Hardening and thickening of the walls of the arteries caused by deposits of fatty material, especially cholesterol.

ath·lete (ăth′lēt′) *n.* A person who participates in physical exercise or sports, especially in competitive events. [From Middle English, from Greek *āthlētēs*, contestant, from *āthlein*, to contend.]

ath·lete's foot (ăth′lēts) *n.* A contagious infection of the feet that usually affects the skin between the toes, causing it to itch, blister, and crack. It is caused by a fungus.

ath·let·ic (ăth-lĕt′ĭk) *adj.* **1.** Relating to athletics or athletes: *athletic ability; an athletic club.* **2.** Characterized by or involving physical activity or exertion: *an athletic workout.* **3.** Physically strong; muscular: *an athletic build.* See Synonyms at **muscular. —ath·let′i·cal·ly** *adv.*

ath·let·ics (ăth-lĕt′ĭks) *n.* *(used with a singular or plural verb)* Competitive sports or other recreational activities that involve physical exercise and typically require strength, speed, endurance, coordination, and agility.

athletic supporter *n.* An elastic support for the male genitals, often worn during athletic activities.

a·thwart (ə-thwôrt′) *prep.* Across: *threw the rope athwart the dock.* ❖ *adv.* From side to side; across.

-ation *suff.* A suffix that means: **1.** Action or process: *strangulation.* **2.** The state, condition, or quality of: *starvation.* **3.** The result of an action or process: *discoloration.* —SEE NOTE.

-ative *suff.* A suffix that means relating to or associated with: *talkative; authoritative.*

At·lan·ta (ăt-lăn′tə) The capital of Georgia, in the northwest part of the state. It was founded in 1837 and almost entirely destroyed by fire on November 15, 1864, before the start of Union general William Tecumseh Sherman's march to the sea.

At·lan·tic Ocean (ăt-lăn′tĭk) The world's second-largest ocean, divided into the **North Atlantic** and the **South Atlantic.** It extends from the Arctic in the north to the Antarctic in the south between the eastern Americas and western Europe and Africa.

Atlantic Standard Time *n.* Standard time in the fourth time zone west of Greenwich, England, used, for example, in Puerto Rico and Nova Scotia.

At·lan·tis (ăt-lăn′tĭs) *n.* A fabled island or continent of ancient times, said to have sunk beneath the sea during an earthquake.

at·las (ăt′ləs) *n., pl.* **at·las·es** A book or bound collection of maps. [Probably from pictures of Atlas holding the world on his shoulders that appeared on the front of early atlases.]

Atlas *n.* In Greek mythology, a Titan who supported the heavens on his shoulders as punishment for revolt against Zeus.

Atlas Mountains A mountain range of northwest Africa extending from southwest Morocco to northern Tunisia. It rises to 13,671 feet (4,167 meters).

ATM (ā′tē′ĕm′) *n.* A computer terminal that allows a bank customer with an identification card to have access to his or her account, especially to withdraw or deposit money.

at·mos·phere (ăt′mə-sfîr′) *n.* **1.** The mixture of gases that surrounds the earth or some other celestial object and is held by the force of gravity. The atmosphere of

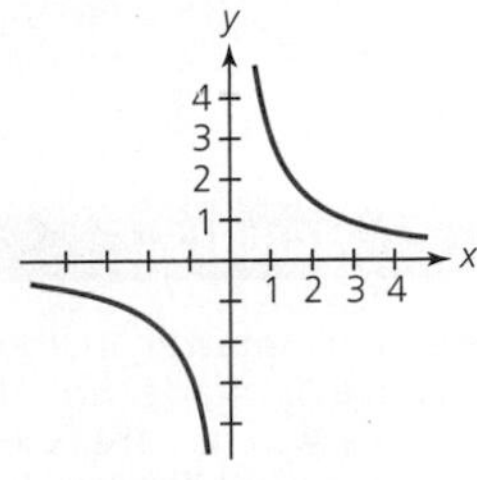

asymptote
The *x*-axis and *y*-axis are asymptotes of the hyperbola $xy = 3$.

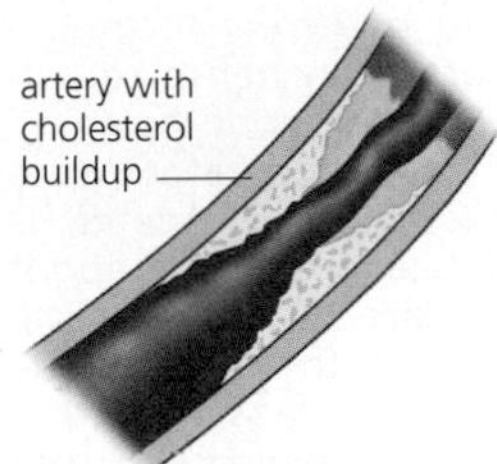

atherosclerosis

WORD BUILDING

-ation The very common suffix **-ation,** which comes from Latin, is used to change a verb to a noun. In English, *-ation* nouns were at first formed from verbs that ended in *-ate,* like the noun *creation* from the verb *create.* But *-ation* became so popular that it is now used to form nouns from verbs that do not end in *-ate,* such as *civilization* from the verb *civilize* and *starvation* from the verb *starve.*

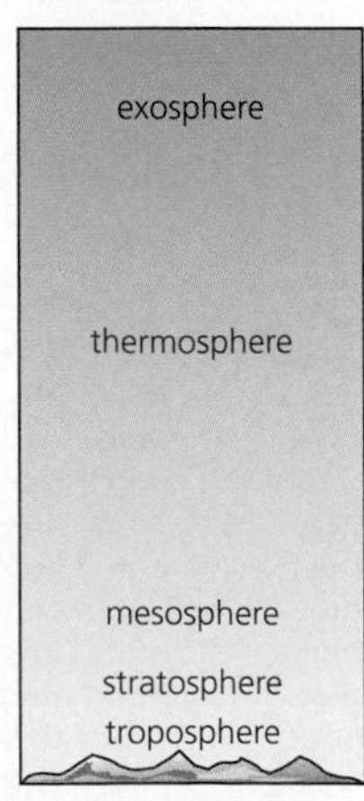

atmosphere

the earth is rich in nitrogen; that of Venus is mainly carbon dioxide. **2.** A unit of pressure equal to the pressure of the air at sea level, about 14.7 pounds per square inch or 1,013 millibars. **3.** The air or climate of a place: *the dry atmosphere of the desert.* **4.** A general feeling or mood: *the library's quiet atmosphere.* [From New Latin *atmosphaera* : Greek *atmos*, vapor + Latin *sphaera*, sphere.]

at·mos·pher·ic (ăt′mə-**sfĕr′**ĭk *or* ăt′mə-**sfîr′**ĭk) *adj.* **1.** Relating to, in, or from the atmosphere: *atmospheric disturbances; atmospheric flight.* **2.** Evoking some mood or aesthetic quality: *a restaurant with atmospheric lighting.* **—at′mos·pher′i·cal·ly** *adv.*

atmospheric pressure *n.* Pressure caused by the weight of the air. At sea level it has an average value of one atmosphere, but it diminishes with increasing altitude.

at. no. *abbr.* An abbreviation of atomic number.

a·toll (**ăt′**ôl′ *or* **ā′**tôl′) *n.* An island or chain of islets connected by a coral reef that nearly or entirely encloses a lagoon. [Probably ultimately from Sanskrit *antara-*, interior.]

at·om (**ăt′**əm) *n.* The smallest unit of an element, consisting of protons and neutrons in a dense central nucleus orbited by a number of electrons. In electrically neutral atoms, the number of protons equals the number of electrons. Atoms remain intact in chemical reactions, except for the removal, transfer, or exchange of certain electrons. [From Middle English *attome*, from Greek *atomos*, indivisible, atom : *a-*, not + *tomos*, cuttable (from *temnein*, to cut).] —SEE NOTE.

SCIENCE

atom All matter in the universe is made up of **atoms.** Atoms are extremely small. The smallest bacterium that can be seen with an ordinary microscope contains about one trillion atoms. Each atom consists of even tinier particles. *Protons* and *neutrons* form the nucleus, a dense region at the center of the atom. If a hydrogen atom were two miles in diameter, its nucleus would be about the size of a tennis ball. Outside the nucleus, the atom is mostly empty space in which *electrons* are orbiting at fantastic speeds. The atoms of every element have a unique number of protons. The nucleus of a hydrogen atom, for example, is made up of just one proton. The nucleus of a lead atom is much bigger, with 82 protons and usually 126 neutrons.

atom bomb *n.* An atomic bomb.

a·tom·ic (ə-**tŏm′**ĭk) *adj.* **1.** Relating to atoms. **2.** Using or produced by atomic energy; nuclear: *an atomic power plant.*

atomic age *n.* The present age considered as the time of the discovery and use of atomic energy; the nuclear age.

atomic bomb *n.* A very destructive bomb that gets its explosive power from the energy released by the fission of atomic nuclei, usually of plutonium or uranium, in an uncontrolled chain reaction.

atomic clock *n.* An extremely precise clock that is regulated by atomic vibrations.

atomic energy *n.* Nuclear energy.

atomic mass *n.* The mass of an atom, usually expressed in atomic mass units.

atomic mass unit *n.* A unit of mass equal to $\frac{1}{12}$ the mass of the most abundant kind of carbon atom, carbon-12; approximately 1.6604×10^{-24} gram.

atomic number *n.* The number of protons in the atomic nucleus of a chemical element.

atomic theory *n.* The physical theory of the structure, properties, and behavior of atoms.

atomic weight *n.* The average weight of an atom of an element, usually expressed relative to the most abundant isotope of carbon, which is assigned 12 atomic mass units.

at·om·ize (**ăt′**ə-mīz′) *tr.v.* **at·om·ized, at·om·iz·ing, at·om·iz·es 1.** To break apart or separate into atoms. **2.** To reduce (a liquid) into a fine spray. **—at′om·i·za′tion** (ăt′ə-mĭ-**zā′**shən) *n.*

at·om·iz·er (**ăt′**ə-mī′zər) *n.* A device for producing a fine spray, especially of a perfume or medicine.

atom smasher *n.* A particle accelerator.

a·ton·al (ā-**tō′**nəl) *adj.* In music, having no key or tonality. **—a·ton′al·ly** *adv.*

a·to·nal·i·ty (ā′tō-**năl′**ĭ-tē) *n., pl.* **a·to·nal·i·ties** The absence of a tonal center and of harmonies using a diatonic scale.

a·tone (ə-**tōn′**) *intr.v.* **a·toned, a·ton·ing, a·tones** To make amends for a sin, fault, or other wrong: *atone for bad manners by apologizing.* [From Middle English *atonen*, to be reconciled, from *at one*, in agreement.]

a·tone·ment (ə-**tōn′**mənt) *n.* **1.** The act of atoning; amends. **2. Atonement** In Christianity, the reconciliation between God and humans brought about by the life and death of Jesus.

a·top (ə-**tŏp′**) *prep.* On top of: *The Supreme Court stands atop our judicial court system.*

ATP (ā′tē′**pē′**) *n.* An organic compound, having the formula $C_{10}H_{16}N_5O_{13}P_3$, that acts as an energy source in cell metabolism. [From the chemical name *a(denosine) t(ri)p(hosphate).*]

A·treus (**ā′**tro͞os′ *or* **ā′**trē-əs) *n.* In Greek mythology, a king of Mycenae and the father of Agamemnon and Menelaus.

a·tri·um (**ā′**trē-əm) *n., pl.* **a·tri·a** (**ā′**trē-ə) or **a·tri·ums 1a.** A central area in some modern buildings that often has skylights and contains plants. **b.** The open entrance court of an ancient Roman house. **2.** A cavity or chamber of the body, especially one of the chambers of the heart that receives blood from the veins and pumps it into a ventricle. **—a′tri·al** *adj.*

a·tro·cious (ə-**trō′**shəs) *adj.* **1.** Extremely evil or cruel; wicked. **2.** Very bad; abominable: *atrocious weather.* [From Latin *atrōx*, cruel.] **—a·tro′cious·ly** *adv.* **—a·tro′cious·ness** *n.*

a·troc·i·ty (ə-**trŏs′**ĭ-tē) *n., pl.* **a·troc·i·ties 1.** The condition of being atrocious. **2.** An act of extreme cruelty and violence.

at·ro·phy (**ăt′**rə-fē) *n., pl.* **at·ro·phies** The wasting away of a body part, most commonly caused by disease, injury, or lack of use. ❖ *tr. & intr.v.* **at·ro·phied, at·ro·phy·ing, at·ro·phies** To waste away or cause to waste away: *A month of inactivity had atrophied the patient's body.*

at·ro·pine (**ăt′**rə-pēn′ *or* **ăt′**rə-pĭn) *n.* A very poisonous bitter alkaloid that is obtained from belladonna and is used as a medicine to control muscle spasms and relax the pupils in examining the eye.

at sign *n.* The symbol (@) for the word *at.*

at·tach (ə-**tăch′**) *v.* **at·tached, at·tach·ing, at·tach·es** *—tr.* **1.** To fasten or join; connect: *attached the wires to the post.* **2.** To add (something) at the end; append: *The lawyer had us attach our signatures to the document.* **3.** To think of as belonging to something; ascribe: *I attach no importance to our different points of view.* **4.** To bind by ties of affection or loyalty: *The brother and sister are very attached to each other.* **5.** To assign (military personnel) to a unit on a temporary basis: *attach soldiers to an expeditionary force.* **6.** To take or seize (property) by court order: *The bank attached the debtor's salary.* *—intr.* **1.** To adhere or belong: *Acclaim attaches to the hero.* **2.** To be attached or attachable: *The helmet's chin strap attaches on the side just below the ear.* [From Middle English *attachen*, from Old French *estachier*, from *estache*, stake, of Germanic origin.] **—at·tach′a·ble** *adj.*

attaché case

at·ta·ché (ăt′ə-**shā′**) *n.* A person assigned to the staff of a diplomatic mission to serve in some particular capacity: *a cultural attaché to the American Embassy.*

attaché case *n.* A briefcase resembling a small suitcase, with hinges and flat sides.

at·tach·ment (ə-**tăch′**mənt) *n.* **1.** The act of attaching or condition of being attached: *attachment of a horse to a wagon.* **2.** A supplementary part; an accessory: *This vacuum cleaner has several attachments.* **3.** A supplementary document attached to a main document. **4.** A bond of affection or loyalty: *a strong attachment to a friend.*

at·tack (ə-**tăk′**) *v.* **at·tacked, at·tack·ing, at·tacks** *—tr.* **1.** To set upon with violent force: *Even large animals will not attack elephants.* **2.** To criticize strongly or in a hostile manner: *The candidates attacked each other in their*

ă	pat	ôr	core
ā	pay	oi	boy
âr	care	ou	out
ä	father	o͝o	took
ĕ	pet	o͝or	lure
ē	be	o͞o	boot
ĭ	pit	ŭ	cut
ī	bite	ûr	urge
îr	pier	th	thin
ŏ	pot	*th*	this
ō	toe	zh	vision
ô	paw	ə	about

debate. **3.** To cause harm to; affect harmfully: *a disease that attacks the nervous system.* **4.** To start work on with purpose and vigor: *attack the problem of costly health care.* —*intr.* To launch an assault: *The troops attacked at dawn.* ❖ *n.* **1.** The act of violent attacking; an assault. **2.** An expression of strong criticism. **3.** An occurrence or onset of a disease, especially when sudden: *an attack of asthma.* **4.** The manner in which a musical tone, phrase, or passage is begun: *a hard, cutting attack.* **5.** In sports, offensive play: *Even the defenders got involved in the attack.* [From Old French *attaquer*, of Germanic origin.] **—at·tack′er** *n.*

at·tain (ə-tān′) *tr.v.* **at·tained, at·tain·ing, at·tains 1.** To gain, accomplish, or achieve by effort: *attain a diploma by hard work.* See Synonyms at **reach. 2.** To arrive at or reach, as through time, growth, or movement: *Today many people attain the age of 80.* [From Middle English *atteinen*, from Old French *ataindre*, to reach to : Latin *ad-*, to + Latin *tangere*, to touch.] **—at·tain′a·bil′i·ty** *n.* **—at·tain′a·ble** *adj.*

at·tain·ment (ə-tān′mənt) *n.* **1.** The act of attaining: *Despite attainment of independence, the United States remained closely associated with Great Britain.* **2.** often **attainments** Something attained; an acquirement, as a skill or an ability: *Eleanor Roosevelt is noted for her attainments in diplomacy.*

at·tar (ăt′ər) *n.* A fragrant oil obtained from the petals of flowers, especially roses, and used in making perfume.

at·tempt (ə-tĕmpt′) *tr.v.* **at·tempt·ed, at·tempt·ing, at·tempts 1.** To try (to do something): *He attempted to run a mile in under six minutes.* **2.** To try to perform, make, or achieve: *She attempted a difficult dive.* ❖ *n.* **1.** An effort or a try: *an attempt to solve the mystery.* **2.** An attack; an assault: *an attempt on the king's life.* [From Middle English *attempten*, from Latin *attemptāre* : *ad-*, toward + *temptāre*, to test.]

at·tend (ə-tĕnd′) *v.* **at·tend·ed, at·tend·ing, at·tends** —*tr.* **1.** To be present at; go to: *In some countries, students attend school on Saturdays.* **2.** To follow as a result or occur as a circumstance of: *The speech was attended by wild applause.* **3.** To accompany and assist: *The squire attended the knight during the joust.* **4.** To take care of: *Two nurses attended the sick boy.* **5.** To pay attention to; heed: *We attended the words of the instructor.* —*intr.* **1.** To be present at an event: *I wanted to go, but was ill and could not attend.* **2.** To apply oneself; give care and thought: *Please attend to the matter at hand.* **3.** To pay attention; heed: *The audience attended to the lecture with great interest.* [From Middle English *attenden*, from Latin *attendere*, to heed : *ad-*, toward + *tendere*, to stretch.]

at·ten·dance (ə-tĕn′dəns) *n.* **1.** The act or practice of being present: *The child's attendance at school has been perfect.* **2.** The people or number of people who are present: *an attendance of 50,000 at the football game.* **3.** The act or state of taking care of someone or something, as at a hospital: *a physician in attendance.*

at·ten·dant (ə-tĕn′dənt) *n.* A person who attends or waits on another: *a parking lot attendant.* ❖ *adj.* Accompanying or following as a result: *attendant circumstances.*

at·ten·tion (ə-tĕn′shən) *n.* **1.** The act of close or careful observing or listening: *Read the article carefully and pay attention to the details.* **2.** Concentration of the mental powers upon something or someone: *The speaker held the listeners' attention for more than an hour.* **3.** Observant consideration; notice: *Your suggestion has come to our attention.* **4. attentions** Acts of courtesy or consideration, especially in trying to win a person's affection: *Do you think his attentions are sincere?* **5.** The posture taken by a soldier, with the body erect, eyes to the front, arms at the sides, and heels together: *Stand at attention.* ❖ *interj.* An expression used as a command to assume an erect military posture.

attention deficit disorder *n.* Attention deficit hyperactivity disorder.

attention deficit hyperactivity disorder *n.* A condition whose symptoms include impulsiveness, a short attention span, and often hyperactivity. It is usually diagnosed in childhood and can interfere with performance at school, in the workplace, and in social situations.

attention span *n.* The length of time during which a person can concentrate on a subject or idea.

at·ten·tive (ə-tĕn′tĭv) *adj.* **1.** Giving attention to something; alert: *Only the most attentive students understood the explanation.* **2.** Giving or marked by careful attention to the comfort of others; considerate: *an attentive host.* **—at·ten′tive·ly** *adv.* **—at·ten′tive·ness** *n.*

at·ten·u·ate (ə-tĕn′yo͞o-āt′) *v.* **at·ten·u·at·ed, at·ten·u·at·ing, at·ten·u·ates** —*tr.* **1.** To make slender or thin: *The drought attenuated the river to a narrow channel.* **2.** To reduce, as in strength, force, or power; weaken: *Medicine attenuated the effect of the fever.* —*intr.* To become thin or weak. **—at·ten′u·a′tion** *n.*

at·test (ə-tĕst′) *v.* **at·test·ed, at·test·ing, at·tests** —*tr.* **1.** To declare or state to be true, correct, or genuine, especially by signing one's name as a witness: *attest a will.* **2.** To give evidence or proof of; prove: *Their rounded shapes attest the great age of the mountains.* —*intr.* To bear witness: *I can attest to his presence at the concert.*

at·test·ed (ə-tĕs′tĭd) *adj.* Recorded in written form: *Use of the word* helicopter *is first attested in English in 1887.*

at·tic (ăt′ĭk) *n.* A story or room just below the roof of a building. [From *Attic story*, story of a building enclosed by one decorative structure placed above another, much taller decorative structure, usually involving the Attic order, an architectural order having square columns of any of the basic five orders, from Latin *Atticus*, of Attica, the region in Greece of which Athens was the capital.]

At·ti·la (ăt′l-ə *or* ə-tĭl′ə) AD 406?–453. King of the Huns (433?–453). He reigned over a large empire and led a successful invasion of the Roman Empire.

at·tire (ə-tīr′) *tr.v.* **at·tired, at·tir·ing, at·tires** To dress, especially in fine or formal clothing: *an emperor attired in ceremonial robes.* ❖ *n.* Clothing, costume, or apparel: *white tennis attire.*

at·ti·tude (ăt′ĭ-to͞od′) *n.* **1.** A state of mind with regard to someone or something: *She has a positive attitude about school.* **2.** A position of the body indicative of a mood or condition: *The kids sprawled on the couch in a relaxed attitude.* **3.** An arrogant or hostile state of mind or disposition: *We tried to help him, but so far he's given us nothing but attitude.* **4.** The position of an aircraft or spacecraft in relation to its direction of motion.

at·tor·ney (ə-tûr′nē) *n., pl.* **at·tor·neys** A person who is legally qualified and licensed to represent a person in a legal matter, such as a transaction or lawsuit.

at·tor·ney-at-law (ə-tûr′nē-ət-lô′) *n., pl.* **attorneys-at-law** An attorney.

attorney general *n., pl.* **attorneys general** or **attorney generals** The chief law officer of a state or national government.

at·tract (ə-trăkt′) *v.* **at·tract·ed, at·tract·ing, at·tracts** —*tr.* To cause to draw near or adhere; direct to oneself or itself by some quality or action: *A magnet attracts nails by the physical force of magnetism. The fine beaches attract many tourists.* —*intr.* To have the power to draw to oneself or itself: *attract by magnetic force.* [From Middle English *attracten*, from Latin *attrahere* : *ad-*, toward + *trahere*, to pull.] **—at·tract′er, at·trac′tor** *n.* —SEE NOTE AT **detract.**

at·trac·tion (ə-trăk′shən) *n.* **1.** The act or power of attracting: *the attraction of a magnet.* **2.** Something that attracts: *Its many theaters and museums are some of New*

WRITERS CHOOSE THEIR WORDS

He looked as dry as dust and no more kindly than a silver ink-pot, but he was as polite and **attentive** to those two little girls as if they'd been the Duchess of Savoy and her twin sister.

—Philip Pullman
Count Karlstein

auger

WRITERS CHOOSE THEIR WORDS

Ay me! for **aught** that I could ever read, / Could ever hear by tale or history, / The course of true love never did run smooth.

—William Shakespeare
A Midsummer Night's Dream

Aung San Suu Kyi

ă	pat	ôr	core
ā	pay	oi	boy
âr	care	ou	out
ä	father	o͝o	took
ĕ	pet	o͝or	lure
ē	be	o͞o	boot
ĭ	pit	ŭ	cut
ī	bite	ûr	urge
îr	pier	th	thin
ŏ	pot	*th*	this
ō	toe	zh	vision
ô	paw	ə	about

York's greatest attractions. **3a.** The electric or magnetic force exerted by oppositely charged particles, as a proton and an electron, tending to draw them together. **b.** The gravitational force exerted by one body on another, as by Earth on the moon.

at·trac·tive (ə-**trăk′**tĭv) *adj.* **1.** Pleasing to the eye or mind; appealing: *an attractive young couple; an attractive offer that should be profitable.* **2.** Having the power to attract: *the attractive forces of magnetism and gravity.* **—at·trac′tive·ly** *adv.* **—at·trac′tive·ness** *n.*

at·trib·ute (ə-**trĭb′**yo͞ot) *tr.v.* **at·trib·ut·ed, at·trib·ut·ing, at·trib·utes** To consider (something) as belonging to or resulting from someone or something; ascribe: *We attribute much air pollution to trucks and buses. This piece is attributed to Mozart.* ❖ *n.* **at·tri·bute** (**ăt′**rə-byo͞ot′) A quality or characteristic belonging to a person or thing; a distinctive feature: *One of her best attributes is her quick wit.* See Synonyms at **quality.** [From Latin *attribuere* : *ad-*, to + *tribuere*, to allot.] **—at·trib′ut·a·ble** *adj.* **—at·trib′ut·er, at·trib′u·tor** *n.* **—at′tri·bu′tion** (ăt′rə-**byo͞o′**shən) *n.*

at·trib·u·tive (ə-**trĭb′**yə-tĭv) *n.* A word or phrase placed next to the noun it modifies. In the phrase *city streets,* the word *city* is an attributive. ❖ *adj.* **1.** In grammar, relating to an attributive. **2.** Relating to an attribution or an attribute. —SEE NOTE AT **adjective.**

at·tri·tion (ə-**trĭsh′**ən) *n.* **1.** A wearing away or rubbing down by friction: *The rocks became sand by attrition.* **2.** A gradual loss of number or strength due to constant stress. **3.** A gradual natural reduction in membership or personnel, as through retirement, resignation, or death.

At·tucks (**ăt′**əks), **Crispus** 1723?–1770. American patriot who was among the five people killed in the Boston Massacre.

at·tune (ə-**to͞on′**) *tr.v.* **at·tuned, at·tun·ing, at·tunes** To bring into a harmonious relationship; adjust: *a person attuned to the times.* **—at·tune′ment** *n.*

Atty. *abbr.* An abbreviation of attorney.

at. wt. *abbr.* An abbreviation of atomic weight.

a·typ·i·cal (ā-**tĭp′**ĭ-kəl) *adj.* Not typical; abnormal: *atypical behavior.* **—a·typ′i·cal·ly** *adv.*

Au The symbol for the element **gold.**

au·burn (**ô′**bərn) *n.* A reddish brown. ❖ *adj.* Reddish brown: *auburn hair.*

Auck·land (**ôk′**lənd) The largest city of New Zealand, on an isthmus of northwest North Island. It is a major port.

auc·tion (**ôk′**shən) *n.* A public sale in which goods or property is sold to the highest bidder. ❖ *tr.v.* **auc·tioned, auc·tion·ing, auc·tions** To sell at an auction.

auc·tion·eer (ôk′shə-**nîr′**) *n.* A person who conducts an auction.

au·da·cious (ô-**dā′**shəs) *adj.* **1.** Fearlessly daring: *an audacious explorer.* **2.** Arrogant; impudent: *a showoff's audacious behavior.* **—au·da′cious·ly** *adv.* **—au·da′cious·ness** *n.*

au·dac·i·ty (ô-**dăs′**ĭ-tē) *n., pl.* **au·dac·i·ties 1.** Courage and resolution; boldness. **2.** Insolence; impudence: *the customs official's audacity in demanding a bribe.*

au·di·ble (**ô′**də-bəl) *adj.* Loud enough to be heard: *Speak in an audible voice so that others may hear you.* [From Late Latin *audībilis*, from Latin *audīre*, to hear.] **—au′di·bil′i·ty, au′di·ble·ness** *n.* **—au′di·bly** *adv.*

au·di·ence (**ô′**dē-əns) *n.* **1.** The people gathered to see and hear a play, movie, concert, or other performance. **2.** The readers, hearers, or viewers reached by a book, radio broadcast, television program, or online source: *The audience for this TV series has been growing.* **3.** A formal hearing or conference: *an audience with the pope.* **4.** An opportunity to be heard; a hearing: *The planning committee gave the builders an audience before voting on the project.*

au·di·o (**ô′**dē-ō′) *adj.* **1.** Relating to sound that is recorded, transmitted, or reproduced: *an MP3 player and other audio equipment.* **2.** Relating to sound that can be heard: *audio signals used in a hearing test.* ❖ *n., pl.* **au·di·os 1.** Audible sound. **2.** Recorded or reproduced sound. [From Latin *audīre*, to hear.]

audio frequency *n.* A frequency corresponding to audible sound vibrations, usually between 20 hertz and 20,000 hertz for humans.

au·di·ol·o·gy (ô′dē-**ŏl′**ə-jē) *n.* The study of hearing, especially hearing defects and their treatment. **—au·di·ol′o·gist** *n.*

au·di·om·e·ter (ô′dē-**ŏm′**ĭ-tər) *n.* An instrument used to measure how well a person can hear.

au·di·o·tape (**ô′**dē-ō-tāp′) *n.* A magnetic tape used to record sound for later playback. ❖ *tr.v.* **au·di·o·taped, au·di·o·tap·ing, au·di·o·tapes** To record (sound) on magnetic tape: *audiotaped the lecture.*

au·di·o·vis·u·al also **au·di·o·vis·u·al** (ô′dē-ō-**vĭzh′**o͞o-əl) *adj.* **1.** Relating to both hearing and sight. **2.** Conveying information through media, such as audio and video recordings, that are perceivable by both hearing and sight.

au·dit (**ô′**dĭt) *n.* **1.** An examination of financial records or accounts to check their accuracy. **2.** A thorough evaluation: *an audit of home energy use.* ❖ *tr.v.* **au·dit·ed, au·dit·ing, au·dits 1.** To examine and verify (financial records or accounts). **2.** To attend (a college course) without receiving academic credit.

au·di·tion (ô-**dĭsh′**ən) *n.* **1.** A trial performance, as by an actor, dancer, or musician, to demonstrate suitability or skill. **2.** The sense or power of hearing: *audition in bats.* ❖ *v.* **au·di·tioned, au·di·tion·ing, au·di·tions** —*intr.* To perform in an audition: *Several musicians auditioned for a place in the orchestra.* —*tr.* To give (a performer) an audition: *The director of the movie auditioned many actors.*

au·di·tor (**ô′**dĭ-tər) *n.* **1.** A person who audits financial records or accounts. **2.** A person who audits courses in college. **3.** A hearer or listener, especially of musical auditions.

au·di·to·ri·um (ô′dĭ-**tôr′**ē-əm) *n., pl.* **au·di·to·ri·ums** or **au·di·to·ri·a** (ô′dĭ-**tôr′**ē-ə) **1.** A room to seat a large audience in a building, such as a school. **2.** A large building used for public meetings or performances. [From Middle English *auditorie*, from Latin *audītōrium*, from *audīre*, to hear.]

au·di·to·ry (**ô′**dĭ-tôr′ē) *adj.* Relating to hearing or the organs of hearing: *the auditory canal of the ear.*

auditory nerve *n.* The nerve that carries impulses associated with hearing and balance from the inner ear to the brain.

Au·du·bon (**ô′**də-bŏn′), **John James** 1785–1851. Haitian-born American naturalist who wrote and illustrated *The Birds of America* (1827–1838).

au·ger (**ô′**gər) *n.* **1.** A tool for boring holes. **2.** A screwlike shaft that has a continuous, spiraling blade and is rotated to move material, such as snow in a snowblower. ❖ *tr.v.* **au·gered, au·ger·ing, au·gers** To drill or bore a hole using an auger. [From Old English *nafogār*, altered to Middle English *(an) auger*, from the phrase *(a) nauger.*]

❑ *These sound alike:* **auger, augur** (predict).

aught[1] also **ought** (ôt) *pron.* Anything at all. [From Old English *āuht.*]

❑ *These sound alike:* **aught[1]** (anything), **aught[2]** (zero), **ought** (be obliged).

aught[2] also **ought** (ôt) *n.* The digit zero. [From *(an) aught*, alteration of *(a) naught.*]

❑ *These sound alike:* **aught[2]** (zero), **aught[1]** (anything), **ought** (be obliged).

aug·ment (ôg-**mĕnt′**) *tr.v.* **aug·ment·ed, aug·ment·ing, aug·ments** To make larger; increase: *The library's collection has been augmented by 5,000 new books.*

—**aug·ment′a·ble** *adj.* —**aug′men·ta′tion** *n.*

au gra·tin (ō **grät′**n) *adj.* Topped with bread crumbs and often grated cheese and browned in an oven.

au·gur (**ô′**gər) *n.* A religious official of ancient Rome who foretold events by omens from the entrails of birds, thunder, and other natural signs. ❖ *v.* **au·gured, au·gur·ing, au·gurs** —*tr.* **1.** To predict (something), especially from signs or omens. **2.** To be a sign of; give promise of: *Early returns augured victory for the young candidate.* —*intr.* **1.** To make predictions from signs or omens. **2.** To be a sign or omen: *A smooth dress rehearsal augured well for the play.*

❑ *These sound alike:* **augur, auger** (drill).

au·gu·ry (**ô′**gyə-rē) *n., pl.* **au·gu·ries 1.** The art or practice of auguring. **2.** A sign or an omen.

au·gust (ô-**gŭst′**) *adj.* Inspiring awe or reverence; majestic: *the august bearing of the king.* [From Latin *augustus.*] —**au·gust′ly** *adv.*

Au·gust (**ô′**gəst) *n.* The eighth month of the year in the Gregorian calendar, having 31 days. [From Old English, from Latin *(mēnsis) Augustus,* (month) of Augustus.]

Au·gus·ta (ô-**gŭs′**tə) The capital of Maine, in the southwest part of the state north-northeast of Portland. A trading post was established here in 1628.

Au·gus·tine (**ô′**gə-stēn′ *or* ô-**gŭs′**tĭn), Saint. AD 354–430. Early Christian philosopher whose writings, especially *Confessions* (397) and *City of God* (413–426), profoundly influenced Christianity.

Au·gus·tus (ô-**gŭs′**təs) Originally **Oc·ta·vi·an** (ŏk-**tā′**-vē-ən). 63 BC–AD 14. First emperor of Rome (27 BC–AD 14). He defeated Mark Antony and Cleopatra in 31 and then gained control over Rome and its territories.

au jus (ō **zhōōs′** *or* ō **zhü′**) *adj.* Served with its own gravy or juice from cooking: *roast beef au jus.*

auk (ôk) *n.* Any of several black-and-white northern seabirds having a plump body and short wings. [From Old Norse *ālka.*]

auld (ôld) *adj. Scots* Old.

auld lang syne (ôld′ lăng **zīn′**) *n.* The times gone past; the good old days.

Aung San Suu Kyi (**ông′ sän′ sōō′ chē′**) Born 1945. Burmese political leader who became an outspoken proponent of democracy after a military junta seized power in her country in 1988.

aunt (ănt *or* änt) *n.* **1.** The sister of one's father or mother. **2.** The wife of a sibling of one's mother or father. [From Middle English *aunte,* from Latin *amita,* paternal aunt.]

❑ *These sound alike:* **aunt, ant** (insect).

au·ra (**ôr′**ə) *n., pl.* **au·ras** or **au·rae** (**ôr′**ē) A distinctive air or quality that characterizes a person or thing: *an aura of mystery about the old house.* [From Middle English, gentle breeze, from Latin, from Greek *aurā,* breath.]

au·ral (**ôr′**əl) *adj.* Relating to or perceived by the ear: *aural stimulation.* —**au′ral·ly** *adv.*

❑ *These sound alike:* **aural, oral** (of the mouth).

au·re·ole (**ôr′**ē-ōl′) *n.* **1.** In art, an area of light around the head of a sacred figure; a halo. **2.** A glow that surrounds the sun or the moon, especially when seen through a fog or haze.

au·ri·cle (**ôr′**ĭ-kəl) *n.* **1.** The external part of the ear. **2.** An atrium of the heart.

❑ *These sound alike:* **auricle, oracle** (prophet).

au·ric·u·lar (ô-**rĭk′**yə-lər) *adj.* **1.** Relating to hearing or the organs of hearing. **2.** Relating to an auricle of the heart.

au·rochs (**ou′**rŏks′ *or* **ôr′**ŏks′) *n., pl.* **aurochs** A wild ox of Europe, northern Africa, and western Asia that became extinct in the 1600s and is believed to be the ancestor of domestic cattle.

au·ro·ra (ə-**rôr′**ə) *n.* A brilliant display of bands or streamers of light visible in the night sky, chiefly in the polar regions. It is thought to be caused by electrically charged particles from the sun that are drawn into the atmosphere by the earth's magnetic field. [From Middle English, dawn, from Latin *aurōra,* dawn.]

Aurora *n.* In Roman mythology, the goddess of the dawn, identified with the Greek Eos.

aurora aus·tra·lis (ô-**strā′**lĭs) *n.* The aurora of the Southern Hemisphere; the southern lights.

aurora bo·re·al·is (bôr′ē-**ăl′**ĭs) *n.* The aurora of the Northern Hemisphere; the northern lights.

aus·pi·ces (**ô′**spĭ-sĭz *or* **ô′**spĭ-sēz′) *pl.n.* Protection and support; patronage: *The marathon was organized under the auspices of local athletic clubs.*

aus·pi·cious (ô-**spĭsh′**əs) *adj.* Showing signs of a successful outcome or result; favorable: *Their first large orders were an auspicious beginning for the new business.* —**aus·pi′cious·ly** *adv.* —**aus·pi′cious·ness** *n.*

Aus·ten (**ô′**stən), **Jane** 1775–1817. British writer whose novels include *Pride and Prejudice* (1813). —SEE NOTE.

aus·tere (ô-**stîr′**) *adj.* **aus·ter·er, aus·ter·est 1.** Having a stern personality or appearance; somber: *an unsmiling, austere judge.* **2.** Living very simply, with few comforts: *a desert nomad's austere life.* **3.** Lacking decoration; plain or bare: *Their austere living quarters had no pictures on the walls.* —**aus·tere′ly** *adv.* —**aus·tere′ness** *n.*

aus·ter·i·ty (ô-**stĕr′**ĭ-tē) *n., pl.* **aus·ter·i·ties 1.** The condition of being austere. **2.** Lack of luxury; extreme restraint in spending: *wartime austerity.*

Aus·tin (**ô′**stən *or* **ŏs′**tən) The capital of Texas, in the south-central part of the state northeast of San Antonio. Made the capital of the Republic of Texas in 1839, it became the capital of the state of Texas in 1872.

Aus·tra·lia (ô-**strāl′**yə) **1.** The world's smallest continent, southeast of Asia between the Pacific and Indian Oceans. **2.** A commonwealth made up of the continent of Australia and the island of Tasmania. The first Australian federation was formed in 1901. Canberra is the capital and Sydney the largest city.

Aus·tra·lian (ô-**strāl′**yən) *adj.* Relating to Australia or its peoples, languages, or cultures. ❖ *n.* **1.** A native or inhabitant of Australia. **2.** A member of any of the Aboriginal peoples of Australia. **3.** Any of the languages of the Aboriginal peoples of Australia.

aus·tra·lo·pith (**ô′**strə-lə-pĭth′) *n.* Any of several extinct humanlike primates known from fossils dating from about four million to about one million years ago. Fossil remains of australopiths have been found in southern and eastern Africa.

Aus·tri·a (**ô′**strē-ə) A landlocked country of central Europe south of Germany and the Czech Republic. Austria was annexed by Adolf Hitler in 1938, and full independence was restored in 1955. Vienna is the capital.

Aus·tri·a-Hun·ga·ry (ô′strē-ə-**hŭng′**gə-rē) A former dual monarchy of central Europe formed in 1867 and lasting until 1918.

au·then·tic (ô-**thĕn′**tĭk) *adj.* **1.** Being so in fact; not counterfeit or copied; genuine: *an authentic medieval sword.* **2.** In accord with fact and worthy of belief; true or credible: *an authentic account of the events.* [From Middle English *autentik,* from Greek *authentikos,* from *authentēs,* author.] —**au·then′ti·cal·ly** *adv.*

SYNONYMS authentic, genuine, real, true These adjectives mean not counterfeit or copied. *An expert assured us that the chair is an authentic antique from the 1700s. The recipe calls for genuine Italian olive oil, but the store sells only American brands. The bouquets were made with silk flowers instead of real ones. A true friend would be more understanding.*

au·then·ti·cate (ô-**thĕn′**tĭ-kāt′) *tr.v.* **au·then·ti·cat·ed, au·then·ti·cat·ing, au·then·ti·cates 1.** To establish as being true; prove: *Witnesses will authenticate our account*

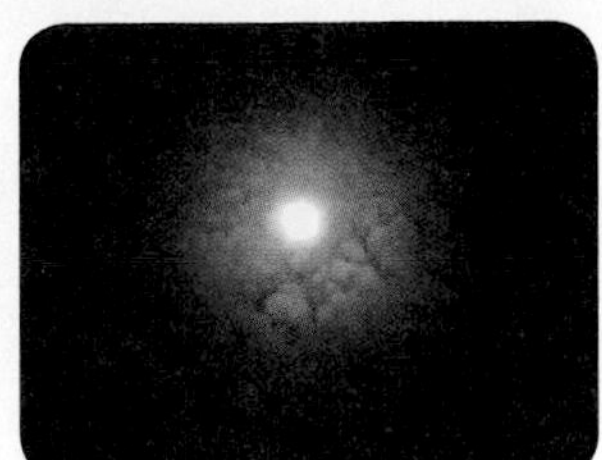

aureole

Jane Austen

BIOGRAPHY

Jane Austen Jane **Austen** lived a short and mostly uneventful life, yet she wrote six of the best-loved novels in the English language, novels whose popularity has endured for two centuries. Austen was born in a village in southern England, where her father was a clergyman. She began writing fiction as a teenager, mostly for her own entertainment and that of her immediate family, producing several drafts of novels which she reworked in her adult years for publication. Her books, such as *Pride and Prejudice* (published in 1813) and *Emma* (1816), are remarkable for the wit, realism, and affectionate irony with which they depict the social life of her day.

of the accident. **2.** To establish (a painting, an antique, or another object) as being genuine: *Experts can authenticate the old violin.* **—au·then′ti·ca′tion** *n.* **—au·then′ti·ca′tor** *n.*

au·then·tic·i·ty (ô′thĕn-tĭs′ĭ-tē) *n.* The condition or quality of being authentic: *The authenticity of our claim is established by these old records.*

au·thor (ô′thər) *n.* **1.** A person who writes a book, story, article, or other written work. **2.** A person who writes or constructs an electronic document or system, such as a website. **3.** The creator or originator of something: *the author of an idea.* ❖ *tr.v.* **au·thored, au·thor·ing, au·thors** To be the author of: *She has authored several books.* [From Middle English *auctour,* from Latin *auctor,* creator, from *augēre,* to create.]

au·thor·i·tar·i·an (ə-thôr′ĭ-târ′ē-ən) *adj.* Characterized by, favoring, or demanding absolute obedience to authority: *the authoritarian government of a dictator.* ❖ *n.* A person who believes in or practices authoritarian behavior. **—au·thor′i·tar′i·an·ism** *n.*

au·thor·i·ta·tive (ə-thôr′ĭ-tā′tĭv) *adj.* **1.** Having or arising from proper authority; official: *an authoritative ruling.* **2.** Known to be accurate; reliable: *authoritative sources for the newspaper article.* **—au·thor′i·ta′tive·ly** *adv.* **—au·thor′i·ta′tive·ness** *n.*

au·thor·i·ty (ə-thôr′ĭ-tē) *n., pl.* **au·thor·i·ties 1a.** The power to enforce laws, command obedience, determine, or judge: *Our principal has the authority to close the school.* **b.** A person or organization having this power: *government authorities.* **2.** An accepted source of expert information, as a book or person: *an authority on history.* **3.** Power to influence or affect resulting from knowledge or experience: *She writes about science with authority.*

au·thor·i·za·tion (ô′thər-ĭ-zā′shən) *n.* **1.** The act of authorizing. **2.** An expression of official consent: *needed written authorization from his commanding officer.*

au·thor·ize (ô′thə-rīz′) *tr.v.* **au·thor·ized, au·thor·iz·ing, au·thor·iz·es 1.** To grant authority or power to: *The school authorizes teachers to hold class outside.* **2.** To approve or give permission for: *The legislature authorized a highway project.* **—au′thor·iz′er** *n.*

au·thor·ship (ô′thər-shĭp′) *n.* The origin, as of a book: *a book of unknown authorship.*

au·tism (ô′tĭz′əm) *n.* A developmental disorder, marked by difficulty in communicating and in relating to other people, and often by the presence of repetitive behaviors. **—au·tis′tic** (ô-tĭs′tĭk) *adj.*

au·to (ô′tō) *n., pl.* **au·tos** An automobile.

auto– or **aut–** *pref.* A prefix that means: **1.** Self; same: *autobiography.* **2.** Automatic: *autopilot.*

au·to·bi·og·ra·phy (ô′tō-bī-ŏg′rə-fē) *n., pl.* **au·to·bi·og·ra·phies** The story of a person's life written by that person. **—au′to·bi·og′ra·pher** *n.* **—au′to·bi′o·graph′i·cal** (ô′tō-bī′ə-grăf′ĭ-kəl) *adj.* **—au′to·bi′o·graph′i·cal·ly** *adv.*

au·to·clave (ô′tō-klāv′) *n.* A tank used especially for antiseptic sterilizing under high-pressure steam.

au·to·com·plete (ô′tō-kəm-plēt′) *n.* A function, as on a search engine, that supplies options of predicted words or phrases based on the characters that a user has already entered.

au·toc·ra·cy (ô-tŏk′rə-sē) *n., pl.* **au·toc·ra·cies 1.** Government by a person having absolute power. **2.** A country having this form of government.

au·to·crat (ô′tə-krăt′) *n.* **1.** A ruler having unlimited power. **2.** An arrogant person with unlimited power: *The boss is an autocrat.*

au·to·crat·ic (ô′tə-krăt′ĭk) *adj.* **1.** Relating to autocracy: *an autocratic government.* **2.** Like an autocrat; arrogant: *The professor has a very autocratic manner.* **—au′to·crat′i·cal·ly** *adv.*

au·to·fill (ô′tō-fĭl′) *n. Computers* A feature, as in a spreadsheet, that automatically fills certain boxes with data based on information the user has entered elsewhere.

au·to·graph (ô′tə-grăf′) *n.* **1.** A signature, usually of a famous person and saved by an admirer or collector. **2.** A manuscript in the author's own handwriting. ❖ *tr.v.* **au·to·graphed, au·to·graph·ing, au·to·graphs** To write one's name or signature on. [From Late Latin *autographum,* from Greek *autographos,* written with one's own hand : *auto-,* self + *graphein,* to write.] **—au′to·graph′ic, au′to·graph′i·cal** *adj.*

Au·to·harp (ô′tō-härp′) A trademark for a musical instrument that is somewhat like a zither with a set of keys to play different chords.

au·to·im·mune (ô′tō-ĭ-myo͞on′) *adj.* Relating to a reaction of the immune system in which antibodies are produced that attack the body's own cells and tissues, often causing illness: *an autoimmune disease.* **—au′to·im·mu′ni·ty** (ô′tō-ĭ-myo͞o′nĭ-tē) *n.*

au·to·mak·er (ô′tō-mā′kər) *n.* A manufacturer of automobiles.

au·tom·a·ta (ô-tŏm′ə-tə) *n.* A plural of **automaton.**

au·to·mate (ô′tə-māt′) *v.* **au·to·mat·ed, au·to·mat·ing, au·to·mates** *—tr.* To operate (a process, factory, or machine) with automatic machinery or processes: *automate an assembly line with robots.* *—intr.* To make use of automatic machinery and processes: *Costs of manufacturing were reduced after the factory automated.*

au·to·mat·ed teller machine (ô′tə-mā′tĭd) *n.* An ATM.

au·to·mat·ic (ô′tə-măt′ĭk) *adj.* **1.** Acting or operating without the control of a human: *an automatic elevator.* **2.** Done or produced by the body without conscious control or awareness; involuntary: *the automatic shrinking of the pupils in bright light.* **3.** Capable of firing continuously until ammunition is gone or the trigger is released: *an automatic rifle.* ❖ *n.* A device or machine, especially a firearm, that is completely or partially automatic. [From Greek *automatos* : *auto-,* self + *-matos,* willing.] **—au′to·mat′i·cal·ly** *adv.*

automatic pilot *n.* A navigation device that automatically keeps to a preset course.

au·to·ma·tion (ô′tə-mā′shən) *n.* The automatic operation or control of a process, machine, or system, often by electronic devices, such as computers or robots: *Automation has replaced many workers in manufacturing.*

au·tom·a·ton (ô-tŏm′ə-tŏn′ *or* ô-tŏm′ə-tən) *n., pl.* **au·tom·a·tons** or **au·tom·a·ta** (ô-tŏm′ə-tə) **1.** An automatic machine, especially a robot. **2.** A person who behaves in a mechanical way.

au·to·mo·bile (ô′tə-mō-bēl′ *or* ô′tə-mō′bēl′) *n.* A passenger vehicle generally moving on four wheels and propelled by a gasoline engine on land.

au·to·mo·tive (ô′tə-mō′tĭv) *adj.* **1.** Relating to self-propelled vehicles, such as automobiles and trucks. **2.** Self-propelled or self-propelling.

au·to·nom·ic nervous system (ô′tə-nŏm′ĭk) *n.* The part of the vertebrate nervous system that regulates involuntary actions, as in the heart, digestive system, and glands. It is divided into two parts, the sympathetic nervous system and the parasympathetic nervous system.

au·ton·o·mous (ô-tŏn′ə-məs) *adj.* **1.** Acting independently: *an autonomous organization.* **2.** Self-governing with respect to local or internal affairs: *an autonomous region of a country.* **—au·ton′o·mous·ly** *adv.*

au·ton·o·my (ô-tŏn′ə-mē) *n., pl.* **au·ton·o·mies** The ability or right to act independently.

au·to·pi·lot (ô′tō-pī′lət) *n.* An automatic pilot.

au·top·sy (ô′tŏp′sē) *n., pl.* **au·top·sies** A medical examination of a dead human body to determine the cause of death. —SEE NOTE AT **triceratops.**

au·to·troph (ô′tə-trŏf′ *or* ô′tə-trōf′) *n.* An organism that

CHRIS VAN ALLSBURG

10 · 17 · 06

autograph

ă	pat	ôr	core
ā	pay	oi	boy
âr	care	ou	out
ä	father	o͝o	took
ĕ	pet	o͝or	lure
ē	be	o͞o	boot
ĭ	pit	ŭ	cut
ī	bite	ûr	urge
îr	pier	th	thin
ŏ	pot	*th*	this
ō	toe	zh	vision
ô	paw	ə	about

manufactures its own food from inorganic substances, such as carbon dioxide and nitrogen, using light or chemical energy. Green plants, algae, and some bacteria are autotrophs. **—au′to·troph′ic** *adj.*

au·tumn (ô′təm) *n.* The season of the year occurring between summer and winter. In the Northern Hemisphere, it lasts from the autumnal equinox until the winter solstice, or in ordinary usage, from September until December. In the Southern Hemisphere, it lasts from March until June. ❖ *adj.* Occurring in or appropriate to the season of autumn: *autumn colors.* [From Middle English *autumpne*, from Latin *autumnus.*]

au·tum·nal (ô-tŭm′nəl) *adj.* Relating to, occurring in, or appropriate to the autumn. **—au·tum′nal·ly** *adv.*

autumnal equinox *n.* The equinox that occurs on September 22 or 23, when the sun crosses the celestial equator while moving in a southwesterly direction, marking the beginning of autumn in the Northern Hemisphere and spring in the Southern Hemisphere.

aux·il·ia·ry (ôg-zĭl′yə-rē *or* ôg-zĭl′ə-rē) *adj.* **1.** Giving assistance or support: *a sailboat with an auxiliary engine.* **2.** Additional, subsidiary, or supplementary: *auxiliary branches of the fire department in outlying areas.* ❖ *n., pl.* **aux·il·ia·ries 1.** A person or thing that helps; an assistant. **2.** An auxiliary verb. **3.** An organization that is subsidiary to a larger one: *Members of the hospital auxiliary visit patients and run errands.* **4.** A member of a body of foreign troops serving a country in war.

auxiliary verb *n.* A verb that comes first in a verb phrase and helps form the tense, mood, or voice of the main verb. *Have, may, can, must* and *will* can act as auxiliary verbs.

aux·in (ôk′sĭn) *n.* Any of various plant hormones that regulate growth and development.

aux. v. *abbr.* An abbreviation of auxiliary verb.

AV *abbr.* An abbreviation of audio-visual.

av. *abbr.* An abbreviation of: **1.** average. **2.** avoirdupois.

Av. *abbr.* An abbreviation of avenue.

a·vail (ə-vāl′) *v.* **a·vailed, a·vail·ing, a·vails** *—tr.* To be of use or advantage to; help: *Nothing can avail us now.* *—intr.* To be of use or value; help: *A calculator avails little if you don't understand the problem.* ❖ *n.* Use, benefit, or advantage: *Since all the doors were locked, the burglar's efforts were to no avail.* ◆ **avail (oneself) of** To make use of; take advantage of: *While visiting Paris you must avail yourself of the museums.* [From Middle English *availen* : Latin *ad-*, intensive prefix + Old French *valoir*, to be worth (from Latin *valēre*).]

a·vail·a·ble (ə-vā′lə-bəl) *adj.* **1.** Capable of being obtained: *Tickets are available at the box office.* **2.** Close by and ready for use: *Keep a calculator available during the test.* **3.** Willing to serve: *All available volunteers were asked to help.* **—a·vail′a·bil′i·ty, a·vail′a·ble·ness** *n.* **—a·vail′a·bly** *adv.*

av·a·lanche (ăv′ə-lănch′) *n.* **1.** The fall or slide of a large mass of material, as of snow or rock, down the side of a mountain. **2.** A massive or overwhelming amount: *an avalanche of mail.* [From French; akin to Provençal *lavanca*, ravine, perhaps ultimately from Latin *lābī*, to slip.]

Av·a·lon (ăv′ə-lŏn′) *n.* In legend, an island paradise in the western seas to which King Arthur was taken after he was mortally wounded in battle.

a·vant-garde (ä′vänt-gärd′) *n.* A group of people who are the leaders in promoting new or unconventional styles, ideas, or methods, especially in the arts. ❖ *adj.* Exhibiting new or unconventional styles, ideas, or methods: *an avant-garde magazine.*

av·a·rice (ăv′ə-rĭs) *n.* Extreme desire for getting money or wealth; greed.

av·a·ri·cious (ăv′ə-rĭsh′əs) *adj.* Extremely desirous of money or wealth; greedy. **—av′a·ri′cious·ly** *adv.* **—av′a·ri′cious·ness** *n.*

a·vast (ə-văst′) *interj.* An expression used as a command aboardship to stop an activity.

av·a·tar (ăv′ə-tär′) *n.* An image used by a member of an online community to represent himself or herself.

a·vaunt (ə-vônt′ *or* ə-vänt′) *interj. Archaic* An expression used as a command to get out or away.

Ave. *abbr.* An abbreviation of avenue.

A·ve Ma·ri·a (ä′vā mə-rē′ə) *n.* The Hail Mary prayer in Latin. [From Middle English, from Medieval Latin *Avē Maria*, Hail, Mary!]

a·venge (ə-vĕnj′) *tr.v.* **a·venged, a·veng·ing, a·veng·es 1.** To take revenge or satisfaction for: *The hockey team vowed to avenge the loss to their rivals.* **2.** To take revenge on behalf of: *avenge a betrayed friend.* **—a·veng′er** *n.*

av·e·nue (ăv′ə-no͞o′) *n.* **1.** A wide street or thoroughfare. **2.** A means of reaching or achieving something: *We must seek many avenues for peace.*

a·ver (ə-vûr′) *tr.v.* **a·verred, a·ver·ring, a·vers** To state positively and firmly; assert; affirm.

av·er·age (ăv′ər-ĭj *or* ăv′rĭj) *n.* **1.** A number, especially the arithmetic mean, that is derived from and considered typical or representative of a set of numbers. **2.** A typical kind or usual level or degree: *That musician's abilities are above average.* ❖ *tr.v.* **av·er·aged, av·er·ag·ing, av·er·ag·es 1.** To compute the average of (a set of numbers): *After the trip we averaged the number of miles we went each day.* **2.** To have or attain as an average: *The temperature averages about 75 degrees in the summer.* ❖ *adj.* **1.** Computed or determined as an average: *On our trip across the country our average speed was 50 miles per hour.* **2a.** Typical, usual, or ordinary: *an average American family.* **b.** Not exceptional; mediocre: *a bright boy who was only an average student in math.* ◆ **on the average** Using the average as a basis for judgment. [From Middle English, charge above the cost of freight, from Arabic *'awārīya*, damaged goods.]

a·verse (ə-vûrs′) *adj.* Opposed; unwilling: *Cats are averse to getting wet.* **—a·verse′ly** *adv.* **—a·verse′ness** *n.*

a·ver·sion (ə-vûr′zhən *or* ə-vûr′shən) *n.* A strong dislike: *I have an aversion to crowds.*

a·vert (ə-vûrt′) *tr.v.* **a·vert·ed, a·vert·ing, a·verts 1.** To turn away or aside: *When we were stared at we averted our eyes.* **2.** To keep from happening; prevent: *She averted an accident by staying well behind the truck.* **—a·vert′a·ble, a·vert′i·ble** *adj.*

avg. *abbr.* An abbreviation of average.

a·vi·an (ā′vē-ən) *adj.* Relating to birds.

a·vi·ar·y (ā′vē-ĕr′ē) *n., pl.* **a·vi·ar·ies** A large cage or enclosure for birds, as in a zoo.

a·vi·a·tion (ā′vē-ā′shən) *n.* **1.** The art of operating and navigating aircraft. **2.** The design, development, and production of aircraft.

a·vi·a·tor (ā′vē-ā′tər) *n.* A pilot of an aircraft.

av·id (ăv′ĭd) *adj.* Having or marked by keen interest and enthusiasm: *an avid golfer; an avid interest in cooking.* **—av′id·ly** *adv.*

a·vid·i·ty (ə-vĭd′ĭ-tē) *n.* Eagerness or enthusiasm.

a·vi·on·ics (ā′vē-ŏn′ĭks) *n. (used with a singular verb)* The science and technology of electronics as applied to aircraft and spacecraft.

av·o·ca·do (ăv′ə-kä′dō *or* ä′və-kä′dō) *n., pl.* **av·o·ca·dos 1.** An edible, tropical American fruit having leathery green or blackish skin, mild-tasting yellow-green flesh, and a single large seed. **2.** The tree that bears such fruit. [From Spanish *aguacate*, from Nahuatl *ahuacatl.*]

av·o·ca·tion (ăv′ō-kā′shən) *n.* An interest or activity that is done for enjoyment in addition to one's regular work.

A·vo·ga·dro's number (ä′və-gä′drōz) *n.* The number

WRITERS CHOOSE THEIR WORDS

The old man suddenly scowled. "A curse on Duke Raymond. When he betrayed us and sank the *Black Falcon,* he condemned us to this life of poverty. I am too old to begin the pirate life again, but you, you will go far. And you will **avenge** us all, myself and the crew." "I will **avenge** us all," Erik replied dutifully.

—Conor Kostick
Epic

avocado

awning

axe

axolotl

ă	pat	ô r	core
ā	pay	oi	boy
âr	care	ou	out
ä	father	o͝o	took
ĕ	pet	o͝or	lure
ē	be	o͞o	boot
ĭ	pit	ŭ	cut
ī	bite	ûr	urge
îr	pier	th	thin
ŏ	pot	*th*	this
ō	toe	zh	vision
ô	paw	ə	about

of items in a mole of a given substance, approximately 6.0221 × 10^{23}. [After Amedeo *Avogadro* (1776–1856), Italian physicist.]

a·void (ə-**void′**) *tr.v.* **a·void·ed, a·void·ing, a·voids 1.** To keep away from; stay clear of; shun: *avoid too many sweets; avoid the crowds at the mall.* **2.** To prevent; keep from happening: *avoid an accident.* **—a·void′a·ble** *adj.* **—a·void′a·bly** *adv.* **—a·void′ance** *n.*

av·oir·du·pois weight (ăv′ər-də-**poiz′**) *n.* A system of weights based on a pound equal to 16 ounces, traditionally used in English-speaking countries to weigh everything except gems, precious metals, and drugs.

a·vow (ə-**vou′**) *tr.v.* **a·vowed, a·vow·ing, a·vows** To acknowledge openly; admit freely: *We avowed our support for the controversial law.* **—a·vow′a·ble** *adj.*

a·vow·al (ə-**vou′**əl) *n.* An open admission or acknowledgment: *avowal of an unpopular opinion.*

a·vowed (ə-**voud′**) *adj.* Openly acknowledged: *Policies that are openly arrived at are the avowed platform of our democratic government.* **—a·vow′ed·ly** *adv.*

a·vun·cu·lar (ə-**vŭng′**kyə-lər) *adj.* **1.** Relating to an uncle. **2.** Resembling an uncle, especially in kindliness.

aw (ô) *interj.* An expression used to show sympathy, doubt, or disapproval.

❑ *These sound alike:* **aw, awe** (wonder).

a·wait (ə-**wāt′**) *tr.v.* **a·wait·ed, a·wait·ing, a·waits 1.** To wait for: *We sat up awaiting news of the election results.* **2.** To be in store for: *The meeting with the principal awaits us at the end of the week.*

a·wake (ə-**wāk′**) *v.* **a·woke** (ə-**wōk′**) or **a·waked, a·waked** or **a·wok·en** (ə-**wō′**kən), **a·wak·ing, a·wakes** *—tr.* **1.** To rouse from sleep; waken: *The alarm clock awoke me at seven.* **2.** To make (someone) aware of something: *The report awoke him to the possibilities of a compromise.* **3.** To stir up (memories, for example): *Seeing the old car awoke memories of my grandfather.* *—intr.* **1.** To wake up: *I awoke at dawn.* **2.** To become aware of something: *Americans are awaking to the need for recycling.* ❖ *adj.* **1.** Not asleep: *He was awake all night.* **2.** Alert, vigilant, or watchful: *awake to the dangers of an unhealthy diet.* [From Middle English *awaken*, from Old English *āwacan* : *ā-*, intensive prefix + *wacan*, wake.]

a·wak·en (ə-**wā′**kən) *v.* **a·wak·ened, a·wak·en·ing, a·wak·ens** *—intr.* **1.** To wake up: *I awakened early because of the noise.* **2.** To become aware of something: *We finally awakened to the fact that our team needed more practice.* *—tr.* **1.** To cause to wake up: *A barking dog awakened me during the night.* **2.** To stir up or produce (a feeling or memory, for example): *Becoming an aunt awakened in her a sense of responsibility.* **—a·wak′en·er** *n.*

a·wak·en·ing (ə-**wā′**kə-nĭng) *n.* **1.** The act of waking up. **2.** The act or process of rousing from inactivity or indifference; a stirring up: *a great awakening of interest in our environment.*

a·ward (ə-**wôrd′**) *tr.v.* **a·ward·ed, a·ward·ing, a·wards 1.** To give or bestow (a prize, medal, or other honor) for outstanding performance or quality: *The committee awarded a ribbon to the best dog in the show.* **2.** To give or grant by legal or governmental decision: *award damages to the injured driver; award a contract to the lowest bidder.* ❖ *n.* **1.** Something, such as a prize or medal, awarded for outstanding performance or quality: *an award for bravery.* **2.** Something judged as due by legal decision. **—a·ward′a·ble** *adj.* **—a·ward′er** *n.*

a·ware (ə-**wâr′**) *adj.* Mindful or conscious: *be aware of the abilities of each staff member.* **—a·ware′ness** *n.*

a·wash (ə-**wŏsh′**) *adv. & adj.* **1.** Level with or washed by waves: *The rocks were awash in the tide.* **2.** Floating on waves: *The wrecked ship's cargo was awash in the sea.*

a·way (ə-**wā′**) *adv.* **1.** From a particular thing or place: *They got in the car and drove away.* **2.** At or to a distance: *We live two miles away from the beach.* **3.** In a different direction: *Don't look away now.* **4.** Into storage or a safe place: *Please put the toys away.* **5.** From one's presence or possession: *They gave away that old bicycle.* **6.** Out of existence: *The music faded away.* **7.** Continuously: *working away.* **8.** Freely; at will: *Fire away!* ❖ *adj.* **1.** Absent: *My brother is away from home.* **2.** Distant, as in space or time: *Those mountains are miles away. The game is a week away.* **3.** Played on the opposing team's home grounds: *home games and away games.* **4.** In baseball, out: *two away in the ninth.* [From Old English *aweg* : *a-*, on + *weg*, way.]

❑ *These sound alike:* **away, aweigh** (free of the bottom).

awe (ô) *n.* A feeling of wonder, fear, and respect inspired by something mighty or majestic: *gazing in awe at the mountains.* ❖ *tr.v.* **awed, aw·ing, awes** To fill with awe: *The size of the huge plane awed everyone.* [From Middle English *aue*, from Old Norse *agi.*]

❑ *These sound alike:* **awe, aw** (interjection).

a·weigh (ə-**wā′**) *adj.* Hanging clear of the bottom: *With the anchor aweigh, the boat began to drift.*

❑ *These sound alike:* **aweigh, away** (at a distance).

awe·some (**ô′**səm) *adj.* **1.** Inspiring awe: *an awesome sight.* **2.** Remarkable; outstanding: *an awesome party.* **—awe′some·ly** *adv.* **—awe′some·ness** *n.*

awe·struck (**ô′**strŭk′) also **awe·strick·en** (**ô′**strĭk′ən) *adj.* Full of awe: *awestruck by the beauty of the mountains.*

aw·ful (**ô′**fəl) *adj.* **1.** Very bad or unpleasant; horrible: *awful weather; an awful book.* **2.** Inspiring awe or fear; fearsome: *the awful stillness before the tornado.* **3.** Great; considerable: *an awful lot of homework.* ❖ *adv. Informal* Very; extremely: *awful sick.* **—aw′ful·ness** *n.*

❑ *These sound alike:* **awful, offal** (rubbish).

aw·ful·ly (**ô′**fə-lē) *adv.* **1a.** In a manner that inspires awe; terribly: *The wind blew awfully.* **b.** *Informal* Very badly: *She behaved awfully.* **2.** *Informal* Very: *The tourists seemed awfully confused.*

a·while (ə-**wīl′**) *adv.* For a short time: *We waited awhile until they returned.*

awk·ward (**ôk′**wərd) *adj.* **1.** Not graceful; clumsy: *an awkward dancer.* **2.** Causing embarrassment; trying: *An awkward silence fell over the shy students.* **3.** Difficult to handle or manage; cumbersome: *a large and awkward bundle to carry.* [From Middle English *awkeward*, in the wrong way : *awke*, wrong (from Old Norse *öfugr*, backward) + *-ward*, -ward.] **—awk′ward·ly** *adv.* **—awk′ward·ness** *n.*

awl (ôl) *n.* A pointed tool for making holes, as in wood or leather. [From Old English *æl.*]

❑ *These sound alike:* **awl, all** (everything).

awn·ing (**ô′**nĭng) *n.* A protective structure set up over a window or door like a roof.

a·woke (ə-**wōk′**) *v.* A past tense of **awake.**

a·wok·en (ə-**wō′**kən) *v.* A past participle of **awake.**

AWOL or **awol** (**ā′**wôl′) *adj.* Absent without leave, as from an army base. ❖ *n.* A person who is absent without leave.

a·wry (ə-**rī′**) *adv.* **1.** Turned or twisted to one side or out of shape; askew: *The wind blew the curtains awry.* **2.** Wrong; amiss: *Our plans went awry.*

axe or **ax** (ăks) *n., pl.* **ax·es** (**ăk′**sĭz) A tool consisting of a head with a sharp blade on a long handle, used for cutting trees or chopping wood. ❖ *tr.v.* **axed, ax·ing, ax·es** To cut or chop (something) with an axe. ◆ **axe to grind** A selfish or personal aim.

ax·el (**ăk′**səl) *n.* In figure skating, a jump in which the skater takes off while moving forward, makes one and one-half midair turns, and lands on one skate moving backward. [After *Axel Paulsen* (1856–1938), Norwegian figure skater.]

ax·es¹ (ăk′sēz′) *n.* Plural of **axis.**

ax·es² (ăk′sĭz) *n.* Plural of **axe.**

ax·i·al (ăk′sē-əl) *adj.* On, around, forming, or relating to an axis: *A wheel turns by axial motion.*

ax·il (ăk′sĭl) *n.* The angle between the upper side of a leaf and the stem it is attached to. Each axil contains a bud.

ax·i·om (ăk′sē-əm) *n.* **1.** A statement that is accepted as true or assumed to be true without proof. "The whole is greater than any of its parts" is an example of an axiom. **2.** An established rule, principle, or law: *One of the axioms of driving in the United States is to stay to the right.* [From Latin *axiōma*, from Greek, something that is worthy, from *axios*, worthy.]

ax·i·o·mat·ic (ăk′sē-ə-măt′ĭk) *adj.* Relating to or resembling an axiom; self-evident: *That all people are equal under the law is axiomatic.* **—ax′i·o·mat′i·cal·ly** *adv.*

ax·is (ăk′sĭs) *n., pl.* **ax·es** (ăk′sēz′) **1.** A straight line around which an object rotates or can be imagined to rotate: *The axis of the earth passes through both of its poles.* **2.** In geometry, a line, ray, or line segment with respect to which a figure or object is symmetrical: *the axis of a cone.* **3.** A reference line from which or along which distances or angles are measured in a system of coordinates: *the x-axis.* **4. Axis** The alliance of Germany, Italy, Japan, and other nations that opposed the Allies in World War II.

ax·le (ăk′səl) *n.* **1.** A shaft on which one or more wheels revolve. **2.** The spindle of an axletree.

ax·le·tree (ăk′səl-trē′) *n.* A crossbar or rod supporting a vehicle and having a spindle at each end on which a wheel turns.

ax·o·lotl (ăk′sə-lŏt′l) *n.* Any of several salamanders of Mexico and the western United States that unlike most amphibians do not go through metamorphosis. They continue to live in water and breathe with external gills when mature.

ax·on (ăk′sŏn′) *n.* The long extension of a nerve cell that carries impulses away from the body of the cell.

ay (ī) *n. & adv.* Variant of **aye.**

a·ya·tol·lah (ī′yə-tō′lə) *n.* A high-ranking Shiite religious teacher of religious law and interpretation. [From Persian *āyatollāh*, from Arabic *'āyatu llāh*, sign of god.]

aye also **ay** (ī) *n.* **1.** A vote of yes. **2. ayes** Those who vote yes: *The ayes have it; the motion is approved.* ❖ *adv.* Yes; yea.

❑ *These sound alike:* **aye, eye** (organ of sight), **I¹** (personal pronoun).

Ay·ma·ra (ī′mä-rä′) *n., pl.* **Aymara** or **Ay·ma·ras 1.** A member of a South American Indian people inhabiting Bolivia and Peru. **2.** The language of this people. **—Ay′ma·ran′** *adj.*

Ayr·shire (âr′shîr *or* âr′shər) *n.* Any of a breed of reddish-brown and white dairy cattle originally raised in Scotland.

Ayrshire

AZ *abbr.* An abbreviation of Arizona.

a·zal·ea (ə-zāl′yə) *n.* Any of various shrubs that are related to the rhododendrons and are often cultivated for their funnel-shaped, brightly colored flowers.

A·zer·bai·jan (ăz′ər-bī-jän′ *or* ä′zər-bī-jän′) A country of southwest Asia on the Caspian Sea north of Iran and south of Russia. It was formerly a kingdom that extended into northwest Iran. Azerbaijan was part of the USSR from 1922 to 1991. Baku is the capital.

A·zer·bai·ja·ni (ăz′ər-bī-jä′nē *or* äz′ər-bī-jä′nē) *adj.* Relating to Azerbaijan or its people, language, or culture. ❖ *n., pl.* **A·zer·bai·ja·nis 1.** A native or inhabitant of Azerbaijan. **2.** The Turkic language of Azerbaijan.

A·zer·i (ə-zĕr′ē) *adj.* Relating to Azerbaijan or its people, language, or culture. ❖ *n., pl.* **A·zer·is 1.** An Azerbaijani. **2.** The Azerbaijani language.

az·i·muth (ăz′ə-məth) *n.* An arc measured clockwise from a reference point, usually the northern point of the horizon, to the point where a vertical circle passing through a celestial object crosses the horizon. [From Middle English *azimut*, from Arabic *as-sumūt*, plural of *as-samt*, the way, compass bearing, from Latin *sēmita*, path.]

A·zores (ā′zôrz *or* ə-zôrz′) A group of Portuguese islands in the northern Atlantic Ocean about 900 miles (1,450 kilometers) west of mainland Portugal.

Az·tec (ăz′tĕk′) *n.* **1.** A member of an American Indian people of central Mexico whose civilization was at its height at the time of the Spanish conquest in the early 1500s. **2.** The Nahuatl language of the Aztecs. [From Nahuatl *Aztecatl*, one who comes from the place of the cranes.] **—Az′tec′** *adj.*

Aztec
basalt calendar stone, 1479, excavated in Mexico City in 1790

az·ure (ăzh′ər) *n.* A bright blue, as of a clear sky.

baboon

b or **B** (bē) *n., pl.* **b's** or **B's** also **bs** or **Bs** **1.** The second letter of the English alphabet. **2. B** The second-best or second-highest grade: *get a B on a test.* **3. B** In music, the seventh tone in the scale of C major. **4. B** One of the four types of blood in the ABO system.

B The symbol for the element **boron.**

Ba The symbol for the element **barium.**

BA *abbr.* An abbreviation of: **1.** Bachelor of Arts. **2.** batting average.

baa (bă *or* bä) *intr.v.* **baaed, baa·ing, baas** To bleat, as a sheep does. ❖ *n.* The bleating sound made by a sheep.

bab·ble (băb′əl) *v.* **bab·bled, bab·bling, bab·bles** *—intr.* **1.** To utter indistinct or meaningless words or sounds: *Babies babble before they can talk.* **2.** To talk idly or foolishly; chatter: *babble on about neighborhood gossip.* **3.** To make a continuous low murmuring sound, as flowing water. *—tr.* **1.** To utter indistinctly: *babble an answer to a teacher.* **2.** To disclose without consideration; blurt out. ❖ *n.* **1.** Indistinct or meaningless words or sounds: *a babble of voices as we walked through the crowd.* **2.** Idle or foolish talk; chatter. **3.** A continuous low murmuring sound, as of flowing water. [From Middle English *babelen.*] **—bab′bler** *n.*

babe (bāb) *n.* **1.** A baby; an infant. **2.** *Informal* Sweetheart; dear.

ba·bel also **Ba·bel** (băb′əl *or* bā′bəl) *n.* A confusion of sounds, voices, or languages: *a babel of voices in the street below.* [After the Tower of *Babel.*]

Ba·bel (bā′bəl *or* băb′əl) In the Bible, a city, now thought to be Babylon, where God stopped the construction of a tower to heaven by changing the language of the builders into many different languages.

ba·boon (bă-**bo͞on′**) *n.* Any of several large monkeys of Africa and Arabia that have a face with a projecting muzzle like that of a dog and spend most of their time on the ground rather than in trees. [From Middle English *babewin,* from Old French *babuin,* gargoyle.]

ba·bush·ka (bə-**bo͝osh′**kə) *n.* A woman's headscarf, folded in a triangle and worn tied under the chin. [From Russian, grandmother.]

ba·by (bā′bē) *n., pl.* **ba·bies** **1.** A very young child; an infant: *Babies are not able to care for themselves.* **2.** A very young animal: *We went to the zoo to see the chimpanzee's new baby.* **3.** The youngest member of a family: *My sister in second grade is the baby of the family.* **4.** A person who behaves in an immature or selfish manner: *Don't be a baby and pout.* **5.** *Informal* A lover or sweetheart. ❖ *tr.v.* **ba·bied, ba·by·ing, ba·bies** To treat like a baby; coddle: *baby a spoiled child.* See Synonyms at **pamper.** [From Middle English *babe.*]

baby boom *n.* A large increase in the number of babies born in a population, especially the one in the United States from the later 1940s through the early 1960s.

baby boomer *n.* A person who is born during a baby boom, especially a person born in the United States between the later 1940s and the early 1960s.

baby carriage *n.* A four-wheeled carriage, often with a hood that folds back, used for transporting an infant.

baby grand *n.* A small grand piano about 5 feet (1.5 meters) long.

ba·by·hood (bā′bē-ho͝od′) *n.* The time or condition of being a baby.

ba·by·ish (bā′bē-ĭsh) *adj.* **1.** Resembling a baby; childlike: *a babyish whimper.* **2.** Childish; immature: *a babyish attitude about sharing.*

Bab·y·lon (băb′ə-lən *or* băb′ə-lŏn′) The capital of ancient Babylonia in Mesopotamia on the Euphrates River. Babylon was the site of the Hanging Gardens, one of the Seven Wonders of the World.

Bab·y·lo·ni·a (băb′ə-**lō′**nē-ə) An ancient empire of Mesopotamia in the Euphrates River valley in modern-day southern Iraq. It fell to the Persians in 539 BC.

Bab·y·lo·ni·an (băb′ə-**lō′**nē-ən) *adj.* Relating to Babylonia or Babylon or their people, language, or culture. ❖ *n.* **1.** A native or inhabitant of Babylonia or Babylon. **2.** The Semitic language of the Babylonians.

ba·by·proof (bā′bē-pro͞of′) *adj.* Made safe for babies or young children; childproof. ❖ *tr.v.* **ba·by·proofed, ba·by·proof·ing, ba·by·proofs** To make safe for babies or young children; childproof: *babyproofed the room by placing plastic plugs in the electrical sockets.*

ba·by's breath (bā′bēz) *n.* Any of several plants having branching clusters of small white flowers.

ba·by·sit (bā′bē-sĭt′) *v.* **ba·by·sat** (bā′bē-săt′), **ba·by·sit·ting, ba·by·sits** *—intr.* To take care of a child or children in the absence of a parent or guardian: *babysit for the neighbors next door.* *—tr.* To take care of (a child): *He babysat his younger brother.*

ba·by·sit·ter (bā′bē-sĭt′ər) *n.* A person who babysits.

baby tooth *n.* Any of the temporary teeth that first grow in the mouth of a young mammal.

bac·ca·lau·re·ate (băk′ə-**lôr′**ē-ĭt) *n.* **1.** A bachelor's degree. **2.** A farewell address delivered to a graduating class at a college or university.

Bac·chus (băk′əs) *n.* Dionysus.

Bach (bäкн *or* bäk), **Johann Sebastian** 1685–1750. German composer and organist. He wrote cantatas, orchestral works, and numerous works for organ, harpsichord, other solo instruments, and chamber ensembles.

bach·e·lor (băch′ə-lər *or* băch′lər) *n.* **1.** A man who has never been married. **2.** A person who has a bachelor's degree. [From Middle English *bacheler,* from Medieval Latin *baccalārius,* tenant farmer.]

Bachelor of Arts *n.* A bachelor's degree in liberal arts.

Bachelor of Science *n.* A bachelor's degree in science or mathematics.

bach·e·lor's button (băch′ə-lərz *or* băch′lərz) *n.* The cornflower.

bachelor's degree *n.* A degree given by a college or university to a person who has completed a four-year undergraduate program or its equivalent.

ă	pat	ôr	core
ā	pay	oi	boy
âr	care	ou	out
ä	father	o͝o	took
ĕ	pet	o͝or	lure
ē	be	o͞o	boot
ĭ	pit	ŭ	cut
ī	bite	ûr	urge
îr	pier	th	thin
ŏ	pot	*th*	this
ō	toe	zh	vision
ô	paw	ə	about

ba·cil·lus (bə-sĭl′əs) *n., pl.* **ba·cil·li** (bə-sĭl′ī′) **1.** Any of various rod-shaped bacteria. **2.** A bacterium. [From Late Latin, diminutive of Latin *baculum,* rod.]

back (băk) *n.* **1.** The rear part of the human body between the neck and the pelvis. **2.** The part of another animal that corresponds to this part in humans: *a bird with a red head and black back.* **3.** The spine or backbone. **4.** The part or area farthest from the front: *the back of the theater.* **5.** The part or side that is not usually seen or used; the reverse side: *the back of a photograph.* **6.** A part that supports the back of a person: *the back of a chair.* **7.** In certain sports such as football and soccer, a player who is positioned behind the front line of other players. ❖ *v.* **backed, back·ing, backs** —*tr.* **1.** To cause to move backward or in a reverse direction: *backed the car out of the driveway.* **2.** To furnish or strengthen with a back or backing: *back a poster with cardboard.* **3a.** To support or aid: *We backed our team by going to all their games.* **b.** To be in favor of: *A poll found that a majority of students backed the proposal.* **4.** To provide with musical accompaniment: *The singer was backed up by a pianist.* —*intr.* To move backward: *We backed away from the barking dog.* ❖ *adj.* **1.** Located at the back or rear: *the back porch.* **2.** Distant from a center of activity; remote: *a back road.* **3.** Overdue: *trying to pay the back rent.* **4.** Of a past date; not current: *a back issue of the magazine.* **5.** Being in a backward direction: *a back flip.* ❖ *adv.* **1.** At, to, or toward the rear: *Move back, please.* **2.** In, to, or toward a former place, time, or condition: *They went back to their old home.* **3.** In reserve or concealment: *It is dishonest to hold back the truth.* **4.** In reply or return: *If you send me a letter, I'll write back.* **5.** In check: *The firefighter kept back the flames.* ◆ **back away** To withdraw from a position; retreat: *He backed slowly away from the skunk.* **back down** To withdraw from a stand that one has taken: *There was an argument because neither side was willing to back down.* **back off** To retreat or fall back, as from something dangerous or risky: *The senator backed off from his support of the unpopular bill.* **back out** To withdraw from something one has agreed to: *They accepted the invitation but backed out at the last minute.* **back to back** In a series, without interruption: *broadcast six episodes of the sitcom back to back.* **back up 1.** To make a copy of (a computer program or file). **2.** To accumulate: *Traffic backed up at the intersection.* **behind (one's) back** When one is not present: *Don't talk about me behind my back.* [From Old English *bæc.*]

back·ache (băk′āk′) *n.* An ache or pain in the region of the spine or back, especially the lower back.

back and forth *adv.* **1.** Backward and forward: *pushed the child back and forth in the swing.* **2.** From side to side or end to end: *paced back and forth in the waiting room.* **3.** From one to another and back again: *I emailed back and forth with my sister all summer.*

back·beat (băk′bēt′) *n.* A strong accent on the second and fourth beats of a measure with four beats, characteristic of rock music.

back·bit·ing (băk′bī′tĭng) *n.* The saying of mean or spiteful things about an absent person. —**back′bit′er** *n.*

back·board (băk′bôrd′) *n.* **1.** In basketball, an elevated vertical sheet of wood or other material to which the basket is attached. **2a.** A board forming or placed at the back of something: *mounted the photos on a backboard.* **b.** A board used to support an injured person's back, especially when the person is being moved.

back·bone (băk′bōn′) *n.* **1.** The system of bones that forms the main support of a vertebrate; the spinal column. **2.** A principal support; a mainstay: *Manufacturing is the backbone of the economy.* **3.** Strength of character; courage; fortitude: *It takes backbone to refuse to go along with the crowd.*

back·break·ing (băk′brā′kĭng) *adj.* Requiring great physical exertion; exhausting: *backbreaking work.*

back-check (băk′chĕk′) *intr.v.* **back-checked, back-check·ing, back-checks** In ice hockey, to check or defend against an opponent while skating back toward one's own goal.

back·coun·try (băk′kŭn′trē) *n.* An uninhabited or sparsely inhabited region, especially one that is not accessible by road.

back·court (băk′kôrt′) *n.* **1.** In tennis and similar net sports, the part of a court between the service line and the baseline. **2.** In basketball: **a.** The half of the court that a team defends. **b.** The portion of the frontcourt farthest from the basket.

back·date (băk′dāt′) *v.* **back·dat·ed, back·dat·ing, back·dates** To supply with a date that is earlier than the actual date: *He backdated his rent check to the first of the month.*

back dive *n.* A dive in which the diver stands with the back to the water, leaps up, and rotates backward.

back·drop (băk′drŏp′) *n.* **1.** A painted cloth hung at the back of a stage set. **2.** A background or setting: *The action of the novel takes place against the backdrop of the Civil War.*

back·er (băk′ər) *n.* A person who supports or gives aid to a person, group, or enterprise.

back·field (băk′fēld′) *n.* **1.** In football, the players who are positioned some distance behind the line of scrimmage. **2.** The area in which these players are positioned.

back·fire (băk′fīr′) *n.* **1.** In a gasoline engine, an explosion of fuel that ignites too soon or an explosion of unburned fuel in the exhaust system. **2.** A controlled fire started in the path of an oncoming uncontrolled fire in order to deprive it of fuel and thereby extinguish it. ❖ *intr.v.* **back·fired, back·fir·ing, back·fires 1.** To explode in or make the sound of a backfire. **2.** To lead to a result opposite to that intended: *Their scheme to raise money backfired and everybody lost in the end.*

back·flip (băk′flĭp′) *intr.v.* **back·flipped, back·flip·ping, back·flips** To perform a backward somersault, especially in the air. ❖ *n.* A backward somersault.

back-for·ma·tion (băk′fôr-mā′shən) *n.* **1.** A new word formed from an older word by dropping the ending or beginning of the older word, as the verb *burgle* formed from the noun *burglar* or the noun *flab* formed from the adjective *flabby.* **2.** The process of forming new words in this way. —SEE NOTE AT **enthuse.**

back·gam·mon (băk′găm′ən) *n.* A game for two people played on a specially marked board with pieces whose moves are determined by throws of dice. The object is to move all of one's pieces to an end point where they are removed from the board.

back·ground (băk′ground′) *n.* **1a.** The part of a picture, scene, or view that is or appears to be in the distance: *The painting was of a town with a line of mountains in the background.* **b.** The general scene or surface upon which designs, figures, or other forms are seen or represented: *The banner had a blue background covered with white stars.* **2.** An inconspicuous position: *The police remained in the background during the demonstration.* **3.** The circumstances or events surrounding or leading up to something: *The judge asked for more details on the background of the case.* **4.** A person's experience, training, and education: *had a perfect background for the job.* **5.** The social or cultural environment in which a person was brought up: *a class with students from many different backgrounds.*

background music *n.* Soft music played to accompany an activity, such as shopping, or to enhance the mood or emotions in a play or motion picture.

background radiation *n.* A low level of naturally occurring radiation that is continuously present in the environment.

backboard

backflip

backgammon

backsplash

USAGE

bacterium Bacteria is the plural of **bacterium** and is never singular. Saying *a bacteria* is incorrect. It is correct to say *The soil sample contains millions of bacteria,* and *Tetanus is caused by a bacterium.*

ă	pat	ôr	core
ā	pay	oi	boy
âr	care	ou	out
ä	father	o͝o	took
ĕ	pet	o͝or	lure
ē	be	o͞o	boot
ĭ	pit	ŭ	cut
ī	bite	ûr	urge
îr	pier	th	thin
ŏ	pot	*th*	this
ō	toe	zh	vision
ô	paw	ə	about

back·hand (băk′hănd′) *n.* **1.** In sports, a stroke, as of a racket, made with the back of the hand facing forward. **2.** In hockey, a shot made with the back of the stick blade. **3.** In baseball, a catch made by reaching across the body with the palm turned toward the ball. **4.** Handwriting with letters that slant to the left. ❖ *adj.* Backhanded. ❖ *adv.* With a backhand stroke or motion: *hit the ball backhand.*

back·hand·ed (băk′hăn′dĭd) *adj.* **1.** With the motion or direction of a backhand: *a backhanded stroke in tennis.* **2.** Indirect or insincere: *a backhanded compliment.* —**back′hand′ed·ly** *adv.* —**back′hand′ed·ness** *n.*

back·hoe (băk′hō′) *n.* A machine used for digging, having a bucket attached to a hinged arm that is drawn back toward the operator when in use.

back·ing (băk′ĭng) *n.* **1.** Material that forms the back of something: *a table mat with a felt backing.* **2a.** Support or aid: *financial backing for a new business.* **b.** Approval or endorsement: *a request with official backing from the mayor.*

back·lash (băk′lăsh′) *n.* **1.** A strong and hostile reaction to an earlier action or event: *There was an angry public backlash against the unpopular law.* **2.** A sudden or violent backward whipping motion.

back·log (băk′lôg′) *n.* An accumulation, especially of unfinished work: *a backlog of unfilled orders due to a shortage of parts.*

back·pack (băk′păk′) *n.* **1.** A sturdy bag designed for carrying articles on a person's back, having shoulder straps and often mounted on a lightweight frame. **2.** A piece of equipment made to be used while being carried on the back: *a firefighter's backpack.* ❖ *intr.v.* **back·packed, back·pack·ing, back·packs** To hike while carrying a backpack: *The children and their guide backpacked to the lake.* —**back′pack′er** *n.*

back·ped·al (băk′pĕd′l) *intr.v.* **back·ped·aled, back·ped·al·ing, back·ped·als** or **back·ped·alled, back·ped·al·ling, back·ped·als 1.** To move the pedals of a bicycle or similar vehicle backward, especially to apply a brake. **2.** To retreat or withdraw from a previous stand: *The governor backpedaled after the proposals in his speech were criticized.*

back·rest (băk′rĕst′) *n.* A rest or support for the back.

back·seat driver (băk′sēt′) *n.* **1.** A passenger in a car who frequently advises, corrects, or nags the driver. **2.** A person who persists in giving unwanted advice.

back·side (băk′sīd′) *n. Informal* The buttocks.

back·slash (băk′slăsh′) *n.* A diagonal mark (\) used especially in computer commands and website addresses.

back·slide (băk′slīd′) *intr.v.* **back·slid** (băk′slĭd′), **back·slid·ing, back·slides** To return to a bad habit or behavior after one had previously given it up. —**back′slid′er** *n.*

back·space (băk′spās′) *intr.v.* **back·spaced, back·spac·ing, back·spac·es 1.** To move the cursor on a computer screen to the left by hitting the backspace key, usually deleting the character that is there. **2.** To move the carriage of a typewriter to the left one space by hitting the backspace key. ❖ *n.* A backspace key.

backspace key *n.* A computer or typewriter key used for backspacing.

back·spin (băk′spĭn′) *n.* In sports, a spin on a ball that tends to slow or reverse its forward motion.

back·splash (băk′splăsh′) *n.* An upright surface or border, as of tile, that protects the wall behind a sink or stove.

back·stab·bing (băk′stăb′ĭng) *n.* The practice of saying critical or mean things about someone, especially when that person is not present. —**back′stab′** *v.* —**back′stab′ber** *n.*

back·stage (băk′stāj′) *adv.* **1.** In or toward the area of a theater that is behind the stage, especially the area where the dressing rooms are located. **2.** In or toward a place closed to public view: *backstage at a political convention.* ❖ *adj.* (băk′stāj′) **1.** Relating to or situated behind the stage: *a backstage orchestra.* **2.** Not open or known to the public: *backstage political dealings.*

back·stop (băk′stŏp′) *n.* **1.** In baseball, a screen or fence used to prevent the ball from being thrown or hit far behind or to the sides of home plate. **2.** In baseball, a catcher.

back·stretch (băk′strĕch′) *n.* The part of an oval racecourse farthest from the spectators and opposite the homestretch.

back·stroke (băk′strōk′) *n.* A swimming stroke made while lying on the back and moving the arms alternately upward and backward.

back·swing (băk′swĭng′) *n.* The first part of a stroke, in which a person moves a tennis racket or golf club, for instance, to the position from which to start forward motion.

back talk or **back·talk** (băk′tôlk′) *n.* Rude and disrespectful remarks.

back·track (băk′trăk′) *intr.v.* **back·tracked, back·track·ing, back·tracks 1.** To return over the route by which one has come: *We backtracked to find the side trail we had missed.* **2.** To return to a previous point or subject, as in a lecture. **3.** To reverse one's position or policy: *The president backtracked on his pledge not to raise taxes.*

back·up (băk′ŭp′) *n.* **1.** Something reserved for use in case of emergency or additional need: *If this generator fails, we have another one we can use as a backup.* **2.** People who act to help or support others: *Arriving on the scene of the trouble, the police officer called for backup.* **3.** A copy of a computer program or file that is stored separately from the original. **4.** An accumulation or overflow caused by the blockage or clogging of something: *a backup in the drain.* ❖ *adj.* Ready and available as a substitute or in a case of emergency; extra; standby: *a backup pilot.*

back·ward (băk′wərd) *adj.* **1.** Directed or moving toward the rear: *a backward glance; a backward tumble.* **2.** Done or arranged in a manner that is opposite to normal use or practice: *alphabetized the books in backward order, starting with Z.* **3.** Behind others, as in economic or social progress: *backward technology.* **4.** Unwilling to act; reluctant or shy. ❖ *adv.* or **back·wards** (băk′wərdz) **1.** To or toward the back or rear. **2.** With the back or rear first: *With its hind legs a toad can dig its way into the ground backward.* **3.** In reverse order or direction: *count backward from 100; wore my T-shirt backward.* **4.** Toward a worse condition: *During the Depression many people slipped backward.* **5.** To, toward, or into the past: *The study looks backward to discover the source of the problem.* —**back′ward·ly** *adv.*

back·wash (băk′wŏsh′) *n.* **1.** The backward flow of water produced by the oars or propeller of a boat. **2.** The backward flow of air from a propeller of an aircraft.

back·wa·ter (băk′wô′tər) *n.* **1.** Water that is held back, as by a dam, or pushed upstream, as by a current. **2.** A place or situation regarded as stagnant or backward: *When the factory closed, people moved away and the town became a backwater.*

back·woods (băk′wo͝odz′) *pl.n. (used with a singular or plural verb)* **1.** Heavily wooded, uncultivated, remote areas. **2.** An area that is far from population centers, often regarded as backward; a backwater.

back·woods·man (băk′wo͝odz′mən) *n.* A person who lives in the backwoods.

back·yard also **back yard** (băk′yärd′) *n.* A yard at the back of a house.

ba·con (bā′kən) *n.* The salted and smoked meat from the back and sides of a pig.

Ba·con (bā′kən), **Francis** First Viscount Saint Albans. 1561–1626. English philosopher, writer, and politician. His writings include *The Advancement of Learning* (1605).

bac·te·ri·a (băk-tîr′ē-ə) *n.* Plural of **bacterium.**

bac·te·ri·al (băk-tîr′ē-əl) *adj.* Relating to or caused by bacteria: *a bacterial enzyme; a bacterial disease.*

bac·te·ri·ol·o·gy (băk-tîr′ē-ŏl′ə-jē) *n.* The scientific study of bacteria. **—bac·te′ri·o·log′i·cal** (băk-tîr′ē-ə-lŏj′ĭ-kəl) *adj.* **—bac·te·ri·ol′o·gist** *n.*

bac·te·ri·um (băk-tîr′ē-əm) *n., pl.* **bac·te·ri·a** (băk-tîr′-ē-ə) Any of a large group of very small one-celled organisms that lack a nucleus and reproduce by fission or by forming spores. Some kinds live in the digestive system or in soil or water, and some kinds can cause disease. [From Greek *baktērion*, diminutive of *baktron*, rod.] —SEE NOTE.

Bac·tri·an camel (băk′trē-ən) *n.* A two-humped camel widely used to carry loads in desert regions of central and southwest Asia.

bad (băd) *adj.* **worse** (wûrs), **worst** (wûrst) **1.** Being below an acceptable standard; inferior; poor: *a bad book; a bad painter.* **2.** Evil or wicked; sinful. **3.** Disobedient; naughty: *bad behavior.* **4.** Vulgar or obscene: *bad language.* **5.** Unfavorable: *bad luck; bad weather.* **6.** Disagreeable, unpleasant, or disturbing: *a bad odor; bad news.* **7.** Faulty; incorrect; improper: *a bad choice of words.* **8.** Not working properly; defective: *a bad telephone connection.* **9.** Rotten; spoiled: *bad fish.* **10.** Harmful in effect; detrimental: *Candy is bad for your teeth.* **11.** Being in poor health or condition: *I feel bad today. The jogger has a bad knee.* **12.** Severe; violent; intense: *a bad cold; a bad snowstorm.* **13.** Sorry; regretful: *I feel very bad about what happened.* **14. bad·der, bad·dest** *Slang* Very good; great. ❖ *n.* Something bad: *You must learn to accept the bad with the good.* ◆ **my bad** *Slang* Used to admit that one is at fault. **not half bad** or **not so bad** *Informal* Reasonably good. **too bad** Regrettable; unfortunate: *It's too bad you can't come along.* **—bad′ness** *n.*

❑ *These sound alike:* **bad, bade** (commanded).

bad blood *n.* Bitterness or hostility between people or groups.

bad breath *n.* The condition of having breath that smells unpleasant.

bade (băd *or* bād) *v.* A past tense of **bid.**

❑ *These sound alike:* **bade, bad** (inferior).

badge (băj) *n.* **1.** An emblem worn to show rank, office, or membership. **2.** An emblem given as an award or honor.

badg·er (băj′ər) *n.* **1.** Any of several stocky burrowing mammals having short legs, long claws on the front feet, and thick grayish fur. Badgers feed mostly at night on worms, insects, and small animals. **2.** The fur of such a mammal. ❖ *tr.v.* **badg·ered, badg·er·ing, badg·ers** To bother with many questions or demands; pester: *The fans badgered the celebrity for her autograph.*

bad·lands (băd′lăndz′) *pl.n.* An area of barren land typically having rough, deeply eroded terrain.

bad·ly (băd′lē) *adv.* **worse** (wûrs), **worst** (wûrst) **1.** In a bad manner; poorly: *a job badly done.* **2.** Very much; greatly: *He misses his brother badly.*

bad·min·ton (băd′mĭn′tən *or* băd′mĭt′n) *n.* A game in which players use a light long-handled racket to hit a shuttlecock back and forth over a high net. [After *Badminton*, the Duke of Beaufort's country seat in western England.]

bad-mouth (băd′mouth′ *or* băd′mouth′) *tr.v.* **bad·mouthed, bad·mouth·ing, bad·mouths** *Slang* To criticize or belittle, often unfairly or spitefully: *Why are you always badmouthing the coach behind her back?*

Baf·fin Island (băf′ĭn) An island of northeast Nunavut, Canada, west of Greenland. It is the fifth-largest island in the world.

baf·fle (băf′əl) *tr.v.* **baf·fled, baf·fling, baf·fles 1.** To confuse (someone) in a way that frustrates or prevents further action from being taken; puzzle: *The patient's condition baffled the doctors.* **2.** To interfere with or impede the force or movement of (a gas, sound, or liquid). ❖ *n.* A partition or enclosure that stops or regulates the movement of a gas, sound, or liquid: *A baffle covering part of the opening prevents the air conditioner from blowing directly onto me.* [Perhaps blend of Scottish Gaelic *bauchle*, to denounce, revile publicly, and French *bafouer*, to ridicule.] **—baf′fle·ment** *n.* **—baf′fler** *n.*

bag (băg) *n.* **1.** A container made of flexible material, such as paper, cloth, or plastic, used for carrying various articles. **2a.** A bag with something in it: *buy a bag of onions.* **b.** The amount that a bag can hold: *ate a whole bag of peanuts.* **3.** A purse, handbag, or suitcase: *Many passengers carry their bags right onto the airplane.* **4.** The amount of game caught or killed in a hunting expedition. **5.** Something that is shaped like a bag or hangs loosely like a bag: *bags under one's eyes.* **6.** In baseball, a base. **7.** *Slang* An area of interest or skill: *Cooking is not my bag.* ❖ *v.* **bagged, bag·ging, bags** *—tr.* **1.** To put into a bag: *I bag groceries at the supermarket.* **2.** To capture and kill, as in hunting. **3.** *Slang* **a.** To fail to attend purposely; skip: *bagged class for the afternoon.* **b.** To stop doing or considering; abandon: *bagged their suggestion.* *—intr.* To hang loosely like a bag: *pants that bag at the knees.* ◆ **in the bag** Assured of a successful outcome; virtually accomplished or won.

bag·a·telle (băg′ə-tĕl′) *n.* An unimportant or insignificant thing; a trifle.

ba·gel (bā′gəl) *n.* A ring-shaped roll with a chewy texture. [From Yiddish *beygl*, from Middle High German *bouc*, ring.]

bag·gage (băg′ĭj) *n.* **1.** The trunks, bags, suitcases, or boxes in which one carries one's belongings while traveling; luggage. **2.** The movable equipment and supplies of an army. **3.** Emotions or thoughts that stem from painful or unpleasant past experiences and that affect one's outlook or behavior.

bag·gy (băg′ē) *adj.* **bag·gi·er, bag·gi·est** Bulging or hanging loosely; loose-fitting: *bought a pair of baggy pants.* **—bag′gi·ness** *n.*

Bagh·dad or **Bag·dad** (băg′dăd′) The capital of Iraq, in the central part of the country on the Tigris River. It was founded in the eighth century.

bag·pipe (băg′pīp′) *n.* often **bagpipes** A musical instrument that consists of a reed pipe for playing melodies and several other pipes that play continuous single tones, all being supplied with air from a large bag that is filled by the player's breath or by a bellows. **—bag′pip′er** *n.*

ba·guette (bă-gĕt′) *n.* A long narrow loaf of French bread.

bah (bä *or* bă) *interj.* An expression used to show contempt or disgust.

Ba·ha·mas (bə-hä′məz) An island country in the Atlantic Ocean east of Florida and Cuba made up of some 700 islands and islets. Nassau is the capital.

Bah·rain (bä-rān′) A country made up of a group of low sandy islands in the Persian Gulf between Qatar and Saudi Arabia. Manama, on **Bahrain Island,** is the capital.

baht (bät) *n.* The basic monetary unit of Thailand.

Bai·kal (bī-kôl′), **Lake** A lake of south-central Russia. It is the world's deepest lake, with a maximum depth of 5,370 feet (1,637 meters).

bail[1] (bāl) *n.* **1.** Money supplied for the temporary release of an arrested person and guaranteeing a person's

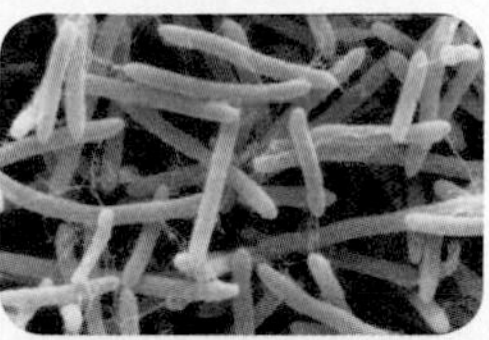

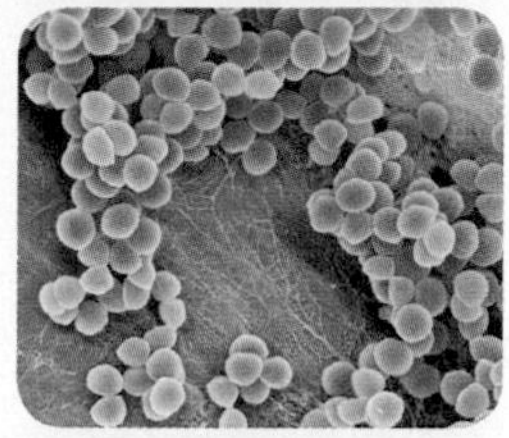

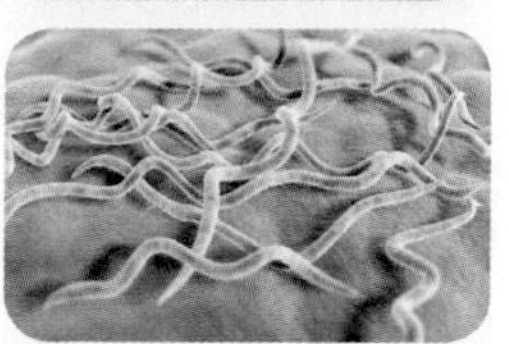

bacterium

top: rod-shaped bacteria
center: sphere-shaped bacteria
bottom: spiral-shaped bacteria

badger

baguette

bail[3]
on a teakettle

Ella Baker

appearance for trial: *Friends posted bail of $500 for the accused thief.* **2.** The release so obtained: *The accused thief was out on bail until the trial.* **3.** A person who supplies the money for such a release. ❖ *tr.v.* **bailed, bail·ing, bails 1.** To secure the release of (an arrested person) by providing bail. **2.** To release or deliver from a difficult situation: *The bank loan bailed out her business when sales dropped.* [From Middle English *bail,* custody, from Old French *baillier,* to take charge of, from Latin *bāiulāre,* to carry a load.]

❑ *These sound alike:* **bail[1]** (money), **bail[2]** (remove water), **bail[3]** (handle), **bale** (bundle).

bail[2] (bāl) *tr.v.* **bailed, bail·ing, bails 1.** To remove (water) from a boat by repeatedly filling a container and emptying it: *bail water with a coffee can.* **2.** To empty (a boat) of water by this means. ◆ **bail out 1.** To parachute from an aircraft; eject. **2.** To abandon a project or enterprise. [From Middle English *baille,* bucket, from Latin *bāiulāre,* to carry a load.]

❑ *These sound alike:* **bail[2]** (remove water), **bail[1]** (money), **bail[3]** (handle), **bale** (bundle).

bail[3] (bāl) *n.* **1.** The arched handle of a pail, kettle, or similar container. **2.** The pivoting U-shaped part of a fishing reel that guides the line during rewinding. **3.** A small, usually metal loop that is attached to a pendant to enable it to be strung on a necklace or bracelet. [From Middle English *beil,* possibly of Scandinavian origin or from Old English *bēgel.*]

❑ *These sound alike:* **bail[3]** (handle), **bail[1]** (money), **bail[2]** (remove water), **bale** (bundle).

bail·iff (bā′lĭf) *n.* An official who guards prisoners and maintains order in a courtroom. [From Middle English *baillif,* from Latin *bāiulus,* carrier.]

bail·i·wick (bā′lə-wĭk′) *n.* **1.** A person's specific area of interest, skill, or authority: *Responding to customer complaints is the superviser's bailiwick.* **2.** The office or district of a bailiff.

bail·out (bāl′out′) *n.* A rescue from financial difficulties: *The company, facing bankruptcy, turned to the government for a bailout.*

bairn (bârn) *n. Scots* A child.

bait (bāt) *n.* **1.** Food placed on a hook or in a trap to lure fish, birds, or other animals: *I always use worms for bait.* **2.** Something used to lure or entice: *A free book was the bait to get people to attend the book fair.* ❖ *tr.v.* **bait·ed, bait·ing, baits 1.** To put bait on: *bait a fishhook.* **2.** To set dogs upon (a chained animal) for sport. **3.** To torment with repeated verbal attacks, insults, or ridicule. [From Middle English, from Old Norse *beita,* food, and *beita,* to hunt with dogs.]

baize (bāz) *n.* A thick, often green, woolen or cotton cloth that looks like felt, used chiefly on billiard tables.

Ba·ja California (bä′hä) A mountainous peninsula of western Mexico bordering on the Pacific Ocean.

bake (bāk) *v.* **baked, bak·ing, bakes** —*tr.* **1.** To cook in an oven with dry heat: *We baked several loaves of bread.* **2.** To harden or dry by heating in or as if in an oven: *bake bricks in the sun.* —*intr.* **1.** To cook food by dry heat: *He loves to bake bread.* **2.** To become hardened or dry by or as if by baking: *The ground baked in the hot sun.* [From Old English *bacan.*]

bak·er (bā′kər) *n.* A person who bakes and sells bread, cakes, and pastries.

Ba·ker (bā′kər), **Ella** 1903–1986. American social reformer who worked to organize the civil rights movement of the 1950s and 1960s.

bak·er's dozen (bā′kərz) *n.* A group of thirteen; one dozen plus one. [From the former custom among bakers of adding an extra roll as a safeguard against the possibility of 12 weighing light.]

bak·er·y (bā′kə-rē) *n., pl.* **bak·er·ies** A place where products such as bread, cake, and pastries are baked or sold.

bak·ing powder (bā′kĭng) *n.* Any of several powdered mixtures of baking soda, starch, and a slightly acid compound such as cream of tartar, that are used to leaven biscuits and other baked goods.

baking soda *n.* A white crystalline compound having the formula $NaHCO_3$, used especially in beverages and as an ingredient in baking powder; sodium bicarbonate.

Ba·ku (bä-ko͞o′) The capital of Azerbaijan, in the eastern part of the country on the Caspian Sea.

bal·a·lai·ka (băl′ə-lī′kə) *n.* A Russian musical instrument that is somewhat like a guitar but has a triangular body and three strings.

bal·ance (băl′əns) *n.* **1.** A device in which the weight of an object is measured by putting it at one end of a rod that swings on a pivot at its center and adding known weights to the other side until the rod is level and motionless: *Chemists use a balance to weigh ingredients of a formula.* **2.** A condition in which forces or influences are canceled or matched by opposite forces or influences: *She tried to maintain a balance between work and play.* **3a.** A state of bodily stability, as when standing erect: *I was thrown off balance by the gust of wind.* **b.** The ability to maintain bodily stability: *The gymnast has good balance.* **4.** Mental or emotional stability; sanity. **5.** A condition in which an equation represents a correct statement in mathematics or chemistry: *The balance in the equation is maintained as equal quantities are added to each side.* **6a.** An equality between the debit and credit sides of an account: *Our bookkeeper achieves a balance in books of account at the end of the month.* **b.** The difference between such sides: *There is a balance due of $50.00.* **7.** Something left over; a remainder: *After dinner the balance of the evening was spent playing cards.* **8.** A satisfying proportion or arrangement achieved between parts or elements; harmony: *The red curtains destroyed the balance of color in the room.* **9.** An action or influence that results in even, suitable, or fair distribution: *Part of the US system of checks and balances is the division of power between Congress and the president.* ❖ *v.* **bal·anced, bal·anc·ing, bal·anc·es** —*tr.* **1.** To bring into or keep in a condition of balance: *I balanced the book on my head.* **2.** To compare in the mind: *We tried to balance the pros and cons before deciding.* **3.** To act as an equalizing weight or factor to; offset: *Your skill in languages balances your lack of experience in foreign countries.* **4.** To equalize the sums of the debits and credits of (an account): *balance a checkbook.* **5.** In mathematics and chemistry, to bring (an equation) into balance. —*intr.* **1.** To be equal or equivalent, as in weight, force, or parts: *rewards that don't balance with the risks.* **2.** To be or come into a state of balance or stability: *He balanced on the top of the wall.* **3.** To be equal in accounts of debit and credit. ◆ **in the balance** In an undetermined and often critical position. **on balance** Taking everything into consideration; all in all. [From Middle English *balaunce,* from Latin *bilānx,* (scale) with two pans.]

balance beam *n.* A horizontal raised beam on which competitors in gymnastics perform balancing feats.

balance of payments *n.* The amount of a nation's total payments to foreign countries after calculating the total receipts from abroad.

balance of power *n.* A distribution of power whereby no one nation is able to dominate or interfere with others.

balance of trade *n.* The difference in value between the total exports and the total imports of a nation.

balance sheet *n.* A statement that lists the assets and debts of a business or institution.

balance wheel *n.* A wheel that regulates the speed of a machine, as in a clock or watch.

Bal·an·chine (băl′ən-chēn′), **George** 1904–1983. Russian-born American ballet director and choreogra-

ă	pat	ôr	core
ā	pay	oi	boy
âr	care	ou	out
ä	father	o͝o	took
ĕ	pet	o͝or	lure
ē	be	o͞o	boot
ĭ	pit	ŭ	cut
ī	bite	ûr	urge
îr	pier	th	thin
ŏ	pot	*th*	this
ō	toe	zh	vision
ô	paw	ə	about

pher who choreographed more than 100 ballets, including Igor Stravinsky's *Firebird* (1949).

bal·bo·a (băl-bō′ə) *n.* The basic monetary unit of Panama. [After Vasco Núñez de *Balboa*.]

Bal·bo·a (băl-bō′ə), **Vasco Núñez de** 1475–1517. Spanish explorer who in 1513 crossed the Isthmus of Panama and claimed the Pacific Ocean for Spain.

bal·co·ny (băl′kə-nē) *n., pl.* **bal·co·nies 1.** A platform projecting from the wall of a building and surrounded by railing. **2.** An upper section of seats in a theater or auditorium.

bald (bôld) *adj.* **bald·er, bald·est 1.** Lacking hair on the head. **2.** Lacking a natural or usual covering: *a bald mountaintop without any vegetation.* **3.** Lacking treads: *replaced the bald tire.* **4.** Plain; blunt: *a bald statement of unpleasant facts.* **—bald′ness** *n.*

bald eagle *n.* A North American eagle having brownish-black feathers with a white head and tail.

bal·der·dash (bôl′dər-dăsh′) *n.* Nonsense.

bald·ing (bôl′dĭng) *adj.* Becoming bald.

bal·dric (bôl′drĭk) *n.* A belt worn over one shoulder across the chest to the opposite hip, used to support a sword or bugle.

Bald·win (bôld′wĭn), **James Arthur** 1924–1987. American writer and outspoken critic of racism whose works include *Go Tell it on the Mountain* (1953) and *Notes of a Native Son* (1955).

bale (bāl) *n.* A large bound package or bundle of raw or finished material: *a bale of hay.* ❖ *tr.v.* **baled, bal·ing, bales** To wrap in bales: *bale cotton.* **—bal′er** *n.*

❑ *These sound alike:* **bale, bail¹** (money), **bail²** (remove water), **bail³** (handle).

Bal·e·ar·ic Islands (băl′ē-ăr′ĭk) A group of islands in the western Mediterranean Sea off the eastern coast of Spain. The islands are noted for their scenery and mild climate.

ba·leen (bə-lēn′) *n.* Whalebone. [From Middle English *bleine*, from Greek *phallaina*, whale.]

bale·ful (bāl′fəl) *adj.* **1.** Threatening; menacing: *a baleful look.* **2.** Producing evil or harm; harmful: *a baleful influence.* **—bale′ful·ly** *adv.* **—bale′ful·ness** *n.*

Ba·li (bä′lē) An island of southern Indonesia just east of Java. It is largely mountainous with a tropical climate.

balk (bôk) *v.* **balked, balk·ing, balks** *—intr.* **1.** To stop short and refuse to go on: *The horse balked and wouldn't jump the fence.* **2.** To refuse; recoil; shrink: *The workers balked at the low terms of the wage settlement.* **3.** In baseball, to make an illegal motion before pitching, allowing base runners to advance a base. *—tr.* To check or thwart: *The police balked the prisoners' plans to escape.* ❖ *n.* **1.** A hindrance, check, or defeat. **2.** In baseball, the act of balking.

Bal·kan (bôl′kən) *adj.* **1.** Relating to the Balkan Peninsula. **2.** Relating to the Balkan States or their inhabitants. ❖ *pl.n.* **Bal·kans** (bôl′kənz) The Balkan States.

Balkan Peninsula A peninsula of southeast Europe bounded by the Black Sea, the Sea of Marmara, and the Aegean, Mediterranean, and Adriatic Seas.

Balkan States Albania, Bosnia and Herzegovina, Bulgaria, Croatia, continental Greece, Kosovo, Macedonia, Montenegro, southeast Romania, Serbia, and European Turkey.

balk·y (bô′kē) *adj.* **balk·i·er, balk·i·est 1.** Given to stopping short and refusing to go on; stubborn: *a balky mule.* **2.** Difficult to start or operate: *She spent half an hour trying to start the balky engine.*

ball¹ (bôl) *n.* **1a.** Something that is spherical or nearly spherical; a round object: *The earth is a great round ball.* **b.** A round movable object used in various sports and games: *a tennis ball.* **c.** Such an object moving, thrown, hit, or kicked in a certain way: *a fly ball; a curve ball.* **2.** A game, especially baseball or basketball, played with such an object. **3.** In baseball, a pitch that does not pass through the strike zone and is not swung at by the batter. **4.** A rounded part of the body: *the ball of the foot.* **5.** A solid projectile or shot for a firearm: *a cannon ball.* ❖ *tr. & intr.v.* **balled, ball·ing, balls** To form into a ball: *ball yarn for knitting.* ◆ **on the ball** *Informal* Alert, competent, or efficient. [From Middle English *bal*.]

❑ *These sound alike:* **ball¹** (round object), **ball²** (dance), **bawl** (cry).

ball² (bôl) *n.* **1.** A formal social dance. **2.** *Informal* A wonderful time: *had a ball at the beach.* [From French *bal*, from Greek *ballizein*, to dance.]

❑ *These sound alike:* **ball²** (dance), **ball¹** (round object), **bawl** (cry).

bal·lad (băl′əd) *n.* **1.** A poem that tells a story in simple stanzas, often intended to be sung. **2.** The music for such a poem. **3.** A popular love song.

ball-and-sock·et joint (bôl′ən-sŏk′ĭt) *n.* **1.** A joint formed by a rounded part of one bone fitting into a hollow part of another bone, permitting rotary motion, as in the shoulder or hip joint. **2.** A similar joint in a mechanical device.

bal·last (băl′əst) *n.* **1.** Heavy material carried especially in the hold of a ship or the gondola of a balloon to provide weight and steadiness: *Submarines use water as ballast in order to submerge.* **2.** Gravel or small stones used to form a foundation for a roadway or for railroad tracks. ❖ *tr.v.* **bal·last·ed, bal·last·ing, bal·lasts** To provide with or stabilize with ballast: *They used heavy stones to ballast the ship.*

ball bearing *n.* **1.** A bearing in which a ring-shaped track packed with small, freely revolving steel balls is used to reduce friction between a stationary part and a moving part, such as a rotating shaft or axle. **2.** A small steel ball used in such a bearing.

bal·le·ri·na (băl′ə-rē′nə) *n.* A female dancer in a ballet company.

bal·let (bă-lā′ *or* băl′ā′) *n.* **1.** An artistic form of dance characterized by very precise, graceful movements based on established steps, poses, and gestures. **2.** A theatrical performance of dancing to music, usually in costume, to convey a story or theme. **3.** Music written or used for ballet. [From French, from Italian *balletto*, diminutive of *ballo*, dance, from *ballare*, to dance.]

ball game or **ball·game** (bôl′găm′) *n.* A game, especially baseball, that is played with a ball.

bal·lis·tic (bə-lĭs′tĭk) *adj.* Relating to ballistics or projectiles. ◆ **go ballistic** *Slang* To become very angry or irrational.

ballistic missile *n.* A missile that is guided by an internal system as it is propelled upward and then allowed to fall without further guidance or power toward its target.

bal·lis·tics (bə-lĭs′tĭks) *n. (used with a singular verb)* **1.** The scientific study of the characteristics of projectiles, such as bullets or missiles, and the way they move in flight. **2.** The study of firearms and ammunition.

ball joint *n.* A ball-and-socket joint in a mechanical device.

bal·loon (bə-lo͞on′) *n.* **1.** A large flexible bag filled with helium, hot air, or some other gas that is lighter than the surrounding air and designed to rise and float in the atmosphere. Balloons often carry a gondola or scientific instruments. **2.** A similar bag that is shaped like a figure or object when inflated; an inflatable. **3.** A small brightly colored rubber or plastic bag that is inflated and used for decoration or as a toy. ❖ *intr.v.* **bal·looned, bal·loon·ing, bal·loons 1.** To swell out like a balloon: *The tire ballooned as it was inflated with air.* **2.** To increase or rise quickly: *John's debt ballooned while he was out of work.* **3.** To ride in a gondola suspended from a balloon: *We ballooned over the beautiful desert scenery.*

Vasco Núñez de Balboa

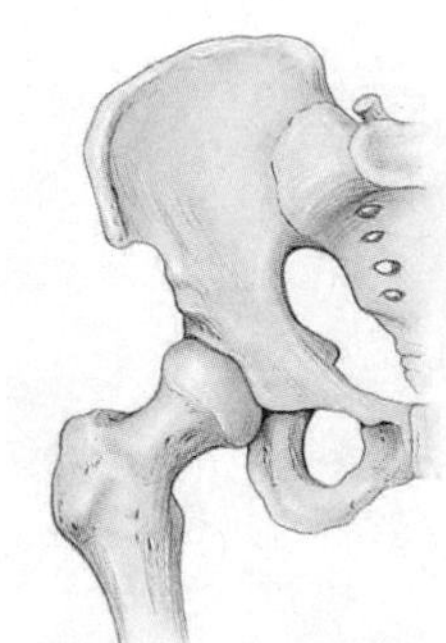

ball-and-socket joint
hip ball-and-socket joint

ballet

bamboo

banana

ă	pat	ôr	core
ā	pay	oi	boy
âr	care	ou	out
ä	father	o͝o	took
ĕ	pet	o͝or	lure
ē	be	o͞o	boot
ĭ	pit	ŭ	cut
ī	bite	ûr	urge
îr	pier	th	thin
ŏ	pot	*th*	this
ō	toe	zh	vision
ô	paw	ə	about

bal·lot (băl′ət) *n.* **1.** A piece of paper used to cast a vote, especially a secret vote. **2.** The act, process, or method of voting: *In a democracy, many decisions are made by the ballot.* **3.** A list of candidates running for office in an election. **4.** The total of all votes cast in an election: *The ballot is especially heavy in the year of a presidential election.* **5.** The right to vote; franchise: *Many countries do not have the ballot.* ❖ *intr.v.* **bal·lot·ed, bal·lot·ing, bal·lots** To cast a ballot or ballots; vote. [From Italian *ballotta*, a small ball used to register a vote, diminutive of dialectal *balla*, ball.]

ball·park (bôl′pärk′) *n.* A stadium for playing baseball. ❖ *adj. Informal* Being approximately right or in the right range: *They gave us a ballpark estimate for what a new computer would cost.* ◆ **in the ballpark** *Informal* Approximately right or within the right range.

ball·play·er (bôl′plā′ər) *n.* A baseball player.

ball·point pen (bôl′point′) *n.* A pen having as its writing point a small ball bearing that transfers ink from a cartridge onto a writing surface.

ball·room (bôl′ro͞om′ *or* bôl′ro͝om′) *n.* A large room for dancing.

bal·ly·hoo (băl′ē-ho͞o′) *n., pl.* **bal·ly·hoos** Extravagant advertising or publicity. ❖ *tr.v.* **bal·ly·hooed, bal·ly·hoo·ing, bal·ly·hoos** To advertise or publicize in an extravagant manner.

balm (bäm) *n.* **1.** Any of several plants related to mint and having a pleasant scent. **2.** Any of various fragrant resins obtained from several trees and shrubs. **3.** A fragrant ointment or oil. **4.** Something that soothes or comforts: *Her apology was balm to his hurt feelings.*

balm·y (bä′mē) *adj.* **balm·i·er, balm·i·est** Mild and pleasant: *balmy subtropical climates.* **—balm′i·ly** *adv.* **—balm′i·ness** *n.*

ba·lo·ney[1] (bə-lō′nē) *n., pl.* **ba·lo·neys** Variant of **bologna.**

ba·lo·ney[2] (bə-lō′nē) *n. Slang* Nonsense. ❖ *interj.* An expression used to show disagreement or annoyance.

bal·sa (bôl′sə) *n.* **1.** A tropical American tree having wood that is unusually light in weight. **2.** The buoyant wood of this tree, used for rafts and floats and in making model airplanes. [From Spanish.]

bal·sam (bôl′səm) *n.* **1.** Any of several fragrant resins obtained from various trees and used in medicines and perfumes. **2.** A tree, especially the balsam fir, that yields such a resinous substance. **3.** A garden plant having colorful flowers.

balsam fir *n.* **1.** An evergreen cone-bearing tree of northern North America, widely used for pulpwood. Turpentine and varnish are made from its resin. **2.** The wood of such a tree.

bal·sam·ic vinegar (bôl-săm′ĭk) *n.* A dark, sweet vinegar that has been aged in wooden barrels.

Balt (bôlt) *n.* **1.** A member of a Baltic-speaking people. **2.** A native or inhabitant of Estonia, Latvia, or Lithuania.

Bal·tic (bôl′tĭk) *adj.* **1.** Relating to the Baltic Sea or to the Baltic States. **2.** Relating to Baltic or a people that speaks Baltic. ❖ *n.* A group of Indo-European languages that includes Lithuanian and Latvian.

Baltic Sea An arm of the Atlantic Ocean in northern Europe bounded by Denmark, Sweden, Finland, Russia, Estonia, Latvia, Lithuania, Poland, and Germany. It opens to the North Sea by way of channels and canals.

Baltic States Estonia, Latvia, and Lithuania, on the eastern coast of the Baltic Sea. They were formerly provinces of Russia and republics of the Soviet Union.

Bal·ti·more (bôl′tə-môr′) The largest city of Maryland, in the northern part of the state on an arm of Chesapeake Bay northeast of Washington, DC.

bal·us·ter (băl′ə-stər) *n.* One of the posts supporting a railing, as of a porch or banister.

bal·us·trade (băl′ə-strād′) *n.* A handrail and the row of posts supporting it, as on a balcony or the edge of a staircase.

Ba·ma·ko (bä′mə-kō′) The capital of Mali, in the southwest part of the country on the Niger River.

bam·bi·no (băm-bē′nō) *n., pl.* **bam·bi·nos** or **bam·bi·ni** (băm-bē′nē) A baby or young child.

bam·boo (băm-bo͞o′) *n., pl.* **bam·boos 1.** Any of numerous grasses that often grow very tall and have jointed, tough, hollow stems. **2.** The strong stems of these plants, used for construction, for making fabric, and for many other purposes. The young shoots of some types are used as food. [Ultimately of Malay or Dravidian origin.]

bam·boo·zle (băm-bo͞o′zəl) *tr.v.* **bam·boo·zled, bam·boo·zling, bam·boo·zles** *Informal* To deceive by elaborate trickery; hoodwink: *She bamboozled me into buying her worthless magazine collection.*

ban (băn) *tr.v.* **banned, ban·ning, bans 1.** To prohibit (an action) or forbid the use of (something), especially by official decree: *The city council banned billboards on most streets.* **2.** To refuse to allow (someone) to do something, go somewhere, or be a participant; exclude: *The player was banned from the tournament for violating the rules.* ❖ *n.* A prohibition made by law or official decree: *a ban on cigarette smoking on airplanes.*

ba·nal (bə-năl′ *or* bā′nəl *or* bə-näl′) *adj.* Commonplace; dull; trite: *Always remarking on the weather makes banal conversation.* **—ba·nal′ly** *adv.*

ba·nal·i·ty (bə-năl′ĭ-tē *or* bā-năl′ĭ-tē) *n., pl.* **ba·nal·i·ties 1.** The quality or condition of being banal; triteness: *The banality of the speaker's remarks put the audience to sleep.* **2.** Something that is banal: *Television commercials are full of banalities.*

ba·nan·a (bə-năn′ə) *n.* **1.** A crescent-shaped fruit having sweet soft flesh and yellow to reddish skin that peels off easily. **2.** Any of several tropical plants that bear such fruit. [Of African origin.]

ba·nan·as (bə-năn′əz) *adj. Slang* Crazy.

banana split *n.* A dessert consisting of ice cream and usually flavored syrups, nuts, and whipped cream served over a banana that has been split lengthwise.

band[1] (bănd) *n.* **1a.** A strip of metal, cloth, or other flexible material, used to bind, trim, support, or hold things together: *Metal bands hold the slats of the wooden barrel together.* **b.** A stripe, mark, or area suggestive of such a strip: *the band of colors forming the rainbow.* **c.** A simple ring, especially a wedding ring. **2.** A specific range of wavelengths or frequencies in the electromagnetic spectrum, as those used in radio broadcasting: *the shortwave band.* ❖ *tr.v.* **band·ed, band·ing, bands 1.** To tie, bind, or encircle with a band: *band a skirt with a red ribbon.* **2.** To mark or identify with a band: *a program to band migrating birds.* [From Middle English *band*, from Old Norse *band*, bond, band, and from Middle English *bende* Old French *bande*, band, strip, of Germanic origin.]

band[2] (bănd) *n.* **1.** A group of people or animals: *a band of wild dogs roaming the desert.* **2.** A group of musicians who perform as an ensemble. **3.** A group of people or families who belong to a tribe but who live on their own for at least part of the year. ❖ *tr. & intr.v.* **band·ed, band·ing, bands** To form or gather in a group or association: *The homesteaders banded together for protection.* [From Old French *bande*, banner, troop identified by its banner, of Germanic origin.]

band·age (băn′dĭj) *n.* A strip of cloth or other material used to bind, cover, or protect a wound or other injury. ❖ *tr.v.* **band·aged, band·ag·ing, band·ag·es** To cover or bind with a bandage: *bandage a wound.*

Band-Aid (bănd′ād′) A trademark for an adhesive bandage with a gauze pad in the center.

ban·dan·na or **ban·dan·a** (băn-dăn′ə) *n.* A large handkerchief usually patterned and brightly colored. [From Hindi *bāndhnā*, to tie.]

Ban·dar Se·ri Be·ga·wan (bŭn′dər sĕr′ē bə-gä′wən) The capital of Brunei, on the northern coast of Borneo.

band·box (bănd′bŏks′) *n.* A light round box used to hold small articles of apparel.

ban·di·coot (băn′dĭ-ko͞ot′) *n.* **1.** Any of several large rats of Asia and the Middle East that are often destructive to food crops. **2.** Any of several burrowing Australian marsupials that resemble a rat, have a long tapering snout, and feed on insects and plants.

ban·dit (băn′dĭt) *n.* A robber, often one who is a member of a gang of outlaws. ◆ **make out like a bandit** *Slang* To be highly successful in a given enterprise.

ban·di·try (băn′dĭ-trē) *n.* The activity of a bandit.

band·lead·er (bănd′lē′dər) *n.* The conductor of a musical band.

ban·do·leer or **ban·do·lier** (băn′də-lîr′) *n.* A military belt that has small pockets or loops for carrying cartridges and is worn over the shoulder and across the chest. [From French *bandoulière*.]

band saw *n.* A power saw consisting of a toothed metal band driven around two wheels in a loop.

band·stand (bănd′stănd′) *n.* An outdoor platform, usually with a roof, for a musical band to give concerts.

band·wag·on (bănd′wăg′ən) *n.* **1.** A brightly decorated wagon for carrying musicians in a parade. **2.** *Informal* A popular cause, party, or trend: *Supermarkets began jumping on the organic foods bandwagon once they realized how many customers wanted to buy them.*

band·width (bănd′wĭdth′ *or* bănd′wĭth′) *n.* The amount of digital information that can be passed along a communications channel in a given period of time.

ban·dy (băn′dē) *tr.v.* **ban·died, ban·dy·ing, ban·dies 1.** To toss, throw, or strike back and forth: *We bandied the ball over the net.* **2.** To give and take; exchange: *The opposing groups bandied insults at each other.* **3.** To say or discuss in a casual manner: *The movie star's name was bandied about in idle gossip.* ❖ *adj.* Bent or curved outward; bowed: *bandy legs.*

ban·dy-leg·ged (băn′dē lĕg′ĭd *or* băn′dē-lĕgd′) *adj.* Bowlegged.

bane (bān) *n.* A cause of great trouble or annoyance: *Fleas were the bane of the cat's existence.* [From Old English *bana*, killer, slayer.]

bane·ber·ry (bān′bĕr′ē) *n.* Any of several plants having clusters of white flowers and poisonous red, white, or blackish berries.

bane·ful (bān′fəl) *adj.* Causing harm, ruin, or death; harmful: *the baneful effect of pollution on the environment.*

bang[1] (băng) *n.* **1.** A loud, sharp, sudden noise: *The door slammed with a bang.* **2.** A sudden forceful blow; a thump: *a bang on the knee.* **3.** *Slang* A feeling of excitement; thrill: *Most kids get a real bang out of the circus.* ❖ *v.* **banged, bang·ing, bangs** —*tr.* **1.** To strike or hit with a loud sharp noise: *The cook banged the pots and pans together.* **2.** To strike, hit, or move suddenly and with great force: *I banged my knee against the table.* **3.** To close suddenly and loudly; slam. —*intr.* **1.** To make a loud, sharp, sudden noise: *Firecrackers banged in the distance.* **2.** To crash noisily against or into something: *The toy car banged into the wall.* ❖ *interj.* Used to indicate the sound of an explosion or collision. ◆ **bang up** To damage extensively. [Probably from Old Norse, a hammering.]

bang[2] (băng) *n.* often **bangs** Hair cut straight across the forehead. [From *bang*, abruptly.]

Bang·kok (băng′kŏk′ *or* băng-**kŏk′**) The capital of Thailand, in the southwest part of the country near an arm of the South China Sea.

Bang·la·desh (bäng′glə-**dĕsh′** *or* băng′glə-**dĕsh′**) A country of southern Asia on the Bay of Bengal. Formerly part of Pakistan, it became independent in 1971. Dhaka is the capital.

ban·gle (băng′gəl) *n.* **1.** A rigid bracelet or anklet, especially one with no clasp. **2.** An ornament that hangs from a bracelet or necklace.

Ban·gui (bäng-**gē′**) The capital of Central African Republic, in the southern part of the country near the border of the Democratic Republic of the Congo.

bang-up (băng′ŭp′) *adj. Slang* Very good; great: *a bang-up party.*

ban·ish (băn′ĭsh) *tr.v.* **ban·ished, ban·ish·ing, ban·ish·es 1.** To force to leave a country or place by official decree; exile: *The king banished the outlaw.* **2.** To drive away; cast out: *Banish all doubts from your mind.* —**ban′ish·ment** *n.*

ban·is·ter also **ban·nis·ter** (băn′ĭ-stər) *n.* **1.** A handrail, especially on a staircase. **2.** One of the posts supporting a handrail on a staircase.

ban·jo (băn′jō) *n., pl.* **ban·jos** or **ban·joes** A musical instrument having a narrow neck, a hollow circular body with a covering of skin or plastic on one side, and four or sometimes five strings that are strummed or plucked. [Akin to Jamaican English *banja*, fiddle, probably of African origin.]

Ban·jul (bän′jo͞ol′) The capital of Gambia, on an island in the Atlantic Ocean south of Dakar, Senegal.

bank[1] (băngk) *n.* **1.** A hillside or slope: *the steep bank leading down to the valley.* **2.** often **banks a.** The rising ground bordering a body of water, especially bordering a river. **b.** An elevated area of a sea floor. **3.** A mound, pile, or ridge of earth or other solid material: *a snow bank.* **4.** A pile or mass, as of clouds or fog. **5.** The sideways tilt of an aircraft in making a turn. ❖ *v.* **banked, bank·ing, banks** —*tr.* **1.** To pile up (earth, snow, or other matter) in a ridge or sloping surface: *The plows banked snow along the edge of the road.* **2.** To pile ashes or fuel onto (a fire) to make it burn slowly: *bank a fire in the fireplace for the night.* **3.** To tilt (an aircraft) in making a turn. **4.** In sports, to propel (a ball or puck) in such a way as to make it bounce off a surface at an angle. —*intr.* To tilt an aircraft in making a turn: *The pilot banked to the left before descending.* [From Middle English, of Scandinavian origin.]

bank[2] (băngk) *n.* **1.** A place or organization in which money is kept for saving or business purposes or is invested, supplied for loans, or exchanged. **2.** The funds held by a dealer or banker in certain games, especially gambling games. **3.** A supply or stock for future use: *the blood bank of a hospital.* **4.** A place of safekeeping or storage: *a computer's memory bank.* ❖ *v.* **banked, bank·ing, banks** —*tr.* **1.** To put (money) in a bank: *Many workers bank a part of their salary.* **2.** To store (something) for future use. —*intr.* To have an account or savings at a particular bank. ◆ **bank on** To rely on; count on: *I'm banking on you to get the job done.* [From Middle English *banke*, from Old High German *banc*, bench, moneychanger's table.]

bank[3] (băngk) *n.* **1.** A set or group arranged in a row: *a bank of elevators.* **2.** A row of keys on a keyboard instrument, especially on an organ. **3.** A row of oars in a galley. [From Middle English, bench, from Late Latin *bancus*, of Germanic origin.]

bank·book (băngk′bo͝ok′) *n.* A book held by a depositor in which a bank enters the amounts added to or taken out of the depositor's account; a passbook.

bank·card (băngk′kärd′) *n.* A plastic card given by a bank to a customer for use at an ATM.

bank·er (băng′kər) *n.* A person who owns or is an executive of a bank.

Ban Ki Moon or **Ban Ki-moon** (**bän′ gē′ mo͞on′** *or* **bän′ kē′ mo͞on′**) Born 1944. South Korean diplomat

WRITERS CHOOSE THEIR WORDS

I do not know whether Father Linares saw it again or not, but I do know that while it lived there in the sea it lost the claws and forked tongue and the evil smell. It became the most beautiful creature I have ever seen. Yes, beautiful. And still it was the same evil thing that Father Linares **banished** from our land many years ago. This is strange.

—Scott O'Dell
The Black Pearl

banister

baobab

who served as secretary-general of the United Nations from 2007 to 2016.

bank·ing (băng′kĭng) *n.* The business or occupation of running a bank.

bank·note (băngk′nōt′) *n.* A piece of paper currency, such as a dollar bill, that is issued by a government's central bank.

bank·roll (băngk′rōl′) *tr.v.* **bank·rolled, bank·roll·ing, bank·rolls** To provide funds or financial support for: *The corporation agreed to help bankroll the new arts center.*

bank·rupt (băngk′rŭpt′) *adj.* **1.** Legally declared unable to pay one's debts because of lack of money. The property of someone who is bankrupt is controlled by or divided among the people who are owed money. **2.** Completely without money; financially ruined: *a gambler who went bankrupt.* **3.** Lacking in or depleted of valuable qualities: *a book that is bankrupt of original ideas.* ❖ *n.* A person who is bankrupt. ❖ *tr.v.* **bank·rupt·ed, bank·rupt·ing, bank·rupts** To cause to become bankrupt: *The stock market crash bankrupted him.* [From Italian *banca rotta*, broken table (from the practice of breaking the tables of bankrupt bankers) : *banca*, moneychanger's table + *rotta*, broken.]

bank·rupt·cy (băngk′rəpt-sē *or* băngk′rəp-sē) *n.* The condition of being bankrupt.

bank shot *n.* **1.** A shot in billiards in which the player causes a ball to rebound off a cushion. **2.** A shot in basketball in which the ball glances off the backboard before reaching the basket.

Ban·ne·ker (băn′ĭ-kər), **Benjamin** 1731–1806. American mathematician and astronomer who helped survey the District of Columbia in 1791. Largely self-taught, Banneker published an astronomical almanac from 1791 to 1797.

ban·ner (băn′ər) *n.* **1.** A flag or piece of cloth, often having words or a special design on it: *They marched in the parade with a banner for women's rights.* **2.** A headline spanning the width of a newspaper page. ❖ *adj.* Unusually good; outstanding: *a banner year for our team.*

ban·nis·ter (băn′ĭ-stər) *n.* Variant of **banister.**

banns also **bans** (bănz) *pl.n.* An announcement in a church that a particular couple intends to be married.

ban·quet (băng′kwĭt) *n.* **1.** A large elaborate meal; a feast. **2.** A ceremonial dinner honoring a person or group: *The school invited this year's honor students and their parents to the awards banquet.* ❖ *tr. & intr.v.* **ban·quet·ed, ban·quet·ing, ban·quets** To honor (someone) at or eat a banquet.

ban·shee (băn′shē) *n.* In Gaelic folklore, a female spirit supposed to warn of a death in a family by wailing loudly. [From Irish Gaelic *bean sídhe*, woman of the fairies, banshee.]

ban·tam (băn′təm) *n.* **1.** A chicken of any of various small breeds. **2.** A small, aggressive person.

ban·tam·weight (băn′təm-wāt′) *n.* A professional boxer weighing more than 112 and not more than 118 pounds (about 50–53 kilograms).

ban·ter (băn′tər) *n.* Playful good-humored conversation. ❖ *intr.v.* **ban·tered, ban·ter·ing, ban·ters** To exchange joking or teasing remarks: *She bantered with her friends during lunch hour.* —**ban′ter·er** *n.*

Ban·ting (băn′tĭng), Sir **Frederick Grant** 1891–1941. Canadian physiologist who isolated the hormone insulin, used in the treatment of diabetes.

Ban·tu (băn′to͞o) *n., pl.* **Bantu** or **Ban·tus 1.** A member of a large group of peoples native to southern and central Africa. **2.** A family of languages spoken by these people, including Swahili and Zulu. —**Ban′tu** *adj.*

ban·yan (băn′yən) *n.* A tropical Indian fig tree having large oval leaves and spreading branches from which aerial roots grow to the ground to form new trunks.

ban·zai (bän-zī′) *n.* A Japanese battle cry or patriotic cheer. [From Japanese, (may you live) ten thousand years.]

ba·o·bab (bā′ō-băb′ *or* bä′ō-băb′) *n.* A tree of tropical Africa, having a very thick trunk and large, hard-shelled fruit with edible pulp.

bap·tism (băp′tĭz′əm) *n.* **1.** A Christian sacrament in which a person is sprinkled with or dipped in water as a sign of being cleansed of sin and admitted to membership in a Christian church. **2.** A first experience. —**bap·tis′mal** (băp-tĭz′məl) *adj.*

Bap·tist (băp′tĭst) *n.* A member of a Protestant church that believes in baptism only for people old enough to understand its meaning. Baptists are usually baptized by placing the whole body in water. —**Bap′tist** *adj.*

bap·tis·ter·y also **bap·tis·try** (băp′tĭ-strē) *n., pl.* **bap·tis·ter·ies** also **bap·tis·tries** A part of a church or a separate building in which baptism is performed.

bap·tize (băp-tīz′ *or* băp′tīz′) *tr.v.* **bap·tized, bap·tiz·ing, bap·tiz·es** To admit (a person) into Christianity or a particular Christian church by baptism. [From Middle English *baptisen*, from Greek *baptizein*, from *baptein*, to dip.]

bar[1] (bär) *n.* **1.** A narrow, straight, rigid piece of solid material, often used to close an opening or as part of a machine or other device: *That long iron bar serves as an axle for the wagon.* **2.** A solid oblong piece of a substance: *a chocolate bar; a bar of soap.* **3.** A narrow marking, such as a stripe or band: *Some owls have bars of white on their feathers.* **4a.** A horizontal rod that marks the height to be cleared in the high jump or pole vault. **b.** A standard, expectation, or degree of requirement: *His work raised the bar for other musicians.* **5.** Something that prevents entry or progress; a barrier; an obstacle: *The fallen tree was a bar to our progress along the old dirt road.* **6.** A ridge of sand or gravel on a shore or stream bed, formed by the action of tides or currents. **7a.** A high counter at which drinks, especially alcoholic drinks, and sometimes food, are served. **b.** A place having such a counter. **8a.** The railing in a courtroom separating the participants in a legal proceeding from the spectators. **b.** A court or courtroom: *a case argued at the bar.* **c.** The occupation of a lawyer; the legal profession: *She chose the bar for her career.* **d.** Lawyers considered as a group: *a meeting of the local bar.* **9.** Variant of **barre. 10a.** A vertical line dividing a musical staff into equal measures. **b.** A measure of music: *Let's practice the final bars of this march.* ❖ *tr.v.* **barred, bar·ring, bars 1.** To close or fasten with a bar or bars: *barred the gate.* **2.** To block; close off; obstruct: *Fallen branches barred the way.* **3.** To keep out; exclude: *Hunters are barred from wildlife sanctuaries.* **4.** To prohibit (someone) from doing something: *Failing the eye test barred him from driving.* **5.** To rule out; except: *wrestling with no holds barred.* **6.** To mark with stripes or narrow bands. ◆ **bar none** With no exceptions: *This is the best pizza I've ever had, bar none.* **behind bars** In prison: *put the criminal behind bars.* [From Middle English *barre*, from Old French.]

bar[2] (bär) *n.* A unit used to measure atmospheric pressure. It is equal to a force of 100,000 newtons per square meter of surface area, or 0.987 atmosphere.

barb (bärb) *n.* **1.** A sharp point projecting backward, as on a fishhook or arrow. **2.** One of the hairlike branches on the shaft of a feather. **3.** A cutting or biting remark: *The author saved her best barbs for her critics.*

Bar·ba·dos (bär-bā′dōs′ *or* bär-bā′dōz′) A country on the easternmost island of the West Indies. The island gained its independence from Great Britain in 1966. Bridgetown is the capital.

bar·bar·i·an (bär-bâr′ē-ən) *n.* **1.** A member of a people considered by those of another nation or group to be uncivilized or culturally inferior. **2.** A crude, uncivilized,

ă	pat	ôr	core
ā	pay	oi	boy
âr	care	ou	out
ä	father	o͝o	took
ĕ	pet	o͝or	lure
ē	be	o͞o	boot
ĭ	pit	ŭ	cut
ī	bite	ûr	urge
îr	pier	th	thin
ŏ	pot	*th*	this
ō	toe	zh	vision
ô	paw	ə	about

or brutal person: *The pirates were barbarians.* [From French *barbarien,* from Latin *barbarus,* barbarous, from Greek *barbaros,* foreign.] —SEE NOTE.

bar·bar·ic (bär-**băr′**ĭk) *adj.* **1.** Relating to or characteristic of barbarians: *The native peoples considered the explorers barbaric.* **2.** Cruel or brutal: *a barbaric dictator; torture and other barbaric punishments.* **3.** Marked by crudeness or lack of restraint: *barbaric eating habits.*

bar·ba·rism (**bär′**bə-rĭz′əm) *n.* **1.** A barbarous uncivilized state. **2.** A barbarous act or custom: *Imprisoning debtors is now considered a barbarism.* **3.** A word or expression regarded as being incorrect and showing lack of education or refinement.

bar·bar·i·ty (bär-**băr′**ĭ-tē) *n., pl.* **bar·bar·i·ties 1.** Cruel or savage behavior: *a dictatorship known for its barbarity toward its people.* **2.** A cruel or savage act: *accused the army of committing barbarities against civilians during the war.*

bar·ba·rize (**bär′**bə-rīz′) *tr. & intr.v.* **bar·ba·rized, bar·ba·riz·ing, bar·ba·riz·es** To make or become crude, savage, or barbarous.

bar·ba·rous (**bär′**bər-əs) *adj.* **1.** Primitive in culture and customs; uncivilized: *The barbarous invaders burned the library.* **2.** Brutal; cruel: *animals that were held in cramped, barbarous conditions.* **3.** Uncultured or unrefined, especially in language: *barbarous writing.* **—bar′ba·rous·ly** *adv.* **—bar′ba·rous·ness** *n.*

Bar·ba·ry Coast (**băr′**bə-rē *or* **băr′**brē) The Mediterranean coastal area of northern Africa, including the coastlines of Egypt, Libya, Tunisia, Algeria, and Morocco.

bar·be·cue (**bär′**bĭ-kyo͞o′) *n.* **1.** A grill, pit, or fireplace for roasting meat, often outdoors. **2.** A whole animal or a piece of it roasted over an open fire. **3.** A social gathering at which food is cooked over an open fire: *Everybody came to the neighborhood barbecue.* ❖ *tr.v.* **bar·be·cued, bar·be·cu·ing, bar·be·cues** To cook (food) over an open fire, often with a spicy sauce: *We barbecued ribs.* [From Spanish *barbacoa,* of Taíno origin.]

barbed (bärbd) *adj.* **1.** Having barbs: *the barbed head of a harpoon.* **2.** Cutting; stinging: *barbed criticism.*

barbed wire *n.* Twisted strands of wire with barbs at regular intervals, used in making fences.

bar·bel (**bär′**bəl) *n.* A slender feeler extending from the head of certain fishes, such as the catfishes.

bar·bell (**bär′**bĕl′) *n.* A bar with adjustable weights at each end, lifted for sport or exercise.

bar·ber (**bär′**bər) *n.* A person whose work is cutting hair and shaving or trimming beards. ❖ *tr.v.* **bar·bered, bar·ber·ing, bar·bers** To cut the hair of or shave or trim the beard of (someone).

bar·ber·ry (**bär′**bĕr′ē) *n.* Any of various shrubs having small leaves, yellowish flowers, and small red, orange, or blackish berries.

bar·ber·shop (**bär′**bər-shŏp′) *n.* A barber's place of business. ❖ *adj. Informal* Relating to singing sentimental songs for unaccompanied, usually male voices in four-part harmony: *a barbershop quartet.*

bar·bi·can (**bär′**bĭ-kən) *n.* A tower at a gate or drawbridge at the entrance to a medieval castle or town. [From Middle English, from Old French *barbacane,* ultimately from Persian *barbārkhān* : *barbār,* guard + *khān,* house.]

bar·bi·tu·rate (bär-**bĭch′**ər-ĭt *or* bär-**bĭch′**ə-rāt′ *or* bär-**bĭch′**ə-wĭt) *n.* Any of a group of drugs that reduce the activity of the central nervous system and are used as sedatives. Barbiturates are highly addictive.

barb·wire (**bärb′**wīr′) *n.* Barbed wire.

bar·ca·role also **bar·ca·rolle** (**bär′**kə-rōl′) *n.* **1.** A song of a Venetian gondolier with a rhythm that suggests rowing. **2.** A musical composition imitating such a song.

Bar·ce·lo·na (bär′sə-**lō′**nə) A city of northeast Spain on the Mediterranean Sea. It was founded by the Carthaginians.

bar·code (**bär′**kōd′) *n.* A series of vertical bars of varying widths printed on a consumer product to allow a computer scanner to verify the product's price and to keep track of inventory.

bard (bärd) *n.* **1.** A poet of ancient times who composed and recited verses about heroes and heroic deeds. **2.** A poet. [Of Celtic origin.]

bare (bâr) *adj.* **bar·er, bar·est 1.** Lacking clothing or covering; naked: *bare feet; a bare hillside.* **2.** Lacking the usual or expected furnishings, equipment, or supplies: *bare shelves; bare walls.* **3.** Having no addition or restriction; simple or plain: *the bare facts.* **4.** Just sufficient or adequate; mere: *the bare necessities of life.* ❖ *tr.v.* **bared, bar·ing, bares** To uncover; expose to view: *The dog bared its teeth and growled.* [From Old English *bær.*] **—bare′ness** *n.*

❑ *These sound alike:* **bare, bear**[1] (support), **bear**[2] (animal).

bare·back (**bâr′**băk′) *adv. & adj.* On a horse or other animal with no saddle: *riding bareback; a bareback rider.*

bare·faced (**bâr′**fāst′) *adj.* Shameless; bold; brazen: *a barefaced lie.*

bare·foot (**bâr′**fo͝ot′) also **bare·foot·ed** (**bâr′**fo͝ot′ĭd) *adv. & adj.* Without shoes or other covering on the feet: *running barefoot through the grass; a barefoot child.*

bare·hand·ed (**bâr′**hăn′dĭd) *adv. & adj.* With the hand or hands alone; without a glove, tool, weapon, or protection: *catching fish barehanded; a barehanded catch of a baseball.*

bare·head·ed (**bâr′**hĕd′ĭd) *adv. & adj.* Without a hat or other head covering: *walking bareheaded in the rain; bareheaded hikers.*

bare·leg·ged (**bâr′**lĕg′ĭd *or* **bâr′**lĕgd′) *adv. & adj.* With the legs uncovered: *ran barelegged through the surf; barelegged children at the beach.*

bare·ly (**bâr′**lē) *adv.* **1.** By very little; hardly; just: *We could barely see the shore in the dark.* **2.** In a bare or scanty manner; sparsely: *a barely furnished room.*

bar·gain (**bär′**gĭn) *n.* **1.** An arrangement or agreement between two sides, often involving payment or trade; a deal: *We made a bargain that I would cut the grass for twenty dollars.* **2.** Something offered or bought at a low price: *The elegant dress that's now on sale is a bargain.* ❖ *intr.v.* **bar·gained, bar·gain·ing, bar·gains** To argue over or discuss the terms of an agreement, especially a price to be paid: *The hotel's cook bargained for vegetables in the market.* ◆ **bargain for** or **bargain on** To count on; expect: *That old car gave us more trouble than we bargained for.* **into the bargain** or **in the bargain** Over and above what is expected; in addition: *We bought the large-size bag of dog food and got a dog toy into the bargain.*

barge (bärj) *n.* **1.** A large flatbottom boat that is usually towed or pushed and is used to carry loads on rivers, canals, and coastal waters. **2.** A large open boat used for parties and ceremonies. ❖ *intr.v.* **barged, barg·ing, barg·es 1.** To intrude or interrupt, especially rudely: *He barged into our conversation and told us what happened.* **2.** To move clumsily: *They barged through the crowded city square.* [From Middle English, from Latin *barca,* boat.]

bar graph *n.* A graph consisting of parallel bars or rectangles drawn at lengths that are in proportion to the quantities they represent.

bar·ite (**bâr′**īt) *n.* A white or colorless crystalline mineral of barium sulfate that is the chief source of barium.

bar·i·tone (**băr′**ĭ-tōn′) *n.* **1.** A moderately low singing voice of a man, higher than a bass and lower than a tenor. **2.** A singer whose voice lies within this range. **3.** An instrument whose sound falls within this range,

WORD HISTORY

barbarian Our word **barbarian,** "a member of an uncivilized people," comes from the ancient Greek word for "foreigner," *barbaros.* Originally this word was probably an imitation of the unintelligible speech of non-Greeks ("bar-bar-bar"). It later came to mean "uncultured." The Romans borrowed the word from the Greeks and used it to mean "neither Greek nor Roman, outside the Roman Empire," and later "uncivilized."

barbed wire

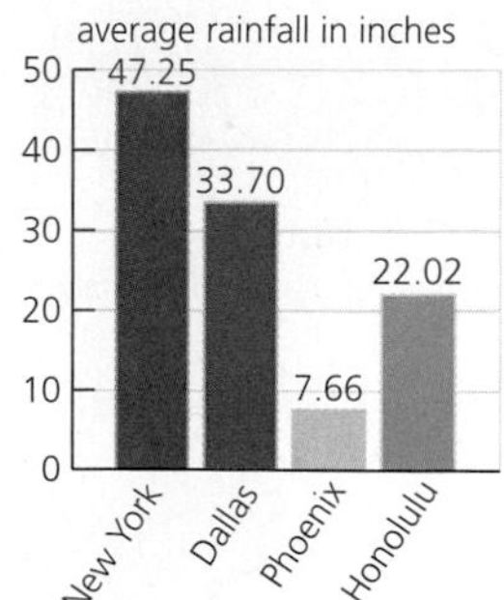

bar graph
average annual rainfall in several US cities

barnacle

baroque
Trevi Fountain, Rome, Italy

ă	pat	ôr	core
ā	pay	oi	boy
âr	care	ou	out
ä	father	o͝o	took
ĕ	pet	o͝or	lure
ē	be	o͞o	boot
ĭ	pit	ŭ	cut
ī	bite	ûr	urge
îr	pier	th	thin
ŏ	pot	*th*	this
ō	toe	zh	vision
ô	paw	ə	about

especially a valved brass instrument similar to but larger than the euphonium. **4.** A part written in this range. [From Greek *barutonos*, deep-sounding.]

bar·i·um (bâr′ē-əm) *n. Symbol* **Ba** A soft, silvery-white metallic element that occurs only in combination with other elements, especially in barite. Barium compounds are used in making fireworks and white pigments. Atomic number 56. See **Periodic Table.**

barium sulfate *n.* A compound of barium, sulfur, and oxygen that occurs as a fine white powder. It is used in taking x-rays of the digestive tract and in making textiles, rubber, and plastic.

bark[1] (bärk) *n.* **1.** The harsh sound made by a dog and certain other animals such as seals and coyotes. **2.** A sound similar to this, such as a cough or the firing of a gun. ❖ *v.* **barked, bark·ing, barks** *—intr.* **1.** To make the sound of a bark: *The neighbor's dog barked all night.* **2.** To speak gruffly or sharply; snap: *The sergeant barked at the new recruits.* *—tr.* To say in a loud harsh voice: *The team captain barked commands.* ◆ **bark up the wrong tree** To misdirect one's energies or attention. [From Middle English *berken*, to bark, from Old English *beorcan*.]

bark[2] (bärk) *n.* The protective outer covering of the trunk, branches, and roots of trees and other woody plants. ❖ *tr.v.* **barked, bark·ing, barks** To bump or rub so as to scrape the skin from: *I barked my shin on the rocks.* [From Middle English, from Old Norse *börkr*.]

bark[3] also **barque** (bärk) *n.* A sailing ship with three to five masts, all of them square-rigged except the after mast, which is fore-and-aft rigged. [From Middle English *barke*, boat, from Latin *barca*, ultimately from Egyptian *byr*.]

bar·keep·er (bär′kē′pər) *n.* **1.** A person who owns or runs a bar for the sale of alcoholic beverages. **2.** A bartender.

bar·ken·tine (bär′kən-tēn′) *n.* A sailing ship with three to five masts, of which only the foremast is square-rigged, the other masts being fore-and-aft rigged.

bark·er (bär′kər) *n.* **1.** A person or animal that barks: *That dog is a loud barker.* **2.** A person who makes a loud entertaining sales pitch at the entrance to a show, carnival, or other attraction.

bar·ley (bär′lē) *n.* **1.** The grain of a grass that grows in cool regions, used as food for humans and livestock and for making beer and whiskey. **2.** The plant that produces such grain.

bar·ley·corn (bär′lē-kôrn′) *n.* A grain of barley.

bar·maid (bär′mād′) *n.* A woman who serves drinks in a bar.

bar·man (bär′mən) *n.* A man who serves drinks in a bar.

bar mitz·vah (bär mĭts′və) *n.* **1.** A ceremony in which a Jewish boy who is at least 13 years old is admitted as an adult into the religious community. **2.** The boy for whom this ceremony is held. ❖ *tr.v.* **bar mitz·vahed, bar mitz·vah·ing, bar mitz·vahs** To recognize (a boy) in such a ceremony. [From Hebrew *bar miṣwâ* : Aramaic *bar*, son + Hebrew *miṣwâ*, command, commandment.]

barn (bärn) *n.* **1.** A large farm building used for storing grain, hay, and other farm products and for sheltering livestock. **2.** A large shed for the housing of vehicles: *a bus barn.* [From Old English *berærn* : *bere*, barley + *ærn*, house.]

bar·na·cle (bär′nə-kəl) *n.* Any of various small hard-shelled sea animals that have feathery structures used for filtering food particles from the water and that attach themselves to underwater objects such as rocks, pilings, and the bottoms of ships.

barn dance *n.* A social gathering, often held in a barn, with music and square dancing.

barn·storm (bärn′stôrm′) *tr. & intr.v.* **barn·stormed, barn·storm·ing, barn·storms** To travel about the countryside making political speeches or appearing in exhibits or sporting events. **—barn′storm′er** *n.*

barn swallow *n.* A widely distributed bird having a deeply forked tail, a dark-blue back, and a tan underside. Barn swallows often build their nests in the eaves of barns.

Bar·num (bär′nəm), **P(hineas) T(aylor)** 1810–1891. American entrepreneur and entertainer who established The Greatest Show on Earth (1871), which later became the Barnum and Bailey Circus.

barn·yard (bärn′yärd′) *n.* The yard or area of ground around a barn. ❖ *adj.* Crude or indecent: *barnyard jokes.*

bar·o·graph (băr′ə-grăf′) *n.* A barometer that automatically records changes in air pressure.

ba·rom·e·ter (bə-rŏm′ĭ-tər) *n.* **1.** An instrument for measuring atmospheric pressure, used to determine height above sea level and in weather forecasting. **2.** Something that shows shifts and changes like those of the weather; an indicator: *Opinion polls are used as a barometer of public mood.* [From Greek *baros*, weight + Greek *metron*, measure.]

bar·o·met·ric (băr′ə-mĕt′rĭk) *adj.* Relating to or measured by a barometer: *take a barometric reading.*

barometric pressure *n.* Atmospheric pressure.

bar·on (băr′ən) *n.* **1a.** A British nobleman of the lowest rank. **b.** A nobleman of other parts of Europe, ranked differently in various countries. **2.** In feudal times, a man holding rights, lands, and a title directly from a king or another high-ranking nobleman. **3.** A businessman of great wealth and influence: *an oil baron.*

❑ *These sound alike:* **baron, barren** (not productive).

bar·on·ess (băr′ə-nĭs) *n.* **1.** The wife or widow of a baron. **2.** A woman holding the title to a barony.

bar·on·et (băr′ə-nĭt *or* băr′ə-nĕt′) *n.* In Great Britain, a man holding a hereditary title of honor reserved for commoners, ranking just below the barons.

bar·on·et·ess (băr′ə-nĭ-tĭs *or* băr′ə-nĕt′ĭs) *n.* In Great Britain, a woman holding a hereditary title of honor reserved for commoners, ranking just below the barons.

ba·ro·ni·al (bə-rō′nē-əl) *adj.* **1.** Relating to a baron or a barony. **2.** Suitable for a baron; stately or splendid: *a large baronial home.*

bar·o·ny (băr′ə-nē) *n., pl.* **bar·o·nies** The rank or domain of a baron.

ba·roque (bə-rōk′) *adj.* **1.** also **Baroque** Relating to or characteristic of a style of art and architecture developed in Europe from about 1600 to 1750, characterized by elaborate curving forms and intricate detail. **2.** also **Baroque** Relating to or characteristic of a style of musical composition that flourished in Europe from about 1600 to 1750 and was notable for its strict form and elaborate patterns. **3.** Elaborate and fantastic; outlandish: *a baroque plot with many twists and turns.* **4.** Irregular in shape: *a baroque pearl.* ❖ *n.* also **Baroque** The baroque style or period in art, architecture, or music. [From French, from Italian *barocco*, imperfect pearl, and from Portuguese *barroco*.]

ba·rouche (bə-ro͞osh′) *n.* A horse-drawn carriage with a folding top, two double passenger seats inside facing one another, and a driver's seat outside.

barque (bärk) *n.* Variant of **bark[3]**.

bar·rack (băr′ək) *n.* often **barracks** A building or group of buildings used to house soldiers, workers, or a large number of other people: *cleaned the barracks daily.*

bar·ra·cu·da (băr′ə-ko͞o′də) *n., pl.* **barracuda** or **bar·ra·cu·das** Any of various ocean fishes having a long narrow body and a projecting lower jaw with very sharp teeth, found mostly in tropical waters.

bar·rage (bə-räzh′) *n.* **1.** A concentrated firing of artillery, missiles, or other firearms directed at an enemy position. **2.** An overwhelming outpouring: *a barrage of customer complaints.* ❖ *tr.v.* **bar·raged, bar·rag·ing,**

bar·rag·es To direct a barrage at: *Gunboats barraged the fort. Reporters barraged the speaker with questions.*

barre also **bar** (bär) *n.* **1.** In ballet, a horizontal rail used as a support in exercises. **2.** A technique in which a finger is laid across the fingerboard of a stringed instrument to stop several strings at once.

barred (bärd) *adj.* **1.** Having been secured with bars: *barred windows.* **2.** Having stripes: *a bird with barred plumage.*

bar·rel (băr′əl) *n.* **1.** A large container of wood, metal, plastic, or cardboard with round flat ends of equal size. Wooden barrels usually have sides that bulge out slightly and are held together by hoops. **2.** The amount that a barrel can hold: *spread a barrel of sawdust over the floor.* **3.** Any of various measures of volume or capacity ranging from 31 to 42 gallons (117 to 159 liters). **4a.** The long tube of a gun, through which a bullet or shell travels. **b.** A cylindrical machine part. **5.** *Informal* A great amount: *a barrel of fun.* ❖ *v.* **bar·reled, bar·rel·ing, bar·rels** or **bar·relled, bar·rel·ling, bar·rels** —*tr.* To put or pack in a barrel: *barrel vinegar for shipping to market.* —*intr. Informal* To move at great speed: *The express train barreled along the tracks.* [From Middle English *barel,* from Old French *baril.*] —**bar′rel·ful′** *n.*

barrel organ *n.* A portable musical instrument, similar to a small organ, in which air from a bellows is directed to the pipes by turning a barrel with a hand crank. Pins inside the barrel open the pipe valves in a particular sequence to play the notes of a tune.

bar·ren (băr′ən) *adj.* **1.** Lacking plants or crops: *a barren desert; barren soil.* **2.** Unable to bear offspring or fruit: *an orchard of barren trees.* **3.** Not useful or productive: *barren efforts.* **4.** Empty; bare: *a life barren of pleasure.* ❖ *n.* often **barrens** An area of barren or unproductive land. —**bar′ren·ness** *n.*

❑ *These sound alike:* **barren, baron** (nobleman).

bar·rette (bə-rĕt′) *n.* A bar-shaped or oval clip used to hold the hair in place.

bar·ri·cade (băr′ĭ-kād′ *or* băr′ĭ-kād′) *n.* **1.** A structure set up hastily to obstruct the passage of an enemy. **2.** A barrier or obstruction. ❖ *tr.v.* **bar·ri·cad·ed, bar·ri·cad·ing, bar·ri·cades** To close off, block, or protect with a barricade: *barricade streets to control the crowd at a parade.*

bar·ri·er (băr′ē-ər) *n.* **1.** A structure, such as a fence or wall, built to obstruct passage: *Police set up a barrier at each end of the street the night before the fair began.* **2.** Something that obstructs; an obstacle: *Lack of education can be a barrier to success.*

barrier island *n.* A long, narrow sand island that is parallel to the mainland and serves to protect the coast from erosion.

barrier reef *n.* A long narrow ridge of coral deposits parallel to the mainland and separated from it by a deep lagoon.

bar·ring (bär′ĭng) *prep.* Apart from the occurrence of; excepting: *Barring a last-minute change, we'll be the first to arrive.*

bar·ri·o (bä′rē-ō′) *n., pl.* **bar·ri·os 1.** A chiefly Spanish-speaking community or neighborhood in a US city. **2.** A village or district in a Spanish-speaking country.

bar·ris·ter (băr′ĭ-stər) *n. Chiefly British* A lawyer who argues cases in a court of law.

bar·room (bär′ro͝om′ *or* bär′ro͞om′) *n.* A room or building in which alcoholic beverages are sold at a counter or bar.

bar·row[1] (băr′ō) *n.* **1.** A flat rectangular tray or cart with handles at each end, used for carrying loads. **2.** A wheelbarrow. [From Old English *bearwe,* basket.]

bar·row[2] (băr′ō) *n.* A large mound of earth or stones placed over a grave in ancient times. [From Old English *beorg,* hill.]

Barrow, Point The northernmost point of Alaska, on the Arctic Ocean.

bar·tend·er (bär′tĕn′dər) *n.* A person who mixes and serves alcoholic drinks at a bar. —**bar′tend′** *v.*

bar·ter (bär′tər) *v.* **bar·tered, bar·ter·ing, bar·ters** —*intr.* To trade goods or services without using money. —*tr.* To trade (goods or services) without using money: *We bartered home-grown vegetables for firewood.* ❖ *n.* The act or practice of bartering. ❖ *adj.* Relating to or being something based on bartering: *a barter economy.*

Bar·thol·o·mew (bär-thŏl′ə-myo͞o′), Saint. Sometimes called **Na·than·ael** (nə-thăn′yəl). First century AD. One of the 12 Apostles.

Bar·ton (bär′tn), **Clara** 1821–1912. American administrator who did battlefield emergency work during the Civil War and organized the American Red Cross (1881).

bas·al (bā′səl *or* bā′zəl) *adj.* **1.** Located at, relating to, or forming a base: *a plant having a tuft of basal leaves.* **2.** Basic; fundamental; primary: *Most schools use basal readers in the early grades.*

basal metabolism *n.* The amount of energy used by an organism at complete rest.

ba·salt (bə-sôlt′ *or* bā′sôlt′) *n.* A dark, fine-grained igneous rock consisting mostly of feldspar, iron, and magnesium. Basalt makes up most of the ocean floor and commonly forms when volcanic lava becomes solid.

base[1] (bās) *n.* **1.** The lowest or bottom part: *the base of a cliff.* **2a.** A part or layer on which something rests or is placed for support; a foundation: *a skyscraper built on a base of solid rock.* **b.** A fundamental part: *The theory of evolution forms the base of modern biology.* **3.** A chief ingredient or element of something; a basis: *a paint with an oil base.* **4.** A starting point or central place; a headquarters: *The explorers established a base at the foot of the glacier.* **5.** A center of supplies or operations for a military force: *The army has many bases around the country.* **6a.** A starting point, safety area, or goal in certain games. **b.** In baseball, one of the four corners of the infield that must be touched by a runner to score a run. **7.** The side or face of a geometric figure to which an altitude can be drawn. **8a.** In a number system, the factor by which each place value of a number is multiplied to generate the next place value to the left. For example, 10 is the base of the decimal system and 100 represents $1 \times 10 \times 10$; 1000 represents $1 \times 10 \times 10 \times 10$. Two is the base of the binary system and 100 represents $1 \times 2 \times 2$; 1000 represents $1 \times 2 \times 2 \times 2$. **b.** A number that is raised to an exponent. For example, if $6^2 = 6 \times 6 = 36$, 6 is the base. **c.** The number to which the percent is applied in a percentage problem. In the example *20 percent of 40 is 8,* 40 is the base. **9.** A word or word part to which affixes or other word parts may be added. For example, in *filled, refill,* and *filling, fill* is the base. **10.** Any of a class of chemical compounds that are capable of neutralizing acids in solution and that react with acids and certain metals to form water and salts. Bases turn red litmus paper blue, have a bitter taste, and have a pH of greater than 7. **11.** One of the purines (adenine and guanine) or pyrimidines (cytosine, thymine, and uracil) that are found in DNA or RNA. ❖ *adj.* **1.** Forming or serving as a base: *a base layer of soil.* **2.** Situated at or near the bottom: *a base camp for the mountain climbers.* ❖ *tr.v.* **based, bas·ing, bas·es 1.** To find a basis for; establish: *base an opinion on facts.* **2.** To form or provide a base for: *The composer based this song on an old folk melody.* **3.** To locate; station: *The general based the troops in Europe.* ◆ **off base** Badly mistaken: *Your criticism of me is off base.* [From Middle English *bas,* from Greek *basis.*]

❑ *These sound alike:* **base**[1] (lowest part), **base**[2] (mean), **bass**[2] (lowest tones in music).

barre

WRITERS CHOOSE THEIR WORDS

There are people in this world who are naturally open and easy to get to know, and there are difficult people, the ones who put up **barricades** and expect you to climb over them.

—Janet Taylor Lisle
The Art of Keeping Cool

Clara Barton
photographed c. 1904

basketweave

bas-relief
bas-relief sculpture at the ruins of the palace at Persepolis, Iran

bass clef

base[2] (bās) *adj.* **bas·er, bas·est 1.** Having or showing a lack of decency; mean; contemptible: *a base act.* **2.** Being a metal that is of little value. [From Middle English *bas,* low, from Medieval Latin *bassus.*] **—base′ly** *adv.* **—base′ness** *n.*

❑ *These sound alike:* **base[2]** (mean), **base[1]** (lowest part), **bass[2]** (lowest tones in music).

base·ball (bās′bôl′) *n.* **1.** A game played with a bat and ball on a field with four bases laid out in a diamond pattern. Two teams of nine players take turns at bat and in the field, the members of the team at bat trying to score runs by touching all four bases. **2.** The ball used in this game.

base·board (bās′bôrd′) *n.* A molding along the lower edge of a wall, where it meets the floor of a room.

base hit *n.* In baseball, a hit by which the batter reaches base safely without an error or a force play being made.

base·less (bās′lĭs) *adj.* Having no basis or foundation in fact; unfounded: *The manufacturers were forced to withdraw the baseless claims for their product.*

base·line or **base line** (bās′līn′) *n.* **1a.** A line serving as a base, as for measurement. **b.** A measurement, calculation, or location used as a basis for comparison: *The latest census figures will provide a baseline for measuring population growth in the next decade.* **2.** In baseball, an area within which a base runner must stay when running between bases. **3.** The boundary line at the back end of each side of a court, as in basketball or tennis.

base·man (bās′mən) *n.* In baseball, a player who plays at or near first, second, or third base.

base·ment (bās′mənt) *n.* The lowest story of a building, often below ground level.

base on balls *n., pl.* **bases on balls** In baseball, an advance to first base awarded to a batter who takes four pitches that are balls.

base runner *n.* A baseball player on the team at bat who has safely reached or is trying to reach a base.

ba·ses (bā′sēz′) *n.* Plural of **basis.**

bash (băsh) *v.* **bashed, bash·ing, bash·es** *—tr.* **1.** To strike or collide with (something) with a great force: *The car skidded off the road and bashed the fence.* **2.** *Informal* To criticize (a person or thing) harshly: *She's always bashing the kids from other schools.* *—intr.* To strike or collide with something with great force: *The bus bashed into the railing.* ❖ *n.* **1.** *Informal* A forceful blow. **2.** *Slang* A party or celebration.

bash·ful (băsh′fəl) *adj.* Timid and embarrassed with other people; shy: *Some children are bashful around strangers.* **—bash′ful·ly** *adv.* **—bash′ful·ness** *n.*

ba·sic (bā′sĭk) *adj.* **1.** Relating to or forming a base or basis; fundamental: *The basic idea of chess is to checkmate your opponent's king. Philosophy seeks to understand the basic truths of human experience.* **2.** Serving as a starting point; elementary: *a basic course in Chinese; a set of basic woodworking tools.* **3a.** Being or containing a chemical base. **b.** Alkaline. ❖ *n.* often **basics** Something basic or fundamental: *learn the basics of arithmetic before studying algebra.*

BASIC or **Basic** *n.* A simple computer programming language.

ba·si·cal·ly (bā′sĭ-klē) *adv.* In a basic way; fundamentally; essentially.

bas·il (băz′əl *or* bā′zəl) *n.* A fragrant plant related to mint, having leaves used as a seasoning.

ba·sil·i·ca (bə-sĭl′ĭ-kə) *n.* **1.** A type of ancient Roman building having two rows of columns dividing the interior into a central hall with two side aisles, and an arched semicircular space at one end. **2.** A Christian church built in this design.

bas·i·lisk (băs′ə-lĭsk′ *or* băz′ə-lĭsk′) *n.* **1.** A legendary serpent or dragon that could kill with its breath and glance. **2.** Any of various tropical American lizards having a crest on the head and back.

ba·sin (bā′sĭn) *n.* **1.** An open, shallow, usually round container used especially for holding liquids: *soaked our feet in a basin of hot water.* **2.** A sink, as in a bathroom: *Take the plug out of the basin.* **3.** An enclosed part of a river or harbor where the water remains relatively calm and level: *went swimming in the basin at the foot of the falls.* **4.** A geographical region drained by a river and the streams that flow into it: *the Amazon basin.*

ba·sis (bā′sĭs) *n., pl.* **ba·ses** (bā′sēz′) **1.** The foundation for something, such as a plan or idea: *On what basis did you make this decision?* **2.** The main part or basic ingredient: *The basis for most liquids is water.* **3a.** A pattern of behavior or action in time: *The teacher reviews student papers on a weekly basis.* **b.** A condition for relating or proceeding: *We are on a first-name basis.* [From Middle English, base of a pyramid, from Greek.]

bask (băsk) *intr.v.* **basked, bask·ing, basks 1.** To expose oneself to or enjoy a pleasant warmth: *turtles basking in the sun.* **2.** To take pleasure; live happily: *We basked in the glory of our team's success.*

bas·ket (băs′kĭt) *n.* **1.** A container made of interwoven strips, as of cane, wood, or other plant material. **2.** Something resembling such a container in shape or function: *a wastepaper basket.* **3.** The amount that a basket can hold: *a basket of peaches.* **4a.** A metal hoop from which an open net is hung, used as a goal in basketball. **b.** A score made by throwing the ball through this hoop.

bas·ket·ball (băs′kĭt-bôl′) *n.* **1.** A game played by two teams of five players in which players try to throw a ball through an elevated basket on the opponent's end of a rectangular court. **2.** The ball used in this game.

bask·et·ful (băs′kĭt-fo͝ol′) *n.* The amount that a basket can hold.

bas·ket·ry (băs′kĭ-trē) *n.* **1.** The craft or process of making baskets, especially by weaving. **2.** Baskets considered as a group.

bas·ket·weave or **basket weave** (băs′kĭt-wēv′) *n.* A pattern resembling that of a woven basket.

bas mitz·vah (bäs mĭts′və) *n. & v.* Variant of **bat mitzvah.**

Basque (băsk) *n.* **1.** A member of a people who live in the western Pyrenees of France and Spain. **2.** The language of the Basques, unrelated to any other known language. **—Basque** *adj.*

bas-re·lief (bä′rĭ-lēf′) *n.* **1.** A sculptural technique in which figures or letters are raised slightly from a flat background: *The tombstone was carved in bas-relief.* **2.** A sculpture made using this technique.

bass[1] (băs) *n., pl.* **bass** or **bass·es** Any of several freshwater or saltwater fishes, often having spiny fins, caught for food or sport. [From Old English *bærs.*]

bass[2] (bās) *n.* **1.** A male singing voice in the lowest range. **2.** A singer who has such a voice. **3.** An instrument whose sound falls within this range. **4.** A part written in this range. **5.** A low-pitched sound or tone. [From Middle English *bas,* from *bas,* low.]

❑ *These sound alike:* **bass[2]** (lowest tones in music), **base[1]** (lowest part), **base[2]** (mean).

bass clef (bās) *n.* A symbol on a musical staff indicating that the note on the fourth line from the bottom of the staff is F below middle C.

bass drum (bās) *n.* A large cylindrical double-headed drum that makes a deep booming sound when struck.

Basse·terre (bäs-târ′ *or* bäs-târ′) The capital of St. Kitts and Nevis, in the Leeward Islands of the West Indies.

Basse-Terre (bäs-târ′ *or* bäs-târ′) The capital of Guadeloupe, on **Basse-Terre Island** in the Leeward Islands of the West Indies.

bas·set hound (băs′ĭt) *n.* A dog of a breed originally

ă	pat	ôr	core
ā	pay	oi	boy
âr	care	ou	out
ä	father	o͝o	took
ĕ	pet	o͝or	lure
ē	be	o͞o	boot
ĭ	pit	ŭ	cut
ī	bite	ûr	urge
îr	pier	th	thin
ŏ	pot	*th*	this
ō	toe	zh	vision
ô	paw	ə	about

bred for hunting, having a long body, short legs, and long drooping ears.

bas·si·net (băs′ə-nĕt′ or băs′ə-nĕt′) *n.* A bed for a small baby, resembling a basket and sometimes having a hood at one end.

bas·so (băs′ō or bä′sō) *n., pl.* **bas·sos** or **bas·si** (bä′sē) A bass singer, especially in opera.

bas·soon (bə-so͞on′) *n.* A low-pitched woodwind instrument having a long wooden body connected to a double reed by a U-shaped metal tube. **—bas·soon′ist** *n.*

bass viol (bās) *n.* A double bass.

bass·wood (băs′wo͝od′) *n.* **1.** Any of several North American linden trees, having heart-shaped leaves and clusters of fragrant yellowish flowers. **2.** The soft light wood of such a tree.

bast (băst) *n.* A strong fiber found in the stalks of certain plants, such as flax and hemp, used for making rope, cord, and some textiles.

bas·tard (băs′tərd) *n.* Used as a disparaging term for a child born to parents who are not married to each other.

baste[1] (bāst) *tr.v.* **bast·ed, bast·ing, bastes** To sew with long loose stitches meant to be taken out when the final sewing is done: *baste a hem.* [From Middle English *basten*, from Old French *bastir*.]

baste[2] (bāst) *tr.v.* **bast·ed, bast·ing, bastes** To moisten (meat) with liquid such as melted fat while roasting. [From Middle English *basten*.]

Bas·tille Day (bă-stēl′) *n.* July 14, celebrated as a holiday in France in memory of the invasion by French citizens of the Bastille, a fortress used as a prison, in 1789.

bas·tion (băs′chən or băs′tē-ən) *n.* **1.** A projecting part of a fort or rampart that enables defenders to aim at attackers who have advanced to the foot of a wall. **2.** A strongly protected or well-defended position; a stronghold: *That magazine is a bastion of freedom of speech.*

bat[1] (băt) *n.* **1.** A wooden stick or club, especially one used for hitting a ball, as in baseball or cricket. **2.** A hard hit, such as one delivered with a stick. ❖ *v.* **bat·ted, bat·ting, bats** *—tr.* **1.** To hit, especially with a swinging motion or a bat: *The cat batted the toy mouse around the room.* **2.** In baseball, to have (a certain percentage) as a batting average: *He is batting .276 this season.* *—intr.* **1.** To use a bat: *She's batting well this season.* **2.** To be at bat: *Our team batted first.* ◆ **at bat** Taking one's turn to bat, as in baseball. **go to bat for** To give assistance to; defend: *The student went to bat for his friend who was wrongly accused.* **right off the bat** Without hesitation; immediately: *We liked the new student right off the bat.* [From Middle English, perhaps partly of Celtic origin and partly from Old French *batte*, tool for pounding.]

bat[2] (băt) *n.* Any of various flying mammals that have thin leathery wings that extend from long thin bones of the forelimbs to the hind legs and tail. Bats are active at night, and some kinds eat fruit while others eat insects or other foods. [From Middle English *bakke*, of Scandinavian origin.] —SEE NOTE.

bat[3] (băt) *tr.v.* **bat·ted, bat·ting, bats** To move with a flapping motion; blink: *bat one's eyelashes.* ◆ **not bat an eye** To show no change of expression: *They didn't bat an eye when the firecracker exploded.* [Probably from Old French *batre*, to beat.]

bat·boy (băt′boi′) *n.* A boy who takes care of a baseball team's bats and equipment.

batch (băch) *n.* **1.** An amount prepared at one time: *baked a batch of cookies; mixed a batch of cement.* **2.** A group or number of similar things: *recycle a batch of old newspapers.* **3.** In computer science, a set of data to be processed in a single run. ❖ *tr.v.* **batched, batch·ing, batch·es** To assemble or process as a batch: *The author batched all the maps in a section at the back of the book.*

bate (bāt) *tr.v.* **bat·ed, bat·ing, bates** To lessen the force or intensity of; moderate: *My parents bated their enthusiasm when they saw how much summer camp cost.* ◆ **with bated breath** In a frightened or excited way, as if holding one's breath.

ba·teau (bă-tō′) *n., pl.* **ba·teaux** (bă-tōz′) A light flat-bottom boat or rowboat used on rivers and lakes, especially in Canada and Louisiana.

Bates (bāts), **Katharine Lee** 1859–1929. American educator and writer best known for her poem "America the Beautiful" (1895).

bat·girl (băt′gûrl′) *n.* A girl who takes care of a baseball team's bats and equipment.

bath (băth) *n., pl.* **baths** (bă*th*z or băths) **1a.** The act of washing or soaking the body, as in water or steam: *give the baby a bath.* **b.** The water used for a bath: *run a hot bath.* **2.** A bathtub or bathroom: *an apartment with three rooms and a bath.* **3.** A building equipped for bathing. **4.** often **baths** A resort providing therapeutic baths; a spa. **5.** A liquid in which an object is dipped or soaked in order to process it in some way: *dipped the cloth in a bath of dye.*

bathe (bā*th*) *v.* **bathed, bath·ing, bathes** *—intr.* **1.** To take a bath: *bathe before breakfast.* **2.** To go into the water for swimming or recreation: *bathe in the surf.* *—tr.* **1.** To wash in water; give a bath to: *bathe the baby.* **2.** To apply a liquid to, as for medicinal purposes: *bathed the wound in disinfectant.* **3.** To make wet; moisten: *Tears bathed the baby's cheeks.* **4.** To seem to wash or pour over; flood: *Moonlight bathed the side of the building.* **—bath′er** *n.*

ba·thet·ic (bə-thĕt′ĭk) *adj.* Marked by bathos: *a bathetic passage in a novel.*

bath·house (băth′hous′) *n.* **1.** A building equipped for bathing. **2.** A building, as at a beach, used by swimmers for changing clothes.

bath·ing cap (bā′*th*ĭng) *n.* A tight elastic cap worn to keep the hair dry or away from the face while swimming.

bathing suit *n.* A swimsuit.

bath·mat (băth′măt′) *n.* A mat for use in a bathtub or on a bathroom floor to absorb water or prevent slipping.

bath·o·lith (băth′ə-lĭth′) *n.* A large mass of igneous rock that has melted and flowed into surrounding rock layers deep below the earth's surface.

ba·thos (bā′thŏs′) *n.* A sudden change from a dignified or serious style to one that is very commonplace, producing a ridiculous effect.

bath·robe (băth′rōb′) *n.* A loose robe worn before and after bathing and for lounging.

bath·room (băth′ro͞om′ or băth′ro͝om′) *n.* **1.** A room equipped for taking a bath or shower and usually also containing a sink and toilet. **2.** A room containing a toilet and sink.

bath·tub (băth′tŭb′) *n.* A tub for bathing, especially one installed in a bathroom.

bath·y·scaphe (băth′ĭ-skăf′ or băth′ĭ-skāf′) also **bath·y·scaph** (băth′ĭ-skăf′) *n.* A deep-sea research vessel having a large flotation hull and an observation capsule attached to its underside. A bathyscaphe operates under its own power and is capable of diving to great ocean depths.

bath·y·sphere (băth′ĭ-sfîr′) *n.* A strong spherical chamber in which a crew can be lowered by cable deep into the ocean to make underwater observations.

ba·tik (bə-tēk′ or băt′ĭk) *n.* **1.** A method of dyeing a design on cloth by putting removable wax over the parts of the cloth not meant to be dyed. **2.** Cloth dyed by batik. **—ba·tik′** *v.*

ba·tiste (bə-tēst′) *n.* A fine light fabric, usually of cotton or linen. [From Old French, perhaps after *Baptiste* of Cambrai, textile maker of the 1200s.]

bat mitz·vah (bät mĭts′və) or **bas mitz·vah** (bäs mĭts′-və) *n.* **1.** A ceremony in which a Jewish girl who is 12

Bastille Day
a depiction of the invasion of the Bastille

SCIENCE

bat[2] Bats are the only mammals that can truly fly, and they have been very successful: there are over 1000 different species. Many eat insects or fruit, but some species have evolved to feed on nectar, small vertebrates, or blood. Most bats navigate using a form of natural radar called *echolocation*. The bat emits a series of very high-pitched squeaks, inaudible to human ears, which reflect off objects in its path. Relying on the pattern of echoes it hears, the bat can then avoid obstacles or head for a specific target, such as a tasty moth.

batik

battering ram

or 13 years old is admitted as an adult into the religious community. **2.** A girl for whom such a ceremony is celebrated. ❖ *tr.v.* **bat mitz·vahed, bat mitz·vah·ing, bat mitz·vahs** or **bas mitz·vahed, bas mitz·vah·ing, bas mitz·vahs** To recognize (a girl) in such a ceremony. [From Hebrew *bat miṣwâ* : *bat*, daughter + *miṣwâ*, commandment.]

ba·ton (bə-tŏn′ *or* băt′n) *n.* **1.** A thin tapered stick often used by a conductor in leading a band, chorus, or orchestra. **2.** A stick or staff such as that twirled by a drum major, passed in a relay race, or carried as a symbol of office.

Bat·on Rouge (băt′n ro͞ozh′) The capital of Louisiana, in the southeast-central part of the state on a bluff above the Mississippi River. It was founded in 1719 as a French fort.

bats·man (băts′mən) *n.* A batter in baseball or cricket.

bat·tal·ion (bə-tăl′yən) *n.* **1.** A large group of soldiers organized as a unit, usually consisting of a headquarters and two or more companies of infantry or artillery. **2.** A large number: *a battalion of ants.*

bat·ten[1] (băt′n) *intr.v.* **bat·tened, bat·ten·ing, bat·tens 1.** To feed and grow fat. **2.** To thrive and prosper, often at another's expense: *politicians battening on a corrupt system.* [Ultimately from Old Norse *batna*, to improve.]

bat·ten[2] (băt′n) *n.* A narrow strip of wood or plastic, such as one used on a boat or ship to fasten a covering over a hatch or to stiffen the edge of a sail. ❖ *tr.v.* **bat·tened, bat·ten·ing, bat·tens** To furnish, fasten, or secure with such strips: *batten down the hatch before the storm.* ◆ **batten down the hatches** To prepare for an approaching disaster or emergency. [From Old French *batant*, wooden strip, clapper.]

battlement

bat·ter[1] (băt′ər) *v.* **bat·tered, bat·ter·ing, bat·ters** —*tr.* **1.** To strike or hit forcefully and repeatedly: *Heavy wind and rain battered the windows.* **2.** To injure or damage by rough treatment or hard wear: *The dented old car was badly battered.* **3.** To subject to repeated beatings or physical abuse. —*intr.* To hit forcefully and repeatedly; pound: *Waves battered against the pier.* [From Middle English *bateren*, from Latin *battuere*.]

bat·ter[2] (băt′ər) *n.* The player at bat in baseball or cricket.

bat·ter[3] (băt′ər) *n.* A beaten mixture, as of flour, milk, and eggs, used in cooking: *a bowl of cake batter.* ❖ *tr.v.* **bat·tered, bat·ter·ing, bat·ters** To coat in batter: *battered the chicken before frying it.* [From Middle English *bature*, probably from Old French *bateure*, a beating, from *batre*, to beat.]

bat·ter·ing ram (băt′ər-ĭng) *n.* **1.** A heavy wooden beam used in ancient and medieval warfare to batter down walls and gates. **2.** A heavy metal bar used by firefighters and law enforcement officers to break down walls and doors.

bat·ter·y (băt′ə-rē) *n., pl.* **bat·ter·ies 1a.** Two or more connected electric cells that supply a direct current by converting chemical energy to electrical energy. **b.** A small dry cell designed to power a flashlight or other portable electric device. **2a.** A group or set of large guns, as of artillery: *The fort had a battery of cannons.* **b.** A place where such guns are set up: *the old battery at the end of Manhattan Island.* **c.** A unit of soldiers in the artillery, corresponding to a company in the infantry. **3.** A group of things or people used or doing something together: *The celebrities faced a battery of cameras and reporters.* **4.** In baseball, the pitcher and catcher. **5.** The unlawful touching or beating of another person, with the intention of doing harm.

bat·ting (băt′ĭng) *n.* Cotton or wool fibers wadded into rolls or sheets, used to stuff mattresses or furniture or to line quilts.

batting average *n.* A measure of a baseball batter's performance obtained by dividing the number of base hits by the number of times at bat, not including walks.

bat·tle (băt′l) *n.* **1.** A fight between two armed forces, usually on a large scale. **2.** Armed fighting; combat: *wounded in battle.* **3.** A struggle or sharp conflict: *a political battle; a battle of wits.* ❖ *v.* **bat·tled, bat·tling, bat·tles** —*intr.* To fight in or as if in battle; struggle: *The firefighters battled bravely against the flames.* —*tr.* To fight against: *The sailors battled the storm for hours.* **—bat′tler** *n.*

bat·tle-axe or **bat·tle-ax** (băt′l-ăks′) *n.* A heavy axe with a broad head, used formerly as a weapon.

battle cry *n.* **1.** A shout to spur on fighting, uttered by troops in battle. **2.** A slogan used by the supporters of a cause: *The campaign's battle cry was "Lower Taxes."*

bat·tle·dore (băt′l-dôr′) *n.* **1.** An early form of badminton played with a flat wooden paddle and a shuttlecock. **2.** The paddle used in this game.

bat·tle·field (băt′l-fēld′) *n.* A field or area where a battle is or was fought: *the Civil War battlefield at Gettysburg.*

bat·tle·front (băt′l-frŭnt′) *n.* The line or area in which armed forces engage opponents in battle.

bat·tle·ground (băt′l-ground′) *n.* A battlefield.

bat·tle·ment (băt′l-mənt) *n.* A top part of a wall, especially on a castle or fortress, having notched openings through which soldiers defend the structure against attack.

battle royal *n., pl.* **battles royal 1.** A battle in which many people take part. **2.** A bitter or intense quarrel: *a battle royal over spending for public works.*

bat·tle·ship (băt′l-shĭp′) *n.* Any of a class of warships of largest size, having the heaviest guns and armor.

bat·ty (băt′ē) *adj.* **bat·ti·er, bat·ti·est** *Slang* Crazy or eccentric: *My uncle is kind of batty.*

bau·ble (bô′bəl) *n.* A showy ornament or trinket of little value.

baud (bôd) *n.* A unit of speed in data transmission equal to one change in a carrier signal per second. [After Jean Maurice Emile *Baudot* (1845–1903), French engineer.]

baux·ite (bôk′sīt′) *n.* A mixture of minerals, often resembling clay, that is the principal ore of aluminum.

Ba·var·i·a (bə-vâr′ē-ə) A region and former duchy of southern Germany. Bavaria was one of the most important duchies of medieval Germany.

bawd·y (bô′dē) *adj.* **bawd·i·er, bawd·i·est** Humorously coarse; ribald: *bawdy jokes.* **—bawd′i·ly** *adv.* **—bawd′i·ness** *n.*

bawl (bôl) *v.* **bawled, bawl·ing, bawls** —*intr.* **1.** To cry or weep loudly; wail: *The unhappy baby kicked and bawled.* **2.** To cry out loudly; shout: *I could hear the coach bawling from the sidelines.* —*tr.* To utter or call in a loud strong voice: *The sentry bawled an order to halt.* ◆ **bawl out** *Informal* To scold loudly or harshly.

❑ *These sound alike:* **bawl, ball[1]** (round object), **ball[2]** (dance).

bay[1] (bā) *n.* A body of water partially enclosed by land but having a wide outlet to the sea. A bay is usually smaller than a gulf and larger than a cove. [From Middle English *bai*, from Old French *baie*.]

❑ *These sound alike:* **bay[1]** (body of water), **bay[2]** (part of a room), **bay[3]** (reddish brown), **bay[4]** (bark), **bay[5]** (laurel), **bey** (Turkish governor).

bay[2] (bā) *n.* **1.** A part of a building divided by vertical supports such as columns or pillars: *an arcade with ten bays.* **2.** A bay window. **3.** A section or compartment, as of a building or aircraft, set off for a specific purpose: *The cargo was stored in a loading bay.* **4.** A sickbay. [From Middle English *bai*, from Old French *baee*, an opening, from *baer*, to gape.]

❑ *These sound alike:* **bay[2]** (part of a room), **bay[1]**

ă	pat	ôr	core
ā	pay	oi	boy
âr	care	ou	out
ä	father	o͝o	took
ĕ	pet	o͝or	lure
ē	be	o͞o	boot
ĭ	pit	ŭ	cut
ī	bite	ûr	urge
îr	pier	th	thin
ŏ	pot	*th*	this
ō	toe	zh	vision
ô	paw	ə	about

(body of water), **bay³** (reddish brown), **bay⁴** (bark), **bay⁵** (laurel), **bey** (Turkish governor).

bay³ (bā) *adj.* Reddish-brown: *a bay horse.* ❖ *n.* **1.** A reddish brown. **2.** A reddish-brown horse with a black mane. [From Middle English *bai*, from Latin *badius.*]

❑ *These sound alike:* **bay³** (reddish brown), **bay¹** (body of water), **bay²** (part of a room), **bay⁴** (bark), **bay⁵** (laurel), **bey** (Turkish governor).

bay⁴ (bā) *n.* **1.** A deep, prolonged bark, such as the sound made by a hound. **2.** A position of or like that of an animal cornered by and facing its pursuers: *The barking hounds kept the stag at bay. The policeman chased the dog and brought it to bay.* **3.** The position of being kept at a distance: *Lights around the factory kept intruders at bay.* ❖ *intr.v.* **bayed, bay·ing, bays** To make deep, prolonged barks. [From Middle English *abai*, cornering a hunted animal, from Old French *abaiier*, to bark.]

❑ *These sound alike:* **bay⁴** (bark), **bay¹** (body of water), **bay²** (part of a room), **bay³** (reddish brown), **bay⁵** (laurel), **bey** (Turkish governor).

bay⁵ (bā) *n.* **1.** An evergreen tree of the Mediterranean region having glossy fragrant leaves that are used as a flavoring in cooking. **2.** Any of certain other trees or shrubs having fragrant leaves. [From Middle English *bai*, from Latin *bāca*, berry.]

❑ *These sound alike:* **bay⁵** (laurel), **bay¹** (body of water), **bay²** (part of a room), **bay³** (reddish brown), **bay⁴** (bark), **bey** (Turkish governor).

bay·ber·ry (bā′bĕr′ē) *n.* **1.** The gray, waxy, aromatic berries of a North American shrub, used to make candles. **2.** The shrub that bears such berries.

bay leaf *n.* The dried leaf of the bay, used as a flavoring in cooking.

Bay of For the names of actual bays, see the specific proper name; for example, **Biscay, Bay of.**

bay·o·net (bā′ə-nĕt′ *or* bā′ə-nĭt) *n.* A knife attached to the muzzle of a rifle for use in close combat. ❖ *tr.v.* **bay·o·net·ed, bay·o·net·ing, bay·o·nets** or **bay·o·net·ted, bay·o·net·ting, bay·o·nets** To stab or prod with a bayonet.

bay·ou (bī′o͞o *or* bī′ō) *n.* A sluggish marshy stream connected with a river, lake, or gulf, common in the southern United States.

bay rum *n.* A fragrant lotion made from the leaves of a tropical American tree.

bay window *n.* A window or group of windows projecting from the outer wall of a building and forming an alcove within.

ba·zaar (bə-zär′) *n.* **1.** A market, usually consisting of a street lined with shops and stalls, especially in the Middle East. **2.** A store where various kinds of things are sold. **3.** A fair or sale, often to raise money for a charity: *a hospital bazaar.* [From Italian *bazarro* and Urdu *bāzār*, both from Persian *bāzār*.]

ba·zoo·ka (bə-zo͞o′kə) *n.* A portable military weapon consisting of a tube for launching antitank rockets. [After a crude wind instrument made of pipes, invented and named by Bob Burns (1896–1956), American comedian.]

BB¹ (bē′bē) *n.* A metal pellet measuring $^7/_{40}$ of an inch (0.44 centimeter) in diameter, used in air rifles.

BB² *abbr.* An abbreviation of base on balls.

BBC *abbr.* An abbreviation of British Broadcasting Corporation.

BB gun *n.* A small air rifle that shoots BBs.

BC *abbr.* An abbreviation of: **1.** or **BC** before Christ (in a specified year before the birth of Jesus). **2.** British Columbia.

BCE or **BCE** *abbr.* An abbreviation of before Common Era. —SEE NOTE AT **Common Era.**

B cell *n.* Any of the lymphocytes that are involved in the formation and secretion of antibodies. In mammals, B cells mature in the bone marrow.

B complex *n.* Vitamin B complex.

bd. ft. *abbr.* An abbreviation of board foot.

be (bē) *v. Present tense first person singular* **am** (ăm), *second person singular* **are** (är), *third person singular* **is** (ĭz), *plural* **are,** *present participle* **be·ing** (bē′ĭng). *Past tense first and third person singular* **was** (wŭz *or* wŏz), *second person singular* **were** (wûr), *plural* **were,** *past participle* **been** (bĭn). —*intr.* **1.** To exist; have life or reality: *There are no longer any dinosaurs.* **2.** To occupy a position: *The food is on the table.* **3.** To take place; occur: *When is the show?* **4.** To come or go: *Have you ever been to Ohio?* **5a.** To equal in identity or meaning: *That experiment was a complete success.* **b.** To signify or stand for: *A is excellent; C is passing.* **c.** To belong to a specified class or group: *Snakes are reptiles.* **d.** To have or show a specified quality or characteristic: *Skyscrapers are tall.* **6.** To belong; befall: *Woe is me.* —*aux.* **1.** Used to form the passive voice in combination with the past participle of transitive verbs: *Elections are held annually.* **2.** Used to express a continuing action in combination with the present participle of a verb: *We are working on the project.* **3.** Used to indicate duty, possibility, or a future event with the infinitive of another verb: *I am to inform you that the package has arrived. How am I to know the answer? They are to be married Monday.* [From Old English *bēon.*]

❑ *These sound alike:* **be, bee** (insect).

Be The symbol for the element **beryllium.**

be– *pref.* A prefix that means: **1.** Completely; thoroughly: *bemoan.* **2.** On; around; over: *bespatter.* **3.** Make; cause to become: *becloud.* **4.** About; to: *bespeak.* **5.** Affect or provide with: *befriend.*

beach (bēch) *n.* The area of accumulated sand, stone, or gravel deposited above the water line at a shore by the action of waves. ❖ *tr.v.* **beached, beach·ing, beach·es** To haul or run ashore: *We beached our canoes on a sandbar. The whale beached itself in shallow water.*

❑ *These sound alike:* **beach, beech** (tree).

beach ball *n.* A large ball that can be inflated and used for games, especially at a beach or swimming pool.

beach·front (bēch′frŭnt′) *adj.* Located at or on a strip of land facing or running along a beach: *beachfront hotels.*

beach·head (bēch′hĕd′) *n.* A military position on an enemy shoreline captured by advance troops of an invading force.

bea·con (bē′kən) *n.* **1.** A guiding or warning signal, such as a lighthouse located on a coast. **2.** A radio transmitter that sends a guidance signal for aircraft. **3.** A source of guidance or inspiration: *Her achievements were a beacon to others.* [From Old English *bēacen.*]

bead (bēd) *n.* **1.** A small, often round piece of glass, wood, plastic, or other material that is pierced for placing on a string or wire. **2. beads** A necklace of beads on a string. **3. beads** A rosary. **4.** A small round object, such as a drop of moisture: *beads of sweat on one's forehead.* **5.** A small knob of metal located at the muzzle of a rifle or pistol and used in taking aim. ❖ *tr. & intr.v.* **bead·ed, bead·ing, beads** To furnish with or collect into beads: *bead the collar around a sweater; water beading on the soda can.* [From Old English *gebed*, prayer.]

bead·ing (bē′dĭng) *n.* Ornamentation using beads; beadwork: *moccasins with colorful beading on top.*

bea·dle (bēd′l) *n.* A minor official in an English church, whose duties include keeping order and ushering during services.

bead·work (bēd′wûrk′) *n.* Decorative work in beads.

bead·y (bē′dē) *adj.* **bead·i·er, bead·i·est** Small, round, and shining: *beady eyes.*

bea·gle (bē′gəl) *n.* A small hound of a breed having drooping ears and a smooth coat with white, black, and tan markings.

beadwork

beak
top to bottom: black skimmer, pileated woodpecker, and American goldfinch

bearskin

ă	pat	ôr	core
ā	pay	oi	boy
âr	care	ou	out
ä	father	o͝o	took
ĕ	pet	o͝or	lure
ē	be	o͞o	boot
ĭ	pit	ŭ	cut
ī	bite	ûr	urge
îr	pier	th	thin
ŏ	pot	*th*	this
ō	toe	zh	vision
ô	paw	ə	about

beak (bēk) *n.* **1.** A bird's bill, especially a strong curved one such as that of a hawk or a finch. **2.** A similar, often horny, part in other animals, such as turtles and octopuses. **3.** A projecting part that resembles a bird's beak. [From Middle English *bek,* from Latin *beccus,* of Celtic origin.] **—beaked** (bēkt) *adj.*

beak·er (bē′kər) *n.* **1.** A cylindrical glass container with a pouring lip, used especially in laboratories. **2.** A large drinking cup with a wide mouth. [From Middle English *biker,* from Medieval Latin *bicārius, bicārium.*]

beam (bēm) *n.* **1.** A long rigid piece of wood or metal used especially as a horizontal support in construction. **2.** One of the main horizontal supports of a building or ship. **3.** The width of a ship at its widest part. **4.** In a balance, the bar from which the weights are hung. **5.** A stream of particles or waves, as of light, sound, or other radiation: *the beam of a flashlight; a laser beam.* **6.** A radio beam used to help ships or aircraft navigate. ❖ *v.* **beamed, beam·ing, beams** *—intr.* **1.** To give off light; shine: *The sun is beaming in the sky.* **2.** To smile broadly: *His face beamed with delight. —tr.* To emit or transmit: *beam a TV program to Europe by satellite.* [From Old English *bēam.*]

beam·ing (bē′mĭng) *adj.* **1.** Shining; bright: *the beaming sun.* **2.** Smiling broadly; cheery; joyful: *a beaming face.*

bean (bēn) *n.* **1a.** Any of various plants related to the pea, having seeds in pods that are usually long and narrow. **b.** The edible seed or pod of such a plant. **2.** A seed or pod similar to a bean: *a coffee bean; a vanilla bean.* **3.** *Slang* A person's head: *got hit on the bean with a snowball.* ❖ *tr.v.* **beaned, bean·ing, beans** *Slang* To hit (a person) on the head with a thrown object, especially a pitched baseball. ◆ **full of beans** Energetic; lively: *The children were too full of beans to sit still.* **spill the beans** To disclose a secret. [From Old English *bēan.*]

bean·bag (bēn′băg′) *n.* **1.** A small bag filled with pellets or dried beans and used as a toy for throwing in games. **2.** A large bag filled with pellets or dried beans and used as a chair or other piece of furniture.

bean ball *n.* In baseball, a pitch aimed at the batter's head.

bean curd *n.* Tofu.

bean·ie (bē′nē) *n.* A small brimless cap.

bean sprouts *pl.n.* The tender shoots of certain bean plants, used as food.

bean·stalk (bēn′stôk′) *n.* The stem of a bean plant.

bear[1] (bâr) *v.* **bore** (bôr), **borne** (bôrn) or **born** (bôrn), **bear·ing, bears** *—tr.* **1.** To carry on one's person from one place to another: *He bore the heavy suitcase from the car into the house.* **2.** To move while containing or supporting (something); convey or transport: *a train bearing grain.* **3.** To have in the heart or mind: *bear a grudge.* **4.** To have as a visible characteristic; show: *buildings bearing the scars of time; twins bearing a strong resemblance to each other.* **5.** To carry (oneself) in a specified way: *Members of both teams bore themselves with pride.* **6.** To hold up; support: *a floor able to bear the weight of heavy machinery.* **7.** To be accountable for; assume: *We all shared in bearing the blame for our actions.* **8.** To put up with; endure: *I can't bear his smug attitude.* **9.** To call for; warrant: *This case bears investigation.* **10.** To bring forth; produce: *Some trees bear fruit early in the spring. My savings account bears interest.* **11.** To give birth to: *The woman bore three children.* **12.** To give or offer; provide: *bear witness in a written statement. —intr.* **1.** To yield fruit; produce: *fruit trees that bear well.* **2.** To have influence or relevance; apply: *The police brought pressure to bear upon the accused. Your remark does not bear upon the problem.* **3.** To extend, turn, or be turned in a given direction: *After the bridge, the road bears to the left. At the corner, bear right. The cannons were brought to bear on the pirate ship.* ◆ **bear down 1.** To exert pressure; press down: *Concern about water bears down heavily in times of drought.* **2.** To exert oneself; make a special effort: *By bearing down the staff was able to complete the job on time.* **bear down on 1.** To affect in a harmful way: *The large amount of work was bearing down on the entire staff.* **2.** To move toward or approach rapidly: *The runners bore down on the finish line.* **bear in mind** To hold in one's mind; remember: *Bear in mind that we're reporting, not taking sides.* **bear out** To prove right; confirm: *The test results bear out our theory.* **bear up** To withstand difficulty or stress: *The patient bore up well during a long illness.* **bear with** To be patient or indulgent with: *Please bear with me while I find out where to go.* [From Old English *beran.*]

❑ *These sound alike:* **bear**[1] (support), **bare** (uncovered), **bear**[2] (animal).

bear[2] (bâr) *n.* **1.** Any of various large mammals having a shaggy coat, a very short tail, and a flat-footed walk. Bears usually eat both plants and animals, such as insects and small rodents. **2.** A large clumsy person. **3.** *Slang* Something that is difficult or unpleasant: *That exam was a bear!* **4.** A person who sells stocks or other securities expecting their price to fall. ❖ *adj.* Characterized by falling prices: *a bear market in stocks.* [From Old English *bera.*]

❑ *These sound alike:* **bear**[2] (animal), **bare** (uncovered), **bear**[1] (support).

bear·a·ble (bâr′ə-bəl) *adj.* Capable of being borne; tolerable: *Resting from time to time made the long hike bearable.* **—bear′a·bly** *adv.*

beard (bîrd) *n.* **1.** A growth of hair on a man's chin, cheeks, and throat. **2.** A tuft or growth of hairs, bristles, or other hairlike threads on a plant or animal. [From Old English.]

bear·er (bâr′ər) *n.* **1.** A person who carries or supports something: *a stretcher bearer; a message bearer.* **2.** A person who holds or presents a check, money order, bond, or other note for payment: *Checks direct a bank to pay the bearer a certain sum of money.*

bear·ing (bâr′ĭng) *n.* **1.** The manner or way in which one carries oneself: *The judge has a dignified bearing.* **2.** Relevance or relationship: *That issue has no bearing on my situation.* **3.** A supporting part of a structure. **4.** A mechanical part that supports a moving part, especially a turning shaft, and allows it to move with little friction: *a wheel bearing.* **5.** Direction, especially angular direction as used in navigation: *The ship took a bearing on the lighthouse.* **6.** often **bearings** The knowledge of one's position in relation to one's surroundings: *The hikers lost their bearings in the dark.*

bear·ish (bâr′ĭsh) *adj.* **1.** Rough, clumsy, or rude. **2.** Expecting or characterized by falling prices: *a bearish outlook on the bond market.* **—bear′ish·ly** *adv.*

bear·skin (bâr′skĭn′) *n.* **1.** The skin of a bear. **2.** A rug made from the skin of a bear. **3.** A tall military hat made of black fur.

beast (bēst) *n.* **1.** An animal other than a human, especially a large four-footed animal: *the beasts of the forest.* **2.** A cruel or brutal person. [From Middle English *beste,* from Latin *bēstia.*]

beast·ly (bēst′lē) *adj.* **beast·li·er, beast·li·est 1.** Wicked or offensive: *beastly behavior.* **2.** Unpleasant; disagreeable: *a beastly drive through heavy rain.* ❖ *adv. Chiefly British* To an extreme degree; very: *a beastly hot day.* **—beast′li·ness** *n.*

beast of burden *n., pl.* **beasts of burden** An animal, such as a horse, ox, or camel, used to carry loads or pull vehicles.

beat (bēt) *v.* **beat, beat·en** (bēt′n) or **beat, beat·ing, beats** *—tr.* **1.** To strike or hit repeatedly: *The baby beat the table with a spoon.* **2.** To punish or abuse by striking; batter. **3a.** To produce sound by striking, hitting, or tapping (something) repeatedly: *beat a drum.* **b.** To mark or count (a rhythm or pulse) by tapping, moving, or striking, as with a part of the body: *beat time with one's foot.* **4.** To shape or break by pounding: *Ancient artisans beat copper into spearheads.* **5.** To flap repeatedly: *Hummingbirds beat their wings very fast.* **6.** To mix rapidly with a utensil: *beat egg whites.* **7a.** To defeat or overcome, as in a contest or battle. **b.** To surpass or be superior to: *Riding a bike beats walking.* **c.** To force to retreat; drive away: *The soldiers beat back the enemy.* **8.** To act ahead of or arrive before: *We beat you to the restaurant.* **9.** To forge or make by treading over: *The early settlers beat a path across the wilderness.* **10.** *Slang* To baffle or perplex: *How the magician did that trick beats me.* **11.** *Informal* To avoid or counter the effects of: *Let's leave early to beat the traffic.* —*intr.* **1.** To pound forcefully and repeatedly; dash: *Huge waves beat against the pier.* **2.** To fall in torrents: *The rain beat down on the field.* **3.** To shine or glare intensely: *The summer sun beat down on the thirsty bikers.* **4.** To make a sound when struck: *The drums beat loudly.* **5.** To throb; pulsate: *My heart beat faster with excitement.* **6.** To sail against the wind by tacking in a zigzag course. ❖ *n.* **1.** A stroke or blow, especially one that makes a sound: *the beat of the drums in the parade.* **2.** A pulsation or throb: *the beat of your heart.* **3a.** One of the succession of units that make up meter in music: *There are four beats in this measure.* **b.** A gesture with the hand, foot, or a baton that marks one of these units. **4.** An area regularly covered by a police officer, guard, or reporter: *The police officer patrolled her beat on a bicycle. The new reporter was given the arts beat.* ❖ *adj.* **1.** *Informal* Tired; worn-out: *I'm really beat after a full day's work.* **2.** Relating to the beatniks of the 1950s and 1960s. ◆ **beat around the bush** To avoid a subject; delay in coming to the point. **beat it** *Slang* To leave hurriedly. [From Old English *bēaten.*]

❑ *These sound alike:* **beat, beet** (vegetable).

beat·en (bēt′n) *adj.* **1.** Thinned or formed by hammering: *a beaten copper bracelet.* **2.** Much traveled: *beaten paths.*

beat·er (bē′tər) *n.* **1.** A person or thing that beats, especially an instrument for beating: *Use an electric beater to mix bread dough.* **2.** A person who drives wild game from under cover in a hunt.

be·a·tif·ic (bē′ə-tĭf′ĭk) *adj.* Showing extreme happiness; joyful: *a beatific smile.* **—be′a·tif′i·cal·ly** *adv.*

be·at·i·fy (bē-ăt′ə-fī′) *tr.v.* **be·at·i·fied, be·at·i·fy·ing, be·at·i·fies** In the Roman Catholic Church, to declare (a deceased person) to be blessed and worthy of public veneration.

beat·ing (bē′tĭng) *n.* **1.** An act of repeated hitting or striking. **2.** An instance of rough or injurious treatment: *The car took a beating on the rough back roads.* **3.** A defeat: *The defending champions gave our team a beating.* **4.** A throbbing or pulsation, as of the heart.

be·at·i·tude (bē-ăt′ĭ-to͞od′) *n.* **1.** Supreme blessedness. **2. Beatitude** Any of the declarations made by Jesus in the Sermon on the Mount, beginning with the words "Blessed are."

beat·nik (bēt′nĭk) *n.* A person who breaks convention in behavior, political opinions, and often style of dress, especially a member of a defiantly unconventional literary movement in the 1950s and early 1960s.

Be·a·trix (bā′ə-trĭks′ *or* bē′ə-trĭks′) Born 1938. Queen of the Netherlands who ascended to the throne in 1980 and abdicated in 2013.

beat-up (bēt′ŭp′) *adj. Slang* In bad condition; rundown: *a beat-up old car.*

beau (bō) *n., pl.* **beaus** or **beaux** (bōz) **1.** The boyfriend of a woman or girl. **2.** A dandy; a fop.

❑ *These sound alike:* **beau, bow³** (weapon to shoot arrows).

Beau·fort scale (bō′fərt) *n.* A scale of wind velocities ranging from 0 (calm) to 12 (hurricane). [After Sir Francis *Beaufort* (1774–1857), British naval officer.]

beau·te·ous (byo͞o′tē-əs) *adj.* Beautiful. **—beau′te·ous·ly** *adv.* **—beau′te·ous·ness** *n.*

beau·ti·cian (byo͞o-tĭsh′ən) *n.* A person who is skilled in the cosmetic services offered by a beauty parlor.

beau·ti·ful (byo͞o′tə-fəl) *adj.* **1.** Showing or having beauty; pleasing to the senses or the mind: *beautiful scenery; beautiful music.* **2.** Excellent; wonderful: *made a beautiful jump shot to win the game.* **—beau′ti·ful·ly** *adv.* **—beau′ti·ful·ness** *n.*

beau·ti·fy (byo͞o′tə-fī′) *tr.v.* **beau·ti·fied, beau·ti·fy·ing, beau·ti·fies** To make beautiful: *Green parks and wide boulevards help to beautify the city.* **—beau′ti·fi·ca′tion** (byo͞o′tə-fĭ-kā′shən) *n.* **—beau′ti·fi′er** *n.*

beau·ty (byo͞o′tē) *n., pl.* **beau·ties 1.** A pleasing quality, especially with regard to form, that delights the senses and appeals to the mind: *the beauty of the snowcapped mountains.* **2.** A person or thing that is beautiful: *Helen of Troy was a great beauty.* **3.** A feature that is most gratifying or effective: *The beauty of this scheme is that we come out ahead either way.* [From Middle English *bealte,* from Latin *bellus,* pretty.]

beauty contest *n.* **1.** A contest in which a number of people are judged with regard to their physical beauty and often their talents. **2.** A competition or comparison based mostly on superficial factors: *The election proved to be little more than a beauty contest.*

beauty parlor *n.* A beauty salon.

beauty salon *n.* A business offering hair styling, manicures, facial treatments, and other cosmetic services, especially for women.

beauty shop *n.* A beauty salon.

Beau·voir (bō-vwär′), **Simone de** 1908–1986. French writer and feminist whose works include *The Second Sex* (1949).

beaux (bōz) *n.* A plural of **beau.**

beaux arts (bō-zär′ *or* bō-zärt′) *pl.n.* The fine arts.

bea·ver¹ (bē′vər) *n.* **1a.** Either of two rodents of North America or Eurasia having thick fur, a flat broad tail, and large strong front teeth. Beavers live in and near lakes and streams and gnaw down trees to build dams and lodges. **b.** The fur of a beaver. **2.** A top hat, originally made of beaver fur. [From Old English *beofor.*]

bea·ver² (bē′vər) *n.* **1.** A piece of armor attached to a helmet or breastplate to protect the throat or lower face. **2.** The visor on a helmet. [From Middle English *bavier,* from Old French *bave,* saliva.]

bea·ver·board (bē′vər-bôrd′) *n.* A light building material of compressed wood pulp, used for walls, partitions, and bulletin boards.

be·bop (bē′bŏp′) *n.* A style of jazz that developed in the 1940s and 1950s and is characterized by complex rhythms and harmonies and by improvised solo performances. [After a two-note phrase in this style of music.]

be·calmed (bĭ-kämd′) *adj.* Motionless for lack of wind: *The becalmed sailboat waited for a breeze.*

be·came (bĭ-kām′) *v.* Past tense of **become.**

be·cause (bĭ-kôz′ *or* bĭ-kŭz′) *conj.* For the reason that; since: *The room is uncomfortable because it is too hot.*

because of *prep.* On account of; by reason of: *I stayed home because of illness.*

beck (bĕk) *n.* A gesture of beckoning. ◆ **at (someone's) beck and call** Willingly obedient; ready to perform a service: *The staff of the hotel are generally at the beck and call of the guests.*

beck·on (bĕk′ən) *v.* **beck·oned, beck·on·ing, beck·ons** —*tr.* **1.** To signal (a person) to come, as by nodding or waving: *The principal beckoned us to her office.* **2.** To attract because of an inviting appearance: *The lake beck-*

WRITERS CHOOSE THEIR WORDS

Isabel, with a **beatific** grin, expects to see something romantic, while Harriet, her face all pinched and practical, is viewing the proceedings scientifically.

—Delia Ephron
Frannie in Pieces

Beatrix
photographed in 2010

beaver¹

WRITERS CHOOSE THEIR WORDS

His gray uniform, plentifully **bedaubed** with Virginia mud, was torn in a hundred places, and hung in tatters upon his emaciated frame.

—Oliver Optic
The Soldier Boy

beech
American beech

ă	pat	ôr	core
ā	pay	oi	boy
âr	care	ou	out
ä	father	o͝o	took
ĕ	pet	o͝or	lure
ē	be	o͞o	boot
ĭ	pit	ŭ	cut
ī	bite	ûr	urge
îr	pier	th	thin
ŏ	pot	*th*	this
ō	toe	zh	vision
ô	paw	ə	about

oned me to dive in and cool off. —*intr.* **1.** To signal to come: *The guide beckoned at the mouth of the cave.* **2.** To attract or entice: *Adventure beckoned down every road.* [From Old English *bīecnan.*]

be·cloud (bĭ-**kloud′**) *tr.v.* **be·cloud·ed, be·cloud·ing, be·clouds** To darken with or as if with clouds; obscure: *The candidates' debate was beclouded by passionate emotions.*

be·come (bĭ-**kŭm′**) *v.* **be·came** (bĭ-**kām′**), **be·come, be·com·ing, be·comes** —*intr.* To grow or come to be: *As winter approaches the temperature becomes colder.* —*tr.* **1.** To be appropriate or suitable to: *It becomes a judge to act with dignity.* **2.** To look good with or cause to look good on: *The new coat becomes you.* ◆ **become of** To be the fate of; happen to: *What ever became of your friend that moved away?*

be·com·ing (bĭ-**kŭm′**ĭng) *adj.* **1.** Appropriate; suitable: *a helpful and cheerful manner becoming to a nurse.* **2.** Pleasing or attractive to look at: *the baby's becoming smile.* —**be·com′ing·ly** *adv.*

bec·que·rel (bĕ-**krĕl′** *or* bĕk′ə-**rĕl′**) *n.* A unit for measuring radioactivity, equal to the decay of one atomic nucleus per second. [After Antoine Henri *Becquerel* (1852–1908), French physicist.]

bed (bĕd) *n.* **1a.** A piece of furniture for resting and sleeping, consisting usually of a flat rectangular frame and a mattress resting on springs. **b.** A mattress: *a feather bed.* **c.** A mattress and bedclothes: *make up a bed on the floor.* **2.** A place where one may sleep; lodging: *I have a bed for the night at the inn.* **3.** The time at which one goes to sleep: *I drank a glass of water before bed.* **4a.** A small plot for cultivating or growing things: *a bed of flowers.* **b.** A similar plot on the bottom of a body of water: *an oyster bed.* **5.** The bottom of a body of water: *a stream bed.* **6.** A supporting, underlying, or securing part: *Underneath the brick path is a bed of sand.* **7.** The part of a truck, trailer, or railroad car designed to carry loads. **8.** A layer of sediments or rock that extends under a large area and has other layers below: *a bed of coal.* ❖ *tr.v.* **bed·ded, bed·ding, beds 1.** To provide with a bed or sleeping quarters: *We bedded the guests in the living room.* **2.** To set or plant in a bed of soil: *bed tulip bulbs before the ground freezes.* [From Old English.]

bed and breakfast *n.* A private residence that offers overnight lodging and breakfast as part of the charge.

be·daub (bĭ-**dôb′**) *tr.v.* **be·daubed, be·daub·ing, be·daubs** To smear; soil: *The chimney sweep was bedaubed with soot.*

be·daz·zle (bĭ-**dăz′**əl) *tr.v.* **be·daz·zled, be·daz·zling, be·daz·zles** To dazzle completely; confuse; bewilder: *The magician bedazzled the audience with tricks.* —**be·daz′zle·ment** *n.*

bed·bug (**bĕd′**bŭg′) *n.* A small wingless insect with a flat reddish body that lives in dwellings and bedding and bites humans to feed on their blood.

bed·cham·ber (**bĕd′**chām′bər) *n.* A bedroom.

bed·clothes (**bĕd′**klōz′ *or* **bĕd′**klō*th*z′) *pl.n.* Coverings, such as sheets and blankets, used on a bed.

bed·ding (**bĕd′**ĭng) *n.* **1.** Sheets, blankets, and mattresses for beds. **2.** Material, such as straw or hay, for animals to sleep on. **3.** A foundation or bottom layer: *a bedding of gravel supporting the road.* **4.** The way in which layers of sedimentary rock are arranged.

be·deck (bĭ-**dĕk′**) *tr.v.* **be·decked, be·deck·ing, be·decks** To cover with decorations; adorn: *a hero bedecked with medals.*

be·dev·il (bĭ-**dĕv′**əl) *tr.v.* **be·dev·iled, be·dev·il·ing, be·dev·ils** or **be·dev·illed, be·dev·il·ling, be·dev·ils 1.** To plague; trouble; harass: *The project was bedeviled with accidents and injuries.* **2.** To possess with or as if with a devil; bewitch. —**be·dev′il·ment** *n.*

be·dew (bĭ-**do͞o′**) *tr.v.* **be·dewed, be·dew·ing, be·dews** To wet with or as if with dew: *cheeks bedewed with tears.*

bed·fel·low (**bĕd′**fĕl′ō) *n.* **1.** A person with whom one shares a bed. **2.** An associate or ally: *The opponents made strange bedfellows in their efforts to secure the agreement.*

bed·lam (**bĕd′**ləm) *n.* **1.** A place or situation of confusion, disorder, or noisy uproar: *the bedlam of a one-day sale in the department store.* **2.** *Archaic* A place where people with mental illness were once forced to stay. [From Middle English *Bedlem*, the Hospital of Saint Mary of *Bethlehem*, an institution in London for the mentally ill.]

Bed·ou·in (**bĕd′**o͞o-ĭn *or* **bĕd′**wĭn) *n., pl.* **Bedouin** or **Bed·ou·ins** An Arab belonging to any of the nomadic tribes of the Arabian, Syrian, or Sahara Deserts. [From Middle English *Bedoin*, from Old French *beduin*, from Arabic *badāwīyīn*, plural of *badāwī*, nomadic, from *badw*, desert nomads.]

bed·pan (**bĕd′**păn′) *n.* A container used as a toilet by a bedridden person.

bed·post (**bĕd′**pōst′) *n.* An upright post at the corner of a bed.

be·drag·gled (bĭ-**drăg′**əld) *adj.* **1.** Wet, drenched, or messy: *bedraggled clothes.* **2.** Run-down; deteriorated: *the bedraggled condition of the old buildings.*

bed·rid·den (**bĕd′**rĭd′n) *adj.* Confined to bed because of sickness or weakness.

bed·rock (**bĕd′**rŏk′) *n.* **1.** The solid rock that lies beneath the soil and other loose material on the surface of the earth. **2.** The basis or foundation: *A free press is the bedrock of democracy.*

bed·roll (**bĕd′**rōl′) *n.* Blankets or a sleeping bag rolled up to be carried by a camper or a person who sleeps outdoors.

bed·room (**bĕd′**ro͞om′ *or* **bĕd′**ro͝om′) *n.* A room in which to sleep.

bed·side (**bĕd′**sīd′) *n.* The side of a bed or the space alongside a bed: *The nurse stood at the patient's bedside.* ❖ *adj.* Near the side of a bed: *a bedside table; a bedside conversation.*

bedside manner *n.* The attitude and conduct of a physician in the presence of a patient.

bed·sore (**bĕd′**sôr′) *n.* An ulcer of the skin caused by pressure, occurring in people who are bedridden for long periods.

bed·spread (**bĕd′**sprĕd′) *n.* A covering for a bed.

bed·spring (**bĕd′**sprĭng′) *n.* One of the springs supporting the mattress of a bed.

bed·stead (**bĕd′**stĕd′) *n.* The frame supporting the springs and mattress of a bed.

bed·time (**bĕd′**tīm′) *n.* The time when a person usually goes to bed.

bee (bē) *n.* **1.** Any of numerous winged, often stinging insects that have a hairy body and gather pollen and nectar from flowers. Some bees, such as the honeybee, live in colonies. **2.** A gathering where people work together or compete against one another: *a quilting bee; a spelling bee.* ◆ **a bee in (one's) bonnet** An idea or plan that persistently occupies one's mind; a notion: *Once he has a bee in his bonnet about something, there's no stopping him.* [From Old English *bēo.*]

❑ *These sound alike:* **bee, be** (exist).

beech (bēch) *n.* **1.** Any of several trees having smooth gray bark, small edible nuts, and strong heavy wood. **2.** The wood of such a tree.

❑ *These sound alike:* **beech, beach** (area of sand).

beech·nut (**bēch′**nŭt′) *n.* The edible nut of a beech tree, encased in a prickly husk.

beef (bēf) *n., pl.* **beeves** (bēvz) or **beef 1a.** The flesh of a full-grown steer, bull, ox, or cow, used as meat. **b.** An animal raised to produce such meat. **2.** *Informal* Human muscle; brawn: *football players with plenty of beef.* **3.** *pl.* **beefs** *Slang* A complaint: *has a beef against the teacher.* ❖ *intr.v.* **beefed, beef·ing, beefs** *Slang* To complain: *What are you beefing about now?* ◆ **beef up** *Informal* To make greater or stronger: *beef up efforts to combat crime.*

beef·steak (bēf′stāk′) *n.* A slice of beef suitable for broiling or frying.

beef·y (bē′fē) *adj.* **beef·i·er, beef·i·est** Heavy, strong, and muscular; brawny: *a beefy wrestler.* **—beef′i·ness** *n.*

bee·hive (bē′hīv′) *n.* **1.** A hive for bees. **2.** A very busy place: *The bus terminal is always a beehive of activity.* **3.** A woman's hairstyle in which the hair is arranged in a tall, rounded peak on top of the head.

bee·keep·er (bē′kē′pər) *n.* A person who cares for and raises bees for commercial or agricultural purposes.

bee·line (bē′līn′) *n.* The fastest and most direct course, as one that might be taken by a bee going to its hive: *At noontime everybody made a beeline for the lunchroom.*

Be·el·ze·bub (bē-ĕl′zə-bŭb′) *n.* The Devil. [From Old English *Belzebub,* from Hebrew *ba'al zəbûb,* lord (of the) fly, mocking alteration of *ba'al zəbûl,* exalted lord (name of a Philistine god).]

been (bĭn) *v.* Past participle of **be.**

❑ *These sound alike:* **been, bin** (container).

beep (bēp) *n.* A short sound, as from an automobile's horn or a radio transmitter. ❖ *v.* **beeped, beep·ing, beeps** *—intr.* To make a beep: *The transmitter beeped steadily.* *—tr.* **1.** To cause to make a beep: *The drivers stuck in traffic beeped their horns.* **2.** To activate the beeper of (a person) by telephoning its number.

beep·er (bē′pər) *n.* **1.** A person or thing that beeps. **2.** A small electronic device that beeps or vibrates to alert the person carrying it that someone is trying to contact him or her by telephone.

beer (bîr) *n.* **1.** A fermented alcoholic beverage brewed from malt and hops. **2.** A nonalcoholic drink flavored with extracts of roots or plants: *ginger beer.*

❑ *These sound alike:* **beer, bier** (stand for a coffin).

bees·wax (bēz′wăks′) *n.* **1.** The yellowish or brownish wax produced by honeybees for making their honeycombs. **2.** A processed and purified form of this wax used in making candles, crayons, and polishes.

beet (bēt) *n.* **1a.** A leafy plant having edible leaves and a rounded, usually red root eaten as a vegetable. **b.** A form of this plant having a large whitish root from which sugar is made; the sugar beet. **2.** The root of either of these plants.

❑ *These sound alike:* **beet, beat** (strike).

Bee·tho·ven (bā′tō′vən), **Ludwig van** 1770–1827. German composer whose works include symphonies, sonatas, string quartets, Masses, and one opera. Many of his works were composed after he became partially and then totally deaf.

bee·tle¹ (bēt′l) *n.* Any of numerous insects that have biting or chewing mouthparts and hard front wings that fold over the delicate hind wings when at rest. Scientists have described over 350,000 species of beetles. [From Old English *bitula,* from *bītan,* to bite.]

❑ *These sound alike:* **beetle¹** (insect), **beetle²** (overhang), **beetle³** (mallet), **betel** (plant).

bee·tle² (bēt′l) *intr.v.* **bee·tled, bee·tling, bee·tles** To overhang; jut: *cliffs beetling over the valley below.* [From Middle English *bitel-brouwed,* grim-browed.]

❑ *These sound alike:* **beetle²** (overhang), **beetle¹** (insect), **beetle³** (mallet), **betel** (plant).

bee·tle³ (bēt′l) *n.* A heavy wooden mallet. [From Old English *bīetel.*]

❑ *These sound alike:* **beetle³** (mallet), **beetle¹** (insect), **beetle²** (overhang), **betel** (plant).

beeves (bēvz) *n.* A plural of **beef.**

be·fall (bĭ-fôl′) *v.* **be·fell** (bĭ-fĕl′), **be·fall·en** (bĭ-fô′lən), **be·fall·ing, be·falls** *—intr.* To come to pass by chance; happen. *—tr.* To happen to: *Many serious mishaps befell the explorers.*

be·fit (bĭ-fĭt′) *tr.v.* **be·fit·ted, be·fit·ting, be·fits** To be suitable to or appropriate for: *He wore a tuxedo to befit the formal occasion.*

be·fog (bĭ-fôg′) *tr.v.* **be·fogged, be·fog·ging, be·fogs** **1.** To cover or obscure with fog: *Clouds befogged the airport.* **2.** To cause confusion in; muddle: *His rambling explanation only befogged the issue.*

be·fore (bĭ-fôr′) *adv.* **1.** Earlier in time: *I told you about this before.* **2.** In front; ahead: *The people who went before were turned away.* ❖ *prep.* **1.** Previous to; earlier than: *They got there before me.* **2.** In front of: *Eat what's set before you.* **3.** In store for; awaiting: *You've got a great future before you.* **4.** Into or in the presence of: *Each prisoner was brought before the judge.* **5.** Under the consideration of: *The case is now before the court.* **6.** In preference to or in higher esteem than: *I'd take a hamburger before a hot dog any day.* ❖ *conj.* **1.** In advance of the time when: *See me before you leave.* **2.** Sooner than; rather than: *I'd die before I'd give in.* [From Old English *beforan.*]

be·fore·hand (bĭ-fôr′hănd′) *adv.* In advance; ahead of time: *The class starts at 9 o'clock, but I always get there beforehand.*

be·foul (bĭ-foul′) *tr.v.* **be·fouled, be·foul·ing, be·fouls** To make dirty; soil: *smokestacks befouling the air.*

be·friend (bĭ-frĕnd′) *tr.v.* **be·friend·ed, be·friend·ing, be·friends** To act as a friend to; assist: *A perfect stranger befriended the lost tourists.*

be·fud·dle (bĭ-fŭd′l) *tr.v.* **be·fud·dled, be·fud·dling, be·fud·dles** To confuse; perplex: *The problem befuddled even the experts.* **—be·fud′dle·ment** *n.*

beg (bĕg) *v.* **begged, beg·ging, begs** *—tr.* **1.** To ask (someone) for something in an urgent or humble manner: *We begged her for help.* **2.** To ask for (something) in an urgent or humble manner: *Could I beg a favor of you?* *—intr.* To ask for something, especially money or food, in an urgent or humble manner. ◆ **beg off** To ask to be excused from something: *We had to beg off the invitation to the party.* [From Middle English *beggen.*]

be·gan (bĭ-găn′) *v.* Past tense of **begin.**

be·gat (bĭ-găt′) *v. Archaic* A past tense of **beget.**

be·get (bĭ-gĕt′) *tr.v.* **be·got** (bĭ-gŏt′), **be·got·ten** (bĭ-gŏt′n) or **be·got, be·get·ting, be·gets** **1.** To father; sire. **2.** To cause to exist; produce: *Violence often begets more violence.* **—be·get′ter** *n.*

beg·gar (bĕg′ər) *n.* **1.** A person who begs as a means of living. **2.** A person who is very poor; a pauper. ❖ *tr.v.* **beg·gared, beg·gar·ing, beg·gars** **1.** To make very poor; ruin: *They feared that the stock market crash would beggar them.* **2.** To outdo; go beyond: *The beauty of the Grand Canyon beggars description.*

beg·gar·ly (bĕg′ər-lē) *adj.* **1.** Relating to or befitting a beggar; poor or meager: *a sweatshop that paid its workers beggarly wages.* **2.** Mean; contemptible: *a beggarly remark of envy.* **—beg′gar·li·ness** *n.*

beg·gar·y (bĕg′ə-rē) *n.* Extreme poverty.

be·gin (bĭ-gĭn′) *v.* **be·gan** (bĭ-găn′), **be·gun** (bĭ-gŭn′), **be·gin·ning, be·gins** *—intr.* **1.** To do or undergo the first part of an action; start: *When I clean my room, I begin with my desk. The rain began around noon.* **2.** To come into being; originate: *Education begins at home.* **3.** To have as a first element or part: *The movie begins with a car chase.* **4.** To have as a first position, stage, or job: *The restaurant began as an ice-cream shop. The principal began as a math teacher.* *—tr.* **1.** To take the first step in doing (something); start: *She began the project last month. When did you begin taking photos? We began to eat lunch.* **2.** To say as the first in a series

Ludwig van Beethoven

begonia

of remarks: *"I bought some plane tickets," he began.* **3.** To bring into being; originate: *The owner's grandfather began the newspaper many years ago.* **4.** To come first in: *The letter A begins the alphabet.* [From Old English *beginnan.*]

SYNONYMS **begin, start, commence, launch, initiate** These verbs mean to take the initial step in doing something. **Begin** and **start** are the most general words: *My teacher began the class after everyone arrived. I had just started to eat dinner when the lights went out.* **Commence** is a more formal word, and it often indicates that what is beginning is serious or important: *Our meetings always commence with a call to order.* **Launch** suggests beginning something with energy and expectation: *She looked for a job that could launch her career as a journalist.* **Initiate** applies to taking the first steps in a process or procedure: *My mother initiated a lawsuit against the driver who hit her car.*
ANTONYM **end**

be·gin·ner (bĭ-gĭn′ər) *n.* A person who is just starting to learn or do something; a novice: *A beginner at the piano plays simple pieces.*

be·gin·ning (bĭ-gĭn′ĭng) *n.* **1.** The act or process of bringing or being brought into existence; a start: *The Founding Fathers assumed responsibility for the beginning of the nation.* **2.** The time or point when something begins or is begun: *was born at the beginning of the twenty-first century.* **3.** The place where something begins or is begun; an initial section, division, or part: *started rehearsing at the beginning of the play.* **4a.** A source or origin: *An early fort served as the beginning of the city of Chicago.* **b.** often **beginnings** An early phase or rudimentary period: *the beginnings of life on the earth.*

be·gone (bĭ-gôn′) *v.* Used in the imperative to order someone to go away.

be·go·nia (bĭ-gōn′yə) *n.* Any of various plants grown for their showy, colorful flowers. [After Michel *Bégon* (1638–1710), French governor in the West Indies.]

be·got (bĭ-gŏt′) *v.* Past tense and a past participle of **beget.**

be·got·ten (bĭ-gŏt′n) *v.* A past participle of **beget.**

be·grime (bĭ-grīm′) *tr.v.* **be·grimed, be·grim·ing, be·grimes** To soil with dirt or grime: *boots that were begrimed with mud.*

be·grudge (bĭ-grŭj′) *tr.v.* **be·grudged, be·grudg·ing, be·grudg·es 1.** To envy (someone) for the possession or enjoyment of (something): *A generous person does not begrudge others their good fortune.* **2.** To give with reluctance: *He begrudged every penny spent on the repairs.* **—be·grudg′ing·ly** *adv.*

be·guile (bĭ-gīl′) *tr.v.* **be·guiled, be·guil·ing, be·guiles 1.** To deceive; trick: *The salesman beguiled me into buying more than I wanted.* **2.** To amuse; delight: *She beguiled us with song.* **3.** To pass pleasantly: *stories written to beguile the time during a journey.* **—be·guile′ment** *n.* **—be·guil′er** *n.*

be·gun (bĭ-gŭn′) *v.* Past participle of **begin.**

be·half (bĭ-hăf′) *n.* Interest; benefit: *On whose behalf did they act?* ◆ **in behalf of** For the benefit of; in the interest of: *We raised money in behalf of the Red Cross.* **on behalf of** As the agent of; on the part of: *The principal thanked the parents for their help on behalf of the entire teaching staff.*

be·have (bĭ-hāv′) *v.* **be·haved, be·hav·ing, be·haves** —*intr.* **1a.** To conduct oneself in a specified way: *behave badly.* **b.** To conduct oneself properly: *The babysitter told the child to behave.* **2.** To act, react, perform, or function in a certain way: *The car behaves well on rough roads.* —*tr.* **1.** To conduct (oneself) properly. **2.** To conduct (oneself) in a specified way: *They behaved themselves with dignity at the wedding.* [From Middle English *behaven* : *be-*, be- + *haven*, to have.]

be·hav·ior (bĭ-hāv′yər) *n.* **1.** The way in which a person behaves; conduct: *on one's best behavior.* **2a.** The actions or reactions of people or things under specified circumstances: *the behavior of matter at very low temperatures.* **b.** One of these actions or reactions: *the nesting behaviors of birds.* **—be·hav′ior·al** (bĭ-hāv′yər-əl) *adj.* **—be·hav′ior·al·ly** *adv.*

behavioral science *n.* A branch of science that studies human behavior. Psychology is a behavioral science.

be·hav·iour (bĭ-hāv′yər) *n. Chiefly British* Variant of **behavior.**

be·head (bĭ-hĕd′) *tr.v.* **be·head·ed, be·head·ing, be·heads** To cut off the head of; decapitate.

be·held (bĭ-hĕld′) *v.* Past tense and past participle of **behold.**

be·he·moth (bĭ-hē′məth *or* bē′ə-məth) *n.* **1.** Something enormous in size or power. **2.** often **Behemoth** A huge animal, possibly the hippopotamus, mentioned in the Bible. [From Middle English *behemoth*, from Hebrew *bəhēmôt*, plural of *bəhēmâ*, beast.]

be·hest (bĭ-hĕst′) *n.* A command or urgent request: *At the behest of the principal, no radios will be allowed in school.*

be·hind (bĭ-hīnd′) *adv.* **1.** In, to, or toward the rear: *They did not see me because I was walking behind.* **2.** In a place or condition that has been passed or left: *I left my gloves behind.* **3.** In or into an inferior position; below the standard or acceptable level: *The sick student fell behind in the class.* **4.** Slow: *That clock is running behind.* ❖ *prep.* **1.** At the back or in the rear of: *the shed behind the barn.* **2.** On the farther side of or on the other side of: *The broom is behind the door.* **3.** In a place or time that has been passed or left by: *Their worries are behind them.* **4.** In a state less advanced than: *Many nations are behind the United States in space technology.* **5.** In the background of; underlying: *Behind the theory there is much research and observation.* **6.** In a position or attitude of support: *Most of the people are behind the president.* **7.** In pursuit of: *The fox raced for the woods with the dogs fast behind it.* ❖ *n. Informal* The buttocks or backside. [From Old English *behindan.*]

be·hind·hand (bĭ-hīnd′hănd′) *adj.* Being late or slow in doing something: *That tenant is always behindhand with the rent.*

be·hold (bĭ-hōld′) *tr.v.* **be·held** (bĭ-hĕld′), **be·hold·ing, be·holds** To gaze upon; look at; see: *In a tomb the treasure hunters beheld a rich store of gold and jewels.* **—be·hold′er** *n.*

be·hold·en (bĭ-hōl′dən) *adj.* Indebted: *We were beholden to our neighbors for shelter in the storm.*

be·hoove (bĭ-ho͞ov′) *tr.v.* **be·hooved, be·hoov·ing, be·hooves** To be necessary or proper for: *It behooves you to study for the test.*

beige (bāzh) *n.* A light grayish or yellowish brown. ❖ *adj.* Light grayish or yellowish brown. [From French, perhaps from Old Italian *bambagia*, cotton wool.]

Bei·jing (bā′jĭng′) The capital of China, in the northeast part of the country. Formerly known as Peking, it is an important industrial, educational, and cultural center.

be·ing (bē′ĭng) *n.* **1.** The state or quality of existing; existence: *Rock 'n' roll music came into being in the 1950s.* **2a.** A living organism, especially a person. **b.** An imaginary or supernatural creature: *extraterrestrial beings.* **3.** One's basic or essential nature: *an experience that became part of my very being.*

Bei·rut (bā-ro͞ot′) The capital of Lebanon, in the western part of the country on the Mediterranean Sea.

be·jew·eled (bĭ-jo͞o′əld) *adj.* Decorated with jewels.

bel (bĕl) *n.* A unit for measuring the difference in inten-

ă	pat	ôr	core
ā	pay	oi	boy
âr	care	ou	out
ä	father	o͝o	took
ĕ	pet	o͝or	lure
ē	be	o͞o	boot
ĭ	pit	ŭ	cut
ī	bite	ûr	urge
îr	pier	th	thin
ŏ	pot	*th*	this
ō	toe	zh	vision
ô	paw	ə	about

sity of sounds, equal to ten decibels. [After Alexander Graham *Bell*.]

be·la·bor (bĭ-lā′bər) *tr.v.* **be·la·bored, be·la·bor·ing, be·la·bors 1.** To go over repeatedly; harp on: *The audience got bored as the politician belabored the point.* **2.** To attack verbally; assail: *The candidate belabored her opponent on his weak record.* **3.** To attack with blows; beat.

Bel·a·rus (bĕl′ə-ro͞os′ *or* bĕl′ə-ro͞os′) Formerly **Be·lo·rus·sia** (bĕl′ō-rŭsh′ə) also **Bye·lo·rus·sia** (byĕl′ō-rŭsh′ə). A country of Eastern Europe east of Poland and west of Russia. It was part of the USSR from 1922 to 1991. Minsk is the capital.

be·lat·ed (bĭ-lā′tĭd) *adj.* Done or sent too late; tardy: *belated birthday wishes.* **—be·lat′ed·ly** *adv.* **—be·lat′ed·ness** *n.*

be·lay (bĭ-lā′) *v.* **be·layed, be·lay·ing, be·lays** *—tr.* **1.** To secure (a rope) by winding it around a cleat or pin. **2.** To secure (a mountain climber) against a potential fall by using a rope that can be drawn in or let out in a controlled manner. *—intr.* Used in the imperative as an order to stop: *Belay there!*

be·lay·ing pin (bĭ-lā′ĭng) *n.* A pin on the rail of a ship used to secure ropes.

belch (bĕlch) *v.* **belched, belch·ing, belch·es** *—intr.* **1.** To expel gas noisily from the stomach through the mouth; burp. **2.** To gush forth; pour out: *smoke belching from the truck's tailpipe.* *—tr.* To send out or eject (smoke or flames) violently: *The burning house belched smoke from its windows.* ❖ *n.* The act or an instance of belching: *The old car stopped with a belch of smoke.* [From Old English *bealcettan*.]

be·lea·guer (bĭ-lē′gər) *tr.v.* **be·lea·guered, be·lea·guer·ing, be·lea·guers 1.** To persecute constantly, as by threats or demands; harass: *During the power outage the electric company was beleaguered by its customers.* **2.** To surround with troops; besiege: *The king's troops beleaguered the city until the rebels surrendered.* [Probably from Dutch *belegeren* : *be-*, around + *leger*, camp.]

Bel·fast (bĕl′făst′ *or* bĕl-făst′) The capital of Northern Ireland, in the eastern part on an inlet of the Irish Sea. After many years of conflict between Protestants and Catholics, a peace settlement was signed here in 1998.

bel·fry (bĕl′frē) *n., pl.* **bel·fries** A tower or steeple in which one or more bells are hung.

Bel·gian (bĕl′jən) *adj.* Relating to Belgium or its people or culture. ❖ *n.* A native or inhabitant of Belgium.

Bel·gium (bĕl′jəm) A country of northwest Europe on the North Sea north of France. It is culturally divided into the Flemish-speaking area north of Brussels and the French-speaking area to the south. Brussels is the capital.

Bel·grade (bĕl′grăd′ *or* bĕl′gräd′) The capital of Serbia, in the north-central part on the Danube River. It was founded in the third century BC.

Be·li·al (bē′lē-əl) *n.* In the Bible, the Devil.

be·lie (bĭ-lī′) *tr.v.* **be·lied, be·ly·ing, be·lies 1.** To give a wrong or false idea of: *Her soft-spoken manner belied her strong feelings on the subject.* **2.** To be inconsistent with; contradict: *The rise in crime belied the city's reputation for being safe.*

be·lief (bĭ-lēf′) *n.* **1.** Mental acceptance or conviction of the truth or existence of something: *His explanation of what happens defies belief.* **2.** The mental act or condition of placing trust or confidence in a person: *My belief in you is as strong as ever.* **3.** Something believed or accepted as true, especially by a group of people: *We sometimes take our beliefs for granted until we meet someone who does not share them.*

be·lieve (bĭ-lēv′) *v.* **be·lieved, be·liev·ing, be·lieves** *—tr.* **1.** To accept (something) as true or real: *Do you believe his version of what happened?* **2.** To consider (someone) to be truthful or accurate in what they are saying: *I believe you when you say she is angry.* **3.** To expect or suppose; think: *I believe it will snow tomorrow. I believe the letters to be authentic.* *—intr.* **1.** To have religious faith: *believe in God.* **2.** To have faith, trust, or confidence: *We believe in their ability to solve the problem.* **3.** To consider something to be important, worthwhile, or valuable: *I believe in free speech.* [From Old English *belȳfan*.] **—be·liev′a·ble** *adj.* **—be·liev′er** *n.*

be·lit·tle (bĭ-lĭt′l) *tr.v.* **be·lit·tled, be·lit·tling, be·lit·tles** To represent or speak of as trivial or unimportant; disparage: *They belittled her accomplishments out of jealousy.*

Be·lize (bə-lēz′) A country of Central America on the Caribbean Sea east of Guatemala. Formerly the colony of British Honduras, Belize gained its independence in 1981. Belmopan is the capital.

bell (bĕl) *n.* **1.** A hollow metal musical instrument, usually cup-shaped with a flared opening, that makes a metallic tone when struck. **2.** Something having a flared opening like that of a bell: *the bell of a trumpet.* **3. bells** A musical instrument consisting of metal tubes that emit tones when struck. ❖ *tr.v.* **belled, bell·ing, bells** To put a bell on: *bell a cat that lives outdoors.* [From Old English *belle*.]

❑ *These sound alike:* **bell, belle** (girl or woman).

Bell (bĕl), **Alexander Graham** 1847–1922. British-born American inventor who received the first patent for the telephone (1876). He also invented the audiometer and an early hearing aid.

bel·la·don·na (bĕl′ə-dŏn′ə) *n.* **1.** A poisonous plant native to Eurasia and northern Africa, having purplish bell-shaped flowers and small black berries; deadly nightshade. **2.** A medicinal substance that contains the drug atropine and is derived from this plant. [From Italian : *bella*, beautiful + *donna*, lady.]

bell-bot·tom (bĕl′bŏt′əm) *adj.* Having legs that flare out at the bottom: *bell-bottom pants.*

bell-bot·toms (bĕl′bŏt′əmz) *pl.n.* Pants that flare out at the bottom.

bell·boy (bĕl′boi′) *n.* A male bellhop.

bell curve *n.* A bell-shaped curve representing the distribution and frequency of data in a set.

belle (bĕl) *n.* A popular, attractive girl or woman, especially the most attractive one of a group: *the belle of the ball.*

❑ *These sound alike:* **belle, bell** (musical instrument).

belles-let·tres (bĕl-lĕt′rə) *pl.n.* *(used with a singular verb)* Literature regarded for its artistic value rather than for its information or teaching content.

bell·flow·er (bĕl′flou′ər) *n.* Any of various plants having bell-shaped, usually purplish-blue flowers.

bell·hop (bĕl′hŏp′) *n.* A person employed by a hotel to carry luggage, run errands, and do other chores.

bel·li·cose (bĕl′ĭ-kōs′) *adj.* Warlike in manner or disposition; belligerent: *the demands of a bellicose nation.* **—bel′li·cos′i·ty** (bĕl′ĭ-kŏs′ĭ-tē) *n.*

bel·lig·er·ence (bə-lĭj′ər-əns) *n.* A warlike or hostile attitude, nature, or disposition.

bel·lig·er·en·cy (bə-lĭj′ər-ən-sē) *n.* **1.** The state of being at war or engaged in a conflict. **2.** Belligerence: *The lawyer was known for his belligerency toward witnesses during cross-examination.*

bel·lig·er·ent (bə-lĭj′ər-ənt) *adj.* **1.** Inclined to fight; hostile; aggressive: *a belligerent bully.* **2.** Relating to or engaged in warfare: *a belligerent nation.* ❖ *n.* A person, group, or nation engaged in war or a conflict. **—bel·lig′er·ent·ly** *adv.*

bell jar *n.* A large bell-shaped glass container with an open bottom, placed over delicate instruments to protect them and used in experiments to provide a space that is sealed off from the atmosphere.

belaying pin

belfry

Alexander Graham Bell

bellows

bench press

bel·low (bĕl′ō) *v.* **bel·lowed, bel·low·ing, bel·lows** —*intr.* **1.** To roar as a bull does. **2.** To shout in a deep loud voice. —*tr.* To utter in a loud voice: *The crowd bellowed its disapproval of the umpire's call.* ❖ *n.* **1.** The loud roaring sound made by a bull or certain other large animals. **2.** A loud deep shout or cry.

bel·lows (bĕl′ōz) *pl.n.* *(used with a singular or plural verb)* A device for pumping air, consisting of a chamber with openings controlled by valves so that air enters at one opening and leaves at another as the chamber is forced to expand and contract.

bell·weth·er (bĕl′wĕ*th*′ər) *n.* A person or thing that leads or begins something else: *a state that could be the bellwether for the country's economic recovery.*

bel·ly (bĕl′ē) *n., pl.* **bel·lies 1.** In humans and other mammals, the front part of the body below the chest; the abdomen. **2.** The stomach: *I ate until my belly was full.* **3.** The underside of the body of certain vertebrates, such as snakes and fish. **4.** A part that bulges or protrudes: *the belly of a sail.* **5.** The hollow interior of something: *the belly of an airplane.* ❖ *intr. & tr.v.* **bel·lied, bel·ly·ing, bel·lies** To swell; bulge: *The sails bellied in the breeze.* [From Old English *bælig*, bag.]

bel·ly·ache (bĕl′ē-āk′) *n.* Pain in the stomach or abdomen. ❖ *intr.v.* **bel·ly·ached, bel·ly·ach·ing, bel·ly·aches** *Slang* To grumble or complain, especially in a whining way. **—bel′ly·ach′er** *n.*

bel·ly·band (bĕl′ē-bănd′) *n.* A band passed around the belly of an animal to secure something, such as a saddle.

bel·ly·but·ton (bĕl′ē-bŭt′n) *n.* *Informal* The navel.

bel·ly-land (bĕl′ē-lănd′) *intr.v.* **bel·ly-land·ed, bel·ly-land·ing, bel·ly-lands** To crash-land an airplane without the aid of landing gear, so that the underside comes in direct contact with the land or water. **—belly landing** *n.*

belly laugh *n.* A deep laugh.

Bel·mo·pan (bĕl′mō-**păn′**) The capital of Belize, in the central part of the country. It became the capital in 1970.

be·long (bĭ-**lông′**) *intr.v.* **be·longed, be·long·ing, be·longs 1.** To be owned by someone: *This watch belonged to my grandmother.* **2a.** To be a member of a group: *Many of the workers belong to a labor union.* **b.** To fit into a group naturally or comfortably: *I feel like I just don't belong at this school.* **3a.** To be proper or suitable: *Blue jeans don't belong at a formal dinner.* **b.** To be properly or suitably placed: *Dictionaries belong in the library's reference section.*

be·long·ings (bĭ-**lông′**ĭngz) *pl.n.* The things that belong to someone; possessions: *We took all of our belongings when we moved out of state.*

Be·lo·rus·sia (bĕl′ō-**rŭsh′**ə) See **Belarus.**

be·lov·ed (bĭ-**lŭv′**ĭd *or* bĭ-**lŭvd′**) *adj.* Dearly loved: *my beloved grandparents; her beloved pets.* ❖ *n.* A person who is dearly loved.

be·low (bĭ-**lō′**) *adv.* **1.** In or to a lower place or level: *They paused on the bridge to admire the rapids below.* **2.** On or to a lower floor or deck: *The trunks were stowed in a compartment below.* **3.** Further down, as along a slope or stream: *There is a cabin in the valley below.* **4.** Following or farther down on a page: *A diagram is printed below with an explanation.* **5.** In a lower rank or class: *a decision of the courts below.* **6.** On the earth: *all creatures here below.* ❖ *prep.* **1.** Underneath; beneath: *We stood at the window watching the street below us.* **2.** Lower than, as in degree or rank: *temperatures below zero.* **3.** Unworthy of: *actions below contempt.* **4.** South of: *Arizona is below Utah.* [From Middle English *biloghe* : *bi*, by + *loghe*, low.]

be·low·ground (bĭ-**lō′**ground′) *adv. & adj.* Situated or occurring below the surface of the ground.

belt (bĕlt) *n.* **1.** A band of leather, cloth, or plastic worn around the waist to hold up pants, weapons, or tools, or to serve as decoration. **2.** A broad strip or band: *a belt of trees along the highway.* **3.** A seat belt or safety belt. **4.** A band that passes over two or more wheels or pulleys to transmit motion from one to another or to convey objects: *A belt connects the car motor to the fan.* **5.** A band of tough reinforcing material beneath the tread of a tire. **6.** A geographical region that is distinctive in some specific way: *the corn belt.* ❖ *tr.v.* **belt·ed, belt·ing, belts 1.** To support or attach with a belt: *The hikers belted canteens around their waists.* **2.** To strike; hit: *He belted three home runs in one game.* **3.** *Informal* To sing loudly and forcefully: *The audience belted out our school song.* ◆ **below the belt** Not according to the rules; unfair or unfairly: *The candidate's false accusations were below the belt.* **tighten (one's) belt** To become thrifty and frugal: *We can save money if we tighten our belts.* [From Old English, ultimately from Latin *balteus.*]

belt·way (**bĕlt′**wā′) *n.* A high-speed highway that encircles an urban area.

be·lu·ga (bə-**lo͞o′**gə) *n.* **1.** A large white sturgeon of the Black and Caspian Seas, whose roe is used for caviar. **2.** A small white or grayish whale living in northern waters. [From Russian *belukha*, white whale, and *beluga*, sturgeon, both from *belyĭ*, white.]

be·moan (bĭ-**mōn′**) *tr.v.* **be·moaned, be·moan·ing, be·moans** To mourn over; lament; grieve for: *bemoan one's fate.*

be·mused (bĭ-**myo͞ozd′**) *adj.* **1.** Confused; bewildered: *bemused by all the conflicting opinions.* **2.** Lost in thought or showing that one is lost in thought: *She remembered her old neighborhood with a bemused smile.*

bench (bĕnch) *n.* **1.** A long seat, often without a back, for two or more people. **2.** A sturdy table on which a carpenter, shoemaker, or other skilled person works. **3a.** The seat for judges in a courtroom. **b.** The office or position of a judge: *appointed to the bench.* **c.** often **Bench** The judge or judges on a court. **4a.** The place where the members of an athletic team sit when they are not actively participating in a game. **b.** The reserve players on an athletic team. ❖ *tr.v.* **benched, bench·ing, bench·es** To remove or keep (a player) from a game: *benched the goalie after she let in three quick goals.* [From Old English *benc.*]

bench·mark (**bĕnch′**märk′) *n.* **1.** A standard by which something can be measured or judged: *a hybrid car whose fuel economy is considered a benchmark for the automotive industry.* **2.** A surveyor's mark made on some stationary object, such as a boulder, used as a reference point in measuring elevation.

bench press *n.* In weightlifting, a lift done while lying face-up on a bench, in which a weight is pushed up from the chest to arm's length and then lowered back to the chest. **—bench′-press′** (**bĕnch′**prĕs′) *v.*

bend (bĕnd) *v.* **bent** (bĕnt), **bend·ing, bends** —*tr.* **1.** To make curved or crooked: *Bend the wire around the post.* **2.** To cause to deviate from a straight line; deflect: *Light is bent as it passes through water.* **3.** To turn or direct: *bend one's steps toward home; bend their attention to the problem.* **4.** To force to yield; subdue: *He bent his employees to his will.* **5.** To change deceptively; distort: *You must not bend the facts to fit a conclusion.* **6.** To make an exception to: *bent the rules.* —*intr.* **1.** To deviate from a straight line or position: *The road bends to the right at the bridge.* **2.** To assume a curved, crooked, or angular form or direction: *The saplings bent in the wind.* **3.** To incline the body; stoop: *I bent over to pick up the ball.* **4.** To submit; yield: *bend to someone's wishes.* ❖ *n.* **1.** A turn, curve, or bent part: *a bend in the river.* **2. bends** *(used with a singular or plural verb)* Decompression sickness. Used with *the.* ◆ **bend over backward** To make an effort greater than is required: *They bent over backward to be fair.* [From Old English *bendan.*]

ă	pat	ôr	core
ā	pay	oi	boy
âr	care	ou	out
ä	father	o͝o	took
ĕ	pet	o͝or	lure
ē	be	o͞o	boot
ĭ	pit	ŭ	cut
ī	bite	ûr	urge
îr	pier	th	thin
ŏ	pot	*th*	this
ō	toe	zh	vision
ô	paw	ə	about

be·neath (bĭ-**nēth′**) *adv.* In a lower place; below: *From the top of the hill, we looked down at the valley beneath.* ❖ *prep.* **1a.** Lower than; below: *a drawer beneath the cabinet.* **b.** To or into a lower position than: *moved the picture beneath the light.* **2.** Covered or concealed by: *Most oil lies beneath the ground.* **3.** Under the force, control, or influence of: *The supervisor has six workers beneath her.* **4.** Unworthy of: *Lying is beneath me.* [From Old English *beneothan* : *be*, by + *neothan*, below.]

Ben·e·dict XVI (**bĕn′**ĭ-dĭkt′) Born 1927. Pope (2005–2013) noted for his advocacy of conservative doctrine and his efforts to improve the Vatican's relations with other countries and religious organizations, including China and the Eastern Orthodox Church.

Ben·e·dic·tine (bĕn′ĭ-**dĭk′**tĭn *or* bĕn′ĭ-**dĭk′**tēn′) *n.* A Roman Catholic monk or nun belonging to the order founded around 529 by Saint Benedict of Nursia (480?–547?). **—Ben′e·dic′tine** *adj.*

ben·e·dic·tion (bĕn′ĭ-**dĭk′**shən) *n.* A blessing, especially one recited at the close of a religious service by a member of the clergy.

ben·e·fac·tor (**bĕn′**ə-făk′tər) *n.* A person who gives financial or other aid.

be·nef·i·cence (bə-**nĕf′**ĭ-səns) *n.* **1.** The quality or condition of being kind or charitable. **2.** A charitable act or gift: *The contributor's beneficence was large enough to complete the church building.*

be·nef·i·cent (bə-**nĕf′**ĭ-sənt) *adj.* Doing or bringing about good: *beneficent legislation that improved working conditions for low-paid laborers.* **—be·nef′i·cent·ly** *adv.*

ben·e·fi·cial (bĕn′ə-**fĭsh′**əl) *adj.* Bringing benefit; advantageous: *Many bacteria are beneficial to human life.* **—ben′e·fi′cial·ly** *adv.*

ben·e·fi·ci·ar·y (bĕn′ə-**fĭsh′**ē-ĕr′ē *or* bĕn′ə-**fĭsh′**ə-rē) *n., pl.* **ben·e·fi·ci·ar·ies 1.** A person who derives benefit from something: *We are all beneficiaries of the large new library.* **2.** A person who is designated to receive funds or property from an insurance policy or a will.

ben·e·fit (**bĕn′**ə-fĭt) *n.* **1.** Something that is of help; an advantage: *The field trip was of great benefit to the students.* **2.** A payment or favorable allowance made in accordance with a wage agreement, insurance policy, or public assistance program: *Her new job's benefits include three weeks of paid vacation.* **3.** A theatrical performance or social event held to raise money for a cause. ❖ *v.* **ben·e·fit·ed, ben·e·fit·ing, ben·e·fits** also **ben·e·fit·ted, ben·e·fit·ting, ben·e·fits** —*tr.* To be helpful or beneficial to: *The clean-air program will benefit the environment.* —*intr.* To receive help; profit: *You can benefit from your brother's example.* ◆ **benefit of the doubt** A favorable judgment made in the absence of more complete information. [From Middle English *benefet*, from Latin *benefactum*, good deed, from *benefacere*, to do a service.]

be·nev·o·lence (bə-**nĕv′**ə-ləns) *n.* **1.** An inclination to do good; kindliness; good will. **2.** A kindly act.

be·nev·o·lent (bə-**nĕv′**ə-lənt) *adj.* **1.** Characterized by doing good; kindly: *a benevolent king; a benevolent attitude.* **2.** Relating to or organized for charitable purposes: *a benevolent fund.* **—be·nev′o·lent·ly** *adv.*

Ben·gal (bĕn-**gôl′**) A region of eastern India and Bangladesh on the **Bay of Bengal,** an arm of the Indian Ocean. It was a province of India until 1947.

Ben·ga·li (bĕn-**gô′**lē) *adj.* Relating to Bengal or its people, language, or culture. ❖ *n., pl.* **Bengali** or **Ben·ga·lis 1.** A native or inhabitant of Bengal. **2.** The Indic language of Bangladesh and western Bengal.

Ben Gur·i·on (bĕn **go͝or′**ē-ən), **David** 1886–1973. Polish-born Israeli politician. He became the first prime minister of Israel, serving from 1948–1953 and again from 1955–1963.

be·night·ed (bĭ-**nī′**tĭd) *adj.* Resulting from or in a state of moral or intellectual backwardness; ignorant or unenlightened: *benighted prejudice; a benighted population whose rulers denied it access to basic education.*

be·nign (bĭ-**nīn′**) *adj.* **1a.** Causing little or no real harm; harmless: *a benign chemical.* **b.** Not likely to spread or get worse; not malignant: *a benign tumor.* **2a.** Kind; gentle: *a benign ruler.* **b.** Showing or expressing kindness or gentleness: *a benign smile.* **3.** Mild; favorable: *a benign climate.* [From Middle English *benigne*, from Latin *benignus*.]

be·nig·ni·ty (bĭ-**nĭg′**nĭ-tē) *n.* The quality or condition of being benign: *a dynasty noted for the benignity of its rulers.*

Be·nin (bə-**nĭn′** *or* bĕ-**nēn′**) **1.** A former kingdom of western Africa, now part of Nigeria. **2.** Formerly **Da·ho·mey** (də-**hō′**mē). A country of western Africa west of Nigeria. Porto-Novo is the capital.

Ben·ja·min (**bĕn′**jə-mən) In the Bible, the younger son of Jacob and Rachel and the ancestor of one of the tribes of Israel.

bent (bĕnt) *v.* Past tense and past participle of **bend.** ❖ *adj.* **1.** Curved or crooked: *a bent nail.* **2.** Resolved; determined: *a runner bent on becoming a champion.* ❖ *n.* A tendency or inclination: *a strong bent for studying science.*

ben·thic (**bĕn′**thĭk′) *adj.* Relating to or inhabiting the bottom of a sea, lake, or river: *benthic invertebrates.*

ben·thos (**bĕn′**thŏs′) *n.* **1.** The bottom of the sea, a lake, or a river. **2.** The organisms living on sea, lake, or river bottoms.

be·numb (bĭ-**nŭm′**) *tr.v.* **be·numbed, be·numb·ing, be·numbs** To make numb; deprive of feeling: *Cold benumbed our fingers.* [From Middle English *binomen*, taken away (as to one's senses), past participle of *binimen*, to take away, from Old English *beniman*.]

ben·zene (**bĕn′**zēn′ *or* bĕn-**zēn′**) *n.* A clear colorless liquid that burns easily and has the formula C_6H_6. It is derived from petroleum and used to make detergents, insect poisons, motor fuels, and other chemical products.

ben·zine (**bĕn′**zēn′ *or* bĕn-**zēn′**) *n.* Naphtha.

ben·zo·ate of soda (**bĕn′**zō-āt′) *n.* Sodium benzoate.

ben·zo·ic acid (bĕn-**zō′**ĭk) *n.* A white crystalline acid that is used as an antiseptic and a food preservative.

ben·zo·in (**bĕn′**zō-ĭn *or* **bĕn′**zoin′) *n.* Any of various fragrant resins that are obtained from certain Southeast Asian trees and contain benzoic acid. They are used in making incense, perfumes, ointments, and cough medicines. [Ultimately from Arabic *lubān jāwī*, frankincense of Java.]

Be·o·wulf (**bā′**ə-wo͝olf′) *n.* **1.** An Old English epic poem probably composed in the early 700s. **2.** The hero of this poem, who killed two water monsters and died in a fight with a dragon.

be·queath (bĭ-**kwēth′** *or* bĭ-**kwēth′**) *tr.v.* **be·queathed, be·queath·ing, be·queathes 1.** To leave or give (personal property) by will. **2.** To pass on or hand down: *One generation bequeaths its knowledge to the next.* [From Old English *becwethan* : *be-*, about + *cwethan*, to speak.]

be·quest (bĭ-**kwĕst′**) *n.* **1.** The act of bequeathing: *From her bequest, he inherited great wealth.* **2.** Something that is bequeathed in a will: *The will included a bequest of $1,000 to a local charity.*

be·rate (bĭ-**rāt′**) *tr.v.* **be·rat·ed, be·rat·ing, be·rates** To scold severely or angrily.

Ber·ber (**bûr′**bər) *n.* **1.** A member of any of several Muslim peoples of North Africa. **2.** Any of the Afro-Asiatic languages of the Berbers. **—Ber′ber** *adj.*

be·reave (bĭ-**rēv′**) *tr.v.* **be·reaved** or **be·reft** (bĭ-**rĕft′**), **be·reav·ing, be·reaves** To leave alone or desolate, especially by death: *She was bereaved by the death of her*

Benedict XVI
photographed in 2011

beret

husband. [From Old English *berēafian.*] **—be·reave′ment** *n.*

be·reft (bĭ-rĕft′) *v.* A past tense and a past participle of **bereave.** ❖ *adj.* Deprived of something: *an act that left him bereft of dignity.*

be·ret (bə-rā′) *n.* A round, soft, brimless cap that fits snugly. [From French *béret,* from Late Latin *birrus,* hooded cloak.]

berg (bûrg) *n.* An iceberg.

ber·i·ber·i (bĕr′ē-bĕr′ē) *n.* A disease caused by a lack of thiamine in the diet. It causes nerve damage, problems with the circulation, and loss of weight. [From Sinhalese, from *beri,* weakness.]

Ber·ing Sea (bîr′ĭng *or* bâr′ĭng) A northward extension of the Pacific Ocean between Siberia and Alaska, lying north of the Aleutian Islands and connected with the Arctic Ocean by the Bering Strait.

Bering Strait A narrow stretch of water separating Alaska from Siberia. It is believed that the strait once formed a land bridge by which the original inhabitants of North America arrived from Asia.

ber·ke·li·um (bər-kē′lē-əm *or* **bûrk′**lē-əm) *n. Symbol* **Bk** A radioactive element that has been artificially produced by scientists. The half-life of its longest-lived isotope is about 1,380 years. Atomic number 97. See **Periodic Table.** [After *Berkeley,* California.]

Ber·lin (bûr-lĭn′) The capital of Germany, in the northeast part of the country. It was divided between 1945 and 1990 into **East Berlin** and **West Berlin.** The **Berlin Wall,** a wire and concrete barrier, was built by the East German government in 1961 and dismantled in 1989.

Ber·lu·sco·ni (bûr′lə-**skō′**nē), **Silvio** Born 1936. Italian politician who served as prime minister (1994–1995, 2004–2006, and 2008–2011).

berm (bûrm) *n.* **1.** A raised bank or path, such as one along a canal. **2.** A bank of earth placed against the wall of a building to provide protection or insulation. **3.** The flat space between the edge of a moat and the wall of a castle or other fortification.

Ber·mu·da (bər-**myo͞o′**də) A self-governing British colony on a cluster of coral islands in the Atlantic Ocean southeast of Cape Hatteras. Hamilton, on **Bermuda Island,** is the capital.

Bermuda shorts *pl.n.* Shorts that end slightly above the knees.

Bern or **Berne** (bûrn *or* bĕrn) The capital of Switzerland, in the west-central part of the country. It was founded as a military post in 1191.

Ber·ners-Lee (bûr′nûrz-lē′), Sir **Timothy John** Known as "Tim." Born 1955. British computer scientist who proposed the World Wide Web and developed the first website (1989–1991).

Bern·stein (**bûrn′**stīn′ *or* **bûrn′**stēn′), **Leonard** 1918–1990. American composer whose works include the musical *West Side Story* (1957).

ber·ry (bĕr′ē) *n., pl.* **ber·ries 1.** A fruit having many seeds in fleshy pulp, such as a strawberry, blueberry, or raspberry. **2.** In botany, a fleshy fruit that develops from a single plant ovary, such as a tomato, avocado, or grape. **3.** A seed or dried kernel of certain grains or other plants, such as wheat or coffee. ❖ *intr.v.* **ber·ried, ber·ry·ing, ber·ries** To hunt for or gather berries. [From Old English *berie.*]

❑ *These sound alike:* **berry, bury** (cover with earth).

ber·serk (bər-**sûrk′** *or* bər-**zûrk′**) *adv. & adj.* In or into a crazed or violent frenzy. [From *berserker,* a frenzied Norse warrior, from Old Norse *berserkr,* one wearing a bearskin, berserker.]

berth (bûrth) *n.* **1.** A built-in bed or bunk in a ship or train. **2.** A space at a wharf for a ship to dock or anchor. **3.** A job or position: *have a berth on the US Olympic Team.* ❖ *v.* **berthed, berth·ing, berths** *—tr.* **1.** To bring (a ship) to a berth. **2.** To provide with a berth. *—intr.* To come to a berth; dock: *berth at a pier along the river.*

❑ *These sound alike:* **berth, birth** (act of being born).

ber·yl (bĕr′əl) *n.* A transparent to translucent mineral of varied colors that is a silicate of beryllium and aluminum. It is the chief source of beryllium. Transparent varieties, such as emeralds and aquamarines, are valued as gems.

be·ryl·li·um (bə-rĭl′ē-əm) *n. Symbol* **Be** A grayish-white, hard, lightweight metallic element found in various minerals, especially beryl. Beryllium is used to make sturdy, lightweight alloys and to control the speed of neutrons in nuclear reactors. Atomic number 4. See **Periodic Table.**

be·seech (bĭ-sēch′) *tr.v.* **be·sought** (bĭ-sôt′) or **be·seeched, be·seech·ing, be·seech·es** To ask earnestly; entreat; implore: *beseech the authorities for help.* **—be·seech′ing·ly** *adv.*

be·seem (bĭ-sēm′) *tr.v.* **be·seemed, be·seem·ing, be·seems** *Archaic* To be appropriate for; befit.

be·set (bĭ-sĕt′) *tr.v.* **be·set, be·set·ting, be·sets 1.** To trouble persistently; harass: *I was beset by doubts about the right course to follow.* **2.** To attack from all sides: *Enemy troops beset the fort.* **3.** To hem in; surround: *Rising floodwaters beset the town.*

be·side (bĭ-sīd′) *prep.* **1.** At the side of; next to: *The cat sat down beside the radiator.* **2.** In comparison with: *Your test score looks pretty good beside mine.* **3.** Not relevant to: *a remark that was beside the point.* **4.** In addition to; besides: *Four dogs beside my own started to bark.* ◆ **beside (oneself)** In a state of extreme excitement or emotion: *The winners were beside themselves with joy.*

be·sides (bĭ-sīdz′) *adv.* **1.** In addition; also: *We had dinner and a late-night snack besides.* **2.** Moreover; furthermore: *It was time to go; besides, I was getting bored.* ❖ *prep.* **1.** In addition to: *Dentists do other things besides drilling cavities.* **2.** Other than; except for: *There's nothing to eat here besides a little cheese.* —SEE NOTE AT **together.**

be·siege (bĭ-sēj′) *tr.v.* **be·sieged, be·sieg·ing, be·sieg·es 1.** To surround and blockade in order to capture; lay siege to: *The king's troops besieged the city until it surrendered.* **2.** To crowd around and hem in: *A crowd of fans besieged the movie star.* **3.** To harass, as with requests: *The reporters besieged the police for information.* **—be·sieg′er** *n.*

be·smirch (bĭ-**smûrch′**) *tr.v.* **be·smirched, be·smirch·ing, be·smirch·es** To soil or tarnish; stain: *besmirch someone's good name by repeating slanderous remarks.*

be·sought (bĭ-sôt′) *v.* A past tense and a past participle of **beseech.**

be·spat·ter (bĭ-spăt′ər) *tr.v.* **be·spat·tered, be·spat·ter·ing, be·spat·ters** To spatter: *The dripping paint bespattered the floor.*

be·speak (bĭ-spēk′) *tr.v.* **be·spoke** (bĭ-spōk′), **be·spo·ken** (bĭ-spō′kən) or **be·spoke, be·speak·ing, be·speaks** To be or give a sign of; indicate: *a shake of the head that bespoke disbelief.*

be·spec·ta·cled (bĭ-spĕk′tə-kəld) *adj.* Wearing eyeglasses.

be·sprin·kle (bĭ-sprĭng′kəl) *tr.v.* **be·sprin·kled, be·sprin·kling, be·sprin·kles** To sprinkle.

Bes·se·mer process (bĕs′ə-mər) *n.* A method for making steel by forcing compressed air through molten iron to burn out excess carbon and impurities. [After Sir Henry *Bessemer* (1813–1898), British inventor.]

best (bĕst) *adj.* Superlative of **good. 1.** Surpassing all others in excellence, quality, or achievement: *the best singer in the choir.* **2.** Most satisfactory, suitable, or useful: *the best place to dig a well.* **3.** Largest or greatest: *We talked for the best part of the journey.* ❖ *adv.*

ă	pat	ôr	core
ā	pay	oi	boy
âr	care	ou	out
ä	father	o͝o	took
ĕ	pet	o͝or	lure
ē	be	o͞o	boot
ĭ	pit	ŭ	cut
ī	bite	ûr	urge
îr	pier	th	thin
ŏ	pot	*th*	this
ō	toe	zh	vision
ô	paw	ə	about

Superlative of **well²**. **1.** In the most excellent way; most properly or successfully: *Which of the three jackets fits best?* **2.** To the greatest degree or extent; most: *What do you like to eat best?* ❖ *n.* **1.** A person or thing that surpasses all others: *That skier is surely the best in the race.* **2.** The best part or value: *The best is yet to come.* **3.** One's best effort or appearance: *do your best; look your best.* **4.** One's nicest clothing: *She put on her best and went to the dance.* **5.** One's warmest wishes or regards: *Give them my best.* ❖ *tr.v.* **best·ed, best·ing, bests** To get the better of; defeat: *besting their rivals in every game.* ◆ **at best 1.** Viewed most favorably; at the most: *There were 20 people in the theater at best.* **2.** Under the most favorable conditions: *This car has a top speed of 40 miles per hour at best.* **for the best** With an ultimately positive or preferable result. **get the best of** or **have the best of** To outdo or outwit; defeat: *Nobody's ever gotten the best of me at checkers.* [From Old English *betst.*]

Best (bĕst), **Charles Herbert** 1899–1978. American-born Canadian physiologist noted for his work with Frederick Banting on the use of insulin to treat diabetes.

bes·tial (bĕs′chəl *or* bēs′chəl) *adj.* **1.** Characteristic of a beast: *a bestial roar.* **2.** Brutal or cruel: *bestial crimes.* —**bes′tial·ly** *adv.*

be·stir (bĭ-stûr′) *tr.v.* **be·stirred, be·stir·ring, be·stirs** To stir to action; rouse: *He finally bestirred himself to look for a job.*

best man *n.* The chief attendant of the bridegroom at a wedding.

be·stow (bĭ-stō′) *tr.v.* **be·stowed, be·stow·ing, be·stows** To give or present, especially as a gift or honor; confer: *bestowed awards on the best actors and plays each season.* —**be·stow′al** *n.*

be·strew (bĭ-stro͞o′) *tr.v.* **be·strewed, be·strewed** or **be·strewn** (bĭ-stro͞on′), **be·strew·ing, be·strews 1.** To scatter (a surface) with things so as to cover it: *The crowd bestrewed the street with confetti.* **2.** To lie or be scattered over: *Dead leaves bestrewed the yard.*

be·stride (bĭ-strīd′) *tr.v.* **be·strode** (bĭ-strōd′), **be·strid·den** (bĭ-strĭd′n), **be·strid·ing, be·strides** To sit or stand on with one leg on each side; straddle: *bestride a horse.*

best·sell·er (bĕst′sĕl′ər) *n.* A product, such as a book, that is among those sold in the largest numbers.

best-sell·ing (bĕst′sĕl′ĭng) *adj.* Selling in the largest numbers at a given time: *a best-selling novel.*

bet (bĕt) *n.* **1.** An agreement, usually between two people or groups, that the one who has made an incorrect prediction about an event will give something, such as a sum of money, to the other: *We made a bet that I could beat him at checkers.* **2.** An object or amount of money risked in a wager; a stake: *People were placing bets of $10 on the outcome of the tournament.* **3.** A person, animal, or event on which a wager is or can be made: *That horse is a good bet to win the race.* **4.** A plan or option considered with regard to its likely outcome: *The short route is probably your best bet to get home on time.* ❖ *v.* **bet** or **bet·ted, bet·ting, bets** —*tr.* **1.** To risk (something) in a bet: *He bet $20 on the race.* **2.** To make a bet with (a person or group): *I bet my sister that she couldn't eat the hot pepper.* **3.** To state with confidence, as in a bet: *I bet you did well on the exam.* —*intr.* To make or place a bet. ◆ **you bet** *Informal* Of course; surely.

be·ta (bā′tə *or* bē′tə) *n.* **1.** The second letter of the Greek alphabet, written Β, β. In English it is represented as *B, b.* **2.** The second item in a series. ❖ *adj.* Being the version of a software program used in a beta test.

beta carotene *n.* A form of carotene found in yellow fruits and vegetables and leafy green vegetables that is converted to vitamin A in the liver.

be·take (bĭ-tāk′) *tr.v.* **be·took** (bĭ-to͝ok′), **be·tak·en** (bĭ-tā′kən), **be·tak·ing, be·takes** To cause (oneself) to go or move: *They betook themselves to the distant kingdom.*

beta particle *n.* A high-speed electron or positron, especially one emitted by an atomic nucleus undergoing radioactive decay.

beta ray *n.* A stream of beta particles.

beta test *n.* The final stage in the testing of a new software or computer hardware product before its commercial release.

be·ta·tron (bā′tə-trŏn′ *or* bē′tə-trŏn′) *n.* A particle accelerator that uses a changing magnetic field to accelerate electrons to very high speeds.

beta version *n.* The version of software used in a beta test.

be·tel (bēt′l) *n.* An evergreen vine of South and Southeast Asia whose leaves are used to wrap betel nuts. [From Portuguese, from Malayalam *vettila,* from Tamil *verrilai.*]

❑ *These sound alike:* **betel, beetle¹** (insect), **beetle²** (mallet), **beetle³** (overhang).

Be·tel·geuse (bēt′l-jo͞oz′) *n.* A bright-red star in the constellation Orion. [Ultimately from Arabic *yad al-jawzā',* hand of Gemini (later, also used for Orion).]

betel nut *n.* The seed of a tropical Asian palm, chewed with leaves from the betel plant as a mild stimulant.

bête noire (bĕt nwär′) *n.* A person or thing that is particularly disliked: *Speaking in public has long been my bête noire.*

Beth·le·hem (bĕth′lĭ-hĕm′) A town in the West Bank south of Jerusalem. It is the traditional birthplace of Jesus.

Be·thune (bə-tho͞on′), **Mary McLeod** 1875–1955. American educator and reformer. In 1935 she founded the National Council of Negro Women, serving as its president until 1949.

Mary McLeod Bethune
photographed in 1949

be·tide (bĭ-tīd′) *tr.v.* **be·tid·ed, be·tid·ing, be·tides** To happen to: *Woe betide anyone who is late for class.*

be·times (bĭ-tīmz′) *adv.* In good time; early: *I awoke betimes and got ready to go.*

be·to·ken (bĭ-tō′kən) *tr.v.* **be·to·kened, be·to·ken·ing, be·to·kens** To be a sign of; point to: *Public concern betokens a new attitude about our environment.*

be·took (bĭ-to͝ok′) *v.* Past tense of **betake.**

be·tray (bĭ-trā′) *tr.v.* **be·trayed, be·tray·ing, be·trays 1.** To give aid or information to an enemy of (a country, for example). **2.** To be disloyal to: *betray a friend; a corrupt politician betraying the confidence of the voters.* **3.** To make known in a breach of trust; divulge: *betray a secret.* **4.** To give evidence of; indicate: *The redness of her face betrayed embarrassment.* [From Middle English *bitraien.*] —**be·tray′er** *n.*

be·tray·al (bĭ-trā′əl) *n.* The act of betraying, especially through disloyalty and deception.

be·troth·al (bĭ-trō′*th*əl *or* bĭ-trô′thəl) *n.* A promise to marry; an engagement.

be·trothed (bĭ-trō*thd*′ *or* bĭ-trôtht′) *adj.* Engaged to be married. ❖ *n.* A person to whom one is engaged to be married.

bet·ter (bĕt′ər) *adj.* Comparative of **good. 1.** Greater in excellence or higher in quality than another of the same kind: *Which of the twins is the better skater?* **2.** More useful, suitable, or desirable: *I know a better way to go.* **3.** Larger; greater: *It took the better part of an hour to get there.* **4.** Healthier than before: *Many days passed before I began to feel better.* ❖ *adv.* Comparative of **well². 1.** In a more excellent way: *He sings better than his father.* **2.** To a greater extent or larger degree: *I like fish better when it's broiled.* **3.** More: *The play was first performed better than 20 years ago.* ❖ *n.* **1.** The superior of two: *Both are good, but which is the better?* **2.** A superior: *I leave the delicate work to my betters.* ❖ *v.* **bet·tered, bet·ter·ing, bet·ters** —*tr.* **1.**

USAGE

better In writing, the phrase *had better,* meaning "must, ought to," is correct only as long as the *had* (or *'d,* the contraction of *had*), is present. You can say *You had better do it* or *You'd better do it* but not *You better do it.*

USAGE

between When two people or objects are discussed, **between** is correct and **among** is wrong: *the friendship between Jill and Jane.* When more than two people or objects are involved, however, or when the number is unspecified, use *between* to suggest pairs of distinct individuals and *among* for a group or mass. *Friendship between team members* emphasizes that there are friendships between different pairs of teammates, but *friendship among team members* suggests that many or even all team members are friendly with each other.

ă	pat	ôr	core
ā	pay	oi	boy
âr	care	ou	out
ä	father	o͝o	took
ĕ	pet	o͝or	lure
ē	be	o͞o	boot
ĭ	pit	ŭ	cut
ī	bite	ûr	urge
îr	pier	th	thin
ŏ	pot	*th*	this
ō	toe	zh	vision
ô	paw	ə	about

To make better; improve: *The purpose of education is to better ourselves.* **2.** To surpass or exceed: *The old record stood until another athlete bettered it.* —*intr.* To become better: *Conditions bettered with time.* ◆ **better off** In a better condition: *With vaccines, people are better off than they were years ago.* **for the better** Resulting in or aiming at an improvement. **had better** Ought to; must: *We had better leave before dark.* [From Old English *betera.*] —SEE NOTE.

❑ *These sound alike:* **better, bettor** (one who bets).

bet·ter·ment (bĕtʹər-mənt) *n.* An improvement: *work for the betterment of our children.*

bet·tor also **bet·ter** (bĕtʹər) *n.* A person who bets.

❑ *These sound alike:* **bettor, better** (greater).

be·tween (bĭ-twēnʹ) *prep.* **1a.** In or through the position or interval separating: *between the trees; between 11:00 and 12:00; waters flowing between the banks.* **b.** Intermediate to, as in amount or degree: *costs between $5 and $10.* **2.** Connecting over or through a space that is separating: *a long path between the cabin and the lake.* **3.** By the combined effect or effort of: *Between them, the friends finished the job.* **4.** In the combined ownership of: *We have $25 between us.* **5.** As measured against: *choose between milk and water; not much to choose between the two cars.* ❖ *adv.* In an intermediate space, position, or time: *The plane went from New York to Los Angeles, and several cities between.* ◆ **between you and me** In the strictest confidence: *We can surprise the others if we keep the plans between you and me.* **in between** In an intermediate situation: *There are two cities near each other, with a river running in between.* **in between times** During an intervening period; in the meantime. [From Old English *betwēonum.*] —SEE NOTE.

be·twixt (bĭ-twĭkstʹ) *adv. & prep.* Between. ◆ **betwixt and between** In an intermediate position; neither wholly one thing nor another.

BeV *abbr.* An abbreviation of billion electron volts.

bev·el (bĕvʹəl) *n.* **1.** A surface cut so that it is not at a right angle to another surface: *The edge of the counter has a bevel.* **2.** The angle at which such a surface is cut. **3.** A tool used to measure or mark such angles. ❖ *tr.v.* **bev·eled, bev·el·ing, bev·els** or **bev·elled, bev·el·ling, bev·els** To cut a bevel on (something): *bevel the edges of the picture frame.*

bev·er·age (bĕvʹər-ĭj *or* bĕvʹrĭj) *n.* A liquid for drinking, such as milk, tea, or juice. [From Middle English, from Old French *bevrage,* from *beivre,* to drink, from Latin *bibere.*]

bev·y (bĕvʹē) *n., pl.* **bev·ies** A group of living things or objects that are all of the same kind: *a bevy of poets; a bevy of quail; a bevy of mistakes.*

be·wail (bĭ-wālʹ) *tr.v.* **be·wailed, be·wail·ing, be·wails** To express sorrow or regret over; bemoan: *bewail one's fate.*

be·ware (bĭ-wârʹ) *v.* **be·wared, be·war·ing, be·wares** —*tr.* To watch out for; be on guard against: *Beware the smooth talk of the salesman.* —*intr.* To be cautious: *Beware of the dog.* [From Middle English *ben war,* to be on guard.]

be·wil·der (bĭ-wĭlʹdər) *tr.v.* **be·wil·dered, be·wil·der·ing, be·wil·ders** To confuse greatly; puzzle. **—be·wilʹ·dered·ly** *adv.* **—be·wilʹder·ment** *n.*

be·witch (bĭ-wĭchʹ) *tr.v.* **be·witched, be·witch·ing, be·witch·es 1.** To cast a spell over: *The prince was bewitched by a fairy.* **2.** To captivate completely; fascinate; charm: *Her piano solo bewitched the audience.*

be·witch·ing (bĭ-wĭchʹĭng) *adj.* Fascinating; enchanting: *a bewitching smile.* **—be·witchʹing·ly** *adv.*

bey (bā) *n.* **1.** A governor of a province in the former Ottoman Empire. **2.** A ruler of the former kingdom of Tunis.

❑ *These sound alike:* **bey, bay¹** (body of water), **bay²** (part of a room), **bay³** (reddish brown), **bay⁴** (bark), **bay⁵** (laurel).

be·yond (bē-ŏndʹ *or* bĭ-yŏndʹ) *prep.* **1.** On the far side of; past: *I planted carrots just beyond the fence.* **2.** To a degree or amount greater than: *rich beyond his wildest dreams.* **3.** Later than: *Don't stay up beyond midnight.* **4.** Past the reach, scope, or understanding of: *beyond hope; beyond recall.* ❖ *adv.* Farther along: *We walked under the trees into the bright sunlight beyond.* [From Old English *begeondan.*]

BFF *abbr.* An abbreviation of: **1.** best friend forever. **2.** best friends forever.

Bh The symbol for the element **bohrium.**

Bhu·tan (bo͞o-tănʹ *or* bo͞o-tänʹ) An isolated country of South Asia in the eastern Himalaya Mountains north of Bangladesh. Thimphu is the capital.

Bi The symbol for the element **bismuth.**

bi–¹ or **bin–** *pref.* A prefix that means: **1.** Two: *bifocal.* **2.** Both sides, parts, or directions: *biconcave.* **3.** Occurring at intervals of two: *bicentennial.* **4.** Occurring twice during: *bimonthly.* —SEE NOTE AT **biweekly.**

bi–² *pref.* Variant of **bio–.**

bi·a·ly (bē-äʹlē) *n., pl.* **bi·a·lys** A flat roll topped with onion flakes. [After *Białystok* in northeast Poland.]

bi·an·nu·al (bī-ănʹyo͞o-əl) *adj.* **1.** Happening twice each year; semiannual. **2.** Occurring every two years; biennial. **—bi·anʹnu·al·ly** *adv.* —SEE NOTE AT **biweekly.**

bi·as (bīʹəs) *n.* **1.** The direction of a piece of fabric as it runs diagonal to the grain: *cut cloth on the bias.* **2.** A preference for or hostile feeling against a person or thing that interferes with impartial judgment; a prejudice. ❖ *tr.v.* **bi·ased, bi·as·ing, bi·as·es** or **bi·assed, bi·as·sing, bi·as·ses** To cause to have a bias: *His stubbornness biased the employer against him.* [From French *biais,* slant, perhaps ultimately from Greek *epikarsios,* slanted.]

bi·ased also **bi·assed** (bīʹəst) *adj.* Marked by or showing bias; prejudiced.

bi·ath·lon (bī-ăthʹlŏnʹ) *n.* **1.** A competition that combines events in cross-country skiing and rifle shooting. **2.** An athletic contest in which participants compete in two successive events, such as long-distance swimming and running.

bib (bĭb) *n.* **1.** A piece of cloth or plastic worn under the chin, especially by small children, to protect the clothes while eating. **2.** The part of an apron or a pair of overalls worn over the chest.

Bi·ble (bīʹbəl) *n.* **1.** The sacred book of Christianity, a collection of ancient writings including both the Old Testament and the New Testament. **2.** The Hebrew Scriptures, the sacred book of Judaism. **3.** often **bible** A book considered authoritative in its field: *the bible of French cooking.* [From Middle English, from Greek *biblia,* plural of *biblion,* book.]

bib·li·cal also **Bib·li·cal** (bĭbʹlĭ-kəl) *adj.* **1.** Relating to or contained in the Bible. **2.** Very great in extent; enormous: *a disaster of biblical proportions.* **—bibʹli·cal·ly** *adv.*

bib·li·o·graph·i·cal (bĭbʹlē-ə-grăfʹĭ-kəl) or **bib·li·o·graph·ic** (bĭbʹlē-ə-grăfʹĭk) *adj.* Relating to bibliography: *the vast bibliographical resources of a great library.* **—bibʹli·o·graphʹi·cal·ly** *adv.*

bib·li·og·ra·phy (bĭbʹlē-ŏgʹrə-fē) *n., pl.* **bib·li·og·ra·phies 1.** A list of the works of a specific author or publisher. **2.** A list of the writings on a specific subject: *a bibliography of Latin American history.* [From Greek *biblion,* book.]

bi·cam·er·al (bī-kămʹər-əl) *adj.* Composed of two chambers or branches, as a legislature: *The United States Congress is a bicameral legislature consisting of the Senate and the House of Representatives.* [From *bi-,* two + Latin *camera,* chamber.]

bi·car·bon·ate (bī-kärʹbə-nātʹ *or* bī-kärʹbə-nĭt) *n.* The radical HCO_3 or a compound containing it, such as sodium bicarbonate.

bicarbonate of soda *n.* Sodium bicarbonate.

bi·cen·ten·ni·al (bī′sĕn-**tĕn′**ē-əl) *adj.* **1.** Relating to a 200th anniversary: *a bicentennial celebration.* **2.** Occurring once every 200 years. ❖ *n.* A 200th anniversary or its celebration.

bi·ceps (**bī′**sĕps′) *n., pl.* **biceps** A muscle that has two points of attachment at one end, especially: **a.** The muscle at the front of the upper arm that bends the forearm. **b.** The muscle at the back of the thigh that bends the knee. [From Latin *biceps,* two-headed : *bi-,* two + *caput,* head.] —SEE NOTE.

bick·er (**bĭk′**ər) *intr.v.* **bick·ered, bick·er·ing, bick·ers** To argue or quarrel over an unimportant matter; squabble: *We bickered over whose turn it was to wash dishes.* ❖ *n.* A petty quarrel; a squabble. **—bick′er·er** *n.*

bi·con·cave (bī′kŏn-**kāv′** *or* bī-**kŏn′**kāv′) *adj.* Concave on both sides or surfaces: *a biconcave lens.*

bi·con·vex (bī′kŏn-**vĕks′** *or* bī-**kŏn′**vĕks′) *adj.* Convex on both sides or surfaces: *a biconvex lens.*

bi·cus·pid (bī-**kŭs′**pĭd) *adj.* Having two points or cusps, as a crescent moon. ❖ *n.* A double-pointed premolar tooth that tears and grinds food. An adult human has eight bicuspids.

bi·cy·cle (**bī′**sĭk′əl *or* **bī′**sĭ-kəl) *n.* A vehicle consisting of a light metal frame mounted on two wheels one behind the other and having a seat for the rider, who steers the front wheel by handlebars and pushes pedals that drive the rear wheel. ❖ *intr.v.* **bi·cy·cled, bi·cy·cling, bi·cy·cles** To ride on a bicycle: *bicycle down to the store.* **—bi′cy·cler, bi′cy·clist** *n.*

bid (bĭd) *v.* **bade** (băd *or* bād) or **bid, bid·den** (**bĭd′**n) or **bid, bid·ding, bids** *—tr.* **1.** *past tense and past participle* **bid a.** To offer (an amount of money) as a price for something: *The collector bid $5,000 for the antique desk.* **b.** To state one's intention to take (a certain number of tricks) in card games, as in bridge. **2.** To say or express (a greeting, wish, or farewell): *He bade us good night.* **3.** To give a command to; direct: *The queen bid the courtiers rise.* **4.** To request to come; invite: *The host bid the guests come to dinner.* *—intr. past tense and past participle* **bid 1.** To make an offer to pay a certain price: *We bid on the old lamp.* **2.** To try to win or achieve something: *Both candidates bid for election to Congress.* ❖ *n.* **1a.** An offer to pay a certain amount of money for something: *The auctioneer called for bids on the antique desk.* **b.** An amount bid: *He made a bid of $5,000.* **2.** A declaration of the number of tricks one expects to win in certain card games such as bridge: *My bid is three hearts.* **3.** An effort to win or attain something: *Several candidates made a bid for the presidency.* ◆ **bid out** To offer (work) for bids from outside contractors. [From Old English *biddan,* from Old English *bēodan.*]

bid·der (**bĭd′**ər) *n.* A person who makes a bid at an auction, in seeking a contract, or in a card game.

bid·ding (**bĭd′**ĭng) *n.* **1.** An order or command: *Orchestras start to play at the conductor's bidding.* **2.** A request to appear; an invitation: *At my bidding, they accepted.* **3.** Bids considered as a group.

bid·dy (**bĭd′**ē) *n., pl.* **bid·dies** A hen; a fowl.

bide (bīd) *tr. & intr.v.* **bid·ed** or **bode** (bōd), **bid·ed, bid·ing, bides** To wait or wait for. ◆ **bide (one's) time** To wait for further developments: *If you bide your time, you too shall have a chance.*

bi·en·ni·al (bī-**ĕn′**ē-əl) *adj.* **1.** Lasting or living for two years: *biennial plants.* **2.** Occurring every second year: *biennial elections to Congress.* ❖ *n.* A plant that grows and produces leaves in its first year and that flowers, produces seeds, and dies in its second year. Carrots are biennials. **—bi·en′ni·al·ly** *adv.*

bier (bîr) *n.* A stand on which a corpse or a coffin containing a corpse is placed before burial.
❏ *These sound alike:* **bier, beer** (alcoholic drink).

bi·fo·cal (bī-**fō′**kəl *or* **bī′**fō′kəl) *adj.* **1.** Focusing light rays at two different points: *a bifocal lens.* **2.** Having one section that corrects for distant vision and another that corrects for near vision: *bifocal eyeglasses.* ❖ *n.* **bi·fo·cals** (bī-**fō′**kəlz *or* **bī′**fō′kəlz) A pair of eyeglasses having bifocal lenses to correct both near and distant vision.

bi·fur·cate (**bī′**fər-kāt′ *or* bī-**fûr′**kāt′) *tr. & intr.v.* **bi·fur·cat·ed, bi·fur·cat·ing, bi·fur·cates** To divide or be divided into two parts or branches. **—bi′fur·ca′tion** (bī′fər-**kā′**shən) *n.*

big (bĭg) *adj.* **big·ger, big·gest 1.** Of great size, number, quantity, or extent; large: *a big house; a big city; a big appetite.* See Synonyms at **large. 2a.** Grown-up; adult: *Most big people are kind to young children.* **b.** Older or eldest. Used especially of a brother or sister. **3.** Prominent; influential: *a big banker.* **4.** Of great significance; momentous: *a big day in my life; practice for the big game.* **5.** Loud; resounding: *a big voice.* **6.** Full of self-importance; boastful: *a big talker.* ❖ *adv.* **1.** With an air of self-importance; boastfully: *talk big about what one is going to do.* **2.** With considerable success: *made it big.* ◆ **big on** Enthusiastic about; partial to: *She's big on volleyball.* [From Middle English, perhaps of Scandinavian origin.] **—big′ness** *n.*

big·a·mist (**bĭg′**ə-mĭst) *n.* A person who practices bigamy.

big·a·mous (**bĭg′**ə-məs) *adj.* **1.** Relating to bigamy. **2.** Guilty of bigamy.

big·a·my (**bĭg′**ə-mē) *n.* The crime of marrying one person while still being legally married to another. [From Middle English *bigamie,* from Late Latin *bigamus,* twice married : Latin *bi-,* two + Greek *gamos,* marriage.]

Big Bang theory *n.* The scientific theory that the universe originated approximately 13.7 billion years ago in a violent expansion of a singular point of extremely high density and temperature. —SEE NOTE.

big business *n.* Large businesses and corporations considered as a group: *The proposed regulations were opposed by Wall Street and big business.*

Big Dipper *n.* A group of seven stars in the constellation Ursa Major, four forming the bowl and three the handle in the shape of a dipper.

big·heart·ed (**bĭg′här′**tĭd) *adj.* Generous; kind. **—big′heart′ed·ly** *adv.* **—big′heart′ed·ness** *n.*

big·horn (**bĭg′**hôrn′) *n., pl.* **big·horn** or **big·horns** The bighorn sheep.

bighorn sheep *n.* A wild sheep of the mountains of western North America, the male of which has very large curved horns.

bight (bīt) *n.* **1a.** A loop in a rope. **b.** The middle or slack part of an extended rope. **2a.** A long curve, especially in a shoreline. **b.** A wide bay formed by such a curve.

big league *n.* **1.** A major league in a professional sport, especially in baseball. **2.** often **big leagues** *Informal* The highest level of accomplishment in a field: *Getting nominated for the award is a sign that an actor has made it to the big leagues.* **—big′-league′** *adj.*

big·mouth (**bĭg′**mouth′) *n. Slang* A person who talks very loudly or who gossips a lot.

big·ot (**bĭg′**ət) *n.* A person who is intolerant of people who are different, as in religion, race, or politics. [From Old French.]

big·ot·ed (**bĭg′**ə-tĭd) *adj.* Characteristic of a bigot; intolerant; prejudiced.

big·ot·ry (**bĭg′**ə-trē) *n.* The attitude or behavior of a bigot; intolerance; prejudice.

big shot *n. Slang* A very important person.

USAGE

biceps Each of our arms has a muscle called a **biceps**. The plural of *biceps* looks like the singular: *Since he started lifting weights, his biceps have become huge.* Some people say *bicep,* thinking that the *-s* on the end is like the *-s* in the plural word *weights,* and the singular is made by dropping the *-s*. But *bicep* is a mistake.

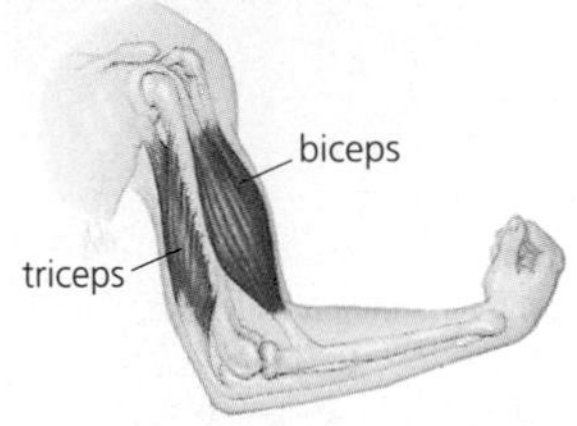

biceps

SCIENCE

Big Bang theory It seems impossible to know how the universe began, or even if it had a beginning at all. But since the 1960s, most evidence suggests that the universe began with something like a massive explosion. In the 1920s, astronomers found that wherever we look in the sky, galaxies are moving rapidly away from us. In other words, the universe is expanding. By studying the speed of the galaxies' motion at various distances from Earth, astronomers calculated that all galaxies had begun moving away from each other approximately 13.7 billion years ago. These galaxies, and indeed all matter, must originally have been compressed into a point that was infinitesimally small and infinitely dense. According to the **Big Bang theory,** space, time, matter, and energy came into being at that time, when the universe was born and began to expand.

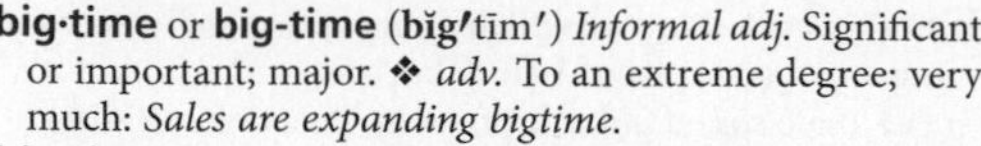

big·time or **big-time** (bĭg′tīm′) *Informal adj.* Significant or important; major. ❖ *adv.* To an extreme degree; very much: *Sales are expanding bigtime.*

big time *n. Informal* The highest level of attainment in a field, such as the arts, business, or sports.

big top *n.* **1.** The main tent of a circus. **2.** The circus: *worked as a clown in the big top for ten years.*

big·wig (bĭg′wĭg′) *n. Slang* An important person; a dignitary.

bike (bīk) *n.* **1.** A bicycle. **2.** A motorbike or motorcycle. ❖ *intr.v.* **biked, bik·ing, bikes** To ride a bike.

bik·er (bī′kər) *n.* A person who rides a bicycle, motorbike, or motorcycle.

bike·way (bīk′wā′) *n.* A lane or path for bicycles.

bi·ki·ni (bĭ-kē′nē) *n.* **1.** A very small two-piece bathing suit worn by women. **2.** A very small bathing suit worn by men. [After *Bikini*, an atoll in the Marshall Islands.]

bi·lat·er·al (bī-lăt′ər-əl) *adj.* **1.** Having two sides; two-sided. **2.** Affecting or undertaken by two sides or parties: *bilateral negotiations.* **3.** Relating to both the right and left sides of the body or of a body structure: *bilateral brain damage.* **—bi·lat′er·al·ly** *adv.*

bilateral symmetry *n.* Symmetrical arrangement of right and left halves along a central axis, as in an organism or body part.

bile (bīl) *n.* **1.** A bitter, alkaline, greenish liquid that is produced by the liver and stored in the gallbladder. Bile aids digestion in the duodenum by neutralizing acids and emulsifying fats. **2.** Bitterness of temper; ill humor: *sarcastic remarks full of bile.*

bilge (bĭlj) *n.* **1.** The lowest inner part of a ship's hull. **2.** Bilge water. [Probably from *bulge*.]

bilge water *n.* **1.** Water that collects in the bilge of a ship. **2.** *Slang* Nonsense.

bi·lin·gual (bī-lĭng′gwəl) *adj.* **1.** Able to use two languages equally well: *Many diplomats are bilingual.* **2.** Relating to or expressed in two languages: *a bilingual dictionary.* **—bi·lin′gual·ly** *adv.*

bil·ious (bĭl′yəs) *adj.* **1.** Relating to or containing bile. **2.** Relating to or characterized by an excess of bile. **3.** Relating to or suggestive of bilious distress or disease: *a bilious complexion.* **4.** Having a peevish disposition; ill-humored: *Our bilious neighbor is always complaining about one thing or another.* **—bil′ious·ly** *adv.* **—bil′ious·ness** *n.*

bilk (bĭlk) *tr.v.* **bilked, bilk·ing, bilks** To cheat, defraud, or swindle: *The art dealer bilked unsuspecting clients out of millions.*

bill[1] (bĭl) *n.* **1.** A statement of charges for goods supplied or work performed: *a telephone bill.* **2.** A piece of paper money worth a certain amount: *a ten-dollar bill.* **3.** The entertainment offered by a theater. **4.** An advertising poster: *Post no bills!* **5.** A draft of a law presented for approval to a legislature: *a conservation bill.* ❖ *tr.v.* **billed, bill·ing, bills 1a.** To give or send a statement of charges to: *Bill me for the amount due.* **b.** To enter on a statement of charges; prepare a bill of: *Please bill these purchases to our account.* **2.** To advertise or schedule by public notice or as part of a program: *I see that the play is billed as a comedy.* [From Middle English *bille*, from Medieval Latin *bulla*, seal on a document.]

bill[2]
on a baseball cap

bill[2] (bĭl) *n.* **1.** The horny, projecting structure that extends forward from the head of a bird and has an upper and a lower part. Birds that eat different kinds of food have bills of different sizes and shapes. **2.** The visor of a cap. [From Old English *bile*.]

bill·board (bĭl′bôrd′) *n.* A large upright board for the display of advertisements in public places or alongside highways.

bil·let (bĭl′ĭt) *n.* Lodging for soldiers in a civilian building such as a private house or hotel. ❖ *v.* **bil·let·ed, bil·let·ing, bil·lets** *—tr.* To house (soldiers), especially in civilian buildings: *The army billeted the soldiers in the village.* *—intr.* To be housed; lodge: *The soldiers billeted in an old farmhouse.*

bill·fold (bĭl′fōld′) *n.* A small case that folds flat, used for carrying paper money and personal documents, as in a pocket or handbag.

bil·liard (bĭl′yərd) *n.* A shot in billiards in which the cue ball strikes two balls; a carom. ❖ *adj.* Relating to or used in billiards: *a billiard table; a billiard cue.*

bil·liards (bĭl′yərdz) *pl.n. (used with a singular verb)* **1.** A game played on a rectangular cloth-covered table with raised cushioned edges, in which a cue is used to hit three balls against one another or the side cushions of the table. **2.** One of several similar games, such as pool. [From French *billard*, from *bille*, log.]

bill·ing (bĭl′ĭng) *n.* **1.** Relative prominence in publicity, as in the order in which the names of performers are listed: *The two actors share top billing in the new play.* **2.** Advertising; promotion: *The movie did not live up to its advance billing.*

Bil·lings (bĭl′ĭngz) The largest city of Montana, in the southern part of the state on the Yellowstone River east-southeast of Helena.

bil·lion (bĭl′yən) *n.* **1.** The number, written as 10^9 or 1 followed by nine zeros, that is equal to one thousand times one million. **2.** *Chiefly British* The number, written as 10^{12} or 1 followed by 12 zeros, that is equal to one million times one million. [From French, a million million : blend of *bi-*, to the second power, squared, and *million*, million.] **—bil′lionth** *n.*

bil·lion·aire (bĭl′yə-nâr′) *n.* A person whose wealth amounts to at least a billion dollars, pounds, or similar units in another currency.

bill of exchange *n., pl.* **bills of exchange** A written order directing that a specified sum of money be paid to a particular person.

bill of fare *n., pl.* **bills of fare** A menu.

bill of health *n., pl.* **bills of health** A certificate stating whether there is infectious disease aboard a ship or in a port of departure, given to the ship's master for presentation at the next port of arrival. ◆ **clean bill of health** *Informal* A good report based on a past record or condition.

bill of lading *n., pl.* **bills of lading** A document listing and acknowledging receipt of goods for shipment.

bill of rights *n., pl.* **bills of rights 1.** A formal statement of those rights and liberties considered essential to a people or group of people: *a consumer bill of rights.* **2. Bill of Rights** The first ten amendments to the Constitution of the United States, guaranteeing certain rights and privileges to citizens, such as freedom of speech.

bill of sale *n., pl.* **bills of sale** A document that transfers ownership of something to a new owner.

bil·low (bĭl′ō) *n.* **1.** A great wave or surge of water. **2.** A great swell or mass of something: *billows of smoke.* ❖ *v.* **bil·lowed, bil·low·ing, bil·lows** *—intr.* **1.** To rise or surge in or as if in billows: *Flames and smoke billowed through the whole building.* **2.** To swell out; bulge: *At the open window there were curtains billowing in the wind.* *—tr.* To cause to swell out: *The wind billowed the ship's sails.* [From Old Norse *bylgja*, a wave.] **—bil′low·y** *adj.*

bil·ly club (bĭl′ē) *n.* A short stick or club, especially a police officer's club.

billy goat *n. Informal* A male goat.

bi·month·ly (bī-mŭnth′lē) *adj.* **1.** Occurring once every two months: *There are six bimonthly meetings of the club each year.* **2.** Occurring twice a month. ❖ *adv.* **1.** Once every two months. **2.** Twice a month: *Many businesses pay bimonthly, on the first and the fifteenth.* ❖ *n., pl.* **bi·month·lies** A publication issued bimonthly. —SEE NOTE AT **biweekly.**

ă	pat	ôr	core
ā	pay	oi	boy
âr	care	ou	out
ä	father	o͝o	took
ĕ	pet	o͝or	lure
ē	be	o͞o	boot
ĭ	pit	ŭ	cut
ī	bite	ûr	urge
îr	pier	th	thin
ŏ	pot	*th*	this
ō	toe	zh	vision
ô	paw	ə	about

bin (bĭn) *n.* A container or enclosed space for holding or storing something: *a coal bin; a recycle bin.*
❑ *These sound alike:* **bin, been** (existed).

bin– *pref.* Variant of **bi–**[1].

bi·na·ry (**bī′**nə-rē) *adj.* **1.** Relating to or based on the number 2 or the binary number system: *a binary numeral.* **2.** Relating to a system of encoding data using only 0's and 1's. **3.** Consisting of or involving two different parts, kinds, or things: *a binary chemical compound.* [From Middle English *binarie,* from Latin *bīnī,* two at a time.]

binary digit *n.* Either of the digits 0 or 1, used in the binary number system.

binary fission *n.* A form of asexual reproduction in bacteria and other one-celled organisms that involves the dividing of a cell into two cells of approximately the same size.

binary number system *n.* A method of representing numbers as sums of powers of 2 in which all numbers can be written using just the digits 0 and 1.

binary star *n.* A pair of stars revolving around a common center of gravity, often appearing to observers as a single star.

bin·au·ral (bī-**nôr′**əl *or* bĭn-**ôr′**əl) *adj.* **1.** Having or hearing with two ears. **2.** Relating to sound coming from two sources in a way that causes a stereophonic effect.

bind (bīnd) *v.* **bound** (bound), **bind·ing, binds** —*tr.* **1a.** To fasten, tie, or secure by tying, as with a rope or cord: *bind a package with string; bind a prisoner in chains.* **b.** To hold or restrain with or as if with bonds: *traditions that bind people to a way of life.* **2.** To bandage: *bound their wounds.* **3a.** To compel, obligate, or unite: *Duty binds me to remain at my post.* **b.** To place under legal obligation: *The terms of the contract bind the author and the publisher.* **c.** To hold or employ as an apprentice or servant; indenture: *The young man was bound out as a servant.* **4.** To form a chemical bond with: *Hydrogen binds with oxygen to form water.* **5.** To cause to stick together in a mass: *Cement binds gravel to make concrete for paving roads.* **6.** To enclose and fasten between covers: *bind a book.* **7.** To cover with a border or edging for added protection or decoration: *bind a seam with tape.* —*intr.* **1.** To tie up or fasten something. **2.** To stick or become stuck: *Will that glue bind to glass?* **3.** To be tight and uncomfortable: *Once a sweater shrinks it binds.* **4.** To become compact or solid; stick together: *Cement will not bind without water.* **5.** To be compelling or unifying: *We have family ties that bind.* **6.** To combine chemically or form a chemical bond. ❖ *n. Informal* A difficult or confining situation: *He was in a bind when his car broke down.* [From Old English *bindan.*]

bind·er (**bīn′**dər) *n.* **1.** A person who binds books. **2.** A notebook cover with rings or clamps for holding sheets of paper. **3.** Something used to tie or fasten, such as cord or rope. **4.** A material added to something to make it hold together: *Water is a binder in bread dough.* **5.** A farm machine that reaps and ties grain in bundles. **6.** A payment or written statement making an agreement legally binding until the completion of a contract, especially an insurance contract.

bind·er·y (**bīn′**də-rē) *n., pl.* **bind·er·ies** A place where books are bound.

bind·ing (**bīn′**dĭng) *n.* **1.** The cover that holds together the pages of a book: *an expensive book with leather binding.* **2.** A strip of tape or fabric sewn over an edge or seam to protect or decorate it. **3.** A fastening on a ski for securing the boot, especially when designed to release the boot in case of a fall. ❖ *adj.* Imposing a firm obligation; obligatory: *a binding agreement.*

binding energy *n.* The net energy necessary to break a molecule, atom, or nucleus into its smaller component parts.

bind·weed (**bīnd′**wēd′) *n.* Any of various plants having twining stems and pink or white trumpet-shaped flowers.

binge (bĭnj) *n.* A period of excessive or unrestrained activity, especially of eating or drinking. ❖ *intr.v.* **binged, binge·ing** or **bing·ing, bing·es** To indulge in some activity, especially eating, excessively or immoderately: *I felt a little sick after bingeing on chocolate.*

bin·go (**bĭng′**gō) *n.* A game of chance played by covering numbers on a printed card as they are called out. The winner is the player who covers the first five numbers in a row in any direction.

bin La·den (bĭn **lä′**dən), **Osama** 1957–2011. Saudi Arabian–born leader of al-Qaeda.

bin·na·cle (**bĭn′**ə-kəl) *n.* The case that supports a ship's compass, usually located near the helm.

binnacle

bin·oc·u·lar (bə-**nŏk′**yə-lər *or* bī-**nŏk′**yə-lər) *adj.* Relating to or involving both eyes at once: *binocular vision.* [From Latin *bīnī,* two at a time + English *ocular.*]

bin·oc·u·lars (bə-**nŏk′**yə-lərz *or* bī-**nŏk′**yə-lərz) *pl.n.* A distance-viewing device consisting of two small telescopes mounted next to each other, designed for use by both eyes at the same time.

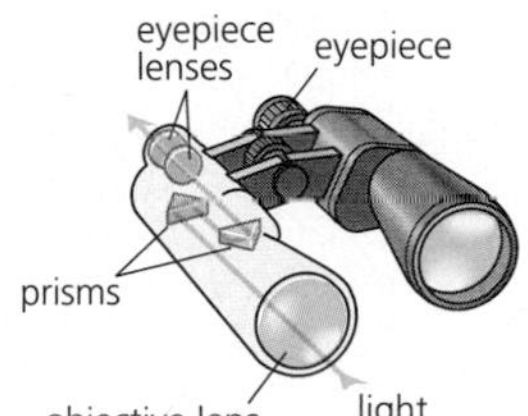

binoculars

bi·no·mi·al (bī-**nō′**mē-əl) *adj.* Consisting of or relating to two names or terms: *a binomial expression in math.* ❖ *n.* A polynomial that is composed of two terms, such as $3a + 2b$.

bio– or **bi–** *pref.* A prefix that means: **1.** Life or living organism: *biome.* **2.** Biology or biological: *biophysics.* —SEE NOTE.

bi·o·chem·i·cal (bī′ō-**kĕm′**ĭ-kəl) *adj.* Relating to biochemistry. **—bi′o·chem′i·cal·ly** *adv.*

bi·o·chem·ist (bī′ō-**kĕm′**ĭst) *n.* A scientist who specializes in biochemistry.

bi·o·chem·is·try (bī′ō-**kĕm′**ĭ-strē) *n.* The study of the chemical composition of substances that form living matter and of chemical processes that go on in living matter.

bi·o·de·grad·a·ble (bī′ō-dĭ-**grā′**də-bəl) *adj.* Capable of being decomposed by biological agents, especially bacteria: *a biodegradable detergent.*

bi·o·di·ver·si·ty (bī′ō-dĭ-**vûr′**sĭ-tē) *n.* The number and variety of species found within a particular geographic region.

bi·o·eth·ics (bī′ō-**ĕth′**ĭks) *n.* *(used with a singular verb)* The study of the ethical and moral questions raised by new biological and medical research, as in the fields of genetic engineering and cloning.

bi·o·feed·back (bī′ō-**fēd′**băk′) *n.* The use of monitoring devices in an attempt to gain some voluntary control over involuntary bodily functions, such as the heartbeat or blood pressure.

bi·o·fuel (**bī′**ō-fyo͞o′əl) *n.* Fuel that is produced from renewable resources, especially plants or treated municipal and industrial wastes.

bi·og·ra·pher (bī-**ŏg′**rə-fər) *n.* A person who writes a biography.

bi·o·graph·i·cal (bī′ə-**grăf′**ĭ-kəl) also **bi·o·graph·ic** (bī′ə-**grăf′**ĭk) *adj.* **1.** Relating to or based on a person's life: *The interviewer asked the singer for some biographical information.* **2.** Relating to biography: *the biographical section of a bookstore.*

bi·og·ra·phy (bī-**ŏg′**rə-fē) *n., pl.* **bi·og·ra·phies** An account of a person's life written by someone else.

bi·o·haz·ard (**bī′**ō-hăz′ərd) *n.* A substance that can cause harm to humans because it contains infectious organisms such as bacteria or viruses. Medical waste, for example, often contains biohazards.

bi·o·log·i·cal (bī′ə-**lŏj′**ĭ-kəl) *adj.* **1.** Relating to or affecting living organisms: *biological processes such as growth and digestion.* **2.** Relating to biology: *the biological sciences.* **3.** Related because of sharing genes transmitted

WORD BUILDING

bio– The prefix **bio–** comes from the Greek word *bios,* meaning "life." When used to form words in English, *bio–* generally refers to living organisms or to biology, the science of living organisms. Many of the words that begin with *bio–* only came into being in the 1900s, such as *bioethics* and *biotechnology.* Sometimes before an *o, bio–* becomes *bi–*: *biopsy.*

by a parent or other ancestor: *He has one biological sister and one adoptive sister.* **—bi′o·log′i·cal·ly** *adv.*

biological clock *n.* An internal mechanism in organisms that controls the cycle of various functions, such as sleep cycles in mammals and photosynthesis in plants.

biological warfare *n.* The use of disease-producing microorganisms or biological toxins as a weapon of war.

bi·ol·o·gy (bī-ŏl′ə-jē) *n.* The scientific study of life and of living organisms, including growth, structure, reproduction, and evolution. Botany, zoology, and bacteriology are all branches of biology. [From German *Biologie* : Greek *bios*, life + Greek *-logiā*, study.] **—bi·ol′o·gist** *n.*

bi·o·lu·mi·nes·cence (bī′ō-lo͞o′mə-**nĕs′**əns) *n.* Emission of light by living organisms, such as fireflies, certain fungi, and many sea animals. **—bi′o·lu′mi·nes′cent** *adj.*

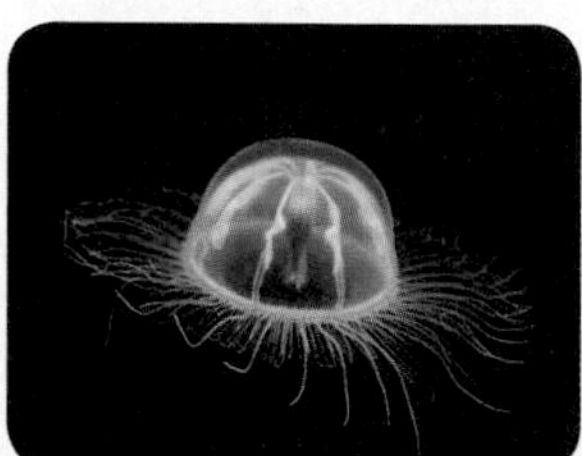

bioluminescence
jellyfish

bi·o·mass (**bī′**ō-măs′) *n.* **1.** The total amount of living material in a given area. **2.** Crops, algae, agricultural waste, or other organic materials used as a fuel or energy source.

bi·ome (**bī′**ōm′) *n.* A large community of organisms occupying a distinct region, such as a grassland or desert, that is defined chiefly by its climate and vegetation.

bi·o·me·chan·ics (bī′ō-mĭ-**kăn′**ĭks) *n.* *(used with a singular verb)* The scientific study of the mechanics of motion in humans and other animals. **—bi′o·me·chan′i·cal** *adj.*

bi·o·met·rics (bī′ō-**mĕt′**rĭks) *n.* *(used with a singular verb)* The statistical study of biological phenomena.

bi·on·ic (bī-**ŏn′**ĭk) *adj.* **1.** Relating to a body part that has been wholly or partly replaced by electronic or mechanical devices. **2.** Relating to bionics.

bi·on·ics (bī-**ŏn′**ĭks) *n.* *(used with a singular verb)* The use of a system or design found in nature, such as the ability of plants to store solar energy, as a model for designing artificial systems, especially mechanical or electronic systems.

bi·o·phys·ics (bī′ō-**fĭz′**ĭks) *n.* *(used with a singular verb)* The scientific study of biological systems and processes using the methods of physics.

bi·op·sy (**bī′**ŏp′sē) *n., pl.* **bi·op·sies 1.** The surgical removal of a sample of tissue from a living body for examination and diagnosis. **2.** A tissue sample obtained by surgery.

bi·o·re·me·di·a·tion (bī′ō-rĭ-mē′dē-**ā′**shən) *n.* The use of biological materials, such as bacteria or plants, to reduce the amount of contamination in polluted soil or water.

bi·o·re·serve (bī′ō-rĭ-**zûrv′**) *n.* An area set up as a wildlife preserve in which only limited visits by the public are allowed.

bi·o·sphere (**bī′**ə-sfîr′) *n.* The part of the earth and its atmosphere in which living organisms exist, along with all those organisms.

bi·o·tech·nol·o·gy (bī′ō-tĕk-**nŏl′**ə-jē) *n.* **1.** The use of living organisms or biological processes to develop certain agricultural, industrial, or medical products. **2.** The science of equipment design; ergonomics. **—bi′o·tech′no·log′i·cal** (bī′ō-tĕk′nə-**lŏj′**ĭ-kəl) *adj.*

bi·o·ter·ror·ism (bī′ō-**tĕr′**ə-rĭz′əm) *n.* The use of biological substances that cause disease for the purposes of terrorism.

bi·ot·ic (bī-**ŏt′**ĭk) *adj.* Relating to living organisms: *the biotic components of an ecosystem.*

bi·o·tin (**bī′**ə-tĭn) *n.* A vitamin belonging to the vitamin B complex and important in the metabolism of carbohydrates and fats. It is found in liver, egg yolks, milk, yeast, and some vegetables.

bi·par·ti·san (bī-**pär′**tĭ-zən *or* bī-**pär′**tĭ-sən) *adj.* Composed of or supported by two political parties, especially the Republican and Democratic parties: *a bipartisan bill to fight crime.*

WRITERS CHOOSE THEIR WORDS

It would be more than a year before Congress passed the Civil Rights Act of 1964. In the meantime, President Kennedy worried that any further demonstrations threatened his ability to secure sufficient **bipartisan** support for the legislation.

—Vincent Harding, Robin D.G. Kelley, and Earl Lewis
We Changed the World: African Americans, 1945–1970

ă	pat	ôr	core
ā	pay	oi	boy
âr	care	ou	out
ä	father	o͝o	took
ĕ	pet	o͝or	lure
ē	be	o͞o	boot
ĭ	pit	ŭ	cut
ī	bite	ûr	urge
îr	pier	th	thin
ŏ	pot	*th*	this
ō	toe	zh	vision
ô	paw	ə	about

bi·par·tite (bī-**pär′**tīt′) *adj.* **1.** Having or consisting of two parts. **2.** Drawn up in two corresponding parts, one for each party: *a bipartite treaty.*

bi·ped (**bī′**pĕd′) *n.* An animal having two feet, such as a bird or human. **—bi·ped′al** *adj.*

bi·plane (**bī′**plān′) *n.* An airplane having two sets of wings, one above the other.

bi·po·lar disorder (bī-**pō′**lər) *n.* A mood disorder characterized by periods of depression alternating with mania.

bi·ra·cial (bī-**rā′**shəl) *adj.* **1.** For, consisting of, or relating to members of two racial groups: *a biracial committee for cooperation between black and white residents.* **2.** Having parents of two different races.

birch (bûrch) *n.* **1.** Any of various trees of the Northern Hemisphere having toothed leaves and papery bark that peels easily. **2.** The hard wood of such a tree. [From Old English *birce.*]

bird (bûrd) *n.* **1.** Any of numerous warm-blooded, egg-laying vertebrate animals that have wings, a body covered with feathers, and a bill used for gathering food. **2.** A shuttlecock. **3.** *Slang* A person, especially one who is odd or unusual: *a strange bird.* ❖ *intr.v.* **bird·ed, bird·ing, birds** To observe and identify birds in their natural surroundings. ◆ **birds of a feather** People who are similar, as in character, personality, or tastes. **for the birds** Worthless or objectionable. [From Old English *brid*, young bird.] —SEE NOTE AT **pretty.**

bird·bath (**bûrd′**băth′) *n.* A basin filled with water for birds to drink or bathe in.

bird·cage (**bûrd′**kāj′) *n.* A cage for birds.

bird·call (**bûrd′**kôl′) *n.* **1.** The song or cry of a bird. **2a.** An imitation of the song or cry of a bird. **b.** A small device for producing this sound.

bird dog *n.* A dog trained to hunt game birds.

bird·er (**bûr′**dər) *n.* A bird watcher.

bird·house (**bûrd′**hous′) *n.* A box, often shaped like a house, that is provided as a nesting place for birds.

bird·ie (**bûr′**dē) *n.* **1.** *Informal* A small bird. **2.** In golf, a score of one stroke under par for a hole.

bird·lime (**bûrd′**līm′) *n.* A sticky substance smeared on twigs to catch small birds.

bird of paradise *n., pl.* **birds of paradise 1.** Any of various birds of New Guinea and Australia, usually having brightly colored, showy feathers in the male. **2.** Any of several African plants grown for their showy orange and blue flowers that emerge from a beak-shaped structure.

bird of prey *n., pl.* **birds of prey** Any of various birds, such as a hawk, eagle, owl, or vulture, that hunt and kill other animals for food or feed on dead animals.

bird·seed (**bûrd′**sēd′) *n.* Seed that is provided as food for caged or wild birds.

bird's-eye (**bûrdz′**ī′) *adj.* Seen from high above: *a bird's-eye view of the countryside.*

bird watcher *n.* A person who observes and identifies birds in their natural surroundings. **—bird watching** *n.*

bi·ret·ta (bə-**rĕt′**ə) *n.* A stiff square cap worn by members of the Roman Catholic clergy. Birettas are black for priests, purple for bishops, and red for cardinals.

Bir·ming·ham (**bûr′**mĭng-hăm′) **1.** (*also* **bûr′**mĭng-əm) A city of central England northwest of London. **2.** The largest city of Alabama, in the north-central part of the state northwest of Montgomery.

birr (bûr) *n.* The basic monetary unit of Ethiopia.

birth (bûrth) *n.* **1.** The emergence and separation of offspring from the body of the mother: *At birth she weighed seven pounds.* **2.** The act or process of bearing young: *A second birth is usually easier than the first.* **3.** A beginning or origin: *the birth of an idea.* **4.** Family background; ancestry: *an heir of noble birth.* ❖ *tr.v.* **birthed,**

birth·ing, births To deliver (a baby). [From Middle English, of Scandinavian origin.]
❑ *These sound alike:* **birth, berth** (bed).

birth certificate *n.* An official record of the date and place of a person's birth, usually including the names of the parents.

birth control *n.* **1.** Control of the number of children conceived or born, especially by the use of contraception. **2.** A contraceptive device or technique.

birth·day (bûrth′dā′) *n.* **1.** The day of a person's birth. **2.** The anniversary of that day.

birth defect *n.* A physical defect or abnormality of the body that is present at the time of birth. Birth defects can be caused by heredity or by the injury or faulty development of the fetus before or during birth.

birth·mark (bûrth′märk′) *n.* A mark or blemish present on the body from birth.

birth name *n.* **1.** The name given to a person at birth, especially that of an adopted child before he or she is renamed. **2.** A maiden name.

birth·place (bûrth′plās′) *n.* The place where someone is born or where something originates.

birth·rate (bûrth′rāt′) *n.* The ratio of total live births to total population in a specified area or community over a particular period of time, usually one year.

birth·right (bûrth′rīt′) *n.* A right to which a person is entitled because of birth or origin: *Freedom of speech is an American birthright.*

birth·stone (bûrth′stōn′) *n.* A jewel associated with the specific month of a person's birth.

Bis·cay (bĭs′kā), **Bay of** An arm of the Atlantic Ocean on the western coast of Europe from northwest France to northwest Spain.

bi·scot·ti (bĭ-skŏt′ē) *pl.n.* Italian cookies traditionally baked in hard oblong slices and often containing almonds or other nuts. [From Italian, from Medieval Latin *bis coctus*, twice cooked.]

bis·cuit (bĭs′kĭt) *n., pl.* **bis·cuits 1.** A small flaky cake of bread leavened with baking powder or soda. **2.** *Chiefly British* **a.** A cracker. **b.** A cookie. [From Middle English *bisquit*, from Medieval Latin *bis coctus*, twice cooked.]

bi·sect (bī′sĕkt′ *or* bī-sĕkt′) *tr.v.* **bi·sect·ed, bi·sect·ing, bi·sects** To cut or divide into two equal parts: *bisect a triangle.* **—bi·sec′tion** *n.* —SEE NOTE AT **segment.**

bi·sec·tor (bī′sĕk′tər *or* bī-sĕk′tər) *n.* A straight line that bisects an angle or line segment.

bi·sex·u·al (bī-sĕk′sho͞o-əl) *adj.* **1.** Having a sexual orientation toward people of both sexes. **2.** Having male and female reproductive organs in a single individual; hermaphroditic: *Earthworms are bisexual.* ❖ *n.* A bisexual person. **—bi′sex·u·al′i·ty** (bī′sĕk-sho͞o-ăl′ĭ-tē) *n.*

Bish·kek (bĭsh′kĕk *or* bēsh′kĕk) Formerly **Frun·ze** (fro͞on′zə). The capital of Kyrgyzstan, in the north-central part of the country.

bish·op (bĭsh′əp) *n.* **1.** A high-ranking Christian cleric, in modern churches usually in charge of a diocese. **2.** A chess piece that can move diagonally across any number of unoccupied spaces of the same color. [From Old English *biscop*, from Greek *episkopos*, overseer.]

Bish·op (bĭsh′əp), **Elizabeth** 1911–1979. American poet whose works include *Questions of Travel* (1965).

bish·op·ric (bĭsh′ə-prĭk) *n.* The office, rank, or diocese of a bishop.

Bis·marck (bĭz′märk′) The capital of North Dakota, in the south-central part of the state on hills overlooking the Missouri River.

Bismarck, Prince. **Otto Eduard Leopold von** 1815–1898. First chancellor of the German Empire (1871–1890). He set in motion sweeping social reforms.

bis·muth (bĭz′məth) *n. Symbol* **Bi** A brittle, pinkish-white metallic element that occurs in nature as a free metal and in various ores. It is used in making low-melting alloys for fire-safety devices. Atomic number 83. See **Periodic Table.** [From obsolete German *Bismuth.*]

bi·son (bī′sən *or* bī′zən) *n., pl.* **bison 1.** A large mammal of western North America that has a massive head, a shaggy dark-brown mane, and short curved horns; a buffalo. **2.** A similar but smaller European animal. [From Latin *bisōn*, of Germanic origin.] —SEE NOTE AT **buffalo.**

bis·phe·nol A (bĭs′fē′nôl′) *n.* A white solid with an odor similar to phenol, used as a monomer for polycarbonate and epoxy resins, and in other plastics. It is suspected of being toxic by interfering with the body's hormones.

bisque (bĭsk) *n.* A thick cream soup: *lobster bisque.*

Bis·sau (bĭ-sou′) The capital of Guinea-Bissau, on the Atlantic Ocean southeast of Banjul, Gambia. It was founded in 1687.

bis·tro (bē′strō *or* bĭs′trō) *n., pl.* **bis·tros** A small restaurant, bar, or nightclub.

bit[1] (bĭt) *n.* **1.** A small piece or amount: *a bit of lint; a bit of luck.* **2.** A brief amount of time; a moment: *Wait a bit.* **3.** An entertainment routine given regularly by a performer; an act. **4.** *Informal* An amount equal to one eighth of a dollar: *two bits.* ◆ **a bit** To a small degree; somewhat: *The soup is a bit hot.* **bit by bit** Little by little; gradually: *My piano playing improved bit by bit.* [From Old English *bita.*]

bit[2] (bĭt) *n.* **1.** A pointed tool for drilling that fits into a brace or electric drill. **2.** The sharp part of a tool, such as the cutting edge of a knife. **3.** The metal mouthpiece of a bridle, used to control the horse. **4.** The part of a key that enters the lock and works the mechanism. [From Old English *bite*, act of biting.]

bit[3] (bĭt) *n.* The smallest unit of computer memory. A bit holds one of two possible values, either of the binary digits 0 or 1. [From *b(inary) (dig)it.*]

bit[4] (bĭt) *v.* Past tense and a past participle of **bite.**

bitch (bĭch) *n.* A female dog or related animal, such as a coyote.

bite (bīt) *v.* **bit** (bĭt), **bit·ten** (bĭt′n) or **bit, bit·ing, bites** *—tr.* **1.** To use the teeth to cut, tear, or hold: *He bit the bread and tore off a piece.* **2a.** To pierce the skin of (a person or animal) with the teeth, fangs, or mouthparts: *Did the snake bite you?* **b.** To sting with a stinger: *I got bitten by a wasp.* **3.** To tear or cut into. Used especially of implements: *The axe bit the tree trunk.* **4.** To seize (bait or a lure) with the mouth: *The fish just won't bite this lure.* **5.** To gain traction on or apply pressure that does not slip to; grip: *Couldn't get the wrench to bite the pipe.* **6.** To cause sharp pain to: *The cold wind was biting my face.* *—intr.* **1.** To use the teeth to tear or cut something: *I bit into the pizza.* **2.** To cut or tear something: *The chainsaw bit into the log.* **3.** To grip a surface: *The tires can't bite when the road is icy.* **4.** To seize bait or a lure with the mouth: *Fish seem to bite more just before it starts to rain.* **5.** To be deceived by a trick or scheme: *She tried to pass off the old car as a bargain, but no one would bite.* ❖ *n.* **1.** The act of biting: *The dog's bark is worse than his bite.* **2.** A wound or injury resulting from biting: *a mosquito bite.* **3.** An amount of food taken into the mouth at one time; a mouthful: *Let me have a bite of your sandwich.* **4.** *Informal* A light meal or snack: *We stopped at the coffee shop for a bite.* **5.** A secure grip or hold, as by a tool: *The pliers had a good bite on the nut.* **6.** The angle at which the upper and lower teeth meet: *He wore braces to correct his bite.* ◆ **bite off more than (one) can chew** To decide or agree to do more than one can accomplish. **bite the dust** *Slang* **1.** To fall dead. **2.** To come to an end. **bite the hand that feeds (one)** To repay generosity or

bird of paradise

biscotti

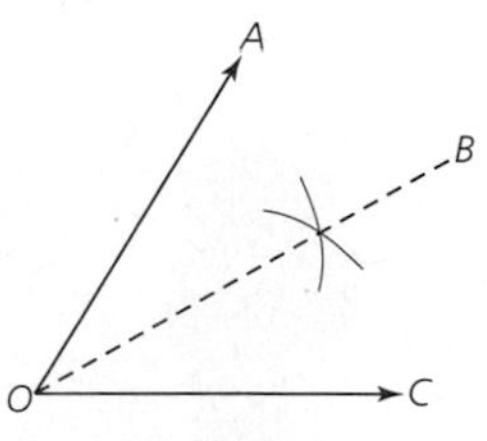

bisector
Line *OB* bisects angle *AOC.*

bison
North American bison

bitterroot

USAGE

biweekly Properly speaking, the word **biweekly** means "once every two weeks" and **bimonthly** means "once every two months." **Semiweekly** means "twice a week" and **semimonthly** means "twice a month." Because many people mix up these *bi–* and *semi–* words, it is safest to use phrases like *every two weeks* or *twice a month.* A publication that comes out every two weeks, however, is always called a *biweekly.* One appearing every two months is a *bimonthly.*

Black Hawk
c. 1837 lithograph by Charles Bird King (1785–1862)

ă	pat	ôr	core
ā	pay	oi	boy
âr	care	ou	out
ä	father	o͝o	took
ĕ	pet	o͝or	lure
ē	be	o͞o	boot
ĭ	pit	ŭ	cut
ī	bite	ûr	urge
îr	pier	th	thin
ŏ	pot	*th*	this
ō	toe	zh	vision
ô	paw	ə	about

kindness with ingratitude and injury. [From Old English *bītan.*] **—bit′er** *n.*

❑ *These sound alike:* **bite, byte** (unit of computer measure).

bit·ing (bī′tĭng) *adj.* **1.** Causing a stinging sensation: *a biting wind blew across the field.* **2.** Injuring or capable of injuring the feelings: *biting criticism.* **3.** Capable of wounding with the teeth, fangs, or mouthparts: *biting flies.* **—bit′ing·ly** *adv.*

bit·map (bĭt′măp′) *n.* A set of bits forming a graphic image generated by a computer. Each bit or group of bits corresponds to a pixel in the image. **—bit′mapped′** (bĭt′măpt′) *adj.*

bit part *n.* A small or insignificant role, as in a play or movie, usually with very few spoken lines.

bit·ten (bĭt′n) *v.* A past participle of **bite.**

bit·ter (bĭt′ər) *adj.* **bit·ter·er, bit·ter·est 1.** Having or being a taste that is sharp or unpleasant: *a bitter drink.* **2.** Causing sharp pain to the body; harsh: *a bitter wind.* **3.** Hard to accept, admit, or bear: *the bitter truth.* **4.** Showing or proceeding from strong dislike or animosity: *bitter foes; a bitter fight.* **5.** Resulting from severe grief, anguish, or disappointment: *cry bitter tears.* **6.** Having or showing a resentful feeling: *bitter about being cheated.* ❖ *n.* **1. bitters** A bitter, usually alcoholic liquid used in cocktails and as a tonic. **2.** *Chiefly British* A sharp-tasting beer made with hops. [From Old English *biter.*] **—bit′ter·ly** *adv.* **—bit′ter·ness** *n.*

bit·tern (bĭt′ərn) *n.* Any of several long-necked wading birds having mottled brownish feathers and a deep booming cry.

bit·ter·root (bĭt′ər-ro͞ot′ *or* bĭt′ər-ro͝ot′) *n.* A plant of western North America having showy pink or white flowers and a bitter but edible root.

bit·ter·sweet (bĭt′ər-swēt′) *n.* **1.** Any of several woody vines having yellow-orange fruits that split open and expose seeds with red coverings. **2.** A kind of nightshade plant that has violet flowers and poisonous red berries. ❖ *adj.* **1.** Bitter and sweet at the same time: *bittersweet chocolate.* **2.** Pleasant and unpleasant at the same time: *bittersweet memories.*

bit·ty (bĭt′ē) *adj.* **bit·ti·er, bit·ti·est** *Informal* Tiny.

bi·tu·men (bĭ-to͞o′mən) *n.* Any of various flammable mixtures of hydrocarbons and other substances found in asphalt and tar. They occur naturally or are produced from petroleum and coal. [From Middle English, a kind of mineral pitch or asphalt, from Latin *bitūmen,* perhaps of Celtic origin.]

bi·tu·mi·nous (bĭ-to͞o′mə-nəs) *adj.* **1.** Resembling or containing bitumen. **2.** Relating to bituminous coal.

bituminous coal *n.* A grade of coal that contains a high percentage of bitumen and burns with much smoke and a yellow flame; soft coal.

bi·valve (bī′vălv′) *n.* Any of numerous mollusks, such as a clam, oyster, or scallop, having a shell that consists of two parts hinged together. ❖ *adj.* Having a hinged shell: *a bivalve mollusk.*

biv·ou·ac (bĭv′o͞o-ăk′ *or* bĭv′wăk′) *n.* A temporary camp made by soldiers in the field. ❖ *intr.v.* **biv·ou·acked, biv·ou·ack·ing, biv·ou·acs** also **biv·ou·acks** To camp in a bivouac.

bi·week·ly (bī-wēk′lē) *adj.* **1.** Occurring every two weeks. **2.** Occurring twice a week: *biweekly meetings on Tuesday and Thursday.* ❖ *n., pl.* **bi·week·lies** A publication issued every two weeks. ❖ *adv.* **1.** Once every two weeks: *The company gives out paychecks biweekly.* **2.** Twice a week. —SEE NOTE.

bi·zarre (bĭ-zär′) *adj.* Very strange or odd: *a bizarre hat; a bizarre idea.*

Bk The symbol for the element **berkelium.**

blab (blăb) *v.* **blabbed, blab·bing, blabs** *—tr.* To tell (a secret), especially through careless talk. *—intr.* **1.** To reveal secret matters: *The secret was out when I blabbed without thinking.* **2.** To chatter indiscreetly.

blab·ber (blăb′ər) *intr.v.* **blab·bered, blab·ber·ing, blab·bers** To chatter. ❖ *n.* **1.** Idle chatter. **2.** A person who blabs.

blab·ber·mouth (blăb′ər-mouth′) *n. Informal* A person who talks carelessly and at length.

black (blăk) *adj.* **black·er, black·est 1.** Being of the color black, producing or reflecting comparatively little light and having no predominant hue. **2.** Without light: *a black moonless night.* **3.** also **Black a.** Relating to or belonging to a racial group having dark skin, especially a group of African origin. **b.** Relating to or belonging to an American group of people descended from African peoples having dark skin; African-American. **4.** Evil; wicked: *black deeds.* **5.** Gloomy; depressing: *a black day; black thoughts.* **6.** Angry; sullen: *He gave me a black look.* **7.** Portraying tragic or unhappy events in a satirical or humorous way: *a black comedy about war.* **8.** Marked by disaster: *The stock market crashed on Black Friday.* **9.** Deserving of or indicating censure or dishonor: *the industry's blackest record as a polluter of the rivers.* **10.** Served without cream or milk: *black coffee.* ❖ *n.* **1a.** The darkest extreme of the series of colors that runs through all the shades of gray to white, being the opposite of white. **b.** A black paint, dye, or pigment. **2.** Clothing of this color, especially clothing worn for mourning: *At the funeral everyone was dressed in black.* **3.** also **Black a.** A member of a racial group having dark skin, especially one of African origin. **b.** An American descended from peoples of African origin having dark skin; an African American. ❖ *tr.v.* **blacked, black·ing, blacks** To make black: *blacked the pair of scuffed shoes.* ◆ **black out 1.** To lose consciousness or memory temporarily: *He felt lightheaded and then blacked out.* **2.** To prevent the transmission of (a television program). **3.** To cover or make illegible with black marking: *The names in the report had been blacked out.* **4.** To turn off or conceal all lights in (a building or area) in order to make it difficult for enemy aircraft to find a target during an air raid. **5.** To cause a failure of electrical power in: *The storm blacked out the street lights.* **in the black** Making a profit; prosperous. [From Old English *blæc.*] **—black′ly** *adv.* **—black′ness** *n.*

black-and-blue (blăk′ən-blo͞o′) *adj.* Discolored from broken blood vessels and clotted blood under the skin; bruised.

black and white *n.* **1.** Writing or printing: *She did not believe it until she read it in black and white.* **2.** Photography or printmaking that uses only black and white, or black, white, and values of gray: *a movie shot in black and white.*

black-and-white (blăk′ən-wīt′) *adj.* **1.** Being done, drawn, or photographed in shades of black and white: *a black-and-white picture.* **2.** Partly black and partly white: *a black-and-white cow.* **3.** Making judgments based on two rigid categories, such as right and wrong: *black-and-white opinions.*

black art *n.* Black magic.

black·ball (blăk′bôl′) *n.* A negative vote. ❖ *tr.v.* **black·balled, black·ball·ing, black·balls 1.** To vote against and prevent (someone) from being admitted to an organization, as by placing a black ball in a ballot box. **2.** To shut out from participation: *actors who were blackballed for their political views.*

black bean *n.* A type of bean that has small, blackish seeds.

black bear *n.* **1.** A North American bear that lives in forests and has thick black or dark-brown fur. **2.** An Asian bear having a pointed snout and black or dark-brown fur with a white V-shaped mark on the chest.

black belt *n.* The rank of expert in a system of self-defense, such as judo or karate.

black·ber·ry (blăk′bĕr′ē) *n.* **1.** A blackish, glossy, many-seeded fruit of any of various plants with long prickly stems. **2.** A shrub that bears such berries.

black·bird (blăk′bûrd′) *n.* Any of various birds having black or mostly black feathers.

black·board (blăk′bôrd′) *n.* A hard, smooth, dark-colored panel for writing on with chalk; a chalkboard.

black·bod·y (blăk′bŏd′ē) *n., pl.* **black·bod·ies** A theoretical object that completely absorbs any radiation that strikes it.

black box *n.* A flight recorder.

black·damp (blăk′dămp′) *n.* A suffocating gas, mostly a mixture of carbon dioxide and nitrogen, found in mines after fires and explosions.

Black Death *n.* A widespread outbreak of bubonic plague that killed large numbers of people throughout Europe and much of Asia in the 1300s.

black·en (blăk′ən) *v.* **black·ened, black·en·ing, black·ens** —*tr.* **1.** To make black: *Smoke blackened the sky.* **2.** To speak evil of; defame: *The scandal blackened the athlete's reputation.* **3.** To sear (meat or fish that has been coated with pepper and other spices) in a very hot skillet: *blackened the salmon and served it with rice.* —*intr.* To become dark or black: *The sky blackened before the storm.*

Black English *n.* **1.** African American Vernacular English. **2.** Any of the nonstandard varieties of English spoken by black people throughout the world.

black eye *n.* **1.** A bruised discoloration of the skin around the eye, resulting from a blow. **2.** A bad name; a dishonored reputation: *Involvement in the scandal gave the politician a black eye.*

black-eyed pea (blăk′īd′) *n.* The cowpea.

black-eyed Su·san (so͞o′zən) *n.* Any of several North American plants having hairy stems and leaves and showy flowers with orange-yellow rays surrounding a dark-brown center.

Black·foot (blăk′fo͝ot′) *n., pl.* **Blackfoot** or **Black·feet** (blăk′fēt′) **1.** A member of a Native American people of Montana, Alberta, and Saskatchewan. **2.** The Algonquian language of the Blackfoot. [Translation of Blackfoot *siksiká*, perhaps from the blackening of their moccasins from painting them or from walking near prairie fires.]

black·guard (blăg′ərd *or* blăg′ärd′) *n.* A low unprincipled person; a scoundrel.

Black Hawk Originally **Makataimeshekiakiak.** 1767–1838. Sauk leader who organized the resistance of the Fox and Sauk against white settlement of Native American ancestral lands that ended in the Black Hawk War (1832).

black·head (blăk′hĕd′) *n.* A mass of fatty material and dirt that collects in and blocks one of the pores of the skin.

black hole *n.* An extremely dense celestial object that has a gravitational field so strong that nothing can escape, not even light. A black hole is formed by the collapse of a massive star's core in a supernova.

black ice *n.* A thin, nearly invisible coating of ice that forms on paved surfaces.

black·ing (blăk′ĭng) *n.* A black paste or liquid used as a polish, as for shoes or stoves.

black·ish (blăk′ĭsh) *adj.* Somewhat black in color.

black·jack (blăk′jăk′) *n.* **1.** A small leather-covered club with a flexible handle. **2.** A card game in which the object is to hold cards with a higher count than that of the dealer but not exceeding 21. ❖ *tr.v.* **black·jacked, black·jack·ing, black·jacks** To strike or threaten with a blackjack.

black-legged tick (blăk′lĕgd′) *n.* A deer tick.

black light *n.* Invisible ultraviolet or infrared light. Black light causes fluorescent materials to emit visible light.

black·list (blăk′lĭst′) *n.* A list of people or organizations to be disapproved, boycotted, or penalized. ❖ *tr.v.* **black·list·ed, black·list·ing, black·lists** To place (a name) on a blacklist: *The government blacklisted the political dissidents.*

black lung *n.* A disease of the lungs caused by inhaling coal dust over a long period of time.

black magic *n.* Magic practiced for evil purposes, especially when invoking the help of evil spirits.

black·mail (blăk′māl′) *n.* **1.** The extortion of money or something of value from a person by the threat of exposing something criminal or discreditable about the person. **2.** Money or something of value paid or demanded as blackmail: *The official refused to pay blackmail.* ❖ *tr.v.* **black·mailed, black·mail·ing, black·mails** To subject (someone) to blackmail. **—black′mail′er** *n.*

black market *n.* **1.** The illegal business of buying or selling goods that are banned or restricted by a government. **2.** A place where this illegal business is carried on.

Black Muslim *n.* A member of a black American group, the Nation of Islam, that professes Islamic beliefs.

black·out (blăk′out′) *n.* **1.** A cutoff of electric power, especially as a result of a shortage, a mechanical failure, or overuse by consumers. **2.** The act of putting out or concealing all lights that might be visible to enemy aircraft during a night raid. **3.** A temporary loss of consciousness or memory: *The driver's blackout caused the crash.* **4.** A suppression by censorship: *a news blackout.* **5.** The suppression of a television broadcast, as of a popular sports event, in a particular area, often to support ticket sales within that area.

Black Power *n.* A movement among black Americans emphasizing racial pride and social equality.

Black Sea An inland sea between Europe and Asia. It is connected with the Aegean Sea by the Bosporus, the Sea of Marmara, and the Dardanelles.

black sheep *n.* **1.** A sheep with black fleece. **2.** An undesirable or disgraceful member of a family or group.

black·smith (blăk′smĭth′) *n.* A person who forges and shapes iron into horseshoes and other objects of metal. —SEE NOTE.

black·snake (blăk′snāk′) *n.* Any of various dark-colored, chiefly nonvenomous snakes of eastern North America.

black·thorn (blăk′thôrn′) *n.* A thorny shrub of Eurasia having white flowers and small bluish-black fruit.

black tie *n.* **1.** A black bow tie worn with a tuxedo or dinner jacket. **2.** A style of evening dress that includes a black bow tie with a tuxedo or dinner jacket for men and an evening gown or other formal dress for women. **—black′-tie′** *adj.*

black·top (blăk′tŏp′) *n.* A bituminous material, such as asphalt, used to pave roads. ❖ *tr.v.* **black·topped, black·top·ping, black·tops** To pave with blacktop.

Blackwell, Elizabeth 1821–1910. British-born American physician who was the first woman to earn an MD from an American medical school (1849).

black widow *n.* Any of several spiders with a black shiny body, the female of which is venomous and often has red markings in the shape of an hourglass on the underside.

blad·der (blăd′ər) *n.* **1.** A sac with an elastic membrane that stores urine secreted by the kidneys and is found in most vertebrates except birds. **2.** Any of other similar sacs in animals, such as a swim bladder. **3.** A hollow structure or sac in a plant, such as an air bladder in certain seaweeds. **4.** Something that is hollow and inflatable: *the bladder of a football.* [From Old English *blǣdre.*]

blade (blād) *n.* **1.** The flat sharp-edged part of a cutting tool or weapon. **2.** A sword. **3a.** The thin flat part of something: *the blade of an oar.* **b.** A long, thin, often

WORD HISTORY

blacksmith Originally, a *smith* was a skilled worker in metal, wood, or cloth, but the meaning of *smith* has narrowed to "a worker in metal." A **blacksmith** is "a smith who works with iron," the black metal, especially with forging iron, which is at the beginning of the metalworking process. A **whitesmith,** by contrast, is a person who works with white metal (any of various light-colored alloys usually containing tin or lead) or who polishes or otherwise finishes metal products.

Elizabeth Blackwell

black widow

curved piece, as of metal or rubber, used for plowing, clearing, or wiping. **4.** The broad flattened part of a leaf, extending from the stalk. **5.** The metal part of an ice skate that makes contact with the ice. **6.** A dashing young man. [From Old English *blæd*, leaf.]

blah (blä) *Informal n.* **1. blahs** A general feeling of dissatisfaction or depression: *She's had the blahs all week.* **2.** Meaningless or uninteresting remarks; blah-blah. ❖ *adj.* **1.** Dull and uninteresting: *The party turned out to be very blah.* **2.** Low in spirits or health: *I'm feeling blah.*

blah-blah (**blä′blä′**) *Informal n.* Meaningless or uninteresting remarks: *The opening presentation was nothing but a lot of blah-blah.*

Blair (blâr), **Anthony Charles Lynton** Known as "Tony." Born 1945. British politician who served as prime minister (1997–2007).

Blair, Bonnie Born 1964. American speedskater who won five gold medals and one bronze medal in the 1988, 1992, and 1994 Olympics.

Blake (blāk), **William** 1757–1827. British poet and artist who printed many of his own volumes, including *Songs of Innocence* (1789).

blame (blām) *tr.v.* **blamed, blam·ing, blames 1.** To hold (a person or thing) responsible or at fault: *The driver blamed the icy road for the accident.* **2.** To find fault with; censure: *I can't blame you for wanting your fair share.* **3.** To place responsibility for (something) on a cause: *The article blamed the crisis on poor planning.* ❖ *n.* The state of being responsible for a fault or error: *I had to accept the blame for my mistake.* ◆ **to blame 1.** Deserving censure; at fault: *Who is to blame for this mess?* **2.** Being the cause or source of something: *The snowstorm was to blame for the cancellation of the flight.* [From Middle English *blamen*, from Old French *blasmer*, from alteration of Late Latin *blasphēmāre*, to reproach.] **—blam′a·ble** *adj.*

blame·less (**blām′**lĭs) *adj.* Free from blame or guilt; innocent: *Neither side is blameless in the dispute.* **—blame′less·ly** *adv.* **—blame′less·ness** *n.*

blame·wor·thy (**blām′**wûr′*th*ē) *adj.* **blame·wor·thi·er, blame·wor·thi·est** Deserving blame: *All of us were blameworthy for leaving such a mess in the kitchen.* **—blame′wor′thi·ness** *n.*

Blanc (blăngk *or* bläɴ), **Mont** The highest peak of the Alps, rising to 15,771 feet (4,807 meters) in southeast France on the Italian border.

blanch (blănch) *v.* **blanched, blanch·ing, blanch·es** *—tr.* **1.** To make lighter in color; bleach or whiten. **2.** To place (almonds or tomatoes, for example) briefly in boiling water in order to remove the skins more easily. **3.** To scald (vegetables) by plunging into boiling water, as before freezing. **4.** To cause to become pale: *Fear blanched the startled child's face.* *—intr.* To turn pale: *They blanched at the awful news.* [From Middle English *blaunchen*, from Old French *blanc*, white.]

bland (blănd) *adj.* **bland·er, bland·est 1.** Pleasant or soothing in manner; gentle: *a bland smile.* **2.** Having a moderate, soft, or soothing quality; not irritating or stimulating: *a bland climate; a bland diet.* **3.** Having little or no distinctive flavor: *bland cooking.* **4.** Lacking distinctive character; dull; flat: *a bland speech.* **—bland′ly** *adj.* **—bland′ness** *n.*

blan·dish (**blăn′**dĭsh) *tr.v.* **blan·dished, blan·dish·ing, blan·dish·es** To coax by flattery or wheedling; cajole.

blan·dish·ment (**blăn′**dĭsh-mənt) *n.* often **blandishments** A word or act meant to coax or flatter: *The diplomat used a variety of blandishments to bring the two sides together.*

blank (blăngk) *adj.* **blank·er, blank·est 1.** Free of marks or writing: *a blank wall; a blank piece of paper.* **2.** Containing no information: *a blank tape.* See Synonyms at **empty. 3.** Having empty spaces to be filled in: *Fill in this blank application.* **4.** Showing no expression or interest: *a blank stare.* **5.** Lacking thought or attention: *a blank mind.* ❖ *n.* **1a.** An empty space on a document to be filled in with an answer or comment. **b.** A document or form with empty spaces to be filled in: *a pad of order blanks.* **2.** An empty space or place; a void: *My mind was a complete blank on the subject.* **3.** A gun cartridge having a charge of powder but no bullet. ❖ *v.* **blanked, blank·ing, blanks** *—tr.* To prevent (an opponent) from scoring in a game: *Our team blanked theirs 4–0.* *—intr.* To fail to find or remember something: *I blanked when I tried to remember her name.* [From Middle English *blaunk*, white, from Old French *blanc*.] **—blank′ly** *adv.* **—blank′ness** *n.*

blan·ket (**blăng′**kĭt) *n.* **1.** A large piece of cloth or other woven material used as a covering for warmth. **2.** A layer that covers: *a blanket of snow.* ❖ *adj.* Covering a wide range of topics, conditions, or requirements: *They gave the proposals a blanket approval.* ❖ *tr.v.* **blan·ket·ed, blan·ket·ing, blan·kets** To cover with or as if with a blanket: *Snow blanketed the countryside.* [From Middle English, from Old French *blankete*, an unbleached soft cloth, from *blanc*, white.]

blank verse *n.* Verse written in unrhymed lines, usually of iambic pentameter.

blare (blâr) *v.* **blared, blar·ing, blares** *—intr.* To sound loudly and stridently: *horns blaring in the traffic jam.* *—tr.* To cause to sound loudly and stridently: *A brass band blared the national anthem.* ❖ *n.* A loud strident noise: *the blare of a radio from the open window.*

blar·ney (**blär′**nē) *n.* Smooth flattering talk.

Blarney Stone A famous stone located in the ruins of Blarney Castle, Ireland, supposed to impart great powers of eloquence and persuasion to anyone who kisses it.

bla·sé (blä-**zā′**) *adj.* Uninterested or unexcited because of constant exposure or indulgence: *People who live on the coast tend to be blasé about the ocean.* [From past participle of French *blaser*, to cloy, from French dialectal, to be chronically hung over.]

blas·pheme (blăs-**fēm′** *or* **blăs′**fēm′) *v.* **blas·phemed, blas·phem·ing, blas·phemes** *—tr.* To speak of (God or something sacred) in a disrespectful way. *—intr.* To speak blasphemy. **—blas·phem′er** *n.*

blas·phe·mous (**blăs′**fə-məs) *adj.* Committing or containing blasphemy: *a blasphemous critic; a blasphemous speech.* **—blas′phe·mous·ly** *adv.*

blas·phe·my (**blăs′**fə-mē) *n., pl.* **blas·phe·mies** The act of saying or doing something that is disrespectful of God or of something considered sacred.

blast (blăst) *n.* **1a.** An explosion: *a blast of dynamite.* **b.** The force of an explosion: *The blast of the explosion blew out the windows.* **2.** A strong gust of wind or air. **3.** A strong stream of air, gas, or steam from an opening. **4.** A loud sudden sound, especially one produced by forced air: *the blast of the steam whistle.* **5.** *Slang* A very exciting or pleasurable experience or event: *We had a blast at the amusement park. Summer camp was a blast.* ❖ *v.* **blast·ed, blast·ing, blasts** *—tr.* **1a.** To knock down or tear apart with an explosive: *blasting rocks in a quarry.* **b.** To make or open by an explosion: *blast a road through the mountain.* **2.** To destroy or shatter: *Defeat blasted our hopes.* **3.** To cause to shrivel or wither before flowering or bearing fruit or seeds: *A severe drought blasted the crops.* **4.** To cause to sound loudly; blare: *Buglers blasted their horns. The radio blasted music out the window.* **5.** To criticize severely: *The reviewer blasted the movie.* *—intr.* **1.** To emit a loud unpleasant sound: *Car horns blasted from the street below.* **2.** To criticize or attack: *The paper blasted away at the corrupt city government.* ◆ **blast off** To take off, as a rocket. **full blast** At full speed, volume, or capacity: *turned the radio up full blast.*

ă	pat	ôr	core
ā	pay	oi	boy
âr	care	ou	out
ä	father	ŏŏ	took
ĕ	pet	ŏŏr	lure
ē	be	ōō	boot
ĭ	pit	ŭ	cut
ī	bite	ûr	urge
îr	pier	th	thin
ŏ	pot	*th*	this
ō	toe	zh	vision
ô	paw	ə	about

blast furnace *n.* A furnace in which combustion is made more intense by a forced stream of air.

blast·off also **blast-off** (**blăst′**ôf′) *n.* The launching of a rocket or spacecraft.

blas·tu·la (**blăs′**chə-lə) *n., pl.* **blas·tu·las** or **blas·tu·lae** (**blăs′**chə-lē′) An embryo at the stage immediately following the division of the fertilized egg cell, consisting of a ball-shaped layer of cells around a fluid-filled cavity. [From Greek *blastos*, bud.]

bla·tant (**blāt′**nt) *adj.* Done with no attempt to disguise or hide wrongdoing; so obvious or shameless as to be offensive: *a blatant lie; a blatant attempt to rig the election.* **—bla′tan·cy** (**blāt′**n-sē) *n.* **—bla′tant·ly** *adv.*

blath·er (**blăth′**ər) *intr.v.* **blath·ered, blath·er·ing, blath·ers** To talk too much in a boring or nonsensical manner; babble. ❖ *n.* Nonsense; drivel.

blaze¹ (blāz) *n.* **1a.** A brightly burning fire: *make a blaze out of a pile of twigs.* **b.** A destructive fire: *A blaze destroyed the building.* **2.** A bright or steady glare: *the blaze of the sun.* **3.** A brilliant or striking display: *The flowers were a blaze of color.* **4.** A sudden outburst, as of activity or emotion: *in a blaze of speed; a blaze of anger.* ❖ *intr.v.* **blazed, blaz·ing, blaz·es 1.** To burn brightly: *a fire blazing in the fireplace.* **2.** To shine brightly: *The hot noonday sun blazed down on the beach.* **3.** To be resplendent: *The garden blazed with colorful flowers.* **4.** To flare up suddenly: *My temper blazed at the insulting remark.* [From Old English *blæse.*]

blaze² (blāz) *n.* **1.** A white or light-colored spot on the face of an animal, such as a horse. **2.** A mark to indicate a trail, usually painted on or cut into a tree. ❖ *tr.v.* **blazed, blaz·ing, blaz·es 1.** To indicate (a trail) by marking trees. **2.** To prepare or lead (the way in an endeavor): *blazed the way in space exploration.*

blaze³ (blāz) *tr.v.* **blazed, blaz·ing, blaz·es** To make known publicly; proclaim. [From Middle English *blasen*, from Middle Dutch *blāsen*, to blow up, swell.]

blaz·er (**blā′**zər) *n.* A lightweight sports coat having pockets and a notched lapel.

blaz·ing (**blā′**zĭng) *adj.* **1.** Flaming: *a blazing fire.* **2.** Shining; glaring: *the blazing sun.*

bla·zon (**blā′**zən) *tr.v.* **bla·zoned, bla·zon·ing, bla·zons 1.** To decorate (a flag, for example) with a coat of arms. **2.** To decorate brightly; emblazon: *Stars blazoned the night sky.* **3.** To announce; proclaim: *Demonstrators marched with signs blazoning their protest.* ❖ *n.* A coat of arms.

bldg. *abbr.* An abbreviation of building.

bleach (blēch) *v.* **bleached, bleach·ing, bleach·es** *—tr.* **1.** To remove the color from (fibers or fabrics, for example) by means of sunlight or chemicals; whiten: *bleach a shirt in the wash; old jeans bleached by the sun.* **2.** To lighten the color of (hair). *—intr.* To turn white or lose color: *boards bleaching in the desert sun.* ❖ *n.* A chemical agent used for bleaching. [From Old English *blǣcan.*]

bleach·ers (**blē′**chərz) *pl.n.* Tiers of wooden planks or pieces of flat metal used as seating by spectators at a public event, especially a sports contest.

bleach·ing powder (**blē′**chĭng) *n.* A white powder made by treating slaked lime with chlorine and used as a bleach and disinfectant.

bleak (blēk) *adj.* **bleak·er, bleak·est 1.** Gloomy; dreary; depressing: *The prospects for success are bleak.* **2.** Cold and harsh: *a damp bleak wind.* **3.** Exposed to the elements; barren and windswept: *bleak treeless moors.* [From Middle English *bleik*, pale, from Old Norse *bleikr*, white.] **—bleak′ly** *adv.* **—bleak′ness** *n.*

blear (blîr) *tr.v.* **bleared, blear·ing, blears 1.** To blur or redden (the eyes), as with tears. **2.** To blur; dim: *Mist rising from the lake bleared our vision.*

blear·y (**blîr′**ē) *adj.* **blear·i·er, blear·i·est 1.** Blurred by or as if by tears: *bleary eyes.* **2.** Vague or indistinct; blurred: *a bleary photograph.* **—blear′i·ness** *n.*

bleat (blēt) *n.* The characteristic cry of a goat or sheep. ❖ *intr.v.* **bleat·ed, bleat·ing, bleats** To utter the cry of a goat or sheep.

bleed (blēd) *v.* **bled** (blĕd), **bleed·ing, bleeds** *—intr.* **1.** To lose blood: *My finger bled when I cut it on the glass.* **2.** To feel sympathetic grief: *My heart bleeds for you in your sorrow.* **3.** To lose sap or other fluid, as a plant does that has been cut. **4.** To be lost or depleted gradually: *Their savings were bleeding away during the recession.* **5.** To become mixed and run, as dye in wet cloth: *When I washed my new jeans, the dye bled and ruined a white shirt.* **6.** To show through a layer of paint as a stain in wood. *—tr.* **1a.** To take or remove blood from: *Long ago, doctors bled patients as a cure.* **b.** To remove sap or juice from (a plant). **2a.** To draw off (a liquid or gas) from a container or pipe: *bleed air from tires that are overly inflated.* **b.** To draw liquid or gas from; drain: *bleed radiators to stop them from knocking.* **3.** To drain of a valuable resource: *Runaway inflation is bleeding the economy.*

bleed·ing heart (**blē′**dĭng) *n.* Any of various garden plants having nodding pink, red, or white heart-shaped flowers.

bleep (blēp) *n.* A brief high-pitched sound, as from an electronic device. ❖ *v. —intr.* **bleeped, bleep·ing, bleeps** To make a bleep. *—tr.* To remove (spoken material) from a broadcast or recording, especially by replacing with a bleep: *The vulgar words were bleeped out of the recording.*

blem·ish (**blĕm′**ĭsh) *tr.v.* **blem·ished, blem·ish·ing, blem·ish·es** To impair or mar by a flaw; disfigure: *Scratches blemished the table.* ❖ *n.* Something that impairs or mars; a flaw: *skin blemishes; a blemish on one's reputation.*

blench (blĕnch) *intr.v.* **blenched, blench·ing, blench·es** To draw back or shy away, as from fear; flinch.

blend (blĕnd) *v.* **blend·ed, blend·ing, blends** *—tr.* **1.** To combine so that the parts are not distinct; mix thoroughly: *The cook blended milk and flour.* **2.** To combine (varieties or grades of something) to make a mixture with unique qualities: *We blended the two coffees.* **3.** To combine (different elements) into a single entity: *a college program that blends economics and liberal arts.* *—intr.* **1.** To form a mixture; be combined: *Oil does not blend with water.* **2.** To become merged into one; unite: *The blue blends into the green in this painting.* **3.** To be in harmony; go together: *Your tie blends with your jacket.* ❖ *n.* **1.** Something blended; a harmonious mixture or combination: *a blend of colors; a blend of teas.* **2.** A word produced by combining parts of other words, as *smog* from *smoke* and *fog.* [From Middle English *blenden*, probably from Old Norse *blanda.*]

blend·er (**blĕn′**dər) *n.* An electrical appliance with whirling blades, used to blend or purée foods.

bless (blĕs) *tr.v.* **blessed** or **blest** (blĕst), **bless·ing, bless·es 1.** To make holy; consecrate: *The minister blessed the water for baptism.* **2.** To call divine favor upon. **3.** To make the sign of the cross over: *The priest blessed the congregation.* **4.** To praise as holy; glorify: *Bless the Lord.* **5.** To endow, favor, or enrich: *The artist was blessed with unusual talent.* [From Old English *blētsian*, to consecrate.]

bless·ed (**blĕs′**ĭd) also **blest** (blĕst) *adj.* **1.** Worthy of worship; holy. **2.** Enjoying happiness; very fortunate: *I feel blessed.* **3.** Bringing happiness; pleasurable: *A new baby in a family is a blessed event.* **—bless′ed·ly** *adv.* **—bless′ed·ness** *n.*

bless·ing (**blĕs′**ĭng) *n.* **1.** A prayer calling for divine favor. **2.** A short prayer given at mealtime; grace. **3.** often **blessings** Something that brings happiness or well-being: *the blessings of liberty.* **4.** Approval; sanction:

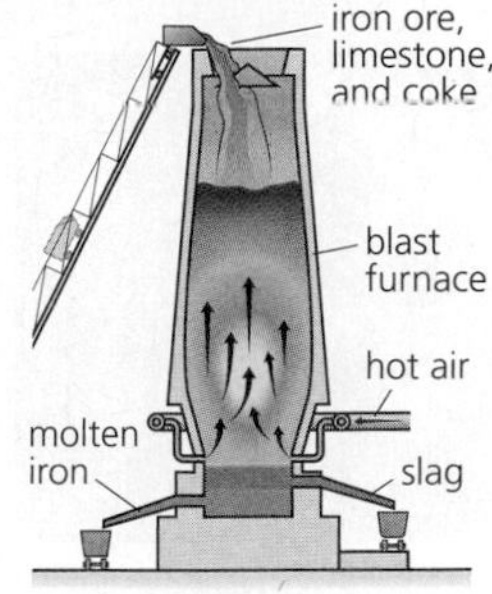

blast furnace

blaze²
painted trail marker on a tree

bleeding heart

blight
tomato blight

blinders

The expedition to explore the Northwest had the government's blessing.

blest (blĕst) *v.* A past tense and a past participle of **bless**. ❖ *adj.* Variant of **blessed**.

blew¹ (blo͞o) *v.* Past tense of **blow¹**.
❑ *These sound alike:* **blew¹** (expelled air), **blew²** (bloomed), **blue** (color).

blew² (blo͞o) *v.* Past tense of **blow³**.
❑ *These sound alike:* **blew²** (bloomed), **blew¹** (expelled air), **blue** (color).

blight (blīt) *n.* **1.** Any of numerous plant diseases that cause leaves, stems, or fruits to wither and die. **2.** The organism, such as a bacterium, fungus, water mold, or virus, that causes such a disease. **3.** Something that is harmful, destructive, or unattractive: *That abandoned house is a blight on the neighborhood.* ❖ *tr.v.* **blight·ed, blight·ing, blights** To ruin, damage, or destroy: *Several losses blighted the team's hopes of becoming county champions.*

blimp (blĭmp) *n.* An airship that does not have a rigid framework.

blind (blīnd) *adj.* **blind·er, blind·est 1a.** Lacking the sense of sight; sightless. **b.** Having a visual acuity of one-tenth normal vision or less while wearing corrective lenses. **2.** Performed by instruments and without the use of sight: *blind navigation.* **3.** Unwilling or unable to perceive or understand: *Many people are blind to their own faults.* **4.** Not based on reason or evidence: *blind faith.* **5.** Immoderate or unrestrained: *blind rage.* **6.** Performed without access to information that might prejudice the results: *a blind taste test in which participants were not told which brands they were sampling.* **7.** Performed without preparation or knowledge: *a blind attempt to fix the washing machine.* **8.** Hidden or screened from sight: *a blind driveway.* **9.** Closed at one end: *a blind alley.* ❖ *n.* **1.** *(used with a plural verb)* People who are sightless or have very little ability to see: *an organization that makes recorded books for the blind.* **2.** Something that shuts out light or hinders vision: *We pull the blinds over the windows at night.* **3.** A shelter for concealing hunters, photographers, or observers of wildlife. **4.** Something that conceals the true nature of an activity, especially of an illegal or improper one; a subterfuge: *The spies used the restaurant as a blind for their operations.* ❖ *adv.* Without being able to see: *The pilot had to fly blind in the fog.* ❖ *tr.v.* **blind·ed, blind·ing, blinds 1.** To deprive of sight: *Lights from the oncoming cars blinded me.* **2.** To deprive (a person) of judgment or reason: *Prejudice blinds them to the advantages of the plan.* **—blind′ly** *adv.* **—blind′ness** *n.*

blind date *n.* A date between two people who have not previously met.

blind·ers (blīn′dərz) *pl.n.* A pair of leather flaps attached to a horse's bridle to prevent it from seeing things on either side.

blind·fold (blīnd′fōld′) *tr.v.* **blind·fold·ed, blind·fold·ing, blind·folds** To cover the eyes of with a strip of cloth or other material: *blindfold a prisoner.* ❖ *n.* A strip of cloth put over the eyes and tied around the head to keep someone from seeing. **—blind′fold′ed** *adj.*

blind·man's bluff or **blind·man's buff** (blīnd′mănz′) *n.* A game in which a blindfolded person tries to catch and identify one of the other players.

blind spot *n.* **1.** The point on the retina, not sensitive to light, where the optic nerve leaves the eyeball. **2.** An area that one cannot see because of an obstruction or because of insufficient range of view: *the blind spot along the side of the car, which does not appear in the driver's mirror.* **3.** An area where radio or television reception is poor. **4.** An area about which a person is noticeably unaware or prejudiced: *He has a blind spot where his children are concerned—he thinks they can do no wrong.*

blink (blĭngk) *v.* **blinked, blink·ing, blinks** *—intr.* **1.** To close and open the eye or eyes rapidly: *blink at the bright light.* **2.** To flash off and on: *holiday lights blinking in the window.* *—tr.* **1.** To close and open (the eye or eyes) rapidly; wink: *The cat blinked its eyes in the bright light.* **2.** To make flash off and on: *blink the lights of a car.* ❖ *n.* A very quick closing and opening of the eye or eyes. ◆ **on the blink** Out of working order.

blink·er (blĭng′kər) *n.* **1.** A light that blinks as a means of sending a message or warning. **2. blinkers** Blinders.

blintz (blĭnts) *n.* A thin rolled pancake with a filling such as cream cheese or fruit. [From Yiddish *blintse,* of Russian origin.]

blip (blĭp) *n.* **1.** A spot of light on a radar or sonar screen indicating the position of a detected object, such as an aircraft. **2.** A high-pitched electronic sound; a bleep. **3.** A temporary, sharp increase or decrease: *a blip in stock prices.*

bliss (blĭs) *n.* Extreme happiness; joy.

bliss·ful (blĭs′fəl) *adj.* Full of or causing bliss: *a blissful afternoon at the beach; blissful ignorance of the problem.* **—bliss′ful·ly** *adv.* **—bliss′ful·ness** *n.*

blis·ter (blĭs′tər) *n.* **1.** A thin fluid-filled sac that forms on the skin as a result of a burn or irritation. **2.** A raised bubble, as on a painted surface. ❖ *intr. & tr.v.* **blis·tered, blis·ter·ing, blis·ters** To form or cause to form blisters: *Her skin blistered from poison ivy. Tight shoes blistered the hiker's feet.* [From Middle English, probably from Old French *blestre,* of Germanic origin.] **—blis′ter·y** *adj.*

blis·ter·ing (blĭs′tər-ĭng) *adj.* **1.** Extremely hot: *a blistering summer sun.* **2.** Very strong; intense: *blistering criticism.* **3.** Extremely rapid: *a blistering pace.*

blithe (blīth *or* blīth) *adj.* **blith·er, blith·est 1.** Carefree and lighthearted: *the blithe atmosphere of the birthday party.* **2.** Showing a lack of concern: *a blithe disregard of danger.* **—blithe′ly** *adv.* **—blithe′ness** *n.*

blithe·some (blīth′səm *or* blīth′səm) *adj.* Cheerful; merry; lighthearted. **—blithe′some·ly** *adv.* **—blithe′some·ness** *n.*

blitz (blĭts) *n.* **1.** A blitzkrieg. **2.** An intense campaign: *an advertising blitz.* **3.** In football, a charge upon the quarterback by one or more of the linebackers or defensive backs after the ball is snapped. ❖ *v.* **blitzed, blitz·ing, blitz·es** *—tr.* **1.** To subject to a blitz. **2.** In football, to run toward (the quarterback) in a blitz. *—intr.* In football, to carry out a blitz. [Short for *blitzkrieg.*]

blitz·krieg (blĭts′krēg′) *n.* A swift, sudden military attack, usually by air and land forces. [From German : *Blitz,* lightning + *Krieg,* war.]

bliz·zard (blĭz′ərd) *n.* **1.** A very heavy snowstorm with strong winds. **2.** A great number or an unusually heavy flow: *a blizzard of phone calls congratulating the winning candidate.*

bloat (blōt) *intr. & tr.v.* **bloat·ed, bloat·ing, bloats** To swell or cause to swell or puff up, as with liquid or gas: *a stomach bloated by overeating.* [From Middle English *blot, blout,* soft, puffed, from Old Norse *blautr,* soft, soaked.]

blob (blŏb) *n.* A soft formless mass: *a blob of wax fell from the burning candle.*

bloc (blŏk) *n.* A group of nations, parties, or people united by common interests or political aims: *representatives forming the farm bloc in Congress.* [From Old French *bloc,* block.]
❑ *These sound alike:* **bloc, block** (flat-sided object).

block (blŏk) *n.* **1.** A solid piece of wood or another hard substance having one or more flat sides: *Blocks of marble form the front of that building.* **2.** One of a set of small wooden or plastic pieces, such as a cube or bar, used as a building toy. **3.** Such a piece on which chopping or cutting is done: *a butcher's block.* **4.** A stand from which articles are displayed at an auction. **5.** A mold or form

ă	pat	ôr	core
ā	pay	oi	boy
âr	care	ou	out
ä	father	o͝o	took
ĕ	pet	o͝or	lure
ē	be	o͞o	boot
ĭ	pit	ŭ	cut
ī	bite	ûr	urge
îr	pier	th	thin
ŏ	pot	*th*	this
ō	toe	zh	vision
ô	paw	ə	about

upon which something is shaped or displayed: *a hat block.* **6.** A pulley or set of pulleys set in a casing. **7.** The metal casing that contains the cylinders of an engine. **8.** A set of like items sold or handled as a unit: *a block of tickets in the balcony.* **9a.** An obstacle or hindrance: *Road work caused a block in traffic.* **b.** In medicine, an obstruction of a bodily function: *an intestinal block.* **10a.** A usually rectangular section of a city or town enclosed by connecting streets: *Walk the dog around the block.* **b.** The part of a street that lies between two successive cross streets: *Our home is in the middle of the block.* **11.** A large building divided into separate units, such as apartments. **12.** In sports, an act of obstructing an opponent, especially in football a legal act of using one's body to obstruct an opponent and thus protect the teammate who has the ball. ❖ *v.* **blocked, block·ing, blocks** —*tr.* **1a.** To stop the movement or progress of: *Road work was blocking traffic. The opposing members blocked every attempt at reform.* **b.** To stop movement through: *The stalled car blocked the intersection.* **2.** To be in the way of; obstruct visually: *You're blocking my view.* **3.** In medicine, to obstruct the functioning of (a nerve, for example). **4.** To shape or form with or on a block: *block a sweater after washing it.* **5.** In sports, to stop or hinder the movement of (an opponent or the ball) by physical interference. **6.** To indicate in a general way; sketch: *block out a plan of action.* —*intr.* In sports, to interfere with the movement of an opponent. [From Middle English *blok,* from Old French *bloc,* from Middle Dutch.]

❑ *These sound alike:* **block, bloc** (group).

block·ade (blŏ-kād′) *n.* **1.** The closing off of a city, harbor, or country by troops or warships in order to prevent people and supplies from going in and out. **2.** The forces used in a blockade. **3.** Something that closes off or obstructs; an obstacle. ❖ *tr.v.* **block·ad·ed, block·ad·ing, block·ades** To set up a blockade against. —**block·ad′er** *n.*

block·ade-run·ner (blŏ-kād′rŭn′ər) *n.* A ship or person that attempts to go through or past an enemy blockade.

block·age (blŏk′ĭj) *n.* **1.** The act of obstructing. **2.** An obstruction: *an intestinal blockage.*

block and tackle *n.* An arrangement of pulleys and ropes used for lifting heavy objects.

block·bust·er (blŏk′bŭs′tər) *n.* **1.** Something, such as a movie or book, that is very popular or sells in large numbers. **2.** A large bomb capable of great destruction.

block·head (blŏk′hĕd′) *n.* A stupid person; a dolt.

block·house (blŏk′hous′) *n.* **1.** A fort made of heavy timbers, with a projecting upper story and loopholes for firing. **2.** A fortification made of concrete with slits for firing or observation. **3.** A heavily reinforced building from which the launching of rockets or space vehicles is observed and controlled.

blog (blŏg) *n.* A website that displays postings by one or more individuals in the order they were written and usually has links to comments on specific postings. ❖ *intr.v.* **blogged, blog·ging, blogs** ❖ To write entries in, add material to, or maintain a blog. —**blog′ger** *n.*

bloke (blōk) *n. Chiefly British Slang* A fellow; a man.

blond also **blonde** (blŏnd) *adj.* **blond·er, blond·est** **1.** Having fair hair and skin: *a blond baby.* **2.** Having a pale yellow or golden color: *blond hair.* **3.** Light-colored: *blond furniture.* ❖ *n.* A blond person. [From Middle English *blounde,* from Old French *blonde,* of Germanic origin.] —**blond′ness** *n.*

blood (blŭd) *n.* **1a.** The red fluid that is circulated through the body of vertebrate animals by the action of the heart, distributing oxygen, nutrients, and hormones to the tissues and carrying away wastes. **b.** A similar fluid in invertebrate animals. **2.** Temperament or disposition: *a person of hot blood and a fiery temper.* **3.** Descent from a particular ancestor or ancestors; parental lineage: *Does the prince's wife have any royal blood?* ◆ **in cold blood** Deliberately, coldly, and dispassionately: *The judge was murdered in cold blood.* [From Old English *blōd.*]

blood bank *n.* **1.** A place where blood or blood plasma is classified according to blood type for use in transfusions. **2.** Blood or blood plasma stored in such a place.

blood·bath (blŭd′băth′) *n.* Savage and widespread killing; a massacre.

blood cell *n.* Any of the cells contained in blood; a red blood cell or white blood cell.

blood clot *n.* A mass of coagulated blood that consists of red blood cells, white blood cells, platelets, and fibrin. —**blood clotting** *n.*

blood count *n.* A count of the number of red and white blood cells and platelets in a sample of a person's blood.

blood·cur·dling (blŭd′kûrd′lĭng) *adj.* Causing great horror; terrifying.

blood·ed (blŭd′ĭd) *adj.* **1.** Having blood or a temperament of a specified kind: *a cold-blooded reptile; a hot-blooded delinquent.* **2.** Thoroughbred: *blooded racehorses.*

blood group *n.* A blood type.

blood·hound (blŭd′hound′) *n.* A hound of a breed having a smooth coat, drooping ears, loose folds of skin around the face, and a keen sense of smell.

blood·less (blŭd′lĭs) *adj.* **1.** Having no blood. **2.** Pale and anemic in color: *cold and bloodless hands.* **3.** Accomplished without killing: *a bloodless revolution.* **4.** Lacking spirit: *a dull bloodless tale.* —**blood′less·ly** *adv.* —**blood′less·ness** *n.*

blood·line (blŭd′līn′) *n.* A direct line of descent.

blood·mo·bile (blŭd′mə-bēl′) *n.* A motor vehicle equipped for collecting blood from donors.

blood orange *n.* A sweet orange having pulp that is red or streaked with red.

blood plasma *n.* The yellowish, liquid part of the blood, composed mainly of water and proteins, in which the blood cells are suspended.

blood poisoning *n.* A disease caused by microorganisms or their toxins in the blood; septicemia.

blood pressure *n.* The pressure that the blood exerts on the walls of the arteries or other blood vessels. Blood pressure varies with the strength of the heartbeat, the volume of the blood, the elasticity of the arteries, and the person's health, age, and physical condition.

blood·root (blŭd′ro͞ot′ *or* blŭd′ro͝ot′) *n.* A woodland plant of eastern North America having a fleshy root with poisonous red sap, a single lobed leaf, and a single white flower.

blood sausage *n.* A sausage made of pig's blood, diced pork fat, and other ingredients.

blood·shed (blŭd′shĕd′) *n.* The shedding of blood, especially the injuring or killing of people.

blood·shot (blŭd′shŏt′) *adj.* Inflamed and overfilled with blood, often with the small blood vessels enlarged: *bloodshot eyes.*

blood·stained (blŭd′stānd′) *adj.* Stained or spotted with blood: *a bloodstained handkerchief.*

blood·stone (blŭd′stōn′) *n.* A deep-green, cloudy form of quartz that is flecked with red. It is used as a gem.

blood·stream (blŭd′strēm′) *n.* The blood as it flows through the circulatory system.

blood·suck·er (blŭd′sŭk′ər) *n.* An animal, such as a leech, that sucks blood.

blood test *n.* An examination of a sample of blood to determine its contents, as for ascertaining the blood group or diagnosing illness.

blood·thirst·y (blŭd′thûr′stē) *adj.* Eager to cause or see the shedding of blood; cruel. —**blood′thirst′i·ly** *adv.* —**blood′thirst′i·ness** *n.*

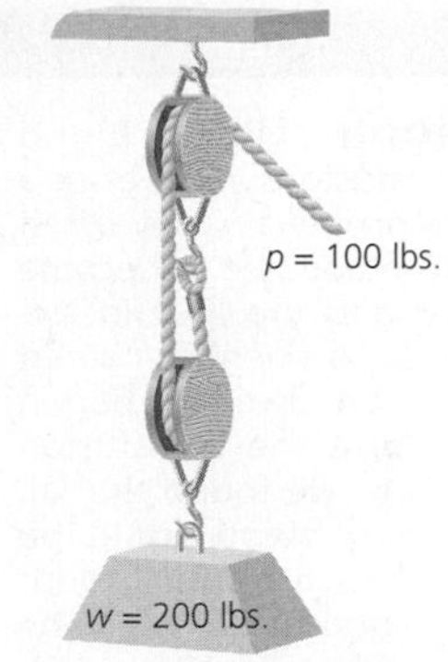

block and tackle

Half the pull *(p)* is required to lift the weight *(w)* with this block and tackle unit.

SCIENCE

blood type Blood transfusions were once a big problem—they often caused people to become sick and die. But in the 1890s, a scientist named Karl Landsteiner began to solve the transfusion puzzle. He found that all human blood could be divided into four groups or **blood types,** which he named A, B, AB, and O. The letters A and B refer to substances, called *antigens*, that are found on the surface of red blood cells. If a person receives a transfusion of blood of the wrong type, the person's antibodies bind to the antigens on the mismatched red blood cells, causing clumping of the cells. So the key to the puzzle is to give a person blood that matches his or her blood type. Blood of type O can be given to anyone because its red blood cells have no antigens on the surface.

bloomers

ă	pat	ôr	core
ā	pay	oi	boy
âr	care	ou	out
ä	father	o͝o	took
ĕ	pet	o͝or	lure
ē	be	o͞o	boot
ĭ	pit	ŭ	cut
ī	bite	ûr	urge
îr	pier	th	thin
ŏ	pot	*th*	this
ō	toe	zh	vision
ô	paw	ə	about

blood type *n.* Any of the four main types, A, B, AB, and O, into which human blood is divided on the basis of the presence or absence of certain proteins and antibodies; blood group. —SEE NOTE.

blood vessel *n.* An elastic tubular structure in the body through which blood circulates; an artery, vein, or capillary.

blood·y (blŭd′ē) *adj.* **blood·i·er, blood·i·est 1.** Bleeding: *a bloody nose.* **2.** Stained with blood: *bloody bandages.* **3.** Causing or marked by bloodshed: *a bloody fight.* **4.** Bloodthirsty; cruel. ❖ *adv. Chiefly British Slang* Used as an intensive: *You're bloody right.* ❖ *tr.v.* **blood·ied, blood·y·ing, blood·ies** To make bloody: *My elbow was bloodied in the fall.* **—blood′i·ly** *adv.* **—blood′i·ness** *n.*

bloom (blo͞om) *n.* **1.** The flower or blossom of a plant. **2.** The condition or time of flowering: *a rosebush in bloom.* **3.** A condition or time of great development, vigor, or beauty: *a boy in the full bloom of youth.* **4.** A fresh rosy complexion: *a fine bloom to the cheeks.* **5.** A waxy or powdery coating sometimes occurring on fruits, leaves, or stems: *the bloom on a plum.* ❖ *intr.v.* **bloomed, bloom·ing, blooms 1.** To bear flowers; blossom: *Tulips bloom in the spring.* **2.** To grow or flourish: *Volunteer groups to teach reading are blooming.* **3.** To show in a healthy or vigorous way; glow: *Joy bloomed in her face.* [From Middle English *blom*, from Old Norse *blōm*.]

bloom·ers (blo͞o′mərz) *pl.n.* **1.** Baggy pants gathered at the knee, once worn by women and girls for sports, such as riding bicycles. **2.** Similar pants worn as underwear. [After Amelia Jenks *Bloomer* (1818–1894), American social reformer.]

bloom·ing (blo͞o′mĭng) *adv. & adj. Chiefly British Slang* Used as an intensive: *a blooming hot day; a blooming idiot.*

bloop·er (blo͞o′pər) *n.* **1.** A clumsy mistake, especially one made in public. **2.** In baseball, a weakly hit ball that carries just past the infield.

blos·som (blŏs′əm) *n.* **1.** A flower or cluster of flowers: *apple blossoms.* **2.** The condition or time of flowering: *spring flowers in blossom.* ❖ *intr.v.* **blos·somed, blos·som·ing, blos·soms 1.** To come into flower; bloom. **2.** To develop and do well; flourish: *The public's interest in science blossomed with space flight.* [From Old English *blōstm*.]

blot (blŏt) *n.* **1.** A stain or spot: *an ink blot.* **2.** A stain on one's character or reputation; a disgrace. ❖ *v.* **blot·ted, blot·ting, blots** *—tr.* **1.** To spot or stain: *Greasy fingerprints blotted the page.* **2.** To dry or soak up with absorbent material: *blot a spill with paper towels.* *—intr.* **1.** To spill or spread in a spot or stain. **2.** To become blotted or absorbed: *Watercolors blot easily.* ◆ **blot out 1.** To hide from view; obscure: *Storm clouds blotted out the sun.* **2.** To destroy completely; annihilate: *The frost blotted out the tomatoes.* [From Middle English.]

blotch (blŏch) *n.* **1.** A spot or blot; a splotch. **2.** A discoloration on the skin; a blemish. ❖ *tr. & intr.v.* **blotched, blotch·ing, blotch·es** To mark or become marked with blotches. **—blotch′y** *adj.*

blot·ter (blŏt′ər) *n.* **1.** A piece or pad of thick absorbent paper used to soak up excess ink from a surface that has been written on. **2.** A book containing daily records of occurrences or transactions: *A blotter kept at a police station records the arrests made.*

blouse (blous *or* blouz) *n.* **1.** A woman's or child's loosely fitting shirt that extends to the waist. **2.** A loose garment resembling a smock, worn by some workmen and peasants in Europe. **3.** The jacket of a military uniform.

blow[1] (blō) *v.* **blew** (blo͞o), **blown** (blōn), **blow·ing, blows** *—intr.* **1.** To be in motion. Used of the air or of wind: *The wind blew hard all night.* **2.** To be moved by a current of air: *My hat blew off.* **3.** To send out a current of air: *Blow on your soup to cool it.* **4.** To spout water and air from the blowhole, as a whale does. **5.** To sound: *The whistle blows at noon.* **6.** To burst suddenly: *The tire blew when we hit a rock.* **7a.** To fail or break down: *The furnace blew.* **b.** To burn out or melt: *We were left in darkness when the fuse blew.* **8.** *Informal* To move very fast in relation to something: *She blew by me on the final lap of the race.* *—tr.* **1.** To cause to move by a current of air: *The gale blew a tree across the power lines.* **2.** To expel (air) from the mouth. **3a.** To cause (a wind instrument) to sound by forcing breath through it: *blow a trumpet.* **b.** To sound (a melody): *a bugle blowing taps.* **4.** To cause to explode: *To build the tunnel they blew rock out of the way with dynamite.* **5.** To have or cause air or gas to be expelled suddenly from: *We blew a tire when we hit the curb.* **6.** To clear by forcing air through: *blowing his nose noisily.* **7.** To shape (a pliable material, such as molten glass) by forcing air into it. **8a.** To cause to fail or break down. **b.** To cause (an electrical fuse) to melt and open a circuit. **9.** *Slang* **a.** To spend (money) freely or foolishly: *He blew all his savings on a video game.* **b.** To spoil or lose by inept performance: *We blew a two-goal lead in the third period.* ❖ *n.* **1.** A blast of air or wind. **2.** A storm. **3.** The act or an instance of blowing. ◆ **blow away** *Slang* **1.** To kill by shooting, especially with a firearm. **2.** To defeat decisively. **3.** To affect intensely; overwhelm: *That concert blew me away.* **blow in** *Slang* To arrive, especially when unexpected. **blow off 1.** To relieve or release (pressure); let off. **2.** *Slang* To choose not to attend or accompany: *They blew off the meeting and went for a walk.* **blow off steam** To express pent-up emotion. **blow (one's) top** or **blow (one's) stack** To lose one's temper. **blow out 1.** To extinguish or be extinguished by a gust of air: *blow out the candles.* **2.** To fail, as an electrical apparatus: *The fuse blew out.* **blow over** To subside or pass over with little lasting effect: *The storm will blow over soon.* **blow up 1.** To come into being: *A storm blew up.* **2.** To fill with air; inflate: *blowing up balloons.* **3.** To enlarge (a photograph). **4.** To explode: *The gas tank blew up.* **5.** To lose one's temper. [From Old English *blāwan*.]

blow[2] (blō) *n.* **1.** A sudden hard stroke or hit, as with the fist or a weapon. **2.** A sudden unexpected shock or great misfortune: *The closing of the museum was a blow to our weekend plans.* **3.** A sudden unexpected attack; an assault. [From Middle English *blou*.]

blow[3] (blō) *intr. & tr.v.* **blew** (blo͞o), **blown** (blōn), **blow·ing, blows** To bloom or cause to bloom. [From Old English *blōwan*.]

blow-dry (blō′drī′) *tr.v.* **blow-dried, blow-dry·ing, blow-dries** To dry and often style (hair) with a blow dryer.

blow dryer *n.* A handheld electric blower for drying and styling hair.

blow·er (blō′ər) *n.* A device that produces a flow of air or other gas through a duct or an enclosed space.

blow·fly (blō′flī′) *n.* Any of several flies that deposit their eggs in the bodies of dead animals or in wounds.

blow·gun (blō′gŭn′) *n.* A long narrow pipe through which pellets or poison darts can be blown; a blowpipe.

blow·hole (blō′hōl′) *n.* **1.** An opening or one of a pair of openings for breathing in the top of the head of a whale, porpoise, or dolphin. **2.** A hole in the ice to which sea mammals such as seals and whales come to breathe.

blown[1] (blōn) *v.* Past participle of **blow**[1].

blown[2] (blōn) *v.* Past participle of **blow**[3].

blow·out (blō′out′) *n.* **1.** A sudden and violent loss of air pressure, as from an automobile tire. **2.** A sudden escape of a confined gas or liquid, as from an oil well. **3.** A lopsided victory: *The score was 45 to 0—a real blowout!*

blow·pipe (blō′pīp′) *n.* **1.** A narrow tube for blowing air or gas into a flame to increase its heat, used especially in the identification of minerals. **2.** A long narrow iron pipe used to gather, work, and blow molten glass. **3.** A blowgun.

blow·torch (blō′tôrch′) *n.* A torch in which a pressurized mix of air and gas produces a very hot flame, used for soldering, welding, and glass blowing.

blow·up (blō′ŭp′) *n.* **1.** An explosion. **2.** A photographic enlargement. **3.** An outburst of temper: *The coach had a blowup over the referee's call.* **4.** An angry argument or confrontation: *We avoided a blowup between the administration and the teachers.*

blow·zy also **blow·sy** (blou′zē) *adj.* **blow·zi·er, blow·zi·est** also **blow·si·er, blow·si·est** Not tidy; disheveled; messy: *blowzy hair.*

BLT (bē′ĕl-tē′) *n.* A bacon, lettuce, and tomato sandwich.

blub·ber[1] (blŭb′ər) *v.* **blub·bered, blub·ber·ing, blub·bers** —*intr.* To cry or sob in a noisy manner. See Synonyms at **cry.** —*tr.* To say while crying and sobbing: *The boy blubbered his name.* [From Middle English *bluberen*, to bubble, from *bluber*, foam.] **—blub′ber·er** *n.*

blub·ber[2] (blŭb′ər) *n.* The fat of whales and some other sea animals, lying under the skin and over the muscles, from which oil is obtained. Blubber insulates the animal from heat loss and serves as a food reserve. [From Middle English *blober*, foam.]

bludg·eon (blŭj′ən) *n.* A short heavy club with one end heavier or thicker than the other. ❖ *tr.v.* **bludg·eoned, bludg·eon·ing, bludg·eons** To beat or strike with or as if with a bludgeon.

blue (blo͞o) *n.* **1.** The color of the sky on a clear day. In the spectrum it is between green and indigo. **2.** often **Blue a.** A Union soldier in the US Civil War. **b.** The Union Army. **3a.** The sea. **b.** The sky. ❖ *adj.* **blu·er, blu·est 1.** Of the color blue. **2.** Having a gray or purplish color, as from cold or a bruise: *lips blue from the chill.* **3.** Gloomy; depressed: *a sailor far from home, lonely and blue.* ❖ *tr. & intr.v.* **blued, blu·ing, blues** To make or become blue. ◆ **out of the blue 1.** From an unexpected or unforeseen source: *a problem that came out of the blue.* **2.** At a completely unexpected time: *My friend showed up out of the blue last night.* [From Middle English *bleu*, from Old French, of Germanic origin.] **—blue′ly** *adv.* **—blue′ness** *n.*

❑ *These sound alike:* **blue, blew**[1] (expelled air), **blew**[2] (bloomed).

blue baby *n.* A newborn baby having a bluish tint to its skin because of a heart or lung defect, resulting in too little oxygen in its blood.

blue·bell (blo͞o′bĕl′) also **blue·bells** (blo͞o′bĕlz′) *n.* Any of several plants having bell-shaped, usually blue flowers.

blue·ber·ry (blo͞o′bĕr′ē) *n.* **1.** A round, juicy, edible blue or blue-black berry. **2.** Any of various plants that bear such berries.

blue·bird (blo͞o′bûrd′) *n.* Any of several North American songbirds having blue feathers and usually a rust-colored breast in the male.

blue blood *n.* **1.** Noble or aristocratic descent. **2.** A member of the aristocracy or other high social group.

blue·bon·net (blo͞o′bŏn′ĭt) *n.* Any of several North American plants that have clusters of blue flowers.

blue·bot·tle (blo͞o′bŏt′l) *n.* Any of several large blowflies having a bright metallic-blue body.

blue cheese *n.* A tangy semisoft cheese with greenish-blue mold.

blue-col·lar (blo͞o′kŏl′ər) *adj.* Relating to wage earners whose jobs are performed in work clothes and often involve manual labor.

blue·fish (blo͞o′fĭsh′) *n.* A silvery bluish or greenish ocean fish caught for food or sport.

blue·gill (blo͞o′gĭl′) *n., pl.* **bluegill** or **blue·gills** A sunfish of North American lakes and streams, eaten as food.

blue·grass (blo͞o′grăs′) *n.* **1.** Any of various lawn and pasture grasses often having bluish leaves or flower heads. **2.** A type of country music that originated in the southern United States, typically played on stringed instruments such as banjos and guitars.

blue-green alga (blo͞o′grēn′) *n.* A cyanobacterium.

blue·ing (blo͞o′ĭng) *n.* Variant of **bluing.**

blue·ish (blo͞o′ĭsh) *adj.* Variant of **bluish.**

blue jay *n.* A North American bird having a crested head, blue feathers with white and black markings, and a harsh noisy cry.

blue jeans *pl.n.* Pants of blue denim or similar cloth.

blue law *n.* **1.** A law restricting certain activities, especially shopping, on Sunday. **2.** A law passed in colonial New England to govern personal behavior and particularly to prohibit certain forms of recreation on Sunday.

blue·line or **blue line** (blo͞o′līn′) *n.* Either of two blue lines running across an ice-hockey rink, dividing the rink into defensive, neutral, and offensive zones.

blue·print (blo͞o′prĭnt′) *n.* **1.** A photographic copy of architectural plans or technical drawings, typically appearing as white lines on a blue background. **2.** A carefully worked-out plan: *a blueprint for success.*

blue ribbon *n.* An award made from a blue ribbon, given to a competitor who finishes in first place.

Blue Ridge Mountains also **Blue Ridge** A range of the Appalachian Mountains extending from southern Pennsylvania to northern Georgia. It rises to 6,684 feet (2,038 meters).

blues (blo͞oz) *pl.n. (used with a singular or plural verb)* **1.** A type of popular music that developed from southern African-American songs and usually has a slow tempo, a strong 4/4 rhythm, and flatted third and seventh tones in its scale. **2.** Lowness of spirit; melancholy: *The rainy weather is giving people the blues.*

blue state *n.* A US state in which a majority has voted for the Democratic candidate in a statewide election. [From the fact that states electing Democratic candidates are often blue on maps in the news.]

blu·ets (blo͞o′ĭts) *pl.n. (used with a singular or plural verb)* Any of several low-growing plants of North America having small light-blue flowers with a yellow center.

blue whale *n.* A very large whale having a bluish-gray back and grooves on the throat. It is thought to be the largest animal ever to have lived on earth, reaching a length of up to 100 feet (30.5 meters).

bluff[1] (blŭf) *v.* **bluffed, bluff·ing, bluffs** —*intr.* **1.** To engage in a false display of confidence or aggression in order to deceive or intimidate someone: *The reporter was bluffing when she said she knew the movie star.* **2.** To make a display of aggression, as by charging or baring the teeth, as a means of intimidating another animal. **3.** To try to mislead opponents in a card game by betting a lot on a poor hand or by little or no betting on a good hand. —*tr.* To deceive or mislead by a false display of confidence or aggression: *He bluffed the guard into thinking he worked for the bank.* ❖ *n.* The act or an example of bluffing. ◆ **call (someone's) bluff** To force someone to reveal that he or she is bluffing. [Probably from Dutch *bluffen*, from Low German.] **—bluff′er** *n.*

bluff[2] (blŭf) *n.* A steep headland, cliff, or riverbank. ❖ *adj.* **bluff·er, bluff·est 1.** Gruff or blunt in manner but not unkind: *bluff speech.* **2.** Having a broad steep front: *bluff cliffs along the riverbanks.* [Probably from obsolete Dutch *blaf* or Middle Low German *blaff*, broad.] **—bluff′ly** *adv.* **—bluff′ness** *n.*

blu·ing also **blue·ing** (blo͞o′ĭng) *n.* A blue powder or liquid added to rinse water to prevent white fabrics from turning yellow during laundering.

blu·ish also **blue·ish** (blo͞o′ĭsh) *adj.* Somewhat blue.

blun·der (blŭn′dər) *n.* A foolish or careless mistake: *Using the wrong wax was a serious blunder.* ❖ *intr.v.*

blowpipe

bluebonnet

WRITERS CHOOSE THEIR WORDS

He was growling way down deep and showing his teeth to that squalling monkey. A full minute went by before it dawned on me that I was still in one piece. When I realized this, I began noticing things. Every time the big monkey ran at me he only came a little way, then he would turn and shuffle back. He was **bluffing.**

—Wilson Rawls
Summer of the Monkeys

BIOGRAPHY

Nellie Bly Elizabeth Cochrane Seaman, who wrote under the pen name Nellie **Bly,** was an ambitious and idealistic young newspaper reporter when she agreed to go undercover to write an exposé of conditions at New York City's public mental hospital. By feigning mental illness, Bly had herself admitted to the hospital as a patient, where for ten days she witnessed firsthand the abusive treatment and unsanitary conditions the patients were subjected to. Her written account of this experience in the *New York World* raised a public outcry for reform and made her instantly famous. Two years later, she undertook a record-breaking journey in which she traveled around the world in 72 days by steamship and train, the fastest that anyone had ever performed such a trip.

Nellie Bly

ă	pat	ôr	core
ā	pay	oi	boy
âr	care	ou	out
ä	father	o͝o	took
ĕ	pet	o͝or	lure
ē	be	o͞o	boot
ĭ	pit	ŭ	cut
ī	bite	ûr	urge
îr	pier	th	thin
ŏ	pot	*th*	this
ō	toe	zh	vision
ô	paw	ə	about

blun·dered, blun·der·ing, blun·ders 1. To make a foolish mistake: *We blundered in estimating the cost of the curtains.* **2.** To move clumsily or blindly; stumble: *blunder through the bushes into a stream.*

blun·der·buss (**blŭn′**dər-bŭs′) *n.* A short musket with a wide muzzle for scattering shot at close range. [Alteration of Dutch *donderbus* : *donder*, thunder + *bus*, gun.]

blunt (blŭnt) *adj.* **blunt·er, blunt·est 1.** Having a thick dull edge or end; not sharp. **2.** Abrupt and frank in manner: *a blunt reprimand.* ❖ *tr. & intr.v.* **blunt·ed, blunt·ing, blunts** To make or become less sharp or keen; dull: *The knife was blunted from so much use.* **—blunt′ly** *adv.* **—blunt′ness** *n.*

blur (blûr) *v.* **blurred, blur·ring, blurs** *—tr.* **1.** To make indistinct or hazy in outline; obscure: *Clouds blurred the mountain peak.* **2.** To make dim or unclear; cloud: *Tears blurred my vision.* **3.** To make less distinct to the mind: *a book that blurs the line between fiction and nonfiction.* *—intr.* **1.** To become indistinct, vague, or hazy: *The streetlights blurred in the snowstorm. My memories of childhood have blurred with time.* **2.** To become unclear or clouded: *As he got sleepy his vision began to blur.* ❖ *n.* Something that is indistinct and hazy: *The crowd was a blur of colors in the distance.*

blurb (blûrb) *n.* A brief favorable publicity notice, as on the jacket of a book.

blur·ry (**blûr′**ē) *adj.* **blur·ri·er, blur·ri·est 1.** Unclear or out of focus: *a blurry picture.* **2.** Not clearly distinguished; indistinct: *a blurry line between categories.*

blurt (blûrt) *tr.v.* **blurt·ed, blurt·ing, blurts** To say suddenly and without thought: *She blurted out the secret.*

blush (blŭsh) *intr.v.* **blushed, blush·ing, blush·es 1.** To become suddenly red in the face from modesty, embarrassment, or shame. **2.** To feel ashamed: *I blushed to think how rude I must have seemed to them.* ❖ *n.* **1.** A sudden reddening of the face caused by modesty, embarrassment, or shame. **2.** A reddish or rosy color: *the blush of dawn.* **3.** A blusher.

blush·er (**blŭsh′**ər) *n.* A cosmetic used to give the cheeks a rosy tint.

blus·ter (**blŭs′**tər) *intr.v.* **blus·tered, blus·ter·ing, blus·ters 1.** To blow in loud violent gusts: *Winds blustered on the mountaintop.* **2.** To utter noisy boasts or threats: *The angry customer blustered at the sales clerk.* ❖ *n.* **1.** A violent gusty wind: *the bluster of a March storm.* **2.** Loud boastful or aggressive talk, often full of empty threats: *The candidate's speech was full of bluster, but no one took it very seriously.* **—blus′ter·er** *n.* **—blus′ter·ous** *adj.* **—blus′ter·y** *adj.*

Blvd. *abbr.* An abbreviation of boulevard.

Bly (blī), **Nellie** Pen name of **Elizabeth Cochrane Seaman.** 1864?–1922. American journalist whose articles in the *New York World* included an exposé on conditions in mental institutions. —SEE NOTE.

bo·a (**bō′**ə) *n.* **1.** Any of various large nonvenomous snakes of tropical regions, including the anacondas and the boa constrictor, that coil around and suffocate their prey. **2.** A long fluffy scarf made of soft material, such as fur or feathers.

boa constrictor *n.* A large boa of tropical America that has dark brown markings on a lighter background.

Bo·ad·i·ce·a (bō′ăd-ĭ-**sē′**ə) See **Boudicca.**

boar (bôr) *n.* **1.** A male pig. **2.** A wild pig native to Eurasia and northern Africa, having dark bristles and short tusks.

❑ *These sound alike:* **boar, bore¹** (drill), **bore²** (make weary), **bore³** (tidal wave), **bore⁴** (supported).

board (bôrd) *n.* **1.** A flat thin length of sawed lumber; a plank: *The side of the hut was finished with old boards.* **2a.** A flat piece of wood or similar material adapted for some special use: *a bulletin board; a chess board.* **b.** A blackboard or similar upright flat surface used for writing. **c.** A flat piece of material designed to be ridden as a sport, such as a snowboard or skateboard. **d.** A diving board. **3.** Food served daily to paying guests: *room and board.* **4.** A group of people organized to transact or administer some particular business: *the board of trustees.* **5.** A backboard in basketball. **6. boards** The wooden structure enclosing a skating rink or similar playing area. **7.** A circuit board. ❖ *v.* **board·ed, board·ing, boards** *—tr.* **1.** To close with boards: *boarding up the windows.* **2.** To provide (someone) with food and lodging for a charge. **3.** To go aboard (a ship, train, or plane). *—intr.* To live as a paying guest: *board at the local hotel.* [From Old English *bord*, table, shield, side of a ship.]

❑ *These sound alike:* **board, bored** (wearied).

board·er (**bôr′**dər) *n.* **1.** A person who pays for and receives both meals and lodging at another person's home. **2.** A person who rides a board, such as a snowboard or surfboard, as a sport.

❑ *These sound alike:* **boarder, border** (edge).

board foot *n., pl.* **board feet** A unit of measure for lumber, equal to the volume of an unplaned board one foot long, one foot wide, and one inch thick; 144 cubic inches of wood.

board game *n.* A game of strategy, such as chess or backgammon, played by moving pieces on a board.

board·ing house (**bôr′**dĭng) *n.* A private home that provides meals and lodging for paying guests.

boarding school *n.* A school where pupils are provided with meals and lodging.

board shorts also **board·shorts** (**bôrd′**shôrts′) *pl.n.* Shorts, usually knee-length but sometimes shorter, that are worn for surfing or other water sports.

board·walk (**bôrd′**wôk′) *n.* A public walk or promenade along a beach, usually made of wooden planks.

boast (bōst) *v.* **boast·ed, boast·ing, boasts** *—intr.* To speak about oneself in a proud or self-admiring way; brag. *—tr.* **1.** To say (something about oneself) in a proud or self-admiring way: *The doctors boasted that their discovery would lead to a cure for cancer.* **2.** To have as a desirable feature: *The mall boasted 70 stores and an arcade with games and rides.* ❖ *n.* A bragging or boastful statement: *a boast not supported by fact.* **—boast′er** *n.*

boast·ful (**bōst′**fəl) *adj.* Tending to boast or brag. **—boast′ful·ly** *adv.*

boat (bōt) *n.* **1.** A small open craft for traveling on water. **2.** A large seagoing vessel; a ship or submarine. **3.** A dish shaped like a boat: *a gravy boat.* ❖ *intr. & tr.v.* **boat·ed, boat·ing, boats** To travel by boat; row or sail: *boat across the lake.* ◆ **in the same boat** In the same situation as someone else. [From Old English *bāt.*]

boat·house (**bōt′**hous′) *n.* A house in which boats are kept, often near the water's edge.

boat·load (**bōt′**lōd′) *n.* The number of passengers or the amount of cargo that a boat can hold.

boat·man (**bōt′**mən) *n.* A person who works on, deals with, or operates boats.

boat people *pl.n.* Refugees who attempt to flee their country by boat and seek asylum in another country.

boat·swain also **bo's'n** or **bo·sun** (**bō′**sən) *n.* A warrant officer or petty officer in charge of a ship's deck crew, rigging, and anchors.

bob¹ (bŏb) *v.* **bobbed, bob·bing, bobs** *—intr.* **1.** To move up and down: *a cork bobbing on the water.* **2.** To grab at floating or hanging objects with the teeth: *bob for apples.* **3.** To fish with a bobber. *—tr.* To cause to move up and down: *bobbed their heads.* ❖ *n.* **1.** A quick jerking movement of the head or body. **2.** A bobber used in fishing. ◆ **bob up** To appear or arise unexpectedly or suddenly. [From Middle English *bobben*, to move up and down.]

bob² (bŏb) *n.* **1.** A small hanging weight, such as a plumb bob. **2.** A small lock or curl of hair. **3.** A short haircut on a woman or child. ❖ *tr.v.* **bobbed, bob·bing, bobs** To cut short or reshape: *bobbed her hair; had his nose bobbed.* [From Middle English *bobbe*, cluster of fruit.]

bob³ (bŏb) *n., pl.* **bob** *Chiefly British* A shilling.

bob·ber¹ (bŏb′ər) *n.* **1.** A buoyant object used to suspend a fishing line. **2.** A person who fishes with such an object. [From *bob*, to move up and down.]

bob·ber² (bŏb′ər) *n.* A person who reshapes or trims something, especially hair. [From *bob*, to cut short.]

bob·bin (bŏb′ĭn) *n.* A spool or reel that holds something, such as thread or yarn, for spinning, weaving, knitting, sewing, or making lace.

bob·ble (bŏb′əl) *v.* **bob·bled, bob·bling, bob·bles** —*intr.* To bob up and down. —*tr.* To lose one's grip on (a ball) momentarily. ❖ *n.* A mistake or blunder.

bob·by (bŏb′ē) *n., pl.* **bob·bies** *Chiefly British* A policeman. [After Sir *Robert* Peel (1788–1850), home secretary of England when the Metropolitan Police Force was created in 1829.]

bobby pin *n.* A small metal hairpin having springy ends pressed tightly together to hold the hair in place.

bobby socks also **bobby sox** *pl.n. Informal* Short thick socks worn by girls or women.

bob·cat (bŏb′kăt′) *n.* A North American wildcat having spotted reddish-brown fur, tufted ears, and a short tail.

bob·o·link (bŏb′ə-lĭngk′) *n.* A songbird of the Americas that has black, white, and yellowish feathers in the male and is usually found in fields and grasslands.

bob·sled (bŏb′slĕd′) *n.* **1.** A long racing sled with a steering device that controls the front runners. **2a.** A long sled made of two shorter sleds joined one behind the other. **b.** Either of these two smaller sleds. ❖ *intr.v.* **bob·sled·ded, bob·sled·ding, bob·sleds** To ride or race in a bobsled. —**bob′sled·der** *n.*

bob·tail (bŏb′tāl′) *n.* **1.** A short tail or a tail that has been cut short. **2.** An animal, especially a horse, having such a tail.

bob·white (bŏb-wīt′) *n.* A brown and white North American quail having a call that sounds like its name.

bode¹ (bōd) *tr.v.* **bod·ed, bod·ing, bodes** To be a sign or omen of (something to come): *A heavy sea boded trouble for the passengers on board.* ◆ **bode ill** To be a bad sign: *The coming hurricane bodes ill for many store owners along the beach.* **bode well** To be a good sign: *A clear sky boded well for our trip to the mountains.* [From Middle English *boden*, from Old English *bodian*, to announce.]

bode² (bōd) *v.* A past tense of **bide.**

bo·de·ga (bō-dā′gə) *n.* A small grocery store that specializes in Caribbean and Latin American products. —SEE NOTE AT **boutique.**

bod·ice (bŏd′ĭs) *n.* **1.** The fitted upper part of a dress. **2.** A woman's vest that laces in front, worn over a blouse. [Alteration of *bodies.*]

bod·i·less (bŏd′ē-lĭs) *adj.* Having no body, form, or substance: *a bodiless spirit.*

bod·i·ly (bŏd′l-ē) *adj.* Relating or belonging to the body: *bodily ailments; food and other bodily needs.* ❖ *adv.* **1.** In the flesh; in person: *a sleepy student that was present bodily but not mentally.* **2.** As a complete body; as a whole: *carried the child bodily up the stairs.*

bod·kin (bŏd′kĭn) *n.* **1.** A small pointed instrument for punching holes in cloth or leather. **2.** A blunt needle for pulling tape or ribbon through loops or a hem. **3.** A small dagger. **4.** A long ornamental hairpin.

bod·y (bŏd′ē) *n., pl.* **bod·ies 1a.** The entire physical structure and substance of a living thing, especially of a human or other animal. **b.** A corpse or carcass: *The body of the drowned sailor was never found.* **2.** The main part of a person or other animal excluding the head and limbs; the trunk or torso: *After a feint to the head, the boxer landed a punch on his opponent's body.* **3.** A mass or collection of matter that is distinct from other masses: *a celestial body; a body of water.* **4.** A number of people or things considered as a group: *the student body; a body of information.* **5.** The main or central part of something: *the body of a ship.* **6.** A collection or quantity, as of material or information: *The investigators examined the body of evidence.* [From Old English *bodeg.*]

bod·y·board (bŏd′ē-bôrd′) *n.* A very short surfboard with one straight end, usually ridden by lying on one's chest. —**bod′y·board′** *v.*

bod·y·build·ing (bŏd′ē-bĭl′dĭng) *n.* The process of building one's muscles through diet and exercise, such as weightlifting. —**bod′y·build′er** *n.*

bod·y·guard (bŏd′ē-gärd′) *n.* A person or group of persons responsible for the safety of someone else.

body language *n.* Gestures, facial expressions, and postures of the body by which a person communicates nonverbally or manifests various physical, mental, or emotional states: *I could tell by his body language that he was upset.*

body politic *n.* The whole people of a nation or state, regarded as a political unit.

body shop *n.* A shop or garage where the bodies of automotive vehicles are repaired.

bod·y·surf (bŏd′ē-sûrf′) *intr.v.* **bod·y·surfed, bod·y·surf·ing, bod·y·surfs** To ride a wave to shore without a surfboard.

Boer (bôr *or* bō′ər) *n.* A Dutch colonist or a descendant of a Dutch colonist in South Africa. —**Boer** *adj.*

bog (bôg) *n.* An area of wet spongy ground that usually consists of a thick mat of decaying moss. ❖ *intr.v.* **bogged, bog·ging, bogs** To be hindered or slowed: *The plan to restore the building bogged down in government red tape.*

bo·gey also **bo·gy** or **bo·gie** (bō′gē) *n., pl.* **bo·geys** also **bo·gies 1.** (*also* **bŏŏg′ē** *or* **bōō′gē**) An evil or mischievous spirit; a hobgoblin. **2.** In golf, a score of one stroke over par on a hole.

bog·ey·man (bŏŏg′ē-măn′) *n.* Variant of **boogeyman.**

bog·gle (bŏg′əl) *v.* **bog·gled, bog·gling, bog·gles** —*intr.* To be staggered or overwhelmed, as with astonishment or dismay: *My mind boggles at the amount of studying I still have to do.* —*tr.* To stagger or overwhelm, as with astonishment or dismay: *The vast number of stars in our galaxy boggles the mind.*

bo·gie (bō′gē *or* bŏŏg′ē) *n.* A variant of **bogey.**

Bo·go·tá (bō′gə-tä′) The capital of Colombia, in the central part of the country on a high plain in the eastern Andes.

bo·gus (bō′gəs) *adj.* **1.** Counterfeit; fake: *It is a crime to pass bogus money.* **2.** *Slang* Highly objectionable; senseless; pointless: *assigned us a task that was totally bogus.*

bo·gy (bō′gē *or* bŏŏg′ē) *n.* A variant of **bogey.**

Bo·he·mi·a (bō-hē′mē-ə) A historical region and former kingdom of present-day western Czech Republic. The Czechs settled in the area between the fifth and sixth centuries AD. Bohemia became part of Czechoslovakia in 1918.

bo·he·mi·an (bō-hē′mē-ən) *n.* A person, especially an artist, who does not follow conventional standards of behavior. [From French *bohémien*, from *Bohême*, Bohemia (from the unconventional lifestyle of the Romani people, who were once thought to have come from Bohemia).]

Bohr (bôr), **Niels Henrik David** 1885–1962. Danish physicist who investigated atomic structure and radiation.

bohr·i·um (bôr′ē-əm) *n. Symbol* **Bh** A radioactive element that has been artificially produced by scientists. The longest confirmed half-life of any of its isotopes is

boa

board shorts

bob²

bobsled

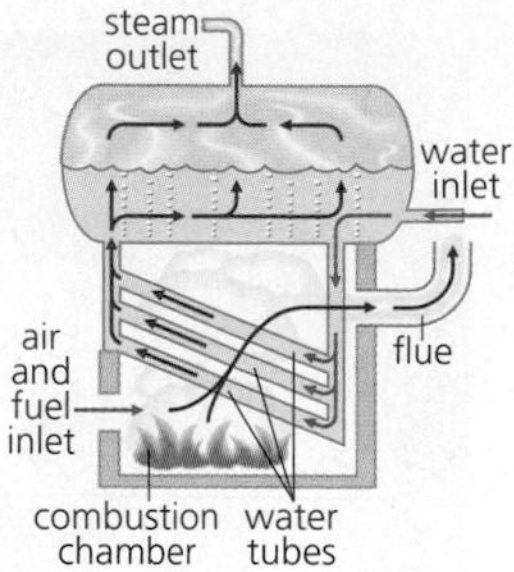

boiler
water-tube boiler

about 1.3 seconds. Atomic number 107. See **Periodic Table.**

boil¹ (boil) *v.* **boiled, boil·ing, boils** —*intr.* **1.** To change from a liquid state to a gaseous state by being heated to the boiling point: *Water boils at 212°F.* **2.** To be cooked by boiling or putting into boiling water: *I set the table while the potatoes were boiling.* **3.** To have the contents at a boil: *The kettle is boiling on the stove.* **4.** To be stirred up or greatly excited, especially in anger: *boil with anger at the insult.* **5.** To rush or churn: *The water boiled through the rapids.* —*tr.* **1.** To heat (a liquid) to a temperature at which it turns into a gaseous state, with bubbles breaking though the liquid's surface. **2.** To cook by boiling: *boil an egg; boil syrup.* ❖ *n.* The condition or act of being boiled: *First you should bring the soup to a rapid boil.* ◆ **boil down 1.** To reduce in volume or amount by boiling: *boil down maple sap into maple syrup.* **2.** To reduce or be reduced to a simpler form: *Let's boil the problem down to its basic elements. The problem boils down to a lack of money.* **boil over 1.** To overflow while boiling. **2.** To explode in rage; lose one's temper. [From Middle English *boillen*, from Latin *bullīre.*]

boil² (boil) *n.* A painful pus-filled swelling of the skin and the tissue beneath it, caused by a local bacterial infection. [From Old English *b*ȳ*le.*]

boil·er (**boi′**lər) *n.* **1.** A vessel in which a liquid, usually water, is heated and often vaporized for use in an engine, turbine, or heating system. **2.** A container, such as a kettle, for boiling liquids. **3.** A storage tank for hot water.

boil·ing point (**boi′**lĭng) *n.* The temperature at which a liquid boils, especially as measured at sea level.

Boi·se (**boi′**sē *or* **boi′**zē) The capital of Idaho, in the southwest part of the state. The city was founded in 1863 after gold was discovered nearby.

bois·ter·ous (**boi′**stər-əs *or* **boi′**strəs) *adj.* Noisy and unruly or unrestrained: *a playground full of boisterous children; the boisterous cheers of an excited crowd.* **—bois′ter·ous·ly** *adv.* **—bois′ter·ous·ness** *n.*

bo·la (**bō′**lə) also **bo·las** (**bō′**ləs) *n.* A rope with weights attached, used in South America to catch cattle or game by entangling their legs. [From Spanish *bolas*, plural of Spanish *bola*, ball, probably from Latin *bulla.*]

bold (bōld) *adj.* **bold·er, bold·est 1a.** Having little fear; brave; courageous: *bold explorers.* **b.** Showing or requiring courage; daring; audacious: *a bold voyage to unknown lands.* See Synonyms at **brave. 2.** Lacking respectful restraint in behavior; arrogant or overbearing: *a bold, sassy child.* **3.** Strikingly different or unconventional; arresting or provocative: *a bold new way to tackle the problem of homelessness.* **4.** Clear and distinct to the eye; vivid; clear: *bold colors; a bold pattern.* **5.** Being in boldface: *bold type.* **—bold′ly** *adv.* **—bold′ness** *n.*

bold·face (**bōld′**fās′) *n.* Type that has thick heavy lines: *Entry words in this dictionary are in boldface.* **—bold′face′** *adj.*

bold-faced (**bōld′**fāst′) *adj.* **1.** Shamelessly bold and disrespectful; brazen: *a bold-faced lie.* **2.** Printed in boldface.

bole (bōl) *n.* The trunk of a tree.

❏ *These sound alike:* **bole, boll** (seed capsule), **bowl¹** (dish), **bowl²** (roll a ball).

bo·le·ro (bō-**lâr′**ō) *n., pl.* **bo·le·ros 1.** A very short jacket of Spanish origin, worn open in the front. **2a.** A lively Spanish dance or the music for this dance, in triple meter. **b.** A slow Latin American dance or the music for this dance, in triple meter.

Bol·eyn (**bo͝ol′**ĭn *or* bo͝o-**lĭn′**), **Anne** 1507?–1536. Queen of England (1533–1536) as the second wife of Henry VIII. She was the mother of Elizabeth I.

bo·li·var (bō-**lē′**vär *or* **bŏl′**ə-vər) *n., pl.* **bo·li·vars** or **bo·li·var·es** (bō-**lē′**vä-rēs′) A basic monetary unit of Venezuela. [After Simón *Bolívar.*]

Bo·lí·var (bō-**lē′**vär), **Simón** Known as "the Liberator." 1783–1830. South American revolutionary leader who defeated the Spanish in 1819 and became president of Greater Colombia (now Colombia, Venezuela, Ecuador, and Panama). He also helped liberate (1823–1834) Peru and Bolivia. —SEE NOTE.

Bo·liv·i·a (bə-**lĭv′**ē-ə *or* bō-**lĭv′**ē-ə) A landlocked country of western South America north of Argentina. Sucre is the legal capital. La Paz is the administrative center and the largest city.

bo·li·vi·a·no (bə-lĭv′ē-**ä′**nō) *n., pl.* **bo·li·vi·a·nos** The basic monetary unit of Bolivia.

boll (bōl) *n.* The rounded seed-bearing capsule of certain plants, especially cotton and flax.

❏ *These sound alike:* **boll, bole** (tree trunk), **bowl¹** (dish), **bowl²** (roll a ball).

boll weevil *n.* A long-snouted beetle that causes damage to cotton plants by feeding on and laying its eggs in the buds and bolls of the plants.

bo·lo·gna also **ba·lo·ney** (bə-**lō′**nē) *n.* A large sausage of finely ground pork or other meat, usually served as cold cuts. [After *Bologna*, Italy.]

Bo·lo·gna (bə-**lōn′**yə) A city of north-central Italy at the foot of the Apennines north-northeast of Florence. It was originally an Etruscan town.

Bo·lo·gnese (bō′lə-**nēz′** *or* bō′lə-**nēs′**) *adj.* **1.** Relating to or characteristic of Bologna, Italy. **2.** Being or served with a sauce containing meat, tomatoes and other vegetables, and often wine and cream: *spaghetti Bolognese.* ❖ *n.* **1.** A native or inhabitant of Bologna, Italy. **2.** Bolognese sauce. [From Italian.]

Bol·she·vik (**bōl′**shə-vĭk′) *n.* **1.** A member of the Russian Social Democratic Workers' Party that adopted Lenin's ideas and seized control of the Russian government in November 1917. **2.** A Communist. [From Russian *Bol'shevik*, from *bol'she*, comparative of *bol'shoĭ*, large.]

Bol·she·vism also **bol·she·vism** (**bōl′**shə-vĭz′əm) *n.* **1.** The theories and practices developed by the Bolsheviks between 1903 and 1917 with a view to seizing governmental power and establishing the world's first Communist state. **2.** Communism in the Soviet Union.

Bol·she·vist also **bol·she·vist** (**bōl′**shə-vĭst) *n.* A Bolshevik. **—Bol′she·vist′** *adj.*

bol·ster (**bōl′**stər) *n.* A long narrow pillow or cushion. ❖ *tr.v.* **bol·stered, bol·ster·ing, bol·sters** To support or reinforce: *Visitors bolstered the patient's morale.*

bolt (bōlt) *n.* **1.** A rod or pin with a head at one end and threads onto which a nut is screwed at the other end, used to hold two parts together. **2.** A sliding bar of wood or metal for fastening a door or gate. **3.** A metal bar or rod in a lock that is pushed out or withdrawn at a turn of the key. **4.** A sliding bar that positions the cartridge in a rifle and closes the breech. **5.** A large roll of cloth, especially as it comes from the loom. **6.** A short heavy arrow used with a crossbow. **7.** A flash of lightning; a thunderbolt. **8.** A sudden movement toward or away from something: *Our cat made a bolt for the open door.* ❖ *v.* **bolt·ed, bolt·ing, bolts** —*tr.* **1.** To attach or fasten with a bolt or bolts: *bolted the rack to the wall.* **2.** To lock with a bolt: *Bolt the door.* **3.** To eat hurriedly and with little chewing; gulp. **4.** To break away from (a political party). —*intr.* **1.** To move or spring suddenly: *bolting from the room.* **2.** To break from a rider's control and run away: *a horse that shied and bolted.* **3.** To break away from an affiliation, as from a political party. ◆ **bolt from the blue** A sudden, usually shocking surprise: *The news came as a bolt from the blue.* **bolt upright** Stiff and straight: *Realizing he was late, he sat bolt upright in bed.* [From Old English *bolt*, heavy arrow.]

bomb (bŏm) *n.* **1.** An explosive weapon constructed to go off by striking something, by a timing mechanism, or by some other means. **2.** A weapon exploded to re-

ă	pat	ôr	core
ā	pay	oi	boy
âr	care	ou	out
ä	father	o͝o	took
ĕ	pet	o͝or	lure
ē	be	o͞o	boot
ĭ	pit	ŭ	cut
ī	bite	ûr	urge
îr	pier	th	thin
ŏ	pot	*th*	this
ō	toe	zh	vision
ô	paw	ə	about

lease gas or other destructive materials: *a smoke bomb.* **3.** In football, a long forward pass. **4.** A container for holding a substance under pressure, as a preparation for killing insects, that can be released as a spray or gas. **5.** *Slang* A dismal failure: *That new movie is a bomb.* **6.** *Slang* One that is excellent or superior. Used with *the: That new movie is the bomb.* ❖ *v.* **bombed, bomb·ing, bombs** —*tr.* To attack, damage, or destroy with a bomb or bombs: *bomb a bridge.* —*intr. Slang* To fail miserably: *That new movie bombed and closed after one week in the theaters.* [From Italian *bomba*, probably from Latin *bombus*, a booming sound, from Greek *bombos*, of imitative origin.]

bom·bard (bŏm-**bärd′** *or* bəm-**bärd′**) *tr.v.* **bom·bard·ed, bom·bard·ing, bom·bards 1.** To attack with bombs, shells, or missiles: *bombard an enemy position.* **2.** To barrage or shower, as with words: *Reporters bombarded the police with questions.* **3.** To strike (the nucleus of an atom) with a stream of subatomic particles in order to study the structure of the nucleus. **—bom·bard′ment** *n.*

bom·bar·dier (bŏm′bər-**dîr′**) *n.* The member of a bomber crew who works the bombsight and releases the bombs.

bom·bast (**bŏm′**băst′) *n.* Extravagant or pompous speech or writing: *a politician full of bombast and bluster.*

bom·bas·tic (bŏm-**băs′**tĭk) *adj.* Having an extravagant pompous style: *a bombastic speech denouncing the government's policies.* **—bom·bas′ti·cal·ly** *adv.*

Bom·bay (bŏm-**bā′**) See **Mumbai.**

bomb bay *n.* The compartment in a bomber from which bombs are dropped.

bomb·er (**bŏm′**ər) *n.* **1.** A military airplane that carries and drops bombs. **2.** A person who makes and sets off bombs.

bomb·proof (**bŏm′**pro͞of′) *adj.* Designed to resist destruction by a bomb: *a bombproof bunker.*

bomb·shell (**bŏm′**shĕl′) *n.* **1.** A bomb. **2.** Something that is shocking, surprising, or amazing: *The news that our teacher was resigning came as a bombshell.*

bomb·sight (**bŏm′**sīt′) *n.* A device in a military aircraft for aiming bombs.

bo·na fide (**bō′**nə fīd′ *or* **bŏn′**ə fīd′) *adj.* **1.** Done or made in good faith; sincere: *a bona fide offer to buy.* **2.** Genuine; authentic: *a bona fide painting by Rembrandt.* [From Latin *bonā fidē*, in good faith.]

Bo·naire (bô-**nâr′**) An island territory of the Netherlands in the Caribbean Sea off the northern coast of Venezuela.

bo·nan·za (bə-**năn′**zə) *n.* **1.** A rich mine or vein of ore. **2.** A source of great wealth: *The rise in stock prices was a bonanza to shareholders.* [From Spanish, from Medieval Latin *bonacia*, calm sea, blend of Latin *bonus*, good, and Medieval Latin *malacia*, calm sea.]

Bo·na·parte (**bō′**nə-pärt′) Corsican family, all brothers of Napoleon I, including **Joseph** (1768–1844), who was king of Naples (1806–1808) and Spain (1808–1813), and **Louis** (1778–1846), who was king of Holland (1806–1810).

bon·bon (**bŏn′**bŏn′) *n.* A piece of candy, often with a creamy center and a chocolate coating. [From French, from *bon*, good, from Latin *bonus*.]

bond (bŏnd) *n.* **1.** Something, such as a cord or band, that binds or holds things together: *They tied bonds around the prisoner's wrists.* **2.** A force that unites; a tie: *a strong familial bond; a bond of affection between the two friends.* **3.** A force of attraction that holds atoms or groups of atoms together in a molecule, produced in general by a transfer or sharing of one or more electrons. **4.** A union of objects or parts created by an adhesive substance: *The glue formed a tight bond between the two surfaces.* **5.** A binding agreement; a covenant: *My word is my bond.* **6.** Money paid as bail: *The bond for the prisoner's release was set at $100,000.* **7.** A certificate of debt issued by a government or corporation that guarantees repayment of the original investment with interest by a specified date. **8.** An insurance contract that guarantees payment to an employer in the event of financial loss caused by the actions of an employee. ❖ *v.* **bond·ed, bond·ing, bonds** —*tr.* **1.** To join securely, as with glue: *bonded the poster to the wall with paste.* **2.** To connect by strong emotional or social ties: *The adventures we shared bonded us for life.* **3.** To place (an employee) under bond so as to insure his or her employer against loss. —*intr.* To be joined together with a bond: *Oxygen bonds to hydrogen to form water.*

bond·age (**bŏn′**dĭj) *n.* The condition of being bound as a slave or serf; slavery or servitude.

bond·hold·er (**bŏnd′**hōl′dər) *n.* The owner of a government or corporate bond.

bond·man (**bŏnd′**mən) *n.* A male bondservant.

Bonds (bŏndz), **Barry Lamar** Born 1964. American baseball player (1986–2007) who hit a single-season record of 73 home runs in 2001 and retired with 762 career home runs.

bond·ser·vant (**bŏnd′**sûr′vənt) *n.* A person who is obligated to work for another without wages; a slave or serf.

bonds·man (**bŏndz′**mən) *n.* **1.** A male bondservant. **2.** A person who provides bail for another.

bond·wom·an (**bŏnd′**wo͝om′ən) *n.* A female bondservant.

bone (bōn) *n.* **1a.** The hard, dense, calcified tissue that forms the skeleton of most vertebrate animals. **b.** One of the many distinct structures making up such a skeleton: *the bones of the foot.* **2. bones a.** A corpse or skeleton: *buried his bones in the cemetery.* **b.** The body: *Sit down and rest your bones.* ❖ *tr.v.* **boned, bon·ing, bones** *Informal* In cooking, to remove the bones from: *bone fish.* ◆ **bone of contention** The subject of a dispute: *Who goes first is often a bone of contention.* **bone to pick** A reason for a complaint or dispute. **bone up** *Informal* To study a subject intensively, especially to prepare for something: *boned up for the final exam.* **in (one's) bones** In one's innermost feelings: *I knew in my bones that I was wrong.* [From Old English *bān*.]

bone-dry (**bōn′**drī′) *adj.* Without a trace of moisture.

bone·head (**bōn′**hĕd′) *n. Informal* A stupid person.

bone marrow *n.* The soft tissue that fills the cavities inside most bones. In adult mammals, cells in the bone marrow produce red blood cells, white blood cells, and platelets.

bone meal *n.* Bones crushed and ground to a coarse powder, used as fertilizer and animal feed.

bon·fire (**bŏn′**fīr′) *n.* A large fire built outdoors. [From Middle English *bonfir* : *bon*, bone + *fir*, fire.]

bon·gos (**bŏng′**gōz) *pl.n.* A pair of small drums, usually tuned to different pitches, that are played by beating with the hands. [From Spanish, probably of West African origin.]

bo·ni·to (bə-**nē′**tō) *n., pl.* **bonito** or **bo·ni·tos** Any of several ocean fishes that resemble a small tuna and are caught for food and sport.

Bonn (bŏn) A city of western Germany on the Rhine River. Founded by the Romans in the first century AD, it was the capital of West Germany from 1949 until 1990.

bon·net (**bŏn′**ĭt) *n.* **1.** A hat tied with ribbons under the chin and traditionally worn by women or children. **2.** A cap without a brim, worn by men or boys in Scotland. **3.** *Chiefly British* The hood of an automobile.

bon·ny also **bon·nie** (**bŏn′**ē) *adj.* **bon·ni·er, bon·ni·est** *Scots* Pleasing to the eye; pretty: *a bonny lass.*

bo·no·bo (bə-**nō′**bō) *n., pl.* **bo·no·bos** A dark-haired African ape that is closely related to and resembles the chimpanzee but has a more slender build. Bonobos are

BIOGRAPHY

Simón Bolívar Simón **Bolívar** was born in South America at a time when nearly the entire continent was controlled by the kingdom of Spain. He belonged to a prominent family and received a good education. Inspired in part by Thomas Jefferson, George Washington, and the other American patriots who had fought to win independence for the British colonies in North America, Bolívar joined the independence movement in his own country (what is now Venezuela), fighting a series of campaigns between 1811 and 1824 that eventually resulted in independence not only for Venezuela but also for Colombia, Ecuador, Peru, and the country high in the Andes that was eventually named Bolivia in his honor.

Simón Bolívar

bolt

found only in the Democratic Republic of the Congo, south of the Congo River.

bon·sai (bŏn-sīʹ *or* **bŏnʹ**sīʹ) *n., pl.* **bonsai 1.** The art of growing miniature trees in small pots or dishes. **2.** A tree grown in this way. [From Japanese *bonsai,* potted plant : *bon,* basin + *sai,* to plant.]

bonsai

bo·nus (**bōʹ**nəs) *n., pl.* **bo·nus·es** Something given or paid in addition to what is usual or expected: *Each worker got a bonus of three extra days off for the holidays.*

bon voy·age (bŏnʹ voi **äzhʹ**) *interj.* An expression used to wish a departing traveler a pleasant journey.

bon·y or **bon·ey** (**bōʹ**nē) *adj.* **bon·i·er, bon·i·est** or **bon·ey·er, bon·ey·est 1.** Relating to, resembling, or consisting of bone. **2.** Full of bones: *a bony piece of fish.* **3.** Having bones that stick out or show through; thin; gaunt: *bony arms.* **—bonʹi·ness** *n.*

bony fish *n.* Any of numerous fishes that have a bony skeleton, in contrast to the cartilaginous fishes, such as sharks.

boo (bo͞o) *n., pl.* **boos** A sound uttered to show dislike or disapproval: *There was a mix of cheers and boos when the speaker was finished.* ❖ *interj.* An expression used to show dislike or disapproval or to frighten or surprise. ❖ *v.* **booed, boo·ing, boos** *—intr.* To utter a boo: *The fans booed angrily. —tr.* To say "boo" to; jeer: *The spectators booed the umpire's decision.*

boob (bo͞ob) *n. Slang* A stupid or foolish person; a dunce.

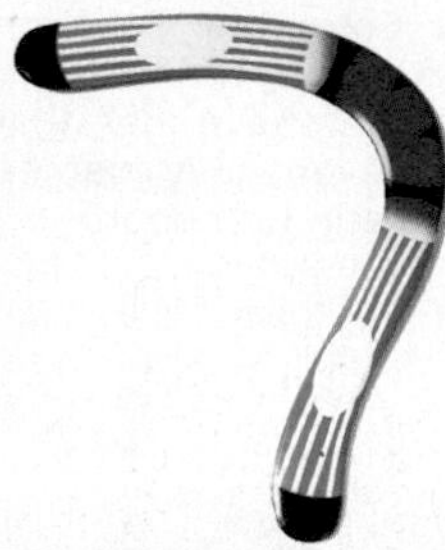
boomerang

boo-boo also **boo·boo** (**bo͞oʹ**bo͞o) *n., pl.* **boo-boos** also **boo·boos** *Informal* **1.** A foolish or thoughtless mistake. **2.** A slight physical injury, such as a scratch.

boo·by (**bo͞oʹ**bē) *n., pl.* **boo·bies** Any of several large usually tropical seabirds having long pointed wings and a long bill.

booby prize *n.* An award given to the person who performs worst in a game or contest.

booby trap *n.* **1.** A device, often containing an explosive, designed to injure or kill an unsuspecting person who moves a seemingly harmless object. **2.** A situation for catching a person off-guard; a trap.

boog·ey·man or **bog·ey·man** (**bo͝ogʹ**ē-mănʹ) *n.* A terrifying spirit; a hobgoblin.

boog·ie-woog·ie (bo͝ogʹē-**wo͝ogʹ**ē *or* bo͞oʹgē-**wo͞oʹ**gē) *n.* A style of blues piano playing characterized by a quick tempo, a repeated bass line, and a series of improvised variations in the treble. [Perhaps ultimately of West African origin.]

book (bo͝ok) *n.* **1a.** A set of printed, written, or blank pages fastened together along one edge and enclosed between covers. **b.** An e-book or other electronic source of information structured like a book. **2a.** A printed or written literary work: *She's writing a new book about Mexico.* **b.** A main division of a larger written or printed work: *a book of the Bible.* **3. Book a.** The Bible. **b.** The Koran. **4a.** A volume for recording financial transactions: *an account book.* **b. books** Financial records in which an accounting is kept of money received, owed, and paid: *A bookkeeper keeps books.* **5.** A set of established rules: *She runs the company by the book.* **6.** A small packet of similar things bound together: *a book of matches.* **7.** The words or script of a play, musical, or opera. ❖ *tr.v.* **booked, book·ing, books 1.** To arrange for in advance; reserve or schedule: *We booked tickets to the show.* **2.** To write down charges against (a person) in a police record: *book a suspect.* ◆ **in (one's) book** In one's opinion: *In my book she was one of the all-time greats.* **like a book** Thoroughly; completely: *I know the town like a book.* **throw the book at 1.** To make all possible charges against (an offender). **2.** To scold or punish severely. [From Old English *bōc.*]

book·bag (**bo͝okʹ**băgʹ) *n.* A small backpack or bag used to carry books and papers.

book·bind·er (**bo͝okʹ**bīnʹdər) *n.* A person whose business is binding books.

book·case (**bo͝okʹ**kāsʹ) *n.* A piece of furniture with shelves for holding books.

book club *n.* **1.** A business organization that sells books to its members at a discount from a selected list. **2.** A group of readers who meet periodically to discuss assigned books.

book·end (**bo͝okʹ**ĕndʹ) *n.* An often decorative prop placed at the end of a row of books to keep them upright.

book·ie (**bo͝okʹ**ē) *n.* A person who accepts and pays off bets; a bookmaker.

book·ish (**bo͝okʹ**ĭsh) *adj.* **1.** Fond of books and study; studious: *a bookish scholar.* **2.** Depending too much on books rather than experience: *a bookish notion of the world.* **3.** Scholarly or formal in a dull, dry way: *bookish writing.*

book·keep·ing (**bo͝okʹ**kēʹpĭng) *n.* The work or skill of keeping records of money received, owed, or paid by a business. **—bookʹkeepʹer** *n.*

book·let (**bo͝okʹ**lĭt) *n.* A small book or pamphlet, usually with paper covers.

book·mak·er (**bo͝okʹ**māʹkər) *n.* **1.** A person or business that edits, prints, or publishes books. **2.** A person who accepts and pays off bets, especially on sporting events such as horse races. **—bookʹmakʹing** *n.*

book·mark (**bo͝okʹ**märkʹ) *n.* **1.** An object, such as a ribbon or a strip of leather, placed between the pages of a book to mark the reader's place. **2.** A link in a web browser that allows a user to easily return to a webpage.

book·mo·bile (**bo͝okʹ**mō-bēlʹ) *n.* A truck or van with shelves of books in it, used as a traveling library.

Book of Common Prayer *n.* The book of services and prayers used in the Anglican Church.

Book of Mormon *n.* A sacred book of the Mormon Church, published in 1830 and believed by Mormons to be a sacred history of the Americas revealed by the prophet Mormon to Joseph Smith.

book·plate (**bo͝okʹ**plātʹ) *n.* A label pasted inside a book and bearing the owner's name.

book·sell·er (**bo͝okʹ**sĕlʹər) *n.* A person or business that sells books.

book·shelf (**bo͝okʹ**shĕlfʹ) *n., pl.* **book·shelves** A shelf or set of shelves for holding books.

book·shop (**bo͝okʹ**shŏpʹ) *n.* A bookstore.

book·stand (**bo͝okʹ**stăndʹ) *n.* **1.** A small counter where books are sold. **2.** A frame for holding an open book.

book·store (**bo͝okʹ**stôrʹ) *n.* A store where books are sold.

book·worm (**bo͝okʹ**wûrmʹ) *n.* A person who spends much time reading or studying.

Bool·e·an algebra (**bo͞oʹ**lē-ən) *n.* A form of algebra in which variables may have one of two values and the operations defined on them are logical OR, a type of addition, and logical AND, a type of multiplication. Boolean algebra is fundamental to computer programming. [After George *Boole* (1815–1864), English mathematician.]

boom¹ (bo͞om) *v.* **boomed, boom·ing, booms** *—intr.* **1.** To make a deep resonant sound: *The cannon boomed across the valley.* **2.** To grow, develop, or progress rapidly; thrive; flourish: *Business is booming. —tr.* To say or give forth with such a sound: *Rescuers boomed a message over their loudspeaker.* ❖ *n.* **1.** A deep hollow sound, as from an explosion. **2.** A sudden increase, as in growth or production: *a boom in farm production filled the markets.* **3.** A time of economic prosperity: *California had a boom after gold was discovered.* [From Middle English *bomben.*]

boom² (bo͞om) *n.* **1.** A long pole extending from the mast of a boat to hold or stretch out the bottom of a sail. **2a.** A long pole or similar structure that extends upward

ă	pat	ôr	core
ā	pay	oi	boy
âr	care	ou	out
ä	father	o͝o	took
ĕ	pet	o͝or	lure
ē	be	o͞o	boot
ĭ	pit	ŭ	cut
ī	bite	ûr	urge
îr	pier	th	thin
ŏ	pot	*th*	this
ō	toe	zh	vision
ô	paw	ə	about

and outward from the mast of a derrick and supports the object being lifted. **b.** A similar support that holds a microphone. **3.** A chain, cable, or line of timbers that keeps logs from floating away. **4.** A floating barrier used to contain an oil spill. [From Dutch *boom*, tree, pole.]

boom·er (bo͞o**′**mər) *n. Informal* A baby boomer.

boo·mer·ang (bo͞o**′**mə-răng′) *n.* **1.** A flat curved piece of wood that can be thrown so that it returns to the thrower. **2.** Something that comes back to harm or surprise the originator. ❖ *intr.v.* **boo·mer·anged, boo·mer·ang·ing, boo·mer·angs** To have the opposite effect of that intended; backfire: *The advertising campaign boomeranged when people found out that the claims weren't entirely true.* [From Dharuk (Aboriginal language of southeast Australia) *bumarin*ʸ.]

boom·town (bo͞om**′**toun′) *n.* A town that experiences sudden growth and prosperity, as after a discovery of gold, silver, or oil.

boon[1] (bo͞on) *n.* Something that provides a benefit or advantage: *Delay would be a blow to us and a boon to our competitors.* [From Middle English *bon*, from Old Norse *bōn*, prayer.]

boon[2] (bo͞on) *adj.* Friendly and jolly; sociable: *a boon companion.* [From Middle English *bon*, good, from Latin *bonus*.]

boon·docks (bo͞on**′**dŏks′) *pl.n. Slang* **1.** Rough uncleared country. **2.** Rural country; the backwoods.

Boone (bo͞on), **Daniel** 1734–1820. American pioneer and folk hero who helped lead new settlers to what is now Kentucky.

boor (bo͝or) *n.* A crude person with rude or clumsy manners.

boor·ish (bo͝or**′**ĭsh) *adj.* Crude, rude, and offensive: *loud boorish behavior.* **—boor′ish·ly** *adv.* **—boor′ish·ness** *n.*

boost (bo͞ost) *tr.v.* **boost·ed, boost·ing, boosts 1.** To lift by pushing up from below: *My friend boosted me into the tree.* **2.** To increase; raise: *Advertising often boosts sales.* **3.** To increase the strength of (an electric current or signal). **4.** To stir up enthusiasm for; promote: *She writes articles that boost her hometown.* ❖ *n.* **1.** A push upward or ahead: *Give me a boost up the pole.* **2.** An encouraging act or comment. **3.** An increase: *A boost in salary.*

boost·er (bo͞o**′**stər) *n.* **1.** Something that increases the power or effectiveness of a system or device: *a battery booster.* **2.** An amplifier for radio or television signals: *a television booster.* **3.** A rocket used to launch a missile or space vehicle. **4.** A booster shot. **5.** A person or thing that boosts: *The holiday was a morale booster.*

booster shot *n.* An additional dose of a vaccine or serum given in order to sustain the immunity provided by an earlier dose of the same vaccine or serum.

boot[1] (bo͞ot) *n.* **1.** A kind of shoe that covers the foot and ankle and usually part of the lower calf, often made of leather or rubber. **2.** Something shaped like a boot, as a peninsula: *the boot of Italy.* **3.** A kick: *give a ball a good boot.* **4.** *Slang* The state of being fired from a job: *Half the staff was given the boot.* **5.** *Chiefly British* The trunk of an automobile. **6.** The process of starting or restarting a computer. ❖ *tr.v.* **boot·ed, boot·ing, boots 1.** To kick: *The soccer player booted the ball down the field.* **2.** To put boots on: *The soldiers carrying flags were booted.* **3.** To start (a computer) by loading the operating system. **4.** In baseball, to misplay (a ground ball). [From Middle English *bote*, from Old French.]

boot[2] (bo͞ot) *intr.v.* **boot·ed, boot·ing, boots** To benefit, help, or avail: *It boots you little to worry.* ◆ **to boot** In addition; besides: *He got a T-shirt and a baseball cap to boot.* [From Old English *bōtian*, from *bōt*, help.]

boot·black (bo͞ot**′**blăk′) *n.* A person who cleans and polishes shoes for a living.

boot camp *n.* **1.** A training camp for soldiers or sailors who have just joined the armed services. **2.** A facility, similar to a military boot camp, where convicted criminals undergo intense physical workouts as part of a program to teach self-discipline and respect for the law.

boo·tee also **boo·tie** (bo͞o**′**tē) *n.* A soft, usually knitted baby shoe.

❑ *These sound alike:* **bootee, booty** (loot).

Bo·ö·tes (bō-ō**′**tēz) *n.* A constellation in the Northern Hemisphere near the handle of the Big Dipper, traditionally pictured as a herdsman.

booth (bo͞oth) *n., pl.* **booths** (bo͞o*th*z *or* bo͞oths) **1.** A small enclosed or partially enclosed compartment, usually for a single person: *a telephone booth; a voting booth.* **2.** A small enclosed compartment with a window, at which a service is provided: *a ticket booth; an information booth.* **3.** A small stall where merchandise is sold: *a booth at the market selling gourmet foods.* **4.** A seating compartment consisting of a table enclosed by two facing benches with high backs: *We ate in a booth at the restaurant.*

Booth (bo͞oth), **John Wilkes** 1838–1865. American actor who killed President Abraham Lincoln.

boot·jack (bo͞ot**′**jăk′) *n.* A forked device that holds a boot while the foot is pulled out of it.

boot·leg (bo͞ot**′**lĕg′) *v.* **boot·legged, boot·leg·ging, boot·legs** *—tr.* To make, sell, or transport (a product, especially alcoholic liquor) illegally. *—intr.* To engage in bootlegging a product, especially alcoholic liquor. ❖ *n.* A product that is illegally made, sold, or transported. ❖ *adj.* Made, sold, or transported illegally: *bootleg music tapes.* **—boot′leg′ger** *n.*

boot·less (bo͞ot**′**lĭs) *adj.* Without advantage or benefit; useless; fruitless: *a bootless effort.*

boo·ty (bo͞o**′**tē) *n., pl.* **boo·ties 1.** Plunder taken from an enemy in war: *Soldiers often carry off the booty of war.* **2.** Seized or stolen goods: *pirates' booty.* **3.** A valuable prize; a treasure: *Divers brought up booty from a sunken ship.*

❑ *These sound alike:* **booty, bootee** (baby shoe).

booze (bo͞oz) *Slang n.* Alcoholic drink. ❖ *intr.v.* **boozed, booz·ing, booz·es** To drink alcoholic beverages to excess. **—booz′er** *n.*

bop[1] (bŏp) *Informal tr.v.* **bopped, bop·ping, bops** To hit or strike. ❖ *n.* A blow or punch. [Of imitative origin.]

bop[2] (bŏp) *n.* Bebop. [Short for *bebop*.]

bo·rate (**bôr′**āt′) *n.* A salt or ester of boric acid.

bo·rax (**bôr′**ăks′) *n.* A white crystalline powder and mineral, used as an antiseptic, as a cleansing agent, in fusing metals, and in making heat-resistant glass. The mineral is an ore of boron.

Bor·deaux[1] (bôr-**dō′**) A city of southwest France southwest of Paris. It is the trading center of a wine-producing region.

Bor·deaux[2] (bôr-**dō′**) *n., pl.* **Bor·deaux** (bôr-**dō′** *or* bôr-**dōz′**) A red or white wine made in the region around Bordeaux, France.

bor·der (**bôr′**dər) *n.* **1.** The line where one country, state, or region ends and another begins; a boundary: *the border between the United States and Canada.* **2.** A margin or edge: *They picnicked on the border of the pond.* **3.** A strip put on or around an edge, as for ornament: *a border of lace around the tablecloth.* ❖ *tr.v.* **bor·dered, bor·der·ing, bor·ders 1.** To lie along or next to: *Canada and Mexico border the United States.* **2.** To put a border or an edging on: *border a collar with lace.* ◆ **border on** or **border upon 1.** To be next to; touch: *France borders on Germany.* **2.** To come close to; approach: *This weather borders on the ideal.* [From Middle English *bordure*, from Old French *bordure*, to border, from *bort*, border, of Germanic origin.]

❑ *These sound alike:* **border, boarder** (lodger).

Daniel Boone
1820 portrait by Chester Harding (1792–1866)

WRITERS CHOOSE THEIR WORDS

"Mr. Lewis!" he said sternly. "I've had to tolerate your increasingly **boorish** behavior throughout this semester, and, frankly, I'm getting tired of it."

—Paul Baczewski
Just for Kicks

John Wilkes Booth

USAGE

borrow The word **borrow** means "to take (something) temporarily with the promise of returning it"; **lend** means "to give (something) temporarily on condition of having it returned." A library *lends* books; readers *borrow* them. Another verb very similar to "lend" is **loan,** meaning "to lend money or an object." *Lend* also has a figurative use, but *loan* does not: *The music lent spirit to the party. Lend us your enthusiasm.*

ă	pat	ôr	core
ā	pay	oi	boy
âr	care	ou	out
ä	father	o͝o	took
ĕ	pet	o͝or	lure
ē	be	o͞o	boot
ĭ	pit	ŭ	cut
ī	bite	ûr	urge
îr	pier	th	thin
ŏ	pot	*th*	this
ō	toe	zh	vision
ô	paw	ə	about

SYNONYMS **border, edge, margin, brink, rim** These nouns mean the line or narrow area that marks the outside limit of something. **Border** can mean a boundary line: *He built a fence along his property's border.* **Edge** can mean the precise bounding line where two different surfaces meet: *She curled her toes over the diving board's edge.* **Margin** refers to a strip that runs along an edge or border: *Cornflowers grow along the margin of the meadow.* **Brink** means the upper edge of something steep: *The car teetered on the brink of the canyon.* **Rim** often means the edge of something that is circular or curved: *The rim of the telescope lens had a small nick.*

border collie *n.* A dog of a medium-sized, agile breed developed on the border between England and Scotland for herding sheep, often having a wavy black coat with white markings.

bor·der·land (bôr**′**dər-lănd′) *n.* **1.** Land on or near a border or frontier. **2.** An indefinite area or condition in which two different things seem to overlap: *the borderland between dreams and reality.*

bor·der·line (bôr**′**dər-līn′) *n.* **1.** A dividing line; a border or boundary. **2.** An indefinite line between two different conditions: *on the borderline between good and excellent.* ❖ *adj.* **1.** Relating to an indefinite or uncertain area between two different conditions: *a borderline medical diagnosis.* **2.** Barely acceptable; nearly unacceptable or abnormal: *borderline behavior.*

Border States The slave states bordering the free states of the North during the Civil War. After Virginia joined the Confederacy in 1861, its western counties formed the new state of West Virginia, which remained in the Union along with the other Border States of Delaware, Maryland, Kentucky, and Missouri.

bore[1] (bôr) *v.* **bored, bor·ing, bores** —*tr.* **1.** To make (a hole, tunnel, or well) by drilling or digging: *bore a tunnel through a mountain.* **2.** To make a hole in or through (something), as with a drill or auger: *bore a mountain to make a tunnel.* —*intr.* To make a hole by drilling or digging: *The miners bored through the rock to get at the coal.* ❖ *n.* **1.** The inside diameter of a hole, tube, cylinder, or other hollow object: *a pipe with a bore of three inches.* **2.** A bored hole, as in a pipe or the barrel of a firearm. [From Old English *borian.*]

❑ *These sound alike:* **bore[1]** (drill), **boar** (male pig), **bore[2]** (make weary), **bore[3]** (tidal wave), **bore[4]** (supported).

bore[2] (bôr) *tr.v.* **bored, bor·ing, bores** To make weary by being dull or repetitive: *The speaker bored the audience by talking too long.* ❖ *n.* An uninteresting person or thing.

❑ *These sound alike:* **bore[2]** (make weary), **boar** (male pig), **bore[1]** (drill), **bore[3]** (tidal wave), **bore[4]** (supported).

bore[3] (bôr) *n.* A sudden high tidal wave that rushes upstream, with great force, at the mouth of a river. [From Middle English *bare,* wave, from Old Norse *bāra.*]

❑ *These sound alike:* **bore[3]** (tidal wave), **boar** (male pig), **bore[1]** (drill), **bore[2]** (make weary), **bore[4]** (supported).

bore[4] (bôr) *v.* Past tense of **bear[1].**

❑ *These sound alike:* **bore[4]** (supported), **boar** (male pig), **bore[1]** (drill), **bore[2]** (make weary), **bore[3]** (tidal wave).

bore·dom (bôr**′**dəm) *n.* The condition of being bored; weariness of mind.

bor·er (bôr**′**ər) *n.* **1.** A tool used for boring or drilling. **2.** Any of various insects or insect larvae that bore into the stems or trunks of plants. **3.** Any of various mollusks that bore into soft rock or wood.

bo·ric acid (bôr**′**ĭk) *n.* A white or colorless crystalline compound occurring in nature or made from borax and composed of hydrogen, boron, and oxygen. It is used as an antiseptic, as a preservative, and in cements and enamels.

bor·ing (bôr**′**ĭng) *adj.* Uninteresting; dull: *a long boring speech.* —**bor′ing·ly** *adv.*

SYNONYMS **boring, dull, tedious, tiresome** These adjectives mean lacking in interest, liveliness, or imagination. **Boring** describes something that makes one feel tired and unhappy: *The movie was so boring that most of the audience left before the end.* **Dull** means uninteresting and unsurprising: *The lecturer managed to give an enthusiastic presentation on a dull topic.* **Tedious** describes something that is boring because of its slowness: *You might think train travel is romantic, but I find it tedious.* **Tiresome** means tedious and repetitious: *I don't mind the tiresome job of returning empty cans because I want to help keep the environment clean.*
ANTONYM **interesting**

born (bôrn) *v.* A past participle of **bear[1].** ❖ *adj.* **1.** Brought into life or existence: *a political movement born in the last century.* **2.** Having a natural talent from birth: *a born artist.* **3.** Destined from birth: *She was born to sing.* **4.** Coming or resulting: *wisdom born of experience.*

born-a·gain (bôrn**′**ə-gĕn′) *adj.* **1.** Having discovered or renewed a commitment to Jesus as one's personal savior: *a born-again Christian.* **2.** Marked by renewed activity or revived interest or enthusiasm: *a born-again supporter of free speech.*

borne (bôrn) *v.* A past participle of **bear[1].**

Bor·ne·o (bôr**′**nē-ō′) An island of the western Pacific Ocean east of Sumatra and southwest of the Philippines. Brunei is on the northern coast; the rest of the island is divided between Indonesia and Malaysia.

bo·ron (bôr**′**ŏn′) *n. Symbol* **B** A nonmetallic element extracted chiefly from borax and occurring as a brown powder or black crystalline solid. It is used in flares, in nuclear reactors to control the speed of neutrons, in abrasives, and in hard metallic alloys. Atomic number 5. See **Periodic Table.**

bor·ough (bûr**′**ō) *n.* **1.** A self-governing incorporated town, as in certain states of the United States. **2.** One of the five administrative units of New York City. **3.** A governmental district in Alaska, corresponding to a county. **4.** A town in Great Britain that sends one or more representatives to Parliament.

❑ *These sound alike:* **borough, burro** (donkey), **burrow** (hole).

bor·row (bŏr**′**ō) *v.* **bor·rowed, bor·row·ing, bor·rows** —*tr.* **1.** To obtain (something) with the promise of returning or replacing it later: *borrow a library book; borrow money.* **2.** To take (a word, idea, or method) from another source and use it as one's own: *We borrowed the word "kindergarten" from German in the 1800s.* **3.** In mathematics, to subtract (one) from a digit in a number in order to add ten to the value of the digit to the right. When subtracting 6 from 93, you borrow 1 from 9 to make 3 into 13, and then subtract 6, leaving 87. —*intr.* To obtain or receive something, especially money on loan: *I borrowed from the bank to buy a new car.* —**bor′row·er** *n.* —SEE NOTE.

bor·row·ing (bŏr**′**ō-ĭng) *n.* Something that is borrowed, especially a word or phrase borrowed from another language: *The English word "plateau" is a borrowing from French.*

borscht (bôrsht) also **borsch** (bôrsh) *n.* A beet soup served hot or cold, often with sour cream. [From Yiddish *borsht,* from Russian *borshch.*]

bor·zoi (bôr**′**zoi′) *n., pl.* **bor·zois** A large slender dog of a breed developed in Russia to hunt wolves, having a narrow pointed head and silky coat.

bosk·y (bŏs′kē) *adj.* **bosk·i·er, bosk·i·est 1.** Wooded. **2.** Having many bushes and trees: *a bosky stretch of land along the river.*

bo's'n (bō′sən) *n.* Variant of **boatswain.**

Bos·ni·a (bŏz′nē-ə) **1.** A region making up the northern part of Bosnia and Herzegovina. It was settled by Serbs in the 7th century and has been joined with Herzegovina since the 1400s. **2.** See **Bosnia and Herzegovina.** **—Bos′ni·an** *adj. & n.*

Bosnia and Her·ze·go·vi·na (hĕrt′sə-gō-**vē′**nə *or* hûrt′sə-gō-**vē′**nə) also **Bosnia-Herzegovina** Commonly known as **Bosnia.** A country of the northwest Balkan Peninsula west of Serbia. It was part of Yugoslavia from 1946 to 1991, when it declared its independence. Sarajevo is the capital.

bos·om (bŏŏz′əm *or* bōō′zəm) *n.* **1a.** The chest: *He held the sleepy child to his bosom.* **b.** A woman's breast or breasts. **2.** The part of a garment that covers the breast: *the starched bosom of a shirt.* **3.** The human breast regarded as the center of emotion: *empty one's bosom of sorrow.* **4.** Emotional closeness and comfort: *We welcomed her into the bosom of our family.* ❖ *adj.* Close; intimate: *bosom friends.*

Bos·po·rus (bŏs′pər-əs) A narrow strait separating European and Asian Turkey and joining the Black Sea with the Sea of Marmara.

boss[1] (bôs) *n.* **1.** A person who employs or directs workers. **2.** A person who is in charge or makes decisions: *Who is boss around here?* **3.** A powerful person who controls a political party or organization. ❖ *tr.v.* **bossed, boss·ing, boss·es** To give orders to; order around: *Their older cousin tried to boss the children around.* [From Dutch *baas,* master.]

boss[2] (bôs) *n.* A raised ornament projecting from a flat surface. ❖ *tr.v.* **bossed, boss·ing, boss·es** To decorate with bosses; emboss. [From Middle English *boce,* from Old French.]

boss·ism (bô′sĭz′əm) *n.* The control of a political party or organization by a boss.

boss·y (bô′sē) *adj.* **boss·i·er, boss·i·est** Inclined to order others around; domineering.

Bos·ton (bô′stən) The capital of Massachusetts, in the eastern part of the state on an inlet of the Atlantic Ocean. It was founded in 1600.

Boston terrier *n.* A small dog of a breed developed in New England, having a short muzzle and a black or brindled coat with white markings.

bo·sun (bō′sən) *n.* Variant of **boatswain.**

bot (bŏt) *n.* A software program that imitates human behavior, as by responding to questions and comments in chatrooms.

bo·tan·i·cal (bə-tăn′ĭ-kəl) *adj.* Relating to plants or botany: *a collection of botanical specimens.* **—bo·tan′i·cal·ly** *adv.*

botanical garden *n.* A place for the study, cultivation, and exhibition of plants.

bot·a·nist (bŏt′n-ĭst) *n.* A scientist who specializes in botany.

bot·a·ny (bŏt′n-ē) *n., pl.* **bot·a·nies 1.** The branch of biology that deals with plants. **2.** The plant life of a particular area: *the botany of Arizona.* [From Greek *botanē,* fodder, plants.]

botch (bŏch) *tr.v.* **botched, botch·ing, botch·es** To spoil by careless or clumsy work; bungle: *botch a repair job.* ❖ *n.* A bad job or poor piece of work; a mess: *made a botch of the paint job.*

both (bōth) *adj.* One as well as the other; relating to or being two: *Both sides of the board are painted.* ❖ *pron.* The one as well as the other: *Both of them skate well.* ❖ *conj.* As well; equally: *The baby both walks and talks.* [From Middle English *bothe,* from Old Norse *bādhar.*] —SEE NOTE.

both·er (bŏ*th*′ər) *v.* **both·ered, both·er·ing, both·ers** *—tr.* **1.** To disturb or anger; annoy: *Noise in the hall bothered the teacher while she was teaching.* **2.** To make nervous or upset: *Being in high places bothers some people.* **3.** To take the trouble (to do something): *My brother didn't bother to take out the trash. —intr.* To take the trouble; concern oneself: *He was in too much of a hurry to bother with the formalities.* ❖ *n.* An annoying thing; a nuisance: *Having to wait so long was a bother.* [Probably from dialectal *bodder,* possibly of Celtic origin.]

both·er·some (bŏ*th*′ər-səm) *adj.* Causing trouble; troublesome: *He raised several bothersome questions about the details of the plan.*

bot·net (bŏt′nĕt′) *n.* A network of maliciously installed bots running on multiple computers.

Bot·swa·na (bŏt-**swä′**nə) A country of south-central Africa. Gaborone is the capital.

bot·tle (bŏt′l) *n.* **1.** A container, usually made of glass or plastic, having a narrow neck and a mouth that can be corked or capped. **2a.** A bottle with something in it: *buy a bottle of ketchup.* **b.** The amount that a bottle holds: *A whole bottle of perfume spilled on the table.* **3.** A bottle filled with milk or formula with a nipple for feeding a baby. ❖ *tr.v.* **bot·tled, bot·tling, bot·tles** To put in a bottle or bottles: *a machine that bottles water.* ◆ **bottle up** To hold in or back; restrain: *bottle up one's anger; bottle up traffic for hours.* [From Middle English *botel,* from Medieval Latin *butticula,* diminutive of Late Latin *buttis,* cask.] **—bot′tler** *n.*

bot·tle·neck (bŏt′l-nĕk′) *n.* **1.** A narrow route or passage where movement is slowed down: *Highway construction caused a bottleneck that slowed traffic to a crawl.* **2.** A condition that slows or hinders progress: *The staff shortage created a bottleneck in the processing of applications.*

bot·tom (bŏt′əm) *n.* **1.** The lowest or deepest part of something: *the bottom of a page; the bottom of the hill.* **2.** The underside of something: *the bottom of a boot.* **3.** The solid surface under a body of water: *The diver went to the bottom of the lake.* **4.** The underlying truth or cause; the basis or heart: *get to the bottom of the mystery.* **5.** often **bottoms** The low land that adjoins a river. **6.** The seat of a chair: *a cane bottom.* **7.** The part of a ship's hull below the water line: *barnacles growing on the bottom of a boat.* **8.** The second half of an inning in baseball. **9.** *Informal* The buttocks. ❖ *adj.* **1.** Situated at the bottom: *the bottom shelf.* **2.** Of the lowest degree, quality, rank, or amount: *the bottom team in the league.* ❖ *intr.v.* **bot·tomed, bot·tom·ing, bot·toms** To have or strike the underside against something: *The car bottomed on the gravel.* ◆ **at bottom** Basically: *Though gruff, at bottom the store owner was a kindly person.* **bottom out** To reach the lowest point possible, after which only a rise may occur: *Sales of personal computers have bottomed out.* [From Old English *botm.*]

bot·tom·land (bŏt′əm-lănd′) *n.* often **bottomlands** Low-lying land along a river: *Ohio River bottomlands.*

bot·tom·less (bŏt′əm-lĭs) *adj.* **1.** Having no bottom: *a bottomless container that rests on the ground.* **2.** Too deep to be measured: *a bottomless lake.* **3.** Having no limitations; boundless: *bottomless sympathy; a bottomless supply of money.*

bottom line *n.* **1.** The last line in a financial statement that shows the amount of profit or loss for a business. **2.** The final result or statement; the upshot: *The bottom line was that the play was a success.* **3.** The main or essential point: *The bottom line is that he forgives you.*

bot·tom-line (bŏt′əm-līn′) *adj.* **1.** Concerned mainly with costs and profits: *bottom-line business decisions.* **2.** Essential; crucial: *Plenty of exercise is a bottom-line requirement for good health.*

Boston terrier

USAGE

both The word **both** means "each of two, taken individually." *Both books weigh more than five pounds* means that each book weighs more than five pounds by itself, not that the two books weighed together come to more than five pounds. When *both* is used with *and* to link two words or phrases in a sentence, these words or phrases should be grammatically parallel. The phrases *in both India and China* and *both in India and in China* are parallel. The phrase *both in India and China* is not.

bouquet

WORD HISTORY

boutique The word **boutique,** "a small, specialized retail shop," comes from French, as its spelling and pronunciation suggest. The French word *boutique* comes from Latin *apothēca,* "storehouse, warehouse." The same Latin word became *bodega* in Spanish, meaning "wine cellar, pantry, storeroom." In the United States the word *bodega* refers to a grocery store in a Spanish-speaking neighborhood.

ă	pat	ôr	core
ā	pay	oi	boy
âr	care	ou	out
ä	father	o͝o	took
ĕ	pet	o͝or	lure
ē	be	o͞o	boot
ĭ	pit	ŭ	cut
ī	bite	ûr	urge
îr	pier	th	thin
ŏ	pot	*th*	this
ō	toe	zh	vision
ô	paw	ə	about

bot·u·lism (**bŏch′**ə-lĭz′əm) *n.* A serious, often fatal form of food poisoning usually caused by bacteria that grow in improperly canned or preserved foods and produce poisons that act on the nervous system. [From German *Botulismus,* from Latin *botulus,* sausage.]

Bou·dic·ca (bo͞o-**dĭk′**ə) also **Bo·ad·i·ce·a** (bō′ăd-ĭ-**sē′**ə) First century AD. Queen of ancient Britain who led a revolt against the Roman army.

bou·doir (**bo͞o′**dwär′ *or* **bo͞o′**dwôr′) *n.* A woman's private sitting room, dressing room, or bedroom.

bouf·fant (bo͞o-**fänt′**) *adj.* Full and puffed-out, as a hairdo, skirt, or sleeve.

bough (bou) *n.* A large or main branch of a tree.
❑ *These sound alike:* **bough, bow¹** (front of a ship), **bow²** (bend).

bought (bôt) *v.* Past tense and past participle of **buy.**

bouil·la·baisse (bo͞o′yə-**bās′** *or* **bo͞ol′**yə-bās′) *n.* A highly seasoned thick soup made with several kinds of fish and shellfish.

bouil·lon (**bo͝ol′**yŏn′ *or* **bo͝ol′**yən) *n.* A clear thin broth usually made by simmering meat in water with seasonings: *beef bouillon.*
❑ *These sound alike:* **bouillon, bullion** (gold).

boul·der (**bōl′**dər) *n.* A large rounded mass of rock lying on the ground or imbedded in the soil.

boul·e·vard (**bo͝ol′**ə-värd′) *n.* A broad city street, often lined with trees. [From Old French *bollevart,* rampart converted to a promenade, from Middle Dutch *bolwerc,* bulwark.]

bounce (bouns) *v.* **bounced, bounc·ing, bounc·es** —*intr.* **1.** To hit a surface and spring back from it; rebound: *The ball bounced off the wall.* **2.** To move with a bobbing, jolting, or vibrating motion: *Cars bounced down the dirt road.* **3.** To jump, spring, or bound: *The excited children bounced out of the room.* **4.** To be reflected: *Sunlight bounced off the water into my eyes.* **5.** To be left unpaid because of insufficient money in an account: *The check bounced because of insufficient funds.* —*tr.* **1.** To cause to bounce: *Bounce the ball to me.* **2.** To present or propose for comment or approval: *bounced an idea off my teacher.* **3.** *Slang* To throw (someone) out forcefully: *The rowdy group was bounced from the movie theater.* ❖ *n.* **1.** An act of bouncing or a bouncing movement; a bound or rebound: *catch a ball off the first bounce.* **2.** Capacity to bounce; springiness: *a rubber ball with plenty of bounce.* ◆ **bounce back** To return to a normal condition; recover or begin anew: *bounce back after a serious illness.*

bounc·er (**boun′**sər) *n. Slang* A person employed to remove disorderly people from a nightclub, bar, or similar place of entertainment.

bounc·ing (**boun′**sĭng) *adj.* Big and strong; healthy; thriving: *a happy bouncing baby.*

bounc·y (**boun′**sē) *adj.* **bounc·i·er, bounc·i·est 1.** Tending to bounce: *a bouncy ball.* **2.** Springy; elastic: *bouncy hair.* **3.** Lively; energetic: *bouncy tunes.* **—bounc′i·ly** *adv.*

bound¹ (bound) *intr.v.* **bound·ed, bound·ing, bounds** **1.** To leap, jump, or spring: *The dog bounded over the gate.* **2.** To move forward by leaps or springs: *The deer bounded into the woods.* ❖ *n.* **1.** A leap or jump: *The deer was away in a single bound.* **2.** A rebound; a bounce. [From French *bondir,* to bounce, perhaps from Latin *bombitāre,* to hum, from *bombus,* a humming sound, from Greek *bombos.*]

bound² (bound) *n.* **1.** often **bounds** A limit; a boundary: *Their enthusiasm knew no bounds.* **2. bounds** The territory on, within, or near limiting lines: *the bounds of the kingdom.* ❖ *tr.v.* **bound·ed, bound·ing, bounds** To enclose or be the boundary of: *Water bounds the city on three sides.* ◆ **in bounds** In sports, within the area marked as the playing surface. **out of bounds 1.** In sports, outside the area marked as the playing surface. **2.** In a way that is unacceptable: *behavior that was out of bounds.* [From Middle English, from Medieval Latin *bodina,* of Celtic origin.]

bound³ (bound) *v.* Past tense and past participle of **bind.** ❖ *adj.* **1.** Being under obligation; obliged: *bound by a promise.* **2.** Certain: *If we leave after dark, we are bound to be late for dinner.* **3.** Confined by bonds; tied: *the bound hands of the prisoner.* **4.** Enclosed in a cover or binding: *a bound book.* ◆ **bound up with** Closely associated or connected with: *The migration of birds is bound up with change in the seasons.*

bound⁴ (bound) *adj.* Headed or intending to go in a certain direction: *We are bound for Quebec.* [From Middle English *boun,* ready, from Old Norse *būinn,* past participle of *būa,* to get ready.]

bound·a·ry (**boun′**də-rē *or* **boun′**drē) *n., pl.* **bound·a·ries** A border or limit: *the southern boundary of Montana; the boundary between right and wrong.*

bound·en (**boun′**dən) *adj.* Being an obligation; required: *a soldier's bounden duty.*

bound·less (**bound′**lĭs) *adj.* **1.** Without any known limits; infinite: *the boundless reaches of outer space.* **2.** Very great; enormous: *her boundless energy.* **—bound′less·ness** *n.*

boun·te·ous (**boun′**tē-əs) *adj.* Existing in or producing great abundance: *a bounteous feast; a bounteous harvest.* **—boun′te·ous·ly** *adv.* **—boun′te·ous·ness** *n.*

boun·ti·ful (**boun′**tə-fəl) *adj.* **1.** Plentiful; abundant: *bountiful crops.* **2.** Giving generously and kindly: *a bountiful donor.* **—boun′ti·ful·ly** *n.* **—boun′ti·ful·ness** *n.*

boun·ty (**boun′**tē) *n., pl.* **boun·ties 1.** Generosity in giving: *an artist dependent on the bounty of patrons.* **2.** Plentiful gifts or provisions: *the bounty of the earth in a rich harvest.* **3.** A reward for performing a service for the government, as for capturing an outlaw or killing a destructive animal.

bou·quet (bō-**kā′** *or* bo͞o-**kā′**) *n.* **1.** A cluster or arrangement of flowers. **2.** A pleasant odor, especially of a wine.

bour·bon (**bûr′**bən) *n.* A whiskey distilled mainly from fermented corn mash.

Bour·bon (**bo͝or′**bən *or* bo͞or-**bôN′**) French royal family descended from Louis I, Duke of Bourbon (1270?–1342), whose members have ruled in France, Spain, and Naples and Sicily.

bour·geois (bo͝or-**zhwä′** *or* **bo͝or′**zhwä′) *n., pl.* **bourgeois** A member of the middle class or bourgeoisie. ❖ *adj.* **1.** Relating to or typical of the middle class: *bourgeois merchants and shopkeepers.* **2.** Caring too much about respectability and possessions: *bourgeois attitudes about social standing.*

bour·geoi·sie (bo͝or′zhwä-**zē′**) *n.* **1.** The middle class in a society. **2.** In the political theory of Karl Marx, the social group opposed to the lower classes, consisting of landowners and other capitalists.

bourn¹ also **bourne** (bôrn *or* bo͝orn) *n.* A stream or brook. [From Old English *burna.*]

bourn² also **bourne** (bôrn *or* bo͝orn) *n. Archaic* **1.** A boundary or limit. **2.** A goal or destination. [From Old French *bodne,* from Medieval Latin *bodina.*]

bour·rée (bo͞o-**rā′** *or* bo͞o-**rā′**) *n.* **1.** A lively French dance of the 1600s, resembling the gavotte. **2.** Music written for this dance.

bout (bout) *n.* **1.** A contest, such as a boxing match. **2.** A period or spell: *a severe bout of the flu.*

bou·tique (bo͞o-**tēk′**) *n.* A small retail shop that sells gifts, fashionable clothes, or other specialized merchandise. —SEE NOTE.

bou·ton·niere (bo͞o′tə-**nîr′**) *n.* A flower worn in a buttonhole, usually on the lapel of a man's jacket.

bo·vine (**bō′**vīn′) *adj.* **1.** Relating to or resembling a cow or a cowlike mammal, such as a yak. **2.** Dull and placid:

He sat in front of the TV with a bovine stare on his face. ❖ *n.* A cow or a cowlike mammal. [From Late Latin *bovīnus*, from Latin *bōs*, cow.]

bow¹ (bou) *n.* **1.** The front section of a ship or boat. **2.** Either of the sides of this front section: *the starboard bow.* [From Middle English *boue*, probably of Low German origin.]

❑ *These sound alike:* **bow¹** (front of a ship), **bough** (branch), **bow²** (bend).

bow² (bou) *v.* **bowed, bow·ing, bows** —*intr.* **1.** To bend the body, head, or knee, as in greeting or agreement: *bow politely from the waist.* **2.** To bend downward; stoop: *The mover bowed beneath the heavy load.* **3.** To give in; yield: *They refused to bow to pressure.* —*tr.* **1.** To bend (the body, head, or knee), as in greeting, agreement, or respect: *bow the head in prayer.* **2.** To express by bowing: *They bowed their agreement.* ❖ *n.* A bending of the body or head, as when showing respect or accepting applause. ◆ **bow out** To remove oneself; withdraw: *The candidate bowed out of the race for mayor.* **take a bow** To acknowledge or accept applause, as by standing up or coming out on stage: *The cast took a bow before the audience.* [From Old English *būgan*.]

❑ *These sound alike:* **bow²** (bend), **bough** (branch), **bow¹** (front of a ship).

bow³ (bō) *n.* **1.** A weapon used to shoot arrows, consisting of a flexible curved strip, usually of wood or plastic, with a string stretched tightly from end to end. **2.** A slender rod having horsehair stretched between two raised ends, used in playing the violin, viola, and other stringed instruments. **3.** A knot usually having two loops and two ends: *tie shoes with a bow.* **4.** A curve or arch, as of lips or eyebrows. **5.** A rainbow. ❖ *v.* **bowed, bow·ing, bows** —*tr.* **1.** To play with a bow: *bow a fiddle.* **2.** To bend into a curved shape: *The heavy snow bowed the branches until they broke.* —*intr.* **1.** To play a stringed instrument with a bow. **2.** To bend into a curved shape: *The branches bowed and snapped in the high wind.* [From Old English *boga*.]

❑ *These sound alike:* **bow³** (weapon), **beau** (suitor).

bow·el (bou′əl) *n.* **1.** often **bowels** The intestine, especially of a human. **2.** A part of the intestine: *the large bowel.* **3. bowels** The interior part of something: *the bowels of a ship.*

bow·er (bou′ər) *n.* A leafy shaded nook or shelter; an arbor.

bow·ie knife (bō′ē *or* bo͞o′ē) *n.* A long heavy knife with a single-edged blade, carried in a sheath and used for hunting. [After James *Bowie* (1799–1836), American-born Mexican colonist.]

bowl¹ (bōl) *n.* **1.** A rounded hollow container or dish that can hold liquid or food: *a soup bowl; a mixing bowl.* **2.** The amount that a bowl holds: *Eat a bowl of cereal.* **3.** Something shaped like a bowl, such as the hollow part of a spoon or a valley. **4a.** A stadium or outdoor theater shaped like a bowl. **b.** One of several special football games played after the regular season ends. [From Old English *bolla*.]

❑ *These sound alike:* **bowl¹** (dish), **bole** (tree trunk), **boll** (seed capsule), **bowl²** (ball).

bowl² (bōl) *n.* **1.** A wooden or plastic ball shaped to roll in a curving line, used in the game of lawn bowling. **2.** A throwing or rolling of the ball in various bowling games. ❖ *v.* **bowled, bowl·ing, bowls** —*intr.* **1.** To play the game of bowling: *Do you like to bowl?* **2.** To roll or throw a ball in bowling: *You bowl first.* **3.** To move smoothly and rapidly: *Huge trucks bowled along the superhighway.* —*tr.* **1.** To play (a game) of bowling. **2.** To make (a score) in bowling: *The champion bowled a high score.* **3.** To knock down with or as if with a rolling ball: *The swimmer was bowled by the wave.* ◆ **bowl over** To take by surprise or overwhelm: *The unexpected announcement bowled them over.* [From Middle English *boule*, from Latin *bulla*, round object.]

❑ *These sound alike:* **bowl²** (ball), **bole** (tree trunk), **boll** (seed capsule), **bowl¹** (dish).

bow·leg·ged (bō′lĕg′ĭd *or* bō′lĕgd′) *adj.* Having legs that curve outward near the knee: *a bowlegged horseman.*

bowl·er¹ (bō′lər) *n.* A person who bowls.

bowl·er² (bō′lər) *n.* A derby hat.

bow·line (bō′lĭn *or* bō′līn′) *n.* A knot forming a loop that does not slip.

bowl·ing (bō′lĭng) *n.* **1.** A game played by rolling a ball down a bowling alley to knock down ten wooden pins at the opposite end; tenpins. **2.** A similar game, such as ninepins or skittles. **3.** Lawn bowling.

bowling alley *n.* **1.** A smooth level wooden lane used in bowling. **2.** A building or room containing lanes for bowling.

bowling green *n.* A smooth grassy area on which the game of lawn bowling is played.

bow·man (bō′mən) *n.* A person who shoots with a bow and arrow; an archer.

bow·sprit (bou′sprĭt′ *or* bō′sprĭt′) *n.* A long pole sticking out of the front of a sailing ship, to which lines are attached for fastening sails.

bow·string (bō′strĭng′) *n.* The string of a bow that is pulled back to shoot an arrow.

bow tie (bō) *n.* A small necktie tied in a bow.

box¹ (bŏks) *n.* **1a.** A stiff container having four sides, a bottom, and often a top or lid. **b.** The amount that a box can hold: *eat a box of crackers.* **2.** A rectangle or square: *Draw a box around the right answer.* **3a.** A separated compartment holding seats in a theater or stadium. **b.** A small building serving as a shelter: *a sentry box.* **4.** A signaling device enclosed in a casing: *a fire-alarm box.* **5a.** A post office box. **b.** An inbox or outbox. **6.** An area on a baseball field marked by lines to show where the batter, catcher, or coach may stand. **7.** The driver's seat on a carriage, coach, or other horse-drawn vehicle. ❖ *tr.v.* **boxed, box·ing, box·es 1.** To put or pack in a box: *box fruit before shipping.* **2.** To enclose in something shaped like a box: *box the title of the story.* **3.** To hinder or impede, as by blocking or restricting: *The bus was boxed in by the traffic jam.* ◆ **outside the box** In a very unconventional or original way: *Solving this puzzle requires thinking outside the box.* [From Old English, from Late Latin *buxis*, from Greek *puxis*, from *puxos*, box tree.]

box² (bŏks) *n.* A hit or slap with the hand: *a box on the ear.* ❖ *v.* **boxed, box·ing, box·es** —*tr.* **1.** To take part in a boxing match with (an opponent). **2.** To hit or slap with the hand. —*intr.* To fight with the fists in a boxing match. [From Middle English.]

box³ (bŏks) *n., pl.* **box** or **box·es 1.** Any of several shrubs or trees having small evergreen leaves and hard yellowish wood, used for hedges and ornamental borders. **2.** The wood of such a shrub. [From Old English, from Latin *buxus*, from Greek *puxos*.]

box·car (bŏks′kär′) *n.* An enclosed railroad car used to carry freight that is loaded through a sliding door on each side.

box cutter *n.* A utility knife.

box elder *n.* A small maple tree of North America having compound leaves with toothed or lobed leaflets.

box·er¹ (bŏk′sər) *n.* A person who fights with the fists as a sport.

box·er² (bŏk′sər) *n.* A medium-sized dog having a short, smooth, brownish coat and a square-jawed face.

box·ers (bŏk′sərz) *pl.n.* Boxer shorts.

boxer shorts *pl.n.* Loose-fitting shorts worn especially as underwear or for sport.

bow³

bowline

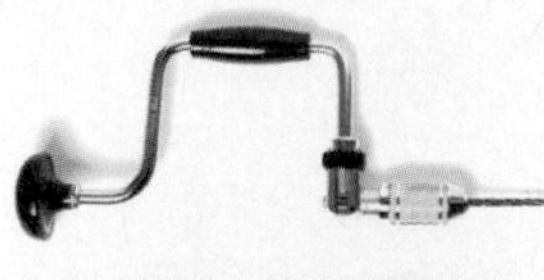

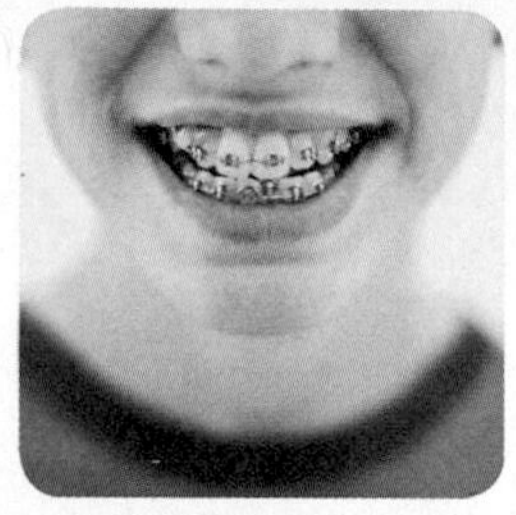

brace
top: boring brace
bottom: dental braces

WRITERS CHOOSE THEIR WORDS

In my nostrils, the faint hay smell of the grass mingled with that of the **brackish** water of the Bay, while the spring wind chilled the tips of my ears and raised goosebumps along my arms.

—Katherine Paterson
Jacob Have I Loved

ă	pat	ôr	core
ā	pay	oi	boy
âr	care	ou	out
ä	father	o͝o	took
ĕ	pet	o͝or	lure
ē	be	o͞o	boot
ĭ	pit	ŭ	cut
ī	bite	ûr	urge
îr	pier	th	thin
ŏ	pot	*th*	this
ō	toe	zh	vision
ô	paw	ə	about

box·ing (bŏk′sĭng) *n.* The sport of fighting with the fists, especially when boxing gloves are worn and blows must be landed on the front or sides and above the waist of the opponent.

boxing glove *n.* One of a pair of heavily padded leather mittens worn for boxing.

box office *n.* A booth where tickets are sold in a theater, auditorium, or stadium.

box score *n.* In sports, a printed summary of a game in the form of a table recording each player's performance.

box seat *n.* A seat in a box at a theater or stadium.

box spring *n.* A cloth-covered frame containing rows of coiled springs, usually placed under a mattress for support.

box turtle *n.* **1.** Any of several North American land turtles, having a high-domed shell into which they can withdraw entirely. **2.** Any of several similar land or water turtles of Asia.

box·wood (bŏks′wo͝od′) *n.* The box plant or its wood.

box·y (bŏk′sē) *adj.* **box·i·er, box·i·est** Resembling a box, as in shape: *The square rear end gave the car a boxy look.*

boy (boi) *n.* **1.** A male child. **2a.** A son: *her youngest boy.* **b.** *Informal* A fellow; a guy: *a night out with the boys.* **3.** *Offensive* A male servant. ❖ *interj.* An expression used to show astonishment, elation, or disgust: *Boy! What a great car!*

boy·cott (boi′kŏt′) *tr.v.* **boy·cott·ed, boy·cott·ing, boy·cotts** To act together in refusing to use, buy from, or deal with, especially as an expression of protest: *boycott a store; boycott a meeting.* ❖ *n.* The act or an instance of boycotting. [After Charles C. *Boycott* (1832–1897), English land agent in Ireland.]

boy·friend (boi′frĕnd′) *n. Informal* **1.** A male sweetheart or favored companion. **2.** A male friend.

boy·hood (boi′ho͝od′) *n.* The time of being a boy: *spent his boyhood on a farm.*

boy·ish (boi′ĭsh) *adj.* Characteristic of or suitable for a boy: *a boyish sense of humor; boyish colors.* **—boy′ish·ly** *adv.* **—boy′ish·ness** *n.*

Boyle (boil), **Robert** 1627–1691. Irish-born British physicist and chemist whose work, which precisely defined chemical elements and reactions, began the separation of chemistry from alchemy.

Boyle's law (boilz) *n.* The physical principle that at a constant temperature the volume of a confined gas decreases as its pressure increases and increases as its pressure decreases. [After Robert *Boyle.*]

Boy Scout *n.* A member of an organization for boys, having the goals of developing self-reliance, good citizenship, and outdoor skills.

boy·sen·ber·ry (boi′zən-bĕr′ē) *n.* **1.** A large dark-red to nearly black fruit that is similar to a blackberry. **2.** The plant that bears such fruit. [After Rudolph *Boysen* (1895–1950), American botanist.]

BPA *abbr.* An abbreviation of bisphenol A.

Br The symbol for the element **bromine.**

bra (brä) *n.* A brassiere.

brace (brās) *n.* **1.** A device that holds parts together or in place; a clamp. **2.** A supporting beam in a building or a connecting wire that holds something steady. **3.** An orthopedic device used to support or align a body part in the correct position. **4.** A handle that holds a drill or bit and is turned to bore holes. **5.** Either of the symbols, { or }, used in printing and writing to connect several lines of text or staves of music and in mathematics to enclose members of a set. **6. braces** Wires and bands attached to the teeth to straighten them. **7. braces** *Chiefly British* Suspenders. **8.** A pair; a couple: *a brace of dogs.* ❖ *tr.v.* **braced, brac·ing, brac·es 1.** To give support to; make firm; strengthen: *brace a tent with poles.* **2.** To prepare for a shock or difficulty: *The candidates braced themselves for the coming election.* [From Middle English, from Old French *brace,* the two arms, from Latin *brācchia,* plural of *brācchium,* arm.]

brace·let (brās′lĭt) *n.* A band or chain worn around the wrist or arm as an ornament.

bra·chi·o·pod (brā′kē-ə-pŏd′ *or* brăk′ē-ə-pŏd′) *n.* Any of various sea animals having paired shells attached to a stalk and a ring of hollow tentacles covered with cilia that sweep food into the mouth. Most brachiopods are extinct, but they are often found as fossils.

bra·chi·o·sau·rus (brā′kē-ə-**sôr′**əs *or* brăk′ē-ə-**sôr′**əs) *n.* A very large plant-eating dinosaur of the Jurassic Period, having forelegs longer than the hind legs.

brac·ing (brā′sĭng) *adj.* Giving strength and energy; refreshing: *a bracing wind.*

brack·en (brăk′ən) *n.* **1.** A fern having large fronds divided into three parts. **2.** An area with dense thickets of this fern.

brack·et (brăk′ĭt) *n.* **1.** A support or fixture fastened to a wall and sticking out to hold something, such as a shelf. **2.** A shelf supported by brackets. **3.** Either of the pair of symbols, [or], used to enclose printed or written material or to enclose a set of mathematical symbols that are to be considered a single expression. **4.** A group, class, or range within a numbered or graded series: *the 9-to-12 age bracket.* ❖ *tr.v.* **brack·et·ed, brack·et·ing, brack·ets 1.** To support with a bracket or brackets: *bracket shelves to strengthen them.* **2.** To place within brackets: *bracket words inserted in a quotation.* **3.** To classify or group together: *The law bracketed taxpayers according to their earnings.*

brack·ish (brăk′ĭsh) *adj.* Slightly salty; briny: *brackish marsh waters near the ocean.*

bract (brăkt) *n.* A small plant part resembling a leaf and growing at the base of a flower or a flower cluster. Most bracts are small and inconspicuous, but some, as in the poinsettia, are showy or brightly colored and resemble petals.

brad (brăd) *n.* A thin nail with a small head. ❖ *tr.v.* **brad·ded, brad·ding, brads** To fasten with brads.

Brad·bur·y (brăd′bĕr′ē *or* brăd′bə-rē), **Ray Douglas** 1920–2012. American writer of science fiction whose works include *Fahrenheit 451* (1953).

Brad·dock (brăd′ək), **Edward** 1695–1755. British general in the American colonies during the French and Indian War.

Brad·ford (brăd′fərd), **William** 1590–1657. English colonist in America. He served as governor of Plymouth colony and led the settlement through its difficult early years.

Brad·street (brăd′strēt′), **Anne Dudley** 1612–1672. English-born colonial American poet whose published works include *The Tenth Muse Lately Sprung Up in America* (1650).

brae (brā) *n. Scots* A hillside; a slope.

brag (brăg) *v.* **bragged, brag·ging, brags** *—intr.* To talk boastfully; boast: *brag about one's accomplishments. —tr.* To boast about; say boastfully: *He bragged that he could outrun all of us.* ❖ *n.* A boast. **—brag′ger** *n.*

brag·gart (brăg′ərt) *n.* A person who brags a lot.

Brahe (brä *or* brä′hē *or* brä′ə), **Tycho** 1546–1601. Danish astronomer who made the most accurate and extensive observations of the planets and stars in the age before the telescope.

Brah·ma (brä′mə) *n.* **1a.** One of the principal Hindu gods, worshipped as the creator of worlds. **b.** Variant of **Brahman** (sense 1). **2.** Variant of **Brahman** (sense 3).

Brah·man (brä′mən) *n.* **1.** also **Brah·ma** (-mə) **a.** In Hinduism, the holy or sacred power that created and sustains the universe. **b.** In Hinduism, the single absolute being that is found throughout the universe and within the individual. **2.** also **Brahmin** (-mĭn) A member of the highest class in traditional Indian society, responsible for officiating at religious rites. **3.** also **Brah·ma** (brä′mə) or **Brah·min** (-mĭn) Any of a breed of beef cattle developed in the southern United States from cattle imported from India, having a hump between the shoulders and a fold of loose skin hanging below the neck.

Brah·man·ism (brä′mə-nĭz′əm) *n.* **1.** The religion of ancient India. **2.** The religious and social system of the Brahmins of India.

Brah·ma·pu·tra (brä′mə-po͞o′trə) A river of southern Asia rising in the Himalaya Mountains of southwest Tibet and flowing about 1,800 miles (2,900 kilometers) to join the Ganges River in central Bangladesh.

Brah·min (brä′mĭn) *n.* **1.** Variant of **Brahman** (sense 2). **2.** A member of the upper social class, especially a member of one of the old New England families: *a Boston Brahmin.* **3.** Variant of **Brahman** (sense 3).

Brahms (brämz), **Johannes** 1833–1897. German composer. His works include concertos, four symphonies, chamber music, and choral compositions.

braid (brād) *tr.v.* **braid·ed, braid·ing, braids 1.** To weave or twist together three or more strands of (hair, fiber, or fabric); plait: *She braided her long hair.* **2.** To make by weaving strands together: *braid a straw rug.* **3.** To decorate or edge with an ornamental trim. ❖ *n.* **1.** A segment of braided hair, fabric, or other material. **2.** Ornamental cord or ribbon, used especially for trimming clothes. **—braid′er** *n.*

Braille or **braille** (brāl) *n.* A system of writing and printing for visually impaired or blind people in which raised dots representing letters, numbers, and punctuation are read by touching them. [After Louis *Braille.*]

Braille, Louis 1809–1852. French educator who invented a writing and printing system for visually impaired or blind people (1829).

brain (brān) *n.* **1.** The large mass of gray and white nerve tissue enclosed in the skull of humans and other vertebrates. It interprets impulses from sense organs, coordinates and controls bodily activities and functions, and is the center of memory, thought, and feeling. **2.** A similar part of an invertebrate animal. **3.** The mind: *The plan took shape in his brain.* **4.** often **brains** Intellectual power; intelligence: *It takes brains to be an economist.* **5.** *Informal* **a.** A highly intelligent person: *That new student is a brain.* **b.** often **brains** The main director or planner, as of an organization: *She is the brains of the business.* **6.** An electronic device, especially a computer, that is used to control a machine or vehicle, such as a ship. ❖ *tr.v.* **brained, brain·ing, brains** *Informal* To hit (someone) on the head. ◆ **rack (one's) brain** *Informal* To think long and hard. [From Old English *brægen.*]

brain·child (brān′chīld′) *n.* *Informal* The product of a person's mind; an original plan, idea, or invention: *The telephone was Bell's brainchild.*

brain death *n.* Complete and irreversible loss of brain function. **—brain′-dead′** (brān′dĕd′) *adj.*

brain·less (brān′lĭs) *adj.* Without thought; stupid; foolish: *I regretted my brainless reply.* **—brain′less·ly** *adv.* **—brain′less·ness** *n.*

brain stem or **brain·stem** (brān′stĕm′) *n.* The part of the brain connecting the spinal cord to the forebrain.

brain·storm (brān′stôrm′) *n.* A sudden inspiration or clever idea. ❖ *v.* **brain·stormed, brain·storm·ing, brain·storms** —*intr.* To propose and discuss, usually in an informal group setting, a variety of ideas for accomplishing something or solving a problem. —*tr.* To consider or produce (an idea, for example) by brainstorming.

brain·teas·er (brān′tē′zər) *n.* A puzzle or problem that is very difficult to solve.

brain·wash (brān′wŏsh′) *tr.v.* **brain·washed, brain·wash·ing, brain·wash·es 1.** To indoctrinate (a person) forcibly so that his or her basic convictions are replaced with a different set of beliefs: *The prisoner was brainwashed into rejecting his country's ideals.* **2.** To persuade (a person) by intense means, such as repeated suggestions, to adopt a belief or behave in a certain way: *TV commercials brainwashed them into buying junk food.*

brain·wash·ing (brān′wŏsh′ĭng) *n.* The act or process by which someone is brainwashed. [Translation of Chinese (Mandarin) *xǐ nǎo* : *xǐ*, to wash + *nǎo*, brain.]

brain wave *n.* A rhythmic electric fluctuation arising from the brain and capable of being measured between points on the scalp. Brain waves are recorded by an electroencephalograph and are used to detect abnormalities in the brain.

brain·y (brā′nē) *adj.* **brain·i·er, brain·i·est** *Informal* Intelligent; smart.

braise (brāz) *tr.v.* **braised, brais·ing, brais·es** To brown (meat or vegetables) in fat and then simmer in a small amount of liquid in a covered container.

❑ *These sound alike:* **braise, braze** (join metal).

brake[1] (brāk) *n.* **1.** A device for slowing or stopping motion, as of a vehicle or machine: *The brakes failed and the car ran off the road.* **2.** Something that slows or stops an action or process: *A bout of flu put a brake on my sightseeing.* ❖ *v.* **braked, brak·ing, brakes** —*tr.* To slow or stop with a brake or brakes: *brake a train.* —*intr.* To operate or apply a brake or brakes: *Slow down and brake before turning.* [From Middle Dutch or Middle Low German, nose ring, curb.]

❑ *These sound alike:* **brake[1]** (device for stopping), **brake[2]** (fern), **brake[3]** (thicket), **break** (split).

brake[2] (brāk) *n.* Any of various ferns that have compound leaves and are often grown as houseplants. [From Middle English, probably from *braken,* bracken.]

❑ *These sound alike:* **brake[2]** (fern), **brake[1]** (device for stopping), **brake[3]** (thicket), **break** (split).

brake[3] (brāk) *n.* An area overgrown with dense bushes or briers; a thicket. [From Middle English, from Middle Low German.]

❑ *These sound alike:* **brake[3]** (thicket), **brake[1]** (device for stopping), **brake[2]** (fern), **break** (split).

brake light *n.* A light on the rear of a vehicle that goes on when the brakes are applied.

brake·man (brāk′mən) *n.* A member of a train crew who assists the conductor, as by uncoupling freight cars and checking on the operation of the train's brakes.

bram·ble (brăm′bəl) *n.* A prickly vine or shrub, such as a blackberry or raspberry. **—bram′bly** *adv.*

bran (brăn) *n.* The outer husks of wheat, rye, and other grains, sifted out from the flour after milling. Bran is used in animal feed and in some cereals and bread as a source of dietary fiber.

branch (brănch) *n.* **1a.** A woody stem or limb growing from the trunk or main stem of a tree or shrub or from another limb. **b.** A smaller part that extends from or connects to a main part: *the west branch of the river; the branches of an artery.* **2.** A part or division of a larger whole: *Botany and zoology are branches of biology. Congress is the legislative branch of the US government.* **3.** A subdivision of a family of languages. **4.** A local unit or office: *a bank branch.* ❖ *intr.v.* **branched, branch·ing, branch·es 1.** To put forth branches. **2.** To develop as a branch or division; diverge: *A small road branches to the left at the bottom of the hill.* **3.** To expand one's interests, business, or activities: *The newspaper publisher branched out into television.*

brand (brănd) *n.* **1.** A particular kind or make of product, especially as shown by a trademark: *a popular brand of soap; a good brand of coffee.* **2.** A trademark or distinctive name that identifies a product, service, or organization: *This company owns several brands of breakfast*

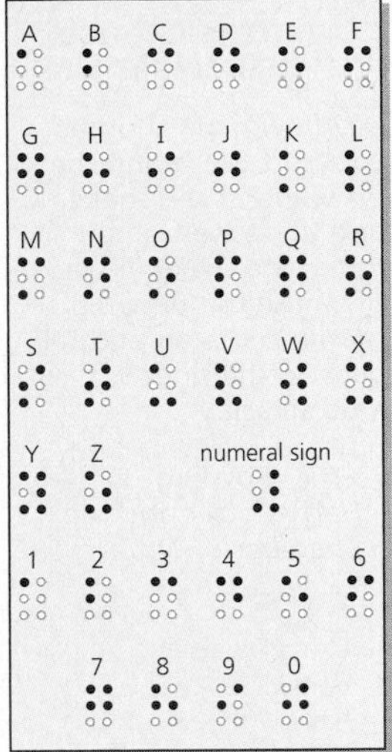

Braille

Braille alphabet and numerals

Louis Braille

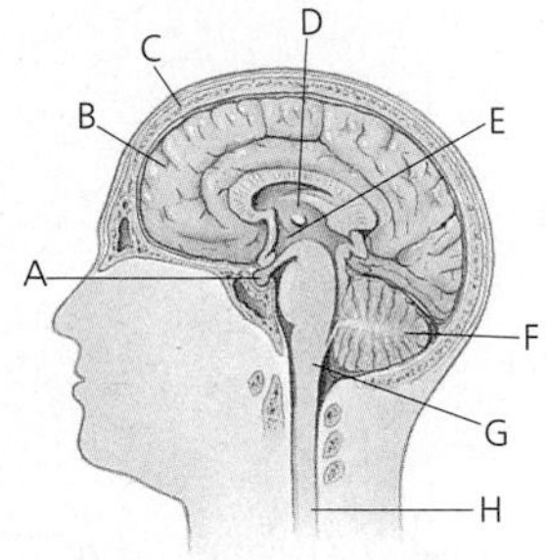

brain

A. pituitary gland, B. cerebrum, C. skull, D. thalamus, E. hypothalamus, F. cerebellum, G. medulla, H. spinal cord

WRITERS CHOOSE THEIR WORDS

"Allow me!" shouted Lockhart. He **brandished** his wand at the snake and there was a loud bang; the snake, instead of vanishing, flew ten feet into the air and fell back to the floor with a loud smack.

—J.K. Rowling
Harry Potter and the Chamber of Secrets

cereal. **3.** A distinctive category or kind: *That comedian is known for a rough brand of slapstick humor.* **4a.** A mark indicating ownership burned into the hide of cattle with a hot iron. **b.** An iron used to make such a mark. **5.** A mark formerly burned into the flesh of criminals. **6.** A mark of disgrace; a stigma: *That store owner bears the brand of having defrauded customers.* **7.** A piece of burning or charred wood. ❖ *tr.v.* **brand·ed, brand·ing, brands 1.** To mark with a hot iron: *Cowhands branded the calves.* **2.** To mark with a label of disgrace; stigmatize: *The court branded the spies as traitors.* **3.** To provide with or publicize using a brand name or other readily recognized identifier: *branded the video game after a popular adventure story.* —**brand′er** *n.*

bran·dish (brăn′dĭsh) *tr.v.* **bran·dished, bran·dish·ing, bran·dish·es** To wave or exhibit in a dramatic or threatening way: *brandish one's fist in defiance.*

brand-new (brănd′no͞o′) *adj.* Completely new; not used.

bran·dy (brăn′dē) *n., pl.* **bran·dies** An alcoholic liquor distilled from wine or fermented fruit juice. ❖ *tr.v.* **bran·died, bran·dy·ing, bran·dies** To mix, flavor, or preserve with brandy.

brant (brănt) *n., pl.* **brant** or **brants** A small wild goose that breeds in Arctic regions and has a black head and neck.

brash (brăsh) *adj.* **brash·er, brash·est 1.** Lacking respectful restraint in behavior; arrogant or overbearing: *disliked the brash newcomer on the team.* **2.** Hasty and unthinking; rash: *a brash move.* —**brash′ly** *adv.* —**brash′ness** *n.*

Bra·sí·lia (brə-zĭl′yə) The capital of Brazil, in the central part of the country northwest of Rio de Janeiro. It became the capital in 1960.

brass (brăs) *n.* **1.** A yellow alloy of copper and zinc. **2.** Ornaments, objects, or utensils made of such metal: *Polish all the brass including the doorknobs.* **3.** often **brasses** Wind instruments made of brass or some other metal, including the French horn, trumpet, trombone, and tuba. **4.** *Informal* Lack of respectful restraint in behavior; impudence or nerve: *She had the brass to ask for more money right after she got her allowance.* **5.** *Slang* Military officers or civilian officials of high rank. [From Old English *bræs.*]

bras·siere (brə-zîr′) *n.* A woman's undergarment worn to support the breasts.

brass instrument *n.* A wind instrument, such as the trumpet or trombone, made of brass or other metal. Sound is produced through vibration of the lips and is modified by means of valves or a slide.

brass tacks *pl.n. Informal* Essential facts; basics: *Let's get down to brass tacks.*

brass·y (brăs′ē) *adj.* **brass·i·er, brass·i·est 1.** Made of, decorated with, or having the color of brass. **2.** Resembling or featuring the sound of brass instruments: *a brassy voice.* **3.** *Informal* Lacking respectful restraint in behavior; impudent: *the brassy behavior of a showoff.* —**brass′i·ly** *adv.* —**brass′i·ness** *n.*

brat (brăt) *n.* **1.** An ill-mannered or spoiled child. **2.** A child of a career military person.

Bra·ti·sla·va (brăt′ĭ-**slä′**və *or* brä′tĭ-**slä′**və) The capital of Slovakia, in the southwest part of the country on the Danube River. It was the capital of Hungary from 1541 to 1784.

brat·wurst (**brăt′**wûrst′) *n.* A sausage made of seasoned pork.

bra·va·do (brə-vä′dō) *n., pl.* **bra·va·dos** or **bra·va·does** A show of pretended or defiant courage; false bravery: *Their noisy threats were nothing but bravado.*

brave (brāv) *adj.* **brav·er, brav·est** Having or showing courage: *a brave defiance of danger.* ❖ *n.* A Native American warrior. ❖ *tr.v.* **braved, brav·ing, braves** To undergo or face with courage: *Firefighters brave many dangers in the line of duty.* [From Old French, probably from Latin *barbarus*, like a barbarian.] —**brave′ly** *adv.* —**brave′ness** *n.*

SYNONYMS brave, courageous, fearless, bold, valiant These adjectives mean having or showing courage in a difficult or dangerous situation. **Brave,** the most general, often refers to an inner quality: *I'm not brave enough to speak in front of such a large crowd.* **Courageous** means consciously drawing on one's inner strength to face peril: *The courageous captain guided the ship through the terrible storm.* **Fearless** emphasizes the absence of fear: *The fearless tightrope walker does not use a net.* **Bold** often means being brave and showing a tendency to seek out danger: *The bolder members of the search party went into the cave first.* **Valiant** suggests heroic bravery in service of a noble cause: *The valiant firefighters had rescued everyone from the burning building.*
ANTONYM cowardly

brav·er·y (brā′və-rē *or* **brāv′**rē) *n.* The quality or condition of being brave; courage.

bra·vo (brä′vō *or* brä-vō′) *interj.* An expression used to show approval, as for a musical performance. ❖ *n., pl.* **bra·vos** A shout or cry of "bravo."

bra·vu·ra (brə-**vo͝or′**ə) *n.* **1.** Excellent technique or style in a musical performance. **2.** A showy display: *Special effects gave the movie a visual bravura that critics raved about.*

brawl (brôl) *n.* A noisy quarrel or fight. ❖ *intr.v.* **brawled, brawl·ing, brawls** To quarrel or fight noisily. [From Middle English *braul*, from *braullen*, to quarrel.]

brawn (brôn) *n.* Muscular strength and power.

brawn·y (brô′nē) *adj.* **brawn·i·er, brawn·i·est** Strong and muscular. See Synonyms at **muscular.** —**brawn′i·ness** *n.*

bray (brā) *intr.v.* **brayed, bray·ing, brays** To utter the loud harsh cry of a donkey. ❖ *n.* The loud harsh cry of a donkey.

braze (brāz) *tr.v.* **brazed, braz·ing, braz·es** To join (pieces of metal) together using a hard solder with a high melting point.
❑ *These sound alike:* **braze, braise** (cook meat).

bra·zen (brā′zən) *adj.* **1.** Rudely bold; impudent; insolent: *made a brazen remark.* **2.** Having a loud harsh sound: *the sound of a brazen bell.* **3.** Made of or resembling brass: *the brazen sky at sunset.* ❖ *tr.v.* **bra·zened, bra·zen·ing, bra·zens** To face or undergo with bold self-assurance: *The sailors brazened out the storm.* —**bra′zen·ly** *adv.* —**bra′zen·ness** *n.*

bra·zier (brā′zhər) *n.* A metal pan for holding burning coals or charcoal.

Bra·zil (brə-**zĭl′**) A country of eastern South America on the Atlantic Ocean. It is the largest country in the continent. Brasília is the capital and São Paulo the largest city.

Brazil nut *n.* The edible oily seed of a tropical South American tree, having a hard, three-sided, dark-brown shell.

Braz·za·ville (**brăz′**ə-vĭl′ *or* brä-zä-**vēl′**) The capital of the Republic of the Congo, in the southern part of the country on the Congo River. It is a major port.

breach (brēch) *n.* **1.** A gap or hole, especially in a solid structure: *The crowd poured through a breach in the barrier.* **2.** A violation or infraction, as of a contract, law, legal obligation, or promise. **3.** A disruption of friendly relations; an estrangement: *An argument caused a breach between the friends.* ❖ *tr.v.* **breached, breach·ing, breach·es 1.** To make a hole or gap in; break through: *Floodwaters breached the dike.* **2.** To break or violate (an agreement, for example). [From Old English *brēc.*]

ă	pat	ôr	core
ā	pay	oi	boy
âr	care	ou	out
ä	father	o͝o	took
ĕ	pet	o͝or	lure
ē	be	o͞o	boot
ĭ	pit	ŭ	cut
ī	bite	ûr	urge
îr	pier	th	thin
ŏ	pot	*th*	this
ō	toe	zh	vision
ô	paw	ə	about

❑ *These sound alike:* **breach, breech** (rear of a gun barrel).

bread (brĕd) *n.* **1.** A food made from flour or meal mixed with water and other ingredients, usually combined with a leavening agent, and kneaded and baked in a loaf. **2.** Food in general, regarded as necessary to sustain life: *A farm family works long hours for its daily bread.* **3.** The necessities of life; livelihood: *earn one's bread as a writer.* **4.** *Slang* Money. ❖ *tr.v.* **bread·ed, bread·ing, breads** To coat (food) with bread crumbs before cooking. [From Old English *brēad*.]

❑ *These sound alike:* **bread, bred** (produced offspring).

bread-and-but·ter (brĕd′n-bŭt′ər) *adj.* Reliable, as in producing a desired outcome: *a bread-and-butter product that sells well throughout the year.*

bread·bas·ket (brĕd′băs′kĭt) *n.* **1.** A basket for serving bread. **2.** A region serving as a principal source of grain supply: *Iowa, Nebraska, and Kansas are part of America's breadbasket.* **3.** *Slang* The stomach.

bread·box (brĕd′bŏks′) *n.* A container for storing baked goods to maintain their freshness.

bread·fruit (brĕd′fro͞ot′) *n.* **1.** A large, round, edible fruit that has a rough skin and starchy flesh resembling bread when roasted. **2.** The tropical tree that bears such fruit.

bread·line (brĕd′līn′) *n.* A line of people waiting to receive a free meal given out by a charitable organization or the government.

bread·stuff (brĕd′stŭf′) *n.* **1.** Bread. **2.** Flour, meal, or grain used in the baking of bread.

breadth (brĕdth) *n.* **1a.** The distance from side to side of something; width: *The wall has a breadth of 20 feet and a height of 10 feet.* **b.** A piece of something having a regular width: *a breadth of cloth.* **2.** Freedom from narrowness, as of interests or attitudes: *a judge's great breadth and wisdom.* **3.** Wide extent or scope: *Her breadth of knowledge is impressive.*

bread·win·ner (brĕd′wĭn′ər) *n.* A person who earns money to support a household.

break (brāk) *v.* **broke** (brōk), **bro·ken** (brō′kən), **break·ing, breaks** —*tr.* **1.** To cause to separate into two or more pieces as the result of force: *broke the vase.* **2.** To snap off or detach: *break a twig from a branch.* **3.** To fracture a bone of: *break an arm.* **4.** To separate into components or parts: *broke the assignment into smaller tasks.* **5a.** To destroy the regularity, order, or completeness of: *hills that break the plain; a collector willing to break a set of books.* **b.** To exchange for smaller monetary units: *broke a dollar for change to pay the bus fare.* **6.** To create a gap across which electricity cannot pass: *break a circuit.* **7a.** To force a way through; puncture or penetrate: *The blade broke the skin.* **b.** To part or pierce the surface of: *break ground for a new building; fish breaking the water.* **8.** To produce (a sweat) copiously on the skin, as from exercise. **9.** To make or bring about by cutting or forcing: *break a trail through the brush.* **10.** To find the solution or key to: *break a code.* **11.** To make known, as news: *broke the sad news gently.* **12.** To surpass or outdo: *broke the league's home-run record.* **13.** To put an end to, as by force, opposition, or change: *One vote broke the tie.* **14.** To make unusable; ruin: *I accidentally broke the radio by dropping it.* **15.** To lessen or diminish in force or effect: *A big bush broke my fall.* **16.** To weaken or destroy; overwhelm: *Defeat broke the champion's spirit.* **17.** To call off; cancel: *break a date.* **18.** To violate by failing to follow, conform, or observe; fail to keep: *break a law; break a promise.* **19.** To give up (a habit). **20.** To reduce in rank; demote: *break a sergeant to a private.* **21.** To cause to be without money; bankrupt: *Big bills and few customers broke the new business.* **22.** To train to obey; tame: *The horse was difficult to break.* —*intr.* **1.** To become separated into pieces or fragments: *Glass breaks easily. The string broke with a snap.* **2.** To become unusable: *The radio broke.* **3.** To give way; collapse: *The bridge broke under the weight of the truck.* **4.** To burst: *The blister broke.* **5.** To scatter or disperse: *The clouds broke after the storm.* **6.** To move or escape suddenly: *The cattle broke out of their pen.* **7.** To change direction suddenly: *The fullback broke to the right.* **8.** To come into being or appear suddenly: *Crocuses broke from the soil.* **9.** To become known or noticed: *The story broke in the afternoon news.* **10.** To interrupt or cease an activity or association: *Let's break for five minutes.* **11.** To decrease rapidly: *Hot summer temperatures often break after a rainstorm.* **12.** To come to an end: *The cold spell finally broke.* **13.** To collapse or crash into surf or spray: *waves breaking on the beach.* **14.** To change suddenly in musical tone or pitch: *Her voice broke with emotion.* **15.** In baseball, to curve suddenly at or near home plate: *The pitch broke sharply.* ❖ *n.* **1.** A result of breaking; a fracture or crack: *a break in a bone.* **2a.** A gap or opening: *a break in the clouds.* **b.** The beginning or start: *the break of day.* **3.** An interruption or disruption of regularity or continuity: *a break in the conversation; a break in an electrical circuit.* **4.** A pause or interval, as from work: *Take a break for a few minutes.* **5.** A sudden run; a dash: *The rabbit made a break for cover.* **6.** An attempt to escape: *a jail break.* **7.** A sudden change: *a break in the weather.* **8.** A severing of ties: *a break between families.* **9.** An unexpected occurrence or chance: *a lucky break.* ◆ **break down 1.** To cause to collapse; destroy: *break down a wall.* **2.** To fail to function: *The truck broke down on the highway.* **3a.** To decompose chemically: *Plastic takes years to break down.* **b.** To analyze or consider in parts: *Break the exercise down into several steps.* **4.** To become distressed or upset: *They broke down and cried when they got lost.* **break even** To gain an amount equal to that invested, as in a business. **break in 1.** To enter a building or property forcibly or illegally: *The burglars broke in but could not find the jewels.* **2.** To interrupt a conversation: *The operator broke in to tell us our time was up.* **3.** To train or instruct for some purpose: *break in a new worker.* **4.** To soften with use: *break in new shoes.* **break into 1.** To enter forcibly and illegally: *The bear broke into the cabin.* **2.** To begin suddenly: *He broke into song.* **3.** To interrupt: *She broke into our discussion to tell us it was time to go.* **break off 1.** To stop suddenly, as in speaking: *break off in the middle of a sentence.* **2.** To stop being friendly: *When the soldiers left the army they broke off with their old buddies.* **break out 1.** To be affected with a skin irritation, such as a rash: *An allergy to wool makes me break out.* **2.** To begin or develop suddenly: *Fire broke out during the night.* **3.** To ready for action or use: *Firefighters broke out the hoses.* **4.** To emerge or escape: *We repaired the fence, but the horses broke out anyway.* **break (someone's) heart** To disappoint or dispirit someone severely. **break up 1a.** To scatter; disperse: *The clouds are breaking up.* **b.** To separate into smaller parts: *break up a word into syllables.* **2.** To bring or come to an end: *The police broke up a fight. Their partnership broke up.* **3.** To interrupt: *break up the long day by going swimming.* [From Old English *brecan*.]

❑ *These sound alike:* **break, brake**[1] (device for stopping), **brake**[2] (fern), **brake**[3] (thicket).

SYNONYMS break, crack, fracture, splinter, shatter These verbs mean to cause to separate into parts or pieces. **Break** is the most general: *He accidentally broke the glass while cleaning it.* **Crack** means to break, often with a sharp snapping sound, without dividing into parts: *A small pebble cracked our windshield while we were driving.* **Fracture** applies to a break or crack in a rigid body: *She fractured her hip in the accident.* **Splinter** means to split into long, thin, sharp pieces: *Lightning*

WRITERS CHOOSE THEIR WORDS

As young children, in **brazen** disregard of their parents' instructions, they had often sneaked out of the house.

—Roderick Gordon and Brian Williams
Deeper

breadfruit

breaker

breakwater

ă	pat	ôr	core
ā	pay	oi	boy
âr	care	ou	out
ä	father	o͝o	took
ĕ	pet	o͝or	lure
ē	be	o͞o	boot
ĭ	pit	ŭ	cut
ī	bite	ûr	urge
îr	pier	th	thin
ŏ	pot	*th*	this
ō	toe	zh	vision
ô	paw	ə	about

struck the tree and splintered it. **Shatter** means to break into many loose scattered pieces: *She dropped the vase and shattered it.*

---

break·a·ble (brā′kə-bəl) *adj.* Capable of being broken; fragile.

break·age (brā′kĭj) *n.* **1.** The act of breaking something, or the fact of being broken: *They had to pay for the breakage of the window.* **2.** A quantity broken: *Breakage during shipping was extensive.*

break·down (brāk′doun′) *n.* **1.** The act or process of failing to function properly: *The communications satellite suffered a total breakdown when it collided with a piece of debris.* **2.** The condition resulting from this process: *There was a breakdown in communication when the satellite stopped working.* **3.** A collapse of physical or mental health: *Not getting enough sleep will eventually cause a breakdown in health.* **4.** Decomposition or disintegration into parts or elements: *Bacteria are used in the breakdown of sewage.* **5.** An analysis or summary consisting of itemized data: *The sticker on the car window shows a breakdown of accessories.*

break·er (brā′kər) *n.* **1.** A person or thing that breaks: *a breaker of promises.* **2.** A circuit breaker. **3.** A wave that turns into foam when it crests.

break·fast (brĕk′fəst) *n.* The first meal of the day. ❖ *intr.v.* **break·fast·ed, break·fast·ing, break·fasts** To eat breakfast. [From Middle English *brekefaste* : from *breken*, to break + *faste*, a fast (from Old Norse *fasta*, to fast).]

break-in (brāk′ĭn′) *n.* The act of entering a room or building by force for an illegal purpose: *The alarm went off because of a break-in.*

break·ing and entering (brā′kĭng) *n.* The illegal act of forcibly going into someone else's house or building without permission.

break·neck (brāk′nĕk′) *adj.* Dangerously fast: *The ambulance drove at breakneck speed.*

break·out (brāk′out′) *n.* **1.** A forceful exit from a condition or situation that restricts or confines: *The prisoners were caught shortly after their breakout.* **2.** A sudden appearance or increase, as of a disease or condition; an outbreak: *a breakout of acne.*

break·through (brāk′thro͞o′) *n.* A major achievement or success that permits further progress, as in technology.

break·up (brāk′ŭp′) *n.* **1.** The act or an instance of breaking up; a separation or dispersal: *the breakup of an iceberg; the breakup of a large corporation.* **2.** The ending of a relationship, as of friends.

break·wa·ter (brāk′wô′tər) *n.* A barrier that protects a harbor or shore from the full impact of waves.

bream (brēm *or* brĭm) *n., pl.* **bream** or **breams 1.** Any of several European freshwater fishes having a flattened body and silvery scales. **2.** Any of various freshwater sunfishes. [From Middle English *breme*, from Old French, of Germanic origin.]

breast (brĕst) *n.* **1.** In mammals, especially humans, one of the glands in which a female produces milk to feed her young offspring. **2.** A corresponding but undeveloped gland in a male mammal. **3a.** The upper part of the front surface of the human body, extending from the neck to the abdomen. **b.** A corresponding part in other animals. **4.** The seat of affection or emotion: *Deep in his breast he felt an abiding sorrow.*

breast·bone (brĕst′bōn′) *n.* The sternum.

breast·feed (brĕst′fēd′) *tr.v.* **breast·fed** (brĕst′fĕd′), **breast·feed·ing, breast·feeds** To feed (a baby) mother's milk from the breast; nurse.

breast·plate (brĕst′plāt′) *n.* A piece of metal armor worn over the chest.

breast·stroke (brĕst′strōk′) *n.* A swimming stroke in which a person lies face down and extends the arms in front of the head, then sweeps them back to the sides under the surface of the water while performing a frog kick.

breast·work (brĕst′wûrk′) *n.* A temporary, hastily constructed fortification, usually breast-high.

breath (brĕth) *n.* **1.** A single act of breathing, especially an inhalation: *Take a deep breath.* **2.** The air inhaled into and exhaled from the lungs: *let out the breath in his lungs.* **3.** The ability to breathe, especially with ease: *I got short of breath as I ran up the hill.* **4.** Exhaled air, as shown by vapor, odor, or heat: *You can see your breath in the cold winter air.* **5.** A slight breeze: *Not a breath of air stirred the leaves.* **6.** A trace or suggestion: *the first breath of spring.* ◆ **out of breath** Breathing with difficulty, as from exertion; gasping: *I was out of breath when I got to the top of the hill.* **under (one's) breath** In a muted voice or whisper. [From Old English *brǣth*.]

breathe (brē*th*) *v.* **breathed, breath·ing, breathes** —*intr.* **1.** To inhale and exhale air: *As we climbed higher, it got harder to breathe.* **2.** To exhale air: *Breathe on the window and see if it fogs up.* **3.** To exchange gases as part of respiration or photosynthesis: *Fish breathe with their gills. Stomata allow leaves to breathe.* **4.** To be alive; live: *As long as the dog breathed, it was loyal to its master.* **5.** To pause to rest or to regain breath, as after action: *Give me a moment to breathe.* —*tr.* **1.** To inhale and exhale (air, for example). **2.** To exhale; emit: *breathe a sigh of relief after the danger passed.* **3.** To impart (a quality) as if by breathing: *The artist breathed life into the painting of the children.* **4.** To utter, especially quietly; whisper: *Don't breathe a word of this.* **5.** To allow (a person or animal) to rest: *breathe a horse after a race.* ◆ **breathe down (someone's) neck** To watch or monitor closely, often annoyingly. **breathe (one's) last** To die.

breath·er (brē′*th*ər) *n. Informal* A short rest period.

breath·less (brĕth′lĭs) *adj.* **1.** Breathing with difficulty; gasping: *The runners were breathless after the race.* **2.** Holding the breath from excitement or suspense: *The audience was breathless as the acrobats performed.* **3.** Inspiring or marked by excitement that makes one hold the breath: *the breathless beauty of the mountains.* **—breath′less·ly** *adv.* **—breath′less·ness** *n.*

breath·tak·ing (brĕth′tā′kĭng) *adj.* **1.** Inspiring awe; very exciting: *The fireworks are always a breathtaking spectacle.* **2.** Astonishing; astounding: *breathtaking stupidity.*

bred (brĕd) *v.* Past tense and past participle of **breed.** ❖ *adj.* Raised or brought-up: *a country-bred politician.*
❑ *These sound alike:* **bred, bread** (food).

breech (brēch) *n.* **1.** The lower rear part of the human trunk; the buttocks. **2.** The part of a firearm behind the barrel.
❑ *These sound alike:* **breech, breach** (gap).

breech·cloth (brēch′klôth′) *n.* A cloth worn to cover the loins; a loincloth.

breech·es (brĭch′ĭz *or* brē′chĭz) *pl.n.* **1.** Pants extending to or just below the knees. **2.** *Informal* Pants of any kind.

breeches buoy *n.* A device used for rescue at sea, made up of pants attached to a life preserver that is suspended from a line strung from ship to ship or ship to shore. A person sits in the pants and is transported to safety along the line by means of a pulley.

breed (brēd) *v.* **bred** (brĕd), **breed·ing, breeds** —*tr.* **1.** To produce (offspring): *Mice breed large litters.* **2a.** To arrange the mating of (animals) so as to produce offspring: *We hope to breed the dogs and sell the puppies.* **b.** To produce new varieties of (organisms) especially by selecting individuals with desired traits to mate with each other: *Scientists are hoping to breed disease-resistant crops.* **3.** To bring about; give rise to: *Poverty breeds crime.* **4.** To produce (fissionable material) in a breeder reactor. *—intr.* **1.** To produce offspring: *Mosquitoes breed rapidly.* **2.** To originate and grow: *Discontent breeds under a repressive government.* ❖ *n.* **1.** A group of organisms having common ancestors and certain characteristics, often produced by mating selected parents: *a hardy breed of cattle; a breed of hybrid corn.* **2.** A type or kind: *a new breed of politician.* [From Old English *brēdan.*] **—breed′er** *n.*

breeder reactor *n.* A nuclear reactor that produces more fissionable material than it consumes.

breed·ing (brē′dĭng) *n.* **1.** Upbringing or education, especially in proper social behavior: *Good manners are evidence of good breeding.* **2.** The producing of offspring or young: *measures to control the breeding of mosquitoes.* **3.** The intentional propagation of a type of organism, especially to produce new or improved varieties: *the breeding of laboratory mice for experiments.*

breeze (brēz) *n.* **1.** A light current of air; a gentle wind. **2.** *Informal* Something that is easy to do. ❖ *intr.v.* **breezed, breez·ing, breez·es** *Informal* To make rapid progress without effort: *We breezed through the homework.*

breeze·way (brēz′wā′) *n.* A roofed, open-sided passageway connecting two buildings, such as a house and a garage.

breez·y (brē′zē) *adj.* **breez·i·er, breez·i·est 1.** Characterized by or full of breezes: *a warm breezy day.* **2.** Exposed to breezes; windy: *a breezy point along the shore.* **3.** Lively; sprightly: *a writer's breezy style.* **—breez′i·ly** *adv.* **—breez′i·ness** *n.*

breth·ren (brĕ*th*′rən) *n.* A plural of **brother** (sense 3).

Bret·on (brĕt′n) *adj.* Relating to Brittany or its people, language, or culture. ❖ *n.* **1.** A native or inhabitant of Brittany. **2.** The Celtic language of Brittany.

breve (brĕv *or* brēv) *n.* **1.** A mark (˘) placed over a vowel to show that it has a short sound, as in *ă*, the vowel sound in *bat.* **2.** A similar mark used to indicate that a syllable is unstressed in a foot of verse.

bre·vi·ar·y (brē′vē-ĕr′ē *or* brĕv′ē-ĕr′ē) *n., pl.* **bre·vi·ar·ies** In the Roman Catholic and Anglican churches, a book containing the daily prayers, hymns, and other readings for priests and members of certain religious orders.

brev·i·ty (brĕv′ĭ-tē) *n.* Briefness, as of expression; shortness: *The brevity of the speaker's remarks prevented boredom.*

brew (bro͞o) *v.* **brewed, brew·ing, brews** *—tr.* **1.** To make (beer or ale) from malt and hops. **2.** To make (a beverage) by boiling, steeping, or mixing ingredients: *brew tea.* **3.** To devise or plan; concoct: *Members of the opposing party brewed a plot to disgrace the president.* *—intr.* **1.** To be brewed: *The tea brewed quickly.* **2.** To be imminent; threaten to occur: *A storm brewed on the horizon.* ❖ *n.* **1.** A beverage made by brewing. **2.** A serving of such a beverage. [From Old English *brēowan.*] **—brew′er** *n.*

brew·er·y (bro͞o′ə-rē *or* bro͝or′ē) *n., pl.* **brew·er·ies** A place where malt liquors, such as beer and ale, are made.

brew·ing (bro͞o′ĭng) *n.* The act, process, or business of making malt liquors, such as beer and ale.

Brey·er (brī′ər), **Stephen Gerald** Born 1938. American jurist who was appointed an associate justice of the US Supreme Court in 1994.

Brezh·nev (brĕzh′nĕf), **Leonid Ilyich** 1906–1982. Soviet politician who served as general secretary of the Communist Party (1964–1982). Under his leadership, the Soviet Union invaded Czechoslovakia (1968) and Afghanistan (1979) to suppress anti-Communist revolts.

bri·ar[1] also **bri·er** (brī′ər) *n.* **1.** A Mediterranean shrub or small tree having a hard woody root used to make tobacco pipes. **2.** A pipe made from the root of this shrub. [From French *bruyère*, heath, from Late Latin *brūcus*, heather, of Celtic origin.]

bri·ar[2] (brī′ər) *n.* Variant of **brier[1]**.

bribe (brīb) *n.* **1.** Something, such as money, property, or position, offered or given to someone in order to influence that person to act dishonestly: *Corrupt officials were dismissed for accepting bribes.* **2.** Something offered or serving to influence or persuade: *He used dessert as a bribe to get the child to behave.* ❖ *tr.v.* **bribed, brib·ing, bribes** To give or offer a bribe to: *It is a criminal act to bribe a judge.*

brib·er·y (brī′bə-rē) *n., pl.* **brib·er·ies** The act of giving, offering, or taking a bribe.

bric-a-brac (brĭk′ə-brăk′) *n.* Small objects displayed in a room as ornaments.

brick (brĭk) *n.* **1.** A rectangular block of clay, baked by the sun or in a kiln until hard and used as a building and paving material. **2.** Such blocks of clay used as a building material: *a house made of brick.* **3.** An object shaped like such a block: *a brick of cheese.* ❖ *tr.v.* **bricked, brick·ing, bricks 1.** To build, line, or pave with bricks. **2.** To close, wall, or fill with bricks: *The mason bricked up the window opening.* [From Middle English *brike*, from Middle Dutch *bricke.*]

brick-and-mor·tar (brĭk′ənd-môr′tər) *adj.* Existing or operating in a building, rather than as an online Internet service: *a brick-and-mortar pet store.*

brick·bat (brĭk′băt′) *n.* **1.** A piece of brick thrown as a weapon. **2.** An unfavorable remark; a criticism: *The candidates exchanged brickbats during the debate.*

brick·lay·er (brĭk′lā′ər) *n.* A person who builds walls or other structures with bricks. **—brick′lay′ing** *n.*

brick·work (brĭk′wûrk′) *n.* **1.** The technique or work of constructing with bricks and mortar. **2.** A structure made of bricks.

brick·yard (brĭk′yärd′) *n.* A place where bricks are made or sold.

bri·dal (brīd′l) *adj.* Relating to a bride or a marriage ceremony: *a bridal veil; the bridal party.*

❑ *These sound alike:* **bridal, bridle** (straps for a horse's head).

bride (brīd) *n.* A woman who is about to be married or has recently been married.

bride·groom (brīd′gro͞om′ *or* brīd′gro͝om′) *n.* A man who is about to be married or has recently been married. [Alteration of Middle English *bridegome*, from Old English *brȳdguma* : *brȳd*, bride + *guma*, man.]

brides·maid (brīdz′mād′) *n.* A woman who attends the bride at a wedding.

bridge[1] (brĭj) *n.* **1.** A structure providing a way across a gap or obstacle, such as a river, railroad, or gorge. **2a.** The upper bony ridge of the human nose. **b.** The part of a pair of eyeglasses that rests against this ridge. **3.** A thin piece of wood that supports the strings above the sounding board in a violin, cello, and some other stringed instruments. **4.** A structure that replaces one or more missing teeth, usually anchored to teeth at both ends. **5.** A platform or enclosed area above the main deck of a ship from which the ship is controlled. **6.** A musical passage that connects two sections of a song or composition. **7.** A long stick with a notched plate at one end, used to steady the cue stick in billiards. ❖ *tr.v.* **bridged, bridg·ing, bridg·es 1.** To build a bridge over: *bridge a river.* **2.** To cross by or as if by a bridge: *His career bridged two generations of technology.* [From Old English *brycg.*]

bridge[2] (brĭj) *n.* Any of several card games usually for four players, derived from whist. [From earlier *biritch*, from Russian *birich*, a call.]

bridge·head (brĭj′hĕd′) *n.* A military position seized by advancing troops in enemy territory as a place for launching further attacks.

Bridge·port (brĭj′pôrt′) The largest city of Connecticut, in the southwest part of the state on Long Island Sound. It was settled in 1639.

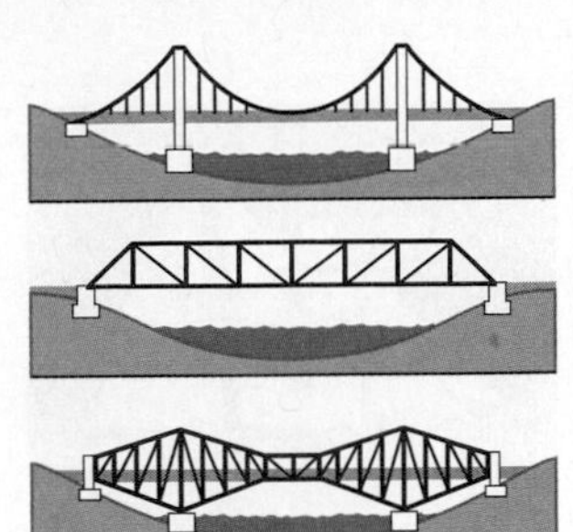

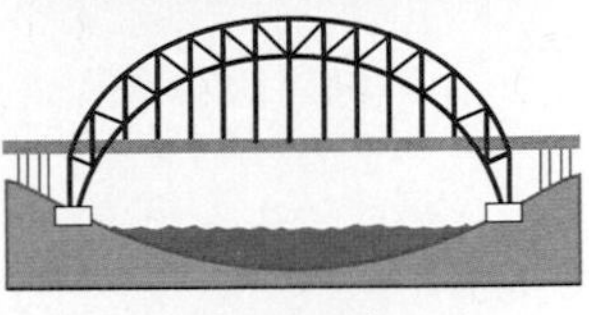

bridge[1]
top to bottom: suspension, through truss, cantilever, and steel arch bridge profiles

brigantine

brindled
brindled greyhound

Bridge·town (brĭj′toun′) The capital of Barbados, in the West Indies. It was founded by the British in 1628.

bridge·work (brĭj′wûrk′) *n.* One or more dental bridges used to replace missing teeth.

bri·dle (brīd′l) *n.* **1.** A harness, consisting of straps, a bit, and reins, fitted about a horse's head and used to control the animal. **2.** A restraint or control: *The committee called for a bridle on new government spending.* ❖ *v.* **bri·dled, bri·dling, bri·dles** —*tr.* **1.** To put a bridle on: *bridle a horse.* **2.** To control with or as if with a bridle: *Bridle your temper!* —*intr.* To show anger; take offense: *The author bridled at the criticism.*
❑ *These sound alike:* **bridle, bridal** (of a bride).

bridle path *n.* A trail for horseback riding.

brief (brēf) *adj.* **brief·er, brief·est 1.** Short in time or duration: *I took a brief nap.* **2.** Short in length or extent: *a brief report taking only one page.* **3.** Covering only a small part of the body: *a brief undergarment.* ❖ *n.* **1.** A short statement or summary, especially a lawyer's summary of the facts relating to a case or argument. **2. briefs** Short, tight-fitting underpants. ❖ *tr.v.* **briefed, brief·ing, briefs** To give instructions, information, or advice to: *The pilot was briefed on weather conditions before takeoff.* [From Middle English *bref*, from Latin *brevis*.] —**brief′ly** *adv.* —**brief′ness** *n.*

brief·case (brēf′kās′) *n.* A flat rectangular case for carrying books or papers.

brief·ing (brē′fĭng) *n.* **1a.** The act or procedure of giving instructions or information: *Staff members gave the president a briefing before his news conference.* **b.** A meeting at which instructions or information are given: *There were 20 reporters at the briefing.* **2.** The instructions or information given during a briefing: *The briefing included a number of classified secrets.*

bri·er[1] also **bri·ar** (brī′ər) *n.* Any of various prickly vines or shrubs. [From Old English *brēr*.]

bri·er[2] (brī′ər) *n.* Variant of **briar**[1].

brig (brĭg) *n.* **1.** A two-masted sailing vessel having one or more square sails on each mast and a fore-and-aft sail attached by a gaff to the aft mast. **2.** A ship's prison. **3.** A guardhouse or jail on a military base. [Short for *brigantine*.]

bri·gade (brĭ-gād′) *n.* **1.** A large army unit, especially such a unit composed of two or more battalions or regiments. **2.** A group organized for a specific purpose: *a fire brigade.* [From Old Italian *brigata*, from *brigare*, to fight, from *briga*, strife, of Celtic origin.]

brig·a·dier (brĭg′ə-dîr′) *n.* A brigadier general.

brigadier general *n.* An officer ranking above a colonel and below a major general in the US Army, Air Force, or Marine Corps.

brig·and (brĭg′ənd) *n.* A member of a roving band of robbers. [From Middle English *brigaunt*, from Old Italian *brigante*, skirmisher, from *brigare*, to fight.]

brig·an·tine (brĭg′ən-tēn′) *n.* A two-masted sailing vessel having a square-rigged foremast and a fore-and-aft-rigged mainsail. [From Old Italian *brigantino*, skirmishing ship, from *brigante*, skirmisher.]

bright (brīt) *adj.* **bright·er, bright·est 1.** Emitting or reflecting light readily or in large amounts; shining: *the bright sun shining in a cloudless sky; a cat's bright glistening eyes.* **2.** Containing little or no black, white, or gray; vivid or intense: *bright green.* **3.** Full of light: *a bright day.* **4.** Quick to learn or understand; smart: *a bright attractive little child; a bright idea.* See Synonyms at **intelligent. 5.** Happy; cheerful: *a bright face.* **6.** Full of promise and hope: *a bright future.* ❖ *adv.* In a bright manner: *The moon shines bright on a clear night.* [From Old English *berht*.] —**bright′ly** *adv.*

bright·en (brīt′n) *tr. & intr.v.* **bright·ened, bright·en·ing, bright·ens 1.** To make or become bright or brighter: *Sunlight brightened the room. Stars brighten as the sun goes down.* **2.** To make or become happy or more cheerful: *Their faces brightened at the clown's approach.*

bright·ness (brīt′nĭs) *n.* **1.** The quality or condition of being bright: *Brightness in the sky announced the dawn.* **2.** The amount of light that appears to come from an object or color: *an instrument that measures the brightness of a star.*

bril·liance (brĭl′yəns) *n.* **1.** Extreme brightness: *the brilliance of the noonday sun.* **2.** Sharpness and clarity of musical tone: *Trumpets are noted for their brilliance.* **3.** Splendor; magnificence: *the brilliance of the palace.* **4.** Exceptional intelligence or inventiveness: *a discovery of great brilliance.*

bril·liant (brĭl′yənt) *adj.* **1.** Full of light; shining brightly: *A brilliant sun blazed in the sky.* **2.** Very vivid in color: *The sky was a brilliant blue.* **3.** Clear and penetrating, as a musical sound: *The trumpet has a firm brilliant tone.* **4.** Splendid; magnificent: *the brilliant court life of the kings of France.* **5.** Excellent; wonderful: *The musicians gave a brilliant performance.* **6.** Having or showing unusual and impressive intelligence: *a brilliant mind; a brilliant solution to the problem.* See Synonyms at **intelligent.** ❖ *n.* A precious gem, especially a diamond, cut so that it catches the light and sparkles. —**bril′liant·ly** *adv.*

brim (brĭm) *n.* **1.** The uppermost edge of a hollow container or natural basin: *The pail was filled to the brim. We peered over the brim of the canyon.* **2.** A projecting rim on a hat. **3.** Full capacity: *a room full to the brim with people.* ❖ *intr.v.* **brimmed, brim·ming, brims 1.** To be full to the brim, often to overflowing. **2.** To be abundantly filled or supplied: *workers who brimmed with pride.* [From Middle English *brimme*.]

brim·ful (brĭm′fo͝ol′) *adj.* Full to the brim; completely full: *a glass brimful of milk.*

brim·stone (brĭm′stōn′) *n.* Sulfur, especially when associated with the torments of hell in Christianity. [From Middle English *brimston*.]

brin·dle (brĭn′dl) *n.* A brindled color.

brin·dled (brĭn′dld) *adj.* Tan or gray with streaks or spots of a darker color.

brine (brīn) *n.* **1.** Water that contains a large amount of dissolved salt, especially sodium chloride. **2.** The water of a sea or ocean. **3.** Salt water used for preserving or pickling foods.

bring (brĭng) *tr.v.* **brought** (brôt), **bring·ing, brings 1.** To carry, convey, lead, or cause to go along to another place: *I brought the books upstairs.* **2.** To cause to occur as a result: *The flood brought much property damage.* **3.** To persuade; convince: *People were having such a good time they could not bring themselves to leave.* **4.** To cause to come; attract: *Smoke from the barn brought the neighbors.* **5.** To call to mind; recall: *This song brings back memories.* **6.** To put or force into a particular situation, location, or condition: *His refusal brought the project to a halt. Bring the potatoes to a boil.* **7.** To put forward (a legal action or charge) against someone in court: *bring suit.* **8.** To sell for: *Diamonds always bring high prices.* ◆ **bring about** To cause to happen: *Hard work brought about the success of the play.* **bring around 1.** To cause to adopt an opinion or take a certain course of action: *We tried to bring him around, but he did what he wanted anyway.* **2.** To cause to recover consciousness. **bring down 1.** To cause to fall or collapse: *The revolution brought down the king.* **2.** To kill. **3.** To disappoint; let down. **bring forth 1.** To give rise to; produce: *The bulbs brought forth flowers in the spring.* **2.** To give birth to (young). **bring forward** To present; produce: *bring forward proof.* **bring in 1.** To give or submit (a verdict) to a court. **2.** To produce, yield, or earn (profits or income). **bring off** To accomplish: *We brought off a successful play.* **bring on** To cause to appear: *Working in the rain brought on a cold.* **bring out 1.** To reveal

ă pat	ôr core		
ā pay	oi boy		
âr care	ou out		
ä father	o͝o took		
ĕ pet	o͝or lure		
ē be	o͞o boot		
ĭ pit	ŭ cut		
ī bite	ûr urge		
îr pier	th thin		
ŏ pot	*th* this		
ō toe	zh vision		
ô paw	ə about		

or expose: *The article in the newspaper brought out the seriousness of the problem.* **2.** To produce or publish: *The company is bringing out a new book.* **3.** To nurture and develop (a quality, for example) to best advantage: *She brings out the best in us.* **bring to** To cause to recover consciousness: *The patient was brought to after surgery.* **bring up 1.** To take care of and educate (a child); rear. **2.** To introduce into discussion; mention: *I was surprised when they brought up the subject of my painting.* [From Old English *bringan.*] —SEE NOTE.

brink (brĭngk) *n.* **1.** The upper edge of a steep or vertical slope: *He stood at the brink of the crater.* See Synonyms at **border. 2.** The point at which something is likely to begin; the verge: *on the brink of extinction; at the brink of success.* [From Middle English *brinke*, probably of Scandinavian origin.]

brin·y (brī′nē) *adj.* **brin·i·er, brin·i·est** Relating to or resembling brine; salty.

bri·quette also **bri·quet** (brĭ-kĕt′) *n.* A block of compressed coal dust, charcoal, or sawdust, used for fuel.

bris (brĭs) *n., pl.* **bris·es** The rite of male circumcision in Judaism.

brisk (brĭsk) *adj.* **brisk·er, brisk·est 1.** Moving or acting quickly; lively; energetic: *a brisk walk to get to school on time.* **2.** Very active; not sluggish: *Business is brisk when the store has a sale.* **3.** Fresh and invigorating: *a brisk fall morning.* **4.** Sharp in speech or manner: *He gave us a friendly but brisk reply.* [Probably of Scandinavian origin.] **—brisk′ly** *adv.* **—brisk′ness** *n.*

bris·ket (brĭs′kĭt) *n.* **1.** The chest of an animal. **2.** Meat from the chest of an animal: *a brisket of beef.*

bris·ling (brĭz′lĭng *or* brĭs′lĭng) *n.* The sprat.

bris·tle (brĭs′əl) *n.* **1.** A short stiff hair. **2.** A short, stiff structure resembling a hair: *the plastic bristles of a hairbrush.* ❖ *intr.v.* **bris·tled, bris·tling, bris·tles 1.** To raise the bristles, as in anger or fright: *The dog bristled and showed his teeth.* **2.** To stand out stiffly like bristles: *The hair on the dog's neck bristled.* **3.** To show sudden anger or annoyance: *The artist bristled at the criticism of his work.* **4.** To be thick with bristles or similar structures: *The path bristled with thorns.* [From Middle English *bristel*, from Old English *byrst*, bristle.]

bris·tly (brĭs′lē) *adj.* **bris·tli·er, bris·tli·est 1.** Consisting of or similar to bristles: *a dog with a short bristly coat.* **2.** Easily angered or irritated: *gets bristly when interrupted.*

Brit. *abbr.* An abbreviation of: **1.** Britain. **2.** British.

Brit·ain (brĭt′n) See **Great Britain.**

Bri·tan·nia (brĭ-tăn′yə) *n.* A female personification of Great Britain.

britch·es (brĭch′ĭz) *pl.n. Informal* Breeches. ◆ **too big for (one's) britches** Overconfident; cocky.

Brit·i·cism (brĭt′ĭ-sĭz′əm) *n.* A word, phrase, or idiom characteristic of or peculiar to English as used in Great Britain.

Brit·ish (brĭt′ĭsh) *adj.* Relating to Great Britain or its people, language, or culture. ❖ *n.* **1.** *(used with a plural verb)* The people of Great Britain. **2.** British English. **3.** The Celtic language of the ancient Britons.

British Columbia A province of western Canada on the Pacific Ocean south of Yukon Territory. It joined the Canadian confederation in 1871. Victoria is the capital and Vancouver the largest city.

British Commonwealth See **Commonwealth of Nations.**

British Empire The countries and territories that were formerly ruled by Great Britain. It once included about one quarter of the world's land area and population.

British English *n.* The English language as used in Great Britain.

Brit·ish·er (brĭt′ĭ-shər) *n. Informal* A native or inhabitant of Great Britain.

British Isles A group of islands off the northwest coast of Europe made up of Great Britain, Ireland, and adjacent smaller islands.

British thermal unit *n.* The amount of energy that is needed to raise the temperature of one pound of water by one degree Fahrenheit. This unit is used mainly to measure heat.

British Virgin Islands A British colony in the eastern Caribbean Sea east of Puerto Rico and the US Virgin Islands. Road Town is the capital.

British West Indies A historic term for the British island colonies in the West Indies. Most of the islands gained their independence in the late 1900s.

Brit·on (brĭt′n) *n.* **1.** A native or inhabitant of Great Britain. **2.** A member of the Celtic people of ancient Britain.

Brit·ta·ny (brĭt′n-ē) A historical region and former province of northwest France on a peninsula between the English Channel and the Bay of Biscay.

brit·tle (brĭt′l) *adj.* **brit·tler, brit·tlest 1.** Likely to break or snap: *a brittle porcelain plate.* **2.** Easily ruined or disrupted: *a brittle friendship.* **—brit′tle·ness** *n.*

Bro. *abbr.* An abbreviation of brother (religious title).

broach (brōch) *tr.v.* **broached, broach·ing, broach·es 1.** To talk or write about for the first time; begin to discuss: *broach a subject tactfully.* **2.** To pierce in order to draw off liquid: *broach a keg of cider.* ❖ *n.* A pointed tool used to shape or enlarge a hole.

❑ *These sound alike:* **broach, brooch** (pin).

broad (brôd) *adj.* **broad·er, broad·est 1.** Wide from side to side: *a broad river.* **2.** Large in expanse; spacious: *broad fields of wheat.* **3.** Clear; bright: *broad daylight.* **4.** Covering a wide scope; general: *a broad rule; a broad topic.* **5.** Main or essential: *the broad sense of a word.* **6.** Plain and obvious: *a broad hint.* **7.** Liberal; tolerant: *a broad point of view.* [From Old English *brād.*] **—broad′ly** *adv.* **—broad′ness** *n.*

broad·axe or **broad·ax** (brôd′ăks′) *n.* An axe with a wide flat head and a short handle; a battle-axe.

broad·band (brôd′bănd′) *n.* A telecommunications system that allows large amounts of data to be transmitted very quickly.

broad·cast (brôd′kăst′) *v.* **broad·cast** or **broad·cast·ed, broad·cast·ing, broad·casts** —*tr.* **1.** To transmit (a television program, for example) to many recipients at the same time over a communications network: *The news station will broadcast the president's speech.* **2.** To make known over a wide area: *Rumors were broadcast all over town.* **3.** To sow (seed) over a wide area; scatter. —*intr.* To transmit a signal to many recipients at the same time over a communications network: *Many stations broadcast from tall buildings.* ❖ *n.* A signal, message, or audio or video program that is broadcast over a communications network: *We watched a live broadcast of the playoffs.* ❖ *adj.* Relating to the broadcasting of audio or video content: *Broadcast time for commercials is expensive.* **—broad′cast′er** *n.*

broad·cloth (brôd′klôth′) *n.* **1.** A fine woolen cloth with a smooth glossy texture, used especially in making suits. **2.** A closely woven silk, cotton, or synthetic cloth with a narrow rib, used especially in making shirts.

broad·en (brôd′n) *tr. & intr.v.* **broad·ened, broad·en·ing, broad·ens** To make or become broad or broader: *a trip that broadened our view of the world; a river that broadens as it nears the sea.*

broad jump *n.* The long jump.

broad·loom (brôd′lo͞om′) *adj.* Woven on a wide loom. ❖ *n.* A carpet woven on a wide loom.

broad-mind·ed (brôd′mīn′dĭd) *adj.* Having liberal and tolerant views and opinions: *I try to keep a broad-minded attitude toward other people's beliefs.* **—broad′mind′ed·ly** *adv.* **—broad′mind′ed·ness** *n.*

broad·side (brôd′sīd′) *n.* **1.** A ship's side above the water

USAGE

bring The verbs **bring** and **take** are very close in meaning, but they can reflect different points of view. *Bring* suggests that the motion is *toward* the place of speaking: *Bring the book over here. Take* suggests that the motion is *away* from the place of speaking: *Take the book to the library.*

Britannia
World War I poster

brocade

brogue[1]

Brontë

c. 1834 painting of the Brontë sisters by their brother Patrick Branwell Brontë (1817–1848)

ă	pat	ôr	core
ā	pay	oi	boy
âr	care	ou	out
ä	father	ŏŏ	took
ĕ	pet	ŏŏr	lure
ē	be	ōō	boot
ĭ	pit	ŭ	cut
ī	bite	ûr	urge
îr	pier	th	thin
ŏ	pot	*th*	this
ō	toe	zh	vision
ô	paw	ə	about

line. **2.** A firing of all the guns on one side of a warship. **3.** A forceful written or verbal attack, as in an editorial or speech. ❖ *adv.* With the side turned to a given point or object: *The wave caught them broadside and filled the canoe.*

broad·sword (**brôd′**sôrd′) *n.* A sword with a broad blade for cutting rather than thrusting.

Broad·way (**brôd′**wā′) The principal theater and amusement district of New York City, on the west side of midtown Manhattan centered on Broadway, a major thoroughfare.

bro·cade (brō-**kād′**) *n.* A heavy cloth with a rich raised design. ❖ *tr.v.* **bro·cad·ed, bro·cad·ing, bro·cades** To weave with a raised design.

broc·co·li (**brŏk′**ə-lē) *n.* A plant having dense clusters of green flower buds that are eaten as a vegetable.

bro·chure (brō-**shŏŏr′**) *n.* A small pamphlet or booklet: *a travel brochure.*

bro·gan (**brō′**gən) *n.* A heavy work shoe extending to the ankle.

brogue[1] (brōg) *n.* **1.** A heavy oxford shoe decorated with rows of tiny holes on top. **2.** A heavy shoe of untanned leather, formerly worn in Scotland and Ireland. [From Irish and Scottish Gaelic *bróg*, from Old Irish *bróc*, shoe.]

brogue[2] (brōg) *n.* A strong dialectal accent, especially an Irish or Scottish accent when speaking English. [Probably from the brogues worn by farmers.]

broil (broil) *v.* **broiled, broil·ing, broils** —*tr.* **1.** To cook close to a flame or other direct source of heat: *broiled the fish on the grill.* **2.** To expose to great heat: *The desert sun broiled the hikers.* —*intr.* **1.** To be cooked by direct heat: *The fish broiled for ten minutes.* **2.** To be exposed to great heat: *The tourists broiled under the tropical sun.* [From Middle English, from Old French *brusler.*]

broil·er (**broi′**lər) *n.* **1.** A grill or a part of an oven used for broiling. **2.** A young chicken suitable for broiling.

broil·ing (**broi′**lĭng) *adj.* Burning; very hot: *The broiling sun withered the plants.*

broke (brōk) *v.* **1.** Past tense of **break. 2.** *Nonstandard* A past participle of **break.** ❖ *adj. Informal* **1.** Bankrupt: *They were completely broke after they lost their money in the stock market crash.* **2.** Lacking money: *Can you pay for lunch? I'm broke.*

bro·ken (**brō′**kən) *v.* Past participle of **break.** ❖ *adj.* **1.** Separated into pieces by force; fractured: *broken pieces of glass; a broken leg.* **2.** Out of order; not functioning: *a broken watch.* **3.** Not kept; violated: *a broken promise.* **4.** Spoken with gaps and errors: *broken English.* **5.** Overwhelmed, as by sadness or hardship: *a broken heart.* **6.** In a weakened condition: *broken health.* **7.** Stopping and starting at intervals having gaps; not continuous: *a broken line on a highway.* **8.** Rough; uneven: *patches of broken ground.* **—bro′ken·ly** *adv.*

bro·ken-down (brō′kən-**doun′**) *adj.* **1.** Not in working order: *a broken-down car.* **2.** In poor condition, as from old age: *a broken-down cart horse.*

bro·ken·heart·ed (**brō′**kən-**här′**tĭd) *adj.* Overwhelmed with sadness; very sad. **—bro′ken·heart′ed·ly** *adv.*

broken home *n.* A home in which the parents have separated or divorced.

bro·ker (**brō′**kər) *n.* A person who acts as an agent for others by negotiating contracts, purchases, or sales in return for a fee or commission: *a commodities broker.* [From Middle English *brokour*, from Anglo-Norman *brocour, abrocour*; akin to Spanish *alboroque*, ceremonial gift at conclusion of a business deal, from colloquial Arabic *al-barka*, the blessing.]

bro·ker·age (**brō′**kər-ĭj) *n.* **1.** The business of a broker. **2.** A fee or commission paid to a broker.

bro·mide (**brō′**mīd′) *n.* **1.** A compound containing bromine and at least one other element, especially potassium, that is used as a sedative drug. **2.** A commonplace remark or notion; a platitude: *an editorial filled with the usual bromides about the importance of team spirit.*

bro·mine (**brō′**mēn) *n. Symbol* **Br** A reddish-brown nonmetallic liquid element that gives off a highly irritating vapor. It is used to make dyes, water purification compounds, and photographic chemicals. Atomic number 35. See **Periodic Table.** [From Greek *brōmos*, stench.]

bron·chi (**brŏng′**kī′) *n.* Plural of **bronchus.**

bron·chi·al (**brŏng′**kē-əl) *adj.* Relating to the bronchi, or the bronchioles.

bronchial tube *n.* A bronchus or any of the tubes branching from a bronchus.

bron·chi·ole (**brŏng′**kē-ōl′) *n.* Any of the fine thin-walled tubes that extend from a bronchus.

bron·chi·tis (brŏn-**kī′**tĭs *or* brŏng-**kī′**tĭs) *n.* Inflammation of the mucous membrane of the bronchial tubes. **—bron·chit′ic** (brŏng-**kĭt′**ĭk) *adj.*

bron·cho·scope (**brŏng′**kə-skōp′) *n.* A slender tube with a small light on the end, used to examine the inside of the bronchi.

bron·chus (**brŏng′**kəs) *n., pl.* **bron·chi** (**brŏng′**kī′) Either of the two large tubes branching from the trachea and leading to the lungs, where they divide into smaller branches.

bron·co (**brŏng′**kō) *n., pl.* **bron·cos** An untrained horse or pony of western North America that bucks when someone tries to ride it.

Bron·të (**brŏn′**tē) Family of British writers including **Charlotte** (1816–1855), **Emily** (1818–1848), and **Anne** (1820–1849). In 1846 they issued *Poems by Currer, Ellis, and Acton Bell.* In 1847 Charlotte published *Jane Eyre,* Emily published *Wuthering Heights,* and Anne published *Agnes Gray.*

bron·to·sau·rus (brŏn′tə-**sôr′**əs) *n.* An earlier name for the apatosaurus. [From Greek *brontē*, thunder + Greek *sauros*, lizard.] —SEE NOTE.

Bronx (brŏngks) A borough of New York City on the mainland north of Manhattan. The Bronx became part of New York City in 1898.

bronze (brŏnz) *n.* **1a.** An alloy of copper and tin, sometimes with traces of other metals. **b.** An alloy of copper and certain metals other than tin, such as aluminum. **2.** A work of art made of bronze: *The sculptor was known for his miniature bronzes of horses and riders.* **3.** A medal made of bronze, awarded for third place in a competition. **4.** A yellowish or olive brown. ❖ *adj.* **1.** Yellowish or olive brown. **2.** Made of or containing bronze: *bronze tools; a bronze statue.* ❖ *tr.v.* **bronzed, bronz·ing, bronz·es** To give the appearance of bronze to: *The sun had bronzed the faces of the lifeguards.* **—bronz′y** *adj.*

Bronze Age *n.* The period of human culture between the Stone Age and the Iron Age, characterized by the use of bronze implements and weapons. In Europe, it began around 3500 BC.

brooch (brōch *or* brōōch) *n.* A large pin worn as an ornament, fastened to the clothing with a clasp.

❑ *These sound alike:* **brooch, broach** (begin to discuss).

brood (brōōd) *n.* **1.** The young of certain animals, especially a group of young birds hatched at one time and cared for together. **2.** The children in one family: *The little house was too small for the Bensons' brood.* ❖ *v.* **brood·ed, brood·ing, broods** —*intr.* **1.** To think at length and unhappily about something; worry: *It seems pointless to brood about the past.* **2a.** To sit on or protect eggs until they hatch or develop into larvae. **b.** To protect young. —*tr.* **1.** To sit on or protect (eggs) until they hatch or develop into larvae. **2.** To protect (young).

brood·er (**brōō′**dər) *n.* **1.** A person or animal that broods. **2.** A heated enclosure in which young chickens or other young birds or livestock are raised.

brook[1] (bro͝ok) *n.* A small natural stream of fresh water; a creek. [From Old English *brōc.*]

brook[2] (bro͝ok) *tr.v.* **brooked, brook·ing, brooks** To put up with; tolerate: *We were late and not in the mood to brook further delay.* [From Old English *brūcan,* to use, enjoy.]

brook·let (bro͝ok′lĭt) *n.* A small brook.

Brook·lyn (bro͝ok′lĭn) A borough of New York City on western Long Island. The community became part of New York City in 1898.

Brooks (bro͝oks), **Gwendolyn Elizabeth** 1917–2000. American poet known for her verses relating the dreams and struggles of African Americans.

brook trout *n.* A speckled freshwater food fish that is native to eastern North America.

broom (bro͞om *or* bro͝om) *n.* **1.** An implement for sweeping, usually consisting of strands of straw or plastic bound together and attached to a long stick. **2.** Any of various European shrubs having yellow flowers, small leaves, and many slender, flexible branches formerly used for sweeping. [From Old English *brōm.*]

❑ *These sound alike:* **broom, brougham** (carriage).

broom·corn (bro͞om′kôrn′ *or* bro͝om′kôrn′) *n.* A variety of sorghum having a flower cluster with many stiff branches, which are used to make brooms and brushes.

broom·stick (bro͞om′stĭk′ *or* bro͝om′stĭk′) *n.* The long handle of a broom.

bros. *abbr.* An abbreviation of brothers.

broth (brôth) *n., pl.* **broths** (brôths *or* brôthz) A clear soup made from the water in which meat, fish, or vegetables have been boiled.

broth·er (brŭ*th*′ər) *n.* **1a.** A boy or man having the same mother and father as someone else. **b.** A boy or man having one parent in common with someone else; a half brother. **c.** A stepbrother. **2a.** A boy or man who shares common ancestors, a common allegiance to a country, or a common purpose with another or others. **b.** A fellow male member of a group, such as a profession, fraternity, or labor union. **3.** *plural* **broth·ers** or **breth·ren** (brĕ*th*′rən) **a.** A member of a men's Christian religious order who is not a priest. **b.** A fellow male member of a Christian church. [From Old English *brōthor.*]

broth·er·hood (brŭ*th*′ər-ho͝od′) *n.* **1.** The relationship of being a brother or brothers. **2.** Brotherly feelings or friendship toward other humans; fellowship. **3.** A group of people united for a common purpose, such as those belonging to a fraternity, labor union, or a profession.

broth·er-in-law (brŭ*th*′ər-ĭn-lô′) *n., pl.* **broth·ers-in-law 1.** The brother of one's spouse. **2.** The husband of one's sibling. **3.** The husband of the sibling of one's spouse.

broth·er·ly (brŭ*th*′ər-lē) *adj.* Characteristic of or appropriate to brothers; affectionate: *a warm brotherly greeting.* **—broth′er·li·ness** *n.*

brougham (bro͞om *or* bro͞o′əm) *n.* **1.** A four-wheeled carriage with a closed compartment for passengers and an open driver's seat. **2.** An automobile with an open driver's seat. [After Henry Peter *Brougham,* First Baron Brougham and Vaux (1778–1868), Scottish-born jurist.]

❑ *These sound alike:* **brougham, broom** (sweeping implement).

brought (brôt) *v.* Past tense and past participle of **bring.**

brow (brou) *n.* **1.** The forehead. **2.** An eyebrow. **3.** The upper edge of a steep place: *We stood on the brow of a hill overlooking the valley.*

brow·beat (brou′bēt′) *tr.v.* **brow·beat, brow·beat·en** (brou′bēt′n), **brow·beat·ing, brow·beats** To bully or intimidate, as with frightening looks or harsh words.

brown (broun) *n.* The color of chocolate or coffee. ❖ *adj.* **brown·er, brown·est 1.** Of the color brown. **2.** Suntanned. ❖ *tr. & intr.v.* **browned, brown·ing, browns 1.** To make or become brown: *Silt browned the stream after the heavy rains.* **2.** To cook until brown on the outside: *The chef browned the meat.* **—brown′ness** *n.*

Brown (broun), **John** 1800–1859. American abolitionist who was tried and hanged in 1859 after capturing the US arsenal at Harper's Ferry as part of an effort to free Southern slaves.

brown bear *n.* A large bear of western North America and northern Eurasia, having dark brown to yellowish fur. There are several types of brown bear, including the grizzly bear.

brown Bet·ty (bĕt′ē) *n.* A baked pudding of apples, bread crumbs, brown sugar, butter, and spices.

brown coal *n.* Lignite.

brown dwarf *n.* A starlike celestial object that does not emit light because it does not have enough mass for nuclear fusion to occur.

brown·field (broun′fēld′) *n.* An abandoned commercial property that is usually polluted but can be reclaimed and developed for new uses.

brown·ie (brou′nē) *n.* **1.** A bar of moist chocolate cake that often has bits of nuts in it. **2. Brownie** A member of the Girl Scouts between six and eight years old. **3.** In folklore, a small elf said to do helpful work such as household chores while people are asleep.

Brown·ing (brou′nĭng), **Elizabeth Barrett** 1806–1861. British poet. Her best-known work, *Sonnets from the Portuguese* (1850), is a series of love poems written to her husband, the poet **Robert Browning** (1812–1889), who published *Men and Women* in 1855.

brown·ish (brou′nĭsh) *adj.* Somewhat brown.

brown·out (broun′out′) *n.* A dimming or partial loss of electric lights and power, especially as the result of a shortage, a mechanical failure, or overuse by consumers.

brown rice *n.* Rice that still has the outer layer of bran on the grain.

brown sauce *n.* A sauce made from butter and flour that have been browned together and mixed with stock.

brown·stone (broun′stōn′) *n.* **1.** A brownish-red sandstone used as a building material. **2.** A house built or faced with such stone.

brown sugar *n.* **1.** Unrefined or partially refined sugar that retains some molasses, giving it a brownish color. **2.** Refined white sugar with molasses added to it, sold as a commercial product.

browse (brouz) *v.* **browsed, brows·ing, brows·es** *—intr.* **1.** To look at something in a leisurely and casual way: *browse through a book; browse through a department store.* **2.** To look for information on the Internet. **3.** To feed on leaves, young shoots, twigs, and other vegetation: *The deer have been browsing on the shrubs.* *—tr.* **1.** To look through (something) casually: *browse the newspaper.* **2.** To read (websites) casually on the Internet. **3.** To nibble at; graze on: *Cattle browsed the pasture.* ❖ *n.* Vegetation, such as leaves, young shoots, and twigs, eaten by animals: *Very little browse is available after a heavy snowfall.*

brows·er (brou′zər) *n.* **1.** A person or thing that browses. **2.** A computer program that accesses and displays files and other data available on the Internet and other networks.

bru·in (bro͞o′ĭn) *n.* A bear. [From Middle Dutch *bruun, bruin,* brown, name of the bear in the fable *History of Reynard the Fox.*]

bruise (bro͞oz) *v.* **bruised, bruis·ing, bruis·es** *—tr.* **1.** To injure (a part of the body) without breaking the skin, as by a blow: *When my bike tipped over I bruised my knees.* **2.** To hurt one's feelings; offend: *Criticism bruised the actor's pride.* *—intr.* To become bruised: *My skin bruises easily.* ❖ *n.* **1.** An injury in which small blood vessels in the skin are broken by pressure or a blow, producing discoloration but leaving the skin itself unbroken:

WORD HISTORY

brontosaurus Take a little deception, add a little excitement, stir them with a century-long mistake, and you have the mystery of the **brontosaurus.** Specifically, you have the mystery of its name. For 100 years this 70-foot-long, 30-ton vegetarian giant had two names. This case of double identity began in 1877, when bones of a large dinosaur were discovered. The creature was dubbed **Apatosaurus,** a name that meant "deceptive lizard" or "unreal lizard." Two years later, bones of a larger dinosaur were found, and in all the excitement, scientists named it *Brontosaurus,* or "thunder lizard." This name stuck until scientists decided it was all a mistake—the two sets of bones actually belonged to the same type of dinosaur. Since it is a rule in taxonomy that the first name given to a newly discovered organism is the one that must be used, scientists have had to use the name *Apatosaurus.* But "thunder lizard" had popular appeal, and many people still prefer to call the beast a brontosaurus.

John Brown

brownstone

Brussels sprouts

get a bruise from a fall. **2.** A similar injury to a fruit, vegetable, or plant.

bruis·er (**broo͞′**zər) *n. Informal* A large powerfully built man.

bruit (bro͞ot) *tr.v.* **bruit·ed, bruit·ing, bruits** To spread news of; repeat: *The rumor was bruited about all over town.*

❑ *These sound alike:* **bruit, brute** (beast).

brunch (brŭnch) *n.* A meal eaten in the late morning or early afternoon that combines breakfast and lunch. [From br(*eakfast*) + (*l*)*unch*.]

Bru·nei (bro͞o-**nī′**) A sultanate of northern Borneo on the South China Sea. Bandar Seri Begawan is the capital.

bru·nette also **bru·net** (bro͞o-**nĕt′**) *adj.* Having dark or brown hair. ❖ *n.* A woman or girl with dark or brown hair.

brunt (brŭnt) *n.* The main impact, force, or burden: *Towns along the shore bore the brunt of the hurricane.*

brush (brŭsh) *n.* **1.** An implement consisting of bristles, hairs, or wire fastened to a handle, used especially for scrubbing, applying paint, or grooming the hair. **2.** An application of a brush: *give one's hair a good brush.* **3.** A sweeping movement or light touch: *the brush of a branch against my coat.* **4.** A brief encounter with something undesirable or dangerous: *a brush with the law.* **5.** Dense vegetation consisting of shrubs or small trees: *The explorers hacked a trail through the brush.* **6.** Broken or cut branches; brushwood: *Pile the brush at the curb.* **7.** A sliding connection completing a circuit between a fixed and a moving conductor, as in a motor or generator. ❖ *v.* **brushed, brush·ing, brush·es** —*tr.* **1.** To clean, polish, or groom with a brush: *brush shoes until they shine.* **2.** To apply with a brush: *brush paint on evenly.* **3.** To remove with a brush or with sweeping strokes: *brush dirt off one's jacket.* **4.** To treat as unimportant; dismiss: *He brushed aside her objections and carried on.* **5.** To touch lightly in passing: *Their arms brushed in the crowded hall.* —*intr.* To touch something lightly in moving past it: *The wet paint got on my clothes when I brushed against it.* ◆ **brush up** To refresh one's memory or renew one's skill regarding something: *I'll have to brush up on my Spanish before going to Mexico.* **—brush′y** *adj.*

James Buchanan

brush·fire also **brush fire** (**brŭsh′**fīr′) *n.* A fire in an area of small trees, bushes, or other low-growing vegetation.

brush·off also **brush-off** (**brŭsh′**ôf′) *n.* An abrupt dismissal; a snub: *She gave him the brushoff.*

brush·wood (**brŭsh′**wo͝od′) *n.* **1.** Cut or broken branches. **2.** Dense, low-growing vegetation; brush.

brush·work (**brŭsh′**wûrk′) *n.* The way in which a painter applies paint with a brush: *a painter known for his detailed brushwork.*

brusque (brŭsk) *adj.* Rudely abrupt in manner or speech; curt; blunt: *The speaker gave a brusque reply to the heckler.* **—brusque′ly** *adv.* **—brusque′ness** *n.*

Brus·sels (**brŭs′**əlz) The capital of Belgium, in the central part of the country south of Antwerp. It is officially bilingual (Flemish and French).

Brussels sprouts *pl.n. (used with a singular or plural verb)* **1.** Buds that resemble small cabbages growing on a long thick stem, eaten as a vegetable. **2.** The plant that bears such buds.

bru·tal (**bro͞ot′**l) *adj.* **1.** Cruel; ruthless: *a brutal attack.* **2.** Harsh; severe: *a brutal Arctic winter.* **3.** Unpleasantly direct or plain: *He is known for his brutal honesty.* **—bru′tal·ly** *adv.*

bru·tal·i·ty (bro͞o-**tăl′**ĭ-tē) *n., pl.* **bru·tal·i·ties 1.** The quality or condition of being brutal: *The brutality of boxing offends many people.* **2.** A ruthless, cruel, or harsh act.

bru·tal·ize (**bro͞ot′**l-īz′) *tr.v.* **bru·tal·ized, bru·tal·iz·ing, bru·tal·iz·es 1.** To make brutal. **2.** To treat cruelly or harshly: *The animal trainer was accused of brutalizing the dogs by locking them in narrow cages.*

brute (bro͞ot) *n.* **1.** An animal other than a human; a beast: *debates about whether brutes have souls.* **2.** A brutal person. ❖ *adj.* **1.** Having to do with animals other than humans. **2.** Lacking reason or intelligence: *a brute craving.* **3.** Entirely physical: *the brute force of the storm.* [From Middle English *brut*, like a beast, nonhuman, from Latin *brūtus*, stupid.]

❑ *These sound alike:* **brute, bruit** (repeat).

brut·ish (**bro͞o′**tĭsh) *adj.* Resembling a brute; coarse, stupid, or cruel: *the brutish behavior of a gangster.* **—brut′ish·ly** *adv.*

Bru·tus (**bro͞o′**təs), **Marcus Junius** 85?–42 BC. Roman politician and general who conspired to assassinate Julius Caesar. He later killed himself.

Bry·an (**brī′**ən), **William Jennings** 1860–1925. American lawyer and politician who ran unsuccessfully for president in 1896, 1900, and 1908.

Bry·ant (**brī′**ənt), **William Cullen** 1794–1878. American poet, critic, and editor known especially for his early nature poems, such as "To a Waterfowl" (1821).

bry·o·phyte (**brī′**ə-fīt′) *n.* Any of numerous nonvascular plants that reproduce by spores, such as the mosses and liverworts.

BS *abbr.* An abbreviation of Bachelor of Science.

BSA *abbr.* An abbreviation of Boys Scouts of America.

Btu *abbr.* An abbreviation of British thermal unit.

bu. *abbr.* An abbreviation of bushel.

bub·ble (**bŭb′**əl) *n.* **1.** A rounded thin film of liquid enclosing an amount of air or other gas: *soap bubbles.* **2.** A small rounded amount of gas that rises to the surface of a liquid or remains trapped in a solid or plastic material: *bubbles of air in ice cubes.* **3.** A glass or plastic dome: *a package of batteries enclosed under a plastic bubble.* **4.** A rounded or irregularly shaped outline containing the words that a character in a cartoon is represented to be saying. **5.** An increase in the price of something, such as housing, resulting from purchases by people expecting that the price will increase further. ❖ *intr.v.* **bub·bled, bub·bling, bub·bles 1.** To form or give off bubbles: *Steam rose as water bubbled in the vat.* **2.** To move or flow with a gurgling sound: *a brook bubbling over the rocks.* **3.** To show lively activity or emotion: *As they entered the theater, the little kids were bubbling with excitement.*

bubble chamber *n.* A device for detecting the paths of charged atomic particles by observation of the trails of gas bubbles that the particles leave in a superheated liquid.

bubble gum *n.* Chewing gum that can be blown into bubbles.

bub·bly (**bŭb′**lē) *adj.* **1.** Full of or producing bubbles. **2.** Resembling bubbles. **3.** Full of high spirits; animated and lively: *a bubbly personality.*

bu·bon·ic plague (bo͞o-**bŏn′**ĭk) *n.* An often fatal disease caused by bacteria transmitted to humans by fleas from infected rats or other rodents. Its symptoms include chills, fever, vomiting, diarrhea, and enlarged lymph nodes.

buc·ca·neer (bŭk′ə-**nîr′**) *n.* A pirate. [From French *boucanier*, a hunter of wild oxen, from *boucaner*, to cure meat, from *boucan*, barbecue frame, of Tupian origin.]

Bu·chan·an (byo͞o-**kăn′**ən *or* bə-**kăn′**ən), **James** 1791–1868. The 15th president of the United States (1857–1861). He was unable to prevent the secession of South Carolina in 1860.

Bu·cha·rest (**bo͞o′**kə-rĕst′) The capital of Romania, in the southeast part of the country on a tributary of the Danube River. It was founded in the 1300s.

buck¹ (bŭk) *n.* **1.** The adult male of certain animals, such as deer, antelopes, and rabbits. **2.** A sudden leap forward

ă	pat	ôr	core
ā	pay	oi	boy
âr	care	ou	out
ä	father	o͝o	took
ĕ	pet	o͝or	lure
ē	be	o͞o	boot
ĭ	pit	ŭ	cut
ī	bite	ûr	urge
îr	pier	th	thin
ŏ	pot	*th*	this
ō	toe	zh	vision
ô	paw	ə	about

and upward, as by a horse or mule. ❖ *v.* **bucked, buck·ing, bucks** —*intr.* **1.** To leap upward while arching the back: *The bronco bucked and kicked.* **2.** To resist or defy a rule or expectation, for example: *bucking against the trend in fashion.* —*tr.* **1.** To throw off (a rider) by bucking. **2.** To struggle against; resist or defy: *a rebel who often bucks the rules.* ◆ **buck up** To summon one's courage or spirits; hearten: *urged the runner to buck up and keep going.* [From Old English *buc*, male deer, and *bucca*, male goat.]

buck² (bŭk) *n. Informal* A dollar. [Short for *buckskin* (from its use in trade).]

Buck (bŭk), **Pearl Sydenstricker** 1892–1973. American writer whose life as a missionary in China influenced her novels, including *The Good Earth* (1931).

buck·a·roo (bŭk′ə-**ro͞o′**) *n., pl.* **buck·a·roos** A cowboy. [Alteration of Spanish *vaquero*, from *vaca*, cow.]

buck·board (**bŭk′**bôrd′) *n.* An open four-wheeled carriage with the seat attached to a flexible board running between the front and rear axles.

buck·et (**bŭk′**ĭt) *n.* **1.** A round open container with a curved handle, used for carrying liquids or solids; a pail. **2a.** The amount that a bucket holds: *pour a bucket of sand on an icy sidewalk.* **b.** An unexpectedly great amount or quantity: *The rain came down in buckets.* **3.** Something resembling a bucket, such as the scoop on a steam shovel. ◆ **a drop in the bucket** An insufficient or trifling amount in comparison with what is needed.

buck·et·ful (**bŭk′**ĭt-fo͝ol′) *n.* The amount that a bucket can hold.

bucket seat *n.* A single, usually low seat with a rounded padded back, as in certain automobiles.

buck·eye (**bŭk′**ī′) *n.* **1.** Any of various North American trees or shrubs having large divided leaves, reddish or white flower clusters, and a leathery capsule containing one or more large seeds. All parts of the plant are poisonous. **2.** The glossy brown seed of such a tree.

buck·le (**bŭk′**əl) *n.* **1.** A clasp used to fasten one end of a strap or belt to the other: *the buckle on the strap of a watch.* **2.** An ornament that looks like such a clasp, as one on top of a shoe. **3.** A bend, bulge, warp, or other distortion: *A buckle in the dike showed it was soon going to break.* ❖ *v.* **buck·led, buck·ling, buck·les** —*tr.* **1.** To fasten with a buckle: *Buckle your seat belt before the car starts.* **2.** To cause to bend, warp, or crumple, as by pressure or heat: *Too much pressure buckled the sides of the box.* —*intr.* To sag, bend, or collapse: *Walls buckled in the heat of the fire.* ◆ **buckle down** To apply oneself with determination. [From Middle English *bokel*, from Latin *buccula*, cheek strap of a helmet, diminutive of *bucca*, cheek.]

buck·ler (**bŭk′**lər) *n.* A small round shield that is either carried or worn on the arm.

buck·min·ster·ful·ler·ene (bŭk′mĭn-stər-**fo͝ol′**ə-rēn′) *n.* An extremely stable, ball-shaped carbon molecule that is shaped like a geodesic dome, and believed to occur naturally in soot. It was the first fullerene to be discovered. [After Richard *Buckminster Fuller* (1895–1983), American architect.]

buck·ram (**bŭk′**rəm) *n.* A coarse cotton cloth stiffened with glue, used especially for binding books.

buck·saw (**bŭk′**sô′) *n.* A saw usually set in an H-shaped frame, used for cutting wood.

buck·shot (**bŭk′**shŏt′) *n.* The large lead shot used in shotgun shells, especially for hunting large game.

buck·skin (**bŭk′**skĭn′) *n.* **1.** A soft, grayish-yellow leather, made from the skins of deer or sheep. **2. buckskins** Breeches or shoes made of this leather.

buck·tooth (**bŭk′**to͞oth′) *n.* A prominent projecting upper front tooth. **—buck′toothed′** *adj.*

buck·wheat (**bŭk′**wēt′) *n.* **1.** The small, starchy, triangular seeds of an annual plant native to Asia. The seeds are often ground into flour or used as livestock feed. **2.** The plant that bears such seeds.

buck·y·ball (**bŭk′**e-bôl′) *n.* A buckminsterfullerene. [Shortening and alteration of *buckminsterfullerene* + *ball*.]

bu·col·ic (byo͞o-**kŏl′**ĭk) *adj.* **1.** Relating to or characteristic of shepherds; pastoral: *bucolic poetry.* **2.** Relating to or characteristic of country life; rustic: *a bucolic scene.*

bud (bŭd) *n.* **1.** A small swelling or structure on a branch or stem containing an undeveloped flower, shoot, or leaf. **2.** A small outgrowth on a simple organism, such as a yeast or hydra, that grows into a complete new organism of the same species. **3.** A small part or organ, such as a taste bud, that is shaped somewhat like a bud. **4.** An earbud. **5.** A stage of early or incomplete development: *the bud of a new idea.* ❖ *intr.v.* **bud·ded, bud·ding, buds 1.** To form or produce a bud or buds: *Tulips bud in the very early spring.* **2.** To be in an early stage; begin to develop: *Businesses using new research are budding near the university.*

Bu·da·pest (**bo͞o′**də-pĕst′ *or* **bo͞o′**də-pĕsht′) The capital of Hungary, in the north-central part of the country on the Danube River.

Bud·dha¹ (**bo͞o′**də *or* **bo͝od′**ə) 563?–483? BC. See Siddhartha **Gautama.**

Bud·dha² (**bo͞o′**də *or* **bo͝od′**ə) *n.* **1.** In Buddhism, one who has achieved perfect spiritual enlightenment, thereby attaining Nirvana. **2.** A representation or likeness of a Buddha.

Buddha²

Bud·dhism (**bo͞o′**dĭz′əm *or* **bo͝od′**ĭz′əm) *n.* The religion, based on the teachings of Siddhartha Gautama, that holds that suffering is unavoidable in life and that freeing oneself from worldly desires leads to a state of enlightenment called Nirvana. **—Bud′dhist** *n. & adj.*

bud·dy (**bŭd′**ē) *Informal n., pl.* **bud·dies** A close friend; a comrade.

buddy system *n.* An arrangement in which people pair up, as during a hike, swim, or similar activity, to look out for each other's safety.

budge (bŭj) *intr. & tr.v.* **budged, budg·ing, budg·es 1.** To move or cause to move slightly: *The boulder did not budge. We cannot budge the boulder.* **2.** To alter or cause to alter a position or attitude: *They won't budge once they have reached a decision. After the prime minister had made up her mind, no one could budge her.*

budg·er·i·gar (**bŭj′**ə-rē-gär′) *n.* A small green, blue, or yellow parakeet often kept as a pet.

budgerigar

budg·et (**bŭj′**ĭt) *n.* **1.** A plan or estimate of the amount of money that will be spent and received in a given period: *Congress must approve the government's budget each year.* **2.** The amount of money included in a budget: *a project with an annual budget of two million dollars.* ❖ *tr.v.* **budg·et·ed, budg·et·ing, budg·ets 1.** To plan in advance how to spend: *budget an allowance; did not budget my time wisely.* **2.** To enter or plan for in a budget: *We need to budget repairs into the estimated car expenses.* ❖ *adj.* **1.** Relating to a budget: *Were these budget items approved by Congress?* **2.** Appropriate to a restricted budget; inexpensive: *a budget car; budget meals.* **—bud′get·ar′y** (**bŭj′**ĭ-tĕr′ē) *adj.*

budg·ie (**bŭj′**ē) *n. Informal* A budgerigar.

Bue·nos Ai·res (**bwā′**nəs **âr′**ēz *or* **bwā′**nəs **ī′**rĭz) The capital of Argentina, in the eastern part of the country on the Río de la Plata. The city was founded in 1536.

buff¹ (bŭf) *n.* **1.** A soft, thick, yellowish leather made from the skins of buffalo, elk, or oxen. **2.** The color of this leather; a yellowish tan. **3.** A piece of soft material used for polishing. ❖ *tr.v.* **buffed, buff·ing, buffs** To polish or shine with a piece of soft material: *waxed and buffed the car.* ❖ *adj.* **1.** Made of buff. **2.** Of the color buff. **3. buff·er, buff·est** Physically fit and trim. [From French *buffle*, from Late Latin *būfalus*, buffalo.]

WORD HISTORY

buffalo Many of the English names of North American animals, like *moose* and *skunk,* come from Native American languages, but the term **buffalo** is not one of these. It can be traced back through Latin to the Greek word *boubalos,* meaning "an antelope or buffalo." The buffalo referred to by the Greek or Latin word was not of course the North American one, but an Asian or African animal such as the water buffalo. Scientists prefer to use the word **bison** for the North American animal, but the word *buffalo* is so much a part of the history of the Wild West that the name lives on in everyday speech.

buffalo
African buffalo

ă	pat	ôr	core
ā	pay	oi	boy
âr	care	ou	out
ä	father	o͝o	took
ĕ	pet	o͝or	lure
ē	be	o͞o	boot
ĭ	pit	ŭ	cut
ī	bite	ûr	urge
îr	pier	th	thin
ŏ	pot	*th*	this
ō	toe	zh	vision
ô	paw	ə	about

buff² (bŭf) *n. Informal* A person who has great interest in, and some knowledge of, a subject; an enthusiast: *a train buff.* [From the buff-colored uniform once worn by New York City volunteer firemen, originally applied to an enthusiast of fires and firefighting.]

buf·fa·lo (bŭf′ə-lō′) *n., pl.* **buffalo** or **buf·fa·loes** or **buf·fa·los 1.** The North American bison. **2.** Any of several large African or Asian mammals having large curving horns, such as the water buffalo. [From Late Latin *būfalus,* from Latin *būbalus,* antelope, buffalo, from Greek *boubalos,* antelope.] —SEE NOTE.

Buffalo A city of western New York at the eastern end of Lake Erie on the Canadian border.

Buffalo Bill See William Frederick **Cody.**

Buffalo wing *n.* A fried chicken wing served with a spicy sauce and blue cheese dressing.

buff·er¹ (bŭf′ər) *n.* A soft pad or a tool having such a pad, used to polish or shine objects.

buff·er² (bŭf′ər) *n.* **1.** Something that reduces or absorbs the shock of a blow or collision: *hung tires along the dock as a buffer to protect boats when docking.* **2.** A substance that minimizes change in the acidity of a solution when an acid or a base is added to the solution. **3.** Something that separates two potential rivals and reduces the danger of conflict: *The railroad tracks served as a buffer between the two hostile neighborhoods.* **4.** A device or area of a computer that is used to store data temporarily. ❖ *tr.v.* **buff·ered, buff·er·ing, buff·ers** To treat (a solution) with a buffer. [Probably from obsolete *buff,* to make a sound like a soft body being hit, of imitative origin.]

buffer state *n.* A country that lies between two countries that are rivals or enemies.

buf·fet¹ (bə-fā′ *or* bo͞o-fā′) *n.* **1.** A large piece of furniture with drawers and cupboards for storing china, silverware, and table linens. **2.** A meal at which guests serve themselves from dishes arranged on a table or counter. **3.** A counter from which food is served. ❖ *adj.* Being a meal where diners serve themselves: *a buffet lunch.* [From French.]

buf·fet² (bŭf′ĭt) *n.* A hit or blow, especially one made with the hand. ❖ *tr.v.* **buf·fet·ed, buf·fet·ing, buf·fets** To hit or strike against forcefully; batter: *The rough sea buffeted the small boat.* [From Middle English, from Old French *bufet,* diminutive of *buffe,* blow.]

buf·foon (bə-fo͞on′) *n.* **1.** A clown or jester. **2.** A person given to making jokes. **3.** A bumbling or ridiculous person; a fool. **—buf·foon′er·y** *n.*

bug (bŭg) *n.* **1.** An insect having mouthparts used for piercing and sucking, such as an aphid or a bedbug. **2.** An insect of any kind, such as a cockroach or a ladybug, or another small invertebrate that looks like an insect, such as a spider or a centipede: *Let's go inside; there are too many bugs out here.* **3a.** A microorganism or virus that causes disease; a germ: *The bug that causes cholera.* **b.** A disease caused by such a microorganism or virus: *She's had that bug for a week.* **4a.** A fault or defect in a system or device: *work the bugs out of a plan.* **b.** An error or defect in a computer program. **5.** A hidden electronic device that allows private conversations to be overheard. **6.** *Slang* An enthusiast; a buff: *a model train bug.* ❖ *v.* **bugged, bug·ging, bugs** *—intr.* To grow large; bulge: *Their eyes bugged out with surprise. —tr. Slang* **1.** To annoy, pester, or trouble: *Stop bugging her to do the dishes.* **2.** To equip (a room or telephone circuit, for example) with a concealed electronic listening device. ◆ **bug off** *Slang* To leave someone alone; go away. —SEE NOTE.

bug·a·boo (bŭg′ə-bo͞o′) *n., pl.* **bug·a·boos** An imaginary or real object of fear: *Speaking in public is my biggest bugaboo.*

bug·bear (bŭg′bâr′) *n.* **1.** A recurring or persistent problem: *Spelling has always been my bugbear in school.* **2.** A bugaboo. [From obsolete *bug,* hobgoblin + *bear.*]

bug·gy (bŭg′ē) *n., pl.* **bug·gies 1.** A small light carriage with a single seat and four wheels, drawn by a horse. **2.** A baby carriage. **3.** A motor vehicle, usually with oversized tires, designed for off-road use.

bu·gle (byo͞o′gəl) *n.* A brass wind instrument similar to a trumpet but lacking valves. It is often used to sound signals in the military, such as reveille. ❖ *intr.v.* **bu·gled, bu·gling, bu·gles** To play a bugle. [From Middle English, from Late Latin *būgula,* from Latin *buculus,* ox, from the idea that early bugles were made from ox horns.] **—bu′gler** *n.*

build (bĭld) *v.* **built** (bĭlt), **build·ing, builds** *—tr.* **1.** To make or form by fitting together materials or parts; construct: *It takes a long time to build a skyscraper. The body needs iron in the diet to build hemoglobin.* **2.** To develop according to a plan or process; create: *people working together to build a better society.* **3.** To increase or strengthen by adding gradually to: *Reading helps build a rich vocabulary. —intr.* To progress toward a climax; grow steadily; develop: *A good mystery builds from the first chapters to its climax. Scientific discoveries build on the work of others.* ❖ *n.* The physical make-up of a person or thing: *a muscular athletic build.* ◆ **build in** or **build into** To construct as a permanent part of: *build in kitchen cabinets.* **build on** or **build onto** To use as a basis or foundation: *We must build on our success.* **build up 1.** To cause to develop in stages or by degrees: *build up a business; build up a strong vocabulary.* **2.** To cover with buildings: *The downtown area is getting built up.* **3.** To accumulate gradually: *sediments building up on the ocean floor.* [From Old English *byldan.*]

build·er (bĭl′dər) *n.* **1.** A person or animal that builds: *Beavers are great dam builders.* **2.** A person who constructs new buildings or develops land: *the architects and builders of a great city.*

build·ing (bĭl′dĭng) *n.* **1.** Something that is built; a structure. **2.** The act, process, or occupation of constructing.

build·up also **build-up** (bĭld′ŭp′) *n.* **1.** The act or process of building up or accumulating: *the buildup of ashes in a fireplace.* **2.** Widely favorable publicity; high praise: *The newspaper gave the fund-raising committee a nice buildup.*

built (bĭlt) *v.* Past tense and past participle of **build.**

built-in (bĭlt′ĭn′) *adj.* Constructed as a permanent part of a larger unit: *a built-in cupboard.*

built-up (bĭlt′ŭp′) *adj.* **1.** Made by fastening layers or sections one on top of the other: *a built-up roof.* **2.** Filled with buildings; developed: *a built-up neighborhood.*

Bu·jum·bu·ra (bo͞o′jəm-bo͝or′ə) The capital of Burundi, in the western part of the country south-southwest of Kigali, Rwanda.

bulb (bŭlb) *n.* **1.** A rounded underground stem surrounded by fleshy modified leaves, from which a shoot emerges that will grow into a new plant. Tulips and onions grow from bulbs. **2.** A similar underground structure, such as a corm, rhizome, or tuber. **3.** A rounded part of something: *the bulb of a thermometer.* **4.** A light bulb. **5.** Any of various rounded structures in the body of an animal. [From Latin *bulbus,* from Greek *bolbos,* bulbous plant.]

bul·bous (bŭl′bəs) *adj.* **1.** Growing from or producing a bulb: *The tulip is a bulbous plant.* **2.** Bulb-shaped: *a bulbous nose.*

Bul·gar·i·a (bŭl-gâr′ē-ə *or* bo͝ol-gâr′ē-ə) A country of southeast Europe on the Black Sea south of Romania. It was subject to the Ottoman Empire from the 1300s until 1908, when it gained independence. Sofia is the capital.

Bul·gar·i·an (bŭl-gâr′ē-ən *or* bo͝ol-gâr′ē-ən) *adj.* Relating to Bulgaria or its people, language, or culture. ❖ *n.*

1. A native or inhabitant of Bulgaria. 2. The Slavic language of the Bulgarians.

bulge (bŭlj) *n.* A protruding part; an outward curve or a swelling: *A blister causes a bulge in the skin.* ❖ *intr. & tr.v.* **bulged, bulg·ing, bulg·es** To swell or cause to swell beyond the usual size: *eyes bulging with surprise; groceries bulging a bag.* —**bulg′y** *adj.*

bul·gur also **bul·ghur** (bŭl′gər *or* bo͝ol-**go͞or′**) *n.* Cracked wheat grains, often used in Middle Eastern dishes. [From Ottoman Turkish *bulğur*, from Arabic *burġul*, from Persian *barghūl*.]

bu·li·mi·a (bo͞o-**lē′**mē-ə) *n.* An eating disorder in which the eating of large amounts of food is followed by vomiting or other measures to prevent gaining weight.

bulk (bŭlk) *n.* **1.** Great size, mass, or volume: *the whale's enormous bulk.* **2.** The major portion of something; greater part: *The bulk of the evidence is negative.* ◆ **in bulk 1.** Unpackaged; loose: *That store sells apples in bulk.* **2.** In large numbers, amounts, or volume: *Flour mills buy wheat in bulk.* [From Middle English, perhaps partly alteration of *bouk*, belly, trunk of the body (from Old English *būc*), and partly from Old Norse *bulki*, cargo, heap.]

bulk·head (**bŭlk′**hĕd′) *n.* **1.** One of the vertical walls that divide the inside of a ship or aircraft into compartments. **2.** A wall or embankment, as in a mine or along a waterfront, built to protect against earth slides, fire, water, or gas.

bulk·y (**bŭl′**kē) *adj.* **bulk·i·er, bulk·i·est 1.** Extremely large; massive: *Elephants and whales are bulky animals.* **2.** Taking up much space; clumsy; unwieldy: *The new lamp came in a bulky package.* —**bulk′i·ly** *adv.* —**bulk′i·ness** *n.*

bull[1] (bo͝ol) *n.* **1a.** The uncastrated adult male of domestic cattle. **b.** The adult male of bovine mammals, such as bison or yaks, or of certain other large animals, such as alligators, elephants, moose, or whales. **2.** A person who buys stock or other securities expecting their price to rise. ❖ *adj.* **1.** Male: *a bull seal.* **2.** Characterized by rising prices, especially in the stock market: *a bull market.* [From Old English *bula*, probably from Old Norse *boli*.]

bull[2] (bo͝ol) *n.* An official document issued by the pope. [From Middle English *bulle*, from Medieval Latin *bulla*, blister, seal on a papal decree.]

bull·dog (**bo͝ol′**dôg′) *n.* A stocky short-haired dog of a breed originally developed in England, having a large head with strong, square jaws.

bull·doze (**bo͝ol′**dōz′) *tr.v.* **bull·dozed, bull·doz·ing, bull·doz·es 1.** To clear, dig up, or move with a bulldozer: *bulldoze land for a new development.* **2.** To bully, intimidate, or coerce: *bulldoze a committee into action.*

bull·doz·er (**bo͝ol′**dō′zər) *n.* A large powerful tractor equipped with treads and a metal blade in front for moving earth and grading land.

bul·let (**bo͝ol′**ĭt) *n.* **1.** A small, rounded, usually pointed piece of metal to be fired from a firearm such as a rifle or pistol. **2.** A heavy dot (•) used to highlight printed information.

bul·le·tin (**bo͝ol′**ĭ-tn) *n.* **1.** A statement on a matter of public interest, as in a newspaper, on television, or on radio: *a weather bulletin.* **2.** A newspaper, magazine, or pamphlet published regularly by an organization, such as a society or club: *Did you read the school bulletin this week?*

bulletin board *n.* **1.** A board on which notices are posted. **2.** A service for computer users that enables participants to send or read messages or files that are of general public interest.

bul·let·proof (**bo͝ol′**ĭt-pro͞of′) *adj.* Designed to stop or repel bullets: *bulletproof glass.*

bullet train *n.* A high-speed passenger train.

bull·fight (**bo͝ol′**fīt′) *n.* A spectacle, especially in Spain, Portugal, and Mexico, in which a matador typically engages a bull in traditional maneuvers with a cape and kills it with a sword. —**bull′fight′er** *n.* —**bull′fight′ing** *n.*

bull·finch (**bo͝ol′**fĭnch′) *n.* A European songbird having a short thick bill and in the male a red breast.

bull·frog (**bo͝ol′**frôg′) *n.* Any of several large frogs native to eastern North America, having a deep hollow croak.

bull·head (**bo͝ol′**hĕd′) *n.* **1.** Any of several North American freshwater catfishes having a large head. **2.** Any of several other large-headed fishes.

bull·head·ed (**bo͝ol′hĕd′**ĭd) *adj.* Very stubborn; headstrong. —**bull′head′ed·ness** *n.*

bull·horn (**bo͝ol′**hôrn′) *n.* A portable electric device resembling a megaphone and used to make the voice louder.

bul·lion (**bo͝ol′**yən) *n.* Gold or silver in the form of bars or ingots.

❑ *These sound alike:* **bullion, bouillon** (soup).

bull·ish (**bo͝ol′**ĭsh) *adj.* **1.** Aggressive or bullheaded. **2a.** Causing, expecting, or characterized by rising stock market prices. **b.** Optimistic or confident: *bullish on the prospects for a negotiated settlement.* —**bull′ish·ly** *adv.* —**bull′ish·ness** *n.*

bul·lock (**bo͝ol′**ək) *n.* **1.** A castrated bull; a steer. **2.** A young ox or bull.

bull·pen (**bo͝ol′**pĕn′) *n.* **1.** An area in a baseball park where relief pitchers warm up during a game. **2.** The relief pitchers of a baseball team considered as a group: *a team with an excellent bullpen.*

bull·ring (**bo͝ol′**rĭng′) *n.* A circular arena for bullfighting.

Bull Run A small stream of northeast Virginia southwest of Washington, DC. It was the site of two Civil War battles (July 21, 1861, and August 29–30, 1862), both Confederate victories.

bull's-eye or **bull's eye** (**bo͝olz′**ī′) *n.* **1a.** The small central circle on a target, as in archery or small arms practice. **b.** A shot that hits this circle. **2.** A direct hit: *scored a bull's-eye on the window with a snowball.*

bull terrier *n.* A dog of a breed developed in England from a cross between a bulldog and a terrier, having a short coat and a flat head with a tapering muzzle.

bul·ly (**bo͝ol′**ē) *n., pl.* **bul·lies** A person who is habitually cruel or aggressive toward smaller, weaker, or less popular people. ❖ *tr.v.* **bul·lied, bul·ly·ing, bul·lies** To hurt or intimidate (someone) as a bully does. [Possibly from Middle Dutch *boele*, sweetheart, probably alteration of *broeder*, brother.]

bul·rush (**bo͝ol′**rŭsh′) *n.* Any of several tall plants that resemble grasses and grow in wet places.

bul·wark (**bo͝ol′**wərk *or* **bo͝ol′**wôrk′) *n.* **1.** A wall or barrier serving as a fortification: *An extensive bulwark protected the city from attack.* **2.** Something that serves as a defense: *Freedom of speech is the citizen's bulwark against the power of government.* **3.** A breakwater. **4.** often **bulwarks** The part of a ship's side that is above the upper deck. [From Middle English *bulwerk*, from Middle Dutch *bolwerk*.]

bum (bŭm) *n.* **1.** A tramp; a vagrant. **2.** A person who avoids work; a loafer or beggar. ❖ *v.* **bummed, bum·ming, bums** —*intr.* **1.** To wander about or pass the time idly: *spent the summer bumming around with friends.* **2.** To live by begging or scavenging. —*tr.* To obtain by begging; mooch: *bum a ride to the next town.* ❖ *adj.* **bum·mer, bum·mest 1.** Worthless: *bum directions.* **2.** Disabled: *a bum knee.* **3.** Unfavorable or unfair: *Breaking your leg before vacation was a bum deal.* ◆ **bum out** *Slang* To depress, dishearten, or dismay: *Not winning the game bummed me out.*

bum·ble·bee (**bŭm′**bəl-bē′) *n.* Any of various large

SCIENCE

bug In everyday language, people use the word **bug** to refer to all insects, such as aphids, mosquitoes, and beetles, as well as a variety of small many-legged animals that are not insects, such as spiders, ticks, and centipedes. But for scientists, the word has a much narrower meaning. In strictest terms, bugs are insects with mouthparts that are used for piercing and sucking and are contained in a beak-shaped structure. Entomologists often call these insects "true bugs," to distinguish them better from what everyone else calls "bugs." Examples of true bugs are bedbugs, which feed on blood, and aphids and cicadas, which suck plant juices.

bulldog
English bulldog

bulldozer

bullet train

bungee jumping

WRITERS CHOOSE THEIR WORDS

I knew from experience that it's not always a good idea to rehearse what you're going to say ahead of time. That can go either way—either you say a thing just the way you wanted to, or you **bungle** it real bad. It depends on the person you're talking to, and whether or not he lets you go ahead and get it out. If there's any interruption, I tend to get all confused, lose track of what I was saying, and end up sounding like a blithering idiot.

—Valerie Sherrard
Sam's Light

hairy bees that fly with a humming sound and nest in underground colonies.

bum·mer (bŭm′ər) *n. Slang* An unpleasant or disappointing experience or situation.

bump (bŭmp) *v.* **bumped, bump·ing, bumps** *—tr.* **1.** To come up or knock against (a person or thing) forcefully: *They bumped heads as they both stooped to pick up the dime.* **2.** To cause (something) to knock against an obstacle: *I bumped the vacuum cleaner against the table.* **3.** To cause to move or shift by knocking or colliding: *bumped the box out of the way with my knee.* **4.** To deprive (a passenger) of a reserved seat due to overbooking, usually offering a seat on another conveyance: *The airlines bumped us to a later flight.* *—intr.* **1.** To hit or knock against something forcefully: *My knee bumped against the wall.* **2.** To proceed with jerks and jolts: *The car bumped slowly over the rutted road.* ❖ *n.* **1.** A light blow, collision, or jolt: *fall and get a bump on the chin.* **2.** A small swelling, as from a blow or an insect sting. **3.** A small place that rises above the level of the surface surrounding it: *a bump in the road.* ◆ **bump into** To meet by chance. [Of imitative origin.]

bump·er¹ (bŭm′pər) *n.* A horizontal metal or rubber bar attached to the front or rear of an automobile to absorb the impact of a collision. [From *bump.*]

bump·er² (bŭm′pər) *n.* A drinking vessel filled to the top. ❖ *adj.* Abundant: *a bumper crop.* [Perhaps from *bump.*]

bumper sticker *n.* A sticker with a printed message to display on the bumper of a car or truck.

bump·kin (bŭmp′kĭn *or* bŭm′kĭn) *n.* An awkward or unsophisticated person: *a country bumpkin.*

bump·y (bŭm′pē) *adj.* **bump·i·er, bump·i·est 1.** Full of bumps: *a bumpy road.* **2.** Marked by or causing jerks and jolts: *a bumpy ride.* **—bump′i·ly** *adv.* **—bump′i·ness** *n.*

bun (bŭn) *n.* **1.** A small bread roll: *a hamburger bun.* **2.** A roll or coil of hair worn at the back of the head.

bunch (bŭnch) *n.* **1.** A group of things that are alike and growing, fastened, or placed together: *a bunch of fresh grapes; a bunch of keys.* **2.** *Informal* A group of people having a common interest: *My brother and his bunch like video games.* **3.** *Informal* A considerable number or amount: *a whole bunch of work.* ❖ *v.* **bunched, bunch·ing, bunch·es** *—tr.* To gather into a bunch: *bunch flowers into a bouquet.* *—intr.* To form a cluster or group: *The cold hikers bunched around the campfire.*

bun·dle (bŭn′dl) *n.* **1.** A number of objects bound, tied, or wrapped together: *a bundle of sticks.* **2.** Something tied up for carrying; a package. ❖ *tr.v.* **bun·dled, bun·dling, bun·dles 1.** To tie, wrap, or bind securely together: *bundle newspapers for recycling.* **2.** To send quickly; hustle: *bundle the children off to school.* **3.** To dress (a person) warmly: *She bundled up the baby and went outside.*

bundt cake (bŭnt *or* bo͝ont) *n.* A ring-shaped cake with grooved sides, baked in a mold.

bung (bŭng) *n.* A stopper for the hole in a cask.

bun·ga·low (bŭng′gə-lō′) *n.* A small one-story house or cottage. [From Hindi *baṅglā*, Bengali, bungalow.]

bun·gee cord (bŭn′jē′) *n.* An elasticized rubber cord used to secure things and to engage in bungee jumping.

bungee jumping *n.* The sport of jumping from a great height while attached to a bungee cord.

bung·hole (bŭng′hōl′) *n.* The hole in a cask through which liquid is poured in or drained out.

bun·gle (bŭng′gəl) *tr.v.* **bun·gled, bun·gling, bun·gles** To do or manage (an action or task) poorly; botch: *He bungled the mixing of the ingredients, and his pancakes were terrible.* **—bun′gler** *n.*

bun·ion (bŭn′yən) *n.* A painful inflamed swelling in the joint at the base of the big toe.

bunk¹ (bŭngk) *n.* **1.** A narrow bed built like a shelf against a wall. **2.** A bunk bed. ❖ *intr.v.* **bunked, bunk·ing, bunks 1.** To sleep, especially in a makeshift bed: *had to bunk on the sofa last night.* **2.** To stay the night as a guest: *bunk over at a friend's house.*

bunk² (bŭngk) *n.* Empty talk; nonsense.

bunk bed *n.* Either of a pair of narrow beds stacked one on top of the other.

bun·ker (bŭng′kər) *n.* **1.** An underground room or shelter, often having a fortified structure above ground for positioning guns. **2.** A bin or tank for storing fuel, especially on a ship. **3.** An obstacle on a golf course consisting of a depression filled with sand.

Bunker Hill A hill, 107 feet (33 meters) high, in Boston, Massachusetts. The first major Revolutionary War battle took place nearby on June 17, 1775.

bunk·house (bŭngk′hous′) *n.* A building having bunks or beds, used as sleeping quarters for a ranch or camp.

bun·ny (bŭn′ē) *n., pl.* **bun·nies** A rabbit, especially a young one.

Bun·sen burner (bŭn′sən) *n.* A gas burner used in laboratories. It consists of a vertical tube with adjustable holes at its base that allow air to mix with the gas in order to make a very hot flame. [After Robert Wilhelm *Bunsen* (1811–1899), German chemist.]

bunt (bŭnt) *v.* **bunt·ed, bunt·ing, bunts** *—tr.* **1.** In baseball, to bat or tap (a pitched ball) lightly so that the ball rolls in the infield. **2.** To push or strike with the horns or head; butt. *—intr.* In baseball, to bat a pitched ball by tapping it lightly. ❖ *n.* **1.** An act of bunting. **2.** A ball that is bunted. **—bunt′er** *n.*

bunt·ing¹ (bŭn′tĭng) *n.* **1.** A light cotton or woolen cloth used for making flags. **2.** Flags considered as a group. **3.** Long strips of cloth with stripes or colors, used for decoration. [Perhaps from German *bunt*, colored.]

bunt·ing² (bŭn′tĭng) *n.* Any of various birds having a short cone-shaped bill. Some kinds of buntings have brightly colored feathers. [From Middle English.]

bunt·ing³ (bŭn′tĭng) *n.* A snug-fitting, hooded sleeping bag or one-piece garment for an infant, usually made of heavy cloth. [Perhaps from Scots *buntin*, plump, short.]

buoy (bo͞o′ē *or* boi) *n.* **1.** A float placed in water and usually moored, as to mark a location, enable retrieval of a sunken object, or record oceanographic data. **2.** A life buoy. ❖ *tr.v.* **buoyed, buoy·ing, buoys 1.** To keep afloat or aloft: *The kite was buoyed by a strong breeze.* **2.** To cheer; hearten: *The good news buoyed our spirits.*

buoy·an·cy (boi′ən-sē *or* bo͞o′yən-sē) *n.* **1.** The tendency or capacity to float in a liquid or to rise in air or other gas: *the buoyancy of wood in water.* **2.** The upward force that a fluid exerts on an object less dense than itself: *the buoyancy of salt water.* **3.** Lightness of spirit; cheerfulness: *The nurse's buoyancy cheered up the patient.*

buoy·ant (boi′ənt *or* bo͞o′yənt) *adj.* **1.** Having buoyancy; floating or tending to float: *a buoyant cork.* **2.** Lighthearted; cheerful: *a buoyant mood.* **—buoy′ant·ly** *adv.*

bur¹ also **burr** (bûr) *n.* **1.** A rough prickly covering enclosing a seed or fruit, as that of a chestnut or burdock. **2.** A plant that bears burs. [From Middle English *burre*, of Scandinavian origin.]

bur² (bûr) *n. & v.* Variant of **burr².**

Bur·bank (bûr′băngk′), **Luther** 1849–1926. American scientist who developed many new varieties of fruits, vegetables, and flowers.

bur·ble (bûr′bəl) *intr.v.* **bur·bled, bur·bling, bur·bles** To bubble; gurgle: *The stream burbled over the mossy rocks.*

bur·den¹ (bûr′dn) *n.* **1.** Something that is carried; a load: *mules carrying their heavy burden uphill.* **2.** Something that is endured or assumed, especially as a difficult duty or responsibility: *Citizens carry the burden of taxation.* ❖ *tr.v.* **bur·dened, bur·den·ing, bur·dens 1.** To load or overload: *heavy snow burdening the tree branches.* **2.** To cause difficulty or distress to: *burdened him with cares.* [From Old English *byrthen.*]

ă	pat	ôr	core
ā	pay	oi	boy
âr	care	ou	out
ä	father	o͝o	took
ĕ	pet	o͝or	lure
ē	be	o͞o	boot
ĭ	pit	ŭ	cut
ī	bite	ûr	urge
îr	pier	th	thin
ŏ	pot	*th*	this
ō	toe	zh	vision
ô	paw	ə	about

bur·den² (bûr′dn) *n.* **1.** A main idea or recurring theme: *the burden of the argument rests on this central point.* **2.** *Archaic* **a.** The chorus or refrain of a song. **b.** A bass accompaniment for a song. [From Middle English, variant of *bourdon*, bass pipe of a bagpipe, from Old French.]

burden of proof *n.* In a legal case, the responsibility of providing evidence in proof of a charge or allegation.

bur·den·some (bûr′dn-səm) *adj.* Imposing a burden; hard to bear; heavy; arduous.

bur·dock (bûr′dŏk′) *n.* Any of several plants having large leaves and pink or purplish flower heads surrounded by prickly bracts that form burs.

bu·reau (byo͝or′ō) *n., pl.* **bu·reaus** or **bu·reaux** (byo͝or′ōz) **1.** A chest of drawers, especially for holding clothes. **2.** An office for a specific kind of business: *a travel bureau.* **3.** A department of a government: *the Federal Bureau of Investigation.*

bu·reauc·ra·cy (byo͝o-rŏk′rə-sē) *n., pl.* **bu·reauc·ra·cies 1a.** The administration of a government or other organization through a hierarchy of departments with appointed officials instead of elected representatives. **b.** The officials of such a government or organization considered as a group: *promised to reorganize the federal bureaucracy.* **2.** Administration, as of a government or other organization, in which the need to follow rules and regulations slows or prevents effective action: *The accounting department's bureaucracy delayed our refund.*

bu·reau·crat (byo͝or′ə-krăt′) *n.* **1.** An official of a bureaucracy. **2.** An official who insists on rigid adherence to rules and routines. **—bu′reau·crat′ic** *adj.*

burg (bûrg) *n. Informal* A city or town.

bur·geon (bûr′jən) *intr.v.* **bur·geoned, bur·geon·ing, bur·geons 1.** To put forth new buds, leaves, or shoots; begin to sprout or grow. **2.** To develop as if by sprouting or growing; flourish: *New ideas burgeon when people are allowed to talk freely.*

burg·er (bûr′gər) *n.* **1.** A hamburger or cheeseburger. **2.** A similar sandwich with a nonbeef filling: *a tofu burger.*

bur·gess (bûr′jĭs) *n.* A member of the lower house of colonial legislature of Virginia or Maryland.

burgh·er (bûr′gər) *n.* A citizen of a town, especially a merchant or trader in a medieval town.

bur·glar (bûr′glər) *n.* A person who commits burglary; a housebreaker.

bur·glar·ize (bûr′glə-rīz′) *tr.v.* **bur·glar·ized, bur·glar·iz·ing, bur·glar·iz·es** To enter and steal from (a building or home, for example).

bur·gla·ry (bûr′glə-rē) *n., pl.* **bur·gla·ries** The crime of breaking into a building with the intention of stealing.

bur·gle (bûr′gəl) *tr.v.* **bur·gled, bur·gling, bur·gles** To burglarize.

Bur·goyne (bûr-goin′ *or* bûr′goin′), **John** 1722–1792. British general. In the American Revolution he captured Fort Ticonderoga (July 6, 1777) but lost the Battle of Saratoga (October 17, 1777).

Bur·gun·dy¹ (bûr′gən-dē) A historical region and former province of eastern France. It became a part of France in 1477. **—Bur·gun′di·an** (bər-gŭn′dē-ən) *adj. & n.*

Bur·gun·dy² (bûr′gən-dē) *n., pl.* **Bur·gun·dies 1.** A red or white wine made in Burgundy. **2.** A similar wine made in another place.

bur·i·al (bĕr′ē-əl) *n.* The act of placing a dead body in a grave, a tomb, or the sea.

bur·ka (bo͝or′kə) *n.* Variant of **burqa.**

Bur·ki·na Fa·so (bər-kē′nə fä′sō) A landlocked country of western Africa north of Ghana. It was known as Upper Volta until 1984. Ouagadougou is the capital.

bur·ki·ni (bûr-kē′nē) *n.,* pl. **bur·ki·nis** A two-piece swimsuit worn by Muslim women, covering the entire body except for the hands, feet, and face. [Blend of *burqa* and *bikini.*]

burl (bûrl) *n.* **1.** A large rounded outgrowth on a tree trunk or branch. **2.** Wood from such a growth, usually with a marked grain.

bur·lap (bûr′lăp′) *n.* A coarse cloth made of hemp, jute, or flax, used to make bags, sacks, curtains, and coverings.

bur·lesque (bər-lĕsk′) *n.* **1.** An imitation of something, especially in a play, story, or song, that makes it seem ridiculous by treating it too seriously or too frivolously. **2.** A variety show with singing, dancing, and ribald comedy. ❖ *tr.v.* **bur·lesqued, bur·les·quing, bur·lesques** To imitate mockingly: *Many comedies burlesque traditional stories of success.*

Bur·ling·ton (bûr′lĭng-tən) The largest city of Vermont, in the northwest part of the state on Lake Champlain.

bur·ly (bûr′lē) *adj.* **bur·li·er, bur·li·est** Heavy and strong; muscular: *burly football players.* See Synonyms at **muscular. —bur′li·ness** *n.*

Bur·ma (bûr′mə) See **Myanmar.**

Bur·mese (bər-mēz′ *or* bər-mēs′) *adj.* Relating to Myanmar (Burma) or its people, language, or culture. ❖ *n., pl.* **Burmese 1.** A native or inhabitant of Myanmar. **2.** The Sino-Tibetan language of Myanmar.

burn¹ (bûrn) *v.* **burned** or **burnt** (bûrnt), **burn·ing, burns** *—intr.* **1.** To undergo combustion or be consumed as fuel: *Wood and paper burn easily.* **2.** To be damaged, injured, or destroyed by fire, heat, a chemical, or radiation: *The house burned to the ground. The eggs burned in the pan.* **3.** To produce light and heat by fire or energy: *The sun burned bright in the sky.* **4.** To feel or look hot: *burning with fever.* **5.** To be irritated or painful, as by inflammation: *My eyes are burning from the smoke.* **6.** To become sunburned or windburned: *Fair skin burns easily.* **7.** To be full of strong emotion: *burn with anger; burning with a desire to win.* *—tr.* **1.** To cause to undergo combustion: *We burned the logs in the fireplace.* **2.** To damage, injure, or destroy with fire, heat, a chemical, or radiation: *Our town burns trash to generate electricity. The acid burned my fingers.* **3.** To use as fuel: *This furnace burns oil.* **4.** To produce by fire, heat, a chemical, or radiation: *The sparks burned holes in the rug.* **5.** To use up or process for energy: *How many calories do you burn when you run for 20 minutes?* **6a.** To give a feeling of heat to: *Some highly seasoned food burns my mouth.* **b.** To make angry: *Their nasty remarks burned me up.* **7.** To affect with a sunburn or windburn: *My face got burned while I was skiing.* **8.** To swindle or deceive; cheat: *investors who were burned in a stock fraud.* **9.** To record data on (a compact disc). ❖ *n.* **1.** An injury produced by fire, heat, a chemical, or radiation: *I got a blister from the burn.* **2.** A burned place or area: *a burn in the tablecloth.* **3.** In aerospace, a firing of a rocket: *The rocket made a good burn.* **4.** A sunburn or windburn. ◆ **burn out 1.** To stop burning from lack of fuel: *The campfire slowly burned out.* **2.** To wear out or fail, especially because of heat: *The fan motor burned out from the short.* **3.** To make or become exhausted, especially as a result of long-term stress: *Working overtime finally burned her out. She burned out from years of overwork.* [From Old English *beornan.*] **—burn′a·ble** *adj.*

burn² (bûrn) *n. Scots* A small stream or brook. [From Old English *burna.*]

burn·er (bûr′nər) *n.* **1.** A furnace or other device in which something is burned: *An oil burner heats the house.* **2.** The part of a stove, furnace, or lamp in which a flame or heat is produced.

burn·ing (bûr′nĭng) *adj.* **1.** On fire; flaming; hot: *a burning candle.* **2.** Inflamed with strong emotion; heated: *a burning desire; a burning issue.*

bur·nish (bûr′nĭsh) *tr.v.* **bur·nished, bur·nish·ing, bur·nish·es** To make smooth and glossy by or as if by rubbing; polish: *burnish a brass plate.* ❖ *n.* A smooth glossy finish or appearance; luster.

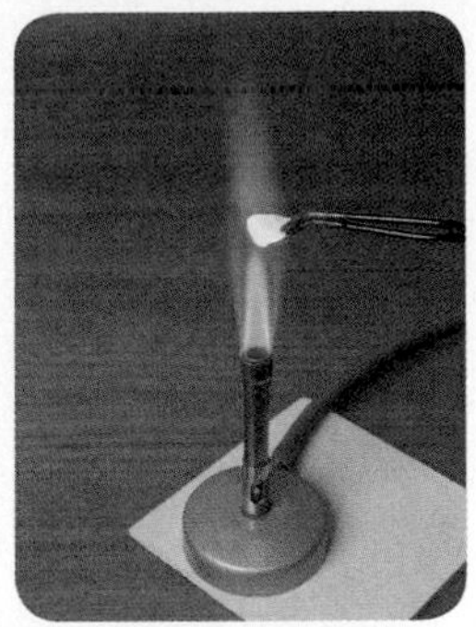

Bunsen burner

buoy

burdock

burqa

burrito

bur·nous also **bur·noose** (bər-**no͞os′**) *n.* A long cloak with a hood, worn especially by Arabs and Berbers.

burn·out (**bûrn′**out′) *n.* **1.** A failure of a device because of burning, heat, or friction. **2.** The end of a burn in a rocket engine, especially when the fuel has been exhausted or shut off. **3.** Exhaustion of physical or emotional strength.

Burns (bûrnz), **Robert** 1759–1796. British poet whose songs and poems, written in English and Scots, celebrate love, patriotism, and country life.

burnt (bûrnt) *v.* A past tense and a past participle of **burn**[1].

burp (bûrp) *n.* A belch. ❖ *intr. & tr.v.* **burped, burp·ing, burps** To belch or cause to belch: *Chris burped and said "Excuse me." Pat burped the baby after her feeding.*

bur·qa or **bur·ka** (**bo͝or′**kə) *n.* A loose, usually black or light blue outer garment worn by Muslim women that covers the head and face and sometimes the entire body.

burr[1] (bûr) *n.* **1.** A rough edge or spot left on metal or other material after it has been cast, cut, or drilled. **2.** Variant of **bur**[1].

burr[2] also **bur** (bûr) *n.* **1.** The trilled "r" of Scottish pronunciation. **2.** A whirring sound. [Of imitative origin.]

Burr (bûr), **Aaron** 1756–1836. American politician who was vice president of the United States (1801–1805) under Thomas Jefferson. In 1804 Burr mortally wounded his rival Alexander Hamilton in a duel.

bur·ri·to (bo͞o-**rē′**tō) *n., pl.* **bur·ri·tos** A dish consisting of a flour tortilla wrapped around a filling, as of beef, beans, or cheese.

bur·ro (**bûr′**ō *or* **bo͝or′**ō) *n., pl.* **bur·ros** A small donkey, usually used for carrying loads.

bur·row (**bûr′**ō) *n.* A hole or tunnel dug in the ground by a small animal, such as a rabbit or mole. ❖ *v.* **bur·rowed, bur·row·ing, bur·rows** *—intr.* **1.** To make a tunnel, hole, or shelter by digging or tunneling: *gophers burrowing in the fields.* **2.** To move as if making a burrow: *burrowed under the covers. —tr.* To press or push (something) as though making a burrow: *She burrowed her toes into the sand.* **—bur′row·er** *n.*

bur·sa (**bûr′**sə) *n., pl.* **bur·sae** (**bûr′**sē) or **bur·sas** A body cavity resembling a sac, especially one containing a lubricating fluid that reduces friction between a muscle or tendon and a bone.

bur·sar (**bûr′**sər *or* **bûr′**sär′) *n.* A treasurer, as at a college or university.

bur·si·tis (bər-**sī′**tĭs) *n.* Inflammation of a bursa, especially in the shoulder, elbow, or knee.

burst (bûrst) *v.* **burst, burst·ing, bursts** *—intr.* **1.** To break open suddenly and violently: *The balloon may burst.* **2.** To come forth, emerge, or arrive suddenly and in full force: *The police burst into the room.* **3.** To be or seem to be full to the point of breaking open; swell: *He's bursting with pride.* **4.** To give sudden utterance or expression: *burst out laughing; burst into tears. —tr.* To cause to break open suddenly and violently: *The heat of the lamp burst the balloon.* ❖ *n.* **1.** A sudden outbreak or outburst; an explosion: *a burst of laughter.* **2.** A firing of bullets from an automatic weapon. **3.** A sudden and intense increase; a rush: *a burst of speed.* **4.** A period of intense activity: *worked on the project in short bursts.*

Bu·run·di (bo͞o-**ro͞on′**dē) A country of east-central Africa south of Rwanda. Bujumbura is the capital.

bur·y (**bĕr′**ē) *tr.v.* **bur·ied, bur·y·ing, bur·ies 1.** To place in the ground: *The dog buried a bone.* **2.** To place (a dead body) in a grave, a tomb, or the sea. **3.** To conceal; hide: *She buried her face in the pillow.* **4.** To occupy (oneself) with deep concentration; absorb: *I buried myself in my homework.* **5.** To put an end to; abandon: *Let's shake hands and bury our quarrel.* [From Old English *byrgan.*]
❑ *These sound alike:* **bury, berry** (fruit).

bus (bŭs) *n., pl.* **bus·es** or **bus·ses 1.** A long motor vehicle with rows of seats for carrying passengers. **2.** A circuit that connects the major components of a computer, allowing the transfer of electric impulses from one component to another. ❖ *v.* **bused, bus·ing, bus·es** or **bussed, bus·sing, bus·ses** *—tr.* **1.** To carry or transport in a bus: *The club bused us to the beach.* **2.** To transport (students) by bus to schools outside their neighborhoods, especially to achieve racial integration. **3.** To clear dishes from (a table). *—intr.* To travel in a bus: *Many people bus to work and school.*

bus·boy also **bus boy** (**bŭs′**boi′) *n.* A waiter's helper who sets and clears the table in a restaurant.

bush (bo͝osh) *n.* **1.** A shrub, especially one having many separate branches starting from or near the ground. **2.** Vegetation consisting of a thick growth of shrubs: *We walked in a single file through the thick bush.* **3.** Land that is remote from human settlement: *a journey through the Australian bush.*

Bush (bo͝osh), **George Herbert Walker** Born 1924. The 41st president of the United States (1989–1993) and vice president (1981–1989) under Ronald Reagan. As president he led the United States during the Gulf War (1991).

Bush, George Walker Born 1946. The 43rd president of the United States (2001–2009). His presidency was marked by an American-led invasion of Afghanistan in response to the terrorist attacks of September 11, 2001, and by the Iraq War.

bushed (bo͝osht) *adj. Informal* Extremely tired.

bush·el (**bo͝osh′**əl) *n.* **1.** A unit of volume or capacity, used in dry measure in the United States and equal to 4 pecks (about 35.24 liters or 2,150 cubic inches): *Many fruits and vegetables are measured by the bushel for market.* **2.** A container that holds this amount.

bush·ing (**bo͝osh′**ĭng) *n.* A metal tube that serves as a guide for or reduces wear on a moving part, as in machinery.

Bush·man (**bo͝osh′**mən) *n.* A member of the San people.

bush·mas·ter (**bo͝osh′**măs′tər) *n.* A large venomous snake of Central and South America having brown and gray markings.

bush pilot *n.* A pilot who flies a small airplane to and from remote areas where larger planes cannot land.

bush·whack (**bo͝osh′**wăk′) *v.* **bush·whacked, bush·whack·ing, bush·whacks** *—tr.* To attack suddenly from a place of hiding; ambush. *—intr.* To force one's way through an overgrown area where no path exists.

bush·y (**bo͝osh′**ē) *adj.* **bush·i·er, bush·i·est 1.** Consisting of or covered with bushes: *bushy plants; a bushy area.* **2.** Thick and shaggy: *bushy eyebrows.* **—bush′i·ness** *n.*

bus·i·ly (**bĭz′**ə-lē) *adv.* In a busy manner.

busi·ness (**bĭz′**nĭs) *n.* **1.** The occupation, trade, or work that provides a person with a means of living: *a group of salespersons in the automobile business.* **2.** Commercial, industrial, and professional dealings considered as a group: *Computers are now being used throughout business and industry.* **3.** A commercial establishment, such as a store or factory: *Will you go into the family business?* **4.** The volume or amount of trade: *Business falls off when summer begins.* **5.** One's rightful or proper concern: *Where he goes is none of our business.* **6.** An affair; a matter: *The committee dealt with the business at hand.* **7.** Serious work: *Let's get down to business.*

business card *n.* A small card printed with a person's name, business affiliation, and contact information.

busi·ness·like (**bĭz′**nĭs-līk′) *adj.* Systematic; efficient; orderly: *a friendly but businesslike manner.*

busi·ness·man (**bĭz′**nĭs-măn′) *n.* A man engaged in business.

busi·ness·per·son (**bĭz′**nĭs-pûr′sən) *n.* A businessman or businesswoman.

busi·ness·wom·an (**bĭz′**nĭs-wo͝om′ən) *n.* A woman engaged in business.

ă	pat	ôr	core
ā	pay	oi	boy
âr	care	ou	out
ä	father	o͝o	took
ĕ	pet	o͝or	lure
ē	be	o͞o	boot
ĭ	pit	ŭ	cut
ī	bite	ûr	urge
îr	pier	th	thin
ŏ	pot	*th*	this
ō	toe	zh	vision
ô	paw	ə	about

bus·load (bŭs′lōd′) *n.* The number of passengers or the quantity of cargo that a bus can carry.

bus·ses (bŭs′ĭz) *n.* A plural of **bus**.

bust¹ (bŭst) *n.* **1.** A sculpture of a person's head, shoulders, and upper chest: *a marble bust of Lincoln.* **2.** A woman's breasts. [From French *buste*, from Italian *busto*, possibly from Latin *bustum*, sepulchral monument.]

bust² (bŭst) *v.* **bust·ed, bust·ing, busts** —*tr.* **1.** *Slang* To smash or break: *I busted the ice with a hatchet.* **2.** *Slang* To make unusable; break: *He busted the vending machine by putting in foreign coins.* **3.** To break or tame (a horse). **4.** To cause to become bankrupt or short of money: *The long drought busted many farmers.* **5.** *Slang* To reduce the rank of; demote: *bust a sergeant to corporal.* **6.** To hit; punch. **7.** *Slang* To place under arrest: *The cops busted the thief.* —*intr.* **1.** *Slang* To become broken or unusable; break: *The bicycle chain busted as I went up the hill.* **2.** To become bankrupt or short of money. ❖ *n.* **1.** A failure; a flop: *That movie is a real bust.* **2.** A financial depression: *times of boom and bust.* **3.** A punch or blow. **4.** *Slang* An arrest: *a drug bust.* [Variant of *burst*.]

bus·tard (bŭs′tərd) *n.* Any of various large brownish or grayish birds of Africa, Asia, and Australia that have a long neck and legs and live in dry grassy plains.

bust·ed (bŭs′tĭd) *adj. Slang* **1a.** Broken or fractured: *a busted window.* **b.** Not working; inoperable: *a busted car.* **2.** Bankrupt or out of funds. **3.** Captured or held by law enforcement; arrested: *a busted thief.*

bus·tle¹ (bŭs′əl) *intr.v.* **bus·tled, bus·tling, bus·tles** To move busily and energetically: *The mechanics bustled about the airplane.* ❖ *n.* Excited activity; commotion: *the hustle and bustle of city streets.* [Possibly variant of obsolete *buskle*, from *busk*, to prepare oneself.]

bus·tle² (bŭs′əl) *n.* A pad or frame worn by women in earlier times to puff out the back of a long skirt.

bus·y (bĭz′ē) *adj.* **bus·i·er, bus·i·est 1.** Occupied with work; active: *The doctor was busy with a patient.* **2.** Crowded with activity: *the doctor's busy morning.* **3.** In use, as a telephone line: *The doctor's phone is busy.* ❖ *tr.v.* **bus·ied, bus·y·ing, bus·ies** To make (oneself) busy; occupy (oneself): *I busied myself with my chores.* **—bus′y·ness** *n.*

bus·y·bod·y (bĭz′ē-bŏd′ē) *n., pl.* **bus·y·bod·ies** A nosy or meddling person interested in the affairs of others.

bus·y·work (bĭz′ē-wûrk′) *n.* An activity that takes up time but does not necessarily produce anything.

but (bŭt; bət *when unstressed*) *conj.* **1a.** On the contrary: *My bike is old, but yours is new. They have not two dogs but three.* **b.** Nevertheless; yet: *The plan may not work, but we must try. She was tired but happy.* **2.** That. Used in negative statements: *There is no doubt but right will win out.* **3.** With the exception that; except that: *I would have stayed longer but I was getting sleepy.* **4.** Without the result that: *It never rains but it pours.* ❖ *prep.* Other than; except: *No one went but me.* ❖ *adv.* Only; merely: *This is but one case in many.* ◆ **but for** Were it not for: *We would have gone but for the weather.* [From Old English *būtan*, around the outside of.] —SEE NOTE AT **not.**

❑ *These sound alike:* **but, butt¹** (hit), **butt²** (object of scorn), **butt³** (end).

bu·tane (byo͞o′tān′) *n.* A gaseous hydrocarbon having the formula C_4H_{10}. It is produced from petroleum and is used as a fuel and in the making of synthetic rubber.

butch·er (bo͝och′ər) *n.* **1.** A person who slaughters animals and prepares their meat for food. **2.** A person who sells meat: *buy a steak from the local butcher.* **3.** A person who kills cruelly or without reason. ❖ *tr.v.* **butch·ered, butch·er·ing, butch·ers 1.** To slaughter or prepare (animals) for market. **2.** To kill brutally and without reason. **3.** To botch up; bungle: *The bad actor butchered the role.*

butch·er·y (bo͝och′ə-rē) *n., pl.* **butch·er·ies** Cruel or savage killing; slaughter.

but·ler (bŭt′lər) *n.* The chief male servant of a household.

butt¹ (bŭt) *tr.v.* **butt·ed, butt·ing, butts** To hit or push with the head or horns: *The goat butted the farmer.* ❖ *n.* A push or blow with the head or horns. ◆ **butt in** *Informal* To meddle; intrude: *Don't butt in on other people's conversations.* [From Middle English *butten*, from Old French *bouter*, to strike, of Germanic origin.]

butt² (bŭt) *n.* A person or thing that is an object of ridicule or scorn: *The clown was the butt of his own jokes.* [From Middle English *but*, target, from Old French.]

butt³ (bŭt) *n.* **1.** The thicker end of something: *the butt of a rifle.* **2.** An unused or unburned end, especially of a cigarette. **3.** *Informal* The buttocks. [From Middle English, of Germanic origin.]

butte (byo͞ot) *n.* A steep-sided hill with a flat top, often standing alone.

but·ter (bŭt′ər) *n.* **1.** A soft, yellowish, fatty food churned from milk or cream. **2.** A similar substance, such as a fruit spread: *There are many fruit butters such as apple butter.* ❖ *tr.v.* **but·tered, but·ter·ing, but·ters** To put butter in or on. ◆ **butter up** To flatter: *He's always buttering up the boss.* [From Old English *butere*, from Greek *boutūron* : *bous*, cow + *tūros*, cheese.]

butter bean *n.* A lima bean or a wax bean.

but·ter·cup (bŭt′ər-kŭp′) *n.* **1.** Any of numerous plants having cup-shaped flowers that are usually yellow. **2.** A flower of this plant.

but·ter·fat (bŭt′ər-făt′) *n.* The fat that is contained in milk and from which butter is made.

but·ter·fin·gers (bŭt′ər-fĭng′gərz) *pl.n.* *(used with a singular verb)* A clumsy person who is apt to drop things.

but·ter·fish (bŭt′ər-fĭsh′) *n.* Any of various fishes having oily flesh or slippery skin, especially a silvery edible ocean fish of the Atlantic coast of North America.

but·ter·fly (bŭt′ər-flī′) *n.* **1.** Any of numerous insects having four broad, often colorful wings, a narrow body, and slender antennae with knobs at the tips. **2.** A swimming stroke in which the swimmer draws both arms upward out of the water and forward while kicking the legs up and down in unison.

but·ter·milk (bŭt′ər-mĭlk′) *n.* The thick sour liquid that remains after butter has been churned from milk.

but·ter·nut (bŭt′ər-nŭt′) *n.* **1.** The oily edible nut of a kind of walnut tree native to eastern North America. **2.** The tree that bears such nuts.

but·ter·scotch (bŭt′ər-skŏch′) *n.* A syrup, sauce, candy, or flavoring made from brown sugar and butter.

but·ter·y (bŭt′ə-rē) *adj.* **1.** Containing or spread with butter: *hot buttery muffins.* **2.** Resembling butter.

but·tock (bŭt′ək) *n.* Either of the rounded fleshy parts of the human body situated between the lower back and the upper thighs.

but·ton (bŭt′n) *n.* **1a.** A usually disk-shaped fastener used to join two parts of a garment by fitting through a buttonhole or loop. **b.** Such an object used on a garment for decoration. **2.** A part that is pushed to work a switch, as to ring a bell, turn on a light, or start a machine: *Push the button to get the elevator.* **3.** Something resembling a button, as a round flat pin with words or a design on it: *a campaign button.* **4.** A distinct area, such as a small box, on a computer screen that can be clicked to execute a command. ❖ *v.* **but·toned, but·ton·ing, but·tons** —*tr.* To fasten with a button or buttons: *button up a coat.* —*intr.* To become fastened with a button or buttons: *a coat that buttons down the front.* [From Middle English *bouton*, from Old French *bouter*, to thrust, of Germanic origin.]

but·ton·hole (bŭt′n-hōl′) *n.* A slit in a garment or in cloth used to fasten a button. ❖ *tr.v.* **but·ton·holed, but·ton·hol·ing, but·ton·holes 1.** To make a buttonhole in. **2.** To make (a person) stop and listen, as if grabbing the buttonhole in a garment.

George H.W. Bush

George W. Bush

butte

George Gordon Byron

Byzantine
Church of Saints Jason and Sosipater, Corfu, Greece

ă	pat	ôr	core
ā	pay	oi	boy
âr	care	ou	out
ä	father	ŏŏ	took
ĕ	pet	ŏŏr	lure
ē	be	ōō	boot
ĭ	pit	ŭ	cut
ī	bite	ûr	urge
îr	pier	th	thin
ŏ	pot	*th*	this
ō	toe	zh	vision
ô	paw	ə	about

but·ton·wood (bŭt′n-wŏŏd′) *n.* **1.** The sycamore tree of North America. **2.** An evergreen shrub or tree of coastal wetlands of tropical America and western Africa, having small buttonlike heads of greenish flowers.

but·tress (bŭt′rĭs) *n.* **1.** A structure, often of brick or stone, built against a wall as a support. **2.** Something that serves to support or reinforce: *Testimony of witnesses was a strong buttress to our side of the story.* ❖ *tr.v.* **but·tressed, but·tress·ing, but·tress·es 1.** To brace or reinforce with a buttress: *buttress the roof of a tunnel with timbers.* **2.** To sustain or bolster: *buttress an argument with evidence.*

bux·om (bŭk′səm) *adj.* Having large breasts.

buy (bī) *v.* **bought** (bôt), **buy·ing, buys** —*tr.* **1.** To get in exchange for money or something of equal value: *go to the store to buy groceries; buy land through a bank.* **2.** To be capable of purchasing: *Money can buy comfort but not happiness.* **3.** To bribe (someone): *Money will not buy an honest judge.* **4.** *Informal* To accept as true; believe: *The coach didn't buy my excuse for missing practice.* —*intr.* To purchase goods: *Looked at the shoes but decided not to buy.* ❖ *n.* Something cheaper than usual; a bargain: *The coats on sale are a good buy.* ◆ **buy off** To bribe: *It is illegal to try to buy off a government official.* **buy out** To purchase the stock, rights, or interests of: *buy out a company.* **buy time** To increase the time available for a specific purpose: *We stayed with our friends so we could buy time in looking for a new apartment.* **buy up** To purchase all that is available: *bought up all the newspapers.* [From Old English *bycgan.*]

buy·er (bī′ər) *n.* **1.** A person who buys goods; a customer. **2.** A person who buys merchandise for a retail store.

buy·out (bī′out′) *n.* The purchase of a business by buying all of its stock.

buzz (bŭz) *v.* **buzzed, buzz·ing, buzz·es** —*intr.* **1.** To make a low droning sound like that of a bee: *Flies buzzed near the cherries.* **2.** To talk in excited low tones: *The audience buzzed in anticipation of the show.* —*tr.* **1.** To signal, as with a buzzer: *The patient buzzed the nurse.* **2.** *Informal* To fly a plane low over: *The pilot buzzed the stadium.* ❖ *n.* **1.** A low droning sound, such as the one made by a bee: *the buzz of a fly.* **2.** A buzzcut. **3.** *Slang* Excited interest or attention: *There was a lot of buzz surrounding the new movie.* ◆ **buzz off** *Informal* To leave quickly; go away.

buz·zard (bŭz′ərd) *n.* **1.** Any of various North American vultures. **2.** *Chiefly British* Any of various hawks having broad wings and a broad tail. [From Middle English *busard*, hawk, from Latin *būteō.*]

buzz·cut (bŭz′kŭt′) *n.* A haircut in which the hair is cut very close to the scalp.

buzz·er (bŭz′ər) *n.* An electrical device that makes a buzzing noise to give a signal or warning.

buzz saw *n.* A circular saw.

by (bī) *prep.* **1.** Close to; near: *the chair by the window; sitting by the wall.* **2.** Up to and beyond; past: *A car drove by us.* **3.** At or to: *came by the house; stopped by the bakery.* **4.** Through the agency or action of: *a building destroyed by fire; a novel by a young author.* **5.** With the help or use of; through: *come by the back road; crossing by ferry.* **6.** According to: *playing by the rules; by their own account.* **7.** With respect to: *related by blood.* **8.** In the course of; during: *sleeping by night and working by day.* **9.** In the amount of: *The president receives letters by the thousands.* **10.** Not later than: *finish by noon.* **11.** In the matter of; concerning: *They are storekeepers by trade.* **12.** After; following: *One by one they left.* **13.** Combined in multiplication, division, or measurement with: *Multiply 4 by 6. The room measures 12 by 20 feet. Divide 4 by 2.* **14.** With the difference of; to the extent of: *shorter by three inches.* ❖ *adv.* **1.** Close at hand; nearby: *We just stood by watching.* **2.** Aside; away: *putting some money by for later.* **3.** Up to and beyond; past: *The car raced by.* **4.** At or to one's home or location: *Stop by later on.* **5.** Into the past: *as time goes by.* ◆ **by and by** Before long; later: *The weather always changes by and by.* **by and large** On the whole; mostly: *By and large people are honest.* **by oneself 1.** Alone: *I walked by myself in the woods.* **2.** Without help: *I repaired the car by myself.* **by the way** Incidentally. [From Old English *bī.*]

by– or **bye–** *pref.* A prefix that means: **1.** Near; at hand: *bystander.* **2.** Out of the way; aside: *bypass.* **3.** Secondary: *byproduct.* **4.** Past: *bygone.*

bye (bī) *interj.* An expression used to say goodbye.

bye-bye (bī′bī′ *or* bī-**bī′**) *interj.* An expression used to say goodbye.

Bye·lo·rus·sia (byĕl′ō-**rŭsh′**ə) See **Belarus.**

by·gone (bī′gôn′) *adj.* Gone by; past: *bygone days.* ❖ *n.* often **bygones** A past occurrence: *Let bygones be bygones.*

by·law (bī′lô′) *n.* A law or rule made by a local government, corporation, club, or other organization governing its own affairs. [From Middle English *bi-laue*, body of local regulations.]

by·line (bī′līn′) *n.* A printed line at the head of a newspaper or magazine article giving the writer's name.

by·pass also **by-pass** (bī′păs′) *n.* **1.** A highway that passes around a city or other congested area. **2.** A path that leads around some component of a system, as in an electric circuit or a system of pipes. **3.** A surgical operation to make a new passage for blood around old vessels that are blocked: *a bypass around a blood vessel of the heart.* ❖ *tr.v.* **by·passed, by·pass·ing, by·pass·es** To go or send around by or as if by means of a bypass: *We can bypass the salespeople if we see the manager directly.*

by·path (bī′păth′) *n.* An indirect or little-used path.

by·prod·uct or **by-prod·uct** (bī′prŏd′əkt) *n.* **1.** Something produced in the making of something else: *Asphalt and paraffin are byproducts of refining crude oil into gasoline.* **2.** A secondary result; a side effect: *Increased unemployment is a byproduct of the economic downturn.*

Byrd (bûrd), **Richard Evelyn** 1888–1957. American naval officer and explorer. He established a scientific research base in Antarctica (1928) and was the first person to fly over the South Pole (1929).

by·road (bī′rōd′) *n.* A side road; a back road.

By·ron (bī′rən), **George Gordon** Sixth Baron Byron of Rochdale. 1788–1824. British romantic poet. His works include *Don Juan* (1819–1824).

by·stand·er (bī′stăn′dər) *n.* A person who is present at an event but does not take part.

byte (bīt) *n.* A sequence of adjacent bits operated on as a unit by a computer. A byte usually consists of eight bits. [Alteration and blend of *bit*, single character, and *bite.*]
❑ *These sound alike:* **byte, bite** (grip with the teeth).

by·way (bī′wā′) *n.* A road not often used; a side road.

by·word (bī′wûrd′) *n.* **1.** A well-known saying; a proverb. **2.** A person or thing thought of as representing a type, class, or quality: *That newspaper is the byword for honest reporting.*

Byz·an·tine (bĭz′ən-tēn′ *or* bĭz′ən-tīn′ *or* bĭ-**zăn′**tĭn) *adj.* **1.** Relating to Byzantium, its inhabitants, or their culture. **2.** Relating to the Byzantine Empire. **3.** Relating to the style of architecture developed in Byzantium, characterized by round arches, massive domes, and the extensive use of mosaic designs. **4. byzantine** Highly complicated; intricate and involved. ❖ *n.* An inhabitant of Byzantium or the Byzantine Empire.

Byzantine Empire The eastern part of the later Roman Empire, dating from AD 395 and focused around the Balkan Peninsula and Asia Minor. The empire collapsed in 1453.

By·zan·ti·um (bĭ-**zăn′**shē-əm *or* bĭ-**zăn′**tē-əm) A city of ancient Greece on the site of present-day Istanbul, Turkey. It was founded in the seventh century BC.

c or **C** (sē) *n., pl.* **c's** or **C's** also **cs** or **Cs** **1.** The third letter of the English alphabet: *There are two c's in the word "clock."* **2.** **C** The third best or third highest grade: *get a C on a test.* **3.** **C** In music, the first tone in the scale of C major. —SEE NOTE.

C[1] **1.** The symbol for the element **carbon.** **2.** also **c** The symbol for the Roman numeral one hundred. **3.** **c** The symbol for the speed of light in a vacuum.

C[2] *abbr.* An abbreviation of: **1.** Celsius. **2.** centigrade. **3.** cold. **4.** consonant.

c. *abbr.* An abbreviation of: **1.** cent. **2.** also **C.** century. **3.** circa (approximately). **4.** copyright.

ca *abbr.* An abbreviation of circa (approximately).

Ca The symbol for the element **calcium.**

CA *abbr.* An abbreviation of California.

cab (kăb) *n.* **1.** A taxicab. **2.** A one-horse carriage for public hire. **3.** A covered compartment for the operator or driver of a heavy vehicle or machine, such as a locomotive, truck, or crane. [Short for *cabriolet*, a two-wheeled carriage, from French *cabriole*, caper.]

ca·bal (kə-bäl′ *or* kə-băl′) *n.* **1.** A small group of people organized to carry out a secret plot or conspiracy. **2.** A plot organized by such a group.

ca·ba·la (kăb′ə-lə *or* kə-bä′lə) *n.* Variant of **kabbalah.**

cab·al·le·ro (kăb′ə-lâr′ō *or* kä′bä-yĕ′rō) *n., pl.* **cab·al·le·ros** **1.** A Spanish gentleman; a cavalier. **2.** A skilled horseman.

ca·ban·a (kə-băn′ə) *n.* **1.** A shelter on a beach or at a swimming pool used as a bathhouse. **2.** A cabin or hut.

cab·a·ret (kăb′ə-rā′) *n.* **1.** A restaurant or nightclub providing short programs of live entertainment. **2.** The entertainment presented in such a place.

cab·bage (kăb′ĭj) *n.* Any of several plants having a large rounded head of tightly overlapping green or reddish leaves eaten as a vegetable. [From Middle English *caboche*, from Old North French, head, possibly from Latin *caput*.]

cab·by or **cab·bie** (kăb′ē) *n., pl.* **cab·bies** A cabdriver.

cab·driv·er (kăb′drī′vər) *n.* A driver of a taxicab.

cab·in (kăb′ĭn) *n.* **1.** A small, simply built house; a cottage or hut. **2.** A room in a ship used as living quarters for a passenger or officer. **3.** An enclosed compartment in a boat that serves as a shelter or as living quarters. **4.** The enclosed compartment in an airplane or spacecraft for passengers, crew, or cargo.

cabin boy *n.* A male servant who serves the officers and passengers on a ship.

cabin cruiser *n.* A large motorboat having a cabin equipped with living facilities.

cab·i·net (kăb′ə-nĭt) *n.* **1.** A case or cupboard with shelves, drawers, or compartments for storing or displaying objects: *a kitchen cabinet; a filing cabinet.* **2.** The box that houses the main parts of a computer. **3.** often **Cabinet** A group of people appointed by a head of state or prime minister to act as official advisers and to head the various departments of state.

cab·i·net·mak·er (kăb′ə-nĭt-mā′kər) *n.* A person who makes fine articles of wooden furniture.

cab·i·net·work (kăb′ə-nĭt-wûrk′) *n.* Fine woodwork made by a cabinetmaker.

cabin fever *n.* An uneasy or distressed feeling that results from a long stay in a remote area or in a small enclosed space.

ca·ble (kā′bəl) *n.* **1.** A strong thick rope made of steel wires or fiber. **2.** A group of insulated electrical wires or optical fibers that are bound together. **3a.** Cable television. **b.** A similar service that provides Internet access. **4.** A cablegram. ❖ *adj.* Relating to a subscription television or Internet service that uses cables to carry signals between local distribution antennas and the subscriber's location. ❖ *tr.v.* **ca·bled, ca·bling, ca·bles** **1.** To send a cablegram to (a person, for example): *Several reporters cabled their newspapers about the earthquake.* **2.** To transmit (a message) by telegraph. [From Middle English, from Late Latin *capulum*, lasso.]

cable box *n.* An electronic device that allows channels transmitted by cable to be viewed on a television.

cable car *n.* A vehicle pulled by a cable that runs in an endless loop either overhead or beneath rails.

ca·ble·gram (kā′bəl-grăm′) *n.* A telegram sent by submarine cable.

cable television *n.* A subscription television service that uses cables to carry signals between local distribution antennas and the subscriber's location.

ca·boose (kə-bo͞os′) *n.* The last car of a freight train, having living facilities for the train crew and used as a vantage point for spotting problems on the train. The introduction of electronic sensors has made the caboose unnecessary. [Possibly from obsolete Dutch *cabuse*, ship's galley.]

Cab·ot (kăb′ət), **John** 1450?–1498? Italian-born explorer who commanded the first English expedition to the North American mainland in 1497.

cab·ri·o·let (kăb′rē-ə-lā′) *n.* A two-wheeled carriage pulled by one horse, having two seats and a folding top.

ca·ca·o (kə-kä′ō *or* kə-kā′ō) *n., pl.* **ca·ca·os** **1.** The seeds from the pods of a tropical American evergreen tree, used to make chocolate, cocoa, and cocoa butter. **2.** The tree that bears such seeds. [From Spanish, from Nahuatl *cacahuatl*.]

cach·a·lot (kăsh′ə-lŏt′ *or* kăsh′ə-lō′) *n.* The sperm whale.

cache (kăsh) *n.* **1.** A hiding place, as for a supply of provisions or weapons. **2.** A supply of something hidden in such a place: *a cache of food.* **3.** A fast storage buffer in the central processing unit of a computer. ❖ *tr.v.* **cached, cach·ing, cach·es** To hide or store away in a cache: *squirrels caching nuts for winter.*

❑ *These sound alike:* **cache, cash** (money).

ca·chet (kă-shā′) *n.* **1a.** A mark or quality, as of distinc-

WORD HISTORY

C Have you ever wondered why **c** is sometimes pronounced like a *k* and sometimes like an *s*, as in *candy* and *cereal*? Our letter *c* comes from the Roman alphabet, which was used to represent the sounds of Latin and was later adopted for English. In languages derived from Latin, such as Italian and French, the hard *c* sound (k) of Latin gradually changed before the vowels e, *i*, and *y* to (ch) or the soft *c* sound (s). When the Normans conquered England in 1066, they brought their French language and spelling with them. For this reason, scribes in England continued to write *c* for the soft sound before e, *i*, and *y* in words like *center* and *circle*, and they introduced *k* for the hard *c* sound in many words like *keep* and *king*. In Modern English, *c* is still usually soft before e, *i*, and *y* and hard before *a*, *o*, *u*, and consonants. (The letter *g* has a similar history to the letter *c*, which is why it is sometimes pronounced hard, as in *got*, and sometimes soft, as in *gene*.)

cabriolet

caduceus

Julius Caesar

cairn

ă	pat	ôr	core
ā	pay	oi	boy
âr	care	ou	out
ä	father	ŏŏ	took
ĕ	pet	ŏŏr	lure
ē	be	ōō	boot
ĭ	pit	ŭ	cut
ī	bite	ûr	urge
îr	pier	th	thin
ŏ	pot	*th*	this
ō	toe	zh	vision
ô	paw	ə	about

tion or individuality: *Doctors have a certain cachet in America.* **b.** Great prestige or appeal: *a designer label with cachet.* **2.** A seal on a letter or document.

cack·le (kăk′əl) *v.* **cack·led, cack·ling, cack·les** *—intr.* **1.** To make the shrill cry of a hen that has just laid an egg. **2.** To laugh or speak in a shrill manner. *—tr.* To utter in cackles: *He cackled a sarcastic reply.* ❖ *n.* **1.** The act or sound of cackling. **2.** Shrill laughter or foolish chatter.

ca·coph·o·nous (kə-**kŏf′**ə-nəs) *adj.* Harsh and unpleasant in sound; dissonant. [From Greek *kakophōnos* : *kakos*, bad + *phōnē*, sound.]

ca·coph·o·ny (kə-**kŏf′**ə-nē) *n., pl.* **ca·coph·o·nies** Harsh unpleasant sound; dissonance: *the cacophony of horns in city traffic.*

cac·tus (**kăk′**təs) *n., pl.* **cac·ti** (**kăk′**tī′) or **cac·tus·es** Any of various plants that have thick, leafless, usually spiny stems and that grow in hot dry places, chiefly in the Americas. [From Greek *kaktos*.]

cad (kăd) *n.* A man whose behavior is unprincipled or dishonorable.

CAD *abbr.* An abbreviation of computer-aided design.

ca·dav·er (kə-**dăv′**ər) *n.* A dead body, especially one that is to be dissected and studied.

ca·dav·er·ous (kə-**dăv′**ər-əs) *adj.* Resembling a corpse; pale and gaunt.

cad·die also **cad·dy** (**kăd′**ē) *n., pl.* **cad·dies** A person hired by a golfer to carry golf clubs. ❖ *intr.v.* **cad·died, cad·dy·ing, cad·dies** To serve as a caddie.

cad·disfly or **cad·dis fly** (**kăd′**ĭs-flī′) *n.* Any of numerous insects that have long antennae and four wings covered with short hairs and that are usually found near lakes and streams. The larvae live in tubular cases covered with grains of sand or tiny pieces of wood or shell.

Cad·do (**kăd′**ō) *n., pl.* **Caddo** or **Cad·dos 1.** A member of a group of Native American peoples living in central Oklahoma. **2.** Their Caddoan language.

Cad·do·an (**kăd′**ō-ən) *n.* A family of Native American languages spoken nowadays in North Dakota and Oklahoma.

cad·dy[1] (**kăd′**ē) *n., pl.* **cad·dies** A small container, such as a box, used especially for holding tea.

cad·dy[2] (**kăd′**ē) *n. & v.* Variant of **caddie.**

ca·dence (**kād′**ns) *n.* **1.** Measured rhythmic flow, as of poetry or music: *poetry written in short quick cadences.* **2.** The measure or beat of movement, as in marching. **3.** A progression of chords that brings a phrase or other division of a musical composition to a close. **4.** The general rise and fall of the voice in speaking, as at the end of a question.

ca·den·za (kə-**dĕn′**zə) *n.* An elaborate section for the soloist, usually near the end of a concerto's movement.

ca·det (kə-**dĕt′**) *n.* A student who is training to be an officer in the military or the police. [From French dialectal *capdet*, captain, from Late Latin *capitellum*, diminutive of Latin *caput*, head.]

cad·mi·um (**kăd′**mē-əm) *n. Symbol* **Cd** A soft, bluish-white metallic element resembling tin that occurs only in combination with other elements. It is used in plating metals to prevent corrosion and in making alloys and storage batteries. Atomic number 48. See **Periodic Table.**

cad·re (**kä′**drā *or* **kăd′**rē) *n.* A group of people trained to establish and teach new members in a larger organization.

ca·du·ce·us (kə-**dōō′**sē-əs) *n., pl.* **ca·du·ce·i** (kə-**dōō′**sē-ī′) **1.** In Greek mythology, a winged staff with two serpents coiled around it carried by Hermes. **2.** A similar staff used as a symbol of the medical profession.

cae·cil·ian (sə-**sĭl′**yən *or* sə-**sēl′**yən) *n.* Any of various legless, burrowing amphibians that have numerous grooved rings encircling the body and are found mostly in tropical regions. [From Latin *caecilia*, a kind of lizard, from *caecus*, blind (from its small eyes).]

cae·cum (**sē′**kəm) *n.* Variant of **cecum.**

cae·sar also **Cae·sar** (**sē′**zər) *n.* **1.** A title of Roman emperors after the reign of Augustus. **2.** A dictator or other ruler having absolute power. [From Middle English *cesar*, from Latin *Caesar*, after Julius *Caesar*.]

Caesar, Julius 100–44 BC. Roman general and politician who was given a mandate by the people to rule as dictator for life (45). On March 15 of the following year he was murdered by a group who feared he intended to establish a monarchy.

cae·sar·e·an (sĭ-**zâr′**ē-ən) *adj. & n.* Variant of **cesarean.**

caesar salad *n.* A tossed salad of greens, croutons, grated cheese, and sometimes anchovies, with a dressing of olive oil, lemon juice, garlic, and a raw or coddled egg.

cae·su·ra (sĭ-**zhŏŏr′**ə *or* sĭ-**zŏŏr′**ə) *n., pl.* **cae·su·ras** or **cae·su·rae** (sĭ-**zhŏŏr′**ē *or* sĭ-**zŏŏr′**ē) A short pause in a line of verse or in a melody.

ca·fé also **ca·fe** (kă-**fā′**) *n.* A restaurant where coffee and baked goods or light meals are served. [From French *café*, coffee, café, from Italian *caffè*, coffee, from Ottoman Turkish *qahveh*.]

caf·e·te·ri·a (kăf′ĭ-**tîr′**ē-ə) *n.* **1.** A dining area, as at a school, where meals may be purchased or brought from home and eaten. **2.** A restaurant where customers are served at a counter and carry their meals to tables.

caf·feine also **caf·fein** (kă-**fēn′** *or* **kăf′**ēn′) *n.* A bitter white alkaloid that acts as a stimulant and is found in coffee, tea, and cola beverages.

caf·fe lat·te (**kăf′**ā **lä′**tā) *n.* A strong espresso coffee topped with steamed frothed milk. [From Italian *caffè (e) latte*, coffee (with) milk.]

caf·tan or **kaf·tan** (**kăf′**tăn′ *or* kăf-**tăn′**) *n.* A full-length robe or tunic having long sleeves and worn mainly in eastern Mediterranean countries.

cage (kāj) *n.* **1.** An enclosure for confining birds or other animals, having a grating of wires or bars on at least one side to let in air or light. **2.** Something similar to a cage: *a ticket seller's cage at the stadium.* **3.** A wire backstop or enclosure placed around home plate, used to stop balls batted during practice. **4.** An enclosure to confine prisoners. ❖ *tr.v.* **caged, cag·ing, cag·es** To put in a cage: *cage a wild animal.*

ca·gey also **ca·gy** (**kā′**jē) *adj.* **ca·gi·er, ca·gi·est** Wary; shrewd; crafty: *a cagey lawyer with much experience.* **—cag′i·ly** *adv.* **—cag′i·ness** *n.*

ca·hoots (kə-**hōōts′**) *pl.n. Informal* Secret partnership: *a surprise party that she planned in cahoots with friends.* [Perhaps from French *cahute*, cabin.]

cai·man also **cay·man** (**kā′**mən) *n., pl.* **cai·mans** also **cay·mans** Any of various large tropical American reptiles that resemble and are related to alligators and crocodiles and that live in rivers and wetlands.

Cain (kān) In the Bible, the eldest son of Adam and Eve, who murdered his brother Abel.

cairn (kârn) *n.* A mound of stones built as a landmark or memorial. [From Old Irish *carn*.]

Cai·ro (**kī′**rō) The capital of Egypt, in the northeast part of the country on the Nile River.

cais·son (**kā′**sŏn′ *or* **kā′**sən) *n.* **1.** A watertight structure inside of which construction work is done under water, as in the building of tunnels, bridges, or dams. **2.** A watertight container used to raise a sunken vessel by attaching it to the hull and filling it with air. **3.** A floating structure used to close the entrance of a dock or canal lock. **4.** A two-wheeled horse-drawn vehicle formerly used to carry military ammunition.

ca·jole (kə-**jōl′**) *tr.v.* **ca·joled, ca·jol·ing, ca·joles** To persuade by flattery or insincere talk; coax: *Immigrants were cajoled into going west by promises of great wealth and land.*

ca·jol·er·y (kə-jō′lə-rē) *n., pl.* **ca·jol·er·ies** Persuasion by flattery or insincere talk.

Ca·jun (kā′jən) *n.* A member of a group of people living in Louisiana and descended from French colonists exiled from Acadia in the 1700s. **—Ca′jun** *adj.*

cake (kāk) *n.* **1.** A sweet baked food made of flour, liquid, eggs, and other ingredients. **2.** A flat rounded mass of dough or batter that is baked or fried: *a wheat cake.* **3.** A flat rounded mass of chopped food that is baked or fried: *a fish cake.* **4.** A shaped or molded piece, as of soap. ❖ *v.* **caked, cak·ing, cakes** *—tr.* To cover or fill with a thick layer; encrust: *My shoes are caked with mud. —intr.* To form into a compact mass: *The melted cheese caked on the counter as it cooled.*

cake·walk (kāk′wôk′) *n.* **1.** Something that is easily accomplished. **2.** A public entertainment among African Americans in the 1800s in which dancers performing the most accomplished or amusing steps won cakes as prizes. **—cake′walk′er** *n.*

cal or **Cal** *abbr.* An abbreviation of calorie.

cal·a·bash (kăl′ə-băsh′) *n.* **1a.** A large gourd having a hard rind. **b.** The vine that bears such gourds. **2a.** The similar fruit of a tropical American tree. **b.** The tree that bears such fruit. **3.** A bowl, ladle, or other article made from the hollowed-out shell of either of these fruits.

cal·a·boose (kăl′ə-bo͞os′) *n.* A jail. [From Spanish *calabozo*, dungeon.]

Ca·lais (kă-lā′ *or* kăl′ā) A city of northern France southeast of Dover, England.

cal·a·mar·i (kä′lə-**mä′**rē *or* kăl′ə-**mä′**rē) *n.* Squid eaten as food.

ca·la·ma·ta olive (kä′lə-**mä′**tə *or* kăl′ə-**mä′**tə) *n.* Variant of **kalamata olive.**

cal·a·mine (kăl′ə-mīn′ *or* kăl′ə-mĭn) *n.* A pink powder used in skin lotions and composed of zinc oxide mixed with a small amount of ferric oxide.

ca·lam·i·tous (kə-lăm′ĭ-təs) *adj.* Causing or resulting in a calamity; disastrous. **—ca·lam′i·tous·ly** *adv.*

ca·lam·i·ty (kə-lăm′ĭ-tē) *n., pl.* **ca·lam·i·ties 1.** An event that causes great distress and suffering; a disaster: *The long drought was a calamity for farmers.* **2.** Distress or misfortune: *the calamity of unemployment.*

cal·car·e·ous (kăl-kâr′ē-əs) *adj.* Composed of or containing limestone, calcium, or calcium carbonate; chalky.

cal·ci·fi·ca·tion (kăl′sə-fĭ-**kā′**shən) *n.* **1.** The process of calcifying: *Calcification of cartilage often causes stiffness in the joints of the body.* **2.** A calcified part, such as tissue or an organ.

cal·ci·fy (kăl′sə-fī′) *tr. & intr.v.* **cal·ci·fied, cal·ci·fy·ing, cal·ci·fies** To make or become stony or chalky by the deposit of calcium salts.

cal·ci·mine (kăl′sə-mīn′) *n.* A white or tinted mixture of zinc oxide, water, and glue, formerly used to coat walls and ceilings.

cal·cine (kăl-sīn′ *or* kăl′sīn′) *tr.v.* **cal·cined, cal·cin·ing, cal·cines** To dry, reduce, or oxidize (a substance) by heating it to a high temperature without causing it to melt: *a furnace to calcine limestone.* ❖ *n.* A substance produced by calcining. **—cal′ci·na′tion** (kăl′sə-**nā′**shən) *n.*

cal·cite (kăl′sīt′) *n.* A crystalline mineral that is the main component of chalk, limestone, and marble. It is a natural form of calcium carbonate.

cal·ci·um (kăl′sē-əm) *n. Symbol* **Ca** A silvery-white, moderately hard metallic element found in limestone, gypsum, milk, and bone. It is essential for the normal growth and development of most plants and animals, and is used in alloys, plaster, and cement. Atomic number 20. See **Periodic Table.** [From Latin *calx*, lime.]

calcium carbide *n.* A crystalline grayish-black compound of carbon and calcium that has the formula CaC_2 and reacts with water to form acetylene gas.

calcium carbonate *n.* A white or colorless crystalline compound of calcium, carbon, and oxygen that has the formula $CaCO_3$ and occurs naturally in chalk, limestone, and marble. It is used in the manufacture of toothpaste, white paint, and Portland cement.

calcium chloride *n.* A white crystalline salt composed of calcium and chlorine and having the formula $CaCl_2$. It attracts water very strongly and is used in refrigeration and on roads to settle dust or melt ice.

calcium hydroxide *n.* A soft white powder composed of calcium, hydrogen, and oxygen and having the formula $Ca(OH)_2$. It is made by adding water to lime and used in making mortar, cement, and a variety of industrial products.

calcium oxide *n.* A white lumpy powder composed of calcium and oxygen and having the formula CaO; lime. It is obtained by heating limestone and used in making steel, glass, and insecticides and as an industrial alkali.

cal·cu·la·ble (kăl′kyə-lə-bəl) *adj.* Capable of being calculated or estimated. **—cal′cu·la·bil′i·ty** *n.*

cal·cu·late (kăl′kyə-lāt′) *v.* **cal·cu·lat·ed, cal·cu·lat·ing, cal·cu·lates** *—tr.* **1.** To find or determine (an answer or result) by using mathematics; reckon: *calculate the total cost of the trip.* **2.** To make an estimate of; evaluate: *calculate the possibilities of succeeding.* **3.** To make for a specific purpose; design: *His remarks were calculated to please the stockholders. —intr.* **1.** To perform a mathematical process, such as addition; figure. **2.** *Informal* To count, depend, or rely: *We are calculating on your help.* [From Latin *calculus*, small stone used for counting.]

cal·cu·lat·ed (kăl′kyə-lā′tĭd) *adj.* **1.** Carefully estimated in advance: *a calculated risk.* **2.** Made or planned to accomplish a specific purpose: *a smile calculated to win favor.* **3.** Determined by mathematical calculation.

cal·cu·lat·ing (kăl′kyə-lā′tĭng) *adj.* **1.** Used in or for performing calculation: *a calculating machine.* **2.** Shrewd; crafty: *the calculating defense of an experienced attorney.* **3.** Selfish; scheming: *a cold and calculating criminal.*

cal·cu·la·tion (kăl′kyə-**lā′**shən) *n.* **1.** The act, process, or result of calculating: *All the calculations in my math homework turned out to be correct.* **2.** Careful thinking or planning: *They won the game by clever calculation.*

cal·cu·la·tor (kăl′kyə-lā′tər) *n.* **1.** A person who calculates. **2.** An electronic or mechanical device that performs mathematical calculations.

cal·cu·lus (kăl′kyə-ləs) *n., pl.* **cal·cu·li** (kăl′kyə-lī′) or **cal·cu·lus·es 1.** An abnormal hard mass, usually of mineral salts, that forms in the body and is often found in the urinary bladder, gallbladder, or kidney. **2.** The branch of mathematics that extends the use of algebra to problems that involve rates of change in quantities. [From Latin *calculus*, small stone used for counting.]

Cal·cut·ta (kăl-kŭt′ə) See **Kolkata.**

Cal·de·rón (käl′də-**rōn′**), **Felipe** Born 1962. Mexican politician who took office as president in 2006, following a close, contested election, and served until 2012.

Cal·e·do·ni·a (kăl′ĭ-**dō′**nē-ə) A poetic name for Scotland.

cal·en·dar (kăl′ən-dər) *n.* **1.** A chart showing the months, weeks, and days of a certain year. **2.** Any of various systems of reckoning time in which the beginning, length, and divisions of a year are defined, sometimes along with multiyear cycles: *Many of the world's calendars divide the year into twelve months.* **3.** A list of dates, as of events or things to be done, arranged in order of time of occurrence: *a court calendar.* [From Middle English *calender*, from Latin *kalendārium*, account book.]

❑ *These sound alike:* **calendar, calender** (machine for treating paper).

cal·en·der (kăl′ən-dər) *n.* A machine in which paper or cloth is given a smooth glossy finish by being pressed between rollers. ❖ *tr.v.* **cal·en·dered, cal·en·der·ing,**

calabash

GEOGRAPHY

California The name of the state of **California** was first used in a Spanish poem written around 1500. In the poem it was the name of a legendary island said to be located "near Paradise." Baja California was the first part of California reached by the Spaniards; it was thought to be an island and so was named after the poetic island. Since the author of the poem probably made up the name, its meaning is not known for certain.

calligraphy

ă	pat	ôr	core
ā	pay	oi	boy
âr	care	ou	out
ä	father	o͝o	took
ĕ	pet	o͝or	lure
ē	be	o͞o	boot
ĭ	pit	ŭ	cut
ī	bite	ûr	urge
îr	pier	th	thin
ŏ	pot	*th*	this
ō	toe	zh	vision
ô	paw	ə	about

cal·en·ders To press (paper or cloth) with a calender. ❑ *These sound alike:* **calender, calendar** (time chart).

calf¹ (kăf) *n., pl.* **calves** (kăvz) **1.** A young cow or bull. **2.** One of the young of certain other mammals, such as a moose, elephant, or whale. **3.** A type of leather made from the hide of a calf; calfskin. [From Middle English, from Old English *cælf.*]

calf² (kăf) *n., pl.* **calves** (kăvz) The muscular back part of the human leg between the knee and ankle. [From Middle English, from Old Norse *kālfi.*]

calf·skin (**kăf′**skĭn′) *n.* The hide of a calf or leather made from it.

Cal·ga·ry (**kăl′**gə-rē) The largest city of Alberta, Canada, in the southern part of the province south of Edmonton. The 1988 Winter Olympics were held here.

Cal·houn (kăl-**ho͞on′**), **John Caldwell** 1782–1850. American politician who served as vice president of the United States (1825–1832) under John Quincy Adams and Andrew Jackson and as a senator (1832–1843). He defended slavery and was an advocate of states' rights.

cal·i·ber (**kăl′**ə-bər) *n.* **1a.** The diameter of the inside of a tube. **b.** The inside diameter or bore of a firearm, usually expressed in decimal fractions. **2.** The diameter of a bullet or other projectile intended for a firearm: *a .45-caliber bullet.* **3.** Degree of worth; quality: *A judge should be a citizen of high caliber.*

cal·i·brate (**kăl′**ə-brāt′) *tr.v.* **cal·i·brat·ed, cal·i·brat·ing, cal·i·brates 1.** To check, adjust, or standardize (a measuring instrument), usually by comparing with an accepted model: *calibrate an oven thermometer.* **2.** To determine the caliber of (a tube). **—cal′i·bra′tion** *n.*

cal·i·co (**kăl′**ĭ-kō′) *n., pl.* **cal·i·coes** or **cal·i·cos 1.** A cotton cloth with a brightly colored or closely printed pattern. **2.** An animal, such as a cat, having a coat that has patches of fur of different colors, often reddish-orange, white, and black.

Cal·i·for·nia (kăl′ĭ-**fôr′**nyə) A state of the western United States on the Pacific Ocean south of Oregon. It was admitted as the 31st state in 1850. Sacramento is the capital and Los Angeles the largest city. —SEE NOTE.

California, Gulf of An arm of the Pacific Ocean in northwest Mexico separating Baja California from the mainland.

cal·i·for·ni·um (kăl′ə-**fôr′**nē-əm) *n. Symbol* **Cf** A radioactive element that has been artificially produced by scientists. The half-lives of its isotopes is range from 21 milliseconds to 898 years. Atomic number 98. See **Periodic Table.**

cal·i·per (**kăl′**ə-pər) *n.* **1.** often **calipers** An instrument having two hinged legs that can be adjusted to measure diameter, thickness, or the distance between two points, as on a map or scale. **2.** The assembly housing or applying brake pads, as in a disc brake or on a bicycle.

ca·liph (**kā′**lĭf *or* **kăl′**ĭf) *n.* A leader of an Islamic nation, by tradition always male. [From Middle English *calife*, from Arabic *ḫalīfa*, successor (to Muhammad), from *ḫalafa*, to succeed.]

cal·is·then·ics (kăl′ĭs-**thĕn′**ĭks) *n.* **1.** *(used with a plural verb)* Gymnastic exercises usually done without special equipment to develop muscular strength and general health. **2.** *(used with a singular verb)* The practice of such exercises. [From Greek *kalli-*, beautiful + Greek *sthenos*, strength.] **—cal′is·then′ic** *adj.*

calk (kôk) *n.* A pointed piece of metal on the bottom of a horseshoe, designed to prevent slipping. [From Middle English *kakun*, possibly from Latin *calcāneum*, heelbone.]

call (kôl) *v.* **called, call·ing, calls** *—tr.* **1.** To say in a loud voice; announce: *call the dog; call directions in a square dance.* **2.** To send for; summon: *call the fire department; call the guests in to dinner.* **3.** To summon to a particular career or pursuit: *felt he was called to the priesthood.* **4.** To order or invite to assemble; convoke: *call a meeting.* **5.** To bring into being, effect, or action, as by giving an order: *Either country could call an end to the trade agreements.* **6a.** To give a name to; name: *What did they call the baby?* **b.** To describe as; designate: *We call her the athlete of the family.* **7.** To estimate as being; regard as; consider: *I would call him a great writer.* **8a.** To speak with or attempt to speak with (someone) by telephone: *call a friend and chat.* **b.** To dial (a telephone number). **9.** To halt or postpone; suspend: *call a game on account of rain.* **10.** To predict accurately: *The reporter called the outcome of the election.* **11.** To demand payment of: *The bank called the loan.* **12.** In baseball, to indicate a decision in regard to (a pitch, ball, or player): *The umpire called him safe.* **13.** To choose or select (plays to be made), as in football. **14.** In poker, to equal the bet of (the preceding bettor). *—intr.* **1.** To attract attention by shouting: *call until help comes.* **2.** To utter a characteristic cry: *pheasants calling to each other.* **3.** To telephone someone: *You've already called several times.* **4.** To pay a short visit: *We called to pay our respects.* **5.** In poker, to place a bet equal to the bet of the preceding bettor. ❖ *n.* **1.** A shout or loud cry: *A frightened call came from the woods.* **2a.** The typical cry of an animal, especially a bird: *the call of the blue jay.* **b.** An instrument or sound made to imitate such a cry, used as a lure: *a duck call used by hunters.* **c.** A word habitually used as a signal or direction: *Square dancing calls can be hard to follow.* **3.** A signal, such as one made by a horn or bell: *a bugle call to meals.* **4.** The act or an instance of communicating or trying to communicate by telephone: *an afternoon spent making calls to friends.* **5.** A short visit: *a friendly call on new neighbors.* **6a.** A strong urge or feeling: *felt she had a call to become a teacher.* **b.** Attraction or appeal; fascination: *the call of camping in the wilderness.* **7.** Need, reason, or cause: *There was no call to be unpleasant.* **8a.** Demand, as for a certain product: *There isn't much call for inkstands today.* **b.** A claim on one's time: *the call of duty.* **9.** In sports, a decision made by an official. ◆ **call back 1.** To telephone in return. **2.** To summon (a person) to return: *The company called us back to work.* **call for 1.** To go and get: *The taxi will call for you at eight.* **2.** To require; demand: *The recipe calls for half a cup of flour.* **call in 1.** To summon for help or consultation: *call in a specialist.* **2.** To take out of circulation: *call in old dollar bills.* **call into question** To raise doubt about: *The whole story is called into question by the lack of evidence.* **call off 1.** To cancel: *call off a game.* **2.** To restrain or recall: *Call off your dogs!* **call on 1.** To ask or order (someone) to speak: *The teacher called on the new student first.* **2.** To appeal to (someone) to do something: *The principal called on each of us to contribute something.* **call out 1.** To say in a loud voice; yell: *The rescuers called out for more people to help.* **2.** To cause to assemble; summon: *The governor called out the National Guard after the earthquake struck.* **call to account** To demand an explanation from: *The student was called to account for being late.* **call to mind** To cause one to think of (something), especially by being similar: *The movie calls to mind other adventure stories.* **call up** To summon into military service: *Reserve units are being called up for active duty.* **on call** Available when summoned; ready: *a nurse on call.* [From Middle English *callen*, probably from Old Norse *kalla.*]

cal·la lily (**kăl′**ə) *n.* Any of several southern African plants that are cultivated for their showy white, yellow, pink, or purple flowers.

call box *n.* A telephone by the side of a highway or road for the use of motorists to report an emergency.

call·er (**kô′**lər) *n.* **1.** A person who calls, especially by paying a short visit or making a telephone call: *Several* *callers came by to see the new baby.* **2.** A person who calls out numbers or directions, as in bingo or square dancing.

caller ID *n.* A telephone service that displays an incoming caller's name and telephone number.

cal·lig·ra·phy (kə-lĭg′rə-fē) *n.* **1.** The art of fine handwriting. **2.** Handwriting. **—cal·lig′ra·pher** *n.*

call·ing (kô′lĭng) *n.* **1.** An inner urge or strong impulse, especially one that is believed to be divinely inspired: *felt a calling to become a priest.* **2.** An occupation, profession, or career: *Writing poetry is her calling.*

calling card *n.* **1.** A phone card. **2.** A small engraved card that has a person's full name printed on it.

cal·li·o·pe (kə-lī′ə-pē′ *or* **kăl′**ē-ōp′) *n.* A musical instrument having a keyboard that controls a set of steam whistles, used mostly at carnivals and circuses. [From *Calliope*.]

Cal·li·o·pe (kə-lī′ə-pē′) *n.* In Greek mythology, the Muse of epic poetry.

call letters *pl.n.* The letters that identify a radio or television station.

call number *n.* A number used in libraries to classify a book and indicate its location on the shelves.

cal·los·i·ty (kə-lŏs′ĭ-tē) *n., pl.* **cal·los·i·ties 1.** A hard growth or mass, such as a callus. **2.** Lack of feeling; hardheartedness.

cal·lous (**kăl′**əs) *adj.* **1.** Having calluses: *the callous hands of a logger.* **2.** Unfeeling; unsympathetic. [From Middle English, from Latin *callōsus*, from *callum*, hard skin.] **—cal′lous·ly** *adv.*

❑ *These sound alike:* **callous, callus** (hard skin).

cal·low (**kăl′**ō) *adj.* Not completely developed; immature; inexperienced: *a callow youngster.* **—cal′low·ly** *adv.* **—cal′low·ness** *n.*

call-up (**kôl′**ŭp′) *n.* An order to report for military service.

cal·lus (**kăl′**əs) *n., pl.* **cal·lus·es** An area of the skin that has become hardened and thick, usually because of prolonged pressure or rubbing.

❑ *These sound alike:* **callus, callous** (unfeeling).

call waiting *n.* A telephone service that alerts someone using the phone that another call is incoming and allows switching between calls.

calm (käm) *adj.* **calm·er, calm·est 1.** Peacefully quiet; not excited; composed: *We remained calm throughout the storm.* **2.** Nearly motionless; undisturbed; still: *the calm lake waters.* ❖ *n.* **1.** A condition of being peaceful; tranquility; serenity: *Her calm was broken by the shouts in the street.* **2.** Lack of motion; stillness: *a calm in the air just before the storm hit.* ❖ *tr. & intr.v.* **calmed, calm·ing, calms** To make or become calm or quiet: *calm a crying baby; calm down after an argument.* [From Middle English *calme*, from Late Latin *cauma*, resting place in the heat of the day, from Greek *kauma*, burning heat.] **—calm′ly** *adv.* **—calm′ness** *n.*

SYNONYMS **calm, peaceful, placid, serene, tranquil** These adjectives describe the absence of excitement or disturbance. *The streets of the capital were eerily calm after days of popular unrest. We took a long hike through the peaceful forest. The author lived a placid life in a small town. The artist rendered the serene valley in the painting. I'm looking forward to some tranquil days at a cabin on a lake.*

ANTONYMS **turbulent, upset**

---

cal·o·mel (**kăl′**ə-mĕl′ *or* **kăl′**ə-məl) *n.* A white tasteless compound of mercury and chlorine, formerly used as a purgative and insecticide.

ca·lor·ic (kə-lôr′ĭk) *adj.* Relating to heat or calories.

cal·o·rie (**kăl′**ə-rē) *n.* **1.** A unit of energy equal to the amount of heat needed to raise the temperature of one gram of water one degree Celsius. **2.** A unit that is used to measure the energy supplied by food, equal to the amount of heat needed to raise the temperature of 1,000 grams of water one degree Celsius; a kilocalorie. [From Latin *calor*, heat.]

cal·o·rif·ic (kăl′ə-**rĭf′**ĭk) *adj.* Relating to or generating heat.

cal·o·rim·e·ter (kăl′ə-**rĭm′**ĭ-tər) *n.* An apparatus for measuring the quantity of heat given off by or present in a body, such as the specific heat of different substances or the heat generated by a chemical reaction.

cal·u·met (**kăl′**yə-mĕt′ *or* kăl′yə-**mĕt′**) *n.* A sacred or ceremonial pipe used by certain Native American peoples. [From Latin *calamus*, reed.]

ca·lum·ni·ate (kə-**lŭm′**nē-āt′) *tr.v.* **ca·lum·ni·at·ed, ca·lum·ni·at·ing, ca·lum·ni·ates** To make false statements about; slander. **—ca·lum′ni·a′tion** *n.* **—ca·lum′ni·a′tor** *n.*

ca·lum·ni·ous (kə-**lŭm′**nē-əs) *adj.* Containing or implying calumny; slanderous: *a calumnious attack.* **—ca·lum′ni·ous·ly** *adv.*

cal·um·ny (**kăl′**əm-nē) *n., pl.* **cal·um·nies 1.** A false statement made to injure another person's reputation: *calumnies springing from jealousy.* **2.** The making of such statements; slander.

Cal·va·ry (**kăl′**və-rē *or* **kăl′**vrē) also **Gol·go·tha** (**gŏl′**gə-thə) A hill outside ancient Jerusalem where Jesus was crucified.

calve (kăv) *intr.v.* **calved, calv·ing, calves 1.** To give birth to a calf. **2.** To break and drop off a large mass of ice: *Glaciers calving into the sea.*

calves[1] (kăvz) *n.* Plural of **calf**[1].

calves[2] (kăvz) *n.* Plural of **calf**[2].

Cal·vin (**kăl′**vĭn), **John** 1509–1564. French-born Swiss Protestant whose theology is known today as Calvinism.

Cal·vin·ism (**kăl′**vĭ-nĭz′əm) *n.* The Protestant doctrines of John Calvin, emphasizing God's omnipotence and the predestination of souls to heaven and hell. **—Cal′vin·ist** *n. & adj.* **—Cal′vin·is′tic** *adj.*

Ca·lyp·so or **ca·lyp·so** (kə-**lĭp′**sō) *n.* A type of music that originated in Trinidad, characterized by improvised lyrics about humorous or timely subjects.

ca·lyx (**kā′**lĭks *or* **kăl′**ĭks) *n., pl.* **ca·lyx·es** or **ca·ly·ces** (**kā′**lĭ-sēz′ *or* **kăl′**ĭ-sēz′) The sepals of a flower considered as a group.

cal·zo·ne (kăl-**zō′**nē *or* kăl-**zōn′**) *n.* A baked or fried turnover filled with vegetables, meat, or cheese.

cam (kăm) *n.* A wheel with a projecting part that is attached to a rotating shaft and changes a regular circular motion into a back-and-forth motion in a connected part.

ca·ma·ra·der·ie (kä′mə-**rä′**də-rē *or* käm′**rä′**də-rē) *n.* Goodwill and warm feeling between or among friends; comradeship.

cam·ber (**kăm′**bər) *n.* A slightly arched surface, as of a road or a ship's deck.

cam·bi·um (**kăm′**bē-əm) *n., pl.* **cam·bi·ums** or **cam·bi·a** (**kăm′**bē-ə) A tissue in the stems and roots of many seed-bearing plants that consists of cells that divide to form new layers of tissue toward the inside and toward the outside of the plant.

Cam·bo·di·a (kăm-**bō′**dē-ə) or **Kam·pu·che·a** (kăm′-po͞o-**chē′**ə) A country of southeast Asia southeast of Thailand. Phnom Penh is the capital.

Cam·bri·an (**kăm′**brē-ən *or* **kām′**brē-ən) *n.* The first period of the Paleozoic Era, from about 542 to 488 million years ago. During the Cambrian, there was a great increase in the numbers and kinds of invertebrate marine animals. See table at **geologic time.** **—Cam′bri·an** *adj.*

cam·bric (**kām′**brĭk) *n.* A fine white linen or cotton cloth.

John Calvin

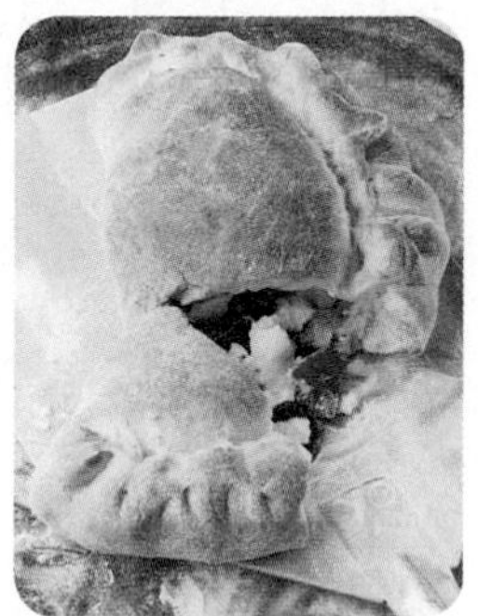

calzone

WRITERS CHOOSE THEIR WORDS

He watched the young kids in Petra's army, fresh out of their launch groups, watched how they played, how they made fun of their leaders when they thought no one was looking. He watched the **camaraderie** of old friends who had known each other in the Battle School for years, who talked and laughed about old battles and long-graduated soldiers and commanders.

—Orson Scott Card
Ender's Game

camel
Bactrian camel *(top)* and dromedary *(bottom)*

cameo

camouflage
insect camouflaged as a leaf

ă	pat	ôr	core
ā	pay	oi	boy
âr	care	ou	out
ä	father	o͝o	took
ĕ	pet	o͝or	lure
ē	be	o͞o	boot
ĭ	pit	ŭ	cut
ī	bite	ûr	urge
îr	pier	th	thin
ŏ	pot	*th*	this
ō	toe	zh	vision
ô	paw	ə	about

cambric tea *n.* A hot drink made from milk, sugar, water, and usually a small amount of tea.

Cam·bridge (kām**′**brĭj) **1.** A city of east-central England north-northeast of London. It is the site of the University of Cambridge, established in the 1200s. **2.** A city of eastern Massachusetts northwest of Boston. It is the site of Harvard University, founded in 1636.

cam·cord·er (**kăm′**kôr′dər) *n.* A camera that records video on a storage device.

came (kām) *v.* Past tense of **come.**

cam·el (**kăm′**əl) *n.* Either of two cud-chewing mammals, the Bactrian camel or the dromedary, that have a humped back and long neck and are widely used in northern Africa, the Middle East, and Asia to carry loads and as a source of wool, milk, and meat. [From Old English, from Greek *kamēlos*, of Semitic origin.]

cam·el·hair (**kăm′**əl-hâr′) also **cam·el's hair** (**kăm′**əlz) *n.* **1.** The soft fine hair of a camel or a substitute for it. **2.** A soft, heavy, usually light tan cloth made chiefly of the hair of a camel.

ca·mel·lia (kə-**mēl′**yə) *n.* **1.** Any of several shrubs or small trees having glossy evergreen leaves and red, pink, or white roselike flowers. **2.** The flower of such a plant. [After George Josef *Kamel* (1661–1706), Jesuit missionary.]

Cam·e·lot (**kăm′**ə-lŏt′) *n.* In Arthurian legend, the site of King Arthur's court.

Cam·em·bert (**kăm′**əm-bâr′) *n.* A creamy rich cheese that softens on the inside as it matures.

cam·e·o (**kăm′**ē-ō′) *n., pl.* **cam·e·os 1.** A gem, shell, or medallion usually having a carved design that projects from a background of a different color. **2.** A brief appearance of a prominent actor, as in a motion picture.

cam·er·a (**kăm′**ər-ə *or* **kăm′**rə) *n.* A usually portable device containing a light-sensitive surface that records images through a lens. [From Late Latin *camera*, chamber, from Greek *kamarā*, vault.]

cam·er·a·man (**kăm′**ər-ə-măn′ *or* **kăm′**rə-măn′) *n.* A man who operates a television or movie camera.

cam·er·a·per·son (**kăm′**ər-ə-pûr′sən *or* **kăm′**rə-pûr′-sən) *n.* A person who operates a television or movie camera.

cam·er·a·wom·an (**kăm′**ər-ə-wo͝om′ən *or* **kăm′**rə-wo͝om′ən) *n.* A woman who operates a television or movie camera.

Cam·er·on (**kăm′**ər-ən *or* **kăm′**rən), **David William Donald** Born 1966. British politician who served as prime minister from 2010 to 2016.

Cam·e·roon (kăm′ə-**ro͞on′**) A country of west-central Africa on the Atlantic Ocean southeast of Nigeria. Yaoundé is the capital.

cam·i (**kăm′**ē) *n., pl.* **cam·is** A camisole.

cam·i·sole (**kăm′**ĭ-sōl′) *n.* A woman's short, sleeveless undergarment, often having thin shoulder straps.

cam·o (**kăm′**ō) *n. Slang* Camouflage.

cam·ou·flage (**kăm′**ə-fläzh′ *or* **kăm′**ə-fläj′) *n.* **1.** A method of concealing troops or equipment by making them blend in with their surroundings. **2.** A shape or coloring that conceals: *An alligator's camouflage makes it look like a floating log.* **3a.** Cloth or other material used for camouflage: *planes covered with camouflage.* **b.** Fabric or clothing having a pattern often used for camouflage, usually with green, brown, and tan splotches: *hunters wearing camouflage.* ❖ *tr.v.* **cam·ou·flaged, cam·ou·flag·ing, cam·ou·flag·es** To conceal or hide by camouflage.

camp (kămp) *n.* **1.** A place where a group of people, such as vacationers, miners, or soldiers, live temporarily in tents, cabins, or other rough shelters. **2.** A cabin or shelter or group of such buildings: *They have a camp on a lake.* **3.** A place in the country that offers recreational activities or instruction, as for children on vacation. ❖ *intr.v.* **camped, camp·ing, camps 1.** To make or set up a camp: *We camped next to the river.* **2.** To live in or as if in a camp: *Our friends camped for a month in the Rocky Mountains.* [From Latin *campus*, field.]

cam·paign (kăm-**pān′**) *n.* **1.** A series of military operations undertaken to achieve an important objective during a war: *Grant's campaign secured the Mississippi River for the Union.* **2.** Organized activity to attain a political, social, or commercial goal: *an advertising campaign.* ❖ *intr.v.* **cam·paigned, cam·paign·ing, cam·paigns** To engage in a campaign: *The candidates campaigned on television.* [From Late Latin *campānia*, battlefield, from *campus*, field.] **—cam·paign′er** *n.*

cam·pa·ni·le (kăm′pə-**nē′**lē) *n.* A bell tower, especially one near but not attached to a church or other building.

Camp·bell (**kăm′**bəl), **(Avril) Kim** Born 1947. Canadian prime minister (1993).

camp·er (**kăm′**pər) *n.* **1.** A person who camps outdoors. **2.** A boy or girl who attends a summer camp. **3.** A motor vehicle having a space equipped as a dwelling place for camping on long trips.

camp·fire (**kămp′**fīr′) *n.* An outdoor fire in a camp, used for warmth or cooking.

camp·ground (**kămp′**ground′) *n.* An area used for setting up a camp or holding a camp meeting.

cam·phor (**kăm′**fər) *n.* A white crystalline compound that is obtained from plants or made from turpentine and is used as an insect repellent, in making plastics, and in medicine as an external preparation to relieve mild pain and itching.

camp meeting *n.* An evangelistic gathering held in a tent or outdoors and often lasting a number of days.

camp·site (**kămp′**sīt′) *n.* An area used for camping.

cam·pus (**kăm′**pəs) *n., pl.* **cam·pus·es** The grounds and buildings of a school, college, university, business, or hospital: *Yesterday I saw our new math professor on campus for the first time.*

cam·shaft (**kăm′**shăft′) *n.* A shaft fitted with one or more cams, as in a gasoline engine.

can[1] (kăn; kən *when unstressed*) *aux.v. Past tense* **could** (ko͝od) **1.** To know how to: *My cousin can speak Arabic.* **2.** To be able to: *I can skate backward.* **3.** To possess the right or power to: *The president can veto bills passed by Congress.* **4.** To have permission to; be allowed to: *You can borrow my pen if you like.* [From Old English *cunnan*, to know, know how.]

can[2] (kăn) *n.* **1a.** An airtight metal container in which food and beverages are preserved: *Put the empty cans in the trash.* **b.** The contents of such a container: *This chili recipe calls for a can of pinto beans and a can of kidney beans.* **2.** A usually cylindrical metal container: *a garbage can.* ❖ *tr.v.* **canned, can·ning, cans** To preserve (food) in a sealed container: *spent the morning canning beans.* [From Old English *canne*, container.]

Ca·naan (**kā′**nən) An ancient region of the Middle East lying mostly between the Jordan River and the Mediterranean Sea.

Ca·naan·ite (**kā′**nə-nīt′) *n.* **1.** A member of a group of Semitic peoples inhabiting Canaan from late prehistoric times, including the Israelites and Phoenicians. **2.** In the Bible, a member of any of these peoples other than the Israelites. **—Ca′naan·ite′** *adj.*

Can·a·da (**kăn′**ə-də) A country of northern North America. The Dominion of Canada was formed in 1867. Ottawa is the capital and Toronto the largest city. **—Ca·na′di·an** (kə-**nā′**dē-ən) *adj. & n.*

Canada Day *n.* July 1, observed in Canada to commemorate the formation of the Dominion of Canada in 1867.

Canada goose or **Canadian goose** *n.* A North American wild goose having gray, black, and white feathers and a white patch on the throat and the sides of the face.

Canadian bacon *n.* Cured, rolled, and very lean bacon from the loin of a pig.

Canadian French *n.* The French language as spoken in Canada.

ca·nal (kə-năl′) *n.* **1.** An artificial waterway used for irrigation, drainage, or navigation. **2.** A tube or duct in the body of an organism, as for the passage of liquid, air, food, or other matter: *the alimentary canal; the ear canal.*

Canal Zone A strip of land, about 10 miles (16 kilometers) wide, through which the Panama Canal runs. It was administered by the United States until 1979.

can·a·pé (kăn′ə-pā′ *or* kăn′ə-pē) *n.* A cracker or piece of bread with meat, cheese, or other food spread on top, served as an appetizer.

ca·nard (kə-närd′) *n.* An unfounded or false, deliberately misleading story.

ca·nar·y (kə-nâr′ē) *n., pl.* **ca·nar·ies** A small greenish to yellow finch that is originally from the Canary Islands and is popular as a pet. [From Spanish *canario,* of the Canary Islands, from Late Latin *Canāriae (Īnsulae),* (islands) of dogs, from Latin *canis,* dog.]

Canary Islands A group of Spanish islands in the Atlantic Ocean off the northwest coast of Africa.

ca·nas·ta (kə-năs′tə) *n.* A card game for two to six players that uses two decks and is related to rummy.

Ca·nav·er·al (kə-năv′ər-əl *or* kə-năv′rəl) A sandy promontory extending into the Atlantic Ocean from a barrier island on the east-central coast of Florida. Named Cape Kennedy from 1963 to 1973, it is the site of NASA's launching area for US space missions.

Can·ber·ra (kăn′bər-ə *or* kăn′bĕr′ə) The capital of Australia, in the southeast part of the country southwest of Sydney. It was settled in 1824.

can·cel (kăn′səl) *v.* **can·celed, can·cel·ing, can·cels** also **can·celled, can·cel·ling, can·cels** —*tr.* **1.** To cross out with lines or other markings: *cancel items on a shopping list.* **2a.** To decide or announce that (an event) will not take place as scheduled: *cancel an appointment; cancel the performance.* **b.** To make invalid: *cancel a credit card.* **3.** To mark or perforate (a postage stamp, for example) to indicate that it may not be used again. **4.** To make up for; offset; balance: *Two opposing votes cancel each other out.* **5a.** To remove (a common factor) from the numerator and denominator of a fraction. **b.** To remove (a common term or factor) from both sides of an equation. —*intr.* To balance or offset each other: *Spending and saving often cancel out.*

can·cel·la·tion (kăn′sə-lā′shən) *n.* **1.** The act or process of canceling. **2.** A mark made, as on a stamp or check, to indicate that it has been canceled.

can·cer (kăn′sər) *n.* **1.** A disease in which cells of a body part become abnormal and multiply without limit, sometimes spreading to and damaging other tissues of the body. **2.** A tumor, especially a malignant one. **3.** A destructive spreading evil: *Poverty is a fearful social cancer.* [From Old English *cancer,* spreading sore, from Latin, crab, disease.] —**can′cer·ous** *adj.*

Cancer *n.* **1.** A constellation in the Northern Hemisphere, traditionally pictured as a crab. **2.** The fourth sign of the zodiac in astrology.

can·del·a (kăn-dĕl′ə) *n.* A unit used to measure the brightness of a source of light. See table at **measurement.**

can·de·la·bra (kăn′dl-ä′brə *or* kăn′dl-ăb′rə) *n.* A candelabrum.

can·de·la·brum (kăn′dl-ä′brəm *or* kăn′dl-ăb′rəm) *n., pl.* **can·de·la·bra** (kăn′dl-ä′-brə *or* kăn′dl-ăb′rə) or **can·de·la·brums** A large decorative candlestick with several arms or branches for holding candles.

can·did (kăn′dĭd) *adj.* **1.** Direct and frank; straightforward; open: *a candid opinion.* **2.** Free from prejudice; impartial: *a candid judgment.* **3.** Not posed or rehearsed: *a candid photograph.* [From Latin *candidus,* glowing, white, pure.] —**can′did·ly** *adv.* —**can′did·ness** *n.*

can·di·da·cy (kăn′dĭ-də-sē) *n., pl.* **can·di·da·cies** The fact or condition of being a candidate.

can·di·date (kăn′dĭ-dāt′ *or* kăn′dĭ-dĭt) *n.* **1.** A person who seeks or is nominated for an office, prize, or honor. **2.** A student who has nearly completed the requirements for a degree: *a master's degree candidate.* [From Latin *candidātus,* clothed in white (from the white togas worn by Romans seeking office), candidate, from *candidus,* white.]

can·died (kăn′dēd) *adj.* Cooked in or coated with a glaze of sugar: *candied sweet potatoes; candied fruit.*

can·dle (kăn′dl) *n.* **1.** A solid stick of wax, tallow, or other fatty substance with a wick inside that is lit and burned to provide light. **2.** An obsolete unit of luminous intensity, replaced by the candela. ❖ *tr.v.* **can·dled, can·dling, can·dles** To examine (an egg) for freshness by holding it in front of a bright light. [From Old English *candel,* from Latin *candēla,* from *candēre,* to shine.]

can·dle·light (kăn′dl-līt′) *n.* **1.** The light given off by a candle. **2.** Dusk; twilight.

Can·dle·mas (kăn′dl-məs) *n.* February 2, celebrated in some Christian churches to commemorate the purification of the Virgin Mary and presentation of the infant Jesus in the Temple.

can·dle·pow·er (kăn′dl-pou′ər) *n.* The brightness or intensity of a source of light as expressed in candelas.

can·dle·snuff·er (kăn′dl-snŭf′ər) *n.* An instrument with a small cup and often a long slender handle, used to extinguish the flame of a candle.

can·dle·stick (kăn′dl-stĭk′) *n.* A usually tall holder with a cup or spike for a candle.

can·dle·wick (kăn′dl-wĭk′) *n.* The wick of a candle.

can-do (kăn′do͞o′) *adj.* Marked by willingness to tackle a job and confidence in the ability to finish it: *the can-do spirit of volunteers.*

can·dor (kăn′dər) *n.* **1.** The quality of saying freely what one thinks; openness; frankness: *criticize in all candor without regard to feelings.* **2.** Freedom from prejudice; fairness: *judge a matter in complete candor.*

can·dy (kăn′dē) *n., pl.* **can·dies 1.** A sweet food made with sugar and often combined with fruit or nuts. **2.** A single piece of this food. ❖ *v.* **can·died, can·dy·ing, can·dies** —*tr.* To cook, preserve, or coat with sugar or syrup: *candy apples.* —*intr.* To turn into sugar: *The molasses candied along the edges of the jar.* [From Middle English *candi,* crystallized cane sugar, ultimately from Arabic *qand,* cane sugar.]

candy cane *n.* A stick of peppermint candy, often white with red stripes, having a curved top like a walking cane.

candy strip·er (strī′pər) *n.* A volunteer worker in a hospital.

can·dy·tuft (kăn′dē-tŭft′) *n.* Any of several garden plants that have clusters of white, red, or light purple flowers.

cane (kān) *n.* **1.** A stick used as an aid in walking. **2a.** A thin hollow or woody plant stem that usually has joints and is easily bent. **b.** A plant, such as bamboo or sugar cane, having such stems. **c.** Strips of such stems woven together to make chair seats or other objects. **3.** A rod used in flogging. ❖ *tr.v.* **caned, can·ing, canes 1.** To beat or flog with a cane. **2.** To make or repair (furniture, for example) with cane.

cane·brake (kān′brāk′) *n.* A dense growth of cane plants.

cane sugar *n.* Sugar obtained from sugar cane.

ca·nine (kā′nīn) *adj.* Relating to or resembling a dog or a doglike mammal, such as a wolf, fox, or coyote. ❖ *n.* **1.** A dog or a doglike mammal. **2.** One of the four pointed teeth next to the incisors; a cuspid. [From Latin *canis,* dog.]

candelabrum

cane

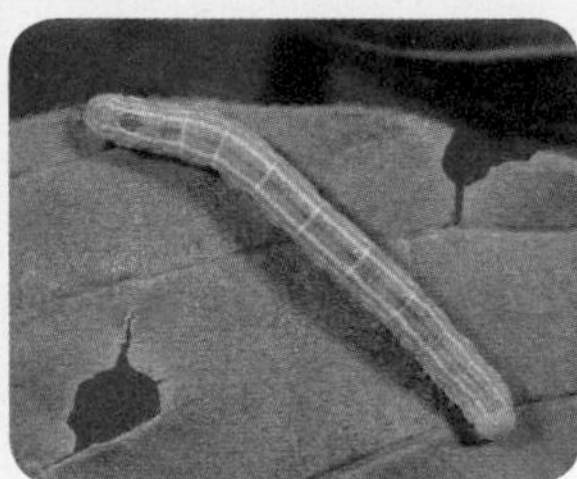
cankerworm

cannoli

canoe

canopy
canopy bed

ă pat	ô r core
ā pay	oi boy
âr care	ou out
ä father	ŏŏ took
ĕ pet	ŏŏr lure
ē be	ōō boot
ĭ pit	ŭ cut
ī bite	ûr urge
îr pier	th thin
ŏ pot	*th* this
ō toe	zh vision
ô paw	ə about

can·is·ter (kăn′ĭ-stər) *n.* A usually cylindrical container used to hold dry foods such as flour and coffee, film, or other materials.

can·ker (kăng′kər) *n.* A sore similar to an ulcer on the lips or in the mouth. [From Old English *cancer*, from Latin *cancer*, crab, disease.]

can·ker·ous (kăng′kər-əs) *adj.* **1.** Marked by or affected with a canker; ulcerous: *cankerous gums.* **2.** Tending to cause a canker: *a cankerous irritant.*

canker sore *n.* A canker.

can·ker·worm (kăng′kər-wûrm′) *n.* Either of two moth caterpillars that damage fruit trees and shade trees by feeding on the leaves.

can·na (kăn′ə) *n.* Any of various plants native to the tropics, having large leaves and showy red or yellow flowers.

can·na·bis (kăn′ə-bĭs) *n.* **1.** The hemp plant. **2.** The dried leaves or flowers of the hemp plant; marijuana.

canned (kănd) *adj.* **1.** Preserved and sealed in an airtight can or jar: *canned vegetables.* **2.** *Informal* Recorded or taped: *canned music.*

can·ner·y (kăn′ə-rē) *n., pl.* **can·ner·ies** A factory where fish, fruit, vegetables, or other foods are canned.

can·ni·bal (kăn′ə-bəl) *n.* **1.** A person who eats the flesh of other humans. **2.** An animal that feeds on others of its own kind. [From Spanish *Caníbalis*, name (as recorded by Christopher Columbus) of the supposedly cannibalistic Caribs of Cuba and Haiti, from earlier Carib *karibna*, person, Carib.]

can·ni·bal·ism (kăn′ə-bə-lĭz′əm) *n.* The practices of a cannibal. **—can′ni·bal·is′tic** *adj.*

can·ni·bal·ize (kăn′ə-bə-līz′) *tr.v.* **can·ni·bal·ized, can·ni·bal·iz·ing, can·ni·bal·iz·es 1.** To remove useful parts from (a machine or equipment) to use in the repair of other equipment: *cannibalize an old truck for its motor.* **2.** To practice cannibalism on.

can·no·li (kə-nō′lē) *n., pl.* **can·no·lis** A pastry roll with a creamy sweet filling.

can·non (kăn′ən) *n., pl.* **cannon** or **can·nons** A large gun that is mounted on wheels or on a fixed base and fires heavy projectiles. [From Middle English *canon*, from Old Italian *cannone*, large tube, from Latin *canna*, reed, cane, from Greek *kanna*.]

❑ *These sound alike:* **cannon, canon¹** (law), **canon²** (cleric).

can·non·ade (kăn′ə-**nād′**) *tr. & intr.v.* **can·non·ad·ed, can·non·ad·ing, can·non·ades** To assault or bombard with heavy artillery fire. ❖ *n.* A long heavy artillery assault or bombardment.

can·non·ball also **cannon ball** (kăn′ən-bôl′) *n.* **1.** An iron or steel ball fired from a cannon. **2.** A jump into water made with the arms grasping the knees, usually intended to make a big splash.

can·not (kăn′ŏt *or* kə-**nŏt′** *or* kă-**nŏt′**) *aux.v.* The negative form of **can¹**.

can·ny (kăn′ē) *adj.* **can·ni·er, can·ni·est** Careful and shrewd in one's actions and dealings: *a canny investor.* **—can′ni·ly** *adv.* **—can′ni·ness** *n.*

ca·noe (kə-nōō′) *n.* A light, open, narrow boat that has pointed ends and is propelled by paddles. ❖ *intr.v.* **ca·noed, ca·noe·ing, ca·noes** To paddle or travel in a canoe. **—ca·noe′ist** *n.*

ca·no·la oil (kə-nō′lə) *n.* An oil made from the seeds of certain varieties of the rape plant, used in cooking and in industry as a lubricant.

can·on¹ (kăn′ən) *n.* **1.** A law or code of laws enacted by a church. **2.** A principle or standard: *the canons of good behavior.* **3.** The books of the Bible accepted by a Christian church as authentic. **4.** A group of literary works generally accepted as important in a field: *the canon of Latin American literature.* **5.** A musical composition or passage in which a melody is repeated by different, overlapping voices. [From Middle English *canoun*, from Old English *canon*, from Latin *canōn*, rule, from Greek *kanōn*, measuring rod, rule.]

❑ *These sound alike:* **canon¹** (law), **cannon** (gun), **canon²** (cleric).

can·on² (kăn′ən) *n.* **1.** A cleric serving in a cathedral or collegiate church. **2.** A member of certain religious communities living according to established rules. [From Middle English *canoun*, from Late Latin *canōnicus*, one living under a rule, from Greek *kanōn*, measuring rod.]

❑ *These sound alike:* **canon²** (cleric), **cannon** (gun), **canon¹** (law).

ca·non·i·cal (kə-nŏn′ĭ-kəl) also **ca·non·ic** (kə-nŏn′ĭk) *adj.* **1.** Relating to or required by canon law. **2.** Relating to or appearing in the biblical canon. **3.** Relating to a literary canon: *canonical works of Romantic poetry.* **4.** Conforming to well-established rules or patterns.

can·on·ize (kăn′ə-nīz′) *tr.v.* **can·on·ized, can·on·iz·ing, can·on·iz·es** To declare (a dead person) to be a saint. **—can′on·i·za′tion** (kăn′ə-nĭ-zā′shən) *n.*

canon law *n.* The body of laws governing matters of faith and practice in a religious denomination, especially a Christian church.

can·o·py (kăn′ə-pē) *n., pl.* **can·o·pies 1.** A covering, usually of cloth, hung above a bed or throne or supported by poles above an important person or a sacred object. **2.** A similar covering: *a canopy of leafy branches.* **3.** The transparent movable enclosure over the cockpit of certain aircraft. ❖ *tr.v.* **can·o·pied, can·o·py·ing, can·o·pies** To cover with a canopy.

canst (kănst) *aux.v. Archaic* A second person singular present tense of **can¹**.

cant¹ (kănt) *n.* **1.** A slant or slope: *The cant of the roof makes the rain run off.* **2a.** A push or motion that causes something to tilt to one side. **b.** The tilt resulting from such a push or motion. ❖ *v.* **cant·ed, cant·ing, cants** *—tr.* **1.** To give a slanted edge to; bevel. **2.** To cause to slant or tilt to one side: *A gust of wind canted the sailboat so that it capsized.* *—intr.* **1.** To tilt or slant to one side or turn over: *The sailboat's masts cant slightly as it sails.* **2.** To swing around: *In a sudden turn the boat canted off toward the south.* [From Middle English *cant*, side, from Latin *canthus*, rim of a wheel, tire, of Celtic origin.]

❑ *These sound alike:* **cant¹** (slope), **cant²** (talk), **can't** (can not).

cant² (kănt) *n.* **1.** Insincere or trite talk, especially about moral or religious behavior: *hollow words that are mere cant.* **2.** The special vocabulary used by a certain group or class of people; jargon: *"Deadheading" is railroad cant for running without passengers or freight.* [From Anglo-Norman *canter*, to sing, from Latin *cantāre*.]

❑ *These sound alike:* **cant²** (talk), **cant¹** (slope), **can't** (can not).

can't (kănt) Contraction of *cannot.*

❑ *These sound alike:* **can't, cant¹** (slope), **cant²** (talk).

can·ta·loupe also **can·ta·loup** (kăn′tl-ōp′) *n.* A variety of melon having a rough rind and sweet orange flesh.

can·tan·ker·ous (kăn-tăng′kər-əs) *adj.* Quarrelsome and ill-tempered; disagreeable: *a cantankerous professor who is difficult to study with.* **—can·tan′ker·ous·ly** *adv.* **—can·tan′ker·ous·ness** *n.*

can·ta·ta (kən-tä′tə) *n.* A musical composition, often using a sacred text, containing recitatives, arias, and choruses.

can·teen (kăn-tēn′) *n.* **1.** A container for carrying water or other liquid to drink. **2.** A store, restaurant, or recreational facility meant for the use of soldiers, especially on a military base. **3.** A place to get food or drinks in a school, factory, or camp.

can·ter (kăn′tər) *n.* A slow easy gallop. ❖ *intr. & tr.v.* **can·tered, can·ter·ing, can·ters** To move or cause to move at a canter: *The horse and rider cantered down the road. She cantered her horse across the field.*

❑ *These sound alike:* **canter, cantor** (singer).

Can·ter·bur·y (**kăn′**tər-bĕr′ē) A city of southeast England east-southeast of London. Its cathedral was an important medieval pilgrimage site.

can·ti·cle (**kăn′**tĭ-kəl) *n.* A song or chant, especially a hymn whose words are taken from a biblical text other than the Book of Psalms.

can·ti·le·ver (**kăn′**tl-ē′vər *or* **kăn′**tl-ĕv′ər) *n.* A projecting structure, such as a beam, that is supported only at one end and carries a load at the other end or along its length. ❖ *tr.v.* **can·ti·le·vered, can·ti·le·ver·ing, can·ti·le·vers** To support by a cantilever.

cantilever bridge *n.* A bridge formed by two cantilevers each supported at one end by a pier and joined in the center by a connecting piece.

can·tle (**kăn′**tl) *n.* The raised part at the back of some saddles.

can·to (**kăn′**tō) *n., pl.* **can·tos** A principal division of a long poem.

can·ton (**kăn′**tən *or* **kăn′**tŏn′) *n.* A small division of a country, especially one of the states of Switzerland.

Can·ton (**kăn′**tŏn′ *or* kăn′**tŏn′**) See **Guangzhou.**

Can·ton·ese (kăn′tə-**nēz′** *or* kăn′tə-**nēs′**) *n., pl.* **Cantonese 1.** A native or inhabitant of Guangzhou (formerly Canton). **2.** The variety of Chinese spoken in and around Guangzhou. **—Can′ton·ese′** *adj.*

can·ton·ment (kăn-**tōn′**mənt *or* kăn-**tŏn′**mənt) *n.* **1.** A group of structures for housing soldiers, often on a temporary basis. **2.** A military installation in India.

can·tor (**kăn′**tər) *n.* **1.** The official who leads the congregation in the musical part of a Jewish religious service. **2.** The person who leads a church choir or congregation in singing.

❑ *These sound alike:* **cantor, canter** (gait of a horse).

can·vas (**kăn′**vəs) *n.* **1.** A heavy coarse cloth of cotton, hemp, or flax, used for making tents and sails. **2a.** A piece of canvas used for painting. **b.** An oil painting on canvas: *That artist has several canvases hanging in this museum.*

❑ *These sound alike:* **canvas, canvass** (survey).

can·vas·back (**kăn′**vəs-băk′) *n.* A North American duck having a reddish head and neck and a whitish back in the male.

can·vass (**kăn′**vəs) *v.* **can·vassed, can·vass·ing, can·vass·es** *—tr.* **1.** To visit (a person or region) asking for votes, opinions, sales, or contributions. **2.** To examine or discuss thoroughly: *canvass the newspapers for a job; canvass ideas in a meeting.* *—intr.* To go about a region asking for votes, sales, opinions, or contributions: *canvassed for votes.* ❖ *n.* **1.** The act of canvassing. **2.** A thorough examination or discussion. **—can′vass·er** *n.*

❑ *These sound alike:* **canvass, canvas** (cloth).

can·yon (**kăn′**yən) *n.* A deep narrow valley with steep cliff walls, cut into the earth by running water; a gorge. [From Spanish *cañón.*]

caou·tchouc (**kou′**cho͝ok′ *or* **kou′**cho͝ok′) *n.* Crude natural rubber.

cap¹ (kăp) *n.* **1a.** A usually soft, close-fitting head covering, either having no brim or with a visor. **b.** A special covering for the head worn to show rank, occupation, or membership in a group: *a soldier's cap.* **2.** A protective cover or seal: *a bottle cap; a cap on a tooth.* **3.** A truck cap. **4.** The umbrella-shaped or rounded cap of a mushroom, where the spores are produced. **5a.** The top or highest part: *the polar cap.* **b.** A limit or restraint: *a cap on government spending.* **6a.** A percussion cap. **b.** A small explosive charge enclosed in paper for use in a toy gun. ❖ *tr.v.* **capped, cap·ping, caps 1.** To cover, protect, or seal with a cap: *cap a bottle; hills capped with snow.* **2.** To outdo; excel: *Each joke capped the one before.*
◆ **cap in hand** Humbly or submissively.

cap² (kăp) *n.* A capital letter.

cap. *abbr.* An abbreviation of: **1.** capacity. **2.** capital. **3.** capital letter.

ca·pa·bil·i·ty (kā′pə-**bĭl′**ĭ-tē) *n., pl.* **ca·pa·bil·i·ties 1.** The quality of being capable; ability: *prove one's capability for the job.* **2.** often **capabilities** Potential ability: *live up to one's capabilities.* **3.** The capacity to be used or developed for a specific purpose: *To become more energy-efficient we must make full use of our technological capability.*

ca·pa·ble (**kā′**pə-bəl) *adj.* **1.** Having capacity or ability; able; competent: *a capable teacher.* **2.** Having the tendency or disposition: *She's just not capable of saying such a thing.* **3.** Having qualities that permit an action to be performed: *a statement capable of several interpretations.* **—ca′pa·bly** *adv.*

ca·pa·cious (kə-**pā′**shəs) *adj.* Capable of containing a large quantity; roomy: *a capacious dining room.* **—ca·pa′cious·ly** *adv.*

ca·pac·i·tance (kə-**păs′**ĭ-təns) *n.* The capacity of a device to collect and store electric charge. Capacitance is equal to the amount of stored charge divided by the electrical potential of the device.

ca·pac·i·tor (kə-**păs′**ĭ-tər) *n.* A device used in an electric circuit to store charge temporarily.

ca·pac·i·ty (kə-**păs′**ĭ-tē) *n., pl.* **ca·pac·i·ties 1.** The ability to hold, receive, or contain: *a can with a capacity of three quarts; a theater with a small seating capacity.* **2.** The maximum amount that can be contained: *a trunk filled to capacity.* **3.** The ability to perform or produce; capability: *a comedian's capacity to make people laugh.* **4.** The maximum amount that can be produced: *a machine operating at full capacity.* **5.** Mental ability: *a person's capacity for learning.* **6.** The position in which a person functions; a role: *in your capacity as sales manager.*

ca·par·i·son (kə-**păr′**ĭ-sən) *n.* **1.** An ornamental covering for a horse or harness. **2.** Rich or fancy clothing; finery. ❖ *tr.v.* **ca·par·i·soned, ca·par·i·son·ing, ca·par·i·sons 1.** To put a caparison on: *caparison a horse.* **2.** To dress in splendid clothes.

cape¹ (kāp) *n.* **1.** A sleeveless outer garment fastened at the throat and worn hanging loose over the shoulders. **2.** A brightly colored cloth used by a matador to maneuver the bull in a bullfight. [From Late Latin *cappa,* cloak.]

cape² (kāp) *n.* A point of land projecting into a body of water. [From Middle English *cap,* from Latin *caput,* head.]

Cape or **Cape of** For the names of actual capes, see the specific proper name; for example, **Cod, Cape.**

Cape Bret·on Island (**brĕt′**n) An island forming the northeast part of Nova Scotia, Canada.

ca·per¹ (**kā′**pər) *n.* **1.** A playful leap or hop: *the capers of a frisky pony.* **2.** A prank: *Halloween capers.* **3.** *Slang* A criminal plot or act, especially one involving theft. ❖ *intr.v.* **ca·pered, ca·per·ing, ca·pers** To jump about playfully; gambol: *The lambs capered about the meadow.* [Alteration of French *capriole,* a leap by a horse, from Italian *capriola,* somersault, from Latin *caper,* goat.]

ca·per² (**kā′**pər) *n.* **1.** A pickled flower bud of a spiny shrub of the Mediterranean region. Capers are used to flavor sauces and relishes. **2.** The shrub that bears such buds. [From Middle English *capar,* from Greek *kapparis.*]

Cape Town or **Cape·town** (**kāp′**toun′) The legislative capital of South Africa, in the extreme southwest part of the country on the Atlantic Ocean. It was founded in 1652.

Cape Verde (vûrd) An island country of the Atlantic Ocean west of Senegal. Praia is the capital.

cap·il·lar·i·ty (kăp′ə-**lăr′**ĭ-tē) *n.* Capillary action.

cantaloupe

cantilever bridge
Forth railway bridge over the firth of Forth, Scotland

cantle
cantle on an English-style saddle

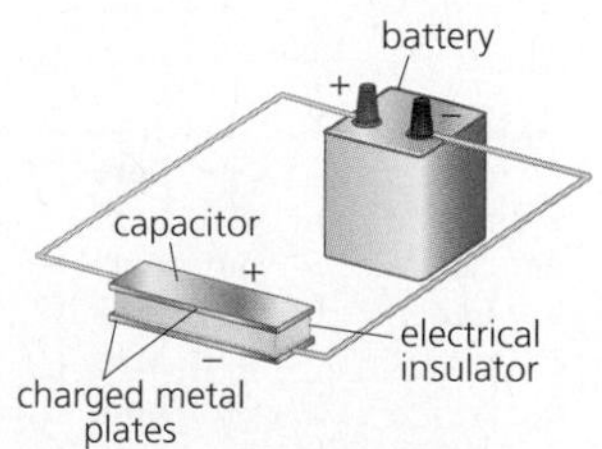

capacitor

USAGE

capital The word for a town or city that serves as a seat of government is **capital**: *Sacramento is the capital of California.* The term for the building in which a legislative assembly meets is **capitol**: *Daily tours of the capitol are offered.*

cap·il·lar·y (kăp′ə-lĕr′ē) *adj.* **1.** Relating to or resembling a hair; fine; slender. **2.** Having a very small inside diameter. **3.** Relating to the capillaries in the body. ❖ *n., pl.* **cap·il·lar·ies 1.** One of the tiny blood vessels that connect the smallest arteries to the smallest veins. **2.** A tube that has a very small inside diameter.

capillary action *n.* The tendency of the surface of a liquid to rise or fall where it is in contact with a solid, as in a capillary tube.

capillary attraction *n.* The force that causes a liquid to rise in a narrow tube or when in contact with a porous substance. It is the force that allows a paper towel to soak up a liquid or plants to draw up water from the ground.

cap·i·tal[1] (**kăp′**ĭ-tl) *n.* **1.** A city that is the seat of a state or national government: *Every state has a capital.* **2.** Wealth in the form of money or property that has accumulated in a business and is often used to create more wealth. **3.** Assets or resources that can be used to accomplish something: *Does the president have the political capital to get the law passed?* **4.** A capital letter. ❖ *adj.* **1.** First and foremost; principal: *a decision of capital importance.* **2.** Excellent; first-rate: *a capital idea.* **3.** Punishable by or involving death: *a capital offense.* **4.** Relating to or involving wealth and its use in investment: *capital improvements in the plant site.* **5.** Relating to a seat of government: *a capital city.* [From Middle English *capital*, principal, from Latin *capitālis*, from *caput*, head, money laid out.] —SEE NOTE.

❑ *These sound alike:* **capital[1]** (city), **capital[2]** (top of a column), **capitol** (building).

capital[2]
Corinthian capital

cap·i·tal[2] (**kăp′**ĭ-tl) *n.* The top part of a pillar or column. [From Middle English, from Late Latin *capitellum*, diminutive of Latin *caput*, head.]

❑ *These sound alike:* **capital[2]** (top of a column), **capital[1]** (city), **capitol** (building).

capital gain *n.* The profit made by selling an investment, such as a stock or piece of property.

cap·i·tal·ism (**kăp′**ĭ-tl-ĭz′əm) *n.* An economic system in which the means of production and distribution are privately owned by individuals or groups, and competition for business establishes the price of goods and services. The means of production include labor, land, factories, and services. The means of distribution include trains, trucks, and airlines.

Capitol
US Capitol building, Washington, DC

cap·i·tal·ist (**kăp′**ĭ-tl-ĭst) *n.* **1a.** A person who invests capital in business, especially a large investor in an important business. **b.** A person of great wealth. **2.** A person who supports capitalism. ❖ *adj.* Relating to capitalism or capitalists: *a capitalist country.* **—cap′i·tal·is′tic** *adj.* **—cap′i·tal·is′ti·cal·ly** *adv.*

cap·i·tal·ize (**kăp′**ĭ-tl-īz′) *v.* **cap·i·tal·ized, cap·i·tal·iz·ing, cap·i·tal·iz·es** *—tr.* **1.** To write or print with a capital letter or letters: *capitalize the title of a report.* **2.** To supply with capital or funds. *—intr.* To turn to advantage; profit by: *capitalize on an opponent's errors.* **—cap′i·tal·i·za′tion** (kăp′ĭ-tl-ĭ-**zā′**shən) *n.*

capital letter *n.* A letter, such as A or B, written or printed in a size larger than and often in a form differing from its corresponding lowercase letter.

cap·i·tal·ly (**kăp′**ĭ-tl-ē) *adv.* In an excellent manner; admirably.

capital punishment *n.* The legal punishment of putting a person to death for certain crimes, such as murder or treason.

capital ship *n.* A warship of the largest class, such as a battleship or an aircraft carrier.

capital stock *n.* The total amount of stock issued by a corporation, including common and preferred stock.

cap·i·tol (**kăp′**ĭ-tl) *n.* **1. Capitol** The building in Washington DC where the Congress of the United States meets. **2.** A building in which a state legislature assembles. [From Middle English *Capitol*, Jupiter's temple in Rome, from Latin *Capitōlium*.] —SEE NOTE AT **capital[1]**.

❑ *These sound alike:* **capitol, capital[1]** (city), **capital[2]** (top of a column).

ca·pit·u·late (kə-**pĭch′**ə-lāt′) *intr.v.* **ca·pit·u·lat·ed, ca·pit·u·lat·ing, ca·pit·u·lates** To surrender under stated conditions; give in; yield: *The soldiers capitulated to the enemy after a long siege.*

ca·pit·u·la·tion (kə-pĭch′ə-**lā′**shən) *n.* **1.** The act of capitulating: *capitulation in the face of defeat.* **2.** A statement of the main points of a topic; an outline.

cap·let (**kăp′**lĭt) *n.* A tablet of medicine coated to make it easy to swallow.

ca·pon (**kā′**pŏn′ *or* **kā′**pən) *n.* A male chicken that has been castrated when young to improve the quality of its flesh for food.

cap·puc·ci·no (kăp′ə-**chē′**nō) *n., pl.* **cap·puc·ci·nos** A drink made with espresso coffee and steamed milk.

ca·price (kə-**prēs′**) *n.* An impulsive change of mind; a whim: *the caprices of a vain and immature person.* [From Italian *capriccio*, from *caporiccio*, fright, sudden start : *capo*, head + *riccio*, curly.]

ca·pri·cious (kə-**prĭsh′**əs *or* kə-**prē′**shəs) *adj.* Subject to sudden unpredictable changes: *a capricious child; capricious weather.* **—ca·pri′cious·ly** *adv.* **—ca·pri′cious·ness** *n.*

Cap·ri·corn (**kăp′**rĭ-kôrn′) *n.* **1.** A constellation in the Southern Hemisphere, traditionally pictured as a goat with the body of a fish. **2.** The tenth sign of the zodiac in astrology. [From Middle English, from Latin *Capricornus* : *caper*, goat + *cornū*, horn.]

ca·pri pants (kə-**prē′**) *pl.n.* Tight-fitting, calf-length pants, usually worn by women.

ca·pris (kə-**prēz′**) *pl.n.* Capri pants.

cap·size (**kăp′**sīz′ *or* kăp-**sīz′**) *intr. & tr.v.* **cap·sized, cap·siz·ing, cap·siz·es** To overturn or cause to overturn: *Our boat did not capsize in the storm. A huge wave capsized the ship.*

cap·stan (**kăp′**stən *or* **kăp′**stăn′) *n.* An apparatus used for lifting an anchor or other heavy weight, consisting of a vertical cylinder that is rotated manually or by machine and around which a cable is wound.

cap·stone (**kăp′**stōn′) *n.* **1.** The top stone of a structure or wall. **2.** A crowning achievement; a culmination: *The Pulitzer Prize was the capstone of her long career in journalism.*

cap·su·lar (**kăp′**sə-lər *or* **kăp′**syo͞o-lər) *adj.* Relating to or enclosed in a capsule: *a medicine in capsular form.*

cap·sule (**kăp′**səl *or* **kăp′**so͞ol) *n.* **1.** A small container, usually of gelatin or another soluble material, that contains a dose of a medicine to be taken by mouth. **2.** A covering, such as a membrane, that encloses an organ or another part of the body. **3.** An outer shell composed of carbohydrates that surrounds a microscopic organism, especially a bacterium. **4.** A seed case that opens when ripe. **5.** A space capsule. ❖ *adj.* Very brief; condensed: *a capsule description.* [From Latin *capsula*, diminutive of *capsa*, box.]

Capt. or **CAPT** *abbr.* An abbreviation of captain.

cap·tain (**kăp′**tən) *n.* **1.** The leader of a group; chief: *the captain of the football team.* **2.** The person in command of a ship, aircraft, or spacecraft: *the captain of a tugboat; the captain of a 747 jet.* **3.** An officer in the US Army, Air Force, or Marine Corps ranking above a first lieutenant and below a major. **4.** An officer in the US Navy or Coast Guard ranking above a commander and below a commodore. **5.** An officer in a police or fire department ranking above a lieutenant. **6.** A person who is in the forefront of an enterprise; a leader: *a captain of industry.* ❖ *tr.v.* **cap·tained, cap·tain·ing, cap·tains** To command or direct; lead: *captain a soccer team; captain a*

ă	pat	ôr	core
ā	pay	oi	boy
âr	care	ou	out
ä	father	o͝o	took
ĕ	pet	o͝or	lure
ē	be	o͞o	boot
ĭ	pit	ŭ	cut
ī	bite	ûr	urge
îr	pier	th	thin
ŏ	pot	*th*	this
ō	toe	zh	vision
ô	paw	ə	about

ship. [From Middle English *capitain*, from Late Latin *capitāneus*, chief, from Latin *caput*, head.]

cap·tain·cy (kăp′tən-sē) *n., pl.* **cap·tain·cies** The rank, authority, or skill of a captain.

cap·tain's chair (kăp′tənz) *n.* A wooden chair having a low back with extensions that curve forward to provide armrests.

cap·tion (kăp′shən) *n.* **1a.** A short explanation accompanying an illustration or photograph. **b.** Written dialogue placed at the bottom of television or movie frames. **2.** A heading, as of a legal document or a chapter of a book. ❖ *tr.v.* **cap·tioned, cap·tion·ing, cap·tions** To furnish a caption for.

cap·tious (kăp′shəs) *adj.* **1.** Inclined to criticize or find faults: *a captious movie critic.* **2.** Designed to confuse or ensnare, especially in an argument: *a captious question.* **—cap′tious·ly** *adv.* **—cap′tious·ness** *n.*

cap·ti·vate (kăp′tə-vāt′) *tr.v.* **cap·ti·vat·ed, cap·ti·vat·ing, cap·ti·vates** To fascinate or charm, as with wit, beauty, or intelligence: *The movie captivated audiences everywhere.* **—cap′ti·va′tion** *n.*

cap·tive (kăp′tĭv) *n.* A person held under restraint or in bondage; a prisoner. ❖ *adj.* **1.** Held as a prisoner, as in war. **2.** Kept under restraint or control; confined: *saw captive tigers at the zoo.*

cap·tiv·i·ty (kăp-tĭv′ĭ-tē) *n., pl.* **cap·tiv·i·ties** The condition or period of being held captive: *Few wild animals thrive in captivity.*

cap·tor (kăp′tər *or* kăp′tôr′) *n.* A person who takes or holds another as a captive.

cap·ture (kăp′chər) *tr.v.* **cap·tured, cap·tur·ing, cap·tures 1.** To get hold of, as by force or craft; seize: *Troops captured the rebel barricade.* **2.** To gain possession or control of: *The winner captured first prize.* **3.** To get or hold the interest of: *a mystery story that captures the imagination.* **4.** To hold or preserve in permanent form: *capture the sound of a howling wolf on tape.* ❖ *n.* **1.** The act of capturing or the process of being captured: *The capture of first prize was a triumph for our side.* **2.** Someone or something that has been captured: *The British warship was a great capture for the Colonial Navy.* [From Latin *captūra*, a catching of animals, from *capere*, to seize.]

cap·u·chin (kăp′yə-chĭn *or* kə-pyo͞o′chĭn) *n.* **1.** A member of an order of Franciscan friars that wear long pointed hoods. **2.** Any of several long-tailed monkeys of Central and South America that have a black or brown cap of hair on top of the head.

cap·y·ba·ra (kăp′ə-bär′ə *or* kăp′ə-băr′ə) *n.* A short-tailed South American rodent that lives in or near water and may grow to a length of 4 feet (1.2 meters). It is the largest living rodent.

car (kär) *n.* **1.** An automobile. **2.** A vehicle, such as a railroad car, that moves on rails. **3.** The part of an elevator or hot-air balloon that holds passengers or cargo. [From Middle English *carre*, cart, from Latin *carrus, carrum*, wagon, of Celtic origin.] —SEE NOTE.

car·a·bao (kä′rə-bou′) *n., pl.* **car·a·baos** A water buffalo of the Philippine Islands.

car·a·bi·ner (kăr′ə-bē′nər) *n.* An oblong metal ring with a hinged gate, used in activities such as mountaineering to secure ropes.

Ca·ra·cas (kə-rä′kəs) The capital of Venezuela, in the northern part of the country near the coast of the Caribbean Sea. It was founded by the Spanish in 1567.

ca·rafe (kə-răf′) *n.* **1.** A glass bottle for serving water or wine. **2.** A glass or metal container with a pouring spout, used in making or serving coffee.

car·a·mel (kăr′ə-məl *or* kär′məl) *n.* **1.** A smooth chewy candy made with sugar, butter, and cream or milk. **2.** Sugar heated to a brown syrup and used for coloring and sweetening foods.

car·a·pace (kăr′ə-pās′) *n.* A shell or bony covering on the back part of an animal such as a turtle or a lobster.

car·at (kăr′ət) *n.* **1.** A unit of weight for precious stones, equal to 200 milligrams or about 1/140 of an ounce. **2.** Variant of **karat.** [From Middle English, from Medieval Latin *quarātus*, from Arabic *qīrāṭ*, weight of four grains, from Greek *kerātion*, weight of four grains, diminutive of *keras*, horn.]

❑ *These sound alike:* **carat, caret** (proofreader's mark), **carrot** (plant), **karat** (measure of gold).

car·a·van (kăr′ə-văn′) *n.* **1.** A group of travelers journeying together for safety in hostile regions such as the desert. **2.** A group of vehicles or pack animals traveling together in single file: *The caravan of trucks crossed over the mountains.* **3.** *Chiefly British* A home on wheels, as a trailer or camper. [From Persian *kārvān*.]

car·a·van·sa·ry (kăr′ə-văn′sə-rē) also **car·a·van·se·rai** (kăr′ə-văn′sə-rī′) *n., pl.* **car·a·van·sa·ries** also **car·a·van·se·rais** An inn with a large courtyard for the accommodation of caravans in central and western Asia.

car·a·vel (kăr′ə-vĕl′) *n.* A small light sailing ship with two to four masts used by the Spanish and Portuguese in the 1400s and 1500s.

car·a·way (kăr′ə-wā′) *n.* A plant native to Eurasia, having strong-tasting crescent-shaped seeds used as a flavoring in baking and cooking. [From Middle English *carewei*, from Arabic *karawyā*, from Greek *karō*.]

car·bide (kär′bīd′) *n.* A chemical compound, especially calcium carbide, consisting of carbon and a metal.

car·bine (kär′bēn′ *or* kär′bīn′) *n.* A light rifle with a short barrel.

car·bo·hy·drate (kär′bō-hī′drāt′) *n.* Any of a large class of organic compounds consisting of only carbon, hydrogen, and oxygen and serving as a major source of food in animal diets. Carbohydrates are produced in green plants by photosynthesis. Sugars, starches, and cellulose are carbohydrates.

car·bo·lat·ed (kär′bə-lā′tĭd) *adj.* Containing or treated with carbolic acid.

car·bol·ic acid (kär-bŏl′ĭk) *n.* Phenol.

car bomb *n.* An explosive device that is placed in a motor vehicle and detonated in order to kill people or destroy nearby property, especially as an act of terrorism.

car·bon (kär′bən) *n.* **1.** *Symbol* **C** A nonmetallic element that occurs in all organic compounds and many inorganic compounds, and can be found in all living things. Diamonds and graphite are pure carbon in the form of crystals; coal and charcoal are mostly carbon in uncrystallized form. Atomic number 6. See **Periodic Table. 2.** A gas containing carbon, such as carbon dioxide, or a collection of such gases, especially when considered as a contributor to the greenhouse effect: *equipment for measuring the carbon produced by power plants.* [From Latin *carbō*, a coal, charcoal.] **—car′bo·na′ceous** (kär′bə-nā′shəs), **car·bon′ic** (kär-bŏn′ĭk) *adj.*

car·bon-12 (kär′bən-twĕlv′) *n.* The most common isotope of carbon, used as the standard for determining atomic weights.

car·bon-14 (kär′bən-fôr-tēn′) *n.* A radioactive isotope of carbon that has an atomic mass of 14 and that occurs in all objects that contain carbon, notably animal and plant matter. Because the half-life of carbon-14 is 5,730 years, scientists can figure the age of archaeological materials and geologic formations that contain organic matter using radiocarbon dating.

car·bon·ate (kär′bə-nāt′) *tr.v.* **car·bon·at·ed, car·bon·at·ing, car·bon·ates** To add carbon dioxide gas to (a beverage) so that bubbles are produced upon release from a container: *Soda water is carbonated.* ❖ *n.* (kär′bə-nāt′ *or* kär′bə-nĭt) A salt or ester of carbonic acid. **—car′bon·a′tion** *n.* **—car′bon·a′tor** *n.*

car·bon·at·ed water (kär′bə-nā′tĭd) *n.* Water that has

capri pants

capuchin

WORD HISTORY

car Our word **car** comes from the Latin word *carrus*, "heavy two-wheeled wagon." Until the early 1800s, *car* meant "chariot" and was associated with dignity, solemnity, and splendor: *the sun rides in a celestial car in his orbit; the heroes of myth ride to battle in horse-drawn cars.* In about 1826 in the United States, *car* was used for a carriage pulled by a railway locomotive. *Motor car* first appears around 1895 for a horseless carriage. *Car* later came to mean any kind of wheeled vehicle and could be modified by words such as *passenger, freight,* and *street.*

been charged with carbon dioxide under pressure, used in various drinks and refreshments.

carbon copy *n.* **1a.** A duplicate of something written or typed, made by using carbon paper or a photocopier. **b.** A copy of an electronic document sent to people in addition to the addressed recipient. **2.** A person or thing that closely resembles another. ❖ *tr.v.* **carbon cop·ied, carbon cop·y·ing, carbon cop·ies 1a.** To reproduce something written or typed as a carbon copy. **b.** To send an electronic document as a carbon copy. **2.** To designate someone as the recipient of a carbon copy: *Carbon copy the lawyer on all correspondence regarding the contract.*

carbon cycle *n.* The circulation of carbon in nature through processes such as photosynthesis, respiration, decay, and combustion. For example, plants take in carbon dioxide from the atmosphere and convert it to carbohydrates through photosynthesis, and animals eat carbohydrates and release carbon dioxide through respiration.

carbon dating *n.* Radiocarbon dating.

carbon dioxide *n.* A colorless, odorless gas that does not burn, composed of carbon and oxygen in the proportion CO_2 and present in the atmosphere or formed when any fuel containing carbon is burned. It is exhaled from an animal's lungs during respiration and is used by plants in photosynthesis. Carbon dioxide is used in refrigeration, in fire extinguishers, and in carbonated drinks.

carbon footprint *n.* The amount of greenhouse gases containing carbon that are released into the environment by an activity, process, individual, or group, especially by the burning of fossil fuels.

carbonic acid *n.* A weak acid having the formula H_2CO_3. It exists only in solution and decomposes readily into carbon dioxide and water.

car·bon·if·er·ous (kär′bə-**nĭf′**ər-əs) *adj.* Producing or containing carbon or coal.

Carboniferous *n.* The geologic time comprising the Mississippian (or Lower Carboniferous) and Pennsylvanian (or Upper Carboniferous) Periods of the Paleozoic Era, from about 360 to 299 million years ago. During the Carboniferous, widespread swamps formed in which plant remains accumulated and later hardened into coal. See table at **geologic time.** **—Carboniferous** *adj.*

car·bon·ize (**kär′**bə-nīz′) *tr.v.* **car·bon·ized, car·bon·iz·ing, car·bon·iz·es 1.** To change an organic compound into carbon by heating. **2.** To treat, coat, or combine with carbon. **—car′bon·i·za′tion** (kär′bə-nĭ-**zā′**shən) *n.*

carbon monoxide *n.* A colorless odorless gas that is extremely poisonous and has the formula CO. Carbon monoxide is formed when carbon or a compound that contains carbon burns incompletely. It is present in the exhaust gases of automobile engines.

car·bon-neu·tral (kär′bən-**no͞o′**trəl) *adj.* Relating to a process or activity in which the total amount of carbon in carbon-containing gases released into the environment is offset by the amount of carbon in such gases removed from the environment.

carbon paper *n.* A lightweight paper coated on one side with a dark coloring matter, placed between two sheets of blank paper so that the bottom sheet will receive a copy of what is typed or written on the top sheet.

carbon tet·ra·chlo·ride (tĕt′rə-**klôr′**īd′) *n.* A colorless poisonous liquid composed of carbon and chlorine that does not burn, although it vaporizes easily. It is used in fire extinguishers and as a dry-cleaning fluid.

Car·bo·run·dum (kär′bə-**rŭn′**dəm) A trademark for an abrasive made of silicon carbide, used to cut, grind, and polish.

car·bun·cle (**kär′**bŭng′kəl) *n.* **1.** A painful inflammation in the tissue under the skin that is somewhat like a boil but releases pus from several openings. **2.** A red precious stone, especially a deep-red garnet.

car·bu·re·tor (**kär′**bə-rā′tər *or* **kär′**byə-rā′tər) *n.* A device in a gasoline engine that vaporizes the gasoline with air to form an explosive mixture. [From *carburet*, carbide, from Latin *carbō*, carbon.]

car·cass (**kär′**kəs) *n.* **1.** The dead body of an animal. **2.** The body of a human. **3.** The remains of something: *the carcasses of old cars in a junkyard.*

car·cin·o·gen (kär-**sĭn′**ə-jən) *n.* A substance or agent that can cause cancer. Asbestos and tobacco products are examples of carcinogens. **—car′cin·o·gen′ic** (kär′sə-nə-**jĕn′**ĭk) *adj.*

car·ci·no·ma (kär′sə-**nō′**mə) *n., pl.* **car·ci·no·mas** or **car·ci·no·ma·ta** (kär′sə-**nō′**mə-tə) A cancerous growth on the surface of the skin, blood vessels, or other organ or structure. [From Greek *karkinōma*, from *karkinos*, cancer.]

card[1] (kärd) *n.* **1.** A small, usually rectangular piece of stiff paper, cardboard, or plastic: *The address file is filled with cards.* **2.** One of a set of 52 pieces of stiff heavy paper bearing numbers or figures and divided into four suits, used for various games and for telling fortunes; a playing card. **3. cards** *(used with a singular or plural verb)* **a.** A game played with one or more sets of 52 cards. **b.** The playing of such games. **4a.** A piece of stiff paper, often printed with a picture or message, used to send a note or greeting. **b.** A postcard. **5.** A stiff piece of paper bearing information, such as a person's name and email address or a book's title and author, and used for identification or classification: *a business card.* **6.** A stiff piece of paper bearing the image and often the statistics of a sports figure. **7.** A credit card or bankcard. **8.** A circuit board, especially for use in a computer. **9.** *Informal* An amusing or eccentric person: *Our cousin is quite a card and entertains everyone with jokes.* ◆ **in the cards** Likely; probable. **put (one's) cards on the table** or **lay (one's) cards on the table** To be frank and clear, as in one's intentions. [From Middle English *carde*, from Greek *khartēs*, paper made from papyrus.]

card[2] (kärd) *n.* A brush with teeth of wire, used to comb fibers of wool, flax, or cotton before spinning. ❖ *tr.v.* **card·ed, card·ing, cards** To comb with a card: *card wool.* [From Middle English, from Latin *carduus*, thistle.]

card·board (**kärd′**bôrd′) *n.* A material similar to thick, stiff, heavy paper and made of pressed paper pulp or pasted sheets of paper.

card catalog *n.* An alphabetical listing, especially of books in a library, containing information about each item. A card catalog usually exists as separate cards kept in a series of drawers or as a collection of electronic records.

card·hold·er (**kärd′**hōl′dər) *n.* A person who owns a card, especially a credit card.

car·di·ac (**kär′**dē-ăk′) *adj.* Relating to the heart: *a cardiac disorder.* [From Middle English *cardiac*, vein associated with the heart, from Greek *kardiakos*, from *kardiā*, heart.]

cardiac arrest *n.* Sudden stoppage of the heartbeat.

Car·diff (**kär′**dĭf) The capital of Wales, in the southeast part west of London, England.

car·di·gan (**kär′**dĭ-gən) *n.* A knitted sweater or jacket that opens down the full length of the front. [After the Seventh Earl of *Cardigan*, James Thomas Brudenell (1797–1868), British army officer.]

car·di·nal (**kär′**dn-əl *or* **kärd′**nəl) *adj.* Of primary importance; chief; foremost: *A good design is the cardinal element of a successful building.* ❖ *n.* **1.** An official of the Roman Catholic Church who is appointed by a pope and whose rank is just below that of the pope. **2.** A North American bird having a crested head and bright

cardigan

cargo pants

ă	pat	ôr	core
ā	pay	oi	boy
âr	care	ou	out
ä	father	o͝o	took
ĕ	pet	o͝or	lure
ē	be	o͞o	boot
ĭ	pit	ŭ	cut
ī	bite	ûr	urge
îr	pier	th	thin
ŏ	pot	*th*	this
ō	toe	zh	vision
ô	paw	ə	about

red feathers in the male. **3.** A cardinal number. [From Middle English, from Late Latin *cardinālis*, principal, pivotal, from Latin *cardō*, hinge.]

cardinal flower *n.* A plant of eastern North America that bears a cluster of brilliant scarlet flowers.

cardinal number *n.* A number, such as 3 or 11 or 412, used in counting to indicate quantity but not order.

cardinal point *n.* One of the four principal directions on a compass; north, south, east, or west.

card·ing (**kär′**dĭng) *n.* The cleaning and combing of fibers, such as wool, cotton, or flax, to prepare them for spinning into yarn.

car·di·o·gram (**kär′**dē-ə-grăm′) *n.* An electrocardiogram.

car·di·ol·o·gist (kär′dē-**ŏl′**ə-jĭst) *n.* A physician who specializes in cardiology.

car·di·ol·o·gy (kär′dē-**ŏl′**ə-jē) *n.* The branch of medicine that deals with the diagnosis and treatment of disorders of the heart.

car·di·o·pul·mo·nar·y (kär′dē-ō-**pŏŏl′**mə-nĕr′ē *or* kär′-dē-ō-**pŭl′**mə-nĕr′ē) *adj.* Relating to the heart and lungs.

cardiopulmonary resuscitation *n.* A procedure used to restore normal breathing and circulation after a person's heart has stopped beating. It employs mouth-to-mouth resuscitation, pushing on the chest to force blood from the heart, and sometimes drugs.

car·di·o·vas·cu·lar (kär′dē-ō-**văs′**kyə-lər) *adj.* Relating to or involving the heart and blood vessels: *cardiovascular disease.*

care (kâr) *n.* **1a.** A feeling of fear, doubt, or anxiety; worry: *on vacation and free from care.* **b.** An object or source of worry, attention, or concern: *The cares of running a business are many.* **2a.** Close attention, as in doing something well or avoiding harm: *did his homework with care; handled the package with care.* **b.** Upkeep; maintenance: *products for hair care.* **c.** Watchful oversight; charge or supervision: *The patient was left in the care of a nurse.* **3.** Attentive assistance or treatment to those in need: *a hospital that provides emergency care.* ❖ *v.* **cared, car·ing, cares** —*intr.* **1.** To be concerned or interested: *I don't care about going.* **2.** To provide protection or help: *Who will care for the dog while we are away?* **3.** To object or mind: *Would you care if I turned on the radio?* **4a.** To have a liking; like: *Do you really care for that person? Some people don't care for fish.* **b.** To have a wish; be inclined: *Would you care for another helping of peas?* —*tr.* **1.** To wish; desire: *Would you care to go for a walk?* **2.** To be concerned or interested in: *I don't care what they think.* ◆ **in care of** At the address of or in the name of: *Address all letters for the club in care of the secretary.*

SYNONYMS care, charge, keeping, trust These nouns refer to the function of watching, guarding, or overseeing something. *My neighbors left their dog in my care when they went on vacation. Who is in charge of the team's equipment? I left the key in my sister's keeping. My parents committed their important papers to the bank's trust.*

---

ca·reen (kə-**rēn′**) *v.* **ca·reened, ca·reen·ing, ca·reens** —*intr.* **1.** To lurch or swerve while in motion: *The car careened on the icy road.* **2.** To lean to one side, as a ship: *The ship careened wildly in the heavy winds.* —*tr.* **1.** To lean (a ship) onto its side for cleaning or repairing. **2.** To cause to lean to one side: *Strong winds will careen a small sailboat.*

ca·reer (kə-**rîr′**) *n.* **1.** A profession or occupation: *considering a career in medicine.* **2.** The general progress or course of one's life, especially in one's profession: *a police officer with a distinguished career.* ❖ *intr.v.* **ca·reered, ca·reer·ing, ca·reers** To move or run at full speed: *The startled horse went careering off through the meadow.*

care·free (**kâr′**frē′) *adj.* Free of worries or responsibilities: *a carefree vacation.*

care·ful (**kâr′**fəl) *adj.* **1.** Attentive to possible danger; cautious; prudent: *Be careful not to eat too much.* **2.** Done with care; thorough; conscientious: *a careful job on one's homework.* **3.** Showing concern; mindful; solicitous: *being careful of other people's feelings.* —**care′ful·ly** *adv.* —**care′ful·ness** *n.*

care·giv·er (**kâr′**gĭv′ər) *n.* A person who cares for older people, children, or people who are ill.

care·less (**kâr′**lĭs) *adj.* **1.** Taking insufficient care; negligent: *a careless worker; careless about one's appearance.* **2.** Done or made without care or attention: *a careless mistake.* **3.** Said or done without thought; inconsiderate: *a careless remark.* **4.** Free from cares; cheerful: *a careless smile.* —**care′less·ly** *adv.* —**care′less·ness** *n.*

ca·ress (kə-**rĕs′**) *n.* A gentle touch or gesture of fondness, tenderness, or love: *The child's caresses reassured the frightened cat.* ❖ *tr.v.* **ca·ressed, ca·ress·ing, ca·ress·es** To touch or stroke affectionately.

car·et (**kăr′**ĭt) *n.* A proofreading symbol (^) used to indicate where something is to be inserted in a line of printed or written material.

❑ *These sound alike:* **caret, carat** (weight of gems), **carrot** (plant), **karat** (measure of gold).

care·tak·er (**kâr′**tā′kər) *n.* A person employed to look after and take care of a thing, place, or person: *We hired a caretaker for our elderly aunt because she can't live alone anymore.*

care·worn (**kâr′**wôrn′) *adj.* Showing signs of worry or anxiety; haggard: *the parent's careworn face.*

car·fare (**kär′**fâr′) *n.* The amount charged for a ride, as on a subway or bus.

car·go (**kär′**gō) *n., pl.* **car·goes** or **car·gos** The freight carried by a ship, airplane, or other vehicle: *The freighter delivered its cargo at the wharf.* [From Spanish, from *cargar*, to load, from Late Latin *carricāre*, from Latin *carrus*, Gaulish wagon.]

cargo pants *pl.n.* Loose-fitting, usually cotton pants having large exterior pockets partway down the sides.

car·hop (**kär′**hŏp′) *n.* A person who waits on customers in their cars at a drive-in restaurant.

Car·ib (**kăr′**ĭb) *n., pl.* **Carib** or **Car·ibs 1.** also **Car·i·ban** (**kăr′**ə-bən *or* kə-**rē′**bən) A member of a group of American Indian peoples of northern South America and the Lesser Antilles in the Caribbean. **2.** Any of the languages of the Carib.

Car·i·ban (**kăr′**ə-bən *or* kə-**rē′**bən) *n., pl.* **Cariban** or **Car·i·bans 1.** Variant of **Carib** (sense 1). **2.** A family of American Indian languages spoken by the Carib. —**Car′i·ban** *adj.*

Car·ib·be·an (kăr′ə-**bē′**ən *or* kə-**rĭb′**ē-ən) *adj.* **1.** Relating to the Caribbean Sea, its islands, or coastal lands. **2.** Relating to the peoples or cultures of this region. **3.** Relating to the Carib or their language or culture. ❖ *n.* **1.** A Carib. **2.** The Caribbean Sea.

Caribbean Sea An arm of the western Atlantic Ocean bounded by the coasts of Central and South America and the West Indies.

car·i·bou (**kăr′**ə-bōō′) *n., pl.* **caribou** or **car·i·bous** A large deer of the Arctic tundra and northern forest regions of North America, having large spreading antlers in both the male and the female. Caribou and reindeer belong to the same species. [From Mi'kmaq *ĝalipu*.]

car·i·ca·ture (**kăr′**ĭ-kə-chŏŏr′ *or* **kăr′**ĭ-kə-chər) *n.* **1.** A picture or description of a person or thing in which certain distinctive features are greatly exaggerated or distorted to produce a comic effect. **2.** The art of creating such pictures or descriptions: *The cartoonist is a master of caricature.* ❖ *tr.v.* **car·i·ca·tured, car·i·ca·tur·ing, car·i·ca·tures** To represent in caricature: *He caricatures political figures.* —**car′i·ca·tur′ist** *n.*

caribou

caricature
photograph (*top*) and caricature (*bottom*) of author Charles Dickens

carob

ă pat | ā pay | âr care | ä father | ĕ pet | ē be | ĭ pit | ī bite | îr pier | ŏ pot | ō toe | ô paw | ôr core | oi boy | ou out | o͝o took | o͝or lure | o͞o boot | ŭ cut | ûr urge | th thin | *th* this | zh vision | ə about

car·ies (kâr′ēz) *n., pl.* **caries 1.** Decay of a bone or tooth. **2.** A cavity formed by decay in a tooth.

car·il·lon (kăr′ə-lŏn′ *or* kăr′ə-lən) *n.* A set of bells hung in a tower, usually played from a keyboard. [From French, alteration of Old French *quarregnon*, from Late Latin *quaterniō*, set of four.]

car·ing (kâr′ĭng) *adj.* Feeling and showing concern and compassion for others: *caring volunteers who helped raise money for charity.*

car·jack (kâr′jăk′) *tr.v.* **car·jacked, car·jack·ing, car·jacks** To seize or steal (a motor vehicle) from its driver. **—car′jack′er** *n.*

car·load (kär′lōd′) *n.* The number of passengers or the amount of cargo that a car can carry: *took a carload of children to the zoo.*

Car·mel·ite (kär′mə-līt′) *n.* **1.** A monk or friar belonging to a Roman Catholic order founded in 1155. **2.** A member of a community of nuns in this order, founded in 1452. **—Car′mel·ite′** *adj.*

car·mine (kär′mĭn *or* kär′mīn′) *n.* A deep or purplish red.

car·nage (kär′nĭj) *n.* Great slaughter, especially in war: *the carnage of battle.*

car·nal (kär′nəl) *adj.* **1.** Relating to bodily appetites; sensual. **2.** Worldly or earthly. **3.** Relating to the body: *carnal remains.* **—car′nal·ly** *adv.*

car·na·tion (kär-nā′shən) *n.* **1.** Any of numerous forms of a garden plant cultivated for its fragrant many-petaled white, pink, or red flowers. **2.** A flower of this plant.

car·nel·ian (kär-nēl′yən) *n.* A pale to deep red type of clear quartz used as a gem.

car·ni·val (kär′nə-vəl) *n.* **1.** A traveling amusement show that offers rides, games, and sideshows. **2.** often **Carnival** A period of celebrating and feasting just before Lent. **3.** A time of merrymaking; a festival.

car·ni·vore (kär′nə-vôr′) *n.* **1.** An animal that feeds on the flesh of other animals and generally has large sharp teeth. Dogs, cats, raccoons, and seals are carnivores. **2.** A plant that traps insects and absorbs nutrients from them.

car·niv·o·rous (kär-nĭv′ər-əs) *adj.* **1.** Feeding on the flesh of other animals: *Wolves are carnivorous.* **2.** Having leaves or other parts that trap insects and absorb nutrients from them: *carnivorous plants.* [From Latin *carnivorus* : *carō*, flesh + *-vorus*, eating.] **—car·niv′o·rous·ly** *adv.*

car·ob (kăr′əb) *n.* An evergreen tree of the Mediterranean region that has compound leaves and bears long pods used as food.

car·ol (kăr′əl) *n.* A song of joy, especially for Christmas. ❖ *intr.v.* **car·oled, car·ol·ing, car·ols** also **car·olled, car·ol·ling, car·ols 1.** To sing joyously. **2.** To go from house to house singing Christmas carols. **—car′ol·er, car′ol·ler** *n.*

❑ *These sound alike:* **carol, carrel** (library nook).

Car·o·li·nas (kăr′ə-lī′nəz) The colonies (after 1729) or present-day states of North Carolina and South Carolina.

Car·o·line Islands (kăr′ə-līn′ *or* kăr′ə-lĭn) A group of islands of the western Pacific Ocean east of the Philippines, consisting of Palau and the Federated States of Micronesia.

car·om (kăr′əm) *n.* **1.** A collision followed by a rebound, as of a ball bouncing off a wall. **2.** A shot in billiards or similar games in which the cue ball successively strikes two other balls. ❖ *intr.v.* **car·omed, car·om·ing, car·oms** To collide and rebound; make a carom: *The golf ball caromed off the tree.*

car·o·tene (kăr′ə-tēn′) *n.* An organic compound that occurs as an orange-yellow to red pigment in many plants and in animal tissue. It is converted to vitamin A by the liver.

ca·rot·id (kə-rŏt′ĭd) *n.* Either of the two large arteries in the neck that carry blood to the head. ❖ *adj.* Relating to either of these arteries.

ca·rous·al (kə-rou′zəl) *n.* A noisy riotous drinking party.

ca·rouse (kə-rouz′) *intr.v.* **ca·roused, ca·rous·ing, ca·rous·es** To have a noisy and enjoyable time with others, often while drinking alcohol. **—ca·rous′er** *n.*

car·ou·sel or **car·rou·sel** (kăr′ə-sĕl′) *n.* **1.** A merry-go-round. **2.** A circular conveyor on which objects are displayed or presented: *the baggage carousel at the airport.*

carp¹ (kärp) *intr.v.* **carped, carp·ing, carps** To find fault or complain in a petty or disagreeable way. [From Middle English *carpen*, from Old Norse *karpa*, to boast.]

carp² (kärp) *n., pl.* **carp** or **carps 1.** A large freshwater fish of Eurasia, often bred in ponds and lakes and used as food. **2.** Any of various related fishes. [From Middle English *carpe*, from Medieval Latin *carpa*, of Germanic origin.]

car·pal (kär′pəl) *adj.* Relating to the carpus or wrist. ❖ *n.* A bone of the carpus.

❑ *These sound alike:* **carpal, carpel** (flower pistil).

carpal tunnel syndrome *n.* A condition marked by pain and numbness in the hand, caused by compression of a nerve in the wrist.

car·pel (kär′pəl) *n.* A part of the pistil of a seed-bearing plant in which the seeds develop.

❑ *These sound alike:* **carpel, carpal** (bone).

car·pen·ter (kär′pən-tər) *n.* A person who builds or repairs wooden objects and structures such as cabinets, houses, and ships.

car·pen·try (kär′pən-trē) *n.* **1.** The work or trade of a carpenter. **2.** Woodwork done by a carpenter: *The palace is renowned for its intricate interior carpentry.*

car·pet (kär′pĭt) *n.* **1.** A thick heavy covering for a floor, usually made of woven wool or synthetic fibers; a rug. **2.** The fabric used for floor covering: *a roll of carpet.* **3.** Something that covers a surface like a carpet: *a carpet of pine needles on the forest floor.* ❖ *tr.v.* **car·pet·ed, car·pet·ing, car·pets** To cover with or as if with a carpet: *carpet the stairs.*

car·pet·bag (kär′pĭt-băg′) *n.* A traveling bag made of carpet fabric that was used chiefly in the United States during the 1800s.

car·pet·bag·ger (kär′pĭt-băg′ər) *n.* **1.** A Northerner who went to the South after the Civil War to make money by taking advantage of the unsettled conditions there. **2.** An outsider who aggressively seeks a position of advantage in a new place.

car·pet·ing (kär′pĭ-tĭng) *n.* **1.** Material used for carpets: *pretty red carpeting.* **2.** A carpet or carpets: *a room with wall-to-wall carpeting.*

car·pool also **car pool** (kär′po͞ol′) *n.* **1.** An arrangement among a number of car owners who agree to take turns driving each other or their children to a regular destination, such as work or school. **2.** A group of people forming a car pool.

car-pool (kär′po͞ol′) *v.* **car-pooled, car-pool·ing, car-pools** *—intr.* To travel in a car pool: *Four of us car-pool to work every day.* *—tr.* To transport by means of a car pool: *Several families car-pool their children to school.* **—car′-pool′er** *n.*

car·port (kär′pôrt′) *n.* A shelter for a car, usually formed by a roof projecting from the side of a building.

car·pus (kär′pəs) *n., pl.* **car·pi** (kär′pī′) **1.** The group of eight bones forming the joint between the hand and the forearm in humans; the wrist. **2.** The corresponding joint in four-footed animals.

Car·ran·za (kə-răn′zə *or* kä-rän′sä), **Venustiano** 1859–1920. Mexican revolutionary politician who was the first president (1915–1920) of the new Mexican Republic after the overthrow of Porfirio Díaz (1911).

car·rel (kăr′əl) *n.* A small enclosed area with a desk for study in a library.

❑ *These sound alike:* **carrel, carol** (song).

car·riage (kăr′ĭj) *n.* **1.** A wheeled passenger vehicle, usually drawn by horses. **2.** A small vehicle for a baby or a doll that is pushed by someone walking behind it. **3.** A wheeled structure on which a heavy object, such as a cannon, is moved. **4.** A movable part of a machine that often holds or shifts another part: *Many typewriters have a carriage that holds the paper and moves it in front of the keys.* **5.** The manner in which one's head or body is held; posture. **6.** The act of transporting: *The explorers used porters for the carriage of supplies up the mountain.* **7.** The costs of transporting: *Carriage was added to the bill.*

car·ri·er (kăr′ē-ər) *n.* **1.** A person or thing that transports or conveys: *a baggage carrier.* **2.** A person or business that deals in transporting passengers or goods: *Airlines, railroads, bus lines, and other carriers see an increase in business during holidays.* **3.** An aircraft carrier. **4.** A device or mechanism for moving or carrying something: *We attached our bikes to the carrier on top of the car.* **5a.** An organism that carries a disease agent in its body and is capable of transmitting it to others but usually shows no symptoms of disease. People who are carriers of typhoid, for example, can pass the bacteria on to others even though they do not feel sick. **b.** An organism that has one copy of a gene for a trait but shows no physical signs of the trait, usually because the gene is recessive. If two people who are carriers of a gene for cystic fibrosis have a child, for example, there is a chance that the child will inherit one copy of the gene from each parent and will develop the disease. **6.** A carrier wave. **7.** An organization that issues insurance policies or guarantees to pay off debts in case of a business failure. **8.** A telecommunications company.

carrier pigeon *n.* A homing pigeon.

carrier wave *n.* An electromagnetic wave whose amplitude or frequency is modulated to transmit speech, music, images, or other signals, as in radio broadcasting.

car·ri·on (kăr′ē-ən) *n.* The decaying flesh of dead animals: *Vultures feed on carrion.* [From Middle English *careine*, from Latin *carō*, flesh.]

Car·roll (kăr′əl), **Lewis** See Charles Lutwidge **Dodgson.**

car·rot (kăr′ət) *n.* **1.** A plant having feathery leaves and a long, tapering, yellow-orange root. **2.** The root of this plant, eaten as a vegetable. [From Greek *karōton.*]

❑ *These sound alike:* **carrot, carat** (weight of gems), **caret** (proofreader's mark), **karat** (measure of gold).

car·rou·sel (kăr′ə-sĕl′) *n.* Variant of **carousel.**

car·ry (kăr′ē) *v.* **car·ried, car·ry·ing, car·ries** —*tr.* **1.** To hold or support while moving; bear: *carry the groceries into the house.* **2.** To take from one place to another; transport: *Airlines carry passengers and freight.* **3.** To serve as a means of conveying; transmit: *The pipes carry water from the reservoir.* **4.** To cause to move; propel: *The wind carried the ball over the fence.* **5.** To sustain the weight or responsibility of; bear: *She is carrying a heavy load of courses this semester.* **6.** To keep or have on one's person: *carry an umbrella.* **7.** To be pregnant with (a child). **8.** To hold and move (oneself, one's body or a part of it) in a certain way: *Dancers carry themselves very gracefully.* **9.** To have in stock; have for sale: *Drugstores carry many different health products.* **10.** To sing (a tune or melody) in key: *carry a tune.* **11.** To put (a digit) into the next column to the left, as in performing addition. **12.** To have as an attribute, consequence, or effect; involve: *The washing machine carries a guarantee for one year.* **13.** To express or contain: *The engineer's report carried a grim warning about unsafe bridges.* **14a.** To win a majority of the votes in: *The president carried almost all the states.* **b.** To win support or acceptance for: *The proposition is carried by a large majority of votes.* **15.** To prolong, extend, or continue: *carry a joke too far.* **16.** To print or broadcast: *All the papers carried the story.* **17.** To be propelled over (a distance) or advance beyond (a point or object), as in a golf stroke: *Did my shot carry the trees?* **18.** In sports, to control and advance (a ball or puck). **19.** In basketball, to palm (the ball) in violation of the rules. —*intr.* **1.** To act as a bearer: *The dog could fetch and carry.* **2.** To be transmitted or conveyed: *a voice that carries well.* **3.** To be approved or accepted: *The proposal carried by a wide margin.* ❖ *n., pl.* **car·ries 1.** The range of a gun or a projectile: *The first cannons had a short carry of only a few hundred feet.* **2.** The distance covered by a ball or projectile. **3.** An act of carrying something from one place to another: *A short overland carry was necessary to canoe down the whole length of the river.* **4.** In football, an act of running with the ball from the line of scrimmage: *The halfback averages four yards per carry.* ◆ **carry away** To arouse great emotion or excitement in: *I was carried away by the music.* **carry off 1.** To win: *He carried off first prize.* **2.** To handle successfully: *The debate was carried off without any difficulty.* **3.** To cause the death of; kill: *The epidemic carried off hundreds of sheep.* **carry on 1.** To engage in or conduct: *carry on a conversation; carry on a correspondence.* **2.** To continue despite difficulties; persevere: *carry on even with a bad cold.* **3.** To behave in an excited or improper manner: *What are they carrying on about?* **carry out 1.** To execute or accomplish: *carry out a plan.* **2.** To follow or obey: *carry out orders.* [From Middle English *carien*, from Old North French *carier*, from *carre*, cart.]

car·ry·all (kăr′ē-ôl′) *n.* A large bag, basket, or pocketbook.

car·ry·ing capacity (kăr′ē-ĭng) *n.* **1.** The maximum number of people or things that a vehicle or a receptacle can carry: *a van with a carrying capacity of 12.* **2.** The maximum number of individuals, as of humans or deer, that can be supported by the resources available in a given environment.

car·ry-on (kăr′ē-ŏn′) *adj.* Small or compact enough to be carried aboard an airplane, train, or bus by a passenger: *carry-on luggage.* ❖ *n.* A carry-on bag or piece of luggage.

car·ry-out (kăr′ē-out′) *adj.* Intended to be eaten off the premises; takeout: *carry-out pizza.*

car seat *n.* A small seat for securing and protecting young children that can be fastened to the seat of a vehicle and that contains a restraining device or harness.

car·sick (kär′sĭk′) *adj.* Nauseated by the motion of a car, bus, or other vehicle. **—car′sick′ness** *n.*

Car·son (kär′sən), **Christopher** Known as "Kit." 1809–1868. American pioneer who was a guide for western expeditions, an agent for the Ute, and a Union commander in the Civil War.

Kit Carson

Carson, Rachel Louise 1907–1964. American environmentalist and writer whose *Silent Spring* (1962) condemns the use of pesticides that are hazardous to wildlife.

Rachel Carson
photographed c. 1952

Carson City The capital of Nevada, in the western part of the state near the California border. It was named in honor of Kit Carson.

cart (kärt) *n.* **1.** A small wheeled vehicle pushed by hand: *placed the eggs in the grocery cart.* **2.** A two-wheeled, usually wooden vehicle pulled by a draft animal or tractor and used to transport goods or people. **3.** The amount that a cart holds: *bought three carts of apples.* **4.** A light motorized vehicle: *a golf cart.* ❖ *tr.v.* **cart·ed, cart·ing, carts** To transport in or as if in a cart: *Trucks cart goods across the country.*

cart·age (kär′tĭj) *n.* **1.** The act or process of transporting or carting: *Many movers offer cartage overseas.* **2.** The cost of transporting or carting: *overseas cartage in the amount of $2,000.*

Jimmy Carter
photographed in 2011

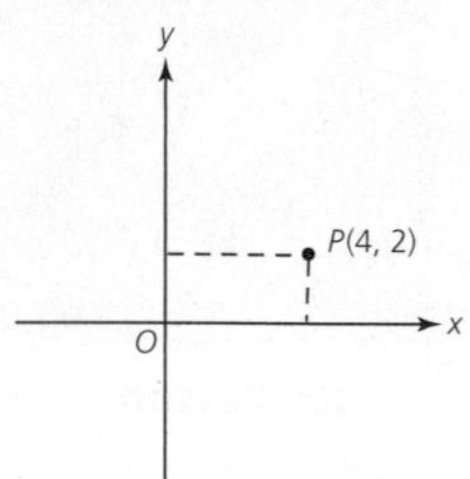

Cartesian coordinate system
two-dimensional coordinate system

cartwheel

ă	pat	ôr	core
ā	pay	oi	boy
âr	care	ou	out
ä	father	o͝o	took
ĕ	pet	o͝or	lure
ē	be	o͞o	boot
ĭ	pit	ŭ	cut
ī	bite	ûr	urge
îr	pier	th	thin
ŏ	pot	*th*	this
ō	toe	zh	vision
ô	paw	ə	about

carte blanche (kärt **bläNsh′** *or* kärt **blänch′**) *n., pl.* **cartes blanches** (kärt **bläNsh′** *or* kärts **blänch′**) Complete freedom of action: *The teacher gave us carte blanche to organize the party.* [From French *carte blanche* : *carte*, ticket + *blanche*, blank.]

car·tel (kär-**tĕl′**) *n.* An association of independent businesses, often from different countries, organized to control prices, production, and sales by its members. [From Italian *cartello*, placard, from Medieval Latin *cartellus*, charter.]

Car·ter (**kär′**tər), **James Earl, Jr.** Known as "Jimmy." Born 1924. The 39th president of the United States (1977–1981), who established energy-conservation measures and negotiated peace talks between Egypt and Israel (1979).

Car·te·sian (kär-**tē′**zhən) *adj.* Relating to the philosophy or methods of René Descartes.

Cartesian coordinate system *n.* A system in which the location of a point is given by coordinates that represent its distances from perpendicular lines that intersect at a point called the origin. A Cartesian coordinate system in a plane has two perpendicular lines; in three-dimensional space, it has three.

Car·thage (**kär′**thĭj) An ancient city and state of northern Africa northeast of modern Tunis. It was founded in the ninth century BC. **—Car′tha·gin′i·an** (kär′thə-**jĭn′**ē-ən) *adj. & n.*

Car·tier (kär-**tyā′**), **Jacques** 1491–1557. French explorer who navigated the St. Lawrence River (1535) and claimed the region for France.

car·ti·lage (**kär′**tl-ĭj) *n.* A tough white connective tissue that in humans and most other vertebrates forms the major part of the skeleton of the embryo but changes largely to bone as the individual matures. It is more flexible than bone but not as hard.

car·ti·lag·i·nous (kär′tl-**ăj′**ə-nəs) *adj.* Relating to or consisting of cartilage.

cartilaginous fish *n.* Any of various fishes that have a skeleton consisting mainly of cartilage rather than bone. The sharks, skates, and rays are cartilaginous fishes.

car·tog·ra·phy (kär-**tŏg′**rə-fē) *n.* The art of making maps or charts. **—car·tog′ra·pher** *n.*

car·ton (**kär′**tn) *n.* **1.** A cardboard or plastic box made in various sizes: *an egg carton.* **2.** The contents of a carton: *drink a carton of milk.* [From Italian *cartone*, pasteboard.]

car·toon (kär-**to͞on′**) *n.* **1.** A drawing, often accompanied by a caption, showing a humorous situation or illustrating an opinion on a public issue. **2a.** A usually short, animated movie or television program. **b.** An animated character in a movie or television program. **3.** A comic strip. [From Italian *cartone*, pasteboard.]

car·toon·ist (kär-**to͞on′**ĭst) *n.* A person who draws cartoons.

car·tridge (**kär′**trĭj) *n.* **1a.** A cylindrical casing of metal or cardboard that holds the powder to propel a bullet or shot. **b.** Such a casing fitted with a bullet or containing shot. **2.** A small unit designed to be inserted into a larger piece of equipment: *an ink cartridge.* [Alteration of French *cartouche*, from Italian *cartuccio*, variant of *cartoccio*, roll of paper.]

cart·wheel (**kärt′**wēl′) *n.* **1.** The wheel of a cart. **2.** A handspring in which the body turns over sideways with the arms and legs spread like the spokes of a wheel.

carve (kärv) *v.* **carved, carv·ing, carves** *—tr.* **1.** To make or form by cutting: *The settlers carved beams out of logs. We carved our initials in the board.* **2.** To cut (a piece of material) in order to form or decorate something: *carve a block of marble into a statue.* **3.** To cut (meat or poultry) into pieces to be eaten: *carve a turkey. —intr.* To slice meat or poultry to eat: *My grandfather is always in charge of carving at Thanksgiving dinner.* ◆ **carve out 1.** To make from something bigger: *a town that was carved out of the wilderness.* **2.** To make or accomplish by strenuous or persistent effort: *settlers carving out a living in the mountains.* [From Old English *ceorfan.*] **—carv′er** *n.*

Car·ver (**kär′**vər), **George Washington** 1864?–1943. American botanist, agricultural chemist, and educator whose work was instrumental in improving the agricultural efficiency of the United States.

carv·ing (**kär′**vĭng) *n.* **1.** The act or process of carving, especially of cutting wood or stone to form an object or design. **2.** An object or design formed by cutting: *a wood carving.*

car wash *n.* A place or business equipped for washing cars or other vehicles.

ca·sa·ba also **cas·sa·ba** (kə-**sä′**bə) *n.* A melon having a yellow rind and sweet whitish flesh.

Cas·a·blan·ca (kăs′ə-**blăng′**kə *or* kä′sə-**bläng′**kə) The largest city of Morocco, in the northwest part of the country on the Atlantic Ocean south-southwest of Tangier. It was founded in the 1500s.

cas·cade (kăs-**kād′**) *n.* **1.** A waterfall or a series of small waterfalls that flows over steep rocks. **2.** Something resembling a cascade: *a cascade of sparks from a grinding wheel.* ❖ *intr.v.* **cas·cad·ed, cas·cad·ing, cas·cades** To fall in or in the manner of a cascade: *The river cascades over a shelf of granite rock. The cards cascaded to the floor.*

Cascade Range A mountain chain of western Canada and the United States extending about 700 miles (1,100 kilometers) south from British Columbia to northern California, where it joins the Sierra Nevada. It rises to 14,411 feet (4,392 meters).

case[1] (kās) *n.* **1.** An instance of something; an occurrence or example: *It was a case of mistaken identity.* **2.** A situation or state of affairs: *In that case there is nothing more we can do.* **3.** A situation that requires investigation: *the case of the missing diamonds.* **4.** An occurrence of a disease or disorder: *a case of chickenpox.* **5.** A person being assisted, treated, or studied, as by a doctor or social worker. **6a.** A legal action; a lawsuit: *The Supreme Court is the last court to consider a case.* **b.** A statement of facts by an attorney, for a court to consider: *The case was clearly presented by the defense.* **7.** A set of reasons or arguments offered in support of something: *There is a good case for changing the law.* **8.** In grammar, a distinct form of a noun, pronoun, or adjective that shows syntactic relationships among words in a sentence. English has three cases: nominative, objective, and possessive. ◆ **in any case** No matter what happens; in any event: *In any case, we will have to leave soon.* **in case 1.** As a precaution: *brought along an umbrella just in case.* **2.** If it happens that: *brought some water in case I got thirsty.* **in case of** If there should happen to be; in the event of: *In case of emergency, call the police.* [From Middle English *cas*, from Latin *cāsus*, from past participle of *cadere*, to fall.]

case[2] (kās) *n.* **1.** A container or protective cover: *a packing case; a case for eyeglasses.* **2.** A container and its contents: *We bought a case of soda.* **3.** The form of a written, printed, or keyed letter that distinguishes it as being lowercase or uppercase: *typed my password using the wrong case.* ❖ *tr.v.* **cased, cas·ing, cas·es 1.** To put into or cover with a case. **2.** *Slang* To examine carefully, as in planning a crime: *cased the bank before robbing it.* [From Middle English, from Norman French *casse*, from Latin *capsa*.]

case history *n.* A detailed list of the facts affecting the condition of a person or group under treatment or study, especially in medicine or psychology.

ca·sein (**kā′**sēn′ *or* **kā′**sē-ĭn) *n.* A white, tasteless, odorless protein derived from milk and cheese, used in making foods, plastics, adhesives, and paints.

case·load (**kās′**lōd′) *n.* The number of cases handled in a given period, as by a lawyer or a social services agency.

case·ment (kās′mənt) *n.* **1.** A window sash that opens outward on hinges. **2.** A window fitted with such sashes.

case·work (kās′wûrk′) *n.* Social work devoted to individual people or cases. —**case′work′er** *n.*

cash (kăsh) *n.* **1.** Money in the form of bills and coins: *I have five dollars in cash in my pocket.* **2.** Payment in the form of currency or a check: *I paid in cash.* ❖ *tr.v.* **cashed, cash·ing, cash·es** To exchange for or convert into money in the form of bills or coins: *cash a check.* ◆ **cash in on** *Informal* To take advantage of: *cash in on the sunshine and go to the beach.*
❑ *These sound alike:* **cash, cache** (hiding place).

cash crop *n.* A crop that is grown for sale rather than for use by the producer.

cash·ew (kăsh′o͞o *or* kə-sho͞o′) *n.* **1.** The kidney-shaped edible nut of a tropical American tree. **2.** The evergreen tree that bears such nuts.

cash·ier[1] (kă-shîr′) *n.* A person employed to receive and pay out money, as in a store, restaurant, hotel, or bank. [From French *caisse*, money box, from Latin *capsa*, case.]

ca·shier[2] (kă-shîr′) *tr.v.* **ca·shiered, ca·shier·ing, ca·shiers** To dismiss in disgrace from a position of command or responsibility: *cashier a soldier for neglect of duty.* [From Dutch *casseren*, from Old French *casser*, to annul, dismiss.]

ca·shier's check (kă-shîrz′) *n.* A check drawn by a bank on its own funds and signed by the bank's cashier.

cash machine *n.* An ATM.

cash·mere (kăzh′mîr′ *or* kăsh′mîr′) *n.* **1.** Fine soft wool growing beneath the outer hair of a goat native to the mountains of India and Tibet. **2.** Yarn or fabric made from this wool. [After *Kashmir.*] —**cash′mere′** *adj.*

cash register *n.* A machine that records the amount of each sale and contains a drawer for holding money.

cas·ing (kā′sĭng) *n.* **1.** A protective case or covering, as for an automobile tire or a rocket. **2.** A case usually made of animal intestines and used as a wrapping for sausage meat. **3.** The frame or framework for a door or window.

ca·si·no (kə-sē′nō) *n., pl.* **ca·si·nos 1.** A business providing gambling and other entertainment. **2.** A building or room where such gambling and entertainment takes place. **3.** A card game for two to four players in which cards on the table are matched with cards in the hand.

cask (kăsk) *n.* **1.** A barrel for holding liquids: *a cask of cider.* **2.** The amount that a cask can hold.

cas·ket (kăs′kĭt) *n.* **1.** A coffin. **2.** A small case used to hold jewels or other valuables.

Cas·pi·an Sea (kăs′pē-ən) A saline lake between southeast Europe and western Asia. It is the largest landlocked body of water on earth.

casque (kăsk) *n.* A helmet or other armor for the head.

Cas·san·dra (kə-săn′drə) *n.* In Greek mythology, a daughter of Priam, endowed with the gift of prophecy but fated by Apollo never to be believed.

Cas·satt (kə-săt′), **Mary Stevenson** 1844?–1926. American painter noted for her studies of mothers and their children, such as *The Bath* (1891–1892).

cas·sa·va (kə-sä′və) *n.* **1.** A tropical American plant having a large starchy root. **2.** The root of this plant, eaten as a staple food in the tropics after preparation to remove toxins. Cassava starch is also the source of tapioca.

cas·se·role (kăs′ə-rōl′) *n.* **1.** A dish, usually of pottery or glass, in which food is both baked and served. **2.** Food baked in such a dish.

cas·sette (kə-sĕt′) *n.* A magnetic tape contained in a plastic case and used to make audio or video recordings and to store data in digital form. [From French, small box, from Norman French *casse*, case.]

Cas·si·o·pe·ia (kăs′ē-ə-pē′ə) *n.* A constellation in the Northern Hemisphere, traditionally pictured as a seated queen.

cas·sock (kăs′ək) *n.* A robe reaching to the feet, worn by the clergy and others assisting in church services.

cas·so·war·y (kăs′ə-wĕr′ē) *n., pl.* **cas·so·war·ies** Any of several large flightless birds of New Guinea and Australia that resemble an ostrich and have a bony projection on the top of the head.

cast (kăst) *v.* **cast, cast·ing, casts** —*tr.* **1.** To throw, fling, or hurl: *Tourists cast coins into the fountain.* **2.** To throw or force (a person) onto the ground, as in wrestling. **3.** To shed or molt: *The snake casts its skin as it grows.* **4a.** To cause to fall on something: *cast a shadow.* **b.** To cause to be associated with something: *cast doubt on the report.* **5.** To turn or direct: *cast a glance in the mirror.* **6.** To deposit or indicate (a ballot or vote). **7.** To assign a role to: *The director cast the actor as a judge.* **8a.** To form (an object) by pouring molten or soft material into a mold and allowing it to harden: *The artist cast the sculpture in bronze.* **b.** To pour (a liquid metal) in forming an object this way: *The factory casts molten iron into pipe.* —*intr.* **1.** To throw or force out something, especially a fishing line: *The fisherman cast in the river all morning.* **2.** To be shaped in a mold: *Some metals, such as lead, cast easily.* ❖ *n.* **1.** The act or an instance of throwing or casting: *a cast of the dice; a cast of the fishing line.* **2.** The distance thrown: *a winning cast of 40 meters.* **3.** The actors in a play or movie: *There were only four people in the cast.* **4.** A hard stiff bandage, usually of gauze and plaster, used to keep an injured bone or joint from moving. **5a.** An object cast in a mold: *a cast of a statue.* **b.** An impression formed in a mold: *a plaster cast of a face.* **6.** A hue or shade: *The cloth has a slightly reddish cast.* **7.** Outward form, quality, or appearance: *New facts put a different cast on the matter.* **8.** A slight squint or turning of the eye in a certain direction: *a cast in the left eye.* ◆ **cast about** To make a search; look around: *cast about for a way to escape.* **cast aside** To discard or abandon: *cast aside a suggestion.* **cast lots** To draw lots to determine something by chance. **cast off** To release a ship from being tied to a dock. [From Middle English *casten*, from Old Norse *kasta.*]
❑ *These sound alike:* **cast, caste** (social class).

cas·ta·nets (kăs′tə-nĕts′) *pl.n.* A rhythm instrument consisting of a pair of hollowed-out shells of wood or ivory, struck together with the fingers to make a sharp click. [From Spanish *castañeta*, from *castaña*, chestnut, from Latin *castanea.*]

cast·a·way (kăst′ə-wā′) *adj.* **1.** Cast adrift or ashore; shipwrecked. **2.** Discarded; thrown away: *castaway clothes.* ❖ *n.* **1.** A shipwrecked person. **2.** A person or thing that has been discarded.

caste (kăst) *n.* **1.** In India, one of the hereditary social classes in Hindu society. **2.** A social class as distinguished by rank, profession, or wealth: *the priestly caste of Aztec civilization.* **3.** A social system based on caste.
❑ *These sound alike:* **caste, cast** (throw).

cas·tel·lat·ed (kăs′tə-lā′tĭd) *adj.* Having turrets and battlements like a castle.

cast·er (kăs′tər) *n.* **1.** A person or thing that casts: *a caster of fishing nets.* **2.** also **castor** A small roller or wheel attached under a piece of furniture or other heavy object to make it easier to move. **3.** also **castor a.** A small bottle, pot, or shaker for holding vinegar, mustard, salt, or a similar seasoning. **b.** A stand for a set of these containers.

cas·ti·gate (kăs′tĭ-gāt′) *tr.v.* **cas·ti·gat·ed, cas·ti·gat·ing, cas·ti·gates** To criticize severely; rebuke; berate: *should be castigated for neglecting one's duty.* —**cas′ti·ga′tion** *n.* —**cas′ti·ga′tor** *n.*

WRITERS CHOOSE THEIR WORDS

Tears began to **cascade** down her cheeks once more. She didn't seem to notice, making no attempt to wipe them away, just staring silently into the fire as the horror of it all came back to her. When she spoke once more, her voice was almost inaudible.

—John Flanagan
The Burning Bridge

cashew

Mary Cassatt

casserole

Fidel Castro
photographed in 2003

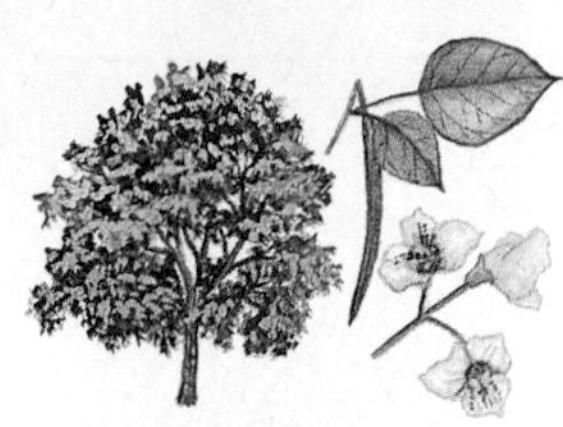
catalpa

ă	pat	ôr	core
ā	pay	oi	boy
âr	care	ou	out
ä	father	o͝o	took
ĕ	pet	o͝or	lure
ē	be	o͞o	boot
ĭ	pit	ŭ	cut
ī	bite	ûr	urge
îr	pier	th	thin
ŏ	pot	*th*	this
ō	toe	zh	vision
ô	paw	ə	about

Cas·tile (kăs-tēl′) A region and former kingdom of central and northern Spain. It joined with Aragon in 1479, thus forming the core of modern Spain.

Castile soap *n.* An odorless soap made with sodium hydroxide and a vegetable oil, usually olive oil.

Cas·til·ian (kă-**stĭl′**yən) *adj.* Relating to Castile, its people, language, or culture. ❖ *n.* **1a.** The Spanish dialect of Castile. **b.** The standard form of Spanish, based on this dialect. **2.** A native or inhabitant of Castile.

cast·ing (**kăs′**tĭng) *n.* **1.** The act or process of making casts or molds. **2.** An object that has been formed in a mold. **3.** The selection of actors or performers, as for a play.

cast iron *n.* A hard brittle alloy of iron that contains carbon and small amounts of silicon, sulfur, manganese, and phosphorus.

cast-i·ron (**kăst′ī′**ərn) *adj.* **1.** Made of cast iron. **2.** Rigid or inflexible: *a cast-iron rule.* **3.** Hardy; strong: *With your cast-iron stomach you could eat anything!*

cas·tle (**kăs′**əl) *n.* **1.** A large building or group of buildings with high thick walls, towers, and other defenses against attack, such as battlements or a moat. **2.** A building that resembles a castle in size or appearance. **3.** A rook in chess. ❖ *intr.v.* **cas·tled, cas·tling, cas·tles** In chess, to move the king two squares toward a rook and place the rook on the square next past the king. [From Old English *castel*, from Latin *castellum*.]

cast·off (**kăst′**ôf′) *n.* A person or thing that has been discarded or thrown away. **—cast′-off′** *adj.*

cas·tor (**kăs′**tər) *n.* Variant of **caster** (senses 2, 3).

Castor *n.* In Greek mythology, one of the twin sons of Leda, who along with his brother Pollux was transformed by Zeus into the constellation of Gemini.

castor oil *n.* An oil pressed from the seeds of a tropical plant, used as a light lubricant and in medicine as a laxative.

cas·trate (**kăs′**trāt′) *tr.v.* **cas·trat·ed, cas·trat·ing, cas·trates** To remove the testicles of; geld or emasculate. **—cas·tra′tion** *n.*

Cas·tries (**kăs′**trēz′ *or* **kăs′**trēs′) The capital of St. Lucia, in the Windward Islands of the British West Indies. It was founded in 1650.

Cas·tro (**kăs′**trō *or* **kä′**strō), **Fidel** 1926–2016. Cuban revolutionary leader who overthrew a corrupt regime in 1959 and established a socialist government. He led Cuba until 2008, when he retired and passed control of the government to his brother Raúl.

ca·su·al (**kăzh′**o͞o-əl) *adj.* **1.** Suited for everyday wear or use; informal: *casual dress.* **2.** Not serious or thorough; superficial: *a casual inspection.* **3a.** Showing little interest; unconcerned; nonchalant: *a breezy casual manner.* **b.** Not thought about beforehand; passing: *a casual remark about the weather.* **4.** Happening by chance; not planned; accidental: *a casual meeting of friends on a street corner.* **5.** Not close or intimate: *a casual friendship.* **—cas′u·al·ly** *adv.* **—cas′u·al·ness** *n.*

ca·su·al·ty (**kăzh′**o͞o-əl-tē) *n., pl.* **ca·su·al·ties 1a.** A person who is killed or injured in an accident. **b.** A person who is killed, wounded, captured, or missing during a military action. **2.** A serious accident, especially one in which someone is seriously injured or killed.

cat (kăt) *n.* **1.** A small domesticated mammal having soft fur and sharp claws, kept as a pet or for catching mice and rats. **2.** Any of various related mammals, such as a lion, tiger, leopard, or lynx. ◆ **let the cat out of the bag** To give away a secret; let a secret be known. [From Old English *catt.*]

ca·tab·o·lism (kə-**tăb′**ə-lĭz′əm) *n.* The phase of metabolism that yields energy by breaking down complex molecules, such as proteins and fats, into simpler ones. **—cat′a·bol′ic** (kăt′ə-**bŏl′**ĭk) *adj.*

cat·a·clysm (**kăt′**ə-klĭz′əm) *n.* **1.** A sudden and violent change in the earth's crust, such as an earthquake or volcanic eruption. **2.** A great upheaval or disaster, such as a revolution or war. **—cat′a·clys′mic** (kăt′ə-**klĭz′**mĭk) *adj.*

cat·a·combs (**kăt′**ə-kōmz′) *pl.n.* An underground cemetery consisting of chambers or tunnels with recesses used as graves.

Cat·a·lan (**kăt′**l-ăn′ *or* kăt′l-**ăn′**) *adj.* Relating to Catalonia, its people, language, or culture. ❖ *n.* **1.** A native or inhabitant of Catalonia. **2.** The Romance language of Catalonia and the surrounding region.

cat·a·lep·sy (**kăt′**l-ĕp′sē) *n., pl.* **cat·a·lep·sies** A condition in which the muscles of the body become rigid and a person is unaware of his or her surroundings and does not respond to stimuli. Catalepsy has been associated with epilepsy, schizophrenia, and certain other mental disorders. **—cat′a·lep′tic** (kăt′l-**ĕp′**tĭk) *adj.*

cat·a·log or **cat·a·logue** (**kăt′**l-ôg′) *n.* **1.** A list of items, usually in alphabetical order, with a description of each item: *a library card catalog.* **2.** A book or pamphlet containing such a list: *a mail order catalog of merchandise.* ❖ *tr.v.* **cat·a·loged, cat·a·log·ing, cat·a·logs** or **cat·a·logued, cat·a·logu·ing, cat·a·logues** To list in a catalog; make a catalog of: *catalog the books in a library.* [From Middle English *cathaloge*, list, register, from Greek *katalogos* : *kata-*, down, off + *legein*, to count.] **—cat′a·log′er, cat′a·logu′er** *n.*

Cat·a·lo·nia (kăt′l-**ōn′**yə) A region of northeast Spain bordering on France and the Mediterranean Sea.

ca·tal·pa (kə-**tăl′**pə *or* kə-**tôl′**pə) *n.* Any of several trees of North America and Asia having large heart-shaped leaves, showy white flower clusters, and long slender pods.

ca·tal·y·sis (kə-**tăl′**ĭ-sĭs) *n.* The starting, speeding up, or changing of a chemical reaction by the action of a catalyst.

cat·a·lyst (**kăt′**l-ĭst) *n.* **1.** A substance that starts or speeds up a chemical reaction while undergoing no permanent change itself. The enzymes in saliva, for example, are catalysts in digestion. **2.** A person or thing that causes or speeds up a process or event. **—cat·a·lyt·ic** (kăt′l-**ĭt′**ĭk) *adj.*

catalytic converter *n.* A device that changes harmful exhaust gases of an automotive engine from hydrocarbons and carbon monoxide into carbon dioxide and water vapor.

cat·a·lyze (**kăt′**l-īz′) *tr.v.* **cat·a·lyzed, cat·a·lyz·ing, cat·a·lyz·es** To change or bring about by catalysis: *The enzyme catalyzes the synthesis of a large molecule.*

cat·a·ma·ran (kăt′ə-mə-**răn′**) *n.* **1.** A boat with two parallel hulls. **2.** A long raft of logs tied together. [From Tamil *kaṭṭumaran* : *kaṭṭu*, to tie + *maram*, wood, log.]

cat·a·mount (**kăt′**ə-mount′) *n.* A cougar.

cat·a·pult (**kăt′**ə-pŭlt′ *or* **kăt′**ə-po͝olt′) *n.* **1.** Any of various ancient military machines used to hurl stones, spears, arrows, or other missiles at an enemy. **2.** A mechanism for launching aircraft from the deck of a ship. ❖ *v.* **cat·a·pult·ed, cat·a·pult·ing, cat·a·pults** —*tr.* To hurl or launch from or as if from a catapult: *The volcano catapulted large boulders high into the air.* —*intr.* **1.** To be catapulted or hurled: *The rider catapulted over the handlebars as her bike hit the curb.* **2.** To jump or spring: *When the firefighters heard the alarm, they catapulted out of bed.* [From Greek *katapaltēs.*]

cat·a·ract (**kăt′**ə-răkt′) *n.* **1.** A large steep waterfall. **2.** A great downpour. **3.** A condition in which the lens of an eye or the membrane that covers it turns cloudy, causing total or partial blindness.

ca·tarrh (kə-**tär′**) *n.* Abnormal discharge of mucus related to inflammation of mucous membranes, especially those of the nose and throat. **—ca·tarrh′al** *adj.*

ca·tas·tro·phe (kə-**tăs′**trə-fē) *n.* **1.** A great and sudden calamity, such as an earthquake or flood. **2.** A complete failure: *The dry and crumbly cake was a catastrophe.*

cat·a·stroph·ic (kăt′ə-strŏf′ĭk) *adj.* Relating to or resulting in a catastrophe: *a catastrophic fire.* **—cat′a·stroph′i·cal·ly** *adv.*

Ca·taw·ba (kə-tô′bə) *n., pl.* **Catawba** or **Ca·taw·bas 1.** A member of a Native American people of North and South Carolina. **2.** The Siouan language of the Catawba.

cat·bird (kăt′bûrd′) *n.* A dark-gray North American songbird having a call resembling the mewing of a cat.

cat·boat (kăt′bōt′) *n.* A small sailboat with a single sail on a mast set far forward in the bow.

cat burglar *n.* A stealthy burglar.

cat·call (kăt′kôl′) *n.* A loud shrill call or whistle expressing disapproval or derision, usually directed from an audience toward a speaker or performer. ❖ *intr.v.* **cat·called, cat·call·ing, cat·calls** To make catcalls.

catch (kăch *or* kĕch) *v.* **caught** (kôt), **catch·ing, catch·es** *—tr.* **1.** To get and hold (something that has been in motion), especially by using the hands or an implement: *catch a ball.* **2.** To capture or seize, especially after a chase: *The cat caught a mouse.* **3.** To discover or come upon suddenly: *We caught the puppy stealing the cat's food.* **4.** To reach in time to board: *Can we still catch the 3:00 train?* **5.** To become infected with; contract: *catch a cold.* **6.** To cause to be hooked, entangled, or fastened: *I caught my shirt on a nail.* **7.** To hit; strike: *The falling tree caught a corner of the porch.* **8.** To attract: *They tried to catch our attention by yelling and waving their arms.* **9.** To take in or get momentarily: *catch sight of a deer; catch what was said over the noise.* **10.** To go to see (a play, motion picture, or other entertainment). **11.** To stop or check (oneself) before or during an action: *I caught myself before laughing.* **12.** In baseball, to play (a game) as catcher. *—intr.* **1.** To become hooked, entangled, or fastened: *My coat caught in the car door.* **2.** To burn; ignite: *The fire caught quickly.* **3.** In baseball, to play as catcher. ❖ *n.* **1.** The act or an instance of catching: *The center fielder made a diving catch.* **2.** The amount of something caught, especially fish: *a huge catch of tuna.* **3.** A device, such as a hook or latch, for fastening or closing something: *a door catch.* **4.** A game in which two or more people throw a ball back and forth to each other: *They played catch until supper.* **5.** *Informal* A hidden or tricky condition; a pitfall: *The offer is generous but there must be a catch.* ◆ **catch fire 1.** To begin to burn. **2.** To become popular: *a hobby that has caught fire around the country.* **catch on 1.** *Informal* To understand; get the idea: *The dancers caught on to the new steps quickly.* **2.** To become fashionable or popular. **catch (one's) breath** To rest so as to be able to continue: *We caught our breath for a minute before climbing to the top of the mountain.* **catch up 1.** To move fast enough to reach another; draw even: *We've almost caught up with them.* **2.** To become up-to-date: *We have to catch up on the latest news.* **3.** To absorb completely; captivate: *The scientist was caught up in challenging research.* [From Middle English *cacchen*, from Anglo-French *cachier*, to chase, hunt, from Latin *captāre*, to grasp at.]

Catch-22 also **catch-22** (kăch′twĕn-tē-**too͞′** *or* kĕch′-twĕn-tē-**too͞′**) *n.* A situation in which a desired outcome is impossible because the apparent ways of achieving the outcome are directly contradictory and end up causing failure for one another.

catch·all (kăch′ôl′ *or* kĕch′ôl′) *n.* **1.** A place for keeping odds and ends, as a box, shelf, or closet. **2.** Something that covers many different situations, as a phrase, word, or law.

catch·er (kăch′ər *or* kĕch′ər) *n.* A person or thing that catches, especially the baseball player stationed behind home plate who catches pitches.

catch·ing (kăch′ĭng *or* kĕch′ĭng) *adj.* **1.** Easily transmitted; contagious: *Flu is catching.* **2.** Attractive; catchy: *a catching tune; a catching idea.*

catch phrase *n.* An often repeated word or slogan: *"No new taxes" is a catch phrase often heard at election time.*

catch·word (kăch′wûrd′ *or* kĕch′wûrd′) *n.* A well-known word or phrase, especially one that sums up an idea or group.

catch·y (kăch′ē *or* kĕch′ē) *adj.* **catch·i·er, catch·i·est 1.** Attractive or appealing: *a catchy idea for a new book.* **2.** Easily remembered: *a catchy tune.* **3.** Tricky; deceptive: *a catchy question.*

cat·e·chism (kăt′ĭ-kĭz′əm) *n.* **1.** A series of questions along with the correct answers to them, used as a way of teaching the basic doctrines of a Christian denomination. **2.** A series of questions and answers used to examine something.

cat·e·chize (kăt′ĭ-kīz′) *tr.v.* **cat·e·chized, cat·e·chiz·ing, cat·e·chiz·es 1.** To teach Christian doctrine to (a person) by means of questions and answers. **2.** To question closely: *The coach catechized the team on the new plays until everyone knew them perfectly.*

cat·e·gor·i·cal (kăt′ĭ-**gôr′**ĭ-kəl) *adj.* Being without exception or qualification; absolute: *a categorical rejection of an offer.* **—cat′e·gor′i·cal·ly** *adv.*

cat·e·go·rize (kăt′ĭ-gə-rīz′) *tr.v.* **cat·e·go·rized, cat·e·go·riz·ing, cat·e·go·riz·es** To put into a category; classify: *categorize news reports into those about domestic matters and those about international affairs.* **—cat′e·go·ri·za′tion** (kăt′ĭ-gər-ĭ-**zā′**shən) *n.*

cat·e·go·ry (kăt′ĭ-gôr′ē) *n., pl.* **cat·e·go·ries** A class or division in a system of classification.

ca·ter (kā′tər) *v.* **ca·tered, ca·ter·ing, ca·ters** *—intr.* **1.** To provide and serve food and drinks: *His business caters for functions at the statehouse.* **2.** To try to satisfy or appeal to the wants and needs of someone: *The governor was accused of catering to big business.* *—tr.* To supply and serve food and drinks for: *cater a wedding.*

cat·er·cor·nered (kăt′ər-kôr′nərd) also **cat·er·cor·ner** (kăt′ər-kôr′nər) or **cat·ty-cor·nered** (kăt′ē-kôr′nərd) or **cat·ty-cor·ner** (kăt′ē-kôr′nər) or **kit·ty-cor·nered** (kĭt′ē-kôr′nərd) or **kit·ty-cor·ner** (kĭt′ē-kôr′nər) *adj.* Diagonal. ❖ *adv.* In a diagonal position.

ca·ter·er (kā′tər-ər) *n.* A person or business that provides and serves food and drinks for weddings, banquets, meetings, and other occasions.

cat·er·pil·lar (kăt′ər-pĭl′ər *or* kăt′ə-pĭl′ər) *n.* The wormlike larva of a butterfly or moth.

cat·er·waul (kăt′ər-wôl′) *intr.v.* **cat·er·wauled, cat·er·waul·ing, cat·er·wauls** To utter a shrill cry or screech like that of a cat. ❖ *n.* A shrill or howling cry.

cat·fish (kăt′fĭsh′) *n.* Any of numerous scaleless, mostly freshwater fishes having feelers that resemble whiskers near the mouth.

cat·gut (kăt′gŭt′) *n.* A tough thin cord made from the dried intestines of certain animals, especially sheep, and used in making strings for musical instruments and tennis rackets and in sewing up surgical wounds.

ca·thar·tic (kə-**thär′**tĭk) *adj.* **1.** Tending to stimulate the intestines as a laxative. **2.** Purifying or cleansing the emotions: *a cathartic experience.* ❖ *n.* A cathartic drug or medicine.

Ca·thay (kă-**thā′**) A medieval name for China, usually applied only to the area north of the Yangtze River.

ca·the·dral (kə-**thē′**drəl) *n.* **1.** The principal church of a bishop's diocese. **2.** A large or important church.

Cath·er (kă*th*′ər), **Willa Sibert** 1873–1947. American author whose novels include *My Ántonia* (1918).

Cath·e·rine II (kăth′ər-ĭn *or* kăth′rĭn) Known as "Catherine the Great." 1729–1796. Empress of Russia (1762–1796) who greatly increased the territory of the empire.

Catherine of Ar·a·gon (ăr′ə-gŏn′) 1485–1536. The first

catboat

Catherine II

catkin
catkins of a birch tree

Carrie Chapman Catt
photographed c. 1914

wife of Henry VIII of England (1508–1533). Henry's insistence on divorcing her caused his break with Roman Catholicism.

cath·e·ter (kăth′ĭ-tər) *n.* A thin, hollow, flexible tube inserted into a duct of the body to remove a blockage or drain fluid.

cath·ode (kăth′ōd′) *n.* **1.** A negative electrode. **2.** The positive terminal in a battery or other device that is supplying current. [From Greek *kathodos*, descent : *kata-*, down + *hodos*, way, path.]

cathode ray *n.* A beam of electrons from the cathode in a vacuum tube. When cathode rays strike a solid substance, they produce x-rays.

cath·ode-ray tube (kăth′ōd-rā′) *n.* A vacuum tube in which a beam of electrons is directed against a phosphorescent screen where, under the influence of electric or magnetic fields, it forms an image. Cathode-ray tubes were standard in TVs and computer screens before the introduction of flat-screen technology.

cath·o·lic (kăth′ə-lĭk *or* kăth′lĭk) *adj.* **1.** Broad in sympathies, interests, and understanding: *a person with catholic tastes.* **2. Catholic a.** Relating to the Roman Catholic Church. **b.** Relating to all Christians or the universal Christian church. ❖ *n.* **Catholic** A Roman Catholic. [From Middle English *catholik*, universally accepted, from Greek *katholikos*, from *katholou*, in general.]

Ca·thol·i·cism (kə-thŏl′ĭ-sĭz′əm) *n.* The faith, doctrine, practice, and organization of the Roman Catholic Church.

cat·i·on (kăt′ī′ən) *n.* A positively charged ion that moves toward the negative electrode in electrolysis.

cat·kin (kăt′kĭn) *n.* A dense, often drooping cluster of very small flowers without petals, found especially in willows, birches, and oaks. [From obsolete Dutch *katteken*, kitten.]

cat·nap (kăt′năp′) *n.* A short nap. ❖ *intr.v.* **cat·napped, cat·nap·ping, cat·naps** To take a short nap.

cat·nip (kăt′nĭp′) *n.* A plant related to mint, having a strong smell that is very attractive to cats. [From *cat* + *nip*, catnip (from Old English *nepte*, from Latin *nepeta*, aromatic herb).]

cat-o'-nine-tails (kăt′ə-nīn′tālz′) *n., pl.* **cat-o'-nine-tails** A whip consisting of nine knotted cords fastened to a handle, used for flogging.

CAT scan (kăt) *n.* A CT scan. [From *c(omputerized) a(xial) t(omography).*] **—CAT scanner** *n.*

cat's cradle (kăts) *n.* A child's game in which a loop of string is woven in patterns over the fingers of both hands and often transferred back and forth between the hands of two players.

Cats·kill Mountains (kăt′skĭl′) An upland region in southeast New York west of the Hudson River. The Catskills rise to 4,180 feet (1,275 meters).

cat's-paw also **cats·paw** (kăts′pô′) *n.* **1.** A person who is used by another to do something risky or illegal. **2.** A light breeze that ruffles small areas of water, as in a pool or pond. [From a fable about a monkey that used a cat's paw to pull chestnuts out of a fire.]

cat·sup (kăt′səp *or* kăch′əp *or* kĕch′əp) *n.* Variant of **ketchup.**

Catt (kăt), **Carrie (Lane) Chapman** 1859–1947. American suffragist who was an organizer and president of the National American Woman Suffrage Association. She organized the League of Women Voters in 1920.

cat·tail (kăt′tāl′) *n.* Any of various tall marsh plants having long leaves and a dense cylindrical cluster of tiny brownish flowers.

cat·tle (kăt′l) *pl.n.* Large hoofed mammals that have been domesticated and are often raised for meat and dairy products. Cows, bulls, and oxen are cattle. [From Middle English *catel*, property, livestock, from Medieval Latin *capitāle*, holdings, funds, from Latin *caput*, head.]

cat·tle·man (kăt′l-mən) *n.* A man who tends or raises cattle.

cat·ty (kăt′ē) *adj.* **cat·ti·er, cat·ti·est 1.** Spiteful; mean; malicious: *catty gossip.* **2.** Like a cat; stealthy. **—cat′ti·ly** *adv.* **—cat′ti·ness** *n.*

cat·ty-cor·nered (kăt′ē-kôr′nərd) or **cat·ty-cor·ner** (kăt′ē-kôr′nər) *adj. & adv.* Variants of **cater-cornered.**

cat·walk (kăt′wôk′) *n.* A narrow elevated platform or pathway, as on the sides of a bridge or above a stage.

Cau·ca·sian (kô-kā′zhən) *adj.* **1a.** Relating to a racial group having light skin; white. **b.** Relating to a human racial classification distinguished especially by light or brown skin color and straight, wavy, or curly hair. This classification, which includes peoples native to Europe, northern Africa, southwest Asia, and the Indian subcontinent, is no longer in scientific use. **2.** Relating to the Caucasus region or its peoples, languages, or cultures. ❖ *n.* **1a.** A white person. **b.** A person belonging to the Caucasian racial division. **2.** A native or inhabitant of the Caucasus.

Cau·ca·sus (kô′kə-səs) A region between the Black and Caspian Seas that includes Georgia, Azerbaijan, Armenia, and part of southwest Russia. Much of the region consists of the **Caucasus Mountains,** rising to 18,510 feet (5,642 meters).

cau·cus (kô′kəs) *n., pl.* **cau·cus·es** or **cau·cus·ses** A meeting of members of a political party to decide on a question of policy or to choose a candidate for office. ❖ *intr.v.* **cau·cused, cau·cus·ing, cau·cus·es** or **cau·cussed, cau·cus·sing, cau·cus·ses** To gather in or hold a caucus. [After the *Caucus*, Club of Boston (in the 1760s).]

cau·dal (kôd′l) *adj.* **1.** At or near the tail or hind parts of an animal: *a fish's caudal fin.* **2.** Resembling a tail.

caught (kôt) *v.* Past tense and past participle of **catch.**

caul·dron (kôl′drən) *n.* **1.** A large kettle for boiling. **2.** A situation of turmoil or unrest: *a cauldron of political intrigue.* [From Middle English *caudron*, from Late Latin *caldāria*.]

cau·li·flow·er (kô′lĭ-flou′ər *or* kŏl′ĭ-flou′ər) *n.* A plant having a compact whitish head of undeveloped flowers that is eaten as a vegetable. [Probably alteration (influenced by *flower*) of New Latin *cauliflōra* : Latin *caulis*, stem + Latin *flōs*, flower.]

caulk (kôk) *n.* A material, such as a compound containing polyurethane, acrylic, or silicone, that is used to fill or seal narrow spaces, such as cracks around a window or the seams of a boat. ❖ *v.* **caulked, caulk·ing, caulks** *—tr.* To make watertight or airtight by filling or sealing with caulking: *caulk the cracks around the door.* *—intr.* To apply caulking: *The plumber caulked around the bathtub to keep it from leaking.* [From Middle English *cauken*, to press, from Latin *calcāre*, to tread, from *calx*, heel.] **—caulk′er** *n.*

caulk·ing (kô′kĭng) *n.* Caulk.

caus·al (kô′zəl) *adj.* Being or constituting a cause: *the causal connection between a scarcity of goods and higher prices.* **—caus′al·ly** *adv.*

cause (kôz) *n.* **1.** A person or thing that makes something happen: *Scientists are investigating the cause of the extinction of the dinosaurs.* **2.** A basis for a certain feeling, action, or decision; a reason: *There is no cause for alarm.* **3.** An idea or goal to which many people are dedicated: *the noble cause of peace.* ❖ *tr.v.* **caused, caus·ing, caus·es** To be the cause of; make happen; bring about: *Many bacteria cause disease.* [From Middle English, from Latin *causa*, reason, purpose.]

cause·way (kôz′wā′) *n.* A raised roadway, as across marshland or water.

caus·tic (kô′stĭk) *adj.* **1.** Capable of burning, corroding, dissolving or destroying other substances, such as living tissue or metal. **2.** Sarcastic; biting; cutting: *caustic re-*

ă	pat	ôr	core
ā	pay	oi	boy
âr	care	ou	out
ä	father	o͝o	took
ĕ	pet	o͝or	lure
ē	be	o͞o	boot
ĭ	pit	ŭ	cut
ī	bite	ûr	urge
îr	pier	th	thin
ŏ	pot	*th*	this
ō	toe	zh	vision
ô	paw	ə	about

marks. ❖ *n.* A caustic material or substance. **—caus′ti·cal·ly** *adv.*

caustic soda *n.* Sodium hydroxide.

cau·ter·ize (kô′tə-rīz′) *tr.v.* **cau·ter·ized, cau·ter·iz·ing, cau·ter·iz·es** To burn or sear (a wound or dead tissue, for example), as with a caustic substance or a hot instrument, in order to stop bleeding or prevent infection. **—cau′ter·i·za′tion** (kô′tər-ĭ-zā′shən) *n.*

cau·tion (kô′shən) *n.* **1.** Care to avoid danger or trouble: *climb icy steps with caution.* **2.** A warning: *My doctor ended his advice with a caution about not getting enough sleep.* ❖ *tr.v.* **cau·tioned, cau·tion·ing, cau·tions** To warn against possible trouble or danger: *The sign cautioned drivers to go slowly.*

cau·tious (kô′shəs) *adj.* Showing or having caution; careful: *a slow and cautious driver.* **—cau′tious·ly** *adv.* **—cau′tious·ness** *n.*

cav·al·cade (kăv′əl-kād′ *or* kăv′əl-kād′) *n.* **1.** A ceremonial procession of people on horseback, in carriages, or in automobiles: *The president and his cavalcade drove through town.* **2.** A succession of notable people, scenes, or events: *The actress starred in a cavalcade of hit movies.*

cav·a·lier (kăv′ə-lîr′) *n.* **1.** An armed horseman; a knight. **2.** A gallant or chivalrous gentleman, especially one who escorts a lady. **3. Cavalier** A supporter of King Charles I during the English civil war (1642-52). ❖ *adj.* Casual and indifferent, often in an arrogant manner: *The official gave a cavalier answer to our demands for more information.* [From Late Latin *caballārius*, horseman, from Latin *caballus*, horse.] **—cav′a·lier′ly** *adv.* —SEE NOTE AT **chivalry.**

cav·al·ry (kăv′əl-rē) *n., pl.* **cav·al·ries 1.** A military unit using armored vehicles, such as tanks and helicopters. **2.** Troops trained to fight on horseback. [From Italian *cavalleria*, from *cavaliere*, cavalier.] —SEE NOTE AT **chivalry.**

cave (kāv) *n.* A hollow or natural passage under the earth or in the side of a hill or mountain with an opening to the surface. ❖ *v.* **caved, cav·ing, caves** —*tr.* To cause to collapse or fall: *A surge of water caved in the banks of the river.* —*intr.* **1.** To fall in; collapse: *The ground above the old mine caved in.* **2.** To give up all opposition: *caved in to our demands.* **3.** To explore caves. [From Middle English, from Latin *cava*, from *cavus*, hollow.]

ca·ve·at (kăv′ē-ăt′ *or* kä′vē-ät′) *n.* A warning or restriction: *The recommendation comes with several caveats.*

caveat emp·tor (ĕmp′tôr′) *n.* Let the buyer beware; a warning to buyers to be sure of the quality of a product before purchasing it.

cave bear *n.* A large extinct bear of the Pleistocene Epoch. Most fossils have been found in caves in Europe.

cave dweller *n.* A person who lives in a cave, especially in prehistoric times.

cave-in (kāv′ĭn′) *n.* **1.** A collapse, as of a tunnel or structure. **2.** A place where something has collapsed.

cave·man also **cave man** (kāv′măn′) *n.* A prehistoric cave dweller.

cav·er (kā′vər) *n.* A person who explores or studies caves.

cav·ern (kăv′ərn) *n.* A very large cave.

cav·ern·ous (kăv′ər-nəs) *adj.* Resembling a cavern; huge, deep, and hollow: *the cavernous interior of a great cathedral.*

cav·i·ar (kăv′ē-är) *n.* The eggs of a sturgeon or other large fish, prepared with salt and eaten as a delicacy.

cav·il (kăv′əl) *intr.v.* **cav·iled, cav·il·ing, cav·ils** also **cav·illed, cav·il·ling, cav·ils** To find fault unnecessarily; raise unimportant objections: *Let's not waste time caviling about the rules instead of getting on with the game.* ❖ *n.* A trivial objection.

cav·i·ta·tion (kăv′ĭ-tā′shən) *n.* The sudden formation and collapse of bubbles in a liquid caused by mechanical forces, such as the moving blades of a ship's propeller.

cav·i·ty (kăv′ĭ-tē) *n., pl.* **cav·i·ties 1.** A hollow or hole. **2.** A hollow area within the body: *the abdominal cavity.* **3.** A pocket of decay in a tooth.

ca·vort (kə-vôrt′) *intr.v.* **ca·vort·ed, ca·vort·ing, ca·vorts 1.** To leap about playfully; romp; frolic: *lambs cavorting in a pen.* **2.** To have lively or noisy fun: *The children cavorted in the pool.*

ca·vy (kā′vē) *n., pl.* **ca·vies** Any of various tailless South American rodents, such as the guinea pig.

caw (kô) *n.* The hoarse harsh sound made by a crow. ❖ *intr.v.* **cawed, caw·ing, caws** To make this sound.

cay (kē *or* kā) *n.* A small low island composed largely of coral or sand.

❑ *These sound alike:* **cay, key**[1] (island), **key**[2] (lock opener), **quay** (wharf).

Cay·enne (kī-ĕn′ *or* kā-ĕn′) The capital of French Guiana, in the northeast part on the Atlantic Ocean. It was founded in 1643.

cayenne pepper *n.* A very strong sharp-tasting seasoning made from the ground pods of any of several red peppers. [Alteration (by folk etymology from *Cayenne*) of *kian*, from Tupí *quiínia*, hot pepper.]

cay·man (kā′mən) *n.* Variant of **caiman.**

Cay·man Islands (kā′mən) A British-administered island group in the Caribbean Sea northwest of Jamaica. Georgetown, on the island of Grand Cayman, is the capital.

Ca·yu·ga (kā-yo͞o′gə *or* kī-yo͞o′gə) *n., pl.* **Cayuga** or **Ca·yu·gas 1.** A member of a Native American people of western New York State. **2.** The Iroquoian language of the Cayuga.

cay·use (kī-yo͞os′ *or* kī′yo͞os′) *n.* A small sturdy horse, especially one of the western United States.

Cayuse *n., pl.* **Cayuse** or **Cay·us·es 1.** A member of a Native American people of Oregon and Washington. **2.** The extinct language of the Cayuse.

CB *abbr.* An abbreviation of citizens band.

cc *abbr.* An abbreviation of: **1.** carbon copy. **2.** cubic centimeter.

C clef *n.* A sign used to indicate which line of a musical staff represents middle C.

C clef

Cd The symbol for the element **cadmium.**

CD *abbr.* An abbreviation of: **1.** certificate of deposit. **2.** civil defense. **3.** compact disc.

CD-ROM (sē′dē′rŏm′) *n.* A compact disc whose data cannot be erased or changed.

Ce The symbol for the element **cerium.**

CE or **CE** *abbr.* An abbreviation of Common Era. —SEE NOTE AT **Common Era.**

cease (sēs) *intr. & tr.v.* **ceased, ceas·ing, ceas·es** To come or bring to an end; stop: *The noise ceased. The factory ceased production.* See Synonyms at **stop.**

cease-fire or **cease·fire** (sēs′fīr′) *n.* A suspension of fighting in a war; a truce.

cease·less (sēs′lĭs) *adj.* Having no pause; constant or continual. **—cease′less·ly** *adv.* **—cease′less·ness** *n.*

ce·cro·pi·a moth (sĭ-krō′pē-ə) *n.* A large North American moth having brownish wings with red and white markings.

ce·cum also **cae·cum** (sē′kəm) *n.* pl. **ce·ca** *also* **cae·ca** (sē′kə) A pouch that constitutes the beginning of the large intestine. [From Middle English, from Latin *(intestīnum) caecum*, blind (intestine).]

ce·dar (sē′dər) *n.* **1.** Any of various evergreen trees related to the pines and firs, having hard fragrant wood. **2.** The wood of such a tree, used to make furniture, shingles, chests, and pencils. [From Middle English *cedre*, from Latin *cedrus*, from Greek *kedros*.]

cedar waxwing

Cedar Rapids A city of east-central Iowa east-northeast of Des Moines.

cedar waxwing *n.* A grayish-brown North American

bird having a crested head, a yellow-tipped tail, and bright red tips on the wing feathers.

cede (sēd) *tr.v.* **ced·ed, ced·ing, cedes** To surrender possession of, especially by treaty; yield; give up: *France ceded Canada to Great Britain at the end of the French and Indian War.* See Synonyms at **yield.**

❑ *These sound alike:* **cede, seed** (part that plants grow from).

ce·di (sä′dē) *n., pl.* **cedi** or **ce·dis** The basic monetary unit of Ghana.

ce·dil·la (sĭ-dĭl′ə) *n.* A mark (¸) placed beneath the letter *c* in French and Portuguese and in certain words in English, such as *façade,* indicating that the letter is to be pronounced like (s), as *c* in *cent.* [From obsolete Spanish, diminutive of *ceda,* the letter *z* (so called because a small *z* was formerly written after a *c,* and later below it, to indicate that it was to be pronounced as a sibilant, like *s* or *z,* and not as a normal hard *c*), from Late Latin *zēta,* zeta.]

ceil·ing (sē′lĭng) *n.* **1.** The inside upper surface of a room: *lights hung from the ceiling.* **2.** The distance between the earth and the lowest clouds: *A ceiling of less than 500 feet gives poor visibility for an aircraft.* **3.** The maximum altitude at which an airplane can fly. **4.** A maximum limit: *a ceiling on gasoline prices; a ceiling on crop production; a debt ceiling.*

Cel·e·bes (sĕl′ə-bēz′ *or* sə-lē′bēz′) See **Sulawesi.**

cel·e·brant (sĕl′ə-brənt) *n.* **1.** A person who performs the official or religious duties of a ceremony or rite. **2.** The priest who conducts the celebration of the Mass. **3.** A participant in a celebration.

cel·e·brate (sĕl′ə-brāt′) *v.* **cel·e·brat·ed, cel·e·brat·ing, cel·e·brates** —*tr.* **1.** To have a party or engage in other festive activity in honor of (a special occasion): *celebrate one's birthday.* **2.** To perform (a religious ceremony): *The priest celebrated Mass.* **3.** To praise publicly; honor; extol: *a poem that celebrates friendship.* —*intr.* To have a good time with others to mark a special occasion or an important event: *celebrate after hearing the good news.* **—cel′e·bra′tion** *n.*

cel·e·brat·ed (sĕl′ə-brā′tĭd) *adj.* Known and praised by many people: *a celebrated musician.* See Synonyms at **famous.**

ce·leb·ri·ty (sə-lĕb′rĭ-tē) *n., pl.* **ce·leb·ri·ties 1.** A famous person: *The singer is a celebrity wherever he goes.* **2.** Fame; renown: *She achieved celebrity as an architect.*

ce·ler·i·ty (sə-lĕr′ĭ-tē) *n.* Quickness; speed: *move with celerity.*

cel·er·y (sĕl′ə-rē) *n.* **1.** The crisp, juicy, light-green stems of a plant related to parsley, eaten raw or cooked. **2.** The plant that bears such stems.

ce·les·ta (sə-lĕs′tə) also **ce·leste** (sə-lĕst′) *n.* A musical instrument with a keyboard and metal plates that are struck by hammers and produce bell-like tones.

ce·les·tial (sə-lĕs′chəl) *adj.* **1.** Relating to the sky or the astronomical universe: *Stars and planets are celestial objects.* **2.** Of heaven: *Angels are celestial beings.* **—ce·les′tial·ly** *adv.*

celestial equator *n.* A great circle on the celestial sphere in the plane of Earth's equator.

celestial pole *n.* Either of the points at which the imaginary extensions of Earth's axis intersect the celestial sphere.

celestial sphere *n.* An imaginary sphere, having Earth as its center, on which the sun, moon, and stars appear to be located.

ce·li·ac disease (sē′lē-ăk′) *n.* A long-lasting disease of the stomach and intestines that is characterized by sensitivity to gluten and poor absorption of nutrients.

cel·i·ba·cy (sĕl′ə-bə-sē) *n.* The condition of being unmarried or of abstaining from sexual intercourse, especially for religious reasons.

cel·i·bate (sĕl′ə-bĭt) *n.* A person who remains unmarried or abstains from sexual intercourse, especially for religious reasons. ❖ *adj.* Unmarried or abstaining from sexual intercourse, especially for religious reasons.

cell (sĕl) *n.* **1.** The basic unit of living matter in all organisms, consisting of cytoplasm and various organelles, all surrounded by a membrane. All cells except bacteria and archaea have a distinct nucleus that is also enclosed by a membrane. Some organisms consist of single cells, while others consist of vast numbers of cells. **2.** A single unit that is capable of changing some form of energy, such as chemical energy or radiant energy, into electricity. A flashlight battery is a single cell. **3.** A cell phone. **4.** A small confining room, as in a prison or convent. **5.** A small enclosed cavity or space, such as a compartment in a honeycomb. [From Middle English *celle,* from Latin *cella,* chamber.]

❑ *These sound alike:* **cell, sell** (give for money).

cel·lar (sĕl′ər) *n.* **1.** A storage room beneath a house. **2.** A cool dark room for storing wines. [From Middle English *celer,* from Late Latin *cellārium,* pantry, from Latin *cella,* storeroom.]

❑ *These sound alike:* **cellar, seller** (one who gives something for money).

cell·block (sĕl′blŏk′) *n.* A group of cells that make up a section of a prison.

cell division *n.* The process by which a cell divides into two or more cells. Mitosis and meiosis are two types of cell division. —SEE NOTE.

cel·list (chĕl′ĭst) *n.* A person who plays the cello.

cell line *n.* A group of identical cells that come from a single cell or set of cells of the same type and are used for scientific and medical research. Under certain conditions, the cells can grow and divide for many years.

cell membrane *n.* The thin membrane that surrounds the cytoplasm of a cell and regulates the passage of materials in and out of the cell.

cel·lo (chĕl′ō) *n., pl.* **cel·los** A large musical instrument of the violin family, held upright between the knees and having four strings tuned an octave below those of a viola.

cel·lo·phane (sĕl′ə-fān′) *n.* **1.** A thin, flexible, transparent material made from cellulose that is obtained from wood pulp, used as a moistureproof wrapping. **2.** Plastic wrap.

cell phone or **cell·phone** (sĕl′fōn′) *n.* A portable telephone that sends and receives calls through a network of short-range radio transmitters and relay stations that make connections to telephone lines.

cel·lu·lar (sĕl′yə-lər) *adj.* **1.** Relating to or involving cells: *cellular division.* **2.** Made of or containing cells: *the cellular structure of the brain.* **3.** Relating to cell phones or to a cell phone network: *We get spotty cellular service in the mountains.*

cellular respiration *n.* A process of cell metabolism that produces energy in the form of ATP, usually involving the use of oxygen to break down nutrients (such as glucose) and the release of carbon dioxide and water as byproducts.

cellular telephone *n.* A cell phone.

cel·lu·lite (sĕl′yə-līt′) *n.* A fatty deposit, as under the skin around the thighs.

cel·lu·loid (sĕl′yə-loid′) *n.* A colorless flammable material made from cellulose and formerly used in making photographic film.

cel·lu·lose (sĕl′yə-lōs′) *n.* A carbohydrate that is insoluble in water, forms the main component of the cell walls of plants, and is used in making products such as paper, insulation, cellophane, and textiles.

Golgi apparatus chloroplast
vacuole cell wall cell membrane
mitochondrion nucleolus
nucleus endoplasmic reticulum

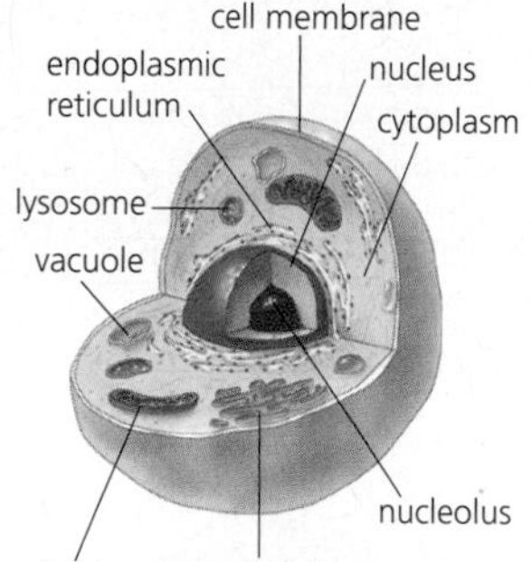

cell
top: plant cell
bottom: animal cell

ă	pat	ôr	core
ā	pay	oi	boy
âr	care	ou	out
ä	father	ŏŏ	took
ĕ	pet	ŏŏr	lure
ē	be	ōō	boot
ĭ	pit	ŭ	cut
ī	bite	ûr	urge
îr	pier	th	thin
ŏ	pot	*th*	this
ō	toe	zh	vision
ô	paw	ə	about

cellulose acetate *n.* Any of several durable materials made from cellulose and used in making magnetic tape, plastic film for wrapping and packaging, and textile fibers.

cell wall *n.* The rigid outer layer that surrounds the cell membrane in plants, fungae, and most algae and bacteria.

Cel·si·us (sĕl′sē-əs *or* sĕl′shəs) *adj.* Relating to a temperature scale on which water freezes at 0° and boils at 100° under normal atmospheric pressure. See table at **measurement.** [After Anders *Celsius.*]

Celsius, Anders 1701–1744. Swedish astronomer who invented the centigrade thermometer in 1742.

Celt (kĕlt *or* sĕlt) also **Kelt** (kĕlt) *n.* **1.** A member of an ancient Indo-European people inhabiting central and much of western Europe and the British Isles, especially a Briton or Gaul. **2.** A native speaker of a modern Celtic language or a descendant of such a speaker. [From Latin *Celtae*, the Celts, from Greek *Keltoi.*]

Celt·ic (kĕl′tĭk *or* sĕl′tĭk) also **Kelt·ic** (kĕl′tĭk) *adj.* Relating to the Celts and their languages. ❖ *n.* A group of Indo-European languages including Welsh, Irish Gaelic, Scottish Gaelic, Breton, and the extinct languages Manx, Cornish, and Gaulish.

ce·ment (sĭ-mĕnt′) *n.* **1.** A building material made by grinding heated limestone with clay to form a powder that can be mixed with water and poured to harden as a solid mass. **2.** Concrete. **3.** A substance that hardens to hold things together; glue: *use cement to mend a broken cup.* **4.** Something that unites or joins: *Mutual respect for each other's opinions was the cement of their friendship.* ❖ *tr.v.* **ce·ment·ed, ce·ment·ing, ce·ments 1.** To join or cover with cement: *cement bricks in a wall.* **2.** To make binding; establish or strengthen: *Signing the contract cemented the partners' agreement.* [From Middle English *ciment*, from Latin *caementum*, rough-cut stone, rubble used to make concrete, from *caedere*, to cut.]

cem·e·ter·y (sĕm′ĭ-tĕr′ē) *n., pl.* **cem·e·ter·ies** A place for burying the dead; a graveyard. [From Middle English *cimiterie*, from Greek *koimētērion*, from *koimān*, to put to sleep.]

Cen·o·zo·ic (sĕn′ə-zō′ĭk *or* sē′nə-zō′ĭk) *n.* The most recent era of geologic time, from about 66 million years ago to the present. During the Cenozoic, birds and mammals diversified, and the continents developed into their present forms. See table at **geologic time.** —**Cen′o·zo′ic** *adj.*

cen·ser (sĕn′sər) *n.* A container for burning incense, especially in a religious ceremony.

❑ *These sound alike:* **censer, censor** (remover of material considered harmful).

cen·sor (sĕn′sər) *n.* **1.** A person who is authorized by a government or organization to examine books, movies, or other materials and to remove or prevent from becoming available anything that is considered improper or harmful. **2.** One of two officials in ancient Rome responsible for taking the public census and supervising public behavior and morals. ❖ *tr.v.* **cen·sored, cen·sor·ing, cen·sors** To remove material from or prevent the publication of: *censor classified information in a letter.*

❑ *These sound alike:* **censor, censer** (incense container).

cen·so·ri·ous (sĕn-sôr′ē-əs) *adj.* Very critical: *The critic's censorious review seemed unfair.* —**cen·so′ri·ous·ly** *adv.* —**cen·so′ri·ous·ness** *n.*

cen·sor·ship (sĕn′sər-shĭp′) *n.* **1.** The act or practice of censoring. **2.** The office or authority of a Roman censor.

cen·sure (sĕn′shər) *n.* An expression of strong disapproval or harsh criticism. ❖ *tr.v.* **cen·sured, cen·sur·ing, cen·sures** To express strong disapproval of; criticize: *The press censured the city government for corruption.* —**cen′sur·er** *n.*

cen·sus (sĕn′səs) *n.* An official counting of population, usually made at regular intervals and often including statistics on age, sex, occupation, and other information.

cent (sĕnt) *n.* **1.** A coin of the United States, Canada, Australia, New Zealand, and various other countries, that is 1⁄100 of a dollar. **2.** A coin of various other countries equal to 1⁄100 of the basic monetary unit. **3.** A small sum of money: *I haven't a cent to my name.* [From Middle English, from Latin *centum*, hundred.]

❑ *These sound alike:* **cent, scent** (smell), **sent** (transmitted).

cent. *abbr.* An abbreviation of: **1.** centigrade. **2.** central. **3.** century.

cen·taur (sĕn′tôr′) *n.* In Greek mythology, a creature having the head, arms, and trunk of a human and the body and legs of a horse.

cen·ta·vo (sĕn-tä′vō) *n., pl.* **cen·ta·vos** A unit of money equal to 1⁄100 of the basic monetary unit in many Spanish-speaking or Portuguese-speaking countries.

cen·te·nar·i·an (sĕn′tə-nâr′ē-ən) *n.* A person who is one hundred years old or older.

cen·ten·a·ry (sĕn-tĕn′ə-rē *or* sĕn′tə-nĕr′ē) *n., pl.* **cen·ten·a·ries 1.** A period of 100 years. **2.** A centennial. ❖ *adj.* Centennial.

cen·ten·ni·al (sĕn-tĕn′ē-əl) *n.* A 100th anniversary or a celebration of it. ❖ *adj.* **1.** Relating to a period of 100 years. **2.** Happening once every 100 years: *The United States has had two centennial celebrations of its founding.* —**cen·ten′ni·al·ly** *adv.*

cen·ter (sĕn′tər) *n.* **1a.** A point within a circle or sphere that is equally distant from all points on the circumference or surface. **b.** A point that is equally distant from each vertex of a regular polygon. **2.** The middle position, part, or place of something: *the center of a table; chocolates with soft centers.* **3.** A place of concentrated activity: *a shopping center; a port that is a trading center.* **4.** A person or thing that is the chief object of attention, interest, activity, or emotion: *Our guest was the center of the party.* **5.** often **Center** A political party or set of policies representing a moderate view between those of the right and left. **6.** A player on a team positioned in or near the middle of a playing area or forward line, as in football, basketball, and hockey. ❖ *v.* **cen·tered, cen·ter·ing, cen·ters** —*tr.* **1.** To place in or at the center: *center a picture on a page.* **2.** To consider, treat, or have as a main theme, interest, or concern: *The moderator centered the discussion on the most urgent problems.* —*intr.* **1.** To be concentrated: *Support for the political opposition centered in the cities.* **2.** To have something as a main theme, interest, or concern; focus: *The conversation centered on air pollution.*

cen·ter·board (sĕn′tər-bôrd′) *n.* A flat board or metal plate that can be lowered through the bottom of a sailboat to prevent it from drifting.

center field *n.* **1.** In baseball, the middle part of the outfield, behind second base. **2.** The position played by the center fielder.

center fielder *n.* In baseball, the player who defends center field.

center of gravity *n., pl.* **centers of gravity** The point in a body around which its weight is evenly balanced.

center of mass *n., pl.* **centers of mass** The point in a body that moves as though the body's entire mass were concentrated in it. It is usually in the same place as the center of gravity.

cen·ter·piece (sĕn′tər-pēs′) *n.* **1.** An ornamental object, such as a vase of flowers, placed at the center of a dining table. **2.** The central or most important feature: *the centerpiece of the president's speech.*

cen·tes·i·mal (sĕn-tĕs′ə-məl) *adj.* Relating to or divided into hundredths. —**cen·tes′i·mal·ly** *adv.*

SCIENCE

cell division As you grow from a baby to an adult, your body forms new tissues through the amazing process of **cell division.** Even after you become an adult, your body is constantly forming new cells to replace those that are shed or die. To make sure that you stay you, each new cell has to be identical to the old cell it is replacing. In plants, animals, and other many-celled organisms, the process of cell division leading to the formation of new cells with the identical genetic material is called *mitosis.* If you scrape your knee, the cells in your skin divide in this way to repair and replace the damaged cells. Reproduction involves different types of cell division. In most animals and plants, reproductive cells such as eggs and sperm are formed by a type of cell division called *meiosis.* Bacteria reproduce by splitting down the middle in a process known as *fission,* yet another type of cell division.

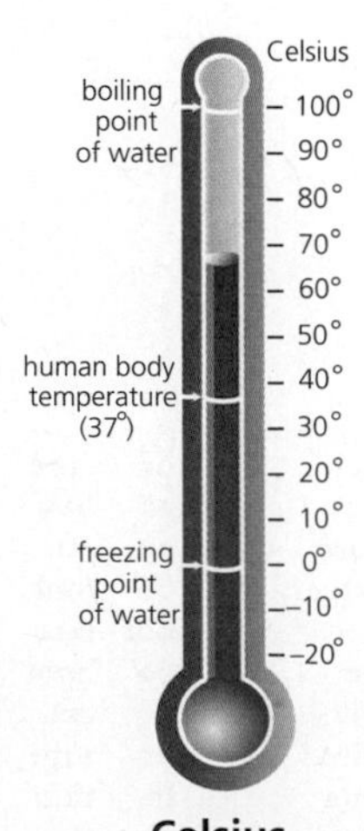

Celsius

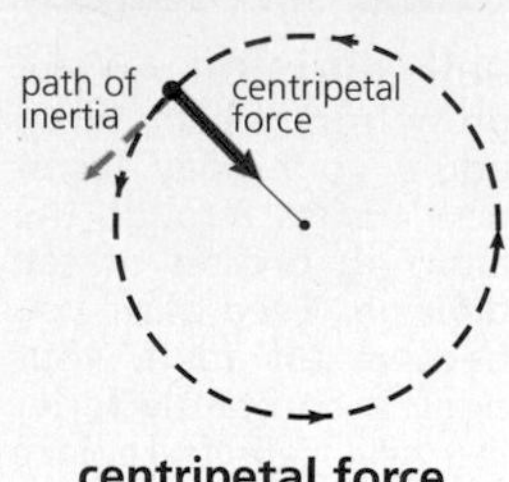

centripetal force

centi– *pref.* A prefix that means one hundredth: *centigram.*

cen·ti·grade (sĕn**′**tĭ-grād′) *adj.* Celsius. [From French : Latin *centum*, hundred + Latin *gradus*, step, degree.]

cen·ti·gram (sĕn**′**tĭ-grăm′) *n.* A unit of mass or weight in the metric system equal to ¹⁄₁₀₀ gram.

cen·ti·li·ter (sĕn**′**tə-lē′tər) *n.* A metric unit of volume equal to ¹⁄₁₀₀ of a liter.

cen·ti·me·ter (sĕn**′**tə-mē′tər) *n.* A unit of length in the metric system equal to ¹⁄₁₀₀ meter. See table at **measurement.**

cen·ti·pede (sĕn**′**tə-pēd′) *n.* Any of various small invertebrate animals having a body divided into many segments, each with a pair of legs. The front legs are used to inject venom into prey. [From Latin *centipeda* : *centi-*, hundred + *pēs*, foot.]

cen·tral (sĕn**′**trəl) *adj.* **1.** Situated at, near, or in the center: *a central position from which to view the game.* **2.** Forming the center: *the central part of the state.* **3a.** Having the dominant or controlling power: *the central office of the corporation.* **b.** Controlling all parts of a system from a particular place: *central air conditioning; central heating.* **4.** Essential or principal: *the central topic of a story.* **5.** Easily reached from many places: *a central location for the new grocery store.* **—cen′tral·ly** *adv.*

Central African Republic A country of central Africa east of Cameroon. Bangui is the capital.

Central America A region of southern North America extending from the southern border of Mexico to the northern border of Colombia. It is linked to South America by the Isthmus of Panama.

central angle *n.* An angle formed by two lines extending from the center of a circle.

Central Asia A landlocked region of Asia consisting of Kazakhstan, Kyrgyzstan, Tajikistan, Turkmenistan, and Uzbekistan. The term sometimes also includes Afghanistan, Mongolia, and western China including Tibet.

central bank *n.* A nation's primary banking authority, which controls the amount of money circulating in the economy, especially by printing new bills and setting interest rates on borrowing.

Central Intelligence Agency *n.* An agency of the US government that gathers information on matters affecting national security.

cen·tral·ize (sĕn**′**trə-līz′) *v.* **cen·tral·ized, cen·tral·iz·ing, cen·tral·iz·es** *—tr.* **1.** To draw into or toward a center; consolidate: *centralize records in one office.* **2.** To bring under a central controlling authority: *The Constitution centralizes political power in the federal government.* *—intr.* To come together at a center; concentrate: *Their attention centralized on the basic problem.* **—cen′tral·i·za′tion** (sĕn′trə-lĭ-**zā′**shən) *n.*

central nervous system *n.* The part of the vertebrate nervous system that consists of the brain and spinal cord.

Central Powers *n.* The alliance of Germany, Austria-Hungary, Bulgaria, and the Ottoman Empire that fought against the Allies in World War I.

central processing unit *n.* The part of a computer that interprets and carries out instructions.

Central Standard Time *n.* Standard time in the sixth time zone west of Greenwich, England, used in the central United States.

cen·tre (sĕn**′**tər) *n.* & *v.* *Chiefly British* Variant of **center.**

cen·trif·u·gal (sĕn-**trĭf′**yə-gəl *or* sĕn-**trĭf′**ə-gəl) *adj.* Moving or directed away from a center: *the centrifugal action of a spinning top.* [From Latin *centrum*, center + Latin *fugere*, to flee.] **—cen·trif′u·gal·ly** *adv.*

centrifugal force *n.* The apparent force that seems to cause a body turning around a center to move away from the center. Centrifugal force is not a true force but is actually an example of inertia.

ă pat	ôr core		
ā pay	oi boy		
âr care	ou out		
ä father	ŏŏ took		
ĕ pet	ŏŏr lure		
ē be	ōō boot		
ĭ pit	ŭ cut		
ī bite	ûr urge		
îr pier	th thin		
ŏ pot	*th* this		
ō toe	zh vision		
ô paw	ə about		

cen·tri·fuge (sĕn**′**trə-fyōōj′) *n.* A machine for separating substances of different densities, as cream from milk or bacteria from a fluid, by rotating them at very high speeds so that the denser substances move further outward. ❖ *tr.v.* **cen·tri·fuged, cen·tri·fug·ing, cen·tri·fug·es** To rotate (something) in a centrifuge.

cen·tri·ole (sĕn**′**trē-ōl′) *n.* Either of a pair of rod-shaped bodies within the centrosome of an animal cell. Centrioles organize other materials in the cell and help determine the arrangement of chromosomes during cell division.

cen·trip·e·tal (sĕn-**trĭp′**ĭ-tl) *adj.* Directed or moving toward a center or axis. [From Latin *centrum*, center + Latin *petere*, to seek.] **—cen·trip′e·tal·ly** *adv.*

centripetal force *n.* The force that pulls an object moving in a circle toward the center of the circle and causes the object to follow a curving path. Earth's gravity acts as a centripetal force on the moon.

cen·trist (sĕn**′**trĭst) *n.* A person who has moderate political views, such as views midway between liberal and conservative. ❖ *adj.* Marked by or holding moderate political views: *a centrist policy; a centrist representative.*

cen·tro·mere (sĕn**′**trə-mîr′) *n.* A region near the center of a chromosome that plays an important role in the separation of chromosomes during cell division.

cen·tro·some (sĕn**′**trə-sōm′) *n.* A region of the cytoplasm next to the nucleus of a cell that in animal cells contains the centrioles.

cen·tu·ri·on (sĕn-**tŏŏr′**ē-ən) *n.* An officer commanding a unit of a hundred men in the army of ancient Rome.

cen·tu·ry (sĕn**′**chə-rē) *n., pl.* **cen·tu·ries 1.** A period of 100 years. **2.** Each of the 100-year periods counted forward or backward since the time of Jesus's birth: *the 20th century.* [From Middle English *centurie*, a group of one hundred soldiers, from Latin *centuria*, from *centum*, hundred.]

century plant *n.* Any of various tropical American agave plants having long thick stiff leaves and a tall flower stalk. Century plants live for 10 to 30 years and then die after flowering once.

CEO *abbr.* An abbreviation of chief executive officer.

ce·phal·ic (sə-**făl′**ĭk) *adj.* Relating to or located on, near, or in the head. [From French *céphalique*, from Greek *kephalē*, head.]

ceph·a·lo·pod (**sĕf′**ə-lə-pŏd′) *n.* Any of various ocean mollusks, such as a squid, octopus, or nautilus, having long arms or tentacles around the mouth, a large head, a pair of large eyes, and a sharp beak.

ceph·a·lo·tho·rax (sĕf′ə-lə-**thôr′**ăks′) *n.* The combined head and thorax of some animals, such as crabs and spiders.

Ce·phe·id (**sē′**fē-ĭd *or* **sĕf′**ē-ĭd) *n.* A type of star whose brightness varies in a regular periodic way.

ce·ram·ic (sə-**răm′**ĭk) *n.* **1.** A hard brittle material that resists heat and corrosion and is made by treating clay or some other nonmetallic mineral with extreme heat. Ceramic is used in making pottery, electrical insulators, and other products. **2.** An object made of this material. **3. ceramics** *(used with a singular verb)* The art or technique of making things from this material: *She took a class in ceramics and made several vases.* [From Greek *keramos*, potter's clay.] **—ce·ram′ic** *adj.*

ce·re·al (**sîr′**ē-əl) *n.* **1.** The seeds of certain grasses, such as wheat, oats, barley, rice, or corn, used as food. **2.** A grass bearing such seeds. **3.** A food, especially a breakfast food such as corn flakes or oatmeal, prepared from such seeds. [From Latin *cereālis*, of grain, from *Cerēs*, Ceres.]

❑ *These sound alike:* **cereal, serial** (a series).

cer·e·bel·lum (sĕr′ə-**bĕl′**əm) *n., pl.* **cer·e·bel·lums** or **cer·e·bel·la** (sĕr′ə-**bĕl′**ə) A part of the brain, located at the rear of the skull, that regulates balance and coordinates muscle activity.

cer·e·bra (sĕr′ə-brə *or* sə-rē′brə) *n.* A plural of **cerebrum.**

cer·e·bral (sĕr′ə-brəl *or* sə-rē′brəl) *adj.* **1.** Relating to the brain or cerebrum: *a cerebral blood vessel.* **2.** Concerned with the intellect rather than the emotions: *a cerebral kind of poetry that does not stir the heart.*

cerebral cortex *n.* The outer layer of gray tissue that covers the two parts of the cerebrum, responsible for most of the higher functions of the nervous system, such as learning and memory.

cerebral palsy *n.* A disorder caused by brain injury usually at or before birth, resulting in symptoms that affect a person's ability to move the muscles in a coordinated way.

cer·e·bro·spi·nal (sĕr′ə-brō-**spī′**nəl *or* sə-rē′brō-**spī′**nəl) *adj.* Relating to the brain and spinal cord: *cerebrospinal fluid.*

cer·e·brum (sĕr′ə-brəm *or* sə-rē′brəm) *n., pl.* **cer·e·brums** or **cer·e·bra** (sĕr′ə-brə *or* sə-rē′brə) The large rounded structure of the brain that fills most of the skull, divided by a deep groove into two parts that are joined at the bottom. It integrates information coming in from the senses and controls voluntary movements of the muscles and mental functions such as thought and emotion.

cer·e·mo·ni·al (sĕr′ə-**mō′**nē-əl) *adj.* **1.** Relating to or appropriate to a ceremony: *ceremonial dances.* **2.** Characterized by or involved in ceremony: *ceremonial robes; ceremonial duties.* ❖ *n.* A set of ceremonies established for a specific occasion; a ritual.

cer·e·mo·ni·ous (sĕr′ə-**mō′**nē-əs) *adj.* **1.** In accordance with a set of customary forms or rites; formal: *Inauguration of the president is a ceremonious occasion.* **2.** Careful about ceremony and formality; formally polite: *a fancy restaurant with ceremonious waiters.* **—cer′e·mo′ni·ous·ly** *adv.* **—cer′e·mo′ni·ous·ness** *n.*

cer·e·mo·ny (sĕr′ə-mō′nē) *n., pl.* **cer·e·mo·nies 1.** A formal act or set of acts performed in honor or celebration of an occasion, such as a wedding, funeral, or national event. **2.** Proper or polite behavior; formality: *the ceremony of shaking hands when introduced.* [From Middle English *cerimonie*, from Latin *caerimōnia*, religious rite.]

Ce·res (sîr′ēz) *n.* **1.** In Roman mythology, the goddess of agriculture, identified with the Greek Demeter. **2.** The closest dwarf planet to the sun. The orbit of Ceres is between Mars and Jupiter, and it was the first object in the asteroid belt to be discovered. —SEE NOTE AT **planet.**

ce·ri·um (sîr′ē-əm) *n. Symbol* **Ce** A grayish metallic element that occurs only in combination with other elements and is used in porcelain, glass, and alloys. Atomic number 58. See **Periodic Table.**

cer·tain (**sûr′**tn) *adj.* **1.** Established or agreed upon; definite: *We save a certain amount each month.* **2.** Sure to come or happen; inevitable: *If the temperature keeps dropping, it is certain that the rain will turn to snow.* **3.** Established beyond doubt; indisputable: *It is certain that the planets revolve around the sun.* **4.** Reliable; dependable: *a certain remedy to the problem.* **5.** Confident; assured: *Are you certain that you left the book here?* **6.** Not named or specified but assumed to be known: *certain kinds of farm animals.* **7.** Named but not familiar or known: *a certain Mr. Smith.* **8.** Some but not much; limited: *The report is accurate to a certain degree.* ❖ *pron.* A certain number; some: *Certain of the watches are waterproof.* ◆ **for certain** Without doubt; definitely: *Winter will come for certain.* [From Middle English, from Latin *certus*, past participle of *cernere*, to determine.]

cer·tain·ly (**sûr′**tn-lē) *adv.* Surely; definitely: *I am certainly going to the movies if I get a chance.*

cer·tain·ty (**sûr′**tn-tē) *n., pl.* **cer·tain·ties 1.** The condition or quality of being certain; freedom from doubt; sureness: *There is no certainty that the package will arrive today.* **2.** A clearly established fact: *It is a certainty that the moon affects the tides.*

cer·tif·i·cate (sər-**tĭf′**ĭ-kĭt) *n.* **1.** An official document that is proof of some fact, such as a date of birth. **2.** A document stating that a person has completed the requirements to practice a certain profession. **3.** A document that certifies ownership: *an automobile registration certificate; a stock certificate.*

certificate of deposit *n., pl.* **certificates of deposit** A certificate from a bank stating that a certain amount of money has been deposited at that bank by a particular person, usually paying a specified rate of interest over a stated period of time.

cer·ti·fi·ca·tion (sûr′tə-fĭ-**kā′**shən) *n.* **1.** The act of certifying or the condition of being certified: *All states require the certification of doctors.* **2.** A certified document or statement; a certificate: *Our doctor's certification hung in a frame on the wall.*

Cer·ti·fied Mail (**sûr′**tə-fīd′) A trademark used for a mail service that provides proof of delivery to the sender.

cer·ti·fy (**sûr′**tə-fī′) *tr.v.* **cer·ti·fied, cer·ti·fy·ing, cer·ti·fies 1.** To guarantee to be true or valid by an official document: *Your license certifies that you know how to drive a car.* **2.** To guarantee the quality, value, or standard of: *The inspector certified the elevator as safe.* **3.** To issue a license or certificate to: *This document certifies that she can practice dentistry in this state.* [From Middle English *certifien*, from Late Latin *certificāre*, from Latin *certus*, certain.]

cer·ti·tude (**sûr′**tĭ-to͞od′) *n.* The condition of being certain; confidence; complete assurance: *the doctor's certitude about my good health.*

ce·ru·le·an (sə-**ro͞o′**lē-ən) *adj.* Sky-blue; azure.

Cer·van·tes (sər-**văn′**tēz), **Miguel de** 1547–1616. Spanish writer whose works include *Don Quixote* (1605–1615), which influenced the development of the novel.

Miguel de Cervantes

cer·vi·cal (**sûr′**vĭ-kəl) *adj.* Relating to the neck or to a cervix: *the cervical vertebrae of the upper backbone.*

cer·vix (**sûr′**vĭks) *n., pl.* **cer·vix·es** or **cer·vi·ces** (**sûr′**vĭ-sēz′) **1.** A neck-shaped part of the body, especially the narrow outer end of the uterus. **2.** The neck.

ce·sar·e·an also **cae·sar·e·an** (sĭ-**zâr′**ē-ən) *n.* A cesarean section. ❖ *adj.* Relating to a cesarean section.

cesarean section *n.* A surgical procedure in which an incision is made through the abdominal wall and uterus in order to deliver a baby. [From the traditional belief that Julius *Caesar* or one of his ancestors was born by this operation.]

ce·si·um (**sē′**zē-əm) *n. Symbol* **Cs** A soft, silvery metallic element that becomes liquid just above room temperature and is used in photoelectric cells. The rate of vibration of cesium atoms is used as a standard for measuring time. Atomic number 55. See **Periodic Table.**

ces·sa·tion (sĕ-**sā′**shən) *n.* The act of ceasing or stopping; a halt: *A computer failure caused a cessation of stock trading.*

ces·sion (**sĕsh′**ən) *n.* A giving up or yielding to another: *the French cession of Acadia to Great Britain.*

cess·pool (**sĕs′**po͞ol′) *n.* A covered hole or pit in the ground for receiving drainage or sewage.

ce·ta·cean (sĭ-**tā′**shən) *n.* Any of various sea mammals having an almost hairless body resembling that of a fish, a flat notched tail, and forelimbs modified into broad flippers. Whales, dolphins, and porpoises are cetaceans. ❖ *adj.* Relating to or characteristic of cetaceans.

Cey·lon (sĭ-**lŏn′**) See **Sri Lanka.**

Cé·zanne (sā-**zăn′**), **Paul** 1839–1906. French artist. His most famous paintings include *Mont Sainte-Victoire* (1885–1887) and *The Card Players* (1890–1892).

WRITERS CHOOSE THEIR WORDS

A cold dampness seeped into her socks, and the wet wool began to **chafe** her ankles. Caroline ducked her head against the wind ... and when Mother and Joseph stopped abruptly, Caroline bumped headfirst into the folds of Mother's long gray coat.

—Maria D. Wilkes
Little Town at the Crossroads

chainlink fence

chairlift

ă	pat	ôr	core
ā	pay	oi	boy
âr	care	ou	out
ä	father	o͝o	took
ĕ	pet	o͝or	lure
ē	be	o͞o	boot
ĭ	pit	ŭ	cut
ī	bite	ûr	urge
îr	pier	th	thin
ŏ	pot	*th*	this
ō	toe	zh	vision
ô	paw	ə	about

Cf The symbol for the element **californium.**

CF *abbr.* An abbreviation of: **1.** center field. **2.** cystic fibrosis.

cf. *abbr.* An abbreviation of compare.

CFC *abbr.* An abbreviation of chlorofluorocarbon.

CFO *abbr.* An abbreviation of chief financial officer.

cg *abbr.* An abbreviation of centigram.

CG *abbr.* An abbreviation of: **1.** coast guard. **2.** commanding general. **3.** consul general.

CGI *abbr.* An abbreviation of computer-generated imagery.

cgm. *abbr.* An abbreviation of centigram.

ch. *abbr.* An abbreviation of chapter.

Ch. *abbr.* An abbreviation of: **1.** chaplain. **2.** church.

chad (chăd) *n.* **1.** Scraps or bits of paper, such as the tiny rectangles punched out from cards once commonly used to enter data into computers. **2.** One of these scraps or bits of paper.

Chad (chăd) A country of north-central Africa west of Sudan. N'Djamena is the capital.

chafe (chāf) *v.* **chafed, chaf·ing, chafes** —*tr.* **1.** To cause irritation by friction or rubbing: *The starched collar chafed his neck.* **2.** To annoy; vex: *The fans' taunts chafed the pitcher.* **3.** To warm by rubbing: *The skaters chafed their cold hands.* —*intr.* **1.** To become irritated or sore from rubbing: *My hands chafed from washing them with harsh soap.* **2.** To feel irritation or impatience: *chafe at the delay.* [From Middle English *chaufen*, to warm, from Latin *calefacere* : *calēre*, to be warm + *facere*, to make.]

chaff[1] (chăf) *n.* **1.** The husks of grain separated from the seeds by threshing. **2.** Finely cut straw or hay used as fodder. **3.** Trivial or worthless matter: *The art exhibit had a few good paintings, but the rest were chaff.* [From Old English *ceaf.*]

chaff[2] (chăf) *tr.v.* **chaffed, chaff·ing, chaffs** To make good-natured fun of; tease: *My classmates chaffed me about my picture in the newspaper.* ❖ *n.* Good-natured teasing; banter. [Possibly alteration of *chafe* or *chaff*, husks.]

chaf·finch (**chăf′**ĭnch) *n.* A small European songbird often kept as a pet, the male of which has reddish-brown feathers and a blue-gray cap.

chaf·ing dish (**chā′**fĭng) *n.* A pan set above a heating device, used to cook food or keep it warm at the table.

cha·grin (shə-**grĭn′**) *n.* A strong feeling of unease or annoyance caused by disappointment, embarrassment, or humiliation, especially at a mistake or failure. ❖ *tr.v.* **cha·grined, cha·grin·ing, cha·grins** To cause to feel chagrin; annoy greatly: *I was chagrined at being corrected in front of my friends.*

chai (chī) *n.* A beverage made from spiced black tea, milk, and honey or sugar.

chain (chān) *n.* **1.** A series of connected links, usually of metal, used especially to bind or hold something or to transmit mechanical power. **2.** A set of such links used as an ornament. **3.** A series of connected or related things: *a chain of events; a chain of mountains.* **4.** A number of stores, restaurants, theaters, or other establishments under common ownership or management: *a chain of supermarkets around the state.* **5. chains** Something that restrains or confines: *They threw off the chains of slavery.* **6.** A unit of length used in land surveying, equal to 66 feet (20.1 meters). ❖ *tr.v.* **chained, chain·ing, chains** To bind or confine with or as if with a chain or chains: *chain an elephant to a stake; be chained to one's job.* [From Middle English *chaine*, from Latin *catēna*.]

chain gang *n.* A group of convicts chained together when doing heavy labor outside their prison.

chain letter *n.* A letter, email, or other message sent to a certain number of people, asking each of them to copy and send it to the same number of people.

chain·link fence (**chān′**lĭngk′) *n.* A fence made of thick steel wire woven together in a diamond pattern.

chain mail *n.* Flexible armor made of metal rings that are connected like links in a chain.

chain-re·act (chān′rē-**ăkt′**) *intr.v.* **chain-re·act·ed, chain-re·act·ing, chain-re·acts** To undergo a chain reaction.

chain reaction *n.* **1.** A series of events each of which causes or influences the next: *The car crash caused a chain reaction on the highway that involved a number of other cars in accidents.* **2.** A continuous series of nuclear fissions in which neutrons released from the splitting of one atomic nucleus collide with nearby nuclei, which in turn release more neutrons to collide with more nuclei, thus keeping the reaction going.

chain·saw (**chān′**sô′) *n.* A power saw with teeth set on a circular chain.

chain store *n.* One store of a number of retail stores under the same ownership or management.

chair (châr) *n.* **1.** A piece of furniture on which one may sit, usually consisting of a seat, back, legs, and sometimes arms at the sides. **2.** A position of authority, as that of a professor: *The head of the department has the chair of ancient history.* **3.** A chairperson: *address questions to the chair.* ❖ *tr.v.* **chaired, chair·ing, chairs** To preside over: *chair a meeting; chair a committee.* [From Middle English *chaiere*, from Latin *cathedra*.]

chair·lift (**châr′**lĭft′) *n.* A series of chairs or bars suspended from an endless cable and used to carry skiers and others up or down a slope.

chair·man (**châr′**mən) *n.* **1.** A man who is a chairperson. **2.** A chairperson.

chair·man·ship (**châr′**mən-shĭp′) *n.* The office of a chairperson or the period during which a chairperson is in office.

chair·per·son (**châr′**pûr′sən) *n.* A person who is in charge of a meeting or is the head of a committee, board, or college department.

chair·wom·an (**châr′**wo͝om′ən) *n.* A woman who is a chairperson.

chaise (shāz) *n.* **1.** A light, usually two-wheeled carriage with a folding top, drawn by one horse. **2.** A chaise longue.

chaise longue (shāz **lông′**) *n., pl.* **chaise longues** or **chaises longues** (shāz **lông′**) A chair having a long seat on which one can sit and stretch out one's legs.

chal·ced·o·ny (kăl-**sĕd′**n-ē) *n., pl.* **chal·ced·o·nies** A type of quartz that has a waxy luster and varies from transparent to translucent. It is used as a gemstone. Agate and onyx are forms of chalcedony.

Chal·de·a or **Chal·dae·a** (kăl-**dē′**ə) An ancient kingdom of southern Mesopotamia. It was founded in about 1000 BC.

cha·let (shă-**lā′** *or* **shăl′**ā) *n.* **1.** A wooden house with a gently sloping roof and overhanging eaves. **2.** The hut of a herder in the Swiss Alps.

chal·ice (**chăl′**ĭs) *n.* **1.** A cup or goblet. **2.** A cup for the consecrated wine of the Eucharist.

chalk (chôk) *n.* **1.** A soft white, gray, or yellow limestone formed chiefly from fossil seashells. **2.** A piece of this material or a similar substance, used especially for making marks on a chalkboard or other surface: *make a picture using colored chalk.* ❖ *tr.v.* **chalked, chalk·ing, chalks 1.** To mark, draw, or write with chalk: *chalk math problems on the blackboard.* **2.** To treat or cover with chalk: *chalk a field in order to neutralize its acid soil.* ◆ **chalk up 1.** To earn or score: *The team chalked up one victory after another.* **2.** To credit: *chalk up a success to pure luck.*

chalk·board (**chôk′**bôrd′) *n.* A smooth hard surface, usually green or black, for writing on with chalk.

chalk·y (**chô′**kē) *adj.* **chalk·i·er, chalk·i·est 1.** Containing chalk: *chalky water from washing the blackboards.* **2.** Resembling chalk: *chalky bits of dried paint.* **—chalk′i·ness** *n.*

chal·lah (KHä′lə *or* hä′lə) *n.* A bread made with eggs, usually baked in the shape of a braid and traditionally eaten by Jews on the Sabbath.

chal·lenge (chăl′ənj) *n.* **1.** A call to take part in a contest or fight: *a challenge to a duel.* **2.** Something that tests a person's skills, efforts, or resources: *the challenge of studying advanced mathematics.* **3.** A calling into question; a demand for an explanation: *The new scientific evidence poses a challenge to their theory.* **4.** A sentry's call for identification: *"Who goes there?" was the challenge of the soldier.* **5.** A formal objection, especially to the qualifications of a juror or to certain evidence or rulings in a trial. ❖ *tr.v.* **chal·lenged, chal·leng·ing, chal·leng·es 1.** To call to engage in a contest or fight: *We challenged the other class to a game of basketball.* **2.** To question or dispute the truth or rightness of: *We challenged his claim.* **3.** To order to halt and be identified: *The sentries challenged everybody who walked by.* **4.** To summon to action, effort, or use; stimulate: *a problem that challenges the imagination.* **5.** To make a formal objection to (a person being considered as a juror). [From Middle English *chalenge*, from Latin *calumnia*, trickery, false accusation.] **—chal′leng·er** *n.*

chal·leng·ing (chăl′ən-jĭng) *adj.* **1.** Requiring the full use of one's abilities, skills, or attention: *a challenging job; a challenging homework assignment.* **2.** Arousing one's interest or curiosity; intriguing: *a challenging idea.*

chal·lis (shăl′ē) *n.* A lightweight fabric of wool, cotton, or rayon, usually having a printed pattern.

cham·ber (chām′bər) *n.* **1.** A private room, especially a bedroom. **2.** A room in which a person of high rank receives visitors: *the pope's audience chamber.* **3. chambers** A judge's office in a courthouse: *Before the trial the lawyers met in the judge's chambers.* **4a.** The hall used by a group of lawmakers or judges: *Inside the Capitol are the two chambers where the laws are made, the Senate and the House of Representatives.* **b.** A legislative or judicial body: *The Senate is called the upper chamber of the legislature.* **5a.** An enclosed space or compartment in a machine or other device: *a bullet in the chamber of a rifle.* **b.** An enclosed space in the body of an organism, as in the brain or heart. ❖ *tr.v.* **cham·bered, cham·ber·ing, cham·bers** To put into a chamber, as in a firearm: *chambered a bullet.* [From Middle English *chaumbre*, from Latin *camera*, vault, from Greek *kamarā*.]

cham·ber·lain (chām′bər-lĭn) *n.* **1.** An official who manages the household of a monarch or noble. **2.** A treasurer.

cham·ber·maid (chām′bər-mād′) *n.* A woman who is employed to clean and take care of bedrooms, as in a hotel.

chamber music *n.* Music written for a small group of instruments and suitable for performance in a private home or small concert hall.

chamber of commerce *n., pl.* **chambers of commerce** An association of businesspersons and merchants for the promotion of business interests in the community.

chamber pot *n.* A portable container used as a toilet, especially in a bedroom.

cham·bray (shăm′brā′) *n.* A fine, lightweight fabric woven with white threads crossing colored ones.

cha·me·leon (kə-mēl′yən) *n.* **1.** Any of various tropical lizards chiefly of Africa and Madagascar, having a grasping tail, eyes that can move independently, and the ability to change color. **2.** Any of several other lizards that can change color. [From Middle English *camelioun*, from Greek *khamaileōn* : *khamai*, on the ground + *leōn*, lion.]

cham·ois (shăm′ē) *n., pl.* **cham·ois** (shăm′ēz) **1.** Either of two animals of mountainous regions of Europe and western Asia that are similar to goats and antelopes. **2.** Soft yellowish material originally made from the skin of this animal, used as a drying or polishing cloth.

cham·o·mile (kăm′ə-mīl′ *or* kăm′ə-mēl′) *n.* A strong-smelling plant having flowers similar to daisies and feathery leaves. The dried flowers can be steeped in hot water to make chamomile tea. [From Middle English *camomille*, from Greek *khamaimēlon* : *khamai*, on the ground + *mēlon*, apple.]

champ[1] (chămp) *tr. & intr.v.* **champed, champ·ing, champs** To chew or bite upon noisily: *a horse champing its oats; a horse chewing and champing with great vigor.* ◆ **champ at the bit** To be impatient at being delayed: *The team was champing at the bit to start the game.* [Probably of imitative origin.]

champ[2] (chămp) *n. Informal* A champion. [From *champion.*]

cham·pagne (shăm-pān′) *n.* **1.** A sparkling white wine produced in Champagne, a region of France. **2.** A similar wine made in another area.

cham·pi·on (chăm′pē-ən) *n.* **1.** A person or thing that holds first place or wins first prize in a contest, especially in sports. **2.** A person who fights for or defends something, such as a cause or movement: *a champion of human rights.* ❖ *tr.v.* **cham·pi·oned, cham·pi·on·ing, cham·pi·ons** To fight for or defend; support actively: *champion the rights of poor people.* ❖ *adj.* Holding first place or prize: *the champion team.* [From Middle English *championn*, combatant, athlete, from Medieval Latin *campiō*, from Latin *campus*, field.]

cham·pi·on·ship (chăm′pē-ən-shĭp′) *n.* **1a.** The position or title of a champion: *hold the championship.* **b.** A contest held to determine a champion: *attend the championship.* **2.** Defense or support: *the championship of civil rights.*

Cham·plain (shăm-plān′), **Lake** A lake of northeast New York, northwest Vermont, and southern Quebec, Canada.

Cham·plain (shăm-plān′), **Samuel de** 1567?–1635. French explorer who founded a settlement on the site of present-day Quebec in 1608.

chance (chăns) *n.* **1.** The unknown or uncertain course of events that has no apparent cause: *Most card games are games of chance. By chance did you find your glasses?* **2.** often **chances** The likelihood that something will happen; possibility or probability: *Chances are good that it will rain tonight. Is there any chance of getting a ride in your car?* **3.** An opportunity: *We never miss a chance to go to the movies.* **4.** A risk or gamble: *You're taking a chance that the store will still be open.* ❖ *adj.* Caused by chance; not planned: *a chance meeting.* ❖ *v.* **chanced, chanc·ing, chanc·es** *—intr.* To do or experience something by accident: *I chanced to find a quarter on the sidewalk.* —*tr.* To take a chance with; risk: *They chanced crossing the river in a canoe.* ◆ **chance on** or **chance upon** To find or meet accidentally; happen upon: *I chanced on an old friend yesterday.*

chan·cel (chăn′səl) *n.* The space around the altar of a church for the clergy and choir, often set apart by a railing, lattice, or screen.

chan·cel·ler·y or **chan·cel·lor·y** (chăn′sə-lə-rē *or* chăn′slə-rē) *n., pl.* **chan·cel·ler·ies** or **chan·cel·lor·ies 1.** The rank or position of a chancellor. **2.** The office or building in which a chancellor is located. **3.** The office of an embassy or consulate.

chan·cel·lor (chăn′sə-lər *or* chăn′slər) *n.* **1a.** The chief minister of state in some European countries. **b.** In the British government, any of various high officials, such as the Chancellor of the Exchequer. **2.** The president of certain American universities. **3.** The presiding judge of

chalet

chalice

challah

chandelier

chaps

ă	pat	ôr	core
ā	pay	oi	boy
âr	care	ou	out
ä	father	o͝o	took
ĕ	pet	o͝or	lure
ē	be	o͞o	boot
ĭ	pit	ŭ	cut
ī	bite	ûr	urge
îr	pier	th	thin
ŏ	pot	*th*	this
ō	toe	zh	vision
ô	paw	ə	about

a court of equity in some states of the United States and in Great Britain.

Chancellor of the Exchequer *n.* The highest minister of finance in the British government and a member of the prime minister's cabinet.

chan·cel·lor·ship (**chăn′**sə-lər-shĭp′ *or* **chăn′**slər-shĭp′) *n.* The position or term of office of a chancellor.

chan·cer·y (**chăn′**sə-rē) *n., pl.* **chan·cer·ies 1.** A court dealing with cases that are not covered by common law and that have to be tried according to a special body of laws. **2.** An office for the collection and safekeeping of official documents. **3.** A chancellery, especially a country's embassy or consulate.

chan·cre (**shăng′**kər) *n.* A sore or ulcer that forms on the skin, usually as an early indication of a diseased condition.

chanc·y (**chăn′**sē) *adj.* **chanc·i·er, chanc·i·est** Uncertain as to outcome; risky: *a chancy undertaking.*

chan·de·lier (shăn′də-**lîr′**) *n.* A lighting fixture that holds a number of bulbs or candles on branches and is suspended from a ceiling.

chan·dler (**chănd′**lər) *n.* **1.** A person who makes or sells candles. **2.** A person who sells goods or equipment for use on a ship.

change (chānj) *v.* **changed, chang·ing, chang·es** *—tr.* **1.** To cause to be different; alter: *change the rules; change the color of a room.* **2.** To take, put, or use (something) in place of another, usually of the same kind: *The company changed its name.* **3a.** To give and receive (one thing for another); exchange; switch: *The twins changed places to fool everybody.* **b.** To exchange (a unit of money) for smaller units or for a different currency: *The machine changes a dollar bill into coins.* **4.** To transfer from (one vehicle) to another: *We have to change planes in Denver on our way home.* **5.** To put fresh clothes or coverings on: *It's your turn to change the baby. I'll show you how to change the bed. —intr.* **1.** To become different or altered: *The town grew and changed over the years.* **2.** To make an exchange; switch: *If you would rather sit in this seat, I'll change with you.* **3.** To put on other clothing: *They changed into work clothes.* **4.** To transfer from one vehicle to another: *We changed in Chicago on our way to the coast.* **5.** To become deeper in tone: *His voice began to change.* ❖ *n.* **1.** The act, process, or result of changing: *a change in the schedule.* **2a.** Money of smaller denomination exchanged for a unit of higher denomination: *Will you give me change of four quarters for a dollar?* **b.** The money returned when the amount given in paying for something is more than what is due: *The change was only a dime.* **c.** A number of coins: *a purse full of change.* **3.** Something different; a break in one's routine: *We finished dinner early for a change.* **4.** A fresh article or set of clothing: *a change of shirts.* ◆ **change hands** To pass from one owner to another: *The store changed hands this year.* **change (one's) mind** To alter a decision or opinion. [From Middle English *chaungen*, from Latin *cambiāre*, to exchange.] **—chang′er** *n.*

change·a·ble (**chān′**jə-bəl) *adj.* **1.** Likely to change; capricious: *changeable moods.* **2.** Capable of being altered: *changeable habits.* **3.** Changing color or appearance when seen from different angles: *the hummingbird's changeable, vivid plumage.* **—change′a·bil′i·ty, change′a·ble·ness** *n.* **—change′a·bly** *adv.*

change·ful (**chānj′**fəl) *adj.* Having the tendency or ability to change; variable: *a changeful sky at sunset.* **—change′ful·ly** *adv.* **—change′ful·ness** *n.*

change·less (**chānj′**lĭs) *adj.* Never changing; constant: *He was changeless in his opposition to our proposal.* **—change′less·ly** *adv.* **—change′less·ness** *n.*

change·ling (**chānj′**lĭng) *n.* **1.** In folklore, a child of the fairies secretly exchanged for a human child. **2.** A human child secretly exchanged for another.

change·o·ver (**chānj′**ō′vər) *n.* A change from one way of doing something to another: *a changeover from typewriters to computers.*

change·up (**chānj′**ŭp′) *n.* In baseball, a pitch that is thrown with the same motion as a fastball but actually moves more slowly, causing the batter to swing too early.

Chang·jiang (**chäng′jyäng′**) See **Yangtze.**

chan·nel (**chăn′**əl) *n.* **1.** The bed or deepest part of a stream or river. **2.** A part of a river or harbor deep enough to form a passage for ships and often maintained by dredging. **3.** A broad strait: *a channel between islands.* **4.** A passage or conduit for liquids: *Each side of the road had a channel for water to run off.* **5.** A course or way through which something, such as news, messages, or ideas, may be transmitted: *opening new channels of information; a channel of thought.* **6a.** A band of frequencies reserved for broadcasting or communication: *a television channel.* **b.** A station that distributes audio or video content on television, radio, or the Internet: *a sports channel.* **7.** A site on a computer network where people hold online conversations in real time. **8. channels** Official routes of communication: *go through channels to get permission to enter the secluded forest.* **9.** The sound recorded by a separate microphone and played back through a single loudspeaker in a stereo system. ❖ *tr.v.* **chan·neled, chan·nel·ing, chan·nels** also **chan·nelled, chan·nel·ling, chan·nels 1.** To form a channel in or through: *The stream channeled the limestone.* **2.** To direct or guide along a desired route: *channel her thoughts towards making a movie.* [From Middle English *chanel*, from Latin *canālis*, canal.]

Channel Islands A group of British islands in the English Channel off the coast of Normandy, France. The islands became part of England with the Norman Conquest of 1066.

chan·nel-surf (**chăn′**əl-sûrf′) *intr.v.* **chan·nel-surfed, chan·nel-surf·ing, chan·nel-surfs** To watch different television channels in rapid succession.

chant (chănt) *n.* **1.** A simple melody in which many words or syllables are sung on the same note or a limited range of notes. **2.** A religious text sung to such a melody. **3.** A sustained rhythmic call or shout: *the chant of the crowd at a football game.* ❖ *v.* **chant·ed, chant·ing, chants** *—tr.* **1.** To sing to a chant: *The monks chanted psalms.* **2.** To call out in a sustained rhythmic way: *chant a slogan at a rally. —intr.* **1.** To call in a chant: *The crowd chanted for the president.* **2.** To sing a chant: *The monks chanted during the service.* **—chant′er** *n.*

chan·tey (**shăn′**tē *or* **chăn′**tē) *n., pl.* **chan·teys** also **chan·ties** A work song sung by sailors in earlier times to the rhythm of their work.

❑ *These sound alike:* **chantey, shanty** (shack).

Cha·nu·kah (**ᴋʜä′**nə-kə *or* **hä′**nə-kə) *n.* Variant of **Hanukkah.**

cha·os (**kā′**ŏs′) *n.* **1.** Great disorder or confusion: *The street was in chaos after the car accident.* **2.** often **Chaos** The shapeless and disordered state of unformed matter and infinite space supposed to have existed before the creation of the universe.

cha·ot·ic (kā-**ŏt′**ĭk) *adj.* In a state of chaos; in great disorder or confusion. **—cha·ot′i·cal·ly** *adv.*

chap[1] (chăp) *tr. & intr.v.* **chapped, chap·ping, chaps** To make or become dry, scaly, and cracked: *Harsh soaps will chap your hands. My lips chap easily in the cold weather.* ❖ *n.* A roughness and soreness of the skin, caused especially by cold. [From Middle English *chappen.*]

chap[2] (chăp) *n. Chiefly British* A man or boy; a fellow. [Short for *chapman*, peddler, from Old English *cēapman* : *cēap*, trade + *man*, man.]

chap. *abbr.* An abbreviation of chapter.

chap·ar·ral (shăp′ə-**răl′**) *n.* An area covered by a dense growth of mostly small-leaved evergreen shrubs, especially in central and southern California. [From Spanish, from *chaparro*, evergreen oak, from Basque *txapar*.]

cha·peau (shă-**pō′**) *n., pl.* **cha·peaus** or **cha·peaux** (shă-**pōz′**) A hat.

chap·el (**chăp′**əl) *n.* **1a.** A small church: *a little chapel in the hills.* **b.** A small place within a church with its own altar, reserved for special services: *The cathedral had a chapel dedicated to soldiers and sailors.* **2.** A place for religious services, as in a school, hospital, or military base. **3.** Religious services held at a chapel: *Students attended chapel before the holidays.*

chap·er·one or **chap·er·on** (**shăp′**ə-rōn′) *n.* **1.** An older person who attends and supervises a social gathering for young people. **2.** A person, especially an older or married woman, who accompanies a young unmarried woman in public. ❖ *tr.v.* **chaper·oned, chaper·on·ing, chaper·ones** To act as a chaperone for: *chaperone a party.* See Synonyms at **accompany.**

chap·lain (**chăp′**lĭn) *n.* **1.** A member of the clergy who conducts religious services and provides counseling for an institution, such as a prison or hospital. **2.** A lay person who provides counseling on spiritual matters to members of an organization or institution, such as a college.

chap·let (**chăp′**lĭt) *n.* **1.** A wreath for the head. **2.** A short rosary. **3.** A string of beads.

chaps (chăps) *pl.n.* Heavy leather coverings worn over pants by cowhands to protect their legs. Chaps buckle around the waist and have no seat. [Short for Spanish *chaparreras*, from *chaparro*, chaparral.]

chap·ter (**chăp′**tər) *n.* **1.** A main division of a book. **2.** A series of related events or a part of a person's life: *That was an exciting chapter in my life.* **3.** A local branch of a club, fraternity, or other organization.

Cha·pul·te·pec (chə-**pŏŏl′**tə-pĕk′) A rocky hill south of Mexico City, Mexico. It was the site of a major American victory (1847) during the Mexican War.

char (chär) *v.* **charred, char·ring, chars** —*tr.* To burn the surface or edge of; burn partially: *The fire charred the papers.* —*intr.* To become burned on the surface or edge: *The edge of the paper charred when it was held next to a burning match.*

char·ac·ter (**kăr′**ək-tər) *n.* **1.** The combination of qualities or features that makes one person, group, or thing different from another: *The character of the town is calm and peaceful.* **2.** One's moral nature: *an honest and upstanding student of fine character.* **3.** Moral strength; integrity: *a respected citizen of character.* **4.** A person portrayed in a work of art, such as a novel, play, or movie: *The hero is the chief character in the play.* **5.** *Informal* An odd or eccentric person. **6a.** A letter in a writing system. **b.** A symbol, letter, or number used in a computer code. **7.** A physical feature of an organism. ◆ **in character** Consistent with someone's general character or usual behavior. **out of character** Not consistent with one's general character or usual behavior: *Teasing friends is quite out of character for him.* [From Middle English *caracter*, distinctive mark, imprint on the soul, from Greek *kharaktēr*, from *kharassein*, to inscribe.]

char·ac·ter·is·tic (kăr′ək-tə-**rĭs′**tĭk) *adj.* Being a feature or quality that distinguishes a person or thing; typical: *the zebra's characteristic stripes; my friend's characteristic laugh.* ❖ *n.* **1.** Something that distinguishes a person or thing; a typical feature or quality: *A curved bill is a characteristic of parrots.* See Synonyms at **quality. 2.** The whole number in a logarithm. For example, if 2.713 is a logarithm, 2 is the characteristic. **—char′ac·ter·is′ti·cal·ly** *adv.*

char·ac·ter·i·za·tion (kăr′ək-tər-ĭ-**zā′**shən) *n.* **1.** The act or an instance of characterizing. **2.** A description of qualities: *This book has characterizations of all the restaurants in town.* **3.** Representation of a character or characters in literature or drama: *The author uses very realistic characterization in the novel.*

char·ac·ter·ize (**kăr′**ək-tə-rīz′) *tr.v.* **char·ac·ter·ized, char·ac·ter·iz·ing, char·ac·ter·iz·es 1.** To describe the character or qualities of; portray: *The supervisor's report characterized the nurse as very efficient.* **2.** To be a characteristic or quality of: *Spruce and birch forests characterize that region.*

cha·rade (shə-**rād′**) *n.* *(used with a singular or plural verb)* **1. charades** A game in which words or phrases are acted out in pantomime, often syllable by syllable, until guessed by the other players. **2.** Something done as a deception; a pretense: *Laughter is often a charade to cover up nervousness.*

char·broil (**chär′**broil′) *tr.v.* **char·broiled, char·broil·ing, char·broils** To broil (food) over charcoal or another heat source: *charbroiled some steaks.*

char·coal (**chär′**kōl′) *n.* **1.** A black porous material composed chiefly of carbon, produced by heating wood or sometimes bone until the lighter materials in it are burned away. It is used as a fuel, a filtering material, and for drawing. **2a.** A stick of this material, used for drawing. **b.** A drawing made with charcoal.

chard (chärd) *n.* A variety of beet having large succulent leaves that are eaten as a vegetable; Swiss chard.

charge (chärj) *v.* **charged, charg·ing, charg·es** —*tr.* **1a.** To ask as a price: *The shop charges three dollars to sharpen skates.* **b.** To demand payment from: *The store will charge you for wrapping the gift.* **2.** To postpone payment on (a purchase) by recording the amount owed: *We can charge school supplies to our account at the bookstore.* **3.** To rush toward or attack (someone or something): *The soldiers charged the hill.* **4.** In sports, to bump, check, or rush into (an opposing player) illegally. **5.** To accuse; blame: *The police charged the driver with reckless driving.* **6.** To command; order: *The judge charged the jury to consider all the evidence.* **7.** To entrust with a duty, task, or responsibility: *The reporter was charged with the task of discovering what really happened.* **8.** To load or fill: *They charged the furnace with coal.* **9.** To be present in every part of; fill: *The last scene of the movie was charged with excitement.* **10.** To fill with an amount of electrical energy; energize: *We can charge the car battery at the gas station.* —*intr.* **1.** To demand or ask payment: *They didn't charge for the repair.* **2a.** To rush forward in an attack: *The dog charged toward the stranger.* **b.** To move quickly or abruptly forward: *The children charged out of the room.* **3.** To postpone payment for a purchase. **4.** To become energized: *Don't unplug the battery while it's charging.* ❖ *n.* **1.** An amount asked or made as payment: *There is no charge for this delivery.* **2.** Care; supervision; control: *the scientist in charge of the laboratory.* See Synonyms at **care. 3.** A person or thing for which one is responsible: *The camp counselors took their charges to the amusement park.* **4.** A duty or task; a responsibility: *My charge is to find out what happened.* **5.** An order or command: *received a written charge to attend the hearing.* **6.** An accusation, especially one made formally, as in a legal case: *The charge against the defendant was dismissed.* **7.** A rushing forceful attack: *the charge of a bull elephant.* **8.** The amount of electrical energy contained in an object, particle, or region of space. A charge is positive if the object or space contains fewer electrons than protons. A charge is negative if the object or space contains more electrons than protons. **9.** The quantity that an apparatus or container can hold: *They gave the battery a full charge.* **10.** An amount of explosive to be set off at one time: *a box of dynamite charges.* **11.** *Informal* A feeling of excitement; a thrill: *They got a real charge from seeing the Grand Canyon.* ◆ **in charge** In a position of authority or management; in command: *The manager of the store is in charge.* **in charge of** Having control over or

SCIENCE

charge Electric **charge** is a basic property of elementary particles of matter. The protons in an atom have a positive charge, while the electrons have a negative charge. In an ordinary atom, the number of protons equals the number of electrons, so the atom is electrically neutral. If an atom gains some electrons, it becomes negatively charged. If it loses some electrons, it becomes positively charged. Atoms that become charged are called *ions*. Particles with the opposite charge attract one another, and those with the same charge repel one another. *Static electricity* consists of charged particles at rest. Electric *current* consists of moving charged particles, especially electrons or ions. Electric currents provide energy for the appliances you use every day and operate in your body, too, carrying impulses along nerve cells.

chariot

chateau
Chateau Azay-le-Rideau, near Tours, France

ă	pat	ôr	core
ā	pay	oi	boy
âr	care	ou	out
ä	father	o͝o	took
ĕ	pet	o͝or	lure
ē	be	o͞o	boot
ĭ	pit	ŭ	cut
ī	bite	ûr	urge
îr	pier	th	thin
ŏ	pot	*th*	this
ō	toe	zh	vision
ô	paw	ə	about

responsibility for: *The recreation department is in charge of the annual fireworks display.* [From Middle English *chargen*, to load, from Late Latin *carricāre*, from Latin *carrus*, Gaulish wagon, of Celtic origin.] —SEE NOTE.

char·gé d'af·faires (shär-zhā′ dä-**fâr′**) *n., pl.* **char·gés d'affaires** (shär-zhā′ dä-**fâr′** *or* shär-**zhāz′** dä-**fâr′**) **1.** A government official who temporarily takes over the duties of an absent ambassador or minister. **2.** A diplomat of the lowest rank.

charg·er[1] (**chär′**jər) *n.* **1.** A device used to charge electric storage batteries. **2.** A horse ridden in battle.

charg·er[2] (**chär′**jər) *n.* A large shallow dish; a platter. [From Middle English *chargeour*, from Old French *chargier*, to load.]

char·i·ot (**chăr′**ē-ət) *n.* A horse-drawn two-wheeled vehicle used in ancient times in battles, races, and processions.

char·i·o·teer (chăr′ē-ə-**tîr′**) *n.* A person who drives a chariot.

cha·ris·ma (kə-**rĭz′**mə) *n., pl.* **cha·ris·ma·ta** (kə-**rĭz′**-mə-tə) A special quality of individuals who show an exceptional ability to lead and win the devotion of large numbers of people.

char·is·mat·ic (kăr′ĭz-**măt′**ĭk) *adj.* Having or showing charisma: *a charismatic leader.*

char·i·ta·ble (**chăr′**ĭ-tə-bəl) *adj.* **1.** Concerned with helping the needy: *a charitable organization.* **2.** Showing love or goodwill; full of kindness: *a warm charitable spirit.* **3.** Generous in giving money or help to the needy. **4.** Tolerant or lenient in judging others or their work: *a charitable review of the movie.* **—char′i·ta·ble·ness** *n.* **—char′i·ta·bly** *adv.*

char·i·ty (**chăr′**ĭ-tē) *n., pl.* **char·i·ties 1.** Help or relief to the needy: *raising money for charity.* **2.** An institution or fund established to help the needy: *a ten-dollar donation to a charity.* **3.** Goodwill or kind feelings toward others: *known for her charity and generosity of spirit.* **4.** Tolerance and leniency in judging others: *Lincoln urged charity for all after the Civil War.* [From Middle English *charite*, from Latin *cāritās*.]

char·la·tan (**shär′**lə-tən) *n.* A person who deceives others by falsely claiming to have expert knowledge or skill; a quack. [From Italian *ciarlatano*, probably alteration of *cerretano*, inhabitant of *Cerreto*, a city of Italy once famous for its quacks.]

Char·le·magne (**shär′**lə-mān′) 742?–814. King of the Franks (768–814) whose court was the center of a cultural rebirth in Europe.

Charles I (chärlz) 1600–1649. King of England, Scotland, and Ireland (1625–1649) who was tried for treason and beheaded.

Charles II 1630–1685. King of England, Scotland, and Ireland (1660–1685) who reigned during the Restoration.

Charles·ton[1] (**chärl′**stən) **1.** A city of southeast South Carolina northeast of Savannah, Georgia. The Civil War began in 1861 with the Confederate attack on Fort Sumter in Charleston Harbor. **2.** The capital of West Virginia, in the west-central part of the state.

Charles·ton[2] (**chärl′**stən) *n.* A quick lively dance popular in the 1920s.

char·ley horse (**chär′**lē) *n. Informal* A muscle cramp or stiffness, especially in the leg.

Char·lotte (**shär′**lət) The largest city of North Carolina, in the southern part of the state near the South Carolina border west-southwest of Raleigh. It was settled in about 1750.

Charlotte A·ma·lie (ə-**mäl′**yə) The capital of the US Virgin Islands, on St. Thomas Island in the West Indies east of Puerto Rico.

Char·lotte·town (**shär′**lət-toun′) The capital of Prince Edward Island, Canada, on the southern coast of the island. It was founded in about 1720.

charm (chärm) *n.* **1.** The power or ability to please or delight; appeal: *The old house had a lot of charm.* **2.** A quality or manner that pleases or attracts: *Her wit is one of her many charms.* **3.** A saying, action, or thing supposed to have magical power, as in warding off evil. **4.** A trinket or small ornament worn hanging on a bracelet or chain. ❖ *tr.v.* **charmed, charm·ing, charms 1.** To please greatly; delight: *The audience was charmed by the young pianist.* **2.** To attract and delight (someone) or cause (someone to do something) by being attractive or pleasant: *The children's laughter charmed us into playing the game again.* **3.** To cast a magical spell on; bewitch. ◆ **like a charm** Exceedingly well. [From Middle English *charme*, magic spell, from Latin *carmen*, incantation.] **—charm′er** *n.*

charm·ing (**chär′**mĭng) *adj.* Delightful; attractive; very pleasing: *a charming person; charming manners.* **—charm′ing·ly** *adv.*

char·nel house (**chär′**nəl) *n.* A building, room, or vault in which the bodies or bones of the dead are placed.

Char·on (**kâr′**ən) *n.* In Greek mythology, the ferryman who carried the dead over the river Styx to Hades.

chart (chärt) *n.* **1.** Something written or drawn, as a table or graph, that presents information in an organized, easily viewed form: *a chart showing rainfall for the last ten years.* **2.** A map showing coastlines, water depths, or other information of use to navigators. **3.** often **charts** A list of best-selling recorded music: *The song reached the top of the charts only a few weeks after it was released.* ❖ *tr.v.* **chart·ed, chart·ing, charts 1.** To show or record on a chart; make a chart of: *chart the daily changes in temperature.* **2.** To plan in detail: *I hope to chart a course for success.* [From Latin *charta*, sheet of paper made from papyrus.]

char·ter (**chär′**tər) *n.* **1.** A written grant or document from a ruler, government, or other group, giving certain rights to a person, corporation, or entire people: *The Magna Carta is a famous charter granted by King John of England in 1215 to his nobles.* **2.** A document, such as a constitution, stating the principles, function, and form of a governing body or organization: *The United Nations is governed by a charter.* **3.** The hiring or renting of a bus, aircraft, boat, or other vehicle for a special use. ❖ *tr.v.* **char·tered, char·ter·ing, char·ters 1.** To grant a charter to; establish by charter: *Congress chartered the bank for twenty years.* **2.** To hire or rent for private use: *The travel club chartered a plane.* **—char′ter·er** *n.*

charter school *n.* An independent public school, often with a distinct curriculum and educational philosophy.

char·treuse (shär-**tro͞oz′** *or* shär-**tro͞os′**) *n.* A light yellowish green.

char·wom·an (**chär′**wo͝om′ən) *n.* A woman hired to do cleaning, usually in an office or a large building.

char·y (**châr′**ē) *adj.* **char·i·er, char·i·est 1.** Cautious; wary: *chary of walking on thin ice.* **2.** Not giving freely; sparing: *chary of compliments.* **—char′i·ly** *adv.* **—char′i·ness** *n.*

Cha·ryb·dis (kə-**rĭb′**dĭs) *n.* In Greek mythology, a whirlpool opposite the cave of Scylla near Sicily, personified as a monster because of its ability to destroy ships.

chase (chās) *v.* **chased, chas·ing, chas·es** *—tr.* **1.** To follow quickly and try to catch or overtake; pursue: *Our dog chased the cat.* **2.** To drive away: *chased the rabbits from the garden.* *—intr.* **1.** To go or follow in pursuit: *chase after a loose dog.* **2.** *Informal* To hurry; rush: *chasing about town doing last-minute errands.* ❖ *n.* **1.** The act of chasing; rapid pursuit: *The police arrested the driver after a wild chase.* **2a.** The hunting of wild animals. **b.** Something that is hunted; quarry: *The hunters drove their chase into the open.* [From Middle English *chacen*, to hunt, from Latin *captāre*, to capture.]

chas·er (**chā′**sər) *n.* **1.** A person or thing that chases or pursues. **2.** *Informal* A drink of water, beer, or other liquid taken after a drink of hard liquor.

chasm (kăz′əm) *n.* **1.** A deep crack or opening in the surface of the earth; a gorge. **2.** A gap, such as that caused by a difference of opinion or attitude: *a chasm in communication.* [From Greek *khasma.*]

chas·sis (chăs′ē) *n., pl.* **chas·sis** (chăs′ēz) **1.** The frame of an automotive vehicle that supports the body and includes the motor, gears, axles, and wheels. **2.** The landing gear of an aircraft. **3.** The structure that holds and supports the parts of an electronic device.

chaste (chāst) *adj.* **chast·er, chast·est 1a.** Having never experienced sexual intercourse; virginal. **b.** Abstaining from sexual intercourse; celibate. **2.** Not involving or suggestive of sexual desire or indecency: *a chaste conversation.* **3.** Not ornate or extreme; pure in style or simple in design. **—chaste′ly** *adv.* **—chaste′ness** *n.*

chas·ten (chā′sən) *tr.v.* **chas·tened, chas·ten·ing, chas·tens 1.** To discipline or correct (someone) by punishment. **2.** To cause to become subdued or meek; restrain: *a spirit chastened by hard experience.* **—chas′ten·er** *n.*

chas·tise (chăs-tīz′ *or* chăs′tīz′) *tr.v.* **chas·tised, chas·tis·ing, chas·tis·es** To punish or criticize severely for misbehavior or wrongdoing. **—chas·tise′ment** *n.* **—chas·tis′er** *n.*

chas·ti·ty (chăs′tĭ-tē) *n.* The condition or quality of being chaste or pure.

chat (chăt) *intr.v.* **chat·ted, chat·ting, chats 1.** To converse in a relaxed, friendly, informal manner: *chat with friends.* **2.** To exchange remarks over a computer network in real time. ❖ *n.* **1.** A relaxed, friendly, informal conversation. **2.** An exchange of remarks that takes place on a computer network and happens in real time. **3.** Any of several songbirds having a chattering call.

chat·bot (chăt′bŏt′) *n.* A bot that mimics human conversation. Some chatbots are used by businesses for interacting with customers, and others are used by criminals to commit fraud.

cha·teau also **châ·teau** (shă-tō′) *n., pl.* **cha·teaus** or **cha·teaux** (shă-tōz′) **1.** A French castle or manor house. **2.** A large country house. [From Old French *chastel,* from Latin *castellum,* castle.]

chat·e·laine (shăt′l-ān′) *n.* **1.** The woman who is in charge of a castle or large house. **2.** A clasp or chain worn at the waist for holding keys, a watch, or a purse.

chat·room (chăt′ro͝om′ *or* chăt′ro͞om′) *n.* A site on a computer network where online conversations are held in real time.

Chat·ta·noo·ga (chăt′ə-no͞o′gə) A city of southeast Tennessee on the Georgia border southeast of Nashville. It was strategically important during the Civil War.

chat·tel (chăt′l) *n.* **1.** An article of personal property that can be moved from place to place, as a piece of furniture or an animal. **2.** A slave. [From Middle English *chatel,* from Old French, from Medieval Latin *capitāle.*]

chat·ter (chăt′ər) *v.* **chat·tered, chat·ter·ing, chat·ters** *—intr.* **1.** To make short rapid sounds that resemble speech, as some animals and birds do: *Monkeys chattered in the trees.* **2.** To talk rapidly and at length about something unimportant; jabber. **3.** To make a rapid series of rattling or clicking noises: *My teeth chattered with cold.* *—tr.* To utter in a rapid and thoughtless way: *chatter nonsense.* ❖ *n.* **1.** Idle talk about unimportant matters: *All of that gossip is just neighborhood chatter.* **2.** The sharp rapid sounds made by some birds and animals. **3.** A series of quick rattling or clicking sounds: *the chatter of a typewriter.*

chat·ter·box (chăt′ər-bŏks′) *n.* A person who seems to talk all the time.

chat·ty (chăt′ē) *adj.* **chat·ti·er, chat·ti·est 1.** Known for chatting, especially about unimportant things: *a chatty person full of gossip.* **2.** Having the tone or style of informal conversation: *a chatty website about current celebrities.* **—chat′ti·ly** *adv.* **—chat′ti·ness** *n.*

Chau·cer (chô′sər), **Geoffrey** 1340?–1400. English poet whose writing presents a detailed picture of life and values in late-medieval England. His works include *The Canterbury Tales* (1387–1400).

Geoffrey Chaucer
portrait from an early 15th-century manuscript of the *Canterbury Tales*

chauf·feur (shō′fər *or* shō-fûr′) *n.* A person who is hired to drive an automobile. ❖ *tr.v.* **chauf·feured, chauf·feur·ing, chauf·feurs** To serve as a driver for: *chauffeuring visiting relatives to see the local sights.* [From French, stoker, from Old French *chaufer,* to heat, stoke.]

chau·vin·ism (shō′və-nĭz′əm) *n.* **1.** Extreme devotion to one's country or a cause; fanatical patriotism. **2.** Unwarranted belief in the superiority of one's own group. [From French *chauvinisme,* after Nicolas *Chauvin,* a legendary French soldier famous for his devotion to Napoleon.] **—chau′vin·ist** *n.* **—chau′vin·is′tic** *adj.*

Chá·vez (chä′vĕz′ *or* shä′vĕz′), **César** 1927–1993. American labor organizer and cofounder of the United Farm Workers (1962).

César Chávez
photographed in 1990

cheap (chēp) *adj.* **cheap·er, cheap·est 1.** Low in price; inexpensive or comparatively inexpensive: *Tomatoes are cheap and plentiful in the summer months.* **2.** Charging low prices: *a cheap restaurant.* **3.** Requiring little effort; easily gotten: *a cheap victory.* **4.** Of little value or poor quality; inferior: *cheap shoes that wear out quickly.* **5.** Worthy of no respect; contemptible: *cheap humor.* **6.** Not spending or giving money generously; stingy: *a miser's cheap ways.* ❖ *adv.* **cheaper, cheapest** At a low price: *an old car that we bought cheap.* [From Middle English *(god) chep,* (good) price, purchase, bargain, from Old English *cēap,* trade, from Latin *caupō,* shopkeeper.] **—cheap′ly** *adv.* **—cheap′ness** *n.*

❑ *These sound alike:* **cheap, cheep** (chirp).

cheap·en (chē′pən) *tr. & intr.v.* **cheap·ened, cheap·en·ing, cheap·ens** To make or become cheap or cheaper: *Rude behavior tends to cheapen one's reputation.*

cheap shot *n.* An unfair statement directed especially at a vulnerable person or group.

cheap·skate (chēp′skāt′) *n. Slang* A stingy person; a miser. [From *cheap* + *skate,* obsolete term for mean person.]

cheat (chēt) *v.* **cheat·ed, cheat·ing, cheats** *—tr.* **1.** To deceive by trickery: *The grocer cheated customers by selling old bread at full prices.* **2.** To deprive of something dishonestly or unfairly; swindle: *The grain dealer cheated farmers out of their profits.* **3.** To elude or escape as if by trickery or deception: *The daring mountain climbers cheated death.* *—intr.* To act dishonestly: *cheat to pass a test; cheat at cards.* ❖ *n.* **1.** A person who cheats; a swindler. **2.** An act of cheating; a fraud or swindle: *a scheme that was nothing but a big cheat.* **—cheat′er** *n.*

Chech·en (chĕch′ən) *n.* **1a.** A native or inhabitant of Chechnya. **b.** A member of the predominant, traditionally Muslim ethnic group of Chechnya. **2.** The language of this people. **—Chech′en** *adj.*

Chech·nya (chĕch′nē-ə *or* chĕch-nyä′) A region of southwest Russia in the northern Caucasus. Chechnya declared its independence from the USSR in 1991, but after two wars (1994–1996 and 1999–2000), Russia regained control of most of the region.

check (chĕk) *v.* **checked, check·ing, checks** *—tr.* **1.** To test, examine, or make sure of: *Check your answers after finishing the math problems. I will check the address before we go.* **2.** To mark with a check: *Check each item on the list that is missing on the shelf.* **3.** To cause to stop suddenly; halt: *The farmers checked erosion by building terraces across their sloping fields.* **4.** To restrain or control: *The angry driver checked a sudden urge to shout.* **5.** In sports such as hockey, to block or hinder (an opposing player with the puck) by using one's body or one's stick. **6.** In chess, to move a piece so as to place

checkered
checkered flooring

cheetah

(an opponent's king) under direct attack. **7.** To place for temporary safekeeping or shipping: *They checked their baggage at the airport.* **8.** To mark with a pattern of squares: *A pattern of blue and white squares checked the floor.* —*intr.* **1.** To make an examination; be sure something is true or correct: *check on departure times; check with the teacher before leaving.* **2.** To correspond item for item; agree: *Our two lists checked exactly.* ❖ *n.* **1.** A careful examination or investigation to see that something is being done or working properly: *A check of the math homework revealed several errors.* **2.** Something that stops motion or expression; a restraint: *The snowstorm was a check on all air travel.* **3.** The condition of being stopped or held back: *The dry weather kept the mosquitoes in check.* **4.** A mark made to show that something has been noted, selected, or is accurate. **5.** A ticket or slip for identifying and claiming something: *a baggage check.* **6.** A written order to a bank to pay a certain amount from funds on deposit in an account: *write a check to pay a bill.* **7.** A bill at a restaurant: *The waiter gave us our check at the end of the meal.* **8.** In chess, the situation of the king when under direct attack by an opponent's piece. **9.** In hockey, the action of checking an opposing player. **10a.** A pattern of squares resembling a checkerboard. **b.** A single square in such a pattern: *a floor made of black and white checks.* **c.** A fabric printed or woven with such a pattern. ◆ **check in** To register or sign in, as at a hotel: *check in before the flight.* **check out 1.** To leave, as after paying a hotel bill. **2a.** To take after having paid the amount owed: *check out groceries at a supermarket.* **b.** To take after having recorded what is being taken: *check out books from the library.* **3.** To be confirmed as true: *The suspect's story checks out.* [From Middle English *chek*, check in chess, from Old French *eschec*, from Arabic *šāh*, from Persian *shāh*, king, shah, king in chess, check.]

check·book (chĕk′bo͝ok′) *n.* A book containing blank checks, given by a bank to a depositor who has a checking account.

check card *n.* A debit card that enables the user to withdraw money from a checking account.

checked (chĕkt) *adj.* Having a pattern of squares; checkered: *a checked shirt.*

check·er (chĕk′ər) *n.* **1.** A person or thing that checks, as for accuracy: *Our word processor has a checker for spelling.* **2.** A person who receives items for safekeeping or shipping: *a baggage checker.* **3.** A cashier in a supermarket. **4.** One of the pieces used in the game of checkers. **5a.** A pattern of many squares. **b.** One of the squares in such a pattern. ❖ *tr.v.* **check·ered, check·er·ing, check·ers** To mark with a pattern of squares. [From Middle English *cheker*, chessboard, from Old French *eschequier*, from *eschec*, check in chess.]

check·er·board (chĕk′ər-bôrd′) *n.* A game board divided into 64 squares of alternating colors, on which games of checkers are played.

check·ered (chĕk′ərd) *adj.* **1.** Marked with or divided into squares: *a checkered floor.* **2.** Varied in experiences, including some suspicious or immoral incidents: *a checkered career.*

check·ers (chĕk′ərz) *pl.n. (used with a singular verb)* A game played on a checkerboard by two players, each using 12 round, flat pieces. Each player tries to capture all of the opponent's pieces.

check·ing account (chĕk′ĭng) *n.* A bank account from which payments may be made by writing checks against the amount on deposit.

check·list (chĕk′lĭst′) *n.* A list of items to be checked, noted, or remembered.

check mark *n.* A mark placed next to an item to show that it has been noted, verified, approved, or otherwise dealt with.

check·mate (chĕk′māt′) *tr.v.* **check·mat·ed, check·mat·ing, check·mates 1.** In chess, to move so as to place (an opponent's king) under threat of being taken on the next move with no chance of escape or defense, thus ending the game. **2.** To defeat completely. ❖ *n.* **1.** In chess, a move or situation that checkmates an opponent's king. **2.** A situation in which one is completely defeated. [From Middle English *chekmat*, from Old French *eschec mat*, from Arabic *šāh māt*, the king is dead : *šāh*, king + *māt*, died.]

check·out (chĕk′out′) *n.* **1.** The act or process of checking out, as at a supermarket, library, or hotel. **2.** A test or inspection, as of a machine, for working condition or accuracy.

check·point (chĕk′point′) *n.* A place where pedestrians or vehicles are stopped for inspection.

check·room (chĕk′ro͞om′ *or* chĕk′ro͝om′) *n.* A room where coats, packages, or baggage may be left temporarily.

check·up (chĕk′ŭp′) *n.* A thorough examination or inspection, as for health or general working condition: *regular medical checkups; an engine checkup.*

Ched·dar also **ched·dar** (chĕd′ər) *n.* A firm, smooth, usually yellowish cheese first made in Cheddar, a village of southwest England.

cheek (chēk) *n.* **1.** The part of either side of the face below the eye and between the nose and ear. **2.** Rudely assertive behavior; disrespectful boldness: *have the cheek to tell one's elders what to do.* **3.** *Informal* A buttock. [From Old English *cēce*.]

cheek·bone (chēk′bōn′) *n.* A small bone on the side of the face just below the eye, forming the outermost point of the cheek.

cheek pouch *n.* A pocketlike fold of skin in the cheeks of various animals in which food can be carried.

cheek·y (chē′kē) *adj.* **cheek·i·er, cheek·i·est** Impudent; impertinent: *a cheeky smart aleck.* **—cheek′i·ly** *adv.* **—cheek′i·ness** *n.*

cheep (chēp) *n.* A high-pitched chirp, like that of a young bird. ❖ *intr.v.* **cheeped, cheep·ing, cheeps** To make such a sound.

❑ *These sound alike:* **cheep, cheap** (inexpensive).

cheer (chîr) *n.* **1.** A shout of happiness, approval, encouragement, or enthusiasm: *The crowd gave a loud cheer for the winning team.* **2.** A slogan or chant shouted in encouragement or approval, as for a school's team at a game. **3.** Happiness; good spirits: *full of cheer.* **4.** Something that gives joy or happiness: *Friends sent words of cheer and encouragement.* **5.** Food and drink: *came over for some holiday cheer.* ❖ *v.* **cheered, cheer·ing, cheers** —*intr.* **1.** To shout in happiness, approval, encouragement, or enthusiasm: *The audience cheered and clapped.* **2.** To become cheerful: *In spite of my disappointment, I soon cheered up.* —*tr.* **1.** To praise, encourage, or urge by shouting: *The fans cheered the runner on.* **2.** To make happier or more cheerful: *A warm fire soon cheered us up.* [From Middle English *chere*, expression, mood, from Late Latin *cara*, face, from Greek *kara*, head.]

cheer·ful (chîr′fəl) *adj.* **1.** In good spirits; good-humored or happy: *Everyone was cheerful at breakfast.* See Synonyms at **glad. 2.** Producing a feeling of cheer: *a cheerful hello; a cozy, cheerful room.* **—cheer′ful·ly** *adv.* **—cheer′ful·ness** *n.*

cheer·lead·er (chîr′lē′dər) *n.* **1.** A person who leads the cheering of spectators, as at a football game. **2.** A member of a group that performs coordinated routines combining gymnastic and dance moves, often in competition with similar groups. **—cheer′lead′** *v.*

cheer·less (chîr′lĭs) *adj.* Lacking cheer; gloomy and depressing: *a cheerless rainy day.* **—cheer′less·ly** *adv.* **—cheer′less·ness** *n.*

cheer·y (chîr′ē) *adj.* **cheer·i·er, cheer·i·est** Bright and

ă	pat	ôr	core
ā	pay	oi	boy
âr	care	ou	out
ä	father	o͝o	took
ĕ	pet	o͝or	lure
ē	be	o͞o	boot
ĭ	pit	ŭ	cut
ī	bite	ûr	urge
îr	pier	th	thin
ŏ	pot	*th*	this
ō	toe	zh	vision
ô	paw	ə	about

cheerful: *a cheery smile; a cheery fire.* —**cheer′i·ly** *adv.* —**cheer′i·ness** *n.*

cheese (chēz) *n.* A food made from pressed curds of milk, often seasoned and aged. [From Old English *cēse, cȳse*, from Latin *cāseus*.]

cheese·burg·er (chēz′bûr′gər) *n.* A hamburger topped with melted cheese.

cheese·cake (chēz′kāk′) *n.* A cake made with sweetened cream cheese or cottage cheese and often with various flavorings.

cheese·cloth (chēz′klôth′) *n.* A thin, loosely woven cotton cloth resembling gauze, originally used for wrapping cheese.

chees·y (chē′zē) *adj.* **chees·i·er, chees·i·est 1.** Containing or resembling cheese. **2.** *Informal* **a.** Of poor quality; shoddy: *a cheap room with cheesy furniture.* **b.** Lacking in refinement or subtlety: *a cheesy movie.* —**chees′i·ly** *adv.* —**chees′i·ness** *n.*

chee·tah (chē′tə) *n.* A long-legged, swift-running wild cat of Africa and southwest Asia that has tawny fur with black spots. [From Hindi *cītā*, from Sanskrit *citrakāyaḥ*, tiger, leopard.]

chef (shĕf) *n.* A cook, especially the chief cook of a large kitchen staff, as in a restaurant.

che·la (kē′lə) *n., pl.* **che·lae** (kē′lē) A pincerlike claw of a scorpion or a crustacean such as a lobster or crab. [From New Latin *chēla*, from Greek *khēlē*, claw.]

che·lic·er·a (kĭ-lĭs′ər-ə) *n., pl.* **che·lic·er·ae** (kĭ-lĭs′ə-rē′) Either of the first pair of fanglike appendages near the mouth of an arachnid, such as a spider, or a horseshoe crab, used for grasping, piercing, or injecting venom. [From New Latin : English *chela* + Greek *keras*, horn.]

chem·i·cal (kĕm′ĭ-kəl) *adj.* **1.** Relating to chemistry: *a chemical discovery.* **2.** Used in or produced by means of chemistry: *a chemical symbol; a chemical change.* ❖ *n.* A substance obtained by or used in a chemical process. —**chem′i·cal·ly** *adv.*

chemical engineering *n.* The branch of engineering that deals with the industrial production of chemicals and chemical products. —**chemical engineer** *n.*

chemical weapon *n.* A poisonous chemical agent, usually a gas or aerosol, that has been prepared for release on the battlefield or within a civilian population in order to cause widespread illness or death.

che·mise (shə-mēz′) *n.* **1.** A woman's undergarment that resembles a short, loose slip. **2.** A loosely fitting dress that hangs straight from the shoulders.

chem·ist (kĕm′ĭst) *n.* **1.** A scientist who specializes in chemistry. **2.** *Chiefly British* A pharmacist. [From Medieval Latin *alchymista*, alchemist, from *alchymia*, alchemy.]

chem·is·try (kĕm′ĭ-strē) *n., pl.* **chem·is·tries 1.** The science that deals with the structure, properties, and reactions of the elements and the compounds they form. **2.** The chemical properties of a substance or a system of substances: *the chemistry of the blood.* **3.** Mutual trust or understanding: *The two partners started a business, but there was no chemistry between them.*

che·mo·syn·the·sis (kē′mō-sĭn′thĭ-sĭs) *n.* The formation of carbohydrates from carbon dioxide and water using energy obtained from chemical reactions rather than from light, as in photosynthesis. Certain bacteria, especially those that live deep in the ocean, use chemosynthesis for making their own food. —**che′mo·syn·thet′ic** (kē′mo-sĭn-thĕt′ĭk) *adj.*

che·mo·ther·a·py (kē′mō-thĕr′ə-pē) *n.* The treatment of disease with chemicals that have a specific poisonous effect on the disease-causing organisms or cells. Chemotherapy is used especially to stop the spread or growth of certain cancers. —**che′mo·ther′a·peu′tic** *adj.*

che·nille (shə-nēl′) *n.* **1.** Cord or yarn of silk, cotton, wool, or rayon with a fuzzy velvety pile, used for making fringes, tassels, or embroidery. **2.** Fabric made with this cord, used for bedspreads, rugs, and curtains.

Chen·nai (chə-nī′) Formerly **Ma·dras** (mə-drăs′ *or* mə-dräs′). A city of southeast India on the Bay of Bengal southeast of Mumbai (Bombay). It was founded in 1639.

Che·ops (kē′ŏps) 2609–2584 BC. A king of Egypt who is famous as the builder of the Great Pyramid.

cheque (chĕk) *n. Chiefly British* Variant of **check** (sense 6).

cher·ish (chĕr′ĭsh) *tr.v.* **cher·ished, cher·ish·ing, cher·ish·es 1.** To treat with affection and tenderness; hold dear: *The children cherished the little kittens.* **2.** To keep fondly in mind; treasure: *She cherished the memories from her childhood.* See Synonyms at **appreciate.**

Cher·o·kee (chĕr′ə-kē′ *or* chĕr′ə-kē′) *n., pl.* **Cherokee** or **Cher·o·kees 1.** A member of a Native American people formerly living in the Appalachian Mountains of the western Carolinas, northern Georgia, and eastern Tennessee, now living mainly in Oklahoma and western North Carolina. **2.** The Iroquoian language of the Cherokee.

cher·ry (chĕr′ē) *n., pl.* **cher·ries 1.** Any of various small, round, fleshy fruits having smooth skin and a hard pit. Cherries range in color from yellow to bright red to dark purple and can be sour or sweet. **2.** A tree that bears such fruit. **3.** The wood of such a tree. **4.** A deep or bright red. [From Middle English *cheri*, ultimately from Greek *kerasiā*, cherry tree.] —SEE NOTE AT **kudos.**

cherry bomb *n.* A round, red firecracker that explodes with a loud bang.

cherry tomato *n.* A small variety of tomato.

cher·ub (chĕr′əb) *n., pl.* **cher·u·bim** (chĕr′ə-bĭm) **1.** An angel of high rank. **2.** *pl.* **cher·ubs a.** An angel, usually shown in pictures as a beautiful winged child with a chubby face. **b.** A sweet, pretty, or innocent-looking child. —**che·ru′bic** (chə-ro͞o′bĭk) *adj.*

Ches·a·peake Bay (chĕs′ə-pēk′) An inlet of the Atlantic Ocean cutting through coastal Virginia and Maryland.

chess (chĕs) *n.* A game played on a chessboard by two players, each starting with 16 pieces that are moved in various ways. The object of the game is to checkmate the opponent's king. [From Middle English *ches*, short for Old French *esches*, plural of *eschec*, check in chess.]

chess·board (chĕs′bôrd′) *n.* A game board with 64 squares in alternating colors, used in playing chess.

chess·man (chĕs′măn′) *n.* One of the pieces used in the game of chess; a king, queen, bishop, knight, rook, or pawn.

chest (chĕst) *n.* **1a.** The part of the body between the neck and the abdomen, enclosed by the ribs and breastbone. **b.** The front portion of this part of the body: *a man with a tattoo on his chest.* **2.** A sturdy box with a lid, used especially for holding or storing things: *a tool chest.* **3.** A small cabinet with shelves used to store things: *Bandages are kept in the medicine chest above the sink.* **4.** A chest of drawers.

ches·ter·field (chĕs′tər-fēld′) *n.* **1.** An overcoat, usually with a velvet collar. **2.** A large sofa with rounded armrests.

chest·nut (chĕs′nŭt′) *n.* **1.** A smooth, reddish-brown, edible nut of any of several trees of northern regions that is enclosed in a prickly husk. **2.** A tree that bears such nuts. **3.** The wood of such a tree. **4.** A reddish brown. **5.** A reddish-brown horse. **6.** Something lacking freshness or originality, such as an old stale joke or story. ❖ *adj.* Reddish-brown.

chest of drawers *n., pl.* **chests of drawers** A piece of furniture with several drawers, used chiefly for keeping clothes; a bureau or dresser.

chev·a·lier (shĕv′ə-lîr′) *n.* **1.** A knight or nobleman. **2.** A member of certain male honorary groups or orders. [From Middle English *chevaler*, from Late Latin

chess

chestnut
American chestnut

chevron

Chiang Kai-shek

WRITERS CHOOSE THEIR WORDS

A tiny dog who looked like a hairy beetle sat on [Madame Joanna's] lap all through dinner. She fed him the best pieces of meat picked from the serving bowls. Sometimes the dog sniffed or licked a piece of meat and then would not eat it, so she'd put it back in the bowl. No one dared **chide** her, her being the cousin of the king!

—Karen Cushman
Catherine, Called Birdy

ă	pat	ôr	core
ā	pay	oi	boy
âr	care	ou	out
ä	father	o͝o	took
ĕ	pet	o͝or	lure
ē	be	o͞o	boot
ĭ	pit	ŭ	cut
ī	bite	ûr	urge
îr	pier	th	thin
ŏ	pot	*th*	this
ō	toe	zh	vision
ô	paw	ə	about

caballārius, horseman, from Latin *caballus*, horse.] —SEE NOTE AT **chivalry**.

chev·ron (shĕv′rən) *n.* A badge of stripes meeting at an angle, worn on the sleeve, as of a military or police uniform, to show rank, merit, or length of service.

chew (cho͞o) *v.* **chewed, chew·ing, chews** —*tr.* To bite and grind with the teeth: *chew food thoroughly.* —*intr.* To make crushing or grinding motions with the teeth. ❖ *n.* **1.** The act of chewing: *puppies having a good chew on a bone.* **2.** Something held in the mouth and chewed. [From Old English *cēowan*.] **—chew′a·ble** *adj.* **—chew′er** *n.*

chew·ing gum (cho͞o′ĭng) *n.* A sweet flavored gum for chewing, formerly made of chicle, but now made of synthetic substances.

chew·y (cho͞o′ē) *adj.* **chew·i·er, chew·i·est** Needing much chewing in order to swallow: *tough chewy steak.* **—chew′i·ness** *n.*

Chey·enne[1] (shī-ĕn′ *or* shī-ăn′) *n., pl.* **Cheyenne** or **Chey·ennes 1.** A member of a Native American people formerly living in parts of the eastern Rocky Mountains and the western Great Plains, now living mainly in Oklahoma and Montana. **2.** The Algonquian language of the Cheyenne. **—Chey·enne′** *adj.*

Chey·enne[2] (shī-ăn′ *or* shī-ĕn′) The capital of Wyoming, in the southeast part of the state near the Nebraska and Colorado borders. It was founded in 1867.

chi[1] (kī *or* kē) *n.* The 22nd letter of the Greek alphabet, written X, χ. In English, it is represented as *Kh, kh* or *Ch, ch.*

chi[2] (chē) *n.* The vital force believed in Taoism and other Chinese philosophy to exist as part of all things.

Chiang Kai-shek (chăng′ kī′shĕk′) 1887–1975. Chinese military and political figure who led the Nationalists from 1928 until his defeat by Communist forces in 1949. He fled to Taiwan, where he served as president of Nationalist China until his death.

chic (shēk) *adj.* **chic·er, chic·est** Attractive and stylish; fashionable: *a chic gown; a chic crowd.* ❖ *n.* Style and elegance in dress or manner. [From French, probably from German *Schick*, skill, fitness, elegance.]
❑ *These sound alike:* **chic, sheikh** (Arab leader).

Chi·ca·go (shĭ-kä′gō *or* shĭ-kô′gō) The largest city of Illinois, in the northeast part of the state on Lake Michigan. It is the commercial, financial, industrial, and cultural center of the Midwest.

Chi·ca·na (chĭ-kä′nə *or* shĭ-kä′nə) *n.* A Mexican-American woman or girl. **—Chi·ca′na** *adj.*

chi·can·er·y (shĭ-kā′nə-rē *or* chĭ-kā′nə-rē) *n., pl.* **chi·can·er·ies** Deception by trickery.

Chi·ca·no (chĭ-kä′nō *or* shĭ-kä′nō) *n., pl.* **Chi·ca·nos** A Mexican American, especially a man or boy. [Variant of Spanish *mexicano*, Mexican.] **—Chi·ca′no** *adj.*

chick (chĭk) *n.* A young bird, especially a young chicken.

chick·a·dee (chĭk′ə-dē′) *n.* Any of several small plump birds that are mostly gray with a darker marking on the head.

Chick·a·mau·ga (chĭk′ə-mô′gə) A city of extreme northwest Georgia south of Chattanooga, Tennessee. It is the site of a Confederate victory in the Civil War (September 19–20, 1863).

Chick·a·saw (chĭk′ə-sô′) *n., pl.* **Chickasaw** or **Chick·a·saws 1.** A member of a Native American people formerly living in Mississippi and Alabama and now living in Oklahoma. **2.** The Muskogean language of the Chickasaw.

chick·en (chĭk′ən) *n.* **1.** The common domesticated fowl raised for eggs or food. **2.** The meat of this fowl. **3.** Any of various similar birds. **4.** *Slang* A person who is afraid or acts in a cowardly manner. ❖ *adj. Slang* Afraid; cowardly. ❖ *intr.v.* **chick·ened, chick·en·ing, chick·ens** *Slang* To lose one's nerve; act in a cowardly manner: *chicken out at the last moment.* [From Old English *cīcen*.]

chick·en-heart·ed (chĭk′ən-här′tĭd) *adj.* Cowardly; timid.

chick·en·pox or **chicken pox** (chĭk′ən-pŏks′) *n.* A contagious viral disease, mainly of young children, in which the skin breaks out in a rash and mild fever occurs.

chicken wire *n.* A hexagonal wire mesh used as light fencing.

chick·pea (chĭk′pē′) *n.* **1.** The round edible seed of a bushy plant related to the pea; the garbanzo. **2.** The plant that bears such seeds.

chick·weed (chĭk′wēd′) *n.* Any of various low-growing weeds having small white flowers.

chic·le (chĭk′əl *or* chē′klĕ) *n.* The thickened milky sap of a tropical evergreen American tree, formerly used as the main ingredient of chewing gum.

chic·o·ry (chĭk′ə-rē) *n., pl.* **chic·o·ries 1.** A plant having blue flowers that resemble daisies. Some varieties are grown for their leaves, which are used as salad greens. **2.** The root of this plant, dried, roasted, and ground and added to or used as a substitute for coffee.

chide (chīd) *tr.v.* **chid·ed, chid·ing, chides** To scold or reproach; reprove: *The coach chided me for being late for practice.*

chief (chēf) *n.* A person with the highest rank or authority; a leader: *the chief of a Scottish clan; the chief of the fire department.* ❖ *adj.* **1.** Highest in rank or authority: *The chief engineer is in charge of the power station.* **2.** Most important; main; principal: *What is the country's chief crop?* ◆ **in chief** With the highest rank or greatest authority: *Our editor-in-chief determines this newspaper's policies.* [From Middle English *chef*, from Latin *caput*, head.]

Chief Executive *n.* The President of the United States.

chief justice also **Chief Justice** *n.* A judge who presides over a court having several judges, especially the United States Supreme Court.

chief·ly (chēf′lē) *adv.* **1.** Above all; especially: *They went home early, chiefly to avoid the storm.* **2.** For the most part; mostly; mainly: *grassy land used chiefly for grazing.*

chief of staff *n., pl.* **chiefs of staff 1.** The highest ranking officer of the US Army or Air Force, responsible to the secretary of his or her branch of service and to the president. **2.** The senior military officer on the staff of a general or admiral. **3.** The senior staff member at an organization or institution: *the president's chief of staff.*

chief of state *n., pl.* **chiefs of state** A person who is the formal head of a nation, but is not the head of the government: *In Great Britain the monarch is the chief of state.*

chief·tain (chēf′tən) *n.* The leader or head of a group, especially of a clan or tribe. [From Middle English *chevetain*, from Late Latin *capitāneus*, from Latin *caput*, head.]

chif·fon (shĭ-fŏn′ *or* shĭf′ŏn′) *n.* A soft, sheer, light fabric of silk, cotton, or rayon, used for scarves, veils, dresses, and blouses. ❖ *adj.* **1.** Relating to or resembling chiffon. **2.** Made light and fluffy by the addition of beaten egg whites or gelatin: *lemon chiffon pie.*

chif·fo·nier (shĭf′ə-nîr′) *n.* A narrow high chest of drawers, often with a mirror attached.

chig·ger (chĭg′ər) *n.* **1.** Any of various tiny mite larvae that parasitize humans and other vertebrates and whose bite causes intense itching. **2.** The chigoe.

chi·gnon (shēn-yŏn′ *or* shēn′yŏn′) *n.* A roll or knot of hair worn at the back of the head or nape of the neck.

chig·oe (chĭg′ō *or* chē′gō) *n.* **1.** A small tropical flea, the female of which burrows under the skin of humans and other mammals, causing intense itching and sores. **2.** Any of various mite larvae that cause itching; a chigger.

Chi·hua·hua[1] (chĭ-wä′wä) A city of northern Mexico

south of El Paso, Texas. It is the rail and commercial center for the northern part of Mexico.

Chi·hua·hua² (chĭ-**wä′**wä) *n.* A very small dog of a breed developed in Mexico, having a smooth, usually tan or black coat and pointed ears.

chil·blain (**chĭl′**blān′) *n.* An itchy redness and soreness of the hands, feet, or ears, caused by exposure to damp cold.

child (chīld) *n., pl.* **chil·dren** (**chĭl′**drən) **1.** A person between birth and physical maturity. **2a.** A son or daughter; an offspring: *There are several children in that big family.* **b.** An infant; a baby: *a newborn child.* **c.** An unborn baby; a fetus: *She is carrying a child in her womb.* **3.** An older person who behaves like a child; an immature person: *Most adults act the child now and then.* **4.** A descendant: *children of Abraham.* **5.** A person or thing considered as the product or result of something: *a child of the 20th century.* ◆ **with child** Pregnant. [From Old English *cild.*]

child·bear·ing (**chīld′**bâr′ĭng) *n.* Pregnancy and childbirth. ❖ *adj.* Relating to childbearing, especially with regard to the ability to become pregnant: *women of childbearing age.*

child·birth (**chīld′**bûrth′) *n.* The act or process of giving birth to a child.

child·hood (**chīld′**ho͝od′) *n.* The time or condition of being a child: *Friends are easily made during childhood.*

child·ish (**chīl′**dĭsh) *adj.* **1.** Relating to or suitable for a child: *a high childish voice; childish games.* **2.** Immature; foolish or silly: *childish behavior.* **—child′ish·ly** *adv.* **—child′ish·ness** *n.*

child·like (**chīld′**līk′) *adj.* Similar to or suitable for a child; innocent and simple: *childlike faith in others.*

child·proof (**chīld′**pro͞of′) *adj.* **1.** Designed to resist tampering by young children: *a childproof medicine bottle.* **2.** Made safe for young children: *Is the living room childproof?* ❖ *tr.v.* **child·proofed, child·proof·ing, child·proofs** To make safe for young children: *childproofed the kitchen by placing all the cleaning products on high shelves.*

chil·dren (**chĭl′**drən) *n.* Plural of **child.**

child's play (chīldz) *n.* Something very easy to do: *These problems of addition are mere child's play.*

Chil·e (**chĭl′**ē *or* **chē′**lĕ) A country of southwest South America west of Argentina with a long Pacific coastline. Santiago is the capital.

chil·i (**chĭl′**ē) *n., pl.* **chil·ies 1.** The fresh or dried fruit of any of several red peppers, used especially as a flavoring in cooking; chili pepper. **2.** A stew made of meat or beans (or both) and usually tomatoes, spiced with chili peppers or chili powder. [From Spanish *chile*, from Nahuatl *chīlli.*]

❑ *These sound alike:* **chili, chilly** (cold).

chili con car·ne (kŏn **kär′**nē) *n.* Chili made with meat, usually beef.

chili powder *n.* A seasoning consisting of chilies that are ground and mixed with other spices, such as cumin and oregano.

chill (chĭl) *n.* **1.** A moderate but penetrating coldness: *a chill in the fall air.* **2.** A feeling of coldness: *Chills and sneezing are signs of a cold.* **3.** A discouraging of enthusiasm or depressing of spirit: *The bad news put a chill on the celebration.* **4.** A feeling of fear: *We all felt a chill when the lights went out.* ❖ *adj.* **1.** Moderately cold; chilly: *a chill north wind.* **2.** Not warm and friendly: *a chill greeting.* **3.** Discouraging: *My suggestions met with a chill response.* ❖ *v.* **chilled, chill·ing, chills** *—tr.* **1.** To make cold: *The icy wind chilled our faces.* **2.** To produce a feeling of cold, fear, or dismay in: *The eerie story chilled all who heard it.* **3.** To discourage; dampen: *Bad luck has chilled their enthusiasm.* *—intr.* **1.** To become cold: *Put the dessert in the refrigerator to chill.* **2.** To feel cold or be affected by a cold feeling: *The skaters chilled quickly in harsh wind.* **3.** *Slang* **a.** To calm down or relax: *needed to chill after a long day at school.* **b.** To pass time idly; loiter. [From Old English *cele.*] **—chill′er** *n.*

chill·y (**chĭl′**ē) *adj.* **chill·i·er, chill·i·est 1.** Cold enough to cause or feel discomfort: *Damp chilly weather is common along the seacoast.* See Synonyms at **cold. 2.** Feeling cold; shivering. **3.** Not enthusiastic: *a chilly reaction to the new plan.* **4.** Unfriendly: *a chilly greeting.* **—chill′i·ness** *n.*

❑ *These sound alike:* **chilly, chili** (seasoning).

chime (chīm) *n.* **1.** often **chimes** A set of bells tuned to different pitches and rung to make musical sounds. **2.** often **chimes** An orchestral instrument consisting of a set of metal tubes tuned to a musical scale and struck to make bell-like sounds. **3.** A single bell: *The chime in that clock strikes on the hour.* **4.** A musical sound produced by or as if by bells or chimes: *hear the chime of the church clock.* ❖ *v.* **chimed, chim·ing, chimes** *—intr.* To ring, as a bell or set of chimes. *—tr.* **1.** To strike (a bell) to produce music: *chime the church bells in celebration of peace.* **2.** To announce (the time of day) by ringing bells: *The clock chimed three o'clock.* ◆ **chime in** To join in, as in song or conversation: *The audience chimed in on the chorus.* [From Middle English *chimbe*, from Latin *cymbalum*, cymbal.]

Chi·me·ra (kī-**mîr′**ə *or* kĭ-**mîr′**ə) *n.* **1.** In Greek mythology, a fire-breathing female monster having the head of a lion, the body of a goat, and the tail of a serpent. **2a.** A frightening imaginary monster made up of wildly different parts. **b.** A fantastic or impossible idea or fancy.

chi·mer·i·cal (kī-**mĕr′**ĭ-kəl *or* kĭ-**mĕr′**ĭ-kəl) *adj.* Imaginary; fantastic: *chimerical notions with little basis in reality.*

chim·ney (**chĭm′**nē) *n., pl.* **chim·neys 1.** A hollow, usually vertical structure for the passage of smoke and gases rising from a fireplace, stove, or furnace. **2.** The part of such a structure that rises above a roof. **3.** The glass tube, often wide at the center and narrow at the top, placed around the flame of a lamp. **4.** Something resembling a chimney, as a narrow cleft in a cliff. [From Middle English *chimene*, from Late Latin *camīnāta*, fireplace.]

chimney sweep or **chimney sweeper** *n.* A person employed to clean soot from chimneys.

chimney swift *n.* A small dark bird of North America, somewhat resembling a swallow, that often nests in unused chimneys.

chimp (chĭmp) *n. Informal* A chimpanzee.

chim·pan·zee (chĭm′păn-**zē′** *or* chĭm-**păn′**zē) *n.* A dark-haired African ape that is smaller than a gorilla and is found in central and western Africa north of the Congo River.

chin (chĭn) *n.* The front part of the face below the lips formed by the lower jaw and extending to the neck. ❖ *tr.v.* **chinned, chin·ning, chins** To grasp an overhead horizontal bar and pull (oneself) up with the arms until the chin clears the bar. [From Old English *cin.*]

chi·na (**chī′**nə) *n.* **1.** A fine hard porcelain, originally made in China from a type of white clay, baked at high temperatures and often decorated with colored designs. **2.** Articles made from this porcelain or a similar material, especially dishes used at the table.

Chi·na (**chī′**nə) A country of eastern Asia south of Mongolia and Russia. Its ancient civilization traditionally dates to around 2700 BC. Beijing is the capital and Shanghai the largest city.

chi·na·ber·ry (**chī′**nə-bĕr′ē) *n.* A spreading tree of Asia that has been widely planted in warm climates for its shade and attractive purplish flowers.

Chi·na·town (**chī′**nə-toun′) *n.* A part of a city that is inhabited chiefly by Chinese people.

chignon

Chihuahua²

chinchilla

Chinese lantern

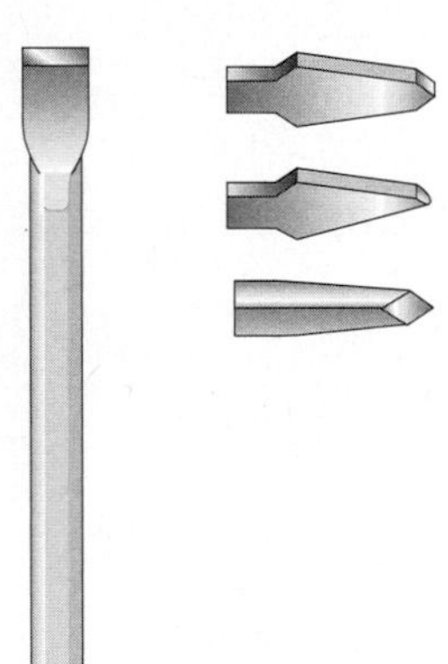

chisel
left: cold metal chisel with a flat head
right, top to bottom: cape, roundnose, and diamond-point metal chisel heads

ă	pat	ôr	core
ā	pay	oi	boy
âr	care	ou	out
ä	father	o͝o	took
ĕ	pet	o͝or	lure
ē	be	o͞o	boot
ĭ	pit	ŭ	cut
ī	bite	ûr	urge
îr	pier	th	thin
ŏ	pot	*th*	this
ō	toe	zh	vision
ô	paw	ə	about

chi·na·ware (chī**′**nə-wâr′) *n.* Dishes and other articles made of china or similar pottery.

chinch (chĭnch) *n.* A bedbug.

chinch bug *n.* A small black-and-white insect that feeds on and damages wheat and other grains and grasses in dry weather.

chin·chil·la (chĭn-**chĭl′**ə) *n.* **1.** Either of two rodents native to the mountains of South America, resembling a squirrel and having soft pale-gray fur. **2.** The fur of either of these animals.

Chi·nese (chī-**nēz′** *or* chī-**nēs′**) *adj.* Relating to China or to its people, languages, or culture. ❖ *n., pl.* **Chinese 1.** A native or inhabitant of China. **2a.** A group of Sino-Tibetan languages and dialects spoken by the Chinese people, including Mandarin and Cantonese. **b.** The official national language of China; Mandarin.

Chinese checkers *pl.n. (used with a singular or plural verb)* A game for two to six players in which marbles are moved from holes of one point of the star-shaped board to a set of holes on the opposite side.

Chinese lantern *n.* A decorative lantern of thin brightly colored paper made in such a way that it can be collapsed.

Chinese puzzle *n.* A very complicated puzzle or difficult problem.

chink[1] (chĭngk) *n.* A narrow crack or opening. ❖ *tr.v.* **chinked, chink·ing, chinks** To seal or close narrow cracks or openings by filling: *They chinked the spaces between the logs of the cabin wall with mud.* [From Old English *cine.*]

chink[2] (chĭngk) *n.* A short clinking sound, as of metal striking together: *the chink of coins.* ❖ *intr. & tr.v.* **chinked, chink·ing, chinks** To make or cause to make such a sound: *Coins chinked in my pocket. I chinked the coins in my pocket.* [Of imitative origin.]

chi·no (chē**′**nō) *n., pl.* **chi·nos 1.** A strong cotton cloth used chiefly for uniforms and work clothes. **2. chinos** Pants made of this material.

chi·nook (shĭ-**no͝ok′** *or* chĭ-**no͝ok′**) *n.* **1.** A moist warm wind that blows from the ocean in the Pacific Northwest. **2.** A warm dry wind that comes down from the eastern slopes of the Rocky Mountains.

Chinook *n., pl.* **Chinook** or **Chi·nooks 1.** A member of a Native American people living in the state of Washington. **2.** The language of this people.

Chinook Jargon *n.* A blend of English, French, Chinook, and other Native American languages, formerly used by traders in the Pacific Northwest.

chintz (chĭnts) *n.* A printed, usually brightly colored cotton fabric.

chintz·y (**chĭnt′**sē) *adj.* **chintz·i·er, chintz·i·est 1.** Relating to or decorated with chintz. **2.** Gaudy; cheap: *chintzy trinkets.*

chin-up (**chĭn′**ŭp′) *n.* The act or exercise of chinning oneself on an overhead bar.

chip (chĭp) *n.* **1.** A small broken or cut off piece; a fragment: *a chip of wood.* **2.** A dent or mark left when a small piece is broken off: *a chip in the marble.* **3a.** A thin slice of food: *a potato chip.* **b. chips** French fries: *fish and chips.* **4.** An integrated circuit. **5.** A small disk that is used in poker and other games to represent money. **6.** A chip shot in golf. ❖ *v.* **chipped, chip·ping, chips** *—tr.* **1.** To break off a small piece from (something), as by hitting, jarring, or scraping: *chip the edge of the glass.* **2.** To shape or carve by cutting or chopping: *chipped my name in stone. —intr.* **1.** To become broken off: *These dishes chip if you are not careful.* **2.** To make a chip shot in golf. ◆ **a chip off the old block** A child that closely resembles one parent or the other. **chip in** To contribute money or labor: *How many people chipped in for the present?* **chip on (one's) shoulder** An aggressive or hostile attitude: *My cousin has had a chip on his shoulder ever since our argument.*

Chip·e·wy·an (chĭp′ə-**wī′**ən) *n., pl.* **Chipewyan** or **Chip·e·wy·ans 1.** A member of a Native American people living in north-central Canada. **2.** The Athabascan language of the Chipewyan.

chip·munk (**chĭp′**mŭngk′) *n.* Any of several burrowing rodents of North America that resemble a small squirrel and have a striped back. [Alteration of obsolete *chitmunk*, perhaps from Ojibwa *ajidamoon?*, red squirrel.]

chipped beef (chĭpt) *n.* Dried beef, smoked and thinly sliced.

chip·per (**chĭp′**ər) *adj.* Active; cheerful; sprightly.

Chip·pe·wa (**chĭp′**ə-wô′ *or* **chĭp′**ə-wä′) *n., pl.* **Chippewa** or **Chip·pe·was 1.** An Ojibwa. **2.** The Ojibwa language.

chip shot *n.* A short lofted golf stroke, used in approaching the green.

Chi·rac (shē-**räk′**), **Jacques** Born 1932. French politician who served as president (1995–2007). He was a strong champion of the European Union.

Chi·ron (**kī′**rŏn′) *n.* In Greek mythology, the wise centaur who tutored Achilles, Hercules, and Asclepius.

chi·rop·o·dy (kĭ-**rŏp′**ə-dē) *n.* Podiatry. **—chi·rop′o·dist** *n.*

chi·ro·prac·tic (**kī′**rə-prăk′tĭk) *n.* A method of treating diseases by manipulating the spine and certain other structures of the body, usually without the use of drugs or surgery.

chi·ro·prac·tor (**kī′**rə-prăk′tər) *n.* A person who practices chiropractic.

chirp (chûrp) *n.* A short high-pitched sound, such as the one made by a small bird or a cricket. ❖ *intr.v.* **chirped, chirp·ing, chirps** To make such a sound: *The crickets chirped noisily.*

chir·rup (**chûr′**əp *or* **chĭr′**əp) *n.* The sound of repeated chirping, clicking, or clucking; a series of chirps, clicks, or clucks. ❖ *intr.v.* **chir·ruped, chir·rup·ing, chir·rups** To make or utter such a sound.

chis·el (**chĭz′**əl) *n.* A metal tool with a sharp beveled edge across the end of a thick blade, used to cut and shape stone, wood, or metal. ❖ *v.* **chis·eled, chis·el·ing, chis·els** or **chis·elled, chis·el·ling, chis·els** *—tr.* **1.** To cut into or shape with a chisel: *The sculptor chiseled the statue out of stone.* **2.** *Informal* To cheat or obtain by deception. *—intr.* To use a chisel. **—chis′el·er** *n.*

Chis·holm (**chĭz′**əm), **Shirley Anita Saint Hill** 1924–2005. American politician who served as a US representative from New York State (1969–1983) and in 1972 was the first African American to seek the presidential nomination of a major party.

Chi·şi·nău (**kĭsh′**ə-nou′) or **Ki·shi·nev** (**kĭsh′**ə-nĕf′) The capital of Moldova, in the south-central part of the country northwest of Odessa, Ukraine. It was founded as a monastery center in the early 1400s.

chit·chat (**chĭt′**chăt′) *n.* **1.** Casual conversation; small talk. **2.** Gossip: *neighborhood chitchat.* ❖ *intr.v.* **chit·chat·ted, chit·chat·ting, chit·chats** To engage in chitchat.

chi·tin (**kīt′**n) *n.* A tough substance that is the main component of the external skeletons of crustaceans, insects, and spiders. It is also found in the cell walls of fungi. **—chi′tin·ous** *adj.*

chi·ton (**kīt′**n *or* **kī′**tŏn′) *n.* A loosely draped gown or tunic worn by men and women in ancient Greece.

chit·ter·lings also **chit·lins** or **chit·lings** (**chĭt′**lĭnz) *pl.n.* The small intestine of a pig, fried as food.

chiv·al·rous (**shĭv′**əl-rəs) *adj.* **1.** Relating to the age of chivalry: *the chivalrous adventures of King Arthur's knights.* **2.** Having or showing the qualities of the ideal knight; brave, honorable, and courteous: *a chivalrous act of self-sacrifice.* **—chiv′al·rous·ness** *n.*

chiv·al·ry (**shĭv′**əl-rē) *n., pl.* **chiv·al·ries 1.** The medieval institution of knighthood and its customs: *the code of chivalry.* **2.** The qualities of the ideal knight, such as bravery, courtesy, honor, and gallantry towards women: *the victorious general's chivalry toward the welfare of defeated enemy troops.* **3.** A group of knights or gallant gentlemen. [From Middle English *chevalrie*, from Old French *chevalier*, knight.] —SEE NOTE.

chive (chīv) *n.* **1.** A plant related to the onion, having long narrow leaves. **2. chives** The onion-flavored leaves of this plant, used as a seasoning. [From Middle English *cive*, from Latin *cēpa*, onion.]

chla·myd·i·a (klə-**mĭd′**ē-ə) *n., pl.* **chla·myd·i·ae** (klə-**mĭd′**ē-ē′) Any of several sexually transmitted diseases caused by bacteria, often resulting in inflammation of the reproductive organs.

chlo·ral hydrate (**klôr′**əl) *n.* A colorless crystalline compound used as a sedative.

chlo·ride (**klôr′**īd′) *n.* A chemical compound of chlorine and another element or radical.

chlo·ri·nate (**klôr′**ə-nāt′) *tr.v.* **chlo·ri·nat·ed, chlo·ri·nat·ing, chlo·ri·nates** To treat or combine with chlorine or one of its compounds, especially in order to kill bacteria in water. **—chlo′ri·na′tion** *n.*

chlo·rine (**klôr′**ēn′ *or* **klôr′**ĭn) *n. Symbol* **Cl** A greenish-yellow gaseous element found chiefly in combination with sodium as common salt. It is very poisonous and is used in water purification, sewage treatment, and the manufacture of bleach. Atomic number 17. See **Periodic Table.** [From Greek *khlōros*, greenish-yellow.]

chlo·ro·fluor·o·car·bon (klôr′ō-flo͝or′ō-**kär′**bən *or* klôr′ō-flôr′ō-**kär′**bən) *n.* Any of various compounds consisting of carbon, hydrogen, chlorine, and fluorine, formerly used as aerosol propellants and refrigerants. Chlorofluorocarbons are believed to cause depletion of the atmospheric ozone layer.

chlo·ro·form (**klôr′**ə-fôrm′) *n.* A clear, colorless, heavy liquid having the formula $CHCl_3$. It is used in refrigeration, in industrial chemicals, and sometimes as an anesthetic. ❖ *tr.v.* **chlo·ro·formed, chlo·ro·form·ing, chlo·ro·forms** To make unconscious or kill with chloroform.

chlo·ro·phyll (**klôr′**ə-fĭl) *n.* Any of several green pigments that are found in green plants, algae, and certain bacteria and that capture light energy which is used in photosynthesis to convert carbon dioxide and water into food molecules. Chlorophyll molecules are composed of carbon, hydrogen, magnesium, nitrogen, and oxygen.

chlo·ro·plast (**klôr′**ə-plăst′) *n.* A structure in the cells of green plants and algae that contains chlorophyll and is the site where photosynthesis takes place.

chock (chŏk) *n.* A block or wedge placed under something, such as a boat, barrel, or wheel, to keep it from moving. ❖ *tr.v.* **chocked, chock·ing, chocks** To hold in place with a chock or chocks: *chock the wheels of a truck parked on a hill.*

chock-full (**chŏk′fo͝ol′**) *adj.* Completely filled; stuffed: *a bus chock-full of people at rush hour.*

choc·o·late (**chô′**kə-lĭt *or* **chôk′**lĭt) *n.* **1.** A food made from cacao seeds that have been roasted and ground and often mixed with sweeteners and flavoring. Chocolate for cooking is sold in powdered or block form. **2.** A candy made from or covered with this substance, often with a soft filling. ❖ *adj.* Made of or flavored with chocolate: *a chocolate cake.* [From Spanish, from Nahuatl *chicolātl*, frothy beverage made from water, cornmeal, and ground cacao and kapok tree seeds : probably *chicol-*, of unknown meaning and origin + *atl*, water.]

Choc·taw (**chŏk′**tô) *n., pl.* **Choctaw** or **Choc·taws 1.** A member of a Native American people formerly living in parts of Mississippi and Alabama, now living mainly in Oklahoma, Mississippi, and Alabama. **2.** The Muskogean language of the Choctaw.

choice (chois) *n.* **1.** The act of choosing; selection: *Did price influence your choice?* **2.** The power, right, or possibility to choose; option: *You leave me no choice in this matter.* **3.** Someone or something chosen: *The customer's choices were roast beef, mashed potatoes, and peas.* **4.** A variety from which to choose: *The cafeteria has a wide choice of sandwiches.* **5.** An alternative: *There is no choice but to obey the rules.* ❖ *adj.* **choic·er, choic·est 1.** Of fine quality; very good; select: *choice tidbits; choice vegetables.* **2.** Selected with care: *reply in a few choice words.* **—choice′ly** *adv.*

SYNONYMS choice, alternative, option, preference, selection These nouns mean the act, power, or right of choosing. **Choice** suggests the freedom to choose from a set of things: *The ice cream vendor offered a wide choice of flavors.* **Alternative** often means a choice between only two possibilities: *The only alternative to keeping this job is to look for another.* **Option** often means a power to choose that has been granted by someone else: *That school gives you the option of studying either French or Spanish.* **Preference** means a choice based on one's values, bias, or tastes: *The designer inquired about our preference of colors.* **Selection** suggests a variety of things or people to choose from: *The choir director was careful in her selection of singers during the audition.*

---

choir (kwīr) *n.* **1.** An organized group of singers, especially one that performs regularly in a church: *a children's choir; a cathedral choir.* **2.** The part of a church especially for the use of such singers. [From Middle English *quer*, from Old French *cuer*, from Latin *chorus*, choral dance, from Greek *khoros.*] —SEE NOTE.

❑ *These sound alike:* **choir, quire** (unit of paper).

choir·boy (**kwīr′**boi′) *n.* A boy who is a member of a choir.

choir·girl (**kwīr′**gûrl′) *n.* A girl who is a member of a choir.

choir·mas·ter (**kwīr′**măs′tər) *n.* The director of a choir.

choke (chōk) *v.* **choked, chok·ing, chokes** *—tr.* **1.** To interfere with the breathing of (a person or animal) by squeezing or blocking the windpipe. **2.** To reduce the amount of air supplied to (a gasoline engine) so that it will start and warm up more easily. **3.** To check or slow down the movement, growth, or action of: *Weeds are choking the garden.* **4.** To stop or suppress by or as if by strangling: *Sobs choked her words.* **5.** To clog up; congest: *Traffic choked the highway.* *—intr.* **1.** To be unable to breathe, swallow, or speak normally, as when the throat is blocked: *choke on a piece of bread.* **2.** To be blocked up or obstructed: *The drain choked up with kitchen scraps.* **3.** To fail to perform effectively, especially in a game or contest: *He choked when he missed a two-foot putt to win the match.* ❖ *n.* **1.** The act or sound of choking. **2.** A device that controls the amount of air taken in by a gasoline engine. ◆ **choke back** To hold back; control; suppress: *choke back tears.* **choke off** To put an end to; stop: *Closing the train station would choke off business in the area.* **choke up 1.** To be unable to speak because of strong emotion. **2.** To shorten one's grip on the handle, as of a baseball bat.

choke·cher·ry (**chōk′**chĕr′ē) *n.* **1.** A shrub or small tree having narrow clusters of small white flowers and bitter-tasting dark-red or black fruit. **2.** The fruit of this plant.

chok·er (**chō′**kər) *n.* **1.** A person or thing that chokes: *Many dogs are trained on restraining collars that are chokers.* **2.** A short necklace that fits closely around the throat.

chol·er (**kŏl′**ər) *n.* Anger; irritability.

❑ *These sound alike:* **choler, collar** (neck band).

chol·er·a (**kŏl′**ər-ə) *n.* An infectious, often fatal disease of the intestines that is caused by bacteria and is often

WORD HISTORY

chivalry The words **cavalry** and **cavalier** are first cousins to **chivalry** and **chevalier.** They all come from the Roman soldier's slang word *caballus,* "horse, pack horse, nag," and from a very late Latin noun *caballārius,* "horseman, rider." A *caballārius* became a *cavaliere* in Italian, and he rides in the *cavalleria,* "troop of horse soldiers, cavalry." Both *cavaliere* and *cavalleria* were taken into English as *cavalier* and *cavalry.* In French, however, *caballārius* became *chevalier,* "horseman, knight," who rides in a *chevalerie* or *chivalerie,* "troop of men-at-arms, knighthood." *Chevalier* and *chivalerie* came into English with knightly overtones as *chevalier* and *chivalry.*

chock

WORD HISTORY

choir Why don't we spell the word **choir** as *quire*? In fact, English did once spell it this way. Its spelling was changed because in the 1600s, a group of scholars in England decided that many words should be respelled to make them look more like Latin or Greek. Latin and Greek were the languages of classical learning, and their spelling was thought to be "proper." Since our word comes from Latin *chorus,* "dance, musical composition, band of singers or dancers," *quire* was respelled as *choir* to make it look more like *chorus.*

chopsticks

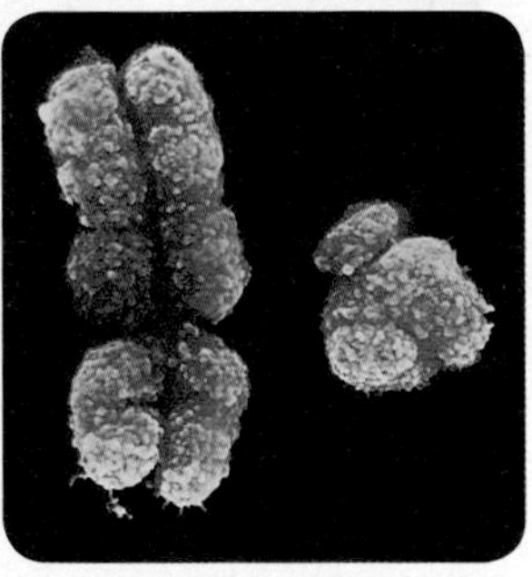

chromosome
replicated x-chromosome (*left*) and y-chromosome (*right*) during cell division

ă	pat	ôr	core
ā	pay	oi	boy
âr	care	ou	out
ä	father	o͝o	took
ĕ	pet	o͝or	lure
ē	be	o͞o	boot
ĭ	pit	ŭ	cut
ī	bite	ûr	urge
îr	pier	th	thin
ŏ	pot	*th*	this
ō	toe	zh	vision
ô	paw	ə	about

epidemic. It is caught from contaminated water and food and causes severe diarrhea, vomiting, and dehydration.

chol·er·ic (kŏl′ə-rĭk *or* kə-lĕr′ĭk) *adj.* Easily made angry; bad-tempered. —SEE NOTE AT **humor.**

cho·les·ter·ol (kə-lĕs′tə-rôl′) *n.* A white fatty substance that is found chiefly in animals and is important in metabolism and hormone production. It is manufactured by the body and taken in by eating foods such as meat, cheese, and eggs. High levels of certain kinds of cholesterol are thought to be a factor in developing heart disease.

chomp (chŏmp) *v.* **chomped, chomp·ing, chomps** —*tr.* To chew or bite on noisily: *a horse chomping oats.* —*intr.* To chew or bite on something: *chomping on a carrot.*

choose (cho͞oz) *v.* **chose** (chōz), **cho·sen** (chō′zən), **choos·ing, choos·es** —*tr.* **1.** To decide on and pick out from a greater number of people or things; select: *I chose a book in the library.* **2.** To decide: *We chose to walk to work.* —*intr.* To make a choice; select: *They had to choose for themselves.* **—choos′er** *n.*

choos·y also **choos·ey** (cho͞o′zē) *adj.* **choos·i·er, choos·i·est** Very careful in choosing: *She's very choosy about the clothes that she wears.*

chop (chŏp) *v.* **chopped, chop·ping, chops** —*tr.* **1.** To cut by striking with a heavy sharp tool, such as an axe: *chop wood.* **2.** To make by cutting in this way: *chop a path through the woods.* **3.** To cut up into small pieces; mince: *chop onions.* **4.** To cut short; reduce: *chop a report that is too long.* **5.** In sports, to hit or hit at with a short swift downward stroke: *The batter chopped a grounder through the infield.* —*intr.* To make heavy cutting strokes: *chop away at a block of ice.* ❖ *n.* **1.** A quick short cutting stroke or blow: *A chop of the axe split the log.* **2.** A small cut of meat that usually contains a bone: *Ribs from lamb and pork make nice chops.* **3.** A short irregular movement of waves. [From Middle English *choppen*, probably variant of *chappen*, to split.]

Cho·pin (shō′păn′ *or* shō-păɴ′), **Frédéric François** 1810–1849. Polish-born French composer and pianist. Many of his works adopt the rhythms of Polish folk music.

chop·per (chŏp′ər) *n.* **1.** *Informal* A helicopter. **2.** A person or thing that chops: *a food chopper.*

chop·pers (chŏp′ərz) *pl.n. Slang* Teeth, especially a set of false teeth.

chop·ping block (chŏp′ĭng) *n.* A wooden block on which food or wood is chopped.

chop·py¹ (chŏp′ē) *adj.* **chop·pi·er, chop·pi·est** Having many short irregular waves: *choppy seas.* [From *chop*, to cut.] **—chop′pi·ness** *n.*

chop·py² (chŏp′ē) *adj.* **chop·pi·er, chop·pi·est 1.** Shifting quickly; variable: *choppy winds.* **2.** Not smooth; jerky: *choppy prose.* [From *chop*, to shift.]

chops (chŏps) *pl.n.* The jaws, cheeks, or jowls.

chop·sticks (chŏp′stĭks′) *pl.n.* A pair of slender sticks usually made of wood or plastic and held between the fingers, used as an eating utensil in eastern Asia. [From Chinese (Cantonese) *kuaì*, quick.]

chop su·ey (so͞o′ē) *n.* A Chinese-American dish made with bits of meat, bean sprouts, and other vegetables and served with rice. [From Cantonese *zaap seoi*, miscellaneous bits.]

cho·ral (kôr′əl) *adj.* Relating to, intended for, or sung by a chorus or choir: *a choral society; a choral passage.*

cho·rale also **cho·ral** (kə-răl′) *n.* **1.** A harmonized arrangement of a hymn melody, especially one forming part of a larger work. **2.** A chorus or choir.

❑ *These sound alike:* **chorale, corral** (fenced-in area).

chord¹ (kôrd) *n.* A combination of three or more musical pitches sounded at the same time. [From Old French *acorde*, agreement, harmony.] **—chord′al** *adj.*

❑ *These sound alike:* **chord¹** (musical tones), **chord²** (line segment), **cord** (string).

chord² (kôrd) *n.* A line segment whose end points lie on a curve or on the circumference of a circle. [Alteration of *cord*, string.]

❑ *These sound alike:* **chord²** (line segment), **chord¹** (musical tones), **cord** (string).

chor·date (kôr′dāt′ *or* kôr′dĭt) *n.* Any of a large group of animals having at some stage of development a spinal column or a strip of cartilage along the back and openings to allow water to pass over the gills. Chordates include all vertebrates and certain other sea animals, such as the lancelets and the tunicates.

chore (chôr) *n.* **1.** A routine or minor task: *Feeding the cat is a daily chore.* See Synonyms at **task. 2.** An unpleasant task: *Taking out the garbage is a chore I'd like to forget.*

cho·re·a (kô-rē′ə) *n.* Any of various disorders of the nervous system that cause the arms, legs, and face to twitch and move uncontrollably.

cho·re·o·graph (kôr′ē-ə-grăf′) *v.* **cho·re·o·graphed, cho·re·o·graph·ing, cho·re·o·graphs** —*tr.* To create the choreography of (a ballet or other stage work). —*intr.* To engage in choreography.

cho·re·og·raph·er (kôr′ē-ŏg′rə-fər) *n.* Someone who creates, arranges, and directs ballets or dances.

cho·re·og·ra·phy (kôr′ē-ŏg′rə-fē) *n., pl.* **cho·re·og·ra·phies** The art of creating and arranging ballets or dances.

cho·ri·on (kôr′ē-ŏn′) *n.* The outer membrane that encloses the embryo or fetus of a reptile, bird, or mammal. In placental mammals it contributes to the development of the placenta. **—cho′ri·on′ic** (kôr′ē-ŏn′ĭk) *adj.*

cho·ris·ter (kôr′ĭ-stər) *n.* **1.** A person who sings in a choir. **2.** A choir leader.

cho·roid (kôr′oid′) *n.* A delicate membrane between the sclera and the retina of the eyeball.

chor·tle (chôr′tl) *n.* A snorting chuckle. ❖ *intr.v.* **chor·tled, chor·tling, chor·tles** To laugh in a snorting joyful manner.

cho·rus (kôr′əs) *n., pl.* **cho·rus·es 1.** An organized group of singers who perform together. **2.** A musical composition or a part of a musical composition written for such a group. **3.** A group of people who speak or sing a part in a play all at the same time. **4.** A group of singers and dancers who play a supporting role in an opera, musical comedy, or other stage production. **5.** A section of music that is repeated after each verse of a song; a refrain. **6.** Something uttered by many people at one time: *a chorus of laughter.* ❖ *tr.v.* **cho·rused, cho·rus·ing, cho·rus·es** or **cho·russed, cho·rus·sing, cho·rus·ses** To sing or utter at the same time. ◆ **in chorus** All together: *The group responded to the suggestion in chorus.*

chose (chōz) *v.* Past tense of **choose.**

cho·sen (chō′zən) *v.* Past participle of **choose.** ❖ *adj.* **1.** Selected from or preferred above others: *the chosen few.* **2.** Selected by God; elect: *the chosen people.*

chow¹ (chou) *n.* A dog of a breed developed in China, having a large head, a thick reddish-brown or black coat, and a blackish tongue. [Perhaps from *chow-chow*, miscellaneous knick-knacks exported from China.]

chow² (chou) *Slang n.* Food. [Possibly from Cantonese *zaap*, food, miscellany.]

chow chow *n.* A chow dog.

chow·der (chou′dər) *n.* **1.** A thick soup or stew containing fish or shellfish, especially clams, and vegetables in a milk base. **2.** A thin soup of seafood with tomatoes in a meat broth. **3.** A soup similar to either of these soups, made with a vegetable, such as corn, as the main ingredient. [From Late Latin *caldāria*, stew pot, caldron.]

chow mein (chou′ mān′) *n.* A Chinese-American dish of bits of meat and cooked vegetables served over fried noodles. [From Chinese dialectal form related to Cantonese *caau min*, to stir-fry noodles.]

Chré·tien (krā-**tyăN′**), **Jean** Born 1934. Canadian politician who was prime minister from 1993 to 2003.

Christ (krīst) *n.* **1.** The Messiah, as foretold by the prophets of the Bible. **2.** Jesus as considered in Christianity to be the Messiah.

chris·ten (**krĭs′**ən) *tr.v.* **chris·tened, chris·ten·ing, chris·tens 1.** To baptize into a Christian church. **2.** To give a name to at baptism: *They christened him Joseph.* **3.** To name, especially at a ceremony: *christen a ship.* **4.** *Informal* To use for the first time: *christen a new car with a ride around the block.*

Chris·ten·dom (**krĭs′**ən-dəm) *n.* **1.** Christians considered as a group. **2.** The countries of the world where Christianity is the principal religion.

chris·ten·ing (**krĭs′**ə-nĭng) *n.* **1.** The Christian ceremony of baptizing and naming a child. **2.** A ceremony at which something is named and declared ready for use, especially a ship.

Chris·tian (**krĭs′**chən) *adj.* **1.** Believing in Jesus as Christ or in the religion based on his teachings: *a Christian congregation.* **2.** Relating to or characteristic of Christianity or Christians: *Easter is a Christian holiday.* **3.** Showing qualities considered characteristic of Jesus, such as gentleness or humility: *a Christian act of forgiveness.* ❖ *n.* A person who believes in Jesus as Christ or follows a religion based on his teachings.

Chris·ti·an·i·ty (krĭs′chē-**ăn′**ĭ-tē *or* krĭs′tē-**ăn′**ĭ-tē) *n.* **1.** The Christian religion, based on the life and teachings of Jesus. **2.** Christians considered as a group; Christendom: *Christianity celebrates Christmas.* **3.** The condition or fact of being a Christian.

Chris·tian·ize (**krĭs′**chə-nīz′) *tr.v.* **Chris·tian·ized, Chris·tian·iz·ing, Chris·tian·iz·es** To convert (another) to Christianity: *Missionaries tried to Christianize the native peoples of North America.* **—Chris′tian·i·za′tion** (krĭs′chə-nĭ-**zā′**shən) *n.* **—Chris′tian·iz′er** *n.*

Christian name *n.* **1.** A name that is given at baptism. **2.** A name that precedes a person's family name, especially a first name.

Christian Science *n.* The church and religious system founded by Mary Baker Eddy that emphasizes healing through spiritual means. **—Christian Scientist** *n.*

Christ·mas (**krĭs′**məs) *n.* **1.** A festival celebrated by Christians in commemoration of the birth of Jesus. **2.** December 25, the day on which this festival is observed as a public holiday in many countries. **3.** The period around Christmas, traditionally the period from December 24 (Christmas Eve) to January 5 (the eve of Epiphany).

Christmas Eve *n.* The day or evening before Christmas.

Christ·mas·time (**krĭs′**məs-tīm′) *n.* The season of Christmas.

Christmas tree *n.* An evergreen or artificial tree decorated with ornaments and lights at Christmastime.

chro·mat·ic (krō-**măt′**ĭk) *adj.* **1.** Relating to color or colors. **2.** Relating to or based on the chromatic scale, as a melody or chord. **—chro·mat′i·cal·ly** *adv.*

chromatic scale *n.* A musical scale consisting of twelve notes, each separated from the next by a semitone.

chro·ma·tid (**krō′**mə-tĭd) *n.* Either of the two strands formed when a chromosome duplicates itself during cell division.

chro·ma·tin (**krō′**mə-tĭn) *n.* A substance in the nucleus of a cell that consists of DNA and proteins. During cell division the chromatin becomes dense and compact, forming individual chromosomes.

chro·ma·tog·ra·phy (krō′mə-**tŏg′**rə-fē) *n.* A technique that separates the components of a chemical mixture by moving the mixture along a stationary material such as gelatin. The components are taken up and held in the material at different rates, thus forming isolated bands that scientists can further separate and analyze.

chrome (krōm) *n.* **1.** Chromium. **2.** A material plated with chromium or one of its alloys.

chro·mic (**krō′**mĭk) *adj.* Relating to or containing chromium.

chro·mi·um (**krō′**mē-əm) *n. Symbol* **Cr** A grayish, hard, brittle metallic element that does not rust or become dull easily. Chromium is used in plating other metals, in making stainless steel and other alloys, and in making dyes and paints. Atomic number 24. See **Periodic Table.**

chro·mo·some (**krō′**mə-sōm′) *n.* A cellular structure that is composed mainly of DNA and includes the genes that determine heredity. In plants, animals, and other eukaryotic organisms, the chromosomes are located in the nucleus. **—chro′mo·so′mal** (krō′mə-**sō′**məl) *adj.*

chro·mo·sphere (**krō′**mə-sfîr′) *n.* **1.** A glowing transparent layer of gas surrounding the photosphere of the sun. It is several thousand miles thick and is rich in hydrogen, helium, and calcium. **2.** A similar layer around a star.

chron·ic (**krŏn′**ĭk) *adj.* **1.** Lasting for a long time or recurring frequently: *chronic bronchitis.* **2.** Subject to a habit for a long time: *a chronic complainer.* **—chron′i·cal·ly** *adv.*

chron·i·cle (**krŏn′**ĭ-kəl) *n.* **1.** A record of historical events arranged in order of occurrence. **2. Chronicles** *(used with a singular verb)* Either of two books of the Bible that tell the history of the Israelite kings. ❖ *tr.v.* **chron·i·cled, chron·i·cling, chron·i·cles** To record, as in a chronicle: *Medieval monks chronicled the events of each year.* **—chron′i·cler** *n.*

chron·o·log·i·cal (krŏn′ə-**lŏj′**ĭ-kəl) *adj.* Arranged in order of time in which the events took place: *keep all historical facts in chronological order.* **—chron′o·log′i·cal·ly** *adv.*

chro·nol·o·gy (krə-**nŏl′**ə-jē) *n., pl.* **chro·nol·o·gies 1.** The science that deals with determining the dates and order of events. **2.** A chronological list or table: *a detailed chronology of modern history.* **3.** The arrangement of events in time.

chro·nom·e·ter (krə-**nŏm′**ĭ-tər) *n.* A very accurate clock or other timepiece, especially as used in scientific experiments, navigation, or astronomical observations.

chrys·a·lis (**krĭs′**ə-lĭs) *n., pl.* **chrys·a·lis·es** or **chry·sal·i·des** (krĭ-**săl′**ĭ-dēz′) A pupa of a butterfly, consisting of a tough case enclosing the insect as it undergoes metamorphosis and eventually emerges as a fully developed adult. [From Greek *khrūsallis*, gold-colored pupa, from *khrūsos*, gold.]

chry·san·the·mum (krĭ-**săn′**thə-məm) *n.* **1.** Any of various plants having many cultivated forms with showy, round, variously colored flowers. **2.** The flower of such a plant.

chub (chŭb) *n., pl.* **chub** or **chubs 1.** Any of various freshwater fishes of Europe and North America that are related to the carps and minnows. **2.** Any of various other freshwater fishes of North America.

chub·by (**chŭb′**ē) *adj.* **chub·bi·er, chub·bi·est** Round and plump: *a chubby face.* **—chub′bi·ness** *n.*

chuck¹ (chŭk) *tr.v.* **chucked, chuck·ing, chucks 1.** To pat affectionately, especially under the chin. **2a.** To throw or toss: *chuck a stone in the pond.* **b.** *Informal* To throw out; discard: *chuck an old shoe; chuck a poor plan.* ❖ *n.* **1.** An affectionate pat, especially under the chin. **2.** A toss or throw. [Possibly from French *choc*, knock, blow.]

chuck² (chŭk) *n.* **1.** A cut of beef extending from the neck to the ribs. **2.** In a machine such as a drill or lathe, a rotating clamp that holds either a tool or the work. [Perhaps variant of *chock*, wedge, lump.]

chrysalis

chuckwalla

Winston Churchill

ciabatta

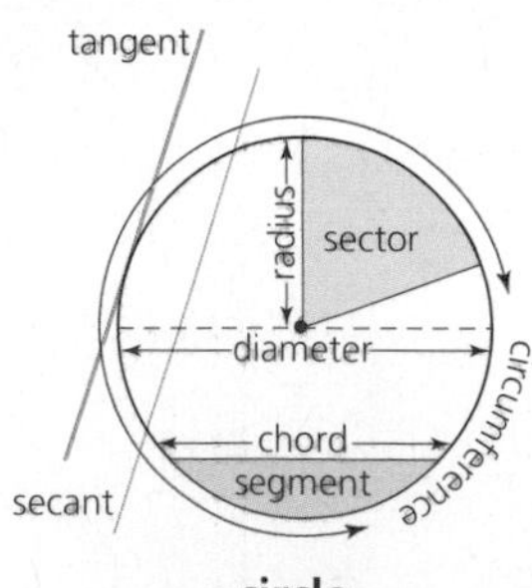

circle

ă	pat	ôr	core
ā	pay	oi	boy
âr	care	ou	out
ä	father	o͝o	took
ĕ	pet	o͝or	lure
ē	be	o͞o	boot
ĭ	pit	ŭ	cut
ī	bite	ûr	urge
îr	pier	th	thin
ŏ	pot	*th*	this
ō	toe	zh	vision
ô	paw	ə	about

chuck·le (chŭk′əl) *intr.v.* **chuck·led, chuck·ling, chuck·les** To laugh quietly or to oneself. ❖ *n.* A quiet laugh of amusement or satisfaction.

chuck wagon *n.* A wagon with food and cooking utensils for a group of workers, especially those moving from place to place, as on a cattle drive.

chuck·wal·la (chŭk′wŏl′ə) *n.* Any of several large plant-eating lizards of the southwest United States and Mexico.

chug (chŭg) *n.* A dull explosive sound, especially a sound made by an engine working hard. ❖ *intr.v.* **chugged, chug·ging, chugs 1.** To make such sounds: *The old truck's motor chugged under the hood.* **2.** To move while making such sounds: *The little train chugged up the mountain.*

chum¹ (chŭm) *n.* A close friend or companion; a pal. ❖ *intr.v.* **chummed, chum·ming, chums** To spend time together as friends; keep company: *Those kids chum around a lot after school.* [Perhaps short for *chamber fellow*, roommate.]

chum² (chŭm) *n.* Bait consisting of cut-up fish scattered on the water. ❖ *intr.v.* **chummed, chum·ming, chums** To fish with chum.

chum·my (chŭm′ē) *adj.* **chum·mi·er, chum·mi·est** Friendly; intimate: *a chummy bunch.*

chump (chŭmp) *n. Informal* A foolish or stupid person.

chunk (chŭngk) *n.* **1.** A thick piece of something: *a chunk of ice.* **2.** A large portion or amount: *They spent a chunk of their free time making music.*

chunk·y (chŭng′kē) *adj.* **chunk·i·er, chunk·i·est 1.** Short, strong, and somewhat fat; stocky: *a chunky horse.* **2.** Containing small thick pieces: *chunky soup.* **—chunk′i·ness** *n.*

Chun·nel (chŭn′əl) *n.* A railroad tunnel under the English Channel that connects Great Britain and France.

church (chûrch) *n.* **1.** A building for public worship, especially Christian worship. **2.** A Christian congregation: *Her church holds a children's fair each spring.* **3.** Religious service in a church: *They go to church every week.* **4.** often **Church** A specified Christian denomination: *the Baptist Church.* **5.** often **Church** All Christians regarded as a single spiritual body: *the Church and its beliefs.* **6.** The clerical profession; clergy. **7.** Ecclesiastical power as distinguished from secular power: *The separation of church and state is firmly established by the First Amendment to the Constitution.* ❖ *adj.* Relating to the church: *church music.* [From Old English *cirice*, from Late Greek *kūriakon (dōma)*, the Lord's (house), from *kūrios*, lord.]

church·go·er (chûrch′gō′ər) *n.* A person who attends church services regularly.

Chur·chill (chûr′chĭl′), Sir **Winston Leonard Spencer** 1874–1965. British politician and writer. He served as prime minister of Great Britain twice (1940–1945 and 1951–1955) and led the country through World War II. Churchill published several historical works, including *The Second World War* (1948–1953).

church·man (chûrch′mən) *n.* **1.** A man who is a cleric. **2.** A man who is a member of a church.

Church of Christ, Scientist *n.* Christian Science.

Church of England *n.* The national Christian church of England, which split off from the Roman Catholic Church in 1534 under the leadership of Henry VIII.

Church of Jesus Christ of Latter-day Saints *n.* The Mormon Church.

church·war·den (chûrch′wôr′dn) *n.* A lay officer in an Anglican or Episcopal Church who helps manage parish business or legal affairs.

church·wom·an (chûrch′wo͝om′ən) *n.* **1.** A woman who is a cleric. **2.** A woman who is a member of a church.

church·yard (chûrch′yärd′) *n.* A yard adjacent to a church, often used as a cemetery.

churl (chûrl) *n.* **1.** A rude surly person; a boor. **2.** A medieval English peasant.

churl·ish (chûr′lĭsh) *adj.* Rude; surly; boorish: *The criminal's churlish answer offended the judge.* **—churl′ish·ly** *adv.* **—churl′ish·ness** *n.*

churn (chûrn) *n.* A container in which milk or cream is stirred or beaten vigorously in order to make butter. ❖ *v.* **churned, churn·ing, churns** *—tr.* **1.** To stir or beat (milk or cream) in a churn to make butter. **2.** To move or swirl about violently: *Wind churned the leaves into piles.* *—intr.* **1.** To make butter in a churn. **2.** To stir or move violently: *waves churning in a storm.* [From Old English *cyrn, cyrin.*]

chute (sho͞ot) *n.* **1.** A vertical or inclined trough or passage down which things can be dropped or slid: *a laundry chute; a chute for toboggans.* **2.** A waterfall or rapid. **3.** A parachute.

❑ *These sound alike:* **chute, shoot** (fire a weapon).

chut·ney (chŭt′nē) *n.* A spicy relish made of fruits and herbs.

chutz·pah (ᴋʜo͝ot′spə *or* ho͝ot′spə) *n.* Shameless boldness; impudence; gall.

chyme (kīm) *n.* The thick soft mass of partly digested food that is passed from the stomach to the small intestine.

CIA *abbr.* An abbreviation of Central Intelligence Agency.

ci·a·bat·ta (chə-bä′tə) *n.* A porous bread with a crispy crust, baked in a flattish, usually oblong loaf. [From Italian, slipper (from the fact the loaf is slipper-shaped).]

ci·ca·da (sĭ-kā′də) *n., pl.* **ci·ca·das** or **ci·ca·dae** (sĭ-kā′dē′) Any of various insects having a broad head and transparent wings, the males of which produce a high-pitched droning sound from specialized organs. Some kinds of cicadas live underground as nymphs and emerge after 13 or 17 years.

Cic·e·ro (sĭs′ə-rō′), **Marcus Tullius** 106–43 ʙᴄ. Roman politician and orator known for his superb prose.

–cide *suff.* A suffix that means: **1.** A killer of: *insecticide.* **2.** An act of killing: *suicide.*

ci·der (sī′dər) *n.* The juice pressed from apples, used as a beverage or to produce vinegar. [From Middle English *sider*, from Greek *sikera*, of Semitic origin.]

ci·gar (sĭ-gär′) *n.* A tight roll of tobacco leaves prepared for smoking. [From Spanish *cigarro*, possibly from Maya *sik*, tobacco.]

cig·a·rette (sĭg′ə-rĕt′ *or* sĭg′ə-rĕt′) *n.* A small roll of finely cut tobacco enclosed in a wrapper of thin paper for smoking.

ci·lan·tro (sĭ-lăn′trō *or* sĭ-län′trō) *n.* The stems and leaves of the coriander plant, used as a flavoring and garnish.

ciliary body (sĭl′ē-ĕr′ē) *n.* A ring-shaped structure inside the eye that adjusts the shape of the lens and produces the fluid of the aqueous humor.

cil·i·ate (sĭl′ē-ĭt *or* sĭl′ē-āt′) *adj.* Having cilia. ❖ *n.* A microorganism, such as a paramecium, having cilia.

cil·i·um (sĭl′ē-əm) *n., pl.* **cil·i·a** (sĭl′ē-ə) One of usually many hairlike projections found on the outside of certain cells and capable of a whipping motion. Some microorganisms use cilia to move themselves. The respiratory tract in humans is lined with cilia that remove foreign matter from air before it reaches the lungs.

cinch (sĭnch) *n.* **1.** A strap that encircles a horse's body and is used for holding a saddle or pack. **2.** Something easy to accomplish: *Riding a bike is a cinch once you know how.*

cin·cho·na (sĭng-kō′nə *or* sĭn-chō′nə) *n.* Any of several evergreen trees and shrubs of South America whose bark is the source of quinine. [Reputedly after Francisca Henríquez de Ribera (1576–1639), Countess of *Chinchón*.]

Cin·cin·na·ti (sĭn′sə-năt′ē) A city of extreme southwest Ohio near the borders of Kentucky and Indiana. It was founded in 1788.

Cin·co de Ma·yo (sēng′kō də mä′yō) *n.* May 5, observed by Mexican communities in the Americas in celebration of the 1862 defeat of French troops at the Battle of Puebla.

cinc·ture (sĭngk′chər) *n.* A belt or sash worn around the waist.

cin·der (sĭn′dər) *n.* **1a.** A burned or partly burned material, such as coal or wood, that cannot be burned further. **b.** A partly charred material that can burn further but without flame. **2. cinders** Ashes.

cinder block or **cin·der·block** (sĭn′dər-blŏk′) *n.* A hollow concrete block made with coal cinders and used in building.

cin·e·ma (sĭn′ə-mə) *n.* **1a.** A film or movie. **b.** A movie theater: *the local cinema.* **2a.** The movie industry: *looking for a job in cinema.* **b.** The art of making movies or films: *studied cinema in college.* **—cin′e·mat′ic** (sĭn′ə-măt′ĭk) *adj.*

cin·e·ma·tog·ra·pher (sĭn′ə-mə-tŏg′rə-fər) *n.* A movie photographer, especially one who is in charge of shooting a movie.

cin·e·ma·tog·ra·phy (sĭn′ə-mə-tŏg′rə-fē) *n.* The art or technique of movie photography.

cin·na·bar (sĭn′ə-bär′) *n.* **1.** A red or brown mineral that is the chief source of mercury. **2.** Red mercuric sulfide used as a pigment. [From Middle English *cinabare*, from Greek *kinnabari.*]

cin·na·mon (sĭn′ə-mən) *n.* **1.** A reddish-brown spice made from the dried and ground inner bark of certain tropical Asian trees. **2.** A tree from which this bark is obtained. ❖ *adj.* Having the flavor of cinnamon. [From Middle English *cinamome*, from Greek *kinnamōmon*, probably of Semitic origin.]

ci·pher also **cy·pher** (sī′fər) *n.* **1.** The numerical symbol 0 representing zero. **2.** A person or thing without influence or value. **3a.** A system of writing in which letters are changed or substituted for other letters according to a code. **b.** A message in secret code. ❖ *v.* **ci·phered, ci·pher·ing, ci·phers** also **cy·phered, cy·pher·ing, cy·phers** *—tr.* To put (a message) into a cipher. *—intr.* To do arithmetic: *a one-room school where pupils learned to read and cipher.* [From Middle English *cifre*, from Arabic *ṣifr*, from *ṣafira*, to be empty.]

cir·ca (sûr′kə) *prep.* About: *a little-known painter who was born circa 1790.*

cir·ca·di·an (sər-kā′dē-ən) *adj.* Functioning or recurring in cycles of 24 hours: *Jet lag results from a disruption in a person's circadian rhythm.*

Cir·ce (sûr′sē) *n.* In Greek mythology, a goddess who detained Odysseus on an island for a year and turned his men into swine.

cir·cle (sûr′kəl) *n.* **1.** A closed curve that has all of its points at the same distance from a fixed point called the center. **2.** A flat surface or area bounded by such a closed curve: *colored the circles blue and yellow.* **3.** Something having the shape of a circle: *sit in a circle around a campfire.* **4.** A group of people sharing common interests or activities: *an astronomer well known in scientific circles.* ❖ *v.* **cir·cled, cir·cling, cir·cles** *—tr.* **1.** To draw or form a circle around: *Circle the right answer.* **2.** To move or travel in a circle around: *A helicopter circled the city. Magellan's expedition circled the globe.* *—intr.* To move in a circle: *A hawk circled overhead.* [From Middle English *cercle*, from Latin *circulus*, from Greek *kirkos, krikos.*]

circle graph *n.* A pie chart.

cir·clet (sûr′klĭt) *n.* A small circle, especially a circular band worn on the head as an ornament.

cir·cuit (sûr′kĭt) *n.* **1a.** A circular or elliptical line or route, especially a path that forms a circle around something: *the moon's elliptical circuit around Earth.* **b.** The act of following or completing such a route: *It takes a full year for Earth to make a circuit around the sun.* **2.** A closed path through which an electric current flows or may flow: *Using too many appliances at once blew the circuit to the kitchen.* **3.** A system of electrically connected parts or devices: *A microchip contains all the circuits for this computer.* **4a.** A regular route followed from place to place: *a salesperson on the West Coast circuit.* **b.** The district or area covered by such a route, especially the area under the jurisdiction of a judge who tries cases in various places. **5.** An association of theaters in which plays, shows, or films move from theater to theater for presentation: *The summer circuit brought good plays to many small towns.* **6.** A series of athletic competitions held in different places: *the professional tennis circuit.*

circuit board *n.* An insulated board on which circuits and electronic components are mounted.

circuit breaker *n.* A safety device that automatically switches off the flow of electricity in a circuit if the current becomes too strong.

circuit court *n.* In some states, a court holding sessions in various places in the area over which it has jurisdiction.

cir·cu·i·tous (sər-kyōō′ĭ-təs) *adj.* Not direct; roundabout: *take a circuitous route to the store; a confusing and circuitous argument.* **—cir·cu′i·tous·ly** *adv.* **—cir·cu′i·tous·ness** *n.*

cir·cuit·ry (sûr′kĭ-trē) *n., pl.* **cir·cuit·ries 1.** The plan for an electric or electronic circuit. **2.** Electric circuits considered as a group: *The circuitry of television sets is complicated.*

cir·cu·lar (sûr′kyə-lər) *adj.* **1.** Relating to or shaped like a circle: *Most coins are circular pieces of metal.* **2.** Forming or moving in a circle: *circular motion.* **3.** Using a premise to prove a conclusion that in turn is used to prove the premise: *a circular argument.* ❖ *n.* A printed advertisement, notice, or other statement intended for public distribution: *During the campaign, candidates sent out circulars explaining their political viewpoints.* **—cir′cu·lar·ly** *adv.*

cir·cu·lar·ize (sûr′kyə-lə-rīz′) *tr.v.* **cir·cu·lar·ized, cir·cu·lar·iz·ing, cir·cu·lar·iz·es** To send circulars to: *Candidates circularize their districts for votes.*

circular saw *n.* A power saw whose blade is a toothed metal disk that cuts as the blade rotates at a high speed.

cir·cu·late (sûr′kyə-lāt′) *v.* **cir·cu·lat·ed, cir·cu·lat·ing, cir·cu·lates** *—intr.* **1.** To move or flow in a closed path: *Blood circulates through the body.* **2.** To move or flow freely: *The fan helps the air circulate.* **3.** To spread widely among people or places: *Rumors tend to circulate quickly.* *—tr.* **1.** To cause to move or flow: *The heart circulates blood throughout the body.* **2.** To spread or distribute among: *A topic that has been widely circulated in public discussion.*

cir·cu·la·tion (sûr′kyə-lā′shən) *n.* **1a.** The act or process of circulating: *Opening the window will help the circulation of air.* **b.** The passage of something, such as money or news, from person to person or from place to place: *There aren't many two-dollar bills in circulation.* **2.** The flow of the blood from the heart through the arteries and veins back to the heart: *a person with poor circulation.* **3a.** The distribution of printed matter, such as newspapers and magazines: *This popular magazine has a wide circulation.* **b.** The number of copies of a newspaper, magazine, book, or other printed matter, sold or distributed to the public: *a newspaper with a daily circulation of 400,000.*

cir·cu·la·to·ry (sûr′kyə-lə-tôr′ē) *adj.* **1.** Relating to or involving circulation. **2.** Relating to the circulatory system: *Hardening of the arteries is a circulatory disease.*

circulatory system *n.* The system consisting of the heart

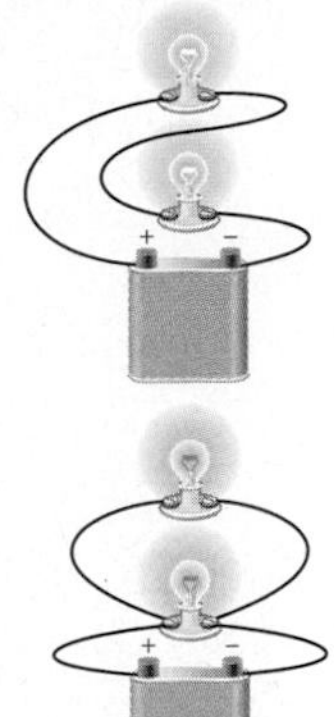

circuit

top: Bulbs in a series circuit are dim because electricity has to pass through every bulb in the circuit before returning to the battery. *bottom:* Bulbs in a parallel circuit shine brightly because each bulb has its own circuit that connects directly to the battery.

circular saw

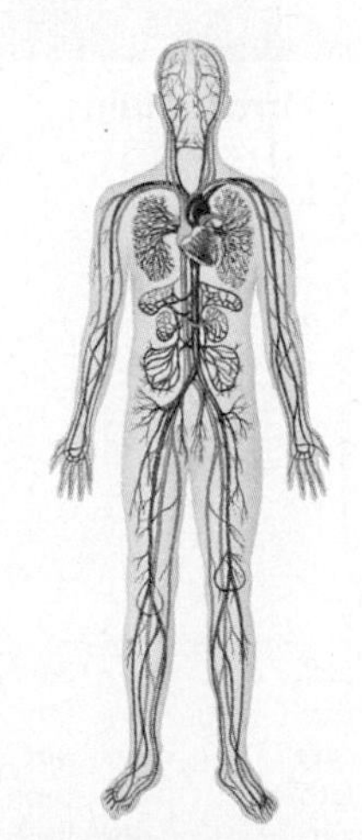

circulatory system

Arteries (*red*) carry blood rich in oxygen from the heart to tissues of the body. Veins (*blue*) carry blood low in oxygen back to the heart.

and blood vessels that circulates blood throughout the body.

circum– *pref.* A prefix that means around or about: *circumnavigate.*

cir·cum·cise (sûr′kəm-sīz′) *tr.v.* **cir·cum·cised, cir·cum·cis·ing, cir·cum·cis·es** To remove the foreskin of (a male).

cir·cum·ci·sion (sûr′kəm-**sĭzh′**ən) *n.* The act or process of circumcising.

cir·cum·fer·ence (sər-**kŭm′**fər-əns) *n.* **1.** The boundary of a circle. **2.** The boundary line of an area or object: *walked around the circumference of the island.* **3.** The length of such a boundary: *The circumference of the moon is about 6,800 miles.* [From Middle English, from Latin *circumferre*, to carry around : *circum-*, around + *ferre*, to carry.]

cir·cum·flex (**sûr′**kəm-flĕks′) *n.* The mark (^) used over a vowel in certain languages or in a pronunciation key to indicate that the vowel is pronounced differently from the ordinary way.

cir·cum·lo·cu·tion (sûr′kəm-lō-**kyo͞o′**shən) *n.* **1.** The use of wordy and indirect language: *The politician was a master of circumlocution.* **2.** A wordy or roundabout expression; for example, *the husband of my mother's sister* is a circumlocution for *my uncle.*

cir·cum·nav·i·gate (sûr′kəm-**năv′**ĭ-gāt′) *tr.v.* **cir·cum·nav·i·gat·ed, cir·cum·nav·i·gat·ing, cir·cum·nav·i·gates** To go completely around; circle: *an attempt to circumnavigate the earth in a balloon.* **—cir′cum·nav′i·ga′tion** *n.*

cir·cum·scribe (**sûr′**kəm-skrīb′) *tr.v.* **cir·cum·scribed, cir·cum·scrib·ing, cir·cum·scribes 1a.** To draw (a figure) around another figure so as to touch as many points as possible: *A circle that is circumscribed around a triangle touches it at three points called the vertices of the triangle.* **b.** To enclose within a line or surface: *A circle will circumscribe a square but not a trapezoid.* **2.** To confine within or as if within bounds; limit: *Their plans for the future were circumscribed by their lack of money.* [From Middle English *circumscriben*, from Latin *circumscrībere* : *circum-*, around + *scrībere*, to write.]

cirrocumulus

cir·cum·spect (**sûr′**kəm-spĕkt′) *adj.* Careful of circumstances or consequences; cautious; prudent: *The president must be circumspect about statements made to reporters.* **—cir′cum·spec′tion** *n.* **—cir′cum·spect′ly** *adv.*

cir·cum·stance (**sûr′**kəm-stăns′) *n.* **1.** A condition, fact, or event connected with and usually affecting another event: *I'm not familiar with the circumstances of the case. We were delayed by weather and other circumstances.* **2.** A set of determining factors that are beyond one's control: *She tried hard, but in the end she was a victim of circumstance.* **3. circumstances** Financial condition: *a wealthy family in comfortable circumstances.* **4.** Formal display; ceremony: *the pomp and circumstance of graduation.* ◆ **under no circumstances.** In no case; never: *Under no circumstances should you touch these two wires together.* **under the circumstances** or **in the circumstances** Given these conditions; such being the case: *A storm was brewing, and under the circumstances we left for home.*

cir·cum·stan·tial (sûr′kəm-**stăn′**shəl) *adj.* **1.** Relating to or dependent on circumstances: *the flexibility to react to any circumstantial developments.* **2.** Not of primary importance; incidental: *circumstantial matters having little bearing on the main plan.* **3.** Full of detail; complete: *a circumstantial account of what happened last night.*

circumstantial evidence *n.* Evidence not directly relevant to the facts in a legal case but describing known circumstances from which one might draw a conclusion about the facts in a case.

cir·cum·vent (sûr′kəm-**vĕnt′**) *tr.v.* **cir·cum·vent·ed, cir·cum·vent·ing, cir·cum·vents 1.** To avoid or get around by cleverness or ingenuity: *They tried to circumvent the building code when remodeling the garage.* **2.** To avoid by or as if by going around: *take side roads to circumvent construction.* **—cir′cum·ven′tion** *n.*

cir·cus (**sûr′**kəs) *n.* **1a.** A public entertainment featuring acrobats, clowns, and trained animals. **b.** The traveling company of performers, animals, and workers that puts on the circus: *ran away to join the circus.* **2.** A roofless arena used by the ancient Romans for athletic contests and public spectacles. **3.** *Informal* Something suggestive of a circus, as in activity or disorder: *Holidays are a regular circus in our house.* [From Middle English, from Latin, circle, circus.]

cir·rho·sis (sĭ-**rō′**sĭs) *n.* A chronic disease of the liver, in which normal tissue is gradually replaced by scar tissue so that its function is destroyed and the entire organ shrinks and hardens in the process.

cir·ri (**sîr′**ī′) *n.* Plural of **cirrus.**

cir·ro·cu·mu·lus (sîr′ō-**kyo͞om′**yə-ləs) *n.* A high-altitude cloud formation made up of many small puffy clouds, typically in the form of ripples or closely spaced patches.

cir·ro·strat·us (sîr′ō-**străt′**əs *or* sîr′ō-**strā′**təs) *n.* A thin hazy cloud formation made up of high-altitude ice crystals, often covering the sky and producing a halo effect.

cir·rus (**sîr′**əs) *n., pl.* **cir·ri** (**sîr′**ī′) A high-altitude cloud formation made up of feathery white patches, bands, or streamers of ice crystals. [From Latin *cirrus*, curl of hair.]

cis·tern (**sĭs′**tərn) *n.* A large tank or reservoir for holding liquid, especially for the collection and storage of rainwater.

cit·a·del (**sĭt′**ə-dəl) *n.* **1.** A fortress overlooking a city. **2.** A stronghold or safe place: *The United States is often referred to as a citadel of democracy.*

ci·ta·tion (sī-**tā′**shən) *n.* **1.** A reference or quotation: *a report full of citations from books and scholarly articles.* **2.** A summons to appear in court: *The police officer issued a citation to the speeding driver.* **3.** An official recommendation for bravery. **4.** The act of citing: *Citation of diaries and official documents made the book seem authoritative.*

cite (sīt) *tr.v.* **cit·ed, cit·ing, cites 1a.** To quote as an authority or example. **b.** To mention or bring forward as support, illustration, or proof: *Let me cite two cases of what I have in mind.* **2.** To summon (someone) to appear in a court of law: *The police officer cited the juveniles for defacing public property.* **3.** To mention and commend for meritorious action: *The firefighter was cited for bravery beyond the call of duty.* —SEE NOTE AT **quote.**

❑ *These sound alike:* **cite, sight** (vision), **site** (place).

cit·i·zen (**sĭt′**ĭ-zən) *n.* **1.** A person owing loyalty to and entitled to the protection of a given country. **2.** A resident of a city or town, especially one entitled to vote and enjoy other privileges there. [From Middle English *citisein*, from Old French *cite*, city.]

cit·i·zen·ry (**sĭt′**ĭ-zən-rē) *n., pl.* **cit·i·zen·ries** Citizens considered as a group.

cit·i·zens band (**sĭt′**ĭ-zənz) *n.* A radio frequency band available for private use, as by truck drivers or motorists.

cit·i·zen·ship (**sĭt′**ĭ-zən-shĭp′) *n.* The status of a citizen with its duties, rights, and privileges.

cit·rate (**sĭt′**rāt′) *n.* A salt or ester of citric acid.

cit·ric acid (**sĭt′**rĭk) *n.* A white odorless acid with a sour taste, found in oranges, grapefruit, lemons, and other fruit. It is used in medicine and as a flavoring.

cit·ron (**sĭt′**rən) *n.* **1a.** A yellowish thick-skinned fruit similar to a lemon. **b.** A tree that bears such fruit. **c.** The candied rind of this fruit, used especially in fruitcake, plum pudding, and other baked goods. **2.** A melon having white flesh and a thick hard rind. The rind and sometimes the flesh are pickled or preserved.

ă	pat	ôr	core
ā	pay	oi	boy
âr	care	ou	out
ä	father	o͝o	took
ĕ	pet	o͝or	lure
ē	be	o͞o	boot
ĭ	pit	ŭ	cut
ī	bite	ûr	urge
îr	pier	th	thin
ŏ	pot	*th*	this
ō	toe	zh	vision
ô	paw	ə	about

cit·ro·nel·la (sĭt′rə-**nĕl′**ə) *n.* **1.** A pale yellow aromatic oil obtained from the leaves of a tropical Asian grass and used in insect repellents and perfumes. **2.** The plant from which this oil is obtained.

cit·rus (**sĭt′**rəs) *n., pl.* **citrus** or **cit·rus·es 1.** The fruit of any of various related evergreen trees or shrubs, having juicy flesh and a thick rind, such as an orange, lemon, lime, or grapefruit. **2.** A tree or shrub that bears such fruit. [From Latin *citrus*, citron tree.] **—cit′rus** *adj.*

cit·y (**sĭt′**ē) *n., pl.* **cit·ies 1.** A center of population, commerce, and culture; a large and important town: *Many people go into the city to work each day.* **2.** In the United States, a division of local government with stated boundaries of jurisdiction set forth in a charter granted by the state: *Our city is governed by the mayor and his council.* **3.** The people living in a city considered as a group: *The city will vote in a special election next week.* [From Middle English *cite*, from Latin *cīvitās*, from *cīvis*, citizen.]

city hall *n.* **1.** The building in which the offices of a city government are located. **2.** A city government, especially its officials considered as a group: *City hall released a statement about the new budget.*

city manager *n.* An administrator appointed by a city council to manage the affairs of city government.

cit·y·scape (**sĭt′**ē-skāp′) *n.* **1.** A part of a city that can be seen from one place. **2.** A painting or a picture that shows such a view.

cit·y-state (**sĭt′**ē-**stāt′**) *n.* An independent state consisting of a city and its surrounding territory: *Sparta was a city-state of ancient Greece.*

cit·y·wide (**sĭt′**ē-wīd′) *adj.* Including or occurring in all parts of a city: *citywide busing; a citywide strike.*

civ·et (**sĭv′**ĭt) *n.* **1.** Any of various often spotted mammals of Africa and Asia that resemble a cat and have scent glands that produce a fluid with a strong musky odor. **2.** This yellowish fluid, used in making perfumes. [From Medieval Latin *zibethus*, from Arabic *zabād*, civet perfume.]

civ·ic (**sĭv′**ĭk) *adj.* **1.** Relating to or belonging to a city: *The town's Fourth of July parade is our chief civic event.* **2.** Relating to or belonging to a citizen or citizenship: *It is a civic duty to vote in elections.* **—civ′i·cal·ly** *adv.*

civ·ics (**sĭv′**ĭks) *n.* *(used with a singular verb)* The study of the purpose and function of local and national government and of the rights and duties of citizens.

civ·il (**sĭv′**əl) *adj.* **1.** Relating to a citizen or citizens: *voting and other civil responsibilities.* **2.** Relating to citizens and their relations to the government: *Most departments of the government are concerned with civil affairs.* **3.** Relating to the general public rather than to military or religious matters: *a couple married in a civil ceremony at city hall.* **4.** Following accepted social usage or manners, often just barely; polite enough: *a civil reply.* See Synonyms at **polite. 5.** Relating to the rights of private individuals and legal proceedings concerning these rights, especially as distinguished from criminal proceedings. [From Middle English, from Latin *cīvīlis*, from *cīvis*, citizen.] **—civ′il·ly** *adv.*

civil defense *n.* The emergency measures to be taken for the protection of civilian life and property in the case of a natural disaster or enemy attack.

civil disobedience *n.* Nonviolent refusal by members of the public to obey laws, done in an effort to cause change in government policy or legislation.

civil engineer *n.* An engineer trained in the design and construction of projects such as bridges, roads, and dams. **—civil engineering** *n.*

ci·vil·ian (sĭ-**vĭl′**yən) *n.* A person not serving in the armed forces or the police. ❖ *adj.* Relating to civilians: *civilian clothes; a civilian career.*

ci·vil·i·ty (sĭ-**vĭl′**ĭ-tē) *n., pl.* **ci·vil·i·ties 1.** Courteous behavior; politeness: *Civility in daily affairs creates a harmonious atmosphere.* **2.** An act or expression of courtesy: *Saying "Good morning" is a pleasant civility.*

civ·i·li·za·tion (sĭv′ə-lĭ-**zā′**shən) *n.* **1.** A condition of human society in which there is a high level of development in political and social organizations and in the arts and sciences. **2.** The kind of culture and society developed by a particular people or nation in some period of history: *Mayan civilization.* **3.** *Informal* Modern society with its conveniences: *returned to civilization after two weeks of camping.*

civ·i·lize (**sĭv′**ə-līz′) *tr.v.* **civ·i·lized, civ·i·liz·ing, civ·i·liz·es 1.** To bring to a higher level of development in the arts, sciences, culture, and political organization. **2.** To refine by education and training: *civilize young minds.*

civ·i·lized (**sĭv′**ə-līzd′) *adj.* **1.** Having or indicating a highly developed society and culture; not primitive: *civilized life.* **2.** Polite or cultured; refined: *a civilized person.*

civil law *n.* The body of law dealing with the rights of private citizens, as distinguished from military law and criminal law.

civil libertarian *n.* A person who is actively concerned with protecting civil liberties.

civil liberties *pl.n.* Fundamental individual rights, such as freedom of speech and religion, especially as guaranteed to citizens by a constitution.

civil rights *pl.n.* The rights belonging to an individual as a citizen, especially of the United States, including civil liberties and freedom from discrimination.

civil servant *n.* A person employed in the civil service.

civil service *n.* **1.** All branches of government service that are not legislative, judicial, or military. **2.** Those people employed by the civil branches of the government: *Most of the civil service in the US government is appointed after competitive examination.*

civil union *n.* A legally sanctioned relationship between two people, especially of the same sex, having many of the rights and responsibilities of marriage.

civil war *n.* **1.** A war between opposing groups of the same country. **2. Civil War a.** The war in the United States between the Union and the Confederacy from 1861 to 1865. **b.** The war in England between the supporters of Parliament and the supporters of the king, lasting from 1642 to 1648.

Cl The symbol for the element **chlorine.**

clab·ber (**klăb′**ər) *n.* Sour curdled milk. ❖ *tr. & intr.v.* **clab·bered, clab·ber·ing, clab·bers** To curdle.

clack (klăk) *intr. & tr.v.* **clacked, clack·ing, clacks** To make or cause to make a sudden sharp sound, as that of objects struck together. ❖ *n.* A sudden sharp sound: *the clack of wooden clogs on a tile floor.* [From Middle English *clakken*, from Old Norse *klaka*, of imitative origin.]
❑ *These sound alike:* **clack, claque** (applauding group).

clad (klăd) *v.* A past tense and a past participle of **clothe.**

claim (klām) *tr.v.* **claimed, claim·ing, claims 1.** To demand, ask for, or take (something) as one's own; assert one's right to: *claim luggage; claim a reward.* **2.** To declare to be true; assert: *The witnesses claim that they saw the accident.* **3.** To deserve or call for; require: *Studying for an exam should claim all your attention.* ❖ *n.* **1.** A demand for something as one's rightful due: *file an insurance claim for losses from the fire.* **2.** A statement of something as fact; an assertion: *an advertisement that makes false claims concerning certain products.* **3.** A basis for demanding something; a right: *a sailor whose claim to fame was being the youngest to sail solo around the world.* **4.** Something claimed, especially a tract of land claimed by a miner or homesteader. ◆ **lay claim to** To assert one's right to or ownership of: *laid claim to the land along the river.* [From Middle English *claimen*, from Latin *clāmāre*, to call.]

claim·ant (**klā′**mənt) *n.* A person making a claim.

clair·voy·ance (klâr-**voi′**əns) *n.* The supposed power to

cirrus

WRITERS CHOOSE THEIR WORDS

"You are a very discourteous Giant," answered the stranger quietly, "and I shall probably have to teach you a little **civility,** before we part."

—Nathaniel Hawthorne "The Pygmies" in *Tanglewood Tales*

clam

clapboard

clarinet

ă	pat	ôr	core
ā	pay	oi	boy
âr	care	ou	out
ä	father	o͝o	took
ĕ	pet	o͝or	lure
ē	be	o͞o	boot
ĭ	pit	ŭ	cut
ī	bite	ûr	urge
îr	pier	th	thin
ŏ	pot	*th*	this
ō	toe	zh	vision
ô	paw	ə	about

see objects or events that cannot be perceived by the senses.

clair·voy·ant (klâr-**voi′**ənt) *n.* A person said to have power of clairvoyance. ❖ *adj.* Relating to or having the power of clairvoyance. [From French : *clair*, clear (from Latin *clārus*) + *voir*, to see (from Latin *vidēre*).]

clam (klăm) *n.* Any of various freshwater or saltwater mollusks that have a hinged shell and burrow into sand or mud. Many kinds of clams are used as food. ❖ *intr.v.* **clammed, clam·ming, clams** To dig or hunt for clams: *clamming along the seashore at low tide.* ◆ **clam up** *Informal* To refuse to talk; stop talking: *The suspect clammed up when the police started asking questions.* [From *clam*, clamp, vise, from Old English *clamm*, bond.]

clam·bake (**klăm′**bāk′) *n.* A picnic at which clams and other kinds of seafood are served.

clam·ber (**klăm′**bər *or* **klăm′**ər) *intr.v.* **clam·bered, clam·ber·ing, clam·bers** To climb with difficulty, especially on all fours: *clamber up a rocky slope.*

clam·my (**klăm′**ē) *adj.* **clam·mi·er, clam·mi·est** Unpleasantly damp, sticky, and usually cold: *clammy basement walls; clammy feet in wet boots.* **—clam′mi·ness** *n.*

clam·or (**klăm′**ər) *n.* **1.** A loud, continuous, and usually confused noise: *the clamor of fans at a football game.* **2.** A strong or loud demand; an outcry: *a public clamor for clean air.* ❖ *intr.v.* **clam·ored, clam·or·ing, clam·ors** To make a clamor: *The excited crowd clamored for an encore.* [From Middle English *clamour*, from Latin *clāmor*, shout, from *clāmāre*, to cry out.]

clam·or·ous (**klăm′**ər-əs) *adj.* **1.** Loud and noisy: *a clamorous birthday party.* **2.** Making or full of strong or loud demands: *a clamorous crowd of protesters.* **—clam′or·ous·ly** *adv.* **—clam′or·ous·ness** *n.*

clamp (klămp) *n.* A device for gripping or fastening things together, consisting of two parts that can be tightened together by pressure of a spring or by turning a screw. ❖ *tr.v.* **clamped, clamp·ing, clamps** To grip or fasten with or as if with a clamp: *glue and clamp two boards together; clamped her fingers tightly around the rope.* ◆ **clamp down** To become more strict or repressive: *The government clamped down on dissent by closing several newspapers.*

clam·shell (**klăm′**shĕl′) *n.* **1.** The shell of a clam. **2.** Any of various devices that have two hinged jaws and are used for dredging or digging.

clan (klăn) *n.* **1.** A group of families, as in the Scottish Highlands, claiming a common ancestor: *the MacIntyre clan.* **2.** A division of a tribe often claiming descent from a common ancestor. **3.** A group of relatives, friends, or others having a common background or interest: *a clan of local politicians.* [From Scottish Gaelic *clann*, family, from Old Irish *cland*, offspring, from Latin *planta*, plant, sprout.]

clan·des·tine (klăn-**dĕs′**tĭn) *adj.* Done secretly or kept secret, often for some unlawful purpose: *a clandestine meeting of conspirators.* **—clan·des′tine·ly** *adv.*

clang (klăng) *tr. & intr.v.* **clanged, clang·ing, clangs** To make or cause to make a loud metallic ringing sound: *Bells clanged to announce the new year.* ❖ *n.* A clanging sound: *the clang of an alarm.*

clan·gor (**klăng′**ər *or* **klăng′**gər) *n.* A loud repeated clanging or banging; a din: *wore earplugs against the incessant clangor of the assembly line.* **—clan′gor·ous** *adj.* **—clan′gor·ous·ly** *adv.*

clank (klăngk) *n.* A loud, metallic ringing sound: *The gate closed with a clank.* ❖ *intr.v.* **clanked, clank·ing, clanks** To make a clank: *The old car clanked and sputtered down the road.*

clan·nish (**klăn′**ĭsh) *adj.* **1.** Relating to or characteristic of a clan. **2.** Inclined to cling together as a group and exclude outsiders. **—clan′nish·ly** *adv.*

clans·man (**klănz′**mən) *n.* A man belonging to a clan.

clans·wom·an (**klănz′**wo͝om′ən) *n.* A woman belonging to a clan.

clap (klăp) *v.* **clapped, clap·ping, claps** *—intr.* **1.** To strike the hands together with a sudden loud sound: *The audience clapped at the end of the play.* **2.** To make a sudden sharp sound: *The door clapped shut.* *—tr.* **1.** To strike (the hands) together with an abrupt loud sound: *We clapped our hands in rhythm to the music.* **2.** To make (something) come together suddenly with a sharp noise: *The baby clapped the spoon on the table.* **3.** To tap with the open hand, as in hearty greeting: *clap a friend on the shoulder.* **4.** To put or place suddenly: *I clapped the lid on the box before the cricket could jump out.* ❖ *n.* **1.** The act or sound of clapping the hands. **2.** A loud, sharp, or explosive noise: *a clap of thunder.* **3.** A slap: *a friendly clap on the back.*

clap·board (**klăb′**ərd *or* **klăp′**bôrd′) *n.* A long narrow board with one edge thicker than the other, overlapped to cover the outside walls of a building. ❖ *tr.v.* **clap·board·ed, clap·board·ing, clap·boards** To cover with clapboards.

clap·per (**klăp′**ər) *n.* **1.** The tongue of a bell. **2.** A person or thing that claps. **3. clappers** Two flat pieces of wood that are held between the fingers and struck together as a percussion instrument.

clap·trap (**klăp′**trăp′) *n.* Insincere, empty speech or writing.

claque (klăk) *n.* **1.** A group of people hired to applaud at a performance. **2.** A group of fawning admirers.
❑ *These sound alike:* **claque, clack** (sharp sound).

clar·et (**klăr′**ĭt) *n.* **1.** A dry red wine. **2.** A dark purplish red.

clar·i·fy (**klăr′**ə-fī′) *v.* **clar·i·fied, clar·i·fy·ing, clar·i·fies** *—tr.* **1.** To make clear or easier to understand: *gave a detailed explanation to clarify the instructions.* **2.** To make (a liquid, butter, or other substance) clear or pure by removing unwanted solid matter: *clarify butter by heating it; clarify vinegar by straining it.* *—intr.* To become clear. **—clar′i·fi·ca′tion** (klăr′ə-fĭ-**kā′**shən) *n.*

clar·i·net (klăr′ə-**nĕt′**) *n.* A woodwind instrument having a cylindrical body, a flaring bell, and a mouthpiece with a single reed. It is played by covering holes in its body and pressing keys with the fingers. [From Old French *clarin*, clarion, from Latin *clārus*, clear.] **—clar′i·net′ist** *n.*

clar·i·on (**klăr′**ē-ən) *adj.* Shrill and clear: *the clarion call of a trumpet.* ❖ *n.* **1.** A medieval trumpet with a clear shrill tone. **2.** The sound made by this trumpet or a similar sound.

clar·i·ty (**klăr′**ĭ-tē) *n.* The condition or quality of being clear: *clarity of speech; complex ideas presented with great clarity.*

Clark (klärk), **George Rogers** 1752–1818. American military leader and pioneer who led numerous raids in the Northwest Territory during the Revolutionary War.

Clark, William 1770–1838. American explorer who with Meriwether Lewis led an expedition from St. Louis to the mouth of the Columbia River (1804–1806).

clash (klăsh) *v.* **clashed, clash·ing, clash·es** *—intr.* **1.** To strike or collide with a loud harsh sound: *The cymbals clashed loudly.* **2.** To meet in violent conflict: *The armies clashed repeatedly with no clear victor.* **3.** To be in sharp disagreement: *The researcher's data clashed with previously published results.* **4.** To create an unpleasant or jarring effect: *That striped shirt clashes with your plaid pants.* *—tr.* To strike together or collide with a loud harsh noise: *At the end of the march I clashed the cymbals together.* ❖ *n.* **1.** A conflict, opposition, or disagreement: *a clash between political parties.* **2.** A loud, harsh, metallic sound: *a clash of cymbals.*

clasp (klăsp) *n.* **1.** A fastener, such as a hook or buckle, used to hold two objects or parts together. **2.** A firm grasp or embrace: *took my hand with a firm clasp.* ❖ *tr.v.* **clasped, clasp·ing, clasps 1.** To fasten with a clasp: *clasp a necklace.* **2.** To grasp or embrace tightly: *clasped each other after their long separation.* [From Middle English *claspe*, probably ultimately from Old English *clyppan*, to grasp, hold.]

class (klăs) *n.* **1.** A group of people or things that are generally alike in some way; a kind or category: *the class of odd numbers; a class of ships.* **2.** A group of people having approximately the same economic and social standing: *the working class.* **3.** A taxonomic category of organisms that share certain characteristics, ranking above an order and below a phylum: *All mammals belong to the same class of animals.* See table at **taxonomy. 4a.** A group of people who graduated in the same year: *a reunion of the class of 1990.* **b.** A group of students who meet regularly to study the same subject: *Our biology class has 20 students.* **c.** The period during which such a group meets: *eat lunch before class; meet after class.* **d.** A course of instruction: *wants to take a ballet class next year.* **5a.** A grade of mail: *A letter is sent first class and a magazine third class.* **b.** The quality of accommodations on a public vehicle: *They flew by business class to Tokyo.* **6.** *Informal* Great style or quality: *This restaurant has a lot of class.* ❖ *tr.v.* **classed, class·ing, class·es** To assign to a class; classify: *class a novel as a murder mystery.* [From Latin *classis*, class of citizens.]

clas·sic (klăs′ĭk) *adj.* **1.** Long regarded as a model; serving as an outstanding example of its kind: *a classic example of abstract art; a classic horror film.* **2.** Well-known and typical: *A runny nose and a cough are classic signs of a cold.* **3.** Simple and refined in form or in style: *the classic lines of a luxury automobile.* **4.** Relating to ancient Greece and Rome or their literature or art; classical: *a film based on a classic Greek tragedy.* ❖ *n.* **1.** A work of literature, music, or art generally considered to be of the highest rank: *Many early rock 'n' roll recordings are now classics.* **2. classics** The languages and literature of ancient Greece and Rome. **3.** A traditional event held annually, as in sports: *The World Series is baseball's fall classic.* [From Latin *classicus*, belonging to the higher class of citizens, from *classis*, class.]

clas·si·cal (klăs′ĭ-kəl) *adj.* **1.** Relating to the art, architecture, literature, and way of life of ancient Greece and Rome: *classical architecture of the Roman forum; a classical scholar.* **2a.** Relating to a style of European music during the second half of the 1700s and early 1800s. **b.** Relating to music in the educated European tradition, such as symphony, concerto, and opera, as opposed to popular or folk music. **3.** Standard or traditional rather than new or experimental; established: *The calculator has displaced the classical methods of arithmetic computation.* **4.** Well-known; typical; classic: *Blue jeans, bandannas, and cowboy boots are classical items of western clothing.* **—clas′si·cal·ly** *adv.*

clas·si·cism (klăs′ĭ-sĭz′əm) *n.* **1.** The rules and ideals that form the basis of the art, architecture, and literature of ancient Greece and Rome. They include the use of regular order in design, simplicity in style, and restraint or proportion in form. **2.** The use of such rules or principles in artistic creation. **3.** The scholarly study of the art, languages, and cultures of ancient Greece and Rome.

clas·si·cist (klăs′ĭ-sĭst) *n.* A student of or an authority on the art, architecture, literature, languages, and cultures of ancient Greece and Rome.

clas·si·fi·ca·tion (klăs′ə-fĭ-kā′shən) *n.* **1.** The act or process of classifying; grouping by categories: *The classification of books according to subject is the work of a librarian.* **2a.** The result of classifying, as by category, name, or rating; a systematic arrangement: *chemical elements arranged in a classification by atomic weight.* **b.** In biology, the systematic grouping of organisms by similarity of characteristics, often thought to reflect evolutionary relationships.

clas·si·fied (klăs′ə-fīd′) *adj.* **1.** Arranged in separate classes or categories; categorized: *"For Sale" and "Wanted" are common categories in the classified section of a newspaper.* **2.** Available only to authorized people; secret: *classified information.*

classified advertisement *n.* An advertisement, usually brief and in small type, printed in a newspaper along with others of the same category.

clas·si·fy (klăs′ə-fī′) *tr.v.* **clas·si·fied, clas·si·fy·ing, clas·si·fies 1.** To arrange in classes or assign to a class; sort; categorize: *A librarian classifies books according to subject matter.* **2.** To designate (information) as available only to authorized people. **—clas′si·fi′a·ble** *adj.* **—clas′si·fi′er** *n.*

class·mate (klăs′māt′) *n.* A member of the same class in a school or college.

class·room (klăs′ro͝om′ *or* klăs′ro͞om′) *n.* A room in which classes are held in a school or college.

class·y (klăs′ē) *adj.* **class·i·er, class·i·est** *Informal* Stylish; elegant: *a classy suit; classy manners.*

clat·ter (klăt′ər) *v.* **clat·tered, clat·ter·ing, clat·ters** —*intr.* **1.** To make a rattling sound: *The shutters clattered in the wind.* **2.** To move with a rattling sound: *A rickety old truck clattered down the road.* —*tr.* To cause to make a rattling sound: *The cook clattered pots and pans in the kitchen.* ❖ *n.* A rattling sound: *the clatter of dishes falling to the floor.*

clause (klôz) *n.* **1.** In grammar, a group of words containing a subject and a finite verb. In the complex sentence *The dog ran off before we caught it,* the words *The dog ran off* constitute an independent clause and the words *before we caught it* constitute a subordinate clause. **2.** A separate part of a document containing some distinct provision: *The contract had several clauses, each outlining the duties of the partners.* [From Middle English, from Medieval Latin *clausa*, close of a rhetorical period, from Latin, from *claudere*, to close.]

claus·tro·pho·bi·a (klô′strə-fō′bē-ə) *n.* An abnormal fear of being in small or confined spaces.

clav·i·chord (klăv′ĭ-kôrd′) *n.* A keyboard musical instrument with a soft sound made by small metal hammers that strike the strings as keys are pushed. The modern piano was developed from it.

clav·i·cle (klăv′ĭ-kəl) *n.* The collarbone.

cla·vier (klə-vîr′ *or* klā′vē-ər *or* klăv′ē-ər) *n.* **1.** The keyboard of a musical instrument, such as a piano or organ. **2.** A stringed keyboard instrument, such as a harpsichord.

claw (klô) *n.* **1.** A sharp, curved, hard structure on the end of the toe of a vertebrate animal. **2a.** A pincer, as of a lobster or crab, used for grasping. **b.** A small curved structure at the tip of an appendage of an insect or other invertebrate animal. **3.** Something resembling a claw: *I pulled out the bent nail with the claw of the hammer.* ❖ *tr. & intr.v.* **clawed, claw·ing, claws** To scratch, dig, tear, or pull with the claws or fingernails: *The cat clawed the chair. She clawed at the package to open it.* [From Old English *clawu*.]

clay (klā) *n.* An earthy material that is soft and sticky when wet but that hardens when heated, consisting mainly of various silicates of aluminum. It is widely used in making bricks, pottery, and tiles. [From Old English *clæg*.]

Clay (klā), **Cassius Marcellus** See Muhammad **Ali.**

Clay, Henry 1777–1852. American politician who served numerous terms as a US representative and senator between 1806 and 1852. Noted for his skill as a compromiser, he exerted his influence to pass legislation that was agreeable to both Free and Slave States.

claw
of an eagle (*left*) and of a crab (*right*)

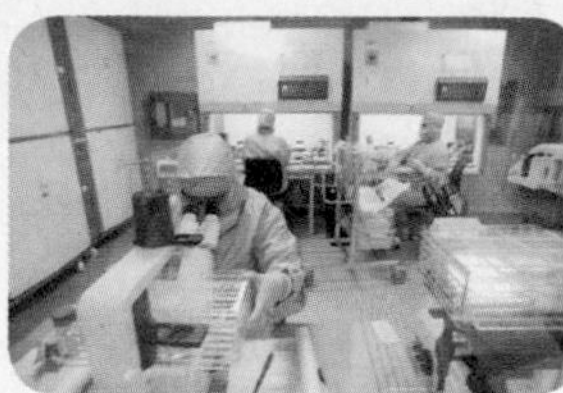

clean room

cleat

cleaver

ă	pat	ôr	core
ā	pay	oi	boy
âr	care	ou	out
ä	father	o͝o	took
ĕ	pet	o͝or	lure
ē	be	o͞o	boot
ĭ	pit	ŭ	cut
ī	bite	ûr	urge
îr	pier	th	thin
ŏ	pot	*th*	this
ō	toe	zh	vision
ô	paw	ə	about

clay pigeon *n.* A clay disk hurled as a flying target in skeet and trapshooting.

clean (klēn) *adj.* **clean·er, clean·est 1.** Free from dirt, stain, or impurities; unsoiled: *clean clothing; drinking from a clean glass.* **2a.** Free from pollution or contamination: *clean drinking water.* **b.** Producing little pollution: *The new law calls for clean fuels in all cars.* **3.** Having a smooth edge or surface; even; regular: *A clean break in the bone heals quickly.* **4.** Entire; thorough; complete: *They made a clean escape, leaving no clues as to where they went.* **5.** Free from wrongdoing; honorable: *a clean life of hard work; a clean record.* **6.** Free from clumsiness; skillful; adroit: *a clean hit to center field.* **7.** Fit for all readers, listeners, or audiences; not ribald or obscene: *a clean joke.* **8.** Blank: *a clean page.* ❖ *adv.* **cleaner, cleanest 1a.** So as to be unsoiled: *We washed the wall clean.* **b.** In a fair manner: *They played the game clean.* **2.** *Informal* Entirely; completely: *I clean forgot about the test.* ❖ *v.* **cleaned, clean·ing, cleans** —*tr.* **1.** To rid of dirt, stain, or disorder: *clean a room.* **2.** To get rid of (dirt, for example); remove: *Let's clean the dirt from the floor.* **3.** To prepare (fowl or other food) for cooking, as by removing entrails: *clean a fish.* **4.** To remove the contents from; empty: *I cleaned my plate.* —*intr.* To undergo or perform cleaning: *A wool rug cleans easily. A damp rag cleans well.* ◆ **clean house** *Slang* To get rid of what is unwanted: *The new boss cleaned house and fired the unproductive workers.* **clean out 1.** To rid of dirt, trash, or disorder: *clean out the garage.* **2.** To empty of contents: *cleaned out the refrigerator to make sandwiches.* **3.** *Slang* To deprive completely, as of money; remove everything from: *Shopping cleaned out my savings.* **clean up 1.** To rid of dirt or disorder: *clean up one's room; clean up the city government.* **2.** *Slang* To make a large sum of money in a short period of time: *We cleaned up on the spring sale.* [From Old English *clǣne.*] —**clean′ness** *n.*

clean and jerk *n.* A lift in weightlifting in which a weight is raised to shoulder height, held there briefly, and then pushed overhead in a rapid motion.

clean-cut (klēn′kŭt′) *adj.* **1.** Having a distinct sharp outline: *a racing car with clean-cut lines.* **2.** Neat and trim in appearance: *a clean-cut soldier.*

clean·er (klē′nər) *n.* **1.** A person whose work is cleaning: *We moved the furniture before the rug cleaner arrived.* **2.** often **cleaners** A business that cleans clothes, often by dry cleaning: *took the shirts to the cleaners.* **3.** A machine or substance used in cleaning: *Ammonia is a good household cleaner.*

clean·li·ness (klĕn′lē-nĭs) *n.* The state of being clean: *Personal cleanliness is important for good health.*

clean·ly (klēn′lē) *adv.* In a clean manner: *The fruit stems had been severed cleanly by a knife.* ❖ *adj.* (klĕn′lē) **clean·li·er, clean·li·est** Habitually and carefully neat and clean: *Cats are thought of as cleanly animals.*

clean room *n.* A room that is kept free of dust, bacteria, or other contaminants. Clean rooms are used in laboratory work and in the making of electronic and aerospace products.

cleanse (klĕnz) *tr.v.* **cleansed, cleans·ing, cleans·es** To free from dirt or guilt; clean or purge: *cleanse a wound.* [From Old English *clǣnsian*, from *clǣne*, pure, clean.]

cleans·er (klĕn′zər) *n.* A substance used for cleaning.

clean·up (klēn′ŭp′) *n.* **1.** The act or process of cleaning up: *a trash cleanup.* **2.** The fourth position in a baseball batting order. —**clean′up′** *adj.*

clear (klîr) *adj.* **clear·er, clear·est 1.** Free from clouds, mist, or haze: *a clear sky.* **2.** Free from anything that dims, darkens, or obscures; transparent: *a glass of cool clear water.* **3.** Free from obstruction or hindrance; open: *We had a clear view of the valley from the mountains. The road was clear of snow.* **4a.** Easily perceived by the eye or ear; distinct: *a clear picture on the TV; the clear sound of church bells; a crisp clear voice.* **b.** Plain or evident to the mind; easily understood: *a clear explanation; clear directions.* **5.** Obvious; unmistakable: *a clear case of the flu.* **6.** Free from doubt or confusion; certain: *Are you clear about what has to be done?* **7.** Free from guilt; untroubled: *a clear conscience.* **8.** Free from flaw or blemish: *clear skin.* **9.** Free from charges or deductions; net: *earned a small but clear profit after paying for expenses.* ❖ *adv.* **1.** Out of the way: *The deer jumped clear of the oncoming car.* **2.** Distinctly; clearly: *spoke loud and clear before the audience.* **3.** *Informal* All the way; entirely: *The baby cried clear through the night.* ❖ *v.* **cleared, clear·ing, clears** —*tr.* **1.** To make clear, light, or bright: *The fan cleared the room of smoke.* **2a.** To make free of objects or obstructions: *clear the table after dinner; clear the road of snow.* **b.** To remove (objects or obstructions): *clear the dishes from the table; clear snow from the sidewalk.* **3.** To pass by, under, or over without contact: *The runner cleared every hurdle.* **4.** To free from a legal charge; acquit: *The jury cleared the accused of all charges.* **5.** To rid of confusion or doubt: *cleared up the questions surrounding the lost book.* **6.** To win the approval of: *The bill cleared the Senate.* **7.** To pass (a check or bill of exchange) through a clearing-house: *Banks clear checks every day.* **8.** To earn (an amount of money) as net profit or earnings: *cleared $45 selling pies.* —*intr.* **1.** To become clear, light, or bright: *The sky cleared in the afternoon.* **2.** To go away; disappear: *The fog cleared.* **3.** To pass through a clearing-house: *My check to pay the rent cleared today.* ◆ **clear out** *Informal* To leave a place, often quickly: *The raccoons cleared out before the campers returned.* **clear the air** To dispel emotional tensions or differences: *A joke cleared the air.* **in the clear** Free from burdens, dangers, guilt, or responsibility: *Once the facts were known, the suspect was in the clear.* [From Middle English *cler*, bright, from Latin *clārus*, clear, bright.] —**clear′ly** *adv.* —**clear′ness** *n.*

clear·ance (klîr′əns) *n.* **1.** The act of clearing: *The city has begun land clearance where the abandoned buildings are.* **2.** A sale to dispose of old merchandise at reduced prices: *Department stores often have a clearance after the holidays.* **3.** The height or width of a passage: *This underpass has a clearance that is too low for many trucks.* **4.** Permission for an airplane, ship, or other vehicle to proceed: *The control tower gave us clearance to take off.* **5.** Official certification of blamelessness, trustworthiness, or suitability: *You need clearance to handle classified material.*

clear-cut (klîr′kŭt′) *adj.* Not vague or confused; obvious: *a clear-cut case of fraud.* ❖ *tr.v.* **clear-cut, clear-cut·ting, clear-cuts** To remove all of the trees in (a wooded area) at one time.

clear·ing (klîr′ĭng) *n.* An open space in a wooded or overgrown area: *a clearing in the forest where the trees were cut down.*

clear·ing-house or **clear·ing·house** (klîr′ĭng-hous′) *n.* An office where banks exchange checks, drafts, and other notes and settle accounts.

cleat (klēt) *n.* **1a.** A projecting piece of iron, rubber, or leather attached to the sole of a shoe to keep it from slipping. **b. cleats** A pair of shoes having such projecting pieces. **2.** A piece of metal or wood with projecting arms or ends on which a rope can be wound.

cleav·age (klē′vĭj) *n.* **1.** The act of splitting or state of being split: *Earthquakes are often accompanied by cleavage of the ground.* **2.** The breaking of certain minerals along specific planes, making smooth surfaces. **3a.** The series of cell divisions by which a fertilized egg becomes a blastula. **b.** A stage in this series of divisions.

cleave[1] (klēv) *tr.v.* **cleft** (klĕft) or **cleaved** or **clove** (klōv), **cleft** or **cleaved** or **clo·ven** (klō′vən), **cleav·ing, cleaves 1.** To split, as by a sudden blow: *The axe* *cleft the piece of wood.* **2.** To make or proceed through as if by cutting: *a ship cleaving its way through the ice.* [From Old English *clēofan.*]

cleave² (klēv) *intr.v.* **cleaved, cleav·ing, cleaves 1.** To cling; adhere; stick fast: *Barnacles cleave to a hull.* **2.** To remain faithful: *cleave to old beliefs.* [From Old English *cleofian.*]

cleav·er (**klē′**vər) *n.* A tool with a broad heavy blade and a short handle, used especially by butchers for cutting meat.

clef (klĕf) *n.* A symbol on a musical staff indicating the pitch of one of the lines in relation to middle C. The pitch of the other lines and spaces on the staff can be determined accordingly. [From Latin *clāvis,* key.]

cleft (klĕft) *v.* A past tense and a past participle of **cleave¹**. ❖ *adj.* Divided; split: *a cleft chin.* ❖ *n.* A crack or split: *My canteen fell into a cleft in the rock.*

cleft lip *n.* A split or cleft in the upper lip that sometimes occurs together with a cleft palate.

cleft palate *n.* A split in the roof of the mouth, occurring when the two parts of the developing palate do not close before birth.

clem·a·tis (**klĕm′**ə-tĭs *or* klĭ-**măt′**ĭs) *n.* Any of various climbing plants having white, pink, or purplish flowers and feathery seeds. [From Greek *klēmatis.*]

clem·en·cy (**klĕm′**ən-sē) *n., pl.* **clem·en·cies 1.** Mercy, as toward an offender or enemy; leniency: *The judge showed clemency in sentencing the defendant.* **2.** Mildness, especially of weather.

Clem·ens (**klĕm′**ənz), **Samuel Langhorne** Pen name Mark Twain. 1835–1910. American writer who used his childhood along the Mississippi River as a source for his books, including *Tom Sawyer* (1876).

clem·ent (**klĕm′**ənt) *adj.* **1.** Inclined to be lenient or merciful: *a clement ruler.* **2.** Pleasant; mild: *clement spring weather.* **—clem′ent·ly** *adv.*

clem·en·tine (**klĕm′**ən-tīn′) *n.* A deep red-orange, often seedless mandarin orange. [From French *clémentine,* after Father *Clément* Rodier (1829–1904), French missionary.]

clench (klĕnch) *tr.v.* **clenched, clench·ing, clench·es 1.** To close (a hand or the teeth) tightly: *I clenched my fists in anger.* **2.** To grasp or grip tightly: *clenched the steering wheel.*

Cle·o·pat·ra (klē′ə-**păt′**rə *or* klē′ə-**pä′**trə) 69–30 BC. Egyptian queen (51–49 and 48–30) whose defeat by Octavian in 31 ended the rule of the Ptolemy dynasty.

cler·gy (**klûr′**jē) *n., pl.* **cler·gies** The group of people ordained or recognized by a religious community as spiritual leaders, as ministers, mullahs, or rabbis. —SEE NOTE AT **collective noun.**

cler·gy·man (**klûr′**jē-mən) *n.* A man who is a member of the clergy.

cler·gy·wom·an (**klûr′**jē-wo͝om′ən) *n.* A woman who is a member of the clergy.

cler·ic (**klĕr′**ĭk) *n.* A member of the clergy. [From Late Latin *clēricus,* clerk.]

cler·i·cal (**klĕr′**ĭ-kəl) *adj.* **1.** Relating to clerks or office workers: *typing and other clerical work.* **2.** Relating to the clergy: *dressed in clerical garb.* **—cler′i·cal·ly** *adv.*

clerk (klûrk) *n.* **1.** A person who works in an office doing such jobs as keeping records, filing, and typing. **2.** A person who keeps the records and performs the regular business of a court, legislative body, or municipal district. **3.** A person who sells merchandise in a store or works at a service desk, as in a hotel. ❖ *intr.v.* **clerked, clerk·ing, clerks** To work or serve as a clerk: *My sister clerked in a supermarket as a summer job.* [From Old English *clerc, clēric,* clergyman, from Greek *klērikos,* belonging to the clergy.]

Cleve·land (**klēv′**lənd) A city of northeast Ohio on Lake Erie. A port and industrial center, the city was laid out in 1796.

Cleveland, (Stephen) Grover 1837–1908. The 22nd and 24th president of the United States (1885–1889 and 1893–1897). He was known as an honest, independent president who opposed corruption.

clev·er (**klĕv′**ər) *adj.* **clev·er·er, clev·er·est 1.** Having the capacity to learn and think quickly; bright; quick-witted: *a clever student.* **2.** Showing wit or ingenuity: *a clever plan; a clever trick.* **3.** Skilled at doing something, especially with the hands: *a clever magician.* **—clev′er·ly** *adv.* **—clev′er·ness** *n.*

clew (klo͞o) *Chiefly British n. & v.* Variant of **clue.**

cli·ché (klē-**shā′**) *n.* An overused expression or idea that has lost its original quality or effect: *The expression "as sharp as a tack" is a cliché.*

click (klĭk) *n.* A short sharp sound: *the click of train wheels over the tracks.* ❖ *v.* **clicked, click·ing, clicks** —*intr.* **1.** To produce a click or a series of clicks: *The wheels of the train clicked over the rails.* **2.** To press down and release a button on a computer mouse or other pointing device, as to activate a program or highlight text: *clicked on the icon.* **3.** *Slang* To be a success: *The new comedian clicked with the audience.* **4.** *Slang* To work well together or be in harmony: *We clicked as soon as we met.* **5.** *Slang* To become understandable; make sense: *The name clicked when I saw the actor's picture.* —*tr.* **1.** To cause to make such a sound: *clicked his ballpoint pen and started to write.* **2.** To press down and release (a button on a pointing device): *Click the left button to open the file.*

click·er (**klĭk′**ər) *n.* A thing that clicks or can be clicked, as a remote control for a television.

cli·ent (**klī′**ənt) *n.* **1.** A person who uses the services of a professional person: *The lawyer defended his client in court.* **2.** A customer or patron: *That jewelry store has several wealthy clients.* **3.** A computer or program that can download files from a file server.

cli·en·tele (klī′ən-**tĕl′**) *n.* The group of regular clients or customers, as of a store.

cliff (klĭf) *n.* A high, steep, or overhanging face of rock or earth: *stand on the cliffs overlooking the sea far below.*

cliff dweller *n.* A member of certain prehistoric peoples of the southwest United States who built rock or adobe dwellings on sheltered ledges in the sides of cliffs. The Pueblo peoples are their descendants.

cliff·hang·er (**klĭf′**hăng′ər) *n.* **1.** A melodrama presented in serial episodes, with each episode ending in high suspense. **2.** A suspenseful situation at the end of a chapter, scene, or episode. **3.** A contest whose outcome is uncertain until the end: *The game was a cliffhanger—tied until the last minute.*

cli·mac·tic (klī-**măk′**tĭk) *adj.* Relating to or forming a climax: *climactic events leading to the end of the mystery story.*

cli·mate (**klī′**mĭt) *n.* **1.** The general or average weather conditions of a certain region, including temperature, rainfall, and wind: *Southern California has a year-round climate of warm temperatures, low rainfall, and sunshine.* **2.** A region having certain weather conditions: *They live in tropical climate.* **3.** A general condition or attitude: *After the Berlin Wall came down, there was a climate of joy in Europe.* [From Middle English *climat,* from Greek *klima,* surface of the earth, region.]

cli·mat·ic (klī-**măt′**ĭk) *adj.* Relating to climate: *climatic changes; distinct climatic regions.* **—cli·mat′i·cal·ly** *adv.*

cli·ma·tol·o·gy (klī′mə-**tŏl′**ə-jē) *n.* The scientific study of climates.

cli·max (**klī′**măks′) *n.* **1.** The point in a series of events that is of greatest intensity or effect, usually occurring near the end: *Winning the presidency was the climax of a long political career.* **2.** The turning point in a plot or dramatic action: *The climax of the novel occurs when the*

clematis

Grover Cleveland
photographed in 1888

Bill Clinton
photographed in 2010

clipper

ă	pat	ôr	core
ā	pay	oi	boy
âr	care	ou	out
ä	father	ŏŏ	took
ĕ	pet	ŏŏr	lure
ē	be	ōō	boot
ĭ	pit	ŭ	cut
ī	bite	ûr	urge
îr	pier	th	thin
ŏ	pot	*th*	this
ō	toe	zh	vision
ô	paw	ə	about

main character meets his father for the first time.

climax community *n.* An ecological community in which there is little change in the kinds and numbers of organisms present until a disturbance such as a fire occurs.

climb (klīm) *v.* **climbed, climb·ing, climbs** —*intr.* **1a.** To move upward, especially by using the hands and feet; ascend: *The hikers climbed all day to reach the top of the mountain.* **b.** To move in a stated direction, especially by means of the hands and feet: *The firefighter climbed across the roof and down the ladder.* **2.** To go higher; rise: *The morning sun climbed in the sky. The patient's fever began to climb. The executive climbed to the top of her profession.* **3.** To slant or slope upward: *The trail climbs to the top of the cliff.* **4.** To grow upward by clinging to or twining around something: *The vine climbs around the tree.* —*tr.* **1.** To go up, over, or through (something), especially by using the hands and feet; ascend: *Leopards can climb trees. The hikers climbed the mountain.* **2.** To grow up on (something): *Roses climbed the trellis.* ❖ *n.* **1.** The act of climbing: *a hard climb up the mountain; an executive's climb to power.* **2.** A place to be climbed: *That hill was a steep climb.* [From Old English *climban.*] **—climb′a·ble** *adj.*

❑ *These sound alike:* **climb, clime** (climate).

climb·er (klī′mər) *n.* **1.** A person or thing that climbs: *a mountain climber.* **2.** A plant, such as a vine, that climbs.

clime (klīm) *n.* Climate: *moved to a sunny clime.*

❑ *These sound alike:* **clime, climb** (move up).

clinch (klĭnch) *v.* **clinched, clinch·ing, clinch·es** —*tr.* **1.** To fix or secure (a nail or bolt) by bending down or flattening the end that sticks out. **2.** To fasten securely, as with a nail or bolt: *clinch rafters in place.* **3.** To settle definitely; confirm or complete: *clinch a deal.* **4.** To secure (a divisional championship, for example) before the end of regular season play by having an unbeatable lead. —*intr.* In boxing, to hold the opponent's body with one or both arms. ❖ *n.* In boxing, the act or an instance of clinching: *The boxers went into a clinch at the end of the second round.*

clinch·er (**klĭn′**chər) *n.* **1.** Something that clinches, especially a nail or bolt. **2.** A final and decisive point, fact, or remark, as in an argument.

cling (klĭng) *intr.v.* **clung, cling·ing, clings 1.** To hold tight to something: *clung to the rope to keep from falling.* **2.** To stick or adhere to something: *fabrics that cling to the body.* **3.** To stay near; remain close: *We clung together during the storm.* **4.** To remain attached emotionally; hold on: *cling to old beliefs; cling to a hope.*

cling·stone (**klĭng′**stōn′) *n.* A fruit, such as a peach or apricot, having flesh that adheres to the pit.

clin·ic (**klĭn′**ĭk) *n.* **1.** A medical facility that provides diagnosis and treatment to patients who do not stay overnight. **2.** A place where medical specialists work together in research and treatment of particular illnesses: *an eye and ear clinic for the treatment of children.* **3.** A group offering special counseling or training: *an acting clinic; a tennis clinic.* **4.** A training session for medical students in which they observe while patients are examined and treated.

clin·i·cal (**klĭn′**ĭ-kəl) *adj.* **1.** Relating to or connected with a clinic: *a doctor on the clinical staff.* **2.** Involving or based on direct examination and treatment of patients: *a clinical diagnosis of disease.* **3.** Very objective; not emotional; analytical: *a clinical account of the state's economic problems.* **—clin′i·cal·ly** *adv.*

clinical depression *n.* A psychiatric disorder characterized by extreme and persistent sadness, and often feelings of guilt or helplessness, difficulty concentrating and sleeping, loss of appetite, and the inability to experience pleasure.

clink[1] (klĭngk) *tr. & intr.v.* **clinked, clink·ing, clinks** To make or cause to make a light, sharp, ringing sound: *They clinked glasses after the toast. The ice clinked in the glass.* ❖ *n.* A light, sharp, ringing sound: *the clink of glasses on a tray.* [From Middle English *clinken*, probably from Middle Dutch *klinken*, of imitative origin.]

clink[2] (klĭngk) *n. Slang* A prison or prison cell. [After *Clink*, a district of London famous for its prison.]

clink·er (**klĭng′**kər) *n.* **1.** A lump of incombustible matter left over after coal has burned. **2.** *Slang* A mistake; a blunder.

Clin·ton (**klĭn′**tən), **Hillary Rodham** Born 1947. American politician and first lady of the United States (1993–2001) as the wife of Bill Clinton. She later served as a US senator (2001–2009) and was appointed secretary of state in 2009.

Clinton, William Jefferson Known as "Bill." Born 1946. The 42nd president of the United States (1993–2001). His presidency was marked by economic expansion. In 1999 he was impeached but was found not guilty.

clip[1] (klĭp) *v.* **clipped, clip·ping, clips** —*tr.* **1.** To cut, cut off, or cut out with scissors or shears: *clip a picture out of the newspaper.* **2.** To shorten by cutting; trim: *clip a hedge; clip a fingernail.* **3.** To shorten (a word or words) by leaving out letters or syllables: *clip one's words when speaking excitedly.* **4.** *Informal* To hit or strike with a quick sharp blow: *Their car clipped ours in the front fender.* **5.** In football, to block (an opposing player) illegally from behind. —*intr.* **1.** To cut or trim something. **2.** *Informal* To move rapidly: *The sailboat clipped along in the strong wind.* ❖ *n.* **1.** The act of clipping: *Just a few clips of the scissors will even your bangs.* **2.** The wool clipped from sheep at one shearing. **3.** Something clipped off, as a sequence clipped from a movie film. **4.** *Informal* A quick sharp blow: *a clip on the chin.* **5.** *Informal* A brisk pace: *The train sped along at a good clip.* **6.** In football, an act of clipping. [From Middle English *clippen*, from Old Norse *klippa.*]

clip[2] (klĭp) *n.* **1.** A device, such as a paper clip, for gripping or holding things together. **2.** A holder for cartridges to be loaded into an automatic rifle or pistol. **3.** A piece of jewelry, such as a pin, that fastens with a clasp or clip. ❖ *tr.v.* **clipped, clip·ping, clips** To fasten with a clip: *clip the papers together.* [From Middle English, hook, from *clippen*, to clasp, embrace, from Old English *clyppan.*]

clip art *n.* Ready-made computerized graphic art used in decorating documents.

clip·board (**klĭp′**bôrd′) *n.* **1.** A small writing board with a spring-loaded clip at the top for holding papers or a writing pad. **2.** A computer file or an area in computer memory where the user can store text or graphics before inserting them into another document or file.

clip·per (**klĭp′**ər) *n.* **1.** A person who clips, cuts, or shears. **2. clippers** A tool for clipping, cutting, or shearing: *nail clippers; a barber's clippers.* **3.** A sailing vessel built for great speed, having tall masts and sharp lines.

clip·ping (**klĭp′**ĭng) *n.* **1.** Something cut or trimmed off, especially an article or photograph clipped from a newspaper or magazine. **2.** A word formed by dropping one or more syllables from a longer word, such as *app*, a clipping formed from *application.*

clique (klēk *or* klĭk) *n.* A small group of people who stick together and remain aloof from others.

cliqu·ish (**klē′**kĭsh *or* **klĭk′**ĭsh) *adj.* Relating to or characteristic of a clique. **—cliqu′ish·ly** *adv.* **—cliqu′ish·ness** *n.*

clit·o·ris (**klĭt′**ər-ĭs *or* **klī′**tər-ĭs) *n.* A sex organ that is composed of erectile tissue and forms part of the external reproductive system in female mammals and some other animals.

clo·a·ca (klō-**ā′**kə) *n.* The common cavity that serves as the opening for the intestinal, genital, and urinary tracts in many vertebrates, including amphibians, reptiles, birds, and some fishes.

cloak (klōk) *n.* **1.** A loose outer garment or wrap, usually having no sleeves. **2.** Something that covers or conceals: *A cloak of mystery surrounds their disappearance.* ❖ *tr.v.* **cloaked, cloak·ing, cloaks** To cover with or as if with a cloak: *A dense fog cloaked the city. The situation was cloaked in mystery.* [From Middle English *cloke*, from Medieval Latin *clocca*, bell, cloak (from its shape).]

cloak·room (**klōk′**rōōm′ *or* **klōk′**rŏŏm′) *n.* A room where coats and other outdoor clothing may be left temporarily.

clob·ber (**klŏb′**ər) *tr.v.* **clob·bered, clob·ber·ing, clob·bers** *Slang* **1.** To hit or pound with great force: *The batter clobbered the ball for a triple.* **2.** To defeat completely: *Our team was clobbered by theirs.*

clock (klŏk) *n.* **1.** An instrument other than a watch for measuring and indicating time, often having a digital display or a numbered dial with moving hands that point to the numbers. **2.** A time clock. ❖ *tr.v.* **clocked, clock·ing, clocks** To record the time or speed of: *The bicyclist was clocked at 30 miles per hour.* ◆ **around the clock** Continuously: *Some convenience stores are open around the clock.* [From Middle English *clokke*, from Old North French *cloque*, bell, or from Middle Dutch *clocke*, bell, clock, both from Medieval Latin *clocca*, of imitative origin.]

clock radio *n.* A radio with a built-in clock that can be set to turn the radio on automatically.

clock·wise (**klŏk′**wīz′) *adv. & adj.* In the same direction as the rotating hands of a clock: *turn clockwise; a clockwise movement.*

clock·work (**klŏk′**wûrk′) *n.* A mechanism of gears driven by a spring, as in a mechanical clock. ◆ **like clockwork** With perfect regularity and precision: *The assembly line in the factory operates like clockwork.*

clod (klŏd) *n.* **1.** A lump of earth or clay. **2.** A dull or stupid person; a dolt.

clod·hop·per (**klŏd′**hŏp′ər) *n.* **1.** A clumsy country fellow; a bumpkin. **2. clodhoppers** Big heavy shoes.

clog (klôg) *n.* **1.** Something that obstructs or hinders: *a clog in the drain; a clog in the flow of traffic.* **2.** A heavy shoe, usually having a wooden sole. ❖ *v.* **clogged, clog·ging, clogs** —*tr.* To cause to become obstructed or blocked up: *Heavy traffic clogged the highway.* —*intr.* To become obstructed or blocked up: *The drain clogs easily.*

clois·ter (**kloi′**stər) *n.* **1.** A covered walk along the side of a building, such as a convent or church, with open arches facing into a courtyard. **2.** A place of religious seclusion, as a monastery or convent. **3.** A quiet secluded place. ❖ *tr.v.* **clois·tered, clois·ter·ing, clois·ters** To shut away or confine in or as if in a cloister; seclude: *The author was cloistered in the library all morning.*

clomp (klŏmp) *intr.v.* **clomped, clomp·ing, clomps** To walk heavily and noisily.

clone (klōn) *n.* **1.** An organism or a group of organisms produced asexually from a single ancestor and genetically identical to it. Cloning can occur naturally, as by fission in one-celled organisms, or can be performed artificially, as by taking the nucleus from the cell of an adult organism and placing it into an egg cell so that it grows into an adult with the same genes as the original organism. **2.** A person or thing that is copied from or closely resembles another: *The new governor is a clone of the previous one.* ❖ *tr.v.* **cloned, clon·ing, clones 1.** To produce a clone of (an organism, cell, or DNA sequence). **2.** To produce a copy of (a person or thing): *The criminals had cloned several cell phones.* [From Greek *klōn*, twig.]

clop (klŏp) *n.* A sharp hollow sound, as of a horse's hoof striking the pavement. ❖ *intr.v.* **clopped, clop·ping, clops** To move with such a sound: *The team of horses clopped steadily along.*

close (klōs) *adj.* **clos·er, clos·est 1.** Near in space or time: *The airport is close to town.* **2.** Near in relationship: *They are close relatives.* **3.** Bound by loyalties or affection; intimate: *close friends.* **4.** Having little space in between: *chairs arranged in close rows.* **5.** Very short or near to the surface: *a close haircut; a close shave.* **6.** Fitting tightly: *a jacket with a close fit.* **7.** Very much like another or the original: *a close copy of an ancient statue.* **8.** Attentive or rigorous: *During the drought rangers kept a close watch for forest fires.* **9.** Confining; narrow; crowded: *The little cabin was close quarters for the three of us.* **10.** Lacking fresh air; stuffy: *It's very close in this room with the window shut.* **11.** Almost even, as in a contest: *a close race; a close election.* ❖ *v.* (klōz) **closed, clos·ing, clos·es** —*tr.* **1.** To move (a door, for example) so that an opening or a passage is blocked; shut. **2.** To prevent passage through; obstruct: *closed the bridge for repairs.* **3.** To stop the operations of: *Most shopkeepers close their stores around six o'clock.* **4.** To fill up or stop up: *Close the cracks in the wall with plaster.* **5.** To bring to an end; conclude: *close a letter; close a meeting.* See Synonyms at **complete. 6.** To draw together the edges of: *It took eight stitches to close the wound.* —*intr.* **1.** To become shut: *The window closed with a bang.* **2.** To come to an end: *The book closes with a reunion of friends.* **3.** To cease operation: *The museum closes on Wednesdays.* **4.** To draw near: *Our boat was closing fast on the one in front.* **5.** To come together: *The child's arms closed around the stuffed animal.* **6.** To be priced at a specified amount when trading ends: *Stocks closed higher today.* ❖ *n.* (klōz) A conclusion; an end: *Sunset marks the close of day. The meeting came to a quick close.* ❖ *adv.* (klōs) **closer, closest** In a close position or manner: *Let's stick close together.* ◆ **close down** To stop operating: *The old factory finally closed down.* **close in** To surround and advance upon: *The fog was quickly closing in on us.* **close out** To sell at a reduced price in order to dispose of quickly: *The store closed out all winter clothes in March.* **close to** On the brink of: *He was close to tears.* **—close′ly** *adv.* **—close′ness** *n.*

❑ *These sound alike:* **close, clothes** (garments).

close call (klōs) *n. Informal* A narrow escape.

closed (klōzd) *adj.* **1.** Blocked to passage or entry: *a closed door; a tunnel closed off for repairs.* **2.** Not open for business or visitation: *The museum is closed on Mondays.* **3.** Not open to the public; conducted in secrecy: *a closed meeting of Congress.* **4.** Not open to new ideas; prejudiced: *a closed mind.* **5.** Relating to a curve, such as a circle, having no endpoints. **6.** Producing only elements of the same set in a given mathematical operation. The set of whole numbers is closed under addition because adding whole numbers to each other only produces other whole numbers. The set of whole numbers is not closed under division, since dividing whole numbers by each other can produce fractions. **7.** Allowing electricity to flow or pass: *a closed switch.*

closed-cap·tioned (klōzd′**kăp′**shənd) *adj.* Having titles or captions that explain action or give dialogue on a television program but that can be seen only on a specially equipped receiver: *a closed-captioned news program for the hearing-impaired.*

closed circuit *n.* **1.** An electric circuit through which current can flow in an uninterrupted path. **2.** A television system in which the signal is usually sent by cable to a limited number of receivers.

closed shop *n.* A company or business in which only union members or people who agree to join the union within a certain time may be hired.

close-fist·ed (**klōs′fĭs′**tĭd) *adj.* Stingy: *a close-fisted business manager.*

close-knit (**klōs′**nĭt′) *adj.* Closely joined by a common

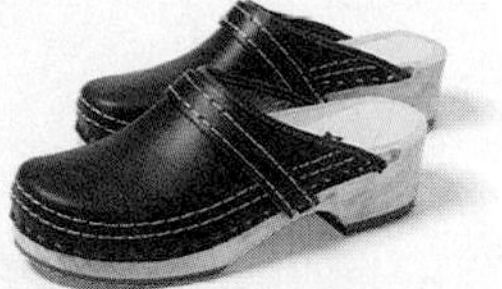

clog
pair of clogs

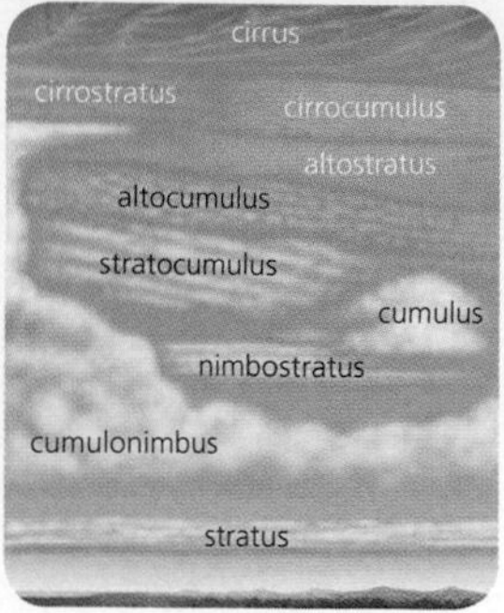

cloud

clove hitch

cloverleaf

ă	pat	ôr	core
ā	pay	oi	boy
âr	care	ou	out
ä	father	o͝o	took
ĕ	pet	o͝or	lure
ē	be	o͞o	boot
ĭ	pit	ŭ	cut
ī	bite	ûr	urge
îr	pier	th	thin
ŏ	pot	*th*	this
ō	toe	zh	vision
ô	paw	ə	about

bond, as a relationship or interest: *a close-knit family.*

close-mouthed (**klōs′mouthd′** *or* **klōs′moutht′**) *adj.* Not talking much; giving away little information: *He was close-mouthed about his whereabouts last week.*

close·out (**klōz′**out′) *n.* A sale in which goods are offered at greatly reduced prices in order to dispose of them.

clos·er (**klō′**zər) *n.* **1.** A person or thing that closes something: *an automatic door closer.* **2.** In baseball, a relief pitcher who tries to protect a lead late in a game.

clos·et (**klŏz′**ĭt *or* **klô′**zĭt) *n.* **1.** A small room or cabinet for hanging clothes, storing linens or supplies, or keeping food: *a clothes closet; a broom closet.* **2.** A small private room for study or prayer. ❖ *tr.v.* **clos·et·ed, clos·et·ing, clos·ets** To enclose in a private room, as for discussion: *The lawyers closeted themselves in conference for hours.* ❖ *adj.* Keeping something secret to avoid embarrassment or being accused of acting inconsistently with one's beliefs or positions: *a closet smoker.*

close-up (**klōs′**ŭp′) *n.* **1.** A photograph or a view in a film or videotape in which the subject is shown at close range: *The portrait was a close-up of the president.* **2.** A close or intimate look or view: *The article presented a close-up of the daily life of a street vendor.*

clos·ing (**klō′**zĭng) *n.* **1.** A concluding part: *In the closing of his letter, he thanks us.* **2.** A meeting for concluding something, especially a real estate transaction: *The buyers brought their lawyer to the closing.*

clo·sure (**klō′**zhər) *n.* **1.** The act of closing: *Closure of the incision ended the operation.* **2.** Something that closes or shuts something: *a plastic bag with a resealable closure.* **3.** In mathematics, the property of being closed.

clot (klŏt) *n.* A thickened or solid mass formed from a liquid, such as a blood clot. ❖ *intr. & tr.v.* **clot·ted, clot·ting, clots** To form or cause to form into clots: *Blood clots when exposed to air.*

cloth (klôth) *n., pl.* **cloths** (klôths *or* klô*th*z) **1.** Fabric or material made by weaving, knitting, or matting fibers together. **2.** A piece of cloth used for a special purpose, as for a tablecloth. **3.** The clergy: *a man of the cloth.* [From Old English *clāth.*]

clothe (klō*th*) *tr.v.* **clothed** or **clad** (klăd), **cloth·ing, clothes 1.** To put clothes on or provide clothes for; dress: *feed and clothe a family.* **2.** To cover, as if with clothing: *trees clothed in their fall colors.*

clothes (klōz *or* klō*th*z) *pl.n.* **1.** Coverings worn on the body; garments, such as shirts, pants, dresses, and coats. **2.** Bedclothes.

❑ *These sound alike:* **clothes, close** (shut).

clothes·horse (**klōz′**hôrs′ *or* **klō*th*z′**hôrs′) *n.* **1.** A frame on which clothes are hung to dry or air. **2.** A person who has an excessive interest in clothes and frequently wears new outfits.

clothes·line (**klōz′**līn′ *or* **klō*th*z′**līn′) *n.* A rope or wire on which clothes are hung to dry.

clothes moth *n.* Any of several small moths whose larvae feed on wool and fur.

clothes·pin (**klōz′**pĭn′ *or* **klō*th*z′**pĭn′) *n.* A clip of wood or plastic used to fasten clothes on a clothesline.

cloth·ier (**klō*th*′**yər *or* **klō′***th*ē-ər) *n.* A person who makes or sells clothing or cloth.

cloth·ing (**klō′***th*ĭng) *n.* Clothes or garments considered as a group: *wore warm clothing for the hike.*

cloud (kloud) *n.* **1a.** A visible mass of very fine water droplets or ice particles floating in the air at heights ranging up to several miles above sea level. **b.** A similar mass formed of suspended particles or droplets, as of dust, steam, or smoke. **2.** A collection of things on the ground, in the water, or in the air that is so large and dense that it appears to resemble a cloud: *A cloud of locusts swarmed above the field. A cloud of silt made it impossible to see the river bottom.* **3.** A state or cause of sadness or worry: *The bad news cast a cloud over the celebration.* **4.** A state or cause of suspicion or disgrace: *A cloud of mistrust hung over the stockbroker until he resigned.* **5.** The collection of data and services available through the Internet: *storing data in the cloud.* ❖ *v.* **cloud·ed, cloud·ing, clouds** —*tr.* **1.** To cover with clouds: *Heavy mist clouded the hills.* **2.** To make less clear or transparent; darken or obscure: *Steam clouded the bathroom mirror.* **3.** To make gloomy or confused: *Superstition clouded their thinking.* **4.** To taint; tarnish; sully: *A charge of corruption clouded the mayor's reputation.* —*intr.* **1.** To become covered with clouds: *The sky clouded over.* **2.** To become dark, obscure, or less transparent: *The water in the bowl clouded up.* [From Middle English, hill, cloud, from Old English *clūd*, rock, hill.]

cloud·burst (**kloud′**bûrst′) *n.* A sudden heavy rainstorm; a downpour.

cloud chamber *n.* A device in which the paths of charged subatomic particles are made visible as trails of droplets. A cloud chamber contains a supersaturated vapor that condenses on the ions formed along the path of the charged particle.

cloud seeding *n.* A method of making a cloud give up its moisture as rain, especially by releasing particles of dry ice or silver iodide into the cloud.

cloud·y (**klou′**dē) *adj.* **cloud·i·er, cloud·i·est 1.** Full of or covered with clouds; overcast: *a cloudy sky.* **2.** Not clear; murky: *cloudy water.* **3.** Confused, gloomy, or uncertain: *cloudy thinking; a project with a cloudy future.* —**cloud′i·ly** *adv.* —**cloud′i·ness** *n.*

clout (klout) *n.* **1.** A heavy blow, as with the fist: *a clout on the chin.* **2.** Power, prestige, or influence: *The president has great political clout.* ❖ *tr.v.* **clout·ed, clout·ing, clouts** To hit hard: *The batter clouted the ball over the fence.*

clove[1] (klōv) *n.* **1.** The dried aromatic flower bud of a tropical Southeast Asian tree, used whole or ground as a spice. **2.** The plant that bears such flower buds. [From Middle English *clow (de gilofre)*, from Old French *clou (de girofle)*, nail (of the clove tree), from Latin *clāvus*, nail.]

clove[2] (klōv) *n.* One of the sections of a garlic bulb or a similar plant bulb. [From Old English *clufu.*]

clove[3] (klōv) *v.* **1.** A past tense of **cleave**[1]. **2.** *Archaic* A past participle of **cleave**[1].

clove hitch *n.* A knot, often used to tie a rope to a post, consisting of two half hitches.

clo·ven (**klō′**vən) *v.* A past participle of **cleave**[1]. ❖ *adj.* Split or divided into two parts: *the cloven hooves of deer or cattle.*

clo·ver (**klō′**vər) *n.* Any of various plants having leaves divided into three leaflets and tightly clustered heads of small, often fragrant flowers. Many kinds of clover are grown to feed cattle and horses. [From Old English *clāfre.*]

clo·ver·leaf (**klō′**vər-lēf′) *n.* A highway interchange whose exit and entrance ramps resemble a four-leaf clover and enable vehicles to go from one highway to the other in either direction.

clown (kloun) *n.* **1.** A performer, as in a circus or carnival, who jokes and does tricks or humorous stunts. **2.** A person who is always making jokes or acting foolishly: *the office clown.* ❖ *intr.v.* **clowned, clown·ing, clowns 1.** To perform as a clown in a circus or other show. **2.** To behave like a clown; act foolishly: *Practical jokers are always clowning around.*

clown·ish (**klou′**nĭsh) *adj.* Resembling or characteristic of a clown: *the baby's clownish antics.* —**clown′ish·ly** *adv.*

cloy·ing (**kloi′**ĭng) *adj.* Unpleasant because of an excess of a quality, such as sweetness, that in itself is pleasant.

club (klŭb) *n.* **1.** A heavy stick, usually thicker at one end than at the other, used as a weapon. **2.** A stick designed to drive a ball in certain games, especially golf. **3a.** A black figure, shaped like a trefoil or the leaf of a clover, on a playing card. **b.** A card bearing this figure. **c. clubs** The suit in a deck of cards having this figure as its symbol. **4a.** A group of people organized for a common purpose: *a chess club.* **b.** The room, building, or other facility used by such a group. ❖ *v.* **clubbed, club·bing, clubs** —*tr.* To strike or beat with or as if with a club. —*intr.* To join together for a common purpose: *All the tenants clubbed together to clean up the apartment building.* [From Middle English, from Old Norse *klubba.*]

club·foot (klŭb′fo͝ot′) *n.* **1.** A deformity of the foot, usually marked by a curled or twisted shape, that arises as a birth defect. **2.** A foot that has such a deformity. **—club′foot′ed** *adj.*

club·house (klŭb′hous′) *n.* **1.** A building occupied by a club. **2.** A locker room used by an athletic team.

club moss *n.* Any of various low-growing evergreen plants that have small leaves resembling needles and do not have flowers or seeds.

club sandwich *n.* A sandwich made of two or three slices of bread with a filling of meat, tomato, lettuce, and mayonnaise.

club soda *n.* Carbonated water.

cluck (klŭk) *n.* The low short sound made by a hen sitting on eggs or calling for its chicks. ❖ *intr.v.* **clucked, cluck·ing, clucks** To make this sound or a similar sound.

clue (klo͞o) *n.* A fact or object that helps to solve a problem or mystery: *Today's powerful telescopes can give us clues about the origin of the universe.* ❖ *tr.v.* **clued, clue·ing** or **clu·ing, clues** To give (someone) information: *Clue me in on what's happening.*

clue·less (klo͞o′lĭs) *adj.* Lacking understanding or knowledge.

clump (klŭmp) *n.* **1.** A thick group or cluster, as of trees or bushes. **2.** A thick mass, as of dirt or sod. **3.** A heavy dull sound, as of footsteps. ❖ *v.* **clumped, clump·ing, clumps** —*intr.* **1.** To walk with a heavy dull sound. **2.** To form clumps: *Blood clumps as it forms a scab.* —*tr.* To gather into or form clumps of: *clumped all the boots by the door.* **—clump′y** *adj.*

clum·sy (klŭm′zē) *adj.* **clum·si·er, clum·si·est 1.** Lacking grace or deftness; awkward: *a clumsy walk; clumsy newborn puppies.* **2.** Difficult to handle or maneuver: *thick clumsy gloves; a big clumsy package.* **3.** Done without skill; inept: *a clumsy drawing of a horse.* **—clum′si·ly** *adv.* **—clum′si·ness** *n.*

clung (klŭng) *v.* Past tense and past participle of **cling.**

clus·ter (klŭs′tər) *n.* **1.** A group of similar things growing, grouped, or occurring close together: *a cluster of flowers; a cluster of break-ins in the neighborhood.* **2.** Two or more consonants in a row, as *str* and *ct* in the word *strict.* ❖ *intr.v.* **clus·tered, clus·ter·ing, clus·ters** To gather, grow, or occur in clusters: *Everyone clustered around the fire.*

clutch[1] (klŭch) *v.* **clutched, clutch·ing, clutch·es** —*tr.* To hold or grasp tightly: *I clutched the railing as I started down the stairs.* —*intr.* To try to grasp or seize something: *I clutched at the chair as I started to fall.* ❖ *n.* **1.** A tight hold or grip. **2.** often **clutches** Control or power; possession: *fall into the clutches of the enemy.* **3a.** A device used to connect and disconnect a driveshaft in a transmission system. **b.** The lever, pedal, or other control that operates such a device, as in an automobile or truck. **4.** A critical situation: *our best hitter in the clutch.* [From Old English *clyccan.*]

clutch[2] (klŭch) *n.* **1.** The eggs produced at a single laying by a bird, turtle, or other animal. **2.** A brood of chicks hatched from such eggs. [From Middle English *clekken*, to hatch, from Old Norse *klekja.*]

clut·ter (klŭt′ər) *n.* A collection of things scattered about in a disorderly fashion; a jumble: *She stumbled over the clutter on the floor.* ❖ *tr.v.* **clut·tered, clut·ter·ing, clut·ters** To fill in such a way as to block movement or action or to create disorder: *On Sundays our living room floor is cluttered up with newspapers.*

Cly·tem·nes·tra (klī′təm-nĕs′trə) *n.* In Greek mythology, the wife of Agamemnon, who murdered him on his return from the Trojan War and was later murdered by her son, Orestes.

cm *abbr.* An abbreviation of centimeter.

Cm The symbol for the element **curium.**

Cn The symbol for the element **copernicium.**

cni·dar·i·an (nī-dâr′ē-ən) *n.* Any of various ocean-dwelling invertebrate animals that have a body with radial symmetry, tentacles, and a sac-like internal cavity. They include the jellyfishes, corals, and sea anemones.

Co The symbol for the element **cobalt.**

CO *abbr.* An abbreviation of Colorado.

Co. *abbr.* An abbreviation of: **1.** company. **2.** county.

c/o *abbr.* An abbreviation of care of.

co– *pref.* A prefix that means: **1.** Together; jointly: *coexist.* **2.** Partner or associate: *coauthor.* **3.** To the same extent or degree: *coextensive.* —SEE NOTE.

coach (kōch) *n.* **1.** A large closed carriage on four wheels, pulled by horses. **2.** A railroad passenger car. **3.** A bus. **4.** A low-priced class of passenger accommodations on a train, airplane, or bus. **5.** A person who trains or instructs athletes or athletic teams. **6.** A person who gives private instruction, as in singing or acting. ❖ *v.* **coached, coach·ing, coach·es** —*tr.* To train or teach: *coach a lacrosse team.* —*intr.* To act as a coach. [From Hungarian *kocsi*, after *Kocs*, a town of northwest Hungary (where such carriages were first made).]

coach·man (kōch′mən) *n.* A man who drives a coach.

co·ag·u·lant (kō-ăg′yə-lənt) *n.* A substance that causes coagulation.

co·ag·u·late (kō-ăg′yə-lāt′) *v.* **co·ag·u·lat·ed, co·ag·u·lat·ing, co·ag·u·lates** —*tr.* To change (a liquid) into a solid or nearly solid mass; clot: *Cooking an egg coagulates both the yolk and the white.* —*intr.* To become solid or nearly solid: *Blood coagulates when exposed to air.* [From Middle English *coagulaten*, from Latin *coāgulum*, something that coagulates, from *cōgere*, to condense : *co-*, together + *agere*, to drive.]

co·ag·u·la·tion (kō-ăg′yə-lā′shən) *n.* **1.** The act or process of coagulating. **2.** A mass or clot that results from coagulation.

coal (kōl) *n.* **1a.** A natural, dark-brown to black, solid substance formed from fossilized plants under conditions of great pressure, high humidity, and lack of air. Coal consists mainly of carbon and is widely used as a fuel and raw material. **b.** A piece of this substance: *There were only a few coals left in the bin.* **2.** A glowing or charred piece of wood, coal, or other solid fuel; an ember: *Coals continue to give off heat long after the flame is out.* ❖ *tr. & intr.v.* **coaled, coal·ing, coals** To supply with or take on a supply of coal: *coal a ship.* [From Old English *col.*]

co·a·lesce (kō′ə-lĕs′) *intr.v.* **co·a·lesced, co·a·lesc·ing, co·a·lesc·es 1.** To come or grow together into a single mass: *materials that coalesced to form stars.* **2.** To come together so as to form one whole; unite: *local groups that coalesced into a powerful national organization.* [From Latin *coalēscere* : *co-*, together + *alēscere*, to grow.] **—co′a·les′cence** *n.*

coal gas *n.* **1.** The mixture of gases given off when bituminous coal is heated without air, used as a fuel. **2.** The mixture of gases released when coal burns.

co·a·li·tion (kō′ə-lĭsh′ən) *n.* An alliance of people, parties, or nations for some special purpose: *a coalition of small business owners to defeat a sales tax.*

coal tar *n.* A thick sticky black liquid obtained by heating

WRITERS CHOOSE THEIR WORDS

I left the mirror and approached the bottles of scent, watching with absorption as the mother and daughter, wearing an elaborate system of scarves and jackets, huddled and gasped over the various perfumes, applying them to their wrists and squealing as they smelled them. The intense, almost **cloying** scent of flowers distressed me.

—Regina McBride
The Fire Opal

WORD BUILDING

co– The prefixes **co–** and **com–** are similar in meaning, and both go back to Latin prefixes that meant "with." In English, *co–* means "together, joint, jointly." It can be used to form nouns like *costar* or *coworker,* and it can also be used to form verbs like *cosign* or *coedit.* If you find a noun or a verb beginning with *co–* that you've never seen before, you can probably guess its meaning correctly.

coat of arms
coat of arms of the town of Carlisle, England

cobblestone

ă	pat	ôr	core
ā	pay	oi	boy
âr	care	ou	out
ä	father	o͝o	took
ĕ	pet	o͝or	lure
ē	be	o͞o	boot
ĭ	pit	ŭ	cut
ī	bite	ûr	urge
îr	pier	th	thin
ŏ	pot	*th*	this
ō	toe	zh	vision
ô	paw	ə	about

coal in the absence of air. It is used as a raw material for many dyes, drugs, and paints.

coarse (kôrs) *adj.* **coars·er, coars·est 1.** Not smooth; rough: *coarse skin; coarse material.* **2.** Consisting of large particles: *coarse sand.* **3.** Not refined; crude; rude: *coarse and vulgar language.* **4.** Of low, common, or inferior quality: *coarse lumber fit only for planking.* **—coarse′ly** *adv.* **—coarse′ness** *n.*
❑ *These sound alike:* **coarse, course** (route).

coars·en (kôr′sən) *tr. & intr.v.* **coars·ened, coars·en·ing, coars·ens** To make or become coarse: *Hard work coarsened the laborer's hands. Wool fabric often coarsens with long use.*

coast (kōst) *n.* **1.** The land next to the sea; the seashore. **2.** The water near this land: *fishes of the Pacific coast.* ❖ *intr.v.* **coast·ed, coast·ing, coasts 1.** To slide or move without the use of power: *The car coasted to a stop.* See Synonyms at **slide. 2.** To move ahead or through with little effort: *Some students coast through math class.*

coast·al (kō′stəl) *adj.* Relating to or being on or near a coast: *a coastal town; shallow coastal waters.*

coast·er (kō′stər) *n.* **1.** A small flat object, such as a disk or plate, placed under a bottle or glass to protect a surface, especially of a table. **2.** A ship engaged in coastal trade. **3.** A roller coaster.

coast guard also **Coast Guard** *n.* A military organization whose job is to patrol the coast of a nation, carry out rescue operations of ships in trouble, and enforce immigration, navigation, and custom laws.

coast·line (kōst′līn′) *n.* The shape, outline, or boundary of a coast.

coast-to-coast (kōst′tə-kōst′) *adj.* Reaching, airing, or traveling from one coast to another: *a coast-to-coast broadcast of the president's speech.*

coast·ward (kōst′wərd) *adj.* Directed toward a coast: *a coastward current.* ❖ *adv.* also **coast·wards** (kōst′-wərdz) Toward a coast: *The boat sailed coastward.*

coat (kōt) *n.* **1a.** An outer garment with sleeves, usually worn for warmth or protection. **b.** A jacket usually forming the top part of a suit. **2.** The hair or fur of an animal: *a dog with a short coat.* **3a.** The outer covering of a biological structure or organ: *a seed coat.* **b.** The outer covering of a virus. **4.** A layer of something spread over a surface: *a coat of paint.* ❖ *tr.v.* **coat·ed, coat·ing, coats** To cover with a layer: *Dust coated the table.*
❑ *These sound alike:* **coat, cote** (shed).

co·a·ti (kō-ä′tē) *n., pl.* **coati** or **co·a·tis** Any of several mammals of South and Central America and the southwest United States that have a long flexible snout and a ringed tail.

co·a·ti·mun·di (kō-ä′tē-mŭn′dē) *n., pl.* **coatimundi** or **co·a·ti·mun·dis** A coati.

coat·ing (kō′tĭng) *n.* A layer of a substance spread over a surface, as for protection or decoration: *a sticky coating of varnish; a thin coating of ice on the streets.*

coat of arms *n., pl.* **coats of arms 1.** An emblem on a shield that serves as the insignia of a nation, family, institution, or group. **2.** A shield or drawing that represents such an emblem.

coat of mail *n., pl.* **coats of mail** A coat made of chain mail or overlapping metal plates, worn as armor during the Middle Ages.

coat·room (kōt′ro͞om′ or kōt′ro͝om′) *n.* A cloakroom.

coat·tail (kōt′tāl′) *n.* The loose rear flap of a coat that hangs below the waist. ◆ **on (someone's) coattails** As a result of the success of another: *When the governor won the election in a landslide, several local candidates from the same party were elected on her coattails.*

co·au·thor (kō-ô′thər) *n.* One of two or more people who work together in writing a book, story, report, or other piece of writing. ❖ *tr.v.* **co·au·thored, co·au·thor·ing, co·au·thors** To be the coauthor of.

coax (kōks) *tr.v.* **coaxed, coax·ing, coax·es 1.** To persuade or try to persuade by gently urging: *The trainer coaxed the lion into the cage.* **2.** To obtain by gentle persuasion: *I couldn't coax the secret out of my little brother.* **3.** To move gently or gradually toward a desired end; nudge: *coaxed the heavy girder into place.* **—coax′er** *n.*

co·ax·i·al cable (kō-ăk′sē-əl) *n.* A cable made of a conducting outer metal tube insulated from an inner conducting core. Coaxial cables are used to carry telephone, telegraph, and television signals.

cob (kŏb) *n.* **1.** The long hard central part of an ear of corn; a corncob. **2.** A male swan. **3.** A stocky short-legged horse.

co·balt (kō′bôlt′) *n. Symbol* **Co** A hard, silver-white metallic element that occurs widely in ores containing other metals. Cobalt is used in making alloys and pigments. Atomic number 27. See **Periodic Table.**

cobalt-60 *n.* A radioactive isotope of cobalt having a mass number of 60. It is an intense source of gamma rays and is used in the treatment of cancer.

cobalt blue *n.* **1.** A blue to green pigment consisting of a mixture of cobalt oxide and aluminum oxide. **2.** A deep vivid blue.

cob·ble¹ (kŏb′əl) *n.* A cobblestone. ❖ *tr.v.* **cob·bled, cob·bling, cob·bles** To pave with cobblestones. [From Middle English *cobelston*, cobblestone, from *cob*, round object.]

cob·ble² (kŏb′əl) *tr.v.* **cob·bled, cob·bling, cob·bles** To make or mend (boots or shoes). [Probably from *cobbler*, shoemaker.]

cob·bler¹ (kŏb′lər) *n.* A shoemaker. [From Middle English *cobeler*.]

cob·bler² (kŏb′lər) *n.* A fruit pie topped with a biscuit crust and baked in a deep dish.

cob·ble·stone (kŏb′əl-stōn′) *n.* A naturally rounded stone formerly used for paving streets.

co·bra (kō′brə) *n.* Any of several venomous Asian or African snakes capable of spreading out the skin of the neck to form a flattened hood.

cob·web (kŏb′wĕb′) *n.* A spider web, especially an old one that is covered in dust. [From Middle English *coppeweb* : *coppe*, spider + *web*, web.]

co·ca (kō′kə) *n.* Any of certain trees or shrubs native to South America whose leaves are chewed as a stimulant or processed for cocaine.

co·caine (kō-kān′ or kō′kān′) *n.* A drug obtained from coca leaves that stimulates the nervous system and is highly addictive. It is sometimes used in medicine as a local anesthetic.

coc·cus (kŏk′əs) *n., pl.* **coc·ci** (kŏk′sī or kŏk′ī) Any of various bacteria that are shaped like a sphere and are usually grouped together in chains or clusters.

coc·cyx (kŏk′sĭks) *n., pl.* **coc·cy·ges** (kŏk-sī′jēz or kŏk′-sĭ-jēz′) or **coc·cyx·es** A small triangular bone found at the base of the spinal column in humans and other apes.

coch·i·neal (kŏch′ə-nēl′ or kōch′ə-nēl′) *n.* A bright-red dye made from the dried bodies of a tropical American insect.

Co·chise (kō-chēs′ or kō-chēz′) Died 1874. Apache leader who organized resistance to US troops in the Southwest (1861–1872).

coch·le·a (kŏk′lē-ə) *n., pl.* **coch·le·ae** (kŏk′lē-ē′) also **coch·le·as** A spiral tube of the inner ear that resembles a snail shell and contains the nerve endings necessary for hearing. **—coch′le·ar** *adj.*

coch·le·ar implant (kŏk′lē-ər) *n.* An electronic device that is implanted in the inner ear and allows people with severe hearing loss to recognize some sounds, especially speech.

cock¹ (kŏk) *n.* **1.** A full-grown male chicken; a rooster. **2.** An adult male of various other birds. **3.** A faucet or valve for regulating the flow of a liquid or gas. **4.** The hammer of a gun. **5.** A tilting or jaunty turning upward: *the cock of a sailor's cap.* ❖ *tr.v.* **cocked, cock·ing, cocks 1.** To set the hammer of (a gun) in position to fire. **2.** To tilt or turn up to one side: *He cocked his head and thought about the question.* [From Middle English *cok*, from Old English *cocc*, probably from Late Latin *coccus*.]

cock² (kŏk) *n.* A cone-shaped pile of straw or hay. ❖ *tr.v.* **cocked, cock·ing, cocks** To arrange (straw or hay) in such piles. [From Middle English *cok*.]

cock·a·too (kŏk′ə-to͞o′) *n., pl.* **cock·a·toos** Any of various large parrots of Australia and adjacent areas, having feathers on the head that can be raised in a crest.

cocked hat (kŏkt) *n.* A hat with the brim turned up in two or three places.

cock·er·el (kŏk′ər-əl) *n.* A young rooster.

cock·er spaniel (kŏk′ər) *n.* A dog of an American or an English breed having long drooping ears and a silky coat.

cock·eyed (kŏk′īd′) *adj. Informal* **1.** Tilted or crooked; askew: *The picture hung at a cockeyed angle on the wall.* **2.** Ridiculous; absurd: *cockeyed schemes that are sure to fail.*

cock·fight (kŏk′fīt′) *n.* A fight between two gamecocks with metal spurs attached to their legs.

cock·horse (kŏk′hôrs′) *n.* A rocking horse or hobbyhorse.

cock·le (kŏk′əl) *n.* **1.** Any of various mollusks having a pair of heart-shaped shells with narrow ribbed markings. **2.** A cockleshell. ◆ **cockles of one's heart** One's innermost feelings: *Their thoughtfulness warmed the cockles of my heart.*

cock·le·bur (kŏk′əl-bûr′) *n.* **1.** Any of several large weedy plants that have prickly burs. **2.** The bur of such a plant.

cock·le·shell (kŏk′əl-shĕl′) *n.* **1.** A shell of a cockle. **2.** A small light boat used in shallow waters.

Cock·ney (kŏk′nē) *n., pl.* **Cock·neys 1.** A native of the eastern section of London. **2.** The distinctive dialect or accent of the Cockneys. **—Cock′ney** *adj.*

cock·pit (kŏk′pĭt′) *n.* **1.** The space in an airplane that has seats for the pilot and copilot and sometimes passengers. **2.** The space in a small boat from which the boat is steered. **3.** An area used for cockfights.

cock·roach (kŏk′rōch′) *n.* Any of numerous usually dark-colored insects that have a flat oval body and lay their eggs in hardened cases. Several kinds of cockroaches are common household pests.

cocks·comb (kŏks′kōm′) *n.* **1.** The fleshy red comb on the head of a rooster. **2.** A jester's cap, topped with a strip of red cloth notched like the comb of a rooster. **3.** A garden plant having dense fan-shaped clusters of red, purple, or yellow flowers.

cock·sure (kŏk′sho͝or′) *adj.* Completely sure, especially too sure of oneself: *a cocksure young upstart.* **—cock′sure′ness** *n.*

cock·tail (kŏk′tāl′) *n.* **1.** An alcoholic drink consisting of a liquor mixed with fruit juice, soda, or another liquor. **2.** An appetizer such as seafood, juice, or fruit: *a shrimp cocktail.*

cock·y (kŏk′ē) *adj.* **cock·i·er, cock·i·est** Too sure of oneself; arrogant; conceited: *a cocky showoff.* **—cock′i·ly** *adv.* **—cock′i·ness** *n.*

co·coa (kō′kō) *n.* **1.** A powder made of roasted ground cacao seeds from which much of the fat has been removed. **2.** A drink made by mixing this powder with sugar and hot milk or water. [Alteration of *cacao*.]

cocoa butter *n.* A yellowish waxy solid obtained from cacao seeds and used in making soap, cosmetics, and confections.

co·co·nut (kō′kə-nŭt′) *n.* **1.** The large hard-shelled nut of the coconut palm, having white meat and a hollow center filled with liquid. **2.** The edible white meat of this nut, often shredded and used as food and in confections. **3.** The coconut palm. [From Portuguese *côco*, grinning skull, goblin.]

coconut milk *n.* A milky liquid extracted from the meat of a coconut.

coconut oil *n.* A semisolid or liquid oil obtained from coconut meat and used in foods, soaps, and cosmetics.

coconut palm *n.* A palm tree of tropical regions that bears coconuts as fruits.

co·coon (kə-ko͞on′) *n.* **1.** A protective case of silky strands spun by the larva of a moth or other insect as a cover for the pupa. **2.** A similar protective covering or structure: *wrapped in a cocoon of blankets.*

cod (kŏd) *n., pl.* **cod** or **cods** Any of various large food fishes of the northern Atlantic and Pacific Oceans; a codfish.

Cod, Cape A hook-shaped peninsula of southeast Massachusetts extending east and north into the Atlantic Ocean.

COD *abbr.* An abbreviation of cash on delivery.

co·da (kō′də) *n.* A passage that ends a musical movement or composition. [From Italian, from Latin *cauda*, tail.]

cod·dle (kŏd′l) *tr.v.* **cod·dled, cod·dling, cod·dles 1.** To cook in water just below the boiling point: *coddle eggs.* **2.** To treat indulgently; baby. See Synonyms at **pamper.**

code (kōd) *n.* **1.** A system of signals used to represent the letters and numerals in a message that is to be transmitted: *a telegraphic code.* **2.** A system of words, symbols, or letters given arbitrary meanings, usually used to keep messages secret. **3.** A system of symbols and rules used to represent instructions to a computer; a computer program. **4.** A special command, such as a sequence of keystrokes, that allows a user to activate a hidden or accidental feature in a computer program or video game. **5.** A system or collection of laws or rules and regulations: *a building code; an honor code.* ❖ *tr.v.* **cod·ed, cod·ing, codes** To put (a text, numbers, or information) into a code: *code information to store in a computer.* [From Middle English, from Latin *cōdex*, book.]

co·deine (kō′dēn′) *n.* A drug obtained from opium or morphine and used especially to relieve coughing or pain.

code name *n.* A name assigned to conceal the identity or existence of something or someone.

code word *n.* A secret word or phrase used as a code name or password.

cod·fish (kŏd′fĭsh′) *n.* **1.** A cod. **2.** The flesh of a cod, used as food.

codg·er (kŏj′ər) *n. Informal* An odd or somewhat eccentric old man.

cod·i·cil (kŏd′ə-sĭl) *n.* A supplement or appendix, especially to a will.

cod·i·fy (kŏd′ĭ-fī′ *or* kō′də-fī′) *tr.v.* **cod·i·fied, cod·i·fy·ing, cod·i·fies** To arrange (laws, for example) in a systematic way. **—cod′i·fi·ca′tion** (kŏd′ĭ-fĭ-kā′shən) *n.* **—cod′i·fi′er** *n.*

cod·ling moth (kŏd′lĭng) *n.* A small moth whose caterpillars feed on and damage apples and other fruits.

cod-liv·er oil (kŏd′lĭv′ər) *n.* An oil rich in vitamins A and D, obtained from the livers of cod and related fishes.

Co·dy (kō′dē), **William Frederick** Known as "Buffalo Bill." 1846–1917. American frontier scout and performer who toured the United States and Europe with his Wild West Show.

co·ed or **co-ed** (kō′ĕd′) *Informal n.* A woman who attends a coeducational college or university. ❖ *adj.* Relating to coeducation: *a coed school.*

co·ed·u·ca·tion (kō-ĕj′ə-kā′shən) *n.* The system of education in which both male and female students take

cobra

cockatoo

Cape Cod
satellite image of Cape Cod, Massachusetts

coffee

cogwheel

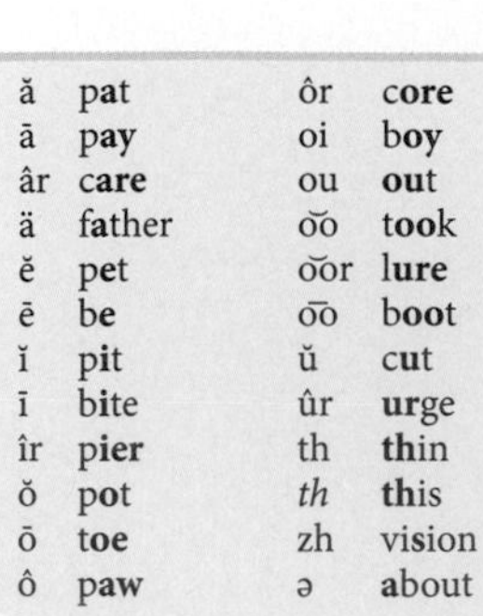

ă	pat	ôr	core
ā	pay	oi	boy
âr	care	ou	out
ä	father	o͝o	took
ĕ	pet	o͝or	lure
ē	be	o͞o	boot
ĭ	pit	ŭ	cut
ī	bite	ûr	urge
îr	pier	th	thin
ŏ	pot	*th*	this
ō	toe	zh	vision
ô	paw	ə	about

classes together at a school or college. **—co′ed·u·ca′tion·al** *adj.*

co·ef·fi·cient (kō′ə-**fĭsh′**ənt) *n.* A number or symbol multiplying a variable or an unknown quantity in an algebraic term. In the term $4x$, 4 is the coefficient. In $x(a + b)$, x is the coefficient.

coe·la·canth (**sē′**lə-kănth′) *n.* Any of various fishes having lobed fleshy fins and several characteristics not found in other vertebrate animals. They were known only from fossil remains until a living specimen was caught off the coast of southern Africa in 1938. A second species was discovered in 1999 in Indonesia.

coe·len·ter·ate (sĭ-**lĕn′**tə-rāt′ *or* sĭ-**lĕn′**tər-ĭt) *n.* A cnidarian.

coe·lom (**sē′**ləm) *n.* The fluid-filled cavity within the body of most multicellular animals, except some invertebrates such as flatworms, that lies between the body wall and the digestive tract and contains the internal organs. [From German *Koelom*, from Greek *koilōma*, cavity, from *koilos*, hollow.]

co·erce (kō-**ûrs′**) *tr.v.* **co·erced, co·erc·ing, co·erc·es** To force or compel (someone) to do something by pressure, threats, or intimidation: *The suspect claimed that the police coerced her to confess by intimidating her.* **—co·erc′er** *n.* **—co·er′cion** (kō-**ûr′**zhən) *n.*

co·er·cive (kō-**ûr′**sĭv) *adj.* Tending to coerce: *Public opinion has a coercive effect on elected officials.* **—co·er′cive·ly** *adv.*

co·ev·o·lu·tion (kō′ĕv-ə-**lo͞o′**shən *or* kō′ē-və-**lo͞o′**shən) *n.* The process by which two or more interacting species evolve together, each changing as a result of changes in the other or others. It occurs, for example, between predators and prey and between insects and the flowers that they pollinate. **—co′e·volve′** (kō′ĭ-**vŏlv′**) *v.*

co·ex·ist (kō′ĭg-**zĭst′**) *intr.v.* **co·ex·ist·ed, co·ex·ist·ing, co·ex·ists** To live or exist together, at the same time, or in the same place: *Bears and wolves coexist in the Alaskan wilderness. Many nations coexist on the European continent.* **—co′ex·is′tence** *n.* **—co′ex·is′tent** *adj.*

co·ex·ten·sive (kō′ĭk-**stĕn′**sĭv) *adj.* Occupying the same space; having the same limits or boundaries: *The habitat of certain mammals is coextensive with the Great Plains.*

cof·fee (**kô′**fē) *n.* **1.** A brown drink prepared from the ground seeds of any of various tropical plants native to Africa. **2.** The dried whole or ground seeds of any of these plants. **3.** Any of various trees or shrubs that bear such seeds and are widely cultivated in the tropics. [From Arabic *qahwa*.]

cof·fee·cake (**kô′**fē-kāk′) *n.* A cake made of sweetened dough with yeast, often containing nuts and raisins and covered with sugar or icing.

cof·fee·house (**kô′**fē-hous′) *n.* A restaurant where coffee and other refreshments are served.

cof·fee·pot (**kô′**fē-pŏt′) *n.* A covered pot with a handle and spout, for making and pouring coffee.

coffee shop *n.* A small restaurant in which coffee and light meals are served.

coffee table *n.* A low table, often placed in front of a sofa.

cof·fer (**kô′**fər) *n.* **1.** A strongbox for holding money or other valuables. **2. coffers** A treasury, as of a nation; financial resources: *The state coffers were opened to aid the flood victims.*

cof·fin (**kô′**fĭn) *n.* A box in which a dead person is buried. [From Middle English *coffin*, basket, from Greek *kophinos*.]

cog (kŏg) *n.* **1.** One of a series of teeth on the rim of a wheel that fit between the teeth on another wheel so that one wheel can move the other. **2.** A cogwheel.

co·gent (**kō′**jənt) *adj.* Forceful and convincing: *a cogent argument based on facts.* **—co′gen·cy** (**kō′**jən-sē) *n.* **—co′gent·ly** *adv.*

cog·i·tate (**kŏj′**ĭ-tāt′) *intr.v.* **cog·i·tat·ed, cog·i·tat·ing, cog·i·tates** To think carefully; reflect; ponder. **—cog′i·ta′tion** *n.*

co·gnac (**kōn′**yăk′) *n.* A brandy made from white wine near Cognac, a town in western France.

cog·nate (**kŏg′**nāt′) *adj.* **1.** Related in origin: *French and Spanish are cognate languages.* **2.** Related by blood; having a common ancestor: *cognate branches of the same family.* ❖ *n.* A cognate person or thing, especially a word related to one in another language. For example, the English word *cup*, the Dutch word *kopje*, and the Italian word *coppa* are cognates from the Late Latin word *cuppa*. [From Latin *cognātus* : *co-*, together + *gnātus*, born.]

cog·ni·tion (kŏg-**nĭsh′**ən) *n.* The mental process of gaining knowledge, including the ability to perceive, reason, and be aware.

cog·ni·tive (**kŏg′**nĭ-tĭv) *adj.* Relating to cognition: *the cognitive development of young children.*

cog·ni·zance (**kŏg′**nĭ-zəns) *n.* **1.** Observation; notice: *The government was slow to take cognizance of the growing unrest.* **2.** Ability to understand: *The origins of life are still beyond the cognizance of modern science.*

cog·ni·zant (**kŏg′**nĭ-zənt) *adj.* Aware; conscious: *Until they heard a weather report, none of the sailors was cognizant of the approaching storm.*

cog·wheel (**kŏg′**wēl′) *n.* A wheel with cogs on its rim that mesh with those of another wheel so that one wheel can move the other.

co·hab·it (kō-**hăb′**ĭt) *intr.v.* **co·hab·it·ed, co·hab·it·ing, co·hab·its** To live together in a sexual relationship, especially when not legally married. **—co·hab′i·ta′tion** *n.*

co·here (kō-**hîr′**) *intr.v.* **co·hered, co·her·ing, co·heres** **1.** To stick together in a mass, as dough or wet clay does. **2.** To be logically connected: *The plot elements of that movie just don't cohere.*

co·her·ence (kō-**hîr′**əns *or* kō-**hĕr′**əns) *n.* The quality or state of being coherent. **—co·her′en·cy** (kō-**hîr′**ən-sē *or* kō-**hĕr′**ən-sē) *n.*

co·her·ent (kō-**hîr′**ənt *or* kō-**hĕr′**ənt) *adj.* **1.** Sticking together: *A snowball is a coherent mass of soft wet snow.* **2.** Logically connected; easy to understand: *wrote a coherent argument for nuclear disarmament.* **3.** Composed of waves that oscillate together and travel in the same direction: *the coherent red light of a laser.* **—co·her′ent·ly** *adv.*

co·he·sion (kō-**hē′**zhən) *n.* **1.** The attraction between molecules of the same kind: *The cohesion of molecules of H_2O produces drops of water.* **2.** The condition of cohering; a tendency to stick together; unity: *The cohesion of so many different groups is the result of common beliefs.*

co·he·sive (kō-**hē′**sĭv) *adj.* **1.** Tending to cohere; sticking together: *the cohesive nature of water molecules.* **2.** Producing cohesion: *the cohesive force of glue.* **—co·he′sive·ly** *adv.* **—co·he′sive·ness** *n.*

co·hort (**kō′**hôrt′) *n.* **1.** A companion or associate: *My cohorts on the newspaper staff agreed to publish the article.* **2.** A group or band: *A cohort of protesters assembled in front of city hall.* **3.** One of the divisions of a legion in the army of ancient Rome.

coif (koif) *n.* **1.** A tight-fitting cap worn under a veil, as by nuns. **2.** A skullcap, such as one worn under a knight's helmet or an English lawyer's wig. **3.** (*also* kwäf) A coiffure. ❖ *tr.v.* **coifed, coif·ing, coifs** (*also* kwäf) To arrange or dress (the hair): *hair coifed in an elaborate style.*

coif·fure (kwä-**fyo͝or′**) *n.* A way of arranging the hair; a hairstyle.

coil (koil) *n.* **1.** A series of connected spirals or gathered loops: *a coil of rope.* **2.** A spiral or loop in such a series. **3.** An electrical device consisting of a number of turns of insulated wire, used as an electromagnet or to store energy in the form of a magnetic field. **4.** A winding pipe or series of pipes through which a fluid is circulated for heating or cooling, as in a radiator or refrigerator. ❖ *v.* **coiled, coil·ing, coils** *—tr.* To wind into a series of spirals or loops: *The snake coiled itself around a branch. —intr.* **1.** To form spirals or loops: *The hose that I was using coiled and knotted.* **2.** To move in a spiral course: *The smoke coiled up into the sky.* [Probably from Latin *colligere*, gather together, collect.]

coin (koin) *n.* **1.** A piece of metal, usually flat and round, issued by a government for use as money. **2.** Pieces of metal money considered as a group: *Only the government can issue coin.* ❖ *tr.v.* **coined, coin·ing, coins 1.** To make (coins) from metal; mint: *The government coins dimes and quarters.* **2.** To make coins from (metal): *coin copper into pennies.* **3.** To invent (a word or phrase): *The computer industry has had to coin many new terms.* [From Middle English, from Latin *cuneus*, wedge.]
❑ *These sound alike:* **coin, quoin** (corner).

coin·age (koi′nĭj) *n.* **1.** The process of making coins: *the coinage of silver.* **2.** Coins considered as a group. **3a.** A new word or phrase. **b.** The invention of new words: *words of recent coinage.*

co·in·cide (kō′ĭn-sīd′) *intr.v.* **co·in·cid·ed, co·in·cid·ing, co·in·cides 1.** To occur at the same time or during the same period of time: *The date of your party coincides with my birthday.* **2.** To agree; be identical: *Our opinions of the movie coincided.* **3.** To be in the same position or occupy the same space: *The park coincides with the site of an old settlement.*

co·in·ci·dence (kō-ĭn′sĭ-dəns) *n.* **1.** A combination of events or circumstances that is accidental but seems to have been planned or arranged: *By a strange coincidence, John Adams and Thomas Jefferson both died on the 50th anniversary of the signing of the Declaration of Independence.* **2.** The state or fact of coinciding: *A curious coincidence of events brought the two nations together in agreement.*

co·in·ci·dent (kō-ĭn′sĭ-dənt) *adj.* **1.** Happening at the same time: *coincident elections in three different countries.* **2.** Very similar; agreeing: *coincident opinions.* **3.** Matching point for point; coinciding: *coincident circles.* **—co·in′ci·dent·ly** *adv.*

co·in·ci·den·tal (kō-ĭn′sĭ-**dĕn′**tl) *adj.* Occurring as or resulting from coincidence: *a coincidental meeting of old friends.* **—co·in′ci·den′tal·ly, co·in′ci·dent′ly** *adv.*

co·i·tus (kō′ĭ-təs *or* kō-ē′təs) *n.* Sexual union between a female and a male in which the penis enters the vagina.

coke (kōk) *n.* The solid material, chiefly carbon, that remains after the coal gas and coal tar have been removed from bituminous coal by heat. It is used as a fuel and in making steel.

col. *abbr.* An abbreviation of column.

col– *pref.* Variant of **com–**.

Col. also **COL** *abbr.* An abbreviation of colonel.

co·la[1] (kō′lə) *n.* A carbonated drink made with an extract from cola nuts or similar flavorings. [From *cola*, nut of the cola tree.]

co·la[2] also **ko·la** (kō′lə) *n.* Any of several tropical African evergreen trees having reddish fragrant nutlike seeds that are chewed as a stimulant and that yield an extract used in beverages and medicines. [Of West African origin.]

col·an·der (kŏl′ən-dər *or* kŭl′ən-dər) *n.* A bowl-shaped kitchen utensil with holes in the bottom, used for rinsing and draining off liquids from foods.

cold (kōld) *adj.* **cold·er, cold·est 1a.** Having a low temperature: *cold water; a cold day.* **b.** Having a temperature lower than normal or desirable: *cold hands and feet; cold oatmeal.* **2.** Feeling no warmth; chilled: *I am cold without a jacket.* **3a.** Not friendly; aloof: *a cold and businesslike manner.* **b.** Showing no enthusiasm or interest: *a cold audience.* **4.** Having lost freshness; faint; weak: *The bear's trail was cold.* **5.** Characterized by repeated failure, as in a sport: *He has been cold shooting from the three-point line.* ❖ *adv.* **1.** Completely; thoroughly; absolutely: *Our suggestion was turned down cold. The player was stopped cold on the 40-yard line.* **2.** Without preparation or prior notice: *We took the test cold.* ❖ *n.* **1.** Relative lack of warmth: *Cold slows down chemical reactions.* **2.** The feeling resulting from lack of warmth; chill. **3.** Cold weather: *We were out in the cold all day.* **4.** A viral infection that causes a runny or stuffy nose, coughing, sneezing, and fever. ◆ **catch cold** or **take cold** To become sick with a cold. **get cold feet** or **have cold feet** To lack courage; be or become timid or fearful: *Their friends got cold feet and wouldn't go skiing with them.* **out in the cold** Lacking benefits given to others; neglected: *Because she had just been hired, she was left out in the cold when raises were given.* [From Old English *ceald*.] **—cold′ly** *adv.* **—cold′ness** *n.*

SYNONYMS cold, chilly, frigid, frosty, icy These adjectives describe something at a very low temperature. *The cold wind made me wish I had worn a coat. He could see his breath in the chilly air. She brought the portable heater into the frigid room. This frosty weather is perfect for sledding. The travelers warmed their icy hands by the fire.*
ANTONYM hot

---

cold-blood·ed (kōld′blŭd′ĭd) *adj.* **1.** Having a body temperature that is maintained by external rather than internal sources of heat. Most fishes, amphibians, and reptiles are cold-blooded. **2a.** Having no feeling or emotion; cruel. **b.** Done without feeling or emotion: *a cold-blooded dismissal of an employee.* **—cold′-blood′ed·ly** *adv.* **—cold′-blood′ed·ness** *n.*

cold cream *n.* A creamy cosmetic for cleansing and softening the skin.

cold cuts *pl.n.* Slices of cold cooked or cured meat.

cold feet *pl.n. Slang* The condition of being fearful or timid, resulting in the inability to complete a course of action: *He got cold feet before the talent show and refused to go onto the stage.*

cold front *n.* The forward edge of a mass of cold air in the atmosphere that replaces a mass of warm air, often accompanied by heavy showers.

cold-heart·ed (kōld′här′tĭd) *adj.* Lacking sympathy or feeling; callous: *a cold-hearted decision to evict the tenants.* **—cold′-heart′ed·ly** *adv.* **—cold′-heart′ed·ness** *n.*

cold shoulder *n. Informal* Deliberate coldness or disregard; a snub: *He gave me the cold shoulder after our quarrel.*

cold sore *n.* A small sore on the lips that often accompanies a fever or cold; a fever blister.

cold storage *n.* The storage of food, furs, or other perishable things in a refrigerated place.

cold sweat *n.* Perspiration and cold moist skin resulting from pain, shock, or fear: *broke out into a cold sweat upon hearing the strange cry.*

cold war or **Cold War** *n.* A state of political tension and military rivalry between nations that stops short of full-scale war, especially that which existed between the United States and its allies and the Soviet Union and other Communist countries from the end of World War II until the fall of the Berlin Wall in 1989 and the collapse of the Soviet Union in 1991.

Cole·ridge (kōl′rĭj *or* kō′lə-rĭj), **Samuel Taylor** 1772–1834. British poet and critic who was a leader of the romantic movement.

cole·slaw (kōl′slô′) *n.* A salad that is made of shredded raw cabbage with mayonnaise or a vinaigrette; a slaw.

colander

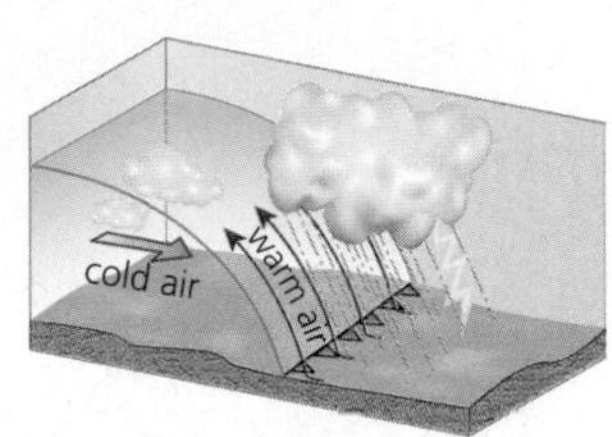

cold front

coliseum
ruins of the Flavian Amphitheater, Rome, Italy

USAGE

collective noun When referring to a collection as a whole, a **collective noun** takes a singular verb: *The family was united on this question.* A collective noun takes a plural verb when it refers to the members of the group as individuals, as in *My family are all good skiers.* Among the common collective nouns are *committee, clergy, company, enemy, group, family, flock, public,* and *team.*

ă	pat	ôr	core
ā	pay	oi	boy
âr	care	ou	out
ä	father	o͝o	took
ĕ	pet	o͝or	lure
ē	be	o͞o	boot
ĭ	pit	ŭ	cut
ī	bite	ûr	urge
îr	pier	th	thin
ŏ	pot	*th*	this
ō	toe	zh	vision
ô	paw	ə	about

[From Dutch *koolsla* : *kool*, cabbage + *sla*, salad.]

co·le·us (kō′lē-əs) *n.* Any of various plants grown for their colorful leaves, which are often marked with red, purple, or yellow.

col·ic (kŏl′ĭk) *n.* Severe pain or cramping in the abdomen. [From Middle English *colik*, affecting the colon, from Greek *kōlikos*, from *kolon*, colon.] **—col′ick·y** *adj.*

col·i·se·um also **col·os·se·um** (kŏl′ĭ-sē′əm) *n.* A large stadium or hall for sports events, exhibitions, or other public entertainment.

co·li·tis (kə-lī′tĭs) *n.* Inflammation of the colon.

coll. *abbr.* An abbreviation of: **1.** college. **2.** colloquial.

col·lab·o·rate (kə-lăb′ə-rāt′) *intr.v.* **col·lab·o·rat·ed, col·lab·o·rat·ing, col·lab·o·rates 1.** To work together on a project: *The scientists collaborated by sharing their discoveries and planning a new experiment.* **2.** To cooperate with an enemy that has invaded one's country: *Some Southerners collaborated with the Union during the Civil War.* **—col·lab′o·ra′tion** *n.* **—col·lab′o·ra′tor** *n.*

col·lage (kə-läzh′) *n.* A work of art made by pasting materials or objects, such as pieces of cloth, metal, colored paper, string, and pictures, onto a surface. [From French, from *coller*, to glue.]

col·la·gen (kŏl′ə-jən) *n.* The tough fibrous protein found in bone, cartilage, and connective tissue.

col·lapse (kə-lăps′) *v.* **col·lapsed, col·laps·ing, col·laps·es** *—intr.* **1.** To fall down or inward suddenly; cave in: *Part of the roof collapsed after the fire.* **2.** To break down or fail suddenly and completely: *collapse from overwork and fatigue; negotiations collapsing in disagreement.* **3.** To fold together compactly: *This folding chair collapses very easily.* *—tr.* To cause to collapse: *The weight of the books collapsed the flimsy shelf.* ❖ *n.* **1.** The act or an example of collapsing: *the collapse of the decrepit building; the collapse of a business deal.* **2.** A sudden and complete loss of strength or stamina; a breakdown: *suffered a collapse and was rushed to the hospital.* [From Latin *collābī*, to fall together : *com-*, together + *lābī*, to fall.]

col·laps·i·ble (kə-lăp′sə-bəl) *adj.* Capable of being collapsed or folded compactly: *a collapsible tent.*

col·lar (kŏl′ər) *n.* **1.** The part of a shirt, coat, or dress that encircles the neck. **2.** A separate band for the neck, as one of lace, linen, or jewels. **3.** A leather, metal, or plastic band put around the neck of an animal, such as a dog. **4.** The cushioned part of a harness that presses against the shoulders of a draft animal, such as a horse. **5.** A band or marking, as around the neck of an animal, resembling a collar: *The buzzard has a collar of white feathers.* **6.** A device shaped like a ring and used to guide or secure a machine part. ❖ *tr.v.* **col·lared, col·lar·ing, col·lars 1.** To put a collar on: *collar a sheep to attach a bell.* **2.** *Slang* To seize, capture, or arrest: *The police collared the thief a few blocks away.* [From Middle English *coler*, from Latin *collāre*, from *collum*, neck.]

❑ *These sound alike:* **collar, choler** (anger).

col·lar·bone (kŏl′ər-bōn′) *n.* A bone that connects the breastbone and the shoulder blade; the clavicle.

col·lard (kŏl′ərd) *n.* **1.** A plant having large, smooth, spreading leaves. **2. collards** The leaves of this plant, eaten as a vegetable.

col·late (kō′lāt′ *or* kŏl′āt′) *tr.v.* **col·lat·ed, col·lat·ing, col·lates 1.** To examine and compare carefully (copies of texts or books, for example) in order to discover differences between them: *The scholar collated the early editions of the poem to determine which version was the original.* **2.** To arrange in proper sequence: *a photocopier that collates pages as it prints them.* **—col·la′tion** *n.*

col·lat·er·al (kə-lăt′ər-əl) *adj.* **1.** Additional; supporting: *Further experiments provided collateral evidence for the theory.* **2.** Of a secondary nature, especially occurring as an unintended consequence: *The missile destroyed its target but caused collateral damage to nearby buildings.* **3.** Guaranteed by something that has been pledged as security: *a collateral loan.* **4.** Situated or running side by side; parallel: *the collateral lines of a parallelogram.* ❖ *n.* Property, such as jewelry or bonds, pledged as security for a loan. **—col·lat′er·al·ly** *adv.*

col·league (kŏl′ēg′) *n.* A fellow member of a profession, staff, or organization; an associate.

col·lect (kə-lĕkt′) *v.* **col·lect·ed, col·lect·ing, col·lects** *—tr.* **1.** To bring together in a group; gather; assemble: *We collected firewood.* See Synonyms at **gather. 2.** To pick up and take away: *collect garbage.* **3.** To accumulate as a hobby or for study: *collect stamps; collect specimens for a report about beetles.* **4.** To obtain payment of: *We collected a dollar from each student for the gift.* **5.** To recover control of; pull together: *They finally collected themselves after the accident.* *—intr.* **1.** To come together; congregate: *A group of bystanders collected on the sidewalk.* **2.** To build up; accumulate: *A pile of snow collected by the door.* **3.** To take in payments or donations: *The band collected for new uniforms.* ❖ *adv. & adj.* With payment to be made by the receiver: *call home collect; a collect call.* [From Middle English *collecten*, from Latin *colligere* : *com-*, together + *legere*, to gather.] **—col·lect′a·ble, col·lect′i·ble** *adj.*

col·lect·ed (kə-lĕk′tĭd) *adj.* **1.** In full control of oneself; composed; calm: *He did his best to remain cool and collected when speaking to a crowd.* **2.** Gathered together: *the collected works of Shakespeare.* **—col·lect′ed·ly** *adv.* **—col·lect′ed·ness** *n.*

col·lec·tion (kə-lĕk′shən) *n.* **1.** The act or process of collecting: *Trash collection is on Tuesday.* **2.** A group of things brought or kept together for study or use or as a hobby: *a collection of folk songs; a coin collection.* **3.** An accumulation; a deposit: *the collection of dust on the piano.* **4a.** The act of seeking and obtaining money, as during a church service. **b.** The amount of money so obtained.

col·lec·tive (kə-lĕk′tĭv) *adj.* **1.** Assembled into or viewed as a whole: *the collective accomplishments of the past.* **2.** Relating to a number of people or nations acting as a group: *the collective opinion of the committee; our collective security.* **3.** Owned, managed, or operated by a group: *collective farming in China.* ❖ *n.* **1.** A business or undertaking owned and controlled by its workers, usually under the supervision of a government. **2.** A collective noun. **—col·lec′tive·ly** *adv.*

collective bargaining *n.* Negotiation between the representatives of organized workers and their employer or employers to determine wages and working conditions.

collective farm *n.* A farm or a group of farms managed and worked by a group of laborers, usually under the supervision of a communist government.

collective noun *n.* A noun that refers to a collection of people or things regarded as a unit. —SEE NOTE.

col·lec·tiv·ism (kə-lĕk′tə-vĭz′əm) *n.* The theory or system in which the means of producing and distributing goods are owned and managed by the people as a group, especially under the control of a government. **—col·lec′tiv·ist** *adj. & n.*

col·lec·tiv·ize (kə-lĕk′tə-vīz′) *tr.v.* **col·lec·tiv·ized, col·lec·tiv·iz·ing, col·lec·tiv·iz·es** To organize (an economy, industry, or business) on the basis of collectivism. **—col·lec′tiv·i·za′tion** (kə-lĕk′tə-vĭ-zā′shən) *n.*

col·lec·tor (kə-lĕk′tər) *n.* **1.** A person or thing that collects: *a garbage collector; a solar collector.* **2.** A person assigned to collect money: *a tax collector.* **3.** A person who assembles a collection: *a collector of autographs.*

col·leen (kŏ-lēn′ *or* kŏl′ēn′) *n.* An Irish girl. [From Irish Gaelic *cailín*, diminutive of *caile*, girl.]

col·lege (kŏl′ĭj) *n.* **1.** A school of higher learning, entered after high school, that grants a bachelor's degree. **2.** An undergraduate division within a university. **3.** A school for special study, often connected with a university: *a teachers' college.* **4.** A body of people having a common purpose or shared duties: *a college of surgeons.* [From Middle English, from Latin *collēgium*, association.]

col·le·gian (kə-lē′jən *or* kə-lē′jē-ən) *n.* A college student.

col·le·giate (kə-lē′jĭt *or* kə-lē′jē-ĭt) *adj.* Relating to or typical of a college or college students: *collegiate activities.*

col·lide (kə-līd′) *intr.v.* **col·lid·ed, col·lid·ing, col·lides** **1.** To strike or bump together with violent direct impact: *The car was badly damaged when it collided with the tree.* **2.** To meet in opposition or conflict; clash: *The interests of the two nations collided over fishing rights in coastal waters.* [From Latin *collīdere* : *com-*, together + *laedere*, to strike.]

col·lie (kŏl′ē) *n.* A medium-sized to large dog of a breed originally developed in Scotland to herd sheep, having long white and tan hair and a narrow snout. [From Scots, perhaps variant of *colly*, like coal, from Middle English *col*, coal.]

col·lier (kŏl′yər) *n.* **1.** A coal miner. **2.** A ship for carrying coal.

col·lin·e·ar (kə-lĭn′ē-ər) *adj.* **1.** Lying on the same straight line, as a set of points. **2.** Sharing a common line, as two intersecting planes.

col·li·sion (kə-lĭzh′ən) *n.* The act or process of colliding; a crash or conflict.

col·loid (kŏl′oid′) *n.* A mixture in which very small particles of one substance are distributed evenly throughout another substance. Paints, milk, and fog are colloids. ❖ *adj.* Colloidal.

col·loi·dal (kə-loid′l) *adj.* Relating to or containing a colloid: *Foam rubber is a colloidal suspension of air in a rubber mixture.*

col·lo·qui·al (kə-lō′kwē-əl) *adj.* Characteristic of or suitable to spoken language or to writing that resembles speech; informal. **—col·lo′qui·al·ly** *adv.* **—col·lo′qui·al·ness** *n.*

col·lo·qui·al·ism (kə-lō′kwē-ə-lĭz′əm) *n.* **1.** Colloquial style or quality: *That writer uses colloquialism to make her characters sound more natural.* **2.** A colloquial expression: *"Up a tree" is a colloquialism meaning "in a difficult situation."*

col·lo·quy (kŏl′ə-kwē) *n., pl.* **col·lo·quies** A conversation or conference, especially a formal one. [From Middle English *colloquie*, discourse, from Latin *colloquium*, conversation : *com-*, together + *loquī*, to speak.]

col·lu·sion (kə-lo͞o′zhən) *n.* A secret agreement between people seeking to deceive or cheat someone else. **—col·lu′sive** (kə-lo͞o′sĭv) *adj.*

co·logne (kə-lōn′) *n.* A scented liquid made of alcohol and fragrant oils, used as light perfume.

Co·logne (kə-lōn′) A city of western Germany on the Rhine River north of Bonn. It was a Roman settlement after AD 50.

Co·lom·bi·a (kə-lŭm′bē-ə) A country of northwest South America north of Ecuador and Peru with coastlines on the Pacific Ocean and the Caribbean Sea. Bogotá is the capital.

Co·lom·bo (kə-lŭm′bō) The capital of Sri Lanka, on the western coast of the island on the Indian Ocean.

co·lon[1] (kō′lən) *n.* **1.** A punctuation mark (:) used after a word introducing a quotation, explanation, example, or series. **2.** The sign (:) used between numbers or groups of numbers in expressions of time (2:30 AM, read as "two thirty AM") and ratios (1:2, read as "one to two"). [From Greek *kōlon*, limb, member, metrical unit.]

co·lon[2] (kō′lən) *n.* The section of the large intestine, extending from the cecum to the rectum, in which solid waste is accumulated and prepared for excretion. [From Middle English, from Greek *kolon*, large intestine.]

co·lon[2] (kō-lōn′) *n., pl.* **co·lons** or **co·lo·nes** (kō-lō′nās′) The basic monetary unit of Costa Rica and El Salvador. [From Spanish *colón*, after Cristóbal *Colón*, Christopher Columbus.]

colo·nel (kûr′nəl) *n.* An officer in the US Army, Air Force, or Marine Corps ranking below a brigadier general and above a major. [From Old Italian *colonello*, from Latin *columna*, column.]

❑ *These sound alike:* **colonel, kernel** (seed).

co·lo·ni·al (kə-lō′nē-əl) *adj.* **1.** Relating to, forming, or possessing a colony or colonies: *France and England were colonial powers in Africa and Asia. Most corals are colonial animals.* **2.** often **Colonial** Relating to the 13 British colonies that became the United States of America: *the Colonial period of British rule before the Revolutionary War.* **3.** often **Colonial** Relating to the style of architecture and furniture often found in the British colonies in America. ❖ *n.* A person who lives in a colony: *French colonials in Vietnam.* **—co·lo′ni·al·ly** *adv.*

co·lo·ni·al·ism (kə-lō′nē-ə-lĭz′əm) *n.* A governmental policy of acquiring or maintaining foreign territory as colonies.

col·o·nist (kŏl′ə-nĭst) *n.* **1.** An original settler or founder of a colony. **2.** A person who lives in a colony.

col·o·nize (kŏl′ə-nīz′) *tr.v.* **col·o·nized, col·o·niz·ing, col·o·niz·es** **1.** To establish or settle a colony in: *Norwegian Vikings originally colonized Iceland.* **2.** To spread or proliferate in: *the birds that colonized Madagascar; beetles that colonize dead trees.* **—col′o·ni·za′tion** (kŏl′ə-nĭ-zā′shən) *n.* **—col′o·niz′er** *n.*

col·on·nade (kŏl′ə-nād′) *n.* A series of columns placed at regular intervals to support a roof or other structure of a building.

col·o·ny (kŏl′ə-nē) *n., pl.* **col·o·nies** **1.** A group of people who settle in a distant land but remain subject to their native country: *The English Pilgrims founded a colony at Plymouth.* **2.** A territory ruled by a distant power: *The government built railroads in each of its colonies.* **3. Colonies** The Thirteen Colonies. **4.** A group of people of the same nationality, religion, or interests, living together in one area: *the American colony in Paris; an artists' colony.* **5.** A group of the same kind of organisms living or growing together: *a colony of ants; a colony of bacteria.* [From Middle English *colonie*, from Latin *colōnia*.]

col·or (kŭl′ər) *n.* **1.** The property by which objects reflect, transmit, or emit particular wavelengths of light. Colors can be described in terms of their hue, their saturation, and their lightness or brightness. **2.** The distinct sensation produced when light of a particular wavelength or combination of wavelengths strikes the retina of the eye. **3.** A color other than black, white, or gray. **4.** A dye, pigment, paint, or other coloring substance. **5.** The general appearance of the skin, especially an appearance indicating good health: *The patient regained her color after a few days' rest.* **6a.** Skin pigmentation considered as a racial characteristic: *people of all colors; laws against discrimination based on color.* **b.** Racial identity other than white: *Blacks, Asians, and other people of color.* **7. colors a.** A flag or banner, as of a country or military unit: *At the beginning of the ceremony, they raised the colors.* **b.** A distinguishing symbol, badge, ribbon, color, or mark of something: *a tie with the college's colors on it.* **8.** Vivid and interesting detail, as of a scene or of an event in writing: *The author's description of the political campaign had a great deal of color.* **9.** Traits of personality or behavior that are appealing. ❖ *v.* **col·ored, col·or·ing, col·ors** *—tr.* **1.** To give color to or change the color of: *color a picture with crayons.* **2.** To give a distinctive character or quality to: *A sense of humor colored the author's writing.* **3.** To influence, especially by distortion or misrepresentation: *Anger colored the witness's account of the accident.* *—intr.* **1.** To take on or change color. **2.** To

collie

colonnade
courtyard of the Palace of the Legion of Honor, San Francisco, California

GEOGRAPHY

Colorado The name **Colorado** comes from a Spanish word meaning "colored, especially reddish colored." Spanish explorers first gave this name to the Colorado River, on account of its reddish waters. The state took its name from the river.

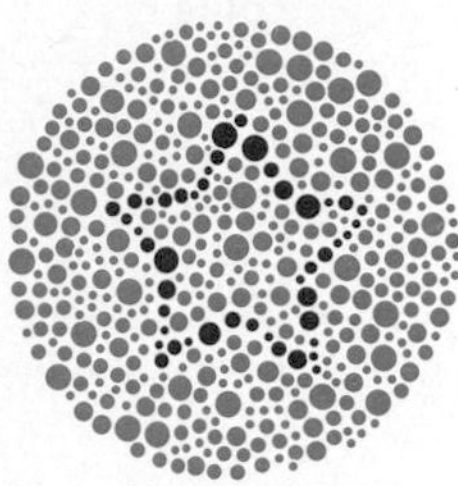

colorblind
A person with red-green colorblindness is unable to distinguish the red star within the green circle.

colossal
Buddha statue in Monywa, Myanmar, standing 423 feet high

ă	pat	ôr	core
ā	pay	oi	boy
âr	care	ou	out
ä	father	o͝o	took
ĕ	pet	o͝or	lure
ē	be	o͞o	boot
ĭ	pit	ŭ	cut
ī	bite	ûr	urge
îr	pier	th	thin
ŏ	pot	*th*	this
ō	toe	zh	vision
ô	paw	ə	about

blush. [From Middle English *colour*, from Latin *color*.] **—col′or·er** *n.*

Col·o·ra·do (kŏl′ə-**răd′**ō *or* kŏl′ə-**rä′**dō) A state of the west-central United States north of New Mexico. It was admitted as the 38th state in 1876. The region was explored by the Spanish in the 1500s and 1600s. Denver is the capital. —SEE NOTE.

Colorado River A river of the southwest United States rising in the Rocky Mountains and flowing about 1,450 miles (2,350 kilometers) southwest to the Pacific Ocean in northwest Mexico. The most spectacular of its many gorges is the Grand Canyon.

col·or·a·tion (kŭl′ə-**rā′**shən) *n.* Arrangement of colors: *Protective coloration helps some animals to hide from their enemies.*

col·or·blind or **col·or-blind** (**kŭl′**ər-blīnd′) *adj.* Partly or totally unable to distinguish certain colors, such as red and green. **—col′or·blind′ness** *n.*

col·or-code (**kŭl′**ər-kōd′) *tr.v.* **col·or-cod·ed, col·or-cod·ing, col·or-codes** To color according to a code for easy identification: *color-code the sections of a telephone directory.*

col·ored (**kŭl′**ərd) *adj.* **1.** Having color. **2.** often **Colored** *Offensive* Relating to or belonging to a racial or ethnic group having dark skin or descended from people with dark skin. **3.** Distorted by prejudice or biased by self-interest: *The drivers each gave a very colored version of the accident.*

col·or·fast (**kŭl′**ər-făst′) *adj.* Having color that will not run or fade with washing or wear: *a colorfast fabric.*

col·or·ful (**kŭl′**ər-fəl) *adj.* **1.** Full of color or colors: *Many butterflies have colorful wings.* **2.** Rich in variety; vivid; distinctive: *a colorful description of life in a medieval castle.* **—col′or·ful·ly** *adv.* **—col′or·ful·ness** *n.*

col·or·ing (**kŭl′**ər-ĭng) *n.* **1.** The manner or process of applying color: *The government regulates the artificial coloring of packaged foods.* **2.** A substance used to color something: *I'm thinking of using a hair coloring.* **3.** Appearance with regard to color: *Some animals are protected by their coloring.*

col·or·ize (**kŭl′**ə-rīz′) *tr.v.* **col·or·ized, col·or·iz·ing, col·or·iz·es** To color (a black and white film) by means of a computer process. **—col′or·i·za′tion** (kŭl′ər-ĭ-**zā′**shən) *n.*

col·or·less (**kŭl′**ər-lĭs) *adj.* **1.** Lacking color: *Air is colorless.* **2.** Weak in color; pallid: *the colorless face of the sick boy.* **3.** Lacking in variety, interest, or distinction; dull: *a colorless account of the event.* **—col′or·less·ly** *adv.* **—col′or·less·ness** *n.*

co·los·sal (kə-**lŏs′**əl) *adj.* Very great in size, extent, or degree; enormous; gigantic: *a city full of colossal buildings; a daring venture requiring colossal self-confidence.* **—co·los′sal·ly** *adv.*

col·os·se·um (kŏl′ĭ-**sē′**əm) *n.* Variant of **coliseum.**

co·los·sus (kə-**lŏs′**əs) *n., pl.* **co·los·si** (kə-**lŏs′**ī′) or **co·los·sus·es 1.** A huge statue. **2.** Something of enormous size or importance: *a colossus among software companies.*

col·our (**kŭl′**ər) *n. & v. Chiefly British* Variant of **color.**

colt (kōlt) *n.* A young male horse.

col·tan (**kŏl′**tăn′) *n.* A dull black mixture of columbite and tantalite, mined as a source of niobium and tantalum.

colt·ish (**kōl′**tĭsh) *adj.* **1.** Relating to a colt: *coltish behavior.* **2.** Resembling a colt; lively; playful: *the coltish antics of the children at the playground.*

Col·trane (**kōl′**trān), **John William** 1926–1967. American jazz saxophonist and composer known for his innovations in jazz improvisation.

Co·lum·bi·a (kə-**lŭm′**bē-ə) The capital of South Carolina, in the central part of the state. It was nearly destroyed in a fire during the Civil War.

Columbia River A river rising in southeast British Columbia, Canada, and flowing about 1,240 miles (2,000 kilometers) south then west along the Washington-Oregon border to the Pacific Ocean.

col·um·bine (**kŏl′**əm-bīn′) *n.* Any of various garden plants that have colorful flowers with five narrow projecting parts. [From Middle English, from Latin *columba*, dove.]

co·lum·bite (kə-**lŭm′**bīt′) *n.* A black, red-brown, or colorless mineral, the principal ore of niobium.

Co·lum·bus (kə-**lŭm′**bəs) The capital of Ohio, in the central part of the state northeast of Cincinnati. It was laid out in 1812.

Columbus, Christopher 1451–1506. Italian explorer in the service of Spain whose attempt to reach Asia by sailing west from Europe instead led him to the Americas in 1492 and began a new era of European exploration and colonization in the Western Hemisphere.

Columbus Day *n.* October 12, celebrated officially on the second Monday in October in honor of Christopher Columbus.

col·umn (**kŏl′**əm) *n.* **1.** A pillar, usually shaped like a cylinder, used in a building as a support or as a decoration. **2.** Something that resembles a pillar in shape or use: *a column of mercury in a thermometer.* **3.** One of two or more vertical sections of a page, lying side by side but separated from each other, in which lines of print are arranged: *Newspapers are often printed in six columns across the page.* **4.** A feature article that appears regularly in a newspaper or magazine: *a sports column; an advice column.* **5.** A formation, as of soldiers or trucks, in which members or rows follow one behind the other. [From Middle English *columpne*, from Latin *columna*.]

co·lum·nar (kə-**lŭm′**nər) *adj.* Having the shape of a column: *the columnar trunks of the redwoods.*

col·um·nist (**kŏl′**əm-nĭst *or* **kŏl′**ə-mĭst) *n.* A person who writes a column for a newspaper or magazine.

Com. *abbr.* An abbreviation of: **1.** commissioner. **2.** commonwealth.

com– or **col–** or **con–** or **cor–** *pref.* A prefix that means together or with: *commingle.* —SEE NOTE.

co·ma[1] (**kō′**mə) *n., pl.* **co·mas** A state of deep unconsciousness resulting from disease, injury, or poisoning. [From Greek *kōma*, deep sleep.]

co·ma[2] (**kō′**mə) *n., pl.* **co·mae** (**kō′**mē) A luminous gaseous cloud around the nucleus of a comet. [From Greek *komē*, hair.]

Co·man·che (kə-**măn′**chē) *n., pl.* **Comanche** or **Co·man·ches 1.** A member of a Native American people formerly of the southern Great Plains and now living in Oklahoma. **2.** The Uto-Aztecan language of the Comanche. **—Co·man′che** *adj.*

co·ma·tose (**kō′**mə-tōs′) *adj.* **1.** Being in a coma; deeply unconscious. **2.** Asleep, inactive, or not responding: *My friends sat comatose in front of the TV.*

comb (kōm) *n.* **1.** A thin toothed strip used to smooth, arrange, or fasten the hair. **2.** Something resembling a comb in shape or use, as a card for arranging and cleaning wool. **3.** The brightly colored ridge of flesh on the top of the head of a rooster, hen, or certain other birds. **4.** A honeycomb. ❖ *v.* **combed, comb·ing, combs** *—tr.* **1.** To move a comb through (the hair) so as to arrange or groom. **2.** To search thoroughly: *combed many books for information.* *—intr.* To make a thorough search: *combed through the documents.* [From Old English *camb, comb.*]

com·bat (kəm-**băt′** *or* **kŏm′**băt′) *tr.v.* **com·bat·ed, com·bat·ing, com·bats** or **com·bat·ted, com·bat·ting, com·bats 1.** To oppose in battle; fight against. **2.** To act or work in order to eliminate, curtail, or stop: *new drugs that combat infection.* See Synonyms at **oppose.** ❖ *n.* (**kŏm′**băt′) Fighting, especially with weapons: *naval* *combat.* [From Late Latin *combattere* : Latin *com-*, with, against + Latin *battere*, to beat.]

com·bat·ant (kəm-**băt′**nt *or* **kŏm′**bə-tnt) *n.* A person engaged in fighting or combat.

combat boot *n.* A boot that laces up the front and has a thick rubber outer sole, worn especially by soldiers.

com·bat·ive (kəm-**băt′**ĭv) *adj.* Ready or disposed to fight; belligerent: *the lawyer's combative disposition.* **—com·bat′ive·ness** *n.*

comb·er (**kō′**mər) *n.* **1.** A person or thing that combs something, such as wool. **2.** A long wave that has reached its peak or broken into foam; a breaker.

com·bi·na·tion (kŏm′bə-**nā′**shən) *n.* **1.** The act of combining or the condition of being combined: *The combination of fresh air and sunshine produced a beautiful day.* **2.** Something that results from combining two or more things: *An alloy is a combination of metals.* **3.** The series of numbers or letters used to open a combination lock. **4.** In mathematics, any of the possible arrangements of numbers or letters in a set.

combination lock *n.* A lock that can be opened only by turning its dial through a particular sequence of numbers or letters.

com·bine (kəm-**bīn′**) *v.* **com·bined, com·bin·ing, com·bines** *—tr.* **1.** To bring together; make united; join: *a movie that combines an interesting story and a moral.* See Synonyms at **join. 2.** To join (two or more substances) to make a single substance; blend; mix: *combine water, gravel, and cement to make concrete.* *—intr.* **1.** To become united; come together: *Friends combined to help the family after the fire.* **2.** To form a compound: *Two atoms of hydrogen combine with one of oxygen to form water.* ❖ *n.* (**kŏm′**bīn′) **1.** A power-operated machine that cuts, threshes, and cleans grain. **2.** A group of people or companies acting together in a business transaction. [From Middle English *combinen*, from Late Latin *combīnāre* : Latin *com-*, together + *bīnī*, two by two.]

com·bin·ing form (kəm-**bī′**nĭng) *n.* A form of a word that combines with other word forms to create new words, as *electro–* (from *electric*) in *electromagnet.*

com·bo (**kŏm′**bō) *n., pl.* **com·bos 1.** A small group of musicians: *a jazz combo.* **2.** *Informal* A combination.

com·bust (kəm-**bŭst′**) *intr.v.* **com·bust·ed, com·bust·ing, com·busts** To catch fire or burn: *The oily rags suddenly combusted.*

com·bus·ti·ble (kəm-**bŭs′**tə-bəl) *adj.* Capable of catching fire and burning. ❖ *n.* A substance that catches fire and burns quickly. **—com·bus′ti·bil′i·ty** *n.* **—com·bus′ti·bly** *adv.*

com·bus·tion (kəm-**bŭs′**chən) *n.* **1.** The process of burning: *the combustion of oil in the furnace.* **2.** A chemical reaction, especially a rapid combination with oxygen, accompanied by heat and light.

Comdr. *abbr.* An abbreviation of commander.

Comdt. *abbr.* An abbreviation of commandant.

come (kŭm) *intr.v.* **came** (kām), **come, com·ing, comes 1.** To advance toward the speaker or toward a specified place; approach: *Come over here.* **2.** To arrive at a particular result or end: *The rivals came to an agreement. Their arrangements finally came to nothing.* **3.** To move toward or arrive at a particular condition: *The new garden is coming along well.* **4.** To move or be brought to a particular position: *The bus came to a stop.* **5.** To extend; reach: *The snow came up to the window ledge.* **6a.** To exist at a particular point or place: *The date of birth comes after the name in this listing.* **b.** To rank; have priority: *Work comes first. A comes before B.* **7a.** To happen: *How did they come to be invited?* **b.** To happen as a result: *Difficulty often comes from stubbornness.* **8.** To occur in the mind: *Sounds of the city come back to me.* **9.** To issue forth: *The giggle came from the back of the class.* **10.** To arise; originate: *Oaks come from acorns.* **11.** To be a native or resident of a particular place: *Her family comes from Chicago.* **12.** To become: *The knot came loose.* **13.** To be available or obtainable: *Shoes come in many styles.* **14.** To prove or turn out to be: *The dream came true.* ◆ **come about 1.** To occur; take place; happen: *It came about that we could go.* **2.** In sailing, to change tack or direction. **come across** To meet or find by chance: *We came across some letters in the attic.* **come around 1.** To recover; revive: *He fainted but came around quickly.* **2.** To change one's opinion or position: *The coach came around after hearing the whole story.* **come back 1.** To remember; recall: *The author's name came back to me.* **2.** To return to past success after a period of misfortune: *The town came back after the flood.* **come by** To acquire; get: *How did you come by that chair?* **come down 1.** To lose wealth or position. **2.** To be handed down by tradition: *a custom that comes down from colonial times.* **come down with** To become sick with (an illness): *came down with a cold.* **come in for** *Informal* To receive; get: *The reporter's work came in for criticism.* **come off** To happen; occur: *The celebration came off on schedule.* **come out 1.** To become known: *The whole story came out in the trial.* **2.** To be issued or brought out: *The author's new book just came out.* **3.** To declare oneself publicly: *The president has come out for the tax proposal.* **4.** To result; end up; turn out: *Everything came out fine.* **5.** To make a formal social debut. **come through** To do what is required or expected: *I asked for their help, and they came through.* **come to 1.** To regain consciousness. **2.** To amount to: *The bill came to $15.* **come up 1.** To show up; arise: *The question didn't come up at the meeting.* **2.** To rise: *The sun came up.* **come up against** To encounter or confront: *We came up against many problems.* **come upon** To discover or meet by accident. **come up with** *Informal* To propose; produce: *The committee came up with some interesting new ideas.* **how come?** *Informal* Why: *How come they left early?* [From Old English *cuman.*]

come·back (**kŭm′**băk′) *n.* **1.** A return to prosperity, popularity, or high rank: *The struggling tennis star made a comeback by winning the latest tournament.* **2.** A reply, especially a quick witty one; a retort.

co·me·di·an (kə-**mē′**dē-ən) *n.* **1.** A professional entertainer who tells jokes or does other things intended to make audiences laugh. **2.** A person who amuses or tries to be amusing; a clown: *the office comedian.* **3.** An actor in comedy.

co·me·di·enne (kə-mē′dē-**ĕn′**) *n.* A woman professional entertainer who tells jokes or does other things intended to make audiences laugh.

come·down (**kŭm′**doun′) *n.* A decline or drop in status or position: *Losing so badly was quite a comedown for the former champion.*

com·e·dy (**kŏm′**ĭ-dē) *n., pl.* **com·e·dies 1.** A play, motion picture, operetta, or other work that has a funny story with humorous characters and usually a happy ending. **2.** The branch of drama made up of such plays or other dramatic works: *The actor found comedy more difficult than tragedy.* **3.** Popular entertainment consisting of jokes, satire, and other things meant to be humorous. **4.** A funny incident. [From Middle English *comedie*, from Greek *kōmōidiā* : *kōmos*, revel + *aoidē*, song.] **—co·me′dic** (kə-**mē′**dĭk) *adj.*

come·ly (**kŭm′**lē) *adj.* **come·li·er, come·li·est** Having a pleasing appearance; attractive: *a comely face.* **—come′li·ness** *n.*

come-on (**kŭm′**ŏn′) *n.* Something offered to allure or attract; an inducement: *The come-on for renting cars was a free tank of gas.*

com·er (**kŭm′**ər) *n.* **1.** A person or thing that arrives or comes: *All comers were welcome at the free soccer clinic.* **2.** A person or thing that shows promise of reaching

columbine

Christopher Columbus

WORD BUILDING

com– The basic meaning of the prefix **com–** is "together, with." It comes from the Latin prefix *com–*. Before the consonants *l* and *r,* Latin *com–* became *col–* and *cor–*, respectively, as we see in our words *collaborate* and *correspond.* Before all other consonants except *p, b,* or *m, com–* became *con–*, as in *confirm, constitution,* and *contribute.* For more information, see Note at **co–.**

combine

comet
Comet Hyakutake

success: *The critics think the young pianist may be a real comer.*

com·et (kŏm′ĭt) *n.* An object in the solar system consisting of a dense nucleus of frozen gases and dust, which develops a luminous halo and tail when near the sun. Comets travel around the sun in an immense elongated orbit. [From Middle English *comete*, from Greek *komētēs*, long-haired (star).]

come·up·pance (kŭm′**ŭp′**əns) *n.* Punishment or retribution that one deserves: *The bully finally got his comeuppance.*

com·fort (**kŭm′**fərt) *tr.v.* **com·fort·ed, com·fort·ing, com·forts 1.** To soothe in time of grief or fear; console: *comfort a lost child.* **2.** To help relieve the pain and suffering of: *A nurse comforted the patient by putting a pillow behind her back.* ❖ *n.* **1.** A condition of ease or well-being: *Pillows are available for the comfort of the passengers.* **2.** Relief in time of pain, grief, or fear: *The frightened child ran to its mother for comfort.* **3.** A person or thing that provides relief, ease, or well-being: *His friends were a comfort to him during his long illness.* **4.** The capacity or ability to give ease or a sense of well-being: *Curtains and soft chairs added to the comfort of the room.* [From Middle English *comforten*, from Late Latin *cōnfortāre*.]

com·fort·a·ble (**kŭm′**fər-tə-bəl *or* **kŭmf′**tə-bəl *or* **kŭmf′**tər-bəl) *adj.* **1.** Providing physical comfort: *a comfortable chair.* **2.** Free from worry or anxiety; at ease: *I felt very comfortable on stage.* **3.** Enough to meet a need; sufficient: *a comfortable income for a small family.* **—com′fort·a·ble·ness** *n.* **—com′fort·a·bly** *adv.*

com·fort·er (**kŭm′**fər-tər) *n.* **1.** A person or thing that comforts: *a comforter of the sick.* **2.** A thick warm quilt used as a bed cover.

comfort food *n.* Food that is simply prepared and associated with a sense of home or contentment.

com·fy (**kŭm′**fē) *adj.* **com·fi·er, com·fi·est** *Informal* Comfortable.

com·ic (**kŏm′**ĭk) *adj.* **1.** Relating to comedy: *comic writing.* **2.** Humorous; amusing: *a comic situation.* ❖ *n.* **1.** A person who is funny or amusing, especially a comedian: *a nightclub where comics tell jokes before an audience.* **2. comics** *Informal* Comic strips. [From Middle English *comice*, from Greek *kōmikos*, from *kōmos*, revel.]

com·i·cal (**kŏm′**ĭ-kəl) *adj.* Causing amusement or laughter; funny: *The dog looked comical wearing a bow tie.* **—com′i·cal·ly** *adv.* **—com′i·cal·ness** *n.*

comic book *n.* A book of comic strips or cartoons, usually telling a story.

comic strip *n.* A series of cartoons that tells a joke or a story, usually printed in a newspaper.

com·ing (**kŭm′**ĭng) *adj.* **1.** Approaching; next: *The coastal towns prepared for the coming storm.* **2.** Showing promise of fame or success: *a young and coming political leader.* ❖ *n.* Arrival: *With the coming of spring, the days become longer.*

com·ma (**kŏm′**ə) *n.* A punctuation mark (,) used to indicate a separation of elements within a sentence. [From Greek *komma*, piece cut off, short clause, from *koptein*, to cut.]

comma fault *n.* The improper use of a comma to join two independent clauses. For example, the sentence *We ran hard, we missed the bus anyway* has a comma fault that could be fixed by adding the conjunction *but* after the comma.

com·mand (kə-**mănd′**) *v.* **com·mand·ed, com·mand·ing, com·mands** *—tr.* **1.** To direct with authority; give orders to: *The control tower commanded the pilot to land elsewhere.* **2.** To have control or authority over; rule: *The general commands thousands of troops.* **3.** To receive as something that has been earned: *His bravery commands respect.* **4.** To occupy a dominant or strategic position over: *The fort commands the approach to the harbor.* *—intr.* **1.** To give orders: *The coach commanded loudly from the sideline.* **2.** To exercise authority as a commander; be in control: *The general commanded through a staff of junior officers.* ❖ *n.* **1.** An order or direction: *Dogs can be trained to follow commands.* **2.** The possession or exercise of authority to command: *The admiral was in command of the navy.* **3.** Ability to control or use; mastery: *She has a command of French and Russian.* **4a.** The extent or range of a commander: *He has command over three battalions.* **b.** A military unit or area under the control of one officer. ❖ *adj.* **1.** Relating to or being a command: *a command decision.* **2.** Done in response to a command: *a command performance.* [From Middle English *commaunden*, from Late Latin *commandāre*.]

com·man·dant (kŏm′ən-**dănt′** *or* kŏm′ən-**dänt′**) *n.* A commanding officer of a military organization.

com·man·deer (kŏm′ən-**dîr′**) *tr.v.* **com·man·deered, com·man·deer·ing, com·man·deers** To seize (property) for public use, especially for military use: *The soldiers commandeered a heavy truck when their own vehicle broke down.*

com·mand·er (kə-**măn′**dər) *n.* **1.** A person who commands, especially a commanding military officer. **2.** An officer in the US Navy or Coast Guard ranking below a captain and above a lieutenant commander.

commander in chief *n., pl.* **commanders in chief 1.** The commander of all the armed forces of a nation: *The president is commander in chief of the armed forces of the United States.* **2.** The officer commanding a major armed force: *the commander in chief of Pacific forces.*

com·mand·ing (kə-**măn′**dĭng) *adj.* **1.** Having command; in charge: *The captain is the commanding member of a ship's crew.* **2.** Dominating, as by reason of position or size: *a commanding lead over an opponent.*

commanding officer *n.* A military officer in charge of a unit, post, camp, base, or station.

com·mand·ment (kə-**mănd′**mənt) *n.* **1. Commandment** One of the Ten Commandments in the Bible. **2.** A command; an order.

com·man·do (kə-**măn′**dō) *n., pl.* **com·man·dos** or **com·man·does** A member of a small fighting force trained for making quick raids into enemy territory. [From Afrikaans *kommando*, from Dutch *commando*, unit of troops, from Spanish *comando*, from *comandar*, to command, from Late Latin *commandāre*.]

com·mem·o·rate (kə-**mĕm′**ə-rāt′) *tr.v.* **com·mem·o·rat·ed, com·mem·o·rat·ing, com·mem·o·rates 1.** To honor the memory of (someone or something), especially with a ceremony: *The crowd gathered in the park to commemorate the firefighters' sacrifice.* **2.** To be a memorial to, as a holiday, ceremony, or statue: *Independence Day commemorates the adoption of the Declaration of Independence.* **—com·mem′o·ra′tion** *n.*

com·mem·o·ra·tive (kə-**mĕm′**ər-ə-tĭv *or* kə-**mĕm′**ə-rā′tĭv) *adj.* Serving to commemorate: *a commemorative plaque; a commemorative service.*

com·mence (kə-**mĕns′**) *intr. & tr.v.* **com·menced, com·menc·ing, com·menc·es** To begin; start: *The festivities commenced with the singing of the national anthem. Has the senate commenced the investigation?* See Synonyms at **begin.** [From Middle English *commencen*, from Old French *comencier* : Latin *com-*, intensive prefix + Late Latin *initiāre*, to begin.]

com·mence·ment (kə-**mĕns′**mənt) *n.* **1.** A beginning; a start: *The commencement of the Olympic Games is marked by a parade.* **2.** A graduation ceremony in which students receive their diplomas.

com·mend (kə-**mĕnd′**) *tr.v.* **com·mend·ed, com·mend·ing, com·mends 1.** To speak highly of; praise: *The principal commended the students for their skill in algebra.* **2.** To recommend: *I commend the book without hesitation.*

ă	pat	ôr	core
ā	pay	oi	boy
âr	care	ou	out
ä	father	ŏŏ	took
ĕ	pet	ŏŏr	lure
ē	be	ōō	boot
ĭ	pit	ŭ	cut
ī	bite	ûr	urge
îr	pier	th	thin
ŏ	pot	*th*	this
ō	toe	zh	vision
ô	paw	ə	about

3. To put in the care of someone: *The sick patient was commended to the care of the doctor.* [From Middle English *commenden*, from Latin *commendare*.]

com·mend·a·ble (kə-**mĕn′**də-bəl) *adj.* Praiseworthy: *a commendable performance of a difficult play.* **—com·mend′a·bly** *adv.*

com·men·da·tion (kŏm′ən-**dā′**shən) *n.* **1.** Praise: *a performance worthy of commendation.* **2.** An official award or citation: *She received a commendation from the mayor for her service to the city.* **—com·men′da·to′ry** (kə-**mĕn′**də-tôr′ē) *adj.*

com·men·sal (kə-**mĕn′**səl) *adj.* Relating to or characterized by commensalism. ❖ *n.* An organism living in a commensal relationship with another. [From Middle English, sharing a meal, from Medieval Latin *commēnsālis* : Latin *com-*, together + Latin *mēnsa*, table.]

com·men·sal·ism (kə-**mĕn′**sə-lĭz′əm) *n.* A relationship between two organisms of different species in which one benefits while the other is unaffected, as when an orchid uses a tree branch for support.

com·men·su·ra·ble (kə-**mĕn′**sər-ə-bəl *or* kə-**mĕn′**shər-ə-bəl) *adj.* Properly proportioned; fitting; suitable: *The judge handed down a heavy sentence commensurable to the seriousness of the crime.* **—com·men′su·ra·bly** *adv.*

com·men·su·rate (kə-**mĕn′**sər-ĭt *or* kə-**mĕn′**shər-ĭt) *adj.* **1.** Of the same size, extent, or length of time as that of another: *Men and women should receive commensurate pay for the same job.* **2.** Corresponding in size or degree; proportionate: *I want a salary commensurate with my performance.* **—com·men′su·rate·ly** *adv.*

com·ment (**kŏm′**ĕnt) *n.* **1.** A written note or a remark that explains, interprets, or gives an opinion on something: *a critic's comment on a play; the newspaper's comments on the governor's speech.* **2.** Talk; gossip: *Their squabbling caused much comment among friends.* ❖ *intr.v.* **com·ment·ed, com·ment·ing, com·ments** To make a comment; remark: *He commented on my new red coat.* [From Middle English, from Late Latin *commentum*, interpretation.]

com·men·tar·y (**kŏm′**ən-tĕr′ē) *n., pl.* **com·men·tar·ies** **1.** A series of explanations or interpretations: *a copy of the Bible that contained a commentary.* **2.** An ongoing series of spoken remarks, especially during a television or radio broadcast of an event: *A retired quarterback does the commentary on the games.* **3.** An illustrating comment: *The scandal is a sad commentary on the state of our city government.*

com·men·ta·tor (**kŏm′**ən-tā′tər) *n.* **1.** A person who makes commentaries: *Many social commentators criticize the state of our cities.* **2.** A writer or broadcaster who explains or gives opinions of events: *The commentators gave opposing views at the end of the newscast.*

com·merce (**kŏm′**ərs) *n.* The buying and selling of goods, especially on a large scale; trade. [From Latin *commercium* : *com-*, together + *merx*, merchandise.]

com·mer·cial (kə-**mûr′**shəl) *adj.* **1.** Relating to commerce: *a commercial loan from the bank.* **2.** Done primarily to make a profit: *The professor writes scholarly books, not commercial ones.* **3.** Sponsored by an advertiser or supported by advertising: *a commercial television station.* ❖ *n.* A paid advertisement on television or radio. **—com·mer′cial·ly** *adv.*

com·mer·cial·ism (kə-**mûr′**shə-lĭz′əm) *n.* The practices of commerce or business, especially those that give chief importance to the making of profit. **—com·mer′cial·is′tic** *adj.*

com·mer·cial·ize (kə-**mûr′**shə-līz′) *tr.v.* **com·mer·cial·ized, com·mer·cial·iz·ing, com·mer·cial·iz·es** **1.** To apply business methods to (something) in order to make a profit: *commercialize agriculture on a large scale.* **2.** To do, make, or exploit mainly for profit: *The town commercialized its beach by putting in a snack shop and video arcade.* **—com·mer′cial·i·za′tion** (kə-mûr′shə-lĭ-**zā′**shən) *n.*

com·min·gle (kə-**mĭng′**gəl) *tr. & intr.v.* **com·min·gled, com·min·gling, com·min·gles** To blend or mix together; combine: *a story that commingles comedy with tragedy; cities where people of many nationalities commingle.*

com·mis·er·ate (kə-**mĭz′**ə-rāt′) *intr.v.* **com·mis·er·at·ed, com·mis·er·at·ing, com·mis·er·ates** To feel or express sorrow or sympathy: *I commiserated with my friend over losing the competition.*

com·mis·er·a·tion (kə-mĭz′ə-**rā′**shən) *n.* A feeling or expression of sorrow or sympathy for the misfortune of another.

com·mis·sar (**kŏm′**ĭ-sär′) *n.* The head of a commissariat in the former Soviet Union.

com·mis·sar·i·at (kŏm′ĭ-**sâr′**ē-ĭt) *n.* **1.** A department of an army in charge of providing food and other supplies for the troops. **2.** A government department of the former Soviet Union, known after 1946 as a ministry.

com·mis·sar·y (**kŏm′**ĭ-sĕr′ē) *n., pl.* **com·mis·sar·ies** **1.** A store maintained by a company or an army post for the sale of food and supplies to its employees or personnel. **2.** A lunchroom or cafeteria that serves the employees of a company or the personnel of an institution, such as a university. **3.** A person to whom a special duty is given by a superior; a deputy.

com·mis·sion (kə-**mĭsh′**ən) *n.* **1.** The act of committing or doing something: *the commission of a crime.* **2.** A group of people who have been given authority by law to perform certain duties: *The president set up a commission to improve education.* **3a.** The act of granting authority to someone to carry out a certain job or duty: *The commission of ambassadors is one of the president's duties.* **b.** The authority given by such a grant: *The secretary of state's commission is to direct US foreign policy.* **4a.** Appointment to the rank of a commissioned officer in the armed forces: *The pilot received a commission in the air force.* **b.** An official document issued by a government conferring such a rank. **5.** Money in the form of a fee or a percentage of a price paid to a salesperson or agent for services: *The dealer's commission on the $500 sale was $50.* ❖ *tr.v.* **com·mis·sioned, com·mis·sion·ing, com·mis·sions** **1.** To grant a commission to: *The monarchs commissioned Columbus to find a western route to India. The Coast Guard commissioned new officers at graduation.* **2.** To place an order for: *The mayor commissioned a new sculpture for City Hall.* **3.** To put (a ship) into active service. ◆ **in commission** **1.** In active service. Used of a ship. **2.** In use or in usable condition: *Only two computers are in commission.* **out of commission** **1.** Not in active service. Used of a ship. **2.** Not in working condition: *Three machines are out of commission and awaiting repair.* [From Middle English *commissioun*, from Latin *commissiō*, from *committere*, to entrust.]

com·mis·sioned officer (kə-**mĭsh′**ənd) *n.* An officer who holds by a commission the rank of a second lieutenant or above in the US Army, Air Force, or Marine Corps or the rank of an ensign or above in the US Navy or Coast Guard.

com·mis·sion·er (kə-**mĭsh′**ə-nər) *n.* **1.** A member of a commission. **2.** An official in charge of a governmental department: *a police commissioner.* **3.** An official chosen by an athletic association or league as administrative head of an organized professional sport: *a baseball commissioner.*

com·mit (kə-**mĭt′**) *tr.v.* **com·mit·ted, com·mit·ting, com·mits** **1.** To do, perform, or be guilty of: *commit a crime; commit a serious blunder.* **2.** To place in the charge or keeping of another; entrust: *commit oneself to the care of a doctor; commit responsibilities to an assistant.* **3.** To place in confinement or custody, as by an

commensalism
epiphyte growing on the trunk of a tree

USAGE

Common Era The traditional system of dating in Europe and the Americas has for its focal point the date of the birth of Jesus (or what was once thought to be the correct date of his birth). Dates for events in the ancient world are thus followed by the abbreviations BC (before Christ) and AD (anno Domini, "in the year of the Lord"). But in the late 1900s many scholars and scientists switched to a dating system that is convenient and familiar but avoids the religious associations of the BC and AD designations. They adopted the term **Common Era.** It is abbreviated CE, with the date 1 CE being the same year as 1 AD. Dates before the Common Era are abbreviated BCE, with 1 BCE being the same year as 1 BC.

ă	pat	ôr	core
ā	pay	oi	boy
âr	care	ou	out
ä	father	o͝o	took
ĕ	pet	o͝or	lure
ē	be	o͞o	boot
ĭ	pit	ŭ	cut
ī	bite	ûr	urge
îr	pier	th	thin
ŏ	pot	*th*	this
ō	toe	zh	vision
ô	paw	ə	about

official act: *The judge committed the criminal to prison for two years.* **4.** To give over, as for future use or for preservation; consign: *commit funds to a project; commit a text to memory.* **5.** To bind or obligate, as by a pledge: *The heirs were committed to follow the terms of the will. New citizens commit themselves to obey the laws of the United States.* **6.** To dedicate (oneself) to someone or something: *The doctor was committed to providing medical services to the poor.* [From Middle English *committen*, from Latin *committere* : *com-*, with + *mittere*, to send.] —**com·mit′ta·ble** *adj.*

com·mit·ment (kə-**mĭt′**mənt) *n.* **1.** The act of committing something: *the commitment of a crime; the commitment of funds to a project.* **2.** A pledge or obligation, as to follow a certain course of action: *The president takes an oath that is a binding commitment to uphold the Constitution.* **3.** Dedication or devotion to another person or to a course of action: *We have a deep commitment to help clean up the environment.*

com·mit·tee (kə-**mĭt′**ē) *n.* A group of people chosen to do a particular job or to fulfill specified duties: *A committee of five members will investigate the best ways of using computers to teach mathematics.* [From Middle English *committe*, trustee, from Anglo-Norman *comité*, past participle of *cometre*, to commit, entrust, from Latin *committere.*] —SEE NOTE AT **collective noun.**

com·mit·tee·man (kə-**mĭt′**ē-mən) *n.* A man who is a member of a committee.

com·mit·tee·wom·an (kə-**mĭt′**ē-wo͝om′ən) *n.* A woman who is a member of a committee.

com·mode (kə-**mōd′**) *n.* **1.** A low cabinet or chest of drawers. **2.** A movable stand containing a washbowl or a chamber pot.

com·mo·di·ous (kə-**mō′**dē-əs) *adj.* Having plenty of room; spacious: *a room with a commodious closet.* —**com·mo′di·ous·ly** *adv.* —**com·mo′di·ous·ness** *n.*

com·mod·i·ty (kə-**mŏd′**ĭ-tē) *n., pl.* **com·mod·i·ties 1.** A product, such as a raw material or an agricultural product, that can be bought and resold, especially in large quantities. Commodities usually do not have brand names or packaging. **2.** Something useful that can be turned to profit or advantage: *Time is a valuable commodity.* [From Middle English *commodite*, from Latin *commoditās*, convenience, from *commodus*, convenient.]

com·mo·dore (**kŏm′**ə-dôr′) *n.* **1.** A former rank in the US Navy that was above captain and below rear admiral. **2.** The presiding officer of a yacht club.

com·mon (**kŏm′**ən) *adj.* **com·mon·er, com·mon·est 1a.** Belonging to or shared equally by two or more: *common interests of the United States and Canada.* **b.** Relating to the community as a whole; public: *health regulations enforced for the common good.* **2a.** Found or occurring often and in many places; widespread: *Cell phones have become common in many parts of the world.* **b.** Usual or expected: *The common reply to "Thank you" is "You're welcome."* **3.** Most widely known of its kind: *the common crow.* **4a.** Having no special rank or status; ordinary: *the common people.* **b.** Of no special quality; standard or regular: *Common sneakers cost less than running shoes.* **5.** Unrefined or coarse in manner; vulgar: *thought her behavior was common.* ❖ *n.* **1.** A tract of land belonging to or used by a community as a whole: *The early New England town had a common for citizens to graze their sheep.* **2. commons** The common people. **3. commons** *(used with a singular or plural verb)* A place for dining, especially at a college or university. **4. Commons** *(used with a singular or plural verb)* The House of Commons. ◆ **in common** Equally with another or others; jointly: *The partners have interests in common.* [From Middle English *commune*, from Latin *commūnis.*] —**com′mon·ness** *n.*

common cold *n.* A viral infection marked by discharge of mucus, sneezing, and watering of the eyes; a cold.

common denominator *n.* A number that is a multiple of the denominators of a group of fractions. For example, since ¼ = ²⁵⁄₁₀₀, ¹⁄₂₅ = ⁴⁄₁₀₀, ³⁄₁₀ = ³⁰⁄₁₀₀, and ⁴⁄₅ = ⁸⁰⁄₁₀₀, the fractions ¼, ¹⁄₂₅, ³⁄₁₀, and ⁴⁄₅ can be expressed with the common denominator 100. By finding a common denominator it is possible to add and subtract fractions.

common divisor *n.* A number that will divide each of a group of numbers without a remainder. For example, 3 is a common divisor of 6, 9, 15, and 24.

com·mon·er (**kŏm′**ə-nər) *n.* A person without noble rank or title.

Common Era *n.* The period of time that coincides with the period beginning with the birth of Jesus. Year 1 CE is the same as year 1 AD. —SEE NOTE.

common factor *n.* A common divisor.

common fraction *n.* A fraction whose numerator and denominator are both whole numbers. For example, ¼, ⁴⁄₅, and ⅞ are common fractions.

common ground *n.* A shared set of beliefs, values, or views that can form the basis for mutual understanding.

common law *n.* The system of law based on court decisions and on customs and usages rather than on an organized body of written laws or statutes. —**com′mon-law′** (**kŏm′**ən-lô′) *adj.*

common logarithm *n.* A logarithm for which the number ten is used as the base.

com·mon·ly (**kŏm′**ən-lē) *adv.* Generally; ordinarily: *Archaic words, such as "methinks," are not commonly used today.*

common multiple *n.* A number divisible by two or more numbers with remainder of zero. For example, 12 is a common multiple of 2, 3, 4, and 6.

common name *n.* An ordinary, everyday name as distinguished from a scientific name, as *sugar maple* for the tree *Acer saccharum.*

common noun *n.* A noun that is the name of a class or group of things or people. Common nouns refer to one or all members, as *teacher, car,* and *crowd,* and are different from proper nouns that name a specific person, place, or thing, as *Iowa, Mozart,* and *Brooklyn Bridge.* —SEE NOTE AT **noun.**

com·mon·place (**kŏm′**ən-plās′) *adj.* Ordinary; common; uninteresting: *a commonplace plot of good guys against bad guys.* ❖ *n.* A statement or remark that is dull or worn out through use.

common sense *n.* Good judgment gained from everyday experience.

common stock *n.* Stock shares in a corporation that entitle the owner to be paid dividends and often assets after payments are made to owners of preferred stock.

common time *n.* In music, a meter in which each measure contains four quarter notes.

com·mon·weal (**kŏm′**ən-wēl′) *n.* **1.** The public good or welfare. **2.** *Archaic* A commonwealth.

com·mon·wealth (**kŏm′**ən-wĕlth′) *n.* **1.** A nation or state governed by the people; a republic. **2. Commonwealth a.** The official title of some US states, specifically Kentucky, Maryland, Massachusetts, Pennsylvania, and Virginia. **b.** The official title of Puerto Rico. **c.** The official title of some democratic countries, such as Australia. **3. Commonwealth** The Commonwealth of Nations.

Commonwealth of Independent States An association of self-governing states including most of the republics of the former Soviet Union. It was formed in 1991.

Commonwealth of Nations also **British Commonwealth** An association made up of the United Kingdom, its dependencies, and many former British colonies.

com·mo·tion (kə-mō′shən) *n.* **1.** A confused and noisy situation; a disturbance: *The argument created a commotion in the hall.* **2.** A condition of turbulent motion: *commotion of the water behind the propeller.*

com·mu·nal (kə-myōō′nəl) *adj.* **1.** Relating to a community or to the common people; public: *our town's communal spirit.* **2.** Shared, owned, or used jointly by the members of a group or community: *communal grazing lands; the communal dining room of a boarding school.* **—com·mu′nal·ly** *adv.*

com·mune[1] (kə-myōōn′) *intr.v.* **com·muned, com·mun·ing, com·munes 1.** To feel a sense of closeness or intimacy: *a hiker communing with nature.* **2.** To receive the Eucharist. [From Middle English *communen*, to have common dealings with, converse, from Old French *communer*, to communicate, share.]

com·mune[2] (**kŏm′**yōōn′ *or* kə-**myōōn′**) *n.* **1.** A small community whose members have common interests and in which property is often shared or owned jointly. **2.** In some European countries, such as France and Italy, the smallest division of local government. [From French, from Medieval Latin *commūnia*, community.]

com·mu·ni·ca·ble (kə-**myōō′**nĭ-kə-bəl) *adj.* Capable of being communicated or transmitted from person to person: *Chickenpox and measles are communicable diseases.* **—com·mu′ni·ca·ble·ness** *n.* **—com·mu′ni·ca·bly** *adv.*

com·mu·ni·cant (kə-**myōō′**nĭ-kənt) *n.* **1.** A person who receives or is entitled to receive the Eucharist. **2.** A person who communicates something.

com·mu·ni·cate (kə-**myōō′**nĭ-kāt′) *v.* **com·mu·ni·cat·ed, com·mu·ni·cat·ing, com·mu·ni·cates** *—tr.* **1.** To make known; impart: *A good speaker communicates thoughts and ideas clearly.* **2.** To transmit (a disease, for example); pass on. *—intr.* **1.** To have an exchange, as of ideas or information: *The telephone makes it possible to communicate over long distances.* **2.** To express oneself effectively, so as to be readily and clearly understood: *The ability to communicate is a valuable job skill.* [From Latin *commūnicāre*, from *commūnis*, common.] **—com·mu′ni·ca′tor** *n.*

com·mu·ni·ca·tion (kə-myōō′nĭ-**kā′**shən) *n.* **1.** The act of communicating; transmission: *Unsanitary conditions contribute to the communication of disease.* **2.** The exchange of thoughts, information, or messages, as by speech, signals, or writing: *Communication between people of different cultures is often difficult.* **3.** Something communicated; a message. **4. communications a.** A system for sending and receiving messages, as by mail, telephone, or radio: *During the earthquake communications broke down with other towns.* **b.** The field of study concerned with the transmission of information by various means, such as print or broadcasting.

communications satellite *n.* An artificial space satellite used to aid communications, as by reflecting or relaying a television or radio signal from one ground station to another.

com·mu·ni·ca·tive (kə-**myōō′**nĭ-kā′tĭv *or* kə-**myōō′**nĭ-kə-tĭv) *adj.* Communicating thoughts or information readily; not secretive: *The frightened child was not very communicative.* **—com·mu′ni·ca′tive·ly** *adv.* **—com·mu′ni·ca′tive·ness** *n.*

com·mun·ion (kə-**myōōn′**yən) *n.* **1.** The act or an instance of sharing, as of thoughts, feelings, or interests: *We felt a communion with the others who had been through the same ordeal.* **2.** A body of Christians with the same religious faith; a denomination. **3. Communion a.** The Christian sacrament of the Eucharist received by a congregation. **b.** The part of the Mass in which the Eucharist is received.

com·mu·ni·qué (kə-myōō′nĭ-**kā′** *or* kə-**myōō′**nĭ-kā′) *n.* An official announcement, such as one issued to the press after a meeting of world leaders.

com·mu·nism or **Communism** (**kŏm′**yə-nĭz′əm) *n.* **1.** A theoretical economic system based on the writings of Karl Marx and Friedrich Engels and characterized by common ownership of property and by the organization of labor for the benefit of society as a whole. **2a.** A system of government in which the state plans and controls the economy and a single party holds power, claiming to make progress toward a society in which all goods are shared equally by the people. **b.** The version of communist theory advanced by Vladimir Lenin that advocates the violent overthrow of capitalism by the proletariat.

com·mu·nist or **Communist** (**kŏm′**yə-nĭst) *n.* A person who believes in or advocates communism, especially a member of a political party that advocates communism. ❖ *adj.* Relating to, characteristic of, or resembling communism or communists.

com·mu·nis·tic (kŏm′yə-**nĭs′**tĭk) *adj.* Based on or favoring the principles of communism. **—com′mu·nis′ti·cal·ly** *adv.*

com·mu·ni·ty (kə-**myōō′**nĭ-tē) *n., pl.* **com·mu·ni·ties 1a.** A group of people living in the same area: *Our community organized a parade.* **b.** The district or locality in which such a group lives: *a small community of only a few square miles.* **2.** A group of people who have close ties, as through common nationality or interests: *an area of controversy within the scientific community.* **3.** Sharing, participation, and fellowship: *Working together to clean up the park showed our sense of community.* **4.** A group of organisms interacting with one another and with the environment in a specific region. [From Middle English *communite*, from Latin *commūnitās*, fellowship, from *commūnis*, common.]

community chest *n.* A fund raised by contributions from residents and businesses of an area and used for charity.

community college *n.* A junior college that does not have residential facilities and is often funded by the government.

community service *n.* Service that is done without pay to benefit a community or its institutions: *In order to graduate, each student had to perform 20 hours of community service.*

com·mu·ta·tion (kŏm′yə-**tā′**shən) *n.* **1.** The act of lessening something or of making something less severe, as a prison sentence: *a commutation of a jail sentence to community service.* **2.** The travel of a commuter, especially to and from work.

com·mu·ta·tive (**kŏm′**yə-tā′tĭv *or* kə-**myōō′**tə-tĭv) *adj.* Relating to the commutative property.

commutative property *n.* The property of addition and multiplication which states that the order in which numbers are added or multiplied will not change the result of the operation. For example, 2 + 3 gives the same sum as 3 + 2, and 2 × 3 gives the same product as 3 × 2.

com·mu·ta·tor (**kŏm′**yə-tā′tər) *n.* A switching device in electric motors and generators that causes a current to reverse direction.

com·mute (kə-**myōōt′**) *v.* **com·mut·ed, com·mut·ing, com·mutes** *—intr.* To travel as a commuter: *commute to work.* *—tr.* To reduce (a legal sentence) to a less severe one: *commute a sentence of imprisonment to home confinement.* ❖ *n.* A trip made by a commuter: *a commute of 15 miles to work.* [From Middle English *commuten*, to transform, from Latin *commūtāre*.]

com·mut·er (kə-**myōō′**tər) *n.* **1.** A person who travels regularly between a home in one community and work or school in another. **2.** A commercial airplane or airline that carries passengers short distances.

WRITERS CHOOSE THEIR WORDS

The day whizzed by, and so did his afternoon chores and dinner. Suddenly he was dressed in his best clothes and standing next to Benny backstage, listening to the **commotion** as the cafeteria filled with school kids and parents.

—Gary Soto
"La Bamba" in *Baseball in April and Other Stories*

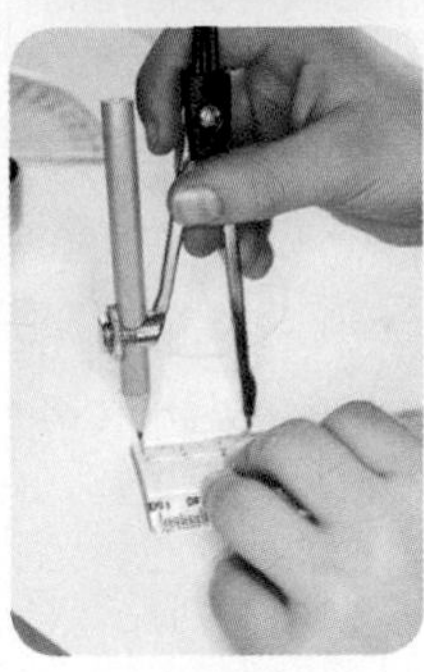

compass
directional *(top)* and drawing *(bottom)* compasses

Com·o·ros (kŏm′ə-rōz′) A country made up of the three main islands and numerous islets of the **Comoro Islands** in the Indian Ocean off southeast Africa between Mozambique and Madagascar. Moroni, on Grand Comoro Island, is the capital.

com·pact[1] (kəm-**păkt′** *or* **kŏm′**păkt′) *adj.* **1.** Closely and firmly united or packed together; solid; dense: *flowers growing in tight compact clusters.* **2.** Occupying little space in comparison with others of the same kind: *a compact camera.* **3.** Brief and to the point; concise: *a compact news summary.* ❖ *tr.v.* (kəm-**păkt′**) **com·pact·ed, com·pact·ing, com·pacts** To press or join firmly together; pack together: *The dirt was compacted by the heavy trucks running over it.* ❖ *n.* (**kŏm′**păkt′) **1.** A small case containing face powder and sometimes blusher. **2.** An automobile that is smaller than a standard model. [From Middle English, from Latin *compāctus*, past participle of *compingere*, to put together : *com-*, together + *pangere*, to fasten.] **—com·pact′ly** *adv.* **—com·pact′ness** *n.*

com·pact[2] (**kŏm′**păkt′) *n.* An agreement or covenant: *a compact between nations to reduce tariffs.* [From Latin *compactum*, past participle of *compacīscī*, to make an agreement : *com-*, together + *pacīscī*, to agree.]

com·pact disc or **com·pact disk** (**kŏm′**păkt′) *n.* A small optical disc containing data, such as music, text, or graphic images, in digital form.

com·pac·tor or **com·pact·er** (kəm-**păk′**tər *or* **kŏm′**-păk′tər) *n.* A machine that compresses trash into small packs for easy disposal.

com·pa·dre (kəm-**pä′**drā) *n. Informal* A close friend; companion.

com·pan·ion (kəm-**păn′**yən) *n.* **1.** A person who accompanies or associates with another; a comrade. **2.** A person hired to assist, live with, or travel with another: *working as a companion to an elderly couple.* **3.** One of a pair or set of things; a mate: *I lost the companion to this sneaker.* [From Middle English *compaignoun*, from Old French *compaignon* : Latin *com-*, together + Latin *pānis*, bread.]

com·pan·ion·a·ble (kəm-**păn′**yə-nə-bəl) *adj.* Suited to be a good companion; friendly: *Most dogs are companionable pets.* **—com·pan′ion·a·bil′i·ty** *n.* **—com·pan′ion·a·bly** *adv.*

com·pan·ion·ship (kəm-**păn′**yən-shĭp′) *n.* The relationship of companions; fellowship.

com·pan·ion·way (kəm-**păn′**yən-wā′) *n.* A staircase leading from a ship's deck to the area below.

com·pa·ny (**kŭm′**pə-nē) *n., pl.* **com·pa·nies 1.** A group of people; a gathering: *A large company of tourists waited outside the White House.* **2.** A guest or guests: *We're having company for dinner.* **3a.** A companion or companions: *I find them very interesting company.* **b.** Companionship: *She went shopping with him, and he was grateful for the company.* **4.** A business enterprise; a firm: *That company makes many useful products.* **5.** A group of performers organized to present stage works, such as plays, operas, and ballets, or to produce motion pictures. **6.** A military unit consisting of two or more platoons. **7.** The officers and crew of a ship: *The ship's company went ashore.* **8.** A unit of firefighters. [From Middle English *compaignie*, from Old French.] —SEE NOTE AT **collective noun.**

com·pa·ra·ble (**kŏm′**pər-ə-bəl) *adj.* **1.** Capable of being compared: *In some ways, the creation of the Internet is comparable to the invention of the printing press.* **2.** Worthy of being compared; similar: *Some photographs are comparable in quality to fine paintings.* **—com′pa·ra·bly** *adv.*

com·par·a·tive (kəm-**păr′**ə-tĭv) *adj.* **1.** Relating to, based on, or involving a comparison: *the comparative study of related languages.* **2.** Estimated or considered in comparison to something else; relative: *He is a comparative beginner in computer skills.* **3.** Relating to or being the intermediate degree of comparison of adjectives or adverbs: *"Bigger" is the comparative form of "big."* ❖ *n.* **1.** In grammar, the comparative degree of an adjective or adverb. **2.** An adjective or adverb expressing the comparative degree. **—com·par′a·tive·ly** *adv.*

com·pare (kəm-**pâr′**) *v.* **com·pared, com·par·ing, com·pares** —*tr.* **1.** To represent as similar; liken: *Shakespeare compared the world to a stage.* **2.** To examine so as to note the similarities and differences of: *Let's compare cooking over heat with cooking in a microwave oven.* **3.** In grammar, to form the positive, comparative, or superlative of (an adjective or adverb). —*intr.* To be worthy of comparison: *His photographs do not compare with yours.* ❖ *n.* Comparison: *Her singing ability is beyond compare.* [From Middle English *comparen*, from Latin *comparāre*, from *compār*, equal : *com-*, with + *pār*, equal.]

com·par·i·son (kəm-**păr′**ĭ-sən) *n.* **1.** The act of comparing: *A comparison of prices shows that you can save money if you shop online.* **2.** The quality of being similar; likeness: *There is no comparison between homemade bread and sliced bread bought in a supermarket.* **3.** In grammar, the changing of the form of the adjective or adverb to indicate the positive, comparative, and superlative degrees.

com·part·ment (kəm-**pärt′**mənt) *n.* **1.** One of the parts or spaces into which something is subdivided: *A cash register drawer is divided into compartments for paper bills and coins.* **2.** A separate room, section, or chamber: *a built-in storage compartment under the stairs.*

com·pass (**kŭm′**pəs *or* **kŏm′**pəs) *n.* **1a.** A device used to determine geographical direction, usually consisting of a magnetic needle mounted so that it points to magnetic north. **b.** Any of several other devices, especially a gyrocompass or a radio compass, used to determine geographical direction. **2.** A device used for drawing circles and arcs and for measuring distances, consisting of two legs hinged together at one end. **3.** Range or scope; extent: *That decision is not within the compass of your authority.* **4.** An enclosing line or boundary; a circumference: *within the compass of the garden.* ❖ *tr.v.* **com·passed, com·pass·ing, com·pass·es 1.** To go around; make a circuit of: *The sailboat compassed the island.* **2.** To surround or encircle: *A ring of hills compasses the valley.* **3.** To succeed in carrying out: *We finally compassed our goal.* **4.** To understand or comprehend: *Scientists tried to compass the implications of the discovery.* [From Middle English *compas*, circle, compass, from Old French, from *compasser*, to measure : Latin *com-*, with + Latin *passus*, step.]

com·pas·sion (kəm-**păsh′**ən) *n.* The deep awareness of the suffering of another, together with a desire to relieve it. [From Middle English *compassioun*, from Late Latin *compassiō*, from *compatī*, to sympathize : Latin *com-*, with + Latin *patī*, to suffer.]

com·pas·sion·ate (kəm-**păsh′**ə-nĭt) *adj.* Feeling or showing compassion; sympathetic: *a compassionate caregiver; compassionate acts.* **—com·pas′sion·ate·ly** *adv.*

com·pat·i·ble (kəm-**păt′**ə-bəl) *adj.* **1.** Capable of living or existing together in agreement or harmony: *They are very compatible with their cousins and enjoyed the trip together.* **2.** Capable of working together in the same system: *Is the printer compatible with the computer?* **3.** Capable of being grafted, transfused, or transplanted from one indivual to another without rejection: *Some blood types are not compatible with each other.* [From Middle English, from Late Latin *compatī*, to sympathize.] **—com·pat′i·bil′i·ty** *n.* **—com·pat′i·bly** *adv.*

com·pa·tri·ot (kəm-**pā′**trē-ət) *n.* A person from one's own country.

ă	pat	ôr	core
ā	pay	oi	boy
âr	care	ou	out
ä	father	ŏŏ	took
ĕ	pet	ŏŏr	lure
ē	be	ōō	boot
ĭ	pit	ŭ	cut
ī	bite	ûr	urge
îr	pier	th	thin
ŏ	pot	*th*	this
ō	toe	zh	vision
ô	paw	ə	about

com·pel (kəm-pĕl′) *tr.v.* **com·pelled, com·pel·ling, com·pels 1.** To make (a person) do something, as by force, necessity, or powerful influence: *Camp rules compelled all campers to pass a water safety test before taking out a boat.* **2.** To make necessary; require or demand: *The teacher compelled obedience from the class. Social change often compels a new way of thinking.* **3.** To exert an irresistible influence on; command: *The book compelled my interest from the very first page.* [From Middle English *compellen*, from Latin *compellere* : *com-*, together + *pellere*, to drive.]

com·pel·ling (kəm-pĕl′ĭng) *adj.* Having a very strong influence or effect; powerful; forceful: *a compelling argument.* **—com·pel′ling·ly** *adv.*

com·pen·di·ous (kəm-pĕn′dē-əs) *adj.* Giving facts or information about a subject in brief but complete form: *News broadcasts are supposed to be compendious reviews of the events of the day.*

com·pen·di·um (kəm-pĕn′dē-əm) *n., pl.* **com·pen·di·ums** or **com·pen·di·a** (kəm-pĕn′dē-ə) **1.** A short but complete summary of something: *a compendium of the committee's views.* **2.** A collection of various items: *a compendium of English poetry.*

com·pen·sate (kŏm′pən-sāt′) *v.* **com·pen·sat·ed, com·pen·sat·ing, com·pen·sates** —*tr.* To make satisfactory payment to; pay or reimburse: *The store compensates its clerks for extra time worked during the holiday season.* —*intr.* To act as or provide a balancing effect; make up: *We worked extra hard to compensate for the hour lost. In baseball speedy running can compensate for weak hitting.* [From Latin *compēnsāre* : *com-*, together + *pēnsāre*, to weigh.] **—com′pen·sa′tor** *n.* **—com·pen′sa·to′ry** (kəm-pĕn′sə-tôr′ē) *adj.*

com·pen·sa·tion (kŏm′pən-sā′shən) *n.* **1.** Something given or received as payment or as a balance for a loss: *The family received little compensation for the loss of their belongings in the fire.* **2.** The act of compensating or the state of being compensated: *The payroll department handles the compensation of workers. We got a free night in a hotel in compensation for our flight that was canceled.*

com·pete (kəm-pēt′) *intr.v.* **com·pet·ed, com·pet·ing, com·petes 1.** To strive against another or others to attain a goal: *compete in a race; compete for someone's business.* **2.** To attempt to use the same resource, such as food, living space, or light, as other organisms: *bacteria competing for nutrients.* [From Late Latin *competere*, to strive together : Latin *com-*, with + Latin *petere*, to seek.]

com·pe·tence (kŏm′pĭ-təns) *n.* **1.** The ability to do what is required; adequate skill or knowledge: *She has great competence as a tennis player.* **2.** A range of ability, skill, or knowledge: *Is this task within his competence?* **3.** The condition of being legally qualified to perform an act.

com·pe·ten·cy (kŏm′pĭ-tən-sē) *n., pl.* **com·pe·ten·cies** Competence.

com·pe·tent (kŏm′pĭ-tənt) *adj.* **1.** Able to do something with adequate skill; capable: *a competent worker.* **2.** Legally qualified to perform an act, especially by mental fitness: *The judge ruled that the defendant was competent to stand trial.* **—com′pe·tent·ly** *adv.*

com·pe·ti·tion (kŏm′pĭ-tĭsh′ən) *n.* **1.** The act of competing, as for a prize; rivalry: *won the race in competition with ten contestants.* **2.** A test of skill or ability; a contest: *a skating competition.* **3.** A competitor: *Is the competition as good as our team?* **4.** Rivalry between businesses for the same customers: *trying to get clients away from the competition.* **5.** The simultaneous demand by two or more organisms for resources such as nutrients, living space, and light: *competition between two predators for food.*

com·pet·i·tive (kəm-pĕt′ĭ-tĭv) *adj.* **1.** Involving or decided by competition: *competitive games.* **2.** Liking competition or inclined to compete: *Most athletes are competitive people.* **—com·pet′i·tive·ly** *adv.* **—com·pet′i·tive·ness** *n.*

com·pet·i·tor (kəm-pĕt′ĭ-tər) *n.* A person, team, business organization, or other group that competes with another or others; an opponent or rival.

com·pi·la·tion (kŏm′pə-lā′shən) *n.* **1.** The act of compiling: *Computers are useful in the compilation of facts and figures.* **2.** Something that has been compiled, such as a collection of written works or a report.

com·pile (kəm-pīl′) *tr.v.* **com·piled, com·pil·ing, com·piles 1.** To put together (facts, information, or other matter from several sources) into a single collection, set, or record. **2.** To write or compose (a book) using material gathered from various sources: *compile a dictionary.* [From Middle English *compilen*, from Old French *compiler*, probably from Latin *compīlāre*, to plunder : *com-*, together + *pīla*, heap (of stone), pillar.] **—com·pil′er** *n.*

com·pla·cence (kəm-plā′səns) *n.* Complacency.

com·pla·cen·cy (kəm-plā′sən-sē) *n.* Contentment or self-satisfaction, especially when combined with a lack of readiness to respond to difficulty or controversy.

com·pla·cent (kəm-plā′sənt) *adj.* Full of complacency or self-satisfaction: *The team had won so often that they began to feel complacent.* [From Latin *complacēre*, to please.] **—com·pla′cent·ly** *adv.*

❑ *These sound alike:* **complacent, complaisant** (willing).

com·plain (kəm-plān′) *intr.v.* **com·plained, com·plain·ing, com·plains 1.** To express feelings of pain, dissatisfaction, or resentment: *They worked hard all day and never complained.* **2.** To make an accusation about something that one considers wrong or troublesome: *complain to the telephone company about a mistake in one's bill.* [From Middle English *compleinen*, from Old French *complaindre*.]

com·plain·ant (kəm-plā′nənt) *n.* A person who makes a formal complaint, as in a court of law.

com·plaint (kəm-plānt′) *n.* **1.** An expression of pain, dissatisfaction, or resentment: *There have been many complaints about the cafeteria food.* **2.** A cause or reason for complaining; a grievance: *The tenants sent a list of their complaints to the landlord.* **3.** A formal charge of the commission of a crime: *The storekeeper signed a complaint accusing the suspect of robbery.* **4.** Something, such as a minor ailment, that causes pain or discomfort: *We all had stomach complaints after eating too much.*

com·plai·sance (kəm-plā′səns *or* kəm-plā′zəns) *n.* The desire to please or oblige others.

com·plai·sant (kəm-plā′sənt *or* kəm-plā′zənt) *adj.* Showing a desire or willingness to please; cheerfully obliging: *The complaisant host was always asking if we needed anything.* **—com·plai′sant·ly** *adv.*

❑ *These sound alike:* **complaisant, complacent** (self-satisfied).

com·ple·ment (kŏm′plə-mənt) *n.* **1.** Something that causes something else to be made into a whole or brought to a level of excellence: *Attractive shrubs are a complement to a fine building.* **2.** The number or amount needed to make something complete: *library shelves with a full complement of books.* **3.** In grammar, a word or group of words that follows a transitive or linking verb and completes a predicate. For example, *worm* in *The robin ate the worm,* and *cold* in *The water feels cold* are complements. **4.** An angle related to another so that their sum is 90°. If an angle measures 30°, its complement is 60°. **5.** A system of proteins found in the serum of the blood that helps antibodies destroy disease-causing bacteria or other foreign substances. **6.** Either of two complementary colors. ❖ *tr.v.* (kŏm′plə-mĕnt′) **com·ple·ment·ed, com·ple·ment·ing, com·ple·ments** To make complete; be a complement to: *That easy chair complements the furnishings of the room.* [From Middle

WRITERS CHOOSE THEIR WORDS

The salty air and warm breeze drifting with the scent of orchids lulled her mind into **complacency,** made her think that they would survive this ordeal after all.

—Alaya Dawn Johnson
Racing the Dark

USAGE

complement The word **complement** means "something that completes or brings to perfection": *The flowers were a perfect complement to the beautifully set table.* **Compliment** means "an expression of courtesy or praise": *They gave us a compliment on our beautiful table.*

English, from Latin *complēmentum*, from *complēre*, to fill out.] —SEE NOTE.

❑ *These sound alike:* **complement, compliment** (praise).

com·ple·men·ta·ry (kŏm′plə-**mĕn′**tə-rē *or* kŏm′plə-**mĕn′**trē) *adj.* Serving as a complement; supplying what is lacking or needed: *The flowers on the dinner table provided a complementary touch.*

❑ *These sound alike:* **complementary, complimentary** (praising).

complementary angles *pl.n.* Two angles whose sum is 90 degrees.

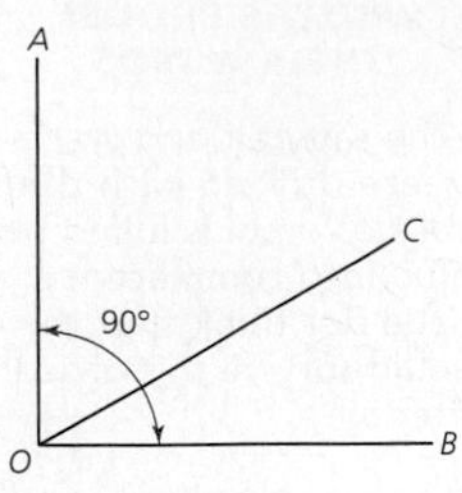

complementary angles
Angles *AOC* + *COB*= 90°.

complementary color *n.* One of two colors, such as red and green, that produce white (in the case of light) or gray (in the case of pigment) when mixed in the proper proportions.

com·plete (kəm-**plēt′**) *adj.* **com·plet·er, com·plet·est 1.** Having all necessary or normal parts; entire: *a complete set of dishes.* **2.** Having come to an end; finished: *The renovation of the kitchen is complete.* **3.** Absolute; total: *complete control of the situation.* **4.** In football, caught in bounds by a receiver: *a complete pass.* ❖ *tr.v.* **com·plet·ed, com·plet·ing, com·pletes 1.** To bring to an end; finish: *The farmers completed the spring planting.* **2.** To add what is missing; make whole: *Fill in the blanks to complete the form.* **3.** In football, to throw (a forward pass) so as to be caught in bounds by a receiver. [From Middle English, from Latin *complētus*, past participle of *complēre*, to fill out.] **—com·plete′ly** *adv.* **—com·plete′ness** *n.* —SEE NOTE AT **replete.**

SYNONYMS complete, conclude, close, end, finish These verbs mean to bring to a stopping point. *The students will complete their science projects next week. We will conclude the program with a song everyone in the audience can sing. The lawyer closed her argument with a plea for mercy. The television program ended the season with a cliffhanger. When you're finished washing the dishes, please dry them.*

WORD BUILDING

compose The word root *pos–* in English comes from the French verb *poser,* "to put." **Compose** therefore literally means "to put together" (using the prefix *com–,* "with, together"); **expose** means "to put out" (*ex–,* "out, out of"); **propose** is literally "to put forward" (*prō,* "forward, in front"); **oppose** is literally "to put against" (*op–,* a form of *ob–,* "toward, against"). The French verb *poser* comes ultimately from the Latin verb *pōnere,* whose present participle was *pōnēns* or *pōnent-*. This is where the English nouns that contain *–ponent* and correspond to verbs containing the *–pos* root come from: **component, exponent, proponent,** and **opponent.**

com·ple·tion (kəm-**plē′**shən) *n.* **1.** The act of completing something or the state of being completed: *Completion of the building took only three weeks.* **2.** In football, a forward pass that is caught in bounds by a receiver.

com·plex (kəm-**plĕks′** *or* **kŏm′**plĕks′) *adj.* **1.** Consisting of many connected or interrelated parts: *the complex wiring of a computer.* **2.** Difficult to understand for being intricate or involved; complicated: *a mystery with a complex plot.* ❖ *n.* (**kŏm′**plĕks′) **1.** A building or group of buildings used for a single purpose: *a sports complex.* **2.** A group of related ideas and emotions that influence a person's behavior and personality. [From Latin *complexus*, past participle of *complectī*, to entwine.] **—com·plex′ly** *adv.*

complex fraction *n.* A fraction having a fraction in the numerator, denominator, or both.

com·plex·ion (kəm-**plĕk′**shən) *n.* **1.** The color, texture, and appearance of the skin, especially of the face: *The skier had a ruddy complexion from being outside.* **2.** General character, aspect, or nature: *The whole complexion of the situation brightened with the good news.*

com·plex·i·ty (kəm-**plĕk′**sĭ-tē) *n., pl.* **com·plex·i·ties 1.** The condition of being complex: *the complexity of modern civilization.* **2.** One of the components in something complicated: *the complexities of the immune system.*

complex number *n.* A number that can be expressed as *a* + *bi,* where *a* and *b* are real numbers and *i* is an imaginary number whose square equals −1.

complex sentence *n.* A sentence containing an independent clause and one or more subordinate clauses, for example, *When the rain ends, we will go home.*

com·pli·ance (kəm-**plī′**əns) *n.* **1.** The act of complying: *Compliance with a country's laws is expected of all citizens.* **2.** A tendency to yield to others.

com·pli·an·cy (kəm-**plī′**ən-sē) *n.* Compliance.

com·pli·ant (kəm-**plī′**ənt) *adj.* **1.** Inclined or willing to yield to the wishes or requests of others. **2.** In compliance, as with a standard or regulation: *a refrigerator that is compliant with federal energy-saving regulations.* **—com·pli′ant·ly** *adv.*

com·pli·cate (**kŏm′**plĭ-kāt′) *tr.v.* **com·pli·cat·ed, com·pli·cat·ing, com·pli·cates** To make more complex or confusing: *The new development only complicates an already serious problem.* [From Latin *complicāre*, to fold together.]

com·pli·cat·ed (**kŏm′**plĭ-kā′tĭd) *adj.* **1.** Not easy to understand or deal with; complex or confusing: *a long complicated explanation; had a complicated problem with her insurance claim.* **2.** Containing intricately combined or involved parts: *a complicated computer program.*

com·pli·ca·tion (kŏm′plĭ-**kā′**shən) *n.* **1.** Something that complicates something else: *Running out of milk was one more complication in trying to get dinner ready on time.* **2.** The state of being complicated or confused: *There is so much complication in these instructions that nobody can understand them.* **3.** A secondary medical condition that occurs during an illness and usually makes it worse.

com·plic·i·ty (kəm-**plĭs′**ĭ-tē) *n., pl.* **com·plic·i·ties** Involvement as an accomplice in a crime or wrongdoing: *Complicity in the scheme cost the accountants their reputation.*

com·pli·ment (**kŏm′**plə-mənt) *n.* **1.** An expression of praise, admiration, or congratulation: *The author received many compliments on the new book.* **2.** An act showing honor or courtesy: *The neighbors paid us the compliment of an invitation to dinner.* **3. compliments** Good wishes; regards: *Please extend my compliments to your parents.* ❖ *tr.v.* **com·pli·ment·ed, com·pli·ment·ing, com·pli·ments** To pay a compliment to: *The critic complimented both artists on their work.* [From French, from Spanish *cumplimiento*, from Latin *complēre*, to fill up.] —SEE NOTE AT **complement.**

❑ *These sound alike:* **compliment, complement** (something that completes).

com·pli·men·ta·ry (kŏm′plə-**mĕn′**tə-rē *or* kŏm′plə-**mĕn′**trē) *adj.* **1.** Expressing, using, or resembling a compliment: *The reviewer was not very complimentary about the movie.* **2.** Given free out of courtesy: *a complimentary copy of a new book.*

❑ *These sound alike:* **complimentary, complementary** (completing).

com·ply (kəm-**plī′**) *intr.v.* **com·plied, com·ply·ing, com·plies** To act in accordance with a request, rule, or order: *The singer complied by giving several encores. Sick people should comply with their doctor's orders.* [From Middle English *complien*, to fulfill, from Latin *complēre*, to complete.]

com·po·nent (kəm-**pō′**nənt) *n.* One of the parts that make up a whole: *Components such as batteries and resistors make up an electric circuit.* ❖ *adj.* Being or functioning as a part or ingredient: *The loudspeakers and amplifiers are component parts of our stereo system.* [From Latin *compōnere*, to put together : *com-*, together + *pōnere*, to put.]

com·port (kəm-**pôrt′**) *v.* **com·port·ed, com·port·ing, com·ports** —*tr.* To conduct or behave (oneself) in a certain way: *The students comported themselves very well in the teacher's absence.* —*intr.* To agree, correspond, or suit: *actions that comport with the dignity of a judge.*

com·port·ment (kəm-**pôrt′**mənt) *n.* A manner of behaving; conduct; bearing: *the solemn comportment of the orchestra's conductor.*

ă	pat	ôr	core
ā	pay	oi	boy
âr	care	ou	out
ä	father	ŏŏ	took
ĕ	pet	ŏŏr	lure
ē	be	ōō	boot
ĭ	pit	ŭ	cut
ī	bite	ûr	urge
îr	pier	th	thin
ŏ	pot	*th*	this
ō	toe	zh	vision
ô	paw	ə	about

com·pose (kəm-**pōz′**) *v.* **com·posed, com·pos·ing, com·pos·es** —*tr.* **1.** To make up the parts of; form: *The heart, veins, arteries, and capillaries compose the circulatory system.* **2.** To make or create by putting parts or elements together: *She composed the speech from entries in her journal.* **3.** To create (a musical or literary work): *compose a symphony.* **4.** To make calm, controlled, or orderly: *compose oneself before making a speech.* **5.** To settle or adjust: *The two nations composed their differences and agreed to share the fishing grounds.* **6.** To arrange or set (type or matter to be printed): *compose type; compose a page.* —*intr.* To create literary or musical pieces: *Chopin composed mostly for the piano.* [From Middle English *composen*, from Old French *composer*, from Latin *compōnere*, to put together.] —SEE NOTE.

com·posed (kəm-**pōzd′**) *adj.* Being in control of one's emotions; calm; serene. **—com·pos′ed·ly** (kəm-**pō′**-zĭd-lē) *adv.*

com·pos·er (kəm-**pō′**zər) *n.* A person who composes, especially a creator of musical works.

com·pos·ite (kəm-**pŏz′**ĭt) *adj.* **1.** Made up of distinctly different parts: *The photograph was a composite picture of several snapshots of family members.* **2.** Relating to or belonging to a plant family having flower heads made up of many small densely clustered flowers that give the impression of a single bloom. ❖ *n.* **1.** Something made by combining different parts: *An almanac is a composite of many facts and tables from different sources.* **2.** A composite plant, such as a daisy or dandelion.

composite number *n.* A whole number that is divisible without a remainder by at least one whole number other than itself and 1.

com·po·si·tion (kŏm′pə-**zĭsh′**ən) *n.* **1.** The act or process of putting together parts or elements to form a whole: *The composition of a symphony can take months.* **2.** A work created by such a process, as a musical work or a short essay: *My composition was six pages long.* **3.** The parts or constituents forming a whole; makeup: *the chemical composition of a mineral.* **4.** The arrangement of parts or elements forming a whole, as in an artistic work: *the orderly and colorful composition of a painting.* **5.** A mixture of substances: *Concrete is a composition of gravel and cement.* **6.** The setting of type for printing.

com·pos·i·tor (kəm-**pŏz′**ĭ-tər) *n.* A person who arranges or sets type for printing; a typesetter.

com·post (**kŏm′**pōst′) *n.* A mixture of decayed organic matter, such as leaves, food waste, or manure, used to enrich the soil.

com·po·sure (kəm-**pō′**zhər) *n.* Control over one's emotions; calmness: *Don't lose your composure over a mistake.*

com·pote (**kŏm′**pōt) *n.* **1.** Sweetened stewed fruit, served as a dessert. **2.** A long-stemmed dish for holding fruit, candy, or nuts.

com·pound[1] (kəm-**pound′** *or* **kŏm′**pound′) *tr.v.* **com·pound·ed, com·pound·ing, com·pounds 1.** To put together to form a whole; combine: *compounded pigments with an oil base to make paint.* **2.** To produce or create by combining parts or ingredients: *The pharmacist compounded the medicine our doctor ordered.* **3.** To compute (interest) on the principal and accumulated interest of a sum of money, as in a savings account. **4.** To add to; increase: *We had compounded our difficulties by making so many mistakes.* ❖ *adj.* (**kŏm′**pound′ *or* kəm-**pound′**) Consisting of two or more parts, ingredients, elements, or substances. ❖ *n.* (**kŏm′**pound′) **1.** Something consisting of a combination of two or more parts or ingredients: *Cough syrup is usually a compound of alcohol, sweet flavoring, and some medicine.* **2.** A word consisting of a combination of two or more other words and forming a single unit with its own meaning. *Loudspeaker, deep-fry,* and *cell division* are compounds. **3.** A substance formed by chemical combination of two or more elements in definite proportions by weight: *Water is a compound of hydrogen and oxygen.* [From Middle English *compounen*, from Latin *compōnere*, to put together.] **—com·pound′a·ble** *adj.* **—com·pound′er** *n.*

com·pound[2] (**kŏm′**pound′) *n.* A group of houses or other buildings, enclosed by a wall, fence, or other barrier. [Alteration of Malay *kampong*, village.]

compound eye *n.* An eye, as of an insect or crustacean, consisting of many small light-sensitive units, each of which forms part of an image.

compound fraction *n.* A complex fraction.

compound fracture *n.* A bone fracture in which a sharp piece of bone cuts through nearby soft tissue and makes an open wound.

compound interest *n.* Interest computed on an amount of money constituting the principal plus all the unpaid interest already earned.

compound leaf *n.* A leaf, as of clover, whose blade is divided into two or more distinct leaflets.

compound sentence *n.* A sentence of two or more independent clauses, usually joined by a conjunction such as *and, but,* or *or.* For example, *The problem was difficult, but I finally found the answer* is a compound sentence.

com·pre·hend (kŏm′prĭ-**hĕnd′**) *tr.v.* **com·pre·hend·ed, com·pre·hend·ing, com·pre·hends 1.** To grasp mentally; understand: *Many people do not comprehend the theory of relativity.* **2.** To take in as a part; include: *The metropolitan area of a city comprehends the surrounding suburbs.* [From Middle English *comprehenden*, from Latin *comprehendere* : *com-*, intensive prefix + *prehendere*, to grasp.]

com·pre·hen·si·ble (kŏm′prĭ-**hĕn′**sə-bəl) *adj.* Readily understood; understandable: *I was able to make the menu comprehensible to our visitor from Japan.* **—com′pre·hen′si·bil′i·ty** *n.* **—com′pre·hen′si·bly** *adv.*

com·pre·hen·sion (kŏm′prĭ-**hĕn′**shən) *n.* **1.** The act or fact of understanding something: *Comprehension of basic chemistry is not as difficult as you think.* **2.** The capacity to understand something: *Algebra is well within your comprehension.*

com·pre·hen·sive (kŏm′prĭ-**hĕn′**sĭv) *adj.* **1.** Including much; broad in scope; thorough: *The last chapter is a comprehensive review of the book's contents.* **2.** Marked by or showing extensive understanding: *comprehensive knowledge.* **—com′pre·hen′sive·ly** *adv.*

com·press (kəm-**prĕs′**) *tr.v.* **com·pressed, com·press·ing, com·press·es 1.** To squeeze or press together: *He compressed his lips into a thin line.* **2.** To make more compact by or as if by squeezing or pressing: *compress one's thoughts into a short statement.* **3.** To transform (data) in order to minimize the space needed to store or transmit it. ❖ *n.* (**kŏm′**prĕs′) A soft pad of gauze, cotton, or other material, often moistened or medicated, applied to some part of the body, especially to a wound or injury. [From Middle English *compressen*, from Late Latin *compressāre*, from Latin *comprimere* : *com-*, together + *premere*, to press.] —SEE NOTE AT **pressure.**

com·pressed (kəm-**prĕst′**) *adj.* Pressed together; made smaller by pressure: *The tank contains compressed gas.*

compressed air *n.* Air that has been put under pressure greater than the pressure of the atmosphere, as in a storage tank. When released, its force is often used to operate a mechanism, such as air brakes.

com·press·i·ble (kəm-**prĕs′**ə-bəl) *adj.* Capable of being compressed. **—com·press′i·bil′i·ty** *n.*

com·pres·sion (kəm-**prĕsh′**ən) *n.* **1.** The act or process of compressing. **2.** The condition of being compressed.

com·pres·sor (kəm-**prĕs′**ər) *n.* Something that compresses, especially a machine used to compress a gas, as in a refrigerator.

compote

compound eye
compound eyes of a fly

compound leaf
left: pinnately compound leaf
right: palmately compound leaf

SCIENCE

computer All modern **computers** are essentially collections of extremely fast electronic switches. Most of the switches are contained on an integrated circuit made of semiconductor materials that stop or release the flow of electrons when a current or change in voltage is applied. Each switch can be either off or on. The either/or nature of a switch fits perfectly with the *binary system* of numbers. Off represents the value 0. On represents the value 1. All data—words, symbols, sounds, pictures, and numbers—that a computer processes must be encoded as a series of 0s and 1s. The digits 0 and 1 are called *bits.* Each pattern of bits that represents a letter, symbol, or number is called a *byte.* Like decimal numbers, binary numbers can be added, subtracted, multiplied, and divided, so a computer can perform arithmetic operations.

com·prise (kəm-**prīz′**) *tr.v.* **com·prised, com·pris·ing, com·pris·es 1.** To consist of; be composed of; include: *The United Nations comprises more than 130 countries.* **2.** To make up; form; constitute: *Milk, butter, and cheese comprise the bulk of dairy products.* [From Middle English *comprisen,* to be included, from Old French *compris,* included, past participle of *comprendre,* to include, from Latin *comprehendere.*]

com·pro·mise (**kŏm′**prə-mīz′) *n.* **1.** A settlement of differences between opposing sides in which each side gives up some claims and agrees to some demands of the other: *By agreeing to share the cost, our neighbors reached a compromise over rebuilding the fence.* **2.** Something that combines qualities or elements of different, often conflicting things: *The design of the car is a compromise between style and safety.* ❖ *v.* **com·pro·mised, com·pro·mis·ing, com·pro·mis·es** —*tr.* **1.** To reduce in quality or value; weaken or lower: *He felt he compromised his standards in rushing through the job.* **2.** To expose to danger or risk: *The secret mission was compromised when news of it was leaked to the press.* **3.** To impair, as by disease or injury: *The patient's immune system was compromised by a viral infection.* —*intr.* To settle a difference by making a compromise: *My parents compromised and let me have one dog but not two, like I wanted.* [From Middle English *compromis,* from Latin *comprōmissum,* mutual promise : *com-,* together + *prōmittere,* to promise.]

comp·trol·ler (kən-**trō′**lər *or* kŏmp-**trō′**lər) *n.* Variant of **controller** (sense 3).

com·pul·sion (kəm-**pŭl′**shən) *n.* **1.** The act of compelling or the state of being compelled: *the compulsion of prisoners to work on a chain gang; residents who were under compulsion to evacuate their homes due to flooding.* **2.** An irresistible urge or impulse: *a compulsion to stay up late.* [From Middle English, from Late Latin *compulsiō,* from Latin *compellere,* to compel.]

com·pul·sive (kəm-**pŭl′**sĭv) *adj.* Relating to, having, or resulting from a strong irresistible impulse: *Some people have a compulsive desire to talk.* **—com·pul′sive·ly** *adv.* **—com·pul′sive·ness** *n.*

com·pul·so·ry (kəm-**pŭl′**sə-rē) *adj.* **1.** Required by law, regulations, or duty: *Education is compulsory for children in most countries.* **2.** Using or involving compulsion: *compulsory powers of the law.*

com·punc·tion (kəm-**pŭngk′**shən) *n.* An uneasy feeling that one has done something wrong; remorse: *The children showed no compunction about eating all the cookies.*

com·pu·ta·tion (kŏm′pyo͝o-**tā′**shən) *n.* The act, process, method, or result of computing; mathematical calculation.

com·pute (kəm-**pyo͞ot′**) *tr.v.* **com·put·ed, com·put·ing, com·putes 1.** To work out (a result, answer, or solution) by mathematics; calculate: *The bank computes the interest on savings accounts.* **2.** To determine by use of a computer: *compute the most efficient design of a sailboat.* [From Latin *computāre* : *com-,* together + *putāre,* to reckon.]

com·put·er (kəm-**pyo͞o′**tər) *n.* A device that computes, especially an electronic device capable of processing information according to a set of instructions stored within the device. —SEE NOTE.

computer graphics *n. (used with a singular or plural verb)* Graphic artwork, such as maps, diagrams, or pictures, produced with a computer.

com·put·er·ize (kəm-**pyo͞o′**tə-rīz′) *tr.v.* **com·put·er·ized, com·put·er·iz·ing, com·put·er·iz·es 1.** To process or store (information) in an electronic computer: *computerize office files.* **2.** To furnish with a computer or a system of computers: *computerize an office.*

computer language *n.* A programming language.

computer literacy *n.* The ability to operate a computer and to understand how a computer works.

computer science *n.* The study of the design and operation of computers, including their software and hardware.

com·rade (**kŏm′**răd′) *n.* **1.** A friend or companion, especially a person who shares one's activities. **2.** often **Comrade** A fellow member of a group, especially a fellow member of the Communist Party. [From Old Spanish *camarada,* from *camara,* room, from Late Latin *camera,* chamber.]

com·rade·ship (**kŏm′**răd-shĭp′) *n.* Association as comrades; companionship: *the comradeship of old friends.*

con¹ (kŏn) *n.* An argument or consideration against something: *discussing the pros and cons of the subject.* ❖ *adv.* In opposition or disagreement; against: *arguing a question pro and con.* ❖ *adj.* Opposing: *the arguments pro and con.* [From Latin *contrā,* against.]

con² (kŏn) *tr.v.* **conned, con·ning, cons** To direct the course of (a ship, for instance). ❖ *n.* **1.** The position from which a vessel's course is directed. **2.** The authority to direct a vessel's course. [From Middle English *conduen,* from Latin *condūcere,* to lead.]

con³ (kŏn) *tr.v.* **conned, con·ning, cons** *Slang* To trick or coax (someone) into doing something by first winning the person's confidence: *con someone into buying a junky old car.* ❖ *n.* A swindle. [From *confidence.*]

con⁴ (kŏn) *n. Slang* A convict. [From *convict.*]

con– *pref.* Variant of **com–.**

Con·a·kry (**kŏn′**ə-krē) The capital of Guinea, in the southwest part of the country on the Atlantic Ocean.

con·cave (kŏn-**kāv′** *or* **kŏn′**kāv′) *adj.* Curved inward like the inside of a circle or sphere: *Many birds build concave nests to hold their eggs.* **—con·cave′ly** *adv.* **—con·cave′ness** *n.*

con·cav·i·ty (kŏn-**kăv′**ĭ-tē) *n., pl.* **con·cav·i·ties 1.** The condition of being concave: *The concavity of the mirror allows it to focus the rays of the sun into a beam.* **2.** A concave surface, line, or body.

con·ceal (kən-**sēl′**) *tr.v.* **con·cealed, con·ceal·ing, con·ceals 1.** To keep from being seen; put out of sight: *A bank of clouds concealed the setting sun.* See Synonyms at **hide¹. 2.** To keep secret: *conceal hurt feelings.* [From Middle English *concelen,* from Latin *concēlāre* : *com-,* intensive prefix + *cēlāre,* to hide.] **—con·ceal′a·ble** *adj.* **—con·ceal′er** *n.* **—con·ceal′ment** *n.*

con·cede (kən-**sēd′**) *v.* **con·ced·ed, con·ced·ing, con·cedes** —*tr.* **1.** To admit as being true or real, often unwillingly; acknowledge: *The losing candidate finally conceded defeat the morning after election day.* **2.** To give, yield, or grant: *After the uprising, the government conceded the right to vote to all citizens.* —*intr.* To make a concession; yield. [From Latin *concēdere* : *com-,* intensive prefix + *cēdere,* to yield.]

con·ceit (kən-**sēt′**) *n.* **1.** An overly high opinion of one's abilities or worth; vanity: *The famous author's conceit was unpleasant.* **2.** A witty expression or fanciful idea. [From Middle English *conceit,* mind, conception, from Late Latin *conceptus,* concept.]

con·ceit·ed (kən-**sē′**tĭd) *adj.* Holding or showing an overly high opinion of oneself: *a conceited braggart.* **—con·ceit′ed·ly** *adv.* **—con·ceit′ed·ness** *n.*

con·ceiv·a·ble (kən-**sē′**və-bəl) *adj.* Capable of being thought of; imaginable: *It is conceivable that life exists on other planets.*

con·ceive (kən-**sēv′**) *v.* **con·ceived, con·ceiv·ing, con·ceives** —*tr.* **1.** To form or develop in the mind: *Albert Einstein conceived the theory of relativity.* **2.** To imagine or think of; consider: *We could not conceive that such a strange place existed.* **3.** To become pregnant with: *conceive a child.* —*intr.* **1.** To have an idea or concept; think: *People in ancient times conceived of the earth as flat.* **2.** To become pregnant. **—con·ceiv′er** *n.*

ă	pat	ôr	core
ā	pay	oi	boy
âr	care	ou	out
ä	father	o͝o	took
ĕ	pet	o͝or	lure
ē	be	o͞o	boot
ĭ	pit	ŭ	cut
ī	bite	ûr	urge
îr	pier	th	thin
ŏ	pot	*th*	this
ō	toe	zh	vision
ô	paw	ə	about

con·cen·trate (kŏn′sən-trāt′) *v.* **con·cen·trat·ed, con·cen·trat·ing, con·cen·trates** —*intr.* **1.** To keep or direct one's thoughts, attention, or efforts: *It's hard to concentrate on doing homework with the TV on.* **2.** To come toward or meet in a common center: *The migrating geese concentrate at ponds and streams.* **3.** To have something as a main point of interest or concern; focus: *The first chapter concentrates on positioning of the hands on the keyboard.* —*tr.* **1.** To draw or gather toward one place or point; focus: *Europe's population is concentrated in large cities.* **2.** To make (a solution or mixture) stronger. ❖ *n.* Something that has been concentrated: *orange juice concentrate.* [Ultimately from Latin *com-*, together + Latin *centrum*, center.]

con·cen·tra·tion (kŏn′sən-trā′shən) *n.* **1.** The act or process of concentrating, especially the directing of close undivided attention: *The secret of doing your work in less time is complete concentration.* **2.** A close gathering or dense grouping: *Lights shone brightly from the concentration of houses in the new development.* **3.** The amount of a particular substance in a given amount of a solution or mixture: *the concentration of salt in sea water.*

concentration camp *n.* An area or camp where people are confined, often under harsh conditions, usually for belonging to a group that a government considers dangerous or undesirable.

con·cen·tric (kən-sĕn′trĭk) *adj.* Having the same center: *a set of concentric circles.* —**con·cen′tri·cal·ly** *adv.*

con·cept (kŏn′sĕpt′) *n.* **1.** A general idea or understanding, especially one based on known facts or observation: *the concept that all people have a right to equal treatment under the law.* See Synonyms at **idea. 2.** A scheme; a plan: *a concept for a new mall.* [From Late Latin *conceptus*, from Latin *concipere*, to conceive.]

con·cep·tion (kən-sĕp′shən) *n.* **1.** A general idea or understanding; a concept: *The study of astronomy has given us some conception of the age of the universe.* See Synonyms at **idea. 2.** A beginning or formation of an idea: *a history of the computer from its earliest conception to the most advanced integrated circuits.* **3.** The formation of a cell that is capable of developing into a new organism by the union of a sperm and egg cell; fertilization.

con·cep·tu·al (kən-sĕp′cho͞o-əl) *adj.* Consisting of or based on a concept or mental conception: *the conceptual difference between a robot and a human being.* —**con·cep′tu·al·ly** *adv.*

con·cep·tu·al·ize (kən-sĕp′cho͞o-ə-līz′) *tr. & intr.v.* **con·cep·tu·al·ized, con·cep·tu·al·iz·ing, con·cep·tu·al·iz·es** To form a general idea or a concept about: *It is difficult to conceptualize what the world will be like in the next century.*

con·cern (kən-sûrn′) *tr.v.* **con·cerned, con·cern·ing, con·cerns 1.** To have to do with; relate to: *The new book concerns urban sprawl.* **2.** To be of importance or interest to; involve: *Cleaning up the environment concerns all of us.* **3.** To fill with care or anxiety; worry; trouble: *The lack of rain deeply concerned the farmers.* ❖ *n.* **1.** Something of interest or importance: *The author's chief concern is to write the history of the plastics industry.* **2.** Worry; anxiety: *the parents' concern for their sick child.* **3.** A business establishment; a firm: *Repair shops and banks are concerns that provide services rather than goods.* [From Middle English *concernen*, from Late Latin *concernere*, to mingle together.]

con·cerned (kən-sûrnd′) *adj.* **1.** Interested or affected; involved: *Most concerned citizens recycle trash.* **2.** Worried; anxious; troubled: *a concerned expression on his face.*

con·cern·ing (kən-sûr′nĭng) *prep.* In reference to; about: *science-fiction stories concerning visitors from outer space.*

con·cert (kŏn′sərt) *n.* A musical performance given in front of an audience. ◆ **in concert** As a single unit or group; together: *Several nearby towns are working in concert to ease rush-hour traffic.* [From Old Italian *concerto*, agreement, harmony, from *concertare*, to bring into agreement.]

con·cert·ed (kən-sûr′tĭd) *adj.* Planned or accomplished together with others; combined: *a concerted fundraising drive.*

con·cer·ti·na (kŏn′sər-tē′nə) *n.* A small accordion in the shape of a hexagon.

con·cer·to (kən-chĕr′tō) *n., pl.* **con·cer·tos** or **con·cer·ti** (kən-chĕr′tē) A musical composition written for one or more solo instruments and an orchestra: *a piano concerto; a concerto for violin and orchestra.*

con·ces·sion (kən-sĕsh′ən) *n.* **1.** An act of yielding or conceding: *settle a dispute by mutual concession.* **2.** Something yielded or conceded: *The workers demanded more time off and other concessions.* **3a.** A right to operate a business in a certain place: *The US government gave land concessions to the railroads to encourage their development.* **b.** A business that has such a right: *We got hot dogs at the food concession in the ballpark.*

con·ces·sion·aire (kən-sĕsh′ə-nâr′) *n.* A person who holds or operates a business concession.

conch (kŏngk *or* kŏnch) *n., pl.* **conchs** (kŏngks) or **conch·es** (kŏn′chĭz) **1.** Any of various tropical marine snails having edible flesh and a large spiral shell. **2.** The shell of such an animal. [From Middle English, from Greek *konkhē*, mussel.]

❑ *These sound alike:* **conch, conk** (hit).

con·cil·i·ate (kən-sĭl′ē-āt′) *tr.v.* **con·cil·i·at·ed, con·cil·i·at·ing, con·cil·i·ates 1.** To overcome the anger or distrust of; win over: *The babysitter tried to conciliate the angry child by reading a story.* **2.** To make harmonious; reconcile: *made an attempt to conciliate the conflicting theories.* [From Latin *conciliāre*, from *concilium*, meeting.] —**con·cil′i·a′tion** *n.* —**con·cil′i·a′tor** *n.*

con·cil·i·a·to·ry (kən-sĭl′ē-ə-tôr′ē) *adj.* Intending to conciliate or having the effect of conciliating: *a conciliatory attitude.*

con·cise (kən-sīs′) *adj.* Expressing much in a few words; brief and clear: *a concise summary of the main points of the meeting.* [From Latin *concīsus*, from *concīdere*, to cut up.] —**con·cise′ly** *adv.* —**con·cise′ness** *n.*

con·clave (kŏn′klāv′) *n.* A private or secret meeting.

con·clude (kən-klo͞od′) *v.* **con·clud·ed, con·clud·ing, con·cludes** —*tr.* **1.** To bring to an end; close; finish: *concluded the rally with the school's alma mater.* See Synonyms at **complete. 2.** To arrange or settle finally: *conclude an agreement on trade between two countries.* **3.** To arrive at (a conclusion, judgment, or opinion) by the process of reasoning: *The scientist concluded that the bones were those of a dinosaur.* —*intr.* To come to an end; close: *The conference concluded with a call for action.* [From Middle English *concluden*, from Latin *conclūdere* : *com-*, intensive prefix + *claudere*, to close.] —**con·clud′er** *n.*

con·clu·sion (kən-klo͞o′zhən) *n.* **1.** The closing or last part of something; the end: *the exciting conclusion of a story.* **2.** A judgment or decision reached by reasoning: *Scientists check their observations thoroughly to arrive at accurate conclusions.* **3.** A final arrangement or settlement, as of a treaty. ◆ **in conclusion** As a last statement; finally.

con·clu·sive (kən-klo͞o′sĭv) *adj.* Putting an end to doubt, question, or uncertainty; decisive: *The new piece of evidence was conclusive and proved that he was guilty.* —**con·clu′sive·ly** *adv.*

con·coct (kən-kŏkt′) *tr.v.* **con·coct·ed, con·coct·ing, con·cocts 1.** To make by mixing or combining ingredients or parts: *concoct a stew from leftover meat and vegetables.* **2.** To make up; invent: *concoct an excuse to avoid going to the concert.* [From Latin *concoquere*, to

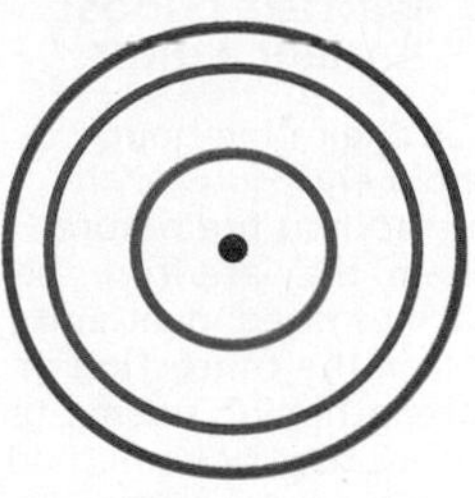

concentric
three concentric circles

concertina

conch

WRITERS CHOOSE THEIR WORDS

She was in no mood to be **conciliatory;** she had several bones to pick with her mother. "I said I would go to the village, and I did. There's no sensible reason why I shouldn't take the tour of the House. It's open to the public, isn't it?"

—Liz Berry
The China Garden

WRITERS CHOOSE THEIR WORDS

In their pine-bough snow enclosure, with a crackling fire before them, they ate from their sack of dried meat and drank the **concoction** of strengthening swamp tea leaves that Nokomis had plucked from bushes as they walked.

— Louise Erdrich
The Porcupine Year

boil together : *com-*, together + *coquere*, to cook.]

con·coc·tion (kən-**kŏk′**shən) *n.* Something concocted, especially a mixture of ingredients: *a concoction of orange juice and soda.*

con·com·i·tant (kən-**kŏm′**ĭ-tənt) *adj.* Happening or existing along with something else; accompanying: *A fever and rash are concomitant symptoms of chickenpox.* ❖ *n.* Something that happens or is found along with something else: *Poor health is often a concomitant of unsanitary living conditions.* **—con·com′i·tant·ly** *adv.*

con·cord (**kŏn′**kôrd′ *or* **kŏng′**kôrd′) *n.* **1.** A friendly or harmonious relationship: *The neighboring nations lived in peace and concord.* **2.** An agreement establishing such a relationship. **3.** The relationship between musical tones that produce a pleasing effect when they are sounded together. [From Middle English, from Latin *concordia*, from *concors*, agreeing : *com-*, together + *cor*, heart.]

Con·cord (**kŏng′**kərd) **1.** A town of eastern Massachusetts on the **Concord River** west-northwest of Boston. An early battle of the Revolutionary War was fought here on April 19, 1775. **2.** The capital of New Hampshire, in the south-central part of the state. It became the capital in 1808.

concourse
Liverpool Street Station, London, England

con·cor·dance (kən-**kôr′**dns) *n.* **1.** A state of agreement or harmony; concord. **2.** An alphabetical index of the words in a written work or collection of works, showing where they occur: *a concordance to the Bible.*

con·course (**kŏn′**kôrs′) *n.* **1.** A large open space in which crowds gather or pass through, as in an airport. **2.** A wide road or avenue. **3.** A large crowd. **4.** The act of coming, moving, or flowing together: *Pittsburgh lies at the concourse of two rivers.*

con·crete (**kŏn′**krēt′ *or* kŏn-**krēt′**) *n.* A building or paving material made of sand and pebbles or crushed stone, held together by cement. ❖ *adj.* (kŏn-**krēt′** *or* **kŏn′**krēt′) **1.** Made of concrete: *The children played jacks on the concrete sidewalk.* **2.** Existing in reality as something that can be perceived by the senses: *concrete objects such as rocks and trees.* **3.** Specific or particular: *concrete evidence that led to a conviction.* [From Middle English *concrete*, solid, real, from Latin *concrētus*, past participle of *concrēscere*, to grow together, harden : *com-*, together + *crēscere*, to grow.] **—con·crete′ly** *adv.* **—con·crete′ness** *n.*

con·cu·bine (**kŏng′**kyə-bīn′) *n.* In certain societies, a woman who cohabits with a man in a similar relationship to marriage but who does not have the full legal status of a wife.

con·cur (kən-**kûr′**) *intr.v.* **con·curred, con·cur·ring, con·curs 1.** To have the same opinion; agree: *Most people concur on the need to stop pollution.* **2.** To occur at the same time: *When rain concurs with melting snow, flooding often develops.* [From Middle English *concurren*, from Latin *concurrere*, to meet, coincide : *com-*, together + *currere*, to run.] —SEE NOTE AT **cursive.**

con·cur·rence (kən-**kûr′**əns) *n.* **1.** Agreement of opinion: *Concurrence among all of the partners led to a satisfactory business arrangement.* **2.** An occurrence, as of events, actions, or efforts, at the same time: *The concurrence of high tide and strong winds caused damage along the coast.*

con·cur·rent (kən-**kûr′**ənt) *adj.* **1.** Happening at the same time: *concurrent events.* **2.** Being in accordance; harmonious: *concurrent opinions.* **3.** Meeting or tending to meet at the same point: *concurrent lines.* **—con·cur′rent·ly** *adv.*

con·cus·sion (kən-**kŭsh′**ən) *n.* **1.** A violent jarring; a shock: *A strong concussion from the blast shattered many windows.* **2.** An injury, especially to the brain, resulting from a hard blow.

con·demn (kən-**dĕm′**) *tr.v.* **con·demned, con·demn·ing, con·demns 1.** To express strong disapproval of; denounce: *The governor condemned the waste of taxpayers' money.* **2a.** To judge to be guilty: *The suspect was condemned by the jury.* **b.** To sentence to a particular punishment: *He was condemned to 15 years in prison.* **3.** To declare unfit for use: *The city condemned the old warehouse after the fire.* **4.** To take over (private property) for public use: *The state condemned farms in the path of the new expressway.* [From Middle English *condempnen*, from Latin *condemnāre* : *com-*, intensive prefix + *damnāre*, to sentence (from *damnum*, penalty).]

con·dem·na·tion (kŏn′dĕm-**nā′**shən) *n.* The act of condemning or state of being condemned: *The angry speech drew strong condemnation from his colleagues. The building was torn down after condemnation.*

con·den·sate (**kŏn′**dən-sāt′ *or* kən-**dĕn′**sāt′) *n.* The liquid produced by the condensation of a gas.

con·den·sa·tion (kŏn′dən-**sā′**shən) *n.* **1.** The change of a gas or vapor to a liquid, either by cooling or by being subjected to increased pressure: *Cooling causes the condensation of steam to water.* **2.** A liquid, especially water, formed by this process: *Breathing on a mirror often causes condensation to form.* **3a.** The act or process of condensing something: *The author spent several months in the condensation of his novel.* **b.** A shortened version of something; an abridgment: *The newspaper printed a condensation of the president's speech.*

con·dense (kən-**dĕns′**) *v.* **con·densed, con·dens·ing, con·dens·es** —*tr.* **1.** To cause (a gas or vapor) to change to a liquid form: *Cool temperatures may condense water vapor in the air into dew.* **2.** To make more concentrated or dense: *We boiled the soup to condense it.* **3.** To make shorter or more concise: *The author condensed the book for use in a magazine.* —*intr.* **1.** To become denser or more compact: *Stars may condense from matter scattered in space.* **2.** To change from a gas to a liquid: *Water vapor often condenses on the bathroom mirror.* [From Middle English *condensen*, from Latin *condēnsāre* : *com-*, intensive prefix + *dēnsāre*, to thicken (from *dēnsus*, thick).] **—con·dens′a·ble** *adj.*

con·densed milk (kən-**dĕnst′**) *n.* Sweetened cow's milk that has been made very thick by evaporation before canning.

con·dens·er (kən-**dĕn′**sər) *n.* **1.** A person or thing that condenses. **2.** An apparatus used to condense a gas or vapor. **3.** A capacitor.

con·de·scend (kŏn′dĭ-**sĕnd′**) *intr.v.* **con·de·scend·ed, con·de·scend·ing, con·de·scends 1.** To agree to do something willingly that is regarded as beneath one's social rank or dignity: *The princess graciously condescended to help at the charity auction.* **2.** To act in a manner that shows one considers oneself superior to others: *The snobbish family in the big house condescends to all their neighbors.*

con·de·scend·ing (kŏn′dĭ-**sĕn′**dĭng) *adj.* Showing that one considers oneself superior to others; patronizing: *a condescending manner.* **—con′de·scend′ing·ly** *adv.*

con·de·scen·sion (kŏn′dĭ-**sĕn′**shən) *n.* **1.** The act of condescending. **2.** An attitude or behavior that shows one considers oneself superior to others; haughtiness.

con·di·ment (**kŏn′**də-mənt) *n.* A substance, such as a relish, vinegar, or spice, used to flavor or complement food. [From Middle English, from Latin *condīmentum*, from *condīre*, to season.]

con·di·tion (kən-**dĭsh′**ən) *n.* **1.** A state of being or existence: *They worked hard to restore the old house to its original condition.* **2. conditions** The existing circumstances: *Economic conditions have improved. What are the latest weather conditions?* **3a.** A state of health or fitness: *Have you exercised enough to get back into condition?* **b.** Readiness for use; working order: *A few repairs will put the car in condition.* **4.** A disease or physical ailment: *a heart condition.* **5.** Something that is necessary

ă	pat	ôr	core
ā	pay	oi	boy
âr	care	ou	out
ä	father	o͝o	took
ĕ	pet	o͝or	lure
ē	be	o͞o	boot
ĭ	pit	ŭ	cut
ī	bite	ûr	urge
îr	pier	th	thin
ŏ	pot	*th*	this
ō	toe	zh	vision
ô	paw	ə	about

to the occurrence of something else: *I'll only go with you on this condition: that you let my sister come too.* ❖ *tr.v.* **con·di·tioned, con·di·tion·ing, con·di·tions 1.** To put into good or proper condition; make fit: *Running five miles a day will condition the track team.* **2.** To adapt; accustom to: *The visitors from Sweden were not conditioned to the hot weather here.* **3.** To train (a person or other animal) to behave or react in a certain way: *The researchers conditioned the chicken to go outside when a light was turned on.* ◆ **on condition that** Provided that: *She gave us permission to use the computer on condition that we report any problems with it.* [From Middle English *condicioun*, from Latin *conditiō*, from *condīcere*, to agree : *com-*, together + *dīcere*, to talk.]

con·di·tion·al (kən-**dĭsh′**ə-nəl) *adj.* **1.** Depending on a condition or conditions: *While awaiting the response of parents, the committee gave conditional approval to the plan.* **2.** In grammar, expressing a condition on which an outcome or possibility depends. For example, *if it's sunny tomorrow* is a conditional clause in the sentence *We'll go swimming if it's sunny tomorrow.*

con·di·tioned (kən-**dĭsh′**ənd) *adj.* **1.** Dependent on a condition or conditions; conditional: *gave the project her conditioned approval.* **2.** Physically fit. **3a.** Determined or established by means of conditioning: *a conditioned reflex.* **b.** Trained by means of conditioning.

con·di·tion·er (kən-**dĭsh′**ə nər) *n.* A device or substance used to improve something in some way: *a leather conditioner; a bottle of hair conditioner.*

con·di·tion·ing (kən-**dĭsh′**ə-nĭng) *n.* A process of behavior modification by which an experimental subject comes to associate a desired behavior with a previously unrelated stimulus.

con·do (**kŏn′**dō′) *n., pl.* **con·dos** *Informal* A condominium.

con·dole (kən-**dōl′**) *intr.v.* **con·doled, con·dol·ing, con·doles** To express sympathy or sorrow: *She condoled with the family over their loss.*

con·do·lence (kən-**dō′**ləns) *n.* Sympathy or an expression of sympathy for a person who has experienced sorrow or misfortune.

con·dom (**kŏn′**dəm) *n.* A flexible cover for the penis to be worn during sexual intercourse to prevent pregnancy and sexually transmitted diseases. Condoms are usually made of thin rubber or latex.

con·do·min·i·um (kŏn′də-**mĭn′**ē-əm) *n.* **1.** A building in which units of property, such as apartments, are owned by individuals. **2.** A unit in such a building. [From *com-*, *con-*, together + Latin *dominium*, ownership, domain.]

con·done (kən-**dōn′**) *tr.v.* **con·doned, con·don·ing, con·dones** To forgive, overlook, or ignore: *The school will not condone bullying in any form.* See Synonyms at **forgive.** [From Latin *condōnāre* : *com-*, intensive prefix + *dōnāre*, to give (from *dōnum*, gift).]

con·dor (**kŏn′**dôr′ *or* **kŏn′**dər) *n.* Either of two very large vultures, one living in the mountains of California and the other in the Andes, having a bare head and a ruff of feathers at the base of the neck. [From Spanish *cóndor*, from Quechua *kuntur*.]

con·duce (kən-**dōōs′**) *intr.v.* **con·duced, con·duc·ing, con·duc·es** To contribute or lead to a specific result: *an atmosphere at home that was conducing to good study habits.*

con·du·cive (kən-**dōō′**sĭv) *adj.* Tending to cause, promote, or help bring about a specific result: *Lax discipline in the classroom can be conducive to cheating.* —**con·du′cive·ness** *n.*

con·duct (kən-**dŭkt′**) *tr.v.* **con·duct·ed, con·duct·ing, con·ducts 1.** To direct the course of; manage: *conduct an experiment; conduct negotiations.* **2.** To lead; guide: *The guide conducted us through the art museum.* See Synonyms at **accompany. 3.** To direct the performance of (musicians or a musical work): *conduct an orchestra; conduct one of Mozart's symphonies.* **4.** To serve as a medium for conveying; transmit: *Most metals conduct electricity well.* ❖ *n.* (**kŏn′**dŭkt′) **1.** The way a person acts; behavior: *rude and disorderly conduct.* **2.** The act of directing or controlling; management: *The president is responsible for the conduct of foreign affairs.* ◆ **conduct (oneself)** To behave in a certain way: *They conducted themselves with dignity during the ceremony.* [From Middle English *conducten*, from Latin *condūcere* : *com-*, together + *dūcere*, to lead.] —**con·duct′i·bil′i·ty** *n.* —**con·duct′i·ble** *adj.*

con·duc·tance (kən-**dŭk′**təns) *n.* A measure of the ability of a material to conduct electric charge.

con·duc·tion (kən-**dŭk′**shən) *n.* The transmission or passage of something through a medium or along a path, especially the transmission of heat or electric charge through a substance. —SEE NOTE AT **convection.**

con·duc·tive (kən-**dŭk′**tĭv) *adj.* Relating to or showing conductivity: *a highly conductive material.*

con·duc·tiv·i·ty (kŏn′dŭk-**tĭv′**ĭ-tē) *n.* The ability or power to conduct heat, electricity, or sound.

con·duc·tor (kən-**dŭk′**tər) *n.* **1.** The person who conducts an orchestra or other group of musical performers. **2.** The person in charge of a train, bus, or streetcar, especially one who collects fares or checks tickets. **3.** A material or object that conducts heat, electricity, light, or sound: *Copper is a good conductor of heat and electricity.*

con·duit (**kŏn′**dōō-ĭt *or* **kŏn′**dĭt) *n.* **1.** A channel or pipe for carrying fluids, such as water or natural gas. **2.** A tube or pipe through which electric wires or cables pass. **3.** A means by which something is transmitted: *The spy served as a conduit of secret information.*

cone (kōn) *n.* **1.** A solid made by extending line segments from a point to the perimeter of a circle at the base. **2.** Something having the shape of such a figure: *an ice-cream cone.* **3.** One of a group of cells in the retina of the eye that are shaped like such a figure and are sensitive to bright light and color. **4.** A rounded or long reproductive structure of certain seed plants, having scales that bear either pollen-containing structures or ovules and seeds. Pines, spruces, cedars, and related plants bear cones. [From Greek *kōnos*.]

Con·es·to·ga wagon (kŏn′ĭ-**stō′**gə) *n.* A heavy covered wagon first built at Conestoga, Pennsylvania, used especially by American pioneers in their westward travel.

co·ney also **co·ny** (**kō′**nē *or* **kŭn′**ē) *n., pl.* **co·neys** also **co·nies 1.** A rabbit, especially the common European rabbit. **2.** The fur of a rabbit.

con·fec·tion (kən-**fĕk′**shən) *n.* A sweet food or preparation, such as candy. [From Middle English *confeccioun*, from Latin *cōnfectiō*, a making, from *cōnficere*, to put together.]

con·fec·tion·er (kən-**fĕk′**shə-nər) *n.* A person who makes or sells candy and other confections.

con·fec·tion·ers' sugar (kən-**fĕk′**shə-nərz) *n.* A fine powdery sugar used especially in frostings and as a topping on desserts.

con·fec·tion·er·y (kən-**fĕk′**shə-nĕr′ē) *n., pl.* **con·fec·tion·er·ies** A confectioner's shop.

con·fed·er·a·cy (kən-**fĕd′**ər-ə-sē) *n., pl.* **con·fed·er·a·cies 1.** A political union of peoples or states: *the confederacy of Native American peoples called the Iroquois Nation.* **2. Confederacy** The Confederate States of America. **3.** A group of people united for unlawful practices; a conspiracy: *A confederacy of dissidents plotted the overthrow of the government.*

con·fed·er·ate (kən-**fĕd′**ər-ĭt) *n.* **1.** An associate in a plot or crime; an accomplice. **2.** A member of a confederacy. **3. Confederate** A supporter of the Confederate States of America. ❖ *adj.* **1.** Belonging to a confederacy. **2. Confederate** Relating to the Confederate States of

condor
California condor

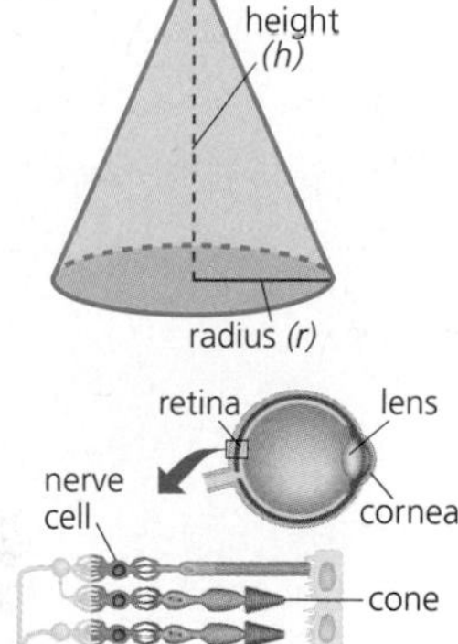

cone
top: right circular cone
bottom: detail of a retina showing cones and rods

confluence
confluence of the Iguazú and Paraná rivers in South America

ă	pat	ôr	core
ā	pay	oi	boy
âr	care	ou	out
ä	father	ŏŏ	took
ĕ	pet	ŏŏr	lure
ē	be	ōō	boot
ĭ	pit	ŭ	cut
ī	bite	ûr	urge
îr	pier	th	thin
ŏ	pot	*th*	this
ō	toe	zh	vision
ô	paw	ə	about

America. ❖ *tr. & intr.v.* (kən-**fĕd′**ə-rāt′) **con·fed·er·at·ed, con·fed·er·at·ing, con·fed·er·ates** To form into or become part of a confederacy.

Confederate States of America A republic made up of the 11 Southern states that seceded from the United States in 1860 and 1861. It was dissolved in 1865 after being defeated in the American Civil War.

con·fed·er·a·tion (kən-fĕd′ə-**rā′**shən) *n.* **1.** A group of people united for a common purpose; a league: *The teachers formed a national confederation to protect their interests.* **2.** A group of states, provinces, or territories united under a single government. **3.** The act of confederating or the state of being confederated.

con·fer (kən-**fûr′**) *v.* **con·ferred, con·fer·ring, con·fers** —*intr.* To meet in order to discuss something or compare opinions; consult: *The president conferred with cabinet advisers.* —*tr.* To bestow or award: *The mayor conferred a medal on the two heroic firefighters.* [From Latin *cōnferre* : *com-*, together + *ferre*, to bring.] —SEE NOTE AT **transfer.**

con·fer·ence (**kŏn′**fər-əns *or* **kŏn′**frəns) *n.* **1.** A meeting to discuss a subject or a number of subjects: *a peace conference.* **2.** A regional association of churches, athletic teams, or other groups. **3.** The act of conferring: *The principal and teachers were in conference for hours.*

conference call *n.* A conference by telephone in which three or more people participate.

con·fess (kən-**fĕs′**) *v.* **con·fessed, con·fess·ing, con·fess·es** —*tr.* **1.** To state openly or admit (something wrong or bad that one has done): *The children confessed that they had been playing with matches.* **2a.** To make known (one's sins) to a priest or to God. **b.** To hear the confession of (a person). —*intr.* **1.** To admit or acknowledge something wrong or bad that one has done: *The driver confessed to driving too fast.* **2.** To tell one's sins to a priest. [From Middle English *confessen*, from Latin *cōnfitērī*.]

con·fes·sion (kən-**fĕsh′**ən) *n.* **1.** The act of confessing or admitting; acknowledgment: *The suspect's full confession of guilt cleared up the case.* **2.** The act of telling one's sins to a priest or to God. **3.** Something confessed: *Did the prisoner sign her confession?*

con·fes·sion·al (kən-**fĕsh′**ə-nəl) *n.* A small booth in which a priest hears confessions.

con·fes·sor (kən-**fĕs′**ər) *n.* **1.** A priest who hears confession and gives absolution of sins. **2.** A person who accepts intimate confidences and consoles: *The counselor acted as confessor to the whole group.* **3.** A person who confesses.

con·fet·ti (kən-**fĕt′**ē) *pl.n.* *(used with a singular verb)* Small pieces of colored paper that are scattered about on festive occasions. [From Italian, plural of *confetto*, candy, from Latin *cōnficere*, to prepare.]

con·fi·dant (**kŏn′**fĭ-dănt′ *or* **kŏn′**fĭ-dänt′) *n.* A person to whom another person confides personal matters or secrets.

con·fide (kən-**fīd′**) *v.* **con·fid·ed, con·fid·ing, con·fides** —*tr.* **1.** To tell (something) in confidence: *confide a secret to a friend.* **2.** To put into another's care; entrust: *Before going on vacation, he confided the task of mowing the lawn to a friend.* —*intr.* To tell or share one's secrets with: *Can I confide in you?* **—con·fid′er** *n.*

con·fi·dence (**kŏn′**fĭ-dəns) *n.* **1.** Belief in the effectiveness of one's own abilities or in one's favorable acceptance by others; self-confidence: *She finally developed the confidence to sing in public.* **2.** Trust or faith: *We are placing our confidence in you to solve the problem.* **3.** A trusting relationship: *I have decided to take you into my confidence.* **4.** A feeling of assurance that someone will keep a secret: *I am telling you this in strict confidence.* **5.** Something confided; a secret: *the many confidences of close friends.*

con·fi·dent (**kŏn′**fĭ-dənt) *adj.* Feeling or showing confidence, especially in being sure of oneself; certain: *The lawyer is confident of winning the case. The surgeon approached the operation with a confident air.* [From Latin *cōnfīdere*, to rely on : *com-*, intensive prefix + *fīdere*, to trust.] **—con′fi·dent·ly** *adv.*

con·fi·den·tial (kŏn′fĭ-**dĕn′**shəl) *adj.* **1.** Told in confidence; secret: *A person's medical history is confidential information shared only with a doctor.* **2.** Entrusted with the confidence of someone else: *a confidential secretary.* **3.** Showing confidence or intimacy: *a confidential tone of voice.* **—con′fi·den′tial·ly** *adv.*

con·fid·ing (kən-**fī′**dĭng) *adj.* Having a tendency to confide; trusting: *a confiding nature.*

con·fig·u·ra·tion (kən-fĭg′yə-**rā′**shən) *n.* The form or arrangement of the parts of something: *a configuration of dots that form a picture when connected; the configuration of a computer system.*

con·fine (kən-**fīn′**) *tr.v.* **con·fined, con·fin·ing, con·fines 1.** To keep within bounds; restrict; limit: *Firefighters confined the fire to the roof.* **2.** To shut or keep inside, as in prison: *The dogs were confined to a kennel.* [From Latin *cōnfīnis*, adjoining : *com-*, together + *fīnis*, border.]

con·fine·ment (kən-**fīn′**mənt) *n.* **1.** The act of confining or condition of being confined: *The prisoner was held in solitary confinement.* **2.** The period of childbirth.

con·fines (**kŏn′**fīnz′) *pl.n.* The limits of a space or area; the borders: *The dog wandered beyond the confines of the yard.*

con·firm (kən-**fûrm′**) *tr.v.* **con·firmed, con·firm·ing, con·firms 1.** To support or establish the certainty or validity of: *The results of the experiment confirmed the theory.* **2.** To make firmer; strengthen: *Reading about famous scientists confirmed her intention to study chemistry.* **3.** To make valid or binding by a formal or legal act; ratify: *The judge's appointment to the Supreme Court was confirmed by the Senate.* **4.** To admit to full membership in a church or synagogue by the rite of confirmation. [From Middle English *confermen*, from Latin *cōnfirmāre* : *com-*, intensive prefix + *firmāre*, to strengthen (from *firmus*, strong).]

con·fir·ma·tion (kŏn′fər-**mā′**shən) *n.* **1.** The act of confirming: *The president needs the Senate's confirmation to appoint an ambassador.* **2.** Something that confirms; proof: *The license was confirmation of the doctor's qualification to practice medicine.* **3.** A Christian ceremony in which a baptized person is made a full member of a church. **4.** A Jewish ceremony marking the completion of a young person's religious training.

con·firmed (kən-**fûrmd′**) *adj.* **1.** Firmly established; proved: *a confirmed theory.* **2.** Settled in a habit or condition: *a confirmed gossip.* **—con·firm′ed·ly** (kən-**fûr′**mĭd-lē) *adv.*

con·fis·cate (**kŏn′**fĭ-skāt′) *tr.v.* **con·fis·cat·ed, con·fis·cat·ing, con·fis·cates 1.** To seize (private property) from someone for the public treasury: *The government confiscated the boat and its illegal goods.* **2.** To seize by authority; take away: *The teacher confiscated the pack of chewing gum.* **—con′fis·ca′tion** *n.*

con·fla·gra·tion (kŏn′flə-**grā′**shən) *n.* A large fire.

con·flict (**kŏn′**flĭkt′) *n.* **1.** A state of fighting; a battle or war. **2.** A state of disagreement, as between people, ideas, or interests: *a conflict between two sets of instructions.* ❖ *intr.v.* (kən-**flĭkt′**) **con·flict·ed, con·flict·ing, con·flicts** To be in opposition; differ; clash: *The meeting conflicts with my dental appointment.* [From Middle English, from Latin *cōnflīctus*, collision, from *cōnflīgere*, to strike together.]

conflict of interest *n., pl.* **conflicts of interest** A conflict between a person's private interests and public obligations: *To avoid a conflict of interest, the judge refused to hear a trial involving a company owned by her brother.*

con·flu·ence (kŏn′flo͞o-əns) *n.* **1.** The point at which two or more rivers or streams come together: *The city is located at the confluence of two important rivers.* **2.** A gathering, flowing, or joining together of people, causes, or events: *A confluence of factors led to the financial collapse.* [From Middle English, from Latin *cōnfluere*, to flow together.]

con·flu·ent (kŏn′flo͞o-ənt) *adj.* Flowing or running together; blending into one: *confluent rivers.*

con·form (kən-fôrm′) *intr.v.* **con·formed, con·form·ing, con·forms 1.** To be or act in agreement with established customs, expectations, or rules: *Many young people do not like to conform to the way older people dress.* See Synonyms at **adapt. 2.** To be similar in form or pattern: *a tarp that conforms to the shape of the boat.* **—con·form′er** *n.*

con·for·ma·tion (kŏn′fər-mā′shən) *n.* **1.** The way something is formed; shape or structure: *The conformation of a snake's skeleton is elongated.* **2.** The act of conforming or the state of being conformed.

con·form·ist (kən-fôr′mĭst) *n.* A person who conforms to current customs, rules, or styles.

con·form·i·ty (kən-fôr′mĭ-tē) *n., pl.* **con·form·i·ties 1.** Agreement; harmony: *practices that are in conformity with standards set by the industry.* **2.** Action or behavior that is in agreement with current customs, rules, or styles: *a policy that encouraged originality among employees rather than blind conformity.*

con·found (kən-found′ *or* kŏn-found′) *tr.v.* **con·found·ed, con·found·ing, con·founds 1.** To bewilder, puzzle, or perplex: *The dog's strange behavior confounded its master.* **2.** To mistake (one thing) for another; mix up: *The confused witness confounded fiction and fact.* [From Middle English *confounden*, from Latin *cōnfundere*, to mix together, confuse : *com-*, together + *fundere*, to pour.]

con·front (kən-frŭnt′) *tr.v.* **con·front·ed, con·front·ing, con·fronts 1.** To come face to face with, especially in opposition: *She finally confronted her rival on the tennis court.* **2.** To bring face to face with; cause to encounter: *The defendant was confronted with all the evidence and confessed.* **3.** To come up against; encounter: *The scientists confronted many difficulties in creating the new vaccine.* [From Medieval Latin *cōnfrontāre*, to adjoin.]

con·fron·ta·tion (kŏn′frŭn-tā′shən) *n.* **1.** The act of confronting or the state of being confronted: *The lawyer's confrontation of the witnesses proved their testimony was unreliable.* **2.** A direct encounter, especially a conflict or a clash, as of opponents: *The hikers hoped to avoid any confrontations with wild animals.*

Con·fu·cian (kən-fyo͞o′shən) *adj.* Relating to a set of principles of conduct that are based on the teaching of Confucius and that stress social harmony, justice, and devotion to family ancestors. **—Con·fu′cian·ism** *n.*

Con·fu·cius (kən-fyo͞o′shəs) c. 551–479 BC. Chinese philosopher who promoted a system of social and political ethics emphasizing order and moderation. The *Analects* contains a collection of his sayings and dialogues.

con·fuse (kən-fyo͞oz′) *tr.v.* **con·fused, con·fus·ing, con·fus·es 1.** To cause to be unable to understand or think clearly; perplex or bewilder: *The audience was confused by the poorly organized presentation.* **2.** To mistake (a person or thing) for someone or something else; fail to identify correctly: *The coach confused me with my brother.* [From Middle English *confusen*, from Latin *cōnfūsus*, past participle of *cōnfundere*, to mix together.] **—con·fus′ing·ly** *adv.*

con·fused (kən-fyo͞ozd′) *adj.* **1.** Bewildered; perplexed: *a confused look.* **2.** Mixed up; disordered: *a confused situation; a confused story.* **—con·fus′ed·ly** (kən-fyo͞o′zĭd-lē) *adv.*

con·fu·sion (kən-fyo͞o′zhən) *n.* **1.** The act of confusing: *The confusion of the addresses meant the package was not delivered to the right place.* **2.** The state of being confused: *The unexpected news threw us all into confusion.*

con·fute (kən-fyo͞ot′) *tr.v.* **con·fut·ed, con·fut·ing, con·futes** To prove to be wrong or false; refute: *The facts confuted his testimony. An expert confuted the speaker.* **—con′fu·ta′tion** (kŏn′fyo͞o-tā′shən) *n.*

con·geal (kən-jēl′) *v.* **con·gealed, con·geal·ing, con·geals** *—intr.* **1.** To become thicker or turn into a solid: *Fat congealed in globs on the surface of the soup.* **2.** To come together and form a whole or produce a result: *Popular discontent finally congealed into political opposition.* *—tr.* To cause to congeal: *The cool air congealed the fat.* [From Middle English *congelen*, from Latin *congelāre* : *com-*, together + *gelāre*, to freeze.] **—con·geal′ment** *n.*

con·gen·ial (kən-jēn′yəl) *adj.* **1.** Having similar tastes, habits, or dispositions: *two congenial people.* **2.** Of a pleasant disposition; friendly; amiable: *a congenial host.* **3.** Suited to one's nature; pleasant; agreeable: *The bright, airy room provided congenial surroundings.* **—con·ge′ni·al′i·ty** (kən-jē′nē-ăl′ĭ-tē) *n.* **—con·gen′ial·ly** *adv.*

con·gen·i·tal (kən-jĕn′ĭ-tl) *adj.* Existing at or before birth: *Many congenital defects can now be corrected by surgery.* **—con·gen′i·tal·ly** *adv.*

con·ger (kŏng′gər) *n.* Any of various large ocean eels, often caught for food in Europe.

con·gest (kən-jĕst′) *v.* **con·gest·ed, con·gest·ing, con·gests** *—tr.* **1.** To overfill; overcrowd: *Heavy traffic congested the highway.* **2.** To cause an abnormally large amount of fluid to collect in (a vessel or organ of the body). *—intr.* To become congested: *Pneumonia causes the lungs to congest with fluid.* **—con·ges′tive** *adj.*

con·ges·tion (kən-jĕs′chən) *n.* **1.** A condition of overcrowding: *traffic congestion during rush hour.* **2.** A condition in which fluid collects in an organ or tissue of the body: *Colds often produce bronchial congestion.*

con·ges·tive heart failure (kən-jĕs′tĭv) *n.* A medical condition characterized usually by shortness of breath, congestion in the lungs, fatigue, and fluid buildup resulting from the inability of a damaged heart to adequately pump blood to body tissues.

con·glom·er·ate (kən-glŏm′ə-rāt′) *intr. & tr.v.* **con·glom·er·at·ed, con·glom·er·at·ing, con·glom·er·ates** To form or cause to form into a mass; cluster. ❖ *n.* (kən-glŏm′ər-ĭt) **1.** A business corporation made up of a number of different companies that operate in widely diversified fields. **2.** A mass of material that clings together. **3.** A sedimentary rock that consists of pebbles, gravel, or seashells cemented together by hardened clay or a similar material. ❖ *adj.* (kən-glŏm′ər-ĭt) **1.** Formed together into a mass: *conglomerate rock formed of sand and pebbles.* **2.** Made up of many parts: *The reformers were a conglomerate group from several political parties.*

con·glom·er·a·tion (kən-glŏm′ə-rā′shən) *n.* A collection or accumulation of many different things or people.

Con·go (kŏng′gō) **1.** Officially **Democratic Republic of the Congo,** formerly **Za·ire** (zī′îr *or* zä-îr′). A country of central Africa astride the equator. Kinshasa is the capital. **2.** Officially **Republic of the Congo.** A country of west-central Africa with a short coastline on the Atlantic Ocean. Brazzaville is the capital.

Con·go·lese (kŏng′gō-lēz′ *or* kŏng′gō-lēs′) *adj.* Relating to the Democratic Republic of the Congo or the Republic of the Congo. ❖ *n., pl.* **Con·go·lese** A native or inhabitant of either of these countries.

Congo River A river of central Africa flowing about 2,920 miles (4,700 kilometers) north, west, and southwest through the Democratic Republic of the Congo to the Atlantic Ocean.

con·grat·u·late (kən-grăch′ə-lāt′ *or* kən-grăj′ə-lāt′) *tr.v.* **con·grat·u·lat·ed, con·grat·u·lat·ing, con·grat·**

Confucius

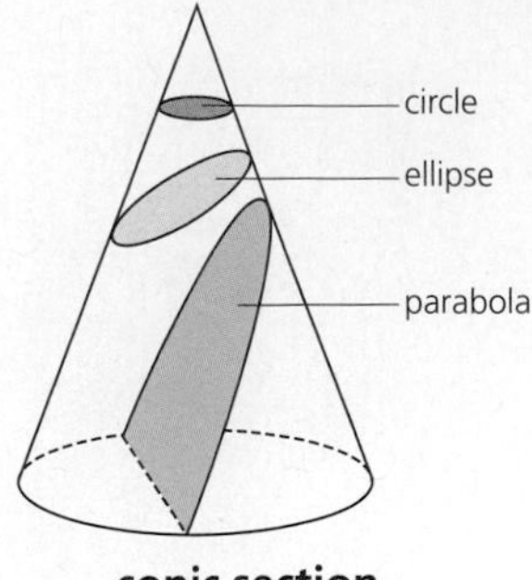

conic section

ă	pat	ôr	core
ā	pay	oi	boy
âr	care	ou	out
ä	father	o͝o	took
ĕ	pet	o͝or	lure
ē	be	o͞o	boot
ĭ	pit	ŭ	cut
ī	bite	ûr	urge
îr	pier	th	thin
ŏ	pot	*th*	this
ō	toe	zh	vision
ô	paw	ə	about

u·lates To express joy or good wishes to (someone) for an achievement or good fortune: *The crowd congratulated the newly elected mayor.* [From Latin *congrātulārī* : *com-*, with + *grātulārī*, to rejoice.]

con·grat·u·la·tion (kən-grăch′ə-**lā′**shən *or* kən-grăj′-ə-**lā′**shən) *n.* often **congratulations** An expression of joy or acknowledgement: *I shook the winner's hand in congratulation. We sent a card with our congratulations to the new parents.* ❖ *interj.* **congratulations** An expression used to show joy or acknowledgement: *You won first prize. Congratulations!*

con·grat·u·la·to·ry (kən-**grăch′**ə-lə-tôr′ē *or* kən-**grăj′**ə-lə-tôr′ē) *adj.* Expressing congratulations: *a congratulatory message.*

con·gre·gate (**kŏng′**grĭ-gāt′) *intr.v.* **con·gre·gat·ed, con·gre·gat·ing, con·gre·gates** To come together in a crowd or mass; assemble: *Salmon congregate at the falls in large numbers.* [From Middle English *congregaten*, from Latin *congregāre* : *com-*, together + *gregāre*, to assemble (from *grex*, herd).] **—con′gre·ga′tor** *n.*

con·gre·ga·tion (kŏng′grĭ-**gā′**shən) *n.* **1a.** A group of people gathered for religious worship: *The congregation bowed their heads in prayer.* **b.** The members of a specific religious group who regularly worship at a church or synagogue. **2.** A gathering of people or things: *The congregation of tourists crowded around the exhibit.* **3.** The act of assembling: *the congregation of birds on their nesting grounds.*

con·gre·ga·tion·al (kŏng′grĭ-**gā′**shə-nəl) *adj.* **1.** Relating to a congregation: *congregational worship.* **2. Congregational** Relating to Congregationalism or Congregationalists.

con·gre·ga·tion·al·ism (kŏng′grĭ-**gā′**shə-nə-lĭz′əm) *n.* **1.** Church government in which each local congregation governs itself. **2. Congregationalism** The system of government and religious beliefs of a Protestant denomination in which each member church is self-governing. **—con′gre·ga′tion·al·ist, Con′gre·ga′tion·al·ist** *adj. & n.*

con·gress (**kŏng′**grĭs) *n.* **1.** A formal meeting of people representing various nations, organizations, or professions to discuss problems: *a medical congress of heart specialists.* **2.** The lawmaking body of a republic. **3. Congress** The national legislative body of the United States, consisting of the Senate and the House of Representatives. [From Middle English *congresse*, body of attendants, from Latin *congressus*, meeting, from past participle of *congredī*, to meet : *com-*, together + *gradī*, to go.] **—con·gres′sion·al** (kən-**grĕsh′**ə-nəl *or* kəng-**grĕsh′**ə-nəl) *adj.*

con·gress·man (**kŏng′**grĭs-mən) *n.* A man who is a member of the United States Congress, especially of the House of Representatives.

con·gress·wom·an (**kŏng′**grĭs-wo͝om′ən) *n.* A woman who is a member of the United States Congress, especially of the House of Representatives.

con·gru·ence (**kŏng′**gro͞o-əns *or* kən-**gro͞o′**əns) *n.* The condition of being congruent.

con·gru·en·cy (**kŏng′**gro͞o-ən-sē *or* kən-**gro͞o′**ən-sē) *n., pl.* **con·gru·en·cies** Congruence.

con·gru·ent (**kŏng′**gro͞o-ənt *or* kən-**gro͞o′**ənt) *adj.* **1.** In geometry, matching exactly; having the same size and shape: *congruent triangles.* **2.** Corresponding or agreeing; harmonious: *congruent objectives of policy.* [From Middle English, from Latin *congruere*, to agree.] **—con′gru·ent·ly** *adv.*

con·gru·i·ty (kən-**gro͞o′**ĭ-tē) *n., pl.* **con·gru·i·ties 1.** Agreement; harmony: *The two leaders worked in congruity to achieve world peace.* **2.** The state or fact of being congruent: *the congruity of superimposed triangles.*

con·ic (**kŏn′**ĭk) *adj.* Conical.

con·i·cal (**kŏn′**ĭ-kəl) *adj.* Relating to or shaped like a cone. **—con′i·cal·ly** *adv.*

conic section *n.* A curve, such as a circle, ellipse, hyperbola, or parabola, formed by the intersection of a plane with a cone.

con·i·fer (**kŏn′**ə-fər *or* **kō′**nə-fər) *n.* Any of various trees or shrubs that bear cones. Conifers are usually evergreen and include the pines, firs, spruces, hemlocks, and yews. [From Latin *cōnifer*, cone-bearing.]

co·nif·er·ous (kō-**nĭf′**ər-əs *or* kə-**nĭf′**ər-əs) *adj.* **1.** Bearing cones: *coniferous trees such as pines and hemlocks.* **2.** Relating to conifers: *a coniferous forest.*

conj. *abbr.* An abbreviation of conjunction.

con·jec·tur·al (kən-**jĕk′**chər-əl) *adj.* Based on or inclined to conjecture: *a conjectural forecast of economic improvement.*

con·jec·ture (kən-**jĕk′**chər) *n.* **1.** The formation of an opinion or conclusion from incomplete or insufficient evidence; guesswork: *The origin of language is a matter of conjecture.* **2.** A statement, opinion, or conclusion based on guesswork; a guess: *make a conjecture about the election's outcome.* ❖ *intr.v.* **con·jec·tured, con·jec·tur·ing, con·jec·tures** To make a conjecture; guess: *The radio commentator conjectured on who would be the new mayor.*

con·join (kən-**join′**) *tr. & intr.v.* **con·joined, con·join·ing, con·joins** To join or become joined; connect; unite: *A strip of sand conjoined the two islands at low tide. The two parties conjoined into one.* **—con·join′er** *n.*

conjoined twin (kən-**joind′**) *n.* One of a pair of identical twins born with parts of their bodies joined together. Conjoined twins develop when an early embryo divides incompletely into two parts.

con·joint (kən-**joint′**) *adj.* Joined together; combined: *a conjoint military action involving air and naval forces.*

con·ju·gal (**kŏn′**jə-gəl) *adj.* Relating to marriage or the relationship of spouses: *conjugal happiness.* **—con′ju·gal·ly** *adv.*

con·ju·gate (**kŏn′**jə-gāt′) *v.* **con·ju·gat·ed, con·ju·gat·ing, con·ju·gates** —*tr.* To give the inflected forms of a verb, usually in a set order. For example, the verb "to have" is conjugated *I have, you have, she has, we have, you have, they have.* —*intr.* In biology, to unite or fuse in conjugation. ❖ *adj.* (**kŏn′**jə-gĭt *or* **kŏn′**jə-gāt′) Joined together, especially in pairs; coupled. [From Latin *coniugāre*, to join together : *com-*, together + *iugāre*, to join (from *iugum*, yoke).]

con·ju·ga·tion (kŏn′jə-**gā′**shən) *n.* **1a.** The inflection of a particular verb. **b.** A presentation of the complete set of inflected forms of a verb. **c.** A class of verbs having similar inflected forms. **2a.** A type of sexual reproduction in which single-celled organisms of the same species join together and exchange nuclear material before each organism undergoes cell division. **b.** The union of reproductive cells to form a fertilized cell.

con·junc·tion (kən-**jŭngk′**shən) *n.* **1.** The act of joining or state of being joined; combination: *A happy conjunction of circumstances strengthened the economy.* **2a.** A part of speech that connects words, phrases, clauses, or sentences. **b.** A word belonging to this part of speech. *And, but, or,* and *yet* are examples of conjunctions in English. **3.** In astronomy, an arrangement in which a planet or the moon lies on a straight line from Earth to or through the sun. When the moon is in conjunction, it is a new moon. [From Middle English *conjunccioun*, from Latin *coniūnctiō*, from *coniungere*, to join together.]

con·junc·ti·va (kŏn′jŭngk-**tī′**və) *n., pl.* **con·junc·ti·vas** or **con·junc·ti·vae** (kŏn′jŭngk-**tī′**vē) The mucous membrane that lines the inside of the eyelid and covers the surface of the eyeball.

con·junc·tive (kən-**jŭngk′**tĭv) *adj.* **1.** Joined or serving to join together. **2.** In grammar, connecting or serving as a conjunction. Conjunctive adverbs, such as *however* and *therefore,* are used to connect sentences. —**con·junc′tive·ly** *adv.*

con·junc·ti·vi·tis (kən-jŭngk′tə-**vī′**tĭs) *n.* Inflammation of the conjunctiva, often in the form of pinkeye.

con·jure (**kŏn′**jər *or* kən-**jŏŏr′**) *v.* **con·jured, con·jur·ing, con·jures** —*tr.* **1.** To summon (a devil or spirit) by a magic or supernatural power. **2.** To influence or bring about as if by magic: *In saving the patient our doctor conjured a miracle.* **3.** To call to mind: *The mention of Kansas conjures up images of fields of grain.* —*intr.* To practice magic; perform magic tricks. [From Middle English *conjuren,* to summon under oath, from Late Latin *coniūrāre,* to pray by something holy : Latin *com-,* together + Latin *iūrāre,* to swear.]

con·jur·er also **con·jur·or** (**kŏn′**jər-ər *or* **kŭn′**jər-ər) *n.* A magician or sorcerer.

conk (kŏngk) *Informal n.* A blow, especially on the head. ❖ *tr.v.* **conked, conk·ing, conks** To hit, especially on the head. ◆ **conk out 1.** To fail suddenly; break down: *The engine conked out.* **2.** To fall asleep, especially suddenly: *He conked out while watching television.*
❑ *These sound alike:* **conk, conch** (mollusk).

con·nect (kə-**nĕkt′**) *v.* **con·nect·ed, con·nect·ing, con·nects** —*tr.* **1.** To join or fasten together; link: *A new road connects the two towns.* See Synonyms at **join. 2.** To consider as related; associate in the mind: *We connect summer with picnics and swimming.* **3.** To plug in (an electrical cord or device) to an outlet: *connect a TV set.* **4.** To link by telephone or other communications circuit: *The operator connected me with the order department. Her computer is connected to the Internet.* —*intr.* **1.** To be or become joined: *The two streams connected to form a river.* **2.** To be scheduled so that passengers can transfer from one bus, train, or airplane to another: *The bus connected with the train at the station.* [From Middle English *connecten,* from Latin *cōnectere* : *cō-,* together + *nectere,* to bind.] —**con·nect′er, con·nec′tor** *n.* —**con·nect′i·ble** *adj.*

Con·nect·i·cut (kə-**nĕt′**ĭ-kət) A state of the northeast United States south of Massachusetts. It was admitted as one of the original Thirteen Colonies in 1788. In 1635 colonists from Massachusetts began to settle in the **Connecticut River** valley. Hartford is the capital and Bridgeport the largest city. —SEE NOTE.

con·nec·tion (kə-**nĕk′**shən) *n.* **1.** The act of connecting or the condition of being connected: *Connection of the telephone cables took several hours. That doctor's connection to the hospital has benefited many patients.* **2.** Something that connects or joins; a link: *a telephone connection; rail connections between the two cities.* **3.** An association or relationship: *There is a connection between good health and eating well.* **4.** A person with whom one is associated, as by kinship, common interests, or marriage: *I heard about the job through family connections.* **5.** A usually influential or important person with whom one is associated: *used my connections to get a job in the newsroom.* **6.** A means of continuing transportation: *I missed my connection in Chicago.*

con·nec·tive (kə-**nĕk′**tĭv) *adj.* Connecting or serving to connect. ❖ *n.* **1.** Something that connects. **2.** In grammar, a word such as a conjunction that connects words, phrases, clauses, or sentences.

connective tissue *n.* Tissue that forms the framework and supporting structures of the body, including bone, cartilage, mucous membrane, and fat.

con·ning tower (**kŏn′**ĭng) *n.* **1.** A raised, enclosed structure on the deck of a submarine, used for observation and as an entrance or exit. **2.** The armored pilothouse of a warship.

con·nive (kə-**nīv′**) *intr.v.* **con·nived, con·niv·ing, con·nives 1.** To cooperate secretly in an illegal or wrongful action: *The traitor connived with the enemy.* **2.** To pretend not to notice or fail to deal with something that should be reported or condemned: *The mayor connived at the bribery of city officials.* —**con·niv′ance** (kə-**nī′**vəns) *n.*

con·nois·seur (kŏn′ə-**sûr′** *or* kŏn′ə-**sŏŏr′**) *n.* A person who has expert knowledge or excellent judgment of something, such as art or fine food. [From Old French *connoisseor,* from *connoistre,* to know, from Latin *cognōscere.*]

con·no·ta·tion (kŏn′ə-**tā′**shən) *n.* A meaning suggested by a certain word in addition to its literal or most exact meaning: *The word "lamb" has connotations of simplicity and innocence.*

con·note (kə-**nōt′**) *tr.v.* **con·not·ed, con·not·ing, con·notes** To suggest or imply in addition to literal or exact meaning: *In a political leader, hesitation is apt to connote weakness.*

con·nu·bi·al (kə-**nōō′**bē-əl) *adj.* Relating to marriage or the relationship between spouses; conjugal: *connubial bliss.*

con·quer (**kŏng′**kər) *tr.v.* **con·quered, con·quer·ing, con·quers 1.** To get control of or subdue by military force: *In 1066 the Norman French conquered England.* **2.** To eliminate or overcome: *Scientists have conquered many diseases by developing vaccines. You must conquer your fear if you want to learn to fly.* [From Middle English *conqueren,* from Latin *conquīrere,* to procure : *com-,* intensive prefix + *quaerere,* to seek.] —**con′quer·or, con′quer·er** *n.*

con·quest (**kŏn′**kwĕst′ *or* **kŏng′**kwĕst′) *n.* **1.** An act of conquering: *the Spanish conquest of lands in the New World.* **2.** Something conquered: *one of the empire's conquests.* [From Middle English, from Old French.]

con·quis·ta·dor (kŏn-**kwĭs′**tə-dôr′ *or* kŏng-**kē′**stə-dôr′) *n., pl.* **con·quis·ta·dors** or **con·quis·ta·dor·es** (kŏng-**kē′**stə-dôr′ās) One of the Spanish conquerors of Mexico, Central America, and Peru in the 1500s.

con·science (**kŏn′**shəns) *n.* A sense of right and wrong that urges one to act morally: *Listen to your conscience and you'll be glad in the long run.*

con·sci·en·tious (kŏn′shē-**ĕn′**shəs) *adj.* **1.** Guided by or done with a sense of what is right or proper: *a conscientious decision.* **2.** Careful and thorough: *a conscientious worker.* —**con′sci·en′tious·ly** *adv.* —**con′sci·en′tious·ness** *n.*

conscientious objector *n.* A person who on the basis of religious belief or moral principle refuses to serve in the armed forces or take up arms.

con·scious (**kŏn′**shəs) *adj.* **1.** Able to perceive what is happening around oneself; awake: *The patient was fully conscious throughout the operation.* **2a.** Having an awareness of one's own existence, sensations, thoughts, and surroundings: *People are not always conscious of their talents.* **b.** Known to oneself or felt by oneself: *filled with conscious remorse.* **3.** Intentionally done; deliberate: *make a conscious effort to speak more distinctly.* [From Latin *cōnscius* : *com-,* together + *scīre,* to know.] —**con′scious·ly** *adv.*

con·scious·ness (**kŏn′**shəs-nĭs) *n.* **1.** The condition of being conscious: *The doctor asked if the patient had lost consciousness.* **2.** The sense of identity, especially the ideas, opinions, and feelings, held by a person or shared by a group: *Love of freedom runs deep in the national consciousness.*

con·script (**kŏn′**skrĭpt′) *n.* A person who is drafted, especially into the armed forces. ❖ *tr.v.* (kən-**skrĭpt′**) **con·script·ed, con·script·ing, con·scripts** To enroll by force into service in the armed forces; draft: *Some volunteered for the army, while others were conscripted.* —**con·scrip′tion** (kən-**skrĭp′**shən) *n.*

con·se·crate (**kŏn′**sĭ-krāt′) *tr.v.* **con·se·crat·ed, con·se·crat·ing, con·se·crates 1.** To declare or set apart as sacred: *consecrate a new church.* **2.** To dedicate to a

GEOGRAPHY

Connecticut The name for the state of **Connecticut** comes from a Mohegan word meaning "by the long river." The name was given to the Connecticut River, from which the state then takes its name. The silent second *c* was not in the earliest spelling of the word; it was put in by someone who may have thought the name began with the word *connect.*

WORD BUILDING

consent The word roots *sent–* and *sens–* in English words come from the Latin verb *sentīre,* "to feel, sense, judge," which has the past participle *sēnsus.* **Consent** therefore means "to feel with, agree" (using the prefix *con–,* a form of *com–,* "with, together"). **Dissent** is literally "to judge differently" (*dis–,* "apart"). A **consensus** is "a feeling all together, universal agreement"; **dissension** is the exact opposite—general disagreement.

WORD HISTORY

consommé The rich, thick, heavy broth we call **consommé** is soup that is all used up. *Consommé* in French means "finished, used up, completed," because the meat in the soup is slowly boiled to get all the nourishment out of it. *Consommé* is the past participle of the French verb *consommer,* "to finish, complete, end," and comes from the Latin word *consummāre,* "to finish up, finish off." From *consummāre* we also get the verb *consummate,* the adjective *consummate,* and the noun *consummation.*

ă	pat	ôr	core
ā	pay	oi	boy
âr	care	ou	out
ä	father	o͝o	took
ĕ	pet	o͝or	lure
ē	be	o͞o	boot
ĭ	pit	ŭ	cut
ī	bite	ûr	urge
îr	pier	th	thin
ŏ	pot	*th*	this
ō	toe	zh	vision
ô	paw	ə	about

worthy purpose: *The nurse's life was consecrated to caring for the ill.* [From Middle English *consecraten,* from Latin *cōnsecrāre* : *com-,* intensive prefix + *sacrāre,* to make sacred.] **—con′se·cra′tion** *n.* **—con′se·cra′tor** *n.*

con·sec·u·tive (kən-**sĕk′**yə-tĭv) *adj.* Following in order, without a break or interruption; successive: *It rained this week for five consecutive days.* [From Medieval Latin *cōnsecūtīvus,* from Latin *cōnsequī,* to follow closely.] **—con·sec′u·tive·ly** *adv.*

con·sen·sus (kən-**sĕn′**səs) *n.* An opinion reached by a group as a whole; general agreement: *The consensus among voters is for building the new school.* —SEE NOTE AT **consent.**

con·sent (kən-**sĕnt′**) *intr.v.* **con·sent·ed, con·sent·ing, con·sents** To give permission; agree: *My parents finally consented to let me go skiing.* ❖ *n.* Agreement and acceptance; permission: *Our teacher got the principal's consent to let us go early.* [From Middle English *consenten,* from Latin *cōnsentīre* : *com-,* together + *sentīre,* to feel.] —SEE NOTE.

con·se·quence (**kŏn′**sĭ-kwĕns′) *n.* **1.** Something that follows from an action or condition; an effect: *Having a large vocabulary was a consequence of so much reading.* **2.** Importance; significance: *a minor matter of no consequence.* [From Middle English, from Latin *cōnsequī,* to follow closely.]

con·se·quent (**kŏn′**sĭ-kwĕnt′) *adj.* Following as an effect or result: *heavy rains and the consequent flooding of the farmlands.*

con·se·quen·tial (kŏn′sĭ-**kwĕn′**shəl) *adj.* **1.** Important; significant: *a consequential decision that affected us all.* **2.** Distinguished; influential: *She is the most consequential film critic writing today.* **3.** Consequent: *a downturn in the markets with a consequential rise in unemployment.* **—con′se·quen′tial·ly** *adv.*

con·se·quent·ly (**kŏn′**sĭ-kwĕnt′lē) *adv.* As a result; therefore: *I forgot my key and consequently was locked out of the house.*

con·ser·va·tion (kŏn′sûr-**vā′**shən) *n.* **1.** The act or process of conserving. **2.** Preservation from loss or damage, especially the protection, management, or restoration of wildlife and of natural resources, such as forests, soil, and water. **3.** The continuance of a physical quantity, such as mass, in the same amount during a physical or chemical change.

con·ser·va·tion·ist (kŏn′sûr-**vā′**shə-nĭst) *n.* A person who advocates or practices conservation, especially of natural resources.

conservation of energy *n.* A principle of physics stating that the total energy in any closed system does not vary, although energy can be changed from one form into another.

conservation of mass *n.* A principle of physics stating that the total mass of a closed system remains constant regardless of reactions within the system. In a chemical reaction, matter is thought to be neither created nor destroyed but changed from one substance to another.

conservation of mass-energy *n.* Mass-energy equivalence.

con·ser·va·tism (kən-**sûr′**və-tĭz′əm) *n.* **1.** Conservative political views and policies. **2.** Caution or moderation, as in behavior or outlook: *an investor who practiced conservatism in managing her money.*

con·ser·va·tive (kən-**sûr′**və-tĭv) *adj.* **1.** Favoring things as they are; opposing change: *a conservative attitude toward manners.* **2.** Traditional in style; not showy: *a conservative dark suit.* **3.** Moderate; cautious; restrained: *a conservative estimate of expenses.* **4.** often **Conservative** Relating to or belonging to a political party or group that emphasizes respect for traditional institutions and that generally opposes the attempt to bring about social change through legislation or government programs. **5.** **Conservative** Relating to or belonging to Conservative Judaism. ❖ *n.* **1.** A person who is conservative. **2.** often **Conservative** A member of a conservative party. **—con·serv′a·tive·ly** *adv.*

Conservative Judaism *n.* The branch of Judaism that allows for changes in Jewish law that are authorized by rabbis.

con·ser·va·to·ry (kən-**sûr′**və-tôr′ē) *n., pl.* **con·ser·va·to·ries 1.** A greenhouse in which plants are arranged for display. **2.** A school of music, theater, or dance.

con·serve (kən-**sûrv′**) *tr.v.* **con·served, con·serv·ing, con·serves 1.** To protect from loss or harm; preserve: *conserve one's energy; conserve forests and other natural resources.* **2.** To use carefully; avoid wasting: *We turned down the thermostat to conserve energy.* **3.** To preserve (fruits) by cooking with sugar. **4.** To keep (a physical quantity, such as mass) in the same amount during a physical or chemical change. ❖ *n.* (**kŏn′**sûrv′) A jam made of fruits stewed in sugar. [From Middle English *conserven,* from Latin *cōnservāre.*]

con·sid·er (kən-**sĭd′**ər) *v.* **con·sid·ered, con·sid·er·ing, con·sid·ers** *—tr.* **1.** To think about (something) carefully, especially before making a decision: *I will consider what you said and respond later.* **2.** To regard as; believe to be: *She considers this the most beautiful park in town.* **3.** To take into account; keep in mind: *He sings well if you consider the fact that he never had lessons.* **4.** To be thoughtful of; show consideration for: *Consider the feelings of other people.* *—intr.* To think carefully; reflect: *Give me time to consider.* [From Middle English *consideren,* from Latin *cōnsīderāre,* to observe attentively (probably originally meaning "to observe the stars attentively") : *com-,* intensive prefix + *sīdus,* star.]

con·sid·er·a·ble (kən-**sĭd′**ər-ə-bəl) *adj.* **1.** Large or great in amount, extent, or degree: *They gave considerable thought to the matter.* **2.** Worth considering; important; significant: *a considerable issue.* **—con·sid′er·a·bly** *adv.*

con·sid·er·ate (kən-**sĭd′**ər-ĭt) *adj.* Taking into account other people's feelings; thoughtful: *quiet and considerate neighbors.* **—con·sid′er·ate·ly** *adv.* **—con·sid′er·ate·ness** *n.*

con·sid·er·a·tion (kən-sĭd′ə-**rā′**shən) *n.* **1.** Careful thought; deliberation: *The matter is complicated and needs consideration.* **2.** A factor to be considered in making a judgment or decision: *The health of the public is an important consideration when allocating tax dollars.* **3.** Thoughtful concern: *consideration for people's feelings.* **4.** A payment for a service rendered; a fee: *I agreed to take care of their dog for a small consideration.* ◆ **in consideration of 1.** In view of; on account of: *a medal awarded in consideration of bravery.* **2.** In return for: *payment in consideration of extra work.*

con·sid·ered (kən-**sĭd′**ərd) *adj.* Reached after careful thought: *my considered opinion.*

con·sid·er·ing (kən-**sĭd′**ər-ĭng) *prep.* In view of; taking into consideration: *Considering the mistakes that were made, it is amazing that the job was completed.*

con·sign (kən-**sīn′**) *tr.v.* **con·signed, con·sign·ing, con·signs 1.** To give or hand over, especially to the care of another: *The criminals have been consigned to prison.* **2.** To deliver (merchandise) for sale: *The manufacturer consigned the cars to the dealer.* **—con·sign′a·ble** *adj.*

con·sign·ment (kən-**sīn′**mənt) *n.* **1.** The delivery of something, as for sale or safekeeping: *The consignment of food for the earthquake victims was a top priority.* **2.** Something that is consigned, as for sale: *The store received a consignment of umbrellas.* ◆ **on consignment** With the agreement that payment is expected only after sales have been made and that unsold items may be returned: *The store owner accepted the shipment on consignment.*

con·sist (kən-**sĭst′**) *intr.v.* **con·sist·ed, con·sist·ing, con·**

sists 1. To be made up or composed: *The United States consists of 50 states.* **2.** To have a basis; lie: *The beauty of the author's style consists in its simplicity.* [From Latin *cōnsistere*, to stand still, to be composed of.]

con·sis·ten·cy (kən-sĭs′tən-sē) *n., pl.* **con·sis·ten·cies 1.** Agreement or harmony among things or parts: *A polite greeting is in consistency with good manners.* **2.** Adherence to or agreement with the same principles or course of action: *The game was confusing because the rules lacked consistency.* **3.** The degree of firmness, density, or thickness: *mix water and clay to the consistency of thick cream.*

con·sis·tent (kən-sĭs′tənt) *adj.* **1.** In agreement; compatible: *The experimental results were consistent with the theory.* **2.** Continually adhering to the same principles or course of action: *a consistent supporter of women's rights.* **—con·sis′tent·ly** *adv.*

con·sis·to·ry (kən-sĭs′tə-rē) *n., pl.* **con·sis·to·ries 1.** A council of the cardinals of the Roman Catholic Church, presided over by the pope. **2.** The governing assembly of certain Protestant churches.

con·so·la·tion (kŏn′sə-lā′shən) *n.* **1.** The act or an instance of consoling or comforting. **2.** Something that consoles: *The one consolation in having my wisdom teeth out is that I'll get lots of ice cream.*

consolation prize *n.* A prize given to someone who participates in but does not win a contest.

con·sole¹ (kən-sōl′) *tr.v.* **con·soled, con·sol·ing, con·soles** To comfort in time of disappointment or sorrow: *Friends consoled the widow at the funeral.* [From Latin *cōnsōlārī*.]

con·sole² (**kŏn′**sōl′) *n.* **1.** A cabinet for a radio, television set, or stereo system, designed to stand on the floor. **2.** A small storage compartment mounted between bucket seats in an automobile. **3.** A panel housing the controls for a system of electronic or mechanical equipment. **4.** A computer system designed to play a specific format of video game using special controllers. **5.** The part of an organ facing the player, containing the keyboard, stops, and pedals. **6.** A decorative bracket for supporting a cornice or shelf. [From French, perhaps short for *consolider*, to strengthen, from Latin *cōnsolidāre*.]

con·sol·i·date (kən-sŏl′ĭ-dāt′) *v.* **con·sol·i·dat·ed, con·sol·i·dat·ing, con·sol·i·dates** —*tr.* **1.** To combine into one; unite: *The ranch was formed when four small farms were consolidated.* **2.** To make secure and strong: *She consolidated her power during her first year in office.* —*intr.* To be united or combined: *The two businesses consolidated into one large firm.* [From Latin *cōnsolidāre* : *com-*, intensive prefix + *solidāre*, to make firm (from *solidus*, firm).] **—con·sol′i·da′tion** *n.*

con·som·mé (kŏn′sə-**mā′** *or* **kŏn′**sə-mā′) *n.* A clear soup made of meat or vegetable broth. —SEE NOTE.

con·so·nance (**kŏn′**sə-nəns) *n.* **1.** Agreement; harmony; accord. **2.** A combination of musical tones that are regarded as pleasing.

con·so·nant (**kŏn′**sə-nənt) *n.* **1.** A speech sound made by partially or completely blocking the flow of air through one's mouth. **2.** A letter of the alphabet representing such a sound, as *b, m, s,* and *t.* ❖ *adj.* **1.** Consonantal: *a consonant sound.* **2.** Being in agreement or accord: *Her remarks were consonant with her stated principles.* **3.** Musically harmonious. [From Middle English, from Latin *cōnsonāre*, to agree : *com-*, together + *sonāre*, to sound.]

con·so·nan·tal (kŏn′sə-**năn′**tl) *adj.* Relating to or containing a consonant or consonants.

con·sort (**kŏn′**sôrt′) *n.* A husband or wife, especially of a monarch. ❖ *intr.v.* (kən-**sôrt′**) **con·sort·ed, con·sort·ing, con·sorts** To keep company; associate: *a musician who consorts with movie stars.*

con·spic·u·ous (kən-spĭk′yōō-əs) *adj.* **1.** Easily seen; obvious: *a conspicuous spot on the front of my shirt.* **2.** Attracting attention; striking; remarkable: *a conspicuous achievement.* [From Latin *cōnspicuus*, from *cōnspicere*, to observe : *com-*, intensive prefix + *specere*, to look.] **—con·spic′u·ous·ly** *adv.*

con·spir·a·cy (kən-**spîr′**ə-sē) *n., pl.* **con·spir·a·cies 1.** The act of secretly planning with others to do something unlawful: *The prisoner was charged with conspiracy and treason.* **2.** A secret plan to commit an unlawful act; a plot: *A conspiracy to overthrow the government was uncovered.* **3.** A group planning such a secret act: *He was thought to be the leader of the conspiracy.*

con·spir·a·tor (kən-**spîr′**ə-tər) *n.* A person who takes part in a conspiracy; a plotter.

con·spire (kən-**spīr′**) *intr.v.* **con·spired, con·spir·ing, con·spires 1.** To plan together secretly to commit an illegal or wrongful act: *Traitors conspired to assassinate the military leader.* **2.** To work together; combine: *Good weather and a reliable car conspired to make the trip a happy one.* [From Middle English *conspiren*, from Latin *cōnspīrāre* : *com-*, together + *spīrāre*, to breathe, whisper.] **—con·spir′er** *n.*

con·sta·ble (**kŏn′**stə-bəl *or* **kŭn′**stə-bəl) *n.* **1.** A public officer in a town or village having somewhat less authority than a sheriff. **2.** *Chiefly British* A police officer. [From Middle English, from Late Latin *comes stabulī*, officer of the stable : Latin *comes*, officer, companion + Latin *stabulum*, stable.]

con·stab·u·lar·y (kən-**stăb′**yə-lĕr′ē) *n., pl.* **con·stab·u·lar·ies 1a.** The body of constables of a certain district. **b.** The district under the jurisdiction of a constable. **2.** An armed police force organized like a military unit.

con·stan·cy (**kŏn′**stən-sē) *n.* **1.** The quality of remaining constant; changelessness: *the constancy of the stars.* **2.** Faithfulness; steadfastness: *constancy in friendship.*

con·stant (**kŏn′**stənt) *adj.* **1.** Not changing or varying; continuous: *a constant gentle rain; drove at a constant speed.* **2.** Happening regularly or repeatedly; continual: *the constant barking of the dog next door; constant interruptions.* **3.** Steadfast in loyalty or affection; faithful: *a constant friend.* ❖ *n.* **1.** Something that never changes. **2.** In mathematics: **a.** A number that has a fixed value in a specific situation: *In averaging final grades for the semester, the number of tests is a constant for each student.* **b.** A number that never varies: *The ratio of the circumference to the diameter of a circle is π, a constant.* [From Middle English *constaunt*, from Latin *cōnstāre*, to stand firm : *com-*, intensive prefix + *stāre*, to stand.] **—con′stant·ly** *adv.*

Con·stan·tine I (**kŏn′**stən-tēn′ *or* **kŏn′**stən-tīn′) AD 285?–337. Emperor of Rome (306–337) who adopted Christianity and suspended the persecution of Christians.

Con·stan·ti·no·ple (kŏn′stăn-tə-**nō′**pəl) See **Istanbul.**

con·stel·la·tion (kŏn′stə-**lā′**shən) *n.* **1.** A group of stars, especially one perceived as a design or mythological figure: *Orion and Cassiopeia are two well-known constellations.* **2.** A group or gathering of distinguished people or things: *The Nobel Prize ceremony is usually attended by a constellation of scientists and scholars.* [From Middle English, from Late Latin *cōnstēllātiō* : *com-*, together + *stēlla*, star.]

con·ster·na·tion (kŏn′stər-**nā′**shən) *n.* Great fear or dismay: *To our consternation the dog darted out into the road.*

con·sti·pate (**kŏn′**stə-pāt′) *tr.v.* **con·sti·pat·ed, con·sti·pat·ing, con·sti·pates** To cause constipation in.

con·sti·pa·tion (kŏn′stə-**pā′**shən) *n.* Difficult or infrequent movement of the bowels.

con·stit·u·en·cy (kən-**stĭch′**ōō-ən-sē) *n., pl.* **con·stit·u·en·cies** A body of voters in a district represented by an

WRITERS CHOOSE THEIR WORDS

The fifth-grade boys, bursting with new importance, ordered the fourth graders this way and that, while the smaller boys tried to include themselves without being **conspicuous.**

—Katherine Paterson
Bridge to Terabithia

Constantine I
4th-century AD bronze sculpture

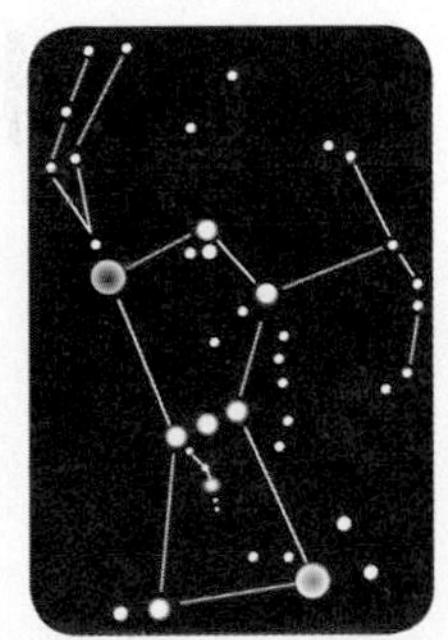

constellation
the constellation Orion (the Hunter); Orion's belt can be seen in the middle of the figure, and his sword hangs from the belt

elected representative or official: *The constituency repeatedly returned the senator to office.*

con·stit·u·ent (kən-**stĭch′**o͞o-ənt) *adj.* **1.** Making up part of a whole: *An atom is a constituent element of a molecule.* **2.** Authorized to draw up or change a constitution: *a constituent assembly.* ❖ *n.* **1.** A constituent part; a component: *Flour is the main constituent of bread.* **2.** A person represented by an elected official: *The congresswoman asked her constituents for their opinions on the pending legislation.*

con·sti·tute (**kŏn′**stĭ-to͞ot′) *tr.v.* **con·sti·tut·ed, con·sti·tut·ing, con·sti·tutes 1.** To be the elements or parts of; compose: *Four quarters constitute a dollar.* **2.** To set up; establish: *Police departments are constituted to maintain law and order.* **3.** To appoint, elect, or designate: *The assembly was constituted to write a new city charter.* [From Middle English, from Latin *cōnstituere*, to set up.]

con·sti·tu·tion (kŏn′stĭ-**to͞o′**shən) *n.* **1.** The system of fundamental laws or principles by which a nation, government, or group is organized. **2.** A document in which such a system is written. **3. Constitution** The fundamental law of the US, framed in 1787, ratified in 1789, and variously amended since. **4.** The way in which something or someone is made up, especially the physical makeup of a person or organization; nature: *a healthy person with a strong constitution.* **5.** The act of setting up: *Many lawyers participated in the constitution of a new legal society.*

con·sti·tu·tion·al (kŏn′stĭ-**to͞o′**shə-nəl) *adj.* **1.** Relating to a constitution: *a constitutional amendment.* **2.** Consistent with or permissible according to a constitution: *The proposed law restricting the press is not constitutional.* **3.** Established by or operating under a constitution: *a constitutional government.* **4.** Basic or inherent in one's makeup: *a constitutional weakness in his health.* ❖ *n.* A walk taken regularly for one's health. **—con′sti·tu′tion·al·ly** *adv.*

con·sti·tu·tion·al·i·ty (kŏn′stĭ-to͞o′shə-**năl′**ĭ-tē) *n.* Accordance with a constitution: *The Supreme Court will decide on the constitutionality of the new law.*

con·strain (kən-**strān′**) *tr.v.* **con·strained, con·strain·ing, con·strains 1.** To keep (something) within certain limits; confine or limit: *We must constrain our spending.* **2.** To compel by physical force or moral obligation: *I felt constrained to ask why the park was closed down.* **—con·strain′ed·ly** (kən-**strā′**nĭd-lē) *adv.* **—con·strain′er** *n.*

con·straint (kən-**strānt′**) *n.* **1.** Something that restricts, limits, or regulates: *Without moral constraints we would live in social chaos.* **2.** The holding back of one's natural feelings or behavior: *The new mayor showed constraint in the presence of television cameras.*

con·strict (kən-**strĭkt′**) *tr. & intr.v.* **con·strict·ed, con·strict·ing, con·stricts 1.** To make or become smaller or narrower, as by contracting; compress: *This drug constricts blood vessels. I could feel the muscles in my body constrict with fright.* **2.** To limit or restrict: *Their lives were constricted by lack of education.* **—con·stric′tive** *adj.*

con·stric·tion (kən-**strĭk′**shən) *n.* **1.** The act or process of constricting. **2.** A feeling of pressure or tightness: *a constriction in one's throat.* **3.** Something that constricts: *The oppressive law was a constriction on their freedom.*

con·stric·tor (kən-**strĭk′**tər) *n.* **1.** A muscle that contracts or compresses a part or organ of the body. **2.** Any of various snakes, such as a boa or python, that kill their prey by coiling around it and squeezing.

con·struct (kən-**strŭkt′**) *tr.v.* **con·struct·ed, con·struct·ing, con·structs** To build or put together; erect or compose: *construct new houses; construct an argument.* **—con·struc′tor** *n.*

con·struc·tion (kən-**strŭk′**shən) *n.* **1.** The act or process of constructing: *Two new hotels are under construction.* **2.** A thing that is put together; a structure: *The treehouse we built was an odd-looking construction.* **3.** The way in which something is put together; a design: *The shed is a building of simple construction.* **4.** An interpretation or explanation given to a certain statement: *I put a favorable construction on his reply.* **5a.** The arrangement of words to form a meaningful phrase, clause, or sentence. **b.** A group of words arranged in a meaningful way. **—con·struc′tion·al** *adj.* **—con·struc′tion·al·ly** *adv.*

construction paper *n.* A heavy paper used in artwork, especially for designs that are folded and cut out.

con·struc·tive (kən-**strŭk′**tĭv) *adj.* Serving a useful purpose or helping to improve something: *My teacher gave me constructive suggestions on my work.* **—con·struc′tive·ly** *adv.* **—con·struc′tive·ness** *n.*

con·strue (kən-**stro͞o′**) *tr.v.* **con·strued, con·stru·ing, con·strues** To determine or explain the meaning of; interpret: *construed her smile as approval.*

con·sul (**kŏn′**səl) *n.* **1.** An official appointed by a government to live in a foreign city, look after the government's interest, and give assistance to its citizens who live or travel there. **2.** Either of the two chief magistrates of the ancient Roman republic, elected for a term of one year. **—con′su·lar** (**kŏn′**sə-lər) *adj.*

con·su·late (**kŏn′**sə-lĭt) *n.* The building or offices occupied by a consul.

con·sult (kən-**sŭlt′**) *v.* **con·sult·ed, con·sult·ing, con·sults** *—tr.* **1.** To seek information or advice from: *Consult your doctor.* **2.** To refer to: *We consulted the dictionary to settle the question.* **3.** To have regard for; consider: *Consult the feelings of others before going ahead.* *—intr.* To exchange views; confer: *The United States consulted with the Canadian government.* [From Latin *cōnsultāre*, from *cōnsulere*, to take counsel.]

con·sul·tant (kən-**sŭl′**tənt) *n.* **1.** A person who gives expert or professional advice: *A lawyer is a consultant in legal matters.* **2.** A person who consults someone else.

con·sul·ta·tion (kŏn′səl-**tā′**shən) *n.* **1.** An act of consulting: *Close consultation between the nurses and the doctor saved the patient.* **2.** A conference at which advice is given or views are exchanged: *Lawyers for the opposing sides in the case held a heated consultation.*

con·sul·ta·tive (kən-**sŭl′**tə-tĭv) *adj.* For the purpose of consultation; advisory: *a consultative council.*

con·sume (kən-**so͞om′**) *v.* **con·sumed, con·sum·ing, con·sumes** *—tr.* **1.** To take in as food; eat or drink up: *The guests consumed all the spaghetti, so we made more.* **2.** To use up; expend: *The experiment consumed her entire summer.* **3.** To purchase (goods or services) for personal use or ownership. **4.** To destroy totally, as by fire: *Flames consumed the factory.* **5.** To occupy the attention of; engross: *The book consumed me for hours.* *—intr.* To purchase goods or services: *People often consume less during an economic downturn.* [From Middle English *consumen*, from Latin *cōnsūmere*.] **—con·sum′a·ble** (kən-**so͞o′**mə-bəl) *adj.*

con·sum·er (kən-**so͞o′**mər) *n.* **1.** A person or thing that consumes, especially a person who buys and uses goods and services: *The manufacturers passed on the price increase to consumers.* **2.** An organism that feeds on other organisms or particles of organic matter.

con·sum·er·ism (kən-**so͞o′**mə-rĭz′əm) *n.* **1.** A movement seeking to protect consumers by requiring honest advertising and packaging, fair prices, and improved safety standards of products. **2.** Attachment to materialistic values or possessions: *The social critic spoke out against the rampant consumerism gripping the nation.*

con·sum·mate (**kŏn′**sə-māt′) *tr.v.* **con·sum·mat·ed, con·sum·mat·ing, con·sum·mates** To bring to completion; conclude: *consummate a business deal.* ❖ *adj.* (kən-**sŭm′**ĭt *or* **kŏn′**sə-mət) **1.** Highly skilled; polished: *a consummate musician.* **2.** Complete or perfect

ă	pat	ôr	core
ā	pay	oi	boy
âr	care	ou	out
ä	father	o͝o	took
ĕ	pet	o͝or	lure
ē	be	o͞o	boot
ĭ	pit	ŭ	cut
ī	bite	ûr	urge
îr	pier	th	thin
ŏ	pot	*th*	this
ō	toe	zh	vision
ô	paw	ə	about

in every respect: *consummate happiness.* **—con·sum′mate·ly** *adv.* **—con′sum·ma′tion** *n.* —SEE NOTE AT **consommé.**

con·sump·tion (kən-sŭmp′shən) *n.* **1.** The act or process of consuming: *Much manufacturing is based on the consumption of oil.* **2.** A quantity consumed: *The consumption of wood used for paper can be reduced by recycling.* **3.** Tuberculosis of the lungs, especially the wasting of the body caused by this disease. This term is no longer used in medicine.

con·sump·tive (kən-sŭmp′tĭv) *adj.* **1.** Tending to consume or use up, especially at an excessive or wasteful rate: *the consumptive use of natural resources.* **2.** Relating to tuberculosis of the lungs. This term is no longer used in medicine. ❖ *n.* A person with tuberculosis of the lungs. This term is no longer used in medicine.

cont. *abbr.* An abbreviation of continued.

con·tact (kŏn′tăkt′) *n.* **1a.** The touching or coming together of people or things: *Avoid any contact with the wet paint.* **b.** The state or condition of touching: *I have a rash where my skin came in contact with the poison ivy.* **2.** The condition of being in communication: *We lost contact with our former neighbors after they moved away.* **3.** *Informal* A person who is in a position to be of help; a connection: *His aunt has many contacts in politics.* **4a.** A connection between two conductors that allows an electric current to flow. **b.** A part or device that makes or breaks a connection in an electrical circuit: *the contacts of a switch.* **5.** A contact lens. ❖ *v.* (**kŏn′tăkt′** *or* kən-**tăkt′**) **con·tact·ed, con·tact·ing, con·tacts** *—tr.* **1.** To bring or put into contact with; touch: *If water contacts the paper, it will leave a mark.* **2.** To get in touch with; communicate with: *I contacted my grandmother by email.* *—intr.* To be or come into contact: *Bare wires that contact will cause a short circuit.* [From Latin *contāctus,* from past participle of *contingere,* to touch.]

contact lens *n.* A thin plastic or glass lens designed to correct a defect in vision, worn directly on the cornea of the eye.

con·ta·gion (kən-tā′jən) *n.* **1.** The transmission of disease by direct or indirect contact between individuals: *Lack of sanitary conditions may lead to widespread contagion.* **2.** A disease that is or can be transmitted in this way: *The flu is a common contagion of the winter months.* **3.** Something, such as a virus, that causes a contagious disease. **4.** The tendency to spread, as of an influence or emotional state: *the contagion of panic.*

con·ta·gious (kən-tā′jəs) *adj.* **1.** Capable of being transmitted by direct or indirect contact: *Chickenpox is a highly contagious disease.* **2.** Capable of carrying disease: *He stayed home until he was no longer contagious.* **3.** Tending to spread from person to person: *contagious laughter.* [From Middle English, from Latin *contāgiō,* a touching, contagion, from *contingere,* to touch.] **—con·ta′gious·ly** *adv.*

con·tain (kən-tān′) *tr.v.* **con·tained, con·tain·ing, con·tains 1.** To have within; hold: *This bottle contains drinking water. The document contains important information.* **2.** To consist of; comprise; include: *A gallon contains four quarts.* **3.** To hold back; restrain: *I could scarcely contain my laughter.* **4.** To halt the spread or development of: *a method of containing disease.* [From Middle English *conteinen,* from Latin *continēre* : *com-,* together + *tenēre,* to hold.] **—con·tain′a·ble** *adj.* —SEE NOTE AT **tenacious.**

con·tain·er (kən-tā′nər) *n.* Something, such as a box, can, jar, or barrel, used to hold something; a receptacle.

con·tain·ment (kən-tān′mənt) *n.* **1.** The act or fact of containing something: *underground storage facilities for the containment of radioactive waste.* **2.** The policy of attempting to prevent the expansion of an hostile country or ideology.

con·tam·i·nant (kən-tăm′ə-nənt) *n.* Something that contaminates: *Contaminants polluted the nearby stream.*

con·tam·i·nate (kən-tăm′ə-nat′) *tr.v.* **con·tam·i·nated, con·tam·i·nat·ing, con·tam·i·nates 1.** To make impure or unclean by mixture or contact; pollute; foul: *The waters were contaminated with oil from a leaking tanker.* **2.** To expose to or permeate with radioactivity: *A leak from the damaged reactor contaminated the air for miles around.* **—con·tam′i·na′tor** *n.*

con·tam·i·na·tion (kən-tăm′ə-nā′shən) *n.* **1.** The act of contaminating or the condition of being contaminated: *Dumping chemicals nearby caused contamination of the lake.* **2.** Something that contaminates; an impurity.

contd. *abbr.* An abbreviation of continued.

con·tem·plate (kŏn′təm-plāt′) *v.* **con·tem·plat·ed, con·tem·plat·ing, con·tem·plates** *—tr.* **1.** To think about (something) carefully; ponder: *I contemplated the offer of a job.* **2.** To think about doing (something); consider, intend, or expect: *We contemplated a trip to Africa.* **3.** To look at carefully and thoughtfully: *contemplate the stars in wonder.* *—intr.* To ponder; meditate: *He sat in the garden contemplating.* [From Latin *contemplārī* : *com-,* intensive prefix + *templum,* space for observing auguries.]

con·tem·pla·tion (kŏn′təm-plā′shən) *n.* **1.** The act of looking at or thinking about something thoughtfully. **2.** Meditation on spiritual or religious matters.

con·tem·pla·tive (kən-tĕm′plə-tĭv *or* kŏn′təm-plā′tĭv) *adj.* Characterized by or given to contemplation: *the contemplative life of a monk.* **—con·tem′pla·tive·ly** *adv.* **—con·tem′pla·tive·ness** *n.*

con·tem·po·ra·ne·ous (kən-tĕm′pə-rā′nē-əs) *adj.* Originating, existing, or occurring at the same time as something else. **—con·tem′po·ra′ne·ous·ly** *adv.* **—con·tem′po·ra′ne·ous·ness** *n.*

con·tem·po·rar·y (kən-tĕm′pə-rĕr′ē) *adj.* **1.** Living or occurring during the same period of time: *contemporary figures in ancient Greek history.* **2.** Current; modern: *a trendy new store selling contemporary clothing.* ❖ *n., pl.* **con·tem·po·rar·ies 1.** A person living at the same time as another: *Emily Dickinson and Walt Whitman were contemporaries.* **2.** A person of the present age.

con·tempt (kən-tĕmpt′) *n.* **1a.** A feeling that a person or thing is inferior, base, or worthless; scorn: *She has contempt for hypocrites.* **b.** The condition of being despised or dishonored: *a traitor who was held in contempt by his compatriots.* **2.** Open disobedience or disrespect to a court of law or to a legislative body: *Failure to appear before the judge put the witness in contempt.*

con·tempt·i·ble (kən-tĕmp′tə-bəl) *adj.* Deserving contempt; despicable: *a contemptible tyrant.* **—con·tempt′i·ble·ness** *n.* **—con·tempt′i·bly** *adv.*

con·temp·tu·ous (kən-tĕmp′cho͞o-əs) *adj.* Feeling or showing contempt: *a haughty and contemptuous refusal.* **—con·temp′tu·ous·ly** *adv.* **—con·temp′tu·ous·ness** *n.*

con·tend (kən-tĕnd′) *v.* **con·tend·ed, con·tend·ing, con·tends** *—intr.* **1.** To struggle against difficulties: *Doctors contend with disease. Holiday shoppers had to contend with long lines at the checkout counters.* **2.** To compete; vie: *The two teams contended for the championship.* *—tr.* To claim or maintain: *The lawyer contended that the evidence was inadmissible in court.* **—con·tend′er** *n.*

con·tent[1] (kŏn′tĕnt′) *n.* **1.** often **contents** Something that is contained in a receptacle: *empty a jar of its contents.* **2.** often **contents** The subject matter of a written work, as a document or book: *The contents of the report were not revealed.* **3.** The substantive or meaningful part: *The content of the paper is fine, but the style needs work.* **4.** The amount of a substance contained in something: *the fat content of milk.* [From Middle English, from Me-

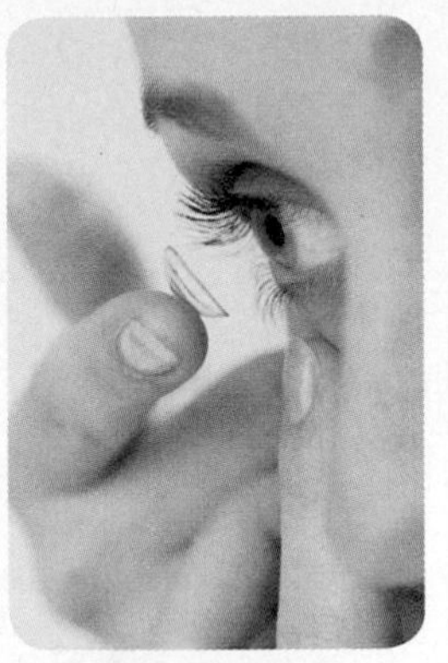

contact lens

Continental Divide

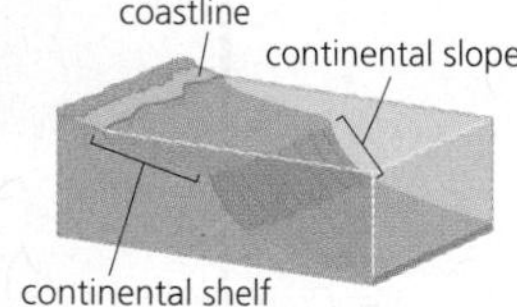

continental shelf

ă	pat	ôr	core
ā	pay	oi	boy
âr	care	ou	out
ä	father	o͝o	took
ĕ	pet	o͝or	lure
ē	be	o͞o	boot
ĭ	pit	ŭ	cut
ī	bite	ûr	urge
îr	pier	th	thin
ŏ	pot	*th*	this
ō	toe	zh	vision
ô	paw	ə	about

dieval Latin *contentum*, from Latin *continēre*, to contain.]

con·tent² (kən-tĕnt′) *adj.* Desiring no more than what one has; satisfied: *He was content to live in the small apartment.* ❖ *n.* A feeling of satisfied ease; contentment; satisfaction. ❖ *tr.v.* **con·tent·ed, con·tent·ing, con·tents** To make content or satisfied: *I contented myself with a cup of tea and a book.* [From Middle English, from Latin *contentus*, past participle of *continēre*, to restrain.]

con·tent·ed (kən-tĕn′tĭd) *adj.* Satisfied with things as they are; content: *The baby looked perfectly contented after his meal.* **—con·tent′ed·ly** *adv.* **—con·tent′ed·ness** *n.*

con·ten·tion (kən-tĕn′shən) *n.* **1.** The act of striving or contending: *The rival teams played in fierce but friendly contention.* **2.** A statement put forward in an argument: *The lawyer's contention was that the evidence was misleading.*

con·ten·tious (kən-tĕn′shəs) *adj.* Inclined to argue; quarrelsome: *a contentious troublemaker.* **—con·ten′tious·ly** *adv.* **—con·ten′tious·ness** *n.*

con·tent·ment (kən-tĕnt′mənt) *n.* The condition of being contented; satisfaction.

con·test (kŏn′tĕst′) *n.* **1.** A struggle for victory or superiority between rivals: *The struggle for American independence was a long contest.* **2.** A competition, usually between entrants who perform separately and are rated by judges: *an essay contest; a skating contest.* ❖ *v.* (kən-tĕst′ *or* kŏn′tĕst′) **con·test·ed, con·test·ing, con·tests** —*tr.* **1.** To compete or strive for: *a strategic waterway that was contested by several different countries.* **2.** To dispute; challenge: *contest a parking ticket; contest a will.* —*intr.* To struggle or compete: *rival teams contesting for first place.* [Probably from French *contester*, to dispute, from Latin *contestārī*, to call to witness : *com-*, together + *testis*, witness.] **—con·test′a·ble** *adj.*

con·tes·tant (kən-tĕs′tənt *or* kŏn′tĕs′tənt) *n.* A person who takes part in a contest.

con·text (kŏn′tĕkst′) *n.* **1.** The part of a statement or text that surrounds a particular word or passage and makes clear its meaning: *In some contexts "mad" means "crazy"; in other contexts it means "angry."* **2.** A general setting or set of circumstances in which a particular event occurs; a situation: *Horses are out of place in the context of modern city life.* [From Middle English *context*, composition, from Latin *contextus*, from past participle of *contexere*, to join together : *com-*, together + *texere*, to weave.]

con·tex·tu·al (kən-tĕks′cho͞o-əl) *adj.* Relating to or depending on context. **—con·tex′tu·al·ly** *adv.*

con·tig·u·ous (kən-tĭg′yo͞o-əs) *adj.* **1.** Having a common boundary; adjoining: *Arizona is contiguous with New Mexico.* **2a.** Connected without a break: *the 48 contiguous states.* **b.** Connected in time; uninterrupted: *served three contiguous terms.* **—con·tig′u·ous·ly** *adv.* **—con·tig′u·ous·ness** *n.*

con·ti·nent¹ (kŏn′tə-nənt) *n.* **1.** One of the seven great land masses of the earth, including Africa, Antarctica, Asia, Australia, Europe, North America, and South America. **2. Continent** The mainland of Europe: *left England by boat for the Continent.* [From Middle English, from Latin *(terra) continēns*, continuous (land), present participle of *continēre*, to hold together.]

con·ti·nent² (kŏn′tə-nənt) *adj.* **1.** Self-restrained in behavior. **2.** Able to keep normal control of urination or defecation. [From Middle English, from Latin *continēns*, present participle of *continēre*, to restrain.] **—con′ti·nence** *n.*

con·ti·nen·tal (kŏn′tə-nĕn′tl) *adj.* **1.** Relating to or characteristic of a continent: *continental weather patterns; the continental United States.* **2.** often **Continental** Relating to the mainland of Europe. **3. Continental** Relating to the American colonies during and just after the Revolutionary War: *the Continental Army.* ❖ *n.* **1.** often **Continental** An inhabitant of the mainland of Europe. **2. Continental** A soldier in the Continental Army during the Revolutionary War. **3.** A piece of paper money issued by the Continental Congress during the Revolutionary War.

continental breakfast *n.* A light breakfast consisting usually of coffee or tea and a roll, pastry, or other baked good.

Continental Congress *n.* Either of two legislative assemblies of the Thirteen Colonies and then of the United States. The first met in 1774; the second was the legislative and executive body of the federal government from 1775 until the Constitution took effect in 1789.

continental divide *n.* A region of high ground from each side of which the river systems of a continent flow in opposite directions.

Continental Divide A watershed line that extends through North America, dividing the areas that drain into the Atlantic and Arctic Oceans from those that drain into the Pacific. It is often called the **Great Divide** in the United States.

continental drift *n.* The gradual movement of the earth's continents toward or away from each other. —SEE NOTE AT **plate tectonics.**

continental shelf *n.* The part of the edge of a continent covered by shallow ocean waters and extending to the steep slopes that descend into the deep part of the ocean.

con·tin·gen·cy (kən-tĭn′jən-sē) *n., pl.* **con·tin·gen·cies** **1.** An event that may occur but is not likely or intended; a possibility: *People who work in emergency medical service must be prepared for any contingency.* **2.** The condition of being contingent: *Whether we will be able to drive through the mountain pass is a matter of contingency.*

con·tin·gent (kən-tĭn′jənt) *adj.* **1.** Possible but not certain to occur; uncertain: *a contingent move of company offices.* **2.** Dependent on circumstances not yet known; conditional: *Our picnic's success is contingent on the weather.* **3.** Happening by chance; accidental; unexpected: *a quick contingent meeting in the hall.* ❖ *n.* **1.** A representative group forming part of a gathering; a delegation: *the Maine contingent at the Democratic national convention.* **2.** A share, as of troops, contributed to a general effort: *The medical team at the earthquake site included a contingent of American doctors.* **—con·tin′gent·ly** *adv.*

con·tin·u·al (kən-tĭn′yo͞o-əl) *adj.* **1.** Repeated regularly and frequently: *the continual banging of the shutters in the wind.* **2.** Not broken or stopping; continuing over a long period of time; steady: *continual noise; made continual progress up the river.* **—con·tin′u·al·ly** *adv.*

con·tin·u·ance (kən-tĭn′yo͞o-əns) *n.* **1.** The act, fact, or duration of continuing; continuation: *a continuance of good relations between the two countries.* **2.** Adjournment of legal proceedings to a future date: *The judge gave the defense a continuance until witnesses could be found.*

con·tin·u·a·tion (kən-tĭn′yo͞o-ā′shən) *n.* **1a.** The act or fact of going on or persisting: *The continuation of the heavy rain will cause flooding.* **b.** The act or fact of beginning again after stopping; resumption: *a continuation of the game after a rain delay.* **2.** Something by which another thing is continued; an extension to a further point; an added part: *There is a continuation of the story in the author's next book.*

con·tin·ue (kən-tĭn′yo͞o) *v.* **con·tin·ued, con·tin·u·ing, con·tin·ues** —*intr.* **1.** To keep on or persist in doing something: *We continue in our efforts to improve the quality of our products.* **2.** To go on after stopping; resume: *Our program continues after these commercials.* **3.** To remain in the same condition, place, or direction: *The* *rainy weather continued for weeks.* —*tr.* **1.** To carry on or persist in: *The police continued their investigation.* **2.** To begin with again after stopping; resume: *We will continue our discussion tomorrow.* **3.** To cause to remain or last; retain; maintain: *continue a family business.* [From Middle English *continuen*, from Latin *continuāre*, from *continuus*, continuous, from *continēre*, to hold together.]

con·ti·nu·i·ty (kŏn′tə-**no͞o′**ĭ-tē) *n., pl.* **con·ti·nu·i·ties 1.** An uninterrupted succession: *A telephone call broke the continuity of my thoughts.* **2.** The condition of being continuous: *His erratic thoughts lacked continuity.*

con·tin·u·ous (kən-**tĭn′**yo͞o-əs) *adj.* Continuing without interruption; unbroken: *the continuous line of the horizon; a continuous supply of oxygen to the blood.* **—con·tin′u·ous·ly** *adv.* **—con·tin′u·ous·ness** *n.*

continuous spectrum *n.* A spectrum that covers a range of wavelengths without breaks or gaps.

con·tin·u·um (kən-**tĭn′**yo͞o-əm) *n., pl.* **con·tin·u·a** (kən-**tĭn′**yo͞o-ə) *or* **con·tin·u·ums** Something that continues or extends without interruption but can be divided into arbitrary units for analysis: *The past is a continuum that we divide into periods for historical study.*

con·tort (kən-**tôrt′**) *tr.v.* **con·tort·ed, con·tort·ing, con·torts** To twist or bend severely out of shape; wrench: *The pain of a toothache contorted his face.*

con·tor·tion (kən-**tôr′**shən) *n.* A twist, turn, or distortion in the shape of something.

con·tor·tion·ist (kən-**tôr′**shə-nĭst) *n.* An acrobat or entertainer who twists into contorted positions.

con·tour (**kŏn′**to͝or′) *n.* **1.** The outline of a figure, body, or mass: *the twisted contour of the coastline.* See Synonyms at **outline. 2.** A contour line. ❖ *adj.* **1.** Following the contour lines of uneven terrain to limit erosion of topsoil: *contour plowing.* **2.** Shaped to fit the outline or form of something: *contour sheets on a bed.* ❖ *tr.v.* **con·toured, con·tour·ing, con·tours 1.** To make or shape so as to fit something else: *The seats are contoured to fit your body.* **2.** To build (a road, for example) to follow the contour of the land. [From French, from Italian *contornare*, to draw in outline.]

contour line *n.* A line on a map joining points of the same elevation.

contour map *n.* A map that shows elevations above sea level and surface features of the land by means of contour lines.

contra– *pref.* A prefix that means against or opposite: *contradistinction.*

con·tra·band (**kŏn′**trə-bănd′) *n.* **1.** Goods that are prohibited by law from being imported or exported. **2.** Smuggling: *The suspect was arrested for contraband and forgery.* ❖ *adj.* Prohibited from being imported or exported: *a contraband shipment.* [From Italian *contrabbando* : *contra-*, against + *bando*, legal ruling.]

con·tra·bass (**kŏn′**trə-bās′) *n.* A double bass. ❖ *adj.* Pitched an octave below the normal bass range.

con·tra·bas·soon (kŏn′trə-bə-**so͞on′**) *n.* A large bassoon pitched about an octave below an ordinary bassoon.

con·tra·cep·tion (kŏn′trə-**sĕp′**shən) *n.* The intentional prevention of conception and pregnancy, as by the use of drugs or a device such as a condom.

con·tra·cep·tive (kŏn′trə-**sĕp′**tĭv) *adj.* Capable of preventing conception. ❖ *n.* A contraceptive substance or device.

con·tract (**kŏn′**trăkt′) *n.* **1.** An agreement between two or more people or groups, especially one that is written and enforceable by law: *The athlete negotiated a two-year contract with her new team.* **2.** A document stating the terms of such an agreement: *Both sides signed the new labor contract.* ❖ *v.* (kən-**trăkt′** *or* **kŏn′**trăkt′) **con·tract·ed, con·tract·ing, con·tracts** —*tr.* **1.** To make smaller by drawing together: *Hot water contracted the wool fibers in my sweater, and it shrank.* **2.** To arrange or settle by a formal agreement: *contract a business deal.* **3.** To get; acquire: *contract the mumps; contract a debt.* **4.** To shorten (a word or words) by omitting or combining some of the letters or sounds: *Most people contract "I am" to "I'm" when they speak.* —*intr.* **1.** To draw together; become smaller: *The pupils of the cat's eyes contracted in the light.* **2.** To arrange by a formal agreement: *The developers contracted for construction of several new houses.* [From Middle English, from Latin *contractus*, past participle of *contrahere*, to draw together, make a contract : *com-*, together + *trahere*, to draw.]

con·trac·tile (kən-**trăk′**təl *or* kən-**trăk′**tīl′) *adj.* Capable of contracting or causing contraction: *contractile muscle fibers; contractile forces of cooling.*

contractile vacuole *n.* A vacuole in one-celled organisms that discharges a fluid by contracting.

con·trac·tion (kən-**trăk′**shən) *n.* **1.** The act of contracting or the condition of being contracted: *The pupil of the eye usually undergoes contraction in strong light.* **2.** A condensed word or phrase, formed by omitting or combining some of the letters or sounds. For example, *isn't* is a contraction of *is not.* **3.** The shortening and thickening of a muscle in action.

con·trac·tor (**kŏn′**trăk′tər *or* kən-**trăk′**tər) *n.* A person who contracts to do something, especially to provide materials and labor for a construction job.

con·trac·tu·al (kən-**trăk′**cho͞o-əl) *adj.* Relating to a contract: *a contractual arrangement between a worker and an employer.* **—con·trac′tu·al·ly** *adv.*

con·tra·dict (kŏn′trə-**dĭkt′**) *tr.v.* **con·tra·dict·ed, con·tra·dict·ing, con·tra·dicts 1.** To assert or express the opposite of (a statement): *The witness gave information that contradicted previous testimony.* **2.** To deny the statement of: *The two scientists contradicted each other in heated debate.* **3.** To be contrary to or inconsistent with: *The results of the experiments contradicted his predictions.* [From Latin *contrādīcere* : *contrā-*, against + *dīcere*, to speak.] —SEE NOTE AT **predict.**

con·tra·dic·tion (kŏn′trə-**dĭk′**shən) *n.* **1.** The act of contradicting or the condition of being contradicted: *His persistent contradiction of the teacher embarrassed us.* **2.** An inconsistency; a discrepancy: *There's a contradiction between what you say and what your report states.* **3.** A statement that contradicts something: *The politician issued a contradiction of the allegations reported in the press.*

con·tra·dic·to·ry (kŏn′trə-**dĭk′**tə-rē) *adj.* **1.** Involving or having the nature of a contradiction; opposing; contrary: *Contradictory reports about the vaccine's effectiveness perplexed the doctors.* **2.** Given to contradicting: *a quarrelsome and contradictory nature.* **—con′tra·dic′to·ri·ly** *adv.* **—con′tra·dic′tor·i·ness** *n.*

con·tra·dis·tinc·tion (kŏn′trə-dĭ-**stĭngk′**shən) *n.* Distinction by contrasting or by opposing qualities: *The critic called the new composition mere noise in contradistinction to music.*

con·tral·to (kən-**trăl′**tō) *n., pl.* **con·tral·tos 1.** The lowest female singing voice or voice part, lower than soprano and higher than tenor. **2.** A woman having such a voice.

con·trap·tion (kən-**trăp′**shən) *n.* A mechanical device; a gadget.

con·trar·i·wise (**kŏn′**trĕr′ē-wīz′ *or* kən-**trâr′**ē-wīz′) *adv.* **1.** In an opposite way or reverse order. **2.** On the contrary.

con·trar·y (**kŏn′**trĕr′ē) *adj.* **1.** Completely different; opposed: *The debaters held contrary points of view.* **2.** Adverse; unfavorable: *Contrary economic conditions caused the business to go bankrupt.* **3.** (*also* kən-**trâr′**ē) Stubbornly opposed to others; willful: *Little children often become contrary when they need a nap.* ❖ *n., pl.* **con·trar·ies** Something that is opposite: *Their theory made sense at first, but experimentation proved the contrary to*

WRITERS CHOOSE THEIR WORDS

If you look at old pictures in the *Two Mills Times*, you see that the Knot was about the size and shape of a lopsided volleyball. It was made of string, but it had more **contortions,** ins and outs, twists and turns and dips and doodles than the brain of Albert Einstein himself.

—Jerry Spinelli
Maniac Magee

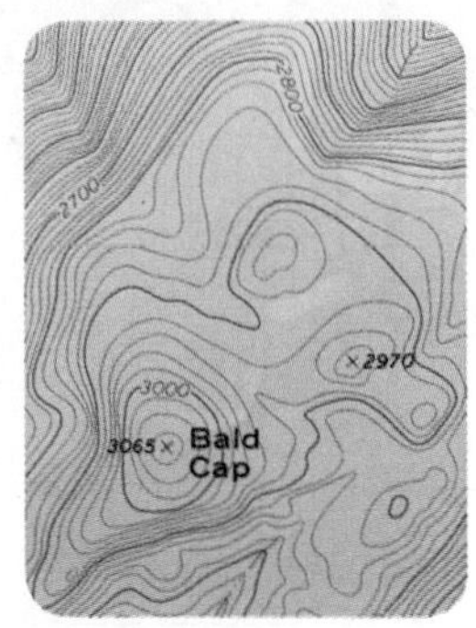

contour map

WRITERS CHOOSE THEIR WORDS

At last she perceived that there was not going to be any peace for her until she should devise a test that should prove, clearly and without question, whether this lad was her son or not, and so banish these wearing and worrying doubts. Ah yes, this was plainly the right way out of the difficulty; therefore she set her wits to work at once to **contrive** that test. But it was an easier thing to propose than to accomplish.

—Mark Twain
The Prince and the Pauper

convection
Air heated by a space heater rises and is replaced by cool air, creating a convection current that circulates warm air throughout a room.

be true. ◆ **on the contrary** In opposition to the previous statement; conversely: *I'm not sick; on the contrary, I'm feeling quite healthy.* **—con′trar′i·ly** *adv.* **—con′trar′i·ness** *n.*

con·trast (kən-**trăst′** *or* **kŏn′**trăst′) *v.* **con·trast·ed, con·trast·ing, con·trasts** *—tr.* To compare in order to reveal differences: *The essay contrasts city and country life.* *—intr.* To show differences when compared: *light colors that contrast with a dark background.* ❖ *n.* (**kŏn′**trăst′) **1.** Comparison, especially in order to reveal differences: *the author's contrast of rural and urban America.* **2.** The state of being different when viewed in comparison: *Let's consider pioneer life in contrast to modern life.* **3.** Something that is strikingly different from something else: *Driving a truck is quite a contrast to driving a compact car.* **4.** The difference in brightness between the light and dark areas of a picture, such as a photograph. [From Medieval Latin *contrāstāre* : Latin *contrā-*, against + Latin *stāre*, to stand.]

con·trib·ute (kən-**trĭb′**yo͞ot) *v.* **con·trib·ut·ed, con·trib·ut·ing, con·trib·utes** *—tr.* **1.** To give or supply in common with others: *contribute money to a charity; contributed a lot of my time to the project.* **2.** To submit (something written) for publication: *contribute an article to the school newspaper.* *—intr.* **1.** To give or supply something along with others: *contribute to the Red Cross.* **2.** To help in bringing about a result: *Exercise contributes to better health.* **3.** To submit material for publication. **—con·trib′u·tor** *n.*

con·tri·bu·tion (kŏn′trĭ-**byo͞o′**shən) *n.* **1.** The act of contributing: *A good discussion requires the contribution of several people.* **2.** Something contributed: *We made a contribution of food to the poor.*

con·trib·u·to·ry (kən-**trĭb′**yə-tôr′ē) *adj.* Contributing toward a result; helping to bring about a result: *Carelessness was a contributory factor in the accident.*

con·trite (kən-**trīt′** *or* **kŏn′**trīt′) *adj.* **1.** Feeling deep regret and sorrow for one's wrongdoing: *a contrite sinner.* **2.** Arising from or showing deep regret or sorrow: *contrite tears.* [From Middle English *contrit*, from Latin *contrītus*, past participle of *conterere*, to crush : *com-*, intensive prefix + *terere*, to grind.] **—con·trite′ly** *adv.* **—con·trite′ness** *n.*

con·tri·tion (kən-**trĭsh′**ən) *n.* Sincere remorse for wrongdoing; repentance.

con·triv·ance (kən-**trī′**vəns) *n.* **1.** The act of contriving: *the contrivance of friends to give a surprise party.* **2.** Something that is contrived, as a mechanical device or a clever plan: *Causing a commotion was only a contrivance to divert attention.*

con·trive (kən-**trīv′**) *tr.v.* **con·trived, con·triv·ing, con·trives 1.** To plan or devise cleverly: *contrive an excuse for being late.* **2.** To bring about, especially by scheming: *contrive a victory by surprise attack.* [From Middle English *contreven*, from Medieval Latin *contropāre*, to compare.] **—con·triv′er** *n.*

con·trived (kən-**trīvd′**) *adj.* Obviously planned or calculated; unnatural: *a movie with a contrived plot.*

con·trol (kən-**trōl′**) *tr.v.* **con·trolled, con·trol·ling, con·trols 1.** To exercise authority or influence over; direct: *The mayor controls the city government.* **2.** To adjust or regulate: *This valve controls the flow of water.* **3.** To hold in check; restrain: *control one's anger.* **4.** To reduce or prevent the spread of: *controlled the fire..* ❖ *n.* **1.** Authority or power to regulate, direct, or dominate: *the coach's control over the team.* **2.** A means of restraint; a check: *A leash is a control over a dog.* **3.** A standard of comparison for testing the results of a scientific experiment. **4.** often **controls** A device or set of devices used to operate, regulate, or guide a machine or vehicle: *The pilot was sitting at the controls of the airplane.* [From Middle English *countrollen*, from Medieval Latin *contrārotulāre*, to check by duplicate register : Latin *contrā-*, against, opposite + Latin *rotulus*, roll, diminutive of *rota*, wheel.] **—con·trol′la·ble** *adj.*

control key *n.* A key on a computer keyboard that is pressed in combination with other keys to perform a command.

con·trol·ler (kən-**trō′**lər) *n.* **1.** A person who controls or regulates something, such as air traffic. **2.** A mechanism or device that regulates or operates something: *a video game controller.* **3.** also **comp·trol·ler** (kən-**trō′**lər *or* kŏmp-**trō′**lər) An officer who supervises the financial affairs of a business or a governmental body.

control tower *n.* An observation tower at an airport from which the landing and takeoff of aircraft are controlled by radio and radar.

con·tro·ver·sial (kŏn′trə-**vûr′**shəl *or* kŏn′trə-**vûr′**sē-əl) *adj.* Relating to, producing, or marked by argument or sharp disagreement: *controversial writing; a controversial issue.* **—con′tro·ver′sial·ly** *adv.*

con·tro·ver·sy (**kŏn′**trə-vûr′sē) *n., pl.* **con·tro·ver·sies 1.** A dispute, especially a public one between sides holding sharply opposing views: *A controversy arose over the size of the school budget.* **2.** The act of engaging in such disputes: *Their lawyers are skilled at controversy.* [From Middle English *controversie*, from Latin *contrōversus*, disputed : *contrā-*, against + *vertere*, to turn.]

con·tro·vert (**kŏn′**trə-vûrt′ *or* kŏn′trə-**vûrt′**) *tr.v.* **con·tro·vert·ed, con·tro·vert·ing, con·tro·verts** To raise arguments against; dispute: *The prosecutor controverted the defendant's testimony.* **—con′tro·vert′i·ble** *adj.*

con·tu·sion (kən-**to͞o′**zhən) *n.* A bruise.

co·nun·drum (kə-**nŭn′**drəm) *n.* A baffling or insoluble problem.

con·va·lesce (kŏn′və-**lĕs′**) *intr.v.* **con·va·lesced, con·va·lesc·ing, con·va·lesc·es** To regain health and strength after illness or injury; recuperate. [From Latin *convalēscere* : *com-*, intensive prefix + *valēscere*, to grow strong.]

con·va·les·cence (kŏn′və-**lĕs′**əns) *n.* **1.** Gradual return to health after illness or injury. **2.** The time needed for this: *a short convalescence in bed.* **—con′va·les′cent** *adj.*

con·vec·tion (kən-**vĕk′**shən) *n.* The transfer of heat from one place to another by the circulation of heated currents within a gas or liquid. —SEE NOTE.

con·vene (kən-**vēn′**) *intr. & tr.v.* **con·vened, con·ven·ing, con·venes** To assemble or cause to assemble: *Members of the committee convene monthly to decide on club business. The governor convened the legislature.* [From Middle English *convenen*, from Latin *convenīre* : *com-*, together + *venīre*, to come.] —SEE NOTE AT **intervene.**

con·ven·ience (kən-**vēn′**yəns) *n.* **1.** The quality of being convenient; suitability: *the convenience of shopping at a supermarket.* **2.** Personal comfort or advantage: *Each hotel room has a telephone for the guests' convenience.* **3.** Something that provides comfort or saves effort, as a device or service: *A microwave oven is a modern convenience.* **4.** A suitable or agreeable time: *Please respond at your convenience.*

convenience store *n.* A small retail store that is open long hours and that typically sells snacks and basic groceries.

con·ven·ient (kən-**vēn′**yənt) *adj.* **1.** Suited or favorable to one's comfort, needs, or purpose: *An electric mixer is a convenient kitchen appliance.* **2.** Easy to reach or close by: *a bank with many convenient locations.* **—con·ven′ient·ly** *adv.*

con·vent (**kŏn′**vənt) *n.* **1.** A community of nuns. **2.** The building or buildings occupied by nuns; a nunnery.

con·ven·tion (kən-**vĕn′**shən) *n.* **1a.** A formal meeting of a group for a particular purpose: *a political conven-*

ă	pat	ôr	core
ā	pay	oi	boy
âr	care	ou	out
ä	father	o͝o	took
ĕ	pet	o͝or	lure
ē	be	o͞o	boot
ĭ	pit	ŭ	cut
ī	bite	ûr	urge
îr	pier	th	thin
ŏ	pot	*th*	this
ō	toe	zh	vision
ô	paw	ə	about

tion for nominating candidates. **b.** The group of people attending such an assembly: *The convention will nominate its candidate tonight.* **2a.** General agreement on or acceptance of certain practices or attitudes: *Convention formerly required some judges to wear white wigs.* **b.** A widely accepted practice; a custom: *the convention of shaking hands.* **3.** A formal agreement or compact, as between nations. —SEE NOTE AT **intervene.**

con·ven·tion·al (kən-vĕn**′**shə-nəl) *adj.* **1a.** Based on or approved by general usage; customary: *Saying "Hello" is a conventional way of answering the telephone.* **b.** Following accepted practice, customs, or taste: *a conventional white wedding dress.* **2.** Following accepted practice so closely as to be dull or unimaginative: *a boring movie with a conventional love story.* **3.** Using means other than nuclear weapons or energy: *conventional warfare; conventional power plants.* **—con·ven′tion·al′i·ty** (kən-vĕn′shə-**năl′**ĭ-tē) *n.* **—con·ven′tion·al·ly** *adv.*

con·verge (kən-**vûrj′**) *v.* **con·verged, con·verg·ing, con·verg·es** *—intr.* **1.** To come together in one place; meet: *The three roads converge in the center of town.* **2.** To tend or move toward each other or toward the same conclusion or result: *Their minds converged on the same point.* *—tr.* To cause to converge: *A magnifying glass converges rays of light.* [From Late Latin *convergere,* to incline together.]

con·ver·gence (kən-**vûr′**jəns) *n.* **1.** The act or process of converging; tendency to meet in one point. **2.** The point of converging; a meeting place: *Pittsburgh was built at the convergence of three rivers.* **—con·ver′gent** *adj.*

con·ver·sant (kən-**vûr′**sənt *or* **kŏn′**vər-sənt) *adj.* Familiar, as by study or experience: *She is conversant with medieval history.* **—con·ver′sant·ly** *adv.*

con·ver·sa·tion (kŏn′vər-**sā′**shən) *n.* A spoken exchange of thoughts and feelings; a talk.

con·ver·sa·tion·al (kŏn′vər-**sā′**shə-nəl) *adj.* **1.** Relating to conversation: *in a normal conversational tone.* **2.** Adept at or given to conversation: *Outgoing people are generally more conversational than others.* **—con′ver·sa′tion·al·ly** *adv.*

con·ver·sa·tion·al·ist (kŏn′vər-**sā′**shə-nə-lĭst) *n.* A person who is fond of or skilled at conversation.

con·verse[1] (kən-**vûrs′**) *intr.v.* **con·versed, con·vers·ing, con·vers·es** To talk informally with others: *converse about family matters.* [From Middle English *conversen,* to associate with, from Latin *conversārī* : *com-,* with + *versārī,* to occupy oneself.]

con·verse[2] (kən-**vûrs′** *or* **kŏn′vûrs′**) *adj.* Reversed, as in order; contrary: *The converse order of the alphabet is hard to repeat.* ❖ *n.* (**kŏn′**vûrs′) Something that has been reversed; an opposite: *Dark is the converse of light.* [From Latin *conversus,* past participle of *convertere,* to turn around.] **—con·verse′ly** *adv.*

con·ver·sion (kən-**vûr′**zhən *or* kən-**vûr′**shən) *n.* **1.** The act or process of changing one thing, use, or purpose into another: *A generator is used for the conversion of water power into electricity.* **2.** A change in which a person adopts a new belief, opinion, or religion. **3.** The expression of a quantity in alternative units, as of length or weight: *conversion of miles to kilometers.*

con·vert (kən-**vûrt′**) *v.* **con·vert·ed, con·vert·ing, con·verts** *—tr.* **1.** To change into another form, substance, or condition: *convert water into ice by freezing; a solar cell that converts sunlight into electricity.* **2.** To change from one use to another; adapt to a new purpose: *convert a bedroom into a study.* **3.** To persuade (a person) to adopt a particular religion or belief: *Missionaries tried to convert the native peoples to Christianity.* **4a.** To exchange for something of equal value: *Since we are going to France, we need to convert our dollars into euros.* **b.** To express (a quantity) in alternative units: *convert 100 yards into meters.* *—intr.* **1.** To undergo a change; be converted: *This sofa converts easily into a bed.* **2.** To adopt a particular religion or belief: *Many pagans converted to Christianity in the Middle Ages.* ❖ *n.* (**kŏn′**vûrt′) A person who has adopted a new religion or belief. [From Middle English *converten,* from Latin *convertere,* to turn around : *com-,* intensive prefix + *vertere,* to turn.]

con·vert·er (kən-**vûr′**tər) *n.* **1.** A machine that changes alternating current to direct current or direct current to alternating current. **2.** An electronic device that changes the frequency of a radio or other electromagnetic signal. **3.** A furnace in which pig iron is changed into steel by the Bessemer process.

con·vert·i·ble (kən-**vûr′**tə-bəl) *adj.* **1.** Capable of being converted: *The convertible couch is also a bed.* **2.** Having a top that can be folded back or removed: *a convertible sports car.* ❖ *n.* **1.** An automobile whose top can be folded back or removed. **2.** Something, such as a piece of furniture, that can be converted. **—con·vert′i·bil′i·ty** *n.* **—con·vert′i·bly** *adv.*

con·vex (**kŏn′**vĕks′ *or* kən-**vĕks′**) *adj.* Curving outward like the outside of a circle or sphere: *Rain rolled off the convex surface of the dome.* **—con·vex′ly** *adv.* **—con·vex′ness** *n.*

con·vex·i·ty (kən-**vĕk′**sĭ-tē) *n., pl.* **con·vex·i·ties 1.** The condition of being convex. **2.** A convex surface, line, or body.

con·vey (kən-**vā′**) *tr.v.* **con·veyed, con·vey·ing, con·veys 1.** To take or carry from one place to another; transport: *A helicopter conveyed the skiers to the top of the glacier.* **2.** To serve as a means of transmission for; transmit: *Cables convey electrical power.* **3.** To make known; communicate: *His smile conveyed his pleasure.* **4.** To transfer ownership of: *The deed conveyed the land to a close relative.*

con·vey·ance (kən-**vā′**əns) *n.* **1.** The act of conveying: *Airlines now serve as the chief means of conveyance for transatlantic passengers.* **2.** Something used to convey, especially a vehicle such as an automobile or a bus. **3a.** The transfer of ownership from one person to another. **b.** A legal document that brings about such a transfer.

con·vey·or also **con·vey·er** (kən-**vā′**ər) *n.* **1.** A person or thing that conveys: *a conveyor of good news.* **2.** A mechanical device, such as a continuous moving belt, that carries things from one place to another: *put the groceries on the conveyor.*

con·vict (kən-**vĭkt′**) *tr.v.* **con·vict·ed, con·vict·ing, con·victs** To find or prove guilty of an offense, especially in a court of law: *The judge convicted the polluter of endangering public health.* ❖ *n.* (**kŏn′**vĭkt′) **1.** A person who has been found guilty of a crime. **2.** A person who has been sentenced to prison. [From Middle English *convicten,* from Latin *convincere,* to convince.]

con·vic·tion (kən-**vĭk′**shən) *n.* **1.** The judgment of a judge or jury that a person is guilty of a crime. **2.** The state of being found or proven guilty: *a trial ending in the swindler's conviction.* **3.** A strong opinion or belief: *act according to one's true convictions.*

con·vince (kən-**vĭns′**) *tr.v.* **con·vinced, con·vinc·ing, con·vinc·es** To cause (someone) to believe or feel certain; persuade: *More clues convinced us we were on the right track.* [From Latin *convincere,* to prove wrong : *com-,* intensive prefix + *vincere,* to conquer.]

con·vinc·ing (kən-**vĭn′**sĭng) *adj.* Serving to convince; persuasive: *a convincing argument.* **—con·vinc′ing·ly** *adv.*

con·viv·i·al (kən-**vĭv′**ē-əl) *adj.* **1.** Fond of food, drink, and good company; sociable. **2.** Festive: *a convivial reunion of old friends.* **—con·viv′i·al′i·ty** (kən-vĭv′ē-**ăl′**ĭ-tē) *n.* **—con·viv′i·al·ly** *adv.*

con·vo·ca·tion (kŏn′və-**kā′**shən) *n.* **1.** The act of convoking: *the convocation of church leaders to enact new*

SCIENCE

convection Heat is a form of energy that results in the motion of molecules. Heat travels by **conduction, convection,** or **radiation.** In *conduction,* heat spreads through a solid by making its molecules vibrate faster. As faster molecules bump into slower ones, they cause them to vibrate faster as well, so that the solid becomes hotter overall. This is how the handle of a teaspoon in a cup of hot tea gets hot. When liquids and gases are heated, their molecules, which are free to move about, move farther apart. The hotter portions of the liquid or gas expand and rise, and cooler portions move into their place. This movement is called *convection.* The currents of the ocean are convection currents caused by the uneven heating of waters by the sun. *Radiation* carries heat in the form of waves through space. A hot object, like a heat lamp, gives off energy waves called infrared rays. When these rays strike an object, like your face, its molecules absorb the rays' energy and vibrate faster, and so the object becomes hotter.

convertible

conveyor
conveyor belt in a pasta-making factory

James Cook
c. 1776 portrait by Nathaniel Dance-Holland (1735–1811)

Calvin Coolidge

ă	pat	ôr	core
ā	pay	oi	boy
âr	care	ou	out
ä	father	o͝o	took
ĕ	pet	o͝or	lure
ē	be	o͞o	boot
ĭ	pit	ŭ	cut
ī	bite	ûr	urge
îr	pier	th	thin
ŏ	pot	*th*	this
ō	toe	zh	vision
ô	paw	ə	about

policy. **2.** A summoned assembly, as of members of a college community.

con·voke (kən-vōk′) *tr.v.* **con·voked, con·vok·ing, con·vokes** To call together; cause to assemble: *the president convoked the new Congress.*

con·vo·lut·ed (kŏn′və-lo͞o′tĭd) *adj.* **1.** Having many twists or coils: *a convoluted path winding around streams and boulders.* **2.** Complicated; intricate: *a convoluted argument that is difficult to understand.*

con·vo·lu·tion (kŏn′və-**lo͞o′**shən) *n.* **1.** A part or development in something complicated, such as a story or explanation; a twist: *I couldn't follow the convolutions of the movie's plot.* **2.** A fold or coil: *the convolutions of a coiled snake.* **3.** One of the folds on the surface of the brain.

con·voy (**kŏn′**voi′) *n.* **1.** A group, as of ships or motor vehicles, traveling with a protective military force or for safety or convenience. **2.** An accompanying and protecting force: *a convoy of warships protecting the supply ships.* [From Middle English *conveien, convoyen,* to escort, convey, from Old French *convoier.*]

con·vulse (kən-**vŭls′**) *v.* **con·vulsed, con·vuls·ing, con·vuls·es** —*tr.* **1.** To cause (a human or other animal) to have violent involuntary muscle contractions: *The patient was convulsed by high fever.* **2.** To cause to laugh uproariously: *Her impersonations convulsed the audience.* **3.** To disturb violently; rock: *An earthquake convulsed the area.* —*intr.* To become affected by or as if by convulsions; shake: *The audience convulsed with laughter.* [From Latin *convellere,* to pull violently.]

con·vul·sion (kən-**vŭl′**shən) *n.* **1.** A violent involuntary muscular contraction: *convulsions resulting from high fever.* **2.** An uncontrolled fit of laughter: *The audience went into convulsions watching the clown's antics.* **3.** A violent upheaval: *convulsions of the earth's crust.*

con·vul·sive (kən-**vŭl′**sĭv) *adj.* **1.** Marked by or resembling convulsions: *convulsive movements.* **2.** Having or causing convulsions: *a convulsive disorder.*

co·ny (**kō′**nē *or* **kŭn′**ē) *n.* Variant of **coney.**

coo (ko͞o) *intr.v.* **cooed, coo·ing, coos 1.** To make the murmuring sound of a pigeon or dove or a sound similar to it: *The baby laughed and cooed.* **2.** To speak softly, with affection or approval: *Everyone cooed over her new dress.*

❑ *These sound alike:* **coo, coup** (stratagem).

COO *abbr.* An abbreviation of chief operating officer.

cook (ko͝ok) *v.* **cooked, cook·ing, cooks** —*tr.* To prepare (food) for eating by using heat. —*intr.* **1.** To undergo cooking: *Fish cooks quickly.* **2.** To prepare food for eating by using heat: *A short-order chef must cook quickly.* ❖ *n.* A person who prepares food for eating. ◆ **cook up** *Informal* To concoct; invent: *cook up an excuse.* [From Middle English *coken,* from *coke,* a cook, from Old English *cōc,* from Latin *coquere,* to cook.]

Cook (ko͝ok), **James** Known as "Captain Cook." 1728–1779. British navigator and explorer who commanded three major voyages, charting and naming many islands of the Pacific Ocean.

cook·book (**ko͝ok′**bo͝ok′) *n.* A book containing recipes and other information about cooking.

cook·er (**ko͝ok′**ər) *n.* An appliance used for cooking.

cook·er·y (**ko͝ok′**ə-rē) *n.* The art or practice of preparing food.

cook·ie also **cooky** (**ko͝ok′**ē) *n., pl.* **cook·ies 1.** A small, usually flat and crisp cake made from sweetened dough. **2.** A collection of information about a person using the Internet that is stored on the user's computer and used by a website to identify the user on subsequent visits.

cook·out (**ko͝ok′**out′) *n.* A meal cooked and eaten outdoors.

cook·top (**ko͝ok′**tŏp′) *n.* A flat cooking surface, as on a stove, usually consisting of electric heating elements that are covered with glass.

cool (ko͞ol) *adj.* **cool·er, cool·est 1.** Moderately cold; neither warm nor very cold: *cool fall weather.* **2.** Giving or allowing relief from heat: *a cool summer breeze; a cool light blouse.* **3.** Calm; unexcited: *a cool head in a crisis.* **4.** Indifferent or disdainful; unenthusiastic: *They were cool to the idea of hosting the party.* **5.** *Slang* **a.** Excellent; first-rate: *saw a really cool movie.* **b.** Acceptable; satisfactory: *It's cool with me if you want to go to the mall.* **6.** *Slang* Entire; full: *a deal worth a cool million in profit.* ❖ *tr. & intr.v.* **cooled, cool·ing, cools 1.** To make or become less warm: *cool a room by opening a window; let the pie cool.* **2.** To make or become less intense: *Having to wait cooled their enthusiasm. My anger cooled as time went by.* ❖ *n.* **1.** A cool place, part, or time: *the cool of the evening.* **2.** *Slang* Calmness of mind; composure: *When told there were no tickets left, several people lost their cool.* ◆ **cool it** *Slang* To calm down; relax. **cool (one's) heels** *Informal* To wait or be kept waiting. [From Old English *cōl.*] —**cool′ly** *adv.* —**cool′ness** *n.*

cool·ant (**ko͞o′**lənt) *n.* Something that cools, especially a fluid that circulates through a machine or over some of its parts in order to draw off heat.

cool·er (**ko͞o′**lər) *n.* A device or container for cooling something: *a water cooler.*

cool-head·ed (**ko͞ol′hĕd′**ĭd) *adj.* Not easily excited or flustered; calm. —**cool′-head′ed·ly** *adv.* —**cool′-head′ed·ness** *n.*

Coo·lidge (**ko͞o′**lĭj), **(John) Calvin** 1872–1933. The 30th president of the United States (1923–1929), who encouraged business ventures that led to a stock market boom in the 1920s, followed by economic collapse.

coon (ko͞on) *n. Informal* A raccoon.

coon·skin (**ko͞on′**skĭn′) *n.* The pelt of a raccoon.

coop (ko͞op) *n.* An enclosure or cage for poultry. ❖ *tr.v.* **cooped, coop·ing, coops** To confine; shut in: *We were cooped up inside all day because of the bad weather.*

❑ *These sound alike:* **coop, coupe** (two-door automobile).

co-op (**kō′**ŏp′ *or* kō-**ŏp′**) *n.* A cooperative.

coop·er (**ko͞o′**pər) *n.* A person who makes or repairs wooden barrels, casks, and tubs.

Coo·per (**ko͞o′**pər *or* **ko͝op′**ər), **James Fenimore** 1789–1851. American writer who is known for his novels of frontier life, such as *The Last of the Mohicans* (1826).

co·op·er·ate (kō-**ŏp′**ə-rāt′) *intr.v.* **co·op·er·at·ed, co·op·er·at·ing, co·op·er·ates 1.** To work or act with another or others for a common purpose: *Everyone cooperated in decorating the gym.* **2.** To agree or yield willingly; go along: *The parents asked the children to cooperate and get ready for bed.*

co·op·er·a·tion (kō-ŏp′ə-**rā′**shən) *n.* The act of working together toward a common end or purpose: *international cooperation to reduce air pollution.*

co·op·er·a·tive (kō-**ŏp′**ər-ə-tĭv *or* kō-**ŏp′**ə-**rā′**tĭv *or* kō-**ŏp′**rə-tĭv) *adj.* **1.** Done in cooperation with others: *a cooperative effort.* **2.** Willing to help or cooperate: *a cooperative and helpful assistant.* **3.** Relating to a cooperative: *a cooperative apartment.* ❖ *n.* **1.** A business, farm, store, or residence owned jointly by those who use its facilities or services: *That apartment house is a cooperative in which the residents share the costs of operating the building.* **2.** An apartment in a building jointly owned by the residents: *a three-room cooperative on the first floor.* —**co·op′er·a·tive·ly** *adv.* —**co·op′er·a·tive·ness** *n.*

co-opt (kō-**ŏpt′** *or* **kō′**ŏpt′) *tr.v.* **co-opt·ed, co-opt·ing, co-opts 1.** To cause (someone) to stop criticizing or opposing a person, group, or institution, especially by offering a job or some advantage through association: *By promising pay raises, the company co-opted many strikers.* **2.** To adopt or make use of (something such as an idea or practice) for one's own purposes, especially when originally used by an opposing person or group.

co·or·di·nate (kō-ôr′dn-ĭt′ *or* kō-ôr′dn-āt′) *n.* In mathematics, one of a set of numbers that determines the position of a point. If the point is on a line, only one coordinate is needed; if the point is in a plane, two are needed; and if the point is in space, three are required. ❖ *adj.* **1.** Of equal importance, rank, or degree: *A compound sentence has two or more coordinate clauses.* **2.** Relating to or involving coordinates: *a coordinate system.* ❖ *v.* (kō-ôr′dn-āt′) **co·or·di·nat·ed, co·or·di·nat·ing, co·or·di·nates** —*tr.* To arrange or cause to work efficiently in a common cause or effort: *the agency that is coordinating the relief efforts in the flood zone.* —*intr.* **1.** To work efficiently with others in a common cause or effort: *If we can coordinate with the bands at your school, we can hold a joint concert.* **2.** To be in a harmonious arrangement; harmonize: *Do the curtains coordinate with the rest of room?* **—co·or′di·nate·ly** *adv.*

co·or·di·nat·ed universal time (kō-ôr′dn-ā′tĭd) *n.* An international time standard calculated by atomic clock and serving as the basis for standard time around the world.

co·or·di·nat·ing conjunction (kō-ôr′dn-ā′tĭng) *n.* A conjunction that connects two grammatical elements having identical construction, for example, *and* in *books and pencils*, or *or* in *out of sight or out of mind.*

co·or·di·na·tion (kō-ôr′dn-ā′shən) *n.* **1.** An act of coordinating or a condition or being coordinated: *Coordination among the rescue workers saved many of the earthquake victims.* **2.** The organized action of muscles or groups of muscles in the performance of complicated movements or tasks: *Gymnastics requires a great deal of coordination.*

co·or·di·na·tor (kō-ôr′dn-ā′tər) *n.* A person or thing that coordinates: *The mayor served as coordinator of the relief efforts.*

coot (ko͞ot) *n.* **1.** Any of several waterbirds of North America and Europe having dark-gray feathers and a short often white bill. **2.** *Informal* An eccentric or ornery person, especially an eccentric old man. [From Middle English *cote*, possibly from Middle Dutch *coet.*]

coo·tie (ko͞o′tē) *n. Slang* A body louse.

cop (kŏp) *n. Informal* A police officer. [Short for *copper*, probably from *cop*, to catch, capture, variant of *cap*, from Latin *capere.*]

cope[1] (kōp) *intr.v.* **coped, cop·ing, copes** To contend or deal, especially successfully: *Computers help us cope with vast amounts of information.* [From Middle English *copen*, to strike, fight against, from Old French *couper*, from Late Latin *colpus*, a blow, from Greek *kolaphos.*]

cope[2] (kōp) *n.* A long cloak worn by priests or bishops during special ceremonies or processions. [From Middle English, from Old English *-cāpe*, from Medieval Latin *cāpa*, cloak.]

Co·pen·ha·gen (kō′pən-hā′gən *or* kō′pən-hä′gən) The capital of Denmark, in the eastern part of the country. It became the capital in 1443.

co·pe·pod (kō′pə-pŏd′) *n.* Any of numerous very small animals that live in fresh water or salt water and are often parasitic on other organisms. Copepods are crustaceans.

co·per·ni·ci·um (kō′pər-nē′sē-əm *or* kō′pər-nē′shē-əm) *n. Symbol* **Cn** A radioactive element that has been artificially produced by scientists. The half-life of its most stable isotope is about 34 seconds. Atomic number 112. See **Periodic Table.** [After Nicolaus *Copernicus.*]

Co·per·ni·cus (kō-pûr′nə-kəs), **Nicolaus** 1473–1543. Polish astronomer whose theory that Earth and other planets revolve around the sun provided the foundation for modern astronomy. **—Co·per′ni·can** *adj.*

cop·i·er (kŏp′ē-ər) *n.* **1.** A machine that makes photocopies; a photocopier. **2.** A person who makes written copies; a copyist.

co·pi·lot (kō′pī′lət) *n.* The second or relief pilot of an aircraft.

cop·ing (kō′pĭng) *n.* The top layer of a stone or brick wall, usually slanted so as to shed rainwater or snow.

coping saw *n.* A saw with a narrow short blade stretched across a U-shaped frame, used for cutting designs in wood.

co·pi·ous (kō′pē-əs) *adj.* Large in quantity; abundant: *Rainfall is copious in the tropics.* [From Middle English, from Latin *cōpiōsus*, from *cōpia*, abundance.] **—co′pi·ous·ly** *adv.*

co·pla·nar (kō-plā′nər) *adj.* Lying in the same plane: *coplanar points.*

Cop·land (kōp′lənd), **Aaron** 1900–1990. American composer whose works include the ballet *Appalachian Spring* (1944).

Cop·ley (kŏp′lē), **John Singleton** 1738–1815. American painter who is known for his emotionally revealing portraits of prominent Bostonians such as Samuel Adams, John Hancock, and Paul Revere.

cop-out (kŏp′out′) *n. Slang* An excuse for avoiding a commitment or responsibility: *Saying you didn't try out for the team because of the practice schedule was just a cop-out; in fact, you were afraid you wouldn't be chosen.*

cop·per (kŏp′ər) *n.* **1.** *Symbol* **Cu** A reddish-brown metallic element that is an excellent conductor of heat and electricity. It is widely used for electrical wiring, water piping, and rust-resistant parts, either in pure form or in alloys such as brass and bronze. Atomic number 29. See **Periodic Table. 2.** A small coin made of copper or an alloy of copper. **3.** A reddish brown. ❖ *tr.v.* **cop·pered, cop·per·ing, cop·pers** To coat or finish with a layer of copper. [From Old English *coper*, from Late Latin *cuprum*, from Greek *Kupros*, Cyprus.] **—cop′per·y** *adj.*

cop·per·head (kŏp′ər-hĕd′) *n.* **1.** A venomous snake of the eastern and central United States, having a tan body with reddish-brown markings. **2. Copperhead** A Northerner who sympathized with the South during the Civil War.

cop·per·plate (kŏp′ər-plāt′) *n.* **1.** A copper printing plate engraved or etched with a pattern of the picture or other design to be printed. **2.** A print or engraving made with a copperplate.

cop·per·smith (kŏp′ər-smĭth′) *n.* A worker or manufacturer of objects in copper.

cop·pice (kŏp′ĭs) *n.* A copse.

co·pra (kō′prə *or* kŏp′rə) *n.* Dried coconut meat from which coconut oil is extracted.

copse (kŏps) *n.* A thicket of small tress or bushes.

Copt (kŏpt) *n.* **1.** A member of a historically Christian people of Egypt. **2.** A member of the Coptic Church.

cop·ter (kŏp′tər) *n. Informal* A helicopter.

Cop·tic (kŏp′tĭk) *n.* The language of the Copts, related to the Semitic languages and now used only in the Coptic Church. ❖ *adj.* Relating to the Copts, the Coptic Church, or the Coptic language.

Coptic Church *n.* The Christian church of Egypt that believes that Jesus had a single nature that was simultaneously divine and human.

cop·u·la (kŏp′yə-lə) *n.* A linking verb.

cop·u·late (kŏp′yə-lāt′) *intr.v.* **cop·u·lat·ed, cop·u·lat·ing, cop·u·lates 1.** To engage in sexual intercourse. **2.** To transfer male reproductive cells from one individual to another, usually into an internal organ or cavity, as in birds. **—cop′u·la′tion** *n.*

cop·y (kŏp′ē) *n., pl.* **cop·ies 1.** An imitation or reproduction of something original; a duplicate. **2.** One specimen or example of a printed text or picture: *a copy of the June issue of the magazine.* **3.** Written material to be set in type and printed: *The reporter submitted her copy for the newspaper article.* **4.** The words that are to be printed

copepod

Nicolaus Copernicus

coping saw

copperhead

coral
top: brain coral
bottom: staghorn coral

corduroy

Corinthian

ă	pat	ôr	core
ā	pay	oi	boy
âr	care	ou	out
ä	father	ŏŏ	took
ĕ	pet	ŏŏr	lure
ē	be	ōō	boot
ĭ	pit	ŭ	cut
ī	bite	ûr	urge
îr	pier	th	thin
ŏ	pot	*th*	this
ō	toe	zh	vision
ô	paw	ə	about

or spoken in an advertisement. ❖ *v.* **cop·ied, cop·y·ing, cop·ies** —*tr.* **1.** To make a reproduction of an original: *I copied my report on clean paper.* **2.** To follow as a model or pattern; imitate: *The builder copied the house next door.* See Synonyms at **imitate.** —*intr.* To make a copy or copies: *Good authors don't copy from others.* [From Middle English *copie*, from Medieval Latin *cōpia*, transcript, from Latin *cōpia*, profusion.]

cop·y·book (kŏp′ē-bo͝ok′) *n.* A book with models of handwriting to imitate.

cop·y·cat (kŏp′ē-kăt′) *n.* A person who mimics or imitates others, as in speech, dress, or action.

cop·y·ist (kŏp′ē-ĭst) *n.* A person who makes written copies, as of a manuscript.

cop·y·right (kŏp′ē-rīt′) *n.* The legal right to be the only one to publish, produce, sell, or distribute a literary, musical, dramatic, or artistic work. ❖ *tr.v.* **cop·y·right·ed, cop·y·right·ing, cop·y·rights** To secure a copyright for: *She copyrighted her novel.*

cop·y·writ·er (kŏp′ē-rī′tər) *n.* A person who writes advertising copy.

co·quet·ry (kō′kĭ-trē *or* kō-kĕt′rē) *n., pl.* **co·quet·ries** The behavior of a coquette; flirtation.

co·quette (kō-kĕt′) *n.* A woman who flirts. —**co·quet′tish** *adj.* —**co·quet′tish·ly** *adv.*

co·qui·na (kō-kē′nə) *n.* **1.** Any of various small clams having brightly colored shells. **2.** A soft porous limestone containing shells and coral, used for building.

cor– *pref.* Variant of **com–.**

cor·a·cle (kôr′ə-kəl) *n.* A small rounded boat made of hide or other waterproof material stretched over a wicker or wooden frame.

cor·al (kôr′əl) *n.* **1.** A hard stony substance formed by the skeletons of tiny, usually tropical invertebrate sea animals that live together in large colonies. It is often white, pink, or reddish, and some kinds are used for making jewelry. **2.** Any of the various animals that form this substance. [From Middle English, from Greek *korallion.*]

coral reef *n.* A reef consisting mainly of coral that has been compacted together with algae and minerals such as calcium carbonate.

coral snake *n.* Any of various venomous American snakes marked with bright red, black, and yellow bands.

Cor·bin (kôr′bĭn), **Margaret Cochran** 1751–1800. American Revolutionary figure. She fought at the Battle of Fort Washington (1776) until she was seriously wounded.

cord (kôrd) *n.* **1.** A string or small rope of twisted strands. **2.** An insulated flexible electric wire fitted with a plug or plugs. **3.** A structure of the body, such as a nerve or tendon, that resembles a cord. **4.** A unit of measure for cut firewood, equal to a stack that measures 4 feet by 4 feet by 8 feet or 128 cubic feet (3.6 cubic meters). **5a.** A raised ridge or rib on the surface of cloth. **b.** Cloth, such as corduroy, having raised ridges or ribs. **6. cords** *Informal* Pants made of corduroy. ❖ *tr.v.* **cord·ed, cord·ing, cords 1.** To fasten or bind with a cord: *Please cord the newspapers into bundles.* **2.** To cut and stack (firewood) in cords. [From Middle English *corde*, from Latin *chorda*, from Greek *khordē.*]

❑ *These sound alike:* **cord, chord[1]** (musical notes), **chord[2]** (line segment).

cord·age (kôr′dĭj) *n.* **1.** Cords or ropes, especially the ropes in a ship's rigging. **2.** An amount of wood measured in cords.

cord·ed (kôr′dĭd) *adj.* **1.** Tied or bound with cords: *a corded bundle.* **2.** Ribbed or twilled, as corduroy. **3.** Stacked in cords, as firewood.

cor·dial (kôr′jəl) *adj.* Warm and sincere; hearty: *cordial relations with the neighbors.* ❖ *n.* A liqueur. [From Middle English *cordial*, of the heart, from Medieval Latin *cordiālis*, from Latin *cor*, heart.] —**cor·dial′i·ty** *n.* —**cor′dial·ly** *adv.*

cor·dil·le·ra (kôr′dl-yâr′ə) *n.* An extensive chain of mountains, especially the main mountain range of a large land mass.

cord·less (kôrd′lĭs) *adj.* Having no cord, usually using batteries as a source of power: *a cordless telephone.*

cor·do·ba (kôr′də-bə) *n.* The basic monetary unit of Nicaragua. [After Francisco Fernández de *Córdoba* (1475?–1526?), Spanish explorer.]

Cór·do·ba (kôr′də-bə) A city of southern Spain east-northeast of Seville. Córdoba was renowned under the Moors as a cultural and intellectual center.

cor·don (kôr′dn) *n.* **1.** A line of military posts, people, or ships stationed around an area to enclose or guard it. **2.** A rope or tape stretched around an area, usually by the police, in order to restrict access. ❖ *tr.v.* **cor·doned, cor·don·ing, cor·dons** To form a cordon around: *The firefighters had cordoned off the burned-out building.*

cor·do·van (kôr′də-vən) *n.* **1.** A soft fine leather used for shoes and other leather goods. **2.** A shoe made from this leather.

cor·du·roy (kôr′də-roi′) *n.* **1.** A heavy cotton fabric with raised ribs or ridges. **2. corduroys** Pants made of this fabric.

cord·wood (kôrd′wo͝od′) *n.* **1.** Wood cut and piled in cords. **2.** Wood sold by the cord.

core (kôr) *n.* **1.** The innermost part of something; the heart: *the hard elastic core of a baseball.* **2.** The basic or most important part of something; the essence: *The core of the problem was a lack of funds.* **3.** The hard or stringy central part of certain fruits, such as an apple or pear, containing the seeds. **4.** The central or innermost portion of the earth below the mantle, probably consisting of iron and nickel. **5.** A piece of magnetic material, such as a rod of soft iron, placed inside an electrical coil or transformer to intensify and provide a path for the magnetic field produced by the windings. **6.** A long, cylindrical sample of soil, rock, or ice, collected with a drill to study the layers of material that are not visible from the surface. **7.** The central part of a nuclear reactor where atomic fission occurs. **8.** A computer memory or one of the magnetic devices in a computer memory. ❖ *tr.v.* **cored, cor·ing, cores** To remove the core of: *core apples.* [From Middle English.] —**cor′er** *n.*

❑ *These sound alike:* **core, corps** (military unit).

cor·gi (kôr′gē) *n., pl.* **cor·gis** A Welsh corgi. [From Welsh : *cor*, dwarf + *ci*, dog.]

co·ri·an·der (kôr′ē-ăn′dər) *n.* **1.** A plant related to and resembling parsley, having aromatic seedlike fruits. **2.** The dried fruits of this plant, used whole or ground as a seasoning. **3.** The leaves of this plant, often known as cilantro, used as a flavoring and garnish.

Cor·inth (kôr′ĭnth) A city of southern Greece west of Athens. It is near the site of the ancient city of **Corinth,** which was a maritime power in the seventh and sixth centuries BC.

Co·rin·thi·an (kə-rĭn′thē-ən) *adj.* **1.** Relating to ancient Corinth or its people, language, or culture. **2.** Relating to an order of ancient Greek and Roman architecture characterized by a slender column with an ornate bell-shaped top decorated with a design of acanthus leaves. ❖ *n.* **1.** A native or inhabitant of ancient Corinth. **2. Corinthians** Either of two books of the New Testament, containing letters from the Apostle Paul to the Christians in Corinth.

cork (kôrk) *n.* **1.** The light spongy outer bark of the cork oak, used for bottle stoppers and in insulation, life rafts, and flooring. **2a.** Something made of cork, especially a bottle stopper. **b.** A bottle stopper made of other material, such as plastic. **3.** A protective tissue of dead cells that forms the outermost layer of the bark of woody plants. ❖

tr.v. **corked, cork·ing, corks** To close up or stop with a cork: *cork a bottle.* [From Middle English, probably from Arabic dialectal *qūrq*, cork, from Latin *quercus*, oak.]

cork·er (kôr′kər) *n. Slang* A remarkable or astounding person or thing.

cork oak *n.* An evergreen oak tree of the Mediterranean region, having thick bark that is the source of cork.

cork·screw (kôrk′skrōō′) *n.* A device for drawing corks from bottles, consisting of a pointed metal spiral attached to a handle. ❖ *adj.* Spiral in shape; twisted: *the corkscrew motion of a slowly spinning top.*

corm (kôrm) *n.* A short, thick underground stem in which food is stored in the form of starch, as in a crocus.

cor·mo·rant (kôr′mər-ənt) *n.* Any of several large waterbirds having blackish feathers, webbed feet, and a slender hooked bill.

corn[1] (kôrn) *n.* **1a.** The ears or grains, called kernels, of any of several varieties of a tall grass first cultivated in Mexico and used as food for humans and livestock and as a source of edible oil or starch. **b.** The plant that bears such ears or kernels, called maize in much of the world. **2.** *Chiefly British* Any of various cereal plants or grains, such as wheat or rye. **3.** *Slang* Something considered trite, outdated, or too melodramatic or sentimental. ❖ *tr.v.* **corned, corn·ing, corns** To preserve and season with salt or in brine: *corn beef.* [From Old English *corn*, grain.] —SEE NOTE.

corn[2] (kôrn) *n.* A horny thickening of the skin, usually on or near a toe, resulting from pressure or rubbing. [From Middle English *corne*, from Latin *cornū*, horn.]

corn bread or **corn·bread** (kôrn′brĕd′) *n.* Bread made from cornmeal.

corn·cob (kôrn′kŏb′) *n.* The long hard central part of an ear of corn, bearing the kernels.

corn·crib (kôrn′krĭb′) *n.* A bin or building for storing and drying ears of corn.

corn dog *n.* A baked or fried frankfurter encased in corn bread.

cor·ne·a (kôr′nē-ə) *n.* The tough transparent membrane of the outer coat of the eyeball that covers the iris and the pupil.

corned (kŏrnd) *adj.* Preserved in strong salty water or with dry salt: *corned beef.*

cor·ner (kôr′nər) *n.* **1a.** The point at which two lines, edges, or surfaces meet: *the upper left-hand corner of the page; the corner of a table.* **b.** The area enclosed by the intersection of two lines, edges, or surfaces: *I sat in the corner.* **2.** The place where two roads or streets meet: *Meet me at the corner of Oak and Pine.* **3.** A remote or secluded place: *Americans have come from all corners of the world.* **4.** A threatening or difficult position: *I got myself in a corner by boasting I could outrun everybody.* **5.** A monopoly, as of a stock or commodity, that enables the supplier to control the price: *tried to get a corner on the wheat market.* ❖ *tr.v.* **cor·nered, cor·ner·ing, cor·ners 1.** To force or drive into a corner: *The dog cornered the cat in a closet.* **2.** To gain a monopoly over: *He attempted to corner the market in silver.* ❖ *adj.* **1.** Located at a street corner: *the corner convenience store.* **2.** Designed for or used in a corner: *a corner cupboard for dishes.* [From Middle English, from Latin *cornua*, horns.]

corner kick *n.* In soccer, a free kick from a corner of the field given to the offense when the defense has driven the ball out of bounds beyond the goal line.

cor·ner·stone (kôr′nər-stōn′) *n.* **1.** A stone at one of the corners of a building's foundation, often inscribed and set in place with a special ceremony. **2.** The basis or foundation of something: *Good nutrition is the cornerstone of a healthy life.*

cor·net (kôr-nĕt′) *n.* A brass instrument that is similar to the trumpet but has a mellower tone. [From Middle English, from Old French, from Latin *cornū*, horn.]

cor·net·ist also **cor·net·tist** (kôr-nĕt′ĭst) *n.* A person who plays a cornet.

corn flakes *pl.n.* A crisp, flaky, cold cereal prepared from coarse cornmeal and other ingredients.

corn·flow·er (kôrn′flou′ər) *n.* An annual plant of gardens and fields, having flowers that are usually deep blue, but sometimes white or pink.

corn·husk (kôrn′hŭsk′) *n.* The leafy covering surrounding an ear of corn.

cor·nice (kôr′nĭs) *n.* **1.** A projection of stone or molding at the top of a wall or column. **2.** The molding at the top of the walls of a room, just below the ceiling. **3.** A horizontal frame used to conceal curtain rods.

Cor·nish (kôr′nĭsh) *adj.* Relating to Cornwall, its inhabitants, or the Cornish language. ❖ *n.* A Celtic language spoken in Cornwall until about 1800.

corn·meal also **corn meal** (kôrn′mēl′) *n.* Coarse meal made from ground corn kernels.

corn·pone or **corn pone** (kôrn′pōn′) *n.* Corn bread that is made without milk or eggs, baked in rounded patties.

corn·rows (kôrn′rōz′) *pl.n.* Tight braids of hair in narrow parallel rows lying close to the scalp.

corn·starch (kôrn′stärch′) *n.* A starchy flour made from corn, used as a thickener in cooking.

corn syrup *n.* A thick sweet syrup that is made from corn starch and consists chiefly of glucose. It is often processed into high-fructose corn syrup for use in commercial foods and beverages.

cor·nu·co·pi·a (kôr′nə-kō′pē-ə) *n.* **1.** A cone-shaped container overflowing with fruit, vegetables, and flowers, symbolizing prosperity; a horn of plenty. **2.** An overflowing supply; an abundance: *The candidate offered a cornucopia of new ideas.*

Corn·wall (kôrn′wôl′) A peninsula of extreme southwest England. Its tin and copper mines were known in ancient times.

Corn·wal·lis (kôrn-wŏl′ĭs), **Charles** First Marquis Cornwallis. 1738–1805. British military leader who commanded forces during the American Revolution and surrendered to George Washington at Yorktown (1781).

corn·y (kôr′nē) *adj.* **corn·i·er, corn·i·est** *Slang* Trite, melodramatic, or sentimental: *a corny love scene.*

co·rol·la (kə-rō′lə *or* kə-rŏl′ə) *n.* The petals of a flower considered as a group.

cor·ol·lar·y (kôr′ə-lĕr′ē) *n., pl.* **cor·ol·lar·ies 1.** A statement that follows with little or no proof required from an already proven statement: *If we know A equals B, then the corollary is that B equals A.* **2.** A natural consequence or effect; a result: *Disease is a corollary of unsanitary living conditions.*

co·ro·na (kə-rō′nə) *n., pl.* **co·ro·nas** or **co·ro·nae** (kə-rō′nē) **1.** The extremely hot outer atmosphere of the sun, visible as a halo of light during a solar eclipse. **2.** A faintly colored shining ring seen around a celestial object, especially the moon or sun, when seen through a thin cloud or haze. **3.** A crown-shaped appendage on the inner side of the corolla in some flowers, such as the daffodil. [From Latin *corōna*, crown.]

cor·o·nar·y (kôr′ə-nĕr′ē) *adj.* **1.** Relating to the coronary arteries. **2.** Relating to the heart: *Many hospitals have coronary care units.* ❖ *n., pl.* **cor·o·nar·ies** A coronary thrombosis or heart attack.

coronary artery *n.* Either of the two arteries that supply blood directly to the heart.

coronary thrombosis *n.* The blockage of a coronary artery by a blood clot.

cor·o·na·tion (kôr′ə-nā′shən) *n.* The act or ceremony of crowning a sovereign, such as a king or queen.

cor·o·ner (kôr′ə-nər) *n.* A public official who investigates any death not clearly due to natural causes.

corm
gladiolus corms

WORD HISTORY

corn Throughout the English-speaking world, people eat **corn,** but they don't eat the same thing. In Old English *corn* meant "any small, hard particle or grain, as of sand or salt, or of a cereal or a seed." The cereal grains include wheat, oats, barley, maize, and so forth, and *corn* is used for the cereal grain most commonly grown in a given place. In most of England that crop is *wheat,* so *corn* usually means "wheat." In Ireland and Scotland that crop is *oats,* and *corn* means "oats" there. In the United States and Canada *corn* means "maize" because it is short for *Indian corn. Corn* in the sense of "grain of salt" appears in *corned beef*; in the sense of "seed," it appears in *peppercorn.*

cornrows

cor·o·net (kôr′ə-nĕt′) *n.* **1.** A small crown worn by princes, princesses, and other nobles. **2.** A band for the head, decorated with gold or jewels. [From Middle English *corounet*, from Old French, diminutive of *corone*, crown.]

corp. *abbr.* An abbreviation of corporation.

cor·po·ra (**kôr′**pər-ə) *n.* Plural of **corpus.**

cor·po·ral[1] (**kôr′**pər-əl *or* **kôr′**prəl) *adj.* Relating to the body. [From Middle English, from Latin *corporālis*, from *corpus*, body.]

cor·po·ral[2] (**kôr′**pər-əl *or* **kôr′**prəl) *n.* A noncommissioned officer in the US Army or Marine Corps ranking below a sergeant. [From Old Italian *caporale*, from *capo*, head, from Latin *caput*.]

cor·po·rate (**kôr′**pər-ĭt *or* **kôr′**prĭt) *adj.* **1.** Formed into a corporation; incorporated: *the corporate companies of industrial America.* **2.** Relating to a corporation: *The government taxes corporate profits.* **3.** United or combined; collective: *The team made a corporate effort to finish the project on time.* **—cor′po·rate·ly** *adv.*

corrosion

cor·po·ra·tion (kôr′pə-**rā′**shən) *n.* A group of people or an organization that has a charter recognizing it as a separate legal unit with rights, privileges, and liabilities that are separate from those of its individual members. Corporations act under the law as if they were a single person, as in entering into contracts or buying and selling property.

cor·po·re·al (kôr-**pôr′**ē-əl) *adj.* **1.** Relating to the body: *corporeal needs of food and water.* **2.** Of a material nature; tangible: *buildings, land, and other corporeal property.* **—cor·po′re·al·ly** *adv.*

corps (kôr) *n., pl.* **corps** (kôrz) **1.** A section or branch of the armed forces having a special function: *The Medical Corps is trained to take care of the wounded.* **2.** A large military unit composed of two or more divisions along with supporting units and commanded by a lieutenant general. **3.** A group of people acting together: *the press corps.*

❑ *These sound alike:* **corps, core** (central part).

corps de bal·let (kôr′ də bă-**lā′**) *n.* The dancers in a ballet troupe who perform as a group with no solo parts.

corpse (kôrps) *n.* A dead body, especially that of a human. [From Middle English *cors*, from Latin *corpus*, body.]

corrugation
metal roofing

corps·man (**kôr′**mən *or* **kôrz′**mən) *n.* An enlisted person in the US Navy or Marines who is trained as a medical assistant.

cor·pu·lent (**kôr′**pyə-lənt) *adj.* Having an abundance of fat or flesh; heavy or overweight. **—cor′pu·lence** *n.*

cor·pus (**kôr′**pəs) *n., pl.* **cor·po·ra** (**kôr′**pər-ə) A large collection of writings of a specific kind or on a specific subject: *a corpus of legal documents.*

cor·pus·cle (**kôr′**pŭs′əl) *n.* **1.** A cell, such as a blood cell, that circulates freely in the body. **2.** A very small particle.

cor·ral (kə-**răl′**) *n.* **1.** An enclosed area for keeping cattle, horses, or sheep. **2.** An enclosed area formed by a circle of wagons for defense against attack. ❖ *tr.v.* **cor·ralled, cor·ral·ling, cor·rals 1.** To drive into and hold in a corral: *corral cattle for shipment to market.* **2.** To arrange (wagons) in a corral. **3.** To surround or seize: *The soldiers corralled the revolutionaries.* [From Spanish, from Latin *currus*, cart, from *currere*, to run.]

❑ *These sound alike:* **corral, chorale** (hymn tune).

cor·rect (kə-**rĕkt′**) *tr.v.* **cor·rect·ed, cor·rect·ing, cor·rects 1a.** To remove the mistakes from: *Correct your paper before you hand it in.* **b.** To indicate or mark the errors in: *The teacher corrected our tests.* **2.** To change or adjust so as to bring improvement or meet a standard: *Glasses will correct your vision. A kind word corrected a wrong impression.* **3.** To rebuke or punish for the purpose of improving: *Our teacher corrected us for running in the halls.* ❖ *adj.* **1.** Free from error; accurate: *Your answers are absolutely correct.* **2.** Conforming to approved standards; proper: *the correct way to give artificial respiration.* [From Middle English *correcten*, from Latin *corrigere*.] **—cor·rect′ly** *adv.* **—cor·rect′ness** *n.*

cor·rec·tion (kə-**rĕk′**shən) *n.* **1.** The act or process of correcting: *Correction of all my spelling mistakes did not take long.* **2.** Something that is offered or substituted for a mistake or fault; an improvement: *Several corrections are written in the margin.* **3a.** Punishment intended to rehabilitate or improve a wrongdoer. **b.** often **corrections** A system for restoring legal offenders to a law-abiding and productive life, involving imprisonment, rehabilitation, parole, and probation. **4.** A brief or small decline in stock-market activity or prices following a period of increases. **—cor·rec′tion·al** *adj.*

cor·rec·tive (kə-**rĕk′**tĭv) *adj.* Intended or tending to correct: *corrective lenses.* **—cor·rec′tive·ly** *adv.*

cor·re·late (**kôr′**ə-lāt′) *v.* **cor·re·lat·ed, cor·re·lat·ing, cor·re·lates** *—tr.* To put or bring into a systematic relation: *We correlated the new data with the old and revised our theory.* *—intr.* To have systematic connection; be related: *The new data correlates perfectly with earlier studies.*

cor·re·la·tion (kôr′ə-**lā′**shən) *n.* **1.** A relation or connection: *a proven correlation between smoking and lung disease.* **2.** An act of correlating or a condition of being correlated: *The navigator's correlation of speed and position kept the ship on course.*

cor·rel·a·tive (kə-**rĕl′**ə-tĭv) *adj.* **1.** Related; corresponding: *Reading and writing are correlative language skills.* **2.** In grammar, indicating a relation and usually used in pairs. In the sentence *Neither Jim nor Joe went along, neither* and *nor* are correlative conjunctions. **—cor·rel′a·tive·ly** *adv.*

correlative conjunction *n.* A conjunction that regularly occurs as part of a pair of conjunctions and that indicates a relation, such as *both* and *and* (as in *feeling both tired and discouraged*) or *either* and *or* (as in *either laughing or crying.*)

cor·re·spond (kôr′ĭ-**spŏnd′**) *intr.v.* **cor·re·spond·ed, cor·re·spond·ing, cor·re·sponds 1.** To be in agreement; match or compare closely: *This rainy weather hardly corresponds with yesterday's sunny forecast.* **2.** To be very similar or equivalent: *A camera's shutter corresponds to an eyelid.* **3.** To communicate by letter, usually over a period of time: *Even though you will be away we can correspond over the summer.*

cor·re·spon·dence (kôr′ĭ-**spŏn′**dəns) *n.* **1.** Agreement; conformity: *Correspondence in the wording of the documents shows one is a copy of the other.* **2.** Resemblance, as in function or structure; similarity: *There is a close correspondence between the human arm and a seal's flipper.* **3a.** Communication by the exchange of letters. **b.** The letters exchanged: *a drawer full of old correspondence.*

cor·re·spon·dent (kôr′ĭ-**spŏn′**dənt) *n.* **1.** A person who communicates by letter, often on a regular basis. **2.** A person hired by a newspaper or radio or television station to report on news from a particular place: *the London correspondent for an American newspaper.* ❖ *adj.* Corresponding.

cor·re·spond·ing (kôr′ĭ-**spŏn′**dĭng) *adj.* Matching closely; similar: *the corresponding function of feathers and fur.* **—cor′re·spond′ing·ly** *adv.*

cor·ri·dor (**kôr′**ĭ-dər) *n.* **1.** A hall or passageway, often with rooms opening onto it. **2.** A tract of land forming a passageway: *a corridor for trains through the city.* [From Italian *corridore*, from *correre*, to run, from Latin *currere*.]

cor·rob·o·rate (kə-**rŏb′**ə-rāt′) *tr.v.* **cor·rob·o·rat·ed, cor·rob·o·rat·ing, cor·rob·o·rates** To support or confirm by new or additional evidence; make certain: *Similar results of several experiments corroborated the new*

ă	pat	ôr	core
ā	pay	oi	boy
âr	care	ou	out
ä	father	o͝o	took
ĕ	pet	o͝or	lure
ē	be	o͞o	boot
ĭ	pit	ŭ	cut
ī	bite	ûr	urge
îr	pier	th	thin
ŏ	pot	*th*	this
ō	toe	zh	vision
ô	paw	ə	about

scientific theory. —**cor·rob′o·ra′tion** *n.* —**cor·rob′o·ra′tive** *adj.*

cor·rode (kə-**rōd′**) *v.* **cor·rod·ed, cor·rod·ing, cor·rodes** —*tr.* To dissolve or wear away (a metal or alloy), especially by chemical action. —*intr.* To be dissolved or worn away: *Most metals corrode in a solution of salt.* [From Middle English *corroden*, from Latin *corrōdere*, to gnaw away.]

cor·ro·sion (kə-**rō′**zhən) *n.* **1.** The process of corroding metal: *Corrosion caused the pipe to leak.* **2.** The product or result of such a process: *We found some corrosion on the car door.*

cor·ro·sive (kə-**rō′**sĭv) *adj.* Capable of producing or tending to produce corrosion: *The salt used to melt snow and ice on the highways is corrosive to the metal rods in the concrete.* ❖ *n.* A corrosive substance. —**cor·ro′sive·ly** *adv.* —**cor·ro′sive·ness** *n.*

cor·ru·gat·ed (**kôr′**ə-gā′tĭd) *adj.* Having parallel ridges and grooves: *a roof of corrugated tin.*

cor·ru·ga·tion (kôr′ə-**gā′**shən) *n.* A groove or ridge in a corrugated surface.

cor·rupt (kə-**rŭpt′**) *adj.* **1.** Immoral; wicked; depraved: *the corrupt life of a swindler.* **2.** Willing to accept bribes; dishonest: *a corrupt government.* **3.** Containing errors or changes, as in a text: *A corrupt translation of the poem made it incomprehensible.* ❖ *v.* **cor·rupt·ed, cor·rupt·ing, cor·rupts** —*tr.* **1.** To ruin morally; cause to behave wickedly: *Greed corrupts some people.* **2.** To destroy the honesty or integrity of, as by bribing: *They corrupted the senator with offers of shares in their company.* **3.** To taint; infect; spoil: *Several chemical spills corrupted the water supply.* **4.** To change the original form of (a text, word, or language): *Careless copying corrupted later versions of the poem.* **5.** To damage (data) in a computer file or on a disk. —*intr.* To become corrupt: *Absolute power corrupts absolutely.* [From Middle English *corrupt*, from Latin *corruptus*, past participle of *corrumpere*, to destroy : *com-*, intensive prefix + *rumpere*, to break.] —**cor·rupt′er** *n.* —**cor·rupt′ly** *adv.*

cor·rupt·i·ble (kə-**rŭp′**tə-bəl) *adj.* Capable of being corrupted, as by bribery. —**cor·rupt′i·bil′i·ty** *n.* —**cor·rupt′i·bly** *adv.*

cor·rup·tion (kə-**rŭp′**shən) *n.* **1.** The act or process of corrupting by making wicked or dishonest: *money's corruption of a powerful official.* **2.** Dishonesty or improper behavior, as by a person in a position of authority: *The legislature was riddled with corruption.* **3.** Decay; rot.

cor·sage (kôr-**säzh′** *or* kôr-**säj′**) *n.* A small bouquet of flowers worn at the shoulder or waist or on the wrist, especially by women.

cor·sair (**kôr′**sâr′) *n.* **1.** A pirate, especially along the Barbary Coast. **2.** A pirate ship, often acting with the approval of a government.

cor·se·let (**kôr′**slĭt) *n.* Metal armor worn to protect the body, especially the upper body.

cor·set (**kôr′**sĭt) *n.* A close-fitting undergarment, worn by women to support or shape the waist and hips.

Cor·si·ca (**kôr′**sĭ-kə) An island of France in the Mediterranean Sea north of Sardinia. Napoleon Bonaparte was born here. —**Cor′si·can** *adj. & n.*

cor·tege (kôr-**tĕzh′**) *n.* **1.** A ceremonial procession, especially a funeral procession. **2.** A procession of attendants; a retinue.

Cor·tés (kôr-**tĕz′**), **Hernando** or **Hernán** 1485–1547. Spanish explorer who conquered Aztec Mexico.

Hernando Cortés

cor·tex (**kôr′**tĕks′) *n., pl.* **cor·ti·ces** (**kôr′**tĭ-sēz′) or **cor·tex·es 1.** The outer layer of an organ or part of the body, as of the adrenal glands. **2.** The cerebral cortex. **3.** A layer of tissue under the outermost part of plant stems and roots. [From Latin *cortex*, bark.]

cor·ti·cal (**kôr′**tĭ-kəl) *adj.* **1.** Relating to or consisting of a cortex: *the rind and other cortical tissue of an orange.* **2.** Relating to, associated with, or depending on the cerebral cortex: *the cortical functions of the brain.* —**cor′ti·cal·ly** *adv.*

cor·ti·sone (**kôr′**tĭ-sōn′ *or* **kôr′**tĭ-zōn′) *n.* A hormone produced by the adrenal gland or produced synthetically, used in treating arthritis, allergies, and gout.

co·run·dum (kə-**rŭn′**dəm) *n.* An extremely hard mineral composed mainly of aluminum oxide. It occurs in gem varieties such as ruby and sapphire and in a dark-colored variety that is used for polishing and scraping.

cor·vette (kôr-**vĕt′**) *n.* **1.** A fast gunboat often used to protect convoys from submarines. **2.** A small sailing warship armed with one tier of guns.

cor·ymb (**kôr′**ĭmb) *n.* A flat-topped flower cluster in which the outer flowers have longer stalks than the inner flowers.

corymb

cos *abbr.* An abbreviation of cosine.

co·se·cant (kō-**sē′**kănt′) *n.* In a right triangle, the ratio of the length of the hypotenuse to the length of the side opposite an acute angle.

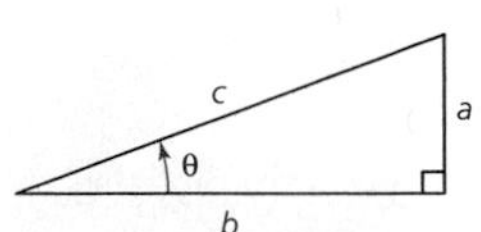

cosecant
csc θ = c/a

co·sign (kō-**sīn′**) *tr.v.* **co·signed, co·sign·ing, co·signs** To sign (a legal document) with another or others.

co·sine (**kō′**sīn′) *n.* In a right triangle, a function of an acute angle equal to the length of the side adjacent to the angle divided by the length of the hypotenuse.

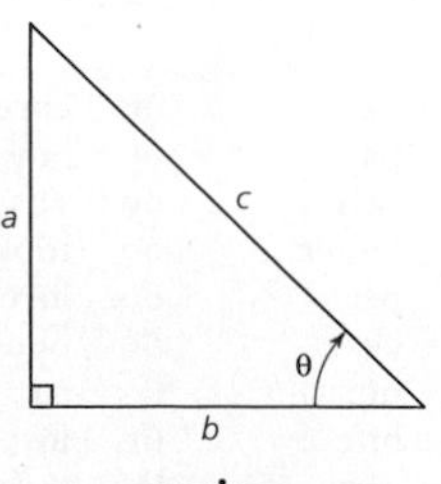

cosine
cos θ = b/c

cos·met·ic (kŏz-**mĕt′**ĭk) *n.* A preparation, such as face powder or skin cream, designed to beautify the body. ❖ *adj.* Done or used to improve the outward appearance, as of a person or building: *cosmetic surgery to remove a scar; a little paint and some other cosmetic repairs on a porch.*

cos·mic (**kŏz′**mĭk) *adj.* **1.** Relating to the universe: *telescopes that reveal the cosmic past.* **2.** Infinitely extended; vast: *Overpopulation of the planet is an issue of cosmic importance.* —**cos′mi·cal·ly** *adv.*

cosmic dust *n.* Clouds of fine solid particles of matter in outer space.

cosmic ray *n.* A very rapidly moving particle, especially a proton or alpha particle, that enters the atmosphere from outer space.

cos·mol·o·gy (kŏz-**mŏl′**ə-jē) *n.* The branch of astronomy that deals with the history and structure of the universe.

cos·mo·naut (**kŏz′**mə-nôt′) *n.* A Russian or Soviet astronaut. [From Russian *kosmonavt* : Greek *kosmos*, universe + Greek *nautēs*, sailor.]

cos·mo·pol·i·tan (kŏz′mə-**pŏl′**ĭ-tn) *adj.* **1.** Composed of people or elements from many different parts of the world: *Montreal is a cosmopolitan city.* **2.** Having broad interests or wide experience of the world; sophisticated: *A cosmopolitan guest made the party interesting.* ❖ *n.* A cosmopolitan person.

cos·mos (**kŏz′**məs *or* **kŏz′**mōs′) *n.* **1.** The universe regarded as an orderly and harmonious whole. **2.** Any of various tall garden plants having pink, white, or red flowers that resemble daisies. [From Middle English, from Greek *kosmos*, order.]

cos·play (**kŏz′**plā) *n.* **1.** The hobby of dressing up as a fictional character, as from a science fiction movie or comic book.

Cos·sack (**kŏs′**ăk) *n.* A member of a people of southern Russia, whose men often served in the cavalry during the rule of the czars. —**Cos′sack′** *adj.*

cost (kôst) *n.* **1.** An amount paid or charged for a purchase; a price: *The cost of a fishing license is going up.* **2.** The loss or sacrifice necessary to attain a goal: *He worked day and night at the cost of his health.* **3.** **costs** The expenses of a lawsuit. ❖ *tr.v.* **cost, cost·ing, costs 1.** To have or require as a price: *A subscription to the magazine costs $35.* **2.** To cause to lose or sacrifice: *Years of drought cost them their farm.*

cos·tal (**kŏs′**təl) *adj.* Relating to or near the ribs.

co·star also **co-star** (**kō′**stär′) *n.* A starring actor given

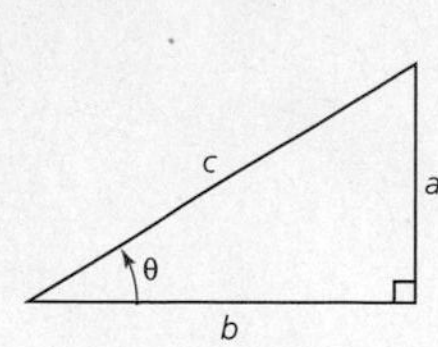

cotangent
$\cot \theta = b/a$

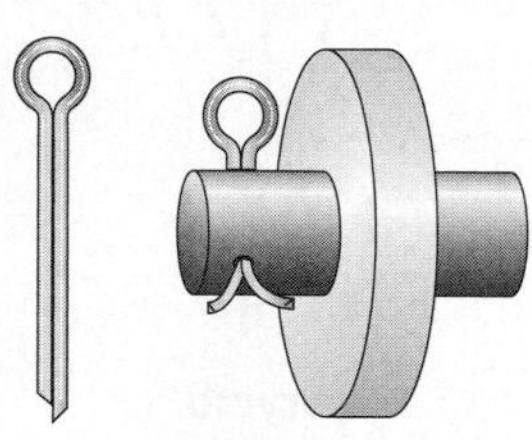
cotter pin

cottonwood

equal status with another or others in a play or film. **—co′star′** *v.*

Cos·ta Ri·ca (kŏs′tə rē′kə *or* kō′stə rē′kə) A country of Central America between Panama and Nicaragua. San José is the capital.

cost·ly (kôst′lē) *adj.* **cost·li·er, cost·li·est 1.** High-priced; expensive: *costly jewelry.* **2.** Involving great loss or sacrifice: *Going west was a costly decision for many pioneer families.* **—cost′li·ness** *n.*

cost of living *n.* The average cost of basic necessities, such as food, clothing, and shelter.

cos·tume (kŏs′to͞om′) *n.* **1.** An outfit or disguise worn on special occasions such as Halloween. **2.** The style of clothing and hair typical of a certain time, place, or people: *The costume of the ancient Romans included togas and sandals.* **3.** A set of clothes suitable for a certain occasion or season: *a skating costume.* ❖ *tr.v.* (kŏ-sto͞om′) **cos·tumed, cos·tum·ing, cos·tumes** To dress in a costume: *Everyone was costumed for our Halloween party.* [From Italian, style, fashion, from Latin *cōnsuētūdō*, custom, habit.]

costume jewelry *n.* Jewelry made from inexpensive metals and imitation gems or semiprecious stones.

cos·tum·er (kŏs′to͞o′mər) *n.* A person who makes or supplies costumes, as for plays.

cot[1] (kŏt) *n.* A narrow bed usually made of canvas stretched over a folding frame.

cot[2] *abbr.* An abbreviation of cotangent.

co·tan·gent (kō-tăn′jənt) *n.* In a right triangle, a function of an acute angle equal to the length of the side adjacent to the angle divided by the length of the opposite side.

cote (kōt) *n.* A small shed or coop for sheep or birds.
❑ *These sound alike:* **cote, coat** (garment).

Côte d'I·voire (kōt′ dē-vwär′) also **Ivory Coast** A country of western Africa on the Atlantic Ocean west of Ghana. Yamoussoukro is the capital and Abidjan the largest city.

co·ter·ie (kō′tə-rē *or* kō′tə-rē′) *n.* A group of people who share interests and associate frequently.

co·til·lion (kō-tĭl′yən) *n.* A formal ball, especially one at which young women are presented to society.

cot·tage (kŏt′ĭj) *n.* **1.** A small house, usually in the country. **2.** A small house for vacation use.

cottage cheese *n.* A soft white cheese made of curds of sour skim milk.

cot·tag·er (kŏt′ĭ-jər) *n.* A person who lives in a cottage.

cot·ter pin (kŏt′ər) *n.* A split pin that fits through a hole in order to fasten parts together and is secured by bending back the ends.

cot·ton (kŏt′n) *n.* **1.** Any of various shrubby plants grown in warm regions for the downy white fibers that surround their oil-rich seeds. **2.** The soft fine fibers of any of these plants, used in making textiles and other products. **3.** Thread or cloth made of cotton fibers. ❖ *intr.v.* **cot·toned, cot·ton·ing, cot·tons** *Informal* To take a liking; become friendly: *Our dog doesn't cotton to strangers.* [From Middle English *cotoun*, from Arabic *quṭn*.]

cotton candy *n.* A candy made of sugar spun into thin fibers that form a fluffy mass.

cotton gin *n.* A machine that separates the seeds, hulls, and other small objects from cotton fibers.

cot·ton·mouth (kŏt′n-mouth′) *n.* The water moccasin.

cot·ton·seed (kŏt′n-sēd′) *n.* The seed of the cotton plant, the source of cottonseed oil.

cottonseed oil *n.* An oil obtained by pressing cottonseed, used in food products, paints, and soaps.

cot·ton·tail (kŏt′n-tāl′) *n.* Any of several rabbits of the Americas, having grayish or brownish fur and a short fluffy white tail.

cot·ton·wood (kŏt′n-wo͝od′) *n.* Any of several American poplar trees having triangular leaves and seeds with cottony tufts.

cot·ton·y (kŏt′n-ē) *adj.* Resembling cotton; fluffy or downy: *cottony clouds.*

cot·y·le·don (kŏt′l-ēd′n) *n.* A leaf of the embryo of a seed-bearing plant. A cotyledon contains stored food and is the first leaf or the first of a pair of leaves in a newly developing plant.

couch (kouch) *n.* A sofa. ❖ *tr.v.* **couched, couch·ing, couch·es** To word in a certain manner; phrase: *The negotiators couched their demands in tactful language.* [From Middle English *couche*, from Old French *couchier*, to lay down, lie down.]

couch potato *n. Slang* A person who spends much time sitting or lying down, usually watching television.

cou·gar (ko͞o′gər) *n.* A large wild cat chiefly of mountainous regions of the Americas, having a long tail and a tawny coat; a mountain lion.

cough (kôf) *v.* **coughed, cough·ing, coughs** *—intr.* **1.** To force air from the lungs suddenly and noisily, usually to clear mucus or other matter from the throat or lungs: *cough from breathing smoke.* **2.** To make a noise similar to coughing: *The engine coughed and died.* *—tr.* To clear from the respiratory tract by coughing: *cough up mucus.* ❖ *n.* **1.** The act of coughing: *The student's cough disturbed the class.* **2.** An illness marked by coughing: *A deep cough kept me out of school.*

could (ko͝od) *aux.v.* Past tense of **can**[1]. **1.** Used to indicate ability in the past: *I could run faster back then.* **2.** Used to indicate permission in the past: *Only friends of the musicians could go backstage after the concert.* **3.** Used to indicate possibility: *It could rain tomorrow.* **4.** Used to indicate politeness: *Could you help me?* —SEE NOTE AT **should.**

could·n't (ko͝od′nt) Contraction of *could not.*

couldst (ko͝odst) *aux.v. Archaic* A second person singular past tense of **can**[1].

cou·lee (ko͞o′lē) *n.* A deep gulch or ravine in the western United States, often dry in summer.

cou·lomb (ko͞o′lŏm′ *or* ko͞o′lōm′) *n.* A unit used to measure electric charge. One coulomb is equal to the quantity of charge that passes a point in an electric circuit in one second when a current of one ampere is flowing through the circuit. [After Charles Augustin de *Coulomb* (1736–1806), French physicist.]

coul·ter (kōl′tər) *n.* A blade or wheel attached to a plow to cut the soil in front of the plowshare.

coun·cil (koun′səl) *n.* **1.** A gathering of people called together to discuss a problem or give advice. **2.** A body of people elected or appointed to make laws, policies, or decisions: *The president has a council of economic advisers.* [From Middle English *counseil, councel*, from Latin *concilium*.] —SEE NOTE.
❑ *These sound alike:* **council, counsel** (advice).

coun·cil·man (koun′səl-mən) *n.* A member of a council, especially of the group that makes the laws of a city.

coun·cil·or also **coun·cil·lor** (koun′sə-lər *or* koun′slər) *n.* A member of a council. —SEE NOTE AT **council.**
❑ *These sound alike:* **councilor, counselor** (adviser).

coun·cil·wom·an (koun′səl-wo͝om′ən) *n.* A woman who is a member of a council, especially of the group that makes the laws of a city.

coun·sel (koun′səl) *n.* **1.** The act of exchanging opinions and ideas; consultation: *Frequent counsel among the members kept the committee informed.* **2.** Advice; guidance: *I will not make a decision without your counsel.* **3.** A lawyer or group of lawyers giving legal advice. ❖ *tr.v.* **coun·seled, coun·sel·ing, coun·sels** or **coun·selled, coun·sel·ling, coun·sels 1.** To give (a person) advice; advise: *The school counseled parents to keep children at home during the storm.* **2.** To recommend: *counsel swift*

ă	pat	ôr	core
ā	pay	oi	boy
âr	care	ou	out
ä	father	o͝o	took
ĕ	pet	o͝or	lure
ē	be	o͞o	boot
ĭ	pit	ŭ	cut
ī	bite	ûr	urge
îr	pier	th	thin
ŏ	pot	*th*	this
ō	toe	zh	vision
ô	paw	ə	about

action. [From Middle English *counseil,* from Latin *consilium.*] —SEE NOTE AT **council.**

❑ *These sound alike:* **counsel, council** (group).

coun·sel·or also **coun·sel·lor** (koun′sə-lər *or* **koun′**-slər) *n.* **1.** A person who advises or guides; an advisor: *a high-school counselor.* **2.** A lawyer. **3.** A person who supervises children at a summer camp. —SEE NOTE AT **council.**

❑ *These sound alike:* **counselor, councilor** (member of a council).

count¹ (kount) *v.* **count·ed, count·ing, counts** —*tr.* **1.** To find the total of; add up: *Count your change before leaving the store. Count the books before you return them to the library.* **2.** To name the numbers in order up to and including (a particular number): *Count three and jump.* **3.** To take account of; include: *There are seven in my family, counting me.* **4.** To regard; consider: *Count yourself lucky that you didn't get sick.* —*intr.* **1.** To name numbers in order or list items: *count from 1 to 10.* **2.** To have importance or value: *It is not how much you write but how well you write that counts.* **3.** To keep time in music by counting beats. ❖ *n.* **1.** The act of counting or calculating: *A count showed that two members were absent.* **2.** A number reached by counting: *The count of nesting birds was lower than last year.* **3.** In law, any of the separate charges listed in an indictment: *The thief was tried on five counts of robbery.* ◆ **count in** To include: *If you are going camping, count me in.* **count off** To separate into groups by counting: *count off by twos.* **count on 1.** To rely on: *You can count on me to help.* **2.** To be confident of; anticipate: *I am counting on an A in history.* **count out** To exclude: *If there's going to be any roughness, you can count me out.* [From Middle English *counten,* from Latin *computāre,* to calculate.]

count² (kount) *n.* A nobleman in some European countries, corresponding to an English earl. [From Middle English *counte,* from Late Latin *comes,* occupant of any state office, from Latin *comes,* companion.]

count·down (**kount′**doun′) *n.* **1.** The counting backward from a starting number to indicate the time remaining before a scheduled event, such as the launching of a rocket. **2.** The checks and preparations carried out during this process.

coun·te·nance (**koun′**tə-nəns) *n.* The face or the expression on the face: *The question left him with a puzzled countenance.* ❖ *tr.v.* **coun·te·nanced, coun·te·nanc·ing, coun·te·nanc·es** To accept or give support to; tolerate or approve: *The school will not countenance cheating.*

coun·ter¹ (**koun′**tər) *adj.* Contrary; opposing: *views counter to public opinion.* ❖ *n.* **1.** A person or thing that counters; an opposite. **2.** A blow given in return, as in boxing. **3.** A stiff piece of leather around the heel of a shoe. ❖ *v.* **coun·tered, coun·ter·ing, coun·ters** —*tr.* **1.** To move or act in opposition to; oppose: *They countered our plan with one of their own.* **2.** To return (a blow) with another blow. **3.** To offer or say in response: *She countered that she was too busy to write a long paper.* —*intr.* **1.** To move, act, or respond in opposition: *They countered with a weak argument.* **2.** To give a blow in return, as in boxing. ❖ *adv.* In a contrary manner or direction: *a new method that runs counter to the regular way.* [From Middle English *countre,* from Latin *contrā,* against.]

count·er² (**koun′**tər) *n.* **1.** A flat surface on which goods are sold, money is counted, or food is prepared or served. **2.** A small object, such as a stone or bead, used for counting, as on an abacus, or for marking a place in a game. ◆ **over the counter** Without a doctor's prescription being legally required: *aspirin is usually sold over the counter.* [From Middle English *contour,* from Medieval Latin *computātōrium,* counting house, from Latin *computāre,* to calculate.]

count·er³ (**koun′**tər) *n.* A person or thing that counts, especially a mechanical or electronic device that automatically counts.

counter– *pref.* A prefix that means: **1.** Contrary or opposite: *counteract; counterclockwise.* **2.** In return or opposing: *counterattack.* **3.** Complementary; corresponding: *countersign.*

coun·ter·act (koun′tər-**ăkt′**) *tr.v.* **coun·ter·act·ed, coun·ter·act·ing, coun·ter·acts** To oppose and lessen the effects of by contrary action; check: *Aspirin often counteracts a fever.*

coun·ter·at·tack (**koun′**tər-ə-tăk′) *n.* An attack made in return for another attack. ❖ *intr. & tr.v.* (koun′tər-ə-**tăk′**) **coun·ter·at·tacked, coun·ter·at·tack·ing, coun·ter·at·tacks** To attack in return.

coun·ter·bal·ance (**koun′**tər-băl′əns) *n.* **1.** A force or an influence that counteracts another. **2.** A weight that balances another. ❖ *tr.v.* (koun′tər-**băl′**əns) **coun·ter·bal·anced, coun·ter·bal·anc·ing, coun·ter·bal·anc·es** To act as a counterbalance to.

coun·ter·claim (**koun′**tər-klām′) *n.* A claim made in opposition to another claim.

coun·ter·clock·wise (koun′tər-**klŏk′**wīz′) *adv. & adj.* In a direction opposite to that of the movement of the hands of a clock: *move counterclockwise; counterclockwise motion.*

coun·ter·feit (**koun′**tər-fĭt′) *v.* **coun·ter·feit·ed, coun·ter·feit·ing, coun·ter·feits** —*tr.* **1.** To make a copy of (something) in order to deceive: *The defendant was found guilty of counterfeiting money.* **2.** To pretend; fake: *We counterfeited surprise to please the host.* —*intr.* **1.** To carry on a deception; pretend. **2.** To make fraudulent copies, especially of money. ❖ *adj.* **1.** Made in imitation of what is genuine in order to deceive: *a counterfeit dollar bill.* **2.** Pretended; simulated: *counterfeit friendliness.* ❖ *n.* Something counterfeited: *That $20 bill is a counterfeit.* [From Middle English *contrefeten,* from Old French *contrefait,* made in imitation : *contre-,* against + *faire,* to make (from Latin *facere*).] **—coun′ter·feit′·er** *n.*

coun·ter·in·sur·gen·cy (koun′tər-ĭn-**sûr′**jən-sē) *n.* Actions taken by a government to oppose or suppress an insurgency.

coun·ter·in·tel·li·gence (koun′tər-ĭn-**tĕl′**ə-jəns) *n.* Actions taken by a government to deceive enemy agents or prevent them from gathering political or military secrets.

coun·ter·mand (**koun′**tər-mănd′ *or* koun′tər-**mănd′**) *tr.v.* **coun·ter·mand·ed, coun·ter·mand·ing, coun·ter·mands** To cancel or reverse (a command or order).

coun·ter·meas·ure (**koun′**tər-mĕzh′ər) *n.* A measure or action taken to oppose or offset another.

coun·ter·move (**koun′**tər-mo͞ov′) *n.* A move in opposition to another move: *countermoves in chess.*

coun·ter·of·fen·sive (**koun′**tər-ə-fĕn′sĭv) *n.* A large-scale attack by an army, intended to stop the offensive of an enemy force.

coun·ter·of·fer (**koun′**tər-ô′fər) *n.* An offer made in return by a person who rejects an unsatisfactory offer.

coun·ter·pane (**koun′**tər-pān′) *n.* A bedspread or quilt.

coun·ter·part (**koun′**tər-pärt′) *n.* **1.** A person or thing that corresponds to another, as in function, relation, or position: *The ancient counterpart to the car was the chariot.* **2.** A person or thing that is a natural complement to another: *He has one sock but lost its counterpart.*

coun·ter·point (**koun′**tər-point′) *n.* **1.** A musical technique in which two or more distinct melodies are combined in harmony while at the same time keeping their distinctness. **2.** A secondary melody designed to go along with a principal melody.

coun·ter·pro·duc·tive (koun′tər-prə-**dŭk′**tĭv) *adj.* Tending to hinder rather than help one's purpose.

USAGE

council The word **council** refers to a decision-making assembly, as in *city council* or *student council*; its members are known as *councilors.* The word **counsel,** on the other hand, means "advice and guidance"; a person who provides such counsel, as at a summer camp or in a legal dispute, is a *counselor.*

WRITERS CHOOSE THEIR WORDS

The shells, which had ceased to trouble the regiment for a time, came swirling again, and exploded in the grass or among the leaves of the trees. They looked to be strange war flowers bursting into fierce bloom. The men groaned. The luster faded from their eyes. Their smudged **countenances** now expressed a profound dejection.

—Stephen Crane
The Red Badge of Courage

WRITERS CHOOSE THEIR WORDS

Claudia, who had eaten cereal and drunk pineapple juice, scolded him about the need to eat properly. Breakfast food for breakfast, and lunch food for lunch. Jamie **countered** with complaints about Claudia's narrow-mindedness.

—E.L. Konigsburg
From the Mixed-up Files of Mrs. Basil E. Frankweiler

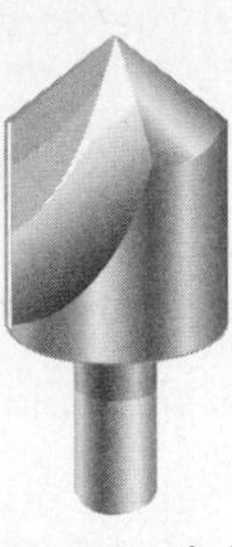
countersink

coupler
railroad car coupler

coun·ter·rev·o·lu·tion (koun′tər-rĕv′ə-**lo͞o′**shən) *n.* A movement arising in opposition to a revolution and aiming to restore the conditions before the revolution.

coun·ter·rev·o·lu·tion·ar·y (koun′tər-rĕv′ə-**lo͞o′**shə-nĕr′ē) *adj.* Relating to or tending to promote counterrevolution. ❖ *n.* A person who is engaged in or supports counterrevolution.

coun·ter·sign (**koun′**tər-sīn′) *tr.v.* **coun·ter·signed, coun·ter·sign·ing, coun·ter·signs** To sign (a document previously signed by another), as to guarantee authenticity: *The property deed was signed by the new owner and countersigned by a notary public.* ❖ *n.* **1.** A second or confirming signature. **2a.** A sign or signal to be given to a sentry in order to pass; a password. **b.** A secret sign or signal given in answer to another.

coun·ter·sink (**koun′**tər-sĭngk′) *n.* **1.** A hole with the top part enlarged so that the head of a screw or bolt will lie flush with or below the surface. **2.** A tool for making such a hole. ❖ *tr.v.* **coun·ter·sunk** (**koun′**tər-sŭngk′), **coun·ter·sink·ing, coun·ter·sinks 1.** To enlarge the top part of (a hole) so that the head of a screw or bolt will lie flush with or below the surface. **2.** To drive (a screw or bolt) into a hole so that the screw or bolt sits flush with or below the surface.

coun·ter·spy (**koun′**tər-spī′) *n., pl.* **coun·ter·spies** A spy working to uncover or oppose enemy espionage.

coun·ter·ten·or (**koun′**tər-tĕn′ər) *n.* **1.** A man's singing voice with a range above that of tenor. **2.** A singer having such a voice.

coun·ter·ter·ror·ism (koun′tər-**tĕr′**ə-rĭz′əm) *n.* Actions taken by a government to prevent terrorist attacks or to defeat terrorists.

coun·ter·top (**koun′**tər-tŏp′) *n.* The top of a counter, as in a kitchen: *placed the groceries on the countertop.*

coun·ter·weight (**koun′**tər-wāt′) *n.* **1.** A weight used as a counterbalance. **2.** A force or influence that counteracts another: *The new conservative judge will provide a counterweight to the court's most liberal members.*

count·ess (**koun′**tĭs) *n.* **1.** A woman holding the title of count or earl. **2.** The wife or widow of a count or earl.

count·ing number (**koun′**tĭng) *n.* A number used to count objects; a whole number greater than zero. The numbers 1, 5, and 29 are counting numbers, but ¼ and −7 are not.

count·less (**kount′**lĭs) *adj.* Too many to be counted; innumerable: *the countless stars.*

count noun *n.* A noun, such as *chair* or *pen,* that refers to a single object and can form a plural or occur with the article *a* or *an.*

coun·tri·fied (**kŭn′**trĭ-fīd′) *adj.* **1.** Resembling or having the characteristics of country life; rural; rustic: *The wide-brimmed hat gave the actor a countrified look.* **2.** Lacking in sophistication: *simple, countrified manners.*

coun·try (**kŭn′**trē) *n., pl.* **coun·tries 1a.** A nation or state: *Mexico and Canada are two countries in the Western Hemisphere.* **b.** The land of a nation or state: *Switzerland is a mostly mountainous country.* **2.** The land of one's birth or citizenship: *The sailors returned to their country at the end of the voyage.* **3.** The people of a nation or state: *The country will benefit from his invention.* **4.** A large area of land distinguished by certain physical, geographic, or cultural features: *hill country.* **5.** The region outside of cities or heavily populated districts; a rural area: *go to the country for a vacation.* **6.** Country music: *The new album is a mix of pop and country.* ❖ *adj.* **1.** Relating to or typical of the country: *country life.* **2.** Relating to country music. [From Middle English *contre,* from Latin *contrā,* opposite.]

country and western *n.* Country music.

country club *n.* A suburban club with facilities for social and sports activities, usually having a golf course.

coun·try·man (**kŭn′**trē-mən) *n.* **1.** A person from one's own country; a compatriot. **2.** A native or inhabitant of a particular country. **3.** A man who lives in the country.

country music *n.* Popular music based on the folk style of the southern rural United States or on the music of cowboys in the American West.

coun·try·side (**kŭn′**trē-sīd′) *n.* **1.** A rural region. **2.** The inhabitants of the countryside: *The whole countryside resisted building the highway.*

coun·try·wom·an (**kŭn′**trē-wo͝om′ən) *n.* **1.** A woman from one's own country; a compatriot. **2.** A woman who was born in or lives in a particular country. **3.** A woman who lives in the country.

coun·ty (**koun′**tē) *n., pl.* **coun·ties 1.** The largest administrative division of most states in the United States. **2.** A major territorial division in Great Britain and Ireland. **3.** The people living in a county: *The county will vote on the school proposal.* [From Middle English *counte,* territorial division, from Old French *conte,* the territory of a count, from Late Latin *comitātus,* the office of count.]

county seat *n.* A town or city that is the center of government in its county.

coup (ko͞o) *n., pl.* **coups** (ko͞oz) **1.** A brilliantly executed move or action that achieves the desired results: *Quickly restoring peace between the enemy nations was a real coup for the ambassador.* **2.** A coup d'état. **3.** Among certain Native American peoples, a feat of bravery performed in battle, especially the touching of an enemy's body without causing injury. [From French *coup,* from Late Latin *colpus.*]

❑ *These sound alike:* **coup, coo** (murmuring sound).

coup d'é·tat (ko͞o′ dā-**tä′**) *n., pl.* **coups d'état** (ko͞o′ dā-**tä′**) or **coup d'é·tats** (ko͞o′ dā-**täz′**) The sudden overthrow of a government, bringing a new group into power: *The dictatorship started as a coup d'état.* [From French *coup d'état,* stroke of state.]

coupe (ko͞op) *n.* **1.** A closed two-door automobile. **2.** A closed four-wheel carriage with two seats inside and one outside.

❑ *These sound alike:* **coupe, coop** (cage).

cou·ple (**kŭp′**əl) *n.* **1.** Two things of the same kind; a pair: *a couple of shoes.* **2a.** Two people united, as by marriage: *a young couple just starting a family.* **b.** Two people together: *a dance couple.* **3.** *Informal* A few; several: *vacation for a couple of days; have only a couple of dollars.* ❖ *v.* **cou·pled, cou·pling, cou·ples** —*tr.* To link together; attach; join: *couple the cars of a train.* —*intr.* To form pairs; join: *The dancers coupled up as the music began.* [From Middle English, from Latin *cōpula,* bond, pair.]

cou·pler (**kŭp′**lər) *n.* A person or thing that couples, especially a device that holds two railroad cars together.

cou·plet (**kŭp′**lĭt) *n.* A unit of verse consisting of two successive lines that usually rhyme and have the same meter.

cou·pling (**kŭp′**lĭng) *n.* A device that links or connects.

cou·pon (**ko͞o′**pŏn′ *or* **kyo͞o′**pŏn′) *n.* **1a.** A detachable part of a ticket, card, or advertisement that entitles the person holding it to certain benefits, such as a cash refund or a gift. **b.** A printed form to be used to order something or to obtain a discount. **2.** One of a number of small certificates attached to a bond that represent sums of interest that can be collected at specified dates. [From Old French *colpon,* piece cut off.]

cour·age (**kûr′**ĭj) *n.* The quality of mind or spirit that enables one to face danger or hardship with confidence, resolution, and firm control of oneself; bravery: *It takes courage to defend people who hold unpopular beliefs.* [From Middle English *corage,* from Old French, from Latin *cor,* heart.]

cou·ra·geous (kə-**rā′**jəs) *adj.* Having or characterized by courage. See Synonyms at **brave.** —**cou·ra′geous·ly** *adv.* —**cou·ra′geous·ness** *n.*

ă	pat	ôr	core
ā	pay	oi	boy
âr	care	ou	out
ä	father	o͝o	took
ĕ	pet	o͝or	lure
ē	be	o͞o	boot
ĭ	pit	ŭ	cut
ī	bite	ûr	urge
îr	pier	th	thin
ŏ	pot	*th*	this
ō	toe	zh	vision
ô	paw	ə	about

cou·ri·er (ko͝or′ē-ər *or* **kûr′**ē-ər) *n.* A messenger, especially one on official diplomatic business: *Government requests for a truce were sent by courier.*

course (kôrs) *n.* **1a.** Development in a particular way: *the course of events.* **b.** Onward movement in time; duration: *in the course of a week.* **2.** The route or direction taken by something or someone: *the course of a stream; strike a course due south.* **3.** An area of land or water on which a race is held or a sport is played: *the course of a marathon; a golf course.* **4.** A way of behaving or acting: *Your best course is to do what was asked.* **5.** A typical manner of proceeding; regular development: *The law took its steady course.* **6.** An orderly sequence: *a course of medical treatments.* **7a.** A complete body of studies in a subject in a school, college, or university: *a four-year course in engineering.* **b.** A unit of such studies: *an algebra course.* **8.** A part of a meal served as a unit at one time: *Soup was our first course.* ❖ *intr.v.* **coursed, cours·ing, cours·es** To flow or move swiftly: *Blood courses through the veins.* ◆ **in due course** At the proper or right time. **of course 1.** As is to be expected under the circumstances; naturally or obviously: *Of course the milk will spoil if you leave it out.* **2.** Without any doubt; certainly: *Of course we'll come to your party.* [From Middle English *cours*, from Latin *cursus*, from past participle of *currere*, to run.]

❑ *These sound alike:* **course, coarse** (rough).

cours·er (kôr′sər) *n.* A swift horse.

court (kôrt) *n.* **1.** An area of open ground partly or completely enclosed by walls or buildings; a courtyard. **2.** A short street, especially an alley enclosed by buildings on three sides. **3a.** A person or body of officials who hear and make decisions on legal cases. **b.** The room or building in which such cases are heard; a courthouse or courtroom. **c.** The regular session of a judicial assembly: *Court is not held on a holiday.* **4a.** A sovereign's governing body of ministers and state advisers: *The British monarchy is often called the Court of St. James.* **b.** An official meeting of this body, presided over by the sovereign: *hold court to try a traitor.* **5a.** The people who attend a monarch, including family, servants, advisers, and friends: *In medieval days the court moved several times a year.* **b.** A royal mansion or palace. **6.** An open level area marked with lines for games such as tennis, handball, or basketball. ❖ *v.* **court·ed, court·ing, courts** —*tr.* **1.** To seek the affection of, especially with hopes of marrying: *He courted her for a year before proposing.* **2.** To seek the support or favor of; try to please: *Columbus courted the queen and king of Spain to help pay for his expeditions.* **3.** To try to gain; seek, often foolishly or unwittingly: *court danger.* **4.** To behave in such a way as to attract (a mate): *Male birds often court females by singing.* —*intr.* To pay loving attention to one other: *They courted in secret for a year.* [From Middle English, from Latin *cohors*, courtyard, retinue.]

cour·te·ous (kûr′tē-əs) *adj.* Considerate toward others; gracious; polite: *a courteous manner.* See Synonyms at **polite.** —**cour′te·ous·ly** *adv.*

cour·te·san (kôr′tĭ-zən) *n.* A woman who is a prostitute to men of high social standing, especially in a royal court.

cour·te·sy (kûr′tĭ-sē) *n., pl.* **cour·te·sies 1.** Polite behavior: *We try to treat all of our customers with courtesy.* **2.** An act or gesture showing politeness: *Our host's many courtesies made the stay very enjoyable.*

court·house (kôrt′hous′) *n.* **1.** A building in which courts of law are held. **2.** A building that houses a county government.

court·i·er (kôr′tē-ər) *n.* **1.** An attendant at the court of a king or other ruler. **2.** A person who seeks favor, especially by flattery.

court·ly (kôrt′lē) *adj.* **court·li·er, court·li·est** Suitable for a royal court; dignified and elegant: *courtly manners.* —**court′li·ness** *n.*

court-mar·tial (kôrt′mär′shəl) *n., pl.* **courts-mar·tial 1.** A military court of officers who are appointed to try people for offenses under military law. **2.** A trial by such a court. ❖ *tr.v.* **court-mar·tialed, court-mar·tial·ing, court-mar·tials** or **court-mar·tialled, court-mar·tial·ling, court-mar·tials** To try (someone) by court-martial.

court order *n.* An order issued by a court that requires a person to do or refrain from doing something.

court·room (kôrt′ro͞om′ *or* **kôrt′**ro͝om′) *n.* A room in which the proceedings of a court of law are held.

court·ship (kôrt′shĭp′) *n.* **1.** The act or period of courting. **2.** Specialized behavior in animals that leads to mating.

court·yard (kôrt′yärd′) *n.* An open space that is partly or completely surrounded by walls or buildings.

cous·cous (ko͞os′ko͞os′) *n.* A pasta of North African origin made of granules of crushed wheat.

cous·in (kŭz′ĭn) *n.* **1.** A child of one's aunt or uncle. **2.** A relative descended from a common ancestor, such as a grandparent, by two or more generations. **3.** A member of a country or group having similar origins or interests: *our Canadian cousins.* **4.** Something similar in quality or character: *Cricket is the British cousin of baseball.* [From Middle English *cosin*, a relative, from Latin *cōnsōbrīnus*, cousin.]

❑ *These sound alike:* **cousin, cozen** (deceive).

co·va·lent bond (kō-vā′lənt) *n.* A chemical bond formed when electrons are shared between two atoms.

cove (kōv) *n.* **1.** A small sheltered bay or inlet. **2a.** A recess or a small valley in the side of a mountain. **b.** A cave or cavern.

cov·en (kŭv′ən) *n.* A gathering or meeting of witches.

cov·e·nant (kŭv′ə-nənt) *n.* A formal binding agreement made by two or more people or parties: *Marriage is a legal covenant between two people.*

cov·er (kŭv′ər) *v.* **cov·ered, cov·er·ing, cov·ers** —*tr.* **1.** To place something upon or over, so as to protect or conceal: *cover a table with a tablecloth; covered her smile with her hand.* **2.** To spread over the surface of: *Dust covered the furniture.* **3.** To hide from view or knowledge: *He tried to cover up his mistakes.* **4.** To extend over; include: *a farm covering 100 acres.* **5.** To travel or journey over: *We covered 200 miles a day.* **6.** To have as a subject; deal with: *This course covers basic first aid.* **7.** To be responsible for reporting the details of (an event or situation), as for a newspaper: *The reporter covered the crisis in the Middle East.* **8.** To be enough for: *Will five dollars cover the cost of it?* **9.** To protect, as from loss: *We have fire insurance to cover our belongings.* **10a.** To aim a firearm at: *The police officer covered the suspect.* **b.** To protect by having within range or by firing a gun at an enemy: *The entrance to the harbor is covered by the guns of the fort.* **11.** In sports: **a.** To guard (an opponent playing offense). **b.** To defend (an area or position): *The pitcher covers first base when the first baseman fields a grounder.* —*intr.* **1.** *Informal* To act as a substitute for someone absent: *The stand-in covered for the ailing star of the play.* **2.** To hide something in order to save someone from punishment, embarrassment, or loss: *cover for a friend's mistake.* ❖ *n.* **1.** Something placed on or attached to something else, as for protection: *the covers on a bed; the cover of a book.* **2.** Vegetation covering an area: *The rabbits hid in the dense cover.* **3.** Shelter or protection: *seek cover in a cave during a storm.* **4.** Something that conceals or disguises: *The enemy retreated under the cover of darkness.* **5.** A recording of a song that was previously recorded or made popular by another singer or musician. ◆ **take cover** To seek a hiding place or protection, as from enemy fire. **under cover** Secretly: *Spies work under cover.* [From Middle English *coveren*, from Latin *cooperīre*, to cover completely.]

courtyard
aerial photograph of Christ Church College, Oxford, England

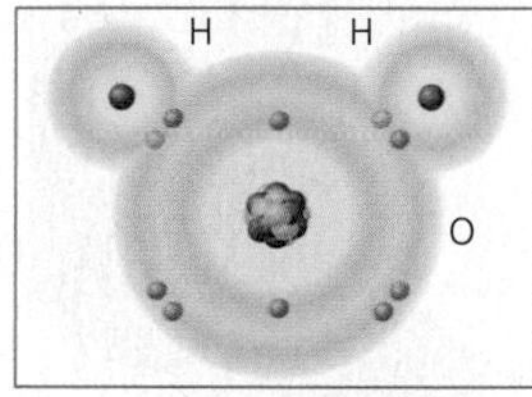

covalent bond
In a water molecule, each hydrogen atom (H) shares an electron (yellow) with the oxygen atom (O).

cowboy boot
pair of cowboy boots

cowcatcher

coxswain
rower *(left)* and coxswain *(right)*

ă	pat	ôr	core
ā	pay	oi	boy
âr	care	ou	out
ä	father	ŏŏ	took
ĕ	pet	ŏŏr	lure
ē	be	ōō	boot
ĭ	pit	ŭ	cut
ī	bite	ûr	urge
îr	pier	th	thin
ŏ	pot	*th*	this
ō	toe	zh	vision
ô	paw	ə	about

cov·er·age (kŭv′ər-ĭj) *n.* **1.** The extent to or way in which something is analyzed and reported: *television news coverage of local events.* **2.** The extent of protection given by an insurance policy: *We carry accident and theft coverage on our car.*

cov·er·alls (kŭv′ər-ôlz′) *pl.n.* A one-piece garment of pants and shirt, worn over other clothes to protect them.

cover crop *n.* A crop planted to prevent soil erosion in winter and to enrich the soil when plowed into the ground in the spring.

cov·ered wagon (kŭv′ərd) *n.* A large wagon covered with an arched canvas top, used by American pioneers for travel across the prairie.

cov·er·ing (kŭv′ər-ĭng) *n.* Something that covers, protects, or hides: *a covering for a bed.*

cov·er·let (kŭv′ər-lĭt) *n.* A bedspread.

cover slip *n.* A small thin piece of glass used to cover a specimen on a microscope slide.

cov·ert (kŭv′ərt *or* kō′vərt) *adj.* Concealed; secret: *a covert mission behind enemy lines.* ❖ *n.* **1.** A covered or sheltered place; a hiding place. **2.** Thick underbrush that provides cover for game animals or birds. **—cov′ert·ly** *adv.* **—cov′ert·ness** *n.*

cov·er-up or **cov·er·up** (kŭv′ər-ŭp′) *n.* An effort or strategy designed to conceal something, such as a crime or scandal, that could be harmful or embarrassing if revealed.

cov·et (kŭv′ĭt) *tr.v.* **cov·et·ed, cov·et·ing, cov·ets 1.** To desire (something belonging to another). **2.** To wish for strongly; crave: *an ambitious person who coveted success.*

cov·et·ous (kŭv′ĭ-təs) *adj.* Very desirous of something belonging to another. **—cov′et·ous·ly** *adv.* **—cov′et·ous·ness** *n.*

cov·ey (kŭv′ē) *n., pl.* **cov·eys** A small group of partridges, grouse, or similar birds.

cow[1] (kou) *n.* **1.** The mature female of domestic cattle or other bovine mammals. **2.** The mature female of certain other large mammals, such as elephants or moose. **3.** A domestic bovine mammal of any sex or age: *a farm with cows, sheep, and chickens.* [From Old English *cū.*]

cow[2] (kou) *tr.v.* **cowed, cow·ing, cows** To frighten or subdue with threats or a show of force: *The approach of the troops cowed the rioting crowd.* [Probably of Scandinavian origin.]

cow·ard (kou′ərd) *n.* A person who lacks courage to face danger or pain, or shows fear in a shameful way. [From Middle English *couard,* from Old French *coue,* tail, from Latin *cauda.*]

cow·ard·ice (kou′ər-dĭs) *n.* Lack of courage or a shameful show of fear when facing danger or pain.

cow·ard·ly (kou′ərd-lē) *adj.* **1.** Lacking courage: *a cowardly liar.* **2.** Characteristic of a coward: *cowardly behavior.* ❖ *adv.* In the manner of a coward: *acted cowardly under pressure.* **—cow′ard·li·ness** *n.*

cow·bell (kou′bĕl′) *n.* A bell hung from a collar around a cow's neck to help in finding it.

cow·bird (kou′bûrd′) *n.* Any of various blackbirds that lay their eggs in the nests of other birds and are often found near herds of grazing cattle.

cow·boy (kou′boi′) *n.* A hired man who tends cattle, especially in the western United States, performing many of his duties on horseback.

cowboy boot *n.* A high leather boot often having tooled designs or ornamental stitching.

cowboy hat *n.* A felt hat having a tall crown and a very wide brim.

cow·catch·er (kou′kăch′ər *or* kou′kĕch′ər) *n.* An iron grille or heavy metal plate on the front of a locomotive to clear away obstacles from the track.

cow·er (kou′ər) *intr.v.* **cow·ered, cow·er·ing, cow·ers** To crouch or draw back, as from fear or pain; cringe: *The dog cowered under the table in the thunderstorm.*

cow·girl (kou′gûrl′) *n.* A hired woman who tends cattle, especially in the western United States, performing many of her duties on horseback.

cow·hand (kou′hănd′) *n.* A cowboy or cowgirl.

cow·herd (kou′hûrd′) *n.* A person who herds or tends cattle.

cow·hide (kou′hīd′) *n.* **1.** The skin or hide of a cow. **2.** Leather made from this hide.

cowl (koul) *n.* **1a.** The hood worn especially by a monk. **b.** A robe or cloak having such a hood. **2.** The part of the front of an automobile body that supports the windshield and dashboard. **3.** The cowling on an aircraft.

cow·lick (kou′lĭk′) *n.* A tuft of hair that stands up from the head and will not lie flat.

cowl·ing (kou′lĭng) *n.* A removable metal cover for an engine, especially an engine of an aircraft.

cow·man (kou′mən) *n.* **1.** A man who owns cattle or a cattle ranch. **2.** A cowboy.

co·work·er (kō′wûr′kər) *n.* A person with whom one works; a fellow worker.

cow·poke (kou′pōk′) *n.* A cowboy or cowgirl.

cow·pox (kou′pŏks′) *n.* A contagious skin disease of cattle that is caused by a virus. When cowpox is transmitted to humans it provides immunity to smallpox.

cow·punch·er (kou′pŭn′chər) *n.* A cowboy or cowgirl.

cow·rie or **cow·ry** (kou′rē) *n., pl.* **cow·ries** Any of various tropical sea mollusks having glossy, often brightly marked shells that were formerly used as money in some parts of Africa and Asia.

cow·slip (kou′slĭp′) *n.* **1.** A primrose usually having fragrant yellow flowers and used in herbal medicine. **2.** A marsh marigold.

cox·comb (kŏks′kōm′) *n.* A vain and often foolish person; a conceited dandy; a fop.

cox·swain (kŏk′sən *or* kŏk′swān′) *n.* A person who steers a boat or racing shell or has charge of its crew.

coy (koi) *adj.* **coy·er, coy·est 1.** Pretending to be shy or modest, especially in a flirtatious way. **2.** Unwilling to make a commitment or give information; evasive: *He was always coy when asked how old he was.* [From Middle English *coi,* from Old French *quei, coi,* quiet, still, from Latin *quiētus.*] **—coy′ly** *adv.* **—coy′ness** *n.*

coy·o·te (kī-ō′tē *or* kī′ōt′) *n.* A wolflike mammal having grayish-brown or yellowish fur, large erect ears, and a drooping bushy tail. [From Nahuatl *cóyotl.*]

coy·pu (koi′pōō) *n., pl.* **coy·pus** The nutria.

coz·en (kŭz′ən) *tr.v.* **coz·ened, coz·en·ing, coz·ens** To deceive by means of a petty trick. **—coz′en·er** *n.*
❑ *These sound alike:* **cozen, cousin** (relative).

co·zy (kō′zē) *adj.* **co·zi·er, co·zi·est 1.** Snug and comfortable: *a cozy spot by the fire.* **2.** Friendly; intimate: *a cozy circle of friends.* **3.** *Informal* Marked by close association for devious purposes: *a cozy deal between management and union leaders.* ❖ *n., pl.* **co·zies** A padded or knitted covering placed over a teapot to keep the tea hot. **—co′zi·ly** *adv.* **—co′zi·ness** *n.*

cp *abbr.* An abbreviation of candlepower.

cp. *abbr.* An abbreviation of compare.

CPA *abbr.* An abbreviation of certified public accountant.

Cpl. or **CPL** *abbr.* An abbreviation of corporal.

CPR *abbr.* An abbreviation of cardiopulmonary resuscitation.

cps *abbr.* An abbreviation of: **1.** characters per second. **2.** cycles per second.

CPU *abbr.* An abbreviation of central processing unit.

Cr The symbol for the element **chromium.**

crab[1] (krăb) *n.* **1.** Any of various primarily marine animals related to the lobsters and shrimps, having a broad flattened hard-shelled body and five pairs of legs, the front pair of which are claws. **2.** Any of various similar animals, such as a horseshoe crab or a hermit crab. **3.** A crab louse. ❖ *intr.v.* **crabbed, crab·bing, crabs** To hunt or catch crabs. [From Middle English *crabbe*, from Old English *crabba*.] **—crab′ber** *n.*

crab[2] (krăb) *n.* **1.** A crabapple tree or its fruit. **2.** *Informal* A bad-tempered complaining person; a grouch. ❖ *intr.v.* **crabbed, crab·bing, crabs** *Informal* To complain irritably. [From Middle English *crabbe*, possibly from *crabbe*, crab (shellfish).]

coyote

crab·ap·ple or **crab apple** (krăb′ăp′əl) *n.* **1.** Any of various small trees having clusters of white, pink, or reddish flowers. **2.** The small sour fruit of such a tree, sometimes used to make jelly and preserves.

crab·bed (krăbd *or* krăb′ĭd) *adj.* **1.** Difficult to read; cramped: *crabbed handwriting.* **2.** Crabby; ill-tempered. **—crab′bed·ly** *adv.* **—crab′bed·ness** *n.*

crab·by (krăb′ē) *adj.* **crab·bi·er, crab·bi·est** *Informal* Irritable and difficult to please; grouchy. **—crab′bi·ly** *adv.* **—crab′bi·ness** *n.*

crab·grass or **crab grass** (krăb′grăs′) *n.* Any of various grasses that spread rapidly and grow as weeds in lawns and agricultural fields.

crab louse *n.* A louse that infests the pubic region and causes severe itching.

crab·meat (krăb′mēt′) *n.* The edible flesh of a crab.

crack (krăk) *v.* **cracked, crack·ing, cracks** ❖ *intr.v.* **1a.** To break without dividing into parts: *The mirror cracked when I bumped it.* **b.** To break or snap apart: *The branch cracked off and fell.* **2.** To make a sharp snapping sound: *The pond ice cracked.* **3.** To have a mental or physical breakdown: *The young doctor cracked under the strain of long hours.* **4.** To change sharply in pitch or timbre; break: *The reporter's voice cracked with emotion.* —*tr.* **1a.** To cause to break without dividing into parts: *The pebble cracked the car's windshield.* See Synonyms at **break. b.** To break with a sharp sound: *We cracked walnuts.* **2a.** To strike with a sudden sharp sound: *I cracked my head on the cabinet door.* **b.** To cause to make a sharp snapping sound: *The coach driver cracked a whip.* **3.** To open to a slight extent: *cracked the window to air out the room.* **4.** To break open or into: *Thieves cracked the safe.* **5.** To solve: *We cracked the spies' code.* **6.** *Informal* To tell or say (a joke or something witty). **7.** To break down (a complex substance, especially petroleum) into simpler chemical compounds: *crack oil into gasoline.* ❖ *n.* **1a.** A partial split or break: *a crack in a plate.* **b.** A narrow space: *The door was opened just a crack.* **2.** A sharp snapping sound: *a loud crack of thunder.* **3.** A sharp blow: *a crack on the head.* **4.** A cracking tone or sound: *a crack in the singer's voice.* **5.** An attempt: *Take a crack at the job.* **6.** A witty or sarcastic remark. **7.** An instant; a moment: *the crack of dawn.* ❖ *adj.* Excelling in skill; first-rate: *a crack shot.* ◆ **crack down** To become more severe or strict: *The principal cracked down on tardiness.* **crack up** *Informal* **1.** To damage or wreck: *cracked up the car.* **2.** To have a mental or physical breakdown: *started to crack up from overwork.* **3.** To experience or cause to experience a great deal of amusement: *I cracked up when I heard the funny joke.* [From Old English *cracian*.]

crack·down (krăk′doun′) *n.* An action taken to stop an illegal or disapproved activity: *a crackdown on gambling.*

cracked (krăkt) *adj.* **1.** Having a crack or cracks: *a cracked dish.* **2.** Broken into pieces: *cracked ice.* **3.** Changing in pitch or timbre; uneven: *a cracked voice.* **4.** *Informal* Crazy or deranged.

crack·er (krăk′ər) *n.* **1.** A thin crisp wafer or biscuit: *cheese and crackers.* **2.** A firecracker. **3.** A person who uses a computer without permission, especially in order to tamper with data or programs.

crack·er·jack (krăk′ər-jăk′) *Slang n.* A person or thing of excellent quality or ability. ❖ *adj.* Of the highest quality or ability: *a crackerjack pilot.*

crack·ing (krăk′ĭng) *n.* The process of breaking down a complex substance, especially petroleum, into simpler compounds by means of heat and often various catalysts.

crack·le (krăk′əl) *intr.v.* **crack·led, crack·ling, crack·les** To make slight sharp snapping or rustling sounds: *The fire crackled in the fireplace. The cellophane crackled as I crushed it.* ❖ *n.* **1.** The act or sound of crackling: *the crackle of dry leaves underfoot.* **2.** A network of fine cracks on the surface of glazed pottery, china, or glassware.

crack·ling (krăk′lĭng) *n.* **1.** Sharp snapping sounds like those produced by a fire or by the crushing of paper. **2. cracklings** Crisp bits remaining after fat from meat has been melted down, as in making lard.

crack·ly (krăk′lē) *adj.* Making or likely to make a crackling sound: *a crackly fire.*

crack·pot (krăk′pŏt′) *n.* A person with very strange ideas. ❖ *adj.* Foolish; harebrained: *a crackpot theory.*

–cracy *suff.* A suffix that means government or rule: *meritocracy.*

crab[1]

cra·dle (krād′l) *n.* **1.** A small bed for a baby, usually mounted on rockers. **2.** A place of origin; a birthplace: *Boston was the cradle of the American Revolution.* **3.** Infancy: *The great pianist showed an interest in music almost from the cradle.* **4.** A framework of wood or metal used to support something, such as a ship, being built or repaired. **5.** The part of a telephone on which the handset rests when not in use. **6.** A box on rockers, used for washing dirt that might contain gold. ❖ *tr.v.* **cra·dled, cra·dling, cra·dles 1.** To place or hold in or as if in a cradle: *cradle a baby in one's arms.* **2.** To hold or support in a construction cradle: *cradle a ship in drydock.* **3.** To wash (dirt believed to contain gold) in a cradle. [From Old English *cradol*.]

cra·dle·board (krād′l-bôrd′) *n.* A board or frame on which an infant can be secured, carried on the back by certain Native American peoples as a portable cradle.

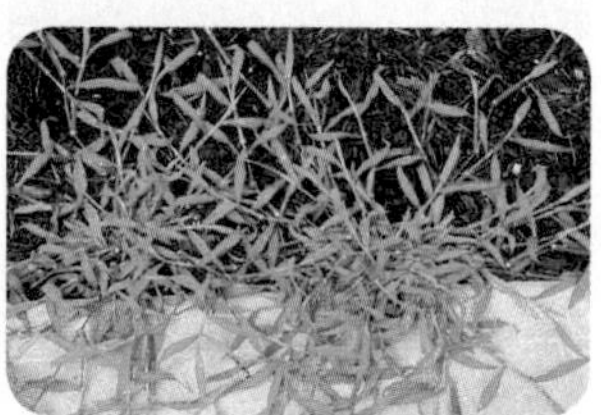

crabgrass

craft (krăft) *n.* **1.** Special skill or ability: *a table made with craft; the craft of fine needlework.* **2.** Skill in deception or evasion; cunning: *With great craft the spy escaped capture.* **3a.** An occupation or trade requiring special skill: *learning his craft as a printer.* **b.** The members of an occupation or trade. **4.** *pl.* **craft** A boat, ship, aircraft, or spacecraft. **5. crafts** Items made by hand; handicrafts. ❖ *tr.v.* **craft·ed, craft·ing, crafts 1.** To make by hand: *craft fine watches.* **2.** To make or devise with great care and skill: *craft an agreement between the warring nations.* [From Old English *cræft*.]

crafts·man (krăfts′mən) *n.* A man who practices a craft with great skill. **—crafts′man·ship′** *n.*

crafts·wom·an (krăfts′wo͝om′ən) *n.* A woman who practices a craft with great skill.

craft·y (krăf′tē) *adj.* **craft·i·er, craft·i·est** Skilled in underhanded dealing and deceit; cunning. **—craft′i·ly** *adv.* **—craft′i·ness** *n.*

crag (krăg) *n.* A steep projection of rock forming part of a cliff or mountain. [From Middle English, from Welsh *craig* or Scottish Gaelic *creagh*.]

crag
Crystal Crag, near Mammoth Lakes, California

crag·gy (krăg′ē) *adj.* **crag·gi·er, crag·gi·est 1.** Having crags; steep and rugged: *hiked up the craggy mountain.* **2.** Rugged and uneven: *an old sailor's craggy face.* **—crag′gi·ness** *n.*

cram (krăm) *v.* **crammed, cram·ming, crams** —*tr.* **1.** To force, press, or squeeze (people or things) into a small space: *I crammed my clothes into the suitcase.* **2.** To fill tightly; crowd: *Students crammed the halls between classes.* —*intr.* **1.** To study hastily for an examination. **2.** To move into and fully occupy a space: *Commuters crammed into the subway car.* [From Old English *crammian*.]

crampon

cramp[1] (krămp) *n.* **1.** A sudden painful contraction of a muscle, often resulting from strain or chill: *A leg cramp forced the sprinter to drop out of the race.* **2.** A temporary partial paralysis of muscles that are used too much: *My fingers had writer's cramp after the test.* **3. cramps** Sharp persistent pains in the abdomen: *An upset stomach and cramps made me feel sick.* ❖ *intr. & tr.v.* **cramped, cramp·ing, cramps** To have or cause to have a cramp or cramps: *The runner's leg cramped in the cold. Swimming so many laps eventually cramped her legs.* [From Middle English *crampe,* from Old French, of Germanic origin.]

cramp[2] (krămp) *n.* **1.** An iron bar bent at both ends, used to hold together blocks of stone or timbers. **2.** A force or influence that restrains: *The rain put a cramp in our picnic plans.* ❖ *tr.v.* **cramped, cramp·ing, cramps 1.** To hold together with a cramp. **2.** To confine or restrain: *The riders were cramped together on the crowded bus.* **3.** To jam (the wheels of a car) hard to the right or left: *cramp the wheels into the curb when parking on a hill.* [From Middle English *crampe,* probably from Middle Dutch, hook, cramp.]

cramped (krămpt) *adj.* **1.** Confined and limited in space: *a cramped little apartment.* **2.** Small and difficult to read: *cramped handwriting.*

cram·pon (**krăm′**pŏn′ *or* **krăm′**pən) *n.* A spiked iron or steel framework attached to the bottom of a shoe or boot to prevent slipping when climbing on ice and snow.

cran·ber·ry (**krăn′**bĕr′ē) *n.* **1.** The tart, shiny, red berry of an evergreen shrub that grows in damp places, used in making jellies, beverages, and baked goods. **2.** The plant that bears such berries. [Partial translation of Low German *Kraanbere* : *Kraan,* crane + *bere,* berry.]

crane
top: gray crowned crane
bottom: mechanical crane

crane (krān) *n.* **1.** Any of various large wading birds having a long neck, long legs, and a long bill. **2.** A machine for lifting heavy objects by means of cables attached to a movable boom. **3.** Any of various devices in which a swinging arm or rod is used to support a load: *Colonial fireplaces had a crane to swing heavy pots over the fire.* ❖ *tr.v.* **craned, cran·ing, cranes** To strain and stretch (the neck) in order to get a better view of something.

Crane (krān), **Stephen** 1871–1900. American writer whose works include *The Red Badge of Courage* (1895).

cra·ni·al (**krā′**nē-əl) *adj.* Relating to the skull: *cranial nerves.*

cranial nerve *n.* Any of several paired nerves, 12 of which occur in mammals, that arise from the brain stem and exit through openings in the skull. These nerves are involved with various functions, including sight, hearing, smell and balance.

cra·ni·um (**krā′**nē-əm) *n., pl.* **cra·ni·ums** or **cra·ni·a** (**krā′**nē-ə) **1.** The skull. **2.** The part of the skull that encloses the brain. [From Middle English *craneum,* from Greek *krānion.*]

crater
Meteor Crater, near Winslow, Arizona

crank (krăngk) *n.* **1.** A rod and handle that can be attached to a shaft and turned to start a machine or run some device. **2.** *Informal* **a.** An irritable person; a grouch. **b.** An eccentric person; a person with odd ideas. ❖ *tr.v.* **cranked, crank·ing, cranks 1.** To start or operate (an engine or device) by means of a crank: *Electric starters replaced the need to crank early car motors.* **2.** To move or operate (a window, for example) by or as if by turning a handle. ❖ *adj.* Produced by an irritable or eccentric person: *a crank letter.* ◆ **crank out** To produce, especially mechanically and rapidly: *The printing press is cranking out copies of the pamphlet.*

crank·case (**krăngk′**kās′) *n.* The bottom part of a gasoline engine that covers the crankshaft and holds the oil to lubricate it.

crank·shaft (**krăngk′**shăft′) *n.* A shaft that turns or is turned by a crank. In a gasoline engine it is connected to and rotated by the pistons.

crank·y (**krăng′**kē) *adj.* **crank·i·er, crank·i·est** Easily annoyed; irritable; peevish: *a cranky two-year-old.* —**crank′i·ly** *adv.* —**crank′i·ness** *n.*

cran·ny (**krăn′**ē) *n., pl.* **cran·nies** A small opening, as in a wall or rock face; a crevice.

crape (krāp) *n.* **1.** A light cloth with a crinkled surface; crepe. **2.** An armband of black crepe, worn as a sign of mourning.

crap·pie (**krŏp′**ē) *n., pl.* **crap·pies** Either of two edible North American freshwater fishes related to the sunfishes.

craps (krăps) *pl.n.* *(used with a singular or plural verb)* A gambling game played with a pair of dice.

crash (krăsh) *v.* **crashed, crash·ing, crash·es** —*intr.* **1.** To break violently and noisily: *The dishes crashed to pieces on the floor.* **2.** To be damaged or destroyed by a collision or violent impact: *The car crashed into the tree.* **3.** To move noisily or violently: *The elephants crashed through the trees.* **4.** To undergo a sudden severe decline or downturn: *The stock market crashed in 1929.* **5.** To fail suddenly: *The computer crashed in the middle of an operation.* **6.** To make a sudden loud noise: *The cymbals crashed at the end of the symphony.* —*tr.* **1.** To cause to fall, strike, or collide suddenly, violently, and noisily: *The boy crashed his bike into the garage door.* **2.** *Informal* To join or enter without being invited: *crash a party.* ❖ *n.* **1.** A loud noise, as of a sudden impact or collapse: *a crash of thunder.* **2.** A violent collision: *Their car was destroyed in a crash.* **3.** A sudden severe decline in business: *The Great Depression started with the crash of 1929.* **4.** The sudden failure of a computer or computer program. ❖ *adj.* *Informal* Marked by an intense effort to produce or accomplish something: *a crash diet to lose weight.* [From Middle English *crashen.*]

crash dive *n.* A rapid dive by a submarine, especially in an emergency.

crash helmet *n.* A padded helmet, as one worn by a pilot or racecar driver, to protect the head.

crash-land (**krăsh′lănd′**) *tr. & intr.v.* **crash-land·ed, crash-land·ing, crash-lands** To land (an aircraft) under emergency conditions, often resulting in damage to it.

crass (krăs) *adj.* **crass·er, crass·est** Crude or unfeeling; coarse: *a crass remark.* —**crass′ly** *adv.* —**crass′ness** *n.*

–crat *suff.* A suffix that means one who takes part in or supports a certain form of government: *bureaucrat.*

crate (krāt) *n.* **1.** A container, such as a case made of wooden slats, used for storing or shipping. **2.** A container, such as a metal or plastic cage, used to house or transport an animal. ❖ *tr.v.* **crat·ed, crat·ing, crates** To pack into a crate: *crate a painting to be sent to a museum; crate oranges for shipping.*

cra·ter (**krā′**tər) *n.* **1.** A bowl-shaped depression at the top of a volcano or at the mouth of a geyser. **2.** A shallow, bowl-shaped hole in a surface formed by an explosion or by the impact of a body, such as a meteorite. [From Greek *krātēr,* large mixing bowl.]

cra·vat (krə-**văt′**) *n.* A scarf or band of fabric worn around the neck as a tie.

crave (krāv) *tr.v.* **craved, crav·ing, craves 1.** To have a very strong desire for; long for: *The thirsty runners craved water.* See Synonyms at **desire. 2.** To beg earnestly for; implore: *crave a favor of someone.*

cra·ven (**krā′**vən) *adj.* Very cowardly: *the traitor's craven behavior.* ❖ *n.* A coward. —**cra′ven·ly** *adv.* —**cra′ven·ness** *n.*

crav·ing (**krā′**vĭng) *n.* A very strong desire; a yearning.

craw (krô) *n.* The crop of a bird. ◆ **stick in (one's) craw** To be a continuing cause of discontent or resentment for someone: *The harsh insult stuck in his craw for years afterward.*

craw·fish (**krô′**fĭsh′) *n.* Variant of **crayfish.**

ă	pat	ôr	core
ā	pay	oi	boy
âr	care	ou	out
ä	father	ŏŏ	took
ĕ	pet	ŏŏr	lure
ē	be	ōō	boot
ĭ	pit	ŭ	cut
ī	bite	ûr	urge
îr	pier	th	thin
ŏ	pot	*th*	this
ō	toe	zh	vision
ô	paw	ə	about

crawl (krôl) *intr.v.* **crawled, crawl·ing, crawls 1.** To move slowly on the hands and knees or by dragging the body along the ground: *The baby crawled across the room.* **2.** To move or advance slowly or haltingly: *The bus crawled along in the heavy traffic.* **3a.** To be covered with or as if with crawling things: *The scene was crawling with police.* **b.** To feel as if covered with crawling things: *The story made my skin crawl.* ❖ *n.* **1.** A very slow pace: *Traffic moved at a crawl.* **2.** A rapid swimming stroke performed face down with alternating overarm strokes and a flutter kick. **—crawl′er** *n.*

crawl·space (**krôl′**spās) *n.* A low or narrow space, such as one beneath a floor, that gives workers access to plumbing or wiring equipment.

cray·fish (**krā′**fĭsh′) also **craw·fish** (**krô′**fĭsh′) *n.* Any of various freshwater animals that resemble a small lobster and are often used as food.

cray·on (**krā′**ŏn′ *or* **krā′**ən) *n.* **1.** A stick of colored wax used for drawing. **2.** A drawing made with crayons. ❖ *tr.v.* **cray·oned, cray·on·ing, cray·ons** To draw, color, or decorate with crayons. [From French, from Latin *crēta*, chalk.]

craze (krāz) *tr.v.* **crazed, craz·ing, craz·es** To cause to be mentally or emotionally disturbed or distressed: *The lost explorer was crazed by a lack of contact with other people.* ❖ *n.* Something very popular for a brief time; a fad.

cra·zy (**krā′**zē) *adj.* **cra·zi·er, cra·zi·est 1.** Having a serious mental disorder, especially one that distorts the perception of reality. **2.** Mentally or emotionally agitated or distressed: *The noise of the jackhammer is driving us crazy.* **3.** *Informal* Foolish or impractical; senseless: *a crazy idea for making money fast.* **4.** *Informal* Full of enthusiasm or excitement: *The whole family is crazy about their new car.* ◆ **like crazy** *Informal* To an exceeding degree: *They were running around like crazy, preparing for the holidays.* **—cra′zi·ly** *adv.* **—cra′zi·ness** *n.*

Cra·zy Horse (**krā′**zē **hôrs′**) 1849?–1877. Lakota leader who joined Sitting Bull in the defeat of General George A. Custer at the Battle of Little Bighorn (1876).

crazy quilt *n.* A patchwork quilt made of pieces of cloth of various shapes, colors, and sizes, sewn together in an irregular pattern.

creak (krēk) *intr.v.* **creaked, creak·ing, creaks** To make or move with a grating or squeaking sound: *The rusty gate creaked as it swung open.* ❖ *n.* A grating or squeaking sound: *a stair that makes a creak when stepped on.* ❑ *These sound alike:* **creak, creek** (stream).

creak·y (**krē′**kē) *adj.* **creak·i·er, creak·i·est 1.** Likely to creak or giving off creaks: *a door on creaky hinges.* **2.** Shaky or weak, as with old age: *creaky knee joints.* **—creak′i·ly** *adv.* **—creak′i·ness** *n.*

cream (krēm) *n.* **1.** The yellowish fatty part of milk that is not homogenized, used in cooking and making butter. **2.** Any of various substances containing or resembling cream: *a pudding of lemon cream; hand cream.* **3.** A yellowish white. **4.** The best part: *These juicy tomatoes are the cream of the crop.* ❖ *v.* **creamed, cream·ing, creams** *—intr.* To form cream or a layer of foam or froth on the top. *—tr.* **1.** To prepare (foods) in a cream sauce: *cream spinach.* **2.** To remove the cream from; skim: *creamed the milk before drinking it.* **3.** To take or remove (the best part): *creamed the best jobs for her cronies.* **4.** *Slang* To defeat overwhelmingly: *We creamed them at the last basketball game.* [From Middle English *creme*, from Late Latin *crāmum* (of Celtic origin) and from Greek *khrīsma*, ointment.]

cream cheese *n.* A soft white cheese made of cream and milk.

cream·er (**krē′**mər) *n.* **1.** A small pitcher for cream. **2.** A powdered or liquid substitute for cream, used in coffee or tea.

cream·er·y (**krē′**mə-rē) *n., pl.* **cream·er·ies** A place where dairy products are prepared or sold.

cream of tartar *n.* Potassium bitartrate.

cream·y (**krē′**mē) *adj.* **cream·i·er, cream·i·est 1.** Rich in cream: *a creamy filling.* **2.** Resembling cream, as in richness, texture, or color: *a creamy lotion; a creamy yellow.* **—cream′i·ly** *adv.* **—cream′i·ness** *n.*

crease (krēs) *n.* **1.** A line or mark made by pressing or folding: *a crease in his pants.* **2.** A wrinkle: *creases on the old man's face.* ❖ *tr. & intr.v.* **creased, creas·ing, creas·es** To make or become creased, folded, or wrinkled: *crease a piece of paper; a face creased with age.* [Alteration of *creaste*, perhaps from Middle English *creste*, ridge.]

cre·ate (krē-**āt′**) *tr.v.* **cre·at·ed, cre·at·ing, cre·ates 1.** To bring into being; cause to exist: *She created the school to teach practical skills to girls.* See Synonyms at **establish. 2.** To give rise to; produce: *The rumor created a panic among stockholders.* **3.** To produce through artistic effort: *create a poem.* [From Middle English *createn*, from Latin *creāre*.]

cre·a·tion (krē-**ā′**shən) *n.* **1.** The act or process of creating: *the creation of a canyon by erosion.* **2.** Something produced by invention and imagination: *The x-ray machine and the computer are creations of modern science.* **3. Creation** In various religions, the divine act by which the world was brought into existence. **4.** The world and all things in it.

cre·a·tion·ism (krē-**ā′**shə-nĭz′əm) *n.* Belief in the literal interpretation of the account of the creation of the universe contained in the Bible.

cre·a·tive (krē-**ā′**tĭv) *adj.* **1.** Having the ability or power to create things; original: *a creative writer.* **2.** Showing imagination or originality: *a creative design.* **—cre·a′tive·ly** *adv.* **—cre·a′tive·ness** *n.*

cre·a·tiv·i·ty (krē′ā-**tĭv′**ĭ-tē) *n.* The quality of being creative; originality and inventiveness.

cre·a·tor (krē-**ā′**tər) *n.* **1.** A person who creates: *creators of sculpture.* **2. Creator** God.

crea·ture (**krē′**chər) *n.* **1.** A living being, especially a nonhuman animal: *birds, rabbits, and other creatures of the woods.* **2.** A human; a person: *What a handsome creature he is in that tuxedo!* **3.** An imaginary or fantastical being: *a creature from outer space.* —SEE NOTE AT **critter.**

crèche (krĕsh) *n.* A model of the Nativity with statues of the infant Jesus, Mary, Joseph, and others. [From Old French *cresche*, crib, of Germanic origin.]

cre·dence (**krēd′**ns) *n.* Acceptance of something as true; belief: *Don't put any credence in that rumor.*

cre·den·tial (krĭ-**dĕn′**shəl) *n.* **1.** Something that entitles a person to confidence, credit, or authority: *An honest face was the borrower's only credential.* **2. credentials** Letters or other written evidence of a person's qualifications or status: *The new ambassador presented his credentials to the foreign government.*

cred·i·bil·i·ty (krĕd′ə-**bĭl′**ĭ-tē) *n.* The condition, quality, or power of being credible: *The leader lost his credibility by failing to back up his threats with action.*

cred·i·ble (**krĕd′**ə-bəl) *adj.* Worthy of confidence or belief; believable: *a credible news report; a credible witness.* [From Middle English, from Latin *crēdibilis*, from *crēdere*, to believe.] **—cred′i·bly** *adv.*

cred·it (**krĕd′**ĭt) *n.* **1.** Belief or confidence; trust: *We place full credit in our employees.* **2.** Reputation or standing: *It is to their credit that they worked so hard without complaining.* **3.** A source of honor or distinction: *This exceptional athlete is a credit to our team.* **4.** Recognition or approval for an act, ability, or quality: *The two authors shared the credit for the book's success.* **5a.** Certification that a student has fulfilled a requirement by completing a course of study: *She received full credit for her studies at a previous school.* **b.** A unit of study certified as properly

crazy quilt
c. 1875 crazy quilt

WORD HISTORY

creature Difficult as it is to believe, the word **creature** is historically the same word as **critter,** a word that you may have heard used for cows or horses in cowboy movies. We now pronounce the *-ture* suffix with a (ch) sound (-chər), but people used to pronounce it with a (t) sound (-tər). This older pronunciation is still used in some parts of the United States. The most common meaning of *critter* is "a living creature," whether wild or domestic.

creel

crepe

crevasse

ă	pat	ôr	core
ā	pay	oi	boy
âr	care	ou	out
ä	father	o͝o	took
ĕ	pet	o͝or	lure
ē	be	o͞o	boot
ĭ	pit	ŭ	cut
ī	bite	ûr	urge
îr	pier	th	thin
ŏ	pot	*th*	this
ō	toe	zh	vision
ô	paw	ə	about

completed: *Advanced courses are worth four credits.* **6.** often **credits** An acknowledgment of work done, as in the production of a motion picture or play: *There was a long list of credits at the end of the movie.* **7.** Reputation for repaying debts and being financially honest that entitles a person to be trusted in buying and borrowing: *I have good credit at all the local stores.* **8a.** A system of buying goods or services by requiring payment at a later time: *buy a car on credit.* **b.** The terms governing such payments: *a store that offers easy credit.* **9.** The amount of money in the account of a person or group, as at a bank. **10.** In accounting: **a.** The amount paid on a debt. **b.** The right-hand side of an account, on which such payments are entered. ❖ *tr.v.* **cred·it·ed, cred·it·ing, cred·its 1.** To believe in; trust: *They credited my explanation of what happened.* **2a.** To regard (a person) as having done something: *Two Canadian scientists are credited with the discovery of insulin.* **b.** To attribute (something) to a person: *Some credit the song to Haydn.* **3.** To give educational credits to (a student). **4.** In accounting: **a.** To give credit for (a payment) in an account: *The store credited $100 to my account.* **b.** To give credit to (a person's account). [From Latin *crēditum*, loan, from neuter past participle of *crēdere*, to entrust.]

cred·it·a·ble (krĕd′ĭ-tə-bəl) *adj.* Deserving praise or credit: *They made a creditable attempt to solve the problem.* **—cred′it·a·bil′i·ty, cred′it·a·ble·ness** *n.* **—cred′it·a·bly** *adv.*

credit card *n.* A plastic card issued by a bank or business authorizing the holder to buy goods or services on credit.

cred·i·tor (krĕd′ĭ-tər) *n.* A person or business to whom money is owed.

cre·do (krē′dō *or* krā′dō) *n., pl.* **cre·dos** A statement of belief; a creed: *The store owner's credo is "The customer always comes first."*

cre·du·li·ty (krĭ-do͞o′lĭ-tē) *n.* The tendency to believe too readily; gullibility: *Her credulity led her to believe stories that weren't true.*

cred·u·lous (krĕj′ə-ləs) *adj.* Tending to believe too readily; gullible: *A credulous person is easily fooled.* **—cred′u·lous·ly** *adv.* **—cred′u·lous·ness** *n.*

Cree (krē) *n., pl.* **Cree** or **Crees 1.** A member of a Native American people living across a large area of Canada. **2.** The Algonquian language of the Cree.

creed (krēd) *n.* **1.** A formal statement of religious belief. **2.** A system of belief or principles that guides a person's actions: *His creed is to help others as much as possible.*

creek (krēk *or* krĭk) *n.* **1.** A small stream, often a shallow tributary to a river. **2.** *Chiefly British* A small inlet in a shoreline. [From Middle English *crike*, probably from Old Norse *kriki*, bend.]

❑ *These sound alike:* **creek, creak** (squeak).

Creek (krēk) *n., pl.* **Creek** or **Creeks 1.** A member of a Native American people formerly living in eastern Alabama, Georgia, and northern Florida and now located in Oklahoma and southern Alabama. **2.** The Muskogean language of these people. **3.** A member of a Native American confederacy made up of the Creek and various other southeast peoples.

creel (krēl) *n.* A wicker basket used for carrying fish. [From Middle English *crel*, from Latin *crātīcula*, gridiron, diminutive of *crātis*, wickerwork.]

creep (krēp) *intr.v.* **crept** (krĕpt), **creep·ing, creeps 1.** To move slowly or cautiously with the body close to the ground: *The cat crept toward the mouse.* **2.** To move in a timid, cautious, or stealthy way: *The embarrassed host crept out of the room.* **3.** To advance or spread slowly: *Traffic crept along the freeway at rush hour. The ivy crept up the wall of the mansion.* **4.** To have a tingling sensation, as if covered with crawling things: *Thinking of ghosts makes my flesh creep.* ❖ *n.* **1.** The act of creeping: *the silent creep of a tiger.* **2.** *Slang* An unpleasant or annoying person. **3. creeps** *Informal* A sensation of fear and repugnance, as if things were crawling on one's skin: *This old house gives me the creeps.*

creep·er (krē′pər) *n.* **1.** A person or thing that creeps. **2.** A plant having stems that grow along the ground or cling to a surface for support.

creep·y (krē′pē) *adj.* **creep·i·er, creep·i·est** *Informal* Producing a tingling sensation of uneasiness or fear, as if things were creeping on one's skin. **—creep′i·ly** *adv.* **—creep′i·ness** *n.*

cre·mate (krē′māt′ *or* krĭ-māt′) *tr.v.* **cre·mat·ed, cre·mat·ing, cre·mates** To burn (a corpse) to ashes. [From Latin *cremāre*.] **—cre·ma′tion** *n.*

cre·ma·to·ri·um (krē′mə-tôr′ē-əm) *n., pl.* **cre·ma·to·ri·ums** or **cre·ma·to·ri·a** (krē′mə-tôr′ē-ə) A furnace or building with a furnace for burning corpses.

cre·ma·to·ry (krē′mə-tôr′ē *or* krĕm′ə-tôr′ē) *n., pl.* **cre·ma·to·ries** A crematorium.

Cre·ole (krē′ōl′) *n.* **1.** A person of European ancestry born in the Caribbean or Latin America. **2a.** A descendant of the original French settlers of the southern United States, especially Louisiana. **b.** The French dialect spoken by these people. **3. creole** A language formed when two or more groups of people speaking different languages have prolonged contact with one another: *Haitian Creole is a mixture of French and various West African languages.* **4.** A person of mixed African and European ancestry who speaks such a language, especially one based on French or Spanish. ❖ *adj.* **1.** Relating to the Creoles or their languages and cultures. **2. creole** Cooked with a spicy sauce containing tomatoes, green peppers, and onions: *shrimp creole.*

cre·o·sote (krē′ə-sōt′) *n.* A yellow to brown oily liquid obtained from coal tar and used as a wood preservative and disinfectant. ❖ *tr.v.* **cre·o·sot·ed, cre·o·sot·ing, cre·o·sotes** To treat with creosote.

crepe also **crêpe** (krāp) *n.* **1.** A light, soft, thin cloth with a crinkled surface, made of silk, cotton, or another fiber. **2.** A band of black crepe, worn or hung as a sign of mourning. **3.** (*also* krĕp) A very thin pancake, usually served folded with a filling. [From Old French *crespe*, curly, from Latin *crīspus*.]

crepe paper *n.* Paper with crinkles or puckers in it, used especially for decoration.

crept (krĕpt) *v.* Past tense and past participle of **creep.**

cres·cen·do (krə-shĕn′dō) *n., pl.* **cres·cen·dos** or **cres·cen·di** (krə-shĕn′dē) **1.** In music, a gradual increase in loudness. **2.** A musical passage performed with a gradual increase in loudness. **3.** A steady increase in force or intensity: *The new movie received a crescendo of publicity after it was nominated for three awards.* ❖ *adj. & adv.* Gradually increasing in loudness: *a crescendo passage; played the passage crescendo.*

cres·cent (krĕs′ənt) *n.* **1.** The figure of the moon as it appears in its first or last quarter, with concave and convex edges ending in points. **2.** Something shaped like a crescent: *The ancient Middle East is known as the Fertile Crescent.* ❖ *adj.* **1.** Shaped like a crescent. **2.** Increasing; waxing: *the crescent phase of the moon.* [From Middle English *cressaunt*, from Anglo-Norman, from Old French *creistre*, to grow, from Latin *crēscere*.]

cress (krĕs) *n.* Any of several plants, such as watercress, having strong-tasting leaves used in salads.

crest (krĕst) *n.* **1.** A projecting tuft or outgrowth on the head of a bird or other animal. **2a.** The top of something, such as a mountain or wave. **b.** The highest point, as of a process or action: *The crest of a flood; had reached the crest of her career.* **3.** A plume worn as a decoration on top of a helmet. **4.** A design placed above the shield on a coat of arms. ❖ *v.* **crest·ed, crest·ing, crests** *—tr.* **1.** To reach the top of: *The climbers crested the mountain.*

2. To decorate or furnish with a crest. *—intr.* **1.** To form into a crest: *Waves crested over the sea wall.* **2.** To reach a crest: *The river crested after the heavy rain.*

crest·fall·en (**krĕst′**fô′lən) *adj.* Dejected; depressed: *Crestfallen over the loss, the team met to discuss what went wrong.* **—crest′fall′en·ly** *adv.*

Cre·ta·ceous (krĭ-**tā′**shəs) *n.* The third and last period of the Mesozoic Era, from about 146 to 66 million years ago. During the Cretaceous, flowering plants developed. The period ended with the sudden mass extinction of dinosaurs and many other forms of life. See table at **geologic time.** ❖ *adj.* **1.** Relating to the Cretaceous. **2. cretaceous** Relating to, containing, or resembling chalk.

Cre·tan (**krēt′**n) *adj.* Relating to Crete or its people or culture. ❖ *n.* A native or inhabitant of Crete.

Crete (krēt) An island of southeast Greece in the eastern Mediterranean Sea. Its civilization, one of the earliest in the world, reached the height of its wealth and power around 1600 BC.

cre·tonne (krĭ-**tŏn′** *or* **krē′**tŏn′) *n.* A heavy cotton, linen, or rayon cloth with colorful printed patterns, used for curtains and slipcovers.

cre·vasse (krĭ-**văs′**) *n.* **1.** A deep crack, as in a glacier; a chasm. **2.** A crack in a dike or levee.

crev·ice (**krĕv′**ĭs) *n.* A narrow crack or opening; a fissure or cleft: *Snow seeped through the crevice under the door.*

crew (kro͞o) *n. (used with a singular or plural verb)* **1.** A group of people who work together: *A stage crew is needed to put on the new play.* **2.** The people working together to operate a ship, aircraft, spacecraft, or train: *The ship's crew were very helpful during the cruise.* **3a.** A team of rowers. **b.** The sport of rowing. ❖ *tr.v.* **crewed, crew·ing, crews** To provide (a boat, for example) with a crew. [From Middle English *creue,* military reinforcement, from Old French, increase, from *creistre,* to grow, from Latin *crēscere.*]

crew·cut or **crew cut** (**kro͞o′**kŭt′) *n.* A closely cropped haircut.

crew·el (**kro͞o′**əl) *n.* A loosely twisted worsted yarn used for a kind of embroidery.

crew·el·work (**kro͞o′**əl-wûrk′) *n.* Needlework made with crewel.

crew neck *n.* **1.** A round, close-fitting neckline. **2.** A garment, especially a sweater, with such a neckline.

crib (krĭb) *n.* **1.** A small bed with high sides for a baby or young child. **2.** A small building for storing grain. **3.** A rack or trough from which cattle or horses eat. **4.** A framework to support or strengthen a mine or mine shaft. **5.** *Informal* A list of answers or information consulted dishonestly during an examination. **6.** *Slang* One's home. ❖ *v.* **cribbed, crib·bing, cribs** *—intr. Informal* To use a list of answers or information in an examination; cheat: *was caught cribbing on the test.* *—tr.* To copy dishonestly; plagiarize: *cribbed the answers straight from the book.*

crib·bage (**krĭb′**ĭj) *n.* A card game in which the score is kept by inserting small pegs into holes arranged in rows on a small board.

crick (krĭk) *n.* A painful cramp or muscular spasm, especially in the back or the neck. ❖ *tr.v.* **cricked, crick·ing, cricks** To cause a crick in, as by turning or wrenching: *cricked my back getting out of the car.* [From Middle English *crike.*]

Crick (krĭk), **Francis Harry Compton** 1916–2004. British biologist who with James D. Watson identified the structure of DNA.

crick·et¹ (**krĭk′**ĭt) *n.* Any of various small insects that have long antennae and long legs used for leaping. The male produces a chirping sound by rubbing the front wings together. [From Middle English *criket,* from Old French *criquet,* from *criquer,* to click.]

crick·et² (**krĭk′**ĭt) *n.* **1.** A game played with bats, a ball, and wickets by two teams of 11 players each. **2.** *Informal* Good sporting behavior and fair conduct: *Cheating is simply not cricket.* [From Old French *criquet,* stick for a bowling game.] **—crick′et·er** *n.*

cried (krīd) *v.* Past tense and past participle of **cry.**

cri·er (**krī′**ər) *n.* A person who cries, especially: **a.** An official who announces the orders of a court of law. **b.** A town crier. **c.** A hawker.

cries (krīz) *v.* Third person singular present tense of **cry.** ❖ *n.* Plural of **cry.**

crime (krīm) *n.* **1.** A violation of the law in which a person either acts in a way the law forbids or fails to act as the law requires: *Armed robbery is a serious crime.* **2.** Unlawful activity: *There is too much crime in our society.* **3.** A shameful or senseless act: *It's a crime to waste good food.* [From Middle English, from Latin *crīmen.*]

Cri·me·a (krī-**mē′**ə *or* krĭ-**mē′**ə) A peninsula of southern Ukraine on the Black Sea. The peninsula was the scene of the Crimean War (1853–1856).

crim·i·nal (**krĭm′**ə-nəl) *adj.* **1.** Relating to or involving crime: *criminal behavior.* **2.** Relating to criminal law and the punishment of crime: *criminal court.* **3.** Guilty of crime: *a criminal offender.* **4.** *Informal* Shameful; disgraceful: *a criminal waste of energy.* ❖ *n.* A person who has committed or been convicted of a crime: *The judge sentenced the criminal to jail for burglary.* **—crim′i·nal·ly** *adv.*

criminal law *n.* Law involving crime and its punishment.

crim·i·nol·o·gist (krĭm′ə-**nŏl′**ə-jĭst) *n.* A person who specializes in criminology.

crim·i·nol·o·gy (krĭm′ə **nŏl′**ə-jē) *n.* The scientific study of crime and criminals.

crimp (krĭmp) *tr.v.* **crimped, crimp·ing, crimps** To press or bend into small regular folds or ridges: *crimp a pie crust.* ❖ *n.* **1.** Something produced by crimping, as a fold or crease. **2.** Something that hinders or obstructs; a snag: *The bad weather put a crimp in our plans.*

crim·son (**krĭm′**zən) *n.* A vivid purplish red. [From Middle English *cremesin,* from Arabic *qirmizī,* from *qirmiz,* an insect used to make red dye.] **—crim′son** *adj.*

cringe (krĭnj) *intr.v.* **cringed, cring·ing, cring·es 1.** To shrink back, as in fear; cower: *The puppy cringed when I tried to pet it.* **2.** To behave in a slavish manner; fawn: *The new secretary cringed before the boss.* ❖ *n.* An act or an instance of cringing. **—cring′er** *n.*

crin·kle (**krĭng′**kəl) *v.* **crin·kled, crin·kling, crin·kles** *—intr.* **1.** To form wrinkles or creases: *Her face crinkles when she smiles.* **2.** To make a crackling sound; rustle: *The foil crinkled as I wrapped the leftovers.* *—tr.* **1.** To cause to form wrinkles or creases: *I crinkled the wrapping paper when my hand slipped.* **2.** To cause to crackle. ❖ *n.* A wrinkle or crease: *Crinkles form around the eyes from laughter.* **—crin′kly** *adj.*

cri·noid (**krī′**noid′) *n.* Any of various sea animals having a cup-shaped body, feathery arms, and a stalk by which they can attach themselves to a surface. Crinoids belong to the same group as the starfishes and sea urchins.

crin·o·line (**krĭn′**ə-lĭn) *n.* **1.** A cloth used to stiffen collars, linings, hats, and petticoats. **2.** A stiff petticoat of this cloth, worn to make a skirt stand out. **3.** A hoop skirt.

crip·ple (**krĭp′**əl) *n.* **1.** *Offensive* A person who is partially disabled, especially one who is not able to walk easily. **2.** An animal that is unable to use a limb or limbs. ❖ *tr.v.* **crip·pled, crip·pling, crip·ples 1.** To cause to lose the use of a limb or limbs. **2.** To damage or disable: *The storm crippled the ship.* **—crip′pler** *n.*

cri·sis (**krī′**sĭs) *n., pl.* **cri·ses** (**krī′**sēz) **1.** A situation of great difficulty or danger: *The sudden resignation of the president created a political crisis. She faced a crisis when she lost her job.* **2.** A point of change in the course of something; a decisive or crucial time: *The turmoil in that*

crew

cricket¹

crinoid

USAGE

criteria The word **criteria** is a plural form of **criterion.** It is correct to say *The scientists used several criteria for determining water quality.* It is incorrect to say *Only one criteria was used in the study.*

crocus

croissant

ă	pat	ôr	core
ā	pay	oi	boy
âr	care	ou	out
ä	father	ŏŏ	took
ĕ	pet	ŏŏr	lure
ē	be	ōō	boot
ĭ	pit	ŭ	cut
ī	bite	ûr	urge
îr	pier	th	thin
ŏ	pot	*th*	this
ō	toe	zh	vision
ô	paw	ə	about

country has finally reached a crisis. **3.** A sudden change in the course of a serious illness: *Fever often marks the crisis of measles, mumps, and pneumonia.* [From Middle English *crise*, from Greek *krisis*, decisive point, from *krīnein*, to separate, decide.]

crisp (krĭsp) *adj.* **crisp·er, crisp·est 1.** Firm but easily broken or crumbled: *crisp toast; crisp fried chicken.* **2.** Fresh and firm: *crisp lettuce.* **3.** Clean and new; not wrinkled: *a crisp dollar bill.* **4.** Refreshing; bracing: *a walk in the crisp autumn air.* **5.** Sharp, clear, and concise: *a crisp reply.* ❖ *tr. & intr.v.* **crisped, crisp·ing, crisps** To make or become crisp, as by heating or cooking. [From Old English *crisp*, curly, from Latin *crīspus*.] **—crisp′ly** *adv.* **—crisp′ness** *n.*

crisp·y (**krĭs′**pē) *adj.* **crisp·i·er, crisp·i·est** Firm but easily broken or crumbled; crisp. **—crisp′i·ness** *n.*

criss·cross (**krĭs′**krôs′) *v.* **criss·crossed, criss·cross·ing, criss·cross·es** *—tr.* **1.** To mark with a pattern of crossing lines: *Animal trails crisscross the woods.* **2.** To move back and forth over or through: *Ships crisscrossed the sea.* *—intr.* To move back and forth: *Our paths crisscrossed throughout the day.* ❖ *n.* A mark or pattern made of crossing lines. ❖ *adj.* Crossing one another: *crisscross lines.* ❖ *adv.* In crossing directions: *umbrellas leaning crisscross in the stand.* [From Middle English *Crist cros*, Christ's cross.]

cri·te·ri·on (krī-**tîr′**ē-ən) *n., pl.* **cri·te·ri·a** (krī-**tîr′**ē-ə) A rule or standard on which a judgment can be based: *Clarity of expression and organization of thought are two important criteria for judging the quality of an essay.* —SEE NOTE.

crit·ic (**krĭt′**ĭk) *n.* **1.** A person who forms and expresses judgments about the qualities of something, especially in a report on an artistic work or performance: *a movie critic.* **2.** A person who tends to make harsh judgments; a faultfinder. [From Greek *kritikos*, able to discern, from *kritēs*, judge, from *krīnein*, to separate, judge.]

crit·i·cal (**krĭt′**ĭ-kəl) *adj.* **1.** Inclined to judge severely; likely to find fault: *A critical person is seldom pleased with anything.* **2.** Marked by or exercising careful evaluation and judgment: *critical analysis of a poem.* **3.** Extremely important or decisive: *a critical point in the political campaign.* **4a.** Relating to or being the crisis stage of a disease: *High fever is the critical point of pneumonia.* **b.** Extremely serious or dangerous: *a critical injury.* **5.** Being in a state of crisis or emergency: *a critical shortage of food.* **—crit′i·cal·ly** *adv.*

crit·i·cism (**krĭt′**ĭ-sĭz′əm) *n.* **1.** Unfavorable judgment; faultfinding; disapproval: *constant criticism with no encouragement.* **2.** The art or profession of forming and expressing judgments, especially about literary or artistic works. **3.** A comment, article, or review that expresses judgments: *Several reporters wrote criticisms of the new movie.*

crit·i·cize (**krĭt′**ĭ-sīz′) *v.* **crit·i·cized, crit·i·ciz·ing, crit·i·ciz·es** *—tr.* **1.** To judge the merits and faults of; evaluate: *The painter stepped back to criticize her last hour's work.* **2.** To judge severely; find fault with: *Newspapers criticized the library closing.* *—intr.* To express or utter criticism, especially negative criticism: *Those two are always criticizing while others do the work.* **—crit′i·ciz′er** *n.*

cri·tique (krĭ-**tēk′**) *n.* A critical review or commentary, such as an evaluation of an artistic work.

crit·ter (**krĭt′**ər) *n. Informal* A creature, especially an animal. —SEE NOTE.

croak (krōk) *n.* A low hoarse sound, such as that made by a frog or crow. ❖ *intr.v.* **croaked, croak·ing, croaks 1.** To make such a sound: *Bullfrogs croaked in the pond.* **2.** To speak with a low hoarse voice.

Croat (**krō′**ăt′ *or* krōt) *n.* **1.** A native or inhabitant of Croatia. **2.** The Croatian language. **—Croat** *adj.*

Cro·a·tia (krō-**ā′**shə) A country of southern Europe along the northeast coast of the Adriatic Sea. It was part of Yugoslavia from 1946 until 1991, when it declared its independence. Capital, Zagreb.

Cro·a·tian (krō-**ā′**shən) *adj.* Relating to Croatia or its people, language, or culture. ❖ *n.* **1.** A Croat. **2.** The Slavic language of Croatia, written in the Latin alphabet and closely related to Serbian.

cro·chet (krō-**shā′**) *v.* **cro·cheted** (krō-**shād′**), **cro·chet·ing** (krō-**shā′**ĭng), **cro·chets** (krō-**shāz′**) *—tr.* To make by looping thread or yarn into connected links with a hooked needle: *crochet a sweater.* *—intr.* To crochet a piece of needlework. ❖ *n.* Needlework made by crocheting. [From Old French, hook, diminutive of *croche*, of Germanic origin.]

crock (krŏk) *n.* A pot or jar of earthenware.

crock·er·y (**krŏk′**ə-rē) *n.* Earthenware.

Crock·ett (**krŏk′**ĭt), **David** Known as "Davy." 1786–1836. American pioneer and politician who died at the siege of the Alamo.

croc·o·dile (**krŏk′**ə-dīl′) *n.* **1.** Any of various large reptiles having rough thick skin, sharp teeth, and powerful jaws, living in lakes, rivers, and coastal areas of tropical regions. A crocodile's snout is longer and thinner than an alligator's. **2.** Leather made from crocodile skin. [From Middle English *cocodril*, from Latin *cocodrillus*, from Greek *krokodīlos*.]

crocodile tears *pl.n.* A display of grief that is not sincere. [From the belief that crocodiles weep either to lure a victim or when eating one.]

cro·cus (**krō′**kəs) *n., pl.* **cro·cus·es** Any of various small garden plants having purple, yellow, or white flowers that bloom in early spring.

Croe·sus (**krē′**səs) Died c. 546 BC. The last king of Lydia in Asia Minor (560–546).

croft (krôft) *n. Chiefly British* **1.** A small enclosed field or pasture near a house. **2.** A small tenant farm.

croft·er (**krôf′**tər) *n. Chiefly British* A person who rents and cultivates a croft.

crois·sant (krə-**sänt′**) *n.* A rich crescent-shaped roll.

Cro-Mag·non (krō-**măg′**nən *or* krō-**măn′**yən) *n.* An early form of modern human that lived throughout Europe from about 35,000 to 10,000 years ago. The Cro-Magnons made tools of stone and bone and decorated cave walls with elaborate paintings. **—Cro-Mag′non** *adj.*

Crom·well (**krŏm′**wĕl′), **Oliver** 1599–1658. English military, political, and religious figure who led the Parliamentarian victory in the English Civil War (1642–1649).

crone (krōn) *n.* **1.** An old woman considered to be ugly; a hag. **2.** A woman respected for her wisdom and experience.

Cro·nus (**krō′**nəs) *n.* In Greek mythology, a Titan who ruled the universe until he was overthrown by his son Zeus.

cro·ny (**krō′**nē) *n., pl.* **cro·nies** A close friend or companion.

crook (krŏŏk) *n.* **1.** An implement or tool, such as a shepherd's staff, with a hook or hooked part. **2.** Something bent or curved: *a bag of groceries held in the crook of one's arm.* **3.** A curve or bend; a turn: *a crook in the road.* **4.** *Informal* A person who makes a living dishonestly; a thief or swindler. ❖ *tr. & intr.v.* **crooked, crook·ing, crooks** To curve or become curved; bend: *crook one's arm around a package; a road that crooks sharply to the right.* [From Middle English *crok*, from Old Norse *krōkr*.]

crook·ed (**krŏŏk′**ĭd) *adj.* **1.** Not straight; bent or curved: *a crooked street.* **2.** *Informal* Dishonest; underhanded: *a crooked merchant.* **—crook′ed·ly** *adv.* **—crook′ed·ness** *n.*

croon (krōōn) *v.* **crooned, croon·ing, croons** *—tr.* To sing or hum softly: *croon a lullaby to the baby.* —*intr.* **1.** To sing or hum a melody softly. **2.** To sing popular songs in a sentimental manner. ❖ *n.* A soft singing, humming, or murmuring. [From Middle English *cronen*, from Middle Dutch *krōnen*, to lament.] —**croon′er** *n.*

crop (krŏp) *n.* **1a.** A cultivated plant or plant product such as a grain, fruit, or vegetable: *Wheat and other crops are grown here.* **b.** The amount of such a product grown or gathered in a single season or place: *Our orchard produced a huge crop of cherries last year.* **2.** A group or quantity appearing at one time: *training the crop of new volunteers.* **3.** A short whip with a loop used in horseback riding. **4.** An enlargement near the beginning of a bird's or insect's digestive tract where food is stored before digestion. **5.** A short haircut. ❖ *tr.v.* **cropped, crop·ping, crops 1.** To cut or bite off the tops or ends of: *Sheep cropped the grass very short.* **2.** To cut (hair, for example) short. **3.** To trim (a photograph, for example). ◆ **crop up** To appear unexpectedly: *We thought we had fixed everything, but then more problems cropped up.* [From Old English *cropp*, ear of grain.]

crop-dust·ing (krŏp′dŭs′tĭng) *n.* The practice of spraying crops with powdered insecticide and fungicide from an airplane.

crop·land (krŏp′lănd′) *n.* Land for or suitable for growing crops.

crop·per¹ (krŏp′ər) *n.* A sharecropper.

crop·per² (krŏp′ər) *n.* **1.** A heavy fall: *As the horse reared the rider took a cropper.* **2.** A disastrous failure. ◆ **come a cropper** To fail suddenly or disastrously; come to grief. [Perhaps from the phrase *neck and crop*, completely.]

crop rotation *n.* The practice of planting a sequence of different crops on the same land in order to prevent nutrients in the soil from being depleted and to control insects and disease.

cro·quet (krō-kā′) *n.* An outdoor game in which each player uses a mallet to hit a wooden ball through a course of wickets. [From Old North French, shepherd's crook.]

cro·quette (krō-kĕt′) *n.* A small cake of minced food, often coated with bread crumbs and fried in deep fat: *chicken croquettes.*

cro·sier (krō′zhər) *n.* A staff with a crook or cross at the end, carried as a symbol of office by or before an abbot, bishop, or archbishop.

cross (krôs) *n.* **1a.** An upright post with a piece across it near the top, on which condemned people were executed in ancient times. **b.** often **Cross** The cross upon which Jesus was crucified. **c.** A representation of this cross; a crucifix. **d.** Any of various medals or emblems in the shape of a cross. **2.** A mark or pattern formed by the intersection of two lines, especially such a mark (X) used as a signature by a person who cannot read or write. **3.** A trial or affliction: *Having a talented older sibling can be a heavy cross to bear.* **4a.** The process of crossbreeding. **b.** An animal or plant produced by crossbreeding; a hybrid: *A mule is a cross between a horse and a donkey.* **5.** A combination of two different things: *The novel is a cross between a romance and a satire.* **6.** In soccer, a pass made into the center of the field when attempting to score. ❖ *v.* **crossed, cross·ing, cross·es** —*tr.* **1.** To go or extend across: *The chicken crossed the road. The bridge crosses the river.* **2.** To intersect: *at the corner where Elm crosses Main Street.* **3.** To place crosswise: *cross one's legs.* **4.** To thwart or betray; double-cross: *You will regret it if you cross me.* **5.** To crossbreed or cross-fertilize: *cross a horse with a donkey; cross two varieties of carnation.* **6.** To draw a line across: *Cross your t's.* **7.** To make the sign of the cross on or over: *They crossed themselves and entered the chapel.* **8.** To delete or eliminate by or as if by drawing a line through: *cross the names off the list.* **9.** To meet and pass: *We crossed each other on the way to the market.* **10.** To turn (the eyes) inward toward the nose. **11.** In soccer, to pass (the ball) in a cross. —*intr.* **1.** To extend across; intersect: *The stream crosses through our yard.* **2.** To move across something; make a crossing: *We crossed into Mexico.* **3.** To meet in or as if in passing: *Our letters crossed in the mail.* **4.** To crossbreed or cross-fertilize. ❖ *adj.* **1.** Lying crosswise; intersecting: *a cross street.* **2.** Showing anger or irritation; annoyed: *Teasing makes some people very cross.* **3.** Contrary or opposite: *opponents having cross interests.* [From Old English *cros*, probably from Old Norse *kross*, from Old Irish *cros*, from Latin *crux*.] —**cross′ly** *adv.* —**cross′ness** *n.*

cross·bar (krôs′bär′) *n.* A horizontal bar, line, or stripe.

cross·beam (krôs′bēm′) *n.* A horizontal beam or girder that crosses another or goes from one wall to another.

cross·bill (krôs′bĭl′) *n.* Any of various songbirds having a curved bill with narrow crossed tips.

cross·bones (krôs′bōnz′) *pl.n.* A representation of two bones placed crosswise, usually under a skull, used as a symbol of death or a warning of danger.

cross·bow (krôs′bō′) *n.* A weapon consisting of a bow fixed across a wooden stock, with grooves on the stock to direct an arrow or other projectile.

cross·breed (krôs′brēd′) *v.* **cross·bred** (krôs′brĕd′), **cross·breed·ing, cross·breeds** —*tr.* To produce (an organism) by mating individuals of different breeds or varieties. —*intr.* To mate with an individual of a different breed or variety. ❖ *n.* An organism produced by crossbreeding; a hybrid or cross.

cross-coun·try (krôs′kŭn′trē) *adj.* **1.** Moving or directed across open countryside rather than following roads or tracks: *a cross-country race.* **2.** Going from one side of a country to the other: *a cross-country trip.* —**cross′-coun′try** *adv.*

cross-country skiing *n.* The sport of skiing over the countryside rather than downhill.

cross·cut (krôs′kŭt′) *tr.v.* **cross·cut, cross·cut·ting, cross·cuts 1.** To cut across (the grain of a piece of wood). **2.** To cut (a piece of wood) using a crosscut saw. ❖ *adj.* Used for cutting crosswise: *crosscut teeth on a saw.* ❖ *n.* **1.** A course or cut going crosswise. **2.** A shortcut.

crosscut saw *n.* A handsaw for cutting wood across the grain.

cross-ex·am·ine (krôs′ĭg-zăm′ĭn) *tr.v.* **cross-ex·am·ined, cross-ex·am·in·ing, cross-ex·am·ines 1.** To question (a witness already examined by the opposing side) in court. **2.** To question (someone) very closely, especially in order to check the answers against other answers given previously. —**cross′-ex·am′i·na′tion** *n.* —**cross′-ex·am′in·er** *n.*

cross-eyed (krôs′īd′) *adj.* Having one or both of the eyes turned inward toward the nose.

cross-fer·til·i·za·tion (krôs′fûr′tl-ĭ-zā′shən) *n.* Fertilization by the union of gametes from different individuals, sometimes of different varieties or species.

cross-fer·til·ize (krôs′fûr′tl-īz′) *intr. & tr.v.* **cross-fer·til·ized, cross-fer·til·iz·ing, cross-fer·til·iz·es** To undergo or cause to undergo cross-fertilization.

cross·fire (krôs′fīr′) *n.* **1.** Lines of fire from two or more positions, crossing each other at a single point: *soldiers caught in a crossfire.* **2.** A rapid, often heated discussion: *The meeting erupted into a crossfire of threats and accusations.*

cross-grained (krôs′grānd′) *adj.* Having an irregular, transverse, or diagonal grain: *a piece of cross-grained wood.*

cross·hairs (krôs′hârz′) *pl.n.* The two fine strands of wire crossed at right angles in the focus of the eyepiece of an optical instrument, such as the periscope of a submarine.

cross·hatch (krôs′hăch′) *tr.v.* **cross·hatched, cross·**

croquet

crosier
16th-century painting of St. Thomas of Farfa holding a crosier

cross-country skiing

cross-stitch

crosswalk

crucible

ă	pat	ôr	core
ā	pay	oi	boy
âr	care	ou	out
ä	father	o͝o	took
ĕ	pet	o͝or	lure
ē	be	o͞o	boot
ĭ	pit	ŭ	cut
ī	bite	ûr	urge
îr	pier	th	thin
ŏ	pot	*th*	this
ō	toe	zh	vision
ô	paw	ə	about

hatch·ing, cross·hatch·es To mark or shade with two or more sets of intersecting parallel lines: *crosshatched the mountainous regions on the map.*

cross·ing (krô′sĭng) *n.* **1.** A place at which something, such as a street, railroad, or river, may be crossed: *a crossing for cattle along the highway.* **2.** A place where two or more things cross; an intersection: *a traffic light at the street crossing.* **3.** The act of crossing, especially a voyage or flight across an ocean.

cross-leg·ged (**krôs′lĕg′**ĭd) *adv. & adj.* **1.** With legs or ankles crossed and knees spread wide, as when sitting on the ground: *sitting cross-legged around the fire.* **2.** With one leg lying across the other.

cross·o·ver (**krôs′**ō′vər) *n.* Something, such as a bridge over a highway or a short stretch of connecting railroad track, that makes a crossing. ❖ *adj.* Using or incorporating two or more styles, so as to appeal to a broader audience: *a crossover artist who blended country music with contemporary rock.*

cross·piece (**krôs′**pēs′) *n.* A crossing or horizontal piece, such as a crossbeam.

cross-pol·li·na·tion (krôs′pŏl′ə-**nā′**shən) *n.* The transfer of pollen from the anther of one flower to the stigma of another flower on a different plant of the same species. Insects and wind are agents of cross-pollination. **—cross-pol′li·nate′** *v.* —SEE NOTE AT **pollinate.**

cross-pur·pose (**krôs′pûr′**pəs) *n.* A conflicting or contrary purpose. ◆ **at cross-purposes** Misinterpreting or failing to understand each other's purposes: *The two committees were at cross-purposes due to a lack of communication.*

cross-ref·er·ence (**krôs′rĕf′**ər-əns) *n.* A note directing the reader from one part of a book, catalogue, index, or file to another part containing related information.

cross·road (**krôs′**rōd′) *n.* **1.** A road that crosses another road. **2. crossroads** *(used with a singular or plural verb)* **a.** A place, often in the countryside, where two or more roads meet: *The bus for the city stops at the crossroads near our farm.* **b.** A crucial point or place, especially one where different courses of action may be taken: *I'm at a crossroads in my career.*

cross section *n.* **1a.** A slice or section of an object made by cutting through it in a plane, usually at right angles to an axis: *The growth rings are visible in the cross section of a tree trunk.* **b.** A piece cut in this way or a picture or drawing of such a piece: *The picture is a cross section of the eye.* **2.** A sample of something meant to be representative of the whole: *A popular show usually appeals to a cross section of the people.*

cross-stitch (**krôs′**stĭch′) *n.* **1.** A stitch shaped like an X, used in sewing and embroidery. **2.** Needlework made with the cross-stitch. ❖ *tr. & intr.v.* **cross-stitched, cross-stitch·ing, cross-stitch·es** To make or embroider with cross-stitches.

cross·town or **cross-town** (**krôs′**toun′) *adj.* Running, extending, or going across a city or town: *a crosstown bus.* ❖ *adv.* Across a city or town: *get snarled in traffic going crosstown.*

cross-train (**krôs′**trān′) *intr.v.* **cross-trained, cross-train·ing, cross-trains** To train in different sports, by alternating workouts in different activities such as bicycling, running, and swimming.

cross-trainer also **cross trainer** (**krôs′**trā′nər) *n.* **1.** A person who cross-trains, especially in different sports. **2.** An athletic shoe designed for cross-training, as for running and court sports.

cross·walk (**krôs′**wôk′) *n.* A path marked off on a street to show where pedestrians should cross.

cross·wise (**krôs′**wīz′) also **cross·ways** (**krôs′**wāz′) *adv.* So as to be or lie in a cross direction; across: *logs laid crosswise on the fire.*

cross·word (**krôs′**wûrd′) *n.* A puzzle in which an arrangement of numbered squares running both across and down is to be filled with words in answer to clues that are numbered in the same sequence as the squares.

crotch (krŏch) *n.* **1.** The place where something, such as a tree trunk, divides into two or more parts or branches. **2a.** The part of the human body where the legs extend from the trunk. **b.** The part of a pair of pants that is between the legs.

crotch·et·y (**krŏch′**ĭ-tē) *adj.* Irritable or temperamental: *The frustrations of the day left me feeling crotchety.* **—crotch′et·i·ness** *n.*

crouch (krouch) *intr.v.* **crouched, crouch·ing, crouch·es 1.** To lower the body by bending or squatting: *The tiger crouched in the grass waiting for its prey.* **2.** To bend down or squat in fear; cringe: *The cats crouched in the corner while the dog growled at them.* ❖ *n.* The act or posture of crouching: *skiing in a crouch.* [From Middle English *crouchen*, from Old French *crochir*, to be bent, from *croche*, hook.]

croup (kro͞op) *n.* A diseased condition that affects the throat and windpipe, especially in children, producing difficult and noisy breathing and a hoarse cough. **—croup′y** *adj.*

crou·ton (**kro͞o′**tŏn′ *or* kro͞o-**tŏn′**) *n.* A small piece of toasted or fried bread, used as a garnish in soups and salads. [From French *croûton*, from Old French *crouste*, crust, from Latin *crūsta*.]

crow[1] (krō) *n.* Any of several large birds having glossy black feathers and a harsh hoarse call. ◆ **as the crow flies** In a straight line: *The store is two miles from here as the crow flies, but it's five miles by car because you have to go around the lake.* [From Old English *crāwe*.]

crow[2] (krō) *intr.v.* **crowed, crow·ing, crows 1.** To utter the loud shrill cry of a rooster: *A rooster crowed at dawn.* **2.** To make a loud sound of pleasure or delight: *The happy baby kicked and crowed in its crib.* **3.** To boast, especially about someone else's defeat: *The winners crowed over their victory to all their friends.* ❖ *n.* **1.** The loud high-pitched cry of a rooster. **2.** A loud sound expressing pleasure or delight. [From Old English *crāwan*.]

Crow *n., pl.* **Crow** or **Crows 1.** A member of a Native American people formerly living on the northern Great Plains and now settled in Montana. **2.** The Siouan language of the Crow.

crow·bar (**krō′**bär′) *n.* A straight iron or steel bar, usually having one end bent or curved with a wedge-shaped edge, used as a lever for lifting or prying.

crowd (kroud) *n.* **1.** A large number of people gathered together; a throng. **2.** The common people; the masses: *Do what you want to do and don't follow the crowd.* **3.** A particular group of people: *the college crowd; fall in with a bad crowd.* ❖ *v.* **crowd·ed, crowd·ing, crowds** *—tr.* **1.** To fill to overflowing: *Shoppers crowded the store.* **2.** To press tightly or cram together: *He crowded his old magazines in a cabinet.* **3.** To press or shove: *subway riders crowding each other at rush hour.* *—intr.* **1.** To gather together in a limited space: *Fans crowded around the rock star.* **2.** To move forward by shoving: *Everybody crowded into the cafeteria.* [From Middle English *crouden*, to crowd, from Old English *crūdan*, to hasten, press.]

crown (kroun) *n.* **1.** A head covering, often made of gold set with jewels, worn by a sovereign as a symbol of ruling power. **2.** often **Crown a.** The authority, power, or position of a sovereign: *the heir to the Crown.* **b.** The sovereign of a country: *The crowns of Europe signed the peace treaty.* **3.** A wreath worn on the head: *a crown of laurel.* **4.** The top part of something, especially of the head. **5.** The head itself. **6.** The top part of a hat. **7.** The upper, spreading part of a tree or shrub. **8a.** The part of a tooth that projects beyond the gum. **b.** An artificial substitute for the natural crown of a tooth. **9.** A former British coin worth five shillings. **10.** A title, distinction, or reward: *win the heavyweight boxing crown.* ❖ *tr.v.* **crowned, crown·ing, crowns 1.** To place a crown or wreath on the head of: *crown the victor of the marathon.* **2.** To give regal power to; enthrone: *The king was crowned at the age of 15.* **3.** To give honor or recognition to (someone), especially as the best in an endeavor: *The critics crowned her as the best pianist of all.* **4.** To cover or form the topmost part of: *Snow crowned the mountain peaks.* **5.** To hit (someone) on the head. **6.** To put a crown on (a tooth). [From Middle English *coroune*, from Latin *corōna*, wreath, garland, crown.]

crown prince *n.* The male heir to a throne.

crown princess *n.* **1.** The female heir to a throne. **2.** The wife of a crown prince.

crow's-feet (**krōz′fēt′**) *pl.n.* Small wrinkles at the outer corner of the eye.

crow's-nest (**krōz′nĕst′**) *n.* A small lookout platform located near the top of a ship's mast.

cru·ces (**kro͞o′**sēz) *n.* A plural of **crux.**

cru·cial (**kro͞o′**shəl) *adj.* Of the utmost importance; decisive; critical: *The crucial moment in the trial came when the witness contradicted himself.* [From New Latin *(īnstantia) crucis*, crossroads (case), from Latin *crux*, cross.] **—cru′cial·ly** *adv.*

cru·ci·ate (**kro͞o′**shē-āt′) *adj.* Shaped like a cross: *the cruciate ligaments of the knee.*

cru·ci·ble (**kro͞o′**sə-bəl) *n.* **1.** A container that can withstand very high temperatures, used to melt ores, metals, and other materials. **2.** A severe test or trial: *His strength of character was shaped during the crucible of the war years.*

cru·ci·fix (**kro͞o′**sə-fĭks′) *n.* **1.** An image or a figure of Jesus on the cross. **2.** A cross viewed as a symbol of Jesus's crucifixion.

cru·ci·fix·ion (kro͞o′sə-**fĭk′**shən) *n.* **1.** The act of executing a person on a cross. **2. Crucifixion a.** The execution of Jesus on the cross. **b.** A representation of Jesus on the cross.

cru·ci·form (**kro͞o′**sə-fôrm′) *adj.* Having the shape of a cross.

cru·ci·fy (**kro͞o′**sə-fī′) *tr.v.* **cru·ci·fied, cru·ci·fy·ing, cru·ci·fies 1.** To put (a person) to death by nailing or binding to a cross. **2.** To persecute or torment, as by harsh criticism: *The press crucified the senator for his moral failings.* **—cru′ci·fi′er** *n.*

crude (kro͞od) *adj.* **crud·er, crud·est 1.** Being in an unrefined or natural state; raw: *crude oil; crude cotton.* **2.** Lacking tact or refinement; coarse or offensive: *a crude person with no manners; a crude remark made with little feeling.* **3.** Not carefully or skillfully made; rough: *a crude sketch on a paper napkin.* [From Middle English, from Latin *crūdus*.] **—crude′ly** *adv.* **—crude′ness** *n.*

cru·di·ty (**kro͞o′**dĭ-tē) *n.* The condition or quality of being crude; crudeness.

cru·el (**kro͞o′**əl) *adj.* **cru·el·er, cru·el·est** or **cru·el·ler, cru·el·lest 1.** Given to causing pain or suffering: *the reign of a cruel dictator.* **2.** Causing suffering; painful or distressing: *a cruel act; cruel words.* [From Middle English, from Latin *crūdēlis*.] **—cru′el·ly** *adv.* **—cru′el·ness** *n.*

cru·el·ty (**kro͞o′**əl-tē) *n., pl.* **cru·el·ties 1.** The condition or quality of being cruel: *cruelty to animals.* **2.** A cruel act or remark.

cru·et (**kro͞o′**ĭt) *n.* **1.** A small glass bottle for holding a condiment, such as vinegar. **2.** A small vessel for water and wine used in the consecration of the Eucharist.

cruise (kro͞oz) *v.* **cruised, cruis·ing, cruis·es** *—intr.* **1.** To sail or travel about in an unhurried way: *A patrol boat cruised along the coast.* **2.** To move or travel about with no special destination: *Taxis cruised through the business district looking for fares.* **3.** To travel at steady efficient speed: *After takeoff the plane cruised at a high altitude.* *—tr.* To travel about or journey over: *A police car cruised the streets of the town.* ❖ *n.* A sea voyage for pleasure: *We enjoyed our cruise to Bermuda.* [From Dutch *kruis*, cross, from Latin *crux*.]

❑ *These sound alike:* **cruise, cruse** (small bottle).

cruise control *n.* A system in a motor vehicle for maintaining a constant speed.

cruise missile *n.* A guided missile having short wings that allow it to fly at low altitude along a preset course to its target.

cruis·er (**kro͞o′**zər) *n.* **1.** A medium-sized warship of high speed and a large cruising range, with less armor and firepower than a battleship. **2.** A cabin cruiser. **3.** A squad car.

cruis·er·weight (**kro͞o′**zər-wāt′) *n.* **1.** A boxer weighing more than 175 pounds and not more than 190 pounds (about 79–86 kilograms). **2.** A contestant in other sports in a similar weight class.

crul·ler (**krŭl′**ər) *n.* A small, usually ring-shaped or twisted cake of sweet dough fried in deep fat. [From obsolete Dutch *krulle-koken*, rolled-up cake, from Middle Dutch *crulle*, curly.]

crumb (krŭm) *n.* **1.** A tiny piece or particle of food: *We tossed crumbs of bread to the squirrels.* **2.** A little bit; a fragment; a scrap: *She didn't have a crumb of sympathy for him.*

crum·ble (**krŭm′**bəl) *v.* **crum·bled, crum·bling, crum·bles** *—tr.* To break into small pieces or crumbs: *He always crumbles crackers into his soup.* *—intr.* **1.** To break up into small pieces: *The lump of dry dirt crumbled easily.* **2.** To fall apart; disintegrate: *The old barn finally crumbled in decay.*

crum·bly (**krŭm′**blē) *adj.* **crum·bli·er, crum·bli·est** Easily crumbled: *crumbly cake.* **—crum′bli·ness** *n.*

crum·my (**krŭm′**ē) *adj.* **crum·mi·er, crum·mi·est** *Slang* **1.** Of poor quality: *a crummy movie.* **2.** Miserable; wretched: *I felt crummy when I thought of the hurtful things I'd said.*

crum·pet (**krŭm′**pĭt) *n.* A light soft bread similar to a muffin, baked on a griddle and often toasted.

crum·ple (**krŭm′**pəl) *v.* **crum·pled, crum·pling, crum·ples** *—tr.* To crush so as to form creases or wrinkles: *Don't crumple that freshly ironed shirt.* *—intr.* **1.** To become wrinkled or crushed: *Tissue paper crumples easily.* **2.** To collapse: *Stomach cramps caused the runner to crumple to the ground.*

crunch (krŭnch) *v.* **crunched, crunch·ing, crunch·es** *—tr.* **1.** To chew with a noisy crackling sound: *crunch peanuts.* **2.** To crush, grind, or tread noisily: *crunch ice in a blender.* *—intr.* **1.** To chew noisily: *crunch on celery.* **2.** To move with a crushing or cracking sound: *We crunched through the snow.* **3.** To make a crushing or cracking sound: *The snow crunched under my boots.* ❖ *n.* **1.** The act of crunching. **2.** A crushing or cracking sound: *the crunch of gravel as the car drove up the driveway.* **3.** A critical situation, especially one resulting from a shortage of time, money, or resources: *A disruption in the supply of oil created an energy crunch.*

crunch·y (**krŭn′**chē) *adj.* **crunch·i·er, crunch·i·est** Crisp; brittle: *crunchy potato chips.* **—crunch′i·ness** *n.*

cru·sade (kro͞o-**sād′**) *n.* **1.** often **Crusade** Any of a series of military expeditions undertaken by European Christians in the 11th, 12th, and 13th centuries to recover the Holy Land from the Muslims. **2.** A campaign or movement for a reform, cause, or ideal: *a crusade for women's rights.* ❖ *intr.v.* **cru·sad·ed, cru·sad·ing, cru·sades** To take part in a crusade: *The parents crusaded for better schools.* [From Latin *crux*, cross.] **—cru·sad′er** *n.*

cruse (kro͞oz *or* kro͞os) *n.* A small jar or pot for holding oil, wine, or vinegar.

❑ *These sound alike:* **cruse, cruise** (travel).

cruet

cruller

crumpet

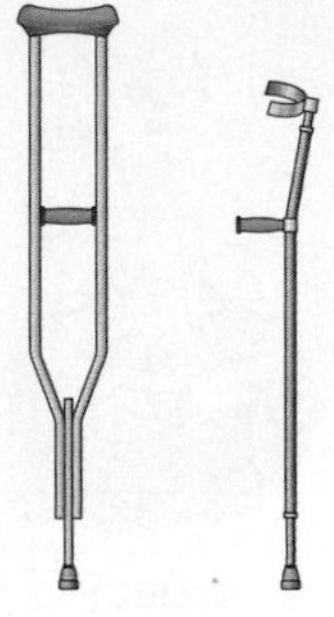

crutch
underarm *(left)* and forearm *(right)* crutches

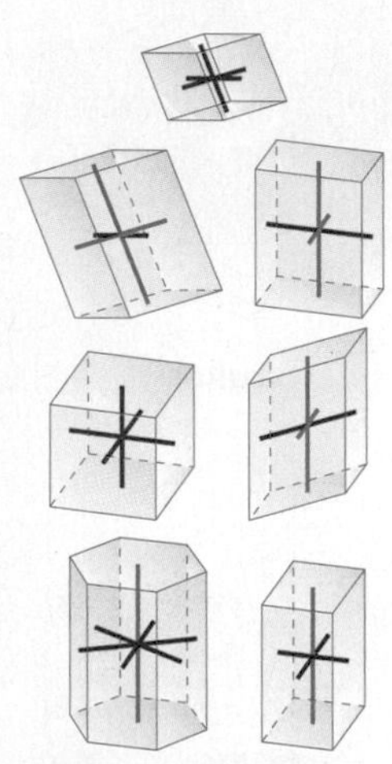

crystal
Axes of symmetry in the seven main crystal systems are depicted using different colors. Within each crystal, axes having the same color are of equal length.

ă	pat	ôr	core
ā	pay	oi	boy
âr	care	ou	out
ä	father	ŏŏ	took
ĕ	pet	ŏŏr	lure
ē	be	ōō	boot
ĭ	pit	ŭ	cut
ī	bite	ûr	urge
îr	pier	th	thin
ŏ	pot	*th*	this
ō	toe	zh	vision
ô	paw	ə	about

crush (krŭsh) *v.* **crushed, crush·ing, crush·es** *—tr.* **1.** To press or squeeze with enough force to break or injure: *The tree limb crushed the front of the car.* **2.** To break, grind, or pound into small pieces or powder: *crush rocks into gravel.* **3.** To crumple; wrinkle: *Packing the suitcase too tight will crush your clothes.* **4.** To shove, crowd, or press: *I was crushed against the wall of the crowded elevator.* **5a.** To put down; subdue: *crush a rebellion.* **b.** To overwhelm; oppress: *The failure of the experiment did not crush the spirit of the researchers. —intr.* **1.** To be or become crushed: *The ice crushed under my feet.* **2.** To proceed or move by crowding or pressing: *The commuters crushed into the train.* ❖ *n.* **1.** The act of crushing; extreme pressure: *The crush of the collision destroyed the car's engine.* **2.** A great crowd: *I was caught in the crush and couldn't get across the square.* **3.** A substance prepared by or as if by crushing: *orange crush.* **4.** *Informal* A strong, often foolish and brief liking for someone. **—crush′er** *n.*

crust (krŭst) *n.* **1a.** The hard outer layer of bread. **b.** A hard dry piece of bread: *had only a few crusts of bread for breakfast.* **2.** A pastry shell, as of a pie. **3.** A hard outer layer or covering: *a layer of snow with a firm crust.* **4.** The solid outer layer of the earth, lying above the mantle. ❖ *v.* **crust·ed, crust·ing, crusts** *—tr.* To cover with a crust; encrust: *Snow and ice crusted the mountain trail. —intr.* To become covered with a crust: *The gravy cooled and crusted over.*

crus·ta·cean (krŭ-**stā′**shən) *n.* Any of a group of arthropods, including the lobsters, crabs, shrimps, and barnacles, that usually live in water and have a segmented body, a hard shell, paired jointed limbs, and two pairs of antennae. [From New Latin *crūstāceus,* hard-shelled, from Latin *crūsta,* shell.]

crust·y (**krŭs′**tē) *adj.* **crust·i·er, crust·i·est 1.** Having a crust: *crusty bread.* **2.** Abrupt in speech or manner; gruff; harsh; curt: *The crusty old soldier was easy to provoke.* **—crust′i·ly** *adv.* **—crust′i·ness** *n.*

crutch (krŭch) *n.* A support used usually as one of a pair by an injured or disabled person as an aid to walking, having a vertical shaft that is sometimes forked and a horizontal grip for the hand. Crutches normally have a crosspiece that is positioned under the armpit or a cuff that wraps around the forearm. [From Old English *crycc.*]

crux (krŭks *or* kro͝oks) *n., pl.* **crux·es** or **cru·ces** (**kro͞o′**sēz) A basic or essential point: *Let's not lose sight of the crux of the problem.*

cry (krī) *v.* **cried** (krīd), **cry·ing, cries** (krīz) *—intr.* **1.** To shed tears, especially as a result of strong emotion such as grief, sorrow, pain, or joy. **2.** To call loudly; shout: *We cried to our friends across the street.* **3.** To utter a characteristic sound or call: *The monkeys cried in the treetops. —tr.* **1.** To call out loudly; shout: *The umpire cried "Strike!"* **2.** To proclaim or announce in public: *The peddlers cry their wares in the streets.* **3.** To bring (oneself) into a particular condition by shedding tears: *She cried herself to sleep.* ❖ *n., pl.* **cries** (krīz) **1.** A loud call; a shout: *a cry of warning.* **2.** A loud sound expressive of fear, grief, distress, or pain. **3.** A fit of weeping: *After a short cry the baby was fast asleep.* **4.** The characteristic sound or call of an animal: *the cry of an eagle swooping down on its prey.* **5.** A public or general demand or complaint; an outcry: *a cry for reform in city politics.* **6.** A call to action; a slogan: *a cry to arms.* **7.** A shout or call for help: *A neighbor heard their cries and called the police.* ◆ **cry over spilled milk** To regret what cannot be undone or fixed. **cry wolf** To raise a false alarm. [From Middle English *crien,* from Latin *quirītāre,* to cry out.]

SYNONYMS cry, weep, wail, blubber, sob These verbs mean to make sounds that show grief, unhappiness, or pain. **Cry** and **weep** both involve the shedding of tears: *Loud, sudden noises make the baby cry. We all wept when the old dog died.* **Wail** refers to crying that is loud and sustained: *Many of the mourners at the funeral wailed throughout the service.* **Blubber** refers to noisy crying mixed with speech that is broken or cannot be understood: *The child blubbered over the broken toy.* **Sob** refers to weeping and broken speech marked by gasps: *Stop sobbing for a minute and catch your breath!*
ANTONYM laugh

cry·ba·by (**krī′**bā′bē) *n., pl.* **cry·ba·bies** A person who cries, whines, or complains frequently with little cause.

cry·ing (**krī′**ĭng) *adj.* **1.** Demanding immediate action or remedy: *a crying need for a new hospital.* **2.** Abominable; reprehensible: *a crying shame.*

cry·o·gen·ics (krī′ə-**jĕn′**ĭks) *n.* *(used with a singular or plural verb)* The branch of physics dealing with the production of low temperatures or the study of matter at low temperatures.

crypt (krĭpt) *n.* An underground vault or chamber, especially one that is used as a tomb beneath a church. [From Latin *crypta,* from Greek *kruptos,* hidden.] —SEE NOTE AT **grotto.**

cryp·tic (**krĭp′**tĭk) *adj.* Having a hidden meaning or secret nature; mysterious; puzzling: *a cryptic message.* **—cryp′ti·cal·ly** *adv.*

cryp·to·gram (**krĭp′**tə-grăm′) *n.* Something written in a secret code or cipher.

cryp·to·graph (**krĭp′**tə-grăf′) *n.* **1.** A cryptogram. **2.** A system or device used to encode and decode messages and documents.

cryp·tog·ra·pher (krĭp-**tŏg′**rə-fər) *n.* A person who specializes in cryptography.

cryp·tog·ra·phy (krĭp-**tŏg′**rə-fē) *n.* The study and use of secret codes and ciphers.

crys·tal (**krĭs′**təl) *n.* **1a.** A solid composed of atoms, molecules, or ions arranged in regular patterns that are repeated throughout the structure to form a characteristic network: *Sugar crystals and salt crystals can be distinguished by the differences in their structure.* **b.** A transparent mineral, especially a transparent form of pure quartz. **c.** A crystalline material that is a semiconductor or has piezoelectric properties. **2a.** A clear colorless glass of high quality. **b.** An object, such as a drinking glass or an ornament, made of this glass. **c.** Such objects considered as a group: *The table was set with fine china and crystal.* **3.** A transparent cover that protects the face of a watch or clock. ❖ *adj.* Clear; transparent: *I could see to the bottom in the crystal water of the lake.*

crystal ball *n.* A globe of crystal or glass in which images believed to predict the future are supposed to appear.

crys·tal·line (**krĭs′**tə-lĭn *or* **krĭs′**tə-līn′) *adj.* **1.** Composed of crystals: *a crystalline semiconductor.* **2.** Made of crystals: *Snowflakes are crystalline.* **3.** Clear; transparent: *crystalline waters.*

crystalline lens *n.* The lens of an eye.

crys·tal·lize (**krĭs′**tə-līz′) *v.* **crys·tal·lized, crys·tal·liz·ing, crys·tal·liz·es** *—tr.* **1.** To cause to form crystals or take on crystalline structure: *The researchers had to crystallize the protein before they could determine its structure.* **2.** To give a definite and permanent form to: *The scientists finally crystallized their ideas about the structure of the protein. —intr.* **1.** To take on crystalline form. **2.** To take on a definite and permanent form: *The writer performed months of research before the book finally crystallized in his mind.* **—crys′tal·li·za′tion** (krĭs′tə-lĭ-**zā′**shən) *n.*

crys·tal·log·ra·phy (krĭs′tə-**lŏg′**rə-fē) *n.* The science that deals with the structure and properties of crystals.

Cs The symbol for the element **cesium.**
CSA *abbr.* An abbreviation of Confederate States of America.
csc *abbr.* An abbreviation of cosecant.
CST *abbr.* An abbreviation of Central Standard Time.
CT *abbr.* An abbreviation of Connecticut.
ct. *abbr.* An abbreviation of cent.
Ct. *abbr.* An abbreviation of court.
ctrl *abbr.* An abbreviation of control key.
CT scan (**sē′tē′**) *n.* A three-dimensional image of a part of the body, made by a computer that assembles a series of two-dimensional x-ray images that are taken at angles around a single axis. [From *c(omputed) t(omography).*] **—CT scanner** *n.*
Cu The symbol for the element **copper.**
cu. *abbr.* An abbreviation of cubic.
cub (kŭb) *n.* **1.** One of the young of certain animals, such as bears, wolves, lions, and pandas. **2.** A beginner, especially in newspaper reporting.
Cu·ba (**kyo͞o′**bə) An island country in the Caribbean Sea south of Florida. Havana is the capital.
cub·by·hole (**kŭb′**ē-hōl′) *n.* A small and sometimes cramped space or room: *work in a cluttered cubbyhole of an office.*
cube (kyo͞ob) *n.* **1.** A solid having six equal square faces or sides. **2.** Something having this shape or almost this shape: *a bouillon cube.* **3.** A cubicle, used for work or study. **4.** The product that results when the same number is used three times as a factor. For example, the cube of 4, written 4^3, is equal to $4 \times 4 \times 4$. ❖ *tr.v.* **cubed, cub·ing, cubes 1.** To form the cube of (a number). **2.** To cut or form into a cube or cubes: *The cook cubed beets for a salad.* [From Greek *kubos.*]
cube root *n.* The number whose cube is equal to a given number. For example, the cube root of 125 is 5.
cu·bic (**kyo͞o′**bĭk) *adj.* **1.** Shaped like or nearly like a cube: *Dice have a cubic form.* **2.** Having three dimensions, especially having equal length, breadth, and thickness: *bought a cubic yard of mulch.* **3.** Relating to or involving a number or a variable that has been raised to the third power: *a cubic equation.*
cu·bi·cal (**kyo͞o′**bĭ-kəl) *adj.* **1.** Cubic: *a room of cubical shape.* **2.** Relating to volume: *cubical dimensions.*
❑ *These sound alike:* **cubical, cubicle** (small room).
cu·bi·cle (**kyo͞o′**bĭ-kəl) *n.* A small compartment, as for work or study.
❑ *These sound alike:* **cubicle, cubical** (cubic).
cubic measure *n.* A system for measuring volume using units, such as cubic inches or cubic centimeters, that are the cubes of linear units.
cub·ism also **Cub·ism** (**kyo͞o′**bĭz′əm) *n.* A style of painting and sculpture in the early 1900s that portrays the subject matter as fragmented geometric forms, especially flat, sharply angled planes. **—cub′ist** *adj. & n.*
cu·bit (**kyo͞o′**bĭt) *n.* An ancient unit of linear measure originally equal to the distance from the tip of the middle finger to the elbow, or about 17 to 22 inches (43 to 56 centimeters).
Cub Scout or **cub scout** *n.* A member of the junior division of the Boy Scouts, for boys of ages eight through ten.
cuck·oo (**ko͞o′**ko͞o *or* **ko͝ok′**o͞o) *n., pl.* **cuck·oos 1.** A bird of Eurasia and Africa having grayish feathers and a call of two notes that sounds like its name. Cuckoos lay their eggs in the nests of birds of other species. **2.** Any of various related birds, including several North American species. ❖ *adj. Slang* Crazy; foolish.
cuckoo clock *n.* A wall clock that marks the time by sounding a mechanical whistle imitating the cuckoo's call while a toy bird emerges from a small door.
cu·cum·ber (**kyo͞o′**kŭm′bər) *n.* **1.** The long cylindrical fruit of a climbing plant, having a green rind and white watery flesh, eaten in salads and used for making pickles. **2.** The vine that bears such fruit.
cud (kŭd) *n.* Food that has been partly digested and brought up from the first stomach to the mouth again for further chewing by mammals such as cattle and sheep.
cud·dle (**kŭd′**l) *v.* **cud·dled, cud·dling, cud·dles** *—tr.* To hold fondly or hug tenderly: *cuddle a baby in one's arms. —intr.* To nestle; snuggle: *The two cats cuddled up near the fire.* ❖ *n.* A hug or embrace.
cud·dly (**kŭd′**lē) *adj.* **1.** Fond of cuddling or of being cuddled: *The cuddly kitten curled up in my lap.* **2.** Pleasant to cuddle or snuggle with: *a big cuddly teddy bear.*
cudg·el (**kŭj′**əl) *n.* A short, heavy club. ❖ *tr.v.* **cudg·eled, cudg·el·ing, cudg·els** or **cudg·elled, cudg·el·ling, cudg·els** To strike or beat with a cudgel.
cue[1] (kyo͞o) *n.* A long tapered stick used to strike the cue ball in billiards and pool. [From Latin *cauda*, tail.]
❑ *These sound alike:* **cue[1]** (stick), **cue[2]** (signal), **queue** (line of people).
cue[2] (kyo͞o) *n.* **1.** A word or signal prompting an actor or singer to speak, sing, or do something during a performance. **2.** A signal for action; a reminder. **3.** A hint or suggestion as to how to behave or what should be done: *Our host's yawn was a cue that it was time to go home.* ❖ *tr.v.* **cued, cu·ing, cues 1.** To give (a person) a cue: *cue me when it's my turn.* **2.** To position (an audio or video recording) in readiness for playing: *cued the DVD to the chase scene.* [Perhaps from abbreviation of Latin *quandō*, when, used for actors' copies of plays.]
❑ *These sound alike:* **cue[2]** (signal), **cue[1]** (stick), **queue** (line of people).
cue ball *n.* The white ball used to strike other balls in billiards and pool.
cuff[1] (kŭf) *n.* **1.** A band or fold of cloth at the bottom of a sleeve, often having a button and buttonhole. **2.** The turned-up fold at the bottom of a trouser leg. **3.** A handcuff. ◆ **off the cuff** With little or no preparation; not rehearsed: *remarks made off the cuff.* [From Middle English *cuffe*, mitten.]
cuff[2] (kŭf) *tr.v.* **cuffed, cuff·ing, cuffs** To strike with or as if with the open hand; slap: *The bear cuffed her cubs.* ❖ *n.* A blow or slap made with or as if with the open hand.
cuff link or **cuff·link** (**kŭf′**lĭngk′) *n.* One of a pair of fasteners for shirt cuffs having a chain or shank that passes through the buttonholes.
cui·rass (kwĭ-**răs′**) *n.* **1.** A piece of armor consisting of a breastplate and a piece for the back that are buckled together. **2.** The breastplate alone.
cui·sine (kwĭ-**zēn′**) *n.* **1.** A style of cooking or preparing food: *French cuisine.* **2.** Food; fare: *a restaurant with excellent cuisine.*
cul-de-sac (**kŭl′**dĭ-**săk′**) *n., pl.* **cul-de-sacs** or **culs-de-sac** (**kŭlz′**dĭ-**săk′**) A blind alley or dead-end street.
cu·li·nar·y (**kyo͞o′**lə-nĕr′ē *or* **kŭl′**ə-nĕr′ē) *adj.* Relating to a kitchen or cookery: *a chef of great culinary skill.*
cull (kŭl) *tr.v.* **culled, cull·ing, culls 1.** To pick out from others; gather selectively: *cull the prettiest flowers in the garden.* **2.** To remove undesirable members or parts from: *cull a herd of wild deer to keep the population healthy.*
culm (kŭlm) *n.* The stem of a grass, sedge, or other similar plant.
cul·mi·nate (**kŭl′**mə-nāt′) *v.* **cul·mi·nat·ed, cul·mi·nat·ing, cul·mi·nates** *—intr.* To reach the highest point or degree, often just before ending; climax: *The celebration culminated in a huge display of fireworks. —tr.* To bring to the highest point or degree, often just before completion: *An appearance by the president culminated the political convention.* [From Latin *culmen*, summit.] **—cul′mi·na′tion** *n.*

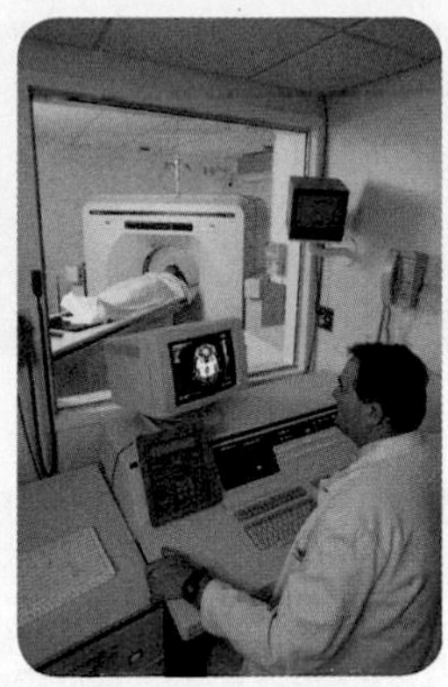
CT scan

cuckoo clock

cumulonimbus

cumulus

cuneiform

WRITERS CHOOSE THEIR WORDS

Not that his whole year at Hogwarts had been fun. At the very end of last term, Harry had come face-to-face with none other than Lord Voldemort himself. Voldemort might be a ruin of his former self, but he was still terrifying, still **cunning,** still determined to regain power.

—J.K. Rowling
Harry Potter and the Chamber of Secrets

ă	pat	ôr	core
ā	pay	oi	boy
âr	care	ou	out
ä	father	o͝o	took
ĕ	pet	o͝or	lure
ē	be	o͞o	boot
ĭ	pit	ŭ	cut
ī	bite	ûr	urge
îr	pier	th	thin
ŏ	pot	*th*	this
ō	toe	zh	vision
ô	paw	ə	about

cu·lottes (ko͞o′lŏts′) *pl.n.* Women's pants cut to resemble a skirt.

cul·pa·ble (kŭl′pə-bəl) *adj.* Deserving blame; blameworthy: *Neglect of one's duty is culpable behavior.* [From Middle English *coupable*, from Latin *culpābilis*, from *culpa*, fault, blame.] —**cul′pa·bil′i·ty** *n.* —**cul′pa·bly** *adv.*

cul·prit (kŭl′prĭt) *n.* **1.** A person or thing guilty of a fault or crime: *We never found the culprit who sprayed graffiti on the school bus.* **2.** A person charged with a crime in a court of law.

cult (kŭlt) *n.* **1a.** A system of religious worship and ritual: *the ancient cults of nature worship.* **b.** A religion or religious sect whose followers live in an unconventional manner under the guidance of a leader who demands strict obedience. **2.** A great or excessive attachment or devotion to a person, principle, or thing: *A cult of physical fitness has created large numbers of joggers and bikers nationwide.* **3.** A group of people sharing a usually artistic or intellectual interest.

cul·ti·vate (kŭl′tə-vāt′) *tr.v.* **cul·ti·vat·ed, cul·ti·vat·ing, cul·ti·vates 1a.** To prepare and improve (land), as by plowing or fertilizing, for raising crops; till. **b.** To loosen or dig soil around (growing plants). **2.** To grow, tend, or raise (plants or certain animals, for example): *cultivate wheat; cultivate oysters.* **3.** To encourage or foster: *The coach cultivates an atmosphere of respect.* **4.** To seek the acquaintance or goodwill of (a person): *cultivate the new neighbors.* [From Medieval Latin *cultīvāre*, from Latin *cultus*, tilled.]

cul·ti·vat·ed (kŭl′tə-vā′tĭd) *adj.* **1.** Planted with crops or prepared for the planting of crops: *cultivated land.* **2.** Grown by cultivation; not wild: *Many roses are cultivated flowers.* **3.** Cultured; refined: *cultivated people with a love of opera.*

cul·ti·va·tion (kŭl′tə-**vā′**shən) *n.* **1.** The process of tilling soil and growing or raising crops: *the cultivation of fruits and vegetables.* **2.** The process of raising certain animals: *the commercial cultivation of sea urchins.* **3.** Encouragement, fostering, or development: *the cultivation of her talents; the cultivation of friendly relations.* **4.** Culture; refinement: *a person of great cultivation.*

cul·ti·va·tor (kŭl′tə-vā′tər) *n.* **1.** A person who cultivates. **2.** An implement or machine for loosening the earth and destroying weeds around growing plants: *A cultivator works faster than a hoe.*

cul·tur·al (kŭl′chər-əl) *adj.* Relating to culture: *Paris is the cultural center of France.* —**cul′tur·al·ly** *adv.*

cul·ture (kŭl′chər) *n.* **1a.** The arts, beliefs, customs, institutions, and all other products of human work and thought at a particular time: *the culture of Renaissance Italy.* **b.** The main attitudes that characterize a group or organization: *Hollywood culture; corporate culture.* **2.** The qualities of mind and the tastes that result from appreciation of the arts and sciences: *a writer of great culture.* **3.** The breeding or cultivation of animals or plants for food or other purposes: *wheat culture in Nebraska; silkworm culture.* **4a.** The growing of microorganisms or tissues in a specially prepared nutrient substance for scientific study or medicinal use. **b.** Such a growth, as of bacteria or tissue: *a culture of penicillin-producing mold.* ❖ *tr.v.* **cul·tured, cul·tur·ing, cul·tures** To grow (microorganisms, tissues, or other living matter) in a specially prepared substance for scientific study. [From Middle English *culture*, cultivation, from Latin *cultūra*, from *cultus*, past participle of *colere*, to cultivate.]

cul·tured (kŭl′chərd) *adj.* **1.** Well-educated; refined: *a cultured supporter of the arts.* **2.** Grown or produced under artificial and controlled conditions: *cultured pearls.*

culture shock *n.* A condition of confusion and anxiety that can affect an individual suddenly exposed to an unfamiliar culture or environment.

cul·vert (kŭl′vərt) *n.* A water drain crossing under a road or embankment.

cum·ber (kŭm′bər) *tr.v.* **cum·bered, cum·ber·ing, cum·bers** To burden or trouble: *cumber a person with worries.*

Cum·ber·land Gap (kŭm′bər-lənd) A natural passage through the **Cumberland Mountains,** a range of the southern Appalachians, near the junction of the Kentucky, Virginia, and Tennessee borders. It was part of the principal route of westward migration starting in the late 1700s.

cum·ber·some (kŭm′bər-səm) *adj.* Difficult to carry or manage: *cumbersome baggage; a cumbersome application process.* —**cum′ber·some·ly** *adv.* —**cum′ber·some·ness** *n.*

cum·in (kŭm′ĭn *or* ko͞o′mĭn *or* kyo͞o′mĭn) *n.* The aromatic seeds of a Mediterranean plant that is related to parsley, used whole or ground as a seasoning.

cum lau·de (ko͝om lou′də) *adv. & adj.* With honor: *She graduated cum laude. He is a cum laude graduate.*

cum·mer·bund (kŭm′ər-bŭnd′) *n.* A broad sash worn around the waist, especially as part of a tuxedo.

cu·mu·la·tive (kyo͞om′yə-lā′tĭv *or* kyo͞om′yə-lə-tĭv) *adj.* Increasing or growing by steady addition or in stages: *The cumulative efforts of many people helped control the epidemic.* —**cu′mu·la′tive·ly** *adv.* —**cu′mu·la′tive·ness** *n.*

cu·mu·lo·nim·bus (kyo͞om′yə-lō-**nĭm′**bəs) *n., pl.* **cu·mu·lo·nim·bus·es** or **cu·mu·lo·nim·bi** (kyo͞om′yə-lō-**nĭm′**bī) A very dense cloud with massive projections that billow upward to great heights, usually producing heavy rains, thunderstorms, or hailstorms.

cu·mu·lus (kyo͞om′yə-ləs) *n., pl.* **cu·mu·li** (kyo͞om′yə-lī′) A dense, white, fluffy cloud that billows upward from a flat base. [From Latin *cumulus*, heap.]

cu·ne·i·form (kyo͞o′nē-ə-fôrm′ *or* kyo͞o-**nē′**ə-fôrm′) *adj.* Relating to or being a kind of writing made with wedge-shaped characters, used by the Babylonians, Assyrians, Persians, and other peoples of the ancient Near East: *a cuneiform text written on a clay tablet.* ❖ *n.* Cuneiform writing.

cun·ning (kŭn′ĭng) *adj.* Sly; crafty; clever: *a cunning scheme.* ❖ *n.* Skill in deception; guile: *It takes great cunning to be a spy.* —**cun′ning·ly** *adv.*

cup (kŭp) *n.* **1.** A small open container, usually having a handle, from which to drink liquids: *The baby can now drink from a cup.* **2.** The contents of such a container: *drink a cup of cocoa.* **3.** In cooking, a measure equal to ½ pint, 8 ounces, or 16 tablespoons (237 milliliters). **4.** Something similar in shape to a cup: *the cup of a flower.* **5.** A cup-shaped vessel awarded as a prize or trophy: *We won the soccer cup.* **6.** In golf, a hole or the metal container inside a hole. ❖ *tr.v.* **cupped, cup·ping, cups 1.** To form in such a way as to resemble a cup: *cup one's hands to get a drink.* **2.** To place in or as if in a cup: *I cupped my ear with my hand to show I couldn't hear her.* [From Old English *cuppe*, from Late Latin *cuppa*, drinking vessel.]

cup·board (kŭb′ərd) *n.* A closet or cabinet, usually having shelves for storing food, dishes, or other small items: *a kitchen cupboard.*

cup·cake (kŭp′kāk′) *n.* A small cake baked in a cup-shaped container.

cup·ful (kŭp′fo͝ol′) *n.* The amount that a cup can hold.

Cu·pid (kyo͞o′pĭd) *n.* **1.** In Roman mythology, the god of love, identified with the Greek Eros. **2. cupid** A figure of a winged boy used as a symbol of love.

cu·pid·i·ty (kyo͞o-**pĭd′**ĭ-tē) *n.* Extreme desire for something, especially wealth; greed.

cu·po·la (kyo͞o′pə-lə) *n.* **1.** A small domelike structure on top of a roof. **2.** A domed roof or ceiling.

cur (kûr) *n.* **1.** A mongrel dog. **2.** A despicable or cowardly person.

cur·a·ble (kyo͝or′ə-bəl) *adj.* Capable of being healed or cured: *a curable illness.* **—cur′a·bil′i·ty** *n.*

Cu·ra·çao (ko͝or′ə-sou′ *or* kyo͝or′ə-sou′) An island territory of the Netherlands in the southern Caribbean Sea off the northwest coast of Venezuela. It was colonized by the Spanish in 1527.

cu·rate¹ (kyo͝or′ĭt) *n.* A member of the clergy who has charge of a parish or who assists a rector or vicar.

cu·rate² (kyo͝or′āt′) *tr.v.* **cur·at·ed, cur·at·ing, cur·ates** To act as curator of; organize and oversee. [Back-formation from *curator*.]

cu·ra·tive (kyo͝or′ə-tĭv) *adj.* Serving or tending to cure: *curative medicine.* ❖ *n.* Something that cures; a remedy.

cu·ra·tor (kyo͞o-rā′tər *or* kyo͝or′ə-tər) *n.* A person who manages an exhibition or collection at a museum or library.

curb (kûrb) *n.* **1.** A concrete or stone border along the edge of a street: *Don't trip over the curb!* **2.** Something that checks or restrains: *a curb on spending.* **3.** A chain or strap used together with a bit to restrain a horse. ❖ *tr.v.* **curbed, curb·ing, curbs** To check, restrain, or control: *curb one's temper.*

curb·ing (kûr′bĭng) *n.* **1.** The material used to construct a curb. **2.** A curb.

curb·side (kûrb′sīd′) *n.* The side of a pavement or street bordered by a curb. ❖ *adj.* Located or occurring at or along the sidewalk or curb: *curbside trash collection; curbside check-in of luggage at the airport.*

curb·stone (kûrb′stōn′) *n.* A stone or row of stones used to make up a curb.

curd (kûrd) *n.* **1.** The thick part of milk that separates from the whey and is used to make cheese. **2.** A lumpy liquid that resembles curd.

cur·dle (kûr′dl) *v.* **cur·dled, cur·dling, cur·dles** *—intr.* **1.** To form into curd: *The milk curdled overnight.* **2.** To seem to thicken and stop running, as because of fear or shock: *My blood curdled at the scream in the night.* *—tr.* To cause to form into curd: *You'll curdle the milk if you leave it out too long.*

cure (kyo͝or) *n.* **1.** Restoration of health; recovery from illness: *The patient returned to work soon after her cure.* **2.** A medical treatment or a series of such treatments used to restore health: *Penicillin is used as a cure for infections.* **3.** Something that restores health or improves a condition: *A trip was the perfect cure for overwork.* ❖ *v.* **cured, cur·ing, cures** *—tr.* **1.** To restore to health: *Strong medicine cured the patient quickly.* **2.** To bring about a recovery from: *cure an infection.* **3.** To remove (a harmful condition or influence): *cure a social problem.* **4.** To use a chemical, physical, or natural process in preparing, preserving, or finishing (a substance or material): *cure fish in a smokehouse; cure leather by tanning it.* *—intr.* **1.** To be or become restored to good health: *The patient cured quickly with the new treatment.* **2.** To be prepared, preserved, or finished by a chemical or physical process: *The fish cured in the sun.* [From Middle English, from Latin *cūra*, medical treatment.]

cu·ré (kyo͞o-rā′ *or* kyo͝or′ā′) *n.* A parish priest.

cure-all (kyo͝or′ôl′) *n.* Something that cures all diseases or ills; a panacea.

cur·few (kûr′fyo͞o) *n.* **1.** A regulation requiring certain people to be off the streets and indoors at a certain hour. **2.** The time at which such a regulation is in effect: *a 10 PM curfew.* **3.** The signal, such as the ringing of a bell, announcing the beginning of this regulation. [From Middle English *curfeu*, from Old French *cuevrefeu* : *covrir*, to cover + *feu*, fire.]

cu·rie (kyo͝or′ē *or* kyo͞o-rē′) *n.* A unit for measuring the intensity of radioactivity. In 1975, the curie was replaced by the becquerel as the standard unit of radioactivity. [After Marie *Curie*.]

Cu·rie (kyo͝or′ē *or* kyo͞o-rē′), **Marie** 1867–1934. Polish-born French chemist noted for her pioneering research in radioactivity and her discovery and study of radium and polonium. —SEE NOTE.

cu·ri·o (kyo͝or′ē-ō′) *n., pl.* **cu·ri·os** A rare or unusual object: *a cupboard filled with miniature teapots and other curios.*

cu·ri·os·i·ty (kyo͝or′ē-ŏs′ĭ-tē) *n., pl.* **cu·ri·os·i·ties** **1.** A desire to know or learn: *She was full of curiosity over who had sent the letter.* **2.** Something unusual or extraordinary: *The explorer brought back many curiosities from his travels.*

cu·ri·ous (kyo͝or′ē-əs) *adj.* **1.** Eager to learn more: *curious detectives.* **2.** Arousing interest because of strangeness: *We found a curious shell at the beach.* [From Middle English, from Latin *cūriōsus*, careful, inquisitive, from *cūra*, care.] **—cu′ri·ous·ly** *adv.* **—cu′ri·ous·ness** *n.*

cu·ri·um (kyo͝or′ē-əm) *n.* *Symbol* **Cm** A radioactive element that has been artificially produced by scientists. The half-life of its most stable isotope is about 15.6 million years. Atomic number 96. See **Periodic Table.** [After Marie *Curie* and Pierre *Curie* (1859–1906), French chemists.]

curl (kûrl) *v.* **curled, curl·ing, curls** *—tr.* **1.** To twist or form into coils or ringlets: *curl one's hair.* **2.** To make curved or twisted: *I curled the string around a pencil.* *—intr.* **1.** To form ringlets or curls: *Her hair curls when it dries.* **2.** To move in a curve or spiral: *Smoke curled from the chimney.* ❖ *n.* **1.** A coil or ringlet of hair. **2.** Something with a spiral or coiled shape: *a curl of smoke.* **3.** A weightlifting exercise in which a barbell is raised to the chest or shoulder and lowered without moving the upper arms, shoulders, or back. ◆ **curl up** To sit or lie down with the legs drawn up: *He curled up on the sofa to read.*

curl·er (kûr′lər) *n.* A pin or roller on which strands of hair are wound for curling.

cur·lew (kûrl′yo͞o *or* kûr′lo͞o) *n.* Any of several shorebirds that have brownish feathers, long legs, and a long downward-curving bill.

curl·i·cue (kûr′lĭ-kyo͞o′) *n.* A fancy twist or curl, such as a flourish in a signature.

curl·ing (kûr′lĭng) *n.* A game played on ice in which two teams of four players slide heavy rounded stones toward a mark in the center of a circle.

curling iron *n.* A rod-shaped metal tool that is electrically heated in order to curl the hair.

curl·y (kûr′lē) *adj.* **curl·i·er, curl·i·est** **1.** Having curls or tending to curl: *curly hair.* **2.** Having a wavy grain or markings: *curly maple wood.* **—curl′i·ness** *n.*

cur·mudg·eon (kər-mŭj′ən) *n.* An ill-tempered person, especially one who is older. **—cur·mudg′eon·ly** *adj.*

cur·rant (kûr′ənt) *n.* **1a.** The small, usually red or black fruit of any of various shrubs, used especially for making jelly. **b.** A shrub that bears such fruit. **2.** A seedless raisin, used chiefly in baking. [From Middle English *(reisins of) corauns*, (raisins of) Corinth, currant.]

❏ *These sound alike:* **currant, current** (belonging to the present time).

cur·ren·cy (kûr′ən-sē) *n., pl.* **cur·ren·cies** **1.** Money in any form when in actual use in a country: *US currency is in dollars, and Japanese currency is in yen.* **2.** General acceptance or use: *Many slang words and expressions have currency for only a short time.* **3.** A passing from one person to another; circulation: *By spreading gossip, people give currency to rumors.* **4.** The state of being current; up-to-dateness: *Can you check the currency of this address?*

cur·rent (kûr′ənt) *adj.* **1.** Belonging to the present time; present-day: *current events; my current address.* **2.** Commonly accepted or used; prevalent: *Cell phones are increasingly current throughout the world.* **3.** Passing from one to another; circulating, as money or a rumor. ❖ *n.*

Marie Curie

BIOGRAPHY

Marie Curie Marie Curie was the first woman to win a Nobel prize (in 1903) and the first person to win a second Nobel prize (1911). The first award, which she shared with her husband Pierre and another scientist, was for her investigation of radioactivity (a word she coined). This work changed scientists' view of the nature of the atom, showing that it was made of small particles that could be emitted as powerful rays. The second award was for her discovery of the elements polonium (named for her native country, Poland) and radium. Marie Curie later founded the Radium Institute in France and advocated the use of radium for medical purposes. The dark side of radiation cut short her own life, however; she died at the age of 67 from the effects of years of exposure to radium.

curling

SCIENCE

current You listen to your portable music player thanks to direct **current,** but you turn on the lights thanks to alternating current. *Direct current,* or *DC,* is electricity that flows at a constant voltage directly from a source, such as a battery with a stored electric charge. Batteries are great when you're on the move, but DC has a fundamental problem: it tends to waste a significant portion of its current as heat. *Alternating current,* or *AC,* on the other hand, is what flows from outlets in your walls. It can be transmitted at very high voltage over long distances with little heat loss, and the voltage can be efficiently reduced to a low, safe level for home use. AC's name reflects the fact that the current alternates its direction of flow. One complete period of flow first in one direction and then in the reverse direction is called a *cycle.* On average, the power system in the United States operates at 60 cycles per second and delivers about 120 volts from an ordinary outlet. Other countries have different AC standards. That's why when you travel, you often need to use an adapter when you plug in electric appliances.

ă	pat	ôr	core
ā	pay	oi	boy
âr	care	ou	out
ä	father	o͝o	took
ĕ	pet	o͝or	lure
ē	be	o͞o	boot
ĭ	pit	ŭ	cut
ī	bite	ûr	urge
îr	pier	th	thin
ŏ	pot	*th*	this
ō	toe	zh	vision
ô	paw	ə	about

1. A mass of liquid or gas that is in motion: *a current of cool air flowing through the room.* **2a.** A flow of electric charge. **b.** The amount of electric charge that passes a point in a unit of time, usually expressed in amperes. **3.** A general tendency or movement, as of events or opinions: *The current of voter opinion supports the president.* [From Middle English *curraunt,* from Old French *corant,* present participle of *courre,* to run, from Latin *currere.*] —SEE NOTE.

❑ *These sound alike:* **current, currant** (fruit).

cur·rent·ly (kûr′ənt-lē) *adv.* At the time now passing; at present: *a movie currently showing at the theater.*

cur·ric·u·lum (kə-rĭk′yə-ləm) *n., pl.* **cur·ric·u·la** (kə-rĭk′yə-lə) or **cur·ric·u·lums** A set of courses of study offered at a particular educational institution or department: *The school has recently updated its science curriculum.* [From Latin *curriculum,* course, from *currere,* to run.] **—cur·ric′u·lar** *adj.*

cur·ry¹ (kûr′ē) *tr.v.* **cur·ried, cur·ry·ing, cur·ries** To groom (a horse) with a currycomb. ◆ **curry favor** To seek or gain favor by flattery: *The new worker tried to curry favor with the boss.* [From Middle English *curreien,* from Anglo-Norman *curreier.*]

cur·ry² (kûr′ē) *n., pl.* **cur·ries 1.** Curry powder. **2.** A pungent sauce or dish seasoned with curry powder: *We ate lamb curry for dinner.* ❖ *tr.v.* **cur·ried, cur·ry·ing, cur·ries** To season (food) with curry powder. [From Tamil *kaṟi.*]

cur·ry·comb (kûr′ē-kōm′) *n.* A comb with plastic or metal teeth used for grooming horses. ❖ *tr.v.* **cur·ry·combed, cur·ry·comb·ing, cur·ry·combs** To curry (a horse).

curry powder *n.* A pungent seasoning prepared from cumin, coriander, turmeric, and other spices.

curse (kûrs) *n.* **1.** A remark or prayer that expresses a wish for evil or harm to happen to a person or thing: *The sorcerer placed a curse on the royal family.* **2.** A coarse or profane utterance; a swearword. **3.** Something that causes great evil or harm; a scourge: *The royal family was destroyed by the curse of madness.* ❖ *v.* **cursed** or **curst** (kûrst), **curs·ing, curs·es** *—tr.* **1.** To wish evil or harm on (a person, for example) with a curse. **2.** To bring great harm to; afflict: *The farmers were cursed with bad weather at harvest time.* **3.** To swear at: *The driver cursed the traffic in front of him.* *—intr.* To utter swearwords. [From Old English *curs.*]

cur·sive (kûr′sĭv) *adj.* Written or printed with connected letters; flowing: *cursive handwriting.* ❖ *n.* A cursive character or letter. —SEE NOTE.

cur·sor (kûr′sər) *n.* A movable indicator, such as a thin bar or small square, on a computer screen that marks the position where a character can be entered or deleted or where an option can be selected.

cur·so·ry (kûr′sə-rē) *adj.* Hasty and superficial; not thorough: *A cursory search of the file showed that many folders were out of order.* **—cur′so·ri·ly** *adv.*

curst (kûrst) *v.* A past tense and a past participle of **curse.** ❖ *adj.* Variant of **cursed.**

curt (kûrt) *adj.* **curt·er, curt·est** Rudely brief and abrupt in speech or manner; brusque: *My former friend gave me a curt nod as we passed.* **—curt′ly** *adv.* **—curt′ness** *n.*

cur·tail (kər-tāl′) *tr.v.* **cur·tailed, cur·tail·ing, cur·tails** To cut short; reduce: *We had to curtail our spending on the rest of the trip.* **—cur·tail′ment** *n.*

cur·tain (kûr′tn) *n.* **1.** Cloth or other material hanging in a window or door as a decoration, shade, or screen: *The wind was blowing the curtains at the open window.* **2.** Something that acts as a screen or cover: *mountains hidden by a thick curtain of fog.* **3.** The movable cloth or screen in a theater that separates the stage from the audience. **4.** The time at which a theatrical performance begins or is scheduled to begin. ❖ *tr.v.* **cur·tained, cur·tain·ing, cur·tains** To provide or shut off with or as if with a curtain. [From Middle English *curtein,* from Late Latin *cōrtīna.*]

curt·sy or **curt·sey** (kûrt′sē) *n., pl.* **curt·sies** or **curt·seys** A gesture of respect made chiefly by women by bending the knees with one foot forward and lowering the body. ❖ *intr.v.* **curt·sied, curt·sy·ing, curt·sies** or **curt·seyed, curt·sey·ing, curt·seys** To make a curtsy: *The singer curtsied before the audience.* [Variant of *courtesy.*]

cur·va·ture (kûr′və-cho͝or′ *or* kûr′və-chər) *n.* **1a.** The act of curving or the condition of being curved: *the curvature of the moon's orbit.* **b.** The degree to which something is curved: *a slight curvature in several warped boards.* **2.** A curving or bending of a body part, especially when abnormal: *curvature of the spine.*

curve (kûrv) *n.* **1.** A line or surface that bends in a smooth continuous way without sharp angles. **2.** Something that has the shape of a curve: *a curve in the road.* **3.** In baseball, a curve ball. ❖ *v.* **curved, curv·ing, curves** *—intr.* To move in or take the shape of a curve: *The ball curved to the right. The road curves sharply just ahead.* *—tr.* To cause to curve: *curve a metal band.* [From Middle English *curve,* curved, from Latin *curvus.*]

curve ball or **curve·ball** (kûrv′bôl′) *n.* **1.** A pitched baseball that veers to one side as it nears the batter. **2.** Something that is unexpected or designed to trick or deceive: *The last question on the exam was a curve ball—only one student got it right.*

cush·ion (ko͝osh′ən) *n.* **1.** A pad or pillow with a soft filling, used to sit, lie, or rest on. **2.** Something used as a rest, support, or shock absorber. **3.** Something shaped like or used as a cushion: *He slept on a cushion of spruce boughs.* **4.** Something used to lessen a bad effect: *We have a savings account as a cushion against hard times.* **5.** The raised rim that borders the playing surface of a billiard table. ❖ *tr.v.* **cush·ioned, cush·ion·ing, cush·ions 1.** To place or seat on a cushion: *The cat cushioned itself on our pillows.* **2.** To furnish with a cushion or cushions: *Soft pillows cushioned the chair.* **3.** To lessen or soften the impact of: *My thick coat cushioned the fall.*

cusp (kŭsp) *n.* A pointed end or rounded projection, as on the crescent moon or a tooth. ◆ **on the cusp** At the point where something is about to begin or change: *an actor on the cusp of a successful career.*

cus·pid (kŭs′pĭd) *n.* A tooth having a single cusp; a canine.

cus·pi·dor (kŭs′pĭ-dôr′) *n.* A spittoon.

cuss (kŭs) *Informal intr. & tr.v.* **cussed, cuss·ing, cuss·es** To curse. ❖ *n.* **1.** An odd or perverse person: *an unpleasant cuss.* **2.** A curse.

cus·tard (kŭs′tərd) *n.* A pudding of milk, sugar, eggs, and flavoring that is baked or boiled.

Cus·ter (kŭs′tər), **George Armstrong** 1839–1876. American soldier. He was killed by Sioux and Cheyenne led by Sitting Bull and Crazy Horse at the Battle of Little Bighorn in southern Montana (1876).

cus·to·di·an (kŭ-stō′dē-ən) *n.* **1.** A person who has charge of something; a caretaker or guardian: *the custodian of a museum collection.* **2.** A person who takes care of a building; a janitor.

cus·to·dy (kŭs′tə-dē) *n., pl.* **cus·to·dies 1.** Supervision; care: *The children were in the custody of their aunt and uncle while their parents were away.* **2.** The condition of being detained or held under guard, especially by the police: *The suspect was held in custody for questioning.*

cus·tom (kŭs′təm) *n.* **1.** An accepted practice or usual way followed by people of a particular group or region: *Shaking hands when meeting someone is a traditional custom.* **2.** A usual practice of an individual; a habit: *Their custom is to go to bed early.* See Synonyms at **habit. 3. customs a.** Duties or taxes imposed on goods imported from another country: *There were no customs due on our purchases on this trip.* **b.** *(used with a singular verb)* The government agency that collects these duties and inspects imported goods. **c.** *(used with a singular verb)* The place where goods and baggage entering a country are inspected by this agency: *We got through customs quickly.* ❖ *adj.* **1.** Made to order: *custom suits made to the instructions of the buyer.* **2.** Making or selling things to order: *a custom tailor.* [From Middle English *custume*, from Latin *cōnsuētūdo*.]

cus·tom·ar·y (**kŭs′**tə-mĕr′ē) *adj.* Established by custom; usual; habitual: *The customary place for a judge to sit is at the head of a courtroom.* **—cus′tom·ar′i·ly** (kŭs′tə-**mâr′**ə-lē) *adv.*

cus·tom-built (**kŭs′**təm-**bĭlt′**) *adj.* Built according to the specifications of the buyer: *custom-built cabinets.*

cus·tom·er (**kŭs′**tə-mər) *n.* **1.** A person who buys goods or services, especially on a regular basis. **2.** *Informal* A person with whom one must deal: *a tough customer.*

cus·tom·house (**kŭs′**təm-hous′) also **cus·toms·house** (**kŭs′**təmz-hous′) *n.* A government building where customs duties are collected and ships are given permission to enter and leave a country.

cus·tom·ize (**kŭs′**tə-mīz′) *tr.v.* **cus·tom·ized, cus·tom·iz·ing, cus·tom·iz·es** To make or alter to suit an individual.

cus·tom-made (kŭs′təm-**mād′**) *adj.* Made according to the specifications of the buyer: *custom-made draperies.*

cut (kŭt) *v.* **cut, cut·ting, cuts** *—tr.* **1.** To make an opening in with a sharp edge or instrument: *I cut my finger on a piece of broken glass.* **2.** To separate or divide by using a sharp instrument: *cut paper with scissors.* **3.** To separate from the main body of something; detach: *cut a limb from a tree.* **4.** To pass through or across; cross: *The path cuts the neighbor's yard.* **5.** To shorten; trim: *cut hair; cut the lawn.* **6.** To make or shape by using a sharp instrument: *I cut a hole in the board. I cut a doll from the paper.* **7.** To reap; harvest: *cut wheat.* **8.** To cause to fall by sawing: *Each year loggers cut millions of trees.* **9.** To have (a new tooth) grow through the gums: *The baby cut two new teeth last week.* **10.** To interrupt or stop: *A bad storm cut our electric power for two hours.* **11.** To reduce the size or amount of: *The governor cut taxes.* **12.** To lessen the strength of; dilute: *The waiter cut the strong iced tea by adding water.* **13.** To eliminate; remove: *The director cut several scenes from the play.* **14.** To edit (film or audio tape). **15.** To remove (a segment) from a computer document or graphics file for storage in a buffer. **16.** To hurt the feelings of: *Their unfriendly remarks cut me deeply.* **17.** *Informal* To fail to attend purposely: *I cut my rehearsal today.* **18.** To divide (a deck of cards) in two, as before dealing. *—intr.* **1.** To make an opening or separation: *The knife cut right through the rind. Swirling water cut under the rocks.* **2.** To allow an opening or severing: *Butter cuts easily.* **3.** To be like a sharp instrument: *The cold wind cut through my thin jacket.* **4a.** To go by a short or direct route: *cut across the park to get home quickly.* **b.** To go across; cross: *This road cuts through the mountains.* **5.** To change direction abruptly: *The driver suddenly cut to the right.* **6.** To divide a deck of cards into two: *The dealer cuts first.* ❖ *n.* **1.** The result of cutting; an opening or a wound. **2.** A blow or stroke, as with an axe: *The tree fell with a few cuts of the axe.* **3.** A part that has been cut from a main body or part: *an expensive cut of beef; a cut of cloth.* **4.** A passage made by excavating or drilling: *The highway runs through a cut in the mountain.* **5.** A removal of a part: *He made several cuts in the speech.* **6.** A reduction: *had to take a cut in pay.* **7.** The style in which a garment is cut: *The fine cut of my suit made it fit well.* **8.** *Informal* A share of profits or earnings: *The salesman got a 5 percent cut at the end of the year.* **9.** A wounding remark; an insult: *That was an unkind cut you directed at me.* **10.** A transition from one scene to another in a film, video, or television program. **11a.** An engraved block or plate. **b.** A print made from such a block: *old cuts of life along the Mississippi River.* ◆ **cut back 1.** To shorten by cutting; prune: *cut back a tree limb.* **2.** To reduce or decrease: *cut back prices in a sale.* **cut down 1.** To kill or strike down: *The cannon fire cut down the charging troops.* **2.** To reduce or curtail: *cut down one's spending.* **cut in 1.** To move into a line of people or things out of turn: *The truck cut in at the head of the line for the tollbooth.* **2.** To interrupt: *cut in on our conversation.* **3.** To interrupt a dancing couple in order to dance with one of them. **cut it** *Informal* To be or perform up to expectations or a standard; be acceptable. **cut off 1.** To stop suddenly; shut off or discontinue: *cut off the electricity.* **2.** To disinherit: *The rich landowner will cut off most of the family without a cent.* **3.** To separate or isolate: *We were cut off from the mainland during the storm.* **cut out 1.** To remove by cutting: *cut out a long sentence from the paragraph.* **2.** To form or shape by cutting: *cut out pieces for a coat.* **3.** To assign or determine as necessary: *I have my work cut out for me.* **4.** To be suited: *Many people are not cut out for city life.* **5.** To stop; cease: *Cut out the noise right now!* **6.** To deprive or disinherit: *cut a relative out of a will.* **cut up** *Informal* To behave in a playful or noisy way; clown. [From Middle English *cutten*.]

cut-and-dried (kŭt′n-**drīd′**) also **cut-and-dry** (kŭt′n-**drī′**) *adj.* **1.** Prepared and arranged in advance: *There are no cut-and-dried rules for good writing.* **2.** Lacking freshness or imagination; ordinary: *His advice was full of cut-and-dried old phrases.*

cu·ta·ne·ous (kyo͞o-**tā′**nē-əs) *adj.* Relating to or affecting the skin: *cutaneous blood vessels.*

cut·back (**kŭt′**băk′) *n.* A decrease; a curtailment: *a cutback in government spending.*

cute (kyo͞ot) *adj.* **cut·er, cut·est 1.** Delightfully pretty or dainty: *a cute puppy.* **2.** Attractive; good-looking: *a cute boyfriend.* **3.** Witty or clever, especially in a teasing or disrespectful way: *made a remark that was a little too cute.* [Short for *acute*.] **—cute′ly** *adv.* **—cute′ness** *n.*

cu·ti·cle (**kyo͞o′**tĭ-kəl) *n.* **1.** The waxy outer surface of a plant. **2.** The hard skin around the sides and base of a fingernail or toenail.

cut·lass also **cut·las** (**kŭt′**ləs) *n.* A heavy sword with a curved single-edged blade. [From Old French *coutelasse*, from Latin *cultellus*, small knife.]

cut·ler·y (**kŭt′**lə-rē) *n.* **1.** Knives, forks, and spoons used as tableware. **2.** Cutting instruments and tools, such as knives and scissors.

cut·let (**kŭt′**lĭt) *n.* **1.** A thin slice of meat, as of veal, cut from the leg or ribs. **2.** A patty of chopped meat or fish. [From Old French *costelette*, diminutive of *coste*, rib, from Latin *costa*.]

cut·off (**kŭt′**ôf′) *n.* **1.** An indicated limit or stopping point: *Saturday is the cutoff for new job applications.* **2.** The act or an instance of cutting something off: *a cutoff of electricity.* **3.** A device used to stop a flow, as of a liquid or gas: *That valve is the cutoff for our water.* **4.** A shortcut or bypass: *use the cutoff through the park.* **5. cutoffs** Pants made into shorts by cutting off part of the legs. ❖ *adj.* Indicating a limit or deadline: *a cutoff date.*

cut·out (**kŭt′**out′) *n.* **1.** Something cut out or intended to be cut out from something else: *cutouts of paper dolls.* **2.** A device that acts as a bypass or cutoff, especially in an electric circuit.

cut-rate (**kŭt′rāt′**) *adj.* Sold or on sale at a reduced price.

cut·ter (**kŭt′**ər) *n.* **1.** A worker whose job involves cutting some material, such as cloth, glass, or stone. **2.** A cutting device or machine: *a cookie cutter.* **3.** A small, lightly armed boat used by the Coast Guard. **4.** A ship's boat, powered by a motor or pulled with oars, used for

WORD BUILDING

cursive Words in English having the elements *cur–, curr–,* and *curs–* all go back to the Latin verb *currere* (past participle *cursus*), "to run." **Cursive** handwriting is therefore literally "running" script, as opposed to printed letters that do not run together in a continuous line. If two people **concur,** they "run together" or agree. An army that makes an **incursion** into a country is literally "running into" it, while a **precursor** is something that "runs before or ahead of" something else. The **currents** of a river or ocean are the parts of it that "run" in a particular direction, as are—figuratively speaking—the currents of the times or of politics.

George Armstrong Custer

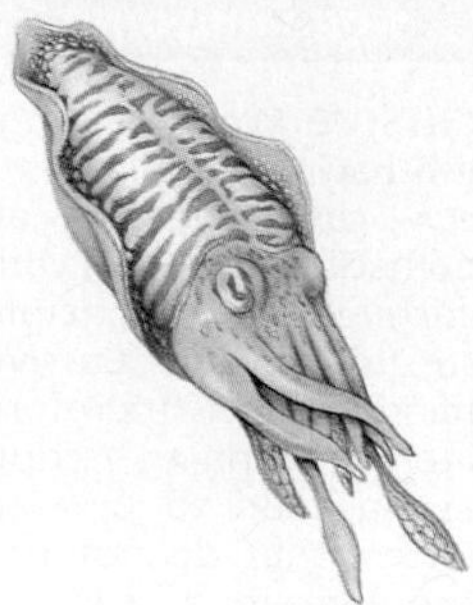
cuttlefish

cyclamen

transporting stores or passengers. **5.** A fast single-masted sailing vessel.

cut·throat (kŭt′thrōt′) *n.* A murderer, especially one who cuts throats. ❖ *adj.* **1.** Cruel; murderous: *a cutthroat band of thieves.* **2.** Ruthless or merciless in competition: *a cutthroat business.*

cut·ting (kŭt′ĭng) *adj.* **1.** Capable of or designed for cutting: *a cutting blade.* **2.** Injuring the feelings of others; insulting: *a cutting remark.* ❖ *n.* **1.** A part cut off from a main body: *cuttings and scrapings.* **2.** A stem, twig, or leaf removed from a plant and placed in soil, sand, or water to form roots and develop into a new plant.

cutting edge *n.* The position of greatest advancement or innovation; the forefront: *medical research on the cutting edge.*

cut·tle·bone (kŭt′l-bōn′) *n.* The chalky shell inside the body of a cuttlefish, used to supply calcium to caged birds or as a mold for metal casting.

cut·tle·fish (kŭt′l-fĭsh′) *n.* Any of various sea mollusks related to the squids and octopuses, having eight arms and two tentacles, a chalky internal shell, and the ability to squirt a dark inky liquid when frightened.

cut·up (kŭt′ŭp′) *n. Informal* A mischievous person.

cut·worm (kŭt′wûrm′) *n.* Any of various moth caterpillars that damage crops, often by cutting through plant stems at the soil surface.

cwt *abbr.* An abbreviation of hundredweight.

–cy *suff.* A suffix that means: **1.** State; condition; quality: *bankruptcy.* **2.** Rank; office: *captaincy.*

cy·a·nide (sī′ə-nīd′) *n.* Any of a large group of salts and esters containing a chemical unit with carbon and nitrogen bonded to each other, especially the very poisonous salts sodium cyanide and potassium cyanide. Cyanides are used in making plastics and extracting and treating metals. [From Greek *kuanos*, dark blue.]

cy·a·no·bac·te·ri·um (sī′ə-nō-băk-tîr′ē-əm) *n., pl.* **cy·a·no·bac·te·ri·a** (sī′ə-nō-băk-tîr′ē-ə) Any of various bacteria that are blue-green in color and are capable of photosynthesis. Cyanobacteria are usually found in water.

cyber– *pref.* A prefix that means computer or computer network: *cyberspace.*

cy·ber·bul·ly (sī′bər-bo͝ol′ē) *n., pl.* **cy·ber·bul·lies** A person who engages in cyberbullying.

cy·ber·bul·ly·ing (sī′bər-bo͝ol′ē-ĭng) *n.,* The use of computer networks and other forms of digital communication, such as text messages or social networks, to bully a person or people.

cy·ber·ca·fe (sī′bər-kă-fā′) *n.* **1.** A cafe from which customers can access the Internet. **2.** A chatroom.

cy·ber·cast (sī′bər-kăst′) *n.* A news or entertainment program transmitted over the Internet.

cy·ber·net·ics (sī′bər-nĕt′ĭks) *n. (used with a singular verb)* The theoretical study of communication and control processes in biological, mechanical, and electronic systems. [From Greek *kubernētēs*, governor, from *kubernān*, to steer.]

cy·ber·space (sī′bər-spās′) *n.* The interconnected system of computer networks in which online communication takes place.

cy·borg (sī′bôrg′) *n.* In science fiction, a person who has a built-in mechanical or electronic device that controls or enhances a part of the body, especially the brain.

cy·cad (sī′kăd′ *or* sī′kəd) *n.* Any of various tropical evergreen plants that bear cones and have large leaves that resemble those of a palm tree.

cy·cla·men (sī′klə-mən *or* sĭk′lə-mən) *n.* Any of various plants having heart-shaped leaves and showy pink, red, or white flowers with petals that are turned outward.

cy·cle (sī′kəl) *n.* **1a.** A series of events that is periodically repeated: *New moon and full moon are two phases of the moon's cycle.* **b.** The time during which such a series of events occurs: *The moon's appearance changes daily throughout its cycle of 29.5 days.* **2.** A set of poems or stories about a central theme or hero: *the Arthurian cycle.* **3.** A bicycle, motorcycle, or similar vehicle. ❖ *intr.v.* **cy·cled, cy·cling, cy·cles 1.** To occur in or pass through a cycle: *The earth cycles through the seasons every year.* **2.** To ride a bicycle, motorcycle, or similar vehicle. [From Middle English *cicle*, from Greek *kuklos*, circle.]

cy·clic (sĭk′lĭk *or* sī′klĭk) or **cy·cli·cal** (sĭk′lĭ-kəl *or* sī′klĭ-kəl) *adj.* **1.** Relating to or occurring in cycles: *the cyclic motion of the tides; a cyclical weather pattern.* **2.** Relating to or containing an arrangement of atoms in a ring or closed chain.

cy·cling (sī′klĭng) *n.* The act or sport of riding or racing on a bicycle, motorcycle, or similar vehicle.

cy·clist (sī′klĭst) *n.* A person who rides a bicycle, motorcycle, or similar vehicle.

cy·clone (sī′klōn′) *n.* **1.** A system of winds spiraling inward around a region of low atmospheric pressure, often producing storms. In the Southern Hemisphere the winds circle clockwise, while in the Northern Hemisphere they circle counterclockwise. **2.** A violent rotating windstorm, such as a hurricane or tornado. [From Greek *kuklōn*, moving in a circle, from *kuklos*, circle.] **—cy·clon′ic** (sī-klŏn′ĭk) *adj.*

Cy·clops (sī′klŏps) *n., pl.* **Cy·clo·pes** (sī-klō′pēz) In Greek mythology, any of a race of giants having one eye in the middle of the forehead.

cy·clo·tron (sī′klə-trŏn′) *n.* A device that uses alternating electric and magnetic fields to accelerate charged subatomic particles, such as protons and electrons, in an outwardly spiraling path. Cyclotrons are used to bring about high-speed particle collisions in order to study subatomic structures.

cyg·net (sĭg′nĭt) *n.* A young swan.

❑ *These sound alike:* **cygnet, signet** (seal).

cyl·in·der (sĭl′ən-dər) *n.* **1.** A solid figure bounded by a curved surface and two parallel circles of equal size at the ends. The curved surface is formed by all the line segments joining corresponding points of the two parallel circles. In a right circular cylinder the circles are perpendicular to the line segments; in an oblique circular cylinder they are not. **2.** An object or container, such as a can, having such a shape. **3.** The chamber in which a piston moves up and down, as in an engine or pump. **4.** The rotating chamber of a revolver that holds the cartridges. [From Greek *kulindros*.]

cy·lin·dri·cal (sə-lĭn′drĭ-kəl) also **cy·lin·dric** (sə-lĭn′drĭk) *adj.* Relating to or having the shape of a cylinder. **—cy·lin′dri·cal·ly** *adv.*

cym·bal (sĭm′bəl) *n.* One or a pair of musical instruments made into the shape of a dish from coils of brass fused together. Cymbals are sounded either by striking two of them together or by hitting one with a drumstick or brush. [From Old English, from Greek *kumbalon*, from *kumbē*, bowl.]

❑ *These sound alike:* **cymbal, symbol** (sign).

cyme (sīm) *n.* A flower cluster in which the main stem and each branch end in a flower that opens before the flowers below or to the side of it.

cyn·ic (sĭn′ĭk) *n.* A person who is scornfully negative and believes that people act mostly out of selfishness. [From Greek *kunikos*, cynic philosopher, from *kuōn*, dog.] **—cyn′i·cal** *adj.* **—cyn′i·cal·ly** *adv.*

cyn·i·cism (sĭn′ĭ-sĭz′əm) *n.* A scornful attitude that comes from a deep distrust of the honesty and motives of others: *Recent scandals have increased cynicism about politics.*

cy·no·sure (sī′nə-sho͝or′ *or* sĭn′ə-sho͝or′) *n.* A center of attention or interest: *The early astronauts were the cynosure of the nation.*

cy·pher (sī′fər) *n. & v.* Variant of **cipher.**

ă	pat	ôr	core
ā	pay	oi	boy
âr	care	ou	out
ä	father	o͝o	took
ĕ	pet	o͝or	lure
ē	be	o͞o	boot
ĭ	pit	ŭ	cut
ī	bite	ûr	urge
îr	pier	th	thin
ŏ	pot	*th*	this
ō	toe	zh	vision
ô	paw	ə	about

cy·press (sī′prĭs) *n.* **1a.** Any of various evergreen trees chiefly of Eurasia and western North America, having small scalelike leaves and roundish cones. **b.** The hard wood of any of these trees, used in making shingles and doors. **2.** Any of several similar trees of the southern United States and Mexico that grow in wetlands and shed their needles each year.

Cyp·ri·ot (sĭp′rē-ət) also **Cyp·ri·ote** (sĭp′rē-ōt′) *adj.* Relating to Cyprus or its people, language, or culture. ❖ *n.* **1.** A native or inhabitant of Cyprus. **2.** The ancient Greek or modern Greek dialect of Cyprus.

Cy·prus (sī′prəs) An island country in the eastern Mediterranean Sea south of Turkey. The northern part of the island declared its independence from the rest of the country in 1983, a move that failed to gain international recognition. Nicosia is the capital of Cyprus.

Cy·ril·lic alphabet (sə-rĭl′ĭk) *n.* An alphabet derived from the Greek alphabet and used in writing Russian, Bulgarian, and several other languages of Eastern Europe and the former Soviet Union.

Cy·rus II (sī′rəs) Known as "Cyrus the Great." 600?–529? BC. King of Persia (550–529) and founder of the Persian Empire who conquered Lydia and Babylon.

cyst (sĭst) *n.* **1.** An abnormal sac in the body, composed of a membrane surrounding a fluid or a soft material. **2.** A protective capsule in which certain organisms enclose themselves during inactive or reproductive periods.

cys·te·ine (sĭs′tə-ēn′) *n.* A nonessential amino acid that is found in most proteins.

cys·tic (sĭs′tĭk) *adj.* **1.** Relating to or having the characteristics of a cyst: *a cystic growth.* **2.** Having, containing, or enclosed in a cyst: *a cystic stage of an organism's development.* **3.** Relating to or involving the gallbladder or urinary bladder.

cystic fi·bro·sis (fī-brō′sĭs) *n.* A hereditary disease that causes thick mucus to build up in certain organs of the body, such as the lungs and pancreas. It makes breathing and digesting food difficult, and it makes people more likely to get infections.

cys·ti·tis (sĭ-stī′tĭs) *n.* Inflammation of the urinary bladder.

cy·to·chrome (sī′tə-krōm′) *n.* Any of various proteins that are important in cell metabolism and respiration.

cy·to·ki·ne·sis (sī′tō-kə-nē′sĭs) *n.* The division of the cytoplasm of a cell following the division of the nucleus.

cy·tol·o·gy (sī-tŏl′ə-jē) *n.* The branch of biology that deals with the formation, structure, and function of cells. **—cy·tol′o·gist** *n.*

cy·to·plasm (sī′tə-plăz′əm) *n.* All the material enclosed by a cell membrane, excluding the nucleus. **—cy′to·plas′mic** *adj.*

cy·to·sine (sī′tə-sēn′) *n.* A base that is a component of DNA and RNA.

czar (zär *or* tsär) *n.* **1.** also **tsar** or **tzar** Any of the emperors who ruled Russia until the revolution of 1917. **2.** A person who has great authority or power: *The president named an energy czar to oversee the administration's energy policy.* [From Russian *tsar'*, from Latin *Caesar*, emperor.]

cza·ri·na (zä-rē′nə *or* tsä-rē′nə) *n.* The wife of a Russian czar.

czar·ist (zär′ĭst) *adj.* Relating to or in the time of the czars: *czarist Russia.*

cza·rit·za (zä-rĭt′sə *or* tsä-rēt′sə) *n.* Any of the empresses who ruled Russia until the revolution of 1917.

Czech (chĕk) *adj.* Relating to the Czech Republic or its people, language, or culture. ❖ *n.* **1.** A native or inhabitant of the Czech Republic or of Czechoslovakia. **2.** The Slavic language of the Czechs.

Czech·o·slo·va·ki·a (chĕk′ə-slə-vä′kē-ə) A former country of central Europe south of Poland. It was formed in 1918 and divided in 1993 into the Czech Republic and Slovakia. **—Czech′o·slo′vak, Czech′o·slo·va′ki·an** *adj.*

Czech Republic A landlocked country of central Europe north of Austria. It was part of Czechoslovakia from 1918 until 1993. Prague is the capital.

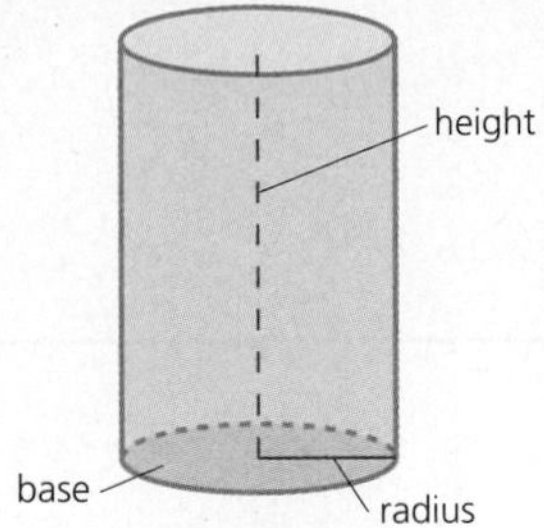

cylinder

To calculate the volume of a right circular cylinder, multiply the area of the base by the height.

D

daffodil

daguerreotype

ă	pat	ôr	core
ā	pay	oi	boy
âr	care	ou	out
ä	father	o͝o	took
ĕ	pet	o͝or	lure
ē	be	o͞o	boot
ĭ	pit	ŭ	cut
ī	bite	ûr	urge
îr	pier	th	thin
ŏ	pot	*th*	this
ō	toe	zh	vision
ô	paw	ə	about

d or **D** (dē) *n., pl.* **d's** or **D's** also **ds** or **Ds 1.** The fourth letter of the English alphabet. **2. D** The lowest passing grade in school. **3. D** In music, the second tone in the scale of C major.

D[1] also **d** The symbol for the Roman numeral 500.

D[2] *abbr.* An abbreviation of: **1.** day **2.** democrat.

d. *abbr.* An abbreviation of: **1.** date. **2.** daughter. **3.** died. **4.** *Chiefly British* penny (1/12 of a shilling).

DA *abbr.* An abbreviation of district attorney.

dab (dăb) *v.* **dabbed, dab·bing, dabs** —*tr.* **1.** To apply with short light strokes: *dabbed some paint on the worn spots.* **2.** To pat quickly and lightly, especially in covering with a moist substance: *dabbed his nose with sunscreen.* —*intr.* To make light patting or stroking motions: *dabbed at her eyes with a tissue.* ❖ *n.* **1.** A small amount: *a dab of butter.* **2.** A light poking stroke or pat: *a kitten making dabs at a string.*

dab·ble (dăb′əl) *v.* **dab·bled, dab·bling, dab·bles** —*tr.* To splash in and out of water: *The children dabbled their feet in the pool.* —*intr.* **1.** To splash or play in water: *The puppies dabbled in the stream.* **2.** To do or work on something casually or without serious intent: *I dabbled in photography for a time.* **—dab′bler** *n.*

dab hand *n.* A person skilled in a particular activity: *a dab hand at gardening.*

da ca·po (dä kä′pō) *adv.* In music, from the beginning. Used as a direction to repeat a section of a composition.

Dac·ca (dăk′ə *or* dä′kə) See **Dhaka.**

dace (dās) *n., pl.* **dace** or **dac·es** Any of various small freshwater fishes of Eurasia and North America, related to the minnows.

dachs·hund (däk′sənd *or* däk′sənt) *n.* A small dog of a breed developed in Germany for hunting badgers, having a long body, a dark coat, drooping ears, and very short legs. [From German : *Dachs*, badger + *Hund*, dog.]

dac·tyl (dăk′təl) *n.* In poetry, a metrical foot consisting of one accented syllable followed by two unaccented syllables, as in *flattery.*

dad (dăd) *n. Informal* Father.

dad·dy (dăd′ē) *n., pl.* **dad·dies** *Informal* Father.

daddy long·legs (lông′lĕgz′) *n., pl.* **daddy longlegs** Any of various spiderlike arachnids having a small rounded body and long slender legs.

da·do (dā′dō) *n., pl.* **da·does 1.** The section of a pedestal between the base and the crown or cap. **2.** The lower part of the wall of a room decorated with wooden panels or other material that is different from the rest of the wall.

Dae·da·lus (dĕd′l-əs) *n.* In Greek mythology, an artist and inventor who built the Labyrinth in Crete. He was imprisoned with his son Icarus and fashioned wings for them to escape by flying.

daf·fo·dil (dăf′ə-dĭl) *n.* A garden plant that grows from a bulb and has long slender leaves and showy, usually yellow flowers with a trumpet-shaped central part. [From Middle English *affodil*, from Latin *asphodelus*, asphodel.]

daf·fy (dăf′ē) *adj.* **daf·fi·er, daf·fi·est** *Informal* Silly or crazy: *That's a daffy idea.* **—daf′fi·ly** *adv.* **—daf′fi·ness** *n.*

daft (dăft) *adj.* **daft·er, daft·est 1.** Foolish; stupid: *a daft reply.* **2.** Crazy: *He must be daft!* **—daft′ly** *adv.* **—daft′ness** *n.*

dag·ger (dăg′ər) *n.* **1.** A short pointed weapon, used for stabbing. **2.** A dagger-shaped symbol (‡) often used as a reference to a footnote in a book or to some special category before a word in a list.

da·guerre·o·type (də-gâr′ə-tīp′) *n.* **1.** An early photographic process in which an image is formed on a silver-coated metal plate that is sensitive to light. **2.** A photograph made by this process. [After Louis *Daguerre* (1789–1851), French artist and inventor.]

dahl·ia (dăl′yə *or* däl′yə) *n.* Any of several garden plants having thick roots and showy flowers of various colors. [After Anders *Dahl* (1751–1787), Swedish botanist.]

Da·ho·mey (də-hō′mē) See **Benin** (sense 2).

dai·ly (dā′lē) *adj.* **1.** Done, happening, or appearing every day or weekday: *a daily walk.* **2.** For each day: *a daily record.* ❖ *adv.* Every day: *Exercise daily.* ❖ *n., pl.* **dai·lies** A newspaper published every day or every weekday.

dain·ty (dān′tē) *adj.* **dain·ti·er, dain·ti·est 1.** Delicately beautiful and usually small: *dainty slippers.* **2.** Very careful in choosing; fussy; finicky: *The cat is a dainty eater.* **3.** Delicious or choice; tasty: *a dainty dish of fancy sandwiches.* ❖ *n., pl.* **dain·ties** A choice delicious food; a delicacy. **—dain′ti·ly** *adv.* **—dain′ti·ness** *n.*

dair·y (dâr′ē) *n., pl.* **dair·ies 1.** A room or building where milk and cream are stored, prepared for use, or made into butter and cheese. **2.** A business or store that prepares or sells milk and milk products. **3.** A dairy farm. **4.** Food containing or based on milk: *How much dairy should you have in your diet?* ❖ *adj.* For or relating to milk or milk products. [From Middle English *daierie*, from *daie*, dairymaid, from Old English *dǣge*, bread kneader.]

dairy cattle *pl.n.* Cows bred and raised for milk rather than meat.

dairy farm *n.* A farm for producing milk and milk products.

dair·y·ing (dâr′ē-ĭng) *n.* The business of running a dairy or a dairy farm.

dair·y·maid (dâr′ē-mād′) *n.* A woman or girl who works in a dairy.

dair·y·man (dâr′ē-mən) *n.* A man who owns, manages, or works in a dairy.

dair·y·wom·an (dâr′ē-wo͝om′ən) *n.* A woman who owns, manages, or works in a dairy.

da·is (dā′ĭs *or* dī′ĭs) *n.* A raised platform for a throne, a speaker, or a group of honored guests.

dai·shi·ki (dī-shē′kē) *n.* Variant of **dashiki.**

dai·sy (dā′zē) *n., pl.* **dai·sies** Any of several plants having flowers with many narrow, usually white rays surrounding a flat, usually yellow center. [From Old English *dæges ēage* : *dæges*, of the day + *ēage*, eye.]

Da·kar (də-**kär′** *or* **dăk′**är′) The capital of Senegal, in the western part of the country on the Atlantic Ocean.

Da·ko·ta (də-**kō′**tə) *n., pl.* **Dakota** or **Da·ko·tas 1.** A member of any of the Sioux peoples, especially of the Santee branch. **2.** The Siouan language of the Dakota. **—Da·ko′tan** *adj. & n.*

Da·ko·tas (də-**kō′**təz) The states of North Dakota and South Dakota.

Da·lai La·ma (dä′lī **lä′**mə) *n.* The traditional leader of the dominant sect of Buddhism in Tibet and Mongolia. [From Tibetan : Mongolian *dalai*, ocean + Tibetan *bla-ma*, monk (so called because he is known as the ocean of compassion).]

da·la·si (dä-**lä′**sē) *n., pl.* **dalasi** The basic monetary unit of the Gambia.

dale (dāl) *n.* A valley.

Da·lit (**dä′**lĭt) *n.* A member of the lowest class in traditional Indian society. Dalits fall outside the Hindu caste categories and are subject to extensive social restrictions. [From Hindi, crushed, oppressed.]

Dal·las (**dăl′**əs) A city of northeast Texas north-northeast of Austin. It was founded in 1841.

dal·li·ance (**dăl′**ē-əns) *n.* **1.** Playful flirting. **2.** A brief romantic relationship. **3.** A brief involvement or interest in something: *a dalliance with radical ideas.*

dal·ly (**dăl′**ē) *intr.v.* **dal·lied, dal·ly·ing, dal·lies 1.** To spend time doing something in a careless or unserious fashion: *For a while she dallied with the notion of becoming a dancer.* **2.** To waste time; dawdle: *Don't dally or we'll miss the train.* **3.** To flirt playfully: *We saw the two friends dallying during lunch.*

Dal·ma·tian (dăl-**mā′**shən) *n.* A dog of a large breed having a short smooth white coat with many small black spots.

dam[1] (dăm) *n.* A barrier across a waterway to control the flow or raise the level of the water. ❖ *tr.v.* **dammed, dam·ming, dams 1.** To hold back by means of a dam: *Engineers dammed the river.* **2.** To hold back or restrain: *dam up emotions.* [From Middle English.]

❑ *These sound alike:* **dam**[1] (barrier), **dam**[2] (female animal), **damn** (condemn).

dam[2] (dăm) *n.* The mother of an animal, especially a domesticated animal such as a horse. [From Middle English *dame*, from Latin *domina*, lady.]

❑ *These sound alike:* **dam**[2] (female animal), **dam**[1] (barrier), **damn** (condemn).

dam·age (**dăm′**ĭj) *n.* **1.** Destruction or loss in value, usefulness, or ability resulting from an action or event: *damage done to a car in an accident.* **2. damages** In law, money to be paid to make up for an injury or wrong: *sue for damages.* ❖ *tr.v.* **dam·aged, dam·ag·ing, dam·ag·es** To harm, hurt, or injure: *Some insects damage plants.* [From Middle English, from Latin *damnum*, financial loss.]

Da·mas·cus (də-**măs′**kəs) The capital of Syria, in the southwest part of the country southeast of Beirut, Lebanon. It has been inhabited since prehistoric times.

Damascus steel *n.* An early form of steel having fine wavy markings, developed in the Near East and used mainly for making sword blades.

dam·ask (**dăm′**əsk) *n.* **1.** A rich glossy fabric woven with patterns that show on both sides, such as a silk used for draperies or a linen used for tablecloths. **2.** Damascus steel.

dame (dām) *n.* **1.** Used formerly as a title for a woman in authority or a mistress of a household. **2.** *Chiefly British* **a.** A woman holding a nonhereditary title given by the queen or king to honor personal merit or service to the country. **b.** The wife or widow of a knight.

damn (dăm) *v.* **damned, damn·ing, damns** *—tr.* **1a.** To condemn to everlasting punishment in the afterlife. **b.** To cause (something) to fail; ruin: *Without money the project was damned.* **2.** To condemn (something) as being very bad: *Reviewers damned the new movie.* **3.** To swear at or curse at. *—intr.* To swear; curse. ❖ *interj.* An expression used to show anger, irritation, or disappointment. ❖ *adj. & adv. Informal* Very; damned: *a damn fool.* ❖ *n. Informal* The least bit; a jot: *not worth a damn.* [From Middle English *dampnen*, from Latin *damnāre*, to impose a fine on, pronounce guilty, from *damnum*, loss, fine.]

❑ *These sound alike:* **damn, dam**[1] (barrier), **dam**[2] (female animal).

dam·na·ble (**dăm′**nə-bəl) *adj.* Deserving to be strongly condemned; hateful: *a damnable traitor.* **—dam′na·bly** *adv.*

dam·na·tion (dăm-**nā′**shən) *n.* The act of damning or the condition of being damned to everlasting punishment.

damned (dămd) *adj.* **damned·er** (**dăm′**dər), **damned·est** (**dăm′**dĭst) **1.** In various religions, condemned to eternal punishment. **2.** Destined to an unhappy fate: *We're damned if we do, and damned if we don't.* **3.** *Informal* Dreadful; awful: *this damned weather.* **4.** Used as an intensive: *a damned fool.* ❖ *adv. Informal* Very; damn: *a damned good idea.*

Da·mon (**dā′**mən) *n.* A legendary Greek man who pledged his life as a guarantee that his condemned friend Pythias would return from arranging his affairs to face execution. Both Damon and Pythias were later pardoned.

damp (dămp) *adj.* **damp·er, damp·est** Slightly wet; moist; humid: *a damp towel; damp air.* See Synonyms at **wet.** ❖ *n.* **1.** Moisture in the air; humidity: *Don't go out in the damp.* **2.** A foul or poisonous gas that pollutes the air in a coal mine. ❖ *tr.v.* **damped, damp·ing, damps 1.** To make damp; moisten. **2.** To extinguish (a fire, for example) by cutting off air. **3.** To restrain or check: *He tried to damp down his anger.* [From Middle English *damp*, poison gas, perhaps from Middle Dutch, vapor.] **—damp′ly** *adv.* **—damp′ness** *n.*

damp·en (**dăm′**pən) *v.* **damp·ened, damp·en·ing, damp·ens** *—tr.* **1.** To moisten: *dampen a sponge.* **2.** To diminish or depress, as in strength or feeling: *The delay dampened their excitement.* *—intr.* To become damp. **—damp′en·er** *n.*

damp·er (**dăm′**pər) *n.* **1.** A movable plate in the flue of a furnace, stove, or fireplace for controlling the draft. **2.** A device for reducing or deadening vibrations, especially a pad that presses against the strings of a keyboard instrument. **3.** A depressing or restraining influence: *The rain put a damper on our vacation.*

dam·sel (**dăm′**zəl) *n.* A young woman or girl.

dam·sel·fly (**dăm′**zəl-flī′) *n.* Any of various often brightly colored insects related to the dragonflies, having a slender body and transparent wings that are folded together when at rest.

dam·son (**dăm′**zən *or* **dăm′**sən) *n.* **1.** A small, egg-shaped, dark-purple plum. **2.** A tree that bears such plums.

Dan (dăn) In the Bible, a son of Jacob and the ancestor of one of the tribes of Israel.

dance (dăns) *v.* **danced, danc·ing, danc·es** *—intr.* **1.** To move with rhythmic steps and motions, especially in time to music. **2.** To leap, skip, or prance about: *excited children dancing about the room.* **3.** To bob up and down: *Moonlight danced on the water.* *—tr.* **1.** To engage in or perform (a dance): *dance a waltz.* **2.** To cause to dance: *He danced her across the room.* ❖ *n.* **1.** A series of rhythmic steps and motions, usually performed to music. **2.** A social gathering at which people dance: *Are you going to*

Dalai Lama

dam[1]
Shasta Dam, near Redding, California

damask

WRITERS CHOOSE THEIR WORDS

He had never in his life felt so good. He felt as huge as the land around him and as clear and bright as the air. No laboring in **dank** tunnels here; no running through dark streets to escape pursuit. Now he was out in the open, free.

—Jeanne DuPrau
The People of Sparks

dappled

Darius I

ă	pat	ôr	core
ā	pay	oi	boy
âr	care	ou	out
ä	father	o͝o	took
ĕ	pet	o͝or	lure
ē	be	o͞o	boot
ĭ	pit	ŭ	cut
ī	bite	ûr	urge
îr	pier	th	thin
ŏ	pot	*th*	this
ō	toe	zh	vision
ô	paw	ə	about

the dance? **3.** One round or turn of dancing: *May I have this dance?* **4.** The art of dancing: *study dance at a ballet school.* **5.** A piece of music composed as an accompaniment for dancing or in a dance rhythm. [From Middle English *dauncen*, from Old French *danser*, perhaps of Germanic origin.]

danc·er (dăn′sər) *n.* A person who dances, especially as a performer.

dan·de·li·on (dăn′dl-ī′ən) *n.* A common weedy plant having bright yellow flowers and long notched leaves that are sometimes eaten in salads. After the flowers have bloomed, the ripe seeds form a fluffy rounded mass. [From Middle English *dent-de-lioun*, from Old French *dentdelion*, from Medieval Latin *dēns leōnis*, lion's tooth (from its sharply indented leaves).]

dan·der¹ (dăn′dər) *n. Informal* Temper or anger: *What got their dander up?* [Perhaps alteration of *dunder*, fermented cane juice used in rum-making, fermentation.]

dan·der² (dăn′dər) *n.* Tiny particles from the coat or feathers of various animals, sometimes causing allergies in humans. [Alteration of *dandruff*.]

dan·dle (dăn′dl) *tr.v.* **dan·dled, dan·dling, dan·dles** To move (a small child) up and down on the knee or in the arms in a playful way.

dan·druff (dăn′drəf) *n.* Small white scales of dead skin that are shed from the scalp.

dan·dy (dăn′dē) *n., pl.* **dan·dies 1.** A man who prides himself on his elegant clothes and fine appearance; a fop. **2.** Something very good of its kind: *This horse is a dandy.* ❖ *adj.* **dan·di·er, dan·di·est** Very good; fine; first-rate: *That's a dandy idea!*

Dane (dān) *n.* A native or inhabitant of Denmark.

dan·ger (dān′jər) *n.* **1.** The chance or risk of harm or destruction: *a house in danger of being swept into the sea.* **2.** A possible cause or chance of harm; a threat or hazard: *Fog is a danger to pilots.* [From Middle English *daunger*, power, dominion, peril, from Latin *dominium*, dominion, from *dominus*, master.]

dan·ger·ous (dān′jər-əs) *adj.* **1.** Involving danger; hazardous: *Mining is a dangerous job.* **2.** Able or likely to cause harm: *The crocodile is a dangerous animal.* **—dan′ger·ous·ly** *adv.* **—dan′ger·ous·ness** *n.*

dan·gle (dăng′gəl) *v.* **dan·gled, dan·gling, dan·gles** *—intr.* To hang loosely and swing or sway: *A key dangled from the chain.* *—tr.* To cause to swing loosely: *The children sat dangling their feet in the water.* **—dan′gler** *n.*

dan·gling participle (dăng′glĭng) *n.* A participle that is not clearly connected with the subject of the sentence that it is supposed to modify. For example, in the sentence *Sitting at my desk, a loud noise startled me,* the word *sitting* is a dangling participle. —SEE NOTE AT **participle.**

Dan·iel¹ (dăn′yəl) A Hebrew prophet of the sixth century BC.

Dan·iel² (dăn′yəl) *n.* A book of the Bible, traditionally believed to have been written by Daniel, which tells of Daniel's adventures and prophetic dreams.

Dan·ish (dā′nĭsh) *adj.* Relating to Denmark or its people, language, or culture. ❖ *n.* **1.** The Germanic language of the Danes. **2.** A Danish pastry.

Danish pastry *n.* A sweet buttery pastry made with raised dough.

dank (dăngk) *adj.* **dank·er, dank·est** Uncomfortably damp; chilly and wet: *a dank and musty cellar.* **—dank′ly** *adv.* **—dank′ness** *n.*

Dan·te A·li·ghie·ri (dän′tā ä′lē-gyĕ′rē) 1265–1321. Italian poet known for *The Divine Comedy* (completed 1321).

Dan·ube (dăn′yo͞ob) A river of south-central Europe rising in southwest Germany and flowing about 1,770 miles (2,850 kilometers) southeast to the Black Sea.

Dan·zig (dăn′sĭg) See **Gdańsk.**

Daph·ne (dăf′nē) *n.* In Greek mythology, a nymph who turned into a laurel tree in order to escape from Apollo.

dap·per (dăp′ər) *adj.* **1.** Neatly dressed; trim; spruce: *dapper soldiers on parade.* **2.** Brisk and jaunty: *The horses trotted at a dapper pace.*

dap·ple (dăp′əl) *tr.v.* **dap·pled, dap·pling, dap·ples** To mark with spots, streaks, or patches of a different color or shade: *Sunlight filtering through the leaves dappled the ground.* ❖ *adj.* Dappled: *dapple horses.*

dap·pled (dăp′əld) *adj.* Marked with spots, streaks, or patches of a different color or shade: *a dappled fawn.*

Dar·da·nelles (där′dn-ĕlz′) Formerly **Hel·les·pont** (hĕl′ĭ-spŏnt′). A strait connecting the Aegean Sea with the Sea of Marmara.

dare (dâr) *v.* **dared, dar·ing, dares** *—tr.* **1.** To have the courage necessary for; be bold enough to try: *She dared her most difficult dive. I didn't dare go into the cave.* **2.** To challenge (someone) to do something requiring courage: *They dared me to dive off the high board.* **3.** To confront boldly; brave: *The rescuers dared the freezing waters in their search.* *—intr.* To be courageous enough to do something. ❖ *n.* A challenge: *I took their dare and swam across the pond.* [From Old English *dearr*, first and third singular present tense of *durran*, to venture, dare.]

Dare (dâr), **Virginia** 1587–1587? The first child of English parents born in America, who disappeared with the Lost Colony of Roanoke Island in Virginia.

dare·dev·il (dâr′dĕv′əl) *n.* A person who takes risks with reckless boldness. ❖ *adj.* Recklessly bold; fearless: *daredevil acrobatic feats.*

dare·say (dâr′sā′) *intr. & tr.v.* To think very likely or almost certain; suppose. Used only in the present tense with *I* or *we: I daresay you're right.*

Dar es Sa·laam (där′ ĕs sə-läm′) The largest city and former capital of Tanzania, in the eastern part of the country on an arm of the Indian Ocean.

dar·ing (dâr′ĭng) *adj.* **1.** Willing to take risks; bold: *a daring test pilot.* **2.** Involving great risk or danger: *a daring rescue.* ❖ *n.* Fearless bravery; boldness; courage: *Climbing the mountain requires great daring.* **—dar′ing·ly** *adv.*

Da·ri·us I (də-rī′əs) Known as "Darius the Great." 550?–486 BC. King of Persia (521–486) who expanded the empire and invaded Greece, only to be was defeated at the Battle of Marathon in 490.

dark (därk) *adj.* **dark·er, dark·est 1a.** Lacking light or having very little light: *a dark tunnel.* **b.** Reflecting only a small amount of light; tending toward black: *dark clothing.* **2a.** Gloomy; dismal: *a dark view of the future.* **b.** Portraying tragic or unhappy events in a satirical or humorous way: *dark comedy.* **3a.** Secret; mysterious: *Keep our plans dark.* **b.** Lacking knowledge, understanding, or culture: *a dark age in the history of medicine.* **4.** Evil or sinister: *a story full of dark deeds.* ❖ *n.* **1.** Absence of light; darkness: *groping around in the dark.* **2.** Night or nightfall: *Come home before dark.* **3.** A dark shade or color: *the darks and lights in a photograph.* ◆ **in the dark 1.** In secret: *The coach kept his game plan in the dark until yesterday.* **2.** In a state of ignorance; uninformed: *We were kept in the dark about the surprise.* [From Old English *deorc.*] **—dark′ly** *adv.* **—dark′ness** *n.*

SYNONYMS **dark, dim, murky, dusky, shadowy** These adjectives describe the absence of light. **Dark** means not lighted enough to see well: *The room was so dark, I thought there had been a blackout.* **Dim** means so dark that the outlines of things cannot be seen clearly: *I stumbled down the dim hallway.* **Murky** means dark as in a smoky or foggy way: *The lighthouse beacon cut through the murky air.* **Dusky** describes decreasing light, as at twilight: *He hurried down the dusky streets,*

trying to get home by dinnertime. **Shady** describes something sheltered from light, especially sunlight: *We found a shady spot in the park for our picnic.* **Shadowy** often describes blocked light or shifting, mysterious shadows: *She shone her flashlight into the shadowy well.*
ANTONYM light

Dark Ages *pl.n.* The early part of the Middle Ages from about AD 476 to about the year 1000, thought of as a time when learning was neglected in Europe.

dark·en (där′kən) *tr. & intr.v.* **dark·ened, dark·en·ing, dark·ens 1.** To make or become dark or darker: *Clouds darkened the sky. Twilight darkens into night.* **2.** To make or grow gloomy, sad, or somber: *News of the defeat darkened their faces.* **—dark′en·er** *n.*

dark horse *n.* **1.** A little-known, unexpectedly successful competitor, as in a horse race. **2.** A person who receives unexpected support and success as a political candidate, especially during a convention.

dar·kling (där′klĭng) *adj.* Dim; obscure; in the dark: *a darkling sky.*

dark matter *n.* Physical objects, such as very dim stars, that emit no light or other radiation but are believed to exist based on their gravitational effects on visible objects, such as galaxies.

dark·room (därk′ro͝om′ *or* därk′ro͞om′) *n.* A room in which photographs are developed, either in total darkness or in colored light to which they are not sensitive.

dar·ling (där′lĭng) *n.* **1.** A dearly loved person. **2.** A favorite: *That star was a darling of the theater for years.* ❖ *adj.* **1.** Dearest; beloved: *my darling child.* **2.** *Informal* Charming; adorable: *The little kittens are darling.* [From Old English *dēorling*, from *dēore*, dear.]

darm·stadt·i·um (därm′shtät′ē-əm) *n. Symbol* **Ds** A radioactive element that has been artificially produced by scientists. The half-life of its most stable isotope is about 10 seconds. Atomic number 110. See **Periodic Table.** [After *Darmstadt*, Germany.]

darn[1] (därn) *v.* **darned, darn·ing, darns** *—tr.* To mend (cloth) by weaving new thread across a hole: *darn socks.* *—intr.* To repair a hole, as in a garment, by weaving thread across it. ❖ *n.* A place repaired by darning. [Perhaps from Norman French *darne*, piece, from Breton *darn.*] **—darn′er** *n.*

darn[2] (därn) *interj.* An expression used to show displeasure or annoyance. ❖ *adv. & adj.* Damn. ❖ *tr. & intr.v.* **darned, darn·ing, darns** To damn. [Alteration of *damn.*]

darn·ing needle (där′nĭng) *n.* A long, often blunt needle with a large eye, used in darning.

dart (därt) *n.* **1.** A thin object with a sharp point, thrown at a target by hand or shot from a blowgun, crossbow, or other device. **2. darts** *(used with a singular or plural verb)* A game in which darts are thrown at a board or other target. **3.** A quick rapid movement: *The cat made a sudden dart at the mouse.* **4.** A tapered tuck sewn to adjust the fit of a garment. ❖ *v.* **dart·ed, dart·ing, darts** *—intr.* To move suddenly and swiftly: *A squirrel darted across the path.* *—tr.* To shoot out or send forth with a swift sudden movement: *The bear darted a paw at the fish. They darted frightened glances behind them.* [From Middle English, from Old French, of Germanic origin.]

dart·board (därt′bôrd′) *n.* A circular board, often made of cork, used as the target in a game of darts.

dash (dăsh) *v.* **dashed, dash·ing, dash·es** *—intr.* **1.** To race or rush with sudden speed: *The children dashed down the stairs.* **2.** To strike, knock, or hurl with violent force: *Heavy rain dashed against the car windshield.* *—tr.* **1.** To break or smash by striking violently: *The ship was dashed upon the rocks.* **2.** To hurl, knock, or thrust with sudden force: *He dashed the cup against the wall.* **3.** To splash: *A car passing through a puddle dashed water all over my clothes.* **4.** To destroy; wreck: *Illness dashed their hopes for a vacation.* **5.** To write hastily: *I dashed off an email before leaving.* ❖ *n.* **1.** A swift forceful stroke: *She knocked the cup to the floor with a dash of her hand.* **2.** A sudden movement; a rush: *a dash for shelter from a cloudburst.* **3.** A short footrace: *the 100-yard dash.* **4.** A small amount; a bit: *a dash of salt.* **5.** Lively spirit or style: *entertainers full of dash.* **6.** A punctuation mark (—) used to show a pause, break, or omission or to set off part of a sentence from the rest. **7.** A long sound or signal used in Morse code in combination with the dot and silent intervals to represent letters, numbers, or punctuation. **8.** A dashboard.

Dar·win (där′wĭn), **Charles Robert** 1809–1882. British naturalist who proposed the theory of evolution by natural selection (1859), which revolutionized the study of biology. —SEE NOTE.

dash·board (dăsh′bôrd′) *n.* The panel beneath the windshield in an automobile, containing instruments, dials, and controls.

da·shi·ki (də-shē′kē) also **dai·shi·ki** (dī-shē′kē) *n., pl.* **da·shi·kis** also **dai·shi·kis** A loose, brightly colored garment worn especially in West Africa.

dash·ing (dăsh′ĭng) *adj.* **1.** Brave, bold, and daring: *a dashing hero.* **2.** Showy or stylish: *The band wore dashing uniforms.*

das·tard (dăs′tərd) *n.* A sneaking, malicious coward.

das·tard·ly (dăs′tərd-lē) *adj.* Cowardly, low, and mean: *dastardly deeds.* **—das′tard·li·ness** *n.*

da·ta (dā′tə *or* dăt′ə) *pl.n. (used with a singular or plural verb)* **1.** Facts that can be analyzed or used in an effort to gain knowledge or make decisions; information. **2.** Statistics or other information represented in a form suitable for processing by computer. [From Latin, plural of *datum*, something given.]

da·ta·base (dā′tə-bās′ *or* dăt′ə-bās′) *n.* A collection of data arranged for easy and speedy retrieval.

data processing *n.* The storing or processing of data by a computer.

date[1] (dāt) *n.* **1a.** Time stated in terms of the day, month, and year: *What is the date of your birthday?* **b.** A specified day of the month: *Is today's date June 15 or 16?* **c.** A statement of calendar time: *There is no date stamped on this coin.* **2.** A point or period of time in history: *At that date radio was unknown.* **3a.** An agreement to meet someone or be somewhere at a particular time, especially as a social engagement: *We made a date to have lunch on Thursday.* **b.** The experience or socializing that occurs as a result of such an agreement: *What did you do on your date?* **c.** A person with whom one has a social engagement: *Who is her date to the prom?* ❖ *v.* **dat·ed, dat·ing, dates** *—tr.* **1.** To mark with a date: *He dated the letter May 1.* **2.** To determine the age, time, or origin of: *They dated the rock by studying the fossils in it.* **3.** *Informal* To go on dates with: *She's been dating him for two months.* *—intr.* **1.** To come from a particular time in the past: *This statue dates from about 500 BC.* **2.** To go on dates: *They dated a lot during vacation.* ◆ **to date** Up to the present time: *a new theory based on our observations to date.* [From Middle English, from Latin *data (Romae)*, issued (at Rome) (on a certain day).]

date[2] (dāt) *n.* **1.** The sweet, one-seeded, oval or oblong fruit of the date palm. **2.** The date palm. [From Middle English, from Latin *dactylus*, from Greek *daktulos*, finger, date (from its shape).]

dat·ed (dā′tĭd) *adj.* **1.** Marked with a date: *a dated receipt.* **2.** Old fashioned: *a dated style.*

date·less (dāt′lĭs) *adj.* **1.** Having no date; lacking a date. **2.** Having no limits in time; endless.

date·line (dāt′līn′) *n.* A phrase at the beginning of a news story or report that gives its date and place of origin.

dartboard

Charles Darwin

BIOGRAPHY

Charles Darwin
Charles **Darwin** began his college studies in medicine and then switched to studying for the clergy. All the while his real interest lay in the plants and animals he observed in the countryside. When he was 22 years old he was appointed the ship's naturalist on the HMS *Beagle* and spent five years traveling the world. The observations he made during that voyage laid the groundwork for his theory of evolution by natural selection, presented in eloquent prose in his 1859 book *On the Origin of Species.* Darwin's argument is simple: variations among individual organisms are often inherited, and those organisms best suited to their environment will produce the most offspring; over millions of years this "selection" of the best-adapted individuals will result in the evolution of numerous species, or, in Darwin's own words, "endless forms most beautiful and most wonderful."

date palm

Jefferson Davis

Miles Davis
photographed c. 1948

ă	pat	ôr	core
ā	pay	oi	boy
âr	care	ou	out
ä	father	o͝o	took
ĕ	pet	o͝or	lure
ē	be	o͞o	boot
ĭ	pit	ŭ	cut
ī	bite	ûr	urge
îr	pier	th	thin
ŏ	pot	*th*	this
ō	toe	zh	vision
ô	paw	ə	about

date line *n.* The International Date Line.

date palm *n.* A very tall tropical palm having a crown of feathery leaves and bearing clusters of dates.

da·tive (dā′tĭv) *adj.* Relating to the grammatical case that indicates the recipient of the action of a verb, the indirect object of the verb, or the object of a preposition. The dative case is used in Latin, Russian, and various other languages, and corresponds to phrases in English beginning with *to* or *for.* ❖ *n.* **1.** The dative case. **2.** A word or form in the dative case.

da·tum (dā′təm *or* dăt′əm) *n.* The singular of **data.**

daub (dôb) *v.* **daubed, daub·ing, daubs** —*tr.* **1.** To cover or smear with a soft sticky substance such as clay, plaster, or mud: *daub the cracks in the wall with mortar.* **2.** To spread or smear (a soft sticky substance): *daub mortar in the cracks.* **3.** To paint (something) with crude or careless strokes. —*intr.* To paint in a crude or amateurish fashion. ❖ *n.* **1.** Something daubed on: *A daub of glue will mend the cup.* **2.** A spot or smear, as of paint. **3.** An amateurish painting.

daugh·ter (dô′tər) *n.* **1.** A person's female child. **2.** A female descendant. **3.** A woman or girl regarded as if in a relationship of child to parent: *daughters of the revolution.* [From Old English *dohtor.*]

daughter cell *n.* Either of two cells formed when a cell undergoes cell division.

daugh·ter-in-law (dô′tər-ĭn-lô′) *n., pl.* **daugh·ters-in-law** The wife of one's child.

daunt (dônt *or* dänt) *tr.v.* **daunt·ed, daunt·ing, daunts** To frighten, discourage, or dishearten: *The chance of failure did not daunt the inventor.*

daunt·less (dônt′lĭs *or* dänt′lĭs) *adj.* Not easily frightened or discouraged; fearless: *a dauntless explorer.* **—daunt′less·ly** *adv.* **—daunt′less·ness** *n.*

dau·phin (dô′fĭn) *n.* The eldest son of a king of France from 1349 to 1830.

dav·en·port (dăv′ən-pôrt′) *n.* A large sofa, often convertible into a bed. [Probably from the name of the manufacturer.]

Da·vid (dā′vĭd) Died about 962 BC. The second king of Israel, traditionally considered the author of many of the Psalms. In the Bible, he slew Goliath.

da Vin·ci (də vĭn′chē), **Leonardo** See **Leonardo da Vinci.**

Da·vis (dā′vĭs), **Jefferson** 1808–1889. American soldier and president of the Confederacy (1861–1865).

Davis, Miles Dewey, Jr. 1926–1991. American trumpeter noted for his innovative style, which mixed jazz and rock.

dav·it (dăv′ĭt *or* dā′vĭt) *n.* A small crane that projects over the side of a ship, used for lowering and hoisting boats.

Da·vy Jones (dā′vē jōnz′) *n.* The bottom of the sea, as personified in songs and stories.

Davy Jones's locker (jōn′zĭz *or* jōnz) *n.* The bottom of the sea, regarded as the grave of people drowned or buried at sea.

daw·dle (dôd′l) *v.* **daw·dled, daw·dling, daw·dles** —*intr.* To take more time than necessary: *If you dawdle over your work, it will take you hours to finish.* —*tr.* To waste (time): *dawdle the day away.* **—daw′dler** *n.*

dawn (dôn) *n.* **1.** The time of the first appearance of daylight in the morning: *get up at dawn.* **2.** A first appearance of something; a beginning: *the dawn of recorded history.* ❖ *intr.v.* **dawned, dawn·ing, dawns 1.** To begin to grow light in the morning: *We rose when the day dawned.* **2.** To come into existence; begin; start: *a new age dawned with the first flights into space.* **3.** To begin to be seen or understood; come as a realization: *As they stood there, it dawned on me they were waiting for an answer.* [From Middle English *daunen*, to dawn, from Old English *dagung*, daybreak, from *dagian*, to dawn.]

day (dā) *n.* **1.** The period of light between sunrise and sunset: *a clear sunny day.* **2.** The 24-hour period during which the earth makes one complete rotation on its axis: *It rained for three days without stopping.* **3.** The part of the day devoted to work or study: *work a seven-hour day; the school day.* **4.** A period that is filled with a certain activity: *a day of fishing.* **5.** A particular period of time: *before the days of automobiles.* ◆ **day after day** For many days in succession: *Day after day they marched across the desert.* **day in, day out** Every day without a break: *Feeding a pet must be done day in, day out.* [From Old English *dæg.*]

Day (dā), **Dorothy** 1897–1980. American journalist and reformer who cofounded the *Catholic Worker* to promote peace and social justice.

day·break (dā′brāk′) *n.* The time each morning when light first appears; dawn: *Farmers often get up before daybreak.*

day·care or **day care** (dā′kâr′) *n.* Daytime care for infants, toddlers, and children of preschool age or for the elderly or the disabled.

day·dream (dā′drēm′) *n.* The act of thinking in a dreamy way, often about things one wishes would come true. ❖ *intr.v.* **day·dreamed** or **day·dreamt** (dā′drĕmt′), **day·dream·ing, day·dreams** To have daydreams: *daydreaming of faraway places.* **—day′dream′er** *n.*

day·light (dā′līt′) *n.* **1.** The light of day; sunlight. **2.** Dawn: *at work before daylight.* **3.** Daytime. **4.** Knowledge or understanding of something that was formerly unknown: *They began to see daylight concerning the cause of the epidemic.*

day·light-sav·ing time (dā′līt-sā′vĭng) *n.* Time during which clocks are set one hour ahead of standard time to provide extra daylight at the end of the working day during spring, summer, and fall.

day·long (dā′lông′) *adj.* Lasting through the whole day: *a daylong seminar.* ❖ *adv.* Through the day; all day.

Day of Atonement *n.* Yom Kippur.

day one *n. Informal* The very beginning; the first day: *I liked my science class from day one.*

days (dāz) *adv.* During the daytime on every day or most days: *works days as a bank teller.*

day school *n.* **1.** A private school for pupils living at home. **2.** A school that holds classes during the day.

day·star (dā′stär′) *n.* **1.** A planet, especially Venus, that is visible in the east just before daylight. **2.** The sun.

day·time (dā′tīm′) *n.* The time between sunrise and sunset. **—day′time′** *adj.*

day-to-day (dā′tə-dā′) *adj.* **1.** Happening every day; daily: *day-to-day routine.* **2.** Surviving one day at a time with little regard for the future: *The lost mountain climbers were existing on a day-to-day basis.*

daze (dāz) *tr.v.* **dazed, daz·ing, daz·es** To stun or confuse, as with a blow, shock, or surprise: *The explosion dazed and deafened them.* ❖ *n.* A stunned or confused condition: *The news left us all in a daze.* [From Middle English *dasen*, of Scandinavian origin.] **—daz′ed·ly** (dā′zĭd-lē) *adv.*

daz·zle (dăz′əl) *tr.v.* **daz·zled, daz·zling, daz·zles 1.** To make nearly or momentarily blind with too much bright light: *The ranger's searchlight dazzled the eyes of the campers.* **2.** To amaze, impress, or astonish with a spectacular display: *The pianist dazzled us with his superb technique.* ❖ *n.* Blinding brightness; glare: *the dazzle of sunlight on the water.*

daz·zling (dăz′lĭng) *adj.* Brilliant or spectacular: *dazzling sunlight; a dazzling burst of speed.* **—daz′zling·ly** *adv.*

dB *abbr.* An abbreviation of decibel.

Db The symbol for the element **dubnium.**

DC *abbr.* An abbreviation of: **1.** direct current. **2.** District of Columbia.

DDS *abbr.* An abbreviation of Doctor of Dental Surgery.

DDT (dē′dē-tē′) *n.* A powerful insecticide that is also poisonous to humans, birds, and other animals when swallowed or absorbed through the skin. It remains active in the environment for many years and has been banned in the United States for most uses since 1972.

DE *abbr.* An abbreviation of Delaware.

de– *pref.* A prefix that means: **1.** Reverse: *decode.* **2.** Remove: *defrost.* **3.** Reduce: *demote.* **4.** Out of: *deplane.* **5.** Down: *descend.* —SEE NOTE.

dea·con (dē′kən) *n.* **1.** A layperson who assists a Protestant minister. **2.** In certain churches, a cleric ranking below a priest. [From Old English *dīacon*, from Greek *diākonos*, attendant.]

dea·con·ess (dē′kə-nĭs) *n.* A laywoman who assists a Protestant minister.

de·ac·ti·vate (dē-ăk′tə-vāt′) *tr.v.* **de·ac·ti·vat·ed, de·ac·ti·vat·ing, de·ac·ti·vates 1.** To make inactive or ineffective: *deactivate a bomb.* **2.** To remove from active military duty: *deactivate soldiers in time of peace.*

dead (dĕd) *adj.* **dead·er, dead·est 1.** No longer alive or living: *The dead tree is starting to decay.* **2.** Having no life or living things; lifeless: *a dead planet.* **3.** Lacking feeling; numb: *My cold toes felt dead.* **4.** Not moving or circulating; motionless: *the dead air in a closed room.* **5a.** No longer important or relevant: *a dead issue.* **b.** No longer learned as a first language: *Latin is a dead language.* **c.** No longer active: *a dead volcano.* **d.** Unexciting: *a dead party.* **6a.** No longer functioning or in operation: *The pump is dead.* **b.** Lacking electric power or charge: *a dead circuit; a dead battery.* **7.** Weary and worn-out; exhausted: *After finishing work I was dead on my feet.* **8.** Complete; absolute: *dead silence.* **9.** Sudden; abrupt: *a dead stop.* **10.** In sports, out of play: *When it crosses the sideline, the ball is dead.* **11.** Exact: *hit the dead center of the target.* ❖ *n.* **1.** Those who have died; dead people: *The soldiers buried the dead.* **2.** The darkest, quietest, or coldest part: *the dead of night; the dead of winter.* ❖ *adv.* **1.** Completely; absolutely: *You can be dead sure of that.* **2.** Straight; directly: *A huge boulder lay dead ahead.* **3.** Suddenly: *We stopped dead in our tracks.* [From Old English *dēad*.]

dead·beat (dĕd′bēt′) *n. Informal* **1.** A person who avoids paying debts. **2.** A lazy person; a loafer.

dead·bolt (dĕd′bōlt′) *n.* A bolt on a lock that is moved by turning the key or knob without activating a spring.

dead·en (dĕd′n) *tr.v.* **dead·ened, dead·en·ing, dead·ens 1.** To make less sensitive, intense, or strong: *Anesthetics deaden pain.* **2.** To make soundproof: *Rugs helped deaden the room.*

dead end *n.* **1.** A street, alley, or other passage that is closed or blocked off at one end. **2.** A situation or subject that allows for no development or progress: *We reached a dead end in our argument.*

dead heat *n.* A race in which two or more contestants finish at the same time; a tie.

dead language *n.* A language, such as Latin, that is no longer learned as a person's native language.

dead letter *n.* A letter that is not delivered or claimed, usually because the address is wrong or impossible to read.

dead·line (dĕd′līn′) *n.* A set time by which something must be done, finished, or settled; a time limit: *No one could enter the contest after the deadline.*

dead·lock (dĕd′lŏk′) *n.* **1.** A standstill that occurs when opposing forces are equally strong and neither will give way. **2.** A tie between opponents, especially in a sporting event. ❖ *tr. & intr.v.* **dead·locked, dead·lock·ing, dead·locks** To bring or come to a deadlock: *The peace talks deadlocked over treaty terms.*

dead·ly (dĕd′lē) *adj.* **dead·li·er, dead·li·est 1.** Causing or capable of causing death: *a deadly weapon.* **2.** Unable to be appeased; unyielding: *deadly enemies.* **3.** Suggesting death: *a total and deadly silence.* **4.** Absolute; extreme; utter: *deadly earnestness.* **5.** Very accurate or effective: *The hunter is a deadly shot.* **6.** Very dull and boring: *a deadly play.* **7.** Causing or capable of causing spiritual death: *Envy is a deadly sin.* ❖ *adv.* **1.** Extremely; utterly: *I'm deadly serious.* **2.** So as to suggest death: *turned deadly pale at the scream.* **—dead′li·ness** *n.*

deadly nightshade *n.* Belladonna.

dead-man's float (dĕd′mănz′) *n.* A floating position in which a person lies face down and extends the arms forward.

dead-on (dĕd′ôn′) *adj. Informal* Precisely accurate: *criticisms that were dead-on; a dead-on imitation of the teacher.*

dead·pan (dĕd′păn′) *adj.* Characterized by or showing no emotion or amusement: *a deadpan expression.* [From *dead* + *pan*, face.]

dead reckoning *n.* A method of estimating the position of a ship or aircraft without astronomical observations, as by determination from its speed, time traveled, and winds and currents encountered.

Dead Sea A salt lake, about 1,380 feet (420 meters) below sea level, between Israel and Jordan. It is the lowest point on the earth.

Dead Sea Scrolls *pl.n.* A number of ancient parchment and papyrus scrolls containing passages from the Hebrew Scriptures and other writings, found in caves near the Dead Sea.

dead·wood (dĕd′wo͝od′) *n.* **1.** Dead wood, including fallen or standing trees, branches, and stumps. **2.** People or things that are burdensome and no longer useful: *getting rid of the deadwood in the company.*

deaf (dĕf) *adj.* **deaf·er, deaf·est 1.** Partially or completely lacking the ability to hear: *Many deaf people learn to use sign language.* **2. Deaf** Relating to the Deaf or their culture. **3.** Unwilling to listen: *The principal was deaf to our complaints.* ❖ *n. (used with a plural verb)* **1.** Deaf people considered as a group. **2. Deaf** The community of deaf people who use American Sign Language as their main means of communication. [From Old English *dēaf*.] **—deaf′ly** *adv.* **—deaf′ness** *n.*

deaf·en (dĕf′ən) *tr.v.* **deaf·ened, deaf·en·ing, deaf·ens** To make deaf: *The explosion deafened us temporarily.*

deal (dēl) *v.* **dealt** (dĕlt), **deal·ing, deals** *—intr.* **1.** To be occupied or concerned: *This book deals with the architecture of Los Angeles.* **2.** To behave in a certain way toward another or others: *The counselor dealt fairly with the campers.* **3.** To take action regarding something: *deal with an emergency.* **4.** *Informal* To cope or contend: *I don't deal well with stress.* **5.** To do business; trade: *a merchant who deals in diamonds.* **6.** To distribute playing cards: *It's your turn to deal.* *—tr.* **1.** To give out in shares or portions: *We dealt out cookies to the children.* See Synonyms at **distribute. 2.** To give or deliver: *The champion dealt the opponent a hard blow.* **3.** To hand out (cards) to players in a card game: *Deal the cards.* ❖ *n.* **1.** *Informal* **a.** An agreement, as in business or politics: *We made a deal with our neighbors to buy their car.* **b.** A favorable sale; a bargain: *I got a real deal on a TV at sale prices.* **2.** A corrupt or secret arrangement: *The inspector made a deal with the builder to pass inferior materials.* **3.** Treatment; conduct: *a fair deal from the judge.* **4a.** The distribution of playing cards. **b.** A player's turn to deal: *It's your deal.* ◆ **a good deal** or **a great deal 1.** A considerable amount; a lot: *We learned a great deal.* **2.** Much; considerably: *a good deal thinner.* [From Old English *dǣlan*, to divide, share.]

deal·er (dē′lər) *n.* **1.** A person engaged in buying and selling: *a furniture dealer.* **2.** A person who distributes the playing cards in a game of cards.

deal·ing (dē′lĭng) *n.* **1. dealings** Agreements or rela-

davit

WORD BUILDING

de– The prefix **de–** can be traced back through Middle English and Old French to Latin *dē–*, meaning "from, off, apart, away, down, out." In English, *de–* usually indicates reversal, removal, or reduction. Thus *deactivate* means "to make inactive," *decontaminate* means "to remove the contamination from," and *decompress* means "to remove or reduce pressure."

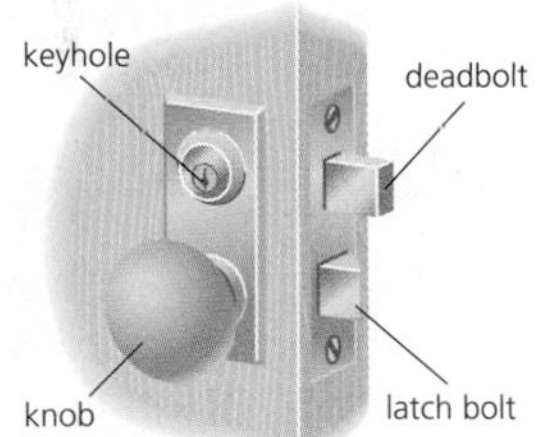

deadbolt

Dead Sea Scrolls

WORD HISTORY

debonair The word **debonair** comes ultimately from the Old French phrase *de bon aire,* meaning "of good lineage or disposition." The *aire* in the phrase is not the air we breathe but comes from the Latin word *ārea,* "area, open space," and developed in Old French to mean "place, stock, disposition."

WRITERS CHOOSE THEIR WORDS

There was a shadowy alcove at the other end of the cellar, filled with old furniture and other stuff. Adam recognized old wicker chairs they had used long ago in the summer, in the backyard. His mother waded through this **debris** of other years, clearing a path to a box tied with an old rope, about four feet square, in the corner.

—Robert Cormier
I Am the Cheese

ă	pat	ôr	core
ā	pay	oi	boy
âr	care	ou	out
ä	father	o͝o	took
ĕ	pet	o͝or	lure
ē	be	o͞o	boot
ĭ	pit	ŭ	cut
ī	bite	ûr	urge
îr	pier	th	thin
ŏ	pot	*th*	this
ō	toe	zh	vision
ô	paw	ə	about

tions with others, especially when involving money or trade: *business dealings.* **2.** A way of acting or doing business; conduct toward others: *That store is known for its fair dealing.*

dealt (dĕlt) *v.* Past tense and past participle of **deal.**

dean (dēn) *n.* **1.** An official of a college or university in charge of a certain school or faculty: *dean of the medical school.* **2.** An official of a college or high school who counsels students and enforces rules. **3.** The head clergyman in charge of a cathedral. **4.** The oldest or most respected member of a group or profession: *the dean of American tennis.* [From Middle English *den,* from Late Latin *decānus,* chief of ten, from Greek *deka,* ten.]

dear (dîr) *adj.* **dear·er, dear·est 1.** Loved and cherished: *my dear friend.* **2.** Greatly valued; precious: *Her dearest possessions are in the cabinet.* **3.** Highly esteemed or regarded, as in speaking to or writing letters: *my dear fellow.* **4.** High in price; expensive. **5.** Heartfelt; sincere: *my dearest wish.* ❖ *adv.* **1.** At a high cost: *You will pay dear for that mistake.* **2.** Fondly or affectionately: *memories of old friends held dear to one's heart.* ❖ *n.* A dearly loved person or animal: *the poor dear.* ❖ *interj.* An expression used to show distress or surprise: *Oh dear!* [From Old English *dēore.*] **—dear′ly** *adv.* **—dear′ness** *n.*

❑ *These sound alike:* **dear, deer** (animal).

dearth (dûrth) *n.* A lack or scarcity: *a dearth of knowledge about the ocean floor.*

death (dĕth) *n.* **1.** The fact or process of dying; the end of life: *remained busy and active until death.* **2.** The condition of being dead: *where the body lay in death.* **3.** A cause of dying: *Such a fall is certain death.* **4.** The ending, destruction, or extinction of something: *the death of Communism.* ◆ **put to death** To kill; execute. **to death** To an unbearable degree; extremely: *We were bored to death by the presentation.* [From Old English *dēath.*]

death·bed (dĕth′bĕd′) *n.* **1.** The bed on which a person dies. **2.** A person's last hours of life.

death·blow (dĕth′blō′) *n.* **1.** A fatal blow. **2.** A destructive event: *The scandal was the deathblow for the previous government.*

death·less (dĕth′lĭs) *adj.* Enduring forever; undying; immortal: *His fame is deathless.* **—death′less·ness** *n.*

death·ly (dĕth′lē) *adj.* Resembling or characteristic of death: *a deathly pallor.* ❖ *adv.* **1.** So as to resemble death: *She was deathly pale.* **2.** Very; extremely: *deathly ill.*

death penalty *n.* A sentence of punishment by execution.

death rate *n.* The ratio of total deaths to total population in a given community over a specified period of time.

death row *n.* The part of a prison for housing inmates who have received the death penalty: *a murderer on death row.*

death's-head (dĕths′hĕd′) *n.* The human skull as a symbol of death.

Death Valley An arid desert basin of eastern California and western Nevada. It includes the lowest point in North America, 282 feet (86 meters) below sea level.

de·ba·cle (dĭ-bä′kəl *or* dĕb′ə-kəl) *n.* **1.** A sudden disastrous collapse, downfall, or defeat; a rout: *The party in power suffered a complete debacle in the election.* **2.** A total, often ridiculous failure.

de·bar (dē-bär′) *tr.v.* **de·barred, de·bar·ring, de·bars** To forbid, prohibit, exclude, or bar: *A person not born a US citizen is debarred from running for the presidency.*

de·base (dĭ-bās′) *tr.v.* **de·based, de·bas·ing, de·bas·es** To lower in character, quality, or worth: *Don't debase yourself by feeling envious.* **—de·base′ment** *n.*

de·bat·a·ble (dĭ-bā′tə-bəl) *adj.* Open to question, argument, or dispute: *an unproven and debatable theory.*

de·bate (dĭ-bāt′) *v.* **de·bat·ed, de·bat·ing, de·bates** *—intr.* **1.** To consider something; try to decide about something: *We debated about which trail to take.* **2.** To present or discuss arguments for and against something: *We debated about the fairness of the school's dress code.* *—tr.* **1.** To consider; try to decide: *I debated what to do next.* **2.** To discuss or argue about (something): *We debated whether the play was truly a tragedy.* ❖ *n.* **1.** A discussion or consideration of the arguments for and against something: *the debate about reforming the health care system.* **2.** A formal contest in which opponents argue for opposite sides of an issue: *Two local schools held a debate on whether to register bicycles.* [From Middle English *debaten,* from *debat,* debate, from Old French *debatre,* to beat down, fight.] **—de·bat′er** *n.*

de·bauch (dĭ-bôch′) *v.* **de·bauched, de·bauch·ing, de·bauch·es** *—tr.* To lead away from good toward evil; corrupt morally. *—intr.* To indulge in too much eating, drinking, and other sensual pleasures. ❖ *n.* An act or a period of debauchery.

de·bauch·er·y (dĭ-bô′chə-rē) *n., pl.* **de·bauch·er·ies** Too much indulgence in eating, drinking, and other sensual pleasures.

de·bil·i·tate (dĭ-bĭl′ĭ-tāt′) *tr.v.* **de·bil·i·tat·ed, de·bil·i·tat·ing, de·bil·i·tates** To make feeble; weaken: *A long illness usually debilitates the body.* [From Latin *dēbilis,* weak.] **—de·bil′i·ta′tion** *n.*

de·bil·i·ty (dĭ-bĭl′ĭ-tē) *n., pl.* **de·bil·i·ties** The condition of abnormal bodily weakness; feebleness.

deb·it (dĕb′ĭt) *n.* **1.** A debt charged to and recorded in an account. **2.** An entry of a sum in the debit or left-hand side of an account. **3.** The sum of such entries. ❖ *tr.v.* **deb·it·ed, deb·it·ing, deb·its** To charge with or as a debt: *The bank debited my account for the checks that I wrote.*

debit card *n.* A bank card that allows a customer to make purchases or get cash by transferring funds electronically from an account.

deb·o·nair also **deb·o·naire** (dĕb′ə-nâr′) *adj.* Gracious and charming in a cheerful carefree way: *Adoring fans mobbed the debonair movie star.* **—deb′o·nair′ly** *adv.* **—deb′o·nair′ness** *n.* —SEE NOTE.

de·bone (dē-bōn′) *tr.v.* **de·boned, de·bon·ing, de·bones** To remove the bones from; to bone: *debone a chicken breast.*

de·brief (dē-brēf′) *tr.v.* **de·briefed, de·brief·ing, de·briefs** To question in order to obtain knowledge, especially knowledge gathered on a mission: *The astronauts were debriefed after returning from their mission.*

de·bris (də-brē′) *n.* The scattered remains of something broken, destroyed, or discarded: *Debris from the storm was spread all over the beach.*

Debs (dĕbz), **Eugene Victor** 1855–1926. American labor organizer and socialist leader who ran unsuccessfully for US president five times between 1900 and 1920.

debt (dĕt) *n.* **1.** Something, such as money, owed by one person to another: *I will pay my debts as soon as I get paid. We owe a debt of gratitude to those who have died defending our country.* **2.** The condition of owing; indebtedness: *They are in debt to the bank for their loan.*

debt·or (dĕt′ər) *n.* A person who owes something to another.

de·bug (dē-bŭg′) *tr.v.* **de·bugged, de·bug·ging, de·bugs** To search for and fix errors in (a computer program).

de·bunk (dē-bŭngk′) *tr.v.* **de·bunked, de·bunk·ing, de·bunks** To expose or ridicule the falseness or exaggerated claims of: *It took centuries to debunk the theory that the planets revolve around Earth.*

De·bus·sy (dĕb′yo͞o-sē′), **Claude Achille** 1862–1918. French composer who is best known for impressionist works.

de·but also **dé·but** (dā-byo͞o′ *or* də-byo͞o′) *n.* **1.** The first public appearance: *a new actor's stage debut; the debut of a new line of computers.* **2.** The formal presentation of a young woman into society.

deb·u·tante (dĕb′yo͞o-tänt′) *n.* A young woman making a formal debut into society.

deca– *pref.* A prefix that means ten: *decaliter.*

dec·ade (dĕk′ād′) *n.* A period of ten years. [From Middle English *decade,* a group of ten, from Greek *dekas,* from *deka,* ten.]

dec·a·dence (dĕk′ə-dəns) *n.* A process, condition, or period of deterioration, decay, or decline, as in morals or art.

dec·a·dent (dĕk′ə-dənt) *adj.* Marked by or in a condition of deterioration or decline; decaying: *a decadent society.* ❖ *n.* A person who is in the process of mental or moral decay. **—dec′a·dent·ly** *adv.*

de·caf·fein·at·ed (dē-kăf′ə-nā′tĭd) *adj.* Having the caffeine removed: *decaffeinated coffee.*

dec·a·gon (dĕk′ə-gŏn′) *n.* A polygon with ten sides and ten angles. **—dec·ag′o·nal** (dĭ-kăg′ə-nəl) *adj.*

dec·a·he·dron (dĕk′ə-hē′drən) *n., pl.* **dec·a·he·drons** or **dec·a·he·dra** (dĕk′ə-hē′drə) A solid geometric figure having ten faces.

de·cal (dē′kăl′ *or* dĭ-kăl′) *n.* A picture or design printed on specially treated paper to be transferred to another surface such as glass, metal, or plastic.

dec·a·li·ter (dĕk′ə-lē′tər) *n.* A metric unit of volume equal to 10 liters, 11 dry quarts, or 2.6 gallons.

Dec·a·logue or **Dec·a·log** (dĕk′ə-lôg′) *n.* The Ten Commandments.

de·camp (dĭ-kămp′) *intr.v.* **de·camped, de·camp·ing, de·camps 1.** To pack up and leave a camping ground; break camp: *The battalion decamped at dawn.* **2.** To leave secretly or suddenly; run away: *The thief decamped while it was still dark outside.* **—de·camp′ment** *n.*

de·cant (dĭ-kănt′) *tr.v.* **de·cant·ed, de·cant·ing, de·cants 1.** To pour off (a liquid, especially wine) without disturbing the sediment at the bottom. **2.** To pour (a liquid) from one container into another.

de·cant·er (dĭ-kăn′tər) *n.* A decorative glass bottle with a stopper, used for holding liquids such as wine.

de·cap·i·tate (dĭ-kăp′ĭ-tāt′) *tr.v.* **de·cap·i·tat·ed, de·cap·i·tat·ing, de·cap·i·tates** To cut off the head of a person or animal; behead. [From Late Latin *dēcapitāre* : Latin *dē-,* off + Latin *caput,* head.] **—de·cap′i·ta′tion** *n.*

de·cath·lon (dĭ-kăth′lŏn′) *n.* A track-and-field event usually for men that includes the 100-meter, 400-meter, and 1,500-meter runs; the 110-meter high hurdles; the discus and javelin throws; the shot put; the pole vault; the high jump; and the long jump. [From Greek *deka-,* ten + Greek *āthlon,* contest.]

de·cay (dĭ-kā′) *intr.v.* **de·cayed, de·cay·ing, de·cays 1.** To rot or become rotten; decompose: *Leaves fall to the forest floor and decay.* **2.** To undergo radioactive decay. **3.** To fall apart or deteriorate: *The bridge is decaying and will have to be rebuilt.* ❖ *n.* **1.** The act or process of rotting: *tooth decay; decay of a corpse.* **2.** The natural disintegration of a radioactive substance by the emission of particles and radiation from its nuclei. **3.** A gradual deterioration or decline: *the decay of traditional values.* [From Middle English *decaien,* from Old French *decair* : Latin *dē-,* off, down + Latin *cadere,* to fall.]

de·cease (dĭ-sēs′) *intr.v.* **de·ceased, de·ceas·ing, de·ceas·es** To die. ❖ *n.* The act or fact of dying; death.

de·ceased (dĭ-sēst′) *adj.* No longer living; dead: *my deceased grandparents.* ❖ *n., pl.* **deceased** A dead person or dead people: *members of the deceased's family.*

de·ce·dent (dĭ-sēd′nt) *n.* In law, the deceased.

de·ceit (dĭ-sēt′) *n.* **1.** The act or practice of deceiving; deception: *A successful spy is an expert in deceit.* **2.** A trick used to deceive someone else. **3.** The quality of being deceitful: *a swindler full of deceit.*

de·ceit·ful (dĭ-sēt′fəl) *adj.* **1.** Practicing deceit: *a deceitful person.* **2.** Deliberately misleading; deceptive: *a deceitful excuse to avoid punishment.* **—de·ceit′ful·ly** *adv.* **—de·ceit′ful·ness** *n.*

de·ceive (dĭ-sēv′) *v.* **de·ceived, de·ceiv·ing, de·ceives** *—tr.* To make (a person) believe something that is not true; mislead; trick: *He deceived her into thinking he was innocent when in fact he was guilty.* *—intr.* **1.** To use deceit. **2.** To give a false impression: *appearances can deceive.* **—de·ceiv′er** *n.*

de·cel·er·ate (dē-sĕl′ə-rāt′) *v.* **de·cel·er·at·ed, de·cel·er·at·ing, de·cel·er·ates** *—tr.* To decrease the speed or rate of: *decelerated the car by jamming on the brakes.* *—intr.* To decrease in speed; slow down: *The spinning top decelerated slowly.* **—de·cel′er·a′tion** *n.* **—de·cel′er·a′tor** *n.*

De·cem·ber (dĭ-sĕm′bər) *n.* The 12th month of the year in the Gregorian calendar, having 31 days. [From Middle English *Decembre,* from Latin *December,* the tenth month of the early Roman calendar : *decem,* ten + *mēnsis,* month.]

de·cen·cy (dē′sən-sē) *n., pl.* **de·cen·cies 1.** The state or condition of being decent: *the decency to act in an honest and proper manner.* **2. decencies a.** Decent or proper acts; proper observances: *the social decencies such as courtesy and good manners.* **b.** The things needed for a respectable and proper way of living: *A refrigerator is one of the decencies of life in a developed nation.*

de·cent (dē′sənt) *adj.* **1.** Conforming to the standards of proper behavior or to the rules and conventions of society: *Decent people abide by the law.* **2.** Kind; considerate: *It was very decent of you to help in time of trouble.* **3.** Adequate; passable: *a decent salary.* **4.** *Informal* Properly or modestly dressed. **—de′cent·ly** *adv.*

de·cen·tral·ize (dē-sĕn′trə-līz′) *tr.v.* **de·cen·tral·ized, de·cen·tral·iz·ing, de·cen·tral·iz·es 1.** To distribute the functions or powers of (a government or central authority) among several local authorities. **2.** To reorganize into smaller units of operation: *decentralize a school system.* **—de·cen′tral·i·za′tion** (dē-sĕn′trə-lĭ-zā′shən) *n.*

de·cep·tion (dĭ-sĕp′shən) *n.* **1.** The use of deceit: *fraudulent advertising and other forms of deception.* **2.** The condition of being deceived: *The magician achieved complete deception of the audience.* **3.** Something that deceives, as a trick or lie: *The scarecrow was a deception to frighten away the deer.*

de·cep·tive (dĭ-sĕp′tĭv) *adj.* Deceiving or tending to deceive: *a deceptive advertisement.* **—de·cep′tive·ly** *adv.* **—de·cep′tive·ness** *n.*

deci– *pref.* A prefix that means one tenth: *deciliter.*

de·ci·bel (dĕs′ə-bəl *or* dĕs′ə-bĕl′) *n.* A unit used in measuring the loudness of sounds: *The speaking voice of most people ranges from 45 to 75 decibels.* —SEE NOTE AT **sound**[1].

de·cide (dĭ-sīd′) *v.* **de·cid·ed, de·cid·ing, de·cides** *—tr.* **1a.** To reach a conclusion or form a judgment about (something) by reasoning or consideration: *decide what to do.* **b.** To bring to a conclusion by removing uncertainty or resolving a conflict: *The court decided the case.* **2.** To influence or determine the outcome of: *A single goal decided the game.* *—intr.* **1.** To give a judgment: *The judge decided against the defendant.* **2.** To reach a decision; make up one's mind: *What took you so long to decide?* [From Middle English *deciden,* from Latin *dēcīdere,* to cut off, decide : *dē-,* off, away + *caedere,* to cut.]

de·cid·ed (dĭ-sī′dĭd) *adj.* **1.** Clear-cut; definite; undoubted: *a decided advantage.* **2.** Free from hesitation; resolute: *The general has a decided manner of talking.* **—de·cid′ed·ly** *adv.* **—de·cid′ed·ness** *n.*

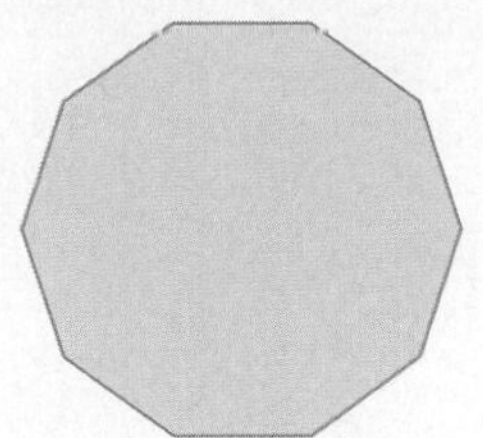

decagon

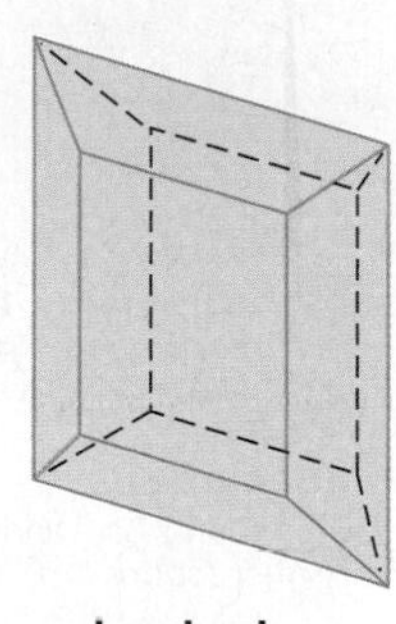

decahedron

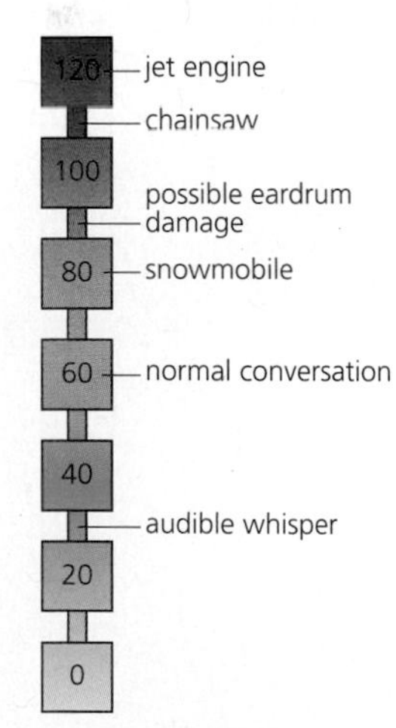

decibel

range of human hearing in decibels

deciduous
oak tree in spring *(top)* and in winter *(bottom)*

de·cid·u·ous (dĭ-**sĭj′**o͞o-əs) *adj.* **1.** Shedding leaves at the end of the growing season: *deciduous trees.* **2.** Falling off at the end of a season or growing period: *deciduous antlers.* [From Latin *dēciduus*, from *dēcidere*, to fall off : *dē-*, down, off + *cadere*, to fall.]

dec·i·li·ter (**dĕs′**ə-lē′tər) *n.* A metric unit of volume equal to one-tenth of a liter.

dec·i·mal (**dĕs′**ə-məl) *n.* **1.** A number containing a decimal fraction, such as 3.1415, 0.099, or −1.04. **2.** A decimal fraction. ❖ *adj.* Based on 10; proceeding by tens: *The system of decimal notation is an invention of mathematicians in India.* [From Latin *decima (pars)*, a tenth (part), from *decem*, ten.]

decimal fraction *n.* A fraction in which the denominator is 10 or a power of 10. Expressed as decimal fractions, 29/100 is 0.29, and 29/1000 is 0.029.

decimal place *n.* The position of a digit in a decimal fraction. In .079, for example, 0 is in the first decimal place, 7 is in the second decimal place, and 9 is in the third decimal place.

decimal point *n.* A dot written in a decimal number, used to separate whole numbers from fractions. For example, 1.3 represents 1 plus 3/10.

decimal system *n.* **1.** A number system based on units of 10. **2.** A system of measurement in which all derived units, such as the deciliter, are multiples of 10 of the fundamental units, such as the liter.

dec·i·mate (**dĕs′**ə-māt′) *tr.v.* **dec·i·mat·ed, dec·i·mat·ing, dec·i·mates** To destroy or kill a large part of: *The hurricane decimated the island's bird population.* [From Latin *decimāre*, to punish every tenth person, from *decimus*, tenth, from *decem*, ten.] **—dec′i·ma′tion** *n.*

dec·i·me·ter (**dĕs′**ə-mē′tər) *n.* A unit of length equal to one-tenth of a meter.

de·ci·pher (dĭ-**sī′**fər) *tr.v.* **de·ci·phered, de·ci·pher·ing, de·ci·phers 1.** To change (a message) from a code or cipher to ordinary language; decode: *Telegraph operators must be able to decipher dots and dashes.* **2.** To read or interpret (something hard to understand or illegible). **—de·ci′pher·a·ble** *adj.*

de·ci·sion (dĭ-**sĭzh′**ən) *n.* **1.** A conclusion or judgment reached after consideration: *Our friends have not come to a decision about going on the trip with us.* **2.** The act of deciding or making up one's mind: *The judge's decision is taking a long time.* **3.** In boxing, a victory won on points awarded by judges when the loser has not been knocked out.

de·ci·sive (dĭ-**sī′**sĭv) *adj.* **1.** Settling a matter or conflict; conclusive: *a decisive argument.* **2.** Characterized by decision and firmness; resolute: *a decisive leader.* **—de·ci′sive·ly** *adv.* **—de·ci′sive·ness** *n.*

deck[1] (dĕk) *n.* **1.** A platform extending from one side of a ship to the other. **2a.** A platform resembling the deck of a ship: *a parking deck on the roof of the building.* **b.** A roofless, floored structure, typically with a railing, that adjoins a house. **3.** A pack of playing cards: *shuffle the deck and deal.* **4.** A tape deck. ❖ *tr.v.* **decked, deck·ing, decks 1.** To provide with a deck: *deck a ship.* **2.** To knock down with force. ◆ **on deck 1.** On hand; present. **2.** Waiting to take one's turn, especially as a batter in baseball. [From Middle English *dekke*, from Middle Dutch *dec*, roof, covering.]

deck[2] (dĕk) *tr.v.* **decked, deck·ing, decks 1.** To put fine clothes on: *She decked herself out for the party.* **2.** To decorate: *decked the halls for the holidays.* [From Dutch *dekken*, to cover.]

deck hand *n.* A member of a ship's crew who performs manual labor.

de·claim (dĭ-**klām′**) *v.* **de·claimed, de·claim·ing, de·claims** *—intr.* **1.** To deliver a speech, especially in a formal way. **2.** To speak loudly, pompously, or in a theatrical manner: *Everyone declaims against inefficient government, but few will do anything about it.* *—tr.* To recite formally: *declaim a poem.* **—de·claim′er** *n.*

dec·la·ma·tion (dĕk′lə-**mā′**shən) *n.* **1.** The act of declaiming: *a sincere declamation of patriotism.* **2.** Something declaimed.

de·clam·a·to·ry (dĭ-**klăm′**ə-tôr′ē) *adj.* **1.** Suitable for declaiming: *a declamatory poem.* **2.** Pretentious and bombastic: *a long declamatory explanation.*

dec·la·ra·tion (dĕk′lə-**rā′**shən) *n.* **1.** The act or process of declaring. **2.** A formal statement or announcement: *the declaration of one's candidacy for office.* **3.** A document listing goods that are taxable or subject to duty: *Travelers made out declarations before going through customs.*

Declaration of Independence *n.* A proclamation, adopted on July 4, 1776, by the Second Continental Congress, declaring the Thirteen Colonies independent of Great Britain.

de·clar·a·tive (dĭ-**klâr′**ə-tĭv) *adj.* Making a statement, as opposed to a question or order: *a declarative sentence such as "I'm going home."*

de·clare (dĭ-**klâr′**) *v.* **de·clared, de·clar·ing, de·clares** *—tr.* **1.** To state with emphasis; affirm: *The teacher declared that cheating would be severely punished.* **2.** To state officially or formally: *Congress has the power to declare new national holidays.* **3.** To make a full statement of (dutiable goods) when entering a country at customs. *—intr.* To announce one's choice or opinion: *The senator declared against raising taxes.* [From Middle English *declaren*, from Latin *dēclārāre*, from *clārus*, clear.]

de·clen·sion (dĭ-**klĕn′**shən) *n.* **1.** In certain languages, the inflection of nouns, pronouns, and adjectives with respect to categories such as case, number, and gender. **2.** A class of words of one language with the same or a similar system of inflections, such as the first declension in Latin.

dec·li·na·tion (dĕk′lə-**nā′**shən) *n.* **1.** The angle between magnetic north and true north at a given point. **2.** The angular distance of a star or planet from the celestial equator.

de·cline (dĭ-**klīn′**) *v.* **de·clined, de·clin·ing, de·clines** *—intr.* **1.** To refuse politely to do or accept something: *I asked them home for a snack, but they declined.* **2.** To become less or decrease, as in strength, value, or importance: *Her health declined until she saw the doctor. Prices tend to decline when business is poor.* **3.** To slope or bend downward: *The hills decline into a hidden valley.* *—tr.* **1.** To refuse politely: *They declined my offer to help. I have to decline the kitten, because we can't have pets.* **2.** In certain languages, to give the inflected forms of (a noun, pronoun, or adjective). ❖ *n.* **1.** The process or result of declining, as in strength or importance; deterioration: *The country was in a period of decline.* **2.** A change to a lower level or state, as in value: *a decline in prices.* **3.** The period when something is coming to an end: *Frost and bare trees marked the decline of fall.* **4.** A downward slope. [From Middle English *declinen*, from Latin *dēclīnāre*, to turn away : *dē-*, away + *-clīnāre*, to lean, bend.]

de·cliv·i·ty (dĭ-**klĭv′**ĭ-tē) *n., pl.* **de·cliv·i·ties** A downward slope, as of a hill.

de·code (dē-**kōd′**) *tr.v.* **de·cod·ed, de·cod·ing, de·codes 1.** To change (information) from a form that is in code into ordinary language; decipher: *decode Egyptian hieroglyphics.* **2.** To convert (a scrambled electronic signal) into one that can be understood. **—de·cod′er** *n.*

de·com·pose (dē′kəm-**pōz′**) *v.* **de·com·posed, de·com·pos·ing, de·com·pos·es** *—tr.* **1.** To separate (a substance) into simpler substances or basic elements: *Heat decomposes chalk into lime and carbon dioxide.* **2.** To cause to rot; decay: *Microbes decomposed the dead plants on the forest floor.* *—intr.* **1.** To separate into component parts: *Sunlight decomposes into the colors of the*

ă	pat	ôr	core
ā	pay	oi	boy
âr	care	ou	out
ä	father	o͝o	took
ĕ	pet	o͝or	lure
ē	be	o͞o	boot
ĭ	pit	ŭ	cut
ī	bite	ûr	urge
îr	pier	th	thin
ŏ	pot	*th*	this
ō	toe	zh	vision
ô	paw	ə	about

spectrum as it passes through a prism. **2.** To decay; rot: *Paper decomposes more quickly than plastic.*

de·com·pos·er (dē′kəm-**pō′**zər) *n.* An organism, often a bacterium or fungus, that feeds on and breaks down dead organic matter.

de·com·po·si·tion (dē-kŏm′pə-**zĭsh′**ən) *n.* The act or process of decomposing: *Leaves undergo decomposition after they fall to the forest floor.*

de·com·press (dē′kəm-**prĕs′**) *tr.v.* **de·com·pressed, de·com·press·ing, de·com·press·es** To bring (a person exposed to increased pressure) gradually to normal atmospheric pressure.

de·com·pres·sion (dē′kəm-**prĕsh′**ən) *n.* The act or process of bringing a person exposed to increased pressure back to normal atmospheric pressure in gradual stages: *Divers and workers building deep tunnels must undergo decompression.*

decompression sickness *n.* A disorder, seen especially in deep-sea divers, caused by the formation of nitrogen bubbles in the blood following a rapid drop in pressure and characterized by severe pain in the joints and chest, cramps, and paralysis.

de·con·ges·tant (dē′kən-**jĕs′**tənt) *n.* A medication or treatment that decreases congestion in the nose or bronchial passages.

de·con·tam·i·nate (dē′kən-**tăm′**ə-nāt′) *tr.v.* **de·con·tam·i·nat·ed, de·con·tam·i·nat·ing, de·con·tam·i·nates** To free of contamination, especially by removing harmful substances, such as bacteria, poisonous chemicals, or radioactive materials. **—de′con·tam′i·na′tion** *n.*

de·con·trol (dē′kən-**trōl′**) *tr.v.* **de·con·trolled, de·con·trol·ling, de·con·trols** To free from control, especially from government control: *The government decontrolled the airlines, letting them set their own ticket prices.*

de·cor (dā-**kôr′**) or **dé·cor** (**dā′**kôr′) *n.* **1.** The decorative style of a room, home, restaurant, or other area. **2.** Scenery in a theatrical or television show.

dec·o·rate (**dĕk′**ə-rāt′) *tr.v.* **dec·o·rat·ed, dec·o·rat·ing, dec·o·rates 1.** To make (something) attractive or impressive by adding things to it or altering its appearance: *The students decorated the auditorium with flowers for graduation.* **2.** To give a medal or other honor to: *The chief decorated the firefighter for bravery.*

dec·o·ra·tion (dĕk′ə-**rā′**shən) *n.* **1.** The act or process of decorating: *Decoration of the auditorium for graduation took most of the morning.* **2.** Something that adorns or beautifies; an ornament: *We put up wreaths, streamers, and other decorations.* **3.** A medal, badge, or ribbon awarded as an honor: *The police officer received a decoration for bravery.*

dec·o·ra·tive (**dĕk′**ər-ə-tĭv *or* **dĕk′**ə-rā′tĭv) *adj.* Serving to decorate; ornamental: *a decorative design in the ceiling.* **—dec′o·ra·tive·ly** *adv.*

dec·o·ra·tor (**dĕk′**ə-rā′tər) *n.* A person who decorates, especially an interior decorator.

dec·o·rous (**dĕk′**ər-əs *or* dĭ-**kôr′**əs) *adj.* Characterized by decorum; proper: *decorous behavior.* **—dec′o·rous·ness** *n.*

de·co·rum (dĭ-**kôr′**əm) *n.* Proper behavior or conduct; propriety.

de·coy (**dē′**koi′ *or* dĭ-**koi′**) *n.* **1.** A model of a duck or other bird, used by hunters to attract wild birds or animals. **2.** A person or thing used to lead another into danger or a trap: *A false delivery of money was a decoy to catch the robbers.* ❖ *tr.v.* (dĭ-**koi′**) **de·coyed, de·coy·ing, de·coys 1.** To lure (wild animals such as birds) into a trap or position to be hunted: *decoy geese into a marsh.* **2.** To lure (a person) into danger or a trap by a trick or temptation. [Possibly from Dutch *de kooi*, the cage : *de*, the + *kooi*, cage (from Latin *cavea*).]

de·crease (dĭ-**krēs′**) *tr. & intr.v.* **de·creased, de·creas·ing, de·creas·es** To become or cause to become gradually less or smaller; diminish: *Oil supplies decreased during the winter. We must decrease spending to conserve our money.* ❖ *n.* (**dē′**krēs′) **1.** The act or process of decreasing; a decline: *A decrease in sales forced the owners to close the store.* **2.** The amount by which something becomes less or smaller: *a decrease in the price of gasoline of five cents a gallon.*

SYNONYMS **decrease, lessen, diminish, dwindle** These verbs mean to become smaller or less. **Decrease** and **lessen** both mean to become smaller or less at a steady, gradual rate: *City traffic decreases on holidays. The demand for gloves lessens as the weather gets warmer.* **Diminish** stresses the idea of loss or depletion: *The scandal diminished the administration's credibility.* **Dwindle** means to decrease bit by bit until no more is left: *Their savings dwindled over the years.*

ANTONYM **increase**

---

de·cree (dĭ-**krē′**) *n.* An authoritative order; an edict: *The falsely accused prisoner was released by court decree.* ❖ *tr.v.* **de·creed, de·cree·ing, de·crees** To order, establish, or decide by decree: *The governor decreed a state holiday.*

dec·re·ment (**dĕk′**rə-mənt) *n.* In mathematics, the amount by which the value of a variable decreases.

de·crep·it (dĭ-**krĕp′**ĭt) *adj.* Weakened, worn-out, or broken down because of old age or long use: *a decrepit old car.* **—de·crep′it·ly** *adv.*

de·crep·i·tude (dĭ-**krĕp′**ĭ-to͞od′) *n.* The condition of being decrepit; weakness: *The abandoned house was in a state of decrepitude.*

de·cre·scen·do (dā′krə-**shĕn′**dō *or* dē′krə-**shĕn′**dō) *adv. & adj.* In music, with gradually diminishing force or loudness. ❖ *n., pl.* **de·cre·scen·dos 1.** A gradual decrease in musical force or loudness. **2.** A musical passage performed with a decrescendo.

de·crim·i·nal·ize (dē-**krĭm′**ə-nə-līz′) *tr.v.* **de·crim·i·nal·ized, de·crim·i·nal·iz·ing, de·crim·i·nal·iz·es** To reduce or abolish the legal penalties for doing or possessing (something): *Betting was decriminalized in many states.*

de·cry (dĭ-**krī′**) *tr.v.* **de·cried, de·cry·ing, de·cries 1.** To condemn as being wrong or bad; disapprove of strongly: *The judge decried the criminal's behavior.* **2.** To cause to seem unimportant or inferior; belittle: *decry watching television as a waste of time.*

ded·i·cate (**dĕd′**ĭ-kāt′) *tr.v.* **ded·i·cat·ed, ded·i·cat·ing, ded·i·cates 1.** To keep for a special purpose or honor: *This chapel is dedicated to the memory of sailors lost at sea.* **2.** To give or apply (one's time or self, for example) to a particular activity, pursuit, cause, or person; devote: *Nurses dedicate their lives to the care of the sick.* **3.** To address or inscribe (a book, performance, or other creative work) to someone as a mark of respect or affection: *The composer dedicated the new symphony to a friend.* [From Middle English *dedicaten*, from Latin *dēdicāre*, from *dicāre*, to proclaim.]

ded·i·ca·tion (dĕd′ĭ-**kā′**shən) *n.* **1.** The act of dedicating or the state of being dedicated: *her dedication to helping others.* **2.** A ceremony dedicating something: *We went to the dedication of the new library.* **3.** A note in a book, musical composition, or other creative work dedicating it to someone. **—ded′i·ca·to′ry** (**dĕd′**ĭ-kə-tôr′ē) *adj.*

de·duce (dĭ-**do͞os′**) *tr.v.* **de·duced, de·duc·ing, de·duc·es** To reach (a conclusion) by reasoning, especially from a general principle: *The engineers deduced from the laws of physics that the new airplane would fly.* [From Middle English *deducen*, from Latin *dēdūcere*, to lead away or down : *dē-*, down, away + *dūcere*, to lead.] —SEE NOTE AT **produce.**

deer
white-tailed deer

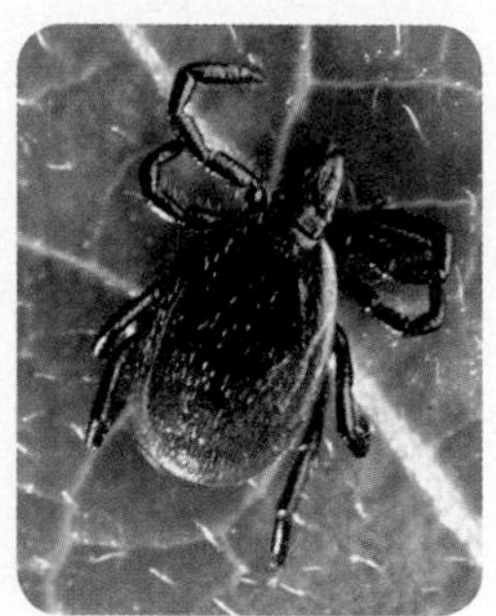

deer tick

de·duct (dĭ-dŭkt′) *tr.v.* **de·duct·ed, de·duct·ing, de·ducts** To take away (a quantity from another); subtract: *The dealer deducted the amount of our earlier deposit from the final payment for the car.* [From Middle English *deducten*, from Latin *dēdūcere*, to lead away or down : *dē-*, down, away + *dūcere*, to lead.]

de·duct·i·ble (dĭ-dŭk′tə-bəl) *adj.* Capable of being deducted, especially from inclusion in one's taxable income.

de·duc·tion (dĭ-dŭk′shən) *n.* **1.** The act of deducting; subtraction: *The salesman's deduction of the cost of installation persuaded us to buy the dishwasher.* **2.** An amount that is or may be deducted: *a deduction from one's taxable income for medical expenses.* **3a.** The process of reaching a conclusion by reasoning, especially from general principles. **b.** A conclusion reached by this process: *the judge's deduction that the law violated the Fourteenth Amendment.*

de·duc·tive (dĭ-dŭk′tĭv) *adj.* Involving logical deduction: *deductive reasoning.* **—de·duc′tive·ly** *adv.*

deed (dēd) *n.* **1.** An act or action: *Returning the lost money was a good deed.* **2.** A legal document showing ownership of property. ❖ *tr.v.* **deed·ed, deed·ing, deeds** To transfer or give (property) by means of a deed: *The government deeded land to the miners.* [From Old English *dǣd*.]

dee·jay (dē′jā′) *Informal n.* A disc jockey.

deem (dēm) *tr.v.* **deemed, deem·ing, deems** To regard as, consider, or believe: *The doctor deemed it essential for me to get more exercise.*

deep (dēp) *adj.* **deep·er, deep·est 1.** Extending far down below a surface: *a deep hole in the river ice.* **2.** Extending from front to rear, or from the outside to the inside: *a deep closet.* **3.** Extending a specified distance in a given direction: *snow three feet deep.* **4.** Far distant down or back: *The hunters were deep in the woods.* **5.** Extreme; profound; intense: *a deep silence; a deep sleep.* **6.** Very much absorbed or involved: *She was deep in thought.* **7.** Showing much thought or feeling; strongly felt: *a deep understanding; a deep love of books.* **8.** Difficult to understand; mysterious: *a deep theory.* **9.** Rich and vivid in shade of color: *a deep red.* **10.** Low in pitch: *a deep voice.* ❖ *adv.* **deeper, deepest 1.** To a great depth: *dig deep into the earth.* **2.** Well along in time; late: *The researchers worked deep into the night.* ❖ *n.* **1.** A deep place, such as the ocean or a place in the ocean: *We know little of life in the deep.* **2.** The most intense or extreme part: *the deep of night.* **—deep′ly** *adv.* **—deep′ness** *n.*

deep-dish (dēp′dĭsh′) *adj.* Made or used in a deep baking dish.

deep·en (dē′pən) *tr. & intr.v.* **deep·ened, deep·en·ing, deep·ens** To make or become deep or deeper: *More digging slowly deepened the hole. Floodwaters deepened as the rain continued.*

deep-fry (dēp′frī′) *tr.v.* **deep-fried, deep-fry·ing, deep-fries** To fry by immersing in a deep container filled with oil or fat: *deep-fried the chicken wings.*

deep-root·ed (dēp′ro͞o′tĭd *or* dēp′ro͝ot′ĭd) *adj.* **1.** Firmly implanted below the surface: *a deep-rooted oak.* **2.** Firmly fixed; deep-seated: *deep-rooted beliefs.*

deep-sea (dēp′sē′) *adj.* Relating to deep parts of the sea: *a deep-sea diver.*

deep-seat·ed (dēp′sē′tĭd) *adj.* **1.** Deeply implanted below the surface: *a deep-seated infection.* **2.** Firmly fixed; deeply rooted; strongly entrenched: *a deep-seated problem of long standing.*

Deep South A region of the southeast United States, usually made up of the states of Alabama, Georgia, Louisiana, Mississippi, and South Carolina.

deep space *n.* **1.** The regions of space that are beyond the gravitational influence of Earth. **2.** The regions of space that are beyond our solar system.

deer (dîr) *n., pl.* **deer** Any of various hoofed mammals, such as the elk or white-tailed deer, that chew their cud and have antlers, usually only in the male. [From Old English *dēor*, beast.]

❑ *These sound alike:* **deer, dear** (loved one).

deer·skin (dîr′skĭn′) *n.* **1.** The skin of a deer. **2.** Leather made from this skin.

deer tick *n.* Either of two small North American ticks that are parasitic on deer and other animals and that transmit the bacteria that cause Lyme disease.

de-es·ca·late (dē-ĕs′kə-lāt′) *tr.v.* **de-es·ca·lat·ed, de-es·ca·lat·ing, de-es·ca·lates** To reduce the scale, size, or intensity of: *Calm words de-escalated the crisis.* **—de-es′ca·la′tion** *n.*

de·face (dĭ-fās′) *tr.v.* **de·faced, de·fac·ing, de·fac·es** To mar or spoil the surface or appearance of; disfigure: *deface a poster with a crayon.* **—de·face′ment** *n.*

de fac·to (dĭ făk′tō *or* dā făk′tō) *adj.* Existing in fact, especially when contrary to or not established by law: *housing practices that resulted in de facto segregation; a de facto government.*

def·a·ma·tion (dĕf′ə-mā′shən) *n.* The act of making a statement that will damage a person's reputation; slander or libel: *defamation of a person's character.* **—de·fam′a·to′ry** (dĭ-făm′ə-tôr′ē) *adj.*

de·fame (dĭ-fām′) *tr.v.* **de·famed, de·fam·ing, de·fames** To attack or damage the reputation of by slander or libel: *He defamed her good name by spreading false rumors.*

de·fault (dĭ-fôlt′) *n.* **1.** A failure to do what is required, especially a failure to pay a debt: *The bankrupt company is guilty of default on its loans.* **2.** The failure of one or more competitors or teams to participate in or complete a contest: *win a contest by default.* **3.** A setting, such as the typeface for text, used by a computer unless the operator chooses a different setting. ❖ *intr.v.* **de·fault·ed, de·fault·ing, de·faults 1.** To fail to do what is required: *default on a business contract.* **2.** To fail to pay money when it is due: *default on a loan.* **3.** To lose a contest by failing to participate in or complete it: *Illness caused the tennis star to default in the match.* **—de·fault′er** *n.*

de·feat (dĭ-fēt′) *tr.v.* **de·feat·ed, de·feat·ing, de·feats 1.** To win victory over; beat: *The mayor defeated all opponents in the last election.* **2.** To prevent the success of; thwart: *A misunderstanding defeated our efforts at a compromise.* **3a.** To dishearten or discourage: *The last setback defeated her, and she gave up.* **b.** To be beyond the comprehension of; mystify: *How the children found their way back home defeats me.* ❖ *n.* **1.** The act of defeating or the state of being defeated: *The veto was a defeat of the new environmental measures.* **2.** Failure to win: *admit defeat.* [From Middle English *defeten*, from Medieval Latin *disfacere*, to undo, mutilate.]

de·feat·ism (dĭ-fē′tĭz′əm) *n.* Acceptance of or resignation to the prospect of defeat: *Defeatism can prevent success.* **—de·feat′ist** *n.*

def·e·cate (dĕf′ĭ-kāt′) *intr.v.* **def·e·cat·ed, def·e·cat·ing, def·e·cates** To empty the bowels of waste matter. **—def′e·ca′tion** *n.*

de·fect (dē′fĕkt′ *or* dĭ-fĕkt′) *n.* A lack of something necessary or desirable for completion or perfection; a deficiency: *A defect in the engine made it sputter and stall.* ❖ *intr.v.* (dĭ-fĕkt′) **de·fect·ed, de·fect·ing, de·fects 1.** To disavow allegiance to one's country and take up residence in another: *a Chinese pilot who defected to Russia.* **2.** To abandon a position or association, often to join an opposing group: *The American general Benedict Arnold defected to the British side.* [From Middle English, from Latin *dēficere*, to desert, be wanting.] **—de·fec′tor** *n.*

de·fec·tion (dĭ-fĕk′shən) *n.* The act of deserting one's country, party, or cause, especially to join or take up residence in another.

ă	pat	ôr	core
ā	pay	oi	boy
âr	care	ou	out
ä	father	o͝o	took
ĕ	pet	o͝or	lure
ē	be	o͞o	boot
ĭ	pit	ŭ	cut
ī	bite	ûr	urge
îr	pier	th	thin
ŏ	pot	*th*	this
ō	toe	zh	vision
ô	paw	ə	about

de·fec·tive (dĭ-fĕk′tĭv) *adj.* Having a defect or flaw; faulty: *The defective clock never kept time well.* **—de·fec′tive·ly** *adv.*

de·fence (dĭ-fĕns′) *n. Chiefly British* Variant of **defense.**

de·fend (dĭ-fĕnd′) *v.* **de·fend·ed, de·fend·ing, de·fends** *—tr.* **1.** To make or keep safe from attack, harm, or danger; guard: *The ants defended their colony against the invading predators.* **2.** To support or maintain, as by argument; justify: *The scientist defended the theory that germs cause disease.* **3.** To represent (a defendant) in a civil or criminal lawsuit: *People accused of a crime have the right to be defended by a lawyer.* **4.** In sports, to compete against a challenger in an attempt to retain (a championship). *—intr.* In sports, to play defense: *tried to defend against the fast break.* **—de·fend′er** *n.*

SYNONYMS **defend, protect, guard, preserve, shield** These verbs mean to make or keep safe from danger, attack, or harm. **Defend** suggests taking measures to drive back an attack: *The army was prepared to defend the island against invasion.* **Protect** suggests the providing of some kind of cover for safety or comfort: *Wear goggles to protect your eyes from the chlorine in the swimming pool.* **Guard** means to keep watch over something: *The family bought a big dog to guard the house.* **Preserve** means to act to keep something safe: *Scientists are working to preserve gorillas in Africa.* **Shield** means to protect in the way that armor does, by standing in between the threat and the threatened: *The suspect's lawyers shielded him from the intrusive reporters.*

de·fen·dant (dĭ-fĕn′dənt) *n.* The person or party against which a legal action or claim is brought.

de·fense (dĭ-fĕns′) *n.* **1.** The act of defending against attack, harm, or danger: *The patriots fought in defense of their freedom.* **2a.** A means or method of defending or protecting: *A heavy coat is a good defense against the cold.* **b.** An argument in support or justification of something: *This newspaper editorial is a strong defense for freedom of the press.* **3a.** The act of defending a legal case. **b.** The defendant and his or her legal counsel: *Where does the defense sit in the courtroom?* **4.** (*often* dē′fĕns′) In sports: **a.** The means or tactics used in trying to keep the opposition from scoring. **b.** The players or the team trying to keep the opposition from scoring.

de·fense·less (dĭ-fĕns′lĭs) *adj.* Having no defense; unprotected: *a defenseless infant.*

de·fen·si·ble (dĭ-fĕn′sə-bəl) *adj.* Capable of being defended, protected, or justified: *Blaming others for one's mistakes is not a defensible position.*

de·fen·sive (dĭ-fĕn′sĭv) *adj.* **1.** Intended to or appropriate for defense: *a defensive moat surrounding the castle; a successful defensive move in chess.* **2a.** Intended to withstand or deter aggression or attack: *developed a defensive shield to protect against missiles.* **b.** Performed so as to avoid risk or danger: *took defensive measures to prevent exposure to mercury.* **3.** Constantly protecting oneself from criticism or other real or perceived threats: *It's hard to say anything to you because you always get so defensive.* ◆ **on the defensive** Prepared to withstand or counter aggression or attack. **—de·fen′sive·ly** *adv.* **—de·fen′sive·ness** *n.*

de·fer¹ (dĭ-fûr′) *tr.v.* **de·ferred, de·fer·ring, de·fers** To put off; postpone: *defer going until we know what the weather will be.* [From Middle English *differren*, from Latin *differre* : *dis-*, off + *ferre*, to carry, put.] **—de·fer′ra·ble** *adj.* —SEE NOTE AT **transfer.**

de·fer² (dĭ-fûr′) *intr.v.* **de·ferred, de·fer·ring, de·fers** To submit to the wishes, opinion, or decision of another, as through recognition of authority or knowledge: *Let's defer to an expert on that matter.* [From Middle English *deferen*, from Latin *dēferre*, to refer to : *dē-*, away + *ferre*, to carry.]

def·er·ence (dĕf′ər-əns *or* dĕf′rəns) *n.* **1.** Submission or courteous yielding to the opinion, wishes, or judgment of another. **2.** Courteous respect: *The guests showed deference to their host by standing until he was seated.*

def·er·en·tial (dĕf′ə-rĕn′shəl) *adj.* Marked by or showing deference; respectful: *deferential behavior.* **—def′er·en′tial·ly** *adv.*

de·fer·ment (dĭ-fûr′mənt) *n.* The act or an example of delaying or putting off: *the deferment of payments on a loan.*

de·fi·ance (dĭ-fī′əns) *n.* Bold resistance to an opposing force or authority: *shook their fists in a gesture of defiance.* ◆ **in defiance of** In spite of; contrary to: *We went on the picnic in defiance of bad weather forecasts.*

de·fi·ant (dĭ-fī′ənt) *adj.* Acting with or marked by defiance; boldly resisting: *The rebels took a defiant stance.* **—de·fi′ant·ly** *adv.*

de·fi·cien·cy (dĭ-fĭsh′ən-sē) *n., pl.* **de·fi·cien·cies 1.** The quality or condition of being deficient. **2.** A lack or shortage, especially of something essential to health: *A vitamin deficiency made the patient weak.*

deficiency disease *n.* A disease, such as pellagra or rickets, that results from a diet lacking in one or more vitamins or from an inability of the body to absorb or use certain essential nutrients.

de·fi·cient (dĭ-fĭsh′ənt) *adj.* **1.** Lacking an essential quality or element: *a diet deficient in vitamin D.* **2.** Lacking in amount or degree; insufficient: *a deficient education.*

def·i·cit (dĕf′ĭ-sĭt) *n.* **1.** Inadequacy or insufficiency: *a deficit in grain production.* **2.** The amount by which a sum of money falls short of the required or expected amount; a shortage: *The deficit in the government's budget can be eliminated by raising taxes or reducing spending.*

de·file¹ (dĭ-fīl′) *tr.v.* **de·filed, de·fil·ing, de·files 1.** To make filthy or dirty; pollute: *Sewage seeping into the lake defiled the water.* **2.** To spoil the sacredness or purity of: *defile a temple.* [From Middle English *defilen*, alteration of *defoulen*, to trample on, abuse, pollute, from Old French *defouler*, to beat, trample down.] **—de·file′ment** *n.*

de·file² (dĭ-fīl′) *intr.v.* **de·filed, de·fil·ing, de·files** To march in single file or in columns. ❖ *n.* A narrow gorge or pass that requires a group, as of soldiers, to move in file. [From French *défiler*, to march in rows : *dé-*, away, off + *file*, line, file.]

de·fine (dĭ-fīn′) *tr.v.* **de·fined, de·fin·ing, de·fines 1.** To state the precise meaning of (a word or phrase, for example): *Dictionaries define words.* **2.** To describe; specify distinctly: *The Constitution defines the powers of the president. She defined the properties of the new drug.* **3.** To make distinct or clear in outline: *The hills were defined against the bright morning sky.*

def·i·nite (dĕf′ə-nĭt) *adj.* **1.** Clearly defined or firmly decided: *a definite plan; a definite time.* **2.** Direct and clear in expression; forthright: *The doctor was definite about getting more exercise.* **3.** Indisputable; certain: *We are at a definite disadvantage without our best player.* **—def′i·nite·ly** *adv.* **—def′i·nite·ness** *n.*

definite article *n.* A word used to introduce and refer to a particular noun or noun phrase, especially one that has already been mentioned or is assumed to be known. In English *the* is the definite article.

def·i·ni·tion (dĕf′ə-nĭsh′ən) *n.* **1.** A statement that explains the meaning of something, such as a word or phrase, as in a dictionary entry. **2.** The act or process of stating a precise meaning or significance: *The textbook begins with the definition of key terms.* **3.** The level of detail in a recording, production, or digital encoding of an image or sound: *The mountains in the snapshots had poor definition.*

de·fin·i·tive (dĭ-fĭn′ĭ-tĭv) *adj.* **1.** Serving to define or identify something as distinct from others: *plot twists*

WRITERS CHOOSE THEIR WORDS

Strange images were floating around Tiffany's mind. There were scraps of voices, fragments of memories . . . and one little voice that was her own, small and **defiant** and getting fainter: You're not me. You just think you are! Someone help me!

—Terry Pratchett
A Hat Full of Sky

Daniel Defoe

Charles de Gaulle
photographed c. 1945

ă	pat	ôr	core
ā	pay	oi	boy
âr	care	ou	out
ä	father	ŏŏ	took
ĕ	pet	ŏŏr	lure
ē	be	ōō	boot
ĭ	pit	ŭ	cut
ī	bite	ûr	urge
îr	pier	th	thin
ŏ	pot	*th*	this
ō	toe	zh	vision
ô	paw	ə	about

that are definitive of the genre of horror movies. **2.** Serving to settle, decide, or put an end to; conclusive: *a definitive answer; a definitive victory.* **3.** Authoritative and complete: *a definitive biography based on diaries and personal papers.* **—de·fin′i·tive·ly** *adv.*

de·flate (dĭ-flāt′) *v.* **de·flat·ed, de·flat·ing, de·flates** *—tr.* **1.** To release contained air or gas from: *A pin deflated the balloon.* **2.** To reduce or lessen the size or importance of: *The crowd's jeers soon deflated the speaker's confidence.* **3.** To reduce the amount or availability of (currency or credit), causing a decline in prices. *—intr.* To be or become deflated: *As the tire deflated, we pulled off to the side of the road.*

de·fla·tion (dĭ-flā′shən) *n.* **1.** The act of deflating or the condition of being deflated: *Deflation made the balloon slowly sink toward the ground.* **2.** A persistent decrease in the level of consumer prices or a persistent increase in the purchasing power of money.

de·flect (dĭ-flĕkt′) *intr. & tr.v.* **de·flect·ed, de·flect·ing, de·flects** To turn aside or cause to turn aside; bend or deviate: *Constant interruptions deflected the speaker's thoughts from his main purpose.* [From Latin *dēflectere* : *dē-*, away, from + *flectere*, to bend.] **—de·flec′tor** *n.*

de·flec·tion (dĭ-flĕk′shən) *n.* **1.** The act of deflecting or the condition of being deflected. **2a.** The movement of something from its normal or zero position. **b.** The amount of this movement.

De·foe (dĭ-fō′), **Daniel** 1660–1731. English writer whose most famous novel, *Robinson Crusoe* (1719), was inspired by the exploits of a Scottish sailor and castaway, Alexander Selkirk.

de·fo·li·ant (dē-fō′lē-ənt) *n.* A chemical sprayed or dusted on plants to cause the leaves to fall off.

de·fo·li·ate (dē-fō′lē-āt′) *tr.v.* **de·fo·li·at·ed, de·fo·li·at·ing, de·fo·li·ates** To cause the leaves of (a plant or plants) to fall off, especially by the use of a chemical dust or spray. **—de·fo′li·a′tion** *n.*

de·for·est (dē-fôr′ĭst) *tr.v.* **de·for·est·ed, de·for·est·ing, de·for·ests** To cut down and clear away the trees or forests from. **—de·for′es·ta′tion** *n.*

de·form (dĭ-fôrm′) *v.* **de·formed, de·form·ing, de·forms** *—tr.* **1.** To alter from previous, proper, or natural form; misshape: *The heat of the fire deformed the candles.* **2.** To spoil the beauty or appearance of; disfigure. *—intr.* To become deformed.

de·for·ma·tion (dē′fôr-mā′shən *or* dĕf′ər-mā′shən) *n.* **1.** The act or process of deforming: *the deformation of plastic by heat.* **2.** The condition of being deformed. **3.** A change in form for the worse: *deformations in plants caused by poor growing weather.*

de·formed (dĭ-fôrmd′) *adj.* Misshapen or distorted in form.

de·for·mi·ty (dĭ-fôr′mĭ-tē) *n., pl.* **de·for·mi·ties 1.** The condition of being deformed: *discarded the plastic parts because of their deformity.* **2.** Something that is misshapen or deformed: *Fish that are exposed to pollution sometimes have deformities.*

de·fraud (dĭ-frôd′) *tr.v.* **de·fraud·ed, de·fraud·ing, de·frauds** To take something from by fraud; swindle: *defrauded the prospectors by selling them worthless land claims.*

de·fray (dĭ-frā′) *tr.v.* **de·frayed, de·fray·ing, de·frays** To undertake the payment of (a cost or expense): *Contributions will defray the cost of the political campaign.*

de·frost (dē-frôst′) *v.* **de·frost·ed, de·frost·ing, de·frosts** *—tr.* **1.** To remove ice or frost from: *defrost a windshield.* **2.** To thaw (frozen food): *We need to defrost the frozen burgers.* *—intr.* **1.** To become free of ice or frost: *a refrigerator that defrosts quickly.* **2.** To become thawed: *Has the meat defrosted?*

de·frost·er (dē-frô′stər) *n.* A heating device that removes frost or prevents its formation, as on a car windshield.

deft (dĕft) *adj.* **deft·er, deft·est** Quick and skillful; adroit: *the deft hands of a magician.* [From Middle English *dafte*, gentle, humble, from Old English *dafte*, meek.] **—deft′ly** *adv.* **—deft′ness** *n.*

de·funct (dĭ-fŭngkt′) *adj.* No longer in existence or use; dead: *a defunct business that failed years ago.*

de·fuse (dē-fyōōz′) *tr.v.* **de·fused, de·fus·ing, de·fus·es 1.** To remove the fuse from (an explosive device): *defused the bomb.* **2.** To make less dangerous, tense, or hostile: *The mediator defused the hostage crisis.*

de·fy (dĭ-fī′) *tr.v.* **de·fied, de·fy·ing, de·fies 1.** To resist openly or refuse to comply with: *He defied the court order by leaving the country.* **2.** To be beyond the power of: *That story defies belief.* **3.** To challenge or dare (someone) to do something: *I defy you to find an error in this report.* [From Middle English *defien*, from Old French *desfier* : Latin *dis-*, not + Latin *fidus*, faithful.]

deg. *abbr.* An abbreviation of degree.

de Gaulle (də gōl′ *or* də gôl′), **Charles André Joseph Marie** 1890–1970. French general and politician who gained popularity during World War II as the leader of Free French forces in exile. He served as president from 1959 to 1969.

de·gen·er·a·cy (dĭ-jĕn′ər-ə-sē) *n.* The process of degenerating or the state of being degenerate.

de·gen·er·ate (dĭ-jĕn′ər-ĭt) *adj.* **1.** Having declined, as in function or nature, from a former or original state: *a degenerate form of ancient tool-making.* **2.** Having fallen into an inferior or undesirable state, especially in mental or moral qualities. ❖ *n.* A corrupt or depraved person. ❖ *intr.v.* (dĭ-jĕn′ə-rāt′) **de·gen·er·at·ed, de·gen·er·at·ing, de·gen·er·ates** To deteriorate into an undesirable condition, especially functionally or morally: *The discussion degenerated into a nasty argument.* **—de·gen′er·ate·ly** *adv.* **—de·gen′er·a′tion** (dĭ-jĕn′ə-rā′shən) *n.*

de·gla·ci·a·tion (dē-glā′shē-ā′shən *or* dē-glā′sē-ā′shən) *n.* The uncovering of land because of the melting of a glacier.

de·grad·a·ble (dĭ-grā′də-bəl) *adj.* Capable of being degraded or decomposed by stages: *degradable plastic.*

deg·ra·da·tion (dĕg′rə-dā′shən) *n.* **1.** The act or process of degrading: *The erosion of rich soil causes the degradation of farmlands.* **2.** The state of being degraded: *the degradation of imprisonment.* **3.** A decline to a lower quality, condition, or level: *Pollution has caused the degradation of our air.*

de·grade (dĭ-grād′) *tr.v.* **de·grad·ed, de·grad·ing, de·grades 1.** To lower in quality or value; make worse or less valuable: *The virus quickly degraded the computer's performance.* **2.** To reduce in grade, rank, or status; demote: *The officer was degraded to private.* **3.** To lower in dignity; dishonor or disgrace: *I refuse to degrade myself by arguing over trivia.*

de·gree (dĭ-grē′) *n.* **1.** One of a series of steps in a process, course, or progression. **2.** Relative social position or official rank: *An ambassador is a person of high degree.* **3.** Relative amount or extent: *a high degree of accuracy; various degrees of skill in acting.* **4.** A unit of measurement on a temperature scale: *The temperature of water at freezing is 32 degrees Fahrenheit.* **5a.** A unit for measuring an angle or an arc of a circle. One degree is $1/360$ of the circumference of a circle. **b.** This unit used to measure latitude or longitude on the earth's surface. **6a.** In a single algebraic term, the sum of the exponents of all the variables. For example, a^2b is a term of the third degree. **b.** In a polynomial, the degree of the term of highest degree. For example, $x^3 + 2xy + x$ is of the third degree. **7a.** An academic title awarded by a college or university after completion of a required course of study: *a bachelor's degree in chemistry.* **b.** A similar title granted as an honorary distinction: *an honorary degree awarded to the senator.* **8.** In law, classification of a crime according to its seriousness: *Accidental murder is murder in the second degree.* **9.** One of the forms used in the comparison of an adjective or adverb: *The superlative degree of* new *is* newest. ◆ **by degrees** Little by little; gradually: *improved on the fiddle by degrees.* [From Middle English *degre,* from Old French : Latin *dē-,* down, off + Latin *gradus,* step.]

de·gree-day (dĭ-**grē′**dā′) *n.* A unit used in estimating the amount of fuel or power required for heating buildings. It is equal to the number of degrees by which the average temperature on a given day falls below some standard temperature, usually 65°F (18°C).

de·hu·man·ize (dē-**hyo͞o′**mə-nīz′) *tr.v.* **de·hu·man·ized, de·hu·man·iz·ing, de·hu·man·iz·es** To deprive of human qualities such as individuality or compassion: *Do you think that computers dehumanize our lives?* **—de·hu′man·i·za′tion** (dē-hyo͞o′mə-nĭ-**zā′**shən) *n.*

de·hu·mid·i·fy (dē′hyo͞o-**mĭd′**ə-fī′) *tr.v.* **de·hu·mid·i·fied, de·hu·mid·i·fy·ing, de·hu·mid·i·fies** To decrease the humidity of: *An air conditioner dehumidifies the air.* **—de′hu·mid′i·fi′er** *n.*

de·hy·drate (dē-**hī′**drāt′) *v.* **de·hy·drat·ed, de·hy·drat·ing, de·hy·drates** *—tr.* **1.** To cause the loss of water or body fluids in: *The hot sun was dehydrating the plants.* **2.** To preserve by removing water from: *dehydrated the vegetables.* *—intr.* To lose water or body fluids: *I started dehydrating toward the end of the race.*

de·hy·dra·tion (dē′hī-**drā′**shən) *n.* **1.** The act or process of dehydrating. **2.** A condition in which an organism loses a large amount of water.

de·ice (dē-**īs′**) *tr.v.* **de·iced, de·ic·ing, de·ic·es** To make or keep free of ice: *deice the wings of an airplane.* **—de·ic′er** *n.*

de·i·fi·ca·tion (dē′ə-fĭ-**kā′**shən *or* dā′ə-fĭ-**kā′**shən) *n.* **1.** The act or process of deifying: *Deification of a great leader was common in early societies.* **2.** The condition of being deified: *After deification, the queen became the center of the religion.*

de·i·fy (**dē′**ə-fī′ *or* **dā′**ə-fī′) *tr.v.* **dei·fied, dei·fy·ing, dei·fies 1.** To make a god of: *Some religions deify volcanoes and stars.* **2.** To worship or revere as a god: *deify a great leader.*

deign (dān) *v.* **deigned, deign·ing, deigns** *—intr.* To be willing to do something that one considers beneath one's dignity; condescend: *The speaker deigned to answer the hecklers' questions.* *—tr.* To condescend to give; vouchsafe: *They didn't deign so much as a nod in our direction.*

de·i·ty (**dē′**ĭ-tē *or* **dā′**ĭ-tē) *n., pl.* **de·i·ties 1.** A god or goddess. **2.** The condition or nature of being a god; divinity: *The ancient Romans believed in the deity of Ceres, goddess of the harvest.* **3. Deity** God. [From Middle English *deite,* from Late Latin *deitās,* divine nature, from Latin *deus,* god.]

dé·jà vu (dā′zhä **vo͞o′**) *n.* The illusion of having already experienced something that is actually being experienced for the first time.

de·ject·ed (dĭ-**jĕk′**tĭd) *adj.* Being low in spirits; depressed: *The students felt dejected when it was announced that the holiday was canceled.* **—de·ject′ed·ly** *adv.* **—de·ject′ed·ness** *n.* —SEE NOTE AT **inject.**

de·jec·tion (dĭ-**jĕk′**shən) *n.* The condition of being dejected; low spirits: *experienced dejection after hearing the bad news.* [From Middle English *dejeccioun,* from Latin *dēicere,* to cast down : *dē-,* down + *iacere,* to throw.]

de ju·re (dē **jo͝or′**ē) *adv. & adj.* According to law; by right.

Del·a·ware[1] (**dĕl′**ə-wâr′) *n., pl.* **Delaware** or **Del·a·wares 1.** A member of a Native American people formerly living in the Delaware and Hudson River valleys, now living in Oklahoma, Kansas, Wisconsin, and Ontario. **2.** Either of the two Algonquian languages of the Delaware. **—Del′a·war′e·an** *adj.*

Del·a·ware[2] (**dĕl′**ə-wâr′) A state of the eastern United States on the Atlantic Ocean east of Maryland. It was admitted as the first of the original Thirteen Colonies in 1787. Dover is the capital and Wilmington the largest city. —SEE NOTE.

de·lay (dĭ-**lā′**) *v.* **de·layed, de·lay·ing, de·lays** *—tr.* **1.** To put off until a later time; postpone: *We will have to delay dinner an hour.* **2.** To cause to be late or slower than expected or desired: *A traffic jam delayed me in getting home.* *—intr.* To act or move slowly; put off an action or decision. ❖ *n.* **1.** The act of delaying or the condition of being delayed: *Your order will be filled without delay.* **2.** A period of time during which one is delayed: *a delay of 15 minutes waiting for the bus to arrive.* [From Middle English *delaien,* from Old French *deslaier* : *des-,* off + *laier,* to leave.] **—de·lay′er** *n.*

de·lec·ta·ble (dĭ-**lĕk′**tə-bəl) *adj.* Greatly pleasing or delicious; enjoyable: *a delectable hot biscuit.*

del·e·gate (**dĕl′**ĭ-gāt′ *or* **dĕl′**ĭ-gĭt) *n.* **1.** A person chosen to speak and act for another; a representative or agent: *Delegates to the convention were elected at the meeting.* **2.** A representative of a US territory in the House of Representatives who is entitled to speak but not vote. ❖ *tr.v.* (**dĕl′**ĭ-gāt′) **del·e·gat·ed, del·e·gat·ing, del·e·gates 1.** To authorize and send (another person) as one's representative: *The class delegated six students to serve on the committee.* **2.** To give or entrust to another: *delegate responsibility for feeding the animals.* [From Middle English *delegat,* from Medieval Latin *dēlēgāre,* to dispatch : *dē-,* away + *lēgāre,* to send.]

del·e·ga·tion (dĕl′ĭ-**gā′**shən) *n.* **1.** The act of delegating: *delegation of power to an attorney.* **2.** The condition of being delegated; appointment. **3.** A person or persons chosen to represent another or others: *Each state sends a delegation to the convention.*

de·lete (dĭ-**lēt′**) *tr.v.* **de·let·ed, de·let·ing, de·letes 1.** To remove (something) from a document or record: *delete the last sentence of a paragraph.* **2.** To remove (a file, for example) from a hard drive or other storage medium. [From Latin *dēlēre,* to wipe out.]

del·e·te·ri·ous (dĕl′ĭ-**tîr′**ē-əs) *adj.* Harmful; injurious: *the deleterious effects of smoking.* **—del′e·te′ri·ous·ly** *adv.* **—del′e·te′ri·ous·ness** *n.*

de·le·tion (dĭ-**lē′**shən) *n.* **1.** The act of deleting. **2.** A part that has been deleted, such as a word, sentence, or paragraph.

delft (dĕlft) *n.* Glazed earthenware of a usually blue-and-white style originally made in the city of Delft in the Netherlands.

Del·hi (**dĕl′**ē) A city of north-central India south-southeast of Islamabad, Pakistan. The new part of the city (New Delhi) became the capital of India in 1947.

del·i (**dĕl′**ē) *n., pl.* **del·is** *Informal* A delicatessen.

de·lib·er·ate (dĭ-**lĭb′**ər-ĭt) *adj.* **1.** Done or said on purpose; intentional: *a deliberate lie.* **2.** Arising from or marked by careful consideration: *a deliberate choice.* **3.** Slow and careful: *crossed the bridge with deliberate steps.* ❖ *v.* (dĭ-**lĭb′**ə-rāt′) **de·lib·er·at·ed, de·lib·er·at·ing, de·lib·er·ates** *—intr.* **1.** To think carefully and often slowly; reflect: *He deliberated over buying a new car.* **2.** To talk with others in an attempt to reach a decision: *The Senate deliberated throughout the night.* *—tr.* To consider (something) carefully and often slowly: *He deliberated the consequences of his act.* [From Middle English, from Latin *dēlīberāre,* to consider, weigh : *dē-,* off + *lībrāre,* to balance (from *lībra,* a balance, scales).] **—de·lib′er·ate·ly** *adv.*

de·lib·er·a·tion (dĭ-lĭb′ə-**rā′**shən) *n.* **1.** The act or process of deliberating. **2. deliberations** Formal discussion and consideration of all sides of an issue: *The deliberations of Congress are printed in the* Congressional Record. **3.** Thoughtfulness in decision or action: *The mountain climber took each step with deliberation.*

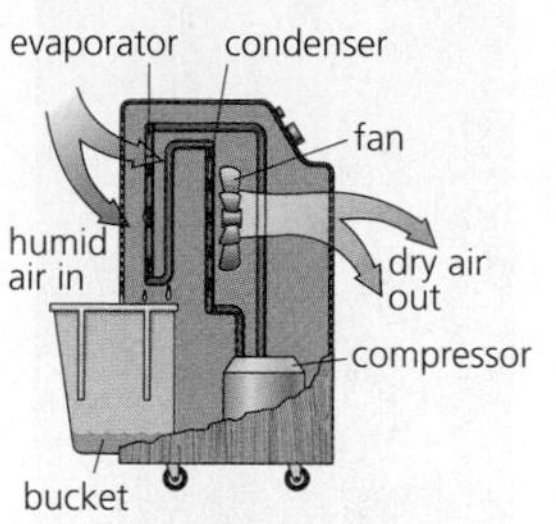

dehumidify

As air is drawn through the unit by the fan, its moisture collects on the cool evaporator and drips into the bucket.

GEOGRAPHY

Delaware[2] The state of Delaware gets its name from Thomas West, Lord de la Warr (1577–1618), who became the colonial governor of Virginia in 1610. During that year a cape was sighted by English explorers and named *Lawar* in his honor. Its name was later changed to *Delaware* and applied also to the river and the bay next to it. In 1664, Delaware Bay and Delaware River gave their name to the colony that had grown up to their west, and this eventually became the state we know as Delaware.

delft

delphinium

ă	pat	ôr	core
ā	pay	oi	boy
âr	care	ou	out
ä	father	o͝o	took
ĕ	pet	o͝or	lure
ē	be	o͞o	boot
ĭ	pit	ŭ	cut
ī	bite	ûr	urge
îr	pier	th	thin
ŏ	pot	*th*	this
ō	toe	zh	vision
ô	paw	ə	about

de·lib·er·a·tive (dĭ-lĭb**′**ə-rā′tĭv *or* dĭ-lĭb**′**ər-ə-tĭv) *adj.* Assembled or organized for deliberation or debate: *A legislature is a deliberative body.*

del·i·ca·cy (dĕl**′**ĭ-kə-sē) *n., pl.* **del·i·ca·cies 1.** The quality of being delicate. **2.** A choice food: *Truffles are considered delicacies.* **3.** Fineness of quality, appearance, construction, or execution: *embroidery of great delicacy.* **4.** Frailty of body or health: *The delicacy of small children makes them subject to many diseases.* **5.** Sensitivity of perception, discrimination, or taste. **6.** Sensitivity to the feelings of others; tact: *phrased the apology with delicacy.* **7.** Sensitivity to or undue concern for what is offensive or improper.

del·i·cate (dĕl**′**ĭ-kĭt) *adj.* **1.** Very fine in quality or appearance; dainty: *delicate lace.* **2.** Easily broken or damaged; fragile: *a delicate china figurine.* **3.** Frail in health: *The patient is delicate and must get plenty of rest.* **4.** Requiring careful or tactful treatment: *a delicate matter that could embarrass one's friends.* **5.** Fine or soft in touch or skill: *a delicate surgeon.* **6.** Very responsive or sensitive: *a delicate thermometer to measure small variations.* **7.** Pleasing to the senses, especially in a subtle way: *a delicate pink; a delicate flavor.* [From Middle English *delicat*, from Latin *dēlicātus*, pleasing; akin to *dēlicia*, pleasure.] **—del′i·cate·ly** *adv.*

del·i·ca·tes·sen (dĕl′ĭ-kə-**tĕs′**ən) *n.* A store that sells cooked or prepared foods ready for serving, such as cheeses, salads, and smoked meats. [From German *Delikatessen*, from French *délicatesse*, delicacy, from Latin *dēlicātus*, pleasing.]

de·li·cious (dĭ-**lĭsh′**əs) *adj.* Very pleasing or agreeable, especially to the senses of taste or smell: *delicious fresh fruit; a delicious supper.* **—de·li′cious·ly** *adv.* **—de·li′cious·ness** *n.*

de·light (dĭ-**līt′**) *n.* **1.** Great pleasure; joy: *The clown's face beamed with delight.* **2.** Something that gives great pleasure or enjoyment: *The birthday party was a delight to the whole family.* ❖ *v.* **de·light·ed, de·light·ing, de·lights** *—intr.* To take great pleasure or joy: *Most people delight in going to the zoo.* *—tr.* To please greatly: *Paris cannot fail to delight the visitor.* [From Middle English *delit*, from Old French *delitier*, to please, charm, from Latin *dēlectāre*.]

de·light·ed (dĭ-**lī′**tĭd) *adj.* Filled with delight: *The delighted winner waved to the crowd.* **—de·light′ed·ly** *adv.*

de·light·ful (dĭ-**līt′**fəl) *adj.* Greatly pleasing: *We had a delightful time at the party.* **—de·light′ful·ly** *adv.* **—de·light′ful·ness** *n.*

De·li·lah (də-**lī′**lə) In the Bible, the lover of Samson who betrayed him by having his hair, the source of his strength, cut off while he slept.

de·lim·it (dĭ-**lĭm′**ĭt) *tr.v.* **de·lim·it·ed, de·lim·it·ing, de·lim·its** To establish the limits or boundaries of: *delimited the line between our property and theirs.*

de·lin·e·ate (dĭ-**lĭn′**ē-āt′) *tr.v.* **de·lin·e·at·ed, de·lin·e·at·ing, de·lin·e·ates 1.** To draw or trace the outline of: *delineate the state of California on a map.* **2.** To represent in a picture; depict: *an artist who delineates sunsets in watercolors.* **3.** To state or describe in words or gestures: *The instructions delineate my duties carefully.* **4.** To show the distinguishing characteristics of: *The audition is supposed to delineate the best dancers from the others.* **—de·lin′e·a′tion** *n.*

de·lin·quen·cy (dĭ-**lĭng′**kwən-sē) *n., pl.* **de·lin·quen·cies 1.** Juvenile delinquency. **2.** Failure to do what law or duty requires. **3.** An offense or a misdeed.

de·lin·quent (dĭ-**lĭng′**kwənt) *adj.* **1.** Failing to do what law or duty requires: *The delinquent owners let their dog run free.* **2.** Overdue in payment: *a delinquent account.* ❖ *n.* **1.** A juvenile delinquent. **2.** A person who fails to do what law or duty requires. **—de·lin′quent·ly** *adv.*

de·lir·i·ous (dĭ-**lîr′**ē-əs) *adj.* **1.** Suffering from or characteristic of delirium: *a delirious patient with a high fever.* **2.** Marked by uncontrolled excitement; ecstatic: *delirious happiness.* **—de·lir′i·ous·ly** *adv.* **—de·lir′i·ous·ness** *n.*

de·lir·i·um (dĭ-**lîr′**ē-əm) *n., pl.* **de·lir·i·ums** or **de·lir·i·a** (dĭ-**lîr′**ē-ə) **1.** A temporary state of mental confusion and clouded consciousness resulting from high fever, poisoning, or shock: *the delirium of patients suffering from malaria.* **2.** A state of uncontrolled excitement or emotion: *the delirium of great success.*

de·liv·er (dĭ-**lĭv′**ər) *v.* **de·liv·ered, de·liv·er·ing, de·liv·ers** *—tr.* **1.** To take or carry (something) to the proper place or person: *deliver the mail; deliver a package.* **2.** To surrender (a person or thing); hand over: *deliver a criminal to the authorities.* **3.** To throw or hurl; pitch: *Our pitcher delivers a good fastball.* **4.** To strike (a blow): *The logger delivered a blow of the axe that split the log completely.* **5.** To provide or achieve (something desired or expected): *The senate leader delivered the votes necessary to pass the bill.* **6.** To express in words; utter: *deliver a speech to an audience.* **7a.** To give birth to: *She delivered a baby girl.* **b.** To assist in the birth of: *The midwife delivered the baby.* **8.** To set free, as from captivity, peril, or evil: *deliver a captive from slavery.* *—intr.* **1.** To make deliveries: *Few stores deliver nowadays.* **2.** To provide or achieve what is desired or expected: *The senator delivered on her pledge.* **3.** To give birth. [From Middle English *deliveren*, from Late Latin *dēlīberāre* : Latin *dē-*, off, away + Latin *līberāre*, to free (from *līber*, free).] **—de·liv′er·er** *n.*

de·liv·er·ance (dĭ-**lĭv′**ər-əns *or* dĭ-**lĭv′**rəns) *n.* **1.** The act of delivering or the condition of being delivered. **2.** Rescue from danger or slavery.

de·liv·er·y (dĭ-**lĭv′**ə-rē *or* dĭ-**lĭv′**rē) *n., pl.* **de·liv·er·ies 1a.** The act of conveying or delivering: *The post office makes deliveries every day but Sunday.* **b.** Something that is delivered: *There is a delivery for you downstairs.* **2.** The act of giving up; surrender: *delivery of a ransom for the king.* **3.** The act or manner of throwing or discharging: *an overhand delivery.* **4.** The act of giving birth: *The woman had a natural delivery of a healthy baby.* **5.** The act or manner of speaking or singing: *The content of his speech was excellent, but his delivery was poor.* **6.** The act of releasing or rescuing: *delivery for all prisoners captured in war.*

dell (dĕl) *n.* A small secluded valley.

Del·phi (**dĕl′**fī′) An ancient town of central Greece northwest of Athens. It was the site of a famous oracle of Apollo.

Del·phic (**dĕl′**fĭk) *adj.* **1.** Relating to Delphi or the oracle of Apollo at Delphi: *a Delphic prophesy.* **2.** Obscurely prophetic: *ambiguous Delphic words.*

del·phin·i·um (dĕl-**fĭn′**ē-əm) *n.* A tall garden plant having long clusters of flowers that are usually blue but are sometimes white, purple, or pink.

del·ta (**dĕl′**tə) *n.* **1.** The fourth letter of the Greek alphabet, written Δ, δ. In English it is represented as *D, d.* **2.** An object resembling a triangle in shape. **3.** A mass of sand, mud, and earth that accumulates at the mouth of a river, usually shaped like a triangle.

delta wing *n.* A single-wing configuration in the shape of an isosceles triangle used on certain aircraft.

del·toid (**dĕl′**toid′) *n.* A thick triangular muscle covering the shoulder joint, used to raise the arm from the side. ❖ *adj.* **1.** Triangular. **2.** Relating to the deltoid.

de·lude (dĭ-**lo͞od′**) *tr.v.* **de·lud·ed, de·lud·ing, de·ludes** To cause (someone) to hold a false belief; deceive thoroughly: *The fans were deluded into believing the team could win without its best pitcher.*

del·uge (**dĕl′**yo͞oj *or* **dā′**lo͞oj) *n.* **1.** A great flood or heavy downpour: *The deluge from spring rains flooded fields and roads for miles around.* **2.** Something that overwhelms as if by a great flood: *a deluge of mail in response to the editorial.* **3. Deluge** In the Bible, the great flood that occurred in the time of Noah. ❖ *tr.v.* **del·uged, del·ug·ing, del·ug·es 1.** To flood with water. **2.** To inundate with an overwhelming number or amount: *deluged with messages of congratulation.*

de·lu·sion (dĭ-lo͞o′zhən) *n.* **1.** The act or process of deluding or the state of being deluded: *the delusion of a swindler's victim.* **2.** A false belief or opinion: *under the delusion that might makes right.*

de·lu·sive (dĭ-lo͞o′sĭv) *adj.* Tending to delude; deceptive: *delusive claims about easy cures.* **—de·lu′sive·ly** *adv.*

de·luxe also **de luxe** (dĭ-lŭks′ *or* dĭ-lo͝oks′) *adj.* Particularly elegant, luxurious, or elaborate for its kind; of superior quality: *stayed in a deluxe hotel as part of the grand prize; ordered a hamburger deluxe.* [From French : *de*, of + *luxe*, luxury.]

delve (dĕlv) *intr.v.* **delved, delv·ing, delves 1.** To search deeply and laboriously: *delved into the court records.* **2.** To research or make inquiries into something: *scientists delving into promising cancer treatments.* **3.** To enter or move into an area in which movement is difficult: *The explorers delved into the jungle.* **—delv′er** *n.*

Dem. *abbr.* An abbreviation of: **1.** Democrat. **2.** democratic.

de·mag·net·ize (dē-măg′nĭ-tīz′) *tr.v.* **de·mag·net·ized, de·mag·net·iz·ing, de·mag·net·iz·es 1.** To remove magnetic properties from. **2.** To erase (a magnetic tape or disk).

dem·a·gog·ic (dĕm′ə-gŏj′ĭk) *adj.* Relating to or characteristic of a demagogue: *a demagogic leader.*

dem·a·gogue (dĕm′ə-gôg′) *n.* A leader who wins people's favor by appealing to their emotions and prejudices: *The demagogue's speech worked the crowd into a frenzy.* [From Greek *dēmagōgos*, popular leader : *dēmos*, people + *agōgos*, leading.]

dem·a·gogu·er·y (dĕm′ə-gô′gə-rē) *n.* The practices or emotional style of speech of a demagogue.

dem·a·gog·y (dĕm′ə-gŏj′ē *or* dĕm′ə-gôg′ē) *n.* The character or practices of a demagogue.

de·mand (dĭ-mănd′) *tr.v.* **de·mand·ed, de·mand·ing, de·mands 1.** To ask for urgently or insistently: *She demanded that they leave immediately.* **2.** To claim as just or due: *demand repayment of a loan.* **3.** To require as useful, just, proper, or necessary: *A lawyer's work demands skill and concentration.* ❖ *n.* **1.** The act of demanding. **2.** Something demanded: *striking workers making new wage demands.* **3.** A requirement, need, or claim: *This project has made many demands on my time.* **4.** The state of being sought after: *Firewood is in great demand during winter months.* **5.** A desire or readiness to purchase a certain commodity or service: *a demand for heating oil in the winter.* ◆ **on demand** When needed or asked for: *fed the baby on demand.* [From Middle English *demaunden*, from Latin *dēmandāre*, to entrust.] **—de·mand′a·ble** *adj.*

de·mand·ing (dĭ-măn′dĭng) *adj.* **1.** Requiring much effort or attention: *a very demanding task.* **2.** Requiring others to work hard or meet high expectations: *a demanding teacher.* **—de·mand′ing·ly** *adv.*

de·mar·cate (dĭ-mär′kāt′ *or* dē′mär-kāt′) *tr.v.* **de·mar·cat·ed, de·mar·cat·ing, de·mar·cates 1.** To set the boundaries of: *A river demarcates the border between the two states.* **2.** To separate clearly as if by boundaries; distinguish: *demarcate categories of art.*

de·mar·ca·tion (dē′mär-kā′shən) *n.* **1.** The setting or marking of boundaries or limits: *the demarcation of fishing rights.* **2.** A separation; a distinction: *There is a fine demarcation between daring and foolishness.*

de·mean¹ (dĭ-mēn′) *tr.v.* **de·meaned, de·mean·ing, de·means** To conduct or behave (oneself) in a particular manner: *The knights demeaned themselves well in battle.* [From Middle English *demeinen*, from Old French *demener.*]

de·mean² (dĭ-mēn′) *tr.v.* **de·meaned, de·mean·ing, de·means** To lower in status or character; degrade or humble: *demean oneself by continually asking for favors.* [From *mean*, inferior.]

de·mean·or (dĭ-mē′nər) *n.* The way in which a person behaves; deportment: *As head librarian, she has a demeanor of quiet authority.*

de·ment·ed (dĭ-mĕn′tĭd) *adj.* **1.** Having a serious mental disorder; insane. **2.** Suffering from dementia. **—de·ment′ed·ly** *adv.*

de·men·tia (dĭ-mĕn′shə) *n.* A condition in which the ability to think, remember, and understand is impaired as a result of disease.

de·mer·it (dĭ-mĕr′ĭt) *n.* **1.** A quality or characteristic deserving of blame; a fault: *work that has the demerits of sloppiness and inaccuracy.* **2.** A mark against one's record for a fault or misconduct.

De·me·ter (dĭ-mē′tər) *n.* In Greek mythology, the goddess of the harvest, identified with the Roman Ceres.

demi– *pref.* A prefix that means partly: *demigod.* —SEE NOTE AT **semi–.**

dem·i·god (dĕm′ē-gŏd′) *n.* A male divine being of lower power or standing than certain other gods, often the offspring of a god and a human.

dem·i·god·dess (dĕm′ē-gŏd′ĭs) *n.* A female divine being of lower power or standing than certain other gods, often the offspring of a god and a human.

dem·i·john (dĕm′ē-jŏn′) *n.* A large bottle with a narrow neck, usually encased in wicker.

demijohn

de·mil·i·ta·rize (dē-mĭl′ĭ-tə-rīz′) *tr.v.* **de·mil·i·ta·rized, de·mil·i·ta·riz·ing, de·mil·i·ta·riz·es** To remove or forbid military troops in (an area): *demilitarized the former war zone.* **—de·mil′i·ta·ri·za′tion** (dē-mĭl′ĭ-tər-ĭ-zā′shən) *n.*

de·mise (dĭ-mīz′) *n.* **1.** Death. **2.** The end of existence or activity; termination: *The invasion of the barbarians signaled the demise of the empire.*

dem·i·tasse (dĕm′ē-tăs′ *or* dĕm′ē-täs′) *n.* **1.** A small cup of strong black coffee. **2.** The small cup used to serve this drink.

dem·o (dĕm′ō) *n., pl.* **dem·os** *Informal* **1a.** A demonstration, as of a product or service. **b.** A recording that shows the abilities of a musician or other performer. **2.** A product used for demonstration and often sold later at a discount.

de·mo·bil·ize (dē-mō′bə-līz′) *tr.v.* **de·mo·bil·ized, de·mo·bil·iz·ing, de·mo·bil·iz·es** To discharge from military service or use: *demobilize an artillery unit.* **—de·mo′bi·li·za′tion** (dē-mō′bə-lĭ-zā′shən) *n.*

de·moc·ra·cy (dĭ-mŏk′rə-sē) *n., pl.* **de·moc·ra·cies 1a.** Government by the people, exercised either directly or through representatives. **b.** A political or social unit that has such a government. **2.** The principles of social equality and respect for the individual in a community. [From Greek *dēmokratiā* : *dēmos*, people + *kratos*, power.]

dem·o·crat (dĕm′ə-krăt′) *n.* **1.** A person who advocates democracy. **2. Democrat** A member of the Democratic Party.

dem·o·crat·ic (dĕm′ə-krăt′ĭk) *adj.* **1.** Characteristic of or advocating democracy. **2.** Relating to or for the people in general; popular: *a democratic movement.* **3. Democratic** Relating to or characteristic of the Democratic Party. **—dem′o·crat′i·cal·ly** *adv.*

Democratic Party *n.* One of the two major political parties of the United States, dating from 1828.

Dem·o·crat·ic-Re·pub·li·can Party *n.* A US political party founded by Thomas Jefferson in 1792 in opposition to the Federalist Party.

de·moc·ra·tize (dĭ-mŏk′rə-tīz′) *tr.v.* **de·moc·ra·tized, de·moc·ra·tiz·ing, de·moc·ra·tiz·es** To make democratic. **—de·moc′ra·ti·za′tion** (dĭ-mŏk′rə-tĭ-zā′shən) *n.*

demolition

dendrite
a mineral dendrite

ă	pat	ôr	core
ā	pay	oi	boy
âr	care	ou	out
ä	father	o͝o	took
ĕ	pet	o͝or	lure
ē	be	o͞o	boot
ĭ	pit	ŭ	cut
ī	bite	ûr	urge
îr	pier	th	thin
ŏ	pot	*th*	this
ō	toe	zh	vision
ô	paw	ə	about

dem·o·graph·ics (dĕm′ə-**grăf′**ĭks) *n. (used with a plural verb)* The characteristics of human populations, especially when used to identify consumer markets. **—dem′o·graph′ic** *adj.*

de·mog·ra·phy (dĭ-**mŏg′**rə-fē) *n.* The study of the characteristics of human populations, such as growth, density, distribution, and birth and death rates.

de·mol·ish (dĭ-**mŏl′**ĭsh) *tr.v.* **de·mol·ished, de·mol·ish·ing, de·mol·ish·es 1.** To tear down or break apart the structure of; raze: *demolish an old building.* See Synonyms at **destroy. 2.** To do away with completely; put an end to: *demolish an argument.* [From Latin *dēmōlīrī* : *dē-*, away, off, un- + *mōlīrī*, to build (from *mōlēs*, mass).]

dem·o·li·tion (dĕm′ə-**lĭsh′**ən *or* dē′mə-**lĭsh′**ən) *n.* The act or process or wrecking or destroying, especially by means of explosives.

de·mon (**dē′**mən) *n.* **1.** An evil supernatural being; a devil. **2.** A tormenting person, force, or passion: *He was never able to deal with his demons.* **3.** A person who is very energetic, skillful, or diligent: *was working like a demon.* [From Middle English, from Greek *daimōn*, divine power, spirit.] **—de·mon′ic** (dĭ-**mŏn′**ĭk) *adj.*

de·mo·ni·ac (dĭ-**mō′**nē-ăk′) *adj.* **1.** Possessed, produced, or influenced by a demon. **2.** Resembling or suggestive of a demon. ❖ *n.* A person who is or seems to be possessed by a demon. **—de′mo·ni′a·cal·ly** (dē′mə-**nī′**ə-kə-lē) *adv.*

de·mon·stra·ble (dĭ-**mŏn′**strə-bəl) *adj.* Capable of being demonstrated or proved: *a demonstrable truth.*

dem·on·strate (**dĕm′**ən-strāt′) *v.* **dem·on·strat·ed, dem·on·strat·ing, dem·on·strates** *—tr.* **1.** To show clearly and deliberately; manifest: *She demonstrated her skill as a gymnast.* **2.** To show to be true; prove: *demonstrate one's ability to do the job.* **3a.** To describe or explain by experiment, practical application, or example: *demonstrate the effect of light on plants.* **b.** To show the use of (a product), as to a prospective buyer: *demonstrate a washing machine.* *—intr.* To take part in a public display of opinion: *demonstrated against the new highway.* [From Latin *dēmōnstrāre* : *dē-*, completely + *mōnstrāre*, to show.]

dem·on·stra·tion (dĕm′ən-**strā′**shən) *n.* **1.** The act of showing that something is true or evident: *a demonstration of the medicine's effectiveness.* **2.** An exemplification or explanation of something, carried out in practice: *a demonstration of ballroom dancing.* **3.** A display or outward show, as of one's feelings: *The frown was another demonstration of her displeasure.* **4.** A public display of group opinion, as by a rally or march.

de·mon·stra·tive (dĭ-**mŏn′**strə-tĭv) *adj.* **1.** Serving to manifest or prove. **2.** Openly expressing one's feelings, especially affection: *Her demonstrative friend wept when she received the award.* **3.** In grammar, specifying or singling out the person or thing referred to; for example, the word *these* is a demonstrative pronoun in *These are my books* and a demonstrative adjective in *These books are mine.* ❖ *n.* A demonstrative pronoun or adjective. **—de·mon′stra·tive·ly** *adv.* **—de·mon′stra·tive·ness** *n.*

dem·on·stra·tor (**dĕm′**ən-strā′tər) *n.* **1.** A person who demonstrates, such as a participant in a public display of opinion. **2.** An article or product used in a demonstration.

de·mor·al·ize (dĭ-**môr′**ə-līz′ *or* dĭ-**mŏr′**ə-līz′) *tr.v.* **de·mor·al·ized, de·mor·al·iz·ing, de·mor·al·iz·es 1.** To weaken the confidence or morale of; dishearten: *Reading the negative reviews of the movie demoralized its director.* **2.** To weaken the morals of; corrupt: *Offers of favors have demoralized many politicians.* **—de·mor′al·i·za′tion** (dĭ-môr′ə-lĭ-**zā′**shən *or* dĭ-mŏr′ə-lĭ-**zā′**shən) *n.*

De·mos·the·nes (dĭ-**mŏs′**thə-nēz′) 384–322 BC. Greek orator who urged the people of Athens to rebel against Philip II of Macedon.

de·mote (dĭ-**mōt′**) *tr.v.* **de·mot·ed, de·mot·ing, de·motes** To reduce in rank, grade, or status: *demoted from captain to lieutenant.* **—de·mo′tion** *n.*

de·mur (dĭ-**mûr′**) *intr.v.* **de·murred, de·mur·ring, de·murs** To raise objections; object: *demur at working such late hours.* ❖ *n.* An objection; a demurral.

de·mure (dĭ-**myo͝or′**) *adj.* **de·mur·er, de·mur·est** Reserved and modest, as in manner or behavior: *a pleasant and demure person.* **—de·mure′ly** *adv.* **—de·mure′ness** *n.*

de·mur·ral (dĭ-**mûr′**əl) *n.* The act of demurring, especially a mild or polite expression of opposition.

den (dĕn) *n.* **1.** The place where a wild animal lives; a lair: *The fox was safe in its den.* **2.** A hidden or secret place where people such as criminals gather: *a den of thieves.* **3.** A room used for relaxation or study. [From Old English *denn.*]

De·na·li (də-**nä′**lē) See Mount **McKinley.**

den·ar (**dĕn′**är) *n., pl.* **den·a·ri** (**dĕn′**är-ē) The basic monetary unit of Macedonia.

de·na·ture (dē-**nā′**chər) *tr.v.* **de·na·tured, de·na·tur·ing, de·na·tures 1.** To change (alcohol) so that it is unfit for drinking but is still useful for other purposes. **2.** To change the structure of (a protein) so that its biological properties are reduced or eliminated. **—de·na′tur·a′tion** *n.*

den·drite (**dĕn′**drīt′) *n.* **1.** A branching extension of a nerve cell that receives impulses from other cells and transmits them inward toward the body of the cell. **2.** A mineral that crystallizes in another mineral in the form of a branching pattern. [From Greek *dendron*, tree.]

de·ni·al (dĭ-**nī′**əl) *n.* **1.** A refusal to comply with or satisfy a request. **2.** A refusal to grant the truth of an accusation or allegation: *The charges of corruption prompted an immediate denial from the mayor.* **3.** A rejection of a doctrine or belief: *denial of a new theory of the origin of the universe.*

de·ni·er (dĭ-**nī′**ər) *n.* A person who denies.

den·i·grate (**dĕn′**ĭ-grāt′) *tr.v.* **den·i·grat·ed, den·i·grat·ing, den·i·grates** To attack the reputation or character of; speak ill of; defame. [From Latin *dēnigrāre*, to blacken, defame, from *niger*, black.] **—den′i·gra′tion** *n.*

den·im (**dĕn′**ĭm) *n.* **1.** A coarse, twilled cotton fabric, often blue, traditionally used for overalls and work clothes and now used for jeans and casual wear. **2. denims** Pants or another garment made of this fabric. [From French *(serge) de Nîmes*, (serge) of Nîmes, after *Nîmes*, a city in France.]

den·i·zen (**dĕn′**ĭ-zən) *n.* A person or animal that lives in a particular place; an inhabitant: *Lions and jackals are denizens of the African plains.* [From Middle English *denisein*, from Late Latin *deintus*, from within.]

Den·mark (**dĕn′**märk′) A country of northern Europe north of Germany. It was unified in the tenth century under the Vikings. Copenhagen is the capital.

de·nom·i·nate (dĭ-**nŏm′**ə-nāt′) *tr.v.* **de·nom·i·nat·ed, de·nom·i·nat·ing, de·nom·i·nates** To give a name to; designate.

de·nom·i·nate number (dĭ-**nŏm′**ə-nĭt) *n.* A number used with a unit of measure. In the measures 12 lb., 14¢, and 3 feet, 12, 14, and 3 are denominate numbers.

de·nom·i·na·tion (dĭ-nŏm′ə-**nā′**shən) *n.* **1.** An organized group of religious congregations under a common faith and name: *People of several denominations met to worship together.* **2.** One of a series of kinds, values, or sizes, as in a system of currency: *bills of different denominations.* **3.** A name, especially for a group or class of things; a designation.

de·nom·i·na·tion·al (dĭ-nŏm′ə-**nā′**shə-nəl) *adj.* Related to or under the control of a religious denomination; sectarian.

de·nom·i·na·tor (dĭ-**nŏm′**ə-nā′tər) *n.* The number

below the line in a fraction that indicates the number of equal parts into which one whole is divided. For example, in the fraction 2/7, 7 is the denominator.

de·no·ta·tion (dē′nō-tā′shən) *n.* **1.** The act of denoting. **2.** The most specific or direct meaning of a word, in contrast to its figurative or associated meanings.

de·note (dĭ-nōt′) *tr.v.* **de·not·ed, de·not·ing, de·notes 1.** To be a sign of; mark: *The blue areas on the map denote water.* **2.** To signify directly; refer to specifically.

de·noue·ment also **dé·noue·ment** (dā′no͞o-mäɴ′) *n.* The outcome or resolution of the plot of a drama or novel.

de·nounce (dĭ-nouns′) *tr.v.* **de·nounced, de·nounc·ing, de·nounc·es 1.** To declare openly as being wrong or reprehensible: *The senator denounced the policy as wasteful and foolish.* **2.** To accuse formally; inform against: *denounced the swindler to the police.*

dense (dĕns) *adj.* **dens·er, dens·est 1.** Having relatively high density. **2.** Crowded closely together; compact: *a dense population in the city.* **3.** Difficult to penetrate; thick: *a dense forest; a dense fog.* **4.** Difficult to understand because of complexity or obscurity: *a dense novel.* **5.** Slow to comprehend; thickheaded. [From Middle English, from Latin *dēnsus.*] **—dense′ly** *adv.* **—dense′ness** *n.*

den·si·ty (dĕn′sĭ-tē) *n., pl.* **den·si·ties 1.** In physics, the mass per unit of volume of a substance: *Lead has a greater density than water.* **2.** The amount of something in a unit or measure of length, volume, or area: *The population density in New York City is greater than in many other cities.* **3.** Thickness of consistency; impenetrability: *The density of the grass made the tiger invisible.* **4.** Stupidity; dullness.

dent (dĕnt) *n.* **1.** A hollow place in a surface, usually caused by pressure or a blow: *a dent in a garbage can.* **2.** *Informal* Meaningful progress; headway: *If we work all day we will make a significant dent in this assignment.* ❖ *v.* **dent·ed, dent·ing, dents** *—tr.* To make a dent in: *When I bumped the guard rail, I dented the car's fender.* *—intr.* To become dented: *Aluminum cans dent easily.*

den·tal (dĕn′tl) *adj.* **1.** Relating to the teeth: *a dental drill.* **2.** Relating to dentistry: *a dental school.*

dental floss *n.* A thread used to remove food particles and plaque from the teeth.

dental hygienist *n.* A person trained to provide care for the teeth, gums, and mouth, usually working with a dentist.

den·ti·frice (dĕn′tə-frĭs′) *n.* A powder, paste, or liquid used for cleaning the teeth.

den·tin (dĕn′tĭn) or **den·tine** (dĕn′tēn′) *n.* The hard, bonelike material that forms most of a tooth and lies beneath the enamel.

den·tist (dĕn′tĭst) *n.* A person who is trained and licensed to practice dentistry.

den·tist·ry (dĕn′tĭ-strē) *n.* **1.** The scientific study and treatment of diseases and disorders of the mouth, gums, and teeth. **2.** The practice of this science as a profession.

den·ti·tion (dĕn-tĭsh′ən) *n.* The type, number, and arrangement of the teeth of a human or other vertebrate animal: *the different dentitions of cats and guinea pigs.*

den·ture (dĕn′chər) *n.* **1.** A partial or complete set of artificial teeth for either the upper or lower jaw. **2.** often **dentures** A complete set of removable artificial teeth for both jaws.

de·nude (dĭ-no͞od′) *tr.v.* **de·nud·ed, de·nud·ing, de·nudes** To remove the covering from; make bare: *Cutting down the trees denuded the landscape.*

de·nun·ci·a·tion (dĭ-nŭn′sē-ā′shən) *n.* **1.** The act or an instance of denouncing, especially a public condemnation: *the editorial's denunciation of government corruption.* **2.** The providing of secret or damaging information about someone to the authorities: *the denunciation of the spy.*

Den·ver (dĕn′vər) The capital of Colorado, in the north-central part of the state on the South Platte River. It was settled by gold prospectors in 1858.

de·ny (dĭ-nī′) *tr.v.* **de·nied, de·ny·ing, de·nies 1.** To declare to be untrue; contradict: *deny an accusation.* **2.** To refuse to believe; reject. **3.** To refuse to acknowledge; disavow: *deny a friendship.* **4.** To decline to grant or allow: *We could not deny seed to the hungry birds.* **5.** To restrain (oneself), especially from indulgence in pleasures: *I denied myself an extra scoop of ice cream.* [From Middle English *denien*, from Latin *dēnegāre*, from *negāre*, to say no.]

de·o·dor·ant (dē-ō′dər-ənt) *n.* A preparation used to conceal or suppress odors: *a room deodorant.*

de·o·dor·ize (dē-ō′də-rīz′) *tr.v.* **de·o·dor·ized, de·o·dor·iz·ing, de·o·dor·iz·es** To conceal or neutralize the odor of or in: *deodorized the carpet.* **—de·o′dor·i·za′tion** (dē-ō′dər-ĭ-zā′shən) *n.* **—de·o′dor·iz′er** *n.*

de·ox·i·dize (dē-ŏk′sĭ-dīz′) *tr.v.* **de·ox·i·dized, de·ox·i·diz·ing, de·ox·i·diz·es** To remove oxygen from (a chemical compound). **—de·ox′i·di·za′tion** (dē-ŏk′sĭ-dĭ-zā′shən) *n.* **—de·ox′i·diz′er** *n.*

de·ox·y·ri·bo·nu·cle·ic acid (dē-ŏk′sē-rī′bō-no͞o-klē′-ĭk) *n.* DNA.

de·part (dĭ-pärt′) *intr.v.* **de·part·ed, de·part·ing, de·parts 1.** To go away; leave: *departed for work before dawn.* **2.** To vary, as from a regular course; deviate: *depart from our custom of eating out on Saturdays.*

de·part·ed (dĭ-pär′tĭd) *adj.* **1.** Bygone or past: *the departed days of vacation.* **2.** Dead; deceased. ❖ *n.* **1.** A dead person. **2.** Dead people considered as a group; the dead.

de·part·ment (dĭ-pärt′mənt) *n.* **1.** A distinct division of an organization, such as a government, company, or college: *the fire department; the personnel department; the English department.* **2.** A section of a department store selling a particular line of merchandise: *the shoe department.*

de·part·men·tal (dē′pärt-mĕn′tl) *adj.* **1.** Relating to a department: *a departmental newsletter.* **2.** Separated into departments: *a departmental organization.*

department store *n.* A large store selling many kinds of goods and services and organized in separate departments.

de·par·ture (dĭ-pär′chər) *n.* **1.** The act of going away: *Our departure was delayed by a flat tire.* **2.** A deviation or divergence, as from an established rule, plan, or procedure: *Going to bed early was a departure from our usual habit.* **3.** A starting out, as on a trip or a new course of action.

de·pend (dĭ-pĕnd′) *intr.v.* **de·pend·ed, de·pend·ing, de·pends 1.** To rely, especially for support or maintenance: *Many people depend on a pension when they retire.* **2.** To place trust or confidence: *You can depend on me to be on time.* **3.** To be determined by; hinge or rest on: *Our plans depend on the weather.* [From Middle English *dependen*, from Latin *dēpendēre* : *dē-*, down, from + *pendēre*, to hang.]

de·pend·a·ble (dĭ-pĕn′də-bəl) *adj.* Trustworthy: *a dependable employee who always finishes his work on time.* **—de·pend′a·bil′i·ty** *n.* **—de·pend′a·bly** *adv.*

de·pen·dence (dĭ-pĕn′dəns) *n.* **1.** The state of being determined, influenced, or controlled by something else: *the dependence of a storekeeper on suppliers.* **2.** The state of being dependent on another for financial support. **3.** The condition of being dependent on a substance such as a drug or a given behavior.

de·pen·den·cy (dĭ-pĕn′dən-sē) *n., pl.* **de·pen·den·cies 1.** Dependence. **2.** Something dependent or subordinate. **3.** A minor territory under the jurisdiction of a government.

denim

WRITERS CHOOSE THEIR WORDS

Gundar seized [Will's hand] and shook it hard —not the least because he was relieved to find that he wasn't facing some supernatural **denizen** of the forest.

—John Flanagan
The Siege of Macindaw

de·pend·ent (dĭ-**pĕn′**dənt) *adj.* **1.** Determined or influenced by something else: *The outcome is dependent on the voters.* **2.** Subordinate: *a clause dependent on the main clause.* **3.** Relying on or needing the help of another for support: *Plants are dependent upon sunlight.* **4.** Engaging in a behavior, such as drug use or gambling, that one is unable to stop without suffering physical symptoms or psychological distress. ❖ *n.* A person who relies on another, especially for financial support: *My parents have three dependents including me.* **—de·pend′ent·ly** *adv.*

dependent clause *n.* A subordinate clause.

dependent variable *n.* A mathematical variable whose value is determined by one or more independent variables. For example, in $y = x^2 + 2x$, y is the dependent variable.

de·pict (dĭ-**pĭkt′**) *tr.v.* **de·pict·ed, de·pict·ing, de·picts** To represent in words or pictures; describe or show: *a book depicting life in ancient Rome; a painting that depicts a historical event.* **—de·pic′tion** *n.*

de·pil·a·to·ry (dĭ-**pĭl′**ə-tôr′ē) *adj.* Able to remove hair: *a depilatory lotion.* ❖ *n., pl.* **de·pil·a·to·ries** A preparation in the form of a liquid or cream used to remove unwanted body hair.

de·plane (dē-**plān′**) *intr.v.* **de·planed, de·plan·ing, de·planes** To disembark from an airplane.

de·plete (dĭ-**plēt′**) *tr.v.* **de·plet·ed, de·plet·ing, de·pletes** To consume or reduce to a very low amount: *This cold snap has depleted our oil supplies.* [From Latin *dēplēre*, to empty : *dē-*, down, away + *plēre*, to fill.] **—de·ple′tion** *n.*

de·plor·a·ble (dĭ-**plôr′**ə-bəl) *adj.* **1.** Worthy of strong disapproval or reproach: *rude and deplorable behavior.* **2.** Lamentable; woeful: *The kitchen was in a deplorable state after we finished cooking.* **3.** Wretched; bad: *deplorable run-down housing.* **—de·plor′a·bly** *adv.*

de·plore (dĭ-**plôr′**) *tr.v.* **de·plored, de·plor·ing, de·plores 1.** To feel or express strong disapproval of; condemn: *We deplore cruelty to animals.* **2.** To express sorrow or grief over: *The world deplored the loss of the great actor.* [From Latin *dēplōrāre*, from *plōrāre*, to wail.]

de·ploy (dĭ-**ploi′**) *tr. & intr.v.* **de·ployed, de·ploy·ing, de·ploys 1.** To position or be in position in readiness for combat: *deploy troops for a battle.* **2.** To distribute or be distributed systematically or strategically: *The ships were deployed along the coast to intercept smugglers.* **—de·ploy′ment** *n.*

de·pop·u·late (dē-**pŏp′**yə-lāt′) *tr.v.* **de·pop·u·lat·ed, de·pop·u·lat·ing, de·pop·u·lates** To sharply reduce the population of: *Severe flooding depopulated much of the lowland region.* **—de·pop′u·la′tion** *n.*

de·port (dĭ-**pôrt′**) *tr.v.* **de·port·ed, de·port·ing, de·ports 1.** To expel from a country; banish: *Government authorities deported the spy.* **2.** To behave (oneself) in a certain manner: *Visitors usually deport themselves with quiet respect while in the cathedral.* [From French *déporter*, to banish, from Latin *dēportāre*, to carry away : *dē-*, off, away + *portāre*, to carry.]

de·por·ta·tion (dē′pôr-**tā′**shən) *n.* The act or an instance of deporting someone.

de·port·ment (dĭ-**pôrt′**mənt) *n.* A manner of personal conduct; behavior: *an ambassador with a very dignified deportment.*

de·pose (dĭ-**pōz′**) *tr.v.* **de·posed, de·pos·ing, de·pos·es 1.** To remove from office or power: *The king was deposed because of his misconduct.* **2.** To take a deposition from: *Investigators will depose the witness behind closed doors.*

de·pos·it (dĭ-**pŏz′**ĭt) *tr.v.* **de·pos·it·ed, de·pos·it·ing, de·pos·its 1.** To put or set down; place: *Please deposit books returned to the library at the front desk.* **2.** To lay down or leave behind by a natural process: *The flooding river deposited mud and debris in the roads.* **3.** To put (money) in a bank or financial account. **4.** To give as partial payment or security: *The store will hold the computer if we deposit half the cost now.* ❖ *n.* **1.** Something, especially an amount of money, put in a place for safekeeping, such as a bank. **2a.** A partial or initial payment of a cost or debt: *left a deposit on the coat.* **b.** An amount of money given as security for an item acquired for temporary use: *a deposit on a rented lawn mower.* **3a.** A mass, layer, or collection of material left or laid down by a natural process: *Deposits of mud and sticks choked the stream.* **b.** A mass of naturally occurring mineral material: *deposits of coal in West Virginia.* ◆ **on deposit** Placed somewhere for safekeeping: *money on deposit in a bank account.* [From Latin *dēpositus*, past participle of *dēpōnere* : *dē-*, down + *pōnere*, to put.] **—de·pos′i·tor** (dĭ-**pŏz′**ĭ-tər) *n.*

dep·o·si·tion (dĕp′ə-**zĭsh′**ən) *n.* **1.** The act of deposing, as from high office. **2.** The act of depositing, especially the laying down of matter by a natural process: *deposition of rock by a retreating glacier.* **3.** Something deposited; a deposit. **4.** Sworn testimony recorded for use in court at a later date: *The expert's deposition was read to the court.*

de·pos·i·to·ry (dĭ-**pŏz′**ĭ-tôr′ē) *n., pl.* **de·pos·i·to·ries** A place where something is deposited, as for storage or safekeeping.

de·pot (**dē′**pō *or* **dĕp′**ō) *n.* **1.** A railroad or bus station. **2.** A warehouse or storehouse: *a trucking depot for freight.* **3.** A place where military equipment and supplies are stored: *an army depot.*

de·prave (dĭ-**prāv′**) *tr.v.* **de·praved, de·prav·ing, de·praves** To make morally bad; corrupt.

de·praved (dĭ-**prāvd′**) *adj.* Morally corrupt; perverted.

de·prav·i·ty (dĭ-**prăv′**ĭ-tē) *n., pl.* **de·prav·i·ties 1.** Moral corruption; degradation: *The depravity of the criminals knew no limits.* **2.** A depraved act or condition.

dep·re·cate (**dĕp′**rĭ-kāt′) *tr.v.* **de·pre·cat·ed, de·pre·cat·ing, de·pre·cates 1.** To speak of as having little value; belittle: *He tends to deprecate his own work and praise the work of others.* **2.** To express disapproval of: *Some people deprecated the mayor's handling of the matter.* [From Latin *dēprecārī*, to ward off by prayer : *dē-*, away, off + *precārī*, to pray.] **—dep′re·ca′tion** *n.*

de·pre·ci·ate (dĭ-**prē′**shē-āt′) *v.* **de·pre·ci·at·ed, de·pre·ci·at·ing, de·pre·ci·ates** *—intr.* To become less in price or value: *The longer you own that car the more it will depreciate.* *—tr.* **1.** To reduce the value of the expenditure for (something) in a business's records: *The company depreciates its equipment every year throughout its useful life.* **2.** To think or speak of as being of little worth; belittle. [From Middle English *depreciaten*, from Latin *dēpretiāre* : *dē-*, down + *pretium*, price.] **—de·pre′ci·a′tor** *n.* **—de·pre′ci·a·to′ry** (dĭ-**prē′**shə-tôr′ē) *adj.*

de·pre·ci·a·tion (dĭ-prē′shē-**ā′**shən) *n.* A decrease or loss in value, as because of wear, age, or market conditions.

dep·re·da·tion (dĕp′rĭ-**dā′**shən) *n.* **1.** A predatory attack; a raid: *a bear's depredation of our campsite.* **2.** Damage or loss; ravage.

de·press (dĭ-**prĕs′**) *tr.v.* **de·pressed, de·press·ing, de·press·es 1.** To lower in spirits; deject: *The sad news depressed everyone.* **2.** To press down: *depress the brake pedal to stop the car.* **3a.** To lessen the activity or force of; weaken: *Widespread layoffs have further depressed the economy.* **b.** To lower prices in (a financial market). —SEE NOTE AT **pressure.**

de·pressed (dĭ-**prĕst′**) *adj.* **1.** Low in spirits; sad and dejected: *The news of the accident left me feeling very depressed.* **2.** Suffering from clinical depression. **3.** Sunk below the surrounding region: *the depressed center of a crater.* **4.** Affected by social and economic hardship, as

ă	pat	ôr	core
ā	pay	oi	boy
âr	care	ou	out
ä	father	ŏŏ	took
ĕ	pet	ŏŏr	lure
ē	be	ōō	boot
ĭ	pit	ŭ	cut
ī	bite	ûr	urge
îr	pier	th	thin
ŏ	pot	*th*	this
ō	toe	zh	vision
ô	paw	ə	about

from poverty and unemployment: *a program of aid for depressed areas of the country.*

de·press·ing (dĭ-prĕs′ĭng) *adj.* Causing one to feel sad or despondent: *depressing news.*

de·pres·sion (dĭ-prĕsh′ən) *n.* **1a.** The condition of feeling sad and despondent: *the players' depression after losing in the playoffs.* **b.** A psychiatric disorder characterized by extreme and persistent sadness, and often feelings of guilt or helplessness, difficulty concentrating and sleeping, loss of appetite, and the inability to experience pleasure; clinical depression. **2.** The act of depressing or the state of being depressed: *the depression of typewriter keys.* **3.** An area that is sunk below its surroundings; a hollow: *Depressions in the sidewalk made it hard to walk on.* **4.** A lowering in amount, degree, or position: *a depression in the temperature.* **5a.** A period of drastic decline in an economy: *A depression brings unemployment and hardship to many people.* **b. Depression** The Great Depression.

dep·ri·va·tion (dĕp′rə-vā′shən) *n.* **1.** The act or an instance of depriving; loss. **2.** The condition of being deprived.

de·prive (dĭ-prīv′) *tr.v.* **de·prived, de·priv·ing, de·prives 1.** To take something away from; divest: *Revolution deprived the government of its power.* **2.** To prevent from having or enjoying; deny: *Heavy snow deprived the deer of food.*

dept. *abbr.* An abbreviation of department.

depth (dĕpth) *n.* **1.** The quality or condition of being deep. **2.** The measure or distance downward, backward, or inward: *Each lot reaches to a depth of about 300 feet from the street.* **3.** often **depths** A deep part or place: *the ocean depths.* **4.** The severest or worst part: *in the depth of despair.* **5.** Intellectual complexity or penetration; profundity: *He wrote poetry and plays of unusual depth.* **6.** Lowness of pitch, as of a voice or a musical tone. **7.** Complete detail; thoroughness: *an interview conducted in great depth.*

depth charge *n.* An explosive charge designed for use underwater, especially one launched from a ship's deck for use against submarines.

depth perception *n.* The ability to see spatial relationships, especially distances between objects, in three dimensions.

dep·u·ta·tion (dĕp′yə-tā′shən) *n.* A person or group appointed to act for others; a delegation: *A deputation of staff members urged officials to improve conditions at the hospital.*

de·pute (dĭ-pyo͞ot′) *tr.v.* **de·put·ed, de·put·ing, de·putes** To appoint as an agent or representative: *The president deputes ambassadors to foreign countries.*

dep·u·tize (dĕp′yə-tīz′) *tr. & intr.v.* **dep·u·tized, dep·u·tiz·ing, dep·u·tiz·es** To appoint or serve as a deputy.

dep·u·ty (dĕp′yə-tē) *n., pl.* **dep·u·ties** A person appointed or empowered to act in place of or for another: *The health officer has several deputies to help enforce environmental laws.* [From Middle English *depute*, from Old French *deputer*, to assign as an agent, from Latin *dēputāre*, to consider : *dē-*, from + *putāre*, to ponder.]

de·rail (dē-rāl′) *intr. & tr.v.* **de·railed, de·rail·ing, de·rails** To go off or cause to go off the tracks: *The train derailed near Buffalo. A fallen tree on the tracks derailed the express.* **—de·rail′ment** *n.*

de·rail·leur (dĭ-rā′lər) *n.* A mechanism on a bicycle that moves the pedal chain from one gearwheel to another.

de·range (dĭ-rānj′) *tr.v.* **de·ranged, de·rang·ing, de·rang·es 1.** To cause (someone) to become mentally unbalanced or unsound. **2.** To upset the arrangement, functioning, or order of: *a chemical that deranges the functioning of the heart.* **—de·range′ment** *n.*

de·ranged (dĭ-rānjd′) *adj.* **1.** Mentally unbalanced or unsound. **2.** Not ordered or functioning properly.

der·by (dûr′bē) *n., pl.* **der·bies 1.** Any of various annual horse races usually restricted to three-year-old horses. **2.** A formal race usually allowing anyone to enter: *a motorcycle derby.* **3.** A stiff felt hat with a round crown and a narrow curved brim. [After Edward Smith-Stanley, 12th Earl of *Derby* (1752–1834), host of the first derby in Epsom, England (1780).]

der·e·lict (dĕr′ə-lĭkt′) *adj.* **1.** Neglectful; remiss: *derelict in one's duty.* **2.** Deserted by an owner; abandoned: *a derelict building crumbling with the years.* ❖ *n.* **1.** A homeless or jobless person. **2.** Abandoned property, especially a ship abandoned at sea.

der·e·lic·tion (dĕr′ə-lĭk′shən) *n.* Willful neglect, as of duty or principle.

de·ride (dĭ-rīd′) *tr.v.* **de·rid·ed, de·rid·ing, de·rides** To laugh at, speak of, or write about with contempt or scorn; scoff at or mock: *Many people deride customs they don't understand.*

de·ri·sion (dĭ-rĭzh′ən) *n.* The act of ridiculing or laughing at someone or something.

de·ri·sive (dĭ-rī′sĭv) *adj.* Expressing ridicule; mocking: *Talk of the plan was silenced by derisive laughter.* **—de·ri′sive·ly** *adv.*

der·i·va·tion (dĕr′ə-vā′shən) *n.* **1.** The act or process of deriving. **2.** Something that is derived; a derivative. **3.** The source from which something is derived; origin: *The polka is a dance of eastern European derivation.* **4.** The historical origin and development of a word; an etymology: *Derivations are given for many of the words in this dictionary.* **5.** The process by which words are formed from existing words or bases, chiefly by the addition of prefixes or suffixes or by changing the form of the word or base.

de·riv·a·tive (dĭ-rĭv′ə-tĭv) *adj.* Resulting from or using derivation: *English has many derivative words.* ❖ *n.* **1.** Something derived: *Gasoline is a derivative of oil.* **2.** A word formed from another by derivation, such as *electricity* from *electric.*

de·rive (dĭ-rīv′) *v.* **de·rived, de·riv·ing, de·rives** *—tr.* **1.** To obtain or receive from a source: *derive pleasure from music.* **2.** To demonstrate the origin or development of (a word). *—intr.* To issue from a source; originate: *Rock music derives in part from blues.* [From Middle English *deriven*, from Latin *dērīvāre*, draw off, to derive : *dē-*, away, off + *rīvus*, stream.]

der·mal (dûr′məl) *adj.* Relating to the skin.

der·ma·ti·tis (dûr′mə-tī′tĭs) *n.* Inflammation of the skin.

der·ma·tol·o·gy (dûr′mə-tŏl′ə-jē) *n.* The branch of medicine that deals with the diagnosis and treatment of diseases and disorders of the skin. **—der′ma·tol′o·gist** *n.*

der·mis (dûr′mĭs) *n.* The layer of skin beneath the epidermis, containing nerve endings and blood vessels.

der·o·gate (dĕr′ə-gāt′) *v.* **der·o·gat·ed, der·o·gat·ing, der·o·gates** *—intr.* To detract; take away: *Cheating will derogate from one's reputation.* *—tr.* To belittle; disparage: *The critic derogated the book.* **—der′o·ga′tion** *n.*

de·rog·a·to·ry (dĭ-rŏg′ə-tôr′ē) *adj.* Tending to detract or make seem inferior; disparaging: *a derogatory remark.* **—de·rog′a·to′ri·ly** *adv.*

der·rick (dĕr′ĭk) *n.* **1.** A machine for lifting and moving heavy objects. It consists of a movable boom that is equipped with pulleys and cables and is connected to the base of a stationary vertical beam. **2.** A tall framework that supports the equipment used in drilling an oil well or a similar hole. [After *Derick*, English hangman of the 1500s.]

der·ring-do (dĕr′ĭng-do͞o′) *n.* Daring or reckless action: *an acrobat of derring-do.*

der·rin·ger (dĕr′ĭn-jər) *n.* A small pistol with a short barrel and a large bore. [After Henry *Deringer* (1786–1868), American gunsmith.]

derby

derrick
oil-drilling rig

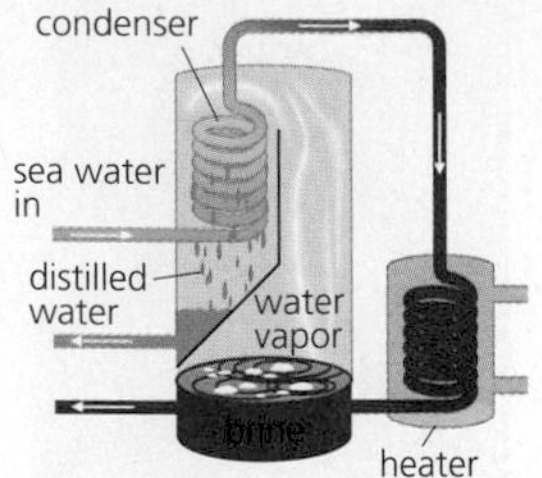

desalination
Sea water enters through the condenser and is then boiled. Pure water vapor rises to the cold condenser and precipitates as distilled (desalinated) water.

desert[1]
top: Monument Valley Navajo Tribal Park, Arizona
bottom: Wright Valley, Antarctica

ă	pat	ôr	core
ā	pay	oi	boy
âr	care	ou	out
ä	father	ŏŏ	took
ĕ	pet	ŏŏr	lure
ē	be	ōō	boot
ĭ	pit	ŭ	cut
ī	bite	ûr	urge
îr	pier	th	thin
ŏ	pot	*th*	this
ō	toe	zh	vision
ô	paw	ə	about

der·vish (dûr′vĭsh) *n.* A member of any of various Muslim religious orders that practice self-denial and poverty. Some engage in chanting and whirling dances as acts of ecstatic devotion.

de·sal·i·na·tion (dē-săl′ə-nā′shən) or **de·sal·i·na·za·tion** (dē-săl′ə-nĭ-zā′shən) *n.* The removal of salt from something, such as seawater or soil. **—de·sal′i·nate′** (dē-săl′ə-nāt′) *v.*

des·cant (dĕs′kănt′) *n.* An ornamental melody played or sung above a theme. ❖ *intr.v.* (dĕs′kănt′ *or* dĕ-skănt′) **des·cant·ed, des·cant·ing, des·cants** To talk at length; discourse: *descant on modern science.*

Des·cartes (dā-kärt′), **René** 1596–1650. French mathematician and philosopher who is considered the founder of analytic geometry.

de·scend (dĭ-sĕnd′) *v.* **de·scend·ed, de·scend·ing, de·scends** *—intr.* **1.** To move from a higher to a lower place; go or come down: *The airplane descended for a landing.* **2.** To slope or incline downward: *The path descended along the side of the cliff.* **3.** To come from an ancestor or ancestry: *Our neighbor descends from New England settlers.* **4.** To pass by inheritance: *The farm descended through several generations to its present owner.* **5.** To lower oneself; stoop: *Both candidates chose not to descend to the level of personal accusations.* **6.** To arrive or attack suddenly or with overwhelming effect: *Our relatives descended on us this weekend.* *—tr.* To move from a higher to a lower part of; go down: *We descended a fire escape.*

de·scen·dant (dĭ-sĕn′dənt) *n.* A person or animal descended from specified ancestors.

de·scent (dĭ-sĕnt′) *n.* **1.** The act or an instance of descending: *the descent from the mountain.* **2.** A downward incline or slope: *Rocks and mud slid down the steep descent.* **3.** Hereditary derivation; lineage: *Many Americans are of a mixed descent.* **4.** A sudden visit or attack; an onslaught: *The descent of the children on the candy store sent the cashier running.*

❑ *These sound alike:* **descent, dissent** (disagreement).

de·scribe (dĭ-skrīb′) *tr.v.* **de·scribed, de·scrib·ing, de·scribes 1.** To give an account of in words; tell or write about: *a newspaper report describing the fire; an oral report describing one's experiences.* **2.** To convey an impression of; characterize: *described him as gentle and kind.* **3.** To trace or draw: *Describe a circle with your compass.* [From Middle English *describen,* from Latin *dēscrībere,* to write down : *dē-,* down + *scrībere,* to write.] **—de·scrib′a·ble** *adj.*

de·scrip·tion (dĭ-skrĭp′shən) *n.* **1.** The act or process of describing: *The writer is so good at description that the characters seem real.* **2.** An account or a statement describing something: *The newspaper carried a description of the plane crash.* **3.** A kind or variety; a sort: *The zoo has animals of every description.*

de·scrip·tive (dĭ-skrĭp′tĭv) *adj.* Involving or characterized by description; serving to describe: *descriptive words; a descriptive passage in a guidebook.* **—de·scrip′tive·ly** *adv.* **—de·scrip′tive·ness** *n.*

de·scry (dĭ-skrī′) *tr.v.* **de·scried, de·scry·ing, de·scries** To catch sight of (something difficult to see): *descry a ship through the mist.*

des·e·crate (dĕs′ĭ-krāt′) *tr.v.* **des·e·crat·ed, des·e·crat·ing, des·e·crates** To violate the sacredness of; profane. **—des′e·crat′er** *n.* **—des′e·cra′tion** *n.*

de·seg·re·gate (dē-sĕg′rĭ-gāt′) *tr.v.* **de·seg·re·gat·ed, de·seg·re·gat·ing, de·seg·re·gates** To abolish racial segregation in (a school or workplace, for example). **—de·seg′re·ga′tion** *n.*

des·ert[1] (dĕz′ərt) *n.* **1.** A dry region that has little or no vegetation. Deserts occur in hot climates, as in western Australia, and also in cold climates, as in Antarctica. **2.** An empty or forsaken place; a wasteland: *a cultural desert.* ❖ *adj.* **1.** Relating to, characteristic of, or inhabiting a desert: *desert conditions; desert plants.* **2.** Uninhabited: *a desert island.* [From Middle English, from Late Latin *dēsertum,* from *dēserere,* to abandon.]

de·sert[2] (dĭ-zûrt′) *n.* often **deserts** Something deserved or merited, especially a punishment: *After conviction the thieves received their just deserts.* [From Middle English, from Old French *deserte,* from *deservir,* to deserve.]

❑ *These sound alike:* **desert**[2] (punishment), **desert**[3] (abandon), **dessert** (last course of a meal).

de·sert[3] (dĭ-zûrt′) *v.* **de·sert·ed, de·sert·ing, de·serts** *—tr.* **1.** To leave empty or alone; abandon: *Miners deserted the valley after the ore ran out.* **2.** To abandon (a military post, for example) in violation of orders or an oath: *The soldiers deserted their posts just before the attack.* *—intr.* To forsake one's duty or post, especially without intending to return. [From Late Latin *dēsertāre,* from Latin *dēserere,* to abandon.] **—de·sert′er** *n.*

❑ *These sound alike:* **desert**[3] (abandon), **desert**[2] (punishment), **dessert** (last course of a meal).

de·sert·ed (dĭ-zûr′tĭd) *adj.* **1.** No longer occupied or used; abandoned: *a deserted sentry post.* **2.** Uninhabited: *a deserted island.*

de·ser·tion (dĭ-zûr′shən) *n.* **1.** The act or an instance of deserting: *Desertion from the military is considered a serious offense.* **2.** The state of being deserted.

de·serve (dĭ-zûrv′) *tr.v.* **de·served, de·serv·ing, de·serves** To be worthy of; merit: *The rescuers deserved a reward for their courageous act.* [From Middle English *deserven,* from Latin *dēservīre,* to serve zealously.]

de·served (dĭ-zûrvd′) *adj.* Merited or earned: *a richly deserved reward.* **—de·serv′ed·ly** (dĭ-zûr′vĭd-lē) *adv.*

de·serv·ing (dĭ-zûr′vĭng) *adj.* Worthy, as of aid, reward, or praise: *Scholarships are available for deserving students.*

des·ic·cate (dĕs′ĭ-kāt′) *tr.v.* **des·ic·cat·ed, des·ic·cat·ing, des·ic·cates** To dry out thoroughly: *A long period of drought desiccated most of the farmland.*

de·sign (dĭ-zīn′) *tr.v.* **de·signed, de·sign·ing, de·signs 1.** To conceive in the mind or make a plan for: *designed an interesting plot for the novel.* **2.** To make a sketch or drawing for: *design a building; design dresses.* **3.** To create or intend for a specific purpose: *This room was designed as a workshop.* ❖ *n.* **1.** A plan, drawing, or sketch, especially a detailed plan showing how something is to be made: *She drew up designs for the new gym.* **2.** The art of creating designs by making patterns, drawings, or sketches: *Engineers and architects are students of design.* **3.** An ornamental pattern: *a design on wallpaper.* **4.** A purpose or intention: *We left early by design to meet the train.* **5.** often **designs** A secretive plan or scheme: *The movie's main character fears that the new student has designs on her boyfriend.* [From Middle English *designen,* from Latin *dēsignāre,* to designate, from *signum,* sign.]

des·ig·nate (dĕz′ĭg-nāt′) *tr.v.* **des·ig·nat·ed, des·ig·nat·ing, des·ig·nates 1.** To indicate or specify; point out: *The fence designates the boundary of our property.* **2.** To give a name or title to; characterize: *a period of history designated as the Space Age.* **3.** To select and set aside for a duty, office, or purpose; appoint: *We designated two delegates to represent us at the meeting.*

des·ig·nat·ed hitter (dĕz′ĭg-nā′tĭd) *n.* In baseball, a player designated at the start of a game to bat instead of the pitcher in the lineup.

des·ig·na·tion (dĕz′ĭg-nā′shən) *n.* **1.** The act of designating; a marking or pointing out: *The designation of the trail is clearly shown on the map.* **2.** Appointment or selection, as for a duty or office. **3.** An identifying name or title: *The designation of the head of a fire department is "Chief."*

de·sign·er (dĭ-zī′nər) *n.* A person who produces designs: *a book designer; a dress designer.*

de·sign·ing (dĭ-zī′nĭng) *adj.* **1.** Conniving; crafty: *fooled by a designing partner.* **2.** Showing or using forethought.

de·sir·a·ble (dĭ-zīr′ə-bəl) *adj.* Worth wanting, seeking, or doing; good: *a desirable neighborhood; desirable changes in the law.* **—de·sir′a·bil′i·ty, de·sir′a·ble·ness** *n.* **—de·sir′a·bly** *adv.*

de·sire (dĭ-zīr′) *tr.v.* **de·sired, de·sir·ing, de·sires** To wish or long for; want; crave: *The puppy seemed to desire only attention. After I graduate, I desire to travel.* ❖ *n.* **1.** A wish or longing: *She had a lifelong desire to fly airplanes.* **2.** A request or petition: *The citizens made their desires known to the mayor.* **3.** The object of longing: *My desire is a trip to Mexico.* [From Middle English *desiren*, from Latin *dēsīderāre* : *dē-*, from + *sīdus*, star.]

SYNONYMS desire, crave, want, wish These verbs mean to feel a strong longing for something. *After many years of war, both nations desire peace. The insecure actor craved fame and fortune. Do you want to come with us to the museum? I wish summer vacation were here.*

---

de·sir·ous (dĭ-zīr′əs) *adj.* Having or showing desire; desiring: *desirous of a vacation.*

de·sist (dĭ-sĭst′ *or* dĭ-zĭst′) *intr.v.* **de·sist·ed, de·sist·ing, de·sists** To cease doing something: *Please desist from interrupting others.*

desk (dĕsk) *n.* **1.** A piece of furniture usually having a flat top for writing and often drawers or compartments. **2.** A table, counter, or booth at which a service is offered: *an information desk; a reservation desk.* **3.** A department of an organization in charge of a specific operation: *The shipping desk keeps track of all mail.*

desk·top (dĕsk′tŏp′) *n.* **1.** The top of a desk. **2.** The area of a computer screen where windows, icons, and other graphical items appear.

desktop publishing *n.* The design and production of publications, such as newsletters and brochures, using personal computers with graphics capability.

Des Moines (dĭ moin′) The capital of Iowa, in the south-central part of the state west-southwest of Cedar Rapids. It was chosen as state capital in 1857.

des·o·late (dĕs′ə-lĭt) *adj.* **1.** Having few or no people, and often causing sadness as a result; deserted: *walked on the desolate moor.* **2.** Feeling or showing sadness or loneliness: *He was desolate when all of his friends went away on vacation.* ❖ *tr.v.* (dĕs′ə-lāt′) **des·o·lat·ed, des·o·lat·ing, des·o·lates 1.** To rid or deprive of people or other forms of life: *A fire desolated the forest.* **2.** To make lonely, forlorn, or wretched: *The loss of our old dog desolated us.* **—des′o·late·ly** *adv.*

des·o·la·tion (dĕs′ə-lā′shən) *n.* **1.** The state of being without people or other forms of life: *The drought brought desolation to the region.* **2.** Loneliness or sadness: *the desolation of being all alone in a foreign land.*

de So·to (dĭ sō′tō), **Hernando** 1496?–1542. Spanish explorer who landed in Florida in 1539 and explored much of southern North America, including the Mississippi River.

de·spair (dĭ-spâr′) *intr.v.* **de·spaired, de·spair·ing, de·spairs** To lose all hope: *despaired of returning on the early train.* ❖ *n.* **1.** Utter lack of hope: *gave up in despair as their supplies began to run out.* **2.** A person or thing despaired of or causing despair: *The leaky boat was the despair of the crew.* [From Middle English *despairen*, from Latin *dēspērāre* : *dē-*, away, off + *spērāre*, to hope.]

de·spair·ing (dĭ-spâr′ĭng) *adj.* Marked by or resulting from despair: *despairing glances.* **—de·spair′ing·ly** *adv.*

des·per·a·do (dĕs′pə-rä′dō) *n., pl.* **des·per·a·does** or **des·per·a·dos** A desperate or bold outlaw.

des·per·ate (dĕs′pər-ĭt) *adj.* **1.** Having lost all hope; despairing. **2.** Willing to do or try anything as the result of an utter lack of hope: *desperate owners looking for their dog.* **3.** Marked by, arising from, or showing despair: *a desperate look.* **4.** Undertaken as a last resort: *desperate measures to save the business from failure.* **5.** Nearly hopeless; critical: *a desperate illness.* **6.** Suffering or driven by a great need for something: *desperate for medical attention.* **7.** Extremely intense: *in desperate need.* **—des′per·ate·ly** *adv.*

des·per·a·tion (dĕs′pə-rā′shən) *n.* **1.** The condition of being desperate. **2.** Recklessness resulting from despair.

de·spic·a·ble (dĭ-spĭk′ə-bəl *or* dĕs′pĭ-kə-bəl) *adj.* Deserving contempt or scorn; hateful. **—de·spic′a·ble·ness** *n.* **—de·spic′a·bly** *adv.*

de·spise (dĭ-spīz′) *tr.v.* **de·spised, de·spis·ing, de·spis·es 1.** To regard with contempt or scorn: *Everyone despises a traitor.* **2.** To dislike intensely; loathe. [From Middle English *despisen*, from Latin *dēspicere* : *dē-*, down + *specere*, to look.]

de·spite (dĭ-spīt′) *prep.* In spite of; notwithstanding: *The movie did well despite the bad reviews.*

de·spoil (dĭ-spoil′) *tr.v.* **de·spoiled, de·spoil·ing, de·spoils** To deprive of something valuable, especially by force; rob: *The pirates despoiled the coastal town.* **—de·spoil′er** *n.* **—de·spo′li·a′tion** (dĭ-spō′lē-ā′shən) *n.*

de·spon·dent (dĭ-spŏn′dənt) *adj.* Feeling depression of spirits from loss of hope, confidence, or courage; dejected: *became despondent during his long absence from home.* **—de·spon′dence, de·spon′den·cy** *n.* **—de·spon′dent·ly** *adv.*

des·pot (dĕs′pət) *n.* **1.** A ruler with absolute power. **2.** A person who wields power oppressively; a tyrant.

des·pot·ic (dĭ-spŏt′ĭk) *adj.* Ruling with absolute power; tyrannical: *a despotic government.* **—des·pot′i·cal·ly** *adv.*

des·pot·ism (dĕs′pə-tĭz′əm) *n.* **1.** Rule by a despot or by someone acting like a despot. **2.** The actions of a despot; tyranny: *the despotism of a dictator.* **3.** A government in which a ruler holds absolute power.

des·sert (dĭ-zûrt′) *n.* The last course of a meal, usually consisting of a sweet dish such as fruit, ice cream, or pastry. [From Old French *desservir*, to clear the table : *des-*, off, away + *servir*, to serve.]

❑ *These sound alike:* **dessert, desert²** (punishment), **desert³** (abandon).

de·sta·bi·lize (dē-stā′bə-līz′) *tr.v.* **de·sta·bi·lized, de·sta·bi·liz·ing, de·sta·bi·liz·es 1.** To upset the stability or smooth functioning of: *The rising temperature of the ocean currents has destabilized the region's weather.* **2.** To undermine the power of (a government or leader) by subversive or terrorist acts.

des·ti·na·tion (dĕs′tə-nā′shən) *n.* The place to which a person or thing is going or is sent: *The destination of that package is written on the label.*

des·tine (dĕs′tĭn) *tr.v.* **des·tined, des·tin·ing, des·tines 1.** To determine beforehand; preordain: *a movie destined to become a classic.* **2.** To set aside for a specific use or purpose: *land destined to be a park.*

des·ti·ny (dĕs′tə-nē) *n., pl.* **des·ti·nies 1.** The fortune, fate, or lot of a particular person or thing, considered as something inevitable or necessary: *Her destiny was to become a playwright.* **2.** The power believed to determine events in advance: *events shaped by destiny.*

des·ti·tute (dĕs′tĭ-to͞ot′) *adj.* **1.** Being without food, shelter, or other basic necessities; completely impoverished. **2.** Having none; void: *a barren land destitute of trees.*

des·ti·tu·tion (dĕs′tĭ-to͞o′shən) *n.* The state of not having basic necessities like food and shelter; extreme poverty.

de·stroy (dĭ-stroi′) *tr.v.* **de·stroyed, de·stroy·ing, de·stroys 1.** To break apart or cause to become unusable, as from damage; ruin completely: *The explosion destroyed*

Hernando de Soto

WRITERS CHOOSE THEIR WORDS

Liyana wore blue jeans with paisley patches on the knees and her aunts pointed and whispered. Poppy admonished her, "They think you're **destitute** if you dress like that." Liyana said, "So?" She repeated the word inside her mind. "Des-ti-tute. Desti-TOOT." She started to like it.

—Naomi Shihab Nye
Habibi

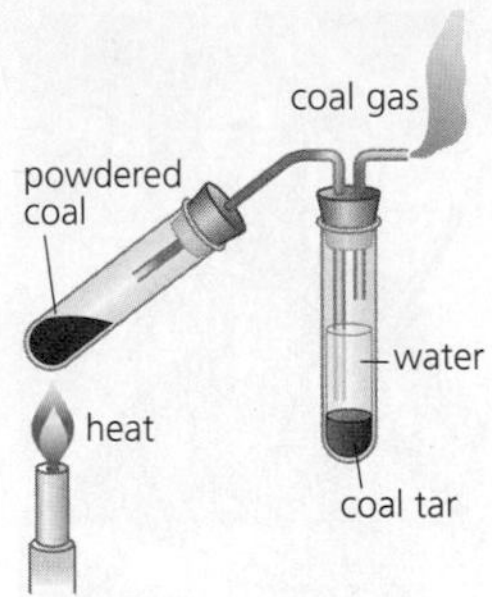

destructive distillation
In the destructive distillation of powdered coal, heated coal turns to coke, ammonia dissolves in water, and coal gas and coal tar are produced.

detail
top: a painting of the Chateau of Chillon by William Baptiste Baird (1847–1899?)
bottom: a detail of the same painting

ă	pat	ôr	core
ā	pay	oi	boy
âr	care	ou	out
ä	father	o͝o	took
ĕ	pet	o͝or	lure
ē	be	o͞o	boot
ĭ	pit	ŭ	cut
ī	bite	ûr	urge
îr	pier	th	thin
ŏ	pot	*th*	this
ō	toe	zh	vision
ô	paw	ə	about

several homes. **2.** To put an end to; eliminate: *Hostile action destroyed all hope of a peaceful settlement.* **3.** To put to death; kill: *The rabid raccoon had to be destroyed.* **4.** To cause emotional trauma to; devastate: *The setback destroyed him.* [From Middle English *destroien*, from Latin *dēstruere* : *dē-*, off, down + *struere*, to pile up.]

SYNONYMS **destroy, raze, demolish, ruin, wreck** These verbs mean to cause the complete ruin or wreckage of something or someone. **Destroy, raze,** and **demolish** all mean that something is damaged so badly that it is completely obliterated: *The explosives destroyed the bridge. The construction company had to raze the old warehouse before they could begin building a new one. A tornado demolished the old barn.* **Ruin** can mean to harm greatly without necessarily bringing about total destruction: *A flood would ruin all the furniture in the basement.* **Wreck** can mean to ruin in or as if in a violent collision: *Six cars were wrecked when the crane fell in the parking lot.*

de·stroy·er (dĭ-**stroi′**ər) *n.* **1.** A person or thing that destroys. **2.** A small, fast, highly maneuverable warship armed with missiles, guns, torpedoes, and depth charges.

de·struc·ti·ble (dĭ-**strŭk′**tə-bəl) *adj.* Breakable or easily destroyed.

de·struc·tion (dĭ-**strŭk′**shən) *n.* **1.** The act of destroying: *Destruction of the old house was completed in two days.* **2.** The condition of having been destroyed; ruin: *The tornado caused great destruction.* **3.** The cause or means of destroying: *An unwillingness to discuss problems is the destruction of many a good friendship.*

de·struc·tive (dĭ-**strŭk′**tĭv) *adj.* **1.** Causing destruction; ruinous: *The coastal residents sought shelter from the destructive storm.* **2.** Designed or intending to disprove or discredit: *Destructive criticism does not offer helpful recommendations.* **—de·struc′tive·ly** *adv.* **—de·struc′tive·ness** *n.*

destructive distillation *n.* A process by which substances such as wood and coal are heated in the absence of air and broken down to produce useful products such as coke, charcoal, and gases.

des·ul·to·ry (**dĕs′**əl-tôr′ē *or* **dĕz′**əl-tôr′ē) *adj.* Moving or jumping from one thing to another; disconnected: *The speaker talked in a desultory manner, skipping from topic to topic.* **—des′ul·to′ri·ly** *adv.* **—des′ul·to′ri·ness** *n.*

de·tach (dĭ-**tăch′**) *tr.v.* **de·tached, de·tach·ing, de·tach·es 1.** To separate or unfasten; disconnect: *detach the trailer from the car; detach a plug from a wall socket.* **2.** To send (troops or ships, for example) on a special mission; assign: *detach a ship to take up patrol.*

de·tach·a·ble (dĭ-**tăch′**ə-bəl) *adj.* Capable of being detached: *The raincoat has a detachable hood.* **—de·tach′a·bly** *adv.*

de·tached (dĭ-**tăcht′**) *adj.* **1.** Standing apart; disconnected; separate: *a house with a detached garage.* **2.** Marked by an absence of emotional involvement; impartial: *a detached view of this problem.*

de·tach·ment (dĭ-**tăch′**mənt) *n.* **1.** The act or process of separating or disconnecting. **2.** Indifference to or remoteness from the concerns of others; aloofness: *attended to various duties with a bored detachment.* **3.** Absence of prejudice or bias: *A judge must consider legal matters with detachment.* **4.** The dispatch of a military unit for a special duty or mission.

de·tail (dĭ-**tāl′** *or* **dē′**tāl′) *n.* **1.** An individual part or item; a particular: *The story has many details about life on a schooner.* **2.** Particulars considered individually and in relation to a whole: *Scientific investigation is concerned with detail.* **3.** A minor or unimportant item or aspect: *Several lawyers are studying the details of the case.* **4a.** A small group assigned to a special duty, usually a fatigue duty. **b.** The duty assigned: *We have cleanup detail all week.* ❖ *tr.v.* (dĭ-**tāl′**) **de·tailed, de·tail·ing, de·tails 1.** To report or relate minutely or in particulars: *The chief detailed the fire to the reporters.* **2.** To assign to a special duty: *The highway department detailed extra plows to clear the snow.* ◆ **in detail** With attention to particulars; minutely: *The planning board examined the design of the new park in detail.* [From Old French *detail*, a piece cut off, from *detaillir*, to cut up : *de-*, off, apart + *tailler*, to cut.]

de·tailed (dĭ-**tāld′** *or* **dē′**tāld′) *adj.* Marked by abundant use of detail or thoroughness of treatment: *a detailed drawing; a detailed study of the legal evidence.*

de·tain (dĭ-**tān′**) *tr.v.* **de·tained, de·tain·ing, de·tains 1.** To keep from going on; delay: *Friends detained me awhile at lunch.* **2.** To keep in custody; confine temporarily: *Police detained several suspects overnight.* [From Old French *detenir*, from Latin *dētinēre* : *dē-*, off, back + *tenēre*, to hold.] **—de·tain′ment** *n.*

de·tect (dĭ-**tĕkt′**) *tr.v.* **de·tect·ed, de·tect·ing, de·tects** To discover or determine the existence, presence, or fact of: *detect the smell of smoke; detect errors in a report.* [From Middle English *detecten*, from Latin *dētegere*, to uncover : *dē-*, off, away + *tegere*, to cover.] **—de·tect′a·ble, de·tect′i·ble** *adj.*

de·tec·tion (dĭ-**tĕk′**shən) *n.* The act or process of detecting; discovery: *the detection of cracks in a vase.*

de·tec·tive (dĭ-**tĕk′**tĭv) *n.* A police officer or private investigator who investigates crimes and obtains evidence or information. ❖ *adj.* **1.** Relating to detectives or their work: *a detective story.* **2.** Suited for or used in detection: *detective methods.*

de·tec·tor (dĭ-**tĕk′**tər) *n.* A person or thing that detects, especially a mechanical, chemical, or electrical device that indicates the presence of a particular substance or agent: *a metal detector in an airport; a smoke detector on the ceiling.*

dé·tente (dā-**tänt′**) *n.* A relaxation or lessening of tensions between nations: *A policy of détente has increased trade.*

de·ten·tion (dĭ-**tĕn′**shən) *n.* **1.** The act of detaining someone: *detention of the suspect by the police at the station.* **2.** The state or a period of being detained in custody while awaiting trial or for other reasons: *The accused thief was held in detention.* **3.** Punishment requiring a student to stay in school after regular hours.

de·ter (dĭ-**tûr′**) *tr.v.* **de·terred, de·ter·ring, de·ters 1.** To prevent or discourage from doing something, as by means of fear: *The threat of rain deterred us from picnicking.* **2.** To make less likely or prevent from happening: *installed surveillance cameras to deter vandalism.* [From Latin *dēterrēre* : *dē-*, away, off + *terrēre*, to frighten.] **—de·ter′ment** *n.*

de·ter·gent (dĭ-**tûr′**jənt) *n.* A cleaning agent that increases the ability of water to penetrate fabric and to break down oils and fats. ❖ *adj.* Having cleansing power: *a detergent soap.*

de·te·ri·o·rate (dĭ-**tîr′**ē-ə-rāt′) *intr.v.* **de·te·ri·o·rat·ed, de·te·ri·o·rat·ing, de·te·ri·o·rates** To become inferior in quality, character, or value; worsen: *The neglected buildings are deteriorating. The state's financial situation is deteriorating.* **—de·te′ri·o·ra′tion** *n.*

de·ter·mi·nant (dĭ-**tûr′**mə-nənt) *adj.* Tending, able, or serving to determine: *a determinant factor in one's thinking.* ❖ *n.* An influencing or determining factor: *A vote is the basic determinant of a democratic government.*

de·ter·mi·na·tion (dĭ-tûr′mə-**nā′**shən) *n.* **1.** Firmness of purpose; resolve: *The determination of the team helped them to win.* **2.** The act of finding out the quality, quantity, position, or character of something: *the determination of the ship's longitude.* **3.** The act or process of making a decision: *After long determination, the judges* *chose a winner.* **4.** A decision reached: *My mother's determination was to buy a new car.*

de·ter·mine (dĭ-tûr′mĭn) *tr.v.* **de·ter·mined, de·ter·min·ing, de·ter·mines 1.** To figure out or establish definitely, as after consideration or investigation: *We determined how much paint we needed for the bedroom.* **2.** To make decisions about; devise or control: *The school board determines athletic policy.* **3.** To be the cause of or be the key factor in: *Climate determines how people in different parts of the world live.* [From Middle English *determinen*, from Latin *dētermināre*, to limit, from *terminus*, boundary.]

de·ter·mined (dĭ-tûr′mĭnd) *adj.* Marked by or showing determination: *a determined leader; a determined effort.* **—de·ter′mined·ly** *adv.*

de·ter·min·er (dĭ-tûr′mə-nər) *n.* A word belonging to a class of noun modifiers that includes articles, demonstrative pronouns, possessive adjectives, and other words such as *any, both,* and *whose.*

de·ter·rence (dĭ-tûr′əns) *n.* The act or a means of deterring: *The fence around the yard served as a deterrence to dogs.*

de·ter·rent (dĭ-tûr′ənt) *adj.* Tending to deter. ❖ *n.* A person or thing that deters: *The supervisor's lack of interest was a deterrent to the rest of us to work hard.*

de·test (dĭ-tĕst′) *tr.v.* **de·test·ed, de·test·ing, de·tests** To dislike strongly; abhor: *Many people detest snakes.*

de·test·a·ble (dĭ-tĕs′tə-bəl) *adj.* Inspiring or deserving hatred or scorn: *Lying is a detestable habit.* **—de·test′a·ble·ness** *n.* **—de·test′a·bly** *adv.*

de·tes·ta·tion (dē′tĕ-stā′shən) *n.* Strong dislike or hatred: *detestation of prejudice.*

de·throne (dē-thrōn′) *tr.v.* **de·throned, de·thron·ing, de·thrones 1.** To remove from the throne; depose. **2.** To remove from a position of power or prominence. **—de·throne′ment** *n.*

det·o·nate (dĕt′n-āt′) *intr. & tr.v.* **det·o·nat·ed, det·o·nat·ing, det·o·nates** To explode or cause to explode: *The explosives detonated in sequence. The miners detonated a charge of explosives.*

det·o·na·tion (dĕt′n-ā′shən) *n.* **1.** The act of exploding. **2.** An explosion.

det·o·na·tor (dĕt′n-ā′tər) *n.* A device used to set off an explosive charge.

de·tour (dē′to͝or′ *or* dĭ-to͝or′) *n.* **1.** A road used temporarily instead of a main route. **2.** A roundabout way or course. ❖ *intr. & tr.v.* **de·toured, de·tour·ing, de·tours** To go or cause to go by a roundabout way: *Police detoured traffic because of heavy flooding.* [From Old French *destor*, from *destorner*, to turn away : *des-*, away + *torner*, to turn.]

de·tox·i·fi·ca·tion (dē-tŏk′sə-fĭ-kā′shən) *n.* The act or process of counteracting or removing poison or other harmful substances: *Some dumps need detoxification.*

de·tox·i·fy (dē-tŏk′sə-fī′) *tr.v.* **de·tox·i·fied, de·tox·i·fy·ing, de·tox·i·fies 1.** To counteract or destroy the toxic properties of. **2.** To remove poison or other harmful substances from.

de·tract (dĭ-trăkt′) *v.* **de·tract·ed, de·tract·ing, de·tracts** *—tr.* To draw or take away; divert: *The controversy over the candidates' personal remarks detracted attention from the serious issues. —intr.* To reduce the value, importance, or quality of something: *Drab curtains detract from the beauty of the room.* **—de·trac′tion** *n.* **—de·trac′tor** *n.* —SEE NOTE.

det·ri·ment (dĕt′rə-mənt) *n.* **1.** Damage, harm, or loss: *was out sick a week without detriment to his grades.* **2.** Something that causes damage, harm, or loss: *Oil spills are a serious detriment to coastal wildlife.*

det·ri·men·tal (dĕt′rə-mĕn′tl) *adj.* Causing damage or harm; injurious: *Being overweight is detrimental to one's health.* **—det′ri·men′tal·ly** *adv.*

de·tri·tus (dĭ-trī′təs) *n.* Loose fragments, such as sand or gravel, that have been worn away from rock. [From Latin *dētrītus*, from past participle of *dēterere*, to wear away.]

De·troit (dĭ-troit′) The largest city of Michigan, in the southeast part of the state on the **Detroit River.** It was founded by French settlers in 1701.

deuce[1] (do͞os) *n.* **1.** A playing card or side of a die bearing two spots; a two. **2.** In tennis, a tied score when a game can be won by winning two successive points. [From Middle English *deus*, from Latin *duōs*, two.]

deuce[2] (do͞os) *Informal n.* The devil. [Probably from Low German *duus*, a throw of two in dice games, bad luck, from Latin *duōs*, two.]

deu·te·ri·um (do͞o-tîr′ē-əm) *n.* An isotope of hydrogen having one proton and one neutron in each atom. Deuterium occurs in heavy water.

Deu·ter·on·o·my (do͞o′tə-rŏn′ə-mē) *n.* The fifth book of the Bible, which includes many Jewish laws.

deut·sche mark (doich′ märk′) *n.* The former basic monetary unit of Germany.

De Va·le·ra (dĕv′ə-lĕr′ə *or* dĕv′ə-lîr′ə), **Eamon** 1882–1975. American-born Irish political leader who served as president of the Republic of Ireland (1959–1973).

de·val·ue (dē-văl′yo͞o) *tr.v.* **de·val·ued, de·val·u·ing, de·val·ues 1.** To lessen or cancel the value of: *The scientist never devalued the contributions of her assistants.* **2.** To lower the exchange value of (a currency). **—de·val′u·a′tion** *n.*

dev·as·tate (dĕv′ə-stāt′) *tr.v.* **dev·as·tat·ed, dev·as·tat·ing, dev·as·tates 1.** To lay waste; destroy: *The storms devastated much of the countryside.* **2.** To overwhelm; confound: *Layoffs devastated the old mill towns.* **—dev′as·tat′ing·ly** *adv.* **—dev′as·ta′tor** *n.*

dev·as·ta·tion (dĕv′ə-stā′shən) *n.* The act of devastating or the condition of being devastated; ruin; destruction: *Dikes saved the land from devastation by flooding.*

de·vel·op (dĭ-vĕl′əp) *v.* **de·vel·oped, de·vel·op·ing, de·vel·ops** *—intr.* **1.** To grow by degrees into a more advanced or mature state: *His musical ability developed with practice. Caterpillars develop into butterflies.* **2.** To increase or expand: *The town developed into a city over the years.* **3.** To come gradually into existence or activity: *A friendship soon developed between the two.* **4.** To come gradually to light; be disclosed: *I'll give you the details as they develop. —tr.* **1.** To cause to grow by degrees into a more advanced or mature state: *I want to develop my computer skills so I can be a programmer.* **2a.** To cause to increase or expand; build up: *She developed the business from a small store into a retail empire.* **b.** To strengthen: *developed his muscles by lifting weights.* **3.** To cause to come into existence or activity: *a researcher who developed a new way to treat the disease.* **4.** To increase the intricacy, complexity, or quality of: *develop one's vocabulary by reading; develop a story.* **5a.** To come to have gradually: *develop a liking for spicy food.* **b.** To become affected with; contract: *develop a rash on the arm.* **6.** To cause (a tract of land or a building) to serve a particular purpose: *developed the site as a community of condominiums.* **7.** To process (photographic film) in order to produce a photographic image. [From Old French *desveloper* : *des-*, off, away + *voloper*, to wrap, roll.]

de·vel·op·er (dĭ-vĕl′ə-pər) *n.* **1.** A person or thing that develops, especially a person who develops real estate by preparing a site for residential or commercial use. **2.** A chemical used in developing a photographic film or similar material.

de·vel·op·ing (dĭ-vĕl′ə-pĭng) *adj.* Having a relatively low level of economic and industrial development: *a developing nation.*

de·vel·op·ment (dĭ-vĕl′əp-mənt) *n.* **1.** The act of developing: *The development of a vaccine requires much*

WORD BUILDING

detract The word root *tract–* in English words comes from the past participle *tractus* of the Latin verb *trahere,* "to pull, drag, draw." Thus **detract** literally means "to drag down" (using the prefix *dē–,* "down"); **extract** means "to pull out" (*ex–,* "out, out of"); **protract** means "to drag forward" (*prō–,* "forward, in front"); **attract** is literally "to draw toward" (*at–,* a form of *ad–,* "to, toward"); and **retract** means "to draw back" (*re–,* "back"). **Tractor** and **traction** come from Latin words meaning "puller" and "pulling."

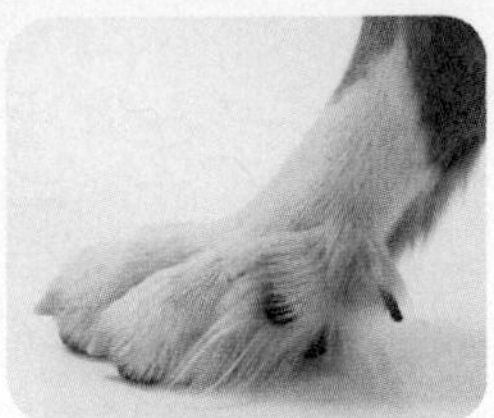
dewclaw
on a dog's foot

dewlap
on a lizard

ă	pat	ôr	core
ā	pay	oi	boy
âr	care	ou	out
ä	father	ŏŏ	took
ĕ	pet	ŏŏr	lure
ē	be	ōō	boot
ĭ	pit	ŭ	cut
ī	bite	ûr	urge
îr	pier	th	thin
ŏ	pot	*th*	this
ō	toe	zh	vision
ô	paw	ə	about

research. **2.** The state of being developed: *The plans for the project are in development.* **3.** The process of change in the structure of an organism, especially as it grows. **4.** A significant event, occurrence, or change: *The newspaper related the latest developments in the peace talks.* **5.** A group of dwellings built by the same contractor: *The development includes homes and a shopping center.* —**de·vel′op·men′tal** *adj.*

de·vi·ant (dē′vē-ənt) *adj.* Differing from a norm or from accepted social standards: *deviant behavior.* ❖ *n.* A person whose attitude, character, or behavior differ from accepted social standards.

de·vi·ate (dē′vē-āt′) *intr.v.* **de·vi·at·ed, de·vi·at·ing, de·vi·ates 1.** To turn aside from a course or way: *hikers who deviated from the main path.* **2.** To change or vary, as from a norm or purpose; depart: *Their plans deviated from our original agreement.* [From Late Latin *dēviāre* : Latin *dē-*, away, off + Latin *via*, road, track.]

de·vi·a·tion (dē′vē-ā′shən) *n.* **1.** The act of deviating or turning aside. **2.** An abnormality; a departure: *Staying up late is a deviation from our routine.*

de·vice (dĭ-vīs′) *n.* **1.** A contrivance or invention designed or used for a particular purpose; a mechanism: *An egg beater is a handy device.* **2.** A plan, scheme, or trick: *used crying and other devices to get his way.* **3.** A decorative design, figure, or pattern, as one used in embroidery. ◆ **leave to (one's) own devices** To allow to do as one pleases: *left the child to her own devices for an hour.*

dev·il (dĕv′əl) *n.* **1.** often **Devil** In many religions, the personified spirit of evil who is often also the ruler of Hell and the enemy of God. **2.** An evil spirit; a demon. **3.** A wicked or bad-tempered person. **4.** A person who is daring, clever, or full of mischief. ❖ *tr.v.* **dev·iled, dev·il·ing, dev·ils** or **dev·illed, dev·il·ling, dev·ils** To season (food) heavily, as with mustard: *devil eggs.* [From Old English *dēofol*, from Greek *diabolos*, slanderer, from *diaballein*, to slander.]

dev·il·fish (dĕv′əl-fĭsh′) *n.* Any of various sea animals having horns or thought to have a sinister appearance, including the manta ray and certain octopuses and squids.

dev·il·ish (dĕv′ə-lĭsh) *adj.* **1.** Resembling or characteristic of a devil; evil. **2.** Mischievous, teasing, or annoying: *That devilish kitten unrolled a ball of string.* —**dev′il·ish·ly** *adv.* —**dev′il·ish·ness** *n.*

dev·il-may-care (dĕv′əl-mā-**kâr′**) *adj.* Very careless; reckless: *His devil-may-care attitude led him to make a lot of mistakes.*

dev·il·ment (dĕv′əl-mənt) *n.* Devilish behavior; mischief.

dev·il·ry (dĕv′əl-rē) *n.* Variant of **deviltry.**

dev·il's advocate (dĕv′əlz) *n.* A person who argues against a position simply for the sake of argument or to test the validity of the position. [Translation of Medieval Latin *advocātus diabolī*, one arguing for the devil's plea against declaring someone a saint.]

dev·il's food cake *n.* A rich chocolate cake.

dev·il·try (dĕv′əl-trē) or **dev·il·ry** (dĕv′əl-rē) *n., pl.* **dev·il·tries** or **dev·il·ries 1.** Reckless mischief: *dangerous deviltry.* **2.** Extreme cruelty; wickedness.

de·vi·ous (dē′vē-əs) *adj.* **1.** Not straightforward; shifty: *a devious character.* **2.** Veering from the correct or accepted way: *They achieved success by devious means.* **3.** Away from the main or direct road or course: *We took a devious route to avoid the traffic.* —**de′vi·ous·ly** *adv.* —**de′vi·ous·ness** *n.*

de·vise (dĭ-vīz′) *tr.v.* **de·vised, de·vis·ing, de·vis·es** To form or arrange in the mind; plan: *devise a way to keep the window open with a stick.* —**de·vis′er** *n.*

de·void (dĭ-void′) *adj.* Completely lacking; destitute or empty: *a person devoid of humor.*

de·volve (dĭ-vŏlv′) *intr. & tr.v.* **de·volved, de·volv·ing, de·volves** To pass or be passed on to another who acts as a substitute or delegate; transfer: *During his illness various duties devolved upon me.*

De·vo·ni·an (dĭ-vō′nē-ən) *n.* The fourth period of the Paleozoic Era, from about 416 to 359 million years ago. During the Devonian, forests, amphibians, and insects first appeared. See table at **geologic time.** —**De·vo′ni·an** *adj.*

de·vote (dĭ-vōt′) *tr.v.* **de·vot·ed, de·vot·ing, de·votes** To give or apply (one's time, attention, or self) entirely to a specified activity, cause, or person: *a musician who devotes time to helping students.* [From Latin *dēvovēre*, to vow.]

de·vot·ed (dĭ-vō′tĭd) *adj.* **1.** Feeling or expressing strong affection or attachment: *a devoted friend.* **2.** Dedicated: *a devoted scientist.* —**de·vot′ed·ly** *adv.* —**de·vot′ed·ness** *n.*

dev·o·tee (dĕv′ə-tē′) *n.* A person who is ardently devoted to something; a fan: *A devotee of fishing will be out in all kinds of weather.*

de·vo·tion (dĭ-vō′shən) *n.* **1.** Affection, concern, and dedication, as to a person or principle: *the devotion of a parent to a child.* **2a.** Religious observance or worship. **b.** often **devotions** An act of religious observance or prayer, especially when private. **3.** The act of devoting: *devotion of time to teaching English to immigrants.*

de·vo·tion·al (dĭ-vō′shə-nəl) *adj.* Relating to or used in devotion, especially religious devotion. —**de·vo′tion·al·ly** *adv.*

de·vour (dĭ-vour′) *tr.v.* **de·voured, de·vour·ing, de·vours 1.** To eat up greedily: *The hungry campers devoured their dinner.* **2.** To destroy or consume: *Flames devoured the building.* **3.** To take in greedily: *devour an exciting mystery story.* [From Middle English *devouren*, from Latin *dēvorāre* : *dē-*, completely + *vorāre*, to swallow.] —**de·vour′ing·ly** *adv.*

de·vout (dĭ-vout′) *adj.* **de·vout·er, de·vout·est 1.** Devoted to religion or to religious obligations: *a devout monk.* **2.** Sincere; earnest: *a devout wish for peace.* —**de·vout′ly** *adv.* —**de·vout′ness** *n.*

dew (do͞o) *n.* **1.** Water droplets condensed from the air, mostly at night, onto cool surfaces. **2.** Something moist, fresh, renewing, or pure. **3.** Moisture appearing in small drops, as tears or perspiration. ❖ *tr.v.* **dewed, dew·ing, dews** To wet with or as if with dew.

❑ *These sound alike:* **dew, do**[1] (perform), **due** (owing).

dew·ber·ry (do͞o′bĕr′ē) *n.* **1.** A purple or black berry from any of several low-growing prickly shrubs related to the blackberry. **2.** A shrub that bears such fruit.

dew·claw (do͞o′klô′) *n.* A short digit that does not reach the ground, found on the feet of dogs and certain other mammals.

dew·drop (do͞o′drŏp′) *n.* A drop of dew.

Dew·ey decimal classification (do͞o′ē) *n.* A system for classifying library books and magazines into subject categories corresponding to three-digit numerals. Each category is subdivided by the addition of decimals to the number. [After Melvil *Dewey* (1851–1931), American librarian.]

dew·lap (do͞o′lăp′) *n.* A loose fold of skin hanging from the neck of certain animals, such as some dogs, cattle, and lizards. Lizards can extend their dewlaps.

dew point *n.* The temperature at which air becomes saturated with water vapor and dew forms.

dew·y (do͞o′ē) *adj.* **dew·i·er, dew·i·est** Moist with dew: *dewy fields of early morning.*

dex·ter·i·ty (dĕk-stĕr′ĭ-tē) *n.* Skill or grace in using the hands, body, or mind.

dex·ter·ous (dĕk′stər-əs *or* dĕk′strəs) also **dex·trous** (dĕk′strəs) *adj.* Skillful in the use of the hands or mind:

a dexterous carpenter. [From Latin *dexter*, on the right, skillful.] **—dex′ter·ous·ly** *adv.* **—dex′ter·ous·ness** *n.*

dex·trose (dĕk′strōs′) *n.* A sugar that is the most common form of glucose. It is found in the cells and tissues of living organisms and can be derived from starch.

Dha·ka also **Dac·ca** (dăk′ə *or* dä′kə) The capital of Bangladesh, in the east-central part of the country.

di– *pref.* A prefix that means two, twice, or double: *dicotyledon; dioxide.*

dia– or **di–** *pref.* A prefix that means through or across: *diaphanous; diagonal.*

di·a·be·tes (dī′ə-**bē′**tĭs *or* dī′ə-**bē′**tēz) *n.* Any of several disorders marked by abnormally high levels of sugar in the blood, caused by the body's inability to produce or use insulin properly. One type of diabetes usually develops in children and is treated with insulin, and another type usually develops in adults and is often managed with changes in exercise and diet.

di·a·bet·ic (dī′ə-**bĕt′**ĭk) *adj.* Relating to or having diabetes. ❖ *n.* A person having diabetes.

di·a·bol·i·cal (dī′ə-**bŏl′**ĭ-kəl) also **di·a·bol·ic** (dī′ə-**bŏl′**ĭk) *adj.* Concerning or characteristic of the devil; satanic. **—di′a·bol′i·cal·ly** *adv.* **—di′a·bol′i·cal·ness** *n.*

di·a·crit·ic (dī′ə-**krĭt′**ĭk) *n.* A diacritical mark.

di·a·crit·i·cal mark (dī′ə-**krĭt′**ĭ-kəl) *n.* A mark, such as a cedilla or acute accent, added to a letter to indicate a certain pronunciation or stress.

di·a·dem (**dī′**ə-dĕm′) *n.* A crown worn as a sign of royalty.

di·aer·e·sis (dī-**ĕr′**ĭ-sĭs) *n.* Variant of **dieresis.**

di·ag·nose (**dī′**əg-nōs′ *or* **dī′**əg-nōz′) *tr.v.* **di·ag·nosed, di·ag·nos·ing, di·ag·nos·es** To make a careful examination of; identify and study: *Doctors diagnose disease, and mechanics diagnose car trouble.*

di·ag·no·sis (dī′əg-**nō′**sĭs) *n., pl.* **di·ag·no·ses** (dī′əg-**nō′**sēz) **1.** The act or process of identifying or determining the nature and cause of a disease or injury by examining a patient, analyzing a patient's medical history, and reviewing the results of laboratory tests: *Today, doctors have many instruments to help them in the diagnosis of diseases.* **2a.** A close analysis of the nature of something. **b.** The conclusions reached by such an analysis: *When the computer broke down, the diagnosis was a short circuit.* [From Greek *diagnōsis*, discernment, from *diagignōskein*, to distinguish : *dia-*, apart + *gignōskein*, to come to know, discern.]

di·ag·nos·tic (dī′əg-**nŏs′**tĭk) *adj.* Relating to or used in diagnosis: *X-ray machines and stethoscopes are diagnostic tools of medicine.* **—di′ag·nos′ti·cal·ly** *adv.*

di·ag·nos·ti·cian (dī′əg-nŏ-**stĭsh′**ən) *n.* A person, especially a physician, who specializes in making medical diagnoses.

di·ag·o·nal (dī-**ăg′**ə-nəl) *adj.* **1a.** Connecting two nonadjacent corners in a polygon: *a diagonal line sloping down across a square.* **b.** Connecting two nonadjacent corners in a polyhedron that do not lie in the same face. **2.** Slanting or oblique: *the diagonal stripes on a tie.* ❖ *n.* **1.** A diagonal line segment. **2.** Something, such as a row, course, or part, that is arranged in a sloping or slanting direction. [From Greek *diagōnios*, from angle to angle : *dia-*, across, through + *gōniā*, angle, corner.] **—di·ag′o·nal·ly** *adv.*

di·a·gram (**dī′**ə-grăm′) *n.* A plan, drawing, or sketch that shows how something works or indicates how parts are put together: *A diagram of the apartment shows where each room is.* ❖ *tr.v.* **di·a·grammed, di·a·gram·ming, di·a·grams** or **di·a·gramed, di·a·gram·ing, di·a·grams** To show or represent by or as if by a diagram: *diagram a floor plan.*

di·a·gram·mat·ic (dī′ə-grə-**măt′**ĭk) *adj.* **1.** In the form of a diagram: *A diagrammatic plan of the tunnel explains how it will be built.* **2.** In outline form only; sketchy: *an essay in diagrammatic form.* **—di′a·gram·mat′i·cal·ly** *adv.*

di·al (**dī′**əl) *n.* **1.** A graduated surface or face on which a measurement, such as speed, is indicated by a moving needle or pointer. **2.** The control that selects the station to which a radio or television is tuned. **3.** A movable disk on a telephone with numbers and letters, used to signal the number to which a call is made. ❖ *v.* **di·aled, di·al·ing, di·als** or **di·alled, di·al·ling, di·als** *—tr.* **1.** To operate by using a dial, as in a combination lock: *We dialed the combination and the lock opened.* **2.** To control or select by means of a dial. **3.** To call (a party) on a telephone: *dialed her friend.* **4.** To make a telephone call to (a specific number): *Dial 911 for emergencies. —intr.* To use a dial, as on a telephone: *dial until you get an answer.* [From Middle English, sundial, clock, from Medieval Latin *diālis*, daily, from *diēs*, day.]

di·a·lect (**dī′**ə-lĕkt′) *n.* A variety of a language that is spoken in a particular region or by a particular group of people: *Cockney is a dialect of English.* —SEE NOTE.

di·a·lec·tal (dī′ə-**lĕk′**təl) *adj.* Relating to a dialect: *dialectal speech.*

dialog box *n.* A window that appears on a computer screen, presenting information or requesting input.

di·a·logue or **di·a·log** (**dī′**ə-lôg′) *n.* **1.** A conversation between two or more people: *a friendly dialogue.* **2.** A discussion of ideas or opinions, especially between groups to resolve a disagreement: *a dialogue on global warming.* **3.** The words spoken by the characters of a play or story: *The dialogue of the comedy was very witty.* **4.** A literary work written in the form of a conversation: *Many students of philosophy have read the dialogues of Plato.*

dial tone *n.* A low steady tone in a telephone receiver, telling the user that a number may be dialed.

di·al-up (**dī′**əl-ŭp′ *or* **dīl′**ŭp′) *adj.* Relating to a network connection, usually to the Internet, made by dialing a phone number: *a dial-up modem.*

di·al·y·sis (dī-**ăl′**ĭ-sĭs) *n., pl.* **di·al·y·ses** (dī-**ăl′**ĭ-sēz′) **1.** The process of separating dissolved substances by diffusion through a membrane that blocks the passage of large molecules but allows smaller molecules to penetrate the membrane. **2.** The removal of wastes from the bloodstream by a machine that performs dialysis when the kidneys do not function properly.

diam. *abbr.* An abbreviation of diameter.

di·am·e·ter (dī-**ăm′**ĭ-tər) *n.* **1.** A straight line segment that passes through the center of a circle or sphere from one side to the other. **2.** The length of such a line segment. [From Middle English *diametre*, from Greek *diametros (grammē)*, diagonal (line) : *dia-*, across, through + *metron*, measure.]

di·a·met·ri·cal (dī′ə-**mĕt′**rĭ-kəl) also **di·a·met·ric** (dī′ə-**mĕt′**rĭk) *adj.* **1.** Relating to or along a diameter: *a diametrical measurement.* **2.** Exactly opposite; contrary: *debaters with diametrical points of view.* **—di·a·met′ri·cal·ly** *adv.*

di·a·mond (**dī′**ə-mənd *or* **dī′**mənd) *n.* **1.** A form of pure carbon that occurs as a clear crystal and is the hardest of all known minerals. It is used as a gemstone in its finer varieties and as an abrasive and an edge on cutting tools. **2a.** A rhombus, particularly when oriented so that one of its diagonals would extend directly ahead of an observer or a point of reference and the other diagonal is perpendicular to it. **b.** A playing card bearing a red figure shaped like this. **c.** often **diamonds** The suit in a deck of cards having this figure as its symbol. **3a.** A baseball infield. **b.** The whole playing field in baseball. [From Middle English *diamaunt*, from Medieval Latin *diamas*, alteration of Greek *adamās*, unconquerable, hard steel, diamond.]

diamondback rattlesnake (**dī′**ə-mənd-băk′ *or* **dī′**-

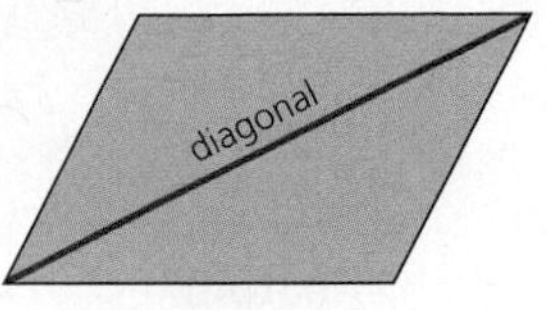

diagonal

USAGE

dialect Everyone who speaks a language speaks some form of **dialect,** which is usually the kind of language spoken by people in the neighborhood where you grow up. A given language may have several dialects that differ from each other in pronunciation, in the names used for certain things, and even in some grammatical constructions. Depending on which part of the country you live in, you probably pronounce words in a certain way and even use certain words because of the dialect spoken. For example, if you live in the northeast United States, you probably call a carbonated soft drink a *soda,* but if you live in the Midwest or farther west, you may call it *pop.* Many people in Boston call it *tonic.* In school you learn to use a variety of English called Standard English that avoids these local variations in speech in favor of a more general language of public communication.

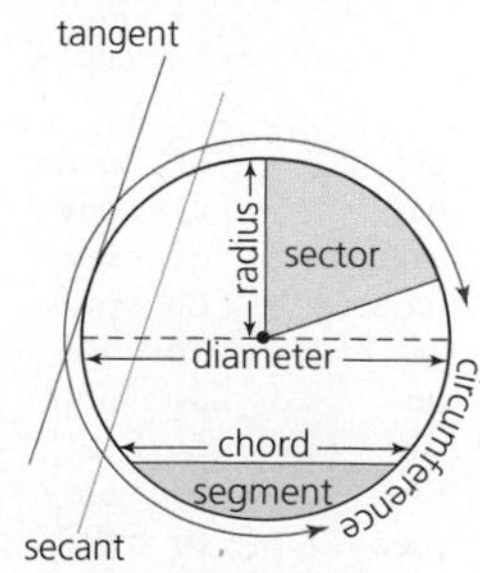

diameter

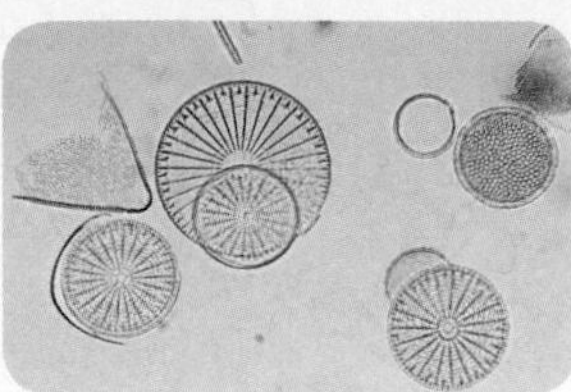

diatom

BIOGRAPHY

Emily Dickinson
Today, Emily **Dickinson** is widely celebrated as one of the most important American poets, but she was virtually unknown during her lifetime. Only a handful of her poems were published during her life (all of them anonymously and some without her consent). The rest came to light after she died in 1886. Her writing was so unlike the standard poetry of the day that the first editors of her work often altered the poems before publishing them in an attempt to make them easier to understand. The poems are short and similar in form to church hymns. They explore the emotional life of the solitary individual and the relation of the soul to God, death, and the afterlife. They employ powerful imagery in unconventional rhythms and sentence structures. These experiments in poetic form greatly influenced many of the modernist poets of the 1900s.

ă	pat	ôr	core
ā	pay	oi	boy
âr	care	ou	out
ä	father	o͝o	took
ĕ	pet	o͝or	lure
ē	be	o͞o	boot
ĭ	pit	ŭ	cut
ī	bite	ûr	urge
îr	pier	th	thin
ŏ	pot	*th*	this
ō	toe	zh	vision
ô	paw	ə	about

mənd-băk′) *n.* Either of two large rattlesnakes of the United States and Mexico, having diamond-shaped markings on the back.

diamondback terrapin *n.* A turtle of coastal regions of the eastern and southern United States, having edible flesh and an upper shell with diamond-shaped ridged or knobby markings.

Di·an·a (dī-**ăn′**ə) *n.* In Roman mythology, the goddess of the moon and the hunt, identified with the Greek Artemis.

di·a·per (**dī′**ə-pər *or* **dī′**pər) *n.* A piece of absorbent material, such as paper or cloth, that is typically placed between the legs and fastened at the waist to contain excretions. ❖ *tr.v.* **di·a·pered, di·a·per·ing, di·a·pers** To put a diaper on (a baby, for example). [From Middle English, a patterned fabric, from Medieval Greek *diaspros*, pure white.]

di·aph·a·nous (dī-**ăf′**ə-nəs) *adj.* Of such fine texture as to allow light to show through: *a diaphanous curtain.* **—di·aph′a·nous·ly** *adv.*

di·a·phragm (**dī′**ə-frăm′) *n.* **1.** A membrane of muscle that separates the chest cavity from the abdominal cavity. As the diaphragm contracts and expands it forces air into and out of the lungs. **2.** A membrane that divides or separates, as in a pump or other type of machinery. **3.** A thin disk, especially in a microphone or telephone receiver, that vibrates in response to sound waves to produce electrical signals or vibrates in response to electrical signals to produce sound waves. **4.** A disk with an opening in the center to regulate the amount of light entering a camera or microscope. **5.** A thin flexible disk, usually made of rubber, that is designed to cover the cervix of the uterus to prevent the entry of sperm during sexual intercourse.

di·ar·rhe·a (dī′ə-**rē′**ə) *n.* A condition in which bowel movements are frequent and watery.

di·a·ry (**dī′**ə-rē) *n., pl.* **di·a·ries 1.** A daily record, especially a personal record of experiences, observations, and events. **2.** A book of blank pages for keeping such a record. [From Latin *diārium*, daily allowance, daily journal, from *diēs*, day.]

di·as·to·le (dī-**ăs′**tə-lē) *n.* The phase of a heartbeat in which the chambers of the heart, especially the ventricles, relax and fill with blood. **—di′a·stol′ic** (dī′ə-**stŏl′**ĭk) *adj.*

di·a·tom (**dī′**ə-tŏm′) *n.* Any of numerous one-celled algae that live in water, make their own food by photosynthesis, and have hard shells containing silica. Diatoms are an important component of plankton.

di·a·tom·ic (dī′ə-**tŏm′**ĭk) *adj.* Made up of two atoms: *a diatomic molecule.*

di·a·ton·ic (dī′ə-**tŏn′**ĭk) *adj.* Relating to or based on a scale using only seven tones, of which five are separated by whole steps and two by half steps. The major and minor scales are diatonic scales.

di·a·tribe (**dī′**ə-trīb′) *n.* A bitter and abusive denunciation: *attack one's enemy in a fierce diatribe.* [From Greek *diatribē*, pastime, lecture, treatise, from *diatrībein*, to wear away, spend time.]

Dí·az (**dē′**äs *or* **dē′**äz), **(José de la Cruz) Porfirio** 1830–1915. Mexican soldier and politician who became president in 1876 and governed the country until 1911 (except for the years 1880–1884).

dibs (dĭbz) *pl.n. Slang* A claim; rights: *I have dibs on the last waffle.*

dice (dīs) *n.* Plural of **die²** (sense 2). ❖ *v.* **diced, dic·ing, dic·es** *—intr.* To play or gamble with dice. *—tr.* To cut (food) into small cubes: *dice vegetables for soup.*

di·chot·o·my (dī-**kŏt′**ə-mē) *n., pl.* **di·chot·o·mies** Division into two parts or things that usually contradict or contrast with each other: *She sees a dichotomy between faith and reason.* **—di·chot′o·mous** (dī-**kŏt′**ə-məs) *adj.*

dick·ens (**dĭk′**ənz) *n. Informal* **1.** A reprimand or an expression of anger: *gave me the dickens for being late.* **2.** Used as an intensive: *Where the dickens did you get that?*

Dick·ens (**dĭk′**ĭnz), **Charles John Huffam** 1812–1870. British writer known for his tales of Victorian life and times, including *Oliver Twist* (1838).

dick·er (**dĭk′**ər) *intr.v.* **dick·ered, dick·er·ing, dick·ers** To bargain; barter: *dickered over the price of the chair.* ❖ *n.* The act or process of bargaining.

dick·ey (**dĭk′**ē) *n., pl.* **dick·eys 1.** A woman's blouse front worn under a suit jacket or sweater. **2.** A man's detachable shirt front.

Dick·in·son (**dĭk′**ĭn-sən), **Emily Elizabeth** 1830–1886. American poet who wrote more than 1,700 verses in her lifetime. The first volume of her poetry was not published until 1890. —SEE NOTE.

di·cot (**dī′**kŏt′) *n.* A dicotyledon.

di·cot·y·le·don (dī′kŏt′l-**ēd′**n) *n.* A flowering plant having two cotyledons and usually other characteristics such as leaf veins that are netlike rather than parallel, flower parts in multiples of four or five, and the capacity for woody growth. Beans, roses, maples, and oaks are dicotyledons, while tulips, onions, grasses, and palms are monocotyledons. **—di′cot′y·le′don·ous** *adj.*

dic·ta (**dĭk′**tə) *n.* A plural of **dictum.**

dic·tate (**dĭk′**tāt′ *or* dĭk-**tāt′**) *v.* **dic·tat·ed, dic·tat·ing, dic·tates** *—tr.* **1.** To say or read aloud to be recorded or written by another: *dictate an order over the phone; dictate a letter.* **2.** To establish with authority; impose: *Hospital rules dictate visiting hours.* *—intr.* **1.** To say or read aloud material to be recorded or written by another: *The reporter dictated into the tape recorder.* **2.** To issue orders or commands. ❖ *n.* (**dĭk′**tāt′) An order; a command. [From Latin *dictāre*, from *dīcere*, to say.]

dic·ta·tion (dĭk-**tā′**shən) *n.* **1a.** The act or process of dictating material to another to be written down or recorded: *dictation of a letter over the telephone.* **b.** The material so dictated. **2.** An authoritative command or order.

dic·ta·tor (**dĭk′**tā′tər *or* dĭk-**tā′**tər) *n.* **1.** An absolute ruler. **2.** A tyrant; a despot.

dic·ta·to·ri·al (dĭk′tə-**tôr′**ē-əl) *adj.* **1.** Tending to tell others what to do in a presumptuous manner: *the chef's dictatorial manner in the kitchen.* **2.** Relating to or characteristic of a dictator or dictatorship: *dictatorial power of an occupying army.* **—dic′ta·to′ri·al·ly** *adv.*

dic·ta·tor·ship (dĭk-**tā′**tər-shĭp′ *or* **dĭk′**tā′tər-shĭp′) *n.* **1.** The office or tenure of a dictator. **2.** A state or government under the rule of a dictator. **3.** Absolute or despotic control or power.

dic·tion (**dĭk′**shən) *n.* **1.** Choice and use of words in speaking or writing: *A mystery writer's diction must be convincing to be successful.* **2.** Degree of clearness and distinctness in pronouncing words; enunciation: *The singer had good diction and so we could enjoy both words and music.* —SEE NOTE AT **predict.**

dic·tion·ar·y (**dĭk′**shə-nĕr′ē) *n., pl.* **dic·tion·ar·ies 1.** A reference work containing an alphabetical list of words, with information given for each word, usually including meaning, pronunciation, and etymology. **2.** A reference work containing an alphabetical list of words in one language with their translations in another language: *a Russian-English dictionary.* **3.** A reference work containing an alphabetical list of words in a particular category or subject with specialized information about them: *a medical dictionary.*

dic·tum (**dĭk′**təm) *n., pl.* **dic·ta** (**dĭk′**tə) or **dic·tums** An authoritative, often formal pronouncement: *Nutrition experts issued a new dictum about junk food.*

did (dĭd) *v.* Past tense of **do¹.**

di·dac·tic (dī-**dăk′**tĭk) *adj.* **1.** Intended to instruct: *Many legends have a didactic purpose.* **2.** Inclined to teach or moralize too much. **—di·dac′ti·cal·ly** *adv.*

did·dle (dĭd′l) *intr.v.* **did·dled, did·dling, did·dles 1.** To toy or fiddle: *diddling with the controls.* **2.** To waste time: *diddled around all day.*

didg·er·i·doo or **didj·er·i·doo** (dĭj′ə-rē-do͞o′) *n., pl.* **didg·er·i·doos** or **didj·er·i·doos** A musical instrument of certain aboriginal peoples of Australia, consisting of a long hollow branch or stick that makes a deep drone when blown into while vibrating the lips.

did·n't (dĭd′nt) Contraction of *did not.*

Di·do (dī′dō) *n.* In Roman mythology, the founder and queen of Carthage who fell in love with Aeneas and killed herself when he abandoned her.

Did·rik·son (dĭd′rĭk-sən), **Mildred Ella** See Mildred Ella Didrikson **Zaharias.**

didst (dĭdst) *v. Archaic* Second person singular past tense of **do[1]**.

die[1] (dī) *intr.v.* **died, dy·ing** (dī′ĭng), **dies 1.** To stop living; become dead: *The sunflowers died in the first frost.* **2.** To cease existing, often gradually: *the conversation died; the sunlight is dying.* **3.** To want something very much: *I'm dying to see that movie.* **4.** To stop working or operating: *The motor died when we ran out of gas.* ◆ **die down** To lose strength; subside: *The winds died down.* **die off** To undergo a sudden sharp decline in population: *Bats are dying off in some regions.* **die out** To cease living or existing completely; become extinct: *Why did the dinosaurs die out? Those customs have died out.* [From Middle English *deien*, probably from Old Norse *deyja*.]

❑ *These sound alike:* **die[1]** (stop living), **die[2]** (device for shaping material), **dye** (color).

die[2] (dī) *n.* **1.** *pl.* **dies** A tool or device that shapes materials by stamping, cutting, or punching: *Dies are used to make coins.* **2.** *pl.* **dice** (dīs) A small cube marked on each side with one to six dots and usually used in pairs in games. [From Middle English *de*, gaming die, from Latin *datum*, given, from *dare*, to give.]

❑ *These sound alike:* **die[2]** (device for shaping material), **die[1]** (stop living), **dye** (color).

die-hard also **die·hard** (dī′härd′) *adj.* Stubbornly resisting change or clinging to a seemingly hopeless cause: *a die-hard supporter.* ❖ *n.* A person who stubbornly refuses to give up a cause or resists change.

di·er·e·sis or **di·aer·e·sis** (dī-ĕr′ĭ-sĭs) *n., pl.* **di·er·e·ses** or **di·aer·e·ses** (dī-ĕr′ĭ-sēz′) **1.** A mark (¨) placed over the second of two adjacent vowels to show that the second vowel is to be pronounced as a separate sound, as in *naïve.* **2.** A mark (¨) placed over a vowel, such as the final vowel in *Brontë*, to indicate that the vowel is not silent.

die·sel (dē′zəl *or* dē′səl) *n.* **1.** A diesel engine. **2.** A vehicle powered by a diesel engine. **3.** A type of fuel designed to power a diesel engine.

diesel engine *n.* An internal-combustion engine in which the fuel oil is ignited by the heat of air that has been highly compressed in the cylinder. [After Rudolph *Diesel* (1858–1913), German engineer.]

di·et[1] (dī′ĭt) *n.* **1.** The usual food and drink eaten by a person or animal. **2.** A regulated selection of foods, as for medical reasons or weight loss: *a diet that excludes milk products.* ❖ *intr.v.* **di·et·ed, di·et·ing, di·ets** To eat and drink according to a regulated system, especially so as to control a medical condition or lose weight. ❖ *adj.* Relating to foods having few or no calories: *diet soft drinks.* [From Middle English *diete*, from Greek *diaita*, way of living.] —**di′et·er** *n.*

di·et[2] (dī′ĭt) *n.* A national or local legislative assembly in certain countries, such as Japan. [From Middle English *diete*, from Medieval Latin *diēta*, day's journey, meeting day, from Latin *diaeta*, daily routine.]

di·e·tar·y (dī′ĭ-tĕr′ē) *adj.* Relating to diet: *a good dietary plan.*

di·e·tet·ic (dī′ĭ-tĕt′ĭk) *adj.* **1.** Relating to diet or its regulation. **2.** Made or processed for restricted diets: *dietetic foods prepared with less salt and sugar.*

di·e·tet·ics (dī′ĭ-tĕt′ĭks) *n.* *(used with a singular verb)* The study of nutrition as it relates to health.

di·e·ti·tian or **di·e·ti·cian** (dī′ĭ-tĭsh′ən) *n.* A person who specializes in dietetics: *The hospital dietitian plans the meals for each patient.*

dif·fer (dĭf′ər) *intr.v.* **dif·fered, dif·fer·ing, dif·fers 1.** To be unlike, as in nature or amount: *The weather often differs from one part of a state to another.* **2.** To be of a different opinion; disagree: *The experts differ on what should be done to fix the economy.* [From Middle English *differren*, from Latin *differre*, to delay, differ : *dis-*, apart + *ferre*, to carry.]

dif·fer·ence (dĭf′ər-əns *or* dĭf′rəns) *n.* **1.** The quality or condition of being unlike or dissimilar: *the difference between summer and winter.* **2.** An instance of being unlike or different: *There is a big difference in sound between a clarinet and an oboe.* **3.** A noticeable change or effect: *Exercise has made a big difference in her health.* **4.** A disagreement or controversy: *We settled our differences amicably.* **5.** The amount by which one quantity is greater or less than another; what is left when one number is subtracted from another: *The difference between 10 and 4 is 6.*

dif·fer·ent (dĭf′ər-ənt *or* dĭf′rənt) *adj.* **1.** Unlike in form, quality, amount, or nature: *The two breeds of dog are very different.* **2.** Distinct or separate: *We ran into each other on three different occasions today.* —**dif′fer·ent·ly** *adv.* —SEE NOTE.

dif·fer·en·tial (dĭf′ə-rĕn′shəl) *adj.* Relating to or showing a difference: *differential rates in air fares.* ❖ *n.* **1.** A differential gear. **2.** A difference in amount, especially in price: *There is a substantial differential between the cost of flying to Florida in the winter and in the summer.* —**dif′fer·en′tial·ly** *adv.*

differential gear *n.* An arrangement of gears used in an automobile or truck that permits the drive shaft to turn the two rear-wheel or front-wheel axle shafts at different speeds, so that the wheels can rotate at different speeds when the vehicle is turning.

dif·fer·en·ti·ate (dĭf′ə-rĕn′shē-āt′) *v.* **dif·fer·en·ti·at·ed, dif·fer·en·ti·at·ing, dif·fer·en·ti·ates** —*tr.* **1.** To be the difference between: *Red shirts and blue shirts differentiate the teams.* **2.** To understand or show the differences between: *differentiated the various wildflowers.* —*intr.* **1.** To become distinct or specialized, especially during the process of biological development: *cells that differentiate into neurons.* **2.** To make distinctions; discriminate: *A doctor can differentiate between a rash and chickenpox.* —**dif′fer·en′ti·a′tion** *n.*

dif·fi·cult (dĭf′ĭ-kŭlt′) *adj.* **1.** Not easy to do or accomplish: *a difficult task.* **2.** Not easy to endure; full of hardship or trouble; trying: *living in difficult times.* **3.** Hard to understand or solve: *a difficult math problem.* **4.** Hard to please, satisfy, or manage: *A perfectionist can be difficult.* [From Middle English, from Latin *difficilis.*]

dif·fi·cul·ty (dĭf′ĭ-kŭl′tē) *n., pl.* **dif·fi·cul·ties 1.** The quality or condition of being difficult: *The difficulty of the subject made the book on botany hard to understand.* **2.** Something that is hard to deal with, accomplish, comprehend, or solve: *Technical difficulties plagued the new website.* **3.** often **difficulties** A troublesome or embarrassing state of affairs, especially financial affairs.

dif·fi·dence (dĭf′ĭ-dəns) *n.* A quality or state of being timid or shy: *Diffidence held him back from calling out the answer.*

dif·fi·dent (dĭf′ĭ-dənt) *adj.* Lacking or marked by a lack of self-confidence; timid and shy. —**dif′fi·dent·ly** *adv.*

dif·fract (dĭ-frăkt′) *intr. & tr.v.* **dif·fract·ed, dif·fract·**

Emily Dickinson

didgeridoo

die[2]
dies used to coin euros

USAGE

different When you are making a comparison between two people or things, **different** should be followed by *from* instead of *than*: *My book is different from* (not *than*) *yours.* When you are making a comparison that ends with a full clause, *different* should be followed by *than* instead of *from*: *The school is different than it was 20 years ago.* However, if the clause starts with a word like *how* or *what*, you should use *from* to make the comparison: *The school is different from what it was 20 years ago.*

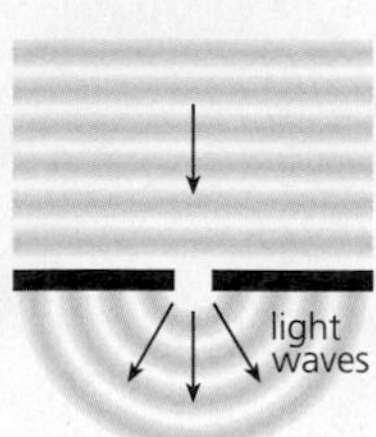

diffraction

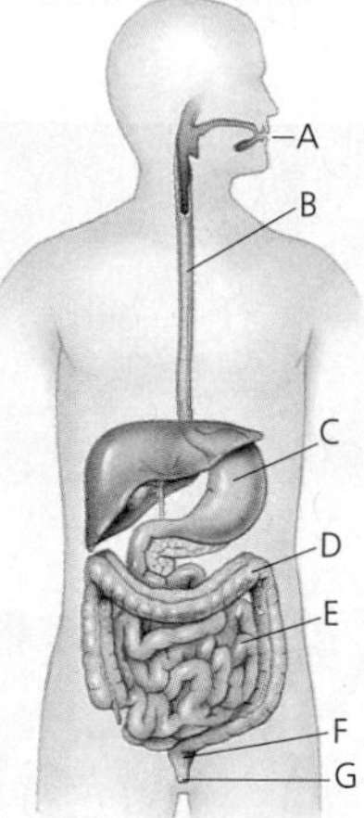

digestive tract
A. mouth
B. esophagus
C. stomach
D. large intestine
E. small intestine
F. rectum
G. anus

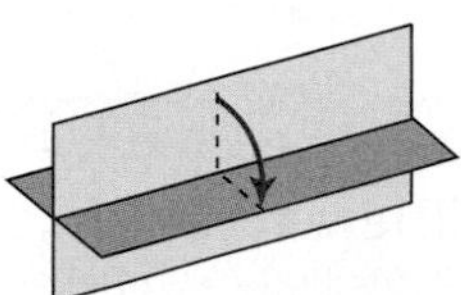

dihedral angle

ă	pat	ôr	core
ā	pay	oi	boy
âr	care	ou	out
ä	father	o͝o	took
ĕ	pet	o͝or	lure
ē	be	o͞o	boot
ĭ	pit	ŭ	cut
ī	bite	ûr	urge
îr	pier	th	thin
ŏ	pot	*th*	this
ō	toe	zh	vision
ô	paw	ə	about

ing, dif·fracts To undergo or cause to undergo diffraction.

dif·frac·tion (dĭ-**frăk′**shən) *n.* **1.** The bending or turning of a wave, such as a light wave, when it encounters an obstacle, such as an edge or a hole, whose size is similar to the wavelength of the wave. The colors of the spectrum can be produced by the diffraction of light. **2.** A similar spreading and bending of sound or other kinds of waves. [From Latin *diffrāctus*, past participle of *diffringere* : *dis-*, apart + *frangere*, to break.]

dif·fuse (dĭ-**fyo͞oz′**) *v.* **dif·fused, dif·fus·ing, dif·fus·es** —*tr.* **1.** To cause to spread out freely: *The lamp diffuses light over the table.* **2.** To scatter; disseminate: *diffuses ideas over the Internet; diffuse knowledge.* —*intr.* **1.** To become spread out or scattered: *A lighthouse beam diffuses far out over the ocean.* **2.** To undergo diffusion: *In the lungs, oxygen diffuses into the bloodstream.* ❖ *adj.* (dĭ-**fyo͞os′**) **1.** Widely spread or scattered: *Diffuse light is often hard to read by.* **2.** Wordy or unclear: *a diffuse description.* [From Middle English, from Latin *diffūsus*, spread out, from *diffundere*, to spread out : *dis-*, apart, out + *fundere*, to pour.] —SEE NOTE AT **transfusion.**

dif·fu·sion (dĭ-**fyo͞o′**zhən) *n.* **1.** The process of diffusing or the condition of being diffused: *the diffusion of knowledge.* **2.** The scattering of light or other radiation as it reflects off a rough surface or passes through a translucent material. **3.** The gradual mixing together of different gases or liquids as a result of the random motions of their atoms or molecules.

dig (dĭg) *v.* **dug** (dŭg), **dig·ging, digs** —*tr.* **1.** To break, turn over, or remove (earth, for example), as with a shovel, a spade, or the hands: *The dog was digging the dirt to crawl under the fence.* **2.** To make or form by removing earth or other material: *A woodchuck dug a hole in the garden.* **3.** To get by digging or by an action similar to digging: *dig clams; dug a quarter out of my pocket.* **4.** To learn or discover by investigation or research: *dig up information in a library.* **5.** To poke, prod, or thrust: *The cat dug its claws into a tree.* **6.** *Slang* **a.** To understand fully: *Do you dig what I mean?* **b.** To like, enjoy, or appreciate: *I dig their music.* **c.** To take notice of: *Dig that fantastic car!* —*intr.* **1.** To loosen, turn over, or remove earth or other material: *I'm going out to the garden to dig.* **2.** To make one's way by or as if by pushing aside or removing material: *dig through the trash to find a lost earring.* **3.** *Slang* To understand something. ❖ *n.* **1.** A poke or thrust: *a dig in the ribs.* **2.** A sarcastic taunting remark: *a nasty dig about my accent.* **3.** An archaeological excavation. **4. digs** *Informal* Lodgings: *liked his new digs.* ◆ **dig in 1.** To dig trenches for protection: *The army dug in for battle.* **2.** To begin to eat heartily: *We were hungry and quickly dug in.* [From Middle English *diggen*; perhaps akin to Old French *digue*, dike, trench.] —**dig′ger** *n.*

dig·er·a·ti (dĭj′ə-**rä′**tē) *pl.n.* People knowledgeable about digital technologies.

di·gest (dī-**jĕst′** *or* dĭ-**jĕst′**) *v.* **di·gest·ed, di·gest·ing, di·gests** —*tr.* **1.** To change (food) chemically into materials that a cell or organism can assimilate, store, or use as nourishment: *As carbohydrates are digested, the body turns them into sugar and starch.* **2.** To absorb mentally; comprehend: *Reporters must digest facts quickly in order to write their stories.* —*intr.* To assimilate or be assimilated as food: *Some foods do not digest easily. The snake is digesting.* ❖ *n.* (**dī′**jĕst′) A collection of previously published materials, such as essays or reports, usually in condensed form: *a website that posts digests of international news.* [From Middle English *digesten*, from Latin *dīgerere*, to separate, arrange : *dī-*, *dis-*, apart + *gerere*, to carry.]

di·gest·i·ble (dī-**jĕs′**tə-bəl *or* dĭ-**jĕs′**tə-bəl) *adj.* Capable of being digested easily or readily. —**di·gest′i·bil′i·ty** *n.*

di·ges·tion (dī-**jĕs′**chən *or* dĭ-**jĕs′**chən) *n.* **1a.** The process of digesting food. **b.** The ability to carry on this process: *poor digestion.* **2.** The decomposition of organic matter in sewage by bacteria.

di·ges·tive (dī-**jĕs′**tĭv *or* dĭ-**jĕs′**tĭv) *adj.* Relating to, aiding, or active in digestion: *digestive juices.* —**di·ges′tive·ly** *adv.*

digestive system *n.* The system of organs that breaks down and absorbs food as nourishment in the body of an animal. In humans, it consists of the digestive tract and the glands, such as the salivary glands, liver, and pancreas, that produce secretions necessary for digestion.

digestive tract *n.* The tube of the digestive system through which food passes, in which digestion takes place, and from which wastes are eliminated. In humans, it extends from the mouth to the anus and includes the pharynx, esophagus, stomach, and small and large intestines.

dig·gings (**dĭg′**ĭngz) *pl.n.* An excavation site, as for mining ore.

dig·it (**dĭj′**ĭt) *n.* **1.** A human finger or toe. **2.** A corresponding part in other vertebrate animals. **3.** One of the ten Arabic numerals, 0 through 9. [From Middle English, from Latin *digitus*.]

dig·i·tal (**dĭj′**ĭ-tl) *adj.* **1.** Relating to the fingers or toes: *digital mobility.* **2.** Expressed in numerical form, especially for use by a computer: *digital information.* **3a.** Relating to or being a device that can read, write, or store information represented in numerical form. **b.** Relating to or being a service that provides information expressed in numerical form: *digital cable.* **4.** Relating to or using digital devices: *digital photography; a digital librarian.* **5.** Using or giving a reading in digits: *a digital clock; a digital speedometer.* —**dig′i·tal·ly** *adv.*

dig·i·tal·is (dĭj′ĭ-**tăl′**ĭs) *n.* A drug prepared from the dried leaves of a kind of foxglove, used as a powerful heart stimulant.

dig·i·tize (**dĭj′**ĭ-tīz′) *tr.v.* **dig·i·tized, dig·i·tiz·ing, dig·i·tiz·es** To put (data, for example) into digital form. —**dig′i·ti·za′tion** (dĭj′ĭ-tĭ-**zā′**shən) *n.*

dig·ni·fied (**dĭg′**nə-fīd′) *adj.* Having or expressing dignity: *the careful and dignified manner of an ambassador.*

dig·ni·fy (**dĭg′**nə-fī′) *tr.v.* **dig·ni·fied, dig·ni·fy·ing, dig·ni·fies 1.** To give dignity or honor to: *The mayor's presence dignified our school ceremony.* **2.** To raise the status of (something unworthy and lowly): *I would not dignify the gossip by responding to it.*

dig·ni·tar·y (**dĭg′**nĭ-tĕr′ē) *n., pl.* **dig·ni·tar·ies** A person of high rank or position.

dig·ni·ty (**dĭg′**nĭ-tē) *n., pl.* **dig·ni·ties 1.** The quality or state of being worthy of esteem or respect. **2.** A stately or poised manner: *The judge maintained his dignity in the court at all times.* **3.** The respect and honor that go with an important position or station. **4.** A high office or rank. [From Middle English *dignite*, from Latin *dignitās*, from *dignus*, worthy.]

di·gress (dī-**grĕs′** *or* dĭ-**grĕs′**) *intr.v.* **di·gressed, di·gress·ing, di·gress·es** To speak or write temporarily about something different from the main subject: *digressed from the sermon to tell a personal story.* —SEE NOTE AT **progress.**

di·gres·sion (dī-**grĕsh′**ən *or* dĭ-**grĕsh′**ən) *n.* **1.** The act of digressing. **2.** An instance of digressing, especially in speech or writing: *tiresome digressions in an otherwise interesting article.*

di·he·dral angle (dī-**hē′**drəl) *n.* An angle formed by two geometric planes that intersect.

dike (dīk) *n.* **1.** A wall or embankment built to hold back water and prevent flooding, as by a river or the sea. **2.** A long mass of igneous rock that cuts across the structure of adjoining rock. ❖ *tr.v.* **diked, dik·ing, dikes** To protect or provide with a dike.

di·lap·i·dat·ed (dĭ-lăp′ĭ-dā′tĭd) *adj.* In a condition of deterioration or disrepair, as through neglect: *The dilapidated building was beyond repair.* [From Latin *dīlapidāre*, to throw stones, bring to ruin : *dī-*, apart + *lapis*, stone.]

di·lap·i·da·tion (dĭ-lăp′ĭ-**dā′**shən) *n.* A condition of deterioration or disrepair: *The run-down house showed signs of dilapidation.*

di·late (dī-**lāt′** *or* **dī′**lāt′) *tr. & intr.v.* **di·lat·ed, di·lat·ing, di·lates** To make or become larger or wider; expand: *When the horse whinnied, its nostrils dilated.* **—di·la′tion** *n.*

dil·a·to·ry (**dĭl′**ə-tôr′ē) *adj.* **1.** Causing or intending to cause delay: *hold up legislation with dilatory tactics such as the filibuster.* **2.** Characterized by or given to delay or slowness: *a dilatory student who always hands her homework in late.*

di·lem·ma (dĭ-**lĕm′**ə) *n.* A situation that requires a person to choose between options that are or seem equally unfavorable: *faced the dilemma of taking a cut in pay or losing her job.*

dil·et·tante (**dĭl′**ĭ-tänt′ *or* dĭl′ĭ-**tänt′**) *n.* A person who dabbles in an art or a branch of knowledge.

Dil·i (**dĭl′**ē) The capital of East Timor, on the northern coast of Timor.

dil·i·gence (**dĭl′**ə-jəns) *n.* Earnest and persistent application or effort: *It took a lot of diligence to stick with such an unrewarding project.*

dil·i·gent (**dĭl′**ə-jənt) *adj.* Marked by persevering painstaking effort: *A diligent search of the records revealed new evidence.* **—dil′i·gent·ly** *adv.*

dill (dĭl) *n.* A perennial plant related to parsley that has aromatic leaves and seeds that are used as seasonings.

dill pickle *n.* A pickled cucumber flavored with dill.

dil·ly-dal·ly (**dĭl′**ē-dăl′ē) *intr.v.* **dil·ly-dal·lied, dil·ly-dal·lying, dil·ly-dal·lies** To waste time, especially in indecision; dawdle.

di·lute (dī-**lo͞ot′** *or* dĭ-**lo͞ot′**) *tr.v.* **di·lut·ed, di·lut·ing, di·lutes 1.** To make thinner or less concentrated by adding a liquid such as water: *dilute thick soup.* **2.** To weaken the force, intensity, purity, or condition of: *A lack of facts diluted the argument.* ❖ *adj.* Weakened; diluted: *a dilute solution of acid.* [From Latin *dīluere* : *dī-*, *dis-*, apart, away + *-luere*, to wash.]

di·lu·tion (dī-**lo͞o′**shən *or* dĭ-**lo͞o′**shən) *n.* **1.** The act of diluting or the condition of being diluted. **2.** A diluted substance: *a 50 percent dilution of a concentrated solution.*

dim (dĭm) *adj.* **dim·mer, dim·mest 1.** Lacking in brightness: *a dim corner of the big room.* See Synonyms at **dark. 2.** Giving off only a small amount of light: *a dim light bulb.* **3.** Lacking luster; dull and subdued: *dim colors faded by the sun.* **4.** Faintly or unclearly perceived; indistinct: *the dim shape of a ship in the mist.* **5.** Lacking sharpness or clearness; vague: *a dim recollection.* **6.** Negative, unfavorable, or disapproving: *took a dim view of my excuses.* **7.** *Slang* Dull or unintelligent. ❖ *tr. & intr.v.* **dimmed, dim·ming, dims** To make or become dim: *Drivers must dim their headlights in traffic. The lights dimmed as the play began.* [From Old English.] **—dim′ly** *adv.* **—dim′ness** *n.*

dime (dīm) *n.* A coin of the United States or Canada worth ten cents. ◆ **a dime a dozen** Overly abundant; commonplace: *Cell phones are a dime a dozen these days.* **on a dime** At a precise point; within a narrowly defined area: *This car stops on a dime.* [From Middle English, tenth part, from Latin *decima (pars)*, tenth (part), from *decem*, ten.]

di·men·sion (dĭ-**mĕn′**shən *or* dī-**mĕn′**shən) *n.* **1.** A measurement of length, width, or thickness: *The dimensions of the window are 2 feet by 4 feet.* **2.** often **dimensions** Extent or magnitude; scope: *a problem of huge dimensions.* **3.** A physical quantity, such as mass, length, or time, on which other measurements are based. [From Middle English *dimensioun*, from Latin *dīmēnsiō*, extent, from *dīmetīrī*, to measure out : *dī-*, *dis-*, off, out + *mētīrī*, to measure.]

di·men·sion·al (dĭ-**mĕn′**shə-nəl) *adj.* **1.** Relating to a dimension or dimensions. **2.** Having a specified number of dimensions: *a two-dimensional picture.*

di·min·ish (dĭ-**mĭn′**ĭsh) *tr. & intr.v.* **di·min·ished, di·min·ish·ing, di·min·ish·es** To make or become smaller or less; reduce or decrease: *A drought diminished their water supply. Light diminished steadily as the sun went down.* See Synonyms at **decrease. —di·min′ish·ing** *adj.*

di·min·u·en·do (dĭ-mĭn′yo͞o-**ĕn′**dō) *n., adj., & adv.* Decrescendo.

dim·i·nu·tion (dĭm′ə-**no͞o′**shən) *n.* The act or process of diminishing; a lessening or reduction: *Lack of exercise contributes to the diminution of strength.*

di·min·u·tive (dĭ-**mĭn′**yə-tĭv) *adj.* **1.** Extremely or extraordinarily small: *diminutive figures in a collection of miniatures.* **2.** Relating to a suffix that expresses smallness, youth, familiarity, affection, or contempt, as *-let* in *booklet* or *-ie* in *dearie.* ❖ *n.* A diminutive suffix, word, or name. For example, *droplet* is a diminutive of *drop.* **—di·min′u·tive·ly** *adv.* **—di·min′u·tive·ness** *n.*

dim·mer (**dĭm′**ər) *n.* A device used to vary the brightness of an electric light.

dim·ple (**dĭm′**pəl) *n.* A small indentation in the flesh on a part of the human body, especially in the chin or on the cheek. ❖ *intr.v.* **dim·pled, dim·pling, dim·ples** To form dimples by smiling.

dim sum (**dĭm′** **so͝om′** *or* **dĭm′** **sŭm′**) *n.* A traditional Chinese meal in which small portions of a variety of foods, such as dumplings, are served.

din (dĭn) *n.* A jumble of loud, usually discordant sounds: *We couldn't hear them over the din of the traffic.* See Synonyms at **noise.**

di·nar (dĭ-**när′** *or* **dē′**när′) *n.* The basic monetary unit of numerous countries, including Algeria, Iraq, Jordan, and Libya.

dine (dīn) *intr.v.* **dined, din·ing, dines** To have dinner: *We dined early.* [From Middle English *dinen*, from Old French *disner* : Latin *dis-*, away, off + Latin *iēiūnium*, fast.]

❑ *These sound alike:* **dine, dyne** (unit of force).

din·er (**dī′**nər) *n.* **1.** A person who dines. **2.** A restaurant that has a long counter and booths, often housed in a building designed to resemble a railroad dining car.

di·nette (dī-**nĕt′**) *n.* **1.** A small dining room or alcove for informal meals. **2.** The table and chairs used to furnish such an area.

ding (dĭng) *intr. & tr.v.* **dinged, ding·ing, dings** To ring or cause to ring with a clanging sound. ❖ *n.* A ringing sound.

ding-dong (**dĭng′**dông′) *n.* The peal of a bell.

din·ghy (**dĭng′**ē) *n., pl.* **din·ghies** A small open boat, especially a rowboat carried by a larger boat. [From Hindi *ḍiṁgī*, diminutive of *ḍeṁgā*, raft.]

din·gle (**dĭng′**gəl) *n.* A small wooded valley; a dell.

din·go (**dĭng′**gō) *n., pl.* **din·goes** A wild dog of Australia, having a yellowish-brown coat.

din·gy (**dĭn′**jē) *adj.* **din·gi·er, din·gi·est** Darkened with grime or soot; dirty or discolored: *a dark and dingy room in need of paint.* **—din′gi·ly** *adv.* **—din′gi·ness** *n.*

din·ing car (**dī′**nĭng) *n.* A railroad car in which meals are served.

dining room *n.* A room, as in a house or hotel, in which meals are eaten.

din·ky (**dĭng′**kē) *adj.* **din·ki·er, din·ki·est** *Informal* Of small size or consequence; insignificant: *a dinky shack in the woods.*

dill

WRITERS CHOOSE THEIR WORDS

He wanted to stay near the lake because he thought the plane, even deep in the water, might show up to somebody flying over and he didn't want to **diminish** any chance he might have of being found.

—Gary Paulsen
Hatchet

WRITERS CHOOSE THEIR WORDS

I told Frankie that taking Luis's **dinghy** out at this time of day was a bad idea. I said, "The fog is still coming in. It's practically dark. Luis will wonder where you are." Things like that. But Frankie kept walking real fast toward the dock, ignoring me, and then stepped into the blue **dinghy** Luis kept tied up there.

—Kathryn Fitzmaurice
The Year the Swallows Came Early

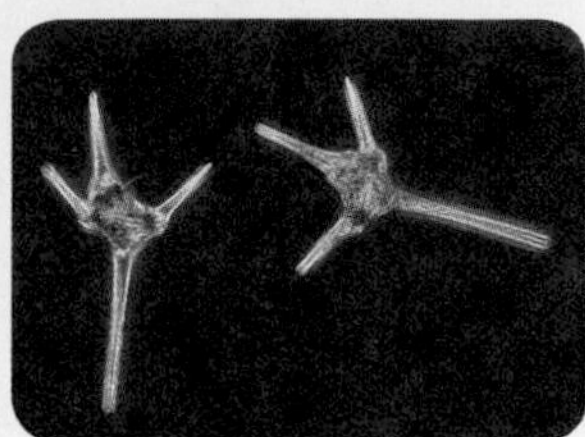

dinoflagellate

ă	pat	ôr	core
ā	pay	oi	boy
âr	care	ou	out
ä	father	o͝o	took
ĕ	pet	o͝or	lure
ē	be	o͞o	boot
ĭ	pit	ŭ	cut
ī	bite	ûr	urge
îr	pier	th	thin
ŏ	pot	*th*	this
ō	toe	zh	vision
ô	paw	ə	about

din·ner (dĭn′ər) *n.* **1.** The main meal of the day, eaten at midday or in the evening. **2.** A banquet or formal meal in honor of a person or event: *held a dinner to celebrate Katie's birthday.*

dinner jacket *n.* A man's short jacket worn with a bow tie for social events in the evening.

din·ner·time (dĭn′ər-tīm′) *n.* The time when dinner is usually eaten.

di·no·flag·el·late (dī′nō-**flăj′**ə-lĭt *or* dī′nō-**flăj′**ə-lāt′) *n.* Any of numerous one-celled organisms found mostly in the ocean, usually having two flagella. Dinoflagellates are one of the main components of plankton.

di·no·saur (**dī′**nə-sôr′) *n.* **1.** One of a large group of extinct meat-eating or plant-eating reptiles that lived on land many millions of years ago, during the Mesozoic Era. The smallest dinosaurs were the size of chickens, and the largest were the largest land animals that have ever lived. **2.** Any of various other large extinct reptiles, such as an ichthyosaur. [From Greek *deinos*, monstrous + Greek *sauros*, lizard.]

dint (dĭnt) *n.* Force or effort; power: *By dint of practice, she became an accomplished musician.*

di·o·cese (**dī′**ə-sĭs *or* **dī′**ə-sēs′) *n.* The district or churches under the authority of a bishop.

di·ode (**dī′**ōd′) *n.* An electron tube or a semiconductor that allows current to flow in one direction only.

di·oe·cious (dī-**ē′**shəs) *adj.* Having male flowers or cones and female flowers or cones on separate plants. Junipers, willows, and hollies are dioecious.

Di·o·ny·sus (dī′ə-**nī′**səs *or* dī′ə-**nē′**səs) *n.* In Greek and Roman mythology, the god of wine and of the power and fertility of nature.

di·o·ram·a (dī′ə-**răm′**ə) *n.* A miniature or life-size scene with lifelike figures and objects set against a painted background.

di·ox·ide (dī-**ŏk′**sīd) *n.* A compound with two atoms of oxygen per molecule.

dip (dĭp) *v.* **dipped, dip·ping, dips** —*tr.* **1.** To plunge briefly in or into a liquid: *dip a cracker into soup.* **2.** To color or dye by putting into a liquid: *dip eggs in dye.* **3.** To immerse (a sheep or other animal) in a disinfecting bath. **4.** To make (a candle) by repeatedly immersing a wick in melted wax or tallow. **5.** To scoop up by plunging the hand or a receptacle below the surface, as of a liquid: *dip water from a stream to get a drink.* **6.** To lower and raise (a flag) in salute. —*intr.* **1.** To plunge briefly into water or other liquid: *The oars dipped in and out of the water.* **2.** To plunge the hand or a receptacle into liquid or a container, especially so as to take something out: *dip into a pickle jar.* **3.** To drop down or sink out of sight suddenly: *The temperature dipped below freezing.* **4.** To slope downward; decline: *The path dips to the river.* ❖ *n.* **1.** A brief plunge, especially a quick swim: *a dip in the pool.* **2.** A liquid into which something is dipped, as for dyeing or disinfecting: *a flea dip for dogs.* **3.** A creamy food mixture into which crackers or other foods may be dipped: *a vegetable dip.* **4.** An amount taken up by dipping; a scoop: *a double dip of ice cream.* **5.** A downward slope; a decline: *a dip in the road.* [From Old English *dyppan.*]

diph·the·ri·a (dĭf-**thîr′**ē-ə *or* dĭp-**thîr′**ē-ə) *n.* A serious contagious disease caused by a bacterium that produces a damaging toxin. Symptoms include fever and the formation of a dark fiberlike covering in the throat that causes difficulty in breathing. [From Greek *diphtherā*, piece of hide, leather.]

diph·thong (**dĭf′**thông′ *or* **dĭp′**thông′) *n.* A speech sound blending two vowels in the same syllable. For example, the speech sounds represented by *oy* in *boy* and *i* in *nice* are diphthongs. [From Middle English *diptonge*, from Greek *diphthongos* : *di-*, two + *phthongos*, sound.]

di·plod·o·cus (dĭ-**plŏd′**ə-kəs) *n.* A very large plant-eating dinosaur having a long, slender neck and tail and a small head. It is one of the longest dinosaurs known, reaching a length of nearly 90 feet (27 meters).

dip·loid (**dĭp′**loid′) *adj.* Being a cell or composed of cells in which there is a pair of each type of chromosome. In animals, all cells except reproductive cells are diploid. ❖ *n.* A diploid cell or organism.

di·plo·ma (dĭ-**plō′**mə) *n.* A document or certificate issued by an educational institution showing that a person has earned a degree or completed a course of study. [From Greek *diplōma*, folded paper, document.]

di·plo·ma·cy (dĭ-**plō′**mə-sē) *n.* **1.** The art or practice of handling international relations. It includes negotiating alliances, treaties, and trade agreements. **2.** Skill in dealing with others; tact: *The lawyer was known for her diplomacy.*

dip·lo·mat (**dĭp′**lə-măt′) *n.* **1.** A person, such as an ambassador, who has been appointed to represent a government in its dealings with other governments. **2.** A person who uses tact and skill in dealing with others.

dip·lo·mat·ic (dĭp′lə-**măt′**ĭk) *adj.* **1.** Relating to or involving diplomacy or diplomats. **2.** Using or marked by skill and tact in dealing with others: *a diplomatic handling of unpleasant matters.* [From French *diplomatique*, from Latin *diplōma*, letter of introduction.] **—dip′lo·mat′i·cal·ly** *adv.*

di·pole (**dī′**pōl′) *n.* A pair of separated electric charges or magnetic poles, equal in strength but opposite in sign or polarity.

dip·per (**dĭp′**ər) *n.* **1.** A person or thing that dips. **2.** A container for scooping up liquids.

dire (dīr) *adj.* **dir·er, dir·est 1.** Warning of or having dreadful or terrible consequences; calamitous: *a dire accident.* **2.** Urgent; desperate: *in dire want.* [From Latin *dīrus*, fearsome.]

di·rect (dĭ-**rĕkt′** *or* dī-**rĕkt′**) *v.* **di·rect·ed, di·rect·ing, di·rects** —*tr.* **1.** To manage or conduct the affairs of; regulate: *direct a business.* **2.** To instruct, order, or command: *The general directed the soldiers to free all prisoners.* **3.** To manage or supervise the performance of (a play, for example). **4.** To cause to move or be turned toward a goal or object; aim: *directed the light toward center stage.* **5.** To show or indicate the way for: *I directed them to the post office.* **6.** To make (remarks, for example) to someone in particular or to an audience: *The principal directed a few words of welcome to the new students.* —*intr.* **1.** To give commands or directions: *police officers directing at an intersection.* **2.** To conduct a performance or rehearsal: *The conductor is directing in front of the orchestra.* ❖ *adj.* **1.** Proceeding in a straight course or line; not roundabout: *The dancers moved in a direct line across the stage.* **2.** Straightforward and candid; frank: *They gave direct answers to my questions.* **3.** Having no intervening people, agencies, or conditions; immediate: *direct sunlight; a direct line to the president.* **4.** Effected by action of the voters rather than through representatives or delegates: *direct election.* **5.** Being of unbroken descent; lineal: *the direct descendant of early settlers.* **6.** Consisting of the exact words of a writer or speaker: *a direct quote from the article.* **7.** Absolute: *direct opposites.* **8.** Varying in the same manner as another quantity; increasing if another quantity increases or decreasing if it decreases. **9.** In soccer, relating to a free kick that can score a goal without the ball being touched by a second player. ❖ *adv.* Straight; directly: *We flew direct from California to New York.* [From Middle English *directen*, from Latin *dīrigere*, to give direction to : *dī-*, *dis-*, apart + *regere*, to guide.] **—di·rect′ness** *n.*

direct current *n.* An electric current flowing in one direction only, as that of a battery. —SEE NOTE AT **current.**

di·rec·tion (dĭ-**rĕk′**shən *or* dī-**rĕk′**shən) *n.* **1.** The management, control, or guidance of an action or operation: *The fire department is under the direction of the chief.* **2.** An order or command: *The supervisor shouted directions to employees in the warehouse.* **3. directions** Instructions for doing or finding something: *I read the directions for starting the snowblower.* **4.** The line or course along which a person or thing moves or lies: *The ship headed in a northerly direction. The old farmhouse is in the direction of the peach orchard.* **5.** A course or area of development: *The orchestra took a different direction by performing contemporary compositions.* [From Middle English *direccioun*, from Latin *dīrēctiō*, from *dīrigere*, to direct.]

di·rec·tion·al (dĭ-**rĕk′**shə-nəl *or* dī-**rĕk′**shə-nəl) *adj.* **1.** Indicating direction: *a car's directional signals.* **2.** Capable of receiving or sending signals in one direction only: *installed a directional radar antenna.* **—di·rec′tion·al·ly** *adv.*

direction finder *n.* A device for finding the direction from which a radio signal is transmitted. It consists of a radio receiver and a compass attached to a coiled antenna that can turn in any direction.

di·rec·tive (dĭ-**rĕk′**tĭv *or* dī-**rĕk′**tĭv) *n.* An order or instruction, especially one issued by someone in authority: *a directive from the coach about attendance at practice.*

di·rect·ly (dĭ-**rĕkt′**lē *or* dī-**rĕkt′**lē) *adv.* **1.** In a direct line or manner; straight: *The cat headed directly for its food.* **2.** Without anything intervening: *The students spoke directly to the superintendent about the issue.* **3.** Exactly or totally: *His views on this issue are directly opposite to mine.* **4.** Without delay; at once: *I'll meet you there directly after work.*

direct mail *n.* Advertising or marketing announcements sent by mail without being requested to residences and workplaces.

direct object *n.* The word or words in a sentence referring to the person or thing receiving the action of a transitive verb. For example, in the sentence *I mailed the letter,* the direct object is *the letter.*

di·rec·tor (dĭ-**rĕk′**tər *or* dī-**rĕk′**tər) *n.* **1.** A person who supervises, controls, or manages: *The magazine has a new art director.* **2.** A member of a group of people chosen to control or govern the affairs of a company or institution: *a meeting of the board of directors.* **3.** A person who supervises and guides the performers and others involved in a dramatic production, film, or other performance.

di·rec·tor·ate (dĭ-**rĕk′**tər-ĭt *or* dī-**rĕk′**tər-ĭt) *n.* **1.** The office or position of a director. **2.** A board of directors, as of a corporation.

di·rec·to·ri·al (dĭ-rĕk′**tôr′**ē-əl *or* dī-rĕk′**tôr′**ē-əl) *adj.* **1.** Relating to a director or directorate: *directorial responsibilities.* **2.** Serving to direct: *a directorial report.*

di·rec·to·ry (dĭ-**rĕk′**tə-rē *or* dī-**rĕk′**tə-rē) *n., pl.* **di·rec·to·ries 1.** A list of names, addresses, or other facts, such as telephone numbers, in alphabetical or other order: *a building directory to the offices of different companies.* **2.** A listing of the data files stored in a computer memory.

dire·ful (**dīr′**fəl) *adj.* Inspiring dread; terrible: *a direful tale of misery and starvation.* **—dire′ful·ly** *adv.*

dirge (dûrj) *n.* A sad solemn piece of music, such as a funeral hymn or lament.

dir·ham (də-**răm′**) *n.* The basic monetary unit of Morocco and the United Arab Emirates.

dir·i·gi·ble (**dĭr′**ə-jə-bəl *or* də-**rĭj′**ə-bəl) *n.* An airship. [From Latin *dīrigere*, to direct.]

dirk (dûrk) *n.* A dagger.

dirn·dl (**dûrn′**dl) *n.* **1.** A dress with a full skirt and tight bodice, that is sleeveless or has short full sleeves. **2.** A full skirt with a gathered waistband. [From German *Dirndlkleid* : German dialectal *Dirndl*, little girl + *Kleid*, dress.]

dirt (dûrt) *n.* **1.** Earth or soil: *Rock and dirt came tumbling down the mountain.* **2.** A substance that soils, such as mud, dust, or grease: *A detergent removes dirt from clothes.* **3.** A person or thing that is mean or contemptible. **4.** Malicious or scandalous gossip: *This magazine publishes all the dirt about movie stars.* [From Middle English *drit*, filth, mud, from Old Norse.]

dirt bike *n.* A lightweight motorcycle for use on rough surfaces, such as dirt roads or trails.

dirt-cheap (**dûrt′chēp′**) *adv. & adj.* Very cheap: *buy a truck dirt-cheap; a dirt-cheap hotel.*

dirt·y (**dûr′**tē) *adj.* **dirt·i·er, dirt·i·est 1a.** Covered or marked with dirt or an unwanted substance; unclean: *dirty water; dirty clothes; a dirty floor.* **b.** Apt to soil with dirt or grime: *Planting a garden is a dirty job.* **c.** Producing radioactive fallout. Used of explosives. **2a.** Mean or contemptible: *a dirty trick.* **b.** Obscene or indecent: *a dirty joke.* **3.** Not playing fair: *a dirty card player.* **4.** Expressing disapproval or hostility: *a dirty look.* ❖ *tr. & intr.v.* **dirt·ied, dirt·y·ing, dirt·ies** To make or become soiled: *I dirtied the tablecloth. White clothes dirty easily.*

SYNONYMS **dirty, filthy, foul, grimy** These adjectives apply to what is unclean, impure, or unkempt. **Dirty,** the most general, describes what is covered or stained with dirt: *Dirty dishes were piled up in the sink.* **Filthy** means disgustingly dirty: *Put that filthy shirt in the washing machine right away.* **Foul** suggests gross offensiveness, particularly to the sense of smell: *A layer of algae covered the foul pond.* **Grimy** describes something whose surface is smudged with dirt such as grime or soot: *I found this grimy pair of gloves near the gardening tools.*

ANTONYM **clean**

---

dis or **diss** (dĭs) *tr.v.* **dissed, diss·ing, diss·es** *Informal* To show disrespect to, often by insult or criticism: *always dissing his neighbor.*

dis– *pref.* A prefix that means: **1.** Not: *dissimilar.* **2.** Absence of: *disfavor.* **3.** Opposite of: *distrust.* **4.** Do the opposite of: *disapprove.* **5.** Deprive of: *disarm.* —SEE NOTE.

dis·a·bil·i·ty (dĭs′ə-**bĭl′**ĭ-tē) *n., pl.* **dis·a·bil·i·ties 1.** The condition of being disabled. **2.** A disadvantage or deficiency, especially a physical or mental impairment that makes certain tasks difficult or impossible. **3.** Financial support provided to people with such impairment: *has been on disability for a month.*

dis·a·ble (dĭs-**ā′**bəl) *tr.v.* **dis·a·bled, dis·a·bling, dis·a·bles** To weaken or impair the capacity, abilities, or effectiveness of; incapacitate: *The storm disabled the steamer's engine.* **—dis·a′ble·ment** *n.*

dis·a·bled (dĭs-**ā′**bəld) *adj.* **1.** Not working or functioning: *a disabled car.* **2.** Impaired in physical or mental functioning: *a disabled veteran.* ❖ *n. (used with a plural verb)* Physically or mentally impaired people: *The new building has access for the disabled.*

dis·a·buse (dĭs′ə-**byōōz′**) *tr.v.* **dis·a·bused, dis·a·bus·ing, dis·a·bus·es** To free from a falsehood or misconception: *disabuse someone of preconceived notions.*

dis·ad·van·tage (dĭs′əd-**văn′**tĭj) *n.* **1.** An unfavorable condition or circumstance: *Some students are at a disadvantage because they don't own computers.* **2.** Something that places one in an unfavorable condition or position: *One disadvantage of river transportation is its slowness.* **3.** Harm or loss: *The road will be closed for six months, to the disadvantage of commuters.*

dis·ad·van·taged (dĭs′əd-**văn′**tĭjd) *adj.* Deprived of some of the basic necessities or advantages of life, such as housing, health care, or education.

dis·ad·van·ta·geous (dĭs-ăd′vən-**tā′**jəs *or* dĭs′ăd-vən-**tā′**jəs) *adj.* Detrimental; unfavorable: *disadvantageous*

dirndl

dirt bike

WORD BUILDING

dis– The prefix **dis–** has several senses, but its basic meaning is "not, not any." Thus *disbelieve* means "to refuse to believe" and *discomfort* means "a lack of comfort." *Dis–* came into English from the Old French prefix *des–*, which in turn ultimately came from the Latin adverb *dis,* meaning "apart, asunder." *Dis–* is an important prefix that occurs very frequently in English in words such as *discredit, disrepair,* and *disrespect.*

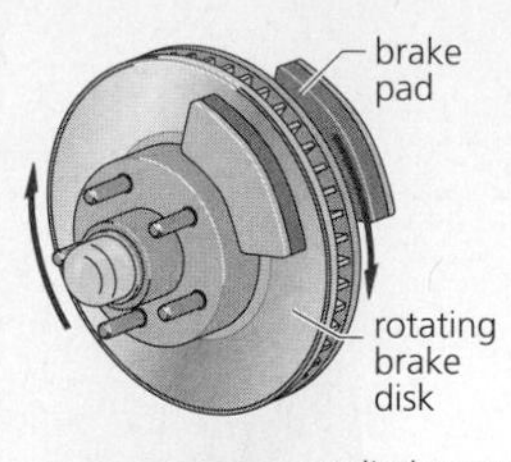

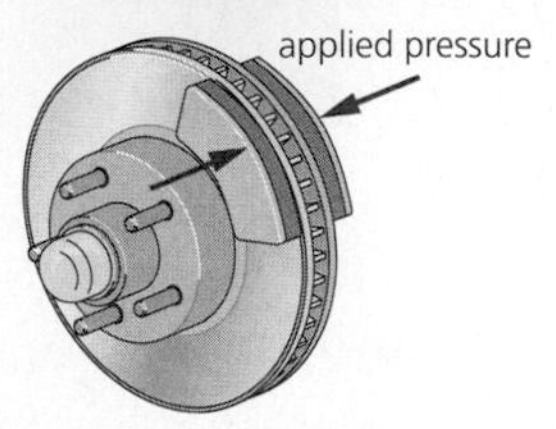

disc brake

ă	pat	ôr	core
ā	pay	oi	boy
âr	care	ou	out
ä	father	ŏŏ	took
ĕ	pet	ŏŏr	lure
ē	be	ōō	boot
ĭ	pit	ŭ	cut
ī	bite	ûr	urge
îr	pier	th	thin
ŏ	pot	*th*	this
ō	toe	zh	vision
ô	paw	ə	about

living conditions. **—dis·ad′van·ta′geous·ly** *adv.*

dis·af·fect (dĭs′ə-**fĕkt′**) *tr.v.* **dis·af·fect·ed, dis·af·fect·ing, dis·af·fects** To cause to lose affection or loyalty. **—dis′af·fec′tion** *n.*

dis·af·fect·ed (dĭs′ə-**fĕk′**tĭd) *adj.* Resentful and rebellious, especially against authority: *The disaffected workers voted to go on strike.*

dis·a·gree (dĭs′ə-**grē′**) *intr.v.* **dis·a·greed, dis·a·gree·ing, dis·a·grees 1.** To have a differing opinion: *Scientists disagree on why dinosaurs died out.* **2.** To dispute or quarrel: *Rival countries often disagree about trade regulations.* **3.** To fail to correspond; differ: *Your answer disagrees with mine.* **4.** To cause bad effects: *Fried food disagrees with me.*

dis·a·gree·a·ble (dĭs′ə-**grē′**ə-bəl) *adj.* **1.** Not to one's liking; unpleasant or offensive: *a strong and disagreeable odor.* **2.** Having a quarrelsome bad-tempered manner: *Many people are disagreeable if they don't get enough sleep.* **—dis′a·gree′a·bly** *adv.*

dis·a·gree·ment (dĭs′ə-**grē′**mənt) *n.* **1.** A failure or refusal to agree. **2.** A conflict or difference of opinion: *Their disagreement ended in loud words.*

dis·al·low (dĭs′ə-**lou′**) *tr.v.* **dis·al·lowed, dis·al·low·ing, dis·al·lows 1.** To refuse to allow: *disallow eating in one's room.* **2.** To reject as invalid, untrue, or improper: *disallow an unsigned will as evidence.*

dis·ap·pear (dĭs′ə-**pîr′**) *intr.v.* **dis·ap·peared, dis·ap·pear·ing, dis·ap·pears 1.** To pass out of sight; vanish: *The ship disappeared over the horizon.* **2.** To cease to be seen; be missing or unfound: *Her purse disappeared from her locker.* **3.** To cease to exist: *Warm weather disappears in the fall.*

SYNONYMS disappear, evaporate, fade, vanish These verbs mean to pass out of sight or existence. *The small plane disappeared in the fog. His courage evaporated when the time came to go to the dentist. As she passed me on the final lap, my hopes of winning the race faded away. No one could figure out how the magician made the coin vanish.*

---

dis·ap·pear·ance (dĭs′ə-**pîr′**əns) *n.* The act or an example of disappearing: *Disappearance of the ship during the storm led most to believe it sank.*

dis·ap·point (dĭs′ə-**point′**) *tr.v.* **dis·ap·point·ed, dis·ap·point·ing, dis·ap·points 1.** To fail to satisfy the hope, desire, or expectation of: *The ads were exciting, but the movie disappointed me.* **2.** To frustrate or thwart: *So far our efforts to get payment have been disappointed.*

dis·ap·point·ed (dĭs′ə-**poin′**tĭd) *adj.* Thwarted in hope, desire, or expectation.

dis·ap·point·ing (dĭs′ə-**poin′**tĭng) *adj.* Not up to expectations or hopes: *He finished the marathon in a disappointing 12th place.*

dis·ap·point·ment (dĭs′ə-**point′**mənt) *n.* **1.** The act of disappointing. **2.** The condition or feeling of being disappointed: *couldn't hide their disappointment.* **3.** A person or thing that disappoints: *The picnic was a disappointment.*

dis·ap·prov·al (dĭs′ə-**prōō′**vəl) *n.* The act of disapproving; censure or condemnation.

dis·ap·prove (dĭs′ə-**prōōv′**) *v.* **dis·ap·proved, dis·ap·prov·ing, dis·ap·proves** *—tr.* **1.** To have an unfavorable opinion of; condemn. **2.** To refuse to approve: *The state disapproved the new zoning proposal.* *—intr.* To have an unfavorable opinion: *disapprove of shouting.*

dis·arm (dĭs-**ärm′**) *v.* **dis·armed, dis·arm·ing, dis·arms** *—tr.* **1.** To take a weapon or weapons from: *The police officer disarmed the robber.* **2.** To make harmless: *disarm a charge of dynamite.* **3.** To overcome the suspicion or unfriendliness of; win the confidence of: *Her kind words disarmed us right away.* *—intr.* **1.** To lay down arms. **2.** To reduce or get rid of armed forces: *The countries voted to disarm.*

dis·ar·ma·ment (dĭs-**är′**mə-mənt) *n.* The reduction or abolition of a country's armed forces or weapons of destruction.

dis·arm·ing (dĭs-**är′**mĭng) *adj.* Serving to remove suspicion or unfriendliness; winning favor or confidence: *a disarming smile.* **—dis·arm′ing·ly** *adv.*

dis·ar·range (dĭs′ə-**rānj′**) *tr.v.* **dis·ar·ranged, dis·ar·rang·ing, dis·ar·rang·es** To upset the proper order or arrangement of: *The wind disarranged my hair.* **—dis′ar·range′ment** *n.*

dis·ar·ray (dĭs′ə-**rā′**) *n.* A state of disorder; confusion: *The mail lay in disarray on the desk.* ❖ *tr.v.* **dis·ar·rayed, dis·ar·ray·ing, dis·ar·rays** To throw into confusion; upset.

dis·as·sem·ble (dĭs′ə-**sĕm′**bəl) *v.* **dis·as·sem·bled, dis·as·sem·bling, dis·as·sem·bles** *—tr.* To take apart: *We have to disassemble the engine to repair it.* *—intr.* To come apart: *This telephone disassembles easily.*

dis·as·ter (dĭ-**zăs′**tər) *n.* **1.** Something that causes widespread destruction and distress; a calamity: *Tornadoes, earthquakes, and floods are natural disasters.* **2.** *Informal* A total failure. [From Italian *disastro* : *dis-*, bad + *astro*, star (from Greek *astron*).]

dis·as·trous (dĭ-**zăs′**trəs) *adj.* Accompanied by or causing disaster; calamitous: *a disastrous earthquake; a disastrous error in judgment.* **—dis·as′trous·ly** *adv.*

dis·a·vow (dĭs′ə-**vou′**) *tr.v.* **dis·a·vowed, dis·a·vow·ing, dis·a·vows** To disclaim knowledge of, responsibility for, or association with.

dis·a·vow·al (dĭs′ə-**vou′**əl) *n.* The act or an example of disavowing; a denial or repudiation.

dis·band (dĭs-**bănd′**) *v.* **dis·band·ed, dis·band·ing, dis·bands** *—tr.* To cause (an organization or group) to break up: *disband an orchestra.* *—intr.* To stop functioning as an organization: *The glee club disbanded last year.*

dis·bar (dĭs-**bär′**) *tr.v.* **dis·barred, dis·bar·ring, dis·bars** To expel (a lawyer) from the practice of law by official action or procedure. **—dis·bar′ment** *n.*

dis·be·lief (dĭs′bĭ-**lēf′**) *n.* Refusal or reluctance to believe: *express disbelief at a fantastic story.*

dis·be·lieve (dĭs′bĭ-**lēv′**) *tr.v.* **dis·be·lieved, dis·be·liev·ing, dis·be·lieves** To refuse or be unable to believe (someone or something): *disbelieved the stories of their fabulous wealth.*

dis·bur·den (dĭs-**bûr′**dn) *tr.v.* **dis·bur·dened, dis·bur·den·ing, dis·bur·dens 1.** To relieve (a pack animal, for example) of a burden. **2.** To free of a trouble or worry: *He disburdened his mind by telling the truth.*

dis·burse (dĭs-**bûrs′**) *tr.v.* **dis·bursed, dis·burs·ing, dis·burs·es** To pay out, as from a fund; expend: *disburse large sums to advertise a product.* [From Old French *desborser* : *des-*, out + *borse*, purse (from Late Latin *bursa*).]

dis·burse·ment (dĭs-**bûrs′**mənt) *n.* **1.** The act or process of disbursing. **2.** Money paid out; expenditure: *small disbursements.*

disc (dĭsk) *n.* Variant of **disk.**

dis·card (dĭ-**skärd′**) *v.* **dis·card·ed, dis·card·ing, dis·cards** *—tr.* **1.** To throw away; reject: *discard old shoes; discard a childish habit.* **2.** In card games, to throw out (a playing card) from one's hand. *—intr.* To throw out a playing card. ❖ *n.* (**dĭs′**kärd′) **1.** The act of discarding in a card game. **2.** A discarded playing card. **3.** Something that is discarded: *Charities will usually accept discards.*

disc brake also **disk brake** *n.* A brake that works by pressing pads against each side of a disk attached to the wheel of a car or truck.

dis·cern (dĭ-**sûrn′** *or* dĭ-**zûrn′**) *tr.v.* **dis·cerned, dis·cern·ing, dis·cerns 1.** To perceive with the eyes; detect: *discern a figure in the shadows.* **2.** To recognize or understand as being different: *Researchers finally discerned* *the purpose of the gene.* [From Middle English *discernen*, from Latin *discernere*, to separate : *dis-*, apart + *cernere*, to perceive.]

dis·cern·i·ble (dĭ-**sûr′**nə-bəl *or* dĭ-**zûr′**nə-bəl) *adj.* Perceptible, as by the faculty of vision or the intellect: *few discernible differences between the two theories.* **—dis·cern′i·bly** *adv.*

dis·cern·ing (dĭ-**sûr′**nĭng *or* dĭ-**zûr′**nĭng) *adj.* Showing keen observation and good judgment; perceptive: *a discerning mind.* **—dis·cern′ing·ly** *adv.*

dis·cern·ment (dĭ-**sûrn′**mənt *or* dĭ-**zûrn′**mənt) *n.* **1.** The act or process of using or showing keen insight and good judgment. **2.** Keenness of insight or judgment: *having great discernment for new art.*

dis·charge (dĭs-**chärj′**) *v.* **dis·charged, dis·charg·ing, dis·charg·es** *—tr.* **1.** To release, as from confinement, care, or duty: *discharge a patient from the hospital.* **2.** To remove from office or employment; dismiss: *The steel plant closed and discharged its workers.* **3.** To send or pour forth: *Pipes discharge water into the lake.* **4.** To shoot: *discharged a volley of arrows.* **5.** To perform the obligations or requirements of (an office, duty, or task): *discharge the duties of mayor.* **6.** To comply with the terms of (a debt or promise, for example): *discharged the loan by making regular payments.* **7.** To take an electric charge from: *We discharged the battery while trying to start the car.* **8.** To unload (cargo, for example) from a ship. *—intr.* **1.** To be fired. Used of a gun: *The musket discharged loudly.* **2.** To pour forth contents: *Several streams discharge into the river.* **3.** To give off or lose an electric charge: *Flashlight batteries discharge when the light is on.* ❖ *n.* (**dĭs′**chärj′ *or* dĭs-**chärj′**) **1.** The act of firing or shooting a gun or projectile: *We could hear the discharges of a distant cannon.* **2.** A pouring out or flowing forth; an emission: *a discharge of pus from an infection.* **3.** Something poured or flowing forth: *a gummy discharge from a tree trunk.* **4.** Fulfillment of the terms of something, such as a debt or promise: *the discharge of the loan.* **5.** Dismissal or release: *got his discharge from the army.* **6a.** A release of electric charge from a capacitor in a circuit or from a conducting body, such as a cloud in a thunderstorm. **b.** The conversion of chemical energy to electric energy in a battery. **c.** The passage of an electric current through a gas. **7.** The act of removing a load from a ship: *a discharge of freight from the ship.*

disc harrow *n.* Variant of **disk harrow.**

dis·ci·ple (dĭ-**sī′**pəl) *n.* **1.** A person who accepts and assists in spreading the teachings of a leader. **2.** often **Disciple** One of the original followers of Jesus. [From Old English *discipul*, from Latin *discipulus*, pupil, from *discere*, to learn.]

dis·ci·pli·nar·i·an (dĭs′ə-plə-**nâr′**ē-ən) *n.* A person who enforces or believes in strict discipline.

dis·ci·pli·nar·y (**dĭs′**ə-plə-nĕr′ē) *adj.* Relating to or used for discipline: *disciplinary measures.*

dis·ci·pline (**dĭs′**ə-plĭn) *n.* **1a.** Training expected to produce a specific skill, behavior, or character. **b.** Controlled behavior resulting from such training. **c.** A systematic method to regulate behavior: *military discipline.* **2.** Punishment intended to correct or train. **3.** A branch of knowledge or of teaching: *Mathematics and computer science are related disciplines.* ❖ *tr.v.* **dis·ci·plined, dis·ci·plin·ing, dis·ci·plines 1.** To train by instruction and practice. **2.** To punish in order to gain control or enforce obedience: *discipline a dog with a quick swat.* [From Middle English, from Latin *disciplīna*, from *discipulus*, pupil.]

disc jockey also **disk jockey** *n.* An announcer who presents popular recorded music, especially on the radio.

dis·claim (dĭs-**klām′**) *tr.v.* **dis·claimed, dis·claim·ing, dis·claims 1.** To deny or repudiate: *He disclaimed any involvement with the criminal group.* **2.** To give up one's legal right or claim to: *disclaimed any part of the inheritance.*

dis·claim·er (dĭs-**klā′**mər) *n.* A repudiation or denial of a responsibility or connection: *issue a disclaimer of involvement in an investment scheme.*

dis·close (dĭ-**sklōz′**) *tr.v.* **dis·closed, dis·clos·ing, dis·clos·es 1.** To expose to view; uncover: *The excavation disclosed remains of an ancient city.* **2.** To make known (something previously kept secret). [From Middle English *disclosen*, from Old French *desclore* : *des-*, away, off + *clore*, to close (from Latin *claudere*).]

dis·clo·sure (dĭ-**sklō′**zhər) *n.* **1.** The act or process of revealing or uncovering: *The company withheld disclosure of information about its new car.* **2.** Something uncovered; a revelation.

dis·co (**dĭs′**kō) *n., pl.* **dis·cos 1.** A discotheque. **2.** Popular dance music, especially of the late 1970s, having strong repetitive bass rhythms. [Short for *discotheque.*]

dis·col·or (dĭs-**kŭl′**ər) *tr. & intr.v.* **dis·col·ored, dis·col·or·ing, dis·col·ors** To alter or become altered in color; stain: *Floodwaters discolored the painting. Metal discolors with rust.*

dis·col·or·a·tion (dĭs-kŭl′ə-**rā′**shən) *n.* **1.** The act of discoloring or the condition of being discolored: *the discoloration of curtains washed in rusty water.* **2.** A stain: *Water damage left several large discolorations on the carpet.*

dis·com·fit (dĭs-**kŭm′**fĭt) *tr.v.* **dis·com·fit·ed, dis·com·fit·ing, dis·com·fits** To make uneasy or confused; embarrass: *Trying to speak a foreign language discomfits many people.*

dis·com·fi·ture (dĭs-**kŭm′**fĭ-cho͝or′) *n.* **1.** Frustration; disappointment: *quit a project in total discomfiture.* **2.** Discomfort; embarrassment: *the discomfiture of a public scolding.*

dis·com·fort (dĭs-**kŭm′**fərt) *n.* **1.** A lack of comfort; uneasiness: *a patient in discomfort.* **2.** Something that disturbs a person's comfort: *A lumpy mattress is a discomfort when sleeping.*

dis·com·pose (dĭs′kəm-**pōz′**) *tr.v.* **dis·com·posed, dis·com·pos·ing, dis·com·pos·es** To disturb the composure or calm of; perturb: *The shouts of a few protesters discomposed the speaker.*

dis·com·po·sure (dĭs′kəm-**pō′**zhər) *n.* The absence of composure; confusion or uneasiness: *The pianist's discomposure was evident from the mistakes made during the performance.*

dis·con·cert (dĭs′kən-**sûrt′**) *tr.v.* **dis·con·cert·ed, dis·con·cert·ing, dis·con·certs** To upset the self-possession of; embarrass or confuse: *All of the horns honking disconcerted the student driver.* [From Old French *desconcerter.*] **—dis′con·cert′ing·ly** *adv.*

dis·con·nect (dĭs′kə-**nĕkt′**) *tr.v.* **dis·con·nect·ed, dis·con·nect·ing, dis·con·nects** To break or interrupt the connection of or between; separate: *Disconnect the TV before you move it. Our phone call was disconnected during the storm.* ❖ *n.* (dĭs′kə-**nĕkt′**) A lack of connection; a disparity: *a disconnect between how legislators view the recession and how voters do.* **—dis′con·nec′tion** *n.*

dis·con·nect·ed (dĭs′kə-**nĕk′**tĭd) *adj.* **1.** Not connected; separate: *disconnected buildings.* **2.** Not clear or logical; disorderly: *a disconnected account of the accident; disconnected bits.* **—dis′con·nect′ed·ly** *adv.*

dis·con·so·late (dĭs-**kŏn′**sə-lĭt) *adj.* Not able to be consoled; very sad or dejected: *We were left disconsolate when our cat disappeared.* **—dis·con′so·late·ly** *adv.* **—dis·con′so·late·ness** *n.*

dis·con·tent (dĭs′kən-**tĕnt′**) *n.* Lack of contentment; dissatisfaction: *Not getting a raise caused discontent among the workers.* ❖ *tr.v.* **dis·con·tent·ed, dis·con·tent·ing, dis·con·tents** To make discontented: *No electricity for*

WRITERS CHOOSE THEIR WORDS

He remained silent for a few moments; and then, removing his hands suddenly from his face, showed, to the unspeakable **discomposure** of Mr. Bumble, that it was much distorted, and discolored.

—Charles Dickens
Oliver Twist

discus

three days discontented everyone. **—dis′con·tent′ment** *n.*

dis·con·tent·ed (dĭs′kən-**tĕn′**tĭd) *adj.* Not contented; unhappy: *Discontented tenants refused to pay rent until they got heat.* **—dis′con·tent′ed·ly** *adv.* **—dis′con·tent′ed·ness** *n.*

dis·con·tin·u·a·tion (dĭs′kən-tĭn′yo͞o-**ā′**shən) *n.* A termination; an ending: *discontinuation of bus service during the storm.* **—dis′con·tin′u·ance** (dĭs′kən-**tĭn′**yo͞o-əns) *n.*

dis·con·tin·ue (dĭs′kən-**tĭn′**yo͞o) *tr.v.* **dis·con·tin·ued, dis·con·tin·u·ing, dis·con·tin·ues 1.** To stop doing or providing (something): *discontinued bus service after midnight.* **2.** To cease making or manufacturing: *This type of computer monitor has been discontinued.*

dis·con·tin·u·ous (dĭs′kən-**tĭn′**yo͞o-əs) *adj.* Not continuous; broken up; interrupted: *a discontinuous supply of natural gas.* **—dis′con·tin′u·ous·ly** *adv.*

dis·cord (**dĭs′**kôrd′) *n.* **1.** Lack of agreement or harmony: *an angry meeting filled with discord.* **2.** A combination of musical tones that sounds harsh or unpleasant; a lack of harmony. **3.** A confused or harsh mingling of sounds: *the early morning discord of rush-hour traffic.* [From Middle English, from Latin *discors*, disagreeing : *dis-*, apart + *cor*, heart.]

dis·cor·dant (dĭ-**skôr′**dnt) *adj.* **1.** Not in agreement; conflicting: *a discordant meeting.* **2.** Disagreeable in sound; harsh: *discordant sounds of the city streets.* **—dis·cor′dance** *n.* **—dis·cor′dant·ly** *adv.*

dis·co·theque (**dĭs′**kə-tĕk′ *or* dĭs′kə-**tĕk′**) *n.* A nightclub that offers dancing to recorded music. [From Italian *discoteca*, record library : *disco*, disk, record (from Latin *discus*, quoit) + *biblioteca*, library (from Latin *bibliothēca*).]

dis·count (**dĭs′**kount′ *or* dĭs-**kount′**) *tr.v.* **dis·count·ed, dis·count·ing, dis·counts 1.** To deduct or subtract (an amount or percentage) from a cost or price of an item, as in a sale: *The dealer discounted 25 percent off the original price of the rug.* **2.** To sell or offer for sale at a reduced price: *The store discounts its coats each spring.* **3.** To disregard or doubt (something) as an exaggeration or not trustworthy: *The scientist discounted the rumors of a new energy source.* ❖ *n.* (**dĭs′**kount′) A reduction from the full amount of a price or debt. ❖ *adj.* (**dĭs′**kount′) **1.** Offering products or services for sale at low or reduced prices: *a discount retailer; a discount airline.* **2.** Sold or offered for sale at low or reduced prices: *discount merchandise.* [From Old French *desconter* : *des-*, away, down + *conter*, to count.]

dis·cour·age (dĭ-**skûr′**ĭj) *tr.v.* **dis·cour·aged, dis·cour·ag·ing, dis·cour·ag·es 1.** To make less hopeful or confident; dishearten: *The size of the job discouraged me.* **2.** To try to prevent by expressing disapproval or raising objections; dissuade: *Friends discouraged them from going.* **3.** To hinder or deter: *Severe penalties are supposed to discourage tax evasion.*

dis·cour·age·ment (dĭ-**skûr′**ĭj-mənt) *n.* **1.** A condition of being or feeling discouraged: *Discouragement and hardship destroyed the hopes of many pioneers.* **2.** Something that discourages: *Harsh winters are a discouragement to living in the far north.* **3.** The act of discouraging: *The discouragement of my family made me more determined to be an actor.*

dis·course (**dĭs′**kôrs′) *n.* **1.** Talking; conversation: *cheerful discourse among friends.* **2.** A series of connected remarks or statements about a subject: *The minister gave a long discourse on morality. The book is a discourse on politics.* ❖ *intr.v.* (dĭ-**skôrs′**) **dis·coursed, dis·cours·ing, dis·cours·es** To speak or write formally and often at length: *The mayor discoursed on the role of the government in improving city life.* [From Middle English *discours*, process of reasoning, from Medieval Latin *discursus* : Latin *dis-*, apart + Latin *currere*, to run.]

dis·cour·te·ous (dĭs-**kûr′**tē-əs) *adj.* Lacking courtesy; not polite; rude. **—dis·cour′te·ous·ly** *adv.* **—dis·cour′te·ous·ness** *n.*

dis·cour·te·sy (dĭs-**kûr′**tĭ-sē) *n., pl.* **dis·cour·te·sies 1.** Lack of courtesy; rudeness. **2.** A rude or impolite act: *the discourtesy of interrupting others.*

dis·cov·er (dĭ-**skŭv′**ər) *tr.v.* **dis·cov·ered, dis·cov·er·ing, dis·cov·ers 1.** To find or see for the first time: *Using the new telescope, astronomers discovered quasars at the edge of the universe.* **2.** To learn of; gain knowledge of: *discover errors by checking.* [From Middle English *discoveren*, to reveal, from Late Latin *discooperīre* : *dis-*, away + *cooperīre*, to cover.] **—dis·cov′er·er** *n.*

dis·cov·er·y (dĭ-**skŭv′**ə-rē) *n., pl.* **dis·cov·er·ies 1.** The act of discovering: *Discovery of a polio vaccine ended fear of the disease.* **2.** Something discovered: *Atomic energy is one of the greatest discoveries of science.*

dis·cred·it (dĭs-**krĕd′**ĭt) *tr.v.* **dis·cred·it·ed, dis·cred·it·ing, dis·cred·its 1.** To damage in reputation; disgrace: *The report of corruption discredits our politicians.* **2.** To cast doubt on; cause to be distrusted: *new scientific evidence that discredits earlier theories.* **3.** To refuse to believe in: *discredit a story as mere gossip.* ❖ *n.* **1.** Loss or damage to one's reputation: *Dishonest officials brought discredit to the city government.* **2.** Lack or loss of trust or belief; doubt: *An eyewitness account that brings earlier testimony into discredit.* **3.** Something that brings disgrace or distrust: *He is a discredit to his family.*

dis·cred·it·a·ble (dĭs-**krĕd′**ĭ-tə-bəl) *adj.* Deserving or bringing discredit; disgraceful: *Lying in court is a discreditable act.* **—dis·cred′it·a·bly** *adv.*

dis·creet (dĭ-**skrēt′**) *adj.* Having or showing caution or self-restraint in one's speech or behavior; prudent: *The teacher was discreet in discussing the student's mistake. Keep a discreet distance from any wild animal.* [From Middle English *discrete*, from Medieval Latin *discrētus*, from Latin *discernere*, to separate, discern.] **—dis·creet′ly** *adv.* **—dis·creet′ness** *n.*

❑ *These sound alike:* **discreet, discrete** (distinct).

dis·crep·an·cy (dĭ-**skrĕp′**ən-sē) *n., pl.* **dis·crep·an·cies** Lack of agreement; inconsistency: *There was a large discrepancy between their statement and the facts.*

dis·crep·ant (dĭ-**skrĕp′**ənt) *adj.* Showing discrepancy; disagreeing. [From Middle English *discrepaunt*, from Latin *discrepāre*, to disagree : *dis-*, apart + *crepāre*, to rattle.]

dis·crete (dĭ-**skrēt′**) *adj.* Separate from others; distinct: *The police commissioner oversees several discrete departments. I have only a few discrete memories of my early childhood.* [From Middle English, from Latin *discrētus*, past participle of *discernere*, to separate.] **—dis·crete′ly** *adv.*

❑ *These sound alike:* **discrete, discreet** (prudent).

dis·cre·tion (dĭ-**skrĕsh′**ən) *n.* **1.** The quality of being discreet; prudence: *Diplomats must use great discretion in negotiating treaties.* **2.** Freedom of action or judgment: *Choosing numbers for their jerseys was left to the players' discretion.*

dis·cre·tion·ar·y (dĭ-**skrĕsh′**ə-nĕr′ē) *adj.* Left to or determined by one's own discretion or judgment: *The governor has a discretionary fund for emergencies.*

dis·crim·i·nate (dĭ-**skrĭm′**ə-nāt′) *v.* **dis·crim·i·nat·ed, dis·crim·i·nat·ing, dis·crim·i·nates** —*intr.* **1.** To make a clear distinction; distinguish: *The art dealer could discriminate among many painters' styles.* **2.** To show preference or prejudice: *It is illegal to discriminate against employees on the basis of age.* —*tr.* To make or see a clear distinction between: *A critic discriminates good books from poor ones.* [From Latin *discrīmen*, distinction.] **—dis·crim′i·na′tor** *n.*

dis·crim·i·nat·ing (dĭ-**skrĭm′**ə-nā′tĭng) *adj.* **1.** Showing

ă	pat	ôr	core
ā	pay	oi	boy
âr	care	ou	out
ä	father	o͝o	took
ĕ	pet	o͝or	lure
ē	be	o͞o	boot
ĭ	pit	ŭ	cut
ī	bite	ûr	urge
îr	pier	th	thin
ŏ	pot	*th*	this
ō	toe	zh	vision
ô	paw	ə	about

careful judgment or fine taste: *a discriminating critic of modern music.* **2.** Serving to distinguish or set apart from others; distinctive: *a discriminating characteristic.* **3.** Marked by or showing bias; discriminatory. **—dis·crim′i·nat′ing·ly** *adv.*

dis·crim·i·na·tion (dĭ-skrĭm′ə-**nā′**shən) *n.* **1.** The ability to recognize or make fine distinctions: *clothes bought without care or discrimination; discrimination of color essential to the work of an artist.* **2.** Treatment of people based on their belonging to a class or category rather than on individual merit; partiality or prejudice: *The Constitution protects citizens from racial and religious discrimination.*

dis·crim·i·na·to·ry (dĭ-**skrĭm′**ə-nə-tôr′ē) *adj.* Showing prejudice; biased. **—dis·crim′i·na·to′ri·ly** *adv.*

dis·cur·sive (dĭ-**skûr′**sĭv) *adj.* **1.** Wandering from one subject to another; rambling: *discursive talk without much point to it.* **2.** Proceeding by means of a logically connected series of statements or ideas: *expressed his opinions in discursive paragraphs; a philosophy that is intuitive rather than discursive.* **—dis·cur′sive·ly** *adv.*

dis·cus (**dĭs′**kəs) *n., pl.* **dis·cus·es** A disk, typically wooden, plastic, or rubber with a metal rim, that is thrown for distance in athletic contests.

dis·cuss (dĭ-**skŭs′**) *tr.v.* **dis·cussed, dis·cuss·ing, dis·cuss·es 1.** To speak with another or others about; talk over: *We met to discuss the plan for the new park.* **2.** To speak or write about (a subject): *In her new book the author discusses recent events in Latin America.* [From Middle English *discussen*, to examine, from Latin *discussus*, past participle of *discutere*, to break apart : *dis-*, apart + *quatere*, to shake.]

dis·cus·sion (dĭ-**skŭsh′**ən) *n.* **1.** A conversation about a subject; an exchange of views: *We had a discussion about what would be fair under the circumstances.* **2.** A usually formal treatment of a subject, as in a speech or book: *Have you read that author's discussion of foreign policy?*

dis·dain (dĭs-**dān′**) *tr.v.* **dis·dained, dis·dain·ing, dis·dains** To consider or treat with contempt; despise: *The playwright disdained the judgments of critics in the press.* ❖ *n.* A show of contempt and aloofness; scorn: *She responded with disdain to his offers of a bribe.* [From Middle English *disdeinen*, from Latin *dēdignārī* : *dē-*, away, off + *dignārī*, to deem worthy (from *dignus*, worthy).]

dis·dain·ful (dĭs-**dān′**fəl) *adj.* Feeling or showing disdain; scornful. See Synonyms at **arrogant. —dis·dain′ful·ly** *adv.*

dis·ease (dĭ-**zēz′**) *n.* A condition of an organism or one of its parts that makes it unable to function in the normal or proper way; sickness. A disease is usually identified by certain signs or symptoms and can result from various causes, such as infection, environmental factors, or a genetic defect.

dis·eased (dĭ-**zēzd′**) *adj.* Affected with or suffering from disease: *a diseased liver.*

dis·em·bark (dĭs′ĕm-**bärk′**) *v.* **dis·em·barked, dis·em·bark·ing, dis·em·barks** *—intr.* To get off a ship or airplane: *After the flight attendant opens the door, you may disembark.* *—tr.* To unload from a ship or airplane: *The ship docked and disembarked the passengers.* **—dis·em′bar·ka′tion** *n.*

dis·em·bod·ied (dĭs′ĕm-**bŏd′**ēd) *adj.* Freed or separated from the body: *disembodied spirits; a disembodied voice coming from somewhere in the dark.*

dis·em·bow·el (dĭs′ĕm-**bou′**əl) *tr.v.* **dis·em·bow·eled, dis·em·bow·el·ing, dis·em·bow·els** or **dis·em·bow·elled, dis·em·bow·el·ling, dis·em·bow·els** To remove the bowels from: *The elephant disemboweled the lion with its tusks.* **—dis′em·bow′el·ment** *n.*

dis·en·chant (dĭs′ĕn-**chănt′**) *tr.v.* **dis·en·chant·ed, dis·en·chant·ing, dis·en·chants** To free from enchantment or false belief; disillusion: *One look at the crumbling house was enough to disenchant any buyer.* **—dis′en·chant′ment** *n.*

dis·en·cum·ber (dĭs′ĕn-**kŭm′**bər) *tr.v.* **dis·en·cum·bered, dis·en·cum·ber·ing, dis·en·cum·bers** To free from something that burdens, hinders, or troubles: *disencumber oneself of worry.*

dis·en·fran·chise (dĭs′ĕn-**frăn′**chīz′) *tr.v.* **dis·en·fran·chised, dis·en·fran·chis·ing, dis·en·fran·chis·es** To disfranchise. **—dis′en·fran′chise′ment** *n.*

dis·en·gage (dĭs′ĕn-**gāj′**) *v.* **dis·en·gaged, dis·en·gag·ing, dis·en·gag·es** *—tr.* **1.** To make free from something that holds fast, entangles, or connects: *disengage the car's clutch.* **2.** To free or release (oneself) from an engagement, promise, or obligation. *—intr.* To become free or detach oneself: *As the brakes disengaged, the car rolled backwards.* **—dis′en·gage′ment** *n.*

dis·en·tan·gle (dĭs′ĕn-**tăng′**gəl) *tr.v.* **dis·en·tan·gled, dis·en·tan·gling, dis·en·tan·gles** To free from tangles or confusion: *disentangle a knotted clothesline; disentangle fact from a web of accusations.* **—dis′en·tan′gle·ment** *n.*

dis·fa·vor (dĭs-**fā′**vər) *n.* **1.** Unfavorable regard; disapproval. **2.** The condition of being regarded with dislike or disapproval: *The governor was in disfavor with voters.* ❖ *tr.v.* **dis·fa·vored, dis·fa·vor·ing, dis·fa·vors** To view or treat with dislike or disapproval: *The company disfavored any expenditure to clean up the environment.*

dis·fig·ure (dĭs-**fĭg′**yər) *tr.v.* **dis·fig·ured, dis·fig·ur·ing, dis·fig·ures** To spoil the appearance of; mar the beauty of: *Vandals disfigured the statue with paint.*

dis·fran·chise (dĭs-**frăn′**chīz′) *tr.v.* **dis·fran·chised, dis·fran·chis·ing, dis·fran·chis·es** To deprive of a privilege or a right, especially the right to vote: *The law disfranchises a person guilty of a felony.* **—dis·fran′chise′ment** *n.*

dis·gorge (dĭs-**gôrj′**) *tr.v.* **dis·gorged, dis·gorg·ing, dis·gorg·es 1.** To bring up and discharge from the throat or stomach; vomit. **2.** To pour forth violently; spew: *The volcano disgorged lava into the ocean.* **3.** To give up (stolen goods, for example) unwillingly. [From Old French *desgorger*, from *gorge*, throat.]

dis·grace (dĭs-**grās′**) *n.* **1.** Loss of honor, respect, or reputation; shame: *The scandal brought disgrace on the politician's family.* **2.** The condition of being strongly disapproved: *in disgrace for telling a secret.* **3.** A person or thing that brings dishonor or disfavor: *The dirty streets are a disgrace to the city.* ❖ *tr.v.* **dis·graced, dis·grac·ing, dis·grac·es 1.** To bring shame or dishonor upon: *The thief's conviction disgraced family and friends.* **2.** To view or treat (someone) with disapproval: *The mayor disgraced the aide for failing to investigate the problem.*

dis·grace·ful (dĭs-**grās′**fəl) *adj.* Causing or deserving disgrace; shameful. **—dis·grace′ful·ly** *adv.*

dis·grun·tle (dĭs-**grŭn′**tl) *tr.v.* **dis·grun·tled, dis·grun·tling, dis·grun·tles** To make discontented; displease or disgust: *Loss of two vacation days disgruntled all the employees.* [From obsolete English *gruntle*, to grumble.] **—dis·grun′tle·ment** *n.*

dis·grun·tled (dĭs-**grŭn′**tld) *adj.* Discontented, dissatisfied or disgusted; cross: *The disgruntled employee filed a complaint.*

dis·guise (dĭs-**gīz′**) *tr.v.* **dis·guised, dis·guis·ing, dis·guis·es 1.** To hide the identity of (someone) by changing the appearance: *The princess disguised herself as a shepherd boy.* **2.** To hide or cause to appear different: *She disguised her embarrassment with a smile.* ❖ *n.* **1.** Clothes or accessories that are worn to conceal one's true identity: *The two spies wore the disguise of repairmen.* **2.** The condition of having concealed one's true identity: *The nurse turned out to be a comedian in disguise.*

dis·gust (dĭs-**gŭst′**) *tr.v.* **dis·gust·ed, dis·gust·ing, dis·gusts** To cause feelings of sickening dislike, distaste, or

WRITERS CHOOSE THEIR WORDS

There was plenty of bread left on the table, but it was sliced bakery bread from the Camerons' shop, wrapped in plastic, and the Boggart looked at it with **disdain.** Compared to the wonderful coarse wholemeal bread the MacDevon had baked once a week, this was poor stuff.

—Susan Cooper
The Boggart

WRITERS CHOOSE THEIR WORDS

By the time I had crossed at the ford, then walked down to Mr. Callender's house, I had ceased sobbing. I imagine I looked pretty **disheveled,** however: I'd left shoes and stockings by the stream and run through the forested countryside, not bothering to avoid bushes. Mr. Callender took one look at me and knelt down beside me. "My dear," he said. His eyes looked gently into mine. "What has happened?"

—Cynthia Voigt
The Callender Papers

disk harrow

ă	pat	ôr	core
ā	pay	oi	boy
âr	care	ou	out
ä	father	ŏŏ	took
ĕ	pet	ŏŏr	lure
ē	be	ōō	boot
ĭ	pit	ŭ	cut
ī	bite	ûr	urge
îr	pier	th	thin
ŏ	pot	*th*	this
ō	toe	zh	vision
ô	paw	ə	about

annoyance: *We are disgusted by your refusal to cooperate.* ❖ *n.* A feeling of extreme dislike, distaste, or annoyance: *The fans showed their disgust by booing the umpire.* [From Old French *desgouster*, to lose one's appetite : *des-*, away, not + *gouster*, to eat, taste (from Latin *gustāre*).]

dis·gust·ed (dĭs-**gŭs′**tĭd) *adj.* Filled with disgust: *a disgusted look.* **—dis·gust′ed·ly** *adv.*

dis·gust·ing (dĭs-**gŭs′**tĭng) *adj.* Causing disgust: *disgusting food; a disgusting remark.* **—dis·gust′ing·ly** *adv.*

dish (dĭsh) *n.* **1a.** A shallow container for holding, cooking, or serving food. **b.** The amount that a dish can hold: *I ate two dishes of fruit.* **2.** A particular kind or preparation of food: *Sushi is a Japanese dish.* **3.** A radio, television, or radar antenna having the shape of a dish. ❖ *tr.v.* **dished, dish·ing, dish·es** To serve (food) in a dish or dishes: *dish out the vegetables.* [From Old English *disc*, from Latin *discus*.]

dish·dash·a (dĭsh-**däsh′**ə) *n.* A loose, long-sleeved garment; a thobe. [From Colloquial Arabic *dišdāša*.]

dis·heart·en (dĭs-**här′**tn) *tr.v.* **dis·heart·ened, dis·heart·en·ing, dis·heart·ens** To cause to lose courage and hope: *Lack of interest in their new battery disheartened the inventors.* **—dis·heart′en·ing·ly** *adv.*

di·shev·eled or **di·shev·elled** (dĭ-**shĕv′**əld) *adj.* Untidy; disorderly: *disheveled clothes; a disheveled look.* [From Middle English *dischevele*, from Old French *descheveler*, to disarrange the hair : *des-*, apart + *chevel*, hair (from Latin *capillus*).]

dis·hon·est (dĭs-**ŏn′**ĭst) *adj.* **1.** Inclined to lie, cheat, or deceive: *a dishonest art dealer.* **2.** Showing or resulting from falseness or fraud: *a dishonest answer; dishonest dealings.* **—dis·hon′est·ly** *adv.*

dis·hon·es·ty (dĭs-**ŏn′**ĭ-stē) *n., pl.* **dis·hon·es·ties 1.** Lack of honesty or integrity. **2.** A dishonest act or statement.

dis·hon·or (dĭs-**ŏn′**ər) *n.* **1.** Loss of honor, respect, or reputation; shame. **2.** A person or thing that causes loss of honor: *a dishonor to the whole team.* ❖ *tr.v.* **dis·hon·ored, dis·hon·or·ing, dis·hon·ors** To bring shame or disgrace on: *His rude behavior dishonors the reputation of his company.*

dis·hon·or·a·ble (dĭs-**ŏn′**ər-ə-bəl) *adj.* Characterized by or causing dishonor: *the dishonorable acts of a swindler.* **—dis·hon′or·a·ble·ness** *n.* **—dis·hon′or·a·bly** *adv.*

dish·tow·el (**dĭsh′**tou′əl) *n.* A towel for drying dishes.

dish·wash·er (**dĭsh′**wŏsh′ər) *n.* **1.** A machine that washes dishes. **2.** A person who washes dishes, especially in a restaurant.

dish·wa·ter (**dĭsh′**wô′tər) *n.* Water in which dishes are or have been washed.

dis·il·lu·sion (dĭs′ĭ-**lōō′**zhən) *tr.v.* **dis·il·lu·sioned, dis·il·lu·sion·ing, dis·il·lu·sions** To free from a false idea or belief: *Many immigrants were disillusioned by the high cost of living.* **—dis′il·lu′sion·ment** *n.*

dis·in·cli·na·tion (dĭs-ĭn′klə-**nā′**shən) *n.* Unwillingness, reluctance, or aversion: *a disinclination to try new foods.*

dis·in·clined (dĭs′ĭn-**klīnd′**) *adj.* Unwilling; reluctant: *I am disinclined to take a job with such long hours.*

dis·in·fect (dĭs′ĭn-**fĕkt′**) *tr.v.* **dis·in·fect·ed, dis·in·fect·ing, dis·in·fects** To cleanse so as to destroy or prevent the growth of microorganisms that can cause disease: *disinfect a cut.* **—dis′in·fec′tion** *n.*

dis·in·fec·tant (dĭs′ĭn-**fĕk′**tənt) *n.* A substance that kills or prevents the growth of microorganisms that cause disease: *wash a wound with disinfectant.* ❖ *adj.* Destroying or preventing the growth of microorganisms that cause disease: *disinfectant soap.*

dis·in·for·ma·tion (dĭs-ĭn′fər-**mā′**shən) *n.* Deliberately misleading information provided by a government, especially by an intelligence agency, to influence public opinion or another nation's government.

dis·in·her·it (dĭs′ĭn-**hĕr′**ĭt) *tr.v.* **dis·in·her·it·ed, dis·in·her·it·ing, dis·in·her·its** To take from (a person) an inheritance or the right to inherit: *The eccentric millionaire disinherited his entire family.*

dis·in·te·grate (dĭs-**ĭn′**tĭ-grāt′) *v.* **dis·in·te·grat·ed, dis·in·te·grat·ing, dis·in·te·grates** —*intr.* **1.** To break into small pieces; separate into bits: *rock disintegrating into sand.* **2.** To lose cohesion or unity: *a family that disintegrated.* **3.** In nuclear physics, to undergo disintegration. —*tr.* To cause to break into separate pieces or bits: *Water disintegrated the cement to pebble-sized pieces.*

dis·in·te·gra·tion (dĭs-ĭn′tĭ-**grā′**shən) *n.* **1a.** The act or process of disintegrating: *Freezing and thawing caused disintegration of the concrete.* **b.** The condition of being disintegrated. **2.** In nuclear physics, the transformation of an atomic nucleus when it loses mass as it throws off particles or rays.

dis·in·ter (dĭs′ĭn-**tûr′**) *tr.v.* **dis·in·terred, dis·in·ter·ring, dis·in·ters 1.** To dig up or remove (a body) from a grave. **2.** To make public; disclose: *disinter old documents from the library.* **—dis′in·ter′ment** *n.*

dis·in·ter·est·ed (dĭs-**ĭn′**trĭ-stĭd *or* dĭs-**ĭn′**tə-rĕs′tĭd) *adj.* **1.** Free of bias and self-interest; impartial: *the disinterested decision of an umpire.* **2.** Uninterested or unconcerned: *My friends are totally disinterested in the movie.* **—dis·in′ter·est·ed·ly** *adv.*

dis·joint (dĭs-**joint′**) *tr.v.* **dis·joint·ed, dis·joint·ing, dis·joints 1.** To take apart at the joints: *The butcher quickly disjointed the chicken for frying.* **2.** To pull out of joint; dislocate: *That tackle disjointed the football player's shoulder.* **3.** To break up; put out of order: *The flooding disjointed the business section of town.* ❖ *adj.* In mathematics, having no common members. {0, 1, 2} and {3, 4, 5} are disjoint sets.

dis·joint·ed (dĭs-**join′**tĭd) *adj.* **1.** Separated at the joints: *a disjointed leg of lamb.* **2.** Lacking order or coherence; disconnected: *a disjointed paragraph.* **—dis·joint′ed·ly** *adv.*

disk also **disc** (dĭsk) *n.* **1.** A thin, flat, circular object, such as a plate or coin. **2.** Something that resembles such an object: *the moon's disk reflected in the pond.* **3a.** A round flat plate coated with a magnetic substance on which computer data is stored. **b.** The data stored on such a disk. **c.** An optical disc, especially a compact disc. **4.** A phonograph record. **5.** A round flattened structure in an animal, such as one made of cartilage and lying between adjacent bones of the spine. [From Greek *diskos*, quoit, from *dikein*, to throw.]

disk brake *n.* Variant of **disc brake.**

disk drive *n.* A device in a computer that reads data stored on a disk and writes data onto the disk for storage.

disk harrow or **disc harrow** *n.* A harrow consisting of a series of sharp, rotating metal disks on one or more axles, used to break up soil for seeding or planting.

disk jockey *n.* Variant of **disc jockey.**

dis·like (dĭs-**līk′**) *tr.v.* **dis·liked, dis·lik·ing, dis·likes** To regard (someone or something) with an unfavorable attitude; not like: *She dislikes lemonade. He dislikes working on Saturday.* ❖ *n.* An unfavorable attitude: *I have a strong dislike of board games.*

dis·lo·cate (**dĭs′**lō-kāt′ *or* dĭs-**lō′**kāt) *tr.v.* **dis·lo·cat·ed, dis·lo·cat·ing, dis·lo·cates 1.** To put (a body part, especially a joint or bone) out of its normal position: *I dislocated my thumb catching the ball barehanded.* **2.** To throw into confusion or disorder; upset: *The drought dislocated the state's economy. The snowstorm dislocated rail and air traffic.* **—dis′lo·ca′tion** *n.*

dis·lodge (dĭs-**lŏj′**) *tr.v.* **dis·lodged, dis·lodg·ing, dis·lodg·es** To move or force out of position: *Heavy rains dislodged boulders from the hillside.*

dis·loy·al (dĭs-**loi′**əl) *adj.* Lacking loyalty; unfaithful. **—dis·loy′al·ly** *adv.*

dis·loy·al·ty (dĭs-**loi′**əl-tē) *n., pl.* **dis·loy·al·ties 1.** Lack of loyalty; unfaithfulness. **2.** A disloyal act: *Taking all the credit for the discovery was a disloyalty to fellow researchers.*

dis·mal (dĭz′məl) *adj.* **1.** Causing gloom or depression; dreary: *a dismal fog.* **2.** Feeling gloomy; depressed; miserable: *feeling dismal from a bad cold.* **—dis′mal·ly** *adv.* **—dis′mal·ness** *n.* —SEE NOTE.

dis·man·tle (dĭs-măn′tl) *tr.v.* **dis·man·tled, dis·man·tling, dis·man·tles 1.** To pull down; take apart: *We dismantled the table to get it through the door.* **2.** To strip of furnishings or equipment: *Movers dismantled the apartment.* [From Old French *desmanteler* : *des-*, off, down + *mantel*, cloak.] **—dis·man′tle·ment** *n.*

dis·may (dĭs-mā′) *tr.v.* **dis·mayed, dis·may·ing, dis·mays 1.** To fill with dread; make anxious or afraid: *The fear of an epidemic dismayed the whole city.* **2.** To discourage or dishearten: *A low grade on the exam dismayed the student.* ❖ *n.* A sudden loss of courage or confidence in the face of danger or trouble: *Being lost in the woods filled the hikers with dismay.* [From Middle English *dismaien*, from Old French *esmaier*, to frighten.]

dis·mem·ber (dĭs-mĕm′bər) *tr.v.* **dis·mem·bered, dis·mem·ber·ing, dis·mem·bers 1.** To cut, tear, or pull off the limbs of: *The fox dismembered the chicken.* **2.** To divide into pieces: *The Roman Empire has been dismembered into numerous states.* **—dis·mem′ber·ment** *n.*

dis·miss (dĭs-mĭs′) *tr.v.* **dis·missed, dis·miss·ing, dis·miss·es 1.** To end the employment or service of; discharge: *Several workers were dismissed for loafing on the job.* **2.** To direct or allow to leave: *The students were dismissed for the holidays.* **3.** To put out of one's mind or consider as unimportant: *We dismissed the story as gossip.* **4.** To put (a claim or action) out of court without further hearing: *The judge dismissed the case due to lack of evidence.* [From Middle English *dismissen*, from Latin *dīmittere* : *dī-*, *dis-*, away + *mittere*, to send.]

dis·miss·al (dĭs-mĭs′əl) *n.* **1.** The act of dismissing someone: *The forecast of a snowstorm led to the principal's dismissal of the students.* **2.** The act of considering something unimportant: *Her dismissal of my concerns annoyed me.* **3.** An order or a notice of discharge: *The laid-off workers received their dismissals by email.*

dis·mount (dĭs-mount′) *v.* **dis·mount·ed, dis·mount·ing, dis·mounts** —*intr.* **1.** To get off or down, as from a horse or bicycle; alight. **2.** To execute a dismount in gymnastics. —*tr.* **1.** To unseat from a horse: *The frightened horse dismounted its rider.* **2.** To remove (a thing) from its support or mounting: *dismounted the old cannon for storage.* **3.** To take apart (a mechanism). ❖ *n.* **1.** The act or manner of dismounting, especially from a horse. **2.** A move in gymnastics whereby the gymnast gets off an apparatus or completes a floor exercise, typically landing on both feet.

dis·o·be·di·ence (dĭs′ə-bē′dē-əns) *n.* Refusal or failure to obey.

dis·o·be·di·ent (dĭs′ə-bē′dē-ənt) *adj.* Refusing or failing to obey: *a disobedient child.* **—dis′o·be′di·ent·ly** *adv.*

dis·o·bey (dĭs′ə-bā′) *tr. & intr.v.* **dis·o·beyed, dis·o·bey·ing, dis·o·beys** To refuse or fail to obey: *Pedestrians sometimes disobey traffic signals. A trained horse seldom disobeys.*

dis·or·der (dĭs-ôr′dər) *n.* **1.** Lack of order or regular arrangement; confusion: *Your desk is always in a state of disorder.* **2.** A public disturbance: *Police responded to a disorder in our neighborhood.* **3.** A sickness or disturbance of the body or mind: *a nervous disorder.* ❖ *tr.v.* **dis·or·dered, dis·or·der·ing, dis·or·ders 1.** To throw into disorder; muddle: *Early arrival of our guests disordered all our arrangements.* **2.** To upset the mental or physical health of: *Rich foods thoroughly disorder my digestion.*

dis·or·der·ly (dĭs-ôr′dər-lē) *adj.* **1.** Lacking regular or orderly arrangement; messy: *a disorderly room.* **2.** Lacking discipline; unruly: *a noisy disorderly crowd.* **—dis·or′der·li·ness** *n.*

dis·or·gan·ize (dĭs-ôr′gə-nīz′) *tr.v.* **dis·or·gan·ized, dis·or·gan·iz·ing, dis·or·gan·iz·es** To destroy the organization or orderly arrangement of; throw into confusion or disorder: *The strike by airline pilots disorganized air schedules.* **—dis·or′gan·i·za′tion** (dĭs-ôr′gə-nĭ-zā′shən) *n.*

dis·or·gan·ized (dĭs-ôr′gə-nīzd′) *adj.* Not organized; without organization or order: *a disorganized person; a disorganized room.*

dis·o·ri·ent (dĭs-ôr′ē-ĕnt′) *tr.v.* **dis·o·ri·ent·ed, dis·o·ri·ent·ing, dis·o·ri·ents** To cause to lose one's sense of direction or bearings; confuse: *Walking around in an unfamiliar part of the city disoriented us.* **—dis·o′ri·en·ta′tion** *n.*

dis·own (dĭs-ōn′) *tr.v.* **dis·owned, dis·own·ing, dis·owns** To refuse to claim or accept as one's own; repudiate; reject: *The father disowned his son for refusing to join the family business.*

dis·par·age (dĭ-spăr′ĭj) *tr.v.* **dis·par·aged, dis·par·ag·ing, dis·par·ag·es 1.** To speak of in an insulting or disrespectful way; belittle: *He disparages the accomplishments of others.* **2.** To lower in regard or position; discredit: *The article disparages environmentalists as busybodies.* [From Middle English *disparagen*, from Old French *desparager* : *des-*, away, down + *parage*, high birth (from *per*, peer).] **—dis·par′age·ment** *n.* **—dis·par′ag·ing·ly** *adv.*

dis·pa·rate (dĭs′pər-ĭt *or* dĭ-spăr′ĭt) *adj.* **1.** Completely distinct or different in kind; entirely dissimilar. **2.** Having dissimilar or opposing elements: *a disparate group.* [From Latin *disparāre*, to separate : *dis-*, apart + *parāre*, to prepare.] **—dis′pa·rate·ly** *adv.*

dis·par·i·ty (dĭ-spăr′ĭ-tē) *n., pl.* **dis·par·i·ties 1.** Inequality; difference: *the disparity in population between one city and another.* **2.** Lack of similarity; unlikeness: *a great disparity in the accounts of what happened.* [From Late Latin *disparitās* : Latin *dis-*, not + Late Latin *paritās*, equality.]

dis·pas·sion·ate (dĭs-păsh′ə-nĭt) *adj.* Not influenced by strong feelings or emotions: *the dispassionate ruling of a judge.* **—dis·pas′sion·ate·ly** *adv.*

dis·patch (dĭ-spăch′) *tr.v.* **dis·patched, dis·patch·ing, dis·patch·es 1.** To send off to a specific destination or on specific business: *dispatch a letter; dispatch a police car to the scene of a disturbance.* **2.** To complete or dispose of promptly: *The police dispatched their duty and left.* **3.** To put to death quickly and without ceremony: *The ranger dispatched the injured deer.* ❖ *n.* **1.** The act of sending off: *the dispatch of a representative to the conference.* **2.** Quickness and efficiency in performance: *The owl killed its prey with dispatch.* **3.** A written message, especially an official communication, sent with speed: *The messenger carried a dispatch from headquarters.* **4.** A news item sent to a news organization, as by a correspondent. [Probably from Old Provençal *empachar*, to impede, from Latin *impingere*, dash against.] **—dis·patch′er** *n.*

dis·pel (dĭ-spĕl′) *tr.v.* **dis·pelled, dis·pel·ling, dis·pels** To drive away, disperse, or cause to disappear: *Light dispelled the fog.* [From Middle English *dispellen*, from Latin *dispellere* : *dis-*, apart, away + *pellere*, to drive.]

dis·pens·a·ble (dĭ-spĕn′sə-bəl) *adj.* Not essential; unimportant: *To shorten the report, I removed all of the dispensable comments.* **—dis·pens′a·bil′i·ty** *n.*

dis·pen·sa·ry (dĭ-spĕn′sə-rē) *n., pl.* **dis·pen·sa·ries 1.** An office in a hospital, school, or other institution where medicines and medical supplies are given out. **2.** A place where medicines and medical treatment are provided, usually at little or no cost.

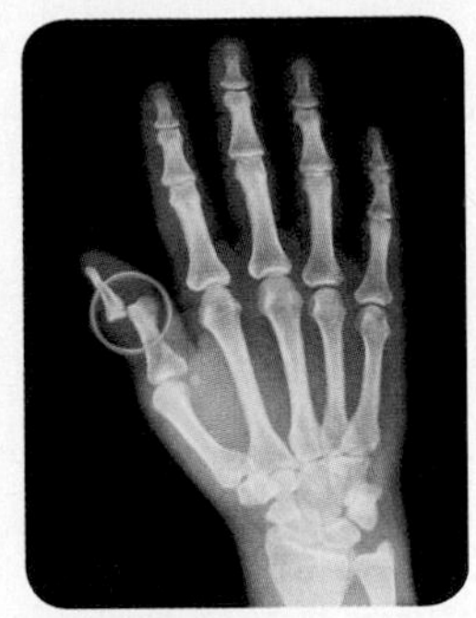

dislocate
x-ray of a hand with a dislocated thumb *(circled)*

WORD HISTORY

dismal The English word **dismal** comes from the medieval French phrase *dis mal,* literally "bad days." The *dis mal* were the two unlucky days of each month, and they also meant unlucky days in general. Those English who didn't understand French spoke of *dismal days,* not realizing that this literally meant "bad days days"; eventually *dismal* was felt to be an adjective meaning "bad, unlucky," and then, ultimately "causing gloom" or "feeling gloom."

WRITERS CHOOSE THEIR WORDS

From the threshold, I saw the glow of the railroad lantern. A fire burned in the little stove, warming the air slightly but not enough to **dispel** the odor of kerosene, damp earth, and old wool.

—Mary Downing Hahn
Stepping on the Cracks

dis·pen·sa·tion (dĭs′pən-**sā′**shən) *n.* **1.** The act or process of dispensing or giving out; distribution: *dispensation of medicine by the local clinic.* **2.** Something given out or distributed: *There were no red pens in this month's dispensation of supplies.* **3.** Freedom or a release from an obligation or rule, granted in a particular case: *a dispensation allowing new businesses relief from taxes.*

dis·pense (dĭ-**spĕns′**) *tr.v.* **dis·pensed, dis·pens·ing, dis·pens·es 1.** To deal out or distribute, especially in parts or portions: *The relief worker dispensed food to the refugees.* See Synonyms at **distribute. 2.** To prepare and give out (medicines). **3.** To carry out; administer: *The judge dispensed justice fairly.* ◆ **dispense with** To manage without; forgo: *Let's dispense with the formalities and get down to business.* [From Middle English *dispensen*, from Latin *dispēnsāre* : *dis-*, out + *pendere*, to weigh.]

dispenser
tape dispenser

dis·pens·er (dĭ-**spĕn′**sər) *n.* A person or thing that dispenses: *a paper cup dispenser.*

dis·per·sal (dĭ-**spûr′**səl) *n.* The act of dispersing or the condition of being dispersed: *the dispersal of a crowd; dispersal of aid among the needy.*

dis·perse (dĭ-**spûrs′**) *v.* **dis·persed, dis·pers·ing, dis·pers·es** —*tr.* **1.** To drive off or scatter in different directions: *The rain dispersed the crowd.* **2.** To cause to vanish or disappear; dispel: *Winds dispersed the clouds.* **3.** To separate (light or other radiation) into its different wavelengths. —*intr.* **1.** To separate and move in different directions; scatter: *The protesters dispersed when the police arrived.* **2.** To vanish or disappear: *The mist had dispersed by noon.* [From Middle English *dispersen*, from Latin *dispergere* : *dis-*, apart + *spargere*, to scatter.]

dis·per·sion (dĭ-**spûr′**zhən *or* dĭ-**spûr′**shən) *n.* **1.** The separation of light or other radiation into components, usually according to wavelength. **2.** The act of dispersing or the state of being dispersed: *Bright sunlight caused dispersion of the fog.*

dis·pir·it (dĭ-**spĭr′**ĭt) *tr.v.* **dis·pir·it·ed, dis·pir·it·ing, dis·pir·its** To lower in spirit; discourage; dishearten.

dis·pir·it·ed (dĭ-**spĭr′**ĭ-tĭd) *adj.* Depressed; disheartened; discouraged: *feeling tired and dispirited.* **—dis·pir′it·ed·ly** *adv.*

dis·place (dĭs-**plās′**) *tr.v.* **dis·placed, dis·plac·ing, dis·plac·es 1.** To change the place or position of: *The goal was displaced by a skater before the puck went in.* **2.** To force to leave a place of residence: *The refugees were displaced by the war.* **3.** To take the place of; replace: *Many workers have been displaced in their jobs by robots.* **4.** To take the space of (a quantity of liquid or gas): *An equal amount of oxygen displaced the carbon dioxide.* **5.** To dismiss from an office or position: *In the election, the voters displaced their representative.*

dis·placed person (dĭs-**plāst′**) *n.* A person who has been driven from his or her home country by war or other calamity; a refugee or evacuee.

dis·place·ment (dĭs-**plās′**mənt) *n.* **1a.** The weight or volume of fluid displaced by a body floating in it. The weight of the body is equal to the weight of the fluid it displaces. **b.** The measure of the distance that a body has been moved from one point to another through space. **2.** The act of displacing or the condition of being displaced: *Flooding caused the displacement of many people.*

dis·play (dĭ-**splā′**) *tr.v.* **dis·played, dis·play·ing, dis·plays 1.** To put in view; exhibit: *The library displays its new books in a case.* **2.** To make noticeable; show evidence of: *a decision that displays poor judgment.* **3.** To show off; flaunt: *proudly displayed his new hat.* ❖ *n.* **1.** The act of displaying: *a display of kindness.* **2.** A public exhibition: *a display of Native American pottery.* **3.** A show designed to impress or to attract attention: *The lavish party was just a display of wealth.* **4.** A specialized pattern of behavior used by an animal to communicate visually: *a male bird spreading its feathers as part of a courtship display.* **5.** A device, such as a computer screen, that gives information in visual form. [From Middle English *displaien*, from Medieval Latin *displicāre*, to unfold : Latin *dis-*, apart + Latin *plicāre*, to fold.]

dis·please (dĭs-**plēz′**) *v.* **dis·pleased, dis·pleas·ing, dis·pleas·es** —*tr.* To cause annoyance or irritation to: *Bad manners displease me.* —*intr.* To cause annoyance or irritation.

dis·pleas·ure (dĭs-**plĕzh′**ər) *n.* The condition of being displeased; dissatisfaction: *The coach showed great displeasure over our performance in the first half.*

dis·port (dĭ-**spôrt′**) *v.* **dis·port·ed, dis·port·ing, dis·ports** —*intr.* To frolic; play. —*tr.* To entertain (oneself) by sport or play.

dis·pos·a·ble (dĭ-**spō′**zə-bəl) *adj.* **1.** Designed to be thrown away after use: *disposable razors.* **2.** Remaining to a person after taxes have been deducted: *disposable income.*

dis·pos·al (dĭ-**spō′**zəl) *n.* **1.** The act of getting rid of something: *The disposal of garbage is a serious problem for cities.* **2.** The act of attending to or settling a matter: *The mayor's decision led to a prompt disposal of the problem.* **3.** The act of transferring something, as by giving or selling: *the disposal of property to his children.* ◆ **at (one's) disposal** Available for one's use: *All of the library books are at the disposal of patrons.*

dis·pose (dĭ-**spōz′**) *tr.v.* **dis·posed, dis·pos·ing, dis·pos·es 1.** To make willing or ready; incline: *Her remorse disposed me to forgive her mistake.* **2.** To place or set in a particular order; arrange: *The gardeners disposed the tulips in circles throughout the park.* ◆ **dispose of 1.** To get rid of: *We disposed of the leftovers in the garbage.* **2.** To sell or give away: *The dealer quickly disposed of the cars.* **3.** To settle or decide: *We disposed of the problem quickly.* [From Middle English *disposen*, from Latin *dispōnere*, to arrange.]

dis·posed (dĭ-**spōzd′**) *adj.* Willing or inclined: *Cats are disposed to nap during the day.*

dis·po·si·tion (dĭs′pə-**zĭsh′**ən) *n.* **1.** The usual mood or attitude of a person or animal; temperament; nature: *a young child's affectionate disposition.* **2.** A tendency or inclination: *We are familiar with her disposition to argue over minor points.* **3.** Arrangement or distribution: *the disposition of books by subject on library shelves.* **4.** An act of settling; settlement: *disposition of legal matters at the lawyer's office.* **5.** An act of transferring: *the disposition of her property to her heirs.*

dis·pos·sess (dĭs′pə-**zĕs′**) *tr.v.* **dis·pos·sessed, dis·pos·sess·ing, dis·pos·sess·es** To deprive (a person) of the possession of something, such as land or a house: *The bank may dispossess a person of land for failure to make loan payments.* **—dis′pos·ses′sion** (dĭs′pə-**zĕsh′**ən) *n.*

dis·proof (dĭs-**pro͞of′**) *n.* **1.** An act of disproving. **2.** Evidence that disproves.

dis·pro·por·tion (dĭs′prə-**pôr′**shən) *n.* A lack of proportion; imbalance: *the disproportion between the size of a piece of balsa wood and its very light weight.*

dis·pro·por·tion·ate (dĭs′prə-**pôr′**shə-nĭt) *adj.* Out of proportion to something else, as in size or shape; not suitably proportioned. **—dis′pro·por′tion·ate·ly** *adv.*

dis·prove (dĭs-**pro͞ov′**) *tr.v.* **dis·proved, dis·prov·ing, dis·proves** To prove to be false or in error; refute: *Shadows of buildings in the photograph disprove the witness's testimony that it was a stormy day.*

dis·put·a·ble (dĭ-**spyo͞o′**tə-bəl *or* **dĭs′**pyə-tə-bəl) *adj.* Open to dispute; debatable: *The facts are well known, but your interpretation of them is disputable.* **—dis·put′a·bil′i·ty** *n.*

dis·pu·tant (dĭ-**spyo͞ot′**nt *or* **dĭs′**pyə-tənt) *n.* A person taking part in an argument, debate, or quarrel.

ă	pat	ôr	core
ā	pay	oi	boy
âr	care	ou	out
ä	father	o͝o	took
ĕ	pet	o͝or	lure
ē	be	o͞o	boot
ĭ	pit	ŭ	cut
ī	bite	ûr	urge
îr	pier	th	thin
ŏ	pot	*th*	this
ō	toe	zh	vision
ô	paw	ə	about

dis·pu·ta·tion (dĭs′pyə-tā′shən) *n.* The act of disputing; debate.

dis·pute (dĭ-spyo͞ot′) *v.* **dis·put·ed, dis·put·ing, dis·putes** —*tr.* **1.** To argue about; debate: *The editors disputed the literary merit of the manuscript.* **2.** To question the truth or validity of; doubt: *We disputed her account of what happened.* **3.** To quarrel or fight over: *The nations disputed the territory.* —*intr.* **1.** To engage in discussion; argue: *The candidates disputed over where city expenses should be cut.* **2.** To quarrel angrily. ❖ *n.* **1.** A debate; an argument: *Each scientist in the dispute had a different theory.* **2.** A quarrel. [From Middle English *disputen*, from Latin *disputāre*, to examine : *dis-*, apart + *putāre*, to reckon.]

dis·qual·i·fi·ca·tion (dĭs-kwŏl′ə-fĭ-kā′shən) *n.* **1.** The act of disqualifying or the condition of being disqualified. **2.** Something that disqualifies: *Very poor vision is a disqualification for getting a driver's license.*

dis·qual·i·fy (dĭs-kwŏl′ə-fī′) *tr.v.* **dis·qual·i·fied, dis·qual·i·fy·ing, dis·qual·i·fies 1.** To make unqualified or unfit: *Poor eyesight disqualifies many people who wish to become pilots.* **2.** To declare to be unqualified or ineligible: *The judges disqualified the swimmer from the race.*

dis·qui·et (dĭs-kwī′ĭt) *tr.v.* **dis·qui·et·ed, dis·qui·et·ing, dis·qui·ets** To make uneasy; trouble; worry: *Strange noises disquieted the guard.* ❖ *n.* Worry, uneasiness, or anxiety: *Rumors of engine trouble caused disquiet among the airplane passengers.*

dis·qui·et·ing (dĭs-kwī′ĭ-tĭng) *adj.* Troubling; worrying; disturbing: *Everyone was upset by the disquieting news.*

dis·qui·e·tude (dĭs-kwī′ĭ-to͞od′) *n.* Worry; uneasiness; anxiety.

Dis·rae·li (dĭz-rā′lē), **Benjamin** First Earl of Beaconsfield. 1804–1881. British politician who served as prime minister in 1868 and from 1874 to 1880. He was instrumental in extending the power of the British Empire.

dis·re·gard (dĭs′rĭ-gärd′) *tr.v.* **dis·re·gard·ed, dis·re·gard·ing, dis·re·gards** To pay little or no attention to; ignore: *They disregarded the warnings not to hike in stormy weather.* ❖ *n.* Lack of attention or regard: *a disregard for safety.*

dis·re·pair (dĭs′rĭ-pâr′) *n.* The condition of being in need of repair: *an abandoned house in disrepair.*

dis·rep·u·ta·ble (dĭs-rĕp′yə-tə-bəl) *adj.* Having a bad reputation; not respectable: *a disreputable building contractor.* **—dis·rep′u·ta·bly** *adv.*

dis·re·pute (dĭs′rĭ-pyo͞ot′) *n.* Damage to or loss of reputation; disgrace.

dis·re·spect (dĭs′rĭ-spĕkt′) *n.* Lack of respect or courtesy; rudeness: *His behavior showed disrespect for the law.*

dis·re·spect·ful (dĭs′rĭ-spĕkt′fəl) *adj.* Having or showing a lack of respect; rude: *disrespectful behavior.* **—dis′re·spect′ful·ly** *adv.* **—dis′re·spect′ful·ness** *n.*

dis·robe (dĭs-rōb′) *tr. & intr.v.* **dis·robed, dis·rob·ing, dis·robes** To undress: *disrobe a doll; disrobe for an x-ray.*

dis·rupt (dĭs-rŭpt′) *tr.v.* **dis·rupt·ed, dis·rupt·ing, dis·rupts** To interrupt or throw into confusion or disorder: *Protesters disrupted the senator's speech.* [From Latin *dīrumpere*, to break apart : *dī-*, *dis-*, apart + *rumpere*, to break.] **—dis·rupt′er** *n.*

dis·rup·tion (dĭs-rŭp′shən) *n.* The act of disrupting or the state of being disrupted: *the storm's disruption of electric power.*

dis·rup·tive (dĭs-rŭp′tĭv) *adj.* Causing disruption: *The street repairs were disruptive to city traffic.* **—dis·rup′tive·ly** *adv.*

diss (dĭs) *v.* Variant of **dis.**

dis·sat·is·fac·tion (dĭs-săt′ĭs-făk′shən) *n.* The feeling of being displeased or dissatisfied; discontent: *dissatisfaction among local residents over the closing of the library.*

dis·sat·is·fied (dĭs-săt′ĭs-fīd′) *adj.* Feeling or showing a lack of contentment or satisfaction: *The dissatisfied customer returned his purchase.*

dis·sat·is·fy (dĭs-săt′ĭs-fī′) *tr.v.* **dis·sat·is·fied, dis·sat·is·fy·ing, dis·sat·is·fies** To fail to satisfy; displease: *Your careless work dissatisfies me.*

dis·sect (dĭ-sĕkt′ *or* dī-sĕkt′ *or* dī′sĕkt′) *tr.v.* **dis·sect·ed, dis·sect·ing, dis·sects 1.** To cut apart or separate (tissue) for study or examination: *dissect an animal in a lab.* **2.** To examine, analyze, or criticize in detail: *We dissected the plan to see where it might go wrong.* [From Latin *dissecāre*, to cut apart : *dis-*, apart + *secāre*, to cut up.]

dis·sec·tion (dĭ-sĕk′shən *or* dī-sĕk′shən) *n.* **1.** The act or process of dissecting: *the complicated dissection of a frog.* **2.** Something that has been dissected, as a tissue being studied. **3.** A thoroughly conducted examination or analysis: *the lawyer's dissection of the evidence.*

dis·sem·ble (dĭ-sĕm′bəl) *v.* **dis·sem·bled, dis·sem·bling, dis·sem·bles** —*intr.* To hide one's real character, feelings, or motives under a false appearance. —*tr.* To conceal or hide behind a false appearance or manner: *dissemble one's disappointment by making a joke.* [From Middle English *dissemblen*, from Old French *dessembler*, to be different : *des-*, apart + *sembler*, to appear, seem (from Latin *simulāre*, to pretend, seem).] **—dis·sem′bler** *n.*

dis·sem·i·nate (dĭ-sĕm′ə-nāt′) *tr.v.* **dis·sem·i·nat·ed, dis·sem·i·nat·ing, dis·sem·i·nates** To make known widely; spread abroad: *Many political blogs disseminated the election news instantly.* **—dis·sem′i·na′tion** *n.*

dis·sen·sion (dĭ-sĕn′shən) *n.* Difference of opinion; disagreement. —SEE NOTE AT **consent.**

dis·sent (dĭ-sĕnt′) *intr.v.* **dis·sent·ed, dis·sent·ing, dis·sents** To think or feel differently; disagree: *Many angry citizens dissented from the government action of raising taxes.* ❖ *n.* **1.** Difference of opinion or feeling; disagreement: *dissent over the British right to tax the American colonists.* **2.** The refusal to conform to the authority or rules of a government or church: *The Puritans' dissent from the Church of England led to their migration to the New World.* [From Middle English *dissenten*, from Latin *dissentīre* : *dis-*, apart + *sentīre*, to feel.] —SEE NOTE AT **consent.**

❏ *These sound alike:* **dissent, descent** (ancestry).

dis·sent·er (dĭ-sĕn′tər) *n.* **1.** A person who dissents. **2.** often **Dissenter** A person who refuses to accept the beliefs and practices of an established or national church, especially a Protestant who dissents from the Church of England.

dis·ser·ta·tion (dĭs′ər-tā′shən) *n.* A lengthy and formal discussion of a subject, especially one written at a university by a candidate for a doctoral degree.

dis·ser·vice (dĭs-sûr′vĭs) *n.* A harmful action, especially one that is undertaken with good intentions.

dis·sev·er (dĭ-sĕv′ər) *tr. & intr.v.* **dis·sev·ered, dis·sev·er·ing, dis·sev·ers** To separate or divide into parts.

dis·si·dence (dĭs′ĭ-dəns) *n.* Disagreement as in opinion or belief; dissent.

dis·si·dent (dĭs′ĭ-dənt) *adj.* Disagreeing, as in opinion or belief; dissenting: *Dissident opinions were voiced before the final vote was taken.* ❖ *n.* A person who disagrees; a dissenter.

dis·sim·i·lar (dĭ-sĭm′ə-lər) *adj.* Unlike; different: *We have dissimilar views.* **—dis·sim′i·lar·ly** *adv.*

dis·sim·i·lar·i·ty (dĭ-sĭm′ə-lăr′ĭ-tē) *n., pl.* **dis·sim·i·lar·i·ties 1.** The quality or condition of being unlike; difference: *There is marked dissimilarity of climate between the wet coastal regions and the arid inland plains.* **2.** A point of distinction or difference: *Even identical twins have little dissimilarities.*

dis·sim·u·late (dĭ-sĭm′yə-lāt′) *v.* **dis·sim·u·lat·ed, dis·sim·u·lat·ing, dis·sim·u·lates** —*tr.* To hide (one's true

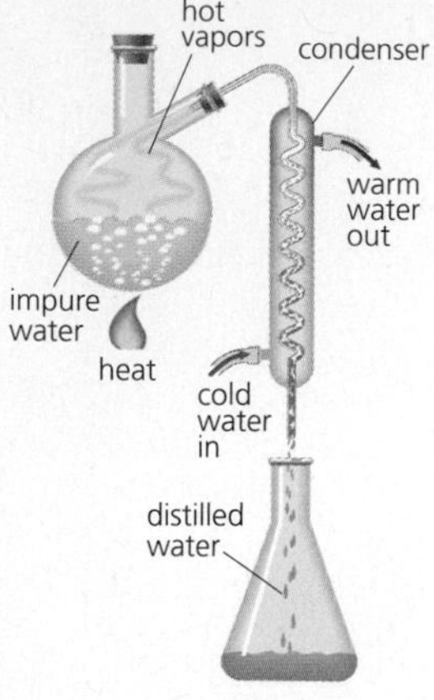

distillation

ă	pat	ôr	core
ā	pay	oi	boy
âr	care	ou	out
ä	father	o͝o	took
ĕ	pet	o͝or	lure
ē	be	o͞o	boot
ĭ	pit	ŭ	cut
ī	bite	ûr	urge
îr	pier	th	thin
ŏ	pot	*th*	this
ō	toe	zh	vision
ô	paw	ə	about

feelings or intentions) under a false appearance. *—intr.* To conceal one's true feelings or intentions. [From Middle English *dissimulaten*, from Latin *dissimulāre* : *dis-*, apart + *simulāre*, to simulate, pretend.] **—dis·sim′u·la′tion** *n.*

dis·si·pate (dĭs′ə-pāt′) *v.* **dis·si·pat·ed, dis·si·pat·ing, dis·si·pates** *—tr.* **1.** To drive away by or as if by dispersing; scatter: *A strong wind dissipated the clouds.* **2.** To use up unwisely; waste; squander: *They dissipated their wealth on needless luxuries.* *—intr.* **1.** To vanish by dispersion; disappear: *The fog dissipated shortly after sunrise.* **2.** To become dispelled; vanish: *His anger dissipated in time.*

dis·si·pat·ed (dĭs′ə-pā′tĭd) *adj.* **1.** Indulging in harmful or destructive pleasures; dissolute: *a dissipated life.* **2.** Wasted; squandered: *a dissipated fortune.*

dis·si·pa·tion (dĭs′ə-pā′shən) *n.* **1.** The act of scattering or the condition of being scattered; dispersion: *the dissipation of storm clouds.* **2.** Wasteful use or expenditure, as of money, energy, or time. **3.** Overindulgence in pleasure.

dis·so·ci·ate (dĭ-sō′shē-āt′ *or* dĭ-sō′sē-āt′) *tr.v.* **dis·so·ci·at·ed, dis·so·ci·at·ing, dis·so·ci·ates** To break association with; separate: *We dissociated ourselves from the committee because we disagree with its report.* **—dis·so′ci·a′tion** *n.*

dis·sol·u·ble (dĭ-sŏl′yə-bəl) *adj.* Capable of being dissolved.

dis·so·lute (dĭs′ə-lo͞ot′) *adj.* Lacking moral restraint; immoral. **—dis′so·lute′ly** *adv.*

dis·so·lu·tion (dĭs′ə-lo͞o′shən) *n.* **1a.** The act or process of breaking up into parts; disintegration: *Failure to take in new members caused the gradual dissolution of the garden club.* **b.** The ending of a formal or legal bond; termination: *dissolution of a business partnership.* **2.** The act or process of changing from a solid to a liquid. **3.** Excessive indulgence in pleasures.

dis·solve (dĭ-zŏlv′) *v.* **dis·solved, dis·solv·ing, dis·solves** *—tr.* **1.** To cause to pass into solution: *dissolve salt in water.* **2.** To change a (solid matter) to a liquid: *Warm weather dissolved the ice on the lake.* **3.** To bring to an end; terminate: *dissolve a partnership; dissolve a meeting.* **4.** To cause to disappear; dispel: *The funny remark dissolved the tension in the room.* *—intr.* **1.** To be taken up into solution: *Alcohol dissolves in water, but oil does not.* **2.** To change from a solid into a liquid: *The ice cubes dissolved in the warm tea.* **3.** To break up; disperse: *The mist dissolved in the wind.* **4.** To fade away; disappear: *The team's confidence dissolved quickly after the loss.* **5.** To be overcome emotionally: *The lost child dissolved into tears.* [From Middle English *dissolven*, from Latin *dissolvere.*] **—dis·solv′a·ble** *adj.*

dis·so·nance (dĭs′ə-nəns) *n.* **1.** A harsh combination of sounds; discord: *the dissonance of horns in heavy traffic.* **2.** Lack of agreement or consistency; conflict: *Dissonance among committee members brought their plans to a halt.*

dis·so·nant (dĭs′ə-nənt) *adj.* **1.** Being or having a harsh combination of sounds: *a dissonant passage in the symphony.* **2.** Lacking agreement: *a dissonant meeting.* [From Middle English *dissonaunt*, from Latin *dissonāre*, to be dissonant : *dis-*, apart + *sonāre*, to sound.] **—dis′so·nant·ly** *adv.*

dis·suade (dĭ-swād′) *tr.v.* **dis·suad·ed, dis·suad·ing, dis·suades** To discourage or keep (a person) from a purpose or course of action by persuasion or advice: *My friends dissuaded me from leaving the party early.* **—dis·sua′sion** (dĭ-swā′zhən) *n.*

dist. *abbr.* An abbreviation of: **1.** distance. **2.** district.

dis·taff (dĭs′tăf′) *n.* A stick holding flax or wool that is pulled off to be spun by hand into yarn or thread. [From Old English *distæf* : *dis-*, bunch of flax + *stæf*, staff.]

distaff side *n.* The female side or branch of a family.

dis·tance (dĭs′təns) *n.* **1.** The extent of space between two points or things: *The distance between my house and the mall is ten miles.* **2.** A stretch of space without definite limits: *The ice covered vast distances.* **3.** A point or area that is far away: *In the distance we could see the whales swimming.* **4.** The full period or length of a contest or game. ❖ *tr.v.* **dis·tanced, dis·tanc·ing, dis·tanc·es** To place or keep at or as if at a distance: *decided to distance herself from the controversy.*

dis·tant (dĭs′tənt) *adj.* **1.** Far away; remote: *a distant peak on the horizon.* **2.** Separate or apart in space: *Our house is two miles distant from the station.* **3.** Far away or apart in time: *the distant past.* **4.** Far apart in relationship: *a distant cousin.* **5.** Unfriendly in manner; aloof: *The new neighbors appeared cold and distant until we got to know them.* [From Middle English *distaunt*, from Latin *distāns*, present participle of *distāre*, to be remote : *dis-*, apart + *stāre*, to stand.] **—dis′tant·ly** *adv.*

dis·taste (dĭs-tāst′) *n.* A dislike or strong objection: *a distaste for modern music.*

dis·taste·ful (dĭs-tāst′fəl) *adj.* Unpleasant; disagreeable; offensive: *Cleaning the basement is a distasteful job.* **—dis·taste′ful·ly** *adv.* **—dis·taste′ful·ness** *n.*

dis·tem·per (dĭs-tĕm′pər) *n.* **1.** An often fatal infection of dogs and certain other animals such as raccoons, caused by a virus and characterized by discharge from the eyes and nose, coughing, fever, and vomiting. **2.** An often fatal infection of cats and certain other animals, caused by a virus and characterized by fever, vomiting, and diarrhea.

dis·tend (dĭ-stĕnd′) *v.* **dis·tend·ed, dis·tend·ing, dis·tends** *—intr.* To swell or expand from or as if from internal pressure: *The puppies ate until their stomachs distended.* *—tr.* To cause to expand by or as if by internal pressure: *Fluid distends a blister.* [From Middle English *distenden*, from Latin *distendere* : *dis-*, out, apart + *tendere*, to stretch.]

dis·till also **dis·til** (dĭ-stĭl′) *v.* **dis·tilled, dis·till·ing, dis·tills** also **dis·tilled, dis·til·ling, dis·tils** *—tr.* **1.** To treat (a substance) by the process of distillation. **2.** To separate (a substance) from a mixture by distillation. **3.** To separate or extract the core or essential part of: *distill the important points of a book in a report.* *—intr.* **1.** To undergo or be produced by distillation. **2.** To fall in drops or small quantities.

dis·til·late (dĭs′tə-lāt′ *or* dĭ-stĭl′ĭt) *n.* A liquid condensed from vapor and collected in distillation.

dis·til·la·tion (dĭs′tə-lā′shən) *n.* **1.** The process of boiling a liquid and condensing and collecting the vapor. Distillation is used to purify liquids, such as sea water, or to separate liquid mixtures, such as petroleum. **2.** Something distilled from another substance or from a more complex form; a distillate.

dis·till·er (dĭ-stĭl′ər) *n.* **1.** A person or thing that distills, especially a condenser. **2.** A person or company that produces alcoholic liquors.

dis·till·er·y (dĭ-stĭl′ə-rē) *n., pl.* **dis·till·er·ies** An establishment for distilling, especially for distilling alcoholic liquors.

dis·tinct (dĭ-stĭngkt′) *adj.* **1.** Different from all others; separate: *We discussed the issue on two distinct occasions.* **2.** Easily perceived by the senses or mind; definite: *Onions have a distinct odor.* **3.** Clearly defined; unquestionable: *Doctors have distinct limitations on their time.* [From Middle English, from Latin *distīnctus*, past participle of *distinguere*, to distinguish.] **—dis·tinct′ly** *adv.* **—dis·tinct′ness** *n.*

dis·tinc·tion (dĭ-stĭngk′shən) *n.* **1.** The act of distinguishing; discrimination: *Employers must hire without distinction of age or race.* **2.** The condition or fact of being distinct; difference: *a distinction between studying* *and casual reading.* **3.** Something that sets one apart; a distinguishing mark or characteristic: *the distinction of being the best singer in the choir.* **4.** Excellence, as of performance, character, or reputation: *a composer of great distinction.* **5.** Recognition of achievement or superiority; honor: *She graduated with distinction.*

dis·tinc·tive (dĭ-stĭngk′tĭv) *adj.* Serving to identify, characterize, or set apart from others: *Your team wears a distinctive uniform.* **—dis·tinc′tive·ly** *adv.* **—dis·tinc′tive·ness** *n.*

dis·tin·guish (dĭ-stĭng′gwĭsh) *v.* **dis·tin·guished, dis·tin·guish·ing, dis·tin·guish·es** *—tr.* **1.** To recognize as being different or distinct: *Counting the number of legs is one way to distinguish spiders from ants.* **2.** To see or hear clearly; make out; discern: *the ear's ability to distinguish musical notes.* **3.** To make noticeable or different; set apart: *The beaver is distinguished by its broad flat tail.* **4.** To cause (oneself) to gain fame, esteem, or honor: *Some artists distinguished themselves as great portrait painters.* *—intr.* To recognize differences; discriminate: *distinguish between right and wrong.* **—dis·tin′guish·a·ble** *adj.*

dis·tin·guished (dĭ-stĭng′gwĭsht) *adj.* **1.** Recognized as excellent; eminent; renowned: *a distinguished composer.* **2.** Dignified in conduct or appearance: *the distinguished air of a great dancer.*

dis·tort (dĭ-stôrt′) *tr.v.* **dis·tort·ed, dis·tort·ing, dis·torts 1.** To twist (something) out of the usual shape; contort: *a grin that distorted the clown's face.* **2.** To give a false account of; misrepresent: *distort the facts.* **3.** To change (an electronic signal) so as to result in poor quality reception or reproduction, as of radio or recorded music. [From Latin *distorquēre* : *dis-*, apart + *torquēre*, to twist.]

dis·tor·tion (dĭ-stôr′shən) *n.* **1a.** The act of distorting: *Distortion of the facts gave a false impression of what actually happened.* **b.** The condition of being distorted: *Playing a record at the wrong speed results in distortion of the sound.* **2.** Something distorted: *Their vague idea of what happened was full of distortions.*

dis·tract (dĭ străkt′) *tr.v.* **dis·tract·ed, dis·tract·ing, dis·tracts 1.** To cause (someone) to have difficulty paying attention to something: *The noise distracted the students in the library.* **2.** To cause (a person's attention) to be diverted from its original focus. **3.** To make (someone) feel uneasy; unsettle: *Worries about moving to a new city distracted the whole family.* [From Middle English *distracten*, from Latin *distrahere*, to pull away : *dis-*, apart, away + *trahere*, to draw.]

dis·trac·tion (dĭ-străk′shən) *n.* **1.** Something that makes it difficult to pay attention or that draws attention away from familiar or everyday concerns: *The new kittens were a continuous distraction from homework.* **2.** The act of distracting someone: *The babysitter's distraction of the child worked well, because the child stopped crying.* **3.** The condition of being distracted, especially from everyday concerns: *people who seek distraction in video games.* **4.** Great mental agitation: *Worry over paying the bills nearly drove the shopkeeper to distraction.*

dis·traught (dĭ-strôt′) *adj.* Very worried or upset: *He was distraught when he lost his wallet.*

dis·tress (dĭ-strĕs′) *tr.v.* **dis·tressed, dis·tress·ing, dis·tress·es 1.** To cause (a person) to suffer in mind or body. **2.** To mar or treat (an object or fabric, for example) to give the appearance of an antique or heavy prior use. ❖ *n.* **1.** Sorrow or anguish: *her distress when her dog ran away.* **2.** Bodily pain or dysfunction: *The accident victim was in severe distress.* **3.** The condition of being in need of immediate assistance: *a motorist in distress.* **4.** Suffering caused by poverty: *government programs to help relieve distress.* **5.** Something that causes discomfort: *Seeing an animal suffering is a great distress to me.*

dis·tress·ful (dĭ-strĕs′fəl) *adj.* Causing or experiencing distress; painful. **—dis·tress′ful·ly** *adv.*

dis·trib·ute (dĭ-strĭb′yo͞ot) *tr.v.* **dis·trib·ut·ed, dis·trib·ut·ing, dis·trib·utes 1.** To give out in portions or shares; parcel out: *distributed the pizza to the kids at the table.* **2.** To supply or give out; deliver: *distribute magazines to local stores.* **3.** To spread, scatter, or divide into portions over an area: *The storm distributed snow over the region. The weight of the roof is distributed evenly along the walls.* **4.** To separate into categories; classify: *This census distributes the population into five income classes.* [From Middle English *distributen*, from Latin *distribuere* : *dis-*, apart, away + *tribuere*, to give.]

SYNONYMS distribute, dispense, deal, ration These verbs mean to give out in portions or shares. **Distribute** is the most general: *In the 1800s, the United States government distributed land to settlers.* **Dispense** often means to give carefully measured or weighed portions: *The pharmacist dispensed the medication carefully.* **Deal** means to distribute in a fair, orderly way: *Each guest was dealt a party hat.* **Ration** means to deal out scarce items: *Every household had to ration water during the drought.*
ANTONYM gather

---

dis·tri·bu·tion (dĭs′trə-byo͞o′shən) *n.* **1.** The act or process of distributing: *the distribution of gifts at the holidays.* **2.** The process of marketing and supplying goods, especially to retailers. **3.** The way in which something occurs or is distributed over an area: *the distribution of wolves in North America.* **4.** Something distributed; a portion: *My grandmother receives distributions from her retirement account.*

dis·trib·u·tive (dĭ-strĭb′yə-tĭv) *adj.* **1.** Relating to or involving distribution: *the distributive function of the blood stream.* **2.** In mathematics, relating to a property stating that the product of a factor and a sum is equal to the sum of the products. For example, $5 \times (6 + 7) = (5 \times 6) + (5 \times 7)$ and $a \times (b + c) = (a \times b) + (a \times c)$. **3.** In grammar, referring to each part or member of a group separately. *Each* and *every* are distributive words. **—dis·trib′u·tive·ly** *adv.*

dis·trib·u·tor (dĭ-strĭb′yə-tər) *n.* **1.** A person or thing that distributes, especially a device that applies electric current at the proper time to each spark plug in an engine. **2.** A person or company that markets or sells merchandise, especially a wholesaler.

dis·trict (dĭs′trĭkt) *n.* **1.** A part of an area marked out by law for a particular purpose: *our school district.* **2.** An area, especially one having a particular characteristic or function: *a shopping district.* ❖ *tr.v.* **dis·trict·ed, dis·trict·ing, dis·tricts** To mark off or divide into districts. [From Medieval Latin *districtus*, from Latin *distringere*, to hinder.]

district attorney *n.* The attorney who conducts the government's side of a case in a judicial district, especially the attorney who prosecutes people accused of a crime.

District of Columbia A federal district of the eastern United States on the Potomac River between Virginia and Maryland. It has the same boundaries as the city of Washington. It was established by congressional acts of 1790 and 1791 on a site chosen by George Washington.

dis·trust (dĭs-trŭst′) *n.* Lack of confidence or trust; suspicion. ❖ *tr.v.* **dis·trust·ed, dis·trust·ing, dis·trusts** To lack confidence or trust in; doubt; suspect: *I distrust commercials that sound too good.*

dis·trust·ful (dĭs-trŭst′fəl) *adj.* Feeling or showing doubt; suspicious. **—dis·trust′ful·ly** *adv.* **—dis·trust′ful·ness** *n.*

dis·turb (dĭ-stûrb′) *tr.v.* **dis·turbed, dis·turb·ing, dis·turbs 1.** To break up or destroy the peace, order, or

distortion
photograph of Tranquility Park, Houston, Texas, taken with a distorting lens

distress
distressed denim

settled state of: *a breeze that disturbed the papers on my desk.* **2.** To make uneasy or anxious; trouble; upset: *I was disturbed when I didn't know where you were.* **3.** To intrude upon; bother: *The visitors disturbed the musician's practice.* [From Middle English *disturben*, from Latin *disturbāre* : Latin *dis-*, apart + Latin *turbāre*, to agitate (from *turba*, confusion).]

dis·tur·bance (dĭ-stûr′bəns) *n.* **1.** The act of disturbing or the condition of being disturbed: *a disturbance in the cable signal.* **2.** Something that disturbs; an interruption or intrusion: *The coughing of a few was a disturbance to the rest of the audience.* **3.** A commotion or scuffle: *Angry fans created a disturbance at the game.*

dis·turbed (dĭ-stûrbd′) *adj.* Having or resulting from emotional problems or mental illness.

di·sul·fide (dī-sŭl′fīd′) *n.* A chemical group that has two sulfur atoms, or a compound in which two sulfur atoms combine with other elements or groups.

dis·un·ion (dĭs-yo͞on′yən) *n.* **1.** The condition of being divided or broken up into parts; separation. **2.** Lack of unity or agreement; discord.

dis·u·nite (dĭs′yo͞o-nīt′) *tr. & intr.v.* **dis·u·nit·ed, dis·u·nit·ing, dis·u·nites** To make or become separate or divided: *differences of opinion that disunited our club.*

dis·u·ni·ty (dĭs-yo͞o′nĭ-tē) *n., pl.* **dis·u·ni·ties** Lack of unity or agreement; discord; dissension.

dis·use (dĭs-yo͞os′) *n.* The condition of not being used or of being no longer in use.

ditch (dĭch) *n.* A long narrow trench dug in the ground. ❖ *tr.v.* **ditched, ditch·ing, ditch·es 1.** To dig or make ditches in or around: *ditch swampy land to drain it.* **2.** To drive (a vehicle) into a ditch. **3.** *Slang* **a.** To throw aside; get rid of: *Why not ditch that old bike and get a new one?* **b.** To get away from (a person in one's company). **c.** To skip (class or school). **4.** To bring (an aircraft) to a forced landing on water.

dith·er (dĭth′ər) *n.* A condition of nervous excitement or indecision: *in a dither about getting ready for the party.* ❖ *intr.v.* **dith·ered, dith·er·ing, dith·ers** To be nervously unable to make a decision or act on something.

dit·to (dĭt′ō) *n., pl.* **dit·tos 1.** The same as stated above or before. **2.** A duplicate or copy, especially a mimeograph. **3.** A pair of marks (") used to indicate that the word, phrase, or figure given directly above it is to be repeated.

dit·ty (dĭt′ē) *n., pl.* **dit·ties** A short simple song.

di·ur·nal (dī-ûr′nəl) *adj.* **1.** Occurring in a 24-hour period; daily: *The diurnal rise of the sun.* **2.** Most active during the daytime rather than at night: *diurnal birds of prey.* **—di·ur′nal·ly** *adv.*

di·va·lent (dī-vā′lənt) *adj.* In chemistry, having valence 2.

di·van (dĭ-văn′ *or* dī-văn′) *n.* A long couch, usually without a back or arms. [From Turkish, from Persian *dīvān*, place of assembly, roster.]

dive (dīv) *v.* **dived** or **dove** (dōv), **dived, div·ing, dives** *—intr.* **1.** To plunge into water, especially headfirst. **2.** To go toward the bottom of a body of water; submerge: *The submarine dived.* **3.** To swim underwater, especially using scuba gear. **4.** To descend rapidly at a steep angle: *The airplane turned and dived.* **5.** To drop sharply and rapidly; plummet: *Stock prices dived over 100 points yesterday.* **6.** To rush headlong and vanish into: *dive into the crowd.* **7.** To engage in something vigorously: *She dove into the project with great enthusiasm.* *—tr.* To cause to dive: *dive a plane.* ❖ *n.* **1.** A plunge into water, especially headfirst. **2.** A sharp downward descent or plunge, as of an airplane or submarine. **3.** A rapid or abrupt decrease: *Stock prices took a dive.* **4.** *Informal* A run-down bar or nightclub. [From Middle English *diven*, from Old English *dȳfan*, to dip, and *dūfan*, to sink.]

div·er (dī′vər) *n.* **1.** A person who dives into water: *a champion diver.* **2.** A person who swims underwater, especially using scuba gear. **3.** Any of several diving birds.

di·verge (dĭ-vûrj′ *or* dī-vûrj′) *intr.v.* **di·verged, di·verg·ing, di·verg·es 1.** To go or extend in different directions from a common point; branch out: *a small dirt road that diverged into two tracks.* **2.** To depart from a set course, standard, or norm; deviate: *Today's class diverged from the usual because we had a fire drill.* **3.** To be different, as in opinion or manner: *The twins diverged in their interests as they grew older.* [From Latin *dīvergere* : Latin *dī-, dis-*, apart, away + Latin *vergere*, to bend.]

di·ver·gence (dĭ-vûr′jəns *or* dī-vûr′jəns) *n.* **1.** The act or process of diverging: *Making a hologram begins with the divergence of a laser beam into two beams.* **2.** Departure from an established course, pattern, or standard: *divergence from the regular schedule.* **3.** Difference, as of opinion: *Divergence among members of the board prevented it from coming to a decision.*

di·ver·gent (dĭ-vûr′jənt *or* dī-vûr′jənt) *adj.* **1.** Moving or extending apart from a common point; diverging. **2.** Differing: *widely divergent views of the problem.* **—di·ver′gent·ly** *adv.*

di·verse (dĭ-vûrs′ *or* dī-vûrs′ *or* dī′vûrs′) *adj.* **1.** Distinct in kind; different or varying: *Members of the same family can have very diverse personalities.* **2.** Relating to or containing people from different ethnicities and social backgrounds: *a diverse student body.* [From Middle English *divers*, from Latin *dīversus*, past participle of *dīvertere*, to divert.] **—di·verse′ly** *adv.*

di·ver·si·fi·ca·tion (dĭ-vûr′sə-fĭ-kā′shən) *n.* The act of diversifying or the condition of being diversified: *Education usually leads to a diversification of interests.*

di·ver·si·fy (dĭ-vûr′sə-fī′ *or* dī-vûr′sə-fī′) *v.* **di·ver·si·fied, di·ver·si·fy·ing, di·ver·si·fies** *—tr.* **1.** To give diversity or variety to; make diverse: *After becoming successful as a portrait photographer, she diversified the kinds of pictures she took.* **2.** To add or produce (new or different products, for example) in different areas: *The cosmetics company diversified its product line by adding allergy treatments.* *—intr.* To become diversified, especially by making or dealing in different products: *The soap company diversified into producing a line of perfumes.*

di·ver·sion (dĭ-vûr′zhən *or* dī-vûr′zhən) *n.* **1.** The act of diverting: *the diversion of a stream for irrigation.* **2.** Something that relaxes or entertains; recreation: *Playing music has been a wonderful diversion for me.* **3.** Something that draws the attention to a different course, direction, or action: *We started yelling to create a diversion from the game.*

di·ver·si·ty (dĭ-vûr′sĭ-tē *or* dī-vûr′sĭ-tē) *n., pl.* **di·ver·si·ties 1.** The condition of being diverse; variety: *There was a considerable diversity of opinion about the new store.* **2.** The condition of having or including people from different ethnicities and social backgrounds: *diversity on campus.*

di·vert (dĭ-vûrt′ *or* dī-vûrt′) *v.* **di·vert·ed, di·vert·ing, di·verts** *—tr.* **1.** To turn aside from a course or direction; deflect: *divert traffic around a fallen tree on the road.* **2.** To draw (the mind or attention) to another direction: *A passing fire truck diverted our attention from the game.* **3.** To amuse or entertain: *divert little children by singing songs on a rainy afternoon.* *—intr.* To turn aside: *The pilot had to divert from the airport closed in by fog.* [From Middle English *diverten*, from Latin *dīvertere* : *dī-, dis-*, away, aside + *vertere*, to turn.] —SEE NOTE.

di·ver·ti·men·to (dĭ-vĕr′tə-mĕn′tō) *n., pl.* **di·ver·ti·men·tos** or **di·ver·ti·men·ti** (dĭ-vĕr′tə-mĕn′tē) A chamber music form, usually in several movements, commonly written during the 1700s.

di·vest (dĭ-vĕst′ *or* dī-vĕst′) *tr.v.* **di·vest·ed, di·vest·ing, di·vests 1.** To deprive, as of rights or property: *A person convicted of a felony is divested of the right to vote.* **2.** To free of, as by selling: *He divested himself of several prop-*

WORD BUILDING

divert The word root *vert–* in English words comes from the Latin verb *vertere*, "to turn." Thus **divert** is literally "to turn aside" (using the prefix *di–*, a form of *dis–*, "apart, aside"), and **revert** means "to turn back" (*re–*, "back"). The past participle of *vertere* was *versus*, from which we form the words **reverse**, "turned around or backwards"; **obverse**, "turned to the front" (*ob–*, "in front of, in the way of"); and **transverse**, "turned sideways" (*trans–*, "across").

Dorothea Dix

ă	pat	ôr	core
ā	pay	oi	boy
âr	care	ou	out
ä	father	o͝o	took
ĕ	pet	o͝or	lure
ē	be	o͞o	boot
ĭ	pit	ŭ	cut
ī	bite	ûr	urge
îr	pier	th	thin
ŏ	pot	*th*	this
ō	toe	zh	vision
ô	paw	ə	about

erties. **3.** To strip, as of clothes: *They divested themselves of their heavy winter coats before sitting down by the fire.*

di·vide (dĭ-vīd′) *v.* **di·vid·ed, di·vid·ing, di·vides** —*tr.* **1a.** To separate into parts, groups, or branches: *The teacher divided the class into four groups.* See Synonyms at **separate. b.** To form a border or barrier between: *A mountain chain divides France and Spain.* **c.** To separate and group according to kind; classify: *divide books into fiction and nonfiction.* **2.** To separate into opposing factions: *Different opinions divided Congress over the issue of air pollution.* **3.** To apportion or distribute among a number: *Volunteers divided the different jobs among themselves.* **4a.** To determine how many times (one number) contains another: *I divided 24 by 4 and got 6.* **b.** To be a divisor of: *3 divides 9 evenly.* **c.** To use (a number) as a divisor: *divide 5 into 35.* —*intr.* **1.** To become separated into parts, groups, or factions: *The country divided on the issue of how to improve the economy.* **2.** To perform the mathematical operation of division. ❖ *n.* A dividing point or line: *hills that form a divide between rivers flowing eastward and westward.* [From Middle English *dividen,* from Latin *dīvidere* : *dī-, dis-,* apart + *-videre,* to separate.]

div·i·dend (dĭv′ĭ-dĕnd′) *n.* **1.** A number or quantity that is to be divided. **2.** A share of profits paid to a stockholder of a company. **3.** A benefit or advantage: *Cleaning up our environment will provide dividends for us all.*

di·vid·er (dĭ-vī′dər) *n.* **1.** A person or thing that divides, especially a screen or other partition: *a room divider.* **2.** A device that is like a compass, used for dividing lines and transferring measurements.

div·i·na·tion (dĭv′ə-nā′shən) *n.* **1.** The art of foretelling the future by interpreting omens or using magic powers. **2.** Something that has been predicted by this art: *There have been numerous divinations about the end of the world.* **3.** A clever guess.

di·vine (dĭ-vīn′) *adj.* **di·vin·er, di·vin·est 1.** Relating to God or a god: *divine wisdom.* **2.** Coming from or given by God or a god: *divine guidance.* **3.** Directed to God or a god; sacred: *divine worship.* ❖ *n.* **1.** A cleric. **2.** A person learned in theology. ❖ *tr.v.* **di·vined, di·vin·ing, di·vines 1.** To foretell or prophesy by divination: *Ancient seers divined disasters from the flights of birds.* **2.** To guess: *The mechanic divined my car's problem after looking at the tires.* [From Middle English, from Latin *dīvīnus,* from *dīvus,* god.] **—di·vine′ly** *adv.* **—di·vine′ness** *n.* **—di·vin′er** *n.*

div·ing bell (dī′vĭng) *n.* A large chamber for people working underwater that is raised and lowered by a cable and supplied with air under pressure to keep water from coming in its open bottom.

diving board *n.* A flexible board from which a person can dive, secured at one end and sticking out over the water at the other.

di·vin·ing rod (dĭ-vī′nĭng) *n.* A forked stick held in the hand and believed to indicate the presence of underground water or minerals by bending downward when over a source.

di·vin·i·ty (dĭ-vĭn′ĭ-tē) *n., pl.* **di·vin·i·ties 1.** The quality or condition of being divine. **2. Divinity a.** God. **b.** A god or goddess. **3.** The study of God and religion; theology: *Ministers study at a school of divinity.*

di·vis·i·ble (dĭ-vĭz′ə-bəl) *adj.* Capable of being divided, especially with no remainder. **—di·vis′i·bil′i·ty** *n.* **—di·vis′i·bly** *adv.*

di·vi·sion (dĭ-vĭzh′ən) *n.* **1.** The act of dividing or the condition of being divided; separation into parts: *the division of a book into chapters.* **2.** The operation of dividing one number or quantity by another; the process of finding out how many times one number or quantity is contained in the other. **3.** One of the parts or groups into which something is divided: *a division in a company.* **4.** Something, such as a partition or boundary, that divides or keeps separate. **5.** Disagreement; disunity: *The meeting was marked by deep division among delegates from different sections of the country.* **6.** An army unit that is smaller than a corps and is composed of several regiments. **7.** The highest taxonomic category within the plant kingdom, made up of one or more related classes and roughly corresponding to a phylum in animal classification. See table at **taxonomy.**

division sign *n.* The symbol (÷) placed between two quantities to indicate that the first is to be divided by the second, as in 12 ÷ 6 = 2.

di·vi·sive (dĭ-vī′sĭv) *adj.* Creating or tending to create disagreement or disunity: *a divisive political issue.* **—di·vi′sive·ly** *adv.* **—di·vi′sive·ness** *n.*

di·vi·sor (dĭ-vī′zər) *n.* The number or quantity by which another is to be divided.

di·vorce (dĭ-vôrs′) *n.* **1.** The legal ending of a marriage. **2.** A complete separation: *His view of the economy is noteworthy chiefly for its divorce from reality.* ❖ *v.* **di·vorced, di·vorc·ing, di·vorc·es** —*tr.* **1.** To end the marriage of (people): *The judge divorced husband and wife.* **2.** To end marriage with (one's spouse) by legal divorce: *She divorced her husband.* **3.** To separate or remove: *We cannot divorce a good diet from fitness.* —*intr.* To obtain a divorce. [From Middle English, from Latin *dīvertere, dīvortere,* to divert.]

di·vor·cé (dĭ-vôr-sā′) *n.* A man who is divorced.

di·vor·cée (dĭ-vôr-sā′) *n.* A woman who is divorced.

div·ot (dĭv′ət) *n.* A piece of turf torn up, especially by a golf club when hitting the ball.

di·vulge (dĭ-vŭlj′) *tr.v.* **di·vulged, di·vulg·ing, di·vulg·es** To make known; reveal; tell: *divulge a secret.* **—di·vulg′er** *n.*

div·vy (dĭv′ē) *tr.v.* **div·vied, div·vy·ing, div·vies** To divide; share: *We divvied up the pizza so that each of us got a piece.*

Dix (dĭks), **Dorothea Lynde** 1802–1887. American reformer who was a pioneer in the movement for specialized treatment of the mentally ill.

Dix·ie (dĭk′se) The southeast region of the United States, consisting of the states that joined the Confederacy during the Civil War.

Dix·ie·land (dĭk′sē-lănd′) *n.* A style of jazz developed in New Orleans in the early 1900s, usually involving improvised passages by multiple musicians.

DIY *abbr.* An abbreviation of do-it-yourself.

diz·zy (dĭz′ē) *adj.* **diz·zi·er, diz·zi·est 1.** Having a sensation of whirling or feeling a tendency to fall; giddy: *A ride on the roller coaster made me feel dizzy.* **2.** Producing or tending to produce giddiness: *a dizzy height.* **3.** Bewildered or confused: *dizzy with excitement.* ❖ *tr.v.* **diz·zied, diz·zy·ing, diz·zies** To make dizzy: *So many facts and figures dizzied my brain.* [From Old English *dysig,* foolish.] **—diz′zi·ly** *adv.* **—diz′zi·ness** *n.*

DJ *abbr.* An abbreviation of disc jockey.

Dja·kar·ta (jə-kär′tə) See **Jakarta.**

Dji·bou·ti (jĭ-bo͞o′tē) **1.** A country of eastern Africa northwest of Somalia. The city of Djibouti is the capital. **2.** The capital of Djibouti, in the southeast part of the country northeast of Addis Ababa, Ethiopia.

DMZ *abbr.* An abbreviation of demilitarized zone.

DNA (dē′ĕn-ā′) *n.* An acid found in all living cells and certain viruses, having a structure resembling a ladder that is twisted into a spiral and forming the main part of chromosomes. DNA contains genes that determine or influence many of an organism's traits and that are passed on to the organism's offspring. [From *d(eoxyribo)-n(ucleic) a(cid).*] —SEE NOTE.

DNA fingerprinting *n.* DNA profiling.

DNA profiling *n.* The determination of the structure

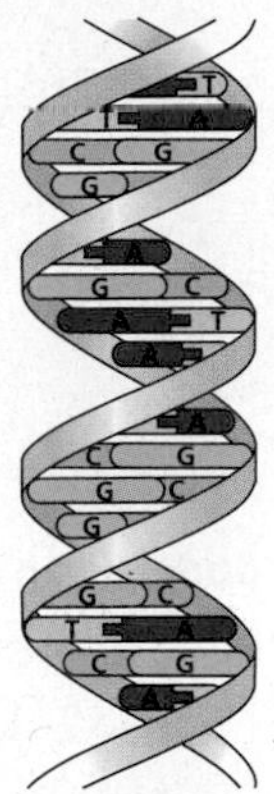

DNA
double-helix DNA model
A. adenine
T. thymine
C. cytosine
G. guanine

SCIENCE

DNA One of the wonders of nature is that the complexity and diversity of life can be contained in a relatively simple molecule with a rather long name—*deoxyribonucleic acid,* commonly called **DNA.** DNA exists in the nucleus of all cells in many-celled organisms. It consists of two long strands linked together in a structure that resembles a ladder twisted into a spiral. This configuration is called a *double helix.* Each rung of the ladder is made up of two different chemical bases that are bonded together. Along the strands, specific sequences of these bases—known as *genes*—form codes that contain all of an organism's genetic information. When other components of a cell "read" this code, they produce proteins, the building blocks of life.

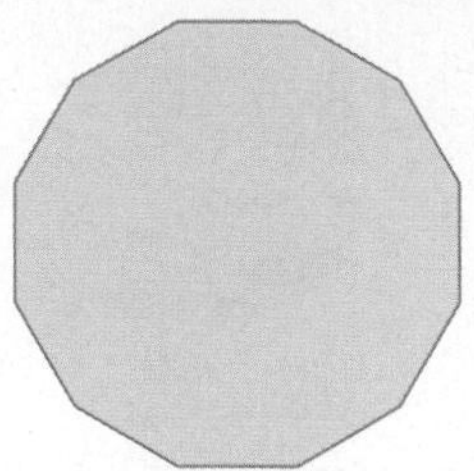
dodecagon

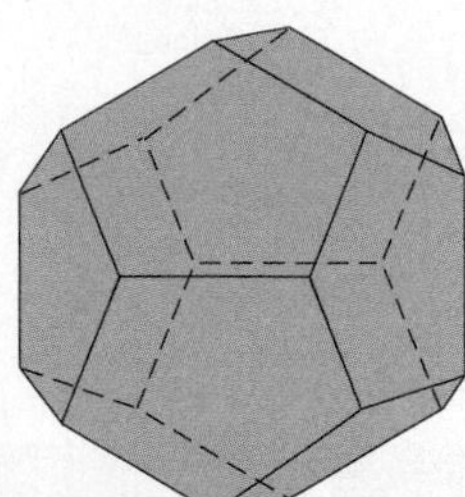
dodecahedron

ă	pat	ôr	core
ā	pay	oi	boy
âr	care	ou	out
ä	father	o͝o	took
ĕ	pet	o͝or	lure
ē	be	o͞o	boot
ĭ	pit	ŭ	cut
ī	bite	ûr	urge
îr	pier	th	thin
ŏ	pot	*th*	this
ō	toe	zh	vision
ô	paw	ə	about

of certain regions of a DNA molecule. DNA profiling can be used to help identify individuals, as by analyzing DNA-containing evidence (such as hair) left at a crime scene.

DNA virus *n.* Any of a group of viruses whose genetic material is composed of DNA, including the viruses that cause chickenpox and herpes.

DNR *abbr.* An abbreviation of: **1.** Department of Natural Resources. **2.** do not resuscitate

do[1] (do͞o) *v.* **did** (dĭd), **done** (dŭn), **do·ing, does** (dŭz) —*tr.* **1.** To perform, carry out, or accomplish: *Do a good job. Do your duty.* **2a.** To create, produce, or make: *do a painting; do a website.* **b.** To create or produce for an audience: *The actors did a new play.* **3.** To bring about; effect: *Crying won't do any good.* **4.** To put into action; exert: *I'll do everything in my power to help you.* **5.** To put into order or take care of: *do one's hair; do the dishes.* **6.** To render or give: *do a favor.* **7.** To work at for a living: *I do house painting in the summer.* **8.** To work out the details of (a problem); solve: *I did this equation.* **9.** Used as a substitute for a preceding verb or verb phrase: *I know it, and she does too.* **10a.** To travel (a specified distance): *do a mile in 7 minutes.* **b.** To travel at a speed of: *He was only doing 50 on the highway.* **11.** To be sufficient or convenient for; suffice: *This room will do us very nicely.* **12.** *Informal* To serve (a prison term): *Both did time for theft.* —*intr.* **1.** To behave or conduct oneself; act: *You did well on the test.* **2.** To get along; manage; get on: *The new student is doing well.* **3.** To serve a purpose: *That old coat will do for now.* **4.** Used instead of a preceding verb: *She reads as much as I do.* —*aux.* **1.** Used to ask questions: *Do you want to go? Did you understand?* **2.** Used to make negative statements: *I did not sleep at all. We do not understand.* **3.** Used to form inverted phrases: *little did I suspect.* **4.** Used to emphasize or make stronger: *We do want to go. I do want to be sure.* ❖ *n., pl.* **dos** or **do's** A statement of what should be done: *a long list of dos and don'ts.* ◆ **do away with 1.** To get rid of; dispose of: *doing away with outmoded laws.* **2.** To kill or destroy: *do away with rats and other vermin.* **do in 1.** *Slang* To exhaust: *That hike really did me in.* **2.** To kill: *Nobody really knows who did him in.* **do over** *Informal* To redecorate: *Professionals are doing over the room.* **do up 1.** To dress lavishly: *all done up for the party.* **2.** To wrap and tie (a package). **do without** To manage despite the absence of (something): *We can do without that kind of help.* [From Old English *dōn.*]

❑ *These sound alike:* **do**[1] (perform), **dew** (water droplets), **due** (owed).

do[2] (dō) *n.* In music, the first tone of a major scale. [From Italian.]

❑ *These sound alike:* **do**[2] (musical tone), **doe** (deer), **dough** (flour mixture).

DOA *abbr.* An abbreviation of dead on arrival.

DOB *abbr.* An abbreviation of date of birth.

dob·bin (dŏb′ĭn) *n.* A horse, especially an old or plodding workhorse.

Do·ber·man pin·scher (dō′bər-mən pĭn′shər) *n.* A large dog of a breed originally developed in Germany, having a short, smooth, usually black coat. [After Ludwig *Dobermann,* German dog breeder of the 1800s + German *Pinscher,* terrier.]

do·bra (dō′brə) *n.* The basic monetary unit of São Tomé and Príncipe.

doc (dŏk) *n. Informal* A doctor.

❑ *These sound alike:* **doc, dock**[1] (platform), **dock**[2] (clip), **dock**[3] (place in court), **dock**[4] (sorrel).

doc·ile (dŏs′əl *or* dŏs′īl′) *adj.* Easy to train or handle; tractable; submissive: *a docile horse with a good disposition.* —**doc′ile·ly** *adv.* —**do·cil′i·ty** (dŏ-sĭl′ĭ-tē *or* dō-sĭl′ĭ-tē) *n.*

dock[1] (dŏk) *n.* **1a.** A structure extending from a shore over water and supported by piles or pillars, used for loading and unloading ships. **b.** A loading platform for loading and unloading trucks or trains. **2.** often **docks** A group of piers that serve as the landing area of a harbor: *We went down to the docks to look at the ships.* **3.** The area of water between or alongside piers for ships. ❖ *v.* **docked, dock·ing, docks** —*tr.* **1.** To maneuver or come into a dock: *dock a big liner.* **2.** To join together (two or more spacecraft) while in space. —*intr.* To come into dock: *The ferry docked in the evening.* [From Early Modern English *dok,* from Middle Dutch *doc.*]

❑ *These sound alike:* **dock**[1] (platform), **doc** (doctor), **dock**[2] (clip), **dock**[3] (place in court), **dock**[4] (sorrel).

dock[2] (dŏk) *tr.v.* **docked, dock·ing, docks 1.** To clip or cut off (an animal's tail, for example). **2a.** To withhold a part of (a salary): *The restaurant docked the waiter's pay to make up for broken dishes.* **b.** To penalize (a worker) by such deduction: *Printers are docked if they make too many mistakes.* [From Middle English *dokken.*]

❑ *These sound alike:* **dock**[2] (clip), **doc** (doctor), **dock**[1] (platform), **dock**[3] (place in court), **dock**[4] (sorrel).

dock[3] (dŏk) *n.* An enclosed place where the defendant stands or sits in a criminal court. [From obsolete Flemish *docke,* cage.]

❑ *These sound alike:* **dock**[3] (place in court), **doc** (doctor), **dock**[1] (platform), **dock**[2] (clip), **dock**[4] (sorrel).

dock[4] (dŏk) *n.* Sorrel. [From Old English *docce.*]

❑ *These sound alike:* **dock**[4] (sorrel), **doc** (doctor), **dock**[1] (platform), **dock**[2] (clip), **dock**[3] (place in court).

dock·et (dŏk′ĭt) *n.* **1.** A calendar or list of cases awaiting court action. **2.** A list of things to be done; an agenda: *several jobs on the docket for today.* **3.** A label or ticket attached to a package and listing its contents. ❖ *tr.v.* **dock·et·ed, dock·et·ing, dock·ets 1.** To enter in a docket; schedule. **2.** To label or ticket (a parcel).

dock·yard (dŏk′yärd′) *n.* A shipyard.

doc·tor (dŏk′tər) *n.* **1.** A person who is trained and licensed to diagnose, treat, and prevent disorders and diseases. **2.** A person who holds the highest degree given by a college or university. ❖ *tr.v.* **doc·tored, doc·tor·ing, doc·tors 1.** *Informal* To give medical treatment to. **2.** To tamper with or falsify: *doctor the results of an experiment.* [From Middle English *doctour,* an expert, authority, from Latin *doctor,* teacher, from *docēre,* to teach.]

doc·tor·al (dŏk′tər-əl) *adj.* Relating to a doctor or doctorate: *a doctoral dissertation.*

doc·tor·ate (dŏk′tər-ĭt) *n.* The degree or status of a doctor as awarded by a university: *a doctorate in Russian literature.*

doc·tri·naire (dŏk′trə-nâr′) *adj.* Characterized by rigid adherence to a theory or belief without considering whether it is practical or applicable: *a doctrinaire approach to a problem.*

doc·trine (dŏk′trĭn) *n.* **1.** A principle or set of principles held and put forward by a religious or philosophical group; dogma. **2.** A statement of government policy, especially in foreign affairs. —**doc′tri·nal** *adj.*

doc·u·ment (dŏk′yə-mənt) *n.* **1.** A written or printed paper that can be used to give evidence or information: *A birth certificate is usually one's first document.* **2.** A piece of work created with a word processor or other computer application. ❖ *tr.v.* (dŏk′yə-mĕnt′) **doc·u·ment·ed, doc·u·ment·ing, doc·u·ments** To prove or support with evidence: *document a report with photographs and letters.*

doc·u·men·ta·ry (dŏk′yə-mĕn′tə-rē) *adj.* **1.** Consisting of, relating to, or based on documents: *documentary evidence.* **2.** Presenting the facts of real events without adding fictional material, as in a movie. ❖ *n., pl.* **doc·u·men·ta·ries** A movie giving a factual account of some subject and often showing actual events.

doc·u·men·ta·tion (dŏk′yə-mĕn-tā′shən) *n.* **1.** The act of supplying documents or supporting references: *Documentation of the scandal took many months to complete.* **2.** The documents or references provided: *Documentation for the trial was stored in several large boxes.*

dod·der (dŏd′ər) *intr.v.* **dod·dered, dod·der·ing, dod·ders** To tremble or move shakily, as from old age; totter. **—dod′der·ing** *adj.*

do·dec·a·gon (dō-**dĕk′**ə-gŏn′) *n.* A polygon with 12 sides and 12 angles. **—do′dec·ag′o·nal** (dō′dĕ-**kăg′**ə-nəl) *adj.*

do·dec·a·he·dron (dō′dĕk-ə-**hē′**drən) *n., pl.* **do·dec·a·he·drons** or **do·dec·a·he·dra** (dō′dĕk-ə-**hē′**drə) A solid geometric figure having 12 faces.

dodge (dŏj) *v.* **dodged, dodg·ing, dodg·es** *—tr.* **1.** To avoid by moving quickly aside or out of the way: *The dog dodged the cars as it ran across the street.* **2.** To evade by cunning, trickery, or other means: *The candidate dodged the reporter's questions.* *—intr.* To move by jumping aside suddenly: *The boy dodged through the crowd.* ❖ *n.* **1.** The act of dodging. **2.** A trick to cheat or avoid: *the dodges of a spy.*

Dodg·son (dŏj′sən), **Charles Lutwidge** Pen name Lewis Carroll. 1832–1898. British writer whose stories about Alice appear in *Alice's Adventures in Wonderland* (1865) and *Through the Looking-Glass* (1872).

do·do (dō′dō) *n., pl.* **do·does** or **do·dos 1.** A large flightless bird that formerly lived on the island of Mauritius in the Indian Ocean but became extinct in the late 1600s. It had a hooked beak and very short wings. **2.** *Informal* A stupid person; an idiot.

Do·do·ma (dō′də-mä′) The capital of Tanzania, in the central part of the country.

doe (dō) *n., pl.* **doe** or **does 1.** A female deer. **2.** The female of various other mammals, such as a kangaroo, mouse, or rabbit. [From Old English *dā*.]

❑ *These sound alike:* **doe, do**[2] (musical tone), **dough** (flour mixture).

do·er (dōō′ər) *n.* A person who does something, especially an active and energetic person: *She is a doer and does not hesitate to act.*

does (dŭz) *v.* Third person singular present tense of **do**[1].

doe·skin (dō′skĭn′) *n.* **1.** The skin of a female deer or of a sheep or lamb. **2.** Soft leather made from such skin, used especially for gloves. **3.** A soft smooth woolen fabric with a nap on it.

does·n't (dŭz′ənt) Contraction of *does not.*

doff (dôf) *tr.v.* **doffed, doff·ing, doffs** To take off; remove: *They doffed their hats in salute to the passing flag.* [From Middle English *doffen*, from *don off*, to do off.]

dog (dôg) *n.* **1.** A domesticated mammal that is related to wolves and is kept as a pet or trained to hunt, herd, or guard. There are many different breeds of dog. **2.** The male of this animal or of a related animal, such as a coyote. **3.** *Informal* **a.** A person regarded as undeserving or contemptible: *I'll never listen to that lying dog again.* **b.** Something considered inferior or of low quality, such as an investment that doesn't return a profit. **4.** *Informal* A hot dog. ❖ *tr.v.* **dogged, dog·ging, dogs** To trail persistently: *The detective dogged the suspect's every move.*

dog·cart (dôg′kärt′) *n.* **1.** A vehicle drawn by one horse and accommodating two people seated back to back. **2.** A small cart pulled by dogs.

dog·catch·er (dôg′kăch′ər) *n.* A person hired to catch stray dogs.

dog days *pl.n.* The hot sultry period between mid-July and early September. [So called from the fact that the Dog Star (Sirius) rises and sets with the sun during this time.]

doge (dōj) *n.* The elected chief magistrate of the former republics of Venice and Genoa.

dog-ear (dôg′îr′) *n.* A turned-down corner of a page in a book. ❖ *tr.v.* **dog-eared, dog-ear·ing, dog-ears** To turn down the corner of (a page in a book). **—dog′-eared′** *adj.*

dog·fight (dôg′fīt′) *n.* **1.** A violent fight between or as if between dogs. **2.** A battle between fighter planes.

dog·fish (dôg′fĭsh′) *n.* Any of various small sharks having two spiny dorsal fins and often found in large schools.

dog·ged (dô′gĭd) *adj.* Not giving up easily; persevering; stubborn: *The doctor's dogged efforts succeeded in discovering a cure for the disease.* **—dog′ged·ly** *adv.* **—dog′ged·ness** *n.*

dog·ger·el (dô′gər-əl) *n.* Simple, trite, or poorly written verse, often having an irregular rhythm.

dog·gy or **dog·gie** (dô′gē) *n., pl.* **dog·gies** A dog, especially a small or a young dog.

doggy bag *n.* A bag for leftover food taken home from a restaurant.

dog·house (dôg′hous′) *n.* A small house or shelter for a dog. ◆ **in the doghouse** *Slang* In disfavor; in trouble: *You'll be in the doghouse for forgetting his birthday.*

dog·ma (dôg′mə) *n., pl.* **dog·mas 1.** A doctrine or system of doctrines that form the basis of a religion. **2.** A belief, opinion, or idea considered to be true: *Political dogmas of the past often seem barbaric today.*

dog·mat·ic (dôg-**măt′**ĭk) *adj.* **1.** Relating to dogma; doctrinal: *a dogmatic idea.* **2.** Asserting or insisting that certain ideas or opinions are true, especially in an overbearing or arrogant way: *a dogmatic person.* **—dog·mat′i·cal·ly** *adv.*

dog·ma·tism (dôg′mə-tĭz′əm) *n.* The tendency to assert that one's opinions or beliefs are true in an overbearing or arrogant way.

do-good·er (dōō′gŏŏd′ər) *n.* *Informal* A person who is eager to make reforms and help people.

dog paddle *n.* A swimming stroke in which a person lies chest down while keeping the head out of the water. The arms remain under the water, and the swimmer pushes them forward and then pulls them back while kicking the legs.

dog·sled (dôg′slĕd′) *n.* A sled pulled by one or more dogs.

Dog Star *n.* Sirius.

dog-tired (dôg′tīrd′) *adj.* Extremely tired: *was dog-tired after swimming practice.*

dog·tooth violet (dôg′tōōth′) *n.* Any of several North American plants having leaves with reddish blotches and nodding, solitary flowers.

dog·trot (dôg′trŏt′) *n.* A steady trot like that of a dog.

dog·watch (dôg′wŏch′) *n.* Either of two periods of watch aboard a ship, from 4 to 6 PM or from 6 to 8 PM.

dog·wood (dôg′wŏŏd′) *n.* A tree having small greenish flowers that are surrounded by showy white or pink bracts resembling petals.

Do·ha (dō′hə) The capital of Qatar, on the Persian Gulf.

doi·ly (doi′lē) *n., pl.* **doi·lies** A small fancy mat, usually of lace, linen, or paper and often used to protect or decorate a table top. [After *Doily* or *Doyly*, London draper of the 1700s.]

do·ings (dōō′ĭngz) *pl.n.* Activities, especially social activities: *doings at the club.*

do-it-your·self (dōō′ĭt-yər-**sĕlf′**) *adj.* Relating to or designed to be done or assembled by an amateur or as a hobby: *do-it-yourself home repairs.*

dol·drums (dōl′drəmz′ *or* dŏl′drəmz′) *pl.n.* *(used with a singular or plural verb)* **1.** A period or condition of depression or inactivity: *in the doldrums over some bad luck.* **2.** A region of the ocean near the equator where there is little or no wind: *Several sailing ships were delayed by being caught in the doldrums.* [From Middle English *dold*, past participle of *dullen*, to dull.]

dodo

dogwood

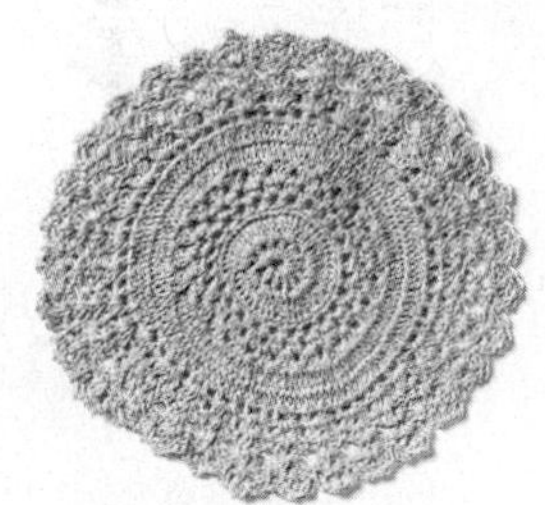
doily

WRITERS CHOOSE THEIR WORDS

Charles turned sadly away. Well, it had been good while it lasted. "What's the matter?" Nirupam asked, catching sight of Charles's **doleful** face as he stood his desk on its legs again. "Nothing," Charles said. "I— I've got detention."

—Diana Wynne Jones *Witch Week*

dolmen

dolphin

ă	pat	ôr	core
ā	pay	oi	boy
âr	care	ou	out
ä	father	o͝o	took
ĕ	pet	o͝or	lure
ē	be	o͞o	boot
ĭ	pit	ŭ	cut
ī	bite	ûr	urge
îr	pier	th	thin
ŏ	pot	*th*	this
ō	toe	zh	vision
ô	paw	ə	about

dole (dōl) *n.* **1.** The distribution by the government of relief payments to people who are unemployed. **2.** A share of money, food, or clothing distributed as charity. ❖ *tr.v.* **doled, dol·ing, doles** To give out, especially in portions or shares; allot or distribute: *The judges of the contest doled out prize money to the winning contestants.* [From Old English *dāl.*]

dole·ful (**dōl′**fəl) *adj.* Filled with or expressing grief; mournful: *the cat's doleful cry in the rain.* [From Middle English *dolful,* from *dol,* grief, from Latin *dolēre,* to suffer.] —**dole′ful·ly** *adv.*

doll (dŏl) *n.* **1.** A child's usually small toy having the likeness of a human. **2.** *Slang* A sweetheart or darling. ◆ **doll up** To dress up elegantly, as for a special occasion: *The guests were dolled up for the party.*

dol·lar (**dŏl′**ər) *n.* The basic monetary unit in the United States and many other countries, including Australia, Canada, Fiji, New Zealand, Taiwan, and Zimbabwe.

dol·lop (**dŏl′**əp) *n.* A lump or mass of something: *a dollop of ice cream.*

dol·ly (**dŏl′**ē) *n., pl.* **dol·lies 1.** *Informal* A child's doll. **2.** A low mobile platform that rolls on small wheels, used for moving heavy loads.

dol·men (**dōl′**mən *or* **dŏl′**mən) *n.* A Neolithic tomb consisting of two or more upright stones with a capstone, believed to have been buried in earth except for a central opening.

dol·o·mite (**dō′**lə-mīt′ *or* **dŏl′**ə-mīt′) *n.* **1.** A white or light-colored mineral consisting mainly of a carbonate of calcium and magnesium. **2.** A rock containing dolomite and resembling limestone, used as a building stone. [After Déodat de *Dolomieu* (1750–1801), French geologist.]

do·lor (**dō′**lər) *n.* Sorrow; grief.

do·lor·ous (**dō′**lər-əs *or* **dŏl′**ər-əs) *adj.* Marked by or showing sorrow, grief, or pain. —**do′lor·ous·ly** *adv.*

dol·phin (**dŏl′**fĭn) *n.* **1.** Any of various marine mammals related to the whales but smaller and having a snout shaped like a beak. Dolphins are noted for their remarkable intelligence. **2.** Either of two edible marine fishes of warm waters, having iridescent coloring when removed from the water.

dolt (dōlt) *n.* A stupid person.

-dom *suff.* A suffix that means: **1.** Condition; state: *stardom.* **2.** Position; rank: *dukedom.*

do·main (dō-**mān′**) *n.* **1.** A territory or range of rule or control; a realm: *the duke's domain.* **2.** A sphere of knowledge or activity; a field: *Ethics is in the domain of philosophy.* **3.** In mathematics, the set of all values that an independent variable can have. **4.** A division of organisms that ranks above a kingdom in systems of classification that are based on similarities in DNA sequences. The three domains are the archaea, the bacteria, and the eukaryotes. See table at **taxonomy. 5.** A group of networked computers whose users have email addresses that are the same to the right of the at sign, such as *hmhpub.com* in the address *host@hmhpub.com.* [From Middle English *demeine, domein,* from Latin *dominium,* property, from *dominus,* lord.]

domain name *n.* A series of letters or numbers separated by periods, such as *www.hmhpub.com,* that is the address of a computer network connection and identifies the owner of the address.

dome (dōm) *n.* **1.** A rounded roof or vault built in the shape of a hemisphere. **2.** A structure or other object resembling such a roof or vault: *the dome of the sky.* ❖ *tr.v.* **domed, dom·ing, domes 1.** To cover with a roof or vault in the shape of a hemisphere. **2.** To shape like such a roof or vault.

do·mes·tic (də-**mĕs′**tĭk) *adj.* **1.** Relating to the family or household: *domestic chores.* **2.** Enjoying or interested in home life and household affairs: *They are very domestic and don't go out much.* **3.** Tame or domesticated. Used of animals: *cats and other domestic animals.* **4.** Relating to a country's internal affairs: *The president has been focusing more on domestic than on international issues.* **5.** Produced in, occurring in, or native to a particular country: *domestic cars; domestic flights.* ❖ *n.* A household servant. —**do·mes′ti·cal·ly** *adv.*

do·mes·ti·cate (də-**mĕs′**tĭ-kāt′) *tr.v.* **do·mes·ti·cat·ed, do·mes·ti·cat·ing, do·mes·ti·cates** To train or adapt (an animal or plant) to live with or to be useful to humans: *Humans domesticated cattle long ago.* —**do·mes′ti·ca′tion** *n.*

do·mes·tic·i·ty (dō′mĕ-**stĭs′**ĭ-tē) *n., pl.* **do·mes·tic·i·ties 1.** The quality or condition of being domestic. **2.** Home life or devotion to it: *the intimate domesticity of a small family.* **3. domesticities** The affairs of a household.

dom·i·cile (**dŏm′**ĭ-sīl′ *or* **dō′**mĭ-sīl′) *n.* **1.** A residence; a home. **2.** A person's legal residence. ❖ *tr.v.* **dom·i·ciled, dom·i·cil·ing, dom·i·ciles** To establish (oneself or another person) in a residence.

dom·i·nance (**dŏm′**ə-nəns) *n.* The condition or fact of being dominant.

dom·i·nant (**dŏm′**ə-nənt) *adj.* **1.** Having the most influence or control: *the dominant dog in a pack.* **2.** Most prominent, as in position: *The tallest buildings are dominant in a city's skyline.* **3.** Relating to a gene that produces its characteristic effect if it is present on either or both of a pair of chromosomes. **4.** Relating to the fifth tone of a musical scale. For example, in the key of C major, a G major chord is said to be dominant. ❖ *n.* **1.** The fifth tone of a musical scale, or a chord based on this tone. **2.** A dominant gene. —**dom′i·nant·ly** *adv.*

dom·i·nate (**dŏm′**ə-nāt′) *v.* **dom·i·nat·ed, dom·i·nat·ing, dom·i·nates** —*tr.* **1.** To rule, control, or govern by superior power or authority: *Great Britain dominated about one-fourth of the world in the 1800s.* **2.** To occupy a commanding controlling position in or over: *The mountain dominates the countryside for miles around.* —*intr.* **1.** To have or exert strong authority or influence. **2.** To have the most prominent or superior position: *Tall people dominate in a crowd.*

dom·i·na·tion (dŏm′ə-**nā′**shən) *n.* Control or power over another or others: *British domination of its colonies.*

dom·i·neer (dŏm′ə-**nîr′**) *intr. & tr.v.* **dom·i·neered, dom·i·neer·ing, dom·i·neers** To rule over or control arbitrarily or arrogantly; tyrannize.

dom·i·neer·ing (dŏm′ə-**nîr′**ĭng) *adj.* Tending to domineer; overbearing: *His domineering manner offended many people.* —**dom′i·neer′ing·ly** *adv.*

Dom·i·ni·ca (dŏm′ə-**nē′**kə *or* də-**mĭn′**ĭ-kə) An island country of the eastern Caribbean between Guadeloupe and Martinique. Roseau is the capital. —**Dom′i·ni′can** *adj. & n.*

Do·min·i·can[1] (də-**mĭn′**ĭ-kən) *adj.* Relating to the Dominican Republic or its people or culture. ❖ *n.* A native or inhabitant of the Dominican Republic.

Do·min·i·can[2] (də-**mĭn′**ĭ-kən) *n.* A member of a Roman Catholic order of preaching friars established in 1216 by Saint Dominic (1170?–1221).

Dominican Republic A country of the West Indies on the eastern part of the island of Hispaniola. Santo Domingo is the capital.

do·min·ion (də-**mĭn′**yən) *n.* **1.** Control or exercise of control; sovereignty. **2.** A territory or sphere of influence or control; a realm: *The dominion of the British monarchy once included part of France.* **3. Dominion** One of the self-governing nations under the nominal rule of the British Commonwealth.

dom·i·no[1] (**dŏm′**ə-nō′) *n., pl.* **dom·i·noes** or **dom·i·nos 1.** A small rectangular block, the face of which is divided into halves. Each half is blank or marked by dots resembling those on dice. **2. dominoes** *(used with a singular or plural verb)* A game played with a set of these small blocks. [Probably from *domino*, mask, perhaps because of the resemblance between the eyeholes and the spots on some of the tiles.]

dom·i·no² (dŏm′ə-nō′) *n., pl.* **dom·i·noes** or **dom·i·nos** **1.** A masquerade costume made up of a hooded robe worn with an eye mask. **2.** The mask so worn. [Probably from Latin *(benedīcāmus) dominō*, (let us praise) the Lord.]

domino theory *n.* A theory that one event will set off a chain of similar events.

don¹ (dŏn) *n.* **1. Don** *(also* dōn) Used as a courtesy title before the name of a man in a Spanish-speaking area. **2.** *Chiefly British* A college or university professor. [From Latin *dominus*, lord.]

don² (dŏn) *tr.v.* **donned, don·ning, dons** To put on (clothing): *don a coat.* [From Middle English, contraction of *do on*, to put on.]

Do·ña (dō′nyä) *n.* Used as a courtesy title before the name of a woman in a Spanish-speaking area.

do·nate (dō′nāt′ *or* dō-**nāt′**) *tr.v.* **do·nat·ed, do·nat·ing, do·nates 1.** To present as a gift to a fund or cause; contribute: *donate clothing to the Red Cross.* **2.** To provide (a body organ or other tissue) for transplant. **3.** To provide (an electron, for example) for combination with an ion, atom, or molecule.

do·na·tion (dō-**nā′**shən) *n.* **1.** The act of giving to a fund or cause. **2.** Something that is donated: *made a small donation to charity; made a blood donation.*

done (dŭn) *v.* Past participle of **do¹**. ❖ *adj.* **1.** Having been completely accomplished or finished: *a done deed.* **2.** Cooked adequately: *Is the fish done?* **3.** Socially acceptable: *Eating with the fingers is not done in certain cultures.* ◆ **done for** Doomed to death or destruction. **done in** Worn out; exhausted: *After the long hike, we were all done in.*

❑ *These sound alike:* **done, dun¹** (ask for payment), **dun²** (grayish-brown).

dong (dông) *n.* The basic monetary unit of Vietnam.

don·jon (dŏn′jən *or* dŭn′jən) *n.* The main tower of a castle; a keep.

don·key (dŏng′kē) *n., pl.* **don·keys** A kind of ass that has been domesticated and is used to carry loads.

Don·na (dŏn′ə *or* dōn′nä) *n.* Used as a courtesy title before the name of a woman in an Italian-speaking area.

don·nish (dŏn′ĭsh) *adj.* Relating to or typical of a university don; bookish.

don·ny·brook (dŏn′ē-bro͝ok′) *n.* A brawl or an uproar.

do·nor (dō′nər) *n.* **1.** A person who contributes something, such as money, to a cause or fund. **2.** A human or other animal from whom blood, tissue, or an organ is taken for use in grafting or in a transfusion or transplant. **3.** An atom, molecule, or ion that provides a component, especially a pair of electrons, to another atom or molecule, in order to form a molecular bond.

do-noth·ing (do͞o′nŭth′ĭng) *Informal adj.* Making no effort for change, especially in politics: *a do-nothing mayor.* ❖ *n.* An idle or lazy person.

Don Qui·xo·te (dŏn′ kē-**hō′**tē) *n.* An impractical idealist who tries to right wrongs. [After *Don Quixote*, hero of a satire of knightly romance by Miguel de Cervantes.]

don't (dōnt) Contraction of *do not.*

do·nut (dō′nŭt′ *or* do′nət) *n.* Variant of **doughnut.**

doo·dle (do͞od′l) *v.* **doo·dled, doo·dling, doo·dles** —*intr.* To draw or sketch aimlessly: *doodle on a pad during a phone call.* —*tr.* To draw (a design or figure) aimlessly. ❖ *n.* A design or figure drawn aimlessly. —**doo′dler** *n.*

doo·dle·bug (do͞od′l-bŭg′) *n.* Any of several insects, especially a pillbug or the larva of an ant lion.

doom (do͞om) *n.* A tragic or ruinous fate: *The events meant doom for the revolution.* ❖ *tr.v.* **doomed, doom·ing, dooms** To cause to have an unhappy end: *The injury doomed the patient to a lifetime of hardship.*

dooms·day (do͞omz′dā′) *n.* Judgment Day. [From Old English *dōmes dæg* : *dōmes*, genitive of *dōm*, judgment + *dæg*, day.]

door (dôr) *n.* **1.** A movable structure used to close off an entrance, typically made of a panel that swings on hinges or slides on a track. **2.** A doorway: *The neighbors stood in the door and talked.* **3.** The room or building to which a door belongs: *The deli is several doors down the street.* **4.** A means of approach or access: *Education can be a door to success.* [From Old English *duru.*]

door·bell (dôr′bĕl′) *n.* A buzzer or bell outside a door that is rung to announce the presence of a visitor.

do-or-die (do͞o′ər-dī′) *adj.* Requiring a great effort to avoid dire consequences: *a do-or-die situation.*

door·jamb (dôr′jăm′) *n.* Either of the two vertical pieces framing a doorway.

door·knob (dôr′nŏb′) *n.* A knob-shaped handle for opening and closing a door.

door·man (dôr′mən) *n.* A man employed to attend the entrance of a hotel, apartment house, or other building.

door·mat (dôr′măt′) *n.* A mat placed before a doorway for wiping the shoes.

door·nail (dôr′nāl′) *n.* A large-headed nail. ◆ **dead as a doornail** Undoubtedly dead.

door·sill (dôr′sĭl′) *n.* The threshold of a doorway.

door·step (dôr′stĕp′) *n.* A step leading to a door.

door·stop (dôr′stŏp′) *n.* **1.** A wedge inserted beneath a door to hold it open at a desired position. **2.** A weight or spring that prevents a door from slamming. **3.** A rubber-tipped projection on a wall to protect it from the impact of an opening door.

door·way (dôr′wā′) *n.* The entrance to a room or building.

door·yard (dôr′yärd′) *n.* A yard in front of the door of a house.

do·pa·mine (dō′pə-mēn′) *n.* A neurotransmitter that is found in the brain and is essential for normal brain function. Decreased concentrations of dopamine are associated wtih Parkinson's disease.

dop·ant (dō′pənt) *n.* A substance added in small amounts to a semiconductor material to change how it conducts electricity.

dope (dōp) *n.* **1.** *Informal* An illegal drug, especially marijuana or a performance-enhancing drug. **2.** *Informal* A stupid person. **3.** *Informal* Information, especially from a person: *He gave me the dope on the new teacher.* **4.** A sticky paste applied to seal pipe joints. ❖ *tr.v.* **doped, dop·ing, dopes 1.** *Informal* To give an illegal drug to: *convicted of doping a racehorse.* **2.** To treat (a semiconductor) with a dopant. [From Dutch *doop*, sauce, from *doopen*, to dip.]

dop·ey (dō′pē) *adj.* **dop·i·er, dop·i·est** *Slang* **1.** Dazed or sleepy. **2.** Stupid or foolish.

dop·ing (dō′pĭng) *n.* The practice of taking a banned substance in an attempt to enhance one's performance as an athlete.

Dop·pler effect (dŏp′lər) *n.* The apparent change in the frequency of waves, as of sound or light, when the source of the waves is moving toward or away from an observer. For example, as the source of sound waves and an observer approach each other, the observer hears a rising pitch. As the source and an observer move apart, the observer hears a falling pitch. [After Christian Johann *Doppler* (1803–1853), Austrian physicist.]

Dor·ic (dôr′ĭk) *adj.* In the style of an order of classical Greek architecture characterized by heavy fluted columns with plain saucer-shaped capitals: *a Doric column.*

dome

domino¹

Doric
Doric columns

dormer

USAGE

double negative The use of a **double negative,** such as *I didn't say nothing,* to express a negative idea should be avoided in Standard English. Instead, use a single negative word, as in *I said nothing* or *I didn't say anything.* A double negative can be used to say something affirmative, as in *I cannot just do nothing,* but such expressions can be confusing.

doublet

ă	pat	ôr	core
ā	pay	oi	boy
âr	care	ou	out
ä	father	o͝o	took
ĕ	pet	o͝or	lure
ē	be	o͞o	boot
ĭ	pit	ŭ	cut
ī	bite	ûr	urge
îr	pier	th	thin
ŏ	pot	*th*	this
ō	toe	zh	vision
ô	paw	ə	about

dork (dôrk) *n. Slang* A foolish, inept, or clumsy person. **—dork′y** *adj.*

dorm (dôrm) *n. Informal* A dormitory.

dor·man·cy (**dôr′**mən-sē) *n.* The condition of being dormant: *dormancy in bacteria.*

dor·mant (**dôr′**mənt) *adj.* **1.** In an inactive state in which growth and development stop, only to start again when conditions are favorable: *dormant seeds.* **2.** Not active but capable of renewed activity: *a dormant volcano.* [From Middle English *dormaunt,* from Old French, from Latin *dormīre,* to sleep.]

dor·mer (**dôr′**mər) *n.* **1.** A small roofed structure projecting outward on a larger, sloping roof. **2.** A window that is set in such a structure.

dor·mi·to·ry (**dôr′**mĭ-tôr′ē) *n., pl.* **dor·mi·to·ries 1.** A building for housing a number of people, especially students. **2.** A room providing sleeping quarters for a number of people. [From Middle English *dormitorie,* from Latin *dormītōrium,* from *dormīre,* to sleep.]

dor·mouse (**dôr′**mous′) *n., pl.* **dor·mice** (**dôr′**mīs′) Any of various small rodents of Eurasia and northern Africa that have long furry tails. Dormice sleep most of the winter. [From Middle English, probably from Old French *dormir,* to sleep.]

dor·sal (**dôr′**səl) *adj.* Relating to or located on the back or upper side of the body of a human or another animal: *the dorsal fin of a fish.* **—dor′sal·ly** *adv.*

do·ry (**dôr′**ē) *n., pl.* **do·ries** A small flatbottom fishing boat with high flaring sides.

dos·age (**dō′**sĭj) *n.* **1.** The administration or application of medicine or some treatment in regulated amounts: *the dosage of a drug three times a day.* **2.** The amount administered or applied at one time: *The doctor reduced my dosage of antihistamine.* **3.** An amount of radiation that a person is exposed to.

dose (dōs) *n.* **1.** The amount of medicine or other substance or treatment given or taken at one time: *a dose of medicine every four hours.* **2.** An amount, especially of something unpleasant, to which one is subjected: *a dose of hard luck.* ❖ *tr.v.* **dosed, dos·ing, dos·es** To give or prescribe (medicine) in specified amounts. [From French, from Greek *dosis,* something given, from *didonai,* to give.]

dos·si·er (**dŏs′**ē-ā′) *n.* A collection of papers giving detailed information about a particular person or subject: *Army records included a dossier on each soldier.* [From Old French, bundle of papers labeled on the back, from *dos,* back, from Latin *dorsum.*]

dost (dŭst) *v. Archaic* A second person singular present tense of **do**[1].

❑ *These sound alike:* **dost, dust** (particles).

Dos·to·yev·sky or **Dos·to·ev·ski** (dŏs′tə-**yĕf′**skē *or* dŏs′toi-**yĕf′**skē), **Feodor Mikhailovich** 1821–1881. Russian writer whose novels include *Crime and Punishment* (1866).

dot (dŏt) *n.* **1.** A small round mark; a spot: *a dot over the small letter i.* **2a.** A decimal point. **b.** A symbol (·) indicating multiplication. **c.** A period used to separate strings of words, as in email addresses and URLs. **3.** The short sound or signal used in Morse code in combination with the dash and silent intervals to represent letters, numbers, or punctuation. ❖ *tr.v.* **dot·ted, dot·ting, dots 1.** To mark with dots. **2.** To cover with or as if with dots: *Dandelions dotted the green field.* ◆ **on the dot** Exactly at the appointed time; punctual or punctually: *I arrived at 9:00 on the dot.*

dot·age (**dō′**tĭj) *n.* A loss of the ability to think clearly as a result of aging.

dot·ard (**dō′**tərd) *n.* An aged person whose mental abilities are declining.

dot-com (**dŏt′kŏm′**) *n.* A business whose services are conducted or provided over the Internet.

dote (dōt) *intr.v.* **dot·ed, dot·ing, dotes** To show excessive love or fondness: *They doted on their only grandchild.*

doth (dŭth) *v. Archaic* A third person singular present tense of **do**[1].

dot·ty (**dŏt′**ē) *adj.* **dot·ti·er, dot·ti·est 1.** Mentally unbalanced; crazy. **2.** Amusingly eccentric or unconventional.

dou·ble (**dŭb′**əl) *adj.* **1.** Twice as much in size, strength, number, or amount: *a double dose.* **2.** Composed of two like parts: *double doors.* **3.** Composed of two unlike parts; dual: *a double meaning.* **4.** Accommodating or designed for two people: *a double hotel room.* **5.** Having more than the usual number of petals, usually in a crowded or overlapping arrangement: *a double chrysanthemum.* ❖ *n.* **1.** An accommodation for two people, as a room in a hotel. **2.** A person or thing that closely resembles another; a duplicate: *She's her sister's double.* **3. doubles** A form of a game, such as tennis or handball, having two players on each side. **4.** In baseball, a hit that enables the batter to reach second base safely. ❖ *v.* **dou·bled, dou·bling, dou·bles** *—tr.* **1.** To make twice as great: *Double the amount of food if both of you go hiking.* **2.** To be twice as much as: *doubled the score of her opponent.* **3.** To fold in two: *double the blanket to get more warmth.* **4.** To clench (one's fist). **5.** To duplicate; repeat: *Double the "t" in "hit" when you spell "hitting."* **6.** To sail around: *double a cape.* *—intr.* **1.** To be increased twofold: *Our rent has doubled in 10 years' time.* **2.** To turn sharply backward; reverse: *The bear doubled back on its trail.* **3.** To serve in an additional capacity: *My bed doubles as a couch.* **4.** To be a substitute: *The assistant doubled for the coach today.* **5.** In baseball, to hit a double. ❖ *adv.* **1.** To twice the amount or extent; doubly: *paid double for the customized car.* **2.** Two together; in pairs: *ride double on a horse.* **3.** In two: *bent double with laughter.* ◆ **double up 1.** To bend suddenly, as in pain or laughter: *The joke made us double up.* **2.** To share accommodations meant for one person. **on the double** Immediately or quickly: *We need help on the double!* [From Middle English, from Latin *duplus.*]

double agent *n.* A person pretending to spy for one government while actually spying for another.

double bar *n.* A pair of vertical lines or a heavy black line drawn through a musical staff to indicate the end of a large section of a composition.

dou·ble-bar·reled (**dŭb′**əl-**băr′**əld) *adj.* **1.** Having two barrels mounted side by side: *a double-barreled shotgun.* **2.** Serving two purposes; twofold: *a double-barreled question.*

double bass (bās) *n.* The largest and lowest pitched of the stringed instruments that are normally played with a bow, related to the violin family but having four strings tuned in intervals of a fourth.

double bassoon *n.* A contrabassoon.

double boiler *n.* A cooking utensil consisting of an upper pot fitted into a lower pot. Water boiling in the lower pot allows the slow even cooking or heating of food in the upper pot.

dou·ble-breast·ed (**dŭb′**əl-**brĕs′**tĭd) *adj.* Having two rows of buttons and fastened by lapping one edge of the front of a garment well over the other: *a double-breasted jacket.*

dou·ble-check (**dŭb′**əl-**chĕk′**) *tr.v.* **dou·ble-checked, dou·ble-check·ing, dou·ble-checks** To inspect or examine again; verify: *double-check one's subtraction.*

double chin *n.* A fold of fatty flesh beneath the chin.

dou·ble-click (**dŭb′**əl-**klĭk′**) *v.* **dou·ble-clicked, dou·ble-click·ing, dou·ble-clicks** *—tr.* To press down and release a button on (a pointing device) twice in rapid succession to activate a command on a computer screen. *—intr.* To double-click a pointing device.

dou·ble-cross (dŭb′əl-krôs′) *tr.v.* **dou·ble-crossed, dou·ble-cross·ing, dou·ble-cross·es** To betray by acting contrary to a prior agreement. ❖ *n.* often **double cross** An act of betrayal. **—dou′ble-cross′er** *n.*

double-deal·er (dŭb′əl-dē′lər) *n.* A person who engages in deceitful or treacherous behavior; a double-crosser.

dou·ble-deal·ing (dŭb′əl-dē′lĭng) *adj.* Duplicitous or deceitful; treacherous. ❖ *n.* Duplicity or deceit; treachery.

dou·ble-deck·er (dŭb′əl-dĕk′ər) *n.* Something, such as a vehicle, structure, or sandwich, that has two decks, floors, or layers.

double digits *pl.n.* A number that is greater than 9 and less than 100: *Our team's center has been shooting in double digits all season.* **—doub′le-dig′it** *adj.*

double dribble *n.* In basketball, an illegal dribble in which a player uses both hands at the same time to dribble the ball or begins to dribble the ball a second time after a complete stop.

dou·ble-edged (dŭb′əl-ĕjd′) *adj.* **1.** Having two cutting edges: *a double-edged knife.* **2.** Effective or capable of being interpreted in two ways: *a double-edged compliment.*

dou·ble-en·ten·dre (dŭb′əl-än-tän′drə) *n.* A word or phrase having a double meaning, especially when the second meaning is indecent or improper.

dou·ble·head·er (dŭb′əl-hĕd′ər) *n.* Two games played one after the other on the same day, especially in baseball.

double helix *n.* A spiral structure that consists of two helixes coiled around each other, especially the two strands of nucleotides that make up a molecule of DNA.

double jeopardy *n.* The condition of being tried a second time for the same offense. It is prohibited by the US Constitution.

dou·ble-joint·ed (dŭb′əl-join′tĭd) *adj.* Having unusually flexible joints, especially of the limbs or fingers.

double knit *n.* A fabric that is somewhat like jersey, knitted so that a double thickness of fabric is produced in which the two sides of the fabric are interlocked. **—doub′ble-knit′** *adj.*

double negative *n.* A construction in which two negatives are used, especially to express one negative thought. —SEE NOTE.

dou·ble-park (dŭb′əl-pärk′) *tr. & intr.v.* **dou·ble-parked, dou·ble-park·ing, dou·ble-parks** To park alongside another vehicle already parked parallel to the curb.

double play *n.* In baseball, a play in which two players are put out.

dou·ble-quick (dŭb′əl-kwĭk′) *adj.* Very quick; rapid. ❖ *n.* A marching cadence; double time.

double reed *n.* A pair of joined reeds that vibrate together to produce sound in certain wind instruments such as the bassoon and oboe.

double standard *n.* A set of standards that allows greater freedom to one group than another, especially one granting more freedom to men than to women.

double star *n.* A binary star.

dou·blet (dŭb′lĭt) *n.* **1.** A close-fitting jacket, with or without sleeves, worn by European men from the late 1300s to around 1650. **2.** One of two words derived from the same source but not through the same route.

double take *n.* A delayed reaction to something unusual: *She did a double take when she saw his strange costume.*

double talk *n.* **1.** Meaningless speech that consists of nonsense syllables mixed with real words. **2.** Talk that is purposefully ambiguous or evasive: *campaign double talk.*

double time *n.* **1.** A rapid marching pace of 180 three-foot steps per minute. **2.** A rate of pay that is twice the regular rate: *was paid double time when working on Saturday.*

dou·ble-time (dŭb′əl-tīm′) *intr. & tr.v.* To move or cause to move in double time.

dou·bloon (dŭ-bloo͞n′) *n.* A gold coin formerly used in Spain and Spanish America. [From Spanish *doblón*, from Latin *duplus*, double.]

dou·bly (dŭb′lē) *adv.* To a double degree; twice: *Make doubly sure the totals are right.*

doubt (dout) *tr.v.* **doubt·ed, doubt·ing, doubts 1.** To be uncertain about (something); not believe in the truth of: *At first many people doubted the rumor.* **2.** To disbelieve (someone): *I should never have doubted such a good friend.* **3.** To regard as unlikely: *I doubt that we'll arrive on time.* ❖ *n.* **1.** The state of being uncertain about the truth or reliability of something: *The reports were met with doubt.* **2.** often **doubts** A feeling of uncertainty or distrust: *She had doubts about the claims made in the article she read online.* **3.** The condition of being unsettled or unresolved: *The outcome of the ball game is still in doubt.* ◆ **beyond doubt** or **without doubt** Without question; certainly; definitely. **no doubt** Certainly or probably. [From Middle English *douten*, from Latin *dubitāre*, to waver.]

doubt·ful (dout′fəl) *adj.* **1.** Subject to or causing doubt: *a doubtful claim.* **2.** Having or showing doubt; questioning: *We were doubtful about the proposed plan.* **3.** Questionable; suspicious: *a shady person with a doubtful past.* **—doubt′ful·ly** *adv.*

doubt·less (dout′lĭs) *adv.* **1.** Certainly; assuredly: *The bad weather was doubtless a factor in the delay.* **2.** Presumably; probably: *They will doubtless reject our proposal.* **—doubt′less·ly** *adv.*

douche (do͞osh) *n.* **1.** A stream of liquid or air applied to a part or cavity of the body in order to cleanse or apply medication. **2.** An instrument for applying a douche. ❖ *tr. & intr.v.* **douched, douch·ing, douch·es** To cleanse or treat by means of a douche.

dough (dō) *n.* **1.** A soft thick mixture of dry ingredients, such as flour or meal, and liquid, such as water, that is kneaded, shaped, and baked, especially as bread or pastry. **2.** *Slang* Money. [From Old English *dāg.*]

❑ *These sound alike:* **dough, do**² (musical tone), **doe** (deer).

dough·nut also **do·nut** (dō′nŭt′ *or* dō′nət) *n.* A small ring-shaped cake made of rich dough that is fried in deep fat.

dough·ty (dou′tē) *adj.* **dough·ti·er, dough·ti·est** Marked by stouthearted courage; very brave. **—dough′ti·ness** *n.*

dough·y (dō′ē) *adj.* **dough·i·er, dough·i·est** Having the appearance or consistency of dough: *a doughy face.* **—dough′i·ness** *n.*

Doug·las (dŭg′ləs), **Stephen Arnold** 1813–1861. American politician who in 1858 took part in a famous series of debates with Abraham Lincoln.

Douglas fir *n.* A tall evergreen tree of western North America having short needles, drooping cones, and strong heavy wood valuable as lumber. [After David *Douglas* (1798–1834), Scottish botanist.]

Doug·lass (dŭg′ləs), **Frederick** 1818–1895. American abolitionist who escaped from slavery (1838) and became an influential lecturer in the North and abroad. He edited the *North Star* (1847–1860), an abolitionist newspaper. —SEE NOTE.

dour (do͝or *or* dour) *adj.* **dour·er, dour·est 1.** Marked by sternness or harshness; forbidding. **2.** Silently ill-humored; gloomy: *had a dour temperament that won him few friends.* **—dour′ly** *adv.* **—dour′ness** *n.*

douse (dous) *tr.v.* **doused, dous·ing, dous·es 1.** To wet thoroughly; drench. **2.** To put out (a light or fire); extinguish: *She doused the campfire with a bucket of water.*

Frederick Douglass

BIOGRAPHY

Frederick Douglass

Born a slave on a Maryland plantation, Frederick **Douglass** was taught to read and write by the wife of his master, and he used these skills to educate himself. At the age of 20, he disguised himself as a sailor and escaped to the North. Douglass soon began giving lectures throughout the North, speaking out publicly about the evils of slavery in the South and the wrongs of racial prejudice in the North. In 1845 he published his *Narrative of the Life of Frederick Douglass, an American Slave,* and then traveled to England to avoid capture as a fugitive slave. While abroad, Douglass gave lectures to raise awareness about slavery. He returned to the United States after British antislavery advocates raised enough money to buy his freedom. In Rochester, New York, in 1847, he founded the *North Star* (named for the star that guided escaping slaves to freedom in the North), a weekly antislavery newspaper. During the Civil War, Douglass called on President Lincoln to abolish slavery and helped recruit black troops to fight for the Union. In his later years, Douglass continued to speak out against racism and lent his support to the women's suffrage movement. Douglass's autobiography is widely read today and remains an outstanding account of the experience of an American slave.

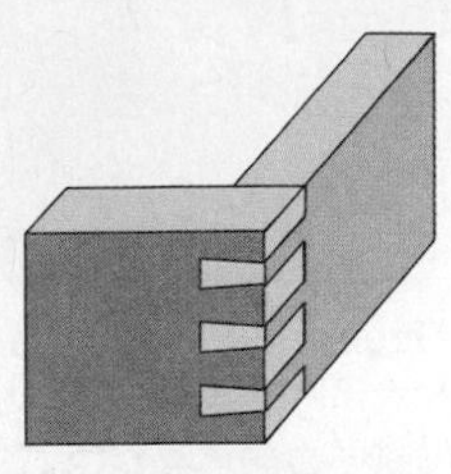
dovetail

dove[1] (dŭv) *n.* **1.** Any of various birds, including the pigeons, having a small head and a characteristic cooing call. **2.** A person who advocates peace or negotiation rather than armed conflict or confrontation: *The doves in Congress opposed military intervention.* [From Middle English *douve.*]

dove[2] (dōv) *v.* A past tense of **dive.**

dove·cote (dŭv′kōt′ *or* dŭv′kŏt′) also **dove·cot** (dŭv′kŏt′) *n.* A small structure, often raised on a pole, for housing domesticated pigeons.

Do·ver (dō′vər) **1.** A town of southeast England on the English Channel opposite Calais, France. It has been a strategic port since Roman times. **2.** The capital of Delaware, in the central part of the state. It was founded in 1683.

dove·tail (dŭv′tāl′) *n.* **1.** One of a series of pieces cut into the end of a board so as to fit into corresponding indentations cut into another board. Both boards together form an interlocking joint. **2.** A joint formed by interlocking such pieces. ❖ *v.* **dove·tailed, dove·tail·ing, dove·tails** —*tr.* **1.** To join or fit together by means of dovetails. **2.** To connect, fit together, or combine harmoniously: *Let's try to dovetail our travel plans so we see each other.* —*intr.* **1.** To be joined or fitted together by means of dovetails. **2.** To be combined or fitted together harmoniously: *Our travel plans dovetail for one weekend.*

dow·a·ger (dou′ə-jər) *n.* **1.** A widow who holds a title or property derived from her dead husband: *a dowager princess.* **2.** An elderly woman of high social station.

dow·dy (dou′dē) *adj.* **dow·di·er, dow·di·est** Lacking stylishness or neatness; shabby: *dowdy old clothes.* **—dow′di·ly** *adv.* **—dow′di·ness** *n.*

dow·el (dou′əl) *n.* **1.** A long thin cylindrical piece of hard material, usually wood. **2.** A round, usually wooden pin that fits into a corresponding hole to fasten or align two adjacent pieces.

dow·er (dou′ər) *n.* The part of a deceased man's real estate allotted by law to his widow for her lifetime.

down[1] (doun) *adv.* **1a.** From a higher to a lower place: *hiked down from the summit.* **b.** To, on, or toward the ground, floor, or bottom: *tripped and fell down.* **2.** In or to a sitting or reclining position: *sat down; lay down on the grass.* **3.** Toward or in the south: *going down to Florida.* **4.** Away from a central place: *down on the farm.* **5.** In or into one's stomach: *washed the bagel down with juice.* **6.** Toward or at a lower point on a scale: *body temperature coming down after a fever.* **7.** To or into an inferior condition: *The mayor went down in defeat.* **8.** From an earlier to a later time: *traditions handed down through the ages.* **9.** In partial payment at the time of purchase: *put $300 down on the TV set.* **10.** In writing: *The reporter took the statement down.* **11.** To the source: *tracking a rumor down.* **12.** Seriously, intensely, or diligently: *Let's get down to work.* **13.** Into a secure position: *nail down the boards.* ❖ *adj.* **1a.** Moving or directed downward: *a down elevator.* **b.** Low or lower: *The room is dark because the blinds are down.* **2.** Sick; not feeling well: *He is down with a bad cold.* **3.** In low spirits; depressed. **4.** Not functioning or operating, especially temporarily: *They can't issue report cards because the school's computers are down.* **5.** Completed; done: *As for the exams, there are two down, and two to go.* **6.** Trailing an opponent, as in a game: *We were down by two points with a minute left.* **7.** In football, having had one's forward progress in carrying the ball stopped, especially by being tackled. **8.** In baseball, retired or put out: *got up to bat with two down and a runner on third base.* ❖ *prep.* **1.** In a descending direction upon, along, through, or into: *ran down the stairs.* **2.** Along the course of: *walking down the road.* ❖ *n.* **1.** A downward movement; a descent. **2.** A misfortune or difficulty: *went through a lot of ups and downs before succeeding.* **3.** In football, any of a series of four plays during which a team must advance at least ten yards to retain possession of the ball. ❖ *tr.v.* **downed, down·ing, downs 1.** To bring, strike, or throw down. **2.** To swallow hastily; gulp: *downed a lot of water before the race.* **3.** In football: **a.** To put (the ball) out of play by throwing it to the ground or touching a knee to the ground. **b.** To stop the advancement of the ball by (a ball carrier), as by tackling. ◆ **down on** *Informal* Hostile or negative toward: *She was down on jogging after her injury.* [From Old English *dūne,* from *dūn,* hill.]

down[2] (doun) *n.* **1.** Soft, fluffy feathers forming the first plumage of a young bird and lying under the outer feathers in certain adult birds: *the down of a chick.* **2.** A covering of soft, short hairs, as on some leaves or fruit. [From Middle English *doun,* from Old Norse *dūnn.*]

down[3] (doun) *n.* often **downs** An expanse of rolling grassy treeless land used for grazing. [From Old English *dūn,* hill.]

down·beat (doun′bēt′) *n.* **1.** The downward stroke made by a conductor to indicate the first beat of a musical measure. **2.** The first beat of a measure. ❖ *adj.* Depressing or pessimistic: *The downbeat economic news sent stock prices lower.*

down·cast (doun′kăst′) *adj.* **1.** Directed downward: *downcast eyes.* **2.** Low in spirits; depressed: *feeling downcast after repeated failure.*

down·court (doun-kôrt′) *adv. & adj.* To, into, or in the far end of a basketball court.

down·er (dou′nər) *n. Slang* A depressing experience, situation, or person: *Not getting to see the movie was a real downer.*

down·fall (doun′fôl′) *n.* **1.** A sudden loss of wealth, reputation, happiness, or status; ruin: *An investigation resulted in the downfall of the corrupt banker.* **2.** A cause of sudden ruin: *Careless spending was the treasurer's downfall.* **3.** A fall of rain or snow, especially one that is heavy or unexpected.

down·field (doun′fēld′) *adv. & adj.* In sports, to, into, or in the defensive team's end of the field.

down·grade (doun′grād′) *tr.v.* **down·grad·ed, down·grad·ing, down·grades 1.** To lower the status or salary of: *downgrade an employee for constant carelessness.* **2.** To minimize the importance, value, or reputation of. ❖ *n.* A descending slope, as in a road; a downward course: *The truck sped up on the downgrade.*

down·heart·ed (doun′här′tĭd) *adj.* Low in spirits; depressed. **—down′heart′ed·ly** *adv.*

down·hill (doun′hĭl′) *adv.* **1.** Down the slope of a hill or mountain: *We raced downhill.* **2.** Toward a worsening condition: *After they lost that sale, the whole business started going downhill.* ❖ *adj.* (doun′hĭl′) **1.** Sloping downward; descending: *a downhill direction.* **2.** Relating to skiing down slopes rather than across the countryside. **3.** Worsening: *a career with a downhill trajectory.* **4.** Easier: *The hardest part of the project is over—it's all downhill from here.*

Down·ing Street (dou′nĭng) A thoroughfare of London, England. Nearly all prime ministers of Great Britain have lived at No. 10 Downing Street since the early 1700s.

down·load (doun′lōd′) *tr.v.* **down·load·ed, down·load·ing, down·loads** To transfer (data or a program) from a central computer or website to another computer or device: *downloaded software from the Internet.* ❖ *n.* **1.** A file that has been downloaded. **2.** An instance of downloading data or a program. **—down·load′a·ble** *adj.*

down payment *n.* A partial payment made at the time of purchase, with the balance to be paid later.

down·play (doun′plā′) *tr.v.* **down·played, down·play·ing, down·plays** To minimize the importance of: *downplayed the severity of the earthquake.*

ă	**pat**	ôr	**core**
ā	**pay**	oi	**boy**
âr	**care**	ou	**out**
ä	**father**	o͝o	**took**
ĕ	**pet**	o͝or	**lure**
ē	**be**	o͞o	**boot**
ĭ	**pit**	ŭ	**cut**
ī	**bite**	ûr	**urge**
îr	**pier**	th	**thin**
ŏ	**pot**	*th*	**this**
ō	**toe**	zh	**vision**
ô	**paw**	ə	**about**

down·pour (**doun′**pôr′) *n.* A heavy fall of rain.

down·right (**doun′**rīt′) *adj.* **1.** Thoroughgoing; unequivocal: *a downright scoundrel.* **2.** Straightforward; candid. ❖ *adv.* Thoroughly; absolutely: *They acted downright unpleasant.*

down·shift (**doun′**shĭft′) *intr.v.* **down·shift·ed, down·shift·ing, down·shifts 1.** To shift a motor vehicle into a lower gear. **2.** To reduce the speed, rate, or intensity of something: *The factory is downshifting as the old products are phased out.*

down·side (**doun′**sīd′) *n.* **1.** The lower side or portion. **2.** A disadvantageous aspect: *weighed the downsides and the benefits before making a decision.*

down·size (**doun′**sīz′) *v.* **down·sized, down·siz·ing, down·siz·es** —*tr.* **1.** To reduce in number or size, especially by eliminating workers: *The department was downsized during a reorganization.* **2.** To make in a smaller size: *cars that were downsized during an era of high gasoline prices.* —*intr.* **1.** To become smaller in size by reductions in personnel or assets: *Corporations continued to downsize after the economy recovered.* **2.** To live in a simpler way, especially by moving into a smaller residence.

down·slope (**doun′**slōp′) *n.* A downward slope. ❖ *adv. & adj.* At or in the direction of a lower point on a slope.

down·spout (**doun′**spout′) *n.* A vertical pipe for carrying rainwater down from a roof gutter.

down·stairs (**doun′stârz′**) *adv.* **1.** Down the stairs: *I slipped going downstairs.* **2.** To or on a lower floor: *I ran downstairs to answer the telephone.* ❖ *adj.* (**doun′**stârz′) Located on a lower floor: *a downstairs bedroom.* ❖ *n.* (**doun′stârz′**) *(used with a singular verb)* The lower or main floor of a building: *The whole downstairs was a mess after the party.*

down·stream (**doun′**strēm′) *adj. & adv.* In the direction of a stream's current: *the downstream rapids are faster than the ones upstream. The raft floated downstream.*

Down syndrome or **Down's syndrome** *n.* A disorder present from birth, characterized by intellectual disabilities, short stature, and a flattened facial profile. It is caused by the presence of an extra chromosome. [After John Langdon Haydon *Down* (1828–1896), English physician.]

down·time (**doun′**tīm′) *n.* **1.** The period of time when something, such as a factory or a piece of machinery, is not in operation. **2.** A period of time when a person is not working or doing a planned activity.

down-to-earth (**doun′**tə-**ûrth′**) *adj.* **1.** Realistic; sensible: *a down-to-earth solution to the problem.* **2.** Not pretentious: *an easygoing, down-to-earth manner.*

down·town (**doun′**toun′) *n.* The business center or the lower part of a city or town. ❖ *adv.* (**doun′toun′**) Toward or in the business center or lower part of a town or city: *Let's walk downtown.* ❖ *adj.* (**doun′**toun′) Being in or going toward the business center of a city or town: *a downtown restaurant; a downtown bus.*

down·trod·den (**doun′**trŏd′n) *adj.* Harshly treated; oppressed.

down·turn (**doun′**tûrn′) *n.* A tendency downward, especially in business or economic activity: *In a recession there is a marked downturn in business.*

down·ward (**doun′**wərd) *adv.* or **down·wards** (**doun′**-wərdz) **1.** In, to, or toward a lower place, level, or position: *floating downward.* **2.** From a prior source or an earlier time: *traditions passed downward through the ages.* ❖ *adj.* Directed toward a lower place or position: *a downward trend.*

down·wind (**doun′wĭnd′**) *adv.* In the direction toward which the wind blows.

down·y (**dou′**nē) *adj.* **down·i·er, down·i·est 1.** Covered with or made of down: *a downy chick.* **2.** Resembling down: *downy white clouds.*

dow·ry (**dou′**rē) *n., pl.* **dow·ries** Money or property brought by a bride to her husband at marriage.

dowse (douz) *intr.v.* **dowsed, dows·ing, dows·es** To use a divining rod to search for underground water or minerals. **—dows′er** *n.*

dox·ol·o·gy (dŏk-**sŏl′**ə-jē) *n., pl.* **dox·ol·o·gies** A hymn or verse in praise of God.

Doyle (doil), Sir **Arthur Conan** 1859–1930. British writer known for his stories featuring the brilliant detective Sherlock Holmes.

Sir Arthur Conan Doyle

doz. *abbr.* An abbreviation of dozen.

doze (dōz) *v.* **dozed, doz·ing, doz·es** —*intr.* To sleep lightly; nap: *doze on the porch in the sun.* —*tr.* To spend (time) dozing or as if dozing: *doze the afternoon hours away.* ❖ *n.* A short light sleep; a nap. ◆ **doze off** To fall into a light sleep: *I dozed off during the play's first act.*

doz·en (**dŭz′**ən) *n.* **1.** *pl.* **dozen** A set of 12: *Two dozen were at the party.* **2. dozens** A large undetermined number: *Dozens of salmon swam below.* ❖ *adj.* Twelve: *a dozen eggs.* [From Middle English *dosein,* from Latin *duodecim,* twelve : *duo,* two + *decem,* ten.]

doz·enth (**dŭz′**ənth) *adj.* Twelfth.

Dr. *abbr.* An abbreviation of: **1.** doctor. **2.** drive (street).

drab (drăb) *adj.* **drab·ber, drab·best 1.** Faded and dull in appearance. **2.** Dull or commonplace in character; dreary: *a drab cheerless house.* ❖ *n.* **1.** A dull grayish to yellowish or light olive brown. **2.** Cloth of this color or of an unbleached natural color. **—drab′ly** *adv.* **—drab′ness** *n.*

drach·ma (**drăk′**mə) *n., pl.* **drach·mas** or **drach·mae** (**drăk′**mē) **1.** The former basic monetary unit of Greece. **2.** A silver coin of ancient Greece. **3.** One of several modern units of weight, especially the dram.

draft (drăft) *n.* **1.** A current of air in an enclosed area: *feel a cold draft on one's feet.* **2.** A device that controls the flow or circulation of air. **3.** The act of pulling loads; traction: *large horses used for draft.* **4.** The depth of a vessel's keel below the water line. **5.** A document for directing the payment of money from an account or fund. **6a.** A gulp, swallow, or inhalation. **b.** The amount taken in by a single act of drinking or inhaling. **7a.** The drawing of a liquid, as from a cask or keg. **b.** An amount of liquid so drawn. **8a.** The process of selecting one or more individuals from a group, as for a service or duty. **b.** Compulsory enrollment in the armed forces; conscription. **c.** A body of people selected or conscripted. **d.** In sports, a system in which the exclusive rights to new players are distributed among professional teams. **9a.** The act of drawing in a fishing net. **b.** The amount of fish caught. **10a.** A preliminary version of a plan, document, or picture. **b.** A representation of something to be constructed: *The architect showed us a draft of the building.* ❖ *tr.v.* **draft·ed, draft·ing, drafts 1a.** To select from a group for some usually compulsory service: *draft citizens for military service.* **b.** To select (a player) in a sports draft. **2.** To draw up a preliminary plan, sketch, or version of: *drafted several versions of a speech.* ❖ *adj.* Suited for or used for drawing heavy loads: *a team of draft horses.* [From Middle English *draught,* act of drawing or pulling.]

draft·ee (drăf-**tē′**) *n.* A person who is drafted, especially into the armed forces.

drafts·man (**drăfts′**mən) *n.* A man who draws plans or designs, as of structures to be built. **—drafts′man·ship′** *n.*

drafts·per·son (**drăfts′**pûr′sən) *n.* A person who drafts plans or designs.

drafts·wom·an (**drăfts′**wo͝om′ən) *n.* A woman who draws plans or designs, as of structures to be built.

draft·y (**drăf′**tē) *adj.* **draft·i·er, draft·i·est** Having or exposed to drafts of air: *a drafty old house.* **—draft′i·ly** *adv.* **—draft′i·ness** *n.*

dragon

Sir Francis Drake
1581 portrait by Nicholas Hilliard (1547–1619)

drag (drăg) *v.* **dragged, drag·ging, drags** —*tr.* **1.** To pull (something) along with difficulty or effort; haul: *dragged the heavy box out of the way.* See Synonyms at **pull. 2.** To cause or allow (something) to trail along the ground: *Don't drag your coat in the mud.* **3.** To cause (oneself) to move in a slow or reluctant fashion: *I dragged myself to the meeting.* **4.** To take or escort (a person, for example), especially in overcoming resistance or reluctance: *dragged my cousin to the reception.* **5.** To move (an item) on a computer screen using a pointing device, such as a mouse: *dragged the document icon into a folder.* **6.** To search the bottom of (a body of water), as with a hook or net: *They dragged the river looking for the suitcase that was thrown from the bridge.* **7.** To prolong tediously: *They dragged the discussion out.* —*intr.* **1.** To trail along the ground: *The chain dragged along behind the tractor.* **2.** To move slowly or with difficulty: *The exhausted hikers dragged back to camp.* **3.** To pass or proceed slowly or tediously: *The long speech dragged on and on.* ❖ *n.* **1.** A person or thing that slows or stops motion or progress: *High interest rates can act as a drag on the economy.* **2.** The force produced by friction that hinders motion through a fluid, such as air or water: *redesigned the race car to reduce drag.* **3.** Something that is pulled along the ground, especially something for carrying loads: *The horse was harnessed to the drag.* **4.** A device for dragging under water, such as a grappling hook. **5.** *Slang* A person or thing that is obnoxiously tiresome. **6.** An act of inhaling something, especially smoke from a cigarette. ◆ **drag (one's) feet** To act or work with intentional slowness: *drag one's feet about completing a chore.* [From Middle English *draggen*, from Old Norse *draga*.]

drag·gle (drăg′əl) *tr. & intr.v.* **drag·gled, drag·gling, drag·gles** To make or become wet and muddy by dragging along the ground.

drag·net (drăg′nĕt′) *n.* **1.** A coordinated system of search used by the police to find criminal suspects. **2.** A net for trawling; a trawl.

drag·on (drăg′ən) *n.* A mythical giant reptile often represented as a winged fire-breathing monster. [From Middle English *dragoun*, from Greek *drakōn*, large serpent.]

drag·on·fly (drăg′ən-flī′) *n.* Any of various flying insects having a long slender body and two pairs of clear wings with fine networks of veins. They feed on other insects, including mosquitoes.

dra·goon (drə-go͞on′) *n.* A heavily armed mounted soldier in some European armies of the 1600s and 1700s. ❖ *tr.v.* **dra·gooned, dra·goon·ing, dra·goons** To compel or force by violent measures: *dragooned the townspeople into supplying the troops with food.* [From French *dragon*, carbine, from Old French *dragon*, dragon.]

drag race *n.* A short race between cars to determine which can accelerate faster from a standstill.

drain (drān) *v.* **drained, drain·ing, drains** —*tr.* **1.** To draw off (a liquid) gradually: *drain water from a sink.* **2.** To make dry or empty by drawing off liquid: *drain the pond.* **3.** To drink all the contents of: *The child drained the cup.* **4.** To deplete gradually, especially to the point of complete exhaustion: *The performance drained the cast and crew.* —*intr.* **1.** To flow off or out: *Melted snow drained off the roof.* **2.** To become empty by the draining off of liquid: *The tub drained slowly.* **3.** To discharge surface or excess water: *Most large rivers drain into the sea.* ❖ *n.* **1.** A pipe or channel by which liquid is drained off: *clog up the drain.* **2.** Something that causes a gradual loss: *Building a new library is a drain on the resources for buying more books.* ◆ **down the drain** To or into the condition of being wasted or lost: *When our first plan went down the drain, we quickly came up with another.* [From Old English *drēahnian*.]

drain·age (drā′nĭj) *n.* **1.** The action or a method of draining: *Drainage in swampland is very poor.* **2.** A natural or artificial system of drains. **3.** Material that is drained off: *Storm sewers carried the drainage away.*

drain·pipe (drān′pīp′) *n.* A pipe for carrying off water or sewage.

drake (drāk) *n.* A male duck.

Drake (drāk), Sir **Francis** 1540?–1596. English explorer who was the first Englishman to sail around the world (1577–1580).

dram[1] (drăm) *n.* **1a.** A unit of weight equal to 1⁄16 of an ounce or 27.3 grains (about 1.8 grams). See table at **measurement. b.** A unit of apothecary weight equal to 1⁄8 of an ounce or 60 grains (about 3.9 grams). **2.** A small drink. [From Middle English *dragme*, a drachma, a unit of weight, from Greek *drakhmē*, drachma.]

dram[2] (dräm) *n.* The basic monetary unit of Armenia. [From Armenian, from Greek *drakhmē*.]

dra·ma (drä′mə) *n.* **1.** A literary work that tells a story in prose or verse and is meant to be performed by actors. **2a.** Theatrical plays of a particular kind or period: *modern drama.* **b.** The art and practice of writing and producing works for the stage. **3.** A situation or a series of events in real life that resemble a play: *the day-by-day drama within Congress.* **4.** The quality or condition of being dramatic: *a confrontation between rivals that was full of drama.*

dra·mat·ic (drə-măt′ĭk) *adj.* **1.** Relating to drama or the theater: *dramatic performances.* **2.** Resembling a drama in action or emotion: *the dramatic events that led to Lincoln's election.* **3.** Arresting or forceful in appearance or effect: *a dramatic mountain range.* [From Greek *drāmatikos*, from *drāma*, from *drān*, to do, perform.] **—dra·mat′i·cal·ly** *adv.*

dra·mat·ics (drə-măt′ĭks) *n.* *(used with a singular or plural verb)* **1.** The art or practice of acting in or staging plays. **2.** Dramatic or exaggerated behavior: *cut the dramatics and get to the point.*

dram·a·tis per·so·nae (drăm′ə-tĭs pər-sō′nē *or* drä′mə-tĭs pər-sō′nī′) *pl.n.* The characters in a play or story.

dram·a·tist (drăm′ə-tĭst *or* drä′mə-tĭst) *n.* A person who writes plays; a playwright.

dram·a·tize (drăm′ə-tīz′ *or* drä′mə-tīz′) *tr.v.* **dram·a·tized, dram·a·tiz·ing, dram·a·tiz·es 1.** To adapt (a literary work) into a play or screenplay. **2.** To present or view in a dramatic or melodramatic way: *The report dramatizes the plight of the flood victims.* **—dram′a·ti·za′tion** (drăm′ə-tĭ-zā′shən *or* drä′mə-tĭ-zā′shən) *n.*

drank (drăngk) *v.* Past tense of **drink.**

drape (drāp) *v.* **draped, drap·ing, drapes** —*tr.* **1.** To cover or hang with or as if with cloth in loose folds: *The artist draped the painting with a cloth.* **2.** To arrange or let fall in loose folds: *draped a long cape over one shoulder.* **3.** To hang or rest limply: *I draped my legs over the back of the chair.* —*intr.* To fall or hang in loose folds: *Silk drapes easily.* ❖ *n.* **1.** A drapery; a curtain: *pull the drapes over the window.* **2.** The way in which cloth falls or hangs: *the drape of fine suit material.* [From Middle English *drapen*, from Old French *draper*, to weave, from *drap*, cloth, from Late Latin *drappus*.]

drap·er (drā′pər) *n.* *Chiefly British* A dealer in cloth or dry goods.

drap·er·y (drā′pə-rē) *n., pl.* **drap·er·ies 1.** A piece or pieces of heavy fabric hanging straight in loose folds, used as a curtain. **2.** Cloth or clothing arranged in loose folds.

dras·tic (drăs′tĭk) *adj.* Severe or radical in nature; extreme: *Calling out troops was a drastic measure to restore order.* [From Greek *drastikos*, active, from *drastos*, to be done, from *drān*, to do.] **—dras′ti·cal·ly** *adv.*

drat (drăt) *interj.* An expression used to show annoyance.

draught (drăft) *n. & v. & adj. Chiefly British* Variant of **draft.**

ă	pat	ôr	core
ā	pay	oi	boy
âr	care	ou	out
ä	father	o͝o	took
ĕ	pet	o͝or	lure
ē	be	o͞o	boot
ĭ	pit	ŭ	cut
ī	bite	ûr	urge
îr	pier	th	thin
ŏ	pot	*th*	this
ō	toe	zh	vision
ô	paw	ə	about

draughts (drăfts *or* dräfts) *n.* *(used with a singular or plural verb) Chiefly British* The game of checkers.

Dra·vid·i·an (drə-vĭd′ē-ən) *n.* **1.** A large family of languages spoken in southern India and northern Sri Lanka. **2.** A member of a people that speaks one of these languages. **—Dra·vid′i·an, Dra·vid′ic** (drə-vĭd′ĭk) *adj.*

draw (drô) *v.* **drew** (dro͞o), **drawn** (drôn), **drawing, draws** *—tr.* **1a.** To pull or move (something) after or toward one by applying force; drag: *a team of horses drawing a load.* See Synonyms at **pull. b.** To cause to move, as by leading: *She drew us into the room to show us her presents.* **c.** To cause to move in a given direction or to a given position: *drew the curtain.* **2.** To cause to flow forth: *a deep scratch that drew blood; draw water for a bath.* **3.** To suck or take in (air, for example): *The singer drew a deep breath.* **4.** To require (a specified depth of water) for floating: *A boat drawing 18 inches.* **5a.** To pull or take out: *draw a sword from a sheath.* **b.** To take (cards) from a dealer or central stack, as in poker. **c.** To extract or take from for one's own use: *drew strength from her example.* **6.** To attract; entice: *Our beaches draw many tourists.* **7.** To get as a response; elicit: *The comic drew laughter from the audience.* **8.** To earn; gain: *draw interest on a savings account.* **9.** To withdraw (money) from an account. **10.** To take or receive by chance: *I drew the lucky number.* **11.** To stretch tight: *draw a string around the package.* **12a.** To inscribe (a line or lines) with a pencil or other marking implement. **b.** To make a picture of, using mostly lines; sketch: *drawing illustrations for a new book.* **c.** To represent in words: *The poet drew scenes of far-off places with words.* **13.** To deduce from evidence at hand; formulate: *We can draw a conclusion from the facts already gathered.* *—intr.* **1.** To proceed or move steadily: *The boat drew near shore.* **2.** To take in a draft of air: *The fireplace chimney doesn't draw well.* **3.** To contract or tighten: *The smile drew into a frown.* **4.** To tie in a contest: *The chess players drew after 32 moves.* **5.** To make a likeness with lines on a surface: *Several students draw especially well.* ❖ *n.* **1.** An act of drawing: *a lucky draw of an ace from the deck of cards.* **2.** Something that attracts interest, customers, or spectators: *The movie is sure to be a good draw at the box office.* **3.** A contest ending in a tie. **4.** A ravine or gully that water drains into. **5.** In football, a play in which the quarterback drops back as if to pass and then runs or hands off to a running back. ◆ **draw down 1.** To reduce or deplete by consuming or spending: *drew down our food reserves.* **2.** To reduce (military forces in a specific deployment). **draw out** To prolong; protract: *drew out the meeting until we were quite bored.* **draw the line** To set a limit, as on behavior. **draw up 1.** To write up in a set form; compose: *draw up a list; draw up an agreement.* **2.** To bring (oneself) into an erect posture. **3.** To bring (troops, for example) into order. **4.** To bring or come to a halt: *The truck drew up at the gate.* [From Old English *dragan.*]

draw·back (drô′băk′) *n.* A disadvantage or inconvenience: *The pay was good but the long hours were a drawback.*

draw·bridge (drô′brĭj′) *n.* A bridge that can be raised or drawn aside either to prevent access or to permit passage beneath it.

draw·er (drô′ər) *n.* **1.** A person who draws. **2.** A boxlike compartment in a piece of furniture that can be pulled in and out. **3. drawers** (drôrz) Underpants.

draw·ing (drô′ĭng) *n.* **1.** The act or an instance of drawing. **2.** The art of representing forms and figures on a surface by means of lines. **3.** A work produced by this art: *There are several fine drawings of horses on the wall.*

drawing room *n.* A large room in which guests are entertained. [Short for earlier *withdrawing room.*]

draw·knife (drô′nīf′) *n.* A knife with a handle at each of the blade, used for shaving wood surfaces.

drawl (drôl) *intr. & tr.v.* **drawled, drawl·ing, drawls** To speak or utter with lengthened or drawn-out vowels. ❖ *n.* The speech or manner of speaking of one who drawls: *spoke with a pronounced drawl.*

drawn (drôn) *v.* Past participle of **draw.** ❖ *adj.* Haggard, as from fatigue or ill health: *The survivors looked drawn after their rescue.*

drawn butter *n.* Melted butter that has been clarified to separate out the milk solids.

draw·string (drô′strĭng′) *n.* A cord or ribbon run through a hem or casing and pulled to tighten or close an opening.

dray (drā) *n.* A low heavy cart without sides, used for hauling. ❖ *tr.v.* **drayed, dray·ing, drays** To haul by means of a dray.

dread (drĕd) *tr.v.* **dread·ed, dread·ing, dreads 1.** To fear intensely: *Many people dread snakes.* **2.** To anticipate with alarm, distaste, or reluctance: *We were dreading the long drive home.* ❖ *n.* **1.** Profound fear; terror. **2.** Fearful or distasteful anticipation: *the dread of saying something foolish on stage.* ❖ *adj.* Causing fear or terror: *a dread disease.* [From Middle English *dreden,* from Old English *adrǣdan,* to fear, from *ondrǣdan,* to advise against, fear : *ond-,* against + *rǣdan,* to advise.]

dread·ful (drĕd′fəl) *adj.* **1.** Causing dread; terrifying: *a dreadful epidemic.* **2.** Extremely unpleasant; distasteful or shocking: *dreadful furniture; dreadful behavior.* **—dread′ful·ly** *adv.* **—dread′ful·ness** *n.*

dread·locks (drĕd′lŏks′) *pl.n.* Long ropelike locks or thin braids of twisted or styled hair extending from the scalp.

dread·nought (drĕd′nôt′) *n.* A heavily armed battleship.

dream (drēm) *n.* **1.** A series of mental images, ideas, and emotions occurring during sleep. **2.** A daydream. **3.** A state of abstraction; a trance: *wandering about in a dream.* **4.** A hope or aspiration: *dreams of world peace.* **5.** Something especially gratifying, excellent, or useful: *The new car runs like a dream.* ❖ *v.* **dreamed** or **dreamt** (drĕmt), **dream·ing, dreams** *—intr.* **1.** To have a dream while sleeping. **2.** To daydream: *dreaming of far-off places.* **3.** To consider as feasible or practical: *I wouldn't even dream of going.* *—tr.* **1.** To have a dream about (something) during sleep: *Did it storm last night, or did I dream it?* **2.** To conceive of; imagine: *We never dreamed it might snow so hard.* ◆ **dream up** To invent; concoct: *dreamed up a plan to get rich quick.* [From Old English *drēam,* joy, music.] **—dream′er** *n.*

dream·land (drēm′lănd′) *n.* **1.** An ideal or imaginary place. **2.** A state of sleep.

dream·y (drē′mē) *adj.* **dream·i·er, dream·i·est 1.** Preoccupied or unattentive; trancelike: *walked around in a dreamy state looking at the trees.* **2.** Having a tendency to daydream: *a dreamy person who seldom pays attention.* **3.** Soothing and serene: *soft dreamy music.* **4.** *Informal* Very pleasant or attractive: *They were all excited about that dreamy new student.* **—dream′i·ly** *adv.* **—dream′i·ness** *n.*

drear (drîr) *adj.* Dreary.

drea·ry (drîr′ē) *adj.* **drea·ri·er, drea·ri·est 1.** Dismal; bleak: *a dreary January rain.* **2.** Boring; dull: *the dreary tasks of housekeeping.* [From Old English *drēorig,* bloody, sad, from *drēor,* gore.] **—drear′i·ly** *adv.* **—drear′i·ness** *n.*

dredge[1] (drĕj) *n.* **1.** A machine equipped with an underwater scooping or suction device, used especially to deepen a harbor or waterway. **2.** A ship or barge equipped with such a machine. ❖ *v.* **dredged, dredg·ing, dredg·es** *—tr.* **1.** To clean, deepen, or widen with a dredge: *dredged the channel.* **2.** To bring up with a

drawbridge

dreidel

driftwood

ă	pat	ôr	core
ā	pay	oi	boy
âr	care	ou	out
ä	father	o͝o	took
ĕ	pet	o͝or	lure
ē	be	o͞o	boot
ĭ	pit	ŭ	cut
ī	bite	ûr	urge
îr	pier	th	thin
ŏ	pot	*th*	this
ō	toe	zh	vision
ô	paw	ə	about

dredge: *dredge dirt and rock out of the river to make a channel.* **3.** To bring to public notice; uncover: *a reporter who dredges up the dirt on celebrities.* —*intr.* To use a dredge. [From Early Modern English *dreg-bot*, a boat used for dredging, from Old English *dragan*, to draw.]

dredge[2] (drĕj) *tr.v.* **dredged, dredg·ing, dredg·es** To sprinkle (food) with fine particles of something, such as flour or bread crumbs. [From Middle English *dragge*, a sweet confection, from Greek *tragēma*.]

dregs (drĕgz) *pl.n.* **1.** The sediment in a liquid: *rinse the dregs out of the coffeepot.* **2.** The basest or least desirable portion.

drei·del also **drei·dl** (drād′l) *n.* A four-sided top spun in games of chance played by children and adults at Hanukkah. [From Yiddish *dreydl*, from *dreyen*, to turn.]

Drei·ser (drī′sər *or* drī′zər), **Theodore Herman Albert** 1871–1945. American writer whose novels include *Sister Carrie* (1900).

drench (drĕnch) *tr.v.* **drenched, drench·ing, drench·es** To wet through and through; soak: *A thunderstorm drenched everyone outside.* [From Old English *drencan*, to give to drink, drown.]

Dres·den (drĕz′dən) A city of east-central Germany on the Elbe River east-southeast of Leipzig.

dress (drĕs) *v.* **dressed, dress·ing, dress·es** —*tr.* **1.** To put clothes on: *Dress the baby warmly.* **2a.** To decorate or adorn: *dress a Christmas tree.* **b.** To arrange a display in: *dress a store window.* **3.** To apply medicine or bandages to (a wound): *After the operation the nurse dressed the incision.* **4.** To arrange or style (the hair). **5.** To groom (an animal); curry. **6.** To clean (fish or fowl) for cooking or sale: *dress a turkey.* **7.** To arrange (troops) in ranks; align: *dress soldiers for a parade.* —*intr.* **1.** To put on clothes: *I got up late and dressed in a hurry.* **2.** To wear clothes of a certain kind or style: *We are allowed to dress casually at the office.* ❖ *n.* **1.** Clothing; apparel: *wore formal dress to the reception.* **2.** A style of clothing: *Bankers often wear conservative dress.* **3.** A one-piece outer garment worn by women and girls. ❖ *adj.* **1.** Suitable for formal occasions: *wear a tie with a dress shirt.* **2.** Calling for formal clothes: *a dress reception.* ◆ **dress down** To scold; reprimand. **dress up** To wear formal or fancy clothes: *They dressed up for the party.* [From Middle English *dressen*, to arrange, put on clothing, from Old French *drecier*, to set up, arrange, from Latin *dīrigere*, to direct.]

dres·sage (drə-säzh′) *n.* The guiding of a horse through a series of complex maneuvers by a rider using very slight movements of the hands, legs, and weight.

dress·er[1] (drĕs′ər) *n.* **1.** A person who dresses: *She is a very chic dresser.* **2.** A wardrobe assistant, as for an actor.

dress·er[2] (drĕs′ər) *n.* **1.** A chest of drawers, often having a mirror above it and typically used for holding clothing and personal items. **2.** A cupboard or set of shelves for dishes or kitchen utensils. [From Middle English *dressour*, table for preparing food, from Old French *drecier*, to set up, arrange.]

dress·ing (drĕs′ĭng) *n.* **1.** A medicinal or protective material applied to a wound. **2.** A sauce for certain dishes, such as salads. **3.** A stuffing, as for poultry or fish.

dressing gown *n.* A robe worn for lounging or before dressing.

dressing room *n.* A room, as in a theater, for changing costumes or clothes and applying makeup.

dressing table *n.* A low table with a mirror at which one sits while applying makeup.

dress·mak·er (drĕs′mā′kər) *n.* A person who makes women's clothing, especially dresses.

dress·mak·ing (drĕs′mā′kĭng) *n.* The act or occupation of making women's clothing, especially dresses.

dress rehearsal *n.* A complete, uninterrupted rehearsal of a play with costumes and stage props.

dress·y (drĕs′ē) *adj.* **dress·i·er, dress·i·est 1.** Requiring or characterized by formal dress: *a dressy party.* **2.** Formal or elegant in style: *dressy shoes.*

drew (dro͞o) *v.* Past tense of **draw.**

drib·ble (drĭb′əl) *v.* **drib·bled, drib·bling, drib·bles** —*intr.* **1.** To flow or fall in drops or an unsteady stream; trickle: *Water dribbled out of the leaky faucet.* **2.** To let saliva drip from the mouth; drool: *Most babies dribble when they are teething.* **3.** To move a ball or puck with repeated light bounces or kicks: *The player dribbled around an opponent.* —*tr.* **1.** To let flow or fall in drops or an unsteady stream: *I dribbled gravy on the potatoes.* **2.** To move (a ball or puck) by repeated light bounces or kicks, as in basketball or soccer: *The forward dribbled the ball right past the defender.* ❖ *n.* **1.** A small quantity; a drop: *a dribble of milk.* **2.** The act of dribbling a ball: *a fast dribble across the court.* **—drib′bler** *n.*

drib·let (drĭb′lĭt) *n.* A small amount or portion: *pay off a loan in driblets.*

dried (drīd) *v.* Past tense and past participle of **dry.**

dri·er[1] also **dry·er** (drī′ər) *n.* **1.** A person or thing that dries: *We did the dishes, and I was the drier.* **2.** A substance added, as to paint, to speed drying.

dri·er[2] (drī′ər) *adj.* A comparative of **dry.**

dries (drīz) *v.* Third person singular present tense of **dry.**

dri·est (drī′ĭst) *adj.* A superlative of **dry.**

drift (drĭft) *v.* **drift·ed, drift·ing, drifts** —*intr.* **1.** To be carried along by a current of water or air: *The boat drifted toward shore.* **2a.** To proceed or move unhurriedly and smoothly: *I drifted among the guests at the party.* **b.** To live or behave without a clear purpose or goal: *He drifted through the summer before applying for jobs in the fall.* **3.** To wander from a course or point of attention; stray: *My attention drifted from my homework.* **4.** To be piled up in banks or heaps by the force of a current: *Snow drifted against the wall.* —*tr.* **1.** To cause to be carried in a current: *Waves drifted debris all along the shore.* **2.** To pile up in heaps or banks: *The winds drifted the snow.* ❖ *n.* **1.** The act or condition of drifting: *a continuous drift of sand.* **2.** Something moving along in a current of air or water. **3.** The mass of material, such as sand or snow, deposited by a current of air or water: *snow drifts six feet high.* **4.** Fragments of rock that are carried and deposited by a glacier: *These drifts appeared at the end of the Ice Age.* **5.** A general meaning or direction of thought: *The drift of the lecture was hard to follow.* **6.** A gradual deviation from an original course, model, method, or intention. [From Middle English *drift*, drove, herd, act of driving.]

drift·er (drĭf′tər) *n.* A person who moves aimlessly from place to place or from job to job.

drift·wood (drĭft′wo͝od′) *n.* Wood floating in or washed up by a body of water.

drill[1] (drĭl) *n.* **1.** A tool used to bore holes in materials, usually by a rotating action or by repeated blows. **2.** Disciplined repetitious exercise as a means of teaching and perfecting a skill or procedure. **3.** A task or exercise for teaching a skill or procedure by repetition: *a fire drill.* ❖ *v.* **drilled, drill·ing, drills** —*tr.* **1.** To make a hole with a drill in (a hard material): *drilling wood.* **2.** To make (a hole) with or as if with a drill. **3.** To teach or train by continuous repetition: *drill a company of soldiers.* —*intr.* **1.** To make a hole with or as if with a drill: *drill into a board.* **2.** To perform a training exercise: *The astronauts drill before attempting repairs in space.* [From Middle Dutch *drillen*, to bore a hole.]

drill[2] (drĭl) *n.* **1.** A shallow trench or furrow in which seeds are planted. **2.** A machine or implement for planting seeds in furrows. [Perhaps from *drill*, rill.]

drink (drĭngk) *v.* **drank** (drăngk), **drunk** (drŭngk), **drink·ing, drinks** —*tr.* **1.** To take into the mouth and swallow (a liquid): *drink water every day.* **2.** To swallow the liquid contents of (a vessel): *I drank a mug of* *hot cocoa.* **3.** To take in or soak up; absorb: *The parched earth drank up the rain.* **4.** To take in eagerly through the senses or intellect: *We drank in the grandeur of the mountains.* **5.** To give or make (a toast): *We drank a toast to happiness.* —*intr.* **1.** To swallow liquid: *The hikers drank from a clear stream.* **2.** To salute a person or occasion with a toast: *We'll drink to your health.* **3.** To drink alcoholic beverages. ❖ *n.* **1.** A liquid for drinking; a beverage: *Iced tea is a satisfying drink.* **2.** An amount of liquid swallowed: *took a drink of water.* **3.** An alcoholic beverage: *The lawyers went out for a drink after work.* [From Old English *drincan.*] **—drink′a·ble** *adj.* **—drink′er** *n.*

drip (drĭp) *intr. & tr.v.* **dripped, drip·ping, drips** To fall or let fall in drops: *Water dripped from the faucet. I dripped paint on the floor.* ❖ *n.* **1.** The process of forming and falling in drops: *the drip of water from leaky gutters.* **2.** Liquid or moisture that falls in drops: *Drips of paint spattered the floor.* **3.** The sound made by liquid falling in drops: *The constant drip of the faucet was annoying.* [From Middle English *dripen.*]

drip-dry (drĭp′drī′) *adj.* Made of a fabric that will not wrinkle when hung dripping wet for drying: *a drip-dry suit.* ❖ *intr.v.* **drip-dried, drip-dry·ing, drip-dries** To dry with no wrinkles when hung dripping wet: *let a shirt drip-dry.*

drip·pings (drĭp′ĭngz) *pl.n.* The fat and juices from roasting meat, often used in making gravy.

drive (drīv) *v.* **drove** (drōv), **driv·en** (drĭv′ən), **driv·ing, drives** —*tr.* **1a.** To push, propel, or press onward forcibly: *drove the horses into the corral.* **b.** To cause to retreat; put to flight: *The dog drove off the raccoon.* **2a.** To guide, control, or direct (a vehicle): *They drive their car to work every day.* **b.** To convey or transport in a vehicle: *The neighbors drove me to the store.* **3a.** To supply the motive force or power to and cause to function: *Electricity drives many motors.* **b.** To cause or sustain, as if by supplying force or power: *an economy that is driven by exports.* **c.** To compel or force to work, often excessively: *The need for recognition drives him to work long hours.* **d.** To force into or from a particular state or act: *Constant interruptions drove me to despair.* **4.** To force to penetrate: *drive a nail into wood.* **5.** To carry through vigorously to a conclusion: *drive home one's point in an argument.* **6.** To hit or propel (a ball, for example) so that it travels with great speed or distance: *The batter drove the ball over the fence in center field.* —*intr.* **1.** To move along or advance quickly as if pushed by a force: *The car drove into the ditch.* **2.** To guide or control a vehicle or animal: *Many people drive too fast on this road.* **3.** To go or be carried in a vehicle: *We drove to the supermarket.* **4.** To make an effort to reach or achieve an objective; aim: *The author drove hard to complete the book on time.* **5.** In basketball, to move directly toward the basket with the ball. ❖ *n.* **1.** A trip or journey in a vehicle: *go for a quiet drive in the country.* **2a.** A road for automobiles and other vehicles: *Cars may use the drive in the park.* **b.** A driveway. **3a.** The means for transmitting motion to a machine: *Lathes often have a belt drive between the motor and the part that holds the piece being shaped.* **b.** The position or operating condition of such a mechanism: *put the car in drive.* **c.** The means by which automotive power is applied to a roadway: *Vehicles used by forest rangers often have four-wheel drive.* **4.** A device in a computer system that reads data from and often writes data onto a storage medium, such as an optical disc. **5a.** An organized effort to accomplish something: *a charity drive.* **b.** A massive and sustained military offensive. **6a.** In basketball, the act of moving with the ball directly to the basket. **b.** In football, a series of downs in which the ball is advanced by the offensive team. **7a.** Energy, push, or aggressiveness: *People who have drive and ambition often achieve their goals.* **b.** A strong motivating instinct: *the basic drive to satisfy one's hunger and thirst.* **8a.** The act of hitting a ball very swiftly. **b.** A golf shot made from a tee with a driver. **9a.** The act of rounding up and driving cattle, as to new pastures. **b.** A gathering and driving of logs down a river. ◆ **drive in** In baseball, to cause (a run) to be scored when batting. **drive at** To mean to do or say: *I'm not sure what you are driving at.* [From Old English *drīfan.*]

drive-in (drīv′ĭn′) *n.* A business, such as an outdoor movie theater, that allows customers to receive services or be entertained while in their vehicles.

driv·el (drĭv′əl) *v.* **driv·eled, driv·el·ing, driv·els** or **driv·elled, driv·el·ling, driv·els** —*intr.* **1.** To slobber; drool. **2.** To talk stupidly or childishly: *drivel on about nothing.* —*tr.* To say (something) stupidly: *driveled their usual empty promises.* ❖ *n.* **1.** Saliva flowing from the mouth. **2.** Stupid or senseless talk. [From Old English *dreflian.*] **—driv′el·er, driv′el·ler** *n.*

driv·en (drĭv′ən) *v.* Past participle of **drive.** ❖ *adj.* **1.** Piled up or carried along by a current: *driven snow.* **2.** Motivated by or having an irresistible inner drive or compulsion to do something: *driven to become the world's richest person.* **3.** Caused, sustained, or stimulated: *an export-driven economic recovery.*

driv·er (drī′vər) *n.* **1.** A person who drives a motor vehicle. **2.** A tool, such as a screwdriver or hammer, that is used to give forceful pressure to another object. **3.** A golf club with a wide head, used for making long shots from the tee. **4.** A machine part that transmits motion or power to something else.

drive shaft *n.* A rotating shaft that transmits mechanical power from a motor or engine to the place where power is applied.

drive-through or **drive-thru** (drīv′thro͞o′) *adj.* Relating to or conducting business with customers who drive up to a window: *drive-through banking.*

drive·way (drīv′wā′) *n.* A private road connecting a house, garage, or other building with the street.

driz·zle (drĭz′əl) *v.* **driz·zled, driz·zling, driz·zles** —*intr.* To rain gently in a fine mist. —*tr.* **1.** To let fall in fine drops: *drizzled sauce onto the meat.* **2.** To moisten with fine drops: *drizzled the asparagus with melted butter.* ❖ *n.* A fine gentle misty rain. **—driz′zly** *adj.*

DRM *abbr.* An abbreviation of digital rights management.

droll (drōl) *adj.* **droll·er, droll·est** Amusingly odd; comical. **—droll′ness** *n.*

drom·e·dar·y (drŏm′ĭ-dĕr′ē *or* drŭm′ĭ-dĕr′ē) *n., pl.* **drom·e·dar·ies** A one-humped camel, widely used for riding and carrying loads in desert regions from northern Africa to western Asia. [From Middle English *dromedarie*, from Late Latin *dromedārius*, from Latin *dromas*, from Greek *dromas*, running.]

drone[1] (drōn) *n.* **1.** A male bee, especially a honeybee that fertilizes the queen. Drones have no stings, do no work, and do not produce honey. **2.** An idle person who lives off others; a loafer. **3.** A person who does tedious or menial work; a drudge. **4.** A usually small or miniature aircraft that has no crew on board and is operated by remote control or by an onboard computer. [From Old English *drān.*]

drone[2] (drōn) *v.* **droned, dron·ing, drones** —*intr.* **1.** To make a continuous low dull humming sound: *An airplane droned far overhead.* **2.** To speak in a monotonous or boring tone: *He droned on about how great his kids were.* —*tr.* To utter in a dull monotone. ❖ *n.* **1.** A continuous low humming or buzzing sound: *the drone of the bumblebee.* **2a.** A bagpipe pipe that has no fingerholes and makes a single continuous tone. **b.** A long sustained tone. [Probably from *drone*, male bee, from its humming sound.]

drool (dro͞ol) *intr.v.* **drooled, drool·ing, drools** **1.** To let saliva dribble from the mouth; drivel. **2.** To show great

dromedary

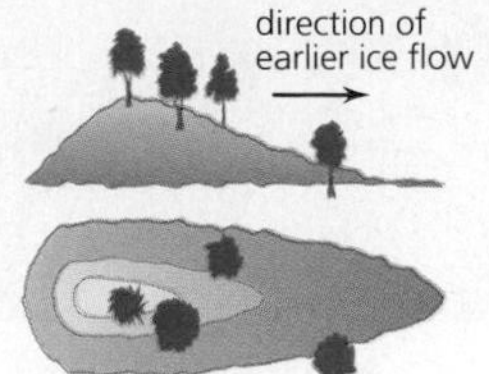

drumlin
top: view in profile
bottom: aerial view

appreciation or desire: *They drooled over the expensive bicycles in the window.* ❖ *n.* Saliva: *wipe the drool from the baby's chin.* [Perhaps alteration of *drivel.*]

droop (dro͞op) *v.* **drooped, droop·ing, droops** —*intr.* **1.** To bend or hang downward; sag: *The flowers are beginning to droop.* **2.** To sag in dejection or exhaustion: *The sightseers began to droop toward the end of the day.* —*tr.* To let bend or hang down: *The dog drooped its ears.* ❖ *n.* The act or condition of drooping. [From Middle English *droupen*, from Old Norse *drūpa.*]
❑ *These sound alike:* **droop, drupe** (fruit).

droop·y (dro͞o′pē) *adj.* **droop·i·er, droop·i·est** Bending or hanging downward; sagging: *droopy eyelids.* **—droop′i·ly** *adv.* **—droop′i·ness** *n.*

drop (drŏp) *n.* **1.** A small mass of liquid in a rounded shape: *drops of paint.* **2. drops** Liquid medicine administered in drops: *eye drops.* **3.** A small quantity of a substance: *There isn't a drop of juice left.* **4.** A trace or hint: *not a drop of pity.* **5.** Something resembling a drop in shape or size, especially a small globular piece of candy: *a lemon drop.* **6.** The act of falling; descent. **7.** A sudden fall or decrease, as in quality, quantity, or intensity: *a drop in temperature; a drop in prices.* **8.** The vertical distance from a higher to a lower level: *a drop of 200 feet.* **9.** A sheer incline, such as the face of a cliff: *The hikers avoided the drop.* **10.** Something that is arranged to fall or be lowered, as a curtain on a stage. ❖ *v.* **dropped, drop·ping, drops** —*intr.* **1.** To fall in drops: *rain dropping from an umbrella.* **2.** To fall from a higher to a lower place or position: *The plate dropped onto the floor.* **3.** To become less, as in intensity or number; decrease: *The temperature dropped as the sun went down.* **4.** To descend from one level to another: *The sun dropped toward the western hills.* **5.** To fall or sink into a state of exhaustion or death: *drop from overexertion.* **6.** To pass or sink into a specified state or condition: *dropped into a doze.* —*tr.* **1.** To let fall by releasing hold of: *I dropped the hot frying pan.* **2.** To let fall in drops: *drop medicine in a baby's ear.* **3.** To say or offer casually: *drop a hint.* **4.** To write at one's leisure: *drop a postcard to a friend.* **5.** To cease consideration or treatment of: *Let's drop the matter.* **6.** To terminate an association or relationship with: *drop one's friends.* **7.** To leave out (a letter, for example) in speaking or writing. **8.** To set down at a particular place; deliver or unload: *drop passengers at their destination; dropped a package off.* **9.** *Informal* To spend, especially lavishly or rashly: *dropped $800 at the mall while shopping.* ◆ **drop behind** To be unable to stay at the same pace as another: *One runner dropped behind as they came around the bend.* **drop by** To stop in for a short visit. **drop off 1.** To fall asleep. **2.** To decrease: *Temperatures usually drop off in the evening.* **drop out** To withdraw from participation, as in a game, club, or school. **drop over** To stop in for a short visit. [From Old English *dropa.*]

drop cloth *n.* A large cloth or sheet of plastic used to cover and protect furniture and floors while a room is being painted.

drop kick *n.* A kick made by dropping a ball to the ground and kicking it just as it starts to rebound.

drop leaf *n.* A hinged wing on a table that can be folded down when not in use.

drop·let (drŏp′lĭt) *n.* A tiny drop.

drop·out (drŏp′out′) *n.* **1.** A person who quits school. **2.** A person who withdraws from a given social group.

drop·per (drŏp′ər) *n.* A small tube with a suction bulb at one end for drawing in a liquid and releasing it in drops.

drop·pings (drŏp′ĭngz) *pl.n.* The excrement of animals.

drop·sy (drŏp′sē) *n.* Edema. This term is no longer used in medicine.

dro·soph·i·la (drə-sŏf′ə-lə) *n.* Any of various small fruit flies, especially a kind used extensively in genetic research.

dross (drŏs) *n.* **1.** The waste material that rises to the surface of a molten metal as it is being smelted or refined. **2.** Worthless, commonplace, or trivial matter.

drought (drout) *n.* A long period of little or no rainfall.

drove[1] (drōv) *v.* Past tense of **drive.**

drove[2] (drōv) *n.* **1.** A flock or herd being driven in a group. **2.** A large mass of people moving or acting as a body: *droves of visitors on their way to the White House.* [From Old English *drāf*, from *drīfan*, drive.]

drov·er (drō′vər) *n.* A person who drives cattle or sheep.

drown (droun) *v.* **drowned, drown·ing, drowns** —*tr.* **1.** To kill by submerging and suffocating in water or another liquid. **2.** To drench thoroughly or cover with or as if with a liquid: *They drowned their meat in gravy.* **3.** To deaden one's awareness of; blot out: *drown disappointment in the company of friends.* **4.** To muffle or mask (a sound) with a louder sound: *Their laughter drowned out the speaker's voice.* —*intr.* To die by suffocating in water or other liquid: *Many animals drowned on the flooded farmland.* [From Middle English *drounen*, probably of Scandinavian origin.]

drowse (drouz) *intr.v.* **drowsed, drows·ing, drows·es** To be half-asleep: *The cat drowsed in the sun.*

drows·y (drou′zē) *adj.* **drows·i·er, drows·i·est 1.** Dull with sleepiness; sluggish: *feeling drowsy after dinner.* **2.** Causing sleepiness: *a drowsy lullaby.* **—drows′i·ly** *adv.* **—drows′i·ness** *n.*

drub (drŭb) *tr.v.* **drubbed, drub·bing, drubs 1.** To beat with a stick. **2.** To instill forcefully: *drubbed the lesson into my head.* **3.** To defeat thoroughly: *drub an opposing team.*

drudge (drŭj) *n.* A person who does tedious, unpleasant, or menial work. ❖ *intr.v.* **drudged, drudg·ing, drudg·es** To do tedious, unpleasant, or menial work.

drudg·er·y (drŭj′ə-rē) *n.* Tedious, unpleasant, or menial work: *Cleaning my room always seems like drudgery.*

drug (drŭg) *n.* **1.** A substance used in medicine especially to cure a disease or relieve its symptoms. **2.** A narcotic or other substance that affects the central nervous system, causing changes in mood and behavior. Narcotic drugs tend to be addictive. ❖ *tr.v.* **drugged, drug·ging, drugs 1.** To administer a drug to: *drug a patient with an anesthetic before an operation.* **2.** To mix a drug into (food or drink). [From Middle English *drogge*, perhaps from Middle Dutch *droge (vate)*, dry (cases).]

drug·gist (drŭg′ĭst) *n.* A pharmacist or person who sells drugs in a store.

drug·store (drŭg′stôr′) *n.* A store where prescriptions are filled and medical supplies and other items are sold.

dru·id also **Dru·id** (dro͞o′ĭd) *n.* A member of an order of pagan priests in ancient Britain and Gaul. [From Latin *druidēs*, druids, of Celtic origin.]

drum (drŭm) *n.* **1.** A musical instrument consisting of a hollow container shaped like a cylinder or bowl with a membrane stretched tightly over one or both ends, played by beating with the hands or sticks. **2.** A sound produced by this instrument or a similar sound. **3.** Something having a shape or structure like a drum: *an oil drum; a cable drum.* ❖ *v.* **drummed, drum·ming, drums** —*intr.* **1.** To play a drum or drums. **2.** To thump or tap rhythmically or continually: *I drummed on the table with my pencil.* —*tr.* **1.** To produce (a beat or rhythm) on a drum. **2.** To make known to or force upon (a person) by constant repetition: *I drummed the facts into my head to pass the test.* **3.** To expel or dismiss in disgrace: *drummed the private out of the corps.* ◆ **drum up** To bring about by continuous persistent effort: *Students drummed up support for their trip.* [From Middle English *drom*, probably from Middle Dutch *tromme*, probably of imitative origin.]

drum·beat (drŭm′bēt′) *n.* The sound produced by beating a drum.

ă	pat	ôr	core
ā	pay	oi	boy
âr	care	ou	out
ä	father	o͝o	took
ĕ	pet	o͝or	lure
ē	be	o͞o	boot
ĭ	pit	ŭ	cut
ī	bite	ûr	urge
îr	pier	th	thin
ŏ	pot	*th*	this
ō	toe	zh	vision
ô	paw	ə	about

drum·head (drŭm′hĕd′) *n.* The material stretched over one or both ends of a drum.

drum·lin (drŭm′lĭn) *n.* A ridge or elongated hill with a smooth summit, formed from glacial deposits.

drum major *n.* A person who leads a marching band or drum corps, often twirling a baton.

drum majorette *n.* A girl or woman who leads a marching band or drum corps, often twirling a baton.

drum·mer (drŭm′ər) *n.* A person who plays a drum, as in a band.

drum·roll (drŭm′rōl′) *n.* A rapid series of short sounds made by beating a drum.

drum·stick (drŭm′stĭk′) *n.* **1.** A stick for beating a drum. **2.** The lower part of the leg of a cooked chicken or turkey.

drunk (drŭngk) *v.* Past participle of **drink.** ❖ *adj.* **1.** Intoxicated with an alcoholic beverage. **2.** Overcome by strong feeling or emotion: *The dictator is drunk with power.* ❖ *n.* **1.** A drunkard. **2.** A drunken spree.

drunk·ard (drŭng′kərd) *n.* A person who is habitually drunk.

drunk·en (drŭng′kən) *adj.* **1.** Drunk; intoxicated. **2.** Relating to, involving, or occurring during intoxication: *a drunken brawl.* **—drunk′en·ly** *adv.* **—drunk′en·ness** *n.*

drupe (dro͞op) *n.* A fleshy fruit, such as a cherry, plum, or peach, whose seed is contained in a hard pit or stone surrounded by soft pulpy flesh.
❑ *These sound alike:* **drupe, droop** (sag).

druth·ers (drŭ*th*′ərz) *pl.n. Informal* A choice or preference.

dry (drī) *adj.* **dri·er** (drī′ər), **dri·est** (drī′ĭst) or **dry·er, dry·est 1.** Free from liquid or moisture: *dry clothes; dry air.* **2.** Having little or no rainfall; arid: *the dry season; a dry area.* **3.** Not under water: *We stepped ashore on dry land.* **4.** Having all or almost all of the liquid or water drained away or used up: *a dry stream; a dry well.* **5.** No longer yielding milk: *a dry cow.* **6.** Not shedding tears: *dry sobs.* **7.** Needing or desiring drink: *My throat is dry.* **8.** Not sweet. Used of wines. **9.** Eaten or served without butter or other spread: *dry toast.* **10.** Having no adornment; plain: *a dry speaker; dry facts.* **11.** Quietly humorous; ironic: *a dry wit.* **12.** Not permitting the sale or consumption of alcoholic beverages: *a dry county.* ❖ *v.* **dried** (drīd), **dry·ing, dries** (drīz) *—tr.* To remove the moisture from; make dry: *We dried the dishes after supper. —intr.* To become dry: *The laundry dried quickly in the sun.* ◆ **dry up** To make or become unproductive, especially to do so gradually: *The stream dried up over the hot arid summer.* [From Old English *drȳge.*] **—dry′ly** *adv.* **—dry′ness** *n.*

dry·ad (drī′əd *or* drī′ăd′) *n.* In Greek mythology, a wood nymph.

dry cell *n.* An electric cell in which the chemical producing the current is a moist paste rather than a liquid.

dry-clean (drī′klēn′) *tr.v.* **dry-cleaned, dry-clean·ing, dry-cleans** To clean (clothing or fabrics) with chemical solvents that have little or no water.

dry cleaner *n.* A person or business that dry-cleans clothes.

dry cleaning *n.* The cleaning of fabrics with chemical solvents.

dry dock *n.* A large dock in the form of a basin from which the water can be emptied, used for building or repairing a ship below its water line.

dry-dock (drī′dŏk′) *tr. & intr.v.* **dry-docked, dry-dock·ing, dry-docks** To place in or go into a dry dock.

dry·er (drī′ər) *n.* **1.** A appliance that removes moisture by heating or another process: *a clothes dryer.* **2.** Variant of **drier¹**.

dry farming *n.* A type of farming practiced in arid regions without irrigation by maintaining a mulch on the surface that protects the natural moisture of the soil from evaporation.

dry goods *pl.n.* Cloth, clothing, and related articles of trade.

dry ice *n.* Carbon dioxide that is compressed and chilled into a solid. It is used as a cooling agent.

dry·ing oil (drī′ĭng) *n.* An organic oil, such as linseed oil, used in paints and varnishes. It dries into a tough elastic layer when exposed to air.

dry measure *n.* A system of units for measuring dry commodities, such as grains, fruits, and vegetables.

dry rot *n.* A decaying of timber that is caused by a fungus and results in the wood becoming brittle and crumbling into powder.

dry run *n.* A trial exercise; a rehearsal.

dry·suit (drī′so͞ot′) *n.* A garment made of rubber or other impermeable material that is sealed to prevent leakage and worn to keep the body warm and dry in cold water, used especially in scuba diving.

dry·wall (drī′wôl′) *n.* **1.** A material consisting of rectangular sheets of plaster bonded to layers of heavy paper, used to cover walls or ceilings. **2.** A stone wall constructed without mortar.

Ds The symbol for the element **darmstadtium.**

DST *abbr.* An abbreviation of daylight-saving time.

du·al (do͞o′əl) *adj.* **1.** Composed of two parts; double: *dual controls for pilot and copilot.* **2.** Having a double character or purpose. **—du′al·ly** *adv.*
❑ *These sound alike:* **dual, duel** (combat).

du·al·i·ty (doo-ăl′ĭ-tē) *n.* The quality or condition of being twofold.

dub¹ (dŭb) *tr.v.* **dubbed, dub·bing, dubs 1.** To confer knighthood on (a man) by tapping him on the shoulder with a sword. **2.** To give a nickname to: *The cat was named Cleo, but the children dubbed it "Mittens."* [From Old English *dubbian,* perhaps from Old French *aduber.*]

dub² (dŭb) *tr.v.* **dubbed, dub·bing, dubs 1.** To transfer (recorded material) onto a new recording medium. **2.** To provide (a film) with a new soundtrack, often with the dialogue in a different language: *The Russian film was dubbed in English for American audiences.* [Short for *double.*]

Du·bai (do͞o-bī′) A city of eastern United Arab Emirates on the Persian Gulf.

du·bi·ous (do͞o′bē-əs) *adj.* **1.** Feeling or showing doubt or uncertainty; uncertain: *I am dubious of the outcome.* **2.** Causing or arousing doubt; doubtful: *an argument based on dubious reasoning.* **3.** Of uncertain morality; questionable or suspicious: *He associates with some very dubious characters.* **—du′bi·ous·ly** *adv.*

Dub·lin (dŭb′lĭn) The capital of Ireland, in the east-central part of the country on the Irish Sea.

dub·ni·um (do͞ob′nē-əm) *n. Symbol* **Db** A radioactive element that has been artificially produced by scientists. Atomic number 105. See **Periodic Table.** [After *Dubna,* Russia.]

Du Bois (do͞o bois′), **William Edward Burghardt** 1868–1963. American civil rights leader who cofounded the NAACP and worked to promote the concerns of African Americans and Africans.

du·cal (do͞o′kəl) *adj.* Relating to a duke or duchy.

duc·at (dŭk′ət) *n.* Any of various gold or silver coins formerly used in Europe.

duch·ess (dŭch′ĭs) *n.* **1.** The wife or widow of a duke. **2.** A woman holding a duchy.

duch·y (dŭch′ē) *n., pl.* **duch·ies** The territory ruled by a duke or duchess.

duck¹ (dŭk) *n.* **1.** Any of various wild or domesticated waterbirds having a broad flat bill, a short neck, short legs, and webbed feet. **2.** A female duck, as distinguished

WRITERS CHOOSE THEIR WORDS

Raffy climbs in and disappears under the dashboard. I lean on the windowsill looking in as she pulls out wires and connects them like someone out of those movies that I have always been so **dubious** about because it's always looked so easy. "You are impressing me like crazy here," I say to her.

—Melina Marchetta
Jellicoe Road

W.E.B. Du Bois

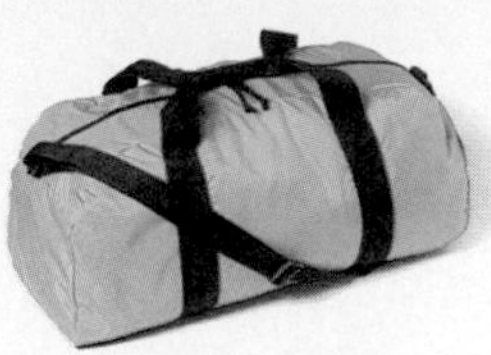

duffle bag

dugong

dumbbell

ă	pat	ôr	core
ā	pay	oi	boy
âr	care	ou	out
ä	father	o͝o	took
ĕ	pet	o͝or	lure
ē	be	o͞o	boot
ĭ	pit	ŭ	cut
ī	bite	ûr	urge
îr	pier	th	thin
ŏ	pot	*th*	this
ō	toe	zh	vision
ô	paw	ə	about

from a drake. **3.** The meat of a duck used as food. [From Old English *dūce*.]

duck² (dŭk) *v.* **ducked, duck·ing, ducks** —*tr.* **1.** To lower (the head and body) quickly: *She ducked her head getting into the car.* **2.** To evade; dodge: *duck a responsibility.* **3.** To push suddenly under water: *duck someone in the pool.* —*intr.* **1.** To lower the head or body quickly: *The boy ducked under the table.* **2.** To push or dip suddenly under water. **3.** *Informal* To enter or leave quickly or temporarily: *duck out of a meeting.* [From Middle English *douken*, to dive.]

duck³ (dŭk) *n.* **1.** A strong cotton or linen cloth that is lighter than canvas. **2. ducks** Pants, especially white ones, made of this fabric. [From Dutch *doek*, cloth.]

duck-billed dinosaur (dŭk′bĭld′) *n.* Any of various plant-eating dinosaurs that had webbed feet, a ducklike bill, and sometimes a crest on the head.

duck-billed platypus *n.* The platypus.

duck·ling (dŭk′lĭng) *n.* A young duck.

duck·weed (dŭk′wēd′) *n.* Any of various small stemless water plants that form floating masses on the surface of ponds and other quiet waters.

duct (dŭkt) *n.* **1.** An enclosed passage used to conduct something, such as a gas or liquid: *installed ducts for the air-conditioning system.* **2.** A tube in the body for carrying a bodily fluid, especially a fluid secreted by a gland: *bile duct.* **3.** A tube or pipe that encloses electric cables or wires. [From Latin *ductus*, act of leading, from *dūcere*, to lead.]

duc·tile (dŭk′təl *or* dŭk′tīl′) *adj.* **1.** Easily drawn out into wire or hammered thin: *Silver is a ductile metal.* **2.** Easily molded or shaped: *Plastic pipe is ductile if heated.* **3.** Readily persuaded or influenced; tractable. **—duc·til′i·ty** (dŭk-tĭl′ĭ-tē) *n.*

duct·less gland (dŭkt′lĭs) *n.* An endocrine gland.

duct tape *n.* A strong, adhesive tape made of cloth mesh coated with a waterproof material, originally designed for sealing heating and air-conditioning ducts.

dud (dŭd) *n.* **1.** A bomb or shell that fails to explode. **2.** A person or thing that turns out to be ineffective or unsuccessful: *Our hasty plan was a real dud.*

dude (do͞od) *Informal n.* **1a.** A man; a fellow. **b.** A person of either sex. **2.** A city person who vacations on a ranch in the American West. ◆ **duded up** Dressed in formal or fancy clothes.

dude ranch *n.* A resort patterned after a Western ranch, featuring horseback riding and other outdoor activities.

dudg·eon (dŭj′ən) *n.* A sullen, angry, or indignant state of mind: *The insulted customer walked out of the shop in high dudgeon.*

due (do͞o) *adj.* **1a.** Owed as a debt: *We must pay the amount still due.* **b.** Required to be submitted: *books due back to the library; homework due tomorrow.* **2.** Fitting or appropriate; suitable: *Every citizen is required to show due respect for the law.* **3.** As much as needed; sufficient; adequate: *We left early, taking due care to be on time.* **4a.** Expected or scheduled: *When is the train due to arrive?* **b.** Expected to give birth: *She's due any day now.* **5.** Expecting or ready for something as part of a normal course or sequence: *We're due for some rain.* ❖ *n.* **1.** Something that is owed or deserved: *a dedicated scholar who finally got his due.* **2. dues** A charge or fee for membership, as in a club. ❖ *adv.* Straight; directly: *The settlers traveled due west.* [From Middle English, from Old French *deu*, from *devoir*, to owe, from Latin *dēbēre*.]

❑ *These sound alike:* **due, dew** (water droplets), **do¹** (perform).

du·el (do͞o′əl) *n.* **1.** A fight using weapons and arranged in advance between two people, usually to settle a matter concerning personal honor. **2.** A struggle between two opponents: *a duel of wits between lawyers in the courtroom.* ❖ *tr. & intr.v.* **du·eled, du·el·ing, du·els** or **du·elled, du·el·ling, du·els** To fight in a duel. [From Middle English *duelle*, from Latin *duellum*, war, variant of *bellum*.] **—du′el·er, du′el·ler, du′el·ist, du′el·list** *n.*

❑ *These sound alike:* **duel, dual** (double).

due process *n.* An established course of proceeding in judicial or other governmental activity that is designed to protect the legal rights of the individual.

du·et (do͞o-ĕt′) *n.* **1a.** A musical composition for two voices or two instruments. **b.** The two performers of such a composition. **2.** A pair.

due to *prep.* Because of: *The cancellation of the concert was due to bad weather.*

duf·fel or **duf·fle** (dŭf′əl) *n.* **1.** A coarse woolen cloth with a nap on both sides. **2.** Clothing and other personal gear carried when camping. [After *Duffel*, a town of northern Belgium.]

duffle bag or **duffel bag** *n.* A large cylindrical cloth bag of canvas or duck for carrying personal belongings.

dug (dŭg) *v.* Past tense and past participle of **dig.**

du·gong (do͞o′gŏng′) *n.* A plant-eating tropical sea mammal having a broad snout, a pair of front flippers, and a flat broad tail.

dug·out (dŭg′out′) *n.* **1.** A boat or canoe made by hollowing out a log. **2.** A rough shelter dug into the ground or on a hillside and used especially in battle for protection from artillery. **3.** Either of two low shelters at the side of a baseball field where the players stay while not on the field.

duh (dŭ) *interj.* An expression used to show scorn, especially for a remark that is considered to be obvious.

DUI *abbr.* An abbreviation of driving under the influence (of drugs or alcohol).

du jour (də **zho͝or′** *or* do͞o **zho͝or′**) *adj.* Offered on a given day: *the soup du jour.*

duke (do͞ok) *n.* **1.** A nobleman of the highest rank, especially a man of the highest level of the British peerage. **2.** A man who rules an independent duchy. **3. dukes** *Slang* The fists: *Put up your dukes and let's fight.*

duke·dom (do͞ok′dəm) *n.* **1.** A duchy. **2.** The rank, office, or title of a duke.

dul·cet (dŭl′sĭt) *adj.* Soothing and agreeable, especially to the ear: *sweet dulcet tones.*

dul·ci·mer (dŭl′sə-mər) *n.* **1.** A narrow, often hourglass-shaped stringed instrument having three or four strings and a fretted neck, typically held flat across the knees and played by plucking or strumming. **2.** A musical instrument with a set of wire strings stretched across a four-sided sound box, played by striking with two padded hammers. [From Middle English *doucemer*, probably from Latin *dulce melos*, sweet song.]

dull (dŭl) *adj.* **dull·er, dull·est 1.** Not sharp or pointed; blunt: *a dull knife; a dull pencil.* **2.** Not interesting; boring: *a dull book; dull work.* See Synonyms at **boring. 3.** Mentally weak; stupid. **4.** Not keenly or intensely felt: *a dull ache in my throat.* **5.** Not bright or vivid; dim: *a dull red.* **6.** Not loud or clear; muffled: *the dull rumble of distant thunder.* ❖ *tr. & intr.v.* **dulled, dull·ing, dulls** To make or become dull: *The saw blade dulled as it cut more wood.* **—dull′ness** *n.* **—dul′ly** *adv.*

dull·ard (dŭl′ərd) *n.* A dull or stupid person.

du·ly (do͞o′lē) *adv.* **1.** In a proper manner; rightfully: *a duly elected candidate.* **2.** At the expected time; punctually: *The loan was duly repaid.*

dumb (dŭm) *adj.* **dumb·er, dumb·est 1.** Lacking the human ability to use speech: *dumb animals.* **2.** *Offensive* Incapable of using speech. Used of humans. **3.** Unwilling to speak; silent: *The witness remained dumb under questioning.* **4.** Temporarily speechless, as with shock or fear: *I was dumb with disbelief.* **5.** Unintelligent; stupid. **—dumb′ly** *adv.* **—dumb′ness** *n.*

dumb·bell (dŭm′bĕl′) *n.* **1.** A weight consisting of a short bar with a metal ball or disk at each end that is lifted to exercise and develop the muscles. **2.** *Slang* A stupid or ignorant person; a dolt.

dumb·found (dŭm′found′) *tr.v.* **dumb·found·ed, dumb·found·ing, dumb·founds** To make speechless with astonishment; amaze or bewilder: *The sophistication of the young man's answers dumbfounded the experts.*

dumb·wait·er (dŭm′wā′tər) *n.* A small elevator used to transport food, dishes, or other articles from one floor to another.

dum·my (dŭm′ē) *n., pl.* **dum·mies 1.** A model of the human body, used as a substitute for a person: *A dummy was used to test the seat belt.* **2.** Something made to look like a real object; an imitation or counterfeit: *The drawer in the cabinet is a dummy.* **3.** A person who acts in business deals on behalf of another person whose identity is concealed. **4.** A stupid person; a dolt. **5.** The player in a card game whose hand is shown and played by a partner. ❖ *adj.* **1.** Made to work like or resemble a real object; imitation; fake: *Dummy cannons fooled the enemy.* **2.** Secretly in the service of another: *a dummy corporation covering up their criminal activities.*

dump (dŭmp) *tr.v.* **dumped, dump·ing, dumps 1.** To release or throw down in a mass: *The factory dumped waste into the river. Don't dump your books on the table.* **2.** To empty out (a container or vehicle): *dump a wastebasket.* **3.** To get rid of or reject: *The president dumped several controversial candidates for the position.* **4.** To sell (goods) in large quantities and at a low price: *The company dumped its old stock of air conditioners in several countries.* **5.** To print out or transfer (information stored in computer memory) without processing it. ❖ *n.* **1.** A place where garbage, trash, or other waste is discarded or kept: *The town dump is nearly full.* **2.** A military storage place: *an ammunition dump.* **3.** A messy or shabby place: *The old house is a dump.*

dump·ling (dŭmp′lĭng) *n.* **1.** A piece of dough, sometimes filled, that is steamed, fried, or cooked in liquid such as water or soup. **2.** Sweetened dough wrapped around fruit, such as an apple, baked and served as dessert.

dumps (dŭmps) *pl.n.* Low gloomy spirits; depression: *down in the dumps.*

Dump·ster (dŭmp′stər) A trademark used for containers designed for receiving, transporting, and dumping waste materials.

dump truck *n.* A heavy-duty truck having a bed that tilts backward to dump loose material.

dump·y (dŭm′pē) *adj.* **dump·i·er, dump·i·est 1.** Messy or shabby: *a dumpy office.* **2.** Short and plump.

dun[1] (dŭn) *tr.v.* **dunned, dun·ning, duns** To make persistent demands of (someone), especially for payment of a debt.

❑ *These sound alike:* **dun**[1] (ask for payment), **done** (finished), **dun**[2] (grayish brown).

dun[2] (dŭn) *n.* **1.** A dull grayish brown. **2.** A horse of this color. [From Old English *dunn,* perhaps of Celtic origin.]

❑ *These sound alike:* **dun**[2] (grayish brown), **done** (finished), **dun**[1] (ask for payment).

dunce (dŭns) *n.* A stupid person. [After John *Duns Scotus* (1265?–1308), Scottish scholastic theologian whose writings and philosophy were ridiculed in the 1500s.]

dune (do͞on) *n.* A hill or ridge of wind-blown sand. [From French, from Middle Dutch *dūne.*]

dune buggy *n.* A light, recreational motor vehicle with oversize tires, designed for use on sand dunes or beaches.

dung (dŭng) *n.* The excrement of animals, especially when used as manure.

dun·ga·ree (dŭng′gə-rē′) *n.* **1.** A sturdy, often blue denim fabric. **2. dungarees** Overalls or pants made from this fabric. [From Hindi *dungrī.*]

dun·geon (dŭn′jən) *n.* A dark, often underground chamber or cell used to confine prisoners.

dunk (dŭngk) *tr.v.* **dunked, dunk·ing, dunks 1.** To dip or briefly submerge (something) in a liquid: *dunk a doughnut in tea.* **2.** To submerge (someone) playfully, as in a swimming pool. **3.** In basketball, to slam (a ball) through the basket from above. ❖ *n.* In basketball, a shot made by jumping and slamming the ball down through the basket.

Dun·kirk (dŭn′kûrk′) A city of northern France on the North Sea. In World War II more than 330,000 Allied troops were evacuated from its beaches (May–June 1940).

du·o (do͞o′ō) *n., pl.* **du·os 1.** A duet, as of musical performers. **2.** Two people or two things that are closely associated.

du·o·dec·i·mal (do͞o′ə-dĕs′ə-məl) *adj.* Relating to or based on twelfths or the number 12: *a duodecimal digit.* [From Latin *duodecim,* twelve : *duo,* two + *decem,* ten.]

duodecimal system *n.* A number system with a base of 12. It uses twelve digits instead of the more familiar ten digits of the decimal system.

du·o·de·num (do͞o′ə-dē′nəm *or* do͞o-ŏd′n-əm) *n., pl.* **du·o·de·na** (do͞o′ə-dē′nə *or* do͞o-ŏd′n-ə) or **du·o·de·nums** The portion of the small intestine starting at the lower end of the stomach and extending to the jejunum. **—du′o·de′nal** *adj.*

dupe (do͞op) *n.* A person who is used or taken advantage of through deception and trickery. ❖ *tr.v.* **duped, dup·ing, dupes** To deceive; trick; fool: *The advertisement duped us into believing the bicycles were on sale.*

du·ple (do͞o′pəl) *adj.* **1.** Consisting of two parts or units; double. **2.** Consisting of two beats or some multiple of two beats to a musical measure.

du·plex (do͞o′plĕks′) *adj.* **1.** Having two parts; twofold; double: *Both plugs will fit in a duplex electrical outlet.* **2.** Having two apartments, divisions, or floors. ❖ *n.* A house divided into two living units, usually with separate entrances. —SEE NOTE.

du·pli·cate (do͞o′plĭ-kĭt) *adj.* Exactly the same as something else, especially because of having been copied from an original: *a duplicate key.* ❖ *n.* **1.** An exact copy; a double: *That letter is a duplicate of the original.* **2.** Something that corresponds exactly to another: *Your bike is a duplicate of mine.* ❖ *tr.v.* (do͞o′plĭ-kāt′) **du·pli·cat·ed, du·pli·cat·ing, du·pli·cates 1.** To make an exact copy of: *duplicate a key.* **2.** To do or perform again; repeat: *duplicate an experiment.* [From Middle English, from Latin *duplicātus,* from *duplicāre,* to double, from *duplex,* twofold.] —SEE NOTE AT **duplex.**

du·pli·ca·tion (do͞o′plĭ-kā′shən) *n.* **1.** The act or condition of being duplicated: *Duplication of the experiment confirmed the original results.* **2.** A duplicate; a replica: *an exact duplication of the document.* **3.** The occurrence of a repeated section of genetic material in a chromosome.

du·pli·ca·tor (do͞o′plĭ-kā′tər) *n.* A machine or device that makes copies of printed or digital material.

du·plic·i·ty (do͞o-plĭs′ĭ-tē) *n., pl.* **du·plic·i·ties** Deliberate deceptiveness in behavior or speech; deceit.

du·ra·ble (do͝or′ə-bəl) *adj.* **1.** Capable of withstanding wear and tear; sturdy: *Denim is a durable fabric used for work clothes.* **2.** Lasting or enduring; stable: *a durable friendship.* [From Middle English, from Latin *dūrāre,* to last.] **—du′ra·bil′i·ty, du′ra·ble·ness** *n.* **—du′ra·bly** *adv.*

durable goods *pl.n.* Manufactured products that can be used for a long time. Furniture, refrigerators, and automobiles are durable goods.

du·ra·tion (do͞o-rā′shən) *n.* The period of time during

WORD BUILDING

duplex The word root *plex–* in English words comes from Latin *–plex,* which meant "multiplied by a specific number." **Duplex** means "twofold, double" (using the word *duo,* "two"); **triplex** is literally "threefold" (*tri–,* "three"); and **multiplex** means "manifold, multiple" (*multi–,* "many"). The Latin *–plex* is related to the verb *plicāre,* "to fold," from whose past participle *plicātus* we form the verb **duplicate** and the noun **multiplication.**

dust storm

which something exists or persists: *the duration of a storm.*

Dü·rer (dŏŏr′ər), **Albrecht** 1471–1528. German painter and engraver who incorporated Italian Renaissance classicism into northern European art.

du·ress (dŏŏ-rĕs′) *n.* The use of force or threat to compel someone to do something: *The prisoner confessed under duress.*

dur·ing (dŏŏr′ĭng) *prep.* **1.** Throughout the course or duration of: *We talked during the entire evening.* **2.** Within the time of; at some time in: *He was born during the last half of the 1800s.*

durst (dûrst) *v. Archaic* A past tense and a past participle of **dare.**

du·rum (dŏŏr′əm) *n.* A kind of wheat having hard grains, used chiefly in making pasta.

Du·shan·be (dōō-shăm′bə *or* dōō-shăm′bə) The capital of Tajikistan, in the western part of the country south of Tashkent, Uzbekistan.

dusk (dŭsk) *n.* The time of evening just before darkness; the darker stage of twilight: *Only a few stars shine at dusk.*

dusk·y (dŭs′kē) *adj.* **dusk·i·er, dusk·i·est 1.** Having little light; dim: *a dusky room.* See Synonyms at **dark. 2.** Rather dark in color: *dusky blue.* **—dusk′i·ly** *adv.*

dust (dŭst) *n.* **1.** Fine dry particles of matter: *clouds of dust raised by a herd of cattle; the dust gathering on old books.* **2.** Pieces of earth or dirt, especially when regarded as the remains of a decayed body. ❖ *v.* **dust·ed, dust·ing, dusts** *—tr.* **1.** To remove dust from by wiping or brushing: *We dusted the shelves.* **2.** To sprinkle with a powdery substance: *I dusted my feet with powder. —intr.* To clean by removing dust: *The cleaning staff dusts every day.* ◆ **dust off** To restore or revise for current use: *dust off an old essay for publication.* **in the dust** Far behind, as in a race or contest: *left her competitors in the dust.* [From Old English *dūst.*]

❑ *These sound alike:* **dust, dost** (do).

dust bowl *n.* **1.** A region in which dry weather and dust storms have produced conditions like those of a desert. **2. Dust Bowl** A region in the south-central United States that was stricken with drought and dust storms in the 1930s.

dust·er (dŭs′tər) *n.* **1.** A person or thing that dusts. **2.** A cloth or brush used to remove dust. **3.** A device for spreading powder on plants. **4.** A coat or smock worn to protect one's clothing from dust.

dust jacket *n.* **1.** A paper cover used to protect the outside of a book. **2.** A cardboard sleeve used to protect a phonograph record.

dust·pan (dŭst′păn′) *n.* A short-handled pan, shaped like a shovel, into which dust is swept.

dust storm *n.* A windstorm that sweeps clouds of dust across a large area, especially in a dry region.

dust·y (dŭs′tē) *adj.* **dust·i·er, dust·i·est 1.** Covered or filled with dust: *a dusty road; a dusty room.* **2.** Consisting of or resembling dust; powdery: *dusty soil.* **3.** Tinged with gray: *a dusty beard.* **—dust′i·ness** *n.*

Dutch (dŭch) *adj.* Relating to the Netherlands or its people, language, or culture. ❖ *n.* **1.** *(used with a plural verb)* The people of the Netherlands. **2.** The Germanic language of the Netherlands. ◆ **go Dutch** To pay one's own expenses, as on a date. [From Middle English *Duch,* German, Dutch, from Middle Dutch *Dūtsch,* relating to the ordinary people.]

Dutch door *n.* A door divided in two horizontally so that one part may be left open or closed.

Dutch East In·dies (ĭn′dēz) See **Indonesia.**

Dutch·man (dŭch′mən) *n.* A man who is a native or inhabitant of the Netherlands.

Dutch oven *n.* **1.** A large heavy pot or kettle with a tight lid, used for slow cooking. **2.** An open metal box equipped with shelves and placed before a fire for baking or roasting food. **3.** A wall oven in which food is baked by means of preheated brick walls.

Dutch treat *n. Informal* An outing, as for dinner or a movie, for which each person pays his or her own expenses.

Dutch·wom·an (dŭch′wŏŏm′ən) *n.* A woman who is a native or inhabitant of the Netherlands.

du·te·ous (dōō′tē-əs) *adj.* Obedient; dutiful: *a duteous and attentive assistant.* **—du′te·ous·ly** *adv.*

du·ti·a·ble (dōō′tē-ə-bəl) *adj.* Subject to a tax when imported into a country: *dutiable goods.*

du·ti·ful (dōō′tĭ-fəl) *adj.* **1.** Careful to perform one's duty; obedient. **2.** Expressing or coming from a sense of duty: *dutiful words.* **—du′ti·ful·ly** *adv.*

du·ty (dōō′tē) *n., pl.* **du·ties 1.** Something that a person ought to or must do; an obligation: *In a democracy one of the chief duties of a citizen is to vote.* **2.** Required action or service: *You must report for jury duty.* **3.** Moral obligation: *It is your duty to tell the truth.* **4.** A task, assignment, or function that is part of one's work: *household duties.* **5.** A tax charged by a government on imported or exported goods. [From Middle English *duete,* from Anglo-Norman, from Old French *deu,* due.]

DVD (dē′vē-dē′) *n.* A high-density optical disc used especially for storing movies.

DVR *abbr.* An abbreviation of digital video recorder.

dwarf (dwôrf) *n., pl.* **dwarfs** or **dwarves** (dwôrvz) **1a.** A person who is much smaller than normal and whose limbs and features are often atypically proportioned or formed. **b.** An atypically small plant or animal. **2.** In fairy tales and legends, a small creature resembling a human who has magical powers. ❖ *tr.v.* **dwarfed, dwarf·ing, dwarfs 1.** To check the natural growth of; stunt: *Lack of water dwarfed the trees.* **2.** To make seem small by comparison: *The skyscraper dwarfed the old church.* [From Middle English *dwergh, dwarf,* from Old English *dweorg.*]

dwarf planet *n.* A celestial object that orbits around the sun, is not a satellite of a planet, and has insufficient gravitational force to pull objects crossing its orbit around the sun into an orbit around it. —SEE NOTE AT **planet.**

dwarf star *n.* A star of relatively small size and mass that emits an average or below average amount of light. The sun is a dwarf star.

dwell (dwĕl) *intr.v.* **dwelt** (dwĕlt) or **dwelled, dwell·ing, dwells 1.** To live as a resident; reside: *dwell in a city.* **2.** To speak or write about at length: *The article dwells on the need for better health care.* **3.** To focus one's attention on; brood about: *Don't dwell on past mistakes.* [From Old English *dwellan,* to mislead, delay.] **—dwell′er** *n.*

dwell·ing (dwĕl′ĭng) *n.* A place to live in; a residence: *Our house is a two-story dwelling.*

DWI *abbr.* An abbreviation of driving while intoxicated.

dwin·dle (dwĭn′dl) *intr.v.* **dwin·dled, dwin·dling, dwin·dles** To become gradually less until little is left: *Their savings dwindled away to nothing over the year.* See Synonyms at **decrease.**

Dy The symbol for the element **dysprosium.**

dye (dī) *n.* **1.** A substance used to color food, hair, cloth, or other materials. **2.** A color produced by dyeing: *The dye in the curtains faded in sunlight.* ❖ *v.* **dyed, dye·ing, dyes** *—tr.* To color with a dye: *dye a fabric red. —intr.* To become colored by a dye: *Some fabrics dye more easily than others.* [From Old English *dēag.*] **—dy′er** *n.*

❑ *These sound alike:* **dye, die[1]** (stop living), **die[2]** (device for shaping material).

dyed-in-the-wool (dīd′ĭn-thə-wŏŏl′) *adj.* Thoroughgoing; outright: *a dyed-in-the-wool conservative.*

ă	pat	ôr	core
ā	pay	oi	boy
âr	care	ou	out
ä	father	ŏŏ	took
ĕ	pet	ŏŏr	lure
ē	be	ōō	boot
ĭ	pit	ŭ	cut
ī	bite	ûr	urge
îr	pier	th	thin
ŏ	pot	*th*	this
ō	toe	zh	vision
ô	paw	ə	about

Dy·er (dī′ər), **Mary** Died 1660. English-born American Quaker martyr who was hanged for her beliefs.

dye·stuff (dī′stŭf′) *n.* A substance used as a dye: *Indigo is a deep blue dyestuff.*

dy·ing (dī′ĭng) *v.* Present participle of **die**[1]. ❖ *adj.* **1.** About to die: *the shriveled leaves of the dying plant.* **2.** Drawing to an end: *a dying day.* **3.** Done or uttered just before death: *dying words.*

Dy·lan (dĭl′ən), **Bob** Originally **Robert Allen Zimmerman.** Born 1941. American singer known for bringing poetic depth to rock-and-roll.

dy·nam·ic (dī-năm′ĭk) *adj.* **1.** Marked by intensity and vigor; forceful: *the dynamic personality of a political leader.* **2.** Changing; active: *a dynamic stock market.* **3.** Relating to energy or to objects in motion. **4.** Relating to the science of dynamics. [From Greek *dunamis*, power, from *dunasthai*, to be able.] **—dy·nam′i·cal·ly** *adv.*

dy·nam·ics (dī-năm′ĭks) *n.* **1.** *(used with a singular verb)* The branch of physics that deals with the effects of forces on the motions of bodies. **2.** *(used with a plural verb)* The forces that produce activity and change in a particular area: *the dynamics that have increased international trade.*

dy·na·mism (dī′nə-mĭz′əm) *n.* Continuous change or activity; vigor; energy: *the dynamism of a new government administration.*

dy·na·mite (dī′nə-mīt′) *n.* A powerful explosive made of nitroglycerin or ammonium nitrate that is combined with an absorbent material and calcium carbonate or another antacid. ❖ *tr.v.* **dy·na·mit·ed, dy·na·mit·ing, dy·na·mites** To blow up or destroy with dynamite: *The old office building was dynamited to make space for new construction.* [From Swedish *dynamit*, from Greek *dunamis*, power.] **—dy′na·mit′er** *n.*

dy·na·mo (dī′nə-mō′) *n., pl.* **dy·na·mos 1.** An electric generator, especially one that produces direct current. **2.** *Informal* An extremely energetic and forceful person.

dy·nas·ty (dī′nə-stē) *n., pl.* **dy·nas·ties 1.** A succession of rulers from the same family: *the Habsburg dynasty.* **2.** A family or group that maintains great power, wealth, or success for a sustained period. **—dy·nas′tic** (dī-năs′tĭk) *adj.*

dyne (dīn) *n.* A unit of force equal to the amount of force required to give a mass of one gram an acceleration of one centimeter per second for each second the force is applied.
❑ *These sound alike:* **dyne, dine** (eat).

dys·en·ter·y (dĭs′ən-tĕr′ē) *n.* Severe diarrhea often with the presence of blood and mucus, usually caused by infection of the intestines by bacteria or parasites.

dys·func·tion (dĭs-fŭngk′shən) *n.* **1.** Abnormal functioning of a system or an organ of the body. **2.** Failure to function normally in social situations or relationships.

dys·lex·i·a (dĭs-lĕk′sē-ə) *n.* A learning disability that interferes with the ability to recognize and understand written words.

dys·lex·ic (dĭs-lĕk′sĭk) *n.* A person who is affected by dyslexia. ❖ *adj.* Relating to or affected with dyslexia.

dys·pep·sia (dĭs-pĕp′shə *or* dĭs-pĕp′sē-ə) *n.* Poor digestion; indigestion.

dys·pep·tic (dĭs-pĕp′tĭk) *adj.* **1.** Relating to or suffering from dyspepsia. **2.** Disgruntled or gloomy: *a dyspeptic outlook on life.*

dys·pla·sia (dĭs-plā′zhə) *n.* Abnormal development or growth of tissues, organs, or cells. **—dys·plas′tic** (dĭs-plăs′tĭk) *adj.*

dys·pro·si·um (dĭs-prō′zē-əm *or* dĭs-prō′zhē-əm) *n.* *Symbol* **Dy** A soft, silvery metallic element that has a high melting point and is used in nuclear reactor control rods and in making laser materials. Atomic number 66. See **Periodic Table.**

dz. *abbr.* An abbreviation of dozen.

Mary Dyer
1959 sculpture by Sylvia Shaw Judson (1897–1978) at the Massachusetts State House

USAGE

each When the subject of a sentence begins with **each,** the verb and following pronouns must be singular: *Each of the hotel rooms has its own bath.* When *each* follows a plural subject, however, the verb and pronouns remain in the plural: *The hotel rooms each have their own baths.*

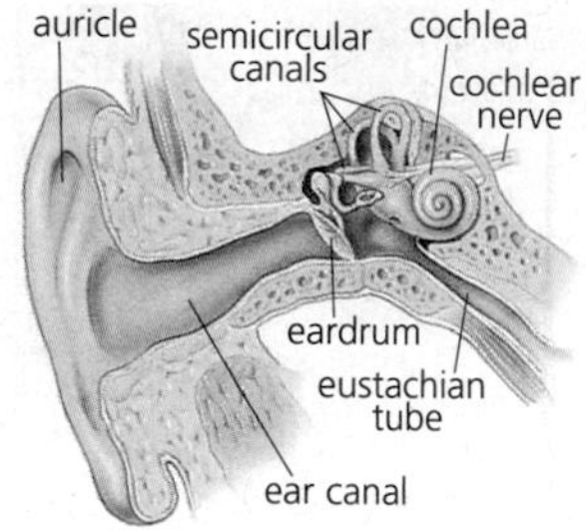

ear¹

ă	pat	ôr	core
ā	pay	oi	boy
âr	care	ou	out
ä	father	o͝o	took
ĕ	pet	o͝or	lure
ē	be	o͞o	boot
ĭ	pit	ŭ	cut
ī	bite	ûr	urge
îr	pier	th	thin
ŏ	pot	*th*	this
ō	toe	zh	vision
ô	paw	ə	about

e or **E** (ē) *n., pl.* **e's** or **E's** also **es** or **Es 1.** The fifth letter of the English alphabet. **2. E** A failing grade in school. **3. E** In music, the third tone in the scale of C major.

E *abbr.* An abbreviation of: **1.** east. **2.** eastern. **3.** energy. **4.** error.

e– *pref.* A prefix that means computer or computer network: *e-commerce.*

ea. *abbr.* An abbreviation of each.

each (ēch) *adj.* Being one of two or more people or things considered individually; every: *The teacher talked to each student for ten minutes.* ❖ *pron.* Every one of a group of people, objects, or things: *Each of us took a turn looking in the telescope.* ❖ *adv.* For or to each one; apiece: *The apples cost 25 cents each.* [From Old English *ǣlce.*] —SEE NOTE.

each other *pron.* Each the other. Used to show that each person or thing does the same as the other: *The girls greeted each other.*

ea·ger (ē′gər) *adj.* **ea·ger·er, ea·ger·est** Having or showing keen interest or desire: *The eager sports fans cheered the team.* **—ea′ger·ly** *adv.* **—ea′ger·ness** *n.*

ea·gle (ē′gəl) *n.* **1.** Any of various large birds of prey having a hooked bill, keen vision, and broad wings. **2.** In golf, a score of two strokes under par on a hole. [From Middle English *egle,* from Latin *aquila.*]

ea·gle-eyed (ē′gəl-īd′) *adj.* Having very keen eyesight: *an eagle-eyed watchdog.*

ea·glet (ē′glĭt) *n.* A young eagle.

ear¹ (îr) *n.* **1a.** The organ of hearing in humans and other animals. In mammals, the ear is divided into the inner ear, the middle ear, and the outer ear. **b.** The part of this organ that shows on the outside of the body: *Some dogs' ears stick up and some flop over.* **2.** The sense of hearing: *The sound of wind in the trees is pleasant to the ear.* **3.** The ability to distinguish tones or sounds very accurately or acutely: *the sensitive ear of a musician.* **4.** Attention; heed: *Give me your ear until I finish the explanation.* ◆ **all ears** Listening eagerly; paying careful attention: *Some people are all ears when they hear gossip.* **in one ear and out the other** Without any influence or effect: *I could tell that my directions went in one ear and out the other.* **give an ear** or **lend an ear** To pay attention; listen carefully. **play by ear 1.** To perform (music) solely from having heard it: *played the sonata by ear without having seen the sheet music.* **2.** To play music on (a musical instrument) solely from having heard the music: *can play the piano by ear.* **play it by ear** To act according to the circumstances; improvise. [From Old English *ēare.*]

ear² (îr) *n.* The part of a cereal plant, such as corn, wheat, oats, barley, or rye, that bears the grains. [From Old English *ēar.*]

ear·ache (îr′āk′) *n.* A pain in the ear.

ear·bud (îr′bŭd′) *n.* A small headphone that fits inside the ear.

ear canal *n.* The narrow, tubelike passage through which sound enters the ear.

ear·drum (îr′drŭm′) *n.* The membrane that separates the middle ear from the outer ear and vibrates when sound waves strike it; the tympanic membrane.

eared (îrd) *adj.* **1.** Having an ear or ears: *an eared seal.* **2.** Having a certain kind or number of ears: *a long-eared puppy.*

ear·ful (îr′fo͝ol′) *n.* **1.** A flow of gossip or information: *I got an earful about the scandal from a neighbor.* **2.** A scolding or strong criticism: *The gardener gave me an earful for walking across the newly seeded grass.*

Ear·hart (âr′härt′), **Amelia** 1897?–1937. American aviator who was the first woman to fly solo across the Atlantic Ocean (1932) and from Hawaii to California (1935). —SEE NOTE.

earl (ûrl) *n.* A British nobleman holding a title and rank below that of a marquis and above that of a viscount. [From Old English *eorl,* nobleman.]

earl·dom (ûrl′dəm) *n.* **1.** The rank of an earl. **2.** The territory of an earl.

ear·lobe (îr′lōb′) *n.* The soft fleshy part at the bottom of the outer ear of humans.

ear·ly (ûr′lē) *adj.* **ear·li·er, ear·li·est 1.** Relating to or happening near the beginning of a time period, series, or course of development: *the early morning; people in their early twenties; the early stages of an animal's growth.* **2.** Relating to or belonging to a previous or distant period of time: *Early humans made simple tools.* **3.** Appearing or happening before the usual or expected time: *We had an early spring this year.* **4.** Happening in the near future: *Lawyers predict an early end to the trial.* ❖ *adv.* **ear·lier, ear·liest 1.** Near the beginning of a period of time or course of events: *The hikers set out early in the morning.* **2.** Before the usual or expected time: *Our guests arrived early.* **3.** Far back in time; long ago: *The Greek islands were settled as early as 5000 BC.* ◆ **early on** At an early stage or point: *Early on in the movie, the main character loses his job.* [From Old English *ǣrlīce.*] **—ear′li·ness** *n.*

early bird *n. Informal* A person who wakes up, arrives, or starts being active before most others.

Early Modern English *n.* English from around 1500 to around 1700.

ear·mark (îr′märk′) *n.* **1.** A notch or mark made on the ear of an animal to show that it belongs to a particular person: *The ranchers find their cattle by their earmarks.* **2.** A special quality or mark that sets a person or thing apart: *Careful observation is one of the earmarks of a good scientist.* **3.** An item in a legislative bill that allots money for a project or institution in a specific place, often the district of a legislator who is sponsoring the bill. ❖ *tr.v.* **ear·marked, ear·mark·ing, ear·marks 1.** To mark the ear of (an animal) for identification: *The ranchers earmarked their sheep.* **2.** To set aside for some purpose: *We earmarked part of the prize money for a new car.* **3.** To allocate (funds) to be spent in a legislative earmark.

ear·muff (îr′mŭf′) *n.* One of a pair of coverings for the ears, often attached to an adjustable headband and typically worn to protect the ears against cold weather.

earn (ûrn) *tr.v.* **earned, earn·ing, earns 1.** To get by working or by supplying a product or service: *earn money by mowing lawns.* **2.** To deserve or win by one's efforts or actions: *earn a reputation for being very thoughtful.* **3.** To produce as income or profit: *A savings account earns interest on your money.* [From Old English *earnian.*] **—earn′er** *n.*

❑ *These sound alike:* **earn, urn** (container).

earned run (ûrnd) *n.* In baseball, a run considered the fault of the pitcher, scored when the pitcher's team has made no errors allowing runners to get on base or to advance to home plate.

earned run average *n.* In baseball, a measure of a pitcher's performance determined by dividing the total of earned runs by the total of innings pitched and multiplying by nine.

ear·nest (ûr′nĭst) *adj.* Showing or expressing sincerity or seriousness: *an earnest offer to help.* ◆ **in earnest** With serious purpose or intent: *After a slow start, we began working on the project in earnest.* [From Old English *eornoste.*] **—ear′nest·ly** *adv.*

earn·ings (ûr′nĭngz) *pl.n.* **1.** Money earned for work; wages. **2.** Profits, as from a business or investment.

ear·phone (îr′fōn′) *n.* A small speaker that is worn over or in the ear.

ear·plug (îr′plŭg′) *n.* An object made of a soft, pliable material and placed in the ear canal to block the entry of water or sound.

ear·ring (îr′rĭng *or* îr′ĭng) *n.* A piece of jewelry worn on or hanging from the ear, especially the earlobe.

ear·shot (îr′shŏt′) *n.* The range or distance within which sound can be heard: *Their shouts were not within earshot and went unnoticed.*

ear·split·ting (îr′splĭt′ĭng) *adj.* Loud enough to hurt the ears; deafening.

earth (ûrth) *n.* **1.** often **Earth** The third planet from the sun and the fifth largest in the solar system. Earth is the only planet known to support life and the only planet on which water in liquid form exists, covering more than 70 percent of its surface. See table at **solar system. 2.** Dry land; the ground: *snowflakes falling to the earth.* **3.** Dirt; soil: *seeds sprouting in the moist earth.* **4.** The human inhabitants of the world: *The earth rejoiced at the news of peace.* [From Old English *eorthe.*]

earth·en (ûr′thən) *adj.* Made of earth or clay: *the earthen floor of a cabin; an earthen pot.*

earth·en·ware (ûr′thən-wâr′) *n.* Pottery made from a porous clay that is fired at relatively low temperatures. Delft is an example of earthenware.

earth·ling (ûrth′lĭng) *n.* A person who lives on the earth; a human.

earth·ly (ûrth′lē) *adj.* **1.** Relating to the earth rather than heaven: *the everyday earthly business of earning a living.* **2.** Possible; imaginable: *a remark with no earthly meaning.* **—earth′li·ness** *n.*

earth·quake (ûrth′kwāk′) *n.* A sudden movement of the earth's crust, followed by a series of shocks. Earthquakes are caused by volcanic action or by the release of built-up stress along geologic faults.

earth science *n.* Any of several sciences, such as geology or meteorology, concerned with the origin, composition, and physical features of the earth.

earth·ward (ûrth′wərd) *adv. & adj.* To or toward the earth: *rain falling earthward.* **—earth′wards** *adv.*

earth·work (ûrth′wûrk′) *n.* An earthen bank or wall used as a fortification.

earth·worm (ûrth′wûrm′) *n.* Any of various worms that have a segmented body and burrow in soil. —SEE NOTE AT **worm.**

earth·y (ûr′thē) *adj.* **earth·i·er, earth·i·est 1.** Relating to or resembling earth or soil: *the earthy smell of the woods after rain.* **2.** Crude; indecent: *earthy humor.* **3.** Hearty; natural: *an earthy enjoyment of life.* **—earth′i·ness** *n.*

ear·wig (îr′wĭg′) *n.* Any of various insects having a pair of movable pincers protruding from the rear of the body.

ease (ēz) *n.* **1.** Freedom from difficulty, strain, or great effort: *I solved the problem with ease.* **2.** Freedom from pain or worry: *Her mind was at ease, knowing the children had returned safely.* **3.** Freedom from awkwardness or embarrassment; naturalness: *She spoke before the crowd with ease.* ❖ *v.* **eased, eas·ing, eas·es** *—tr.* **1.** To free from pain, worry, or agitation: *Knowing she was not offended eased his conscience.* **2.** To make less troublesome or difficult: *The school eased its entrance requirements.* **3.** To lessen the discomfort or pain of; relieve: *The medicine eased the earache.* **4.** To cause to move slowly and carefully: *The captain eased the ship alongside the dock.* **5.** To reduce the pressure or strain of; loosen: *ease the dog's collar. —intr.* To relax; let up: *The tension eased when the angry customer left the store.* [From Middle English *ese*, from Old French *aise*, elbowroom, physical comfort.]

ea·sel (ē′zəl) *n.* An upright stand or rack used to display or support something, such as an artist's canvas. [From Dutch *ezel*, ass, from Latin *asellus*, diminutive of *asinus.*]

eas·i·ly (ē′zə-lē) *adv.* **1.** In an easy manner; with ease: *Libraries are arranged so that you can find books easily.* **2.** Without doubt; surely: *That is easily the best book I have ever read.* **3.** Very likely: *If we beat their team, we could easily win the championship.* **4.** Very quickly or readily: *I am easily embarrassed.*

east (ēst) *n.* **1.** The direction from which the sun is seen to rise, directly opposite west. **2.** often **East** A region or part of a country lying in the east. **3.** often **East a.** The eastern part of the earth, especially eastern Asia. **b.** The part of the United States along the Atlantic coast, especially from Maine to Maryland. ❖ *adj.* **1.** To, toward, facing, or in the east: *the east bank of the river; the east road to town.* **2.** From the east: *An east wind is blowing.* ❖ *adv.* In, from, or toward the east: *a river flowing east.* [From Old English *ēast.*]

east·bound (ēst′bound′) *adj.* Going toward the east.

East China Sea An arm of the western Pacific Ocean bounded by China, South Korea, Taiwan, and parts of Japan.

Eas·ter (ē′stər) *n.* A Christian feast commemorating the Resurrection of Jesus. In the Western Church it is held each year on the first Sunday following the full moon that occurs on or after March 21.

Easter egg *n.* **1.** A dyed or painted egg traditionally given as a gift or hidden and hunted for by children on Easter. **2.** A hidden message or feature, as in a video game or DVD.

Easter Island An island of Chile in the southern Pacific Ocean about 2,300 miles (3,700 kilometers) west of the mainland. Named by Dutch explorers on Easter Day, 1722, the island is famous for its colossal figures carved from volcanic rock.

east·er·ly (ē′stər-lē) *adj.* **1.** Situated toward the east: *an easterly direction.* **2.** Coming from the east: *easterly wind.* ❖ *n., pl.* **east·er·lies** A storm or wind from the east. **—east′er·ly** *adv.*

east·ern (ē′stərn) *adj.* **1.** Situated in, toward, or facing the east: *eastern Europe; the eastern slope of a mountain.* **2.** From the east: *an eastern wind.* **3.** often **Eastern a.** Relating to eastern regions or the East. **b.** Relating to the part of the United States along the Atlantic coast: *a large Eastern vote for the president.*

Eastern Church *n.* The Eastern Orthodox Church.

Eastern equine encephalitis *n.* Encephalitis that is

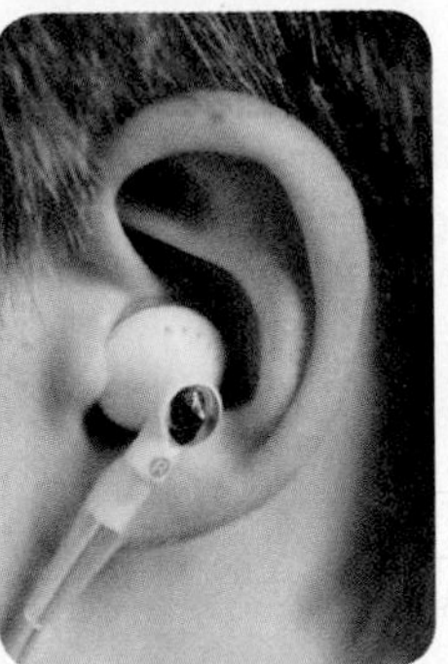

earbud

Amelia Earhart
photographed in 1934

BIOGRAPHY

Amelia Earhart In 1932 Amelia **Earhart** became the first woman to fly alone across the Atlantic Ocean, a flight she made in record time. She went on in 1935 to pilot the first solo flight from Honolulu, Hawaii, to California, as well as the first nonstop solo flight from Mexico City, Mexico, to Newark, New Jersey. In 1937, after completing more than two-thirds of an attempted flight around the world, Earhart lost radio contact with the US Coast Guard while over the Pacific Ocean, and she and her airplane were never found. Her record-breaking achievements greatly advanced early aviation, and her independence and bravery made her an example for other women to follow, encouraging them to pursue their dreams.

WORD HISTORY

eavesdrop The edge of the roof that overhangs the side of the building is the *eaves,* and an **eavesdrop** is the space on the ground where the rainwater falls from the eaves. If you stood in the eavesdrop by a window on the side of a building to listen secretly to a conversation inside, you were said to be *eavesdropping.* The meaning of *eavesdrop* has broadened so that now you can *eavesdrop* anywhere.

echidna

ă	pat	ôr	core
ā	pay	oi	boy
âr	care	ou	out
ä	father	o͝o	took
ĕ	pet	o͝or	lure
ē	be	o͞o	boot
ĭ	pit	ŭ	cut
ī	bite	ûr	urge
îr	pier	th	thin
ŏ	pot	*th*	this
ō	toe	zh	vision
ô	paw	ə	about

caused by a mosquito-borne virus and can occur in small epidemics. It affects humans, horses, and some bird species.

east·ern·er also **East·ern·er** (ē′stər-nər) *n.* A person who lives in or comes from the east, especially the eastern United States.

Eastern Hemisphere The half of the earth including Europe, Africa, Asia, and Australia.

east·ern·most (ē′stərn-mōst′) *adj.* Farthest east.

Eastern Orthodox Church *n.* A group of churches, including the Greek Orthodox and the Russian Orthodox, that trace their origin to the early Christian Church established during the Byzantine Empire.

Eastern Standard Time *n.* Standard time in the fifth time zone west of Greenwich, England, used, for example, in the eastern United States.

Eas·ter·tide (ē′stər-tīd′) *n.* The Easter season.

East Germany See **Germany.**

East In·dies (ĭn′dēz) Indonesia. The term sometimes means all of Southeast Asia.

East Ti·mor (tē′môr) A country of the western Pacific Ocean made up of the eastern part of the island of Timor, a small area in the west of the island, and one offshore island. First colonized by Portugal, it was annexed by Indonesia in 1976 and achieved independence in 2002. Dili is the capital.

east·ward (ēst′wərd) *adv. & adj.* Toward, to, or in the east: *the eastward flow of the current.* ❖ *n.* A direction or region to the east. **—east′wards** *adv.*

eas·y (ē′zē) *adj.* **eas·i·er, eas·i·est 1a.** Requiring or done with little effort or difficulty: *an easy victory; an easy problem.* **b.** Likely to happen by accident or without intention: *It's easy to slip on the wet floor. It's easy to push the wrong button.* **2.** Free from worry, strain, or pain: *an easy life.* **3.** Relaxed in attitude or appearance: *a natural easy manner; an easy smile.* **4.** Not strict or demanding; lenient: *Most teachers are easy on new students.* **5.** Not forced, hurried, or strenuous: *within easy walking distance; an easy drive.* ❖ *adv.* **1.** Without haste or worry: *Take it easy and you'll do a better job.* **2.** With little effort; easily: *Playing the banjo came easy to her.* **3.** Without much hardship or cost: *He got off easy with only a small fine.* [From Middle English *esi,* from Old French *aaisier,* to put at ease.] **—eas′i·ness** *n.*

SYNONYMS **easy, simple, effortless** These adjectives mean requiring little effort: **Easy** describes tasks that are not difficult: *It's easy to take care of a pet hamster.* **Simple** describes something that is easy because it is not complex: *The children were able to follow the game's simple rules.* **Effortless** means seemingly easy because of the strength or skill applied: *The skater performed an effortless jump.*

easy chair *n.* A large comfortable upholstered chair.

eas·y·go·ing (ē′zē-gō′ĭng) *adj.* **1.** Relaxed; carefree: *an artist's easygoing life; an easygoing manner of speech.* **2.** Not hurried; leisurely: *an easygoing pace.*

eat (ēt) *v.* **ate** (āt), **eat·en** (ēt′n), **eat·ing, eats** *—tr.* **1a.** To take into the body through the mouth: *Owls eat mice.* **b.** To take in and absorb as food: *a plant that eats insects.* **2.** To wear away, corrode, or destroy by or as if by eating: *Rust has eaten away the iron pipes.* **3.** To make by eating: *Moths ate holes in the blanket.* *—intr.* **1.** To take food; have a meal: *They usually eat about seven o'clock.* **2.** To wear away; corrode: *Home improvements ate into their savings.* ◆ **eat (one's) words** To retract something that one has said. **eat up** *Slang* To enjoy greatly; be greedy for: *The actor eats up compliments.* [From Old English *etan.*] **—eat′er** *n.*

eat·a·ble (ē′tə-bəl) *adj.* Fit for eating; edible.

eat·er·y (ē′tə-rē) *n., pl.* **eat·er·ies** *Informal* A restaurant.

eat·ing disorder (ē′tĭng) *n.* Any of several disorders, such as anorexia nervosa or bulimia, that are characterized by abnormal eating behaviors.

eau de co·logne (ō′ də kə-lōn′) *n., pl.* **eaux de co·logne** (ō′ də kə-lōn′) A lightly perfumed cologne.

eaves (ēvz) *pl.n.* The part of a roof that forms the lower edge and projects beyond the walls. [From Old English *efes.*]

eaves·drop (ēvz′drŏp′) *intr.v.* **eaves·dropped, eaves·drop·ping, eaves·drops** To listen secretly to the private conversation of others: *hid behind the door to eavesdrop.* **—eaves′drop′per** *n.* —SEE NOTE.

ebb (ĕb) *n.* **1.** Ebb tide. **2.** A period of decline: *The king's fortunes were at their lowest ebb.* ❖ *intr.v.* **ebbed, ebb·ing, ebbs 1.** To flow back; recede: *The floodwaters began to ebb after the storm passed.* **2.** To fade or fall away; decline: *The hooked fish struggled less as its strength ebbed.* [From Old English *ebba.*]

ebb tide *n.* **1.** The tide flowing away from the shore. **2.** The period between high tide and low tide.

eb·on·ite (ĕb′ə-nīt′) *n.* A hard black rubber made by heating rubber in the presence of large amounts of sulfur and used as an electrical insulator.

eb·on·y (ĕb′ə-nē) *n., pl.* **eb·on·ies 1.** The hard black or blackish wood of any of several tropical trees of southern Asia or Africa, used for piano keys and for decorative work. **2.** A tree that yields such wood. **3.** The color black. ❖ *adj.* **1.** Made of ebony: *an ebony cabinet.* **2.** Black: *ebony hair.* [From Middle English *ebenif,* from Greek *ebenos,* ebony tree, from Egyptian *hbny.*]

e-book (ē′bo͝ok) *n.* A book whose contents are in an electronic format.

e·bul·lient (ĭ-bo͝ol′yənt *or* ĭ-bŭl′yənt) *adj.* Full of excitement, enthusiasm, or high spirits: *the ebullient feeling of victory.* **—e·bul′lient·ly** *adv.*

ec·cen·tric (ĭk-sĕn′trĭk) *adj.* **1.** Odd or unusual in appearance, behavior, or manner; strange; peculiar: *an eccentric hat; an eccentric person; an eccentric habit.* **2.** Not perfectly circular; elliptical: *an eccentric orbit.* ❖ *n.* A person who is odd or unusual in behavior. [From Middle English *eccentrik,* planetary orbit that does not have the Earth at its center, from Greek *ekkentros,* not having the same center : *ek-,* out of, away + *kentron,* center.] **—ec·cen′tri·cal·ly** *adv.*

ec·cen·tric·i·ty (ĕk′sĕn-trĭs′ĭ-tē) *n., pl.* **ec·cen·tric·i·ties 1.** The quality or condition of being eccentric: *The eccentricity of the moon's orbit.* **2.** An act or habit that is odd or strange; a peculiarity. **3.** The amount or degree by which something is eccentric.

Ec·cle·si·as·tes (ĭ-klē′zē-ăs′tēz′) *n. (used with a singular verb)* A book of the Bible that stresses the vanity of human wishes and achievements.

ec·cle·si·as·tic (ĭ-klē′zē-ăs′tĭk) *adj.* Ecclesiastical. ❖ *n.* A member of the Christian clergy; a minister or priest.

ec·cle·si·as·ti·cal (ĭ-klē′zē-ăs′tĭ-kəl) *adj.* Relating to a church: *ecclesiastical robes.* **—ec·cle′si·as′ti·cal·ly** *adv.*

ech·e·lon (ĕsh′ə-lŏn′) *n.* **1.** A formation of military aircraft, naval vessels, or soldiers resembling a series of steps. **2.** A level of command or authority: *The president and cabinet officers are among the highest echelons of government.* [From Old French *eschelon,* rung of a ladder, from Latin *scālae,* steps.]

e·chid·na (ĭ-kĭd′nə) *n.* Any of several burrowing, egg-laying mammals of Australia, Tasmania, and New Guinea, having a spiny coat, slender snout, and sticky tongue used for catching insects.

e·chi·no·derm (ĭ-kī′nə-dûrm′) *n.* Any of numerous sea animals, including the starfishes and sea urchins, that have a hard internal skeleton and are often covered with spines. Echinoderms are radially symmetrical.

ech·o (ĕk′ō) *n., pl.* **ech·oes 1.** A repeated sound that is caused by the reflection of sound waves from a surface.

2. A repetition or imitation of something: *New fashions in dress usually have echoes of earlier styles.* **3.** A reflected radio wave. Echoes of radio waves are the basis for radar. ❖ *v.* **ech·oed, ech·o·ing, ech·oes** —*tr.* **1.** To repeat (a sound) by an echo: *The canyon echoed their shouts.* **2.** To repeat or imitate: *She echoed our feelings in her statement to the board.* —*intr.* **1.** To be repeated by an echo: *The shouts echoed from the mountainside.* **2.** To resound with an echo; reverberate: *The long hallway echoed with many footsteps.* [From Middle English *ecco*, from Greek *ēkhō*.]

Echo *n.* In Greek mythology, a nymph whose love for Narcissus was not returned by him, causing her to pine away until nothing but her voice remained.

e·cho·ic (ĕ-kō′ĭk) *adj.* Relating to or resembling an echo.

ech·o·lo·ca·tion (ĕk′ō-lō-kā′shən) *n.* A sensory system in certain animals, such as bats and dolphins, in which the animal sends out high-pitched sounds and uses the echoes to determine the position of objects. —SEE NOTE AT **bat[2]**.

é·clair (ā-klâr′ *or* ā′klâr′) *n.* An elongated pastry filled with custard or whipped cream and usually iced with chocolate.

e·clec·tic (ĭ-klĕk′tĭk) *adj.* Choosing or taking what appears to be the best from various sources: *an eclectic painter blending elements of realism and abstract art.* ❖ *n.* A person whose opinions and beliefs are drawn from several sources. [From Greek *eklektikos*, selective, from *eklegein*, to select : *ek-*, out + *legein*, to gather.] —**e·clec′ti·cal·ly** *adv.*

e·clipse (ĭ-klĭps′) *n.* **1.** The partial or total blocking of light from one celestial object as it passes behind or through the shadow of another celestial object. In a solar eclipse, the moon comes between the sun and Earth. In a lunar eclipse, the moon enters Earth's shadow. **2.** A decline in importance, use, or fame: *The band's popularity suffered an eclipse after their retirement.* ❖ *tr.v.* **e·clipsed, e·clips·ing, e·clips·es 1.** To cause an eclipse of: *When the moon eclipsed the sun, it caused partial darkness.* **2.** To obscure or overshadow in importance, fame, or reputation; surpass: *The war eclipsed all other news for a while.* [From Middle English, from Greek *ekleipsis*, from *ekleipein*, to fail to appear, suffer an eclipse : *ek-*, out + *leipein*, to leave.] —SEE NOTE.

e·clip·tic (ĭ-klĭp′tĭk) *n.* The apparent path of the sun among the stars in one year. The ecliptic is the great circle of the celestial sphere which is cut by the plane containing the orbit of Earth.

E. co·li (ē kō′lī) *n.* A bacterium that is normally found in the intestines of humans and other mammals and is widely used in biological research. Some strains can cause disease. [From New Latin *E(scherichia) colī*, species name : after Theodor *Escherich* (1857–1911), German physician + Latin *colon*, colon.]

e·col·o·gist (ĭ-kŏl′ə-jĭst) *n.* A scientist who specializes in ecology.

e·col·o·gy (ĭ-kŏl′ə-jē) *n.* **1.** The science of the relationships between living things and their environment: *studying ecology.* **2.** The relationship between certain organisms and their environment: *the ecology of reef fishes.* [From German *Ökologie* : Greek *oikos*, house + Greek *-logiā*, study, science.] —**ec′o·log′i·cal** (ĕk′ə-lŏj′ĭ-kəl *or* ē′kə-lŏj′ĭ-kəl) *adj.* —**ec′o·log′i·cal·ly** *adv.*

e-com·merce (ē′kŏm′ərs) *n.* Commerce that takes place electronically, as over the Internet.

ec·o·nom·ic (ĕk′ə-nŏm′ĭk *or* ē′kə-nŏm′ĭk) *adj.* **1.** Relating to the production, development, and management of wealth, as of a country, household, or business: *The state's economic activity increased last month.* **2.** Relating to the science of economics: *economic theories of how money works in society.* **3.** Efficient; economical: *an economic use of home heating oil.*

ec·o·nom·i·cal (ĕk′ə-nŏm′ĭ-kəl *or* ē′kə-nŏm′ĭ-kəl) *adj.* Not wasteful or extravagant; prudent and thrifty: *an economical use of time; an economical way to produce better crops.* —**ec′o·nom′i·cal·ly** *adv.*

ec·o·nom·ics (ĕk′ə-nŏm′ĭks *or* ē′kə-nŏm′ĭks) *n.* **1.** *(used with a singular verb)* The science that deals with the ways in which goods and services are produced, transported, sold, and used. Economics also deals with the effects of taxes and the distribution of money within an economy. **2.** *(used with a singular or plural verb)* Economic matters, especially those relating to cost and profit: *the economics of running a store.*

e·con·o·mist (ĭ-kŏn′ə-mĭst) *n.* A person who specializes in economics.

e·con·o·mize (ĭ-kŏn′ə-mīz′) *v.* **e·con·o·mized, e·con·o·miz·ing, e·con·o·miz·es** —*intr.* To be thrifty; reduce expenses or avoid waste: *economize by bringing your own lunch to work.* —*tr.* To use or manage with thrift: *economize your time to get more done.*

e·con·o·my (ĭ-kŏn′ə-mē) *n., pl.* **e·con·o·mies 1.** The careful use or management of resources, such as money, materials, or labor: *practice economy in running the household.* **2.** An example or result of this; a saving: *the economy of using public transportation.* **3.** The economic system of a country, region, or state: *The rise in housing prices boosted the city's economy.* **4.** A specific kind of economic system: *an industrial economy.* **5.** The least expensive class of accommodations on an airliner or other mode of commercial transportation: *purchased tickets in economy instead of first class.* ❖ *adj.* Economical or inexpensive to buy or use: *an economy car; an economy hotel.* [From Middle English *iconomie*, management of a household, from Greek *oikonomiā* : *oikos*, house + *nemein*, to allot, manage.]

e·co·sys·tem (ē′kō-sĭs′təm *or* ĕk′ō-sĭs′təm) *n.* A biological community, including plants, animals, and microorganisms, considered together with its environment: *A pond is a complex ecosystem.*

ec·ru (ĕk′rōō *or* ā′krōō) *n.* A pale yellowish-brown color.

ec·sta·sy (ĕk′stə-sē) *n., pl.* **ec·sta·sies** Intense joy or delight: *After years of training, the runner was in ecstasy over winning an Olympic medal.*

ec·stat·ic (ĕk-stăt′ĭk) *adj.* **1.** Marked by or expressing intense joy or delight: *the ecstatic final movement of the symphony.* **2.** In a state of ecstasy; enraptured: *I was ecstatic over the chance to go to France.* —**ec·stat′i·cal·ly** *adv.*

ecto– *pref.* A prefix that means outer or external: *ectoderm.*

ec·to·derm (ĕk′tə-dûrm′) *n.* The outer cell layer of an early embryo, developing into the nervous system and the epidermis, such as the skin, hair, and nails.

ec·to·plasm (ĕk′tə-plăz′əm) *n.* The outer portion of the cytoplasm of a cell.

ec·to·therm (ĕk′tə-thûrm′) *n.* A cold-blooded animal. —**ec′to·ther′mic** *adj.*

Ec·ua·dor (ĕk′wə-dôr′) A country of northwest South America on the Pacific Ocean south of Colombia. Quito is the capital.

ec·u·men·i·cal (ĕk′yə-mĕn′ĭ-kəl) *adj.* **1.** Worldwide in range or relevance; universal: *an ecumenical view of environmental planning.* **2.** Relating to the worldwide Christian church: *an ecumenical council.* **3.** Concerned with promoting unity among churches or religions. —**ec′u·men′i·cal·ly** *adv.*

ec·ze·ma (ĕk′sə-mə *or* ĕg′zə-mə) *n.* An inflammation of the skin, marked by redness, itching, and the formation of sores that discharge fluid and become crusted and scaly.

ed (ĕd) *n. Informal* Education: *driver's ed; adult ed.*

ed. *abbr.* An abbreviation of: **1.** edition. **2.** editor.

–ed[1] *suff.* A suffix that forms the past tense of regular verbs: *cared; carried.*

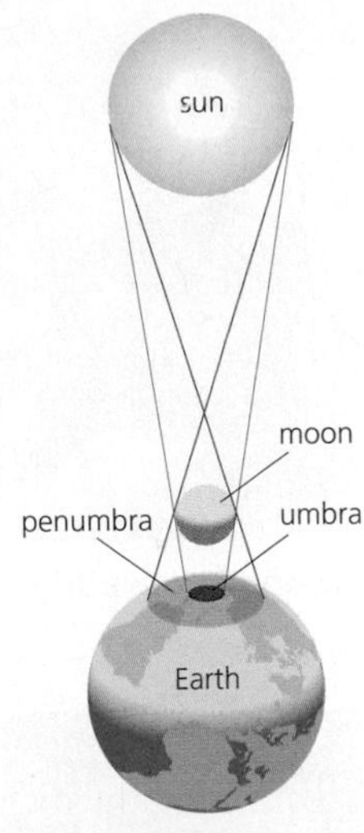

eclipse

An observer of a solar eclipse who is within the umbra will see a total eclipse, while someone within the penumbra will see a partial eclipse.

SCIENCE

eclipse The sun is about 400 times wider than the moon, and it also happens to be about 400 times farther from the earth. For this reason, the sun and the moon appear to be almost exactly the same size in the sky. Our unique vantage point makes for the spectacular phenomenon of a total solar **eclipse,** when the moon blocks out the sun. The orbits of the earth around the sun and of the moon around the earth are not perfect circles. Therefore the sun and moon may vary slightly in how big they appear to us, and the length of total solar eclipses can also vary. The longest solar eclipses, which occur when the earth is farthest from the sun and the moon is nearest to the earth, last only seven and a half minutes. Since looking at the sun can cause blindness, it is safest to view any solar eclipse indirectly. A good method is to project the image through a pinhole in a piece of paper onto another piece of paper.

Mary Baker Eddy

Thomas Edison

–ed² *suff.* A suffix that forms the past participle of regular verbs: *ended; expected.*

–ed³ *suff.* A suffix that means having, characterized by, or resembling: *hardhearted; wretched.*

ed·a·ma·me (ĕd′ə-mä′mā) *pl.n.* Fresh green soybeans, typically prepared by boiling in salted water. [From Japanese : *eda,* twig, branch + *mame,* bean.]

ed·dy (ĕd′ē) *n., pl.* **ed·dies** A current, as of water or air, that moves opposite to the direction of a main current, especially in a circular motion. ❖ *intr.v.* **ed·died, ed·dy·ing, ed·dies** To move in or as if in an eddy: *wisps of mist eddying through the valley.*

Ed·dy (ĕd′ē), **Mary (Morse) Baker** 1821–1910. American religious leader who founded Christian Science (1879) based on ideas set forth in her *Science and Health with Key to the Scriptures* (1875).

e·del·weiss (ā′dəl-vīs′ *or* ā′dəl-wīs′) *n.* A small plant native to high mountain areas of Europe, having clusters of small yellow flowers surrounded by bracts that resemble petals. The leaves and flowers are covered with whitish down.

e·de·ma (ĭ-dē′mə) *n.* A condition in which an excess amount of fluid collects in a body part or tissue and causes swelling.

E·den (ēd′n) *n.* **1.** In the Bible, the garden of God and the first home of Adam and Eve, from which they were banished for disobeying God. **2.** A delightful place; a paradise.

edge (ĕj) *n.* **1a.** The thin sharpened side of a blade. **b.** A slight sharpness or harshness: *His voice had an edge to it.* **2a.** The area or part farthest from the middle: *went to the mall at the edge of town.* **b.** The line or point where two surfaces meet: *the edge of a table.* **c.** The point at which something is likely to begin: *on the edge of war.* **3.** A dividing line; a border: *The stone fence marks the edge of their property.* See Synonyms at **border. 4.** An advantage: *We had a slight edge over the other team.* ❖ *v.* **edged, edg·ing, edg·es** —*tr.* **1.** To give an edge to; sharpen. **2.** To be the edge of: *Flowers edged the lawn.* **3.** To put a border or edge on: *edge a sleeve with lace.* **4.** To advance or move gradually; push: *The photographers edged their way through the crowd.* —*intr.* To move gradually: *The child edged slowly toward the door.* ◆ **edge out** To surpass or beat by a small margin. **on edge** Tense or nervous; irritable: *He was on edge from listening to the baby cry.* [From Old English *ecg.*]

edge·wise (ĕj′wīz′) also **edge·ways** (ĕj′wāz′) *adv.* **1.** With the edge forward: *Turn the table edgewise to get it through the door.* **2.** On, by, with, or toward the edge: *The cricket moved edgewise along the side of the box.* ◆ **get a word in edgewise** To manage to say something in a conversation dominated by another person: *The others talked so much I couldn't get a word in edgewise.*

edg·ing (ĕj′ĭng) *n.* Something that forms an edge or border: *an edging of bricks along the path.*

edg·y (ĕj′ē) *adj.* **edg·i·er, edg·i·est 1.** Nervous or irritable: *We got edgy waiting for the concert to begin.* **2.** Daring, provocative, or trend-setting: *an exhibition of edgy paintings.* **—edg′i·ness** *n.*

ed·i·ble (ĕd′ə-bəl) *adj.* Fit to be eaten: *The spoiled cheese was no longer edible.* [From Late Latin *edibilis,* from Latin *edere,* to eat.]

e·dict (ē′dĭkt′) *n.* An order or decree issued by a person in authority. [From Latin *ēdictum,* from past participle of *ēdīcere,* to declare : *ē-, ex-,* out + *dīcere,* to speak.]

ed·i·fi·ca·tion (ĕd′ə-fĭ-kā′shən) *n.* Intellectual, moral, or spiritual improvement; enlightenment: *She wrote the book for the edification of the people.*

ed·i·fice (ĕd′ə-fĭs) *n.* A building, especially one that is very imposing in size or appearance.

ed·i·fy (ĕd′ə-fī′) *tr.v.* **ed·i·fied, ed·i·fy·ing, ed·i·fies** To instruct so as to encourage intellectual, moral, or spiritual improvement: *His poems are intended to edify young readers.*

Ed·in·burgh (ĕd′n-bûr′ə) The capital of Scotland, in the eastern part of the country on an inlet of the North Sea. The city is the site of a yearly international festival of the arts.

Ed·i·son (ĕd′ĭ-sən), **Thomas Alva** 1847–1931. American inventor who took out more than 1,000 patents in his lifetime. His inventions include the microphone (1877) and the light bulb (1879).

ed·it (ĕd′ĭt) *tr.v.* **ed·it·ed, ed·it·ing, ed·its 1.** To make (written material) ready for publication by correcting, revising, or marking directions for a printer: *The staff edited reporters' stories for publication in the newspaper.* **2.** To supervise and be responsible for the publication of (a newspaper or magazine, for example): *edited a literary magazine.* **3.** To put together or cut out parts of (a film or soundtrack, for example): *We edited our videotape of the wedding down to a 30-minute show.* ◆ **edit out** To delete during the course of editing: *A controversial scene was edited out of the film.*

e·di·tion (ĭ-dĭsh′ən) *n.* **1a.** The entire number of copies of a book or newspaper printed at one time and having the same content: *today's edition of the newspaper.* **b.** A single copy from such a number: *I bought this month's edition of the magazine.* **2.** Any of the various forms in which a publication is issued: *a paperback edition of a novel.* **3.** The entire number of like or identical items issued or made as a set: *a limited edition of early jazz recordings.*

ed·i·tor (ĕd′ĭ-tər) *n.* **1.** A person who edits written material for publication. **2.** A person who prepares a recording for viewing or hearing by assembling and deleting various parts. **3.** A person who directs the writing and layout of a newspaper or magazine or supervises one of its departments. **4.** A computer program used to edit text or data files. [From Late Latin *ēditor,* publisher, from *ēdere,* to publish : *ē-, ex-,* out + *dare,* to give.]

ed·i·to·ri·al (ĕd′ĭ-tôr′ē-əl) *n.* **1.** An article in a newspaper or magazine expressing the opinions of its editors or publisher. **2.** A commentary on television or radio expressing the opinion of the owners. ❖ *adj.* **1.** Relating to an editor or editing: *an editorial position in a publishing company.* **2.** Expressing opinion rather than reporting news: *the editorial page of the newspaper.* **—ed′i·to′ri·al·ly** *adv.*

ed·i·to·ri·al·ize (ĕd′ĭ-tôr′ē-ə-līz′) *intr.v.* **ed·i·to·ri·al·ized, ed·i·to·ri·al·iz·ing, ed·i·to·ri·al·iz·es 1.** To express an opinion in or as if in an editorial: *Most newspapers editorialize in each issue.* **2.** To express an opinion or opinions in what is supposed to be a report of facts: *The author feels so strongly about the issue, he cannot keep himself from editorializing.*

ed·i·tor·ship (ĕd′ĭ-tər-shĭp′) *n.* The position, duties, or guidance of an editor.

Ed·mon·ton (ĕd′mən-tən) The capital of Alberta, Canada, in the central part of the province north of Calgary. It was founded as a fort and trading post in 1795.

ed·u·ca·ble (ĕj′ə-kə-bəl) *adj.* Capable of being educated.

ed·u·cate (ĕj′ə-kāt′) *v.* **ed·u·cat·ed, ed·u·cat·ing, ed·u·cates** —*tr.* To provide with knowledge or training, especially through formal schooling; teach. See Synonyms at **teach.** —*intr.* To provide instructions and training: *Their purpose is to educate through the use of visual aids.* [From Middle English *educaten,* from Latin *ēducāre* : *ē-, ex-,* out + *dūcere,* to lead.]

ed·u·cat·ed (ĕj′ə-kā′tĭd) *adj.* **1.** Having an education, especially one above the average: *Librarians are educated people.* **2.** Showing evidence of schooling; cultured; refined: *an educated taste for books and learning.* **3.** Based on experience or factual knowledge: *an educated guess.*

ed·u·ca·tion (ĕj′ə-kā′shən) *n.* **1a.** The process of im-

ă	pat	ôr	core
ā	pay	oi	boy
âr	care	ou	out
ä	father	o͝o	took
ĕ	pet	o͝or	lure
ē	be	o͞o	boot
ĭ	pit	ŭ	cut
ī	bite	ûr	urge
îr	pier	th	thin
ŏ	pot	*th*	this
ō	toe	zh	vision
ô	paw	ə	about

parting or obtaining knowledge or skill: *Many people want to continue their education after high school.* **b.** The knowledge or skill obtained by such a process; learning: *It takes a lot of education to be an engineer.* **2.** A program of instruction of a specified kind or level: *a college education.* **3.** The field of study that is concerned with teaching and learning: *Many teachers are graduates of schools of education.*

ed·u·ca·tion·al (ĕj′ə-**kā′**shə-nəl) *adj.* **1.** Relating to education: *educational standards.* **2.** Serving to give knowledge or skill; instructive: *educational television.* —**ed′u·ca′tion·al·ly** *adv.*

ed·u·ca·tor (**ĕj′**ə-kā′tər) *n.* **1.** A person who is trained in teaching; a teacher. **2.** A specialist in the theory and practice of education.

e·duce (ĭ-**do͞os′**) *tr.v.* **e·duced, e·duc·ing, e·duc·es** To draw or bring out; elicit: *By clever questions the judge educed the facts of the case from the witnesses.* —**e·duc′i·ble** *adj.* —SEE NOTE AT **produce.**

Ed·ward VII (**ĕd′**wərd) 1841–1910. King of Great Britain and Ireland (1901–1910) who improved Britain's international relations.

Edward VIII Later known as Duke of Windsor. 1894–1972. King of Great Britain and Ireland (1936) who gave up the throne in order to marry Wallis Simpson, an American who had been divorced.

–ee *suff.* A suffix that means: **1.** A person who receives or benefits from an action: *appointee; trainee.* **2.** A person or animal that performs an action: *absentee; escapee.* **3.** A person who possesses something: *grantee.*

EEE *abbr.* An abbreviation of Eastern equine encephalitis.

EEG (ē′ē′**jē′**) *n.* An electroencephalogram.

eel (ēl) *n., pl.* **eel** or **eels** Any of various long slender fishes that lack scales and resemble snakes. [From Old English *ǣl.*]

e'en[1] (ēn) *n.* Evening.

e'en[2] (ēn) *adv.* Even.

–eer *suff.* A suffix that means a person who is associated with or involved in: *auctioneer; racketeer.*

e'er (âr) *adv.* Ever.

❑ *These sound alike:* **e'er, air** (gas), **ere** (before), **heir** (inheritor).

ee·rie or **ee·ry** (**îr′**ē) *adj.* **ee·ri·er, ee·ri·est** Inspiring fear without a clear reason; strange and frightening: *The eerie old house made us feel uneasy.* [From Middle English *eri*, fearful, from Old English *earg*, cowardly.] —**ee′ri·ly** *adv.* —**ee′ri·ness** *n.*

ef·face (ĭ-**fās′**) *tr.v.* **ef·faced, ef·fac·ing, ef·fac·es** To remove, as by rubbing out; erase: *Time had effaced the name on the gravestone.* —**ef·face′ment** *n.*

ef·fect (ĭ-**fĕkt′**) *n.* **1.** Something brought about by a cause or agent; a result: *The effect of advertising should be an increase in sales.* **2.** The power to bring about a result; influence: *The tougher laws had no effect on the crime rate.* **3a.** An artistic technique that produces a specific impression: *Thunder and lightning and other special effects can be used in making a movie.* **b.** The impression produced by some artistic technique: *a musical passage that was meant to create the effect of spring.* **4. effects** Movable belongings; goods. ❖ *tr.v.* **ef·fect·ed, ef·fect·ing, ef·fects** To produce as a result; cause to occur: *New technologies have effected many changes in the way people live.* ◆ **in effect 1.** In essence; actually: *By turning off the lights they were in effect telling us to go home.* **2.** In active force: *The new law is now in effect.* [From Middle English, from Latin *effectus*, past participle of *efficere*, to accomplish : *ex-*, out + *facere*, to make.] —SEE NOTE AT **affect**[1]**.**

ef·fec·tive (ĭ-**fĕk′**tĭv) *adj.* **1.** Having an intended or expected effect: *a vaccine that is effective against polio.* **2.** Operative; in effect: *The law will be effective as soon as the governor signs it.* **3.** Producing a strong impression or response: *The president made an effective speech that united the country behind him.* —**ef·fec′tive·ly** *adv.* —**ef·fec′tive·ness** *n.*

ef·fec·tu·al (ĭ-**fĕk′**cho͞o-əl) *adj.* Producing or sufficient to produce a desired effect; fully adequate: *Practice is the only effectual method of learning to play the piano.* —**ef·fec′tu·al·ly** *adv.*

ef·fec·tu·ate (ĭ-**fĕk′**cho͞o-āt′) *tr.v.* **ef·fec·tu·at·ed, ef·fec·tu·at·ing, ef·fec·tu·ates** To bring about; effect: *effectuate a change in the rule.*

ef·fem·i·nate (ĭ-**fĕm′**ə-nĭt) *adj.* Having qualities associated with women rather than men. —**ef·fem′i·na·cy** (ĭ-**fĕm′**ə-nə-sē) *n.* —**ef·fem′i·nate·ly** *adv.*

ef·fer·ent (**ĕf′**ər-ənt) *adj.* Directed away from a central organ or point: *Efferent nerves carry impulses from the brain to the muscles.*

ef·fer·vesce (ĕf′ər-**vĕs′**) *intr.v.* **ef·fer·vesced, ef·fer·vesc·ing, ef·fer·vesc·es 1.** To give off bubbles of gas, as a carbonated liquid. **2.** To show high spirits; be lively. [From Latin *effervēscere* : *ex-*, up, out + *fervēscere*, to start boiling.]

ef·fer·ves·cence (ĕf′ər-**vĕs′**əns) *n.* **1.** The process of giving off small bubbles of gas: *the effervescence of soda water.* **2.** Sparkling high spirits; vivacity. —**ef′fer·ves′cent** *adj.*

ef·fete (ĭ-**fēt′**) *adj.* **1a.** Characterized by extreme refinement or self-indulgence. **b.** Pretentious; snobby. **2.** Having lost vitality, strength, or effectiveness: *an effete period of a once great civilization.* —**ef·fete′ly** *adv.*

ef·fi·ca·cious (ĕf′ĭ-**kā′**shəs) *adj.* Producing or capable of producing the desired effect; effective: *an efficacious treatment of a disease.* —**ef′fi·ca′cious·ly** *adv.*

ef·fi·ca·cy (**ĕf′**ĭ-kə-sē) *n.* Power or capacity to produce a desired effect; effectiveness: *The efficacy of most medicines declines over time.*

ef·fi·cien·cy (ĭ-**fĭsh′**ən-sē) *n., pl.* **ef·fi·cien·cies 1.** The condition or quality of being efficient: *Tired people can't work with efficiency.* **2.** The ratio of the useful work a machine does to the energy required to operate it.

efficiency apartment *n.* A small, usually furnished apartment with a private bathroom and small kitchen area.

ef·fi·cient (ĭ-**fĭsh′**ənt) *adj.* Acting or producing effectively with a minimum of waste, expense, or unnecessary effort: *an efficient worker; an efficient motor.* [From Middle English, from Latin *efficere*, to effect.] —**ef·fi′cient·ly** *adv.*

ef·fi·gy (**ĕf′**ə-jē) *n., pl.* **ef·fi·gies 1.** A crude figure or dummy of a hated person. **2.** A likeness or sculpture of a person or animal: *a stone effigy on a tomb.* ◆ **in effigy** In the form of an effigy: *The colonists burned King George in effigy.*

ef·flo·res·cence (ĕf′lə-**rĕs′**əns) *n.* **1.** A state or period of flowering: *the splendid efflorescence of the roses.* **2.** The highest point in a process of development: *the efflorescence of mercantilism.* **3.** A deposit of salt crystals or powder on a surface, caused by the evaporation of water from a solution containing dissolved salts. —**ef′flo·res′cent** *adj.*

ef·flu·ent (**ĕf′**lo͞o-ənt) *adj.* Flowing out or forth. ❖ *n.* **1.** Something that flows out or forth, such as a stream that flows from a lake. **2.** The liquid waste or sewage that flows from a factory, water purification plant, or other system. [From Middle English, from Latin *effluere*, to flow out : *ex-*, out + *fluere*, to flow.]

ef·fort (**ĕf′**ərt) *n.* **1.** The use of physical or mental energy to do something; exertion: *It took a lot of effort to plant the tree.* **2.** An attempt, especially an earnest attempt: *We made an effort to arrive on time.* **3.** Something done or produced through exertion; an achievement: *This painting is the artist's best and latest effort.* [From French, from Medieval Latin *exfortiāre*, to force, exert : Latin *ex-*, out + Latin *fortis*, strong.]

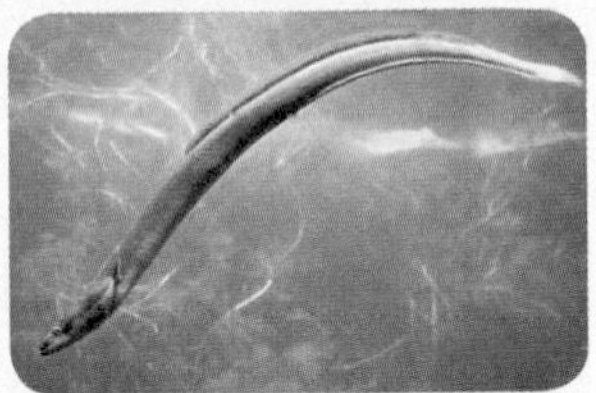
eel

efflorescence

WRITERS CHOOSE THEIR WORDS

We, the fourteen members of the Mouse Council, have discussed your behavior. First, we will give you a chance to defend yourself against these rumors of your **egregious** acts. Did you or did you not sit at the foot of the human king?

—Kate DiCamillo
The Tale of Despereaux

egret

eighth note
left to right: whole, half, quarter, eighth, and sixteenth notes

ă	pat	ôr	core
ā	pay	oi	boy
âr	care	ou	out
ä	father	o͝o	took
ĕ	pet	o͝or	lure
ē	be	o͞o	boot
ĭ	pit	ŭ	cut
ī	bite	ûr	urge
îr	pier	th	thin
ŏ	pot	*th*	this
ō	toe	zh	vision
ô	paw	ə	about

ef·fort·less (ĕf′ərt-lĭs) *adj.* Requiring or showing little or no effort: *Watching TV is an effortless activity. The skater glided in effortless turns around the ice.* See Synonyms at **easy.** —**ef′fort·less·ly** *adv.*

ef·front·er·y (ĭ-frŭn′tə-rē) *n., pl.* **ef·front·er·ies** Shameless or insulting boldness; audacity: *In spite of making several rude remarks they had the effrontery to ask for our help.*

ef·ful·gent (ĭ-fo͝ol′jənt *or* ĭ-fŭl′jənt) *adj.* Shining brilliantly; radiant. —**ef·ful′gence** *n.* —**ef·ful′gent·ly** *adv.*

ef·fu·sion (ĭ-fyo͞o′zhən) *n.* **1.** An outpouring, as of fluid: *The effusion of blood was stopped by a compress.* **2.** An unrestrained outpouring of feeling, as in speech or writing: *Such an effusion of praise embarrassed me.*

ef·fu·sive (ĭ-fyo͞o′sĭv) *adj.* Unrestrained or excessive in emotional expression; gushy: *an effusive display of gratitude.* —**ef·fu′sive·ly** *adv.* —**ef·fu′sive·ness** *n.*

eft (ĕft) *n.* A newt in an immature stage that lives on land.

e.g. *abbr.* An abbreviation of exempli gratia (for example).

egg[1] (ĕg) *n.* **1.** A female reproductive cell of humans and other animals from which an embryo develops; an egg cell or ovum. In animals such as birds, turtles, frogs, fish, and insects, an egg contains nourishment for the developing embryo and may have a protective shell or covering. **2.** A female reproductive cell of plants and most algae; an egg cell. **3.** A hard-shelled egg, the contents of which are used for food, especially a chicken egg: *We had scrambled eggs for breakfast.* **4.** *Informal* A person: *What a good egg!* [From Middle English *eg, egge,* bird's egg, from Old Norse *egg.*]

egg[2] (ĕg) *tr.v.* **egged, egg·ing, eggs** To encourage or urge. Used with *on: egged me on to try to ski down that hill.* [From Middle English *eggen,* from Old Norse *eggja.*]

egg·beat·er (ĕg′bē′tər) *n.* A kitchen utensil with rotating blades for beating eggs, whipping cream, or mixing ingredients together.

egg cell *n.* **1.** A female reproductive cell in animals; an egg. **2.** A female reproductive cell in plants and most algae; an egg.

egg·head (ĕg′hĕd′) *n. Informal* An intellectual.

egg·nog (ĕg′nŏg′) *n.* A drink of milk or cream, sugar, and beaten eggs, often mixed with an alcoholic liquor such as rum or brandy.

egg·plant (ĕg′plănt′) *n.* **1.** The glossy, often egg-shaped fruit of a bushy plant, cooked and eaten as a vegetable. Eggplants are usually purple but can also be white, yellow, or green. **2.** The plant that bears such fruit.

egg roll *n.* A casing of egg dough filled with minced vegetables, sometimes with seafood or meat, and fried.

egg·shell (ĕg′shĕl′) *n.* The thin, often brittle outer covering of the egg of a bird or reptile.

eg·lan·tine (ĕg′lən-tīn′ *or* ĕg′lən-tēn′) *n.* The sweetbrier.

e·go (ē′gō) *n., pl.* **e·gos 1.** The awareness of oneself as separate and different from other things; the self. **2.** Egotism; conceit: *Self-important people are often full of ego.* **3.** Self-confidence; self-esteem: *A leader needs enough ego to take a lot of criticism.* [From Latin *ego,* I.]

e·go·cen·tric (ē′gō-sĕn′trĭk) *adj.* Concerned only with oneself; self-centered: *An egocentric person usually does not work well in a group.*

e·go·ism (ē′gō-ĭz′əm) *n.* **1.** The tendency to think or act with only one's own interests in mind; selfishness. **2.** Conceit; egotism. —**e′go·ist** *n.*

e·go·tism (ē′gə-tĭz′əm) *n.* **1.** The tendency to speak or write about oneself excessively or boastfully. **2.** An exaggerated sense of one's own importance; conceit.

e·go·tist (ē′gə-tĭst) *n.* **1.** A conceited boastful person. **2.** A selfish self-centered person. —**e′go·tis′ti·cal** *adj.* —**e′go·tis′ti·cal·ly** *adv.*

ego trip *n. Slang* An action done to boost one's feeling of importance or to call attention to oneself: *The candidate expected to lose and ran only as an ego trip.*

e·gre·gious (ĭ-grē′jəs) *adj.* Conspicuously bad or offensive: *An egregious error in the computer program caused the spacecraft to fall out of orbit.* —**e·gre′gious·ly** *adv.*

e·gress (ē′grĕs′) *n.* **1.** A path or means of going out; an exit: *When fire blocked the doorway there was no egress from the building.* **2.** The right to leave or go out: *The guard denied them egress.* **3.** The act of going out. —SEE NOTE AT **progress.**

e·gret (ē′grĭt *or* ĕg′rĭt) *n.* Any of several wading birds having a long neck, a pointed bill, and usually white feathers. Many egrets have long drooping plumes during the breeding season. [From Middle English, from Old French *aigrette,* from Old Provençal *aigron,* heron, of Germanic origin.]

E·gypt (ē′jĭpt) A country of northeast Africa north of Sudan on the Mediterranean Sea. Ancient Egypt was the site of one of the word's first civilizations, dating back at least to the fourth millennium BC. Cairo is the capital.

E·gyp·tian (ĭ-jĭp′shən) *adj.* **1.** Relating to Egypt, the Egyptians, or their culture. **2.** Relating to the language of the ancient Egyptians. ❖ *n.* **1.** A native or inhabitant of Egypt. **2.** The extinct Afro-Asiatic language of the ancient Egyptians.

eh (ā *or* ĕ) *interj.* An expression used in asking for agreement or confirmation: *That's not a bad looking car, eh?*

Eid al-Fitr (ēd əl-fĭt′ər) *n.* A festival that ends the fast of Ramadan. [From Arabic *ʿĪd al-Fiṭr,* Feast of Breaking the Fast.]

ei·der (ī′dər) *n.* Any of several large ducks of northern regions of the Atlantic and Pacific Oceans, having a layer of very soft downy feathers under the outer feathers.

ei·der·down (ī′dər-doun′) *n.* **1.** The soft light down of the eider, used for stuffing coats, quilts, pillows, and sleeping bags. **2.** A quilt stuffed with eiderdown.

eight (āt) *n.* **1.** The number, written 8, that is equal to 7 + 1. **2.** The eighth in a set or sequence. [From Old English *eahta.*]
❑ *These sound alike:* **eight, ate** (eat).

eight·een (ā-tēn′) *n.* **1.** The number, written 18, that is equal to 17 + 1. **2.** The 18th in a set or sequence.

eight·eenth (ā-tēnth′) *n.* **1.** The ordinal number matching the number 18 in a series. **2.** One of 18 equal parts.

eighth (ātth *or* āth) *n.* **1.** The ordinal number matching the number eight in a series. **2.** One of eight equal parts.

eighth note *n.* A musical note having one eighth the time value of a whole note.

eight·i·eth (ā′tē-ĭth) *n.* **1.** The ordinal number matching the number 80 in a series. **2.** One of 80 equal parts.

eight·y (ā′tē) *n., pl.* **eight·ies** The number, written 80, that is equal to 8 × 10.

Ein·stein (īn′stīn′), **Albert** 1879–1955. German-born American physicist whose two-part theory of relativity revolutionized scientific understanding on the nature of space and time and on the relationship of mass and energy.

ein·stei·ni·um (īn-stī′nē-əm) *n. Symbol* **Es** A radioactive element that is usually produced artificially by scientists. It was first discovered in the debris of a hydrogen bomb explosion. The half-life of its longest-lived isotope is about 472 days. Atomic number 99. See **Periodic Table.** [After Albert *Einstein.*]

Eir·e (âr′ə *or* ī′rə *or* âr′ē *or* ī′rē) See **Ireland** (sense 2).

Ei·sen·how·er (ī′zən-hou′ər), **Dwight David** Known as "Ike." 1890–1969. American general and the 34th president of the United States (1953–1961). His presidency was marked by the Korean War armistice (1953) and the Cold War with the Soviet Union.

ei·ther (ē′*th*ər *or* ī′*th*ər) *pron.* One or the other of two: *It was a while before either of them spoke.* ❖ *conj.* Used before the first of two or more words or groups of words linked by *or*: *Either we go now or we forget about going.* ❖ *adj.* **1.** One or the other; any one of two: *Wear either coat.* **2.** One and the other; each of the two: *Candles stood on either end of the mantelpiece.* ❖ *adv.* Any more than the other; likewise; also: *I didn't go to the movies, and my friends didn't either.* [From Old English *ǣther.*] —SEE NOTE.

e·jac·u·late (ĭ-jăk′yə-lāt′) *v.* **e·jac·u·lat·ed, e·jac·u·lat·ing, e·jac·u·lates** —*tr.* **1.** To discharge (semen). **2.** To utter suddenly and passionately; exclaim. —*intr.* To eject a body fluid, especially semen.

e·jac·u·la·tion (ĭ-jăk′yə-lā′shən) *n.* **1.** The act or process of ejaculating. **2.** A sudden utterance; an exclamation.

e·ject (ĭ-jĕkt′) *tr.v.* **e·ject·ed, e·ject·ing, e·jects 1.** To throw out with force; expel: *Active volcanoes eject hot ash and lava.* **2.** To force (someone) to leave; drive out: *The noisy people were ejected from the theater.* [From Middle English *ejecten*, from Latin *ēicere* : *ē-, ex-*, out + *iacere*, to throw.]

e·jec·tion (ĭ-jĕk′shən) *n.* **1.** The act of ejecting or the condition of being ejected: *The ejection of the pilot from the stalled plane saved her.* **2.** Something ejected: *Heavy metal nets were laid over the rock to catch ejections from blasting.*

e·jec·tor (ĭ-jĕk′tər) *n.* A person or thing that ejects.

eke (ēk) *tr.v.* **eked, ek·ing, ekes** To get with great effort or strain. Used with *out*: *The farmers managed to eke out an existence during the drought.*

EKG *abbr.* An abbreviation of: **1.** electrocardiogram. **2.** electrocardiograph.

el. *abbr.* An abbreviation of elevation.

e·lab·o·rate (ĭ-lăb′ər-ĭt) *adj.* Planned or made with great attention to numerous parts or details; intricate: *We made elaborate plans for the party.* ❖ *v.* (ĭ-lăb′ə-rāt′) **e·lab·o·rat·ed, e·lab·o·rat·ing, e·lab·o·rates** —*tr.* To work out with care and detail; develop thoroughly: *It may take scientists years to elaborate a theory.* —*intr.* To express oneself at greater length or in greater detail; provide further information: *The author elaborated on the difficulty of writing the book.* [From Latin *ēlabōrāre*, to work out : *ē-, ex-*, out + *labōrāre*, to work (from *labor*, work).] **—e·lab′o·rate·ly** *adv.* **—e·lab′o·ra′tion** *n.*

é·lan (ā-län′) *n.* Enthusiastic liveliness and vigor; zest: *The musicians in the marching band played with élan.*

e·land (ē′lənd) *n., pl.* **eland** also **e·lands** Either of two large African antelopes having long twisted horns. [From Afrikaans, from Dutch, elk, from obsolete German *Elend*, of Baltic origin.]

e·lapse (ĭ-lăps′) *intr.v.* **e·lapsed, e·laps·ing, e·laps·es** To pass; go by: *Months elapsed before I heard from my friend again.* [From Latin *ēlāpsus*, past participle of *ēlābī* : *ē-, ex-*, out, away + *lābī*, to slip.]

e·las·tic (ĭ-lăs′tĭk) *adj.* **1.** Easily returning to an original shape after being stretched, compressed, or otherwise deformed: *Rubber bands are very elastic.* **2.** Capable of adapting or being adapted to change or a variety of circumstances; flexible: *an elastic application of the rules.* ❖ *n.* **1.** A fabric woven with strands of rubber or a similar synthetic fiber to make it stretch: *Elastic held the sleeves of my jacket around my wrists.* **2.** A rubber band. **—e·las′ti·cal·ly** *adv.*

e·las·tic·i·ty (ĭ-lă-stĭs′ĭ-tē *or* ē′lă-stĭs′ĭ-tē) *n.* The condition or property of being elastic: *The rubber band broke when it lost its elasticity.*

e·late (ĭ-lāt′) *tr.v.* **e·lat·ed, e·lat·ing, e·lates** To fill with great joy or happiness; delight: *The news of victory elated the candidate's supporters.*

e·lat·ed (ĭ-lā′tĭd) *adj.* Joyful; happy; in high spirits: *the elated feeling of winning a race.* **—e·lat′ed·ly** *adv.*

e·la·tion (ĭ-lā′shən) *n.* An intense feeling of happiness or joy: *the elation of succeeding after much effort.*

El·ba (ĕl′bə) An island of Italy between Corsica and the mainland. Napoleon Bonaparte spent his first period of exile here (May 1814–February 1815).

El·be (ĕl′bə *or* ĕlb) A river of the Czech Republic and Germany flowing about 725 miles (1,165 kilometers) to the North Sea.

el·bow (ĕl′bō′) *n.* **1a.** The joint or bend between the human forearm and the upper arm. **b.** A corresponding joint in another vertebrate animal. **2.** Something having a bend or sharp angle, such as a length of pipe that has a sharp bend in it. ❖ *tr.v.* **el·bowed, el·bow·ing, el·bows 1.** To poke or push with the elbow: *She elbowed me in the side to get my attention.* **2.** To make (one's way) by pushing with the body, especially the elbows: *The detectives elbowed their way through the crowd.* [From Old English *elnboga.*]

elbow grease *n. Informal* Strenuous physical effort: *Polishing a car requires elbow grease.*

el·bow·room (ĕl′bō-ro͝om′ *or* ĕl′bō-ro͝om′) *n.* Room to move around or function in; ample space: *Their cramped cubicles didn't give the artists enough elbowroom to lay out their work.*

eld·er[1] (ĕl′dər) *adj.* Born before another; older; senior: *my elder sister; an elder statesman.* ❖ *n.* **1.** An older person: *The children rely on their elders for guidance and support.* **2.** An older influential person of a family, tribe, or community: *In colonial times, a council of elders governed the affairs of many settlements.* **3.** One of the officers of certain churches. [From Old English *eldra*, older.]

el·der[2] (ĕl′dər) *n.* The elderberry. [From Old English *ellærn.*]

el·der·ber·ry (ĕl′dər-bĕr′ē) *n.* **1.** Any of various shrubs or small trees having clusters of small white flowers and small red or purplish-black berrylike fruit. **2.** The fruit of certain of these plants, used to make wine or preserves.

eld·er·ly (ĕl′dər-lē) *adj.* Approaching old age; rather old: *an elderly person.* ❖ *n. (used with a plural verb)* Older people considered as a group. **—eld′er·li·ness** *n.*

eld·est (ĕl′dĭst) *adj.* Oldest: *The king's eldest child became the new ruler.*

El Do·ra·do (ĕl də-rä′dō) A legendary city of South America, fabled for its great wealth of gold and precious jewels.

e·lect (ĭ-lĕkt′) *tr.v.* **e·lect·ed, e·lect·ing, e·lects 1.** To choose by vote for an office or for membership: *The citizens of each state vote to elect two senators.* **2.** To select from a group of options; choose: *I elected an art course. I elected to take geology, too.* ❖ *adj.* Elected but not yet installed in office: *The governor-elect will take office in January.* ❖ *n. (used with a plural verb)* A chosen or privileged group: *one of the elect who have power in the state government.* [From Middle English *electen*, from Latin *ēligere*, to select : *ē-, ex-*, out + *legere*, to choose.]

e·lec·tion (ĭ-lĕk′shən) *n.* **1.** The act or process of choosing by vote among candidates to fill an office or position: *The election of representatives takes place every two years.* **2.** Selection or choice: *his election of a course in sculpting.*

e·lec·tion·eer (ĭ-lĕk′shə-nîr′) *intr.v.* **e·lec·tion·eered, e·lec·tion·eer·ing, e·lec·tion·eers** To work actively for a particular candidate or party in an election.

e·lec·tive (ĭ-lĕk′tĭv) *adj.* **1.** Filled or obtained by election: *The presidency is an elective office.* **2.** Chosen by election: *The president is the highest elective official.* **3.** Permitting a choice; not required; optional: *Italian is an elective course in my school.* ❖ *n.* An optional course in school: *My electives are music and woodworking.*

e·lec·tor (ĭ-lĕk′tər) *n.* **1.** A person who has the right to vote in an election. **2.** A member of the Electoral College of the United States.

e·lec·tor·al (ĭ-lĕk′tər-əl) *adj.* **1.** Relating to electors, especially the members of the Electoral College: *The president had a majority of the electoral vote.* **2.** Relating to

Albert Einstein
photographed c. 1931

Dwight Eisenhower

USAGE

either When used as a pronoun, **either** is singular and takes a singular verb: *You can take French or Spanish; either is a good choice.* This rule holds even when *either* is followed by *of* and a plural noun: *Either of the two languages is a good one to study.* In an *either ... or* construction, you use the singular when the words used as the subject of a sentence are singular: *Either Jennifer or June is coming to the party.* When the words are plural, the verb is plural: *Either the Montoyas or the Smiths throw a party every year.* It is best to avoid sentences in which *either* is followed by one singular and one plural.

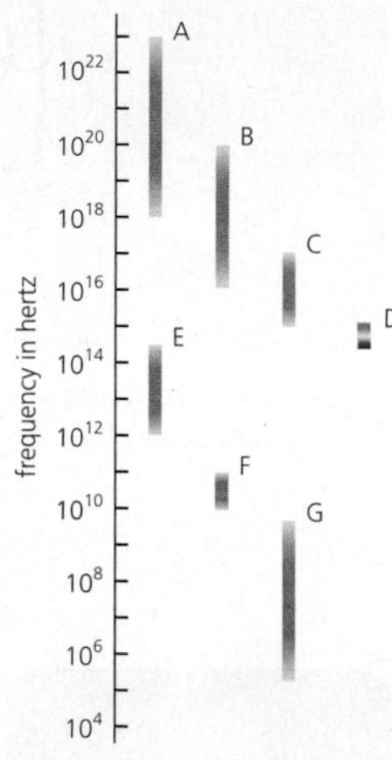

electromagnetic spectrum

electromagnetic spectrum frequencies in hertz
A. gamma rays
B. x-rays
C. ultraviolet rays
D. visible light
E. infrared rays
F. microwaves
G. radio waves

election: *electoral reforms that will make it easier to vote.*

Electoral College *n.* A group of electors chosen by the voters to elect the president and vice president of the United States. The number of electors allotted to each state is based on population.

e·lec·tor·ate (ĭ-**lĕk′**tər-ĭt) *n.* All those people qualified to vote in an election: *The United States has a huge electorate, but many people do not vote.*

e·lec·tric (ĭ-**lĕk′**trĭk) *adj.* **1.** also **e·lec·tri·cal** (ĭ-**lĕk′**trĭ-kəl) Relating to, producing, or operated by electricity: *electric power; an electrical appliance.* **2.** Amplified by an electronic device: *an electric guitar.* **3.** Charged with emotion; exciting; thrilling: *the electric feeling of watching a very close race.* [From New Latin *ēlectricus,* deriving from amber (as by rubbing), from Greek *ēlektron,* amber.] **—e·lec′tri·cal·ly** *adv.*

electrical engineering *n.* The branch of engineering that deals with the practical uses of electricity and their effects. **—electrical engineer** *n.*

electric blanket *n.* A blanket fitted with an electric heating element and a control for regulating its temperature.

electric chair *n.* A device used to electrocute a person sentenced to death by restraining that person in a chair and applying a deadly electrical current to the body.

electric eel *n.* A South American freshwater fish that resembles an eel and can produce a powerful electric discharge, which it uses to stun prey and to defend itself.

electric eye *n.* An electrical device that detects variations in the intensity of a light source by means of a photoelectric cell. If something obscures or blocks the light, the electric eye can activate or turn off another device.

electric field *n.* A region of space characterized by the existence of a force generated by electric charge.

e·lec·tri·cian (ĭ-lĕk-**trĭsh′**ən *or* ē′lĕk-**trĭsh′**ən) *n.* A person who installs, maintains, repairs, or operates electric equipment and electrical circuits.

e·lec·tric·i·ty (ĭ-lĕk-**trĭs′**ĭ-tē *or* ē′lĕk-**trĭs′**ĭ-tē) *n.* **1.** The collection of physical effects resulting from the behavior and interactions of electrons and protons. Particles with like charge repel each other. Particles with opposite charges attract each other. **2.** Electric current used as a source of power: *Electricity lights our homes.* **3.** Emotional excitement: *felt the electricity in the crowd.*

e·lec·tri·fy (ĭ-**lĕk′**trə-fī′) *tr.v.* **e·lec·tri·fied, e·lec·tri·fy·ing, e·lec·tri·fies 1.** To charge with electricity: *throw the switch to electrify a circuit.* **2a.** To wire or equip for the use of electric power: *electrify a building.* **b.** To supply with electric power: *The new power station made it possible to electrify the whole valley.* **3.** To thrill, startle, or shock: *The goalie's play electrified the audience.* **—e·lec′tri·fi·ca′tion** (ĭ-lĕk′trə-fĭ-**kā′**shən) *n.*

electro– or **electr–** *pref.* A prefix that means: **1.** Electric: *electromagnet.* **2.** Electric or electrically: *electrocute.*

e·lec·tro·car·di·o·gram (ĭ-lĕk′trō-**kär′**dē-ə-grăm′) *n.* **1.** A record of the electrical activity of the heart made by an electrocardiograph, used especially in the diagnosis of disease. **2.** The procedure performed to produce such a record.

e·lec·tro·car·di·o·graph (ĭ-lĕk′trō-**kär′**dē-ə-grăf′) *n.* An instrument that records the electrical activity of the heart, usually in the form of a curve traced on paper or on a computer monitor.

e·lec·tro·chem·is·try (ĭ-lĕk′trō-**kĕm′**ĭ-strē) *n.* The study of chemical reactions that involve electricity, especially reactions that occur when an electric current flows through a solution. **—e·lec′tro·chem′i·cal** *adj.* **—e·lec′tro·chem′i·cal·ly** *adv.*

e·lec·tro·cute (ĭ-**lĕk′**trə-kyo͞ot′) *tr.v.* **e·lec·tro·cut·ed, e·lec·tro·cut·ing, e·lec·tro·cutes** To kill or execute with electricity: *The workers shut off the power to avoid any danger of being electrocuted.* [From : *electro-* + *(exe)cute.*]

e·lec·tro·cu·tion (ĭ-lĕk′trə-**kyo͞o′**shən) *n.* Death caused by an electric current.

e·lec·trode (ĭ-**lĕk′**trōd′) *n.* A conductor through which an electric current enters or exits a liquid or gas during electrolysis.

e·lec·tro·en·ceph·a·lo·gram (ĭ-lĕk′trō-ĕn-**sĕf′**ə-lə-grăm′) *n.* **1.** A record of the electrical activity of the brain made by an electroencephalograph, used especially in the diagonsis of disease. **2.** The procedure performed to produce such a record.

e·lec·tro·en·ceph·a·lo·graph (ĭ-lĕk′trō-ĕn-**sĕf′**ə-lə-grăf′) *n.* An instrument that records the electrical activity of the brain, usually in the form of curved lines on a paper chart or a computer monitor.

e·lec·trol·y·sis (ĭ-lĕk-**trŏl′**ĭ-sĭs) *n.* **1.** Chemical change, especially decomposition, produced in a chemical compound that breaks apart into ions when an electric current is passed through it. **2.** Destruction of living tissue, such as the roots of hairs, by an electric current. [From *electro-* + Greek *lusis,* a loosening.]

e·lec·tro·lyte (ĭ-**lĕk′**trə-līt′) *n.* **1.** A substance that when dissolved or melted becomes electrically conductive by breaking apart into ions. **2.** Any of various ions, such as sodium, potassium, or chloride, required by cells to regulate the electric charge and flow of water molecules across the cell membrane.

e·lec·tro·lyt·ic (ĭ-lĕk′trə-**lĭt′**ĭk) *adj.* **1.** Relating to electrolysis. **2.** Relating to or using electrolytes. **—e·lec′tro·lyt′i·cal·ly** *adv.*

e·lec·tro·lyze (ĭ-**lĕk′**trə-līz′) *tr.v.* **e·lec·tro·lyzed, e·lec·tro·lyz·ing, e·lec·tro·lyz·es** To cause to decompose by electrolysis.

e·lec·tro·mag·net (ĭ-lĕk′trō-**măg′**nĭt) *n.* A magnet that consists of a coil of insulated wire wrapped around an iron core that becomes magnetized only when an electric current flows through the wire. —SEE NOTE AT **magnetism.**

e·lec·tro·mag·net·ic (ĭ-lĕk′trō-măg-**nĕt′**ĭk) *adj.* Relating to electromagnetism.

electromagnetic radiation *n.* Energy that moves through space and matter both in the form of electromagnetic waves and in the form of a stream of particles called photons.

electromagnetic spectrum *n.* The entire range of electromagnetic radiation, consisting of radio waves (which have the longest wavelengths and lowest frequencies), microwaves, infrared waves, visible light, ultraviolet rays, x-rays, and gamma rays (which have the shortest wavelengths and highest frequencies).

electromagnetic wave *n.* A wave of energy consisting of electric and magnetic fields that regularly swing back and forth around a central point as they move in a given direction. Radio waves, light waves, and x-rays are electromagnetic waves.

e·lec·tro·mag·net·ism (ĭ-lĕk′trō-**măg′**nĭ-tĭz′əm) *n.* **1.** Magnetism produced by electric charge in motion. **2.** The scientific study of electricity and magnetism and the relationships between them.

e·lec·tro·mo·tive (ĭ-lĕk′trō-**mō′**tĭv) *adj.* Relating to or producing an electric current.

electromotive force *n.* The energy that is converted from chemical, mechanical, or other forms of energy into electrical energy in a battery or dynamo. Electromotive force is measured in volts.

e·lec·tron (ĭ-**lĕk′**trŏn′) *n.* A stable subatomic particle with a negative electric charge equal in strength to the positive charge of a proton. All atoms have at least one electron orbiting the nucleus. Electrons can move freely through space and can flow through a conducting material in an electric current. [From *electr(ic)* + *(i)on.*] —SEE NOTE AT **atom.**

electron gun *n.* A device that generates a beam of high-

ă	pat	ôr	core
ā	pay	oi	boy
âr	care	ou	out
ä	father	o͝o	took
ĕ	pet	o͝or	lure
ē	be	o͞o	boot
ĭ	pit	ŭ	cut
ī	bite	ûr	urge
îr	pier	th	thin
ŏ	pot	*th*	this
ō	toe	zh	vision
ô	paw	ə	about

speed electrons. In the cathode-ray tube of older television sets, the electron gun focuses an electron beam on the screen to create a picture.

e·lec·tron·ic (ĭ-lĕk-**trŏn′**ĭk *or* ē′lĕk-**trŏn′**ĭk) *adj.* **1.** Relating to or produced by means of electronics: *an electronic book.* **2.** Relating to, done with, or controlled by a computer or computer network. **3.** Relating to electrons. **—e·lec·tron′i·cal·ly** *adv.*

e·lec·tron·ics (ĭ-lĕk′**trŏn′**ĭks *or* ē′lĕk-**trŏn′**ĭks) *n.* **1.** *(used with a singular verb)* The science and technology concerned with the study of electrons in motion and the development of devices operated by a controlled flow of electrons, especially by means of integrated circuits: *Electronics has made the computer possible.* **2.** *(used with a plural verb)* Electronic devices and systems: *Most aircraft have very sophisticated electronics.*

electron microscope *n.* A microscope that uses electrons instead of visible light to produce images of objects that are too small to be seen or studied with an ordinary microscope.

electron tube *n.* A sealed glass tube containing either a vacuum or a small amount of gas, in which electrons flow between two or more electrodes.

electron volt *n.* A unit that is used to measure the energy of subatomic particles. It is equal to the energy gained by an electron that is accelerated until its electric potential is one volt greater than it was before being accelerated.

e·lec·tro·plate (ĭ **lĕk′**trə-plāt′) *tr.v.* **e·lec·tro·plat·ed, e·lec·tro·plat·ing, e·lec·tro·plates** To cover or coat with a thin layer of metal by means of electrolysis.

e·lec·tro·scope (ĭ-**lĕk′**trə-skōp′) *n.* An instrument used to detect electric charges and to determine whether they are positive or negative.

e·lec·tro·stat·ic (ĭ-lĕk′trō-**stăt′**ĭk) *adj.* Relating to, produced by, or caused by stationary electric charges.

electrostatic generator *n.* A machine that generates high voltages by accumulating large quantities of static electric charges.

e·lec·tro·ther·mal (ĭ-lĕk′trō-**thûr′**məl) *adj.* **1.** Relating to or involving both electricity and heat. **2.** Relating to the production of heat by electricity.

el·e·gance (**ĕl′**ĭ-gəns) *n.* **1.** Refinement, grace, and beauty in appearance or behavior: *The old castle still had signs of past elegance in its great staircase.* **2.** Something that is elegant: *Expensive jewelry is an elegance few students can afford.*

el·e·gant (**ĕl′**ĭ-gənt) *adj.* Marked by or showing elegance: *elegant clothes; an elegant restaurant.* [From Latin *ēlegāns*, choosing, from *ēligere*, to select.] **—el′e·gant·ly** *adv.*

el·e·gi·ac (ĕl′ə-**jī′**ək) *adj.* Relating to or involving elegy.

el·e·gize (**ĕl′**ə-jīz′) *v.* **el·e·gized, el·e·giz·ing, el·e·giz·es** *—intr.* To compose an elegy. *—tr.* To compose an elegy about.

el·e·gy (**ĕl′**ə-jē) *n., pl.* **el·e·gies** A poem or song that expresses sorrow, especially one composed to lament a person who has died. [From Greek *elegeia*.]

el·e·ment (**ĕl′**ə-mənt) *n.* **1.** A part of a whole, especially a fundamental or essential part: *The story contains elements of a detective novel and a romance.* **2. elements** The basic principles: *Composers must learn the elements of music.* **3.** A substance whose atoms always have the same number of protons in their nuclei. An element cannot be broken down into simpler substances by chemical means. See the **Periodic Table** of elements on pages 700–701. **4.** In mathematics, a member of a set. **5. elements** The forces of the weather, especially the cold, wind, and rain: *The rescuers braved the elements to hunt for the lost children.* **6.** An environment to which a person or thing is suited or adapted: *The sea was as much the sailors' element as the land.* [From Middle English, from Latin *elementum*.]

el·e·men·tal (ĕl′ə-**mĕn′**tl) *adj.* **1.** Relating to an element. **2.** Relating to or resembling a force of nature in power or effect: *the elemental fury of the hurricane.* **3.** Fundamental; basic: *Most students are familiar with the elemental concepts of physics.*

el·e·men·ta·ry (ĕl′ə-**mĕn′**tə-rē *or* ĕl′ə-**mĕn′**trē) *adj.* Relating to or involving the basic or simplest aspects of a subject: *an elementary math textbook.*

elementary particle *n.* Any of the smallest known units of matter, such as quarks and neutrinos. Elementary particles are smaller than atoms, are not made up of smaller units, and cannot be broken apart by collisions with other particles.

elementary school *n.* A school attended for the first four to eight years of a child's formal classroom instruction, often including kindergarten.

el·e·phant (**ĕl′**ə-fənt) *n.* Any of several large mammals of Asia and Africa having thick, almost hairless skin, a long flexible trunk, and long tusks. Elephants are the largest living land animals. [From Middle English *elefaunt*, from Greek *elephās*.]

elephant
top: Asian elephant
bottom: African elephant

el·e·phan·tine (ĕl′ə-**făn′**tēn′ *or* ĕl′ə-**făn′**tīn′) *adj.* Extremely large: *an elephantine problem.*

el·e·vate (**ĕl′**ə-vāt′) *tr.v.* **ele·vat·ed, ele·vat·ing, ele·vates 1.** To raise to a higher place or position; lift up: *A nurse elevated the head of the bed so the patient could sit up to read.* **2.** To promote to a higher rank: *The publisher elevated him to editor-in-chief.* **3.** To bring to a higher moral, cultural, or intellectual level: *By using its melody in a symphony the composer elevated the folk song to heights of great beauty.* [From Middle English *elevaten*, from Latin *ēlevāre* : *ē-*, *ex-*, out, up + *levāre*, to raise.] —SEE NOTE AT **leaven.**

el·e·vat·ed (**ĕl′**ə-vā′tĭd) *adj.* **1.** Raised or placed above a given level: *the elevated speaker's platform.* **2.** Increased in amount or degree: *an elevated temperature.* **3.** Formal; lofty: *an elevated style of prose.* ❖ *n.* An elevated railway.

elevated railway *n.* A railway that operates on a track raised high enough so that vehicles and pedestrians can pass beneath.

el·e·va·tion (ĕl′ə-**vā′**shən) *n.* **1.** An elevated place or position: *That hill is the highest elevation for miles around.* **2.** The height to which something is elevated, especially the height above sea level: *The ridge rises to an elevation of 3,300 feet.* **3.** The act of elevating or the condition of being elevated: *Elevation to a high position in government is a great honor.*

el·e·va·tor (**ĕl′**ə-vā′tər) *n.* **1.** A car, platform, or cage raised or lowered in a vertical shaft to carry freight or people, as from floor to floor in a building. **2.** A grain elevator. **3.** A movable piece attached to a horizontal part of an airplane tail used to turn the nose of the craft upward or downward.

e·lev·en (ĭ-**lĕv′**ən) *n.* **1.** The number, written 11, that is equal to 10 + 1. **2.** The 11th in a set or sequence. [From Old English *endleofan*.]

e·lev·enth (ĭ-**lĕv′**ənth) *n.* **1.** The ordinal number matching the number 11 in a series. **2.** One of 11 equal parts.

eleventh hour *n.* The latest possible time: *They waited until the eleventh hour to buy tickets for the concert.*

elf (ĕlf) *n., pl.* **elves** (ĕlvz) A magical creature in human form but usually smaller, often considered mischievous. [From Old English *ælf*.]

elf·in (**ĕl′**fĭn) *adj.* Relating to or suggestive of an elf or elves: *a mischievous, elfin smile.*

elf·ish (**ĕl′**fĭsh) or **elv·ish** (**ĕl′**vĭsh) *adj.* Elfin.

El Grec·o (ĕl **grĕk′**ō) See El **Greco.**

e·lic·it (ĭ-**lĭs′**ĭt) *tr.v.* **e·lic·it·ed, e·lic·it·ing, e·lic·its** To bring out; draw forth; evoke: *By clever questioning the lawyer elicited the truth from the witness.* [From Latin *ēlicere* : *ē-*, *ex-*, out + *lacere*, to entice.]

❑ *These sound alike:* **elicit, illicit** (illegal).

George Eliot

Elizabeth I
c. 1588 portrait attributed to George Gower (1540–1596)

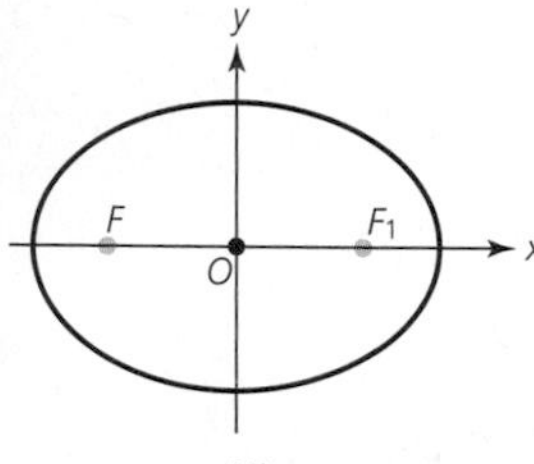

ellipse
The line running through the foci (F and F_1) of an ellipse is the major axis.

ă	pat	ôr	core
ā	pay	oi	boy
âr	care	ou	out
ä	father	ŏŏ	took
ĕ	pet	ŏŏr	lure
ē	be	ōō	boot
ĭ	pit	ŭ	cut
ī	bite	ûr	urge
îr	pier	th	thin
ŏ	pot	*th*	this
ō	toe	zh	vision
ô	paw	ə	about

el·i·gi·ble (ĕl**′**ĭ-jə-bəl) *adj.* Fit or worthy to be chosen; qualified or suited: *Eligible voters may go to the polls to vote on election day.* [From Middle English, from Latin *ēligere*, to select.] **—el′i·gi·bil′i·ty** *n.*

E·li·jah (ĭ-lī**′**jə) Ninth century BC. A Hebrew prophet who according to the Bible did not die but was carried into the sky in a chariot of fire.

e·lim·i·nate (ĭ-lĭm**′**ə-nāt′) *tr.v.* **e·lim·i·nat·ed, e·lim·i·nat·ing, e·lim·i·nates 1.** To get rid of; remove: *The company saved money by eliminating several positions.* **2.** To leave out or omit from consideration; reject: *The police eliminated two of the four suspects in the case.* **3.** To rid the body of (waste products); excrete. [From Latin *ēlīmināre*, to banish : *ē-, ex-*, out, off + *līmen*, threshold.]

e·lim·i·na·tion (ĭ-lĭm′ə-**nā′**shən) *n.* The act of eliminating or the state of being eliminated: *elimination of language barriers; elimination from the contest.*

El·i·ot (ĕl**′**ē-ət), **George** Pen name of Mary Ann Evans. 1819–1880. British writer whose novels include *Silas Marner* (1861) and *Middlemarch* (1872).

Eliot, T(homas) S(tearns) 1888–1965. American-born British writer known for his poems, including *The Waste Land* (1922).

E·li·sha (ĭ-lī**′**shə) Ninth century BC. In the Bible, a Hebrew prophet.

e·lite or **é·lite** (ĭ-lēt**′** *or* ā-lēt**′**) *n. (used with a plural verb)* **1.** Those considered as the best, superior, or wealthiest members of a society or group: *the elite of the sports world.* **2.** A small and privileged group. **—e·lite′** *adj.*

e·lit·ism or **é·lit·ism** (ĭ-lē**′**tĭz′əm *or* ā-lē**′**tĭz′əm) *n.* **1.** The belief that certain people in a group deserve special treatment because they are superior to others. **2.** Rule or domination by an elite. **—e·lit′ist** *adj. & n.*

e·lix·ir (ĭ-lĭk**′**sər) *n.* **1.** A sweetened and flavored solution of alcohol and water containing one or more medicinal substances. **2.** In medieval alchemy, a substance believed to have the power to change base metals into gold. **3.** A substance believed to maintain life indefinitely. **4.** A substance believed to have the power to cure all ills.

E·liz·a·beth I (ĭ-lĭz**′**ə-bəth) 1533–1603. Queen of England and Ireland (1558–1603) who reestablished Protestantism in England. Her reign was marked by the execution of Mary Queen of Scots (1587), the defeat of the Spanish Armada (1588), domestic prosperity, and literary achievement.

Elizabeth II Born 1926. Queen of Great Britain and Northern Ireland. She ascended to the throne in 1952.

E·liz·a·be·than (ĭ-lĭz′ə-**bē′**thən *or* ĭ-lĭz′ə-**bĕth′**ən) *adj.* Relating to or characteristic of the reign of Elizabeth I: *Elizabethan style of dress; Elizabethan drama.*

elk (ĕlk) *n., pl.* **elk** or **elks** A large reddish-brown or grayish deer of western North America, having long, branching antlers in the male. [From Middle English, probably alteration of Old English *eolh*.]

ell[1] (ĕl) *n.* A wing of a building at right angles to the main structure. [From its resemblance to the shape of the capital letter L, or short for *elbow*.]

ell[2] (ĕl) *n.* An English measure of length equal to 45 inches (114 centimeters). [From Old English *eln*, the length from the elbow to the tip of the middle finger.]

El·ling·ton (ĕl**′**ĭng-tən), **Edward Kennedy** Known as "Duke." 1899–1974. American jazz composer, pianist, and bandleader whose compositions include "Mood Indigo" (1930).

el·lipse (ĭ-lĭps**′**) *n.* A figure that forms a closed curve shaped like an oval with both ends alike. The sum of the distances of any point on an ellipse from two fixed points remains constant.

el·lip·sis (ĭ-lĭp**′**sĭs) *n., pl.* **el·lip·ses** (ĭ-lĭp**′**sēz) **1.** The omission of a word or phrase that is needed to make a sentence grammatically complete but that is not necessary to understanding. **2.** A mark or series of marks (for example, . . .) used in writing or printing to show the omission of a word or phrase.

el·lip·tic (ĭ-lĭp**′**tĭk) or **el·lip·ti·cal** (ĭ-lĭp**′**tĭ-kəl) *adj.* **1.** Relating to or shaped like an ellipse: *an elliptic window over a door.* **2.** Containing or characterized by ellipsis: *an elliptic sentence.* **—el·lip′ti·cal·ly** *adv.*

El·li·son (ĕl**′**ĭ-sən), **Ralph Waldo** 1914–1994. American writer whose novel *Invisible Man* (1952) depicts a young African-American man's struggle with issues of identity in American society.

elm (ĕlm) *n.* **1.** Any of various tall trees having arching or curving branches. **2.** The hard strong wood of such a tree. [From Old English.]

El Ni·ño (ĕl nēn**′**yō) *n.* A warming of the surface water of the eastern and central Pacific Ocean, occurring every two to seven years, killing fish and plankton and causing unusual weather patterns.

el·o·cu·tion (ĕl′ə-**kyōō′**shən) *n.* The art of public speaking that emphasizes gestures and vocal delivery. [From Middle English *elocucioun*, from Latin *ēlocūtus*, past participle of *ēloquī*, to speak out : *ē-, ex-*, out + *loquī*, to speak.]

e·lon·gate (ĭ-lông**′**gāt′) *tr. & intr.v.* **e·lon·gat·ed, e·lon·gat·ing, e·lon·gates** To make or grow longer; lengthen: *The artist often elongates faces and figures in cartoons.* ❖ *adj.* or **elongated** Long and thin; lengthened; extended.

e·lon·ga·tion (ĭ-lông′**gā′**shən *or* ē′lông-**gā′**shən) *n.* Something that elongates; an extension.

e·lope (ĭ-lōp**′**) *intr.v.* **e·loped, e·lop·ing, e·lopes** To run away with a lover, especially with the intention of getting married. **—e·lope′ment** *n.*

el·o·quence (ĕl**′**ə-kwəns) *n.* Persuasive, moving, or graceful speaking or writing: *His eloquence brought many to tears.*

el·o·quent (ĕl**′**ə-kwənt) *adj.* Capable of or characterized by eloquence: *an eloquent spokesperson for the cause; an eloquent appeal for justice.* [From Middle English, from Old French, from Latin *ēloquī*, to speak out.] **—el′o·quent·ly** *adv.*

El Pas·o (ĕl păs**′**ō) A city of extreme western Texas on the Rio Grande. It was established by Spanish settlers in the 1600s.

El Sal·va·dor (ĕl săl**′**və-dôr′) A country of Central America northwest of Nicaragua on the Pacific Ocean. San Salvador is the capital.

else (ĕls) *adj.* **1.** Other; different: *Somebody else will see you today.* **2.** Additional; more: *Would you like something else to eat?* ❖ *adv.* **1.** Differently: *How else could it have been done?* **2.** If not; otherwise: *Run, or else you will be caught in the rain.* ◆ **or else 1.** Used to indicate an alternative: *We either need to eat leftovers or else buy more food.* **2.** Used to indicate negative consequences if something isn't done: *We need to pay the bill, or else the electricity will be shut off.* **3.** Used after a command or demand to make a threat: *Be there on time, or else!*

else·where (ĕls**′**wâr′) *adv.* In or to a different or another place: *We decided to go elsewhere.*

e·lu·ci·date (ĭ-lōō**′**sĭ-dāt′) *tr.v.* **e·lu·ci·dat·ed, e·lu·ci·dat·ing, e·lu·ci·dates** To make clear or plain; explain: *She elucidated the meaning of the poem so that everyone could understand it.* **—e·lu′ci·da′tion** *n.*

e·lude (ĭ-lōōd**′**) *tr.v.* **e·lud·ed, e·lud·ing, e·ludes 1.** To avoid or escape from, as by skill, cunning, or daring: *The fox eluded the hunters.* **2.** To be not remembered or understood by: *Very small details often elude us.* [From Latin *ēlūdere* : *ē-, ex-*, out + *lūdere*, to play (from *lūdus*, play).]

e·lu·sive (ĭ-lōō**′**sĭv) *adj.* **1.** Difficult to catch or seize: *an elusive butterfly.* **2.** Difficult or impossible to attain: *an elusive goal.* **3.** Difficult to remember or understand: *an elusive metaphor.* **—e·lu′sive·ly** *adv.*

el·ver (ĕl**′**vər) *n.* A young eel.

elves (ĕlvz) *n.* Plural of **elf.**

elv·ish (ĕl′vĭsh) *adj.* Variant of **elfish.**

el·y·tron (ĕl′ĭ-trŏn′) *n., pl.* **el·y·tra** (ĕl′ĭ-trə) Either of the thickened forewings of a beetle that protect the thin hind wings used in flight.

em– *pref.* Variant of **en–.**

'em (əm) *pron. Informal* Them.

e·ma·ci·at·ed (ĭ-mā′shē-ā′tĭd) *adj.* Very thin, as from disease or starvation: *an emaciated stray dog.*

e·mail or **e-mail** (ē′māl′) *n.* **1.** A system for sending and receiving messages electronically over a computer network: *sent the information by email.* **2.** A message or messages sent or received by such a system: *received a lot of email while on vacation.* ❖ *tr.v.* **e·mailed, e·mail·ing, e·mails** or **e-mailed, e-mail·ing, e-mails** To send (a message) by such a system.

em·a·lan·ge·ni (ĕm′ə-läng-gĕn′ē) *n.* Plural of **lilangeni.**

em·a·nate (ĕm′ə-nāt′) *intr. & tr.v.* **em·a·nat·ed, em·a·nat·ing, em·a·nates** To come or send forth, as from a source: *The sound of a piano emanated from the house. The stove emanated a steady heat.* [From Latin *ēmānāre* : *ē-, ex-,* out + *mānāre,* to flow.]

em·a·na·tion (ĕm′ə-nā′shən) *n.* **1.** The act or an instance of emanating: *the emanation of heat from a fire.* **2.** Something that emanates from a source: *steamy emanations from a kettle of boiling water.*

e·man·ci·pate (ĭ-măn′sə-pāt′) *tr.v.* **e·man·ci·pat·ed, e·man·ci·pat·ing, e·man·ci·pates 1.** To free (someone) from bondage, oppression, or restraint; liberate. **2.** To release (a child) from the legal control of parents or a guardian. [From Latin *ēmancipāre* : *ē-, ex-,* out of + *mancipāre,* to sell, transfer.] **—e·man′ci·pa′tor** *n.*

e·man·ci·pa·tion (ĭ-măn′sə-pā′shən) *n.* The act or an instance of emancipating or the condition of being emancipated: *The emancipation of the slaves happened during the Civil War.*

Emancipation Proclamation *n.* A proclamation issued by President Abraham Lincoln on January 1, 1863, freeing slaves in those areas of the Confederacy still at war against the United States.

e·mas·cu·late (ĭ-măs′kyə-lāt′) *tr.v.* **e·mas·cu·lat·ed, e·mas·cu·lat·ing, e·mas·cu·lates 1.** To castrate. **2.** To deprive of strength; weaken. **—e·mas′cu·la′tion** *n.*

em·balm (ĕm-bäm′) *tr.v.* **em·balmed, em·balm·ing, em·balms** To treat (a corpse) with substances that prevent or slow decay. **—em·balm′er** *n.*

em·bank·ment (ĕm-băngk′mənt) *n.* A mound of earth or stone built up to hold back water or to support a roadway.

em·bar·go (ĕm-bär′gō) *n., pl.* **em·bar·goes 1.** An order by a government prohibiting merchant ships from entering or leaving its ports. **2.** A prohibition by a government on certain or all trade with a foreign nation. **3.** A prohibition; a ban. ❖ *tr.v.* **em·bar·goed, em·bar·go·ing, em·bar·goes** To place an embargo on. [From Spanish *embargar,* to impede, barricade.]

em·bark (ĕm-bärk′) *intr.v.* **em·barked, em·bark·ing, em·barks 1.** To go aboard an aircraft or ship. **2.** To set out on a venture; begin: *embark on a campaign to clean up the environment.* **—em′bar·ka′tion** (ĕm′bär-kā′shən) *n.*

em·bar·rass (ĕm-băr′əs) *tr.v.* **em·bar·rassed, em·bar·rass·ing, em·bar·rass·es 1.** To cause to feel self-conscious or ill at ease; disconcert: *Not knowing the answer to the question embarrassed me.* **2.** To hinder with obstacles or difficulties. [From Italian *imbarazzo,* obstacle, obstruction, from *imbarrare,* to block, bar.]

em·bar·rass·ing (ĕm-băr′ə-sĭng) *adj.* Causing embarrassment: *an embarrassing remark.*

em·bar·rass·ment (ĕm-băr′əs-mənt) *n.* **1.** The condition of being embarrassed: *My face turned red with embarrassment.* **2.** Something that embarrasses: *Their argument in public was an embarrassment.*

em·bas·sy (ĕm′bə-sē) *n., pl.* **em·bas·sies 1.** A building containing the offices of an ambassador and staff. **2.** The position, function, or assignment of an ambassador. **3.** A staff of diplomatic representatives headed by an ambassador.

em·bat·tled (ĕm-băt′ld) *adj.* **1.** Prepared or fortified for battle or engaged in battle: *the embattled countries of Europe during World War II.* **2.** Beset with attackers, criticism, or controversy: *an embattled candidate fighting to win election.*

em·bed (ĕm-bĕd′) *tr.v.* **em·bed·ded, em·bed·ding, em·beds 1.** To fix firmly in a surrounding mass: *The splinter was deeply embedded in my finger.* **2.** To cause to be an integral part of a surrounding whole: *a student who embedded herself in the social life of her school.* **3.** To assign (a journalist) to travel with a military unit during an armed conflict.

em·bel·lish (ĕm-bĕl′ĭsh) *tr.v.* **em·bel·lished, em·bel·lish·ing, em·bel·lish·es 1.** To make beautiful, as by ornamentation; decorate: *embellish a tablecloth with fine embroidery.* **2.** To add fanciful or fictitious details to: *embellish a story with some invented characters.* [From Middle English *embelishen,* from Old French *embellir,* from *bel,* beautiful (from Latin *bellus*).] **—em·bel′lish·ment** *n.*

em·ber (ĕm′bər) *n.* **1.** A piece of glowing coal or wood, as in a dying fire. **2. ember** The smoldering coal or ash of a dying fire: *Embers still glowed in the fireplace.*

em·bez·zle (ĕm-bĕz′əl) *tr.v.* **em·bez·zled, em·bez·zling, em·bez·zles** To take (money that does not belong to one but that one has been entrusted with) for one's own use: *The bank president was caught embezzling funds.* **—em·bez′zle·ment** *n.* **—em·bez′zler** *n.*

em·bit·ter (ĕm-bĭt′ər) *tr.v.* **em·bit·tered, em·bit·ter·ing, em·bit·ters** To arouse bitter feelings in.

em·bla·zon (ĕm-blā′zən) *tr.v.* **em·bla·zoned, em·bla·zon·ing, em·bla·zons 1.** To ornament (a surface) richly with prominent markings: *An embroidered coat of arms emblazoned the tapestry.* **2.** To make brilliant with colors: *Fireworks emblazoned the sky.* **3.** To celebrate; make illustrious.

em·blem (ĕm′bləm) *n.* An object or representation that functions as a symbol: *The bald eagle is the emblem of the United States.*

em·blem·at·ic (ĕm′blə-măt′ĭk) or **em·blem·at·i·cal** (ĕm′blə-măt′ĭ-kəl) *adj.* Relating to or serving as an emblem; symbolic: *The dove is emblematic of peace.*

em·bod·y (ĕm-bŏd′ē) *tr.v.* **em·bod·ied, em·bod·y·ing, em·bod·ies 1.** To give a bodily form to; personify: *A hero embodies our ideal of bravery.* **2.** To make part of a system or whole; incorporate: *The US Constitution embodies a plan for a democracy.* **—em·bod′i·ment** *n.*

em·bold·en (ĕm-bōl′dən) *tr.v.* **em·bold·ened, em·bold·en·ing, em·bold·ens** To foster boldness or courage in; encourage: *Our many supporters emboldened us to present a list of demands.*

em·bo·lism (ĕm′bə-lĭz′əm) *n.* The obstruction of a blood vessel by an embolus.

em·bo·lus (ĕm′bə-ləs) *n., pl.* **em·bo·li** (ĕm′bə-lī′) A substance, such as an air bubble or blood clot, that is carried in the bloodstream and leads to blockage of a blood vessel.

em·boss (ĕm-bôs′) *tr.v.* **em·bossed, em·boss·ing, em·boss·es 1.** To mold or carve in relief: *emboss a head and lettering on a coin.* **2.** To decorate with or as if with a raised design: *emboss a leather belt.*

em·bou·chure (äm′bo͞o-sho͝or′) *n.* **1.** The mouthpiece of a woodwind or brass instrument. **2.** The manner in which the lips and tongue are applied to such a mouthpiece. [From French *emboucher,* to put in the mouth.]

em·brace (ĕm-brās′) *v.* **em·braced, em·brac·ing, em·brac·es** *—tr.* **1.** To clasp or hold close with the arms,

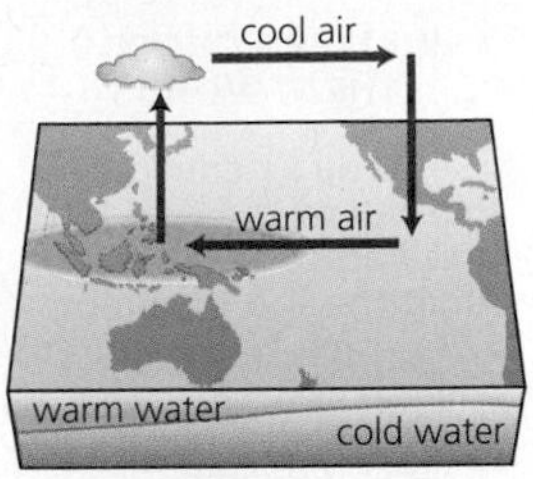

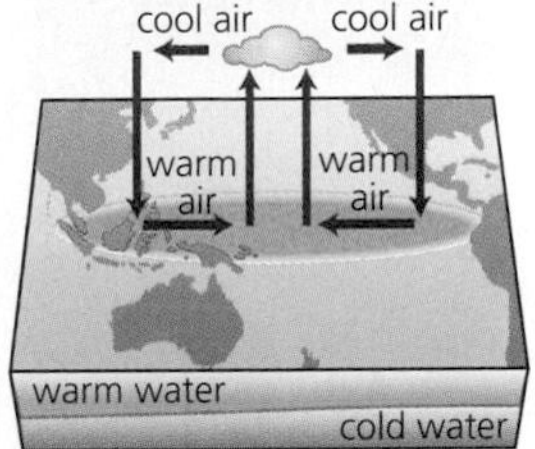

El Niño
top: normal water temperatures, with warm water concentrated in the western Pacific Ocean
bottom: El Niño conditions, with warm water extending from the western Pacific Ocean to the eastern Pacific Ocean

WRITERS CHOOSE THEIR WORDS

Rosa and I were both crying by the time Erika finished speaking. We hugged her and held on tight to her and I knew she was right. My little sister. Tears flow down my face as I think of it now. Timid, silent Erika, who turned out to be the bravest, most **eloquent** of us all.

—Carol Matas
Daniel's Story

WRITERS CHOOSE THEIR WORDS

The barn's loft held over three tons of timothy hay, delivered earlier that day. Flames from the burning hay pushed against the roof and beams, almost as if they were struggling to break free. A shower of burning **embers** greeted Sullivan as he entered the building.

—Jim Murphy
The Great Fire

WRITERS CHOOSE THEIR WORDS

Serafina listened as he told her of the rumors that had swept the town. Amid the fog of rumor, a few facts had begun to **emerge** clearly.

—Philip Pullman
The Subtle Knife

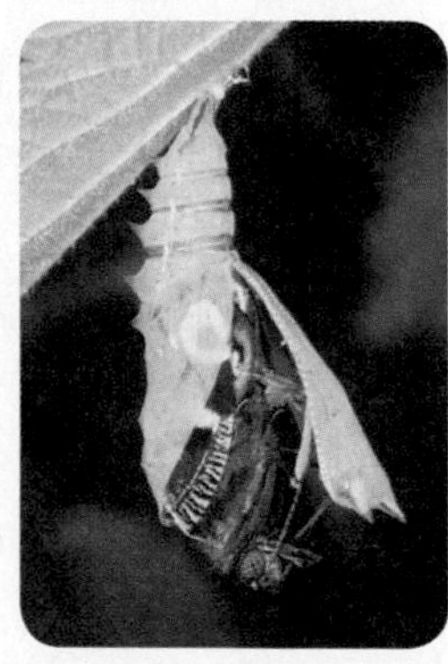

emergence
butterfly emerging from chrysalis

USAGE

emigrate The words **emigrate** and **immigrate** are both used of people involved in a permanent move, generally across a political boundary. *Emigrate* refers to the point of departure: *He emigrated from Germany* (that is, left Germany). By contrast, *immigrate* refers to the new location: *The promise of prosperity in the United States encouraged many people to immigrate* (that is, move to the United States).

ă	pat	ôr	core
ā	pay	oi	boy
âr	care	ou	out
ä	father	o͝o	took
ĕ	pet	o͝or	lure
ē	be	o͞o	boot
ĭ	pit	ŭ	cut
ī	bite	ûr	urge
îr	pier	th	thin
ŏ	pot	*th*	this
ō	toe	zh	vision
ô	paw	ə	about

usually as a sign of affection; hug: *embrace a child.* **2.** To enclose or surround: *The warm water of the pool embraced us.* **3.** To take up willingly; adopt eagerly: *embraced the hectic life of the big city.* **4.** To include as part of something broader: *Her education embraced all the sciences.* —*intr.* To join in an embrace: *The twins embraced at their reunion.* ❖ *n.* **1.** The act of holding close with the arms; a hug. **2.** Eager acceptance: *her embrace of college life.* [From Middle English *embracen*, from Old French *embracer* : *en-*, in + *brace*, the two arms.]

em·bra·sure (ĕm-**brā′**zhər) *n.* **1.** An opening in a thick wall for a window or door. **2.** A flared opening for a gun in a wall or parapet.

em·broi·der (ĕm-**broi′**dər) *v.* **em·broi·dered, em·broi·der·ing, em·broi·ders** —*tr.* **1.** To ornament with needlework: *embroider a shirt.* **2.** To make by means of needlework: *embroider a design on a blouse.* **3.** To add imaginary or fanciful details to: *The author embroidered the his autobiography.* —*intr.* **1.** To make needlework. **2.** To add embellishments or fanciful details. [From Middle English *embrouderen*, from Old English *brogden*, woven, and from Old French *embroder*, to embroider.]

em·broi·der·y (ĕm-**broi′**də-rē) *n., pl.* **em·broi·der·ies 1.** The act or art of embroidering. **2.** A piece of embroidered fabric.

em·broil (ĕm-**broil′**) *tr.v.* **em·broiled, em·broil·ing, em·broils 1.** To involve in argument or contention: *embroiled the candidate in a debate.* **2.** To throw into confusion or disorder; entangle.

em·bry·o (**ĕm′**brē-ō′) *n., pl.* **em·bry·os 1.** An animal in its earliest stages of development, especially before it has reached a distinctively recognizable form. **2.** A plant in its earliest stages of development, especially a partly developed plant within a seed. **3.** An early or beginning stage: *an idea that was the embryo of a short story.*

em·bry·ol·o·gist (ĕm′brē-**ŏl′**ə-jĭst) *n.* A scientist who specializes in embryology.

em·bry·ol·o·gy (ĕm′brē-**ŏl′**ə-jē) *n.* The branch of biology that deals with embryos and their development. —**em′bry·o·log′i·cal** (ĕm′brē-ə-**lŏj′**ĭ-kəl) *adj.*

em·bry·on·ic (ĕm′brē-**ŏn′**ĭk) *adj.* **1.** Relating to an embryo: *embryonic membranes.* **2.** In an early stage of development: *an embryonic democracy.*

em·cee (**ĕm′sē′**) *n.* A master of ceremonies. ❖ *tr. & intr.v.* **em·ceed, em·cee·ing, em·cees** To serve as master of ceremonies of: *That announcer emcees a quiz program.*

e·mend (ĭ-**mĕnd′**) *tr.v.* **e·mend·ed, e·mend·ing, e·mends** To make corrections or improvements to (a text): *emended the preface so that it reads more smoothly.*

e·men·da·tion (ĭ-mĕn′**dā′**shən *or* ē′mĕn-**dā′**shən) *n.* **1.** The act of emending. **2.** A change made with the purpose of improving: *made emendations to the text.*

em·er·ald (**ĕm′**ər-əld *or* **ĕm′**rəld) *n.* **1.** A brilliant green transparent form of beryl that is used as a gem. **2.** A strong yellowish-green color. ❖ *adj.* Of a strong yellowish-green color. [From Middle English *emeraude*, from Medieval Latin *esmeralda*, from Greek *smaragdos*.]

e·merge (ĭ-**mûrj′**) *intr.v.* **e·merged, e·merg·ing, e·merg·es 1.** To move out or away from a surrounding fluid, covering, or shelter: *The leopard emerged from the forest.* **2.** To come forth from obscurity: *The new nation soon emerged as an important power.* **3.** To become known or evident: *The truth emerged at the hearing.* [From Latin *ēmergere* : *ē-*, *ex-*, out + *mergere*, to immerse.]

e·mer·gence (ĭ-**mûr′**jəns) *n.* The act or process of emerging: *the emergence of a butterfly from a chrysalis; emergence of the truth under questioning.*

e·mer·gen·cy (ĭ-**mûr′**jən-sē) *n., pl.* **e·mer·gen·cies** A serious situation or occurrence that happens suddenly and calls for immediate action: *A fire extinguisher is kept in the hall for use in case of an emergency.*

e·mer·gent (ĭ-**mûr′**jənt) *adj.* Coming into existence, view, or attention: *an emergent political leadership.*

e·mer·i·ta (ĭ-**mĕr′**ĭ-tə) *adj.* Retired but retaining an honorary title corresponding to that held immediately before retirement. Used of a woman: *a professor emerita.*

e·mer·i·tus (ĭ-**mĕr′**ĭ-təs) *adj.* Retired but retaining an honorary title corresponding to that held immediately before retirement: *a professor emeritus.*

Em·er·son (**ĕm′**ər-sən), **Ralph Waldo** 1803–1882. American writer and philosopher whose essays include *Nature* (1836).

em·er·y (**ĕm′**ə-rē *or* **ĕm′**rē) *n.* A dark mineral that is very hard and is used in a crushed or powdered form for grinding and polishing.

e·met·ic (ĭ-**mĕt′**ĭk) *adj.* Causing vomiting. ❖ *n.* An emetic drug or medicine.

EMF *abbr.* An abbreviation of electromotive force.

em·i·grant (**ĕm′**ĭ-grənt) *n.* A person who emigrates: *Many emigrants from Europe traveled to America by ship.*

em·i·grate (**ĕm′**ĭ-grāt′) *intr.v.* **em·i·grat·ed, em·i·grat·ing, em·i·grates** To leave one country or region to settle in another: *My parents emigrated from Italy to the United States.* —**em′i·gra′tion** (ĕm′ĭ-**grā′**shən) *n.* —SEE NOTE.

é·mi·gré (**ĕm′**ĭ-grā′) *n.* A person who has left a native country, especially for political reasons.

em·i·nence (**ĕm′**ə-nəns) *n.* **1.** A position of great distinction or superiority: *She rose to eminence as a scientist.* **2.** A rise of ground; a hill. **3.** also **Eminence** A title and form of address for a cardinal in the Roman Catholic Church: *Your Eminence.*

em·i·nent (**ĕm′**ə-nənt) *adj.* Well-known and respected, especially for achievement in a particular field: *an eminent surgeon.* See Synonyms at **famous.** [From Middle English, from Latin *ēminēre*, to stand out : *ē-*, *ex-*, out + *-minēre*, to jut out.] —**em′i·nent·ly** *adv.*

e·mir also **a·mir** (ĭ-**mîr′** *or* ā-**mîr′**) *n.* A prince, chieftain, or governor, especially in the Middle East. [From Arabic *ʾamīr*, commander, prince, from *ʾamara*, to command.]

em·ir·ate (**ĕm′**-ər-ĭt *or* ĭ-**mîr′**ĭt) *n.* **1.** The office of an emir. **2.** The nation or territory ruled by an emir.

em·is·sar·y (**ĕm′**ĭ-sĕr′ē) *n., pl.* **em·is·sar·ies** A person sent on a mission as the representative of another: *sent an emissary to discuss the new trade agreement.*

e·mis·sion (ĭ-**mĭsh′**ən) *n.* **1.** The act or process of emitting: *The factory worked to reduce the emission of dangerous fumes and smoke.* **2.** Something that is emitted: *harmful emissions from cars.*

e·mis·sive (ĭ-**mĭs′**ĭv) *adj.* Emitting or tending to emit; radiating: *radio signals from a highly emissive star.*

e·mit (ĭ-**mĭt′**) *tr.v.* **e·mit·ted, e·mit·ting, e·mits 1.** To release or send out (matter or energy): *Volcanoes emit lava and hot gases.* **2.** To utter; express: *The baby emitted a cry.* [From Latin *ēmittere* : *ē-*, *ex-*, out + *mittere*, to send.] —**e·mit′ter** *n.*

e·mo·ji (ē-**mō′**jē) *n., pl.* **emoji** also **e·mo·jis** A standardized icon, as of a face or a heart, used especially in electronic messages or on social media. [Japanese *e*, picture : Japanese *moji*, writing.]

e·mol·lient (ĭ-**mŏl′**yənt) *adj.* Softening and soothing, especially to the skin: *an emollient cream.* ❖ *n.* Something that softens and soothes the skin.

e·mo·ti·con (ĭ-**mō′**tĭ-kŏn′) *n.* A series of characters and punctuation marks used to indicate an emotion or attitude, especially in online communication. For example, :-) is an emoticon indicating happiness or friendliness.

e·mo·tion (ĭ-**mō′**shən) *n.* **1.** A mental state arising on its own rather than through conscious effort; a feeling: *Envy is a powerful emotion.* See Synonyms at **feeling.** **2.** Such mental states or the qualities that are associated with them, especially in contrast to reason: *a decision* *based on emotion rather than cold logic; a speech delivered with real emotion.* [From French *émotion*, from Old French *esmovoir*, to excite : Latin *ex-*, out + Latin *movēre*, to move.]

e·mo·tion·al (ĭ-**mō′**shə-nəl) *adj.* **1.** Relating to emotion: *an emotional conflict.* **2.** Easily affected with or stirred by emotion: *an emotional person who is easily upset.* **3.** Arousing or intended to arouse the emotions: *an emotional piece of music.* **4.** Marked by or showing emotion: *their emotional reaction.* —**e·mo′tion·al·ly** *adv.*

em·pa·thy (**ĕm′**pə-thē) *n.* The ability to understand and share the feelings of someone else: *empathy between parent and child.*

em·per·or (**ĕm′**pər-ər) *n.* A man who is the ruler of an empire. [From Middle English *emperour*, from Latin *imperātor*, from *imperāre*, to command.]

em·pha·sis (**ĕm′**fə-sĭs) *n., pl.* **em·pha·ses** (**ĕm′**fə-sēz′) **1.** Special forcefulness of expression that gives importance or significance: *a lecture on computers with an emphasis on the Internet.* **2.** Prominence given to a syllable, word, or phrase. [From Greek, from *emphainein*, to exhibit, display : *en-*, in, on + *phainein*, to show.]

em·pha·size (**ĕm′**fə-sīz′) *tr.v.* **em·pha·sized, em·pha·siz·ing, em·pha·siz·es** To give emphasis to; stress: *emphasize an idea by repeating it in several different ways.*

em·phat·ic (ĕm-**făt′**ĭk) *adj.* **1.** Expressed or performed with emphasis: *an emphatic shake of the head.* **2.** Forceful and definite in expression or action: *an emphatic person.* **3.** Standing out in a striking way: *The party was an emphatic success.* —**em·phat′i·cal·ly** *adv.*

em·phy·se·ma (ĕm′fĭ-**sē′**mə *or* ĕm′fĭ-**zē′**mə) *n.* A condition in which the small air sacs of the lungs become stretched and lose their elasticity, so that one becomes out of breath quickly.

em·pire (**ĕm′**pīr′) *n.* **1.** A group of territories or nations headed by a single supreme authority: *the empire of Alexander the Great.* **2.** The territories included in such a group. **3.** Imperial or imperialistic power and authority. **4.** An extensive enterprise under a unified authority: *a publishing empire of newspapers and magazines.* [From Middle English, from Latin *imperium*, from *imperāre*, to command.]

em·pir·i·cal (ĕm-**pîr′**ĭ-kəl) *adj.* Relying on or derived from observation or experiment rather than theory: *empirical results that support the hypothesis.* [From Greek *empeirikos*, experienced.] —**em·pir′i·cal·ly** *adv.*

em·pir·i·cism (ĕm-**pîr′**ĭ-sĭz′əm) *n.* **1.** The view that experience, especially of the senses, is the only source of knowledge. **2.** The employment of methods based on experience, experiment, and observation. —**em·pir′i·cist** *n.*

em·place·ment (ĕm-**plās′**mənt) *n.* A prepared position for heavy guns, as a mounting or platform, for example.

em·ploy (ĕm-**ploi′**) *tr.v.* **em·ployed, em·ploy·ing, em·ploys 1.** To engage the services of; put to work: *The store employs many salespeople.* **2.** To put to use or service: *They employed all their skills to build the bridge.* **3.** To devote (time, for example) to an activity or purpose: *I employ my free time with bicycling and reading.* ❖ *n.* The condition of being employed: *in the employ of the government.* —**em·ploy′a·ble** *adj.*

em·ploy·ee (ĕm-**ploi′**ē *or* ĕm′ploi-**ē′**) *n.* A person who receives money or other compensation in exchange for work.

em·ploy·er (ĕm-**ploi′**ər) *n.* A person or business that employs people for financial or other compensation.

em·ploy·ment (ĕm-**ploi′**mənt) *n.* **1.** The act of employing or the condition of being employed: *the employment of new technology in industry.* **2.** The work in which a person is engaged; an occupation: *employment as a carpenter.*

em·po·ri·um (ĕm-**pôr′**ē-əm) *n., pl.* **em·po·ri·ums** or **em·po·ri·a** (ĕm-**pôr′**ē-ə) **1.** A place where various goods are bought and sold; a marketplace. **2.** A large retail store or place of business.

em·pow·er (ĕm-**pou′**ər) *tr.v.* **em·pow·ered, em·pow·er·ing, em·pow·ers 1.** To invest with power, especially legal power or official authority: *The state legislature empowered the governor to levy new taxes.* **2.** To equip or supply with an ability; enable: *Getting an education empowered them in the selection of a career.*

em·press (**ĕm′**prĭs) *n.* **1.** A woman who is the ruler of an empire. **2.** The wife or widow of an emperor.

emp·ty (**ĕmp′**tē) *adj.* **emp·ti·er, emp·ti·est 1.** Holding or containing nothing: *an empty box; an empty gas tank.* **2.** Having no occupants or inhabitants; not being used: *an empty house.* **3.** Lacking force or power: *an empty threat.* **4.** Lacking purpose or substance; meaningless: *Everything you said was empty talk.* **5.** Needing food; hungry: *an empty stomach.* ❖ *v.* **emp·tied, emp·ty·ing, emp·ties** —*tr.* **1.** To remove the contents of: *I emptied the dishwasher.* **2.** To transfer or pour off: *Please empty the garbage from the wastebasket.* —*intr.* **1.** To become empty: *The sink emptied when the plumber opened the drain.* **2.** To discharge or flow out: *The river empties into a bay.* ❖ *n., pl.* **emp·ties** *Informal* An empty container. [From Old English *ǣmetig*, unoccupied, from *ǣmetta*, leisure.] —**emp′ti·ly** *adv.* —**emp′ti·ness** *n.*

SYNONYMS empty, vacant, blank, void These adjectives mean without contents that could or should be present. **Empty** means having no contents or substance: *I thought there were some cherries left, but the bowl was empty.* **Vacant** can mean not occupied: *Many vacant seats are left in the auditorium.* **Blank** describes the absence of writing or images on a surface: *The teacher handed each student a blank piece of paper.* **Void** means absolutely empty: *The guard's face was void of all expression.*

---

emp·ty-hand·ed (ĕmp′tē-**hăn′**dĭd) *adj.* **1.** Bearing nothing: *Some guests arrived at the birthday party empty-handed.* **2.** Having received or gained nothing.

empty set *n.* In mathematics, the set that has no members; the null set.

em·py·re·al (ĕm′pī-**rē′**əl *or* ĕm-**pîr′**ē-əl) *adj.* Relating to the sky; celestial.

em·py·re·an (ĕm′pī-**rē′**ən *or* ĕm-**pîr′**ē-ən) *n.* **1.** The highest reaches of heaven. **2.** The sky. ❖ *adj.* Heavenly; celestial.

EMT *abbr.* An abbreviation of emergency medical technician.

e·mu (**ē′**myo͞o) *n.* A large flightless Australian bird that has brown feathers and resembles an ostrich. [From Portuguese *ema*, rhea.]

em·u·late (**ĕm′**yə-lāt′) *tr.v.* **em·u·lat·ed, em·u·lat·ing, em·u·lates** To strive to equal or excel, especially through imitation: *an experienced pianist whose style I tried to emulate.*

em·u·la·tion (ĕm′yə-**lā′**shən) *n.* **1.** Effort or ambition to equal or surpass another: *the young writer's emulation of the famous novelist.* **2.** Imitation of another.

e·mul·si·fy (ĭ-**mŭl′**sə-fī′) *tr.v.* **e·mul·si·fied, e·mul·si·fy·ing, e·mul·si·fies** To make into an emulsion: *Soap emulsifies fats in warm water.* —**e·mul′si·fi·ca′tion** (ĭ-mŭl′sə-fĭ-**kā′**shən) *n.*

e·mul·sion (ĭ-**mŭl′**shən) *n.* **1.** A suspension of small droplets of one liquid in a second liquid with which the first does not mix, as the suspension of cream in homogenized milk. **2.** The coating of a photographic film or paper that is sensitive to light. [From Latin *ēmulsus*, past participle of *ēmulgēre*, to milk out : *ē-*, *ex-*, out + *mulgēre*, to milk.]

en– or **em–** or **in–** *pref.* A prefix that means: **1.** To put

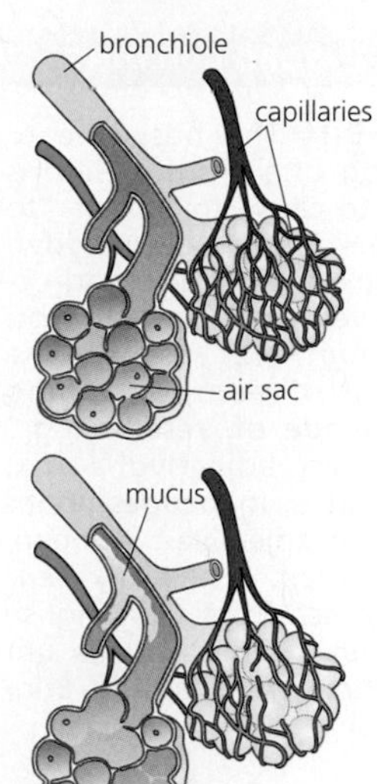

emphysema
top: normal bronchiole and air sacs
bottom: diseased bronchiole with mucus, enlarged air sacs, and fewer capillaries

WORD BUILDING

-en¹ The basic meaning of the suffix **-en¹** is "to cause to be" or "to become." When added to nouns and adjectives, *-en¹* forms verbs: *lengthen, soften.* The suffix **-en²**, meaning "made of; resembling," is an adjective suffix; that is, it changes nouns into adjectives: *wooden, golden.* The suffix *-en¹* comes from Old English *-nian,* and *-en²* is unchanged from Old English *-en.*

enchilada

into or onto: *encapsulate.* **2.** To go into or onto: *entrain.* **3.** To cover or provide with: *encircle.* **4.** To cause to be: *endear.* **5.** Thoroughly: *entangle.* —SEE NOTE AT **in-²**.

-en¹ *suff.* A suffix that means: **1.** To cause to be: *cheapen.* **2.** To become: *redden.* **3.** To cause to have: *hearten.* **4.** To come to have: *lengthen.* —SEE NOTE.

-en² *suff.* A suffix that means made of or resembling: *earthen; wooden.* —SEE NOTE AT **-en¹**.

en·a·ble (ĕ-**nā′**bəl) *tr.v.* **en·a·bled, en·a·bling, en·a·bles** To give the means, ability, or opportunity to do something: *The new computer system enables the store owners to keep close track of inventory.*

en·act (ĕn-**ăkt′**) *tr.v.* **en·act·ed, en·act·ing, en·acts 1.** To make into law: *The Senate enacted legislation to help schools throughout the country.* **2.** To act (something) out, as on a stage: *They enacted the final scene without any mistakes.*

en·act·ment (ĕn-**ăkt′**mənt) *n.* **1.** The act of enacting or the state of being enacted: *the enactment of laws by Congress.* **2.** Something that has been enacted.

e·nam·el (ĭ-**năm′**əl) *n.* **1.** A glassy coating baked onto the surface of metal, porcelain, or pottery for decoration or protection. **2.** A paint that dries to a hard glossy surface. **3.** The hard substance that covers the exposed part of a tooth. ❖ *tr.v.* **e·nam·eled, e·nam·el·ing, e·nam·els** or **e·nam·elled, e·nam·el·ling, e·nam·els** To coat, inlay, or decorate with enamel. [From Middle English *enamelen,* to put on enamel, from Anglo-Norman *enamailler* : *en-,* on + Old French *esmail,* enamel (of Germanic origin).]

e·nam·el·ware (ĭ-**năm′**əl-wâr′) *n.* Objects of metal, porcelain, or pottery that are coated or decorated with enamel.

en·am·or (ĭ-**năm′**ər) *tr.v.* **en·am·ored, en·am·or·ing, en·am·ors** To inspire with love; captivate: *We were enamored with the beautiful landscape.*

en·camp (ĕn-**kămp′**) *v.* **en·camped, en·camp·ing, en·camps** —*intr.* To set up camp or live in a camp: *encamp in the woods.* —*tr.* To provide quarters for in a camp.

en·camp·ment (ĕn-**kămp′**mənt) *n.* **1.** The act of encamping. **2.** The state of being encamped. **3.** A camp or campsite: *The encampment is just down the road.*

en·cap·su·late (ĕn-**kăp′**sə-lāt′) *tr.v.* **en·cap·su·lat·ed, en·cap·su·lat·ing, en·cap·su·lates 1.** To enclose in or as if in a capsule. **2.** To express in a brief summary: *The statement encapsulated the long committee report.* —**en·cap′su·la′tion** *n.*

en·case (ĕn-**kās′**) *tr.v.* **en·cased, en·cas·ing, en·cas·es** To enclose in or as if in a case: *The skull encases the brain.*

-ence *suff.* A suffix that means: **1.** State or condition: *dependence.* **2.** Action: *emergence.*

en·ceph·a·li·tis (ĕn-sĕf′ə-**lī′**tĭs) *n.* Inflammation of the brain, usually caused by viral infection.

en·chant (ĕn-**chănt′**) *tr.v.* **en·chant·ed, en·chant·ing, en·chants 1.** To cast a spell; bewitch. **2.** To attract and delight; entrance: *The play enchanted everyone who saw it.* [From Middle English *enchaunten,* from Latin *incantāre,* to utter an incantation, cast a spell : *in-,* against + *cantāre,* to sing.] —**en·chant′er** *n.*

en·chant·ing (ĕn-**chăn′**tĭng) *adj.* Having the power to enchant; charming: *an enchanting melody.*

en·chant·ment (ĕn-**chănt′**mənt) *n.* **1.** The act of enchanting. **2.** The state of being enchanted. **3.** Something that enchants; a magic spell.

en·chant·ress (ĕn-**chăn′**trĭs) *n.* **1.** A sorceress; a witch. **2.** A woman of great charm or attractiveness.

en·chi·la·da (ĕn′chə-**lä′**də) *n.* A tortilla rolled and stuffed usually with a mixture containing meat or cheese and served with a sauce spiced with chili peppers. [From Spanish : *en-,* in + *chile,* chili pepper + *-ada,* feminine adjective suffix.]

en·cir·cle (ĕn-**sûr′**kəl) *tr.v.* **en·cir·cled, en·cir·cling, en·cir·cles 1.** To form a circle around; surround: *Trees encircled the house.* **2.** To move or go around completely: *It takes Earth one year to encircle the sun.* —**en·cir′cle·ment** *n.*

en·clave (**ĕn′**klāv′ *or* **ŏn′**klāv′) *n.* **1.** A country or part of a country that lies completely within the boundaries of another. **2.** A distinctly separated area enclosed within a larger unit: *ethnic enclaves in a large city.*

en·close (ĕn-**klōz′**) *tr.v.* **en·closed, en·clos·ing, en·clos·es 1.** To surround on all sides; close in: *A high fence encloses the yard.* **2.** To build or equip with a roof and walls: *enclosed the deck for use in the winter.* **3.** To insert in the same envelope or package: *I enclosed a check for $25 with the order.*

en·clo·sure (ĕn-**klō′**zhər) *n.* **1.** The act of enclosing or the state of being enclosed: *enclosure of a payment.* **2.** Something enclosed: *a garden in the middle of the enclosure; a business letter with enclosures.* **3.** Something that encloses, as a wall or fence: *The zoo had a high enclosure to keep the antelopes in.*

en·code (ĕn-**kōd′**) *tr.v.* **en·cod·ed, en·cod·ing, en·codes** To put (a message, for example) into code: *encoded the note.* —**en·cod′er** *n.*

en·co·mi·um (ĕn-**kō′**mē-əm) *n., pl.* **en·co·mi·ums** or **en·co·mi·a** (ĕn-**kō′**mē-ə) A formal expression of praise; a tribute.

en·com·pass (ĕn-**kŭm′**pəs) *tr.v.* **en·com·passed, en·com·pass·ing, en·com·pass·es 1.** To form a circle or ring about; surround. **2.** To constitute or include: *The report encompassed a number of subjects.*

en·core (**ŏn′**kôr′) *n.* **1.** A demand by an audience for an additional performance, usually expressed by applause. **2.** An additional performance in response to such a demand: *Three short songs made the perfect encore.* ❖ *interj.* An expression used to demand an additional performance. [From French *encore,* again.]

en·coun·ter (ĕn-**koun′**tər) *n.* **1.** A chance or unexpected meeting: *a frightening encounter with a bear.* **2.** A hostile or adversarial confrontation: *an encounter between British and Colonial troops.* ❖ *tr.v.* **en·coun·tered, en·coun·ter·ing, en·coun·ters 1.** To experience unexpectedly or by chance: *encounter many problems.* **2.** To meet, especially unexpectedly: *encountered an old friend in the park.* **3.** To confront in battle or contention. [From Middle English *encontre,* from Old French *encontrer,* to meet, from Late Latin *incontrāre.*]

en·cour·age (ĕn-**kûr′**ĭj) *tr.v.* **en·cour·aged, en·cour·ag·ing, en·cour·ag·es 1.** To give hope, courage, or confidence to; hearten: *The favorable report encouraged me somewhat.* **2.** To give support to; foster. **3.** To stimulate; spur: *Fertilizer encourages the growth of plants.*

en·cour·age·ment (ĕn-**kûr′**ĭj-mənt) *n.* **1.** The act of encouraging: *the encouragement of friends to enter a contest.* **2.** A person or thing that encourages: *Kind words are an encouragement.*

en·cour·ag·ing (ĕn-**kûr′**ə-jĭng) *adj.* Giving courage, hope, or confidence: *We were heartened to hear the encouraging news.*

en·croach (ĕn-**krōch′**) *intr.v.* **en·croached, en·croach·ing, en·croach·es 1.** To take another's possessions or rights gradually or stealthily: *encroach on a neighbor's land.* **2.** To advance beyond proper or former limits: *the ocean encroaching on the shore.* —**en·croach′ment** *n.*

en·crust (ĕn-**krŭst′**) *tr.v.* **en·crust·ed, en·crust·ing, en·crusts** To cover with or as if with a crust or hard layer: *Ice encrusted the windowpanes. The crown was encrusted with jewels.* —**en′crus·ta′tion** *n.*

en·crypt (ĕn-**krĭpt′**) *tr.v.* **en·crypt·ed, en·crypt·ing, en·crypts** To put (a message or computer data, for example) into code; encode.

en·cum·ber (ĕn-**kŭm′**bər) *tr.v.* **en·cum·bered, en·cum·ber·ing, en·cum·bers 1.** To put a heavy load on;

ă	pat	ôr	core
ā	pay	oi	boy
âr	care	ou	out
ä	father	o͝o	took
ĕ	pet	o͝or	lure
ē	be	o͞o	boot
ĭ	pit	ŭ	cut
ī	bite	ûr	urge
îr	pier	th	thin
ŏ	pot	*th*	this
ō	toe	zh	vision
ô	paw	ə	about

burden: *The heavy pack encumbered the hiker.* **2.** To hinder or impede the action or performance of: *restrictions that encumber police work.* **3.** To burden with legal or financial obligations.

en·cum·brance (ĕn-**kŭm′**brəns) *n.* A person or thing that encumbers; a burden or obstacle.

–ency *suff.* A suffix that means quality or condition: *dependency; emergency.*

en·cyc·li·cal (ĕn-**sĭk′**lĭ-kəl) *n.* A letter from the pope addressed to the bishops of the Roman Catholic Church or to the hierarchy of a particular country.

en·cy·clo·pe·di·a (ĕn-sī′klə-**pē′**dē-ə) *n.* A large reference work containing articles, usually arranged in alphabetical order and covering one particular field or a wide variety of subjects. [From Greek *enkuklios paideia*, general education : *enkuklios*, circular, general + *paideia*, education (from *pais*, child).]

en·cy·clo·pe·dic (ĕn-sī′klə-**pē′**dĭk) *adj.* **1.** Relating to or characteristic of an encyclopedia. **2.** Having or covering many subjects; comprehensive: *a scholar with encyclopedic knowledge.*

end (ĕnd) *n.* **1a.** Either point where something that has length begins or stops: *They sat at opposite ends of the table.* **b.** The extreme edge or limit of a space or area; a boundary: *Buffalo lies at the eastern end of Lake Erie.* **2.** The point in time when an action, event, or phenomenon ceases or is completed: *Summer vacation is coming to an end. I'll get paid at the end of the month.* **3.** Something toward which one strives; a goal or result: *wanted to be a doctor and studied hard to achieve that end.* **4.** The termination of life or existence; death: *The explorer met his end in the desert.* **5.** The ultimate extent of something; the final limit: *at the end of one's savings; at the end of one's patience.* **6.** A share of a responsibility: *your end of the bargain; the financial end of a business.* **7.** In football, either of two players stationed at the outermost position of a team's line. ❖ *v.* **end·ed, end·ing, ends** —*tr.* **1.** To bring to a conclusion; finish: *a nice way to end a trip.* **2.** To form the last or concluding part of: *the song that ended the performance.* See Synonyms at **complete.** —*intr.* **1.** To come to a finish; cease: *The game ended in a tie.* **2.** To arrive at a place, situation, or condition as a result of a course of action: *His laziness ended up costing him his job. She ended up happier than before.* ◆ **in the end** Eventually; ultimately: *There were many problems, but it worked out in the end.* **no end** A great deal: *We have no end of stories to tell.* [From Old English *ende.*]

en·dan·ger (ĕn-**dān′**jər) *tr.v.* **en·dan·gered, en·dan·ger·ing, en·dan·gers 1.** To put in danger; imperil: *Forest fires endanger wildlife.* **2.** To cause to become nearly extinct: *hunting practices that endangered whales.*

en·dan·gered species (ĕn-**dān′**jərd) *n.* A species present in such small numbers that it is at risk of extinction.

en·dear (ĕn-**dîr′**) *tr.v.* **en·deared, en·dear·ing, en·dears** To make beloved or very sympathetic: *The kitten quickly endeared itself to the whole family.* **—en·dear′·ing·ly** *adv.*

en·dear·ment (ĕn-**dîr′**mənt) *n.* **1.** The act of endearing. **2.** An expression of affection.

en·deav·or (ĕn-**dĕv′**ər) *n.* An earnest effort toward an end; a serious attempt: *her endeavor to start her own business.* ❖ *tr.v.* **en·deav·ored, en·deav·or·ing, en·deav·ors** To make an effort (to do or accomplish something); try: *endeavored to improve their quality of life.* [From Middle English *endevour*, from *endeveren*, to make an effort, from *(putten) in dever*, (to put oneself) in duty, make it one's duty, from Old French *deveir*, duty.]

en·dem·ic (ĕn-**dĕm′**ĭk) *adj.* **1.** Constantly present in a particular region or group of people. Used of a disease: *Lyme disease is endemic in parts of New England.* **2.** Native to a particular region: *the endemic birds of Hawaii.* **3.** Common in or characteristic of an enterprise or situation: *an endemic problem in the energy industry.* ❖ *n.* An endemic organism or disease.

end·ing (**ĕn′**dĭng) *n.* **1.** The concluding part, especially of a book, play, or film: *The comedy has a happy ending.* **2.** A letter or letters added to the end of a word to change the meaning or show some relationship of grammar, as in adding *-ed* to *walk* to make the past tense *walked.*

en·dive (**ĕn′**dīv′ *or* **ŏn′**dēv′) *n.* **1.** A variety of chicory having a narrow pointed cluster of whitish leaves used in salads. **2.** A related plant having curled or ruffled leaves with a bitter flavor, used in salads. [From Middle English, from Greek *entubon.*]

endive

end·less (**ĕnd′**lĭs) *adj.* **1.** Being or seeming to be without an end; infinite: *endless stretches of sandy beaches.* **2.** Formed with the ends joined; continuous: *an endless chain.* **—end′less·ly** *adv.*

end line *n.* In sports, a line that is at right angles to the sidelines and that marks an end boundary of a playing field or court.

end·most (**ĕnd′**mōst′) *adj.* Being at or closest to the end; last: *the endmost rooms on a hall.*

endo– or **end–** *pref.* A prefix that means inside or within: *endoderm; endosperm.*

en·do·car·di·um (ĕn′dō-**kär′**dē-əm) *n., pl.* **en·do·car·di·a** (ĕn′dō-**kär′**dē-ə) The smooth membrane that lines the cavities of the heart.

en·do·crine (**ĕn′**də-krĭn *or* **ĕn′**də-krēn′) *adj.* **1.** Producing secretions, especially hormones, directly into the blood. **2.** Relating to endocrine glands or the hormones they secrete: *an endocrine disease.*

endocrine gland *n.* Any of various glands, such as the thyroid gland or the pituitary gland, that produce hormones that pass directly into the bloodstream. —SEE NOTE AT **hormone.**

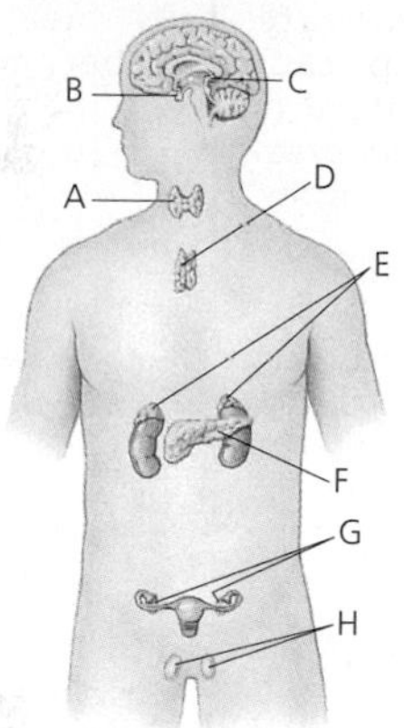

endocrine gland
endocrine glands
A. thyroid gland
B. pituitary gland
C. pineal gland
D. thymus
E. adrenal glands
F. pancreas
G. ovaries (female)
H. testes (male)

endocrine system *n.* The system of endocrine glands in a vertebrate animal that produce hormones that regulate internal body activities and processes.

en·do·cri·nol·o·gy (ĕn′də-krə-**nŏl′**ə-jē) *n.* The branch of medicine that deals with the diagnosis and treatment of diseases and disorders of the endocrine glands.

en·do·cy·to·sis (ĕn′dō-sī-**tō′**sĭs) *n.* A process of cellular ingestion by which a cell membrane folds to surround a substance and bring it into the cell.

en·do·derm (**ĕn′**də-dûrm′) *n.* The innermost of the three layers of cells found in an early embryo, developing into the lining of the digestive system and lungs and certain organs such as the liver and pancreas.

en·do·me·tri·um (ĕn′dō-**mē′**trē-əm) *n., pl.* **en·do·me·tri·a** (ĕn′dō-**mē′**trē-ə) The membrane that lines the uterus, to which a fertilized egg must attach itself in order to develop. [From New Latin *endomētrium* : English *endo-*, inside + Greek *mētrā*, uterus.] **—en′do·me′tri·al** *adj.*

en·do·plasm (**ĕn′**də-plăz′əm) *n.* The central, most fluid portion of the cytoplasm of a cell.

en·do·plas·mic re·tic·u·lum (ĕn′də-**plăz′**mĭk rĭ-**tĭk′**yə-ləm) *n.* A network of membranes within the cytoplasm of many cells that is important in the production and transport of proteins and other large molecules.

en·dor·phin (ĕn-**dôr′**fĭn) *n.* Any of a group of hormones present chiefly in the brain that are involved in regulating various physiological functions and that reduce feelings of pain.

en·dorse (ĕn-**dôrs′**) *tr.v.* **en·dorsed, en·dors·ing, en·dors·es 1.** To give approval of; support: *Many have already endorsed the idea of national health care.* **2.** To recommend (a product), often for payment, as in an advertisement: *The athlete endorsed a new brand of shaving cream.* **3.** To write one's signature on the back of (a check, for example) as evidence of the legal transfer of its ownership: *endorse a check in order to receive payment.* [From Middle English *endosen*, from Medieval

Latin *indorsāre* : Latin *in-*, in, on + Latin *dorsum*, back.] **—en·dors′er** *n.*

en·dorse·ment (ĕn-**dôrs′**mənt) *n.* **1.** Something, such as a signature, that endorses or validates. **2.** Approval; support: *The plan has the endorsement of the mayor.*

en·do·scope (**ĕn′**də-skōp′) *n.* An instrument for viewing the inside of a body canal or a hollow organ such as the colon.

en·do·skel·e·ton (ĕn′dō-**skĕl′**ĭ-tn) *n.* An internal supporting structure within an organism, such as the skeleton in humans and other vertebrates or the rigid framework in a starfish.

en·do·sperm (**ĕn′**də-spûrm′) *n.* The part of a plant seed that contains stored food and supplies nourishment for the developing embryo.

en·do·spore (**ĕn′**də-spôr′) *n.* A thick-walled spore that is formed by some bacteria and can resist harsh environmental conditions.

en·do·therm (**ĕn′**də-thûrm′) *n.* A warm-blooded animal.

en·do·ther·mic (ĕn′dō-**thûr′**mĭk) *adj.* **1.** Causing or characterized by absorption of heat: *an endothermic chemical reaction.* **2.** Warm-blooded: *Mammals are endothermic.*

en·dow (ĕn-**dou′**) *tr.v.* **en·dowed, en·dow·ing, en·dows 1.** To provide with property, income, or a source of income: *endow a school.* **2.** To provide with a talent or quality: *Nature endowed you with a good singing voice.* [From Middle English *endouen*, from Anglo-Norman *endouer*, from Latin *dōtāre*, to provide with a dowry.]

en·dow·ment (ĕn-**dou′**mənt) *n.* **1.** Money or property donated to an institution or person as a source of income: *An endowment pays for new library books.* **2.** A natural gift, ability, or quality.

end·point or **end point** (**ĕnd′**point′) *n.* **1.** Either of two points that mark the ends of a line segment. **2.** A tip or point of termination.

end run *n.* **1.** In football, a play in which the ball carrier tries to run around one end of the defensive line. **2.** *Informal* An action undertaken to get around an obstacle or hindrance: *The manager did an end run around the ban on spending and was able to order additional supplies.*

end table *n.* A small table, usually placed beside a chair or couch.

en·dur·a·ble (ĕn-**do͝or′**ə-bəl) *adj.* Capable of being endured; tolerable: *an endurable pain.* **—en·dur′a·bly** *adv.*

en·dur·ance (ĕn-**do͝or′**əns) *n.* **1.** The act, quality, or power to withstand stress or hardship: *Climbing a high mountain is a test of endurance.* **2.** The state or fact of persevering. **3.** Continuing existence; duration.

en·dure (ĕn-**do͝or′**) *v.* **en·dured, en·dur·ing, en·dures** *—tr.* **1.** To carry on through, despite hardships: *The early settlers of America endured long cold winters.* **2.** To bear with tolerance; put up with: *I could no longer endure such rudeness.* *—intr.* **1.** To continue to exist; last: *a name that will endure forever.* **2.** To suffer patiently without yielding: *The prisoners endured in spite of terrible conditions.* [From Middle English *enduren*, from Latin *indūrāre*, to make hard, from *dūrus*, hard.]

en·dur·ing (ĕn-**do͝or′**ĭng) *adj.* Lasting; durable: *the enduring friendship of the old schoolmates.*

end use *n.* The ultimate application for which a product has been designed.

end user *n.* The consumer of a product seen as the person for whom the product has been designed.

end·wise (**ĕnd′**wīz′) also **end·ways** (**ĕnd′**wāz′) *adv.* **1.** On end; upright: *Stand the books endwise on the shelf.* **2.** With the end forward: *a bookcase standing endwise out into the room.* **3.** Lengthwise: *a couch placed endwise along a wall.* **4.** End to end: *Lay the bricks endwise to make the wall.*

end zone *n.* In football, the area between the goal line and the end line at each end of the playing field.

en·e·ma (**ĕn′**ə-mə) *n.* **1.** The injection of a liquid into the rectum through the anus for cleansing or for stimulating the emptying of the bowels. **2.** The liquid used in this way.

en·e·my (**ĕn′**ə-mē) *n., pl.* **en·e·mies 1.** A person who feels hatred toward, intends injury to, or opposes the interests of another; a foe. **2a.** A hostile power or force, such as a nation: *During a war, neighboring nations may be enemies.* **b.** A unit or member of such a force: *The enemy sailed into battle with guns blazing.* **3.** Something harmful or destructive: *Disease is an enemy of plant and animal life.* ❖ *adj.* Relating to or being a hostile power or force: *enemy soldiers.* [From Middle English *enemi*, from Latin *inimīcus* : *in-*, not + *amīcus*, friend.] —SEE NOTE AT **collective noun.**

en·er·get·ic (ĕn′ər-**jĕt′**ĭk) *adj.* Possessing, exerting, or displaying energy: *The energetic efforts of the crew helped us meet our building deadline.* **—en′er·get′i·cal·ly** *adv.*

en·er·gize (**ĕn′**ər-jīz′) *tr.v.* **en·er·gized, en·er·giz·ing, en·er·giz·es** To give energy to; activate or invigorate: *This switch energizes the electric circuit.* **—en′er·giz′er** *n.*

en·er·gy (**ĕn′**ər-jē) *n., pl.* **en·er·gies 1.** The capacity for work or vigorous activity; vigor; power: *lacked the energy to finish the job.* **2.** Exertion of power or vigor: *Only with a lot of energy were we able to finish the project.* **3.** Usable heat or power: *The town will need more energy as it grows.* **4.** The capacity of a physical system, such as a machine, to do work, as in turning, pushing, or raising something. Energy can be electrical, mechanical, chemical, thermal, or nuclear. It is measured by the amount of work done. [From Greek *energeia*, from *energos*, active : *en-*, in, at + *ergon*, work.]

en·er·vate (**ĕn′**ər-vāt′) *tr.v.* **en·er·vat·ed, en·er·vat·ing, en·er·vates** To weaken or destroy the strength or vitality of: *The prolonged hot weather enervated everyone.* **—en′er·va′tion** *n.* —SEE NOTE.

USAGE

enervate Contrary to what many people think, the verb **enervate** does not mean "to invigorate, energize." In fact, *enervate* means essentially the opposite of *energize*. That's because *enervate* comes from the Latin word *nervus*, "sinew." *Enervate* thus means "to cause to become 'out of muscle,'" that is, "to weaken or sap of strength."

en·fee·ble (ĕn-**fē′**bəl) *tr.v.* **en·fee·bled, en·fee·bling, en·fee·bles** To deprive of strength; make feeble. **—en·fee′ble·ment** *n.*

en·fold (ĕn-**fōld′**) *tr.v.* **en·fold·ed, en·fold·ing, en·folds 1.** To cover with or as if with folds; envelop: *enfold a baby in a blanket.* **2.** To embrace.

en·force (ĕn-**fôrs′**) *tr.v.* **en·forced, en·forc·ing, en·forc·es 1.** To compel observance of or obedience to: *enforce parking regulations.* **2.** To require that people practice (a certain behavior, for example); impose: *Librarians enforce silence in the library.* **3.** To give force to; reinforce: *a documentary film that enforced our opinions.* **—en·force′a·ble** *adj.* **—en·force′ment** *n.*

en·fran·chise (ĕn-**frăn′**chīz′) *tr.v.* **en·fran·chised, en·fran·chis·ing, en·fran·chis·es** To endow with the rights of citizenship, especially the right to vote: *An amendment to the Constitution enfranchised women.* **—en·fran′chise·ment** *n.*

Eng. *abbr.* An abbreviation of: **1.** England. **2.** English.

en·gage (ĕn-**gāj′**) *v.* **en·gaged, en·gag·ing, en·gag·es** *—tr.* **1.** To cause (someone) to participate or be involved in something: *I wanted to engage him in conversation, but he left early.* **2.** To attract and hold (the attention): *The puzzle engaged our attention for an hour.* **3.** To obtain or contract for the services of; employ: *engage a carpenter to build a porch.* **4.** To pledge or promise, especially to marry: *My aunt is engaged to a musician.* **5.** To require the use of; occupy: *Studying engages much of my time.* **6.** To enter or bring into conflict with: *planes that engaged the enemy over the bay.* **7.** To put into working position: *A lever engages the gears.* *—intr.* **1.** To involve oneself or become occupied; participate: *They engaged in a lively conversation.* **2.** To assume an obligation; agree:

ă	pat	ôr	core
ā	pay	oi	boy
âr	care	ou	out
ä	father	o͝o	took
ĕ	pet	o͝or	lure
ē	be	o͞o	boot
ĭ	pit	ŭ	cut
ī	bite	ûr	urge
îr	pier	th	thin
ŏ	pot	*th*	this
ō	toe	zh	vision
ô	paw	ə	about

They engaged to finish the project on schedule. **3.** To enter into conflict or battle: *The armies engaged at dawn.* **4.** To move or be put into working position: *The car's transmission engaged.* [From Middle English *engagen*, to pledge something as security for repayment of debt, from Old French *engagier* : *en-*, in + *gage*, pledge, of Germanic origin.]

en·gaged (ĕn-**gājd′**) *adj.* **1.** Employed, occupied, or busy. **2.** Pledged to marry; betrothed: *an engaged couple.* **3.** Being in working position.

en·gage·ment (ĕn-**gāj′**mənt) *n.* **1.** An act of engaging or the state of being engaged. **2a.** A promise between two people to get married. **b.** The period during which this promise is kept: *the couple's long engagement.* **3.** A promise to be at a particular place at a certain time: *a dinner engagement.* **4.** Employment, especially for a set length of time: *an actor's two-week engagement.* **5.** A battle; a military encounter.

en·gag·ing (ĕn-**gā′**jĭng) *adj.* Charming; attractive: *an engaging smile.* See Synonyms at **interesting.** **—en·gag′ing·ly** *adv.*

Eng·els (**ĕng′**əlz *or* **ĕng′**əls), **Friedrich** 1820–1895. German socialist theorist who collaborated with Karl Marx on *The Communist Manifesto* (1848).

en·gen·der (ĕn-**jĕn′**dər) *tr.v.* **en·gen·dered, en·gen·der·ing, en·gen·ders** To give rise to; bring into existence: *A candid manner engenders trust.*

en·gine (**ĕn′**jĭn) *n.* **1.** A machine that turns energy into mechanical force or motion, especially one that gets its energy from a source of heat, such as the burning of a fuel. **2.** A mechanical appliance, instrument, or tool: *The battering ram is an ancient engine of warfare.* **3.** A railroad locomotive: *The freight train was drawn by a diesel engine.* [From Middle English *engin*, skill, machine, from Latin *ingenium*, innate ability.]

en·gi·neer (ĕn′jə-**nîr′**) *n.* **1.** A person who is specially trained or works in a branch of engineering. **2.** A person who operates an engine: *a locomotive engineer.* **3.** A person who skillfully or shrewdly manages a project: *The head of our advertising department was the engineer of this sales campaign.* ❖ *tr.v.* **en·gi·neered, en·gi·neer·ing, en·gi·neers 1.** To plan, construct, or manage as an engineer: *engineer a new bridge.* **2.** To plan, manage, and accomplish by skill or shrewdness; maneuver: *engineered the entire party.*

en·gi·neer·ing (ĕn′jə-**nîr′**ĭng) *n.* The use of scientific and mathematical principles to design and build structures, machines, and systems. Bridges, cars, and electronic circuits are products of engineering.

Eng·land (**ĭng′**glənd) A former kingdom in the southern part of Great Britain, now joined with Wales, Scotland, and Northern Ireland to form the United Kingdom. London is the historic capital.

Eng·lish (**ĭng′**glĭsh) *adj.* Relating to England or its people, language, or culture. ❖ *n.* **1.** *(used with a plural verb)* The people of England. **2.** The West Germanic language of England, the United States, and other countries that are or have been under English influence or control. **3.** often **english** The spin given to a ball by striking it on one side or releasing it with a sharp twist.

English Channel An arm of the Atlantic Ocean between western France and southern England. It opens into the North Sea.

English horn *n.* A woodwind instrument similar to but larger than the oboe and pitched below it. [Translation of French *cor anglais*, perhaps alteration of *cor anglé*, bent horn (from the curved part to which the mouthpiece is attached).]

Eng·lish·man (**ĭng′**glĭsh-mən) *n.* A man who is a native or inhabitant of England.

English muffin *n.* A flat round muffin made of yeast dough, usually split and served toasted.

English sparrow *n.* The house sparrow.

Eng·lish·wom·an (**ĭng′**glĭsh wo͝om′ən) *n.* A woman who is a native or inhabitant of England.

en·gorge (ĕn-**gôrj′**) *tr.v.* **en·gorged, en·gorg·ing, en·gorg·es 1.** To devour greedily: *engorged a meal in just minutes.* **2.** To congest or overfill with blood or other fluid: *The tick was engorged with blood.* **—en·gorge′·ment** *n.*

en·graft (ĕn-**grăft′**) *v.* **en·graft·ed, en·graft·ing, en·grafts** *—intr.* To become successfully grafted: *The transplanted bone marrow cells have engrafted.* *—tr.* To graft (a shoot) onto a plant.

en·grave (ĕn-**grāv′**) *tr.v.* **en·graved, en·grav·ing, en·graves 1.** To carve, cut, or etch into a material: *engrave a name on a plaque.* **2.** To carve, cut, or etch a design or letters into: *engrave a marble stone with a coat of arms.* **3a.** To carve, cut, or etch into a block or surface used for printing: *engrave a poem into a copper plate using fine tools.* **b.** To print from a block or plate made by such a process. **4.** To have a lasting effect on (a person or a person's mind) as if by carving or etching; impress deeply: *engrave rules of safety in a child's mind.* [From Middle English *ingraved*, engraved, from *graven*, to carve, from Old English *grafan*.] **—en·grav′er** *n.*

en·grav·ing (ĕn-**grā′**vĭng) *n.* **1.** The art or technique of one that engraves. **2.** A design or text engraved on a surface. **3.** An engraved surface for printing. **4.** A print made from an engraved plate or block.

en·gross (ĕn-**grōs′**) *tr.v.* **en·grossed, en·gross·ing, en·gross·es** To occupy the complete attention of; absorb: *The interesting new book engrossed him.* [From Middle English *engrossen*, to collect in large quantity, monopolize, from Old French *en gros*, in large quantity.]

en·gross·ing (ĕn-**grō′**sĭng) *adj.* Occupying one's complete attention; extremely interesting: *an engrossing film.*

en·gulf (ĕn-**gŭlf′**) *tr.v.* **en·gulfed, en·gulf·ing, en·gulfs** To swallow up or overwhelm by or as if by overflowing and enclosing: *Floodwaters engulfed the land near the river.*

en·hance (ĕn-**hăns′**) *tr.v.* **en·hanced, en·hanc·ing, en·hanc·es** To make greater, as in value, beauty, or reputation: *The gardens enhanced the grounds.* [From Middle English *enhauncen*, from Old French *enhaucier*, from Late Latin *inaltāre*, from Latin *altus*, high.] **—en·hance′ment** *n.*

e·nig·ma (ĭ-**nĭg′**mə) *n.* A person or thing that is puzzling, ambiguous, or hard to explain: *The disappearance of the dinosaurs remains an enigma.* [From Middle English *enigmate*, from Greek *ainigma*, from *ainissesthai*, to speak in riddles.]

en·ig·mat·ic (ĕn′ĭg-**măt′**ĭk) *adj.* Resembling an enigma; puzzling: *the enigmatic behavior of an eccentric person.* **—en′ig·mat′i·cal·ly** *adv.*

en·join (ĕn-**join′**) *tr.v.* **en·joined, en·join·ing, en·joins 1.** To urge or order (someone to do something): *The doctor enjoined the patient to walk one mile each day.* **2.** To require or impose (an action or behavior, for example); prescribe. **3.** To prohibit or forbid (someone from doing something): *The court enjoined the company from merging with its competitor.*

en·joy (ĕn-**joi′**) *v.* **en·joyed, en·joy·ing, en·joys** *—tr.* **1.** To receive pleasure or satisfaction from: *I enjoy living in the country.* **2.** To have the use or benefit of: *You seem to enjoy good health.* *—intr.* To have a pleasurable or satisfactory time. ◆ **enjoy (oneself)** To have a good time: *I enjoyed myself at the ball game.* [From Middle English *enjoien*, from Old French *enjoir*, from Latin *gaudēre*.]

en·joy·ment (ĕn-**joi′**mənt) *n.* **1.** The act or state of enjoying. **2.** Use or possession of something beneficial or pleasurable: *the enjoyment of good health.* **3.** Something that gives pleasure: *My grandparents' garden is their chief enjoyment.*

engraving

WRITERS CHOOSE THEIR WORDS

He began wandering around the room, picking things up and putting them down again. "Where's your TV?" he asked after a while. She pretended to be too **engrossed** in her reading to hear. "I *said* where's your TV?"

—Stephanie S. Tolan
Surviving the Applewhites

ensign
on a Swiss vessel

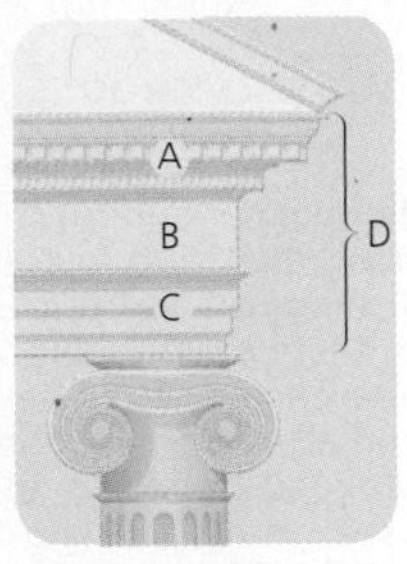

entablature
an Ionic order entablature
A. cornice
B. frieze
C. architrave
D. entablature

ă	pat	ôr	core
ā	pay	oi	boy
âr	care	ou	out
ä	father	o͝o	took
ĕ	pet	o͝or	lure
ē	be	o͞o	boot
ĭ	pit	ŭ	cut
ī	bite	ûr	urge
îr	pier	th	thin
ŏ	pot	*th*	this
ō	toe	zh	vision
ô	paw	ə	about

en·large (ĕn-lärj′) *v.* **en·larged, en·larg·ing, en·larg·es** —*tr.* To make larger in size, scope, or effect: *enlarge a house; enlarge one's understanding.* —*intr.* To become larger; grow: *The town enlarged as new businesses moved in.* See Synonyms at **increase.** ◆ **enlarge on** or **enlarge upon** To speak or write about more thoroughly: *The second article enlarged on the subject of the first.* **—en·larg′er** *n.*

en·large·ment (ĕn-lärj′mənt) *n.* **1.** An act of enlarging or the state of being enlarged: *Enlargement of the theater will permit the school to put on musicals.* **2.** Something that has been enlarged, especially a copy that is larger than the original.

en·light·en (ĕn-līt′n) *tr.v.* **en·light·ened, en·light·en·ing, en·light·ens** To give spiritual or intellectual insight to: *The movie enlightened us about the difficulty of improving health care in developing countries.*

en·light·en·ment (ĕn-līt′n-mənt) *n.* **1.** The act or means of enlightening or the state of being enlightened. **2. Enlightenment** A movement of the 1700s that called for critical examination of previously unchallenged doctrines and beliefs. **3.** In Buddhism and Hinduism, a state in which a person overcomes desire and suffering and attains Nirvana.

en·list (ĕn-lĭst′) *v.* **en·list·ed, en·list·ing, en·lists** —*tr.* **1.** To engage (a person or persons) for service in the armed forces: *The army enlisted three people from the same neighborhood.* **2.** To engage the support or cooperation of: *The minister enlisted our help in giving food to the homeless.* —*intr.* **1.** To join one of the armed forces voluntarily: *enlisted in the army after high school.* **2.** To participate actively in a cause or enterprise: *Many volunteers enlisted as drivers.*

en·list·ed (ĕn-lĭs′tĭd) *adj.* Relating to or being a member of a military rank below a commissioned officer or warrant officer.

en·liv·en (ĕn-lī′vən) *tr.v.* **en·liv·ened, en·liv·en·ing, en·liv·ens** To make lively or spirited; animate: *Music enlivened the party.*

en masse (ŏn măs′) *adv.* In a group or body; all together: *Our guests arrived en masse by taxi.*

en·mesh (ĕn-mĕsh′) *tr.v.* **en·meshed, en·mesh·ing, en·mesh·es** To entangle or catch in or as if in a net: *enmeshed in local politics.*

en·mi·ty (ĕn′mĭ-tē) *n., pl.* **en·mi·ties** Deep-seated, often mutual hatred. [From Middle English *enemite*, from Old French *enemistie*, from Latin *inimīcus*, enemy.]

en·no·ble (ĕn-nō′bəl) *tr.v.* **en·no·bled, en·no·bling, en·no·bles 1.** To make noble: *Working for a good cause ennobles a person's life.* **2.** To confer nobility upon: *ennoble a person for distinguished service.* **—en·no′ble·ment** *n.*

en·nui (ŏn-wē′) *n.* Dissatisfaction resulting from lack of interest; boredom. [From French, from Old French *ennuyer*, to annoy, bore.]

e·nor·mi·ty (ĭ-nôr′mĭ-tē) *n., pl.* **e·nor·mi·ties** The quality of passing all moral bounds; excessive wickedness or outrageousness.

e·nor·mous (ĭ-nôr′məs) *adj.* Very great in size, extent, number, or degree: *an enormous elephant; the enormous cost of building a sports arena.* See Synonyms at **large.** [From Latin *ēnormis*, unusual, huge : *ē-*, *ex-*, out of + *norma*, norm.] **—e·nor′mous·ly** *adv.* **—e·nor′mous·ness** *n.*

e·nough (ĭ-nŭf′) *adj.* Sufficient to meet a need or satisfy a desire: *There is enough food for everybody.* ❖ *pron.* An adequate amount or quantity: *The hungry hiker ate enough for two.* ❖ *adv.* **1.** To a satisfactory amount or degree; sufficiently: *Are you warm enough?* **2.** Very; fully; quite: *We were glad enough to leave after waiting so long.* **3.** Tolerably; rather: *The songs were good enough, but the show didn't draw a big audience.* [From Old English *genōg*.]

en·quir·y (ĕn-kwīr′ē *or* ĕn′kwə-rē) *n., pl.* **en·quir·ies** *Chiefly British* Variant of **inquiry.**

en·rage (ĕn-rāj′) *tr.v.* **en·raged, en·rag·ing, en·rag·es** To put into a rage; infuriate: *The plan to put a highway right through town enraged the residents.*

en·rap·ture (ĕn-răp′chər) *tr.v.* **en·rap·tured, en·rap·tur·ing, en·rap·tures** To fill with rapture or delight: *The music enraptured the audience.*

en·rich (ĕn-rĭch′) *tr.v.* **en·riched, en·rich·ing, en·rich·es 1.** To make rich or richer: *Foreign words have enriched the English language.* **2.** To add fertilizer to (soil). **3.** To add nutrients, such as vitamins and minerals, to (food). **4.** To increase the amount of a radioactive isotope in (a material): *enrich nuclear fuel.* **—en·rich′ment** *n.*

en·roll also **en·rol** (ĕn-rōl′) *v.* **en·rolled, en·roll·ing, en·rolls** also **en·rols** —*tr.* To enter or register in a list, record, or roll: *enrolled the child in kindergarten; enroll new students for an art class.* —*intr.* To place one's name on a roll or register: *enroll as a voter before the elections; enroll in the algebra class.*

en·roll·ment also **en·rol·ment** (ĕn-rōl′mənt) *n.* **1.** The act or process of enrolling. **2.** The number enrolled: *The school has an enrollment of 600.*

en route (ŏn ro͞ot′ *or* ĕn ro͞ot′) *adv. & adj.* On or along the way: *We'll pick you up en route to the theater.*

en·sconce (ĕn-skŏns′) *tr.v.* **en·sconced, en·sconc·ing, en·sconc·es 1.** To settle (oneself) comfortably or snugly: *Our visitors ensconced themselves on the couch.* **2.** To put or hide in a safe place.

en·sem·ble (ŏn-sŏm′bəl) *n.* **1.** A group of musicians, singers, dancers, or actors who perform together. **2.** A musical work for two or more vocalists or instrumentalists. **3.** A coordinated outfit or costume: *a colorful ensemble of dress, shoes, and bag.* [From Middle English, from Late Latin *īnsimul*, at the same time.]

en·shrine (ĕn-shrīn′) *tr.v.* **en·shrined, en·shrin·ing, en·shrines 1.** To enclose in or as if in a shrine. **2.** To cherish as sacred. **—en·shrine′ment** *n.*

en·shroud (ĕn-shroud′) *tr.v.* **en·shroud·ed, en·shroud·ing, en·shrouds** To cover with or as if with a shroud: *Fog enshrouded the city.*

en·sign (ĕn′sən *or* ĕn′sīn′) *n.* **1.** A national flag displayed on ships and aircraft: *the naval ensign of the United States.* **2.** A badge of office or power; a token. **3.** (ĕn′sən) An officer in the US Navy or Coast Guard ranking below lieutenant junior grade. [From Middle English *ensigne*, from Latin *īnsignia*, signal, sign.]

en·slave (ĕn-slāv′) *tr.v.* **en·slaved, en·slav·ing, en·slaves 1.** To make into a slave. **2.** To prevent from acting freely: *addicts enslaved by dependency on drugs.* **—en·slave′ment** *n.*

en·snare (ĕn-snâr′) *tr.v.* **en·snared, en·snar·ing, en·snares** To catch in or as if in a trap or snare: *ensnare customers into buying something they don't need.*

en·snarl (ĕn-snärl′) *tr.v.* **en·snarled, en·snarl·ing, en·snarls** To entangle in or as if in a snare: *The net ensnarled the ship's propeller.*

en·sue (ĕn-so͞o′) *intr.v.* **en·sued, en·su·ing, en·sues 1.** To follow as a consequence or result: *After their angry words a real fight ensued.* **2.** To follow immediately afterward. See Synonyms at **follow.** [From Middle English *ensuen*, from Latin *īnsequī*, to follow closely.]

en·sure (ĕn-sho͝or′) *tr.v.* **en·sured, en·sur·ing, en·sures** To make sure or certain; guarantee: *measures to ensure good health.* —SEE NOTE AT **assure.**

-ent *suff.* A suffix that means: **1.** Performing, promoting, or causing a specified action: *absorbent.* **2.** Being in a specified state or condition: *independent.* **3.** A person or thing that performs, promotes, or causes a specified action: *superintendent; correspondent.*

en·tab·la·ture (ĕn-tăb′lə-cho͝or′) *n.* The upper section of a classical structure, resting on the columns and made up of the architrave, frieze, and cornice.

en·tail (ĕn-**tāl′**) *tr.v.* **en·tailed, en·tail·ing, en·tails** To impose or require as a necessary accompaniment or consequence: *Building a new tunnel will entail great expense.*

en·tan·gle (ĕn-**tăng′**gəl) *tr.v.* **en·tan·gled, en·tan·gling, en·tan·gles 1.** To cause to become twisted together or caught in a snarl or entwining mass: *The fishing line got entangled. My foot got entangled in the hose.* **2.** To involve in a complicated situation or in circumstances from which it is difficult to disengage: *I don't want to get entangled in their feud.* **—en·tan′gle·ment** *n.*

en·ter (**ĕn′**tər) *v.* **en·tered, en·ter·ing, en·ters** *—tr.* **1.** To come or go into: *The train entered the tunnel.* **2.** To become a part of or participant in: *enter a discussion; enter a contest.* **3.** To cause to become a participant, member, or part of; enroll: *enter a child in kindergarten; enter a collie in a dog show.* **4.** To take up; make a beginning in; start: *enter a business as a clerk; enter a medical profession.* **5a.** To write or put in: *enter names in a guest book; enter data into a computer.* **b.** To place formally upon the records; record: *enter a plea of not guilty.* *—intr.* To come or go in: *We entered at the side of the building. Trucks enter from both sides of the road.* ◆ **enter into 1.** To participate in: *enter into a conversation; enter into an agreement.* **2.** To be a factor in: *Many considerations entered into the decision to move.* **enter on** or **enter upon** To begin; start: *The doctor entered on a career after graduating from medical school.* [From Middle English *entren*, from Latin *intrāre*, from *intrā*, inside.]

en·ter·i·tis (ĕn′tə-**rī′**tĭs) *n.* Inflammation of the intestinal tract.

en·ter·prise (**ĕn′**tər-prīz′) *n.* **1.** An undertaking, especially one of some importance, complication, and risk: *a new business enterprise.* **2.** Readiness to undertake new ventures; initiative.

en·ter·pris·ing (**ĕn′**tər-prī′zĭng) *adj.* Showing initiative and willingness to undertake new projects: *An inventor must be an enterprising person.* **—en′ter·pris′ing·ly** *adv.*

en·ter·tain (ĕn′tər-**tān′**) *v.* **en·ter·tained, en·ter·tain·ing, en·ter·tains** *—tr.* **1.** To hold the attention of with something amusing or diverting: *A country music band entertained us.* **2.** To extend hospitality toward: *entertain friends at dinner.* **3.** To consider or keep in mind: *We entertained the idea of holding a fair.* *—intr.* To show hospitality to guests.

en·ter·tain·er (ĕn′tər-**tā′**nər) *n.* A person, such as a singer or comic, who performs for an audience.

en·ter·tain·ing (ĕn′tər-**tā′**nĭng) *adj.* Amusing; agreeably diverting: *The clown told many entertaining stories.* **—en′ter·tain′ing·ly** *adv.*

en·ter·tain·ment (ĕn′tər-**tān′**mənt) *n.* **1.** The act of entertaining: *After a while the expenses of entertainment add up.* **2.** Something intended to amuse or divert, especially a performance or show. **3.** The pleasure that comes from being entertained; amusement: *offered to play the piano for our entertainment.*

en·thrall (ĕn-**thrôl′**) *tr.v.* **en·thralled, en·thrall·ing, en·thralls 1.** To hold spellbound; captivate: *The magic show enthralled the entire audience.* **2.** To enslave. **—en·thrall′ment** *n.*

en·throne (ĕn-**thrōn′**) *tr.v.* **en·throned, en·thron·ing, en·thrones 1.** To place on a throne. **2.** To invest with sovereign power or with the authority of high office. **3.** To raise to a lofty position; exalt. **—en·throne′ment** *n.*

en·thuse (ĕn-**thōōz′**) *tr. & intr.v.* **en·thused, en·thus·ing, en·thus·es** To cause (someone) to become enthusiastic or to show enthusiasm. —SEE NOTE.

en·thu·si·asm (ĕn-**thōō′**zē-ăz′əm) *n.* Great interest in or excitement for a subject or cause: *The audience applauded with enthusiasm.* [From Greek *enthousiasmos*, from *entheos*, possessed : *en-*, in + *theos*, god.]

en·thu·si·ast (ĕn-**thōō′**zē-ăst′) *n.* A person who is ardently absorbed in an interest or pursuit: *a golf enthusiast.*

en·thu·si·as·tic (ĕn-thōō′zē-**ăs′**tĭk) *adj.* Having or showing enthusiasm: *an enthusiastic welcome; enthusiastic support of a team.* **—en·thu′si·as′ti·cal·ly** *adv.*

en·tice (ĕn-**tīs′**) *tr.v.* **en·ticed, en·tic·ing, en·tic·es** To attract by arousing hope or desire; lure: *Advertising entices people to buy things.* **—en·tice′ment** *n.*

en·tire (ĕn-**tīr′**) *adj.* **1.** Having no part missing or excepted; whole: *the entire country; his entire savings.* **2.** Without reservation or limitation; complete: *The plan has my entire approval.* [From Middle English *enter*, from Latin *integer*.]

en·tire·ly (ĕn-**tīr′**lē) *adv.* **1.** Wholly; completely: *an argument entirely forgotten.* **2.** Solely or exclusively: *He was entirely to blame.*

en·tire·ty (ĕn-**tī′**rĭ-tē *or* ĕn-**tīr′**tē) *n., pl.* **en·tire·ties 1.** The condition of being entire; completeness: *I'd like to see the plan in its entirety.* **2.** The entire amount or extent; the whole: *They spent the entirety of their evening playing video games.*

en·ti·tle (ĕn-**tīt′**l) *tr.v.* **en·ti·tled, en·ti·tling, en·ti·tles 1.** To give a name or title to. **2.** To give a right or privilege to something: *This coupon entitles you to a discount.*

en·ti·tle·ment (ĕn-**tīt′**l-mənt) *n.* **1.** The act or process of entitling. **2.** The condition of being entitled. **3.** A government program that guarantees and provides benefits to a particular group.

en·ti·ty (**ĕn′**tĭ-tē) *n., pl.* **en·ti·ties** Something that exists and may be distinguished from other things: *American English and British English are distinct entities.*

en·tomb (ĕn-**tōōm′**) *tr.v.* **en·tombed, en·tomb·ing, en·tombs** To place in or as if in a tomb or grave; bury: *The eruption of the volcano entombed whole buildings.* **—en·tomb′ment** *n.*

en·to·mol·o·gist (ĕn′tə-**mŏl′**ə-jĭst) *n.* A scientist who specializes in entomology.

en·to·mol·o·gy (ĕn′tə-**mŏl′**ə-jē) *n.* The branch of zoology that deals with insects. [From Greek *entomon*, insect.]

en·tou·rage (ŏn′tōō-**räzh′**) *n.* A group of associates or attendants who accompany an important person: *arrived with an entourage of staff members.*

en·trails (**ĕn′**trālz′ *or* **ĕn′**trəlz) *pl.n.* The internal organs of the body, especially the intestines.

en·train (ĕn-**trān′**) *intr. & tr.v.* **en·trained, en·train·ing, en·trains** To go or put aboard a train.

en·trance[1] (**ĕn′**trəns) *n.* **1.** The act or an instance of entering: *an actor's entrance onstage.* **2.** A means or point by which to enter: *Use the back entrance of the building for deliveries.* **3.** The permission or power to enter; admission: *Entrance to the meeting was free.* [From Middle English *entraunce*, right to enter, from Old French, from *entrer*, to enter.]

en·trance[2] (ĕn-**trăns′**) *tr.v.* **en·tranced, en·tranc·ing, en·tranc·es 1.** To put into a trance. **2.** To fill with delight, enchantment, or wonder; fascinate: *The exciting movie entranced us all.* [From *trance*.] **—en·tranc′ing** *adj.*

en·trant (**ĕn′**trənt) *n.* A person or animal that enters a competition, such as a race or contest.

en·trap (ĕn-**trăp′**) *tr.v.* **en·trapped, en·trap·ping, en·traps 1.** To catch in a trap: *A net entrapped the fish.* **2.** To lure into danger or difficulty: *She felt entrapped by her conflicting social commitments.* **3.** To trick or manipulate (someone) into doing something illegal so that he or she can be prosecuted for breaking the law. **—en·trap′ment** *n.*

en·treat (ĕn-**trēt′**) *tr.v.* **en·treat·ed, en·treat·ing, en·treats** To ask earnestly; beg; implore.

WORD HISTORY

enthuse English can form new verbs by dropping a suffix from another word (such as a noun) that already exists. The new verb is then called a *back-formation.* An example is the verb **enthuse,** which was formed from the noun **enthusiasm.** Many writers dislike back-formations at first, but over time they tend to become accepted as everyday words. While *enthuse* is not yet fully accepted by all writers, no one objects to the verbs *donate* and *diagnose,* even though they are back-formations too—from the nouns *donation* and *diagnosis.*

en·treat·y (ĕn-trē′tē) *n., pl.* **en·treat·ies** An earnest request; a plea.

en·trée or **en·tree** (ŏn′trā *or* ŏn-trā′) *n.* **1.** The main course of a meal. **2.** The power, permission, or liberty to enter; admittance: *gained entrée to the meeting.*

en·trench (ĕn-trĕnch′) *tr.v.* **en·trenched, en·trench·ing, en·trench·es 1.** To provide with a trench, especially to fortify or defend: *The general entrenched the forces and waited for an attack.* **2.** To fix firmly or securely: *Their opinions are so entrenched they cannot change.* —**en·trench′ment** *n.*

en·tre·pre·neur (ŏn′trə-prə-nûr′ *or* ŏn′trə-prə-no͝or′) *n.* A person who organizes and operates a business enterprise and assumes the risks involved.

en·trust (ĕn-trŭst′) *tr.v.* **en·trust·ed, en·trust·ing, en·trusts 1.** To turn over (something) to another for safekeeping, care, or action: *Our neighbors entrusted the care of their dog to me.* **2.** To give as a trust to (someone): *entrusted an aide with an important message.*

en·try (ĕn′trē) *n., pl.* **en·tries 1.** The act or right of entering; entrance: *A visa is needed for entry into the country.* **2.** A means or place by which to enter: *The entry is a narrow hall.* **3.** An item written in a diary, register, list, or other record: *Each sale is an entry in this account book.* **4.** A word, phrase, or term entered and defined, as in a dictionary or encyclopedia. **5.** A person or thing entered in a contest: *That horse was a late entry in the race.*

en·try·way (ĕn′trē-wā′) *n.* A passage or opening by which to enter.

entry word *n.* A headword.

en·twine (ĕn-twīn′) *tr.v.* **en·twined, en·twin·ing, en·twines** To twine around or together: *Ivy entwined the pillars of the porch.*

e·nu·mer·ate (ĭ-no͞o′mə-rāt′) *tr.v.* **e·nu·mer·at·ed, e·nu·mer·at·ing, e·nu·mer·ates 1.** To count off or name one by one; list: *My list of objectives is too long to enumerate.* **2.** To determine the number of; count. —**e·nu′mer·a′tion** *n.* —**e·nu′mer·a′tor** *n.*

e·nun·ci·ate (ĭ-nŭn′sē-āt′) *v.* **e·nun·ci·at·ed, e·nun·ci·at·ing, e·nun·ci·ates** —*tr.* **1.** To pronounce; articulate: *The speaker enunciated every word clearly.* **2.** To state or set forth precisely or systematically: *The speech enunciated a new program of education reforms.* —*intr.* To pronounce words; speak aloud: *The professor enunciated so poorly that we hardly understood the lecture.* —**e·nun′ci·a′tion** (ĭ-nŭn′sē-ā′shən) *n.* —**e·nun′ci·a′tor** *n.*

en·vel·op (ĕn-vĕl′əp) *tr.v.* **en·vel·oped, en·vel·op·ing, en·vel·ops** To enclose or encase completely with or as if with a covering: *Fog enveloped the tallest buildings.* [From Middle English *envolupen*, to be involved in, from Old French *envoluper* : *en-*, in + *voloper*, to wrap up.] —**en·vel′op·ment** *n.*

en·ve·lope (ĕn′və-lōp′ *or* ŏn′və-lōp′) *n.* **1.** A flat paper container, especially for a letter. **2.** Something that envelops; a wrapping. **3.** The section of an airship or balloon that is filled with gas. [From French *enveloppe*, from *envelopper*, to envelop.]

en·vi·a·ble (ĕn′vē-ə-bəl) *adj.* Admirable or desirable enough to be envied: *an enviable achievement.* —**en′vi·a·bly** *adv.*

en·vi·ous (ĕn′vē-əs) *adj.* Feeling, expressing, or characterized by envy: *Other contestants were envious of the winner.* —**en′vi·ous·ly** *adv.* —**en′vi·ous·ness** *n.*

en·vi·ron·ment (ĕn-vī′rən-mənt *or* ĕn-vī′ərn-mənt) *n.* **1a.** The entire natural world, often excluding humans: *chemicals that pollute the environment.* **b.** A designated part of the natural world; an ecosystem: *the desert environment.* **2.** The combination of physical and biological conditions that affect the development and survival of an organism or group of organisms: *how whales respond to changes in their environment.* **3.** The social and cultural conditions affecting a person or community: *He grew up in an urban environment.* **4.** The general set of conditions in which an activity is carried out: *a good environment for business.* [From Old French *environ*, round about.]

en·vi·ron·men·tal (ĕn-vī′rən-mĕn′tl *or* ĕn-vī′ərn-mĕn′tl) *adj.* **1.** Relating to or associated with the environment: *climate and other environmental factors.* **2.** Relating to or concerned with the impact of human activities on the natural environment: *the environmental movement.* **3.** Relating to potentially harmful factors originating in the environment: *environmental health.* **4.** —**en·vi′ron·men′tal·ly** *adv.*

en·vi·rons (ĕn-vī′rənz *or* ĕn-vī′ərnz) *pl.n.* A surrounding area, especially of a city: *The historical environs of Boston include Lexington and Concord.*

en·vis·age (ĕn-vĭz′ĭj) *tr.v.* **en·vis·aged, en·vis·ag·ing, en·vis·ag·es** To form a picture of in the mind; conceive of: *envisage world peace.*

en·vi·sion (ĕn-vĭzh′ən) *tr.v.* **en·vi·sioned, en·vi·sion·ing, en·vi·sions** To picture in the mind; imagine.

en·voy (ĕn′voi′ *or* ŏn′voi′) *n.* **1.** A representative of a government who is sent on a special diplomatic mission. **2.** A diplomat who represents a government and ranks next below an ambassador. **3.** A messenger; an agent.

en·vy (ĕn′vē) *n., pl.* **en·vies 1.** A feeling of discontent and resentment caused by wanting something that is possessed by or is achieved by someone else: *felt envy for her friend's new baseball glove.* **2.** The object of such a feeling: *The racing bike was the envy of everyone who saw it.* ❖ *tr.v.* **en·vied, en·vy·ing, en·vies 1.** To feel envy toward: *I envy you for the chance to travel to Mexico.* **2.** To regard with envy: *envy the talent of a great musician.* [From Middle English *envie*, from Latin *invidia*, from *invidēre*, to look at enviously : *in-*, on, at + *vidēre*, to see.]

en·wrap (ĕn-răp′) *tr.v.* **en·wrapped, en·wrap·ping, en·wraps** To wrap up or enclose: *presents enwrapped in beautiful paper.*

en·zyme (ĕn′zīm) *n.* Any of numerous proteins produced in living cells and acting as catalysts in the chemical processes of living organisms. Digestive enzymes, for example, help break down large food molecules into smaller molecules that can be absorbed by the body. [From Medieval Greek *enzūmos*, leavened : Greek *en-*, in + Greek *zūmē*, yeast.]

E·o·cene (ē′ə-sēn′) *n.* The second epoch of the Tertiary Period, from about 56 to 34 million years ago. During the Eocene, climates were warm and most modern families of mammals arose. See table at **geologic time.** —**E′o·cene′** *adj.*

e·o·hip·pus (ē′ō-hĭp′əs) *n.* The hyracotherium.

e·on also **ae·on** (ē′ŏn′ *or* ē′ən) *n.* **1.** An extremely long period of time; an age; eternity. **2.** A division of geologic time that contains two or more eras. [From Greek *aiōn*, age, lifetime.]

E·os (ē′ŏs′) *n.* In Greek mythology, the goddess of the dawn, identified with the Roman Aurora.

ep·au·let also **ep·au·lette** (ĕp′ə-lĕt′ *or* ĕp′ə-lĕt′) *n.* An ornamental strap worn on the shoulder of an officer's uniform.

e·phem·er·al (ĭ-fĕm′ər-əl) *adj.* **1.** Lasting only a brief time; short-lived: *For most people, fame is ephemeral, and their achievements are soon forgotten.* **2.** Living or growing for only a short time, as certain plants or insects do. [From Greek *ephēmeros* : *ep-*, *epi-*, upon + *hēmerā*, day.] —**e·phem′er·al·ly** *adv.*

E·phe·sian (ĭ-fē′zhən) *adj.* Relating to ancient Ephesus or its people, language, or culture. ❖ *n.* **1.** A native or inhabitant of ancient Ephesus. **2. Ephesians** *(used with a singular verb)* A book of the New Testament consisting of a letter from the Apostle Paul to the Christians of Ephesus.

Eph·e·sus (ĕf′ĭ-səs) An ancient city of Greek Asia Minor in present-day western Turkey.

ă	pat	ôr	core
ā	pay	oi	boy
âr	care	ou	out
ä	father	o͝o	took
ĕ	pet	o͝or	lure
ē	be	o͞o	boot
ĭ	pit	ŭ	cut
ī	bite	ûr	urge
îr	pier	th	thin
ŏ	pot	*th*	this
ō	toe	zh	vision
ô	paw	ə	about

epi– or **ep–** *pref.* A prefix that means: **1.** On; upon: *epiphyte.* **2.** Over; above: *epicenter.*

ep·ic (ĕp′ĭk) *n.* **1.** A long poem about the deeds of heroic characters. **2.** A literary or other artistic work that has the qualities of an epic. ❖ *adj.* **1.** Relating to or resembling an epic: *an epic film.* **2.** Resembling something described in an epic; grand; tremendous: *an epic achievement.* [From Greek *epikos*, relating to an epic, from *epos*, song.] **—ep′i·cal·ly** *adv.*

ep·i·cen·ter (ĕp′ĭ-sĕn′tər) *n.* The point of the earth's surface directly above the focus of an earthquake.

ep·i·cure (ĕp′ĭ-kyo͝or′) *n.* A person who knows much about and has excellent taste in good food and drink. [From Middle English, after *Epicurus* (341?–270 BC), Greek philosopher.]

ep·i·cu·re·an (ĕp′ĭ-kyo͝o-**rē′**ən *or* ĕp′ĭ-**kyo͝or′**ē-ən) *adj.* **1.** Devoted to the pursuit of pleasure, especially to the enjoyment of good food and comfort. **2.** Suited to the tastes of an epicure: *an epicurean meal of exotic foods.* ❖ *n.* An epicure.

ep·i·dem·ic (ĕp′ĭ-**dĕm′**ĭk) *n.* **1.** An outbreak of a disease, especially a contagious disease, in a region or among a group of people: *an epidemic of cholera after the earthquake.* **2.** A rapid spread or development: *an epidemic of homelessness.* ❖ *adj.* Spreading rapidly and widely among the inhabitants of an area: *conditions for an outbreak of epidemic typhus.* [From Greek *epidēmos*, prevalent : *epi-*, upon + *dēmos*, people.]

ep·i·de·mi·ol·o·gy (ĕp′ĭ-dē′mē-**ŏl′**ə-jē) *n.* The branch of medicine that deals with the study of the causes, distribution, and control of disease in populations. **—ep′i·de′mi·ol′o·gist** *n.*

ep·i·der·mis (ĕp′ĭ-**dûr′**mĭs) *n.* **1.** The outer protective layer of the skin of vertebrates. **2.** The outer protective layer of cells of the stems, roots, and leaves of plants.

ep·i·glot·tis (ĕp′ĭ-**glŏt′**ĭs) *n.* A thin triangular flap of cartilage at the base of the tongue that covers the glottis during swallowing to keep food from entering the windpipe.

ep·i·gram (**ĕp′**ĭ-grăm′) *n.* **1.** A short witty poem expressing a single thought. **2.** A short witty saying.

ep·i·gram·mat·ic (ĕp′ĭ-grə-**măt′**ĭk) *adj.* **1.** Resembling an epigram; terse; witty. **2.** Containing or inclined to use epigrams. **—ep′i·gram·mat′i·cal·ly** *adv.*

ep·i·graph (**ĕp′**ĭ-grăf′) *n.* **1.** An inscription, as on a building or statue. **2.** A quotation at the beginning of a book or a chapter of a book that suggests its theme.

ep·i·lep·sy (**ĕp′**ə-lĕp′sē) *n.* Any of various disorders of the nervous system characterized by recurring seizures, often resulting in convulsions or the loss of consciousness. [From Greek *epilēpsis*, from *epilambanein*, to lay hold of : *epi-*, upon + *lambanein*, to seize.]

ep·i·lep·tic (ĕp′ə-**lĕp′**tĭk) *adj.* Relating to or affected with epilepsy: *an epileptic attack.* ❖ *n.* A person who has epilepsy.

ep·i·logue also **ep·i·log** (**ĕp′**ə-lôg′) *n.* **1.** A short section at the end of a literary work, often discussing what happens to the characters after the main story. **2.** A short poem or speech spoken directly to the audience at the end of a play. [From Middle English *epiloge*, from Greek *epilogos*, conclusion of a speech : *epi-*, after + *logos*, word, speech.]

ep·i·neph·rine (ĕp′ə-**nĕf′**rĭn) *n.* A hormone secreted by the adrenal glands that quickens the heartbeat and raises blood pressure, thereby preparing the body for vigorous action, as in response to danger or other stress. It is also prepared synthetically and used to treat asthma.

e·piph·a·ny (ĭ-**pĭf′**ə-nē) *n., pl.* **e·piph·a·nies** **1. Epiphany** A Christian feast traditionally held on January 6 that in the Western Church celebrates the visit of the Magi to the infant Jesus and in the Eastern Church celebrates the baptism of Jesus. **2.** A revelatory manifestation of a divine being. **3.** A sudden understanding or perception by means of intuition.

ep·i·phyte (**ĕp′**ə-fīt′) *n.* A plant growing on another plant that provides support but not nutrients. Spanish moss and many orchids are epiphytes. **—ep′i·phyt′ic** (ĕp′ə-**fĭt′**ĭk) *adj.*

e·pis·co·pal (ĭ-**pĭs′**kə-pəl) *adj.* **1.** Relating to or governed by bishops. **2. Episcopal** Relating to the Episcopal Church. [From Middle English, from Late Latin *episcopus*, bishop, from Greek *episkopos*, overseer.]

Episcopal Church *n.* The church in the United States that agrees with the Church of England in doctrine and most practices.

E·pis·co·pa·lian (ĭ-pĭs′kə-**pā′**lē-ən) *adj.* Relating to the Episcopal Church. ❖ *n.* A member of the Episcopal Church.

ep·i·sode (**ĕp′**ĭ-sōd′) *n.* **1a.** An event or incident in the course of a larger series: *Living in India was an exciting episode in her life.* **b.** An incident that forms a distinct part of a story. **2.** A part of a novel or radio or television program presented as a series: *The story was divided into six episodes for TV.* **—ep·i·sod′ic** (ĕp′ĭ-**sŏd′**ĭk) *adj.*

e·pis·tle (ĭ-**pĭs′**əl) *n.* **1.** A letter, especially a formal one. **2. Epistle** One of the letters written by the early Christians and included as books in the New Testament.

ep·i·taph (**ĕp′**ĭ-tăf′) *n.* An inscription on a tombstone or monument in memory of the person buried there.

ep·i·the·li·um (ĕp′ə-**thē′**lē-əm) *n., pl.* **ep·i·the·li·ums** or **ep·i·the·li·a** (ĕp′ə-**thē′**lē-ə) The thin tissue that covers most of the inner and outer surfaces of an animal body and lines the inside of certain organs. **—ep′i·the′li·al** *adj.*

ep·i·thet (**ĕp′**ə-thĕt′) *n.* A term used to describe the nature of a person or thing; for example, *The Big Apple* is an epithet for New York City.

e·pit·o·me (ĭ-**pĭt′**ə-mē) *n.* **1.** A person or thing that is a typical example of an entire class or type: *Her remark was the epitome of good judgment.* **2.** A summary of a book, article, or other literary work; an abstract.

e·pit·o·mize (ĭ-**pĭt′**ə-mīz′) *tr.v.* **e·pit·o·mized, e·pit·o·miz·ing, e·pit·o·miz·es** To be a typical example of: *Daniel Boone epitomizes the independent frontiersman.*

e plu·ri·bus u·num (ē′ **plo͝or′**ə-bəs **yo͞o′**nəm) Out of many, one (the official motto of the seal of the United States).

ep·och (**ĕp′**ək *or* **ē′**pŏk′) *n.* **1.** A period, especially one in history marked by certain important events or developments; an era: *the epoch of space exploration.* **2.** A unit of time that is a division of a geologic period. [From Greek *epokhē*, a point in time.]

ep·och·al (**ĕp′**ə-kəl) *adj.* **1.** Relating to or characteristic of an epoch. **2.** Highly important or significant; momentous: *epochal decisions made by Lincoln during the Civil War.*

ep·ox·y (ĭ-**pŏk′**sē) *n., pl.* **ep·ox·ies** Any of various artificial resins that are tough, strongly adhesive, and resistant to chemicals, used in making protective coatings and glues.

ep·si·lon (**ĕp′**sə-lŏn′) *n.* The fifth letter of the Greek alphabet, written Ε, ε. In English it is represented as *E, e.*

Ep·som salts (**ĕp′**səm) *pl.n.* *(used with a singular verb)* A colorless crystalline compound of magnesium, sulfur, and oxygen, used in making textiles, in fertilizers, and for medical purposes.

eq. *abbr.* An abbreviation of: **1.** equal. **2.** equation. **3.** equivalent.

eq·ua·ble (**ĕk′**wə-bəl *or* **ē′**kwə-bəl) *adj.* **1.** Not varying; steady; even: *the equable climate of the Caribbean.* **2.** Even-tempered; not easily upset; serene: *Our teacher has an equable disposition.* **—eq′ua·bil′i·ty** *n.* **—eq′ua·bly** *adv.*

e·qual (**ē′**kwəl) *adj.* **1a.** Having the same quantity,

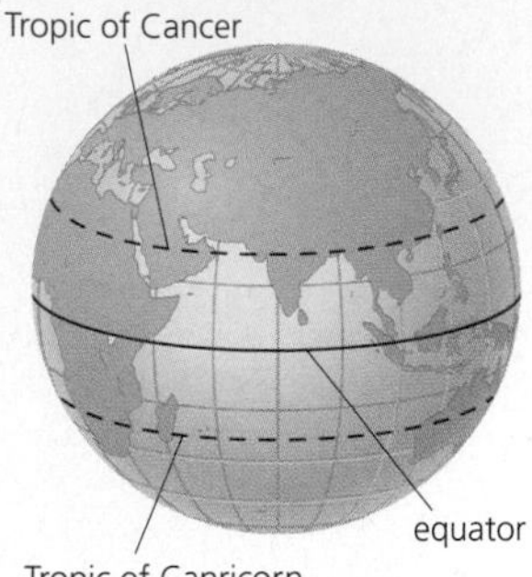

equator

measure, or extent as another: *equal strength; equal size.* **b.** Having the same value, as 3 + 2 and 6 − 1. **2.** Having the same privileges, status, or rights: *All citizens are equal before the law.* **3.** Being the same for all members of a group; even: *Every player had an equal chance to win.* ❖ *n.* A person or thing that is equal to another: *Most people want to be treated as equals.* ❖ *tr.v.* **e·qualed, e·qual·ing, e·quals** or **e·qualled, e·qual·ling, e·quals 1.** To be equal to: *Two pints equal a quart. My ability equals theirs.* **2.** To do, make, or produce something equal to: *The athlete equaled the world's record in the mile run.* [From Middle English, from Latin *aequālis*, from *aequus*, even, level.] —**e′qual·ly** *adv.*

e·qual·i·ty (ĭ-**kwŏl′**ĭ-tē) *n., pl.* **e·qual·i·ties** The condition of being equal, especially the condition of enjoying equal rights: *equality under the law.*

e·qual·ize (**ē′**kwə-līz′) *tr.v.* **e·qual·ized, e·qual·iz·ing, e·qual·iz·es 1.** To make equal: *Opening the bottle equalizes the pressure with the outside air.* **2.** To make uniform: *Move this box to equalize the weight on both sides of the car.* —**e′qual·i·za′tion** (ē′kwə-lĭ-**zā′**shən) *n.* —**e′qual·iz′er** *n.*

equal sign *n.* The symbol (=) used in mathematics to show that something is equal, as in $a = b$ and 2 + 2 = 4.

e·qua·nim·i·ty (ē′kwə-**nĭm′**ĭ-tē *or* ĕk′wə-**nĭm′**ĭ-tē) *n.* The condition or quality of being calm and even-tempered; composure: *Judges are expected to show equanimity in court.*

e·quate (ĭ-**kwāt′**) *tr.v.* **e·quat·ed, e·quat·ing, e·quates** To make equal or consider as equal or equivalent: *Many people equate fame with success.*

e·qua·tion (ĭ-**kwā′**zhən *or* ĭ-**kwā′**shən) *n.* **1.** A mathematical statement asserting that two expressions are equal. For example, 3 × 2 = 6, $y = 2 + 8$, and $x + y = 18$ are all equations. **2.** An expression using chemical formulas and symbols to show the quantities and substances in a chemical reaction. For example, two hydrogen molecules reacting with an oxygen molecule to form two molecules of water is expressed by the equation $2H_2 + O_2 = 2H_2O$.

e·qua·tor (ĭ-**kwā′**tər) *n.* **1.** The imaginary line that circles the earth halfway between the North and South poles. It divides the earth into the Northern Hemisphere and the Southern Hemisphere. **2.** A similar circle on any celestial object: *the sun's equator.* **3.** The celestial equator. [From Middle English, from Medieval Latin *aequātor (diēī et noctis)*, equalizer (of day and night), from Latin *aequāre*, to equalize.]

e·qua·to·ri·al (ē′kwə-**tôr′**ē-əl *or* ĕk′wə-**tôr′**ē-əl) *adj.* **1.** Relating to or near the equator: *an equatorial region of Brazil.* **2.** Characteristic of conditions at the earth's equator: *equatorial heat.*

Equatorial Guin·ea (**gĭn′**ē) A country of west-central Africa north of Gabon including islands in the Gulf of Guinea. Malabo is the capital.

eq·uer·ry (**ĕk′**wə-rē) *n., pl.* **eq·uer·ries 1.** An officer in charge of the horses in a royal or noble household. **2.** In England, a personal attendant to a member of the royal family.

e·ques·tri·an (ĭ-**kwĕs′**trē-ən) *adj.* **1.** Relating to horseback riders or horseback riding: *equestrian ability.* **2.** Mounted or represented as mounted on horseback: *an equestrian statue of the king.* ❖ *n.* A person who rides a horse or performs on horseback. [From Latin *equester*, from *eques*, horseman, from *equus*, horse.]

e·ques·tri·enne (ĭ-kwĕs′trē-**ĕn′**) *n.* A woman who rides a horse or performs on horseback.

equi– *pref.* A prefix that means equal or equally: *equidistant.* —SEE NOTE.

e·qui·an·gu·lar (ē′kwē-**ăng′**gyə-lər) *adj.* Having all angles equal: *Rectangles are equiangular.*

e·qui·dis·tant (ē′kwĭ-**dĭs′**tənt) *adj.* Equally distant. —**e′qui·dis′tant·ly** *adv.*

e·qui·lat·er·al (ē′kwə-**lăt′**ər-əl) *adj.* Having all sides equal: *an equilateral triangle.* —**e′qui·lat′er·al·ly** *adv.*

e·qui·lib·ri·um (ē′kwə-**lĭb′**rē-əm) *n.* **1.** A condition of balance or stability: *Ideally, the supply of a product should be in equilibrium with the demand for it.* **2.** Mental or emotional balance; poise: *The quarrel upset their equilibrium for the whole morning.*

e·quine (**ē′**kwīn′ *or* **ĕk′**wīn′) *adj.* Relating to or resembling a horse.

e·qui·noc·tial (ē′kwə-**nŏk′**shəl *or* ĕk′wə-**nŏk′**shəl) *adj.* **1.** Relating to an equinox. **2.** Occurring at or near the time of an equinox: *an equinoctial storm.*

e·qui·nox (**ē′**kwə-nŏks′ *or* **ĕk′**wə-nŏks′) *n.* Either of the times of year when the sun crosses the celestial equator and day and night are about equal in length. In the Northern Hemisphere, the vernal equinox occurs around March 20 and the autumnal equinox occurs around September 22. [From Middle English, from Latin *aequinoctium* : *aequi-*, equal + *nox*, night.]

e·quip (ĭ-**kwĭp′**) *tr.v.* **e·quipped, e·quip·ping, e·quips** To supply with what is needed; provide: *The expedition was equipped with oxygen tanks for climbing at high altitudes.* [From Old French *esquiper*, of Germanic origin; akin to Old Norse *skipa* (from *skip*, ship).]

eq·ui·page (**ĕk′**wə-pĭj) *n.* **1.** Equipment, as of an army. **2.** An elegantly equipped horse-drawn carriage, usually attended by footmen.

e·quip·ment (ĭ-**kwĭp′**mənt) *n.* **1.** The things needed or used for a particular purpose: *a tent, sleeping bag, and other camping equipment.* **2.** The act of equipping or state of being equipped: *The equipment of the expedition took over a month to complete.*

e·qui·poise (**ē′**kwə-poiz′ *or* **ĕk′**wə-poiz′) *n.* **1.** Equality in distribution, as of weight or force; balance; equilibrium. **2.** A weight or force that balances another; a counterbalance.

eq·ui·ta·ble (**ĕk′**wĭ-tə-bəl) *adj.* Just and impartial: *Judges are expected to make equitable decisions.* —**eq′ui·ta·bly** *adv.*

eq·ui·ty (**ĕk′**wĭ-tē) *n., pl.* **eq·ui·ties 1.** Justice or fairness: *No one questioned the equity of the jury's verdict.* **2a.** The amount that a person's ownership in a business or property is worth after subtracting the debts that are owed by the business or on the property. **b. equities** Common or preferred stock: *How much of their life savings is in equities?*

e·quiv·a·lence (ĭ-**kwĭv′**ə-ləns) *n.* The condition or property of being equivalent.

e·quiv·a·lent (ĭ-**kwĭv′**ə-lənt) *adj.* **1.** Equal, as in value, meaning, or force: *The wish of the king is equivalent to a command.* **2.** Having a one-to-one correspondence, as between parts: *equivalent geometric figures.* ❖ *n.* Something that is equivalent: *A dime is the equivalent of two nickels.* [From Middle English, from Late Latin *aequivalēre*, to have equal force : *aequi-*, equal + *valēre*, to be strong, to be worth.]

e·quiv·o·cal (ĭ-**kwĭv′**ə-kəl) *adj.* **1.** Open to two or more interpretations and often intended to conceal the truth: *The politician gave an equivocal answer to the reporter's question.* See Synonyms at **ambiguous. 2.** Characterized by a mixture of opposing elements and therefore questionable or uncertain: *The experiment gave equivocal results that we could not interpret with certainty.* —**e·quiv′o·cal·ly** *adv.*

e·quiv·o·cate (ĭ-**kwĭv′**ə-kāt′) *intr.v.* **e·quiv·o·cat·ed, e·quiv·o·cat·ing, e·quiv·o·cates** To use language that can be interpreted in more than one way, especially in order to mislead: *Stop equivocating and tell us what you really think.* —**e·quiv′o·ca′tor** *n.*

e·quiv·o·ca·tion (ĭ-kwĭv′ə-**kā′**shən) *n.* **1.** The use of

WORD BUILDING

equi– The prefix **equi–** means "equal" or "equally." *Equi–* is from the Latin prefix *aequi–*, which came from the Latin word *aequus*, meaning "equal." Thus *equidistant* means "equally distant." *Equi–* often occurs in words with Latin elements. For example, *equinox* means "having the night equal (to the day)," from Latin *nox*, "night." *Equivalent* is from *valēre*, "to be worth, amount to," and so is literally "amounting to the same thing."

ă	pat	ôr	core
ā	pay	oi	boy
âr	care	ou	out
ä	father	o͝o	took
ĕ	pet	o͝or	lure
ē	be	o͞o	boot
ĭ	pit	ŭ	cut
ī	bite	ûr	urge
îr	pier	th	thin
ŏ	pot	*th*	this
ō	toe	zh	vision
ô	paw	ə	about

equivocal language. **2.** An equivocal statement: *The defense lawyer's remarks were full of equivocations.*

Er The symbol for the element **erbium.**

–er[1] *suff.* A suffix that means: **1.** A person or thing that does a specified action: *swimmer; blender.* **2.** A person who is born in or lives in a place: *islander; New Yorker.* **3.** A person or thing that is: *foreigner; six-footer.* **4.** A person or thing that is associated or involved with: *banker; gardener.*

–er[2] *suff.* A suffix that forms the comparative degree of adjectives and adverbs: *neater; slower.*

e·ra (îr′ə *or* ĕr′ə) *n.* **1.** A period of time as marked from a specific date or event: *The atomic era and the postwar era began in 1945.* **2.** A period of time characterized by particular circumstances, events, or people: *the Colonial era of American history.* **3.** A major division of geologic time, containing one or more periods. [From Latin *aera,* counters, plural of *aes,* bronze coin.]

e·rad·i·cate (ĭ-răd′ĭ-kāt′) *tr.v.* **e·rad·i·cat·ed, e·rad·i·cat·ing, e·rad·i·cates 1.** To get rid of; eliminate: *a campaign to eradicate smallpox.* **2.** To tear up by the roots. [From Middle English *eradicaten,* from Latin *ērādīcāre* : *ē-, ex-,* out + *rādīx,* root.] **—e·rad′i·ca′tion** *n.*

e·rase (ĭ-rās′) *tr.v.* **e·rased, e·ras·ing, e·ras·es 1.** To remove (something written or drawn) by rubbing, scraping, or wiping: *erase a mistake.* **2a.** To remove (recorded material) from a magnetic tape, computer disk, or other storage medium. **b.** To remove recorded material from (a magnetic tape, for example). **3.** To remove or destroy as if by wiping out: *Time will erase hurt feelings.* [From Latin *ērādere,* to scratch out : *ē-, ex-,* out + *rādere,* to scrape.] **—e·ras′a·ble** *adj.*

e·ras·er (ĭ-rā′sər) *n.* An implement that erases marks made with pencil, ink, or chalk.

E·ras·mus (ĭ-răz′məs), **Desiderius** 1466?–1536. Dutch scholar and theologian whose works include *The Praise of Folly* (1509).

e·ra·sure (ĭ-rā′shər) *n.* **1.** The act of erasing. **2.** Something erased, as a word or number: *The paper had numerous erasures.*

er·bi·um (ûr′bē-əm) *n. Symbol* **Er** A soft, silvery metallic element used in nuclear research and in coloring glass and porcelain. Atomic number 68. See **Periodic Table.**

ere (âr) *prep.* Previous to; before. ❖ *conj.* Sooner than; rather than. [From Old English *ǣr.*]

❑ *These sound alike:* **ere, air** (gas), **e'er** (ever), **heir** (inheritor).

e-read·er (ē′rē′dər) *n.* A device with a screen on which electronic texts may be read.

e·rect (ĭ-rĕkt′) *adj.* **1.** In a vertical or upright position: *a soldier's erect posture; an erect flower stalk.* **2.** Being enlarged and stiff as a result of sexual excitement. ❖ *tr.v.* **e·rect·ed, e·rect·ing, e·rects 1.** To build; put up; construct: *erect a skyscraper.* **2.** To raise upright; set on end: *erect a new telephone pole.* **3.** To set up; establish: *The country erected a model legal system.* **—e·rect′ly** *adv.* **—e·rect′ness** *n.*

e·rec·tile (ĭ-rĕk′təl *or* ĭ-rĕk′tīl′) *adj.* **1.** Capable of being raised to an upright position: *a fish with erectile spines.* **2.** Relating to tissue that is capable of filling with blood and becoming rigid.

e·rec·tion (ĭ-rĕk′shən) *n.* **1.** The act of erecting, building, or raising upright: *The erection of the new temple took nearly two years.* **2.** The stiffening of certain body parts, especially the penis or the clitoris, when the tissues within them fill with blood.

erg (ûrg) *n.* A unit used to measure energy or work, equal to the force of one dyne over a distance of one centimeter. This unit has been mostly replaced by the joule.

er·go (ûr′gō *or* âr′gō) *conj. & adv.* Consequently; therefore. [From Latin *ergō.*]

er·got (ûr′gət *or* ûr′gŏt′) *n.* A fungus that infects rye, wheat, and other grain plants, forming black masses among the seeds. Grain infected with ergot is poisonous and can cause serious illness.

Er·ic·son (ĕr′ĭk-sən), **Leif** Flourished about 1000. Norwegian navigator who went in search of lands west of Greenland. His camp in what he named Vinland was probably the first European settlement in North America.

E·rie (îr′ē) *n., pl.* **Erie** or **E·ries 1.** A member of a Native American people formerly living in the region south of Lake Erie. **2.** The Iroquoian language of the Erie.

Erie, Lake One of the Great Lakes, surrounded by southern Ontario, western New York, northwest Pennsylvania, northern Ohio, and southeast Michigan.

Erie Canal An artificial waterway extending about 360 miles (580 kilometers) across central New York from Albany to Buffalo. It was constructed from 1817 to 1825.

Er·in (ĕr′ĭn) A poetic name for Ireland.

E·rin·y·es (ĭ-rĭn′ē-ēz′) *pl.n.* In Greek mythology, the terrible winged goddesses who pursued and punished those who committed unavenged crimes, identified with the Roman Furies.

E·ris (îr′ĭs *or* ĕr′ĭs) *n.* **1.** In Greek Mythology, the goddess of discord. **2.** A dwarf planet with a diameter of about 1,500 miles (2,400 kilometers). It is the largest known dwarf planet in our solar system and has a moon of its own. —SEE NOTE AT **planet.**

Er·i·tre·a (ĕr′ĭ-trē′ə) A country of northeast Africa on the Red Sea north of Ethiopia. It gained its independence from Ethiopia in 1993. Asmara is the capital. **—Er′i·tre′an** *adj. & n.*

er·mine (ûr′mĭn) *n.* **1.** A weasel of northern regions having brownish fur that turns white in winter. **2.** The valuable white fur of this animal.

e·rode (ĭ-rōd′) *v.* **e·rod·ed, e·rod·ing, e·rodes** *—tr.* **1.** To wear away by or as if by rubbing or scraping: *Wind eroded the hillside.* **2.** To eat into; corrode: *The acidity of the water eroded the pipes.* **3.** To form by wearing away: *The river eroded a deep gorge through the rock.* **4.** To cause to diminish or deteriorate: *The bookkeeper's mistakes eroded their trust in his work.* *—intr.* **1.** To become worn away gradually: *The cliffs along the seashore have eroded over the centuries.* **2.** To diminish or deteriorate: *Public confidence in the mayor eroded.* [From Latin *ērōdere,* to gnaw off, eat away : *ē-, ex-,* off, away + *rōdere,* to gnaw.]

Er·os (ĕr′ŏs′ *or* îr′ŏs′) *n.* In Greek mythology, the god of love, identified with the Roman Cupid.

e·ro·sion (ĭ-rō′zhən) *n.* **1.** The action of eroding or the condition of being eroded: *soil erosion.* **2.** Diminishment or deterioration: *the erosion of public confidence.*

e·ro·sive (ĭ-rō′sĭv) *adj.* Causing erosion: *erosive winds.*

e·rot·ic (ĭ-rŏt′ĭk) *adj.* Relating to or arousing sexual desire. **—e·rot′i·cal·ly** *adv.*

err (ĕr *or* ûr) *intr.v.* **erred, err·ing, errs 1.** To make a mistake or error; be incorrect: *We erred in thinking the bus would be on time.* **2.** To commit an act that is wrong; do wrong.

er·rand (ĕr′ənd) *n.* **1.** A short trip taken to do something, usually for someone else: *Our neighbor asked me to run an errand to the store downtown.* **2.** The purpose or object of such a trip: *My errand was to mail a letter.* [From Old English *ǣrend.*]

er·rant (ĕr′ənt) *adj.* **1.** Roving or wandering: *knights errant seeking adventure.* **2.** Straying from the proper course or correct behavior: *an errant youth.*

er·rat·ic (ĭ-răt′ĭk) *adj.* **1.** Lacking a fixed course; wandering: *a moth's erratic flight.* **2.** Lacking consistency, regularity, or uniformity; irregular: *an erratic heartbeat.* **3.** Straying from the usual course in conduct or opinion; eccentric: *erratic behavior.* **—er·rat′i·cal·ly** *adv.*

er·ro·ne·ous (ĭ-rō′nē-əs) *adj.* Containing or derived

erosion

eruption
Mt. Kilauea, Hawaii

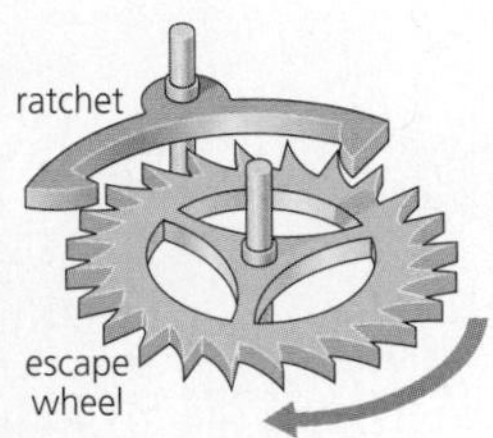

escapement

escutcheon
coat of arms of Christopher Columbus

ă	pat	ôr	core
ā	pay	oi	boy
âr	care	ou	out
ä	father	o͝o	took
ĕ	pet	o͝or	lure
ē	be	o͞o	boot
ĭ	pit	ŭ	cut
ī	bite	ûr	urge
îr	pier	th	thin
ŏ	pot	*th*	this
ō	toe	zh	vision
ô	paw	ə	about

from error; mistaken: *an erroneous belief.* **—er·ro′ne·ous·ly** *adv.*

er·ror (ĕr′ər) *n.* **1.** Something that is incorrect, wrong, or false: *The waiter made an error in adding up our bill.* **2.** The condition of being incorrect or wrong: *The statement is in error.* **3.** The difference between the measured value of a quantity and its exact or true value: *The error in the thermostat was 10 degrees.* **4.** In baseball, a fielding or throwing play in which a player misses the ball or throws it inaccurately, allowing a runner to reach first base or advance one or more bases. [From Middle English *errour*, from Latin *error*, from *errāre*, to err.]

er·satz (ĕr′zäts′) *adj.* Being a substitute or imitation; artificial: *ersatz leather.*

erst·while (ûrst′wīl′) *adv.* In times past; formerly. ❖ *adj.* Former: *an erstwhile foe.*

er·u·dite (ĕr′yə-dīt′ *or* ĕr′ə-dīt′) *adj.* Having or marked by great knowledge or learning; learned: *an erudite book; an erudite person.* **—er′u·dite′ly** *adv.*

er·u·di·tion (ĕr′yə-**dĭsh′**ən *or* ĕr′ə-**dĭsh′**ən) *n.* Extensive learning.

e·rupt (ĭ-rŭpt′) *intr.v.* **e·rupt·ed, e·rupt·ing, e·rupts 1.** To throw or force out something violently, such as lava, ash and gases: *The volcano erupted.* **2.** To be thrown or forced out: *Water erupted from the geyser.* **3.** To develop suddenly: *War erupted between the two nations.* **4.** To express oneself suddenly and loudly: *The audience erupted in laughter.* **5.** To break through the gums in developing. Used of teeth. **6.** To appear on the skin: *A rash erupted on the child's back.* [From Latin *ērumpere* : *ē-*, *ex-*, out + *rumpere*, to break.] **—e·rup′tive** *adj.*

e·rup·tion (ĭ-rŭp′shən) *n.* **1.** The act or an instance of erupting: *the eruption of a geyser.* **2.** A sudden, almost violent outburst: *an eruption of anger.* **3.** A rash or blemish on the skin: *an eruption caused by a virus.*

–ery or **–ry** *suff.* A suffix that means: **1.** A place for: *bakery.* **2.** A collection or class: *greenery.* **3.** A state or condition: *slavery.* **4.** Act or practice: *bribery.* **5.** Characteristics or qualities of: *snobbery*

e·ryth·ro·cyte (ĭ-rĭth′rə-sīt′) *n.* A red blood cell.

Es The symbol for the element **einsteinium.**

–es[1] *suff.* Variant of **–s[1].**

–es[2] *suff.* Variant of **–s[2].**

E·sau (ē′sô) In the Bible, the eldest son of Isaac and Rebecca, who sold his birthright to his twin brother, Jacob, for a dish of stew.

es·ca·late (ĕs′kə-lāt′) *intr. & tr.v.* **es·ca·lat·ed, es·ca·lat·ing, es·ca·lates 1.** To increase or cause to increase: *Rents escalated during the 1990s. The cold weather escalated the number of flu cases.* **2.** To become or cause to become more intense: *Bad feeling between the countries escalated. The diplomatic blunder escalated the crisis.* [From *escalator.*] **—es′ca·la′tion** *n.*

es·ca·la·tor (ĕs′kə-lā′tər) *n.* A moving stairway consisting of steps attached to a continuously circulating belt.

es·ca·pade (ĕs′kə-pād′) *n.* An adventurous, often reckless act or undertaking.

es·cape (ĭ-skāp′) *v.* **es·caped, es·cap·ing, es·capes** —*intr.* **1.** To break loose from confinement; get free: *The prisoners escaped by climbing the wall.* **2.** To avoid capture, danger, or harm: *The thieves escaped every time the police tried to catch them.* **3.** To leak or seep out: *All the air escaped from the balloon.* —*tr.* **1.** To get free of; break loose from: *A vacation will allow me to escape the noise of the city.* **2.** To succeed in avoiding (capture, danger, or harm): *I barely escaped injury when the ladder fell.* **3.** To fail to be noticed or remembered by: *The name of the new worker escapes me.* **4.** To come out of (someone or someone's lips) involuntarily: *A cry of delight escaped the child's lips.* ❖ *n.* **1.** The act or means of escaping: *prisoners planning an escape.* **2.** A means of escaping: *An open gate provided the dog's escape.* **3.** A means of obtaining temporary freedom from worry, care, or unpleasantness: *For her, running provides an escape from everyday problems.* **4.** A key on a computer keyboard pressed to interrupt a command or exit a program. [From Middle English *escapen*, from Old North French *escaper* : Latin *ex-*, out + Medieval Latin *cappa*, cloak.]

es·cap·ee (ĭ-skā′**pē′**) *n.* A person who has escaped, especially an escaped prisoner.

es·cape·ment (ĭ-skāp′mənt) *n.* A device in clocks and watches that controls the speed at which the movement runs. It consists of a gearwheel controlled by a ratchet having teeth that fit into the wheel as the ratchet swings, allowing the wheel to escape or move one tooth at a time.

escape velocity *n.* The minimum velocity that a body, such as a rocket, must achieve to overcome the gravitational pull of the earth or another celestial object.

escape wheel *n.* The rotating notched gearwheel in an escapement.

es·cap·ism (ĭ-**skā′**pĭz′əm) *n.* The tendency to escape from daily routine or responsibilities by engaging in daydreams, entertainment, or other forms of distraction. **—es·cap′ist** *adj. & n.*

es·car·got (ĕs′kär-**gō′**) *n., pl.* **es·car·gots** (ĕs′kär-**gō′**) An edible snail. [From French, probably from Latin *scarabaeus*, beetle.]

es·carp·ment (ĭ-skärp′mənt) *n.* **1.** A steep slope or long cliff formed by erosion or by vertical movement of the earth's crust along a fault. **2.** A steep slope or embankment in front of a fortification.

–escence *suff.* A suffix that means the state or process: *convalescence; luminescence.*

–escent *suff.* A suffix that means beginning to be or becoming: *convalescent; luminescent.*

es·chew (ĕs-**cho͞o′**) *tr.v.* **es·chewed, es·chew·ing, es·chews** To take care to avoid; shun: *eschew bad company.*

es·cort (ĕs′kôrt′) *n.* **1.** One or more people accompanying another to give protection or guidance or to pay honor: *The visiting foreign leader was given a police escort.* **2.** One or more airplanes, warships, or other vehicles accompanying another or others to provide protection. **3.** A man who is the companion of a woman, especially on a social occasion. ❖ *tr.v.* (ĭ-**skôrt′** *or* ĕs′-kôrt′) **es·cort·ed, es·cort·ing, es·corts** To accompany or guide, especially as an escort: *An honor guard escorted the president during the parade.* See Synonyms at **accompany.** [From Italian *scorta*, from *scorgere*, to guide : Latin *ex-*, intensive prefix + Latin *corrigere*, to set right.]

es·crow (ĕs′krō′ *or* ĕ-**skrō′**) *n.* Money, property, a deed, or a bond put into the custody of a third party until certain conditions are fulfilled. ◆ **in escrow** In the care of another until various conditions are met: *The bank is holding the savings account in escrow until the heirs reach their twenty-first birthday.*

es·cu·do (ĭ-sko͞o′dō) *n., pl.* **es·cu·dos** The basic monetary unit of Cape Verde.

es·cutch·eon (ĭ-**skŭch′**ən) *n.* A shield or emblem in the shape of a shield bearing a coat of arms.

–ese *suff.* A suffix that means: **1.** Relating to or originating from a certain place: *Japanese.* **2.** Native or inhabitant of: *Chinese.* **3.** A language or dialect of: *Portuguese.*

es·ker (ĕs′kər) *n.* A ridge of coarse gravel deposited by a stream flowing in or under a sheet of glacial ice.

Es·ki·mo (ĕs′kə-mō′) *n., pl.* **Eskimo** or **Es·ki·mos 1.** A member of a group of peoples inhabiting the Arctic coastal regions of North America and parts of Greenland and northeast Siberia. **2.** Any of the languages of the Eskimo peoples. **—Es′ki·mo′** *adj.*

Eskimo dog *n.* **1.** A dog of a large breed developed in the Canadian Arctic to pull sleds, having a thick coat, erect ears, and a feathery tail. **2.** A dog of a small to medium-sized breed developed in the United States, having a thick white coat, erect ears, and a feathery tail, and formerly popular in circus acts.

ESL *abbr.* An abbreviation of English as a second language.

e·soph·a·ge·al (ĭ-sŏf′ə-**jē′**əl) *adj.* Relating to the esophagus.

e·soph·a·gus (ĭ-**sŏf′**ə-gəs) *n., pl.* **e·soph·a·gi** (ĭ-**sŏf′**ə-jī′) The part of the digestive tract that consists of a muscular tube connecting the throat to the stomach.

es·o·ter·ic (ĕs′ə-**tĕr′**ĭk) *adj.* **1.** Intended for or understood by only a small group: *an esoteric book.* **2.** Not publicly disclosed; confidential. **—es′o·ter′i·cal·ly** *adv.*

ESP (ē′ĕs-**pē′**) *n.* The supposed ability to perceive events and information by means other than the physical senses: *People who seem to know what others are thinking sometimes claim they have ESP.* [From *e(xtra)s(ensory) p(erception).*]

esp. *abbr.* An abbreviation of especially.

es·pa·drille (**ĕs′**pə-drĭl′) *n.* A shoe having a rope sole and a canvas upper part.

es·pe·cial (ĭ-**spĕsh′**əl) *adj.* Of special note; exceptional: *a portrait painted with especial skill.*

es·pe·cial·ly (ĭ-**spĕsh′**ə-lē) *adv.* To an extent or degree deserving of special emphasis; particularly: *We came by especially to visit our friend.*

Es·pe·ran·to (ĕs′pə-**răn′**tō *or* ĕs′pə-**rän′**tō) *n.* An artificial language for international use, based on word roots common to many European languages. [After Dr. *Esperanto,* "one who hopes," pseudonym of Ludwik Lejzer Zamenhof (1859–1917), Polish philologist.]

es·pi·o·nage (**ĕs′**pē-ə-näzh′ *or* **ĕs′**pē-ə-nĭj) *n.* The practice of spying or of using spies to gain secret information about a government or business: *Many countries engage in espionage in time of war.* [From Old Italian *spione,* spy.]

es·pla·nade (**ĕs′**plə-näd′ *or* **ĕs′**plə-**näd′**) *n.* A flat open stretch of pavement or grass used as a promenade, especially along a shore.

es·pous·al (ĭ-**spou′**zəl *or* ĭ-**spou′**səl) *n.* **1.** Adoption of an idea or cause: *espousal of equal rights.* **2a.** A betrothal. **b.** A wedding ceremony.

es·pouse (ĭ-**spouz′**) *tr.v.* **es·poused, es·pous·ing, es·pous·es 1.** To give loyalty or support to (an idea or cause); adopt: *Their government espouses free elections.* **2.** To take in marriage; marry. **3.** To promise or present (a woman) in marriage.

es·pres·so (ĕ-**sprĕs′**ō) *n., pl.* **es·pres·sos** A strong coffee brewed by forcing steam through long-roasted, powdered coffee beans. [From Italian *(caffè) espresso,* espresso (coffee), from past participle of *esprimere,* to press out, from Latin *exprimere* : *ex-,* out + *premere,* to press.]

es·prit (ĕ-**sprē′**) *n.* Liveliness of mind and expression; wit.

esprit de corps (də **kôr′**) *n.* A spirit of devotion and enthusiasm among members of a group for one another, their group, and its cause.

es·py (ĭ-**spī′**) *tr.v.* **es·pied, es·py·ing, es·pies** To catch sight of; glimpse: *The lookout espied a sail on the horizon.*

Esq. *abbr.* An abbreviation of Esquire.

–esque *suff.* A suffix that means in the manner of or resembling: *statuesque.*

es·quire (**ĕs′**kwīr′) *n.* **1.** In medieval times, a man or boy who wished to be a knight and served as a knight's attendant and shield bearer. **2.** A man belonging to the English gentry ranking just below a knight. **3. Esquire** In the United States, a title of courtesy used especially after the name of a lawyer: *John Doe, Esq.* [From Middle English *esquier,* from Late Latin *scūtārius,* shield bearer, from Latin *scūtum,* shield.]

–ess *suff.* A suffix that means female: *heiress; lioness.*

es·say (**ĕs′**ā′ *or* ĕ-**sā′**) *n.* **1.** A short literary composition on a single subject, usually presenting the personal views of the author. **2.** An attempt; a try: *He made a brief essay at politics before settling on a teaching career.* ❖ *tr.v.* (ĕ-**sā′** *or* **ĕs′**ā′) **es·sayed, es·say·ing, es·says** To make an attempt at; try: *The actor essayed a new role on television.*

es·say·ist (**ĕs′**ā′ĭst) *n.* A writer of essays.

es·sence (**ĕs′**əns) *n.* **1.** The quality or qualities of a thing that give it its identity or character: *The essence of democracy is freedom to choose.* **2.** The most important aspect of something: *The essence of her argument is that the policy should be revised.* **3.** A concentrated form or extract of a substance that keeps the basic or most desirable properties: *Turpentine is an essence of pine tar.* **4.** A perfume or scent. [From Middle English *essencia,* from Latin *essentia,* being, from *esse,* to be.]

es·sen·tial (ĭ-**sĕn′**shəl) *adj.* **1.** Relating to or being the essence of something; basic or inherent: *The essential difficulty is getting so many independent thinkers to cooperate.* **2.** Of the greatest importance; indispensable; necessary: *The essential requirements for combustion are heat, oxygen, and fuel.* **3.** Relating to a substance that is necessary for normal functioning but cannot be made by the body and therefore must be included in the diet: *an essential amino acid.* ❖ *n.* Something fundamental, necessary, or indispensable: *Take along only the essentials when traveling.* **—es·sen′tial·ly** *adv.*

essential oil *n.* An oil that evaporates quickly and usually has the odor or flavor of the plant from which it is obtained. Essential oils are used to make perfumes and flavorings.

EST *abbr.* An abbreviation of Eastern Standard Time.

–est[1] *suff.* A suffix that forms the superlative degree of adjectives and adverbs: *greatest; earliest.*

–est[2] *suff.* A suffix that forms the archaic second person singular of verbs: *wherever thou goest.*

es·tab·lish (ĭ-**stăb′**lĭsh) *tr.v.* **es·tab·lished, es·tab·lish·ing, es·tab·lish·es 1a.** To begin or set up; found: *Their ancestors established the company in 1789.* **b.** To bring about; generate or effect: *The dinner established goodwill between the diplomats.* **2.** To settle securely in a position or condition; install: *It took several years for the new family to establish itself in this town.* **3.** To cause to be recognized and accepted: *a discovery that established the researcher's reputation.* **4.** To show to be true; prove: *The defense attorneys established the innocence of the accused.* [From Middle English *establishen,* from Latin *stabilīre,* from *stabilis,* firm.]

SYNONYMS establish, create, found, institute These verbs mean to bring something into existence and set it in operation. *The first public high school for girls in the United States was established in 1824. Our class created a scale model of a feudal manor. Are people who hope to found a colony on Mars being realistic? The library instituted an annual book sale.*

---

es·tab·lish·ment (ĭ-**stăb′**lĭsh-mənt) *n.* **1.** The act of establishing or the condition of being established: *The new government's first priority was the establishment of peace.* **2.** An organization or institution, such as a business, hospital, or school: *Most of the town's commercial establishments contributed to the fund for the new playground.* **3.** often **Establishment** A group of people holding most of the power and influence in a government, society, or field of endeavor.

es·tate (ĭ-**stāt′**) *n.* **1.** A large piece of land, usually with a large house. **2.** Everything one owns, especially all of the property and debts left by a deceased person: *When the shopkeeper died, the family inherited a small estate.* **3.** A class of citizens, such as the nobility, the commons, or the clergy, formerly possessing distinct political rights.

es·teem (ĭ-**stēm′**) *tr.v.* **es·teemed, es·teem·ing, es·**

espadrille

WRITERS CHOOSE THEIR WORDS

Espionage was all about gadgets. Electronic listening devices, computer hacking, lock picking, cameras, photocopiers. Nothing as fancy as you see in the movies. Mrs. Flagg, the ex-KGB **espionage** teacher, always stood in the unheated classroom wearing fur-lined boots, a fur coat, hat, and scarf while the trainees shivered in damp T-shirts. Occasionally she would bang her gloved hands together and moan about the cold not doing her varicose veins any good.

—Robert Muchamore
The Recruit

teems 1. To regard with respect; value: *Judges are esteemed for their fairness and honesty.* **2.** To judge to be; regard as; consider: *Improving public transportation was esteemed the best way to deal with the parking problem.* ❖ *n.* Favorable regard; respect: *The doctor is held in high esteem.*

es·ter (ĕs′tər) *n.* Any of a large group of organic chemical compounds formed when an acid and an alcohol interact. Animal and vegetable fats and oils are esters.

Es·ther[1] (ĕs′tər) In the Bible, the Jewish queen of Persia who saved her people from massacre.

Es·ther[2] (ĕs′tər) *n.* A book of the Bible that tells the story of Esther.

es·ti·ma·ble (ĕs′tə-mə-bəl) *adj.* Worthy of or deserving high regard; admirable: *Patience, honesty, and fairness are estimable characteristics.* **—es′ti·ma·bly** *adv.*

es·ti·mate (ĕs′tə-māt′) *tr.v.* **es·ti·mat·ed, es·ti·mat·ing, es·ti·mates** To make a judgment about the approximate cost, quantity, or extent of; calculate roughly: *I estimate that 25 people will come to the party.* ❖ *n.* (ĕs′tə-mĭt) **1.** A rough calculation: *Our estimate is that we will arrive in about an hour.* **2.** A preliminary calculation of the cost of work to be undertaken: *The plumber's estimate to fix the pipe was reasonable.* [From Latin *aestimāre.*]

es·ti·ma·tion (ĕs′tə-**mā′**shən) *n.* **1.** The act or an instance of estimating: *Estimation of the storm damage took several weeks.* **2.** An opinion; a judgment: *In my estimation that is a good painting.*

es·ti·vate (ĕs′tə-vāt′) *intr.v.* **es·ti·vat·ed, es·ti·vat·ing, es·ti·vates** To be in a dormant or inactive state during a hot dry period, such as the summer months: *Some tortoises estivate in burrows.* **—es′ti·va′tion** (ĕs′tə-vā′-shən) *n.*

Es·to·ni·a (ĕ-stō′nē-ə) A country of northern Europe on the Baltic Sea north of Latvia. Tallinn is the capital.

Es·to·ni·an (ĕ-stō′nē-ən) *adj.* Relating to Estonia or its people, language, or culture. ❖ *n.* **1.** A native or inhabitant of Estonia. **2.** The language of Estonia, related to Finnish.

es·trange (ĭ-strānj′) *tr.v.* **es·tranged, es·trang·ing, es·trang·es** To cause (a person) to change from friendly or affectionate to unfriendly or indifferent: *The neighbors were estranged because of a property dispute.* **—es·trange′ment** *n.*

es·tro·gen (ĕs′trə-jən) *n.* Any of several hormones produced primarily in the ovaries of mammals. They are responsible for the development of female secondary sex characteristics and are involved in the regulation of the female reproductive cycle.

es·trous (ĕs′trəs) *adj.* Relating to estrus.

estrous cycle *n.* The recurrent set of physiological and behavioral changes that take place in a female mammal from one period of estrus to another.

es·trus (ĕs′trəs) *n.* A regularly recurring period during which female mammals, excluding humans and certain other primates, are ready to mate; heat.

es·tu·ar·y (ĕs′cho͞o-ĕr′ē) *n., pl.* **es·tu·ar·ies 1.** The wide lower course of a river where its current is met by the tides. **2.** An arm of the sea that extends inland to meet the mouth of a river.

–et *suff.* A suffix that means small: *eaglet.*

e·ta (ā′tə *or* ē′tə) *n.* The seventh letter of the Greek alphabet, written Η, η. In English it is represented as *Ē, ē.*

et al. *abbr.* An abbreviation of et alii (and others).

etc. *abbr.* An abbreviation of et cetera.

et cet·er·a (ĕt sĕt′ər-ə *or* ĕt **sĕt′**rə) And other things of the same type; and so forth. [From Latin *et cētera* : *et,* and + *cētera,* the rest.]

etch (ĕch) *v.* **etched, etch·ing, etch·es** *—tr.* **1.** To cut into (metal, glass, or other material), especially by using acid. **2.** To make (a picture or pattern) by cutting into a material. **3.** To impress or imprint clearly: *The sight of that waterfall is etched in my memory.* *—intr.* To practice the art of etching. [From Dutch *etsen,* from Old High German *ezzen,* to eat.]

etch·ing (ĕch′ĭng) *n.* **1.** The art or technique of making etched metal plates and printing pictures and designs from them. **2.** A design or picture etched on such a plate: *The artist finished the etching.* **3.** A print made from such a plate: *Several etchings hung on the wall.*

e·ter·nal (ĭ-tûr′nəl) *adj.* **1.** Having no beginning or end; existing outside of time. **2.** Continuing without interruption: *For that favor you have my eternal gratitude.* ❖ *n.* **Eternal** God. [From Middle English, from Latin *aeternus.*] **—e·ter′nal·ly** *adv.*

e·ter·ni·ty (ĭ-tûr′nĭ-tē) *n., pl.* **e·ter·ni·ties 1.** All of time without beginning or end; infinite time: *We cannot measure eternity.* **2a.** The timeless state following death. **b.** The afterlife; immortality. **3.** A very long or seemingly very long time: *It was an eternity before they opened the doors of the theater.*

–eth[1] or **–th** *suff.* A suffix that forms the archaic third person singular of the present tense of verbs: *He leadeth.*

–eth[2] *suff.* Variant of **–th.**

eth·ane (ĕth′ān′) *n.* A colorless odorless gas composed of carbon and hydrogen and having the formula C_2H_6. It occurs in natural gas and is used as a fuel and in refrigeration.

eth·a·nol (ĕth′ə-nôl′) *n.* An alcohol obtained from the fermentation of sugars and starches and also made artificially. It is found in beer, wine, and liquor and is also used as a solvent.

e·ther (ē′thər) *n.* **1.** An organic compound in which two hydrocarbon groups are linked by an oxygen atom. **2.** A colorless flammable liquid that is formed from ethanol and used as a solvent and formerly as an anesthetic. **3.** The region of space beyond the earth's atmosphere; the heavens.

e·the·re·al (ĭ-thîr′ē-əl) *adj.* **1.** Delicate; light and airy: *ethereal music.* **2.** Relating to heaven; heavenly: *Angels are ethereal beings.* **—e·the′re·al·ly** *adv.*

eth·ic (ĕth′ĭk) *n.* **1.** A set of principles of right conduct; a system of moral values. **2. ethics** *(used with a singular verb)* The branch of philosophy that deals with the general nature of morals and specific moral choices. **3. ethics** *(used with a singular or plural verb)* Standards of right behavior or conduct; moral principles: *The code of medical ethics keeps patient records confidential.* [From Middle English *etik,* from Greek *ēthikos,* ethical, from *ēthos,* character.]

eth·i·cal (ĕth′ĭ-kəl) *adj.* **1.** Conforming to accepted standards of right behavior or conduct: *It is not considered ethical for a lawyer to represent both sides in a dispute.* **2.** Relating to or dealing with ethics: *ethical standards of right and wrong.* **—eth′i·cal·ly** *adv.*

E·thi·o·pi·a (ē′thē-ō′pē-ə) A country of northeast Africa southeast of Sudan. A kingdom was established here in the first century AD. Addis Ababa is the capital.

eth·nic (ĕth′nĭk) *adj.* Relating to a group of people that have the same racial, national, religious, linguistic, or cultural background. ❖ *n.* A member of a particular ethnic group. [From Middle English *ethnic,* heathen, from Greek *ethnikos,* from *ethnos,* people, nation.] **—eth′ni·cal·ly** *adv.*

eth·nic·i·ty (ĕth-**nĭs′**ĭ-tē) *n.* The condition of belonging to a particular ethnic group.

eth·no·cen·trism (ĕth′nō-**sĕn′**trĭz′əm) *n.* Belief in the superiority of one's own ethnic group. **—eth′no·cen′tric** *adj.*

eth·nol·o·gy (ĕth-**nŏl′**ə-jē) *n.* The branch of anthropology that studies human cultures, especially their social structure, language, religion, and technology. **—eth′no·log′i·cal** (ĕth′nə-**lŏj′**ĭ-kəl) *adj.*

ă	pat	ôr	core
ā	pay	oi	boy
âr	care	ou	out
ä	father	o͝o	took
ĕ	pet	o͝or	lure
ē	be	o͞o	boot
ĭ	pit	ŭ	cut
ī	bite	ûr	urge
îr	pier	th	thin
ŏ	pot	*th*	this
ō	toe	zh	vision
ô	paw	ə	about

eth·yl (ĕth′əl) *adj.* Relating to or being a hydrocarbon unit, C_2H_5, that is present in many organic compounds, such as ethanol and ether.

ethyl alcohol *n.* Ethanol.

eth·yl·ene (ĕth′ə-lēn′) *n.* A colorless flammable gas having the formula C_2H_4. It is obtained from petroleum and natural gas and is used as a fuel, in ripening and coloring citrus fruits, and as an anesthetic.

ethylene gly·col (glī′kôl′) *n.* A poisonous, syrupy, colorless alcohol composed of carbon, hydrogen, and oxygen. It is used as an antifreeze in heating and cooling systems that use water.

e-tick·et (ē′tĭk′ĭt) *n.* A reservation, as for a seat on an airplane, that exists as an electronic record and that makes a printed ticket unnecessary.

e·ti·ol·o·gy (ē′tē-**ŏl′**ə-jē) *n., pl.* **e·ti·ol·o·gies 1.** The branch of medicine that deals with the causes of diseases. **2.** The cause or origin of a disease.

et·i·quette (ĕt′ĭ-kĕt′ *or* ĕt′ĭ-kĭt) *n.* The forms and rules of proper behavior required by custom among people: *Good etiquette requires a person to thank another for a gift or favor.*

Et·na also **Aet·na** (ĕt′nə), **Mount** An active volcano, 10,974 feet (3,345 meters) high, of eastern Sicily. Since ancient times it has been one of the world's most active volcanoes.

E·trus·can (ĭ-**trŭs′**kən) *n.* **1.** A member of an ancient people who lived in what is now west-central Italy. **2.** The extinct language of the Etruscans. **—E·trus′can** *adj.*

–ette *suff.* A suffix that means: **1.** Small: *kitchenette.* **2.** Female: *majorette.* **3.** Imitation or substitute: *leatherette.*

e·tude (ā′to͞od′) *n.* A piece of music, usually written for a solo instrument, meant to develop some point of playing technique. [From Old French *estudie*, study.]

et·y·mo·log·i·cal (ĕt′ə-mə-**lŏj′**ĭ-kəl) *adj.* Relating to etymology. **—et′y·mo·log′i·cal·ly** *adv.*

et·y·mol·o·gist (ĕt′ə-**mŏl′**ə-jĭst) *n.* A person who specializes in etymology.

et·y·mol·o·gy (ĕt′ə-**mŏl′**ə-jē) *n., pl.* **et·y·mol·o·gies 1.** The origin and development of a word as shown by its earliest use and changes in form and meaning: *Many medical terms have etymologies that go back to ancient Greek.* **2.** The study of the origin and history of words: *Etymology requires a knowledge of many languages.* [From Middle English *etimologie*, from Greek *etumologiā* : *etumon*, true sense of a word + *-logiā*, study.]

Eu The symbol for the element **europium.**

EU *abbr.* An abbreviation of European Union.

eu·ca·lyp·tus (yo͞o′kə-**lĭp′**təs) *n.* Any of numerous Australian evergreen trees that have fragrant leaves and are valued as a source of oil, gum, and wood. [From New Latin : Greek *eu-*, well + Greek *kaluptos*, covered (from *kaluptein*, to cover).]

Eu·cha·rist (yo͞o′kər-ĭst) *n.* **1.** The Christian rite commemorating Jesus's Last Supper in which bread and wine are consecrated and consumed in remembrance of Jesus's death; Communion. **2.** The consecrated bread and wine used in this rite.

Eu·clid (yo͞o′klĭd) Third century BC. Greek mathematician whose book, *Elements,* was used continuously until the 1800s. In it, he organized and systematized all that was known about geometry.

eu·gen·ics (yo͞o-**jĕn′**ĭks) *n. (used with a singular verb)* The study or practice of attempting to improve the genes of the human race as a whole by encouraging the reproduction of people considered to have desirable traits and discouraging or preventing the reproduction of people considered to have undesirable traits. **—eu·gen′ic** *adj.*

eu·gle·na (yo͞o-**glē′**nə) *n.* Any of various green one-celled water organisms that move by means of flagella and produce their own food through photosynthesis.

eu·kar·y·ote (yo͞o-**kăr′**ē-ōt) *n.* Any of numerous organisms whose cells contain a nucleus surrounded by a membrane. All organisms except bacteria and archaea are eukaryotes. **—eu·kar′y·ot′ic** (yo͞o-kăr′ē-**ŏt′**ĭk) *adj.*

eu·lo·gize (yo͞o′lə-jīz′) *tr.v.* **eu·lo·gized, eu·lo·giz·ing, eu·lo·giz·es** To praise highly in speech or writing, especially in a formal eulogy. **—eu′lo·gist** (yo͞o′lə-jĭst) *n.*

eu·lo·gy (yo͞o′lə-jē) *n., pl.* **eu·lo·gies** A speech or piece of writing praising a person or thing, especially a person who has just died: *A lifelong friend delivered the eulogy at the memorial service.* [From Middle English *euloge*, from Greek *eulogiā*, praise : *eu-*, well + *-logiā*, speaking.]

eu·nuch (yo͞o′nək) *n.* A castrated man, especially one who was traditionally employed as a household attendant in certain Asian courts.

eu·phe·mism (yo͞o′fə-mĭz′əm) *n.* An inoffensive or indirect word or expression substituted for one considered harsh, blunt, or offensive; for example, *pass away* is a euphemism for *die.* [From Greek *euphēmismos* : *eu-*, good + *phēmē*, speech.] **—eu′phe·mis′tic** (yo͞o′fə-**mĭs′**tĭk) *adj.*

eu·pho·ni·ous (yo͞o-**fō′**nē-əs) *adj.* Pleasing in sound; agreeable to the ear. **—eu·pho′ni·ous·ly** *adv.*

eu·pho·ni·um (yo͞o-**fō′**nē-əm) *n.* A brass musical instrument that looks like a tuba but has a mellower and higher sound.

eu·pho·ny (yo͞o′fə-nē) *n., pl.* **eu·pho·nies** Agreeable sound, especially in the use of words.

eu·pho·ri·a (yo͞o-**fôr′**ē-ə) *n.* A feeling of happiness and well-being: *After peace was declared, the whole country was in a state of euphoria.*

Eu·phra·tes (yo͞o-**frā′**tēz) A river of southwest Asia flowing about 1,740 miles (2,800 kilometers) from central Turkey through Syria and into Iraq. It was a major source of water for ancient Mesopotamia.

Eur·a·sia (yo͞o-**rā′**zhə) The landmass made up of the continents of Europe and Asia.

Eur·a·sian (yo͞o-**rā′**zhən) *adj.* **1.** Relating to Eurasia. **2.** Of mixed European and Asian ancestry. ❖ *n.* **1.** A native or inhabitant of Eurasia. **2.** A person of mixed European and Asian ancestry.

eu·re·ka (yo͞o-**rē′**kə) *interj.* An expression used to express triumph upon discovering something or finding a solution to a problem. [From Greek *heurēka*, I have found (it) (supposedly exclaimed by Archimedes upon discovering the principle of buoyancy), from *heuriskein*, to find.]

eu·ro or **Eu·ro** (yo͝or′ō) *n., pl.* **euro** or **eu·ros** The basic monetary unit of most of the members of the European Union and several nearby nonmember states.

Eu·ro-A·mer·i·can (yo͝or′ō-ə-**mĕr′**ĭ-kən) *n.* An American of European ancestry. **—Eu′ro-A·mer′i·can** *adj.*

Eu·ro·cen·tric (yo͝or′ō-**sĕn′**trĭk) *adj.* Centered or focused on Europe or European peoples.

Eu·rope (yo͝or′əp) The second-smallest continent, extending west from Asia to the Atlantic Ocean. It is separated from Asia by the Ural Mountains, the Caspian Sea, the Caucasus Mountains, the Black Sea, the Dardanelles, and the Aegean Sea.

Eu·ro·pe·an (yo͝or′ə-**pē′**ən) *n.* **1.** A native or inhabitant of Europe. **2.** A person of European descent. ❖ *adj.* Relating to Europe or its peoples, languages, or cultures.

European Union *n.* An economic and political union established in 1993 by most of the countries of western Europe and since expanded to include numerous central and eastern European nations. The nations of the European Union cooperate on matters pertaining to commerce and security and have mostly adopted a common currency, the euro.

eu·ro·pi·um (yo͞o-**rō′**pē-əm) *n. Symbol* **Eu** A soft, silvery-white metallic element used in making color tele-

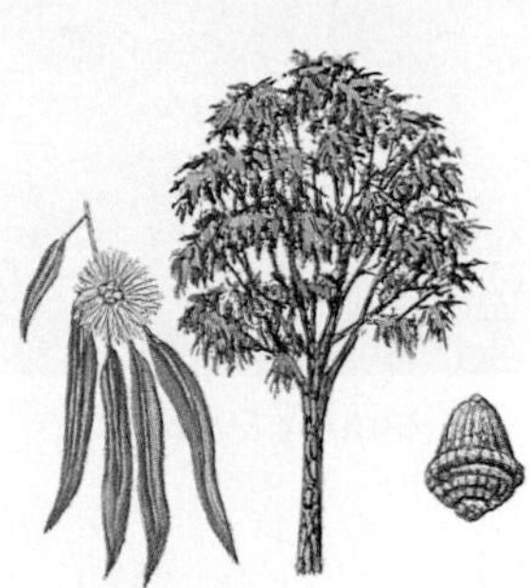

eucalyptus

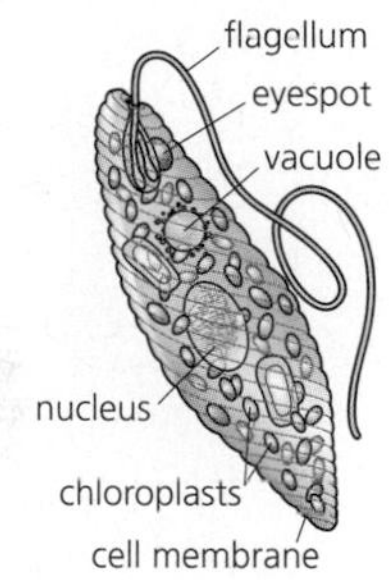

euglena

Mount Everest

vision tubes and lasers and in scientific research. Atomic number 63. See **Periodic Table.**

Eu·ryd·i·ce (yo͝o-**rĭd′**ĭ-sē) *n.* In Greek mythology, the wife of Orpheus, whom he almost rescued from the underworld.

eu·sta·chian tube or **Eu·sta·chian tube** (yo͞o-**stā′**shən *or* yo͞o-**stā′**shē-ən) *n.* The narrow tube that connects the middle ear and the pharynx and serves to equalize air pressure on the two sides of the eardrum. [After Bartolomeo *Eustachio* (1514–1574), Italian anatomist.]

eu·tha·na·sia (yo͞o′thə-**nā′**zhə) *n.* The intentional ending of the life of a person or a domestic animal that is suffering from an incurable illness or has a medical condition that causes unbearable pain.

e·vac·u·ate (ĭ-**văk′**yo͞o-āt′) *v.* **e·vac·u·at·ed, e·vac·u·at·ing, e·vac·u·ates** —*tr.* **1.** To send away or remove (people) from an area: *evacuate a neighborhood threatened by toxic fumes.* **2.** To withdraw or depart from; vacate: *The firefighters quickly evacuated the burning building.* **3.** To discharge waste matter from: *evacuated his bowels.* —*intr.* To withdraw or depart from a place or area, especially as a protective measure: *Residents were ordered to evacuate because of the flood.* [From Latin *ēvacuāre* : *ē-*, *ex-*, out + *vacuus*, empty.]

e·vac·u·a·tion (ĭ-văk′yo͞o-**ā′**shən) *n.* **1.** The act of evacuating or the condition of being evacuated: *The evacuation of children was begun at the first sign of danger.* **2.** Discharge of waste materials from the body, especially from the bowels.

e·vac·u·ee (ĭ-văk′yo͞o-**ē′**) *n.* A person who has been evacuated from a dangerous area.

e·vade (ĭ-**vād′**) *tr.v.* **e·vad·ed, e·vad·ing, e·vades 1.** To escape or avoid, as by cleverness or deceit: *evade arrest.* **2.** To avoid the fulfillment or performance of: *By blaming the source of the information, the reporter evaded responsibility for the mistake.* **3.** To avoid giving a direct answer to: *The mayor evaded the question by talking about something else.* [From Latin *ēvādere* : *ē-*, *ex-*, out, away + *vādere*, to go.]

e·val·u·ate (ĭ-**văl′**yo͞o-āt′) *tr.v.* **e·val·u·at·ed, e·val·u·at·ing, e·val·u·ates 1.** To find out or estimate the value or worth of; examine and appraise: *evaluate a course of action; evaluate paintings for sale.* **2.** To find the numerical value of (an algebraic expression). **—e·val′u·a′tion** *n.*

ev·a·nes·cent (ĕv′ə-**nĕs′**ənt) *adj.* Tending to vanish or last only a short time: *the rainbow's evanescent beauty.* **—ev′a·nes′cence** *n.* **—ev′a·nes′cent·ly** *adv.*

e·van·gel·i·cal (ē′văn-**jĕl′**ĭ-kəl) also **e·van·gel·ic** (ē′-văn-**jĕl′**ĭk) *adj.* **1.** Relating to or in accordance with the Christian gospel, especially the four Gospels of the New Testament. **2. Evangelical** Relating to or being a Protestant group that stresses belief solely in the authority of the Bible and salvation through faith in Jesus. **3.** Ardently advocating something: *an evangelical vegan.* ❖ *n.* **Evangelical** A member of an evangelical church. **—e′van·gel′i·cal·ly** *adv.*

e·van·gel·ism (ĭ-**văn′**jə-lĭz′əm) *n.* **1.** The practice of preaching and spreading the gospel, as through missionary work. **2.** Ardent advocacy of a cause. **—e·van′gel·is′tic** (ĭ-văn′jə-**lĭs′**tĭk) *adj.*

e·van·gel·ist (ĭ-**văn′**jə-lĭst) *n.* **1.** often **Evangelist** Any of the authors of the New Testament Gospels: Matthew, Mark, Luke, or John. **2.** A person who practices evangelism, especially a Protestant preacher or missionary. **3.** One who promotes something enthusiastically. [From Middle English, from Greek *euangelion*, good news : *eu-*, good + *angelos*, messenger.]

e·van·gel·ize (ĭ-**văn′**jə-līz′) *v.* **e·van·gel·ized, e·van·gel·iz·ing, e·van·gel·iz·es** —*tr.* **1.** To convert or try to convert (someone) to Christianity. **2.** To promote (a doctrine or idea, for example) enthusiastically. —*intr.* **1.** To preach the gospel. **2.** To promote something enthusiastically.

Ev·ans (**ĕv′**ənz), **Mary Ann** See George **Eliot.**

e·vap·o·rate (ĭ-**văp′**ə-rāt′) *v.* **e·vap·o·rat·ed, e·vap·o·rat·ing, e·vap·o·rates** —*tr.* **1.** To cause to change from a liquid into a vapor, especially without boiling: *The sun evaporates water from the ocean.* **2.** To extract water or other liquid from: *evaporate milk.* —*intr.* **1.** To change from a liquid into a vapor: *The dew evaporated as the sun came up.* **2.** To disappear; vanish; fade: *My fear evaporated as the airplane took off.* See Synonyms at **disappear. —e·vap′o·ra′tion** *n.*

e·vap·o·rat·ed milk (ĭ-**văp′**ə-rā′tĭd) *n.* Unsweetened milk that has been slightly thickened by evaporation of some of the water in it.

e·va·sion (ĭ-**vā′**zhən) *n.* **1.** The act or an instance of evading: *His evasion of paying taxes led to his imprisonment.* **2.** A means of evading; an excuse: *Every evasion we tried to avoid the test was unsuccessful.*

e·va·sive (ĭ-**vā′**sĭv) *adj.* **1.** Tending or intended to evade: *The submarine took evasive action to elude its pursuers.* **2.** Intentionally misleading or ambiguous: *the candidate's evasive answers to her questions.* **—e·va′sive·ly** *adv.* **—e·va′sive·ness** *n.*

eve (ēv) *n.* **1.** The evening or day preceding a special day, such as a holiday. **2.** The period immediately preceding a certain event: *the eve of war.* **3.** Evening. Used chiefly in poetry.

Eve (ēv) In the Bible, the first woman and the wife of Adam.

e·ven[1] (**ē′**vən) *adj.* **1a.** Having a horizontal surface; flat: *The even lawn is good for playing croquet.* **b.** Having no roughness, dents, or bumps; smooth: *an even board.* **c.** Being in the same plane or line; parallel: *Is your writing even with the top of the page?* **2.** Having no variation; uniform: *an even speed.* **3.** Calm; peaceful: *an even temper.* **4a.** Equally matched: *an even fight.* **b.** Equal in degree, extent or amount: *even portions of a meal.* **5.** Exactly divisible by 2: *6, 20, and −478 are even numbers.* **6.** Having equal probability: *Our team has an even chance of winning.* **7a.** Having an equal score: *The teams are even.* **b.** Being equal for each opponent: *an even score.* **8.** Having nothing due: *Pay me one dollar, and we are even.* **9.** Having an exact amount, extent, or number: *an even pound.* ❖ *adv.* **1.** To a higher or greater degree; yet; still: *an even better idea.* **2.** At the same time as; just: *Even as we watched, the tree fell.* **3.** Indeed; moreover: *She was relieved, even happy, to see us.* **4.** Used to emphasize something that is unexpected: *He refused even to consider our idea.* ❖ *tr.v.* **e·vened, e·ven·ing, e·vens** To make even: *even out a garden with a rake.* ◆ **on an even keel** In a stable or unimpaired state: *The new contract put the relationship between the company and its workers on an even keel.* [From Old English *efen.*] **—e′ven·ly** *adv.* **—e′ven·ness** *n.*

e·ven[2] (**ē′**vən) *n. Archaic* Evening. [From Old English *ǣfen.*]

e·ven·hand·ed (ē′vən-**hăn′**dĭd) *adj.* Dealing fairly with all; impartial.

eve·ning (**ēv′**nĭng) *n.* **1.** The period of decreasing daylight between afternoon and night: *At evening the moon rose over the lake.* **2.** The period between sunset and bedtime: *We spent a quiet evening at home.* **3.** A later period or time: *in the evening of life.*

evening gown *n.* A woman's formal dress, usually reaching to the floor or close to it.

evening star *n.* A planet, especially Venus, that shines brightly in the western sky shortly after sunset.

e·ven·song (**ē′**vən-sông′) *n.* **1.** A daily evening service in the Anglican Church. **2.** A song sung in the evening.

e·vent (ĭ-**vĕnt′**) *n.* **1.** An occurrence, incident, or experience, especially one of significance: *A trip to Brazil was*

ă	pat	ôr	core
ā	pay	oi	boy
âr	care	ou	out
ä	father	o͝o	took
ĕ	pet	o͝or	lure
ē	be	o͞o	boot
ĭ	pit	ŭ	cut
ī	bite	ûr	urge
îr	pier	th	thin
ŏ	pot	*th*	this
ō	toe	zh	vision
ô	paw	ə	about

the great event of her adolescence. **2.** A social gathering or activity: *a fundraising event.* **3.** An item in a program of sports: *I like to watch the jumping events at a horse show.* ◆ **in any event** In any case; anyhow. **in the event** If it should happen; in case: *In the event of the president's death, the vice president takes over.* [From Latin *ēventus,* from past participle of *ēvenīre,* to happen : *ē-, ex-,* out + *venīre,* to come.] —SEE NOTE AT **intervene.**

e·vent·ful (ĭ-**vĕnt′**fəl) *adj.* **1.** Full of events: *an eventful afternoon.* **2.** Important; momentous: *an eventful decision to change jobs.* **—e·vent′ful·ly** *adv.*

e·ven·tide (**ē′**vən-tīd′) *n.* Evening. Used chiefly in poetry.

e·ven·tu·al (ĭ-**vĕn′**cho͞o-əl) *adj.* Occurring at an unspecified future time; ultimate: *We never lost hope of eventual victory.* **—e·ven′tu·al·ly** *adv.*

e·ven·tu·al·i·ty (ĭ-vĕn′cho͞o-**ăl′**ĭ-tē) *n., pl.* **e·ven·tu·al·i·ties** Something that may occur; a possibility: *One prepares for the worst eventuality and hopes for the best outcome.*

ev·er (**ĕv′**ər) *adv.* **1.** At all times; always: *They lived happily ever after.* **2.** At any time: *Have you ever visited Miami?* **3.** By any chance; in any possible case or way: *How could they ever have thought they would get away with that?* **4.** To a great extent or degree. Used for emphasis often with *so: She's ever so sorry.*

Ev·er·est (**ĕv′**ər-ĭst *or* **ĕv′**rĭst), **Mount** A mountain, 29,029 feet (8,848 meters) high, of the central Himalaya Mountains on the border of Tibet and Nepal. It is the highest elevation in the world.

ev·er·glade (**ĕv′**ər-glād′) *n.* A large area of marshland, usually underwater with tall grass growing in places.

Ev·er·glades (**ĕv′**ər-glādz′) A wetland area of southern Florida including **Everglades National Park.** It is noted for its wildlife.

ev·er·green (**ĕv′**ər-grēn′) *adj.* Having leaves that remain green all year: *spruces and other evergreen trees.* ❖ *n.* An evergreen plant: *a nursery that sells evergreens.*

ev·er·last·ing (ĕv′ər-**lăs′**tĭng) *adj.* **1.** Lasting forever; eternal. **2.** Continuing for a long time: *everlasting happiness.* **3.** Lasting too long; wearisome: *everlasting work.* **—ev′er·last′ing·ly** *adv.*

ev·er·more (ĕv′ər-**môr′**) *adv.* Forever; always.

eve·ry (**ĕv′**rē) *adj.* **1.** Each and all without exception: *every student in the class.* **2.** Each in a specified series or at specific intervals: *every third seat; every two hours.* **3.** Being the highest degree or expression of: *I have every confidence they will succeed.* ◆ **every bit** *Informal* In all ways; equally: *every bit as clever as we thought.* **every now and then** or **every now and again** From time to time; occasionally: *The whole family goes camping every now and then.* **every other** Each alternate: *every other seat.* **every so often** At intervals; occasionally: *We exchange letters every so often.* [From Middle English *everi, everich,* from Old English *ǣfre ǣlc,* every one : *ǣfre,* ever, always + *ǣlc,* each.]

eve·ry·bod·y (**ĕv′**rē-bŏd′ē *or* **ĕv′**rē-bŭd′ē) *pron.* Every person; everyone.

eve·ry·day (ĕv′rē-**dā′**) *adj.* **1.** Suitable for ordinary days or occasions: *everyday clothes.* **2.** Ordinary; usual: *an everyday event.*

eve·ry·one (**ĕv′**rē-wŭn′) *pron.* Every person; everybody: *Everyone has bought a ticket.*

eve·ry·thing (**ĕv′**rē-thĭng′) *pron.* **1.** All things or all of a group of things: *Everything in this room must be packed.* **2.** The most important fact or consideration: *When telling a joke, timing is everything.*

eve·ry·where (**ĕv′**rē-wâr′) *adv.* In any or every place; in all places: *People were celebrating the news everywhere in town.*

e·vict (ĭ-**vĭkt′**) *tr.v.* **e·vict·ed, e·vict·ing, e·victs** To put out (a tenant) by legal process; expel: *The landlord evicted the man who was living in that apartment for failure to pay rent.* [From Middle English *evicten,* from Latin *ēvincere,* to vanquish : *ē-, ex-,* intensive prefix + *vincere,* to defeat.] **—e·vic′tion** *n.*

ev·i·dence (**ĕv′**ĭ-dəns) *n.* **1.** A thing or things helpful in making a judgment or coming to a conclusion: *The fossils of seashells were evidence that the region had once been covered by water.* **2.** The statements, objects, and facts accepted for consideration in a court of law: *The evidence was not clear enough to convince the jury that the defendant was guilty.* **3.** Something that indicates; a sign: *Constant laughter was evidence that the show was very funny.* ❖ *tr.v.* **ev·i·denced, ev·i·denc·ing, ev·i·denc·es** To indicate clearly; prove: *Cheers and applause evidenced the audience's approval.* ◆ **in evidence** Plainly visible; to be seen: *The welcome signs were much in evidence among the crowd at the airport.*

ev·i·dent (**ĕv′**ĭ-dənt) *adj.* Easily seen or understood; clear; plain: *From the warm temperature and abundant flowers, it is evident that spring is here.* [From Middle English, from Latin *ēvidēns* : *ē-, ex-,* out + *vidēns,* present participle of *vidēre,* to see.]

ev·i·dent·ly (**ĕv′**ĭ-dənt-lē *or* ĕv′ĭ-**dĕnt′**lē) *adv.* Plainly; clearly: *They evidently did not practice enough and played poorly.*

e·vil (**ē′**vəl) *adj.* **e·vil·er, e·vil·est 1.** Morally bad or wrong; wicked: *evil deeds.* **2.** Causing pain or injury; harmful: *an evil temper; an evil tongue.* **3.** Indicating misfortune: *evil signs.* ❖ *n.* **1.** The quality of being morally bad or wrong; wickedness: *a story about good and evil.* **2.** Something that causes harm: *the social evil of poverty.* [From Old English *yfel.*] **—e′vil·ly** *adv.* **—e′vil·ness** *n.*

e·vil·do·er (**ē′**vəl-do͞o′ər) *n.* A person who does evil things.

evil eye *n.* A gaze or stare believed to cause injury or misfortune.

e·vince (ĭ-**vĭns′**) *tr.v.* **e·vinced, e·vinc·ing, e·vinc·es** To show or demonstrate clearly; exhibit: *The lawyer evinced surprise at the witness's statement.*

e·vis·cer·ate (ĭ-**vĭs′**ə-rāt′) *tr.v.* **e·vis·cer·at·ed, e·vis·cer·at·ing, e·vis·cer·ates 1.** To remove the intestines or other internal organs of. **2.** To take away a vital or essential part of: *Leaving out the facts and figures eviscerated the report.* **—e·vis′cer·a′tion** *n.*

ev·o·ca·tion (ĕv′ə-**kā′**shən *or* ē′və-**kā′**shən) *n.* The act of calling forth: *the evocation of a pleasant memory.*

e·voc·a·tive (ĭ-**vŏk′**ə-tĭv) *adj.* Tending to evoke: *The walk in the woods was evocative of the hikes I took in my childhood.*

e·voke (ĭ-**vōk′**) *tr.v.* **e·voked, e·vok·ing, e·vokes 1.** To summon or call forth; inspire: *The question evoked a complicated reply.* **2.** To call to mind by naming or suggesting: *a song that evokes memories.* [From Latin *ēvocāre* : *ē-, ex-,* out, forth + *vocāre,* to call.]

ev·o·lu·tion (ĕv′ə-**lo͞o′**shən) *n.* **1.** A gradual process by which something changes into a different form: *the evolution of jazz from ragtime to bop.* **2.** Change in the genes of a group of organisms over many generations, so that descendants are different from their ancestors and may develop into a new species. Evolution is caused by natural selection and certain other factors, such as mutation. **3.** The historical development of a related group of organisms: *the evolution of horses.* [From Latin *ēvolūtiō,* from *ēvolvere,* to unroll, evolve.] **—ev′o·lu′tion·ar′y** (ĕv′ə-**lo͞o′**shə-nĕr′ē) *adj.* —SEE NOTE.

e·volve (ĭ-**vŏlv′**) *v.* **e·volved, e·volv·ing, e·volves** *—tr.* **1.** To develop or achieve gradually: *The committee evolved a plan for a new civic center.* **2.** To develop (a characteristic) by biological evolution: *Many bacteria have evolved resistance to antibiotics.* *—intr.* **1.** To undergo biological evolution: *Biologists believe that whales evolved from mammals that lived on land.* **2.** To

evergreen

SCIENCE

evolution Before Charles Darwin developed the theory of **evolution** by natural selection, other naturalists, including Darwin's grandfather Erasmus Darwin, had suggested that organisms might slowly change over long periods of time. But how did that change come about, and how did plants and animals come to be so exquisitely adapted to their environments? Darwin came up with the idea of *natural selection* at about the same time as another naturalist, Alfred Russel Wallace. Both of them realized that if an organism had many offspring that differed slightly from each other, and those offspring that had certain heritable characteristics survived and reproduced more than the others did, then little by little, as each generation differed from the previous one, huge changes could occur over millions of years.

ewer
16th-century ewer by Wenzel Jamnitzer (1507–1585)

WORD BUILDING

ex– In cases where the prefix **ex–** doesn't mean "former," it is usually part of a word of Latin origin and has the meaning "out of, from." Thus combining *ex–* with the Latin verb *tendere,* "to stretch," gives us *extend,* "to stretch out." Similarly, in *express,* it combines with the root *press–,* which comes from the Latin verb *premere,* "to squeeze." Words that use the Latin *ex–* this way usually drop the *x* if the root begins with *b, d, f, g, j, l, m, n,* or *r,* as in *educate, eject, emit,* and *erode.*

ă	pat	ôr	core
ā	pay	oi	boy
âr	care	ou	out
ä	father	ŏŏ	took
ĕ	pet	ŏŏr	lure
ē	be	ōō	boot
ĭ	pit	ŭ	cut
ī	bite	ûr	urge
îr	pier	th	thin
ŏ	pot	*th*	this
ō	toe	zh	vision
ô	paw	ə	about

undergo change or development: *a small company that has evolved into a huge corporation; a bud evolving into a flower.* [From Latin *ēvolvere,* to unroll : *ē-, ex-,* out + *volvere,* to roll.]

ewe (yōō) *n.* A full-grown female sheep. [From Old English *ēowu.*]

❑ *These sound alike:* **ewe, yew** (shrub), **you** (pronoun).

ew·er (yōō′ər) *n.* A large, wide-mouthed pitcher or jug.

ex. *abbr.* An abbreviation of example.

ex– *pref.* A prefix that means former: *ex-president.* —SEE NOTE.

ex·ac·er·bate (ĭg-zăs′ər-bāt′) *tr.v.* **ex·ac·er·bat·ed, ex·ac·er·bat·ing, ex·ac·er·bates** To make worse or more severe; aggravate: *The rumor exacerbated tensions between groups.* —**ex·ac′er·ba′tion** *n.*

ex·act (ĭg-zăkt′) *adj.* **1.** Fully in agreement with fact or an original: *a person's exact words; an exact duplicate.* **2.** Characterized by accurate measurement: *An exact reading of these instruments is necessary in this experiment.* ❖ *tr.v.* **ex·act·ed, ex·act·ing, ex·acts 1.** To force the payment of: *The king exacted new taxes from the people.* **2.** To require or demand, especially by force or authority: *The teacher exacts strict discipline in class.* [From Latin *exāctus,* past participle of *exigere,* to weigh out, demand : *ex-,* out + *agere,* to weigh.] —**ex·act′ness** *n.* —SEE NOTE AT **react.**

ex·act·ing (ĭg-zăk′tĭng) *adj.* **1.** Making great demands: *I learn the most from an exacting teacher.* **2.** Requiring great effort, attention, or care: *A medical operation is an exacting procedure.* —**ex·act′ing·ly** *adv.*

ex·ac·tion (ĭg-zăk′shən) *n.* **1.** The act of exacting or demanding. **2.** Something exacted or demanded, as a tax considered to be excessive.

ex·ac·ti·tude (ĭg-zăk′tĭ-tōōd) *n.* The quality or condition of being exact; exactness.

ex·act·ly (ĭg-zăkt′lē) *adv.* **1.** In an exact manner; precisely: *The cake did not rise because I failed to follow the recipe exactly.* **2.** In all respects; just: *Do exactly as you see fit.* **3.** As you say. Used to indicate agreement: *"Exactly," he replied. "I feel the same way."*

ex·ag·ger·ate (ĭg-zăj′ə-rāt′) *v.* **ex·ag·ger·at·ed, ex·ag·ger·at·ing, ex·ag·ger·ates** —*tr.* To consider, represent, or cause to appear as larger, more important, or more extreme than is actually the case; overstate: *exaggerated his own role in the incident; exaggerated the size of the enemy force; exaggerated how difficult the project would be.* —*intr.* To make overstatements: *It's important not to exaggerate when writing stories for a newspaper.* —**ex·ag′ger·a′tion** *n.*

ex·alt (ĭg-zôlt′) *tr.v.* **ex·alt·ed, ex·alt·ing, ex·alts 1.** To raise in position, status, rank, or regard; elevate: *The emperor exalted the faithful servant to a place among his most trusted advisors.* **2.** To praise; honor; glorify. —**ex′al·ta′tion** (ĕg′zôl-tā′shən) *n.*

ex·alt·ed (ĭg-zôl′tĭd) *adj.* **1.** Having high rank or status; dignified: *The emperor is an exalted personage.* **2.** Elevated as in style or condition; lofty; noble: *the exalted style of epic poetry.*

ex·am (ĭg-zăm′) *n.* An examination; a test.

ex·am·i·na·tion (ĭg-zăm′ə-nā′shən) *n.* **1.** The act of examining or the state of being examined: *Close examination of the diamond showed it was a fake.* **2.** A set of questions or exercises testing knowledge or skill; a test. **3.** A formal interrogation: *the lawyer's examination of the witness in a trial.*

ex·am·ine (ĭg-zăm′ĭn) *tr.v.* **ex·am·ined, ex·am·in·ing, ex·am·ines 1.** To observe carefully; inspect or study: *She examined the plant cells under a microscope.* **2.** To test or check the condition or health of: *The doctor examined the patient.* **3.** To determine the qualifications, aptitude, or skills of (someone) by means of questions or exercises: *examined the job candidates in interviews.* See Synonyms at **ask. 4.** To interrogate or question formally to obtain information or facts: *The prosecutor examined the witness.* [From Middle English *examinen,* from Latin *exāmināre,* from *exāmen,* a weighing out, from *exigere,* to weigh out.] —**ex·am′in·er** *n.*

ex·am·ple (ĭg-zăm′pəl) *n.* **1.** A person or thing that is typical of a whole class or group; a sample or specimen: *The Empire State Building is an example of a graceful skyscraper.* **2.** A person or thing that is worthy of imitation; a model: *This article is an example of good writing.* **3.** A person or thing that is intended to serve as a warning to others: *The court made an example of the fraudulent dealer by imposing heavy fines on him.* **4.** A problem or exercise worked out to illustrate a principle or method: *an example of multiplication; an example of the form of a composition.* ◆ **for example** As an illustration; for instance: *We have several team sports, for example, baseball and soccer.*

ex·as·per·ate (ĭg-zăs′pə-rāt′) *tr.v.* **ex·as·per·at·ed, ex·as·per·at·ing, ex·as·per·ates** To make angry or impatient; irritate greatly: *The dog's constant barking exasperated the neighbors.* —**ex·as′per·a′tion** (ĭg-zăs′pə-rā′shən) *n.*

Ex·cal·i·bur (ĕk-skăl′ə-bər) *n.* In Arthurian legend, the sword of King Arthur.

ex·ca·vate (ĕk′skə-vāt′) *tr.v.* **ex·ca·vat·ed, ex·ca·vat·ing, ex·ca·vates 1.** To make a hole in; hollow out: *excavate a hillside to build a tunnel.* **2.** To form by digging out: *excavate the foundation for a house.* **3.** To remove by digging or scooping out: *The bulldozer excavated ten truckloads of earth.* **4.** To expose or uncover by or as if by digging: *excavated the remains of an ancient settlement.* [From Latin *excavāre,* to hollow out : *ex-,* out + *cavus,* hollow.]

ex·ca·va·tion (ĕk′skə-vā′shən) *n.* **1.** The act or process of excavating: *Excavation of the basement is to begin soon.* **2.** A hole formed by excavation: *a deep excavation for the new skyscraper.*

ex·ca·va·tor (ĕk′skə-vā′tər) *n.* A person or thing that excavates, especially a backhoe.

ex·ceed (ĭk-sēd′) *tr.v.* **ex·ceed·ed, ex·ceed·ing, ex·ceeds 1.** To be greater than; surpass: *The results exceeded everyone's hopes.* **2.** To go beyond the limits of: *Do not exceed the speed limit.*

ex·ceed·ing (ĭk-sē′dĭng) *adj.* Extreme; extraordinary: *a night of exceeding darkness.*

ex·ceed·ing·ly (ĭk-sē′dĭng-lē) *adv.* To an advanced or unusual degree; extremely: *exceedingly hot weather; exceedingly delicate work.*

ex·cel (ĭk-sĕl′) *v.* **ex·celled, ex·cel·ling, ex·cels** —*tr.* To do or be better than; surpass: *Their performance excelled all the others.* —*intr.* To be better than others: *Few people excel at every sport.*

ex·cel·lence (ĕk′sə-ləns) *n.* The condition or quality of excelling; superiority: *artistic excellence; a prize given for excellence in writing.*

Ex·cel·len·cy (ĕk′sə-lən-sē) *n., pl.* **Ex·cel·len·cies** Used as a title and form of address for certain high officials, such as ambassadors, viceroys, or bishops: *Your Excellency.*

ex·cel·lent (ĕk′sə-lənt) *adj.* Of the highest or finest quality; superb: *an excellent report; an excellent book.* —**ex′cel·lent·ly** *adv.*

ex·cept (ĭk-sĕpt′) *prep.* With the exclusion of; but: *All the rooms except one are clean. Everybody went to the movies except for me.* ❖ *conj.* **1.** If it were not for the fact that; only: *I could babysit except that I have to study.* **2.** Otherwise than: *He would not open his mouth except to argue.* ❖ *tr.v.* **ex·cept·ed, ex·cept·ing, ex·cepts** To leave out; exclude: *I had helped earlier and was excepted from staying to clean up.* ◆ **except for** Were it not for:

I would go to the store except for the rain. [From Middle English, from Latin *exceptus*, past participle of *excipere*, to exclude : *ex-*, out + *capere*, to hold.]

ex·cept·ing (ĭk-sĕp′tĭng) *prep.* With the exception of: *No one excepting our father wanted to go fishing in the rain.*

ex·cep·tion (ĭk-sĕp′shən) *n.* **1.** The act of excepting or the condition of being excepted: *All our guests have arrived with the exception of two.* **2.** A person or thing that is excepted: *I like all my classes with one exception. Certain exceptions to the rule will be considered.* **3.** An objection or criticism: *opinions that are open to exception.*

ex·cep·tion·a·ble (ĭk-sĕp′shə-nə-bəl) *adj.* Open or liable to objection or disapproval: *an exceptionable description of their opponents.*

ex·cep·tion·al (ĭk-sĕp′shə-nəl) *adj.* **1.** Being an exception; uncommon: *The speaker discussed the topic with exceptional frankness.* **2.** Well above average; extraordinary: *an exceptional memory.* **—ex·cep′tion·al·ly** *adv.*

ex·cerpt (ĕk′sûrpt′) *n.* A passage or scene selected from a longer work, such as a book, film, or piece of music. ❖ *tr.v.* (ĭk-sûrpt′) **ex·cerpt·ed, ex·cerpt·ing, ex·cerpts** To select or use (a passage or segment from a longer work): *The author excerpted parts of several famous speeches.*

ex·cess (ĭk-sĕs′ *or* ĕk′sĕs′) *n.* **1.** The state of exceeding what is normal or sufficient: *filled my glass to excess.* **2.** An amount or quantity beyond what is normal or sufficient; a surplus. **3.** The amount or degree by which one quantity exceeds another: *an excess of four pounds.* ❖ *adj.* Being more than what is usual, permitted, or required: *Skim off the excess fat.* ◆ **in excess of** Greater than; more than: *a package weighing in excess of 40 pounds.*

ex·ces·sive (ĭk-sĕs′ĭv) *adj.* Exceeding a normal, usual, reasonable, or proper limit: *Excessive rains cause flooding.* **—ex·ces′sive·ly** *adv.* **—ex·ces′sive·ness** *n.*

ex·change (ĭks-chānj′) *tr.v.* **ex·changed, ex·chang·ing, ex·chang·es 1.** To give in return for something received: *I exchanged my pesos for dollars. He exchanged labor for a room to sleep in.* **2.** To give and receive mutually; interchange: *exchange gifts; exchange ideas.* **3.** To give up for a substitute: *She exchanged her job as a professor for a position in the government.* **4.** To turn in for replacement: *exchanged the tie for a belt at the store.* ❖ *n.* **1.** An act or an instance of exchanging: *an exchange of gifts; an exchange of ideas.* **2.** A person or thing that is exchanged: *The watch seemed a fair exchange for the compass.* **3.** A place where things, especially stocks or commodities, are exchanged or traded: *a commodities exchange.* **—ex·change′a·ble** *adj.* **—ex·chang′er** *n.*

exchange rate *n.* A rate of exchange.

exchange student *n.* A high school or college student taking part in a program of arranged exchanges between a local and a foreign institution or group.

ex·cheq·uer (ĕks′chĕk′ər *or* ĭks-chĕk′ər) *n.* **1. Exchequer** The department of the British government in charge of the national revenue. **2.** A treasury, as of a nation or organization.

ex·cise[1] (ĕk′sīz′) *n.* An excise tax. [From Middle Dutch *accijs*, tax, possibly from Latin *cēnsus*, tax.]

ex·cise[2] (ĭk-sīz′) *tr.v.* **ex·cised, ex·cis·ing, ex·cis·es** To remove by or as if by cutting: *excised two scenes from the movie.* [From Latin *excīdere* : *ex-*, out + *caedere*, to cut.] **—ex·ci′sion** (ĭk-sĭzh′ən) *n.*

ex·cise tax (ĕk′sīz′) *n.* A tax on production, sale, or use of certain items or services within a country.

ex·cit·a·ble (ĭk-sī′tə-bəl) *adj.* Easily excited: *a jumpy and excitable cat.* **—ex·cit′a·bil′i·ty, ex·cit′a·ble·ness** *n.* **—ex·cit′a·bly** *adv.*

ex·ci·ta·tion (ĕk′sī-tā′shən) *n.* The act of exciting or the condition of being excited.

ex·cite (ĭk-sīt′) *tr.v.* **ex·cit·ed, ex·cit·ing, ex·cites 1.** To arouse strong feeling in: *The charismatic speaker excited the audience.* **2.** To call forth (a reaction or emotion, for example); elicit: *The news report excited our curiosity.* **3.** To cause to become more active: *Lowering interest rates should excite the market for housing.* **4.** To produce increased activity or response in (an organ or other body part): *The vaccine excites the immune system to produce antibodies against the disease.* **5.** To increase the energy of (an electron, atom, or molecule). [From Middle English *exciten*, from Latin *excitāre*.]

ex·cit·ed (ĭk-sī′tĭd) *adj.* Emotionally aroused; stirred: *The astronomers were very excited about their discovery of a new star.* **—ex·cit′ed·ly** *adv.*

ex·cite·ment (ĭk-sīt′mənt) *n.* The act or an instance of exciting or the state of being excited: *In all of the excitement of the party, I couldn't hear the phone ring.*

ex·cit·ing (ĭk-sī′tĭng) *adj.* Creating or producing excitement: *an exciting rafting trip down the river.* **—ex·cit′ing·ly** *adv.*

ex·claim (ĭk-sklām′) *v.* **ex·claimed, ex·claim·ing, ex·claims** *—tr.* To say or express (something) by crying out suddenly, as from surprise: *"How nice of you to stop by!" he exclaimed.* *—intr.* To cry out suddenly, as from surprise: *She exclaimed with pleasure when she saw the new car.* [From Latin *exclāmāre* : *ex-*, out + *clāmāre*, to call.]

ex·cla·ma·tion (ĕk′sklə-mā′shən) *n.* **1.** Something said suddenly or forcefully: *exclamations of surprise.* **2.** An outcry, as of protest.

exclamation mark *n.* An exclamation point.

exclamation point *n.* A punctuation mark (!) used after an exclamation.

ex·clam·a·to·ry (ĭk-sklăm′ə-tôr′ē) *adj.* Containing, using, or being an exclamation: *a sudden exclamatory remark; an exclamatory sentence.*

ex·clude (ĭk-sklo͞od′) *tr.v.* **ex·clud·ed, ex·clud·ing, ex·cludes 1.** To prevent from entering; keep out: *a rule that excludes young children from the big swimming pool.* **2.** To prevent from being included, considered, or accepted: *Let's not exclude the possibility of rain in making our plans.* [From Middle English *excluden*, from Latin *exclūdere* : *ex-*, out + *claudere*, to shut.]

ex·clu·sion (ĭk-sklo͞o′zhən) *n.* **1.** The act or practice of excluding: *The exclusion of large trucks from some streets eases traffic congestion.* **2.** The condition or fact of being excluded.

ex·clu·sive (ĭk-sklo͞o′sĭv) *adj.* **1.** Not divided or shared with others: *the exclusive owner of the estate.* **2.** Undivided; complete: *The spectators gave the diver their exclusive attention.* **3.** Not including the specified endpoints but only the area between them. For example, "20–25, exclusive" refers to 21, 22, 23 and 24. **4.** Excluding some or most, as from membership or participation; restricted: *an exclusive school.* **—ex·clu′sive·ly** *adv.* **—ex·clu′sive·ness** *n.*

exclusive of *prep.* Not including; besides: *Exclusive of last-minute changes, this report is finished.*

ex·com·mu·ni·cate (ĕks′kə-myo͞o′nĭ-kāt′) *tr.v.* **ex·com·mu·ni·cat·ed, ex·com·mu·ni·cat·ing, ex·com·mu·ni·cates** To deprive of the right of church membership by official authority: *In 1533, the pope excommunicated Henry VIII.*

ex·com·mu·ni·ca·tion (ĕks′kə-myo͞o′nĭ-kā′shən) *n.* **1.** The act of excommunicating. **2.** The state of being excommunicated.

ex·cre·ment (ĕk′skrə-mənt) *n.* Waste matter that is passed from the body after digestion.

ex·cres·cence (ĭk-skrĕs′əns) *n.* An abnormal growth, such as a wart, on a surface.

ex·crete (ĭk-skrēt′) *tr.v.* **ex·cret·ed, ex·cret·ing, ex·cretes** To eliminate (waste matter) from a living organism, organ, or tissue: *Kidneys excrete urea and other waste products of metabolism.*

Excalibur
King Arthur receiving Excalibur from the Lady of the Lake

excavator

ex·cre·tion (ĭk-**skrē′**shən) *n.* **1.** The act or process of excreting. **2.** The waste matter, such as urine or sweat, that is excreted.

ex·cre·to·ry (**ĕk′**skrĭ-tôr′ē) *adj.* Involving or used in excretion: *excretory organs.*

ex·cru·ci·at·ing (ĭk-**skrōō′**shē-ā′tĭng) *adj.* Intensely painful; agonizing: *the excruciating pain of a toothache.* **—ex·cru′ci·at′ing·ly** *adv.*

ex·cur·sion (ĭk-**skûr′**zhən) *n.* **1.** A usually short journey made for pleasure; an outing: *an excursion to the park.* **2.** A roundtrip on a passenger vehicle at a special reduced fare: *Excursions are a cheap way to travel abroad.*

ex·cuse (ĭk-**skyōōz′**) *tr.v.* **ex·cused, ex·cus·ing, ex·cus·es 1.** To seek to remove the blame from: *She excused herself for being late.* **2.** To pardon; forgive: *Excuse me for taking your chair.* See Synonyms at **forgive. 3.** To serve as an apology for; justify: *Nothing excuses such rudeness.* **4.** To free or release, as from a duty, activity, or obligation: *All seniors will be excused from school early today.* ❖ *n.* (ĭk-**skyōōs′**) **1.** An explanation offered to justify a fault or offense: *What is your excuse for being late?* **2.** *Informal* An inferior example: *Their old station wagon is a poor excuse for a car.* ◆ **excuse me 1.** Used to acknowledge and ask forgiveness for an action that could cause offense. **2.** Used to request that a statement be repeated. [From Middle English *excusen*, from Latin *excūsāre* : *ex-*, off, away + *causa*, accusation.] **—ex·cus′a·ble** *adj.* **—ex·cus′a·bly** *adv.* **—ex·cus′er** *n.*

ex·e·cute (**ĕk′**sĭ-kyōōt′) *tr.v.* **ex·e·cut·ed, ex·e·cut·ing, ex·e·cutes 1.** To put into effect; carry out: *The government must execute the law fairly.* **2.** To perform; do: *execute a U-turn.* **3.** To create (a work of art, for example) according to a design. **4.** To make valid, as by signing: *execute a deed.* **5.** To put to death, especially by carrying out a legal sentence: *execute a convicted criminal.* **6.** To run or carry out (a computer program or instruction). [From Middle English *executen*, from Latin *execūtus*, past participle of *exsequī*, to carry out : *ex-*, out + *sequī*, to follow.]

ex·e·cu·tion (ĕk′sĭ-**kyōō′**shən) *n.* **1.** The act of executing something: *administrators responsible for the execution of a new school policy; the execution of a will.* **2.** The manner, style, or result of executing something: *the flawless execution of a plan.* **3a.** The act of putting a person to death, especially as a lawful penalty. **b.** An instance of a person being put to death, especially as a lawful penalty.

ex·e·cu·tion·er (ĕk′sĭ-**kyōō′**shə-nər) *n.* A person who puts someone to death, especially someone convicted of a capital crime.

ex·ec·u·tive (ĭg-**zĕk′**yə-tĭv) *n.* **1.** A person or group that manages the affairs of an organization, especially a corporation: *an executive responsible for the running of a company.* **2.** The chief officer of a government, state, or political division. **3.** The branch of government responsible for putting laws into effect or managing the affairs of a country. ❖ *adj.* **1.** Relating to or capable of carrying out plans, duties, or other tasks: *a committee having executive powers.* **2.** Having, marked by, or relating to administrative or managerial authority. **3.** Relating to the branch of government concerned with putting laws into effect or managing the affairs of a country: *an executive department.*

ex·ec·u·tor (ĭg-**zĕk′**yə-tər *or* **ĕk′**sĭ-kyōō′tər) *n.* A person who is responsible for carrying out the terms of a will.

ex·em·pla·ry (ĭg-**zĕm′**plə-rē) *adj.* **1.** Worthy of imitation; commendable: *exemplary behavior.* **2.** Serving as an illustration; typical: *an exemplary Supreme Court case.* **3.** Serving as a warning: *an exemplary glance.* **—ex·em′pla·ri·ly** *adv.*

ex·em·pli·fy (ĭg-**zĕm′**plə-fī′) *tr.v.* **ex·em·pli·fied, ex·em·pli·fy·ing, ex·em·pli·fies** To serve as an example of; illustrate: *a movie that exemplifies a director's style.* **—ex·em′pli·fi·ca′tion** (ĭg-zĕm′plə-fĭ-**kā′**shən) *n.*

ex·empt (ĭg-**zĕmpt′**) *tr.v.* **ex·empt·ed, ex·empt·ing, ex·empts** To free from a duty or obligation; excuse: *Regulations exempt certain people from serving on juries.* ❖ *adj.* Freed from a duty or obligation required of others; excused: *Church property is exempt from taxes.* [From Middle English *exempten*, from Latin *exemptus*, past participle of *eximere*, to take out.] **—ex·empt′i·ble** *adj.*

ex·emp·tion (ĭg-**zĕmp′**shən) *n.* The act of exempting or the condition of being exempt: *the exemption of food from the sales tax.*

ex·er·cise (**ĕk′**sər-sīz′) *n.* **1a.** Activity that requires physical exertion, especially when performed to develop or maintain fitness: *He swims every day for exercise.* **b.** A specific activity performed to develop or maintain fitness or a skill: *sit-ups and other exercises; a piano exercise.* **2.** The active use or performance of something: *the exercise of good judgment; the exercise of official duties.* **3.** An activity having a specified aspect: *Trying to get him to clean his room is an exercise in futility.* **4.** A military maneuver or training activity. **5. exercises** A program that includes speeches and other ceremonial activities performed before an audience: *high school graduation exercises.* ❖ *v.* **ex·er·cised, ex·er·cis·ing, ex·er·cis·es** *—tr.* **1.** To subject to practice or exertion in order to train, strengthen, or develop: *exercise a horse; exercise your abdominal muscles.* **2.** To make active use of; employ: *By voting we exercise our rights as citizens.* *—intr.* To take exercise: *We exercise for an hour daily.* [From Middle English, from Latin *exercitium*, from *exercēre*, to exercise : *ex-*, away + *arcēre*, to restrain.]

ex·ert (ĭg-**zûrt′**) *tr.v.* **ex·ert·ed, ex·ert·ing, ex·erts 1.** To put to use or effect; put forth: *exerted all my strength to move the box.* **2.** To put (oneself) to strenuous effort: *The hikers exerted themselves to climb the mountain by noon.* [From Latin *exserere*, to put forth, stretch out : *ex-*, out + *serere*, to join.]

ex·er·tion (ĭg-**zûr′**shən) *n.* The act or an instance of exerting, especially a strenuous effort: *the tremendous exertion of running a marathon.*

ex·ha·la·tion (ĕks′hə-**lā′**shən *or* ĕk′sə-**lā′**shən) *n.* **1.** The act or process of exhaling: *exhalation of air from the lungs.* **2.** Something, such as air or vapor, that is exhaled.

ex·hale (ĕks-**hāl′** *or* ĕk-**sāl′**) *v.* **ex·haled, ex·hal·ing, ex·hales** *—intr.* To breathe out. *—tr.* To breathe (something) out or blow (something) forth: *The dragon exhaled fire and smoke. The spring flowers exhaled a delicate perfume.* [From Middle English *exalen*, from Latin *exhālāre* : *ex-*, out + *hālāre*, to breathe.]

ex·haust (ĭg-**zôst′**) *tr.v.* **ex·haust·ed, ex·haust·ing, ex·hausts 1.** To wear out completely; tire: *Moving the heavy furniture exhausted us all.* **2.** To use up completely: *Tickets and snacks exhausted our money.* **3.** To drain the contents of; empty: *exhaust the fuel tank.* **4.** To let out or draw off: *exhaust vaporous wastes through a pipe.* **5.** To treat completely; cover thoroughly: *exhaust a topic of conversation.* ❖ *n.* **1.** The escape or release of waste gases or vapors, as from an engine: *The fan is too small to ensure quick exhaust of the fumes.* **2.** The vapors or gases so released: *A cloud of exhaust came from the bus.* **3.** A device or system that allows vapors or gases to escape: *replaced the exhaust on the truck.* [From Latin *exhaurīre* : *ex-*, out + *haurīre*, to draw.]

ex·haust·ed (ĭg-**zô′**stĭd) *adj.* **1.** Used up; consumed: *The oil reserves are nearly exhausted.* **2.** Worn out completely; very tired: *an exhausted swimmer.* **—ex·haust′ed·ly** *adv.*

ex·haus·tion (ĭg-**zôs′**chən) *n.* **1.** An act or an instance of exhausting: *exhaustion of the water supply.* **2.** The state of being exhausted; extreme fatigue: *The runner collapsed from exhaustion.*

ă	pat	ôr	core
ā	pay	oi	boy
âr	care	ou	out
ä	father	ŏŏ	took
ĕ	pet	ŏŏr	lure
ē	be	ōō	boot
ĭ	pit	ŭ	cut
ī	bite	ûr	urge
îr	pier	th	thin
ŏ	pot	*th*	this
ō	toe	zh	vision
ô	paw	ə	about

ex·haus·tive (ĭg-zô′stĭv) *adj.* Complete; thorough: *an exhaustive search for a solution.* **—ex·haus′tive·ly** *adv.* **—ex·haus′tive·ness** *n.*

ex·hib·it (ĭg-zĭb′ĭt) *tr.v.* **ex·hib·it·ed, ex·hib·it·ing, ex·hib·its 1.** To present for the public to view; display: *exhibit new artworks at a gallery.* **2.** To give evidence of; show; demonstrate: *The doctors exhibited great skill in repairing the patient's knee.* ❖ *n.* **1.** Something exhibited; a display: *She studied the museum's fossil exhibits for her new book.* **2.** A public showing; an exhibition: *The art exhibit will open next month.* **3.** Something formally introduced as evidence in a court of law. [From Middle English *exhibiten,* from Latin *exhibēre* : *ex-,* out + *habēre,* to hold.] **—ex·hib′i·tor, ex·hib′it·er** *n.*

ex·hi·bi·tion (ĕk′sə-**bĭsh′**ən) *n.* **1.** The act or an instance of exhibiting. **2.** Something exhibited; an exhibit. **3.** A large-scale public showing: *attended an exhibition of boating equipment.*

ex·hi·bi·tion·ism (ĕk′sə-**bĭsh′**ə-nĭz′əm) *n.* The act or practice of deliberately behaving so as to attract attention. **—ex′hi·bi′tion·ist** *n.*

ex·hil·a·rate (ĭg-zĭl′ə-rāt′) *tr.v.* **ex·hil·a·rat·ed, ex·hil·a·rat·ing, ex·hil·a·rates 1.** To cause to feel happy; elate: *The victory exhilarated the whole school.* **2.** To invigorate; stimulate: *A walk in the cold will exhilarate us.* [From Latin *exhilarāre,* from *hilaris,* cheerful, from Greek *hilaros.*] **—ex·hil′a·ra′tion** *n.*

ex·hort (ĭg-zôrt′) *tr.v.* **ex·hort·ed, ex·hort·ing, ex·horts** To urge by strong argument or earnest appeal: *The candidate exhorted the crowd to vote.*

ex·hor·ta·tion (ĕg′zôr-**tā′**shən *or* ĕk′sôr-**tā′**shən) *n.* **1.** The act or an instance of exhorting: *No amount of exhortation could persuade them to give up.* **2.** A speech intended to advise or encourage: *delivered a fiery exhortation to her team.*

ex·hume (ĭg-zo͞om′) *tr.v.* **ex·humed, ex·hum·ing, ex·humes 1.** To dig up or remove from a grave: *an order to exhume the body.* **2.** To bring to light; uncover. [From Medieval Latin *exhumāre* : Latin *ex-,* out + Latin *humus,* ground.]

ex·i·gen·cy (**ĕk′**sə-jən-sē) *n., pl.* **ex·i·gen·cies 1.** A pressing or urgent situation. **2.** An urgent requirement; a pressing need: *The exigencies of the schedule meant no holiday.*

ex·i·gent (**ĕk′**sə-jənt) *adj.* Requiring immediate action or remedy; urgent.

ex·ile (**ĕg′**zīl′ *or* **ĕk′**sīl′) *n.* **1a.** The condition or period of being forced to live away from one's native country or home: *Exile was the punishment for opposing political activities.* **b.** The condition or period of self-imposed absence from one's country or home: *The author chose exile over living in a country he found oppressive.* **2.** A person who lives away from his or her native country. ❖ *tr.v.* **ex·iled, ex·il·ing, ex·iles** To send into exile; banish: *The dictator exiled members of the opposition party.* [From Middle English *exil,* from Latin *exilium,* from *exsul,* exiled person, wanderer.]

ex·ist (ĭg-zĭst′) *intr.v.* **ex·ist·ed, ex·ist·ing, ex·ists 1.** To have actual being; be real: *How many chemical elements have been shown to exist?* **2a.** To have life; live: *Dinosaurs existed millions of years ago.* **b.** To live at a minimal level; subsist: *Animals cannot exist without food and water.* **3.** To continue to be; persist: *old traditions that still exist in parts of the country.* **4.** To be present; occur: *A new spirit of cooperation existed on both sides.*

ex·is·tence (ĭg-zĭs′təns) *n.* **1.** The fact or condition of existing; being. **2.** The fact or condition of continued being; life: *our existence on the earth.* **3.** A manner of existing: *lived an ordinary existence.* **4.** Occurrence; presence: *The existence of oil deposits in the rocks brought many people to the region.* [From Middle English, from Latin *existere,* to exist : *ex-,* out + *sistere,* to stand.]

ex·is·tent (ĭg-zĭs′tənt) *adj.* **1.** Having life or being; existing: *existent creatures.* **2.** Occurring or present at the moment; current: *existent customs.*

ex·it (**ĕg′**zĭt *or* **ĕk′**sĭt) *n.* **1.** The act of going away or out: *I made a hasty exit from the snake house at the zoo.* **2.** A passage or way out: *Exits must be clearly marked.* **3.** A performer's departure from the stage. ❖ *v.* **ex·it·ed, ex·it·ing, ex·its** *—intr.* To make one's exit; depart: *Please exit to the left.* *—tr.* **1.** To go out of; leave: *exited the plane through a rear door.* **2.** To stop the execution of and close down (a computer application). [From Latin, third person singular present tense of *exīre,* to go out : *ex-,* out + *īre,* to go.]

exit poll *n.* A poll of voters taken as they leave a polling place.

exo– *pref.* A prefix that means outside or external: *exoskeleton.*

ex·o·crine gland (**ĕk′**sə-krĭn *or* **ĕk′**sə-krēn) *n.* Any of various glands, such as a sweat gland or mammary gland, that discharge their product through a duct that opens onto an external or internal surface rather than directly into the bloodstream.

ex·o·cy·to·sis (ĕk′sō-sī-**tō′**sĭs) *n.* A process by which a cell secretes or excretes a substance by enclosing it in a vesicle which fuses with the cell membrane and discharges its contents outside the cell.

ex·o·dus (**ĕk′**sə-dəs) *n.* **1.** A departure of a large number of people: *an exodus from the cities to the suburbs.* **2. Exodus a.** In the Bible, the departure of the Israelites from Egypt. **b.** The book of the Bible that tells of this departure and of God's giving of the Ten Commandments to Moses. [From Late Latin, from Greek *exodos* : *ex-,* out + *hodos,* way, journey.]

ex of·fi·ci·o (ĕks′ ə-**fĭsh′**ē-ō′) *adv. & adj.* By virtue of the office or position one holds: *The mayor is ex officio a member of the city council.*

ex·on·er·ate (ĭg-**zŏn′**ə-rāt′) *tr.v.* **ex·on·er·at·ed, ex·on·er·at·ing, ex·on·er·ates** To free from blame: *The jury's decision exonerated the defendant.* [From Latin *exonerāre,* to free from a burden : *ex-,* away from + *onus,* burden.] **—ex·on′er·a′tion** *n.*

ex·o·plan·et (**ĕk′**sō-plăn′ĭt) *n.* An extrasolar planet.

ex·or·bi·tant (ĭg-**zôr′**bĭ-tənt) *adj.* Exceeding what is reasonable or customary, especially in cost: *an exorbitant price on an imported car.* **—ex·or′bi·tance** *n.* **—ex·or′bi·tant·ly** *adv.*

ex·or·cise (**ĕk′**sôr-sīz′) *tr.v.* **ex·or·cised, ex·or·cis·ing, ex·or·cis·es 1.** To drive away (an evil spirit), often by incantation, prayer, or command. **2.** To eliminate or suppress (a negative feeling, for example). **3.** To free from evil spirits: *the exorcising of an old house.* [From Middle English *exorcisen,* from Greek *exorkizein* : *ex-,* out of + *horkizein,* to make one swear an oath.] **—ex′or·cis′er** *n.*

ex·or·cism (**ĕk′**sôr-sĭz′əm) *n.* **1.** The act or practice of exorcising. **2.** A formula used in exorcising. **—ex′or·cist** *n.*

ex·o·skel·e·ton (ĕk′sō-**skĕl′**ĭ-tn) *n.* A hard outer covering, such as the shell of a grasshopper or a crab, that provides protection and support. [From Greek *exō,* outside + *skeleton.*]

ex·o·sphere (**ĕk′**sō-sfîr′) *n.* The transitional zone between the thermosphere (the outermost layer of the earth's atmosphere) and outer space. **—ex′o·spher′ic** (ĕk′sō-**sfîr′**ĭk *or* ĕk′sō-**sfĕr′**ĭk) *adj.*

ex·o·ther·mic (ĕk′sō-**thûr′**mĭk) also **ex·o·ther·mal** (ĕk′sō-**thûr′**məl) *adj.* Releasing or giving off heat: *an exothermic chemical reaction.*

ex·ot·ic (ĭg-**zŏt′**ĭk) *adj.* **1.** From another part of the world; foreign: *exotic imported birds.* **2.** Strikingly unfamiliar or unusual; excitingly strange: *the exotic beauty of the Galápagos Islands.* [From Greek *exōtikos,* from *exō,* outside.] **—ex·ot′i·cal·ly** *adv.* **—ex·ot′ic·ness** *n.*

WRITERS CHOOSE THEIR WORDS

Liyana felt **exhilarated** by the skyscrapers. Their glittering lines lifted her out of her worry. She wished she could ride every sleek elevator up and down, punching buttons, seeing who got on and off.

—Naomi Shihab Nye
Habibi

exp. *abbr.* An abbreviation of: **1.** exponent. **2.** express.

ex·pand (ĭk-spănd′) *v.* **ex·pand·ed, ex·pand·ing, ex·pands** —*tr.* **1.** To increase the size, number, volume, or scope of; enlarge: *expand a balloon with air; expanded the business into new areas.* **2.** To express at length or in detail; enlarge upon: *She promised to expand her ideas in her next presentation.* **3.** To open (something) up or out: *The owl expanded its wings and flew away. The article expanded the author's ideas.* **4.** To express or write (a number or mathematical expression) in an extended form: *We expand 452 by writing it as 400 + 50 + 2.* —*intr.* **1.** To become greater in size, volume, quantity, or scope: *Gases expand when heated.* See Synonyms at **increase. 2.** To open up or out; unfold: *The sofa expands into a bed.* **3.** To speak or write at length or in detail: *expanded on the issues at the meeting.* [From Middle English *expanden*, from Latin *expandere* : *ex-*, out + *pandere*, to spread.] —**ex·pand′a·ble** *adj.*

ex·panse (ĭk-spăns′) *n.* A wide and open extent, as of surface, land, or sky: *a vast expanse of desert.*

ex·pan·sion (ĭk-spăn′shən) *n.* **1.** The act or process of expanding: *the growth and expansion of industry.* **2.** Something formed or produced by expansion: *These suburbs are an expansion of the city.* **3.** The extent or amount by which something has expanded: *a 40 percent expansion in sales.* **4.** A number or other mathematical expression written in an extended form; for example, $a^2 + 2ab + b^2$ is the expansion of $(a + b)^2$.

ex·pan·sion·ism (ĭk-spăn′shə-nĭz′əm) *n.* A nation's practice or policy of territorial or economic expansion. —**ex·pan′sion·ist** *adj. & n.*

ex·pan·sive (ĭk-spăn′sĭv) *adj.* **1.** Capable of expanding or tending to expand: *Balloons are made of expansive material.* **2.** Broad in size or extent; comprehensive: *an expansive view of world affairs.* **3.** Disposed to be open, communicative, and generous. **4.** Grand in scale: *the calm expansive lake.* —**ex·pan′sive·ly** *adv.* —**ex·pan′sive·ness** *n.*

ex·pa·ti·ate (ĭk-spā′shē-āt′) *intr.v.* **ex·pa·ti·at·ed, ex·pa·ti·at·ing, ex·pa·ti·ates** To speak or write at length; elaborate: *Our guide expatiated on the history and wildlife of the area.* —**ex·pa′ti·a′tion** *n.*

ex·pa·tri·ate (ĕk-spā′trē-āt′) *tr.v.* **ex·pa·tri·at·ed, ex·pa·tri·at·ing, ex·pa·tri·ates 1.** To send into exile. **2.** To remove (oneself) from residence in one's native land: *Many writers expatriated themselves to France in the 1920s.* ❖ *n.* (ĕk-spā′trē-ĭt) A person who has taken up residence in a foreign country. —**ex·pa′tri·a′tion** *n.*

ex·pect (ĭk-spĕkt′) *tr.v.* **ex·pect·ed, ex·pect·ing, ex·pects 1.** To look forward to the probable occurrence or appearance of: *expecting a telephone call.* **2.** To consider reasonable or due: *The host will expect an apology for breaking the dish.* **3.** *Informal* To presume; suppose: *I expect you're right.* [From Latin *exspectāre* : *ex-*, off, away + *spectāre*, to look at.]

ex·pec·tan·cy (ĭk-spĕk′tən-sē) *n., pl.* **ex·pec·tan·cies 1.** The act or state of expecting; anticipation: *I was filled with expectancy as I waited for my flight.* **2.** Something that is expected.

ex·pec·tant (ĭk-spĕk′tənt) *adj.* **1.** Having or marked by expectation: *an expectant audience; an expectant look.* **2.** Awaiting the birth of a child: *expectant parents.* —**ex·pec′tant·ly** *adv.*

ex·pec·ta·tion (ĕk′spĕk-tā′shən) *n.* **1.** The act of expecting. **2.** Anticipation: *eyes shining with expectation.* **3. expectations** Prospects, especially of success or gain.

ex·pec·to·rant (ĭk-spĕk′tər-ənt) *adj.* Helping to discharge phlegm or mucus from the respiratory tract. ❖ *n.* An expectorant medicine or drug.

ex·pec·to·rate (ĭk-spĕk′tə-rāt′) *v.* **ex·pec·to·rat·ed, ex·pec·to·rat·ing, ex·pec·to·rates** —*tr.* **1.** To force from the mouth; spit. **2.** To cough up and spit (phlegm, for example). —*intr.* To spit. —**ex·pec′to·ra′tion** *n.*

ex·pe·di·ence (ĭk-spē′dē-əns) *n.* Expediency.

ex·pe·di·en·cy (ĭk-spē′dē-ən-sē) *n., pl.* **ex·pe·di·en·cies 1.** Appropriateness to the purpose at hand; fitness. **2.** Adherence to self-serving means: *Their plans seem to be nothing but expediency.* **3.** A means; an expedient.

ex·pe·di·ent (ĭk-spē′dē-ənt) *adj.* **1.** Suitable or efficient for accomplishing a purpose: *Email is the most expedient way to communicate with our distant relatives.* **2.** Convenient but based on a concern for self-interest rather than principle: *She changed her position when it was politically expedient.* ❖ *n.* Something that is a means to an end, especially when based on self-interest: *He compromised only as an expedient to boost his career.* —**ex·pe′di·ent·ly** *adv.*

ex·pe·dite (ĕk′spĭ-dīt′) *tr.v.* **ex·pe·dit·ed, ex·pe·dit·ing, ex·pe·dites** To speed up the progress of or execute quickly: *expedite a loan application.* —**ex′pe·dit′er, ex′pe·di′tor** *n.*

ex·pe·di·tion (ĕk′spĭ-dĭsh′ən) *n.* **1.** A trip made by a group of people with a definite purpose: *a geological expedition through the canyon.* **2.** The group making such a trip: *The expedition set off at dawn.* **3.** Speed in performance; promptness: *The cleanup was done well and with expedition.* [From Middle English *expedicioun*, military campaign, from Latin *expedītiō*, from *expedīre*, to make ready.]

ex·pe·di·tion·ar·y (ĕk′spĭ-dĭsh′ə-nĕr′ē) *adj.* Relating to or being an expedition.

ex·pe·di·tious (ĕk′spĭ-dĭsh′əs) *adj.* Acting or done with speed and efficiency: *The most expeditious transportation over long distances is by airplane.* See Synonyms at **fast**[1]. —**ex′pe·di′tious·ly** *adv.* —**ex′pe·di′tious·ness** *n.*

ex·pel (ĭk-spĕl′) *tr.v.* **ex·pelled, ex·pel·ling, ex·pels 1.** To force or drive out; eject forcefully: *expel air from the lungs.* **2.** To deprive (someone) of membership or rights in an organization; force to leave: *The principal expelled several students for cheating.* [From Middle English *expellen*, from Latin *expellere* : *ex-*, out + *pellere*, to drive.]

ex·pend (ĭk-spĕnd′) *tr.v.* **ex·pend·ed, ex·pend·ing, ex·pends 1.** To lay out; spend: *expend tax money on health care.* **2.** To use up; consume: *expend energy.*

ex·pend·a·ble (ĭk-spĕn′də-bəl) *adj.* **1.** Subject to being used up or consumed: *an expendable source of energy that is not renewable.* **2.** Not worth salvaging or reusing: *expendable rocket boosters.* **3.** Not strictly necessary; dispensable: *an expendable budget item.*

ex·pen·di·ture (ĭk-spĕn′dĭ-chər) *n.* **1.** The act or process of expending; outlay: *the expenditure of city funds for a recycling plant.* **2.** An amount expended.

ex·pense (ĭk-spĕns′) *n.* **1.** Something spent to attain a goal or achieve a purpose: *an expense of time and effort on the project.* **2.** A loss for the sake of something gained; a sacrifice: *outlaw demonstrations at the expense of free speech.* **3.** An expenditure of money; a cost: *With so many visitors, food is our biggest expense.* **4. expenses** Charges brought about by an employee in doing a job or in carrying out an assignment: *My expenses include food and lodging.* **5.** Something requiring the expenditure of money: *Owning a car can be a big expense.* [From Middle English, from Latin *(pecūnia) expēnsa*, (money) paid out, from past participle of *expendere*, to pay out : *ex-*, out + *pendere*, to weigh.]

ex·pen·sive (ĭk-spĕn′sĭv) *adj.* **1.** Requiring a large expenditure; costly: *an expensive limousine.* **2.** Marked by high prices: *an expensive store.* —**ex·pen′sive·ly** *adv.* —**ex·pen′sive·ness** *n.*

ex·pe·ri·ence (ĭk-spîr′ē-əns) *n.* **1a.** Active participation in events or activities, leading to the accumulation of knowledge or skill: *learned more from experience than from reading books.* **b.** The knowledge or skill so derived: *a carpenter with a lot of experience.* **2.** An event or series

ă	pat	ôr	core
ā	pay	oi	boy
âr	care	ou	out
ä	father	o͝o	took
ĕ	pet	o͝or	lure
ē	be	o͞o	boot
ĭ	pit	ŭ	cut
ī	bite	ûr	urge
îr	pier	th	thin
ŏ	pot	*th*	this
ō	toe	zh	vision
ô	paw	ə	about

of events participated in or lived through: *the experience of traveling in space.* ❖ *tr.v.* **ex·per·i·enced, ex·per·i·enc·ing, ex·per·i·enc·es** To participate in personally; undergo: *experience a great adventure; experience the excitement of winning a race.* [From Middle English, from Latin *experientia*, from *experiēns*, present participle of *experīrī*, to try.]

ex·pe·ri·enced (ĭk-spîr′ē-ənst) *adj.* Skilled or knowledgeable through active participation or practice: *an experienced teacher.*

ex·per·i·ment (ĭk-spĕr′ə-mənt) *n.* A test or procedure that is designed to determine the validity of a hypothesis or the effects of something and is carried out under conditions that are carefully controlled: *an experiment to test a theory about plant hormones; conducted an experiment to evaluate a new drug.* ❖ *intr.v.* (ĭk-spĕr′ə-mĕnt′) **ex·per·i·ment·ed, ex·per·i·ment·ing, ex·per·i·ments 1.** To conduct an experiment; make tests or trials. **2.** To try something new, especially in order to gain experience: *They experimented with new ways of growing corn.* [From Middle English, from Latin *experīmentum*, from *experīrī*, to try.] **—ex·per′i·ment′er** *n.*

ex·per·i·men·tal (ĭk-spĕr′ə-**mĕn′**tl) *adj.* **1.** Relating to or based on experiments: *an experimental approach to psychology.* **2.** Not yet proven to work; still being tested: *an experimental drug for diabetes.* **—ex·per′i·men′tal·ly** *adv.*

ex·per·i·men·ta·tion (ĭk-spĕr′ə-mĕn-**tā′**shən) *n.* The act, process, or practice of experimenting: *I discovered how to make good biscuits after much experimentation.*

ex·pert (**ĕk′**spûrt′) *n.* A person with great knowledge of or skill in a particular field: *Doctors are experts in medicine.* ❖ *adj.* Having or showing great knowledge or skill as the result of experience or training: *The forest ranger was an expert guide.* See Synonyms at **proficient.** [From Middle English, from Latin *expertus*, past participle of *experīrī*, to try.] **—ex′pert′ly** *adv.*

ex·per·tise (ĕk′spûr-**tēz′**) *n.* Skill or knowledge in a particular area: *a researcher with expertise in infectious diseases.*

ex·pi·ate (**ĕk′**spē-āt′) *tr.v.* **ex·pi·at·ed, ex·pi·at·ing, ex·pi·ates** To atone or make amends for: *expiate sins by acts of penance.* **—ex′pi·a′tion** *n.*

ex·pi·ra·tion (ĕk′spə-**rā′**shən) *n.* **1.** The act of coming to a close; termination: *the expiration of a contract.* **2.** The act or process of breathing out; exhalation.

ex·pire (ĭk-**spīr′**) *intr.v.* **ex·pired, ex·pir·ing, ex·pires 1.** To come to an end; terminate: *When our dog's license expires, we have to renew it.* **2.** To die: *The injured bird expired before we could get help for it.* **3.** To breathe out; exhale. [From Middle English *expiren*, from Latin *exspīrāre* : *ex-*, out + *spīrāre*, to breathe.]

ex·plain (ĭk-**splān′**) *v.* **ex·plained, ex·plain·ing, ex·plains** *—tr.* **1.** To make plain or comprehensible: *explain the rules of a game; explain a job to a substitute.* **2.** To define or interpret: *The professor explained the meaning of the poem.* **3.** To offer reasons for or a cause of; justify: *We were asked to explain our noisy behavior during class.* *—intr.* To make something plain or comprehensible. ◆ **explain away** To dismiss or minimize the significance of (something) by means of an explanation or excuse: *There is no way to explain away my carelessness.* **—ex·plain′a·ble** *adj.* **—ex·plain′er** *n.*

ex·pla·na·tion (ĕk′splə-**nā′**shən) *n.* **1.** The act or process of explaining. **2.** Something that explains: *Give a simple explanation of how to make a kite. The police looked for an explanation for the crime.*

ex·plan·a·to·ry (ĭk-**splăn′**ə-tôr′ē) *adj.* Serving or intended to explain: *The math book has explanatory notes to go along with some problems.*

ex·ple·tive (**ĕk′**splĭ-tĭv) *n.* An exclamation or oath, especially one that is profane, vulgar, or obscene.

ex·plic·a·ble (ĭk-**splĭk′**ə-bəl *or* **ĕk′**splĭ-kə-bəl) *adj.* Possible to explain: *explicable phenomena.* **—ex·plic′a·bly** *adv.*

ex·pli·cate (**ĕk′**splĭ-kāt′) *tr.v.* **ex·pli·cat·ed, ex·pli·cat·ing, ex·pli·cates** To make clear the meaning of; explain: *explicate a scientific theory.* **—ex′pli·ca′tion** *n.*

ex·plic·it (ĭk-**splĭs′**ĭt) *adj.* **1.** Fully and clearly expressed or defined; having nothing left out: *an explicit statement of their plans for a new school.* **2.** Clear and outspoken: *We were explicit in demanding that the marsh should be preserved.* **—ex·plic′it·ly** *adv.* **—ex·plic′it·ness** *n.*

ex·plode (ĭk-**splōd′**) *v.* **ex·plod·ed, ex·plod·ing, ex·plodes** *—intr.* **1.** To release energy in an explosion; blow up: *Fireworks exploded all around.* **2.** To burst violently as a result of internal pressure: *Suddenly the bottle of soda water exploded.* **3.** To make an emotional outburst: *exploded with anger at the trespassers.* **4.** To increase suddenly and sharply: *The population has exploded in the past decade.* *—tr.* **1.** To cause to undergo an explosion; detonate: *The engineers exploded the dynamite to open a passage through the rock.* **2.** To show to be false or unreliable: *explode a hypothesis.* [From Latin *explōdere*, to drive out by clapping : *ex-*, out + *plaudere*, to clap.] **—ex·plod′er** *n.* —SEE NOTE.

ex·ploit (**ĕk′**sploit′) *n.* An act or deed, especially a brilliant or heroic one: *the exploits of legendary figures such as Robin Hood.* ❖ *tr.v.* (ĭk-**sploit′**) **ex·ploit·ed, ex·ploit·ing, ex·ploits 1.** To use to the greatest possible advantage: *exploit an idea to make a profit.* **2.** To make use of selfishly or unethically: *exploit unskilled workers.* [From Middle English *expleit*, from Latin *explicitum*, past participle of *explicāre*, to unfold.] **—ex·ploit′a·ble** *adj.* **—ex·ploit′er** *n.*

ex·ploi·ta·tion (ĕk′sploi-**tā′**shən) *n.* **1.** The act of using to the greatest possible advantage: *the exploitation of oil fields.* **2.** The use of a person or group for selfish purposes: *the exploitation of immigrant labor.*

ex·plo·ra·tion (ĕk′splə-**rā′**shən) *n.* The act or an instance of exploring: *Arctic exploration; an exploration of new medical treatments.* **—ex·plor′a·to′ry** (ĭk-**splôr′**ə-tôr′ē) *adj.*

ex·plore (ĭk-**splôr′**) *v.* **ex·plored, ex·plor·ing, ex·plores** *—tr.* **1.** To investigate systematically; examine: *explored the possibilities of a new trade agreement.* **2.** To travel in or search into for the purpose of discovery: *explore a vast region of rainforest.* *—intr.* To make a careful examination or search: *Geologists were hired to explore for oil.* [From Latin *explōrāre.*]

ex·plor·er (ĭk-**splôr′**ər) *n.* A person or thing that explores, especially a person who explores a geographic area.

ex·plo·sion (ĭk-**splō′**zhən) *n.* **1.** The act of bursting apart or blowing up with a sudden violent release of energy: *an explosion of fireworks.* **2.** The loud sharp sound made by bursting apart or blowing up: *an explosion heard for miles.* **3.** A sudden, often vehement outbreak: *an explosion of laughter.* **4.** A sudden great increase: *a population explosion.*

ex·plo·sive (ĭk-**splō′**sĭv) *adj.* **1.** Having the nature of an explosion: *an explosive laugh; an explosive fit of temper.* **2.** Tending to explode: *an explosive powder.* ❖ *n.* A substance that tends to explode or is capable of exploding: *Explosives were used to make the tunnel through the mountain.* **—ex·plo′sive·ly** *adv.* **—ex·plo′sive·ness** *n.*

ex·po·nent (ĭk-**spō′**nənt *or* **ĕk′**spō′nənt) *n.* **1.** A person who is an enthusiastic supporter of or advocates something: *exponents of free trade.* **2.** A number or symbol, placed to the right of and above the expression to which it applies, that indicates the number of times a mathematical expression is used as a factor. For example, the exponent 3 in 5^3 indicates $5 \times 5 \times 5$; the exponent 2 in $(x + y)^2$ indicates $(x + y) \times (x + y)$. [From Latin *expōnere*, to

WORD HISTORY

explode The word **explode** has not always had the same meaning as it does today. It comes from the Latin verb *explōdere,* "to drive away by clapping." The modern meaning ultimately comes from the bursting sound made by clapping. The Latin verb is composed of the prefix *ex–*, "out, away," and the verb *plaudere*, "to clap." This verb shows up also in English **applaud,** where the sense of "clapping" is more immediately apparent. *Applaud* comes from Latin *applaudere*, "to clap at" (*ad–*, "to, toward"). We also get the word **plausible** from the same source; it once meant "likely to be applauded or received favorably," and later, "believable."

expound : *ex-*, out, away + *pōnere*, to place.]

ex·po·nen·tial (ĕk′spə-**nĕn′**shəl) *adj.* Containing or involving one or more exponents in a mathematical expression: *an exponential increase.*

ex·port (ĭk-**spôrt′** *or* **ĕk′**spôrt′) *tr.v.* **ex·port·ed, ex·port·ing, ex·ports 1.** To send or transport (goods or products) to another country, especially for trade or sale: *export fruit to England.* **2.** To cause the spread of (an idea, for example) in another part of the world; transmit. ❖ *n.* (**ĕk′**spôrt′) Exportation. [From Middle English *exsporten*, from Latin *exportāre* : *ex-*, out, away + *portāre*, to carry.] **—ex·port′a·ble** *adj.* **—ex·port′er** *n.*

ex·por·ta·tion (ĕk′spôr-**tā′**shən) *n.* The act or an instance of exporting: *The exportation of automobiles is an important element of the Japanese economy.*

ex·pose (ĭk-**spōz′**) *tr.v.* **ex·posed, ex·pos·ing, ex·pos·es 1.** To lay open or subject to an action or an influence: *expose young children to literature; expose a visitor to a cold.* **2.** To subject (a photographic film, for example) to the action of light. **3.** To make visible; reveal: *Paint remover exposed the old wood underneath.* **4.** To make known (something discreditable) or reveal the guilt of: *exposed the criminal activity; expose a dishonest official.* [From Middle English *exposen*, from Old French *exposer*, from Latin *expōnere*, to set forth.] **—ex·pos′er** *n.* —SEE NOTE AT **compose.**

ex·po·sé (ĕk′spō-**zā′**) *n.* An exposure or revelation of something discreditable: *a magazine exposé of corruption in government.*

ex·po·si·tion (ĕk′spə-**zĭsh′**ən) *n.* **1.** An exact and detailed explanation of difficult material: *The astronomer gave a long exposition on the nature of the eclipse.* **2.** The first part of a musical composition in sonata form that introduces the themes. **3.** A large public exhibition or fair: *an international computer exposition.* **—ex·pos′i·to′ry** (ĭk-**spŏz′**ĭ-tôr′ē) *adj.* **—ex·pos′i·tor** *n.*

ex post fac·to (ĕks′ pōst **făk′**tō) *adj.* Enacted after an event but applying to it nonetheless. Used especially of a law.

ex·pos·tu·late (ĭk-**spŏs′**chə-lāt′) *intr.v.* **ex·pos·tu·lat·ed, ex·pos·tu·lat·ing, ex·pos·tu·lates** To reason earnestly with someone, especially in an effort to dissuade or correct: *The parent expostulated with the committee on the need for new computers in school.* **—ex·pos′tu·la′tion** *n.*

ex·po·sure (ĭk-**spō′**zhər) *n.* **1.** The act or an instance of exposing, as: **a.** An act or instance of subjecting or being subjected to an action or influence: *a child's exposure to measles; her exposure to city living.* **b.** Appearance in public or in the mass media. **c.** Revelation, especially of crime or guilt. **2.** A position in relation to climatic or weather conditions or points of the compass: *Our house has a southern exposure.* **3a.** The act of exposing a photographic film or plate. **b.** The amount of light needed to expose a photographic film: *This exposure will not produce a clear image.* **c.** An exposed section of a roll of film: *We took several exposures.*

ex·pound (ĭk-**spound′**) *v.* **ex·pound·ed, ex·pound·ing, ex·pounds** *—tr.* To set forth or give a detailed statement of: *Debaters must always expound their views clearly.* *—intr.* To make a detailed statement: *The candidate expounded on the need for good government.* **—ex·pound′er** *n.*

ex·press (ĭk-**sprĕs′**) *tr.v.* **ex·pressed, ex·press·ing, ex·press·es 1a.** To put into words; state or communicate in words: *Parents expressed their opinions at the school committee meeting.* **b.** To manifest or communicate without using words; show: *The winner's face expressed great joy. He expressed his displeasure by walking out of the room.* **c.** To make known the opinions or feelings of (oneself): *She expressed herself in a letter to the editor.* **2.** To represent by a sign, symbol, number, or formula: *A fraction can be expressed as a decimal.* **3.** To squeeze or press out, as juice from an orange: *a machine that expresses juice from berries and fruits.* **4.** To manifest a trait encoded by (a gene): *a gene that is expressed during fetal development.* ❖ *adj.* **1.** Clearly stated; explicit: *my express wish to go home.* **2.** Particular; specific: *The express object of the exercise was to teach cooperation.* **3a.** Direct, rapid, and usually making few or no stops: *an express train.* **b.** Relating to or sent by rapid transportation: *an express package; an express service.* ❖ *adv.* By express transport or delivery: *send a package express.* ❖ *n.* A means of transportation, such as a train, that travels rapidly and makes few or no stops before its destination: *Take an express to the airport.* [From Middle English *expressen*, from Medieval Latin *expressāre*, from Latin *exprimere* : Latin *ex-*, out + Latin *premere*, to press.] **—ex·press′i·ble** *adj.* —SEE NOTE AT **pressure.**

ex·pres·sion (ĭk-**sprĕsh′**ən) *n.* **1.** The act of expressing something, as in words, art, action, or movement: *the expression of one's opinion by voting.* **2a.** Something that expresses or communicates: *These flowers are an expression of my gratitude.* **b.** A facial aspect or look that indicates a certain mood or feeling: *an expression of joy in his eyes.* **3.** A symbol or arrangement of symbols that indicates a mathematical quantity or relationship between quantities. For example, *x* + *y* is an algebraic expression. **4.** A manner of speaking, depicting, or performing that expresses particular feeling or meaning: *The poet read several poems with great expression.* **5.** A particular word or phrase: Burnt to a crisp *is a familiar expression.* **6.** The act or process of expressing a gene.

ex·pres·sion·ism or **Ex·pres·sion·ism** (ĭk-**sprĕsh′**ə-nĭz′əm) *n.* A movement in the fine arts during the early 1900s that emphasized the expression of artists' feelings and experiences.

ex·pres·sion·less (ĭk-**sprĕsh′**ən-lĭs) *adj.* Lacking expression: *a dull expressionless voice.*

ex·pres·sive (ĭk-**sprĕs′**ĭv) *adj.* **1.** Serving to express or indicate: *The kitten's crying was expressive of its hunger.* **2.** Full of meaning; significant: *an expressive smile.* **—ex·pres′sive·ly** *adv.* **—ex·pres′sive·ness** *n.*

ex·press·ly (ĭk-**sprĕs′**lē) *adv.* **1.** In an express or a definite manner; explicitly: *The rules expressly say that only four can play at a time.* **2.** For a specific purpose; particularly: *scissors made expressly for left-handed people.*

ex·press·way (ĭk-**sprĕs′**wā′) *n.* A major divided highway designed for high-speed travel, having few or no intersections.

ex·pro·pri·ate (ĕk-**sprō′**prē-āt′) *tr.v.* **ex·pro·pri·at·ed, ex·pro·pri·at·ing, ex·pro·pri·ates** To take (a property) for public use: *The government expropriated the farmers' lands to create the national park.* **—ex·pro′pri·a′tion** *n.*

ex·pul·sion (ĭk-**spŭl′**shən) *n.* The act of expelling or the state of being expelled: *the expulsion of gases from a jet engine; a representative faced with expulsion from the legislature.* [From Middle English *expulsioun*, from Old French *expulsion*, from Latin *expulsus*, past participle of *expellere*, to expel.]

ex·punge (ĭk-**spŭnj′**) *tr.v.* **ex·punged, ex·pung·ing, ex·pung·es** To remove completely; delete; erase: *expunge a statement from the records of a trial.* [From Latin *expungere* : *ex-*, out, away + *pungere*, to prick.]

ex·pur·gate (**ĕk′**spər-gāt′) *tr.v.* **ex·pur·gat·ed, ex·pur·gat·ing, ex·pur·gates** To remove objectionable passages from (a book, for example) before publication: *References to several living people were expurgated from the play.* [From Latin *expūrgāre*, to purify, from *pūrgāre*, to cleanse.] **—ex′pur·ga′tion** *n.*

ex·qui·site (**ĕk′**skwĭ-zĭt *or* ĭk-**skwĭz′**ĭt) *adj.* **1.** Characterized by intricate and beautiful design or execution: *an exquisite vase.* **2.** Showing careful judgment or fine taste: *exquisite taste in art.* **3.** Intense; keen: *took exquisite*

ă	pat	ôr	core
ā	pay	oi	boy
âr	care	ou	out
ä	father	o͝o	took
ĕ	pet	o͝or	lure
ē	be	o͞o	boot
ĭ	pit	ŭ	cut
ī	bite	ûr	urge
îr	pier	th	thin
ŏ	pot	*th*	this
ō	toe	zh	vision
ô	paw	ə	about

pleasure in their children's success. [From Middle English *exquisit*, carefully chosen, from Latin *exquīsītus*, past participle of *exquīrere*, to search out : *ex-*, out + *quaerere*, to seek.] **—ex′qui·site·ly** *adv.*

ext. *abbr.* An abbreviation of extension.

ex·tant (ĕk′stənt *or* ĕk-stănt′) *adj.* Still in existence; not destroyed, lost, or extinct: *extant diaries of early settlers.*

ex·tem·po·ra·ne·ous (ĭk-stĕm′pə-rā′nē-əs) *adj.* Done or made with little or no preparation; impromptu: *The scientist stood up and made extemporaneous comments on the situation.* **—ex·tem′po·ra′ne·ous·ly** *adv.* **—ex·tem′po·ra′ne·ous·ness** *n.*

ex·tend (ĭk-stĕnd′) *v.* **ex·tend·ed, ex·tend·ing, ex·tends** *—tr.* **1.** To cause (something) to be longer, wider, or cover more area: *extended the dock to accommodate larger boats.* See Synonyms at **increase. 2.** To increase the scope or effect of: *research that extended our knowledge of the universe.* **3.** To cause (something) to last longer: *extended our visit by a day.* **4.** To open or straighten (something) out: *Extend your left arm.* **5.** To offer or provide: *extend congratulations to the graduates; extend aid to a developing nation.* **6.** To prolong the time allowed for payment of: *The bank extended our loan for another month.* *—intr.* To be or become long, large, or comprehensive: *The beach extends for miles. The influence of our democracy extends around the world.* [From Middle English *extenden*, from Latin *extendere* : *ex-*, out + *tendere*, to stretch.]

ex·tend·ed (ĭk-stĕn′dĭd) *adj.* **1.** Stretched or pulled out: *extended arms.* **2.** Continued for a long period of time; prolonged: *an extended vacation in the Caribbean.* **3.** Enlarged or broad in meaning, scope, or influence: *extended television coverage of the Congressional hearings.* **—ex·tend′ed·ly** *adv.*

extended family *n.* A family that includes parents, children, and other relatives, often living with or near to each other.

ex·ten·sion (ĭk-stĕn′shən) *n.* **1.** The act of extending or the condition of being extended: *extension of the highway farther up the coast.* **2.** The amount, degree, or range to which something extends or can extend: *The wire has an extension of 50 feet.* **3a.** The act of straightening or extending a part of the body by a muscle: *extension of the leg to relieve muscle cramps.* **b.** The position assumed by an extended limb. **4.** Something that extends from a main part; an addition: *An extension was added to the back of the building.* **5.** An additional telephone connected to a main line: *We have two extensions to our telephone.* **6.** A string of letters or numbers following the name of a computer file that identify the kind of file: *The extension .txt indicates that a file is a text file.*

extension cord *n.* An insulated electric wire fitted with a plug and one or more sockets, used to plug in devices whose cords are not long enough to reach a wall outlet.

ex·ten·sive (ĭk-stĕn′sĭv) *adj.* Large in extent, range, or amount: *An extensive park runs along the ocean. We made extensive renovations to the old building.* **—ex·ten′sive·ly** *adv.* **—ex·ten′sive·ness** *n.*

ex·ten·sor (ĭk-stĕn′sər) *n.* A muscle that extends or stretches a limb of the body.

ex·tent (ĭk-stĕnt′) *n.* **1.** The area, magnitude, or distance over which something extends; size: *increased the extent of their lands; underestimated the extent of the damage.* **2.** The degree to which something extends: *prosecuted to the fullest extent of the law.* **3.** An extensive space or area: *an extent of pine forest.*

ex·ten·u·ate (ĭk-stĕn′yo͞o-āt′) *tr.v.* **ex·ten·u·at·ed, ex·ten·u·at·ing, ex·ten·u·ates** To lessen or appear to lessen the seriousness or extent of, especially by providing partial excuses: *Lack of experience extenuated the fault of the goalie in the team's loss.* **—ex·ten′u·a′tor** *n.* **—ex·ten′u·a·to′ry** (ĭk-stĕn′yo͞o-ə-tôr′ē) *adj.*

ex·ten·u·a·tion (ĭk-stĕn′yo͞o-ā′shən) *n.* The act of extenuating or the condition of being extenuated; partial justification.

ex·te·ri·or (ĭk-stîr′ē-ər) *adj.* **1.** Outer; external: *the exterior walls of a castle.* **2.** Originating or acting from the outside: *exterior pressures.* **3.** Suitable for use outside: *an exterior paint able to withstand sun and rain.* ❖ *n.* **1.** A part or surface that is outside: *the exterior of the house.* **2.** An outward appearance: *The town had a cheerful exterior.* [From Latin *exterior*, comparative of *exter*, outward.]

exterior angle *n.* **1.** Any of the four angles on the outside of two straight lines that are intersected by a third line. **2.** The angle formed between a side of a polygon and an extended adjacent side.

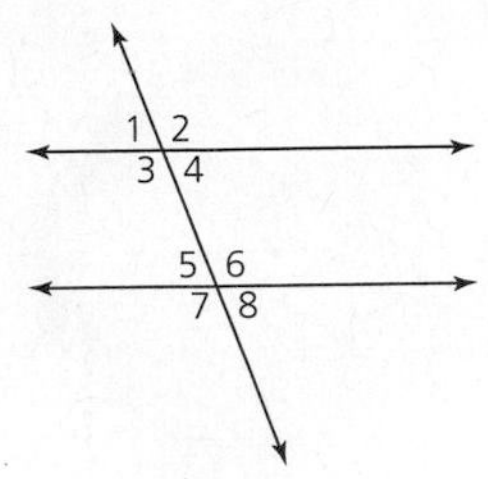

exterior angle
Angles 1, 2, 7, and 8 are exterior angles.

ex·ter·mi·nate (ĭk-stûr′mə-nāt′) *tr.v.* **ex·ter·mi·nat·ed, ex·ter·mi·nat·ing, ex·ter·mi·nates** To get rid of by destroying completely; wipe out: *exterminate a colony of termites.* [From Latin *extermināre*, to drive out : *ex-*, out + *terminus*, boundary.] **—ex·ter′mi·na′tion** *n.*

ex·ter·mi·na·tor (ĭk-stûr′mə-nā′tər) *n.* A person whose occupation is exterminating insects, rodents, or other pests.

ex·ter·nal (ĭk-stûr′nəl) *adj.* **1.** Relating to, existing on, or connected with the outside or an outer part; exterior: *external repairs on a house.* **2.** Suitable for application to an outer surface: *a salve for external use only.* **3.** Acting or coming from the outside: *an external force.* **4.** Relating chiefly to outward appearance; superficial: *an external display of pleasure.* **5.** Relating to foreign affairs or foreign countries. [From Middle English, from Latin *externus*, outward.] **—ex·ter′nal·ly** *adv.*

external ear *n.* The outer ear.

ex·tinct (ĭk-stĭngkt′) *adj.* **1.** No longer existing or living: *an extinct species.* **2.** No longer in use: *extinct languages.* **3.** No longer burning or erupting; no longer active: *an extinct volcano.* [From Middle English, from Latin *exstīnctus*, past participle of *exstinguere*, to extinguish.]

ex·tinc·tion (ĭk-stĭngk′shən) *n.* **1.** The fact of being extinct or the process of becoming extinct: *Colonization by humans has led to the extinction of many plant and animal species on the Hawaiian Islands.* **2.** The act of extinguishing: *Extinction of the fire took many hours.*

ex·tin·guish (ĭk-stĭng′gwĭsh) *tr.v.* **ex·tin·guished, ex·tin·guish·ing, ex·tin·guish·es 1.** To put out (a fire, for example); quench: *extinguish a candle; extinguish the lights.* **2.** To put an end to (hopes, for example); destroy: *Missing the bus extinguished our hope of arriving on time.* [From Latin *exstinguere* : *ex-*, out + *stinguere*, to quench.] **—ex·tin′guish·a·ble** *adj.*

ex·tin·guish·er (ĭk-stĭng′gwĭ-shər) *n.* A portable device for spraying and extinguishing a fire with chemicals.

ex·tir·pate (ĕk′stər-pāt′) *tr.v.* **ex·tir·pat·ed, ex·tir·pat·ing, ex·tir·pates** To destroy totally; exterminate: *extirpate the evils of prejudice.* **—ex′tir·pa′tion** *n.*

ex·tol also **ex·toll** (ĭk-stōl′) *tr.v.* **ex·tolled, ex·tol·ling, ex·tols** or **ex·tolls** To praise highly; laud: *extol the achievements of a great humanitarian.* **—ex·tol′ler** *n.*

ex·tort (ĭk-stôrt′) *tr.v.* **ex·tort·ed, ex·tort·ing, ex·torts** To obtain by coercion, intimidation, or psychological pressure: *The gangsters extorted money from local shopkeepers.* [From Latin *extorquēre*, to wrench out, extort : *ex-*, out + *torquēre*, to twist.] **—ex·tort′er** *n.*

ex·tor·tion (ĭk-stôr′shən) *n.* The act or practice of obtaining something by coercion or intimidation, especially in violation of the law. **—ex·tor′tion·ist** *n.*

ex·tor·tion·ate (ĭk-stôr′shə-nĭt) *adj.* **1.** Characterized by extortion: *the extortionate demands of the rebel forces.* **2.** Exorbitant; immoderate: *extortionate prices for gasoline.* **—ex·tor′tion·ate·ly** *adv.*

ex·tra (ĕk′strə) *adj.* More than what is usual, normal, expected, or necessary; additional: *earn extra money by working part-time.* ❖ *n.* **1.** Something additional,

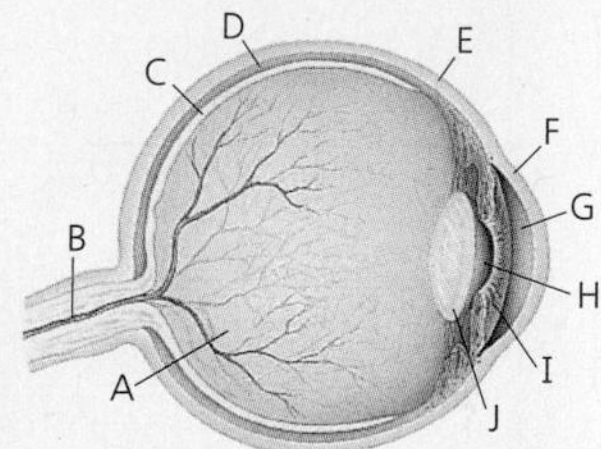

eye
top: cross section of a human eye
A. vitreous humor
B. optic nerve
C. retina
D. choroid
E. sclera
F. cornea
G. aqueous humor
H. pupil
I. iris
J. lens
bottom: the eye of a hurricane

ă	pat	ôr	core
ā	pay	oi	boy
âr	care	ou	out
ä	father	ŏŏ	took
ĕ	pet	ŏŏr	lure
ē	be	ōō	boot
ĭ	pit	ŭ	cut
ī	bite	ûr	urge
îr	pier	th	thin
ŏ	pot	*th*	this
ō	toe	zh	vision
ô	paw	ə	about

for which one pays an added charge: *We bought a new car with all the extras such as a stereo.* **2.** A special edition of a newspaper: *The extra gave the latest news of the crisis.* **3.** A performer hired to play a minor part, as in a crowd scene in a film. ❖ *adv.* To an exceptional extent or degree; unusually: *The audience was extra quiet during the vocalist's solo.* [Probably short for *extraordinary*.]

extra– or **extro–** *pref.* A prefix that means outside or beyond: *extracurricular.*

ex·tra-base hit (**ĕk′**strə-**bās′**) *n.* In baseball, a double, triple, or home run.

ex·tract (ĭk-**străkt′**) *tr.v.* **ex·tract·ed, ex·tract·ing, ex·tracts 1.** To draw or pull out, often with great force or effort: *extract a tooth; extract ore from a mine.* **2.** To obtain despite resistance: *extract a confession.* **3.** To obtain from a substance by a chemical or physical process: *extract aluminum from bauxite; extract the juice of berries.* **4.** To remove for separate consideration or publication; excerpt. **5.** To derive or gain from an experience or source: *extract pleasure from listening to music.* ❖ *n.* (**ĕk′**străkt′) **1.** A passage from a literary work; an excerpt: *The book is made up of extracts from other works.* **2.** A concentrated substance from a food or flavoring: *vanilla extract; an extract of coffee.* [From Middle English *extracten*, from Latin *extractus*, past participle of *extrahere* : *ex-*, out + *trahere*, to draw.] **—ex·trac′tor** *n.* —SEE NOTE AT **detract.**

ex·trac·tion (ĭk-**străk′**shən) *n.* **1.** The act of extracting or the condition of being extracted: *The extraction of impacted wisdom teeth is quite common.* **2.** Something obtained by extraction; an extract. **3.** Descent; origin: *of French-Canadian extraction.*

ex·tra·cur·ric·u·lar (ĕk′strə-kə-**rĭk′**yə-lər) *adj.* Being outside the regular course of study of a school or college: *Debating is an extracurricular activity.*

ex·tra·dite (**ĕk′**strə-dīt′) *tr.v.* **ex·tra·dit·ed, ex·tra·dit·ing, ex·tra·dites** To give up or deliver (a prisoner or fugitive, for example) to the jurisdiction of another government or authority.

ex·tra·di·tion (ĕk′strə-**dĭsh′**ən) *n.* The surrender of an individual by one nation or state to another nation or state where that individual is wanted for trial or punishment for the commission of a crime.

ex·tra·ne·ous (ĭk-**strā′**nē-əs) *adj.* **1.** Not essential; irrelevant: *These minor points are extraneous to my report.* **2.** Coming from the outside; foreign. **—ex·tra′ne·ous·ly** *adv.* **—ex·tra′ne·ous·ness** *n.*

ex·traor·di·nar·y (ĭk-**strôr′**dn-ĕr′ē *or* ĕk′strə-**ôr′**dn-ĕr′ē) *adj.* Very unusual; exceptional; remarkable: *Landing on the moon was an extraordinary accomplishment. Great intelligence is an extraordinary gift.* [From Middle English *extraordinarie*, from Latin *extraōdinārius* : *extrā*, outside + *ōrdō*, order, rule.] **—ex·traor′di·nar′i·ly** (ĭk-strôr′dn-**âr′**ə-lē *or* ĕk′strə-ôr′dn-**âr′**ə-lē) *adv.*

ex·trap·o·late (ĭk-**străp′**ə-lāt′) *v.* **ex·trap·o·lat·ed, ex·trap·o·lat·ing, ex·trap·o·lates** *—tr.* **1.** To infer or estimate (something unknown) on the basis of known information: *We extrapolated next year's expenses from a review of this year's bills.* **2.** In mathematics, to estimate the value of a quantity that falls outside the range in which its values are known. *—intr.* To make an estimate or prediction of something not known on the basis of known information. **—ex·trap′o·la′tion** *n.*

ex·tra·sen·so·ry (ĕk′strə-**sĕn′**sə-rē) *adj.* Outside the normal range of the physical senses: *Extrasensory powers are said to enable some people to predict the future.*

extrasensory perception *n.* ESP.

ex·tra·so·lar (ĕk′strə-**sō′**lər) *adj.* Existing or originating outside the solar system: *an extrasolar planet.*

ex·tra·ter·res·tri·al (ĕk′strə-tə-**rĕs′**trē-əl) *adj.* Beyond the earth or outside its atmosphere: *extraterrestrial bodies such as stars and comets.* ❖ *n.* An extraterrestrial being or life form.

ex·trav·a·gance (ĭk-**străv′**ə-gəns) *n.* **1.** The quality of being extravagant: *the extravagance of the party decorations.* **2.** Immoderate spending: *Such extravagance can lead to debt.* **3.** Something that is excessively costly: *Their latest extravagance is an expensive car.*

ex·trav·a·gant (ĭk-**străv′**ə-gənt) *adj.* **1.** Excessive or unreasonable: *extravagant fees for the service.* **2.** Given to lavish or imprudent spending: *an extravagant executive.* **—ex·trav′a·gant·ly** *adv.*

ex·trav·a·gan·za (ĭk-străv′ə-**găn′**zə) *n.* An elaborate spectacular display or entertainment: *The circus is one huge extravaganza.*

ex·treme (ĭk-**strēm′**) *adj.* **1.** The farthest possible; outermost: *the extreme end of the room.* **2.** Very great or intense: *exercise extreme caution; suffer from the extreme cold.* **3.** Extending far beyond the norm: *hold extreme opinions in politics.* **4.** Drastic; severe: *The doctors took extreme measures to control the baby's temperature.* **5a.** Relating to environmental conditions that normally do not support living organisms. **b.** Adapted to life under such conditions: *extreme microorganisms.* **6a.** Very dangerous or difficult: *extreme sports.* **b.** Participating in a very dangerous or difficult sport: *an extreme skier.* ❖ *n.* **1.** The greatest or utmost degree or point: *eager to the extreme.* **2.** Either of two things set at opposite ends of a range: *the extremes of boiling and freezing.* **3.** A drastic measure: *resort to extremes in an emergency.* **4.** In mathematics, the first or last term of a proportion. [From Middle English, from Latin *extrēmus*.] **—ex·treme′ly** *adv.* **—ex·treme′ness** *n.*

extremely high frequency *n.* A radio frequency between 30,000 and 300,000 megahertz.

extremely low frequency *n.* A radio frequency below 300 hertz.

ex·trem·ist (ĭk-**strē′**mĭst) *n.* A person with views extending far beyond the norm, especially in politics. **—ex·trem′ism** *n.*

ex·trem·i·ty (ĭk-**strĕm′**ĭ-tē) *n., pl.* **ex·trem·i·ties 1.** The outermost or farthest point: *Patagonia is at the southern extremity of South America.* **2.** The greatest or utmost degree or condition: *the extremity of the recent weather.* **3.** An extreme or severe measure: *resort to extremities in a crisis.* **4. extremities** Limbs or appendages, especially the hands and feet: *Boots and gloves protect the extremities from cold.*

ex·tre·mo·phile (ĭk-**strē′**mə-fīl′) *n.* Any of various organisms that thrive only in extreme conditions, such as very hot or very salty environments. Many archaea are extremophiles.

ex·tri·cate (**ĕk′**strĭ-kāt′) *tr.v.* **ex·tri·cat·ed, ex·tri·cat·ing, ex·tri·cates** To set free from an entanglement or difficulty; disengage: *extricate oneself from an embarrassing situation.* [From Latin *extrīcāre* : *ex-*, out + *trīcae*, hindrances, perplexities.] **—ex′tri·ca′tion** *n.*

ex·trin·sic (ĭk-**strĭn′**sĭk *or* ĭk-**strĭn′**zĭk) *adj.* **1.** Not essential or basic; extraneous: *Your arguments are extrinsic to the discussion.* **2.** Originating from the outside; external: *extrinsic forces on the environment.* **—ex·trin′si·cal·ly** *adv.*

ex·tro·vert (**ĕk′**strə-vûrt′) *n.* A person who is sociable and outgoing and who is more interested in external circumstances than in his or her personal thoughts or feelings. **—ex′tro·vert′ed** *adj.*

ex·trude (ĭk-**strōōd′**) *v.* **ex·trud·ed, ex·trud·ing, ex·trudes** *—tr.* **1.** To push or thrust out. **2.** To shape (plastic, for example) by forcing it through a die. *—intr.* To protrude or project: *Lava extruded from a crack in the mountainside.*

ex·tru·sion (ĭk-**strōō′**zhən) *n.* **1.** The act or process of extruding: *Pieces for plastic furniture are often made* *by extrusion.* **2.** Something that has been extruded.

ex·u·ber·ance (ĭg-zo͞o′bər-əns) *n.* The condition or quality of being exuberant: *The crowd cheered in wild exuberance.*

ex·u·ber·ant (ĭg-zo͞o′bər-ənt) *adj.* **1.** Full of unrestrained enthusiasm or joy: *exuberant sports fans; exuberant smiles.* **2.** Lavish or extravagant; overflowing: *exuberant praise of the hero.* [From Middle English, from Latin *exūberāre,* to be exuberant.] **—ex·u′ber·ant·ly** *adv.*

ex·u·da·tion (ĕks′yo͞o-dā′shən) *n.* **1.** The act or an instance of oozing forth: *a slight exudation of blood from a cut.* **2.** Something that has oozed forth.

ex·ude (ĭg-zo͞od′ *or* ĭk-so͞od′) *tr. & intr.v.* **ex·ud·ed, ex·ud·ing, ex·udes** To give or come forth by or as if by oozing: *The body exudes sweat through the pores. Sap exuded from the cuts in the plant's stem. Confidence exuded in their cocky manner.* [From Latin *exsūdāre* : *ex-,* out + *sūdāre,* to sweat.]

ex·ult (ĭg-zŭlt′) *intr.v.* **ex·ult·ed, ex·ult·ing, ex·ults** To rejoice greatly; be jubilant or triumphant: *The entire town exulted in the team's victory.* [From Latin *exsultāre* : *ex-,* out, up + *saltāre,* to dance, leap.]

ex·ul·tant (ĭg-zŭl′tənt) *adj.* Marked by great joy or jubilation: *an exultant victor.* **—ex·ult′ant·ly** *adv.*

ex·ul·ta·tion (ĕk′səl-tā′shən *or* ĕg′zəl-tā′shən) *n.* The act or condition of rejoicing greatly.

–ey *suff.* Variant of **–y¹**.

eye (ī) *n.* **1a.** An organ by means of which an animal is able to see or sense light. In vertebrates the eye consists of a hollow structure containing a lens that focuses incoming light on a photosensitive retina. **b.** The outer visible part of this organ, especially the colored iris: *Tina has brown eyes.* **c.** The area and the structures around the eye, including the eyelids, eyelashes, and eyebrows: *She put her hands over her eyes.* **2.** A light-sensitive organ of an invertebrate animal. **3.** The ability to observe carefully: *A lifeguard must have a sharp eye.* **4.** The ability to estimate, judge, or note: *The coach had an eye for new talent.* **5.** A way of regarding something; a point of view or an opinion: *saw the world with a critical eye.* **6.** Something that resembles an eye, as a bud on a potato or a spot on a peacock's tail feather. **7.** The hole in a needle that the thread goes through. **8.** A loop, as of metal, rope, or thread. **9.** The relatively calm area at the center of a hurricane or similar storm. ❖ *tr.v.* **eyed, eye·ing** or **ey·ing** (ī′ĭng), **eyes** To look at; watch; regard: *The child eyed the big dog suspiciously.* ◆ **an eye for an eye** Punishment in which an offender suffers what the victim has suffered: *Execution of the murderer was defended as an eye for an eye.* **have (one's) eye on** To look at, especially attentively or continuously: *He's got his eye on that piece of cake.* **lay (one's) eyes on** or **set (one's) eyes on** To see: *the cutest dog I've ever laid eyes on.* **eye to eye** In agreement: *see eye to eye on most issues.* **in the public eye** Frequently seen in public or in the media: *celebrities who are constantly in the public eye.* **with an eye to** With a view to: *We left early with an eye to getting home before dark.* [From Old English *ēge.*]

❑ *These sound alike:* **eye, aye** (yes), **I¹** (pronoun).

eye·ball (ī′bôl′) *n.* The ball-shaped part of the eye of a vertebrate animal, enclosed by the socket and covered by the eyelids. It is connected at the rear to the optic nerve.

eye·brow (ī′brou′) *n.* **1.** The bony ridge of the skull that extends over the eye. **2.** The line of short hairs covering this ridge.

eye·cup (ī′kŭp′) *n.* A small cup with a rim shaped to fit over the eye, used for washing the eye or applying liquid medicine to it.

eye·drop·per (ī′drŏp′ər) *n.* A dropper for applying liquid medicine to the eye.

eye·ful (ī′fo͝ol′) *n.* **1.** An amount of something that gets into the eye: *The wind was blowing and I got an eyeful of dust.* **2.** A complete view; a good look: *We got a real eyeful during the tour of the auto plant.*

eye·glass·es (ī′glăs′ĭz) *pl.n.* A pair of lenses worn in front of the eyes to correct vision; glasses.

eye·lash (ī′lăsh′) *n.* **1.** A row of hairs that forms a fringe on the edge of the eyelid. **2.** One of the hairs in this row.

eye·let (ī′lĭt) *n.* **1a.** A small hole for a lace, cord, or hook to fit through: *Shoelaces are threaded through eyelets.* **b.** A metal ring used as a rim to strengthen such a hole: *The eyelets on the flag protected it from tearing.* **2.** A small hole edged with embroidered stitches as part of a design. [From Middle English *oilet,* from Old French *oillet,* diminutive of *oil,* eye.]

❑ *These sound alike:* **eyelet, islet** (small island).

eye·lid (ī′lĭd′) *n.* Either one of a pair of folds of skin and muscle that can be brought together to cover the eyeball.

eye·lin·er (ī′lī′nər) *n.* Makeup used to outline the eyes.

eye opener *n. Informal* A startling or shocking revelation: *The article about the water shortage was a real eye opener.*

eye·piece (ī′pēs′) *n.* The lens or group of lenses closest to the eye in a telescope, microscope, or similar optical instrument.

eye shadow *n.* A cosmetic applied to the eyelids to enhance the eyes.

eye·sight (ī′sīt′) *n.* **1.** The ability to see; vision; sight: *People wear glasses to correct poor eyesight.* **2.** Range of vision; view: *a stream within eyesight of the house.*

eye socket *n.* The bony cavity in the skull that holds the eyeball.

eye·sore (ī′sôr′) *n.* An ugly or unpleasant sight: *That junkyard is an eyesore.*

eye·spot (ī′spŏt′) *n.* **1.** An area that is sensitive to light and functions somewhat like an eye, found in certain one-celled organisms and many invertebrate animals. **2.** A round marking resembling an eye, as on a butterfly's wing.

eye·stalk (ī′stôk′) *n.* A movable structure having an eye on its tip, found on crabs, lobsters, and certain other crustaceans.

eye·strain (ī′strān′) *n.* Pain and fatigue of the eyes, often resulting from prolonged use of the eyes or uncorrected defects of vision.

eye·tooth (ī′to͞oth′) *n.* Either of the two canine teeth of the upper jaw.

eye·wash (ī′wŏsh′) *n.* **1.** A solution used to wash or medicate the eyes. **2.** *Informal* Actions or remarks intended to conceal the facts of a situation.

eye·wit·ness (ī′wĭt′nĭs) *n.* A person who has seen something or someone and can bear witness to the fact.

ey·rie (âr′ē *or* îr′ē) *n.* Variant of **aerie**.

E·ze·ki·el¹ (ĭ-zē′kē-əl) A Hebrew prophet of the 6th century BC.

E·ze·ki·el² (ĭ-zē′kē-əl) *n.* A book of the Bible containing Ezekiel's prophecies on the destruction and restoration of Israel.

Ez·ra¹ (ĕz′rə) A Hebrew priest, scribe, and reformer of the 5th century BC.

Ez·ra² (ĕz′rə) *n.* A book of the Bible describing the return of the Hebrew exiles from Babylon and their efforts to build a temple in Jerusalem.

eyelet

eyespot

eyespots on a moth

WRITERS CHOOSE THEIR WORDS

"Don't tell me," said Allie, "your name is Summer, and you want to know if we're groovy." "My name's Meadow, and I don't say groovy anymore, because I got tired of people making fun of me." "Do you have to insult everybody you meet?" Nick whispered to Allie, then turned back to Meadow. "I'm Nick, and this is Lief. The rude one is Allie." "I wasn't being rude," Allie insisted. "I was being **facetious.** There's a difference." "No sweat," said Meadow, which was almost as bad as groovy.

—Neal Shusterman
Everlost

f or **F** (ĕf) *n., pl.* **f's** or **F's** also **fs** or **Fs** **1.** The sixth letter of the English alphabet: *There are two f's in off.* **2. F** A failing grade in school. **3.** In music, the fourth tone in the scale of C major.

F[1] The symbol for the element **fluorine.**

F[2] *abbr.* An abbreviation of: **1.** Fahrenheit. **2.** fail. **3.** female.

fa (fä) *n.* In music, the fourth tone of a major scale.

fa·ble (fā′bəl) *n.* **1.** A usually short tale or story that teaches a useful lesson about human nature, often with animal characters that speak and act like humans. **2.** A legend or myth. **3.** A falsehood; a lie. [From Middle English, from Latin *fābula,* from *fārī,* to speak.]

fa·bled (fā′bəld) *adj.* **1.** Made known or famous by fables; legendary: *the fabled city of El Dorado.* **2.** Existing only in fables; fictitious.

fab·ric (făb′rĭk) *n.* **1.** Material made of woven, knitted, or matted fibers; cloth: *Lace, felt, and jersey are different types of fabric.* **2.** An underlying structure or framework: *Crime is threatening the very fabric of American society.* [From Middle English *fabryke,* something constructed, from Latin *fabrica,* craft, workshop, from *faber,* craftsman.]

fab·ri·cate (făb′rĭ-kāt′) *tr.v.* **fab·ri·cat·ed, fab·ri·cat·ing, fab·ri·cates** **1.** To make, build, or manufacture, especially by assembling parts: *fabricate refrigerators on an assembly line.* **2.** To make up; invent: *fabricate an excuse for being late.* **—fab′ri·ca′tion** *n.*

fab·u·list (făb′yə-lĭst) *n.* A person who composes fables.

fab·u·lous (făb′yə-ləs) *adj.* **1.** Extremely pleasing or successful; wonderful: *a fabulous vacation.* **2.** Astonishing or remarkable: *a fabulous rise to fame.* **3.** Legendary or mythical: *unicorns and other fabulous beasts.* [From Middle English, from Latin *fābulōsus,* from *fābula,* fable.] **—fab′u·lous·ly** *adv.* **—fab′u·lous·ness** *n.*

fa·çade also **fa·cade** (fə-säd′) *n.* **1.** The face or front of a building: *the decorated façade of a church.* **2.** An artificial or false front: *Her friendliness was only a façade to gain our confidence.* [From Italian *facciata,* from *faccia,* face.]

face (fās) *n.* **1.** The front of the head: *had a mask over her face.* **2a.** The expression of the face; countenance: *a friendly face.* **b.** A twisted facial expression: *The baby learned to make faces.* **3.** The surface presented to view; the front: *the face of a building.* **4.** An outer surface: *the face of the earth.* **5.** The upper or marked side: *the face of a playing card.* **6.** A plane surface that bounds a geometric solid: *the face of a cube.* **7.** The outward appearance; look: *With so many new buildings, the face of the city has changed.* **8.** Value or standing in the eyes of others; dignity; prestige: *They saved face by saying they were misled.* ❖ *v.* **faced, fac·ing, fac·es** *—tr.* **1.** To have or turn the face toward: *The actor faced the audience.* **2.** To have the front toward; look out on: *The cathedral faces the square.* **3.** To meet or confront with self-assurance: *How can I face my parents when I know that I've let them down?* **4.** To acknowledge and accept or deal with: *You've got to face the facts. We must be willing to face our problems.* **5.** To cover a surface with a different material: *face the front of the fireplace with marble.* **6.** To line or trim the edge of: *face a cloth collar with satin.* *—intr.* **1.** To be turned or placed with the front in a certain direction: *The house faces toward the west.* **2.** To turn the face in a certain direction: *I faced into the wind.* ◆ **face off** To start play in ice hockey, lacrosse, and other games by releasing the puck or ball between two opposing players. **face up** To confront an unpleasant situation boldly: *finally faced up to the problem.* **in the face of** In spite of; despite: *The team won in the face of strong competition.* [From Middle English, from Old French, from Latin *faciēs.*]

face card *n.* A king, queen, or jack in a deck of playing cards.

face·less (fās′lĭs) *adj.* **1.** Having no face. **2.** Without identity; anonymous; impersonal: *a huge faceless corporation.*

face-lift also **face·lift** (fās′lĭft′) *n.* **1.** An operation to tighten wrinkles or sagging skin of the face. **2.** A change or renovation to improve the appearance: *a plan to give the old building a face-lift.*

face·mask (fās′măsk′) *n.* **1.** A covering for the face or head that is worn for protection or as a disguise: *Hockey players in our league must wear a helmet with a facemask.* **2.** A transparent, watertight covering for the face used in seeing underwater: *wore a facemask while scuba diving.*

face-off (fās′ôf′) *n.* **1.** A method of starting play in ice hockey, lacrosse, and other games in which an official drops the puck or ball between two opposing players who then try to gain possession of it. **2.** A confrontation.

face·palm (fās′päm′) *n. Informal* The act of putting one's hand over one's face, as in embarrassment or dismay. **—face′palm′** *v.*

fac·et (făs′ĭt) *n.* **1.** One of the flat polished surfaces cut on a gem or occurring naturally on a crystal. **2.** One of the ways of considering something; an aspect: *a complex problem with many facets to consider.* **3.** One of the individual outer visual units or lenses of a compound eye. [From Old French *facette,* diminutive of *face.*]

fa·ce·tious (fə-sē′shəs) *adj.* Trying or meant to be funny; joking or humorous: *a facetious remark.* [From Latin *facētia,* a jest.] **—fa·ce′tious·ly** *adv.* **—fa·ce′tious·ness** *n.*

face value *n.* **1.** The value indicated on postage stamps, money, checks, bonds, or other paper securities: *an old coin worth 10 times its face value.* **2.** The apparent value or meaning: *Take such compliments at face value.*

fa·cial (fā′shəl) *adj.* Relating to the face: *a comic with amusing facial expressions.* ❖ *n.* A treatment for the face, usually including a massage.

fac·ile (făs′əl) *adj.* **1.** Done with little effort or difficulty; easy: *a facile task.* **2.** Working, acting, or speaking effortlessly or quickly: *a facile speaker; a facile writer.* **3.** Arrived at or presented without proper care or effort; superficial: *a facile solution to the problem.*

fa·cil·i·tate (fə-sĭl′ĭ-tāt′) *tr.v.* **fa·cil·i·tat·ed, fa·cil·i·tat·**

ă	pat	ôr	core
ā	pay	oi	boy
âr	care	ou	out
ä	father	ŏŏ	took
ĕ	pet	ŏŏr	lure
ē	be	ōō	boot
ĭ	pit	ŭ	cut
ī	bite	ûr	urge
îr	pier	th	thin
ŏ	pot	*th*	this
ō	toe	zh	vision
ô	paw	ə	about

ing, fa·cil·i·tates 1. To make easier; assist: *The bank loans will facilitate the building of a new sports arena.* **2.** To lead (a discussion). **—fa·cil′i·ta′tion** *n.* **—fa·cil′i·ta′tor** *n.*

fa·cil·i·ty (fə-sĭl′ĭ-tē) *n., pl.* **fa·cil·i·ties 1.** Ease in moving, acting, or doing; aptitude: *She has a real facility for learning foreign languages.* **2.** often **facilities** Something built or designed to provide a service or convenience: *The building has ample storage facilities.*

fac·ing (fā′sĭng) *n.* **1.** A piece of material sewn to the edge of a garment as a lining or decoration. **2.** An outer covering of different material applied to a surface for decoration or protection: *a wood house with a stone facing.*

fac·sim·i·le (făk-sĭm′ə-lē) *n.* **1.** An exact copy or reproduction: *The exhibit contained facsimiles of medieval manuscripts.* **2a.** A fax machine. **b.** A page received or sent by a fax machine. [From Latin *fac simile*, make similar.]

fact (făkt) *n.* **1.** Knowledge or information based on real occurrences: *The account is based on fact. The movie is a mixture of fact and fiction.* **2.** Something whose reality, existence, or occurrence is known: *Genetic engineering is now a fact. That the Civil War happened is a fact. We are unsure of the facts in the case.* **3.** A thing that has been done, especially a crime: *an accessory after the fact.* ◆ **in fact** In reality; in truth. [From Latin *factum*, deed, from past participle of *facere*, to do.]

fac·tion (făk′shən) *n.* **1.** A group of people who have certain interests that are not shared with others in a larger group: *Factions form in organizations when members feel discontented with things as they are.* **2.** Internal discord; conflict within a nation, an organization, or another group: *The town government was torn by faction.*

fac·tion·al (făk′shə-nəl) *adj.* **1.** Relating to factions: *factional disputes.* **2.** Causing conflict or discord: *factional questions arose during the conference.*

fac·tion·al·ism (făk′shə-nə-lĭz′əm) *n.* A condition of discord or conflict; a tendency toward the creation of factions: *Factionalism within the group caused the organization to break up.*

fac·tious (făk′shəs) *adj.* Tending to cause conflict or discord; divisive: *factious members of a group.* **—fac′tious·ly** *adv.* **—fac′tious·ness** *n.*

fac·toid (făk′toid) *n.* **1.** A brief, somewhat interesting fact. **2.** A piece of information that is not true or cannot be verified but which is accepted as true because of frequent repetition.

fac·tor (făk′tər) *n.* **1.** Something that helps bring about a certain result; an element or ingredient: *Many factors contributed to the success of the celebration.* **2.** One of two or more numbers or expressions that are multiplied to obtain a given product. For example, 2 and 3 are factors of 6, and $a + b$ and $a - b$ are factors of $a^2 - b^2$. **3.** A substance found in the body, such as a protein, that is essential to a biological process: *Growth factors are needed for proper cell development.* ❖ *tr.v.* **fac·tored, fac·tor·ing, fac·tors** To find the factors of (a number or expression). ◆ **factor in** To figure in: *We factored in the possibility of getting stuck in traffic when we scheduled the meeting.* [From Middle English *factour*, perpetrator, agent, from Latin *factor*, maker, from *facere*, to make.] **—fac′tor·a·ble** *adj.*

fac·to·ri·al (făk-tôr′ē-əl) *n.* The product of all of the positive integers from 1 to a given positive integer. For example, the factorial of 4, written 4!, is $1 \times 2 \times 3 \times 4 = 24$. ❖ *adj.* Relating to a factorial: *a factorial symbol.*

fac·to·ry (făk′tə-rē) *n., pl.* **fac·to·ries** A building or group of buildings in which goods are manufactured; a plant: *The new automobile factory is filled with automated machines.*

factory farm *n.* A large-scale farming operation designed for efficient production, especially a large complex where animals are kept in small cages. **—factory farming** *n.*

fac·to·tum (făk-tō′təm) *n.* An assistant who does many kinds of work. [From Medieval Latin *factōtum* : Latin *fac*, imperative of *facere*, to do + Latin *tōtum*, everything.]

fac·tu·al (făk′cho͞o-əl) *adj.* Based on or containing facts: *a factual account of what happened.* **—fac′tu·al·ly** *adv.*

fac·ul·ty (făk′əl-tē) *n., pl.* **fac·ul·ties 1.** One of the powers of the mind or body: *the faculty of speech.* **2.** A special ability or skill: *He has a faculty for doing impersonations.* **3.** The teaching staff of a school, college, or university: *How many math teachers are on the school's faculty?*

fad (făd) *n.* Something that is done or adopted with great enthusiasm by many people for a brief period of time; a craze.

fade (fād) *v.* **fad·ed, fad·ing, fades** *—intr.* **1.** To lose brightness or loudness gradually: *The colors faded in the wash. The bird's call faded as we left the forest.* **2.** To lose freshness; wither: *The flowers are beginning to fade.* **3.** To pass out of existence slowly; disappear gradually: *Our chances of winning faded when they scored late in the game.* See Synonyms at **disappear. 4.** In football, to move back from the scrimmage line. Used of a quarterback. *—tr.* To cause to lose brightness: *The sun faded the colors in the quilt.* [From Middle English *faden*, from Old French *fade*, faded, probably from Latin *fatuus*, insipid.]

fade-in or **fade·in** (fād′ĭn′) *n.* A gradual appearance of an image, light or sound, especially as a transition in a film, performance, or audio recording.

fade-out or **fade·out** (fād′out′) *n.* A gradual decrease in intensity of an image, light, or sound, especially as a transition in a film, performance, or audio recording.

fa·er·ie also **fa·er·y** (fā′ə-rē *or* fâr′ē) *n., pl.* **fa·er·ies** A fairy.

fag·ot (făg′ət) *n.* A bundle of twigs, sticks, or branches bound together, especially for firewood.

Fahr·en·heit (făr′ən-hīt′) *adj.* Relating to or based on a temperature scale that indicates the freezing point of water as 32° and the boiling point of water as 212° under standard atmospheric pressure. [After Daniel Gabriel *Fahrenheit* (1686–1736), German physicist.]

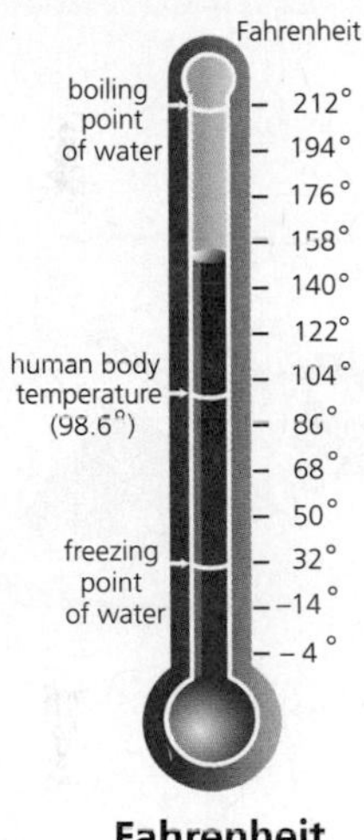

Fahrenheit

fail (fāl) *v.* **failed, fail·ing, fails** *—intr.* **1.** To be unsuccessful in attempting to do something, especially something wanted or expected: *Their first attempt at climbing the mountain failed.* **2.** To be lacking or not enough; fall short: *After months of drought the water supply failed.* **3.** To receive a grade that is less than acceptable in school. **4.** To stop functioning correctly; break down: *The brakes on the car failed.* **5.** To decline, as in strength or effectiveness: *The light began to fail.* **6.** To become bankrupt: *A number of downtown stores failed in the recession.* *—tr.* **1.** To leave (something) undone; neglect: *The defendant failed to appear in court.* **2.** To disappoint or prove undependable to: *I won't fail you this time.* **3.** To abandon; forsake: *His strength failed him on the homestretch.* **4a.** To receive an academic grade that is below the acceptable minimum in (a course, for example): *Did any students fail geometry?* **b.** To give an academic grade indicating unacceptability to: *The professor failed several students in the class.* ◆ **without fail** Definitely; certainly: *The job will be finished tomorrow without fail.* [From Middle English *failen*, from Latin *fallere*, to deceive.]

fail·ing (fā′lĭng) *n.* **1.** A fault or weakness; a shortcoming: *One of my failings is being late with library books.* **2.** The act of a person or thing that fails; a failure: *a failing of the water supply.* ❖ *prep.* In the absence of; without: *Failing directions, we will have to find the office on our own.*

fail-safe or **fail·safe** (fāl′sāf′) *adj.* **1.** Capable of stopping or making safe the operation of a mechanism in

WORD HISTORY

fair[1] The adjective **fair[1]** comes from the Old English adjective *faeger,* "lovely, pleasant, agreeable, beautiful," and the original meanings survive in expressions like "fair weather" and "fair price." *Fair* in the sense "neither very bad nor very good" probably came from people using the word *fair* to avoid hurting other people's feelings about something that was not very well done.

fajita

case of a failure or malfunction: *Fail-safe switches on machinery can save workers' lives.* **2.** Guaranteed not to fail: *a fail-safe plan.*

fail·ure (fāl′yər) *n.* **1.** The condition of not achieving something desired; lack of success: *Early airplane experiments ended in failure.* **2.** The neglect or inability to do something: *My failure to return library books meant a large fine.* **3.** The condition of being insufficient or falling short: *a crop failure during a drought.* **4.** A stopping of function or performance: *an electric power failure.* **5.** Bankruptcy: *The failure of the shop put several people out of work.* **6.** A person or thing that has failed: *I'm a failure as a trombone player.*

fain (fān) *Archaic adv.* Willingly or gladly. ❖ *adj.* Willing or glad.

❑ *These sound alike:* **fain, feign** (pretend).

faint (fānt) *adj.* **faint·er, faint·est 1.** So weak as to be difficult to perceive: *a faint light; a faint odor.* **2.** Small in degree or amount; meager: *a faint hope of getting the part.* **3.** Lacking in strength, energy, or interest: *only a faint attempt to understand their concerns.* **4.** Likely to fall unconscious; dizzy and weak: *Hunger made the hiker feel faint.* ❖ *n.* A sudden, usually short loss of consciousness, often caused by too little blood flowing to the brain. ❖ *intr.v.* **faint·ed, faint·ing, faints** To lose consciousness for a short time; swoon: *The dancer fainted in the heat.* ◆ **faint at heart** Lacking boldness or courage; faint-hearted. **—faint′ly** *adv.* **—faint′ness** *n.*

❑ *These sound alike:* **faint, feint** (pretend).

faint-heart·ed (fānt′här′tĭd) *adj.* Lacking courage; cowardly; timid. **—faint′-heart′ed·ly** *adv.* **—faint′-heart′ed·ness** *n.*

fair[1] (fâr) *adj.* **fair·er, fair·est 1.** Free of favoritism; impartial or just: *a fair price; a fair trial.* **2.** Conforming to the rules or moral standards: *fair play.* **3.** Pleasing to look at; beautiful; lovely: *a fair face.* **4.** Light in color or complexion: *fair hair; fair skin.* **5.** Clear and sunny; free of clouds or storms: *fair weather.* **6.** Somewhat good; acceptable: *The movie was only fair.* **7.** In baseball, lying or falling within the foul lines: *a fair ball.* ❖ *adv.* In a fair manner; properly: *I believe in playing fair.* ◆ **fair and square** Just and honest. **no fair** Something contrary to the rules. [From Old English *fæger,* lovely, pleasant.] **—fair′ness** *n.* —SEE NOTE.

❑ *These sound alike:* **fair[1]** (just), **fair[2]** (market), **fare** (travel cost).

fair[2] (fâr) *n.* **1.** A gathering for the buying and selling of goods, often held at a particular time and place; a market: *We went to the annual book fair.* **2.** An exhibition of home or farm products and skills, usually with competitions and entertainment: *Her pumpkin won first prize at the county fair.* **3.** An exhibition intended to inform people about products or opportunities: *a technology fair; a jobs fair.* **4.** A social event held for charity and usually including the sale of articles; a bazaar: *the hospital fair.* [From Middle English *feire,* from Late Latin *fēria,* holiday.]

❑ *These sound alike:* **fair[2]** (market), **fair[1]** (just), **fare** (travel cost).

fair catch *n.* In football, a catch of a kicked ball by a receiving player who has signaled the intention not to run with the ball. The receiving player may not be hit if no attempt is made to advance the ball after catching it.

fair game *n.* **1.** Animals that can be legally hunted: *Deer are fair game in many states in the fall.* **2.** A person or thing that seems suitable for pursuit or attack: *Politicians are fair game for reporters, especially during a campaign.*

fair·ground (fâr′ground′) *n.* An outdoor space where fairs, exhibitions, or other public events are held.

fair-haired (fâr′hârd′) *adj.* **1.** Having blond hair. **2.** Favorite: *the fair-haired member of the family.*

fair·ly (fâr′lē) *adv.* **1.** In a fair or just manner: *treating everyone fairly.* **2.** Moderately; rather: *I am feeling fairly well today.* **3.** Actually; positively: *The walls fairly shook from the wind.*

fair-mind·ed (fâr′mīn′dĭd) *adj.* Just and impartial; not prejudiced: *a fair-minded judge.* **—fair′-mind′ed·ness** *n.*

fair·way (fâr′wā′) *n.* The part of a golf course covered with short grass and extending from the tee to the putting green.

fair·y (fâr′ē) *n., pl.* **fair·ies** An imaginary being in human form, supposed to have magical powers.

fair·y·land (fâr′ē-lănd′) *n.* **1.** An imaginary place where fairies are supposed to live. **2.** An enchanting place; a wonderland: *Snow turned the woods into a fairyland.*

fairy tale *n.* **1.** A story about fairies, magical creatures, or legendary deeds, usually intended for children. **2.** An explanation that is not true; a very fanciful story.

fait ac·com·pli (fā′tä-kôN-plē′) *n., pl.* **faits ac·com·plis** (fā′tä-kôN-plē′ *or* fā′tä-kôN-plēz′) An accomplished fact; something done that cannot be undone.

faith (fāth) *n.* **1.** Belief in God or in the teachings of a religion: *a person of great faith.* **2.** The set of teachings of a religion: *the Muslim faith.* **3.** Confidence or trust in a person or thing: *You must have faith in yourself.* **4.** Loyalty to a person or thing: *The senator vowed to keep faith with his supporters.* ◆ **on faith** With trust; confidently: *You'll have to accept my promise on faith.* [From Middle English *feith,* from Latin *fidēs.*]

faith·ful (fāth′fəl) *adj.* **1.** Loyal and dutiful; trustworthy: *a faithful friend; faithful performance of duty.* **2.** Keeping trust in a marriage or relationship by having sexual relations solely with one's spouse or romantic partner. **3.** Having or full of faith: *the faithful children in the procession.* **4.** Accurate; exact: *a faithful copy of the manuscript.* ❖ *n. (used with a plural verb)* **1.** The practicing members of a religion considered as a group. **2.** Loyal followers or supporters considered as a group: *The faithful journeyed to the huge rock concert in the park.* **—faith′ful·ly** *adv.* **—faith′ful·ness** *n.*

faith·less (fāth′lĭs) *adj.* **1.** Not trustworthy; disloyal: *The candidate was betrayed by a faithless friend.* **2.** Having no religious faith. **—faith′less·ly** *adv.* **—faith′less·ness** *n.*

fa·ji·ta (fə-hē′tə) *n.* A dish consisting of strips of marinated meat or vegetables grilled over an open fire and wrapped in a tortilla.

fake (fāk) *adj.* Not genuine or real; counterfeit or false: *a fake document; a fake diamond.* ❖ *n.* **1.** A person who deceives others by pretending and making false claims: *The doctor turned out to be a fake.* **2.** Something that looks authentic but is not; a forgery: *Experts discovered a fake in the museum's art collection.* **3.** In sports, a brief action, such as a change of direction, that is intended to mislead an opponent. ❖ *tr.v.* **faked, fak·ing, fakes 1.** To pretend or feign: *fake illness.* **2.** To make in order to deceive; counterfeit: *fake an identification card.* **3.** In sports, to mislead (an opponent) with a fake. **—fak′er** *n.*

fak·er·y (fā′kə-rē) *n.* **1.** The act or process of faking: *An artist was responsible for the fakery of many famous paintings.* **2.** Something faked: *The Roman statue proved to be a complete fakery.*

fa·kir (fə-kîr′ *or* fā-kîr′) *n.* A Muslim or Hindu holy person who lives by begging, especially a Hindu one who performs unusual feats of endurance or magic. [From Arabic *faqīr,* poor.]

fa·la·fel (fə-lä′fəl) *n.* A mixture of ground chickpeas and spices that is shaped into balls and fried.

fal·con (făl′kən *or* fôl′kən *or* fô′kən) *n.* Any of various swift, small to medium-sized birds of prey having a short curved beak, sharp claws, and long pointed wings. Certain falcons can be trained to hunt small animals and

ă	pat	ôr	core
ā	pay	oi	boy
âr	care	ou	out
ä	father	o͝o	took
ĕ	pet	o͝or	lure
ē	be	o͞o	boot
ĭ	pit	ŭ	cut
ī	bite	ûr	urge
îr	pier	th	thin
ŏ	pot	*th*	this
ō	toe	zh	vision
ô	paw	ə	about

birds for sport. [From Middle English *faucoun*, from Late Latin *falcō*.]

fal·con·er (făl′kə-nər *or* fôl′kə-nər *or* fô′kə-nər) *n.* A person who raises, trains, or hunts with falcons.

fal·con·ry (făl′kən-rē *or* fôl′kən-rē *or* fô′kən-rē) *n.* **1.** The sport of hunting with falcons. **2.** The art of training falcons for hunting.

Falk·land Islands (fôk′lənd *or* fôlk′lənd) A group of islands in the southern Atlantic Ocean east of the Strait of Magellan. The islands are controlled by Great Britain but are also claimed by Argentina.

fall (fôl) *intr.v.* **fell** (fĕl), **fall·en** (fô′lən), **fall·ing, falls 1.** To drop or come down without restraint: *The snow fell silently to the ground.* **2a.** To drop oneself to a lower or less upright position: *She fell into a chair.* **b.** To come down from an upright position suddenly: *Several people slipped on the ice and fell.* **c.** To be wounded or killed, especially in battle. **3.** To hang down: *The horse's mane fell smoothly on its neck.* **4.** To be directed toward or come into contact; rest: *Her gaze fell on the letter. Light fell on the book.* **5.** To côme into existence or occur as if by falling: *Darkness fell and all was silent. A hush fell over the crowd.* **6.** To occur at a specific time or place: *The holiday falls on a Thursday. The accent of "control" falls on the last syllable.* **7.** To be uttered; come out: *Angry words fell from my lips.* **8.** To assume a downcast look: *The child's face fell upon seeing the injured puppy.* **9.** To suffer defeat, destruction, capture, or overthrow: *The monarchy fell in the revolution.* **10.** To slope downward: *The fields fall steeply toward the river.* **11.** To become lower or less, as in value, intensity, or amount: *The temperature fell below freezing.* **12.** To decline, as in moral standing; err or sin. **13.** To pass from one state or condition into another: *fall asleep; fall ill.* **14.** To come by chance: *The papers fell into the enemy's hands.* **15.** To be given by assignment or distribution: *The task of cleaning the room fell to us.* **16.** To be divided or put into categories: *The books fall into three categories: novels, biographies, and scholarly works.* ❖ *n.* **1.** A dropping or coming down from a higher place without restraint: *the fall of leaves from trees; a heavy fall of snow.* **2.** A sudden drop from an upright position: *a bad fall on the ice.* **3.** The distance that something falls: *a fall of ten feet.* **4.** An amount of something that has fallen: *We expect a fall of two inches of snow.* **5.** The season of the year occurring between summer and winter; autumn. **6.** A specific place or position: *the fall of an accent on the last syllable.* **7. falls** *(used with a singular or plural verb)* A waterfall; a cascade. **8.** A downward movement or slope: *the gentle fall of fields toward the river.* **9.** A capture, overthrow, or collapse: *the fall of a corrupt government.* **10.** A reduction in amount, intensity, or value: *a fall in water pressure.* **11.** A decline in standing, rank, or importance: *a story of one family's fall from wealth to poverty.* **12.** A moral decline; a lapse. **13. Fall** In the Bible, the loss of humanity's original innocence and happiness resulting from Adam and Eve's eating of the forbidden fruit in the Garden of Eden. **14.** In wrestling, the act of pinning one's opponent to the ground. ❖ *adj.* Occurring in or appropriate to the season of fall: *fall fashions.* ◆ **fall back** To give ground; retreat. **fall back on** To rely on or resort to: *fall back on savings.* **fall behind** To fail to keep up with: *We fell behind the group we were traveling with. They fell behind in paying their bills.* **fall flat** To produce no result; fail: *Their hasty plans fell flat.* **fall for 1.** To become infatuated with; fall in love with. **2.** To be taken in by: *They fell for the swindler's scheme.* **fall in** To take one's place in a military formation. **fall in with 1.** To associate or begin to associate with: *She fell in with a new crowd at school.* **2.** To agree to: *They immediately fell in with my suggestions.* **fall off** To become smaller or fewer; decline: *Attendance fell off in the spring.* **fall on** or **fall upon 1.** To attack suddenly: *The cat fell on the mice.* **2.** To find; come across: *They fell upon the ruins of an ancient city in the desert.* **fall out 1.** To quarrel; become estranged: *The cousins fell out over an inheritance.* **2.** To leave one's place in a military formation. **3.** To be readily explainable; follow logically or naturally: *These facts fall out nicely from the new theory.* **fall short 1.** To fail to reach a specified amount or degree: *Our donations fell short of expectations.* **2.** To be inadequate: *Food supplies fell short.* **fall through** To fail; collapse: *Their plans for a vacation fell through.* **fall to** To begin an activity; start: *The shoppers fell to as soon as the doors were opened.* **fall under** To come under the influence of: *The student fell under the spell of his teacher and became a great cellist.* [From Old English *feallan*.]

fal·la·cious (fə-lā′shəs) *adj.* **1.** Based on a fallacy: *fallacious arguments based on a misunderstanding of the facts.* **2.** Tending to mislead; deceptive: *The dealer made fallacious claims about the car's gas mileage.* **—fal·la′cious·ly** *adv.*

fal·la·cy (făl′ə-sē) *n., pl.* **fal·la·cies 1.** A false notion or mistaken belief: *It is a fallacy that money can buy happiness.* **2.** False reasoning, belief, or argument. [Alternation of Middle English *fallace*, from Latin *fallāx*, deceitful.]

fall·en (fô′lən) *v.* Past participle of **fall.**

fal·li·ble (făl′ə-bəl) *adj.* Capable of making mistakes; tending to err: *Every human is fallible.* **—fal′li·bil′i·ty** *n.* **—fal′li·bly** *adv.*

fall·ing-out (fô′lĭng-out′) *n., pl.* **fall·ings-out** or **fall·ing-outs** A disagreement; a quarrel.

fall·ing star (fô′lĭng) *n.* A meteor.

fall line *n.* **1.** The steepest possible line of descent from a given point on a slope. **2.** A line connecting the waterfalls of upland rivers before they reach a common coastal plain, often indicating a zone of potential water power for industrial purposes.

fal·lo·pi·an tube also **Fal·lo·pi·an tube** (fə-lō′pē-ən) *n.* Either of a pair of tubes found in female mammals that carry egg cells from the ovaries to the uterus. [After Gabriele *Fallopio* (1523–1562), Italian anatomist.]

fall·out (fôl′out′) *n.* **1.** The tiny particles of debris discharged into the atmosphere by an explosion, especially radioactive debris from a nuclear explosion. **2.** The fall of such particles back to the earth.

fal·low (făl′ō) *adj.* Plowed and tilled but left unseeded during a growing season: *The soil in a fallow field will be more fertile when next planted.*

false (fôls) *adj.* **fals·er, fals·est 1.** Not true; incorrect: *The information she gave you is false.* **2.** Deliberately untrue: *false testimony.* **3.** Meant to mislead; deceitful: *false promises.* **4.** Based on mistaken ideas or information: *The early news report raised false hopes.* **5.** Unfaithful; disloyal: *a false friend.* **6.** Not natural or genuine; not real: *a false signature.* **7.** In music, of a pitch that is not correct or within a specific range: *False notes spoiled the singer's performance.* [From Old English *fals*, from Latin *falsus*, from past participle of *fallere*, to deceive.] **—false′ly** *adv.* **—false′ness** *n.*

false·hood (fôls′ho͝od′) *n.* **1.** An untrue statement; a lie or an inaccuracy: *a report filled with falsehoods.* **2.** The quality of being false; untruthfulness: *the falsehood of the accusation.* **3.** The practice of making false statements; lying.

fal·set·to (fôl-sĕt′ō) *n., pl.* **fal·set·tos** A person's voice in a range that is higher than the person's usual range.

fal·si·fy (fôl′sə-fī′) *v.* **fal·si·fied, fal·si·fy·ing, fal·si·fies** *—tr.* **1.** To state untruthfully; misrepresent: *It is a crime to falsify the facts when testifying under oath.* **2.** To change (a document, for example) in order to deceive; counterfeit: *falsify a driver's license.* *—intr.* To make an untrue statement; lie. **—fal′si·fi·ca′tion** (fôl′sə-fĭ-kā′shən) *n.* **—fal′si·fi′er** *n.*

falcon

peregrine falcon

WRITERS CHOOSE THEIR WORDS

The winding key [of the music box] was still revolving, but more and more slowly. The melody **faltered.** Another few widely spaced notes plinked, and then it stopped.

—Natalie Babbitt
Tuck Everlasting

fan¹
top: handheld fan
bottom: electric fan

ă	pat	ôr	core
ā	pay	oi	boy
âr	care	ou	out
ä	father	ŏŏ	took
ĕ	pet	ŏŏr	lure
ē	be	ōō	boot
ĭ	pit	ŭ	cut
ī	bite	ûr	urge
îr	pier	th	thin
ŏ	pot	*th*	this
ō	toe	zh	vision
ô	paw	ə	about

fal·si·ty (fôl′sĭ-tē) *n., pl.* **fal·si·ties 1.** The condition of being false; falseness: *Experiment proved the falsity of that theory.* **2.** Something false; a lie.

fal·ter (fôl′tər) *intr.v.* **fal·tered, fal·ter·ing, fal·ters 1.** To lose confidence or purpose; hesitate or waver: *He never faltered in his efforts to help us.* **2.** To speak hesitatingly; stammer: *Several times the speaker faltered from embarrassment.* **3.** To move haltingly; stumble: *We faltered along the slippery path.* **4.** To continue in an unsteady or weakening manner: *Business was strong during the holidays but faltered afterward.* [From Middle English *falteren*, to stagger, possibly from Old Norse *faltrask*, to be puzzled, hesitate.] **—fal′ter·er** *n.* **—fal′ter·ing·ly** *adv.*

fame (fām) *n.* The state of being widely known, widely recognized, or of great popular interest; renown. [From Middle English, from Latin *fāma.*]

famed (fāmd) *adj.* Widely known; renowned.

fa·mil·ial (fə-mĭl′yəl) *adj.* **1.** Relating to family. **2.** Occurring among the members of a family, usually by heredity: *the familial tendency for diabetes.*

fa·mil·iar (fə-mĭl′yər) *adj.* **1.** Well-known; often encountered; common: *a familiar sight.* **2.** Having some knowledge; acquainted: *I am familiar with those streets in your neighborhood.* **3.** Of established friendship; close: *We are on familiar terms with the neighbors.* **4.** Unduly forward; presumptuous: *It is a mistake to be too familiar with one's boss.* [From Middle English *familier*, from Latin *familiāris*, domestic, from *familia*, family.] **—fa·mil′iar·ly** *adv.*

fa·mil·iar·i·ty (fə-mĭl′yăr′ĭ-tē *or* fə-mĭl′ē-ăr′ĭ-tē) *n., pl.* **fa·mil·iar·i·ties 1.** Acquaintance with or knowledge of something: *Familiarity with the city's streets is a necessity for a cab driver.* **2.** Friendship or informality: *the familiarity of close associates.* **3.** Improper friendliness; forwardness: *I was offended by the salesperson's familiarity on the telephone.*

fa·mil·iar·ize (fə-mĭl′yə-rīz′) *tr.v.* **fa·mil·iar·ized, fa·mil·iar·iz·ing, fa·mil·iar·iz·es 1.** To make acquainted with: *They familiarized themselves with the new library.* **2.** To make (something) known or recognized: *TV familiarized the special vocabulary of the space program.*

fam·i·ly (făm′ə-lē *or* făm′lē) *n., pl.* **fam·i·lies 1.** A social group typically consisting of one or two parents and their children: *She lived with her family until she left home at 21.* **2.** All the members of a household living under one roof: *His family includes his grandmother and his uncle, who live on the first floor.* **3.** The children of the same parents: *They raised a large family.* **4.** A group of people sharing common ancestors; relatives: *Each year our whole family gets together.* **5.** Line of descent; ancestry: *I come from an old Virginia family.* **6.** A group of things that are alike; a class: *The family of brass instruments includes the trumpet and trombone.* **7.** A taxonomic category of organisms that share certain characteristics, ranking above a genus and below an order: *Dogs, wolves, coyotes, and foxes belong to the same family.* See table at **taxonomy. 8.** A group of languages derived from the same parent language: *French, Spanish, and Italian are of the same family.* [From Middle English *familie*, from Latin *familia*, household, servants of a household, from *famulus*, servant.] —SEE NOTE AT **collective noun.**

family leave *n.* A period during which a person is allowed time off of work to take care of a family member, such as a new baby.

family name *n.* A surname.

family planning *n.* The planned timing of children born into a family through the use of birth control.

family tree *n.* A diagram showing the relationships among the ancestors of a family.

fam·ine (făm′ĭn) *n.* A drastic, widespread shortage of food: *Famine may strike after a prolonged drought.* [From Middle English, from Latin *famēs*, hunger.]

fam·ished (făm′ĭsht) *adj.* Extremely hungry; starving.

fa·mous (fā′məs) *adj.* Widely known; famed; renowned: *a famous singer; a country famous for its beautiful mountains.*

SYNONYMS **famous, celebrated, eminent, illustrious, noted, renowned** These adjectives mean known by many people. *Many famous actors came to the charity fundraiser. The concert series features several celebrated musicians. The essay discusses the work of several eminent scholars. An illustrious judge presided over the case. Our library has invited a noted author to read from her new book. To solve the problem, the government sought the opinions of our most renowned scientists.*
ANTONYM **obscure**

fan¹ (făn) *n.* **1.** A collapsible flat implement, usually shaped like a half-circle, waved in the hand to create a cooling breeze. **2.** Something that resembles an open fan: *The turkey's tail feathers spread into a fan.* **3.** An electrical device that moves air, especially for cooling, by means of rotating metal or plastic blades. ❖ *v.* **fanned, fan·ning, fans** *—tr.* **1.** To direct a current of air to blow upon (a person or thing), especially in order to cool: *We sat fanning ourselves under a tree.* **2.** To move or create a current of (air) with or as if with a fan. **3.** To stir up by or as if by fanning: *Rumors fanned smoldering anger in the crowd.* **4.** To open (something) out into the shape of a fan: *The peacock fanned its tail.* **5.** In baseball, to strike out (a batter): *The pitcher fanned three batters in succession. —intr.* **1.** To spread like a fan: *The search parties fanned out in different directions.* **2.** In baseball, to strike out. [From Old English, winnowing device, from Latin *vannus.*]

fan² (făn) *n.* An enthusiastic devotee or admirer: *a baseball fan.* [Short for *fanatic.*]

fa·nat·ic (fə-năt′ĭk) *n.* A person who is excessively or unreasonably devoted to a cause or belief. ❖ *adj.* Fanatical. [From Latin *fānāticus*, relating to a temple, from *fānum*, temple.]

fa·nat·i·cal (fə-năt′ĭ-kəl) *adj.* Unreasonably enthusiastic or zealous. **—fa·nat′i·cal·ly** *adv.*

fa·nat·i·cism (fə-năt′ĭ-sĭz′əm) *n.* Unreasonable or excessive enthusiasm, especially in politics or religion.

fan·cied (făn′sēd) *adj.* Imaginary; invented: *the fancied monsters of dreams.*

fan·ci·er (făn′sē-ər) *n.* A person with a special interest in something: *a cat fancier.*

fan·ci·ful (făn′sĭ-fəl) *adj.* **1.** Created in the mind; imaginary; unreal: *fanciful tales.* **2.** Using or tending to use the imagination: *a fanciful mind.* **3.** Original in design; imaginative: *fanciful figures made with odds and ends of cloth.* **—fan′ci·ful·ly** *adv.* **—fan′ci·ful·ness** *n.*

fan·cy (făn′sē) *adj.* **fan·ci·er, fan·ci·est 1.** Highly decorated; elaborate: *fancy carvings around the door.* **2.** Requiring or done with great skill; complex; intricate: *a tap dancer's fancy footwork.* **3.** Elegantly fashionable or sophisticated: *a fancy restaurant.* **4.** Of superior grade; fine: *fancy fruits and vegetables.* **5.** Exorbitant; excessive: *That store charges very fancy prices.* ❖ *n., pl.* **fan·cies 1.** Imagination, especially of a playful or whimsical sort: *The characters are all creations of the author's fancy.* **2.** An impulsive idea or thought; a whim: *We had a sudden fancy to go to the diner.* **3.** A liking, fondness, or inclination: *The stray dog took a fancy to our family.* ❖ *tr.v.* **fan·cied, fan·cy·ing, fan·cies 1.** To picture in the mind; imagine: *I tried to fancy myself as an actor.* **2.** To have a liking for; enjoy: *Would you fancy a movie tonight?* **3.** To suppose; guess; surmise: *I fancy the meeting will end soon.* [From Middle English *fantasie, fantsy*, imagination, fantasy.] **—fan′ci·ly** *adv.* **—fan′ci·ness** *n.*

fan·cy-free (făn′sē-frē′) *adj.* Having no commitments or restrictions; carefree.

fan·fare (făn′fâr′) *n.* **1.** A short melody played by one or more brass instruments; a flourish. **2.** A spectacular public display or ceremony: *The soldiers were welcomed home with great fanfare.*

fang (făng) *n.* **1.** A long pointed tooth, such as one used by a venomous snake to inject venom into its prey. **2.** Something thin and tapering that is shaped like a fang.

fan mail *n.* Mail that is sent to a public figure by admirers.

fan·tail (făn′tāl′) *n.* **1.** A pigeon, goldfish, or other animal having a fan-shaped tail. **2.** A tail or end resembling a fan. **3.** The stern overhang of a ship.

fan·tas·tic (făn-tăs′tĭk) *adj.* **1.** Based on or existing only in fantasy; unreal: *a fantastic story of life in another galaxy.* **2.** Weird; bizarre: *dancers dressed in fantastic costumes.* **3.** Remarkable; outstanding; superb: *The carpenter did a fantastic job of restoring the old house.* **—fan·tas′ti·cal·ly** *adv.*

fan·ta·sy (făn′tə-sē *or* făn′tə-zē) *n., pl.* **fan·ta·sies 1.** The creative imagination: *Her fantasy is vigorously at work in her latest science fiction novel.* **2.** Something that is a creation of the imagination, such as a fanciful work of fiction. **3.** An imagined event or situation, especially one that fulfills a wish: *He has this fantasy about becoming a movie star.* [From Middle English *fantasie*, from Greek *phantasiā*, appearance, imagination.]

FAQ (făk) *n.* A list of frequently asked questions along with their answers about a given topic.

far (fär) *adv.* **far·ther** (fär′*th*ər), **far·thest** (fär′*th*ĭst) or **fur·ther** (fûr′*th*ər), **fur·thest** (fûr′*th*ĭst) **1.** To, from, or at a great distance in space or time: *My home is situated far from town. The movie takes place far in the future.* **2.** To a great degree; much: *I feel far better today than I did yesterday.* ❖ *adj.* **farther, farthest** or **further, furthest 1.** Being at great distance in space or time: *a far country halfway around the world; the far past.* **2.** More distant than another; opposite: *the far side of the mountain.* **3.** Extensive or long: *a far trek into the jungle.* **4.** Politically extreme: *the far right.* ◆ **as far as** To the distance, extent, or degree that: *As far as I know they left an hour ago.* **by far** To a great degree: *Their grades are better than mine by far.* **far and away** By a wide margin: *This is far and away the best movie we've seen.* **far and wide** Everywhere. **far from** Not at all; anything but: *You are far from a failure.* **so far 1.** Up to the present moment: *We haven't heard from anyone so far.* **2.** To a limited extent: *You can only go so far on $10.*

far·ad (făr′əd *or* făr′ăd′) *n.* A unit used to measure electric capacitance. A capacitor in which a charge of one coulomb can produce a change of one volt between its two storage plates has a capacitance of one farad. [After Michael *Faraday* (1791–1867), British physicist.]

far·a·day (făr′ə-dā′) *n.* A unit of electric charge, equal to about 96,494 coulombs, or the electric charge carried by one mole of electrons. It is used frequently to measure charge in electrolysis. [After Michael *Faraday* (1791–1867), British physicist.]

far·a·way (fär′ə-wā′) *adj.* **1.** Very distant; remote: *The explorer spent years traveling in faraway places.* **2.** Dreamy; preoccupied: *a faraway look in his eyes.*

farce (färs) *n.* **1.** A comic play with an unlikely story and characters exaggerated for humorous effect. **2.** Something ridiculous or laughable; a mockery: *Baseball practice turned into a farce after the coach left.* [From Middle English *fars*, stuffing, from Latin *farcīre*, to stuff.]

far·ci·cal (fär′sĭ-kəl) *adj.* Relating to or resembling a farce; absurd; foolish: *farcical errors.* **—far′ci·cal·ly** *adv.*

fare (fâr) *intr.v.* **fared, far·ing, fares 1.** To get along; progress: *How are you faring with your project?* **2.** To travel; go. ❖ *n.* **1.** The money charged for transportation from one place to another: *The subway fare has gone up.* **2.** A passenger who pays a fare: *The taxi stopped to pick up a fare.* **3.** Food and drink: *The fare at this inn is superb.* [From Old English *faran*.]

❑ *These sound alike:* **fare, fair**[1] (just), **fair**[2] (market).

Far East The countries and regions of eastern and southeast Asia, especially China, Japan, North Korea, South Korea, and Mongolia.

fare·well (fâr-wĕl′) *interj.* An expression used to say goodbye. ❖ *n.* **1.** The act of saying goodbye, usually with good wishes: *a nod of farewell.* **2.** An expression used at parting; goodbye: *It was hard to say our farewells.*

far-fetched (fär′fĕcht′) *adj.* Hard to believe; strained and improbable: *a far-fetched story.*

far-flung (fär′flŭng′) *adj.* Extending over a large area: *the far-flung operations of an international airline.*

Far·go (fär′gō) The largest city of North Dakota, in the eastern part of the state east of Bismarck. It was founded in 1871.

fa·ri·na (fə-rē′nə) *n.* A fine meal used as a cooked cereal or in puddings.

farm (färm) *n.* **1.** An area of land on which crops or domestic animals are raised. **2.** An area of water devoted to raising aquatic animals: *a trout farm.* **3.** A facility for the generation of energy by converting it from a particular source: *a wind farm.* ❖ *v.* **farmed, farm·ing, farms** *—tr.* **1.** To cultivate or produce a crop on: *We farm 1,000 acres.* **2.** To cultivate, breed, or raise (plants or animals): *companies that farm salmon.* *—intr.* To engage in farming; grow crops or raise livestock. ◆ **farm out** To send (work) out to be done by another business: *All the sewing done by hand is farmed out by the manufacturer.*

farm·er (fär′mər) *n.* A person who owns or operates a farm.

farm·ers' market (fär′mərz) *n.* A market at which farmers sell their produce directly to customers.

farm hand *n.* A person who works on a farm.

farm·house (färm′hous′) *n.* A house on a farm.

farm·land (färm′lănd′) *n.* Land suitable or used for farming.

farm·stead (färm′stĕd′) *n.* A farm, including its land and buildings.

farm team *n.* In baseball, a minor-league team that trains young players and supplies players as needed to an affiliated major-league team.

farm·yard (färm′yärd′) *n.* An area surrounded by or next to farm buildings: *Chickens and geese wandered freely in the farmyard.*

far-off (fär′ôf′) *adj.* Faraway; distant: *Home seemed very far-off.*

far-out (fär′out′) *adj. Slang* Extremely unconventional; very unusual: *a far-out movie.*

far-reach·ing (fär′rē′chĭng) *adj.* Having a wide influence or effect: *A tax on energy will have far-reaching effects in the economy.*

far·ri·er (făr′ē-ər) *n.* A person who shoes horses; a blacksmith.

far·row (făr′ō) *n.* A litter of pigs. ❖ *intr.v.* **far·rowed, far·row·ing, far·rows** To give birth to a litter of pigs.

far·see·ing (fär′sē′ĭng) *adj.* **1.** Able to see far; keen-sighted. **2.** Planning wisely for the future; foresighted.

Far·si (fär′sē) *n.* The modern form of the Persian language, especially the western dialect of Persian that is the national language of Iran.

far·sight·ed or **far-sight·ed** (fär′sī′tĭd) *adj.* **1.** Able to see distant objects better than objects at close range: *I am farsighted and wear glasses to read.* **2.** Planning wisely for the future; foresighted. **—far′sight′ed·ly** *adv.* **—far′sight′ed·ness** *n.*

far·ther (fär′*th*ər) *adv.* A comparative of **far. 1.** To or at a greater distance: *We walked farther than we had*

fang
diamondback rattlesnake

USAGE

farther The word **farther** tends to be used in reference to physical distance, while the word **further** tends to be used in reference to nonphysical advancement: *If you are planning to drive any farther, you'd better stop at a gas station. We won't be able to answer these questions until we are further along in our research.*

SCIENCE

fat Many people choose "fat-free" or "reduced fat" foods in an attempt to limit the amount of **fat** in their diets. Fatty foods are hard to resist, though, because they taste good. Many of the chemicals that give food its pleasant taste dissolve easily in fats, so fatty foods often contain more of these flavorful compounds. Fat is also satisfying, which means that if you eliminate it from your diet, you can feel hungry. And some fat is necessary for your body. A gram of fat contains more than twice as much stored energy—calories—as does a gram of either protein or carbohydrate, so it's the most efficient way to store excess food. Fat is also an excellent insulator. Sea mammals, such as whales and seals, have thick layers of fat, called *blubber,* that protect them from the cold and serve as a reserve supply of food. A whale's blubber may be two feet thick—now *that's* fat!

ă	pat	ôr	core
ā	pay	oi	boy
âr	care	ou	out
ä	father	o͝o	took
ĕ	pet	o͝or	lure
ē	be	o͞o	boot
ĭ	pit	ŭ	cut
ī	bite	ûr	urge
îr	pier	th	thin
ŏ	pot	*th*	this
ō	toe	zh	vision
ô	paw	ə	about

expected. **2.** To a greater extent or degree: *I've read farther in the book and I like it now.* ❖ *adj.* A comparative of **far.** More distant; remoter: *at the farther end of the street.* —SEE NOTE.

far·ther·most (fär′*th*ər-mōst′) *adj.* Farthest; most remote: *explore the farthermost corners of the earth.*

far·thest (fär′thĭst) *adj.* A superlative of **far.** Most remote or distant: *the farthest regions of the Arctic.* ❖ *adv.* A superlative of **far. 1.** To or at the greatest distance in space or time: *The tallest people in the photograph stood farthest in the back.* **2.** By the greatest extent or degree; most: *Their research had progressed farthest of all.*

far·thing (fär′*th*ĭng) *n.* **1.** A coin formerly used in Great Britain worth one-fourth of a penny. **2.** Something of very little value. [From Old English *fēorthung,* a fourth.]

far·thin·gale (fär′thĭn-gāl′ *or* fär′*th*ĭng-gāl′) *n.* A framework worn under a skirt or petticoat to make it stand out around the waist, worn by European women in the 1500s and 1600s.

fas·ci·nate (făs′ə-nāt′) *tr.v.* **fas·ci·nat·ed, fas·ci·nat·ing, fas·ci·nates** To capture and hold the interest and attention of; captivate: *This book fascinates me so much I cannot put it down.* [From Latin *fascināre,* from *fascinum,* an evil spell, amulet.]

fas·ci·nat·ing (făs′ə-nā′tĭng) *adj.* Arousing great interest and attention: *a fascinating story.* See Synonyms at **interesting. —fas′ci·nat′ing·ly** *adv.*

fas·ci·na·tion (făs′ə-**nā′**shən) *n.* **1.** The condition of being fascinated: *Everyone watched in fascination as the rocket took off.* **2.** The power of fascinating; charm; attraction: *All the stories are about the fascination of the sea.*

fas·cism or **Fas·cism** (făsh′ĭz′əm) *n.* **1.** A system of government marked by dictatorship, government control of the economy, violent suppression of dissent, and belligerent nationalism. **2.** A political movement advocating such a system of government.

fas·cist or **Fas·cist** (făsh′ĭst) *n.* A person who advocates or believes in fascism. ❖ *adj.* Relating to fascism or fascists: *a fascist regime.*

fash·ion (făsh′ən) *n.* **1.** The current style or custom, as in dress or behavior: *an idea now in fashion.* **2.** Something, such as a garment, that is in the current style: *a store carrying the latest fashions.* **3.** A manner of doing something; a way: *She works in an organized fashion.* ❖ *tr.v.* **fash·ioned, fash·ion·ing, fash·ions** To shape or form into: *fashion figures from clay.* [From Middle English *facioun,* form, appearance, from Latin *factiō,* a making, from *facere,* to make, do.]

fash·ion·a·ble (făsh′ə-nə-bəl) *adj.* **1.** Conforming to the current styles or trends; stylish: *a fashionable wardrobe.* **2.** Adopting or setting current styles or trends: *a fashionable artist.* **3.** Associated with or used by stylish people: *a fashionable hotel.* **—fash′ion·a·bly** *adv.*

fast[1] (făst) *adj.* **fast·er, fast·est 1.** Moving, acting, or capable of moving or acting quickly; swift: *a fast train; a fast computer.* **2.** Accomplished in very little time: *We ate a fast lunch.* **3.** Suitable or made for rapid movement: *a fast racetrack.* **4.** Quick to understand or learn: *a class for the faster students.* **5.** Ahead of the correct time: *My watch is fast.* **6.** Firmly fixed or fastened: *Keep a fast grip on the rope.* **7.** Permanent; not likely to fade: *Fast colors will not run in the wash.* **8.** Loyal; firm: *fast friends.* **9.** Disposed to dissipation; wild: *He hangs out with a fast crowd.* ❖ *adv.* **faster, fastest 1.** Quickly; rapidly: *You are driving too fast.* **2.** Firmly; securely: *Hold fast to the railing.* **3.** Deeply; soundly: *The child is fast asleep.* **4.** So as to run ahead of the correct time: *My watch runs fast.* [From Old English *fæst,* firm, fixed.]

SYNONYMS **fast, rapid, swift, quick, expeditious** These adjectives describe something marked by great speed. **Fast** often describes the person or thing in motion: *You would become a fast runner if you stayed in shape.* **Rapid** often describes the activity or movement involved: *Rapid advances in technology have improved efficiency in business.* **Swift** suggests smoothness of movement: *Be careful of the swift current while you're swimming.* **Quick** usually describes what takes little time: *Her quick reaction prevented the accident.* **Expeditious** suggests speed and efficiency: *We sent the package by the most expeditious means.*

fast[2] (făst) *intr.v.* **fast·ed, fast·ing, fasts** To eat little or no food or only certain foods, especially for religious reasons or as a form of protest. ❖ *n.* The act or a period of fasting. [From Old English *fæstan.*]

fast·ball (făst′bôl′) *n.* In baseball, a pitch that is thrown at maximum speed.

fast break *n.* In sports, a rush by the offense toward the goal before the defense is ready.

fas·ten (făs′ən) *v.* **fas·tened, fas·ten·ing, fas·tens** *—tr.* **1.** To attach firmly to; join; connect: *fasten a button to a shirt; unable to fasten blame on anyone.* **2.** To make fast or secure: *Fasten your seat belts.* **3.** To fix or direct steadily: *She fastened her gaze on the stranger. —intr.* **1.** To become attached, fixed, or joined: *The helmet fastens under your chin.* **2.** To fix or focus steadily: *My eyes fastened on the approaching plane.*

fas·ten·er (făs′ə-nər) *n.* A person or thing that fastens or holds separate things together, such as a zipper, snap, hook, or button.

fas·ten·ing (făs′ə-nĭng) *n.* Something, such as a hook, used to fasten things together.

fast food *n.* Inexpensive food, such as hamburgers, prepared and served quickly. **—fast′-food′** *adj.*

fast-for·ward or **fast forward** (făst-fôr′wərd) *intr.v.* **fast-for·ward·ed, fast-for·ward·ing, fast-for·wards** To advance an audio or video recording rapidly. ❖ *n.* A control mechanism for fast-forwarding an audio or video recording.

fas·tid·i·ous (fă-**stĭd′**ē-əs *or* fə-**stĭd′**ē-əs) *adj.* **1.** Careful in all details: *Reporters must pay fastidious attention to the facts.* **2.** Difficult to please; choosy or finicky: *a fastidious eater.* **—fas·tid′i·ous·ly** *adv.* **—fas·tid′i·ous·ness** *n.*

fast·ness (făst′nĭs) *n.* **1.** A remote or secure place, as a stronghold or fortress: *a mountain fastness.* **2.** The condition or quality of being secure or firmly fixed: *Check the locks for fastness.* **3.** Rapidity; swiftness: *Sport cars are known for their elegance and fastness.*

fat (făt) *n.* **1.** Any of a large class of oily organic compounds that are widely found in animal tissues and in nuts, seeds, and some fruits. Fats serve mainly as a reserve source of energy. **2.** Animal tissue containing such compounds: *cut the fat off the steak.* **3.** A substance of this kind prepared for use in cooking: *potatoes cooked in fat.* **4.** Something that is unnecessary or excessive: *cut the fat from the budget.* ❖ *adj.* **fat·ter, fat·test 1.** Having much body fat: *The cat is too fat, so we are giving her less food.* **2.** Full of fat or oil; greasy: *a menu full of fat foods.* **3.** Big; ample; generous: *a fat paycheck.* ◆ **fat chance** *Slang* Very little or no chance. [From Old English *fǣtt,* fatted.] **—fat′ness** *n.* —SEE NOTE.

fa·tal (fāt′l) *adj.* **1.** Causing or capable of causing death: *a fatal disease.* **2.** Causing ruin or destruction; disastrous: *The investment was a blunder that proved fatal to the business.* **3.** Most decisive; fateful: *the fatal moment of going onstage to perform.* **—fa′tal·ly** *adv.*

fa·tal·ism (fāt′l-ĭz′əm) *n.* **1.** The belief that all events are determined in advance by fate and cannot be altered. **2.** Acceptance of this belief; submission to fate: *His fatalism prevented him from acting to improve the situation.* **—fa′tal·ist** *n.* **—fa′tal·is′tic** *adj.*

fa·tal·i·ty (fā-tăl′ĭ-tē *or* fə-tăl′ĭ-tē) *n., pl.* **fa·tal·i·ties 1.** A death resulting from an accident or disaster: *Three fatalities occurred in the fire.* **2.** The ability to cause death: *a disease known for its fatality.*

fat·back (făt′băk′) *n.* Salt-cured fat from the upper part of a side of pork.

fate (fāt) *n.* **1.** A force or power that is supposed to determine the course of events. **2.** Something supposed to be caused by fate, especially an unfavorable destiny: *It was his fate never to defeat his rival.* **3.** A final result; an outcome: *The fate of the plane remains unknown.* **4. Fates** In Greek and Roman mythology, the three goddesses who governed human destiny.
❑ *These sound alike:* **fate, fete** (festival).

fate·ful (fāt′fəl) *adj.* **1.** Decisively important; momentous: *the colonists' fateful decision to go to war against Great Britain.* **2.** Indicating approaching trouble or disaster; unfavorably prophetic: *The fever was a fateful sign that the patient was getting worse.* **3.** Bringing death or disaster; fatal: *a fateful battle in which thousands died.* **4.** Controlled by or as if by fate: *a fateful journey.* **—fate′ful·ly** *adv.* **—fate′ful·ness** *n.*

fa·ther (fä′*th*ər) *n.* **1.** A male parent or guardian of a child. **2.** A male parent of an animal. **3.** A male ancestor; a forefather: *the land of our fathers.* **4.** A male leader or official: *the city fathers.* **5.** A man who creates, starts, or founds something: *Chaucer is considered the father of English poetry.* **6. Father** In Christianity, another name for God. **7. Father** Used as a title and form of address for a Christian priest or other clergyman. ❖ *tr.v.* **fa·thered, fa·ther·ing, fa·thers 1.** To be the male parent of; beget: *father two children.* **2.** To act or serve as a father to: *He willingly undertook the duties of fathering his new stepchildren.*

fa·ther·hood (fä′*th*ər-ho͝od′) *n.* The condition of being a father.

fa·ther-in-law (fä′*th*ər-ĭn-lô′) *n., pl.* **fa·thers-in-law** The father of one's husband or wife.

fa·ther·land (fä′*th*ər-lănd′) *n.* **1.** A person's native land; the country of one's birth. **2.** The land of one's ancestors.

fa·ther·less (fä′*th*ər-lĭs) *adj.* Having no living or known father.

fa·ther·ly (fä′*th*ər-lē) *adj.* Relating to, like, or appropriate to a father: *a fatherly interest in my progress in school.* **—fa′ther·li·ness** *n.*

Fa·ther's Day (fä′*th*ərz) *n.* The third Sunday in June, observed in the United States in honor of fathers.

fath·om (fă*th*′əm) *n., pl.* **fathom** or **fath·oms** A unit of length equal to six feet (1.8 meters), used for measurements of the depth of water. ❖ *tr.v.* **fath·omed, fath·om·ing, fath·oms 1.** To measure the depth of; sound: *fathom a channel in a river.* **2.** To understand; comprehend: *Motives are very often difficult to fathom.* [From Old English *fæthm*, outstretched arms.] **—fath′om·a·ble** *adj.*

fath·om·less (fă*th*′əm-lĭs) *adj.* **1.** Too deep to be measured: *the fathomless oceans.* **2.** Impossible to understand: *His motivation for leaving seemed fathomless.*

fa·tigue (fə-tēg′) *n.* **1.** Weariness or exhaustion resulting from hard work or great effort. **2.** Manual nonmilitary work, such as barracks cleaning, assigned to soldiers. **3. fatigues** Clothing worn by soldiers for heavy work or field duty. ❖ *tr.v.* **fa·tigued, fa·tigu·ing, fa·tigues** To tire out; exhaust: *The long hike fatigued us.*

fat·ten (făt′n) *intr. & tr.v.* **fat·tened, fat·ten·ing, fat·tens** To make or become fat: *fatten cattle; fatten on a rich diet; fatten one's bank account.*

fat·ty (făt′ē) *adj.* **fat·ti·er, fat·ti·est 1.** Composed of or containing fat: *fatty food.* **2.** Characteristic of fat; greasy. **—fat′ti·ness** *n.*

fatty acid *n.* Any of a large group of organic acids, especially those found in animal and vegetable fats and oils.

fat·u·ous (făch′o͞o-əs) *adj.* Foolish and self-satisfied; silly: *a fatuous smile.* **—fat′u·ous·ly** *adv.* **—fat′u·ous·ness** *n.*

fat·wa (făt′wä′) *n.* A ruling issued by an Islamic scholar.

fau·cet (fô′sĭt) *n.* A device with an adjustable valve that regulates the flow of liquid from a pipe; a tap.

Faulk·ner (fôk′nər), **William** 1897–1962. American writer whose works, such as *The Sound and the Fury* (1929), explore the decay of older Southern culture.

fault (fôlt) *n.* **1.** A defect or shortcoming: *A fault in the book is its small type. Laziness is one of my few faults.* **2.** A mistake; an error: *a fault in addition.* **3.** Responsibility for a mistake or error: *The mix-up was all my fault.* **4.** A crack in a rock mass along which there has been movement caused by a shifting of the earth's crust. **5.** In tennis and other racquet games, a serve that falls outside a boundary. ❖ *tr.v.* **fault·ed, fault·ing, faults** To find fault in; criticize: *No one can fault such a fine performance.* ◆ **at fault** Deserving of blame; guilty: *He admitted to being at fault.* **to a fault** To the highest possible or an excessive degree: *He is polite to a fault.* [From Middle English *faute*, from Old French, from Latin *fallere*, to deceive, fail.]

fault·find·er (fôlt′fīn′dər) *n.* A person who habitually finds fault with and freely criticizes others. **—fault′find′ing** *n. & adj.*

fault·less (fôlt′lĭs) *adj.* Being without fault or flaw: *The lifeguard was faultless in her handling of the emergency.* See Synonyms at **perfect.** **—fault′less·ly** *adv.*

fault·y (fôl′tē) *adj.* **fault·i·er, fault·i·est** Having a fault or faults; imperfect or defective: *faulty electric wiring; a faulty argument.* **—fault′i·ly** *adv.* **—fault′i·ness** *n.*

faun (fôn) *n.* In Roman mythology, one of numerous minor gods dwelling in woods and fields and depicted as having the body of a man and the ears, horns, tail, and sometimes the legs of a goat. [From Middle English, from Latin *Faunus*, Roman god of nature.]
❑ *These sound alike:* **faun, fawn¹** (flatter), **fawn²** (young deer).

fau·na (fô′nə) *n.* *(used with a singular or plural verb)* The animals of a particular region or time period considered as a group: *tropical fauna; prehistoric fauna.*

Faust (foust) also **Faus·tus** (fou′stəs *or* fô′stəs) *n.* A magician in German legend who sold his soul to the devil in exchange for power and knowledge.

faux (fō) *adj.* Artificial; fake: *faux pearls.*

faux pas (fō pä′) *n., pl.* **faux pas** (fō päz′) A social blunder: *Wiping your mouth on the tablecloth is a major faux pas.*

fave (fāv) *Informal n.* A person, animal, or thing that is preferred above others or likely to win; a favorite. ❖ *adj.* Favorite.

fav·i·con (făv′ĭ-kŏn′ *or* fāv′ĭ-kŏn′) *n.* A symbol or graphic associated with a website.

fa·vor (fā′vər) *n.* **1.** A kind or helpful act: *My friend agreed to go with me as a favor.* **2.** Approval or support; liking: *The plan is fast gaining favor.* **3.** A small gift given to each guest at a party. **4.** Friendly regard; partiality: *A judge cannot show favor in the court.* **5.** Behalf; interest: *The cashier made an error in our favor.* ❖ *tr.v.* **fa·vored, fa·vor·ing, fa·vors 1.** To perform a kindness or service for; oblige: *The singer favored us with two more songs.* **2.** To approve or support: *I favor longer vacations.* **3.** To be partial to; indulge: *a father who favored his youngest child.* **4.** To make easier or more likely; aid; promote: *The climate there favors fruit farming.* **5.** To be gentle with; treat with care: *The lineman favored his left leg while walking off the field.* **6.** To resemble; look like: *She favors her father.* ◆ **in favor of 1.** In support of: *All those in favor of the motion say "aye."* **2.** To the advantage of: *The judge decided in favor of the defendant.* [From Middle English *favour*, from Latin *favor*, from *favēre*, to be favorable.]

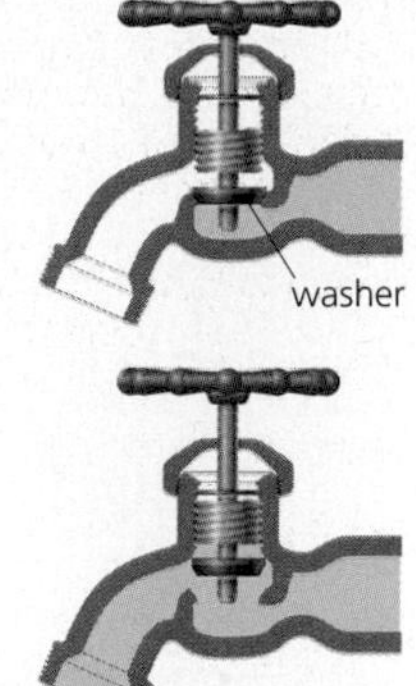

faucet
top: turned off
bottom: turned on

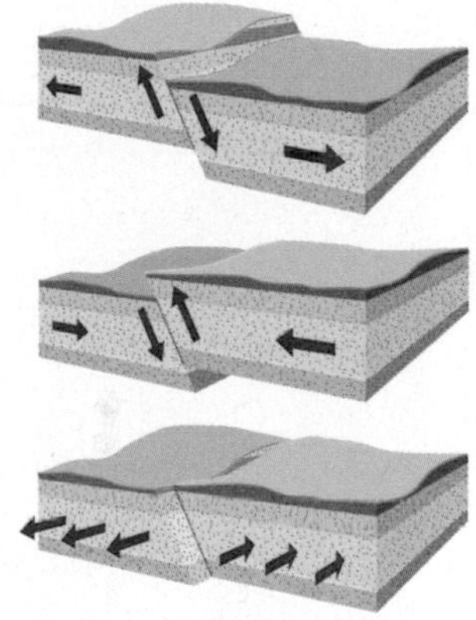

fault
top: normal fault
center: reverse fault
bottom: strike-slip fault

fa·vor·a·ble (fā′vər-ə-bəl *or* fāv′rə-bəl) *adj.* **1.** Helpful; advantageous: *The boat sailed swiftly before favorable winds.* **2.** Pleasing or promising: *The new student made a favorable impression on us.* **3.** Approving or praising: *favorable movie reviews.* **4.** Granting what has been desired or requested: *a favorable reply.* **—fa′vor·a·ble·ness** *n.* **—fa′vor·a·bly** *adv.*

fa·vor·ite (fā′vər-ĭt *or* fāv′rĭt) *n.* **1.** A person or thing viewed or treated with special regard, especially one preferred to all others: *That song is my favorite.* **2.** A contestant believed most likely to win: *Our team is the favorite in today's game.* ❖ *adj.* Liked or preferred above all others: *Green is my favorite color.*

fa·vor·it·ism (fā′vər-ĭ-tĭz′əm *or* fāv′rĭ-tĭz′əm) *n.* Better treatment given to one person or group over another; partiality: *gain promotion by favoritism rather than by skill.*

fawn¹ (fôn) *intr.v.* **fawned, fawn·ing, fawns 1.** To show affection or attempt to please, as a dog does by crawling or whining. **2.** To try to gain favor by flattery or acting submissively: *The clerk fawned on the customer hoping to make a sale.* [From Old English *fagnian*, to rejoice, from *fagen, fægen*, glad.]

❑ *These sound alike:* **fawn¹** (flatter), **faun** (woodland god), **fawn²** (young deer).

fawn² (fôn) *n.* A young deer, especially one less than a year old. [From Middle English *foun*, from Old French *faon*, young animal, from Latin *fētus*, offspring.]

❑ *These sound alike:* **fawn²** (young deer), **faun** (woodland god), **fawn¹** (flatter).

fax (făks) *n.* **1.** A fax machine. **2.** A document sent or received by a fax machine: *a fax of a birth certificate.* ❖ *tr.v.* **faxed, fax·ing, fax·es** To send by a fax machine: *I faxed the contract to my lawyer.*

fax machine *n.* A device that sends and receives exact copies of documents over telephone lines.

fay (fā) *n.* A fairy or elf.

faze (fāz) *tr.v.* **fazed, faz·ing, faz·es** To upset; bother: *Some people do not let anything faze them.*

❑ *These sound alike:* **faze, phase** (aspect).

FBI *abbr.* An abbreviation of Federal Bureau of Investigation.

FCC *abbr.* An abbreviation of Federal Communications Commission.

F clef *n.* In music, a bass clef.

FDA *abbr.* An abbreviation of Food and Drug Administration.

Fe The symbol for the element **iron.**

fe·al·ty (fē′əl-tē) *n., pl.* **fe·al·ties 1.** In feudal times, the loyalty owed by a vassal to his lord. **2.** Loyalty; faithfulness: *the fealty of friends.* [From Middle English *feute*, from Latin *fidēlitās*, faithfulness, from *fidēlis*, faithful.]

fear (fîr) *n.* **1.** A feeling of alarm or fright caused by the expectation of danger. **2.** A state or condition marked by this feeling: *The citizens of the besieged town lived in fear.* **3.** An anxious feeling; concern: *a fear of looking foolish.* **4.** A cause for fear; dread: *My greatest fear is having to finish the job by myself.* ❖ *v.* **feared, fear·ing, fears** *—tr.* **1.** To be afraid of; be frightened of: *The boy does not fear spiders.* **2.** To feel anxious or concerned about; worry about: *We fear mistakes will show up.* *—intr.* **1.** To be afraid; feel fear. **2.** To feel anxious or worried: *The captain feared for the ship near the rocks.*

fear·ful (fîr′fəl) *adj.* **1.** Feeling fear; afraid: *I was fearful of losing my way in the forest.* **2.** Causing fear; terrible: *We heard a fearful explosion.* **3.** Feeling or showing anxiety, fear, or terror: *a fearful driver; a fearful glance.* **4.** Very bad; dreadful: *a fearful blunder.* **—fear′ful·ly** *adv.* **—fear′ful·ness** *n.*

fear·less (fîr′lĭs) *adj.* Having no fear; brave: *a fearless explorer.* See Synonyms at **brave. —fear′less·ly** *adv.* **—fear′less·ness** *n.*

fear·some (fîr′səm) *adj.* **1.** Causing or capable of causing fear; frightening; awesome: *A tornado is a fearsome sight.* **2.** Fearful; afraid. **—fear′some·ly** *adv.* **—fear′some·ness** *n.*

fea·si·ble (fē′zə-bəl) *adj.* **1.** Capable of being done or carried out; possible: *Development of rockets made space exploration feasible.* **2.** Likely; logical: *That answer seems feasible enough.* **—fea′si·bil′i·ty** *n.* **—fea′si·bly** *adv.*

feast (fēst) *n.* **1.** A large elaborate meal, especially one prepared for a special occasion; a banquet. **2.** A religious festival. ❖ *v.* **feast·ed, feast·ing, feasts** *—tr.* **1.** To give a feast for; entertain lavishly: *feasted all their friends with an elaborate dinner party.* **2.** To give pleasure to; delight: *feast one's eyes on the beautiful landscape.* *—intr.* To eat heartily: *feast on the first corn of summer.* [From Middle English *feste*, from Latin *fēstus*, festive.]

Feast of Lights *n.* Hanukkah.

feat (fēt) *n.* An outstanding deed or accomplishment; an exploit that requires much skill or daring: *The dam is a remarkable feat of engineering.* [From Middle English *fet*, action, deed, from Latin *factum*, from past participle of *facere*, to make, do.]

❑ *These sound alike:* **feat, feet** (plural of foot).

feath·er (fĕ*th*′ər) *n.* **1.** One of the light flat structures that cover the skin of birds. A feather is formed of numerous slender, closely arranged parallel barbs forming a vane on either side of a hollow shaft. **2.** A fringe or tuft of long hair, as on the legs or tail of some dogs. ❖ *tr.v.* **feath·ered, feath·er·ing, feath·ers 1.** To cover or fit with a feather or feathers: *feather an arrow.* **2.** To turn (an oar) so that its blade is parallel to the surface of the water between strokes. ◆ **a feather in (one's) cap** Something to be proud of; a great achievement. **feather (one's) nest** To get rich by taking advantage of circumstances. [From Old English *fether.*]

feather bed *n.* A soft mattress or quilt stuffed with feathers or down.

feath·ered (fĕ*th*′ərd) *adj.* Covered or trimmed with feathers: *a feathered headdress.*

feath·er·weight (fĕ*th*′ər-wāt′) *n.* **1.** A boxer weighing more than 118 and not more than 126 pounds (about 53–57 kilograms). **2.** *Informal* A very small or unimportant person or thing.

feath·er·y (fĕ*th*′ə-rē) *adj.* **1.** Made of or covered with feathers. **2.** Resembling or suggestive of a feather or feathers, as in form or lightness: *the feathery leaves of the hemlock.*

fea·ture (fē′chər) *n.* **1.** A prominent part, quality, or characteristic: *Dust and craters are features of the moon's surface. Several features of the plan caught our attention.* See Synonyms at **quality. 2.** Any of the distinct parts of the face: *couldn't make out his features from a distance.* **3.** The main film presentation at a theater. **4.** A special article or column in a newspaper or magazine. ❖ *tr.v.* **fea·tured, fea·tur·ing, fea·tures 1.** To display or offer prominently: *an exhibit that features Native American pottery.* **2.** To have or include as a prominent part or characteristic: *The play featured a famous actor.*

Feb·ru·ar·y (fĕb′ro͞o-ĕr′ē *or* fĕb′yo͞o-ĕr′ē) *n., pl.* **Feb·ru·ar·ies** The second month of the year in the Gregorian calendar, having 28 days, or in leap years, 29 days. [From Middle English *Februarie*, from Latin *Februārius (mēnsis)*, (month) of purification, from *februa*, offerings of atonement.]

fe·cal (fē′kəl) *adj.* Relating to feces.

fe·ces (fē′sēz) *n.* *(used with a singular or plural verb)* Waste matter excreted from the intestine.

feck·less (fĕk′lĭs) *adj.* **1.** Lacking purpose or vitality; weak or ineffective. **2.** Careless and irresponsible: *an idle feckless youth.* **—feck′less·ness** *n.*

fe·cund (fē′kənd *or* fĕk′ənd) *adj.* Productive; fertile; fruitful: *the artist's fecund imagination.*

ă	pat	ôr	core
ā	pay	oi	boy
âr	care	ou	out
ä	father	o͝o	took
ĕ	pet	o͝or	lure
ē	be	o͞o	boot
ĭ	pit	ŭ	cut
ī	bite	ûr	urge
îr	pier	th	thin
ŏ	pot	*th*	this
ō	toe	zh	vision
ô	paw	ə	about

fe·cun·di·ty (fĭ-kŭn′dĭ-tē) *n.* **1.** The ability to produce offspring or seeds, especially in abundance. **2.** Productive or creative power.

fed (fĕd) *v.* Past tense and past participle of **feed.**

Fed *n. Informal* **1.** The Federal Reserve. **2.** often **fed** A federal agent or official.

fed·er·al (fĕd′ər-əl *or* fĕd′rəl) *adj.* **1a.** Relating to or being a form of government in which separate states retain control over local affairs but are united under a central government that manages affairs of common concern to all the states. **b.** Relating to the central government of such a union rather than to the governments of its member states: *federal courts; federal laws applying to all the states.* **2a.** often **Federal** Relating to the central government of the United States: *the Federal Court of Appeals.* **b. Federal** Relating to or supporting the Union during the American Civil War: *a Federal soldier.* **c. Federal** Relating to Federalism or the Federalist Party. ❖ *n.* **Federal** A supporter of the Union during the American Civil War. [From Latin *foedus*, league, treaty.] **—fed′er·al·ly** *adv.*

Federal Bureau of Investigation *n.* An agency of the US Department of Justice responsible for investigating violations of federal law.

fed·er·al·ism (fĕd′ər-ə-lĭz′əm *or* fĕd′rə-lĭz′əm) *n.* **1.** A system of government in which power is divided between a central government and member states. **2.** Advocacy of or belief in such a system of government. **3. Federalism** The principles of the Federalist Party.

fed·er·al·ist (fĕd′ər-ə-lĭst *or* fĕd′rə-lĭst) *n.* **1.** A person who supports federalism. **2. Federalist** A supporter or member of the Federalist Party.

Federalist Party *n.* A US political party that flourished in the 1790s under the leadership of Alexander Hamilton and advocated a strong central government.

fed·er·al·ize (fĕd′ər-ə-līz′ *or* fĕd′rə-līz′) *tr.v.* **fed·er·al·ized, fed·er·al·iz·ing, fed·er·al·iz·es 1.** To unite in a federal union. **2.** To subject to the authority of a federal government; put under federal control: *federalized the local transportation departments.*

Federal Reserve or **Federal Reserve System** *n.* The US central bank, a system consisting of 12 Federal Reserve banks, each of which serves the banks located within its own district. The system has broad powers over US monetary policy and regulation of the banking industry.

fed·er·ate (fĕd′ə-rāt′) *tr. & intr.v.* **fed·er·at·ed, fed·er·at·ing, fed·er·ates** To bring or join together in a league, federal union, or other association: *The unions voted to federate under one national organization.*

fed·er·a·tion (fĕd′ə-**rā′**shən) *n.* **1.** The act of joining together in a league, federal union, or other association. **2.** A league or association formed by federating: *a federation of independent store owners.*

fe·do·ra (fĭ-**dôr′**ə) *n.* A soft felt hat with a crown creased lengthwise and a brim that can be turned up or down.

fed up *adj.* Unable or unwilling to put up with something any longer: *The manager got fed up with his excuses for being late.*

fee (fē) *n.* **1.** A charge or payment for a service or privilege: *an admission fee to the movies; fees for advice from our lawyer; a tuition fee for school.* **2.** In feudal times, an estate of land granted by a lord to a vassal; a fief. [From Middle English *fe*, from Old English *feoh*, cattle, goods, money, and from Anglo-Norman *fee*, fief.]

fee·ble (fē′bəl) *adj.* **fee·bler, fee·blest 1.** Lacking strength; weak: *a very old and feeble person recovering from surgery.* **2.** Without adequate force, power, or intensity; inadequate: *a feeble attempt; a feeble voice.* [From Middle English *feble*, from Latin *flēbilis*, lamentable, from *flēre*, to weep.] **—fee′ble·ness** *n.* **—fee′bly** *adv.*

fee·ble-mind·ed (fē′bəl-**mīn′**dĭd) *adj.* **1.** Lacking intelligence or foresight: *a feeble-minded plan to build housing in the park.* **2.** A term formerly used for people with impaired mental development. **—fee′ble-mind′ed·ly** *adv.*

feed (fēd) *v.* **fed** (fĕd), **feed·ing, feeds** *—tr.* **1.** To give food to; supply with nourishment: *People feed the birds in the park.* **2.** To provide as food or nourishment: *We fed the fish to the cat when we got home.* **3a.** To serve as food for: *a turkey large enough to feed a dozen.* **b.** To produce food for: *This valley feeds an entire country.* **4.** To provide (something) for growth, maintenance, or operation: *We fed more wood to the fire. Scientists fed data into a computer.* *—intr.* To eat or ingest something as food: *Young turtles feed on insects.* ❖ *n.* **1.** Food for animals, especially livestock. **2.** *Informal* A meal, especially a large one. [From Old English *fēdan.*]

feed·back (fēd′băk′) *n.* **1.** The return of a part of the output of a system or process to the input, especially when used to regulate an electrical system or an electronic process. Computers use feedback to regulate their operations. **2.** A response or reaction: *We asked the employees for feedback on the new cafeteria.*

feed·er (fē′dər) *n.* **1.** A person or thing that supplies feed: *a bird feeder on a window ledge.* **2.** A person or thing that eats: *Caterpillars are greedy feeders that damage trees.* **3.** Something that feeds materials into a machine to be processed. **4.** A branch or tributary, as of a river, railroad, or corporation.

feel (fēl) *v.* **felt** (fĕlt), **feel·ing, feels** *—tr.* **1.** To be aware of through the sense of touch: *feel the softness of velvet.* **2.** To be aware of as a physical sensation: *feel a sharp pain; feel the cold.* **3.** To touch or examine by touching in order to find something out: *The nurse felt the patient's forehead for fever.* **4.** To find (one's way) by touching; grope: *In the dark we felt our way up the steps.* **5.** To sense or experience: *They felt my annoyance over their loud music.* **6.** To be affected by: *She still feels the loss of her cat.* **7.** To believe; consider: *We feel the idea is worth trying.* *—intr.* **1.** To experience sensations of touch: *The doctor poked my finger to see if it could feel.* **2.** To produce a particular sensation or feeling: *The sheets felt cool and smooth. It feels good to be home.* **3.** To be aware of a quality or emotional state: *We all felt satisfied with the results of our work.* **4.** To try to find something by touching: *We felt around for the light switch.* **5.** To have compassion or sympathy: *I feel for him.* ❖ *n.* **1.** Awareness or sensation caused by physical touch: *the feel of raindrops.* **2.** A quality that can be sensed by touching: *the smooth and slippery feel of satin.* ◆ **feel in (one's) bones** To have an intuition about: *I feel in my bones that this project will succeed.* **feel like** *Informal* To be in the mood for: *I did not feel like going for a walk.* **feel like (oneself)** To be aware of oneself as being in the usual state of health or spirits: *I don't feel quite myself this morning.* **feel out** To try cautiously to find out the viewpoint of (a person): *We felt them out about playing a football game.* [From Old English *fēlan.*]

feel·er (fē′lər) *n.* **1.** A slender body part, such as the antenna of an insect, used for touching or feeling. **2.** A remark, question, or suggestion used to find out the attitude or intention of others: *The letter was a feeler sent to see if there was any interest in our project.*

feel·ing (fē′lĭng) *n.* **1.** The sense of touch: *I had no feeling in my cut finger.* **2.** A physical sensation, especially one produced by touch: *the feeling of ice.* **3.** An emotion, such as joy or sorrow: *a feeling of excitement.* **4.** Strong emotion or emotional quality: *She plays the violin with real feeling.* **5.** An awareness; an impression: *a feeling of danger nearby.* **6. feelings** The sensitive nature of one's emotions: *His lack of concern hurt my feelings.* **7.** An opinion based strongly on emotion; a sentiment: *What are your feelings about a longer school year?*

fedora

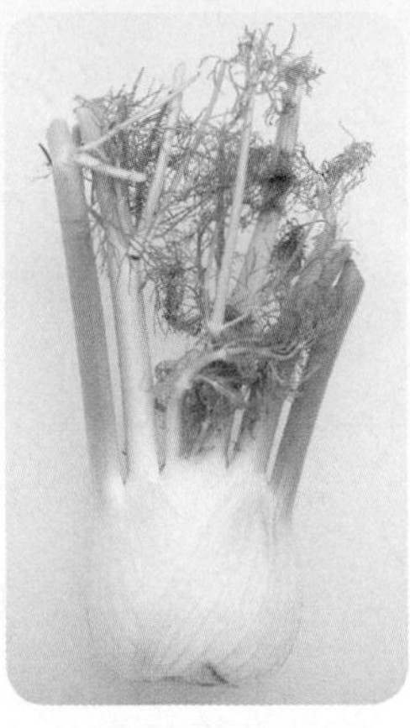
fennel

ă	pat	ôr	core
ā	pay	oi	boy
âr	care	ou	out
ä	father	ŏŏ	took
ĕ	pet	ŏŏr	lure
ē	be	ōō	boot
ĭ	pit	ŭ	cut
ī	bite	ûr	urge
îr	pier	th	thin
ŏ	pot	*th*	this
ō	toe	zh	vision
ô	paw	ə	about

SYNONYMS feeling, emotion, sentiment These nouns refer to an intense, complicated mental state such as love or hate. **Feeling** is the most general and neutral: *A feeling of relief came over us when the tightrope walker regained her balance.* **Emotion** is a stronger term; it often means an excited or agitated feeling: *I was filled with emotion after reading the heartbreaking news article.* **Sentiment** often refers to a delicate, sensitive, refined feeling: *Don't let your sentiments get the better of you.*

feel·ing·ly (fē′lĭng-lē) *adv.* With much emotion or sensitivity: *The poet writes feelingly about liberty.*

feet (fēt) *n.* Plural of **foot.**

❑ *These sound alike:* **feet, feat** (accomplishment).

feign (fān) *v.* **feigned, feign·ing, feigns** *—tr.* To give a false appearance of; pretend: *feign illness. —intr.* To make a false appearance; pretend: *The opossum isn't really dead; it's only feigning to fool the dog.*

❑ *These sound alike:* **feign, fain** (willingly).

feint (fānt) *n.* **1.** A movement or attack that is meant to deceive by diverting attention from the real target or objective: *With a feint to the left, she fooled the goalie and scored.* **2.** An action meant to mislead: *The robbers made a feint of repairing the window they were going to break into.* ❖ *intr.v.* **feint·ed, feint·ing, feints** To make a feint: *My opponent feinted as if to take a shot at the basket.*

❑ *These sound alike:* **feint, faint** (pass out).

feist·y (fī′stē) *adj.* **feist·i·er, feist·i·est 1.** Full of spirit or determination. **2.** Quarrelsome or aggressive.

feld·spar (fĕld′spär′ *or* fĕl′spär′) also **fel·spar** (fĕl′-spär′) *n.* Any of a group of crystalline minerals that occur widely in various rocks and are composed largely of silicates combined with sodium and either potassium or calcium. Feldspars are used in the manufacture of glass.

fe·lic·i·tate (fĭ-lĭs′ĭ-tāt′) *tr.v.* **fe·lic·i·tat·ed, fe·lic·i·tat·ing, fe·lic·i·tates** To wish happiness to; congratulate: *Guests felicitated the newlyweds.*

fe·lic·i·ta·tions (fĭ-lĭs′ĭ-tā′shənz) *pl.n.* Expressions of joy or acknowledgment: *Family and friends offered their felicitations to the graduating senior.*

fe·lic·i·tous (fĭ-lĭs′ĭ-təs) *adj.* **1.** Well-chosen; apt; appropriate: *a felicitous choice of words.* **2.** Having an agreeable manner or style: *the mayor's felicitous greeting to the guests.* **—fe·lic′i·tous·ly** *adv.*

fe·lic·i·ty (fĭ-lĭs′ĭ-tē) *n., pl.* **fe·lic·i·ties 1.** Great happiness; bliss: *the felicity of the moment of victory.* **2.** A source of great happiness: *the felicity of a generous heart.* **3.** An appropriate and pleasing manner or style: *She writes with felicity of expression.* **4.** A pleasing and appropriate expression; a well-chosen phrase: *The felicities of their greeting touched everyone.*

fe·line (fē′līn′) *adj.* **1.** Relating to the family of carnivorous mammals that includes the cats, lions, tigers, and leopards. **2.** Suggestive of a cat: *walking with feline grace.* ❖ *n.* An animal belonging to the feline family. [From Latin *fēlīnus,* from *fēlēs,* cat.]

fell[1] (fĕl) *tr.v.* **felled, fell·ing, fells** To cause to fall; cut or knock down: *They felled trees to build a cabin.* [From Old English *fellan.*]

fell[2] (fĕl) *adj.* **1.** Of a cruel nature; fierce and ruthless: *a fell crew of pirates.* **2.** Capable of destroying; lethal: *a fell potion.* ◆ **at one fell swoop** or **in one fell swoop** All at once. [From Middle English *fel,* from Old French, from *felon,* evil.]

fell[3] (fĕl) *v.* Past tense of **fall.**

fel·low (fĕl′ō) *n.* **1.** A man or boy: *Where are those fellows going?* **2.** A comrade or associate: *Robin Hood and his fellows hid in the forest.* **3.** A member of a learned society or professional organization. **4.** A graduate student who receives a grant of money for further study. **5.** A physician who enters a training program in a medical specialty after completing a residency. **6.** One of a matched pair; a counterpart: *Here's the fellow of your sneaker.* ❖ *adj.* Being of the same kind, group, or class; sharing certain characteristics or interests: *our fellow workers.* [From Old English *fēolaga,* from Old Norse *fēlagi,* business partner, from *fēlag,* partnership : *fē,* property, money + *lag,* a laying down.]

fel·low·ship (fĕl′ō-shĭp′) *n.* **1.** Friendly association of people; companionship: *We enjoyed the fellowship of our neighbors.* **2.** A group of people sharing common interests. **3.** A grant of money awarded a graduate student in a college or university.

fel·on (fĕl′ən) *n.* A person who has committed a felony. [From Middle English *feloun,* from Medieval Latin *fellō.*]

fe·lo·ni·ous (fə-lō′nē-əs) *adj.* Having the nature of a felony: *carrying a gun with felonious intent.*

fel·o·ny (fĕl′ə-nē) *n., pl.* **fel·o·nies** A serious crime, such as murder, rape, or robbery, for which the punishment is more severe than for a misdemeanor.

felt[1] (fĕlt) *n.* A smooth firm cloth made by pressing and matting wool, fur, or other fibers together instead of weaving them. ❖ *adj.* Made of or resembling felt: *a felt hat.* [From Old English.]

felt[2] (fĕlt) *v.* Past tense and past participle of **feel.**

fem. *abbr.* An abbreviation of: **1.** female. **2.** feminine.

fe·male (fē′māl′) *adj.* **1a.** Relating to or characteristic of the sex that produces eggs or gives birth to offspring. **b.** Relating to or being a reproductive organ that produces female gametes: *female flower parts.* **c.** Relating to or being the gamete that is larger and less motile than the other corresponding gamete: *female reproductive cells.* **2.** Composed of women or girls: *a female choir.* **3.** Having a part into which a corresponding male part fits: *a female plug.* ❖ *n.* **1.** A female organism. **2.** A woman or girl. [From Middle English *femele,* from Latin *fēmella,* diminutive of *fēmina,* woman.]

fem·i·nine (fĕm′ə-nĭn) *adj.* **1.** Relating to women or girls. **2.** Marked by or possessing qualities traditionally attributed to a woman: *The lace curtains gave the house a feminine feeling.* **3.** In grammar, relating to or belonging to the gender of nouns that refer to females or to things classified as female: *In German, the word for "world" is feminine.* **—fem′i·nine·ly** *adv.*

fem·i·nin·i·ty (fĕm′ə-nĭn′ĭ-tē) *n.* The quality or condition of being feminine.

fem·i·nism (fĕm′ə-nĭz′əm) *n.* **1.** Belief in or support for the idea that women and men have the same social, political, and economic rights. **2.** The movement organized around this belief. **—fem′i·nist** *n. & adj.*

fem·o·ral (fĕm′ər-əl) *adj.* Relating to or located in the thigh or femur: *femoral arteries and veins.*

fe·mur (fē′mər) *n., pl.* **fe·murs** or **fem·o·ra** (fĕm′ər-ə) **1.** The long bone of the leg between the knee and pelvis in humans; the thighbone. **2.** A corresponding bone in other vertebrate animals.

fen (fĕn) *n.* An area of low wet ground that is usually less acidic than a bog.

fence (fĕns) *n.* **1.** A structure usually made of posts or stakes joined together by wire, boards, or rails, that serves as an enclosure, a boundary, or a barrier. **2.** A person who receives and sells stolen goods. ❖ *v.* **fenced, fenc·ing, fenc·es** *—tr.* To surround or separate with a fence: *fence a pasture to keep cows in; fence in the dog for the night. —intr.* To practice the sport of fencing: *Both actors fenced with skill.* ◆ **on the fence** *Informal* Undecided as to which of two sides to support; uncommitted. **—fenc′er** *n.*

fenc·ing (fĕn′sĭng) *n.* **1.** The art or sport of using a sword, especially a foil, in attack and defense. **2.** Material, such as wire, stakes, and rails, used in building fences: *That lumber yard sells fencing.* **3.** A barrier or enclosure of fences: *Low stone fencing surrounds the park.*

fend (fĕnd) *v.* **fend·ed, fend·ing, fends** —*tr.* To ward off: *fend off an attack.* —*intr.* To attempt to manage without assistance: *I'll have to fend for myself until my parents get home from work.*

fend·er (fĕn′dər) *n.* **1.** A guard over each wheel of an automobile or other vehicle that is shaped and positioned so as to keep mud or water from splashing up. **2.** A device at the front end of a locomotive or streetcar designed to push aside obstructions. **3.** A cushion made of fiber, rubber, or wood and hung over the side of a dock or vessel to absorb friction or impact. **4.** A screen or metal frame placed in front of a fireplace to keep hot coals and debris from falling out.

fend·er-bend·er or **fender bender** (fĕn′dər-bĕn′dər) *n. Informal* A collision between two or more automobiles that results in only minor damage.

fen·nel (fĕn′əl) *n.* An edible perennial plant that has feathery leaves and tastes like licorice. The seeds are used as a flavoring, and the bulbous stalks are eaten as a vegetable.

fer-de-lance (fĕr′dl-äns′ *or* fĕr′dl-äns′) *n., pl.* **fer-de-lance** Any of several large venomous snakes of tropical America, having brown and grayish markings.

Fer·di·nand V (fûr′dn-ănd′) Known as "Ferdinand the Catholic." 1452–1516. King of Castile (1474–1504) who ruled jointly with his wife, Isabella I. Their marriage (1469) marked the beginning of the modern Spanish state.

fer·ment (fər-mĕnt′) *v.* **fer·ment·ed, fer·ment·ing, fer·ments** —*intr.* **1.** To undergo fermentation: *The apple cider had fermented overnight.* **2.** To develop actively or rapidly: *an idea that was fermenting in his mind for months.* —*tr.* To cause to undergo fermentation: *Yeasts ferment sugars.* ❖ *n.* (**fûr′**mĕnt′) A state of agitation, unrest, or rapid development: *It was a time of great intellectual ferment.*

fer·men·ta·tion (fûr′mĕn-**tā′**shən) *n.* A chemical reaction in which enzymes break down complex organic compounds into simpler compounds. Yeasts obtain energy by using fermentation to convert sugar into alcohol and carbon dioxide without the use of oxygen. —SEE NOTE AT **Pasteur, Louis.**

Fer·mi (fĕr′mē), **Enrico** 1901–1954. Italian-born American who led the team that produced the first controlled nuclear chain reaction (1942).

fer·mi·um (fûr′mē-əm) *n. Symbol* **Fm** A radioactive element that has been artificially produced by scientists. The half-life of its longest-lived isotope is about 100 days. Atomic number 100. See **Periodic Table.** [After Enrico *Fermi.*]

fern (fûrn) *n.* Any of numerous plants having feathery fronds usually divided into many leaflets. Ferns do not have flowers or seeds but reproduce by means of spores.

fe·ro·cious (fə-**rō′**shəs) *adj.* **1.** Extremely aggressive or violent: *the tiger's ferocious attack.* **2.** Extreme powerful or destructive: *ferocious heat.* **—fe·ro′cious·ly** *adv.* **—fe·ro′cious·ness** *n.*

fe·roc·i·ty (fə-**rŏs′**ĭ-tē) *n.* The state or quality of being ferocious; fierceness.

fer·ret (fĕr′ĭt) *n.* **1.** A small domesticated mammal with a long slender body, short legs, and brown, black, or whitish fur, often kept as a pet and formerly trained to hunt rats or rabbits. **2.** A North American mammal with a long slender body, short legs, yellowish-brown fur and black feet. ❖ *v.* **fer·ret·ed, fer·ret·ing, fer·rets** —*tr.* **1.** To bring to light by searching; uncover: *ferreted out the solution to the mystery.* **2.** To hunt (rabbits, for example) with ferrets. —*intr.* **1.** To search intensively: *ferreting among old records.* **2.** To engage in hunting with ferrets.

fer·ric (fĕr′ĭk) *adj.* Relating to or containing iron, especially iron with a valence of 3.

ferric oxide *n.* A reddish-brown to black, iron-containing compound that is often used as a pigment.

Fer·ris wheel (fĕr′ĭs) *n.* An amusement ride consisting of an upright wheel having seats suspended from its rim that remain horizontal as the wheel revolves. [After George Washington Gale *Ferris* (1859–1896), American engineer.]

fer·ro·mag·net·ic (fĕr′ō-măg-**nĕt′**ĭk) *adj.* Relating to substances that become magnetic when subjected to a magnetic field under certain conditions. Ferromagnetic substances, such as iron and cobalt, retain the magnetism for some time even after the magnetic field has been removed.

fer·rous (fĕr′əs) *adj.* Relating to or containing iron, especially iron with a valence of 2.

fer·ry (fĕr′ē) *v.* **fer·ried, fer·ry·ing, fer·ries** —*tr.* **1.** To transport (people, vehicles, or goods) by boat across a body of water. **2.** To cross (a body of water) by a ferry: *We ferried the river before a bridge was built.* **3.** To deliver (a vehicle) under its own power to its eventual user. **4.** To transport (people or things) by vehicle: *Volunteers ferried everyone from the disaster area to the hospital.* —*intr.* To cross a body of water on or as if on a ferry: *We ferried across the bay.* ❖ *n., pl.* **fer·ries 1.** A boat used to transport passengers, vehicles, or goods across a body of water; a ferryboat. **2.** A place where passengers or goods are transported across a body of water by a ferry: *There was a crowd waiting at the ferry.* [From Old English *ferian.*]

fer·ry·boat (fĕr′ē-bōt′) *n.* A boat used to transport passengers, vehicles, or goods across a body of water.

fer·tile (fûr′tl) *adj.* **1.** Capable of producing offspring; able to reproduce: *a fertile cow.* **2.** Capable of developing into a complete organism; fertilized: *A fertile egg from a hen will produce a chick.* **3.** Capable of supporting plant life; favorable to the growth of crops or other plants: *fertile soil; a fertile valley.* **4.** Highly productive or active; inventive: *the writer's fertile imagination.*

Fertile Crescent A region of the Middle East extending from the Nile River valley in Egypt to the Tigris and Euphrates Rivers in Iraq. The prehistoric development of agriculture in the region gave rise to many of the world's first civilizations.

fer·til·i·ty (fər-**tĭl′**ĭ-tē) *n.* The quality or condition of being fertile: *the fertility of good soil; factors influencing the fertility of cows.*

fer·til·i·za·tion (fûr′tl-ĭ-**zā′**shən) *n.* **1.** The act or process of fertilizing. **2.** The union of a male reproductive cell and a female reproductive cell to form a cell that is capable of developing into a new organism.

fer·til·ize (fûr′tl-īz′) *tr.v.* **fer·til·ized, fer·til·iz·ing, fer·til·iz·es 1.** To cause (a female reproductive cell) to become able to develop into a new organism, especially by union with a male reproductive cell such as a sperm cell. **2.** To make (soil, for example) fertile: *Manure from grazing animals fertilizes the grasslands.* **3.** To spread fertilizer on: *fertilize the garden.*

fer·til·iz·er (fûr′tl-ī′zər) *n.* A material, such as manure, compost, or a chemical compound, added to soil to increase its productivity or fertility.

fer·ule (fĕr′əl) *n.* A cane or flat stick formerly used in punishing children.

fer·ven·cy (fûr′vən-sē) *n., pl.* **fer·ven·cies** The quality or condition of being fervent.

fer·vent (fûr′vənt) *adj.* Having or showing great emotion or zeal; ardent: *the fervent leaders of the reform movement; a fervent plea for help.* **—fer′vent·ly** *adv.*

fer·vid (fûr′vĭd) *adj.* Marked by great passion or zeal: *a fervid desire to play baseball.* **—fer′vid·ly** *adv.* **—fer′vid·ness** *n.*

Enrico Fermi

photographed in 1942

Ferris wheel

WRITERS CHOOSE THEIR WORDS

The river. The Shenandoah snakes along at the foot of the western slopes in the Blue Ridge, up past Front Royal to join the Potomac at Harper's Ferry. That town and the name of John Brown were not yet infamous in Virginia, but would be within five years. You've read, I'm sure, of the slave rebellion that took place there in 1859. John Brown was a **fervent** abolitionist but, alas, a terrible general, and Robert E. Lee rounded up that desperate small army in only a day.

—Jennifer Armstrong
Steal Away

fetish
a Native American bear fetish, believed to have spiritual powers

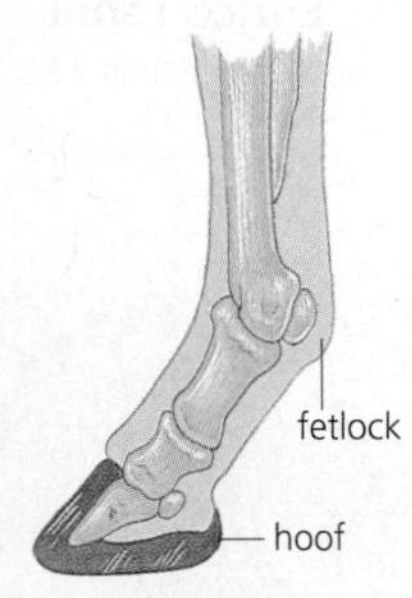

fetlock

USAGE

fewer You use the word **fewer** with words referring to things that can be counted: *Fewer than four players scored in the playoffs.* You use **less** with words referring to things that cannot be counted: *We have less soap than we need. We brought less luggage on this trip.* However, *less* can be used before a plural noun referring to a measure of distance, amount, or time: *We drove less than 50 miles. I have less than ten dollars. There are less than 30 seconds left in the game.*

ă	pat	ôr	core
ā	pay	oi	boy
âr	care	ou	out
ä	father	ŏŏ	took
ĕ	pet	ŏŏr	lure
ē	be	ōō	boot
ĭ	pit	ŭ	cut
ī	bite	ûr	urge
îr	pier	th	thin
ŏ	pot	*th*	this
ō	toe	zh	vision
ô	paw	ə	about

fer·vor (fûr′vər) *n.* Intensity of emotion; ardor.

fes·tal (fĕs′təl) *adj.* Related to a feast or festival; festive: *Flags gave a festal appearance to the village.*

fes·ter (fĕs′tər) *intr.v.* **fes·tered, fes·ter·ing, fes·ters 1.** To form pus, as an infected wound does: *An unclean cut will fester and become painful.* **2.** To be or become a source of irritation; rankle: *bitterness that festered and grew.*

fes·ti·val (fĕs′tə-vəl) *n.* **1.** An occasion for feasting or celebration, especially a day or time of religious significance. **2.** An often regularly recurring series of cultural performances, exhibitions, or competitions: *an international film festival.* [From Middle English *festival,* festive.]

fes·tive (fĕs′tĭv) *adj.* **1.** Relating to a feast or festival. **2.** Merry; joyous: *a festive party; festive decorations.* **—fes′tive·ly** *adv.* **—fes′tive·ness** *n.*

fes·tiv·i·ty (fĕ-stĭv′ĭ-tē) *n., pl.* **fes·tiv·i·ties 1.** The fun and excitement of a celebration or festival: *a holiday full of festivity.* **2. festivities** The activities or events of a festival: *Mardi Gras festivities included parades, banquets, and balls.*

fes·toon (fĕ-stōōn′) *n.* **1.** A string or garland, as of leaves or flowers, suspended in a curve between two points. **2.** A representation of such a string or garland, as in painting or sculpture. ❖ *tr.v.* **fes·tooned, fes·toon·ing, fes·toons 1.** To decorate with or as if with festoons. **2.** To form or make into festoons.

fet·a (fĕt′ə *or* fā′tə) *n.* A white moderately soft cheese usually made of goat's or sheep's milk and often preserved in brine.

fe·tal (fēt′l) *adj.* Relating to or characteristic of a fetus: *a fetal heartbeat.*

fetal position *n.* A position of the body at rest in which the spine is curved, the head is bent forward, and the arms and legs are drawn in toward the chest.

fetch (fĕch) *v.* **fetched, fetch·ing, fetch·es** *—tr.* **1.** To go after and bring or take back; get: *Could you fetch my bags?* **2.** To cause to come; succeed in bringing: *My phone call fetched them home quickly.* **3.** To bring in as a price: *The painting fetched $200 at the auction.* —*intr.* To go after something and return with it: *If you throw the ball, the dog will fetch.* [From Old English *feccan.*]

fetch·ing (fĕch′ĭng) *adj.* Very attractive; charming: *a fetching smile.* **—fetch′ing·ly** *adv.*

fete also **fête** (fāt *or* fĕt) *n.* **1.** A festival or feast. **2.** An elaborate party. ❖ *tr.v.* **fet·ed, fet·ing, fetes** also **fêt·ed, fêt·ing, fêtes** To honor with a festival, feast, or elaborate entertainment: *They feted the veterans on Memorial Day.*

❑ *These sound alike:* **fete, fate** (destiny).

fet·id (fĕt′ĭd *or* fē′tĭd) *adj.* Having an offensive odor. **—fet′id·ly** *adv.* **—fet′id·ness** *n.*

fet·ish (fĕt′ĭsh) *n.* **1.** An object that is believed to have magical or spiritual powers. **2.** An object of too much attention or reverence.

fet·ish·ism (fĕt′ĭ-shĭz′əm) *n.* **1.** Worship of or belief in magical fetishes. **2.** Too much attention to or attachment for something. **—fet′ish·ist** *n.*

fet·lock (fĕt′lŏk′) *n.* **1.** A joint that forms a projection on the back of the leg of a horse or related animal, just above the hoof. **2.** A tuft of hair on this projection.

fet·ter (fĕt′ər) *n.* **1.** A device, usually one of a pair of rings connected to a chain, that is attached to a person's ankles or feet to restrict movement. **2.** often **fetters** Something that restricts or restrains: *the fetters of rigid traditions.* ❖ *tr.v.* **fet·tered, fet·ter·ing, fet·ters 1.** To put fetters on; shackle. **2.** To restrict or restrain: *attempts to fetter free speech.*

fet·tle (fĕt′l) *n.* Proper or sound mental or physical condition or state: *The horse is in fine fettle for today's race.*

fet·tuc·ci·ne (fĕt′ə-chē′nē) *n.* **1.** Pasta in narrow flat strips. **2.** A dish made with such strips of pasta.

fe·tus (fē′təs) *n., pl.* **fe·tus·es** The unborn young of a mammal at the later stages of its development, especially a human embryo from its eighth week of development to its birth.

feud (fyōōd) *n.* A bitter quarrel or state of enmity between two people, families, or groups, often continuing for generations: *An ancient feud came between the two families.* ❖ *intr.v.* **feud·ed, feud·ing, feuds** To carry on a bitter quarrel or state of enmity. [From Middle English *fede,* from Old French *faide,* of Germanic origin.]

feu·dal (fyōōd′l) *adj.* Relating to or characteristic of feudalism. [From Medieval Latin *feudum,* fee, fief.]

feu·dal·ism (fyōōd′l-ĭz′əm) *n.* A political and economic system in Europe during the Middle Ages, in which a landowner granted the use of land to a vassal in exchange for military service and various other duties. **—feu′dal·is′tic** *adj.*

fe·ver (fē′vər) *n.* **1.** A body temperature higher than normal. **2.** A disease in which a high body temperature is one of the main symptoms. **3.** A condition of great activity or excitement: *a fever of enthusiasm during the game.* [From Old English *fefor,* from Latin *febris.*]

fever blister *n.* A cold sore.

fe·ver·ish (fē′vər-ĭsh) *adj.* **1a.** Relating to or resembling a fever. **b.** Having a fever or symptoms characteristic of a fever: *The sick child was feverish.* **c.** Causing or tending to cause fever. **2.** Marked by intense agitation, emotion, or activity: *a feverish worker.* **3.** Intensely excited or active: *a feverish desire to win.* **—fe′ver·ish·ly** *adv.* **—fe′ver·ish·ness** *n.*

few (fyōō) *adj.* **few·er, few·est** Amounting to a small number; not many: *Few people like to swim in cold water.* ❖ *n. (used with a plural verb)* A small number of people or things: *I invited only a few to my party.* ❖ *pron. (used with a plural verb)* A small number of people or things: *Many felt it was an interesting idea, but few seemed willing to do anything about it.* —SEE NOTE.

fez (fĕz) *n., pl.* **fez·zes** A man's brimless felt cap in the shape of a flat-topped cone, usually red with a black tassel, worn chiefly in the eastern Mediterranean region. [From Turkish *fes,* from Fez, Morocco.]

fi·an·cé (fē′än-sā′ *or* fē-än′sā′) *n.* A man to whom one is engaged to be married.

fi·an·cée (fē′än-sā′ *or* fē-än′sā′) *n.* A woman to whom one is engaged to be married.

fi·as·co (fē-ăs′kō) *n., pl.* **fi·as·coes** or **fi·as·cos** A complete failure: *Without enough rehearsal, the play was a fiasco.*

fi·at (fē′ăt′ *or* fē′ät′) *n.* An arbitrary order or decree: *The dictator raised taxes by fiat.*

fib (fĭb) *n.* A lie about something unimportant or small: *She told a fib about why she was late.* ❖ *intr.v.* **fibbed, fib·bing, fibs** To tell a fib: *I think he's fibbing about being a gourmet cook.* **—fib′ber** *n.*

fi·ber (fī′bər) *n.* **1a.** A slender strand; a thread: *wool fibers spun into yarn.* **b.** Material made of such strands: *organic cotton fiber.* **2.** Any of various elongated cells in the body, especially those of muscle or nerve tissue. **3.** Any of the elongated, thick-walled cells that give strength and support to plant tissue. **4a.** The essential character or nature of a person: *She's a person of strong moral fiber.* **b.** An element of a person's character or nature: *He missed her with every fiber of his being.* **5.** The part of vegetable foods such as grains, fruits, and vegetables that contains cellulose and other substances that are not digested in the human intestinal tract. Eating foods with fiber helps stool move through the intestines and is thought to have other health benefits. [From Latin *fibra.*]

fi·ber·board (fī′bər-bôrd′) *n.* A building material made from wood chips or plant fibers bonded together and compressed into rigid sheets.

fi·ber·glass (fī′bər-glăs′) *n.* A material made up of very fine glass fibers, used in making various products, such as building insulation and boat hulls.

fiber optics *n. (used with a singular verb)* The technology of transmitting light through very thin glass or plastic fibers that can be curved. Fiber optics is used for medical imaging instruments and long-distance telephone and computer lines. **—fi′ber-op′tic** (fī′bər-ŏp′tĭk) *adj.*

fi·bre (fī′bər) *n. Chiefly British* Variant of **fiber.**

fib·ril·la·tion (fĭb′rə-lā′shən *or* fī′brə-lā′shən) *n.* A rapid twitching of muscle fibers, especially of the heart.

fi·brin (fī′brĭn) *n.* A fibrous, elastic, and insoluble protein that is formed when blood clots.

fi·brin·o·gen (fī-brĭn′ə-jən) *n.* A soluble protein that is normally present in the plasma of the blood and forms fibrin.

fi·broid (fī′broid′) *adj.* Made up of or resembling fibers or fibrous tissue: *a fibroid tumor.*

fi·brous (fī′brəs) *adj.* Made up of, resembling, or having fibers: *fibrous tissue.*

fib·u·la (fĭb′yə-lə) *n., pl.* **fib·u·lae** (fĭb′yə-lē′) or **fib·u·las 1.** The outer and smaller of the two bones of the leg in humans. It extends from the knee to the ankle. **2.** A similar bone in the hind leg of other vertebrate animals.

–fic *suff.* A suffix that means making or causing: *soporific.*

fick·le (fĭk′əl) *adj.* Changeable; not stable or constant, especially with regard to affections: *a fickle friend.* **—fick′le·ness** *n.*

fic·tion (fĭk′shən) *n.* **1.** The category of literature, drama, or film whose content is imagined and is not necessarily based on fact. **2.** Works, especially novels, in this category: *the fiction of Virginia Woolf.* **3.** Explanation or belief that is not true: *The notion that he was at the scene of the crime is pure fiction.* **4.** An explanation or belief that is not true: *Your explanation for why this keeps happening is a fiction.* [From Middle English *ficcioun,* from Latin *fictiō,* from *fictus,* past participle of *fingere,* to form.] **—fic′tion·al** *adj.*

fic·tion·al·ize (fĭk′shə-nə-līz′) *tr.v.* **fic·tion·al·ized, fic·tion·al·iz·ing, fic·tion·al·iz·es** To treat as fiction or make into fiction: *A writer may fictionalize real-life stories.*

fic·ti·tious (fĭk-tĭsh′əs) *adj.* **1.** Made up, especially in order to mislead: *The criminal used a fictitious name.* **2.** Relating to the characters, settings, or plots created for a work of fiction: *The novel takes place in a fictitious country.* **—fic·ti′tious·ly** *adv.* **—fic·ti′tious·ness** *n.*

fid·dle (fĭd′l) *n.* A violin, especially one used to play folk or country music. ❖ *v.* **fid·dled, fid·dling, fid·dles** *—intr.* **1.** To play the fiddle: *We sang while they fiddled.* **2.** To touch or handle something in a nervous way: *She fiddled with her bracelet while she waited.* **3.** To tinker with something in an attempt to fix or adjust it: *Don't fiddle with the television!* *—tr.* To play (a tune) on a fiddle: *The musicians fiddled a reel.* ◆ **fiddle around** To act foolishly, playfully, or without purpose: *Stop fiddling around and do your homework.* **fiddle away** To waste or squander: *We fiddled away the last week of summer vacation.* **—fid′dler** *n.*

fid·dler crab (fĭd′lər) *n.* Any of various burrowing crabs of warm coastal areas, the male of which has one front claw much larger than the other.

fid·dle·sticks (fĭd′l-stĭks′) *interj.* An expression used to show mild annoyance or impatience.

fi·del·i·ty (fĭ-dĕl′ĭ-tē *or* fī-dĕl′ĭ-tē) *n., pl.* **fi·del·i·ties 1.** Faithfulness to obligations, duties, or observances: *the soldier's fidelity to duty.* **2.** Exact correspondence with the facts; accuracy: *the fidelity of the witness's account of the accident.* **3.** The degree to which an electronic system, such as a tape recorder or compact disc player, reproduces sound without distortion. [From Middle English *fidelite,* from Latin *fidēlitās,* from *fidēlis,* faithful, from *fidēs,* faith.]

fidg·et (fĭj′ĭt) *intr.v.* **fidg·et·ed, fidg·et·ing, fidg·ets** To behave or move nervously or restlessly: *The children fidgeted in their seats.* **—fidg′et·y** *adj.*

fidg·ets (fĭj′ĭts) *pl.n.* Nervousness or restlessness: *had a case of the fidgets while waiting to speak before the class.*

fie (fī) *interj.* An expression used to show distaste or shock.

fief (fēf) *n.* **1.** In feudal times, an estate of land granted by a lord to a vassal. **2.** A group or part of an organization over which one has influence or control. [From Old French *feu, fief,* of Germanic origin.]

fief·dom (fēf′dəm) *n.* A fief.

field (fēld) *n.* **1.** A broad, level, open expanse of land. **2.** An area of land that is cultivated or used for grazing: *cotton fields; cows in the field.* **3.** A portion of land or a geologic formation containing a natural resource: *oil fields; a gold field.* **4.** A wide unbroken expanse, as of ice. **5.** A battleground. **6.** A background area, as on a flag or painting: *white stars on a field of blue.* **7a.** The area in which a game in a team sport such as soccer or football takes place. **b.** The area inside or near to a running track, where events such as the long jump and shotput are held. **8.** All the contestants or participants in an event: *a large field of horses in the Kentucky Derby; the field of candidates running for office.* **9.** An area of human activity, interest, or knowledge: *the field of American history.* **10.** An area or setting of practical work or observation outside an office, school, factory, or laboratory: *experiments done in the field.* **11.** A region of space throughout which a physical force operates: *An electric field surrounds a charged body. The moon is within Earth's gravitational field.* **12.** The area in which an image is visible to the eye or an optical instrument: *the field of a microscope; the field of vision.* **13.** An element in a computer database record in which one item of information is stored: *typed "January 12" in the birthdate field.* ❖ *adj.* **1.** Growing, living, or cultivated in fields or open land: *field poppies.* **2.** Made, used, or done in the field: *field operations.* ❖ *v.* **field·ed, field·ing, fields** *—tr.* **1.** In sports, especially baseball, to stop or catch (a ball): *fielded several fly balls.* **2.** In sports, to place in the field to play: *field a team.* **3.** To respond to: *fielded questions from the reporters.* *—intr.* To play as a fielder: *The team fielded well.* [From Old English *feld.*]

field day *n.* **1.** A day set aside for sports or athletic competition. **2.** A time of great activity, pleasure, or opportunity: *The children had a field day in the toy store.*

field·er (fēl′dər) *n.* In baseball, a player stationed in the field who attempts to put out the team at bat.

field·er's choice (fēl′dərz) *n.* In baseball, a play made on a ground ball in which the fielder chooses to put out an advancing base runner while the batter reaches first base safely.

field event *n.* A throwing or jumping event of a track-and-field meet.

field glasses *pl.n.* Portable binoculars used especially outdoors for viewing distant objects.

field goal *n.* **1.** In football, a score worth three points made on an ordinary down by place-kicking the ball over the crossbar and between the goalposts. **2.** In basketball, a basket made in regulation play, normally worth two points, but worth three points if attempted from beyond a specified distance.

field hockey *n.* A game played on a field in which two teams of players using curved sticks try to drive a ball into each other's goal.

field house *n.* A building at an athletic field having storage and training facilities and locker rooms.

field magnet *n.* A magnet used to produce a magnetic field for the operation of an electrical device such as a motor or generator.

field marshal *n.* An officer in some European armies,

fez

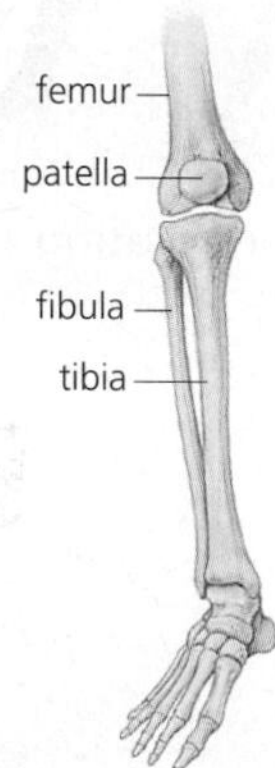

fibula

field hockey

figurehead

figure skating
Maylin Hausch and Daniel Wende of Germany

ă	pat	ôr	core
ā	pay	oi	boy
âr	care	ou	out
ä	father	o͝o	took
ĕ	pet	o͝or	lure
ē	be	o͞o	boot
ĭ	pit	ŭ	cut
ī	bite	ûr	urge
îr	pier	th	thin
ŏ	pot	*th*	this
ō	toe	zh	vision
ô	paw	ə	about

usually ranking just below the commander in chief.

field test *n.* A test of a new product under actual operating conditions.

field-test (fēld′tĕst′) *tr.v.* **field-test·ed, field-test·ing, field-tests** To test (a technique or product) under conditions of actual operation or use: *field-test a new kind of lawnmower.*

field trip *n.* A group excursion for the purpose of first-hand observation, as to a museum, the woods, or a historic place.

fiend (fēnd) *n.* **1.** An evil spirit; a demon. **2.** An evil or wicked person. **3.** *Informal* A person absorbed in or obsessed with a certain thing: *a baseball fiend; a fresh-air fiend.* [From Old English *fēond.*]

fiend·ish (fēn′dĭsh) *adj.* **1.** Relating to or suggestive of a fiend; evil, wicked, or cruel: *a fiendish weapon; a fiendish tyrant.* **2.** Extremely bad, disagreeable, or difficult: *a fiendish problem.* **—fiend′ish·ly** *adv.* **—fiend′ish·ness** *n.*

fierce (fîrs) *adj.* **fierc·er, fierc·est 1.** Having a violent and aggressive nature; ferocious: *a fierce beast.* **2.** Extremely severe or violent; terrible: *a fierce storm.* **3.** Extremely intense or ardent: *fierce loyalty.* [From Middle English *fers,* from Latin *ferus.*] **—fierce′ly** *adv.* **—fierce′ness** *n.*

fier·y (fīr′ē *or* fī′ə-rē) *adj.* **fier·i·er, fier·i·est 1.** Consisting of or containing fire: *the fiery crater of the volcano.* **2.** Having the color of fire: *a fiery sunset.* **3.** Very hot: *the fiery pavements of the city in summer.* **4.** Burning or glowing: *fiery coals.* **5.** Easily excited or provoked; tempestuous: *a fiery temper.* **6.** Charged with emotion; high-spirited: *The candidate delivered a fiery speech.* **—fier′i·ly** *adv.* **—fier′i·ness** *n.*

fi·es·ta (fē-ĕs′tə) *n.* **1.** A festival or religious holiday, especially a saint's day celebrated in Spanish-speaking countries. **2.** A celebration or party. [From Spanish, from Latin *fēstus,* festive.]

FIFA *abbr.* An abbreviation of Fédération Internationale de Football Association (International Federation of Association Football).

fife (fīf) *n.* A small high-pitched musical instrument similar to a flute, often used with drums to accompany military music. [Probably from German *Pfeife,* from Latin *pīpāre,* to chirp.]

fif·teen (fĭf-tēn′) *n.* **1.** The number, written 15, that is equal to 14 + 1. **2.** The 15th in a set or sequence.

fif·teenth (fĭf-tēnth′) *n.* **1.** The ordinal number matching the number 15 in a series. **2.** One of 15 equal parts.

fifth (fĭfth) *n.* **1.** The ordinal number matching the number five in a series. **2.** One of five equal parts. **3.** One fifth of a gallon or four fifths of a quart of liquor. **4a.** The interval covering five tones in a musical scale, as C, D, E, F, and G. **b.** The fifth tone of a musical scale; the dominant. **5.** The transmission gear used to produce speeds next higher than those of fourth in a motor vehicle. **6. Fifth** The Fifth Amendment: *The defendant pled the Fifth.* **—fifth** *adv. & adj.*

Fifth Amendment *n.* An amendment to the Constitution of the United States, ratified in 1791, that deals with the rights of accused criminals by providing for due process of law, forbidding double jeopardy, and stating that no person may be forced to testify as a witness against himself or herself. It also prohibits the government from confiscating private property for public use without fairly compensating the property owner.

fifth column *n.* A secret organization working within a country to further the political and military aims of that country's enemies.

fif·ti·eth (fĭf′tē-ĭth) *n.* **1.** The ordinal number matching the number 50 in a series. **2.** One of 50 equal parts.

fif·ty (fĭf′tē) *n.* **1.** The number, written 50, that is equal to 5 × 10. **2.** A fifty-dollar bill. [From Old English *fīftig.*]

fif·ty-fif·ty (fĭf′tē-fĭf′tē) *adj.* **1.** Divided or shared in two equal portions: *The partners agreed on a fifty-fifty split of the money.* **2.** Being equally likely or unlikely: *I had a fifty-fifty chance of winning the coin toss.* **—fif′ty-fif′ty** *adv.*

fig (fĭg) *n.* **1.** A sweet pear-shaped fruit of any of various trees or shrubs that grow in warm regions. Figs have many seeds and may be eaten fresh or dried. **2.** A tree or shrub that bears such fruit. **3.** A very small or trivial amount: *not worth a fig.* [From Middle English *fige,* from Latin *ficus.*]

fig. *abbr.* An abbreviation of figure.

fight (fīt) *v.* **fought** (fôt), **fight·ing, fights** *—intr.* **1.** To attempt to harm or gain power over an adversary by blows or with weapons: *fought bravely against the invaders.* **2.** To participate in boxing or wrestling: *They fought for the gold medal.* **3.** To engage in a quarrel; argue: *The neighbors fought for years over the boundary.* **4.** To strive vigorously and resolutely: *fought for their rights in court.* See Synonyms at **oppose.** *—tr.* **1.** To contend with physically or in battle: *The Union troops fought the Confederates at Gettysburg.* **2.** To carry on or engage in (a battle). **3.** To box or wrestle against in a ring: *fight a contender in the Olympics.* **4a.** To contend with or struggle against: *fight illiteracy; fight rising floodwaters.* **b.** To try to extinguish (an uncontrolled fire). **5.** To make (one's way) by struggle or striving: *We fought our way through the dense undergrowth.* ❖ *n.* **1a.** A physical conflict between two or more individuals. **b.** A quarrel or conflict: *a fight over who would empty the trash.* **2.** A battle waged between opposing forces. **3.** A boxing or wrestling match. **4.** A struggle to achieve a goal: *the fight for freedom.* **5.** The power or will to battle or struggle: *Is there any fight left in him?* ◆ **fight fire with fire** To combat one evil or one set of negative circumstances by reacting in kind. **fight off** To defend against or drive back (a hostile force, for example): *A fever is one way in which the body fights off germs.* [From Old English *feohtan.*]

fight·er (fī′tər) *n.* **1.** A person who fights, such as a soldier or boxer. **2.** A fast maneuverable airplane that is used in combat. **3.** A person who is unyielding or determined.

fig·ment (fĭg′mənt) *n.* Something invented, made up, or imagined: *a mere figment of the imagination.*

fig·u·ra·tive (fĭg′yər-ə-tĭv) *adj.* **1.** Based on or using figures of speech; metaphorical: *figurative language.* **2.** Containing many figures of speech; ornate. **3.** Represented by a likeness or figure; emblematic: *A light bulb is a figurative representation of an idea.* **—fig′ur·a·tive·ly** *adv.*

fig·ure (fĭg′yər) *n.* **1.** A written or printed symbol, especially a numeral, representing something that is not a letter. **2. figures** Mathematical calculations: *Accountants need to have a good head for figures.* **3.** An amount represented in numbers: *priced at a high figure.* **4.** In geometry, any combination of points, lines, or surfaces: *Circles and triangles are plane figures.* **5.** The shape or form of a human body: *People buy clothes to suit their figures.* **6.** An indistinct object or shape: *I turned and saw a tall figure standing in the doorway.* **7.** A person, especially a well-known one: *The president is an important public figure.* **8.** Impression or appearance made: *cuts an impressive figure in uniform.* **9.** A pictorial or sculptural representation, especially of the human body: *The museum featured many lifelike figures in wax.* **10a.** A diagram: *On that page, the figure shows a bird in flight.* **b.** A design or pattern, as on cloth: *silk with a paisley figure.* **11.** A group of movements in dancing or ice skating: *the lovely figures of the minuet.* **12.** A brief or melodic harmonic unit, often the basis of a larger musical phrase or structure; a motif: *the opening figure of a symphony.* ❖ *v.* **fig·ured, fig·ur·ing, fig·ures** *—tr.* **1.** To calculate with numbers: *She figured the cost of renovating the bathroom.* **2.** *Informal* To conclude, believe, or predict: *I figured that you'd want to go swimming.* —*intr.* **1.** To calculate; compute: *Most store clerks can figure quickly and accurately.* **2.** To be or seem important: *The opening of the store figured in the local news.* **3.** *Informal* To seem reasonable or expected: *It figures that they decided to work as a team because they work well together.* ◆ **figure on** *Informal* To depend on: *You can always figure on some guests to be late.* **figure out** *Informal* To solve, decipher, or discover: *figure out a puzzle.* [From Middle English, from Latin *figūra*.]

fig·ure·head (fĭg′yər-hĕd′) *n.* **1.** A carved figure on the prow of a ship. **2.** A person who is given a position of leadership in name only and who has no actual authority.

figure of speech *n., pl.* **figures of speech** An expression in which words are used in unusual or nonliteral ways to create vivid or dramatic effects. Metaphor, simile, hyperbole, and personification are figures of speech.

figure skating *n.* Ice-skating consisting of sequences of required and optional spins, jumps, and dancelike maneuvers. —**figure skater** *n.*

fig·u·rine (fĭg′yə-rēn′) *n.* A small molded or sculpted figure; a statuette.

Fi·ji (fē′jē) An island country of the southwest Pacific Ocean located southwest of Samoa and made up of about 320 islands. Suva is the capital.

fil·a·ment (fĭl′ə-mənt) *n.* **1.** A fine or slender thread, wire, or fiber. **2.** The slender stalk that bears the anther in the stamen of a flower. **3.** A fine wire that is enclosed in an incandescent light bulb and gives off light when it is heated by the passage of an electric current. [From Late Latin *filāre*, to spin, from Latin *filum*, thread.]

fil·bert (fĭl′bərt) *n.* A hazelnut. [From Middle English, After Saint *Philibert* (died 684), whose feast day in late August coincides with the ripening of the nut.]

filch (fĭlch) *tr.v.* **filched, filch·ing, filch·es** To steal (something, especially something of little value) in a sly manner; pilfer. —**filch′er** *n.*

file[1] (fīl) *n.* **1.** A container, such as a cabinet or folder, for keeping papers in order: *drawings stored in large files.* **2.** A collection of papers or published materials kept or arranged in convenient order. **3.** A collection of related computer data stored as a unit with a single name. **4.** A row or single line of people or things arranged one behind the other: *The ducks waddled across the road in a file.* ❖ *v.* **filed, fil·ing, files** —*tr.* **1.** To put or keep (papers, for example) in useful order for storage or reference. **2.** To submit or send (copy) to a newspaper: *Reporters file stories daily.* **3.** To enter (a legal document) on public official record: *file a claim in court for payment of damages.* —*intr.* **1.** To march or walk in a line: *The nine justices solemnly filed in.* **2.** To submit an application; apply: *Candidates for election must file with the county clerk.* [From Middle English *filen*, to put documents on file, from Old French *filer*, to put documents on a thread, from Latin *filum*, thread.] —**fil′er** *n.* —SEE NOTE.

file[2] (fīl) *n.* Any of several steel tools having a series of sharp ridges, used in smoothing, shaping, or grinding down. ❖ *tr.v.* **filed, fil·ing, files** To smooth, reduce, or remove with or as if with a file: *filed the edge of the blade so it cut better.* [From Old English *fīl.*] —SEE NOTE AT **file[1]**.

file·name (fīl′nām′) *n.* The name of a computer file, often containing an extension that shows what kind of file it is.

file server *n.* A computer connected to a network on which users of the networks can store files.

fi·let[1] (fĭ-lā′ *or* fĭl′ā′) *n.* A net or lace with a simple pattern of squares. [From Old French, diminutive of *fil*, thread, from Latin *filum*.]

fi·let[2] (fĭ-lā′ *or* fĭl′ā′) also **fil·let** (fĭl′ĭt) *n.* A boneless piece of meat or fish, especially the beef tenderloin. ❖ *v.* **fi·let·ed, fi·let·ing, fi·lets** also **fil·let·ed, fil·let·ing, fil·lets** To slice, bone, or make into filets: *I watched the fisherman filet a trout.*

fi·let mi·gnon (fĭ-lā′ mēn-yôN′) *n., pl.* **fi·lets mi·gnons** (fĭ-lā′ mēn-yôN′) A round, very choice cut of beef from the loin.

fil·i·al (fĭl′ē-əl *or* fē′lē-əl) *adj.* Relating to or befitting a son or daughter: *filial duty; filial love.* —**fil′i·al·ly** *adv.*

fil·i·bus·ter (fĭl′ə-bŭs′tər) *n.* **1.** The delaying or obstructing of action in a legislature, especially by making long speeches. **2.** An instance of this. ❖ *v.* **fil·i·bus·tered, fil·i·bus·ter·ing, fil·i·bus·ters** —*intr.* To delay or obstruct the passage of a legislative bill by filibuster. —*tr.* To use a filibuster against (a legislative bill, for example). —**fil′i·bus′ter·er** *n.*

fil·i·gree (fĭl′ĭ-grē′) *n.* **1.** Delicate and intricate ornamental work of twisted gold or silver wire. **2.** A lacy delicate design or pattern. ❖ *tr.v.* **fil·i·greed, fil·i·gree·ing, fil·i·grees** To decorate with or as if with filigree: *Frost filigreed the windowpanes.* [From Italian *filigrana* : Latin *filum*, thread + Latin *grānum*, grain.]

fil·ing (fī′lĭng) *n.* A particle or shaving removed by a file: *metal filings.*

Fil·i·pi·na (fĭl′ə-pē′nə) *n.* A Filipino woman or girl.

Fil·i·pi·no (fĭl′ə-pē′nō) *adj.* Relating to the Philippines or its peoples, languages, or cultures. ❖ *n., pl.* **Fil·i·pi·nos 1.** A native or inhabitant of the Philippines. **2.** The official language of the Philippines, based mostly on Tagalog.

fill (fĭl) *v.* **filled, fill·ing, fills** —*tr.* **1a.** To put as much into (a container, for example) as can be held: *fill a glass with milk.* **b.** To supply or provide to the fullest extent: *filled the mall with new stores.* **2a.** To stop or plug up (an opening, for example): *fill a hole in the road.* **b.** To repair a cavity in (a tooth). **3.** To satisfy or meet; fulfill: *fill the requirements for a job.* **4.** To supply as required: *fill a prescription; fill an order for 20 books.* **5.** To place a person in: *We filled the job with an experienced worker.* **6.** To take up the whole of; occupy: *Music filled the room. A dense fog filled the valley.* **7.** To engage or occupy completely: *Memories of the summer filled my mind.* —*intr.* To become full: *The boat quickly filled with water.* ❖ *n.* **1.** An amount that is needed to make full, complete, or satisfied: *We ate our fill of the blueberries.* **2.** Earth, gravel, or other material used to build up or fill in land. ◆ **fill in 1.** To provide with information that is essential or newly acquired: *We filled in the police chief on the details of the theft.* **2.** To act as a substitute; stand in: *an understudy who filled in at the last minute.* **fill out 1.** To complete (a form, for example) by providing required information: *Did you fill out the job application?* **2.** To become or make more fleshy: *The pup filled out to become a full-grown dog.* **fill (someone's) shoes** To take someone's position or duties: *It will be hard to fill the manager's shoes.* [From Old English *fyllan*.]

fill·er (fĭl′ər) *n.* Something added to increase weight or size or to fill space: *The radio program ended early, so some patriotic music was played as filler.*

fil·let (fĭl′ĭt) *n.* **1.** A narrow band or ribbon, often worn as a headband. **2.** Variant of **filet[2]**. ❖ *tr.v.* Variant of **filet[2]**. [From Middle English *filet*, from Old French, diminutive of *fil*, thread, from Latin *filum*.]

fill-in (fĭl′ĭn′) *n.* *Informal* A person or thing that serves as a substitute: *The understudy was a fill-in for the star.*

fill·ing (fĭl′ĭng) *n.* **1.** Something used to fill a space, cavity, or container: *a gold filling in a tooth.* **2.** An edible mixture used to fill pastries, sandwiches, or cakes: *a pie with a rhubarb filling.*

WORD HISTORY

file The **file** in which we keep things in alphabetical order comes from the Old French word *fil*, "a thread," and refers to the traditional system of running a string or thread through a pile of papers to keep them in order. The **file** we use to roughen or smooth metal is a different word; it comes from the Old English *fīl*, "a file, a cutting tool."

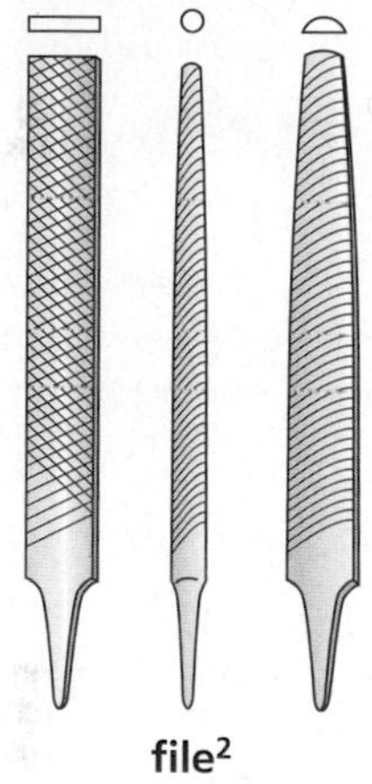

file[2]

filigree
filigree brooch

Millard Fillmore

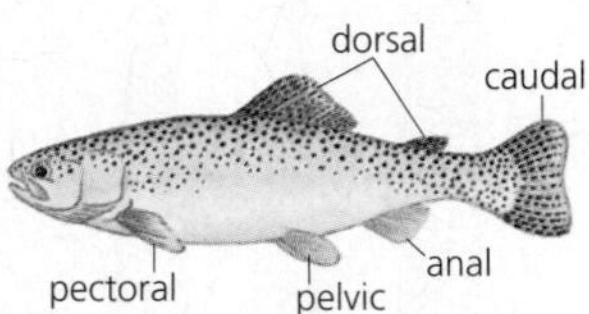

fin
fins on a typical bony fish

fingerboard
of a violin

ă	pat	ôr	core
ā	pay	oi	boy
âr	care	ou	out
ä	father	o͝o	took
ĕ	pet	o͝or	lure
ē	be	o͞o	boot
ĭ	pit	ŭ	cut
ī	bite	ûr	urge
îr	pier	th	thin
ŏ	pot	*th*	this
ō	toe	zh	vision
ô	paw	ə	about

filling station *n.* A gas station.

fil·lip (fĭl′əp) *n.* **1.** Something that mildly excites or leads one to take action. **2.** A snap made by pressing a finger against the thumb and suddenly releasing it.

Fill·more (fĭl′môr′), **Millard** 1800–1874. The 13th president of the United States (1850–1853) who lost his party's support by attempting to enforce the Fugitive Slave Act in the North.

fil·ly (fĭl′ē) *n., pl.* **fil·lies** A young female horse. [From Middle English *filli,* from Old Norse *fylja.*]

film (fĭlm) *n.* **1.** A thin coating, layer, skin, or sheet: *a film of oil over the puddle; a film of dust on a tabletop.* **2.** A thin, flexible, transparent sheet, as of plastic, used in wrapping or packaging. **3.** A thin flexible roll or sheet of material coated with a substance that is sensitive to light, used to make photographs. **4.** A movie, especially one that is recorded on film. ❖ *v.* **filmed, film·ing, films** —*tr.* **1.** To cover with or as if with a film. **2.** To record on film or video using a movie camera: *film a rocket launch; film a scene from a ballet.* —*intr.* **1.** To become coated or obscured with or as if with a film: *My glasses filmed over when I came in from the cold.* **2.** To make or shoot scenes for a movie. [From Old English *filmen,* membrane, skin.]

film·mak·er (fĭlm′mā′kər) *n.* A person who directs or produces movies.

film·strip (fĭlm′strĭp′) *n.* A length of film containing a series of still images prepared for projecting onto a screen or blank wall.

film·y (fĭl′mē) *adj.* **film·i·er, film·i·est 1.** Resembling film in thinness or translucence; gauzy: *filmy curtains.* **2.** Covered with a film: *filmy eyes.* **—film′i·ly** *adv.* **—film′i·ness** *n.*

fil·ter (fĭl′tər) *n.* **1.** A device that strains solid particles from a liquid or gas passing through it. **2.** Paper, sand, screening, charcoal, felt, or other porous material used in such a device. **3.** A device that allows certain frequencies of waves to pass and blocks the passage of others. For example, filters on photographic lenses allow only certain colors of light to enter the camera. **4.** A computer program that blocks access to certain kinds of information: *The filter blocks access to websites that use obscenities.* ❖ *v.* **fil·tered, fil·ter·ing, fil·ters** —*tr.* **1.** To pass (a liquid or gas) through a filter: *filter water for drinking.* **2.** To remove by passing through a filter: *The screen filters leaves from the water.* **3.** To use a data filter to block access to: *a program that filters spam.* —*intr.* **1.** To flow through or as if through a filter: *Light filtered through the blinds.* **2.** To come or go gradually and in small groups: *The audience filtered out after the movie. The students filtered in to the gymnasium.* [From Middle English *filtre,* from Medieval Latin *filtrum,* of Germanic origin.]

❑ *These sound alike:* **filter, philter** (love potion).

filth (fĭlth) *n.* **1.** Foul or dirty matter or refuse. **2.** Something, such as language, considered obscene or immoral.

filth·y (fĭl′thē) *adj.* **filth·i·er, filth·i·est 1.** Covered or smeared with filth; disgustingly dirty: *filthy streets strewn with litter.* See Synonyms at **dirty. 2.** Obscene or offensive: *filthy language.* **—filth′i·ly** *adv.* **—filth′i·ness** *n.*

fil·trate (fĭl′trāt′) *tr. & intr.v.* **fil·trat·ed, fil·trat·ing, fil·trates** To put or go through a filter. ❖ *n.* A liquid or another material that has passed through a filter.

fil·tra·tion (fĭl-trā′shən) *n.* The act or process of filtering.

fin (fĭn) *n.* **1.** One of the movable parts that extends from the body of a fish or other aquatic animal and is used for propelling, steering, and balancing the body in water. **2.** Something shaped or used like a fin, as the tail of an aircraft that keeps it stable in flight. **3.** A rubber or plastic covering for the foot having a flat flexible extension, used in swimming and certain other water sports. [From Old English *finn.*]

fi·na·gle (fə-nā′gəl) *v.* **fi·na·gled, fi·na·gling, fi·na·gles** *Informal* —*tr.* **1.** To get or achieve by indirect, usually deceitful methods: *finagle free tickets to the museum.* **2.** To cheat or swindle: *The dishonest stockbrokers finagled their clients out of millions.* —*intr.* To use crafty or deceitful methods. **—fi·na′gler** *n.*

fi·nal (fī′nəl) *adj.* **1.** Forming or occurring at the end; last: *final preparations before leaving on a trip; the exciting final moments of a game.* **2.** Not to be reconsidered or changed; conclusive: *The judge's decision is final.* ❖ *n.* **1.** The last or one of the last in a series of contests: *the finals of a spelling bee.* **2.** The last examination of an academic course: *Our final covered a whole year's work.* [From Middle English, from Latin *fīnālis,* from *fīnis,* end.]

fi·nal·e (fə-năl′ē *or* fə-nä′lē) *n.* The concluding part, especially of a musical composition.

fi·nal·ist (fī′nə-lĭst) *n.* A contestant in the final session of a competition.

fi·nal·i·ty (fī-năl′ĭ-tē *or* fə-năl′ĭ-tē) *n., pl.* **fi·nal·i·ties** The fact or condition of being final: *a decision given with finality; the finality of leaving.*

fi·nal·ize (fī′nə-līz′) *tr.v.* **fi·nal·ized, fi·nal·iz·ing, fi·nal·iz·es** To put into final form; complete or conclude: *finalize travel plans; finalize an agreement.* **—fi′nal·i·za′tion** (fī′-nə-lĭ-zā′shən) *n.* **—fi′nal·iz′er** *n.*

fi·nal·ly (fī′nə-lē) *adv.* **1.** At last; at the end: *After much delay, the taxi finally arrived.* **2.** Decisively; with finality: *That problem has been disposed of finally.*

fi·nance (fə-năns′ *or* fī′năns′) *n.* **1.** The management of money, banking, investments, and credit: *A banker is a specialist in matters of finance.* **2. finances** Monetary resources; funds: *My finances were getting low.* ❖ *tr.v.* **fi·nanced, fi·nanc·ing, fi·nanc·es** To provide or raise funds or capital for: *We financed our new car with a bank loan.*

finance company *n.* A company that makes loans to clients.

fi·nan·cial (fə-năn′shəl *or* fī-năn′shəl) *adj.* Relating to or involving finance, finances, or financiers: *The treasurer is responsible for the financial affairs of our club.* **—fi·nan′cial·ly** *adv.*

fin·an·cier (fĭn′ən-sîr′ *or* fə-năn′sîr′) *n.* A person who engages in investing or in raising large amounts of money.

finch (fĭnch) *n.* Any of various songbirds having a short thick bill used for cracking seeds.

find (fīnd) *tr.v.* **found** (found), **find·ing, finds 1.** To come upon, often by accident: *I found a quarter on the sidewalk.* **2a.** To come upon or discover by searching or making an effort: *At last I found my glasses. The plumber found the leak in the pipe.* **b.** To discover or ascertain through observation, experience, or study: *Can you find the solution to these problems?* **3.** To perceive to be after observation or experience: *found the book entertaining.* **4.** To recover the use of; regain: *I found my voice and shouted for help.* **5.** To succeed in reaching; arrive at: *The arrow found its mark.* **6.** To obtain or acquire by effort: *find the money to make the trip.* **7.** To decide on and make a declaration about: *The jury found the accused innocent of all charges.* **8.** To furnish; supply: *We can find a bed for you in the house tonight.* **9.** To perceive (oneself) to be in a specific location or condition: *The lost hikers found themselves in difficulty.* ❖ *n.* Something that is found, especially an unexpectedly valuable discovery: *news of oil finds in Alaska.* ◆ **find out 1.** To discover (something), as through examination or inquiry: *I found out when she's arriving.* **2.** To detect the true nature or character of: *The imposter was soon found out.* [From Old English *findan.*]

find·er (fīn′dər) *n.* **1.** A person who finds something. **2.** A device, usually an extra lens or telescope, used to help locate an object or area for a camera or large telescope.

find·ing (fīn′dĭng) *n.* **1.** Something that has been found: *The tomb was a great finding for the archaeologist.* **2.** A conclusion reached after an examination or investigation: *one of the findings in the report about the accident.*

fine[1] (fīn) *adj.* **fin·er, fin·est 1.** Of superior quality, skill, or appearance: *a fine day; a fine performance.* **2.** Very small in size, weight, or thickness: *fine paper.* **3.** Free from impurities: *a fine metal.* **4.** Very sharp; keen: *a fine point on a pencil.* **5.** Very thin; slender: *fine hair.* **6.** Showing delicate and careful artistry: *a fine painting; fine china.* **7.** Consisting of small particles; not coarse: *fine dust; the fine spray of a garden hose.* **8.** Subtle or precise: *the fine differences between a rabbit and a hare.* **9.** Characterized by refinement or elegance: *fine manners.* **10.** Being in a state of good health; quite well; *I'm fine, thank you.* **11.** Satisfactory; acceptable: *It's fine if you want to do it that way instead.* ❖ *adv.* **finer, finest** *Informal* **1.** In small pieces or parts: *Chop the onions fine.* **2.** Very well; splendidly: *The two dogs are getting along fine.* [From Middle English *fin,* from Old French, from Latin *finis,* end.] **—fine′ness** *n.*

fine[2] (fīn) *n.* A sum of money imposed as a penalty for an offense: *a $40 fine for parking too close to an intersection.* ❖ *tr.v.* **fined, fin·ing, fines** To impose a fine on: *fine a borrower who doesn't return library books.* [From Middle English *fin,* from Old French, end of a legal case, settlement, compensation, from Latin *finis,* end.]

fine art *n.* often **fine arts** Any of the art forms, such as painting, sculpture, and music, that are used to create works intended for beauty rather than utility.

fine-drawn (fīn′drôn′) *adj.* **1.** Drawn out to a slender threadlike state: *fine-drawn wire.* **2.** Subtly or precisely fashioned: *a fine-drawn analysis.*

fine-grained (fīn′grānd′) *adj.* **1.** Having a fine, smooth, even grain: *a bookshelf made from fine-grained wood.* **2.** Slightly or subtly different: *a fine-grained distinction.*

fine·ly (fīn′lē) *adv.* **1.** In a fine manner; splendidly: *a finely groomed horse.* **2.** To a small point; discriminatingly. **3.** In small pieces or parts: *finely chopped nuts.*

fine print *n.* The part of a document, especially a contract, containing qualifications or restrictions in small type or obscure language.

fin·er·y (fī′nə-rē) *n., pl.* **fin·er·ies** Elaborate adornment, especially fine clothing and accessories: *a portrait of the captain in naval finery.*

fi·nesse (fə-nĕs′) *n.* **1.** Refinement and delicacy of performance, execution, or artisanship: *the finesse of an experienced glassblower.* **2.** Subtle handling of a situation; tact and skill: *the lawyer's finesse in forging an agreement between the partners.* ❖ *tr.v.* **fi·nessed, fi·ness·ing, fi·ness·es** To accomplish or handle with finesse. [From French, from *fin,* fine.]

fin·ger (fĭng′gər) *n.* **1.** One of the five parts that extend outward from the palm of the hand, especially one other than the thumb. **2.** The part of a glove that covers a finger. **3.** Something, such as an oblong peninsula, that resembles a finger: *a finger of land extending into the ocean.* **4.** The length or width of a finger: *Add about two fingers of juice.* ❖ *tr.v.* **fin·gered, fin·ger·ing, fin·gers 1.** To handle or feel with the fingers; touch: *stooped to finger the dry soil.* **2.** To play (a musical instrument) by using the fingers in a particular way. **3.** *Informal* To inform on; point out as responsible: *finger a thief for the police.* ◆ **have (one's) fingers crossed** or **keep (one's) fingers crossed** To hope for a successful or advantageous outcome: *I'm keeping my fingers crossed until our team has won the game.* **put (one's) finger on** To remember; recall: *I couldn't put my finger on his name.* [From Old English.]

fin·ger·board (fĭng′gər-bôrd′) *n.* A strip of wood on the neck of a stringed instrument against which the strings are pressed in playing.

finger hole *n.* **1.** Any of the holes on a wind instrument that cause a change in pitch when covered by a finger. **2.** A hole or opening for a finger, as on a bowling ball.

fin·ger·ing (fĭng′gər-ĭng) *n.* **1.** The technique used in playing a musical instrument with the fingers: *The fingering for the flute is different from that for the clarinet.* **2.** The symbols on a musical score that show which fingers are to be used in playing.

fin·ger·nail (fĭng′gər-nāl′) *n.* The thin layer of horny transparent material that covers the back of the tip of each finger.

finger painting *n.* **1.** The technique of painting by applying color to paper with the fingers. **2.** A painting made with this technique.

fin·ger·print (fĭng′gər-prĭnt′) *n.* **1.** A mark left on a surface by a person's fingertip: *Why are there dirty fingerprints all over this towel?* **2.** An image of the ridges on a person's fingertip made by putting ink on the fingertip and pressing it against a surface or by using a digital scanning device: *The police obtained the suspect's fingerprints.* ❖ *tr.v.* **fin·ger·print·ed, fin·ger·print·ing, fin·ger·prints** To take the fingerprints of (a person).

fin·ger·tip (fĭng′gər-tĭp′) *n.* The extreme tip or end of a finger. ◆ **at (one's) fingertips** Ready or instantly available: *The Internet puts a vast amount of information at your fingertips.*

fin·ick·y (fĭn′ĭ-kē) *adj.* Very fussy; fastidious: *finicky about certain food.*

fin·is (fĭn′ĭs *or* fē-nē′) *n.* The end; the conclusion.

fin·ish (fĭn′ĭsh) *v.* **fin·ished, fin·ish·ing, fin·ish·es** *—tr.* **1a.** To stop (doing an activity or task) after reaching the point at which there is nothing left to do: *Once we finish raking the leaves, we can play soccer.* **b.** To bring to a desired or required state: *correct the spelling to finish a book report.* See Synonyms at **complete. 2.** To arrive at or attain the end of: *finish a race.* **3.** To consume all of; use up: *finish a bottle of ketchup.* **4.** To give (a surface) a desired texture: *finish a floor with clear varnish.* *—intr.* **1.** To come to an end; stop: *Call me when the washing machine finishes.* **2.** To reach the end of a task, course, or relationship: *The runner finished well ahead of the pack.* ❖ *n.* **1.** The conclusion of something; the end: *The finish of the play was exciting.* **2a.** The surface or texture produced by preparing or coating something: *a shiny finish to the waxed floor.* **b.** The material used in surfacing or finishing something: *Paint is a good finish for wood.* **3.** Completeness, refinement, or smoothness of execution; polish: *The musicians lacked finish.* [From Middle English *finishen,* from Latin *finīre,* from *finis,* end.] **—fin′ish·er** *n.*

fin·ished (fĭn′ĭsht) *adj.* **1.** Brought to a state of completion: *a finished painting.* **2.** In a state of having completed something: *I'm finished with my homework.* **3.** Highly skilled or accomplished: *a finished actor.* **4.** Having no more use, value, or potential; washed-up: *Because of her injury, she is finished as a figure skater.*

fi·nite (fī′nīt′) *adj.* **1.** Having bounds; limited: *a finite list of choices.* **2a.** That can be reached by counting: *The number of whole numbers between 1 and 100 is finite.* **b.** Neither infinite nor infinitesimal: *a finite sum; a finite line segment.* **3.** Relating to any of the forms of a verb that distinguish categories such as person, number, and tense, as the verb *sees* in *She sees the sign.* [From Middle English *finit,* from Latin *fīnītus,* past participle of *finīre,* to limit, from *finis,* end.] **—fi′nite·ly** *adv.*

Fin·land (fĭn′lənd) A country of northern Europe east of Sweden on the **Gulf of Finland,** an arm of the Baltic Sea. Helsinki is the capital.

Finn (fĭn) *n.* A native or inhabitant of Finland.

fin·nan had·die (fĭn′ən hăd′ē) *n.* Smoked haddock.

finned (fĭnd) *adj.* Having a fin or fins: *a finned whale.*

Finn·ish (fĭn′ĭsh) *adj.* Relating to Finland or its people,

WRITERS CHOOSE THEIR WORDS

Angora's cat, Rouge, has a **finicky** system: she is constantly coughing up something or sniffling from allergies, and only bottled water touches that **finicky** tongue.

—Deborah Gregory
Catwalk

fir
balsam fir

fire escape

language, or culture. ❖ *n.* The language of the Finns.

fiord (fyôrd) *n.* Variant of **fjord.**

fir (fûr) *n.* **1.** Any of various evergreen trees having flat needles and bearing cones. **2.** The wood of such a tree. [From Middle English *firre,* probably of Scandinavian origin.]
❑ *These sound alike:* **fir, fur** (pelt).

fire (fīr) *n.* **1.** The flame, light, and heat given off when something is burning: *The fire was bright enough to read by.* **2.** Something that is burning, especially a pile of burning fuel, such as wood: *We started a fire in the fireplace.* **3.** Burning intensity of feeling; ardor: *The veterans played with the fire of rookies.* **4.** The discharge of firearms: *heard the fire of cannon.* ❖ *v.* **fired, fir·ing, fires** —*tr.* **1.** To cause to burn; ignite: *A match fired this pile of leaves.* **2.** To maintain or fuel a fire in: *fire a furnace with oil.* **3.** To bake in a kiln: *fire clay pots to harden them.* **4a.** To arouse or excite (an emotion, for example): *The book fired my interest in science.* **b.** To make (someone) enthusiastic or excited: *The players were all fired up before the big game.* **5.** To discharge (a firearm) or launch (a missile): *fire a cannon; fire a rocket.* **6.** *Informal* To hurl with force and speed: *fire a fast ball across the plate.* **7.** *Informal* To discharge from a job; dismiss: *The company fired several workers today.* —*intr.* **1.** To shoot a weapon: *The soldiers fired into the air as a warning.* **2.** To ignite fuel, as in an engine: *The car motor will not fire properly when it's wet.* ◆ **fire up** To start up (an engine, for example). **on fire 1.** Burning; ablaze. **2.** Filled with enthusiasm or excitement: *The team was on fire after tying the game.* **under fire** Under attack: *The new regulation came under fire.* [From Old English *fȳr.*]

fire alarm *n.* **1.** The signal, especially a loud noise, that warns of fire. **2.** A device, such as a siren, that sets off such a warning.

fire ant *n.* Any of various ants that build large mounds and can inflict a painful burning sting, especially a species that is native to South America and is now present in the southern United States.

fire·arm (fīr′ärm′) *n.* A weapon, especially a pistol or rifle, that uses an explosive charge to propel a projectile.

fire·ball (fīr′bôl′) *n.* **1.** Something that resembles a burning ball, such as a ball of lightning. **2.** The hot, brightly glowing cloud of dust and gases formed by a nuclear explosion. **3.** A very bright meteor.

fire·boat (fīr′bōt′) *n.* A boat equipped to put out fires in harbors and on ships.

fire·brand (fīr′brănd′) *n.* **1.** A person who stirs up trouble or kindles a revolt. **2.** A piece of burning wood.

fire·break (fīr′brāk′) *n.* A strip of land that has been cleared, plowed, or planted with vegetation that is resistant to fire in order to prevent a fire from spreading.

fire·bug (fīr′bŭg′) *n.* *Informal* A person who commits arson; an arsonist.

fire·crack·er (fīr′krăk′ər) *n.* A small explosive charge and a fuse in a heavy paper casing, exploded to make noise, as at celebrations.

fire·damp (fīr′dămp′) *n.* A gas that occurs naturally in coal mines and forms a dangerously explosive mixture with air.

fire drill *n.* An exercise in the use of firefighting equipment or the evacuation of a building in case of a fire.

fire engine *n.* Any of various large motor vehicles that carry firefighters and equipment to a fire.

fire escape *n.* A metal stairway or ladder attached to the outside of a building and used as an emergency exit in case of a fire.

fire extinguisher *n.* A portable container filled with chemicals to spray on a small fire to put it out.

fire·fight (fīr′fīt′) *n.* An exchange of gunfire, as between infantry units.

fire·fight·er also **fire fighter** (fīr′fī′tər) *n.* A member of a fire department who fights fires. —**fire′fight′ing** *n.*

fire·fly (fīr′flī′) *n.* Any of various beetles that fly at night and give off a flashing light from the tip of the abdomen; a lightning bug.

fire·house (fīr′hous′) *n.* A fire station.

fire hydrant *n.* A large upright pipe with a nozzle for drawing water from a water main.

fire·light (fīr′līt′) *n.* The light from a fire, as in a fireplace.

fire·man (fīr′mən) *n.* **1.** A firefighter. **2.** A man who tends fires, as in a steam engine; a stoker. **3.** An enlisted man in the US Navy engaged in the operation of engineering machinery.

Fi·ren·ze (fē-rĕn′dzĕ) See **Florence.**

fire·place (fīr′plās′) *n.* **1.** An open recess in a room for holding a fire at the base of a chimney; a hearth. **2.** A structure, usually of stone or brick, for holding a fire outdoors.

fire·plug (fīr′plŭg′) *n.* A fire hydrant.

fire·pow·er (fīr′pou′ər) *n.* **1.** The capacity, as of a weapon, military unit, or position, for delivering fire. **2.** The ability to deliver fire against an enemy in combat.

fire·proof (fīr′pro͞of′) *adj.* Made of material that is impervious or resistant to fire: *Many fireproof buildings are made of concrete.* ❖ *tr.v.* **fire·proofed, fire·proof·ing, fire·proofs** To make fireproof.

fire·side (fīr′sīd′) *n.* **1.** The area surrounding a fireplace or hearth: *We sat about the fireside and chatted.* **2.** A home.

fire station *n.* A building for firefighters and firefighting equipment.

fire·storm (fīr′stôrm′) *n.* **1.** A fire of great size and intensity that generates and is fed by strong inrushing winds from all sides: *the firestorm that leveled Hiroshima after the atomic blast.* **2.** An intense or violent response.

fire tower *n.* A tower from which a lookout watches for fires, especially forest fires.

fire·trap (fīr′trăp′) *n.* A building that can catch fire easily or is difficult to escape from in the event of fire.

fire truck *n.* A fire engine.

fire·wall (fīr′wôl′) *n.* **1.** A fireproof wall used as a barrier to prevent the spread of fire. **2.** A software program or hardware device that restricts communication between a private network or computer system and outside networks.

fire·wood (fīr′wo͝od′) *n.* Wood used as fuel.

fire·work (fīr′wûrk′) *n.* **1.** An explosive device, often attached to a small rocket, set off to create bright lights and loud noises for amusement. **2. fireworks** A display of such devices.

fir·ing line (fīr′ĭng) *n.* **1.** The line of positions from which gunfire is directed against a target. **2.** The foremost position in a pursuit or activity.

firing pin *n.* The part of the bolt of a firearm that strikes the primer and causes the charge of a projectile to explode.

firm¹ (fûrm) *adj.* **firm·er, firm·est 1.** Resistant to externally applied pressure: *a firm mattress; an athlete's firm muscles.* **2.** Securely fixed in place; not easily moved: *a firm fence post set in concrete.* **3.** Showing or having resolution or determination: *a firm voice; a firm belief.* **4.** Constant; steadfast: *a firm friendship; a firm partnership.* **5.** Not subject to change; fixed and definite: *a firm price on the car.* **6.** Strong and sure: *a firm grip on the handlebars.* ❖ *tr. & intr.v.* **firmed, firm·ing, firms** To make or become firm: *One must firm the dirt around newly potted plants. The gelatin firmed quickly.* ❖ *adv.* **firmer, firmest** Without wavering; resolutely: *stood firm.* [From Middle English *ferm,* from Latin *firmus.*] —**firm′ly** *adv.* —**firm′ness** *n.*

firm² (fûrm) *n.* A business partnership of two or more people. [From Italian *firma,* from *firmare,* to ratify by

ă	pat	ôr	core
ā	pay	oi	boy
âr	care	ou	out
ä	father	o͝o	took
ĕ	pet	o͝or	lure
ē	be	o͞o	boot
ĭ	pit	ŭ	cut
ī	bite	ûr	urge
îr	pier	th	thin
ŏ	pot	*th*	this
ō	toe	zh	vision
ô	paw	ə	about

signature, from Latin *firmāre*, to confirm, from *firmus*, firm.]

fir·ma·ment (fûr′mə-mənt) *n.* The heavens; the sky. [From Middle English, from Latin *firmāmentum*, support, from *firmāre*, to strengthen.]

first (fûrst) *n.* **1.** The ordinal number matching the number one in a series. **2.** A person or thing coming, occurring, or ranking before or above all others. **3.** The beginning; the outset: *At first he was afraid of the water, but now he enjoys swimming.* **4.** The transmission gear used to produce the lowest range of speeds in a motor vehicle. ❖ *adj.* **1.** Corresponding in order to the number one. **2.** Coming before all others in order or location: *January, the first month of the year; the first chapter of the book.* **3.** Ranking above all others, as in importance or quality: *first in her class.* **4.** Being highest in pitch or carrying the principal part: *first soprano; first trumpet.* **5.** Relating to the transmission gear used to produce the lowest range of speeds in a motor vehicle. **6.** Relating to or being a member of the US president's household: *first daughter Sasha Obama.* ❖ *adv.* **1.** Before or above all others: *Who will speak first?* **2.** For the first time: *When did you first meet the new neighbors?* **3.** Rather; preferably: *The musicians said they would quit first and not accept lower pay.* ◆ **first off** From the start; immediately: *First off, let me introduce myself.* [From Old English *fyrst*.]

first aid *n.* Emergency care given to an injured or sick person before professional medical care is available. **—first′-aid′** *adj.*

first base *n.* **1.** In baseball, the base that must be touched first by a batter who has hit a fair ball, located to the right as one looks toward the pitcher from home plate. **2.** The position played by a first baseman. **3.** *Slang* The first step or stage toward completion or success: *The reform bill never got to first base.*

first baseman *n.* The baseball player defending the area near first base.

first·born (fûrst′bôrn′) *adj.* First in order of birth; born first. ❖ *n.* The child in a family who is born first.

first class *n.* **1.** The first, highest, or best group in a system of classification. **2.** The best and most expensive class of accommodations on a train, ship, or airplane. ❖ *adv.* By means of first-class travel accommodations.

first-class (fûrst′klăs′) *adj.* **1.** Relating to the first, highest, or best group in a system of classification: *first-class mail; a first-class hotel.* **2.** Relating to the foremost excellence or highest quality; first-rate: *a first-class poet.*

first-de·gree burn (fûrst′dĭ-grē′) *n.* A mild burn that produces redness of the skin.

first down *n.* In football: **a.** The first in the series of four downs in which an offensive team must advance ten yards to retain possession of the ball. **b.** A gain of ten or more yards entitling the offensive team to a new series of downs.

first·hand (fûrst′hănd′) *adj.* Received from the original source: *firsthand information.* **—first′hand′** *adv.*

first lady *n.* **1.** often **First Lady** The wife or hostess of the chief executive of a country, state, or city. **2.** The foremost woman of a specified group or profession: *the first lady of modern dance.*

first lieutenant *n.* An officer in the US Army, Air Force, or Marine Corps ranking above a second lieutenant and below a captain.

first·ly (fûrst′lē) *adv.* In the first place; to begin with.

First Nation *n.* An organized American Indian group or community in Canada, especially any of the bands officially recognized by the Canadian government.

first person *n.* **1.** A group of words or word forms, such as verbs and pronouns, that designate a speaker or writer referring to himself or herself, either alone or along with other people. *I* and *we* are pronouns in the first person. **2.** The style of writing in which forms in the first person are used: *a novel written in the first person.*

first-rate (fûrst′rāt′) *adj.* Foremost in quality, rank, or importance: *a first-rate hotel; a first-rate mechanic.*

first responder *n.* A police officer, firefighter, or other person trained in emergency medical procedures and prepared to move quickly to an accident or disaster to provide help.

first string *n.* A group of players that play regularly or start games for a sports team. **—first′-string′** *adj.*

First World War *n.* World War I.

firth (fûrth) *n.* A long narrow inlet of the sea. [From Old Norse *fjördhr*.]

fis·cal (fĭs′kəl) *adj.* **1.** Relating to the treasury or finances of a government: *senators debating fiscal policies.* **2.** Relating to finance or finances: *The accountant is our fiscal agent.* **—fis′cal·ly** *adv.*

fiscal year *n.* A twelve-month period for which an organization plans the use of its funds.

fireplace

fish (fĭsh) *n., pl.* **fish** or **fish·es 1.** Any of numerous cold-blooded vertebrate animals that live in water, obtain oxygen through gills, and have fins. Most fish are covered with scales. **2.** The flesh of a fish used as food. ❖ *v.* **fished, fish·ing, fish·es** *—intr.* **1.** To catch or try to catch fish. **2.** To try to find something by using the hands or fingers; grope: *I fished in my pocket for a quarter.* **3.** To try to get someone to say something one wants to hear by being indirect or sly: *He was only fishing for compliments when he mentioned his new skateboard.* *—tr.* **1a.** To catch or try to catch (fish): *to fish salmon.* **b.** To catch or try to catch fish in: *We fished the lake for several hours.* **2.** To remove or pull (something) from water or a container: *fish the keys out of the drawer.* ◆ **like a fish out of water** Completely unfamiliar with one's surroundings or activity: *was like a fish out of water when she tried the new video game for the first time.*

fish and chips *pl.n.* Fried fillets of fish and French fries.

fish·er (fĭsh′ər) *n.* **1.** A person who fishes. **2a.** A North American meat-eating mammal related to the mink and weasel, having thick dark-brown fur. **b.** The fur of this mammal.

❑ *These sound alike:* **fisher, fissure** (crack).

fish·er·man (fĭsh′ər-mən) *n.* A man who fishes as an occupation or for sport.

fish·er·wom·an (fĭsh′ər-wo͝om′ən) *n.* A woman who fishes as an occupation or for sport.

fish·er·y (fĭsh′ə-rē) *n., pl.* **fish·er·ies 1.** The industry or occupation of catching, processing, and selling fish or other aquatic animals. **2.** A place where fish or other aquatic animals are caught: *the cod fisheries of the northwest Atlantic.* **3.** A hatchery for fish.

fish farm *n.* A commercial facility having tanks or ponds where fish are raised for food.

fish hawk *n.* The osprey.

fish·hook (fĭsh′ho͝ok′) *n.* A barbed hook for catching fish.

fish·ing (fĭsh′ĭng) *n.* The act, occupation, or sport of catching fish.

fishing rod *n.* A rod of wood, steel, or fiberglass used with a line for catching fish.

fish·mon·ger (fĭsh′mŏng′gər *or* fĭsh′mŭng′gər) *n.* *Chiefly British* A person who sells fish.

fish·net (fĭsh′nĕt′) *n.* **1.** Netting used to catch fish. **2. fishnets** Stockings made from a mesh fabric resembling such a netting.

fish·pond (fĭsh′pŏnd′) *n.* A pond containing or stocked with fish.

fish stick *n.* An oblong piece of breaded fish fillet.

fish·tail (fĭsh′tāl′) *intr.v.* **fish·tailed, fish·tail·ing, fish·tails** To swerve out of control from side to side. Used of the back end of a vehicle that is moving forward.

fish·wife (fĭsh′wīf′) *n., pl.* **fish·wives** (fĭsh′wīvz′) **1.** A

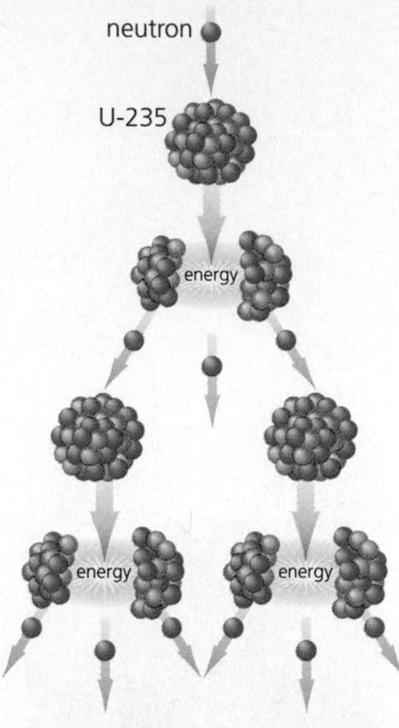

fission
A neutron collides with a uranium-235 atom, splitting it apart and giving off energy and free neutrons. These collide with other uranium-235 atoms, starting a chain reaction.

ă	pat	ôr	core
ā	pay	oi	boy
âr	care	ou	out
ä	father	o͝o	took
ĕ	pet	o͝or	lure
ē	be	o͞o	boot
ĭ	pit	ŭ	cut
ī	bite	ûr	urge
îr	pier	th	thin
ŏ	pot	*th*	this
ō	toe	zh	vision
ô	paw	ə	about

woman who sells fish. **2.** A woman regarded as coarse or abusive.

fish·y (fĭsh′ē) *adj.* **fish·i·er, fish·i·est 1.** Tasting, resembling, or smelling of fish. **2.** Cold or expressionless: *a fishy stare.* **3.** *Informal* Inspiring doubt or suspicion: *something fishy about that excuse.* **—fish′i·ness** *n.*

fis·sion (fĭsh′ən) *n.* **1.** The act or process of splitting into parts. **2.** The splitting of the nucleus of an atom into two or more nuclei either spontaneously or because the nucleus has collided with a free-moving neutron. The splitting of a nucleus releases one or more neutrons and energy in the form of radiation. **3.** A reproductive process in which a single cell splits to form two independent cells that later grow to full size. [From Latin *fissiō*, a cleaving, from *fissus*, past participle of *findere*, to split.]

fis·sion·a·ble (fĭsh′ə-nə-bəl) *adj.* Capable of undergoing fission: *Uranium and plutonium are fissionable elements.*

fis·sure (fĭsh′ər) *n.* **1.** A long narrow crack or opening, as in the face of a rock. **2.** A groove or furrow that divides an organ, such as the brain, into lobes or parts. [From Middle English, from Latin *fissūra*, from *fissus*, past participle of *findere*, to split.]
❑ *These sound alike:* **fissure, fisher** (one that fishes).

fist (fĭst) *n.* The hand closed tightly with the fingers bent against the palm. [From Old English *fȳst*.]

fist·fight (fĭst′fīt′) *n.* A fight with the bare fists.

fist·ful (fĭst′fo͝ol′) *n., pl.* **fist·fuls** The amount a fist can hold.

fist·i·cuffs (fĭs′tĭ-kŭfs′) *pl.n.* **1.** A fistfight. **2.** The activity of fighting with the fists.

fis·tu·la (fĭs′chə-lə) *n., pl.* **fis·tu·las** or **fis·tu·lae** (fĭs′chə-lē′) An abnormal passageway that connects a hollow structure of the body to another hollow structure or to the surface, caused by a disease or wound.

fit¹ (fĭt) *v.* **fit·ted** or **fit, fit·ted, fit·ting, fits** *—tr.* **1.** To be the proper size and shape for: *These shoes fit me.* **2.** To cause to be the proper size and shape: *The tailor fitted the new pants perfectly.* **3.** To be appropriate for or suitable to: *listened to music that fit her mood.* **4.** To equip or provide: *She fitted the car with new tires.* **5.** To provide a place or time for: *He fit all of his books in one bag.* *—intr.* **1.** To be the proper size and shape: *If the key fits, open the door.* **2.** To be suited; agree; belong: *Their happy mood fit in with the joyous occasion.* ❖ *adj.* **fit·ter, fit·test 1.** Suited, adapted, or acceptable for a given purpose or circumstance: *Late at night is hardly a fit time for a meeting. The dinner was not fit to eat.* **2.** Appropriate; proper: *Do as you see fit.* **3.** Physically sound; healthy: *Fresh air and exercise help keep people fit.* ❖ *n.* **1.** The state, quality, or way of being fitted: *a perfect fit.* **2.** The way something fits: *The fit of the sweater was too tight.* [From Middle English *fitten*.]

fit² (fĭt) *n.* **1.** A seizure or convulsion, especially one caused by epilepsy. **2.** A sudden appearance of coughing, sneezing, laughing, or a similar physical outburst: *I had a fit of coughing from the smoke.* **3.** A sudden outbreak of emotion or activity: *a fit of jealousy; a fit of organizing.* ◆ **by fits and starts** or **in fits and starts** With irregular intervals of action and inaction; intermittently: *slept in fits and starts.* [From Middle English, hardship, probably from Old English *fitt*, struggle.]

fit·ful (fĭt′fəl) *adj.* Occurring in or marked by intermittent bursts, as of activity; irregular: *fitful coughing; fitful sleep.* **—fit′ful·ly** *adv.* **—fit′ful·ness** *n.*

fit·ness (fĭt′nĭs) *n.* The state or condition of being physically fit, especially as the result of exercise and proper nutrition.

fit·ting (fĭt′ĭng) *adj.* Being in keeping with a situation; appropriate: *a fitting remark.* ❖ *n.* **1.** The act of trying on clothes whose fit is being adjusted. **2.** A small part for a machine or mechanical device: *a box of nuts, washers, and other fittings.*

Fitz·ger·ald (fĭts-jĕr′əld), **Ella** 1917–1996. American jazz singer known for her expressive interpretations of lyrics.

Fitzgerald, F(rancis) Scott (Key) 1896–1940. American writer whose novels include *The Great Gatsby* (1925) and *Tender Is the Night* (1934).

five (fīv) *n.* **1.** The number, written 5, that is equal to 4 + 1. **2.** The fifth in a set or sequence. **3.** A five-dollar bill. [From Old English *fīf*.]

five-and-ten (fīv′ən-tĕn′) *n.* A store selling a wide variety of inexpensive articles.

Five Nations *pl.n.* The Iroquois confederacy as it originally existed, consisting of the Cayuga, Mohawk, Oneida, Onondaga, and Seneca peoples.

fix (fĭks) *tr.v.* **fixed, fix·ing, fix·es 1a.** To correct or set right: *fixed the mistakes in my math homework.* **b.** To restore to proper condition or working order; repair: *fixed a flat tire.* **2.** To make ready; prepare: *We are fixing dinner for ourselves.* **3.** To place securely; make stable or firm: *fix a post in the ground.* **4.** To direct steadily: *We fixed our eyes on the screen.* **5.** To establish definitely; specify: *fix a time for the meeting; fix a price on a house.* **6.** To attribute; assign: *A witness fixed the blame on the careless driver.* **7.** To convert (nitrogen or carbon) into compounds that can be used by an organism: *bacteria that fix atmospheric nitrogen.* **8.** To treat (a photographic image) with a chemical that prevents it from fading or changing color. **9.** *Informal* To take revenge upon (someone); get even with. **10.** *Informal* To influence the outcome of by unlawful means: *fix a horse race.* ❖ *n.* **1.** The act of adjusting, correcting, or repairing: *His fix of the computer problem took an hour.* **2.** The position, as of a ship or aircraft, determined by visual observations or by radio signals: *get a fix on a disabled ship.* **3.** A difficult or embarrassing situation; a predicament: *We lost our oars and were in a fix out in the middle of the lake.* **4.** *Slang* An amount of something that is craved, especially an intravenous injection of a narcotic. ◆ **fix up 1.** To improve the appearance or condition of: *They fixed up the old house with a fresh coat of paint.* **2.** To supply; provide: *We fixed up a bed for our guests.* [From Middle English *fixen*, from Latin *fixus*, past participle of *figere*, to fasten.] **—fix′a·ble** *adj.* **—fix·er** *n.* —SEE NOTE.

fix·a·tion (fĭk-sā′shən) *n.* **1.** The act or process of fixing something chemically: *the fixation of nitrogen by bacteria.* **2.** An obsessive preoccupation or emotional attachment: *The child had a fixation on a particular blanket.*

fix·a·tive (fĭk′sə-tĭv) *n.* A substance used to treat something and make it permanent or resistant to change: *Fixative keeps chalk drawings from smudging.*

fixed (fĭkst) *adj.* **1.** Firmly in position; stationary: *a row of fixed desks.* **2.** Not subject to change or variation; constant: *living on a fixed income.* **3.** Firmly held; steady: *a fixed stare; old and fixed ideas.* **4.** Illegally prearranged as to outcome: *a fixed election.*

fixed star *n.* A star that appears to remain in the same position in relation to other celestial objects, in contrast to the planets and celestial objects whose changes in position are readily observable by telescope or by the unaided eye. All stars except the sun are considered fixed stars.

fix·er-up·per (fĭk′sər-ŭp′ər) *n.* A house or other dwelling that is badly in need of repair, usually for sale at a low price.

fix·ings (fĭk′sĭngz) *pl.n.* *Informal* Side dishes and condiments accompanying the main dish at a meal; trimmings: *a Thanksgiving dinner with all the fixings.*

fix·ture (fĭks′chər) *n.* **1.** Something that is installed in a permanent location: *a plumbing fixture; a lighting fixture.* **2.** A person or thing that stays or seems to stay in one place: *After 30 years of teaching, he seems like a fixture at the middle school.*

fizz (fĭz) *intr.v.* **fizzed, fizz·ing, fizz·es** To make a hissing or bubbling sound: *Baking soda will fizz if you pour water on it.* ❖ *n.* **1.** A hissing or bubbling sound: *the fizz of soda.* **2.** Effervescence. **—fizz′y** *adj.*

fiz·zle (fĭz′əl) *intr.v.* **fiz·zled, fiz·zling, fiz·zles 1.** To make a hissing or sputtering sound: *The hot coals of our campfire fizzled in the rain.* **2.** *Informal* To fail or end weakly, especially after a hopeful beginning. ❖ *n. Informal* A failure; a fiasco.

fjord or **fiord** (fyôrd) *n.* A long narrow inlet from the sea between steep slopes. [From Old Norse *fjördhr.*]

Fl The symbol for the element **flerovium.**

FL *abbr.* An abbreviation of Florida.

fl. *abbr.* An abbreviation of: **1.** fluid. **2.** flourished.

flab (flăb) *n.* Soft fatty body tissue. [Back-formation from *flabby.*]

flab·ber·gast (flăb′ər-găst′) *tr.v.* **flab·ber·gast·ed, flab·ber·gast·ing, flab·ber·gasts** To cause to be overcome with astonishment; astound: *The news flabbergasted us.*

flab·by (flăb′ē) *adj.* **flab·bi·er, flab·bi·est 1.** Soft and hanging loosely in folds: *a flabby belly.* **2.** Fleshy and soft, as though slightly overweight: *flabby around the waist.* **—flab′bi·ness** *n.*

flac·cid (flăs′ĭd *or* flăk′sĭd) *adj.* **1.** Lacking firmness; hanging limply: *flaccid muscles.* **2.** Lacking force or vigor: *a flaccid acting performance.* **—flac·cid′i·ty** *n.* **—flac′cid·ly** *adv.*

flag¹ (flăg) *n.* **1.** A piece of cloth of a particular color or design, used as a symbol for a nation, an emblem for a monarch or organization, or a signal. **2.** A marking device attached to an object to make it more noticeable: *placed a flag on each page that had a revision.* ❖ *tr.v.* **flagged, flag·ging, flags 1.** To signal with or as if with a flag: *flagged a motorist to get help.* **2.** To signal to stop: *flag down a passing car.*

flag² (flăg) *intr.v.* **flagged, flag·ging, flags** To lose vigor or strength; weaken: *Our spirits flagged when we saw how much we had to do.* [Possibly of Scandinavian origin; akin to Old Norse *flögra.*]

Flag Day *n.* June 14, observed in commemoration of the adoption in 1777 of the official US flag.

flag·el·late (flăj′ə-lāt′) *tr.v.* **flag·el·lat·ed, flag·el·lat·ing, flag·el·lates** To whip or flog. ❖ *adj.* (flăj′ə-lĭt *or* flăj′ə-lāt′) **1.** Having a flagellum, as certain one-celled organisms. **2.** Resembling a flagellum. ❖ *n.* (flăj′ə-lĭt *or* flăj′ə-lāt′) A one-celled organism, such as a euglena, having one or more flagella used for moving through the water and for obtaining food. **—flag′el·la′tion** *n.*

fla·gel·lum (flə-jĕl′əm) *n., pl.* **fla·gel·la** (flə-jĕl′ə) A slender part extending from certain cells or single-celled organisms that moves rapidly back and forth to produce movement.

flag·ger (flăg′ər) *n.* A person who holds a sign or a flag to direct traffic, especially around a construction project.

flag·man (flăg′mən) *n.* A man who is employed as a flagger.

flag·on (flăg′ən) *n.* **1.** A large container for liquids, usually of metal or pottery, having a handle, a spout, and often a lid. **2.** The amount of liquid that such a container can hold. [From Middle English, from Late Latin *flascō,* bottle.]

flag·pole (flăg′pōl′) *n.* A pole on which a flag is raised.

fla·grant (flā′grənt) *adj.* Conspicuously offensive; notorious or scandalous: *a flagrant misuse of public funds.* **—fla′grant·ly** *adv.*

flag·ship (flăg′shĭp′) *n.* A ship that carries a fleet or squadron commander and bears the commander's flag.

flag·staff (flăg′stăf′) *n.* A flagpole.

flag·stone (flăg′stōn′) *n.* A flat stone slab used as a paving material.

flail (flāl) *n.* A tool for threshing grain by hand, having a long wooden handle and a shorter and heavier free-swinging stick attached to its end. ❖ *v.* **flailed, flail·ing, flails** *—tr.* **1.** To beat or strike vigorously: *He flailed the horse with the reins.* **2.** To wave or swing vigorously: *I flailed my arms to get their attention.* *—intr.* **1.** To move vigorously or erratically; thrash about: *The swimmer flailed about until the lifeguard arrived.* **2.** To hit about or lash out violently: *a boxer flailing away in the center of the ring.* **3.** To make a vigorous but unproductive effort: *flailed about in search of a better solution.*

flair (flâr) *n.* A natural talent or aptitude; a knack: *a flair for imitating voices.*

❑ *These sound alike:* **flair, flare** (blaze).

flak (flăk) *n.* **1a.** Antiaircraft artillery. **b.** The bursting shells fired from such artillery: *many planes hit by flak.* **2.** *Informal* Criticism; opposition: *Our plan got a lot of flak.* [From German, from *Fl(ieger)a(bwehr)k(anone),* aircraft-defense gun.]

flake (flāk) *n.* **1.** A flat thin piece or layer; a chip: *Large flakes of paint had fallen on the floor.* **2.** A snowflake. **3.** *Slang* A person who is somewhat eccentric. ❖ *intr.v.* **flaked, flak·ing, flakes** To come off in flakes: *The paint is flaking off the fence.*

flak·y (flā′kē) *adj.* **flak·i·er, flak·i·est 1.** Forming or tending to form flakes or thin crisp fragments: *flaky crackers.* **2.** *Slang* Eccentric; odd. **—flak′i·ly** *adv.* **—flak′i·ness** *n.*

flam·boy·ant (flăm-boi′ənt) *adj.* **1.** Exaggerated or showy in style or manner: *the wild gestures of the flamboyant performer.* **2.** Brilliant; vivid: *flamboyant colors.* **—flam·boy′ance, flam·boy′an·cy** *n.* **—flam·boy′ant·ly** *adv.*

flame (flām) *n.* **1.** The hot, glowing mixture of burning gases and tiny particles that arises from combustion. **2.** The condition of active blazing combustion: *burst into flame.* **3.** A burning or intense feeling; a passion: *a flame of enthusiasm.* **4.** *Informal* A sweetheart. ❖ *intr.v.* **flamed, flam·ing, flames 1.** To burn brightly; blaze: *The logs flamed as I fanned them.* **2.** To flush; acquire color: *My cheeks flamed with embarrassment.* ◆ **flame out** To fail: *The business was only open for three months before it flamed out.*

fla·men·co (flə-mĕng′kō) *n., pl.* **fla·men·cos 1.** A dance style of the Romani of Andalusia, characterized by forceful rhythms and the clicking of castanets. **2.** The guitar music for this dance style.

flame·throw·er (flām′thrō′ər) *n.* A weapon that shoots out a steady stream of burning fuel.

flam·ing (flā′mĭng) *adj.* **1.** On fire; blazing: *flaming logs.* **2.** Resembling a flame in brilliance, color, or form: *flaming red and yellow autumn leaves.*

fla·min·go (flə-mĭng′gō) *n., pl.* **fla·min·gos** or **fla·min·goes** Any of several long-legged, long-necked tropical wading birds having reddish or pinkish feathers and a large bill that curves downward. [Probably from Old Provençal *flamenc,* from Latin *flamma,* flame.]

flam·ma·ble (flăm′ə-bəl) *adj.* Easily ignited and capable of burning rapidly: *Kerosene is flammable.*

Flan·ders (flăn′dərz) A historical region of northwest Europe including parts of northern France, western Belgium, and southwest Netherlands along the North Sea.

flange (flănj) *n.* A projecting rim or edge, as on a wheel or a pipe, used to strengthen an object, hold it in place, or attach it to something.

flank (flăngk) *n.* **1a.** The side of the body between the ribs and the hip. **b.** A cut of meat from this part of an animal. **2.** A side part: *The flank of the mountain rose steeply from the valley.* **3.** The right or left side of a military formation or a fort. ❖ *tr.v.* **flanked, flank·ing, flanks 1.** To protect or guard the flank of. **2.** To attack or maneuver around the flank of: *flank an opposing force.* **3.** To occupy a place at the side of: *Two chairs flanked the*

USAGE

fix The phrase *fixing to* is used in the South to mean "on the verge of or in preparation for (doing a given thing)." The phrase can refer only to events that immediately follow the point in time that the speaker is referring to. You cannot say *I'm fixing to go to college in a few years,* but you would say *I'm fixing to leave in a few minutes.*

fjord
Geirangerfjord, Norway

flagstone

flamingo

flask

flatbed

flatboat

ă	pat	ôr	core
ā	pay	oi	boy
âr	care	ou	out
ä	father	o͝o	took
ĕ	pet	o͝or	lure
ē	be	o͞o	boot
ĭ	pit	ŭ	cut
ī	bite	ûr	urge
îr	pier	th	thin
ŏ	pot	*th*	this
ō	toe	zh	vision
ô	paw	ə	about

fireplace. [From Old English *flanc*, from Old French, of Germanic origin.]

flank·er (flăng′kər) *n.* **1.** A person or thing that protects a flank. **2.** In football, a halfback stationed to the side of the linemen, used chiefly as a pass receiver.

flan·nel (flăn′əl) *n.* **1.** A soft woven cloth of wool or a blend of wool and cotton or synthetic material. **2. flannels** Pants and other clothes made out of flannel. **3.** Flannelette.

flan·nel·ette (flăn′ə-lĕt′) *n.* Soft cotton flannel.

flap (flăp) *n.* **1.** A flat piece attached along one side of something: *the flap of an envelope.* **2.** A section of the rear edge of an aircraft wing that moves up and down in order to control the lift and drag. **3.** The sound or action of waving or fluttering: *the flap of a bird's wings.* **4.** *Informal* A state of disturbance or nervous excitement: *We all got into a flap when no one could find the car keys.* ❖ *v.* **flapped, flap·ping, flaps** —*tr.* **1.** To move (the wings or arms) up and down; beat. **2.** To cause to move with a waving or fluttering motion: *A brisk wind flapped the clothes on the line.* —*intr.* **1.** To wave the arms or wings up and down. **2.** To wave about while attached to something stationary; flutter: *A flag flapped softly in the breeze.* [From Middle English *flappe*, slap.]

flap·jack (flăp′jăk′) *n.* A pancake.

flap·per (flăp′ər) *n.* **1.** A broad part that flaps: *the flapper on an exhaust pipe.* **2.** A young woman of the 1920s who rebelled against conventional ideas of ladylike behavior and dress.

flare (flâr) *intr.v.* **flared, flar·ing, flares 1.** To burn with a sudden or unsteady flame: *The candle flared briefly and went out.* **2.** To burst out or erupt: *Tempers flared during the tense meeting.* **3.** To spread outward in shape: *A horn flares at the end.* ❖ *n.* **1.** A brief wavering blaze of light. **2.** A device that produces a bright light for signaling or lighting. **3.** An outbreak, as of emotion or activity: *a flare of anger.* **4.** A shape or form that spreads out: *the flare of a trumpet.* **5.** In football, a quick pass to a running back heading toward the sideline.

❑ *These sound alike:* **flare, flair** (talent).

flare-up (flâr′ŭp′) *n.* **1.** A sudden outbreak of flame or light. **2.** An outburst or eruption: *a flare-up of anger.* **3.** A recurrence of a disease or condition: *a flare-up of acne.*

flash (flăsh) *v.* **flashed, flash·ing, flash·es** —*intr.* **1.** To give off a sudden bright light: *Bursts of fireworks flashed in the sky.* **2.** To be lighted on and off: *A lighthouse flashed in the distance.* **3.** To appear or occur suddenly: *an idea for a story flashed through my mind.* **4.** To move rapidly: *A shooting star flashed across the sky.* —*tr.* **1.** To send forth suddenly or for an instant: *flash a light into a cave.* **2.** To make known or signal by flashing lights: *The yellow light flashed its warning.* **3.** To send (a message) at great speed: *flash a news bulletin to the world capitals.* ❖ *n.* **1.** A short sudden display of light: *a flash of lightning.* **2.** A sudden brief burst: *a flash of insight.* **3.** A split second; an instant: *I ran to the phone in a flash.* **4.** A brief important item of very current news: *The political website published news flashes about the election all day.* ◆ **flash in the pan** A person or thing that promises great success but fails: *Their latest idea was just another flash in the pan.* [From Middle English *flashen*, to splash, of imitative origin.] **—flash′er** *n.*

flash·back (flăsh′băk′) *n.* **1.** The insertion of an earlier event into a story, play, or movie. **2.** A scene or an episode showing an earlier event that is inserted in a story, play, or movie. **3.** A recurring, vivid mental image of a past experience.

flash·bulb (flăsh′bŭlb′) *n.* An electric bulb that produces a flash of light for taking photographs.

flash card *n.* One of a set of cards marked with words, numbers, or other symbols to be learned through drill.

flash drive *n.* A portable, thumb-sized data storage device that can be plugged into a computer component and uses flash memory.

flash flood *n.* A sudden violent flood after a heavy rain.

flash·light (flăsh′līt′) *n.* A portable electric light that is powered by batteries.

flash memory *n.* A type of computer memory that can be erased and rewritten and is smaller and lighter than a hard drive.

flash point *n.* **1.** The lowest temperature at which the vapor of a flammable liquid can be made to catch fire in air. **2.** The point at which something, such as a disagreement or quarrel, becomes an open conflict.

flash·y (flăsh′ē) *adj.* **flash·i·er, flash·i·est 1.** Creating a brief impression of brilliance; eye-catching: *the acrobat's flashy performance.* **2.** Cheap and showy; gaudy: *a flashy tie.* **—flash′i·ly** *adv.* **—flash′i·ness** *n.*

flask (flăsk) *n.* **1.** A small bottle with a flattened shape, made to fit in one's pocket. **2.** A rounded container with a long neck, used in laboratories. [From Middle English, cask, keg, from Late Latin *flascō*, of Germanic origin.]

flat[1] (flăt) *adj.* **flat·ter, flat·test 1.** Having a smooth even surface; level: *flat land.* **2.** Having a broad surface and little thickness or depth: *a flat dish.* **3.** Extending or lying full length; horizontal: *flat on my back in bed.* **4.** Having lost air; deflated: *a flat tire.* **5.** Lacking interest or excitement; dull: *a flat performance.* **6.** Having lost effervescence or sparkle: *flat soda.* **7.** Complete; absolute: *a flat refusal to help.* **8.** Not changing; fixed: *The taxi charges a flat rate.* **9.** Not glossy; dull: *finished with a flat paint.* **10a.** Lower in musical pitch than is correct. **b.** Lower in pitch by a half step than a corresponding natural tone or key: *D flat.* ❖ *adv.* **1.** On or against a flat surface: *press dough flat.* **2.** Exactly: *He ran the race in 50 seconds flat.* **3.** Completely: *I bought a new cell phone, and now I'm flat broke.* **4.** Below the correct pitch: *Don't sing flat.* ❖ *n.* **1.** A flat surface or part: *the flat of my hand.* **2.** often **flats** An area of level low-lying ground: *dig clams in the mud flats.* **3.** A deflated tire: *The car has a flat.* **4.** A shoe with a flat heel. **5.** A shallow box or frame for growing seeds. **6a.** A musical note or tone that is a half step lower than a corresponding natural tone or key. **b.** A sign (♭) used to indicate that a note is to be lowered by a half step. ❖ *tr. & intr.v.* **flat·ted, flat·ting, flats** To sing or play flat. [From Middle English, from Old Norse *flatr*.] **—flat′ly** *adv.* **—flat′ness** *n.*

flat[2] (flăt) *n.* An apartment usually on one floor of a building. [From Old English *flet*, floor, dwelling.]

flat·bed (flăt′bĕd′) *n.* **1.** An open truck bed or trailer with no sides, used to carry large objects. **2.** A railroad flatcar. **3.** A wide, flat surface onto which documents or other materials are placed for printing or scanning.

flat·boat (flăt′bōt′) *n.* A flatbottom barge for transporting freight in shallow rivers or canals.

flat·bot·tom (flăt′bŏt′əm) or **flat·bot·tomed** (flăt′bŏt′əmd) *adj.* Having a flat bottom: *a flatbottom boat.*

flat·bread (flăt′brĕd′) *n.* Any of various breads that are made from usually unleavened dough and are baked in loaves that are flat and often round.

flat·car (flăt′kär′) *n.* A railroad car without sides or a roof, used for carrying bulky freight.

flat·fish (flăt′fĭsh′) *n.* Any of numerous fishes, such as the flounder, halibut, or sole, that have a flattened body and both eyes on one side.

flat-foot·ed (flăt′fo͝ot′ĭd) *adj.* **1.** Having a condition in which the arch of the foot is very low and most or all of the sole touches the ground. **2.** Unable to react quickly; unprepared: *The question caught me flat-footed.* **—flat′foot′ed·ness** *n.*

Flat·head (flăt′hĕd′) *n., pl.* **Flathead** or **Flat·heads 1.** A member of a Native American people living in western Montana and northern Idaho. **2.** The Salishan language of the Flathead.

flat·i·ron (flăt′ī′ərn) *n.* An iron for pressing clothes.

flat·land (flăt′lănd′) *n.* **1.** Land that has almost no hills or valleys. **2. flatlands** A geographic area made up chiefly of flatland.

flat-screen (flăt′skrēn′) *adj.* Relating to or being a thin computer monitor or television, such as a liquid-crystal display.

flat·ten (flăt′n) *v.* **flat·tened, flat·ten·ing, flat·tens** —*tr.* **1.** To make flat or flatter: *A rolling pin flattens dough.* **2.** To knock down; lay low: *The wind flattened the old shed.* —*intr.* To become flat or flatter: *All the wrinkles flattened out when the shirt was ironed.* **—flat′ten·er** *n.*

flat·ter (flăt′ər) *v.* **flat·tered, flat·ter·ing, flat·ters** —*tr.* **1.** To compliment too much or praise insincerely, especially in order to win favor. **2.** To please or gratify: *The award flattered me.* **3.** To portray or show favorably: *This photograph flatters her.* —*intr.* To use flattery. [From Middle English *flateren*, from Old French *flater*, of Germanic origin.] **—flat′ter·er** *n.*

flat·ter·y (flăt′ə-rē) *n., pl.* **flat·ter·ies** Excessive or insincere praise.

flat·top (flăt′tŏp′) *n. Informal* **1.** An aircraft carrier. **2.** A short haircut in which the hair is brushed straight up and cut flat across the top of the head.

flat·u·lent (flăch′ə-lənt) *adj.* Having excessive gas in the digestive tract. **—flat′u·lence** *n.*

flat·ware (flăt′wâr′) *n.* **1.** Tableware that is fairly flat, as plates. **2.** Table utensils such as knives, forks, and spoons.

flat·worm (flăt′wûrm′) *n.* Any of various worms, such as a tapeworm or planarian, having a flattened body and living in water or as a parasite in a human or other animal.

flaunt (flônt) *tr.v.* **flaunt·ed, flaunt·ing, flaunts** To display (something) in order to impress others: *flaunt one's knowledge.* **—flaunt′ing·ly** *adv.* —SEE NOTE.

fla·vor (flā′vər) *n.* **1.** Distinctive taste of something; savor: *the spicy flavor of applesauce.* **2.** A seasoning or flavoring: *Vanilla is a common flavor.* **3.** A quality felt to be characteristic of a thing: *a story full of the flavor of India.* ❖ *tr.v.* **fla·vored, fla·vor·ing, fla·vors** To give flavor to: *Vinegar flavored the salad.* [From Middle English *flavour*, aroma, from Old French *flaor*, from Latin *flāre*, to blow.] **—fla′vor·ful, fla′vor·some** *adj.*

fla·vor·ing (flā′vər-ĭng) *n.* A substance, such as an extract or a spice, used to flavor food: *raspberry flavoring.*

flaw (flô) *n.* A defect or imperfection: *The dish broke where it had a flaw. Their argument had many flaws and was unconvincing.* ❖ *tr.v.* **flawed, flaw·ing, flaws** To make defective: *The report was flawed with several errors.*

flaw·less (flô′lĭs) *adj.* Without a flaw; perfect: *The singer gave a flawless performance.* See Synonyms at **perfect. —flaw′less·ly** *adv.*

flax (flăks) *n.* **1.** The light-colored fibers from which linen is made. **2.** The plant from which such fibers are obtained, having blue flowers and seeds that yield linseed oil. [From Old English *fleax.*]

flax·en (flăk′sən) *adj.* **1.** Made of flax: *flaxen thread.* **2.** Having the pale-yellow color of flax fiber: *flaxen hair.*

flax·seed (flăks′sēd′) *n.* The seed of the flax plant, used to obtain linseed oil and as a dietary supplement.

flay (flā) *tr.v.* **flayed, flay·ing, flays 1.** To strip off the skin of: *flay a deer.* **2.** To criticize or scold harshly.

flea (flē) *n.* Any of various small, wingless, jumping insects that live on the bodies of humans and other animals and suck their blood. [From Old English *flēah.*]

❑ *These sound alike:* **flea, flee** (run away).

flea collar *n.* A collar, especially for a cat or dog, that contains a substance for killing fleas.

fleck (flĕk) *n.* **1.** A small mark or spot: *flecks of gray paint on the floor.* **2.** A small bit or flake: *a fleck of paper.* ❖ *tr.v.* **flecked, fleck·ing, flecks** To mark with flecks; spot.

fled (flĕd) *v.* Past tense and past participle of **flee.**

fledge (flĕj) *v.* **fledged, fledg·ing, fledg·es** —*intr.* To develop feathers and leave the nest: *Robins fledge in just a few weeks.* —*tr.* **1.** To take care of (a young bird) until it is ready to fly: *The pair of birds fledged two chicks.* **2.** To provide or cover with feathers: *fledge an arrow.*

fledg·ling (flĕj′lĭng) *n.* **1.** A young bird that has just left the nest. **2.** A young or inexperienced person. ❖ *adj.* New and inexperienced: *a fledgling skier.*

flee (flē) *v.* **fled** (flĕd), **flee·ing, flees** —*intr.* **1.** To run away, as from trouble or danger: *The thieves fled when they heard the police siren.* **2.** To pass swiftly away; vanish: *The night fled and the sky brightened.* —*tr.* To run away from; escape from: *flee the burning house.* [From Old English *flēon.*]

❑ *These sound alike:* **flee, flea** (insect).

fleece (flēs) *n.* **1.** The coat of wool of a sheep or similar animal. **2.** The amount of wool sheared from a sheep or similar animal at one time. **3a.** A soft, warm, lightweight, usually synthetic fabric with a deep pile, often used for lining coats, boots, and other outer clothing. **b.** A garment, especially a shirt or jacket, made of such fabric. ❖ *tr.v.* **fleeced, fleec·ing, fleec·es 1.** To shear the fleece from. **2.** To swindle or cheat (a person) of money or belongings: *fleeced the car buyer.*

fleec·y (flē′sē) *adj.* **fleec·i·er, fleec·i·est** Relating to or resembling fleece: *fleecy blankets; fleecy clouds.* **—fleec′i·ness** *n.*

fleet[1] (flēt) *n.* **1.** A group of warships under one commander. **2.** A number of boats or vehicles owned or operated as a group: *a fishing fleet; a fleet of taxis.* [From Old English *flēot*, from *flēotan*, to float.]

fleet[2] (flēt) *adj.* **fleet·er, fleet·est** Moving swiftly; nimble: *fleet as a deer.* ❖ *intr.v.* **fleet·ed, fleet·ing, fleets** To move or pass swiftly: *clouds fleeting across the sky.* [Probably from Old Norse *fljōtr.*] **—fleet′ly** *adv.* **—fleet′ness** *n.*

Fleet Admiral *n.* Admiral of the Fleet.

fleet·ing (flē′tĭng) *adj.* Passing quickly; very brief: *a fleeting glimpse of the eclipse.* **—fleet′ing·ly** *adv.*

Flem·ing (flĕm′ĭng) *n.* **1.** A native or inhabitant of Flanders. **2.** A Belgian who is a native speaker of Flemish.

Fleming, Sir **Alexander** 1881–1955. British bacteriologist who discovered penicillin in 1928.

Flem·ish (flĕm′ĭsh) *adj.* Relating to Flanders, the Flemings, or their language or culture. ❖ *n.* **1.** *(used with a plural verb)* The people of Flanders; the Flemings. **2.** A group of Dutch dialects spoken in the southwestern Netherlands, northwest Belgium, and parts of northern France.

flense (flĕns) *tr.v.* **flensed, flens·ing, flens·es** To strip the blubber or skin from: *flense a whale.*

fle·ro·vi·um (flə-rō′vē-əm) *n. Symbol* **Fl** A radioactive element that has been artificially produced by scientists. The half-life of its most stable isotope is about 2.7 seconds. Atomic number 114. See **Periodic Table.** [After Georgy *Flyorov* (1913–1990), Russian physicist.]

flesh (flĕsh) *n.* **1.** The soft tissue of the body of a vertebrate animal, composed mostly of muscles and fat and covering the bones. **2.** Such tissue used as food: *fish with white flesh.* **3.** The pulpy part of a fruit or vegetable used as food: *the sweet flesh of a ripe melon.* **4.** The body as distinguished from the mind or soul: *The spirit is willing, but the flesh is weak.* ◆ **flesh and blood** A blood relative or relatives; kin. **in the flesh** In person; actually present: *I met the celebrity in the flesh.*

flesh·ly (flĕsh′lē) *adj.* **flesh·li·er, flesh·li·est 1.** Relating to the body; physical: *fleshly need of nourishment.* **2.** Not spiritual; sensual or worldly: *fleshly pleasures.*

flesh·y (flĕsh′ē) *adj.* **flesh·i·er, flesh·i·est 1.** Relating to, consisting of, or having flesh. **2.** Having much flesh; plump: *fleshy cheeks.*

USAGE

flaunt The verbs **flaunt** and **flout** sound similar but have different meanings. *Flaunt* means "to display in a proud or showy manner": *They flaunted their wealth by driving an expensive car. Flout* means "to show contempt for": *an artist who flouted conventional styles.*

Sir Alexander Fleming

fleur-de-lis

flipper

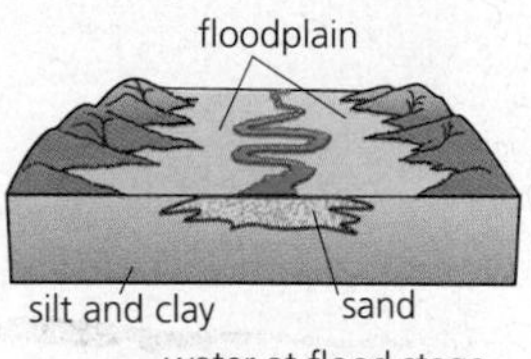

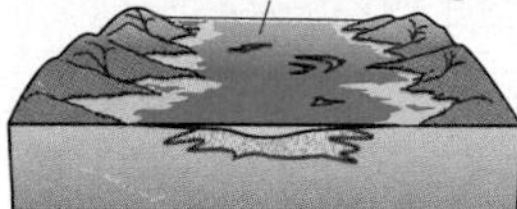

floodplain

ă	pat	ôr	core
ā	pay	oi	boy
âr	care	ou	out
ä	father	ŏŏ	took
ĕ	pet	ŏŏr	lure
ē	be	ōō	boot
ĭ	pit	ŭ	cut
ī	bite	ûr	urge
îr	pier	th	thin
ŏ	pot	*th*	this
ō	toe	zh	vision
ô	paw	ə	about

fleur-de-lis or **fleur-de-lys** (flûr′də-lē′) *n., pl.* **fleurs-de-lis** or **fleurs-de-lys** (flûr′də-lēz′) **1a.** A design in heraldry that has a three-petaled iris flower, used to symbolize the royal family of France. **b.** A similar design used as a decorative motif. **2.** An iris.

flew (flo͞o) *v.* Past tense of **fly¹**.
❑ *These sound alike:* **flew, flu** (influenza), **flue** (pipe).

flex (flĕks) *tr.v.* **flexed, flex·ing, flex·es 1.** To bend: *Flex your elbow.* **2.** To cause (a muscle) to contract. **3.** To exhibit or use (power): *The powerful country flexed its military might.*

flex·i·ble (flĕk′sə-bəl) *adj.* **1.** Capable of bending or being bent; supple; pliable: *a flexible hose.* **2.** Capable of or responsive to change; adaptable: *Our plans are flexible.* **—flex′i·bil′i·ty** *n.* **—flex′i·bly** *adv.*

flex·ion (flĕk′shən) *n.* **1.** The act of bending a part of the body by a muscle: *flexion of the leg.* **2.** The position assumed by a flexed limb.

flex·or (flĕk′sər) *n.* A muscle that bends a joint in the body.

flick (flĭk) *n.* **1.** A light quick motion in striking or touching something: *turn on a light with a flick of the finger.* **2.** The sound made by such a motion: *We heard the flick of the switch.* ❖ *tr.v.* **flicked, flick·ing, flicks 1.** To touch or hit with a light quick motion: *The horse flicked flies with its tail.* **2.** To cause to move with a light quick motion: *flick a switch.* **3.** To remove with a light quick motion: *flick a bug off the table.* [Of imitative origin.]

flick·er¹ (flĭk′ər) *intr.v.* **flick·ered, flick·er·ing, flick·ers 1.** To burn or shine waveringly: *The candles flickered in the breeze.* **2.** To move unevenly; flutter: *Shadows flickered on the wall.* ❖ *n.* **1.** An uneven or wavering light: *only the flicker of a candle to light our way.* **2.** A brief or slight indication or sensation: *a flicker of disappointment.* **3.** A short quick movement; a tremor: *the flicker of a butterfly's wings.* [From Old English *flicerian.*]

flick·er² (flĭk′ər) *n.* Any of various large woodpeckers of the Americas that have a spotted breast and often forage on the ground. [Perhaps from *flick.*]

flied (flīd) *intr.v.* Past tense and past participle of **fly¹** (sense 7).

fli·er also **fly·er** (flī′ər) *n.* **1.** A person or thing that flies, especially: **a.** A pilot or aviator. **b.** A passenger on an aircraft. **2.** *Informal* A pamphlet or circular; a handbill: *We distributed fliers for the candidate.*

flies¹ (flīz) *v.* Third person singular present tense of **fly¹**. ❖ *n.* Plural of **fly¹**.

flies² (flīz) *n.* Plural of **fly²**.

flight¹ (flīt) *n.* **1.** The act or process of flying: *a bird's flight.* **2.** A scheduled airline trip: *My flight to Milwaukee is set for Friday.* **3.** The distance covered in such a trip: *The flight was 3,000 miles.* **4.** A group, especially of birds or aircraft, flying together. **5.** An effort that soars above the ordinary: *a brilliant flight of the imagination.* **6.** A series of stairs, as between floors: *We climbed three flights to get to the top floor.* [From Middle English, from Old English *flyht.*]

flight² (flīt) *n.* An act of running away; an escape. [From Middle English.]

flight attendant *n.* A person who assists passengers in an aircraft.

flight·less (flīt′lĭs) *adj.* Incapable of flying: *Ostriches and penguins are flightless birds.*

flight recorder *n.* An electronic device that records information about the operation of each flight of an aircraft and is kept in a sealed box for recovery after a crash.

flight·y (flī′tē) *adj.* **flight·i·er, flight·i·est 1.** Exhibiting unsteady or fickle behavior. **2.** Irresponsible, especially in a silly way. **—flight′i·ness** *n.*

flim·sy (flĭm′zē) *adj.* **flim·si·er, flim·si·est 1.** Thin or light: *flimsy cloth.* **2.** Not solid or strong; likely to fall apart: *a flimsy table.* **3.** Not believable; unconvincing: *a flimsy excuse.* **—flim′si·ly** *adv.* **—flim′si·ness** *n.*

flinch (flĭnch) *intr.v.* **flinched, flinch·ing, flinch·es** To shrink or wince, as from pain or fear; draw back: *I flinched when the nurse put iodine on my injury.*

fling (flĭng) *tr.v.* **flung** (flŭng), **fling·ing, flings 1.** To throw with violence or force: *flung the dishes against the wall.* See Synonyms at **throw. 2.** To put or send suddenly or unexpectedly: *fling troops into battle.* ❖ *n.* **1.** The act of flinging; a throw. **2.** The Highland fling. **3.** A brief period of doing whatever one wants; a spree or binge. **4.** A brief romantic relationship.

flint (flĭnt) *n.* **1.** A very hard, gray to black form of quartz found in sedimentary rocks that makes sparks when it is struck with steel. **2.** A piece of flint used to produce sparks, as in a musket. [From Old English.]

flint·lock (flĭnt′lŏk′) *n.* A musket in which the powder charge is ignited when a flint strikes a metal plate, producing a spark.

flint·y (flĭn′tē) *adj.* **flint·i·er, flint·i·est 1.** Composed of or containing flint: *gray flinty hills.* **2.** Unyielding; stony: *a cold flinty look.* **—flint′i·ness** *n.*

flip (flĭp) *v.* **flipped, flip·ping, flips** *—tr.* **1.** To toss with a light quick motion, especially with a spin or turn: *flip a coin.* **2.** To turn over with a light quick motion: *flip the pages of a magazine.* **3.** To buy and sell (a house, for example) in a short period of time for profit. *—intr.* **1.** To turn over: *The canoe flipped in the rapids.* **2.** To move in twists and turns: *The fish flipped in the net.* **3.** To turn a somersault, especially in the air: *This dog flips for treats.* ❖ *n.* **1.** An act of flipping, especially a quick turning movement: *give the pancake a flip.* **2.** A somersault. ❖ *adj.* **flip·per, flip·pest** *Informal* Flippant: *a flip attitude.*

flip-flop (flĭp′flŏp′) *n.* **1.** The movement or sound of repeated flapping: *the flip-flop of a shade against a window.* **2.** A reversal of opinion or direction: *The mayor's flip-flop on the important issue left everyone wondering.* **3.** A backward somersault or handspring. **4.** A backless, often foam rubber sandal held to the foot at the big toe by means of a thong. ❖ *intr.v.* **flip-flopped, flip-flop·ping, flip-flops 1.** To reverse a stand or position: *a politician who flip-flopped on legalized gambling.* **2.** To move back and forth between two conditions: *the weather flip-flopped between searing heat and storms.*

flip·pant (flĭp′ənt) *adj.* Casually or humorously disrespectful: *He took offense because he thought she was being flippant.* **—flip′pan·cy** *n.* **—flip′pant·ly** *adv.*

flip·per (flĭp′ər) *n.* **1.** A wide flat limb, as of a seal, walrus, or sea turtle, used for swimming. **2.** A fin worn when swimming, snorkeling, or doing certain other water sports.

flirt (flûrt) *v.* **flirt·ed, flirt·ing, flirts** *—intr.* **1.** To act as if one is sexually attracted to another person, usually in a playful manner. **2.** To deal with (something) in a playful way as being of little importance; trifle: *a daredevil who flirts with danger.* *—tr.* To toss or move abruptly or jerkily; flick: *The bird flirted its tail.* ❖ *n.* **1.** A person given to romantic flirting. **2.** An abrupt jerking movement: *The squirrel gave a flirt of its tail and ran off.*

flir·ta·tion (flûr-tā′shən) *n.* **1.** The act or practice of flirting. **2.** A casual or brief romance.

flir·ta·tious (flûr-tā′shəs) *adj.* **1.** Given to flirting: *a flirtatious person.* **2.** Indicating that one is sexually attracted to someone, especially in a playful way: *a flirtatious look.* **—flir·ta′tious·ly** *adv.*

flit (flĭt) *intr.v.* **flit·ted, flit·ting, flits 1.** To move quickly and nimbly: *Birds flitted about in the thicket.* **2.** To pass quickly: *A smile flitted across his face.*

float (flōt) *v.* **float·ed, float·ing, floats** *—intr.* **1.** To rest within or on the surface of a fluid without sinking: *The raft floated down the river. The balloon floated in the sky.* **2.** To move or drift through space as if supported by a fluid: *The spacecraft floated toward the distant planet.* —*tr.* **1.** To cause to float or move on the surface of a fluid: *float logs down the river.* **2.** To offer for sale: *float a new company.* **3.** To arrange for (a loan). **4.** To offer for consideration; suggest: *floated an idea about a camping trip.* ❖ *n.* **1.** An object designed to float, especially: **a.** A buoy or raft fixed in place. **b.** A cork or ball on a fishing line that keeps the line up in the water and bobs when a fish bites. **c.** A hollow ball attached to a lever to regulate the water level in a tank, as in a toilet tank. **2.** An air-filled sac that keeps an aquatic organism afloat. **3.** A decorated exhibit displayed on a large flat vehicle in a parade. **4.** A soft drink with ice cream in it. [From Old English *flotian.*] —**float′er** *n.*

float·ing rib (flō′tĭng) *n.* A rib that has one end not connected to cartilage or bone. The lowest two pairs of human ribs are floating ribs.

flock (flŏk) *n.* **1.** A group of animals, such as birds or sheep, that live, travel, or feed together. **2.** The members of a church. **3.** A large crowd or number: *A flock of weekend visitors crowded into the museum.* ❖ *intr.v.* **flocked, flock·ing, flocks** To gather or travel in a flock or crowd: *People flocked to the cities for jobs.* —SEE NOTE AT **collective noun.**

floe (flō) *n.* A mass or sheet of floating ice.
❑ *These sound alike:* **floe, flow** (run freely).

flog (flŏg) *tr.v.* **flogged, flog·ging, flogs** To beat harshly with a whip or rod. —**flog′ger** *n.*

flood (flŭd) *n.* **1a.** An overflowing of water onto land that is normally dry. **b. Flood** In the Bible, the covering of the earth with water in the time of Noah. **2.** A large amount or number: *a flood of job applications.* ❖ *v.* **flood·ed, flood·ing, floods** —*tr.* **1.** To cover or submerge with water: *The heavy rain flooded the cellar.* **2.** To fill or overwhelm with too much of something: *Telephone calls flooded the electric company during the power outage.* **3.** To put too much fuel into the carburetor of (an engine), with the result that the engine will not start. —*intr.* **1.** To become covered or submerged with water: *That field floods every spring.* **2.** To overflow; pour forth: *The stream floods after a heavy rain.* [From Old English *flōd.*]

flood·gate (flŭd′gāt′) *n.* A gate used to control the flow of water, as from a lake or a river.

flood·light (flŭd′līt′) *n.* **1.** An electric lamp that produces a broad, intensely bright beam of light. **2.** The beam of light produced by such a lamp: *The fountain sparkled in the floodlight.* ❖ *tr.v.* **flood·light·ed** or **flood·lit** (flŭd′lĭt′), **flood·light·ing, flood·lights** To light with a floodlight.

flood·plain (flŭd′plān′) *n.* A plain that borders a river and is subject to flooding.

flood tide *n.* The incoming or rising tide.

flood·wa·ter (flŭd′wô′tər) *n.* often **floodwaters** The water of a flood.

floor (flôr) *n.* **1.** The surface of a room on which one stands. **2.** The ground or bottom surface, as of a forest or ocean. **3.** A story or level of a building: *Our apartment is on the fifth floor.* **4.** The part of a building where the members of a legislature meet and carry on their business. **5.** The right to address an assembly: *The representative from Hawaii has the floor.* ❖ *tr.v.* **floored, floor·ing, floors 1.** To provide with a floor: *floor a deck with planks.* **2.** To knock down: *The boxer was floored twice.* **3.** To stun; overwhelm: *The thrilling news floored me.*

floor·board (flôr′bôrd′) *n.* **1.** A board in a floor. **2.** The floor of a motor vehicle.

floor exercise *n.* An event in competitive gymnastics that consists of various tumbling maneuvers on a mat.

floor·ing (flôr′ĭng) *n.* **1.** A floor: *The house had flooring of fine wood.* **2.** Material, such as lumber, used to make floors.

floor plan *n.* A diagram of a room or building drawn as if seen from above.

floor·show (flôr′shō′) *n.* A series of entertainments, such as singing or comedy acts, presented in a nightclub.

floor·walk·er (flôr′wô′kər) *n.* An employee of a large store who supervises salespeople and helps customers.

flop (flŏp) *v.* **flopped, flop·ping, flops** —*intr.* **1.** To fall or lie down heavily and noisily; plop: *I flopped on my bed.* **2.** To move about loosely or limply: *The dog's ears flopped as it ran along.* **3.** *Informal* To fail: *The musical comedy totally flopped in New York.* —*tr.* To drop or lay (something) down heavily or drop noisily: *I flopped the heavy package on the table.* ❖ *n.* **1.** The action or sound of flopping. **2.** *Informal* A failure: *The play was a complete flop.*

flop·py (flŏp′ē) *adj.* **flop·pi·er, flop·pi·est** Tending to flop: *floppy ears; big floppy sleeves.* —**flop′pi·ness** *n.*

floppy disk *n.* A flexible plastic disk coated with magnetic material and covered by a protective jacket, formerly used to store computer data.

flo·ra (flôr′ə) *n.* *(used with a singular or plural verb)* **1.** The plants of a particular region or time period considered as a group: *desert flora.* **2.** The bacteria and other microorganisms that normally inhabit a bodily organ or part: *intestinal flora.*

flo·ral (flôr′əl) *adj.* Relating to or suggestive of flowers: *a floral arrangement; floral perfume.*

Flor·ence (flôr′əns) also **Fi·ren·ze** (fē-rĕn′dzĕ) A city of central Italy east of Pisa. Florence was an important artistic center during the Renaissance.

flo·ret (flôr′ĭt *or* flôr′ĕt) *n.* **1.** A small or reduced flower, especially one in the flower cluster of a grass or sedge or in the flower head of a composite plant such as a daisy or dandelion. **2.** One of the clusters of flower buds that together form a head of cauliflower or broccoli.

flor·id (flôr′ĭd) *adj.* **1.** Flushed with rosy color; ruddy: *a florid complexion.* **2.** Elaborate; flowery: *a florid style of writing.*

Flor·i·da (flôr′ĭ-də) A state of the southeast United States south of Georgia bordering on the Atlantic Ocean and the Gulf of Mexico. It was admitted as the 27th state in 1845. Tallahassee is the capital. —SEE NOTE.

flor·in (flôr′ĭn) *n.* **1.** A guilder. **2.** Any of several former European gold or silver coins.

flo·rist (flôr′ĭst) *n.* A person who raises or sells ornamental plants and flowers.

floss (flôs) *n.* **1.** Dental floss. **2.** Soft, loosely twisted silk or cotton thread used in embroidery. ❖ *v.* **flossed, floss·ing, floss·es** —*tr.* To clean with dental floss: *Floss your teeth carefully.* —*intr.* To clean the teeth with dental floss. —**floss′y** *adj.*

flo·til·la (flō-tĭl′ə) *n.* A fleet of boats or ships.

flot·sam (flŏt′səm) *n.* Floating wreckage or cargo from a shipwreck.

flounce¹ (flouns) *n.* A strip of decorative cloth gathered or pleated along one edge and sewn to a curtain or clothing as a trimming. ❖ *tr.v.* **flounced, flounc·ing, flounc·es** To trim with a flounce or flounces. [From Middle English *frounce*, pleat, from Old French *fronce*, of Germanic origin.]

flounce² (flouns) *intr.v.* **flounced, flounc·ing, flounc·es 1.** To move in a lively or bouncy manner: *The children flounced about the room.* **2.** To move with exaggerated or affected motions: *flounce out of the room in a huff.* [Possibly of Scandinavian origin.]

floun·der¹ (floun′dər) *intr.v.* **floun·dered, floun·der·ing, floun·ders 1.** To move clumsily or with difficulty: *The children floundered through deep snow.* **2.** To act or function with confusion or without direction: *flounder through a speech.* [Probably alteration of *founder*, to sink.] —SEE NOTE AT **founder¹.**

floun·der² (floun′dər) *n., pl.* **flounder** or **floun·ders**

GEOGRAPHY

Florida The Spanish explorer Juan Ponce de León gave **Florida** its name when he landed there in 1513 during the Easter season. He was thinking of the Spanish expression for Easter, *Pascua florida,* which means "flowery feast." *Florida* is the first name we know of that was given by Europeans to a place now in US territory. The state of Florida is still a "flowery" place today.

flounder²

WORD BUILDING

fluent The word roots *flu–, flux–,* and *fluc–* in English words come from the Latin verb *fluere,* "to flow." The Latin present participle of *fluere* has the form *fluent–* and meant "flowing." It is the source of the English word **fluent,** "flowing, graceful, smooth." The Latin noun *influentia,* meaning "an inflow" (using the prefix *in–*[2], "in, into") is the source of our word **influence.** The past participle of *fluere* was *flūxus,* from which we form the word **influx,** "an inflow." Latin also had a noun *flūctus* meaning "wave," from which the verb *flūctuāre* was made, meaning "to make waves"; this is the source of the word **fluctuate.**

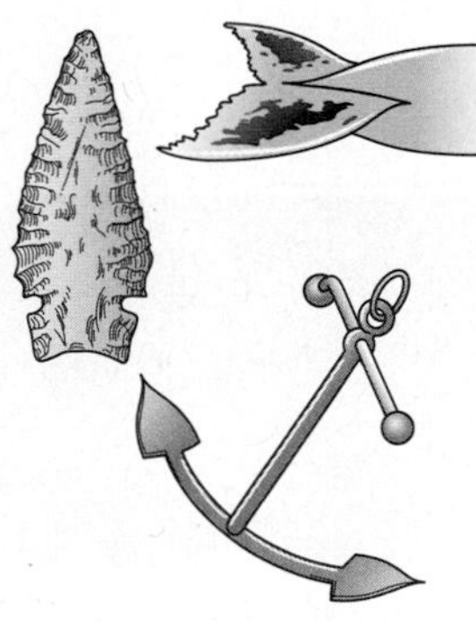

fluke[2]
top: arrowhead and whale flukes
bottom: anchor flukes

ă	pat	ôr	core
ā	pay	oi	boy
âr	care	ou	out
ä	father	o͝o	took
ĕ	pet	o͝or	lure
ē	be	o͞o	boot
ĭ	pit	ŭ	cut
ī	bite	ûr	urge
îr	pier	th	thin
ŏ	pot	*th*	this
ō	toe	zh	vision
ô	paw	ə	about

Any of various flatfishes used as food. [From Middle English, from Anglo-Norman *floundre,* of Scandinavian origin.]

flour (flou′ər *or* flour) *n.* **1.** A fine powdery foodstuff made by grinding and sifting the meal of a grain, especially wheat. **2.** Any of various similar powdery foods, as that made from cassavas or potatoes. ❖ *tr.v.* **floured, flour·ing, flours** To cover or coat with flour: *flour chicken before frying.*
❑ *These sound alike:* **flour, flower** (plant).

flour·ish (flûr′ĭsh) *v.* **flour·ished, flour·ish·ing, flour·ish·es** —*intr.* **1.** To grow or develop well or luxuriantly; thrive: *Most flowers flourish in full sunlight.* **2.** To do well; prosper: *The lawyer's practice flourished.* **3.** To be actively working, especially in a period of great accomplishment: *a writer who flourished in the later 1600s.* —*tr.* To wave vigorously or dramatically: *Marchers flourished their hats in front of the reviewing stand.* ❖ *n.* **1.** A dramatic action or gesture: *the flourish of a sword.* **2.** An added decorative touch; an embellishment: *handwriting with many flourishes.* **3.** In music, a showy passage or a fanfare: *Trumpets played a flourish.*

flout (flout) *tr.v.* **flout·ed, flout·ing, flouts** To ignore or disregard (a rule or convention, for example) in an open or defiant way: *a rebel who flouted convention.* [Possibly from Middle English *flouten,* to play the flute, from Old French *flauter,* from *flaute,* flute.] **—flout′er** *n.* —SEE NOTE AT **flaunt.**

flow (flō) *intr.v.* **flowed, flow·ing, flows 1.** To move or run smoothly in a stream: *Oil flowed from the well. Blood flows through the arteries and veins of the body. Traffic flowed through the tunnel.* **2.** To proceed steadily and easily: *The preparations for the party flowed smoothly.* **3.** To be plentiful: *a river flowing with fish.* **4.** To be full or overflow: *Their hearts flowed with warm feelings.* **5.** To hang loosely and gracefully: *The judges' robes flowed behind them.* **6.** To rise. Used of the tide. ❖ *n.* **1.** A stream or current: *a lava flow.* **2.** A continuous movement: *the flow of traffic.* **3.** The act of flowing: *Downstream the flow is much slower.* **4.** The rising of the tide: *the ocean's flow towards shore.* **5.** A general movement or tendency: *policies that followed the flow of general opinion.*
❑ *These sound alike:* **flow, floe** (ice mass).

flow chart also **flow·chart** (flō′chärt′) *n.* A diagram that shows the order of operations or sequence of tasks for solving a problem or managing a complex project.

flow·er (flou′ər) *n.* **1.** The reproductive part of a large group of plants (the angiosperms), having female or male reproductive structures or both and in its complete form including a pistil and stamens, sepals, and petals. **2.** A plant that is grown mainly for its flowers: *planted irises and other flowers in the garden.* **3.** The best example or representative of something: *Shakespeare and other writers who were the flower of Elizabethan England.* ❖ *intr.v.* **flow·ered, flow·er·ing, flow·ers 1.** To produce flowers; bloom: *Some maple trees flower early in the spring.* **2.** To develop fully; reach a peak: *His artistic talents flowered late in life.* [From Middle English *flour,* from Latin *flōs.*]
❑ *These sound alike:* **flower, flour** (ground wheat).

flow·er·ing plant (flou′ər-ĭng) *n.* A plant that produces flowers and fruit; an angiosperm.

flow·er·y (flou′ə-rē) *adj.* **flow·er·i·er, flow·er·i·est 1.** Full of or suggestive of flowers: *flowery meadows; a flowery fragrance.* **2.** Full of fancy words or expressions: *a flowery speech.* **—flow′er·i·ness** *n.*

flown (flōn) *v.* Past participle of **fly**[1].

fl. oz. *abbr.* An abbreviation of fluid ounce.

flu (flo͞o) *n.* Influenza.
❑ *These sound alike:* **flu, flew** (moved through the air), **flue** (pipe).

flub (flŭb) *tr.v.* **flubbed, flub·bing, flubs** To botch or bungle: *He flubbed the pass and dropped the ball.* ❖ *n.* A blunder; an error.

fluc·tu·ate (flŭk′cho͞o-āt′) *intr.v.* **fluc·tu·at·ed, fluc·tu·at·ing, fluc·tu·ates** To change or vary irregularly; waver: *In summer the temperature fluctuates a great deal.* **—fluc′tu·a′tion** *n.* —SEE NOTE AT **fluent.**

flue (flo͞o) *n.* A pipe, tube, or other channel for carrying smoke, steam, or waste gases, as from a fireplace to a chimney.
❑ *These sound alike:* **flue, flew** (moved through the air), **flu** (influenza).

flu·en·cy (flo͞o′ən-sē) *n.* Smoothness and ease, especially in speaking or writing.

flu·ent (flo͞o′ənt) *adj.* **1.** Capable of expressing oneself smoothly and effortlessly: *a fluent speaker; fluent in German and French.* **2.** Flowing effortlessly; polished: *speaks fluent Russian.* **—flu′ent·ly** *adv.* —SEE NOTE.

fluff (flŭf) *n.* **1.** Light down or fuzz: *the fluff from a woolen sweater.* **2.** Something having a very light or downy appearance: *The ducklings were little balls of fluff.* **3.** Something having very little substance, meaning, or importance: *The report was mostly fluff, with very little new information.* **4.** *Informal* An error; a flub. ❖ *tr.v.* **fluffed, fluff·ing, fluffs 1.** To make light and puffy by patting or shaking: *fluff a pillow.* **2.** *Informal* To ruin or spoil by making a mistake: *fluff an exam; fluff a speech.*

fluff·y (flŭf′ē) *adj.* **fluff·i·er, fluff·i·est 1.** Relating to, resembling, or covered with fluff or down: *a fluffy blanket.* **2.** Light and airy; soft: *fluffy whipped potatoes; fluffy curls.* **—fluff′i·ness** *n.*

flu·id (flo͞o′ĭd) *n.* A substance, such as air or water, that flows easily and takes on the shape of its container. All liquids and gases are fluids. ❖ *adj.* **1.** Capable of flowing; liquid or gaseous: *The waters of this lake remain fluid all winter.* **2.** Smooth and flowing; graceful: *the fluid motion of a ballet dancer.* **3.** Easily changed or tending to change: *Our vacation plans remained fluid until we knew how much time we had.* **—flu·id′i·ty** *n.*

fluid ounce *n.* A liquid measure equal to $\frac{1}{16}$ of a pint (29.57 milliliters).

fluke[1] (flo͞ok) *n.* **1.** Any of numerous parasitic flatworms, especially a trematode. **2.** Any of various flatfishes, especially a flounder. [From Old English *flōc,* flounder, flatfish.]

fluke[2] (flo͞ok) *n.* **1.** The triangular blade at the end of either arm of an anchor, designed to dig into the ocean bottom to hold the anchor in place. **2.** The barbed head of a harpoon, lance, or arrow. **3.** Either of the two flattened fins of a whale's tail. [Possibly from *fluke,* flounder, flatfish.]

fluke[3] (flo͞ok) *n.* Something happening by chance, especially a stroke of good luck: *It was a fluke that we all arrived at the same time.*

flume (flo͞om) *n.* **1.** A narrow gorge with a stream flowing through it. **2.** An artificial channel or chute for flowing water, as for floating logs or furnishing waterpower.

flum·mox (flŭm′əks) *tr.v.* **flum·moxed, flum·mox·ing, flum·mox·es** *Informal* To confuse; perplex: *I was flummoxed by a question I could not answer.*

flung (flŭng) *v.* Past tense and past participle of **fling.**

flunk (flŭngk) *Informal v.* **flunked, flunk·ing, flunks** —*intr.* To fail, especially in an examination or a course. —*tr.* **1.** To fail (a test or subject in school). **2.** To give (a person) a failing grade.

flun·ky also **flun·key** (flŭng′kē) *n., pl.* **flun·kies** also **flun·keys 1.** A person who submissively obeys and fawns on someone in order to win that person's favor. **2.** A person who does menial or trivial work. **3.** A servant in uniform.

fluo·resce (flo͝o-rĕs′ *or* flô-rĕs′) *intr.v.* **fluo·resced, fluo·resc·ing, fluo·resc·es** To produce or show fluorescence.

fluo·res·cence (flo͝o-rĕs′əns *or* flô-rĕs′əns) *n.* **1.** The giving off of electromagnetic radiation, especially visible light, by a substance when it is exposed to electromagnetic radiation having shorter wavelengths, such as ultraviolet rays. Light is emitted only as long as the exposure continues. **2.** The light produced in this way.

fluo·res·cent (flo͝o-rĕs′ənt *or* flô-rĕs′ənt) *adj.* Relating to, showing, or produced by fluorescence: *fluorescent light.*

fluorescent light *n.* A device that produces visible light by fluorescence, especially a glass tube coated on the inside with a fluorescent material and filled with an ionized gas that emits ultraviolet rays.

fluor·i·date (flo͝or′ĭ-dāt′ *or* flôr′ĭ-dāt′) *tr.v.* **fluor·i·dat·ed, fluor·i·dat·ing, fluor·i·dates** To add a compound of fluorine to (drinking water) in order to prevent tooth decay. **—fluor′i·da′tion** *n.*

fluor·ide (flo͝or′īd′ *or* flôr′īd′) *n.* A chemical compound of fluorine and another element or radical. It is added to the water supply to prevent tooth decay.

fluor·ine (flo͝or′ēn′ *or* flôr′ēn′) *n. Symbol* **F** A pale-yellow, poisonous, gaseous element that is highly corrosive. Atomic number 9. See **Periodic Table.**

fluo·ros·co·py (flə-rŏs′kə-pē) *n.* A technique used in medicine that involves passing x-rays through the body to create an image on a fluorescent surface. It is used to view internal parts of the body, especially during movement or during medical procedures. **—fluor′o·scop′ic** (flo͝or′ə-skŏp′ĭk *or* flôr′ə-skŏp′ĭk) *adj.*

flur·ry (flûr′ē) *n., pl.* **flur·ries 1.** A brief light fall of snow. **2.** A sudden gust of wind. **3.** A sudden burst of confusion, excitement, or activity; a stir: *a flurry of interest in the new product.* ❖ *tr.v.* **flur·ried, flur·ry·ing, flur·ries** To confuse, excite, or agitate; fluster: *Unexpected questions flurried the speaker.*

flush1 (flŭsh) *v.* **flushed, flush·ing, flush·es** *—intr.* **1.** To turn red in the face: *Her face flushed with anger.* **2.** To be emptied or cleaned by a rapid gush of water. *—tr.* **1.** To cause to redden or glow: *The disappointed customer was flushed with annoyance.* **2.** To excite or elate, as with a feeling of pride or accomplishment: *The winning team was flushed with victory.* **3.** To wash, empty, or purify with a sudden rapid flow of water: *We flushed the pipe of debris with a hose.* **4.** To drive away with a rapid flow of a liquid: *We flushed the debris from the pipe.* ❖ *n.* **1.** A flow or rush of water. **2.** A blush or rosy glow. **3.** A rush of strong feeling or excitement; exhilaration: *a flush of enthusiasm.* **4.** A state of freshness or vigor: *the first flush of youth.* ❖ *adj.* **flush·er, flush·est 1.** Having an abundant supply of money: *The company was flush with cash from sales of its latest product.* **2.** Marked by abundance; plentiful: *rivers flush with spring rains.* **3.** Having surfaces that are even, level, or close together: *sections of the sidewalk that are flush.* **4.** Aligned evenly with a margin, as along the left or right edge of a document; not indented. ❖ *adv.* So as to be even or aligned: *The figures are written flush down the column.* [Probably from *flush,* to dart out.]

flush2 (flŭsh) *n.* In card games, a hand in which all of the cards are of the same suit. [From Latin *flūxus,* flux.]

flush3 (flŭsh) *v.* **flushed, flush·ing, flush·es** *—tr.* **1.** To cause (an animal, especially one that is being hunted) to run or fly up from a hiding place: *The dog flushed several ducks from the tall grass.* **2.** To drive or force into the open: *The police threw tear gas in the building to flush out the criminals.* *—intr.* To run out or fly up from a hiding place: *The dog barked and the geese flushed from the thicket.* [From Middle English *flusshen.*]

flus·ter (flŭs′tər) *tr.v.* **flus·tered, flus·ter·ing, flus·ters** To make nervous, excited, or confused: *Shouts from the protesters flustered the speaker.* ❖ *n.* A state of excitement, confusion, or agitation: *The heavy city traffic put the driver in a fluster.*

flute (flo͞ot) *n.* **1.** A woodwind instrument consisting of a tube with finger holes and keys on the side, sounded by blowing across a hole near one end. **2.** A rounded groove, especially one carved on the shaft of a column. **3.** A groove in cloth, as in a pleated ruffle. ❖ *tr.v.* **flut·ed, flut·ing, flutes** To make grooves in: *A carpenter fluted the tops of the new columns.*

flut·ing (flo͞o′tĭng) *n.* A series of rounded grooves, as on a column of a building.

flut·ist (flo͞o′tĭst) *n.* A person who plays the flute.

flut·ter (flŭt′ər) *v.* **flut·tered, flut·ter·ing, flut·ters** *—intr.* **1.** To wave or flap rapidly with an irregular motion: *curtains fluttered in the breeze.* **2a.** To fly with a quick light flapping of the wings. **b.** To flap the wings while making short hops: *The chicken fluttered across the yard.* **3.** To vibrate or beat rapidly or irregularly: *When I was scared, my heart fluttered wildly.* **4.** To move quickly in a nervous, restless, or excited fashion; flit: *Clerks fluttered about trying to look busy.* *—tr.* To cause to flutter: *A light breeze fluttered the curtain.* ❖ *n.* **1.** An act of fluttering: *the flutter of a butterfly.* **2.** A condition of nervous excitement or agitation: *We were in a flutter getting ready for the party.*

flutter kick *n.* A swimming kick used in crawl and backstroke in which the legs are extended straight back and alternately moved up and down.

flux (flŭks) *n.* **1.** Continual change: *The price of gold is in flux.* **2.** A flow or flowing of a fluid: *the flux of the outgoing tide.* **3.** A substance applied to a metal surface that is to be soldered or welded. Flux cleans the surface, improves the flow of solder, and prevents the formation of oxides that would weaken the joint. **4.** A substance used in a smelting furnace to make metals melt more easily. **5a.** The rate of flow of fluids, particles, or energy across a given surface or area. **b.** Magnetic flux. **6.** A heavy discharge of fluid from the body, especially the discharge of watery waste material from the intestines.

fly1 (flī) *v.* **flew** (flo͞o), **flown** (flōn), **fly·ing, flies** (flīz) *—intr.* **1.** To move through the air by means of wings: *Birds fly south in winter.* **2a.** To move or travel by air: *We flew to Seattle for vacation.* **b.** To pilot an aircraft or spacecraft: *The crew flew from New York to Tokyo.* **3a.** To rise in or be carried through the air by the wind: *Dust and pollen flew through the air.* **b.** To float or flutter in the air: *pennants flying from buildings.* **4.** To be sent or driven through the air with great speed or force: *The plate flew from my hands when I tripped.* **5.** To move with great speed; rush; flee: *flew down the hall; fly from danger.* **6.** To pass by swiftly: *a vacation flying by.* **7.** *past tense and past participle* **flied** In baseball, to hit a fly ball. **8.** To react explosively; burst: *fly into a rage.* *—tr.* **1.** To cause to float or flutter in the air: *fly a kite.* **2a.** To pilot (an aircraft or spacecraft). **b.** To carry or transport in an aircraft or spacecraft: *fly supplies to a remote area.* **c.** To pass over in flight: *fly the ocean.* **3.** To flee from: *Many people flew the country.* ❖ *n., pl.* **flies 1.** A fly ball in baseball. **2.** A cloth flap covering a zipper or set of buttons, especially one on the front of pants. **3.** A piece of protective fabric secured over a tent and often extended over the entrance. **4. flies** The area directly over a theater's stage where lights and curtains are hung and equipment for raising and lowering sets is located. ◆ **fly at** To attack fiercely; assault. **let fly 1.** To shoot, hurl, or release (a weapon). **2.** To lash out; criticize harshly: *The mayor let fly with an attack on her critics.* **on the fly 1.** On the run; in a hurry: *I got a sandwich on the fly.* **2.** While in the air; in flight: *The bird was singing on the fly.* [From Old English *flēogan.*]

fly2 (flī) *n., pl.* **flies 1a.** Any of numerous two-winged insects, especially a housefly. Fruit flies and mosquitoes are also flies. **b.** Any of various other flying insects, such as a mayfly or a caddisfly. **2.** A fishhook made to look

flume
Leutasch Gorge, near Mittenwald, Germany

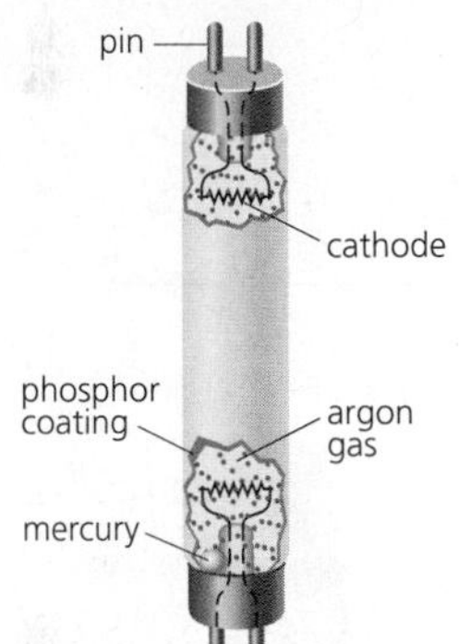

fluorescent light

flute

fly1
dome tent

flycatcher

flying buttress

like such an insect, as by attaching bits of feathers. [From Old English *flēoge, flȳge.*]

fly ball *n.* In baseball, a ball that is batted high in the air, usually to the outfield.

fly·catch·er (flī′kăch′ər *or* flī′kĕch′ər) *n.* Any of various birds that catch insects while flying, such as the phoebe.

fly·er (flī′ər) *n.* Variant of **flier.**

fly-fish·ing (flī′fĭsh′ĭng) *n.* The art or sport of fishing using artificial flies for bait.

fly·ing (flī′ĭng) *adj.* **1.** Relating to aviation: *flying lessons.* **2.** Capable of or engaged in flight: *a flying insect.* **3.** Swiftly moving: *the pianist's flying fingers.* **4.** Brief; hurried: *a flying visit.* ❖ *n.* **1.** Flight, as in an aircraft: *Flying is an exciting way to travel.* **2.** The operation of an aircraft: *A pilot is an expert in flying.*

flying buttress *n.* An arched masonry support that leans against the outside of a building to counteract forces, such as the weight of a vaulted ceiling, that tend to push the wall outwards.

flying fish *n.* Any of various ocean fishes having large side fins that spread out like wings as they leap from the water and make brief gliding flights.

flying jib *n.* A light triangular sail that extends beyond the jib.

flying saucer *n.* An unidentified flying object, usually described as a glowing disk and thought to be from another planet.

flying squirrel *n.* Any of various squirrels that make long gliding leaps between trees with the aid of broad folds of skin that stretch along each side of the body between the front and hind legs.

fly·leaf (flī′lēf′) *n.* A blank or specially printed page at the beginning or end of a book.

fly·pa·per (flī′pā′pər) *n.* Paper coated with a sticky, sometimes poisonous substance, used to catch flies.

fly swatter *n.* An implement used to kill flies or other insects, usually consisting of a piece of plastic or wire mesh attached to a long handle.

fly·way (flī′wā′) *n.* A route followed by migrating birds.

fly·weight (flī′wāt′) *n.* **1.** A boxer of the lightest weight class, weighing not more than 112 pounds (about 50 kilograms). **2.** *Informal* A very small or unimportant person or thing: *The new product proved to be a flyweight in the market and was soon discontinued.*

fly·wheel (flī′wēl′) *n.* **1.** A wheel with a heavy rim, attached to a shaft of a machine to keep it turning at a steady speed. **2.** A similar device used to regulate the speed of the mechanisms inside a clock.

Fm The symbol for the element **fermium.**

FM *abbr.* An abbreviation of frequency modulation.

foal (fōl) *n.* The young offspring of a horse, zebra, or similar animal, especially one less than a year old. ❖ *intr.v.* **foaled, foal·ing, foals** To give birth to a foal: *a mare ready to foal.* [From Old English *fola.*]

foam (fōm) *n.* **1.** A mass of bubbles formed in a liquid, as in surf or liquid soap, from shaking, boiling, or fermenting; froth. **2.** Frothy saliva or sweat: *wiped the froth from the horse's back.* **3.** A light, porous, flexible or spongy material full of small holes, used as a building material, for insulation, or to absorb shock in packaging. ❖ *intr.v.* **foamed, foam·ing, foams** To form foam or come forth in foam; froth: *The milk foamed and boiled over.*

foam rubber *n.* A light spongy rubber used for cushioning, packaging, and insulation.

foam·y (fō′mē) *adj.* **foam·i·er, foam·i·est** Relating to, full of, covered with, or resembling foam: *foamy suds.* **—foam′i·ly** *adv.* **—foam′i·ness** *n.*

fob¹ (fŏb) *n.* **1.** A small pocket in a man's pants or a vest, used to hold a watch, change, or other small items. **2.** A short chain or ribbon attached to a watch carried in a pocket. **3.** An ornament attached to a chain or ribbon. **4.** A key fob. [Probably of Germanic origin.]

fob² (fŏb) *tr.v.* **fobbed, fob·bing, fobs** *Archaic* To cheat someone. ◆ **fob off 1.** To get rid of by some trick or dishonest scheme: *fob off a copy as an original.* **2.** To put (a person) off by trickery: *He fobbed off the bill collector with a phony excuse.* [From Middle English *fobben,* probably from *fob,* trickster.]

fo·cac·ci·a (fə-kä′chē-ə *or* fə-kä′chə) *n.* A flat Italian bread flavored with olive oil and often topped with onions, herbs, or other items. [From Italian, hearth-cake.]

fo·cal (fō′kəl) *adj.* Relating to a focus: *The focal point of the discussion was rights for minority groups.* **—fo′cal·ly** *adv.*

focal length *n.* The distance from the surface of a mirror or lens to its point of focus.

fo'c's'le (fōk′səl) *n.* Variant of **forecastle.**

fo·cus (fō′kəs) *n., pl.* **fo·cus·es** or **fo·ci** (fō′sī′ *or* fō′kī′) **1a.** A point at which rays of light come together or from which they appear to spread apart, as after passing through a lens. **b.** Focal length. **2a.** The degree of clarity with which an eye or optical instrument produces an image: *a telescope with excellent focus.* **b.** The condition or adjustment in which an eye or optical instrument gives its best image: *The camera is out of focus.* **3.** A center of interest, attention, or activity: *The senator was the focus of attention at the assembly.* **4.** Concentration or emphasis: *The narrator's focus is on the characters in the story rather than the action.* **5.** A central point or region, such as the point at which an earthquake starts or a region of the body in which an infection is largely confined. **6.** A fixed point or one of a pair of fixed points used in constructing a curve such as an ellipse, a parabola, or a hyperbola. ❖ *v.* **fo·cused, fo·cus·ing, fo·cus·es** or **fo·cussed, fo·cus·sing, fo·cus·ses** *—tr.* **1a.** To bring (an object or image) into focus by adjusting the eyes or an optical instrument. **b.** To adjust (the eyes or an optical instrument) to produce a clear image: *Focus the telescope on the moon.* **2.** To concentrate or center: *Focus your attention on the bass guitar part in the song.* *—intr.* **1.** To adjust one's eyes or an optical instrument to produce a clear image. **2.** To concentrate attention or energy: *Let's focus on the problem at hand.*

fod·der (fŏd′ər) *n.* **1.** Food, such as chopped corn stalks or hay, for livestock. **2.** Raw material: *The scandal provided fodder for his political enemies.*

foe (fō) *n.* An enemy, opponent, or adversary: *Foes of the new city dump met to fight the plan.* [From Old English *gefā,* from *fāh,* hostile.]

fog (fôg) *n.* **1.** Condensed water vapor in cloudy masses lying close to the surface of the ground or water. It is difficult to see very far in fog. **2.** A cloud of material, such as dust or smoke, that floats in the air: *a fog of insect spray.* **3.** A confused or unthinking condition: *I was so sleepy I was walking around in a fog.* ❖ *v.* **fogged, fog·ging, fogs** *—tr.* **1.** To cover with fog or a similar substance: *Steam fogged the bathroom mirror.* **2.** To make uncertain or unclear; confuse: *The strong medicine fogged the patient's mind.* *—intr.* To become covered with fog or a similar substance: *The car windows fogged up in the rain.*

fog·gy (fô′gē) *adj.* **fog·gi·er, fog·gi·est 1.** Full of or surrounded by fog: *a foggy valley.* **2.** Confused or vague; clouded: *I have only a foggy memory of what happened.* **—fog′gi·ly** *adv.* **—fog′gi·ness** *n.*

fog·horn (fôg′hôrn′) *n.* A horn, usually having a deep tone, blown to warn ships of danger in foggy weather.

fo·gy also **fog·ey** (fō′gē) *n., pl.* **fo·gies** also **fo·geys** A person with old-fashioned or conventional habits or attitudes.

foi·ble (foi′bəl) *n.* A minor personal fault or failing: *Laughing too loudly is an annoying foible.*

ă	pat	ôr	core
ā	pay	oi	boy
âr	care	ou	out
ä	father	o͝o	took
ĕ	pet	o͝or	lure
ē	be	o͞o	boot
ĭ	pit	ŭ	cut
ī	bite	ûr	urge
îr	pier	th	thin
ŏ	pot	*th*	this
ō	toe	zh	vision
ô	paw	ə	about

foil¹ (foil) *tr.v.* **foiled, foil·ing, foils** To prevent from being successful; frustrate; thwart: *an alarm system to foil thieves.* [From Middle English *foilen,* to trample, defile, variant of *filen,* to defile.]

foil² (foil) *n.* **1.** A thin flexible sheet of metal: *aluminum foil.* **2.** A person or thing that makes another stand out by contrast: *The serious official was a perfect foil for the comedian.* ❖ *tr.v.* **foiled, foil·ing, foils** To wrap (strands of hair) in pieces of foil to isolate them after applying bleach or color. [From Middle English, from Latin *folia,* plural of *folium,* leaf.]

foil³ (foil) *n.* A long thin sword used in fencing, having a blunt point to prevent injury.

foist (foist) *tr.v.* **foist·ed, foist·ing, foists** To pass off as genuine, valuable, or worthy; palm off: *The dishonest merchant tried to foist damaged goods on his customers.*

fold¹ (fōld) *v.* **fold·ed, fold·ing, folds** —*tr.* **1.** To bend over or double up so that one part lies over another: *Fold your paper in half.* **2.** To close or flatten by bending, pressing, or doubling jointed or connected parts: *The bird folded its wings. The sunbathers folded their chairs and left.* **3a.** To clasp or embrace: *I folded the infant in my arms.* **b.** To enclose or wrap: *fold the garbage in a newspaper.* **4.** To blend (an ingredient) into a mixture by gently turning one part over another: *Fold the beaten egg whites into the batter.* **5.** To withdraw (one's hand) in defeat, as by laying cards face down on the table: *folded her hand instead of calling the bet.* —*intr.* **1.** To be folded or be capable of being folded: *My wallet folds in the middle.* **2.** *Informal* To fail and close: *The business folded during the recession.* **3.** To withdraw one's hand of cards in defeat: *The first player next to the dealer folded.* ❖ *n.* **1.** A line or crease formed by folding: *Tear the paper along the fold.* **2.** A folded edge or part: *The little child hid in the folds of the curtain.* **3.** A bend in a layer or in several layers of rock. Folds occur in rocks when they are compressed by plate-tectonic forces. ◆ **fold out** To put in an extended position; unfold: *fold out a map.* [From Old English *fealdan.*]

fold² (fōld) *n.* **1.** A fenced area for livestock, especially sheep. **2.** An established group, such as a church or political party, whose members share the same beliefs, aims, or interests. [From Old English *fald.*]

–fold *suff.* A suffix that means: **1.** Divided into a specified number of parts: *a threefold problem.* **2.** Multiplied by a specified number: *a fivefold increase in sales.*

fold·er (fōl′dər) *n.* **1.** A folded sheet of cardboard or heavy paper used as a holder for loose papers: *a file folder.* **2.** An organizational unit for computer files kept on a storage device. **3.** A person or machine that folds things.

fo·li·age (fō′lē-ĭj *or* fō′lĭj) *n.* Plant leaves considered as a group: *colorful fall foliage.* [From Middle English *foilage,* from Old French *foillage,* from *foille,* leaf.]

fo·lic acid (fō′lĭk *or* fŏl′ĭk) *n.* A vitamin belonging to the vitamin B complex that is important in cell growth and metabolism and in the formation of red blood cells. It is found especially in leafy green vegetables and fresh fruit.

fo·li·o (fō′lē-ō′) *n., pl.* **fo·li·os 1a.** A large sheet of paper folded once, making two leaves or four pages of a book. **b.** A book of the largest common size, consisting of such folded sheets, usually about 15 inches (38 centimeters) high. **2.** A page number in a book. [From Middle English, from Late Latin *folium,* leaf of paper, from Latin *folium,* leaf.]

folk (fōk) *n., pl.* **folk** or **folks 1.** The common people of a nation or region, considered as representing a distinctive culture and preserving traditional customs, beliefs, and arts. **2.** People: *city folk; honest folk.* **3. folks** *Informal* **a.** People considered as a group: *The warning sign scared folks away.* **b.** One's family or relatives, especially one's parents: *My folks are coming to visit.* ❖ *adj.* Relating to, occurring in, or coming from the common people or their culture: *a folk hero; a folk tune.* [From Old English *folc.*]

folk etymology *n.* Change in the form of a word in order to make part of it sound like another word that it is associated with or mistakenly thought to contain. For example, some varieties of English have changed the word *asparagus* by folk etymology to *sparrow-grass,* because it was thought to contain the word *sparrow* and to be a type of grass.

folk·lore (fōk′lôr′) *n.* The traditional beliefs, legends, and customs, handed down by a people from generation to generation.

folk music *n.* Traditional music of the people of a country or region, usually passed down from generation to generation.

folk-rock (fōk′rŏk′) *n.* A variety of popular music that combines elements of rock music and folk music.

folk·sing·er (fōk′sĭng′ər) *n.* A singer of folk songs. —**folk singing** *n.*

folk song or **folk·song** (fōk′sông′) *n.* **1.** A song that is part of the folk music of a people. **2.** A song composed in the style of such a song.

folk·sy (fōk′sē) *adj.* **folk·si·er, folk·si·est** *Informal* Simple and informal: *folksy people.*

folk·tale (fōk′tāl′) *n.* A traditional story or legend handed down by the people of a country or region from one generation to the next.

fol·li·cle (fŏl′ĭ-kəl) *n.* **1.** A small cavity, sac, or gland in the body. Hairs grow from follicles. **2.** A dry one-celled fruit that splits open along one seam only, such as the fruit of a milkweed.

focaccia

fol·low (fŏl′ō) *v.* **fol·lowed, fol·low·ing, fol·lows** —*tr.* **1.** To go or come after (a person, for example): *Follow the usher to your seats.* **2.** To go behind (a person or thing) while watching closely and often while trying not to be noticed: *The detectives followed the suspect at a distance.* **3.** To move along the same course as: *We followed a path to the beach.* **4.** To come after (something) in order, time, or position: *Night follows day.* **5.** To occur as a result of: *General agreement followed the discussion.* **6a.** To act in agreement with; obey: *follow the rules of the game.* **b.** To use as a guide or model: *Follow my example. Follow the recipe carefully.* **7.** To accept, believe in, or support: *follow a religion.* **8.** To work at (a trade or occupation): *follow a trade such as carpentry.* **9.** To listen to or watch closely: *Weather forecasters followed the progress of the storm on their radar screen.* **10.** To keep up with; stay informed about: *Scientists follow new developments in genetics.* **11.** To grasp the meaning of; understand: *Do you follow what I'm saying?* —*intr.* **1.** To come, move, or take place after another person or thing in order or time: *A picnic followed after the baseball game.* **2.** To occur as a result: *Success will follow if you keep practicing.* ◆ **follow through 1.** To carry something to completion: *She followed through on her promise.* **2.** In sports, to continue a stroke beyond the point of hitting the ball: *The batter followed through with a full swing.* **follow up 1.** To make (a previous action) more effective by doing something else: *He followed up his interview with a thank-you letter.* **2.** To carry to completion: *We followed up their recommendation with a plan.* [From Old English *folgian.*]

SYNONYMS **follow, succeed, ensue, result** These verbs mean to come after something or someone in time or order. **Follow** is the most general: *We followed their car to the restaurant because I didn't know the way.* **Succeed** means to follow, especially in a planned order determined by rank, inheritance, or election: *His daughter succeeded him as publisher of the local newspaper.* **Ensue** means to follow as an effect or logical development: *If you do not clean the wound, an infection may*

fondue
cheese fondue

orca
↑
seal
↑
squid
↑
copepods
↑
algae

food chain

ă	pat	ôr	core
ā	pay	oi	boy
âr	care	ou	out
ä	father	o͝o	took
ĕ	pet	o͝or	lure
ē	be	o͞o	boot
ĭ	pit	ŭ	cut
ī	bite	ûr	urge
îr	pier	th	thin
ŏ	pot	*th*	this
ō	toe	zh	vision
ô	paw	ə	about

ensue. **Result** means to follow as a direct effect: *Failure to return a library book on time will result in a fine.*

---

fol·low·er (fŏl′ō-ər) *n.* **1.** A person or thing that follows. **2.** A person who follows the beliefs or ideas of another. **3.** A person who has a strong interest or pays close attention to something; a fan: *a follower of new developments in technology.*

fol·low·ing (fŏl′ō-ĭng) *adj.* **1.** Coming next in order or time: *the following afternoon.* **2.** Now to be listed: *The following people should report to the gymnasium.* ❖ *n.* **1.** A group of admirers, supporters, or disciples: *a popular politician with a large following.* **2.** The item or items to be mentioned next: *Please buy the following: milk, bread, and eggs.* ❖ *prep.* After: *Following dinner, we watched a movie.*

fol·low-up or **fol·low·up** (fŏl′ō-ŭp′) *n.* Something that reinforces or enhances a previous action or event: *The software was a successful follow-up to the original product.*

fol·ly (fŏl′ē) *n., pl.* **fol·lies 1.** Lack of good sense or judgment; foolishness. **2.** A foolish act or idea. **3. follies** *(used with a singular or plural verb)* An elaborate theatrical revue with music, dance, and skits. **4.** A pavilion or other structure that is chiefly decorative rather than practical in purpose. [From Middle English *folie*, from Old French, from *fol*, foolish, from Late Latin *follis*, windbag, fool.]

fo·ment (fō-mĕnt′) *tr.v.* **fo·ment·ed, fo·ment·ing, fo·ments** To stir up; arouse; provoke: *The protesters were charged with fomenting a riot.* [From Middle English *fomenten*, to apply warm liquids to the skin, from Latin *fōmentum*, poultice, from *fovēre*, to warm.]

fond (fŏnd) *adj.* **fond·er, fond·est 1.** Having a strong liking: *Are you fond of gardening?* **2.** Loving or affectionate: *a fond embrace.* **3.** Strongly or foolishly held dear: *my fondest hopes.* **—fond′ly** *adv.*

fon·dle (fŏn′dl) *tr. & intr.v.* **fon·dled, fon·dling, fon·dles** To touch or stroke lovingly; caress.

fond·ness (fŏnd′nĭs) *n.* **1.** Liking or inclination: *a fondness for the outdoors.* **2.** Warm affection.

fon·due (fŏn-do͞o′) *n.* A dish consisting of a hot sauce, such as melted cheese or chocolate, or hot oil in which pieces of food are dipped and then eaten. [From French, melted.]

font¹ (fŏnt) *n.* **1.** A basin that holds holy water or water used in baptism. **2.** A source or origin: *The professor is a font of knowledge.* [From Old English, from Latin *fōns*, fountain.]

font² (fŏnt) *n.* A complete set of printing type of one size and style. [From French *fonte*, casting, from Latin *fundere*, to pour forth.]

food (fo͞od) *n.* **1.** Material, especially carbohydrates, fats, and proteins, that an organism uses for energy, growth, and maintaining the processes of life. Plants, algae, and some bacteria make their own food through photosynthesis, while animals and most other organisms obtain food by eating other organisms. **2.** A supply of things to eat: *Is there any food in the house?* **3.** A particular kind of nourishment: *plant food; dog food.* **4.** Something that stimulates or encourages some activity or growth: *The movie gave them food for thought.* [From Old English *fōda.*]

food bank *n.* An organization that collects and distributes donated food for free or at low cost to organizations that serve people in need.

food chain *n.* A succession of organisms in an ecological community that are linked to each other through the transfer of energy and nutrients, beginning with an organism, such as a plant, that makes its own food and continuing with each organism being eaten by one higher in the chain.

food court *n.* An area within a mall or other public space where prepared food is sold from counters or booths clustered around a common eating area.

food·ie (fo͞o′dē) *n. Informal* A person who has a passionate or refined interest in food; a gourmet.

food pantry *n.* **1.** An organization or group that sorts and packages donated foodstuffs for distribution directly to people in need. **2.** The building or location where such distribution takes place.

food poisoning *n.* Illness that results from eating food that has become contaminated with bacteria or viruses.

food processor *n.* An appliance with interchangeable blades that processes food, as by slicing or shredding, at high speeds.

food stamp *n.* A coupon that is worth a certain amount of money or a debit card that gives access to a certain amount of money in an account, issued by a government to people with low incomes so that they can buy food at stores.

food·stuff (fo͞od′stŭf′) *n.* A substance that can be used or prepared for use as food.

food web *n.* A group of interrelated food chains in a particular ecological community.

fool (fo͞ol) *n.* **1.** A person who lacks judgment or good sense. **2.** A member of a royal or noble household who provided entertainment, as by telling jokes and clowning; a jester. ❖ *v.* **fooled, fool·ing, fools** *—tr.* **1.** To deceive or trick; mislead: *They fooled me into thinking they had left.* **2.** To surprise (someone) or prove (someone) wrong: *We were sure their plan would fail, but they fooled us.* *—intr.* **1.** To act frivolously or idly: *If you continue fooling, you'll never finish your homework.* **2.** To act or speak in jest; joke: *My friend thought I was serious, but I was only fooling.* **3.** To play or meddle foolishly: *Don't fool with the knobs on the oven.* ◆ **fool around** To act frivolously or idly; waste time: *fooling around with friends on a summer afternoon.* [From Middle English *fol*, from Old French, from Late Latin *follis*, windbag, fool, from Latin *follis*, bellows.] —SEE NOTE.

fool·har·dy (fo͞ol′här′dē) *adj.* **fool·har·di·er, fool·har·di·est** Unwisely bold or daring; rash: *a foolhardy beginner trying to ski down the steepest slopes.* **—fool′har′di·ness** *n.*

fool·ish (fo͞o′lĭsh) *adj.* **1.** Lacking in good sense or judgment; unwise: *a foolish choice.* **2.** Absurd; ridiculous: *I looked foolish dressed as a clown.* **—fool′ish·ly** *adv.* **—fool′ish·ness** *n.*

fool·proof (fo͞ol′pro͞of′) *adj.* So safe, simple, and reliable that error or misuse is impossible: *a foolproof toaster; a foolproof plan.*

fools·cap (fo͞olz′kăp′) *n.* Writing paper in large sheets about 13 inches (33 centimeters) wide and 16 inches (41 centimeters) long.

fool's gold (fo͞olz) *n.* Any of several minerals, especially pyrite, sometimes mistaken for gold.

foot (fo͝ot) *n., pl.* **feet** (fēt) **1.** The part of the leg of a vertebrate animal that rests on or touches the ground or floor in standing or walking. **2.** A similar part used for moving or attachment in an invertebrate animal, such as the muscular organ extending from the shell of a snail or clam. **3.** A part or base resembling a foot, as the end of a table leg. **4.** The lowest part of something high or long; the bottom: *the foot of the stairs; the foot of the page.* **5.** The end opposite the head in position or rank: *the foot of the bed; the foot of the class.* **6.** The part of a boot or stocking that covers the foot. **7.** A unit of length equal to ⅓ of a yard or 12 inches (about 30.48 centimeters). See table at **measurement. 8.** A unit of poetry, such as an iamb or dactyl, consisting of a combination of stressed and unstressed syllables. ❖ *tr.v.* **foot·ed, foot·ing, foots** To pay: *I'll foot the bill.* ◆ **on foot** or **by foot** Walking or running: *We're going to the restaurant on foot.*

foot·age (fo͝ot′ĭj) *n.* **1.** Length, extent, or amount of something as measured in feet: *estimated the square footage of the apartment.* **2.** Recorded film or video, especially of a specific kind or topic: *news footage; footage of the royal wedding.*

foot-and-mouth disease (fo͝ot′n-**mouth′**) *n.* A highly contagious disease of cattle and other hoofed animals, marked by fever and blisters around the mouth and hooves.

foot·ball (fo͝ot′bôl′) *n.* **1a.** A game played with an oval ball by two teams of 11 players each on a rectangular field with goals at either end. The object is to carry the ball across the opponent's goal line or to kick it between the opponent's goalposts. **b.** The inflated oval ball used in this game. **2.** *Chiefly British* **a.** Soccer or rugby. **b.** The ball used in soccer or rugby.

foot·board (fo͝ot′bôrd′) *n.* **1.** An upright board across the foot of a bedstead. **2.** A board or small platform on which to support or rest the feet.

foot·bridge (fo͝ot′brĭj′) *n.* A bridge used only by people on foot.

foot-can·dle (fo͝ot′kăn′dl) *n.* A unit of light intensity equal to one lumen per square foot. Originally, this unit was defined with respect to a standardized candle burning a foot away from the illuminated surface.

foot·ed (fo͝ot′ĭd) *adj.* Having a foot or feet: *a footed sofa; a four-footed animal.*

foot·er (fo͝ot′ər) *n.* **1.** A person or thing that is a certain number of feet in length or height: *a six-footer.* **2.** Printed information at a page's bottom margin, usually repeated throughout a document.

foot·fall (fo͝ot′fôl′) *n.* The sound made by a footstep.

foot·hill (fo͝ot′hĭl′) *n.* A low hill located near the base of a mountain or mountain range.

foot·hold (fo͝ot′hōld′) *n.* **1.** A place to put the foot so that it won't slip, especially when climbing. **2.** A firm secure position from which it is possible to advance: *He got a foothold in business by first working as an assistant.*

foot·ing (fo͝ot′ĭng) *n.* **1.** A firm placing of the feet allowing one to stand or move without falling: *lose one's footing.* **2.** A secure place to put the foot; a foothold. **3.** The condition of a surface for walking or running: *The road was icy and the footing treacherous.* **4.** A basis or standing: *You'll be on an equal footing with the others.*

foot·lights (fo͝ot′līts′) *pl.n.* Lights placed in a row along the front of a stage floor.

foot·loose (fo͝ot′lo͞os′) *adj.* Having no attachments or responsibilities; free to do as one pleases.

foot·man (fo͝ot′mən) *n.* A man employed as a servant to open doors, run errands, or serve food and drinks, as in a palace.

foot·note (fo͝ot′nōt′) *n.* A note at the bottom of a page explaining something in the text or giving the source of a quotation, fact, or idea.

foot·path (fo͝ot′păth′) *n.* A narrow path for people to walk on.

foot-pound (fo͝ot′**pound′**) *n.* A unit of work equal to the work or energy needed to lift a one-pound weight a distance of one foot against the force of the earth's gravity.

foot·print (fo͝ot′prĭnt′) *n.* **1.** A mark left by a foot or shoe, as in sand or snow. **2.** The surface space occupied by a building. **3.** The area affected or covered by a device or phenomenon: *the footprint of a communications satellite.*

foot·race (fo͝ot′rās′) *n.* A race run by people on foot.

foot·rest (fo͝ot′rĕst′) *n.* A low stool, metal bar, or other support on which to rest the feet.

foot soldier *n.* A soldier in the infantry.

foot·sore (fo͝ot′sôr′) *adj.* Having sore or tired feet from much walking.

foot·step (fo͝ot′stĕp′) *n.* **1.** A step with the foot. **2.** The sound of a foot stepping: *I heard their footsteps on the stairs.* **3.** A footprint. ◆ **follow in (someone's) footsteps** To carry on the behavior, work, or tradition of.

foot·stool (fo͝ot′sto͞ol′) *n.* A low stool on which to rest the feet while sitting.

foot·wear (fo͝ot′wâr′) *n.* Coverings for the feet, such as shoes or boots.

foot·work (fo͝ot′wûrk′) *n.* The movement of the feet, as in boxing or dancing.

fop (fŏp) *n.* A man who is vain about his clothes and manners; a dandy. **—fop′pish** *adj.* **—fop′pish·ly** *adv.*

fop·per·y (fŏp′ə-rē) *n., pl.* **fop·per·ies** The dress or manner of a fop.

for (fôr; fər *when unstressed*) *prep.* **1a.** With the purpose, goal, or object of: *swimming for exercise; studying for the exam; eager for fame.* **b.** In order to go toward or arrive at: *Let's head for home.* **2.** On behalf of: *She spoke for all of us.* **3.** In favor or support of: *Are you for the idea or not?* **4.** In place of: *She used her coat for a blanket.* **5.** In the amount of; at the price of: *a bill for $50; a camera bought for $150.* **6.** To the extent of or through the duration of: *We drove for miles. We talked for an hour.* **7.** At the stated time of: *I have an appointment for 2:00.* **8.** With the indicated number of attempts: *shot three for four from the foul line.* **9.** As a result of: *They were rewarded for their hard work.* **10a.** As regards; concerning: *He's a stickler for neatness.* **b.** Considering the usual character of: *It's a warm day for October.* **c.** In honor of: *She was named for her aunt.* **11.** Suitable to: *It's really for her to decide.* **12.** In spite of: *For all his complaining, he seems to like his job.* ❖ *conj.* Because; since: *We must be careful measuring the windows, for it's easy to make mistakes.* [From Old English, on account of.]

❑ *These sound alike:* **for, fore** (at the front), **four** (number).

for·age (fôr′ĭj) *n.* Plant material that livestock graze or that is cut and fed to them. ❖ *v.* **for·aged, for·ag·ing, for·ag·es** *—intr.* To search for something, especially food: *She foraged in the woods for mushrooms. I foraged for clean socks. —tr.* **1.** To get by searching about: *We foraged cookies from the pantry.* **2.** To obtain food, supplies, or other goods from, often by force; plunder: *Pirates foraged the coastal towns.* [From Middle English, from Old French *fourrage*, from *forrer*, to forage, from *feurre*, fodder, of Germanic origin.] **—for′ag·er** *n.*

for·as·much as (fôr′əz-**mŭch′**) *conj.* Inasmuch as; since.

for·ay (fôr′ā′) *n.* **1.** A sudden raid or military expedition. **2.** A venture or the beginning of an attempt, especially outside one's usual area: *the actor's foray into politics.* ❖ *intr.v.* **for·ayed, for·ay·ing, for·ays** To make a raid: *foray into enemy territory.* [From Middle English *forrai*, from Old French *forrer*, to forage.]

for·bad (fôr-**băd′**) *v.* A past tense of **forbid.**

for·bade (fôr-**băd′** *or* fôr-**bād′**) *v.* A past tense of **forbid.**

for·bear[1] (fôr-**bâr′**) *v.* **for·bore** (fôr-**bôr′**), **for·borne** (fôr-**bôrn′**), **for·bear·ing, for·bears** *—intr.* **1.** To keep oneself from doing something; hold back; refrain: *forbear from replying.* **2.** To be patient or tolerant: *Forbear with my misunderstanding. —tr.* To keep from; refrain from; resist: *I could not forbear telling him the truth.* [From Old English *forberan*, to endure.]

for·bear[2] (fôr′bâr′) *n.* Variant of **forebear.**

for·bear·ance (fôr-**bâr′**əns) *n.* **1.** Patience, tolerance, or restraint: *He showed forbearance in disciplining the unruly children.* **2.** The act of giving one who has a debt that is due more time to pay rather than enforcing immediate repayment.

for·bid (fôr-**bĭd′**) *tr.v.* **for·bade** (fôr-**băd′** *or* fôr-**bād′**) or **for·bad** (fôr-**băd′**), **for·bid·den** (fôr-**bĭd′**n) or **for·bid, for·bid·ding, for·bids 1.** To order (a person) not to do something: *I forbid you to go.* **2.** To refuse to allow;

WORD HISTORY

fool Our word *fool* goes back to a Latin word that meant "a bag or sack, an inflated ball, a bellows." Even speakers of Latin saw the resemblance between an empty bag and a person who is silly or unintelligent. A fool then is someone who is full of (hot) air, as we say today—a windbag or an airhead.

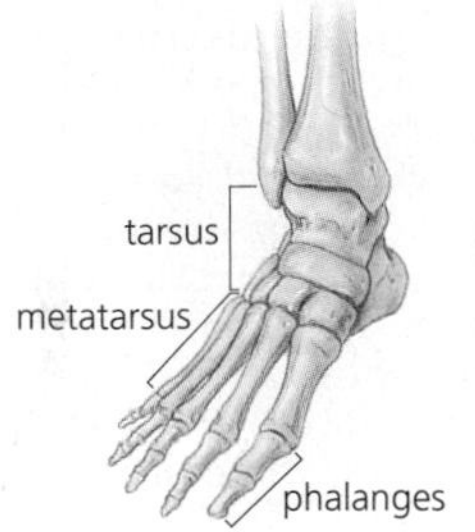

foot

SCIENCE

force In the mid-1600s, the English scientist Isaac Newton figured out that the amount of **force** needed to move an object is directly related to both the mass of the object and how much it is accelerated. This might seem obvious: pushing a pebble takes less force than pushing a boulder, and pushing a boulder quickly takes more force than pushing it slowly. But Newton set this relationship down quantitatively in what is now known as Newton's second law of motion: *Force* equals *mass* times *acceleration,* or *F* = *ma.* Acceleration here means a change in direction or in speed, either faster or slower. If a boat bumps into a dock, you can determine the force of the impact by multiplying the decrease in the boat's speed by the boat's mass. If you swing a rock around your head on a string, the rock is constantly accelerating as its direction changes, and your hand is exerting a force. The bigger the rock, the more force needed!

prohibit or deny: *The law forbids robbery.* [From Old English *forbēodan.*]

for·bid·ding (fôr-**bĭd′**ĭng) *adj.* Looking threatening, dangerous, or unfriendly: *a forbidding desert.*

for·bore (fôr-**bôr′**) *v.* Past tense of **forbear**[1].

for·borne (fôr-**bôrn′**) *v.* Past participle of **forbear**[1].

force (fôrs) *n.* **1.** The capacity to do work or cause physical change; energy, strength, or active power: *the force of an explosion.* See Synonyms at **strength. 2.** Power, pressure, or violence used on a person or thing that resists: *a promise obtained by force.* **3.** Something that causes a body to move, changes its speed or direction, or distorts its shape. One force may be counteracted by another, so that there is no change or distortion. **4a.** A group of people organized or available for a certain purpose: *a large labor force; a police force.* **b. forces** Military units, as of an army: *Napoleon's forces.* **5.** A strong influence acting as an urge or a restraint: *forces affecting modern life.* **6.** The power to influence or persuade; verbal effectiveness: *We felt his argument had considerable force.* ❖ *tr.v.* **forced, forc·ing, forc·es 1.** To cause (a person) to do something, as through pressure or necessity: *The storm forced us to postpone our meeting.* **2.** To get by the use of force: *I forced the ball from his hand.* **3.** To impose or inflict: *The invaders forced their laws on the peoples they conquered.* **4.** To move, push, or drive by pressure: *The pump forces water through the pipe.* **5.** To bring on or bring about through effort or pressure: *I forced a smile on my face.* **6.** To make (one's way) by pushing, thrusting, or breaking: *They forced their way through the thorn hedge.* **7.** To break open or pry open by using violence: *force the door; force a lock.* **8.** To cause to grow or bloom rapidly by artificial means: *force flowers in a greenhouse.* ◆ **in force 1.** In effect; in operation; valid: *a rule no longer in force.* **2.** In full strength: *The protesters turned out in force.* [From Middle English, from Medieval Latin *fortia*, from Latin *fortis*, strong.] **—forc′er** *n.* —SEE NOTE.

forced (fôrst) *adj.* **1.** Done under force, not by free choice; compulsory: *forced labor* **2.** Not natural; strained: *forced laughter.*

force·ful (**fôrs′**fəl) *adj.* Full of force; effective: *The winning candidate is a forceful speaker.* **—force′ful·ly** *adv.* **—force′ful·ness** *n.*

force play *n.* In baseball, a play in which a runner is put out when forced by the batter to move to the next base.

for·ceps (**fôr′**səps) *n., pl.* **forceps** A pair of special pincers or tongs used especially by surgeons or dentists for grasping, holding, or pulling. [From Latin *forceps*, fire tongs, pincers.]

forc·i·ble (**fôr′**sə-bəl) *adj.* **1.** Accomplished through the use of force: *The firefighters broke in by forcible entry.* **2.** Having force; forceful: *a forcible personality.* **—for′ci·bly** *adv.*

ford (fôrd) *n.* A shallow place in a stream or river where one can walk, ride, or drive across. ❖ *tr.v.* **ford·ed, ford·ing, fords** To cross (a stream or river) by wading, riding, or driving through a ford. [From Old English.] **—ford′a·ble** *adj.*

Ford (fôrd), **Gerald Rudolph, Jr.** 1913–2006. The 38th president of the United States (1974–1977), who became president after Richard Nixon's resignation over the Watergate scandal. As president, Ford granted a full pardon to Nixon (1974).

Ford, Henry 1863–1947. American automobile manufacturer who founded the Ford Motor Company (1903) and produced the Model T (1908–1927), the first widely available and affordable car.

fore (fôr) *adj.* In, at, or toward the front; forward: *The fore part of the new building faces the avenue.* ❖ *n.* **1.** Something that is located at or toward the front. **2.** The front part: *checked the ropes at the fore.* ❖ *adv.* At, toward, or near the front; forward: *ran fore to check the damage.* ❖ *interj.* An expression used by golfers to warn others on the course that a ball is headed in their direction. ◆ **to the fore** In, into, or toward a position of prominence: *New issues bring new leaders to the fore.* [From Old English.]

❑ *These sound alike:* **fore, for** (with the purpose of), **four** (number).

fore– *pref.* A prefix that means: **1.** Before; earlier: *foresight; forefather.* **2.** Front; in front of: *forepaw; foremast.* —SEE NOTE.

fore and aft *adv.* **1.** From the bow of a ship to the stern; lengthwise: *sails rigged fore and aft.* **2.** In, at, or toward both ends of a ship.

fore-and-aft (fôr′ən-**ăft′**) *adj.* Extending lengthwise along a structure, such as a ship; from bow to stern: *the fore-and-aft sails of a sloop.*

fore·arm[1] (fôr-**ärm′**) *tr.v.* **fore·armed, fore·arm·ing, fore·arms** To arm or prepare in advance of a conflict. [From *fore-*, before + *arm*, to arm.]

fore·arm[2] (**fôr′**ärm′) *n.* The part of the arm between the wrist and elbow. [From *fore-*, before + *arm*, body part.]

fore·bear also **for·bear** (**fôr′**bâr′) *n.* An ancestor. [From older Scots : *for-*, before + *beer*, one who is (from *ben*, to be).]

fore·bode (fôr-**bōd′**) *tr.v.* **fore·bod·ed, fore·bod·ing, fore·bodes 1.** To indicate the likelihood of; portend: *A dark sky sometimes forebodes a storm.* **2.** To have a sense or feeling of (something bad to come): *The scowls on their faces foreboded a fight.* **—fore·bod′er** *n.*

fore·bod·ing (fôr-**bō′**dĭng) *n.* A sense of impending evil or misfortune.

fore·brain (**fôr′**brān′) *n.* The part of the brain that includes the cerebrum, the thalamus, and the hypothalamus.

fore·cast (**fôr′**kăst′) *tr.v.* **fore·cast** or **fore·cast·ed, fore·cast·ing, fore·casts** To tell in advance what might or will happen, especially to predict weather conditions: *forecast snow for the weekend.* ❖ *n.* A prediction, as of coming events or conditions: *the weather forecast.* [From Middle English *forecasten*, to plan beforehand : *fore-*, before + *casten*, to throw, calculate, prepare.] **—fore′cast′er** *n.*

fore·cas·tle (**fōk′**səl *or* **fôr′**kăs′əl) also **fo′c′s′le** (**fōk′**səl) *n.* **1.** The section of a ship's upper deck located forward of the foremast. **2.** The crew's quarters at the bow of a merchant ship.

fore·close (fôr-**klōz′**) *v.* **fore·closed, fore·clos·ing, fore·clos·es** *—tr.* **1.** To take away the right to pay off (a mortgage), as when payments have not been made: *The bank foreclosed the mortgage and took away the property.* **2.** To shut out or rule out; bar. *—intr.* To bar a right to redeem a mortgage: *The bank foreclosed on the property.* [From Middle English *forclosen*, from Old French *forclos*, shut out, past participle of *forclore*, to exclude : Latin *forīs*, outside + Latin *claudere*, to close.]

fore·clo·sure (fôr-**klō′**zhər) *n.* The act of foreclosing, especially a legal proceeding by which a mortgage is foreclosed.

fore·doom (fôr-**do͞om′**) *tr.v.* **fore·doomed, fore·doom·ing, fore·dooms** To doom or condemn beforehand.

fore·fa·ther (**fôr′**fä′*th*ər) *n.* **1.** An ancestor. **2.** A person from an earlier time who has originated or contributed to a common tradition shared by a particular group.

fore·fin·ger (**fôr′**fĭng′gər) *n.* The finger next to the thumb; the index finger.

fore·foot (**fôr′**fo͝ot′) *n.* One of the front feet of a four-legged animal.

fore·front (**fôr′**frŭnt′) *n.* **1.** The part or area at the very front. **2.** The most important or most advanced position: *at the forefront in the fight against crime.*

fore·gath·er (fôr-**găth′**ər) *v.* Variant of **forgather.**

ă	pat	ôr	core
ā	pay	oi	boy
âr	care	ou	out
ä	father	o͝o	took
ĕ	pet	o͝or	lure
ē	be	o͞o	boot
ĭ	pit	ŭ	cut
ī	bite	ûr	urge
îr	pier	th	thin
ŏ	pot	*th*	this
ō	toe	zh	vision
ô	paw	ə	about

fore·go¹ (fôr-gō′) *tr.v.* **fore·went** (fôr-wĕnt′), **fore·gone** (fôr-gôn′), **fore·go·ing, fore·goes** (fôr-gōz′) To precede, as in time or place.

fore·go² (fôr-gō′) *v.* Variant of **forgo.**

fore·go·ing (fôr-gō′ĭng *or* fôr′gō′ĭng) *adj.* Said, written, or encountered just before; previous: *Refer to the foregoing figures.*

fore·gone *v.* (fôr-gôn′) Past participle of **forego¹.** ❖ *adj.* (fôr′gôn′) Having gone before; previous.

fore·ground (fôr′ground′) *n.* The part of a scene or picture that is nearest to and in front of the viewer.

fore·hand (fôr′hănd′) *n.* In sports, a stroke, as of a racket, made or done with the palm of the hand turned forward. —**fore′hand′** *adj.*

fore·head (fôr′hĕd′ *or* fôr′ĭd) *n.* The part of the face above the eyebrows.

for·eign (fôr′ĭn) *adj.* **1.** Located away from one's own country: *a foreign country.* **2.** Relating to or from another country or place: *a foreign language; foreign customs.* **3.** Conducted or involved with other nations or governments: *foreign trade.* **4.** Not naturally or normally belonging; alien: *Jealousy is foreign to my nature.* [From Middle English *forein*, from Late Latin *forānus*, on the outside.]

for·eign·er (fôr′ə-nər) *n.* **1.** A person from a foreign country or place: *Millions of foreigners have immigrated to the United States.* **2.** An outsider.

fore·know (fôr-nō′) *tr.v.* **fore·knew** (fôr-no͞o′), **fore·known** (fôr-nōn′), **fore·know·ing, fore·knows** To have knowledge of something before its existence or occurrence.

fore·knowl·edge (fôr-nŏl′ĭj *or* fôr′nŏl′ĭj) *n.* Knowledge of something before its occurrence or existence.

fore·leg (fôr′lĕg′) *n.* One of the front legs of a four-legged animal.

fore·limb (fôr′lĭm′) *n.* A front limb such as an arm, wing, foreleg, or flipper.

fore·lock (fôr′lŏk′) *n.* A lock of hair that grows from or falls on the forehead.

fore·man (fôr′mən) *n.* **1.** A man who has charge of a group of workers, as in a factory. **2.** A man who chairs and speaks for a jury.

fore·mast (fôr′məst *or* fôr′măst′) *n.* The forward mast on a sailing ship.

fore·most (fôr′mōst′) *adj.* First in time, place, rank, or position; most important or leading: *the world's foremost authority on the subject.* ❖ *adv.* In the first or front position.

fore·noon (fôr′no͞on′ *or* fôr-no͞on′) *n.* The period of time between sunrise and noon; morning.

fo·ren·sic (fə-rĕn′sĭk *or* fə-rĕn′zĭk) *adj.* **1.** Relating to, used in, or appropriate for courts of law or for public discussion. **2.** Relating to the techniques used in investigating facts or acquiring evidence, as in a criminal case: *a forensic laboratory.*

fore·or·dain (fôr′ôr-dān′) *tr.v.* **fore·or·dained, fore·or·dain·ing, fore·or·dains** To determine or appoint beforehand; predestine: *They believed their fate was foreordained.*

fore·part (fôr′pärt′) *n.* The first, early, or front part.

fore·paw (fôr′pô′) *n.* The paw of an animal's foreleg.

fore·quar·ter (fôr′kwôr′tər) *n.* The front part of a side of beef, lamb, or other animal carcass.

fore·run·ner (fôr′rŭn′ər) *n.* **1.** A person or thing that precedes, as in time; a predecessor: *Roller skates were the forerunners of skateboards.* **2.** A person who announces the coming of another; a herald. **3.** A warning sign or symptom: *A sore throat is often the forerunner of a cold.*

fore·sail (fôr′səl *or* fôr′sāl′) *n.* **1.** The principal sail on the foremast of a square-rigged ship. **2.** The principal fore-and-aft sail on the foremast of a fore-and-aft rigged vessel.

fore·see (fôr-sē′) *tr.v.* **fore·saw** (fôr-sô′), **fore·seen** (fôr-sēn′), **fore·see·ing, fore·sees** To see or know beforehand: *As the mountain got steeper, the hikers foresaw a difficult climb.* —**fore·see′a·ble** *adj.* —**fore·se′er** *n.*

fore·shad·ow (fôr-shăd′ō) *tr.v.* **fore·shad·owed, fore·shad·ow·ing, fore·shad·ows** To present an indication or suggestion of beforehand: *Everyone hoped that the border dispute did not foreshadow a wider war.*

fore·short·en (fôr-shôr′tn) *tr.v.* **fore·short·ened, fore·short·en·ing, fore·short·ens** To shorten the lines of (an object) in a drawing or painting so as to give the illusion of depth or distance.

fore·sight (fôr′sīt′) *n.* **1.** Perception of the importance and nature of events before they occur. **2.** Care in providing for the future: *Spending all of your money at once shows little foresight.* —**fore′sight′ed** *adj.*

fore·skin (fôr′skĭn′) *n.* The loose fold of skin that covers the end of the penis; the prepuce.

for·est (fôr′ĭst) *n.* **1.** A growth of trees and other plants covering a large area. **2.** A large number of objects bearing a similarity to such a growth, especially a dense collection of tall objects: *a forest of skyscrapers.* [From Middle English, from Medieval Latin *forestis (silva)*, outside (forest), from Latin *forīs*, outside.] —**for′es·ta′tion** *n.*

fore·stall (fôr-stôl′) *tr.v.* **fore·stalled, fore·stall·ing, fore·stalls 1.** To prevent, delay, or hinder by acting in advance: *ended the news conference to forestall any more questions.* **2.** To deal with or think of beforehand; anticipate. —**fore·stall′er** *n.*

for·est·er (fôr′ĭ-stər) *n.* A person trained in forestry.

for·est·ry (fôr′ĭ-strē) *n.* The science or work of cultivating, developing, and maintaining forests.

fore·taste (fôr′tāst′) *n.* A slight taste or sample of something to come: *Her first published story was a foretaste of later successful novels.*

fore·tell (fôr-tĕl′) *tr.v.* **fore·told** (fôr-tōld′), **fore·tell·ing, fore·tells** To tell or indicate beforehand; predict: *Can you foretell what will happen?*

fore·thought (fôr′thôt′) *n.* Thought, planning, or consideration for the future; foresight.

for·ev·er (fər-ĕv′ər) *adv.* **1.** For everlasting time; eternally: *No one can live forever.* **2.** At all times; incessantly: *The baby is forever fussing.* ❖ *n.* A seemingly very long time: *The bus is taking forever to come.*

for·ev·er·more (fər-ĕv′ər-môr′) *adv.* Forever.

fore·warn (fôr-wôrn′) *tr.v.* **fore·warned, fore·warn·ing, fore·warns** To warn in advance: *Dark clouds forewarned them of an approaching storm.*

fore·went (fôr-wĕnt′) *v.* Past tense of **forego¹.**

fore·wing (fôr′wĭng′) *n.* Either of a pair of front wings of a four-winged insect, such as a butterfly, dragonfly, or beetle.

fore·wom·an (fôr′wo͝om′ən) *n.* **1.** A woman who has charge of a group of workers, as in a factory. **2.** The woman who chairs and speaks for a jury.

fore·word (fôr′wərd) *n.* A preface or an introductory note, as for a book.

for·feit (fôr′fĭt) *tr.v.* **for·feit·ed, for·feit·ing, for·feits** To surrender or give up the right to (something) as a penalty or punishment for a crime, error, or offense: *By failing to appear, the opposing team forfeited the game.* ❖ *n.* **1.** Something surrendered or paid as a punishment or penalty. **2.** The act of forfeiting: *The team lost the game by forfeit.* [From Middle English *forfet*, crime, penalty, from Old French *forfaire*, to commit a crime, act outside the law.]

for·fei·ture (fôr′fĭ-cho͝or′ *or* fôr′fĭ-chər) *n.* **1.** The act of surrendering something as a forfeit. **2.** Something that is forfeited; a penalty.

for·gath·er also **fore·gath·er** (fôr-găth′ər) *intr.v.* **for·**

Gerald Ford
photographed in 1974

WORD BUILDING

fore– The prefix **fore–** means "before, in front." A *forerunner* is "one that goes before," and a *foreleg* is "a front leg of an animal." It is important not to confuse *fore–* with the prefix *for–*, which appears in many English words but is no longer used to form new words. *For–* bears the meaning of exclusion or rejection, and survives in words like *forbid* and *forget.*

forehand
Ryan Harrison of the United States

forelock

forget-me-not

formation

gath·ered, for·gath·er·ing, for·gath·ers To gather together; assemble.

for·gave (fər-gāv′ *or* fôr-gāv′) *v.* Past tense of **forgive.**

forge[1] (fôrj) *n.* A furnace or hearth where metal is heated so that it can be hammered into shape; a smithy. ❖ *tr.v.* **forged, forg·ing, forg·es 1.** To form (metal, for example) by heating in a forge and hammering into shape. **2.** To give form or shape to, especially by means of careful effort: *The coach forged a close relationship with her players.* **3.** To reproduce or copy for fraudulent purposes; counterfeit: *forge a signature.* [From Middle English, from Latin *fabrica*, from *faber*, worker.] **—forg′er** *n.*

forge[2] (fôrj) *intr.v.* **forged, forg·ing, forg·es 1.** To move forward gradually but steadily: *The explorers forged through the swamp.* **2.** To advance with an abrupt increase in speed: *forged into first place.* [Probably from *forge*, furnace.]

for·ger·y (fôr′jə-rē) *n., pl.* **for·ger·ies 1.** The act of forging, especially the illegal production of something counterfeit: *the forgery of a painting.* **2.** Something counterfeit, forged, or fraudulent.

for·get (fər-gĕt′ *or* fôr-gĕt′) *tr.v.* **for·got** (fər-gŏt′ *or* fôr-gŏt′), **for·got·ten** (fər-gŏt′n *or* fôr-gŏt′n) or **for·got, for·get·ting, for·gets 1.** To be unable to remember (something): *I forgot her email address. He completely forgot his lines in the play.* **2.** To fail to remember (to do something): *I forgot to give you the message.* **3.** To leave behind unintentionally: *I forgot my toothbrush.* ◆ **forget oneself** To lose one's reserve, temper, or self-restraint: *The bystanders forgot themselves and ran to ask the celebrity for an autograph.* [From Old English *forgytan.*] **—for·get′ta·ble** *adj.* **—for·get′ter** *n.*

for·get·ful (fər-gĕt′fəl *or* fôr-gĕt′fəl) *adj.* **1.** Tending or likely to forget: *When I am sleepy I can be forgetful.* **2.** Neglectful; thoughtless: *forgetful of one's responsibilities.* **—for·get′ful·ly** *adv.* **—for·get′ful·ness** *n.*

for·get-me-not (fər-gĕt′mē-nŏt′ *or* fôr-gĕt′mē-nŏt′) *n.* Any of various low-growing garden plants having clusters of small blue flowers.

for·give (fər-gĭv′ *or* fôr-gĭv′) *v.* **for·gave** (fər-gāv′ *or* fôr-gāv′), **for·giv·en** (fər-gĭv′ən *or* fôr-gĭv′ən), **for·giv·ing, for·gives** *—tr.* **1.** To excuse for a fault or offense; pardon: *Our friends forgave us for making them late.* **2.** To absolve from payment of (a debt, for example). *—intr.* To grant forgiveness: *A parent usually forgives easily.* [From Old English *forgiefan.*] **—for·giv′a·ble** *adj.* **—for·giv′er** *n.*

SYNONYMS **forgive, pardon, excuse, condone** These verbs mean to decide not to punish an offender. **Forgive** means to grant pardon without resentment: *He forgave you because he knew you didn't mean what you said.* **Pardon** means to free from a penalty: *After the revolution all political prisoners were pardoned.* **Excuse** means to forgive in effect by overlooking a mistake or fault: *Please excuse the children for their bad manners.* **Condone** means to excuse an offense, usually a serious one: *I cannot condone such horrible behavior by ignoring it.*

for·give·ness (fər-gĭv′nĭs *or* fôr-gĭv′nĭs) *n.* The act of forgiving; pardon.

for·giv·ing (fər-gĭv′ĭng *or* fôr-gĭv′ĭng) *adj.* Inclined or able to forgive: *a kind, forgiving person.*

for·go also **fore·go** (fôr-gō′) *tr.v.* **for·went** (fôr-wĕnt′), **for·gone** (fôr-gôn′ *or* fôr-gŏn′), **for·go·ing, for·goes** To give up; do without: *I will forgo the day at the beach and finish my work instead.*

for·got (fər-gŏt′ *or* fôr-gŏt′) *v.* Past tense and a past participle of **forget.**

for·got·ten (fər-gŏt′n *or* fôr-gŏt′n) *v.* A past participle of **forget.**

fo·rint (fôr′ĭnt′) *n., pl.* **forint** The basic monetary unit of Hungary.

fork (fôrk) *n.* **1.** A utensil with two or more prongs, used to serve or eat food. **2.** A large farm tool of similar shape, used to pick up hay or turn up ground. **3a.** The place where something, such as a stream or road, divides into two or more branches: *stood at the fork in the road.* **b.** One of the branches beginning at such a place: *the right fork of the road.* ❖ *v.* **forked, fork·ing, forks** *—tr.* **1.** To raise, carry, pitch, or pierce with a fork. **2.** *Informal* To pay: *forked over the money for the bill.* *—intr.* To divide into two or more branches: *The road forks beyond the hill.* [From Old English *forca*, from Latin *furca.*]

forked (fôrkt *or* fôr′kĭd) *adj.* Having a fork or forks; divided: *a forked river; a snake's forked tongue.*

fork·lift (fôrk′lĭft′) *n.* A small, power-operated, wheeled device having two flat prongs that can be slid under a load to be lifted and moved.

for·lorn (fər-lôrn′ *or* fôr-lôrn′) *adj.* **1.** Appearing sad or lonely because deserted or abandoned: *a forlorn puppy.* **2.** Wretched or pitiful in appearance or condition: *a forlorn shack.* [From Middle English *forloren*, past participle of *forlesen*, to abandon, from Old English *forlēosan.*] **—for·lorn′ly** *adv.*

form (fôrm) *n.* **1.** The shape and structure of an object: *the form of a snowflake.* **2.** The body or outward appearance of a person or animal; figure: *In the fog we could see two forms standing on the bridge.* **3.** The manner in which a thing exists, acts, or manifests itself: *an element usually found in the form of a gas.* **4.** A kind or sort: *What form of dessert did you make?* **5.** The manner in which an artistic, musical, or literary work is arranged or put together: *in sonata form; arranged my ideas in outline form.* **6.** A document with blanks that are to be filled in: *The patient's condition is recorded on a medical form.* **7.** Fitness or good condition of mind or body: *The athlete is in top form this season.* **8.** A mold for the setting of concrete. **9.** A grade in a British school or in some American private schools. **10.** One of the ways a word may be spelled or pronounced: *"Feet" is the plural form of "foot."* ❖ *v.* **formed, form·ing, forms** *—tr.* **1.** To give form to; shape: *form clay into figures.* **2.** To develop in the mind; conceive: *form an opinion.* **3.** To organize or arrange: *form a students' committee.* **4.** To come to have; develop or acquire: *form a bad habit.* **5a.** To produce (a tense, for example) by adding certain elements: *form a plural by adding an "s" to the singular.* **b.** To make (a word) by combining different word elements: *form a word by adding "-tion" to the root.* *—intr.* To come into being by taking form; arise: *Buds form in the spring.* [From Middle English *forme*, from Latin *fōrma.*]

for·mal (fôr′məl) *adj.* **1.** Relating to outward form rather than structure. **2.** Structured according to forms or conventions: *a formal meeting.* **3.** Executed, carried out, or done in proper or regular form: *a formal document.* **4.** Stiffly ceremonious: *a formal manner.* ❖ *n.* Something, such as a gown or a social affair, that is formal in nature. [From Middle English, from Latin *fōrma*, shape.] **—for′mal·ly** *adv.*

for·mal·de·hyde (fôr-măl′də-hīd′) *n.* A colorless gas with the formula CH_2O. It is used in making plastics, fertilizers, and building materials, and is mixed with water to form a solution for preserving biological specimens.

for·mal·ism (fôr′mə-lĭz′əm) *n.* Strict observance of accepted or recognized forms, as in religion or art.

for·mal·i·ty (fôr-măl′ĭ-tē) *n., pl.* **for·mal·i·ties 1.** Strict observance of accepted rules, forms, or customs: *There was no formality at our dinner table.* **2.** An established rule, form, or custom, especially one followed merely for the sake of procedure: *the legal formalities of a trial.*

for·mal·ize (fôr′mə-līz′) *tr.v.* **for·mal·ized, for·mal·iz·**

ă	pat	ôr	core
ā	pay	oi	boy
âr	care	ou	out
ä	father	o͝o	took
ĕ	pet	o͝or	lure
ē	be	o͞o	boot
ĭ	pit	ŭ	cut
ī	bite	ûr	urge
îr	pier	th	thin
ŏ	pot	*th*	this
ō	toe	zh	vision
ô	paw	ə	about

ing, for·mal·iz·es 1. To give a definite form or shape to: *formalize the style of a book report.* 2. To make formal or official: *They formalized the treaty by signing it.* —for′-mal·iz′er *n.*

for·mat (fôr′măt′) *n.* **1.** A plan for the organization or arrangement of something: *The format of the new television program was a series of interviews.* **2.** The form or layout of a publication: *the format of a newspaper.* **3.** The arrangement of computer data for storage or display. ❖ *tr.v.* **for·mat·ted, for·mat·ting, for·mats 1.** To plan or arrange in a specified form: *format a conference; formatted the document to have large margins.* **2.** To divide (a computer disk) into sectors so that it may store data.

for·ma·tion (fôr-mā′shən) *n.* **1.** The act or process of forming something or of taking form: *the formation of political parties.* **2a.** Something formed: *a cloud formation.* **b.** A layer of sediments or rocks that look alike and were formed at the same time. **3.** A specified arrangement: *The geese flew overhead in a V formation.*

for·ma·tive (fôr′mə-tĭv) *adj.* **1.** Forming or capable of forming: *Childhood experiences often have a formative influence on writers.* **2.** Relating to growth or development: *The growth of industry marked a formative period in the history of the United States.*

for·mer (fôr′mər) *adj.* **1.** Relating to or taking place in the past: *the tools of former civilizations; our former president.* **2.** Being the first of two mentioned.

for·mer·ly (fôr′mər-lē) *adv.* At an earlier time; once: *Machines do work formerly done by people.*

For·mi·ca (fôr-mī′kə) A trademark for several types of plastic sheets that are used especially as surfaces for tables and counters.

for·mi·da·ble (fôr′mĭ-də-bəl *or* fôr-mĭd′ə-bəl) *adj.* **1.** Frightening or difficult to undertake or deal with: *a formidable challenge; a formidable opponent.* **2.** Admirable; awe-inspiring: *a formidable musical talent.* [From Middle English, from Latin *formidāre*, to fear.] —**for′-mi·da·bil′i·ty** *n.* —**for′mi·da·bly** *adv.*

form·less (fôrm′lĭs) *adj.* **1.** Having no definite form; shapeless: *a formless mist.* **2.** Having no material existence: *a formless void.* —**form′less·ly** *adv.* —**form′less·ness** *n.*

For·mo·sa (fôr-mō′sə) See **Taiwan.**

for·mu·la (fôr′myə-lə) *n., pl.* **for·mu·las** or **for·mu·lae** (fôr′myə-lē′) **1.** An established set of words or symbols used in a ceremony or procedure. **2.** A set of symbols showing the composition of a chemical compound; for example, H_2O is the formula for water. **3.** A set of symbols in mathematics that expresses a rule or principle; for example, the formula for the area of a rectangle is $a = lw$, where a is the area, l the length, and w the width. **4.** A list of the ingredients and processes used in making something; a recipe: *the formula for making toothpaste.* **5.** A liquid food for infants, containing many of the nutrients in human milk. —**for′mu·la′ic** (fôr′myə-lā′ĭk) *adj.*

for·mu·late (fôr′myə-lāt′) *tr.v.* **for·mu·lat·ed, for·mu·lat·ing, for·mu·lates** To express in or as if in a formula; plan in an orderly way: *formulate a process; formulate an idea.* —**for′mu·la′tion** *n.*

for·sake (fôr-sāk′) *tr.v.* **for·sook** (fôr-so͝ok′), **for·sak·en** (fôr-sā′kən), **for·sak·ing, for·sakes 1.** To give up (something formerly held dear); renounce. **2.** To leave altogether; abandon: *Do not forsake us when we need help.* [From Old English *forsacan*.]

for·sooth (fôr-so͞oth′ *or* fər-so͞oth′) *adv.* In truth; indeed.

for·swear (fôr-swâr′) *tr.v.* **for·swore** (fôr-swôr′), **for·sworn** (fôr-swôrn′), **for·swear·ing, for·swears 1.** To decide or state that one will not or no longer engage in (an activity or habit, for example): *forswore violence.* **2.** To decide or state that one will not or no longer use or be associated with (something): *forswore junk food.*
◆ **be forsworn** To lie under oath; commit perjury. **forswear (oneself)** To lie under oath; commit perjury.

for·syth·i·a (fôr-sĭth′ē-ə *or* fər-sĭth′ē-ə) *n.* Any of several shrubs having yellow flowers that bloom in early spring. [After William *Forsyth* (1737–1804), Scottish horticulturist.]

fort (fôrt) *n.* A fortified place or position stationed with troops; a fortification. [From Middle English, strength, stronghold, from Latin *fortis*, strong.]

Fort-de-France (fôr-də-fräɴs′) The capital of Martinique, on the western coast of the island.

for·te[1] (fôr′tā′ *or* fôrt) *n.* Something in which a person excels; a strong point: *The trumpet player's forte was jazz.* [From Old French *fort*, strong, from Latin *fortis*.]

for·te[2] (fôr′tā′) *adv. & adj.* In music, in a loud forceful manner. [From Italian *forte*, strong, from Latin *fortis*.]

forth (fôrth) *adv.* **1.** Forward in time, place, or order: *from this time forth.* **2.** Out into view: *After the movie the audience poured forth from the theater.*
❑ *These sound alike:* **forth, fourth** (number).

forth·com·ing (fôrth-kŭm′ĭng) *adj.* **1.** About to appear or take place; approaching: *The authors gave an interview about their forthcoming book.* **2.** Available when required or as promised: *More funds were not forthcoming.*

forth·right (fôrth′rīt′) *adj.* Direct and without evasion; straightforward: *gave a forthright answer to my question.*

forth·with (fôrth-wĭth′ *or* fôrth-wĭth′) *adv.* At once; immediately.

for·ti·eth (fôr′tē-ĭth) *n.* **1.** The ordinal number matching the number 40 in a series. **2.** One of 40 equal parts.

for·ti·fi·ca·tion (fôr′tə-fĭ-kā′shən) *n.* **1.** The act or process of fortifying: *the fortification of the city against enemy invaders.* **2.** Something that fortifies or defends, especially military works erected to fortify a position or place.

for·ti·fy (fôr′tə-fī′) *tr.v.* **for·ti·fied, for·ti·fy·ing, for·ti·fies 1.** To strengthen and secure (a position) with fortifications: *They fortified the castle with a deep moat.* **2.** To strengthen physically; invigorate: *The hikers fortified themselves with a hearty breakfast.* **3.** To strengthen or improve (food, for example), as by adding vitamins; enrich. [From Middle English *fortifien*, from Late Latin *fortificāre*, from Latin *fortis*, strong.] —**for′ti·fi′er** *n.*

for·tis·si·mo (fôr-tĭs′ə-mō′) *adv. & adj.* In music, in a very loud manner.

for·ti·tude (fôr′tĭ-to͞od′) *n.* Strength of mind that allows one to deal with pain or adversity with courage.

fort·night (fôrt′nīt′) *n.* A period of two weeks.

fort·night·ly (fôrt′nīt′lē) *adj.* Appearing or happening once in or every two weeks. ❖ *adv.* Once every two weeks.

for·tress (fôr′trĭs) *n.* A fortified place, especially a large military stronghold.

for·tu·i·tous (fôr-to͞o′ĭ-təs) *adj.* **1.** Happening by accident or chance; unplanned. **2.** Lucky; fortunate: *A fortuitous change in the weather made the picnic possible.* [From Latin *fortuītus*.] —**for·tu′i·tous·ly** *adv.*

for·tu·nate (fôr′chə-nĭt) *adj.* **1.** Bringing something good and unforeseen. **2.** Having good fortune; lucky: *I am fortunate in having good friends.* [From Latin *fortūnātus*, from *fortūna*, chance.] —**for′tu·nate·ly** *adv.*

for·tune (fôr′chən) *n.* **1.** The chance happening of fortunate or adverse events; chance: *I had the good fortune to meet interesting people during my visit.* **2.** Extensive amounts of material possessions or wealth; riches. **3.** Destiny; fate: *told fortunes at the fair.* [From Middle English, from Latin *fortūna*.]

fortune cookie *n.* A cookie made from a thin layer of dough that is folded and baked around a slip of paper bearing a prediction of fortune or a maxim.

WRITERS CHOOSE THEIR WORDS

By the time Shirley and the angry one [Mabel] had gotten to their feet, all the other players had fled the scene. Shirley stood her ground, but it took all her courage not to run, too. Mabel was a **formidable** sight. She was the tallest and the strongest and the scariest girl in all of the fifth grade.

—Bette Bao Lord
In the Year of the Boar and Jackie Robinson

forsythia

Dian Fossey

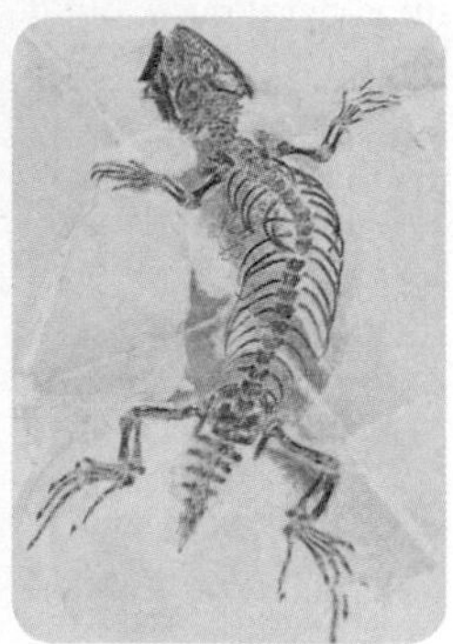
fossil

USAGE

founder[1] Because they have similar meanings, the verbs **founder[1]** and **flounder[1]** are often confused. *Founder* means "to come to ruin, fail utterly." It is used of plans and enterprises, such as businesses: *The effort to build a new ballpark has foundered. Flounder* means "to struggle or proceed with difficulty." It is usually used of people: *My friend has gotten a tutor because he is floundering in math.*

ă	pat	ôr	core
ā	pay	oi	boy
âr	care	ou	out
ä	father	o͝o	took
ĕ	pet	o͝or	lure
ē	be	o͞o	boot
ĭ	pit	ŭ	cut
ī	bite	ûr	urge
îr	pier	th	thin
ŏ	pot	*th*	this
ō	toe	zh	vision
ô	paw	ə	about

for·tune·tell·er (fôr′chən-tĕl′ər) *n.* A person who claims to predict future events. **—for′tune·tell′ing** *n.*

Fort Worth A city of northeast Texas west of Dallas. It was built on the site of a military post established in 1849.

for·ty (fôr′tē) *n., pl.* **for·ties** The number, written 40, that is equal to 4 × 10.

for·ty-nin·er (fôr′tē-**nī′**nər) *n.* A person who took part in the California gold rush of 1849.

fo·rum (fôr′əm) *n., pl.* **fo·rums 1.** The public square of an ancient Roman city, especially the public square of ancient Rome. **2.** A public meeting or presentation involving a discussion usually among experts and often including audience participation. **3.** A public medium for the discussion of ideas, such as a newspaper, radio program, or website. [From Middle English, from Latin.]

for·ward (fôr′wərd) *adj.* **1.** At, near, or belonging to the front of something: *the forward section of an airplane.* **2.** Going or moving toward the front: *a bad forward fall.* **3a.** Enthusiastically inclined: eager: *a forward student wanting to answer every question.* **b.** Lacking restraint or modesty; pushy or presumptuous: *I resented the clerk's forward manner in suggesting a choice.* **4.** Being ahead of current economic, political, or technological trends; progressive: *forward ideas about recycling.* ❖ *adv.* or **for·wards** (fôr′wərdz) **1.** Toward or tending to the front; frontward: *All volunteers please step forward.* **2.** In or toward the future: *I look forward to my vacation.* **3.** In the direction or sequence for normal use: *clicked forward through the slide show.* ❖ *n.* A player in certain sports, such as basketball or soccer, who is part of the front line of offense. ❖ *tr.v.* **for·ward·ed, for·ward·ing, for·wards 1.** To send on to a further destination or address: *forward letters to a new address.* **2.** To promote or advance: *forward one's own interests.* **—for′ward·ly** *adv.* **—for′ward·ness** *n.*

forward dive *n.* A dive in which the diver leaves the board facing the open water and rotates the body forward.

for·went (fôr-wĕnt′) *v.* Past tense of **forgo.**

Fos·sey (fŏs′ē), **Dian** 1932–1985. American zoologist whose studies of gorillas brought about a new understanding of the gorilla's behavior and habitat.

fos·sil (fŏs′əl) *n.* **1.** The hardened remains or imprint of an organism that lived long ago. Fossils are often found in layers of sedimentary rock and along the beds of rivers that flow through them. **2.** A person or thing that is regarded as old-fashioned or outdated. [From Latin *fossilis,* dug up, from *fossus,* past participle of *fodere,* to dig.]

fossil fuel *n.* A fuel that comes from the remains of organisms that lived millions of years ago and were buried in the earth. Petroleum, coal, and natural gas are examples of fossil fuels.

fos·sil·ize (fŏs′ə-līz′) *tr. & intr.v.* **fos·sil·ized, fos·sil·iz·ing, fos·sil·iz·es** To change into or become a fossil: *The shells of many prehistoric sea animals have fossilized in layers of rock.* **—fos′sil·i·za′tion** (fŏs′ə-lĭ-**zā′**shən) *n.*

fos·ter (fô′stər) *tr.v.* **fos·tered, fos·ter·ing, fos·ters 1.** To bring up; nurture: *foster a child.* **2.** To promote the development or growth of; cultivate: *The teacher fostered the students' interest in writing.* ❖ *adj.* Giving or receiving parental care or nurture to or from those not legally related: *a foster child; a foster parent.*

Fos·ter (fô′stər), **Stephen Collins** 1826–1864. American songwriter whose works, such as "Oh! Susannah" (1848), reflect the sentiment of pre-Civil War America.

fought (fôt) *v.* Past tense and past participle of **fight.**

foul (foul) *adj.* **foul·er, foul·est 1.** Offensive or unpleasant to the taste or smell: *the foul flavor of spoiled food; a foul smell of automobile exhaust.* **2.** Full of dirt or mud; dirty: *the foul fur of the stray dog.* See Synonyms at **dirty. 3.** Morally offensive; wicked: *foul rumors.* **4.** Bad or unfavorable: *foul weather.* **5.** Of a vulgar or obscene nature: *foul language.* **6.** In sports, contrary to the rules of a game: *A foul blow in boxing is one below the waist.* **7.** In baseball, outside the foul lines: *a foul fly ball.* ❖ *n.* **1.** In sports, a violation of the rules of play: *a foul in a game of basketball.* **2.** In baseball, a foul ball. ❖ *adv.* In a foul manner. ❖ *v.* **fouled, foul·ing, fouls** *—tr.* **1.** To make dirty or foul: *Factory smoke fouls the air.* **2.** To clog or obstruct: *Leaves fouled the drainpipe.* **3.** To entangle or catch (a rope, for example): *The dog fouled its leash in trying to get at the cat.* **4.** In sports, to commit a foul against (a player). **5.** In baseball, to hit (a ball) outside the foul lines. *—intr.* To become entangled or twisted: *The anchor line fouled on a rock.* ◆ **foul out 1.** In sports such as basketball, to be put out of a game for exceeding the number of permissible fouls. **2.** In baseball, to be put out by hitting a fly ball that is caught outside the foul lines. **foul up** To blunder or cause to blunder because of mistakes or poor judgment; botch: *I fouled up the recipe by adding too much milk.* [From Old English *fūl.*]

❑ *These sound alike:* **foul, fowl** (bird).

foul ball *n.* In baseball, a batted ball that touches the ground outside of fair territory.

foul line *n.* **1.** In baseball, one of two lines extending from home plate to the outfield barriers to indicate the area in which a fair ball can be hit. **2.** In basketball, a line 15 feet in front of the backboard from which a fouled player shoots a free throw. **3.** In sports, a boundary limiting the playing area, as in tennis or soccer.

foul play *n.* Unfair or treacherous action, especially when involving violence.

foul shot *n.* In basketball, an unobstructed shot from the foul line that is awarded to a player who has been fouled. It is scored as one point if successful.

foul-up (foul′ŭp′) *n.* **1.** A condition of confusion caused by mistakes or poor judgment. **2.** A mechanical failure.

found[1] (found) *tr.v.* **found·ed, found·ing, founds 1.** To originate or establish (something); create; set up: *founded the college in 1871.* See Synonyms at **establish. 2.** To establish the foundation or basis of: *found a report on concrete facts.* [From Middle English *founden,* from Latin *fundāre,* from *fundus,* bottom.]

found[2] (found) *tr.v.* **found·ed, found·ing, founds 1.** To melt (metal) and pour into a mold. **2.** To make (objects) by pouring molten material into a mold; cast. [From Middle English *founden,* from Latin *fundere.*]

found[3] (found) *v.* Past tense and past participle of **find.**

foun·da·tion (foun-**dā′**shən) *n.* **1.** The act of founding or establishing. **2.** The basis on which something stands, is founded, or is supported: *the foundations of modern science; the foundation of a building.* **3.** Funds for the support of an institution; an endowment. **4.** An institution that is founded and supported by an endowment. **5.** A cosmetic used as a base for facial makeup.

foun·der[1] (foun′dər) *intr.v.* **foun·dered, foun·der·ing, foun·ders 1.** To sink below the water: *The ship foundered in the gale.* **2.** To fail: *Their business foundered.* **3.** To stumble, especially to stumble and go lame: *The horse foundered on the muddy ground.* [From Middle English *fondren,* to sink to the ground, from Old French *fondrer,* from Latin *fundus,* bottom.] —SEE NOTE.

found·er[2] (foun′dər) *n.* A person who founds or establishes something: *the founders of the school; the founder of the theory.*

Found·ing Father (foun′dĭng) *n.* **1.** A member of the convention that drafted the US Constitution in 1787. **2. founding father** A man who founds or establishes something.

found·ling (found′lĭng) *n.* A deserted or abandoned child of unknown parentage.

foun·dry (foun′drē) *n., pl.* **foun·dries** A place where metals are cast and molded. [From French *fonderie,* from *fondre,* to cast, found, from Latin *fundere.*]

fount (fount) *n.* **1.** A fountain. **2.** A person or thing that initiates or dispenses; a source.

foun·tain (foun′tən) *n.* **1a.** An artificially created jet or stream of water. **b.** A structure, often decorative, from which such a jet or stream rises and flows: *the beautiful fountains of Rome; a drinking fountain.* **2.** A spring, especially the source of a stream. **3.** A device equipped with a nozzle that provides a stream of drinking water for public use. **4.** A point of origin; a source: *The zookeeper was a fountain of knowledge about animals.* [From Middle English, from Latin *fontānus,* of a spring, from *fōns,* spring.]

foun·tain·head (foun′tən-hĕd′) *n.* **1.** A spring that is the source of a stream. **2.** A chief source or an originator: *The old philosopher was a fountainhead of wisdom.*

fountain pen *n.* A pen having a refillable or replaceable ink reservoir that feeds ink to the writing point.

four (fôr) *n.* **1.** The number, written 4, that is equal to 3 + 1. **2.** The fourth in a set or sequence. **3.** Something having four parts or units, such as a musical quartet. ◆ **all fours** All four limbs of an animal or person: *crawled on all fours.* [From Old English *fēower.*]
❑ *These sound alike:* **four, for** (with the purpose of), **fore** (front part).

4-H Club (fôr′āch′) *n.* An organization for young people that offers instruction in agriculture and home economics. [From its four goals: to improve head, heart, hands, and health.]

four-leaf clover (fôr′lēf′) *n.* A clover leaf that has four leaflets instead of the usual three, considered a sign of good luck.

four-o'clock (fôr′ə-klŏk′) *n.* Any of several garden plants having variously colored flowers that have a funnel shape and open in the late afternoon.

401(k) (fôr′ō-wŭn kā′) *n.* A retirement plan in which a person invests a part of his or her wages in an account that is not taxed until he or she retires and takes money from it.

four-post·er (fôr′pō′stər) *n.* A bed with tall corner posts originally intended to support curtains or a canopy.

four·score (fôr′skôr′) *n.* Four times twenty; eighty.

four·some (fôr′səm) *n.* **1.** A group of four people or things, especially two couples. **2.** An activity involving four people, such as a golf match.

four·square (fôr′skwâr′) *adj.* **1.** Having four equal sides and four right angles; square. **2.** Firm and unwavering; forthright: *a foursquare refusal to yield.* ❖ *adv.* In a forthright manner; squarely. ❖ *n.* A game in which each of four players stands in one of four boxes drawn on the ground in a two-by-two grid and must bounce a ball into another player's box without holding the ball or stepping out of bounds.

four·teen (fôr-tēn′) *n.* **1.** The number, written 14, that is equal to 13 + 1. **2.** The 14th in a set or sequence.

four·teenth (fôr-tēnth′) *n.* **1.** The ordinal number matching the number 14 in a series. **2.** One of 14 equal parts.

fourth (fôrth) *n.* **1.** The ordinal number matching the number four in a series. **2.** One of four equal parts. **3a.** The interval covering four tones in a musical scale, as C, D, E, and F. **b.** The fourth tone in a musical scale; the subdominant. **4.** The transmission gear used to produce speeds next higher than those of third in a motor vehicle. **5. Fourth** The Fourth of July; Independence Day: *went to a parade on the Fourth.*
❑ *These sound alike:* **fourth, forth** (forward).

fourth dimension *n.* In physics, time regarded as a dimension along with the three spatial dimensions of length, width, and height.

fourth estate *n.* Journalists considered as a group.

Fourth of July *n.* Independence Day.

four-wheel drive (fôr′wēl′) *n.* An automotive drive system in which mechanical power is transmitted from the drive shaft to all four wheels.

fowl (foul) *n., pl.* **fowl** or **fowls 1a.** A chicken or related bird, such as a duck or turkey. **b.** The meat of any of these birds used as food. **2.** A bird of any kind: *a diet of fish and fowl.* [From Old English *fugel.*]
❑ *These sound alike:* **fowl, foul** (rotten).

fox (fŏks) *n.* **1.** *pl.* **fox·es** also **fox** Any of various meat-eating mammals related to the dogs and wolves, having a pointed snout, upright ears, and a long bushy tail. **2.** The fur of any of these mammals. **3.** A crafty, clever, or sly person: *The old fox outwitted everyone.*

Fox *n.* **1.** A member of a Native American people formerly inhabiting parts of Michigan, Wisconsin, Illinois, and Iowa, now living in Iowa and Oklahoma. **2.** The Algonquian language of the Fox.

Fox (fŏks), **Vicente** Born 1942. Mexican politician who served as president (2000–2006).

fox·glove (fŏks′glŭv′) *n.* Any of several plants having a long cluster of tubular purplish, yellow, or white flowers, used as a source of digitalis.

fox·hole (fŏks′hōl′) *n.* A shallow pit dug by a soldier for protection in combat.

fox·hound (fŏks′hound′) *n.* Any of various short-haired dogs originally developed for fox hunting.

fox terrier *n.* Any of various small terriers having a smooth or wiry white coat with black and tan markings, originally used to drive foxes from their burrows.

fox·trot (fŏks′trŏt′) *intr.v.* **fox·trot·ted, fox·trot·ting, fox·trots** To dance the fox trot.

fox trot *n.* **1.** A ballroom dance in 4/4 time, consisting of a combination of fast and slow steps. **2.** The music for this dance.

fox·y (fŏk′sē) *adj.* **fox·i·er, fox·i·est** Slyly clever; crafty: *a foxy scheme.* —**fox′i·ly** *adv.* —**fox′i·ness** *n.*

foy·er (foi′ər *or* foi′ā′) *n.* **1.** A lobby or anteroom, as of a theater or hotel. **2.** An entrance hall, as of a private house or apartment.

fpm *abbr.* An abbreviation of feet per minute.

fps *abbr.* An abbreviation of: **1.** feet per second. **2.** frames per second.

Fr The symbol for the element **francium.**

fr. *abbr.* An abbreviation of from.

Fr. *abbr.* An abbreviation of father (religious title).

fra·cas (frā′kəs *or* frăk′əs) *n.* A noisy, disorderly fight or quarrel.

frack·ing (frăk′ĭng) *n.* Hydraulic fracturing.

frac·tal (frăk′təl) *n.* A geometric pattern repeated at ever smaller scales and used especially in computer modeling of irregular patterns and structures in nature.

frac·tion (frăk′shən) *n.* **1.** A number that is written in the form $^a/_b$, where *a* and *b* are whole numbers and *b* is not zero. Fractions are used to compare parts to a whole, as in *Joe ate ¼ of the cake.* **2.** A small part or bit of something: *The dress was on sale for a fraction of the original price.* —SEE NOTE AT **fragile.**

frac·tion·al (frăk′shə-nəl) *adj.* **1.** Relating to or composed of a fraction or fractions. **2.** Very small; insignificant: *a fractional share of the popular vote.* —**frac′tion·al·ly** *adv.*

frac·tious (frăk′shəs) *adj.* **1.** Likely to make trouble; unruly. **2.** Cross; peevish; cranky. —**frac′tious·ly** *adv.*

frac·ture (frăk′chər) *n.* **1.** The act or process of breaking: *enough pressure to cause the fracture of solid rock.* **2.** A break, rupture, or crack, as in bone. ❖ *tr. & intr.v.* **frac·tured, frac·tur·ing, frac·tures** To break or cause

foxglove

fox terrier

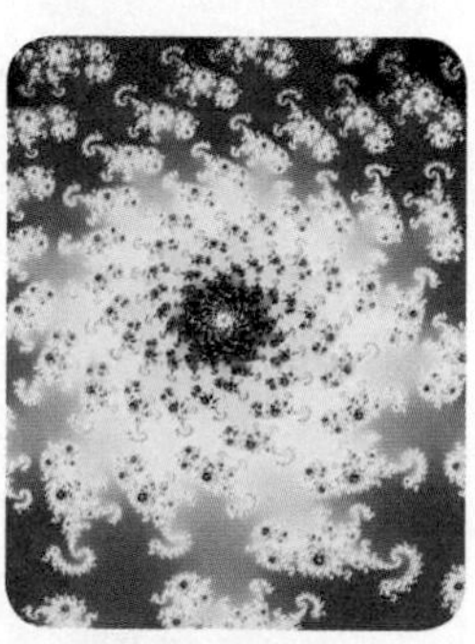

fractal

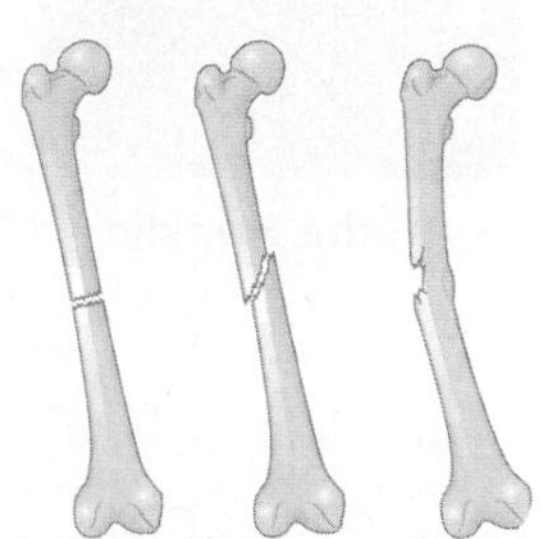

fracture
various types of leg bone fractures

WORD BUILDING

fragile The word root *frag–* in English words comes from a form of the Latin verb *frangere,* "to break." That verb gave rise to the Latin adjective *fragilis,* "breakable," the source of our **fragile.** The same Latin adjective became *frele* in Old French, from which we get the word **frail.** The past participle of *frangere* was *frāctus,* from which the Latin nouns *frāctiō,* "a breaking," and *frāctūra,* "a break," were formed. From these words we get **fraction** and **fracture.**

Anne Frank
photographed in 1942

Aretha Franklin

ă	pat	ôr	core
ā	pay	oi	boy
âr	care	ou	out
ä	father	o͝o	took
ĕ	pet	o͝or	lure
ē	be	o͞o	boot
ĭ	pit	ŭ	cut
ī	bite	ûr	urge
îr	pier	th	thin
ŏ	pot	*th*	this
ō	toe	zh	vision
ô	paw	ə	about

to break: *I fractured my arm in the fall. The foundation of the building fractured in the earthquake.* See Synonyms at **break.** —SEE NOTE AT **fragile.**

frag·ile (frăj′əl *or* frăj′īl′) *adj.* **1.** Easily damaged or broken; frail: *a fragile glass vase.* **2.** Lacking physical or emotional strength; delicate. **3.** Lacking substance; flimsy: *a fragile claim.* [From Latin *fragilis,* from *frangere,* to break.] **—frag′ile·ly** *adv.* **—fra·gil′i·ty** (frə-jĭl′ĭ-tē) *n.* —SEE NOTE.

frag·ment (frăg′mənt) *n.* **1.** A small part that is broken off or detached from a whole: *a fragment of a shattered china plate.* **2.** An incomplete or isolated portion; a bit: *We could overhear fragments of their conversation.* ❖ *tr. & intr.v.* (frăg′mĕnt′) **frag·ment·ed, frag·ment·ing, frag·ments** To break or become broken into fragments: *An explosion had fragmented the sinking ship. After the election, the committee fragmented.* —SEE NOTE AT **fragile.**

frag·men·tar·y (frăg′mən-tĕr′ē) *adj.* Consisting of small disconnected parts: *Only fragmentary sentences of the damaged document were legible.*

frag·men·ta·tion (frăg′mən-tā′shən) *n.* The act or process of fragmenting or breaking into pieces: *the fragmentation of rocks under pressure.*

fra·grance (frā′grəns) *n.* **1.** A sweet or pleasant odor; a scent: *the fresh fragrance of pine.* **2.** A substance, such as a perfume, designed to give off a pleasant odor.

fra·grant (frā′grənt) *adj.* Having a pleasant odor; sweet-smelling: *a fragrant flower garden.* **—fra′grant·ly** *adv.*

frail (frāl) *adj.* **frail·er, frail·est 1.** Physically weak; not robust. **2.** Easily broken or destroyed; fragile: *a flower with a frail stem.* **3.** Easily led astray; morally weak. [From Middle English *frele,* from Old French, from Latin *fragilis,* from *frangere,* to break.] **—frail′ness** *n.* —SEE NOTE AT **fragile.**

frail·ty (frāl′tē) *n., pl.* **frail·ties 1.** The quality or condition of being frail; weakness. **2.** A fault arising from human weakness: *Envy is a common human frailty.*

frame (frām) *n.* **1a.** A structure that shapes or supports: *the frame of a car.* **b.** An open structure or rim used to encase, hold, or border: *a door frame; a picture frame.* **c.** The structure of a human or animal body: *a lanky frame.* **2.** A general structure or system: *the frame of government.* **3.** A round of play in some games, such as bowling. **4a.** One of the set of still images that makes up a film or video. **b.** An individual drawing within a comic strip or graphic novel. **5.** A rectangular area in which text or graphics can be shown, especially one of several rectangular areas on a web page displaying different documents simultaneously. ❖ *tr.v.* **framed, fram·ing, frames 1.** To build by putting together the structural parts of: *frame an agreement; frame a house.* **2.** To enclose in a frame: *frame a picture.* **3.** To put into words, especially in a way that does not acknowledge another point of view: *The questionnaire framed the question to get a favorable response.* **4.** *Informal* To make up evidence so as to incriminate (someone) falsely: *The witness was paid to frame an innocent bystander.* **—fram′a·ble, frame′a·ble** *adj.* **—fram′er** *n.*

frame-up (frām′ŭp′) *n. Informal* A plot to incriminate an innocent person.

frame·work (frām′wûrk′) *n.* **1.** A structure that shapes or supports; a frame: *The building was constructed on a framework of steel girders.* **2.** A fundamental structure, as for a written work or a system of ideas: *Education is the framework on which to build a productive life.* **3.** A set of assumptions, concepts, values, and practices that constitutes a way of viewing or thinking about something.

franc (frăngk) *n.* **1.** The former basic monetary unit of Belgium, France, and Luxembourg. **2.** The basic monetary unit of Mali, Niger, Switzerland, and many other countries. [From Middle English *frank,* from Old French *franc,* from Medieval Latin *Francōrum rēx,* king of the Franks (from the legend on the first of these coins).]

❑ *These sound alike:* **franc, frank¹** (sincere), **frank²** (frankfurter).

France (frăns) A country of western Europe northeast of Spain and southwest of Germany. Founded as a Frankish kingdom after the collapse of the Roman Empire, it became a republic after a revolution in 1789. After several periods of monarchy in the 1800s, France returned to democratic rule in 1870. Paris is the capital.

fran·chise (frăn′chīz′) *n.* **1.** The right to vote; suffrage: *In earlier times only landowners had the franchise.* **2a.** Authorization that is granted to someone to sell or distribute a company's goods or services in a certain area: *The franchise for collecting trash in the town was awarded to a private company.* **b.** A business or group of businesses established or operated under such authorization. **c.** A professional sports team: *Our town does not have a baseball franchise.* ❖ *tr.v.* **fran·chised, fran·chis·ing, fran·chis·es** To grant a franchise to (someone).

Fran·cis (frăn′sĭs) Born 1936. Pope (elected 2013).

Fran·cis·can (frăn-sĭs′kən) *n.* A member of a Roman Catholic order established in 1209 by Saint Francis of Assisi (1182?–1226) and dedicated to the virtues of humility and poverty.

fran·ci·um (frăn′sē-əm) *n. Symbol* **Fr** A radioactive element that has been artificially produced by scientists. The half-life of its longest-lived isotope is about 22 minutes. Atomic number 87. See **Periodic Table.**

Fran·co (frăng′kō *or* fräng′kō), **Francisco** 1892–1975. Spanish political leader who directed the rebel armed forces in the Spanish Civil War (1936–1939) and ruled the country as dictator from 1939 to 1975.

Fran·co·phone also **fran·co·phone** (frăng′kə-fōn′) *n.* A person who speaks French, especially in a country or region where at least one other language besides French is spoken. **—Fran′co·phone′** *adj.*

frank¹ (frăngk) *adj.* **frank·er, frank·est** Open and sincere in expression; straightforward: *made several frank remarks about the quality of their work.* ❖ *tr.v.* **franked, frank·ing, franks 1.** To put an official mark on (mail) so that it can be sent free of charge. **2.** To send (mail) free of charge. ❖ *n.* **1.** A mark placed on a piece of mail to indicate the right to send it free of charge. **2.** The right to send mail free of charge. [From Middle English *franc,* free, open, from Late Latin *Francus,* a Frank.] **—frank′ness** *n.*

❑ *These sound alike:* **frank¹** (sincere), **franc** (money), **frank²** (frankfurter).

frank² (frăngk) *n. Informal* A frankfurter. [From *frankfurter.*]

❑ *These sound alike:* **frank²** (frankfurter), **franc** (money), **frank¹** (sincere).

Frank (frăngk) *n.* A member of a Germanic tribe that conquered Gaul around AD 500 and established a large empire. [From Old English *Franca,* from Late Latin *Francus,* of Germanic origin.]

Frank (frăngk *or* frängk), **Anne** 1929–1945. German Jewish diarist who fled from Nazi Germany to Amsterdam with her family (1933) and kept a diary during her years in hiding (1942–1944). She died of typhus in a concentration camp in 1945. Her diary was published in 1947.

Frank·fort (frăngk′fərt) The capital of Kentucky, in the north-central part of the state northwest of Lexington. It was chosen as capital in 1792.

Frank·furt (frănk′fərt *or* frängk′fo͝ort′) A city of west-central Germany southeast of Cologne. It was founded in the first century BC by the Romans.

frank·furt·er (frăngk′fər-tər) *n.* A sausage usually made of beef or beef and pork. [After *Frankfurt,* Germany.]

frank·in·cense (frăng′kĭn-sĕns′) *n.* A fragrant gum

resin obtained from certain African and Asian trees, used as incense and in perfumes.

Frank·ish (frăng′kĭsh) *adj.* Relating to the Franks or their language. ❖ *n.* The West Germanic language of the Franks.

Frank·lin (frăngk′lĭn), **Aretha** Born 1942. American singer known for her recordings of soul and gospel music. Her popular songs include "Respect" (1967) and "Chain of Fools" (1968).

Franklin, Benjamin 1706–1790. American public official, scientist, inventor, and writer who published *Poor Richard's Almanac* (1732–1757). Franklin signed the Treaty of Paris ending the American Revolution (1783) and helped draft the Constitution (1787–1789). His experiments with electricity and his invention of the lightning rod earned him international fame as a scientist.

frank·ly (frăngk′lē) *adv.* **1.** In a frank manner; candidly: *Speaking frankly, the principal warned the students about their bad behavior.* **2.** Honestly; in truth: *Frankly, I don't know.*

fran·tic (frăn′tĭk) *adj.* Very excited with fear or anxiety; desperate; frenzied: *frantic with worry.* [From Middle English *frenetik*, from Latin *phrenēticus*, frenetic, from Greek *phrenītis*, inflammation of the brain.] **—fran′ti·cal·ly** *adv.* **—fran′tic·ness** *n.*

frappe (frăp) *n.* A milkshake.

frap·pé (fră-pā′) *n.* A fruit drink served almost frozen or poured over crushed ice.

fra·ter·nal (frə-tûr′nəl) *adj.* **1a.** Relating to brothers: *a close fraternal tie.* **b.** Showing comradeship: *a fraternal greeting.* **2.** Relating to or consisting of a fraternity: *The Masons are a fraternal society.* **3.** Relating to twins that develop from egg cells that have been fertilized by two different sperm. Fraternal twins, in contrast to identical twins, can be of different sexes and do not share all of the same genes. **—fra·ter′nal·ly** *adv.*

fra·ter·ni·ty (frə-tûr′nĭ-tē) *n., pl.* **fra·ter·ni·ties 1.** A group of people associated or linked by similar interests, backgrounds, or occupations: *the local business fraternity; the medical fraternity.* **2.** A social organization at a college or university, traditionally consisting of male students. **3.** The quality or condition of being brothers.

frat·er·nize (frăt′ər-nīz′) *intr.v.* **frat·er·nized, frat·er·niz·ing, frat·er·niz·es 1.** To associate with others in a brotherly or friendly way: *Teachers and students fraternize in the cafeteria.* **2.** To associate on friendly terms with the people of an enemy or opposing group. **—frat′er·ni·za′tion** (frăt′ər-nĭ-zā′shən) *n.*

frat·ri·cide (frăt′rĭ-sīd′) *n.* **1.** The killing of one's brother or sister. **2.** Someone who kills his or her brother or sister. **—frat′ri·cid′al** *adj.*

Frau (frou) *n., pl.* **Frau·en** (**frou′**ən) Used as a title in a German-speaking area before the surname or professional title of a woman.

fraud (frôd) *n.* **1.** Deception carried out in order to get something, usually money or property, from someone: *a government agency with the purpose of protecting consumers against fraud in advertising.* **2.** A person who tries to deceive others, especially by claiming to have abilities that he or she does not possess. [From Middle English *fraude*, from Latin *fraus*.]

fraud·u·lent (frô′jə-lənt) *adj.* Relating to, gained by, or engaging in fraud: *a fraudulent scheme; a fraudulent merchant.* **—fraud′u·lence** *n.* **—fraud′u·lent·ly** *adv.*

fraught (frôt) *adj.* Filled with something specified; charged: *an incident fraught with danger.*

Fräu·lein (froi′līn′ *or* **frou′**līn′) *n., pl.* **Fräulein** Used as a title for an unmarried woman or a girl in a German-speaking area.

fray[1] (frā) *n.* A scuffle; a brawl: *Several bystanders were caught up in the fray.* [From Middle English *frai*, shortening of *affrai*, from Old French *esfraier*, to disturb.]

fray[2] (frā) *v.* **frayed, fray·ing, frays** *—tr.* **1.** To wear away (the edges of fabric, for example) by rubbing. **2.** To strain; chafe: *The constant noise of traffic frayed the driver's nerves.* *—intr.* To become worn away or tattered along the edges. [From Middle English *fraien*, to wear, bruise, from Latin *fricāre*, to rub.]

fraz·zle (frăz′əl) *Informal v.* **fraz·zled, fraz·zling, fraz·zles** *—tr.* **1.** To wear away along the edges; fray. **2.** To exhaust physically or emotionally: *frazzled by hard work and pressure.* *—intr.* To become frazzled. ❖ *n.* **1.** A frayed or tattered condition. **2.** A condition of exhaustion: *The long perilous climb wore us to a frazzle.*

freak (frēk) *n.* **1.** A thing or occurrence that is markedly unusual or irregular: *The summer snowstorm was a freak of nature.* **2.** *Slang* An enthusiast: *a movie freak; a running freak.* ❖ *adj.* Highly unusual or irregular: *a freak accident.*

freak·ish (frē′kĭsh) *adj.* Markedly abnormal or unusual; strange: *freakish warm weather in winter.* **—freak′ish·ly** *adv.*

freck·le (frĕk′əl) *n.* Any of the small brownish spots on the skin that often turn darker or increase in number when the skin is exposed to the sun. ❖ *tr. & intr.v.* **freck·led, freck·ling, freck·les** To mark or become marked with freckles or spots of color. [From Middle English *frakles*, freckles, alteration of *fraknes*, probably of Scandinavian origin.]

Fred·er·ick II (frĕd′rĭk *or* **frĕd′**ər-ĭk) Known as "Frederick the Great." 1712–1786. King of Prussia (1740–1786) who was successful in the Seven Years' War (1756–1763) and brought Prussia great military prestige in Europe.

Fred·er·ic·ton (frĕd′rĭk-tən *or* **frĕd′**ər-ĭk-tən) The capital of New Brunswick, Canada, in the south-central part of the province northwest of Halifax, Nova Scotia. It became the capital in 1785.

free (frē) *adj.* **fre·er, fre·est 1.** Not imprisoned or confined; at liberty. **2.** Not controlled or enslaved by another person: *You're free to go.* **3a.** Having political independence: *a free country.* **b.** Not subject to arbitrary interference by a government: *a free press.* **4a.** Not affected by a given condition or circumstance: *free of germs; free from worry.* **b.** Not subject to taxes or other charges; exempt: *Medicine is free of sales tax.* **5.** Not literal or exact: *a free translation.* **6.** Costing nothing; gratuitous: *a free meal.* **7.** Unobstructed; clear: *a free lane.* **8a.** Not occupied or used: *free space.* **b.** Not taken up by scheduled activities: *a free hour at lunchtime.* **9.** Unguarded in expression or manner; frank. **10.** Liberal or lavish: *very free with the inherited money.* **11.** In chemistry, not combined with something else: *Oxygen exists free in air.* ❖ *adv.* **1.** In a free manner; without restraint: *The rope swung free.* **2.** Without charge: *We were admitted free.* ❖ *tr.v.* **freed, free·ing, frees 1.** To make free, as from confinement or oppression: *The convict was freed from prison.* **2.** To relieve of a burden, obligation, or restraint: *Vacation frees us from daily jobs for a short time.* **3.** To unfasten or untangle; detach: *We freed the rope caught on a nail.* ◆ **for free** *Informal* Without charge: *I used a coupon to get tickets for free.* [From Old English *frēo*.] **—free′ly** *adv.* **—free′ness** *n.*

free·boot·er (frē′bo͞o′tər) *n.* A person who plunders, especially a pirate. [From Dutch *vrijbuiter* : *vrij*, free + *buit*, booty.]

freed·man (frēd′mən) *n.* A man who has been freed from slavery.

free·dom (frē′dəm) *n.* **1.** The condition of not being in captivity: *After ten years in prison, he regained his freedom.* **2.** The condition of being free from restraints; the power to act without restraint: *freedom of assembly.* **3.** The ability of a country or group to govern itself; political independence. **4.** The capacity to exercise choice; free will: *the freedom to do what we want.* **5.** Frankness

Benjamin Franklin
c. 1785 portrait by Joseph Siffred Duplessis (1725–1802)

freckle

WORD HISTORY

French The foreign language that has had the most influence on English is probably **French**. Perhaps 60 percent of our common, everyday vocabulary comes from French, including such words as *aim, car, chief, gain, guard, hour, quite, real, sure, use,* and *very.* French was the language of the English royal court for close to 200 years during the Middle Ages. English people outside the nobility would use French words whenever they wanted to sound fancy, a pattern that has continued into modern times. Many of the older French borrowings into English, however, have been around so long now that they no longer seem fancy, like the ones listed above. Others, like *cordial* and *vale,* still have a formal or poetic flavor.

French curve

ă	pat	ôr	core
ā	pay	oi	boy
âr	care	ou	out
ä	father	ŏŏ	took
ĕ	pet	ŏŏr	lure
ē	be	ōō	boot
ĭ	pit	ŭ	cut
ī	bite	ûr	urge
îr	pier	th	thin
ŏ	pot	*th*	this
ō	toe	zh	vision
ô	paw	ə	about

or boldness; lack of reserve: *a casual freedom in their manner.* **6.** Ease or facility of movement: *The paved paths gave us the freedom to skateboard throughout the park.* **7.** The use of or access to something: *Investigators were given the freedom of the files.*

freedom of speech *n.* The right to express any opinion in public without censorship or restraint by the government. The freedom of speech is protected in the United States as a right under the First Amendment to the US Constitution.

freedom rider *n.* One of a group of civil rights activists in the early 1960s who rode buses through parts of the southern United States for the purpose of challenging racial segregation.

freed·wom·an (frēd′wŏŏm′ən) *n.* A woman who has been freed from slavery.

free enterprise *n.* The freedom of private businesses to operate competitively for profit with minimal government regulation.

free fall *n.* **1.** The fall of a body toward the earth without any force restraining it other than the drag produced by the atmosphere. **2.** Rapid, uncontrolled decline: *the news sent the company's stock price into a free fall.*

free-for-all (frē′fər-ôl′) *n.* A disorderly fight, argument, or competition in which everyone present participates.

free·hand (frē′hănd′) *adj.* Drawn by hand without the aid of tracing or drafting tools. —**free′hand′** *adv.*

free kick *n.* In soccer and rugby, a kick of a stationary ball that a referee grants to one team after the other team has committed a foul or violated a rule.

free·lance (frē′lăns′) *intr.v.* **free·lanced, free·lanc·ing, free·lanc·es** To work as a freelancer: *a journalist who freelances.* —**free′lance** *adv. & adj.*

free·lanc·er (frē′lăn′sər) *n.* A person who sells his or her services to employers without a long-term commitment.

free·man (frē′mən) *n.* **1.** A person not in slavery or serfdom. **2.** A person who possesses the rights and privileges of a citizen.

Free·ma·son (frē′mā′sən) *n.* A member of the Free and Accepted Masons, an international fraternal and charitable organization.

Free·ma·son·ry (frē′mā′sən-rē) *n.* The institutions, precepts, and rites of the Freemasons.

free-range (frē′rānj′) *adj.* Relating to or produced by animals, especially poultry, that range freely for food rather than being confined: *free-range eggs.*

free-soil (frē′soil′) *adj.* **1.** Prohibiting slavery: *free-soil states.* **2. Free-Soil** Relating to or being a US political party founded in 1848 to oppose the spread of slavery into US Territories and the admission of slave states into the Union.

free speech *n.* **1.** Freedom of speech. **2.** Speech protected by the law from being restrained or curtailed by the government.

free·stand·ing (frē′stăn′dĭng) *adj.* Standing without support or attachment; able to stand alone: *a freestanding garage.*

Free State *n.* Any state of the Union in which slavery was illegal before the Civil War.

free·stone (frē′stōn′) *n.* A fruit, such as a peach or apricot, having flesh that separates easily from the pit.

free·style (frē′stīl′) *n.* **1.** A rapid swimming stroke performed face down with alternating overarm strokes and a flutter kick; the crawl. **2.** A competitive sports event in which any style, maneuver, or movement may be used by the competitor. —**free′style′** *adv. & adj.*

free·think·er (frē′thĭng′kər) *n.* A person who forms opinions independently and does not follow traditional dogma, especially in matters of religion. —**free′think′ing** *adj. & n.*

free throw *n.* A foul shot in basketball.

Free·town (frē′toun′) The capital of Sierra Leone, in the western part of the country on the Atlantic Ocean. It was settled in 1792 by freed slaves from England.

free verse *n.* Poetry that does not have a regular meter or rhyme scheme.

free·ware (frē′wâr′) *n.* Free software, usually available over the Internet.

free·way (frē′wā′) *n.* A highway for high-speed travel, having several lanes.

free·wheel·ing (frē′wē′lĭng) *adj.* Free of restraints or limits; acting freely: *freewheeling advertising campaigns.*

free·will (frē′wĭl′) *adj.* Done of one's own accord; voluntary.

free will *n.* The power to make free choices that are not limited by people or things beyond one's control.

freeze (frēz) *v.* **froze** (frōz), **fro·zen** (frō′zən), **freez·ing, freez·es** —*intr.* **1.** To change from a liquid to a solid by loss of heat: *Pure water freezes at a higher temperature than salt water.* **2.** To have ice form in or on: *The pond freezes early in winter. The pipes froze.* **3.** To be harmed or killed by cold or frost: *Many fruits freeze in very cold weather.* **4.** To be or feel very cold: *We froze without sweaters.* **5.** To stop functioning, usually temporarily: *The computer screen froze when I opened the infected program.* **6.** To become motionless or unable to move: *The climber froze with fear on the slippery rocks.* —*tr.* **1.** To convert (a liquid substance) into ice. **2.** To cause ice to form upon: *The cold snap froze the river.* **3.** To preserve (food, for example) by subjecting to a freezing temperature: *freeze vegetables.* **4.** To harm or kill by cold: *The deep cold froze the oranges.* **5.** To make very cold: *The winter wind froze my fingers.* **6.** To make motionless or unable to move: *Fear froze the deer in the beam of our lights.* **7.** To keep (prices or wages) from changing: *The company froze wages at last year's levels.* ❖ *n.* **1a.** The act of freezing: *a freeze on hiring.* **b.** The state of being frozen: *a price freeze.* **2.** A period of cold weather; a frost: *crops ruined by the early freeze.* ◆ **freeze out** To shut out or exclude, as by cold or unfriendly treatment: *large chain stores that freeze out small merchants.* [From Old English *frēosan.*]

❑ *These sound alike:* **freeze, frieze** (horizontal band).

freeze-dry (frēz′drī′) *tr.v.* **freeze-dried, freeze-dry·ing, freeze-dries** To preserve (food, for example) by rapid freezing and drying in a vacuum.

freez·er (frē′zər) *n.* A refrigerated compartment that is kept at a very low temperature for freezing and storing items that spoil easily, especially food.

freez·ing point (frē′zĭng) *n.* The temperature at which a liquid freezes.

freight (frāt) *n.* **1.** Goods carried as cargo by truck, train, ship, or aircraft. **2a.** Commercial transportation of goods. **b.** The charge for transporting goods. **3.** A railway train carrying goods only. ❖ *tr.v.* **freight·ed, freight·ing, freights 1.** To transport commercially as cargo. **2.** To load or fill with cargo: *ships waiting to be freighted.* [From Middle English *fraught,* from Middle Dutch or Middle Low German *vracht, vrecht.*]

freight car *n.* A railroad car designed to carry freight.

freight·er (frā′tər) *n.* **1.** A vehicle, especially a ship, for carrying freight. **2.** A shipper of cargo.

freight train *n.* A railroad train made up of an engine and freight cars.

Fré·mont (frē′mŏnt′), **John Charles** 1813–1890. American explorer and politician who mapped much of the American West and Northwest.

French (frĕnch) *adj.* Relating to France or its people, language, or culture. ❖ *n.* **1.** *(used with a plural verb)* The people of France. **2.** The Romance language of France and parts of Switzerland, Belgium, Canada, and certain other countries. [From Old English *frencisc,* Frankish, from *Franca,* Frank.] —SEE NOTE.

French and Indian War *n.* A war (1756–1763) fought in North America between England and France and involving some Native Americans as allies of the French.

French braid *n.* A hairstyle in which the hair is gathered in increasingly greater amounts into one braid that begins at the crown and extends down the back of the head.

French bread *n.* Bread made with water, flour, and yeast and baked in long crusty loaves.

French Canadian *n.* A Canadian of French ancestry. **—French′-Ca·na′di·an** *adj.*

French curve *n.* A flat drafting instrument with curved edges and scroll-shaped cutouts, used as a guide in drawing curves.

French door *n.* A door, usually one of a pair, with glass panes extending for most of its length.

French dressing *n.* **1.** A salad dressing of oil, vinegar, and seasonings. **2.** A commercially prepared creamy salad dressing that is usually pinkish in color and often sweet.

french fry or **French fry** *n.* A thin strip of potato fried in deep fat: *squirted ketchup onto my french fries.*

french-fry (frĕnch′frī′) *tr.v.* **french-fried, french-fry·ing, french-fries** To fry (potato strips, for example) in deep fat.

French Gui·a·na (gē-ăn′ə *or* gē-ä′nə) A French territory of northeast South America on the Atlantic Ocean east of Suriname. Cayenne is the capital.

French horn *n.* A brass musical instrument that has valves and a long, coiled tube ending in a wide bell.

French·man (frĕnch′mən) *n.* A man who is a native or inhabitant of France.

French toast *n.* Sliced bread soaked in a batter of milk and egg and lightly fried.

French·wom·an (frĕnch′wo͝om′ən) *n.* A woman who is a native or inhabitant of France.

fre·net·ic (frə-nĕt′ĭk) *adj.* Wildly active or excited; frantic; frenzied: *worked at a frenetic pace to get the project done.* **—fre·net′i·cal·ly** *adv.*

fren·zied (frĕn′zēd) *adj.* Affected with or marked by frenzy; frantic: *There was a frenzied rush for the nearest exit.* **—fren′zied·ly** *adv.*

fren·zy (frĕn′zē) *n., pl.* **fren·zies** A state of violent agitation or wild excitement: *The frightened horses dashed about in a frenzy.*

fre·quen·cy (frē′kwən-sē) *n., pl.* **fre·quen·cies 1.** The condition of occurring repeatedly at short intervals: *annoyed at the frequency of the telemarketers' calls.* **2.** The number of times some event occurs within a given period; rate of occurrence. **3.** The number of complete cycles of a wave, such as a radio wave, that occur per second. **4.** The ratio of the number of occurrences of some event to the number of opportunities for its occurrence.

frequency modulation *n.* A method of broadcasting in which the frequency of the carrier wave is varied according to the signal being transmitted. Frequency modulation reduces static in radio transmission.

fre·quent (frē′kwənt) *adj.* Occurring or appearing quite often or at close intervals: *frequent visits to the doctor; a frequent visitor.* ❖ *tr.v.* (*also* frē-**kwĕnt′**) **fre·quent·ed, fre·quent·ing, fre·quents** To pay frequent visits to; be in or at often: *They frequented the museum on weekends.* **—fre′quent·ly** *adv.*

fres·co (frĕs′kō) *n., pl.* **fres·coes** or **fres·cos 1.** The art of painting on fresh moist plaster. **2.** A painting done in this manner.

fresh (frĕsh) *adj.* **fresh·er, fresh·est 1.** New to one's experience; not known before: *fresh reports from the scene of the earthquake.* **2.** Being unusual or different; novel: *a fresh approach to old problems.* **3.** Recently made, produced, or gathered; not stale or spoiled: *fresh bread; fresh fruit.* **4.** Not preserved, as by canning, smoking, or freezing: *fresh vegetables.* **5.** Not saline or salty: *fresh water.* **6.** Not yet used or soiled; clean: *fresh paper towels.* **7.** Free from impurity or pollution; pure: *fresh air.* **8.** Bright and clear; not dull or faded: *recent experiences that are fresh in one's memory.* **9.** Fairly strong; brisk: *a fresh morning breeze.* **10.** New or additional; further: *a fresh coat of paint.* **11.** Not tired; refreshed; rested: *felt fresh after a short nap.* **12.** Having the glowing unspoiled appearance of youth: *a bright fresh face.* **13.** *Informal* Lacking respect or restraint in behavior; impudent. **—fresh′ly** *adv.* **—fresh′ness** *n.*

fresh·en (frĕsh′ən) *v.* **fresh·ened, fresh·en·ing, fresh·ens** *—intr.* To become fresh, as in vigor or appearance. *—tr.* To make fresh: *Rain freshened the air.*

fresh·et (frĕsh′ĭt) *n.* **1.** A sudden overflow of a stream as a result of a heavy rain or a thaw. **2.** A stream of fresh water that runs into a body of salt water.

fresh·man (frĕsh′mən) *n.* A student in the first-year class of a high school, college, or university.

fresh·wa·ter (frĕsh′wô′tər) *adj.* Relating to, living in, or consisting of water that is not salty: *freshwater fish; a freshwater pond.*

fret[1] (frĕt) *v.* **fret·ted, fret·ting, frets** *—intr.* To be uneasy, troubled, or worried: *fretted over each detail.* *—tr.* To cause to be uneasy; vex: *I tried not to fret my parents unnecessarily.* [From Old English *fretan*, to eat up.]

fret[2] (frĕt) *n.* One of several ridges set across the fingerboard of certain stringed instruments, such as guitars. **—fret′ted** *adj.*

fret[3] (frĕt) *n.* An ornamental design within a band or border, consisting of repeated and symmetrical designs. ❖ *tr.v.* **fret·ted, fret·ting, frets** To provide with such a design. [From Middle English, interlaced work, from Old French *frete.*]

fret·ful (frĕt′fəl) *adj.* Feeling or showing worry and distress; troubled. **—fret′ful·ly** *adv.* **—fret′ful·ness** *n.*

fret saw *n.* A saw with a narrow, fine-toothed blade, used for cutting thin wood or metal.

fret·work (frĕt′wûrk′) *n.* Ornamental work consisting of three-dimensional frets; geometric openwork.

Freud (froid), **Sigmund** 1856–1939. Austrian founder of psychoanalysis whose theories significantly influenced modern thought. **—Freud·i·an** *adj.*

fri·a·ble (frī′ə-bəl) *adj.* Easily crumbled; brittle: *friable stone.* **—fri′a·bil′i·ty, fri′a·ble·ness** *n.*

fri·ar (frī′ər) *n.* A man who is a member of certain Roman Catholic orders. [From Middle English *frere*, from Old French, from Latin *frāter*, brother.]
❑ *These sound alike:* **friar, fryer** (young chicken).

fric·as·see (frĭk′ə-sē′ *or* frĭk′ə-sē′) *n.* Poultry or meat cut up and stewed in a thick gravy. ❖ *tr.v.* **fric·as·seed, fric·as·see·ing, fric·as·sees** To prepare as a fricassee.

fric·tion (frĭk′shən) *n.* **1.** The rubbing of one object or surface against another: *Friction of flint and steel can produce sparks.* **2.** The force that resists motion between two objects in contact: *By oiling the wheels, we reduced the friction.* **3.** The conflict or irritation that occurs between people who have different opinions or beliefs: *The debate caused friction between the two senators.* **—fric′tion·al** *adj.* **—fric′tion·al·ly** *adv.*

Fri·day (frī′dē *or* frī′dā′) *n.* The sixth day of the week. [From Old English *Frīgedæg*, day of Frigg (goddess of love).] **—Fri′days** *adv.* —SEE NOTE AT **friend.**

fried (frīd) *v.* Past tense and past participle of **fry[1].**

friend (frĕnd) *n.* **1.** A person who is known and liked by another: *My friends came to my birthday party.* **2.** A person who supports a group, cause, or movement; a person on the same side: *Their support of conservation made them friends of the environmental agency.* **3.** **Friend** A member of the Society of Friends; a Quaker.

French door

Sigmund Freud
photographed in 1909

WORD HISTORY

friend You already know that friends love friends, and in fact the word **friend** originally meant "loving, one who loves another." It comes from a word in Old English, the language spoken in England over 1,000 years ago. This word can be traced back to the present participle of an old verb meaning "to love." Though that verb no longer exists, it has a hidden relative in the name of the last day of the week, **Friday**. This day was named for Frigg, the goddess of love in the mythology of the Germanic peoples of northern Europe. The name of our day *Friday* or "Frigg's day" came about as a translation of the Latin name for the same day, *Veneris diēs*, "day of Venus," after Venus, the Roman goddess of love.

frigatebird
male frigatebird during courtship display, with red inflated throat pouch

ă	pat	ôr	core
ā	pay	oi	boy
âr	care	ou	out
ä	father	o͝o	took
ĕ	pet	o͝or	lure
ē	be	o͞o	boot
ĭ	pit	ŭ	cut
ī	bite	ûr	urge
îr	pier	th	thin
ŏ	pot	*th*	this
ō	toe	zh	vision
ô	paw	ə	about

❖ *tr.v.* **friend·ed, friend·ing, friends** *Informal* To add (someone) as a friend on a social networking website. [From Old English *frēond*.] —SEE NOTE.

friend·ly (frĕnd′lē) *adj.* **friend·li·er, friend·li·est 1.** Characteristic or behaving as a friend: *a friendly greeting.* **2.** Outgoing and pleasant: *a friendly clerk.* **3.** Not feeling or showing enmity or hostility: *a government friendly to our interests.* **4.** Welcoming to or accommodating a particular sort of user: *a vegan-friendly restaurant; a child-friendly hotel.* **—friend′li·ness** *n.*

friend·ship (frĕnd′shĭp′) *n.* **1.** The condition or fact of being friends: *a friendship from childhood.* **2.** A feeling of warmth toward another; friendliness: *friendship between people who like the same things.*

fri·er (frī′ər) *n.* Variant of **fryer.**

fries (frīz) *v.* Third person singular present tense of **fry**[1]. ❖ *n.* Plural of **fry**[1].

frieze (frēz) *n.* **1.** In classical architecture, a plain or decorated horizontal band that is above the columns and below the roof. **2.** A decorative horizontal band, as along the upper part of a wall in a room. [From Medieval Latin *frisium*, embroidery, from Latin *Phrygium (opus)*, (work) of Phrygia (ancient region of Asia Minor).]
❑ *These sound alike:* **frieze, freeze** (form ice).

frig·ate (frĭg′ĭt) *n.* **1.** A warship used as an escort and to destroy submarines. **2.** A fast square-rigged warship of the 1600s, 1700s, and 1800s.

frig·ate·bird (frĭg′ĭt-bûrd′) *n.* Any of various tropical seabirds having long powerful wings, dark feathers, and a forked tail. Frigatebirds snatch food from other birds in flight.

Frigg (frĭg) also **Frig·ga** (frĭg′ə) *n.* In Norse mythology, the goddess of the heavens and the wife of Odin.

fright (frīt) *n.* **1.** Sudden intense fear, as of something immediately threatening; alarm: *Fright caused the flock of birds to take flight.* **2.** *Informal* Something very unsightly or alarming: *Their dirty wind-blown hair looked a fright.* [From Old English *fyrhto*.]

fright·en (frīt′n) *v.* **fright·ened, fright·en·ing, fright·ens** *—tr.* **1.** To fill with fear; alarm or startle: *A loud noise frightened me.* **2.** To drive or force by arousing fear: *frightened him into making a confession.* *—intr.* To become afraid: *I fear for your safety.*

SYNONYMS **frighten, scare, alarm, terrify, panic** These verbs mean to cause fear in a person or thing. **Frighten** and **scare** are the most general: *It's hard to believe that elephants are frightened of mice. Don't let the amount of homework scare you.* **Alarm** means to frighten suddenly: *The appearance of a rash on her arm alarmed her.* **Terrify** means to overwhelm with fear: *We were terrified that the footbridge would collapse as we walked on it.* **Panic** refers to a sudden fear that causes a person to rush or think unclearly: *False reports of an invasion panicked the citizens.*

fright·en·ing (frīt′n-ĭng) *adj.* Causing fright or sudden alarm: *a frightening thunderstorm.* **—fright′en·ing·ly** *adv.*

fright·ful (frīt′fəl) *adj.* **1.** Causing disgust or shock; horrifying: *The number of hungry refugees is frightful.* **2.** Causing fright; terrifying: *frightful Halloween masks.* **3.** *Informal* Extreme; excessive: *frightful traffic at rush hour.* **—fright′ful·ly** *adv.*

frig·id (frĭj′ĭd) *adj.* **1.** Extremely cold: *a frigid room.* See Synonyms at **cold. 2.** Lacking warmth of feeling or enthusiasm: *His suggestion received a frigid reception.* **—fri·gid′i·ty** (frĭ-jĭd′ĭ-tē), **frig′id·ness** *n.* **—frig′id·ly** *adv.*

Frigid Zone Either of two extreme latitude zones of the earth, the **North Frigid Zone,** between the North Pole and the Arctic Circle, or the **South Frigid Zone,** between the South Pole and the Antarctic Circle.

fri·jo·les (frē-hō′lĕs *or* frē-hō′lāz) *pl.n.* Beans cultivated and used for food, especially in Latin American cooking. [From Spanish.]

frill (frĭl) *n.* **1.** A ruffled, gathered, or pleated piece of fancy trimming, as on a fabric edge: *frills on a doll's dress.* **2.** *Informal* Something desirable but unnecessary added on as an extra: *a straightforward speech without any frills.* ❖ *tr.v.* **frilled, frill·ing, frills** To put a ruffle or frill on: *frill a skirt.* **—frill′y** *adj.*

fringe (frĭnj) *n.* **1.** A decorative border or edging of hanging threads or cords, often attached to a separate band. **2.** Something that resembles such a border or edging: *a fringe of eyelashes.* **3.** An outer part; a margin; an edge: *stand on the fringe of the crowd.* ❖ *tr.v.* **fringed, fring·ing, fring·es 1.** To decorate with or as if with a fringe: *fringe curtains.* **2.** To form a fringe along the edge of: *Sunlight fringed the horizon.*

fringe benefit *n.* An employment benefit, such as medical care, given in addition to wages or salary.

frip·per·y (frĭp′ə-rē) *n., pl.* **frip·per·ies 1.** Pretentious showy finery. **2.** Pretentious elegance; ostentation.

Fris·bee (frĭz′bē) A trademark used for a plastic disk-shaped toy that players throw and catch.

Fri·sian (frĭzh′ən *or* frē′zhən) *n.* **1.** A native or inhabitant of the Frisian Islands or Friesland, a northern province of the Netherlands. **2.** The West Germanic language of the Frisians. **—Fri′sian** *adj.*

frisk (frĭsk) *v.* **frisked, frisk·ing, frisks** *—tr.* To search (a person) for something concealed, especially a weapon. *—intr.* To move about briskly and playfully; frolic: *Squirrels frisked in the trees.*

frisk·y (frĭs′kē) *adj.* **frisk·i·er, frisk·i·est** Energetic, lively, and playful: *a frisky kitten.* **—frisk′i·ly** *adv.* **—frisk′i·ness** *n.*

frit·ta·ta (frĭ-tä′tə) *n.* An omelet that is not folded over on itself, made with ingredients, such as cheese or vegetables, mixed into the eggs rather than used as a filling. [From Italian, from *fritto*, fried.]

frit·ter[1] (frĭt′ər) *tr.v.* **frit·tered, frit·ter·ing, frit·ters** To reduce or squander little by little; waste: *frittered the day away watching TV.* [Probably from *fritter*, fragment, probably from *fitter*, to break into small pieces.] **—frit′ter·er** *n.*

frit·ter[2] (frĭt′ər) *n.* A small fried cake of batter that often contains fruit, vegetables, or seafood. [From Middle English *friture*, from Late Latin *frīctūra*, from Latin *frīctus*, roasted, fried.]

fri·vol·i·ty (frĭ-vŏl′ĭ-tē) *n., pl.* **fri·vol·i·ties 1.** The quality or condition of being frivolous. **2.** A frivolous act or thing.

friv·o·lous (frĭv′ə-ləs) *adj.* **1.** Not worthy of serious attention; trivial: *wasting time on frivolous ideas.* **2.** Inappropriately silly: *a frivolous purchase.* **—friv′o·lous·ly** *adv.* **—friv′o·lous·ness** *n.*

frizz (frĭz) *tr. & intr.v.* **frizzed, frizz·ing, frizz·es** To form or be formed into small tight tufts or curls. ❖ *n.* A small tight curl or tuft. [From Old French *friser*, possibly from *frire*, to fry.]

friz·zle (frĭz′əl) *tr. & intr.v.* **friz·zled, friz·zling, friz·zles** To form or cause to be formed into small tight curls. ❖ *n.* A small tight curl.

friz·zly (frĭz′lē) *adj.* **friz·zli·er, friz·zli·est** Frizzy.

friz·zy (frĭz′ē) *adj.* **friz·zi·er, friz·zi·est** Tightly curled: *frizzy hair.*

fro (frō) *adv.* Away; back: *A pendulum swings to and fro.*

frock (frŏk) *n.* **1.** A woman's dress. **2.** A long loose outer garment, such as a priest's robe or an artist's smock.

frock coat *n.* A man's dress coat or suit coat that extends to the knees.

frog (frôg) *n.* **1.** Any of numerous tailless amphibians that have a short body, large head, and long legs used for leaping. Most frogs live chiefly in and around water. **2.** An ornamental fastener made of braid or cord with a looped piece that fits around a button. **3.** *Informal* Hoarseness in the throat.

frog kick *n.* A swimming kick in which the legs are drawn up close to the hips and then thrust outward and drawn together when straightened.

frog·man (**frôg′măn′**) *n.* A swimmer provided with breathing apparatus and other equipment to perform underwater maneuvers, especially military maneuvers.

frol·ic (**frŏl′ĭk**) *n.* Playful behavior or merriment. ❖ *intr.v.* **frol·icked, frol·ick·ing, frol·ics** To move about or behave playfully: *The puppies frolicked on the lawn.*

frol·ic·some (**frŏl′ĭk-səm**) *adj.* Full of fun; frisky and playful: *a frolicsome puppy.*

from (frŭm *or* frŏm; frəm *when unstressed*) *prep.* **1.** Used to indicate a specified place or time as a starting point: *walked home from the station; from midnight until dawn.* **2.** Used to indicate a source, agent, or instrument: *a gift from a friend; a note from the teacher.* **3.** Used to indicate a cause: *faint from hunger.* **4.** Out of or off of: *taking a book from the shelf.* **5.** Out of the control or possession of: *They took the ball from us.* **6.** So as not to be engaged in: *kept from playing.* **7.** In contrast to: *knowing right from wrong.*

frond (frŏnd) *n.* **1.** The leaf of a fern or a palm tree, usually divided into smaller leaflets. **2.** A part of a seaweed or lichen that resembles a leaf.

front (frŭnt) *n.* **1.** The forward part or surface, as of a building: *a shirt with buttons down the front; a desk at the front of the room.* **2.** The area, location, or position directly before or ahead: *A crowd gathered in front of the building.* **3.** A person's outward manner, behavior, or appearance: *keeping up a brave front despite misfortune.* **4.** Land bordering a lake, river, or street: *a lake front.* **5.** In warfare, an area where a battle is taking place. **6.** The boundary between two air masses having different temperatures: *a cold front.* **7.** A field of activity: *Conditions on the economic front are poor.* **8.** A group or movement uniting persons or organizations that seek a common goal; a coalition: *Unions and workers formed a labor front.* **9.** An outwardly respectable person or business that serves as a cover for secret or illegal activity. ❖ *adj.* Relating to, aimed at, or located in the front: *the front door; the front pages; the front view.* ❖ *v.* **front·ed, front·ing, fronts** *—tr.* **1.** To face or look out upon: *The building fronts the main street.* **2.** To meet in opposition; directly confront. *—intr.* To have a front; face onto something else: *The motel fronts on the highway.* [From Middle English *frount*, from Latin *frōns*, forehead, front.]

front·age (**frŭn′tĭj**) *n.* **1.** The front part of a piece of property. **2.** The land between a building and the street. **3.** The land adjacent to something, such as a building, street, or body of water.

fron·tal (**frŭn′tl**) *adj.* **1.** Relating to, at, or concerning the front: *a frontal assault.* **2.** Relating to the forehead. **3.** Relating to a weather front. **—fron′tal·ly** *adv.*

frontal bone *n.* A bone of the skull, consisting of a part that corresponds to the forehead and a part that forms the roof of the eye sockets and cavities of the nose.

front·court (**frŭnt′kôrt′**) *n.* In basketball, the half of the court in which the team on offense tries to make baskets.

fron·tier (frŭn-**tîr′** *or* **frŭn′tîr′**) *n.* **1.** A boundary between countries or the land along such a boundary; a border. **2.** A region just beyond or at the edge of a settled area. **3.** An undeveloped area or field of research or interest: *exploring new frontiers in space.* [From Middle English *frounter*, from Old French *frontier*, from *front*, forehead, front.]

fron·tiers·man (frŭn-**tîrz′**mən) *n.* A man who lives on the frontier.

fron·tiers·wom·an (frŭn-**tîrz′**wo͝om′ən) *n.* A woman who lives on the frontier.

fron·tis·piece (**frŭn′**tĭ-spēs′) *n.* An illustration that faces or comes just before the title page of a book.

front·line (**frŭnt′līn′**) *n.* A front or boundary, especially one between political or military positions. ❖ *adj.* **1.** Located or used at a military front. **2.** Relating to the most advanced position in a field or an undertaking: *frontline research.* **3.** Performing the most basic tasks or interacting directly with customers, patients, or clients: *frontline caregivers.*

front-run·ner also **front·run·ner** (**frŭnt′**rŭn′ər) *n.* A person who leads in a race or other competition.

frost (frôst) *n.* **1.** A deposit of small ice crystals, formed from frozen water vapor, covering a surface: *I scraped the frost from the car windshield.* **2.** A period of weather when such deposits form. ❖ *v.* **frost·ed, frost·ing, frosts** *—tr.* **1.** To cover with frost: *frosted the glasses by putting them in the freezer.* **2.** To damage or kill (plants) by frost. **3.** To cover or decorate (a cake, cupcake, or other baked goods) with icing. *—intr.* To become covered with frost: *The windows frosted up.* [From Old English.]

Frost (frôst), **Robert Lee** 1874–1963. American poet whose works, such as "Stopping by Woods on a Snowy Evening" (1923), are often set in rural New England.

frost·bite (**frôst′**bīt′) *n.* Injury to a part of the body as a result of exposure to freezing temperatures. ❖ *tr.v.* **frost·bit** (**frôst′**bĭt′), **frost·bit·ten** (**frôst′**bĭt′n), **frost·bit·ing, frost·bites** To injure (a part of the body) by freezing.

frost·ing (**frô′**stĭng) *n.* **1.** A sweet mixture of sugar and other ingredients, used to cover and decorate cakes or cookies; icing. **2.** A roughened or speckled surface on glass or metal.

frost·y (**frô′**stē) *adj.* **frost·i·er, frost·i·est 1.** Producing or characterized by frost: *A sudden chill made the night frosty and cold.* See Synonyms at **cold. 2.** Covered with frost or having a surface resembling frost: *the frosty bedroom window; a frosty texture.* **3.** Cold in manner; unfriendly: *The hostility between the neighbors was noticeable in their frosty greeting.* **—frost′i·ly** *adv.* **—frost′i·ness** *n.*

froth (frôth) *n.* **1.** A mass of bubbles in or on a liquid; foam. **2.** Something lacking in substance or depth: *Most gossip is mere froth.* ❖ *v.* (*also* frôth) **frothed, froth·ing, froths** *—intr.* To give off or form foam: *The sick dog frothed at the mouth.* *—tr.* **1.** To cover with foam. **2.** To cause to foam. **—froth′i·ly** *adv.* **—froth′i·ness** *n.* **—froth′y** *adj.*

frown (froun) *intr.v.* **frowned, frown·ing, frowns 1.** To wrinkle the brow, as in thought or displeasure; scowl. **2.** To regard something with disapproval or distaste: *frowned on the use of so much salt in the food.* ❖ *n.* An act of wrinkling the brow in thought or displeasure; a scowl. [From Middle English *frounen*, from Old French *frogne*, grimace, of Celtic origin.]

frow·zy (**frou′**zē) *adj.* **frow·zi·er, frow·zi·est 1.** Untidy; slovenly; unkempt: *frowzy wind-blown hair.* **2.** Having an unpleasant smell; musty: *frowzy odors from the old clothes.* **—frow′zi·ness** *n.*

froze (frōz) *v.* Past tense of **freeze.**

fro·zen (**frō′**zən) *v.* Past participle of **freeze.** ❖ *adj.* **1a.** Made into ice: *frozen orange juice.* **b.** Covered with or surrounded by ice: *a frozen pool.* **2.** Very cold: *the frozen North.* **3.** Preserved by freezing: *frozen strawberries.* **4.** Incapable of moving, as from fright: *frozen with fear.* **5.** Unfriendly; cold: *a frozen stare.*

fruc·tose (**frŭk′**tōs′ *or* **fro͝ok′**tōs′) *n.* A simple sugar found in honey, many fruits, and some vegetables.

fru·gal (**fro͞o′**gəl) *adj.* **1.** Careful in spending or in using resources; thrifty: *Frugal use of energy saves natural*

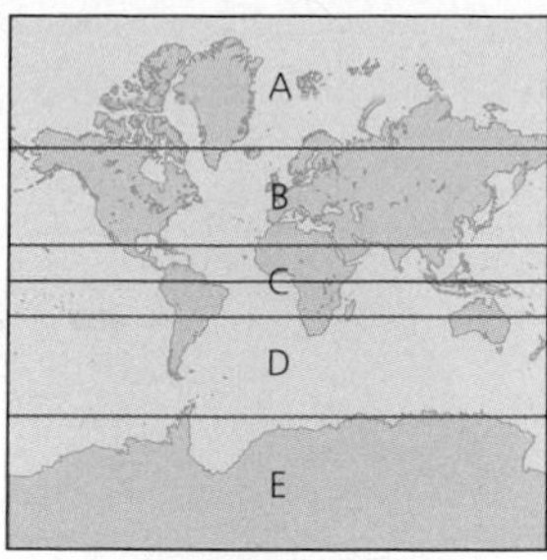

Frigid Zone
A. North Frigid Zone
B. North Temperate Zone
C. Tropics
D. South Temperate Zone
E. South Frigid Zone

frittata

frond

Robert Frost

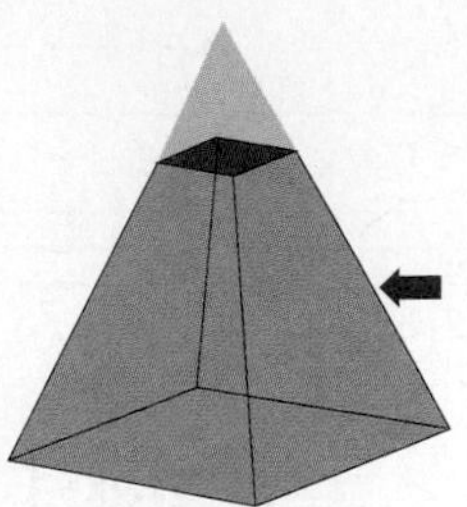
frustum
of a pyramid

fuchsia

resources. **2.** Costing little; inexpensive: *a frugal meal.* —**fru·gal′i·ty** (fro͞o-găl′ĭ-tē) *n.* —**fru′gal·ly** *adv.*

fruit (fro͞ot) *n., pl.* **fruit** or **fruits 1a.** The ripened ovary or ovaries of a seed-bearing plant, occurring in many different forms. Acorns, berries, pods, and squashes are all fruits. **b.** A fleshy, usually sweet plant part of this kind that is eaten as food, such as an apple or a mango. **2.** A result of work or action: *the fruit of their labor.* ❖ *intr. & tr.v.* **fruit·ed, fruit·ing, fruits** To produce or cause to produce fruit: *Apple trees fruit in the fall.* [From Middle English, from Latin *frūctus,* enjoyment, fruit.]

fruit·cake (fro͞ot′kāk′) *n.* A rich spiced cake containing various dried and preserved fruits and nuts.

fruit fly *n.* Any of various small flies whose larvae feed on ripening or decaying plant material, especially fruit.

fruit·ful (fro͞ot′fəl) *adj.* **1.** Producing or bearing fruit. **2.** Producing useful or desired results; productive: *a fruitful approach.* —**fruit′ful·ly** *adv.* —**fruit′ful·ness** *n.*

fru·i·tion (fro͞o-ĭsh′ən) *n.* The achievement of something desired or worked for; accomplishment: *The plan came to fruition after many years of hard work.*

fruit·less (fro͞ot′lĭs) *adj.* **1.** Having little or no result; unproductive: *Only after many fruitless attempts did explorers reach the South Pole.* **2.** Producing no fruit: *a fruitless variety of mulberry.* —**fruit′less·ly** *adv.* —**fruit′less·ness** *n.*

fruit sugar *n.* Fructose.

fruit·y (fro͞o′tē) *adj.* **fruit·i·er, fruit·i·est** Tasting or smelling of fruit: *the fruity smell of ripe peaches.* —**fruit′i·ness** *n.*

Frun·ze (fro͞on′zə) See **Bishkek.**

frus·trate (frŭs′trāt′) *tr.v.* **frus·trat·ed, frus·trat·ing, frus·trates 1.** To prevent (a plan, effort, or desire) from succeeding or being fulfilled: *Bad weather frustrated our plans to go fishing.* **2.** To prevent (someone) from accomplishing something; thwart: *A persistent wind frustrated me as I tried to rake the leaves.* **3.** To cause feelings of discouragement or bafflement in: *The scientists were frustrated by the negative results of the experiment.* [From Middle English *frustraten,* from Latin *frūstrā,* in vain.] —**frus·tra′tion** *n.*

frus·tum (frŭs′təm) *n., pl.* **frus·tums** or **frus·ta** (frŭs′tə) The part of a solid, such as a cone or pyramid, between the base and a plane that cuts through the solid and is parallel to the base.

fry[1] (frī) *v.* **fried** (frīd), **fry·ing, fries** (frīz) ❖ *tr.v.* To cook (food) over direct heat in hot oil or fat: *We fried potatoes in a pan.* ❖ *intr.v.* To be cooked over direct heat in hot oil or fat: *Eggs fry quickly.* ❖ *n., pl.* **fries** (frīz) **1.** A french fry: *ordered a hamburger with fries.* **2.** An informal gathering where food is fried and eaten: *a fish fry.* [From Middle English *frien,* from Latin *frīgere.*]

fry[2] (frī) *pl.n.* Small fish, especially young, recently hatched fish. [From Middle English *fri,* probably from Anglo-Norman *frie,* from *frier,* to rub, from Latin *fricāre.*]

fry·er also **fri·er** (frī′ər) *n.* **1.** A pot or pan having a basket for frying foods. **2.** A small young chicken suitable for frying.

❑ *These sound alike:* **fryer, friar** (member of a religious order).

fry·ing pan (frī′ĭng) *n.* A shallow pan with a long handle, used for frying food.

ft. *abbr.* An abbreviation of foot.

Ft. *abbr.* An abbreviation of fort.

fuch·sia (fyo͞o′shə) *n.* **1.** Any of various tropical plants grown for their drooping, often red, purple, or pink flowers. **2.** A bright purplish red. [After Leonhard *Fuchs* (1501–1566), German botanist.]

fud·dle (fŭd′l) *tr.v.* **fud·dled, fud·dling, fud·dles 1.** To put into a state of confusion; muddle. **2.** To make drunk; intoxicate.

fudge (fŭj) *n.* A soft rich candy, often flavored with chocolate. ❖ *tr.v.* **fudged, fudg·ing, fudg·es 1.** To fake or falsify: *The scientist fudged the results of the experiment to support his hypothesis.* **2.** To be evasive in expressing: *The politican fudged her response to the reporter because she didn't want to commit to a position.*

fu·el (fyo͞o′əl) *n.* **1.** A substance, such as coal, wood, oil, or gas, that is burned to produce useful heat or energy. **2.** A substance that can be made to undergo a nuclear reaction and produce energy. **3.** Material that an organism breaks down to use for energy; food: *I needed fuel for the race, so I ate a big plate of pasta.* **4.** Something that feeds or encourages a feeling: *Being insulted added fuel to his anger.* ❖ *v.* **fu·eled, fu·el·ing, fu·els** also **fu·elled, fu·el·ling, fu·els** —*tr.* To provide with fuel: *She pulled into the gas station and fueled the car.* —*intr.* To take in fuel: *The freighter fueled at the nearest port.* [From Middle English *feuel,* from Old French *feuaile,* from Latin *focus,* hearth, fireplace.]

fuel cell *n.* A device that produces electricity by the chemical reaction between a fuel and an oxidizer.

fu·gi·tive (fyo͞o′jĭ-tĭv) *adj.* **1.** Running or having run away, as from law enforcement agents. **2.** Lasting only a short time; fleeting: *relaxing for a few fugitive hours.* ❖ *n.* A person who flees: *The escaped criminal was a fugitive from the law.* [From Middle English *fugitif,* from Latin *fugitīvus,* from *fugere,* to flee.]

fugue (fyo͞og) *n.* A musical composition in which one or more themes are repeated by different voices or instruments with variations on the themes.

–ful *suff.* A suffix that means: **1.** Full of: *eventful; playful.* **2.** Characterized by: *boastful.* **3.** Tending or able to: *helpful; useful.* **4.** A quantity that fills: *armful; cupful.* —SEE NOTE.

ful·crum (fo͝ol′krəm *or* fŭl′krəm) *n.* The point or support on which a lever pivots.

ful·fill also **ful·fil** (fo͝ol-fĭl′) *tr.v.* **ful·filled, ful·fill·ing, ful·fills** also **ful·fils 1.** To make real; cause to become true: *After many years they fulfilled their lifelong dream.* **2.** To do, perform, or obey (a duty or order): *Citizens should fulfill their duty as voters.* **3.** To meet (a requirement or condition); satisfy: *fulfilling all requirements.* —**ful·fill′ment** *n.*

full (fo͝ol) *adj.* **full·er, full·est 1.** Containing all that is normal or possible; filled: *a full bucket.* **2.** Not deficient; complete: *I need your full attention.* **3.** Of highest degree or development: *at full speed; in full bloom.* **4.** Having a great many or a great deal of: *shelves full of books.* **5.** Rounded in shape; plump: *a full face and figure.* **6.** Having or made with a generous amount of fabric: *a full skirt.* **7.** Filled with food; abundantly fed: *The guests were full after the huge banquet.* **8.** Having depth and body; rich: *a full flavor.* **9.** Having both parents in common: *full sisters; a full brother.* ❖ *adv.* **1.** To a complete extent; entirely: *Fill the pitcher full.* **2.** Exactly; directly: *The tree fell full across the middle of the road.* ◆ **in full** To the maximum amount or degree that is necessary; completely: *a bill paid in full.* [From Middle English *ful,* from Old English, full.] —**full′ness** *n.*

full·back (fo͝ol′băk′) *n.* **1.** In football, a running back usually positioned directly behind the quarterback when the ball is snapped. **2.** In certain sports such as soccer and field hockey, one of usually two defensive players other than the goalie positioned closest to the goal.

full-blood·ed (fo͝ol′blŭd′ĭd) or **full·blood** (fo͝ol′blŭd′) *adj.* Of unmixed ancestry; purebred: *a full-blooded Arabian horse.*

full-blown (fo͝ol′blōn′) *adj.* Fully developed: *a full-blown case of chickenpox.*

full dress *n.* Clothing appropriate or required for formal occasions or ceremonies.

Ful·ler (fo͝olər), **(Sarah) Margaret** 1810–1850. Ameri-

ă	pat	ôr	core
ā	pay	oi	boy
âr	care	ou	out
ä	father	o͝o	took
ĕ	pet	o͝or	lure
ē	be	o͞o	boot
ĭ	pit	ŭ	cut
ī	bite	ûr	urge
îr	pier	th	thin
ŏ	pot	*th*	this
ō	toe	zh	vision
ô	paw	ə	about

can writer known for *Woman in the Nineteenth Century* (1845), a major feminist work.

ful·ler·ene (fo͝ol′ə-rēn′) *n.* Any of various molecules of carbon that always have an even number of carbon atoms, are often shaped like a sphere, and are made of groups of atoms arranged in hexagons and pentagons. [After Richard Buckminster *Fuller* (1895–1983), American architect and designer of the geodesic dome, whose shape is similar to the molecule's.]

full-fledged (fo͝ol′flĕjd′) *adj.* **1.** Having reached full development: *a full-fledged hurricane.* **2.** Having full standing or rank: *a full-fledged lawyer.*

full-length (fo͝ol′lĕngkth′ *or* fo͝ol′lĕngth′) *adj.* **1.** Covering the entire length of a person or thing: *a full-length mirror; a full-length coat.* **2.** Of normal or standard length: *a full-length movie.*

full moon *n.* The moon when the side that faces Earth is fully illuminated by the sun, halfway through a lunar month.

full-scale (fo͝ol′skāl′) *adj.* **1.** Of the actual or full size; not reduced: *The design for the new car was produced in a full-scale model.* **2.** Not limited; complete; all-out: *Everyone turned out for a full-scale demonstration against local water pollution.*

full-size (fo͝ol′sīz′) *adj.* Of the standard or normal size: *a full-size poodle; a full-size car.*

full-time (fo͝ol′tīm′) *adj.* Employed for or involving a standard number of hours of working time: *a full-time editor; a full-time job.* **—full′-time′** *adv.*

ful·ly (fo͝ol′ē) *adv.* **1.** Totally or completely: *The deer was fully aware of our presence.* **2.** At least; no less than: *Fully half the students had to take the test over.*

ful·mi·nate (fo͝ol′mə-nāt′ *or* fŭl′mə-nāt′) *intr.v.* **ful·mi·nat·ed, ful·mi·nat·ing, ful·mi·nates 1.** To make a loud strong verbal attack or denunciation: *The speaker fulminated against the waste of resources.* **2.** To explode with sudden violence or force. ❖ *n.* Any of a number of salts that explode violently at the slightest shock and are used as detonators. [From Middle English *fulminaten,* from Latin *fulmināre,* to strike with lightning, from *fulmen,* lightning that strikes.] **—ful′mi·na′tion** *n.*

ful·some (fo͝ol′səm) *adj.* **1a.** Excessively flattering: *received fulsome praise for her efforts.* **b.** Insincerely earnest. **2.** Disgusting or offensive: *a fulsome smell coming from the garbage bin.* **—ful′some·ly** *adv.* **—ful′some·ness** *n.*

Ful·ton (fo͝ol′tən), **Robert** 1765–1815. American engineer and inventor who developed an experimental submarine (1800) and produced the first commercially successful steamboat (1807).

fum·ble (fŭm′bəl) *v.* **fum·bled, fum·bling, fum·bles** —*intr.* **1.** To touch or handle something nervously or idly: *The driver fumbled with the car keys.* **2.** To feel around awkwardly while searching; grope: *She fumbled for the light switch in the dark.* **3.** In sports, to mishandle or drop a ball. —*tr.* **1.** To handle clumsily or idly: *He fumbled the glass and it broke.* **2.** To make a botch of; bungle: *The bank robber fumbled the job.* **3.** In sports, to mishandle or drop (a ball). ❖ *n.* **1.** An act of fumbling. **2.** A ball that has been fumbled.

fume (fyo͞om) *n.* Smoke, vapor, or gas, especially if irritating, harmful, or smelly: *the choking fumes from a smokestack.* ❖ *intr.v.* **fumed, fum·ing, fumes 1.** To produce or give off fumes. **2.** To feel or show anger or agitation; seethe: *After being put off for the third time, he was fuming.* [From Middle English, from Latin *fūmus.*]

fu·mi·gant (fyo͞o′mĭ-gənt) *n.* A poisonous compound used in fumigating.

fu·mi·gate (fyo͞o′mĭ-gāt′) *tr.v.* **fu·mi·gat·ed, fu·mi·gat·ing, fu·mi·gates** To expose (a room or object) to fumes in order to kill insects, rats, or other pests. **—fu′mi·ga′tion** *n.* **—fu′mi·ga′tor** *n.*

fun (fŭn) *n.* **1.** Enjoyment; amusement: *We had fun at the picnic.* **2.** A source of enjoyment or amusement: *The trampoline was fun.* ❖ *adj. Informal* Enjoyable; amusing: *a fun party.*

Fu·na·fu·ti (fo͞o′nə-fo͞o′tē) The capital of Tuvalu, in the southern Pacific Ocean north of Fiji.

func·tion (fŭngk′shən) *n.* **1.** The normal or proper activity of a person or thing; a purpose: *The function of the heart is to pump blood.* **2.** An assigned duty or activity: *Creating a menu is part of her function as head chef.* **3a.** A quantity whose value depends on the value given to one or more related quantities: *The area of a square is a function of the length of its side.* **b.** A relationship between two sets that matches each member of the first set with a unique member of the second set. **4.** A formal social gathering or official ceremony. —*intr.* **func·tioned, func·tion·ing, func·tions** To have or perform a function; serve: *Posts function as a support for the deck.* [From Latin *fūnctiō,* performance, execution, from *fungī,* to perform, execute.]

func·tion·al (fŭngk′shə-nəl) *adj.* **1.** Relating to a function or functions: *the functional responsibilities of a manager.* **2.** Having or carrying out a function; working: *Is this clock functional?* **3.** Designed for or adapted to a particular purpose or use: *The log cabin is an example of functional architecture.* **—func′tion·al·ly** *adv.*

func·tion·al·i·ty (fŭngk′shə-năl′ĭ-tē) *n.* **1.** The quality or capability of being functional. **2.** A useful function within a computer application or program.

func·tion·ar·y (fŭngk′shə-nĕr′ē) *n., pl.* **func·tion·ar·ies** A person who holds a position of authority or trust; an official: *The tax collector is a functionary in the local government.*

function key *n.* Any of a set of keys on a computer keyboard that is pressed to activate a function.

function word *n.* A word, such as a preposition, auxiliary verb, or conjunction, that expresses relationships between words, clauses, and sentences. In the sentence *It rained and we did not go until later,* the words *and* and *until* are function words.

fund (fŭnd) *n.* **1.** A sum of money raised or set aside for a certain purpose: *Our library has a new book fund each year.* **2. funds** Available money; ready cash: *I'm a little short of funds.* **3.** A source of supply; a stock: *An encyclopedia is a fund of knowledge.* ❖ *tr.v.* **fund·ed, fund·ing, funds** To provide money for: *Several citizens of the town funded our sports program.* [From Latin *fundus,* bottom, piece of land.]

fun·da·men·tal (fŭn′də-mĕn′tl) *adj.* Relating to or forming a foundation; elemental or basic: *The students gained a fundamental understanding of algebra.* ❖ *n.* **1.** Something that is an elemental or basic part; an essential: *the fundamentals of good cooking.* **2.** The lowest frequency of a periodically varying quantity, such as a sound wave. **—fun′da·men′tal·ly** *adv.*

fun·da·men·tal·ism (fŭn′də-mĕn′tl-ĭz′əm) *n.* **1.** A religious movement or point of view characterized by strict following of fundamental principles and often by intolerance of other views. **2.** Belief that the Bible is a completely accurate historical record and statement of prophecy. **—fun′da·men′tal·ist** *n. & adj.*

fund·rais·er (fŭnd′rā′zər) *n.* **1.** A person who raises funds. **2.** A social function or activity, such as a raffle or musical concert, held for raising funds.

fu·ner·al (fyo͞o′nər-əl) *n.* **1.** The ceremonies that accompany burial or cremation of a dead person. **2.** The procession accompanying a body to the grave. [From Middle English *funerelles,* funeral rites, from Medieval Latin *fūnerālia,* from Latin *fūnus,* death rites.]

funeral director *n.* A person whose business is to prepare the dead for burial or cremation and to assist at funerals.

WORD BUILDING

–ful The suffix **–ful** comes from the Old English adjective *full,* meaning "full." *Full* was commonly added to a noun in order to form adjectives meaning "full of, characterized by" whatever quality was denoted by the noun, as in the modern words *playful* and *careful.* The use of *–ful* to form nouns meaning "a quantity that would fill" a particular receptacle (such as *cupful, mouthful*) also goes back to Old English. In modern usage the correct way to form the plural of these nouns is to add an *s* to the end of the suffix rather than the base noun: *cupfuls* (not *cupsful*).

WRITERS CHOOSE THEIR WORDS

"Connor's the newest member of my crew. He's only been with us these past three months but it's hard to imagine a time without him. Why, he's become like a son to me." Connor blushed at Captain Wrathe's **fulsome** praise. Once more, he was struck by the captain's generosity of spirit. "A son, eh?" said Barbarro, shaking Connor's hand. "That's high praise indeed from my brother."

—Justin Somper
Blood Captain

SCIENCE

fungus You probably know that mushrooms are **fungi,** but you might not know about all the different kinds of fungi that affect your daily life. Yeasts that make bread dough rise are fungi, and so are the molds that grow on old bread. Fungi cause athlete's foot and other infections in animals, as well as serious plant diseases, like Dutch elm disease. But fungi also help to cure disease: some of them produce substances that kill bacteria, and these substances can be made into antibiotics. Some fungi live in plant roots and help the plants absorb nutrients. Fungi cannot make their own food. Instead, they grow on living or dead organisms and break down large molecules into smaller molecules that they can absorb. Fungi are neither plants nor animals—they are different enough to be classified by scientists into their own unique kingdom.

WRITERS CHOOSE THEIR WORDS

When he reached the crest I saw the ragged uncouth figure outlined for an instant against the cold blue sky. He looked round him with a **furtive** and stealthy air, as one who dreads pursuit. Then he vanished over the hill.

—Sir Arthur Conan Doyle
The Hound of the Baskervilles

ă	pat	ôr	core
ā	pay	oi	boy
âr	care	ou	out
ä	father	o͝o	took
ĕ	pet	o͝or	lure
ē	be	o͞o	boot
ĭ	pit	ŭ	cut
ī	bite	ûr	urge
îr	pier	th	thin
ŏ	pot	*th*	this
ō	toe	zh	vision
ô	paw	ə	about

funeral home *n.* A building in which the dead are prepared for burial and cremation, and in which wakes and funerals are held.

fu·ne·re·al (fyo͞o-nîr′ē-əl) *adj.* Relating to, suitable for, or suggestive of a funeral: *funereal gloom.* **—fu·ne′re·al·ly** *adv.*

fun·gal (fŭng′gəl) *adj.* Relating to or caused by a fungus or fungi: *fungal hyphae; a fungal disease.*

fun·gi·cide (fŭn′jĭ-sīd′ *or* fŭng′gĭ-sīd′) *n.* A substance that destroys or prevents the growth of fungi.

fun·gus (fŭng′gəs) *n., pl.* **fun·gi** (fŭn′jī *or* fŭng′gī) or **fun·gus·es** Any of a kingdom of organisms, including the mushrooms, molds, yeasts, and certain mildews, that reproduce by spores and obtain their nourishment from other organisms. [From Latin; perhaps akin to Greek *sphongos*, sponge.] —SEE NOTE.

funk[1] (fŭngk) *n.* A strong, usually unpleasant smell. [Probably from a French dialect of northern France *funquer*, to produce smoke.]

funk[2] (fŭngk) *n.* A kind of popular music that has a lively beat and is a mixture of jazz, rock, blues, and often soul. [From *funky*.]

funk[3] (fŭngk) *n.* **1.** A state of fear; panic. **2.** A state of depression: *They were in a funk because their trip was canceled.* [Probably from obsolete Flemish *fonck*, disturbance, agitation.]

funk·y (fŭng′kē) *adj.* **1.** Relating to funk music. **2.** *Slang* Original; unconventional; offbeat: *a funky shirt.* **3.** Having a moldy or musty smell: *funky cheese.* [From *funk*, strong smell.] **—funk′i·ness** *n.*

fun·nel (fŭn′əl) *n.* **1.** A conical utensil with a wide opening at one end and a narrow tube or small hole at the other, used to pour liquids or other substances into a container with a small mouth. **2.** Something shaped like a funnel: *the funnel of a tornado.* **3.** The smokestack of a ship or steam engine. ❖ *v.* **fun·neled, fun·nel·ing, fun·nels** or **fun·nelled, fun·nel·ling, fun·nels** *—intr.* To move through or as if through a funnel: *Tourists funneled through the museum exhibit.* *—tr.* To cause to move through or as if through a funnel: *funnel juice into a pitcher.* [From Middle English *fonel*, from Latin *īnfundibulum*, from *īnfundere*, to pour in.]

fun·nies (fŭn′ēz) *pl.n.* **1.** Comic strips. **2.** A newspaper section containing comic strips.

fun·ny (fŭn′ē) *adj.* **fun·ni·er, fun·ni·est 1.** Causing laughter or amusement: *a funny cartoon.* **2.** Strange; odd; curious: *It's funny that I can't remember where I left my shoes.* **—fun′ni·ly** *adv.* **—fun′ni·ness** *n.*

funny bone *n. Informal* A point near the elbow where a nerve can be pressed against the bone, producing a numb or tingling feeling in the arm.

fur (fûr) *n.* **1.** The thick soft hair covering the body of certain mammals, such as a rabbit, squirrel, or fox. **2.** The skin and hair of such a mammal, treated and used for clothing, trimming, or lining: *gloves lined with fur.* **3.** An item of clothing made of fur: *She gave away her furs.* [From Middle English *furre*, from Old French *fuerre*, lining, of Germanic origin.]
❑ *These sound alike:* **fur, fir** (evergreen).

fur·bish (fûr′bĭsh) *tr.v.* **fur·bished, fur·bish·ing, fur·bish·es 1.** To brighten by cleaning or rubbing; polish: *The jeweler furbished the old silver bracelet.* **2.** To restore to a usable condition; renovate. **—fur′bish·er** *n.*

fu·ri·ous (fyo͝or′ē-əs) *adj.* **1.** Full of or marked by extreme anger; raging. **2.** Full of intensity; energetic or fierce: *the storm's furious winds; worked at a furious pace.* **—fu′ri·ous·ly** *adv.* **—fu′ri·ous·ness** *n.*

furl (fûrl) *v.* **furled, furl·ing, furls** *—tr.* To roll up and fasten (a flag or sail) to a pole, yard, or mast. *—intr.* To become rolled up: *The flag furled around the pole in the wind.* ❖ *n.* **1.** The act of furling. **2.** A rolled section of something furled.

fur·long (fûr′lông′) *n.* A unit for measuring distance, equal to ⅛ mile or 220 yards (201 meters). See table at **measurement.**

fur·lough (fûr′lō) *n.* **1.** A vacation or leave of absence, especially one granted to a member of the armed forces. **2.** A usually temporary suspension of an employee from work. ❖ *tr.v.* **fur·loughed, fur·lough·ing, fur·loughs 1.** To grant a leave to (someone). **2.** To place (an employee) on a furlough.

fur·nace (fûr′nĭs) *n.* An enclosed chamber in which fuel is burned to produce heat. Furnaces are used to heat buildings and to manufacture metal and glass. [From Middle English *furnais*, from Latin *fornāx*, oven.]

fur·nish (fûr′nĭsh) *tr.v.* **fur·nished, fur·nish·ing, fur·nish·es 1.** To outfit with furniture and other necessities: *furnish each room of an apartment.* **2.** To supply; give: *The lamp furnished enough light to read.* **—fur′nish·er** *n.*

fur·nish·ing (fûr′nĭ-shĭng) *n.* **1.** A piece of equipment necessary or useful for comfort or convenience. **2. furnishings** The furniture, appliances, and other movable articles in a house or other building. **3. furnishings** Clothes and accessories: *This store specializes in children's furnishings.*

fur·ni·ture (fûr′nĭ-chər) *n.* The movable articles, such as chairs, tables, or appliances, that make a room fit for living or an office suitable for working.

fu·ror (fyo͝or′ôr′ *or* fyo͝or′ər) *n.* **1.** A noisy outburst; a commotion or uproar: *Rumors of the president's arrival caused a furor of excitement.* **2.** Violent anger; frenzy: *the furor of the mob.*

fur·ri·er (fûr′ē-ər) *n.* A person who deals in fur or makes and repairs fur garments.

fur·row (fûr′ō) *n.* **1.** A long narrow groove made in the ground by a plow or other tool: *furrows cut in the field for planting.* **2.** A rut, groove, or narrow depression: *The car's tires made deep furrows in the dirt road.* ❖ *tr.v.* **fur·rowed, fur·row·ing, fur·rows 1.** To make furrows in; plow: *furrowed the cornfield into neat rows.* **2.** To form deep wrinkles in: *Months of worry had furrowed the banker's brow.*

fur·ry (fûr′ē) *adj.* **fur·ri·er, fur·ri·est 1.** Consisting of or resembling fur: *a furry coat.* **2.** Covered with fur: *a furry kitten.* **—fur′ri·ness** *n.*

fur seal *n.* Any of several seals having thick fur and external ears. Fur seals were heavily hunted for their pelts, but most species are now protected.

fur·ther (fûr′*th*ər) *adj.* A comparative of **far. 1.** More distant in space, time, or degree: *You couldn't be further from the truth.* **2.** Additional; more: *Stay tuned for further bulletins.* ❖ *adv.* A comparative of **far. 1.** To a greater extent; more: *We will explore the matter further at a later time.* **2.** In addition; furthermore; also: *He stated further that he thought the mayor's remarks were unfair.* **3.** At or to a more distant or advanced point: *I read five pages further.* ❖ *tr.v.* **fur·thered, fur·ther·ing, fur·thers** To help the progress of; forward; advance: *The dedicated teacher furthered the careers of many students with sound advice.* —SEE NOTE AT **farther.**

fur·ther·ance (fûr′*th*ər-əns) *n.* The act of advancing or helping forward; advancement.

fur·ther·more (fûr′*th*ər-môr′) *adv.* Moreover; in addition; besides.

fur·ther·most (fûr′*th*ər-mōst′) *adj.* Most distant or remote.

fur·thest (fûr′*th*ĭst) *adj.* A superlative of **far.** Most distant in space, time, or degree: *Radio can transmit to the furthest corners of the earth.* ❖ *adv.* A superlative of **far. 1.** To the greatest extent or degree: *The scientist's explanation went furthest toward providing a solution.* **2.** At or to the most distant or advanced point: *The champion threw the javelin furthest.*

fur·tive (fûr′tĭv) *adj.* Done or acting in a stealthy manner: *He cast a furtive glance at the clock.* [From French *furtif,* from Latin *fūrtum,* theft, from *fūr,* thief.] —**fur′tive·ly** *adv.* —**fur′tive·ness** *n.*

fu·ry (fyo͝or′ē) *n., pl.* **fu·ries 1.** Violent anger; rage. See Synonyms at **anger. 2.** Violent and uncontrolled action; turbulence; agitation: *the blizzard's fury.* **3. Furies** In Roman mythology, the terrible winged goddesses who pursued and punished those who committed unavenged crimes, identified with the Greek Erinyes.

furze (fûrz) *n.* A gorse plant.

fuse[1] also **fuze** (fyo͞oz) *n.* **1.** A cord of easily burned material that is lighted at one end to carry a flame that detonates an explosive charge at the other end. **2.** often **fuze** A mechanical or electronic device used to set off an explosive charge or device, such as a bomb or grenade. [From Italian *fuso,* spindle (originally from its shape), from Latin *fūsus.*]

fuse[2] (fyo͞oz) *v.* **fused, fus·ing, fus·es** —*tr.* **1.** To join (different pieces or elements) together, especially by melting or heating: *fused the metal parts together with a torch.* **2.** To blend or combine: *The music fuses African and Caribbean rhythms.* —*intr.* **1.** To become joined together, especially by melting or heating. **2.** To become blended or combined: *The two cultures fused over the years to produce a new civilization.* ❖ *n.* A safety device that protects an electric circuit from carrying too much current, containing a length of metal that melts and breaks the circuit when the current reaches an unsafe level. [From Latin *fūsus,* past participle of *fundere,* to melt.]

fu·se·lage (fyo͞o′sə-läzh′ *or* **fyo͞o′**zə-läzh′) *n.* The main body of an airplane that holds cargo, passengers, and crew. [From Old French *fusel,* spindle, from Latin *fūsus.*]

fu·si·ble (**fyo͞o′**zə-bəl) *adj.* Capable of being fused or melted. —**fu′si·bil′i·ty** *n.*

fu·sil·lade (**fyo͞o′**sə-läd′ *or* **fyo͞o′**sə-läd′) *n.* **1.** The discharge of many guns at the same time or in rapid succession. **2.** A rapid outburst: *a fusillade of complaints.*

fu·sion (**fyo͞o′**zhən) *n.* **1.** The act or process of melting or mixing different things into one by heat: *the fusion of copper and zinc to produce brass.* **2.** A mixture or blend formed by fusing two or more things: *An alloy is a fusion of two or more metals.* **3.** A union formed by merging different things or groups: *The building is a fusion of different styles of architecture.* **4.** A nuclear reaction in which light nuclei combine to form heavier nuclei, releasing large amounts of energy. Fusion reactions power the sun and stars.

fuss (fŭs) *n.* **1.** Needlessly nervous or useless activity; commotion: *There was a lot of fuss in the confusion of moving to a new office.* **2.** A display of concern or worry, especially over an unimportant matter: *Why make a fuss about a harmless remark?* **3.** A protest; a complaint: *The cancellation of the party provoked a fuss from the workers.* ❖ *intr.v.* **fussed, fuss·ing, fuss·es 1.** To be overly careful or concerned: *The caterer fussed over what to make for dinner.* **2.** To try to adjust or arrange something in a nervous or overly concerned way: *He was fussing with the collar of his shirt all night.* —**fuss′er** *n.*

fuss·y (fŭs′ē) *adj.* **fuss·i·er, fuss·i·est 1.** Easily upset; given to bouts of fussing: *a fussy baby.* **2.** Paying great or too much attention to small details: *She is very fussy about the arrangement of her room.* **3.** Requiring attention to small details: *Organizing a big wedding is a fussy job.* —**fuss′i·ly** *adv.* —**fuss′i·ness** *n.*

fus·ty (fŭs′tē) *adj.* **fus·ti·er, fus·ti·est 1.** Smelling of mildew or decay; musty; moldy: *a fusty smell in the damp basement.* **2.** Old-fashioned or out-of-date. —**fus′ti·ly** *adv.* —**fus′ti·ness** *n.*

fu·tile (**fyo͞ot′**l *or* **fyo͞o′**tīl′) *adj.* Having no useful result; hopeless; vain: *It is futile to argue that the earth is flat.* [From Latin *fūtilis.*] —**fu′tile·ly** *adv.*

fu·til·i·ty (fyo͞o-**tĭl′**ĭ-tē) *n., pl.* **fu·til·i·ties 1.** The condition or quality of being futile; uselessness; ineffectiveness: *The attempt to turn iron into gold was an exercise in futility.* **2.** Lack of importance or purpose.

fu·ton (**fo͞o′**tŏn) *n.* A pad of cotton batting or similar material used on a floor or on a raised platform as a mattress or comforter. [From Japanese : *fu,* cloth + *ton,* ball, mass.]

fu·ture (**fyo͞o′**chər) *n.* **1.** The period of time yet to come: *Let's try to do better in the future.* **2.** Something that will happen in time to come: *The business's future is in the hands of new management.* **3.** Chance of success or advancement; outlook: *The young doctor faced a bright future.* **4.** The future tense. ❖ *adj.* That will be or occur in time to come: *Let's review our progress at some future date.* [From Middle English, from Latin *futūrus,* about to be.]

future perfect tense *n.* A verb tense expressing action or a state completed by a specified time in the future. It is formed in English by combining *will have* or *shall have* with a past participle, as in the sentence *By noon tomorrow the train will have arrived there.*

future tense *n.* A verb tense used to express action or a state in the future. It is formed in English with the auxiliary verbs *will* and *shall,* as in the sentence *They will leave in half an hour.*

fu·tur·is·tic (fyo͞o′chə-**rĭs′**tĭk) *adj.* **1.** Relating to the future. **2.** Characterized by or expressing a vision of the future: *a futuristic movie in which robots rule the world.* —**fu′tur·is′ti·cal·ly** *adv.*

fu·tu·ri·ty (fyo͞o-**to͝or′**ĭ-tē *or* fyo͞o-**cho͝or′**ĭ-tē) *n., pl.* **fu·tu·ri·ties 1.** The time yet to come; the future. **2.** The condition or quality of being in or of the future: *the futurity of experimental car design.* **3.** A future event or possibility.

fuze (fyo͞oz) *n.* Variant of **fuse[1].**

fuzz (fŭz) *n.* Soft short fibers or hairs; down: *the fuzz on a peach.*

fuzz·y (fŭz′ē) *adj.* **fuzz·i·er, fuzz·i·est 1.** Covered with fuzz: *a fuzzy peach.* **2.** Relating to or resembling fuzz: *fuzzy hair of a little kitten.* **3.** Not clear; blurred: *a fuzzy memory.* —**fuzz′i·ly** *adv.* —**fuzz′i·ness** *n.*

–fy or **–ify** *suff.* A suffix that means to make or cause to become: *beautify; solidify.* —SEE NOTE.

FYI *abbr.* An abbreviation of for your information.

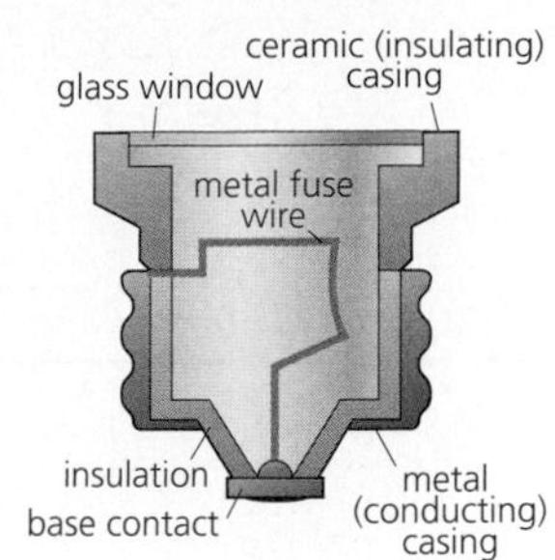

fuse[2]

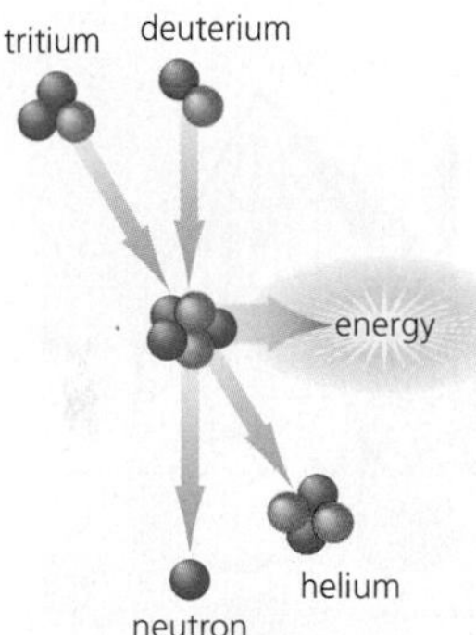

fusion

Tritium and deuterium collide, forming helium and giving off energy and a neutron.

WORD BUILDING

–fy The verb suffix **–fy,** which means "to make or cause to become," derives from Latin *–ficāre,* from the verb *facere,* "to do or make." Thus *purify* means "to make pure, cleanse" (coming from Latin *pūrificāre,* from *pūrus* "clean" + *–ficāre*). In English the suffix *–fy* now normally takes the form *–ify*: *acidify, humidify.* Verbs ending in *–fy* often have related nouns ending in *–fication* or *–faction*: *magnify, magnification; satisfy, satisfaction.*

g[1] or **G** (jē) *n., pl.* **g's** or **G's** also **gs** or **Gs** **1.** The seventh letter of the English alphabet. **2.** In music, the fifth tone in the scale of C major. —SEE NOTE AT **c**[1].

g[2] *abbr.* An abbreviation of: **1a.** gravity. **b.** acceleration due to gravity. **2.** gram.

G[1] A trademark used for a movie rating that allows admission to people of all ages.

G[2] *n. Slang* One thousand dollars: *made 20 Gs on the deal.*

Ga The symbol for the element **gallium.**

GA *abbr.* An abbreviation of Georgia.

gab (găb) *Slang intr.v.* **gabbed, gab·bing, gabs** To talk about unimportant matters; chatter: *The neighbors gabbed over the fence.* ❖ *n.* Idle talk. [From Middle English *gabben,* to speak foolishly, from Old Norse *gabba,* to scoff.]

gab·ar·dine also **gab·er·dine** (**găb′**ər-dēn′ *or* găb′ər-**dēn′**) *n.* A firm woven cloth of cotton, rayon, or wool, having a smooth surface and slanting ribs and used for coats or suits.

gab·by (**găb′**ē) *adj.* **gab·bi·er, gab·bi·est** *Slang* Tending to talk too much. **—gab′bi·ness** *n.*

ga·ble (**gā′**bəl) *n.* **1.** The triangular section of wall between the two slopes of a pitched roof. **2.** The whole end wall of a building or wing having a pitched roof. [From Middle English, from Norman French *gable* (perhaps of Celtic origin) and from Old Norse *gafl.*] **—ga′bled** *adj.*

gable

gable roof *n.* A pitched roof.

Ga·bon (gă-**bŏn′**) A country of west-central Africa on the Atlantic Ocean south of Cameroon. Libreville is the capital.

Ga·bo·ro·ne (gä′bə-**rō′**nē) The capital of Botswana, in the southeast part of the country near the South African border. It was founded in about 1890.

Ga·bri·el (**gā′**brē-əl) *n.* In the Bible, an angel who explained signs from God and announced the conception, birth, and mission of Jesus to Mary.

gad (găd) *intr.v.* **gad·ded, gad·ding, gads** To roam about seeking amusement or social activity.

gad·a·bout (**găd′**ə-bout′) *n.* A person who roams about seeking amusement or social activity.

gad·fly (**găd′**flī′) *n.* **1.** A person who annoys, criticizes, or provokes others: *She is an outspoken gadfly who always raises objections at the meetings.* **2.** Any of various flies that bite and annoy cattle, horses, and other animals.

gadg·et (**găj′**ĭt) *n.* A small mechanical device; a contrivance: *can openers, whisks, and other kitchen gadgets.*

gad·o·lin·i·um (găd′l-**ĭn′**ē-əm) *n. Symbol* **Gd** A silvery-white metallic element used to improve the heat and corrosion resistance of iron, chromium, and several alloys. Atomic number 64. See **Periodic Table.** [After Johan *Gadolin* (1760–1852), Finnish chemist.]

Gae·a (**gā′**ə) *n.* In Greek mythology, the goddess of the earth, who gave birth to and married Uranus and became the mother of the Titans.

Gael (gāl) *n.* **1.** A Gaelic-speaking Celt of Scotland, Ireland, or the Isle of Man. **2.** A Scottish highlander.

Gael·ic (**gā′**lĭk) *adj.* Relating to the Gaels or their culture or languages. ❖ *n.* Any of the Celtic languages of Ireland, Scotland, and the Isle of Man.

gaff (găf) *n.* **1.** An iron hook attached to a pole or handle and used to land large fish. **2.** A spar used to support the top edge of a fore-and-aft sail. ❖ *tr.v.* **gaffed, gaf·fing, gaffs** To hook or land (a fish) with a gaff. [From Middle English *gaffe,* from Old Provençal *gaf,* from *gafar,* to seize, of Germanic origin.]

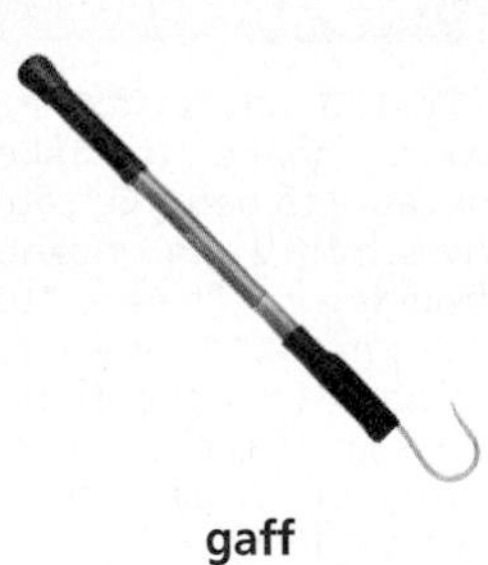

gaff

gaf·fer (**găf′**ər) *n.* **1.** An electrician in charge of the lighting on a movie or television set. **2.** *Chiefly British* An old man.

gag (găg) *n.* **1.** Something put into or over a person's mouth to prevent speaking or crying out. **2.** Something, such as a law or ruling, that limits or censors free speech: *The judge put a gag on press reporting during the trial.* **3a.** A humorous remark intended to make people laugh; a joke. **b.** A practical joke; a hoax. ❖ *v.* **gagged, gag·ging, gags** *—tr.* **1.** To prevent (someone) from speaking or crying out by using a gag. **2.** To prevent (someone) from exercising free speech. **3.** To cause to choke or retch: *The strong gas fumes gagged several passers-by.* *—intr.* To choke or retch: *I gagged on the bitter medicine.* [From Middle English *gaggen,* to suffocate, perhaps of imitative origin.]

Ga·ga·rin (gə-**gär′**ĭn), **Yuri Alekseyevich** 1934–1968. Soviet cosmonaut who in 1961 became the first person to travel in space.

Gage (gāj), **Thomas** 1721?–1787. British general whose efforts to suppress colonial resistance in Massachusetts led to the start of the American Revolution.

gag·gle (**găg′**əl) *n.* **1.** A flock of geese. **2.** A cluster or group: *a gaggle of fans.* [From Middle English *gagel,* from *gagelen,* to cackle, probably of imitative origin.]

gai·e·ty also **gay·e·ty** (**gā′**ĭ-tē) *n., pl.* **gai·e·ties** also **gay·e·ties** **1.** The condition of being merry; cheerfulness: *the gaiety of the laughing children.* **2.** Merrymaking; celebration: *Mardi Gras is a season of gaiety.* **3.** Showiness or brightness in dress or appearance; finery: *The gaiety of the colorful flowers brightened the room.*

gai·ly also **gay·ly** (**gā′**lē) *adv.* **1.** In a joyful, cheerful, or happy manner; merrily. **2.** Brightly; colorfully; showily: *The room for the party was gaily decorated.*

gain (gān) *v.* **gained, gain·ing, gains** *—tr.* **1.** To obtain; acquire: *We gained experience by working during the summer.* **2.** To acquire in competition; win: *The general gained a decisive victory over the enemy.* **3a.** To get an increase of; build up: *gain speed; gain strength after an illness.* **b.** To increase by (a certain amount): *gained 10 pounds over the winter.* **4.** To come to; reach: *gained the top of the mountain.* See Synonyms at **reach.** *—intr.* **1.** To increase; grow: *Has your house gained in value?* **2.** To become better; improve: *The recovering patient is gaining in strength.* **3.** To come nearer; get closer: *The hounds gained on the fleeing fox.* ❖ *n.* **1a.** Something gained

ă	pat	ôr	core
ā	pay	oi	boy
âr	care	ou	out
ä	father	o͝o	took
ĕ	pet	o͝or	lure
ē	be	o͞o	boot
ĭ	pit	ŭ	cut
ī	bite	ûr	urge
îr	pier	th	thin
ŏ	pot	*th*	this
ō	toe	zh	vision
ô	paw	ə	about

or acquired: *territorial gains.* **b.** Progress; advancement: *We have made great social gains since the early 1900s.* **2.** An increase in amount or degree: *a financial gain; a gain in popularity.*

gain·er (gā′nər) *n.* **1.** A person or thing that gains. **2.** A reverse dive.

gain·ful (gān′fəl) *adj.* Providing an income or advantage; profitable: *gainful employment.* **—gain′ful·ly** *adv.*

gain·say (gān-sā′ *or* gān′sā′) *tr.v.* **gain·said** (gān-săd′ *or* gān-sĕd′), **gain·say·ing, gain·says** (gān-săz′ *or* gān-sĕz′) To declare to be false; deny or contradict: *She was the only witness, so there was no one to gainsay her account of the robbery.*

gait (gāt) *n.* **1.** A way of walking or running: *a shuffling gait.* **2.** The way in which a horse moves, as a walk, trot, or gallop. [From Middle English *gate*, path, gait, from Old Norse *gata*, path.]

❑ *These sound alike:* **gait, gate** (entrance).

gai·ter (gā′tər) *n.* **1.** A covering for the lower leg or ankle, worn especially by skiers and hikers. **2.** A tubular collar fitting closely around the neck, often worn by skiers. **3.** An ankle-high shoe with elastic sides. **4.** An overshoe with a cloth top.

gal (găl) *n. Informal* A girl.

gal. *abbr.* An abbreviation of gallon.

ga·la (gā′lə *or* găl′ə *or* gä′lə) *n.* A festive occasion or celebration. ❖ *adj.* Festive: *The city greeted the home team's victory with a gala celebration.*

ga·lac·tic (gə-lăk′tĭk) *adj.* Relating to a galaxy, especially the Milky Way.

Gal·a·had (găl′ə-hăd′) *n.* In Arthurian legend, the most virtuous of King Arthur's knights, who found the Holy Grail.

Ga·lá·pa·gos Islands (gə-lä′pə-gəs *or* gə-lăp′ə-gəs) A group of islands of Ecuador in the Pacific Ocean west of the mainland. The islands are famous for their rare wildlife, including the giant tortoises for which they are named.

Ga·la·tians (gə-lā′shənz) *pl.n. (used with a singular verb)* A book of the New Testament consisting of a letter by Saint Paul to Christians in Galatia, a country in Asia Minor.

gal·ax·y (găl′ək-sē) *n., pl.* **gal·ax·ies 1a.** A vast grouping of stars, gas, and dust held together by the force of gravity. A galaxy has billions of stars. **b.** often **Galaxy** The galaxy that contains our solar system; the Milky Way. **2.** An assembly of brilliant, beautiful, or distinguished people or things: *a galaxy of movie stars.* [From Middle English *galaxie*, the Milky Way, from Greek *galaxiās*, milky, from *gala*, milk.]

gale (gāl) *n.* **1.** A very strong wind. **2.** A storm at sea: *The ship was blown off course by the gale.* **3.** A noisy outburst: *gales of laughter.*

Ga·len (gā′lən) AD 130?–200? Greek physician whose many theories about the structures and functions of the human body formed the basis of European medicine until the Renaissance.

ga·le·na (gə-lē′nə) *n.* A gray mineral, composed of lead and sulfur, that is the main ore of lead.

Gal·i·lee (găl′ə-lē′) A region of northern Israel that was the center of Jesus's ministry. **—Gal′i·le′an** (găl′ə-lē′ən) *n. & adj.*

Galilee, Sea of A freshwater lake of northeast Israel. It is about 705 feet (215 meters) below sea level.

Ga·li·le·o Ga·li·lei (găl′ə-lā′ō găl′ə-lā′) 1564–1642. Italian astronomer and physicist who was the first to use a telescope to study the stars and planets (1609). —SEE NOTE.

gall¹ (gôl) *n.* **1.** Insulting boldness; impudence; nerve: *They had the gall to barge into the party uninvited.* **2.** Bitter feeling; spite: *The feuding neighbors were full of gall.* **3.** A bitter yellow or green liquid secreted by the liver to aid digestion; bile. [From Middle English *galle*, from Old English *gealla, galla.*]

gall² (gôl) *n.* A sore on the skin caused by rubbing: *a saddle gall on a horse.* ❖ *v.* **galled, gall·ing, galls** —*tr.* **1.** To irritate or exasperate: *It galls me to see people littering.* **2.** To make sore or chafed. —*intr.* To become sore by rubbing. [From Middle English *galle*, from Old English *gealla*, possibly from Latin *galla*, nutlike swelling on a tree.]

gall³ (gôl) *n.* An abnormal swelling on a plant, usually caused by insects, bacteria, or mites. [From Middle English *galle*, from Latin *galla*, nutlike swelling on a tree.]

gal·lant (găl′ənt) *adj.* **1.** Stylish in appearance; dashing: *He was very gallant at the ball.* **2.** Brave and noble; courageous; valorous: *a gallant resistance to the invasion.* **3.** Stately or majestic; grand: *a gallant ship.* **4.** (gə-lănt′ *or* gə-länt′) Polite and attentive to women; chivalrous: *our host's gallant manner.* ❖ *n.* (gə-lănt′ *or* gə-länt′ *or* găl′ənt) **1.** A fashionable young man. **2.** A man who is polite and attentive to women. **—gal′lant·ly** *adv.*

gal·lant·ry (găl′ən-trē) *n., pl.* **gal·lant·ries 1.** Heroic courage or brave and noble conduct. **2.** Considerate attention to women; courtliness. **3.** A gallant act or action.

gall·blad·der also **gall bladder** (gôl′blăd′ər) *n.* A small, pear-shaped muscular sac, located near the right lobe of the liver, in which bile is stored.

gal·le·on (găl′ē-ən *or* găl′yən) *n.* A large three-masted sailing ship of the 1400s, 1500s, and 1600s, used especially by the Spanish.

gal·ler·y (găl′ə-rē) *n., pl.* **gal·ler·ies 1.** A long narrow walk or passage, often with a roof and windows along one side. **2.** An enclosed passageway, such as a hall or corridor: *a shooting gallery.* **3.** A narrow balcony, usually with railing, along the outside of a building. **4a.** The balcony in a theater or church: *The gallery in the concert hall has the cheapest seats.* **b.** The seats in such a balcony. **c.** The people occupying these seats: *The gallery applauded and whistled.* **5.** A large audience, as at a sports event: *The golfer tipped his hat toward the gallery.* **6.** A building or hall for displaying works of art. **7.** An underground tunnel or other passageway, as in a mine.

gal·ley (găl′ē) *n., pl.* **gal·leys 1.** A long narrow ship driven by sails and oars and used primarily in the Mediterranean until the 1600s. **2.** The kitchen on a ship, airliner, or camper. **3a.** A long tray for holding metal type that has been set to print a publication. **b.** A galley proof.

galley proof *n.* A trial sheet of printed material; a proof.

gall·fly (gôl′flī′) *n.* Any of various small insects that deposit their eggs on plant stems or in the bark of trees, causing galls to form.

Gal·lic (găl′ĭk) *adj.* Relating to ancient Gaul or to modern France.

gall·ing (gô′lĭng) *adj.* Very irritating or exasperating: *A mechanical problem caused another galling delay in our flight.* **—gall′ing·ly** *adv.*

gal·li·um (găl′ē-əm) *n. Symbol* **Ga** A rare, silvery metallic element that is liquid near room temperature and is used in thermometers, semiconductors, and transistors. Atomic number 31. See **Periodic Table.** [From Latin *gallus*, rooster, translation of surname of Paul Émile *Lecoq* de Boisbaudran (1838–1912), French chemist.]

gal·li·vant (găl′ə-vănt′) *intr.v.* **gal·li·vant·ed, gal·li·vant·ing, gal·li·vants** To travel or roam about in search of pleasure or amusement.

Gal·lo (găl′ō), **Robert Charles** Born 1937. American microbiologist who was one of the first to identify and develop a blood test for the virus later called HIV.

gal·lon (găl′ən) *n.* **1.** A unit of volume or capacity used for measuring liquids, equal to 4 quarts (3.8 liters). See table at **measurement. 2a.** A container having a capacity of one gallon. **b.** The amount that can be held in such a container: *a gallon of milk.*

Yuri Gagarin

galaxy
spiral galaxy

BIOGRAPHY

Galileo Galilei In 1609 **Galileo** heard of the invention of the spyglass, a tube with a piece of glass at each end that made objects appear closer and larger. He set about making his own. Galileo used his telescope (as the device began to be called) to observe the heavens, studying mountains on the moon's surface and discovering Jupiter's four largest moons. Galileo's observations convinced him that Nicolaus Copernicus had been right when he stated that Earth and all the planets orbit the sun. Many people opposed this theory, which contradicted the traditional belief that Earth was the center of the universe. Galileo was called before Roman Catholic Church authorities and forced to declare that Copernicus's theory was false. He was then put under house arrest on his own farm, where he was allowed to continue his scientific work until the end of his life.

gambrel roof

Mohandas Gandhi

gannet

ă	pat	ôr	core
ā	pay	oi	boy
âr	care	ou	out
ä	father	o͝o	took
ĕ	pet	o͝or	lure
ē	be	o͞o	boot
ĭ	pit	ŭ	cut
ī	bite	ûr	urge
îr	pier	th	thin
ŏ	pot	*th*	this
ō	toe	zh	vision
ô	paw	ə	about

gal·lop (găl′əp) *n.* **1.** A fast gait of a horse or other four-footed animal, in which all four feet are off the ground at the same time during each stride. **2.** A ride on a horse going at a gallop. ❖ *v.* **gal·loped, gal·lop·ing, gal·lops** —*tr.* To cause to gallop: *The rider galloped the horse around the track.* —*intr.* **1.** To ride at a gallop: *gallop around the field.* **2.** To move or progress swiftly: *Summer is galloping by.* —**gal′lop·er** *n.*

gal·lows (găl′ōz) *n., pl.* **gallows** or **gal·lows·es 1.** An upright framework from which a noose is suspended, used for execution by hanging. **2.** Execution on a gallows or by hanging: *was sentenced to the gallows.*

gall·stone (gôl′stōn′) *n.* A small hard mass that forms in the gallbladder or in a bile duct.

ga·lore (gə-**lôr′**) *adj.* In great numbers; in abundance: *The streets were filled with shoppers galore during the holiday season.* [From Irish Gaelic *go leór,* enough.]

ga·losh (gə-**lŏsh′**) *n.* A waterproof overshoe.

gal·van·ic (găl-**văn′**ĭk) *adj.* **1.** Relating to electricity that is produced by chemical action. **2.** Producing electricity by chemical action: *a galvanic cell.*

gal·va·nism (**găl′**və-nĭz′əm) *n.* Direct-current electricity produced by chemical action. [After Luigi *Galvani* (1737–1798), Italian physiologist.]

gal·va·nize (**găl′**və-nīz′) *tr.v.* **gal·va·nized, gal·va·niz·ing, gal·va·niz·es 1.** To coat (iron or steel) with zinc as protection against rust. **2.** To stir to action or awareness; spur: *Destruction of important habitats in our state galvanized us to support the conservation law.* —**gal′va·ni·za′tion** (găl′və-nĭ-**zā′**shən) *n.*

gal·va·nom·e·ter (găl′və-**nŏm′**ĭ-tər) *n.* An instrument that detects, measures, and determines the direction of small electric currents.

Ga·ma (**găm′**ə *or* **gä′**mə), **Vasco da** 1460?–1524. Portuguese explorer who sailed to India (1497–1498) and opened the area to Portuguese trade and colonization.

Gam·bi·a (**găm′**bē-ə) A country of western Africa on the Atlantic Ocean surrounded by Senegal. Banjul is the capital.

gam·bit (**găm′**bĭt) *n.* **1.** An opening move in chess in which a pawn or piece is sacrificed in order to gain a favorable position. **2.** An action or remark designed to bring about a desired result.

gam·ble (**găm′**bəl) *v.* **gam·bled, gam·bling, gam·bles** —*intr.* **1.** To bet money on the outcome of a game, contest, or other event. **2.** To take a risk in the hope of gaining an advantage: *The builder is gambling on the need for more houses soon.* —*tr.* **1.** To risk (something) in gambling; wager. **2.** To expose to hazard; risk: *The daredevil gambled his life in his latest stunt.* ❖ *n.* **1.** A bet or wager. **2.** An act of undertaking something uncertain; a risk. [Perhaps from obsolete *gamel,* to play games, from Old English *gamenian,* from *gamen,* fun.] —**gam′bler** *n.*

❑ *These sound alike:* **gamble, gambol** (frolic).

gam·bol (**găm′**bəl) *intr.v.* **gam·boled, gam·bol·ing, gam·bols** or **gam·bolled, gam·bol·ling, gam·bols** To skip or run about playfully; frolic. ❖ *n.* The act of skipping or frolicking about.

❑ *These sound alike:* **gambol, gamble** (bet).

gam·brel roof (**găm′**brəl) *n.* A ridged roof that has two different slopes on each side, with the lower slope steeper than the upper slope.

game[1] (gām) *n.* **1.** An activity that provides entertainment or amusement: *The children made a game of counting cars that passed.* **2.** A sport or contest governed by specific rules: *Tennis is my favorite game.* **3.** A single contest between two opponents or teams: *The game was canceled due to rain.* **4.** The number of points needed to win a game. **5.** The equipment, such as a board and pieces, needed for playing certain games: *The game came with its own box.* **6.** A particular style or ability at a certain game: *A few of the golfers seemed off their game today.* **7a.** Wild animals hunted for food or sport. **b.** The flesh of these animals, used as food. **8.** *Informal* A plan or scheme: *Anyone can see through that old game.* **9.** *Informal* An occupation, profession, or activity: *the game of politics.* ❖ *tr. & intr.v.* **gamed, gam·ing, games** To gamble. ❖ *adj.* **gam·er, gam·est 1.** Courageous; plucky: *They put up a game fight.* **2.** Ready and willing: *I'm game for climbing the mountain.* [From Old English *gamen.*] —**game′ly** *adv.* —**game′ness** *n.*

game[2] (gām) *adj.* **gam·er, gam·est** Lame or injured: *a game leg.*

game bird *n.* A bird, such as a pheasant or grouse, that is widely hunted for sport.

game·cock (**gām′**kŏk′) *n.* A rooster bred and trained for fighting.

game·keep·er (**gām′**kē′pər) *n.* A person employed to protect and maintain game birds and other wildlife, especially on an estate or preserve.

gam·er (**gā′**mər) *n.* A person who plays a game, especially a role-playing or computer game.

game show *n.* A television show in which contestants compete for prizes by playing a game, such as a quiz.

game·ster (**gām′**stər) *n.* A person who plays games, especially a gambler.

gam·ete (**găm′**ēt′) *n.* A cell that unites with another to form a fertilized cell that develops into a new organism; a reproductive cell.

ga·me·to·phyte (gə-**mē′**tə-fīt′) *n.* In plants and most algae, the individual organism or generation of organisms that produces reproductive cells. The life cycle of such an organism involves an alternation between the gametophyte and the sporophyte.

game warden *n.* An official who enforces hunting and fishing regulations.

gam·ing (**gā′**mĭng) *n.* **1.** Gambling. **2.** The playing of games, especially computer or video games.

gam·ma (**găm′**ə) *n.* The third letter of the Greek alphabet, written Γ, γ. In English it is represented as *G, g,* except before *g, k,* or *kh,* when it is often represented as *N, n.*

gamma globulin *n.* A solution of antibodies derived from human blood plasma and used in the treatment of certain diseases.

gamma ray *n.* Electromagnetic radiation with wavelengths shorter than those of x-rays and having greater energy and penetrating power. Gamma rays are given off by unstable nuclei during radioactive decay.

gam·ut (**găm′**ət) *n.* **1.** The entire range of musical tones. **2.** The complete range of something: *the gamut of feelings from high hope to utter despair.*

gam·y (**gā′**mē) *adj.* **gam·i·er, gam·i·est 1.** Having the flavor or odor of game, especially slightly spoiled game. **2.** Showing great spirit; plucky: *a gamy horse that loves to run.* —**gam′i·ly** *adv.* —**gam′i·ness** *n.*

gan·der (**găn′**dər) *n.* **1.** A male goose. **2.** *Informal* A look or glance: *Take a gander at this flat tire and see what you think.*

Gan·dhi (**găn′**dē), **Indira Nehru** 1917–1984. Indian politician who served as prime minister from 1966 to 1977 and from 1980 to 1984.

Gandhi, Mohandas Karamchand Known as "Mahatma." 1869–1948. Indian leader who developed the practice of nonviolent disobedience that led to India's independence from the United Kingdom (1947).

gang (găng) *n.* **1.** An organized group of criminals. **2.** A group of young people who band together, especially a group of delinquents. **3.** *Informal* A group of friends: *The whole gang went to see a movie.* **4.** A group of laborers who work together under a single supervisor: *a road gang filling potholes.* ❖ *intr.v.* **ganged, gang·ing, gangs** To band together in a group or gang: *The reporters ganged around the governor.* ◆ **gang up 1.** To join together in criticism or attack: *The author felt that the critics were ganging up on her.* **2.** To act together as a group: *Researchers ganged up to fight the disease.*

Gan·ges (găn′jēz′) also **Gan·ga** (gŭng′gə) A river of northern India and Bangladesh rising in the Himalaya Mountains and flowing about 1,560 miles (2,510 kilometers) generally east to the Bay of Bengal.

gan·gling (găng′glĭng) *adj.* Tall and awkward; lanky.

gan·gli·on (găng′glē-ən) *n., pl.* **gan·gli·a** (găng′glē-ə) or **gan·gli·ons** A compact group of nerve cells forming a nerve center, especially one located outside the brain or spinal cord.

gang·plank (găng′plăngk′) *n.* A board or ramp used as a bridge between a ship and a pier.

gan·grene (găng′grēn′ *or* găng-**grēn′**) *n.* Decay of tissue in a living body, caused by a stoppage of the blood supply from injury or disease. ❖ *tr. & intr.v.* **gan·grened, gan·gren·ing, gan·grenes** To affect or become affected with gangrene. **—gan′gre·nous** (găng′grə-nəs) *adj.*

gang·ster (găng′stər) *n.* A member of an organized group of criminals.

gang·way (găng′wā′) *n.* **1a.** A gangplank. **b.** An opening in the side of a ship through which passengers may board. **2.** A passage along either side of a ship's upper deck.

gan·net (găn′ĭt) *n.* Any of several large, mostly white seabirds that have long pointed wings and a long bill and that nest in large colonies on rocky coasts. [From Old English *ganot.*]

gant·let¹ (gônt′lĭt *or* gănt′lĭt) *n.* Variant of **gauntlet¹**.

gant·let² (gônt′lĭt *or* gănt′lĭt) *n.* Variant of **gauntlet²**.

gan·try (găn′trē) *n., pl.* **gan·tries 1a.** A large framework designed to carry a crane from one spot to another along a set of rails. **b.** A similar structure on which signals are mounted over railroad tracks. **2.** A large vertical structure somewhat like a scaffold, used in assembling or servicing a rocket, especially on a launching pad.

Gan·y·mede (găn′ə-mēd′) *n.* In Greek mythology, a Trojan boy of great beauty whom Zeus carried away to be cupbearer to the gods.

gaol (jāl) *n. Chiefly British* Variant of **jail.**

gap (găp) *n.* **1.** An opening or break, as in a wall or fence. **2.** A break in something continuous: *There are many gaps in our knowledge of the universe.* **3.** A pass through mountains. **4.** A wide difference or imbalance: *There is a gap between what he says and what he does.* [From Middle English, from Old Norse, chasm.]

gape (gāp *or* găp) *intr.v.* **gaped, gap·ing, gapes 1.** To open the mouth wide, as if to bite or swallow. **2.** To stare in amazement, often with the mouth open: *The fans gaped as the baseball went soaring out of the park.* **3.** To open wide; form a gap: *Cracks gaped in the ground after the earthquake.* ❖ *n.* The act or an instance of gaping: *the wide gape of a lion's yawn.*

gap year *n.* A year taken off from a person's education, especially between high school and college, often to travel or gain practical experience.

gar (gär) *n.* Any of several freshwater fishes of North and Central America having a long body and long narrow jaws with sharp teeth.

ga·rage (gə-räzh′ *or* gə-räj′) *n.* **1.** A building or indoor space in which to park a motor vehicle. **2.** A business where cars are repaired, serviced, or parked. ❖ *tr.v.* **ga·raged, ga·rag·ing, ga·rag·es** To put or keep (a vehicle) in a garage. [From French, from Old French *guerrer, garer,* to shelter, of Germanic origin.]

garage sale *n.* A sale of used household items or clothing held at the home of the seller.

garb (gärb) *n.* A style or form of clothing: *folk dancers in traditional rural garb.* ❖ *tr.v.* **garbed, garb·ing, garbs** To clothe or dress: *The judge was garbed in a long black robe.*

gar·bage (gär′bĭj) *n.* **1.** Food wastes, as from a kitchen. **2.** Worthless or inferior material; trash: *That novel is nothing but garbage.*

gar·ban·zo (gär-**bän′**zō) *n., pl.* **gar·ban·zos** The chickpea.

gar·ble (gär′bəl) *tr.v.* **gar·bled, gar·bling, gar·bles** To distort or mix up: *The report sounded great, but she garbled the facts.* ❖ *n.* The act or an instance of garbling: *a confused garble of voices.*

gar·den (gär′dn) *n.* **1.** A piece of land used for growing flowers, vegetables, herbs, or fruit. **2.** A park or other public place ornamented with flowers and other plants: *a botanical garden.* ❖ *intr.v.* **gar·dened, gar·den·ing, gar·dens** To plant or tend a garden.

gar·den·er (gärd′nər *or* gär′dn-ər) *n.* A person who works in or takes care of a garden.

gar·de·nia (gär-**dēn′**yə) *n.* Any of various shrubs having glossy evergreen leaves and large, fragrant, usually white flowers. [After Alexander *Garden* (1730?–1791), Scottish-born American naturalist.]

gar·den-va·ri·e·ty (gär′dn-və-rī′ĭ-tē) *adj.* Common; unremarkable: *I'm getting bored with the same old garden-variety video games they're making now.*

Gar·field (gär′fēld′), **James Abram** 1831–1881. The 20th president of the United States (1881). He pledged to fight government corruption but was assassinated in his first year in office.

gar·fish (gär′fĭsh′) *n.* A gar.

gar·gan·tu·an (gär-**găn′**cho͞o-ən) *adj.* Of immense size; huge: *a stadium of gargantuan proportions.*

gar·gle (gär′gəl) *v.* **gar·gled, gar·gling, gar·gles** *—intr.* To wash or rinse the mouth or throat by exhaling air through a liquid held there. *—tr.* To circulate (a liquid) in the mouth or throat by gargling. ❖ *n.* A liquid used for gargling. [From Old French *gargouiller.*]

gar·goyle (gär′goil′) *n.* **1.** A drain spout in the form of a grotesque animal or person projecting from the gutter of a building. **2.** A grotesque, usually projecting ornamental figure. [From Middle English *gargoile,* from Old French *gargole, gargouille,* throat, waterspout.]

Gar·i·bal·di (găr′ə-**bôl′**dē), **Giuseppe** 1807–1882. Italian general who led a group of volunteers in the capture of Sicily and Naples (1860). His conquest led to the formation of the kingdom of Italy (1861).

gar·ish (gâr′ĭsh) *adj.* Too bright or ornamented; gaudy: *The clown wore a suit of garish colors.* **—gar′ish·ly** *adv.* **—gar′ish·ness** *n.*

gar·land (gär′lənd) *n.* A wreath or chain, as of flowers or leaves, worn as a crown or used for ornament. ❖ *tr.v.* **gar·land·ed, gar·land·ing, gar·lands** To decorate with a garland.

gar·lic (gär′lĭk) *n.* **1.** The bulb of a plant related to the onion, having a strong taste and odor and used as seasoning. The bulb can be divided into separate parts called cloves. **2.** The plant that bears such a bulb. **—gar′lick·y** *adj.*

gar·ment (gär′mənt) *n.* An article of clothing.

garment bag *n.* A long zippered bag, usually capable of being folded in half, used to carry and protect clothes when traveling.

gar·ner (gär′nər) *tr.v.* **gar·nered, gar·ner·ing, gar·ners** To receive or gather: *The band garnered much praise for their new album.*

gar·net (gär′nĭt) *n.* **1.** A common crystalline silicate mineral of aluminum or calcium. It is usually red and is used as a gem and as an abrasive. **2.** A dark red color. [From Middle English, from Old French *grenate,* probably from Latin *grānātum,* pomegranate.]

gar·nish (gär′nĭsh) *tr.v.* **gar·nished, gar·nish·ing, gar·nish·es 1.** To decorate or embellish: *garnish iced tea with a slice of lemon; mashed potatoes garnished with parsley.* **2.** To take or keep (someone's pay or property)

gantry

James Garfield

WRITERS CHOOSE THEIR WORDS

Every now and then Doon would ask him how it was going, and Edward would get a feverish look in his eyes and say, "Ah! It goes by inches, young Doon. By millimeters. I've done this much"—he held his thumb and forefinger a tiny distance apart—"and this much remains to be done." He stretched his arms as far apart as they would go. "It's a **gargantuan** task. I press forward, but will I finish in my lifetime? It is doubtful."

—Jeanne DuPrau
The People of Sparks

gargoyle

Marcus Garvey

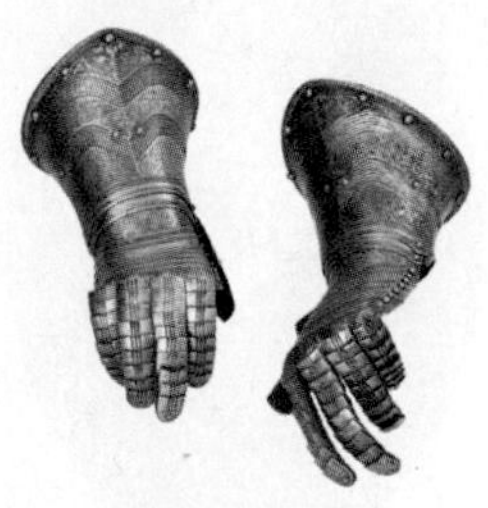
gauntlet[1]

gavel

ă	pat	ôr	core
ā	pay	oi	boy
âr	care	ou	out
ä	father	ŏŏ	took
ĕ	pet	ŏŏr	lure
ē	be	ōō	boot
ĭ	pit	ŭ	cut
ī	bite	ûr	urge
îr	pier	th	thin
ŏ	pot	*th*	this
ō	toe	zh	vision
ô	paw	ə	about

by a legal proceeding in order to use it to pay off a debt. ❖ *n.* A decoration, especially one added to a food or drink to give it extra color or flavor.

gar·ret (găr′ĭt) *n.* A room on the top floor of a house, typically under a pitched roof; an attic.

gar·ri·son (găr′ĭ-sən) *n.* **1.** A military post. **2.** The troops stationed at such a post. ❖ *tr.v.* **gar·ri·soned, gar·ri·son·ing, gar·ri·sons 1.** To assign (troops) to a military post. **2.** To supply (a post or other place) with troops for defense.

Gar·ri·son (găr′ĭ-sən), **William Lloyd** 1805–1879. American abolitionist who founded and published *The Liberator* (1831–1865), an antislavery journal.

gar·ru·li·ty (gə-rōō′lĭ-tē) *n.* The quality of being overly talkative.

gar·ru·lous (găr′ə-ləs *or* găr′yə-ləs) *adj.* Excessively talkative, especially about unimportant matters: *a garrulous neighbor.* **—gar′ru·lous·ness** *n.*

gar·ter (gär′tər) *n.* An elastic band or strap worn on the leg to hold up a stocking or sock. ❖ *tr.v.* **gar·tered, gar·ter·ing, gar·ters** To fasten and hold with a garter.

garter snake *n.* Any of various small nonvenomous North and Central American snakes that usually have a dark body with three lighter-colored lengthwise stripes.

Gar·vey (gär′vē), **Marcus (Moziah) Aurelius** 1887–1940. Jamaican black nationalist who worked in the United States in the 1920s, urging African Americans to establish a country in Africa.

gas (găs) *n., pl.* **gas·es** or **gas·ses 1.** One of the three basic forms of matter, composed of molecules in constant random motion. Unlike a solid, a gas has no fixed shape and will take on the shape of the space available. Unlike a liquid, it has no fixed volume and will expand to fill the space available. **2.** A gas or mixture of gases burned as fuel for cooking or heating. **3.** Gasoline. **4.** A chemical gas that chokes, irritates, or poisons, used as a weapon. **5.** An anesthetic that is in the form of gas. **6.** *Slang* A highly exciting or entertaining person or thing: *That new ride is a gas.* ❖ *tr.v.* **gassed, gas·sing, gas·es** or **gas·ses 1.** To treat chemically with gas. **2.** To injure or poison with gas. ◆ **gas up** To supply a vehicle with gas or gasoline: *We gassed the car up before going on our trip.* [From Dutch *gas*, a hidden physical principle supposed to be present in all bodies, alteration of Greek *khaos*, chaos, empty space.]

gas·e·ous (găs′ē-əs *or* găsh′əs) *adj.* Relating to or existing as a gas: *Water in its gaseous state is called water vapor.*

gas giant *n.* A large planet that has a thick gaseous atmosphere and lacks a solid surface because it has relatively little rock or other solid material. Jupiter, Saturn, Uranus, and Neptune are gas giants.

gash (găsh) *tr.v.* **gashed, gash·ing, gash·es** To make a long deep cut or wound in. ❖ *n.* A long deep cut or wound.

gas·ket (găs′kĭt) *n.* Any of a wide variety of seals or packings placed between machine parts or around pipe joints to prevent the escape of gas or fluid.

gas·light (găs′līt′) *n.* **1.** Light made by burning gas in a lamp. **2.** A lamp that uses gas as fuel.

gas·lit (găs′lĭt′) *adj.* Lighted by gaslight: *a gaslit street in the old section of town.*

gas mask *n.* A mask that covers the face or the face and head and is equipped with an air filter as protection against poisonous gases.

gas·o·hol (găs′ə-hôl′) *n.* A fuel for cars that is a blend of ethyl alcohol and unleaded gasoline.

gas·o·line (găs′ə-lēn′ *or* găs′ə-**lēn′**) *n.* A highly flammable mixture of liquid hydrocarbons that are derived from petroleum. Gasoline is used as a fuel for internal-combustion engines, as in automobiles, motorcycles, and small trucks.

gasp (găsp) *v.* **gasped, gasp·ing, gasps** *—intr.* To inhale in a sudden, sharp, and usually fitful way, as from shock, surprise, or great exertion. *—tr.* To say in a breathless manner: *"Wait!," she gasped.* ❖ *n.* A sudden, violent, or fitful intake of the breath.

gas station *n.* A business at which motor vehicles are refueled.

gas·sy (găs′ē) *adj.* **gas·si·er, gas·si·est** Resembling, containing, or filled with gas.

gas·tric (găs′trĭk) *adj.* Relating to the stomach: *a gastric ulcer.*

gas·tro·en·ter·i·tis (găs′trō-ĕn′tə-**rī′**tĭs) *n.* Inflammation of the mucous membrane of the stomach and intestines.

gas·tro·in·tes·ti·nal (găs′trō-ĭn-**tĕs′**tə-nəl) *adj.* Relating to the stomach and intestines.

gas·tro·nom·ic (găs′trə-**nŏm′**ĭk) also **gas·tro·nom·i·cal** (găs′trə-**nŏm′**ĭ-kəl) *adj.* Relating to gastronomy: *The chef brought out his latest gastronomic creation.* **—gas′tro·nom′i·cal·ly** *adv.*

gas·tron·o·my (gă-**strŏn′**ə-mē) *n.* The art or science of good eating. [From Greek *gastronomiā* : *gastēr*, belly, stomach + *nomos*, rule.]

gas·tro·pod (găs′trə-pŏd′) *n.* Any of numerous mollusks, such as a snail, slug, cowrie, or limpet, having a distinct head with eyes and tentacles, usually a single coiled shell, and a muscular foot on the underside of the body. [From Greek *gastēr*, belly, stomach + Greek *pous*, foot.]

gas·tru·la (găs′trə-lə) *n., pl.* **gas·tru·las** or **gas·tru·lae** (găs′trə-lē′) An embryo at the stage following the blastula, in which the cells are distributed into layers that eventually develop into the different tissues and organs of the body.

gat (găt) *v. Archaic* A past tense of **get.**

gate (gāt) *n.* **1a.** A hinged or sliding barrier that serves as a door in a wall or fence. **b.** An opening in a wall or fence; a gateway. **2.** A device for controlling the flow of water or gas through a pipe, dam, or similar system. **3.** A passageway in an airport through which passengers proceed when boarding or leaving an airplane. **4.** The number of people attending an event or performance: *a gate of 500 people.* **5.** The total amount of money paid for people attending an event or performance: *The gate for the rock concert was $775,000.*
❑ *These sound alike:* **gate, gait** (way of walking).

gate·crash·er (gāt′krăsh′ər) *n. Slang* A person who attends a gathering, performance, private party, or sports event without being invited or without paying.

gat·ed community (gā′tĭd) *n.* A residential neighborhood that is closed off by a gate or other barrier, with entrance permitted only to residents and their guests.

gate·house (gāt′hous′) *n.* A house built over or near a gate, usually lived in by a gatekeeper.

gate·keep·er (gāt′kē′pər) *n.* A person in charge of the passage of people or vehicles through a gate, as on an estate or at a castle.

gate·post (gāt′pōst′) *n.* An upright post on which a gate is hung or against which a gate closes.

Gates (gāts), **Horatio** 1728?–1806. American Revolutionary general who became a hero after winning the Battle of Saratoga (1777) but suffered a humiliating defeat at Camden, South Carolina (1780).

gate·way (gāt′wā′) *n.* **1.** An opening, as in a wall or fence, that may be closed with a gate. **2.** Something that serves as a means of access or an entrance: *Denver is thought of as the gateway to the Rockies.*

gath·er (găth′ər) *v.* **gath·ered, gath·er·ing, gath·ers** *—tr.* **1.** To bring together in a group; convene; assemble: *The teacher gathered the students around the exhibit.* **2.** To pick; collect: *Squirrels gather nuts.* **3.** To accumulate gradually: *The old bureau gathered dust in the attic.* **4.** To summon up; muster (mental or physical powers): *Give me a minute to gather my thoughts.* **5.** To gain or increase gradually: *The avalanche gathered speed.* **6.** To conclude; infer: *I gather that you didn't like the movie.* **7.** To draw (cloth) into small folds or pleats, as by sewing: *gather material at the waist of a full skirt.* **8.** To draw or bring closer: *gather a frightened kitten in one's arms.* —*intr.* **1.** To come together in a group; assemble: *The children gathered to wait for the school bus.* **2.** To grow or increase bit by bit; accumulate: *Dust gathered under the couch.* ❖ *n.* One of the small folds or pleats made in cloth by gathering it. **—gath′er·er** *n.*

SYNONYMS **gather, collect, assemble, accumulate** These verbs mean to bring together in a group or mass. **Gather** is the most general: *I gathered sticks to build a fire.* **Collect** often means to select like or related things that then become part of an organized whole: *She collects stamps and coins from around the world.* **Assemble** means to gather people or things that have a definite and usually close relationship: *The curator is assembling Stone Age artifacts to make an interesting exhibit.* **Accumulate** describes the increase of like or related things over an extended period of time: *He accumulated piles of old newspapers in the basement.*
ANTONYM: **disperse**

gath·er·ing (găth′ər-ĭng) *n.* **1.** An assembly of people; a meeting: *a family gathering.* **2.** The act of a person or thing that gathers.

Gat·ling gun (găt′lĭng) *n.* A machine gun having a cluster of barrels that are fired as the cluster is turned. [After Richard Jordan *Gatling* (1818–1903), American inventor.]

ga·tor (gā′tər) *n. Informal* An alligator.

gauche (gōsh) *adj.* Lacking social grace; tactless; clumsy: *Talking with your mouth full is gauche.*

gau·cho (gou′chō) *n., pl.* **gau·chos** A cowhand of the South American pampas.

gaud·y (gô′dē) *adj.* **gaud·i·er, gaud·i·est** Too brightly colored and showy to be in good taste. **—gaud′i·ly** *adv.* **—gaud′i·ness** *n.*

gauge (gāj) *n.* **1.** A standard dimension, quantity, or capacity, especially: **a.** The distance between the two rails of a railroad. **b.** The thickness or diameter of a material such as sheet metal or wire. **c.** The diameter of a shotgun barrel as determined by the number of lead balls of a size fitting the barrel that make one pound. **2.** An instrument for measuring or testing something: *We checked the air pressure in the tires with a gauge.* **3.** A means of estimating or evaluating; a test: *How a person handles a difficult situation is a good gauge of character.* ❖ *tr.v.* **gauged, gaug·ing, gaug·es 1.** To measure precisely: *gauge the depth of the ocean.* **2.** To evaluate or judge: *gauge a person's ability.* [From Middle English, from Old North French, rod for measuring, of Germanic origin.] **—gauge′a·ble** *adj.*

Gaul[1] (gôl) *n.* **1.** A Celt of ancient Gaul. **2.** A French person.

Gaul[2] (gôl) An ancient region of western Europe south and west of the Rhine River, west of the Alps, and north of the Pyrenees, corresponding roughly to modern-day France and Belgium.

Gaul·ish (gô′lĭsh) *adj.* Relating to Gaul, the ancient Gauls, or their language or customs. ❖ *n.* The Celtic language of ancient Gaul.

gaunt (gônt) *adj.* **gaunt·er, gaunt·est 1.** Thin and bony; haggard; emaciated. **2.** Bleak and desolate; stark: *the gaunt forbidding mountains around the valley.* **—gaunt′ly** *adv.* **—gaunt′ness** *n.*

gaunt·let[1] also **gant·let** (gônt′lĭt *or* gänt′lĭt) *n.* **1.** A heavy protective glove, especially a glove covered with chain mail and worn with medieval armor. **2.** A challenge: *The candidate threw down the gauntlet, daring his opponent to debate him face to face.* [From Middle English *gauntelet*, from Old French, diminutive of *gant*, glove, of Germanic origin.]

gaunt·let[2] also **gant·let** (gônt′lĭt *or* gänt′lĭt) *n.* **1.** A form of punishment in which a person is forced to run between two lines of people and is beaten with clubs, sticks, or other weapons. **2.** An attack from all sides. **3.** A severe trial; an ordeal. ◆ **run the gauntlet** To undergo an ordeal. [From Swedish *gatlopp* : *gata*, lane + *lopp*, course, running.]

Gau·ta·ma (gô′tə-mə *or* gou′tə-mə), **Siddhartha** Known as "the Buddha." 563?–483? BC. Indian mystic and founder of Buddhism. He began preaching at the age of 35.

gauze (gôz) *n.* A loosely woven, somewhat transparent cloth used especially for bandaging.

gauz·y (gô′zē) *adj.* **gauz·i·er, gauz·i·est** Resembling gauze in thinness or transparency. **—gauz′i·ness** *n.*

gave (gāv) *v.* Past tense of **give.**

gav·el (găv′əl) *n.* A small wooden mallet used by a presiding officer to signal for attention or order or by an auctioneer to mark the conclusion of a transaction.

ga·votte (gə-vŏt′) *n.* **1.** A French peasant dance in moderately quick duple meter. **2.** Music written for this dance.

Ga·wain (gə-wān′ *or* gä′wān′ *or* gou′ən) *n.* In Arthurian legend, a nephew of King Arthur and a Knight of the Round Table.

gawk (gôk) *intr.v.* **gawked, gawk·ing, gawks** To stare stupidly; gape. **—gawk·er** *n.*

gawk·y (gô′kē) *adj.* **gawk·i·er, gawk·i·est** Awkward; clumsy: *a gawky colt.* **—gawk′i·ly** *adv.* **—gawk′i·ness** *n.*

gay (gā) *adj.* **gay·er, gay·est 1.** Relating to or having a sexual orientation toward people of the same sex. **2.** Merry; light-hearted: *a gay mood; gay music.* **3.** Bright or lively, especially in color: *The package was tied with gay ribbons.* ❖ *n.* **1.** A person whose sexual orientation is toward people of the same sex. **2.** A man whose sexual orientation is toward men: *an alliance of gays and lesbians.* —SEE NOTE.

gay·e·ty (gā′ĭ-tē) *n.* Variant of **gaiety.**

gay·ly (gā′lē) *adv.* Variant of **gaily.**

Ga·za (gä′zə) A city of southwest Asia in the **Gaza Strip,** a narrow coastal area along the Mediterranean Sea next to Israel and Egypt. The territory passed from British administration to Egypt in 1949 and was occupied by Israel in 1967. Palestinians achieved limited self-rule in the area in 1993.

gaze (gāz) *intr.v.* **gazed, gaz·ing, gaz·es** To look intently, as with wonder or curiosity; stare: *We gazed in awe at the soaring eagle.* ❖ *n.* An intent steady look: *The crowd fixed their gaze on the speaker.*

ga·ze·bo (gə-zā′bō *or* gə-zē′bō) *n., pl.* **ga·ze·bos** or **ga·ze·boes** A small roofed structure, usually having open sides, that provides a shady place to sit or rest.

ga·zelle (gə-zĕl′) *n.* Any of various slender swift-running antelopes of Africa and Asia. [From Arabic *ġazāl.*]

ga·zette (gə-zĕt′) *n.* **1.** A newspaper. **2.** An official journal or periodical.

gaz·et·teer (găz′ĭ-tîr′) *n.* A book with an alphabetical list of geographic names, as of countries, cities, mountains, and bodies of water, often accompanied by a brief description of each name.

gaz·pa·cho (gə-spä′chō) *n.* A chilled soup made with chopped tomatoes, cucumbers, onions, and peppers.

Gb *abbr.* An abbreviation of gigabit.

GB *abbr.* An abbreviation of: **1.** gigabyte. **2.** Great Britain.

gcd *abbr.* An abbreviation of greatest common divisor.

USAGE

gay Although *gay* can refer to either men or women, it is often used to refer solely to men, in contrast to *lesbian,* used for women. *Gay* is generally used not in the singular to refer to an individual person, but rather in the plural to refer collectively either to gay men or to gay men and lesbians.

gazebo

gazelle

gecko

SCIENCE

gene Are you the way you are because of your genes? Yes and no. **Genes** contain the chemical information—in the form of DNA—needed to create proteins, which are essential to the functioning of all living cells. Scientists now know the DNA sequence of the entire human genome—all of the approximately 20,000 genes that are found in each of our cells. The vast majority of a person's genes are identical to those found in all people. We also share genes with other species, such as mice and flies; the more closely related we are evolutionarily, the more we share. Our genes make us human, but what makes each of us unique is a complex interaction of our genes with environmental factors like what we eat, where we were born, and who our friends are.

ă	pat	ôr	core
ā	pay	oi	boy
âr	care	ou	out
ä	father	o͝o	took
ĕ	pet	o͝or	lure
ē	be	o͞o	boot
ĭ	pit	ŭ	cut
ī	bite	ûr	urge
îr	pier	th	thin
ŏ	pot	*th*	this
ō	toe	zh	vision
ô	paw	ə	about

G clef *n.* A treble clef.

Gd The symbol for the element **gadolinium.**

Gdańsk (gə-**dänsk′** *or* gə-**dănsk′**) A city of northern Poland northwest of Warsaw on the **Gulf of Gdańsk,** an inlet of the Baltic Sea. Adolf Hitler's demand that Gdańsk (known as Danzig in German) be turned over to Germany led to his invasion of Poland and the beginning of World War II (September 1939).

GDP *abbr.* An abbreviation of gross domestic product.

Ge The symbol for the element **germanium.**

gear (gîr) *n.* **1a.** A wheel with teeth around its rim that mesh with the teeth of another wheel to transmit motion. **b.** An arrangement of such interlocking wheels, as in an automobile or bicycle, that transmits motion in a particular way that balances speed and power. A low gear results in greater power but less speed, while a high gear results in greater speed but less power. **2.** Equipment used for a particular activity: *fishing gear.* **3.** Personal belongings, including clothing: *The campers stored their gear under their bunks.* ❖ *v.* **geared, gear·ing, gears** —*tr.* **1.** To provide with or connect by gears: *gear a motor to a propeller.* **2.** To adjust or adapt: *The scientists geared their remarks to a youthful audience.* —*intr.* To be or become in gear; mesh: *The cogs of an automobile transmission gear into each other.* ◆ **gear up** To get ready for a coming action or event: *We are geared up for our family's upcoming camping trip.* [From Middle English *gere,* equipment, from Old Norse *gervi;* akin to *gera,* to do, make ready.]

gear·box (**gîr′**bŏks′) *n.* The transmission in a motor vehicle.

gear·shift (**gîr′**shĭft′) *n.* A device for changing from one gear to another in a transmission, as in an automobile.

gear·wheel also **gear wheel** (**gîr′**wēl′) *n.* A wheel having teeth around its rim; a cogwheel.

geck·o (**gĕk′**ō) *n., pl.* **geck·os** or **geck·oes** Any of various small insect-eating lizards of warm climates that have adhesive toe pads with which they cling to walls and other vertical surfaces. [From Javanese *ge'kok.*]

gee[1] (jē) *interj.* An expression used to command an animal pulling a load to turn to the right or to go forward.

gee[2] (jē) *interj.* An expression used as a mild oath or as an exclamation of surprise.

geek (gēk) *n. Slang* **1a.** An inept or clumsy person. **b.** A person who is accomplished in scientific or technical pursuits but is socially awkward or inept. **2.** A person who performs bizarre acts in a carnival show. **—geek′y** *adj.*

geese (gēs) *n.* Plural of **goose.**

ge·fil·te fish (gə-**fĭl′**tə) *n.* Seasoned chopped fish mixed with bread or cracker crumbs and eggs, formed into balls and cooked in a broth.

Gei·ger counter (**gī′**gər) *n.* An electronic instrument that detects and measures nuclear radiation, such as x-rays, gamma rays, or cosmic rays, by counting the ions produced as the radiation passes through a gas-filled tube. [After Hans Wilhelm *Geiger* (1882–1945), German physicist.]

gei·sha (**gā′**shə *or* **gē′**shə) *n., pl.* **geisha** or **gei·shas** A Japanese woman trained to entertain social or professional gatherings of men with singing, dancing, or amusing talk.

gel (jĕl) *n.* **1.** A semisolid mixture formed when particles suspended in a liquid become relatively large, as when boiled fruit juices thicken and cool to form a jelly or colloid. **2.** A jellylike substance used in styling hair. ❖ *intr.v.* **gelled, gel·ling, gels** To become a gel.

❑ *These sound alike:* **gel, jell** (congeal).

gel·a·tin (**jĕl′**ə-tn) *n.* **1.** An odorless, colorless protein substance obtained by boiling a mixture of water and the skin, bones, and tendons of animals. The preparation forms a gel when allowed to cool and is used in foods, drugs, glue, and photographic film. **2.** A flavored jelly made with gelatin, often used as a dessert or in salads. [From Italian *gelatina,* from Latin *gelāre,* to freeze.]

ge·lat·i·nous (jə-**lăt′**n-əs) *adj.* **1.** Similar in texture to gelatin; thick and viscous: *the gelatinous body of a jellyfish.* **2.** Relating to or containing gelatin.

ge·la·to (jə-**lä′**tō) *n., pl.* **ge·la·ti** (jə-**lä′**tē) An Italian ice cream or sorbet. [From Italian, from *gelare,* to freeze.]

geld (gĕld) *tr.v.* **geld·ed, geld·ing, gelds** To remove the testicles of (a horse or another animal).

geld·ing (**gĕl′**dĭng) *n.* A gelded animal, especially a horse.

gem (jĕm) *n.* **1.** A precious or semiprecious stone cut and polished as a jewel. **2.** Something that is much admired or appreciated: *This painting is the gem of the museum's collection.* ❖ *tr.v.* **gemmed, gem·ming, gems** To set or adorn with gems: *The artisan gemmed a gold box with stones of different colors.* [From Middle English *gemme,* from Latin *gemma.*]

Gem·i·ni (**jĕm′**ə-nī′ *or* **jĕm′**ə-nē′) *pl.n. (used with a singular verb)* **1.** A constellation in the Northern Hemisphere, traditionally pictured as the twins Castor and Pollux. **2.** The third sign of the zodiac in astrology.

gem·stone (**jĕm′**stōn′) *n.* A precious or semiprecious stone used as a jewel when cut and polished.

gen. *abbr.* An abbreviation of: **1.** gender. **2.** genitive. **3.** general. **4.** genus.

Gen. *abbr.* An abbreviation of general.

gen·darme (**zhän′**därm′) *n.* A police officer in France and other French-speaking countries.

gen·der (**jĕn′**dər) *n.* **1.** In some languages, a grammatical category, usually feminine, masculine, or neuter, used to classify nouns, pronouns, and adjectives. In Spanish, for example, *casa* (meaning "house") is feminine and *pan* (meaning "bread") is masculine. **2.** Either of the two divisions, designated female and male, by which most organisms are classified on the basis of their reproductive organs and functions; sex. **3.** A person's identity as either female or male or as neither entirely female nor entirely male.

gene (jēn) *n.* A segment of DNA, located at a particular point on a chromosome, that determines hereditary characteristics. Hair and eye color in humans are characteristics controlled by genes. [From Greek *genos,* race, offspring.] —SEE NOTE.

ge·ne·al·o·gist (jē′nē-**ŏl′**ə-jĭst *or* jē′nē-**ăl′**ə-jĭst) *n.* A person who studies and traces genealogies.

ge·ne·al·o·gy (jē′nē-**ŏl′**ə-jē *or* jē′nē-**ăl′**ə-jē) *n., pl.* **ge·ne·al·o·gies 1.** A record of the descent of a family or person from an ancestor or ancestors: *My grandparents gave us a copy of our family genealogy that goes back six generations.* **2.** Direct descent from an ancestor or ancestors; lineage: *There are many websites than can help in researching a family's genealogy.* **3.** The study of ancestry and family histories. [From Middle English *genealogie,* from Greek *genealogiā* : *geneā,* family + *-logiā,* study.] **—ge′ne·a·log′i·cal** (jē′nē-ə-**lŏj′**ĭkəl) *adj.*

gen·er·a (**jĕn′**ər-ə) *n.* Plural of **genus.**

gen·er·al (**jĕn′**ər-əl) *adj.* **1.** Concerned with, applying to, or affecting all members of a category: *An election is supposed to express the general will of the people.* **2.** Affecting a majority of those involved; prevalent; widespread: *general satisfaction.* **3.** Not limited in scope, area, or application: *as a general rule; general studies.* **4.** Involving only the main features of something rather than details or particulars: *The witness could only give a general account of what happened.* **5.** Highest or superior in rank: *the general manager.* ❖ *n.* **1a.** An officer holding any of the ranks above colonel in the US Army, Air Force, or Marine Corps. **b.** An officer holding the rank above lieutenant general in the US Army, Air Force, or Marine Corps. **2.** A person who holds such a rank in another military organization. ◆ **in general** Generally; for the most part. [From Middle English, from Latin *generālis*, from *genus*, kind.]

general assembly *n.* **1.** A legislative body, especially a US state legislature. **2. General Assembly** The main body of the United Nations, in which each member nation is represented and has one vote.

gen·er·al·ist (jĕn′ər-ə-lĭst) *n.* A person with general knowledge and skills in several fields.

gen·er·al·i·ty (jĕn′ə-răl′ĭ-tē) *n., pl.* **gen·er·al·i·ties 1.** The state or quality of being general. **2.** A statement or principle that has general application: *As a generality, hard work is more important than talent in achieving success.* **3.** A statement or idea that is vague or imprecise: *a speech full of generalities and empty phrases.*

gen·er·al·i·za·tion (jĕn′ər-ə-lĭ-zā′shən) *n.* **1.** The act of generalizing: *The judge instructed the jury only to consider the facts of the case and not to engage in generalization.* **2.** A general statement or principle; a generality: *Do you agree with the generalization that money can't buy happiness?*

gen·er·al·ize (jĕn′ər-ə-līz′) *v.* **gen·er·al·ized, gen·er·al·iz·ing, gen·er·al·iz·es** —*tr.* To consider or state in terms of a general form or principle: *The researchers generalized their observations in a report aimed at the average reader.* —*intr.* To draw a general conclusion from particular facts: *Scientists generalize about dinosaurs from their fossilized bones.*

gen·er·al·ly (jĕn′ər-ə-lē) *adv.* **1.** Usually; as a rule: *I generally go for a walk before breakfast.* **2.** Widely; commonly: *The fact is not generally known.* **3.** In general terms: *Generally speaking, there are two ways to handle the problem.*

General of the Air Force *n.* An officer having the highest rank in the US Air Force.

General of the Army *n.* An officer having the highest rank in the US Army.

general practitioner *n.* A doctor who does not specialize in one field but treats a variety of medical problems.

gen·er·al·ship (jĕn′ər-əl-shĭp′) *n.* **1.** The rank of general. **2.** Leadership or skill in the command of an army. **3.** Skillful leadership or management.

gen·er·ate (jĕn′ə-rāt′) *tr.v.* **gen·er·at·ed, gen·er·at·ing, gen·er·ates** To bring into being; produce: *generate heat; generate interest among voters; generate a computer program.* [From Latin *generāre*, to produce, from *genus*, birth.]

gen·er·a·tion (jĕn′ə-rā′shən) *n.* **1.** A group of people who grow up at about the same time, often thought to have similar social and cultural attitudes: *the younger generation; the hippie generation.* **2.** The average length of time between the birth of parents and the birth of their offspring: *Many generations have passed since this land was cleared for a farm.* **3.** All of the offspring that are at the same stage of descent from a common ancestor: *My cousins are in the same generation as I am.* **4.** A class of things derived from an earlier class, usually by making improvements and refinements: *the new generation of computers.* **5.** The act or process of generating: *the generation of electric power; the generation of new ideas.*

generation gap *n.* A difference in values and attitudes between one generation and the next, especially between young people and their parents.

Generation X *n.* The generation following the American baby boom of the 1950s and 1960s, especially people born from the early 1960s to the late 1970s.

Generation Y *n.* The generation following Generation X, especially people born in the United States from the early 1980s to the late 1990s.

gen·er·a·tive (jĕn′ər-ə-tĭv *or* jĕn′ə-rā′tĭv) *adj.* Having the ability to generate, produce, or reproduce: *a generative process; generative cells.*

gen·er·a·tor (jĕn′ə-rā′tər) *n.* A person or thing that generates, especially a machine that converts mechanical energy into electrical energy.

ge·ner·ic (jə-nĕr′ĭk) *adj.* **1.** Relating to an entire group or class; general: *Our teacher gave us some generic advice on how to prepare for a test.* **2.** Relating to a genus: Musca *is the generic name of the housefly* Musca domestica. **3.** Not protected by a trademark and therefore applicable to an entire class of products: *"Aspirin" is the generic name for a painkiller sold under many different brand names.* —**ge·ner′i·cal·ly** *adv.* —SEE NOTE.

gen·er·os·i·ty (jĕn′ə-rŏs′ĭ-tē) *n., pl.* **gen·er·os·i·ties 1.** The quality or condition of being generous: *The charity thanked their donors for their generosity.* **2.** Nobility of thought or behavior: *The coach speaks of our rivals with generosity.* **3.** A generous act.

gen·er·ous (jĕn′ər-əs) *adj.* **1.** Willing to give or share; unselfish: *a generous contributor to worthy causes.* **2.** Large; abundant; ample: *This restaurant serves very generous portions.* **3.** Having or showing high moral character; gracious; kind: *The critic gave a generous review of the inexperienced actor's performance.* [From Latin *generōsus*, from *genus*, birth.] —**gen′er·ous·ly** *adv.*

gen·e·sis (jĕn′ĭ-sĭs) *n., pl.* **gen·e·ses** (jĕn′ĭ-sēz′) **1.** The coming into being of something; the origin: *the genesis of an idea.* **2. Genesis** The first book of the Bible, describing the creation of the world, the banishment of Adam and Eve from the Garden of Eden, and the early history of the Jewish people.

gene splicing *n.* The process in which genetic material from one or more organisms is combined to form recombinant DNA.

gene therapy *n.* The treatment of disease, especially one caused by the inheritance of a defective gene, by replacing defective genes with healthy ones through genetic engineering.

ge·net·ic (jə-nĕt′ĭk) *adj.* **1.** Relating to genetics: *genetic research.* **2.** Involving or determined by the genes: *a genetic disorder; a genetic trait.* —**ge·net′i·cal·ly** *adv.* —SEE NOTE AT **generic.**

genetically modified organism *n.* An organism whose genetic characteristics have been altered by inserting a modified gene or a gene from another organism into its genome.

genetic code *n.* The sequence of chemical compounds in DNA or RNA that determines the order of amino acids when a protein is made. A group of three bases specifies a particular amino acid or designates the beginning or end of a protein.

genetic engineering *n.* The alteration of the genetic material of an organism, usually by inserting a gene from another organism, to produce a new trait, such as resistance to herbicides, or to make a biological substance, such as a protein or hormone.

ge·net·i·cist (jə-nĕt′ĭ-sĭst) *n.* A scientist who specializes in genetics.

ge·net·ics (jə-nĕt′ĭks) *n.* **1.** *(used with a singular verb)* The branch of biology that deals with genes, especially their inheritance and expression and their distribution among different individuals and organisms. **2.** *(used with a plural verb)* The genetic makeup of an individual or group.

Ge·ne·va (jə-nē′və) A city of southwest Switzerland located on **Lake Geneva** and divided by the Rhone River. It was originally an ancient Celtic settlement.

Gen·ghis Khan (jĕng′gĭs kän′ *or* gĕng′gĭs kän′) 1162?–1227. Mongol conqueror who united the Mongol tribes and forged an empire stretching from China to the Danube River and into Persia.

gen·ial (jēn′yəl) *adj.* **1.** Having a pleasant or friendly manner: *an enthusiastic and genial personality.* **2.** Favorable to health or growth; warm and pleasant: *the genial sunshine of springtime.* —**ge′ni·al′i·ty** (jē′nē-ăl′ĭ-tē) *n.* —**gen′ial·ly** *adv.*

WORD BUILDING

generic The word root *gen–* in English words comes both from Latin and from Greek. In Latin the noun *genus* means "type, kind, class, origin, race." A form of the Latin noun *genus,* which occurs for example in the plural *genera,* gives us **general, generic,** and **generation.** From French, which is derived from Latin, we have **genre.** From the Greek noun *genos,* which has the same meanings as Latin *genus,* we have the word **gene.** The Greek adjective *genetikos,* "relating to the origin," is the source of our word **genetic.**

Genghis Khan

WORD BUILDING

geo– The basic meaning of the prefix **geo–** is "earth." It comes from the Greek prefix *geō–*, from the Greek word *gē*, meaning "earth." Thus *geography* (from Greek *geō–* plus *–graphiā*, "writing") is "the study of the earth and its surface features." When used to form words in English, *geo–* can mean either "earth" or "geography." For example, *geomagnetism* refers to the magnetism of the earth, while *geopolitics* refers to the relationship between politics and geography.

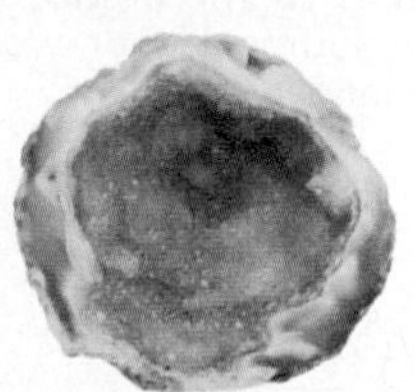

geode

geodesic dome

ă	pat	ôr	core
ā	pay	oi	boy
âr	care	ou	out
ä	father	o͝o	took
ĕ	pet	o͝or	lure
ē	be	o͞o	boot
ĭ	pit	ŭ	cut
ī	bite	ûr	urge
îr	pier	th	thin
ŏ	pot	*th*	this
ō	toe	zh	vision
ô	paw	ə	about

ge·nie (jē′nē) *n.* **1.** A spirit that appears in human form and fulfills wishes with magic powers. **2.** A jinni. [From Latin *genius*, guardian spirit.]

ge·ni·i (jē′nē-ī′) *n.* Plural of **genius** (sense 6).

gen·i·tal (jĕn′ĭ-tl) *adj.* **1.** Relating to biological reproduction: *the genital organs.* **2.** Relating to the genitals.

gen·i·ta·li·a (jĕn′ĭ-tā′lē-ə *or* jĕn′ĭ-tāl′yə) *pl.n.* The genitals.

gen·i·tals (jĕn′ĭ-tlz) *pl.n.* The reproductive organs, especially the external reproductive organs and associated structures in humans and other mammals.

gen·i·tive (jĕn′ĭ-tĭv) *adj.* Relating to the grammatical case that expresses possession or source. ❖ *n.* The genitive case.

gen·ius (jēn′yəs) *n., pl.* **gen·ius·es 1.** A person of extraordinary mental ability or creative power: *The great inventor was a genius.* **2.** Extraordinary mental ability or creative power: *Artists of genius are remembered centuries after their deaths.* **3.** A strong natural talent or ability: *She has a genius for leadership.* **4.** A person who has a natural talent or ability: *My cousin is a mechanical genius.* **5.** The special spirit or character of a person, place, time, or group: *the genius of ancient Rome.* **6.** *pl.* **ge·ni·i** (jē′nē-ī′) In Roman mythology, the guardian spirit of a person or place. [From Middle English, guardian spirit, from Latin.]

Gen·o·a (jĕn′ō-ə) A city of northwest Italy on an arm of the Mediterranean Sea. It is Italy's chief port.

gen·o·cide (jĕn′ə-sīd′) *n.* The systematic extermination or attempted extermination of a national, racial, religious, or ethnic group. **—gen′o·cid′al** (jĕn′ə-sīd′l) *adj.*

Gen·o·ese (jĕn′ō-ēz′ *or* jĕn′ō-ēs′) *adj.* Relating to Genoa or its people. ❖ *n.* A native or inhabitant of Genoa.

ge·nome (jē′nōm) *n.* The total amount of genetic information in the chromosomes of an organism or in the DNA or RNA of viruses.

ge·no·mics (jə-nō′mĭks) *n.* *(used with a singular verb)* The scientific study of the entire genome of an organism.

gen·o·type (jĕn′ə-tīp′ *or* jē′nə-tīp′) *n.* The genetic makeup of an organism, as distinguished from its physical characteristics or phenotype.

gen·re (zhän′rə) *n.* A particular type or class of literary, musical, or artistic composition: *Science fiction and mystery are different genres of literary fiction.* —SEE NOTE AT **generic.**

gent (jĕnt) *n.* *Informal* A man or gentleman.

gen·teel (jĕn-tēl′) *adj.* **1.** Refined or polite, often in an affected or pretentious way. See Synonyms at **polite. 2.** Elegantly stylish: *She had a genteel appearance.* **—gen·teel′ly** *adv.*

gen·tian (jĕn′shən) *n.* Any of numerous plants usually having deep-blue trumpet-shaped flowers. [From Middle English *gencian*, from Latin *gentiāna*, perhaps after *Gentius*, second-century BC king of Illyria, a region on the Balkan Peninsula.]

gen·tile (jĕn′tīl′) *n.* **1.** often **Gentile** A person who is not a Jew. **2.** A person who is not a Mormon. ❖ *adj.* often **Gentile** Relating to a Gentile. [From Middle English, from Late Latin *gentīlis*, pagan.]

gen·til·i·ty (jĕn-tĭl′ĭ-tē) *n.* **1.** Good manners; politeness; refinement. **2.** The condition of coming from a family of high social standing. **3.** People of high social standing considered as a group.

gen·tle (jĕn′tl) *adj.* **gen·tler, gen·tlest 1.** Considerate or kindly in manner; thoughtful and tender: *a gentle nature.* **2.** Not harsh or severe; mild and soft: *a gentle breeze; a gentle tap on the shoulder.* **3.** Not steep or sudden; gradual: *a gentle slope.* **4.** Easily managed or handled; docile: *a gentle horse.* **5.** Of good family; wellborn: *a child of gentle birth.* [From Middle English *gentil*, courteous, noble, from Latin *gentīlis*, of the same clan, from *gēns*, clan.] **—gen′tle·ness** *n.* **—gen′tly** *adv.*

gen·tle·folk (jĕn′tl-fōk′) *pl.n.* People of good family and usually high social standing.

gen·tle·man (jĕn′tl-mən) *n.* **1.** A man of high social standing. **2.** A man with good manners or polite behavior. **3.** A man, especially when spoken of in a polite way: *I believe this gentleman was here first.* **4. gentlemen** (jĕn′tl-mən) Used as a form of address for a group of men: *Good evening, ladies and gentlemen.*

gen·tle·man's agreement or **gen·tle·men's agreement** (jĕn′tl-mənz) *n.* An informal agreement guaranteed only by the promise of the people involved to honor it.

gen·tle·wom·an (jĕn′tl-wo͝om′ən) *n.* **1.** A woman of high social standing. **2.** A woman acting as a personal attendant to a noblewoman.

gen·tri·fi·ca·tion (jĕn′trə-fĭ-kā′shən) *n.* The restoration or upgrading of rundown urban property, especially by middle-class or wealthy people, often resulting in displacement of people with low incomes.

gen·tri·fy (jĕn′trə-fī′) *tr.v.* **gen·tri·fied, gen·tri·fy·ing, gen·tri·fies** To restore (rundown urban property) by gentrification.

gen·try (jĕn′trē) *n., pl.* **gen·tries 1.** People of good family and high social standing. **2.** In England, the class of landowners ranking next below the nobility.

gen·u·flect (jĕn′yə-flĕkt′) *intr.v.* **gen·u·flect·ed, gen·u·flect·ing, gen·u·flects** To bend one knee to or toward the ground, as a gesture of respect and worship. **—gen′u·flec′tion** *n.*

gen·u·ine (jĕn′yo͞o-ĭn) *adj.* **1.** Being so in fact; not spurious or counterfeit: *genuine leather.* See Synonyms at **authentic. 2.** Free from hypocrisy or dishonesty; sincere: *genuine affection.* **—gen′u·ine·ly** *adv.*

ge·nus (jē′nəs) *n., pl.* **gen·er·a** (jĕn′ər-ə) **1.** A taxonomic category of organisms that are closely related and share many characteristics, ranking below a family and above a species: *Dogs, wolves, and coyotes belong to the same genus.* See table at **taxonomy. 2.** A class, group, or kind with common characteristics: *the genus of boats known as pleasure crafts.*

geo– or **ge–** *pref.* A prefix that means: **1.** Earth: *geocentric.* **2.** Geography: *geopolitical.* —SEE NOTE.

ge·o·cen·tric (jē′ō-sĕn′trĭk) *adj.* **1.** Relating to or measured from the earth's center. **2.** Having the earth as the center: *an ancient representation of a geocentric universe.*

ge·o·chem·is·try (jē′ō-kĕm′ĭ-strē) *n.* The study of the chemistry of the earth, including its crust, waters, and atmosphere.

ge·ode (jē′ōd′) *n.* A small, hollow, usually rounded rock lined on the inside with crystals.

ge·o·des·ic (jē′ə-dĕs′ĭk *or* jē′ə-dē′sĭk) *adj.* **1.** Relating to geodesy. **2.** Relating to the branch of geometry that deals with finding the shortest line between two points on a curved surface.

geodesic dome *n.* A structure having the shape of a hemisphere, assembled of straight pieces that form triangles or polygons that fit rigidly together.

ge·od·e·sy (jē-ŏd′ĭ-sē) *n.* The scientific study of the size and shape of the earth.

ge·o·det·ic (jē′ə-dĕt′ĭk) *adj.* Geodesic.

ge·og·ra·pher (jē-ŏg′rə-fər) *n.* A person who specializes in geography.

ge·o·graph·ic (jē′ə-grăf′ĭk) also **ge·o·graph·i·cal** (jē′ə-grăf′ĭ-kəl) *adj.* Relating to geography: *geographic boundaries; geographical names.* **—ge′o·graph′i·cal·ly** *adv.*

geographic mile *n.* A nautical mile.

ge·og·ra·phy (jē-ŏg′rə-fē) *n., pl.* **ge·og·ra·phies 1.** The study of the earth's surface and its various climates, continents, countries, peoples, resources, industries, and products. **2.** The physical features of a region or place: *the rugged geography of the West.* **3.** A book on geography. [From Greek *geōgraphiā* : *gē*, earth + *-graphiā*, writing.]

ge·o·log·ic (jē′ə-lŏj′ĭk) or **ge·o·log·i·cal** (jē′ə-lŏj′ĭ-kəl) *adj.* Relating to geology: *the geologic force of uplift; a geological survey.* **—ge′o·log′i·cal·ly** *adv.*

geologic time *n.* The period of time covering the formation and development of the earth, from about 4.6 billion years ago to today. —SEE TABLE ON pages 410–411.

ge·ol·o·gist (jē-ŏl′ə-jĭst) *n.* A scientist who specializes in geology.

ge·ol·o·gy (jē-ŏl′ə-jē) *n., pl.* **ge·ol·o·gies 1.** The science that studies the origin, history, and structure of the earth. **2.** The structure of a specific region, including its rocks, soils, mountains, and other features. [From Medieval Latin *geōlogiā*, study of earthly things : Greek *gē*, earth + Greek *-logiā*, study.]

ge·o·mag·ne·tism (jē′ō-măg′nĭ-tĭz′əm) *n.* The magnetic properties of the earth. **—ge′o·mag·net′ic** (jē′-ō-măg-**net′**ĭk) *adj.*

ge·o·met·ric (jē′ə-mĕt′rĭk) also **ge·o·met·ri·cal** (jē′ə-**mĕt′**rĭ-kəl) *adj.* **1.** Relating to geometry and its methods and principles: *a geometric problem.* **2.** Increasing or decreasing in a geometric progression. **3.** Consisting of or using simple shapes formed from straight lines or curves: *geometric figures; a geometric design.* **—ge′o·met′ri·cal·ly** *adv.*

geometric progression *n.* A sequence of numbers in which each number is multiplied by the same factor to obtain the next number in the sequence. In the geometric progression 5, 25, 125, 625, each number is multiplied by the factor of 5 to obtain the following number.

ge·om·e·try (jē-ŏm′ĭ-trē) *n., pl.* **ge·om·e·tries 1.** The mathematical study of the properties, measurement, and relationships of points, lines, planes, surfaces, angles, and solids. **2.** A shape or an arrangement of parts, as in a design: *the geometry of a building.* [From Middle English *gemetrie*, from Greek *geōmetriā* : *gē*, earth, land + *metrein*, to measure.]

ge·o·mor·phol·o·gy (jē′ō-môr-fŏl′ə-jē) *n.* The scientific study of the formation and alteration of landforms, such as mountains and valleys.

ge·o·phys·ics (jē′ō-fĭz′ĭks) *n. (used with a singular verb)* The application of physics to the study of the earth and its environment. **—ge′o·phys′i·cal** *adj.*

ge·o·pol·i·tics (jē′ō-pol′ĭtĭks) *n. (used with a singular verb)* The study of how a nation's foreign policy is affected by geography, demographics, and economics. **—ge′o·po·lit′i·cal** (jē′ō-pə-lĭt′i-kəl) *adj.*

George (jôrj), Saint. Died c. AD 303. Christian martyr who, according to legend, killed a fearsome dragon.

George III 1738–1820. King of Great Britain and Ireland (1760–1820) and of Hanover (1815–1820) whose policies fed American discontent, leading to revolution in 1776.

George V 1865–1936. King of Great Britain and Northern Ireland and emperor of India (1910–1936) who gave up his German titles during World War I.

George VI 1895–1952. King of Great Britain and Northern Ireland (1936–1952) and emperor of India (1936–1947) who won popularity by his dedication to his duties, especially during World War II.

George·town (jôrj′toun′) **1.** The capital of the Cayman Islands, in the West Indies west of Jamaica. **2.** The capital of Guyana, in the northern part of the country on the Atlantic Ocean. It was founded in 1781.

Geor·gia (jôr′jə) **1.** A country of southwest Asia on the Black Sea south of Russia. It developed as a kingdom from about the 4th century BC and reached its height in the 1100s and 1200s. Georgia was part of the USSR from 1922 until 1991. Tbilisi is the capital. **2.** A state of the southeast United States on the Atlantic Ocean north of Florida. It was admitted as one of the original Thirteen Colonies in 1788. Atlanta is the capital. —SEE NOTE.

Geor·gian (jôr′jən) *adj.* **1.** Relating to the reigns of the four kings of England named George who ruled from 1714 to 1830: *Georgian architecture.* **2.** Relating to the US state of Georgia or its inhabitants. **3.** Relating to the country of Georgia or its people, language, or culture. ❖ *n.* **1.** A native or inhabitant of the US state of Georgia. **2a.** A native or inhabitant of the country of Georgia. **b.** The language of the Georgians.

ge·o·ther·mal (jē′ō-thûr′məl) *adj.* Relating to the internal heat of the earth: *geothermal energy.*

ge·ot·ro·pism (jē-ŏt′rə-pĭz′əm) *n.* Gravitropism.

ge·ra·ni·um (jə-rā′nē-əm) *n.* **1.** Any of various plants having rounded leaves and showy clusters of red, pink, or white flowers, often grown as potted plants. **2.** Any of various related plants having pink or purplish flowers with five equal petals. [From Latin, crane's bill.]

ger·bil (jûr′bəl) *n.* Any of various small rodents that have long hind legs and a long tail and are native to desert regions of Africa and Asia. One kind of gerbil is often kept as a pet.

ger·i·at·rics (jĕr′ē-ăt′rĭks) *n. (used with a singular verb)* The branch of medicine that deals with the diagnosis and treatment of diseases of old age.

germ (jûrm) *n.* **1.** A bacterium or virus, especially one that causes disease: *The nurse used a disinfectant to kill the germs.* **2.** The earliest form of a living thing; a seed, spore, or bud: *wheat germ.* **3.** Something that serves as the basis of further growth or development: *a germ of an idea.* [From Middle English, bud, sprout, from Latin *germen.*]

Ger·man (jûr′mən) *adj.* Relating to Germany or its people, language, or culture. ❖ *n.* **1.** A native or inhabitant of Germany. **2.** The Germanic language of Germany, Austria, and part of Switzerland.

ger·mane (jər-mān′) *adj.* Closely or naturally related; appropriate; pertinent: *Their comments were not germane to the discussion.* [From Middle English *germain*, closely related, from Latin *germānus.*]

Ger·man·ic (jər-măn′ĭk) *adj.* **1.** Relating to Germany or its people, language, or culture. **2.** Relating to the branch of the Indo-European language family that includes English, German, Dutch, and the Scandinavian languages. **3.** Relating to the ancient Teutons; Teutonic. ❖ *n.* The Germanic branch of the Indo-European language family.

ger·ma·ni·um (jər-mā′nē-əm) *n. Symbol* **Ge** A brittle grayish metallic element found in zinc ores, coal, and certain minerals. It is widely used as a semiconductor. Atomic number 32. See **Periodic Table.**

German measles *n. (used with a singular or plural verb)* Rubella.

German shepherd *n.* A large dog of a breed developed in Germany, having a thick black or brownish coat and often trained to help police officers.

German silver *n.* Nickel silver.

Ger·ma·ny (jûr′mə-nē) A country of north-central Europe west of Poland and bordered on the north by the Baltic and North Seas. From 1949 to 1990 the territory was divided between the countries of **West Germany** and **East Germany.** Berlin is the capital.

germ cell *n.* A reproductive cell of a plant or animal, as an egg or sperm.

ger·mi·cide (jûr′mĭ-sīd′) *n.* A substance that kills germs, especially those that cause disease; a disinfectant. **—ger′mi·cid′al** (gûr′mĭ-sīd′l) *adj.*

ger·mi·nal (jûr′mə-nəl) *adj.* **1.** Relating to or having the nature of a germ cell. **2.** Relating to or occurring in an early stage of development: *a germinal sprout.*

ger·mi·nate (jûr′mə-nāt′) *intr. & tr.v.* **ger·mi·nat·ed, ger·mi·nat·ing, ger·mi·nates** To begin or cause to begin to grow; sprout: *Seeds need water and warmth*

GEOGRAPHY

Georgia The state of **Georgia** is named for King George II of England (reigned 1727–1760), who first gave James Oglethorpe permission to establish a colony there in 1732. A Latin ending was added to the king's name to create the name for the colony, and the state took its name from the colony.

geranium

gerbil

German shepherd

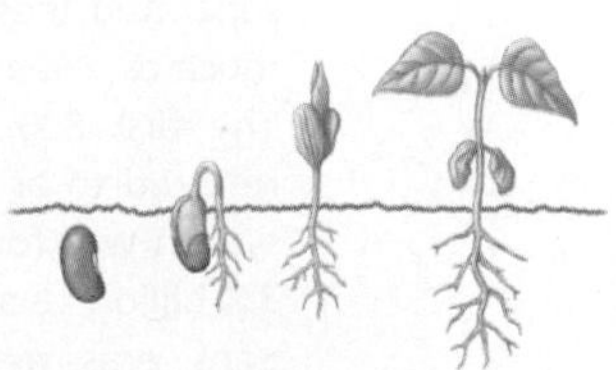
germinate
germination of a bean seed

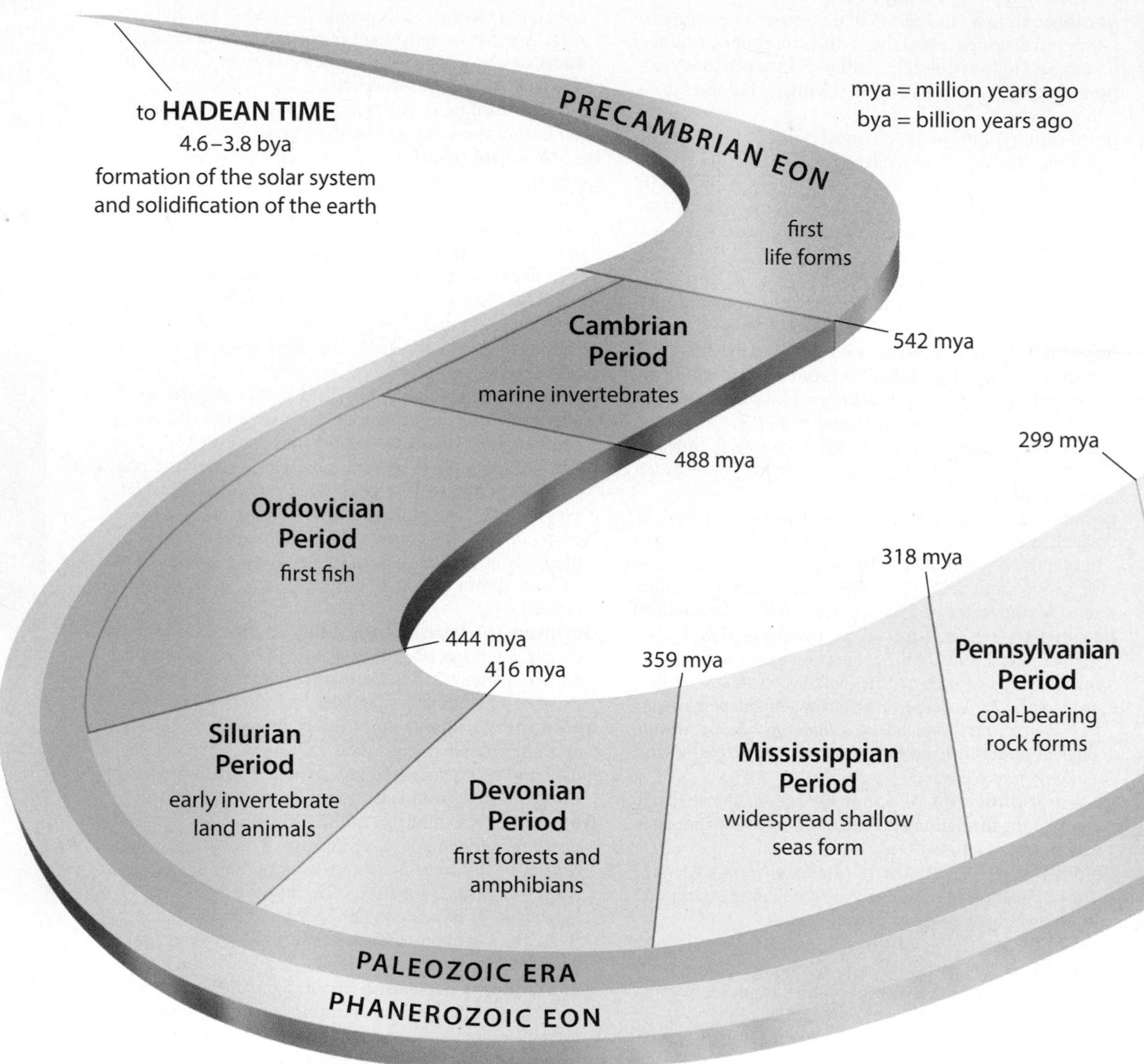

The earth formed approximately 4.6 billion years ago. For the purpose of studying its history, scientists have separated these 4.6 billion years into a set of divisions, much as a year is divided into months, weeks, and days. The first 800 million years of the earth's history are referred to as Hadean Time. During this time the solar system was forming and the earth was solidifying. The 3.8 billion years after Hadean Time are subdivided into eons, eras, periods, and epochs. Eons are the longest divisions of time, and epochs are the shortest. Most of the boundaries between the divisions correspond to visible changes in the types of life forms preserved as fossils in the corresponding rocks. We know a lot more about the earth's recent history than we do about its earlier history because most younger rocks have not yet been destroyed by weathering and earthquakes and other forces the way most older rocks have. This is why most of the geologic time divisions correspond to the last 542 million years (the Phanerozoic Eon), even though most of the earth's history occurred before that time.

Geologic Time

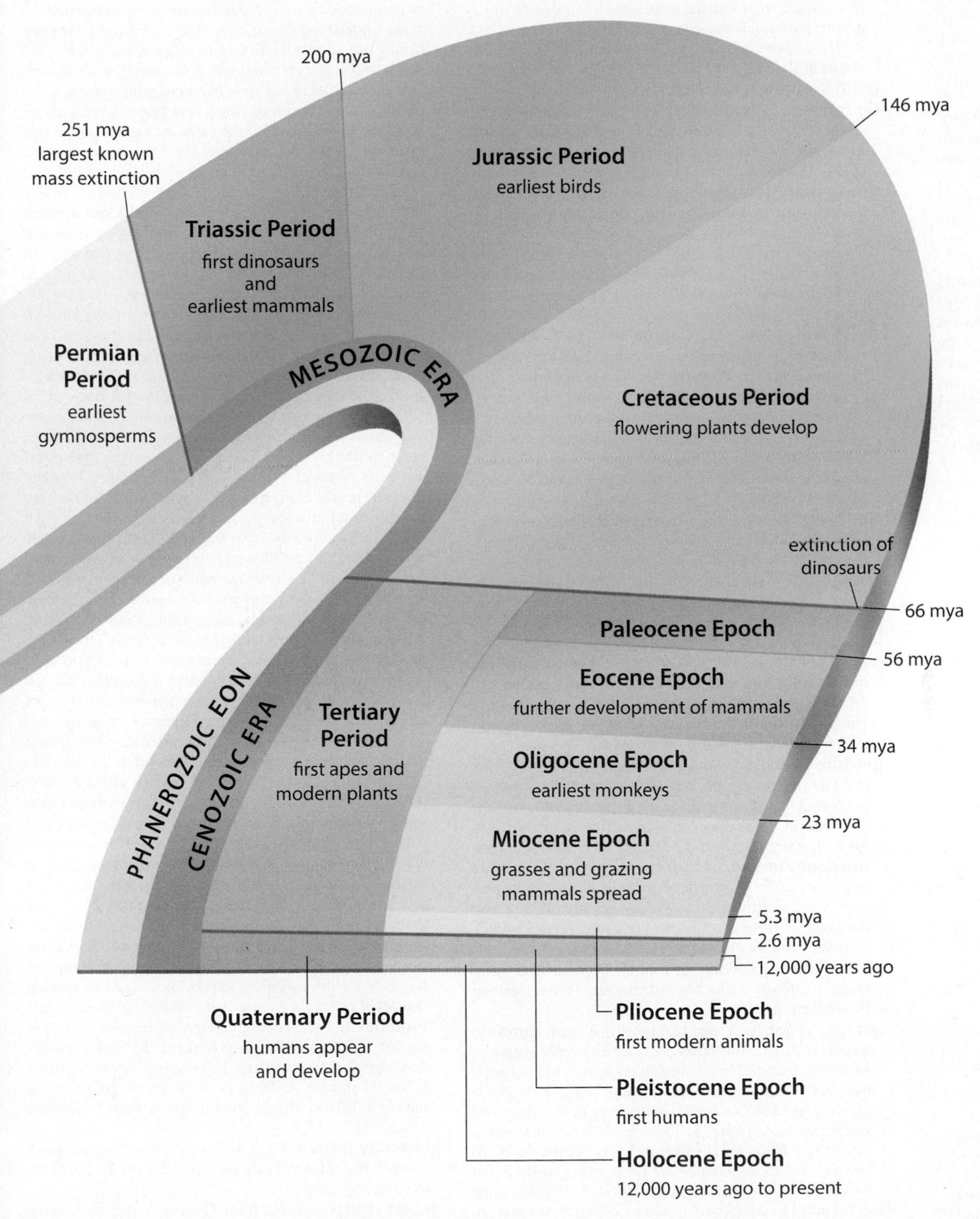

USAGE

get The past participles **got** and **gotten** have some interesting differences in meaning. The phrase *have got* expresses need or obligation. The sentence *She has got to practice tonight* means that she needs to practice. But the sentence *She has gotten to practice tonight* means that she has been given the permission or opportunity to practice. Also, *got* often suggests that you have something in your possession right now (as in *I've got ten dollars*), while *gotten* suggests that you've made an effort to obtain something or been paid for doing or selling something (as in *I've gotten ten dollars for that card; I've gotten ten dollars for mowing their lawn*).

ă	pat	ôr	core
ā	pay	oi	boy
âr	care	ou	out
ä	father	o͝o	took
ĕ	pet	o͝or	lure
ē	be	o͞o	boot
ĭ	pit	ŭ	cut
ī	bite	ûr	urge
îr	pier	th	thin
ŏ	pot	*th*	this
ō	toe	zh	vision
ô	paw	ə	about

to germinate. We germinated the seeds indoors. [From Latin *germinare*, to sprout, from *germen*, seed.] **—ger′mi·na′tion** *n.* **—ger′mi·na′tor** *n.*

germ·line (jûrm′līn′) *n.* **1.** The gamete-producing cells in a sexually reproducing organism, by means of which genetic material is passed on to subsequent generations. **2.** The collection or sequence of such cells in an individual and all its descendants.

germ warfare *n.* Biological warfare.

Ge·ron·i·mo (jə-rŏn′ə-mō′) 1829–1909. Apache leader who resisted the US government and led raids against Mexican and American settlements in the Southwest (1876–1886).

ger·ry·man·der (jĕr′ē-măn′dər) *tr.v.* **ger·ry·man·dered, ger·ry·man·der·ing, ger·ry·man·ders** To divide (voting districts of a state or county) in such a way as to give unfair advantage to one political party. [After Elbridge *Gerry* (1744–1814), American politician + *(sala)mander* (from the shape of an election district created while Gerry was governor of Massachusetts).]

Gersh·win (gûrsh′wĭn), **George** 1898–1937. American composer known for working jazz into classical music in his works, such as *Rhapsody in Blue* (1924).

ger·und (jĕr′ənd) *n.* A noun formed from a verb. In English the gerund ends in *-ing*. In the sentence *Hitting a ball hard requires strength*, the word *hitting* is a gerund. Like a noun, a gerund may be the subject of a sentence, but like a verb it may have a direct object and be modified by an adverb.

Ge·sta·po (gə-stä′pō) *n.* The secret police force of Nazi Germany, known for its ruthlessness against people thought to be disloyal.

ges·ta·tion (jĕ-stā′shən) *n.* **1.** The carrying and development of young in the uterus from conception to birth; pregnancy. **2.** The period of gestation. **3.** The formation or development of a plan or idea.

ges·tic·u·late (jĕ-stĭk′yə-lāt′) *intr.v.* **ges·tic·u·lat·ed, ges·tic·u·lat·ing, ges·tic·u·lates** To make gestures in order to emphasize meaning or express one's feelings: *The angry speaker gesticulated wildly by flailing the air with his hands.* **—ges·tic′u·la′tion** *n.*

ges·ture (jĕs′chər) *n.* **1.** A movement of the limbs, head, or body to help express meaning: *A mime must rely on gestures to tell a story.* **2.** Something done or said for its effect on the feelings or opinions of others: *Sending someone a birthday card is a thoughtful gesture.* ❖ *v.* **ges·tured, ges·tur·ing, ges·tures** *—intr.* To make a gesture or gestures: *The police officer gestured for the car to proceed.* *—tr.* To express or signal by gesture: *With a nod the judge gestured a willingness to listen.* [From Middle English, from Medieval Latin *gestūra*, bearing.]

ge·sund·heit (gə-zo͝ont′hīt′) *interj.* Used to wish good health to a person who has just sneezed. [From German *Gesundheit*, health.]

get (gĕt) *v.* **got** (gŏt), **got·ten** (gŏt′n) or **got, get·ting, gets** *—tr.* **1.** To come to have or use; receive: *She got skates for her birthday.* **2.** To go after and obtain; acquire: *I got a new coat at the store.* **3.** To go after and bring; fetch: *Please get me a pencil.* **4.** To succeed in reaching or boarding: *Did you get the bus on time?* **5.** To earn: *She got an A in math.* **6a.** To become affected with; catch: *I've got the flu.* **b.** To be subjected to; experience: *He got a broken ankle.* **7.** To have; possess: *I've already got that DVD.* **8.** To cause to be or become: *The long journey got the children tired and cross.* **9.** To make ready; prepare: *She got lunch for the children.* **10.** To cause (someone to do something): *got the guide to give us the complete tour.* **11.** To be obligated; need. Used only with a form of *have: We have got to leave early.* **12.** To begin or start (doing something): *We had better get going or we'll be late.* **13.** To hit; strike: *The snowball got me on the arm.* **14.** To understand or comprehend: *I don't get the connection between those ideas.* **15.** To make contact with: *We got the manager on the telephone.* *—intr.* **1.** To reach; come to: *get to the airport; get to shore.* **2.** To be or become: *get well; get stuck in traffic.* **3.** To come or go: *finally got to Wichita; got up the icy steps.* **4.** To be allowed or permitted: *I never got to see the movie.* ◆ **get across** To make understandable or clear: *The principal got her point across.* **get along 1.** To be or remain friendly with: *The two little children got along well.* **2.** To manage with reasonable success: *We're not rich, but we're getting along.* **3.** To advance; make progress: *How's your project getting along?* **4.** To move on; leave: *I think I'll be getting along now.* **get around 1.** To evade; overcome: *Many lazy people try to get around rules.* **2.** To trick: *You can't get around me with that story.* **3.** To travel from place to place. **4.** To become widely known; spread: *The rumor got around quickly.* **get around to** To find the time or occasion for: *A week after we moved, we finally got around to unpacking everything.* **get at 1.** To reach: *The sponge fell behind the sink where I can't get at it.* **2.** To express or mean: *Do you understand what I am getting at?* **get away 1.** To go away: *We want to get away on a trip to the country.* **2.** To escape: *The lion got away from the zoo.* **get away with** To do something without being punished or found out: *get away with a crime.* **get back** To go back or return: *Let's get back to work.* **get back at** To take revenge on. **get by 1.** To manage; survive: *They were unprepared for rain but got by somehow.* **2.** To pass without being noticed: *The prisoners got by the guards.* **get even** To obtain revenge: *After the bully took my money, I thought of a way to get even.* **get even with** To do something to (someone) in response to an act, as for revenge: *I got even with the bully by reporting him to the principal.* **get in 1.** To enter or be allowed to enter: *Can we get in without a ticket?* **2.** To arrive: *The plane gets in at midnight.* **3.** To put in: *I couldn't get in a word during the conversation.* **get it 1.** To understand; comprehend: *I just don't get it.* **2.** *Informal* To be punished or scolded: *You're really going to get it when your mother comes home.* **get nowhere** To make no progress: *After three months, negotiations still had gotten nowhere.* **get off 1.** To get down from or out of: *get off the train.* **2.** To leave; depart: *Tomorrow we get off early in the morning.* **3.** To escape punishment or obligation: *The student got off from detention.* **get on 1.** To climb up onto or into; enter: *Get on the boat before it leaves.* **2.** To be on friendly terms: *The neighbors got on for years and then suddenly had a fight.* **3.** To advance in years: *The old dog is getting on in years.* **4.** To continue, proceed, or progress: *I got on with the work.* **get out 1.** To leave or escape: *Our canary got out.* **2.** To become known: *The secret finally got out.* **3.** To publish: *That author gets out a new book every year.* **get out of** To escape from or be released from: *The cows somehow got out of the pasture.* **get over** To recover from: *get over a cold.* **get through 1.** To finish; complete: *trying to get through a big job.* **2.** To succeed in making contact: *I telephoned twice, but couldn't get through.* **get together 1.** To meet; assemble: *getting together for supper tonight.* **2.** To come to an agreement: *The feuding parties finally got together.* **get up 1.** To arise: *They got up early to see the sunrise.* **2.** To sit or stand up: *He got up out of the chair.* [From Middle English *geten*, from Old Norse *geta*.] —SEE NOTE.

get·a·way (gĕt′ə-wā′) *n.* **1.** The act of getting away; an escape: *The robbers made a quick getaway.* **2.** The start, as of a race.

get-go (gĕt′gō′) *n. Informal* The beginning; the outset: *had trouble from the get-go.*

get-to·geth·er (gĕt′tə-gĕ*th*′ər) *n.* A small party or gathering.

Get·tys·burg (gĕt′ēz-bûrg′) A town of southern Pennsylvania west-southwest of Philadelphia. It was the site of a major Union victory in the Civil War (July 1–3, 1863) and Abraham Lincoln's famous Gettysburg Address (November 19, 1863).

get·up (gĕt′ŭp′) *n. Informal* An outfit or costume, especially one that is odd or different.

get-up-and-go (gĕt′ŭp′ən-gō′) *n. Informal* Ambition and energy.

gew·gaw (gyo͞o′gô′ *or* go͞o′gô′) *n.* A showy trinket of little value; a bauble.

gey·ser (gī′zər) *n.* A natural hot spring that regularly ejects a spray of steam and boiling water into the air.

Gha·na (gä′nə) A country of western Africa on the Gulf of Guinea east of Côte d'Ivoire. Ghana was the site of the ancient Ashanti kingdom. Accra is the capital.

ghast·ly (găst′lē) *adj.* **ghast·li·er, ghast·li·est 1.** Terrifying; horrible: *a ghastly crime.* **2.** Resembling a ghost; pale: *The patient had a ghastly complexion.* **3.** Extremely unpleasant or bad: *His cooking is ghastly.* [From Middle English *gastli*, from *gasten*, to terrify, from Old English *gāst*, spirit.] **—ghast′li·ness** *n.*

Ghent (gĕnt) A city of western Belgium west-northwest of Brussels. It was founded in the seventh century.

gher·kin (gûr′kĭn) *n.* A small cucumber used for making pickles.

ghet·to (gĕt′ō) *n., pl.* **ghet·tos** or **ghet·toes 1.** A usually poor section of a city inhabited primarily by people of the same race, religion, or social background, often because of discrimination. **2.** A section or quarter in a European city where Jews were formerly restricted.

ghost (gōst) *n.* **1.** The spirit of a dead person, especially one that is believed to haunt or appear to living people. **2.** A slight trace; a bit: *a ghost of a smile; a ghost of a chance.* [From Old English *gāst*, breath, spirit.]

ghost·ly (gōst′lē) *adj.* **ghost·li·er, ghost·li·est** Relating to or resembling a ghost: *Dressed all in white, she had a ghostly appearance in the moonlight.* **—ghost′li·ness** *n.*

ghost town *n.* A formerly thriving town, especially a boomtown in the American West, that has been completely abandoned.

ghost·write (gōst′rīt′) *tr.v.* **ghost·wrote** (gōst′rōt′), **ghost·writ·ten** (gōst′rĭt′n), **ghost·writ·ing, ghost·writes** To write (something, such as a speech or autobiography) for another person who is credited as the author. **—ghost′writ′er** *n.*

ghoul (go͞ol) *n.* **1.** In Islamic folklore, an evil spirit believed to plunder graves and feast on corpses. **2.** A person who robs graves. **3.** A person who delights in brutal or horrible things. [From Arabic *ġūl*, from *ġāla*, to snatch.] **—ghoul′ish** *adj.* **—ghoul′ish·ly** *adv.*

GI[1] (jē′ī′) *n.* An enlisted person in or a veteran of any of the US armed forces. ❖ *adj.* Relating to or characteristic of a GI: *a GI uniform.*

GI[2] *abbr.* An abbreviation of: **1.** gastrointestinal. **2.** Government Issue.

gi·ant (jī′ənt) *n.* **1.** A person or thing of great size, ability, or importance: *a musical giant.* **2.** A being of great size and strength having human form and found in myth or folklore. ❖ *adj.* Gigantic; huge: *a giant airport.*

giant star *n.* A very large, bright star of low density.

gib·ber (jĭb′ər) *intr.v.* **gib·bered, gib·ber·ing, gib·bers** To speak rapidly and in a nonsensical way; chatter. ❖ *n.* Gibberish.

gib·ber·ish (jĭb′ər-ĭsh) *n.* Meaningless or nonsensical talk or writing.

gib·bet (jĭb′ĭt) *n.* **1.** A gallows. **2.** A wooden arm that projects from an upright post where the bodies of executed criminals were hung for public viewing. ❖ *tr.v.* **gib·bet·ed, gib·bet·ing, gib·bets** or **gib·bet·ted, gib·bet·ting, gib·bets 1.** To execute by hanging. **2.** To hang on a gibbet for public viewing.

gib·bon (gĭb′ən) *n.* Any of several small tree-dwelling apes of Southeast Asia, having a slender body, long arms, and no tail.

gib·bous (gĭb′əs) *adj.* **1.** More than half but not fully illuminated: *a gibbous moon.* **2.** Curved out; convex.

gibe also **jibe** (jīb) *n.* A scornful remark; a jeer. ❖ *intr.v.* **gibed, gib·ing, gibes** also **jibed, jib·ing, jibes** To make scornful or jeering remarks: *They gibed at my first efforts to water-ski.*

❑ *These sound alike:* **gibe, jibe[1]** (shift a sail), **jibe[2]** (agree).

gib·lets (jĭb′lĭts) *pl.n.* The edible heart, liver, and gizzard of a fowl.

Gi·bral·tar (jə-brôl′tər) A British colony centering on the heavily fortified **Rock of Gibraltar,** a strategically located peninsula on the north side of the **Strait of Gibraltar,** connecting the Mediterranean Sea and the Atlantic Ocean between Spain and northern Africa.

Gib·son (gĭb′sən), **Althea** 1927–2003. American tennis player who was the first African American to play at Wimbledon (1951), where she won singles and doubles titles in 1957 and 1958.

gid·dy (gĭd′ē) *adj.* **gid·di·er, gid·di·est 1a.** Having a whirling sensation in the head; dizzy: *The climber became giddy at the top of the mountain.* **b.** Causing or capable of causing dizziness: *The roller coaster moved at a giddy speed.* **2.** Frivolous; not serious: *The good news put everyone in a giddy mood.* **—gid′di·ly** *adv.* **—gid′di·ness** *n.*

gift (gĭft) *n.* **1.** Something given willingly with no payment in return; a present. **2.** A special talent, aptitude, or ability: *a gift for mathematics.* **3.** The act of giving: *Ownership of the car was transferred by gift.*

gift·ed (gĭf′tĭd) *adj.* Endowed with great natural ability, intelligence, or talent: *a gifted athlete.*

gift-wrap (gĭft′răp′) *tr.v.* **gift-wrapped, gift-wrap·ping, gift-wraps** To wrap (something intended as a gift) with fancy paper, ribbon, or other trimmings.

gig[1] (gĭg) *n.* **1.** A light two-wheeled carriage drawn by one horse. **2.** A long light ship's boat, usually used only by the ship's captain. [Perhaps from obsolete *gig*, spinning top.]

gig[2] (gĭg) *n.* **1.** A set of fishhooks usually dragged through a school of fish to hook them in their bodies. **2.** A pronged fishing spear. ❖ *tr. & intr.v.* **gigged, gig·ging, gigs** To fish with a gig. [From *fishgig*, from Spanish *fisga*.]

gig[3] (gĭg) *n. Slang* A job for a musician, especially at a club.

gig[4] (gĭg *or* jĭg) *n. Informal* A gigabyte. [Short for *gigabyte*.]

giga– *pref.* A prefix that means: **1.** One billion (10^9): *gigahertz; gigabit.* **2.** 1,073,741,824 (2^{30}): *gigabyte.*

gig·a·bit (gĭg′ə-bĭt′) *n.* One billion bits, used as a unit to measure the rate of the transmission of computer data.

gig·a·byte (gĭg′ə-bīt′) *n.* A unit of computer memory equal to 1,024 megabytes (2^{30} bytes).

gig·a·hertz (gĭg′ə-hûrtz′) *n.* A unit of frequency equal to one billion hertz.

gig·a·not·o·saur·us (jĭg′ə-nŏt′ə-sôr′əs) *n.* A very large meat-eating dinosaur that lived during the Cretaceous Period and had a huge skull and large teeth. [From Greek *gigās*, giant + *notos*, south + *sauros*, lizard.]

gi·gan·tic (jī-găn′tĭk) *adj.* Huge; enormous: *a gigantic basketball player; a gigantic factory.* **—gi·gan′ti·cal·ly** *adv.*

gig·gle (gĭg′əl) *intr.v.* **gig·gled, gig·gling, gig·gles** To laugh in a silly or nervous way; titter. ❖ *n.* A short silly laugh. **—gig′gler** *n.* **—gig′gly** *adj.*

Gi·la monster (hē′lə) *n.* A large venomous lizard of the southwest United States and northern Mexico, having a thick body with black and orange, pink, or yellowish beadlike scales.

gild (gĭld) *tr.v.* **gild·ed** or **gilt** (gĭlt), **gild·ing, gilds 1.** To cover with a thin layer of gold: *gild the frame of a mirror.*

gibbon

Althea Gibson
photographed in 1956

Gila monster

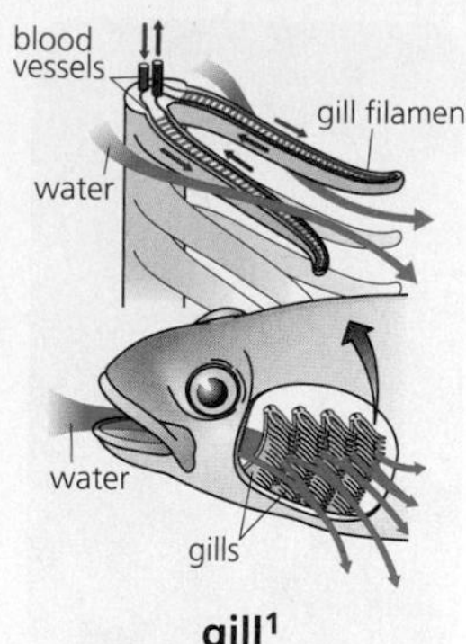

gill[1]
A fish breathes by swallowing water and passing it through gill slits on each side of its head. Blood-filled filaments on the gills take oxygen from the water as it flows through.

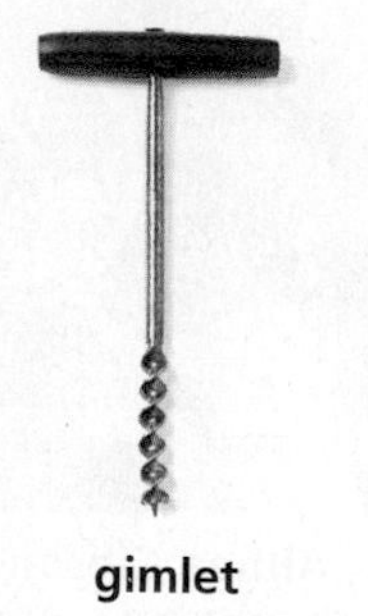

gimlet

WRITERS CHOOSE THEIR WORDS

[Dennys's] bare feet were still tender, and he walked **gingerly.** The girls guided him to the smoothest ways, until the sharp dry grasses and pebbles gave way to sand, and they were in the desert. The sand felt cool to the burning soles of his feet.

—Madeleine L'Engle
Many Waters

ă	pat	ôr	core
ā	pay	oi	boy
âr	care	ou	out
ä	father	o͝o	took
ĕ	pet	o͝or	lure
ē	be	o͞o	boot
ĭ	pit	ŭ	cut
ī	bite	ûr	urge
îr	pier	th	thin
ŏ	pot	*th*	this
ō	toe	zh	vision
ô	paw	ə	about

2. To give a deceptively attractive or improved appearance to (something): *In gilding the facts the author made the commander seem less cruel.*
❑ *These sound alike:* **gild, guild** (association).

gill[1] (gĭl) *n.* **1.** The organ that enables fish and many other water animals to take oxygen from the water. A gill consists of a series of thin membranes that are full of small blood vessels. As water flows across the membranes, oxygen passes into the blood vessels and carbon dioxide passes out of them. **2.** One of the thin plates on the underside of a mushroom cap. ◆ **to the gills** *Informal* As full as possible; completely. [From Middle English *gile,* of Scandinavian origin.]

gill[2] (jĭl) *n.* A unit of volume or capacity used mainly for liquids. It is equal to 4 ounces or 7.2 cubic inches (118 milliliters). See table at **measurement.** [From Middle English *gille,* from Late Latin *gillō,* vessel for cooling liquids.]

gill net (gĭl) *n.* A fishing net set vertically in the water so that fish swimming into it are caught by the gills.

Gil·man (gĭl′mən), **Charlotte Anna Perkins** 1860–1935. American feminist and writer whose works include "The Yellow Wallpaper" (1892).

gilt (gĭlt) *v.* A past tense and a past participle of **gild.** ❖ *n.* A thin layer of gold or something similar to gold, like gold-colored paint, applied to a surface. ❖ *adj.* Covered with gold or something resembling gold; gilded: *a picture in a gilt frame.*
❑ *These sound alike:* **gilt, guilt** (remorse).

gim·crack (jĭm′krăk′) *n.* A cheap and showy object of little or no use.

gim·let (gĭm′lĭt) *n.* A small hand tool with a screw tip, used to bore holes.

gim·mick (gĭm′ĭk) *n.* **1.** A clever idea, scheme, or device, often used to promote something: *an advertising gimmick.* **2.** A hidden or tricky condition; a catch: *My dad says if they're giving away free bicycles, there's probably a gimmick.* **3.** A gadget.

gin[1] (jĭn) *n.* A strong alcoholic liquor distilled from grain and flavored with juniper berries. [From Dutch *jenever,* from Latin *iūniperus,* juniper.]

gin[2] (jĭn) *n.* A cotton gin. ❖ *tr.v.* **ginned, gin·ning, gins** To remove the seeds from (cotton) with a gin. [From Middle English *gin,* device, from Old French *engin,* skill.] **—gin′ner** *n.*

gin[3] (jĭn) *n.* Gin rummy. [From *gin rummy.*]

gin·ger (jĭn′jər) *n.* **1a.** A tropical plant having a root with a sharp spicy flavor. **b.** The root of this plant, often powdered and used for flavoring. **2.** *Informal* Liveliness; vigor: *a kitten full of ginger.* [From Old English *gingifer,* from Greek *zingiberis,* ultimately of Indian or southeast Asian origin.]

ginger ale *n.* A soft drink flavored with ginger.

ginger beer *n.* A nonalcoholic or slightly alcoholic beverage strongly flavored with ginger.

gin·ger·bread (jĭn′jər-brĕd′) *n.* **1.** A cake flavored with ginger and molasses. **2.** A ginger and molasses cookie cut in various shapes, often elaborately decorated with icing. **3.** Elaborate ornamentation, especially in architecture or furniture.

gin·ger·ly (jĭn′jər-lē) *adv.* Cautiously; carefully; warily: *The cat rubbed herself gingerly against the horse's legs.* ❖ *adj.* Cautious; careful: *It is best to offer advice in a gingerly fashion.*

gin·ger·snap (jĭn′jər-snăp′) *n.* A flat crisp cookie made with molasses and ginger.

ging·ham (gĭng′əm) *n.* A light cotton cloth woven with colored thread in checks, stripes, plaids, or solid colors.

gin·gi·va (jĭn′jə-və) *n.* The gums of the mouth. [From Latin *gingīva.*]

gin·gi·vi·tis (jĭn′jə-vī′tĭs) *n.* Inflammation of the gums.

gink·go also **ging·ko** (gĭng′kō) *n., pl.* **gink·goes** also **ging·koes** A tree native to China that has fan-shaped leaves and is widely planted as an ornamental. [From obsolete Japanese *ginkyō.*]

gin rummy *n.* A kind of rummy, usually for two players.

Gins·burg (gĭnz′bərg), **Ruth Bader** Born 1933. American jurist who was appointed an associate justice of the US Supreme Court in 1993.

gin·seng (jĭn′sĕng′) *n.* **1.** Any of several plants of Asia and North America having small greenish flowers and a forked root. **2.** The roots of these plants, used in herbal medicine. [From Mandarin *rén shēn.*]

Giot·to (jō′tō) 1267?–1337. Italian painter whose works depicted natural human expression and movement.

Gip·sy (jĭp′sē) *n.* Variant of **Gypsy.**

gi·raffe (jə-răf′) *n., pl.* **gi·raffes** or **giraffe** An African mammal having a very long neck and legs, a tan coat with brown patches, and short horns. It is the tallest living land animal. [From Arabic dialectal *zirāfa.*]

gird (gûrd) *tr.v.* **gird·ed** or **girt** (gûrt), **gird·ing, girds 1.** To encircle or attach with a belt or band: *The monks girded their robes with a long cord.* **2.** To prepare (oneself) for action: *The employees girded themselves to ask for a raise in pay.* **3.** To encircle or surround: *Bushes and flowers girded the cottage.*

gird·er (gûr′dər) *n.* A beam, as of steel or wood, used as a main horizontal support in a building or bridge.

gir·dle (gûr′dl) *n.* **1.** An elastic undergarment worn over the waist and hips, especially by women, to give the body a more slender appearance. **2.** A belt, sash, or band worn around the waist. **3.** Something that surrounds like a belt: *a girdle of mountains around the valley.* ❖ *tr.v.* **gir·dled, gir·dling, gir·dles 1.** To encircle (the waist) with a belt or cord. **2.** To form a circle around: *The town was girdled by low hills.* **3.** To remove a strip of bark from around the trunk of (a tree), usually as a means of killing it.

girl (gûrl) *n.* **1.** A female child. **2.** A daughter: *our youngest girl.* **3.** *Informal* A woman: *an evening out with the girls.* **4.** *Informal* A female sweetheart; a girlfriend. **5.** *Offensive* A female servant, such as a maid. [From Middle English *girle,* child, girl.]

girl·friend (gûrl′frĕnd′) *n.* **1.** A female sweetheart or favored companion. **2.** A female friend.

girl·hood (gûrl′ho͝od′) *n.* The time of being a girl: *In her girlhood, she studied ballet.*

girl·ish (gûr′lĭsh) *adj.* Characteristic of or suitable for a girl: *a girlish smile; girlish colors.* **—girl′ish·ly** *adv.* **—girl′ish·ness** *n.*

Girl Scout *n.* A member of an organization for girls whose goals include helping girls develop self-reliance, good citizenship, and character.

girt (gûrt) *v.* A past tense and past participle of **gird.**

girth (gûrth) *n.* **1.** The distance around something; the circumference: *the girth of a tree trunk.* **2.** A strap encircling the body of a horse or pack animal in order to hold a load or saddle on its back.

gist (jĭst) *n.* The central idea; main point: *the gist of a message.*

give (gĭv) *v.* **gave** (gāv), **giv·en** (gĭv′ən), **giv·ing, gives** —*tr.* **1.** To make a present of: *My sister gave me a new watch.* **2.** To place in the hands of; hand over; pass: *Please give me the salt.* **3.** To hand over or deliver in exchange or in payment; sell or pay: *We gave them the bike for $75. They gave us $75 for the bike.* **4a.** To bestow; confer; award: *They gave first prize to the best speller.* **b.** To administer: *The doctor gave me a vaccine.* **c.** To convey or deliver by physical action: *She gave me a hug.* **5.** To provide; furnish; supply: *Green vegetables give us vitamins and minerals.* **6.** To grant; let have: *The principal gave us permission to go on the field trip.* **7.** To allot; assign: *The teacher gave me the task of cleaning the blackboard.* **8.** To direct or apply (one's attention or time, for example) to a pursuit or person: *She gave all of her free time to the charity.* **9a.** To offer or present: *Could you give us your ideas on the state of the economy?* **b.** To offer as entertainment: *We gave a party in his honor.* **10.** To emit or issue; put forth; utter: *give an order.* **11.** To be a source of; afford: *Music gives me great pleasure.* **12.** To produce; yield: *Their cows gave milk and cream.* **13.** To yield, as to pressure: *give ground to the enemy.* —*intr.* **1.** To make a gift or donation: *They give generously to local charities.* **2.** To yield to force or pressure: *The door gave when I ran against it.* ❖ *n.* Elasticity; flexibility: *The diving board has a lot of give.* ◆ **give away 1.** To make a gift of: *We gave away many of the vegetables from our garden.* **2.** To present (a bride) to the bridegroom at a wedding ceremony. **3.** To reveal or make known, often by accident: *I gave away the surprise party when I mentioned buying balloons and streamers.* **give back** To return: *Give me back my book.* **give birth to** To bear as offspring. **give in** To surrender; yield: *The babysitter gave in and let the children watch TV.* **give it to** *Informal* To punish or scold severely. **give off** To send forth; emit: *The moon gave off an eerie light.* **give or take** Plus or minus (a small specified amount): *The project should be finished on June 1, give or take a few days.* **give out 1.** To let (something) be known: *gave out the bad news.* **2.** To distribute: *give out paychecks to employees.* **3.** To stop working; fail: *The water pump gave out.* **4.** To become used up; run out: *The runner's energy gave out after five miles.* **give over 1.** To hand over. **2.** To make available for a purpose; devote: *The last part of the program is given over to questions from the audience.* **give rise to** To be the cause or origin of; bring about. **give (someone) the axe** or **give (someone) the boot** To remove (someone) ruthlessly or suddenly: *The owner gave the research department the axe to save money.* **give up 1.** To surrender: *The thieves gave themselves up to the police.* **2.** To stop: *My uncle has given up smoking.* **3.** To admit defeat and stop trying: *They finally gave up and stopped looking for the ring.* **4.** To abandon hope for: *We gave the cat up as lost.* **give way 1.** To withdraw; retreat: *The animals gave way before the advancing fire.* **2.** To abandon oneself: *Don't give way to panic.* **3.** To collapse; break: *The old flooring might give way.* [From Old English *giefan.*] —**giv′er** *n.*

give-and-take also **give and take** (gĭv′ən-tāk′) *n.* **1.** The practice of making concessions in order to secure similar concessions from the other side during a negotiation; compromise: *the give-and-take necessary to reach an agreement.* **2.** A lively exchange of talk: *the give-and-take of a political debate.*

give·a·way (gĭv′ə-wā′) *n.* **1.** *Informal* **a.** The act or an instance of giving something away for free or for very little in return: *the giveaway of free tickets to the concert.* **b.** An act of accidentally revealing something that is otherwise not known: *His refusal to answer the question was a giveaway that he knew more about what happened.* **2.** *Sports* The act of losing possession of the ball or puck to the opposing team.

giv·en (gĭv′ən) *v.* Past participle of **give.** ❖ *adj.* **1.** Specified; stated: *obtain all the facts on one given country.* **2.** Assumed; acknowledged; granted: *Given the condition of the car, it's a wonder it runs at all.* **3.** Having a tendency; inclined: *given to talking too much.* ❖ *n.* Something that is assumed or taken for granted: *It's a given that the test will be hard.*

given name *n.* A name given to a person at birth or at baptism, as distinguished from a surname.

giz·mo (gĭz′mō) *n., pl.* **giz·mos** A gadget whose name is forgotten or not known.

giz·zard (gĭz′ərd) *n.* A muscular pouch behind the stomach in birds. It often contains sand or gravel, which helps to grind up hard pieces of food.

gla·cial (glā′shəl) *adj.* **1.** Relating to or produced by a glacier: *glacial ice; a glacial lake.* **2.** Suggesting the extreme slowness of a glacier: *moved at a glacial pace.* **3.** Extremely cold; icy. **4.** Lacking warmth or friendliness: *a glacial stare.* —**gla′cial·ly** *adv.*

gla·cier (glā′shər) *n.* A large mass of ice slowly moving over a landmass or through a valley, formed over many years from packed snow in areas where snow accumulates faster than it melts. [From Latin *glaciēs,* ice.]

glad (glăd) *adj.* **glad·der, glad·dest 1.** Experiencing or showing joy and pleasure: *We were so glad to get your letter.* **2.** Providing joy and pleasure: *The wedding was a glad occasion.* **3.** Pleased; willing: *I would be glad to help.* —**glad′ly** *adv.* —**glad′ness** *n.*

SYNONYMS **glad, happy, cheerful, lighthearted, joyful** These adjectives mean being in or showing good spirits. **Glad** often means satisfied with immediate circumstances: *I am so glad we finally met.* **Happy** can mean feeling pleasurable contentment, as from a sense of fulfillment: *She is happy with her new job.* **Cheerful** means having good spirits, as from being pleased: *The cheerful children laughed at the clown's antics.* **Lighthearted** means free of cares and worries: *Summertime always puts me in a lighthearted mood.* **Joyful** means having great happiness and liveliness: *Their wedding was a joyful occasion.*

---

glad·den (glăd′n) *tr.v.* **glad·dened, glad·den·ing, glad·dens** To make glad: *The good news gladdened our hearts.*

glade (glād) *n.* An open space in a forest.

glad·i·a·tor (glăd′ē-ā′tər) *n.* In ancient Rome, a person, especially a slave, captive, or criminal, who engaged in mortal combat in an arena to entertain the public. [From Middle English, from Latin *gladiātor,* from *gladius,* sword.]

glad·i·o·lus (glăd′ē-ō′ləs) also **glad·i·o·la** (glăd′ē-ō′lə) *n., pl.* **glad·i·o·li** (glăd′ē-ō′lī) or **glad·i·o·lus·es** also **glad·i·o·las** Any of numerous plants having sword-shaped leaves and long spikes of showy, variously colored flowers. [From Middle English *gladiol,* from Latin *gladiolus,* wild iris, diminutive of *gladius,* sword.]

glad·some (glăd′səm) *adj.* **1.** Glad; joyful. **2.** Causing gladness: *gladsome tidings.* —**glad′some·ly** *adv.*

glam·or (glăm′ər) *n.* Variant of **glamour.**

glam·or·ize also **glam·our·ize** (glăm′ə-rīz′) *tr.v.* **glam·or·ized, glam·or·iz·ing, glam·or·iz·es** also **glam·our·ized, glam·our·iz·ing, glam·our·iz·es** To make glamorous: *Motion pictures have glamorized the life of gangsters.*

glam·or·ous also **glam·our·ous** (glăm′ər-əs) *adj.* Having or showing glamour; charming; alluring: *a glamorous movie star; a glamorous life of wealth and adventure.* —**glam′or·ous·ly** *adv.*

glam·our also **glam·or** (glăm′ər) *n.* An air of romantic charm or excitement surrounding a person or thing; allure: *the glamour of being a famous actor.* [From Scots, magic spell, alteration of *grammar* (from the association of learning with magic).]

glance (glăns) *intr.v.* **glanced, glanc·ing, glanc·es 1.** To look briefly or hastily: *They didn't even glance at my new outfit.* **2.** To strike a surface at such an angle as to fly off to one side: *The axe glanced off the log and struck the ground.* ❖ *n.* **1.** A brief or hasty look: *a quick glance over the shoulder.* **2.** A glancing off; a deflection. ◆ **at first glance** On initial consideration: *At first glance it seemed impossible, but then I saw how we could make it work.*

gland (glănd) *n.* **1.** An organ or group of cells in the body of an animal that produces and secretes a specific substance, such as a hormone or enzyme. The pancreas, pituitary, and thyroid are glands. **2.** A lymph node or

ginkgo

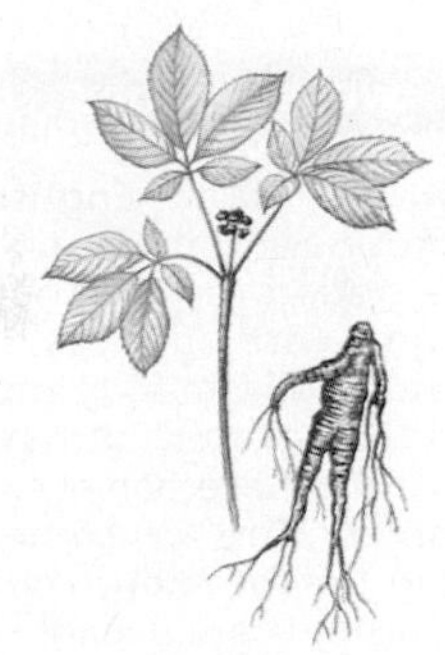
ginseng

girth

glacier
Taku Glacier, Alaska

glass blowing

WORD HISTORY

gleam Many English words having to do with the notion of "shining" begin with *gl*: **glare, gleam, glimmer, glint, glisten, glitter, glossy,** and **glow** are some examples. The *gl* comes from a common root that they share, meaning "shining" or "yellow." This root is also at the source of the word **gold,** "the shining or yellow metal," and of some words suggestive of quick motion, such as **glide** and **glimpse.**

ă	pat	ôr	core
ā	pay	oi	boy
âr	care	ou	out
ä	father	o͝o	took
ĕ	pet	o͝or	lure
ē	be	o͞o	boot
ĭ	pit	ŭ	cut
ī	bite	ûr	urge
îr	pier	th	thin
ŏ	pot	*th*	this
ō	toe	zh	vision
ô	paw	ə	about

other organ of the body that resembles a gland. **3.** An organ or structure in a plant that secretes a substance.

glan·du·lar (glăn′jə-lər) *adj.* **1.** Relating to, affecting, or resembling a gland or its secretion. **2.** Functioning as a gland.

glare (glâr) *v.* **glared, glar·ing, glares** —*intr.* **1.** To stare fiercely or angrily: *The angry customer glared at the sales clerk.* **2.** To shine intensely; dazzle: *The sun glared off the windshield.* —*tr.* To express with a fierce or angry stare: *The prisoners glared defiance at their captors.* ❖ *n.* **1.** A fixed angry stare. **2.** A very strong and blinding light: *the sun's glare.* [From Middle English *glaren,* to glitter.]

glar·ing (glâr′ĭng) *adj.* **1.** Staring fiercely or angrily: *glaring eyes.* **2.** Shining intensely: *a glaring summer sun.* **3.** Too showy; gaudy: *a glaring orange suit.* **4.** Obvious; conspicuous: *a glaring error.* **—glar′ing·ly** *adv.*

glar·y (glâr′ē) *adj.* **glar·i·er, glar·i·est** Dazzlingly bright; glaring.

Glas·gow (glăs′kō *or* glăs′gō *or* glăz′gō) The largest city of Scotland, in the southwest part of the country west of Edinburgh. It was founded in the late sixth century.

glass (glăs) *n.* **1.** A hard material made by melting sand with soda and lime. Glass is generally transparent or translucent and usually breaks or shatters easily. **2.** Something made of glass, as a mirror or a windowpane: *I hit the ball right through the glass.* **3.** A container used for drinking, especially one made of glass. **4.** The amount contained in a drinking container; a glassful: *spilled a whole glass of milk.* **5a. glasses** A pair of lenses mounted in a light frame, used to correct faulty vision or protect the eyes. **b.** A spyglass: *The captain spotted land through the glass.* ❖ *tr.v.* **glassed, glass·ing, glass·es** To cover or enclose with glass: *We glassed in the breezeway.* [From Old English *glæs.*]

glass blowing *n.* The art or process of shaping an object from a mass of molten glass by blowing air into it through a tube. **—glass blower** *n.*

glass·ful (glăs′fo͝ol′) *n.* The quantity that a glass can hold.

glass lizard *n.* Any of several slender legless lizards having a tail that breaks off easily and later grows back. Glass lizards are sometimes called glass snakes.

glass·ware (glăs′wâr′) *n.* Objects, especially containers, made of glass.

glass·y (glăs′ē) *adj.* **glass·i·er, glass·i·est 1.** Resembling glass; smooth: *the glassy surface of a quiet pool.* **2.** Having no expression; lifeless; blank: *a glassy stare.* **—glass′i·ly** *adv.* **—glass′i·ness** *n.*

glau·co·ma (glou-**kō′**mə *or* glô-**kō′**mə) *n.* An eye disease in which the pressure of fluid inside the eyeball becomes abnormally high, often damaging the optic nerve and leading to loss of vision.

glaze (glāz) *n.* **1.** A thin, smooth, shiny coating: *A glaze of ice covered the roads.* **2.** A coating, as of colored material, applied to ceramics before firing in a kiln. ❖ *v.* **glazed, glaz·ing, glaz·es** —*tr.* **1.** To fit or furnish with glass: *glaze a window.* **2.** To apply a glaze to: *The baker glazed the buns with egg white. The potter glazed the mugs and bowls.* —*intr.* To become glassy or blank: *His eyes glazed over from boredom.*

gla·zier (glā′zhər) *n.* A person who cuts and fits glass for windows, doors, and picture frames.

GLBT *abbr.* An abbreviation of gay, lesbian, bisexual, transgender.

gleam (glēm) *n.* **1.** A brief beam or flash of light: *occasional gleams of sunshine through the clouds.* **2.** A steady reflected shininess: *the gleam of polished silver.* **3.** A brief or faint indication; a trace: *a gleam of hope.* ❖ *intr.v.* **gleamed, gleam·ing, gleams 1.** To give off a gleam; shine: *The frost gleamed like diamonds.* **2.** To be reflected as a gleam: *The moon gleamed on the water.* —SEE NOTE.

glean (glēn) *tr.v.* **gleaned, glean·ing, gleans 1.** To gather (grain or other food) left behind after a harvest. **2.** To gather bit by bit: *After weeks of investigation, the reporter gleaned enough information for the article.* **—glean′er** *n.*

glee (glē) *n.* **1.** A feeling of delight; joy. **2.** A song for three or more usually male and unaccompanied voices, popular in the 1700s.

glee club *n.* A group of singers who perform usually short pieces of choral music.

glee·ful (glē′fəl) *adj.* Full of glee; merry. **—glee′ful·ly** *adv.* **—glee′ful·ness** *n.*

glen (glĕn) *n.* A small, secluded valley.

Glenn (glĕn), **John Herschel, Jr.** 1921–2016. American astronaut and politician who was the first American to orbit Earth (1962).

glib (glĭb) *adj.* **glib·ber, glib·best** Speaking or writing smoothly but suggesting lack of thought or sincerity: *a glib reply to a serious question.* **—glib′ly** *adv.* **—glib′ness** *n.*

glide (glīd) *v.* **glid·ed, glid·ing, glides** —*intr.* **1.** To move smoothly and with little effort: *The skaters glided over the ice.* See Synonyms at **slide. 2.** To pass or occur without notice: *The weekend had glided by.* **3.** To fly without using propelling power. —*tr.* **1.** To cause to move smoothly and with little effort: *glided the paintbrush back and forth over the wall.* **2.** To operate or guide (an aircraft) without propelling power. ❖ *n.* **1.** The act or process of gliding. **2.** A smooth effortless movement.

glid·er (glī′dər) *n.* **1.** An aircraft that has no engine and is designed to glide after being towed aloft by an airplane or launched from a catapult. **2.** A swinging sofa, bench, or chair that hangs in a vertical frame.

glim·mer (glĭm′ər) *n.* **1.** A dim or unsteady light; a flicker: *the glimmer of candles in the breeze.* **2.** A faint indication; a trace: *a glimmer of understanding.* ❖ *intr.v.* **glimmered, glim·mer·ing, glim·mers** To give off a dim or flickering light: *A single lamp glimmered in the window.*

glimpse (glĭmps) *n.* A brief incomplete view or look: *a glimpse of the sun on a cloudy day.* ❖ *tr.v.* **glimpsed, glimps·ing, glimps·es** To obtain a brief incomplete view of: *glimpsed a deer through the leaves.*

glint (glĭnt) *n.* **1.** A brief flash of light; a sparkle: *a glint of polished silver in the darkened room.* **2.** A faint indication; a trace: *a glint of suspicion in the guard's face.* ❖ *intr.v.* **glint·ed, glint·ing, glints** To gleam or flash; sparkle: *The creek glinted in the moonlight.*

glis·san·do (glĭ-sän′dō) *n., pl.* **glis·san·di** (glĭ-sän′dē) or **glis·san·dos** In music, a rapid glide from one tone to another.

glis·ten (glĭs′ən) *intr.v.* **glis·tened, glis·ten·ing, glis·tens** To shine with a sparkling reflected light: *The snow glistened in the sunlight.* ❖ *n.* A shine or sparkle.

glitch (glĭch) *n.* A mishap, malfunction, or problem: *a glitch in the computer program.*

glit·ter (glĭt′ər) *n.* **1.** A sparkling light or brightness: *the glitter of a diamond necklace.* **2.** Brilliant, often superficial appeal; showiness: *the glitter of movie stardom.* **3.** Small pieces of shiny decorative material: *tossed handfuls of glitter in the air at the celebration.* ❖ *intr.v.* **glit·tered, glit·ter·ing, glit·ters 1.** To sparkle brilliantly: *The stars glittered in the night sky.* **2.** To be brilliantly, often deceptively attractive: *The chance of making a fortune glittered in front of them.* **—glit′ter·y** *adj.*

gloat (glōt) *intr.v.* **gloat·ed, gloat·ing, gloats** To feel or express great, often spiteful pleasure: *The rival team gloated over their victory.*

glob (glŏb) *n.* A soft rounded mass or lump: *a glob of mashed potatoes.*

glob·al (glō′bəl) *adj.* **1.** Shaped like a globe; spherical. **2.** Of the entire earth; worldwide: *a global population figure.* **3.** Comprehensive; total: *a global approach to the problem.* **—glob′al·ly** *adv.*

Global Positioning System *n.* A system for determining one's exact position on the earth by comparing radio signals received from different satellites.

global warming *n.* An increase in the average temperature of the earth's atmosphere, especially one that is large enough to cause changes in the earth's overall climate. —SEE NOTE AT **greenhouse effect.**

globe (glōb) *n.* **1.** An object having the general shape of a ball or sphere, especially a representation of the earth or the celestial sphere. **2.** The earth: *The space station is designed to circle the globe constantly.* **3.** A spherical container, especially a glass sphere covering a light bulb. [From Middle English, from Latin *globus.*]

glob·u·lar (glŏb′yə-lər) *adj.* **1.** Having the shape of a globe or globule: *A cantaloupe is a globular fruit.* **2.** Made up of globules.

glob·ule (glŏb′yo͞ol) *n.* A very small rounded mass, especially a small drop of liquid.

glob·u·lin (glŏb′yə-lĭn) *n.* Any of a class of simple proteins found in blood, milk, muscle tissue, and plant seeds. Globulins are insoluble in water and coagulate when heated.

glock·en·spiel (glŏk′ən-spēl′ *or* glŏk′ən-shpēl′) *n.* A musical instrument consisting of a series of tuned metal bars and played with two light hammers. [From German : *Glocken*, bells + *Spiel*, play.]

gloom (glo͞om) *n.* **1.** Partial or total darkness; dimness: *He peered into the gloom of the night.* **2.** Sadness; dejection: *I was full of gloom over the loss.*

gloom·y (glo͞o′mē) *adj.* **gloom·i·er, gloom·i·est 1.** Partially or totally dark; dismal: *a gloomy basement.* **2.** Showing or filled with gloom; dejected; sad: *His gloomy face indicated the news was not good.* **3.** Causing low spirits; depressing: *damp gloomy weather; gloomy news.* **—gloom′i·ly** *adv.* **—gloom′i·ness** *n.*

glop (glŏp) *n. Slang* A soft soggy mixture, as of food: *All we can get at the cafeteria is tasteless glop.*

Glo·ri·a (glôr′ē-ə) *n.* **1.** A Christian hymn of praise to God, beginning with the Latin word *Gloria.* **2.** The music for one of these hymns.

glo·ri·fy (glôr′ə-fī′) *tr.v.* **glo·ri·fied, glo·ri·fy·ing, glo·ri·fies 1.** To give glory or honor to, especially through worship; exalt: *a culture that glorifies its ancestors; prayers that glorify God.* **2.** To make seem more glorious or excellent than is actually the case: *Their description glorified the old house as a mansion.* **—glo′ri·fi·ca′tion** (glôr′ə-fĭ-kā′shən) *n.*

glo·ri·ous (glôr′ē-əs) *adj.* **1.** Having or deserving glory; famous: *the glorious achievements of the Renaissance.* **2.** Giving or bringing glory: *a glorious victory.* **3.** Having great beauty or splendor; magnificent: *a glorious sunset.* **—glo′ri·ous·ly** *adv.*

glo·ry (glôr′ē) *n., pl.* **glo·ries 1.** Great honor or praise given by others; fame; renown: *The swimmer won glory by breaking the world record.* **2.** Something that brings honor, praise, or renown: *a symphony that is one of the glories of music of the 1700s.* **3.** Adoration or praise offered in worship: *giving glory to God.* **4.** Great beauty: *The sun was setting in a blaze of glory.* **5.** A period of highest achievement or prosperity: *Rome in its greatest glory.* ❖ *intr.v.* **glo·ried, glo·ry·ing, glo·ries** To rejoice: *The team gloried in its victory.* [From Middle English *gloire*, from Latin *glōria.*]

gloss[1] (glôs) *n.* **1.** A shine on a surface; a sheen: *the gloss of a polished table.* **2.** A cosmetic that adds shine or luster: *lip gloss.* **3.** A superficially attractive appearance intended to hide the real nature of something: *A few new buildings gave the town the gloss of prosperity, but economic problems persisted.* ❖ *tr.v.* **glossed, gloss·ing, gloss·es 1.** To give a bright shine or luster to. **2.** To make attractive or acceptable by concealing or misrepresenting: *The committee glossed over serious problems in its report.* [Perhaps of Scandinavian origin; akin to Icelandic *glossi*, a spark.]

gloss[2] (glôs) *n.* A brief note that explains or translates a difficult word, phrase, or section of a text or manuscript. ❖ *tr.v.* **glossed, gloss·ing, gloss·es** To provide (a text) with glosses: *This science textbook glosses all technical terms.* [From Middle English *glose*, from Late Latin *glōssa*, foreign word requiring explanation, from Greek, tongue, language.]

glos·sa·ry (glô′sə-rē) *n., pl.* **glos·sa·ries** A list of specialized words with their definitions: *a glossary of computer terms.*

gloss·y (glô′sē) *adj.* **gloss·i·er, gloss·i·est** Smooth and shiny: *Satin is a glossy fabric.* **—gloss′i·ly** *adv.* **—gloss′i·ness** *n.*

glot·tal stop (glŏt′l) *n.* A speech sound produced by closing the glottis to hold one's breath momentarily and then releasing it suddenly, as in the middle of the interjection *uh-oh* or between the two *i*'s in some pronunciations of *Hawaii.*

glot·tis (glŏt′ĭs) *n., pl.* **glot·tis·es** or **glot·ti·des** (glŏt′ĭ-dēz′) The space between the vocal cords at the upper part of the larynx. **—glot′tal** (glŏt′l) *adj.*

glove (glŭv) *n.* **1.** A covering for the hand, with a separate section for each finger and the thumb. **2a.** A protective covering for the hand, often made of padded leather, used in playing baseball, handball, or some other sport. **b.** A boxing glove. ❖ *tr.v.* **gloved, glov·ing, gloves 1.** To cover or provide with a glove. **2.** To catch in a baseball glove: *The outfielder gloved a long fly ball.* [From Old English *glōf.*]

glow (glō) *intr.v.* **glowed, glow·ing, glows 1.** To shine brightly and steadily with heat: *The embers glowed in the fireplace.* **2.** To have a bright warm color: *The skier's cheeks glowed in the cold.* **3.** To be radiant with emotion: *glow with happiness.* ❖ *n.* **1.** A light given off by something that is hot: *the glow of molten steel.* **2.** A brilliance or warmth of color: *the rosy glow of an adobe wall in the setting sun.* **3.** A feeling of warmth, especially when caused by emotion: *the glow on a child's happy face.* [From Old English *glōwan.*]

glow·er (glou′ər) *intr.v.* **glow·ered, glow·er·ing, glow·ers** To look or stare angrily: *The unfriendly neighbors glowered at us.* ❖ *n.* An angry or threatening stare.

glow·ing (glō′ĭng) *adj.* **1.** Giving or reflecting brilliant light: *glowing coals.* **2.** Having a rich warm color, as from health or strong emotion: *a glowing complexion.* **3.** Enthusiastic; highly favorable: *the glowing reports of their success.* **—glow′ing·ly** *adv.*

glow·worm (glō′wûrm′) *n.* Any of various beetle larvae or wingless female beetles that give off a glowing light, especially the larva or female of a firefly.

glu·cose (glo͞o′kōs′) *n.* A sugar having the formula $C_6H_{12}O_6$, found in living organisms and created by plants during photosynthesis. It is essential to the animal diet and is the main source of energy for cellular processes.

glue (glo͞o) *n.* A thick sticky substance used to join things together. Glues were originally made from animal skin and bones or from plant resins, but now they are usually made from synthetic chemicals. ❖ *tr.v.* **glued, glu·ing, glues 1.** To stick or fasten together with glue: *glued the broken leg of a chair.* **2.** To fix or hold firmly as if with glue: *The dog glued its eyes on the stranger.*

glum (glŭm) *adj.* **glum·mer, glum·mest** Feeling or appearing sad or dejected; gloomy: *a glum look on his face.* **—glum′ly** *adv.* **—glum′ness** *n.*

glut (glŭt) *tr.v.* **glut·ted, glut·ting, gluts 1.** To fill beyond capacity, especially with food: *The lions slept after glutting themselves on their kill.* **2.** To provide (a market) with too many goods so that the supply is much greater than the demand. ❖ *n.* An excess amount; an oversupply: *A glut of gasoline caused lower prices.*

John Glenn
photographed in 1998

glider

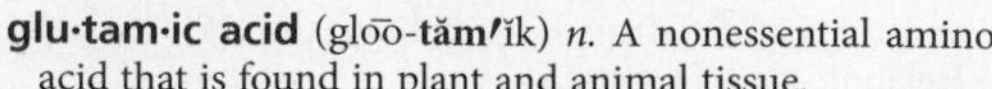

glu·tam·ic acid (glo͞o-**tăm′**ĭk) *n.* A nonessential amino acid that is found in plant and animal tissue.

glu·ta·mine (**glo͞o′**tə-mēn′) *n.* A nonessential amino acid that is found in plant and animal tissue and produced in the laboratory for use in research.

glu·ten (**glo͞ot′**n) *n.* Any of various plant proteins found in cereal grains, especially certain ones in wheat, rye, and barley that can cause digestive disorders.

glu·ti·nous (**glo͞ot′**n-əs) *adj.* Resembling glue; thick and sticky: *a glutinous mixture of flour and water.*

glut·ton (**glŭt′**n) *n.* **1.** A person who eats to excess. **2.** A person with an unusually great capacity to receive or withstand something: *a glutton for work.* **—glut′ton·ous** *adj.* **—glut′ton·ous·ly** *adv.*

glut·ton·y (**glŭt′**n-ē) *n., pl.* **glut·ton·ies** Excess in eating.

glyc·er·in also **glyc·er·ine** (**glĭs′**ər-ĭn) *n.* Glycerol.

glyc·er·ol (**glĭs′**ə-rôl′ *or* **glĭs′**ə-rōl′) *n.* A sweet syrupy liquid obtained from animal fats and oils. It is used as a solvent, sweetener, and antifreeze and in the manufacture of explosives and soaps.

gly·cine (**glī′**sēn′) *n.* A nonessential amino acid that is found in most proteins.

gly·co·gen (**glī′**kə-jən) *n.* A carbohydrate that is stored in the muscles and liver of animals and is converted to glucose for energy.

glyph
curved road ahead

glyph (glĭf) *n.* **1.** A graphic symbol that provides information without using words. An emoticon, such as a smiley, and the arrow on a "ONE WAY" traffic sign are glyphs. **2.** A symbolic figure that is usually engraved or carved.

gm. *abbr.* An abbreviation of gram.

G-man (**jē′**măn′) *n.* An agent of the Federal Bureau of Investigation.

GMO *abbr.* An abbreviation of genetically modified organism.

gnarl (närl) *n.* A knot in wood: *a smooth board without gnarls.* ❖ *tr.v.* **gnarled, gnarl·ing, gnarls** To make knotted or deformed; twist: *Disease gnarled the patient's fingers.* [Probably variant of *knarled,* from *knarl,* tangle, knot, alternation of Middle English *knarre,* knot in wood.] **—gnarl′y** *adj.*

gnarled

gnarled (närld) *adj.* Having gnarls; knotty and misshapen: *gnarled tree roots; gnarled fingers.*

gnash (năsh) *tr.v.* **gnashed, gnash·ing, gnash·es** To grind (the teeth) together. [From Middle English *gnasten,* possibly of Scandinavian origin.]

gnat (năt) *n.* Any of various tiny flies, especially those that form swarms. [From Old English *gnæt.*]

gnaw (nô) *v.* **gnawed, gnaw·ing, gnaws** *—tr.* **1.** To bite, chew, or erode with the teeth: *animals gnawing the bark of trees.* **2.** To produce by gnawing: *Rats gnawed a hole in the wall.* **3.** To reduce gradually as if by gnawing: *The waves gnawed at the base of the cliff.* **4.** To cause distress or pain to. *—intr.* **1.** To bite or chew on: *The dog gnawed on the rope.* **2.** To trouble or distress: *The lack of success gnawed at the scientist for weeks.* [From Old English *gnagan.*]

gneiss (nīs) *n.* A type of metamorphic rock consisting of light-colored layers, usually of quartz and feldspar, alternating with dark-colored layers of other minerals. [From German *Gneis,* probably from Middle High German *ganeist,* spark (from its appearance).]

❑ *These sound alike:* **gneiss, nice** (pleasant).

gne·to·phyte (**nē′**tə-fīt′) *n.* Any of various seed plants that are gymnosperms but have some features similar to those of angiosperms.

gnome (nōm) *n.* In folklore, a dwarf that dwells underground and guards treasure.

gnu (no͞o) *n.* Either of two large African antelopes having a drooping mane, a beard, a long tufted tail, and curved horns. [From Xhosa *i-ngu,* white-tailed gnu.]

❑ *These sound alike:* **gnu, knew** (had knowledge), **new** (not used).

go (gō) *v.* **went** (wĕnt), **gone** (gôn), **go·ing, goes** (gōz) *—intr.* **1.** To move along or forward; proceed: *The bus went along steadily in the rain.* **2.** To move or proceed to a specified place; advance: *I am going to New York.* **3.** To move from a place; depart: *We must go at once.* **4.** To function, operate, move, or work: *A battery makes the watch go.* **5.** To pursue a course of action: *go to a lot of trouble; go through college.* **6a.** To belong in a definite place or position: *This book goes on that shelf.* **b.** To be suitable as an accessory: *Does this tie go with my shirt?* **7.** To extend between two points or in a certain direction: *The windows go from the ceiling to the floor. The road goes north.* **8a.** To extend in time: *The house goes back to the 1800s.* **b.** To pass; elapse: *Time goes quickly when you are busy.* **9.** To be allotted or awarded: *First prize went to my friend. This money goes for food.* **10.** To proceed or end in a particular way; turn out: *How did your day go? How does the rest of the story go?* **11.** To be expressed or phrased: *How does that nursery rhyme go?* **12.** To be typically or in general: *well behaved, as dogs go.* **13a.** To become weak; fail: *My eyes are going.* **b.** To come apart; break up: *The pier looks about ready to go.* **14.** To be sold or auctioned off: *Most of the old books went for high prices.* **15.** To come to be in a certain state or condition: *go mad; go to sleep; a tire going flat.* **16.** Used to indicate future intention or expectation: *I am going to climb that mountain.* *—tr.* **1.** To proceed or move along: *We went separate ways.* **2.** To take part in: *We went swimming.* **3.** *Informal* To say, utter, or produce as sound: *The cow goes moo. Whenever I tell my friend a story, he goes "No way!"* ❖ *n., pl.* **goes 1.** An attempt; an effort: *Let's have a go at the puzzle.* **2.** Something successful; a success: *They tried to make a go of their store.* **3.** *Informal* Energy; vitality: *That athlete has got a lot of go and will be a winner.* **4.** A situation in which a plan is certain to be put into effect: *Our weekend at the lake is still a go.* ❖ *adj. Informal* Ready for action or working correctly: *Everything is go for the parade.* ◆ **go about** To set about to do; undertake: *How does one go about building a house?* **go along** To cooperate: *Why don't you stop criticizing the project and go along?* **go around 1.** To satisfy a demand or requirement: *We have enough food to go around.* **2.** To go here and there; move from place to place. **3.** To circulate: *rumors going around.* **go at 1.** To attack, especially with energy. **2.** To approach; undertake: *He went at the assignment diligently.* **go back on** To fail to honor or keep: *Don't go back on your word!* **go by 1.** To elapse; pass: *Time goes by fast sometimes.* **2.** To be called; be known as: *He goes by Billy.* **go down 1a.** To drop below the horizon; set: *The sun went down.* **b.** To fall to the ground. **c.** To sink. **2.** To be easy to swallow: *This cough syrup goes right down.* **3.** To come to be remembered in posterity: *He went down in history as a famous inventor.* **go for 1.** *Informal* To have a special liking for: *I really go for jazz.* **2.** To attack. **go in for 1.** To have interest in: *I go in for folk music.* **2.** To take part in: *She goes in for water skiing.* **go off 1.** To explode: *fireworks going off.* **2.** To make a noise; sound: *The alarm went off, but it was just a test.* **3.** To leave: *They went off for a hike.* **go on 1.** To take place; happen: *What's going on?* **2a.** To continue: *How long has this discussion been going on?* **b.** To keep on (doing something): *They went on talking.* **c.** To proceed: *She went on to be a famous scientist.* **3.** *Informal* To talk volubly: *He does go on.* **go out 1.** To become extinguished. **2a.** To go outdoors; leave one's residence. **b.** To take part in social life outside the home: *Let's go out for ice cream.* **c.** To be romantically involved: *Are they going out now?* **3.** To become unfashionable: *That dance went out years ago.* **go out of (one's) way** To inconvenience oneself in doing something beyond what is required. **go over 1.** To gain acceptance or ap-

ă	pat	ôr	core
ā	pay	oi	boy
âr	care	ou	out
ä	father	o͝o	took
ĕ	pet	o͝or	lure
ē	be	o͞o	boot
ĭ	pit	ŭ	cut
ī	bite	ûr	urge
îr	pier	th	thin
ŏ	pot	*th*	this
ō	toe	zh	vision
ô	paw	ə	about

proval: *My idea went over well.* **2.** To examine: *Did you go over my paper yet?* **go steady** To date someone exclusively. **go the distance** To carry a course of action through to completion: *He is pitching well, but can he go the distance?* **go through 1.** To examine carefully: *I've gone through your paper and it's great!* **2.** To experience or be subjected to: *We all go through some sad times. The house is going through a renovation.* **go under** To fail: *The business went under.* **go with** To date regularly. **go without saying** To be self-evident: *Some rules go without saying.* **on the go** Constantly busy or active. **to go 1.** To be taken out, as restaurant food or drink: *He ordered a pizza to go.* **2.** Still to be done or taken care of; remaining: *That's one test down and one to go.*

goad (gōd) *n.* **1.** A long stick with a pointed end used for prodding animals, especially cattle. **2.** Something that prods or urges: *Competition is often a goad to hard work.* ❖ *tr.v.* **goad·ed, goad·ing, goads** To stir to action; prod: *The bad grade goaded me to study harder.* [From Old English *gād*.]

go-a·head (gō′ə-hĕd′) *n.* *Informal* Permission to go ahead or proceed.

goal (gōl) *n.* **1.** The purpose toward which one is working; an objective: *The student's goal was to become a doctor.* **2.** The finish of a race. **3a.** In certain sports, a structure or area into which players must propel the ball or puck in order to score. **b.** The score awarded for doing this. [From Middle English *gol*, boundary.]

goal·ie (gō′lē) *n.* A goalkeeper.

goal·keep·er (gōl′kē′pər) *n.* The player who defends the goal in sports such as hockey and soccer.

goal kick *n.* A free kick in soccer awarded to a defensive team when the ball has been driven out of bounds over the goal line by an opponent.

goal line *n.* **1.** A line at either end of a playing area, as in soccer, on which a goal or goalpost is positioned. **2.** In football, a line crossing either end of the playing field over which the ball must be moved to score a touchdown.

goal·post or **goal post** (gōl′pōst′) *n.* **1.** One of a pair of posts usually joined with a crossbar and set at each end of a playing field to form a goal, as in ice hockey or soccer. **2.** A post or a pair of posts supporting a crossbar and either supporting or extending into the uprights of a goal, as in football.

goal·tend·er (gōl′tĕn′dər) *n.* A goalkeeper.

goal·tend·ing (gōl′tĕn′dĭng) *n.* **1.** The act of protecting a goal, as in hockey. **2.** In basketball, an illegal play in which a player touches a ball that is on a downward path to the basket or that is on or within the rim of the basket, resulting in an automatic score when committed by the defense or not scoring the field goal when committed by the offense.

goat (gōt) *n.* **1.** A domesticated hoofed mammal having backward-curving horns and a beard, raised in many parts of the world for wool, milk, and meat. **2.** Any of various similar wild mammals. [From Old English *gāt*.]

goat·ee (gō-tē′) *n.* A small beard, especially one connected to a mustache or trimmed into a point.

goat·skin (gōt′skĭn′) *n.* **1.** The skin of a goat. **2.** Leather made from the skin of a goat. **3.** A container, as for water, made out of this leather.

gob (gŏb) *n.* **1.** A small piece or lump: *a gob of wax.* **2.** often **gobs** *Informal* A large quantity: *a gob of money; gobs of time.* [From Middle English *gobbe*, probably from Old French *gobe*, mouthful.]

gob·ble¹ (gŏb′əl) *tr.v.* **gob·bled, gob·bling, gob·bles** To devour in big greedy gulps. [From Middle English *gobben*, to drink greedily, probably from *gobbe*, lump, mouthful.]

gob·ble² (gŏb′əl) *n.* The throaty chortling sound made by a male turkey. ❖ *intr.v.* **gob·bled, gob·bling, gob·bles** To make this sound. [Of imitative origin.]

gob·ble·dy·gook also **gob·ble·de·gook** (gŏb′əl-dē-go͝ok′) *n.* Unclear, often wordy speech or writing. [Imitative of the gobbling of a turkey.]

gob·bler (gŏb′lər) *n.* A male turkey.

go-be·tween (gō′bĭ-twēn′) *n.* A person who acts as an intermediary or messenger between two sides.

Go·bi (gō′bē) A desert of southeast Mongolia and northern China.

gob·let (gŏb′lĭt) *n.* A drinking glass that has a stem and a base.

gob·lin (gŏb′lĭn) *n.* An ugly elfin creature of folklore, thought to cause mischief or evil. [From Middle English *gobelin*, from the Norman French name of a ghost that supposedly haunted the town of Évreux, France, in the 1100s.]

god (gŏd) *n.* **1. God** A being regarded as the creator and ruler of the universe, forming the object of worship in monotheistic religions. **2.** A being of supernatural powers, worshiped by a people, especially a male being thought to control some part of nature: *the Egyptian sun god Ra; a rain god.* **3.** An image or idol of a god. **4.** Something considered to be of great value or high importance: *Absolute power was his god.* [From Old English.]

god·child (gŏd′chīld′) *n.* A child for whom a person serves as sponsor at baptism.

God·dard (gŏd′ərd), **Robert Hutchings** 1882–1945. American physicist who developed and launched the first successful liquid-fueled rocket (1926) and invented numerous rocketry devices.

god·daugh·ter (gŏd′dô′tər) *n.* A female godchild.

god·dess (gŏd′ĭs) *n.* **1.** A female being of supernatural powers, worshiped by a people: *Venus, the Roman goddess of love and beauty.* **2.** An image or idol of a goddess.

god·fa·ther (gŏd′fä′*th*ər) *n.* A man who serves as sponsor at one's baptism.

god·head (gŏd′hĕd′) *n.* **1.** The essential and divine nature of God; divinity. **2. Godhead** God, especially the Christian Trinity.

god·less (gŏd′lĭs) *adj.* **1.** Not believing in God or a god. **2.** Immoral; wicked. **—god′less·ly** *adv.* **—god′less·ness** *n.*

god·like (gŏd′līk′) *adj.* Resembling or of the nature of God or a god; divine.

god·ly (gŏd′lē) *adj.* **god·li·er, god·li·est** Having great reverence for God; pious. **—god′li·ness** *n.*

god·moth·er (gŏd′mŭ*th*′ər) *n.* A woman who serves as sponsor at one's baptism.

god·par·ent (gŏd′pâr′ənt) *n.* A godfather or godmother.

god·send (gŏd′sĕnd′) *n.* Something wanted or needed that comes or happens unexpectedly: *The $500 holiday bonus was a godsend.*

god·son (gŏd′sŭn′) *n.* A male godchild.

God·speed (gŏd′spēd′) *n.* Success or good fortune: *With a wish of Godspeed they bid me farewell.*

Godt·håb (gôt′hôp′) See **Nuuk.**

Goe·the (gœ′tə), **Johann Wolfgang von** 1749–1832. German writer and scientist who spent 50 years writing his two-part dramatic poem *Faust* (published 1808 and 1832).

go-get·ter (gō′gĕt′ər *or* gō′gĕt′ər) *n.* *Informal* An energetic person with much determination and ambition.

gog·gle (gŏg′əl) *intr.v.* **gog·gled, gog·gling, gog·gles** To stare with wide and bulging eyes.

gog·gle-eyed (gŏg′əl-īd′) *adj.* Having prominent or rolling eyes: *a goggle-eyed frog; tourists who were goggle-eyed with wonder at the Great Wall of China.*

gog·gles (gŏg′əlz) *pl.n.* Eyeglasses worn tight against the head to protect the eyes from hazards such as wind, glare, water, or flying debris.

gneiss

goalkeeper

goatee

goggles

Emma Goldman
photographed c. 1934

gong

WORD HISTORY

goober Most Southerners know that a **goober** is a peanut. The word *goober* is related to *n-guba*, "peanut," in a Bantu language of west-central Africa. *Goober* is one of a small group of words that came into American English from the languages spoken by the Africans who were enslaved and brought to the Americas during the 1600s and 1700s. *Gumbo* is also of Bantu origin, and *okra* and *yam* are of West African origin.

ă	pat	ôr	core
ā	pay	oi	boy
âr	care	ou	out
ä	father	o͝o	took
ĕ	pet	o͝or	lure
ē	be	o͞o	boot
ĭ	pit	ŭ	cut
ī	bite	ûr	urge
îr	pier	th	thin
ŏ	pot	*th*	this
ō	toe	zh	vision
ô	paw	ə	about

Gogh (gō), **Vincent van** See Vincent **van Gogh.**

go·ing (gō**′**ĭng) *n.* **1.** The act of leaving or moving away; departure: *comings and goings of passengers in the terminal.* **2.** The condition of the ground or road as it affects how one walks or rides: *It was rough going over the icy roads, but we made it.* **3.** *Informal* Progress toward a goal: *Learning this new computer program has been easy going.* ❖ *adj.* **1.** Working; running: *The clock is in going order.* **2.** In full operation; flourishing: *Our business is at last a going operation.* **3.** Available or now in existence: *We make the best bikes going.* **4.** Current; prevailing: *The going rates for bank loans will soon increase.*

goi·ter (goi**′**tər) *n.* An enlargement of the thyroid gland, visible as a swelling at the front of the neck and often associated with a diet that contains too little iodine. [From Latin *guttur*, throat.]

gold (gōld) *n.* **1.** *Symbol* **Au** A soft, shiny, yellow metallic element that resists corrosion and is a good conductor of heat and electricity. It is used in making jewelry and in plating electrical and mechanical components. Atomic number 79. See **Periodic Table. 2.** A deep, strong, or metallic yellow: *when fall leaves turn to red and gold.* **3.** Gold coins. **4.** Money; riches. **5.** A medal made of gold, awarded for first place in a competition. **6.** Something thought of as having great value or goodness: *a heart of gold.* ❖ *adj.* **1.** Relating to or containing gold: *a gold ring; a gold coin.* **2.** Having a deep, strong, or metallic yellow color. [From Old English.] —SEE NOTE AT **gleam.**

gold·brick (gōld**′**brĭk′) *Slang n.* A person, especially a soldier, who avoids duties or work. ❖ *intr.v.* **gold·bricked, gold·brick·ing, gold·bricks** To avoid one's duties or work. **—gold′brick′er** *n.*

Gold Coast A section of western Africa along the Gulf of Guinea on the coast of Ghana. It was named for the large quantities of gold found in the area.

gold·en (gōl**′**dən) *adj.* **1.** Relating to, made of, or containing gold: *golden earrings.* **2.** Having the color of gold or a yellow color suggestive of gold: *a golden wheat field.* **3a.** Of great value or importance; precious: *golden memories of a happy childhood.* **b.** Very favorable; excellent: *a golden opportunity.* **4.** Marked by peace, prosperity, and often creativeness: *a golden era in our past.*

golden age *n.* A period usually of peace and prosperity when a nation and its culture are at their height: *Spain's golden age of art and cultural influence was based on the riches of the New World.*

Golden Fleece *n.* In Greek mythology, the fleece of the golden ram, stolen by Jason and the Argonauts.

golden goal *n.* In soccer, a goal that is scored in overtime, resulting in the immediate end of the game.

golden mean *n.* The course between extremes; moderation.

gold·en·rod (gōl**′**dən-rŏd′) *n.* Any of numerous plants having tall stalks with clusters of small, usually yellow flowers that bloom in late summer or fall.

golden rule *n.* The rule of conduct that one should behave toward others as one would have others behave toward oneself.

gold-filled (gōld**′**fĭld**′**) *adj.* Made of inexpensive metal with an outer layer of gold: *gold-filled jewelry.*

gold·finch (gōld**′**fĭnch′) *n.* **1.** Any of several small North American finches, especially a common species in which the male has yellow feathers with a black forehead, wings, and tail. **2.** A European finch having black, yellow, and red markings.

gold·fish (gōld**′**fĭsh′) *n.* A small freshwater fish, usually orange or reddish, often kept in outdoor ponds and home aquariums.

gold leaf *n.* Gold beaten into extremely thin sheets used for gilding.

Gold·man (gōld**′**mən), **Emma** 1869–1940. Lithuanian-born American anarchist who was jailed repeatedly for her advocacy of birth control and opposition to forced enrollment of civilians in the armed forces. Her writings include *Living My Life* (1931).

gold rush *n.* A rush of miners or prospectors and other people to an area where gold has been discovered.

gold·smith (gōld**′**smĭth′) *n.* A person who makes, repairs, or deals in objects of gold.

gold standard *n.* A monetary system in which a country's currency is backed by and exchangeable for gold.

golf (gŏlf) *n.* A game played over a large outdoor course having a series of 9 or 18 holes spaced far apart. A player, using various clubs, tries to take as few strokes as possible in hitting a ball into one hole after another. ❖ *intr.v.* **golfed, golf·ing, golfs** To play golf. [From 15th-century Scots.] **—golf′er** *n.*

golf club *n.* **1.** One of a set of clubs, having a slender shaft and a head usually made of wood or iron, used in golf. **2.** An association of golfers.

golf course *n.* A large tract of land laid out for golf.

Gol·gi apparatus or **Gol·gi complex** (gōl**′**jē) *n.* A structure within many cells that is composed of a series of sacs and plays a role in the storage, modification, and transport of proteins and other large molecules.

Gol·go·tha (gŏl**′**gə-thə) See **Calvary.**

Go·li·ath (gə-lī**′**əth) In the Bible, a giant who was killed by David with a stone and sling.

Go·mor·rah (gə-môr**′**ə) An ancient city of Palestine near Sodom that according to the Bible was destroyed by fire because of its wickedness.

Gom·pers (gŏm**′**pərz), **Samuel** 1850–1924. British-born American labor leader who as president of the American Federation of Labor (1886–1924, except 1895) won higher wages and shorter hours for union members.

–gon *suff.* A suffix that means a figure having a specified number of angles: *octagon.*

go·nad (gō**′**năd′) *n.* An organ, such as an ovary or testis, in which egg cells or sperm cells are produced.

gon·do·la (gŏn**′**dl-ə *or* gŏn-dō**′**lə) *n.* **1.** A long narrow boat with a high pointed prow and stern, propelled from the stern by a single oar and used on the canals of Venice. **2.** An open railroad freight car with low sides. **3.** A basket or cabin attached to the underside of a balloon. **4.** An enclosed car suspended from a cable used for transporting passengers, as up and down a ski slope. [From Old Italian *gondula.*]

gon·do·lier (gŏn′dl-**îr′**) *n.* The person who rows a gondola.

gone (gôn) *v.* Past participle of **go.** ❖ *adj.* **1.** Being away from a place; absent or departed: *I'll be gone for a few days.* **2.** Used up or consumed: *When natural resources are gone they cannot be replaced. Their strength was gone.* **3.** Dead.

gon·er (gô**′**nər) *n. Slang* A person or thing that is ruined or doomed: *A car with a bent frame is usually a goner.*

gong (gông) *n.* A saucer-shaped metal disk that produces a loud ringing tone when struck. [From Malay.]

gon·or·rhe·a (gŏn′ə-rē**′**ə) *n.* A sexually transmitted bacterial disease that causes inflammation of the genitals and urinary tract.

goo (go͞o) *n. Informal* A sticky wet substance.

goo·ber (go͞o**′**bər) *n. Informal* A peanut. [Of Bantu origin.] —SEE NOTE.

good (go͝od) *adj.* **bet·ter** (bĕt**′**ər), **best** (bĕst) **1.** Having positive or desirable qualities; not bad or poor: *a good book; good food.* **2.** Providing a benefit; helpful: *Earthworms are good for our soil.* **3.** Serving the desired purpose; suitable: *Is this a good shirt to wear to the party?* **4.** Superior to average; skilled: *a good painter.* **5.** Not spoiled or ruined: *The milk is still good.* **6.** Genuine; real: *a good dollar bill.* **7.** Valid; true: *a good reason.* **8.** In effect; valid: *The warranty on that car is still good.* **9.**

Providing pleasure; enjoyable: *a good time.* **10.** Attractive; handsome: *good looks.* **11a.** Doing or showing what is right; morally upright: *A good person is honest. It is always good to tell the truth.* **b.** Loyal; devoted: *a good friend.* **c.** Honorable: *a good name.* **12a.** Well-behaved; obedient: *a good dog.* **b.** Proper; correct: *good manners.* **13.** Judged as in play or scoring: *a good tennis return; a good field goal.* **14.** Substantial; ample: *a good income.* **15.** Not less than; full: *It is a good mile to the station.* **16.** Thorough; complete: *a good housecleaning.* **17.** More than a little likely: *Our team has a good chance of winning the competition.* ❖ *n.* **1.** Something good: *You must learn to accept the bad with the good.* **2.** Benefit; welfare: *for the good of the country.* **3.** Value; use: *What good is a bicycle without a chain?* **4. goods a.** Things that can be bought and sold; merchandise. **b.** Personal belongings: *They lost all their household goods in the fire.* **c.** *(used with a singular or plural verb)* Cloth; fabric. ◆ **as good as** Nearly; almost: *This car is as good as new.* **for good** Permanently; forever: *They left town for good.* **good and** *Informal* Very; entirely: *We are good and mad at them.* **no good** Useless; worthless: *It's no good arguing with them.* **to the good** Advantageous; in one's favor. [From Old English *gōd.*] —SEE NOTE.

Good·all (go͝od′ôl), **Jane** Born 1934. British zoologist known for her observations of chimpanzees and her leadership of international conservation efforts.

good·bye or **good-bye** (go͝od-bī′) *n., pl.* **good·byes** also **good-byes 1.** An acknowledgement at parting, especially by saying "goodbye": *Have you said your goodbye to the host yet?* **2.** An act of parting: *There were many long goodbyes among the campers at the end of the summer.* ❖ *interj.* An expression used to make such an acknowledgment. [From *God be with you.*]

good-for-noth·ing (go͝od′fər-nŭth′ĭng) *n.* A person who is considered worthless or useless. ❖ *adj.* Having little worth; useless.

Good Friday *n.* The Friday before Easter, observed by Christians in commemoration of the crucifixion of Jesus.

good·heart·ed (go͝od′här′tĭd) *adj.* Kind and generous: *a goodhearted person.* **—good′heart′ed·ly** *adv.* **—good′heart′ed·ness** *n.*

Good Hope, Cape of A high ridge on the southwest coast of South Africa jutting out into the Atlantic Ocean south of Cape Town.

good-hu·mored (go͝od′hyo͞o′mərd) *adj.* Cheerful; amiable: *He was good-humored about losing the card game.* **—good′-hu′mored·ly** *adv.*

good-look·ing (go͝od′lo͝ok′ĭng) *adj.* Having a pleasing appearance; attractive; handsome: *a good-looking actor; good-looking clothes.*

good·ly (go͝od′lē) *adj.* **good·li·er, good·li·est** Quite large; considerable: *a goodly number of people.*

good-na·tured (go͝od′nā′chərd) *adj.* Having an easygoing, pleasant disposition; cheerful. **—good′-na′tured·ly** *adv.* **—good′-na′tured·ness** *n.*

good·ness (go͝od′nĭs) *n.* **1.** The quality or condition of being good; excellence. **2.** The best or nutritious part. ❖ *interj.* An expression used to show surprise.

Good Samaritan *n.* **1.** In one of Jesus's parables in the New Testament, the only passerby who helped a man who had been beaten and robbed. **2.** A person who unselfishly helps others; a good neighbor.

good-sized (go͝od′sīzd′) *adj.* Of a fairly large size: *a good-sized swimming pool; a good-sized serving.*

good·will also **good will** (go͝od′wĭl′) *n.* **1.** An attitude of kindliness or friendliness: *Her goodwill made us feel welcome in the neighborhood.* **2.** Cheerful consent or willingness: *The lender accepted the risk with goodwill.* **3.** A good relationship of a nation with other nations or a business with its customers.

good·y (go͝od′ē) *Informal interj.* An expression used to show delight. ❖ *n.* also **good·ie** *pl.* **good·ies** Something attractive or delectable, especially something good to eat: *a plate of cupcakes and other goodies.*

goo·ey (go͞o′ē) *adj.* **goo·i·er, goo·i·est** Thick and sticky: *gooey tar.*

goof (go͞of) *Slang n.* **1.** A careless mistake; a slip. **2.** An incompetent or stupid person. ❖ *v.* **goofed, goof·ing, goofs** *—intr.* **1.** To make a careless mistake; blunder. **2.** To waste or kill time: *We goofed off all afternoon. —tr.* To spoil, as through clumsiness; bungle: *He goofed up his lines in the play.*

goof·y (go͞o′fē) *adj.* **goof·i·er, goof·i·est** *Slang* Silly; ridiculous: *a goofy hat.* **—goof′i·ness** *n.*

goo·gol (go͞o′gôl′) *n.* The number 10 raised to the 100th power, written as 10^{100} or as 1 followed by 100 zeros. [Coined at the age of nine by Milton Sirotta, nephew of Edward Kasner (1878–1955), American mathematician.]

goon (go͞on) *n. Slang* **1.** A thug hired to intimidate or harm people, especially workers on strike. **2.** A stupid or oafish person. [Probably from *gooney,* albatross, simpleton.]

goose (go͞os) *n., pl.* **geese** (gēs) **1a.** Any of various waterbirds that resemble ducks but are larger and have a longer neck and a shorter, more pointed bill. **b.** The female of such a bird: *The goose and the gander made a nest by the lake.* **c.** The meat of such a bird, used as food. **2.** *Informal* A silly person. [From Old English *gōs.*]

goose·ber·ry (go͞os′bĕr′ē *or* go͞os′bə-rē) *n.* **1.** A juicy greenish berry that grows on a spiny shrub, used chiefly for making jam or pies. **2.** A shrub that bears such berries.

goose bumps *pl.n.* Small bumps that form around the hairs on the skin as a reaction to cold or fear: *The eerie sound gave me goose bumps.*

goose flesh *n.* Goose bumps.

goose·neck (go͞os′nĕk′) *n.* A slender curved object or part, such as the flexible shaft of a type of desk lamp.

goose step *n.* A marching step made by swinging the legs forward from the hips with the knees unbent.

GOP *abbr.* An abbreviation of Grand Old Party (the Republican Party).

go·pher (gō′fər) *n.* **1.** Any of various burrowing North American rodents having large cheek pouches. **2.** A ground squirrel. [Probably of Muskogean origin.]

Gor·ba·chev (gôr′bə-chôf′), **Mikhail Sergeyevich** Born 1931. Soviet politician who served as general secretary of the Communist Party (1985–1991) and president of the Soviet Union (1989–1991).

gore[1] (gôr) *tr.v.* **gored, gor·ing, gores** To pierce or stab with a horn or tusk. [From Middle English *goren,* probably from *gore,* spear, from Old English *gār.*]

gore[2] (gôr) *n.* A triangular piece of cloth forming a part of something, as in a skirt or sail. [From Old English *gāra,* triangular piece of land.]

gore[3] (gôr) *n.* Blood, especially dried blood from a wound. [From Old English *gor,* filth.]

gorge (gôrj) *n.* A deep narrow canyon with very steep sides: *The river grew swifter as it entered the gorge.* ❖ *v.* **gorged, gorg·ing, gorg·es** *—tr.* **1.** To stuff with food; satiate: *gorged themselves with spaghetti.* **2.** To devour greedily: *gorged my dinner. —intr.* To eat greedily: *We gorged on the local seafood.*

gor·geous (gôr′jəs) *adj.* Dazzlingly beautiful or magnificent: *The snowcapped mountains were gorgeous in the sunset.* **—gor′geous·ly** *adv.* **—gor′geous·ness** *n.*

Gor·gon (gôr′gən) *n.* In Greek mythology, one of three sisters whose hair was made of snakes and who would turn anyone who looked at them into stone.

USAGE

good The adjective **good** is often used with linking verbs such as *be, seem,* or *appear: The future looks good. He seems very good as an actor.* **Good** should not be used as an adverb with other verbs: *The car runs well* (not *good*).

Jane Goodall

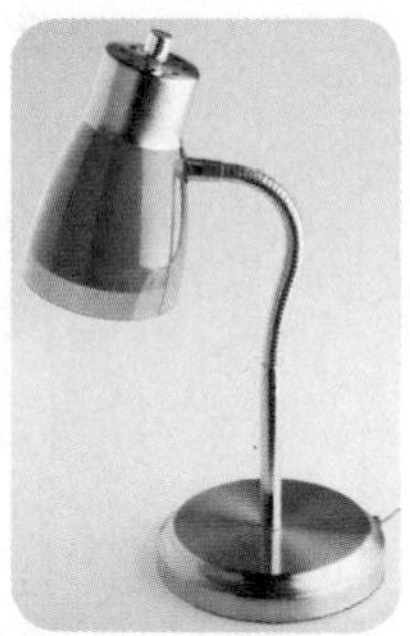

gooseneck

Gorgon

gorilla

Gothic
Cathedral of Notre Dame, Reims, France

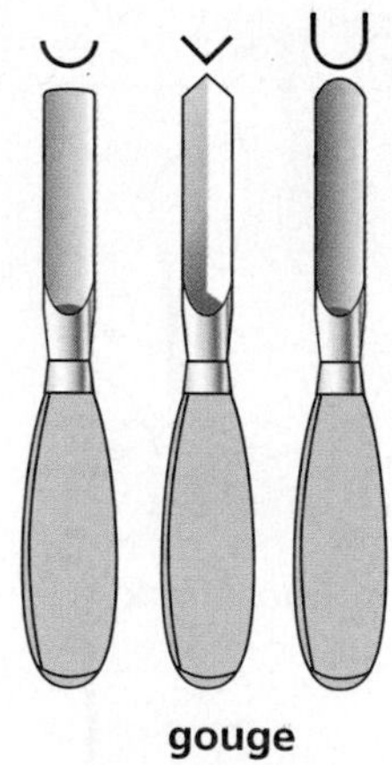

gouge

ă	pat	ôr	core
ā	pay	oi	boy
âr	care	ou	out
ä	father	o͝o	took
ĕ	pet	o͝or	lure
ē	be	o͞o	boot
ĭ	pit	ŭ	cut
ī	bite	ûr	urge
îr	pier	th	thin
ŏ	pot	*th*	this
ō	toe	zh	vision
ô	paw	ə	about

go·ril·la (gə-rĭl′ə) *n.* Either of two large apes of the central African forests and mountains, having a stocky body and dark hair.
❑ *These sound alike:* **gorilla, guerrilla** (fighter).

gorse (gôrs) *n.* Any of several spiny shrubs having fragrant yellow flowers.

gor·y (gôr′ē) *adj.* **gor·i·er, gor·i·est 1.** Covered or stained with gore; bloody. **2.** Full of or marked by bloodshed and violence: *a gory movie.* **—gor′i·ly** *adv.* **—gor′i·ness** *n.*

gosh (gŏsh) *interj.* An expression used to show mild surprise or delight.

gos·hawk (gŏs′hôk′) *n.* Any of various powerful hawks having broad rounded wings and a long tail, especially one found in North America and Europe.

gos·ling (gŏz′lĭng) *n.* A young goose.

gos·pel (gŏs′pəl) *n.* **1.** often **Gospel** The teachings of Jesus and the Apostles. **2. Gospel a.** One of the first four books of the New Testament, describing the life and teachings of Jesus. **b.** A reading from any of the Gospels included as part of a religious service. **3.** Something, such as a principle, believed to be unquestionably true: *They took her explanation as gospel.* **4.** Gospel music. [From Old English *gōdspel* : *gōd*, good + *spel*, news.]

gospel music *n.* A style of Christian music performed especially in African-American churches, marked by strong rhythms and combining elements of American folk music, blues, jazz, and spirituals.

gos·sa·mer (gŏs′ə-mər) *n.* **1.** A fine silky film of cobwebs often seen caught on bushes or grass. **2.** Something that is light, delicate, or sheer, such as fabric. ❖ *adj.* Light, sheer, or delicate. [From Middle English *gossomer* : *gos*, goose + *somer*, summer (probably from the abundance of gossamer in early autumn when geese migrate).]

gos·sip (gŏs′əp) *n.* **1.** Trivial talk, often involving rumors of people and their personal affairs. **2.** A person who habitually engages in such talk. ❖ *intr.v.* **gos·siped, gos·sip·ing, gos·sips** To engage in or spread gossip: *gossip about one's neighbors.* **—gos′sip·er** *n.*

got (gŏt) *v.* Past tense and a past participle of **get.**

goth (gŏth) *n.* **1.** A style of rock music that usually has mournful dark lyrics, evokes a somber mood, and is often written in a minor key. **2.** A performer or follower of this style of music.

Goth *n.* A member of a Germanic people who invaded the Roman Empire in the third, fourth, and fifth centuries AD.

Goth·ic (gŏth′ĭk) *adj.* **1.** Relating to the Goths or their language. **2.** Relating to a style of architecture used in western Europe from the 1100s through the 1400s and characterized by pointed arches, tall windows, and great height overall. **3.** Relating to a style of fiction that emphasizes the grotesque and mysterious: *a Gothic novel.* ❖ *n.* **1.** The extinct Germanic language of the Goths. **2.** Gothic art or architecture.

got·ten (gŏt′n) *v.* A past participle of **get.**

Gou·da (go͞o′də *or* gou′də) *n.* A mild, pale-yellow cheese.

gouge (gouj) *n.* **1.** A chisel with a blade that has a rounded, angled, or troughlike indentation along its length. **2.** A groove or hole made with or as if with such a chisel: *Dragging the heavy couch across the room left a deep gouge in the floor.* ❖ *tr.v.* **gouged, goug·ing, goug·es 1.** To cut or scoop out: *gouge a decorative groove in the table leg; gouged out watermelon seeds with our fingers.* **2.** *Informal* To get (money) from someone by force; extort. **—goug′er** *n.*

gou·lash (go͞o′läsh′) *n.* A meat and vegetable stew seasoned with paprika. [From Hungarian *gulyás (hús)*, herdsman's (meat), goulash, from *gulya*, herdsman.]

gourd (gôrd *or* go͝ord) *n.* **1.** The fruit of any of several vines related to the squashes, having a hard rind and sometimes an irregular shape. **2.** The dried shell of such a fruit, used as a decorative object or as a bowl or ladle. **3.** A vine that bears such fruit. [From Middle English *gourde*, ultimately from Latin *cucurbita*.]

gourde (go͝ord) *n.* The basic monetary unit of Haiti. [From Haitan, from French *gourd*, dull, from Latin *gurdus*, dullard.]

gour·mand (go͝or-mänd′ *or* go͝or′mənd) *n.* **1.** A lover of good food; a gourmet. **2.** A person who often eats too much; a glutton.

gour·met (go͝or-mā′ *or* go͝or′mā′) *n.* A person who enjoys and is knowledgeable about fine food and drink.

gout (gout) *n.* A painful disease in which salts of uric acid are deposited in and near the joints, especially of the feet and hands. **—gout′i·ness** *n.* **—gout′y** *adj.*

Gov. *abbr.* An abbreviation of governor.

gov·ern (gŭv′ərn) *v.* **gov·erned, gov·ern·ing, gov·erns** *—tr.* **1.** To make and administer the public policy and affairs of: *In elections the voters decide who will govern the country.* **2.** To exercise a determining influence on: *The weather governs the success or failure of crops.* **3.** To keep under control; restrain: *a child who could not be governed.* *—intr.* To exercise political authority. [From Middle English *governen*, from Latin *gubernāre*, from Greek *kubernān*, to steer.] **—gov′ern·a·ble** *adj.*

gov·er·ness (gŭv′ər-nĭs) *n.* A woman employed to teach and train the children of a household.

gov·ern·ment (gŭv′ərn-mənt) *n.* **1.** The act or process of governing, especially the control and administration of a political unit: *effective government.* **2.** A system by which a political unit is governed: *democratic government.* **3.** The people who make up a governing body: *The local government has decided to raise taxes.* **—gov′ern·men′tal** (gŭv′ərn-mĕn′tl) *adj.*

gov·er·nor (gŭv′ər-nər) *n.* **1.** The chief executive of a state in the United States. **2.** An official appointed to govern a colony or territory. **3.** A person who directs the operation of a business or organization: *The corporation's board of governors meets every month.* **4.** A device that automatically regulates the speed, pressure, or temperature of a machine.

gov·er·nor·ship (gŭv′ər-nər-shĭp′) *n.* The office or duties of a governor or the period during which a governor is in office.

govt. *abbr.* An abbreviation of government.

gown (goun) *n.* **1.** A long loose flowing garment, such as a nightgown. **2.** A woman's dress, especially a long formal one. **3.** A robe or smock worn in a hospital to guard against contamination: *a surgical gown.* **4.** An outer robe for official ceremonies, worn by scholars and clerics, for example.

Go·ya y Lu·ci·en·tes (goi′ə ē lo͞o-syĕn′tēs), **Francisco José de** 1746–1828. Spanish painter and etcher whose art reflected the political and social turmoil of his times.

GP *abbr.* An abbreviation of general practitioner.

GPA *abbr.* An abbreviation of grade point average.

GPS (jē′pē′ĕs′) *n.* A system of satellites, computers, and receivers that determine the position of a receiver on Earth by calculating the difference in time it takes for signals from different satellites to reach the receiver. [From *G(lobal) P(ositioning) S(ystem).*]

gr. *abbr.* An abbreviation of: **1.** grain (measurement). **2.** gram. **3.** gross.

Gr. *abbr.* An abbreviation of: **1.** Greece. **2.** Greek.

grab (grăb) *v.* **grabbed, grab·bing, grabs** *—tr.* **1.** To take suddenly; snatch: *The monkey grabbed the peanut out of my hand.* **2.** To obtain forcibly: *The dictator grabbed power.* **3.** *Slang* To capture the attention of: *a plot that grabs the reader.* *—intr.* To make a snatch: *She grabbed for the dog's leash.* ❖ *n.* The act of grabbing; a snatch: *I made a grab at the railing.*

grab bag *n.* A container filled with articles, such as party gifts, to be drawn out unseen.

grace (grās) *n.* **1.** Seemingly effortless beauty of movement, form, or manner: *the grace of a swan swimming across a lake.* **2.** A charming or pleasing quality or characteristic: *The prince had not yet mastered the social graces.* **3.** In Christianity, the state of being favored by God, as in being granted redemption from sin. **4.** A short prayer of blessing or thanks said before or after a meal. **5. Grace** A title and form of address for a duke, duchess, or archbishop: *Your Grace.* **6. Graces** In Greek mythology, three sister goddesses who dispensed charm and beauty. ❖ *tr.v.* **graced, grac·ing, grac·es 1.** To give honor to (an event, for example) by one's presence: *The governor's presence graced the meeting.* **2.** To give beauty, elegance, or charm to: *A bouquet of flowers graced the mantelpiece.* ◆ **in the bad graces of** Out of favor with. **in the good graces of** In favor with. [From Middle English, from Latin *grātia*, from *grātus*, pleasing.]

grace·ful (grās′fəl) *adj.* Showing grace of movement, form, or proportion: *a graceful dance; a graceful archway.* **—grace′ful·ly** *adv.* **—grace′ful·ness** *n.*

grace·less (grās′lĭs) *adj.* **1.** Lacking grace; clumsy: *a graceless fall on the ice.* **2.** Lacking charm; ungracious: *a graceless remark.* **—grace′less·ly** *adv.* **—grace′less·ness** *n.*

grace note *n.* A very short musical note added to a melody as an embellishment.

gra·cious (grā′shəs) *adj.* **1.** Characterized by kindness and courtesy: *a gracious host.* **2.** Characterized by tact and propriety: *responded to the insult with gracious good humor.* **3.** Of a merciful or sympathetic nature: *a gracious ruler.* ❖ *interj.* An expression used to show surprise or mild emotion: *Goodness gracious!* **—gra′cious·ly** *adv.* **—gra′cious·ness** *n.*

grack·le (grăk′əl) *n.* Any of several blackbirds of the Americas that have shiny blackish feathers and a harsh call.

grad (grăd) *n. Informal* A graduate of a school or college.

gra·da·tion (grā-dā′shən) *n.* **1.** A series of gradual successive stages or steps: *the gradation in shading from light to dark.* **2.** Any of the stages or steps in such a series.

grade (grād) *n.* **1a.** A position in a scale of size, quality, or intensity: *a poor grade of lumber.* **b.** A group of people or things within the same quality, rank, or value; a class: *several sheets of the finest grade sandpaper.* **2a.** A slope or incline, as of a road: *The truck couldn't stop on the grade.* **b.** The degree to which something, such as a road or railroad track, slopes: *the steep grade of a mountain road.* **3.** A division or section of the course of study in elementary and high school, usually determined as a year's work: *the ninth grade.* **4.** A number, letter, or symbol showing the quality of a student's work: *The test was so hard that no one got a grade above a C.* ❖ *v.* **grad·ed, grad·ing, grades** *—tr.* **1.** To arrange in a series or according to a scale. **2.** To give a grade to (a student or assignment, for example): *grade book reports.* **3.** To level or smooth to a desired or horizontal gradient: *bulldozers grading a road.* *—intr.* To change or progress gradually: *The various piles of gravel grade from coarse to fine.* [From Latin *gradus*.]

grade crossing *n.* An intersection where roads, railroad tracks, or a combination of roads and railroad tracks cross each other at the same level.

grade point *n.* A number that corresponds to the letter grade made in a course or subject.

grade point average *n.* The average grade of a student, determined by dividing the grade points earned by the number of courses taken.

grad·er (grā′dər) *n.* **1.** A student in a specific grade at school: *a fifth grader; a seventh grader.* **2.** A person who grades students' work. **3.** A piece of heavy equipment used to level or smooth road surfaces.

grade school *n.* Elementary school.

gra·di·ent (grā′dē-ənt) *n.* **1.** The degree to which something inclines; a slope: *the steep gradient of the hillside.* **2.** A part that slopes upward or downward; an incline: *skidded on the icy gradient.* **3.** The rate at which a variable, such as temperature or pressure, changes over a distance.

grad·u·al (grăj′o͞o-əl) *adj.* Occurring in small stages or degrees or by even, continuous change: *the gradual increase in prices.* **—grad′u·al·ly** *adv.*

grad·u·ate (grăj′o͞o-āt′) *v.* **grad·u·at·ed, grad·u·at·ing, grad·u·ates** *—intr.* To receive an academic degree or diploma: *graduate from high school.* *—tr.* **1.** To grant an academic degree or diploma to: *Our high school graduated 100 students.* **2.** *Informal* To graduate from: *She graduated law school in 2012.* **3.** To divide or mark into intervals indicating measures, as of length or volume: *A thermometer is graduated into degrees.* ❖ *n.* (grăj′o͞o-ĭt) A person who has received an academic degree or diploma. ❖ *adj.* (grăj′o͞o-ĭt) **1.** Possessing an academic degree or diploma. **2.** Relating to studying beyond the bachelor's degree: *graduate courses.* [From Middle English *graduaten*, to confer a degree, from Medieval Latin *graduārī*, to take a degree, from Latin *gradus*, step.]

graduate school *n.* An institution of higher learning that grants master's degrees or doctorates or both.

grad·u·a·tion (grăj′o͞o-ā′shən) *n.* **1a.** The conferral or receipt of an academic degree or diploma. **b.** A ceremony for giving out academic degrees or diplomas. **2.** Any of the marks made on a container or instrument to show amounts or measures: *The graduations on this thermometer are in red.*

graf·fi·ti (grə-fē′tē) *n.* Drawings or inscriptions made on a wall or other surface, usually so as to be seen by the public: *Graffiti is a problem in some cities.*

graft¹ (grăft) *tr.v.* **graft·ed, graft·ing, grafts 1.** To join (a plant shoot or bud) to another living plant so that the two grow together as a single plant. **2.** To transplant (tissue or an organ) by means of surgery from one part of the body to another or from one person to another. ❖ *n.* **1.** A shoot or bud that has been grafted onto another plant. **2.** An organ or a piece of tissue transplanted by surgery. [From Middle English *graften*, alteration of *graffen*, from Old French *graffe*, stylus, graft (from its shape).]

graft² (grăft) *n.* **1.** The dishonest use of one's position to derive profit or advantage; extortion. **2.** Money or an advantage gained by such use.

Gra·ham (grā′əm *or* grăm), **Martha** 1894–1991. American dancer and choreographer who founded the Dance Repertory Theatre in New York City in 1930.

graham cracker (grăm *or* grā′əm) *n.* A slightly sweet, usually rectangular cracker made with whole-wheat flour. [After Sylvester *Graham* (1794–1851), American social reformer.]

Gra·hame (grā′əm), **Kenneth** 1859–1932. British writer known for his essays and children's books, especially *The Wind in the Willows* (1908).

graham flour *n.* Whole-wheat flour.

Grail (grāl) *n.* In medieval legend, the cup used by Jesus at the Last Supper and the object of many quests by Knights of the Round Table.

grain (grān) *n.* **1a.** A small hard seed of a cereal plant such as wheat, corn, or rice: *picked up one grain of rice.* **b.** The seeds of such plants considered as a group: *buying and selling grain.* **2a.** A cereal grass: *Wheat and rye are grains.* **b.** Cereal plants considered as a group: *a field of grain.* **3a.** A small particle similar to a seed: *a grain of salt.* **b.** A small amount or the smallest possible amount: *There isn't a grain of truth in that statement.* **4.** A unit of weight equal to 1⁄7000 of an ounce (0.07 gram). See table at **measurement.** **5a.** The markings, pattern, or texture in wood: *cherry wood has a fine grain.* **b.** The direction of such markings: *cut a board with the grain.* **6.** The di-

Francisco Goya
1783 self-portrait

graft¹

Martha Graham

granny knot

Ulysses S. Grant

ă	pat	ôr	core
ā	pay	oi	boy
âr	care	ou	out
ä	father	o͝o	took
ĕ	pet	o͝or	lure
ē	be	o͞o	boot
ĭ	pit	ŭ	cut
ī	bite	ûr	urge
îr	pier	th	thin
ŏ	pot	*th*	this
ō	toe	zh	vision
ô	paw	ə	about

rection or texture of fibers in a woven fabric. ◆ **with a grain of salt** With reservations; skeptically: *Take everything he says with a grain of salt.*

grain alcohol *n.* Ethanol.

grain elevator *n.* A tall hollow building for storing grain, equipped with machinery that lifts the grain so that it can be added from the top.

grain·y (grā′nē) *adj.* **grain·i·er, grain·i·est 1.** Consisting of or resembling grains; granular: *grainy flour.* **2.** Resembling the grain of wood: *a grainy surface.* **3.** Having a granular appearance: *a grainy photograph.*

gram (grăm) *n.* A unit of mass or weight in the metric system, equal to about 1/28 of an ounce. See table at **measurement.**

–gram *suff.* A suffix that means something written or drawn: *cardiogram; telegram.*

gram·mar (grăm′ər) *n.* **1.** The study of the structure of words, the relationships between words, and the arrangement of words to make sentences. **2.** The system of rules that allow sentences to be made in a given language: *Latin grammar relies heavily on inflections.* **3.** The use of words with reference to an accepted standard among educated speakers of a language: *The teacher criticized my paper for bad grammar.* **4.** A book containing the rules for making sentences in a given language: *The library has several grammars of French.* [From Middle English *gramere*, from Greek *grammatikos*, of letters, from *gramma*, letter.]

gram·mar·ian (grə-mâr′ē-ən) *n.* A specialist in grammar.

grammar school *n.* **1.** An elementary school. **2.** *Chiefly British* A secondary or preparatory school.

gram·mat·i·cal (grə-măt′ĭ-kəl) *adj.* **1.** Of or relating to grammar: *grammatical principles.* **2.** Conforming to the rules of grammar: *a grammatical sentence.* **—gram·mat′i·cal·ly** *adv.*

gramme (grăm) *n. Chiefly British* Variant of **gram.**

Gra·na·da (grə-nä′də) A city of southern Spain southeast of Córdoba. It was founded in the eighth century.

gran·a·ry (grăn′ə-rē *or* grā′nə-rē) *n., pl.* **gran·a·ries** A building for storing grain.

grand (grănd) *adj.* **grand·er, grand·est 1.** Large and impressive in size, extent, or splendor; magnificent: *The grand entryway of the palace has two curved staircases.* **2.** Very pleasing or wonderful: *The children had a grand time playing in the barn.* **3a.** Having higher rank than others of the same category: *the grand admiral of the fleet.* **b.** Being the most important of a category; principal: *the grand prize.* **4.** Intended to fulfill noble or dignified wishes: *The United Nations has a grand purpose.* **5.** Including or covering all units or aspects: *the grand total.* ❖ *n.* **1.** A grand piano. **2.** *pl.* **grand** *Slang* A thousand dollars: *paid ten grand for the used car.* [From Middle English *graunt*, from Latin *grandis*.] **—grand′ly** *adv.* **—grand′ness** *n.*

SYNONYMS grand, magnificent, majestic, imposing, stately These adjectives mean strikingly large in size, scope, or extent. **Grand** and **magnificent** apply to something that is impressive because of its size, importance, or beauty: *The president welcomed the foreign officials with a grand ceremony. The Taj Mahal is a magnificent example of Indian architecture.* **Majestic** means full of luxurious splendor and grandeur: *The mountain climbers struggled up the majestic slopes of the Alps.* **Imposing** means impressive because of size, bearing, or power: *We stared up at the imposing statue of Abraham Lincoln.* **Stately** often refers to something that is dignified: *The neighborhood where the movie stars live includes many stately mansions.*

---

grand·aunt (grănd′ănt′ *or* grănd′änt′) *n.* A great-aunt.

Grand Banks An area of sandy banks in the western Atlantic Ocean off southeast Newfoundland, Canada. The area is a historic fishing ground.

Grand Canyon A gorge of the Colorado River in northwest Arizona. It is up to 6,000 feet (1,830 meters) deep, over 15 miles (25 kilometers) wide, and about 275 miles (445 kilometers) long.

grand·child (grănd′chīld′ *or* grăn′chīld′) *n.* A child of one's daughter or son.

Grand Coulee A gorge, about 40 miles (65 kilometers) long, of north-central Washington. It is fed by water from the **Grand Coulee Dam.**

grand·dad (grăn′dăd′) *n. Informal* A grandfather.

grand·dad·dy (grăn′dăd′ē) *n., pl.* **grand·dad·dies** *Informal* A grandfather.

grand·daugh·ter (grăn′dô′tər) *n.* A daughter of one's daughter or son.

gran·dee (grăn-dē′) *n.* **1.** A nobleman of the highest rank in Spain or Portugal. **2.** A person of high rank or great importance.

Grande-Terre (grăn′târ′) An island of eastern Guadeloupe in the Leeward Islands of the West Indies.

gran·deur (grăn′jər *or* grăn′jo͝or′) *n.* The quality or condition of being grand; magnificence: *the grandeur of the pyramids in Egypt.*

grand·fa·ther (grănd′fä′*th*ər *or* grăn′fä′*th*ər) *n.* The father of one's mother or father.

grandfather clock *n.* A pendulum clock enclosed in a tall narrow cabinet.

grand·fa·ther·ly (grănd′fä′*th*ər-lē *or* grăn′fä′*th*ər-lē) *adj.* Typical of or befitting a grandfather.

gran·dil·o·quent (grăn-dĭl′ə-kwənt) *adj.* Using lofty words or having a pompous style or manner. **—gran·dil′o·quence** *n.* **—gran·dil′o·quent·ly** *adv.*

gran·di·ose (grăn′dē-ōs′ *or* grăn′dē-ōs′) *adj.* **1.** Characterized by greatness of scope or intent; grand: *The mayor unveiled a grandiose plan to develop the city's waterfront.* **2.** Characterized by excessive self-importance or affected grandeur; pompous: *She was insulted by his grandiose apology.* **—gran′di·ose′ly** *adv.* **—gran′di·os′i·ty** (grăn′dē-ŏs′ĭ-tē), **gran′di·ose′ness** *n.*

grand jury *n.* A jury of 12 to 23 people that meets in private to evaluate accusations against a person charged with a crime and determines whether an indictment should be made.

grand·ma (grănd′mä′ *or* grăn′mä′ *or* grăm′mä′) *n. Informal* A grandmother.

grand·moth·er (grănd′mŭ*th*′ər *or* grăn′mŭ*th*′ər) *n.* The mother of one's father or mother.

grand·moth·er·ly (grănd′mŭ*th*′ər-lē *or* grăn′mŭ*th*′ər-lē) *adj.* Typical of or befitting a grandmother.

grand·neph·ew (grănd′nĕf′yo͞o *or* grăn′nĕf′yo͞o) *n.* A son of one's nephew or niece.

grand·niece (grănd′nēs′ *or* grăn′nēs′) *n.* A daughter of one's nephew or niece.

grand·pa (grănd′pä′ *or* grăn′pä′ *or* grăm′pä′) *n. Informal* A grandfather.

grand·par·ent (grănd′pâr′ənt) *n.* A parent of one's mother or father.

grand piano *n.* A piano whose strings are mounted horizontally in a harp-shaped frame supported usually on three legs.

grand slam *n.* **1.** In baseball, a home run hit when three runners are on base. **2.** The set of major or most prestigious competitions in a sport, especially when won in a single season. **3.** In bridge, the winning of all the tricks in one hand.

grand·son (grănd′sŭn′ *or* grăn′sŭn′) *n.* A son of one's daughter or son.

grand·stand (grănd′stănd′ *or* grăn′stănd′) *n.* **1.** A roofed stand for spectators at a stadium or racetrack.

2. The spectators or audience at an event. ❖ *intr.v.* **grand·stand·ed, grand·stand·ing, grand·stands** To do something showily, especially in front of an audience.

grand·un·cle (grănd′ŭng′kəl) *n.* A great-uncle.

Grange (grānj) *n.* An association of farmers founded in the United States in 1867.

gran·ite (grăn′ĭt) *n.* A common, coarse-grained igneous rock composed mostly of quartz, feldspar, and mica, used in buildings and monuments. [From Italian *granito*, grainy, from *grano*, grain, from Latin *grānum*.]

gran·ny or **gran·nie** (grăn′ē) *n., pl.* **gran·nies** *Informal* A grandmother.

granny knot *n.* A knot resembling a square knot but with the second tie crossed incorrectly.

gra·no·la (grə-nō′lə) *n.* Rolled oats mixed with various ingredients, such as dried fruit, brown sugar, and nuts, and used especially as a breakfast cereal.

grant (grănt) *tr.v.* **grant·ed, grant·ing, grants 1.** To give or allow (something asked for): *grant a request.* **2.** To confer or bestow as a favor, prerogative, or privilege: *The Constitution grants certain powers to the Supreme Court.* **3.** To concede; acknowledge: *I'll grant that it's not the best car, but it still is reliable.* ❖ *n.* **1.** The act of or an example of granting. **2.** Something granted: *The student received a grant of $10,000 for college tuition.* [From Middle English *graunten*, from Old French *creanter*, from Latin *crēdēns*, believing.]

Grant (grănt), **Ulysses Simpson** Originally Hiram Ulysses Grant. 1822–1885. The 18th president of the United States (1869–1877) and a general of the Union Army in the Civil War. His presidency was marked by graft and corruption.

grant·ee (grăn-tē′) *n.* A person to whom a grant is made.

gran·tor (grăn′tər *or* grăn′tôr′) *n.* A person or organization that makes a grant.

gran·u·lar (grăn′yə-lər) *adj.* Made of or appearing to be made of grains or granules: *the granular surface of a rock; clouds with a granular texture.*

gran·u·late (grăn′yə-lāt′) *v.* **gran·u·lat·ed, gran·u·lat·ing, gran·u·lates** —*tr.* **1.** To form into grains or granules. **2.** To roughen the surface of. —*intr.* To become granular or grainy. **—gran′u·la′tion** *n.*

gran·ule (grăn′yo͞ol) *n.* A small grain or pellet, as of sand, sugar, or ice. [From Late Latin *grānulum*, diminutive of Latin *grānum*, grain.]

grape (grāp) *n.* **1.** A small, rounded, juicy fruit having smooth purple, red, or green skin and growing in clusters on a vine. Grapes are eaten fresh, dried as raisins, or used for making wine, juice, and jelly or jam. **2.** A vine that bears such fruit. [From Middle English, from Old French *grape*, bunch of grapes, hook, of Germanic origin.]

grape·fruit (grāp′fro͞ot′) *n.* **1.** A large round fruit of an evergreen tree related to the orange, having a yellow skin and a somewhat sour taste. **2.** The tree that bears such fruit, found in warm climates.

grape·shot (grāp′shŏt′) *n.* A cluster of small iron balls fired as a single shot from a cannon.

grape sugar *n.* Dextrose obtained from grapes.

grape·vine (grāp′vīn′) *n.* **1.** A vine on which grapes grow. **2.** The informal transmission of gossip, rumor, or information from person to person: *We heard through the grapevine that the coach had been fired.*

graph (grăf) *n.* **1.** A diagram showing the relationship of quantities, especially such a diagram in which lines, bars, or proportional areas represent how one quantity depends on or changes with another. **2.** A pictorial device, such as a pie chart, that illustrates quantitative relationships. **3.** A curve or line showing a mathematical function or equation. ❖ *tr.v.* **graphed, graph·ing, graphs** To make a graph of: *graphed seasonal rainfall over a ten-year period.*

-graph *suff.* A suffix that means: **1.** Something that writes or records: *seismograph; telegraph.* **2.** Something written or drawn: *homograph.*

graph·eme (grăf′ēm′) *n.* A letter of an alphabet or combination of letters that represents a phoneme. For example, *f* and *ph* are both graphemes for the phoneme *f* in *fun* and *phone.*

-grapher *suff.* A suffix that means someone who writes or records: *stenographer.*

graph·ic (grăf′ĭk) *adj.* **1a.** Relating to written or drawn representations: *A pronunciation key is a graphic representation of speech sounds.* **b.** Relating to graphics. **c.** Relating to the graphic arts. **2.** Relating to or represented by a graph: *the graphic scale of a map.* **3.** Described or shown in vivid detail: *a witness's graphic description of the incident; graphic violence in a movie.* [From Greek *graphein*, to write.] **—graph′i·cal·ly** *adv.*

graphic arts *pl.n.* **1.** The visual arts that involve the application of lines and strokes to a flat surface. **2.** The visual arts that involve producing images from blocks, plates, or type, as in engraving or lithography.

graphic novel *n.* A novel whose story is told through a combination of words and art, often having the form of a long comic book.

graph·ics (grăf′ĭks) *n.* **1.** *(used with a singular verb)* **a.** The making of drawings in accordance with the rules of mathematics, as in engineering and architecture. **b.** The process by which a computer produces and displays information as pictures, diagrams, and charts, rather than as text. **2.** *(used with a plural verb)* Graphic arts.

graph·ite (grăf′īt′) *n.* A crystalline form of carbon that is steel-gray to black in color and rather soft. It is used in making lubricants, paints, electrodes, and as the writing substance in pencils.

-graphy *suff.* A suffix that means: **1.** Writing or representation produced in a certain way: *photography.* **2.** Writing about a specific subject: *oceanography.*

grap·nel (grăp′nəl) *n.* **1.** A small anchor with three or more claws. **2.** A grappling iron.

grap·ple (grăp′əl) *n.* **1.** A grappling iron. **2.** A grapnel. **3.** The act of grappling. ❖ *v.* **grap·pled, grap·pling, grap·ples** —*tr.* To grasp and hold, as with a grappling iron. —*intr.* **1.** To hold tightly to something. **2.** To grasp someone closely, as in wrestling. **3.** To struggle: *grapple with a difficult problem.*

grap·pling iron (grăp′lĭng) *n.* An iron bar with claws at one end for grasping or holding something.

grasp (grăsp) *v.* **grasped, grasp·ing, grasps** —*tr.* **1.** To seize and hold firmly with or as if with the hands: *grasped the rope and pulled; grasped the chance to play first base.* **2.** To get the full meaning of; understand: *You fail to grasp the problem.* —*intr.* **1.** To make a motion of seizing, snatching, or clutching: *grasped at the loose paddle.* **2.** To show eager acceptance: *grasped at the opportunity to go to college.* ❖ *n.* **1.** A firm hold or grip: *The puppy wriggled out of my grasp.* **2.** The ability to attain; reach: *Victory was within the team's grasp.* **3.** Understanding; comprehension: *The teacher has a thorough grasp of the subject.* [From Middle English *graspen.*]

grasp·ing (grăs′pĭng) *adj.* Eager for material gain; greedy. **—grasp′ing·ly** *adv.* **—grasp′ing·ness** *n.*

grass (grăs) *n.* **1a.** Any of numerous plants having narrow leaves, usually hollow stems, and long clusters of very small flowers. The grasses include wheat, corn, sugar cane, bamboo, and plants grown for pastures and lawns. **b.** These plants considered as a group: *planted grass in the yard.* **2.** A piece of land, such as a lawn, covered with grass: *kids playing on the grass.* [From Old English *græs.*]

grass·hop·per (grăs′hŏp′ər) *n.* Any of numerous insects having two pairs of wings and long hind legs used for

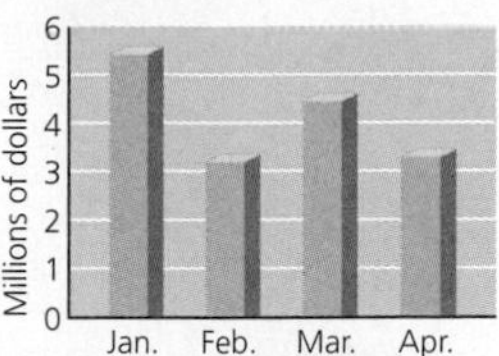

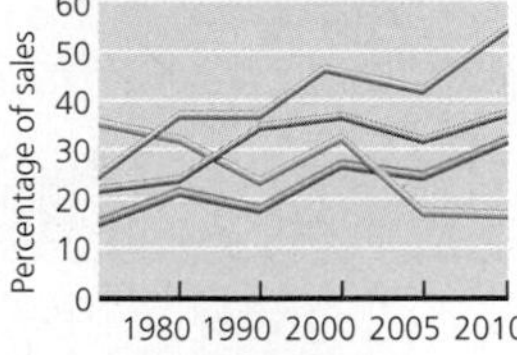

graph
top: bar graph
bottom: line graph

grapnel

grasshopper

grater

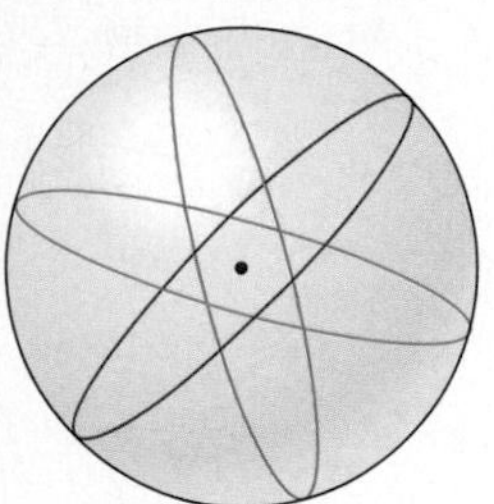

great circle
a sphere with three great circles shown

Great Dane

ă	pat	ôr	core
ā	pay	oi	boy
âr	care	ou	out
ä	father	o͝o	took
ĕ	pet	o͝or	lure
ē	be	o͞o	boot
ĭ	pit	ŭ	cut
ī	bite	ûr	urge
îr	pier	th	thin
ŏ	pot	*th*	this
ō	toe	zh	vision
ô	paw	ə	about

jumping. Grasshoppers feed on plants and sometimes destroy crops.

grass·land (grăs′lănd′) *n.* An area, such as a prairie or meadow, covered with grass.

Gras·so (grăs′ō *or* grä′sō), **Ella Tambussi** 1919–1981. American public official who as governor of Connecticut (1975–1981) was the first woman to hold the office of governor in her own right.

grass·roots (grăs′ro͞ots′ or grăs′ro͝ots′) *pl.n. (used with a singular or plural verb)* Citizens at a local level rather than at the center of political activity: *The candidate received strong support from the grassroots.*

grass·y (grăs′ē) *adj.* **grass·i·er, grass·i·est 1.** Covered with grass: *a grassy plain.* **2.** Resembling or suggestive of grass: *a grassy green; a grassy aroma.*

grate[1] (grāt) *v.* **grat·ed, grat·ing, grates** —*tr.* **1.** To reduce to fragments, shreds, or powder by rubbing against a rough surface: *grated the cabbage for coleslaw.* **2.** To cause to make a harsh grinding or rasping sound by rubbing: *She grated her teeth in anger.* —*intr.* **1.** To make a harsh grinding or rasping sound by rubbing: *The wagon grated on its rusty wheels.* **2.** To cause irritation or annoyance: *Your sarcasm grates on my nerves.* [From Middle English *graten*, from Old French *grater*, to scrape, of Germanic origin.]

❑ *These sound alike:* **grate[1]** (shred), **grate[2]** (framework), **great** (large).

grate[2] (grāt) *n.* **1.** A framework of parallel or interwoven bars for blocking an opening. **2.** A similar framework used to hold fuel or food in a stove, furnace, or fireplace. [From Middle English, from Latin *crātis*, wickerwork.]

❑ *These sound alike:* **grate[2]** (framework), **grate[1]** (shred), **great** (large).

grate·ful (grāt′fəl) *adj.* **1a.** Appreciative of benefits received: *I'm grateful for your help.* **b.** Expressing gratitude: *a grateful look.* **2.** Affording pleasure; agreeable: *grateful relief from the hot sun.* [From obsolete *grate*, pleasing, from Latin *grātus*.] —**grate′ful·ly** *adv.* —**grate′ful·ness** *n.*

grat·er (grā′tər) *n.* A kitchen utensil with slits and perforations, used to grate food.

grat·i·fi·ca·tion (grăt′ə-fĭ-**kā′**shən) *n.* **1.** The act of gratifying or the condition of being gratified. **2.** An instance or a cause of being gratified: *The student's success in mathematics was a great gratification to the teacher.*

grat·i·fy (grăt′ə-fī′) *tr.v.* **grat·i·fied, grat·i·fy·ing, grat·i·fies 1.** To please or satisfy (someone): *The students' performance on the test gratified the teacher.* **2.** To give in to (a desire); indulge: *I gratified my curiosity by trying the hors d'oeuvres.* —**grat′i·fi′er** *n.* —**grat′i·fy′ing** *adj.*

grat·ing (grā′tĭng) *n.* A grill or network of bars set across an opening, such as a window or a street drain; a grate.

grat·is (grăt′ĭs *or* grä′tĭs *or* grā′tĭs) *adv. & adj.* Without charge: *We went to the show gratis. The tickets are gratis.*

grat·i·tude (grăt′ĭ-to͞od′) *n.* The state of being grateful; thankfulness: *The family was full of gratitude for their neighbor's help during the fire.*

gra·tu·i·tous (grə-**to͞o′**ĭ-təs) *adj.* **1.** Given without cost or obligation; free: *gratuitous help.* **2.** Unnecessary or unwarranted: *a gratuitous criticism.* —**gra·tu′i·tous·ly** *adv.* —**gra·tu′i·tous·ness** *n.*

gra·tu·i·ty (grə-**to͞o′**ĭ-tē) *n., pl.* **gra·tu·i·ties** A favor or gift, usually of money, given in return for service; a tip.

grave[1] (grāv) *n.* **1.** A hole dug in the ground for the burial of a corpse. **2.** A place of burial: *The sea is the grave of many sailors.* **3.** Death or extinction. [From Old English *græf*.]

grave[2] (grāv) *adj.* **grav·er, grav·est 1.** Requiring serious thought; momentous: *a grave decision.* **2.** Fraught with danger or harm: *a grave illness.* **3.** Dignified and somber in conduct or character: *The judge looked grave.* [From Latin *gravis*.] —**grave′ly** *adv.* —**grave′ness** *n.*

grave[3] (grāv) *tr.v.* **graved, grav·en** (grā′vən) or **graved, grav·ing, graves** To sculpt or carve; engrave. [From Old English *grafan*.]

grave accent (grāv *or* gräv) *n.* **1.** A mark (`) indicating that an additional syllable is pronounced, as *burnèd.* **2.** A similar mark used in various languages, usually to show how a vowel is pronounced.

grav·el (grăv′əl) *n.* A loose mixture of pebbles or small pieces of rock, often used for roads and walks. ❖ *tr.v.* **grav·eled, grav·el·ing, grav·els** or **grav·elled, grav·el·ling, grav·els** To cover with gravel: *gravel a driveway.*

grav·el·ly (grăv′ə-lē) *adj.* **1.** Covered with or containing gravel: *gravelly soil.* **2.** Having a harsh rasping sound: *a low gravelly voice.*

grav·en (grā′vən) *v.* A past participle of **grave[3]**.

graven image *n.* An idol carved in wood or stone.

grave·side (grāv′sīd′) *n.* The area beside a grave.

grave·site (grāv′sīt′) *n.* The place where a grave is located.

grave·stone (grāv′stōn′) *n.* A stone placed over a grave as a marker; a tombstone.

grave·yard (grāv′yärd′) *n.* A cemetery.

grav·i·tate (grăv′ĭ-tāt′) *intr.v.* **grav·i·tat·ed, grav·i·tat·ing, grav·i·tates 1.** To move under the influence of gravity: *Clumps of mass gravitated together to form the galaxy.* **2.** To moved toward or be attracted by something: *The grazing sheep gravitated toward the greener parts of the hillside.*

grav·i·ta·tion (grăv′ĭ-**tā′**shən) *n.* **1.** The force of attraction that tends to draw together any two objects in the universe. Gravitation increases as the mass of the objects increases and as their distance from each other decreases. **2.** The act or process of gravitating. **3.** A movement toward a source of attraction: *the gravitation of the middle class to the suburbs.* —**grav′i·ta′tion·al** *adj.* —**grav′i·ta′tion·al·ly** *adv.*

gra·vit·ro·pism (grə-**vĭt′**rə-pĭz′əm) *n.* The movement or growth of an organism in response to the earth's gravity. Examples of gravitropism include the downward growth of plant roots and the upward growth of new shoots on a plant. —**grav′i·tro′pic** (grăv′ĭ-**trō′**pĭk) *adj.*

grav·i·ty (grăv′ĭ-tē) *n.* **1a.** The natural force that causes objects to move or tend to move toward the center of the earth as a result of gravitation. **b.** The force of attraction that makes objects move or tend to move toward each other; gravitation. **2.** Grave consequence; seriousness or importance: *The students realized the gravity of the test and its effect on their grades.* [From Latin *gravitās*, heaviness, from *gravis*, heavy.]

gra·vy (grā′vē) *n., pl.* **gra·vies 1.** The juices that drip from cooking meat. **2.** A sauce made by thickening and seasoning these juices.

gray[1] also **grey** (grā) *n.* **1.** A color made by mixing black and white. **2.** often **Gray a.** A Confederate soldier in the US Civil War. **b.** The Confederate Army. ❖ *adj.* **gray·er, gray·est** also **grey·er, grey·est 1.** Having the color gray. **2.** Having gray hair. **3.** Lacking in cheer; gloomy: *a gray mood.* ❖ *tr. & intr.v.* **grayed, gray·ing, grays** also **greyed, grey·ing, greys** To make or become gray: *Age grays the hair. The driftwood grayed in the sun.* —**gray′ly** *adv.* —**gray′ness** *n.*

gray[2] (grā) *n.* A unit used to measure the energy absorbed from radiation, equal to one joule per kilogram, or to 100 rads.

gray·beard (grā′bîrd′) *n.* An old man.

gray·ish (grā′ĭsh) *adj.* Somewhat gray.

gray matter *n.* **1.** The brownish-gray tissue of the brain and spinal cord, made up of nerve cells and fibers and some supporting tissue. **2.** *Informal* Brains; intellect: *Use your gray matter to figure out the answer.*

gray wolf *n.* A wolf of northern North America and Eurasia that ranges in color from whitish to gray to almost black.

graze[1] (grāz) *v.* **grazed, graz·ing, graz·es** —*intr.* To feed on growing grasses and leafy plants: *Cattle grazed in the field.* —*tr.* **1.** To feed on the grass of (a piece of land): *The goats grazed the mountain pasture.* **2.** To put (livestock) out to feed: *grazed their cattle on the plains.* [From Old English *grasian*, from *græs*, grass.]

graze[2] (grāz) *tr.v.* **grazed, graz·ing, graz·es 1.** To touch (something) lightly in passing: *The suitcase just grazed my leg.* **2.** To scrape or scratch (something) slightly: *I fell off my bike and grazed my knees and elbows.* [Perhaps from *graze*, eat grass.]

grease (grēs) *n.* **1.** Animal fat when melted or soft, often used in cooking. **2.** A thick sticky oil or similar material, used to lubricate moving parts, as of a machine. ❖ *tr.v.* (grēs *or* grēz) **greased, greas·ing, greas·es** To apply grease to: *grease the pan before cooking; grease the track of a sliding door.* [From Middle English *grese*, from Latin *crassus*, fat, thick.]

grease·paint also **grease paint** (grēs′pānt′) *n.* Makeup worn by actors, clowns, and other performers.

greas·y (grē′sē *or* grē′zē) *adj.* **greas·i·er, greas·i·est 1.** Coated or soiled with grease: *greasy pots and pans.* **2.** Containing grease; oily: *a greasy hamburger.* **3.** Slippery. **—greas′i·ly** *adv.* **—greas′i·ness** *n.*

great (grāt) *adj.* **great·er, great·est 1.** Very large in size, number, amount, or extent: *a great pile of rubble; a great storm.* See Synonyms at **large. 2.** Remarkable or outstanding in magnitude or degree: *a great crisis.* **3.** Important; significant: *The signing of the treaty was a great moment in history.* **4.** Prominent; distinguished: *a great athlete.* **5.** Being one generation removed from the relative specified: *a great-granddaughter.* **6.** *Informal* Enthusiastic: *a great tennis fan.* **7.** *Informal* **a.** Very good; first-rate: *a great party; a great time.* **b.** Very skillful: *great at algebra.* [From Old English *grēat*, thick, coarse.] **—great′ness** *n.*
❑ *These sound alike:* **great, grate[1]** (shred), **grate[2]** (framework).

great-aunt or **great aunt** (grāt′ănt′ *or* grāt′änt′) *n.* A sister of one's grandparent.

Great Barrier Reef The largest coral reef in the world, about 1,250 miles (2,010 kilometers) long, off the northeast coast of Australia. It is known for its exotic fish and crustaceans.

Great Basin A desert region of the western United States made up of most of Nevada and parts of Utah, California, Idaho, Wyoming, and Oregon.

Great Brit·ain (brĭt′n) **1.** An island off the western coast of Europe east of Ireland and made up of England, Scotland, and Wales. It is separated from the mainland by the English Channel. **2.** See **United Kingdom.**

great circle *n.* A circle on a sphere that has its plane passing through the center of the sphere, as the great circle of the earth's equator does.

great·coat (grāt′kōt′) *n.* A heavy overcoat.

Great Dane *n.* A large dog of a breed developed in Europe to hunt boars, having a muscular body, a smooth short coat, and a narrow head.

Great Depression *n.* The worldwide economic depression from the late 1920s through the 1930s.

Great Divide See **Continental Divide.**

Great·er Antilles (grā′tər) See **Antilles.**

great·est common divisor (grā′tĭst) *n.* The largest number that divides evenly into each of a given set of numbers. For example, the greatest common divisor of 16, 20, and 32 is 4.

great-grand·child (grāt′grănd′chīld′ *or* grāt′grăn′-chīld′) *n.* A child of one's grandchild.

great-grand·daughter (grāt′grăn′dô′tər) *n.* A daughter of one's grandchild.

great-grand·father (grāt′grănd′fä′*th*ər *or* grāt′grăn′-fä′*th*ər) *n.* The father of one's grandparent.

great-grand·mother (grāt′grănd′mŭ*th*′ər *or* grāt′-grăn′mŭ*th*′ər) *n.* The mother of one's grandparent.

great-grand·parent (grāt′grănd′pâr′ənt) *n.* The parent of one's grandparent.

great-grand·son (grāt′grănd′sŭn′ *or* grāt′grăn′sŭn′) *n.* A son of one's grandchild.

great·heart·ed (grāt′här′tĭd) *adj.* **1.** Courageous or noble in spirit. **2.** Generous; magnanimous: *The greathearted landowner donated land for a park.* **—great′-heart′ed·ness** *n.*

Great Lakes A group of five freshwater lakes of central North America between the United States and Canada, including Lakes Superior, Michigan, Huron, Erie, and Ontario. The Great Lakes connect Midwestern ports with the Atlantic Ocean by way of the St. Lawrence Seaway.

great·ly (grāt′lē) *adv.* To a great degree; very much: *Families vary greatly in size.*

Great Plains A vast grassland region of central North America extending from south-central Canada southward to Texas. Much of the area is used for cattle ranching and wheat farming.

Great Salt Lake A shallow body of salt water of northwest Utah northwest of Salt Lake City. The lake is a remnant of a prehistoric lake that covered a large area of the Great Basin. The **Great Salt Lake Desert,** to the west of the lake, is barren and uncultivated.

Great Spirit *n.* The principal god in the religion of many Native American peoples.

great-un·cle or **great uncle** (grāt′ŭng′kəl) *n.* A brother of one's grandparent.

Great Wall of China A line of fortifications across northern China. Originally built in the third century BC by connecting earlier fortifications, it was subsequently rebuilt and altered many times.

greave (grēv) *n.* A piece of armor worn below the knee to protect the front of the leg.

grebe (grēb) *n.* Any of various diving birds having a pointed bill and fleshy membranes along each toe that help them swim.

Gre·cian (grē′shən) *adj.* Greek. ❖ *n.* A native or inhabitant of Greece.

Grec·o (grĕk′ō), **El** 1541–1614. Greek-born Spanish painter of religious works.

Greece (grēs) A country of southeast Europe located on the southern Balkan Peninsula and including numerous islands in the surrounding seas. Greece was an important center of early civilization. Athens is the capital.

greed (grēd) *n.* A selfish desire for more than one needs or deserves.

greed·y (grē′dē) *adj.* **greed·i·er, greed·i·est 1.** Filled with greed; wanting more than one needs or deserves: *The greedy prospector refused to share with his partners.* **2.** Having or showing a desire to consume large amounts of food or drink. [From Old English *grǣdig*.] **—greed′i·ly** *adv.* **—greed′i·ness** *n.*

Greek (grēk) *adj.* Relating to Greece or its people, language, or culture. ❖ *n.* **1.** The Indo-European language of ancient or modern Greece. **2.** A native or inhabitant of Greece. **3.** Something that is unintelligible: *Robotics is Greek to me.*

Greek alphabet *n.* The alphabet of ancient and modern Greece, derived from the alphabet used by the Phoenicians.

Greek Orthodox Church *n.* Any of several branches of the Eastern Orthodox Church that use Greek liturgy, such as the state church of Greece.

Gree·ley (grē′lē), **Horace** 1811–1872. American journalist who founded and edited the *New York Tribune* (1841–1872).

green (grēn) *n.* **1.** The color of most plant leaves and

SCIENCE

greenhouse effect
In a greenhouse, sunlight (relatively short-waved radiation) enters through the glass roof and heats the soil. The soil, in turn, gives off heat (longer-waved infrared radiation) which cannot escape through the glass and therefore warms the air inside. A similar process takes place on the earth as a whole, where the water vapor, carbon dioxide, and other gases in the lower atmosphere act like the glass roof of a greenhouse, letting sunlight in but preventing much of the heat from escaping. Although the **greenhouse effect** was necessary for the development of life on the earth, it has increased since the late 1800s. Most scientists believe that this increase has resulted mainly from the burning of fossil fuels such as coal, oil, and natural gas, and that the carbon dioxide that is being added to the atmosphere from these fuels is causing *global warming*. If global warming continues, sea levels could rise as glaciers and polar ice sheets melt, and patterns of rainfall, storm intensity, and other features of our climate could change drastically.

ă	pat	ôr	core
ā	pay	oi	boy
âr	care	ou	out
ä	father	o͝o	took
ĕ	pet	o͝or	lure
ē	be	o͞o	boot
ĭ	pit	ŭ	cut
ī	bite	ûr	urge
îr	pier	th	thin
ŏ	pot	*th*	this
ō	toe	zh	vision
ô	paw	ə	about

growing grass. In the spectrum it is between yellow and blue. **2. greens a.** The branches and leaves of green plants used for decoration: *decorated the house with greens.* **b.** Leaves that are eaten as vegetables: *salad greens.* **3.** A grassy area located usually at the center of a town or city; a common: *the village green.* **4.** In golf, the area of short smooth grass that surrounds a hole. **5.** often **Green** A person or movement that supports environmental protection. ❖ *adj.* **green·er, green·est 1.** Of the color green: *a green sweater.* **2.** Covered with growing plants, grass, or foliage: *green meadows.* **3.** Not mature or ripe: *a green banana.* **4.** Lacking training or experience: *green musicians.* **5.** Beneficial to the environment or supporting environmentalism: *green recycling laws; green voters.* [From Old English *grēne*.]

green·back (grēn′băk′) *n.* A piece of paper money of US currency.

green bean *n.* A string bean.

green card *n.* A card issued by the US government to citizens of foreign countries, allowing them to work legally in the United States.

Greene (grēn), **Nathanael** 1742–1786. American Revolutionary general who worked to weaken British strength in the South.

green·er·y (grē′nə-rē) *n.* Green plants or leaves, especially when used for decoration.

green·gro·cer (grēn′grō′sər) *n. Chiefly British* A person who sells fresh fruit and vegetables.

green·horn (grēn′hôrn′) *n.* An inexperienced or immature person, especially one who is easily fooled.

green·house (grēn′hous′) *n.* A room or building with the roof and sides made of glass or clear plastic, used for growing plants that need an even, usually warm temperature; a hothouse.

greenhouse effect *n.* The trapping of the sun's radiation in the earth's atmosphere. It is caused by the buildup of carbon dioxide, water vapor, and other gases in the atmosphere, which allows incoming sunlight to pass through but retains heat radiated back from the earth's surface. —SEE NOTE.

greenhouse gas *n.* An atmospheric gas that contributes to the greenhouse effect.

green·ish (grē′nĭsh) *adj.* Somewhat green.

Green·land (grēn′lənd *or* grēn′lănd′) An island northeast of Canada between the Atlantic and Arctic Oceans. The largest island in the world, it became a Danish colony in the 1700s and was granted limited autonomy in 1979. Nuuk is the capital.

green light *n.* **1.** A green light that signals traffic to proceed. **2.** Permission to proceed: *Our teacher gave us the green light to start on our science project.*

green pepper *n.* The unripened green fruit of any of various varieties of the pepper plant.

greens·keep·er (grēnz′kē′pər) *n.* A person who is responsible for maintaining a golf course.

green·strip (grēn′strĭp′) *n.* A strip of land planted with vegetation that is resistant to fire in order to slow the spread of wildfires.

green·sward (grēn′swôrd′) *n.* Ground that is green with grass.

green thumb *n.* An ability to make plants grow well.

Green·wich (grĕn′ĭch *or* grĭn′ĭj) A borough of Greater London in southeast England on the Thames River. The Prime Meridian passes through Greenwich.

Greenwich Mean Time *n.* Coordinated universal time, used as the standard time in the United Kingdom.

greet (grēt) *tr.v.* **greet·ed, greet·ing, greets 1.** To speak to (someone) in a friendly manner to acknowledge their presence or welcome them to a place or gathering: *The hosts greeted their guests.* **2.** To receive or acknowledge (information, for example) with a specified reaction: *Our parents greeted the news with great joy.* **3.** To be perceived by: *A cry of "Surprise!" greeted our ears.*

greet·ing (grē′tĭng) *n.* A gesture or word of welcome or salutation.

gre·gar·i·ous (grĭ-gâr′ē-əs) *adj.* **1.** Seeking out and enjoying the company of others; sociable: *a gregarious person.* **2.** Living in flocks, herds, colonies, or similar groups with others of the same kind: *Zebras are gregarious.* [From Latin *gregārius*, belonging to a flock, from *grex*, flock.] **—gre·gar′i·ous·ly** *adv.* **—gre·gar′i·ous·ness** *n.*

Gre·go·ri·an calendar (grĭ-gôr′ē-ən) *n.* The calendar in use throughout most of the world, sponsored by Pope Gregory XIII (1502–1585) in 1582 as a corrected version of the Julian calendar.

Gregorian chant *n.* A liturgical chant that is sung without accompaniment.

grem·lin (grĕm′lĭn) *n.* An imaginary creature whose mischief is said to cause mechanical failures.

Gre·na·da (grə-nā′də) An island country in the Windward Islands of the West Indies. St. George's is the capital.

gre·nade (grə-nād′) *n.* **1.** A small bomb detonated by a fuse and thrown by hand or fired from a launcher. **2.** A glass bottle filled with a chemical that is scattered when the bottle is thrown and smashed. [From Old French *(pome) grenate*, pomegranate (from its shape).]

gren·a·dier (grĕn′ə-dîr′) *n.* **1.** A soldier equipped with grenades. **2.** A member of the British Grenadier Guards, the first regiment of the royal household infantry.

Gretz·ky (grĕt′skē), **Wayne** Born 1961. Canadian hockey player who became the National Hockey League's all-time leading scorer in 1989. In 1999 he became the all-time leading scorer in North American professional hockey.

grew (gro͞o) *v.* Past tense of **grow.**

grey (grā) *n., adj. & v.* Variant of **gray**[1].

grey·hound (grā′hound′) *n.* A dog of a tall slender breed having a narrow head and a smooth coat. It was originally bred to hunt fast prey and is often used for racing.

grid (grĭd) *n.* **1.** A pattern of regularly spaced horizontal and vertical lines forming squares of equal size, such as those used on a map or graph as a reference for locating points: *The map grid is labeled with letters for ease of reference.* **2.** A framework of parallel or crisscrossed bars; a grating. **3.** Something resembling such a framework, as in organization: *city streets arranged as a grid.* **4.** A network of power stations and wires for the distribution of electricity to buildings, street lights, and other facilities. **5.** A metal conducting plate in a storage battery.

grid·dle (grĭd′l) *n.* A heavy flat metal surface, such as a pan, that is used for cooking by dry heat. [From Middle English *gridel*, gridiron, from Latin *crātīcula*, diminutive of *crātis*, wickerwork hurdle, lattice.]

grid·dle·cake (grĭd′l-kāk′) *n.* A pancake.

grid·i·ron (grĭd′ī′ərn) *n.* **1.** A flat framework of parallel metal bars used to broil meat or fish; a grill. **2.** A football field.

grid·lock (grĭd′lŏk′) *n.* **1.** A complete halt in the movement of motor vehicle traffic, especially at an intersection of major streets. **2.** A complete halt in an activity, resulting in a backup: *Political gridlock between the president and Congress is preventing progress on this year's budget.*

grief (grēf) *n.* **1.** Deep anguish or sorrow, such as that caused by someone's death. **2.** Annoyance, frustration, or difficulty: *The new software has caused us nothing but grief.* **3.** *Informal* Criticism: *They gave him grief for being so late.*

griev·ance (grē′vəns) *n.* **1.** A real or imagined wrong regarded as just cause for complaint: *Lack of affordable* *housing is a legitimate grievance.* **2.** A complaint based on such a circumstance: *delivered a list of grievances to the mayor.*

grieve (grēv) *v.* **grieved, griev·ing, grieves** —*tr.* **1.** To cause to be sorrowful; distress: *The news grieved us deeply.* **2.** To mourn or sorrow for: *grieved the death of his favorite aunt.* —*intr.* To experience or express grief.

griev·ous (grē′vəs) *adj.* **1.** Causing grief, pain, or sorrow: *a grievous loss.* **2.** Serious or grave; dire: *a grievous crime.* **—griev′ous·ly** *adv.* **—griev′ous·ness** *n.*

grif·fin also **grif·fon** or **gryph·on** (grĭf′ən) *n.* A fabled beast with the head and wings of an eagle and the body of a lion.

grill (grĭl) *tr.v.* **grilled, grill·ing, grills 1.** To cook on a grill: *grill fish in the backyard.* **2.** *Informal* To question closely and relentlessly; cross-examine: *The lawyer grilled a witness on the stand.* ❖ *n.* **1.** A cooking utensil of parallel metal bars; a gridiron. **2.** Food cooked by broiling or grilling. **3.** An informal restaurant where grilled foods are served. **4.** Variant of **grille.** [From Latin *crātīcula*, diminutive of *crātis*, wickerwork, lattice.]

grille also **grill** (grĭl) *n.* A metal or wood grating, often of decorative design, that covers a door, window, or other opening or the front end of a motor vehicle.

grim (grĭm) *adj.* **grim·mer, grim·mest 1.** Discouraging or depressing: *The business news has been very grim lately.* **2.** Stern or unnerving in appearance or behavior; forbidding: *The judge was grim when sentencing the criminal.* **3.** Dismal; gloomy: *We started our trip on a grim, rainy morning.* **4.** Repellent or horrifying: *the grim task of searching for survivors of the crash.* **5.** Unrelenting; rigid: *worked with grim determination.* [From Old English, fierce, severe.] **—grim′ly** *adv.* **—grim′ness** *n.*

grim·ace (grĭm′ĭs) *n.* A sharp contortion of the face, expressing pain, disgust, or contempt: *His face contracted in a grimace.* ❖ *intr.v.* **grim·aced, grim·ac·ing, grim·ac·es** To make a sharp contortion of the face: *Most people grimace when tasting a lemon.*

grime (grīm) *n.* Black dirt or soot clinging to or ground into a surface.

Grim·ké (grĭm′kē), **Sarah Moore** 1792–1873. American feminist and abolitionist who with her sister **Angelina Emily Grimké** (1805–1879) lectured widely against slavery and the repression of women.

Grimm (grĭm), **Jakob Ludwig Karl** 1785–1863. German storyteller who with his brother **Wilhelm Karl Grimm** (1786–1859) collected folktales and published them as *Grimm's Fairy Tales* (1812–1815).

Grim Reaper *n.* The personification of death as a cloaked man or skeleton carrying a scythe.

grim·y (grī′mē) *adj.* **grim·i·er, grim·i·est** Covered with grime: *The window was so grimy it was impossible to see through it.* See Synonyms at **dirty. —grim′i·ly** *adv.* **—grim′i·ness** *n.*

grin (grĭn) *v.* **grinned, grin·ning, grins** —*intr.* To smile broadly: *grin with delight.* —*tr.* To express with a grin: *Our host grinned a warm welcome.* ❖ *n.* A broad smile: *a happy grin.*

grind (grīnd) *v.* **ground** (ground), **grind·ing, grinds** —*tr.* **1.** To crush into small bits or a fine powder: *grind wheat into flour; grind coffee.* **2.** To shape, smooth, or sharpen by rubbing on something rough: *grind scissors to a fine edge; grind lenses for eyeglasses.* **3.** To cause (surfaces) to move with great friction: *grind the teeth.* **4.** To bear down on harshly; crush: *The team's spirit was ground down by a string of losses.* **5a.** To operate by turning a crank: *grind a hurdy-gurdy.* **b.** To produce or process by turning a crank: *grinding a pound of beef.* **6.** To produce mechanically or without inspiration: *grinding out cheap novels.* —*intr.* **1.** To become crushed, pulverized, or powdered by friction. **2.** To move noisily or with great friction: *The train ground to a halt.* **3.** *Informal* To devote oneself to study or work: *grind away at a long report.* ❖ *n.* **1.** The action or sound of grinding: *the grind of the brakes.* **2a.** A specific grade or degree of pulverization: *a fine grind of coffee.* **b. grinds** Particles of ground coffee beans for use in making coffee for drinking. **3.** *Informal* A laborious task, routine, or study: *the daily grind of homework.* **4.** *Informal* A student who works or studies all the time. [From Old English *grindan*.] **—grind′ing·ly** *adv.*

grind·er (grīn′dər) *n.* **1.** A person who grinds, especially a person who sharpens scissors, knives, or other tools. **2.** A mechanical device for grinding: *a meat grinder.* **3.** One of the back teeth used for grinding food; a molar. **4.** A submarine sandwich.

grind·stone (grīnd′stōn′) *n.* **1.** A revolving stone disk used for grinding, polishing, or sharpening tools. **2.** A millstone. ◆ **keep (one's) nose to the grindstone** To work hard and steadily.

grip (grĭp) *n.* **1.** A tight hold; a firm grasp: *a good grip on the rope.* **2.** A manner of grasping and holding: *The grip for holding a baseball bat is different from the grip for swinging a golf club.* **3.** A part designed to be grasped and held; a handle: *the grips on the handlebars of a bicycle.* **4.** Ability to function well or properly; competence: *have a good grip on the new technique.* **5.** Understanding; mastery: *He now has a good grip on Spanish.* **6.** A suitcase or valise. ❖ *tr.v.* **gripped, grip·ping, grips 1.** To grasp and hold tightly; seize firmly: *The gymnast gripped the bar as she swung herself back and forth.* **2.** To gain traction on or apply pressure that does not slip to (a surface): *The new tires grip the road really well.* **3.** To hold the interest and attention of: *a real-life drama that gripped the nation.* [From Old English *gripe*, grasp.]

❑ *These sound alike:* **grip, grippe** (influenza).

gripe (grīp) *v.* **griped, grip·ing, gripes** —*intr. Informal* To complain; grumble: *Everyone griped about the new regulations.* —*tr. Informal* To irritate; annoy: *The criticisms really griped me.* ❖ *n.* **1.** *Informal* A complaint: *Everyone has some gripe about winter weather.* **2. gripes** Sharp repeated pains in the bowels. [From Old English *grīpan*, to seize.]

grippe (grĭp) *n.* Influenza. [From Old French *grippe*, claw, quarrel, from *gripper*, to seize, grasp, of Germanic origin.]

❑ *These sound alike:* **grippe, grip** (firm grasp).

gris·ly (grĭz′lē) *adj.* **gris·li·er, gris·li·est** Inspiring repugnance; gruesome. **—gris′li·ness** *n.*

❑ *These sound alike:* **grisly, grizzly** (grayish).

grist (grĭst) *n.* **1.** Grain or a quantity of grain for grinding. **2.** Grain that has been ground.

gris·tle (grĭs′əl) *n.* Tough tissue or cartilage, especially when found in meat.

gris·tly (grĭs′lē) *adj.* **gris·tli·er, gris·tli·est** Composed of, resembling, or containing gristle: *a gristly piece of steak.*

grist·mill (grĭst′mĭl′) *n.* A mill for grinding grain.

grit (grĭt) *n.* **1.** Tiny rough particles, as of sand or stone: *Grit had collected on the chain of my bicycle.* **2.** A coarse sandstone used for grindstones and millstones. **3.** *Informal* Indomitable spirit; great courage and determination: *To be a good athlete one needs plenty of grit.* ❖ *v.* **grit·ted, grit·ting, grits** —*tr.* To clamp or grind (the teeth) together. —*intr.* To make a grinding noise: *Wagon wheels gritted over the lane.*

grits (grĭts) *pl.n.* *(used with a singular or plural verb)* **1.** Coarsely ground hominy or corn kernels cooked and served for breakfast or as a side dish. **2.** Coarsely ground grain, especially corn.

grit·ty (grĭt′ē) *adj.* **grit·ti·er, grit·ti·est 1.** Containing, covered with, or resembling grit. **2.** Showing determination and strength; plucky. **—grit′ti·ness** *n.*

griz·zled (grĭz′əld) *adj.* **1.** Streaked with or partly gray: *a grizzled beard.* **2.** Having fur or hair streaked or tipped with gray.

WRITERS CHOOSE THEIR WORDS

Goblins were very **gregarious.** They lived and ate together, worked together, went on patrol together, and visited one another almost constantly.

—Clare B. Dunkle
Close Kin

Wayne Gretzky
photographed in 1990

grille

grindstone

grommet

grosbeak

WORD HISTORY

grotto The word **grotto** comes from Italian, where its form is *grotta*. This in turn comes from an earlier word *grupta* or *crupta*. *Crupta* comes from the Latin word *crypta*, "an underground vault, chamber, or pit," the source of our word **crypt**.

ă	pat	ôr	core
ā	pay	oi	boy
âr	care	ou	out
ä	father	o͝o	took
ĕ	pet	o͝or	lure
ē	be	o͞o	boot
ĭ	pit	ŭ	cut
ī	bite	ûr	urge
îr	pier	th	thin
ŏ	pot	*th*	this
ō	toe	zh	vision
ô	paw	ə	about

griz·zly (grĭz′lē) *adj.* **griz·zli·er, griz·zli·est** Grayish or flecked with gray. ❖ *n., pl.* **griz·zlies** A grizzly bear.
❑ *These sound alike:* **grizzly, grisly** (horrifying).

grizzly bear *n.* A large brown bear of western North America having grizzled fur.

groan (grōn) *v.* **groaned, groan·ing, groans** —*intr.* **1.** To utter a deep and prolonged sound, as of pain, grief, or displeasure: *groan over a toothache.* **2.** To make a low creaking sound resembling this: *The floorboards groaned.* —*tr.* To utter or communicate by groaning: *The audience groaned their dissatisfaction.* ❖ *n.* The sound made in groaning. **—groan′er** *n.*
❑ *These sound alike:* **groan, grown** (past tense of grow).

groats (grōts) *pl.n. (used with a singular or plural verb)* Grain or seeds, such as oats, barley, or buckwheat, from which the hulls have been removed.

gro·cer (grō′sər) *n.* A storekeeper who sells food and household supplies. [From Middle English, wholesaler, from Late Latin *grossus*, thick, large.]

gro·cer·y (grō′sə-rē) *n., pl.* **gro·cer·ies 1.** A store selling food and household supplies. **2. groceries** The goods sold by a grocer.

grog (grŏg) *n.* Rum or another liquor diluted with water. [After Old *Grog*, nickname of Edward Vernon (1684–1757), British admiral who ordered that diluted rum be served to his sailors. He got this name from his habit of wearing a cloak made of grogram, a kind of coarse fabric.]

grog·gy (grŏg′ē) *adj.* **grog·gi·er, grog·gi·est** Unsteady and dazed; shaky: *still groggy from a bout with the flu.* **—grog′gi·ly** *adv.* **—grog′gi·ness** *n.*

groin (groin) *n.* **1.** The area of the body where the thighs join the trunk of the body. **2.** In architecture, the curved line where two ceiling vaults come together.

grom·met (grŏm′ĭt) *n.* **1.** A reinforced eyelet, as in cloth or leather. **2.** A small metal or plastic ring used to reinforce an eyelet.

groom (gro͞om *or* gro͝om) *n.* **1.** A person employed to take care of horses. **2.** A man who is about to be married or has recently been married. ❖ *tr.v.* **groomed, groom·ing, grooms 1.** To make neat and trim, especially in personal appearance: *groomed themselves in front of the mirror before going to the party.* **2.** To clean and brush (an animal). **3.** To remove dirt and parasites from the skin, fur, or feathers of: *The baboons groomed each other.* **4.** To train (a person), as for a certain job or position: *groom a successor to the manager.* **5.** To prepare (terrain) for use in a sport, as by packing down new snow and leveling bumps for skiers: *groom a ski slope; groom a trail for mountain biking.*

grooms·man (gro͞omz′mən *or* gro͝omz′mən) *n.* A man who accompanies and assists the bridegroom at a wedding.

groove (gro͞ov) *n.* **1.** A long narrow furrow or channel: *The drawer moves in and out on grooves.* **2.** *Slang* A settled or comfortable routine: *We got out of the groove over vacation.* ❖ *tr.v.* **grooved, groov·ing, grooves** To cut a groove or grooves in: *groove the surface of a highway.* ◆ **in the groove** *Informal* **1.** In a condition where a person consistently performs a task well. **2.** In a condition where a person feels good or content.

groov·y (gro͞o′vē) *adj.* **groov·i·er, groov·i·est** *Slang* Very pleasing; wonderful: *a groovy song.* **—groov′i·ly** *adv.* **—groov′i·ness** *n.*

grope (grōp) *v.* **groped, grop·ing, gropes** —*intr.* To reach about or search blindly or uncertainly: *grope for the light switch; grope for an answer.* —*tr.* To make (one's way) by reaching about uncertainly: *grope one's way down a long dark hall.* **—grop′ing·ly** *adv.*

gros·beak (grōs′bēk′) *n.* Any of various birds having a thick rounded bill and often colorful feathers.

gros·grain (grō′grān′) *n.* **1.** A heavy woven silk or rayon fabric having narrow horizontal ribs. **2.** A ribbon made of this fabric.

gross (grōs) *adj.* **gross·er, gross·est 1.** Very easy to see; obvious or glaring: *a gross error.* **2.** On a large scale; not fine or detailed: *gross anatomical similarities between the two species.* **3.** Having nothing subtracted; total: *gross pay of $9.50 an hour.* **4.** Vulgar; coarse: *a gross remark.* **5.** Offensive; disgusting: *They haven't done the dishes in days, and the kitchen is gross.* **6.** Overweight; fat. ❖ *n., pl.* **gross 1.** The entire body or amount, as of income, before the necessary deductions have been made: *The company's gross was impressive, but once expenses were figured in, it didn't seem so great.* **2.** A group of 144 items; 12 dozen: *This box holds a gross of oranges.* ❖ *tr.v.* **grossed, gross·ing, gross·es** To earn as a total income or profit before deductions: *The business grosses about $10,000 each month.* ◆ **gross out** To fill with disgust; nauseate: *The violent scene in the movie grossed me out.* [From Middle English *gros*, large, from Late Latin *grossus*, thick.] **—gross′ly** *adv.* **—gross′ness** *n.*

gross domestic product *n.* The total market value of all the goods and services that are produced inside a nation during a specified period.

gross national product *n.* The total market value of all goods and services produced by a nation during a specified period.

gro·tesque (grō-tĕsk′) *adj.* **1.** Distorted or unattractive in a repulsive or laughable way: *the grotesque features of a gargoyle.* **2.** Outlandish or bizarre, especially in a shocking way: *a grotesque story of a mistreated dog that takes revenge on humans.* **—gro·tesque′ly** *adv.* **—gro·tesque′ness** *n.*

grot·to (grŏt′ō) *n., pl.* **grot·toes** or **grot·tos 1.** A small cave or cavern. **2.** A structure or excavation built to look like a cave or cavern. —SEE NOTE.

grouch (grouch) *n.* **1.** A person who habitually complains or grumbles. **2.** A grumbling or sulky mood: *in a grouch for no good reason.* ❖ *intr.v.* **grouched, grouch·ing, grouch·es** To complain; grumble: *Why grouch about the weather?*

grouch·y (grou′chē) *adj.* **grouch·i·er, grouch·i·est** Tending to complain or grumble; peevish: *Don't be so grouchy!* **—grouch′i·ly** *adv.* **—grouch′i·ness** *n.*

ground¹ (ground) *n.* **1.** The solid surface of the earth; land; soil: *The ground is still frozen.* **2.** often **grounds a.** An area or plot of land set aside for a special purpose: *parade grounds; a burial ground.* **b.** The land surrounding a house or other building: *the school grounds.* **3.** often **grounds** The basis or reason for a belief or action: *grounds for making an accusation.* **4.** An area of reference or discussion; a subject: *covered new ground in today's talk.* **5.** A surrounding area; a background: *The flag has white stars on a blue ground.* **6. grounds a.** The sediment that settles at the bottom of a liquid, such as coffee. **b.** Particles of ground coffee beans for use in making coffee for drinking; grinds. **7.** A connection between an electrical conductor and the earth. ❖ *v.* **ground·ed, ground·ing, grounds** —*tr.* **1.** To place on or cause to touch the ground. **2.** To run (a vessel) aground: *We grounded our boat by accident.* **3.** To instruct in fundamentals or basics: *This class grounds students in basic science.* **4.** To provide a basis for (a theory, for example); justify: *grounded his argument on facts.* **5.** To connect (an electric circuit or conductor) with the earth. **6.** To prevent (an aircraft or pilot) from flying: *Bad weather grounded all flights.* **7.** To restrict (someone) to a certain place as a punishment: *Her parents grounded her for a week because of her bad behavior.* **8.** In baseball, to hit (a ball) onto the ground. —*intr.* **1.** To touch or reach the ground. **2.** To run aground: *The ship grounded in the storm.* **3.** In baseball, to hit a ground ball. ◆ **ground out** In baseball, to be put out by hitting a ground ball that is fielded and thrown to first base. [From Old English *grund.*]

ground² (ground) *v.* Past tense and past participle of **grind.**

ground ball *n.* In baseball, a batted ball that rolls or bounces along the ground.

ground·break·ing (**ground′**brā′kĭng) *n.* The act or ceremony of turning up ground to start construction: *Groundbreaking for the new hospital is happening today.* ❖ *adj.* Characterized by originality and innovation: *groundbreaking technology.*

ground crew *n.* A team of mechanics and technicians that maintain and service aircraft on the ground.

ground·er (**groun′**dər) *n.* A ground ball.

ground floor *n.* **1.** The floor of a building at or nearest ground level. **2.** *Informal* The start of something, as a project or business: *I started in this business on the ground floor as a messenger.*

ground·hog (**ground′**hôg′) *n.* The woodchuck.

Groundhog Day *n.* February 2. According to popular legend, there will be an early spring if the groundhog does not see its shadow when coming out of its burrow on this day, or there will be six more weeks of winter weather if it does see its shadow.

ground·less (**ground′**lĭs) *adj.* Having no ground or foundation; unsupported by the facts: *groundless worries.* **—ground′less·ly** *adv.* **—ground′less·ness** *n.*

ground·nut (**ground′**nŭt′) *n.* **1.** Any of several plants having edible underground tubers that resemble nuts. **2.** Any of several plants, such as the peanut, having edible underground seeds. **3.** The seed or tuber of any of these plants.

ground pine *n.* Any of various low-growing club mosses that look like miniature evergreen trees.

ground rule *n.* often **ground rules** A basic rule: *ground rules for tennis; set ground rules for a club.*

ground squirrel *n.* Any of several small burrowing rodents that have large eyes and small ears and sometimes a spotted or striped back.

ground·swell (**ground′**swĕl′) *n.* **1.** Deep rolling waves in the ocean, often the result of a distant storm or an earthquake. **2.** A sudden gathering of force, as of public opinion: *a groundswell of support for the proposed law.*

ground·wa·ter also **ground water** (**ground′**wô′tər) *n.* Water that flows or seeps beneath the surface of the earth, soaking soil or porous rock and supplying wells and springs.

ground·work (**ground′**wûrk′) *n.* Work that lays the basis for something; a foundation.

group (gro͞op) *n.* **1.** A number of people or things gathered or located together: *a group of students in a museum; a group of islands off the coast of Alaska.* **2.** A number of people or things classed together because of similarities: *The idea has a small group of supporters across the country.* **3.** Two or more atoms bound together that act as a unit in a number of chemical compounds: *a hydroxyl group.* **4.** In the periodic table, a vertical column that contains elements having similar properties. ❖ *v.* **grouped, group·ing, groups** —*tr.* To place or arrange in a group: *group books on the same topic together.* —*intr.* To belong to or form a group: *The class grouped on the steps to pose for a picture.* [From Italian *gruppo,* probably of Germanic origin.] —SEE NOTE.

grou·per (**gro͞o′**pər) *n., pl.* **grouper** or **grou·pers** Any of various large tropical or subtropical ocean fishes, many of which are valued as food.

group·ing (**gro͞o′**pĭng) *n.* **1.** The act or process of uniting in groups: *The grouping of the children into teams took several minutes.* **2.** A collection of things or people united in a group: *There is a large grouping of reference books in the library.*

grouse¹ (grous) *n., pl.* **grouse** or **grous·es** Any of various plump, ground-dwelling birds having mottled brown or grayish feathers on the body and legs, often hunted as game.

grouse² (grous) *Informal intr.v.* **groused, grous·ing, grous·es** To complain; grumble: *groused about the poor hotel service.* [Possibly from Old French *grouchier.*]

grove (grōv) *n.* A group of trees with open ground between them, as in an orchard: *an orange grove.*

grov·el (**grŏv′**əl *or* **grŭv′**əl) *intr.v.* **grov·eled, grov·el·ing, grov·els** also **grov·elled, grov·el·ling, grov·els** **1.** To behave in a servile or demeaning manner; cringe: *Be proud of yourself and do not grovel.* **2.** To lie flat or crawl on one's belly, as in humility or submission: *The dog began to grovel at its owner's feet.* **—grov′el·er, grov′el·ler** *n.*

grow (grō) *v.* **grew** (gro͞o), **grown** (grōn), **grow·ing, grows** —*intr.* **1.** To become bigger by a natural process of development; mature: *The seedlings grew into plants.* **2.** To be capable of growth; thrive; flourish: *Banana trees grow well in tropical climates.* **3.** To increase or spread; expand: *The business grew rapidly.* **4.** To come to be by a gradual process or by degrees: *grow rich; grow dark outside.* —*tr.* **1.** To cause to grow; produce; cultivate: *grow vegetables in a garden.* **2.** To allow (something) to develop or increase by a natural process: *grow a beard.* ◆ **grow out of** To develop or come into existence from: *The book grew out of our scribbled notes.* **grow up** To become an adult. [From Old English *grōwan.*] **—grow′er** *n.*

growl (groul) *n.* **1.** A low, throaty, menacing sound made by an animal: *the growl of a dog.* **2.** A gruff surly utterance: *answered me with a growl.* ❖ *v.* **growled, growl·ing, growls** —*intr.* **1.** To make a low throaty sound or utterance. **2.** To speak in a surly or angry manner. —*tr.* To utter by growling: *The dog growled a warning.*

grown (grōn) *v.* Past participle of **grow.** ❖ *adj.* **1.** Having full growth; mature: *act like a grown person.* **2.** Produced or cultivated: *locally grown produce.*

❑ *These sound alike:* **grown, groan** (moan).

grown·up also **grown-up** (**grōn′**ŭp′) *n.* An adult.

grown-up (**grōn′**ŭp′) *adj.* **1.** Relating to or intended for adults: *a grown-up movie.* **2.** Having or showing maturity in outlook, attitude, or appearance: *Apologizing was a very grown-up thing to do.*

growth (grōth) *n.* **1.** The process of growing; development: *the growth of a child.* **2.** Something that grows or has grown: *A thick growth of weeds covered the yard.* **3.** An amount grown; an increase or expansion: *measure the growth of a country's population.* **4.** An abnormal mass of tissue growing in or on a living organism: *A wart is a growth on the body.*

growth ring *n.* A layer of wood formed in a plant during a single period of growth, appearing as a ring-shaped band when a tree or shrub is cut crosswise.

grub (grŭb) *v.* **grubbed, grub·bing, grubs** —*tr.* **1.** To dig up by the roots: *grub turnips.* **2.** To clear of roots and stumps by digging: *grubbed a small plot.* —*intr.* **1.** To dig in the ground: *grub for potatoes.* **2.** To work hard, especially at menial tasks; drudge: *grub for a living.* ❖ *n.* **1.** The thick wormlike larva of certain beetles and other insects. **2.** *Slang* Food: *buy the grub for a camping trip.*

grub·by (**grŭb′**ē) *adj.* **grub·bi·er, grub·bi·est** Dirty; grimy: *grubby work clothes.* **—grub′bi·ly** *adv.* **—grub′bi·ness** *n.*

grub·stake (**grŭb′**stāk′) *n.* Supplies or funds advanced to a mining prospector or a person starting a business in return for a promised share of the profits. ❖ *tr.v.* **grub·staked, grub·stak·ing, grub·stakes** To supply with a grubstake.

grudge (grŭj) *tr.v.* **grudged, grudg·ing, grudg·es** To be reluctant to give or admit: *grudged me a small dis-*

USAGE

group The word **group** as a *collective noun* can be followed by a singular or plural verb. It takes a singular verb when those making up the group are considered as a body: *The group is all here for the party. Group* takes a plural verb when those making up the group are considered individually: *The group are arguing about where to go for pizza.*

growth ring

WRITERS CHOOSE THEIR WORDS

Machines ran around the clock, and workers were forced to keep up. A typical working day was fourteen hours long. Men, women, and children kept up this **grueling** schedule six days a week, year after year after year. The result was broken bodies, broken spirits, and broken lives.

—Ruth Ashby
Victorian England

count for paying in cash. ❖ *n.* A deep-seated feeling of resentment: *holds a grudge about the accident.* [From Middle English, from *grucchen*, to grumble, complain, from Old French *grouchier*.]

grudg·ing (grŭj′ĭng) *adj.* Reluctant; unwilling: *grudging admiration for his opponent's success.* **—grudg′ing·ly** *adv.*

gru·el (gro͞o′əl) *n.* A thin, watery porridge. [From Middle English, from Old French, of Germanic origin.]

gru·el·ing (gro͞o′ə-lĭng *or* gro͞o′lĭng) *adj.* Physically or mentally exhausting: *Working in a coal mine is a grueling job.*

grue·some (gro͞o′səm) *adj.* Causing horror and shock; frightful: *a gruesome accident.* **—grue′some·ly** *adv.* **—grue′some·ness** *n.*

gruff (grŭf) *adj.* **gruff·er, gruff·est 1.** Brusque or stern in manner or appearance: *a gruff reply.* **2.** Harsh-sounding; hoarse: *a gruff voice.* **—gruff′ly** *adv.* **—gruff′ness** *n.*

grum·ble (grŭm′bəl) *v.* **grum·bled, grum·bling, grum·bles** *—intr.* **1.** To complain in a surly manner; mutter in discontent: *They grumbled about the store's prices.* **2.** To rumble or growl. *—tr.* To express in a grumbling or discontented manner: *grumbled a response.* ❖ *n.* **1.** A muttered complaint. **2.** A rumble; a growl: *the grumble of distant thunder.* **—grum′bler** *n.*

grump·y (grŭm′pē) *adj.* **grump·i·er, grump·i·est** Surly and peevish; cranky: *a grumpy mood.* **—grump′i·ly** *adv.* **—grump′i·ness** *n.*

grunge (grŭnj) *n.* **1.** *Informal* Filth; dirt. **2.** Raucous rock music with lyrics that express dissatisfaction, despair, or apathy.

grun·gy (grŭn′jē) *adj.* **grun·gi·er, grun·gi·est** *Informal* In a dirty, rundown, or inferior condition: *grungy socks.*

grunt (grŭnt) *v.* **grunt·ed, grunt·ing, grunts** *—intr.* **1.** To make a deep throaty sound, as a hog does. **2.** To make a sound similar to a grunt, as in disgust. *—tr.* To utter or express with a deep throaty sound: *The irritated clerk grunted a reply.* ❖ *n.* **1.** A deep throaty sound, as that made by a hog. **2.** Any of the various chiefly tropical ocean fishes that make grunting sounds. **3.** *Slang* A soldier in the infantry, especially during the Vietnam War. **4.** *Slang* A person who performs routine or mundane tasks.

gryph·on (grĭf′ən) *n.* Variant of **griffin.**

gua·ca·mo·le (gwŏk′ə-**mō′**lē) *n.* A thick paste of mashed avocado, usually combined with lemon or lime juice, onion, and seasonings.

Gua·da·la·ja·ra (gwŏd′l-ə-**hä′**rə) A city of west-central Mexico west-northwest of Mexico City. A major commercial center, it is Mexico's second largest city.

Gua·de·loupe (**gwŏd′**l-o͞op′ *or* gwŏd′l-**o͞op′**) A French territory made up of several islands in the Leeward Islands of the West Indies. Basse-Terre is the capital.

Guam (gwäm) A territory of the United States, the largest and southernmost of the Mariana Islands in the western Pacific Ocean. Agana is the capital.

gua·na·co (gwə-**nä′**kō) *n., pl.* **gua·na·cos** or **guanaco** A brownish South American mammal that resembles the llama and has fine, soft wool. [From Quechua *huanaco*.]

Guang·zhou (**gwäng′jō′**) A city of southern China on a delta near the South China Sea. Formerly known as Canton, it is a historic port.

gua·nine (**gwä′**nēn′) *n.* A base that is a component of DNA and RNA.

gua·no (**gwä′**nō) *n.* The dung of certain seabirds or bats, used as fertilizer.

gua·ra·ni (gwä′rə-**nē′**) *n., pl.* **gua·ra·ni·es** The basic monetary unit of Paraguay.

Guarani *n., pl.* **Guarani** or **Guaranis 1.** A member of a South American Indian people of Paraguay, Argentina, and Brazil. **2.** The language of this people.

guar·an·tee (găr′ən-**tē′**) *n.* **1.** Something that assures a particular condition or outcome: *Wealth is not a guarantee of happiness.* **2.** A promise or assurance that attests to the quality or durability of a product or service. **3.** A guaranty. ❖ *tr.v.* **guar·an·teed, guar·an·tee·ing, guar·an·tees 1.** To render certain; make sure: *The rains guarantee a good crop.* **2.** To undertake to accomplish (something) for another: *Jefferson wanted to guarantee freedom of speech for future generations.* **3.** To assume responsibility for the quality or performance of: *The manufacturer guarantees these microwave ovens for two years.* **4.** To provide security for: *Insurance guarantees a car owner against costs of injury or of repairs.* [From Middle English *garant*, warranty, from Old French, of Germanic origin.]

guar·an·tor (găr′ən-**tôr′** *or* **găr′**ən-tər) *n.* A person or business that makes or gives a guarantee or guaranty.

guar·an·ty (**găr′**ən-tē) *n., pl.* **guar·an·ties 1.** An agreement to assume the responsibility of payment or fulfillment of another's debts or obligations: *My cousin signed a guaranty for my bank loan.* **2.** Something given as security for the fulfillment of an obligation or the payment of a debt. **3.** A guarantee, as for a product or service. ❖ *tr.v.* **guar·an·tied, guar·an·ty·ing, guar·an·ties 1.** To provide a guaranty for: *Employers sometimes guaranty loans for trusted employees.* **2.** To guarantee.

guard (gärd) *v.* **guard·ed, guard·ing, guards** *—tr.* **1a.** To watch over (a place or person, for example) in order to keep from being damaged, robbed, or injured: *guard a bank; guard a witness.* See Synonyms at **defend. b.** To supervise the entry and exit through; keep watch at: *guarded the door.* **c.** To watch over so as to prevent escape: *guard a prisoner.* **2.** To keep (an opposing player) from scoring or playing efficiently in certain sports, such as basketball and hockey. *—intr.* To take precautions: *guard against illness by getting exercise.* ❖ *n.* **1.** A person who keeps watch, protects, or acts as a sentinel: *a prison guard.* **2.** Protection or watch: *The sheepdog kept guard over the herd.* **3.** Something that gives protection; a safeguard: *a guard against tooth decay.* **4.** A device or attachment that protects or shields the user: *a helmet with a face guard.* **5.** In football, either of the two players on a team's offensive line on each side of the center. **6.** In basketball, either of two players who usually move the ball up the court and start offensive plays. ◆ **off guard** Unprepared; not alert: *The thunderclap caught me off guard, and I jumped.* **on guard** Alert and watchful; cautious: *Be on guard for patches of ice on the sidewalk.* [From Middle English *garde*, care, custody, and from Old French *garder*, of Germanic origin.]

guard cell *n.* Either of a pair of crescent-shaped cells that control the opening and closing of one of the tiny pores on the surface of a leaf or stem.

guard·ed (**gär′**dĭd) *adj.* **1.** Defended; protected: *a heavily guarded border.* **2.** Cautious; restrained: *give a guarded answer.* **—guard′ed·ly** *adv.*

guard·house (**gärd′**hous′) *n.* **1.** A building that accommodates soldiers on guard. **2.** A jail for military personnel guilty of minor offenses or awaiting court-martial.

guard·i·an (**gär′**dē-ən) *n.* **1.** A person or thing that guards, protects, or watches over: *The courts act as a guardian of the law.* **2.** A person who is legally responsible for the care and management of the person or property of someone who cannot manage his or her own affairs.

guard·rail (**gärd′**rāl′) *n.* A protective railing, as on a highway or staircase.

guard·room (**gärd′**ro͞om′ *or* **gärd′**ro͞om′) *n.* A room used by guards on duty.

guards·man (**gärdz′**mən) *n.* **1.** A person who acts as a guard. **2.** A member of the US National Guard.

Gua·te·ma·la (gwä′tə-**mä′**lə) **1.** A country of north-

guardrail

ă	pat	ôr	core
ā	pay	oi	boy
âr	care	ou	out
ä	father	o͝o	took
ĕ	pet	o͝or	lure
ē	be	o͞o	boot
ĭ	pit	ŭ	cut
ī	bite	ûr	urge
îr	pier	th	thin
ŏ	pot	*th*	this
ō	toe	zh	vision
ô	paw	ə	about

ern Central America west of Honduras. Inhabited by Mayans for more than a thousand years, Guatemala was a Spanish colony from the 1500s to the 1800s. The city of Guatemala is the capital. **2.** also **Guatemala City** The capital of Guatemala, in the south-central part of the country.

gua·va (gwä′və) *n.* **1.** The fruit of a tropical American tree, having greenish skin and sweet pink or white flesh. Guavas are used especially to make jelly and preserves. **2.** The tree that bears such fruit. [From Spanish *guayaba*, of Caribbean Indian origin.]

gu·ber·na·to·ri·al (go͞o′bər-nə-**tôr′**ē-əl) *adj.* Relating to a governor. [From Latin *gubernātor*, governor.]

gudg·eon (gŭj′ən) *n.* A small freshwater fish of Eurasia that is often used for bait.

Guen·e·vere (gwĕn′ə-vîr′) *n.* Variant of **Guinevere.**

Guern·sey (gûrn′zē) *n., pl.* **Guern·seys** Any of a breed of brown and white cattle raised for milk.

guer·ril·la or **gue·ril·la** (gə-rĭl′ə) *n.* A member of a usually indigenous military force operating in small bands in occupied territory to harass the enemy, as by surprise raids. [From Spanish, from *guerra*, war.]

❑ *These sound alike:* **guerrilla, gorilla** (ape).

guess (gĕs) *v.* **guessed, guess·ing, guess·es** —*tr.* **1.** To assume or estimate (a fact or result) without sufficient information: *The reporter guessed that 6,000 people would be at the concert.* **2.** To form a correct statement or estimate regarding (something) without sufficient information or understanding: *I guessed the answer.* —*intr.* To make a guess or estimate: *We can only guess at their reason for staying home.* ❖ *n.* A statement, opinion, or conclusion based on insufficient evidence: *If you're not sure of the answer, at least make a guess.* [From Middle English *gessen*, probably of Scandinavian origin.] **—guess′er** *n.*

guess·ti·mate (gĕs′tə-mĭt) *n. Informal* An estimate based on conjecture.

guess·work (gĕs′wûrk′) *n.* **1.** The process of making guesses: *There is a lot of guesswork involved in predicting sales of a new product.* **2.** An estimate or judgment made by guessing.

guest (gĕst) *n.* **1a.** A person who is a recipient of hospitality at the home or table of another: *We invited several guests for dinner.* **b.** A person who is a recipient of hospitality or entertainment by a host or hostess, as at a party. **2.** A person who pays for meals or accommodations at a restaurant, hotel, or other establishment. **3.** A visiting performer, speaker, or contestant, as on a television program. [From Middle English *gest*, from Old Norse *gestr*.]

guf·faw (gə-fô′) *n.* A hearty, boisterous burst of laughter. ❖ *intr.v.* **guf·fawed, guf·faw·ing, guf·faws** To laugh heartily and boisterously: *The audience guffawed at the jokes.*

Gui·an·a (gē-ăn′ə *or* gē-ä′nə) A region of northeast South America including southeast Venezuela, part of northern Brazil, and French Guiana, Suriname, and Guyana.

guid·ance (gīd′ns) *n.* **1.** The act or process of guiding: *Success of the expedition depended on the guidance of their scouts.* **2.** Counseling, as to help someone make a decision or deal with a personal problem: *Her job is to provide guidance to high school students applying to college.*

guide (gīd) *n.* **1.** A person or thing that shows the way, directs, leads, or advises: *a tour guide; a guide to good manners.* **2.** A person employed to conduct others, as through a museum, and give information. **3.** A guidebook. **4.** A device, such as a ruler, tab, or bar, that acts to regulate operation or direct motion. ❖ *tr.v.* **guid·ed, guid·ing, guides 1.** To serve as a guide for; conduct: *The ranger guided the tourists through the park.* **2.** To direct the course of; steer: *guide a car down a narrow street.* **3.** To exert control or influence over: *Lincoln guided our nation through the Civil War.* [From Middle English, from Old French, from Old Provençal *guidar*, to guide, of Germanic origin.] **—guid′a·ble** *adj.* **—guid′er** *n.*

SYNONYMS guide, lead, shepherd, steer, usher These verbs mean to conduct on the way or direct to the way. *We were guided to our seats. The teacher led the students in a discussion of the novel's themes. The tourists were shepherded to the chartered bus. The secretary steered the applicant to the proper department. The host will now usher the contestants into a soundproof booth.*

---

guide·book (gīd′bo͝ok′) *n.* A handbook of directions and information, especially for travelers and tourists.

guid·ed missile (gī′dĭd) *n.* A missile whose course can be controlled while it is in flight.

guide dog *n.* A dog trained to guide a visually impaired or blind person.

guide dog

guide·line (gīd′līn′) *n.* A statement or other indication of policy or procedure, intended to give practical guidance: *The president presented guidelines for economic development and aid to other countries.*

guide·post (gīd′pōst′) *n.* A signpost.

guide·word (gīd′wûrd′) *n.* A word or term placed at the top of a column or page in a reference book to indicate the first or last entry on the page.

guild (gĭld) *n.* **1.** An association of people who share a trade or pursuit, formed to protect mutual interests and maintain standards. **2.** A similar association, as of merchants or artisans, in medieval times.

❑ *These sound alike:* **guild, gild** (cover with gold).

guil·der (gĭl′dər) *n.* **1.** The former basic monetary unit of the Netherlands. **2.** The basic monetary unit of Suriname.

guild·hall (gĭld′hôl′) *n.* **1.** The meeting hall of a guild. **2.** A town hall.

guile (gīl) *n.* Treacherous cunning; skillful deceit. **—guile′ful** *adj.*

guile·less (gīl′lĭs) *adj.* Free of guile; artless.

guil·lo·tine (gĭl′ə-tēn′ *or* gē′ə-tēn′) *n.* A device consisting of a heavy blade held aloft between two upright guides and dropped to behead a person condemned to die. ❖ *tr.v.* **guil·lo·tined, guil·lo·tin·ing, guil·lo·tines** To behead with a guillotine. [After Joseph Ignace *Guillotin* (1738–1814), French physician.]

guilt (gĭlt) *n.* **1.** The fact of being responsible for committing an offense or error: *The investigation uncovered the suspect's guilt.* **2.** Remorseful awareness of having done something wrong: *Does he feel any guilt for forgetting my birthday?*

❑ *These sound alike:* **guilt, gilt** (layer of gold).

guilt·less (gĭlt′lĭs) *adj.* Free of guilt; innocent.

guilt·y (gĭl′tē) *adj.* **guilt·i·er, guilt·i·est 1.** Having done wrong; deserving of blame; culpable: *The thief was found guilty.* **2.** Burdened with or prompted by a sense of guilt: *a guilty conscience.* **—guilt′i·ly** *adv.* **—guilt′i·ness** *n.*

guin·ea (gĭn′ē) *n.* **1.** A gold coin formerly used in England and worth one pound and one shilling. **2.** The sum of one pound and one shilling.

Guin·ea (gĭn′ē) A country of western Africa on the Atlantic Ocean north of Sierra Leone. Conakry is the capital.

Guinea, Gulf of A broad inlet of the Atlantic Ocean formed by the great bend in the west-central coast of Africa.

Guin·ea-Bis·sau (gĭn′ē-bĭ-**sou′**) A country of western Africa on the Atlantic Ocean south of Senegal. Bissau is the capital.

guinea fowl *n.* Any of several African birds that resemble the pheasants, especially one that has dark feathers with many small white spots and is raised for food.

guitar
electric guitar

guppy

WRITERS CHOOSE THEIR WORDS

In December 1774, Benedict was one of sixty to join the newly formed militia company in New Haven; in March of the following year he was elected captain. He was thirty-four years old but he took command with the same **gusto** as if he'd been fifteen.

—Jean Fritz
Traitor: The Case of Benedict Arnold

ă	pat	ôr	core
ā	pay	oi	boy
âr	care	ou	out
ä	father	ŏŏ	took
ĕ	pet	ŏŏr	lure
ē	be	ōō	boot
ĭ	pit	ŭ	cut
ī	bite	ûr	urge
îr	pier	th	thin
ŏ	pot	*th*	this
ō	toe	zh	vision
ô	paw	ə	about

guinea hen *n.* The guinea fowl, especially a female.

guinea pig *n.* **1.** Any of various small rodents that have short ears, short legs, and little or no tail. They are often kept as pets or used as laboratory animals. **2.** A person who is used as a subject for experimentation.

Guin·e·vere (gwĭn′ə-vîr′) also **Guen·e·vere** (gwĕn′ə-vîr′) *n.* In Arthurian legend, King Arthur's wife, who was loved by Lancelot.

guise (gīz) *n.* **1.** Outward appearance; aspect. **2.** False appearance; pretense: *spoke to me under the guise of friendship.* **3.** Mode of dress; garb: *The spy entered the enemy castle in the guise of a beggar.*

gui·tar (gĭ-tär′) *n.* A stringed musical instrument having a flat-backed, rounded body that narrows in the middle and a long, fretted neck. It is played by plucking or strumming.

gui·tar·ist (gĭ-tär′ĭst) *n.* A person who plays the guitar.

gulch (gŭlch) *n.* A deep narrow ravine, especially one cut by the course of a stream or sudden water flow.

gulf (gŭlf) *n.* **1.** A large body of ocean or sea water that is partly surrounded by land. **2.** A deep wide chasm in the earth; an abyss: *Eruption of the volcano blew a gulf in the side of the mountain.* **3.** A wide gap, as in understanding: *the gulf between one generation and the next.*

Gulf of For the names of actual gulfs, see the specific proper name; for example, **Mexico, Gulf of.**

Gulf Stream *n.* A warm ocean current of the northern Atlantic Ocean off eastern North America. It flows from the Gulf of Mexico up the eastern coast of the United States and then northeast toward Europe.

Gulf War *n.* A war fought in 1990 and 1991 in which a group of countries led by the United States drove the Iraqi army out of Kuwait and destroyed much of Iraq's military capability.

gull[1] (gŭl) *n.* Any of various chiefly coastal seabirds having a strong bill, webbed feet, long wings, and usually gray and white feathers. [From Middle English *gulle.*]

gull[2] (gŭl) *n.* A person who is easily tricked or cheated; a dupe. ❖ *tr.v.* **gulled, gull·ing, gulls** To deceive or cheat. [Probably from Middle English *golen*, to make swallowing motions.]

gul·let (gŭl′ĭt) *n.* **1.** The tube that connects the throat and stomach; the esophagus. **2.** The throat.

gul·li·ble (gŭl′ə-bəl) *adj.* Easily deceived or duped: *He's so gullible that he'll believe anything you tell him.* **—gul′li·bil′i·ty** *n.*

gul·ly (gŭl′ē) *n., pl.* **gul·lies** A ditch or channel cut in the earth by running water, especially after heavy rain.

gulp (gŭlp) *v.* **gulped, gulp·ing, gulps** *—tr.* To swallow greedily or rapidly in large amounts: *We were late and had to gulp our lunch.* *—intr.* To choke, gasp, or swallow air: *She gulped a few times before starting her speech.* ❖ *n.* **1.** The act of gulping: *His bag of peanuts disappeared in just a few gulps.* **2.** An amount swallowed at one time: *a large gulp of water.*

gum[1] (gŭm) *n.* **1a.** Any of various thick sticky substances produced by certain plants that dry into brittle water-soluble solids. **b.** A tree that is a source of gum, such as a eucalyptus tree. **2.** Rubber made from a plant substance. **3.** A sticky or adhesive substance made from the natural gum of plants or from other substances. **4.** Chewing gum. ❖ *tr.v.* **gummed, gum·ming, gums** To cover, clog, seal, or fasten with gum: *gummed the seams of the canoe.* ◆ **gum up** To cause (something) to malfunction or work less efficiently: *A computer glitch is gumming up the processing of orders.* [From Middle English *gomee*, from Late Latin *gumma*, from Greek *kommi.*]

gum[2] (gŭm) *n.* The firm connective tissue that surrounds and supports the bases of the teeth. ❖ *tr.v.* **gummed, gum·ming, gums** To chew (food) with toothless gums. [From Old English *gōma*, palate, jaw.]

gum arabic *n.* A gum produced by certain African acacia trees, used in making pills, cosmetics, various foods, and emulsions.

gum·bo (gŭm′bō) *n., pl.* **gum·bos 1.** The okra plant and its pods. **2.** A soup or stew thickened with okra pods. **3.** A fine soil that contains much clay and becomes sticky when wet. [From Louisiana French *gombo*, of Bantu origin.] —SEE NOTE AT **goober.**

gum·drop (gŭm′drŏp′) *n.* A small sugar-coated candy made of sweetened gum arabic or gelatin.

gum·my (gŭm′ē) *adj.* **gum·mi·er, gum·mi·est 1.** Consisting of, containing, or covered with gum. **2.** Thick and sticky: *gummy tar on my shoes.* **—gum′mi·ness** *n.*

gump·tion (gŭmp′shən) *n.* *Informal* Boldness, initiative, or spunk.

gum resin *n.* A mixture of gum and resin produced by various plants.

gun (gŭn) *n.* **1.** A weapon that shoots bullets, shells, or other projectiles through a heavy metal tube, usually by the explosion of gunpowder. Pistols, rifles, and cannons are guns. **2.** A device that resembles a gun, as in its ability to project something under pressure: *Painting with a spray gun is quick.* **3.** A discharge of a gun as a signal or salute. ❖ *tr.v.* **gunned, gun·ning, guns 1.** To shoot (a person). **2.** To open the throttle of (an engine) so as to accelerate: *gunned the engine and sped away.* ◆ **gun for 1.** To plan or take action to harm or cause trouble for (someone). **2.** To try to obtain (something) with determination or energy: *gunning for a promotion.* **under the gun** Under great pressure to do something.

gun·boat (gŭn′bōt′) *n.* A small armed vessel.

gun control *n.* Government regulation restricting or limiting the sale and possession of handguns and rifles in an effort to reduce violent crime and accidents.

gun·fire (gŭn′fīr′) *n.* The firing of guns.

gung ho (gŭng′ hō′) *adj.* *Slang* Extremely dedicated or enthusiastic: *a gung ho baseball fan.* [From Mandarin *gōnghé*, to work together.]

gun·lock (gŭn′lŏk′) *n.* The mechanism in a gun that explodes the charge of gunpowder.

gun·man (gŭn′mən) *n.* A man armed with a gun, especially a killer or criminal.

gun·ner (gŭn′ər) *n.* **1.** A member of the armed forces who operates a gun. **2.** In the US Marine Corps, a warrant officer in charge of a ship's guns. **3.** A person who hunts with a gun.

gun·ner·y (gŭn′ə-rē) *n.* **1.** The science that deals with the techniques and procedures of operating guns. **2.** The use of guns; shooting.

gun·ny (gŭn′ē) *n., pl.* **gun·nies** A strong coarse cloth made of jute or hemp, used especially for sacks. [From Hindi *goṇī*, from Sanskrit, sack.]

gun·ny·sack (gŭn′ē-săk′) *n.* A bag or sack made of gunny.

gun·pow·der (gŭn′pou′dər) *n.* An explosive powder used in guns, fireworks, and blasting, especially a mixture of potassium nitrate, charcoal, and sulfur.

gun·shot (gŭn′shŏt′) *n.* **1.** Shot fired from a gun. **2.** The range of a gun: *within gunshot.* **3.** The shooting of a gun.

gun·smith (gŭn′smĭth′) *n.* A person who makes or repairs firearms.

gun·wale also **gun·nel** (gŭn′əl) *n.* The upper edge of the side of a ship or boat.

gup·py (gŭp′ē) *n., pl.* **gup·pies** A small tropical American freshwater fish that is bred in many colorful varieties and is often kept in home aquariums. The female does not lay eggs but bears live offspring. [After R.J. Lechmere *Guppy* (1836–1916), clergyman of Trinidad who first supplied specimens to the British Museum.]

gur·gle (gûr′gəl) *v.* **gur·gled, gur·gling, gur·gles** *—intr.* **1.** To flow while making a bubbling sound: *A stream gurgled over the rocks.* **2.** To make such a bubbling sound: *The baby gurgled with contentment.* —*tr.* To express with a bubbling sound: *The baby gurgled her delight.* ❖ *n.* A bubbling sound. [From Middle English *gurguling*, from Latin *gurguliō*, gullet.]

gu·ru (go͝or′o͞o) *n., pl.* **gu·rus 1.** A Hindu, Sikh, or Tibetan Buddhist spiritual teacher. **2.** A person who is followed as a leader or teacher. [From Sanskrit *guruḥ*, from *guru-*, heavy, venerable.]

gush (gŭsh) *v.* **gushed, gush·ing, gush·es** —*intr.* **1.** To flow forth suddenly in great volume: *Water gushed from the broken pipe.* **2.** To make an excessive display of enthusiasm or sentiment: *Be sincere when thanking someone, but don't gush.* —*tr.* To emit abundantly; pour forth: *The new well gushed oil.* ❖ *n.* **1.** A sudden outpouring: *a gush of tears.* **2.** A display of too much enthusiasm or sentiment.

gush·er (gŭsh′ər) *n.* An oil or gas well that pours out a steady flow without pumping.

gush·y (gŭsh′ē) *adj.* **gush·i·er, gush·i·est** Showing excessive enthusiasm or sentiment. **—gush′i·ly** *adv.* **—gush′i·ness** *n.*

gus·set (gŭs′ĭt) *n.* A triangular insert, as in the seam of a garment, for added strength or expansion.

gust (gŭst) *n.* **1.** A sudden strong rush of wind. **2.** A sudden burst, as of rain or smoke. **3.** An outburst of feeling: *a gust of anger.*

gus·ta·to·ry (gŭs′tə-tôr′ē) *adj.* Relating to the sense of taste.

gus·to (gŭs′tō) *n.* Great enjoyment; zest: *We were hungry and ate lunch with gusto.* See Synonyms at **zest.** [From Latin *gustus*, taste.]

gust·y (gŭs′tē) *adj.* **gust·i·er, gust·i·est** Blowing in or marked by gusts: *gusty March weather.* **—gust′i·ly** *adv.* **—gust′i·ness** *n.*

gut (gŭt) *n.* **1.** The digestive tract or any of its parts, especially the stomach or intestines. **2. guts** The intestines; bowels. **3.** Catgut. **4. guts** *Slang* Courage, fortitude, or nerve: *It took guts to stand up to such a powerful foe.* ❖ *tr.v.* **gut·ted, gut·ting, guts 1.** To remove the intestines of; eviscerate: *gutting a deer.* **2.** To destroy the contents or interior of: *The fire gutted their apartment.* ❖ *adj. Slang* Arousing or involving basic emotions: *The student's gut reaction was to protest.*

Gu·ten·berg (go͞ot′n-bûrg′), **Johann** or **Johannes** 1400?–1468? German printer who was the first European to use movable type (c. 1455), in which each character is cast on a separate piece of metal. Movable type made it possible to distribute written information to large numbers of people, which transformed European society.

Guth·rie (gŭth′rē), **Woodrow Wilson** Known as "Woody." 1912–1967. American folksinger and composer whose songs include "This Land Is Your Land" (1940).

gut·less (gŭt′lĭs) *adj. Slang* Lacking courage, drive, or fortitude. **—gut′less·ness** *n.*

gut·ter (gŭt′ər) *n.* **1a.** A channel near a curb for draining off water at the edge of a street. **b.** A trough fixed under or along the eaves for draining water off a roof. **2.** A groove or trough, as the one on either side of a bowling alley. ❖ *intr.v.* **gut·tered, gut·ter·ing, gut·ters** To burn low and unsteadily; flicker: *The candle guttered and then went out.* [From Middle English *goter*, from Old French *gotier*, from Latin *gutta*, drop.]

gut·tur·al (gŭt′ər-əl) *adj.* **1.** Relating to the throat. **2.** Having a harsh sound, as those produced in the back of the mouth: *a deep guttural voice.* **3.** Velar. [From Latin *guttur*, throat.] **—gut′tur·al·ly** *adv.*

guy[1] (gī) *n.* A rope, cord, or cable used to steady, guide, or secure something. [From Middle English *gie*, guide, guy, from Old French *guie*, from *guier*, to guide.]

guy[2] (gī) *n.* **1.** *Informal* A man or boy; a fellow. **2. guys** People of either sex. [After *Guy* Fawkes (1570–1606), English conspirator.]

Guy·a·na (gī-ăn′ə *or* gī-ä′nə) A country of northeast South America on the Atlantic Ocean west of Suriname. Georgetown is the capital.

guz·zle (gŭz′əl) *tr. & intr.v.* **guz·zled, guz·zling, guz·zles** To drink greedily or habitually: *guzzle a can of soda.* **—guz′zler** *n.*

gym (jĭm) *n.* **1.** A gymnasium. **2.** A class in physical education: *I have gym at 10:15.*

gym·na·si·um (jĭm-nā′zē-əm) *n., pl.* **gym·na·si·ums** or **gym·na·si·a** (jĭm-nā′zē-ə) **1.** A room or building equipped for indoor sports: *play basketball in the gymnasium.* **2.** (gĭm-nä′zē-o͞om′) A high school in some European countries, especially Germany.

gym·nast (jĭm′năst′ *or* jĭm′nəst) *n.* A person who is skilled in gymnastics.

gym·nas·tic (jĭm-năs′tĭk) *adj.* Relating to gymnastics: *gymnastic exercise.*

gym·nas·tics (jĭm-năs′tĭks) *n.* Physical exercises designed to develop and display strength, balance, and agility, especially those performed on or with special apparatus.

gym·no·sperm (jĭm′nə-spûrm′) *n.* Any of a group of plants that produce seeds that are not enclosed in an ovary. Conifers and cycads are gymnosperms.

gy·ne·col·o·gist (gī′nĭ-kŏl′ə-jĭst) *n.* A physician who specializes in gynecology.

gy·ne·col·o·gy (gī′nĭ-kŏl′ə-jē) *n.* The branch of medicine that deals with the diagnosis and treatment of disorders of the female reproductive system. **—gy′ne·co·log′i·cal** (gī′nĭ-kə-lŏj′ĭ-kəl) *adj.*

gyo·za (gyō′zə) *n.* A pocket of dough that is stuffed with a filling and fried, steamed, or boiled. [From Japanese *gyōza.*]

gyp (jĭp) *Offensive Slang tr.v.* **gypped, gyp·ping, gyps** To deprive (another person) of something by fraud; cheat or swindle. ❖ *n.* A fraud or swindle.

gyp·sum (jĭp′səm) *n.* A white mineral containing calcium, used in manufacturing plaster of Paris, drywall, and fertilizers.

Gyp·sy also **Gip·sy** (jĭp′sē) *n., pl.* **Gyp·sies** also **Gip·sies 1.** *Often Offensive* A Romani. **2.** One who lives a wandering lifestyle. [From Middle English *Egipcien*, Egyptian (so called because the Romani people were thought to have come from Egypt).]

gypsy moth *n.* A small moth having hairy caterpillars that feed on leaves and do great damage to trees.

gy·rate (jī′rāt′) *intr.v.* **gy·rat·ed, gy·rat·ing, gy·rates 1.** To revolve around a fixed point or axis: *The earth gyrates about its axis.* **2.** To move in a spiral or spiral-like path: *The dancers gyrated around the room.* **—gy·ra′tion** *n.*

gyr·fal·con (jûr′făl′kən *or* jûr′fôl′kən *or* jûr′fô′kən) *n.* A large falcon of northern regions, usually having white and gray feathers.

gy·ro[1] (jī′rō) *n., pl.* **gy·ros** A gyroscope.

gy·ro[2] (jī′rō *or* yē′rō) *n., pl.* **gy·ros** A sandwich made usually of sliced roasted lamb, onion, and tomato on pita bread.

gy·ro·com·pass (jī′rō-kŭm′pəs *or* jī′rō-kŏm′pəs) *n.* A compass using a gyroscope instead of a magnetic needle. It points to true north instead of magnetic north.

gy·ro·scope (jī′rə-skōp′) *n.* An instrument consisting of a disk or wheel that spins rapidly about an axis like a top. The spinning motion keeps the axis fixed, though its base may be turned in any direction, making the gyroscope an accurate navigational instrument and an effective stabilizing device in ships and airplanes. [From Greek *guros*, circle.] **—gy′ro·scop′ic** (jī′rə-skŏp′ĭk) *adj.*

Johann Gutenberg

WRITERS CHOOSE THEIR WORDS

"Want one?" Andy's standing with a couple of cold water bottles in his hand.

"Sure." I take one, unscrew the cap, and **guzzle** half the bottle. I guess I was thirsty.

—Greg Logsted
Alibi Junior High

gyoza

gyroscope

WRITERS CHOOSE THEIR WORDS

Late in the evening, tired and happy and miles from home, they drew up on a remote common far from **habitations,** turned the horse loose to graze, and ate their simple supper sitting on the grass by the side of the cart.

—Kenneth Grahame *The Wind in the Willows*

hacksaw

ă	pat	ôr	core
ā	pay	oi	boy
âr	care	ou	out
ä	father	o͝o	took
ĕ	pet	o͝or	lure
ē	be	o͞o	boot
ĭ	pit	ŭ	cut
ī	bite	ûr	urge
îr	pier	th	thin
ŏ	pot	*th*	this
ō	toe	zh	vision
ô	paw	ə	about

h[1] or **H** (āch) *n., pl.* **h's** or **H's** also **hs** or **Hs** The eighth letter of the English alphabet.

h[2] *abbr.* An abbreviation of: **1.** height. **2.** hour.

H[1] The symbol for the element **hydrogen.**

H[2] *abbr.* An abbreviation of: **1.** high. **2.** hit (in baseball). **3.** hot.

ha also **hah** (hä) *interj.* An expression used to show surprise, wonder, triumph, or puzzlement.

Ha·bak·kuk[1] (**hăb′**ə-ko͝ok′ *or* hə-**băk′**ək) A Hebrew prophet of the seventh century BC.

Ha·bak·kuk[2] (**hăb′**ə-ko͝ok′ *or* hə-**băk′**ək) *n.* A book of the Bible in which Habakkuk prophesies that God will punish oppressors and sustain the innocent.

ha·be·as corpus (**hā′**bē-əs) *n.* **1.** A court order requiring that a person be brought before a court to determine whether he or she has been unlawfully imprisoned. **2.** The right of a citizen to obtain such an order. [From Latin *habeās corpus,* you shall have the body.]

hab·er·dash·er (**hăb′**ər-dăsh′ər) *n.* A dealer in articles of clothing for men.

hab·er·dash·er·y (**hăb′**ər-dăsh′ə-rē) *n., pl.* **hab·er·dash·er·ies 1.** A haberdasher's shop: *get a belt and cuff links at the haberdashery.* **2.** The goods a haberdasher sells.

ha·bil·i·ment (hə-**bĭl′**ə-mənt) *n.* often **habiliments** Clothes or garb, especially that associated with an office or profession: *the habiliments of the theater.*

hab·it (**hăb′**ĭt) *n.* **1.** A recurrent pattern of behavior that is acquired through repetition and is often done without thinking: *the habit of fidgeting in embarrassing situations.* **2.** Customary practice or manner: *the habit of taking an early-morning walk.* **3.** An addiction. **4a.** The distinctive clothing or costume worn by members of a religious order: *a nun's habit.* **b.** A riding habit. [From Middle English, from Latin *habitus,* behavior, custom.]

SYNONYMS habit, practice, custom These nouns refer to a pattern of behavior established by repetition. **Habit** means a way of acting that has been repeated so many times it no longer involves conscious thought: *You have a habit of covering your mouth when you laugh.* **Practice** means a routine, often chosen way of acting: *It is their practice to eat dinner early.* **Custom** means a usually longstanding practice in line with social conventions: *It is a Japanese custom not to wear shoes in the house.*

hab·it·a·ble (**hăb′**ĭ-tə-bəl) *adj.* Suitable or fit to live in or on: *a habitable house; a habitable planet.* **—hab′it·a·bil′i·ty** *n.*

hab·i·tat (**hăb′**ĭ-tăt′) *n.* **1.** The natural environment in which a species or group of species lives: *managing wildlife habitat.* **2.** A particular kind of natural environment: *the birds found in a prairie habitat.*

hab·i·ta·tion (hăb′ĭ-**tā′**shən) *n.* **1.** A place in which to live; a residence. **2.** The act of inhabiting or the condition of being inhabited: *The Antarctic climate is not suitable for human habitation.*

hab·it-form·ing (**hăb′**ĭt-fôr′mĭng) *adj.* Leading to or causing addiction: *a habit-forming drug.*

ha·bit·u·al (hə-**bĭch′**o͞o-əl) *adj.* **1a.** Being a habit: *Matt's habitual lateness annoyed everyone.* **b.** Behaving in a certain manner by habit: *a habitual early riser.* **2.** Established by long use; usual: *her habitual route to the store.* **—ha·bit′u·al·ly** *adv.*

ha·bit·u·ate (hə-**bĭch′**o͞o-āt′) *tr.v.* **ha·bit·u·at·ed, ha·bit·u·at·ing, ha·bit·u·ates** To familiarize by repetition or constant exposure; accustom: *He is habituated to commuting to work every day.* **—ha·bit′u·a′tion** *n.*

Habs·burg or **Haps·burg** (**hăps′**bûrg′ *or* **häps′**bo͝ork′) A royal German family whose members ruled many European states from the late Middle Ages to the 1900s.

ha·ci·en·da (hä′sē-**ĕn′**də) *n.* **1.** A large estate or plantation in a Spanish-speaking region. **2.** The house of the owner of such an estate. [From Spanish, from Latin *facienda,* things to be done.]

hack[1] (hăk) *v.* **hacked, hack·ing, hacks** *—tr.* **1.** To cut or chop with repeated and irregular blows: *hacked down the saplings.* **2.** To make or shape by such blows using a sharp implement: *hack a trail through the thickets.* **3.** *Informal* **a.** To modify (a computer program). **b.** To gain access to (a computer file or network) without authorization. **4.** *Slang* To cut or mutilate as if by hacking: *hacked a large amount off the budget.* **5.** *Slang* To cope with successfully; manage: *Do you think you can hack such responsibilities? —intr.* **1.** To chop or cut by hacking: *hack at a tree stump.* **2.** To work or perform as a hacker. **3.** To cough roughly or harshly: *hacking with a bad cold.* ❖ *n.* **1.** A rough irregular cut or notch made by hacking. **2.** A blow or swing made with a cutting implement. **3.** A rough dry cough. [From Middle English *hakken,* from Old English *haccian.*]

hack[2] (hăk) *n.* **1.** A horse used for routine riding or driving; a hackney. **2.** A person, especially a writer, who does routine work for hire. **3.** A carriage or hackney for hire. **4.** *Informal* A taxicab. [Short for *hackney.*]

hack·er (**hăk′**ər) *n. Informal* **1.** A person skilled in using or programming a computer; a computer buff. **2.** A person who illegally accesses a computer network, as to gain secret information.

hack·le (**hăk′**əl) *n.* **1.** One of the long, slender, often glossy feathers on the neck of a bird, especially a rooster. **2. hackles** The hairs along the back of the neck of an animal, such as a dog, that can be raised upright: *The wolf raised its hackles and bared its teeth.*

hack·ney (**hăk′**nē) *n., pl.* **hack·neys 1.** A horse suited for routine riding or driving. **2.** A coach or carriage for hire.

hack·neyed (**hăk′**nēd) *adj.* Overfamiliar through overuse; trite: *writing full of hackneyed phrases.*

hack·saw (**hăk′**sô′) *n.* A saw with a tough, fine-toothed blade stretched taut in a frame, used especially for cutting metal.

had (hăd) *v.* Past tense and past participle of **have.**

had·dock (hăd′ək) *n., pl.* **haddock** or **had·docks** A food fish of the northern Atlantic Ocean, related to and resembling the cod but having a dark spot on each side.

Ha·de·an Time (hā-dē′ən) *n.* The period of time between 4.6 and 3.8 billion years ago. During Hadean Time, the solar system was forming and the earth was solidifying.

Ha·des (hā′dēz) *n.* **1.** In Greek mythology, the god of the underworld and the dispenser of earthly riches, identified with the Roman Pluto. **2.** In Greek mythology, the underworld kingdom. **3.** also **hades** Hell.

had·n't (hăd′nt) Contraction of *had not.*

had·ro·saur (hăd′rə-sôr′) *n.* A duck-billed dinosaur.

hadst (hădst) *v. Archaic* A second person singular past tense of **have.**

haf·ni·um (hăf′nē-əm) *n. Symbol* **Hf** A silvery metallic element that is found in zirconium ores and is used to control nuclear reactions. Atomic number 72. See **Periodic Table.** [After *Hafnia,* Medieval Latin name for Copenhagen, Denmark.]

haft (hăft) *n.* A handle or hilt, especially the handle of a tool or weapon.

hag (hăg) *n.* **1.** An old woman considered ugly or frightful. **2.** A witch; a sorceress.

hag·fish (hăg′fĭsh′) *n.* Any of various long thin slimy ocean fishes that lack jaws and vertebrae and have a sucking mouth with sharp toothlike projections.

Hag·ga·i[1] (hăg′ē-ī′ *or* hăg′ī′) A Hebrew prophet of the sixth century BC.

Hag·ga·i[2] (hăg′ē-ī′ *or* hăg′ī′) *n.* A book of the Bible that urges the rebuilding of the Temple of Jerusalem.

hag·gard (hăg′ərd) *adj.* Appearing worn and exhausted; gaunt: *a haggard face.* **—hag′gard·ly** *adv.* **—hag′gard·ness** *n.*

hag·gle (hăg′əl) *intr.v.* **hag·gled, hag·gling, hag·gles 1.** To bargain, as over the price of something: *a shopper haggling with a fruit seller.* **2.** To argue in an attempt to come to terms: *The countries haggled over their boundary.* **—hag′gler** *n.*

Hag·i·og·ra·pha (hăg′ē-ŏg′rə-fə *or* hā′jē-ŏg′rə-fə) *n.* The third division of the Hebrew Scriptures; the Writings.

Hague (hāg), **The.** The administrative capital of the Netherlands, in the western part of the country near the North Sea. The Hague is the seat of the country's legislature and supreme court and of the International Court of Justice.

hah (hä) *interj.* Variant of **ha.**

Hai·da (hī′də) *n., pl.* **Haida** or **Hai·das 1.** A member of a Native American people of several islands off the coasts of Alaska and British Columbia. **2.** Any of the languages of the Haida. **—Hai′dan** *adj.*

hai·ku (hī′ko͞o) *n., pl.* **haiku** also **hai·kus** A form of Japanese poetry consisting of three unrhymed lines of five, seven, and five syllables. [From Japanese *haiku* : *hai,* amusement + *ku,* phrase.]

hail[1] (hāl) *n.* **1.** Precipitation in the form of rounded pellets of ice and hard snow that usually falls during thunderstorms. **2.** Something that falls with the force of a shower of hail: *a hail of pebbles; a hail of criticism.* ❖ *v.* **hailed, hail·ing, hails** *—intr.* To fall as hail: *It hailed this afternoon.* *—tr.* To pour (something) down or forth: *The two drivers hailed insults at each other.* [From Old English *hægl.*]

❑ *These sound alike:* **hail**[1] (ice pellets), **hail**[2] (greeting), **hale**[1] (healthy), **hale**[2] (force).

hail[2] (hāl) *tr.v.* **hailed, hail·ing, hails 1.** To salute or greet: *hail a friend across the street.* **2.** To call out or yell in order to catch the attention of: *hail a cab.* ❖ *interj.* An expression used to show a greeting or tribute. ◆ **hail from** To come or originate from: *They hail from Ohio.* [From Middle English *heilen,* from *(wæs) hæil,* (be) healthy.] **—hail′er** *n.* —SEE NOTE AT **heal.**

❑ *These sound alike:* **hail**[2] (greeting), **hail**[1] (ice pellets), **hale**[1] (healthy), **hale**[2] (force).

Hai·le Se·las·sie I (hī′lē sə-lăs′ē *or* hī′lē sə-lä′sē) Title of Ras Tafari Makonnen. 1892–1975. Emperor of Ethiopia (1930–1974) who was deposed in a military coup (1974). He is regarded as a divine figure by the Rastafarians.

Haile Selassie I

Hail Mary *n., pl.* **Hail Marys** A Roman Catholic prayer addressed to the Virgin Mary.

hail·stone (hāl′stōn′) *n.* A pellet of hail.

hail·storm (hāl′stôrm′) *n.* A storm in which hail falls.

hair (hâr) *n.* **1.** One of the fine strands that grow from the skin of humans and other mammals: *She plucked some hairs from her eyebrows.* **2.** A slender growth resembling a mammalian hair, found on insects and other animals. **3.** A mass of such fine strands: *My cat has soft hair. This caterpillar is covered with hair.* **4.** A fine strand growing from the outer layer of a plant. **5.** A tiny distance or narrow margin: *We won by a hair.* [From Old English *hēr.*]

❑ *These sound alike:* **hair, hare** (rabbit).

hair·ball (hâr′bôl′) *n.* A small mass of hair in an animal's stomach or intestine that forms as the animal swallows hair while licking its coat.

hair·breadth (hâr′brĕdth′) *adj.* & *n.* Variant of **hairsbreadth.**

hair·brush (hâr′brŭsh′) *n.* A brush for the hair.

hair·cloth (hâr′klôth′) *n.* A wiry fabric with horsehair or camelhair woven into it, used in upholstery or to stiffen clothing.

hair·cut (hâr′kŭt′) *n.* **1.** The act or an instance of cutting the hair: *You need a haircut.* **2.** A style in which hair is cut: *a short haircut.*

hair·do (hâr′do͞o′) *n., pl.* **hair·dos** A hairstyle.

hair·dress·er (hâr′drĕs′ər) *n.* A person who cuts or styles hair.

hair·less (hâr′lĭs) *adj.* Having little or no hair.

hair·line (hâr′līn′) *n.* **1.** The edge of hair growing above the forehead or around the head. **2.** A very thin line.

hair·net (hâr′nĕt′) *n.* A mesh for holding the hair in place.

hair·piece (hâr′pēs′) *n.* A covering or bunch of human or artificial hair worn to cover a bald spot or as part of a hairdo.

hair·pin (hâr′pĭn′) *n.* A fine metal pin, often bent into the shape of a U, used to secure a hairdo.

hair-rais·ing (hâr′rā′zĭng) *adj.* Causing excitement, terror, or thrills: *a hair-raising ride on a roller coaster.*

hairs·breadth or **hair's-breadth** (hârz′brĕdth′) also **hair·breadth** (hâr′brĕdth′) *n.* A small space, distance, or margin: *win by a hairsbreadth.*

hair·split·ting (hâr′splĭt′ĭng) *n.* The making of distinctions that are too fine to be important: *The hairsplitting between the lawyers annoyed the judge.* **—hair′split′ter** *n.*

hair spray *n.* A preparation sprayed on the hair to keep it in place.

hair·spring (hâr′sprĭng′) *n.* A fine spring that regulates the movement of the balance wheel of a watch or clock.

hair·style (hâr′stīl′) *n.* A style in which hair is cut and arranged.

hair trigger *n.* A gun trigger that responds to a very slight pressure.

hair·y (hâr′ē) *adj.* **hair·i·er, hair·i·est 1.** Covered with hair or projections resembling hair: *a hairy caterpillar.* **2.** Consisting of or resembling hair: *a hairy blanket.* **3.** *Slang* Fraught with difficulties; hazardous: *a hairy escape.* **—hair′i·ness** *n.*

USAGE

half The phrases *a half, half of,* and *half a* or *half an* are all correct. They may differ slightly in meaning. For example, we say *a half day* when *day* has the special sense "a working day," and the phrase then means "4 hours." *Half of a day* and *half a day* are not restricted in this way and can mean either 4 or 12 hours.

half hitch

half note
A. half note
B. quarter note

ă	pat	ôr	core
ā	pay	oi	boy
âr	care	ou	out
ä	father	o͝o	took
ĕ	pet	o͝or	lure
ē	be	o͞o	boot
ĭ	pit	ŭ	cut
ī	bite	ûr	urge
îr	pier	th	thin
ŏ	pot	*th*	this
ō	toe	zh	vision
ô	paw	ə	about

Hai·ti (hā′tē) A country of the West Indies made up of the western part of the island of Hispaniola and two offshore islands. The country gained its independence from France in 1804 following a slave revolt. Port-au-Prince is the capital.

Hai·tian (hā′shən) *adj.* Relating to Haiti or its people or culture. ❖ *n.* **1.** A native or inhabitant of Haiti. **2.** Haitian Creole.

Haitian Creole *n.* A language spoken by the majority of Haitians, based on French and various African languages.

hajj or **haj** (hăj) *n., pl.* **hajj·es** or **haj·es** A pilgrimage to Mecca during the last month of the Islamic calendar. Every Muslim who is capable of it is expected to undertake the hajj at least once in his or her life.

hake (hāk) *n., pl.* **hake** or **hakes** Any of various ocean fishes that closely resemble the cod but are usually smaller.

hal·berd (hăl′bərd *or* hôl′bərd) *n.* A weapon used in the 1400s and 1500s, having an axe blade and a spike mounted on a long pole.

hal·cy·on (hăl′sē-ən) *n.* A fabled bird identified with the kingfisher that is supposed to have the power to calm the wind and the waves while it nests on the sea during the winter solstice. ❖ *adj.* Calm and peaceful; tranquil: *halcyon days.*

hale[1] (hāl) *adj.* **hal·er, hal·est** Free from infirmity or illness; healthy. [From Old English *hāl.*] —SEE NOTE AT **heal.**

❑ *These sound alike:* **hale[1]** (healthy), **hail[1]** (ice pellets), **hail[2]** (greeting), **hale[2]** (force).

hale[2] (hāl) *tr.v.* **haled, hal·ing, hales 1.** To force to go: *hale an offender into court.* **2.** *Archaic* To pull, drag, or hoist. [From Middle English *halen,* to pull, drag, from Old French *haler,* of Germanic origin.]

❑ *These sound alike:* **hale[2]** (force), **hail[1]** (ice pellets), **hail[2]** (greeting), **hale[1]** (healthy).

Hale (hāl), **Nathan** 1755–1776. American Revolutionary soldier who was hanged by the British as a spy.

half (hăf) *n., pl.* **halves** (hăvz) **1a.** One of two equal parts that together make up a whole: *Fifty cents is one half of a dollar.* **b.** One of two approximately equal parts: *the smaller half of a sandwich.* **2.** In football and other sports, either of the two equal time periods that make up a game. **3.** Half an hour: *at half past one.* ❖ *adj.* **1a.** Being one of two equal parts. **b.** Being approximately a half: *a half glass of milk.* **2.** Partial or incomplete: *a half truth.* ❖ *adv.* **1.** To the extent of exactly or nearly 50 percent: *a half empty tank.* **2.** Not completely; partly: *I was still half asleep.* ◆ **in half** Into halves. **not half** Not at all: *not half bad.* [From Old English *healf.*] —SEE NOTE.

half·back (hăf′băk′) *n.* **1.** In football, one of two running backs positioned to the sides behind the quarterback when the ball is snapped. **2.** In certain sports such as soccer and field hockey, one of several players positioned behind the forward line and in front of the fullbacks.

half-baked (hăf′**băkt′**) *adj.* **1.** Only partly baked. **2.** *Informal* Not fully thought out; poorly conceived: *a half-baked idea.*

half brother *n.* A brother who has only one biological parent in common with another sibling.

half-dol·lar (hăf′dŏl′ər) *n.* A US coin worth 50 cents.

half gainer *n.* A dive in which the diver leaves the board facing the water and rotates through half a backward somersault to enter the water headfirst.

half·heart·ed (hăf′här′tĭd) *adj.* Showing or feeling little enthusiasm, interest, or heart; uninspired: *With so much work left, I made only a halfhearted attempt to finish it.* **—half′heart′ed·ly** *adv.*

half hitch *n.* A knot made by looping a rope around an object and then back around itself, bringing the end of the rope through the loop.

half-hour (hăf′**our′**) *n.* **1.** A period of 30 minutes. **2.** The middle point of an hour: *News bulletins are broadcast on the half-hour.*

half-life (hăf′līf′) *n.* The time needed for half the nuclei in a sample of radioactive material to undergo decay.

half-mast (hăf′**măst′**) *n.* The position about halfway up a mast or pole at which a flag is flown as a symbol of mourning for the dead or as a signal of distress.

half-moon (hăf′**mo͞on′**) *n.* The moon when just half of its disk appears lighted, at the end of the first or third quarter.

half nelson *n.* A wrestling hold in which one arm is passed under an opponent's arm from behind to the back of the neck.

half note *n.* A musical note having one half the time value of a whole note.

half·pen·ny (hā′pə-nē *or* hāp′nē) *n., pl.* **half·pence** (hā′pəns) or **half·pen·nies** A former British coin worth one half of a penny.

half-pint (hăf′pīnt′) *Slang n.* A small person or animal.

half-pipe (hăf′pīp′) *n.* A structure that is shaped like a trough and used for stunts in sports such as in-line skating and snowboarding.

half rest *n.* A musical rest having one-half the time value of a whole rest.

half sister *n.* A sister who has only one biological parent in common with another sibling.

half-staff (hăf′**stăf′**) *n.* Half-mast.

half step *n.* A musical interval equal to one half the interval between full tones in a scale. Half steps separate C, C-sharp, and D.

half·time (hăf′tīm′) *n.* The intermission between halves in games of certain sports, such as basketball and football.

half·tone (hăf′tōn′) *n.* **1.** A tone or color between very light and very dark. **2.** A picture in which the shades of light and dark are produced by tiny dots either closely or more widely spaced. **3.** A half step; a semitone.

half-track (hăf′trăk′) *n.* A lightly armored military vehicle that has caterpillar treads in the rear and conventional wheels in front.

half·way (hăf′wā′) *adj.* **1.** Midway between two points or conditions: *the halfway point on the trail to the summit.* **2.** Reaching or including only half or a portion; partial: *halfway measures to control pollution.* ❖ *adv.* **1.** To or at half the distance: *I'll meet you halfway between your house and mine.* **2.** Partially: *I halfway gave in to their demands.*

halfway house *n.* A building providing temporary housing for people who have been released from an institution, where they may receive special services, such as job training and counseling, before living independently.

hal·i·but (hăl′ə-bət *or* hŏl′ə-bət) *n., pl.* **halibut** or **hal·i·buts** Any of several large edible flatfishes of northern ocean waters.

Hal·i·fax (hăl′ə-făks′) The capital of Nova Scotia, Canada, in the south-central part of the province on the Atlantic Ocean. It was founded in 1749.

hal·ite (hăl′īt′ *or* hā′līt′) *n.* Rock salt. [From Greek *hals,* salt.]

hal·i·to·sis (hăl′ĭ-tō′sĭs) *n.* Bad breath.

hall (hôl) *n.* **1.** A corridor or passageway in a building: *The hall had several classrooms off it.* **2.** An entrance room or vestibule in a building; a lobby: *We waited in the hall at the elevators.* **3.** A building where meetings, parties, concerts, or other gatherings are held: *a lecture hall.* **4.** A building used for the meetings, entertainments, or living quarters of a social or religious organization. **5.**

A school, college, or university building: *Students live in three halls at the back of campus.* **6.** The main house of an English landowner. [From Old English *heall,* place covered with a roof.]

❑ *These sound alike:* **hall, haul** (drag).

hal·le·lu·jah (hăl′ə-**lo͞o′**yə) *interj.* An expression used to express praise or joy. ❖ *n.* **1.** An exclamation of "hallelujah." **2.** A song or hymn of praise that is based on the word *hallelujah.* [From Hebrew *halləlû-yāh,* praise Yahweh.]

Hal·ley's comet (**hăl′**ēz *or* **hā′**lēz) *n.* A comet last observed from Earth in 1986, having a period of 76 years. [After Edmund *Halley* (1656–1742), English astronomer.]

hall·mark (**hôl′**märk′) *n.* **1.** A mark that indicates excellence or quality. **2.** A mark indicating a certain level of purity, stamped in England on articles made of gold and silver. **3.** A distinguishing characteristic, feature, or trait: *Good design and quality materials are hallmarks of fine automobiles.*

hal·loo (hə-**lo͞o′**) *interj.* **1.** An expression used to get someone's attention. **2.** An expression used to urge on hounds in a hunt. ❖ *n., pl.* **hal·loos** A shout or call of "halloo."

hal·low (**hăl′**ō) *tr.v.* **hal·lowed, hal·low·ing, hal·lows 1.** To make or set apart as holy: *An ancient burial mound hallows this ground.* **2.** To respect or honor greatly: *hallow the memory of one's ancestors.*

hal·lowed (**hăl′**ōd) *adj.* **1.** Sanctified; consecrated: *hallowed ground.* **2.** Honored; revered: *a hallowed name.*

Hal·low·een also **Hal·low·e'en** (hăl′ə-**wēn′** *or* hŏl′ə-**wēn′**) *n.* October 31, celebrated by children going door to door in costumes and begging treats and playing pranks.

hal·lu·ci·nate (hə-**lo͞o′**sə-nāt′) *intr.v.* **hal·lu·ci·nat·ed, hal·lu·ci·nat·ing, hal·lu·ci·nates** To have hallucinations.

hal·lu·ci·na·tion (hə-lo͞o′sə-**nā′**shən) *n.* An image, sound, or other sensory perception that is experienced mentally but has no basis in reality: *People with high fevers may have hallucinations.*

hal·lu·ci·na·to·ry (hə-**lo͞o′**sə-nə-tôr′ē) *adj.* **1.** Relating to or marked by hallucination: *a hallucinatory experience.* **2.** Hallucinogenic.

hal·lu·ci·no·gen (hə-**lo͞o′**sə-nə-jən) *n.* A drug that produces or tends to produce hallucinations.

hal·lu·ci·no·gen·ic (hə-lo͞o′sə-nə-**jĕn′**ĭk) *adj.* Producing or tending to produce hallucinations: *a hallucinogenic drug.*

hall·way (**hôl′**wā′) *n.* **1.** A corridor in a building. **2.** An entrance hall: *The mail is left in the hallway of our apartment building.*

ha·lo (**hā′**lō) *n., pl.* **ha·los** or **ha·loes 1.** A ring or disk of light surrounding the heads or bodies of sacred figures, such as saints in religious paintings. **2.** A circular band of light that surrounds the sun, the moon, a star, or another light source, resulting from effects such as reflection and refraction of light through ice crystals suspended in air. [From Greek *halōs,* threshing floor, disk around the sun or moon.]

hal·o·gen (**hăl′**ə-jən) *n.* A group of elements with similar properties, including fluorine, chlorine, bromine, iodine, and astatine. Halogens combine directly with most metals to form salts. ❖ *adj.* **1.** Relating to the group of elements that are halogens. **2.** Relating to a bright incandescent light bulb that contains a halogen gas that keeps the filament from falling apart at higher temperatures.

halt (hôlt) *n.* A temporary stop of movement or progress: *The car rolled to a halt when it stalled.* ❖ *intr. & tr.v.* **halt·ed, halt·ing, halts** To stop or cause to stop: *The hikers halted for lunch and some rest. The government hopes to halt air pollution.* See Synonyms at **stop.** [From German *Halt,* from Old High German *haltan,* to hold back.]

hal·ter (**hôl′**tər) *n.* **1.** A device of rope or leather straps that fits around the head or neck of an animal and is used to lead or secure the animal. **2.** A rope with a noose used for execution by hanging. **3.** A woman's top that ties behind the neck, leaving the shoulders and back bare. [From Old English *hælftre.*]

halt·ing (**hôl′**tĭng) *adj.* Hesitant or wavering: *a low and halting voice.*

halve (hăv) *tr.v.* **halved, halv·ing, halves 1.** To divide (something) into two equal portions or parts: *A friend and I halved the remaining apple.* **2.** To reduce or lessen by half: *The storekeeper halved the prices for the sale.* [From Middle English *halven,* from *half,* half.]

❑ *These sound alike:* **halve, have** (possess).

halves (hăvz) *n.* Plural of **half.**

hal·yard (**hăl′**yərd) *n.* A rope that runs through a pulley on a mast or flagpole and is used to raise or lower a sail or a flag.

ham (hăm) *n.* **1.** The hind leg of certain animals, especially of a hog. **2.** A cut of meat from the thigh of a hog. **3. hams** The buttocks and backs of the thighs. **4.** A performer who overacts or exaggerates. **5.** A licensed amateur radio operator. ❖ *intr.v.* **hammed, ham·ming, hams** To exaggerate or overdo a dramatic role, for example; overact. [From Old English *hamm.*]

Ham·burg (**hăm′**bûrg′ *or* **häm′**bo͝org′) A city of northern Germany on the Elbe River northwest of Berlin. It was founded in the early ninth century.

ham·burg·er (**hăm′**bûr′gər) *n.* **1.** Ground meat, usually beef. **2.** A patty of such meat. **3.** A sandwich made with a patty of ground meat usually served in a roll or bun with various toppings. [Short for *Hamburger steak,* after *Hamburg,* Germany.]

Ham·il·ton (**hăm′**əl-tən) **1.** The capital of Bermuda, on Bermuda Island. It was founded in 1790. **2.** A city of southeast Ontario, Canada, at the western end of Lake Ontario southwest of Toronto.

Hamilton, Alexander 1755?–1804. American politician. The first US secretary of the treasury (1789–1795), he established the national bank and public credit system.

ham·let (**hăm′**lĭt) *n.* A small village.

Hamm (hăm), **Mariel Margaret** Known as "Mia." Born 1972. American soccer player who led the US women's soccer team to gold medals at the 1996 and 2004 Olympics.

ham·mer (**hăm′**ər) *n.* **1.** A hand tool consisting of a heavy, usually metal head attached at a right angle to a handle, used chiefly for driving in nails or for pounding and shaping metals. **2.** Something used or shaped like a hammer, such as one of the padded wooden pieces that strikes the strings of a piano, or the device used to strike a gong or bell, or the part of a gun that strikes the firing pin of a gun. **3.** A metal ball weighing 16 pounds and having a long wire or wooden handle by which athletes throw it for distance in track-and-field competitions. **4.** The largest of the three small bones in the middle ear that transmit vibrations to the inner ear; the malleus. **5.** A small mallet used by auctioneers. ❖ *v.* **ham·mered, ham·mer·ing, ham·mers** —*tr.* **1.** To hit, especially repeatedly, with a hammer; pound: *hammer a nail.* **2.** To beat into shape with a hammer: *hammer iron into a horseshoe.* **3.** To accomplish or produce with difficulty or effort: *The two sides in the dispute hammered out an agreement.* **4.** To force upon by constant repetition: *hammered the safety guidelines into the students' heads.* **5.** To defeat soundly: *hammered the visiting team 49–0.* —*intr.* **1.** To hit something repeatedly and firmly, especially with a hammer: *hammer on a door.* **2.** *Informal* To keep doing or trying to do something: *The researchers hammered away at the problem.* [From Old English *hamor.*] —**ham′mer·er** *n.*

Halley's comet

halo

halter

Mia Hamm
photographed in 2011

hammerhead

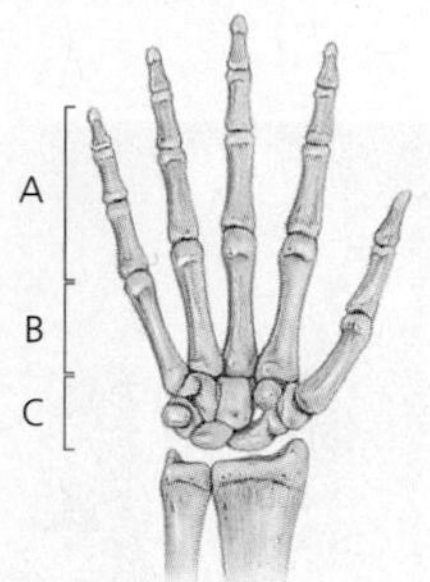

hand
A. phalanges
B. metacarpals
C. carpals

George Handel

ă	pat	ôr	core
ā	pay	oi	boy
âr	care	ou	out
ä	father	o͝o	took
ĕ	pet	o͝or	lure
ē	be	o͞o	boot
ĭ	pit	ŭ	cut
ī	bite	ûr	urge
îr	pier	th	thin
ŏ	pot	*th*	this
ō	toe	zh	vision
ô	paw	ə	about

ham·mer·head (hăm′ər-hĕd′) *n.* Any of several predatory sharks having the sides of the head elongated into fleshy extensions with the eyes at the ends.

ham·mer·lock (hăm′ər-lŏk′) *n.* A wrestling hold in which the opponent's arm is pulled behind the back and twisted upward.

ham·mock (hăm′ək) *n.* A hanging, easily swung length of canvas or heavy netting suspended between two trees or other supports and used as a seat or a bed. [From Taíno.]

Ham·mu·ra·bi (hăm′ə-**rä′**bē *or* hä′mə-**rä′**bē) Died 1750 BC. Babylonian king (1792–1750) who made Babylon the chief Mesopotamian kingdom.

ham·per¹ (hăm′pər) *tr.v.* **ham·pered, ham·per·ing, ham·pers** To prevent the progress, free movement, or action of: *The snowstorm hampered our plane's flight.* [From Middle English *hamperen.*]

ham·per² (hăm′pər) *n.* A large basket, usually with a cover. [From Middle English, from Old French *hanepier*, a case for holding goblets, from *hanap*, goblet.]

ham·ster (hăm′stər) *n.* Any of various small rodents native to Eurasia, having soft fur, large cheek pouches, and a short tail. Hamsters are often kept as pets or used as laboratory animals.

ham·string (hăm′strĭng′) *n.* **1.** Either of two large tendons at the back of the human knee. **2.** Any of the three muscles at the back of the thigh that together act to bend the knee. **3.** A large tendon at the back of the hind leg of a horse or other four-footed animal. ❖ *tr.v.* **ham·strung** (hăm′strŭng′), **ham·string·ing, ham·strings 1.** To cripple (a person or animal) by cutting a hamstring. **2.** To destroy or hinder the efficiency of; frustrate: *A lack of resources hamstrung the company's growth.*

Han·cock (hăn′kŏk′), **John** 1737–1793. American politician and Revolutionary leader who was the first to sign the Declaration of Independence.

hand (hănd) *n.* **1a.** The part of the human arm that is below the wrist. It consists of a palm to which four fingers and a thumb are attached, and is used for holding or grasping. **b.** A similar part in other animals, such as monkeys and other primates. **2.** Something like a hand in shape or use, especially a pointer on a dial, as that of a clock or gauge. **3.** A person's handwriting or a style of handwriting: *The manuscript is written in the author's own hand.* **4.** Side or direction indicated according to the way in which one is facing: *At my right hand you see a box.* **5.** Assistance with a task: *Give me a hand with this heavy carton.* **6.** A person who does manual labor; a laborer: *The field hands picked cotton.* **7.** A member of a group or crew: *All hands on deck!* **8.** An aptitude or ability: *decided to try my hand at painting.* **9.** A manner or way of performing something: *The surgeon works with a delicate hand.* **10.** An influence or effect: *She had a hand in the decision.* **11.** A round of applause: *The audience gave us a tremendous hand.* **12.** A pledge of marriage or permission to marry: *ask for someone's hand.* **13a.** A player in card games: *We need four hands for bridge.* **b.** The cards dealt to and held by such a player: *Don't look at my hand.* **c.** One round of a card game: *I'll play one more hand.* **14.** often **hands** Possession, ownership, or keeping: *The books should be in your hands by noon.* **15.** Participation or involvement: *You can see the hand of the teacher in their class play.* **16.** A unit of length equal to four inches (10.2 centimeters), used especially to indicate the height of horses. ❖ *tr.v.* **hand·ed, hand·ing, hands 1.** To give or pass with or as if with the hands; transmit: *Hand the flashlight to me.* **2.** To lead or help with the hand: *The usher handed the guests to their seats.* ◆ **at hand 1.** Close by; near: *remain close at hand.* **2.** About to occur; imminent: *Spring is at hand.* **at the hand of** or **at the hands of** By the action of: *He died at the hands of an assassin.* **by hand** Performed manually: *These dresses have been sewn by hand.* **hand and foot** With concerted, never-ending effort: *We waited on them hand and foot.* **hand down 1.** To give or pass on, as an inheritance to one's heirs: *The family handed down the painting from generation to generation.* **2.** To make and pronounce an official decision, especially a court verdict. **hand in** To turn in; submit: *Hand in your term papers by May 1.* **hand in glove** In close association or on intimate terms: *The partners worked together hand in glove.* **hand in hand** In cooperation; jointly: *Economic growth and literacy go hand in hand.* **hand off** In football, to put the ball in a teammate's arms without throwing it. **hand out** To give out; distribute: *handed out leaflets to passers-by.* **hand over** To release or relinquish to another: *Hand over the goods.* **hand over fist** *Informal* At a tremendous rate: *making money hand over fist.* **hands down** With no trouble; easily: *win the award hands down.* **in hand 1.** Under control: *We succeeded in keeping the situation in hand.* **2.** Held in one's hand: *I arrived at my exam room with pencil in hand.* **on the one hand** or **on one hand** From one standpoint. **on the other hand** From another standpoint. **out of hand** Out of control: *We can't let our expenses get out of hand.* [From Old English.]

hand·bag (hănd′băg′) *n.* **1.** A woman's purse used to hold money, keys, or other personal items. **2.** A piece of small hand luggage.

hand·ball (hănd′bôl′) *n.* **1.** A game in which two or more players hit a ball against a wall with the hand usually while wearing a special glove. **2.** The small rubber ball used in this game. **3.** often **hand ball** In soccer, a violation of the rules in which a player other than the goalie strikes or carries the ball with the hand or arm.

hand·bill (hănd′bĭl′) *n.* A printed sheet or pamphlet distributed by hand; a leaflet.

hand·book (hănd′bo͝ok′) *n.* A small reference book or manual providing specific information on a certain subject.

hand·cart (hănd′kärt′) *n.* A small, usually two-wheeled cart pushed or pulled by hand.

hand·craft (hănd′krăft′) *n.* Variant of **handicraft.** ❖ *tr.v.* (hănd-**krăft′**) **hand·craft·ed, hand·craft·ing, hand·crafts** To fashion or make by hand: *handcraft wooden toys.*

hand·cuff (hănd′kŭf′) *n.* often **handcuffs** A restraining device consisting of a pair of metal hoops that are chained together and that can be tightened and locked around the wrists. ❖ *tr.v.* **hand·cuffed, hand·cuff·ing, hand·cuffs** To restrain with or as if with handcuffs: *The sheriff handcuffed the prisoner.*

hand·ed (hăn′dĭd) *adj.* **1.** Relating to dexterity, preference, or size with respect to a hand or hands: *left-handed; large-handed.* **2.** Relating to a specified number of people: *a four-handed card game.*

Han·del (hăn′dl), **George Frederick** 1685–1759. German-born British composer whose works include *Messiah* (1742).

hand·ful (hănd′fo͝ol′) *n., pl.* **hand·fuls 1.** The amount that a hand can hold: *a handful of coins.* **2.** A small but unspecified quantity or number: *a handful of people.* **3.** A person or thing that is difficult to control or handle: *That toddler is a real handful.*

hand·gun (hănd′gŭn′) *n.* A firearm that can be used with one hand; a pistol.

hand·held or **hand-held** (hănd′hĕld′) *adj.* Compact enough to be used while being held in the hand or hands: *a handheld video camera.*

hand·i·cap (hăn′dē-kăp′) *n.* **1.** A race or contest in which contestants are given advantages or compensations to equalize the chances of winning. **2.** Such an advantage or disadvantage. **3.** A physical or mental disability. **4.** A hindrance: *Disorganization is my chief handicap.* ❖

tr.v. **hand·i·capped, hand·i·cap·ping, hand·i·caps 1.** To cause to be at a disadvantage; impede: *A sore throat handicapped the singer.* **2.** To give a handicap or handicaps to (a contestant): *handicap a contestant in a golf match.*

hand·i·capped (hăn′dē-kăpt′) *adj.* Physically or mentally disabled. ❖ *n. (used with a plural verb)* People with a physical or mental disability.

hand·i·craft (hăn′dē-krăft′) also **hand·craft** (hănd′-krăft′) *n.* **1.** Skill and facility with the hands. **2.** A craft or occupation requiring skilled use of the hands, as weaving or basketry. **3.** An object produced by skilled hands: *The shop sells handicrafts from Bolivia.*

hand·i·ly (hăn′dĭ-lē *or* hăn′dl-ē) *adv.* **1.** Easily: *The student answered the test questions handily.* **2.** In a convenient manner.

hand·i·work (hăn′dē-wûrk′) *n.* **1.** Work performed by hand: *Knitting is a handiwork that requires dexterity.* **2.** The product of a person's efforts and actions.

hand·ker·chief (hăng′kər-chĭf *or* hăng′kər-chēf′) *n., pl.* **hand·ker·chiefs** also **hand·ker·chieves** (hăng′kər-chĭvz *or* hăng′kər-chēvz′) **1.** A small square of cloth used especially to wipe the nose and mouth. **2.** A kerchief or scarf.

han·dle (hăn′dl) *v.* **han·dled, han·dling, han·dles** —*tr.* **1.** To touch, hold, or lift with the hands: *Please do not handle the merchandise.* **2.** To operate with the hands; manipulate: *know how to handle chopsticks.* **3.** To deal with or treat in a specified way: *handles problems well.* **4.** To manage, direct, or train: *handle a tennis player.* **5.** To deal with, perform, or manage successfully: *I couldn't handle the difficult math test.* **6.** To deal in; buy and sell: *Drugstores handle a wide variety of goods.* —*intr.* To act or function in a given way while in operation: *This new car handles well on the highway.* ❖ *n.* **1.** A part that is designed to be held or operated with the hand: *carry a pail by its handle.* **2.** Understanding or control: *has a handle on the situation.*

han·dle·bar (hăn′dl-bär′) *n.* often **handlebars** A cylindrical, straight or curved steering bar, as on a bicycle: *gripped the handlebars tightly.* ❖ *adj.* Shaped like a long and curved handlebar: *a handlebar mustache.*

han·dler (hănd′lər) *n.* **1.** A person who handles a person or thing: *handlers of food in a restaurant; the mayor's campaign handlers.* **2.** A person who trains an animal and exhibits it in shows: *a dog handler.* **3.** A person who acts as the trainer or second of a boxer.

hand·made (hănd′mād′) *adj.* Made or prepared by hand rather than by machine: *a handmade quilt.*

hand·maid (hănd′mād′) also **hand·maid·en** (hănd′-mād′n) *n.* A woman attendant or servant.

hand-me-down (hănd′mē-doun′) *n.* Something, such as an article of clothing, passed on from one person to another: *The sweater is a hand-me-down from my sister.*

hand·off (hănd′ôf′) *n.* **1.** In football, the act of handing the ball to a teammate during a play. **2.** In track and field, the act of handing a baton to a teammate during a relay race.

hand organ *n.* A barrel organ operated by turning a crank with the hand.

hand·out (hănd′out′) *n.* **1.** A gift to the needy, as of food, clothing, or money. **2.** A folder or leaflet given out free of charge. **3.** A sheet of paper with information that is given out, as at a lecture. **4.** A prepared news or publicity release.

hand·pick (hănd′pĭk′) *tr.v.* **hand·picked, hand·pick·ing, hand·picks 1.** To gather or pick by hand. **2.** To select personally: *handpick members of a committee.*

hand·rail (hănd′rāl′) *n.* A narrow railing to be grasped with the hand for support.

hand·saw (hănd′sô′) *n.* A saw operated with one hand.

hand·set (hănd′sĕt′) *n.* The part of a telephone containing the receiver and transmitter and often a dial or pushbuttons.

hand·shake (hănd′shāk′) *n.* The grasping of hands by two people, as in greeting or leave-taking or to express mutual agreement.

hand·some (hăn′səm) *adj.* **hand·som·er, hand·som·est 1.** Pleasing and dignified in form and appearance: *a handsome couple.* **2.** Generous or liberal: *a handsome reward.* —**hand′some·ly** *adv.* —**hand′some·ness** *n.*
❑ *These sound alike:* **handsome, hansom** (carriage).

hands-on (hăndz′ŏn′) *adj.* Involving active participation; applied, as opposed to theoretical: *We use computers in the classroom in hands-on job training.*

hand·spike (hănd′spīk′) *n.* A bar used as a lever.

hand·spring (hănd′sprĭng′) *n.* A gymnastic feat in which the body is flipped completely forward or backward from an upright position, landing first on the hands and then on the feet.

hand·stand (hănd′stănd′) *n.* The act of balancing on one's hands with one's feet in the air.

hand-to-hand (hănd′tə-hănd′) *adj.* Being at close quarters: *hand-to-hand combat.* —**hand to hand** *adv.*

hand-to-mouth (hănd′tə-mouth′) *adj.* Having or providing only the bare essentials: *a hand-to-mouth existence.* —**hand to mouth** *adv.*

hand·work (hănd′wûrk′) *n.* Work done by hand rather than by machine: *Sewing buttons on is handwork.*

hand·wo·ven (hănd′wō′vən) *adj.* **1.** Woven on a hand-operated loom. **2.** Woven by hand: *handwoven baskets.*

hand·writ·ing (hănd′rī′tĭng) *n.* **1.** Writing done with the hand. **2.** The writing characteristic of a particular person.

hand·y (hăn′dē) *adj.* **hand·i·er, hand·i·est 1.** Skillful in using one's hands: *A carpenter must be handy with tools.* **2.** Readily accessible: *a handy supply of wood for the fireplace; a handy place for the telephone directory.* **3.** Easily or effectively used; convenient or useful: *A can opener is a handy gadget.*

Han·dy (hăn′dē), **W(illiam) C(hristopher)** 1873–1958. American musician and composer who was the first person to publish a blues composition, "The Memphis Blues" (1911).

W.C. Handy

hand·y·man also **handy man** (hăn′dē-măn′) *n.* A man hired to perform various odd jobs.

hang (hăng) *v.* **hung** (hŭng), **hang·ing, hangs** —*tr.* **1.** To fasten from above with no support from below; suspend: *hang a clothesline.* **2.** To fasten so as to allow free movement at or about the point of suspension: *hang a door.* **3.** *Past tense and past participle* **hanged** (hăngd) To execute by suspending by the neck. **4.** To hold or bend downward; let droop: *hang one's head in sorrow.* **5.** To attach to a wall: *hang wallpaper.* **6.** To furnish or decorate by suspending objects around or about: *We've decided to hang the walls with pictures.* **7.** To display by attaching to a wall or other structure: *The museum curator chose which paintings would be hung in the main hall.* **8.** To deadlock (a jury) by failing to come to a unanimous verdict. —*intr.* **1.** To be attached from above with no support from below: *A sign hung over the door.* **2.** To be fastened so as to allow free movement from a hinge or hook: *The gate hangs on its hinges.* **3.** To die as a result of hanging. **4.** To remain unresolved or uncertain: *His future hangs in the balance.* **5.** To be dependent; depend: *A great deal hangs on your decision.* **6.** To incline downward; droop: *The spectators hung over the rail.* **7.** To remain suspended over a place or an object; hover: *A rain cloud hangs over the field.* **8.** To be exhibited: *Many famous paintings hang in this museum.* **9.** To pay strict attention: *The student hung on the teacher's every word.* ❖ *n.* **1.** The way in which something hangs. **2.** *Informal* The proper way of doing, handling, or using something: *I can't get the hang of this new camera.* ◆ **hang**

hang gliding

Lorraine Hansberry
photographed in 1959

hansom

around *Informal* To spend time idly; loiter: *hang around the beach all day.* **hang back** To be averse; hold back: *When the teacher asked a question, several students hung back.* **hang on 1.** To cling tightly to something: *Hang on to the rope and pull yourself up.* **2.** To wait for a short period of time. **3.** To continue persistently; persevere: *This fever keeps hanging on.* **hang out** *Slang* To spend one's free time in a certain place. **hang together 1.** To stand united; stick together: *hang together as a group.* **2.** To make sense as a whole; be understandable: *The sentences hang together to form a good paragraph.* **hang up 1.** To end a telephone conversation. **2.** To suspend on a hook or hanger: *Before class begins, the children hang up their coats.* **3.** To delay or impede; hinder. [From Middle English *hongen*, from Old English *hangian*, to be suspended, and from Old English *hōn*, to hang.]

han·gar (hăng′ər *or* hăng′gər) *n.* A building used for housing or repairing aircraft. [From Old French *hangard*, shed, of Germanic origin.]
❑ *These sound alike:* **hangar, hanger** (hook).

hang·dog (hăng′dôg′) *adj.* Shamefaced or guilty: *a hangdog look on the criminal's face.*

hanged (hăngd) *v.* Past tense and past participle of **hang** (sense 3).

hang·er (hăng′ər) *n.* **1.** A frame or hook on which an article of clothing can be hung. **2.** A person who hangs something: *a wallpaper hanger.*
❑ *These sound alike:* **hanger, hangar** (aircraft building).

hang·er-on (hăng′ər-ŏn′) *n., pl.* **hang·ers-on** A person who cultivates the friendship of an influential person in the hope of achieving personal gain; a parasite.

hang-glide (hăng′glīd′) *intr.v.* **hang-glid·ed, hang-glid·ing, hang-glides** To glide in the air by means of a hang glider.

hang glider *n.* A device resembling a kite from which a rider hangs in a harness while gliding from a height.

hang gliding *n.* The sport of riding a hang glider.

hang·ing (hăng′ĭng) *n.* **1.** Execution on a gallows: *death by hanging.* **2.** Something, such as a tapestry, that is hung: *a wall hanging.* ❖ *adj.* Projecting downward; overhanging: *a hanging lamp; hanging moss.*

hang·man (hăng′mən) *n.* A man who is employed to execute convicted criminals by hanging.

hang·nail (hăng′nāl′) *n.* A small flap of dead skin that hangs from the side or base of a fingernail.

hang·out (hăng′out′) *n. Slang* A frequently visited place: *The mall is a favorite hangout of teenagers.*

hang·o·ver (hăng′ō′vər) *n.* **1.** A condition, often characterized by nausea and a headache, that results from drinking more alcohol than the body can tolerate. **2.** Something left from an earlier time; a holdover.

hang-up (hăng′ŭp′) *n. Informal* **1.** An inhibition or emotional difficulty with something. **2.** An obstacle or inconvenience.

hank (hăngk) *n.* **1.** A coil or loop: *a hank of rope.* **2.** A looped bundle, as of yarn. [From Middle English, from Old Norse *hönk*.]

han·ker (hăng′kər) *intr.v.* **han·kered, han·ker·ing, han·kers** To have a strong, often restless desire: *hanker to travel abroad.* [Perhaps from Dutch dialectal *hankeren*.]

Han·ni·bal (hăn′ə-bəl) 247–183? BC. Carthaginian general who crossed the Alps in 218 with his troops and defeated Roman armies in 217 and 216.

Ha·noi (hă-**noi**′ *or* hə-**noi**′) The capital of Vietnam, in the northern part of the country near the Gulf of Tonkin. It was founded before the seventh century.

Hans·ber·ry (hănz′bĕr-ē), **Lorraine Vivian** 1930–1965. American playwright known for her play *A Raisin in the Sun* (1959).

han·som (hăn′səm) *n.* A two-wheeled, covered carriage with the driver's seat above and behind the passenger compartment. [After Joseph Aloysius *Hansom* (1803–1882), British architect.]
❑ *These sound alike:* **hansom, handsome** (attractive).

Ha·nuk·kah also **Cha·nu·kah** (KHä′nə-kə *or* hä′nə-kə) *n.* A Jewish festival lasting eight days and celebrating the victory in 165 BC of the Maccabees over the king of Syria and the rededication of the Temple at Jerusalem. [From Hebrew *ḥănukkâ*, dedication.]

hap·haz·ard (hăp-hăz′ərd) *adj.* Dependent on or characterized by mere chance; random: *He had left the papers in a haphazard arrangement on the desk.* **—hap·haz′ard·ly** *adv.* **—hap·haz′ard·ness** *n.*

hap·less (hăp′lĭs) *adj.* Unfortunate; unlucky: *a hapless business scheme.* [From *hap*, chance, luck.] **—hap′less·ly** *adv.*

hap·loid (hăp′loid′) *adj.* Being a cell or composed of cells in which there is only one of each type of chromosome. In animals, reproductive cells are haploid. ❖ *n.* A haploid cell or organism.

hap·ly (hăp′lē) *adv.* By chance or accident.

hap·pen (hăp′ən) *intr.v.* **hap·pened, hap·pen·ing, hap·pens 1.** To occur or take place. **2.** To come upon something by chance: *I happened upon an interesting article in the newspaper last week.* [From Middle English *happenen*, from *hap*, chance.]

hap·pen·ing (hăp′ə-nĭng) *n.* Something that happens; an event or occurrence: *an interesting recent happening.*

hap·pen·stance (hăp′ən-stăns′) *n.* A chance circumstance: *By happenstance I met an old friend at the mall.*

hap·pi·ly (hăp′ə-lē) *adv.* **1.** In a happy way; with pleasure, joy, and gladness: *happily married; children playing happily in the swimming pool.* **2.** By luck; with good fortune: *Happily, the parts I needed were all in stock at the hardware store.*

hap·pi·ness (hăp′ē-nĭs) *n.* The state or quality of being happy.

hap·py (hăp′ē) *adj.* **hap·pi·er, hap·pi·est 1.** Having, showing, or marked by a feeling of joy or pleasure: *a happy child; the happiest day of my life.* See Synonyms at **glad. 2.** Cheerful; willing: *We'll be happy to help.* **3.** Characterized by good luck; fortunate: *a happy sequence of events.* **4.** Being especially well adapted or suited: *Their greeting was a happy choice of words.* [From Middle English *happi*, from *hap*, luck.]

hap·py-go-luck·y (hăp′ē-gō-lŭk′ē) *adj.* Taking things easy; carefree: *a happy-go-lucky attitude.*

Haps·burg (hăps′bûrg′) See **Habsburg.**

ha·ra-ki·ri (hăr′ĭ-kîr′ē *or* hä′rē-kîr′ē) *n., pl.* **ha·ra-ki·ris** Suicide by cutting open the abdomen with a dagger or knife, formerly practiced by Japanese samurai. [From Japanese *harakiri* : *hara*, belly + *kiri*, to cut.]

ha·rangue (hə-răng′) *n.* A long loud speech, often one in which the speaker denounces a person, group, or thing: *The dictator delivered a harangue against enemies of the government.* ❖ *tr.v.* **ha·rangued, ha·rangu·ing, ha·rangues** To deliver a harangue to: *harangue one's followers for their shortcomings.*

Ha·ra·re (hə-rär′ā) The capital of Zimbabwe, in the northeast part of the country. It was founded in 1890.

har·ass (hə-răs′ *or* hăr′əs) *tr.v.* **ha·rassed, ha·rass·ing, ha·rass·es 1.** To subject to socially inappropriate remarks or actions: *a boss who was accused of harassing employees.* **2.** To irritate or torment persistently: *harass a speaker with whistles and shouts.* **3.** To carry out repeated attacks and raids against. [From French *harasser*.] **—ha·rass′ment** *n.*

har·bin·ger (här′bĭn-jər) *n.* Something that indicates or foreshadows what is to come; a forerunner: *The robin is a harbinger of spring.*

ă	pat	ôr	core
ā	pay	oi	boy
âr	care	ou	out
ä	father	ŏŏ	took
ĕ	pet	ŏŏr	lure
ē	be	ōō	boot
ĭ	pit	ŭ	cut
ī	bite	ûr	urge
îr	pier	th	thin
ŏ	pot	*th*	this
ō	toe	zh	vision
ô	paw	ə	about

har·bor (här′bər) *n.* **1.** A sheltered part of a body of water deep enough for ships and boats to anchor. **2.** A place of shelter; a refuge: *Home is always a safe harbor.* ❖ *tr.v.* **har·bored, har·bor·ing, har·bors 1.** To give shelter to: *harbor a fugitive.* **2.** To have (a specified thought or feeling): *harboring a grudge against an old enemy.* [From Middle English *herberwe,* probably from Old English *herebeorg,* lodging.]

hard (härd) *adj.* **hard·er, hard·est 1.** Resistant to pressure; not readily penetrated: *a hard surface; hard as a rock.* **2.** Difficult to accomplish or finish: *Was the test hard?* **3.** Difficult to understand, express, or convey: *a hard question; a hard concept to explain.* **4.** Performing or acting with great energy, persistence, or care: *a hard worker.* **5.** Forceful or intense: *a hard blow; a hard twist of the knob.* **6.** Difficult to endure; trying; harsh: *a hard life.* **7.** Bad; adverse: *hard luck.* **8.** Strict and demanding; stern: *My music teacher is a hard taskmaster.* **9.** Making few concessions: *The opposing lawyer drove a hard bargain.* **10.** Realistic or practical: *take a hard look at the facts.* **11.** Definite or real; true and unchangeable: *hard facts of the evidence.* **12.** Causing damage to; tending to wear down quickly: *Freezing weather is hard on a car.* **13.** Bitter; rancorous; resentful: *There is much hard feeling between those old enemies.* **14a.** Designating currency as opposed to checks or notes: *pay in hard cash.* **b.** Readily exchanged for gold or other currency: *hard currency.* **15.** Being the sound of *c* in *cat* or *g* in *go,* rather than in *certain* or *general.* **16a.** Having high alcoholic content; intoxicating: *hard liquor.* **b.** Rendered alcoholic by fermentation: *hard cider.* **17.** In printed rather than electronic form: *The typist made a hard copy of the manuscript.* **18.** Containing dissolved salts that interfere with the action of soap: *hard water of high mineral content.* ❖ *adv.* **hard·er, hard·est 1.** With much effort; intently; earnestly: *work hard.* **2.** With great force, vigor, or energy: *Press hard on the lever.* **3.** In such a way as to cause great damage or hardship: *A number of towns were hit hard by the storm.* **4.** With great distress, grief, pain, or resentment: *took the news hard.* **5.** Toward or into a solid condition: *The little pond is frozen hard all winter.* **6.** Near in space or time; close: *The trees stand hard by the edge of the road.* ◆ **hard and fast** Defined, fixed, and invariable: *a hard and fast rule.* **hard of hearing** Having a partial loss of hearing. **hard put** Undergoing great difficulty: *I'm hard put to explain what he meant.* **hard up** *Informal* In need; poor. [From Old English *heard.*] **—hard′ness** *n.*

hard·back (härd′băk′) *adj. & n.* Hardcover.

hard·ball (härd′bôl′) *n.* **1.** Baseball. **2.** *Informal* The use of tough and aggressive means to obtain an objective: *The negotiator played hardball to get the opposition to cave in.*

hard-bit·ten (härd′bĭt′n) *adj.* Made tough by experience: *a hard-bitten criminal lawyer.*

hard-boiled (härd′boild′) *adj.* **1.** Boiled in the shell to a solid consistency. Used of eggs. **2.** Unsentimental and practical; tough: *a hard-boiled journalist.*

hard·bound (härd′bound′) *adj. & n.* Hardcover.

hard coal *n.* Anthracite.

hard·core or **hard-core** (härd′kôr′) *adj.* **1.** Intensely loyal: *a hardcore golfer.* **2.** Resistant to improvement or change: *a hardcore criminal.*

hard·cov·er (härd′kŭv′ər) *adj.* Bound in cloth, cardboard, or leather rather than paper. Used of books. ❖ *n.* A hardcover book.

hard disk *n.* A rigid magnetic disk fixed within a disk drive and used for storing computer data.

hard drive *n.* A disk drive that reads data stored on hard disks.

hard·en (här′dn) *v.* **hard·ened, hard·en·ing, hard·ens** *—tr.* **1.** To make hard or harder: *harden steel.* **2.** To toughen; make rugged: *harden young athletes by long periods of exercise.* **3.** To make unfeeling, unsympathetic, or callous: *Seeing so much poverty and disease hardened the young doctor's heart.* *—intr.* **1.** To become hard or harder: *Allow the mixture to cool until it hardens.* **2.** To rise and become stable. Used of prices.

hard·hat or **hard-hat** (härd′hăt′) *n.* **1.** A lightweight protective helmet worn by workers in industrial settings. **2.** *Informal* A construction worker.

hard·head·ed (härd′hĕd′ĭd) *adj.* **1.** Stubborn; willful: *a hardheaded mule.* **2.** Pragmatic; realistic: *a hardheaded business manager.* **—hard′head′ed·ly** *adv.* **—hard′head′ed·ness** *n.*

hard·heart·ed (härd′här′tĭd) *adj.* Lacking in feeling or compassion; pitiless. **—hard′heart′ed·ly** *adv.* **—hard′heart′ed·ness** *n.*

har·di·hood (här′dē-ho͝od′) *n.* Boldness and daring.

Har·ding (här′dĭng), **Warren Gamaliel** 1865–1923. The 29th president of the United States (1921–1923). He promised he would help the United States recover from World War I, but his presidency was marred by corruption.

hard line *n.* A firm uncompromising policy, position, or stance: *Our teacher took a hard line on turning in homework late.* **—hard′-line′** *adj.*

hard·ly (härd′lē) *adv.* **1.** Barely; only just: *We hardly noticed it was getting late.* **2.** Probably or almost surely not: *I would hardly expect visitors on such a snowy day.* **3.** With severity; harshly. —SEE NOTE.

hard palate *n.* The hard bony forward part of the roof of the mouth.

hard·pan (härd′păn′) *n.* **1.** A layer of hard, often clayey subsoil. Plant roots do not usually grow through hardpan. **2.** Hard unbroken ground.

hard-pressed (härd′prĕst′) *adj.* Undergoing a difficult time: *was hard-pressed to think of an answer right away.*

hard·ship (härd′shĭp′) *n.* A cause of suffering or difficulty: *The settlers suffered great hardships.*

hard·tack (härd′tăk′) *n.* A hard biscuit or bread made of flour and water.

hard·ware (härd′wâr′) *n.* **1.** Articles made of metal, as tools, locks, and cutlery. **2.** A computer and its equipment, such as the keyboard, monitor, hard drive, and printer. **3.** Machinery used in industry and by the military.

hard·wood (härd′wo͝od′) *n.* **1.** Any of various trees that usually have broad leaves, in contrast to the conifers. Oaks, maples, and mahoganies are hardwoods. **2.** The wood of such a tree, which is usually harder than that of a softwood.

har·dy (här′dē) *adj.* **har·di·er, har·di·est** Capable of withstanding harsh or difficult conditions, such as cold weather or poor food: *hardy plants; hardy explorers.* [From Middle English *hardi,* from Old French, hardened.]

Har·dy (här′dē), **Thomas** 1840–1928. British writer noted for his novels, including *Tess of the d'Urbervilles* (1891).

hare (hâr) *n.* Any of various mammals that are similar to rabbits but have longer ears and give birth to active, furred young. [From Old English *hara.*]

❑ *These sound alike:* **hare, hair** (strands).

hare·bell (hâr′bĕl′) *n.* A plant having slender stems, narrow leaves, and blue flowers shaped like bells.

hare·brained (hâr′brānd′) *adj.* Foolish; flighty: *a harebrained idea.*

hare·lip (hâr′lĭp′) *n.* A cleft lip. This term is no longer used in medicine.

har·em (hâr′əm) *n.* **1.** A house or a section of a house reserved for women members of a Muslim household. **2.** The women who live in a Muslim household. **3.** A

hardhat

Warren Harding
photographed c. 1920

USAGE

hardly The words **hardly, rarely,** and **scarcely** act as if they were negatives and so should not be used with other negatives. You should write *I could hardly believe it* rather than *I couldn't hardly believe it.*

Benjamin Harrison[2]
photographed c. 1896

group of female animals that breed exclusively with a single male. [From Arabic *ḥarīm*, forbidden place, from *ḥarama*, to protect.]

Har·greaves (här′grēvz′), **James** Died 1778. British inventor of a power-operated spinning machine, the spinning jenny (about 1764).

hark (härk) *intr.v.* **harked, hark·ing, harks** To listen carefully. ◆ **hark back** To recall or be reminiscent of a past event or condition.

har·ken (här′kən) *v.* Variant of **hearken.**

Har·lem (här′ləm) A section of New York City in northern Manhattan. In the 1920s it was the site of a flowering of African-American art and literature known as the Harlem Renaissance.

har·le·quin (här′lĭ-kwĭn *or* här′lĭ-kĭn) *n.* **1. Harlequin** A comic pantomime character, usually appearing in a mask and a costume of many colors. **2.** A clown; a buffoon.

har·lot (här′lət) *n.* A woman who is a prostitute.

harm (härm) *n.* **1.** Injury or damage: *Locusts often cause great harm to crops.* **2.** Wrong; evil: *There was no harm meant in their careless mistake.* ❖ *tr.v.* **harmed, harm·ing, harms** To do harm to. [From Old English *hearm.*]

harm·ful (härm′fəl) *adj.* Causing or capable of causing harm; injurious: *Insects can be harmful to plants.* —**harm′ful·ly** *adv.* —**harm′ful·ness** *n.*

harm·less (härm′lĭs) *adj.* **1.** Incapable of causing harm: *a harmless kitten.* **2.** Not meant to harm or offend; inoffensive: *a harmless joke.* —**harm′less·ly** *adv.*

har·mon·ic (här-mŏn′ĭk) *n.* **1.** Any of a series of tones whose frequency is a whole number multiple of that of a fundamental tone, often sounded as overtones of the fundamental. **2. harmonics** *(used with a singular verb)* The theory or study of the physical properties and characteristics of musical sound. ❖ *adj.* **1.** Relating to musical harmony. **2.** Relating to overtones produced when a lower tone occurs or is played. —**har·mon′i·cal·ly** *adv.*

har·mon·i·ca (här-mŏn′ĭ-kə) *n.* A small, rectangular musical instrument consisting of a row of tuned metal reeds set back in air holes, played by exhaling or inhaling.

har·mo·ni·ous (här-mō′nē-əs) *adj.* **1.** Showing accord in feeling or action: *a harmonious neighborhood.* **2.** Having elements pleasingly or appropriately combined: *a harmonious arrangement of colors.* **3.** Characterized by harmony of sound: *the harmonious tones of a handbell choir.* —**har·mo′ni·ous·ly** *adv.*

har·mo·nize (här′mə-nīz′) *v.* **har·mo·nized, har·mo·niz·ing, har·mo·niz·es** —*tr.* **1.** To bring into agreement; make harmonious: *harmonize different ideas into a plan.* **2.** To provide harmony for (a melody). —*intr.* **1.** To be in agreement; be harmonious. **2.** To sing or play in harmony: *The choir harmonized in song.* —**har′mo·ni·za′tion** (här′mə-nĭ-zā′shən) *n.*

har·mo·ny (här′mə-nē) *n., pl.* **har·mo·nies 1.** A pleasing combination of elements that form a whole: *the harmony of a flower arrangement.* **2.** Agreement in feeling or opinion; accord: *a family that lives in harmony.* **3a.** The combination of notes forming a chord: *The piano fills in the harmony for the voice part of the singer.* **b.** The study of the structure, succession, and relationships of chords. **c.** A combination of musical sounds considered to be pleasing. [From Middle English *armonie*, from Greek *harmoniā*, agreement, harmony, from *harmos*, joint.]

har·ness (här′nĭs) *n.* **1.** A set of leather straps and metal pieces by which an animal is attached to and pulls a vehicle or plow. **2.** Something resembling a harness, as the arrangement of straps used to hold a parachute to the body. ❖ *tr.v.* **har·nessed, har·ness·ing, har·ness·es 1.** To put a harness on (a draft animal): *harness a horse to a wagon.* **2.** To bring under control and direct the force of: *Solar panels harness the sun's energy.* ◆ **in harness** At one's work; on duty: *get back in harness after a vacation.* [From Middle English *harneis*, from Old French, of Germanic origin.]

harp (härp) *n.* **1.** A musical instrument consisting of an upright triangular frame on which a series of strings are played by plucking with the fingers. **2.** *Informal* A harmonica. ❖ *intr.v.* **harped, harp·ing, harps** To play a harp. ◆ **harp on** To write or talk about to an excessive or tedious degree: *harping on how expensive movie tickets are.* [From Old English *hearpe.*]

Har·per (här′pər), **Stephen Joseph** Born 1959. Canadian prime minister (2006–2015).

Har·pers Ferry (här′pərz) A town of extreme northeast West Virginia. It was the scene of John Brown's rebellion (1859), in which he briefly seized the US arsenal here.

harp·ist (här′pĭst) *n.* A person who plays the harp.

har·poon (här-po͞on′) *n.* A weapon like a spear with a barbed head that is used in hunting whales and large fish. ❖ *tr.v.* **har·pooned, har·poon·ing, har·poons** To strike, kill, or catch with a harpoon. [Probably from Dutch *harpoen*, from Old French *harpon*, possibly from Greek *harpē*, sickle.] —**har·poon′er** *n.*

harp seal *n.* A seal of the North Atlantic and Arctic Oceans whose young pups have a white coat.

harp·si·chord (härp′sĭ-kôrd′) *n.* A keyboard instrument that resembles a piano, having strings that are plucked by means of quills or plectrums.

Har·py (här′pē) *n., pl.* **Har·pies 1.** In Greek mythology, a hideous monster with the head and trunk of a woman and the tail, wings, and claws of a bird. **2. harpy** A predatory person.

har·que·bus (här′kə-bəs *or* här′kwə-bəs) also **ar·que·bus** (är′kə-bəs *or* är′kwə-bəs) *n.* A heavy portable gun invented during the 1400s.

har·ri·er[1] (hăr′ē-ər) *n.* **1.** A person or thing that harries. **2.** Any of various slender hawks having narrow wings and preying on small animals.

har·ri·er[2] (hăr′ē-ər) *n.* A small hound of a breed originally developed in England to hunt hares and rabbits. [From Middle English *hairer, eirer*, possibly from Old French *errier*, wanderer, from *errer*, to wander, rove.]

Har·ris·burg (hăr′ĭs-bûrg′) The capital of Pennsylvania, in the southeast-central part of the state west-northwest of Philadelphia. It was settled in the early 1700s and became the capital in 1812.

Har·ri·son[1] (hăr′ĭ-sən), **Benjamin** 1726–1791. American Revolutionary leader who served as a member of the Continental Congress (1774–1777).

Har·ri·son[2] (hăr′ĭ-sən), **Benjamin** 1833–1901. The 23rd president of the United States (1889–1893). He approved legislation to fight monopolies and raise tariffs, and he sponsored the first Pan-American Conference (1889).

Harrison, William Henry 1773–1841. The ninth president of the United States (1841). He died of pneumonia after one month in office.

har·row (hăr′ō) *n.* A farm implement consisting of a heavy frame with sharp teeth or upright disks, pulled over plowed fields to break up and even the soil. ❖ *tr.v.* **har·rowed, har·row·ing, har·rows 1.** To break up and level (soil or land) with a harrow. **2.** To inflict great distress or torment on. [From Middle English *harwe.*] —**har′row·er** *n.*

har·row·ing (hăr′ō-ĭng) *adj.* Extremely distressing; agonizing: *a harrowing experience.*

har·ry (hăr′ē) *tr.v.* **har·ried, har·ry·ing, har·ries 1.** To disturb or distress by or as if by repeated attacks; harass: *harried me with constant phone calls.* **2.** To raid, as in war; sack or pillage: *The invading army harried the countryside.*

harsh (härsh) *adj.* **harsh·er, harsh·est 1.** Unpleasantly

ă	pat	ôr	core
ā	pay	oi	boy
âr	care	ou	out
ä	father	o͝o	took
ĕ	pet	o͝or	lure
ē	be	o͞o	boot
ĭ	pit	ŭ	cut
ī	bite	ûr	urge
îr	pier	th	thin
ŏ	pot	*th*	this
ō	toe	zh	vision
ô	paw	ə	about

coarse and rough to the touch: *harsh burlap.* **2.** Unpleasant to the sense of sound or sight: *a harsh angry voice; harsh lighting.* **3.** Unpleasant, uncomfortable, or hostile to survival: *a harsh winter.* **4.** Extremely severe or cruel; stern: *harsh punishment.* **5.** Expressing displeasure or disapproval: *a harsh look.* **—harsh′ly** *adv.* **—harsh′ness** *n.*

hart (härt) *n., pl.* **harts** or **hart** The adult male of various deer.

❑ *These sound alike:* **hart, heart** (organ).

har·te·beest (här′tə-bēst′ *or* härt′bēst′) *n., pl.* **har·te·beests** or **hartebeest** Any of various African antelopes having a brownish coat, a long narrow head, and horns that curve outward in the middle.

Hart·ford (härt′fərd) The capital of Connecticut, in the north-central part of the state on the Connecticut River.

har·um-scar·um (hâr′əm-skâr′əm) *adj.* Lacking a sense of responsibility; reckless. ❖ *adv.* With abandon; recklessly: *ran harum-scarum around the yard.*

har·vest (här′vĭst) *n.* **1.** The act or process of gathering a crop. **2.** The crop that ripens or is gathered in a season: *a large corn harvest.* **3.** The time or season of such gathering: *Harvest lasts about six weeks.* **4.** The result or consequence of an action: *Our trip to the Grand Canyon yielded a rich harvest of memories.* ❖ *v.* **har·vest·ed, har·vest·ing, har·vests** *—tr.* **1.** To gather (a crop): *harvest wheat.* **2.** To gather a crop from: *harvest an apple orchard.* **3.** To take, catch, or remove for a specific purpose: *harvest fish; harvest trees.* **4.** To receive (the benefits or consequences of an action): *harvest the rewards of hard work.* *—intr.* To gather a crop. [From Old English *hærfest.*]

har·vest·er (här′vĭ-stər) *n.* **1.** A person who gathers a crop. **2.** A machine for harvesting crops; a reaper.

harvest moon *n.* The full moon that occurs nearest the beginning of autumn.

Har·vey (här′vē), **William** 1578–1657. English physician who demonstrated (1628) that blood circulates through the human body with the heart acting as a pump.

has (hăz) *v.* Third person singular present tense of **have.**

has-been (hăz′bĭn′) *n., pl.* **has-beens** *Informal* A person whose fame, popularity, or success has passed: *The actor is a has-been.*

hash (hăsh) *n.* **1.** A dish of chopped meat, potatoes, and onions or other vegetables browned and cooked together. **2.** A jumble or hodgepodge: *a hash of disconnected sentences.* ❖ *tr.v.* **hashed, hash·ing, hash·es 1.** To chop into pieces; mince: *hash potatoes.* **2.** *Informal* To discuss carefully; review: *hash over a problem.*

hash browns *pl.n.* Potatoes that are chopped, cooked, and fried until they are brown.

hash·ish (hăsh′ēsh′ *or* hă-shēsh′) *n.* A dry resinous extract prepared from the hemp plant, used as a narcotic or intoxicant.

hash·tag (hăsh′tăg′) *n.* A searchable keyword or sequence of characters starting with the pound sign (#), used in electronic communication to indicate subject matter.

Ha·sid or **Has·sid** (ᴋʜä′sĭd *or* hä′sĭd) *n., pl.* **Ha·si·dim** or **Has·si·dim** (ᴋʜä-sē′dĭm *or* hä-sē′dĭm) A member of a movement of Jewish mysticism founded in Eastern Europe in the 1700s. **—Ha·sid′ic** *adj.*

has·n't (hăz′ənt) Contraction of *has not.*

hasp (hăsp) *n.* A metal fastener with a hinged slotted part that is passed over a staple and secured by a pin, bolt, or padlock.

has·si·um (hä′sē-əm) *n. Symbol* **Hs** A radioactive element that has been artificially produced by scientists. The half-life of its longest-lived isotope is about 16.5 minutes. Atomic number 108. See **Periodic Table.**

has·sle (hăs′əl) *Informal n.* **1.** A cause of annoyance or difficulty: *Driving in the snow is a real hassle.* **2.** An argument or fight. ❖ *v.* **has·sled, has·sling, has·sles** *—intr.* To argue or fight. *—tr.* To bother or harass: *The bully hassled me on my way to school.*

has·sock (hăs′ək) *n.* **1.** A thick cushion used as a footstool or for kneeling. **2.** A dense clump of grass.

hast (hăst) *v. Archaic* Second person singular present tense of **have.**

haste (hāst) *n.* **1.** Swiftness of motion or action; rapidity. **2.** Overeagerness to act: *In their haste they forgot to lock the front door.* ◆ **make haste** To move or act swiftly; hurry: *Make haste to get there on time.*

has·ten (hā′sən) *v.* **has·tened, has·ten·ing, has·tens** *—intr.* To move or act swiftly; hurry: *I hastened to tell them the good news.* *—tr.* **1.** To cause to hurry: *When the rain started, the teacher hastened the children inside.* **2.** To cause (something) to happen faster or sooner: *The medicine hastened my recovery.*

Has·tings (hā′stĭngz) A town of southeast England on the English Channel, near the site where William the Conqueror defeated the Saxons (October 14, 1066).

hast·y (hā′stē) *adj.* **hast·i·er, hast·i·est 1.** Acting with or marked by speed; swift; rapid: *a hasty departure.* **2.** Done or made too quickly to be accurate or wise; rash: *hasty judgments.* **—hast′i·ly** *adv.* **—hast′i·ness** *n.*

hasty pudding *n.* Cornmeal mush served with a sweetener such as maple syrup or brown sugar.

hat (hăt) *n.* A covering for the head, especially one with a crown and brim. ◆ **at the drop of a hat** At the slightest pretext or provocation. **pass the hat** To take up a collection of money: *passed the hat to collect donations.* **take off (one's) hat to** To respect, admire, or congratulate: *I take my hat off to anyone who can pass that test.*

hat·band (hăt′bănd′) *n.* A band of ribbon or cloth worn just above the brim on a hat.

hat·box (hăt′bŏks′) *n.* A box or case for a hat.

hatch[1] (hăch) *n.* **1.** An opening, as in the deck of a ship, in the roof or floor of a building, or in an airplane. **2.** A trap door or cover for such an opening. **3.** A hatchback. [From Old English *hæc.*]

hatch[2] (hăch) *v.* **hatched, hatch·ing, hatch·es** *—intr.* To come out of an egg: *The ducklings hatched today.* *—tr.* **1.** To cause to come out of an egg: *The hen hatched a brood of ten chicks.* **2.** To cause (an egg or eggs) to produce young: *We used an incubator to hatch the eggs.* **3.** To devise or plot, especially in secret: *hatching a plan of escape.* [From Middle English *hacchen.*]

hatch·back (hăch′băk′) *n.* **1.** A door that opens upward on the rear of certain automobiles. **2.** A compact automobile having such a door.

hatch·er·y (hăch′ə-rē) *n., pl.* **hatch·er·ies** A place where eggs, especially those of fish or poultry, are hatched.

hatch·et (hăch′ĭt) *n.* A small axe with a short handle used with one hand. [From Middle English *hachet*, from Old French *hachete*, small axe.]

hatch·ling (hăch′lĭng) *n.* A young animal that has just hatched from an egg.

hatch·way (hăch′wā′) *n.* A passage or opening leading to a hold, compartment, or cellar.

hate (hāt) *v.* **hat·ed, hat·ing, hates** *—tr.* **1.** To have a great dislike for; detest. **2.** To feel dislike or distaste for: *We hate washing dishes.* *—intr.* To feel hatred. ❖ *n.* Intense animosity or dislike; hatred. **—hat′er** *n.*

hate crime *n.* A crime motivated by prejudice.

hate·ful (hāt′fəl) *adj.* **1.** Arousing or deserving hatred. **2.** Feeling or showing hatred; full of hate. **—hate′ful·ly** *adv.* **—hate′ful·ness** *n.*

hath (hăth) *v. Archaic* Third person singular present tense of **have.**

hat·pin (hăt′pĭn′) *n.* A long straight pin used to fasten a hat to the hair.

ha·tred (hā′trĭd) *n.* Intense animosity or hostility.

Hat·shep·sut (hăt-shĕp′so͝ot′) Died about 1482 ʙᴄ.

William Henry Harrison

WRITERS CHOOSE THEIR WORDS

He kept close to the buildings, watching out for a policeman who might stop to ask him what he was doing out alone so late. A clock in the window of a jewelry store showed the hour: 11:50. People walked swiftly, as though they were **hastening** home before something happened.

—Paula Fox
Monkey Island

GEOGRAPHY

Hawaii The name for the state of Hawaii comes from the name that the original Polynesian inhabitants gave to the largest of the Hawaiian Islands. This name probably comes from an earlier Polynesian term, *Sawaiki*, meaning "the underworld" or "ancestral home." Although the English explorer James Cook had named the island group the Sandwich Islands, after the Earl of Sandwich (1718–1792), it joined the United States in 1959 as Hawaii.

Nathaniel Hawthorne

Rutherford B. Hayes

ă	pat	ôr	core
ā	pay	oi	boy
âr	care	ou	out
ä	father	ŏŏ	took
ĕ	pet	ŏŏr	lure
ē	be	ōō	boot
ĭ	pit	ŭ	cut
ī	bite	ûr	urge
îr	pier	th	thin
ŏ	pot	*th*	this
ō	toe	zh	vision
ô	paw	ə	about

Queen of Egypt (1502–1482) who as regent for her stepson took the title of pharaoh.

hat·ter (hăt′ər) *n.* A person who makes, sells, or repairs hats.

Hat·ter·as (hăt′ər-əs), **Cape** A promontory at the southeast point of a long barrier island off the eastern coast of North Carolina in the Atlantic Ocean.

hat trick *n.* Three goals scored by one player in one game, as in ice hockey.

hau·berk (hô′bərk) *n.* A long tunic made of chain mail.

haugh·ty (hô′tē) *adj.* **haugh·ti·er, haugh·ti·est** Scornfully and condescendingly proud: *The haughty waiter offended many customers.* See Synonyms at **arrogant.** [From Middle English *haut*, from Old French *haut, halt*, from Latin *altus*, high.] **—haugh′ti·ly** *adv.* **—haugh′ti·ness** *n.*

haul (hôl) *v.* **hauled, haul·ing, hauls** *—tr.* **1.** To pull or drag forcibly; tug: *We hauled the wood into the shed.* **2.** To transport, as with a truck or cart: *used trucks to haul away the dirt and debris.* *—intr.* To pull or tug. ❖ *n.* **1.** The act of pulling or dragging. **2.** A distance, especially the distance over which something is transported or pulled: *a long haul across country.* **3.** Everything collected or acquired by a single effort; a take: *a big haul of fish.* [From Middle English *halen*, from Old French *haler*, of Germanic origin.] **—haul′er** *n.*

❑ *These sound alike:* **haul, hall** (corridor).

haunch (hônch) *n.* **1.** The hip, rump, and upper thigh of humans and certain other animals: *The dog settled back on its haunches.* **2.** The loin and leg of an animal, especially as used for food: *a haunch of beef.*

haunt (hônt) *tr.v.* **haunt·ed, haunt·ing, haunts 1.** To visit, appear to, or inhabit in the form of a ghost or other supernatural being: *spirits haunting the woods.* **2.** To visit often; frequent: *haunts the local bookstores.* **3.** To come continually to the mind of; obsess: *That bad experience has haunted me ever since.* ❖ *n.* A place that is visited often: *This café is a favorite haunt of artists.* [From Middle English *haunten*, to do habitually, to frequent, from Old French *hanter*.]

haunt·ing (hôn′tĭng) *adj.* Continually recurring to the mind; unforgettable: *a haunting melody.* **—haunt′ing·ly** *adv.*

Hau·sa (hou′sə *or* hou′zə) *n., pl.* **Hausa** or **Hau·sas 1.** A member of a chiefly Muslim people living in Nigeria and Niger. **2.** The language of the Hausa.

haut·boy (hō′boi′ *or* ō′boi′) *n., pl.* **haut·boys** *Archaic* An oboe.

hau·teur (hō-tûr′) *n.* Haughtiness in bearing and attitude; arrogance: *Their hauteur made them unbearable.*

Ha·van·a (hə-văn′ə) The capital of Cuba, in the northwest part of the country on the Gulf of Mexico. It was founded in 1519.

have (hăv) *v.* **had** (hăd), **hav·ing, has** (hăz) *—tr.* **1.** To be in possession of; own: *My family has an old car.* **2.** To display or be capable of displaying a particular characteristic: *That singer has a good voice.* **3.** To feature or contain as a part: *This pencil has an eraser.* **4.** To be in a certain relationship to: *I have a brother and a sister.* **5.** To be trained or experienced in: *This class has had no Spanish at all.* **6.** To hold in the mind: *I have many doubts about this trip. She has a good idea.* **7.** To receive or get: *I had a dozen cards on my birthday.* **8.** To accept; take: *Will you have an orange?* **9.** To go through; experience: *I had a good summer.* **10a.** To cause (someone) to do something, especially by a request or command: *The coach had the students rake the infield.* **b.** To cause (someone or something) to be in a specified place or state: *We had the neighbors over for coffee. In an hour we had the kitchen spotless.* **11.** To allow; permit: *Our teacher won't have sloppy writing.* **12.** To carry on; engage in: *We have arguments but are still good friends.* **13.** To be forced or obliged; must: *We have to leave now.* **14.** To give birth to; bear: *Our cat is having kittens soon.* **15.** To partake of: *I'd like to have a snack.* **16.** *Informal* To get the better of; cheat or deceive: *The travelers were had by the swindler.* *—aux.* Used with a past participle to form the perfect tenses indicating completed action: *They have already had their lunch. We had just finished lunch when they arrived. We will have finished lunch by the time they arrive.* ❖ *n.* A person or country enjoying material wealth: *the gap between the haves and have-nots.* ◆ **have at** To attack: *We watched two birds have at each other over some seeds.* **have done with** To stop; cease: *Let's have done with this nonsense once and for all.* **have had it** To have endured all that one can: *I've had it with this traffic.* **have it in for (someone)** To intend to harm, especially because of a grudge. **have it out** To settle decisively, especially through discussion or argument: *We had it out and decided to share our chores.* **have on** To wear: *The band members have on their uniforms.* **have to do with** To be concerned or associated with: *The book has to do with World War I.*

❑ *These sound alike:* **have, halve** (divide).

Ha·vel (hä′vəl), **Václav** 1936–2011. Czech writer and politician who became a civil rights leader after the Soviet invasion of Czechoslovakia (1968). He served as president of Czechoslovakia (1989–1992) and as the first president of the Czech Republic (1993–2003).

ha·ven (hā′vən) *n.* **1.** A harbor or anchorage; a port. **2.** A place of refuge or safety; a sanctuary: *The library is a haven from noise.*

have-not (hăv′nŏt′) *n.* A person or country enjoying little or no material wealth.

have·n't (hăv′ənt) Contraction of *have not.*

hav·er·sack (hăv′ər-săk′) *n.* A bag worn over one shoulder to carry supplies, as on a hike.

hav·oc (hăv′ək) *n.* Very great destruction; devastation: *The hurricane created havoc throughout the coastal area.*

haw¹ (hô) *n.* A sound made by a speaker who is trying to think of what to say. ❖ *intr.v.* **hawed, haw·ing, haws** To make this sound during a pause in speaking: *The manager hawed before deciding to close early.* [Of imitative origin.]

haw² (hô) *n.* **1.** The fruit of a hawthorn. **2.** A hawthorn or similar tree or shrub. [From Old English *haga.*]

haw³ (hô) *interj.* An expression used to command an animal pulling a load to turn to the left.

Ha·wai·i or **Ha·wai'i** (hə-wä′ē *or* hə-wī′ē *or* hə-vä′ē) A state of the United States in the central Pacific Ocean made up of the Hawaiian Islands. Hawaii was admitted as the 50th state in 1959. Honolulu is the capital. —SEE NOTE.

Ha·wai·ian or **Ha·wai'·ian** (hə-wä′yən) *adj.* Relating to Hawaii or its people, language, or culture. ❖ *n.* **1.** A native or inhabitant of Hawaii. **2.** A Native Hawaiian. **3.** The Polynesian language of the Hawaiians.

Hawaiian Islands A group of volcanic and coral islands in the central Pacific Ocean making up the state of Hawaii. There are eight major islands and more than a hundred minor ones. The islands were settled by Polynesians in the sixth century AD.

Hawaiian shirt *n.* A loose-fitting, collared shirt made of a colorfully printed fabric and usually having short sleeves and buttons down the front.

hawk¹ (hôk) *n.* **1.** Any of various birds having a short hooked bill, keen eyesight, and strong claws with which they catch small birds and other animals for food. **2.** *Informal* A person who favors aggressive action or military intervention rather than negotiation: *The senator is a hawk on national defense.* ❖ *intr.v.* **hawked, hawk·ing, hawks** To hunt with a trained hawk. [From Old English *hafoc.*]

hawk² (hôk) *tr.v.* **hawked, hawk·ing, hawks** To sell

(goods) in the street by calling out; peddle. [From Middle English *hauken*, from Middle Low German *höker*, street peddler.]

hawk³ (hôk) *intr.v.* **hawked, hawk·ing, hawks** To clear or try to clear the throat by coughing up phlegm. [Of imitative origin.]

hawk·er (hô′kər) *n.* A person who peddles goods in the street, especially by calling out.

hawk-eyed (hôk′īd′) *adj.* Having very sharp eyesight.

hawk·moth or **hawk moth** (hôk′môth′) *n.* Any of various moths that have a thick body and long front wings. Hawkmoths feed on the nectar of flowers while hovering.

hawk·weed (hôk′wēd′) *n.* Any of numerous plants that resemble dandelions and have yellow or orange flowers and often hairy stems and leaves.

haw·ser (hô′zər) *n.* A heavy line or cable used to moor or tow a ship.

haw·thorn (hô′thôrn′) *n.* Any of various usually thorny shrubs or trees having white, red, or pinkish flowers and small red fruits.

Haw·thorne (hô′thôrn′), **Nathaniel** 1804–1864. American writer whose novels include *The Scarlet Letter* (1850).

hay (hā) *n.* Grass, clover, alfalfa, and other plants cut and dried as food for horses, cattle, or other animals. ❖ *v.* **hayed, hay·ing, hays** *intr.* To cut and dry grass or other plants so as to make them into hay. —*tr.* To feed with hay.

❑ *These sound alike:* **hay, hey** (expression used to attract attention).

hay·cock (hā′kŏk′) *n. Chiefly British* A cone-shaped mound of hay in a field.

Haydn (hīd′n), **Franz Joseph** 1732–1809. Austrian composer who wrote numerous symphonies, string quartets, operas, and concertos.

Hayes (hāz), **Rutherford Birchard** 1822–1893. The 19th president of the United States (1877–1881), who won the election of 1876 by one electoral vote and removed federal troops from the South (1877).

hay fever *n.* A severe irritation of the eyes, nose, and breathing passages, caused by an allergy to various pollens that are blown about in the air.

hay·fork (hā′fôrk′) *n.* **1.** A pitchfork. **2.** A machine for moving or loading hay.

hay·loft (hā′lôft′) *n.* A loft in a barn or stable for storing hay.

hay·mow (hā′mou′) *n.* **1.** A hayloft. **2.** The hay stored in a hayloft.

hay·rack (hā′răk′) *n.* **1.** A rack from which livestock feed. **2.** A rack mounted on a wagon for carrying hay. **3.** A wagon fitted with such a rack.

hay·rick (hā′rĭk′) *n.* A haystack.

hay·ride (hā′rīd′) *n.* A ride taken for pleasure in a wagon piled with hay.

hay·seed (hā′sēd′) *n.* **1.** Grass seed that is shaken out of hay. **2.** *Slang* A person from the country who is considered unsophisticated.

hay·stack (hā′stăk′) *n.* A large stack of hay, especially one that is left in a field.

hay·wire (hā′wīr′) *n.* Wire used for tying up bales of hay. ❖ *adj. Informal* **1.** Not functioning properly; broken: *The ship went haywire when the rudder broke.* **2.** Mentally confused; upset: *The writer went haywire when told he would have to revise the article again.*

haz·ard (hăz′ərd) *n.* **1a.** A chance of being injured or harmed; danger: *the hazards of sailing.* **b.** A possible source of danger: *The stacks of old newspapers were a fire hazard.* **2.** A sandtrap, pond, or other obstacle on a golf course. ❖ *tr.v.* **haz·ard·ed, haz·ard·ing, haz·ards 1.** To expose to danger; risk: *Firefighters hazard their lives for the safety of others.* **2.** To dare; venture: *hazard a guess.*

haz·ard·ous (hăz′ər-dəs) *adj.* Full of danger; risky; perilous: *a hazardous voyage.*

hazardous waste *n.* A material, such as nuclear or industrial waste products, that can damage the environment and harm the health of humans and other organisms.

haze¹ (hāz) *n.* **1.** Fine dust, smoke, or water vapor suspended in the air: *The skyscrapers were shrouded in haze.* **2.** A vague or confused state of mind: *Many people are in a haze just after waking up.* [Probably from *hazy.*]

haze² (hāz) *tr.v.* **hazed, haz·ing, haz·es** To play rough or humiliating jokes on or force to perform humiliating or unpleasant tasks: *haze new members of the club.* [Perhaps from obsolete French *haser*, to annoy.]

ha·zel (hā′zəl) *n.* **1.** Any of various shrubs or small trees having edible nuts enclosed in a leafy husk. **2.** A light yellowish brown. [From Old English *hæsel.*]

ha·zel·nut (hā′zəl-nŭt′) *n.* **1.** The edible nut of a hazel. **2.** A hazel.

haz·y (hā′zē) *adj.* **haz·i·er, haz·i·est 1.** Marked by the presence of haze; misty: *a hazy sun.* **2.** Not clear; vague: *a hazy recollection of an incident long past.* **—haz′i·ly** *adv.* **—haz′i·ness** *n.*

H-bomb (āch′bŏm′) *n.* A hydrogen bomb.

HD *abbr.* An abbreviation of high definition.

he (hē) *pron.* **1.** The male person or animal previously mentioned: *My brother can't dance, but he can sing. Our dog's toenails click when he walks.* **2.** A person whose gender is not specified or known: *He who laughs last laughs best.* ❖ *n.* A male animal or person: *If the puppy is a he, we'll call him Spot.* [From Old English *hē.*] —SEE NOTE.

He The symbol for the element **helium.**

head (hĕd) *n.* **1.** The uppermost or forwardmost part of the body of a vertebrate animal, containing the brain and the eyes, ears, nose, mouth, and jaws. **2.** A similar part in other organisms: *the head of an ant.* **3.** One's mind: *I can do the addition in my head. These problems are all in your head.* **4.** A mental ability or aptitude: *Our teacher has a good head for mathematics.* **5.** A part of something that sticks out or widens at the end: *the head of a pin.* **6.** The part of a tool used to cut or strike: *the head of a hammer.* **7.** A rounded, tightly clustered mass of leaves, buds, or flowers growing from the main stem: *a head of cabbage.* **8.** A person who leads, rules, or is in charge of something: *the head of the corporation.* **9.** The most important part or leading position: *The girl marched at the head of the parade.* **10.** The uppermost part of something; the top: *Place the appropriate name at the head of each column.* **11.** A distinct topic or category; a heading: *a lengthy report divided into several heads.* **12.** A point when something decisive happens; a turning point: *Continual smog over the city brought the matter of air pollution to a head.* **13a.** An individual; a person: *charged $40 a head for the buffet.* **b.** *pl.* **head** A single animal: *20 head of cattle.* **14.** often **heads** *(used with a singular verb)* The side of a coin having the principal design, often the profile of a political leader's head. **15.** The tip of a boil, pimple, or abscess, in which pus forms. **16.** Water that forms the source of a river or stream: *the little stream that forms the head of a great river.* **17.** The pressure exerted by a liquid or gas: *a head of steam.* **18.** The membrane or skin stretched across an instrument such as a drum or banjo. **19.** A device for recording, playing, or erasing a magnetic tape or electronic disk: *a tape recorder with three heads.* ❖ *adj.* **1.** Most important; ranking first; chief: *the head coach.* **2.** Placed on top or in the front: *the head name on a list; the head truck of a convoy.* ❖ *v.* **head·ed, head·ing, heads** —*tr.* **1.** To aim, point, or turn in a certain direction: *They headed*

haze¹
Shanghai, China

hazel

USAGE

he Many people do not like to use the pronoun **he** to stand for any person, since half of all people are female. This means that *he* and its other forms *him* and *his* should be avoided in sentences like *Any student who hands in his paper early will get extra credit.* The easiest way to avoid this problem is to write in the plural: *Students who hand in their papers early will get extra credit.* For more information, see the notes at **me** and **they.**

headdress
top: Native American headdress
bottom: Vietnamese headdress

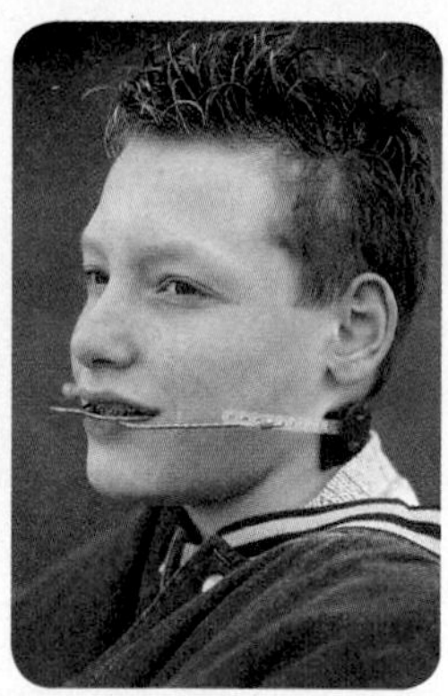

headgear

ă	pat	ôr	core
ā	pay	oi	boy
âr	care	ou	out
ä	father	o͝o	took
ĕ	pet	o͝or	lure
ē	be	o͞o	boot
ĭ	pit	ŭ	cut
ī	bite	ûr	urge
îr	pier	th	thin
ŏ	pot	*th*	this
ō	toe	zh	vision
ô	paw	ə	about

the team of horses up the hill. **2.** To be in charge of; lead: *The mayor headed the delegation.* **3.** To be in the first or foremost position of: *Collins heads the list of candidates for the job.* **4.** To place a heading on: *head each column with a number.* **5.** In soccer, to hit (a ball) in the air with one's head. —*intr.* To proceed or go in a certain direction: *head for home.* ◆ **head off** To block the progress or completion of; intercept: *They tried to head him off before he went home.* **head over heels 1.** Rolling, as in a somersault: *He tripped and fell head over heels.* **2.** Completely; hopelessly: *Those two are head over heels in love.* **over (one's) head 1.** Beyond one's understanding: *At first he thought physics was over his head.* **2.** Beyond one's financial means: *After buying a new house and a luxury car, they were over their heads in debt.*

head·ache (hĕd′āk′) *n.* **1.** A pain in the head. **2.** *Informal* Something that causes trouble: *Their continual interruptions are a real headache.*

head·band (hĕd′bănd′) *n.* A band worn around the head, as to absorb sweat or hold hair in place.

head·board (hĕd′bôrd′) *n.* A board, frame, or panel that stands at the head of a bed.

head count or **head·count** (hĕd′kount′) *n.* **1.** The act of counting people in a group: *After the fire drill, the monitor conducted a head count to make sure everyone left the building.* **2.** The number of people counted in this way.

head·dress (hĕd′drĕs′) *n.* An ornamental covering for the head.

head·ed (hĕd′ĭd) *adj.* **1.** Having a specified kind or number of heads: *a yellow-headed blackbird; a three-headed monster.* **2.** Having a specified kind of disposition: *a cool-headed surgeon.*

head·er (hĕd′ər) *n.* **1.** A beam that supports the ends of joists, studs, or rafters. **2.** A headlong jump or dive. **3.** A shot or pass made in soccer by heading the ball. **4.** Printed information at the top margin of a page.

head·first (hĕd′fûrst′) *adv.* **1.** With the head leading; headlong: *dove headfirst into the water.* **2.** Hastily and with little thought; rashly: *rushing headfirst into a complicated project.*

head·gear (hĕd′gîr′) *n.* **1.** A covering for the head, as a hat or helmet. **2.** A brace extending around the head from one side of the mouth to the other, used to reposition the teeth or to restrict the growth of the upper jaw. **3.** The part of a harness that fits about a horse's head.

head·ing (hĕd′ĭng) *n.* **1.** A title, subtitle, or topic put at the head of a page, chapter, or section of a printed or written work: *Each chapter has a heading on the first page.* **2.** The course or direction in which a ship or aircraft is moving: *The ship's heading was due south.*

head·land (hĕd′lənd *or* hĕd′lănd′) *n.* A point of land, usually high and with a sheer drop, extending out into a body of water; a promontory.

head·less (hĕd′lĭs) *adj.* **1.** Having no head. **2.** Lacking a leader or director.

head·light (hĕd′līt′) *n.* A bright light mounted on the front of an automobile, a train, or another vehicle.

head·line (hĕd′līn′) *n.* The title of a newspaper article, usually printed in large type. ❖ *tr.v.* **head·lined, head·lin·ing, head·lines 1.** To give a headline to (a page or article). **2.** To perform as the main attraction at: *a singer headlining a hip-hop festival.*

head·lock (hĕd′lŏk′) *n.* A wrestling hold in which the head of an opponent is encircled and held tightly between the arm and chest.

head·long (hĕd′lông′) *adv.* **1.** With the head leading; headfirst: *He slid headlong into third base.* **2.** At reckless speed or with uncontrolled force: *The wolf ran headlong in pursuit.* **3.** Hastily and without thinking; rashly. ❖ *adj.* (hĕd′lông′) **1.** Done with the head leading: *a headlong fall down the steps.* **2.** Recklessly fast or uncontrollably forceful: *a headlong race to the finish.* **3.** Done in a rush; caused by or characterized by little thought: *a headlong decision to go.*

head louse *n.* A small parasitic wingless insect that lives on the human scalp, where it bites the skin and feeds on blood, often causing itching.

head·man (hĕd′mən *or* hĕd′măn′) *n.* The male leader or chief, especially of a small village or community.

head·mas·ter (hĕd′măs′tər) *n.* A man who is a school principal, usually of a private school.

head·mis·tress (hĕd′mĭs′trĭs) *n.* A woman who is a school principal, usually of a private school.

head-on (hĕd′ŏn′) *adj.* **1.** Having the front end receiving the impact: *a head-on crash of two cars.* **2.** Facing forward; direct: *the head-on fury of the storm.* ❖ *adv.* **1.** With the head or front first: *The truck ran head-on into the fence.* **2.** In open conflict; directly: *Their opponent attacked the idea head-on.*

head·phone (hĕd′fōn′) *n.* A small speaker that is worn over or in the ear.

head·piece (hĕd′pēs′) *n.* A helmet or cap worn to protect the head.

head·pin (hĕd′pĭn′) *n.* The front or central pin in a group of bowling pins.

head·quar·ters (hĕd′kwôr′tərz) *pl.n.* *(used with a singular or plural verb)* **1.** The building or offices from which a commander, as of a military unit or police force, issues orders. **2.** A center of operations: *That company's headquarters are in Cleveland.*

head·rest (hĕd′rĕst′) *n.* A support for the head, as at the back of a chair.

head·room (hĕd′ro͞om′ *or* hĕd′ro͝om′) *n.* Space above one's head, as in a vehicle or tunnel; clearance.

head·scarf (hĕd′skärf′) *n., pl.* **head·scarfs** or **head·scarves** (hĕd′skärvz) **1.** A scarf worn over or around the head, often folded and tied. **2.** A hijab.

head·set (hĕd′sĕt′) *n.* A pair of headphones, usually equipped with a microphone.

head·stand (hĕd′stănd′) *n.* A position in which one balances oneself vertically on one's head, placing the hands on the floor for support.

head start *n.* **1.** A start before other competitors in a race. **2.** An early start that provides some advantage.

head·stone (hĕd′stōn′) *n.* A memorial stone set at the head of a grave.

head·strong (hĕd′strông′) *adj.* **1.** Determined to have one's own way; stubbornly and often recklessly willful. See Synonyms at **obstinate. 2.** Resulting from willfulness or stubbornness: *a headstrong decision.*

heads up (hĕdz) *interj.* An expression used as a warning to watch out for a source of danger, as at a construction site.

head·wait·er (hĕd′wā′tər) *n.* A waiter who is in charge of other waiters and is often responsible for taking reservations and seating guests.

head·wa·ters (hĕd′wô′tərz) *pl.n.* The water that forms the source of a river.

head·way (hĕd′wā′) *n.* **1.** Movement forward; an advance: *The canoe barely made headway against the strong current.* **2.** Progress toward a goal: *We made a great deal of headway in planning our experiment.* **3.** The distance that separates a bridge, archway, or other overhead structure from the surface beneath it; clearance.

head·wind (hĕd′wĭnd′) *n.* A wind blowing in the direction directly opposite the course of a moving object, such as a ship, aircraft, or runner.

head·word (hĕd′wûrd′) *n.* A word, phrase, or name usually set in bold type and serving as the heading of an entry in a dictionary, encyclopedia, or similar reference work.

head·y (hĕd′ē) *adj.* **head·i·er, head·i·est 1.** Tending to make one dizzy or foolish: *the heady effects of high alti-*

tude. **2.** Characterized by hasty action or willfully rash behavior; headstrong: *a heady outburst of resentment.* **—head′i·ly** *adv.* **—head′i·ness** *n.*

heal (hēl) *v.* **healed, heal·ing, heals** *—tr.* **1.** To make healthy and sound; cure: *heal the sick.* **2.** To set right; amend: *The two friends apologized and healed the rift between them. —intr.* To become healthy and sound: *The small cut healed quickly.* [From Old English *hǣlan,* to make whole.] **—heal′er** *n.* —SEE NOTE.

❑ *These sound alike:* **heal, heel**[1] (foot part), **heel**[2] (tilt), **he'll** (he will).

health (hĕlth) *n.* **1.** The overall condition of an organism or thing at a particular time: *How is your mother's health? Investors are worried about the health of the company.* **2.** Freedom from disease, injury, or defect; soundness of body and mind: *Smoking is bad for your health.* [From Old English *hǣlth.*]

health care also **health·care** (**hĕlth′**kâr′) *n.* The treatment of illness and the preservation of health through the services of medical professionals. ❖ *adj.* also **health-care** (**hĕlth′**kâr′) Relating to health care: *the health care industry.*

health food *n.* Food considered to be especially beneficial to health and usually grown organically and free of chemical additives.

health·ful (**hĕlth′**fəl) *adj.* **1.** Tending to promote good health; beneficial: *a healthful diet.* **2.** Healthy: *a healthful athlete.* **—health′ful·ly** *adv.* **—health′ful·ness** *n.*

health maintenance organization *n.* An HMO.

health·y (**hĕl′**thē) *adj.* **health·i·er, health·i·est 1.** In a state of good health: *a healthy student.* **2.** Promoting good health; healthful: *a healthy climate.* **3.** Indicating or characteristic of good health: *a healthy appearance.* **4.** Great or sizable: *a healthy portion of squash.* **—health′i·ly** *adv.* **—health′i·ness** *n.*

SYNONYMS **healthy, sound, robust, well** These adjectives refer to good physical or mental health. **Healthy** stresses the absence of disease: *The coach encouraged us to eat well so that we would be healthy.* **Sound** indicates freedom from injury or impairment: *When you write a will you must be of sound mind.* **Robust** refers to strength and ruggedness: *The robust soldiers marched for ten hours.* **Well** indicates that a person is not sick or has recovered from a sickness: *My grandfather was in the hospital, but he's back home now that he's well.*

---

heap (hēp) *n.* **1.** A group of things thrown together; a pile: *Why is there a heap of dirty rags thrown in the corner? Please dump these banana peels on the compost heap.* **2.** often **heaps** *Informal* A great amount; a lot: *I have heaps of homework to finish tonight.* ❖ *tr.v.* **heaped, heap·ing, heaps 1.** To put or throw in a heap; pile up: *They heaped wood by the fireplace.* **2.** To fill to overflowing; pile high: *They heaped the cart with groceries.* **3.** To give or bestow in abundance: *The critics heaped compliments on the popular author.* [From Old English *hēap.*]

SYNONYMS **heap, mound, pile, stack** These nouns refer to a group or collection of things lying one on top of the other. *There's a heap of old newspapers on the floor. That mound of boulders indicates that we're on the right trail. Could you take that pile of boxes to the shed? We found a stack of firewood next to the cabin.*

---

hear (hîr) *v.* **heard** (hûrd), **hear·ing, hears** *—tr.* **1.** To be aware of or receive (sound) by the ears: *Did you hear the knock at the door?* **2.** To learn by hearing; be told by others: *We heard the news from a friend.* **3.** To listen to attentively: *They loved to hear their grandmother's stories.* **4.** To listen to officially or formally: *The judge will hear the case in court. —intr.* To be capable of perceiving or receiving by the ear: *I don't hear well.* ◆ **hear from** To get a letter, phone call, email, or other form of communication from: *I haven't heard from her in years.* [From Old English *hīeran.*] **—hear′er** *n.*

❑ *These sound alike:* **hear, here** (at this place).

heard (hûrd) *v.* Past tense and past participle of **hear.**

❑ *These sound alike:* **heard, herd** (cattle).

hear·ing (**hîr′**ĭng) *n.* **1.** The sense by which sound is perceived; the capacity to hear: *Dogs have excellent hearing.* **2.** The region within which sounds from a particular source can be heard; earshot: *They were talking within my hearing.* **3.** An opportunity to be heard: *The protesters deserve a hearing on their concerns.* **4.** A formal session for listening to testimony or arguments: *Congress holds hearings before passing new laws.* ❖ *adj.* Able to hear: *a deaf child born to hearing parents.*

hearing aid *n.* A small electronic device that amplifies sound and is worn in or behind the ear of a person whose hearing is impaired.

hear·ing-im·paired (**hîr′**ĭng-ĭm-pârd′) *adj.* **1.** Having a weakened sense of hearing; hard of hearing. **2.** Completely unable to hear; deaf. ❖ *n. (used with a plural verb)* People who are hard of hearing or are deaf: *The movie was shown with captions to benefit the hearing-impaired.*

hear·ken or **har·ken** (**här′**kən) *intr.v.* **hear·kened, hear·ken·ing, hear·kens** or **har·kened, har·ken·ing, har·kens** *Archaic* To listen attentively; pay close attention. [From Old English *hercnian.*]

hear·say (**hîr′**sā′) *n.* Information that is received from another person and for which the truth cannot be verified.

hearse (hûrs) *n.* A vehicle for carrying a dead person to a church or cemetery. [From Middle English *herse,* a harrow-shaped structure for holding candles over a coffin, from Latin *hirpex,* harrow.]

heart (härt) *n.* **1a.** The hollow muscular organ in vertebrate animals that pumps blood throughout the body by contracting and relaxing. **b.** A similar organ in invertebrate animals. **2.** The general area of the chest containing this organ; the breast. **3.** The vital center and source of one's being, emotions, and sensibilities: *I could feel joy welling up in my heart.* **4a.** Emotional state, disposition, or mood: *I walked to the park with a light heart.* **b.** Love; affection: *The children won their teacher's heart.* **c.** The capacity to feel sympathy, kindness, or concern; compassion: *Have you no heart for these people?* **5.** Courage; determination: *The captain's stirring talk gave the crew heart.* **6a.** The central part; the center: *the heart of the city.* **b.** The essential part; the basis: *the heart of the matter.* **7.** A two-lobed representation of the heart, often colored red or pink. **8a.** A red heart-shaped figure on certain playing cards. **b.** A playing card bearing this figure. **c. hearts** The suit of such playing cards. **9. hearts** A card game in which the object is to avoid hearts in taking tricks or to take all the hearts. ◆ **by heart** Learned by rote; memorized word for word: *He knows that poem by heart.* **from the bottom of (one's) heart** With the deepest appreciation; most sincerely. **have (one's) heart in the right place** To be well-intentioned. **near (one's) heart** or **close to (one's) heart** Loved by or important to one. **take to heart** To take seriously and be affected or troubled by: *Don't take my criticism too much to heart.* **to (one's) heart's content** To one's entire satisfaction; without limitation. **with all (one's) heart** With the deepest feeling or devotion. [From Old English *heorte.*]

❑ *These sound alike:* **heart, hart** (male deer).

heart·ache (**härt′**āk′) *n.* Emotional anguish; deep sorrow.

heart attack *n.* A sudden interruption in the normal functioning of the heart that is often accompanied by

WORD HISTORY

heal The word **heal** belongs to a family of words that all share the basic sense "uninjured." It is related to the adjective *whole* and the less common adjective *hale*[1] (as in the phrase *hale and hearty,* meaning "in good health"). From the verb *heal* is formed the noun *health,* in exactly the same way as the verb *steal* forms the noun *stealth.* The greeting *hail*[2] is also related; it once roughly had the sense "Be healthy!"

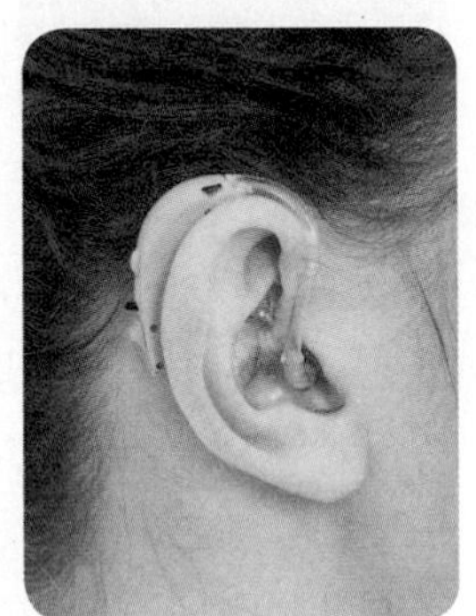

hearing aid

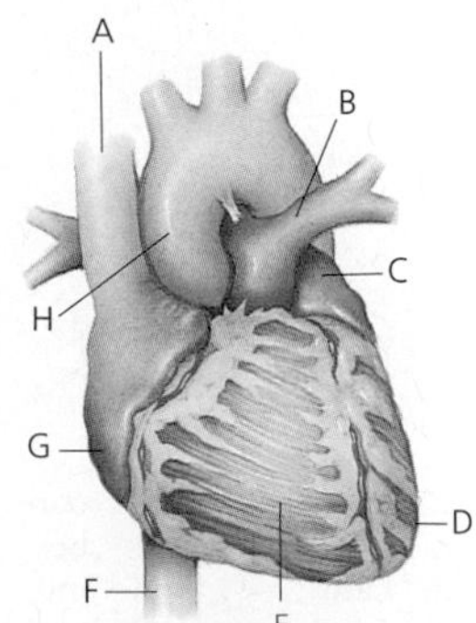

heart

A. superior vena cava
B. pulmonary artery
C. left atrium
D. left ventricle
E. right ventricle
F. inferior vena cava
G. right atrium
H. aorta

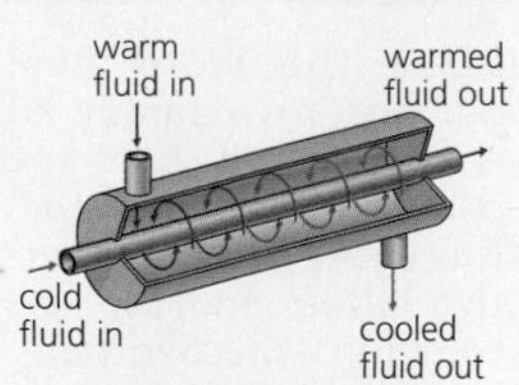

heat exchanger

heather

ă	pat	ôr	core
ā	pay	oi	boy
âr	care	ou	out
ä	father	o͝o	took
ĕ	pet	o͝or	lure
ē	be	o͞o	boot
ĭ	pit	ŭ	cut
ī	bite	ûr	urge
îr	pier	th	thin
ŏ	pot	*th*	this
ō	toe	zh	vision
ô	paw	ə	about

severe pain and is caused by an insufficient supply of blood to the tissues of the heart.

heart·beat (härt′bēt′) *n.* **1.** A single cycle of contraction and relaxation of the heart. **2.** The general nature of the heart's contractions or the rate at which they occur: *a weak and rapid heartbeat.* **3.** An instant: *was ready in a heartbeat.*

heart·break (härt′brāk′) *n.* Great sorrow, grief, or disappointment.

heart·break·er (härt′brā′kər) *n.* **1.** A person or thing that causes sorrow, grief, or disappointment. **2.** A narrow or last-minute defeat, as in a sporting event.

heart·break·ing (härt′brā′kĭng) *adj.* Causing great sorrow, grief, or disappointment: *heartbreaking news.*

heart·bro·ken (härt′brō′kən) *adj.* Suffering from great sorrow, grief, or disappointment; overcome by grief or despair. **—heart′bro′ken·ly** *adv.*

heart·burn (härt′bûrn′) *n.* A burning feeling in the chest area, usually caused by excess acid in the stomach.

heart·en (här′tn) *tr.v.* **heart·ened, heart·en·ing, heart·ens** To give strength or courage to; encourage: *The break in the clouds heartened the campers.*

heart·felt (härt′fĕlt′) *adj.* Deeply felt; sincere: *my heartfelt good wishes.*

hearth (härth) *n.* **1.** The floor of a fireplace, often extending into a room. **2.** Family life; the home: *The weary travelers longed for their own hearth.* **3.** The lower part of a blast furnace, from which the molten metal flows. [From Old English *heorth.*]

hearth·stone (härth′stōn′) *n.* **1.** Stone used in the construction of a hearth. **2.** Family life; the home.

heart·i·ly (här′tl-ē) *adv.* **1.** In a warm and friendly manner; sincerely: *They welcomed their old friends heartily.* **2.** With vigor or enthusiasm: *Everyone plunged heartily into the game.* **3.** Thoroughly; completely: *The mayor heartily disapproved of the plan.* **4.** With much appetite or enjoyment: *After a long day the workers ate heartily.*

heart·land (härt′lănd′) *n.* An important central geographical area considered vital to a nation, region, or culture.

heart·less (härt′lĭs) *adj.* Lacking sympathy or compassion; pitiless. **—heart′less·ly** *adv.* **—heart′less·ness** *n.*

heart of palm *n., pl.* **hearts of palm** The tender edible portion of certain palms of Central and South America, consisting of a bud with small leaves around it or the soft center of a young stem.

heart-rend·ing or **heart·rend·ing** (härt′rĕn′dĭng) *adj.* Causing grief, anguish, or suffering: *a heart-rending story of misfortune.*

hearts·ease also **heart's-ease** (härts′ēz′) *n.* Peace of mind.

heart·sick (härt′sĭk′) *adj.* Profoundly disappointed; very unhappy.

heart·strings (härt′strĭngz′) *pl.n.* A person's deepest feelings: *The actor's lines of grief tugged at the audience's heartstrings.*

heart-to-heart (härt′tə-härt′) *adj.* Personal and sincere; frank: *a heart-to-heart talk.*

heart·warm·ing (härt′wôr′mĭng) *adj.* Causing gladness and tender feelings: *a heartwarming poem.*

heart·wood (härt′wo͝od′) *n.* The older, nonliving central wood of a tree or shrub, usually darker and harder than the sapwood.

heart·y (här′tē) *adj.* **heart·i·er, heart·i·est 1.** Showing warm feelings; cheerful and friendly: *a hearty greeting.* **2.** Complete; thorough: *We gave the team our hearty support.* **3.** Vigorous; robust: *a hearty appearance of health.* **4a.** Giving much nourishment; substantial: *a hearty soup.* **b.** Enjoying or requiring much food: *a hearty appetite.* ❖ *n., pl.* **heart·ies** A good comrade, especially a sailor. **—heart′i·ness** *n.*

heat (hēt) *n.* **1.** A form of energy produced by the motion of molecules that make up a substance. Heat can be transferred from one substance to another through conduction, convection, or radiation. **2.** The condition of being hot; warmth: *feel the heat of the sun.* **3.** A period of hot weather: *We left for the mountains to escape the summer heat.* **4.** A furnace or other source of warmth: *Is the heat on?* **5.** *Informal* Pressure or stress, as from hostile criticism: *Unable to take the heat from the press, the candidate withdrew from the election.* **6.** The most intense or active stage: *In the heat of their debate both candidates were shouting.* **7.** A single contest in a competition, such as a race: *The competition was reduced to six runners after the first heat.* **8.** A regularly recurring period during which female mammals, excluding humans and certain other primates, are ready to mate; estrus. ❖ *tr. & intr.v.* **heat·ed, heat·ing, heats** To make or become warm or hot: *The sun heats the earth. The soup is heating.* ◆ **heat up** *Informal* To become acute or intense: *Their quarrel heated up rapidly.* [From Old English *hǣtu.*] —SEE NOTE AT **temperature.**

heat·ed (hē′tĭd) *adj.* Excited or angry: *a heated debate.* **—heat′ed·ly** *adv.*

heat·er (hē′tər) *n.* An apparatus, such as a furnace or stove, that supplies heat.

heat exchanger *n.* A device, such as an automobile radiator, used to transfer heat from a fluid on one side of a barrier to a fluid on the other side without bringing the fluids into direct contact.

heat exhaustion *n.* A condition caused by exposure to heat, resulting in the loss of body fluids through excessive sweating and causing weakness, dizziness, and nausea.

heath (hēth) *n.* **1.** Any of various usually low-growing shrubs having small evergreen leaves and small, colorful, urn-shaped flowers. **2.** An open uncultivated stretch of land covered with low-growing plants; a moor. [From Old English *hǣth.*]

hea·then (hē′*th*ən) *n., pl.* **hea·thens** or **heathen 1.** *Offensive* **a.** A person who does not believe in the God of Judaism, Christianity, or Islam. **b.** Such people considered as a group: *The missionary had a strong desire to convert the heathen.* **2.** A person regarded as uncivilized or uncultured. [From Old English *hǣthen.*]

heath·er (hĕ*th*′ər) *n.* A low-growing shrub native to Eurasia, having small evergreen leaves and clusters of small, bell-shaped purple or pink flowers. [From Middle English *hather.*]

heat lightning *n.* Distant flashes of light seen near the horizon, especially on hot summer evenings.

heat shield *n.* A barrier that prevents the heating of an object, as a layer of tiles or other coating on a spacecraft to protect it against the tremendous heat of friction caused by reentry into Earth's atmosphere.

heat stroke *n.* A severe illness caused by prolonged exposure to heat and characterized by headache, fever, hot and dry skin, rapid heartbeat, and sometimes loss of consciousness.

heat wave *n.* A period of unusually hot weather.

heave (hēv) *v.* **heaved, heav·ing, heaves** *—tr.* **1a.** To raise or lift with effort or force; hoist: *heaved the pack onto the mule's back.* **b.** *Past tense and past participle* **hove** (hōv) To raise or haul by means of a rope, line, or cable: *They hove anchor and set sail.* **2.** To throw with force or effort; hurl: *heave rocks down the hill.* **3.** To utter painfully or with effort: *heaved a sigh of relief.* *—intr.* **1.** To pull with force or effort; haul: *We heaved on the rope to raise the flag.* **2.** To rise and fall repeatedly: *Seaweed heaved on the gentle waves.* **3.** To be forced upward; bulge: *Parts of the sidewalk heaved after the ground froze.* **4.** To vomit. **5.** *Past tense and past participle* **hove** To move to a specified position: *A tugboat* *hove alongside the huge tanker.* ❖ *n.* **1.** An act or effort of heaving; a throw: *Each heave on the line loosened the anchor a bit more.* **2. heaves** *(used with a singular or plural verb)* A disease of horses affecting the lungs and characterized by coughing and difficulty in breathing. ◆ **heave into sight** or **heave into view** To rise over the horizon into view, as land or a ship. **heave to** To bring a ship at sea to a standstill. [From Old English *hebban.*]

heave-ho (**hēv′hō′**) *n. Slang* Dismissal from one's job or from one's position: *gave him the old heave-ho last week.*

heav·en (**hĕv′**ən) *n.* **1.** often **heavens** The sky or universe as seen from the earth: *a star shooting across the heavens.* **2a.** often **Heaven** In Christianity, the home of God, the angels, and the souls of those who are granted salvation. **b.** Any of the places in or beyond the sky thought of as homes of God or the gods in various religions. **3. Heaven** God: *Thank Heaven you're safe.* **4. heavens** Used in exclamations to express surprise: *Good heavens! Look at that crowd!* **5.** A place or condition of great happiness; bliss: *It'll be heaven to vacation in the quiet of the country.* [From Old English *heofon.*]

heav·en·ly (**hĕv′**ən-lē) *adj.* **1.** Relating to the heavens; celestial: *the planets and other heavenly bodies.* **2.** Relating or belonging to the dwelling place of God; divine. **3.** Very pleasing; delightful; lovely: *a heavenly summer's day.* **—heav′en·li·ness** *n.*

heav·en·ward (**hĕv′**ən-wərd) *adv. & adj.* Toward, to, or in heaven.

heav·y (**hĕv′**ē) *adj.* **heav·i·er, heav·i·est 1.** Having great or unusually great weight: *a heavy package; a heavy skillet.* **2.** Large in amount or intensity: *a heavy rain; heavy traffic.* **3.** Having great power or force; violent: *a heavy blow; heavy seas.* **4a.** Having considerable thickness, density, body, or strength: *a heavy winter coat; drew a heavy line.* **b.** Thick or dense; slow to disperse: *a heavy mist.* **5.** Weighed down, as from weight: *branches heavy with apples; eyelids heavy with sleep.* **6.** Gloomy or sad, as from grief or depression: *a heavy heart.* **7.** Deserving careful consideration; grave; serious: *a heavy issue.* **8a.** Requiring much effort to accomplish; arduous: *heavy reading.* **b.** Hard to endure; severe or burdensome: *a heavy penalty.* **9.** Not easily digested; too rich: *a heavy dessert.* **10.** Moving with or as if with difficulty: *the heavy steps of the movers.* **11.** Involving large-scale manufacturing of basic products, such as steel: *heavy industry.* **12.** Indulging or participating to a great degree: *a heavy eater; a heavy investor.* ❖ *adv.* **heavier, heaviest** Heavily: *These thoughts weigh heavy on his mind.* ❖ *n., pl.* **heav·ies 1.** A serious or tragic role in a play. **2.** A villain in a story or play. [From Old English *hefig.*] **—heav′i·ly** *adv.* **—heav′i·ness** *n.*

heav·y-dut·y (hĕv′ē-**dōō′**tē) *adj.* Made to withstand hard use or wear.

heav·y-hand·ed (**hĕv′**ē-**hăn′**dĭd) *adj.* **1.** Awkward or clumsy: *a heavy-handed performance on the piano.* **2.** Harsh in treating others; oppressive: *heavy-handed discipline.* **—heav′y-hand′ed·ness** *n.*

heav·y-heart·ed (**hĕv′**ē-**här′**tĭd) *adj.* Melancholy; sad; depressed. **—heav′y-heart′ed·ness** *n.*

heavy hydrogen *n.* An isotope of hydrogen with a mass greater than that of ordinary hydrogen; deuterium or tritium.

heavy metal *n.* **1.** A metal that has a high specific gravity, especially one that is greater than 5. Heavy metals, such as lead and mercury, are often poisonous. **2.** Very loud, brash rock music, often having angry or aggressive lyrics.

heav·y·set (**hĕv′**ē-**sĕt′**) *adj.* Having a heavy build; stocky: *The wrestler was heavyset and muscular.*

heavy water *n.* Water formed of oxygen and deuterium. Heavy water is much like ordinary water, but has higher freezing and boiling points and is used in certain nuclear reactors for cooling.

heav·y·weight (**hĕv′**ē-wāt′) *n.* **1.** A person or thing of more than average weight. **2a.** A boxer in the heaviest weight class, usually weighing more than 200 pounds (about 90.7 kilograms). **b.** A contestant in the heaviest weight class in others sports, such as wrestling and weightlifting. **3.** *Informal* A person of great importance or influence: *a heavyweight on the national political scene.*

He·bra·ic (hĭ-**brā′**ĭk) *adj.* Relating to the Hebrews or their language or culture.

He·brew (**hē′**brōō) *n.* **1a.** A member of an ancient Semitic people claiming descent from Abraham, Isaac, and Jacob; an Israelite. **b.** A modern descendant of this people; a Jew. **2a.** The Semitic language of the ancient Hebrews. **b.** The modern form of this language, used especially in Israel. **3. Hebrews** *(used with a singular verb)* A book of the New Testament consisting of an epistle from an unknown writer to a group of Hebrew Christians. **—He′brew** *adj.*

Hebrew Scriptures *pl.n.* The Jewish Bible, consisting of the Torah, the Prophets, and the Writings. The Hebrew Scriptures also form the Old Testament of the Christian Bible.

Heb·ri·des (**hĕb′**rĭ-dēz′) An island group of western and northwest Scotland in the Atlantic Ocean, divided into the **Inner Hebrides,** closer to the Scottish mainland, and the **Outer Hebrides,** to the northwest.

Hec·a·te (**hĕk′**ə-tē *or* **hĕk′**ĭt) *n.* In Greek mythology, an ancient fertility goddess who later became identified with Persephone as queen of Hades and protector of witches.

heck·le (**hĕk′**əl) *tr.v.* **heck·led, heck·ling, heck·les** To harass or bother with questions, annoying remarks, or mocking yells: *The crowd heckled the speaker at the rally.* **—heck′ler** *n.*

hec·tare (**hĕk′**târ′) *n.* A unit of area in the metric system, equal to 2.471 acres.

hec·tic (**hĕk′**tĭk) *adj.* Marked by intense activity, confusion, or excitement: *Constantly changing plans resulted in a hectic departure.* [From Middle English *etik*, feverish, from Greek *hektikos*, habitual.] **—hec′ti·cal·ly** *adv.*

hecto– or **hect–** *pref.* A prefix that means hundred: *hectometer.*

hec·to·me·ter (**hĕk′**tə-mē′tər *or* hĕk-**tŏm′**ĭ-tər) *n.* A unit of length in the metric system, equal to 100 meters.

hec·tor (**hĕk′**tər) *n.* A bully. ❖ *tr.v.* **hec·tored, hec·tor·ing, hec·tors** To try to frighten or control by bullying.

Hector *n.* In Greek mythology, the bravest Trojan warrior and eldest son of Hecuba and Priam, killed by Achilles.

Hec·u·ba (**hĕk′**yə-bə) *n.* In Greek mythology, the wife of Priam and mother of Cassandra, Hector, and Paris.

he'd (hēd) Contraction of *he had* or *he would.*
❑ *These sound alike:* **he'd, heed** (listen).

hedge (hĕj) *n.* **1.** A row of closely planted shrubs or small trees forming a fence or boundary. **2.** A means of protection or defense: *They put some of their savings in stocks as a hedge against inflation.* ❖ *v.* **hedged, hedg·ing, hedg·es** *—tr.* **1.** To enclose or separate with a hedge or hedges: *hedge a yard.* **2.** To restrict or confine; hem in: *The flooded river hedged us in on one side.* **3.** To protect against possible losses on (a bet, investment, or other risk) by balancing one risk against another: *She hedged her investment in stocks by investing in bonds. —intr.* To avoid giving a clear or direct answer or statement. [From Old English *hecg.*]

hedge·hog (**hĕj′**hôg′) *n.* Any of several small mammals of Eurasia and Africa that feed on insects and are covered with short stiff spines. Hedgehogs roll up into a ball for protection when frightened.

WRITERS CHOOSE THEIR WORDS

Louis believed that you could always tell how the team was doing just by the mood in the stadium. During a losing streak the crowd was quick to boo or **heckle** the players, but now, with the team surging, everyone was cheering even though the Yankees were trailing the Washington Senators by a run.

—Wes Tooke
Lucky: Maris, Mantle, and My Best Summer Ever

hedgehog

helicopter

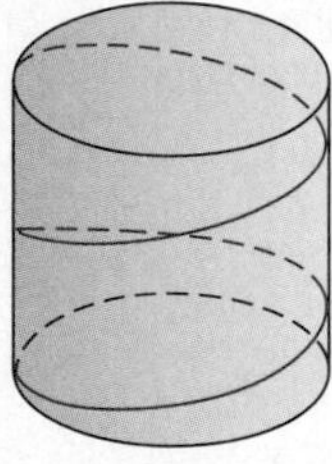

helix
circular helix in a right circular cylinder

ă	pat	ôr	core
ā	pay	oi	boy
âr	care	ou	out
ä	father	ŏŏ	took
ĕ	pet	ŏŏr	lure
ē	be	ōō	boot
ĭ	pit	ŭ	cut
ī	bite	ûr	urge
îr	pier	th	thin
ŏ	pot	*th*	this
ō	toe	zh	vision
ô	paw	ə	about

hedge·row (hĕj′rō′) *n.* A row of bushes or small trees forming a hedge.

heed (hēd) *v.* **heed·ed, heed·ing, heeds** *—tr.* To pay attention to; listen to and consider: *I did not heed his warning. —intr.* To pay attention. ❖ *n.* Close attention or consideration; notice: *They gave no heed to my greeting. Take heed while crossing the highway.* [From Old English *hēdan.*]

❑ *These sound alike:* **heed, he'd** (he had *or* he would).

heed·ful (hēd′fəl) *adj.* Paying close attention; mindful: *The builder was heedful of the architect's advice.*

heed·less (hēd′lĭs) *adj.* Paying little or no attention; unmindful: *heedless of danger.* **—heed′less·ly** *adv.* **—heed′less·ness** *n.*

hee·haw (hē′hô′) *n.* **1.** The loud harsh sound made by a braying donkey. **2.** *Informal* A noisy laugh; a guffaw. ❖ *intr.v.* **hee·hawed, hee·haw·ing, hee·haws** To make such a sound.

heel[1] (hēl) *n.* **1a.** The rounded rear part of the human foot below the ankle. **b.** A similar part of the hind leg of some other vertebrates. **2.** The rounded fleshy base on the palm of the human hand. **3.** The part of a sock, shoe, or stocking that covers the heel of the foot. **4.** The part of a shoe or boot that supports the heel of the foot. **5.** A lower or back part, such as the crusty end of a loaf of bread or the end of a tool next to the handle. **6.** *Informal* A dishonest person; a cad. ❖ *v.* **heeled, heel·ing, heels** *—tr.* To put a heel or heels on: *The cobbler heeled the old shoes. —intr.* To follow at one's heels: *I taught the dog to heel.* ◆ **on the heels of** or **upon the heels of** Directly behind or immediately following: *The first spring birds come on the heels of winter.* **take to (one's) heels** To run away; flee. [From Old English *hēla.*]

❑ *These sound alike:* **heel[1]** (part of a foot), **heel[2]** (tilt), **heal** (make healthy), **he'll** (he will).

heel[2] (hēl) *intr. & tr.v.* **heeled, heel·ing, heels** To tilt or cause to tilt to one side: *Gale winds dangerously heeled the ship. The cargo shifted, and the ship heeled over.* [From Old English *hyldan.*]

❑ *These sound alike:* **heel[2]** (tilt), **heel[1]** (part of a foot), **heal** (make healthy), **he'll** (he will).

heft (hĕft) *n.* Weight; heaviness; bulk. ❖ *tr.v.* **heft·ed, heft·ing, hefts 1.** To lift or hoist up: *Hefting picks and axes, they went to work.* **2.** To lift (something) in order to estimate or test its weight: *I hefted the heavy package and decided I could carry it.*

heft·y (hĕf′tē) *adj.* **heft·i·er, heft·i·est 1.** Weighty; heavy: *a truck carrying a hefty load.* **2.** Big and strong; muscular: *a hefty sailor.* **3.** *Informal* Substantial or considerable: *The cowhand ate a hefty meal.*

he·gem·o·ny (hĭ-jĕm′ə-nē *or* hĕj′ə-mō′nē) *n., pl.* **he·gem·o·nies** The predominance of one nation or social group over others.

he·gi·ra also **he·ji·ra** (hĭ-jī′rə *or* hĕj′ər-ə) *n.* **1.** also **Hegira** The flight of Muhammad from Mecca to Medina in 622, marking the beginning of the Muslim era. **2.** A flight, as from danger or hardship.

heif·er (hĕf′ər) *n.* A young cow that has not given birth to a calf. [From Old English *hēahfore.*]

heigh-ho (hī′hō′ *or* hā′hō′) *interj.* An expression used to show fatigue, boredom, or disappointment.

height (hīt) *n.* **1.** The distance from the top to the bottom of something: *The height of that tree is more than 60 feet.* **2.** Elevation above a given level; altitude: *What is the height of that mountain?* **3.** The condition of being relatively high or tall: *Height is an advantage in basketball.* **4.** often **heights** A high place, such as a hill or mountain. **5.** The highest point or most advanced degree: *the height of the tourist season; the height of an empire's power.* [From Old English *hēhthu, hēahthu.*]

height·en (hīt′n) *tr. & intr.v.* **height·ened, height·en·ing, height·ens 1.** To increase or rise in degree or quantity; intensify: *His angry glare heightened the tension.* **2.** To make or become high or higher; raise or be raised: *The barber heightened the chair for the little boy.*

Hei·long·jiang (hā′lông′jyäng′) See **Amur River.**

Heim·lich maneuver (hīm′lĭk′) *n.* A method of discharging something lodged in the throat of a choking person. It consists of a firm upward thrust just below the rib cage to force air out of the windpipe. [After Henry Jay *Heimlich* (born 1920), American surgeon.]

hei·nous (hā′nəs) *adj.* Very wicked or evil; abominable: *a heinous crime.* [From Middle English *hainous,* from Old French *haine,* hatred.] **—hei′nous·ly** *adv.*

heir (âr) *n.* A person who inherits or is legally entitled to inherit the property or title of another. [From Middle English, from Latin *hērēs.*]

❑ *These sound alike:* **heir, air** (gas), **e'er** (ever), **ere** (before).

heir apparent *n., pl.* **heirs apparent** A person who will inherit property or a title if the owner or ancestor dies first.

heir·ess (âr′ĭs) *n.* A woman who inherits or is legally entitled to inherit the property or title of another.

heir·loom (âr′lo͞om′) *n.* **1.** A possession passed down through succeeding generations of a family. **2.** A variety of fruit or vegetable that was developed in the past and is not widely grown commercially. [From Middle English *heirlome* : *heir,* heir + *lome,* implement.]

heir presumptive *n., pl.* **heirs presumptive** A person who will inherit property or a title unless a relative with a stronger legal claim to the inheritance is born.

he·ji·ra (hĭ-jī′rə *or* hĕj′ər-ə) *n.* Variant of **hegira.**

held (hĕld) *v.* Past tense and past participle of **hold[1].**

Hel·en (hĕl′ən) *n.* In Greek mythology, the wife of Menelaus. Her abduction by Paris caused the Trojan War.

Hel·e·na (hĕl′ə-nə) The capital of Montana, in the west-central part of the state. It was founded in 1864 and became the state capital in 1889.

hel·i·cal (hĕl′ĭ-kəl *or* hē′lĭ-kəl) *adj.* Relating to or having the shape of a helix. **—hel′i·cal·ly** *adv.*

hel·i·ces (hĕl′ĭ-sēz′ *or* hē′lĭ-sēz′) *n.* A plural of **helix.**

hel·i·con (hĕl′ĭ-kŏn′ *or* hĕl′ĭ-kən) *n.* A large circular tuba that fits around the player's shoulder.

hel·i·cop·ter (hĕl′ĭ-kŏp′tər) *n.* A wingless aircraft that is lifted by blades that rotate above the aircraft on a vertical shaft. [From French *hélicoptère* : Greek *helix,* spiral + Greek *pteron,* wing.]

he·li·o·cen·tric (hē′lē-ō-sĕn′trĭk) *adj.* **1.** Relating to or measured from the center of the sun: *a spacecraft with a heliocentric orbit.* **2.** Having the sun as center: *Copernicus's heliocentric model of the solar system.*

He·li·os (hē′lē-ŏs′) *n.* In Greek mythology, the god of the sun, who drives his chariot across the sky from east to west each day.

he·li·o·trope (hē′lē-ə-trōp′) *n.* Any of several garden plants having clusters of small, fragrant, purplish flowers.

he·li·ot·ro·pism (hē′lē-ŏt′rə-pĭz′əm) *n.* Growth or movement of an organism, especially a plant, toward or away from sunlight.

hel·i·port (hĕl′ə-pôrt′) *n.* A place for helicopters to take off and land.

he·li·um (hē′lē-əm) *n.* *Symbol* **He** A very lightweight, colorless, odorless gaseous element. It has the lowest boiling point of any substance and is the second most abundant element in the universe. Atomic number 2. See **Periodic Table.** [From Greek *hēlios,* sun (because its existence was deduced from the solar spectrum).]

he·lix (hē′lĭks) *n., pl.* **he·lix·es** or **hel·i·ces** (hĕl′ĭ-sēz′ *or* hē′lĭ-sēz′) **1.** A three-dimensional curve that lies on a cone or cylinder in such a way that its angle to a plane perpendicular to the axis is constant. **2.** A spiral form or structure, such as the thread of a screw.

hell (hĕl) *n.* **1.** A place, such as Hades, where the spirits of the dead remain for eternity; the underworld. **2.** often **Hell** In certain religions, the place where the souls of the wicked reside in torment after death. **3a.** Misery, torment, or anguish: *the hell of battle.* **b.** A place of misery, torment, or anguish: *City streets are a real hell when choked with traffic.* [From Old English *hel, helle.*]

he'll (hēl) Contraction of *he will.*

❑ *These sound alike:* **he'll, heal** (make healthy), **heel**[1] (part of a foot), **heel**[2] (tilt).

hell·bend·er (hĕl**′**bĕn′dər) *n.* A large salamander of rivers and streams of the eastern United States, having a flattened brownish body.

hel·le·bore (hĕl**′**ə-bôr′) *n.* **1.** Any of various plants of Eurasia having large showy flowers and thick roots formerly used in medicine. **2.** Any of various poisonous plants of North America and Eurasia having large leaves, greenish flowers, and thick roots formerly used in medicine.

Hel·lene (hĕl**′**ēn′) *n.* A Greek.

Hel·len·ic (hĕ-**lĕn′**ĭk) *adj.* Relating to the ancient Greeks or their language or history. ❖ *n.* The Greek branch of the Indo-European family.

Hel·le·nis·tic (hĕl′ə-**nĭs′**tĭk) *adj.* Relating to Greek history and culture from the death of Alexander the Great in 323 BC until the time that Augustus became emperor of Rome in 27 BC.

Hel·les·pont (hĕl**′**ĭ-spŏnt′) See **Dardanelles.**

hell·ish (hĕl**′**ĭsh) *adj.* Relating to, resembling, or worthy of hell; terrible: *hellish confusion and noise.* **—hell′ish·ly** *adv.* **—hell′ish·ness** *n.*

hel·lo (hĕ-**lō′** *or* hə-**lō′**) *interj.* An expression used to greet someone, answer the telephone, or express surprise. ❖ *n., pl.* **hel·los** A call or greeting of "hello."

helm[1] (hĕlm) *n.* **1.** The steering apparatus of a ship, especially the wheel or tiller. **2.** A position of leadership or control: *a new president at the helm.* [From Old English *helma.*]

helm[2] (hĕlm) *Archaic n.* A helmet. [From Old English.]

hel·met (hĕl**′**mĭt) *n.* A covering of metal, plastic, or other hard material worn to protect the head from injury, as in battle, work, or sports.

helms·man (hĕlmz**′**mən) *n.* A man who steers a ship.

helms·per·son (hĕlmz**′**pûr′sən) *n.* A helmsman or helmswoman.

helms·wom·an (hĕlmz**′**wo͝om′ən) *n.* A woman who steers a ship.

hel·o (hĕl**′**ō) *n., pl.* **hel·os** *Informal* A helicopter.

hel·ot (hĕl**′**ət) *n.* **1. Helot** A member of a class of serfs in ancient Sparta. **2.** A serf; a slave.

help (hĕlp) *v.* **helped, help·ing, helps** *—tr.* **1.** To give assistance or support to (someone); aid: *The salesperson helped the customer.* **2.** To make (something) better or more effective; improve or advance: *new ways to help the environment; a remark that didn't help the situation.* **3.** To have a positive effect on (an action or effort). Used with an infinitive: *Your wisecracks are not helping to improve the situation. This program helps create jobs.* **4.** To relieve; ease: *This medicine will help your cold.* **5.** To be able to prevent or change: *I cannot help it if the train is late.* **6.** To refrain from; avoid: *We couldn't help laughing.* *—intr.* To be of service; give assistance: *Do what you can to help.* ❖ *n.* **1.** The act of helping; assistance; aid: *With your help, we can unload these boxes in an hour.* **2.** A person or thing that helps: *A vacuum cleaner is a help in doing housework.* **3.** A person or a group of people hired to work as a helper or helpers: *The restaurant needs kitchen help.* ◆ **cannot help but** To be compelled to; be unable to avoid or resist: *I cannot help but admire their efforts to assist those in need.* **help (oneself) to** To take what one wants, sometimes without permission: *The guests were told to help themselves to the punch.* [From Old English *helpan.*] **—help′er** *n.*

help·ful (hĕlp**′**fəl) *adj.* Providing assistance; useful: *gave me some helpful advice.* **—help′ful·ly** *adv.* **—help′ful·ness** *n.*

help·ing (hĕl**′**pĭng) *n.* A portion of food for one person.

helping verb *n.* An auxiliary verb.

help·less (hĕlp**′**lĭs) *adj.* **1.** Unable to help oneself; powerless: *as helpless as a baby.* **2.** Lacking support or protection: *The townspeople were helpless in the violent storm.* **—help′less·ly** *adv.* **—help′less·ness** *n.*

help·mate (hĕlp**′**māt′) *n.* A helper or helpful companion, especially a husband or wife.

Hel·sin·ki (hĕl**′**sĭng′kē *or* hĕl-**sĭng′**kē) The capital of Finland, in the southern part of the country. It was founded in 1550 and became capital of Finland in 1812.

hel·ter-skel·ter (hĕl′tər-**skĕl′**tər) *adv.* In disorderly haste: *The toys were strewn helter-skelter in the living room.* ❖ *adj.* Hurried and confused: *a helter-skelter retreat from the sudden shower.*

helve (hĕlv) *n.* A handle of a tool, such as an axe or hammer.

hem[1] (hĕm) *n.* An edge or border of a garment or piece of cloth, made by folding the unfinished edge under and sewing it down. ❖ *tr.v.* **hemmed, hem·ming, hems 1.** To fold back and sew down the edge of: *The tailor hems skirts and pants.* **2.** To surround and shut in; enclose: *a valley hemmed in by mountains.* [From Old English.]

hem[2] (hĕm) *n.* A short cough or clearing of the throat made especially to gain attention, hide embarrassment, or fill in a pause when speaking. ❖ *intr.v.* **hemmed, hem·ming, hems** To make this sound. ◆ **hem and haw** To be hesitant and indecisive: *I hemmed and hawed before making a decision.* [From Middle English *heminge,* coughing, of imitative origin.]

he·ma·tite (hē**′**mə-tīt′) *n.* A mineral that is the most abundant iron ore. It is reddish-brown when crushed to powder. [From Middle English *ematite,* from Greek *haima,* blood.]

he·ma·to·ma (hē′mə-**tō′**mə) *n.* An abnormal buildup of blood in a body organ or tissue, caused by a break in a blood vessel.

hemi– *pref.* A prefix that means half: *hemisphere.* —SEE NOTE AT **semi–.**

Hem·ing·way (hĕm**′**ĭng-wā′), **Ernest Miller** 1899–1961. American writer whose short stories and novels, such as *The Sun Also Rises* (1926), have to do with courageous, lonely characters.

hem·i·sphere (hĕm**′**ĭ-sfîr′) *n.* **1.** One half of a sphere formed by a plane that passes through the center of the sphere. **2.** One half of the earth's surface. The Northern and Southern Hemispheres are divided by the equator. The Eastern and Western Hemispheres are divided by a meridian. **3.** Either of the two sides of the brain of a vertebrate animal. **—hem′i·spher′ic, hem′i·spher′i·cal** *adj.*

hem·lock (hĕm**′**lŏk′) *n.* **1a.** Any of various evergreen trees having short flat needles and small cones. **b.** The wood of any of these trees. **2a.** Any of several poisonous plants having feathery leaves and clusters of small white flowers. **b.** A poison made from any of these plants. [From Old English *hymlice.*]

hemo– or **hema–** or **hem–** *pref.* A prefix that means blood: *hemophilia.*

he·mo·glo·bin (hē**′**mə-glō′bĭn) *n.* The iron-containing protein that gives the red blood cells of vertebrate animals their characteristic color. Hemoglobin binds to oxygen and carries it through the bloodstream from the respiratory organs to the body tissues. —SEE NOTE AT **red blood cell.**

he·mo·phil·i·a (hē′mə-**fĭl′**ē-ə *or* hē′mə-**fēl′**yə) *n.* An

helmet

hemlock

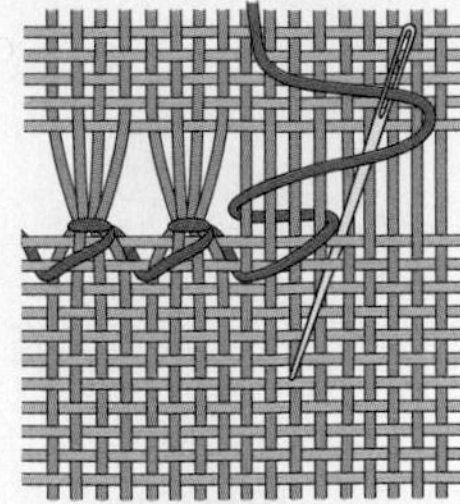
hemstitch

henna

Henry VIII

ă	pat	ôr	core
ā	pay	oi	boy
âr	care	ou	out
ä	father	ŏŏ	took
ĕ	pet	ŏŏr	lure
ē	be	ōō	boot
ĭ	pit	ŭ	cut
ī	bite	ûr	urge
îr	pier	th	thin
ŏ	pot	*th*	this
ō	toe	zh	vision
ô	paw	ə	about

inherited blood disease, principally affecting males, in which the blood does not clot properly, making it very difficult to stop bleeding.

he·mo·phil·i·ac (hē′mə-**fĭl′**ē-ăk′ *or* hē′mə-**fē′**lē-ăk′) *n.* A person who has hemophilia.

hem·or·rhage (**hĕm′**ər-ĭj) *n.* A great amount of bleeding. ❖ *intr.v.* **hem·or·rhaged, hem·or·rhag·ing, hem·or·rhag·es** To have a hemorrhage; bleed heavily.

hem·or·rhoids (**hĕm′**ə-roidz′) *pl.n.* Itching or painful swollen tissue and enlarged veins near the anus.

hemp (hĕmp) *n.* **1.** Tough fibers obtained from the stems of a tall plant and used for making rope, cord, and fabric. **2.** The plant that yields such fibers. Marijuana is made from the leaves and flowers of certain varieties of the hemp plant. [From Old English *hænep*.]

hemp·en (**hĕm′**pən) *adj.* Made of or resembling hemp.

hem·stitch (**hĕm′**stĭch′) *n.* **1.** A fancy stitch that leaves an open design in cloth, made by pulling out several parallel threads and drawing the remaining threads together in even bunches. **2.** Decorative needlework made with hemstitching. ❖ *tr.v.* **hem·stitched, hem·stitch·ing, hem·stitch·es** To hem or decorate with this stitch.

hen (hĕn) *n.* **1.** A female bird, especially an adult female chicken. **2.** The female of certain water animals, such as an octopus or lobster. [From Old English.]

hence (hĕns) *adv.* **1.** For this reason; therefore: *These dolls are handmade and hence expensive.* **2.** From this time; from now: *30 years hence.* **3.** From this place; away from here: *Get thee hence!*

hence·forth (**hĕns′**fôrth′) *adv.* From this time on; from now on.

hence·for·ward (hĕns-**fôr′**wərd) *adv.* Henceforth.

hench·man (**hĕnch′**mən) *n.* **1.** A loyal and trusted follower, as of a politician. **2.** A member of a criminal gang.

hen·ley (**hĕn′**lē) *n., pl.* **hen·leys** A collarless knit shirt with long or short sleeves and buttons extending partway down the front. [After *Henley*, England.]

hen·na (**hĕn′**ə) *n.* **1a.** A reddish-brown dye obtained from the leaves of a shrub of northern Africa and southwest Asia, used especially to color the hair or to make designs on the skin. **b.** The shrub that yields such dye. **2.** A reddish-brown color. ❖ *tr.v.* **hen·naed, hen·na·ing, hen·nas** To dye or color with henna. [From Arabic *ḥinnā'*.]

hen·ry (**hĕn′**rē) *n., pl.* **hen·ries** or **hen·rys** A unit used to measure electrical inductance. When a current varies at the rate of one ampere per second and induces an electromotive force of one volt, the circuit has an inductance of one henry. [After Joseph *Henry* (1797–1878), American physicist.]

Hen·ry I (**hĕn′**rē) 1068–1135. King of England (1100–1135) who conquered Normandy (1106).

Henry VII 1457–1509. King of England (1485–1509). He won the Battle of Bosworth Field (1485) and was proclaimed king, ending more than 30 years of civil war.

Henry VIII 1491–1547. King of England (1509–1547) whose divorce from Catherine of Aragon caused him to break away from the Catholic Church.

Henry the Navigator 1394–1460. Prince of Portugal who directed voyages that enlarged Portugal's empire.

he·pat·ic (hĭ-**păt′**ĭk) *adj.* Relating to the liver. [From Middle English *epatik*, from Greek *hēpatikos*, from *hēpar*, liver.]

he·pat·i·ca (hĭ-**păt′**ĭ-kə) *n.* Any of several low woodland plants having lavender, white, or pink flowers and leaves with three lobes.

hep·a·ti·tis (hĕp′ə-**tī′**tĭs) *n.* Inflammation of the liver, usually caused by a virus and characterized by jaundice and fever. [From Greek *hēpatos*, of the liver.]

Hep·burn (**hĕp′**bûrn′), **Katharine Houghton** 1907–2003. American actress known for her motion pictures, including *The African Queen* (1951).

He·phaes·tus (hĭ-**fĕs′**təs) *n.* In Greek mythology, the god of fire and metalworking, identified with the Roman Vulcan.

hepta– or **hept–** *pref.* A prefix that means seven: *heptagon.*

hep·ta·gon (**hĕp′**tə-gŏn′) *n.* A plane figure with seven sides and seven angles. **—hep·tag′o·nal** (hĕp-**tăg′**ə-nəl) *adj.*

hep·ta·he·dron (hĕp′tə-**hē′**drən) *n., pl.* **hep·ta·he·drons** or **hep·ta·he·dra** (hĕp′tə-**hē′**drə) A solid geometric figure having seven faces.

hep·tath·lon (hĕp-**tăth′**lŏn′) *n.* A track-and-field event usually for women that includes the 200-meter and 800-meter runs, the 100-meter hurdles, the shot put, the javelin throw, the high jump, and the long jump. [From *hepta-* + *(dec)athlon*.]

her (hər; hûr *when stressed*) *adj.* The possessive form of **she.** Relating or belonging to her: *Her greatest pleasure is playing her guitar.* ❖ *pron.* The objective form of **she. 1.** Used as the direct object of a verb: *We brought her to the airport.* **2.** Used as the indirect object of a verb: *I wrote her a letter.* **3.** Used as the object of a preposition: *I gave all the popcorn to her.* —SEE NOTE AT **me.**

He·ra (**hîr′**ə) *n.* In Greek mythology, the chief goddess and the wife and sister of Zeus, worshipped as the goddess of women, marriage, and childbirth. She came to be identified with the Roman Juno.

Her·a·cles or **Her·a·kles** (**hĕr′**ə-klēz′) *n.* Variants of **Hercules.**

her·ald (**hĕr′**əld) *n.* **1.** A person who carries messages or makes announcements. **2.** A person or thing that gives an indication of something to come; a harbinger: *The crocus is a herald of spring.* ❖ *tr.v.* **her·ald·ed, her·ald·ing, her·alds** To indicate the coming of; foretell; announce: *The evening star heralds the arrival of nightfall.* [From Middle English *heraud, herald*, from Anglo-French, of Germanic origin.]

he·ral·dic (hə-**răl′**dĭk) *adj.* Relating to heralds or heraldry.

her·ald·ry (**hĕr′**əl-drē) *n., pl.* **her·ald·ries** The study or art concerned with devising and interpreting coats of arms and tracing the history of families, including the order of succession for aristocratic titles.

herb (ûrb *or* hûrb) *n.* **1.** Any of various usually aromatic plants, such as basil or ginseng, used as a seasoning or for medicinal purposes. **2.** A plant that does not produce a woody stem and often dies back at the end of each growing season. [From Middle English *herbe*, from Latin *herba*.]

her·ba·ceous (hûr-**bā′**shəs *or* ûr-**bā′**shəs) *adj.* Relating to or characteristic of an herb, in contrast to a woody plant.

herb·age (**ûr′**bĭj *or* **hûr′**bĭj) *n.* Grass or other leafy plants having soft stems, especially when grown to be eaten by grazing animals.

herb·al (**ûr′**bəl *or* **hûr′**bəl) *adj.* Relating to or containing aromatic or medicinal herbs: *herbal tea; herbal remedies.* ❖ *n.* A book that describes the kinds and uses of aromatic or medicinal herbs.

herbal medicine *n.* **1.** The use of herbs to prevent or treat disease. **2.** A medicine made from herbs.

her·bar·i·um (hûr-**bâr′**ē-əm *or* ûr-**bâr′**ē-əm) *n., pl.* **her·bar·i·ums** or **her·bar·i·a** (hûr-**bâr′**ē-ə *or* ûr-**bâr′**ē-ə) **1.** A collection of dried plants mounted and labeled for use in scientific study. **2.** A special place or building where such a collection is kept.

her·bi·cide (**hûr′**bĭ-sīd′ *or* **ûr′**bĭ-sīd′) *n.* A chemical substance used to destroy or reduce the growth of plants.

her·bi·vore (**hûr′**bə-vôr′ *or* **ûr′**bə-vôr′) *n.* An animal that feeds mainly on plants.

her·biv·o·rous (hûr-bĭv′ər-əs *or* ûr-bĭv′ər-əs) *adj.* Feeding mainly on plants: *Cattle, deer, and rabbits are herbivorous animals.*

Her·cu·le·an (hûr′kyə-lē′ən *or* hûr-kyo͞o′lē-ən) *adj.* **1.** often **herculean** Demanding great strength or courage; tremendously difficult: *Moving the whole library was a herculean task.* **2.** Relating to or resembling Hercules: *It took Herculean strength to move the fallen tree trunk.*

Her·cu·les (hûr′kyə-lēz′) also **Her·a·cles** or **Her·a·kles** (hĕr′ə-klēz′) *n.* In Greek mythology, a mortal son of Zeus known for his great strength and courage.

herd (hûrd) *n.* **1a.** A group of large domestic animals such as cattle or sheep. **b.** A number of large plant-eating wild animals that stay together as a group: *a herd of elephants.* **2.** A large number of people; a crowd. ❖ *v.* **herd·ed, herd·ing, herds** —*tr.* **1.** To gather or keep (a herd) together: *Dogs herded the sheep into the pen.* **2.** To tend or watch over (a herd): *herding sheep in the mountains.* —*intr.* To come together in a herd: *Buffalo herded together on the plains.* [From Old English *heord.*]
❑ *These sound alike:* **herd, heard** (past tense of hear).

herd·er (hûr′dər) *n.* A person who takes care of or drives a herd, as of sheep or cattle.

herds·man (hûrdz′mən) *n.* A person who owns or breeds livestock.

here (hîr) *adv.* **1.** At or in this place: *Put the package here.* **2.** At this time; now: *Let's stop practicing here and break for lunch.* **3.** To this place; hither: *Come here and sit beside me.* ❖ *interj.* An expression used to answer to one's name in a roll call, to call to an animal, or to get someone's attention. ❖ *n.* **1.** This place: *I went from here to the store.* **2.** This life or this time: *We should think more about the here and now than about what might happen.* ◆ **neither here nor there** Not to the point; off the subject; unimportant: *Their vague remarks were neither here nor there.* [From Old English *hēr.*]
❑ *These sound alike:* **here, hear** (listen).

here·a·bouts (hîr′ə-bouts′) *adv.* In this general area; around here: *I dropped my keys somewhere hereabouts.*

here·af·ter (hîr-ăf′tər) *adv.* From now on; after this: *Hereafter, when you write use my full address.* ❖ *n.* Life after death.

here·by (hîr′bī′) *adv.* By virtue of this; by this means: *All drivers are hereby required to have an eye test.*

he·red·i·tar·y (hə-rĕd′ĭ-tĕr′ē) *adj.* **1.** Passed or capable of being passed from parent to offspring by means of genes: *a hereditary trait.* **2.** Passed down by inheritance to a legal heir: *a hereditary title.* **3.** Passed down from one generation to the next: *a hereditary prejudice.*

he·red·i·ty (hə-rĕd′ĭ-tē) *n.* **1.** The passage of traits or characteristics from parents to offspring by biological inheritance through genes. **2.** The traits or characteristics passed to an offspring in this way. [From Latin *hērēditās*, from *hērēs*, heir.]

Here·ford (hûr′fərd *or* hĕr′ə-fərd) *n.* Any of a breed of cattle originally developed in England and having a reddish-brown coat with a white face, chest, and belly.

here·in (hîr-ĭn′) *adv.* In this thing, matter, fact, or place: *She likes to read, and herein lies the source of her large vocabulary.*

here·of (hîr-ŭv′ *or* hîr-ŏv′) *adv.* Of this: *We will speak no more hereof.*

here·on (hîr-ŏn′) *adv.* On this: *This is the Constitution, and our Bill of Rights was founded hereon.*

her·e·sy (hĕr′ĭ-sē) *n., pl.* **her·e·sies 1.** An opinion or belief that is different from the established beliefs of a religion. **2.** An opinion that is contrary to prevailing views, as in politics or science. **3.** The holding of such a belief or opinion.

her·e·tic (hĕr′ĭ-tĭk) *n.* A person who holds beliefs or opinions that are different from accepted beliefs or opinions, as of a church or a political party.

he·ret·i·cal (hə-rĕt′ĭ-kəl) *adj.* Relating to, characterized by, or revealing heresy: *The speaker's heretical statements made the audience uneasy.*

here·to (hîr-to͞o′) *adv.* To this document or matter: *Attached hereto is my signature.*

here·to·fore (hîr′tə-fôr′) *adv.* Before this; previously: *Such a huge ship had not been seen heretofore.*

here·un·to (hîr-ŭn′to͞o) *adv.* Hereto.

here·up·on (hîr′ə-pŏn′) *adv.* **1.** Immediately after this: *A few bystanders shouted taunts and hereupon began an argument.* **2.** Upon this point; upon this: *We believe in free speech and hereupon the court has remained firm.*

here·with (hîr-wĭth′ *or* hîr-wĭth′) *adv.* **1.** Along with this: *I am sending herewith a snapshot of the baby.* **2.** By means of this; hereby: *I herewith renounce all claim to the estate.*

her·i·ta·ble (hĕr′ĭ-tə-bəl) *adj.* Capable of being inherited: *heritable property; a heritable disease.* —**her′i·ta·bil′i·ty** *n.*

her·i·tage (hĕr′ĭ-tĭj) *n.* **1.** Property that is or can be inherited. **2.** Something other than property passed down from preceding generations; a tradition: *Our country has a great heritage of folk music.*

her·maph·ro·dite (hər-măf′rə-dīt′) *n.* **1.** An organism, such as an earthworm, that typically has both male and female reproductive organs in a single individual. **2.** A person who has both male and female reproductive organs and secondary sexual characteristics.

Her·mes (hûr′mēz) *n.* In Greek mythology, the messenger of the gods and patron of travelers, thieves, and commerce, identified with the Roman Mercury.

her·met·ic (hər-mĕt′ĭk) also **her·met·i·cal** (hər-mĕt′ĭ-kəl) *adj.* Sealed so that air cannot enter or escape; airtight. —**her·met′i·cal·ly** *adv.*

her·mit (hûr′mĭt) *n.* A person who has withdrawn from society and lives a solitary existence. [From Middle English *heremite*, from Greek *erēmītēs*, from *erēmos*, solitary.]

her·mit·age (hûr′mĭ-tĭj) *n.* The home of a hermit.

hermit crab *n.* Any of various crabs that use an empty snail shell or a similar shell to protect their soft bodies.

her·ni·a (hûr′nē-ə) *n., pl.* **her·ni·as** or **her·ni·ae** (hûr′nē-ē′) A condition in which an organ or other structure of the body protrudes through an abnormal opening in the wall that normally contains it; a rupture.

he·ro (hîr′ō) *n., pl.* **he·roes 1.** In mythology and legend, a man of great courage and strength who is celebrated for his bold deeds. **2.** A person noted for courageous acts or significant achievements: *a sports hero.* **3.** The protagonist in a novel, poem, play, or movie. **4.** A submarine sandwich. [From Greek *hērōs.*]

Her·od An·ti·pas (hĕr′əd ăn′tĭ-păs′) Died about AD 40. Ruler of a portion of Judea (4 BC–AD 40) to whom Jesus was sent for judgment.

he·ro·ic (hĭ-rō′ĭk) also **he·ro·i·cal** (hĭ-rō′ĭ-kəl) *adj.* **1.** Having or showing the qualities of a hero; courageous; noble: *heroic deeds; the heroic voyage of Magellan's crew.* **2.** Relating to or resembling the heroes of literature, legend, or myth. ❖ *n.* **heroics** Heroic behavior or action. —**he·ro′i·cal·ly** *adv.*

her·o·in (hĕr′ō-ĭn) *n.* A bitter white crystalline chemical compound derived from morphine. It is a powerful and highly addictive narcotic drug.
❑ *These sound alike:* **heroin, heroine** (courageous woman).

her·o·ine (hĕr′ō-ĭn) *n.* **1.** A woman noted for courageous acts or significant achievements. **2.** The female protagonist in a novel, poem, play, or movie.
❑ *These sound alike:* **heroine, heroin** (drug).

her·o·ism (hĕr′ō-ĭz′əm) *n.* Heroic conduct or action; courage; bravery.

Katharine Hepburn

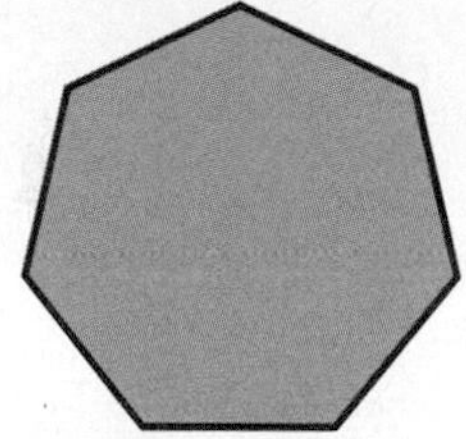

heptagon

heron

herringbone

Caroline Herschel

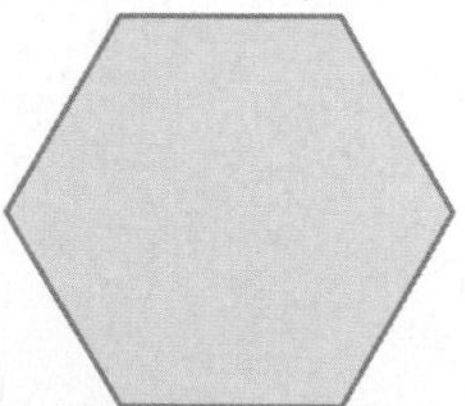
hexagon

ă	pat	ôr	core
ā	pay	oi	boy
âr	care	ou	out
ä	father	o͝o	took
ĕ	pet	o͝or	lure
ē	be	o͞o	boot
ĭ	pit	ŭ	cut
ī	bite	ûr	urge
îr	pier	th	thin
ŏ	pot	*th*	this
ō	toe	zh	vision
ô	paw	ə	about

her·on (**hĕr′**ən) *n.* Any of various wading birds having a long neck, long legs, and a long pointed bill.

her·pes (**hûr′**pēz) *n.* Any of several diseases caused by viruses in which there is an eruption of blisters on the skin or mucous membranes.

her·pe·tol·o·gy (hûr′pĭ-**tŏl′**ə-jē) *n.* The branch of zoology that deals with reptiles and amphibians. **—her′pe·tol′o·gist** *n.*

her·ring (**hĕr′**ĭng) *n., pl.* **herring** or **her·rings** Any of various slivery fishes of northern Atlantic and Pacific waters, caught in large numbers and used as fresh or preserved foods.

her·ring·bone (**hĕr′**ĭng-bōn′) *n.* **1.** A zigzag pattern made up of short parallel lines arranged in rows that slant first one way, then another. **2.** Cloth woven in this pattern.

hers (hûrz) *pron. (used with a singular or plural verb)* The one or ones belonging to her: *If his desk is occupied, use hers.*

Her·schel (**hûr′**shəl) Family of British astronomers. Sir **William Herschel** (1738–1822) discovered Uranus (1781) and cataloged more than 800 binary stars and 2,400 previously unknown nebulae and other celestial objects. His sister **Caroline Herschel** (1750–1848) assisted in his work and discovered numerous comets. His son Sir **John Frederick William Herschel** (1792–1871) cataloged nearly 2,000 more celestial objects and conducted notable research on light, photography, and astrophysics.

her·self (hûr-**sĕlf′**) *pron.* **1.** That one that is the same as her: **a.** Used as the direct object or indirect object of a verb or as the object of a preposition to show that the action of the verb refers back to the subject: *She pulled herself up by the rope. She bought herself a new pen. She had a photograph of herself.* **b.** Used to give emphasis: *Mother herself is going. She herself saw it.* **2.** Her real, normal, or healthy self: *She has not been herself since her friend left town.*

hertz (hûrts) *n., pl.* **hertz** A unit used to measure the frequency of vibrations and waves, equal to one cycle per second. [After Heinrich Rudolf *Hertz* (1857–1894), German physicist.]

Her·ze·go·vi·na (hĕrt′sə-gō-**vē′**nə *or* hûrt′sə-gō-**vē′**nə) A region making up the southern part of Bosnia and Herzegovina. It was conquered by Bosnia in the 1300s and (with Bosnia) by Turkey in the 1400s.

he's (hēz) Contraction of *he is* or *he has.*

hes·i·tan·cy (**hĕz′**ĭ-tən-sē) *n.* The condition or quality of being hesitant: *a hesitancy in speaking one's mind.*

hes·i·tant (**hĕz′**ĭ-tənt) *adj.* Inclined or tending to hesitate; doubtful, uncertain, or reluctant: *We were hesitant to fly in such bad weather.* **—hes′i·tant·ly** *adv.*

hes·i·tate (**hĕz′**ĭ-tāt′) *intr.v.* **hes·i·tat·ed, hes·i·tat·ing, hes·i·tates 1a.** To be slow to act, speak, or decide: *We hesitated about whether to go over the rickety bridge.* **b.** To pause or wait in uncertainty: *I hesitated before answering since I was not sure how he would react.* **2.** To be reluctant or unwilling: *They hesitated to ask for help when they saw how busy I was.* [From Latin *haesitāre,* from *haerēre,* to hold fast.]

hes·i·ta·tion (hĕz′ĭ-**tā′**shən) *n.* The act or an instance of hesitating: *After a short hesitation, we decided to continue the game.*

Hesse (hĕs) A region and former grand duchy of west-central Germany.

Hes·sian (**hĕsh′**ən) *adj.* Relating to Hesse or its people. ❖ *n.* **1.** A native or inhabitant of Hesse. **2.** A German soldier hired to fight in the British army in America during the Revolutionary War.

hetero– or **heter–** *pref.* A prefix that means other or different: *heterogeneous.*

het·er·o·dox (**hĕt′**ər-ə-dŏks′) *adj.* Not in agreement with generally accepted beliefs, especially in religion.

het·er·o·dox·y (**hĕt′**ər-ə-dŏk′sē) *n., pl.* **het·er·o·dox·ies 1.** The condition of being heterodox. **2.** A heterodox belief.

het·er·o·ge·ne·ous (hĕt′ər-ə-**jē′**nē-əs *or* hĕt′ər-ə-**jēn′**-yəs) *adj.* **1.** Consisting of parts that are not alike; having unlike elements: *the museum's vast heterogeneous collection of insects.* **2.** Different in kind; not alike: *the heterogeneous insects in the museum's collection.* **—het′er·o·ge′ne·ous·ly** *adv.* **—het′er·o·ge′ne·ous·ness** *n.*

het·er·o·sex·u·al (hĕt′ə-rō-**sĕk′**sho͞o-əl) *adj.* Relating to or having a sexual orientation toward people of the opposite sex. ❖ *n.* A heterosexual person.

het·er·o·sex·u·al·i·ty (hĕt′ə-rō-sĕk′sho͞o-**ăl′**ĭ-tē) *n.* Sexual orientation toward people of the opposite sex.

het·er·o·troph (**hĕt′**ər-ə-trŏf′ *or* **hĕt′**ər-ə-trōf′) *n.* An organism that cannot manufacture its own food and instead obtains its food and energy by eating other organisms or by taking in parts or remains of other organisms. Animals, fungi, and most bacteria are heterotrophs. **—het′er·o·troph′ic** *adj.*

het·er·o·zy·gous (hĕt′ər-ə-**zī′**gəs) *adj.* Having two different forms of the same gene for a trait such as eye color (for example, brown and blue) at corresponding positions on a pair of chromosomes.

hew (hyo͞o) *v.* **hewed, hewn** (hyo͞on) or **hewed, hew·ing, hews** *—tr.* **1.** To cut with heavy chopping strokes: *hew a log into pieces.* **2.** To make with heavy chopping strokes: *We hewed a path through the jungle.* *—intr.* To adhere; keep; hold: *hew closely to the regulations.*
❑ *These sound alike:* **hew, hue** (color).

hex (hĕks) *n.* **1.** An evil spell; a curse. **2.** A person or thing that brings bad luck: *The new player seemed to be a hex on the team, for we lost four games in a row.* ❖ *tr.v.* **hexed, hex·ing, hex·es 1.** To put a hex on. **2.** To bring bad luck to.

hexa– or **hex–** *pref.* A prefix that means six: *hexagon.*

hex·a·dec·i·mal (hĕk′sə-**dĕs′**ə-məl) *adj.* Relating to or using 16 as the base of a number system.

hex·a·gon (**hĕk′**sə-gŏn′) *n.* A polygon with six sides and six angles. **—hex·a·g′o·nal** (hĕk-**săg′**ə-nəl) *adj.*

hex·a·he·dron (hĕk′sə-**hē′**drən) *n., pl.* **hex·a·he·drons** or **hex·a·he·dra** (hĕk′sə-**hē′**drə) A solid figure having six faces, as a cube.

hex·am·e·ter (hĕk-**săm′**ĭ-tər) *n.* A line of verse made up of six metrical feet.

hey (hā) *interj.* **1.** An expression used to show surprise, appreciation, or wonder: *Hey, that's nice!* **2.** An expression used to attract attention: *Hey, you!* **3.** *Informal* An expression used as a greeting: *Hey, how's it going?* —SEE NOTE.
❑ *These sound alike:* **hey, hay** (dried grass).

hey·day (**hā′**dā′) *n.* The period of greatest popularity, success, or power; prime: *The heyday of very large cars seems to have passed.*

Hf The symbol for the element **hafnium.**

HF *abbr.* An abbreviation of high frequency.

hf. *abbr.* An abbreviation of half.

Hg The symbol for the element **mercury.**

HH *abbr.* An abbreviation of: **1.** Her Highness. **2.** His Highness. **3.** His Holiness.

hi (hī) *interj. Informal* An expression used as a greeting. —SEE NOTE AT **hey.**
❑ *These sound alike:* **hi, hie** (hurry), **high** (elevated).

HI *abbr.* An abbreviation of Hawaii.

hi·a·tus (hī-**ā′**təs) *n., pl.* **hi·a·tus·es** or **hiatus** A gap or interruption in space, time, or continuity; a break: *She took a hiatus from work while on maternity leave.*

Hi·a·wa·tha (hī′ə-**wŏth′**ə *or* hī′ə-**wô′**thə) Flourished about 1550. Onondagan leader who is credited with organizing the Iroquois confederacy.

hi·ba·chi (hĭ-bä′chē) *n., pl.* **hi·ba·chis** A small, portable charcoal-burning stove used for cooking. [From Japanese : *hi*, fire + *bachi*, bowl (ultimately from Sanskrit *pātram*, cup, bowl).]

hi·ber·nate (hī′bər-nāt′) *intr.v.* **hi·ber·nat·ed, hi·ber·nat·ing, hi·ber·nates** To be in an inactive state during a cold period. In cold climates, many animals hibernate during the winter. [From Latin *hībernus*, relating to winter.] **—hi′ber·na′tion** *n.*

Hi·ber·ni·a (hī-bûr′nē-ə) A poetic name for the island of Ireland.

hi·bis·cus (hī-bĭs′kəs) *n.* Any of various tropical shrubs or trees having large trumpet-shaped red, white, or pink flowers.

hic·cup also **hic·cough** (hĭk′əp) *n.* **1.** A sudden and uncontrolled contraction of the muscles of the diaphragm and throat causing the breath to be quickly cut off with a short sharp sound. **2. hiccups** An attack in which spasms of this kind occur repeatedly. ❖ *intr.v.* **hic·cupped, hic·cup·ping, hic·cups** also **hic·coughed, hic·cough·ing, hic·coughs 1.** To make the sound of a hiccup. **2.** To have the hiccups. [Of imitative origin.]

hick (hĭk) *Informal n.* A person regarded as unsophisticated from having lived in the country. ❖ *adj.* Considered rural and unsophisticated: *a hick town.*

hick·o·ry (hĭk′ə-rē) *n., pl.* **hick·o·ries 1.** Any of several mostly North American trees that have compound leaves and bear edible nuts. **2.** The tough, heavy wood of such a tree. [From Virginia Algonquian *pocohiquara*, drink made of pressed hickory nuts.]

Hi·dal·go y Co·stil·la (ē-däl′gō ē kō-stē′yä), **Miguel** 1753–1811. Mexican priest and revolutionary who led a failed revolt (1810) against Spanish rule. He is regarded as a national hero in Mexico's struggle for independence from Spain.

hide[1] (hīd) *v.* **hid** (hĭd), **hid·den** (hĭd′n) or **hid, hid·ing, hides** *—tr.* **1.** To put or keep out of sight; conceal: *I hid his birthday present in my closet.* **2.** To prevent from being known; keep secret: *The disguise was a perfect way to hide her true identity.* **3.** To cut off from sight; cover up: *Clouds hid the stars. —intr.* To keep oneself out of sight: *The lion hid in the tall grass.* ◆ **hide out** To be in hiding, as from a pursuer: *The gangsters hid out in a remote cabin until it was safe to return to the city.* [From Old English *hȳdan*.]

SYNONYMS hide, conceal, secrete, screen These verbs mean to keep from the sight or knowledge of others. **Hide** and **conceal** are the most general: *I smiled to hide my hurt feelings. A throw rug concealed the stain on the carpet.* **Secrete** means to hide in a place unknown to others: *The lioness secreted her cubs in the tall grass.* **Screen** means to shield or block from the view of others: *Tall shrubs screen the actor's home from inquisitive tourists.*

hide[2] (hīd) *n.* The skin of an animal, especially the thick tough skin or pelt of a large animal. [From Old English *hȳd*.]

hide-and-seek (hīd′n-sēk′) *n.* A children's game in which one player tries to find and catch the other players who are hiding.

hide·a·way (hīd′ə-wā′) *n.* **1.** A hideout. **2.** A secluded or isolated place: *Spend a vacation at a hideaway in the mountains.*

hide·bound (hīd′bound′) *adj.* Displaying stubborn attachment to one's own opinions or prejudices; narrow-minded: *a hidebound refusal to change his ways.*

hid·e·ous (hĭd′ē-əs) *adj.* Repulsive, especially to the sight; revoltingly ugly: *a hideous monster; a hideous murder.* **—hid′e·ous·ly** *adv.* **—hid′e·ous·ness** *n.*

hide·out (hīd′out′) *n.* A place of shelter or concealment.

hie (hī) *intr. & tr.v.* **hied, hie·ing** or **hy·ing** (hī′ĭng), **hies** To hasten; hurry. [From Old English *hīgian*, to strive.]
❑ *These sound alike:* **hie, hi** (greeting), **high** (elevated).

hi·er·ar·chi·cal (hī′ə-rär′kĭ-kəl *or* hī-rär′kĭ-kəl) or **hi·er·ar·chic** (hī′ə-rär′kĭk *or* hī′rär′kĭk) *adj.* Relating to or organized in a hierarchy. **—hi′er·ar′chi·cal·ly** *adv.*

hi·er·ar·chy (hī′ə-rär′kē *or* hī′rär′kē) *n., pl.* **hi·er·ar·chies 1.** An arrangement or categorization of people or things according to rank or grade, with each level having less importance or authority than the one above: *We made a chart to show the hierarchy of positions in the corporation.* **2.** A group of people organized in such an arrangement or categorization. [From Middle English *jerarchie*, from Greek *hierarkhēs*, high priest.]

hi·er·o·glyph (hī′ər-ə-glĭf′ *or* hī′rə-glĭf′) *n.* A picture or symbol used in hieroglyphic writing.

hi·er·o·glyph·ic (hī′ər-ə-glĭf′ĭk *or* hī′rə-glĭf′ĭk) *adj.* Related to a system of writing, such as that of ancient Egypt, in which pictures or symbols are used to represent words or sounds: *The ancient Egyptians used hieroglyphic writing.* ❖ *n.* **1.** A hieroglyph. **2. hieroglyphics** Hieroglyphic writing, especially that of the ancient Egyptians. [From Greek *hieros*, holy + Greek *gluphē*, carving.] **—hi′er·o·glyph′i·cal·ly** *adv.*

hi·fa·lu·tin (hī′fə-lo͞ot′n) *adj. Informal* Variant of **highfalutin.**

hi-fi (hī′fī′) *n., pl.* **hi-fis** *Informal* **1.** High fidelity. **2.** An electronic system for reproducing high-fidelity sound from radio or recordings.

hig·gle·dy-pig·gle·dy (hĭg′əl-dē-pĭg′əl-dē) *adv.* In complete disorder or confusion. ❖ *adj.* Disordered; jumbled.

high (hī) *adj.* **high·er, high·est 1a.** Being a relatively great distance above a certain level, as above sea level or the surface of the earth: *These high mountains are over 15,000 feet.* **b.** Extending a specified distance upward: *The cabinet is four feet high.* **2.** Far or farther from a reference point: *too high in the offensive zone to take a shot.* **3.** Greater than usual in degree, amount, quality, force, or intensity: *high temperature; a high standard of living; high winds.* **4.** Above the middle range of musical pitch; shrill; sharp: *the high tones of a flute; a high shriek.* **5.** Being at or near the peak: *Election to the presidency was the high point of a long career in politics.* **6.** Advanced in development or complexity: *higher forms of animal life.* **7.** Greater than others in rank, status, or importance: *a high official; a high priority.* **8.** Serious; grave: *Treason is a high crime.* **9.** Showing joy or excitement: *high spirits.* **10.** Favorable: *The students held their teacher in high regard.* **11.** Expensive; extravagant: *accustomed to high living.* **12.** Situated far from the equator: *high latitudes.* ❖ *adv.* **higher, highest** At, in, or to a high position, level, or degree: *Hawks fly high in the sky. A general ranks high above a private.* ❖ *n.* **1.** A high degree or level: *Gold prices reached a new high.* **2.** A mass of atmospheric air that exerts greater pressure than the air in the regions surrounding it: *This clear dry weather is the result of a high from the west.* **3.** *Informal* An elevated state of good feeling or well-being: *The runner was on a high after winning the race.* **4.** The gear in a transmission that produces the fastest speeds. ◆ **high and dry** Helpless and alone: *When our car broke down in the wilderness we were left high and dry.* **high and low** Everywhere: *I looked high and low for the keys.* [From Old English *hēah*.]
❑ *These sound alike:* **high, hi** (greeting), **hie** (hurry).

high blood pressure *n.* Hypertension.

high·born (hī′bôrn′) *adj.* Of noble birth.

high·boy (hī′boi′) *n.* A tall chest of drawers divided into two sections and supported on four legs.

high·brow (hī′brou′) *adj.* Highly cultured or intellectu-

hexahedron
two types of hexahedrons

USAGE

hey Originally just an exclamation, **hey** is nowadays also used as a greeting. As a short colloquial version of *How are you?* it seems to be replacing its close kin *hi* in many situations. *Hey* once had a distinctly Southern flavor but has become common throughout the United States.

hibiscus

Miguel Hidalgo y Costilla

hieroglyphic

high-top

hijab

hilt

ă	pat	ôr	core
ā	pay	oi	boy
âr	care	ou	out
ä	father	o͝o	took
ĕ	pet	o͝or	lure
ē	be	o͞o	boot
ĭ	pit	ŭ	cut
ī	bite	ûr	urge
îr	pier	th	thin
ŏ	pot	*th*	this
ō	toe	zh	vision
ô	paw	ə	about

al: *highbrow literature.* ❖ *n.* A person who has or seems to have a high degree of culture or learning.

high·chair (hī**′**châr′) *n.* A very young child's feeding chair that has long legs, a footrest, and usually a tray that can be detached.

high definition *n.* A format for recording and displaying video, having wider proportions and a higher resolution than older television formats.

high·er education (hī**′**ər) *n.* Education beyond the high-school level.

high·fa·lu·tin or **hi·fa·lu·tin** (hī′fə-lo͞ot**′**n) *adj. Informal* Pompous or making a showy pretense: *highfalutin words.*

high fidelity *n.* The electronic reproduction of sounds, as on records or magnetic tape, with very little distortion.

high-five (hī**′**fīv**′**) *Slang n.* A gesture used for congratulating or greeting in which one person slaps a raised palm against another person's raised palm.

high-flown (hī**′**flōn**′**) *adj.* **1.** Lofty; exalted: *high-flown ideals.* **2.** Full of showy pretense; inflated: *high-flown language.*

high frequency *n.* A radio wave frequency in the range between 3 and 30 megahertz.

high-fruc·tose corn syrup (hī**′**frŭk**′**tōs′ *or* hī**′**fro͝ok**′**-tōs′) *n.* Corn syrup that has been processed to convert some of the glucose to fructose. It is used to sweeten many foods and beverages.

high-grade (hī**′**grād**′**) *adj.* Of superior quality.

high·hand·ed (hī**′**hăn**′**dĭd) *adj.* Arrogant; overbearing: *The manager's highhanded rejection of my application annoyed me.* **—high′hand′ed·ly** *adv.* **—high′hand′ed·ness** *n.*

high-hat (hī**′**hăt**′**) *Informal tr.v.* **high-hat·ted, high-hat·ting, high-hats** To be condescending or snobbish toward. ❖ *adj.* Snobbish.

high heels *pl.n.* Women's shoes that have long, thin heels.

High Holy Days *pl.n.* The period from Rosh Hashanah until the end of Yom Kippur.

high jump *n.* A jump for height made over a raised horizontal bar in an athletic contest.

high·land (hī**′**lənd) *n.* **1.** Elevated land. **2. highlands** A mountainous or hilly part of a country; a region at a high elevation. ❖ *adj.* Relating to a highland.

high·land·er (hī**′**lən-dər) *n.* A person who lives in the highlands.

Highland fling *n.* A lively folk dance of the Scottish Highlands.

High·lands (hī**′**ləndz) A mountainous region of central and northern Scotland. The area maintained a separate culture until well into the 1800s.

high·light (hī**′**līt′) *n.* **1.** An area in a painting or photograph where light is represented as most intense. **2.** The most outstanding event or part: *The highlight of the trip was visiting the botanical gardens.* **3. highlights** Strands of hair that have been lightened, as by bleaching or coloring. ❖ *tr.v.* **high·light·ed, high·light·ing, high·lights 1.** To cast light on or make brighter with the use of lighter colors: *The artist highlighted the woman's head.* **2.** To make prominent; emphasize: *The article highlighted the painstaking work of the detectives.* **3.** To mark important passages of (text), as with a colored marker, for later reference.

high·light·er (hī**′**lī′tər) *n.* **1.** A usually fluorescent marker that is used for marking passages of text. **2.** A cosmetic for emphasizing areas of the face, such as the eyes or cheekbones.

high·ly (hī**′**lē) *adv.* **1.** To a great degree; extremely; very: *highly developed; highly amusing.* **2.** In a good or favorable way: *I think highly of the candidate.* **3.** In a high position or rank: *a highly placed official of our state.* **4.** At a high price, cost, or rate: *a highly paid executive.*

high-mind·ed (hī**′**mīn**′**dĭd) *adj.* Having lofty ideals; noble: *a mayor with a high-minded approach to politics.*

high·ness (hī**′**nĭs) *n.* **1.** The quality or condition of being tall or high; height. **2. Highness** Used as a title and form of address for a prince or princess: *Her Royal Highness the Princess Margaret.*

high noon *n.* **1.** Exactly noon; the very middle of the day. **2.** The highest stage or most advanced period: *The judge was at the high noon of his career.*

high-pitched (hī**′**pĭcht**′**) *adj.* **1.** High in pitch; shrill: *a high-pitched flute.* **2.** Steeply sloped: *a high-pitched roof.*

high-pres·sure (hī**′**prĕsh**′**ər) *adj.* **1.** Having, using, or withstanding pressures higher than normal: *a high-pressure tire.* **2.** Having a high atmospheric pressure: *a high-pressure area moving across the Great Plains.* **3.** *Informal* Using vigorous and persistent methods of persuasion: *a high-pressure sales pitch.*

high-rise (hī**′**rīz′) *adj.* Very tall and having many stories: *high-rise apartment building.* ❖ *n.* or **high rise** A high-rise building.

high road *n.* **1.** The easiest or surest path or course. **2.** The most positive or ethical path or course.

high school *n.* A secondary school that usually includes grades 9 or 10 through 12. **—high′-school′** *adj.*

high seas *pl.n.* The open waters of an ocean or sea beyond the limits of any nation's jurisdiction.

high-speed (hī**′**spēd**′**) *adj.* **1.** Designed for use at high speed: *a high-speed blender; a high-speed train.* **2.** Taking place at high speed: *a high-speed chase.*

high-spir·it·ed (hī**′**spĭr**′**ĭ-tĭd) *adj.* **1.** Vivacious; lively: *the students' high-spirited antics.* **2.** Having a proud or unbroken spirit: *a high-spirited horse.*

high-stick·ing (hī**′**stĭk**′**ĭng) *n.* The act of carrying a hockey stick so that the blade rises above a specified height, as above an opponent's waist or shoulders, in violation of the rules.

high-strung (hī**′**strŭng**′**) *adj.* Very nervous and easily excited; tense.

high-tech (hī**′**tĕk**′**) *adj. Informal* Relating to high technology: *high-tech electronic gadgets.*

high technology *n.* Technology involving highly advanced or innovative devices, systems, or materials. **—high′-tech·nol′o·gy** *adj.*

high-ten·sion (hī**′**tĕn**′**shən) *adj.* Having a high voltage: *high-tension wires.*

high tide *n.* **1.** The tide when the water reaches its highest level. **2.** The time at which this occurs.

high time *n.* An appropriate time for doing something, especially something that should not be put off any longer: *If you want to catch the train, it's high time we left.*

high-top (hī**′**tŏps′) *adj.* Extending to or above the ankle: *high-top hiking boots.* ❖ *n.* A high-top shoe, especially a sneaker or athletic shoe that laces up to the ankle.

high-wa·ter mark (hī**′**wô′tər) *n.* **1.** A mark showing the highest level reached by a body of water. **2.** The highest point of something; the apex: *The band reached a high-water mark with its third album.*

high·way (hī**′**wā′) *n.* A main public road: *A highway connects the cities.*

high·way·man (hī**′**wā′mən) *n.* A man who robs travelers on a road.

high wire *n.* A tightrope on which acrobats perform, stretched tightly above the ground.

hi·jab (hĭ-jäb**′**) *n.* Any of several cloth head coverings worn by Muslim women. [From Arabic *ḥijāb*, cover, curtain, veil.]

hi·jack (hī**′**jăk′) *tr.v.* **hi·jacked, hi·jack·ing, hi·jacks 1.** To seize or take control of (a moving vehicle) by use of force, especially in order to reach a different destination. **2.** To stop and rob (a vehicle in transit). **3.** To steal (goods) from a vehicle in transit: *The rebels hijacked medical supplies.* **4.** To seize control of (something) and use it for one's own purposes: *spammers who hijacked a computer network.* **—hi′jack′er** *n.*

hike (hīk) *v.* **hiked, hik·ing, hikes** *—intr.* To go on an extended walk, especially for pleasure: *hike through the woods.* *—tr.* **1.** To pull or raise, especially with a sudden motion; hitch: *I hiked up my socks.* **2.** To increase or raise: *The new sales tax will hike up prices.* ❖ *n.* **1.** A long walk or trip on foot. **2.** A hitch or tug upward: *Give your socks a hike.* **3.** A rise; an increase: *a hike in gasoline prices.* **—hik′er** *n.*

hi·la (hī′lə) *n.* Plural of **hilum.**

hi·lar·i·ous (hĭ-lâr′ē-əs) *adj.* Very funny; provoking much laughter: *a hilarious story.* [From Latin *hilaris,* cheerful.] **—hi·lar′i·ous·ly** *adv.*

hi·lar·i·ty (hĭ-lăr′ĭ-tē) *n.* Great merriment or fun.

hill (hĭl) *n.* **1.** A landform that rises above its surroundings but is lower and usually less rugged than a mountain. **2.** A small heap, mound, or pile: *an ant hill.* **3.** A mound of earth that covers seeds or a plant: *hills of corn.* ◆ **over the hill** *Informal* Declining in ability because of age; past one's prime. [From Old English *hyll.*]

hill·bil·ly (hĭl′bĭl′ē) *n., pl.* **hill·bil·lies** *Often Offensive* A person who lives in the backwoods or a mountain area that is remote from settled communities.

hill·ock (hĭl′ək) *n.* A small hill.

hill·side (hĭl′sīd′) *n.* The side of a hill.

hill·top (hĭl′tŏp′) *n.* The top or crest of a hill.

hill·y (hĭl′ē) *adj.* **hill·i·er, hill·i·est** Having many hills: *Northern Missouri is hilly.* **—hill′i·ness** *n.*

hilt (hĭlt) *n.* The handle of a sword or dagger. ◆ **to the hilt** To the limit; completely: *They played their roles to the hilt.* [From Old English.]

hi·lum (hī′ləm) *n., pl.* **hi·la** (hī′lə) A mark or scar on a seed, such as a bean, showing the point of attachment to the plant.

him (hĭm) *pron.* The objective form of **he. 1.** Used as the direct object of a verb: *We helped him.* **2.** Used as the indirect object of a verb: *She gave him a ride.* **3.** Used as the object of a preposition: *This package is for him.* —SEE NOTE AT **he, me.**

❑ *These sound alike:* **him, hymn** (song).

Him·a·la·ya Mountains (hĭm′ə-lā′ə) A mountain system of south-central Asia extending about 1,500 miles (2,400 kilometers) through Kashmir, northern India, southern Tibet, Nepal, and Bhutan. —SEE NOTE.

him·self (hĭm-sĕlf′) *pron.* **1.** That one that is the same as him: **a.** Used as the direct object or indirect object of a verb or as the object of a preposition to show that the action of the verb refers back to the subject: *He dressed himself. He gave himself plenty of time. He saved some popcorn for himself.* **b.** Used to give emphasis: *He took care of his problem himself.* **2.** His real, normal, or healthy self: *He looks more like himself after the vacation.*

hind[1] (hīnd) *adj.* Located at or forming the rear or back, especially of an animal: *a horse's hind legs.* [From Old English *bihindan.*]

hind[2] (hīnd) *n.* The adult female of various deer. [From Old English.]

hind·brain (hīnd′brān′) *n.* The rear part of the brain, consisting of the pons and the medulla oblongata.

hin·der (hĭn′dər) *tr.v.* **hin·dered, hin·der·ing, hin·ders** To prevent the action or progress of; hamper: *Heavy rains hindered traffic on the highway.* [From Old English *hindrian.*]

Hin·di (hĭn′dē) *n.* An Indic language widely spoken in northern India. **—Hin′di** *adj.*

Hin·di-Ur·du (hĭn′dē-o͝or′do͞o *or* hĭn′dē-ûr′do͞o) *n.* Hindi and Urdu, viewed as essentially the same language with respect to their grammar and basic vocabulary, though very different in their literary forms.

hind·most (hīnd′mōst′) *adj.* Farthest to the rear.

hind·quar·ter (hīnd′kwôr′tər) *n.* **1. hindquarters** The rump or haunches of a four-footed animal. **2.** The rear part of a side of beef, lamb, or other animal carcass.

hin·drance (hĭn′drəns) *n.* **1.** A person or thing that hinders; an obstacle: *The heavy backpack was a hindrance to the hiker.* **2.** The act of hindering or the condition of being hindered: *Because of the weather's hindrance, we waited another day to go hiking.*

hind·sight (hīnd′sīt′) *n.* Understanding of the significance of a past event: *In hindsight I know I should have ignored their rude remarks.*

Hin·du (hĭn′do͞o) *adj.* **1.** Relating to Hinduism. **2.** Relating to the Hindus or their culture. ❖ *n.* A believer in Hinduism.

Hin·du·ism (hĭn′do͞o-ĭz′əm) *n.* A diverse body of religion, philosophy, and culture native to India, marked especially by a belief in reincarnation and a supreme being who has many forms and natures.

Hindu Kush (ko͝osh *or* kŭsh) A mountain range of southwest Asia extending more than 500 miles (805 kilometers) westward from northern Pakistan to northeast Afghanistan. It rises to 25,289 feet (7,708 meters).

Hin·du·sta·ni (hĭn′do͞o-stä′nē *or* hĭn′do͞o-stăn′ē) *adj.* Relating to northern India, its people, or their Indic dialects. ❖ *n.* Any of these dialects, especially the spoken form of Hindi-Urdu.

hinge (hĭnj) *n.* **1.** A joint on which a door, gate, lid, or cover turns or swings. **2.** A similar structure or part, such as one that enables the shell of a clam to open and close. ❖ *v.* **hinged, hing·ing, hing·es** *—tr.* To attach by a hinge or hinges: *The carpenter hinged the door.* *—intr.* To depend: *My grade hinges on this exam.* [From Middle English *henge.*]

hint (hĭnt) *n.* **1.** A slight indication or indirect suggestion; a clue: *Can't you give me a hint about the answer to this math problem?* **2.** A small amount; a trace: *There is just a hint of vanilla in these cookies.* ❖ *v.* **hint·ed, hint·ing, hints** *—tr.* To make known or indicate in an indirect manner: *Our host hinted that it was time to leave.* *—intr.* To give a hint: *She refused to hint at what really happened.* [Probably from Old English *hentan,* to grasp.] **—hint′er** *n.*

hin·ter·land (hĭn′tər-lănd′) *n.* **1.** Land away from a seacoast; an inland area. **2.** An area far from cities or towns.

hip[1] (hĭp) *n.* **1.** The projecting part of the human body between the waist and thigh. **2.** A similar part in a four-footed animal, where the hind leg joins the body. **3.** The hipbone or the hip joint. [From Old English *hype.*]

hip[2] (hĭp) *adj.* **hip·per, hip·pest** *Slang* Knowledgeable about or aware of what is new.

hip[3] (hĭp) *n.* A rose hip. [From Old English *hēope.*]

hip·bone (hĭp′bōn′) *n.* Either of the large, flat, irregularly shaped bones that with the lower backbone form the pelvis.

hip boot *n.* A very high boot that goes up to the hip.

hip-hop (hĭp′hŏp′) *n.* **1.** A style of music usually based on rap, often including elements of other styles such as funk or rhythm and blues. **2.** A popular urban youth culture, closely associated with hip-hop music and the style of African Americans living in major cities.

hip joint *n.* The ball-and-socket joint between the hipbone and the femur.

hip·pie (hĭp′ē) *n., pl.* **hip·pies** A member of a social movement originating in the 1960s, typically opposing war and favoring extreme personal freedom in dress and behavior.

hip·po (hĭp′ō) *n., pl.* **hip·pos** A hippopotamus.

Hip·poc·ra·tes (hĭ-pŏk′rə-tēz′) Called "the Father of

WORD HISTORY

Himalaya Mountains
The **Himalaya Mountains** are snowy, and that fact is embedded in their very name. The name comes from Sanskrit, an ancient language of India, and means "dwelling-place of snow." *Hima–* means "cold, winter, snow," and is distantly related to our word **hibernate.** *Ālaya–* means "dwelling-place" and comes from a Sanskrit verb meaning "stick, stay in one place."

WRITERS CHOOSE THEIR WORDS

[Jonathan] laid the loaf of bread on the deck, still in its plastic wrapper. A thin wrapper like that would be no **hindrance** to a bear. And if no bear came, he could wipe off the plastic, bring the bread back to the kitchen, and Dad would never need to know that the bread for his lunch sandwiches had spent the night out in the cold.

—Marion Dane Bauer
A Bear Named Trouble

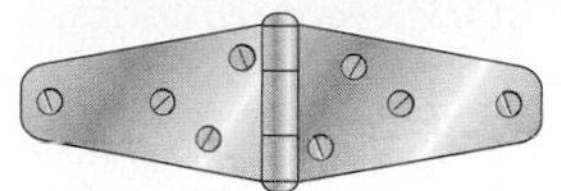

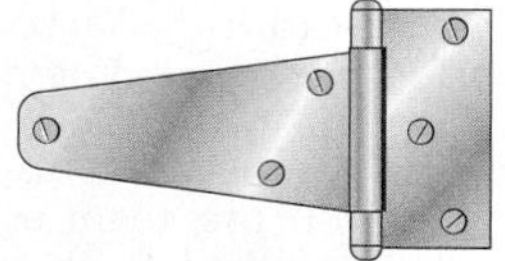

hinge
top: strap hinge
bottom: T-hinge

Hippocrates

hippopotamus

Hirohito
photographed in the 1980s

USAGE

historic The word **historic** refers to what is important in history: *The Revolutionary War was a historic event.* **Historical** refers to whatever existed in the past, whether regarded as important or not: *The author used many historical characters in her novels.* There is overlap in the meanings of these two words, but if you use them as described here, your meaning will be clear.

ă	pat	ôr	core
ā	pay	oi	boy
âr	care	ou	out
ä	father	o͝o	took
ĕ	pet	o͝or	lure
ē	be	o͞o	boot
ĭ	pit	ŭ	cut
ī	bite	ûr	urge
îr	pier	th	thin
ŏ	pot	*th*	this
ō	toe	zh	vision
ô	paw	ə	about

Medicine." 460?–377? BC. Greek physician whose influential writings emphasized that illnesses had natural rather than supernatural causes and that nutrition and the environment were important in shaping health.

Hip·po·crat·ic oath (hĭp′ə-**krăt′**ĭk) *n.* A statement dating from ancient times that sets forth the duties and obligations of a physician. Today many physicians still swear to abide by its principles.

hip·po·drome (**hĭp′**ə-drōm′) *n.* **1.** A stadium with an oval racetrack, used for horse and chariot races in ancient Greece and Rome. **2.** An arena used for horse shows.

Hip·pol·y·ta (hĭ-**pŏl′**ĭ-tə) *n.* In Greek mythology, a queen of the Amazons.

hip·po·pot·a·mus (hĭp′ə-**pŏt′**ə-məs) *n., pl.* **hip·po·pot·a·mus·es** or **hip·po·pot·a·mi** (hĭp′ə-**pŏt′**ə-mī′) A large, heavy African mammal having dark, almost hairless thick skin, short legs, a broad snout, and a wide mouth. Hippopotamuses live in and near rivers and lakes, eating plants and staying under water for long periods of time. [From Greek *hippopotamos* : *hippos*, horse + *potamos*, river.]

hire (hīr) *tr.v.* **hired, hir·ing, hires 1.** To pay (a person) for working or performing a service; employ: *hire teachers for the new school.* **2.** To pay for the use of (something) for a limited time; rent: *hire a car.* ❖ *n.* **1.** A person who has recently become an employee: *The new hires attended a meeting in the human resources office.* **2.** Payment for doing work or for the use of something: *The day's hire for the car is ten dollars.*

hire·ling (**hīr′**lĭng) *n.* A person who works only for money, especially a person willing to do tedious or unpleasant tasks for a fee.

Hi·ro·hi·to (hîr′ō-**hē′**tō) 1901–1989. Emperor of Japan (1926–1989) whose unconditional surrender ended World War II (1945).

Hi·ro·shi·ma (hîr′ə-**shē′**mə *or* hĭ-**rō′**shə-mə) A city of southwest Honshu, Japan, west of Osaka. Founded in the 1500s, it was rebuilt after being destroyed in World War II by an atomic bomb (August 6, 1945).

hir·sute (**hûr′**so͞ot′ *or* **hîr′**so͞ot′) *adj.* Hairy. **—hir′sute′·ness** *n.*

his (hĭz) *adj.* The possessive form of **he.** Belonging to or relating to him: *We were impressed by his dedication to his garden.* ❖ *pron. (used with a singular or plural verb)* The one or ones belonging to him: *If you can't find your hat, take his.* —SEE NOTE AT **he.**

His·pan·ic (hĭ-**spăn′**ĭk) *adj.* **1.** Relating to Spain or Spanish-speaking Latin America. **2.** Relating to a Spanish-speaking people or culture. ❖ *n.* A person of Spanish or Latin-American descent, especially one living in the United States.

His·pan·io·la (hĭs′pən-**yō′**lə) An island of the West Indies east of Cuba, divided between Haiti and the Dominican Republic.

hiss (hĭs) *n.* A sound like that made by pronouncing the letter *s: the hiss of air escaping from a tire.* ❖ *v.* **hissed, hiss·ing, hiss·es** *—intr.* **1.** To make a sound like that of the letter *s*: *A cat will hiss when frightened.* **2.** To express dislike or disapproval with such a sound: *The crowd hissed and booed at the referee's call.* *—tr.* To say or express by hissing: *The audience hissed its displeasure with the comedian.*

his·ta·mine (**hĭs′**tə-mēn′ *or* **hĭs′**tə-mĭn) *n.* A chemical compound found in fungi, plants, and animal tissue and released in allergic reactions in humans, causing expansion of blood vessels and tightening of the airways.

his·ti·dine (**hĭs′**tĭ-dēn′ *or* **hĭs′**tĭ-dĭn) *n.* An essential amino acid that is important for the growth and repair of tissues.

his·tol·o·gy (hĭ-**stŏl′**ə-jē) *n., pl.* **his·tol·o·gies** The scientific study of the structure of plant and animal tissues.

his·to·ri·an (hĭ-**stôr′**ē-ən) *n.* A scholar or writer of history.

his·tor·ic (hĭ-**stôr′**ĭk) *adj.* **1.** Important or famous in history: *the historic city of Williamsburg.* **2.** Historical. —SEE NOTE.

his·tor·i·cal (hĭ-**stôr′**ĭ-kəl) *adj.* **1.** Relating to history: *historical events.* **2.** Based on or concerned with events in history: *a historical novel.* **3.** Historic. **—his·tor′i·cal·ly** *adv.* —SEE NOTE AT **historic.**

his·to·ry (**hĭs′**tə-rē) *n., pl.* **his·to·ries 1.** A written account or record of past events: *I read a history of early aviation.* **2.** The study of past events as a special field of knowledge: *History is her favorite subject.* **3.** The totality of past events in human culture: *printing and other important inventions in history.* **4.** A past that is known and sometimes recorded: *an old building with an interesting history.* **5.** An established pattern of behavior: *a person with a history of getting into trouble.* [From Middle English *histoire*, from Greek *historein*, to inquire, from *histōr*, learned man.]

his·tri·on·ic (hĭs′trē-**ŏn′**ĭk) *adj.* **1.** Excessively dramatic or emotional. **2.** Relating to actors or acting.

his·tri·on·ics (hĭs′trē-**ŏn′**ĭks) *n. (used with a singular or plural verb)* Showy, exaggerated emotional behavior.

hit (hĭt) *v.* **hit, hit·ting, hits** *—tr.* **1.** To strike against with force; crash into: *The car hit the fence.* **2.** To cause an implement or missile to come forcefully into contact with: *I hit the tennis ball with the racket.* **3.** To cause (something) to come against a person or thing: *He hit his fist against the table.* **4a.** To get to; reach: *hit a high note; going smoothly until we hit a bumpy road.* **b.** To be affected by (a negative development): *His career hit a snag.* **5.** In baseball, to make (a base hit): *The batter hit a home run.* **6.** To affect painfully or severely, as if by a blow: *A period of bad business hit the store hard.* *—intr.* **1.** To give or strike a blow: *The post went in deeper every time I hit.* **2.** To come against a person or thing; collide: *The two boats hit in the fog.* **3.** To happen or occur: *The blizzard hit during the night.* **4.** To make an attack: *The enemy hit at midnight.* **5.** To achieve or find something desired or sought: *We hit on the right answer.* ❖ *n.* **1.** A blow that strikes something: *Two or three hits of the hammer will drive the nail in.* **2.** A person or thing that is a popular success: *The new musical is the hit of the season.* **3.** A base hit in baseball. **4a.** A match that is made when searching a collection of data for a particular sequence of characters: *I searched the Web for the phrase "poodle tricks" and got over 40,000 hits.* **b.** A connection made to a website: *My website has received over 1,000 hits since July.* ◆ **hit it off** To get along well together. **hit the nail on the head** To be absolutely right. [From Old English *hyttan*, from Old Norse *hitta.*] **—hit′ter** *n.*

hit-and-run (**hĭt′**n-**rŭn′**) *adj.* Involving a driver of a vehicle who hits someone or damages something and flees to avoid responsibility.

hitch (hĭch) *v.* **hitched, hitch·ing, hitch·es** *—tr.* **1.** To tie or fasten something with a rope, strap, or loop: *hitch a dog team to the sled.* **2.** To raise or pull with a tug or jerk: *hitch up one's pants.* **3.** *Informal* To get (a ride) by hitchhiking: *hitch a lift to the gas station.* **4.** *Slang* To marry: *get hitched.* *—intr.* **1.** To move slowly and in a jerky manner: *The weary climber hitched along the narrow rocky ledge.* **2.** *Informal* To hitchhike. ❖ *n.* **1.** Any of various knots used for temporary fastening, as the timber hitch. **2.** A device used to connect one thing to another; a fastening. **3.** A short pull or jerk; a tug. **4.** A delay or difficulty; a snag: *a hitch in our plans.* **5.** A time period, especially of military service. **6.** *Informal* A ride obtained by hitchhiking. [From Middle English *icchen*, to move, jerk.]

hitch·hike (**hĭch′**hīk′) *intr.v.* **hitch·hiked, hitch·hik·**

ing, hitch·hikes To travel by seeking free rides from drivers of passing vehicles. —**hitch′hik′er** *n.*

hith·er (hĭ*th*′ər) *adv.* To or toward this place: *Come hither.* ◆ **hither and thither** or **hither and yon** In or to many places; here and there: *running hither and thither all day.*

hith·er·to (hĭ*th*′ər-to͞o′) *adv.* Until this time; up to now: *hitherto unobserved stars.*

Hit·ler (hĭt′lər), **Adolf** Known as "Der Führer." 1889–1945. Austrian-born leader of the German Nazi Party who ruled Germany as a dictator after 1934. His regime systematically put to death millions of people, especially European Jews, and caused World War II by attempting to conquer Europe. When Germany was about to be defeated in 1945, Hitler committed suicide.

hit-or-miss (hĭt′ər-mĭs′) *adj.* Careless or unplanned; random.

Hit·tite (hĭt′īt′) *n.* **1.** A member of a people who lived in Asia Minor and northern Syria from 2000 to 1200 BC. **2.** The Indo-European language of this people. ❖ *adj.* Relating to the Hittites or their language or culture.

HIV (āch′ī-vē′) *n.* The virus that causes AIDS by infecting the body's immune system. HIV is transmitted through body fluids such as semen and blood.

hive (hīv) *n.* **1a.** A structure for housing honeybees. **b.** A colony of honeybees living in such a structure. **2.** A place full of people doing things: *The bus station is a hive of activity around the holidays.* ❖ *tr.v.* **hived, hiv·ing, hives** To gather (honeybees) in a hive. [From Old English *hȳf.*]

hives (hīvz) *pl.n.* *(used with a singular or plural verb)* A skin rash characterized by itchy red welts and often resulting from an allergic reaction.

HMO (āch′ĕm-ō′) *n.* A health insurance organization that seeks to control health care costs by requiring people to use only those doctors and facilities on an approved list.

Hmong (hmŏng) *n.* **1.** A member of a group of peoples native to the mountains of southern China and nearby areas of Vietnam, Laos, and Thailand. **2.** The language of the Hmong. —**Hmong** *adj.*

HMS *abbr.* An abbreviation of Her (or His) Majesty's Ship.

ho (hō) *interj.* An expression used to show surprise or to attract attention: *Land ho!*

❏ *These sound alike:* **ho, hoe** (tool).

Ho The symbol for the element **holmium.**

hoa·gie (hō′gē) *n.* A submarine sandwich.

hoar (hôr) *adj.* White or gray; hoary.

❏ *These sound alike:* **hoar, whore** (prostitute).

hoard (hôrd) *n.* A hidden supply that is stored for future use: *the squirrel's hoard of nuts for winter.* ❖ *tr.v.* **hoard·ed, hoard·ing, hoards** To save and store away; accumulate: *The squirrel hoarded nuts for winter.* —**hoard′er** *n.*

❏ *These sound alike:* **hoard, horde** (crowd).

hoar·frost (hôr′frôst′) *n.* A white coating of ice crystals that forms when water vapor in the air freezes on an exposed object.

hoarse (hôrs) *adj.* **hoars·er, hoars·est 1.** Low and gruff in sound; husky: *The cold reduced my voice to a hoarse whisper.* **2.** Having a low gruff voice: *The football fans were hoarse with shouting.* [From Old English *hās.*] —**hoarse′ly** *adv.* —**hoarse′ness** *n.*

❏ *These sound alike:* **hoarse, horse** (animal).

hoar·y (hôr′ē) *adj.* **hoar·i·er, hoar·i·est 1.** White or grayish: *a hoary beard.* **2.** Very old; aged: *hoary ruins of the ancient city.* —**hoar′i·ness** *n.*

hoax (hōks) *n.* A trick or act intended to deceive others, often in the form of a practical joke or false report: *The report that the store was going out of business proved to be a hoax.* ❖ *tr.v.* **hoaxed, hoax·ing, hoax·es** To deceive or cheat by using a hoax. —**hoax′er** *n.*

hob (hŏb) *n.* A shelf at the back or side of a fireplace for keeping food warm.

hob·ble (hŏb′əl) *v.* **hob·bled, hob·bling, hob·bles** —*intr.* To walk with difficulty; limp: *The patient hobbled along with one leg in a cast.* —*tr.* **1.** To put a device around the legs of (an animal) to hamper but not prevent movement. **2.** To impede or hinder: *Quarreling hobbled the efforts of the committee to reach a decision.* ❖ *n.* **1.** An awkward walk or a limp. **2.** A device used to hobble an animal.

hob·by (hŏb′ē) *n., pl.* **hob·bies** An activity, such as collecting stamps or gardening, that is outside one's regular occupation and is engaged in for pleasure. —**hob′by·ist** *n.*

hob·by·horse (hŏb′ē-hôrs′) *n.* **1.** A toy made of a stick with an imitation of a horse's head on one end. **2.** A rocking horse. **3.** A topic that one frequently brings up or dwells on; a fixation.

hob·gob·lin (hŏb′gŏb′lĭn) *n.* **1.** A mischievous or troublesome elf; a goblin. **2.** A source of fear or dread.

hob·nail (hŏb′nāl′) *n.* A short nail with a thick head that is used to protect the soles of shoes or boots.

hob·nob (hŏb′nŏb′) *intr.v.* **hob·nobbed, hob·nob·bing, hob·nobs** To meet, talk, or spend time together in a friendly familiar manner: *hobnobbing with celebrities at a party.*

ho·bo (hō′bō) *n., pl.* **ho·boes** or **ho·bos** A person who wanders from place to place without a permanent home or regular way of making a living.

Ho Chi Minh (hō′ chē′ mĭn′) 1890–1969. Vietnamese leader and first president of North Vietnam (1954–1969).

Ho Chi Minh City The largest city of Vietnam, in the southern part of the country near the South China Sea. Formerly known as Saigon, it is built on the site of an ancient Khmer settlement.

hock[1] (hŏk) *n.* **1.** The joint of the hind leg of certain four-footed animals, such as horses, dogs, and cats, corresponding to the human ankle. **2.** A small cut of meat, especially ham, from the front or hind leg directly above the foot. [From Middle English *hokke,* from Old English *hōh,* heel.]

hock[2] (hŏk) *tr.v.* **hocked, hock·ing, hocks** *Slang* To pawn: *I hocked my ring for some cash.* [Probably from Dutch *hok,* prison.]

hock·ey (hŏk′ē) *n.* **1.** Ice hockey. **2.** Field hockey. **3.** Street hockey.

ho·cus-po·cus (hō′kəs-pō′kəs) *n.* **1.** Meaningless syllables or words used in performing magic tricks. **2.** Meaningless speech or behavior used to deceive: *the hocus-pocus of a swindler.*

hod (hŏd) *n.* **1.** A trough fastened to a long handle and carried over the shoulder for moving bricks, cement, or mortar. **2.** A coal scuttle.

hodge·podge (hŏj′pŏj′) *n.* A mixture of various things; a jumble: *a hodgepodge of items in a desk drawer.* [From Middle English *ochepot,* from Old French *hochepot,* stew.]

Hodg·kin (hŏj′kĭn), **Dorothy Mary Crowfoot** 1910–1994. Egyptian-born British chemist who pioneered x-ray technology to determine the structure of biologically active compounds.

hoe (hō) *n.* A tool with a flat blade on a long handle, used to loosen the soil and weed around plants. ❖ *v.* **hoed, hoe·ing, hoes** —*tr.* To weed or dig up with a hoe: *We hoed the garden.* —*intr.* To use a hoe: *We hoed for an hour.* —**ho′er** *n.*

❏ *These sound alike:* **hoe, ho** (expression of surprise).

hoe·cake (hō′kāk′) *n.* A flat baked or fried cake of cornmeal.

hoe·down (hō′doun′) *n.* **1.** A square dance. **2.** The music for a square dance. **3.** A social gathering at which square dancing takes place.

hitch

hoarfrost

Dorothy Hodgkin
photographed in 1963

hogan

Billie Holiday

holly

hog (hôg) *n.* **1a.** Any of various hoofed mammals having short legs, bristly hair, and a blunt snout used for digging, including the domesticated pig and wild species such as the warthog. **b.** A full-grown pig raised for meat. **2.** A person regarded as greedy, selfish, or filthy. ❖ *tr.v.* **hogged, hog·ging, hogs** *Informal* To take more than one's share of: *Don't hog the sofa!*

ho·gan (hō′gän′ *or* hō′gən) *n.* A one-room Navajo dwelling traditionally built of logs and covered with earth. [From Navajo *hooghan*.]

hog·gish (hô′gĭsh) *adj.* **1.** Very greedy or selfish. **2.** Very dirty; filthy. **—hog′gish·ly** *adv.* **—hog′gish·ness** *n.*

hog·nose snake (hôg′nōz′) *n.* Any of several nonvenomous North American snakes having a thick body and an upturned snout.

hogs·head (hôgz′hĕd′) *n.* A large barrel or cask. In the United States, a hogshead usually holds 63 gallons (238 liters).

hog·tie (hôg′tī′) *tr.v.* **hog·tied, hog·tie·ing** or **hog·ty·ing, hog·ties 1.** To tie together the legs or feet of: *Cowhands usually hogtie cattle to brand them.* **2.** To restrain in movement or disrupt in action; hamper: *The legislature was hogtied in lengthy debate.*

hog·wash (hôg′wŏsh′) *n.* **1.** Worthless or ridiculous speech or writing; nonsense. **2.** Garbage fed to hogs.

hoi pol·loi (hoi′ pə-loi′) *n.* The common people; the masses.

hoist (hoist) *tr.v.* **hoist·ed, hoist·ing, hoists** To raise or haul up, usually with the help of a pulley or machinery: *A tall crane hoisted bricks to the top of the new building.* ❖ *n.* **1.** A device for hoisting, as a crane, winch, or rope and pulley. **2.** A pull or lift: *Let's give the log a hoist onto the wagon.*

Hok·kai·do (hŏ-kī′dō) An island of Japan north of Honshu. It became part of Japan about 1600.

hold[1] (hōld) *v.* **held** (hĕld), **hold·ing, holds** *—tr.* **1.** To have and keep in one's grasp: *The baby can hold a rattle now.* **2.** To keep from moving or getting away: *He held the dog by a leash.* **3.** To restrain, stop, or control: *Hold your tongue!* **4.** To keep in prison or custody: *The suspect is being held in the county jail.* **5.** To occupy by force: *The army held the town for a month.* **6.** To have or take as contents; contain: *This box holds a dozen eggs.* **7.** To support; bear: *Will that bridge hold such a heavy load?* **8.** To have in one's possession: *That family holds hundreds of acres of land.* **9.** To have as a position or privilege: *Thomas Jefferson held the office of president for two terms.* **10.** To have as an achievement: *She holds the school record for goals scored.* **11.** To carry on; engage in: *Hold elections; hold a conversation.* **12.** To keep or capture the attention or interest of: *The speaker held the audience spellbound.* **13.** To keep in the mind: *The teacher holds a high opinion of this class.* **14.** To consider; judge: *That painting was held to be the best.* **15.** To state or affirm: *The court holds that the law is not constitutional.* *—intr.* **1.** To continue in a state or condition; last: *The good weather held for two weeks.* **2.** To remain firm or secure: *The knot held against the strain.* **3.** To continue in the same direction: *The ship held to a southerly course.* **4.** To be true or correct: *The theory holds in all cases.* ❖ *n.* **1.** The act or a means of grasping: *keep a firm hold on the handle.* **2.** Something that may be grasped or used for support: *The rocks had many holds for climbers.* **3.** A very strong influence or power: *England's hold over the American colonies ended with the Revolution.* **4.** In music, a symbol over a note or a rest to show that it should be held for a longer time. **5.** A telephone service that allows one to temporarily interrupt a call without severing the connection. ◆ **get hold of 1.** To get possession of; find: *Where can I get hold of that magazine?* **2.** To communicate with, especially by telephone: *I tried to get hold of you.* **3.** To gain control of: *Get hold of yourself.* **hold a candle to** To have the same stature or abilities as: *Though a good trumpeter, he doesn't hold a candle to Louis Armstrong.* **hold down** To work at and keep: *hold down a job.* **hold forth** To talk at great length; make a long speech. **hold off** To delay or wait: *I hope the rain holds off until after the picnic.* **hold on 1.** To keep a grip; cling. **2.** To continue to do something: *He held on arguing until we were angry.* **3.** To stop or wait for a person or thing: *Hold on a minute.* **hold (one's) own** To do well despite difficulty. **hold out 1.** To last: *How long will our water supply hold out?* **2.** To continue to resist: *The strikers held out against the management.* **hold over 1.** To delay or postpone. **2.** To keep for an additional period of time: *The play was held over for another week.* **hold the bag** To be forced into a state of total responsibility when it ought to have been shared: *She was left holding the bag when the project director quit.* **hold the fort** To assume responsibility, especially in someone's absence: *I'll hold the fort while you're on vacation.* **hold up 1.** To stop or delay. **2.** To remain in good condition; function well: *This car should hold up for many years.* **3.** To show as an example: *The essay was held up as an example of good writing.* **4.** To rob by threatening with harm or force. **no holds barred** Without limits or restraints. **on hold 1.** Into or in a state of temporary interruption without total disconnection during a telephone call: *put someone on hold.* **2.** Into or in a state of delay for an unknown period of time: *The project is on hold until further notice.* [From Old English *healdan*.]

hold[2] (hōld) *n.* The lower inside part of a ship or aircraft, where cargo is stored. [From Middle English *hole*, husk, hull of a ship, from Old English *hulu*.]

hold·er (hōl′dər) *n.* **1.** A person who holds, owns, or possesses something: *a ticket holder; a job holder.* **2.** A device for holding something: *a napkin holder.*

hold·ing (hōl′dĭng) *n.* **1.** often **holdings** Legally owned property, such as land, stocks, or bonds: *has huge holdings in the oil industry.* **2.** In sports, an illegal hampering of an opponent's movements with the hands or arms.

holding company *n.* A company that is formed to own stocks and bonds in other companies, usually for the purpose of controlling them.

hold·out (hōld′out′) *n.* A person or group who refuses to cooperate or agree: *Environmentalists are the last holdouts against building the highway.*

hold·up (hōld′ŭp′) *n.* **1.** A stopping of progress or activity; a delay: *a holdup in production.* **2.** A robbery committed by an armed person.

hole (hōl) *n.* **1.** An opening or open place; a gap or space: *wear a hole in the elbow of a sweater; a hole in a fence; a hole in the clouds.* **2.** A hollowed place in something solid; a cavity or pit: *dug a hole to plant the tree.* **3.** *Informal* A shabby or dismal dwelling: *His apartment is a real hole.* **4.** A bad or troublesome situation; a difficulty: *help a friend out of a hole.* **5.** A fault or defect: *They found holes in her argument.* **6a.** In golf, one of the small cups into which the ball must be hit. **b.** One of the 9 or 18 divisions of a golf course. ❖ *tr.v.* **holed, hol·ing, holes** To hit (a golf ball) into the hole. ◆ **hole up** To sleep, hide, or take shelter in a burrow or other shelter: *The bear has holed up for the winter. She was so angry that she holed herself up in the classroom instead of going out for recess.* [From Old English *hol*.]

❑ *These sound alike:* **hole, whole** (complete).

hole in one *n.* The driving of a golf ball from the tee into the hole in a single stroke.

hol·i·day (hŏl′ĭ-dā′) *n.* **1.** A day on which general business activity is stopped to commemorate or celebrate a particular event. **2.** *Chiefly British* A period of time for relaxing away from work; a vacation. **3.** A religious feast day; a holy day. [From Old English *hālig dæg*, holy day.]

ă	pat	ôr	core
ā	pay	oi	boy
âr	care	ou	out
ä	father	ŏŏ	took
ĕ	pet	ŏŏr	lure
ē	be	ōō	boot
ĭ	pit	ŭ	cut
ī	bite	ûr	urge
îr	pier	th	thin
ŏ	pot	*th*	this
ō	toe	zh	vision
ô	paw	ə	about

Hol·i·day (hŏl′ĭ-dā′), **Eleanora** Known as "Billie." 1915–1959. American singer who was the leading female jazz vocalist of her time.

ho·li·ness (hō′lē-nĭs) *n.* **1.** The condition or quality of being holy. **2. Holiness** Used as a title for the head of certain religions, such as the pope or the Dalai Lama.

Hol·land (hŏl′ənd) **1.** See **Netherlands. 2.** A low-lying region of the Netherlands on the North Sea.

Hol·lande (ō-länd′, -länd′), **François** Born 1954. French politician who served as president from 2012 to 2017.

hol·ler (hŏl′ər) *tr. & intr.v.* **hol·lered, hol·ler·ing, hol·lers** To yell or shout: *She hollered a greeting from across the street.* See Synonyms at **yell.** ❖ *n.* A shout or yell.

hol·low (hŏl′ō) *adj.* **hol·low·er, hol·low·est 1.** Having a space or opening inside: *a hollow log.* **2.** Shaped like a bowl or cup; concave or indented: *A puddle always forms in the hollow spot in the back yard.* **3.** Echoing as if coming from an empty place: *the hollow sound of far-off thunder.* **4.** Not true or sincere; empty: *a hollow promise.* ❖ *n.* **1.** An opening or space; a hole: *The rabbits made a hollow at the foot of the tree.* **2.** A small valley between hills or mountains. ❖ *tr.v.* **hol·lowed, hol·low·ing, hol·lows 1.** To make hollow: *hollow out a pumpkin.* **2.** To scoop or form by making into the shape of a bowl or cup: *The turtle hollowed out a nest in the sand.* [From Middle English *holwe*, from Old English *holh*, hole, burrow.] **—hol′low·ly** *adv.* **—hol′low·ness** *n.*

hol·ly (hŏl′ē) *n., pl.* **hol·lies 1.** Any of numerous shrubs or trees often having evergreen leaves with prickly edges and bright red berries. **2.** Sprigs or branches of such a shrub or tree, traditionally used as Christmas decorations. [From Old English *holen.*]

hol·ly·hock (hŏl′ē-hŏk′) *n.* A tall garden plant having long spikes of showy, variously colored flowers.

Hol·ly·wood (hŏl′ē-wo͝od′) A district of Los Angeles, California. It has long been a film and entertainment center.

Holmes (hōmz *or* hōlmz), **Oliver Wendell, Jr.** 1841–1935. American jurist who served as an associate justice of the US Supreme Court (1902–1932). His opinions defending social legislation established a legal basis for the New Deal. Holmes is also known for his theory that the interpretation of the law should change as society changes.

hol·mi·um (hōl′mē-əm) *n. Symbol* **Ho** A soft, silvery metallic element found in certain minerals and used mainly in scientific research. Atomic number 67. See **Periodic Table.** [After *Holmia* (Stockholm), Sweden.]

hol·o·caust (hŏl′ə-kôst′ *or* hō′lə-kôst′) *n.* **1.** Great or total destruction resulting in massive loss of life, especially by fire. **2. Holocaust** The mass killing of European Jews and other groups by the Nazis during World War II. **3.** A case of widespread destruction or slaughter. **4.** A sacrificial offering that is entirely consumed by flames.

Hol·o·cene (hŏl′ə-sēn′ *or* hō′lə-sēn′) *n.* The more recent of the two epochs of the Quaternary Period, beginning at the end of the last Ice Age, about 12,000 years ago. Human civilizations developed during the Holocene. See table at **geologic time. —Hol′o·cene′** *adj.*

hol·o·gram (hŏl′ə-grăm′ *or* hō′lə-grăm′) *n.* The photographic record of an image produced by holography. —SEE NOTE.

hol·o·graph (hŏl′ə-grăf′ *or* hō′lə-grăf′) *n.* A document, such as a letter, will, or manuscript, written entirely in the handwriting of the person who signs it.

ho·log·raph·y (hō-lŏg′rə-fē) *n.* A method of producing a three-dimensional image of an object by using a divided beam of light from a laser. The laser light is directed by mirrors so that one beam reflects off the object onto a photographic plate or film and the other beam illuminates the plate or film at the same time.

Hol·stein (hōl′stīn′ *or* hōl′stēn′) *n.* Any of a breed of black and white dairy cattle.

hol·ster (hōl′stər) *n.* **1.** A case to hold a pistol, usually made of leather and attached to a belt, strap, or saddle. **2.** A belt with loops or slots for carrying small tools or other equipment.

ho·ly (hō′lē) *adj.* **ho·li·er, ho·li·est 1.** Belonging to, coming from, or associated with a divine power; sacred: *The Bible and the Koran are holy books.* **2.** Living according to highly moral or religious principles; saintly: *a holy person.* **3.** Regarded with special respect or awe; revered: *To music lovers this concert hall is a holy place.* [From Old English *hālig.*]

❑ *These sound alike:* **holy, wholly** (completely).

Holy Ark *n.* The cabinet in a synagogue in which the scrolls of the Torah are kept.

Holy Communion *n.* The Christian rite commemorating Jesus's last supper, in which bread and wine or juice are blessed and eaten in remembrance of Jesus's death.

holy day *n.* A day of a special religious observance.

Holy Ghost *n.* The Holy Spirit.

Holy Grail *n.* In medieval legend, the cup used by Jesus at the Last Supper and the object of many quests by Knights of the Round Table.

Holy Land The biblical region of Palestine.

holy of holies *n.* **1.** The innermost sanctuary of the ancient Temple in Jerusalem, in which the Ark of the Covenant was kept. **2.** A sacred or revered place.

Holy Roman Empire A loosely organized European empire that was founded in 962 and lasted until 1806. The empire was long troubled by religious and political strife.

Holy See *n.* The official position, authority, or court of the pope.

Holy Spirit *n.* The third person of the Christian Trinity.

holy water *n.* Water blessed by a priest and used for baptism and in other religious services.

Holy Week *n.* The week before Easter.

Holy Writ *n.* The Bible.

hom·age (hŏm′ĭj *or* ŏm′ĭj) *n.* **1.** Special honor or respect; reverence: *The president paid homage to the poet by quoting her in his speech.* **2.** The acknowledgment of allegiance made by a vassal to a lord in a ceremony under feudal law. [From Middle English, from Old French, probably from Latin *homō*, person, man.]

hom·bre (ŏm′brā′) *n. Slang* A man; a fellow. [From Spanish, from Latin *homō.*]

home (hōm) *n.* **1.** A place in which a person lives: *Our home is in that apartment building.* **2.** A group of people, especially a family, that lives together in a dwelling place; a household: *Those children come from a loving home.* **3.** The place in which one was born, grew up, or has lived a long time: *No matter where I live, I will always think of Montana as my home.* **4.** The region or place in which a living thing or an object is commonly found: *Coral reefs are home to many different kinds of fish. Where is the stapler's home?* **5.** A place where people are cared for: *a home for the elderly.* **6.** The place, such as a city or stadium, where a sports team originates or plays most of its games. **7.** In certain games, a goal or place of safety that the players try to reach. **8.** In baseball, home plate. ❖ *adj.* **1.** Relating to or taking place in a home: *home life; home cooking.* **2.** Played on the grounds where a team originates or plays most of its games: *a home game.* ❖ *adv.* **1.** At, to, or toward one's home: *The children raced home from school.* **2.** On or into the point or mark at which something is directed: *The arrow struck home.* **3.** To the center or heart of something; deeply: *Their arguments struck home.* ❖ *intr.v.* **homed, hom·ing, homes** To move or advance toward a destination or target: *The missile homed in on the ship.* ◆ **at home 1.** In one's

SCIENCE

hologram If you tear an ordinary photograph in two, each piece shows only a part of the original image. If you break a **hologram** in two, each piece shows the entire original scene, although from slightly different points of view. That's because each spot on a hologram contains enough information to show how the entire scene would look if it were viewed from a particular point of view. Imagine looking at a room through a peephole set in a solid door. What you see depends on where in the door the peephole is placed. Each piece of the hologram is a "peephole" view, and that's what makes the image look three-dimensional: as you move the hologram around or look at different parts of it, you see the original object from different angles, just as if you were walking around it. For this reason, holograms are much harder to copy than simple two-dimensional images, because to forge one you'd have to know what the original object looked like from many angles. And that's why credit cards and other objects that are targets of counterfeiting include holographic stickers as indicators of authenticity.

Homer

home or country: *While we were abroad, we read about problems at home.* **2.** Comfortable and relaxed; at ease: *felt at home with strangers.* **home free** Out of danger; assured of success: *Our hardest exams are first; after they're done we should be home free.* [From Old English *hām.*]

home base *n.* **1.** A goal toward which players of certain games try to make progress. **2.** Home plate. **3.** A center of operations; a headquarters.

home·bod·y (**hōm′**bŏd′ē) *n.* A person whose interests and pleasures center on the home.

home·com·ing (**hōm′**kŭm′ĭng) *n.* **1.** A return to one's home: *The soldier's homecoming was a joyous occasion.* **2.** In some high schools and colleges, a yearly celebration held for returning graduates.

home economics *n. (used with a singular or plural verb)* The art and practice of managing a household. **—home economist** *n.*

home·grown (**hōm′grōn′**) *adj.* **1.** Made or grown at home: *homegrown tomatoes from our garden.* **2.** Coming from or characteristic of a particular place: *homegrown Appalachian music.*

home·land (**hōm′**lănd′) *n.* **1.** The country in which a person was born; a person's native land. **2.** A country, region, or territory that is identified with a particular people or ethnic group.

home·less (**hōm′**lĭs) *adj.* Having no home or haven. ❖ *n. (used with a plural verb)* People who have no home considered as a group. **—home′less·ness** *n.*

home·ly (**hōm′**lē) *adj.* **home·li·er, home·li·est 1.** Not attractive or good-looking. **2.** Simple and plain: *a homely manner.* **—home′li·ness** *n.*

home·made (**hōm′mād′**) *adj.* **1.** Made at home: *delicious homemade bread.* **2.** Crudely or simply made, as if made at home: *rough homemade furniture.*

home·mak·er (**hōm′**mā′kər) *n.* A person who manages a household, especially as one's main daily activity. **—home′mak′ing** *n.*

ho·me·op·a·thy (hō′mē-**ŏp′**ə-thē) *n.* A system for treating disease in which patients are given tiny doses of a drug that, when given in large amounts to healthy people, produces symptoms like those of the disease itself. Homeopathy is a kind of alternative medicine. **—ho′me·o·path′ic** *adj.*

ho·me·o·sta·sis (hō′mē-ō-**stā′**sĭs) *n.* The ability or tendency of an organism or cell to maintain stable internal conditions regardless of changing outside conditions. **—ho′me·o·stat′ic** (hō′mē-ō-**stăt′**ĭk) *adj.*

home·page (**hōm′**pāj′) *n.* The main page of a website, usually providing information about the site.

home plate *n.* In baseball, the base at which the batter stands when hitting and which a base runner must touch in order to score.

hom·er (**hō′**mər) *n.* A home run. ❖ *intr.v.* **ho·mer·ed, ho·mer·ing, ho·mers** To hit a home run.

Ho·mer (**hō′**mər) Flourished about 750 BC. Greek epic poet. The *Iliad* and the *Odyssey* are attributed to him.

home·room (**hōm′**ro͝om′ *or* **hōm′**ro͞om′) *n.* A classroom in which a group of pupils are required to gather each day, as for attendance.

home run *n.* In baseball, a hit that allows the batter to touch all the bases and score a run.

home·school (**hōm′sko͞ol′**) *tr.v.* **home·schooled, home·school·ing, home·schools** To educate (a pupil, for example) at home rather than in an established school. **—home′school′er** *n.*

home·sick (**hōm′**sĭk′) *adj.* Longing for home. **—home′sick′ness** *n.*

home·spun (**hōm′**spŭn′) *adj.* **1.** Spun or woven at home: *homespun cloth.* **2.** Made of homespun cloth: *a homespun shirt.* **3.** Plain and simple; folksy: *homespun humor.* ❖ *n.* A plain coarse cloth woven from homespun yarn, or a similar cloth made from yarn spun by machine.

home·stead (**hōm′**stĕd′) *n.* **1.** A house, especially a farmhouse or similar dwelling, together with the land and buildings belonging to it. **2.** A piece of land given to a settler by the US government, usually with conditions such as clearing and working the land for five years. ❖ *intr.v.* **home·stead·ed, home·stead·ing, home·steads** To settle on land claimed as a homestead. **—home′stead′er** *n.*

home·stretch (**hōm′strĕch′**) *n.* **1.** The part of a racetrack from the last turn to the finish line. **2.** The last stage of something: *I am in the homestretch of writing this report.*

home·ward (**hōm′**wərd) *adv. & adj.* Toward or at home: *They turned their canoe and paddled homeward; the homeward journey.* **—home′wards** *adv.*

home·work (**hōm′**wûrk′) *n.* **1.** Work that is done at home. **2.** School assignments that are done at home or outside the classroom.

hom·ey (**hō′**mē) *adj.* **hom·i·er, hom·i·est** *Informal* Suggesting a home; pleasant, cheerful, and comfortable: *a restaurant with a homey atmosphere.*

hom·i·cide (**hŏm′**ĭ-sīd) *n.* **1.** The killing of one person by another. **2.** A person who kills another person. [From Middle English, from Latin *homicīdium.*] **—hom′i·cid′al** *adj.*

hom·i·ly (**hŏm′**ə-lē) *n., pl.* **hom·i·lies 1.** A sermon, especially one explaining the practical and moral implications of a passage in scripture. **2.** A tiresome lecture or warning that urges virtuous behavior.

hom·ing pigeon (**hō′**mĭng) *n.* A pigeon trained to fly back to its home roost.

hom·i·nid (**hŏm′**ə-nĭd) *n.* Any of various primates belonging to a family that includes orangutans, gorillas, chimpanzees, bonobos, humans, and their extinct relatives. Scientists formerly defined this scientific family as including only humans and their extinct ancestors, and the word *hominid* is still sometimes used in this way. **—hom′i·nid** *adj.*

hom·i·nin (**hŏm′**ĭ-nĭn′) *n.* Any of various primates belonging to a group that includes modern humans and their extinct relatives from the Pliocene and Pleistocene Epochs. The hominins were formerly classified as hominids. [From Latin *homō*, human being, man + New Latin *-īnī*, suffix forming names of taxonomic tribes.] **—hom′i·nin′** *adj.*

hom·i·ny (**hŏm′**ə-nē) *n.* Hulled and dried kernels of corn. [From Virginia Algonquian *uskatahomen.*]

homo– or **hom–** *pref.* A prefix that means same or similar: *homogeneous.*

Ho·mo e·rec·tus (**hō′**mō ĭ-**rĕk′**təs) *n.* An extinct species of humans known from fossil remains found in Africa and Eurasia and dating from about 1.9 million to less than 100,000 years ago. *Homo erectus* is widely regarded as an ancestor of modern humans.

ho·mo·ge·ne·i·ty (hō′mə-jə-**nē′**ĭ-tē *or* hō′mə-jə-**nā′**ĭ-tē) *n., pl.* **ho·mo·ge·ne·i·ties** The state or quality of being homogeneous.

ho·mo·ge·ne·ous (hō′mə-**jē′**nē-əs *or* hō′mə-**jēn′**yəs) *adj.* **1.** Of the same or similar kind; uniform throughout: *a homogeneous class of students having the same abilities.* **2.** Made up of similar parts; having similar elements: *a housing development of homogeneous architecture.* **—ho′mo·ge′ne·ous·ly** *adv.* **—ho′mo·ge′ne·ous·ness** *n.*

ho·mog·e·nize (hə-**mŏj′**ə-nīz′) *tr.v.* **ho·mog·e·nized, ho·mog·e·niz·ing, ho·mog·e·niz·es 1.** To make homogeneous or uniform throughout. **2.** To reduce to particles and disperse throughout a fluid: *homogenize paint.* **3.** To make (milk) uniform in consistency by reducing the fat to small globules so that the fat does not rise to the top as cream. **—ho·mog′e·ni·za′tion** (hə-mŏj′ə-nĭ-**zā′**shən) *n.*

ă	pat	ôr	core
ā	pay	oi	boy
âr	care	ou	out
ä	father	o͝o	took
ĕ	pet	o͝or	lure
ē	be	o͞o	boot
ĭ	pit	ŭ	cut
ī	bite	ûr	urge
îr	pier	th	thin
ŏ	pot	*th*	this
ō	toe	zh	vision
ô	paw	ə	about

hom·o·graph (hŏm′ə-grăf′ *or* hō′mə-grăf′) *n.* A word that has the same spelling as another word but differs in meaning, origin, and sometimes in pronunciation; for example, *ring* (circle) and *ring* (sound), and *bass* (fish) and *bass* (deep tone) are homographs. [From Greek *homos,* same + Greek *graphein,* to write.]

Ho·mo hab·i·lis (hō′mō hăb′ə-ləs) *n.* An extinct species of humans known from fossil remains found in Africa and dating from about 2 million to 1.6 million years ago.

ho·mol·o·gous (hə-mŏl′ə-gəs) *adj.* **1.** Similar in structure and evolutionary origin, as the arm of a human and the flipper of a seal. **2.** Relating to or indicating either of a pair of chromosomes having the same structure, with genes for the same traits arranged in the same order.

hom·o·nym (hŏm′ə-nĭm′ *or* hō′mə-nĭm′) *n.* A word that has the same sound and sometimes the same spelling as another word but a different meaning and origin; for example, *die* (stop living), *die* (stamping), and *dye* (color) are all homonyms. [From Greek *homos,* same + Greek *onuma,* name.] **—ho·mon′y·mous** (hō-mŏn′ə-məs *or* hə-mŏn′ə-məs) *adj.*

hom·o·phone (hŏm′ə-fōn′ *or* hō′mə-fōn′) *n.* A word that has the same sound as another word but differs in spelling, meaning, and origin; for example, *for, fore,* and *four* are homophones. [From Greek *homos,* same + Greek *phōnē,* sound.] **—ho·moph′o·nous** (hō-mŏf′ə-nəs *or* hə-mŏf′ə-nəs) *adj.*

Ho·mo sa·pi·ens (hō′mō sā′pē-ənz) *n.* The modern species of humans. [From Latin *homō,* person, man + Latin *sapiēns,* wise.]

ho·mo·sex·u·al (hō′mə-sĕk′shōō-əl) *adj.* Relating to or having a sexual orientation toward people of the same sex. ❖ *n.* A homosexual person.

ho·mo·sex·u·al·i·ty (hō′mə-sĕk′shōō-ăl′ĭ-tē) *n.* Sexual orientation toward people of the same sex.

ho·mo·zy·gous (hō′mō-zī′gəs) *adj.* Having two identical forms of the same gene for a trait such as eye color at corresponding positions on a pair of chromosomes.

Hon. *abbr.* An abbreviation of: **1.** honorable (title). **2.** honorary.

hon·cho (hŏn′chō) *n., pl.* **hon·chos** *Slang* A person who is in charge; a manager or leader: *the head honcho of the organization.* [From Japanese *hanchō,* squad leader.]

Hon·du·ras (hŏn-dŏŏr′əs) A country of northern Central America east of Guatemala. Tegucigalpa is the capital.

hone (hōn) *tr.v.* **honed, hon·ing, hones 1.** To sharpen (a knife or other sharp tool) on a fine-grained stone. **2.** To make more effective: *Authors must hone their skills by writing a great deal.* ❖ *n.* A fine-grained stone used to sharpen knives or other sharp tools. [From Old English *hān,* stone.]

hon·est (ŏn′ĭst) *adj.* **1.** Not lying, stealing, or cheating; trustworthy: *The bank teller is an honest worker.* **2.** Done or obtained without lying, cheating, or stealing: *an honest profit.* **3.** Not hiding anything; frank; straightforward; sincere: *an honest opinion.* **4.** Being just what it appears to be; not false; true; genuine: *a scale certified to give honest weight.* [From Middle English, from Latin *honestus,* honorable.] —SEE NOTE.

hon·est·ly (ŏn′ĭst-lē) *adv.* **1.** In an honest manner: *answered the question as honestly as I could.* **2.** Really; truly: *Do I honestly look that bad?*

hon·es·ty (ŏn′ĭ-stē) *n., pl.* **hon·es·ties** The quality of being honest; truthfulness, sincerity, or genuineness: *No one questioned the honesty of the judge's statement.*

hon·ey (hŭn′ē) *n., pl.* **hon·eys 1.** A sweet, thick substance made by bees from the nectar of flowers and used as food. **2.** Any of various similar sweet substances. **3.** Sweetness; pleasantness: *Her words flowed with honey.* **4.** *Informal* Sweetheart; dear. [From Old English *hunig.*]

hon·ey·bee (hŭn′ē-bē′) *n.* Any of several bees that produce honey, especially a domesticated bee raised commercially for its honey and beeswax.

hon·ey·comb (hŭn′ē-kōm′) *n.* **1.** A wax structure having many small six-sided compartments, used by honeybees to hold honey, pollen, and eggs. **2.** Something full of openings or spaces like those in a honeycomb: *The building was a honeycomb of small rooms and passages.* ❖ *tr.v.* **hon·ey·combed, hon·ey·comb·ing, hon·ey·combs** To fill with openings or spaces like those in a honeycomb: *Caves and tunnels honeycomb these cliffs.*

hon·ey·dew (hŭn′ē-dōō′) *n.* **1.** A sweet sticky substance given off by aphids and certain other insects that feed on plant juices. **2.** A honeydew melon.

honeydew melon *n.* A melon having a smooth whitish rind and sweet green flesh.

hon·eyed (hŭn′ēd) *adj.* Intended to coax or please: *honeyed words.*

hon·ey·moon (hŭn′ē-mōōn′) *n.* **1.** A trip or vacation taken by a newly married couple. **2.** A period of harmony early in a relationship: *the honeymoon between the new president and Congress.* ❖ *intr.v.* **hon·ey·mooned, hon·ey·moon·ing, hon·ey·moons** To go on a honeymoon. **—hon′ey·moon′er** *n.*

hon·ey·suck·le (hŭn′ē-sŭk′əl) *n.* Any of various vines or shrubs having tubular, often fragrant yellowish, white, or pink flowers.

Hong Kong (hŏng′ kŏng′) A city and administrative region of southeast China on the coast southeast of Guangzhou, including **Hong Kong Island** and adjacent areas. A former British colony, it returned to Chinese rule in 1997.

Ho·ni·a·ra (hō′nē-är′ə) The capital of the Solomon Islands, in the Pacific Ocean east of the island of New Guinea.

honk (hôngk) *n.* A loud harsh sound such as that made by a goose or an automobile horn. ❖ *intr. & tr.v.* **honked, honk·ing, honks** To make or cause to make a honk: *A flock of geese honked overhead. The impatient driver honked the car horn.* **—honk′er** *n.*

Hon·o·lu·lu (hŏn′ə-lōō′lōō) The capital of Hawaii, on the southeast coast of Oahu. In the 1800s it was a whaling and sandalwood port.

hon·or (ŏn′ər) *n.* **1.** Special respect or high regard: *The award is given to show honor to great film directors.* **2.** A source of credit or mark of distinction: *a great writer who is an honor to the profession.* **3.** An act or token that shows respect or high regard: *a hero's funeral with full honors.* **4.** A sense of what is right; high principles; integrity: *A person of honor does not lie, cheat, or steal.* **5.** Good name or reputation: *I must defend my honor.* **6.** Great privilege: *It is an honor to meet you.* **7.** often **Honor** Used as a title and form of address for certain officials, such as judges and some mayors: *her Honor, Judge Jones.* **8. honors a.** Special recognition of a student for unusual achievement: *graduated from high school with honors.* **b.** A program of advanced study for exceptional students. ❖ *tr.v.* **hon·ored, hon·or·ing, hon·ors 1.** To show special respect or recognition to; treat with honor: *We honored the volunteers with a party.* **2.** To think highly of; esteem: *a doctor who was honored everywhere for achievements in medicine.* **3.** To accept as payment: *honor a check.* ◆ **on (one's) honor** Under a solemn pledge to be truthful and do what is right. [From Middle English *honour,* from Latin *honor.*]

hon·or·a·ble (ŏn′ər-ə-bəl) *adj.* **1.** Deserving honor and respect: *Teaching is an honorable profession.* **2.** Bringing distinction or recognition: *honorable efforts to achieve peace.* **3.** Having or showing a sense of what is right or just: *an honorable person; an honorable solution to a difficult problem.* **4.** Done with or accompanied by marks of honor: *an honorable burial.* **5.** Distinguished; illustrious; great: *an honorable family.* **6.** often **Honorable** Used as

WORD HISTORY

honest Why do we pronounce *h* in *hostile* but not in *honest*? The letter *h* comes from the Roman, or Latin, alphabet, which later came to be used for English. The (h) sound was lost in late Latin and in the languages descended from it such as French, although it survived in the spellings of many words. In English, *h* is often silent in words borrowed from French, such as *honor, honest, hour,* and *heir.* In contrast, most words derived directly from Latin, such as *habitat, hibernate, hostile,* and *humus,* are pronounced in English with the (h) sound.

honeydew melon

honeysuckle

hoodie

hoop skirt

Herbert Hoover

ă	pat	ôr	core
ā	pay	oi	boy
âr	care	ou	out
ä	father	o͝o	took
ĕ	pet	o͝or	lure
ē	be	o͞o	boot
ĭ	pit	ŭ	cut
ī	bite	ûr	urge
îr	pier	th	thin
ŏ	pot	*th*	this
ō	toe	zh	vision
ô	paw	ə	about

a title for certain high officials or people of importance. —**hon′or·a·ble·ness** *n.* —**hon′or·a·bly** *adv.*

hon·o·rar·i·um (ŏn′ə-**râr′**ē-əm) *n., pl.* **hon·o·rar·i·ums** or **hon·o·rar·i·a** (ŏn′ə-**râr′**ē-ə) A payment made to a professional person for services, such as a lecture, for which a fee is not legally required.

hon·or·ar·y (**ŏn′**ə-rĕr′ē) *adj.* Given or held as an honor: *an honorary degree from a university.*

honor system *n.* A set of rules by which students are trusted to act properly or honestly without being closely supervised.

hon·our (**ŏn′**ər) *n. & v. Chiefly British* Variant of **honor.**

Hon·shu (**hŏn′**sho͞o) The largest island of Japan, in the central part of the country between the Sea of Japan and the Pacific Ocean.

hood¹ (ho͝od) *n.* **1.** A loose covering for the head and neck, often attached to a coat, cape, or robe: *The Inuit wear heavy parkas with hoods attached.* **2.** The hinged metal lid over the engine of an automobile. **3.** The raised metal cover of a ventilator over a stove. **4.** An expanded part or marking on or near an animal's head, as the flaring skin around a cobra's neck. ❖ *tr.v.* **hood·ed, hood·ing, hoods** To supply or cover with a hood. [From Old English *hōd.*]

hood² (ho͝od) *n. Slang* A hoodlum. [Short for *hoodlum.*]

–hood *suff.* A suffix that means: **1.** Condition or quality: *manhood; falsehood.* **2.** A group sharing a certain condition or quality: *sisterhood; priesthood.*

hood·ed (**ho͝od′**ĭd) *adj.* Covered with or having a hood: *a hooded rider; a hooded cape.*

hood·ie (**ho͝od′**ē) *n. Informal* A piece of clothing with a hood, especially a hooded sweatshirt.

hood·lum (**ho͝od′**ləm *or* **ho͞od′**ləm) *n.* **1.** A gangster or thug. **2.** A tough, often aggressive or violent youth.

hood·wink (**ho͝od′**wĭngk′) *tr.v.* **hood·winked, hood·wink·ing, hood·winks** To deceive or mislead; trick.

hoof (ho͝of *or* ho͞of) *n., pl.* **hooves** (ho͝ovz *or* ho͞ovz) or **hoofs 1.** The tough horny covering on the lower part of the foot of certain mammals, such as horses, cattle, deer, and pigs. **2.** The whole foot of such an animal. ❖ *intr.v.* **hoofed, hoof·ing, hoofs** *Slang* **1.** To dance, especially to tap-dance. **2.** To go on foot; walk. ◆ **hoof it** To walk: *We hoofed it into town.* [From Old English *hōf.*]

hoofed (ho͝oft *or* ho͞oft) *adj.* Having hooves.

hook (ho͝ok) *n.* **1.** A curved or sharply bent piece of metal or other stiff material, used to catch, hold, fasten, or pull something: *Coats hung on hooks in the hall.* **2.** A fishhook. **3.** Something shaped or used like a hook. **4.** A sharp curve or bend, as in a river. **5.** A spit of land with a curved end. **6.** A means of catching or ensnaring; a trap. **7.** In sports, the flight of a ball that goes to the left when propelled by a right-handed player or to the right when propelled by a left-handed player. **8.** In boxing, a short swinging blow delivered with a crooked arm. ❖ *v.* **hooked, hook·ing, hooks** —*tr.* **1.** To catch, hang, or connect with a hook: *hook a tuna while fishing.* **2.** To fasten by means of a hook: *hook a picture on the wall.* **3.** To make (a rug, for example) by looping yarn through a loosely woven material with a hook. **4.** In sports, to hit or throw (a ball) with a hook: *hook a shot in golf; hook the ball into the basket.* **5.** To hit with a hook in boxing. —*intr.* **1.** To move, throw, or extend in a curve: *The road hooks toward the river.* **2.** To be fastened by means of a hook: *The gate hooks on the post.* ◆ **by hook or by crook** By whatever means possible, fair or unfair. **hook up 1.** To connect or make a connection between: *The electricity was hooked up to the house.* **2.** *Slang* To meet: *hooked up after class.* **off the hook** *Informal* Free of blame or obligation. [From Old English *hōc.*]

hook·ah (**ho͝ok′**ə) *n.* A smoking pipe used chiefly in southwest Asia and northern Africa. It has a long tube attached to a container of water that cools the smoke as it is drawn through.

hook and eye *n.* **1.** A fastener for clothes consisting of a small hook and loop which can be linked together. **2.** A latch consisting of a hook that is inserted in a screw eye.

hooked (ho͝okt) *adj.* **1.** Curved or bent like a hook: *the owl's hooked beak.* **2.** Having a hook or hooks: *a hooked spear.* **3.** Made by hooking: *a hooked rug.* **4.** *Slang* Addicted or devoted to something: *She's hooked on canoeing.*

hook·up (**ho͝ok′**ŭp′) *n.* **1.** A system of electrical circuits or equipment designed to operate together: *a nationwide radio and television hookup.* **2.** A connection or arrangement: *a hookup between buyer and seller.*

hook·worm (**ho͝ok′**wûrm′) *n.* Any of numerous parasitic worms that fasten themselves to the inside wall of the intestines of various animals, including humans.

hook·y (**ho͝ok′**ē) *n. Informal* Absence without permission: *play hooky from school.*

hoo·li·gan (**ho͞o′**lĭ-gən) *n. Informal* A tough and aggressive or violent youth.

hoop (ho͞op *or* ho͝op) *n.* **1.** A circular band or ring of wood, metal, bone, or plastic used to hold something together, as the staves of a barrel, or to spread something out, as a piece of embroidery or a fancy skirt. **2.** A large ring of wood, plastic, or metal used as a toy. **3a.** In basketball, the basket. **b.** often **hoops** *Informal* The game of basketball: *shoot some hoop; play some hoops.* ❖ *tr.v.* **hooped, hoop·ing, hoops** To bind or fasten together with a hoop.

hoop·la (**ho͞op′**lä′ *or* **ho͝op′**lä′) *n. Informal* **1.** Noisy or confusing commotion. **2.** Extravagant publicity: *The new book was published with great hoopla.*

hoop skirt *n.* A woman's long skirt worn over a framework of connected flexible hoops that keep it spread out.

hoo·ray (ho͞o-**rā′** *or* hə-**rā′**) also **hur·rah** (ho͞o-**rä′** *or* hə-**rä′**) also **hur·ray** (ho͞o-**rā′** *or* hə-**rā′**) *interj.* An expression used to show approval, pleasure, or victory. ❖ *n.* A shout of "hooray." ❖ *intr.v.* **hoo·rayed, hoo·ray·ing, hoo·rays** also **hur·rahed, hur·rah·ing, hur·rahs** also **hur·rayed, hur·ray·ing, hur·rays** To applaud or cheer with shouts of "hooray."

hoot (ho͞ot) *v.* **hoot·ed, hoot·ing, hoots** —*intr.* **1.** To make the cry of an owl. **2.** To make a shout or loud cry of contempt or disapproval: *Protesters hooted at the speaker.* —*tr.* **1.** To shout at or drive away with scornful cries or jeers: *The hecklers hooted the candidate off the platform.* **2.** To express by hooting: *The fans hooted their anger.* ❖ *n.* **1.** The cry of an owl. **2.** A sound similar to this, especially the sound of a horn. **3.** A shout of scorn or disapproval. **4.** *Informal* A person or thing that is hilariously funny: *The new teacher cracks jokes all the time; she's a real hoot!* ◆ **not give a hoot** or **not care a hoot** To be completely indifferent to: *I don't give a hoot if it rains.*

hoot·en·an·ny (**ho͞ot′**n-ăn′ē) *n., pl.* **hoot·en·an·nies** An informal performance by folksingers, usually with the audience joining in.

Hoo·ver (**ho͞o′**vər), **Herbert Clark** 1874–1964. The 31st president of the United States (1929–1933). During the Great Depression, he was slow to use government funds to ease Americans' financial hardship and create jobs.

hooves (ho͝ovz *or* ho͞ovz) *n.* A plural of **hoof.**

hop¹ (hŏp) *v.* **hopped, hop·ping, hops** —*intr.* **1.** To move with light springing leaps or skips: *The frightened rabbit hopped away.* **2.** To jump on one foot or with both feet at the same time. —*tr.* **1.** To jump over: *hopped the fence in a single bound.* **2.** *Informal* To jump aboard: *hop a freight train.* ❖ *n.* **1.** A hopping motion; a springy jump: *The squirrel crossed the lawn in short hops.* **2.** A trip, especially by air: *It is a short hop between Boston and New York.* **3.** A rebound; a bounce: *The ball took a bad hop.* [From Old English *hoppian.*]

hop² (hŏp) *n.* **1.** A twining vine having green flower clusters that resemble small pine cones. **2. hops** The dried flowers of this plant, used in making beer. [From Middle English *hoppe*, from Middle Dutch.]

hope (hōp) *v.* **hoped, hop·ing, hopes** —*intr.* To desire or wish that something will happen: *I am hoping for a better grade on this test.* —*tr.* **1.** To desire or wish (that something will happen): *I hope that the audience likes our play.* **2.** To expect (to do something) with a feeling of confidence: *I hope to be there by five o'clock.* ❖ *n.* **1.** The longing or desire for something accompanied by the belief that it is possible: *The young composer is full of hope for success.* **2.** An instance of such longing or desire: *My hopes of becoming a doctor are unchanged.* **3.** A reason for or cause of such longing or desire: *A home run is the team's only hope for victory.* [From Old English *hopian*.]

hope·ful (hōp′fəl) *adj.* **1.** Feeling or showing hope; expectant: *The immigrants arrived hopeful of a better life.* **2.** Inspiring hope; encouraging: *We were gladdened by hopeful signs of peace.* ❖ *n.* A person who wishes to succeed or shows promise of succeeding in something: *Several hopefuls tried out for the lead in the play.* —**hope′ful·ness** *n.*

hope·ful·ly (hōp′fə-lē) *adv.* **1.** In a hopeful manner: *We began the new soccer season hopefully.* **2.** *Informal* It is to be hoped that: *Hopefully, there will be enough snow to go sledding.*

hope·less (hōp′lĭs) *adj.* **1.** Having no hope; despairing: *After hours of wandering in the forest the lost hikers felt hopeless.* **2.** Offering or causing no hope: *The search for my wallet proved hopeless.* **3.** Having no hope of improvement; incompetent: *I'm hopeless at crosswords.* —**hope′less·ly** *adv.* —**hope′less·ness** *n.*

Ho·pi (hō′pē) *n., pl.* **Hopi** or **Ho·pis 1.** A member of a Native American people of northeast Arizona. **2.** The Uto-Aztecan language of this people.

hop·per (hŏp′ər) *n.* **1.** A person or thing that hops. **2.** A container having a wide open top and a narrow opening at the bottom through which the contents, such as coal or grain, can be emptied, as for feeding into a machine.

hop·scotch (hŏp′skŏch′) *n.* A children's game in which players toss a small object into the numbered spaces of a pattern of rectangles marked on the ground or pavement and then hop through the spaces to pick up the object and return.

ho·ra (hôr′ə) *n.* A traditional dance of Romania and Israel performed by dancers moving around in a circle.

horde (hôrd) *n.* **1.** A large group, crowd, or swarm: *hordes of people at the fair.* **2.** A wandering tribe or group of people: *In 1264 the Mongol hordes invaded China.*
❑ *These sound alike:* **horde, hoard** (store away).

hore·hound (hôr′hound′) *n.* **1.** An aromatic plant having woolly whitish leaves that yield a bitter substance used in cough medicine and in flavoring. **2.** An extract, medicine, or candy prepared using this plant.

ho·ri·zon (hə-rī′zən) *n.* **1.** The line along which the earth and sky appear to meet. **2.** The limit of one's experience, knowledge, or interests: *Lack of education narrows a person's horizons.* [From Middle English *orisonte*, from Greek *horizōn (kuklos)*, limiting (circle).]

hor·i·zon·tal (hôr′ĭ-zŏn′tl) *adj.* **1.** Parallel to or in the plane of the horizon; level. **2.** Relating to or near the horizon. ❖ *n.* A horizontal line or plane. —**hor′i·zon′tal·ly** *adv.*

hor·mon·al (hôr-mō′nəl) *adj.* Relating to or caused by a hormone or hormones: *a hormonal imbalance.*

hor·mone (hôr′mōn′) *n.* **1.** A substance produced by an endocrine gland in a vertebrate animal and usually carried in the bloodstream to another part of the body, where it acts to regulate, control, or stimulate a specific activity, such as growth or metabolism. **2.** A similar substance in an invertebrate animal or a plant. **3.** A synthetic compound that acts like a hormone in the body. [From Greek *hormōn*, present participle of *horman*, to urge on.] —SEE NOTE.

horn (hôrn) *n.* **1.** One of the hard bony growths on the heads of cattle, sheep, goats, and other hoofed mammals. **2.** A hard growth, such as an antler or a growth on the head of a giraffe, that resembles a horn. **3.** The hard durable substance that forms the outer covering of the horns of cattle and related animals: *old buttons made of horn.* **4.** A container made from an animal's horn: *a powder horn.* **5.** Something shaped like a horn, as either end of a new moon or the pommel of a saddle. **6.** Any of various instruments that are sounded by blowing and vibrating the lips and that usually flare at the end, especially a French horn. Horns can be made of animal horn, metal, wood, or plastic. **7.** A warning device that produces a loud sound: *a car horn.* ❖ *intr.v.* **horned, horn·ing, horns** *Slang* To join in without being invited; intrude: *The older children horned in on the game of tag.* [From Old English.]

Horn, Cape A headland of extreme southern Chile in the Tierra del Fuego islands. It is the southernmost point of South America.

horn·bill (hôrn′bĭl′) *n.* Any of various birds of Africa and tropical Asia that have a large curved bill, often with a horny lump on top.

horn·blende (hôrn′blĕnd′) *n.* A common green to black mineral found in many metamorphic and igneous rocks. Iron, calcium, magnesium, and other metals occur in hornblende.

horn·book (hôrn′bo͝ok′) *n.* An early primer consisting of a single page, usually with the alphabet on it and protected by a transparent sheet of horn.

horned (hôrnd) *adj.* Having a horn, horns, or a hornlike growth: *a horned lark.*

horned lizard *n.* Any of several small lizards of western North America and Central America, having short horns on the head, a wide flattened spiny body, and a short tail.

horned toad *n.* A horned lizard.

hor·net (hôr′nĭt) *n.* Any of various large stinging wasps that live in colonies and build large papery nests.

horn of plenty *n., pl.* **horns of plenty** A cornucopia.

horn·pipe (hôrn′pīp′) *n.* **1.** A wind instrument with a single reed, finger holes, and a bell and mouthpiece made of horn. **2.** A lively dance, usually performed by one person and originally popular among sailors. **3.** Music for this dance.

horn·wort (hôrn′wûrt′ *or* hôrn′wôrt′) *n.* Any of various small plants that are related to the mosses and have a thin, flat plant body from which tall hornlike spore-producing structures grow.

horn·y (hôr′nē) *adj.* **horn·i·er, horn·i·est 1.** Having horns or hornlike projections. **2.** Made of horn or a similar substance: *the horny shell of a lobster.* **3.** Tough and callous: *the horny hands of a mason.*

hor·o·scope (hôr′ə-skōp′) *n.* **1.** The relative position of the planets and stars at a given moment, such as at the hour of a person's birth. **2.** A prediction, especially of a person's future, based on the position of the planets and stars. [From Greek *hōroskopos* : *hōrā*, hour, season + *skopos*, observer.]

hor·ren·dous (hô-rĕn′dəs *or* hə-rĕn′dəs) *adj.* Terrible; dreadful. —**hor·ren′dous·ly** *adv.*

hor·ri·ble (hôr′ə-bəl) *adj.* **1.** Causing horror; dreadful: *a horrible crime.* **2.** Extremely unpleasant: *a horrible noise.* —**hor′ri·ble·ness** *n.* —**hor′ri·bly** *adv.*

hor·rid (hôr′ĭd) *adj.* **1.** Causing horror; horrible. **2.** Extremely disagreeable; offensive. —**hor′rid·ly** *adv.* —**hor′rid·ness** *n.*

hor·ri·fy (hôr′ə-fī′) *tr.v.* **hor·ri·fied, hor·ri·fy·ing, hor·**

WRITERS CHOOSE THEIR WORDS

A **horde** of spiders surrounded them. Gregor watched a gorgeous, gauzy funnel of silk grow up around them as if by magic. It isolated the party and blocked all else from view. The spiders stopped spinning when it reached thirty feet. Two took positions as sentries at the top. It all happened in under a minute.

—Suzanne Collins
Gregor the Overlander

SCIENCE

hormone On the inside, humans are bathing in a sea of **hormones,** chemical compounds that regulate many essential activities in the body. *Endocrine glands,* such as the thyroid and pituitary glands, produce many hormones, which are carried by the bloodstream to their target sites of action. Insulin, secreted by the pancreas, regulates sugar absorption. Estrogen and testosterone control sexual development. Some hormones limit the secretions of other hormones. If your body produces too much or too little of a hormone, you can become sick. People whose thyroids produce too much of the hormone thyroxine, for example, can suffer from weight loss and high blood pressure. Synthetic hormones made in laboratories are used to treat various medical conditions.

horned lizard

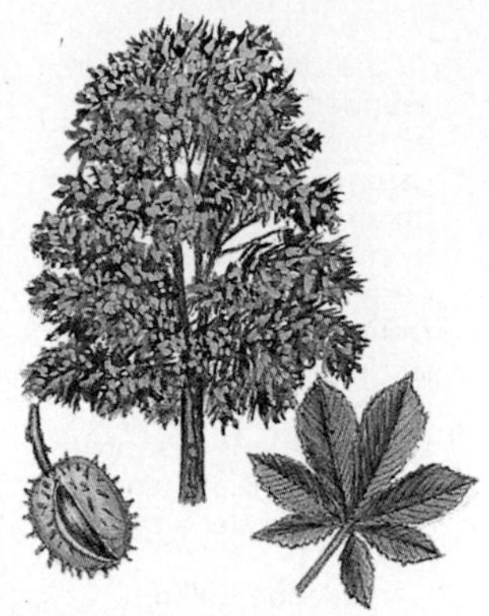
horse chestnut

rifies 1. To cause to feel horror: *The possibility of a violent earthquake horrified people.* **2.** To surprise unpleasantly; shock: *The class's poor performance on the test horrified the teacher.*

hor·ror (hôr′ər) *n.* **1.** A feeling of fear and disgust; terror. **2.** Something that causes horror: *the horrors of war.* **3.** Intense dislike; loathing: *Winston has a horror of rats.*

hors d'oeuvre (ôr dûrv′) *n., pl.* **hors d'oeuvres** (ôr dûrvz′) or **hors d'oeuvre** An appetizer served before a meal.

horse (hôrs) *n.* **1.** A large hoofed mammal having a short coat and a long mane and tail. Horses are used for riding, pulling vehicles, and carrying loads. **2.** An adult male horse. **3.** A frame consisting of a crossbar and four legs, used for supporting or holding. **4.** A pommel horse. ❖ *tr.v.* **horsed, hors·ing, hors·es** To provide with a horse: *After the knights were horsed, they rode off to battle.* ◆ **beat a dead horse 1.** To dwell tiresomely on a matter that has already been decided. **2.** To continue to pursue a cause that has no hope of success. **hold (one's) horses** To restrain oneself. **horse around** *Informal* To indulge in horseplay or frivolous activity. **on (one's) high horse** Self-righteous and disdainful. **the horse's mouth** A source of information regarded as original and beyond doubt: *I know it's true because I got it from the horse's mouth.* [From Old English *hors.*]

❑ *These sound alike:* **horse, hoarse** (husky).

horse·back (hôrs′băk′) *n.* The back of a horse: *police officers on horseback.* ❖ *adv. & adj.* On the back of a horse: *ride horseback; horseback riding.*

horse chestnut *n.* **1.** Any of several large trees having upright clusters of white flowers and shiny brown seeds enclosed in a usually spiny capsule. **2.** The inedible nutlike seed of any of these trees.

horse·fly (hôrs′flī′) *n.* Any of numerous large flies, the female of which bites and sucks blood from horses, cattle, and other animals.

horse·hair (hôrs′hâr′) *n.* **1.** The coarse hair from a horse's mane or tail. **2.** Stiff cloth made of the hair of horses.

horse latitudes *pl.n.* Either of two regions notable for high barometric pressure and calm or light variable wind. They are found over the oceans at about 30 to 35 degrees north and south latitudes.

horse·man (hôrs′mən) *n.* **1.** A man who rides a horse. **2.** A man skilled at riding horses.

horse·man·ship (hôrs′mən-shĭp′) *n.* The skill of riding horses: *Rodeo riders must have superior horsemanship.*

horse·play (hôrs′plā′) *n.* Rough or rowdy play.

horse·pow·er (hôrs′pou′ər) *n.* A unit used to measure the power of engines and motors, equal to the power needed to lift 550 pounds one foot in one second.

horse·rad·ish (hôrs′răd′ĭsh) *n.* **1.** A tall plant having long leaves, white flowers, and a large whitish root with a sharp taste. **2.** A sharp condiment made from the roots of this plant.

horse sense *n. Informal* Common sense.

horse·shoe (hôrs′sho͞o′ *or* hôrsh′sho͞o′) *n.* **1.** A flat U-shaped metal plate fitted and nailed to a horse's hoof for protection. **2.** Something shaped like a horseshoe. **3. horseshoes** *(used with a singular verb)* A game in which the players try to toss horseshoes around or near a stake.

horseshoe crab *n.* Any of various invertebrate sea animals that have a large oval shell and a stiff pointed tail. Horseshoe crabs, like insects and crustaceans, are arthropods.

horse·tail (hôrs′tāl′) *n.* Any of various plants that have a jointed hollow stem and small scalelike leaves and do not have flowers or seeds.

horse·whip (hôrs′wĭp′) *n.* A whip used to drive or control a horse. ❖ *tr.v.* **horse·whipped, horse·whip·ping, horse·whips** To beat with a horsewhip.

horse·wom·an (hôrs′wo͝om′ən) *n.* **1.** A woman who rides a horse. **2.** A woman skilled at riding horses.

hor·ti·cul·ture (hôr′tĭ-kŭl′chər) *n.* **1.** The science or art of cultivating fruits, vegetables, flowers, or ornamental plants. **2.** The cultivation of a garden. **—hor′ti·cul′tur·al** *adj.*

hor·ti·cul·tur·ist (hôr′tĭ-kŭl′chər-ĭst) *n.* A person who specializes in horticulture.

ho·san·na (hō-zăn′ə) *interj.* An expression used to show praise or adoration of God. ❖ *n.* A cry of "hosanna."

hose (hōz) *n.* **1.** *pl.* **hose** Stockings; socks. Used only in the plural. **2.** *pl.* **hose** Tights once worn by men as pants. Used only in the plural. **3.** *pl.* **hos·es** A flexible tube for carrying liquids or gases under pressure: *use an air hose to fill the car tires.* ❖ *tr.v.* **hosed, hos·ing, hos·es** To wash or spray with water from a hose: *hose down a car while washing it.* [From Old English *hosa,* leg covering.]

Ho·se·a[1] (hō-zē′ə *or* hō-zā′ə) A Hebrew prophet of the eighth century BC.

Ho·se·a[2] (hō-zē′ə *or* hō-zā′ə) *n.* A book of the Bible in which Hosea rebukes the Israelites for unfaithfulness and urges repentance.

ho·sier·y (hō′zhə-rē) *n.* Stockings and socks; hose.

hos·pice (hŏs′pĭs) *n.* **1.** A program providing care and support for people who are terminally ill. **2.** A shelter or lodging for travelers or those who are very poor, often maintained by a religious order.

hos·pi·ta·ble (hŏs′pĭ-tə-bəl *or* hŏ-spĭt′ə-bəl) *adj.* **1.** Disposed to treat guests with warmth and generosity: *The hotel staff is extremely hospitable.* **2.** Having an open mind; receptive: *The new manager is hospitable to new ideas.* **—hos′pi·ta·bly** *adv.*

hos·pi·tal (hŏs′pĭ-tl *or* hŏs′pĭt′l) *n.* **1.** An institution providing medical, surgical, or psychiatric care and treatment for sick or injured people. **2.** An institution providing veterinary care and treatment for sick or injured animals. [From Middle English, from Latin *hospitālis,* of a guest.]

hos·pi·tal·i·ty (hŏs′pĭ-tăl′ĭ-tē) *n., pl.* **hos·pi·tal·i·ties** Welcoming or generous treatment of guests.

hos·pi·tal·i·za·tion (hŏs′pĭ-tl-ĭ-zā′shən) *n.* **1.** The act of placing a person in a hospital as a patient. **2.** The condition of being hospitalized: *Hospitalization may increase the chances of recovery from serious illness.* **3.** Insurance that fully or partially covers a patient's hospital expenses.

hos·pi·tal·ize (hŏs′pĭt-l-īz′) *tr.v.* **hos·pi·tal·ized, hos·pi·tal·iz·ing, hos·pi·tal·iz·es** To place in a hospital for treatment, care, or observation: *I was hospitalized for two days with appendicitis.*

host[1] (hōst) *n.* **1a.** A person who receives or entertains guests in a social or official capacity: *The new neighbors were our hosts for the evening.* **b.** The keeper of an inn or hotel. **c.** The emcee or interviewer on a radio or television program. **2a.** An organism on or in which a parasite lives and feeds. **b.** A cell that is infected by a virus. **3.** A computer containing data or programs that another computer can access by network or modem. ❖ *tr.v.* **host·ed, host·ing, hosts 1.** To serve as host to or at: *host a party; host an interview on TV.* **2.** To furnish facilities and resources for (a function or event): *Beijing hosted the Olympic Games in 2008.* [From Middle English, from Late Latin *hospes.*]

host[2] (hōst) *n.* **1.** An army. **2.** A great number; a multitude. [From Middle English, from Latin *hostis,* enemy.]

host[3] also **Host** (hōst) *n.* The consecrated bread or wafer of the Eucharist. [From Middle English, from Latin *hostia,* sacrifice.]

hos·tage (hŏs′tĭj) *n.* **1.** A person who is held by a group or another person in a conflict as security that a specified demand will be met. **2.** A person or thing that serves

ă	pat	ôr	core
ā	pay	oi	boy
âr	care	ou	out
ä	father	o͝o	took
ĕ	pet	o͝or	lure
ē	be	o͞o	boot
ĭ	pit	ŭ	cut
ī	bite	ûr	urge
îr	pier	th	thin
ŏ	pot	*th*	this
ō	toe	zh	vision
ô	paw	ə	about

as security against an implied threat. [From Middle English, from Old French *host*, guest.]

hos·tel (hŏs′təl) *n.* An inexpensive lodging place for travelers, especially young travelers.

❑ *These sound alike:* **hostel, hostile** (antagonistic).

hos·tel·ry (hŏs′təl-rē) *n., pl.* **hos·tel·ries** An inn; a hotel.

host·ess (hō′stĭs) *n.* **1.** A woman who receives or entertains guests in a social or official capacity. **2.** A woman who is the keeper of an inn or hotel. **3.** A woman who is employed to greet and assist patrons, as at a restaurant.

hos·tile (hŏs′təl *or* hŏs′tīl′) *adj.* **1.** Relating to or characteristic of an enemy: *hostile forces.* **2.** Feeling or showing enmity or ill will: *a hostile crowd.* **3.** Unfavorable to health or well-being: *a hostile climate.* [From Latin *hostis*, enemy.] **—hos′tile·ly** *adv.*

❑ *These sound alike:* **hostile, hostel** (lodging).

hos·til·i·ty (hŏ-stĭl′ĭ-tē) *n., pl.* **hos·til·i·ties 1.** The state of being hostile; antagonism or enmity: *The hostility of the former enemies was felt by everyone.* **2. hostilities** Acts of war; open warfare: *Hostilities broke out between the two countries.*

hos·tler (hŏs′lər *or* ŏs′lər) also **os·tler** (ŏs′lər) *n.* **1.** A person who is employed to tend horses, especially at an inn. **2.** A person who maintains and repairs a large vehicle or engine, such as a locomotive.

hot (hŏt) *adj.* **hot·ter, hot·test 1.** Having great heat; being at a high temperature; very warm: *a hot stove; a horse that was hot after working in the sun; a forehead hot with fever.* **2.** Charged with electricity: *a hot wire.* **3.** Radioactive or designed to use radioactive materials. **4.** Causing a burning sensation, as in the mouth; spicy: *hot chile; hot mustard.* **5.** Marked by intense feeling; fiery: *a hot temper; a hot argument.* **6.** Very eager or enthusiastic: *We were hot to go to the beach.* **7.** *Informal* Most recent; new or fresh: *a hot piece of news.* **8.** *Informal* Currently very popular: *a hot topic of conversation.* **9.** Close to a successful solution or conclusion: *hot on the trail of the robbers.* **10.** Having or characterized by repeated successes: *a hot goalie.* **11.** *Slang* Stolen: *a hot DVD player.* ❖ *adv.* In a hot manner; with much heat: *The engine runs hot. The sun shone hot on the pavement.* [From Old English *hāt*.] **—hot′ly** *adv.* **—hot′ness** *n.*

hot air *n. Slang* Empty, exaggerated talk.

hot·bed (hŏt′bĕd′) *n.* **1.** A place that fosters rapid and excessive growth or development, especially of something bad: *a hotbed of intrigue.* **2.** A bed of soil covered with glass or plastic and heated by decaying manure or electricity, used for growing seeds or protecting young plants.

hot-blood·ed (hŏt′blŭd′ĭd) *adj.* Easily excited: *a hot-blooded youth.*

hot·cake (hŏt′kāk′) *n.* A pancake. ◆ **go like hotcakes** or **sell like hotcakes** *Informal* To be disposed of quickly and in great amounts: *The raffle tickets are selling like hotcakes.*

hot chocolate *n.* A drink made by mixing powdered chocolate with a sweetener and hot milk or water; cocoa.

hot cross bun *n.* A sweet bun marked on top with a cross of frosting, traditionally eaten during Lent.

hot dog or **hot·dog** (hŏt′dôg′) *n.* A frankfurter, especially one served hot in a long roll.

ho·tel (hō-tĕl′) *n.* A house or other building that provides lodging and often meals and other services for paying guests.

hot·foot (hŏt′fo͝ot′) *intr.v.* **hot·foot·ed, hot·foot·ing, hot·foots** *Informal* To go in great haste: *hotfoot it to the market before it closes.*

hot·head·ed (hŏt′hĕd′ĭd) *adj.* **1.** Easily angered; quick-tempered: *a crowd of hotheaded protestors.* **2.** Impetuous; rash: *a hotheaded plan.* **—hot′head′ed·ly** *adv.* **—hot′head′ed·ness** *n.*

hot·house (hŏt′hous′) *n.* A heated building with a glass roof and sides, used for growing plants; a greenhouse. ❖ *adj.* Grown in a hothouse: *hothouse tomatoes.*

hot·line (hŏt′līn′) *n.* **1.** A direct and immediate communications link, usually a telephone line, as between heads of governments for use in a crisis. **2.** A telephone line that provides information or help: *the clinic's health hotline.*

hot·ly (hŏt′lē) *adv.* In an intense or fiery manner: *a hotly debated subject.*

hot plate *n.* An electrically heated plate for cooking or warming food.

hot rod *n. Slang* An automobile rebuilt or modified for greater acceleration and speed.

hot·shot (hŏt′shŏt′) *n. Slang* A person with unusual skill and daring, especially one who is highly successful and self-assured.

hot spot *n.* **1.** A place of dangerous unrest or hostile action. **2.** *Slang* A lively and popular place, as a nightclub: *a downtown hot spot for food and dancing.* **3.** In geology, a source of great heat in the earth. **4.** A public place where high-speed access to the Internet is made available.

hot spring *n.* A natural spring of warm water, usually having a temperature greater than that of the human body.

hot toddy *n.* A drink made of whiskey or another liquor mixed with hot water, sugar, and spices.

hot water *n. Informal* A difficult or uncomfortable situation; trouble: *Skipping school got the children into hot water with their parents.*

hound (hound) *n.* **1.** A dog of any of various breeds originally bred and used for hunting, usually having short hair and drooping ears. **2.** A dog of any kind. **3.** A person who is very enthusiastic about something: *She's a serious art hound.* ❖ *tr.v.* **hound·ed, hound·ing, hounds** To pursue or harass: *Reporters hounded the mayor for a statement.* [From Old English *hund*.]

hour (our) *n.* **1.** A unit of time equal to one of the 24 equal parts of a day; 60 minutes. **2.** One of these units of time as shown on a clock or watch or marked by a bell or other signal: *The hour is 3 PM. The church clock strikes on the hour.* **3.** The distance that can be traveled in an hour: *The airport is about an hour from our house by car.* **4.** A particular time of day: *At what hour does the store open?* **5.** A customary or fixed time: *the dinner hour.* **6. hours** A set period of time for a specified activity: *open hours from eight to three; keeps office hours.* [From Middle English *houre*, from Greek *hōrā*, season, time.]

❑ *These sound alike:* **hour, our** (of us).

hour·glass (our′glăs′) *n.* An instrument for measuring time, consisting of two glass chambers connected by a narrow neck and containing an amount of sand or another substance that passes from the top chamber to the bottom one in a fixed amount of time, often one hour.

hour·ly (our′lē) *adj.* **1.** Occurring every hour: *hourly temperature readings; hourly news reports during the hurricane.* **2.** By the hour as a unit: *an hourly wage.* **3.** Frequent; continual: *hourly changes in the weather.* ❖ *adv.* At or during every hour: *doses of medicine given hourly.*

house (hous) *n., pl.* **hous·es** (hou′zĭz *or* hou′sĭz) **1a.** A structure serving as a dwelling for one or more persons, especially for a family. **b.** A dwelling for a group of people, such as students, who live together as a unit: *a sorority house.* **2.** All of the people living in a house; a household. **3.** A building or other structure used for some special purpose: *a movie house; a house of worship.* **4.** The people in an audience: *a full house.* **5.** A noble family including its ancestors and descendants. **6.** A business firm: *a banking house; a publishing house.* **7a.** An assembly having the duty and power of making laws; a legislature. **b. House** The House of Representatives,

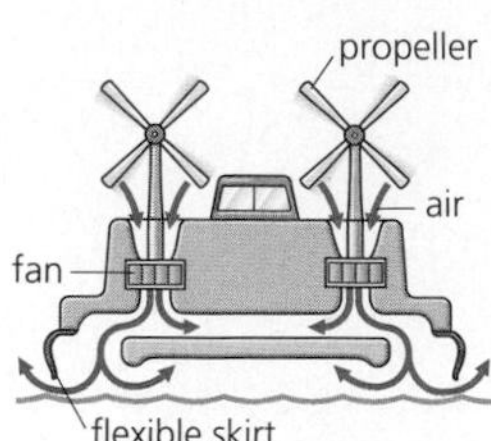

hovercraft

howdah

Julia Ward Howe
photographed c. 1902

ă	pat	ôr	core
ā	pay	oi	boy
âr	care	ou	out
ä	father	o͝o	took
ĕ	pet	o͝or	lure
ē	be	o͞o	boot
ĭ	pit	ŭ	cut
ī	bite	ûr	urge
îr	pier	th	thin
ŏ	pot	*th*	this
ō	toe	zh	vision
ô	paw	ə	about

especially of the US government. ❖ *tr.v.* (houz) **housed, hous·ing, hous·es 1.** To provide living quarters for: *The apartment building houses ten families.* **2.** To keep or store in a house or other shelter or space: *We housed our car in the garage. The electrical controls are housed inside a metal box.* ◆ **on the house** Paid for by the establishment; free. [From Old English *hūs*.]

house arrest *n.* Confinement of a criminal to his or her residence, rather than prison, by court order.

house·boat (**hous′**bōt′) *n.* A barge designed and equipped for use as a floating dwelling.

house·break (**hous′**brāk′) *tr.v.* **house·broke** (**hous′**-brōk′), **house·bro·ken** (**hous′**brō′kən), **house·break·ing, house·breaks** To train (a pet) to have excretory habits that are appropriate for indoor living.

house·break·er (**hous′**brā′kər) *n.* A person who unlawfully breaks into another's house in order to steal or commit some other crime.

house·break·ing (**hous′**brā′kĭng) *n.* The act of unlawfully breaking into and entering another's house.

house·broke (**hous′**brōk′) *v.* Past tense of **housebreak.**

house·bro·ken (**hous′**brō′kən) *v.* Past participle of **housebreak.** ❖ *adj.* Trained to have excretory habits that are appropriate for indoor living: *a housebroken dog.*

house call *n.* A professional visit made to a home, especially by a physician.

house·clean·ing (**hous′**klē′nĭng) *n.* The cleaning and tidying of a house and its contents.

house·fly (**hous′**flī′) *n.* A common fly that is found in all parts of the world around human dwellings and farms. Houseflies breed in manure and garbage and can carry many diseases.

house·hold (**hous′**hōld′) *n.* **1.** The members of a family and others living together as a domestic unit. **2.** The living spaces and possessions belonging to such a unit. ❖ *adj.* Relating to or used in a household: *household appliances; household expenses.*

house·hold·er (**hous′**hōl′dər) *n.* **1.** A person who occupies or owns a house. **2.** The head of a household.

house·hus·band (**hous′**hŭz′bənd) *n.* A married man who manages the household as his main occupation.

house·keep·er (**hous′**kē′pər) *n.* **1.** A person hired to perform or direct the domestic tasks of a household. **2.** An employee of an establishment, such as a hotel, who performs or coordinates housekeeping tasks.

house·keep·ing (**hous′**kē′pĭng) *n.* **1.** Performance or management of household tasks, such as cooking, cleaning, and shopping. **2.** The management of the property and equipment of a hospital, hotel, or similar institution.

house·maid (**hous′**mād′) *n.* A woman or girl employed to do housework.

House of Commons *n.* The lower house of Parliament in the United Kingdom and Canada.

house of correction *n., pl.* **houses of correction** An institution for confining people convicted of minor criminal offenses.

House of Lords *n.* The upper house of Parliament in the United Kingdom, made up of members of the nobility and high-ranking clergy.

House of Representatives *n.* The lower house of the US Congress and of most state legislatures.

house·plant (**hous′**plănt′) *n.* A plant grown indoors, often for decorative purposes.

house sparrow *n.* A small bird having brown and gray feathers and a distinctive black mark on the throat of the male. House sparrows are native to Eurasia but are now found worldwide, usually near human settlements.

house·top (**hous′**tŏp′) *n.* The roof of a house.

house·wares (**hous′**wârz′) *pl.n.* Articles used especially in the kitchen, such as cooking utensils and dishes.

house·warm·ing (**hous′**wôr′mĭng) *n.* A party to celebrate moving into a new home.

house·wife (**hous′**wīf′) *n.* A married woman who manages the household as her main occupation.

house·work (**hous′**wûrk′) *n.* The tasks performed in housekeeping, such as cleaning and cooking.

hous·ing (**hou′**zĭng) *n.* **1.** Buildings or other shelters in which people live. **2.** Provision of lodging or shelter: *The employment agreement included housing.* **3.** Something that covers, contains, or protects a mechanical part.

housing project *n.* A group of publicly funded houses or apartment buildings, usually for people with low incomes.

Hous·ton (**hyo͞o′**stən) The largest city of Texas, in the southeast part of the state east-southeast of Austin. It was founded in 1836.

Houston, Samuel 1793–1863. American soldier and politician who served as president of the Republic of Texas (1836–1838 and 1841–1844).

hove (hōv) *tr.v.* Past tense and past participle of **heave** (sense 1b). ❖ *intr.v.* Past tense and past participle of **heave** (sense 5).

hov·el (**hŭv′**əl *or* **hŏv′**əl) *n.* A small shabby dwelling.

hov·er (**hŭv′**ər *or* **hŏv′**ər) *intr.v.* **hov·ered, hov·er·ing, hov·ers 1.** To stay floating, suspended, or fluttering in the air: *Hummingbirds hover over the flowers they feed on.* **2.** To remain close by: *The mother fox hovered around the den.* **3.** To be in a state of uncertainty; waver: *The patient hovered between recovery and relapse.* [From Middle English *hoveren*.]

hov·er·craft (**hŭv′**ər-krăft′ *or* **hŏv′**ər-krăft′) *n.* A vehicle that travels over land or water on a thin cushion of air created by fans blowing downward.

HOV lane (āch′ō-**vē′**) *n.* An expressway lane restricted to vehicles carrying more than one person, designed to encourage car-pooling and reduce traffic.

how (hou) *adv.* **1.** In what manner or way; by what means: *The teacher showed us how to use a compass.* **2.** In what state or condition: *How do you feel today?* **3.** To what extent, amount, or degree: *How strong is the rope? How much do these gadgets cost?* **4.** For what reason; why: *How did you manage to miss the train?* **5.** With what meaning: *How should I take that remark?* ❖ *conj.* **1.** The manner or way in which: *I forgot how the song goes.* **2.** In whatever way or manner that: *Cook the beans how you like.* ❖ *n.* The way something is done: *I am more interested in the how than the why of a thing.* ◆ **how about** What is your thought, feeling, or desire regarding: *How about some ice cream?* **how come** *Informal* How is it that; why: *How come you're late?*

how·dah (**hou′**də) *n.* A seat for riding on the back of an elephant or camel, usually fitted with a canopy and railing.

how·dy (**hou′**dē) *interj.* An expression used to greet someone.

Howe (hou), **Elias** 1819–1867. American inventor of early sewing machines (1845 and 1846).

Howe, Julia Ward 1819–1910. American writer and suffragist. She wrote "Battle Hymn of the Republic" (1862) and was a founder of the American Woman Suffrage Association (1869).

how·ev·er (hou-**ĕv′**ər) *adv.* **1.** To whatever extent or degree: *However long the process, an education is absolutely necessary.* **2.** In whatever way or manner: *However you manage it, the job must be done.* **3.** Nevertheless; yet: *It was a difficult time; however, there were amusing moments.*

how·it·zer (**hou′**ĭt-sər) *n.* A short cannon that fires shells in a high curving path. [From obsolete German *haufnitz*, catapult.]

howl (houl) *v.* **howled, howl·ing, howls** —*intr.* **1.** To utter or emit a long, mournful, plaintive sound: *The* *dogs howled at the loud siren.* **2.** To cry or wail loudly, as in pain, sorrow, or anger: *The patient howled when the dentist pulled the tooth.* **3.** *Slang* To laugh heartily: *The audience howled at the comedian's jokes.* —*tr.* To express or utter with a howl. See Synonyms at **yell.** ❖ *n.* A long wailing cry. [From Middle English *houlen.*]

how·so·ev·er (hou′sō-ĕv′ər) *adv.* **1.** To whatever extent or degree. **2.** By whatever means.

hp *abbr.* An abbreviation of horsepower.

HPV *abbr.* An abbreviation of human papillomavirus.

HQ *abbr.* An abbreviation of headquarters.

HR *abbr.* An abbreviation of: **1.** home run. **2.** House of Representatives.

hr. *abbr.* An abbreviation of hour.

hryv·nia (hrĭv′nyä) *n.* The basic monetary unit of Ukraine.

Hs The symbol for the element **hassium.**

ht *abbr.* An abbreviation of height.

HTML (āch′tē-ĕm-ĕl′) *n.* A markup language used to structure documents and to set up hypertext links between documents, especially on the World Wide Web.

Huang He (hwäng′ hə′) See **Yellow River.**

hua·ra·che (wə-rä′chē *or* hə-rä′chē) *n.* A flat-heeled sandal whose upper part is made of woven leather strips.

hub (hŭb) *n.* **1.** The center part of a wheel, fan, or propeller. **2.** A center of activity or interest; a focal point: *Nashville is the hub of country music.*

hub·bub (hŭb′ŭb′) *n.* Noisy confusion; uproar: *the hubbub of traffic; the hubbub in a crowded room.*

hub·cap (hŭb′kăp′) *n.* A round covering over an automobile wheel.

huck·le·ber·ry (hŭk′əl-bĕr′ē) *n.* **1.** The edible, usually bluish-black berry of any of various shrubs related to the blueberries. **2.** A shrub that bears such berries.

huck·ster (hŭk′stər) *n.* **1.** A person who sells goods in the street; a peddler. **2.** A person who used aggressive, sometimes devious methods to promote or sell a product. **3.** *Informal* A writer of advertising copy, especially for radio or television.

hud·dle (hŭd′l) *n.* **1.** A densely packed group or crowd, as of people or animals. **2.** In football, a grouping of a team's players behind the line of scrimmage to plan the next play. **3.** A small private conference or meeting: *The two lawyers went into a huddle.* ❖ *v.* **hud·dled, hud·dling, hud·dles** —*intr.* **1.** To crowd together, as from cold or fear: *The pedestrians huddled in doorways until the rain passed.* **2.** To draw one's limbs close to one's body; crouch: *I huddled in the closet playing hide-and-seek.* **3.** In football, to gather in a huddle. **4.** *Informal* To confer; meet: *The two friends huddled and talked over the problem.* —*tr.* To cause to crowd together: *The dog huddled the sheep into a group.* [Possibly from Low German *hudeln,* to crowd together.]

Hud·son (hŭd′sən), **Henry** Died 1611. English navigator who explored the Hudson River in 1609.

Hudson Bay An inland sea of east-central Canada connected to the Atlantic Ocean by **Hudson Strait,** lying between southern Baffin Island and northern Quebec.

Hudson River A river rising in the Adirondack Mountains of northeast New York and flowing about 315 miles (510 kilometers) generally southward to the Atlantic Ocean at New York City.

hue (hyo͞o) *n.* **1.** The property that distinguishes one color in the spectrum of visible light from another, as red from yellow or blue from green: *all the hues of the rainbow; the basic hues of red, blue, and yellow.* **2.** A shade or tint of color: *hues of blue from light to dark.* [From Old English *hīw, hēo.*]

❑ *These sound alike:* **hue, hew** (shape with an axe).

hue and cry *n.* A public clamor, as of protest or demand. [From Middle English *heu and cri,* partial translation of Anglo-Norman *hu e cri* : *hu,* outcry (from Old French *huer,* to shout) + *e,* and + *cri,* cry (from Old French *crier,* to cry).]

Huer·ta (wĕr′tə), **Dolores** Born 1930. American labor organizer and cofounder of the United Farm Workers (1962).

huff (hŭf) *n.* A fit of anger or annoyance: *left the room in a huff.* ❖ *v.* **huffed, huff·ing, huffs** —*intr.* To puff; blow: *I huffed all the way up the hill.* —*tr.* To anger; annoy: *Their snooty attitude huffed me.*

huff·y (hŭf′ē) *adj.* **huff·i·er, huff·i·est 1.** Easily offended; touchy: *Why are you so huffy today?* **2.** Irritated or annoyed; indignant: *Their rude remarks made me huffy.* —**huff′i·ly** *adv.* —**huff′i·ness** *n.*

hug (hŭg) *v.* **hugged, hug·ging, hugs** —*tr.* **1.** To clasp or hold closely; embrace: *hug a child.* **2.** To keep or stay close to: *This car hugs the road well on corners.* **3.** To hold steadfastly to; cherish: *hugs his eccentric ideas.* —*intr.* To cling together closely; embrace: *We hugged and said goodbye.* ❖ *n.* An affectionate or tight embrace.

huge (hyo͞oj) *adj.* **hug·er, hug·est** Of great size, extent, or quantity: *a huge tree; a huge difference.* See Synonyms at **large.** —**huge′ly** *adv.* —**huge′ness** *n.*

Hughes (hyo͞oz), **(James) Langston** 1902–1967. American writer known for his poetry, prose, and drama depicting the lives of urban African Americans.

Hu·go (hyo͞o′gō), **Victor Marie** 1802–1885. French writer whose novels include *The Hunchback of Notre Dame* (1831).

Hu·gue·not (hyo͞o′gə-nŏt′) *n.* A French Protestant of the 1500s to 1700s.

huh (hŭ) *interj.* An expression used to ask a question or show surprise, contempt, or indifference.

hu·la (ho͞o′lə) *n.* A Polynesian dance characterized by swaying movements of the hips and miming movements of the arms and hands. [From Hawaiian.]

hulk (hŭlk) *n.* **1.** The hull of an old, unseaworthy, or wrecked ship. **2.** A heavy unwieldy ship. **3.** A large clumsy person or thing: *a hulk of a football player.* **4.** A wrecked or abandoned shell usually of a large object, such as a building.

hulk·ing (hŭl′kĭng) *adj.* Unwieldy or bulky; massive: *a great hulking St. Bernard.*

hull (hŭl) *n.* **1.** The framework or body of a ship or airplane. **2.** The outer covering of certain seeds or fruits; a husk or pod. **3.** The cluster of green sepals at the stem end of certain fruits, such as the strawberry. ❖ *tr.v.* **hulled, hull·ing, hulls** To remove the hulls of (fruits or seeds): *hull berries.* [From Old English *hulu.*] —**hull′er** *n.*

hul·la·ba·loo (hŭl′ə-bə-lo͞o′) *n., pl.* **hul·la·ba·loos** A great noise or excitement; an uproar.

hul·lo (hə-lō′) *interj. & n. Chiefly British* Variant of **hello.**

hum (hŭm) *v.* **hummed, hum·ming, hums** —*intr.* **1.** To make the continuous droning sound of a bee in flight; buzz: *Bees hummed around the flower. The TV set hums when we turn it on.* **2.** To make a continuous low droning sound like that of the speech sound *m* when prolonged. **3.** To sing without words, with the lips kept closed: *hum while working.* **4.** To be full of or alive with activity: *The street hums with traffic.* —*tr.* To sing (a tune) without opening the lips: *hum a melody.* ❖ *n.* **1.** The act of humming. **2.** The sound produced by humming.

hu·man (hyo͞o′mən) *n.* **1.** A member of the species *Homo sapiens*; a person. **2.** Any of various extinct species that are closely related to modern humans. The first ancient humans are thought to have evolved over 2 million years ago. ❖ *adj.* **1.** Relating to or characteristic of humans: *the human body; the course of human events.* **2.** Relating to or having any of the qualities that are considered characteristic of humans: *human kindness; mistakes that show she's only human.* **3.** Made up of people: *The protesters*

Dolores Huerta
photographed in 2008

Langston Hughes

Victor Hugo

hula

WRITERS CHOOSE THEIR WORDS

Luneta sat alone in her room, staring into the fire, her eyes glowing with excitement. To have arrived for an indefinite stay in this luxurious castle, where she would wear the finest clothes and most of all get to know a real enchantress, was more than she could ever have hoped for. It made her drab and relentlessly **humdrum** childhood at Orkney Hall seem like a dark and unpleasant dream.

—Gerald Morris
The Lioness and Her Knight

hummingbird

ă	pat	ôr	core
ā	pay	oi	boy
âr	care	ou	out
ä	father	o͝o	took
ĕ	pet	o͝or	lure
ē	be	o͞o	boot
ĭ	pit	ŭ	cut
ī	bite	ûr	urge
îr	pier	th	thin
ŏ	pot	*th*	this
ō	toe	zh	vision
ô	paw	ə	about

linked their arms in a human chain. [From Middle English *humain*, from Latin *hūmānus*.] —**hu′man·ness** *n.*

human being *n.* A human; a woman, man, or child.

hu·mane (hyo͞o-**mān′**) *adj.* Marked by kindness, compassion, or mercy: *a humane judge; humane treatment of animals.* —**hu·mane′ly** *adv.* —**hu·mane′ness** *n.*

hu·man·ism (**hyo͞o′**mə-nĭz′əm) *n.* **1.** A system of thought centering on humans and their welfare, interests, and values. **2.** The study of the humanities; learning in the liberal arts. **3.** often **Humanism** The major intellectual movement of the European Renaissance, emphasizing secular concerns and critical ways of thinking as a result of a revival of interest in the art, literature, and civilization of ancient Greece and Rome.

hu·man·ist (**hyo͞o′**mə-nĭst) *n.* **1.** A believer in the principles of humanism. **2.** A student of the liberal arts. **3.** A person who is concerned with the interest, welfare, and values of humans.

hu·man·i·tar·i·an (hyo͞o-măn′ĭ-**târ′**ē-ən) *n.* A person who promotes human welfare and the advancement of social reforms; a philanthropist. ❖ *adj.* Relating to or characteristic of humanitarianism.

hu·man·i·tar·i·an·ism (hyo͞o-măn′ĭ-**târ′**ē-ə-nĭz′əm) *n.* The belief that humans have an obligation to work for the improvement of human welfare.

hu·man·i·ty (hyo͞o-**măn′**ĭ-tē) *n., pl.* **hu·man·i·ties 1.** Humans considered as a group; the human race: *The measles vaccine is of benefit to humanity.* **2.** The quality or fact of being human. **3.** The quality of being humane; kindness: *Taking in the war refugees was an act of great humanity.* **4. humanities** The branches of knowledge, such as art, philosophy, and literature, that are concerned with human thought and culture.

hu·man·ize (**hyo͞o′**mə-nīz′) *tr.v.* **hu·man·ized, hu·man·iz·ing, hu·man·iz·es 1.** To give human characteristics to; make human: *The writer humanizes animal characters by showing how they feel.* **2.** To make humane: *courteous acts that humanize life in the city.* —**hu′man·i·za′tion** (hyo͞o′mə-nĭ-**zā′**shən) *n.*

hu·man·kind (**hyo͞o′**mən-kīnd′) *n.* The human race.

hu·man·ly (**hyo͞o′**mən-lē) *adv.* **1.** In a human way. **2.** Within the scope of human means, abilities, or powers: *as soon as is humanly possible.*

human nature *n.* The sum of qualities and traits shared by all humans.

hu·man·oid (**hyo͞o′**mə-noid′) *adj.* Having human characteristics or form: *a humanoid robot.* ❖ *n.* A being, especially an android, that resembles a human.

human pap·il·lo·ma·vi·rus (păp′ə-**lō′**mə-vī′rəs) *n.* Any of the various viruses that can cause genital warts and several types of cancer, especially cervical cancer.

human rights *pl.n.* The basic rights of all humans, often held to include the right to life and liberty, equality before the law, freedom from torture and slavery, and freedom of thought and expression.

hum·ble (**hŭm′**bəl) *adj.* **hum·bler, hum·blest 1.** Marked by meekness or modesty in behavior, attitude, or spirit: *a humble manner; humble thanks.* **2.** Low in rank, quality, or station: *My career began as a humble clerk.* ❖ *tr.v.* **hum·bled, hum·bling, hum·bles** To cause to be meek or modest in spirit; humiliate: *Defeat humbled the proud general.* [From Middle English, from Latin *humilis*, low, lowly, from *humus*, ground.] —**hum′ble·ness** *n.* —**hum′bly** *adv.*

hum·bug (**hŭm′**bŭg′) *n.* **1.** Nonsense; rubbish: *That argument is simply humbug.* **2.** Something meant to deceive; a hoax. **3.** A person who claims to be other than what he or she is; an impostor. ❖ *tr.v.* **hum·bugged, hum·bug·ging, hum·bugs** To deceive or trick; cheat: *The scheme humbugged many people.*

hum·drum (**hŭm′**drŭm′) *adj.* Lacking variety or excitement; dull: *the humdrum work of filing papers.*

hu·mer·us (**hyo͞o′**mər-əs) *n., pl.* **hu·mer·i** (**hyo͞o′**mə-rī′) **1.** The long bone of the upper arm in humans, extending from the shoulder to the elbow. **2.** A corresponding bone in the forelimb of other vertebrate animals. [From Middle English, from Latin, upper arm.]
❑ *These sound alike:* **humerus, humorous** (funny).

hu·mid (**hyo͞o′**mĭd) *adj.* Having a large amount of water or water vapor; damp; moist: *humid air before a shower of rain.* See Synonyms at **wet.** [From Middle English, from Latin *hūmidus*, from *hūmēre*, to be moist.]

hu·mid·i·fy (hyo͞o-**mĭd′**ə-fī′) *tr.v.* **hu·mid·i·fied, hu·mid·i·fy·ing, hu·mid·i·fies** To make moist or damp: *humidify the air in a greenhouse.* —**hu·mid′i·fi′er** *n.*

hu·mid·i·ty (hyo͞o-**mĭd′**ĭ-tē) *n.* **1.** The condition of being humid; dampness: *The painting was ruined by the humidity of the warehouse.* **2.** Relative humidity.

hu·mil·i·ate (hyo͞o-**mĭl′**ē-āt′) *tr.v.* **hu·mil·i·at·ed, hu·mil·i·at·ing, hu·mil·i·ates** To lower the pride, dignity, or self-respect of: *The parents were humiliated by the rude behavior of their children.*

hu·mil·i·a·tion (hyo͞o-mĭl′ē-**ā′**shən) *n.* **1.** The act of humiliating; degradation: *the humiliation of an opponent.* **2.** The condition of being humiliated; disgrace: *They felt deep humiliation after losing so badly.*

hu·mil·i·ty (hyo͞o-**mĭl′**ĭ-tē) *n.* The quality or condition of being humble: *accept a prize with humility.*

hum·ming·bird (**hŭm′**ĭng-bûrd′) *n.* Any of numerous very small birds of the Americas, having a long slender bill and usually brightly colored feathers. Hummingbirds move their wings so rapidly that they make a humming noise.

hum·mock (**hŭm′**ək) *n.* **1.** A low mound or ridge, as of earth or snow. **2.** A ridge or hill of ice in an ice field.

hum·mus (**ho͝om′**əs *or* **hŭm′**əs) *n.* A smooth mixture of mashed chickpeas, tahini, garlic, and lemon juice, often eaten as a dip for pita.

hu·mor (**hyo͞o′**mər) *n.* **1.** The quality of being funny or comical: *We laughed at the humor of the story.* **2.** The ability to see or express what is funny or comical: *A sense of humor can help a person in a bad situation.* **3.** An often temporary state of mind; a mood: *The beautiful day put me in good humor.* **4.** That which is intended to induce laughter or amusement: *a writer of humor; an actor known for humor.* **5.** In ancient and medieval medicine, one of the four fluids of the body—blood, phlegm, black bile, and yellow bile—thought to determine one's health and character. ❖ *tr.v.* **hu·mored, hu·mor·ing, hu·mors** To go along with the wishes or ideas of; indulge: *The babysitter humored the child.* [From Middle English *humour*, fluid, from Latin *ūmor*.] —SEE NOTE.

hu·mor·ist (**hyo͞o′**mər-ĭst) *n.* A person with a sharp sense of humor, especially a writer or performer of humorous material.

hu·mor·less (**hyo͞o′**mər-lĭs) *adj.* **1.** Lacking a sense of humor: *a dull, humorless person.* **2.** Said or done without humor: *humorless remarks.*

hu·mor·ous (**hyo͞o′**mər-əs) *adj.* Characterized by or expressing humor; funny: *a humorous writer; a humorous story.* —**hu′mor·ous·ly** *adv.* —SEE NOTE AT **humor.**
❑ *These sound alike:* **humorous, humerus** (arm bone).

hu·mour (**hyo͞o′**mər) *n. & v. Chiefly British* Variant of **humor.**

hump (hŭmp) *n.* **1.** A rounded mass or lump, as on the back of a camel. **2.** A low mound; a bump: *a hump in the road.* ❖ *tr.v.* **humped, hump·ing, humps** To bend or make into a hump; arch: *The kitten humped its back.* ◆ **over the hump** Past the worst or most difficult part or stage: *Once exams are finished, we'll be over the hump.*

hump·back (**hŭmp′**băk′) *n.* A hunchback. —**hump′-backed′** *adj.*

humpback whale *n.* A large whale that arches its back when it dives, has long knobby flippers, and communicates with complex songs.

humph (hŭmf *or* həmf) *interj.* An expression used to show doubt, contempt, or displeasure.

hu·mus (**hyōō′**məs) *n.* A dark brown or black substance made up of decayed leaves and other organic material that provides nutrients for plants and increases the ability of soil to retain water. [From Latin, soil.]

Hun (hŭn) *n.* A member of a group of nomadic Central Asian peoples who invaded Europe in the fourth and fifth centuries AD.

hunch (hŭnch) *n.* **1.** A suspicion or intuition; a premonition: *I had a hunch it would get chilly, so I brought a sweater.* **2.** A hump. ❖ *v.* **hunched, hunch·ing, hunch·es** —*tr.* To draw up or bend into a hump: *I hunched my shoulders against the cold wind.* —*intr.* To go into a crouched or cramped posture: *The cat hunched in the corner.*

hunch·back (**hŭnch′**băk′) *n.* **1.** A person whose upper back has a hump in it caused by an abnormally curved spine. **2.** A back having such a hump. **—hunch′-backed′** *adj.*

hun·dred (**hŭn′**drĭd) *n., pl.* **hundred** or **hun·dreds 1.** The number, written as 100 or 10^2, that is equal to 10 × 10. **2.** A one-hundred-dollar bill.

hun·dredth (**hŭn′**drĭdth) *n.* **1.** The ordinal number matching the number 100 in a series. **2.** One of one hundred equal parts.

hun·dred·weight (**hŭn′**drĭd-wāt′) *n., pl.* **hundred-weight** or **hun·dred·weights** A unit of weight equal to 100 pounds (45.36 kilograms) in the United States.

hung (hŭng) *v.* Past tense and a past participle of **hang.**

Hun·gar·i·an (hŭng-**gâr′**ē-ən) *adj.* Relating to Hungary or its people, language, or culture. ❖ *n.* **1.** A native or inhabitant of Hungary. **2.** The language of Hungary, distantly related to Finnish.

Hun·ga·ry (**hŭng′**gə-rē) A country of central Europe east of Austria. Hungary was part of Austria-Hungary from 1867 until 1918, when it gained its independence. Budapest is the capital.

hun·ger (**hŭng′**gər) *n.* **1.** A strong desire or need for food: *Hunger drove the wolves to hunt closer to the town.* **2.** The discomfort, pain, or weakness caused by a lack of food: *faint with hunger.* **3.** A strong desire or craving: *Scholars have a hunger for learning.* ❖ *intr.v.* **hun·gered, hun·ger·ing, hun·gers 1.** To have a need or desire for food: *The hikers hungered for something hot and delicious.* **2.** To have a strong desire or craving: *Our team hungered for victory.* [From Old English *hungor.*]

hun·gry (**hŭng′**grē) *adj.* **hun·gri·er, hun·gri·est 1.** Experiencing a need or desire for food. **2.** Having a strong desire or craving: *The oppressed people were hungry for freedom.* **3.** Showing or feeling hunger or need: *shot a hungry glance at my sandwich.* **—hun′gri·ly** *adv.* **—hun′gri·ness** *n.*

hunk (hŭngk) *n. Informal* A large piece; a chunk: *I broke a hunk of freshly baked bread off the loaf.*

Hunk·pa·pa (**hŭngk′**pä′pä) *n., pl.* **Hunkpapa** or **Hunk·pa·pas** A member of a Native American people that is a subdivision of the Sioux, living in North and South Dakota.

hunt (hŭnt) *v.* **hunt·ed, hunt·ing, hunts** —*tr.* **1.** To attempt to catch or kill (wild animals) for food or sport: *Uncle Ted hunts wild turkeys.* **2.** To search for; seek out: *hunting bargains at the local stores.* **3.** To search (a place) thoroughly in pursuit of something: *The detective hunted the streets for the suspect.* —*intr.* **1.** To attempt to catch or kill wild animals for food or sport: *My uncle loves to hunt.* **2.** To search thoroughly; seek: *I hunted for shoes online.* ❖ *n.* **1.** A hunting expedition: *The town approved a deer hunt in the park.* **2.** A diligent search or pursuit: *She's on a hunt for her missing keys.*

hunt·er (**hŭn′**tər) *n.* **1.** A person who hunts. **2.** A dog or horse bred and trained for use in hunting.

hunt·ing (**hŭn′**tĭng) *n.* The activity of pursuing wild animals for food or sport.

hunts·man (**hŭnts′**mən) *n.* **1.** A man who hunts. **2.** A man who manages a pack of dogs in a hunt.

hur·dle (**hûr′**dl) *n.* **1a.** A light portable barrier over which competitors must leap in certain races. **b. hur·dles** *(used with a singular verb)* A race in which such barriers must be jumped, without the competitors' breaking their stride. **2.** An obstacle or problem to be overcome: *Getting the money was the chief hurdle I had in going to college.* ❖ *v.* **hur·dled, hur·dling, hur·dles** —*tr.* **1.** To jump over (a hurdle or other barrier): *The dog hurdled the fence after the rabbit.* **2.** To overcome or deal with successfully: *hurdled all obstacles.* —*intr.* To jump over a hurdle or other barrier. **—hur′dler** *n.*

hur·dy-gur·dy (hûr′dē-**gûr′**dē) *n., pl.* **hur·dy-gur·dies** A musical instrument played by turning a crank. [Of imitative origin.]

hurl (hûrl) *tr.v.* **hurled, hurl·ing, hurls 1.** To throw with great force; fling: *The volcano hurled smoke and ash high into the air.* See Synonyms at **throw. 2.** To utter vehemently: *The children hurled insults at each other.* **—hurl′er** *n.*

hur·ly-bur·ly (hûr′lē-**bûr′**lē) *n., pl.* **hur·ly-bur·lies** Noisy confusion; uproar.

Hu·ron (**hyōōr′**ən *or* **hyōōr′**ŏn′) *n., pl.* **Huron** or **Hu·rons 1.** A member of a Native American confederacy formerly living in the region east of Lake Huron, with small groups now living in Quebec and Oklahoma. **2.** The Iroquoian language of the Huron.

Huron, Lake The second largest of the Great Lakes, between southeast Ontario, Canada, and eastern Michigan. It is part of the Great Lakes–St. Lawrence Seaway system.

hur·rah (hōō-**rä′** *or* hə-**rä′**) also **hur·ray** (hōō-**rā′** *or* hə-**rā′**) *interj. & n. & intr.v.* Variants of **hooray.**

hur·ri·cane (**hûr′**ĭ-kān′) *n.* A severe swirling tropical storm with heavy rains and winds exceeding 74 miles (119 kilometers) per hour. Hurricanes originate in the tropical parts of the Atlantic Ocean or the Caribbean Sea and move generally northward. [From Spanish *huracán*, from Taíno *hurákan.*]

hur·ried (**hûr′**ēd) *adj.* Done very quickly or in haste; rushed: *Because we got up late, we ate a hurried breakfast.* **—hur′ried·ly** *adv.*

hur·ry (**hûr′**ē) *v.* **hur·ried, hur·ry·ing, hur·ries** —*intr.* To move or act very quickly or in haste: *The children hurried along in the rain.* —*tr.* **1.** To cause to move or act with speed or haste: *Parents hurried their children to the bus stop.* **2.** To cause to move or act too quickly; rush: *hurried me into making a choice.* **3.** To speed the progress or completion of: *Using a computer hurried the job along.* ❖ *n., pl.* **hur·ries 1.** The act or an instance of hurrying: *In my hurry to get to the bus, I forgot my homework.* **2.** The need or wish to hurry; a condition of urgency: *The police were in a hurry to get to the accident.*

Hur·ston (**hûr′**stən), **Zora Neale** 1891–1960. American writer whose novels, such as *Their Eyes Were Watching God* (1937), and nonfiction writings give detailed accounts of African-American life in the South.

hurt (hûrt) *v.* **hurt, hurt·ing, hurts** —*tr.* **1.** To cause physical damage or pain to; injure: *The fall hurt my leg.* **2.** To cause mental or emotional suffering to; distress: *The criticism hurt my feelings.* **3.** To damage: *The dry summer hurt this year's crops.* **4.** To hinder or impair: *The penalties in the first half hurt our chances for victory.* —*intr.* **1.** To have or produce a feeling of physical pain or discomfort: *My feet hurt from walking all day.* **2.** To

WORD HISTORY

humor Doctors in ancient times and in the Middle Ages thought the human body contained a mixture of four substances, called **humors,** that determined a person's health and character. The word *humor* comes from Latin and means "fluid"; the four fluids were blood, phlegm, black bile, and yellow bile. Illnesses and defects in personality were thought to be caused by too much of a particular humor. Too much black bile, for example, was thought to make one gloomy, and too much yellow bile was thought to make one short-tempered. Modern English has words referring to these moods that come from the Greek words for the relevant humors. We call a gloomy person **melancholic,** from the Greek term for "black bile," and we call a short-tempered person **choleric,** from the Greek word for "yellow bile." Our word **humorous,** in fact, originally meant "having changeable moods due to the influence of different humors."

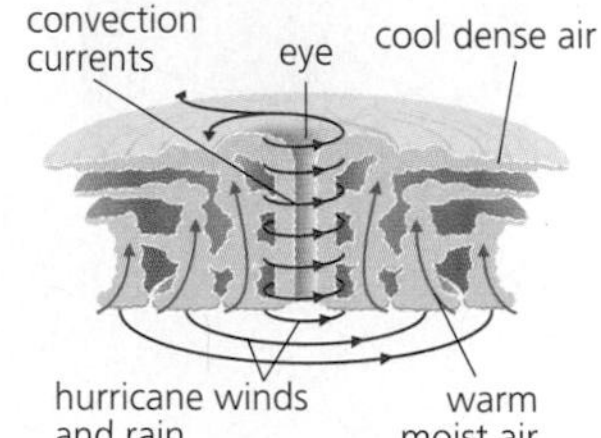

hurricane

WORD HISTORY

husband The Vikings, besides doing a lot of raiding and plundering, also settled peacefully in many places, including England. Because of this, English borrowed many words from Old Norse, the Vikings' language. One of these words is **husband.** Yet the word *wife* is a native Anglo-Saxon (Old English) word. Why should *husband* be Old Norse and *wife* be native English? The reason is that when the Vikings settled in England, they generally took Anglo-Saxon women to be their wives. The men continued to be called by the Old Norse term (it literally means "one bound to a house"), and the women continued to be called by the Anglo-Saxon term (which used to mean just "woman" as well as "wife"). Thus the pairing of *husband* and *wife* shows how historical developments and different social groups can influence the words we use.

hyacinth

ă	pat	ôr	core
ā	pay	oi	boy
âr	care	ou	out
ä	father	o͝o	took
ĕ	pet	o͝or	lure
ē	be	o͞o	boot
ĭ	pit	ŭ	cut
ī	bite	ûr	urge
îr	pier	th	thin
ŏ	pot	*th*	this
ō	toe	zh	vision
ô	paw	ə	about

cause distress or damage: *It hurt not to be picked for the team.* **3.** To have a bad effect: *Their advice hurt more than it helped.* ❖ *n.* **1.** Something that hurts; an injury or wound. **2.** Mental suffering; anguish: *I still feel the hurt of being rejected.* **3.** A wrong; harm: *an incident that caused lasting hurt to the politician's reputation.*

hurt·ful (**hûrt′**fəl) *adj.* Causing injury or suffering; painful: *Air pollution is hurtful to the environment.* **—hurt′ful·ly** *adv.* **—hurt′ful·ness** *n.*

hur·tle (**hûr′**tl) *intr. & tr.v.* **hur·tled, hur·tling, hur·tles** To move or cause to move with great speed: *The speeding train hurtled through the tunnel. The gust of wind hurtled leaves into the air.*

hus·band (**hŭz′**bənd) *n.* A man joined to another person in marriage; a male spouse. ❖ *tr.v.* **hus·band·ed, hus·band·ing, hus·bands** To use sparingly or economically; conserve: *With so many debts, we had to husband our funds.* [From Old English *hūsbōnda*, from Old Norse *hūsbōndi* : *hūs*, house + *bōndi*, householder.] —SEE NOTE.

hus·band·ry (**hŭz′**bən-drē) *n.* **1.** The work of raising crops and farm animals; farming. **2.** Good or careful management; thrift: *practice husbandry of scarce natural resources.*

hush (hŭsh) *v.* **hushed, hush·ing, hush·es** *—tr.* **1.** To make silent or quiet: *The parents tried to hush the infant.* **2.** To keep from public knowledge; suppress: *The mayor tried to hush up news of the city scandal.* *—intr.* To be or become silent or still: *The audience hushed as the curtain went up.* ❖ *n.* A silence or stillness; quiet: *When the teacher returned, a hush fell over the classroom.*

husk (hŭsk) *n.* The dry outer covering of certain seeds or fruits, as of an ear of corn or a nut. ❖ *tr.v.* **husked, husk·ing, husks** To remove the husk from: *husk ears of corn.* **—husk′er** *n.*

husk·y¹ (**hŭs′**kē) *adj.* **husk·i·er, husk·i·est** Hoarse or rough in quality: *a husky voice.* [From *husk*.] **—husk′i·ly** *adv.* **—husk′i·ness** *n.*

husk·y² (**hŭs′**kē) *adj.* **husk·i·er, husk·i·est** Strongly built; burly: *a husky football player.* [Perhaps from *husk*.] **—husk′i·ness** *n.*

hus·ky³ (**hŭs′**kē) *n., pl.* **hus·kies** A strong, thick-coated dog of any of various Arctic breeds that were originally developed as sled dogs, especially the Siberian husky. [Probably from shortening and alteration of *Eskimo*.]

hus·sar (hə-**zär′** *or* hə-**sär′**) *n.* A soldier of the light cavalry in some European armies.

hus·sy (**hŭz′**ē *or* **hŭs′**ē) *n., pl.* **hus·sies** A woman considered to be brazen, impudent, or promiscuous. [Alteration of Middle English *houswif*, housewife.]

hus·tle (**hŭs′**əl) *v.* **hus·tled, hus·tling, hus·tles** *—tr.* **1.** To push or convey in a hurried or rough manner: *The guards hustled the prisoner into a cell.* **2.** To cause to move hurriedly; rush: *They hustled the project to its completion.* *—intr.* **1.** To jostle and push: *We hustled through the busy crowds.* **2.** To work or move energetically and rapidly: *You need to hustle to get the job done.* **3.** *Slang* To obtain something by deceitful or illicit methods. ❖ *n.* **1.** The act or an instance of hustling: *It was a hustle to get to the airport on time.* **2.** Energetic activity; drive: *The new player shows lots of hustle.* [From Middle Dutch *hustelen*.]

hut (hŭt) *n.* A small, crudely made house or shelter; a shack.

hutch (hŭch) *n.* **1.** A pen or coop for small animals, especially rabbits. **2.** A cupboard with drawers for storage and an upper part having open shelves. **3.** A chest or bin for storage.

Hutch·in·son (**hŭch′**ĭn-sən), **Anne** 1591–1643. English-born American religious leader who was banished from Boston (1637) for her religious beliefs.

Hut·ton (**hŭt′**n), **James** 1726–1797. British geologist whose theories of rock and land formation laid the foundation for modern geology.

Hu·tu (**ho͞o′**to͞o′) *n., pl.* **Hutu** or **Hu·tus** A member of a Bantu people inhabiting Rwanda and Burundi.

hwy. *abbr.* An abbreviation of highway.

hy·a·cinth (**hī′**ə-sĭnth) *n.* Any of various plants that grow from a bulb and have narrow leaves and a cluster of fragrant, variously colored flowers. [From Middle English *jacinct*, from Greek *huakinthos*, wild hyacinth.]

hy·brid (**hī′**brĭd) *n.* **1.** An organism that is the result of the mating of individuals of different species or varieties: *A mule is a hybrid between a donkey and a horse.* **2.** Something that is made up of parts that are of two different types: *a movie that is a hybrid between a romance and a thriller; a car that is a hybrid, powered by both an electric motor and an internal combustion engine.* [From Latin *hibrida, hybrida*, mongrel.]

hy·brid·ize (**hī′**brĭ-dīz′) *intr. & tr.v.* **hy·brid·ized, hy·brid·iz·ing, hy·brid·iz·es** To produce or cause to produce hybrids; crossbreed: *Scientists hybridized different varieties of corn. These two oak species sometimes hybridize.* **—hy′brid·i·za′tion** (hī′brĭ-dĭ-**zā′**shən) *n.*

Hy·der·a·bad (**hī′**dər-ə-băd′ *or* **hī′**dər-ə-bäd′) A city of south-central India east-southeast of Mumbai (Bombay). It was founded in 1589.

hydr– *pref.* Variant of **hydro–.**

hy·dra (**hī′**drə) *n.* Any of several small freshwater animals having a tubular body and a mouth opening surrounded by stinging tentacles. Hydras are related to coral and jellyfish and when cut into pieces can form a new individual from each piece.

Hydra *n.* In Greek mythology, a monster that had many heads and grew back two more if one was cut off.

hy·dran·gea (hī-**drān′**jə *or* hī-**drăn′**jə) *n.* Any of various shrubs having large rounded clusters of white, pink, or blue flowers.

hy·drant (**hī′**drənt) *n.* A fire hydrant.

hy·drate (**hī′**drāt′) *n.* A solid compound produced when certain substances unite chemically with water in definite proportions. ❖ *v.* **hy·drat·ed, hy·drat·ing, hy·drates** *—tr.* **1.** To combine (a chemical compound) with water, especially to form a hydrate. **2.** To supply water to (a person, for example) in order to restore or maintain a balance of fluids in the body. *—intr.* To combine with water to form a hydrate. **—hy·dra′tion** *n.*

hy·drau·lic (hī-**drô′**lĭk) *adj.* **1.** Operated by the pressure of water or other fluids. Hydraulic systems transmit mechanical force by pumping the fluid through pipes or tubes: *a hydraulic brake; a hydraulic jack.* **2.** Relating to hydraulics. **3.** Capable of hardening under water: *hydraulic cement.* **—hy·drau′li·cal·ly** *adv.*

hydraulic fracturing *n.* The process of extracting oil or natural gas by injecting a mixture of water, sand or gravel, and certain chemicals under high pressure into well holes in dense rock to create fractures that the sand or gravel holds open, allowing the oil or gas to escape.

hy·drau·lics (hī-**drô′**lĭks) *n.* *(used with a singular verb)* The science that deals with water and other liquids at rest or in motion, their uses in engineering, and the laws of their actions.

hy·dra·zine (**hī′**drə-zēn′ *or* **hī′**drə-zĭn) *n.* A colorless liquid compound of nitrogen and hydrogen, used as a jet and rocket fuel.

hy·dride (**hī′**drīd′) *n.* A chemical compound of hydrogen with another element or radical.

hydro– or **hydr–** *pref.* A prefix that means: **1.** Water: *hydroelectric.* **2.** Hydrogen: *hydrocarbon.* —SEE NOTE.

hy·dro·car·bon (hī′drə-**kär′**bən) *n.* An organic compound that contains only carbon and hydrogen. Hydrocarbons form a large class of chemical compounds and include gasoline, benzene, and butane.

hy·dro·chlo·ric acid (hī′drə-**klôr′**ĭk) *n.* A strong, poisonous, corrosive acid that is a solution of hydrogen chloride gas in water and has the formula HCl. It is used in food processing, metal cleaning, and dyeing.

hy·dro·cy·an·ic acid (hī′drō-sī-**ăn′**ĭk) *n.* A colorless poisonous liquid having an odor of bitter almonds and used in making plastics, pesticides, and dyes.

hy·dro·dy·nam·ic (hī′drō-dī-**năm′**ĭk) *adj.* **1.** Relating to or operated by a moving liquid. **2.** Relating to hydrodynamics. **—hy′dro·dy·nam′i·cal·ly** *adv.*

hy·dro·dy·nam·ics (hī′drō-dī-**năm′**ĭks) *n. (used with a singular verb)* The branch of science that deals with the forces exerted by fluids in motion.

hy·dro·e·lec·tric (hī′drō-ĭ-**lĕk′**trĭk) *adj.* Generating electricity through the use of water power: *a hydroelectric power station.*

hy·dro·foil (**hī′**drə-foil′) *n.* **1.** A winglike structure on the bottom of a boat that lifts the hull partly or completely out of the water at high speeds, decreasing friction and allowing the boat to travel faster and use less fuel. **2.** A boat equipped with hydrofoils.

hy·dro·gen (**hī′**drə-jən) *n. Symbol* **H** A colorless, odorless, highly flammable gaseous element that is the lightest and most abundant element in the universe. It occurs in water in combination with oxygen, in most organic compounds, and in small amounts in the atmosphere. Atomic number 1. See **Periodic Table.** [From French *hydrogène* : Greek *hudō-*, water + Greek *-genēs*, born.]

hy·dro·gen·ate (**hī′**drə-jə-nāt′ *or* hī-**drŏj′**ə-nāt′) *tr.v.* **hy·dro·gen·at·ed, hy·dro·gen·at·ing, hy·dro·gen·ates** To combine chemically with hydrogen. Liquid vegetable oils are often hydrogenated to convert them to a solid fat. **—hy′dro·gen·a′tion** *n.*

hydrogen bomb *n.* An extremely destructive bomb that gets its explosive power from the energy released when hydrogen atoms combine under extreme pressure to form helium atoms in the process called fusion.

hydrogen chloride *n.* A colorless, corrosive, suffocating gas, HCl, used in making plastics and in many industrial processes. When mixed with water, it forms hydrochloric acid.

hydrogen peroxide *n.* A colorless compound of hydrogen and oxygen having the formula H_2O_2. It is an unstable oxidizing agent, and is often used in water solution as an antiseptic and bleaching agent.

hydrogen sulfide *n.* A poisonous chemical compound containing hydrogen and sulfur and having the formula H_2S. It is a flammable gas having a characteristic odor of rotten eggs.

hy·drol·o·gy (hī-**drŏl′**ə-jē) *n.* The scientific study of the distribution and properties of water on and under the earth's surface and in the atmosphere. **—hy′dro·log′ic** (hī′drə-**lŏj′**ĭk) *adj.*

hy·drol·y·sis (hī-**drŏl′**ĭ-sĭs) *n.* Decomposition of a chemical compound by reaction with water. Hydrolysis is an important process in the digestion of food.

hy·dro·lyze (**hī′**drə-līz′) *tr. & intr.v.* **hy·dro·lyzed, hy·dro·lyz·ing, hy·dro·lyz·es** To separate or break down by hydrolysis.

hy·drom·e·ter (hī-**drŏm′**ĭ-tər) *n.* An instrument used to measure the specific gravity of liquids.

hy·dro·pho·bi·a (hī′drə-**fō′**bē-ə) *n.* **1.** Rabies. **2.** An abnormal fear of water.

hy·dro·plane (**hī′**drə-plān′) *n.* **1.** A motorboat with a flattened bottom that skims the surface of the water, allowing it to travel very fast. **2.** A seaplane.

hy·dro·pon·ic (hī′drə-**pŏn′**ĭk) *adj.* Grown in water supplied with nutrients rather than in soil: *hydroponic tomatoes.* **—hy′dro·pon′ics** *n.*

hy·dro·sphere (**hī′**drə-sfîr′) *n.* All the water of the earth, including surface water, groundwater, snow, ice, and the water vapor in the atmosphere.

hy·dro·stat·ics (hī′drə-**stăt′**ĭks) *n. (used with a singular verb)* The branch of physics that deals with fluids at rest and under pressure. **—hy′dro·stat′ic** *adj.*

hy·dro·ther·a·py (hī′drə-**thĕr′**ə-pē) *n., pl.* **hy·dro·ther·a·pies** The use of water to treat pain or the symptoms of disease, as with compresses, therapeutic baths, or whirlpool treatments.

hy·drous (**hī′**drəs) *adj.* Containing water as a constituent: *hydrous salts.*

hy·drox·ide (hī-**drŏk′**sīd′) *n.* A chemical compound consisting of an element or radical joined to one or more hydroxyl radicals. Metal hydroxides are bases and nonmetal hydroxides are acids.

hy·drox·yl (hī-**drŏk′**sĭl) *n.* The radical or group OH with a valence of 1 that is present in bases, certain acids, and alcohols.

hy·dro·zo·an (hī′drə-**zō′**ən) *n.* Any of numerous invertebrate water animals, such as the hydras and the Portuguese man-of-war, that are closely related to jellyfish and sea anemones.

hy·e·na (hī-**ē′**nə) *n.* Any of several meat-eating mammals of Asia or Africa having coarse, sometimes spotted or striped hair. Hyenas have powerful jaws for stripping flesh from dead animals and a piercing cry resembling a laugh. [From Middle English *hiene*, from Greek *huaina*, female pig (because a hyena has a bristly mane resembling a hog's).]

hy·giene (**hī′**jēn′) *n.* **1.** Practices that promote good health and the prevention of disease. **2.** The study of methods that promote and maintain good health and the prevention of disease. [From Greek *hugieinē (tekhnē)*, (art) of health, from *hugiēs*, healthy.]

hy·gien·ic (hī-**jĕn′**ĭk *or* hī-**jē′**nĭk) *adj.* **1.** Relating to hygiene: *hygienic studies.* **2.** Tending to promote good health; clean; sanitary: *a hygienic kitchen; food preparation following hygienic practices.* **—hy′gien′i·cal·ly** *adv.*

hy·gien·ist (hī-**jē′**nĭst *or* hī-**jĕn′**ĭst) *n.* A specialist in hygiene, especially a person who is trained to clean and examine the teeth.

hy·grom·e·ter (hī-**grŏm′**ĭ-tər) *n.* An instrument that measures the humidity of the air.

hy·gro·met·ric (hī′grə-**mĕt′**rĭk) *adj.* Relating to the measurement of moisture in the air.

hy·gro·scope (**hī′**grə-skōp′) *n.* An instrument that records changes in the amount of moisture in the air.

hy·gro·scop·ic (hī′grə-**skŏp′**ĭk) *adj.* Tending to absorb moisture from the air: *a hygroscopic salt.*

hy·ing (**hī′**ĭng) *v.* A present participle of **hie.**

hy·men (**hī′**mən) *n.* A membrane that partly closes the opening of the vagina.

hymn (hĭm) *n.* **1.** A song of praise to God or to another deity. **2.** A song of praise or joy. [From Middle English *imne*, from Greek *humnos.*]

❑ *These sound alike:* **hymn, him** (pronoun).

hym·nal (**hĭm′**nəl) *n.* A book or collection of church hymns.

hy·per (**hī′**pər) *adj. Slang* Excitable; high-strung.

hyper– *pref.* A prefix that means excessively: *hypercritical; hypersensitive.* —SEE NOTE.

hy·per·ac·tive (hī′pər-**ăk′**tĭv) *adj.* **1.** Having or showing greater than normal activity; overactive: *a hyperactive gland; hyperactive children running around the playground.* **2.** Having attention deficit hyperactivity disorder. **—hy′per·ac·tiv′i·ty** (hī′pər-ăk-**tĭv′**ĭ-tē) *n.*

hy·per·bo·la (hī-**pûr′**bə-lə) *n.* A plane curve with two branches that is formed by the intersection of a plane with two similar cones.

hy·per·bo·le (hī-**pûr′**bə-lē) *n.* A figure of speech in which exaggeration is used for effect; for example, the sentence *It rained last night and our yard is a lake* makes use of hyperbole.

WORD BUILDING

hydro– The prefix **hydro–** is from the Greek prefix *hudro–* or *hudr–*, which comes from the noun *hudōr*, "water." The prefix is used frequently to coin technical words, such as *hydroelectric, hydroplane,* and *hydrosphere*. Before a vowel, *hydro–* sometimes becomes *hydr–*, as in *hydrate* and *hydraulic.*

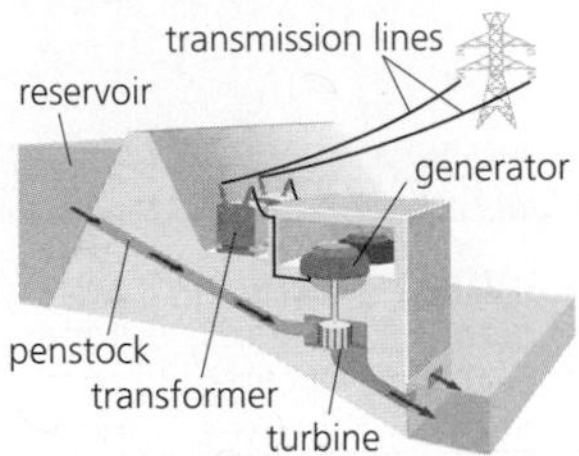

hydroelectric

The mechanical energy of moving water is transferred by a rotating turbine to a generator, where it is converted to electric energy and conveyed along transmission lines.

WORD BUILDING

hyper– The basic meaning of the prefix **hyper–** is "excessive or excessively." For example, *hyperactive* means "highly or excessively active." *Hyper–* comes from the Greek prefix *huper–*, which comes from the preposition *huper,* "over, beyond." *Hyper–* has been used actively in English since the 1600s and is now frequently used to make up new words, such as *hypercritical* and *hypersensitive.* In fact, most of the words in our language beginning with *hyper–* are relatively recent. Only a few, such as *hyperbole,* were formed already in Greek.

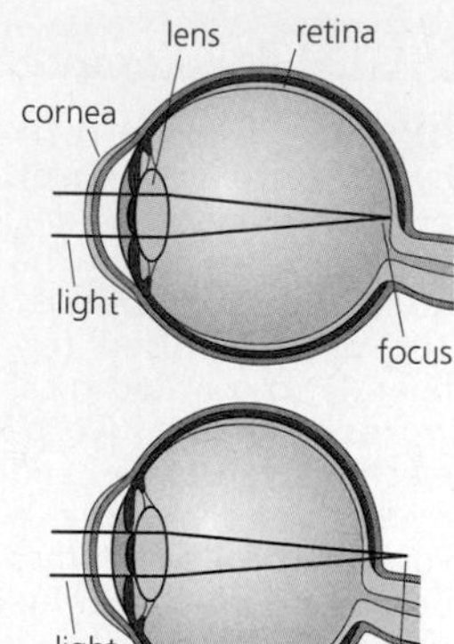

hyperopia
top: normal eye
bottom: hyperopic eye

WORD BUILDING

hypo– The prefix **hypo–** means "beneath, below, or under." It can be traced back to the Greek prefix *hupo–,* from the word *hupo,* "beneath, under." A few English words, such as *hypocrite* and *hypochondria,* come from Greek words; but most English words beginning with *hypo–* have been made up in recent times. In such words, *hypo–* either means "under," as in *hypodermic,* or "less than normal," as in *hypoglycemia.*

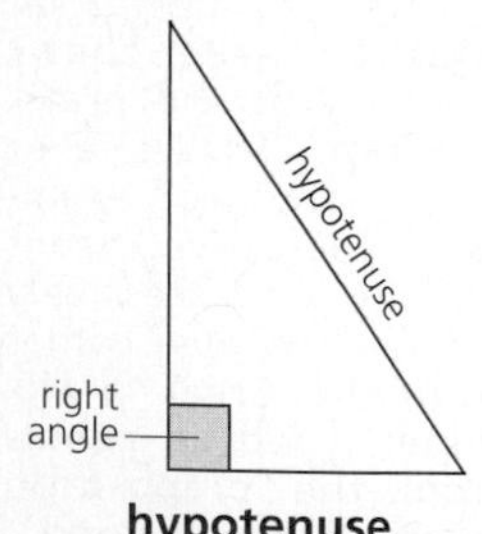

hypotenuse

ă	pat	ôr	core
ā	pay	oi	boy
âr	care	ou	out
ä	father	o͝o	took
ĕ	pet	o͝or	lure
ē	be	o͞o	boot
ĭ	pit	ŭ	cut
ī	bite	ûr	urge
îr	pier	th	thin
ŏ	pot	*th*	this
ō	toe	zh	vision
ô	paw	ə	about

hy·per·bol·ic (hī′pər-**bŏl′**ĭk) *adj.* **1.** Relating to or using hyperbole; exaggerated. **2.** Relating to or shaped like a hyperbola: *a hyperbolic curve.*

hy·per·crit·i·cal (hī′pər-**krĭt′**ĭ-kəl) *adj.* Too ready to find fault; overly critical. **—hy′per·crit′i·cal·ly** *adv.*

hy·per·link (**hī′**pər-lĭngk′) *n.* A link in a webpage or other electronic document.

hy·per·o·pi·a (hī′pə-**rō′**pē-ə) *n.* A defect of the eye that makes near objects appear blurred because their images are focused behind the retina rather than on it; farsightedness. **—hy′per·o′pic** (hī′pər-**ō′**pĭk *or* hī′pər-**ŏp′**ĭk) *adj.*

hy·per·sen·si·tive (hī′pər-**sĕn′**sĭ-tĭv) *adj.* Unusually or overly sensitive: *skin that is hypersensitive to the sun.* **—hy′per·sen′si·tive·ness** *n.* **—hy′per·sen′si·tiv′i·ty** (hī′pər-sĕn′sĭ-**tĭv′**ĭ-tē) *n.*

hy·per·son·ic (hī′pər-**sŏn′**ĭk) *adj.* Moving or able to move at a speed at least five times the speed of sound.

hy·per·ten·sion (hī′pər-**tĕn′**shən) *n.* A condition in which the pressure of the blood, especially in the arteries, is abnormally high; high blood pressure.

hy·per·text (**hī′**pər-tĕkst′) *n.* Digital text that contains hyperlinks to other texts. Hypertext is sometimes used to give stories multiple plots.

hy·per·tro·phy (hī-**pûr′**trə-fē) *n., pl.* **hy·per·tro·phies** An increase in the size of an organ or tissue, resulting from disease or overuse.

hy·pha (**hī′**fə) *n., pl.* **hy·phae** (**hī′**fē) Any of the long slender filaments that form the structural parts of the body of a fungus. Masses of hyphae make up the mycelium.

hy·phen (**hī′**fən) *n.* A punctuation mark (-) used between the parts of a compound word or between syllables of a word that is divided at the end of a line of text. [From Greek *huph' hen*, in one, as one.]

hy·phen·ate (**hī′**fə-nāt′) *tr.v.* **hy·phen·at·ed, hy·phen·at·ing, hy·phen·ates** To divide or connect (syllables, word elements, or names) with a hyphen. **—hy′phen·a′tion** *n.*

hyp·no·sis (hĭp-**nō′**sĭs) *n., pl.* **hyp·no·ses** (hĭp-**nō′**sēz) **1.** A condition resembling sleep in which a person becomes very responsive to suggestions from another. Hypnosis can be self-induced through concentration and relaxation. **2.** Hypnotism. [From Greek *hupnos*, sleep.]

hyp·not·ic (hĭp-**nŏt′**ĭk) *adj.* **1.** Relating to hypnosis. **2.** Relating to hypnotism. **3.** Causing sleep: *the hypnotic effect of television.* ❖ *n.* A drug or other agent that causes sleep. **—hyp·not′i·cal·ly** *adv.*

hyp·no·tism (**hĭp′**nə-tĭz′əm) *n.* **1.** The theory, method, or process of putting a person into a state of hypnosis. **2.** The act of inducing hypnosis.

hyp·no·tist (**hĭp′**nə-tĭst) *n.* A person who practices hypnotism.

hyp·no·tize (**hĭp′**nə-tīz′) *tr.v.* **hyp·no·tized, hyp·no·tiz·ing, hyp·no·tiz·es 1.** To put (a person) into a state of hypnosis: *The patient was hypnotized to relieve pain.* **2.** To fascinate, as if by hypnosis: *The exciting movie hypnotized the audience.* **—hyp′no·tiz′er** *n.*

hypo– or **hyp–** *pref.* A prefix that means: **1.** Beneath or below: *hypodermic.* **2.** Less than normal: *hypoglycemia.* —SEE NOTE.

hy·po·chon·dri·a (hī′pə-**kŏn′**drē-ə) *n.* A condition in which a person believes that he or she is ill or worries too much about becoming ill.

hy·po·chon·dri·ac (hī′pə-**kŏn′**drē-ăk′) *n.* A person with hypochondria. ❖ *adj.* Relating to or exhibiting hypochondria.

hy·poc·ri·sy (hĭ-**pŏk′**rĭ-sē) *n., pl.* **hy·poc·ri·sies 1.** The practice of showing or expressing feelings, beliefs, or virtues that one does not actually hold or possess. **2.** The act or an instance of hypocrisy.

hyp·o·crite (**hĭp′**ə-krĭt′) *n.* A person who practices hypocrisy.

hyp·o·crit·i·cal (hĭp′ə-**krĭt′**ĭ-kəl) *adj.* **1.** Characterized by hypocrisy: *hypocritical praise.* **2.** Being a hypocrite: *a hypocritical politician.* **—hyp′o·crit′i·cal·ly** *adv.*

hy·po·der·mic (hī′pə-**dûr′**mĭk) *adj.* **1.** Beneath the skin: *a hypodermic injection of penicillin.* **2.** Injected or used to inject beneath the skin: *a hypodermic needle.* ❖ *n.* **1.** An injection given under the skin. **2.** A hypodermic syringe. [From Greek *hupo*, under + Greek *derma*, skin.]

hypodermic syringe *n.* A syringe that is fitted with a hollow needle and used especially to inject fluids under the skin.

hy·po·gly·ce·mi·a (hī′pō-glī-**sē′**mē-ə) *n.* An abnormally low level of sugar in the blood, often resulting from too much insulin and causing dizziness and weakness.

hy·pot·e·nuse (hī-**pŏt′**n-o͞os′) *n.* The side of a right triangle opposite the right angle.

hy·po·thal·a·mus (hī′pō-**thăl′**ə-məs) *n.* The region of the brain under the thalamus, controlling temperature, hunger, and thirst, and producing hormones that influence the pituitary gland.

hy·po·ther·mi·a (hī′pə-**thûr′**mē-ə) *n.* Abnormally low body temperature.

hy·poth·e·sis (hī-**pŏth′**ĭ-sĭs) *n., pl.* **hy·poth·e·ses** (hī-**pŏth′**ĭ-sēz′) A statement that appears to explain a set of facts and that can become the basis for a scientific experiment. [From Greek *hupothesis*, basis of an argument, supposition, from *hupotithenai*, to suppose.]

hy·poth·e·size (hī-**pŏth′**ĭ-sīz′) *intr.v.* **hy·poth·e·sized, hy·poth·e·siz·ing, hy·poth·e·siz·es** To make a hypothesis.

hy·po·thet·i·cal (hī′pə-**thĕt′**ĭ-kəl) *adj.* **1.** Relating to or based on a hypothesis; theoretical. **2.** Supposed or made up: *The lawyer used a hypothetical case to prove a point.* ❖ *n.* A hypothetical situation or scenario: *Let's suppose they win this game, just as a hypothetical—what happens then?* **—hy′po·thet′i·cal·ly** *adv.*

hy·ra·co·ther·i·um (hī′rə-kō-**thîr′**ē-əm) *n.* A small extinct horselike mammal that lived about 50 million years ago. It had an arched back, a relatively short neck, four-toed front feet, and three-toed hind feet.

hy·rax (**hī′**răks′) *n., pl.* **hy·rax·es** or **hy·ra·ces** (**hī′**rə-sēz′) Any of several mammals of Africa and Asia that resemble the woodchuck but are more closely related to the hoofed mammals. [From Greek *hurax*, shrew mouse.]

hys·sop (**hĭs′**əp) *n.* **1.** A fragrant plant having clusters of small blue flowers, used in perfumes, as a flavoring, and formerly as a medicine. **2.** In the Bible, a plant that was used in certain purification rituals.

hys·ter·i·a (hĭ-**stĕr′**ē-ə *or* hĭ-**stîr′**ē-ə) *n.* **1.** Uncontrollable excitement or emotion. **2.** A group of feelings and behaviors, such as anxiety and fainting, that were once considered symptoms of a distinct psychiatric disorder. This term is no longer used in medicine.

hys·ter·ic (hĭ-**stĕr′**ĭk) *n.* **1. hysterics** *(used with a singular or plural verb)* A fit of uncontrollable laughing or crying: *The clown's antics sent all of the children into hysterics.* **2.** A person who suffers from hysteria. This term is no longer used in medicine.

hys·ter·i·cal (hĭ-**stĕr′**ĭ-kəl) *adj.* **1.** Laughing or crying for a prolonged period of time: *a screaming and hysterical child.* **2.** *Informal* Extremely funny: *told a hysterical story.* **3.** Relating to or resulting from hysteria. This term is no longer used in medicine. **—hys·ter′i·cal·ly** *adv.*

Hz *abbr.* An abbreviation of hertz.

i or **I** (ī) *n., pl.* **i's** or **I's** also **is** or **Is** The ninth letter of the English alphabet.

I[1] (ī) *pron.* The person who is speaking or writing. [From Old English *ic.*] —SEE NOTE AT **me.**

❑ *These sound alike:* **I**[1], **aye** (yes), **eye** (organ of sight).

I[2] **1.** The symbol for the element **iodine. 2.** also **i** The Roman numeral for 1.

I[3] *abbr.* An abbreviation of: **1.** incomplete. **2.** interstate.

I. *abbr.* An abbreviation of: **1.** island. **2.** isle.

IA *abbr.* An abbreviation of Iowa.

i·amb (īʹămbʹ *or* īʹăm′) *n., pl.* **i·ambs** In poetry, a metrical foot consisting of an unstressed syllable followed by a stressed syllable, as in *delay.* [From Greek *iambos.*] —**i·amʹbic** *adj. & n.*

–ian *suff.* A suffix that means: **1.** Relating to or resembling: *Iberian.* **2.** One relating to, belonging to, or resembling: *pediatrician.*

I·be·ri·an (ī-bîrʹē-ən) *adj.* **1.** Relating to the Iberian Peninsula, its peoples, languages, or cultures. **2.** Relating to the ancient peoples that inhabited the Iberian Peninsula or their languages or cultures.

Iberian Peninsula also **I·be·ri·a** (ī-bîrʹē-ə) A peninsula of southwest Europe occupied by Spain and Portugal. It is separated from the rest of Europe by the Pyrenees and from Africa by the Strait of Gibraltar.

i·bex (īʹbĕks′) *n., pl.* **ibex** or **i·bex·es** Any of several wild goats of mountainous regions of Eurasia and Africa, having long, ridged, backward-curving horns.

i·bi·dem (ĭbʹĭ-dĕm′ *or* ĭ-bīʹdəm) *adv.* In the same place. Used in footnotes and bibliographies, often in its abbreviated form *ibid.*, to refer to something just cited.

i·bis (īʹbĭs) *n., pl.* **ibis** or **i·bis·es** Any of various large wading birds that have a long downward-curving bill. [From Middle English *ibin*, from Greek *ībis*, from Egyptian *hbj.*]

–ible *suff.* Variant of **–able.**

I·bo (ēʹbō) *n.* Variant of **Igbo.**

Ib·sen (ĭbʹsən *or* ĭpʹsən), **Henrik** 1828–1906. Norwegian playwright whose works include *A Doll's House* (1879).

i·bu·pro·fen (ī′byo͞o-prōʹfən) *n.* A drug used to treat pain, fever, or inflammation.

–ic *suff.* A suffix that means: **1.** Relating to or characterized by: *allergic; atomic.* **2.** Having a higher valence or oxidation state in a compound or ion of an element than indicated by the suffix *-ous: ferric; chloric.*

Ic·a·rus (ĭkʹər-əs) *n.* In Greek mythology, the son of Daedalus who, in escaping from Crete on wings made by his father, disobeyed his father by flying too close to the sun. As a result, the wax in his wings melted and he fell into the Aegean Sea.

ice (īs) *n.* **1.** Water frozen solid, normally at or below a temperature of 32 degrees Fahrenheit (0 degrees Celsius). **2.** A surface or mass of frozen water: *Before skating on the pond, test the ice.* **3.** Something resembling frozen water. **4.** A frozen dessert consisting of water, sugar, and a liquid flavoring. ❖ *v.* **iced, ic·ing, ic·es** —*tr.* **1.** To coat or cover with ice: *Sleet iced the road.* **2.** To chill with ice: *After catching the fish, we iced them.* **3.** To decorate (a cake or cookies) with icing. **4.** In ice hockey, to shoot (the puck) from one's defensive half of the rink across the opponent's goal line outside of the goal. —*intr.* To turn into or become covered or blocked with ice; freeze: *The river iced over during the cold spell.* [From Old English *īs.*]

ice age *n.* **1.** Any of several cold periods during which glaciers covered much of the earth. **2. Ice Age** The most recent glacial period, which occurred during the Pleistocene Epoch and ended about 12,000 years ago.

ice·berg (īsʹbûrg′) *n.* A massive body of floating ice that has broken away from a glacier. [Partial translation of Dutch *ijsberg* : *ijs*, ice + *berg*, mountain.]

iceberg lettuce *n.* A variety of lettuce with crisp, pale green leaves that form a compact, round head. [From its pale color.]

ice·boat (īsʹbōt′) *n.* **1.** A vehicle resembling a boat set on runners and having a sail that can propel it at great speed over ice. **2.** An icebreaker.

ice·bound (īsʹbound′) *adj.* **1.** Locked in by surrounding ice: *a ship icebound in the frozen sea.* **2.** Obstructed or covered over by ice: *a harbor icebound during the winter.*

ice·box (īsʹbŏks′) *n.* **1.** An insulated box into which ice is put to cool and preserve food. **2.** A refrigerator.

ice·break·er (īsʹbrā′kər) *n.* A powerful ship with a reinforced hull, built for breaking a passage through icebound water.

ice·cap or **ice cap** (īsʹkăp′) *n.* A year-round cover of ice and snow that spreads over a large area, especially of land or a polar region.

ice-cold (īsʹkōldʹ) *adj.* Extremely cold: *The waiter served us ice-cold lemonade.*

ice cream *n.* A smooth sweet frozen food made of a mixture of milk products, sugar, and flavorings.

ice-cream cone (īsʹkrēm′) *n.* **1.** A cone-shaped wafer used to hold ice cream. **2.** One of these wafers with ice cream in it.

ice-cream soda *n.* A refreshment made of ice cream mixed with carbonated water and syrup.

iced (īst) *adj.* **1.** Covered over with ice: *an iced windshield.* **2.** Chilled with ice: *drank a glass of iced coffee.* **3.** Decorated or coated with icing: *a bakery that sells iced cakes.*

ice field *n.* A large expanse of ice and snow among the peaks of a mountainous region.

ice hockey *n.* A game played on ice in which two teams of skaters use sticks with blades to try to drive a puck into the goal of the opposing team.

Ice·land (īsʹlənd) An island country in the northern Atlantic Ocean near the Arctic Circle east of Greenland. Norse settlers arrived here around 850–875. Reykjavík is the capital.

Ice·land·ic (īs-lănʹdĭk) *adj.* Relating to Iceland or its

Iberian Peninsula
satellite image

Henrik Ibsen

iceboat

GEOGRAPHY

Idaho Nothing has been straightforward in the history of the name of **Idaho.** We do not know what the word originally meant; some think it is a made-up word, while others think it is Native American and related to *Idahi,* the Apache name for the Comanche. The word *Idaho* in fact is first known from a region in what is now Colorado, where the Apache and Comanche lived, and in 1860 it was proposed as a name for the new territory that became the state of Colorado. This proposal did not succeed, but in 1861 *Idaho* was used to name a county in the huge northwest territory called Washington Territory. The area around the county was itself organized into a territory in 1863 and called Idaho—but only after the rejection of an earlier proposal that it be called Montana! This territory became the state of Idaho in 1890.

ă	pat	ôr	core
ā	pay	oi	boy
âr	care	ou	out
ä	father	o͝o	took
ĕ	pet	o͝or	lure
ē	be	o͞o	boot
ĭ	pit	ŭ	cut
ī	bite	ûr	urge
îr	pier	th	thin
ŏ	pot	*th*	this
ō	toe	zh	vision
ô	paw	ə	about

people, language, or culture. ❖ *n.* The Germanic language of Iceland.

ice·mak·er (īs′mā′kər) *n.* A machine, often built into a refrigerator, that freezes water into ice cubes.

ice·man (īs′mən) *n.* A man who delivers or sells ice.

ice pack *n.* **1.** A large mass of floating ice formed from small fragments that have pressed together and frozen solid. **2.** A bag or cloth filled with crushed ice and applied to a sore or swollen part of the body to reduce pain and inflammation.

ice pick *n.* A hand tool with a long sharp point, used for chipping or breaking ice.

ice skate *n.* A boot or shoe with a metal runner or blade attached to the sole, used for skating on ice.

ice-skate (īs′skāt′) *intr.v.* **ice-skat·ed, ice-skat·ing, ice-skates** To skate on ice with ice skates.

ice skater *n.* A person who ice-skates.

ice storm *n.* A storm in which snow or rain freezes on contact, forming a coat of ice on the surfaces it touches.

ich·neu·mon (ĭk-no͞o′mən) *n.* **1.** Any of numerous parasitic wasps whose larvae feed on the larvae of other insects. The females have very long ovipositors. **2.** A large gray mongoose of Africa and southern Europe.

ich·thy·ol·o·gy (ĭk′thē-ŏl′ə-jē) *n.* The branch of zoology that deals with fishes. [From Greek *ikhthūs,* fish.] **—ich′thy·ol′o·gist** *n.*

ich·thy·o·saur (ĭk′thē-ə-sôr′) *n.* Any of various extinct sea reptiles having a long beak, four flippers, a tapering body, and a tail with a large fin.

i·ci·cle (ī′sĭ-kəl) *n.* A hanging spike of ice formed by the freezing of dripping or falling water. [From Middle English *isikel* : *is,* ice + Old English *gicel,* icicle.]

i·ci·ly (ī′sə-lē) *adv.* In an icy or chilling manner: *an icily cold wind; eye an opponent icily.*

i·ci·ness (ī′sē-nĭs) *n.* The condition or quality of being icy.

ic·ing (ī′sĭng) *n.* **1.** A sweet glaze of sugar and egg whites or milk, used to decorate cakes or cookies. **2.** In ice hockey, a minor violation of the rules in which a player ices the puck when the opposing team is not on a power play.

ick·y (ĭk′ē) *adj.* **ick·i·er, ick·i·est** *Informal* **1.** Offensive; distasteful: *icky sentimentality.* **2.** Disagreeably gooey or sticky: *an icky mess on the stove.*

i·con (ī′kŏn′) *n.* **1.** An important and well-known symbol: *The covered wagon is an icon of the pioneer days.* **2.** A picture on a computer screen representing a specific file, directory, window, option, or program that can be opened or activated when the user clicks on it. **3.** A religious image or picture of Jesus, Mary, or a saint, considered sacred in the Eastern Orthodox Church. **—i·con′ic** *adj.*

i·con·o·clast (ī-kŏn′ə-klăst′) *n.* **1.** A person who attacks and opposes popular or traditional ideas, beliefs, or practices. **2.** A person who destroys sacred religious images. [From Medieval Greek *eikonoklastēs,* breaker of religious images : *eikōn,* image + Greek *klān,* to break.] **—i·con′o·clas′tic** *adj.*

–ics *suff.* A suffix that means: **1.** Science, art, study, or knowledge of, or skill in: *graphics; mathematics.* **2.** Activities, actions, or practices of: *athletics; ceramics.* —SEE NOTE AT **politics.**

ic·y (ī′sē) *adj.* **ic·i·er, ic·i·est 1.** Containing or covered with ice; frozen: *an icy sidewalk.* **2.** Very cold: *icy waters.* See Synonyms at **cold. 3.** Unfriendly or hostile: *an icy stare.*

ID[1] (ī′dē′) *Informal n.* A form of identification, especially an ID card. ❖ *tr.v.* **ID'ed, ID'ing, ID's** To check the identification of, especially to verify legal age: *The bouncer ID'ed patrons as they entered the bar.*

ID[2] *abbr.* An abbreviation of: **1.** Idaho. **2.** identification.

I'd (īd) Contraction of *I had* or *I would.*

I·da·ho (ī′də-hō′) A state of the northwest United States west of Montana. It was admitted as the 43rd state in 1890. Boise is the capital. —SEE NOTE.

ID card *n.* A card that gives identifying information about a person, such as name, age, and date of birth, and often includes the person's photograph.

i·de·a (ī-dē′ə) *n.* **1.** A product of mental activity, such as a thought, opinion, belief, or fancy: *She developed her idea for the project over several months.* **2.** A plan, scheme, or method: *My idea is to become a doctor.* **3.** The point or purpose of something: *The idea is to make people aware of the problem by putting up posters.* [From Middle English, from Greek.]

SYNONYMS **idea, thought, notion, concept, conception** These nouns mean something formed or represented in the mind as the product of mental activity. **Idea** is the most general: *Writers sometimes have many ideas before they begin work.* **Thought** can mean an idea produced by contemplation and reason as opposed, for example, to emotion: *I carefully collected my thoughts before responding to the criticism.* **Notion** means a vague, general, or even fanciful idea: *He has a notion that eating beef will make him stronger.* **Concept** means an idea on a large scale: *The concept of time has puzzled many philosophers.* **Conception** refers to a person's understanding or comprehension of an idea: *Einstein's conception of gravity was different from Newton's.*

i·deal (ī-dēl′) *n.* **1.** A conception of something in its perfection: *Equality and justice are some of our society's ideals.* **2.** A person or thing that is regarded as an example of excellence or perfection: *She remains the ideal among mathematics teachers.* **3.** An ultimate or worthy object of endeavor; a goal: *Their ideal is to own their own restaurant.* ❖ *adj.* **1.** Perfect or the best possible: *The hot summer sun made this an ideal day for swimming.* **2.** Existing only in the mind; imaginary: *A line without thickness is an ideal geometric object.*

i·de·al·ism (ī-dē′ə-lĭz′əm) *n.* **1.** The tendency to think of ideas or people in terms of some standard of perfection. **2.** The practice of following one's personal ideals: *His idealism led him to work for world peace.* **3.** A philosophical belief that all things exist only as ideas in the mind, not as objects independent of the mind.

i·de·al·ist (ī-dē′ə-lĭst) *n.* **1.** A person who follows personal ideals, often with little regard for practical considerations. **2.** A person who believes in philosophical idealism.

i·de·al·is·tic (ī-dē′ə-lĭs′tĭk) *adj.* Relating to idealism or idealists: *an idealistic belief; an idealistic philosopher.* **—i′de·al·is′ti·cal·ly** *adv.*

i·de·al·ize (ī-dē′ə-līz′) *tr.v.* **i·de·al·ized, i·de·al·iz·ing, i·de·al·iz·es** To regard as ideal or perfect: *Sometimes we idealize our friends so much that we do not see their faults.* **—i·de′al·i·za′tion** (ī-dē′ə-lĭ-zā′shən) *n.*

i·deal·ly (ī-dē′lē) *adv.* **1.** In agreement with an ideal; perfectly: *The two friends were ideally suited to each other.* **2.** In theory or imagination: *Ideally, each classroom should have its own thermostat to adjust the heat.*

i·den·ti·cal (ī-dĕn′tĭ-kəl) *adj.* **1.** Exactly equal and alike: *We're riding identical bicycles.* **2.** The very same: *The principal used those identical words in his speech.* **3.** Relating to twins developed from the same fertilized egg. Identical twins are always the same sex and have the same genetic traits. [From Late Latin *identitās,* identity, from Latin *idem,* the same.] **—i·den′ti·cal·ly** *adv.*

i·den·ti·fi·ca·tion (ī-dĕn′tə-fĭ-kā′shən) *n.* **1.** The act of identifying or the condition of being identified. **2.** Evidence of a person's identity: *A driver's license is usually accepted as sufficient identification.*

identification card *n.* An ID card.

i·den·ti·fy (ī-dĕn′tə-fī′) *v.* **i·den·ti·fied, i·den·ti·fy·ing, i·den·ti·fies** *—tr.* **1.** To establish or recognize as a certain person or thing: *We identified the bird as a thrush.* **2.** To consider as identical; equate: *The Greek god Ares is identified with the Roman god Mars.* **3.** To associate or connect closely: *That economist is identified with conservative political groups.* —*intr.* **1.** To be or feel closely associated with a person or thing: *He identifies strongly with his grandfather.* **2.** To self-identify. **—i·den′ti·fi′a·ble** *adj.*

i·den·ti·ty (ī-dĕn′tĭ-tē) *n., pl.* **i·den·ti·ties 1.** The condition of being a certain person or thing; individuality: *The police tried to establish the suspect's identity.* **2.** The awareness that an individual or group has of being a distinct, persisting entity: *the main character's identity as an outsider.* **3.** Information, such as an identification number, used to allow a person to prove who he or she is. **4.** The condition of being identical: *The identity of the two signatures was established by a handwriting expert.* **5a.** A mathematical equation that remains true no matter what numbers are substituted for its variables. For example, $x + y = y + x$ is true regardless of the values of x and y. **b.** An identity element.

identity element *n.* An element of a set of numbers that does not change other elements of the set it is combined with in a mathematical operation. For example, 0 is the identity element for addition, since, if a is any real number, $a + 0 = a$. Similarly, 1 is the identity element for multiplication, since $a \times 1 = a$.

id·e·o·gram (ĭd′ē-ə-grăm′ *or* ī′dē-ə-grăm′) *n.* A written character or symbol that represents an idea or thing rather than a particular word or phrase.

id·e·o·graph (ĭd′ē-ə-grăf′) *n.* An ideogram.

i·de·o·log·i·cal (ī′dē-ə-lŏj′ĭ-kəl *or* ĭd′ē-ə-lŏj′ĭ-kəl) *adj.* Relating to ideology: *ideological conflicts.* **—i′de·o·log′i·cal·ly** *adv.*

i·de·ol·o·gy (ī′dē-ŏl′ə-jē *or* ĭd′ē-ŏl′ə-jē) *n., pl.* **i·de·ol·o·gies** A set of doctrines or beliefs that are shared by members of a group, such as a political party or social class.

ides (īdz) *pl.n. (used with a singular or plural verb)* In the ancient Roman calendar, the 15th day of March, May, July, or October or the 13th day of the other months. [From Middle English *idus*, from Latin *Īdūs*.]

id·i·o·cy (ĭd′ē-ə-sē) *n., pl.* **id·i·o·cies 1.** Great foolishness or stupidity. **2.** A foolish or stupid action or remark.

id·i·om (ĭd′ē-əm) *n.* **1.** A phrase or expression having a special meaning that cannot be understood from the individual meanings of its words; for example, *fly off the handle* is an idiom in English meaning *lose one's temper.* **2.** The accepted way in which words are used in a language. **3.** The language or dialect of a particular region or group of people: *the idiom of Cajun French.* [From Late Latin *idiōma*, from Greek *idiousthai*, to make one's own, from *idios*, own, personal, private.]

id·i·o·mat·ic (ĭd′ē-ə-măt′ĭk) *adj.* Following the pattern of word usage particular to a given language: *It takes many years of study to speak idiomatic Chinese.* **—id′i·o·mat′i·cal·ly** *adv.*

id·i·o·syn·cra·sy (ĭd′ē-ō-sĭng′krə-sē) *n., pl.* **id·i·o·syn·cra·sies** A trait or mannerism peculiar to an individual: *One of my brother's idiosyncrasies is never letting the different foods on his plate touch each other.* **—id′i·o·syn·crat′ic** (ĭd′ē-ō-sĭn-**krăt′**ĭk) *adj.* **—id′i·o·syn·crat′i·cal·ly** *adv.*

id·i·ot (ĭd′ē-ət) *n.* A person who is considered stupid or foolish. [From Middle English, from Greek *idiōtēs*, private person, layman, from *idios*, own, private.]

id·i·ot·ic (ĭd′ē-ŏt′ĭk) *adj.* Showing stupidity or foolishness: *an idiotic mistake.* **—id′i·ot′i·cal·ly** *adv.*

i·dle (īd′l) *adj.* **i·dler, i·dlest 1.** Not employed or busy: *idle employees; idle machines; idle time on the holiday.* **2.** Avoiding work; lazy; shiftless. **3.** Not in use or operation: *The presses are idle.* **4.** Lacking substance, value, or basis: *idle talk.* ❖ *v.* **i·dled, i·dling, i·dles** —*intr.* **1.** To pass time without working or in avoiding work: *The men idled on the park benches.* **2.** To run at a low speed or without transmitting power: *The engine idled smoothly.* —*tr.* **1.** To pass (time) without working or in order to avoid work: *I idled the afternoon away without touching my homework.* **2.** To cause to be unemployed or inactive: *The drivers' strike idled every bus in the city.* [From Old English *īdel*.] **—i′dle·ness** *n.* **—i′dler** (īd′lər) *n.* **—i′dly** *adv.*

❑ *These sound alike:* **idle, idol** (image), **idyll** (poem).

i·dol (īd′l) *n.* **1.** An image or object that is worshiped as a god. **2.** A person or thing that is adored or admired, often to fanatical degree: *a pop star who was an idol to her fans.* [From Middle English, from Greek *eidōlon*, from *eidos*, form.]

❑ *These sound alike:* **idol, idle** (not working), **idyll** (poem).

i·dol·a·ter or **i·dol·a·tor** (ī-dŏl′ə-tər) *n.* A person who worships idols.

i·dol·a·trous (ī-dŏl′ə-trəs) *adj.* **1.** Relating to idolatry. **2.** Given to idolatry.

i·dol·a·try (ī-dŏl′ə-trē) *n., pl.* **i·dol·a·tries 1.** The worship of idols. **2.** Fanatical adoration of someone or something: *The fan's idolatry made him blind to the sports star's faults.*

i·dol·ize (īd′l-īz′) *tr.v.* **i·dol·ized, i·dol·iz·ing, i·dol·iz·es 1.** To regard with fanatical adoration: *Many fans idolize their favorite performers.* **2.** To worship or treat as an idol: *Early Egyptians idolized cats.*

i·dyll also **i·dyl** (īd′l) *n.* **1.** A short poem or prose work describing a pleasant scene or event of country life. **2.** A scene or event having a simple peaceful nature.

❑ *These sound alike:* **idyll, idle** (not working), **idol** (image).

i·dyl·lic (ī-dĭl′ĭk) *adj.* **1.** Simple and carefree: *an idyllic childhood.* **2.** Charming and picturesque: *an idyllic tropical beach.* **—i·dyl′li·cal·ly** *adv.*

i.e. *abbr.* An abbreviation of id est. (that is)

–ie *suff.* Variant of **–y**[3].

if (ĭf) *conj.* **1.** In the event that; supposing that: *If it rains, then we won't take a walk.* **2.** On condition that: *I'll go only if you do.* **3.** Even though; although possibly: *a handsome if useless gadget.* **4.** Whether: *I asked if they were coming.* **5.** Indicating a strong wish: *If they had only come sooner!*

iff *abbr.* An abbreviation of if and only if.

if·fy (ĭf′ē) *adj.* **if·fi·er, if·fi·est** *Informal* Doubtful; uncertain: *It's looking iffy for getting concert tickets.*

I formation *n.* In football, an offensive formation in which the running backs line up in single file behind the center and the quarterback.

–ify *suff.* Variant of **–fy.**

Ig·bo (ĭg′bō) also **I·bo** (ē′bō) *n., pl.* **Igbo** or **Ig·bos** also **Ibo** or **I·bos 1.** A member of a people living in southeast Nigeria. **2.** The language of the Igbo.

ig·loo (ĭg′lo͞o) *n., pl.* **ig·loos** A house made of blocks of snow, such as those built by the Inuit. [From Inuit *iglu*, house.]

Ig·na·tius of Loy·o·la (ĭg-**nā′**shəs əv loi-ō′lə), Saint. 1491–1556. Spanish priest who founded the Society of Jesus.

ig·ne·ous (ĭg′nē-əs) *adj.* **1.** Relating to fire. **2.** Formed by the cooling and hardening of molten rock: *Basalt is an igneous rock.* [From Latin *ignis*, fire.]

ig·nite (ĭg-nīt′) *v.* **ig·nit·ed, ig·nit·ing, ig·nites** —*tr.* **1.** To cause to start burning: *A lightning bolt ignited the forest fire.* **2.** To bring about or provoke suddenly; stir up: *His remarks ignited a controversy.* —*intr.* To begin to burn; catch fire: *Wet logs do not ignite easily.* [From Latin *ignis*, fire.]

ig·ni·tion (ĭg-**nĭsh′**ən) *n.* **1.** The act or process of igniting

ideogram
kangaroo crossing

igloo

iguana

GEOGRAPHY

Illinois[2] The state of **Illinois** takes its name from the Illinois River. The river's name comes from the name French explorers used for a Native American people of the region. The French learned this name from an Algonquian language, but it is unclear which one. The name was pronounced (ĭl′ə-**nō′**wä) and meant "ordinary speaker," that is, "one who speaks a similar language." The final *s* at the end of *Illinois* was added by the French to make the word plural when referring to this group. The pronunciation with the final *s* silent comes from the French.

ă	pat	ôr	core
ā	pay	oi	boy
âr	care	ou	out
ä	father	o͝o	took
ĕ	pet	o͝or	lure
ē	be	o͞o	boot
ĭ	pit	ŭ	cut
ī	bite	ûr	urge
îr	pier	th	thin
ŏ	pot	*th*	this
ō	toe	zh	vision
ô	paw	ə	about

a substance. **2.** An electrical system that provides the spark to ignite the fuel mixture of an internal-combustion engine. **3.** A switch that activates this system: *Pump the gas pedal and turn the ignition.*

ig·no·ble (ĭg-**nō′**bəl) *adj.* **1.** Not noble, as in character or purpose; base; dishonorable: *an ignoble act.* **2.** Not of high social rank; common: *Royal princes do not usually marry someone of ignoble birth.* **—ig·no′ble·ness** *n.* **—ig·no′bly** *adv.*

ig·no·min·i·ous (ĭg′nə-**mĭn′**ē-əs) *adj.* **1.** Characterized by shame or disgrace; humiliating: *The candidate suffered an ignominious defeat at the polls.* **2.** Deserving disgrace or shame; despicable: *committing an ignominious crime.* **—ig′no·min′i·ous·ly** *adv.*

ig·no·min·y (**ĭg′**nə-mĭn′ē) *n.* Great personal dishonor or disgrace: *The soldier's brutal act brought ignominy on the entire unit.*

ig·no·ra·mus (ĭg′nə-**rā′**məs) *n., pl.* **ig·no·ra·mus·es** An ignorant person.

ig·no·rance (**ĭg′**nər-əns) *n.* The condition of being ignorant; lack of education or knowledge: *The teacher was surprised by the students' ignorance of geography. Ignorance of the law is no excuse for committing a crime.*

ig·no·rant (**ĭg′**nər-ənt) *adj.* **1.** Lacking education or knowledge. **2.** Showing or arising from a lack of knowledge: *an ignorant mistake.* **3.** Unaware or uninformed: *Many pioneers were ignorant of the hardships they were to face.* **—ig′no·rant·ly** *adv.*

ig·nore (ĭg-**nôr′**) *tr.v.* **ig·nored, ig·nor·ing, ig·nores** To refuse to pay attention to; disregard: *I ignored the sound of the television in the next room.* [From Latin *ignōrāre.*]

i·gua·na (ĭ-**gwä′**nə) *n.* Any of various large plant-eating lizards that have a ridge of spines along the back and are found in the American tropics. [From Arawak *iwana.*]

IL *abbr.* An abbreviation of Illinois.

il–[1] *pref.* Variant of **in–**[1].

il–[2] *pref.* Variant of **in–**[2].

il·e·um (**ĭl′**ē-əm) *n., pl.* **il·e·a** (**ĭl′**ē-ə) The lowest section of the small intestine.

❑ *These sound alike:* **ileum, ilium** (bone).

Il·i·ad (**ĭl′**ē-əd) *n.* An ancient Greek epic poem attributed to Homer, recounting the siege of Troy.

il·i·um (**ĭl′**ē-əm) *n., pl.* **il·i·a** (**ĭl′**ē-ə) The uppermost of the three bones that make up each of the hipbones.

❑ *These sound alike:* **ilium, ileum** (intestine).

Il·i·um (**ĭl′**ē-əm) See **Troy.**

ilk (ĭlk) *n.* Type or kind; sort; class: *Flies, mosquitoes, and other insects of that ilk can be annoying.* [From Old English *ilca,* the same.]

ill (ĭl) *adj.* **worse** (wûrs), **worst** (wûrst) **1.** Not healthy; sick: *went home feeling ill.* **2.** Not normal; unsound: *ill health.* **3.** Resulting in suffering; harmful or distressing: *the ill effects of the storm.* **4.** Having evil intentions; hostile or unfriendly: *ill feeling between rivals.* **5.** Not favorable or promising: *an ill omen.* ❖ *adv.* **worse, worst 1.** In a sickly or unsound manner; unwell. **2.** Scarcely or with difficulty: *We can ill afford another mistake.* ❖ *n.* **1.** Evil; wrongdoing: *the choice between doing good or doing ill.* **2.** Harm; disaster: *The drought was a terrible ill for farmers.* **3.** A source of suffering; an affliction: *the ills of living in an overcrowded city.* **4.** Unfavorable or unkind words: *Do not speak ill of him.* ◆ **ill at ease** Anxious or unsure; uneasy: *Walking through the park alone at night made me feel ill at ease.*

ill. *abbr.* An abbreviation of: **1.** illustrated. **2.** illustration.

I'll (īl) Contraction of *I will.*

❑ *These sound alike:* **I'll, aisle** (passageway), **isle** (island).

ill-ad·vised (ĭl′əd-**vīzd′**) *adj.* Done with bad advice or with insufficient thinking: *an ill-advised scheme to build a pipeline through a region prone to earthquakes.*

ill-bred (**ĭl′brĕd′**) *adj.* Badly brought up; impolite.

il·le·gal (ĭ-**lē′**gəl) *adj.* **1.** Against the law; not legal: *It's illegal to drive over the speed limit.* **2.** Against the official rules, as of a game: *Fouls are illegal acts in basketball.* **—il·le′gal·ly** *adv.*

il·le·gal·i·ty (ĭl′ē-**găl′**ĭ-tē) *n., pl.* **il·le·gal·i·ties 1.** The condition of being illegal; unlawfulness. **2.** An illegal act: *The company was fined for illegalities in their hiring practices.*

il·leg·i·ble (ĭ-**lĕj′**ə-bəl) *adj.* Impossible or very hard to read: *a note written in an illegible scrawl.* **—il·leg′i·bil′i·ty** *n.* **—il·leg′i·bly** *adv.*

il·le·git·i·mate (ĭl′ĭ-**jĭt′**ə-mĭt) *adj.* **1.** Against an established rule or law: *an illegitimate seizure of property.* **2.** *Offensive* Born to parents who are not married to each other. **—il′le·git′i·ma·cy** (ĭl′ĭ-**jĭt′**ə-mə-sē) *n.* **—il′le·git′i·mate·ly** *adv.*

ill-fat·ed (**ĭl′fā′**tĭd) *adj.* **1.** Destined for misfortune; doomed: *The ill-fated ship never reached port.* **2.** Marked by or causing misfortune; unlucky: *an ill-fated decision to act too soon.*

ill-got·ten (**ĭl′gŏt′**n) *adj.* Obtained by evil or dishonest means: *ill-gotten wealth.*

ill-hu·mored (**ĭl′hyo͞o′**mərd) *adj.* Irritable; surly.

il·lib·er·al (ĭ-**lĭb′**ər-əl) *adj.* Narrow-minded; intolerant. **—il·lib′er·al·ly** *adv.*

il·lic·it (ĭ-**lĭs′**ĭt) *adj.* Not permitted by law; unlawful. **—il·lic′it·ly** *adv.* **—il·lic′it·ness** *n.*

❑ *These sound alike:* **illicit, elicit** (evoke).

il·lim·it·a·ble (ĭ-**lĭm′**ĭ-tə-bəl) *adj.* Impossible to limit; limitless. **—il·lim′it·a·bly** *adv.*

Il·li·nois[1] (ĭl′ə-**noi′**) *n., pl.* **Illinois 1.** A member of a group of Native American peoples originally living in Illinois, Iowa, Wisconsin, and Missouri, with a present-day population in Oklahoma. **2.** The Algonquian language of the Illinois.

Il·li·nois[2] (ĭl′ə-**noi′**) A state of the north-central United States west of Indiana. It was admitted as the 21st state in 1818. Springfield is the capital and Chicago the largest city. —SEE NOTE.

il·lit·er·a·cy (ĭ-**lĭt′**ər-ə-sē) *n., pl.* **il·lit·er·a·cies 1.** The condition of being unable to read and write. **2.** A lack of education or knowledge: *scientific illiteracy.*

il·lit·er·ate (ĭ-**lĭt′**ər-ĭt) *adj.* **1.** Unable to read and write. **2.** Showing a lack of knowledge in a certain subject: *illiterate in history.* **—il·lit′er·ate·ly** *adv.*

ill-man·nered (**ĭl′măn′**ərd) *adj.* Showing a lack of good manners; impolite; rude. **—ill′-man′nered·ly** *adv.*

ill-na·tured (**ĭl′nā′**chərd) *adj.* Disagreeable, cross, or mean. **—ill′-na′tured·ly** *adv.*

ill·ness (**ĭl′**nĭs) *n.* **1.** An unhealthy condition; poor health: *often missing school because of illness.* **2.** A disease: *Diphtheria is a serious illness.*

il·log·i·cal (ĭ-**lŏj′**ĭ-kəl) *adj.* **1.** Having or showing a lack of sound reasoning; not logical: *Your argument is illogical.* **2.** Unreasonable; senseless: *an illogical fear of being hit by a meteor.* **—il·log′i·cal·ly** *adv.*

ill-starred (**ĭl′stärd′**) *adj.* Unlucky; ill-fated.

ill-tem·pered (**ĭl′tĕm′**pərd) *adj.* Having a bad temper; irritable. **—ill′-tem′pered·ly** *adv.*

ill-timed (**ĭl′tīmd′**) *adj.* Done or occurring at the wrong time; untimely: *I regretted my ill-timed remark.*

ill-treat (**ĭl′trēt′**) *tr.v.* **ill-treat·ed, ill-treat·ing, ill-treats** To treat badly or cruelly; abuse. **—ill′-treat′ment** *n.*

il·lu·mi·nate (ĭ-**lo͞o′**mə-nāt′) *tr.v.* **il·lu·mi·nat·ed, il·lu·mi·nat·ing, il·lu·mi·nates 1.** To provide with light: *A lamp illuminated the steps.* **2.** To make clear; explain: *The film illuminated the events leading up to the war.* **3.** To decorate with ornamental designs, pictures, or colors: *Medieval manuscripts were often illuminated by monks.*

il·lu·mi·na·tion (ĭ-lo͞o′mə-**nā′**shən) *n.* **1.** The act of illuminating or the state of being illuminated: *the illumination of a dark corner.* **2.** An amount of light; brightness: *the soft illumination of a candle.* **3.** Decoration with lights: *festive outdoor illumination.* **4.** Decoration of a book, manuscript, or other writing. **5.** A design, picture, or other adornment in a book or manuscript.

il·lu·mine (ĭ-lo͞o′mĭn) *tr.v.* **il·lu·mined, il·lu·min·ing, il·lu·mines** To give light to; illuminate.

illus. *abbr.* An abbreviation of illustrated.

ill-use (**ĭl′yo͞oz′**) *tr.v.* **ill-used, ill-us·ing, ill-us·es** To treat badly or unjustly; mistreat. ❖ *n.* (**ĭl′yo͞os′**) Poor or unjust treatment.

il·lu·sion (ĭ-lo͞o′zhən) *n.* **1.** An unreal or misleading appearance or image: *A three-dimensional movie creates an illusion of depth even though the screen is flat.* **2.** An idea or belief that is mistaken or false: *His illusion that he did not need to study for tests did not last long.* [From Middle English *illusioun*, from Late Latin *illūsiō*, ridicule, from Latin *illūdere*, to mock.]

il·lu·so·ry (ĭ-lo͞o′sə-rē *or* ĭ-lo͞o′zə-rē) *adj.* Produced by, based on, or having the nature of an illusion; deceptive: *The sand was so white it had the illusory appearance of snow.*

il·lus·trate (ĭl′ə-strāt′ *or* ĭ-lŭs′trāt′) *tr.v.* **il·lus·trat·ed, il·lus·trat·ing, il·lus·trates 1.** To make clear or explain, as by using examples or comparisons: *The geologist illustrated how the rocks folded by pushing on the ends of a piece of paper.* **2.** To provide with pictures or diagrams that explain or adorn: *The artist illustrated the story.* [From Latin *illūstrāre*, to shed light on : *in-*, into + *lūstrāre*, to make bright.]

il·lus·tra·tion (ĭl′ə-**strā′**shən) *n.* **1.** Something, such as a picture, diagram, or chart, that serves to make clear, explain, or decorate something else: *The illustrations improve the book.* **2.** Something serving as an example, comparison, or proof: *A ball falling to the ground is an illustration of gravity.* **3.** The act of illustrating or the state of being illustrated: *The illustration of the children's book took the artist several months.*

il·lus·tra·tive (ĭ-lŭs′trə-tĭv *or* ĭl′ə-strā′tĭv) *adj.* Serving to illustrate or explain: *a science book with many illustrative photos and diagrams.* **—il·lus′tra·tive·ly** *adv.*

il·lus·tra·tor (ĭl′ə-strā′tər) *n.* An artist who illustrates books, magazines, or other material.

il·lus·tri·ous (ĭ-lŭs′trē-əs) *adj.* Well-known and very distinguished; eminent: *an illustrious author; illustrious deeds.* See Synonyms at **famous.**

ill will *n.* Unfriendly feeling; hostility.

IM (**ī′ĕm′**) *Informal tr.v.* **IMed, IM·ing, IMs** or **IM'ed, IM'·ing, IM's 1.** To send (someone) an instant message: *Matt IMed me to let me know that he would be late.* **2.** To express in an instant message: *Sharon IMed that she wanted to borrow my math textbook.* ❖ *n.* An instant message.

im–¹ *pref.* Variant of **in–¹.**

im–² *pref.* Variant of **in–².**

I'm (īm) Contraction of *I am.*

im·age (**ĭm′**ĭj) *n.* **1.** An artistic representation of a person or thing, especially a painting or statue. **2.** A visual presentation or reproduction of an object, especially by reflection in a mirror or refraction through a lens or lens system: *a microscopic image.* **3.** A mental picture of something not real or present: *Our image of the new apartment did not conform with reality.* **4.** A vivid description in words, especially a metaphor or simile: *The poem is full of images of country life.* **5.** The concept of a person or thing that is held by the public, especially as a result of advertising or publicity: *The toy company has a friendly image.* **6.** A person or thing that closely resembles another: *a child who is the image of a parent.* ❖ *tr.v.* **im·aged, im·ag·ing, im·ag·es** To produce, transmit, or display a visual representation of: *Astronomers set up the telescope to image Mars.* [From Middle English, from Latin *imāgō*.]

im·age·ry (**ĭm′**ĭj-rē) *n., pl.* **im·age·ries 1.** The use of figures of speech or vivid descriptions in writing or speaking: *We discussed the poem's imagery.* **2.** Visual images considered as a group: *imagery of the planet's moons sent back by the probe.*

i·mag·i·na·ble (ĭ-**măj′**ə-nə-bəl) *adj.* Capable of being imagined: *a book that has information on every imaginable topic.* **—i·mag′i·na·bly** *adv.*

i·mag·i·nar·y (ĭ-**măj′**ə-nĕr′ē) *adj.* **1.** Existing only in the imagination; not real: *The book describes an imaginary world of talking animals.* **2.** Relating to an imaginary number.

imaginary number *n.* A number whose square is negative.

i·mag·i·na·tion (ĭ-măj′ə-**nā′**shən) *n.* **1.** The act or ability of forming mental images of something that is not real or present: *Characters for the story were born in the lively imagination of the writer.* **2.** The ability to use the mind effectively; resourcefulness: *The new mayor solved the city's budget problems with imagination.*

i·mag·i·na·tive (ĭ-**măj′**ə-nə-tĭv *or* ĭ-**măj′**ə-nā′tĭv) *adj.* **1.** Having a strong imagination, especially creative imagination: *an imaginative artist.* **2.** Created by or marked by originality and creativity: *an imaginative solution to a problem.* **—i·mag′i·na·tive·ly** *adv.*

i·mag·ine (ĭ-**măj′**ĭn) *v.* **i·mag·ined, i·mag·in·ing, i·mag·ines** *—tr.* **1.** To form a mental picture of: *Can you imagine what weightlessness would feel like?* **2.** To make a guess; suppose: *I imagine this bad weather will make them late.* *—intr.* To use the imagination: *The mind is able to think, remember, and imagine.* [From Middle English *imaginen*, from Latin *imāginārī*, from *imāgō*, image.]

i·ma·go (ĭ-**mā′**gō *or* ĭ-**mä′**gō) *n., pl.* **i·ma·goes** or **i·ma·gi·nes** (ĭ-**mā′**gə-nēz′ *or* ĭ-**mä′**gə-nēz′) An insect in its fully developed adult stage.

i·mam also **I·mam** (ĭ-**mäm′**) *n.* **1.** A male prayer leader in a mosque. **2.** A male Muslim leader regarded as a successor or descendant of Muhammad. **3.** Any of 12 descendants of Muhammad regarded by most Shiite Muslims as forming a divinely appointed succession of leaders.

im·bal·ance (ĭm-**băl′**əns) *n.* A lack of balance, as between amounts or forces: *an imbalance between income and expenditures.*

im·be·cile (**ĭm′**bə-sĭl) *n.* A person who is considered stupid or foolish. [From Latin *imbēcillus*.] **—im′be·cil′ic** *adj.*

im·bibe (ĭm-**bīb′**) *v.* **im·bibed, im·bib·ing, im·bibes** *—tr.* **1.** To drink. **2.** To absorb or take in as if by drinking: *Thirsty plants imbibe moisture through the roots.* **3.** To take or absorb into the mind: *The painter went to Asia to imbibe new ideas.* *—intr.* To drink alcoholic beverages. [From Middle English *embiben*, to soak up, from Latin *imbibere*, to drink in.] **—im·bib′er** *n.*

im·bro·glio (ĭm-**brōl′**yō) *n., pl.* **im·bro·glios** A confused or difficult situation; a predicament.

im·bue (ĭm-**byo͞o′**) *tr.v.* **im·bued, im·bu·ing, im·bues** To fill thoroughly, as with a quality or emotion: *Reading the novel imbued them with a desire to travel to Africa.*

im·i·ta·ble (**ĭm′**ĭ-tə-bəl) *adj.* Capable or worthy of being imitated: *imitable behavior.*

im·i·tate (**ĭm′**ĭ-tāt′) *tr.v.* **im·i·tat·ed, im·i·tat·ing, im·i·tates 1.** To follow as a model or example: *Your little brother imitates you because he admires you.* **2.** To copy the speech or actions of; mimic: *The actor imitated the president perfectly.* **3.** To copy exactly; reproduce: *Few artists can imitate the paintings of Rembrandt.* **4.** To look like; resemble: *a plastic that imitates the look of leather.* [From Latin *imitārī*.] **—im′i·ta′tor** *n.*

WRITERS CHOOSE THEIR WORDS

"There's one thing I didn't tell you about Shoeless Joe," Flip said. "He was **illiterate.**" "You mean he didn't know how to read?" "Or write," Flip explained, turning around to pull out a thick book from the shelf behind him. "It wasn't any secret. A lot of people were **illiterate** back then."

—Dan Gutman
Shoeless Joe & Me

illumination
14th-century illuminated manuscript

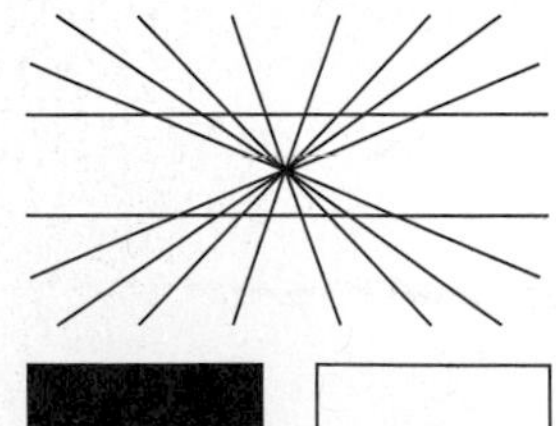

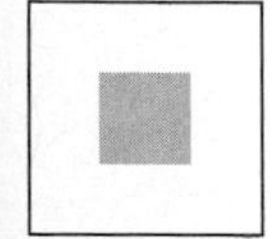

illusion
top: Straight horizontal lines appear curved.
bottom: A gray box against a black background appears lighter than the same gray box against a white background.

SYNONYMS imitate, copy, mimic, simulate These verbs mean to follow something or someone as a model. **Imitate** means to act like another or follow a pattern set by another: *Can you imitate a British accent?* **Copy** means to duplicate an original as closely as possible: *If you were absent, copy the notes from a classmate.* **Mimic** often means to imitate in order to make fun of a person or thing: *The student mimicked the principal in our class skit.* **Simulate** means to falsely take on the appearance or character of something: *They painted the wall to simulate marble.*

im·i·ta·tion (ĭm′ĭ-tā′shən) *n.* **1.** The act or an instance of imitating: *I learned the song through imitation.* **2.** Something made to look like something else; a likeness or copy: *This bell is an imitation of the Liberty Bell.* ❖ *adj.* Made to resemble another: *imitation leather.*

im·i·ta·tive (ĭm′ĭ-tā′tĭv) *adj.* **1.** Involving imitation: *The words* woof *and* meow *are imitative of animal sounds.* **2.** Tending to imitate or copy: *Parrots are imitative birds.* **—im′i·ta′tive·ly** *adv.*

im·mac·u·late (ĭ-măk′yə-lĭt) *adj.* **1.** Impeccably clean; spotless: *an immaculate tablecloth.* **2.** Free from sin. **3.** Free from fault or error; flawless: *an immaculate record on the job.* **—im·mac′u·late·ly** *adv.*

Immaculate Conception *n.* The doctrine of the Roman Catholic Church that the Virgin Mary was conceived free from original sin.

im·ma·nent (ĭm′ə-nənt) *adj.* Existing within; inherent: *They believed that goodness is immanent in all humans.* [From Late Latin *immanēre*, to remain in.]

❑ *These sound alike:* **immanent, imminent** (impending).

im·ma·te·ri·al (ĭm′ə-tîr′ē-əl) *adj.* **1.** Of no importance or consequence; unimportant: *The wedding will be indoors, so it is immaterial what the weather is like.* **2.** Having no physical body or form; spiritual: *ghosts and other immaterial beings.* **—im′ma·te′ri·al·ly** *adv.*

im·ma·ture (ĭm′ə-tyo͝or′ *or* ĭm′ə-cho͝or′) *adj.* **1.** Not fully grown or developed: *immature corn.* **2.** Showing a lack of maturity; childish: *selfish, immature behavior.* See Synonyms at **young. —im′ma·ture′ly** *adv.* **—im′ma·tur′i·ty** *n.*

im·meas·ur·a·ble (ĭ-mĕzh′ər-ə-bəl) *adj.* Impossible to measure: *the immeasurable number of stars in the heavens.* **—im·meas′ur·a·bly** *adv.*

im·me·di·ate (ĭ-mē′dē-ĭt) *adj.* **1.** Taking place at once or very soon; happening without delay: *needing immediate medical care in an emergency room.* **2.** Relating to or near the present time: *the immediate future.* **3.** Close at hand; near: *our immediate surroundings.* **4.** Next in line or relation: *the king's immediate successor.* **5.** Occurring with nothing coming between or interfering; direct: *You should avoid any immediate contact of this glue with the skin.* **—im·me′di·a·cy** (ĭ-mē′dē-ə-sē) *adv.* **—im·me′di·ate·ly** *adv.*

im·me·mo·ri·al (ĭm′ə-môr′ē-əl) *adj.* Reaching beyond the limits of memory or history: *Humans have created art since time immemorial.* **—im′me·mo′ri·al·ly** *adv.*

im·mense (ĭ-mĕns′) *adj.* Of great size, extent, or degree; huge: *immense rocks; an immense length of time.* **—im·mense′ly** *adv.* **—im·men′si·ty** *n.*

im·merse (ĭ-mûrs′) *tr.v.* **im·mersed, im·mers·ing, im·mers·es 1.** To cover completely with a liquid; submerge: *immersed the pans in soapy water.* **2.** To baptize by submerging in water. **3.** To involve deeply; absorb: *I immersed myself in the exciting story.* **—im·mers′i·ble** *adj.*

im·mer·sion (ĭ-mûr′zhən *or* ĭ-mûr′shən) *n.* **1.** An act of immersing or the condition of being immersed. **2.** Baptism performed by immersing a person in water.

im·mi·grant (ĭm′ĭ-grənt) *n.* A person who immigrates: *Immigrants have come to the United States from all over the world.*

im·mi·grate (ĭm′ĭ-grāt′) *intr.v.* **im·mi·grat·ed, im·mi·grat·ing, im·mi·grates** To come into a foreign country to live: *People from many parts of the world immigrate to Europe each year.* **—im′mi·gra′tion** *n.* —SEE NOTE AT **emigrate.**

im·mi·nent (ĭm′ə-nənt) *adj.* About to happen; looming; impending: *It is cold and windy, and snow seems imminent.* [From Middle English *iminent*, from Latin *imminēre*, to overhang.] **—im′mi·nence** *n.* **—im′mi·nent·ly** *adv.*

❑ *These sound alike:* **imminent, immanent** (inherent).

im·mo·bile (ĭ-mō′bəl *or* ĭ-mō′bēl′ *or* ĭ-mō′bīl′) *adj.* **1.** Not able to move; fixed: *A broken axle made the car immobile.* **2.** Not moving; motionless: *The deer stood immobile in the field.* **—im′mo·bil′i·ty** (ĭm′ō-bĭl′ĭ-tē) *n.*

im·mo·bi·lize (ĭ-mō′bə-līz′) *tr.v.* **im·mo·bi·lized, im·mo·bi·liz·ing, im·mo·bi·liz·es** To make immobile; render incapable of moving: *The doctor immobilized the broken finger with a splint.* **—im·mo′bi·li·za′tion** (ĭ-mō′bə-lĭ-zā′shən) *n.*

im·mod·er·ate (ĭ-mŏd′ər-ĭt) *adj.* Going beyond what is normal or proper; extreme: *loud and immoderate laughter.* **—im·mod′er·ate·ly** *adv.*

im·mod·est (ĭ-mŏd′ĭst) *adj.* **1.** Morally offensive or indecent: *Older people considered the new dance immodest.* **2.** Lacking modesty; arrogant or boastful: *She gave an immodest description of her role in the project.* **—im·mod′est·ly** *adv.* **—im·mod′es·ty** *n.*

im·mo·late (ĭm′ə-lāt′) *tr.v.* **im·mo·lat·ed, im·mo·lat·ing, im·mo·lates 1.** To kill (an animal) as a religious sacrifice. **2.** To kill by burning. **—im′mo·la′tion** *n.*

im·mor·al (ĭ-môr′əl *or* ĭ-mŏr′əl) *adj.* Contrary to what is considered moral: *immoral behavior.* **—im·mor′al·ly** *adv.*

im·mor·al·i·ty (ĭm′ô-răl′ĭ-tē) *n., pl.* **im·mor·al·i·ties 1.** The quality or condition of being immoral: *the immorality of war.* **2.** An immoral act or practice: *The immoralities of a few public officials can weaken the public's confidence in government.*

im·mor·tal (ĭ-môr′tl) *adj.* **1.** Never dying; living forever: *The Greek gods were believed to be immortal.* **2.** Having eternal fame: *the immortal words of Shakespeare.* ❖ *n.* **1.** An immortal being: *The ancient Greeks believed their gods were immortals.* **2.** A person with enduring fame: *Mozart and Beethoven are immortals in the field of music.* **—im·mor′tal·ly** *adv.*

im·mor·tal·i·ty (ĭm′ôr-tăl′ĭ-tē) *n.* **1.** The condition of being immortal. **2.** Enduring fame: *the immortality of Michelangelo.*

im·mor·tal·ize (ĭ-môr′tl-īz′) *tr.v.* **im·mor·tal·ized, im·mor·tal·iz·ing, im·mor·tal·iz·es** To make immortal; give enduring fame to: *Longfellow's poem immortalizes the midnight ride of Paul Revere.*

im·mov·a·ble (ĭ-mo͞o′və-bəl) *adj.* **1.** Not capable of moving or of being moved: *Mountains are immovable objects.* **2.** Unyielding; steadfast: *an immovable purpose.* ❖ *n.* **immovables** Property, such as real estate, that cannot be moved. **—im·mov′a·bly** *adv.*

im·mune (ĭ-myo͞on′) *adj.* **1a.** Protected from disease naturally or by vaccination or inoculation: *I'm immune to chickenpox, since I had it when I was young.* **b.** Relating to or producing immunity: *Immune cells help the body resist infections.* **2.** Protected; guarded; safe: *No country is immune from economic problems.* **3.** Not affected by something; unresponsive: *I am immune to your charms.* [From Middle English, from Latin *immūnis*.]

immune response *n.* A response of the immune system to bacteria, viruses, or other substances that are foreign to the body. The immune response usually involves the formation of antibodies.

ă	pat	ôr	core
ā	pay	oi	boy
âr	care	ou	out
ä	father	o͝o	took
ĕ	pet	o͝or	lure
ē	be	o͞o	boot
ĭ	pit	ŭ	cut
ī	bite	ûr	urge
îr	pier	th	thin
ŏ	pot	*th*	this
ō	toe	zh	vision
ô	paw	ə	about

immune system *n.* The system in humans and other animals that enables the body to resist disease, especially by producing white blood cells and antibodies.

im·mu·ni·ty (ĭ-**myo͞o′**nĭ-tē) *n., pl.* **im·mu·ni·ties 1.** The ability of an organism to resist disease, especially through the production of antibodies. **2.** Freedom from certain duties, penalties, or restrictions: *Diplomatic immunity protects ambassadors from being prosecuted for most crimes.* **3.** A condition conferred upon a contestant that prevents him or her from being eliminated from a competition for a certain time period: *The winner of the challenge was given immunity for the following challenge.*

im·mu·ni·za·tion (ĭm′yə-nĭ-**zā′**shən) *n.* **1.** A vaccination: *Have you received your immunization for measles?* **2.** The production of immunity: *rates of immunization in rural areas; undertook a program of immunization.*

im·mu·nize (**ĭm′**yə-nīz′) *tr.v.* **im·mu·nized, im·mu·niz·ing, im·mu·niz·es** To produce immunity in, as by vaccination: *The pediatrician immunized the infant against measles.*

im·mu·no·de·fi·cien·cy (ĭm′yə-nō-dĭ-**fĭsh′**ən-sē *or* ĭ-myo͞o′nō-dĭ-**fĭsh′**ən-sē) *n.* The inability to produce a normal immune response, usually as a result of a disease.

im·mu·nol·o·gy (ĭm′yə-**nŏl′**ə-jē) *n.* The scientific study of the structure and function of the immune system.

im·mure (ĭ-**myo͝or′**) *tr.v.* **im·mured, im·mur·ing, im·mures** To confine within walls; imprison.

im·mu·ta·ble (ĭ-**myo͞o′**tə-bəl) *adj.* Not subject to change; unchangeable: *the immutable laws of nature.* **—im·mu′ta·bil′i·ty, im·mu′ta·ble·ness** *n.* **—im·mu′ta·bly** *adv.*

imp (ĭmp) *n.* **1.** A mischievous child. **2.** A small demon or devil.

imp. *abbr.* An abbreviation of: **1.** imperative. **2.** imperfect. **3.** imported.

im·pact (**ĭm′**păkt′) *n.* **1.** The action of one body striking against another; collision: *The impact of the meteorite left a large crater.* **2.** The effect or impression of something: *the impact of science on modern society; the emotional impact of a poem.* ❖ *tr.v.* **im·pact·ed, im·pact·ing, im·pacts 1.** To strike or collide with forcefully: *The meteorite impacted the earth's surface.* **2.** To have an effect or influence on: *The budget cuts will severely impact the public schools.* [From Latin *impāctus*, past participle of *impingere*, to push against.]

im·pact·ed (ĭm-**păk′**tĭd) *adj.* Wedged into the gum or bone so as not to be able to emerge properly. Used of a tooth: *impacted wisdom teeth.*

im·pair (ĭm-**pâr′**) *tr.v.* **im·paired, im·pair·ing, im·pairs** To diminish in strength, quantity, or quality; weaken: *An ear infection impaired my hearing for a week.* **—im·pair′ment** *n.*

im·pa·la (ĭm-**pä′**lə) *n.* An African antelope having a reddish-brown coat and long curved horns in the male, noted for its ability to leap high. [From Zulu *ím-pàlà*.]

im·pale (ĭm-**pāl′**) *tr.v.* **im·paled, im·pal·ing, im·pales 1.** To pierce with a sharp stake or point: *The salesclerk impaled the receipts on a spike.* **2.** To torture or kill by pushing onto a stake.

im·pal·pa·ble (ĭm-**păl′**pə-bəl) *adj.* **1.** Not perceptible to the touch; intangible: *impalpable shadows.* **2.** Difficult to define or pin down; vague: *There was an impalpable feeling of sadness in the music.* **—im·pal′pa·bil′i·ty** *n.* **—im·pal′pa·bly** *adv.*

im·pan·el (ĭm-**păn′**əl) *tr.v.* **im·pan·eled, im·pan·el·ing, im·pan·els** or **im·pan·elled, im·pan·el·ling, im·pan·els 1.** To enroll or place on a panel or list. **2.** To choose (a jury) from a list or lottery. **—im·pan′el·ment** *n.*

im·part (ĭm-**pärt′**) *tr.v.* **im·part·ed, im·part·ing, im·parts 1.** To give; bestow: *Bright sunlight imparted a cheerful feeling to the room.* **2.** To make known; disclose; reveal: *impart a secret.*

im·par·tial (ĭm-**pär′**shəl) *adj.* Not favoring either side; fair; unprejudiced: *Sports officials must be impartial in their judgments.* **—im′par·ti·al′i·ty** (ĭm′pär-shē-**ăl′**ĭ-tē) *n.* **—im·par′tial·ly** *adv.*

im·pass·a·ble (ĭm-**păs′**ə-bəl) *adj.* Impossible to travel across or over; not passable: *an impassable gorge.* **—im·pass′a·bil′i·ty** *n.* **—im·pass′a·bly** *adv.*

im·passe (**ĭm′**păs′) *n.* **1.** A road or passage that has no exit. **2.** A difficult situation that has no practical solution: *When members could not agree, the committee reached an impasse.*

im·pas·sioned (ĭm-**păsh′**ənd) *adj.* Filled with intense feeling; ardent: *an impassioned plea for human rights.*

im·pas·sive (ĭm-**păs′**ĭv) *adj.* Feeling or showing no emotion; calm: *The judge was impassive through all the lawyer's dramatic arguments.* **—im·pas′sive·ly** *adv.* **—im·pas′sive·ness** *n.*

im·pa·tience (ĭm-**pā′**shəns) *n.* The quality or condition of being impatient.

im·pa·tiens (ĭm-**pā′**shənz *or* ĭm-**pā′**shəns) *n., pl.* **impa·tiens** Any of various garden plants that have colorful flowers and attractive leaves. [From Latin *impatiēns*, impatient (from the fact that the ripe pods burst open when touched).]

im·pa·tient (ĭm-**pā′**shənt) *adj.* **1.** Unable to wait patiently or endure irritation: *When the line for tickets did not move, she grew impatient and left.* **2.** Expressing or produced by impatience: *an impatient answer.* **3.** Restlessly eager: *We were impatient to go home.* **—im·pa′tient·ly** *adv.*

im·peach (ĭm-**pēch′**) *tr.v.* **im·peached, im·peach·ing, im·peach·es 1.** To charge (a public official) formally with misconduct in office: *The president of the United States can be impeached only before Congress.* **2.** To challenge or discredit; attack: *Scientists impeached the report's accuracy.* [From Middle English *empechen*, to impede, accuse, from Late Latin *impedicāre*, to entangle, from Latin *pedica*, fetter.] **—im·peach′ment** *n.*

im·pec·ca·ble (ĭm-**pĕk′**ə-bəl) *adj.* Having no flaws; faultless: *has impeccable table manners.* See Synonyms at **perfect.** [From Latin *impeccābilis* : *in-*, not + *peccāre*, to sin.] **—im·pec′ca·bly** *adv.*

im·pe·cu·ni·ous (ĭm′pĭ-**kyo͞o′**nē-əs) *adj.* Lacking money; penniless. **—im′pe·cu′ni·ous·ly** *adv.*

im·pede (ĭm-**pēd′**) *tr.v.* **im·ped·ed, im·ped·ing, im·pedes** To obstruct or slow down the movement or progress of; hinder: *Road repairs impeded traffic all summer. A lack of funds impeded the research.* [From Latin *impedīre*.]

im·ped·i·ment (ĭm-**pĕd′**ə-mənt) *n.* **1.** Something that impedes or encumbers progress; a hindrance or obstruction: *Youth is no impediment to success in sports and music.* **2.** A physical defect that prevents clear speech.

im·pel (ĭm-**pĕl′**) *tr.v.* **im·pelled, im·pel·ling, im·pels 1.** To urge to action; drive; spur: *Their curiosity impelled them to investigate the noise.* **2.** To drive forward; propel: *A strong current impelled the little boat toward the rocks.* [From Middle English *impellen*, from Latin *impellere* : *in-*, against + *pellere*, to drive.]

im·pend·ing (ĭm-**pĕn′**dĭng) *adj.* About to occur; imminent: *The principal has planned for our teacher's impending retirement.*

im·pen·e·tra·ble (ĭm-**pĕn′**ĭ-trə-bəl) *adj.* **1.** Impossible to penetrate or enter: *an impenetrable fortress.* **2.** Impossible to understand; incomprehensible: *an impenetrable mystery.* **—im·pen′e·tra·bly** *adv.*

im·pen·i·tent (ĭm-**pĕn′**ĭ-tənt) *adj.* Showing no sorrow for having done something wrong; unrepentant. **—im·pen′i·tent·ly** *adv.*

im·per·a·tive (ĭm-**pĕr′**ə-tĭv) *adj.* **1.** Necessary or urgent: *It is imperative that we arrive on time.* **2.** Relating to the mood of a verb that expresses a command, order, or

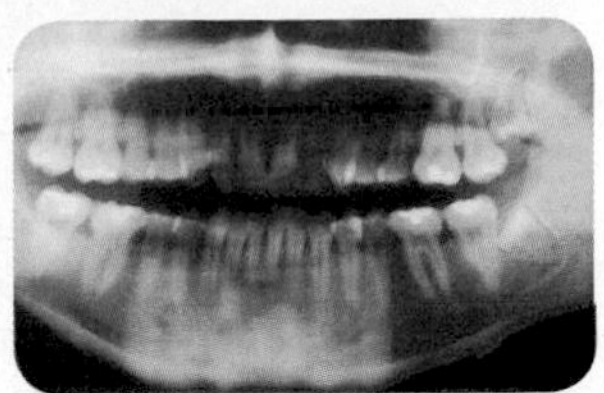

impacted
x-ray of impacted wisdom teeth (highlighted in pink)

impala

WRITERS CHOOSE THEIR WORDS

Throughout the country was the feeling of **impending** evil. It was as if some unknown terror would come out of the deep shadows.

—Marie McSwigan
Snow Treasure

WRITERS CHOOSE THEIR WORDS

The children stood, mouths open, as a stretcher appeared at Mrs. Sharpe's door. The old woman was neatly strapped in under a mound of blankets. . . . "Stop, you carriers! I want to speak with the children. I know them." Mrs. Sharpe's **imperious** tone brought everyone to a standstill.

—Blue Balliett
Chasing Vermeer

ă	pat	ôr	core
ā	pay	oi	boy
âr	care	ou	out
ä	father	ŏŏ	took
ĕ	pet	ŏŏr	lure
ē	be	ōō	boot
ĭ	pit	ŭ	cut
ī	bite	ûr	urge
îr	pier	th	thin
ŏ	pot	*th*	this
ō	toe	zh	vision
ô	paw	ə	about

request. For example, *do* in "Please do it!" and *go* in "Go at once!" are in the imperative mood. ❖ *n.* **1.** Something that is necessary or urgent: *Gaining control of the river was a military imperative.* **2a.** The imperative mood. **b.** A verb form in the imperative mood. [From Middle English *imperatif*, from Late Latin *imperātīvus*, from Latin *imperāre*, to command.] **—im·per′a·tive·ly** *adv.*

im·per·cep·ti·ble (ĭm′pər-**sĕp′**tə-bəl) *adj.* Impossible or difficult to perceive or feel: *an imperceptible difference; the imperceptible movement of the stars overhead.* **—im′per·cep′ti·bil′i·ty** *n.* **—im′per·cep′ti·bly** *adv.*

im·per·fect (ĭm-**pûr′**fĭkt) *adj.* **1.** Not perfect; having faults or defects. **2.** Relating to the imperfect tense. ❖ *n.* **1.** The imperfect tense. **2.** A verb in the imperfect tense. **—im·per′fect·ly** *adv.*

im·per·fec·tion (ĭm′pər-**fĕk′**shən) *n.* **1.** The condition or quality of being imperfect: *human imperfection.* **2.** A defect; a fault or flaw: *scratches and other imperfections in the surface of the table.*

imperfect tense *n.* A verb tense that expresses incomplete or continuous action, especially in the past.

im·pe·ri·al (ĭm-**pîr′**ē-əl) *adj.* Relating to an empire, emperor, or empress: *imperial Rome; the imperial court of Kublai Khan.* **—im·pe′ri·al·ly** *adv.*

im·pe·ri·al·ism (ĭm-**pîr′**ē-ə-lĭz′əm) *n.* **1.** The extension of a nation's authority by acquiring foreign territories or by establishing economic and political dominance over other nations. **2.** A political doctrine or system promoting the dominance of one nation over others in this manner.

im·pe·ri·al·ist (ĭm-**pîr′**ē-ə-lĭst) *n.* A person who believes in or practices imperialism. ❖ *adj.* Relating to or supporting imperialism.

im·pe·ri·al·is·tic (ĭm-pîr′ē-ə-**lĭs′**tĭk) *adj.* Relating to imperialism or imperialists. **—im·pe′ri·al·is′ti·cal·ly** *adv.*

im·per·il (ĭm-**pĕr′**əl) *tr.v.* **im·per·iled, im·per·il·ing, im·per·ils** or **im·per·illed, im·per·il·ling, im·per·ils** To put into peril; endanger: *Pollution imperils the health of the shellfish in the bay.*

im·pe·ri·ous (ĭm-**pîr′**ē-əs) *adj.* Arrogant; overbearing; domineering: *The boss's imperious treatment of the workers caused many to quit.* **—im·pe′ri·ous·ly** *adv.* **—im·pe′ri·ous·ness** *n.*

im·per·ish·a·ble (ĭm-**pĕr′**ĭ-shə-bəl) *adj.* Not perishable: *imperishable food; imperishable hopes.*

im·per·ma·nent (ĭm-**pûr′**mə-nənt) *adj.* Not lasting or durable.

im·per·me·a·ble (ĭm-**pûr′**mē-ə-bəl) *adj.* Impossible to permeate, as by a liquid or gas: *an impermeable raincoat; an impermeable cell wall.*

im·per·son·al (ĭm-**pûr′**sə-nəl) *adj.* **1.** Not referring to or intended for any particular person: *The speaker's remarks were very general and impersonal.* **2.** Showing no emotion; impassive: *an aloof impersonal manner.* **3.** Not existing as a human personality: *A storm is an impersonal force and does not care where it goes.* **4.** Having no subject or having the indefinite *it* as subject. For example, *snow* in the construction *It is snowing* is an impersonal verb. **—im·per′son·al′i·ty** (ĭm-pûr′sə-**năl′**ĭ-tē) *n.* **—im·per′son·al·ly** *adv.*

im·per·son·ate (ĭm-**pûr′**sə-nāt′) *tr.v.* **im·per·son·at·ed, im·per·son·at·ing, im·per·son·ates 1.** To assume the character or appearance of: *He was arrested for impersonating a police officer.* **2.** To imitate the appearance, voice, and manner of: *an entertainer who impersonates Elvis Presley.* **—im·per′son·a′tion** *n.* **—im·per′son·a′tor** *n.*

im·per·ti·nence (ĭm-**pûr′**tn-əns) *n.* **1.** Rudeness; insolence: *I find your impertinence very annoying.* **2.** An impertinent act or statement. **3.** Irrelevance.

im·per·ti·nent (ĭm-**pûr′**tn-ənt) *adj.* **1.** Offensively disrespectful; rude: *The clerk's impertinent manner offended me.* **2.** Not pertinent; irrelevant: *The discussion was interrupted with many impertinent questions and remarks.* **—im·per′ti·nent·ly** *adv.*

im·per·turb·a·ble (ĭm′pər-**tûr′**bə-bəl) *adj.* Unshakably calm and collected: *The senator remained imperturbable even in the heat of the debate.* **—im′per·turb′a·bil′i·ty** *n.* **—im′per·turb′a·bly** *adv.*

im·per·vi·ous (ĭm-**pûr′**vē-əs) *adj.* **1.** Incapable of being penetrated: *A good raincoat should be impervious to water.* **2.** Incapable of being affected: *The racing driver seemed impervious to fear.* [From Latin *impervius* : *in-*, not + *per-*, through + *via*, way.] **—im·per′vi·ous·ly** *adv.*

im·pe·ti·go (ĭm′pĭ-**tī′**gō) *n.* A disease often affecting children, characterized by the formation of pimples and thick yellow crusts on the skin.

im·pet·u·os·i·ty (ĭm-pĕch′ōō-**ŏs′**ĭ-tē) *n., pl.* **im·pet·u·os·i·ties 1.** The quality or condition of being impetuous. **2.** An impetuous act.

im·pet·u·ous (ĭm-**pĕch′**ōō-əs) *adj.* **1.** Characterized by rash or hasty actions; impulsive: *This impetuous decision has brought disaster.* **2.** Marked by violent force or motion: *impetuous waves smashing against the pier.* [From Middle English, from Latin *impetus*, impetus.] **—im·pet′u·ous·ly** *adv.*

im·pe·tus (**ĭm′**pĭ-təs) *n., pl.* **im·pe·tus·es 1.** A driving force; a cause of action: *A sense of fairness is often the impetus for reform.* **2.** The force or energy exhibited by a moving body; momentum: *The impetus of the speeding train made it difficult to stop quickly.* [From Middle English *impetous*, rapid movement, from Latin *impetere*, to attack : *in-*, against + *petere*, to go towards, seek.]

im·pi·e·ty (ĭm-**pī′**ĭ-tē) *n., pl.* **im·pi·e·ties 1.** Lack of piety or reverence. **2.** An impious act.

im·pinge (ĭm-**pĭnj′**) *intr.v.* **im·pinged, im·ping·ing, im·ping·es 1.** To encroach; infringe; trespass: *Censorship impinges on our right of free speech.* **2.** To have an effect or influence: *Have your allergies impinged on your singing ability?* **3.** To collide; strike: *Light rays impinge on the eye.* [From Latin *impingere.*] **—im·pinge′ment** *n.* **—im·ping′er** *n.*

im·pi·ous (**ĭm′**pē-əs *or* ĭm-**pī′**əs) *adj.* Lacking reverence; not pious. **—im′pi·ous·ly** *adv.* **—im′pi·ous·ness** *n.*

imp·ish (**ĭm′**pĭsh) *adj.* Relating to or befitting an imp; mischievous: *impish pranks; an impish grin.* **—imp′ish·ly** *adv.* **—imp′ish·ness** *n.*

im·plac·a·ble (ĭm-**plăk′**ə-bəl *or* ĭm-**plā′**kə-bəl) *adj.* Impossible to placate or appease; unyielding: *an implacable enemy; an implacable demand for justice.* **—im·plac′a·bil′i·ty** *n.* **—im·plac′a·bly** *adv.*

im·plant (ĭm-**plănt′**) *tr.v.* **im·plant·ed, im·plant·ing, im·plants 1.** To establish securely, as in the mind; instill: *The parents implanted a strong sense of values in their children.* **2.** To insert or set in firmly; fix: *implant fence posts in the ground.* **3.** To graft or set (a tissue or device) inside the body: *The doctors implanted a pacemaker in the patient's chest.* ❖ *n.* (**ĭm′**plănt′) A tissue or device that has been surgically grafted or inserted within the body. **—im′plan·ta′tion** (ĭm′plăn-**tā′**shən) *n.*

im·plau·si·ble (ĭm-**plô′**zə-bəl) *adj.* Difficult to believe; not plausible: *an implausible excuse.* **—im·plau′si·bly** *adv.*

im·ple·ment (**ĭm′**plə-mənt) *n.* A tool or piece of equipment used in doing a task: *Rakes and hoes are gardening implements.* ❖ *tr.v.* (**ĭm′**plə-mĕnt′) **im·ple·ment·ed, im·ple·ment·ing, im·ple·ments** To put into effect; carry out: *We need a plan in order to implement your idea.* [From Middle English, supplementary payment, from Latin *implēre*, to fill up.] **—im′ple·men·ta′tion** (ĭm′plə-mən-**tā′**shən) *n.*

im·pli·cate (**ĭm′**plĭ-kāt′) *tr.v.* **im·pli·cat·ed, im·pli·cat·ing, im·pli·cates** To show to be involved or connected with an activity, especially a crime: *The witness's testimony implicated several people in the scandal.* [From

Middle English *implicaten*, to convey a truth bound up in a fable, from Latin *implicāre*, to entangle, unite.]

im·pli·ca·tion (ĭm′plĭ-**kā′**shən) *n.* **1.** Something implied; an indirect indication: *Although he did not say so directly, his implication was that he'd lost his job.* **2.** The act of implying or the condition of being implied: *The writer's thoughts were conveyed more by implication than by direct statement.* **3.** The act of implicating or the condition of being implicated: *The suspect denied any implication in the affair.*

im·plic·it (ĭm-**plĭs′**ĭt) *adj.* **1.** Implied or understood without being directly expressed: *The threat of a lawsuit was implicit in the lawyer's letter.* **2.** Having no doubts; unquestioning: *We have implicit trust in your judgment.* **—im·plic′it·ly** *adv.* **—im·plic′it·ness** *n.*

im·plode (ĭm-**plōd′**) *v.* **im·plod·ed, im·plod·ing, im·plodes** —*intr.* **1.** To collapse inward violently: *The submarine imploded from the deep water pressure.* **2.** To undergo a sudden catastrophic failure: *His political career imploded after the scandal.* —*tr.* To cause to implode: *demolished the old skyscraper by imploding it.* **—im·plo′sion** (ĭm-**plō′**zhən) *n.*

im·plore (ĭm-**plôr′**) *tr.v.* **im·plored, im·plor·ing, im·plores 1.** To ask (a person) earnestly or anxiously; beseech: *The students implored the teacher to postpone the test.* **2.** To plead or beg for (something) earnestly: *The defendant implored the judge's mercy.* [From Latin *implōrāre*.]

im·ply (ĭm-**plī′**) *tr.v.* **im·plied, im·ply·ing, im·plies 1.** To say or convey indirectly; suggest without stating outright: *Our neighbor said something that implied he might be moving soon. The door was closed, which implied that mom was working.* **2.** To involve as a necessary part or consequence: *Life implies growth and eventual death.* [From Middle English *implien*, from Latin *implicāre*.] —SEE NOTE AT **infer.**

im·po·lite (ĭm′pə-**līt′**) *adj.* Not polite; discourteous: *an impolite remark.* **—im′po·lite′ly** *adv.* **—im′po·lite′ness** *n.*

im·port (ĭm-**pôrt′** *or* **ĭm′**pôrt′) *tr.v.* **im·port·ed, im·port·ing, im·ports 1.** To bring in (goods) from a foreign country for sale or use. **2.** To convey as a meaning; mean; signify: *The president's speech imported a major change in the country's foreign policy.* ❖ *n.* (**ĭm′**pôrt′) **1.** Something imported for sale or use. **2.** The act of importing; importation: *The import of fruits and vegetables is strictly regulated.* **3.** Importance; significance: *an event of enormous import.* **4.** Meaning; significance: *Since they found its import unclear, I tried again to explain my letter.*

im·por·tance (ĭm-**pôr′**tns) *n.* The quality or condition of being important; significance: *The trainer stressed the importance of regular workouts.*

im·por·tant (ĭm-**pôr′**tnt) *adj.* **1.** Marked by or having great value, significance, or influence: *Coffee is an important crop in South America.* **2.** Having high social rank or influence; prominent: *government leaders and other important people.* **3.** Believing or acting as if one has high social rank or influence: *Some guests strutted about the party in an important manner.* **—im·por′tant·ly** *adv.*

im·por·ta·tion (ĭm′pôr-**tā′**shən) *n.* **1.** The act of importing, especially as a business: *importation of cars and TVs from Japan.* **2.** Something imported; an import: *Many fine shoes are importations from Italy.*

im·port·er (ĭm-**pôr′**tər) *n.* A person, company, or country that imports goods: *Japan is a large importer of North American timber.*

im·por·tu·nate (ĭm-**pôr′**chə-nĭt) *adj.* Annoyingly persistent in pressing a request or demand: *importunate letters and phone calls from fundraisers.* **—im·por′tu·nate·ly** *adv.* **—im·por′tu·nate·ness** *n.*

im·por·tune (ĭm′pôr-**to͞on′** *or* ĭm-**pôr′**chən) *tr.v.* **im·por·tuned, im·por·tun·ing, im·por·tunes** To beset with frequent requests; ask insistently: *We importuned the management to locate the factory in our town.* **—im′·por·tu′ni·ty** *n.*

im·pose (ĭm-**pōz′**) *v.* **im·posed, im·pos·ing, im·pos·es** —*tr.* **1.** To place (a burden or obligation) on a person: *impose a tax; impose a punishment.* **2.** To bring about by exercising authority; force to prevail: *The United Nations imposed peace on the warring countries.* **3.** To force (oneself) upon another or others: *Our visitors have imposed themselves on us for too long.* —*intr.* To force oneself upon another or others; take unfair advantage: *We don't mean to impose, but could we stay for dinner?* ◆ **impose on** or **impose upon** To take advantage of: *The guests imposed on the good nature of their host by asking to borrow the car.* [From Middle English *imposen*, from Old French *imposer*, from Latin *impōnere*, to place upon.] **—im·pos′er** *n.* —SEE NOTE AT **compose.**

im·pos·ing (ĭm-**pō′**zĭng) *adj.* Impressive, as in size, power, or accomplishment: *an imposing statue; an imposing array of skills.* See Synonyms at **grand. —im·pos′ing·ly** *adv.*

im·po·si·tion (ĭm′pə-**zĭsh′**ən) *n.* **1.** The act of imposing: *the imposition of new taxes.* **2.** Something imposed, such as a tax, burden, or obligation: *The Colonists resented such impositions as the tax on imported tea.* **3.** An unfair demand upon someone's time, friendship, or hospitality: *These daily requests for help have become an imposition.*

im·pos·si·bil·i·ty (ĭm-pŏs′ə-**bĭl′**ĭ-tē) *n., pl.* **im·pos·si·bil·i·ties 1.** The quality or condition of being impossible: *The impossibility of being in two places at once.* **2.** Something that is impossible: *I found being a member of the swimming team and singing in the glee club to be an impossibility.*

im·pos·si·ble (ĭm-**pŏs′**ə-bəl) *adj.* **1.** Not capable of happening or existing: *A square circle is impossible.* **2.** Not capable of being accomplished: *an impossible task.* **3.** Difficult to tolerate or deal with: *That dog is impossible!* **—im·pos′si·bly** *adv.*

im·post (**ĭm′**pōst′) *n.* Something, such as a tax or duty, that is imposed or levied.

im·pos·tor or **im·pos·ter** (ĭm-**pŏs′**tər) *n.* A person who deceives others by pretending to be someone else.

im·pos·ture (ĭm-**pŏs′**chər) *n.* Deception or fraud by the assumption of a false identity.

im·po·tence (**ĭm′**pə-təns) *n.* The quality or condition of being impotent.

im·po·tent (**ĭm′**pə-tənt) *adj.* **1.** Lacking strength, power, or effectiveness: *Loss of popular support left the government impotent to deal with the crisis.* **2.** Incapable of sexual intercourse because of an inability to achieve or sustain an erection. **—im′po·tent·ly** *adv.*

im·pound (ĭm-**pound′**) *tr.v.* **im·pound·ed, im·pound·ing, im·pounds 1.** To seize and hold in legal custody: *A judge can impound all records in a trial.* **2.** To capture and confine in a pound: *The city impounds stray dogs.* **3.** To collect (water) in a natural or artificial lake.

im·pov·er·ish (ĭm-**pŏv′**ər-ĭsh *or* ĭm-**pŏv′**rĭsh) *tr.v.* **im·pov·er·ished, im·pov·er·ish·ing, im·pov·er·ish·es 1.** To make very poor: *Bad harvests impoverished the family.* **2.** To use up the natural richness, strength, or resources of: *Excessive erosion can impoverish the soil.* **—im·pov′er·ish·ment** *n.*

im·pov·er·ished (ĭm-**pŏv′**ər-ĭsht *or* ĭm-**pŏv′**rĭsht) *adj.* Very poor: *hungry and impoverished citizens.*

im·prac·ti·ca·ble (ĭm-**prăk′**tĭ-kə-bəl) *adj.* Impossible to do or carry out: *an impracticable scheme to grow crops in Antarctica.* **—im·prac′ti·ca·bly** *adv.*

im·prac·ti·cal (ĭm-**prăk′**tĭ-kəl) *adj.* **1.** Unwise of foolish to do or carry out: *She suggested that we abandon our impractical plans.* **2.** Incapable of dealing well with practical matters: *an impractical dreamer.* **—im·prac′ti·cal′i·ty** (ĭm-prăk′tĭ-**kăl′**ĭ-tē) *n.*

im·pre·ca·tion (ĭm′prĭ-**kā′**shən) *n.* A curse.

implode
top to bottom: implosion of the Hilton Hotel in Hartford, Connecticut, in 1990

impressionism
Poppy Field, 1873, by Claude Monet (1840–1926)

imprint

ă	pat	ôr	core
ā	pay	oi	boy
âr	care	ou	out
ä	father	ŏŏ	took
ĕ	pet	ŏŏr	lure
ē	be	ōō	boot
ĭ	pit	ŭ	cut
ī	bite	ûr	urge
îr	pier	th	thin
ŏ	pot	*th*	this
ō	toe	zh	vision
ô	paw	ə	about

im·pre·cise (ĭm′prĭ-**sīs′**) *adj.* Not precise or clear: *an imprecise description.* **—im′pre·cise′ly** *adv.*

im·preg·na·ble (ĭm-**prĕg′**nə-bəl) *adj.* **1.** Impossible to capture or enter by force: *an impregnable fort.* **2.** Impossible to refute; firm: *an impregnable argument.* [From Middle English *imprenable,* from Old French : *in-,* not + *prendre,* to seize.] **—im·preg′na·bly** *adv.*

im·preg·nate (ĭm-**prĕg′**nāt) *tr.v.* **im·preg·nat·ed, im·preg·nat·ing, im·preg·nates 1.** To make pregnant. **2.** To fill completely; saturate: *impregnated the cotton ball with alcohol.* **—im′preg·na′tion** *n.*

im·pre·sa·ri·o (ĭm′prĭ-**sär′**ē-ō′ *or* ĭm′prĭ-**sâr′**ē-ō′) *n., pl.* **im·pre·sa·ri·os** A person who organizes, manages, or directs entertainment, such as operas, ballets, or concerts.

im·press[1] (ĭm-**prĕs′**) *tr.v.* **im·pressed, im·press·ing, im·press·es 1.** To have a strong, often favorable effect on the mind or feelings of: *The worker's performance impressed the manager.* **2.** To fix firmly in the mind, as by force or influence: *The coach impressed upon the team the importance of good defense.* **3.** To mark or stamp with pressure: *impress a design on soft clay.* ❖ *n.* (**ĭm′**prĕs′) **1.** The act of impressing. **2.** A mark or imprint made by pressure. [From Middle English *impressen,* to imprint, from Latin *impressus,* past participle of *imprimere,* to press into.] —SEE NOTE AT **pressure.**

im·press[2] (ĭm-**prĕs′**) *tr.v.* **im·pressed, im·press·ing, im·press·es 1.** To force (a person) to serve in the military. **2.** To seize (property): *During the war, the government impressed all foreign funds.* [From obsolete *imprest,* money paid for enlisting.]

im·pres·sion (ĭm-**prĕsh′**ən) *n.* **1.** A marked effect, image, or feeling that stays in the mind: *The new principal made a good impression on everyone.* **2.** A vague notion, memory, or feeling: *I have the impression that we've met before.* **3.** A mark or imprint made on a surface by pressure: *There was an impression left on the cushion where the dog had slept.* **4.** A humorous imitation of a person's speech and manner: *He gave impressions of movie stars.*

im·pres·sion·a·ble (ĭm-**prĕsh′**ə-nə-bəl) *adj.* Easily influenced or affected; suggestible: *The impressionable students were excited by their first trip outside the country.*

im·pres·sion·ism (ĭm-**prĕsh′**ə-nĭz′əm) *n.* **1.** often **Impressionism** A style of painting developed in France in the late 1800s that uses small brush strokes to give the impression of the natural light of a scene or object. **2.** A musical style of the late 1800s and early 1900s that uses unconventional harmonies and tonal effects to create an often dreamy or mysterious mood.

im·pres·sion·ist (ĭm-**prĕsh′**ə-nĭst) *n.* An artist or musician who uses impressionism. ❖ *adj.* Impressionistic: *an impressionist painting.*

im·pres·sion·is·tic (ĭm-prĕsh′ə-**nĭs′**tĭk) *adj.* Relating to impressionism or the impressionists.

im·pres·sive (ĭm-**prĕs′**ĭv) *adj.* Making a strong or vivid impression; commanding attention: *an impressive monument; an impressive science project.* **—im·pres′sive·ly** *adv.* **—im·pres′sive·ness** *n.*

im·print (ĭm-**prĭnt′**) *tr.v.* **im·print·ed, im·print·ing, im·prints 1.** To make (a mark or pattern) on a surface by pressing: *imprint a name with a rubber stamp.* **2.** To produce a mark on (a surface) by pressure. **3.** To establish firmly, as on the mind or memory: *Memories of childhood are often deeply imprinted on our minds.* ❖ *n.* (**ĭm′**prĭnt′) **1.** A mark or pattern made by pressing something on a surface: *the imprints in the sand left by the feet of bathers.* **2.** A marked influence or effect; an impression: *Spanish culture has left its imprint on the Southwestern states.*

im·pris·on (ĭm-**prĭz′**ən) *tr.v.* **im·pris·oned, im·pris·on·ing, im·pris·ons** To put in or as if in prison; confine. **—im·pris′on·ment** *n.*

im·prob·a·ble (ĭm-**prŏb′**ə-bəl) *adj.* Not probable; unlikely: *an improbable tale; an improbable victory.* **—im·prob′a·bil′i·ty** *n.* **—im·prob′a·bly** *adv.*

im·promp·tu (ĭm-**prŏmp′**to͞o) *adj.* Spoken or done with little or no preparation: *The mayor devised an impromptu reply to the unexpected question.* ❖ *adv.* With little or no preparation: *The president commented impromptu on the startling events.* ❖ *n.* Something made or done without rehearsal, as a musical composition or speech.

im·prop·er (ĭm-**prŏp′**ər) *adj.* **1.** Not conforming to accepted standards; incorrect: *an improper diet.* **2.** Not in keeping with circumstances or needs; unsuitable: *A swamp is an improper place to build a house.* **3.** Not conforming to standards of decency; unseemly: *It is improper to interrupt a speaker.* **—im·prop′er·ly** *adv.* **—im·prop′er·ness** *n.*

improper fraction *n.* A fraction in which the numerator is greater than or equal to the denominator. For example, ³⁄₂ and ²⁄₂ are improper fractions.

im·pro·pri·e·ty (ĭm′prə-**prī′**ĭ-tē) *n., pl.* **im·pro·pri·e·ties 1.** The quality or condition of being improper: *the impropriety of playing a radio in the library.* **2.** An improper act or expression.

im·prov (**ĭm′**prŏv′) *n. Informal* **1.** Improvisation: *practiced improv in acting class.* **2.** An improvised sketch or skit: *a funny improv about golf lessons.*

im·prove (ĭm-**pro͞ov′**) *v.* **im·proved, im·prov·ing, im·proves** —*tr.* To make better: *Taking lessons really improved my guitar skills.* —*intr.* To become or get better: *The patient improved after receiving treatment.* [From Middle English *improuen,* to enclose land for cultivation, from Anglo-Norman *emprouwer,* to turn to profit, from *prou,* profit.]

im·prove·ment (ĭm-**pro͞ov′**mənt) *n.* **1.** A change or addition that improves something: *A new kitchen was one of our improvements to the house.* **2.** The act or process of improving: *The student's homework shows great improvement.* **3.** A person or thing that is better than another: *This year's science course is an improvement over the one we had last year.*

im·prov·i·dent (ĭm-**prŏv′**ĭ-dənt) *adj.* Not planning or providing for the future; careless of one's resources: *Given our meager savings we cannot afford improvident expenditures.* **—im·prov′i·dence** *n.* **—im·prov′i·dent·ly** *adv.*

im·prov·i·sa·tion (ĭm-prŏv′ĭ-**zā′**shən *or* ĭm′prə-vĭ-**zā′**shən) *n.* **1.** The act or an instance of improvising: *a pianist famous for his brilliant improvisations.* **2.** Something improvised, such as a comedic skit.

im·pro·vise (**ĭm′**prə-vīz′) *v.* **im·pro·vised, im·pro·vis·ing, im·pro·vis·es** —*tr.* **1.** To invent, compose, or perform without preparation: *The actors improvised a set of scenes based on the audience's suggestions.* **2.** To make or provide on the spur of the moment from materials found nearby: *The hikers improvised a bridge out of fallen logs.* —*intr.* **1.** To invent, compose, or perform something on the spot: *The musicians finished by improvising on the main theme.* **2.** To make do with whatever materials are at hand: *If the tent pole breaks we'll have to improvise.* [From Latin *imprōvīsus,* unforeseen.] **—im′pro·vis′er** *n.*

im·pru·dent (ĭm-**pro͞od′**nt) *adj.* Not prudent; unwise. **—im·pru′dence** *n.* **—im·pru′dent·ly** *adv.*

im·pu·dence (**ĭm′**pyə-dəns) *n.* **1.** The quality of being impudent; insolence. **2.** An impudent act or behavior.

im·pu·dent (**ĭm′**pyə-dənt) *adj.* Rudely or arrogantly disrespectful; insolent: *The impudent student demanded to be assigned another instructor.* [From Middle English, from Latin *impudēns* : *in-,* not + *pudēre,* to be ashamed.] **—im′pu·dent·ly** *adv.*

im·pugn (ĭm-**pyo͞on′**) *tr.v.* **im·pugned, im·pugn·ing, im·pugns** To challenge as false or questionable; cast doubt on: *How dare you impugn my honesty?*

im·pulse (ĭm′pŭls′) *n.* **1.** A driving force: *Customer complaints provided the impulse for the company to improve its product.* **2.** A strong motivation; a drive or instinct: *Most animals have a natural impulse to care for their young.* **3.** A sudden wish or urge: *We had to control our impulse to giggle during the lecture. I try not to buy things on impulse.* **4.** A surge of electrical power in one direction. **5.** A nerve impulse. [From Latin *impulsus,* from *impellere,* to impel.]

im·pul·sion (ĭm-pŭl′shən) *n.* **1.** The act of impelling or the condition of being impelled. **2.** An impelling force; a thrust. **3.** Motion produced by an impelling force; momentum. **4.** A sudden wish or urge; an impulse.

im·pul·sive (ĭm-pŭl′sĭv) *adj.* **1.** Tending to act on impulse rather than careful thought: *An impulsive shopper usually doesn't find the best bargains.* **2.** Motivated or caused by impulse: *The wealthy industrialist was given to impulsive acts of generosity.* **—im·pul′sive·ly** *adv.* **—im·pul′sive·ness** *n.*

im·pu·ni·ty (ĭm-pyōō′nĭ-tē) *n.* Freedom from punishment, harm, or injury: *Did they really expect to break the law with impunity?* [From Latin *impūne,* without punishment.]

im·pure (ĭm-pyŏŏr′) *adj.* **im·pur·er, im·pur·est 1.** Not pure or clean; contaminated: *People were sickened from drinking the impure water.* **2.** Mixed with other substances often of lower value; adulterated: *impure gold.* **3.** Immoral or sinful: *The Puritans viewed gambling as impure.* **—im·pure′ly** *adv.*

im·pu·ri·ty (ĭm-pyŏŏr′ĭ-tē) *n., pl.* **im·pu·ri·ties 1.** The quality or condition of being impure. **2.** A substance that makes another substance impure: *The treatment plant filters all the impurities out of our water.*

im·pute (ĭm-pyōōt′) *tr.v.* **im·put·ed, im·put·ing, im·putes** To assign the blame or credit for (something); attribute: *I impute my mistakes to my own carelessness.* [From Middle English *imputen,* from Latin *imputāre.*] **—im′pu·ta′tion** (ĭm′pyōō-tā′shən) *n.*

in[1] (ĭn) *prep.* **1a.** Within the confines or area of; inside: *The students are all in the classroom.* **b.** From outside to a point within; into: *couldn't get in the house.* **2.** Within the time of; after: *I will finish in an hour.* **3.** To or at the condition or situation of: *in good health.* **4.** Wearing; clothed by: *in a bathing suit.* **5.** Having the activity or function of: *a career in politics.* **6.** With the purpose of; for: *follow in pursuit.* **7.** Made with or through the medium of: *a note written in Spanish.* **8.** With reference to; as to: *10 feet in length.* **9.** Among; out of: *One person in five can play a musical instrument.* ❖ *adv.* **1.** To or toward the inside: *coming in out of the rain.* **2.** To or toward a goal: *The researchers are closing in on a cure.* **3.** So as to score, as by crossing home plate in baseball: *runs driven in.* **4.** Within a place, as of business or residence: *Is the doctor in? The water is cold and the children won't be in long.* **5.** So as to be available or under one's control: *the evidence is now in.* **6.** So as to include: *Did you fold the egg whites in?* **7.** So as to occupy a position of success or favor: *was voted in.* ❖ *adj.* **1.** Located inside; inner. **2.** *Informal* Fashionable; popular; prestigious: *Short haircuts are in.* **3.** Having influence or power: *The in government was made up of a coalition of parties.* **4.** Incoming; inward: *the in bus.* ❖ *n.* **1.** *Informal* A means of access or influence: *the musician has an in with the conductor.* **2.** A person having power or influence: *The ins are always at an advantage over the outs.* ◆ **in for** About to get or have: *We're in for a cold winter.* **in on** Informed about; participating in: *was in on the scheme.* **ins and outs** The details of an activity or process: *had to learn the ins and outs of local politics.* **in that** For the reason that; since: *Their arguments are unconvincing in that their reasons are so weak.* [From Old English.]

❑ *These sound alike:* **in**[1] (inside), **inn** (hotel).

in[2] or **in.** *abbr.* An abbreviation of inch.

In The symbol for the element **indium.**

IN *abbr.* An abbreviation of Indiana.

in–[1] or **il–** or **im–** or **ir–** *pref.* A prefix that means not: *inaccurate; illegible; immoral; irresponsible.* —SEE NOTE.

in–[2] or **il–** or **im–** or **ir–** *pref.* A prefix that means **1.** in, within, or into: *inbound; infield.* **2.** Variant of **en–**[1]. —SEE NOTE.

in·a·bil·i·ty (ĭn′ə-bĭl′ĭ-tē) *n.* Lack of ability or means: *inability to sleep; inability to pay the rent.*

in·ac·ces·si·ble (ĭn′ăk-sĕs′ə-bəl) *adj.* Not accessible; unapproachable: *an inaccessible cave high on the cliff.* **—in′ac·ces′si·bly** *adv.*

in·ac·cu·ra·cy (ĭn-ăk′yər-ə-sē) *n., pl.* **in·ac·cu·ra·cies 1.** The quality or condition of being inaccurate: *The report was criticized for its inaccuracy.* **2.** An error; a mistake: *many inaccuracies in their hasty observations.*

in·ac·cu·rate (ĭn-ăk′yər-ĭt) *adj.* Mistaken or incorrect; not accurate: *an inaccurate answer; an inaccurate description.* **—in·ac′cu·rate·ly** *adv.*

in·ac·tion (ĭn-ăk′shən) *n.* Lack or absence of action.

in·ac·tive (ĭn-ăk′tĭv) *adj.* Not active; not functioning; idle: *an inactive volcano; an inactive life.* **—in·ac′tive·ly** *adv.*

in·ad·e·qua·cy (ĭn-ăd′ĭ-kwə-sē) *n., pl.* **in·ad·e·qua·cies 1.** The quality or condition of being inadequate: *a feeling of inadequacy in math class.* **2.** A failing or lack: *my inadequacies as a musician.*

in·ad·e·quate (ĭn-ăd′ĭ-kwĭt) *adj.* Not enough; insufficient: *We lost the gymnastics competition because of inadequate practice.* **—in·ad′e·quate·ly** *adv.*

in·ad·mis·si·ble (ĭn′əd-mĭs′ə-bəl) *adj.* Not admissible: *Inadmissible evidence cannot be used in a trial.* **—in′ad·mis′si·bil′i·ty** *n.*

in·ad·ver·tent (ĭn′əd-vûr′tnt) *adj.* **1.** Not intended; unintentional: *an inadvertent error in the bill.* **2.** Not paying attention; careless: *The inadvertent captain ran the boat aground.* **—in′ad·ver′tence** *n.*

in·ad·vis·a·ble (ĭn′əd-vī′zə-bəl) *adj.* Not recommended; unwise: *It is inadvisable to swim out past the reef.* **—in′ad·vis′a·bil′i·ty** *n.*

in·al·ien·a·ble (ĭn-āl′yə-nə-bəl *or* ĭn-ā′lē-ə-nə-bəl) *adj.* Impossible to give up or take away: *Life and liberty are two of the inalienable rights listed in the Declaration of Independence.* **—in·al′ien·a·bly** *adv.*

in·ane (ĭn-ān′) *adj.* **in·an·er, in·an·est** Lacking sense or substance: *an inane comment.* [From Latin *inānis,* empty.] **—in·ane′ly** *adv.*

in·an·i·mate (ĭn-ăn′ə-mĭt) *adj.* **1.** Not living: *A stone is an inanimate object.* **2.** Belonging to the class of nouns that stand for nonliving things: *The word "car" is inanimate; the word "dog" is animate.*

in·an·i·ty (ĭ-năn′ĭ-tē) *n., pl.* **in·an·i·ties 1.** The quality or condition of being inane. **2.** Something inane, especially a meaningless statement.

in·ap·pli·ca·ble (ĭn-ăp′lĭ-kə-bəl *or* ĭn′ə-plĭk′ə-bəl) *adj.* Not applicable: *Speed limits are inapplicable to emergency vehicles.* **—in·ap′pli·ca·bil′i·ty** *n.*

in·ap·pre·cia·ble (ĭn′ə-prē′shə-bəl) *adj.* Too small to be noticed or to make a significant difference; negligible: *inappreciable changes in temperature.* **—in′ap·pre′cia·bly** *adv.*

in·ap·pro·pri·ate (ĭn′ə-prō′prē-ĭt) *adj.* Not appropriate to the occasion; unsuitable: *behavior that was inappropriate to the classroom.* **—in′ap·pro′pri·ate·ly** *adv.* **—in′ap·pro′pri·ate·ness** *n.*

in·apt (ĭn-ăpt′) *adj.* **1.** Inappropriate: *an inapt remark.* **2.** Inept. **—in·apt′ly** *adv.* **—in·apt′ness** *n.*

in·ap·ti·tude (ĭn-ăp′tĭ-tōōd′) *n.* **1.** Inappropriateness; unfitness. **2.** Lack of talent or skill; ineptitude.

in·ar·tic·u·late (ĭn′är-tĭk′yə-lĭt) *adj.* **1.** Uttered without

WORD BUILDING

in–[1] The basic meaning of the prefix **in–**[1] is "not." Thus *inactive* means "not active." *In–*[1] is related to and sometimes confused with the prefix *un–*[1], which also means "not." In fact, sometimes *in–*[1] is used interchangeably with *un–*[1], as when *incommunicative* is used instead of *uncommunicative.* Before the consonants *l* and *r, in–*[1] becomes *il–* and *ir–* respectively: *illogical, irregular.* Before the consonants *b, m,* and *p, in–*[1] becomes *im–*: *imbalanced, immeasurable, impossible.* For more information, see Note at **in–**[2].

WORD BUILDING

in–[2] Although **in–**[1] and **in–**[2] are both from Latin, they are not related to each other. The basic meaning of *in–*[2] is "in, within, or into." For example, *inlay* means "to set something in something else." *In–*[2] is also a form of the prefix *en–.* And in pairs such as *enclose/inclose, enquire/inquire, ensure/insure,* the two prefixes can be used somewhat interchangeably. As with the prefix *in–*[1], before the consonants *l* and *r, in–*[2] becomes *il–* and *ir–.* And before the consonants *b, m,* and *p, in–*[2] becomes *im–.*

inauguration
swearing-in ceremony of Barack Obama on January 20, 2009

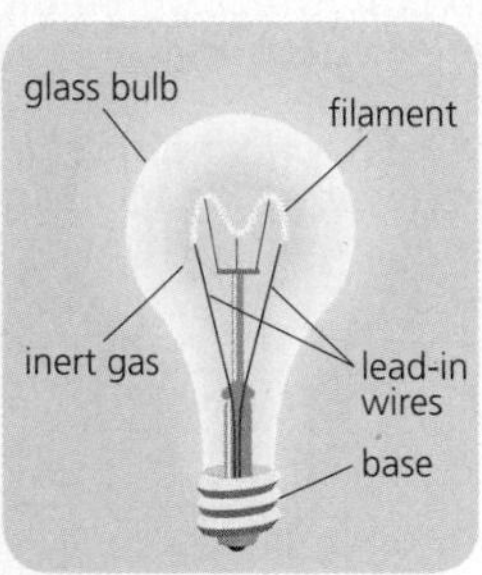

incandescent light

the use of normal words or syllables: *an inarticulate cry.* **2.** Unable to speak; speechless: *I was inarticulate with astonishment.* **3.** Unable to speak clearly or effectively: *He's too inarticulate to be a successful politician.* **4.** Unexpressed: *inarticulate sorrow.* **—in′ar·tic′u·late·ly** *adv.* **—in′ar·tic′u·late·ness** *n.*

in·ar·tis·tic (ĭn′är-tĭs′tĭk) *adj.* Lacking taste or interest in art. **—in′ar·tis′ti·cal·ly** *adv.*

in·as·much as (ĭn′əz-mŭch′) *conj.* Because of the fact that; since: *I decided to go swimming inasmuch as it was hot and sunny.*

in·at·ten·tion (ĭn′ə-tĕn′shən) *n.* Lack of attention, notice, or regard; heedlessness: *careless mistakes caused by inattention to details.*

in·at·ten·tive (ĭn′ə-tĕn′tĭv) *adj.* Showing a lack of attention; negligent: *sleepy and inattentive.* **—in′at·ten′tive·ly** *adv.* **—in′at·ten′tive·ness** *n.*

in·au·di·ble (ĭn-ô′də-bəl) *adj.* Impossible to hear: *Dogs can hear sounds that are inaudible to most humans.* **—in·au′di·bly** *adv.*

in·au·gu·ral (ĭn-ô′gyər-əl) *adj.* **1.** Relating to an inauguration: *the president's inaugural address.* **2.** First; initial: *an inaugural flight of a new airliner.* ❖ *n.* **1.** An inaugural speech, especially that of the president of the United States. **2.** An inaugural ceremony or activity.

in·au·gu·rate (ĭn-ô′gyə-rāt′) *tr.v.* **in·au·gu·rat·ed, in·au·gu·rat·ing, in·au·gu·rates 1.** To install in office by a formal ceremony: *inaugurate a president.* **2.** To open for use with a ceremony; dedicate: *inaugurate a new office building.* **3.** To begin or start officially: *The governor inaugurated a new policy to combat air pollution.* [From Latin *inaugurāre* : *in-*, intensive prefix + *augurāre*, to augur (from *augur*, soothsayer).]

in·au·gu·ra·tion (ĭn-ô′gyə-rā′shən) *n.* **1.** A formal ceremony installing a person in a position or office. **2.** A formal beginning or introduction.

in·aus·pi·cious (ĭn′ô-spĭsh′əs) *adj.* Not auspicious; unfavorable: *Despite an inauspicious weather forecast, we went on the picnic.* **—in′aus·pi′cious·ly** *adv.* **—in′aus·pi′cious·ness** *n.*

in between *prep. & adv.* Between: *mortar in between the bricks; layers with a filling in between.*

in·board (ĭn′bôrd′) *adj.* **1.** In the hull or toward the center of a ship: *an inboard motor.* **2.** Close to the fuselage of an aircraft: *the left inboard engine.*

in·born (ĭn′bôrn′) *adj.* Existing naturally or by heredity rather than being learned through experience: *an inborn talent for music; the inborn ability of a dolphin to swim.*

in·bound (ĭn′bound′) *adj.* Inward bound; coming in: *an inbound ship; inbound traffic.*

in·box (ĭn′bŏks) *n.* **1.** An electronic folder for incoming emails or text messages. **2.** A container for incoming documents, located in or near one's work area.

in·bred (ĭn′brĕd′) *adj.* **1.** Produced by inbreeding: *an inbred dog.* **2.** Firmly fixed, as if by heredity; deep-seated: *an inbred optimism; a painter with an inbred sense of color.*

in·breed (ĭn′brēd′) *v.* **in·bred** (ĭn′brĕd′), **in·breed·ing, in·breeds** *—tr.* To breed by mating closely related individuals in each succeeding generation: *farmers who began inbreeding corn.* *—intr.* To mate or breed with a closely related individual: *plants that often inbreed.*

in·breed·ing (ĭn′brē′dĭng) *n.* The mating of closely related individuals in each succeeding generation.

Inc. *abbr.* An abbreviation of incorporated.

In·ca (ĭng′kə) *n., pl.* **Inca** or **In·cas** A member of the group of Quechuan peoples of highland Peru who established an empire from northern Ecuador to central Chile before being conquered by Spain in the 1500s. **—In′can** *adj.*

in·cal·cu·la·ble (ĭn-kăl′kyə-lə-bəl) *adj.* **1.** Too great or too large to be calculated or described; enormous: *an incalculable number of ants; caused incalculable damage.* **2.** Impossible to foresee. **—in·cal′cu·la·bil′i·ty** *n.* **—in·cal′cu·la·bly** *adv.*

in·can·des·cent (ĭn′kən-dĕs′ənt) *adj.* **1.** Heated to such a high temperature that it gives off light; glowing with heat. **2.** Shining brilliantly; very bright. [From Latin *incandēscere*, to begin to glow.] **—in′can·des′cence** *n.* **—in′can·des′cent·ly** *adv.*

incandescent light *n.* A device that produces light by the glow of a fine wire, or filament, heated by an electric current.

in·can·ta·tion (ĭn′kăn-tā′shən) *n.* **1.** A formula of words or sounds recited or chanted to cast a spell or perform magic. **2.** The act of reciting or chanting such a formula. [From Middle English *incantacioun*, from Latin *incantāre*, to enchant, cast a spell.]

in·ca·pa·ble (ĭn-kā′pə-bəl) *adj.* Lacking the necessary power or ability; not capable: *Humans are incapable of breathing on their own under water.* **—in·ca′pa·bil′i·ty** *n.*

in·ca·pac·i·tate (ĭn′kə-păs′ĭ-tāt′) *tr.v.* **in·ca·pac·i·tat·ed, in·ca·pac·i·tat·ing, in·ca·pac·i·tates** To deprive of power or ability; disable: *A knee injury incapacitated the wrestler.*

in·ca·pac·i·ty (ĭn′kə-păs′ĭ-tē) *n., pl.* **in·ca·pac·i·ties 1.** Inadequate strength or ability: *the incapacity of the small air conditioner to cool such a large space.* **2.** A disability or handicap.

in·car·cer·ate (ĭn-kär′sə-rāt′) *tr.v.* **in·car·cer·at·ed, in·car·cer·at·ing, in·car·cer·ates** To put in jail; imprison. [From Latin *carcer*, prison.] **—in·car′cer·a′tion** *n.*

in·car·nate (ĭn-kär′nĭt) *adj.* Embodied in flesh, especially in human form; personified: *a villain who seemed evil incarnate.* ❖ *tr.v.* (ĭn-kär′nāt′) **in·car·nat·ed, in·car·nat·ing, in·car·nates** To be a perfect embodiment of; personify: *a successful leader who incarnated the ideals of her time.*

in·car·na·tion (ĭn′kär-nā′shən) *n.* **1.** The taking on of bodily form by a supernatural being: *the incarnation of the devil in the form of a serpent.* **2. Incarnation** The Christian doctrine that the Son of God was conceived in the womb of Mary and that Jesus is both true God and true man. **3.** A person or thing thought to be the perfect example of a quality or idea. **4.** A period of time passed in a given bodily form or condition: *hopes for a better life in another incarnation.*

in·cau·tious (ĭn-kô′shəs) *adj.* Not cautious; rash: *an incautious decision to go hiking alone.* **—in·cau′tious·ly** *adv.* **—in·cau′tious·ness** *n.*

in·cen·di·ar·y (ĭn-sĕn′dē-ĕr′ē) *adj.* **1.** Causing or designed to cause fires: *an incendiary bomb.* **2.** Arousing anger or conflict; inflammatory: *an incendiary speech that riled up the mob.* ❖ *n., pl.* **in·cen·di·ar·ies** A bomb or explosive designed to cause fires.

in·cense[1] (ĭn-sĕns′) *tr.v.* **in·censed, in·cens·ing, in·cens·es** To make very angry; enrage: *The factual errors in the article incensed the editor.* [From Middle English *encensen*, from Latin *incēnsus*, set on fire.]

in·cense[2] (ĭn′sĕns′) *n.* **1.** A plant substance, such as a gum or resin, that is burned to produce a pleasant odor. **2.** The smoke or odor produced by the burning of such a substance. **3.** A pleasant smell: *the incense of flowers.* [From Middle English *encens*, from Latin *incēnsum*, from *incendere*, to set on fire.]

in·cen·tive (ĭn-sĕn′tĭv) *n.* Something that prompts action or effort; a stimulus: *Seeing his name in print is incentive enough for him to keep writing.* [From Middle English, from Late Latin *incentīvus*, inciting.]

in·cep·tion (ĭn-sĕp′shən) *n.* The beginning of something; a start: *The telephone has gone through many changes since its inception in 1876.*

in·ces·sant (ĭn-sĕs′ənt) *adj.* Continuing without inter-

ă	pat	ôr	core
ā	pay	oi	boy
âr	care	ou	out
ä	father	ŏŏ	took
ĕ	pet	ŏŏr	lure
ē	be	ōō	boot
ĭ	pit	ŭ	cut
ī	bite	ûr	urge
îr	pier	th	thin
ŏ	pot	*th*	this
ō	toe	zh	vision
ô	paw	ə	about

ruption; constant: *The incessant sound of the traffic made it hard to concentrate.* **—in·ces′sant·ly** *adv.*

in·cest (ĭn′sĕst′) *n.* Sexual relations between people who are so closely related that they cannot be legally married. [From Middle English *inceste*, from Latin *incestus*, impure.]

in·ces·tu·ous (ĭn-**sĕs′**cho͞o-əs) *adj.* **1.** Relating to or involving incest. **2.** Having committed incest.

inch (ĭnch) *n.* **1.** A unit of length equal to 1⁄12 of a foot (2.54 centimeters). See table at **measurement. 2.** A very small degree or amount: *The union would not yield an inch in its demands.* ❖ *intr.v.* **inched, inch·ing, inch·es** To move or proceed very slowly or by small degrees: *We are inching closer to an understanding of the origin of the universe.* ◆ **every inch** In every detail; entirely: *The actor looked every inch a pirate.* **inch by inch** Little by little; very gradually or slowly. **within an inch of** Almost to the point of; very near: *The team was within an inch of gaining the state championship.* [From Old English *ynce*, from Latin *ūncia*, one twelfth.]

inch·worm (**ĭnch′**wûrm′) *n.* A caterpillar that moves by drawing the rear of its body forward to form a loop and then stretching the front forward.

in·ci·dence (**ĭn′**sĭ-dəns) *n.* **1.** The rate or frequency with which something occurs: *The incidence of measles has fallen dramatically since vaccines became available.* **2.** The falling or striking of a ray or beam of light or other radiation upon a surface.

in·ci·dent (**ĭn′**sĭ-dənt) *n.* **1.** A particular occurrence; an event, especially one of minor importance: *I cannot remember all the incidents that happened in my childhood.* **2.** A disturbance or mishap: *The damaged plane managed to land without incident.* ❖ *adj.* Tending to happen at the same time; accompanying or related to something else: *His ankle injuries are incident to a career in basketball.* [From Middle English, from Old French, apt to happen, an incident, from Latin *incidere*, to happen, befall.]

in·ci·den·tal (ĭn′sĭ-**dĕn′**tl) *adj.* **1.** Occurring or likely to occur as a minor consequence; attendant: *Besides the costs of food and lodging there were many incidental expenses.* **2.** Happening unexpectedly: *an incidental encounter with an old friend.* ❖ *n.* A minor item or expense: *Do not spend our entire budget on mere incidentals.*

in·ci·den·tal·ly (ĭn′sĭ-**dĕn′**tl-ē) *adv.* **1.** Apart from the main subject; by the way: *Incidentally, what time is it?* **2.** As a minor matter: *She is a stockbroker and incidentally a runner.*

in·cin·er·ate (ĭn-**sĭn′**ə-rāt′) *tr.v.* **in·cin·er·at·ed, in·cin·er·at·ing, in·cin·er·ates** To destroy by burning; burn to ashes. [From Medieval Latin *incinerāre*, from Latin *cinis*, ashes.] **—in·cin′er·a′tion** *n.*

in·cin·er·a·tor (ĭn-**sĭn′**ə-rā′tər) *n.* A furnace or other device for burning rubbish.

in·cip·i·ent (ĭn-**sĭp′**ē-ənt) *adj.* Beginning to exist or appear: *The gathering clouds were the signs of an incipient storm.* **—in·cip′i·en·cy, in·cip′i·ence** *n.*

in·cise (ĭn-**sīz′**) *tr.v.* **in·cised, in·cis·ing, in·cis·es 1.** To cut into: *incise wood with a chisel.* **2.** To engrave into a surface; carve: *incise a design into leather.*

in·ci·sion (ĭn-**sĭzh′**ən) *n.* **1.** The act of incising: *the incision of a design.* **2.** A cut made into something, especially a surgical cut. [From Middle English *inscicioun*, from Latin *incīdere*, to cut into.]

in·ci·sive (ĭn-**sī′**sĭv) *adj.* Sharp and clear; penetrating: *The incisive analysis was clear and to the point.* **—in·ci′sive·ly** *adv.* **—in·ci′sive·ness** *n.*

in·ci·sor (ĭn-**sī′**zər) *n.* A tooth having a sharp edge adapted for cutting, located in mammals in the front of the mouth between the canine teeth.

in·cite (ĭn-**sīt′**) *tr.v.* **in·cit·ed, in·cit·ing, in·cites** To provoke; stir up; urge on: *The announcement of a cut in pay incited the workers to strike.* [From Middle English *enciten*, from Latin *incitāre*, to urge forward.] **—in·cite′ment** *n.*

incl. *abbr.* An abbreviation of: **1.** including. **2.** inclusive.

in·clem·ent (ĭn-**klĕm′**ənt) *adj.* **1.** Stormy; rough: *inclement weather.* **2.** Unmerciful; harsh: *the severe penalties of inclement justice.* **—in·clem′en·cy** *n.*

in·cli·na·tion (ĭn′klə-**nā′**shən) *n.* **1.** A natural tendency to be or act in a certain way: *Many people have an inclination to sleep late on weekends.* **2.** The act of inclining or the state of being inclined: *The inclination of the child's head suggested that she was tired.* **3.** A slant or slope: *the steep inclination of the roof.*

in·cline (ĭn-**klīn′**) *v.* **in·clined, in·clin·ing, in·clines** *—tr.* **1.** To cause (someone) to have a certain tendency or preference; dispose: *This book might incline you to change your mind on the issue. I am inclined to disagree with you.* **2.** To cause to lean, slant, or slope: *We inclined the boards against the side of the barn.* **3.** To cause to bend or bow: *The conductor inclined his head as a signal for us to get ready to play.* *—intr.* **1.** To slant or slope: *a road that inclines steeply.* **2.** To have a preference; tend: *I incline to a different view of the matter.* ❖ *n.* (**ĭn′**klīn′) A surface that slants; a slope: *The car skidded down the icy incline of the street.* [From Middle English *enclinen*, from Latin *inclīnāre*.]

inclined plane *n.* A plane surface, such as a ramp, set at an acute angle to a horizontal surface. It is a simple machine because it requires less force to slide or roll a load up the plane than to raise the load vertically.

inclined plane
Pushing a box up a gentle slope requires less effort than lifting it.

in·clude (ĭn-**klo͞od′**) *tr.v.* **in·clud·ed, in·clud·ing, in·cludes 1.** To have as a part or member; contain: *The museum's collection includes some masterpieces of modern art.* **2.** To put into a group, class, or total: *I included your whole family in my invitation.* [From Middle English *includen*, from Latin *inclūdere*, to enclose.]

in·clu·sion (ĭn-**klo͞o′**zhən) *n.* **1.** The act of including or the condition of being included: *the inclusion of a story in an anthology.* **2.** Something that is included: *a surprising inclusion in the list of Oscar nominees.*

in·clu·sive (ĭn-**klo͞o′**sĭv) *adj.* **1.** Taking everything into account; comprehensive: *The principal had an inclusive list of all the students in the school.* **2.** Including the specified endpoints as well as what is between them. For example, "ages 10 to 14, inclusive" refers to ages 10, 11, 12, 13, and 14. **—in·clu′sive·ly** *adv.* **—in·clu′sive·ness** *n.*

in·cog·ni·to (ĭn′kŏg-**nē′**tō *or* ĭn-**kŏg′**nĭ-tō′) *adv. & adj.* With one's identity hidden or disguised: *The movie star stayed at the hotel incognito.* [From Latin *incognitus*, unknown.]

in·co·her·ent (ĭn′kō-**hîr′**ənt) *adj.* **1.** Lacking order or logical connection; not coherent: *an incoherent jumble of confused thoughts.* **2.** Unable to think or express one's thoughts in a clear or orderly manner: *The delirious patient was incoherent and confused.* **—in′co·her′ence** *n.* **—in′co·her′ent·ly** *adv.*

in·com·bus·ti·ble (ĭn′kəm-**bŭs′**tə-bəl) *adj.* Incapable of burning. ❖ *n.* An incombustible material.

in·come (**ĭn′**kŭm′) *n.* The amount of money received for labor or services, from the sale of property or goods, or from financial investments: *One's monthly income is all the money one receives in a month.*

income tax *n.* A tax on the income of a person or business.

in·com·ing (**ĭn′**kŭm′ĭng) *adj.* **1.** Coming in or about to come in: *incoming mail.* **2.** About to take an office or position: *the incoming president.*

in·com·men·su·rate (ĭn′kə-**mĕn′**sər-ĭt *or* ĭn′kə-**mĕn′**-shər-ĭt) *adj.* **1.** Not corresponding in size or degree; inadequate: *The salary for the job is incommensurate with the responsibilities.* **2.** Impossible to measure. **—in′com·men′su·rate·ly** *adv.*

in·com·mu·ni·ca·ble (ĭn′kə-**myo͞o′**nĭ-kə-bəl) *adj.* Impossible to communicate: *He found his feelings were so complex as to be incommunicable.*

in·com·mu·ni·ca·do (ĭn′kə-myo͞o′nĭ-**kä′**dō) *adv. & adj.* Without the means or right of communicating with others: *The judge ordered the jurors to remain incommunicado until the trial was over.* [From Spanish *incomunicar*, to deny communication.]

in·com·pa·ra·ble (ĭn-**kŏm′**pər-ə-bəl) *adj.* **1.** Above all comparison; unsurpassed: *the incomparable value of an education.* **2.** Impossible to compare: *two theories of the origin of the universe that are so different as to be incomparable with each other.* **—in·com′pa·ra·bly** *adv.*

in·com·pat·i·ble (ĭn′kəm-**păt′**ə-bəl) *adj.* **1.** Not capable of existing in agreement or harmony with something else: *Speeding is incompatible with safe driving.* **2.** Not capable of living or working together happily or smoothly; antagonistic: *incompatible roommates.* **—in′com·pat′i·bil′i·ty** *n.* **—in′com·pat′i·bly** *adv.*

in·com·pe·tent (ĭn-**kŏm′**pĭ-tənt) *adj.* **1.** Not having adequate abilities or qualifications; incapable: *an apprentice mechanic who was incompetent to do complicated repairs.* **2.** Not qualified under the law: *The judge ruled that the defendant was incompetent to stand trial.* ❖ *n.* An incompetent person. **—in·com′pe·tence** *n.* **—in·com′pe·tent·ly** *adv.*

in·com·plete (ĭn′kəm-**plēt′**) *adj.* **1.** Not complete; unfinished: *The composer's last symphony is incomplete.* **2.** In football, not caught in bounds or intercepted: *an incomplete pass.* **—in′com·plete′ly** *adv.*

in·com·pre·hen·si·ble (ĭn′kŏm-prĭ-**hĕn′**sə-bəl *or* ĭn-kŏm′prĭ-**hĕn′**sə-bəl) *adj.* Difficult or impossible to understand: *an incomprehensible sentence.* **—in′com·pre·hen′si·bil′i·ty** *n.* **—in′com·pre·hen′si·bly** *adv.*

in·con·ceiv·a·ble (ĭn′kən-**sē′**və-bəl) *adj.* Difficult or impossible to understand or imagine: *It was inconceivable for the expedition to turn back when their goal was so close.* **—in′con·ceiv′a·bly** *adv.*

in·con·clu·sive (ĭn′kən-**klo͞o′**sĭv) *adj.* Not conclusive: *The inconclusive election returns left neither candidate sure of victory.* **—in′con·clu′sive·ly** *adv.* **—in′con·clu′sive·ness** *n.*

in·con·gru·i·ty (ĭn′kŏn-**gro͞o′**ĭ-tē) *n., pl.* **in·con·gru·i·ties 1.** The quality or condition of being incongruous. **2.** Something that is incongruous.

in·con·gru·ous (ĭn-**kŏng′**gro͞o-əs) *adj.* **1.** Lacking in harmony; incompatible or inconsistent: *The senator's vote was incongruous with her stated beliefs.* **2.** Not in keeping with what is correct, proper, or logical; inappropriate: *incongruous behavior.* **—in·con′gru·ous·ly** *adv.* **—in·con′gru·ous·ness** *n.*

in·con·se·quen·tial (ĭn-kŏn′sĭ-**kwĕn′**shəl) *adj.* Lacking importance; trivial: *an inconsequential and boring debate.* **—in·con′se·quen′tial·ly** *adv.*

in·con·sid·er·a·ble (ĭn′kən-**sĭd′**ər-ə-bəl) *adj.* Too small or unimportant to be worth attention or consideration; trivial. **—in′con·sid′er·a·bly** *adv.*

in·con·sid·er·ate (ĭn′kən-**sĭd′**ər-ĭt) *adj.* Not considerate; thoughtless: *It is inconsiderate to make noise while we're trying to read.* **—in′con·sid′er·ate·ly** *adv.* **—in′con·sid′er·ate·ness** *n.*

in·con·sis·ten·cy (ĭn′kən-**sĭs′**tən-sē) *n., pl.* **in·con·sis·ten·cies 1.** The quality or condition of being inconsistent. **2.** Something that is inconsistent: *inconsistencies in spelling.*

in·con·sis·tent (ĭn′kən-**sĭs′**tənt) *adj.* **1.** Not in agreement or harmony: *The witness's testimony was inconsistent with the facts.* **2.** Not steady or predictable; erratic: *a baseball team whose biggest problem was inconsistent pitching.* **3.** Lacking in logical relation; contradictory: *inconsistent principles.* **—in′con·sis′tent·ly** *adv.*

in·con·sol·a·ble (ĭn′kən-**sō′**lə-bəl) *adj.* Difficult or impossible to console: *The children were inconsolable at the loss of their pet.* **—in′con·sol′a·bly** *adv.*

in·con·spic·u·ous (ĭn′kən-**spĭk′**yo͞o-əs) *adj.* Not readily noticeable; not obvious: *Fortunately the stain on my shirt was in an inconspicuous spot.* **—in′con·spic′u·ous·ly** *adv.* **—in′con·spic′u·ous·ness** *n.*

in·con·stant (ĭn-**kŏn′**stənt) *adj.* Not constant or steady; changeable or fickle: *inconstant loyalties.* **—in·con′stan·cy** *n.* **—in·con′stant·ly** *adv.*

in·con·ti·nent (ĭn-**kŏn′**tə-nənt) *adj.* **1.** Not restrained, as in behavior: *incontinent rage.* **2.** Unable to keep normal control of urination or defecation. **—in·con′ti·nence** *n.*

in·con·tro·vert·i·ble (ĭn-kŏn′trə-**vûr′**tə-bəl *or* ĭn′kŏn-trə-**vûr′**tə-bəl) *adj.* Impossible to dispute; unquestionable: *incontrovertible evidence pointing to the suspect's guilt.* **—in·con′tro·vert′i·bly** *adv.*

in·con·ven·ience (ĭn′kən-**vēn′**yəns) *n.* **1.** The quality or condition of being inconvenient. **2.** Something that causes difficulty, trouble, or discomfort: *Lack of central heating is an inconvenience.* ❖ *tr.v.* **in·con·ven·ienced, in·con·ven·ienc·ing, in·con·ven·ienc·es** To cause inconvenience to; trouble; bother: *Road construction inconvenienced many drivers.*

in·con·ven·ient (ĭn′kən-**vēn′**yənt) *adj.* Not convenient; causing difficulty: *It is inconvenient to have no cafeteria in this building.* **—in′con·ven′ient·ly** *adv.*

in·cor·po·rate (ĭn-**kôr′**pə-rāt′) *tr.v.* **in·cor·po·rat·ed, in·cor·po·rat·ing, in·cor·po·rates 1.** To include as a part in a whole; combine with something else: *a new car that incorporates features of earlier models.* **2.** To form into a legal corporation: *incorporate a business.* [From Middle English *incorporaten*, from Late Latin *incorporāre*, to form into a body, from Latin *corpus*, body.]

in·cor·po·rat·ed (ĭn-**kôr′**pə-rā′tĭd) *adj.* Organized and maintained as a legal corporation: *an incorporated business.*

in·cor·po·re·al (ĭn′kôr-**pôr′**ē-əl) *adj.* Lacking material form or substance: *Spirits are incorporeal beings.* **—in′cor·po′re·al·ly** *adv.*

in·cor·rect (ĭn′kə-**rĕkt′**) *adj.* **1.** Not correct; faulty; wrong: *The test had many incorrect answers.* **2.** Inappropriate or improper: *incorrect dress for the occasion.* **—in′cor·rect′ly** *adv.* **—in′cor·rect′ness** *n.*

in·cor·ri·gi·ble (ĭn-**kôr′**ĭ-jə-bəl) *adj.* Incapable of being corrected or reformed: *an incorrigible habit.* ❖ *n.* A person who cannot be reformed. **—in·cor′ri·gi·bil′i·ty** *n.* **—in·cor′ri·gi·bly** *adv.*

in·cor·rupt·i·ble (ĭn′kə-**rŭp′**tə-bəl) *adj.* **1.** Incapable of being morally corrupted: *The honest judge is incorruptible.* **2.** Not subject to decay or rot: *Cedar is a nearly incorruptible wood.* **—in′cor·rupt′i·bil′i·ty** *n.* **—in′cor·rupt′i·bly** *adv.*

in·crease (ĭn-**krēs′**) *tr. & intr.v.* **in·creased, in·creas·ing, in·creas·es** To make or become greater or larger in size, number, or power: *Machines increase the rate at which goods are manufactured. The world's population increased rapidly over the last decade.* ❖ *n.* (**ĭn′**krēs′) **1.** The act of increasing; growth: *a steady increase in sales over the last two years.* **2.** The amount or rate by which something is increased: *a ten percent increase in tax rates.* ◆ **on the increase** Becoming greater or more frequent; increasing. [From Middle English *encresen*, from Latin *incrēscere*, to keep growing.] **—in·creas′ing·ly** *adv.*

SYNONYMS increase, expand, enlarge, extend These verbs mean to make greater or larger. **Increase,** the most general, often means to cause to grow steadily: *Better farming practices can help increase crop yields.* **Expand** means to increase in size, volume, or amount: *The pizza parlor expanded its delivery service to cover a wider area.* **Enlarge** means to make larger: *I like that photograph so much that I want to enlarge and frame it.* **Extend** often means to increase in length: *The transit authority extended the subway line to the suburbs.*
ANTONYM decrease

WRITERS CHOOSE THEIR WORDS

In general, Dewey was the best-behaved kitten I had ever seen. He never knocked books or displays off shelves. If I told him not to do something, he usually stopped. He was unfailingly kind to stranger and staffer alike. For a kitten, he was downright mellow. But he was absolutely **incorrigible** when it came to rubber bands. The cat would go anywhere and do anything to sink his teeth into a rubber band.

—Vicki Myron and Bret Witter
Dewey the Library Cat: A True Story

ă	pat	ôr	core
ā	pay	oi	boy
âr	care	ou	out
ä	father	o͝o	took
ĕ	pet	o͝or	lure
ē	be	o͞o	boot
ĭ	pit	ŭ	cut
ī	bite	ûr	urge
îr	pier	th	thin
ŏ	pot	*th*	this
ō	toe	zh	vision
ô	paw	ə	about

in·cred·i·ble (ĭn-**krĕd′**ə-bəl) *adj.* **1.** Astonishing; unbelievable: *The new plane flies at an incredible speed.* **2.** Hard to believe; implausible: *an incredible alibi.* **—in·cred′i·bly** *adv.*

in·cre·du·li·ty (ĭn′krĭ-**do͞o′**lĭ-tē) *n.* The state or quality of disbelief; doubt.

in·cred·u·lous (ĭn-**krĕj′**ə-ləs) *adj.* **1.** Disbelieving or doubtful; skeptical: *We were incredulous of the stories about flying saucers.* **2.** Expressive of disbelief or astonishment: *There were incredulous gasps at the gymnast's performance.* **—in·cred′u·lous·ly** *adv.*

in·cre·ment (**ĭn′**krə-mənt) *n.* **1.** An increase in number, size, amount, or extent: *The increment in sales made the company profitable.* **2.** An added amount, especially one of a series of regular additions: *The crowd grew by increments throughout the day.* [From Middle English, from Latin *incrēmentum*, from *incrēscere*, to increase.]

in·crim·i·nate (ĭn-**krĭm′**ə-nāt′) *tr.v.* **in·crim·i·nat·ed, in·crim·i·nat·ing, in·crim·i·nates 1.** To accuse of a crime or other wrongful act: *The indictment incriminates six conspirators.* **2.** To cause to appear guilty of a crime or fault; implicate: *The new evidence incriminated other suspects in the robbery.* **—in·crim′i·na′tion** *n.* **—in·crim′i·na′tor** *n.*

in·cu·bate (**ĭn′**kyə-bāt′) *v.* **in·cu·bat·ed, in·cu·bat·ing, in·cu·bates** —*tr.* **1.** To sit on (eggs) to provide heat until hatching. **2.** To keep (eggs, organisms, or other living tissue) in conditions favorable for growth and development. **3.** To be infected with (a virus or bacterium) before showing signs or symptoms of disease: *a child who is incubating a cold.* **4.** To form or consider slowly: *She is incubating her outline for a book.* —*intr.* **1.** To sit on eggs; brood. **2.** To go through the process of incubation: *The bacterial cultures have been incubating for two days.* [From Latin *incubāre*, to lie down on.]

in·cu·ba·tion (ĭn′kyə-**bā′**shən) *n.* **1.** The act of incubating or the condition of being incubated. **2.** The development of a disease from the time of infection until the appearance of symptoms. **3.** The maintenance of an infant, especially a premature infant, in an environment of controlled temperature, humidity, and oxygen concentration.

in·cu·ba·tor (**ĭn′**kyə-bā′tər) *n.* **1.** An apparatus in which conditions such as temperature and humidity can be controlled and maintained, used for hatching eggs or for growing cultures of microorganisms. **2.** A similar apparatus supplied with oxygen for the special care of very small or premature babies.

in·cu·des (ĭng-**kyo͞o′**dēz) *n.* Plural of **incus.**

in·cul·cate (ĭn-**kŭl′**kāt′ *or* **ĭn′**kŭl-kāt′) *tr.v.* **in·cul·cat·ed, in·cul·cat·ing, in·cul·cates** To fix in the mind by frequent repetition; impress: *Our science teacher inculcated the importance of being careful when working with chemicals.* [From Latin *inculcāre*, to force upon.] **—in′cul·ca′tion** *n.*

in·cum·ben·cy (ĭn-**kŭm′**bən-sē) *n., pl.* **in·cum·ben·cies 1.** The quality or condition of being incumbent. **2.** The term of an incumbent.

in·cum·bent (ĭn-**kŭm′**bənt) *adj.* **1.** Currently holding a specified office: *the incumbent mayor.* **2.** Imposed as an obligation or duty; required: *It is incumbent on all citizens to pay their taxes.* ❖ *n.* A person currently holding an office. [From Middle English, from Latin *incumbere*, to lean upon, apply oneself to.]

in·cur (ĭn-**kûr′**) *tr.v.* **in·curred, in·cur·ring, in·curs 1.** To acquire or come into (something); sustain: *The investor incurred big losses during the stock market crash.* **2.** To become subject to as a result of one's actions; bring upon oneself: *She incurred her neighbors' anger by playing her music so loud.* [From Middle English *incurren*, from Latin *incurrere*, to run into.]

in·cur·a·ble (ĭn-**kyo͝or′**ə-bəl) *adj.* Impossible to cure: *an incurable disease.* **—in·cur′a·bly** *adv.*

in·cur·sion (ĭn-**kûr′**zhən) *n.* A raid or invasion into a foreign territory: *The Vikings made many incursions along the European coast.* —SEE NOTE AT **cursive.**

in·cus (**ĭng′**kəs) *n., pl.* **in·cu·des** (ĭng-**kyo͞o′**dēz) One of the three small bones in the middle ear; the anvil. [From Latin *incūs*, anvil.]

in·debt·ed (ĭn-**dĕt′**ĭd) *adj.* Owing another money or gratitude for a loan, gift, or useful service; beholden: *We are indebted to you for your hospitality.*

in·debt·ed·ness (ĭn-**dĕt′**ĭd-nĭs) *n.* **1.** The state of being indebted. **2.** Something that is owed to another.

in·de·cen·cy (ĭn-**dē′**sən-sē) *n., pl.* **in·de·cen·cies 1.** The quality or condition of being indecent. **2.** Something that is indecent.

in·de·cent (ĭn-**dē′**sənt) *adj.* **1.** Not in good taste; improper; unsuitable: *Our dinner guests left with indecent haste shortly after the meal.* **2.** Morally offensive; immodest or obscene: *indecent clothing; an indecent joke.* **—in·de′cent·ly** *adv.*

in·de·ci·pher·a·ble (ĭn′dĭ-**sī′**fər-ə-bəl) *adj.* Impossible to decipher: *an indecipherable security code.*

in·de·ci·sion (ĭn′dĭ-**sĭzh′**ən) *n.* The condition of being unable to make up one's mind.

in·de·ci·sive (ĭn′dĭ-**sī′**sĭv) *adj.* **1.** Unable to make up one's mind; wavering; vacillating: *The indecisive executive constantly put off important purchases.* **2.** Having no clear result; inconclusive: *an indecisive election in which no candidate received a clear majority.* **—in′de·ci′sive·ly** *adv.* **—in′de·ci′sive·ness** *n.*

in·dec·o·rous (ĭn-**dĕk′**ər-əs) *adj.* Not in good taste; lacking propriety: *loud and indecorous behavior.* **—in·dec′o·rous·ly** *adv.*

in·deed (ĭn-**dēd′**) *adv.* **1.** Without a doubt; certainly: *They were indeed happy.* **2.** In fact; in reality: *I said the car would break down and indeed it did.* ❖ *interj.* An expression used to show surprise, irony, or disbelief. [From Middle English *in dede.*]

indef. *abbr.* An abbreviation of indefinite.

in·de·fat·i·ga·ble (ĭn′dĭ-**făt′**ĭ-gə-bəl) *adj.* Never giving up or becoming tired; tireless: *indefatigable rescuers who worked through the night searching the wreckage.* **—in′de·fat′i·ga·bly** *adv.*

in·de·fen·si·ble (ĭn′dĭ-**fĕn′**sə-bəl) *adj.* **1.** Vulnerable to attack: *an indefensible town in the middle of a valley.* **2.** Incapable of being justified or excused; inexcusable: *rude and indefensible behavior.* **—in′de·fen′si·bly** *adv.*

in·de·fin·a·ble (ĭn′dĭ-**fī′**nə-bəl) *adj.* Impossible to define, describe, or analyze: *a vague and indefinable feeling of suspicion.* **—in′de·fin′a·bly** *adv.*

in·def·i·nite (ĭn-**dĕf′**ə-nĭt) *adj.* **1.** Not fixed or limited: *an indefinite period of time.* **2.** Not clear or exact; vague: *indefinite outlines of people standing in the shadows.* **3.** Not decided; uncertain: *indefinite plans.* **—in·def′i·nite·ly** *adv.* **—in·def′i·nite·ness** *n.*

indefinite article *n.* An article, in English either *a* or *an*, that does not fix the identity of the noun modified.

indefinite pronoun *n.* A pronoun, as English *any* or *some*, that does not specify the identity of its object.

in·del·i·ble (ĭn-**dĕl′**ə-bəl) *adj.* **1.** Impossible to remove, erase, or wash away; permanent: *an indelible stain.* **2.** Making an indelible mark: *an indelible pen.* **3.** Impossible to forget; memorable: *an indelible memory.* [From Latin *indēlēbilis* : *in-*, not + *dēlēre*, to wipe out.] **—in·del′i·bil′i·ty, in·del′i·ble·ness** *n.* **—in·del′i·bly** *adv.*

in·del·i·ca·cy (ĭn-**dĕl′**ĭ-kə-sē) *n., pl.* **in·del·i·ca·cies 1.** The quality or condition of being indelicate. **2.** Something that is indelicate.

in·del·i·cate (ĭn-**dĕl′**ĭ-kĭt) *adj.* Lacking good taste; crude or improper: *indelicate language.* **—in·del′i·cate·ly** *adv.*

in·dem·ni·fy (ĭn-**dĕm′**nə-fī′) *tr.v.* **in·dem·ni·fied, in·dem·ni·fy·ing, in·dem·ni·fies 1.** To protect against

GEOGRAPHY

Indiana The name **Indiana** comes from *Indian* plus a Latin ending, and means "land of the Indians." It was first used by developers to describe the region, and later by Congress when it created the Indiana Territory (1800) and the state of Indiana (1816).

Indian club

Indian corn

ă	pat	ôr	core
ā	pay	oi	boy
âr	care	ou	out
ä	father	ŏŏ	took
ĕ	pet	ŏŏr	lure
ē	be	ōō	boot
ĭ	pit	ŭ	cut
ī	bite	ûr	urge
îr	pier	th	thin
ŏ	pot	*th*	this
ō	toe	zh	vision
ô	paw	ə	about

possible damage, injury, or loss; insure: *Motorists are indemnified by automobile insurance.* **2.** To make compensation to for damage, injury, or loss suffered: *The shipper indemnified the grower for the lost truckload of fruit.* —**in·dem′ni·fi·ca′tion** (ĭn-dĕm′nə-fĭ-**kā′**shən) *n.*

in·dem·ni·ty (ĭn-**dĕm′**nĭ-tē) *n., pl.* **in·dem·ni·ties 1.** Insurance or other security against possible damage, loss, or injury. **2.** Payment or compensation for damage, loss, or injury.

in·dent[1] (ĭn-**dĕnt′**) *tr.v.* **in·dent·ed, in·dent·ing, in·dents 1.** To set (the first line of a paragraph) in from the margin. **2.** To make notches in the edge of; make jagged: *He indented the board to make a secure joint.* ❖ *n.* (ĭn-**dĕnt′** *or* **ĭn′**dĕnt′) An indentation. [From Middle English *endenten*, to notch, from Medieval Latin *indentāre* : Latin *in-*, in + Latin *dēns*, tooth.]

in·dent[2] (ĭn-**dĕnt′**) *tr.v.* **in·dent·ed, in·dent·ing, in·dents** To make a dent, recess, or other impression in: *The coast is indented with coves.* ❖ *n.* (ĭn-**dĕnt′** *or* **ĭn′**-dĕnt′) An indentation. [From Middle English *endenten*, to decorate, as with precious stones, from *denten*, to make a dent in.]

in·den·ta·tion (ĭn′dĕn-**tā′**shən) *n.* **1.** The act of indenting or the condition of being indented. **2.** The blank space between a margin and the beginning of an indented line. **3.** A recess or notch, as in a border or coastline.

in·den·ture (ĭn-**dĕn′**chər) *n.* A deed or contract between two or more parties, especially one binding a servant or apprentice to another person for a specified period of time. ❖ *tr.v.* **in·den·tured, in·den·tur·ing, in·den·tures** To bind by an indenture: *Many European immigrants in the 1600s were indentured to American landowners.*

in·de·pen·dence (ĭn′dĭ-**pĕn′**dəns) *n.* The quality or condition of being independent: *Many countries of colonial Africa won their independence from European nations in the 1950s and 1960s.*

Independence Day *n.* A national holiday celebrated on July 4 to commemorate the adoption of the Declaration of Independence in 1776.

in·de·pen·dent (ĭn′dĭ-**pĕn′**dənt) *adj.* **1.** Not governed by a foreign country; ruling or governing itself: *The United States became an independent nation after the Revolution.* **2.** Not controlled or guided by others; self-reliant: *an independent mind.* **3.** Not dependent on or connected with a larger or controlling group; separate: *an independent drugstore.* **4.** Not committed to any one political party: *an independent voter.* **5.** Earning one's own living; self-supporting: *With this job I am independent of my parents.* **6.** Providing enough income to allow one to live without working: *a person of independent means.* ❖ *n.* One who is independent, especially a voter, candidate, or officeholder who is not committed to any one political party: *Independents turned out in large numbers during the election.* —**in′de·pen′dent·ly** *adv.*

independent clause *n.* A clause in a sentence that can stand alone as a complete sentence. For example, in the sentence *When the sun came out, we went for a walk,* the clause *we went for a walk* is an independent clause.

in-depth (**ĭn′**dĕpth′) *adj.* Detailed; thorough: *an in-depth interview of the candidate.*

in·de·scrib·a·ble (ĭn′dĭ-**skrī′**bə-bəl) *adj.* Impossible to describe adequately: *indescribable delight.* —**in′de·scrib′a·bly** *adv.*

in·de·struc·ti·ble (ĭn′dĭ-**strŭk′**tə-bəl) *adj.* Impossible to destroy: *a pet toy made of indestructible plastic.* —**in′de·struc′ti·bly** *adv.*

in·de·ter·mi·nate (ĭn′dĭ-**tûr′**mə-nĭt) *adj.* Not precisely determined; not defined; vague: *a person of indeterminate age.* —**in′de·ter′mi·nate·ly** *adv.* —**in′de·ter′mi·nate·ness** *n.*

in·dex (**ĭn′**dĕks′) *n., pl.* **in·dex·es** or **in·di·ces** (**ĭn′**dĭ-sēz′) **1.** A list of names or subjects arranged in alphabetical order and presented at the end of a printed work, along with the page numbers on which each item is mentioned. **2.** Something that reveals or indicates; a sign: *The baby's face is an index to its feelings.* **3.** An indicator or pointer, as the arrow on a dial or other device. ❖ *tr.v.* **in·dexed, in·dex·ing, in·dex·es 1.** To furnish with an index: *index a history textbook.* **2.** To enter (an item) in an index. [From Middle English, forefinger, from Latin.]

index finger *n.* The finger next to the thumb; the forefinger.

index fossil *n.* The fossil remains of an organism that lived in a particular geologic age, used to determine the age of the rock layer in which it is found.

index of refraction *n.* The ratio of the speed of light in a vacuum to the speed of light in another medium, such as water or oil.

In·di·a (**ĭn′**dē-ə) **1.** A peninsula and subcontinent of southern Asia south of the Himalaya Mountains, occupied by India, Nepal, Bhutan, Pakistan, and Bangladesh. **2.** A country of southern Asia on the Indian Ocean. India was the site of one of the oldest civilizations in the world, centered in the Indus River valley from around 2500 to 1500 BC. New Delhi is the capital and Mumbai (Bombay) the largest city.

India ink *n.* Black ink or paint made from lampblack.

In·di·an (**ĭn′**dē-ən) *adj.* **1.** Relating to India or the East Indies or to their peoples, languages, or cultures. **2.** Relating to any of the American Indian peoples. ❖ *n.* **1.** A native or inhabitant of India or the East Indies. **2a.** An American Indian. **b.** Any of the languages of the American Indians. —SEE NOTE AT **Native American.**

In·di·an·a (ĭn′dē-**ăn′**ə) A state of the north-central United States east of Illinois. It was admitted as the 19th state in 1816. Indianapolis is the capital. —SEE NOTE.

In·di·an·ap·o·lis (ĭn′dē-ə-**năp′**ə-lĭs) The capital of Indiana, in the central part of the state. It was founded in 1820.

Indian club *n.* A bottle-shaped wooden club held in the hand and swung for gymnastic exercise.

Indian corn *n.* **1.** The corn plant that is native to the Americas, or its ears or kernels; maize. **2.** Dried ears of corn having colorful kernels, often hung in a cluster for decoration.

Indian Ocean A body of water extending from southern Asia to Antarctica and from eastern Africa to southeast Australia.

Indian paintbrush *n.* **1.** Any of various plants having spikes bearing small greenish flowers surrounded by bright red, yellow, or pink bracts that resemble petals. **2.** A hawkweed with red-orange flowers.

Indian pipe *n.* A waxy whitish woodland plant having a single nodding flower. Indian pipes are parasitic on fungi.

Indian summer *n.* A period of mild weather occurring in late autumn.

Indian Territory A region and former territory of the south-central United States, mainly in present-day Oklahoma. The government set aside this land for forcibly displaced Native Americans between 1834 and 1907. —SEE NOTE AT **Oklahoma.**

India paper *n.* A thin paper used especially in Bibles or in taking impressions of engravings.

In·dic (**ĭn′**dĭk) *adj.* **1.** Relating to India or its people or cultures. **2.** Relating to a branch of the Indo-European language family that includes Sanskrit and the languages descended from it, spoken on the Indian subcontinent and Sri Lanka. ❖ *n.* The Indic branch of Indo-European.

in·di·cate (**ĭn′**dĭ-kāt′) *tr.v.* **indi·cat·ed, indi·cat·ing, indi·cates 1.** To show or point out: *indicate a route on a map.* **2.** To serve as a sign or symptom of: *Dark clouds indicate rain. Fever indicates illness.* **3.** To state or express: *Their faces indicated they did not like spinach at all.*

in·di·ca·tion (ĭn′dĭ-**kā′**shən) *n.* **1.** The act of indicating: *His indication of refusal came in the form of a frown.* **2.** Something that indicates; a sign: *flowers, birds, and other indications of spring.* [From Middle English *indicacioun*, from Latin *indicāre*, to point to, show, from *index*, forefinger.]

in·dic·a·tive (ĭn-**dĭk′**ə-tĭv) *adj.* **1.** Serving to indicate: *A cough is often indicative of a cold.* **2.** Relating to the mood of a verb used in ordinary statements of fact or in factual questions. For example, in *We went* and *Did they go?*, the words *went* and *go* are in the indicative mood. ❖ *n.* **1.** The indicative mood. **2.** A verb form in this mood.

in·di·ca·tor (**ĭn′**dĭ-kā′tər) *n.* **1.** A person or thing that indicates, especially: **a.** A meter or gauge that tells about the operation of an engine or other machine or system. **b.** The needle or dial of such a meter or gauge. **2.** A chemical compound that changes color under certain conditions, used in chemical tests. Litmus is an indicator that shows the amount of acid present in a solution by changes in color.

indicator species *n.* A species whose abundance in a given area is believed to be a sign of certain environmental or ecological conditions, such as the level of pollution.

in·di·ces (**ĭn′**dĭ-sēz′) *n.* A plural of **index.**

in·dict (ĭn-**dīt′**) *tr.v.* **in·dict·ed, in·dict·ing, in·dicts 1.** To accuse of wrongdoing or misconduct: *a protest song that indicts the country's leaders as warmongers.* **2.** To charge with a crime by means of an indictment: *The grand jury indicted the suspect on charges of assault.* [From Middle English *enditen*, ultimately from Latin *dīcere*, to say.] **—in·dict′er, in·dic′tor** *n.*

in·dict·ment (ĭn-**dīt′**mənt) *n.* **1.** The act of indicting or the condition of being indicted: *a bank officer under indictment for embezzlement.* **2.** A written statement issued by a grand jury that charges a person with the commission of a crime.

in·dif·fer·ence (ĭn-**dĭf′**ər-əns *or* ĭn-**dĭf′**rəns) *n.* **1.** Lack of concern or interest: *The regime's indifference to the worsening economic conditions brought about its downfall.* **2.** Lack of importance; insignificance: *Their opinion is a matter of indifference to me.*

in·dif·fer·ent (ĭn-**dĭf′**ər-ənt *or* ĭn-**dĭf′**rənt) *adj.* **1.** Having or showing no interest; not caring one way or the other: *indifferent to the troubles of others; indifferent to weather conditions.* **2.** Being neither good nor bad; mediocre: *The band gave an indifferent performance.* **3.** Showing no preference; impartial: *an indifferent judge.* **—in·dif′fer·ent·ly** *adv.*

in·di·gence (**ĭn′**dĭ-jəns) *n.* The condition of being poor; poverty.

in·dig·e·nous (ĭn-**dĭj′**ə-nəs) *adj.* **1.** Originally living or growing in a particular place or region; native: *The bald eagle is indigenous to North America.* **2.** Originally inhabiting a particular place or region: *the indigenous peoples of Taiwan.* [From Latin *indigena*, a native.]

in·di·gent (**ĭn′**dĭ-jənt) *adj.* Poor; needy. [From Middle English, from Latin *indigēre*, to need.]

in·di·gest·i·ble (ĭn′dĭ-**jĕs′**tə-bəl *or* ĭn′dī-**jĕs′**tə-bəl) *adj.* Difficult or impossible to digest: *indigestible fatty foods.*

in·di·ges·tion (ĭn′dĭ-**jĕs′**chən *or* ĭn′dī-**jĕs′**chən) *n.* Discomfort or illness resulting from difficulty in digesting food: *I got indigestion from eating too many hot dogs.*

in·dig·nant (ĭn-**dĭg′**nənt) *adj.* Feeling or expressing indignation: *I was indignant over their thoughtless remarks.* **—in·dig′nant·ly** *adv.*

in·dig·na·tion (ĭn′dĭg-**nā′**shən) *n.* Anger aroused by something perceived as unfair or wrongful: *The voters expressed their indignation over the government's continuing neglect of serious problems.* See Synonyms at **anger.** [From Middle English *indignacioun*, from Latin *indignātiō*, from *indignārī*, to regard as unworthy, from *indignus*, unworthy.]

in·dig·ni·ty (ĭn-**dĭg′**nĭ-tē) *n., pl.* **in·dig·ni·ties** Something that offends a person's pride and sense of dignity; an insult: *She felt it was an indignity to be asked to do such menial tasks.*

in·di·go (**ĭn′**dĭ-gō′) *n., pl.* **in·di·gos** or **in·di·goes 1a.** Any of various plants that yield a dark violet-blue dye. **b.** A dark violet-blue dye obtained from these plants or an artificial dye of the same color. **2.** A dark violet blue. [From Latin *indicum*, from Greek *Indikon (pharmakon)*, Indian (dye).]

in·di·rect (ĭn′dĭ-**rĕkt′** *or* ĭn′dī-**rĕkt′**) *adj.* **1.** Not following a direct course; roundabout: *an indirect route.* **2.** Not straight to the point, as in talking: *an indirect answer.* **3.** Not directly connected or planned for; secondary: *The boom in bicycle sales was an indirect effect of the new gasoline tax.* **4.** In soccer, relating to a free kick that counts as a goal only if the ball has been touched by a second player. **—in′di·rect′ly** *adv.* **—in′di·rect′ness** *n.*

indirect object *n.* A word or phrase in a sentence referring to a person or thing that is indirectly affected by the action of a transitive verb. For example, in the sentences *Sing me a song* and *We fed the turtle lettuce,* the words *me* and *turtle* are both indirect objects.

in·dis·creet (ĭn′dĭ-**skrēt′**) *adj.* Lacking discretion; unwise or tactless: *an indiscreet remark.* **—in′dis·creet′ly** *adv.* **—in′dis·creet′ness** *n.*

in·dis·cre·tion (ĭn′dĭ-**skrĕsh′**ən) *n.* **1.** Lack of discretion. **2.** An indiscreet act or remark.

in·dis·crim·i·nate (ĭn′dĭ-**skrĭm′**ə-nĭt) *adj.* **1.** Careless in making choices or distinctions: *an indiscriminate shopper.* **2.** Random; haphazard: *indiscriminate violence; an indiscriminate assortment of used books for sale.* **—in′dis·crim′i·nate·ly** *adv.*

in·dis·pens·a·ble (ĭn′dĭ-**spĕn′**sə-bəl) *adj.* Absolutely necessary; essential: *A good education is indispensable to becoming a doctor.* **—in′dis·pens′a·bly** *adv.*

in·dis·posed (ĭn′dĭ-**spōzd′**) *adj.* **1.** Mildly ill: *He was indisposed with a slight cold.* **2.** Unwilling; reluctant: *They were indisposed to help at all.*

in·dis·po·si·tion (ĭn-dĭs′pə-**zĭsh′**ən) *n.* **1.** Unwillingness. **2.** A minor ailment.

in·dis·put·a·ble (ĭn′dĭ-**spyo͞o′**tə-bəl) *adj.* Beyond doubt; unquestionable: *an indisputable fact.* **—in′dis·put′a·bly** *adv.*

in·dis·sol·u·ble (ĭn′dĭ-**sŏl′**yə-bəl) *adj.* **1.** Not capable of being broken or undone; permanent: *an indissoluble bond between friends.* **2.** Impossible to dissolve or disintegrate. **—in′dis·sol′u·bly** *adv.*

in·dis·tinct (ĭn′dĭ-**stĭngkt′**) *adj.* Not clearly heard, seen, or understood: *an indistinct sound heard from far away; saw an indistinct figure in the distance.* **—in′dis·tinct′ly** *adv.* **—in′dis·tinct′ness** *n.*

in·dis·tin·guish·a·ble (ĭn′dĭ-**stĭng′**gwĭ-shə-bəl) *adj.* Lacking clear differences; impossible to tell apart: *a shopping mall indistinguishable from all the others.*

in·di·um (**ĭn′**dē-əm) *n.* *Symbol* **In** A soft, silvery metallic element found mainly in ores of zinc and lead. It is used in making semiconductors and mirrors. Atomic number 49. See **Periodic Table.** [From *indigo* (so called from the indigo-blue lines in its spectrum).]

in·di·vid·u·al (ĭn′də-**vĭj′**o͞o-əl) *adj.* **1.** Relating to a single organism, especially a human: *Each individual child will get a prize.* **2.** By or for one person: *an individual portion of food.* **3.** Existing as a separate unit; distinct: *individual drops of rain.* **4.** Having a special quality; unique; distinct: *Each variety of apple has its individual flavor.* ❖ *n.* A single organism, especially a human: *There were three individuals in the car. Among the redwoods in the grove, two individuals stood out for their great height.* [From Middle English, single, indivisible, from Latin *indīviduus* : *in-*, not + *dīviduus*, divisible.]

in·di·vid·u·al·ism (ĭn′də-**vĭj′**o͞o-ə-lĭz′əm) *n.* **1.** Belief in

WRITERS CHOOSE THEIR WORDS

"The state needs roads for those people [living in surrounding towns] to drive on," Dr. Steve went on. "The little one- and two-lane streets around here aren't cutting it anymore. The state of Pennsylvania has decided to build a state highway, and unfortunately, the plan that makes the most sense for the area cuts right through the center of Camp Lakeview." The room was filled with **indignant** gasps. "They can't do that!" one of the older boys yelled.

—Melissa J. Morgan
Suddenly Last Summer

indigo

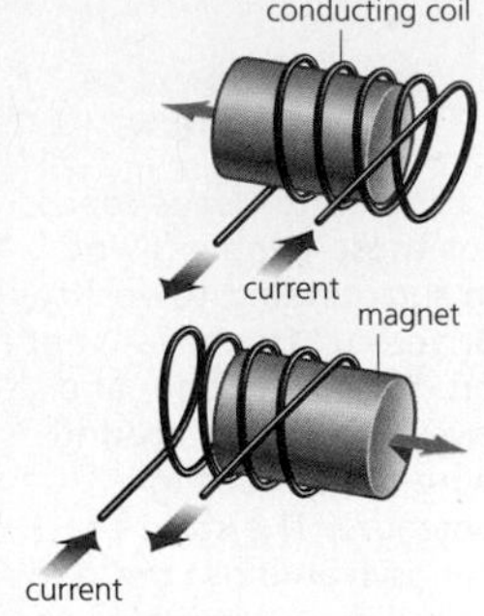

induction
When a magnet is passed through a coil of wire, it produces an electric current. The direction of the flow of the current depends on the direction in which the magnet moves. In the top diagram the current flows from right to left. In the bottom diagram the current flows from left to right.

ă	pat	ôr	core
ā	pay	oi	boy
âr	care	ou	out
ä	father	o͝o	took
ĕ	pet	o͝or	lure
ē	be	o͞o	boot
ĭ	pit	ŭ	cut
ī	bite	ûr	urge
îr	pier	th	thin
ŏ	pot	*th*	this
ō	toe	zh	vision
ô	paw	ə	about

following one's own interests without concern for the opinions of others or the usual way of doing things. **2.** A way of living based on this belief; personal independence. **3.** The doctrine that the interests of an individual are more important than the interests of a group or state.

in·di·vid·u·al·ist (ĭn′də-vĭj**′**o͞o-ə-lĭst) *n.* **1.** A person who is independent in thought and action. **2.** A person who supports or believes in individualism. —**in′di·vid′u·al·is′tic** *adj.* —**in′di·vid′u·al·is′ti·cal·ly** *adv.*

in·di·vid·u·al·i·ty (ĭn′də-vĭj′o͞o-**ăl′**ĭ-tē) *n., pl.* **in·di·vid·u·al·i·ties 1.** The qualities that make a person or thing different from others; identity: *He expresses his individuality in the way he dresses.* **2.** The condition of being individual; distinctness: *At the rock concert, we felt like we had lost our individuality and become part of a larger experience.*

in·di·vid·u·al·ize (ĭn′də-vĭj**′**o͞o-ə-līz′) *tr.v.* **in·di·vid·u·al·ized, in·di·vid·u·al·iz·ing, in·di·vid·u·al·iz·es 1.** To give individuality to: *The artist individualized his painting when he developed a unique style.* **2.** To change to fit or satisfy an individual: *individualize exercises according to each person's need.*

in·di·vid·u·al·ly (ĭn′də-vĭj**′**o͞o-ə-lē) *adv.* As individuals; singly; separately: *The principal knew all the students individually.*

individual retirement account *n.* A personal investment account whose dividends and interest are not taxable until the person making the investment retires.

in·di·vis·i·ble (ĭn′də-vĭz**′**ə-bəl) *adj.* **1.** Incapable of being divided or separated: *states bound together in an indivisible union; childhood friends who seemed indivisible.* **2.** Incapable of being divided without leaving a remainder; for example, 7 is indivisible by 3. —**in′di·vis′i·bil′i·ty** *n.* —**in′di·vis′i·bly** *adv.*

In·do·chi·na (ĭn′dō-**chī′**nə) A peninsula of southeast Asia made up of Vietnam, Laos, Cambodia, Thailand, Myanmar (Burma), and mainland Malaysia.

in·doc·tri·nate (ĭn-**dŏk′**trə-nāt′) *tr.v.* **in·doc·tri·nat·ed, in·doc·tri·nat·ing, in·doc·tri·nates** To instruct (a person) in the doctrines or beliefs of a particular group, especially a political or religious group. —**in·doc′tri·na′tion** *n.*

In·do-Eu·ro·pe·an (ĭn′dō-yo͝or′ə-**pē′**ən) *n.* **1.** A family of languages that includes most of the languages of Europe, along with many languages of Iran, India, and some other parts of Asia. **2.** An unrecorded language that is the ancestor of these languages. **3.** A member of a people speaking an Indo-European language. —**In′do-Eu′ro·pe′an** *adj.*

In·do-I·ra·ni·an (ĭn′dō-ĭ-**rā′**nē-ən) *n.* **1.** A branch of the Indo-European language family that includes many languages spoken in Iran and India, such as Hindi-Urdu and Persian. **2.** A member of any of the peoples speaking an Indo-Iranian language.

in·do·lent (**ĭn′**də-lənt) *adj.* Preferring not to work or be active; habitually lazy. [From Late Latin *indolēns*, painless.] —**in′do·lence** *n.*

in·dom·i·ta·ble (ĭn-**dŏm′**ĭ-tə-bəl) *adj.* Incapable of being overcome or subdued; unconquerable: *an indomitable foe; a determined leader with an indomitable will.* —**in·dom′i·ta·bly** *adv.*

In·do·ne·sia (ĭn′də-**nē′**zhə) A country of southeast Asia in the Malay Archipelago made up of Sumatra, Java, Sulawesi, the Moluccas, parts of Borneo, New Guinea, and Timor, and many smaller islands. Jakarta, on the island of Java, is the capital.

In·do·ne·sian (ĭn′də-**nē′**zhən) *adj.* Relating to Indonesia or its people, languages, or cultures. ❖ *n.* **1.** A native or inhabitant of Indonesia. **2.** A dialect of Malay that is the official language of the Republic of Indonesia.

in·door (**ĭn′**dôr′) *adj.* Situated in or done within a house or other building: *an indoor pool; an indoor party.*

in·doors (ĭn-**dôrz′**) *adv.* In or into a house or building: *staying indoors because of a cold.*

in·du·bi·ta·ble (ĭn-**do͞o′**bĭ-tə-bəl) *adj.* Too obvious or apparent to be doubted; unquestionable: *the indubitable truth of the evidence.* [From Middle English, from Latin *dubitāre*, to hesitate, doubt.] —**in·du′bi·ta·bly** *adv.*

in·duce (ĭn-**do͞os′**) *tr.v.* **in·duced, in·duc·ing, in·duc·es 1.** To prompt or persuade (someone) to do something: *Nothing could induce me to stay in that awful job.* **2.** To cause to occur; bring about: *induce vomiting in a patient who has swallowed poison.* **3.** To arrive at (a conclusion or general principle) by a reasoned examination of particular facts. **4.** To produce (electricity or magnetism) by induction. [From Middle English *enducen*, from Latin *indūcere*, to lead into.] —SEE NOTE AT **produce.**

in·duce·ment (ĭn-**do͞os′**mənt) *n.* **1.** The act or process of inducing: *the inducement of labor in a pregnant woman.* **2.** Something that helps bring about an action; an incentive: *Free samples are an inducement to try new products.*

in·duct (ĭn-**dŭkt′**) *tr.v.* **in·duct·ed, in·duct·ing, in·ducts 1.** To place formally in office; install: *inducted the officer as treasurer.* **2.** To call into military service; draft. **3.** To admit as a member; initiate: *The honor society inducts new students in the spring.*

in·duc·tance (ĭn-**dŭk′**təns) *n.* The property of an electric circuit that makes it possible for an electromotive force to be created in a nearby circuit by a change of current in either circuit.

in·duct·ee (ĭn′dŭk-**tē′**) *n.* A person inducted or about to be inducted into the armed forces.

in·duc·tion (ĭn-**dŭk′**shən) *n.* **1.** The act of installing formally in office: *the induction of the new president.* **2.** The process of being enrolled in the armed forces. **3.** A method of reasoning in which a conclusion is reached or a general principle is discovered on the basis of particular facts. **4.** The process by which an object having electrical or magnetic properties produces similar properties in a nearby object without direct contact.

induction coil *n.* A type of transformer in which an interrupted direct current of low voltage is changed into a high-voltage alternating current.

in·duc·tive (ĭn-**dŭk′**tĭv) *adj.* **1.** Relating to or using logical induction: *inductive reasoning.* **2.** Relating to or caused by electric or magnetic induction. —**in·duc′tive·ly** *adv.*

in·duc·tor (ĭn-**dŭk′**tər) *n.* A part of an electric circuit, typically a coil of wire, that works by or produces inductance.

in·dulge (ĭn-**dŭlj′**) *v.* **in·dulged, in·dulg·ing, in·dulg·es** —*tr.* **1.** To give in to or satisfy (a desire); gratify: *indulge a craving for rich desserts.* **2.** To yield to the desires or whims of (someone): *They always indulge their daughter on her birthday.* See Synonyms at **pamper.** —*intr.* To allow oneself some special pleasure; have or do what one wants: *indulge in a nap; indulge in an afternoon watching old movies.*

in·dul·gence (ĭn-**dŭl′**jəns) *n.* **1.** The act of indulging a desire or a person: *surrender to an occasional indulgence in junk food.* **2.** Something indulged in: *A long vacation is a worthwhile indulgence.* **3.** Liberal or lenient treatment; favor: *The child expects to be treated with indulgence.* **4.** In the Roman Catholic Church, the freeing from non-eternal punishment due for a sin that has been pardoned in confession. [From Middle English, from Latin *indulgēre*, to indulge.]

in·dul·gent (ĭn-**dŭl′**jənt) *adj.* Inclined to pamper or indulge; lenient: *The indulgent owner spoiled the puppy with treats.* —**in·dul′gent·ly** *adv.*

In·dus (**ĭn′**dəs) A river of south-central Asia rising in southwest Tibet and flowing about 1,800 miles (2,900 kilometers) northwest through northern India and southwest through Pakistan to the Arabian Sea. Its valley was the site of an advanced civilization lasting from about 2500 to 1500 BC.

in·dus·tri·al (ĭn-dŭs′trē-əl) *adj.* **1.** Relating to industry: *industrial products.* **2.** Having highly developed industries: *an industrial nation.* **3.** Used in industry: *industrial tools and equipment.* **—in·dus′tri·al·ly** *adv.*

in·dus·tri·al·ist (ĭ-dŭs′trē-ə-lĭst) *n.* A person who owns or runs an industrial enterprise.

in·dus·tri·al·ize (ĭn-dŭs′trē-ə-līz′) *v.* **in·dus·tri·al·ized, in·dus·tri·al·iz·ing, in·dus·tri·al·iz·es** *—tr.* To develop industries in: *a government seeking to industrialize its economy. —intr.* To become industrial: *a country that has been slow to industrialize.* **—in·dus′tri·al·i·za′tion** (ĭn-dŭs′trē-ə-lĭ-**zā′**shən) *n.*

industrial park *n.* An area that is zoned for a group of industries and businesses, usually located on the outskirts of a city.

Industrial Revolution *n.* The gradual shift from hand tools and home manufacturing to power-driven tools and large-scale factory production that began in England in about 1760 and continued into the 1800s.

in·dus·tri·ous (ĭn-dŭs′trē-əs) *adj.* Working hard as a steady habit; diligent: *An industrious student can get good grades.* **—in·dus′tri·ous·ly** *adv.* **—in·dus′tri·ous·ness** *n.*

in·dus·try (**ĭn′**də-strē) *n., pl.* **in·dus·tries 1a.** The manufacture or production of goods on a large scale: *Industry has expanded in many Asian nations.* **b.** A specific branch of such activity: *the computer hardware industry.* **2.** Hard work; steady effort: *Most people admire industry and thrift.* [From Latin *industrius*, diligent.]

in·e·bri·ate (ĭn-ē′brē-āt′) *tr.v.* **in·e·bri·at·ed, in·e·bri·at·ing, in·e·bri·ates** To intoxicate; make drunk. ❖ *n.* (ĭn-ē′brē-ĭt) An intoxicated person, especially a drunkard.

in·ed·i·ble (ĭn-**ĕd′**ə-bəl) *adj.* Unfit to be eaten; not edible: *The peel of a banana is inedible.*

in·ef·fa·ble (ĭn-**ĕf′**ə-bəl) *adj.* Impossible to express adequately; indescribable: *the ineffable majesty of a starlit sky.* **—in·ef′fa·bly** *adv.*

in·ef·fec·tive (ĭn′ĭ-**fĕk′**tĭv) *adj.* **1.** Not effective; not producing results: *Their attempt to patch the bicycle tire proved ineffective.* **2.** Not performing satisfactorily; incompetent: *The corrupt politician was an ineffective governor.* **—in′ef·fec′tive·ly** *adv.* **—in′ef·fec′tive·ness** *n.*

in·ef·fec·tu·al (ĭn′ĭ-**fĕk′**cho͞o-əl) *adj.* **1.** Not having the desired effect; useless: *The pill was ineffectual in relieving my headache.* **2.** Lacking forcefulness or effectiveness; inadequate: *an ineffectual ruler.* **—in′ef·fec′tu·al·ly** *adv.*

in·ef·fi·cien·cy (ĭn′ĭ-**fĭsh′**ən-sē) *n., pl.* **in·ef·fi·cien·cies 1.** The condition, quality, or fact of being inefficient: *The clerk's inefficiency cost the company a great deal of money.* **2.** An inefficient act or procedure: *There are several inefficiencies in the new system for handling business orders.*

in·ef·fi·cient (ĭn′ĭ-**fĭsh′**ənt) *adj.* **1.** Wasteful of time, energy, or materials: *an inefficient gasoline engine.* **2.** Lacking in ability; incompetent: *an inefficient manager.* **—in′ef·fi′cient·ly** *adv.*

in·e·las·tic (ĭn′ĭ-**lăs′**tĭk) *adj.* Not capable of returning to its original shape or dimensions after being stretched or deformed; stiff or unyielding. **—in′e·las·tic′i·ty** (ĭn′-ĭ-lă-**stĭs′**ĭ-tē) *n.*

in·el·e·gant (ĭn-**ĕl′**ĭ-gənt) *adj.* Not elegant; lacking grace or refinement: *inelegant manners.* **—in·el′e·gance** *n.* **—in·el′e·gant·ly** *adv.*

in·el·i·gi·ble (ĭn-**ĕl′**ĭ-jə-bəl) *adj.* Not eligible; not qualified: *ineligible to vote; ineligible for citizenship.* **—in·el′i·gi·bil′i·ty** *n.* **—in·el′i·gi·bly** *adv.*

in·ept (ĭn-**ĕpt′**) *adj.* Awkward or clumsy; lacking skill or competence: *an inept actor; an inept performance.* [From Latin *ineptus* : *in-*, not + *aptus*, suitable.] **—in·ept′ly** *adv.* **—in·ept′ness** *n.*

in·ep·ti·tude (ĭn-**ĕp′**tĭ-to͞od′) *n.* **1.** Lack of skill or competence. **2.** An inept act or remark.

in·e·qual·i·ty (ĭn′ĭ-**kwŏl′**ĭ-tē) *n., pl.* **in·e·qual·i·ties 1.** The condition of being unequal, as in size, rank, or amount: *the growing inequality between rich and poor.* **2.** A mathematical statement that one number is greater than or less than another number.

in·eq·ui·ta·ble (ĭn-**ĕk′**wĭ-tə-bəl) *adj.* Not equitable; unfair; unjust: *inequitable pay; an inequitable division of work.* **—in·eq′ui·ta·bly** *adv.*

in·eq·ui·ty (ĭn-**ĕk′**wĭ-tē) *n., pl.* **in·eq·ui·ties** Lack of equity; injustice; unfairness.

in·ert (ĭn-**ûrt′**) *adj.* **1.** Unable to move or act: *Rock is composed of inert matter.* **2.** Slow to move, act, or respond; sluggish: *the inert forms of lizards sunning on a rock.* **3.** Incapable of reacting with other elements to form chemical compounds: *Helium is an inert gas.* [From Latin *iners* : *in-*, not, without + *ars*, skill, ability.] **—in·ert′ly** *adv.*

in·er·tia (ĭ-**nûr′**shə) *n.* **1.** The tendency of a body at rest to remain at rest, or of a body in motion to continue moving in a straight line at a constant speed unless a force is applied to it. **2.** Resistance to motion, action, or change: *the inertia of a large bureaucracy.*

in·es·cap·a·ble (ĭn′ĭ-**skā′**pə-bəl) *adj.* Incapable of being escaped or avoided; inevitable: *The facts led to an inescapable conclusion.* **—in′es·cap′a·bly** *adv.*

in·es·ti·ma·ble (ĭn-**ĕs′**tə-mə-bəl) *adj.* **1.** Impossible to estimate: *inestimable damage.* **2.** Of immeasurable worth; invaluable: *General Washington performed an inestimable service for the new nation.* **—in·es′ti·ma·bly** *adv.*

in·ev·i·ta·ble (ĭn-**ĕv′**ĭ-tə-bəl) *adj.* Impossible to avoid or prevent; certain to happen: *the inevitable delays in trying to drive across town during rush hour.* [From Middle English : Latin *in-*, not + Latin *ēvitāre*, to avoid.] **—in·ev′i·ta·bly** *adv.*

in·ex·act (ĭn′ĭg-**zăkt′**) *adj.* Not exact; not quite accurate or precise: *Because of inexact measurements, I cut the boards too short.* **—in′ex·act′ly** *adv.*

in·ex·cus·a·ble (ĭn′ĭk-**skyo͞o′**zə-bəl) *adj.* Impossible to excuse, pardon, or justify: *an inexcusable error.* **—in′ex·cus′a·bly** *adv.*

in·ex·haust·i·ble (ĭn′ĭg-**zô′**stə-bəl) *adj.* **1.** Not capable of being used up; unlimited: *an inexhaustible supply of food.* **2.** Tireless; indefatigable: *an inexhaustible rescue worker.* **—in′ex·haust′i·bly** *adv.*

in·ex·o·ra·ble (ĭn-**ĕk′**sər-ə-bəl) *adj.* **1.** Impossible to stop, alter, or resist; inevitable: *the inexorable passage of time.* **2.** Not capable of being persuaded or moderated by pleas: *an inexorable judge.* [From Latin *inexōrābilis* : *in-*, not + *exōrābilis*, pliant, flexible.] **—in·ex′o·ra·bly** *adv.*

in·ex·pe·di·ent (ĭn′ĭk-**spē′**dē-ənt) *adj.* Not expedient; inadvisable. **—in′ex·pe′di·ent·ly** *adv.*

in·ex·pen·sive (ĭn′ĭk-**spĕn′**sĭv) *adj.* Not high in price; cheap. **—in′ex·pen′sive·ly** *adv.* **—in′ex·pen′sive·ness** *n.*

in·ex·pe·ri·ence (ĭn′ĭk-**spîr′**ē-əns) *n.* Lack of experience or of knowledge gained from experience: *mistakes due to inexperience.*

in·ex·pe·ri·enced (ĭn′ĭk-**spîr′**ē-ənst) *adj.* Lacking experience or the knowledge gained from experience: *an inexperienced driver.*

in·ex·pert (ĭn-**ĕk′**spûrt′) *adj.* Not expert; unskilled. **—in·ex′pert′ly** *adv.* **—in·ex′pert′ness** *n.*

in·ex·pli·ca·ble (ĭn-**ĕk′**splĭ-kə-bəl *or* ĭn′ĭk-**splĭk′**ə-bəl) *adj.* Incapable of being explained or understood: *an inexplicable mystery.* **—in·ex′pli·ca·bly** *adv.*

in·ex·press·i·ble (ĭn′ĭk-**sprĕs′**ə-bəl) *adj.* Incapable of being expressed, especially in words; indescribable: *inexpressible joy.* **—in′ex·press′i·bly** *adv.*

in·ex·tin·guish·a·ble (ĭn′ĭk-**stĭng′**gwĭ-shə-bəl) *adj.* Impossible to extinguish or put an end to: *an inextinguishable desire to become a musician.*

in·ex·tri·ca·ble (ĭn-**ĕk′**strĭ-kə-bəl *or* ĭn′ĭk-**strĭk′**ə-bəl) *adj.* **1.** Impossible to escape from: *an inextricable maze.* **2.** Difficult or impossible to disentangle or untie: *an inextricable snarl in my fishing line.* **3.** Too complicated or involved to solve: *an inextricable problem.* —**in·ex′tri·ca·bly** *adv.*

in·fal·li·ble (ĭn-**făl′**ə-bəl) *adj.* **1.** Incapable of making a mistake: *We had an infallible guide on our journey.* **2.** Incapable of failing; sure: *an infallible cure.* —**in·fal′li·bil′i·ty** *n.* —**in·fal′li·bly** *adv.*

in·fa·mous (**ĭn′**fə-məs) *adj.* **1.** Having an exceedingly bad reputation; notorious: *an infamous traitor.* **2.** Deserving condemnation; shocking; outrageous: *infamous deeds.* —**in′fa·mous·ly** *adv.*

in·fa·my (**ĭn′**fə-mē) *n.* **1.** The condition of being infamous: *a name that will live in infamy.* **2.** Evil reputation; disgrace: *The infamy of the dishonest politician was known far and wide.*

in·fan·cy (**ĭn′**fən-sē) *n., pl.* **in·fan·cies 1.** The earliest period of childhood, especially before the ability to walk has been acquired. **2.** The earliest stage of something: *Space exploration was in its infancy in the 1960s.*

in·fant (**ĭn′**fənt) *n.* **1.** A child in the earliest period of life, especially before being able to walk. **2.** In law, a person who has not yet reached the age of majority; a minor. ❖ *adj.* **1.** Relating to an infant: *infant years.* **2.** Intended for infants: *infant clothing.* **3.** Newly begun or formed: *an infant industry.* [From Middle English *infaunt*, from Latin *īnfāns*, not able to speak.]

in·fan·tile (**ĭn′**fən-tīl′ *or* **ĭn′**fən-tĭl) *adj.* **1.** Relating to infants or infancy: *infantile stages of development.* **2.** Lacking in maturity; childish: *The two leaders showed an infantile reluctance to deal with each other.*

infantile paralysis *n.* Poliomyelitis.

in·fan·try (**ĭn′**fən-trē) *n., pl.* **in·fan·tries 1.** Soldiers armed and trained to fight on foot: *The infantry encamped near the town.* **2.** The branch of an army made up of units trained to fight on foot. [From Old Italian *infante*, youth, foot soldier, from Latin *īnfāns*, infant.]

in·fan·try·man (**ĭn′**fən-trē-mən) *n.* A soldier in the infantry.

in·fat·u·ate (ĭn-**făch′**o͞o-āt′) *tr.v.* **in·fat·u·at·ed, in·fat·u·at·ing, in·fat·u·ates** To fill with foolish love or attachment: *The stage assistant was infatuated with the famous actress.* —**in·fat′u·a′tion** *n.*

in·fect (ĭn-**fĕkt′**) *tr.v.* **in·fect·ed, in·fect·ing, in·fects 1.** To enter and grow or multiply in, often resulting in disease. Used of bacteria, viruses, fungi, or other infectious agents: *Many people were infected with salmonella.* **2.** To transmit a disease or an infectious agent to: *The sick child infected the rest of the class.* **3.** To become transmitted to and copied on (a hard drive, for example). Used of a computer virus or other harmful software. **4.** To affect as if by a contagious disease: *Their enthusiasm for baseball infected all of us.* [From Middle English *infecten*, from Latin *īnficere*, to stain, infect.]

in·fec·tion (ĭn-**fĕk′**shən) *n.* **1a.** The invasion of bodily tissue by bacteria, viruses, fungi, or other agents that grow or multipy and often cause disease: *Sterile techniques reduce the chance of infection.* **b.** An instance of being infected: *I have an infection in my toe.* **2.** An instance of a virus or similar software program infecting a computer.

in·fec·tious (ĭn-**fĕk′**shəs) *adj.* **1.** Capable of being spread by infection: *an infectious disease.* **2.** Capable of causing infection: *infectious microorganisms.* **3.** Capable of transmitting a disease; contagious: *an infectious person.* **4.** Tending to spread easily or catch on: *infectious laughter.* —**in·fec′tious·ly** *adv.* —**in·fec′tious·ness** *n.*

infectious mononucleosis *n.* A contagious disease caused by a virus and characterized by fever, sore throat, swollen lymph nodes, and tiredness that may last for several weeks.

in·fer (ĭn-**fûr′**) *tr.v.* **in·ferred, in·fer·ring, in·fers** To decide or conclude by reasoning from evidence: *I inferred from their laughter that the children were having fun.* [From Latin *īnferre*, to bring in.] —SEE NOTE.

in·fer·ence (**ĭn′**fər-əns) *n.* **1.** The act or process of inferring: *arrive at a conclusion by inference.* **2.** Something inferred; a conclusion: *The evidence is too scanty to draw any inferences from it.*

in·fe·ri·or (ĭn-**fîr′**ē-ər) *adj.* **1.** Low or lower in order, rank, or importance: *A lieutenant is inferior to a captain.* **2.** Low or lower in quality, value, or estimation: *That computer is an inferior brand.* ❖ *n.* A person lower in rank, status, or accomplishment than another: *She gave orders to her inferiors.* [From Middle English, from Latin *īnferior*, comparative of *īnferus*, low.]

in·fe·ri·or·i·ty (ĭn-fîr′ē-**ôr′**ĭ-tē) *n.* The fact or quality of being inferior.

inferiority complex *n.* An enduring feeling of being inferior to others, sometimes accompanied by overly aggressive behavior.

in·fer·nal (ĭn-**fûr′**nəl) *adj.* **1.** Relating to hell or a world of the dead: *infernal damnation.* **2.** Abominable; awful: *an infernal nuisance.* [From Middle English, from Late Latin *īnfernus*, hell, from Latin, lower, underground.] —**in·fer′nal·ly** *adv.*

in·fer·no (ĭn-**fûr′**nō) *n., pl.* **in·fer·nos** A place or condition suggestive of hell, as in being chaotic, noisy, or intensely hot: *The fire flared out of control, becoming a raging inferno.* [From Italian *inferno*, hell, from Late Latin *īnfernus*.]

in·fer·tile (ĭn-**fûr′**tl) *adj.* **1.** Not capable of producing offspring; unable to reproduce: *an infertile cow.* **2.** Not capable of developing into a complete organism; unfertilized: *an infertile egg.* **3.** Not capable of supporting plant life; unfavorable to the growth of crops or other plants: *infertile soil.* —**in′fer·til′i·ty** (ĭn′fər-**tĭl′**ĭ-tē) *n.*

in·fest (ĭn-**fĕst′**) *tr.v.* **in·fest·ed, in·fest·ing, in·fests** To live in or overrun in large numbers so as to be harmful or unpleasant: *bedbugs infesting the apartment; a park that was infested with poison ivy.* [From Middle English *infesten*, to distress, from Latin *īnfestus*, hostile.] —**in′fes·ta′tion** *n.*

in·fi·del (**ĭn′**fĭ-dəl *or* **ĭn′**fĭ-dĕl′) *n.* **1.** *Often Offensive* A person who does not believe in a particular religion, especially Christianity or Islam. **2.** A person who has no religious beliefs.

in·fi·del·i·ty (ĭn′fĭ-**dĕl′**ĭ-tē) *n., pl.* **in·fi·del·i·ties 1.** Unfaithfulness to another person, especially by committing adultery. **2.** An unfaithful or adulterous act. **3.** Lack of religious belief.

in·field (**ĭn′**fēld′) *n.* **1.** The area of a baseball field bounded by all four bases. **2.** The four infielders of a baseball team.

in·field·er (**ĭn′**fēl′dər) *n.* A baseball player whose defensive position is first base, second base, shortstop, or third base.

in·fight·ing (**ĭn′**fī′tĭng) *n.* **1.** Strife or competition among associates in a group or organization: *Infighting on the president's staff caused a delay in the policy announcement.* **2.** Fighting or boxing at close range.

in·fil·trate (ĭn-**fĭl′**trāt′ *or* **ĭn′**fĭl-trāt′) *tr.v.* **in·fil·trat·ed, in·fil·trat·ing, in·fil·trates 1a.** To pass (troops) secretly into enemy territory. **b.** To penetrate or slip through with hostile intentions: *Enemy troops infiltrated our border.* **2.** To enter without being noticed for purposes such as spying: *Government agents infiltrated the criminal operation.* **3.** To cause (a liquid or gas) to pass through the small spaces of a substance; filter. **4.** To fill or saturate (a substance) by filtering; permeate. —**in′fil·tra′tion** *n.*

in·fi·nite (**ĭn′**fə-nĭt) *adj.* **1.** Having no limit or bound; endless. **2a.** Greater in value than any countable number,

ă	pat	ôr	core
ā	pay	oi	boy
âr	care	ou	out
ä	father	o͝o	took
ĕ	pet	o͝or	lure
ē	be	o͞o	boot
ĭ	pit	ŭ	cut
ī	bite	ûr	urge
îr	pier	th	thin
ŏ	pot	*th*	this
ō	toe	zh	vision
ô	paw	ə	about

however large: *an infinite number.* **b.** Having an infinite size or measure; unlimited: *an infinite plane; an infinite set of numbers.* **3.** Very great; immense; boundless: *His joy was infinite.* **—in′fi·nite·ly** *adv.* **—in′fi·nite·ness** *n.*

in·fin·i·tes·i·mal (ĭn′fĭn-ĭ-tĕs′ə-məl) *adj.* Immeasurably small; minute: *a high-grade steel with only infinitesimal amounts of impurities.* **—in′fin·i·tes′i·mal·ly** *adv.*

in·fin·i·tive (ĭn-fĭn′ĭ-tĭv) *n.* A verb form that is not inflected to indicate person, number, or tense. In English, it is usually preceded by *to* or by an auxiliary verb. For example, in the phrases *wanted to leave* and *will play tomorrow,* the words *leave* and *play* are infinitives.

in·fin·i·ty (ĭn-fĭn′ĭ-tē) *n., pl.* **in·fin·i·ties 1.** A space, period of time, or quantity that is without a limit. **2.** The quality or condition of being infinite. **3.** A quantity that is greater than any other quantity, however large.

in·firm (ĭn-fûrm′) *adj.* Weak in body, as from sickness; feeble. **—in·firm′ly** *adv.*

in·fir·ma·ry (ĭn-fûr′mə-rē) *n., pl.* **in·fir·ma·ries** A place for the care of sick or injured people, especially a small hospital or dispensary in a large institution.

in·fir·mi·ty (ĭn-fûr′mĭ-tē) *n., pl.* **in·fir·mi·ties 1.** The condition of being infirm; weakness; frailty: *The doctor hesitated to perform surgery because of the patient's infirmity.* **2.** A sickness; an illness.

in·flame (ĭn-flām′) *tr.v.* **in·flamed, in·flam·ing, in·flames 1.** To cause redness, swelling, and soreness in (a body part). **2.** To stir up anger or other strong emotion in (someone); excite: *The speech inflamed the crowd.*

in·flamed (ĭn-flāmd′) *adj.* **1.** Swollen and sore: *an inflamed finger.* **2.** Aroused; stirred up; excited: *an inflamed audience.*

in·flam·ma·ble (ĭn-flăm′ə-bəl) *adj.* **1.** Tending to catch fire easily and burn rapidly; flammable: *Gasoline is very inflammable.* **2.** Quickly or easily aroused to strong emotion: *an inflammable boss.*

in·flam·ma·tion (ĭn′flə-mā′shən) *n.* **1.** The reaction of the immune system to an infection or injury in a body part, marked by pain, redness, swelling, and heat that result from increased blood flow and the leakage of fluid into the tissues. Inflammation is important for helping to heal damaged tissue, but it is also associated with chronic diseases such as rheumatoid arthritis. **2.** The act of inflaming or the condition of being inflamed.

in·flam·ma·to·ry (ĭn-flăm′ə-tôr′ē) *adj.* **1.** Tending to arouse strong emotion: *the speaker's inflammatory language.* **2.** Characterized by or causing inflammation: *Arthritis is an inflammatory disease.*

in·flat·a·ble (ĭn-flā′tə-bəl) *adj.* Capable of being inflated: *an inflatable rubber boat.* ❖ *n.* A large helium or hot-air balloon constructed so as to resemble a figure or object when inflated.

in·flate (ĭn-flāt′) *v.* **in·flat·ed, in·flat·ing, in·flates** *—tr.* **1.** To cause to expand with air or gas: *Did you inflate the tires on your bicycle?* **2.** To enlarge or raise abnormally or improperly: *The flattering attention inflated the athlete's ego.* *—intr.* To become inflated: *The balloon inflated quickly.* [From Middle English *inflaten,* from Latin *īnflāre,* to blow into.] **—in·flat′er, in·fla′tor** *n.*

in·fla·tion (ĭn-flā′shən) *n.* **1.** The act or process of inflating something: *The inflation of the giant balloon took an hour.* **2.** A continuing rise in the price of goods and services in an economy.

in·fla·tion·ar·y (ĭn-flā′shə-nĕr′ē) *adj.* Relating or contributing to inflation: *inflationary policies.*

in·flect (ĭn-flĕkt′) *tr.v.* **in·flect·ed, in·flect·ing, in·flects 1.** To vary the tone or pitch of (the voice), especially in speaking. **2.** To change the form of (a word) to show number, tense, person, comparison, or other grammatical function. For example, *book* is inflected to *books* in the plural. **3.** To bend; curve: *a prism inflects light rays.* [From Middle English *inflecten,* to bend down, from Latin *īnflectere.*]

in·flec·tion (ĭn-flĕk′shən) *n.* **1.** A change in the tone or pitch of the voice, especially in speech: *Questions usually end with a rising inflection.* **2a.** The process that changes the form of a word to indicate number, tense, person, comparison, or other grammatical function. For example, the comparative *quicker* is formed from *quick* by inflection. **b.** A word formed by this process; an inflected form. For example, *drives, drove,* and *driven* are all inflections of the word *drive.* **c.** A suffix used in this process. **3.** The act of inflecting or the condition of being inflected. **4.** A bend or curve: *an inflection at an angle of 45°.* **—in·flec′tion·al** *adj.*

in·flex·i·ble (ĭn-flĕk′sə-bəl) *adj.* **1.** Not flexible; rigid. **2.** Not subject to change or modification: *an inflexible rule.* **3.** Refusing to change; unyielding: *They are inflexible in their demand for better service.* **—in·flex′i·bil′i·ty** *n.* **—in·flex′i·bly** *adv.*

in·flict (ĭn-flĭkt′) *tr.v.* **in·flict·ed, in·flict·ing, in·flicts 1.** To cause (something injurious or harmful) to be endured or suffered, as to a person, group, or area: *claws that inflicted a deep wound; a storm that inflicted widespread damage.* **2.** To force someone to undergo or experience (something unwanted): *The players grew weary of the stern lectures that the coach inflicted on them.* **3.** To give or deliver (a blow). [From Latin *īnflīgere.*]

in·flic·tion (ĭn-flĭk′shən) *n.* **1.** The act or process of inflicting: *the infliction of punishment.* **2.** Something, such as punishment, that is inflicted.

in·flo·res·cence (ĭn′flə-rĕs′əns) *n.* A cluster of flowers arranged in a characteristic way on a stem.

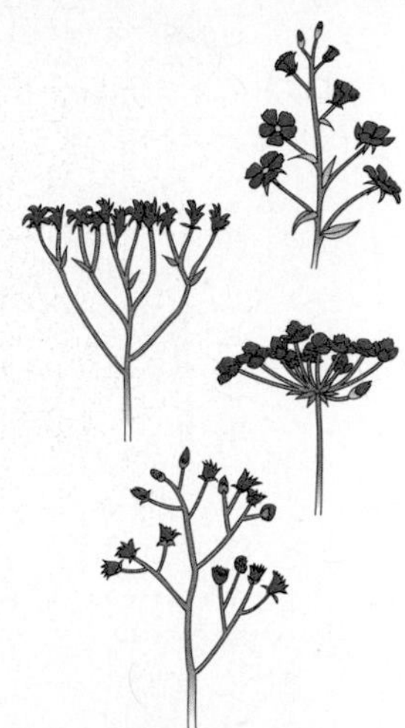

inflorescence
clockwise from top left: corymb, raceme, umbel, and panicle arrangements

in·flow (ĭn′flō′) *n.* **1.** The act or process of flowing in or into: *The inflow of requests has increased.* **2.** Something that flows in or into: *a lake fed by an inflow from the mountains.*

in·flu·ence (ĭn′flo͞o-əns) *n.* **1.** A power that brings about changes or has an effect, especially without any apparent use of force: *Public opinion has a great influence on politicians.* **2.** Power to sway or affect that results from wealth or high position in society: *He got the job because of his uncle's influence.* **3.** A person or thing that brings about change without the use of force: *Travel has had a broadening influence on you.* ❖ *tr.v.* **in·flu·enced, in·flu·enc·ing, in·flu·enc·es** To have an effect on; change: *The automobile has greatly influenced the way people live.* [From Middle English, from Medieval Latin *īnfluentia,* influx, from Latin *īnfluēns,* flowing in.] —SEE NOTE AT **fluent.**

in·flu·en·tial (ĭn′flo͞o-ĕn′shəl) *adj.* Having or exercising influence: *an influential newspaper.* **—in′flu·en′tial·ly** *adv.*

in·flu·en·za (ĭn′flo͞o-ĕn′zə) *n.* A contagious viral disease, characterized by fever, inflammation of the respiratory system, irritation of the intestines, and muscular pain. [From Italian, from Medieval Latin *īnfluentia,* influence (so called apparently from the belief that epidemics were due to the influence of the stars).] —SEE NOTE.

in·flux (ĭn′flŭks′) *n.* A flowing in: *an influx of tourists to the park.* —SEE NOTE AT **fluent.**

in·fo (ĭn′fō) *n. Informal* Information.

in·form (ĭn-fôrm′) *v.* **in·formed, in·form·ing, in·forms** *—tr.* **1.** To give information to; tell; notify: *The notice informed us that the meeting was canceled.* **2.** To acquaint (oneself) with knowledge of a subject: *I watch the news to inform myself about current events.* *—intr.* To give secret or damaging information: *The gang was captured after one of its members informed on the others.*

in·for·mal (ĭn-fôr′məl) *adj.* **1.** Not following or requiring fixed ceremonies or rules; unofficial: *an informal agreement made with a handshake.* **2.** Suitable for everyday use or for casual occasions: *informal dress.* **3.** Not suitable for formal writing but frequently used in conversa-

SCIENCE

influenza Why do people of all ages get vaccinated against **influenza,** commonly called the *flu,* every year, when vaccines against diseases such as measles and mumps are typically given only during childhood? Influenza is caused by a virus that was first isolated in the 1930s, after a worldwide epidemic that killed over 20 million people in the early 1900s. The virus spreads quickly through the air and survives longer in cold weather, which is why flu outbreaks occur in the winter. It is now known that there are many different strains of the influenza virus and that the virus's genes are constantly changing. Every year scientists make vaccines from new strains of the virus, hoping to avert a dangerous flu outbreak.

tion and ordinary writing. For example, the use of *kid* to mean "a child" is informal. **—in·for′mal·ly** *adv.*

in·for·mal·i·ty (ĭn′fôr-**măl′**ĭ-tē) *n., pl.* **in·for·mal·i·ties** **1.** The state or quality of being informal: *the informality of a picnic.* **2.** An informal act; informal behavior.

in·for·mant (ĭn-**fôr′**mənt) *n.* A person who provides information to another.

in·for·ma·tion (ĭn′fər-**mā′**shən) *n.* **1.** Knowledge or facts learned, especially about a certain event or subject: *The newspaper provides information on the day's events.* See Synonyms at **knowledge. 2.** The act of informing or the condition of being informed: *This brochure is for your information.* **3.** Data that a computer transmits, processes, or stores. **4.** Nerve impulses or the perceptions and signals they convey: *information sent from the brain to the fingers.*

in·for·ma·tive (ĭn-**fôr′**mə-tĭv) *adj.* Providing information; instructive: *an informative TV series on dinosaurs.*

in·formed (ĭn-**fôrmd′**) *adj.* Provided with information; knowledgeable: *That reporter is well informed on the facts of the issue.*

in·form·er (ĭn-**fôr′**mər) *n.* A person who notifies authorities of secret and often illegal activities.

infra– *pref.* A prefix that means below or beneath: *infrasonic.*

in·frac·tion (ĭn-**frăk′**shən) *n.* A breach or breaking of a law or rule; a violation.

in·fra·red (ĭn′frə-**rĕd′**) *adj.* Relating to the invisible part of the electromagnetic spectrum with wavelengths longer than those of visible red light but shorter than those of microwaves: *infrared light.* [From Latin *īnfrā*, below + *red.*] —SEE NOTE.

in·fra·son·ic (ĭn′frə-**sŏn′**ĭk) *adj.* Generating or using sound waves that are too low in frequency to be heard by human ears.

in·fra·struc·ture (**ĭn′**frə-strŭk′chər) *n.* An underlying base or foundation for something, especially the basic facilities necessary for a community to function, including roads, bridges, water pipes, and power lines.

in·fre·quent (ĭn-**frē′**kwənt) *adj.* Not occurring often; occasional or rare: *an infrequent visitor.* **—in·fre′quen·cy** *n.* **—in·fre′quent·ly** *adv.*

in·fringe (ĭn-**frĭnj′**) *tr.v.* **in·fringed, in·fring·ing, in·fring·es** To violate or interfere with (a law, right, or obligation); fail to respect: *Censorship infringes the right to free speech.* ◆ **infringe on** or **infringe upon** To intrude or encroach upon; trespass on: *Reading someone else's diary infringes on that person's privacy.* [From Middle English *enfrangen*, from Latin *īnfringere*, to destroy.] **—in·fring′er** *n.* **—in·fringe′ment** *n.*

in·fu·ri·ate (ĭn-**fyo͝or′**ē-āt′) *tr.v.* **in·fu·ri·at·ed, in·fu·ri·at·ing, in·fu·ri·ates** To make furious; enrage: *I was infuriated by their taunts.* **—in·fu′ri·a′tion** *n.*

in·fuse (ĭn-**fyo͞oz′**) *tr.v.* **in·fused, in·fus·ing, in·fus·es** **1.** To fill; inspire: *Winning the game infused us with the hope that we might win the championship.* **2.** To put into or introduce; instill: *The executive infused new vigor into the company.* **3.** To steep or soak without boiling in order to extract a substance: *Tea is made by infusing tea leaves in hot water.* —SEE NOTE AT **transfusion.**

in·fu·sion (ĭn-**fyo͞o′**zhən) *n.* **1.** The act or process of infusing. **2.** Something infused or introduced: *With an infusion of money the business recovered.* **3.** A liquid product obtained by infusing: *drank an infusion of medicinal herbs.*

–ing[1] *suff.* A suffix that forms: **1.** The present participle of verbs: *living.* **2.** Adjectives resembling present participles but not formed from verbs: *swashbuckling.*

–ing[2] *suff.* A suffix that means: **1.** An action, process, or art: *dancing; thinking.* **2.** An instance of an action, process, or art: *a meeting.* **3.** The result of an action or process: *a painting.* **4.** Something used in or connected with an action or process: *roofing.*

in·gen·ious (ĭn-**jēn′**yəs) *adj.* **1.** Clever at devising or making; inventive; creative: *an ingenious storyteller.* **2.** Planned, made, or done with originality and imagination: *The telephone is an ingenious device.* **—in·gen′ious·ly** *adv.* **—in·gen′ious·ness** *n.*

in·gé·nue (**ăɴ′**zhə-no͞o′) *n.* **1.** A naive, innocent girl or young woman. **2.** An actress playing the role of an ingénue.

in·ge·nu·i·ty (ĭn′jə-**no͞o′**ĭ-tē) *n., pl.* **in·ge·nu·i·ties** Inventive skill or imagination; cleverness.

in·gen·u·ous (ĭn-**jĕn′**yo͞o-əs) *adj.* **1.** Frank and open; candid: *They were being quite ingenuous in telling us the whole story.* **2.** Lacking in cunning or guile: *The young child had an ingenuous smile.* **—in·gen′u·ous·ly** *adv.* **—in·gen′u·ous·ness** *n.*

in·gest (ĭn-**jĕst′**) *tr.v.* **in·gest·ed, in·gest·ing, in·gests** To take in or absorb, especially as food or drink: *Do not ingest any water before your surgery.* **—in·ges′tion** *n.*

in·gle·nook (**ĭng′**gəl-no͝ok′) *n.* A nook or corner beside an open fireplace. [From *ingle*, fireplace (perhaps from Scottish Gaelic *aingeal*, fire) + *nook.*]

in·glo·ri·ous (ĭn-**glôr′**ē-əs) *adj.* Shameful; dishonorable: *An inglorious incident of cowardice clouded the soldier's career.*

in·got (**ĭng′**gət) *n.* A mass of metal shaped in the form of a bar or block for convenient storage or transportation.

in·grain (ĭn-**grān′**) *tr.v.* **in·grained, in·grain·ing, in·grains** To fix or impress deeply, as in the mind: *The coach ingrained a sense of fairness into the players.*

in·grained (ĭn-**grānd′**) *adj.* Firmly established; deep-seated: *an ingrained habit.*

in·grate (**ĭn′**grāt′) *n.* An ungrateful person.

in·gra·ti·ate (ĭn-**grā′**shē-āt′) *tr.v.* **in·gra·ti·at·ed, in·gra·ti·at·ing, in·gra·ti·ates** To gain favor for (oneself) from another; make (oneself) agreeable to another: *The class tried to ingratiate itself with the new teacher by being especially attentive.*

in·gra·ti·at·ing (ĭn-**grā′**shē-ā′tĭng) *adj.* **1.** Agreeable; pleasing: *an ingratiating smile.* **2.** Intended to win someone's liking or approval: *an ingratiating remark.* **—in·gra′ti·at′ing·ly** *adv.*

in·grat·i·tude (ĭn-**grăt′**ĭ-to͞od′) *n.* Lack of gratitude; ungratefulness.

in·gre·di·ent (ĭn-**grē′**dē-ənt) *n.* An element in a mixture or compound: *The main ingredient of bread is flour. Sand is an ingredient of concrete.* [From Middle English, from Latin *ingredī*, to go into.]

in·gress (**ĭn′**grĕs′) *n.* **1.** A means or place of going in; an entrance. **2.** The right or permission to enter: *Only employees of the company have ingress to its building.* **3.** The act of going in or entering.

in·grown (**ĭn′**grōn′) *adj.* Grown abnormally into the skin or flesh: *an ingrown toenail.*

in·hab·it (ĭn-**hăb′**ĭt) *tr.v.* **in·hab·it·ed, in·hab·it·ing, in·hab·its** To live in; have as a dwelling place: *Dinosaurs inhabited the earth millions of years ago.*

in·hab·it·a·ble (ĭn-**hăb′**ĭ-tə-bəl) *adj.* Suitable for living in: *an inhabitable land.*

in·hab·i·tant (ĭn-**hăb′**ĭ-tənt) *n.* A permanent resident of a particular place.

in·ha·lant (ĭn-**hā′**lənt) *n.* Something, such as a medicine, that is inhaled.

in·ha·la·tion (ĭn′hə-**lā′**shən) *n.* The act or an instance of inhaling.

in·ha·la·tor (**ĭn′**hə-lā′tər) *n.* A device used to inhale a medicine.

in·hale (ĭn-**hāl′**) *v.* **in·haled, in·hal·ing, in·hales** *—tr.* **1.** To draw (air or a fragrance, for example) into the lungs by breathing: *I inhaled the fresh sea air.* **2.** *Informal* To consume rapidly or eagerly; devour: *We inhaled the pizza.* *—intr.* To breathe in: *inhale deeply.* [From Latin *inhālāre*, to breathe upon.]

WRITERS CHOOSE THEIR WORDS

Father hesitated. I could see that he was uncertain about the etiquette of the situation; in our world, first names were reserved for the family and only the very closest friends. . . . With his most **ingratiating** smile and a little bow, Father introduced us as the Rudomins and the Kaftals.

—Esther Hautzig
The Endless Steppe

ă	pat	ôr	core
ā	pay	oi	boy
âr	care	ou	out
ä	father	o͝o	took
ĕ	pet	o͝or	lure
ē	be	o͞o	boot
ĭ	pit	ŭ	cut
ī	bite	ûr	urge
îr	pier	th	thin
ŏ	pot	*th*	this
ō	toe	zh	vision
ô	paw	ə	about

in·hal·er (ĭn-hā′lər) *n.* A device used to inhale a medicine.

in·har·mo·ni·ous (ĭn′här-mō′nē-əs) *adj.* **1.** Not in harmony; discordant: *inharmonious music.* **2.** Not in accord or agreement: *inharmonious relations between countries.* **—in′har·mo′ni·ous·ly** *adv.*

in·her·ent (ĭn-hîr′ənt *or* ĭn-hĕr′ənt) *adj.* Being part of the basic nature of a person or thing; essential; intrinsic: *The student's inherent curiosity led to an interest in science.* **—in·her′ent·ly** *adv.*

in·her·it (ĭn-hĕr′ĭt) *v.* **in·her·it·ed, in·her·it·ing, in·her·its** —*tr.* **1.** To receive (property or a title) from a person who has died, usually through a will. **2.** To receive or take over from someone else: *Upon taking office, the mayor inherited many serious problems.* **3.** To acquire (characteristics) by genetic transmission from one's parents or ancestors: *I inherited my father's hair color.* —*intr.* To receive an inheritance. [From Middle English *enheriten,* from Late Latin *inhērēditāre,* from Latin *hērēs,* heir.] **—in·her′i·tor** *n.*

in·her·i·tance (ĭn-hĕr′ĭ-təns) *n.* **1.** The act of inheriting: *They gained their wealth by inheritance.* **2.** Something that is inherited or is to be inherited at a person's death. **3.** Something regarded as a heritage: *The concept of democracy is an inheritance from the ancient Greeks.* **4.** The process by which characteristics are acquired by genetic transmission from one's parents or ancestors.

in·hib·it (ĭn-hĭb′ĭt) *tr.v.* **in·hib·it·ed, in·hib·it·ing, in·hib·its** To restrain or hold back; prevent: *Shyness inhibited the new student from talking freely in class.*

in·hi·bi·tion (ĭn′hə-bĭsh′ən *or* ĭn′ə-bĭsh′ən) *n.* **1.** The act of inhibiting or the condition of being inhibited. **2.** A feeling or state of mind that restrains a person from doing something: *My inhibition prevented me from asking a question of the famous writer.*

in·hos·pi·ta·ble (ĭn-hŏs′pĭ-tə-bəl *or* ĭn′hŏ-spĭt′ə-bəl) *adj.* **1.** Showing no hospitality to others; unfriendly. **2.** Not providing shelter or food; barren: *the inhospitable Arctic winter.* **—in·hos′pi·ta·bly** *adv.*

in·hu·man (ĭn-hyo͞o′mən) *adj.* **1.** Lacking kindness or compassion; cruel. **2.** Not suited for human needs: *The moon is an inhuman environment.* **3.** Not of ordinary human form; monstrous. **—in·hu′man·ly** *adv.*

in·hu·mane (ĭn′hyo͞o-mān′) *adj.* Lacking pity or compassion: *The law punishes inhumane treatment of animals.* **—in′hu·mane′ly** *adv.*

in·hu·man·i·ty (ĭn′hyo͞o-măn′ĭ-tē) *n., pl.* **in·hu·man·i·ties 1.** Lack of pity or compassion: *the basic inhumanity of war.* **2.** An inhuman or cruel act.

in·im·i·cal (ĭ-nĭm′ĭ-kəl) *adj.* **1.** Harmful or injurious; adverse: *habits inimical to good health.* **2.** Unfriendly; hostile: *The countries have long been inimical neighbors.* [From Latin *inimīcus,* enemy.] **—in·im′i·cal·ly** *adv.*

in·im·i·ta·ble (ĭ-nĭm′ĭ-tə-bəl) *adj.* Impossible to imitate; unique: *a singer's inimitable style.* **—in·im′i·ta·bil′i·ty** *n.* **—in·im′i·ta·bly** *adv.*

in·iq·ui·tous (ĭ-nĭk′wĭ-təs) *adj.* Unjust; wicked. **—in·iq′ui·tous·ly** *adv.*

in·iq·ui·ty (ĭ-nĭk′wĭ-tē) *n., pl.* **in·iq·ui·ties 1.** Extreme injustice; wickedness: *The iniquity of the crime aroused great public anger.* **2.** An immoral act; a sin.

in·i·tial (ĭ-nĭsh′əl) *adj.* Relating to or occurring at the beginning; first: *the initial phase of a project.* ❖ *n.* **1.** The first letter of a word or name. **2.** A large, often decorated letter, as at the beginning of a chapter. ❖ *tr.v.* **in·i·tialed, in·i·tial·ing, in·i·tials** also **in·i·tialled, in·i·tial·ling, in·i·tials** To mark or sign with initials. **—in·i′tial·ly** *adv.*

in·i·tial·ize (ĭ-nĭsh′ə-līz′) *tr.v.* **in·i·tial·ized, in·i·tial·iz·ing, in·i·tial·iz·es 1.** To prepare (a computer or printer) for use. **2.** To format (a computer disk or other storage medium).

in·i·ti·ate (ĭ-nĭsh′ē-āt′) *tr.v.* **in·i·ti·at·ed, in·i·ti·at·ing, in·i·ti·ates 1.** To cause (something) to begin; start: *The diplomat tried to initiate negotiations.* See Synonyms at **begin. 2.** To introduce (a person) to a new subject, interest, skill, or activity: *My music teacher initiated me into the world of opera.* **3.** To admit into a group, often with a special ceremony: *Several new members were initiated into the club.* ❖ *n.* (ĭ-nĭsh′ē-ĭt) A person who is being or has been initiated. **—in·i′ti·a′tor** *n.*

in·i·ti·a·tion (ĭ-nĭsh′ē-ā′shən) *n.* **1.** The act or process of initiating. **2.** Admission into a club, society, or organization. **3.** A ceremony or ritual with which a new member is initiated.

in·i·tia·tive (ĭ-nĭsh′ə-tĭv) *n.* **1.** The ability to undertake a task or to put a plan of action into effect without getting prior help or direction from others: *Starting one's own business requires much initiative.* **2.** The first step or action, especially when taken before others can; the lead over others: *Seizing the initiative, I applied for the job before it was advertised.* **3.** A proposed law or legal resolution included on a ballot during an election as a result of a petition signed by a certain number of citizens. ◆ **on (one's) own initiative** Without prompting or direction from others; on one's own.

in·ject (ĭn-jĕkt′) *tr.v.* **in·ject·ed, in·ject·ing, in·jects 1a.** To force or drive (a liquid or gas) into something: *a mechanism that injects fuel into a cylinder of an engine.* **b.** To introduce (a fluid or medicine) into a body part, especially by a hypodermic syringe. **2.** To introduce; insert: *By mentioning cost, I injected some realism into our planning.* [From Latin *inicere,* to throw in.] **—in·jec′tor** *n.* —SEE NOTE.

in·jec·tion (ĭn-jĕk′shən) *n.* **1.** The act of injecting. **2.** Something that is injected, especially a dose of a liquid medicine injected into the body.

in·ju·di·cious (ĭn′jo͞o-dĭsh′əs) *adj.* Showing a lack of judgment; unwise: *an injudicious decision.* **—in′ju·di′cious·ly** *adv.* **—in′ju·di′cious·ness** *n.*

in·junc·tion (ĭn-jŭngk′shən) *n.* **1.** An order or command: *The teacher's injunction to be silent quieted the class.* **2.** A court order prohibiting or requiring a specific course of action: *The judge issued an injunction stopping the strike and requiring further negotiations.* [From Middle English *injunccion,* from Latin *iniungere,* to enjoin.]

in·jure (ĭn′jər) *tr.v.* **in·jured, in·jur·ing, in·jures 1.** To cause physical harm to; hurt: *I injured my arm when I fell off my bicycle.* **2.** To harm or impair: *The false accusation injured his reputation.*

in·ju·ri·ous (ĭn-jo͝or′ē-əs) *adj.* Causing injury, damage, or wrong; harmful: *Sunburn is injurious to the skin.* **—in·ju′ri·ous·ly** *adv.* **—in·ju′ri·ous·ness** *n.*

in·ju·ry (ĭn′jə-rē) *n., pl.* **in·ju·ries** Damage or harm done to a person or thing: *I escaped the fall with no serious injuries. The scandal caused lasting injury to the senator's reputation.* [From Middle English *injurie,* from Latin *iniūrius,* unjust.]

injury time *n.* Stoppage time.

in·jus·tice (ĭn-jŭs′tĭs) *n.* **1.** Lack of justice; unfairness: *Tyranny always leads to injustice.* **2.** A specific unjust act; a wrong: *Jailing the protesters was a terrible injustice.*

ink (ĭngk) *n.* **1.** A colored or black liquid used especially for writing or printing. **2.** A dark liquid ejected for protection by squids, octopuses, and similar marine animals. **3.** *Informal* Coverage in the print media; publicity: *Her campaign rallies generated a lot of ink.* **4.** *Informal* A tattoo or tattoos. ❖ *tr.v.* **inked, ink·ing, inks 1.** To cover with ink; spread ink on: *The rubber stamp must be inked often.* **2.** *Informal* To tattoo. [From Middle English *enke,* from Late Latin *encaustum,* purple ink.]

ink·blot (ĭngk′blŏt′) *n.* A blot made of spilled ink.

ink·horn (ĭngk′hôrn′) *n.* A small container made of horn or a similar material, formerly used to hold ink.

ink·jet printer (ĭngk′jĕt′) *n.* A printer that directs streams of electrically charged ink onto a page.

initial

initial letter "A" from the illuminated manuscript *A Natural History* by Pliny the Elder (AD 23–79)

WORD BUILDING

inject The word root *ject–* in English words comes ultimately from the past participle *iactus* of the Latin verb *iacere,* "to throw, shoot." **Inject** thus literally means "to throw or shoot in" (using the prefix *in–*[2], "in, into"). The root also appears in **abject,** literally "thrown away" (*ab–,* "away, away from"); **dejected** is literally "shot down," as we would say informally (*de–,* "down"); **reject** means "to throw back" (*re–,* "back, backward"); and **adjective** comes ultimately from *adiectus,* "thrown to or at, placed near" (*ad–,* "at, to, toward"). Thus, an adjective is a word "placed near" a noun to modify it.

inlay

inline skate

ă	pat	ôr	core
ā	pay	oi	boy
âr	care	ou	out
ä	father	ŏŏ	took
ĕ	pet	ŏŏr	lure
ē	be	ōō	boot
ĭ	pit	ŭ	cut
ī	bite	ûr	urge
îr	pier	th	thin
ŏ	pot	*th*	this
ō	toe	zh	vision
ô	paw	ə	about

in·kling (ĭng′klĭng) *n.* A slight indication or hint; a vague idea: *You haven't an inkling of how much it costs to install solar heating.*

ink·stand (ĭngk′stănd′) *n.* **1.** A tray or rack for pens and bottles of ink. **2.** An inkwell.

ink·well (ĭngk′wĕl′) *n.* A small container or reservoir for ink.

ink·y (ĭng′kē) *adj.* **ink·i·er, ink·i·est 1.** Stained or smeared with ink: *inky fingers.* **2.** Like ink; dark; murky: *inky shadows.* **—ink′i·ness** *n.*

in·laid (ĭn′lād′) *v.* Past tense and past participle of **inlay.** ❖ *adj.* **1.** Set smoothly into a surface to form a pattern or decoration: *inlaid decorative tile in a bathroom wall.* **2.** Decorated with a pattern set into the surface: *a table with an inlaid top of wood.*

in·land (ĭn′lənd) *adj.* Relating to or located in the interior of a country or region: *The Great Lakes are inland waterways.* ❖ *adv.* In, toward, or into the interior of a country or region: *You must travel inland to find the source of a river.* ❖ *n.* (ĭn′lănd′ *or* ĭn′lənd) The interior of a country or region.

in-law (ĭn′lô′) *n.* A relative by marriage.

in·lay (ĭn′lā′ *or* ĭn-**lā′**) *tr.v.* **in·laid** (ĭn′lād′), **in·lay·ing, in·lays 1.** To set (pieces of contrasting material) into a surface to form a design: *inlay strips of gold on a silver bracelet.* **2.** To decorate by setting in such designs: *The jewelry box was inlaid with mother-of-pearl.* ❖ *n.* **1.** Contrasting material set into a surface in pieces to form a design. **2.** An inlaid decoration or design: *a table top with a star-shaped inlay of ivory and gold.* **3.** A filling of gold or other solid material, fitted and cemented into a tooth cavity.

in·let (ĭn′lĕt′ *or* ĭn′lĭt) *n.* **1.** A stream or bay leading inland. **2.** A narrow passage of water, as between two islands. **3.** An opening providing a means of entrance.

in·line skate (ĭn′līn′) *n.* A roller skate whose wheels are arranged in a straight line.

in·mate (ĭn′māt′) *n.* A person confined to an institution, such as a prison or hospital.

in·most (ĭn′mōst′) *adj.* Farthest within; innermost.

inn (ĭn) *n.* **1.** A hotel that serves food and drink to travelers. **2.** A tavern or restaurant. [From Old English.]
❑ *These sound alike:* **inn, in**[1] (inside).

in·nards (ĭn′ərdz) *pl.n. Informal* **1.** The internal organs of the body, especially of the abdomen. **2.** The inner parts, as of a machine.

in·nate (ĭ-**nāt′** *or* ĭn′āt′) *adj.* **1.** Possessed at birth; inborn: *innate intelligence.* **2.** Existing as a basic or essential characteristic; inherent: *Mountain climbing has certain innate dangers.* [From Middle English *innat,* from Latin *innātus,* past participle of *innāscī,* to be born in.] **—in·nate′ly** *adv.* **—in·nate′ness** *n.*

in·ner (ĭn′ər) *adj.* **1.** Located farther inside: *The inner core of the earth lies under the crust and mantle.* **2.** Relating to the spirit or mind: *Sitting beside the brook, he felt an inner peace.* **3.** More exclusive, private, or important: *the inner circles of government.*

inner city *n.* The older central part of a city, especially when run-down and impoverished.

inner ear *n.* The innermost part of the ear, consisting of the cochlea, vestibule, and semicircular canals. The inner ear contains the essential organs of hearing and of balance.

Inner Mongolia An autonomous region of northeast China south of Mongolia. It became part of China in 1911.

in·ner·most (ĭn′ər-mōst′) *adj.* **1.** Located farthest within: *the innermost room in the palace.* **2.** Most private or intimate: *innermost feelings.*

inner tube *n.* A hollow rubber ring that can be inserted inside the casing of a tire and inflated.

in·ning (ĭn′ĭng) *n.* One of the nine divisions of a baseball game during which each team has a turn at bat.

inn·keep·er (ĭn′kē′pər) *n.* A person who owns or manages an inn.

in·no·cence (ĭn′ə-səns) *n.* The condition, quality, or fact of being innocent, especially freedom from guilt.

in·no·cent (ĭn′ə-sənt) *adj.* **1.** Free of evil or wrongdoing; not guilty of a crime or sin: *The jury found the defendant innocent of the crime.* **2.** Unaware of evil or wrongdoing; naive: *We do not remain innocent children for long.* **3.** Not intended to cause harm: *an innocent joke.* ❖ *n.* **1.** A person, especially a child, who is free of evil or sin. **2.** A simple inexperienced person who has no intention of deceiving others. [From Middle English, from Latin *innocēns* : *in-*, not + *nocēns*, harming.] **—in′no·cent·ly** *adv.*

in·noc·u·ous (ĭ-**nŏk′**yōō-əs) *adj.* Harmless; innocent: *an innocuous remark.* **—in·noc′u·ous·ly** *adv.* **—in·noc′u·ous·ness** *n.*

in·no·vate (ĭn′ə-vāt′) *v.* **in·no·vat·ed, in·no·vat·ing, in·no·vates** —*tr.* To begin or introduce for the first time: *innovate a new design for microchips.* —*intr.* To begin or introduce something new. [From Latin *innovāre,* to renew, from *novus,* new.] **—in′no·va′tor** *n.*

in·no·va·tion (ĭn′ə-**vā′**shən) *n.* **1.** The act of innovating: *The Industrial Revolution was a time of great innovation.* **2.** Something newly introduced: *Laptops were a major innovation in computer design.*

in·no·va·tive (ĭn′ə-vā′tĭv) *adj.* Tending to innovate or characterized by innovation: *an innovative architect; an innovative product.*

in·nu·en·do (ĭn′yōō-**ĕn′**dō) *n., pl.* **in·nu·en·does** An indirect hint or suggestion, usually intended to hurt the good name or standing of someone; an insinuation: *The star athlete claimed that the news reports were full of lies and innuendoes.*

in·nu·mer·a·ble (ĭ-**nōō′**mər-ə-bəl) *adj.* Too numerous to be counted: *innumerable difficulties.* **—in·nu′mer·a·ble·ness** *n.* **—in·nu′mer·a·bly** *adv.*

in·oc·u·late (ĭ-**nŏk′**yə-lāt′) *tr.v.* **in·oc·u·lat·ed, in·oc·u·lat·ing, in·oc·u·lates 1.** To inject (a person or animal) with a vaccine or serum, to protect against disease. **2.** To introduce microorganisms into (something, especially a culture): *inculated the broth with bacteria.* [From Middle English *inoculaten,* to graft a scion onto, from Latin *inoculāre,* from *oculus,* eye, bud.]

in·oc·u·la·tion (ĭ-nŏk′yə-**lā′**shən) *n.* **1.** The act of inoculating. **2.** An injection, as of a vaccine, given to make the body resistant to a disease.

in·of·fen·sive (ĭn′ə-**fĕn′**sĭv) *adj.* Giving no offense; harmless: *an inoffensive joke.* **—in′of·fen′sive·ly** *adv.* **—in′of·fen′sive·ness** *n.*

in·op·er·a·ble (ĭn-**ŏp′**ər-ə-bəl *or* ĭn-**ŏp′**rə-bəl) *adj.* **1.** Not suitable for surgery: *an inoperable tumor.* **2.** Not functioning; inoperative.

in·op·er·a·tive (ĭn-**ŏp′**ər-ə-tĭv *or* ĭn-**ŏp′**rə-tĭv) *adj.* **1.** Not working or functioning: *The computer is inoperative at this time.* **2.** No longer in force: *The governor declared her latest policy inoperative.*

in·op·por·tune (ĭn-ŏp′ər-**tōōn′**) *adj.* Coming at the wrong time; inappropriate: *a phone call at a most inopportune moment.*

in·or·di·nate (ĭn-**ôr′**dn-ĭt) *adj.* Exceeding reasonable limits; immoderate; excessive: *The speech lasted an inordinate amount of time.* **—in·or′di·nate·ly** *adv.*

in·or·gan·ic (ĭn′ôr-**găn′**ĭk) *adj.* **1.** Not involving living organisms or the products of their life processes: *Granite is inorganic in origin.* **2.** Relating to compounds that are not organic. Inorganic compounds usually do not contain carbon and are not derived from living organisms. **—in′or·gan′i·cal·ly** *adv.*

in·pa·tient (ĭn′pā′shənt) *n.* A patient who stays overnight in a hospital or clinic for treatment. ❖ *adj.* Relating to inpatients or their care: *an inpatient psychiatric facility.*

in·put (ĭn′po͝ot′) *n.* **1.** Something that is contributed or put into a project or process: *creative input from a design consultant; a new business that will require a large input of money.* **2.** The power supplied to an electronic circuit or device. **3.** The data or programs put into a computer. ❖ *tr.v.* **in·put·ted** or **in·put, in·put·ting, in·puts** To enter (data or a program) into a computer.

input device *n.* A device, such as a keyboard or a mouse, used to enter information into a computer.

in·quest (ĭn′kwĕst′) *n.* **1.** A legal investigation into the cause of a death, especially one made before a jury or an official. **2.** An investigation.

in·quire (ĭn-**kwīr′**) *v.* **in·quired, in·quir·ing, in·quires** —*intr.* **1.** To seek information by asking a question: *If you can't find your size, inquire at the sales desk.* See Synonyms at **ask. 2.** To make a search or study; investigate: *The police inquired into the missing person's whereabouts.* —*tr.* To ask, especially politely or formally: *Our host inquired why we were leaving so soon.* ◆ **inquire after** To ask about the health or condition of (someone). [From Middle English *enqueren,* from Latin *inquīrere.*] —**in·quir′er** *n.* —**in·quir′ing·ly** *adv.*

in·quir·y (ĭn′kwə-rē *or* ĭn-**kwīr′**ē) *n., pl.* **in·quir·ies 1.** The act of inquiring: *engaged in scientific inquiry.* **2.** A request for information; a question: *many inquiries about the new mail rates.* **3.** A detailed examination of a matter; an investigation: *an inquiry into why water bills are so high.*

in·qui·si·tion (ĭn′kwĭ-**zĭsh′**ən) *n.* **1.** An investigation that violates the privacy or rights of individuals. **2.** A thorough harsh questioning: *the reporters' inquisition of the coach during the press conference.* **3. Inquisition** A former tribunal of the Roman Catholic Church established to seek out and punish people considered guilty of heresy.

in·quis·i·tive (ĭn-**kwĭz′**ĭ-tĭv) *adj.* **1.** Eager for learning or knowledge; curious: *an inquisitive mind.* **2.** Prying into the affairs of others; unduly curious. —**in·quis′i·tive·ly** *adv.* —**in·quis′i·tive·ness** *n.*

in·quis·i·tor (ĭn-**kwĭz′**ĭ-tər) *n.* A person who conducts an inquisition. —**in·quis′i·to′ri·al** (ĭn-kwĭz′ĭ-**tôr′**ē-əl) *adj.*

in·road (ĭn′rōd′) *n.* An advance at another's expense; an encroachment: *Foreign companies have made inroads into American markets.*

in·rush (ĭn′rŭsh′) *n.* A sudden rushing in; an influx: *an inrush of commuter traffic to the city.*

in·sane (ĭn-**sān′**) *adj.* **1.** Having a serious mental disorder, especially one that distorts the perception of reality. This term is no longer used in medical diagnosis. **2.** Characteristic of or intended for people with such disorders: *an insane asylum.* **3.** Mentally unfit to be held legally responsible for one's actions or to be able to understand the proceedings at one's trial. **4.** Mentally or emotionally agitated or distressed: *That noisy neighbor has been driving us insane.* **5.** Very foolish; not sensible: *an insane stunt.* —**in·sane′ly** *adv.*

in·san·i·tar·y (ĭn-**săn′**ĭ-tĕr′ē) *adj.* Not sanitary; unclean: *insanitary bandages.*

in·san·i·ty (ĭn-**săn′**ĭ-tē) *n., pl.* **in·san·i·ties 1.** A state of serious mental illness, especially one in which the perception of reality is distorted. This term is no longer used in medical diagnosis. **2.** The condition of having been judged to be legally insane. **3.** Extreme foolishness; utter folly: *Trying to do three jobs at once is sheer insanity.*

in·sa·tia·ble (ĭn-**sā′**shə-bəl *or* ĭn-**sā′**shē-ə-bəl) *adj.* Impossible to satisfy; never satisfied: *an insatiable appetite.* —**in·sa′tia·bly** *adv.*

in·scribe (ĭn-**skrīb′**) *tr.v.* **in·scribed, in·scrib·ing, in·scribes 1a.** To write, print, carve, or engrave (words, letters, or a design) on a surface: *Inscribe the winners' names on a plaque.* **b.** To mark or engrave (a surface) with words, letters, or design: *inscribe a plaque with the names of the winners.* **2.** To sign one's name or write a brief message in or on (a book or picture given as a gift). **3.** To impress deeply on the mind: *Our last day of school is inscribed on my memory.* **4.** To enter in a list; sign up. **5.** To draw (a geometric figure) within another so that the inner figure touches the outer figure at as many points as possible. [From Latin *īnscrībere,* to write on.] —**in·scrib′er** *n.*

in·scrip·tion (ĭn-**skrĭp′**shən) *n.* **1.** The act or an example of inscribing: *The monument has a space for the inscription of the names of the flood victims.* **2.** Something inscribed: *a wall covered with ancient Egyptian inscriptions.* **3.** A short signed message in a book or on a picture given as a gift.

in·scru·ta·ble (ĭn-**skro͞o′**tə-bəl) *adj.* Difficult or impossible to understand or make out; mysterious: *an inscrutable smile; an inscrutable coded message.* —**in·scru′ta·bil′i·ty, in·scru′ta·ble·ness** *n.* —**in·scru′ta·bly** *adv.*

in·seam (ĭn′sēm′) *n.* **1.** The inside seam of a pant leg. **2.** The length or measurement of such a seam.

in·sect (ĭn′sĕkt′) *n.* Any of a large group of arthropods that in the adult stage have six legs, a body with three main divisions, and usually one or two pairs of wings. Flies, bees, grasshoppers, butterflies, and beetles are insects. [From Latin *īnsectum,* from *īnsecāre,* to cut up, divide into segments (translation of Greek *entomon,* segmented, insect).] —SEE NOTE AT **segment.**

in·sec·ti·cide (ĭn-**sĕk′**tĭ-sīd′) *n.* A chemical substance used to kill insects.

in·sec·ti·vore (ĭn-**sĕk′**tə-vôr′) *n.* **1.** Any of a group of small mammals, such as the shrews, moles, and hedgehogs, that feed chiefly on insects and other small invertebrates. **2.** An animal or plant that feeds mainly on insects.

in·sec·tiv·o·rous (ĭn′sĕk-**tĭv′**ər-əs) *adj.* Feeding on insects.

in·se·cure (ĭn′sĭ-**kyo͝or′**) *adj.* **1.** Not sure or certain; doubtful: *an insecure future.* **2.** Not secure or safe; not fully protected: *an insecure post on the frontier; an insecure transaction on the Internet.* **3.** Not firm or sure; shaky: *an insecure hold on the dog's leash.* **4.** Lacking self-confidence: *an insecure person.* —**in′se·cure′ly** *adv.* —**in′se·cu′ri·ty** (ĭn′sĭ-**kyo͝or′**ĭ-tē) *n.*

in·sem·i·nate (ĭn-**sĕm′**ə-nāt′) *tr.v.* **in·sem·i·nat·ed, in·sem·i·nat·ing, in·sem·i·nates** To introduce semen into the reproductive tract of (a female). —**in·sem′i·na′tion** *n.*

in·sen·sate (ĭn-**sĕn′**sāt′ *or* ĭn-**sĕn′**sĭt) *adj.* **1.** Lacking sensation or awareness; inanimate: *rocks, trees, and other insensate objects.* **2.** Unconscious: *The insensate patient was in a deep coma.* **3.** Insensitive; unfeeling: *The insensate official was not interested in my complaints.* **4.** Lacking sense; foolish. —**in·sen′sate′ly** *adv.*

in·sen·si·ble (ĭn-**sĕn′**sə-bəl) *adj.* **1.** Not noticeable; imperceptible: *an insensible change in the weather.* **2.** Lacking the ability to feel sensation; numb: *insensible to cold.* **3.** Not mindful; unaware: *insensible to good advice.* **4.** Emotionally cold; indifferent: *He is insensible to other people's sorrow.* **5.** Unconscious: *The victim lay insensible on the sidewalk.* —**in·sen′si·bil′i·ty** *n.* —**in·sen′si·bly** *adv.*

in·sen·si·tive (ĭn-**sĕn′**sĭ-tĭv) *adj.* **1.** Not physically sensitive; numb: *An injection made the tooth insensitive.* **2.** Lacking in sensitivity for others; cold; unfeeling. **3.** Unresponsive: *We must never be insensitive to the needs of our customers.* —**in·sen′si·tive·ly** *adv.* —**in·sen′si·tive·ness** *n.* —**in·sen′si·tiv′i·ty** *n.*

in·sep·a·ra·ble (ĭn-**sĕp′**ər-ə-bəl *or* ĭn-**sĕp′**rə-bəl) *adj.* Impossible to separate: *inseparable friends.* —**in·sep′a·ra·bil′i·ty, in·sep′a·ra·ble·ness** *n.* —**in·sep′a·ra·bly** *adv.*

in·sert (ĭn-sûrt′) *tr.v.* **in·sert·ed, in·sert·ing, in·serts** To put or set into, between, or among: *insert a key in a lock; insert pictures between chapters in the book.* ❖ *n.* (**ĭn′**sûrt′) Something inserted or meant to be inserted, as into a manuscript: *An advertising insert fell out of the magazine.* [From Latin *īnserere* : *in-*, in + *serere*, to join.]

in·ser·tion (ĭn-**sûr′**shən) *n.* **1.** The act of inserting: *the insertion of a cork into a bottle.* **2.** Something inserted: *Please add this insertion to my report.*

in·set (**ĭn′**sĕt′ *or* ĭn-**sĕt′**) *tr.v.* **in·set, in·set·ting, in·sets** To set in; insert. ❖ *n.* (**ĭn′**sĕt′) Something set in, as a small map or illustration set within a larger one, or a piece of material set into a dress.

in·shore (**ĭn′shôr′**) *adv. & adj.* **1.** Close to a shore. **2.** Toward or coming toward shore: *an inshore wind.*

in·side (ĭn-**sīd′** *or* **ĭn′**sīd′) *n.* **1.** An inner part, side, or surface: *the inside of a house; articles on the inside of a magazine.* **2.** **insides** *Informal* **a.** The inner organs, especially those of the abdomen; entrails. **b.** The inner workings: *the insides of a TV set.* ❖ *adj.* **1.** Inner; interior: *the inside pocket of a jacket.* **2.** Relating to, coming from, or known by those within a group: *inside information; a theft that was definitely an inside job.* **3.** In baseball, passing on the side of home plate nearer the batter: *The first pitch was a fast ball, high and inside.* ❖ *adv.* Into or in the interior; within: *go inside; staying inside.* ❖ *prep.* Into or in the interior of: *inside the package; go inside the house.* ◆ **inside out 1.** With the inner surface turned out; reversed: *wearing his socks inside out.* **2.** *Informal* Thoroughly: *A taxi driver must know the city inside out.*

inside of *prep.* Within: *inside of an hour.*

in·sid·er (ĭn-**sī′**dər) *n.* **1.** An accepted member of a group. **2.** A person who has special knowledge or access to private information.

in·sid·i·ous (ĭn-**sĭd′**ē-əs) *adj.* **1.** Working or spreading harmfully in a subtle or hidden manner: *insidious rumors; an insidious disease.* **2.** Intended to entrap; treacherous: *an insidious plot.* **—in·sid′i·ous·ly** *adv.* **—in·sid′i·ous·ness** *n.*

in·sight (**ĭn′**sīt′) *n.* **1.** The capacity to perceive the true nature of something, especially by intuition: *Einstein's insight into the workings of the universe.* **2.** A perception of the true nature of something: *The critic had a brilliant insight about the meaning of the movie.*

in·sight·ful (ĭn-**sīt′**fəl *or* **ĭn′**sīt′fəl) *adj.* Showing or having insight; perceptive: *an insightful analysis of the painting.*

in·sig·ni·a (ĭn-**sĭg′**nē-ə) *n., pl.* **insignia** or **in·sig·ni·as** A badge of office, rank, membership, or nationality; an emblem. [From plural of Latin *īnsigne*, badge of office, from *īnsignis*, distinguished, marked, from *signum*, sign.]

insignia
of a gunnery sergeant in the US Marine Corps

in·sig·nif·i·cant (ĭn′sĭg-**nĭf′**ĭ-kənt) *adj.* **1.** Of no importance; trivial: *an insignificant detail.* **2.** Small in size, power, or value: *an insignificant contribution; an insignificant job.* **3.** Having little or no meaning: *insignificant doodles on a notepad.* **—in′sig·nif′i·cance** *n.* **—in′sig·nif′i·cant·ly** *adv.*

in·sin·cere (ĭn′sĭn-**sîr′**) *adj.* Not sincere; hypocritical: *an insincere apology.* **—in′sin·cere′ly** *adv.* **—in′sin·cer′i·ty** (ĭn′sĭn-**sĕr′**ĭ-tē) *n.*

in·sin·u·ate (ĭn-**sĭn′**yo͞o-āt′) *tr.v.* **in·sin·u·at·ed, in·sin·u·at·ing, in·sin·u·ates 1.** To introduce or suggest in a sly or indirect way: *Are you insinuating that I'm not good enough for the team?* **2.** To introduce or insert (oneself) by artful means: *The stranger insinuated himself into the wedding reception.*

in·sin·u·a·tion (ĭn-sĭn′yo͞o-**ā′**shən) *n.* An indirect hint or suggestion: *an insinuation of wrongdoing.*

in·sip·id (ĭn-**sĭp′**ĭd) *adj.* **1.** Lacking flavor; bland: *an insipid watery soup.* **2.** Lacking qualities that excite or interest; dull: *an insipid group of people.* [From Late Latin *īnsipidus* : Latin *in-*, not, without + Latin *sapere*, to taste.] **—in·sip′id·ly** *adv.*

in·sist (ĭn-**sĭst′**) *v.* **in·sist·ed, in·sist·ing, in·sists** *—intr.* To be firm in a course or demand; take a strong stand: *I insist on paying my share of the expenses.* *—tr.* To assert or demand vehemently and persistently: *We insist that you stay for dinner.* [From Latin *īnsistere*, to persist : *in-*, on + *sistere*, to stand.]

in·sis·tent (ĭn-**sĭs′**tənt) *adj.* **1.** Firm or persistent in a course or demand: *The doctor was insistent that the water be boiled before use.* **2.** Demanding attention or a response: *my alarm clock's insistent ring.* **—in·sis′tence** *n.* **—in·sis′tent·ly** *adv.*

in·so·far as (ĭn′sō-**fär′**) *conj.* To the extent that: *Insofar as I am able, I will carry out your orders.*

in·sole (**ĭn′**sōl′) *n.* **1.** The inner sole of a shoe or boot. **2.** An extra strip of material put inside a shoe for comfort or protection.

in·so·lent (**ĭn′**sə-lənt) *adj.* Disrespectful and rude; impudent: *an insolent reply.* **—in′so·lence** *n.* **—in′so·lent·ly** *adv.*

in·sol·u·ble (ĭn-**sŏl′**yə-bəl) *adj.* **1.** Not capable of being dissolved: *an insoluble salt.* **2.** Difficult or impossible to solve or explain: *an insoluble riddle.* **—in·sol′u·bil′i·ty** *n.* **—in·sol′u·bly** *adv.*

in·sol·vent (ĭn-**sŏl′**vənt) *adj.* Unable to pay one's debts; bankrupt: *an insolvent business.* **—in·sol′ven·cy** *n.*

in·som·ni·a (ĭn-**sŏm′**nē-ə) *n.* Persistent inability to sleep; sleeplessness. [From Latin *īnsomnis*, sleepless : *in-*, not, without + *somnus*, sleep.]

in·spect (ĭn-**spĕkt′**) *tr.v.* **in·spect·ed, in·spect·ing, in·spects 1.** To examine carefully and critically, especially for flaws: *We inspect all of our products to ensure they are of the highest quality.* **2.** To examine or review formally; evaluate officially: *An officer inspects the troops every Saturday.* —SEE NOTE AT **spectator.**

in·spec·tion (ĭn-**spĕk′**shən) *n.* **1.** The act of inspecting: *Inspection of the wiring will take two days.* **2.** An official examination or review: *Demerits will be given to anyone who is late for inspection.*

in·spec·tor (ĭn-**spĕk′**tər) *n.* **1.** A person who is appointed or employed to inspect something: *Government inspectors try to ensure food safety.* **2.** A police officer ranking next below a superintendent.

in·spi·ra·tion (ĭn′spə-**rā′**shən) *n.* **1.** The excitement of the mind, emotions, or imagination, as in creating something or solving a problem: *Some writers get inspiration for a story from reading the newspaper.* **2.** A person or thing that excites the mind or the emotions: *The brilliant scientist was an inspiration to younger colleagues.* **3.** Something, such as an original idea, that is inspired: *Your suggestion to open a store in town was an inspiration.* **—in′spi·ra′tion·al** *adj.*

in·spire (ĭn-**spīr′**) *v.* **in·spired, in·spir·ing, in·spires 1.** To fill with great emotion: *a singing performance that inspired the entire audience.* **2.** To stimulate to creativity or action: *The story about that great discovery inspired us to look for fossils.* **3.** To cause (a feeling or attitude) in another or others; influence: *The candidate inspired confidence in the voters.* **4.** To be the cause or source of: *The book inspired a movie.* [From Middle English *enspiren*, from Latin *īnspīrāre*, to breathe into.] **—in·spir′er** *n.*

in·spired (ĭn-**spīrd′**) *adj.* Resulting from creative inspiration; extremely well-made or well-done: *an inspired performance.*

in·spir·ing (ĭn-**spīr′**ĭng) *adj.* Causing one to feel creative, uplifted, or motivated; stimulating: *an inspiring story of courage.*

in·sta·bil·i·ty (ĭn′stə-**bĭl′**ĭ-tē) *n., pl.* **in·sta·bil·i·ties** Lack of stability; unsteadiness: *The building was evacuated because of the instability of the roof.*

in·stall (ĭn-**stôl′**) *tr.v.* **in·stalled, in·stall·ing, in·stalls**

ă	pat	ôr	core
ā	pay	oi	boy
âr	care	ou	out
ä	father	o͝o	took
ĕ	pet	o͝or	lure
ē	be	o͞o	boot
ĭ	pit	ŭ	cut
ī	bite	ûr	urge
îr	pier	th	thin
ŏ	pot	*th*	this
ō	toe	zh	vision
ô	paw	ə	about

1. To connect or set in position and prepare for use: *The company installed the new phones yesterday.* **2.** To place in an office, rank, or position, usually with ceremony: *The new mayor was installed soon after election.* **3.** To settle; place: *The mice installed themselves behind the baseboard.* [From Middle English *installen*, to place in office, from Medieval Latin *īnstallāre* : Latin *in-*, in + *stallum*, stall, place.]

in·stal·la·tion (ĭn′stə-**lā′**shən) *n.* **1.** The act of installing: *the installation of telephones.* **2.** A system of machinery or other apparatus set up for use: *A computer system is a complicated installation.* **3.** A military base.

in·stall·ment[1] (ĭn-**stôl′**mənt) *n.* **1.** One of a series of payments in settlement of a debt: *We paid $1,600 for our TV set in four installments of $400 each.* **2.** A portion of something issued or presented at intervals: *The final installment of the trilogy didn't disappoint its audience.* [From Old French *estaler*, to place, fix.]

in·stall·ment[2] (ĭn-**stôl′**mənt) *n.* The act of installing; installation: *the installment of new plumbing.*

in·stance (**ĭn′**stəns) *n.* A case or example: *This is another instance of her great leadership.* ◆ **for instance** As an example; for example.

in·stant (**ĭn′**stənt) *n.* **1.** A period of time almost too brief to detect; a moment. **2.** A precise point in time: *Please call the instant they arrive.* ❖ *adj.* **1.** Immediate: *an instant success.* **2.** Urgent: *an instant need.* **3.** Prepared by a manufacturer for quick preparation by the consumer: *instant cocoa.*

in·stan·ta·ne·ous (ĭn′stən-**tā′**nē-əs) *adj.* Happening without delay; immediate: *an instantaneous reaction.* **—in′stan·ta′ne·ous·ly** *adv.*

in·stant·ly (**ĭn′**stənt-lē) *adv.* At once; immediately: *The frog was instantly transformed into a prince.*

instant message *n.* An electronic message transmitted by instant messaging.

instant messaging *n.* The transmission of an electronic message over a computer network using software that immediately displays the message in a window on the screen when it arrives.

in·stead (ĭn-**stĕd′**) *adv.* In place of something previously mentioned; as a substitute or alternative: *They didn't have cider, so I got apple juice instead.*

instead of *prep.* In place of; rather than: *They walked home instead of taking the bus.*

in·step (**ĭn′**stĕp′) *n.* **1.** The arched middle part of the human foot between the toes and the ankle. **2.** The part of a shoe or stocking covering this part of the foot.

in·sti·gate (**ĭn′**stĭ-gāt′) *tr.v.* **in·sti·gat·ed, in·sti·gat·ing, in·sti·gates 1.** To bring about or initiate: *an incident that instigated an uprising.* **2.** To urge or provoke (someone) to do something. **—in′sti·ga′tion** *n.* **—in′sti·ga′tor** *n.*

in·still (ĭn-**stĭl′**) *tr.v.* **in·stilled, in·still·ing, in·stills** To introduce little by little; implant gradually: *Regular practice instilled a sense of confidence in the players.*

in·stinct (**ĭn′**stĭngkt′) *n.* **1.** An inborn pattern of behavior that is characteristic of a given species: *the salmon's instinct to swim upstream to spawn.* **2.** A natural talent or ability: *an instinct for politics.* [From Middle English, from Latin *īnstinguere*, to incite.]

in·stinc·tive (ĭn-**stĭngk′**tĭv) *adj.* Relating to or arising from instinct: *Building nests is instinctive behavior in most birds.* **—in·stinc′tive·ly** *adv.*

in·sti·tute (**ĭn′**stĭ-to͞ot′) *tr.v.* **in·sti·tut·ed, in·sti·tut·ing, in·sti·tutes** To establish, organize, and set in operation; initiate: *The government instituted a new trade policy.* See Synonyms at **establish.** ❖ *n.* **1.** An organization established to promote a cause: *a research institute.* **2.** An educational institution: *an art institute.* **3.** The building or buildings of such an institution.

in·sti·tu·tion (ĭn′stĭ-**to͞o′**shən) *n.* **1.** The act or process of instituting: *the institution of new school rules for student conduct.* **2.** A custom, practice, or pattern of behavior that is important in the cultural life of a society: *the institution of marriage.* **3a.** An organization or foundation, especially one dedicated to public service: *an educational institution.* **b.** The building or buildings housing such an organization. **c.** A place for the care of people who are destitute, disabled, or mentally ill. **—in′sti·tu′tion·al** *adj.*

in·sti·tu·tion·al·ize (ĭn′stĭ-**to͞o′**shə-nə-līz′) *tr.v.* **in·sti·tu·tion·al·ized, in·sti·tu·tion·al·iz·ing, in·sti·tu·tion·al·iz·es 1.** To place (a person) in the care of an institution. **2.** To make part of a structured system: *rules that were intended to institutionalize nondiscriminatory practices throughout the corporation.*

in·struct (ĭn-**strŭkt′**) *tr.v.* **in·struct·ed, in·struct·ing, in·structs 1.** To give knowledge or skill to; teach: *The teacher will instruct the class in how to use these computers.* See Synonyms at **teach. 2.** To give orders to; direct: *The coach instructed us to run around the track.* [From Middle English *instructen*, from Latin *īnstruere*, to prepare, instruct : *in-*, on + *struere*, to build.]

in·struc·tion (ĭn-**strŭk′**shən) *n.* **1.** Something that is taught; a lesson: *instructions in modern and classical music.* **2.** The act of teaching or instructing; education. **3.** A sequence of code that instructs a computer to perform a particular operation. **4. instructions** Directions; orders: *The model airplane came with clear instructions.* **—in·struc′tion·al** *adj.*

in·struc·tive (ĭn-**strŭk′**tĭv) *adj.* Providing knowledge or information: *an instructive example; an instructive experience.* **—in·struc′tive·ly** *adv.*

in·struc·tor (ĭn-**strŭk′**tər) *n.* **1.** A person who instructs; a teacher. **2.** A college or university teacher ranking below an assistant professor.

in·stru·ment (**ĭn′**strə-mənt) *n.* **1.** An implement used to do work, especially one used by a physician, dentist, or scientist: *surgical instruments.* **2.** A device used for playing or producing music: *the instruments of an orchestra.* **3.** A device for recording or measuring, as in a control system: *A fuel gauge and a compass are important instruments in an aircraft.* **4.** A means by which something is done: *The law to protect jobs was an important instrument of the governor's policy.* **5.** A legal document, such as a deed or will. [From Middle English, from Latin *īnstrūmentum*, from *īnstruere*, to prepare.]

in·stru·men·tal (ĭn′strə-**mĕn′**tl) *adj.* **1.** Serving as the means; useful; helpful: *Our teacher was instrumental in getting the club a place to meet.* **2.** Performed on or written for musical instruments: *instrumental music.* **—in′stru·men′tal·ly** *adv.*

in·stru·men·tal·ist (ĭn′strə-**mĕn′**tl-ĭst) *n.* A person who plays a musical instrument.

in·stru·men·tal·i·ty (ĭn′strə-mĕn-**tăl′**ĭ-tē) *n., pl.* **in·stru·men·tal·i·ties 1.** The quality or condition of being instrumental; usefulness. **2.** A means; a help to achieve an end.

in·stru·men·ta·tion (ĭn′strə-mĕn-**tā′**shən) *n.* **1.** The arrangement or orchestration of music for instruments. **2.** The application or use of instruments.

in·sub·or·di·nate (ĭn′sə-**bôr′**dn-ĭt) *adj.* Not submissive to authority: *punished for being insubordinate to a superior.* **—in′sub·or′di·nate·ly** *adv.* **—in′sub·or′di·na′tion** (ĭn′sə-**bôr′**dn-**ā′**shən) *n.*

in·sub·stan·tial (ĭn′səb-**stăn′**shəl) *adj.* **1.** Not firm or solid; weak or flimsy: *a shed made of insubstantial materials.* **2.** Lacking substance or reality; imaginary: *not facts, but insubstantial visions.* **3.** Not substantial in size or amount: *an insubstantial salary.* **—in′sub·stan′ti·al′i·ty** (ĭn′səb-stăn′shē-**ăl′**ĭ-tē) *n.* **—in′sub·stan′tial·ly** *adv.*

in·suf·fer·a·ble (ĭn-**sŭf′**ər-ə-bəl *or* ĭn-**sŭf′**rə-bəl) *adj.*

WRITERS CHOOSE THEIR WORDS

Twilight had proved himself to be a superb actor. Now, tonight he was going to be an actor no longer. It was Twilight who would **instigate** the fight by uncovering the turnfeather agents.

—Kathryn Lasky
The Siege

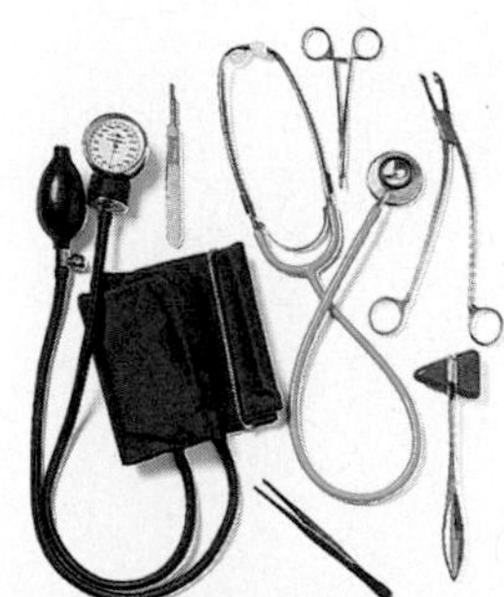

instrument
medical instruments

insulation

ă	pat	ôr	core
ā	pay	oi	boy
âr	care	ou	out
ä	father	o͝o	took
ĕ	pet	o͝or	lure
ē	be	o͞o	boot
ĭ	pit	ŭ	cut
ī	bite	ûr	urge
îr	pier	th	thin
ŏ	pot	*th*	this
ō	toe	zh	vision
ô	paw	ə	about

Difficult or impossible to endure; intolerable: *insufferable rudeness.* —**in·suf′fer·a·bly** *adv.*

in·suf·fi·cien·cy (ĭn′sə-**fĭsh′**ən-sē) *n., pl.* **in·suf·fi·cien·cies** A lack or deficiency: *An insufficiency of funds made it impossible to build a new pool.*

in·suf·fi·cient (ĭn′sə-**fĭsh′**ənt) *adj.* Not enough; inadequate: *insufficient rainfall for a good harvest.* —**in′suf·fi′cient·ly** *adv.*

in·su·lar (**ĭn′**sə-lər *or* **ĭns′**yə-lər) *adj.* **1.** Relating to or forming an island: *England is an insular nation.* **2.** Living or located on an island: *insular people.* **3.** Alone; isolated: *an insular life.* —**in′su·lar′i·ty** (ĭn′sə-**lăr′**ĭ-tē *or* ĭns′yə-**lăr′**ĭ-tē) *n.*

in·su·late (**ĭn′**sə-lāt′) *tr.v.* **in·su·lat·ed, in·su·lat·ing, in·su·lates 1.** To cover or surround with a material that prevents the passage of heat, electricity, or sound into or out of: *We insulated our attic to keep out the cold.* **2.** To detach; isolate: *The mountain valley is insulated from outside influences.* [From Latin *īnsula*, island.]

in·su·la·tion (ĭn′sə-**lā′**shən) *n.* **1a.** The act of insulating: *Insulation of the windows will keep the cold air out.* **b.** The condition of being insulated: *kept warm by insulation.* **2.** Material that is used for insulating: *There is a layer of fiberglass insulation in the attic.*

in·su·la·tor (**ĭn′**sə-lā′tər) *n.* A substance or device that insulates, especially a nonconductor of electricity, heat, or sound.

in·su·lin (**ĭn′**sə-lĭn) *n.* **1.** A hormone that is produced in the pancreas and acts to regulate the amount of sugar in the blood. **2.** A drug containing this hormone, obtained from the pancreas of animals or produced synthetically and used in treating diabetes.

in·sult (ĭn-**sŭlt′**) *tr.v.* **in·sult·ed, in·sult·ing, in·sults** To treat with insensitivity or contempt; offend: *She insulted me by saying hello to everyone but me.* ❖ *n.* (**ĭn′**sŭlt′) An offensive action or remark. [From Latin *īnsultāre*, to leap at, insult.] —**in·sult′ing·ly** *adv.*

in·su·per·a·ble (ĭn-**so͞o′**pər-ə-bəl) *adj.* Impossible to overcome; insurmountable: *insuperable odds.* —**in·su′per·a·bly** *adv.*

in·sup·port·a·ble (ĭn′sə-**pôr′**tə-bəl) *adj.* Unbearable; intolerable: *insupportable pain.*

in·sur·ance (ĭn-**sho͝or′**əns) *n.* **1.** The act or business of guaranteeing to pay for another's future losses or debts, as in the case of damage, theft, illness, or death. Insurance typically involves transferring the risk of a specified loss to another party in exchange for regular payments of an agreed sum of money. **2a.** A contract making such guarantees to a person or group in return for regular payments. **b.** The total amount to be paid to the party insured: *bought $500,000 of life insurance.* **c.** A periodic amount paid for such coverage; a premium: *Our health insurance went up this year.* **3.** A protective measure: *biking helmets that provide insurance against a head injury.*

in·sure (ĭn-**sho͝or′**) *tr.v.* **in·sured, in·sur·ing, in·sures 1a.** To provide or arrange insurance for: *companies that insure homeowners.* **b.** To acquire or have insurance for: *insured her car for theft.* **2.** To make sure or certain; guarantee; ensure: *Proper diet helps to insure good health.* —**in·sur′er** *n.* —SEE NOTE AT **assure.**

in·sured (ĭn-**sho͝ord′**) *n., pl.* **insured** or **in·sureds** A person or thing covered by an insurance policy.

in·sur·gence (ĭn-**sûr′**jəns) *n.* An uprising; a rebellion.

in·sur·gent (ĭn-**sûr′**jənt) *adj.* Rising in revolt: *The insurgent forces overthrew the government.* ❖ *n.* A person who revolts against authority; a rebel.

in·sur·mount·a·ble (ĭn′sər-**moun′**tə-bəl) *adj.* Impossible to overcome; insuperable: *an insurmountable obstacle.*

in·sur·rec·tion (ĭn′sə-**rĕk′**shən) *n.* An uprising against an established authority or government; a rebellion. —**in′sur·rec′tion·ist** *n.*

in·tact (ĭn-**tăkt′**) *adj.* Not weakened, injured, damaged, or separated; whole: *The contents were intact in spite of the damage to the box.*

in·take (**ĭn′**tāk′) *n.* **1.** An opening through which a liquid or gas enters a container or pipe: *an intake clogged with dirt.* **2a.** The act of taking in: *an efficient air intake.* **b.** Something, or the amount of something, taken in: *an adequate intake of food.*

in·tan·gi·ble (ĭn-**tăn′**jə-bəl) *adj.* **1.** Incapable of being touched; lacking physical substance: *Inner satisfaction is one of the intangible rewards of community service.* **2.** Incapable of being defined; vague; elusive: *an intangible change of attitude.* ❖ *n.* Something intangible: *intangibles such as goodwill and dedication.* —**in·tan′gi·bly** *adv.*

in·te·ger (**ĭn′**tĭ-jər) *n.* A positive or negative whole number or zero. [From Latin, whole, complete.]

in·te·gral (**ĭn′**tĭ-grəl *or* ĭn-**tĕg′**rəl) *adj.* **1.** Necessary to form a whole or make something complete: *Rafters are an integral part of a roof.* **2.** Having everything essential; entire. **3.** (**ĭn′**tĭ-grəl) Involving or expressed as an integer or integers. —**in′te·gral·ly** *adv.*

in·te·grate (**ĭn′**tĭ-grāt′) *v.* **inte·grat·ed, inte·grat·ing, inte·grates** —*tr.* **1.** To make into a whole by bringing all parts together; unify: *Our school integrated math and computer courses last fall.* **2.** To open to people of all races or ethnic groups without restriction; desegregate. —*intr.* To become integrated. [From Middle English, from Latin *integrāre*, to make whole, from *integer*, complete.]

in·te·grat·ed (**ĭn′**tĭ-grā′tĭd) *adj.* **1.** Having people of all races; desegregated: *an integrated neighborhood.* **2.** Having all parts combined into a whole; united: *an integrated system.*

integrated circuit *n.* An electronic circuit whose components, such as transistors and resistors, are etched or deposited on a single slice of semiconductor material to produce a chip.

in·te·gra·tion (ĭn′tĭ-**grā′**shən) *n.* **1.** The act or process of integrating. **2.** The bringing of people of different racial or ethnic groups into equal association; desegregation. —**in′te·gra′tion·ist** *n.*

in·teg·ri·ty (ĭn-**tĕg′**rĭ-tē) *n.* **1.** Moral uprightness; honesty: *A judge must be a person of integrity.* **2.** Completeness; unity: *The country maintained its integrity by defending its borders.*

in·teg·u·ment (ĭn-**tĕg′**yo͞o-mənt) *n.* A natural outer covering of an animal or plant, as skin, a seed coat, or a shell.

in·tel·lect (**ĭn′**tl-ĕkt′) *n.* **1.** The power of the mind to think, reason, and learn. **2.** Great intelligence or mental ability: *We admire people of intellect.* **3.** A person of great intellectual ability: *a gathering of scientific intellects.*

in·tel·lec·tu·al (ĭn′tl-**ĕk′**cho͞o-əl) *adj.* **1.** Engaging the intellect: *an intellectual discussion.* **2.** Having or showing intelligence: *an intellectual person.* ❖ *n.* A person of intelligence, especially a person who is informed and interested in many things. —**in′tel·lec′tu·al·ly** *adv.*

in·tel·li·gence (ĭn-**tĕl′**ə-jəns) *n.* **1.** The ability to gain, understand, and use knowledge: *a person of average intelligence.* **2.** Information or news, especially secret information about an enemy. **3.** An agency or office employed in gathering secret information. [From Middle English, from Latin *intellegere*, to perceive.]

intelligence quotient *n.* A number seen as a measure of a person's intelligence. The number is usually derived from a person's score on an intelligence test compared to the scores of others who have taken the same test, with the average score set at 100.

intelligence test *n.* A test used to measure intelligence or mental development.

in·tel·li·gent (ĭn-**tĕl′**ə-jənt) *adj.* **1.** Having intelligence, especially of a high degree: *an intelligent history student.* **2.** Showing intelligence; wise or thoughtful: *an intelligent decision.* **—in·tel′li·gent·ly** *adv.*

SYNONYMS intelligent, bright, brilliant, quick-witted, smart These adjectives refer to the ability to use the mind well to understand or deal with problems. **Intelligent** means able to handle new situations and problems and good at figuring things out: *Only the most intelligent students can keep up with the teacher's rapid pace.* **Bright** means able to learn quickly and easily: *He is so bright, he learned to play chess in one hour.* **Brilliant** means unusually and impressively intelligent: *The most brilliant minds in the country have gathered for this meeting.* **Quick-witted** means mentally alert and quick in response: *The quick-witted student finished the test in half the allotted time.* **Smart** means able to learn quickly and often also able to look out for oneself: *Judy was smart to tune up her bicycle before the long ride.*

in·tel·li·gent·si·a (ĭn-tĕl′ə-**jĕnt′**sē-ə) *n.* The most educated group of people in a society.

in·tel·li·gi·ble (ĭn-**tĕl′**ĭ-jə-bəl) *adj.* Capable of being understood; comprehensible: *We need someone to write intelligible instructions on using this computer program.* **—in·tel′li·gi·bly** *adv.*

in·tem·per·ance (ĭn-**tĕm′**pər-əns *or* ĭn-**tĕm′**prəns) *n.* Lack of self-control, as in giving in to a craving for food or not controlling one's temper.

in·tem·per·ate (ĭn-**tĕm′**pər-ĭt *or* ĭn-**tĕm′**prĭt) *adj.* Not temperate or moderate; excessive. **—in·tem′per·ate·ly** *adv.*

in·tend (ĭn-**tĕnd′**) *tr.v.* **in·tend·ed, in·tend·ing, in·tends 1.** To have as a purpose; have in mind; plan: *We intend to get an early start.* **2.** To design for a specific purpose or use: *This saw is intended to cut metal.* [From Middle English *entenden*, from Latin *intendere.*]

in·tend·ed (ĭn-**tĕn′**dĭd) *adj.* Planned; intentional: *an intended result.* ❖ *n. Informal* A person who is engaged to be married; a fiancé or fiancée: *My sister and her intended came along.*

in·tense (ĭn-**tĕns′**) *adj.* **in·tens·er, in·tens·est 1.** Existing in an extreme degree; very strong: *an intense blue; intense heat.* **2.** Having or showing strong feeling or great seriousness: *an intense look; an intense music teacher.* [From Middle English, from Latin *intēnsus*, stretched, intent, from *intendere*, to stretch, intend.] **—in·tense′ly** *adv.* —SEE NOTE.

in·ten·si·fy (ĭn-**tĕn′**sə-fī′) *tr. & intr.v.* **in·ten·si·fied, in·ten·si·fy·ing, in·ten·si·fies** To make or become intense or more intense: *The police intensified their investigation. Our review sessions intensified as exams drew near.* **—in·ten′si·fi·ca′tion** (ĭn-tĕn′sə-fĭ-**kā′**shən) *n.* **—in·ten′si·fi′er** *n.*

in·ten·si·ty (ĭn-**tĕn′**sĭ-tē) *n., pl.* **in·ten·si·ties 1.** Extreme force, strength, or concentration: *Our team played with emotional intensity.* **2.** The strength of a color: *The two colors vary in intensity.* **3.** The amount of strength of electricity, heat, light, or sound per unit of area, volume, or mass.

in·ten·sive (ĭn-**tĕn′**sĭv) *adj.* **1.** Marked by intensity; deep; concentrated: *intensive study.* **2.** In grammar, giving emphasis: *an intensive adverb.* ❖ *n.* In grammar, a word, phrase, prefix, or suffix that gives force or emphasis. For example, in the sentences *We are very pleased* and *That student is extremely intelligent*, the adverbs *very* and *extremely* are intensives. **—in·ten′sive·ly** *adv.* —SEE NOTE AT **intense.**

intensive care *n.* Health care, especially in a hospital, in which a severely ill or injured person is closely watched at all times.

in·tent (ĭn-**tĕnt′**) *n.* A purpose or aim; an intention: *It was never my intent to start an argument.* ❖ *adj.* **1.** Showing concentration; intense: *an intent expression while studying.* **2.** Firmly fixed on some purpose; determined: *We are intent on securing a new trade agreement.* ◆ **for all intents and purposes** or **to all intents and purposes** In every practical sense; practically. **—in·tent′ly** *adv.* **—in·tent′ness** *n.*

in·ten·tion (ĭn-**tĕn′**shən) *n.* **1.** A plan or purpose in doing something. **2. intentions** Purposes or motives in mind: *with the best of intentions.*

in·ten·tion·al (ĭn-**tĕn′**shə-nəl) *adj.* Done deliberately; meant; intended: *an intentional slight.* **—in·ten′tion·al·ly** *adv.*

in·ter (ĭn-**tûr′**) *tr.v.* **in·terred, in·ter·ring, in·ters** To place in a grave; bury. [From Middle English *enteren*, from Medieval Latin *interrāre* : Latin *in-*, in + Latin *terra*, earth.]

inter– *pref.* A prefix that means: **1.** Between; among: *international.* **2.** Mutually; together: *interact.* —SEE NOTE.

in·ter·act (ĭn′tər-**ăkt′**) *intr.v.* **in·ter·act·ed, in·ter·act·ing, in·ter·acts** To act on or affect each other: *The mechanic's adjustments made the gears interact more smoothly.* **—in′ter·ac′tion** *n.*

in·ter·ac·tive (ĭn′tər-**ăk′**tĭv) *adj.* **1.** Relating to a computer program that responds to user activity: *interactive computer games.* **2.** Relating to a form of television entertainment in which the viewer participates directly.

in·ter·breed (ĭn′tər-**brēd′**) *v.* **in·ter·bred** (ĭn′tər-**brĕd′**), **in·ter·breed·ing, in·ter·breeds** —*intr.* **1.** To breed with an individual of another breed, variety, or species: *Dogs and wolves sometimes interbreed.* **2.** To breed with another individual of the same species, especially as part of a larger group: *found that bullfrogs from different ponds were interbreeding.* —*tr.* To cause (an organism or group of organisms) to breed with one of a different variety or species: *interbreed two varieties of cattle.*

in·ter·cede (ĭn′tər-**sēd′**) *intr.v.* **in·ter·ced·ed, in·ter·ced·ing, in·ter·cedes 1.** To plead on another's behalf; seek some favor for another: *The teacher interceded with my parents to let me go on the trip.* **2.** To act as a mediator in a dispute: *The government can appoint people to intercede in certain labor disputes.*

in·ter·cel·lu·lar (ĭn′tər-**sĕl′**yə-lər) *adj.* Located or occurring between or among cells: *intercellular fluid; intercellular communication.*

in·ter·cept (ĭn′tər-**sĕpt′**) *tr.v.* **in·ter·cept·ed, in·ter·cept·ing, in·ter·cepts 1.** To stop or interrupt the intended course or progress of: *intercept a messenger.* **2.** In sports, to gain possession of (an opponent's pass), as in football or basketball. **3.** To mark off (a space) between two points or lines. ❖ *n.* (**ĭn′**tər-sĕpt′) In a Cartesian coordinate system, the point or coordinate at which a line, curve, or surface intersects a coordinate axis. For example, if a curve intersects the x-axis at (4,0), then 4 is the curve's x-intercept. [From Middle English *intercepten*, from Latin *intercipere* : *inter-*, between + *capere*, to seize.]

in·ter·cep·tion (ĭn′tər-**sĕp′**shən) *n.* **1.** The act or an instance of intercepting: *The interception of an enemy message provided important information.* **2.** In sports, a pass that is intercepted, especially in football.

in·ter·cep·tor also **in·ter·cept·er** (ĭn′tər-**sĕp′**tər) *n.* **1.** A person or thing that intercepts. **2.** A fast-climbing, highly maneuverable fighter plane designed to intercept enemy aircraft.

in·ter·ces·sion (ĭn′tər-**sĕsh′**ən) *n.* **1.** The act of interceding. **2.** An earnest request made in favor of another. **—in′ter·ces′sor** *n.*

in·ter·change (ĭn′tər-**chānj′**) *v.* **in·ter·changed, in·ter·chang·ing, in·ter·chang·es** —*tr.* **1.** To switch each of (two things) into the place of the other: *If you interchange the first and last letters of the word "pal," it becomes "lap."*

USAGE

intense In the two phrases *Mark's intense study of German* and *Mark's intensive study of German,* the words **intense** and **intensive** mean two different things. *Intense* suggests that Mark himself is responsible for his concentrated activity, whereas *intensive* suggests that Mark's concentration of activity is set by a program that covers a great deal of material in a brief period.

WORD BUILDING

inter– The prefix **inter–** comes from the Latin prefix *inter–,* from the preposition *inter,* meaning "between, among." Thus the word *intercede,* in which *inter–* combines with the Latin verb *cēdere,* "to go," means "to go between." Similarly, *interject,* which comes from Latin *iacere,* "to throw," means literally "to throw something between or among others." And *intervene,* coming from Latin *venīre,* "to come," means "to come between people or things." In English, *inter–* is still producing new words, such as *interfaith, intertwine,* and *intercellular.*

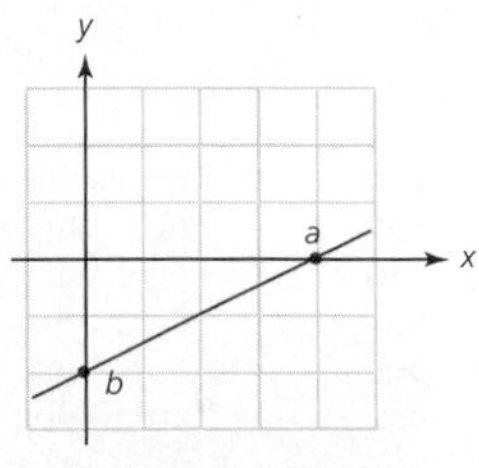

intercept
In this diagram, *a* indicates the intercept on the *x*-axis, and *b* indicates the intercept on the *y*-axis.

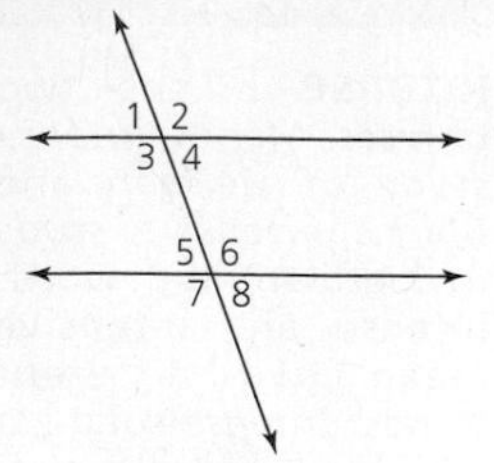

interior angle
Angles 3, 4, 5, and 6 are interior angles.

ă	pat	ôr	core
ā	pay	oi	boy
âr	care	ou	out
ä	father	o͝o	took
ĕ	pet	o͝or	lure
ē	be	o͞o	boot
ĭ	pit	ŭ	cut
ī	bite	ûr	urge
îr	pier	th	thin
ŏ	pot	*th*	this
ō	toe	zh	vision
ô	paw	ə	about

2. To give and receive mutually; exchange: *A vigorous discussion is the best way to interchange ideas.* —*intr.* To change places with each other. ❖ *n.* (**ĭn′**tər-chānj′) **1.** The act of interchanging: *Trade is the interchange of commodities.* **2.** A highway intersection that allows traffic to flow freely from one road to another without crossing another line of traffic.

in·ter·change·a·ble (ĭn′tər-**chān′**jə-bəl) *adj.* Capable of being switched or interchanged: *These two cars have interchangeable parts.* —**in′ter·change′a·bly** *adv.*

in·ter·col·le·giate (ĭn′tər-kə-**lē′**jĭt *or* ĭn′tər-kə-**lē′**jē-ĭt) *adj.* Involving two or more colleges or universities: *an intercollegiate tournament.*

in·ter·com (**ĭn′**tər-kŏm′) *n.* An electronic communication system, as between rooms of a building or areas of a ship.

in·ter·com·mu·ni·cate (ĭn′tər-kə-**myo͞o′**nĭ-kāt′) *intr.v.* **in·ter·com·mu·ni·cat·ed, in·ter·com·mu·ni·cat·ing, in·ter·com·mu·ni·cates** To communicate with each other. —**in′ter·com·mu′ni·ca′tion** *n.*

in·ter·con·nect (ĭn′tər-kə-**nĕkt′**) *intr. & tr.v.* **in·ter·con·nect·ed, in·ter·con·nect·ing, in·ter·con·nects** To connect or be connected with each other. —**in′ter·con·nec′tion** *n.*

in·ter·con·ti·nen·tal (ĭn′tər-kŏn′tə-**nĕn′**tl) *adj.* **1.** Involving or extending between two or more continents: *intercontinental weather patterns.* **2.** Having the capability of traveling from one continent to another: *an intercontinental airline.*

in·ter·course (**ĭn′**tər-kôrs′) *n.* **1.** Sexual intercourse. **2.** Dealings or communication between people or groups: *cafés as places for social intercourse.*

in·ter·de·nom·i·na·tion·al (ĭn′tər-də-nŏm′ə-**nā′**shə-nəl) *adj.* Involving different religious denominations: *an interdenominational service.*

in·ter·de·pen·dent (ĭn′tər-dĭ-**pĕn′**dənt) *adj.* Dependent on one another; mutually dependent. —**in′ter·de·pen′dence** *n.* —**in′ter·de·pen′dent·ly** *adv.*

in·ter·dict (ĭn′tər-**dĭkt′**) *tr.v.* **in·ter·dict·ed, in·ter·dict·ing, in·ter·dicts 1.** To prohibit (an action or thing) or forbid (someone) to do something, especially by order of a legal body or church. **2.** To halt the activities or entry of; block: *were successful in interdicting the smuggled goods.* ❖ *n.* (**ĭn′**tər-dĭkt′) **1.** An authoritative prohibition, especially by court order. **2.** In the Roman Catholic Church, a censure that bars a person, group, or district from participation in most sacraments. —**in′ter·dic′tion** *n.*

in·ter·est (**ĭn′**trĭst *or* **ĭn′**tər-ĭst) *n.* **1a.** A feeling of curiosity or concern about something: *An exciting story will arouse the reader's interest.* **b.** The quality of arousing such a feeling: *a tedious speech that lacked interest for me.* **c.** A subject that arouses such a feeling: *Music, science fiction, and computer games are among my interests.* **2.** often **interests** Advantage; benefit: *The company's decision to burn coal is not in the public interest. She kept her own interests in mind.* **3a.** A right, claim, or legal share in something: *an interest in a business.* **b.** Something in which such a right, claim, or share is held: *American interests in China.* **c.** A group of people holding such a right, claim, or share. **4.** A charge for borrowing money, usually a percentage of the amount borrowed: *a bank with an interest rate of five percent.* **5.** An excess or bonus beyond what is expected or due: *Our host paid back the compliment with interest.* ❖ *tr.v.* **in·ter·est·ed, in·ter·est·ing, in·ter·ests 1.** To arouse the curiosity or hold the attention of: *Modern sculpture interests me a lot.* **2.** To cause to become involved or concerned: *The salesperson tried to interest us in the options on the car.* ◆ **in the interest of** or **in the interests of** To the advantage of; for the sake of: *I agreed to switch chores in the interest of peace.* [From Middle English, from Latin, it is of importance.]

in·ter·est·ed (**ĭn′**trĭ-stĭd *or* **ĭn′**tə-rĕs′tĭd) *adj.* **1.** Having or showing interest, fascination, or concern: *Good teaching usually produces interested students.* **2.** Having a right, claim, or share: *The interested parties met to settle the dispute.* —**in′ter·est·ed·ly** *adv.*

interest group *n.* A group of people working to support a particular cause, such as an item of legislation.

in·ter·est·ing (**ĭn′**trĭ-stĭng *or* **ĭn′**tə-rĕs′tĭng) *adj.* Arousing or holding interest or attention. —**in′ter·est·ing·ly** *adv.*

SYNONYMS **interesting, intriguing, fascinating, engaging** These adjectives all mean capable of capturing and holding one's attention. *You may write your report on any subject you find interesting. She thought my idea was intriguing and wanted to know more about it. Isn't it fascinating that lasers can be used to slow down molecules! All the characters in that movie are engaging.*

---

in·ter·face (**ĭn′**tər-fās′) *n.* **1.** A surface forming a common boundary between any two regions, bodies, or phases. **2.** A point at which two systems or groups interact: *the interface between religion and politics.* **3a.** A system of interaction or communication between a computer and another entity such as a printer, a network, or a human user. **b.** The layout or design of the interactive elements of a computer program, a website, or an electronic device. ❖ *tr. & intr.v.* (ĭn′tər-**fās′**) **in·ter·faced, in·ter·fac·ing, in·ter·fac·es** To work together or communicate, especially with a computer or other electronic device.

in·ter·faith (**ĭn′**tər-fāth′) *adj.* Relating to or involving people of different religious faiths: *attended an interfaith gathering.*

in·ter·fere (ĭn′tər-**fîr′**) *intr.v.* **in·ter·fered, in·ter·fer·ing, in·ter·feres 1.** To get in the way as an obstacle or hindrance: *The rain interfered with our plans to go on a picnic.* **2.** To intrude in the affairs of others; meddle. [From Middle English *enterferen*, from Old French *s'entreferer*, to strike one another : *entre-*, between + *ferir*, to strike.]

in·ter·fer·ence (ĭn′tər-**fîr′**əns) *n.* **1.** The act or an instance of interfering: *Human interference has upset the balance in the environment.* **2.** In sports, the obstruction of an opposing player in a manner prohibited by the rules. **3.** In football, the legal blocking of defensive players to make way for a ball carrier. **4.** The combining of two or more waves of the same frequency, resulting in a new wave or, if the waves match up with each other, the cancellation of both waves. The amplitude of any new wave may be larger or smaller than the amplitude of the combining waves, depending on the differences in their peaks and troughs. **5.** In electronics: **a.** The distortion or interruption of one broadcast signal by others. **b.** The distorted part of a broadcast signal; static.

in·ter·fer·on (ĭn′tər-**fîr′**ŏn′) *n.* Any of a group of proteins that are produced by animal cells in response to infection by a virus and that prevent replication of the virus. Synthetic interferons are used in the treatment of certain diseases.

in·ter·im (**ĭn′**tər-ĭm) *n.* An interval of time between two events, periods, or processes: *During the interim between expeditions, the explorer wrote a book of memoirs.* ❖ *adj.* Relating to or during an interim; temporary: *After an interim job as a cook, he returned to college.* [From Latin, in the meantime.]

in·te·ri·or (ĭn-**tîr′**ē-ər) *adj.* **1.** Relating to or located in the inside; inner: *The interior surfaces of the pipe are corroded.* **2.** Located away from a coast or border; inland: *Interior Australia is sparsely populated.* ❖ *n.* **1.** The inner part of something; the inside: *the interior of a house.* **2.** The inland part of a country or geographical area:

The interior of Alaska is very mountainous. **3.** The affairs within a country; domestic affairs. [From Latin, comparative adjective of *inter*, between.]

interior angle *n.* **1.** Any of the four angles formed inside two straight lines intersected by a third straight line. **2.** An angle formed by two adjacent sides of a polygon and included within the polygon.

interior decorator *n.* A person who specializes in the decoration and furnishing of the interiors of homes, offices, or other buildings.

interj. *abbr.* An abbreviation of interjection.

in·ter·ject (ĭn′tər-**jĕkt′**) *tr.v.* **in·ter·ject·ed, in·ter·ject·ing, in·ter·jects 1.** To say suddenly, often interrupting the remarks of another: *"I disagree," she interjected.* **2.** To put in between or among other things; insert: *The speaker paused in the talk to interject a personal remark.* [From Latin *intericere* : *inter-*, between + *iacere*, to throw.]

in·ter·jec·tion (ĭn′tər-**jĕk′**shən) *n.* **1.** A sudden phrase or remark that is interjected; an exclamation. **2a.** The part of speech that expresses emotion and can stand alone. **b.** A word belonging to this part of speech. *Ouch!* and *Hurrah!* are interjections. **—in′ter·jec′tion·al** *adj.*

in·ter·lace (ĭn′tər-**lās′**) *tr. & intr.v.* **in·ter·laced, in·ter·lac·ing, in·ter·lac·es** To weave, lace, or twine together: *A weaver interlaces threads in order to make cloth.*

in·ter·lard (ĭn′tər-**lärd′**) *tr.v.* **in·ter·lard·ed, in·ter·lard·ing, in·ter·lards** To mix something different into; intersperse: *To illustrate the point, the writer interlarded the report with many examples.*

in·ter·lock (ĭn′tər-**lŏk′**) *tr. & intr.v.* **in·ter·locked, in·ter·lock·ing, in·ter·locks** To unite firmly or join tightly, as by hooking: *The dancers form a circle and interlock hands.*

in·ter·lop·er (**ĭn′**tər-lō′pər) *n.* A person who intrudes or interferes in the affairs of others; a meddler.

in·ter·lude (**ĭn′**tər-lo͞od′) *n.* **1.** An intervening episode or period of time: *There was a brief interlude of sunshine on this mostly cloudy day.* **2.** A short entertainment between the acts of a play. **3.** A short piece of music that occurs between parts of a longer composition. [From Middle English *enterlude*, a dramatic entertainment, from Medieval Latin *interlūdium* : Latin *inter-*, between + Latin *lūdus*, play.]

in·ter·mar·ry (ĭn′tər-**măr′**ē) *intr.v.* **in·ter·mar·ried, in·ter·mar·ry·ing, in·ter·mar·ries 1.** To marry someone of another religion, nationality, or ethnic group. **2.** To be bound together by marriage, as families, religious groups, or ethnic groups, for example. **3.** To marry someone who is a member of one's own family, clan, or tribe. **—in′ter·mar′riage** (ĭn′tər-**măr′**ĭj) *n.*

in·ter·me·di·ar·y (ĭn′tər-**mē′**dē-ĕr′ē) *adj.* **1.** Acting as a mediator: *A labor negotiator plays an intermediary role between management and striking workers.* **2.** Existing or occurring between; intermediate: *A tadpole is an intermediary stage in the development of a frog.* ❖ *n., pl.* **in·ter·me·di·ar·ies** A person or group acting as a mediator between opposing parties to bring about an agreement.

in·ter·me·di·ate (ĭn′tər-**mē′**dē-ĭt) *adj.* Being or occurring between; in the middle: *Middle school is intermediate between high school and elementary school.* ❖ *n.* Something intermediate.

in·ter·ment (ĭn-**tûr′**mənt) *n.* The act of interring; burial.

in·ter·mez·zo (ĭn′tər-**mĕt′**sō *or* ĭn′tər-**mĕd′**zō) *n., pl.* **in·ter·mez·zos** or **in·ter·mez·zi** (ĭn′tər-**mĕt′**sē *or* ĭn′tər-**mĕd′**zē) **1.** A short piece of music played between sections of a long musical work. **2.** A brief entertainment between two acts of a play.

in·ter·mi·na·ble (ĭn-**tûr′**mə-nə-bəl) *adj.* Having or seeming to have no end; endless: *fell asleep during the second act of the interminable play.* **—in·ter′mi·na·bly** *adv.*

in·ter·min·gle (ĭn′tər-**mĭng′**gəl) *tr. & intr.v.* **in·ter·min·gled, in·ter·min·gling, in·ter·min·gles** To mix or become mixed together: *A party presents a good chance to intermingle with others.*

in·ter·mis·sion (ĭn′tər-**mĭsh′**ən) *n.* An interval between periods of activity; a pause: *The orchestra took a short intermission during the concert.* See Synonyms at **pause.**

in·ter·mit·tent (ĭn′tər-**mĭt′**nt) *adj.* Stopping and starting at intervals; not continuous: *The foghorn sounded intermittent blasts at intervals of 15 seconds.* **—in′ter·mit′tent·ly** *adv.*

in·ter·mix (ĭn′tər-**mĭks′**) *tr. & intr.v.* **in·ter·mixed, in·ter·mix·ing, in·ter·mix·es** To mix or become mixed together: *Oil and water do not intermix.*

in·tern (**ĭn′**tûrn′) *n.* An advanced student or recent graduate undergoing practical training, especially a recent medical school graduate who is undergoing supervised training in a hospital or clinic. ❖ *v.* **in·terned, in·tern·ing, in·terns** *—intr.* To train or serve as an intern. *—tr.* (*also* ĭn-**tûrn′**) To detain or confine within a country or place, especially in wartime: *intern an enemy ship.* [From French *interne*, from Latin *internus*, internal.] **—in·tern′ment** *n.*

in·ter·nal (ĭn-**tûr′**nəl) *adj.* **1.** Located within the limits or surface of something; inner; interior: *the internal workings of a clock.* **2.** Located or acting inside the body: *pills and other internal medicines.* **3.** Relating to domestic affairs within a country or organization: *Environmental issues are no longer internal political matters but require global attention.* **—in·ter′nal·ly** *adv.*

in·ter·nal-com·bus·tion engine (ĭn-**tûr′**nəl-kəm-**bŭs′**chən) *n.* An engine whose fuel is burned inside the engine itself rather than in an outside furnace or burner. A gasoline or diesel engine is an internal-combustion engine; a steam engine is not.

internal medicine *n.* The branch of medicine that deals with the diagnosis and treatment of diseases affecting the internal organs of the body.

in·ter·na·tion·al (ĭn′tər-**năsh′**ə-nəl) *adj.* Relating to or involving two or more nations: *The United Nations is an international organization.* **—in′ter·na′tion·al·ly** *adv.*

International Date Line *n.* An imaginary line through the Pacific Ocean roughly along the 180th meridian, agreed upon as the place where each new calendar day begins. The calendar day to the east of the line is one day earlier than to the west.

in·ter·na·tion·al·ism (ĭn′tər-**năsh′**ə-nə-lĭz′əm) *n.* A policy or principle of cooperation among nations for mutual benefit.

in·ter·na·tion·al·ize (ĭn′tər-**năsh′**ə-nə-līz′) *tr.v.* **in·ter·na·tion·al·ized, in·ter·na·tion·al·iz·ing, in·ter·na·tion·al·iz·es** To put under international control; make international: *a peace treaty that internationalized the fishing grounds.*

International System *n.* A system of units that are used as international standards especially in science for measuring length, time, electric current, temperature, light intensity, and mass. For example, in the International System (abbreviated SI), the unit of length is the meter and the unit of time is the second. See table at **measurement.**

in·ter·nec·ine (ĭn′tər-**nĕs′**ēn′ *or* ĭn′tər-**nĕs′**ĭn) *adj.* **1.** Destructive or fatal to both sides: *A long internecine war impoverished both groups in the region.* **2.** Relating to struggle within a nation, organization, or group: *The delegates engaged in an internecine struggle for leadership of the party.*

in·tern·ee (ĭn′tûr-**nē′**) *n.* A person who is interned or confined, especially during a war.

In·ter·net also **in·ter·net** (**ĭn′**tər-nĕt′) *n.* A publicly accessible system of networks that connects computers around the world and that transmits and receives

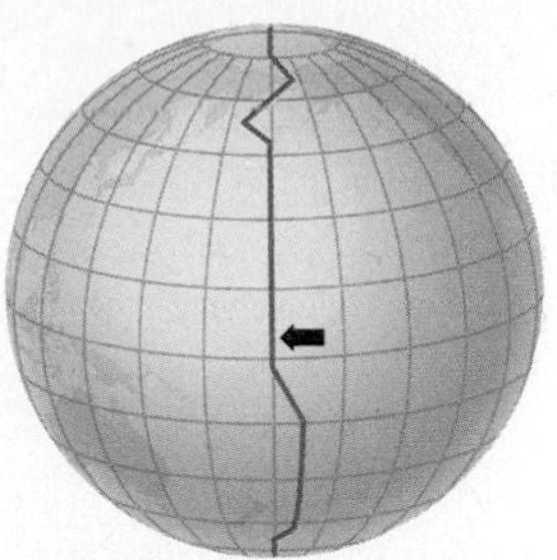

International Date Line

data using a common software protocol called TCP/IP (Transmission Control Protocol/Internet Protocol).

in·ter·nist (ĭn-tûr′nĭst) *n.* A physician who specializes in internal medicine.

in·tern·ship (**ĭn′**tûrn-shĭp′) *n.* A period of service as an intern.

in·ter·phase (**ĭn′**tər-fāz′) *n.* The stage of a cell between two occurrences of cell division.

in·ter·plan·e·tar·y (ĭn′tər-**plăn′**ĭ-tĕr′ē) *adj.* Located or occurring between planets; in the region of the planets: *interplanetary flight.*

in·ter·play (**ĭn′**tər-plā′) *n.* Mutual action or influence; interaction: *The interplay between the two main characters provided most of the humor in the movie.*

in·ter·po·late (ĭn-**tûr′**pə-lāt′) *tr.v.* **in·ter·po·lat·ed, in·ter·po·lat·ing, in·ter·po·lates 1.** In mathematics, to estimate (an unknown value, as of a logarithm or trigonometric function) between two known values. **2.** To change (a text) by inserting new material: *This manuscript has been so interpolated it is hard to recognize the original.* **3.** To insert or add (new material) to a text. [From Latin *interpolis,* refurbished.] **—in·ter′po·la′tion** *n.*

in·ter·pose (ĭn′tər-**pōz′**) *v.* **in·ter·posed, in·ter·pos·ing, in·ter·pos·es** *—tr.* **1.** To put between parts; insert: *Winter ice interposes a barrier between the harbor and the islands.* **2.** To interject (a remark or question) into a conversation. *—intr.* **1.** To come between things. **2.** To come between parties in a dispute; intervene: *The babysitter interposed in the disputes between the children.* **—in′ter·po·si′tion** (ĭn′tər-pə-**zĭsh′**ən) *n.*

in·ter·pret (ĭn-**tûr′**prĭt) *v.* **in·ter·pret·ed, in·ter·pret·ing, in·ter·prets** *—tr.* **1.** To explain the meaning of: *The critic interprets the poem in an essay.* **2.** To understand in one's own way; construe: *We interpreted his smile to be an agreement.* **3.** To present the meaning of, especially through artistic performance: *an actor interpreting a role.* **4.** To translate (something). *—intr.* To serve as an interpreter, especially for speakers of a foreign language. [From Middle English *interpreten,* from Latin *interpretārī,* from *interpres,* negotiator, explainer.]

intertwine
braided hair

in·ter·pre·ta·tion (ĭn-tûr′prĭ-**tā′**shən) *n.* **1.** The act or process of interpreting: *the interpretation of statistical data.* **2.** An explanation of the meaning of something, especially of a work of art: *an unusual interpretation of* Romeo and Juliet. **3.** A performer's unique version of a work of art, such as a song or dance.

in·ter·pret·er (ĭn-**tûr′**prĭ-tər) *n.* **1.** A person who translates from one language to another, especially while a conversation or speech is taking place. **2.** A person who interprets or explains something.

in·ter·pre·tive (ĭn-**tûr′**prĭ-tĭv) also **in·ter·pre·ta·tive** (ĭn-**tûr′**prĭ-tā′tĭv) *adj.* Relating to or marked by interpretation; explanatory: *an interpretive comment.*

in·ter·ra·cial (ĭn′tər-**rā′**shəl) *adj.* Relating to or involving people of different races: *an interracial marriage.*

in·ter·reg·num (ĭn′tər-**rĕg′**nəm) *n., pl.* **in·ter·reg·nums** or **in·ter·reg·na** (ĭn′tər-**rĕg′**nə) The period between the end of one ruler's reign and the beginning of the next ruler's reign.

in·ter·re·late (ĭn′tər-rĭ-**lāt′**) *tr. & intr.v.* **in·ter·re·lat·ed, in·ter·re·lat·ing, in·ter·re·lates** To place in or come into mutual relationship. **—in′ter·re·la′tion** *n.* **—in′ter·re·la′tion·ship′** *n.*

in·ter·re·lat·ed (ĭn′tər-rĭ-**lā′**tĭd) *adj.* Related to each other; affecting one another: *interrelated conditions of starvation and disease.*

in·ter·ro·gate (ĭn-**tĕr′**ə-gāt′) *tr.v.* **in·ter·ro·gat·ed, in·ter·ro·gat·ing, in·ter·ro·gates** To question formally and closely: *The police interrogated witnesses of the accident.* [From Latin *interrogāre* : *inter-,* in the presence of + *rogāre,* to ask.] **—in·ter′ro·ga′tion** *n.* **—in·ter′ro·ga′tor** *n.*

interrogation point *n.* A question mark.

in·ter·rog·a·tive (ĭn′tə-**rŏg′**ə-tĭv) *adj.* **1.** Asking a question or having the nature of a question: *an interrogative sentence.* **2.** Used in asking a question: When, why, *and* where *are interrogative pronouns.* ❖ *n.* **1.** A word or form used in asking a question. For example, in the questions *Where did you go?* and *Whom did you see?* the words *where* and *whom* are interrogatives. **2.** A sentence or expression that asks a question.

in·ter·rog·a·to·ry (ĭn′tə-**rŏg′**ə-tôr′ē) *adj.* Interrogative.

in·ter·rupt (ĭn′tə-**rŭpt′**) *v.* **in·ter·rupt·ed, in·ter·rupt·ing, in·ter·rupts** *—tr.* **1.** To stop (someone engaged in an activity) by saying or doing something: *I was about to finish the joke when my brother interrupted me.* **2.** To cause a sudden or abrupt break in; break the continuity of: *Rain interrupted our baseball game for an hour.* *—intr.* To cause an activity to stop by saying or doing something: *It is impolite to interrupt when others are talking.* [From Middle English *interrupten,* from Latin *interrumpere,* to break off.] **—in′ter·rup′tion** *n.*

in·ter·scho·las·tic (ĭn′tər-skə-**lăs′**tĭk) *adj.* Existing or conducted between or among schools: *an interscholastic tournament.*

in·ter·sect (ĭn′tər-**sĕkt′**) *v.* **in·ter·sect·ed, in·ter·sect·ing, in·ter·sects** *—tr.* To cut across or through; divide: *A fence intersects the pasture.* *—intr.* To cut across each other; overlap: *The road intersects with the highway north of town.* [From Latin *intersecāre* : *inter-,* between + *secāre,* to cut.] —SEE NOTE AT **segment.**

in·ter·sec·tion (ĭn′tər-**sĕk′**shən *or* **ĭn′**tər-sĕk′shən) *n.* **1.** The act or result of intersecting. **2.** A place where two or more things intersect, especially a place where two or more roads cross. **3.** In geometry, the point where one line, surface, or solid crosses another: *The intersection of two planes determines a straight line.* **4.** In mathematics, the set that contains only those elements shared by two or more sets.

in·ter·sperse (ĭn′tər-**spûrs′**) *tr.v.* **in·ter·spersed, in·ter·spers·ing, in·ter·spers·es 1.** To scatter or insert here and there among other things: *The florist interspersed greens among the flowers.* **2.** To vary by distributing things here and there: *The magazine is interspersed with advertisements.*

in·ter·state (**ĭn′**tər-stāt′) *adj.* Involving, existing between, or connecting two or more states: *laws concerning interstate commerce.* ❖ *n.* One of a national system of expressways connecting major population centers in the United States.

in·ter·stel·lar (ĭn′tər-**stĕl′**ər) *adj.* Between or among the stars: *interstellar gases.*

in·ter·tid·al (ĭn′tər-**tīd′**l) *adj.* Relating to or being the region between the highest point that the sea reaches at high tide and the lowest point it reaches at low tide: *the intertidal zone.*

in·ter·twine (ĭn′tər-**twīn′**) *tr. & intr.v.* **in·ter·twined, in·ter·twin·ing, in·ter·twines** To join or become joined by twining together: *She intertwined the strands into a braid. The dancers' arms intertwined.*

in·ter·val (**ĭn′**tər-vəl) *n.* **1.** A space between objects, points, or units, especially when making uniform amounts of separation: *We set up hurdles at intervals of 15 yards around the track.* **2.** An amount of time between events, especially of uniform duration separating events in a series: *We ran laps at 30-second intervals.* **3.** In mathematics and statistics, the set of all numbers between two given numbers. **4.** The difference, usually expressed in the number of steps, between two musical pitches. [From Middle English *intervalle,* from Latin *intervallum* : *inter-,* between + *vallum,* rampart.]

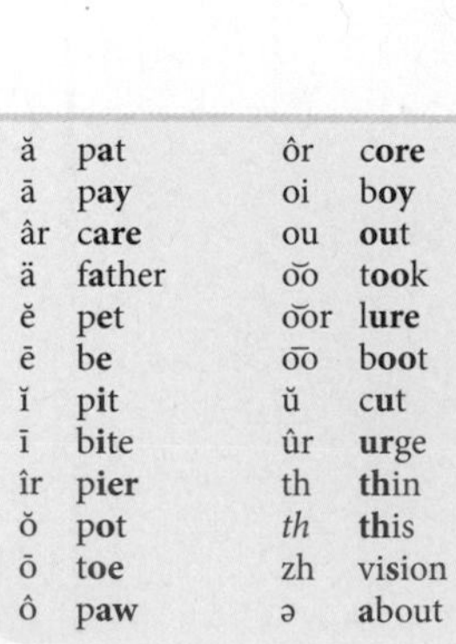

ă	pat	ôr	core
ā	pay	oi	boy
âr	care	ou	out
ä	father	o͝o	took
ĕ	pet	o͝or	lure
ē	be	o͞o	boot
ĭ	pit	ŭ	cut
ī	bite	ûr	urge
îr	pier	th	thin
ŏ	pot	*th*	this
ō	toe	zh	vision
ô	paw	ə	about

in·ter·vene (ĭn′tər-**vēn′**) *intr.v.* **in·ter·vened, in·ter·ven·ing, in·ter·venes 1a.** To come between so as to hinder or change a course of events: *The teacher intervened to settle the dispute.* **b.** To interfere, usually with force, in the affairs of another nation. **2.** To come or lie between two things: *The road goes nearly to the shore, but a farm intervenes.* **3.** To come between two events: *A period of calm intervened between stormy sessions of the legislature.* [From Latin *intervenīre* : *inter-*, between + *venīre*, to come.] —SEE NOTE.

in·ter·ven·tion (ĭn′tər-**vĕn′**shən) *n.* **1.** The act or process of intervening: *The governor's intervention saved the park from development. Congress debated military intervention.* **2.** Steps taken to prevent or correct a social, educational, or developmental problem: *early intervention for toddlers diagnosed with autism.*

in·ter·view (**ĭn′**tər-vyo͞o′) *n.* **1.** A face-to-face meeting for a specified purpose: *an interview for a job.* **2a.** A conversation, such as one between a reporter and another person, for the purpose of obtaining information. **b.** An account or broadcast of such information. ❖ *tr.v.* **in·ter·viewed, in·ter·view·ing, in·ter·views** To have an interview with: *The committee interviewed candidates for the job.* **—in′ter·view′er** *n.*

in·ter·weave (ĭn′tər-**wēv′**) *v.* **in·ter·wove** (ĭn′tər-**wōv′**), **in·ter·wo·ven** (ĭn′tər-**wō′**vən), **in·ter·weav·ing, in·ter·weaves** —*tr.* **1.** To weave together: *Cloth is made by interweaving threads.* **2.** To blend; intermix: *The author skillfully interweaves two plots in a single story.* —*intr.* To intertwine.

in·tes·tate (ĭn-**tĕs′**tāt′ *or* ĭn-**tĕs′**tĭt) *adj.* Having made no legal will: *a person who died intestate.*

in·tes·ti·nal (ĭn-**tĕs′**tə-nəl) *adj.* Relating to or involving the intestines: *an intestinal parasite.* **—in·tes′ti·nal·ly** *adv.*

in·tes·tine (ĭn-**tĕs′**tĭn) *n.* The part of the digestive tract extending from the stomach to the anus, consisting of the large intestine and small intestine.

in·ti·ma·cy (**ĭn′**tə-mə-sē) *n., pl.* **in·ti·ma·cies 1.** The condition of being intimate, especially personal closeness. **2.** An instance of being intimate.

in·ti·mate¹ (**ĭn′**tə-mĭt) *adj.* **1.** Marked by close personal association or familiarity: *intimate friends.* **2.** Very personal; private: *an intimate letter.* **3.** Detailed or thorough: *Cab drivers have an intimate knowledge of the city's streets.* ❖ *n.* A close friend or confidant. [From Latin *intimātus*, from *intimāre*, to make familiar with.] **—in′ti·mate·ly** *adv.*

in·ti·mate² (**ĭn′**tə-māt′) *tr.v.* **in·ti·mat·ed, in·ti·mat·ing, in·ti·mates** To state or express indirectly; imply: *He intimated that the award would go to someone in our class.* [From Latin *intimāre*, to make known, from *intimus*, innermost.] **—in′ti·ma′tion** *n.*

in·tim·i·date (ĭn-**tĭm′**ĭ-dāt′) *tr.v.* **in·tim·i·dat·ed, in·tim·i·dat·ing, in·tim·i·dates** To fill with fear; frighten or discourage: *The rough water intimidated us in our light canoe.* **—in·tim′i·da′tion** *n.* **—in·tim′i·da′tor** *n.*

in·to (**ĭn′**to͞o) *prep.* **1.** To the inside of: *going into the house.* **2.** So as to be in or within: *enter into an agreement.* **3.** To the action or occupation of: *go into banking.* **4.** To the condition or form of: *break into pieces.* **5.** To a time or place in the course of: *It's getting well into the week.* **6.** Toward; in the direction of: *looking into the distance.* **7.** Against: *run into a tree.* **8.** *Informal* Interested in or involved with: *They are into health foods.* **9.** As a divisor of: *5 into 30 is 6.*

in·tol·er·a·ble (ĭn-**tŏl′**ər-ə-bəl) *adj.* Impossible to tolerate; unbearable: *We found the noise in the sawmill intolerable.* **—in·tol′er·a·bly** *adv.*

in·tol·er·ance (ĭn-**tŏl′**ər-əns) *n.* The quality or condition of being intolerant.

in·tol·er·ant (ĭn-**tŏl′**ər-ənt) *adj.* **1.** Unwilling to tolerate opinions or beliefs that differ from one's own. **2.** Unable to endure or tolerate physically: *Allergies can make a person intolerant of certain foods.*

in·to·na·tion (ĭn′tə-**nā′**shən) *n.* **1.** The way in which the speaking voice rises or falls in pitch in order to convey meaning. **2.** An intoned utterance. **3.** The manner in which musical tones are sung or played, especially with regard to accuracy of pitch.

in·tone (ĭn-**tōn′**) *tr. & intr.v.* **in·toned, in·ton·ing, in·tones** To recite in a singing or chanting voice: *The choir intoned prayers at several points during the church service.*

in·tox·i·cant (ĭn-**tŏk′**sĭ-kənt) *n.* Something that intoxicates, especially an alcoholic drink.

in·tox·i·cate (ĭn-**tŏk′**sĭ-kāt′) *tr.v.* **in·tox·i·cat·ed, in·tox·i·cat·ing, in·tox·i·cates 1.** To cause (a person) to lose control of physical or mental powers by means of alcohol or a drug. **2.** To fill with great excitement or enthusiasm; exhilarate: *The grandeur of the mountains intoxicated the tourists.* [From Middle English, to poison, from Latin *toxicum*, poison.]

in·tox·i·cat·ed (ĭn-**tŏk′**sĭ-kā′tĭd) *adj.* **1.** Drunk; stupefied: *an intoxicated driver.* **2.** Very excited; overjoyed.

in·tox·i·ca·tion (ĭn-tŏk′sĭ-**kā′**shən) *n.* **1.** The condition of being intoxicated, especially drunkenness. **2.** Great excitement or enthusiasm.

intr. *abbr.* An abbreviation of intransitive.

intra– *pref.* A prefix that means inside of or within: *intravenous.*

In·tra·coas·tal Waterway (ĭn′trə-**kōs′**təl) A system of artificial and natural channels and canals along the coasts of the Atlantic Ocean and Gulf of Mexico of the eastern and southeast United States. It provides sheltered passage for commercial and pleasure boats.

in·trac·ta·ble (ĭn-**trăk′**tə-bəl) *adj.* **1.** Difficult to manage, deal with, or change: *an intractable conflict; intractable pain.* **2.** Difficult to persuade or keep under control: *an intractable opponent.* **—in·trac′ta·bly** *adv.*

in·tra·mu·ral (ĭn′trə-**myo͝or′**əl) *adj.* Involving members of the same school or institution: *our school's intramural athletic program.*

in·tra·net (**ĭn′**trə-nĕt′) *n.* A privately maintained computer network that can be accessed only by authorized people.

in·tran·si·gent (ĭn-**trăn′**sə-jənt *or* ĭn-**trăn′**zə-jənt) *adj.* Refusing to compromise; stubborn. **—in·tran′si·gence** *n.* **—in·tran′si·gent·ly** *adv.*

in·tran·si·tive (ĭn-**trăn′**sĭ-tĭv *or* ĭn-**trăn′**zĭ-tĭv) *adj.* Relating to a verb that does not require a direct object to complete its meaning. In the sentence *The bell rang loudly*, the verb *rang* is intransitive. **—in·tran′si·tive·ly** *adv.* —SEE NOTE AT **verb.**

in·tra·ve·nous (ĭn′trə-**vē′**nəs) *adj.* Within or into a vein: *an intravenous injection of serum.* **—in′tra·ve′nous·ly** *adv.*

in·trep·id (ĭn-**trĕp′**ĭd) *adj.* Brave; bold; fearless: *Early explorers of Antarctica were intrepid and resourceful.* **—in′tre·pid′i·ty** (ĭn′trə-**pĭd′**ĭ-tē) *n.* **—in·trep′id·ly** *adv.*

in·tri·ca·cy (**ĭn′**trĭ-kə-sē) *n., pl.* **in·tri·ca·cies 1.** The quality or condition of being intricate; complexity: *The intricacy of a maze makes it hard to follow.* **2.** Something intricate; a complication: *The intricacies of human anatomy require years of study.*

in·tri·cate (**ĭn′**trĭ-kĭt) *adj.* Having a complex structure or pattern; elaborate: *the intricate arrangement of gears in a clock.* [From Middle English, from Latin *intrīcāre*, to entangle, perplex, from *trīcae*, perplexities.] **—in′tri·cate·ly** *adv.*

in·trigue (**ĭn′**trēg′ *or* ĭn-**trēg′**) *n.* **1.** Plotting or scheming that is done secretly: *a royal court that was full of intrigue.* **2.** A secret plot or scheme: *the intrigues of foreign spies.* ❖ *v.* (ĭn-**trēg′**) **in·trigued, in·trigu·ing, in·**

WORD BUILDING

intervene The word root *ven–* in English words comes from the Latin verb *venīre*, "to come." Thus **intervene** means literally "to come between, as between two people fighting" (using the prefix *inter–*, "between"). **Convene** means "to come together, as for a meeting or a **convention**" (*com–*, *con–*, "together, with"). *Venīre* has a past participle *ventum*, which provides the word **event**, literally an "outcome" (*ē–*, a form of *ex–*, "out, out of").

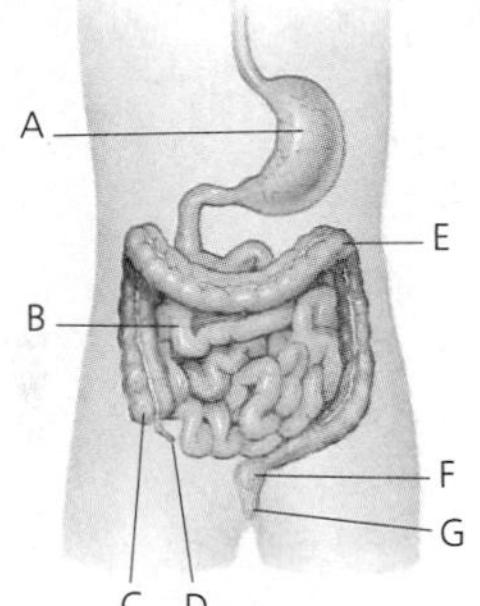

intestine
A. stomach
B. small intestine
C. cecum
D. appendix
E. large intestine
F. rectum
G. anus

WRITERS CHOOSE THEIR WORDS

In front of and around the dwellings was activity and laughter, men and women weaving, making clay from the lake into bowls and dishes, painting the pottery with vivid colors and **intricate** geometrical designs.

—Madeleine L'Engle
A Swiftly Tilting Planet

trigues —*intr.* To plot or scheme secretly: *The political rivals intrigued against one another.* —*tr.* To excite the interest and curiosity of; fascinate: *The mystery of hibernation has long intrigued biologists.* [From Italian *intrigare*, to plot, from Latin *intrīcāre*, to entangle.]

in·trigu·ing (ĭn-**trē′**gĭng) *adj.* Exciting the interest or curiosity; fascinating. See Synonyms at **interesting.**

in·trin·sic (ĭn-**trĭn′**zĭk *or* ĭn-**trĭn′**sĭk) *adj.* Relating to the basic nature of a thing; essential; inherent: *He recommended the adventure movie on its intrinsic merits, not on its special effects.* **—in·trin′si·cal·ly** *adv.*

in·tro (**ĭn′**trō′) *n., pl.* **in·tros** *Informal* An introduction.

intro– *pref.* A prefix that means inward: *introvert.*

in·tro·duce (ĭn′trə-**do͞os′**) *tr.v.* **in·tro·duced, in·tro·duc·ing, in·tro·duc·es 1.** To present (someone) by name to another in order to establish an acquaintance: *Please introduce me to your old friend.* **2.** To bring into use or practice: *That company has introduced several new products.* **3.** To provide (someone) with a first experience of something: *My father introduced me to fishing.* **4.** To present for consideration: *introduce legislation in Congress.* **5.** To talk or write about (something) in advance: *The professor introduced the movie with a short lecture.* **6.** To bring in and establish in a new place or environment: *European starlings were introduced into North America in the late 1800s.* **7.** To put in; insert or inject: *introduce a new character into a story.* [From Middle English *introducen*, to bring into, from Latin *intrōdūcere* : *intrō-*, in + *dūcere*, to lead.] **—in′tro·duc′er** *n.*

in·tro·duc·tion (ĭn′trə-**dŭk′**shən) *n.* **1.** The act or process of introducing: *The introduction of printing made books cheaper and more widely available.* **2.** Something introduced or brought into use: *Like many European introductions, the starling has established itself widely in North America.* **3.** The first part of a book, speech, or musical composition. **4.** A first book in a course of study: *This book is an introduction to physics.*

in·tro·duc·to·ry (ĭn′trə-**dŭk′**tə-rē) *adj.* Serving to introduce a subject or person: *a few introductory remarks by the speaker.*

in·tro·spec·tion (ĭn′trə-**spĕk′**shən) *n.* The examination of one's own thoughts and feelings. —SEE NOTE AT **spectator.**

in·tro·spec·tive (ĭn′trə-**spĕk′**tĭv) *adj.* Given to examining one's own thoughts and feelings: *an introspective philosopher.* **—in′tro·spec′tive·ly** *adv.*

in·tro·vert (**ĭn′**trə-vûrt′) *n.* A person who is not very sociable or outgoing and who tends to be preoccupied with his or her own thoughts and feelings. **—in′tro·vert·ed** *adj.*

in·trude (ĭn-**tro͞od′**) *v.* **in·trud·ed, in·trud·ing, in·trudes** —*intr.* **1.** To break or come in without being wanted or asked: *The new neighbors were always intruding on her quiet afternoons.* **2.** To violate or advance wrongly into the scope or extent of something: *The lawsuit claims that the government intruded on their right to privacy.* —*tr.* **1.** To put or force in without invitation: *They intruded their opinions into our conversation.* **2.** To cause (molten rock) to be forced into existing rock. [From Middle English *intruden*, from Latin *intrūdere*, to thrust in : *in-*, in + *trūdere*, to thrust.] **—in·trud′er** *n.*

in·tru·sion (ĭn-**tro͞o′**zhən) *n.* **1.** The act of intruding: *Your barging into my room is an intrusion on my privacy.* **2.** The forcing of molten rock into an existing rock formation. **3.** The rock mass produced by this process.

in·tru·sive (ĭn-**tro͞o′**sĭv) *adj.* **1.** Intruding or tending to intrude: *a rude intrusive question.* **2.** Relating to or being igneous rock that is forced while molten into cracks or between other layers of rock. **—in·tru′sive·ly** *adv.*

in·tu·i·tion (ĭn′to͞o-**ĭsh′**ən) *n.* **1.** The power of knowing or understanding something without reasoning or proof: *My intuition tells me that the experiment will work if we try it again.* **2.** Knowledge gained immediately without reasoning or proof; an insight.

in·tu·i·tive (ĭn-**to͞o′**ĭ-tĭv) *adj.* **1.** Based on intuition: *an intuitive understanding of musical harmony.* **2.** Having or showing intuition: *an intuitive mind.* **—in·tu′i·tive·ly** *adv.*

In·u·it (**ĭn′**yo͞o-ĭt) *n., pl.* **Inuit** or **In·u·its 1.** *(used with a plural verb)* The members of the Eskimo peoples inhabiting the Arctic from northwest Alaska eastward to eastern Greenland, particularly those inhabiting Canada. **2.** Any or all of the languages of the Inuit. **—In′u·it** *adj.*

in·un·date (**ĭn′**ŭn-dāt′) *tr.v.* **in·un·dat·ed, in·un·dat·ing, in·un·dates 1.** To cover with water; flood: *The storm tide inundated the waterfront.* **2.** To overwhelm as if with a flood: *The store was inundated with shoppers during the holiday sale.* [From Latin *inundāre* : *in-*, in + *undāre*, to surge (from *unda*, wave).] **—in′un·da′tion** *n.*

in·ure (ĭn-**yo͝or′**) *tr.v.* **in·ured, in·ur·ing, in·ures** To make used to; accustom: *Severe winters inured the pioneers to cold.*

in·vade (ĭn-**vād′**) *v.* **in·vad·ed, in·vad·ing, in·vades** —*tr.* **1.** To enter (a place) by force in order to attack or conquer: *The Romans invaded Britain.* **2.** To enter (a cell or tissue), usually multiplying or spreading: *Viruses invaded the cells; bacteria have invaded the lungs.* **3.** To enter (a place) and occupy it in large numbers, often destructively; overrun: *Skiers invaded the mountain town. A South American weed that is invading waterways in Florida.* **4.** To intrude on; violate: *invade someone's privacy.* —*intr.* To make an invasion. **—in·vad′er** *n.*

in·va·lid[1] (**ĭn′**və-lĭd) *n.* A person who is unable to function independently because of severe disease or injury. [From *invalid*, not valid, influenced by French *invalide*, sickly, infirm.]

in·val·id[2] (ĭn-**văl′**ĭd) *adj.* Not valid or proper; without force, foundation, or authority: *Unless a contract is signed, it is invalid.* [From Latin *invalidus*, weak : *in-*, not + *validus*, strong.] **—in·val′id·ly** *adv.*

in·val·i·date (ĭn-**văl′**ĭ-dāt′) *tr.v.* **in·val·i·dat·ed, in·val·i·dat·ing, in·val·i·dates** To make invalid or worthless; nullify: *The lack of a signature invalidated the check.* **—in·val′i·da′tion** *n.*

in·val·u·a·ble (ĭn-**văl′**yo͞o-ə-bəl) *adj.* Of a value greater than can be measured; priceless: *invaluable art treasures.* **—in·val′u·a·bly** *adv.*

in·var·i·a·ble (ĭn-**vâr′**ē-ə-bəl) *adj.* Not changing or varying; constant: *the invariable return of spring.* **—in·var′i·a·bil′i·ty** *n.* **—in·var′i·a·bly** *adv.*

in·va·sion (ĭn-**vā′**zhən) *n.* **1.** The act of invading, especially the entry of an armed force in order to conquer another country. **2.** An intrusion or violation: *The loud music from next door is an invasion of our privacy.*

in·va·sive (ĭn-**vā′**sĭv) *adj.* **1.** Tending to invade, especially tending to invade healthy cells or tissues: *an invasive tumor.* **2.** Involving entry into a part of the body, as by surgical incision: *invasive techniques for curing a heart defect.* **3.** Tending to intrude: *was annoyed by his invasive questions.* **4.** Tending to spread widely in a habitat or ecosystem: *invasive grasses.*

in·vec·tive (ĭn-**vĕk′**tĭv) *n.* Harsh words used to attack; abusive language.

in·veigh (ĭn-**vā′**) *intr.v.* **in·veighed, in·veigh·ing, in·veighs** To protest by speaking out violently and bitterly: *The tenants inveighed against higher rents.*

in·vei·gle (ĭn-**vā′**gəl *or* ĭn-**vē′**gəl) *tr.v.* **in·vei·gled, in·vei·gling, in·vei·gles 1.** To win over by flattery or artful talk: *The saleswoman inveigled me into buying a ring.* **2.** To obtain by flattery or artful talk: *He inveigled free passes from the ticket seller.* **—in·vei′gler** *n.*

in·vent (ĭn-**vĕnt′**) *tr.v.* **in·vent·ed, in·vent·ing, in·vents 1.** To produce or create (something new) by using

ă	pat	ôr	core
ā	pay	oi	boy
âr	care	ou	out
ä	father	o͝o	took
ĕ	pet	o͝or	lure
ē	be	o͞o	boot
ĭ	pit	ŭ	cut
ī	bite	ûr	urge
îr	pier	th	thin
ŏ	pot	*th*	this
ō	toe	zh	vision
ô	paw	ə	about

the imagination: *Thomas Edison invented the light bulb.* **2.** To make up; devise in the mind: *They invented an excuse for having to leave earlier than usual.* [From Latin *invenīre*, to find : *in-*, on, upon + *venīre*, to come.]

in·ven·tion (ĭn-vĕn′shən) *n.* **1.** Something invented, as a new device or process: *The computer is a revolutionary modern invention.* **2.** The act of inventing: *The invention of movable type made books widely available.* **3.** The power or ability to invent: *Only a mystery writer of great invention could create so complicated a plot.* **4.** Something that is made up, especially a falsehood. **—in·ven′tor** *n.*

in·ven·tive (ĭn-vĕn′tĭv) *adj.* **1.** Skillful at inventing; creative: *An inventive writer is able to keep the reader's attention.* **2.** Relating to or characterized by invention. **—in·ven′tive·ly** *adv.*

in·ven·tor (ĭn-vĕn′tər) *n.* A person who invents new ideas, things, or methods.

in·ven·to·ry (ĭn′vən-tôr′ē) *n., pl.* **in·ven·to·ries 1.** A detailed list of goods or possessions, especially a survey of all goods and materials in stock. **2.** The process of making such a survey or list. **3.** The supply of goods on hand; stock: *The store's inventory is getting low.* ❖ *tr.v.* **in·ven·to·ried, in·ven·to·ry·ing, in·ven·to·ries** To make a detailed list of: *Before reordering, the store inventoried its stock.*

in·verse (ĭn-vûrs′ *or* ĭn′vûrs′) *adj.* Opposite or reversed, as in character or order: *CBA is ABC in inverse order.* ❖ *n.* (**ĭn′**vûrs′ *or* ĭn-**vûrs′**) **1.** Something exactly opposite in order or character. **2.** One of a pair of elements in a set whose result under the operation of the set is the identity element. For example, the inverse of 5 under multiplication is ⅕, since 5 × ⅕ = 1. The inverse of 5 under addition is −5, since 5 + −5 = 0. **—in·verse′ly** *adv.*

in·ver·sion (ĭn-vûr′zhən *or* ĭn-vûr′shən) *n.* **1.** The act of inverting or the condition of being inverted. **2.** Something inverted.

in·vert (ĭn-vûrt′) *tr.v.* **in·vert·ed, in·vert·ing, in·verts 1.** To turn upside down: *invert an hourglass.* **2.** To reverse the order, position, or condition of: *A mirror inverts the placement of things in its reflection.* [From Latin *invertere* : *in-*, in + *vertere*, to turn.]

in·ver·te·brate (ĭn-vûr′tə-brĭt *or* ĭn-vûr′tə-brāt′) *adj.* **1.** Having no backbone: *invertebrate animals.* **2.** Relating to invertebrates: *invertebrate fossils; invertebrate anatomy.* ❖ *n.* An animal, such as an insect or octopus, that has no backbone.

in·vest (ĭn-vĕst′) *v.* **in·vest·ed, in·vest·ing, in·vests** —*tr.* **1.** To put (money) into something, such as property, stocks, or a business, in order to earn interest or make a profit: *Many people invest their savings in mutual funds.* **2.** To devote or spend for future advantage or benefit: *The candidates invested much time and energy in the election campaign.* **3.** To entrust with a right or power: *The Constitution invests Congress with the power to make laws.* **4.** To put in office with a formal ceremony: *The president is invested with an inauguration.* **5.** To provide with a certain quality: *The writer invested the novel with many historical details.* —*intr.* To make an investment: *The bank invested heavily in real estate.* [From Latin *investīre*, to clothe, surround.]

in·ves·ti·gate (ĭn-vĕs′tĭ-gāt′) *v.* **in·ves·ti·gat·ed, in·ves·ti·gat·ing, in·ves·ti·gates** —*tr.* To look into or search carefully for facts, knowledge, or information: *The police investigate crimes to determine who commits them.* —*intr.* To make an investigation. [From Latin *investīgāre* : *in-*, in + *vestīgāre*, to track (from *vestīgium*, footprint).]

in·ves·ti·ga·tion (ĭn-vĕs′tĭ-gā′shən) *n.* A careful examination or search in order to discover facts or gain information.

in·ves·ti·ga·tor (ĭn-vĕs′tĭ-gā′tər) *n.* A person who investigates, especially a detective.

in·ves·ti·ture (ĭn-vĕs′tĭ-cho͝or′ *or* ĭn-vĕs′tĭ-chər) *n.* The act or formal ceremony putting a person in a high office or position of authority.

in·vest·ment (ĭn-vĕst′mənt) *n.* **1.** The act of investing money for profit or advantage: *The company made an investment in new equipment.* **2.** A sum of money invested: *interest earned on an investment.* **3.** Something in which money is invested: *Land is a good investment.* **4.** A commitment, as of time or effort: *I've got a big investment in music lessons.*

in·ves·tor (ĭn-vĕs′tər) *n.* A person or group that invests money for profit.

in·vet·er·ate (ĭn-vĕt′ər-ĭt) *adj.* **1.** Fixed in a habit or practice; habitual: *An inveterate reader needs no incentive to pick up a good book.* **2.** Firmly established for a long time; deep-rooted: *Inveterate prejudice is resistant to change or reform.*

in·vid·i·ous (ĭn-vĭd′ē-əs) *adj.* **1.** Likely to produce anger, ill will, or resentment: *She was given the invidious task of identifying the person who had made the error.* **2.** Offensive and unfair: *The article makes invidious comparisons between immigrants and native-born people.* [From Latin *invidia*, envy.] **—in·vid′i·ous·ly** *adv.*

in·vig·or·ate (ĭn-vĭg′ə-rāt′) *tr.v.* **in·vig·or·at·ed, in·vig·or·at·ing, in·vig·or·ates** To fill with energy, strength, or vigor: *The cool autumn air invigorated us.* **—in·vig′or·a′tion** *n.*

in·vin·ci·ble (ĭn-vĭn′sə-bəl) *adj.* Incapable of being defeated or overcome: *an invincible army; invincible courage.* **—in·vin′ci·bil′i·ty** *n.* **—in·vin′ci·bly** *adv.*

in·vi·o·la·ble (ĭn-vī′ə-lə-bəl) *adj.* **1.** Regarded as sacred and not to be violated: *an inviolable promise.* **2.** Incapable of being assaulted or trespassed: *an inviolable castle.* **—in·vi′o·la·bly** *adv.*

in·vi·o·late (ĭn-vī′ə-lĭt) *adj.* Not violated or broken; intact: *Personal integrity requires inviolate honesty in dealing with others.*

in·vis·i·ble (ĭn-vĭz′ə-bəl) *adj.* Impossible to see; not visible: *Air is colorless and invisible.* **—in·vis′i·bil′i·ty** *n.* **—in·vis′i·bly** *adv.*

in·vi·ta·tion (ĭn′vĭ-tā′shən) *n.* **1.** A spoken or written request for a person to come somewhere or do something: *an invitation to a party.* **2.** The act of inviting.

in·vi·ta·tion·al (ĭn′vĭ-tā′shə-nəl) *adj.* Restricted to people who have been invited to participate: *an invitational golf tournament.*

in·vite (ĭn-vīt′) *tr.v.* **in·vit·ed, in·vit·ing, in·vites 1.** To ask (a person or persons) politely to come somewhere or do something: *invite guests to a party.* **2.** To ask; request: *The author invited questions from the audience.* **3.** To tend to bring on; provoke: *Exercising too much invites injury.* **4.** To tempt, lure, or attract: *After days of rain, the bright sun invited us outside.* [From Latin *invītāre*.]

in·vi·tee (ĭn′vī-tē′) *n.* A person who is invited: *The invitees placed their wedding gifts on the table at the reception.*

in·vit·ing (ĭn-vī′tĭng) *adj.* Attractive; tempting: *A swimming pool looks inviting on a hot day.* **—in·vit′ing·ly** *adv.*

in vi·tro (ĭn vē′trō) *adv. & adj.* In an artificial environment, such as a test tube, outside a living organism: *grow tissue in vitro.*

in vitro fertilization *n.* The production of an embryo or embryos by combining egg and sperm cells together outside the body.

in vi·vo (vē′vō) *adv. & adj.* Inside a living organism: *test a new drug in vivo.*

in·vo·ca·tion (ĭn′və-kā′shən) *n.* **1.** The act or an instance of invoking, especially an appeal for help from a higher power: *ancient peoples' invocation of their gods for a bountiful harvest.* **2.** A prayer or appeal used in invoking help or protection, as at the opening of a religious

investiture
investiture of Prince Charles of England as the Prince of Wales in 1969

service. **3.** A set of words spoken as a magic charm to bring forth a spirit.

in·voice (ĭn′vois′) *n.* A detailed list of goods shipped or services rendered, with an account of all costs and charges. ❖ *tr.v.* **in·voiced, in·voic·ing, in·voic·es** To make an invoice of; bill: *The company invoiced the shipment.* [From obsolete *invoyes*, things sent, from French *envoyer*, to send.]

in·voke (ĭn-vōk′) *tr.v.* **in·voked, in·vok·ing, in·vokes 1.** To call on for help or protection: *Viking mariners invoked their gods before long voyages at sea.* **2.** To ask or call for earnestly: *The defendant invoked the mercy of the court.* **3.** To use or apply: *In defending their right to protest, the lawyer invoked the Constitution.* **4.** To call up (a spirit) with magic words or spells. **5.** To activate or start (a computer program, for example). [From Middle English *envoken*, from Latin *invocāre* : *in-*, in, on + *vocāre*, to call.]

in·vol·un·tar·y (ĭn-vŏl′ən-tĕr′ē) *adj.* **1.** Not subject to conscious control; automatic: *Sneezing is involuntary.* **2.** Not done willingly or on purpose; unintentional or accidental: *an involuntary gesture; an involuntary mishap.* **—in·vol′un·tar′i·ly** *adv.*

in·volve (ĭn-vŏlv′) *tr.v.* **in·volved, in·volv·ing, in·volves 1.** To have as a necessary feature or outcome; include or entail: *His new job involves a lot of travel.* **2.** To draw in; mix up; embroil: *By asking my opinion, he involved me in their argument.* **3.** To spread to: *The fire involved the house next door.* **4.** To hold the interest of; absorb: *The children were completely involved in their game.* [From Middle English *involven*, from Latin *involvere*, to enwrap : *in-*, in + *volvere*, to roll, turn.] **—in·volve′ment** *n.*

in·volved (ĭn-vŏlvd′) *adj.* Complicated; complex; intricate: *a long involved sentence.*

in·vul·ner·a·ble (ĭn-vŭl′nər-ə-bəl) *adj.* Impossible to attack, damage, or hurt: *an invulnerable fort; an invulnerable argument.* **—in·vul′ner·a·bil′i·ty** *n.* **—in·vul′ner·a·bly** *adv.*

in·ward (ĭn′wərd) *adj.* **1.** Directed toward the inside: *an inward rush of water into the submarine's holding tanks.* **2.** Located on the inside; inner: *the inward surface of the fuel tank.* **3.** Relating to or existing in the thoughts or mind: *inward feelings.* ❖ *adv.* also **in·wards** (ĭn′wərdz) **1.** Toward the inside or center: *The door swung inward.* **2.** Toward one's own mind or self: *His thoughts turned inward.*

inward dive *n.* A dive in which the diver, standing on the end of the board with the back to the water, leaps up and rotates forward.

in·ward·ly (ĭn′wərd-lē) *adv.* **1.** On or in the inside; internally. **2.** To oneself; privately: *chuckling inwardly.*

IOC *abbr.* An abbreviation of International Olympic Committee.

i·o·dide (ī′ə-dīd′) *n.* A chemical compound of iodine with another element or radical.

i·o·dine (ī′ə-dīn′ *or* ī′ə-dĭn) *n.* **1.** *Symbol* **I** A shiny, purple-black nonmetallic element that is corrosive and poisonous. Small amounts of iodine are essential for proper thyroid function. Iodine compounds are used in antiseptics and dyes. Atomic number 53. See **Periodic Table. 2.** A liquid antiseptic preparation containing iodine, used to treat wounds.

i·o·dize (ī′ə-dīz′) *tr.v.* **i·o·dized, i·o·diz·ing, i·o·diz·es** To treat or combine with iodine or an iodide: *iodize table salt.*

i·on (ī′ŏn′ *or* ī′ən) *n.* An atom or a group of atoms that has an electric charge. Positive ions are formed by the loss of electrons; negative ions are formed by the gain of electrons. [From Greek, something that goes, from *ienai*, to go.] —SEE NOTE AT **charge.**

–ion *suff.* A suffix that means: **1.** Action or process: *completion.* **2.** Result of an action or process: *indentation.* **3.** State or condition: *elation.*

I·o·ni·a (ī-ō′nē-ə) An ancient region of western Asia Minor along the coast of the Aegean Sea. Greek settlers established colonies here before 1000 BC. **—I·o′ni·an** *adj. & n.*

i·on·ic (ī-ŏn′ĭk) *adj.* Containing ions.

Ionic *adj.* **1.** Relating to an order of ancient Greek and Roman architecture characterized by columns with two decorative scrolls at the top. **2.** Relating to ancient Ionia or the Ionians.

i·on·ize (ī′ə-nīz′) *v.* **i·on·ized, i·on·iz·ing, i·on·iz·es** *—tr.* To produce ions in: *Lightning ionizes the air it moves through.* *—intr.* To break apart or change into ions: *Acids, bases, and salts ionize when they are dissolved in a solution.* **—i′on·i·za′tion** (ī′ə-nĭ-zā′shən) *n.*

i·on·o·sphere (ī-ŏn′ə-sfîr′) *n.* A region of the earth's atmosphere extending from about 43 miles (70 kilometers) to more than 250 miles (400 kilometers) above the earth. It is composed of layers of ionized gases that enable radio signals to be transmitted over long distances.

i·o·ta (ī-ō′tə) *n.* **1.** The ninth letter of the Greek alphabet, written Ι, ι. In English it is represented as *I, i.* **2.** A very small amount; a bit: *There is not an iota of truth in that gossip.*

IOU (ī′ō-yo͞o′) *n.* A written promise to pay a debt, bearing the letters IOU, which stand for "I owe you," followed by the amount owed.

I·o·wa¹ (ī′ə-wə) *n., pl.* **Iowa** or **I·o·was 1.** A member of a Native American people formerly living in Iowa and Minnesota, with present-day populations in Nebraska, Kansas, and Oklahoma. **2.** The Siouan language of the Iowa.

I·o·wa² (ī′ə-wə) A state of the north-central United States north of Missouri. It was admitted as the 29th state in 1846. Des Moines is the capital. —SEE NOTE.

ip·e·cac (ĭp′ĭ-kăk′) *n.* A medicine prepared from the root of a South American shrub, used chiefly to induce vomiting. [From Tupí *ipekaaguéne* : from *ipeh*, low + *kaâ*, leaves + *guéne*, vomit.]

IQ *abbr.* An abbreviation of intelligence quotient.

I·qa·lu·it (ī-kăl′o͞o-ĭt) The capital of Nunavut, Canada, on Baffin Island west of Nuuk, Greenland.

Ir The symbol for the element **iridium.**

ir–¹ *pref.* Variant of **in–¹.**

ir–² *pref.* Variant of **in–².**

I·ran (ĭ-răn′ *or* ĭ-rän′ *or* ī-răn′) A country of southwest Asia east of Iraq. Formerly known as Persia, it was the center of a powerful empire from the sixth to the fourth century BC. Tehran is the capital.

I·ra·ni·an (ĭ-rā′nē-ən *or* ĭ-rä′nē-ən) *adj.* **1.** Relating to Iran or its people, languages, or cultures. **2.** Relating to a branch of the Indo-European language family that includes Persian, Kurdish, Pashto, and other languages of Iran, Afghanistan, and western Pakistan. ❖ *n.* **1.** A native or inhabitant of Iran. **2.** The Iranian branch of Indo-European.

I·raq (ĭ-răk′ *or* ĭ-räk′ *or* ī-răk′) A country of southwest Asia north of Saudi Arabia. Iraq was the site of a number of ancient Mesopotamian civilizations. Baghdad is the capital.

I·ra·qi (ĭ-răk′ē *or* ĭ-rä′kē *or* ī-răk′ē) *n., pl.* **I·ra·qis 1.** A native or inhabitant of Iraq. **2.** The modern dialect of Arabic spoken in Iraq. ❖ *adj.* Relating to Iraq, its people, language, or culture.

Iraq War *n.* A war in Iraq that began in 2003 with an attack by a group of forces led by the United States and that resulted in the overthrow of Saddam Hussein's regime. US combat troops were withdrawn in 2010.

i·ras·ci·ble (ĭ-răs′ə-bəl *or* ī-răs′ə-bəl) *adj.* Easily angered;

GEOGRAPHY

Iowa² The name of the state of **Iowa** comes from the Iowa River, which had been named by French settlers for a Native American people who lived on its banks. The French learned the name of the Iowa, earlier pronounced (ī′ə-wā′), from the Illinois, who had in turn adapted it from a Sioux designation meaning "sleepy ones."

iridescent

ă	pat	ôr	core
ā	pay	oi	boy
âr	care	ou	out
ä	father	o͝o	took
ĕ	pet	o͝or	lure
ē	be	o͞o	boot
ĭ	pit	ŭ	cut
ī	bite	ûr	urge
îr	pier	th	thin
ŏ	pot	*th*	this
ō	toe	zh	vision
ô	paw	ə	about

highly irritable: *The long trip made the children very irascible.* **—i·ras′ci·bly** *adv.*

i·rate (ī-rāt′ *or* ī′rāt′) *adj.* Angry; enraged: *A group of irate citizens turned out to protest the tax increase.* **—i·rate′ly** *adv.*

ire (īr) *n.* Anger; wrath. [From Middle English, from Latin *īra*.] **—ire′ful** *adj.*

Ire·land (īr′lənd) **1.** An island in the northern Atlantic Ocean west of Great Britain. After many years under British control, the island was split (1922) into the Irish Free State (now Ireland) and Northern Ireland, which remained in the United Kingdom. **2.** also **Eir·e** (âr′ə *or* ī′rə *or* âr′ē *or* ī′rē) A country occupying most of the island of Ireland. Established as the Irish Free State in 1922, it became Eire in 1937 and the Republic of Ireland in 1949. Dublin is the capital.

ir·i·des·cence (ĭr′ĭ-dĕs′əns) *n.* The quality or state of being iridescent.

ir·i·des·cent (ĭr′ĭ-dĕs′ənt) *adj.* Showing a display of lustrous colors: *iridescent soap bubbles.* [From Latin *īris*, rainbow.] **—ir′i·des′cent·ly** *adv.*

i·rid·i·um (ĭ-rĭd′ē-əm) *n. Symbol* **Ir** A yellowish, very hard and brittle metallic element that is used to make hard alloys of platinum for jewelry and electrical contacts. Atomic number 77. See **Periodic Table.**

i·ris (ī′rĭs) *n., pl.* **i·ris·es** or **i·ri·des** (ī′rĭ-dēz′ *or* ĭr′ĭ-dēz′) **1.** The colored part around the pupil of the eye, located between the cornea and the lens. The iris regulates the amount of light entering the eye. **2.** Any of numerous widely cultivated plants having long sword-shaped leaves and showy flowers of various colors. [From Middle English, from Greek *īris*, rainbow, brightly colored gemstone, iris of the eye.]

I·rish (ī′rĭsh) *adj.* Relating to Ireland or its people, language, or culture. ❖ *n.* **1.** *(used with a plural verb)* The people of Ireland. **2.** Irish Gaelic.

Irish Gaelic *n.* The Celtic language of Ireland.

I·rish·man (ī′rĭsh-mən) *n.* A man who is a native or inhabitant of Ireland.

Irish Sea An arm of the northern Atlantic Ocean between Ireland and Great Britain.

Irish setter *n.* A dog of a breed developed in Ireland for bird hunting, having a silky reddish coat.

Irish stew *n.* A stew of meat and vegetables.

Irish terrier *n.* A dog of a breed developed in Ireland, having a wiry reddish-brown coat.

I·rish·wom·an (ī′rĭsh-wo͝om′ən) *n.* A woman who is a native or inhabitant of Ireland.

irk (ûrk) *tr.v.* **irked, irk·ing, irks** To annoy, bother, or irritate: *Nothing irks a busy person so much as to be kept waiting.* [From Middle English *irken*, to weary, possibly from Old Norse *yrkja*, to work.]

irk·some (ûrk′səm) *adj.* Tiresome; tedious; annoying: *irksome paperwork.* **—irk′some·ly** *adv.* **—irk′some·ness** *n.*

i·ron (ī′ərn) *n.* **1.** *Symbol* **Fe** A silvery-white, hard, brittle metallic element that can be magnetized and is used to make steel. Iron occurs in hemoglobin in red blood cells. Atomic number 26. See **Periodic Table. 2a.** A metal appliance with a handle and flat bottom, used when heated to press wrinkles from cloth. **b.** An implement made of iron or a similar metal: *a branding iron; a curling iron.* **3. irons** Shackles; fetters: *a prisoner restrained by handcuffs and leg irons.* **4.** Any of a series of golf clubs with a bladelike metal head. **5.** Great strength, firmness, or hardness: *a grip of iron; a will of iron.* ❖ *adj.* **1.** Made of or containing iron: *an iron gate.* **2.** Very hard, strong, or determined: *an iron will.* ❖ *v.* **i·roned, i·ron·ing, i·rons** *—tr.* To press or smooth with a heated iron: *iron a shirt.* *—intr.* To press clothes with a heated iron: *She watched television while she was ironing.* ◆ **iron out** To settle through discussion or compromise; work out. [From Old English *īren*.]

Iron Age *n.* The period of human culture following the Bronze Age in Asia, Europe, and Africa, marked by the introduction of iron tools and weapons. In Europe it began around 800 BC.

i·ron·clad (ī′ərn-klăd′) *adj.* **1.** Covered with iron plates for protection: *an ironclad ship.* **2.** Not easily broken or changed; fixed: *an ironclad rule.* ❖ *n.* A warship of the 1800s with protective metal plates.

Iron Curtain *n.* The military and political barrier separating the Soviet Union and the countries under its influence from the western European nations during the Cold War.

iron fist *n.* Strict, tyrannical control: *a dictator who ruled with an iron fist.*

i·ron·ic (ī-rŏn′ĭk) *adj.* Containing or expressing irony: *an ironic comment.* **—i·ron′i·cal·ly** *adv.*

i·ron·ing board (ī′ər-nĭng) *n.* A padded board, usually on collapsible legs, for ironing clothing.

iron lung *n.* A metal tank enclosing the entire body except the head and providing artificial respiration through changes in internal air pressure when normal breathing is impaired.

i·ron·wood (ī′ərn-wo͝od′) *n.* **1.** Any of numerous trees having very hard wood. **2.** The wood of such a tree.

i·ron·work (ī′ərn-wûrk′) *n.* Work in iron, such as gratings and rails.

i·ron·work·er (ī′ərn-wûr′kər) *n.* **1.** A person who makes iron or iron articles. **2.** A construction worker who builds steel structures.

i·ron·works (ī′ərn-wûrks′) *pl.n. (used with a singular or plural verb)* A place where iron is made or articles made of iron are produced.

i·ro·ny (ī′rə-nē *or* ī′ər-nē) *n., pl.* **i·ro·nies 1.** The use of words to express something different to and often opposite from what they mean literally. Referring to a mess as "a pretty sight" is an example of irony. **2.** A conflict between what might be expected and what actually occurs: *We noted the irony that the boy who always complained about the cold weather became a famous skier.* [From Greek *eirōneia*, feigned ignorance.]

Ir·o·quoi·an (ĭr′ə-kwoi′ən) *n.* **1.** A family of Native American languages spoken in Canada and the eastern United States. **2.** A member of an Iroquoian-speaking people. **—Ir′o·quoi′an** *adj.*

Ir·o·quois (ĭr′ə-kwoi′) *n., pl.* **Iroquois** (ĭr′ə-kwoi′ *or* ĭr′ə-kwoiz′) **1.** A member of a Native American confederacy inhabiting New York State and originally including the Cayuga, Mohawk, Oneida, Onondaga, and Seneca peoples. In 1722, the Tuscaroras joined the Iroquois confederacy. **2.** Any or all of the languages of the Iroquois. **—Ir′o·quois′** *adj.*

ir·ra·di·ate (ĭ-rā′dē-āt′) *tr.v.* **ir·ra·di·at·ed, ir·ra·di·at·ing, ir·ra·di·ates 1.** To expose to or treat with radiation: *irradiating food to kill bacteria.* **2.** To shed light on; illuminate: *The morning sun irradiated the room.* **—ir·ra′di·a′tion** *n.*

ir·ra·tion·al (ĭ-răsh′ə-nəl) *adj.* **1.** Not capable of reasoning or thinking clearly. **2.** Not based on or guided by reason; unreasonable; illogical: *an irrational fear of heights.* **3.** Relating to an irrational number. **—ir·ra′tion·al·ly** *adv.*

ir·ra·tion·al·i·ty (ĭ-răsh′ə-năl′ĭ-tē) *n., pl.* **ir·ra·tion·al·i·ties 1.** The condition or quality of being irrational. **2.** Something irrational or absurd.

irrational number *n.* A real number that cannot be written as an integer or as a fraction whose numerator and denominator are both integers; $\sqrt{2}$ and pi (symbolized by π) are irrational numbers.

ir·re·claim·a·ble (ĭr′ĭ-klā′mə-bəl) *adj.* Impossible to reclaim: *irreclaimable land.* **—ir′re·claim′a·bly** *adv.*

ir·rec·on·cil·a·ble (ĭ-rĕk′ən-sī′lə-bəl *or* ĭ-rĕk′ən-sī′lə-bəl) *adj.* Impossible to reconcile: *irreconcilable enemies; irreconcilable differences of opinion.*

WRITERS CHOOSE THEIR WORDS

There are many jobs in a kitchen that even a small child can perform. Because of Togan I found few of them **irksome;** he taught me that there was no work not worth doing well. He was full of truly wise sayings, and if I did not understand them he did not mind spending the time explaining what he meant.

—Erik Christian Haugaard
The Samurai's Tale

iron

ironwork

USAGE

irregardless The word **irregardless** is considered unacceptable by many people because it has both a negative prefix (*ir–*) and a negative suffix (*–less*). It is therefore not considered to be a logical word. The word *regardless,* however, is acceptable: *Regardless of what you say, I still like that song.* For more information, see Note at **nonstandard.**

Isabella I

ă	pat	ôr	core
ā	pay	oi	boy
âr	care	ou	out
ä	father	o͝o	took
ĕ	pet	o͝or	lure
ē	be	o͞o	boot
ĭ	pit	ŭ	cut
ī	bite	ûr	urge
îr	pier	th	thin
ŏ	pot	*th*	this
ō	toe	zh	vision
ô	paw	ə	about

ir·re·cov·er·a·ble (ĭr′ĭ-**kŭv′**ər-ə-bəl) *adj.* Impossible to recover: *irrecoverable losses.* **—ir′re·cov′er·a·bly** *adv.*

ir·re·deem·a·ble (ĭr′ĭ-**dē′**mə-bəl) *adj.* **1.** Not capable of being brought back or paid off: *an irredeemable coupon.* **2.** Impossible to remedy or reform: *an irredeemable loss; an irredeemable sinner.* **3.** Not convertible into coin: *irredeemable Confederate dollar bills.* **—ir′re·deem′a·bly** *adv.*

ir·re·duc·i·ble (ĭr′ĭ-**do͞o′**sə-bəl) *adj.* Impossible to reduce to a smaller or simpler amount or form: *¾ is an irreducible fraction.* **—ir′re·duc′i·bly** *adv.*

ir·ref·u·ta·ble (ĭ-**rĕf′**yə-tə-bəl *or* ĭr′ĭ-**fyo͞o′**tə-bəl) *adj.* Impossible to refute or disprove: *irrefutable facts.* **—ir·ref′u·ta·bly** *adv.*

ir·re·gard·less (ĭr′ĭ-**gärd′**lĭs) *adv. Nonstandard* Regardless. —SEE NOTE.

ir·reg·u·lar (ĭ-**rĕg′**yə-lər) *adj.* **1.** Not done according to rule, accepted order, or general practice: *a highly irregular proceeding.* **2.** Uneven in occurrence or rate: *an irregular heartbeat.* **3.** Not straight, uniform, or balanced: *an irregular coastline.* **4.** In grammar, not following the usual pattern of inflected forms. For example, *do* is an irregular verb, with the irregular principal parts *did* and *done.* **5.** Not up to standard because of flaws or imperfections: *an irregular piece of cloth.* **—ir·reg′u·lar·ly** *adv.*

ir·reg·u·lar·i·ty (ĭ-rĕg′yə-**lăr′**ĭ-tē) *n., pl.* **ir·reg·u·lar·i·ties 1.** The quality or condition of being irregular. **2.** Something irregular: *irregularities in the earth's surface.*

ir·rel·e·vant (ĭ-**rĕl′**ə-vənt) *adj.* Having no relation to the matter at hand; beside the point: *an irrelevant question.* **—ir·rel′e·vance** *n.* **—ir·rel′e·vant·ly** *adv.*

ir·re·li·gious (ĭr′ĭ-**lĭj′**əs) *adj.* **1.** Indifferent to religion. **2.** Contrary or hostile to religion. **—ir′re·li′gious·ly** *adv.*

ir·re·me·di·a·ble (ĭr′ĭ-**mē′**dē-ə-bəl) *adj.* Impossible to remedy, correct, cure, or repair: *an irremediable blunder.* **—ir′re·me′di·a·bly** *adv.*

ir·rep·a·ra·ble (ĭ-**rĕp′**ər-ə-bəl) *adj.* Impossible to repair, remedy, or set right: *The statue has suffered irreparable damage.* **—ir·rep′a·ra·bly** *adv.*

ir·re·place·a·ble (ĭr′ĭ-**plā′**sə-bəl) *adj.* Impossible to replace: *irreplaceable natural resources such as coal and oil.*

ir·re·press·i·ble (ĭr′ĭ-**prĕs′**ə-bəl) *adj.* Impossible to hold back, control, or restrain: *irrepressible laughter.* **—ir′re·press′i·bly** *adv.*

ir·re·proach·a·ble (ĭr′ĭ-**prō′**chə-bəl) *adj.* Perfect or blameless; faultless: *irreproachable behavior.* **—ir′re·proach′a·bly** *adv.*

ir·re·sis·ti·ble (ĭr′ĭ-**zĭs′**tə-bəl) *adj.* Too great or overpowering to be resisted; impossible to resist: *an irresistible impulse.* **—ir′re·sist′i·bil′i·ty** *n.* **—ir′re·sist′i·bly** *adv.*

ir·res·o·lute (ĭ-**rĕz′**ə-lo͞ot′) *adj.* Unsure of how to act; undecided; indecisive: *The irresolute editor was always asking for advice from his colleagues.* **—ir·res′o·lute′ly** *adv.* **—ir·res′o·lute′ness, ir·res′o·lu′tion** *n.*

ir·re·spec·tive of (ĭr′ĭ-**spĕk′**tĭv) *prep.* Regardless of: *Anyone can try out for this play, irrespective of past experience.*

ir·re·spon·si·bil·i·ty (ĭr′ĭ-spŏn′sə-**bĭl′**ĭ-tē) *n.* Lack of responsibility or concern for consequences.

ir·re·spon·si·ble (ĭr′ĭ-**spŏn′**sə-bəl) *adj.* **1.** Showing a lack of responsibility: *Much of our pollution comes from irresponsible manufacturing processes.* **2.** Lacking a sense of responsibility; unreliable or untrustworthy: *an irresponsible driver.* **3.** Not accountable or responsible to a higher authority: *favored representative democracy over irresponsible forms of government such as a dictatorship or monarchy.* **—ir′re·spon′si·bly** *adv.*

ir·re·triev·a·ble (ĭr′ĭ-**trē′**və-bəl) *adj.* Difficult or impossible to retrieve or recover: *After the computer's hard disk crashed, all files were irretrievable.* **—ir′re·triev′a·bly** *adv.*

ir·rev·er·ence (ĭ-**rĕv′**ər-əns) *n.* **1.** Lack of reverence or respect. **2.** A disrespectful act or remark.

ir·rev·er·ent (ĭ-**rĕv′**ər-ənt) *adj.* Having or showing a lack of reverence or respect; disrespectful: *an irreverent attitude toward the ceremony.* **—ir·rev′er·ent·ly** *adv.*

ir·re·vers·i·ble (ĭr′ĭ-**vûr′**sə-bəl) *adj.* Impossible to reverse: *rolling on an irreversible downhill path.* **—ir′re·vers′i·bly** *adv.*

ir·rev·o·ca·ble (ĭ-**rĕv′**ə-kə-bəl) *adj.* Not capable of being changed or undone: *an irrevocable judgment.* **—ir·rev′o·ca·bly** *adv.*

ir·ri·gate (**ĭr′**ĭ-gāt′) *tr.v.* **ir·ri·gat·ed, ir·ri·gat·ing, ir·ri·gates 1.** To supply with water by means of pipes, sprinklers, ditches, or streams: *Ancient Egyptians used water from the Nile to irrigate barren land.* **2.** To wash out (a wound or opening) with water or a medicated solution: *The dentist irrigated the infected area around the tooth.* [From Latin *irrigāre* : *in-*, in + *rigāre*, to water.] **—ir′ri·ga′tion** *n.*

ir·ri·ta·bil·i·ty (ĭr′ĭ-tə-**bĭl′**ĭ-tē) *n.* The quality or condition of being irritable.

ir·ri·ta·ble (**ĭr′**ĭ-tə-bəl) *adj.* **1.** Easily annoyed or angered: *Lack of sleep will make anyone irritable.* **2.** Very sensitive: *irritable skin around a scrape.* **—ir′ri·ta·ble·ness** *n.* **—ir′ri·ta·bly** *adv.*

ir·ri·tant (**ĭr′**ĭ-tənt) *n.* Something that irritates: *They found the city air full of irritants such as dust, soot, and smoke.* ❖ *adj.* Causing irritation.

ir·ri·tate (**ĭr′**ĭ-tāt′) *tr.v.* **ir·ri·tat·ed, ir·ri·tat·ing, ir·ri·tates 1.** To make angry or impatient; annoy: *The reporter's repeated questions on the same subject irritated the speaker.* **2.** To make sore or inflamed: *The smoke irritated the firefighter's eyes.* [From Latin *irrītāre.*] **—ir′ri·tat′ing·ly** *adv.* **—ir′ri·ta′tor** *n.*

ir·ri·ta·tion (ĭr′ĭ-**tā′**shən) *n.* The act of irritating or the state of being irritated: *His irritation was apparent in his scowl. Dust can cause irritation of the eyes.*

IRS *abbr.* An abbreviation of Internal Revenue Service.

Ir·tysh or **Ir·tish** (ĭr-**tĭsh′**) A river rising in northwest China and flowing about 2,650 miles (4,250 kilometers) generally northwest through Kazakhstan and into west-central Russia.

Ir·ving (**ûr′**vĭng), **Washington** 1783–1859. American writer known for his stories, including "Rip Van Winkle," contained in *The Sketch Book* (1820).

is (ĭz) *v.* Third person singular present tense of **be.** [From Old English.]

Is. *abbr.* An abbreviation of: **1.** island. **2.** islands.

I·saac (**ī′**zək) In the Bible, the son of Abraham who was offered as a sacrifice to God but was saved by divine intervention.

Is·a·bel·la I (ĭz′ə-**bĕl′**ə) 1451–1504. Queen of Castile (1474–1504) who ruled jointly with her husband, Ferdinand V. Their marriage (1649) marked the beginning of the modern Spanish state.

I·sa·iah[1] (ī-**zā′**ə) A Hebrew prophet of the eighth century BC.

I·sa·iah[2] (ī-**zā′**ə) *n.* A book of the Bible containing the prophecies of Isaiah, which offer an ethical critique of society and a vision of a perfected world.

is·chi·um (**ĭs′**kē-əm) *n., pl.* **is·chi·a** (**ĭs′**kē-ə) The lowest of the three large bones forming either side of the pelvis.

–ise *suff.* Variant of **–ize.**

I·seult (ĭ-**so͞olt′**) also **I·sol·de** (ĭ-**sōl′**də) *n.* In Arthurian legend, an Irish princess who married the king of Cornwall and fell in love with his knight Tristan.

–ish *suff.* A suffix that means: **1.** Relating to: *Finnish.* **2.** Having the character of; like: *sheepish; childish.* **3.** Approximately; somewhat: *greenish.* **4.** Tending toward; interested in: *selfish.*

Ish·ma·el (**ĭsh′**mē-əl or **ĭsh′**mā-əl) In the Bible, the son of Abraham who was cast out after the birth of Isaac. In Islam, he is considered the ancestor of the Arab people.

Ish·tar (ĭsh′tär′) *n.* The chief Babylonian and Assyrian goddess, associated with love, fertility, and war.

i·sin·glass (ī′zən-glăs′ *or* ī′zĭng-glăs′) *n.* **1.** A transparent, almost pure gelatin obtained from the swim bladders of sturgeon and certain other fishes and used in making glue. **2.** Mica in thin transparent sheets. [From obsolete Dutch *huizenblas*, from Middle Dutch *hūsblase*, sturgeon bladder.]

I·sis (ī′sĭs) *n.* In Egyptian mythology, a goddess of fertility and magic who was the sister and wife of Osiris.

Is·lam (ĭs-läm′ *or* ĭz-läm′ *or* ĭz′läm′ *or* ĭz-lăm′) *n.* **1.** A monotheistic religion marked by the doctrine of absolute submission to God and by reverence for Muhammad as the chief and last prophet of God. **2a.** The people or nations that practice Islam; the Muslim world. **b.** The civilization based on Islam. [From Arabic *'islām*, submission, from *'aslama*, to surrender, resign oneself, from Syriac *'ašlem*, to make peace, surrender.] **—Is·lam′ic** *adj.*

Is·lam·a·bad (ĭs-lä′mə-bäd′ *or* ĭz-lăm′ə-băd′) The capital of Pakistan, in the northeast part of the country east of Kabul, Afghanistan.

Islamic calendar *n.* The lunar calendar used by Muslims reckoned from the year of the Hegira in AD 622.

is·land (ī′lənd) *n.* **1.** A body of land, especially one smaller than a continent, entirely surrounded by water: *Iceland is an island in the Atlantic Ocean.* **2.** Something resembling an island by being separated or different in character from what surrounds it: *The library is an island of quiet in the teeming city.* —SEE NOTE.

is·land·er (ī′lən-dər) *n.* A person who lives on an island.

isle (īl) *n.* An island, especially a small one. [From Middle English *ile*, from Old French *isle*, from Latin *īnsula*.] —SEE NOTE AT **island.**

❑ *These sound alike:* **isle, aisle** (passageway), **I'll** (I will).

Isle of Man See **Man, Isle of.**

is·let (ī′lĭt) *n.* A very small island.

❑ *These sound alike:* **islet, eyelet** (small hole).

is·lets of Lang·er·hans (ī′lĭts əv läng′ər-häns′) *pl.n.* Irregular clusters of endocrine cells in the pancreas that secrete insulin.

ism (ĭz′əm) *n. Informal* A distinctive doctrine, system or theory: *capitalism, communism, and other competing isms.*

–ism *suff.* A suffix that means: **1.** Action, practice, or process: *criticism.* **2.** State or condition: *optimism.* **3.** Characteristic behavior or quality: *heroism.* **4.** A distinctive or characteristic trait, as of a language or people: *Briticism.* **5.** A doctrine, theory, or system: *pacifism.* —SEE NOTE.

is·n't (ĭz′ənt) Contraction of *is not.*

i·so·bar (ī′sə-bär′) *n.* A line on a weather map connecting places having the same barometric pressure. Isobars show the distribution of atmospheric pressure at a given time, and are used in forecasting the weather.

i·so·late (ī′sə-lāt′) *tr.v.* **i·so·lat·ed, i·so·lat·ing, i·so·lates 1.** To separate from others; set apart: *We isolated the new kitten from our other pets for a few days.* **2.** To place in quarantine. [From *isolated*, from Latin *īnsulātus*, made into an island.]

i·so·lat·ed (ī′sə-lā′tĭd) *adj.* Separated from others; solitary: *an isolated cabin deep in the woods.*

i·so·la·tion (ī′sə-lā′shən) *n.* **1.** The condition of being isolated: *living in isolation on a remote island.* **2.** The act of isolating: *the isolation of patients with tuberculosis.*

i·so·la·tion·ism (ī′sə-lā′shə-nĭz′əm) *n.* The policy or principle that a nation should avoid political and economic relationships with other countries. **—i′so·la′tion·ist** *n. & adj.*

I·sol·de (ĭ-sōl′də *or* ĭ-zōl′də) *n.* Variant of **Iseult.**

i·so·leu·cine (ī′sə-lo͞o′sēn′) *n.* An essential amino acid that is found in plant and animal protein. Isoleucine has the same chemical composition as leucine, but the atoms are arranged differently.

i·so·mer (ī′sə-mər) *n.* One of two or more compounds that have the same chemical formula but differ in the way their atoms are arranged or connected, often leading to different properties.

i·so·met·ric (ī′sə-mĕt′rĭk) *adj.* Involving contraction of a muscle under constant tension without change in length: *isometric exercises.*

i·so·pod (ī′sə-pŏd′) *n.* Any of numerous small crustaceans of a group that includes the woodlice, characterized by a flattened segmented body with seven pairs of legs. [From New Latin *Īsopoda*, order name : *iso-*, same, equal + New Latin *-poda*, -pod.]

i·sos·ce·les triangle (ī-sŏs′ə-lēz′) *n.* A triangle having two sides of equal length.

i·so·therm (ī′sə-thûrm′) *n.* A line on a weather map connecting places having the same average temperature.

i·so·tope (ī′sə-tōp′) *n.* One of two or more forms of an element that have the same chemical properties and the same atomic number but different atomic weights and slightly different physical properties because of different numbers of neutrons in their atomic nuclei. [From *iso-*, same, equal + Greek *topos*, place.] **—i′so·top′ic** (ī′sə-tŏp′ĭk) *adj.*

Is·ra·el¹ (ĭz′rē-əl) *n.* **1.** In the Bible, the name given to Jacob by the angel with whom he wrestled. **2.** The Jewish people, regarded in the Bible as the chosen people of God. [From Old English, from Hebrew *yiśrā'ēl*, God has striven, God has saved.]

Is·ra·el² (ĭz′rē-əl) **1.** An ancient kingdom of Palestine, founded around 1025 BC and lasting until it was overthrown by the Assyrians in 721. **2.** A country of southwest Asia on the eastern Mediterranean Sea. It was established in 1948 as a Jewish state on recommendation of the United Nations. Jerusalem is the capital.

Is·rae·li (ĭz-rā′lē) *adj.* Relating to modern Israel or its people. ❖ *n., pl.* **Is·rae·lis** A native or inhabitant of modern Israel.

Is·ra·el·ite (ĭz′rē-ə-līt′) *adj.* Relating to the ancient kingdom of Israel or to its people. ❖ *n.* **1.** A native or inhabitant of ancient Israel. **2.** A descendant of Jacob; a Jew.

is·su·ance (ĭsh′o͞o-əns) *n.* The act of issuing: *the issuance of driver's licenses.*

is·sue (ĭsh′o͞o) *n.* **1.** A subject being discussed or disputed; a question under debate: *the issue of reforming campaign laws.* **2a.** A complaint or objection: *One teacher has issues with the plan to change the curriculum.* **b.** A problem or difficulty: *a movie star who had to deal with some issues before continuing his career.* **3.** The act of distributing or putting out; release: *the government's issue of new postage stamps.* **4.** A newspaper or magazine published at a given time: *the June issue of the news magazine.* **5a.** The act of flowing or giving out: *the issue of water from the spring.* **b.** A place of outflow; an outlet: *a lake with no issue to the sea.* **6.** An outcome or result: *The policy was the issue of extensive debate.* **7.** Offspring; children: *died without issue.* ❖ *v.* **is·sued, is·su·ing, is·sues** —*intr.* **1.** To come out; flow out: *Water issued from the broken pipe.* **2.** To proceed from a source; emerge or result: *ideas that issued from the discussion.* —*tr.* **1.** To give out; distribute: *issue uniforms to members of the team.* **2.** To put in circulation; publish: *The Postal Service issues stamps.* **3.** To cause to flow out: *a chimney that was issuing smoke.* ◆ **at issue** In question; in dispute: *Your conduct is not at issue here.* **take issue** To take an opposing point of view; disagree. [From Middle English, from Old French, from Latin *exīre*, to go out.] **—is′su·er** *n.*

–ist *suff.* A suffix that means: **1.** A person who performs

WORD HISTORY

island Although the words **island** and **isle** look similar, they are not historically related. *Isle* comes from the Old French word *isle,* which comes from the Latin word *īnsula,* meaning "island." The Latin word also shows up in our word *peninsula,* which in both Latin and English means "almost an island" (*paene* in Latin means "almost"). As for *island,* it was originally spelled *iland* or *ilond* in Middle English, and it only acquired an *s* in the 1500s when people confused it with the French word *isle.*

WORD BUILDING

–ism The suffix **–ism** is a noun suffix. That is, when added to words or word roots, it forms nouns. It comes from the Greek noun suffix *–ismos* and means roughly "the act, state, or theory of." Nouns that end in *–ism* often have related verbs that end in *–ize* (*criticism/criticize*), related personal nouns that end in *–ist* (*optimism/optimist*), and related adjectives that end in *–istic* (*optimistic*). For more information, see Note at **–ize.**

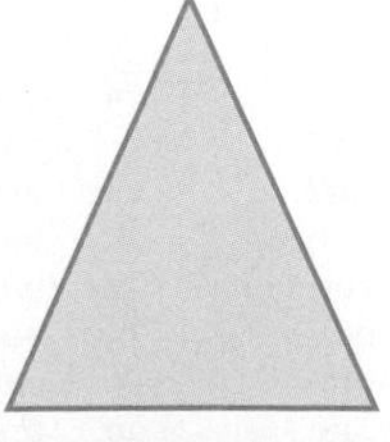

isosceles triangle

USAGE

its The word **its** is the possessive form of the pronoun *it* and is never written with an apostrophe: *I like the park because of its big trees.* The contraction **it's** (for *it is* or *it has*) is always written with an apostrophe: *It's a long way from my house to the park. It's been a long time since we've been to the park.*

WORD BUILDING

–ize The suffix **–ize,** which comes from the Greek verb suffix *–izein,* is used in English to turn nouns and adjectives into verbs. The oldest words in *–ize* exist alongside related words ending in *–ism* or *–ist,* such as *baptize/baptism/Baptist.* But for hundreds of years now, verbs in *–ize* have been coined from almost any source: *legalize, modernize, popularize* from adjectives, and *authorize, computerize, hospitalize* from nouns. These newer verbs form nouns in *–ization* and *–izer* rather than *–ism* and *–ist*: *legalization, hospitalization; authorizer, popularizer.* For more information, see Note at **–ism.**

an action: *lobbyist.* **2.** A person who produces, makes, operates, plays, or is connected with a specified thing: *novelist.* **3.** A person who specializes in a specified art, science, or skill: *biologist.* **4.** A person who believes in a certain doctrine or system: *socialist.* **5.** A person characterized as having a particular trait: *romanticist.*

Is·tan·bul (ĭs′tăn-**bo͞ol′** *or* ĭs′-tän-**bo͞ol′**) The largest city of Turkey, in the northwest part of the country on the Bosporus at its entrance into the Sea of Marmara. Known as Constantinople until 1930, it was the capital of the Byzantine and Ottoman Empires.

isth·mus (ĭs′məs) *n., pl.* **isth·mus·es** or **isth·mi** (ĭs′mī′) A narrow strip of land with water on both sides, connecting two larger masses of land. [From Greek *isthmos.*]

Isthmus of Panama See **Panama, Isthmus of.**

it (ĭt) *pron.* **1.** The thing, being, or action last mentioned or thought to be understood: *I polished the table until it shone. They played with the puppy until it got tired. Whatever you choose, give it your best. I couldn't find out who it was on the telephone.* **2.** Used as the subject of an impersonal verb: *It is snowing.* **3.** Used as the subject of a clause that introduces a phrase or clause that presents the idea of the sentence: *It is important to get enough exercise.* **4.** Used to designate a player in a game, such as tag, who attempts to find or catch the other players. [From Old English *hit.*]

I·tal·ian (ĭ-tăl′yən) *adj.* Relating to Italy or its people, language, or culture. ❖ *n.* **1.** A native or inhabitant of Italy. **2.** The Romance language of Italy and a part of Switzerland.

i·tal·ic (ĭ-tăl′ĭk *or* ī-tăl′ĭk) *adj.* Being a style of printing type with the letters slanting to the right, used chiefly to set off a word or passage within a text of roman print: *This is italic print.* ❖ *n.* often **italics** Italic print or typeface: *The example sentences in this dictionary are printed in italics.* [From Latin *Italicus,* Italian.]

i·tal·i·cize (ĭ-tăl′ĭ-sīz′ *or* ī-tăl′ĭ-sīz′) *tr.v.* **i·tal·i·cized, i·tal·i·ciz·ing, i·tal·i·ciz·es** To print in italic type: *italicize the title of a book.*

It·a·ly (ĭt′l-ē) **1.** A peninsula of southern Europe projecting into the Mediterranean Sea between the Tyrrhenian and Adriatic Seas. **2.** A country of southern Europe made up of the peninsula of Italy, Sardinia, Sicily, and several smaller islands. After the collapse of the Roman Empire, Italy split into many smaller states. It was unified in 1870. Rome is the capital.

itch (ĭch) *n.* **1.** An irritated feeling in the skin that causes a desire to scratch. **2.** Any of various skin diseases that cause a desire to scratch. **3.** A restless craving or desire: *Every summer I get an itch to go to the beach.* ❖ *v.* **itched, itch·ing, itch·es** *—intr.* **1.** To feel, have, or cause an itch: *I itch all over from mosquito bites.* **2.** To have a restless craving or desire: *They were just itching to show the teacher what they had done.* *—tr.* To cause to have an itch: *This wool shirt itches my back.* [From Old English *gicce,* from *giccan,* to itch.]

itch·y (ĭch′ē) *adj.* **itch·i·er, itch·i·est 1.** Having or causing an itch: *an itchy bug bite.* **2.** Restless; jumpy: *I get itchy if I have to sit for a long period of time.* **—itch′i·ness** *n.*

–ite *suff.* A suffix that means: **1.** A native or resident of: *Brooklynite.* **2.** Descendant of: *Israelite.* **3.** Rock; mineral: *graphite.*

i·tem (ī′təm) *n.* **1.** A single thing or unit: *I bought a shirt and several other items of clothing. You must show a receipt for each item purchased.* **2.** A piece of news or information: *an interesting item in the newspaper.* [From Latin *item,* also.]

i·tem·ize (ī′tə-mīz′) *tr.v.* **i·tem·ized, i·tem·iz·ing, i·tem·iz·es** To place or include on a list of items: *itemizing all charges on the bill.*

it·er·ate (ĭt′ə-rāt′) *tr.v.* **it·er·at·ed, it·er·at·ing, it·er·ates** To say or do again; repeat. [From Latin *iterāre,* from *iterum,* again.] **—it′er·a′tion** *n.*

i·tin·er·ant (ī-tĭn′ər-ənt *or* ĭ-tĭn′ər-ənt) *adj.* Traveling from place to place: *At harvest time many farmers employ itinerant workers.* ❖ *n.* A person who travels from place to place.

i·tin·er·ar·y (ī-tĭn′ə-rĕr′ē *or* ĭ-tĭn′ə-rĕr′ē) *n., pl.* **i·tin·er·ar·ies 1.** A schedule of places to be visited in the course of a journey: *The tourists' itinerary includes stops in Denver and Salt Lake City.* **2.** An account or record of a journey. **3.** A traveler's guidebook. [From Middle English *itinerarie,* from Latin *iter,* journey.]

–itis *suff.* A suffix that means an inflammation or inflammatory disease of: *bronchitis.*

it'll (ĭt′l) Contraction of *it will.*

its (ĭts) *adj.* The possessive form of **it.** Belonging to the thing just mentioned: *How does the picture look? We just changed its frame.* —SEE NOTE.

❑ *These sound alike:* **its, it's** (it is).

it's (ĭts) Contraction of *it is* or *it has.* —SEE NOTE AT **its.**

❑ *These sound alike:* **it's, its** (of it).

it·self (ĭt-sĕlf′) *pron.* **1.** That one that is the same as it: **a.** Used as the direct object or indirect object of a verb or as the object of a preposition to show that the action of the verb refers back to the subject: *The cat scratched itself. Congress voted itself a pay raise. The robot moves by itself.* **b.** Used to give emphasis: *The trouble is in the motor itself.* **2.** Its normal or healthy condition or state: *The dog has not been itself since the hot weather began.*

I·tur·bi·de (ē′to͞or-bē′dā), **Agustín de** 1783–1824. Mexican revolutionary leader who established Mexican independence from Spain (1821) and served as emperor of Mexico from 1822 to 1823.

–ity *suff.* A suffix that means a quality or condition: *authenticity.* —SEE NOTE AT **–ty.**

–ive *suff.* A suffix that means tending toward or performing a specified action: *disruptive.*

I've (īv) Contraction of *I have.*

IVF *abbr.* An abbreviation of in vitro fertilization.

i·vied (ī′vēd) *adj.* Overgrown or covered with ivy: *ivied brick walls.*

i·vo·ry (ī′və-rē *or* īv′rē) *n., pl.* **i·vo·ries 1.** The hard, smooth, yellowish-white substance forming the tusks of elephants and the tusks or teeth of certain other animals. It was formerly used for making piano keys and decorative objects. **2.** A yellowish white. **3. ivories** *Slang* **a.** The keys of a piano. **b.** The teeth: *He smiled and flashed his ivories.* ❖ *adj.* **1.** Made of or resembling ivory: *ivory chess pieces.* **2.** Yellowish-white. [From Middle English *ivorie,* from Latin *ebur.*]

Ivory Coast 1. See **Côte d'Ivoire. 2.** A section of coastal western Africa along the Gulf of Guinea roughly corresponding to present-day Côte d'Ivoire. It was named for the large quantities of ivory traded there in precolonial times.

i·vy (ī′vē) *n., pl.* **i·vies** Any of several climbing or trailing plants having evergreen leaves. [From Old English *īfig.*]

I·wo Ji·ma (ē′wə **jē′**mə *or* **ē′**wō **jē′**mə) An island of Japan in the northwest Pacific Ocean east of Taiwan. It was the scene of severe fighting during World War II.

–ize or **–ise** *suff.* A suffix that means: **1.** To cause to be or become: *dramatize.* **2.** To become; become like: *materialize; crystallize.* **3.** To treat like: *idolize.* **4.** To subject to or with: *satirize; anesthetize.* **5.** To perform, engage in, or produce: *fraternize.* —SEE NOTE.

Iz·mir (ĭz-mîr′) Formerly **Smyr·na** (smûr′nə). A city of western Turkey on an inlet of the Aegean Sea.

ă	pat	ôr	core
ā	pay	oi	boy
âr	care	ou	out
ä	father	o͝o	took
ĕ	pet	o͝or	lure
ē	be	o͞o	boot
ĭ	pit	ŭ	cut
ī	bite	ûr	urge
îr	pier	th	thin
ŏ	pot	*th*	this
ō	toe	zh	vision
ô	paw	ə	about

j or **J** (jā) *n., pl.* **j's** or **J's** also **js** or **Js** The tenth letter of the English alphabet.

jab (jăb) *v.* **jabbed, jab·bing, jabs** —*tr.* **1.** To poke or thrust abruptly: *She jabbed the fork into the meat.* **2.** To stab or pierce: *He jabbed the meat with his fork.* **3.** To punch with short quick blows: *The boxer jabbed his opponent.* —*intr.* **1.** To make an abrupt poking or thrusting motion: *He jabbed at the air with his fingers while talking.* **2.** To deliver a quick punch: *She jabbed at the punching bag.* ❖ *n.* **1.** A quick blow or stab: *He gave me a jab in the ribs with his elbow.* **2.** In boxing, a short, straight punch.

jab·ber (jăb′ər) *intr.v.* **jab·bered, jab·ber·ing, jab·bers** To talk rapidly and in a senseless manner; chatter: *They jabbered on about their neighbors.* ❖ *n.* Rapid or babbling talk.

ja·bot (zhă-**bō′** *or* **jăb′**ō) *n.* A series of frills or ruffles down the front of a shirt, blouse, or dress.

jac·a·ran·da (jăk′ə-**răn′**də) *n.* Any of several tropical American trees or shrubs having feathery leaves and clusters of pale purple flowers.

jack (jăk) *n.* **1.** A person who works in a specified manual trade: *a lumberjack; a steeplejack.* **2.** A usually portable device used to raise heavy objects by means of force applied to a lever, screw, or hydraulic press. **3.** A socket into which a plug is inserted in order to make an electrical connection: *a telephone jack.* **4.** A playing card bearing the figure of a young man and ranking below a queen. **5a. jacks** *(used with a singular or plural verb)* A game in which each player in turn bounces and catches a small ball while picking up small six-pointed metal pieces with the same hand. **b.** One of the six-pointed pieces used in this game. **6.** A male donkey. **7.** A small flag flown on a ship, usually to show nationality. ❖ *tr.v.* **jacked, jack·ing, jacks 1.** To hoist by means of a jack: *The mechanic jacked the rear of the car to fix the tire.* **2.** To raise (something) to a higher level, as in cost: *The landlord jacked rents, causing much concern among tenants.* [From Middle English *jakke*, Jack, possibly from Old French *Jacques*.]

jack·al (**jăk′**əl) *n.* Any of several wild dogs of Africa, Asia, and southeast Europe that eat a variety of foods including plants, insects, rodents, and the flesh of dead animals. [From Sanskrit *śṛgālaḥ*.]

jack·a·napes (**jăk′**ə-nāps′) *n.* A vain or disrespectful person.

jack·ass (**jăk′**ăs′) *n.* **1.** A male donkey. **2.** A foolish or stupid person.

jack·boot (**jăk′**bo͞ot′) *n.* **1.** A sturdy military boot extending above the knee. **2.** A person who uses bullying tactics, especially to force compliance.

jack·daw (**jăk′**dô′) *n.* A bird of Eurasia and North Africa that is related to and resembles the crows and has black and gray feathers.

jack·et (**jăk′**ĭt) *n.* **1.** A short coat usually extending to the hips. **2.** An outer covering or casing, as of a book. [From Middle English *jaket*, from Old French *jaquet*.]

Jack Frost *n.* Frost or cold weather personified as an old man.

jack·ham·mer (**jăk′**hăm′ər) *n.* A drill that is powered by compressed air, used especially to drill rock or break up concrete.

jack-in-the-box (**jăk′**ĭn-*thə*-bŏks′) *n., pl.* **jack-in-the-box·es** or **jacks-in-the-box** A toy consisting of a box from which a clownlike puppet springs when the lid is opened.

jack-in-the-pul·pit (jăk′ĭn-*thə*-**po͝ol′**pĭt *or* jăk′ĭn-*thə*-**po͝ol′**pĭt) *n., pl.* **jack-in-the-pulpits** A North American plant having a hood-shaped sheath arching over an upright stalk covered with very small greenish flowers.

jack·knife (**jăk′**nīf′) *n.* **1.** A large pocketknife with blades that can be folded back into the handle. **2.** A forward dive in which the diver bends in midair, touching the feet while keeping the legs straight, and then straightens out before entering the water hands first. ❖ *intr.v.* **jack·knifed, jack·knif·ing, jack·knifes** To fold or bend like a jackknife: *The trailer truck jackknifed on the icy road.*

jack·light (**jăk′**līt′) *n.* A light that is used as a lure in night hunting or fishing. ❖ *intr.v.* **jack·light·ed, jack·light·ing, jack·lights** To hunt or fish with a jacklight.

jack-of-all-trades (jăk′əv-**ôl′trādz′**) *n., pl.* **jacks-of-all-trades** A person who can do many different kinds of work.

jack-o'-lan·tern (**jăk′**ə-lăn′tərn) *n., pl.* **jack-o'-lan·terns** A lantern made from a hollowed-out pumpkin with a carved face, used at Halloween.

jack·pot (**jăk′**pŏt′) *n.* **1.** The collection of bets that grows larger with each stage of a poker game. **2.** The largest prize or award in various games or contests.

jack·rab·bit or **jack rabbit** (**jăk′**răb′ĭt) *n.* Any of several hares of western North America having long ears and long, powerful hind legs.

Jack·son (**jăk′**sən) The capital of Mississippi, in the west-central part of the state west of Montgomery, Alabama. It was chosen as capital in 1821.

Jackson, Andrew 1767–1845. The seventh president of the United States (1829–1837). As president he opposed the Bank of the United States, strengthened federal and presidential powers, and pursued policies that forced thousands of Native Americans to relocate to the western United States.

Jackson, Michael 1958–2009. American singer and songwriter whose album *Thriller* (1982) became the all-time best-selling album. Known for his inventive dance moves, Jackson helped to popularize music videos.

Jackson, Thomas Jonathan Known as "Stonewall." 1824–1863. American Confederate general who commanded troops at both battles of Bull Run (1861 and 1862) and directed the Shenandoah Valley campaign (1862).

Jack·son·ville (**jăk′**sən-vĭl′) A city of northeast Florida near the Atlantic Ocean and the Georgia border. It was settled in 1816.

WRITERS CHOOSE THEIR WORDS

Nerves made her want to **jabber,** to talk to him about inconsequential things, but she could feel that he needed quiet, needed to be able to concentrate on his watching, so she contented herself with saying every couple of minutes, "Not far now. We'll be there soon."

—Gill Arbuthnott
The Keepers' Tattoo

jabot

Andrew Jackson

jalousie

WORD HISTORY

janitor A holiday for **janitors** ought to take place in **January,** for both words are related. They come ultimately from the Latin word *iānus,* which meant "archway, gateway, covered passage." A *iānitor* was a doorkeeper or gatekeeper; the word was borrowed into English several hundred years ago in that meaning and spelled *janitor.* In Scotland, the word came to refer also to a minor school official with maintenance duties, and this is closer to the word's present-day sense. The Latin word *iānus* with which we started was also the name (spelled *Iānus*) of the Roman god of gates, doorways, and beginnings. Our month *January*—a month of beginnings—is named for the god.

ă	pat	ôr	core
ā	pay	oi	boy
âr	care	ou	out
ä	father	o͝o	took
ĕ	pet	o͝or	lure
ē	be	o͞o	boot
ĭ	pit	ŭ	cut
ī	bite	ûr	urge
îr	pier	th	thin
ŏ	pot	*th*	this
ō	toe	zh	vision
ô	paw	ə	about

jack·straw (jăk′strô′) *n.* **1. jackstraws** *(used with a singular verb)* A children's game played with straws or thin sticks thrown in a pile from which the players try in turn to remove single sticks without disturbing the others. **2.** One of the straws or sticks used in this game.

Ja·cob (jā′kəb) In the Bible, the son of Isaac whose 12 sons became the ancestors of the 12 tribes of Israel.

jade (jād) *n.* **1.** A hard mineral that is pale green or white and either carved or used as a gemstone. **2.** A light bluish-green. [From Spanish *piedra de ijada,* stone of the side (from the belief that it cured kidney disease).] —**jade** *adj.*

jad·ed (jā′dĭd) *adj.* **1.** Tired or worn out: *a jaded look.* **2.** Dulled by having had too much of something: *a jaded appetite.* **3.** Cynically callous or unsympathetic: *a jaded attitude.* —**jad′ed·ly** *adv.* —**jad′ed·ness** *n.*

Jaf·fa (jăf′ə *or* yä′fə) also **Yafo** (yä′fō) A former city of west-central Israel on the Mediterranean Sea. Originally an ancient Phoenician city, it has been part of Tel Aviv–Yafo since 1950.

jag (jăg) *n.* A sharp projecting point. ❖ *tr.v.* **jagged, jag·ging, jags** To cut or tear unevenly; notch.

jag·ged (jăg′ĭd) *adj.* Having notches or indentations; irregular: *jagged edges of broken glass; a jagged coastline.* —**jag′ged·ly** *adv.*

jag·uar (jăg′wär′) *n.* A large wild cat that resembles a leopard and has a coat of light-brown fur spotted with black marks. Jaguars are found from Mexico south to Argentina. [From Guaraní *jaguá,* dog.]

jai a·lai (**hī′** lī′ *or* **hī′** ə-lī′ *or* hī′ ə-**lī′**) *n.* A game similar to handball, played on a walled court, in which the players use a long basket strapped to the wrist to catch and throw the ball.

jail (jāl) *n.* A place for lawfully confining people, especially those who are awaiting trial for a crime and have not been released on bail or for those who are serving short sentences after being convicted of a misdemeanor. ❖ *tr.v.* **jailed, jail·ing, jails** To detain in jail.

jail·er also **jail·or** (jā′lər) *n.* A person in charge of a jail.

Ja·kar·ta or **Dja·kar·ta** (jə-**kär′**tə) The capital of Indonesia, on the northwest coast of Java. It was founded in about 1619.

ja·lop·y (jə-**lŏp′**ē) *n., pl.* **ja·lop·ies** *Informal* An old automobile that is in bad condition.

jal·ou·sie (jăl′ə-sē) *n.* A blind or shutter having horizontal slats that can be tilted to admit or keep out air or light.

jam¹ (jăm) *v.* **jammed, jam·ming, jams** —*tr.* **1.** To drive or wedge into a tight space: *jam a cork into a bottle.* **2.** To fill (something) to excess: *Holiday shoppers jammed the store.* **3.** To cause to become unworkable because a part is stuck: *Grass jammed the mower.* **4.** To crush or bruise: *jam one's finger in the door.* **5.** To activate or apply (a brake) suddenly: *My bike skidded when I jammed on the brakes.* **6.** To make (electronic signals) difficult or impossible to receive by broadcasting an interfering signal. —*intr.* **1.** To become wedged or stuck in a tight space: *The coin jammed in the slot.* **2.** To stop working because a part is stuck: *The copier jammed again.* **3.** To force one's way into a limited space: *Everyone jammed into the elevator.* **4.** To participate in a jam session. ❖ *n.* **1.** A crush or congestion of people or things in a limited space, making it difficult or impossible to move: *a traffic jam; a log jam.* **2.** *Informal* A difficult situation: *We're really in a jam.*

❑ *These sound alike:* **jam¹** (wedge), **jam²** (preserve), **jamb** (door post).

jam² (jăm) *n.* A preserve made from whole fruit boiled to a pulp with sugar. [Possibly from *jam,* wedge.]

❑ *These sound alike:* **jam²** (preserve), **jam¹** (squeeze), **jamb** (door post).

Ja·mai·ca (jə-**mā′**kə) An island country in the Caribbean Sea south of Cuba. Kingston is the capital.

jamb (jăm) *n.* One of the vertical posts or pieces that form sides of a door or window. [From Middle English *jaumbe,* from Old French *jambe,* leg.]

❑ *These sound alike:* **jamb, jam¹** (wedge), **jam²** (preserve).

jam·bo·ree (jăm′bə-**rē′**) *n.* **1.** A noisy party or celebration. **2.** A large assembly of Boy Scouts or Girl Scouts.

James (jāmz) *n.* A book of the New Testament, traditionally attributed to James the Just, written in the form of a letter exhorting Christians to act morally.

James¹, Saint. Known as "the Great." Died AD 44. One of the 12 Apostles and brother of John.

James², Saint. Known as "the Just." Died about AD 62. The person traditionally regarded as the brother of Jesus and the author of the Epistle of James in the New Testament.

James³, Saint. Known as "the Less." Flourished first century AD. One of the 12 Apostles.

James I 1566–1625. King of England (1603–1625) and of Scotland as James VI (1567–1625) who was the son of Mary Queen of Scots. He sponsored the King James Bible.

James, Henry 1843–1916. American writer known for his many novels, such as *The Portrait of a Lady* (1881).

James·town (jāmz′toun′) **1.** The capital of St. Helena, in the southern Atlantic Ocean. **2.** A former village of southeast Virginia. The first permanent English settlement in America, it was founded in 1607 and named for James I.

Jam·mu and Kash·mir (jŭm′o͞o ənd **kăsh′**mîr′ *or* kăsh-**mîr′**) A former princely state of northern India and Pakistan. It was divided between India and Pakistan after fierce fighting (1947–1948). Both countries have continued to claim jurisdiction over the territory.

jam session *n.* An informal gathering of musicians to play improvised or unrehearsed music.

Jane Doe (jān) *n.* **1.** A made-up name used in legal proceedings to refer to an unknown or unidentified woman or girl. **2.** An average or ordinary woman.

jan·gle (jăng′gəl) *v.* **jan·gled, jan·gling, jan·gles** —*intr.* To make a harsh metallic sound: *The coins jangled in my pocket.* —*tr.* **1.** To cause to make a harsh metallic sound: *I jangled my keys.* **2.** To have an irritating effect on: *The racket from the street jangled my nerves.* ❖ *n.* A harsh metallic sound.

jan·i·tor (jăn′ĭ-tər) *n.* A person whose job is to clean and take care of a building. [From Latin *iānitor,* doorkeeper, from *iānua,* door.] —SEE NOTE.

Jan·u·ar·y (jăn′yo͞o-ĕr′ē) *n., pl.* **Jan·u·ar·ies** The first month of the year in the Gregorian calendar, having 31 days. —SEE NOTE AT **janitor.**

Ja·nus (jā′nəs) *n.* In Roman mythology, the god that protects doorways and city gates, shown with two faces looking in opposite directions.

Ja·pan (jə-**păn′**) An island country of Asia in the Pacific Ocean off the northeast coast of the mainland. Tokyo is the capital.

Japan, Sea of An enclosed arm of the western Pacific Ocean between Japan and the Asian mainland.

Jap·a·nese (jăp′ə-**nēz′** *or* jăp′ə-**nēs′**) *adj.* Relating to Japan or its people, language, or culture. ❖ *n., pl.* **Japanese 1.** A native or inhabitant of Japan. **2.** The language of Japan.

Japanese beetle *n.* A green and brown beetle native to eastern Asia that is a common plant pest in North America.

jar¹ (jär) *n.* **1.** A cylindrical container of glass or earthenware with a wide mouth and usually no handles. **2.** The amount that a jar can hold: *We ate a jar of peanut butter in two weeks.* [From Middle English *jarre,* a liquid measure, ultimately from Arabic *jarra,* earthen jar.]

jar² (jär) *v.* **jarred, jar·ring, jars** —*intr.* **1.** To cause shaking or vibrations: *The ride over the old road was jarring.* **2.** To have an irritating effect: *The loud music jars on my nerves.* **3.** To be out of harmony; clash or conflict: *The statements of the opposing candidates frequently jarred.* —*tr.* **1.** To bump or cause to shake; rock: *His heavy steps jarred the floor.* **2.** To unsettle or shock: *The defeat jarred everyone on the team.* ❖ *n.* A jolt or shock. [Perhaps of imitative origin.]

jar·gon (jär′gən) *n.* **1.** The specialized language of a trade, profession, or class, especially when viewed as difficult to understand by outsiders: *medical jargon.* **2.** Nonsensical or meaningless talk; gibberish.

jas·mine (jăz′mĭn) also **jes·sa·mine** (jĕs′ə-mĭn) *n.* Any of several vines or shrubs having fragrant, usually yellow or white flowers.

Ja·son (jā′sən) *n.* In Greek mythology, the leader of the Argonauts in quest of the Golden Fleece.

jas·per (jăs′pər) *n.* A red, brown, or yellow variety of opaque quartz.

jaun·dice (jôn′dĭs *or* jän′dĭs) *n.* An abnormal yellow coloration of the tissues of the body, resulting from the accumulation of pigments that are normally excreted in bile. Jaundice can be caused by several conditions, such as liver disease.

jaun·diced (jôn′dĭst *or* jän′dĭst) *adj.* **1.** Affected with jaundice. **2.** Showing or feeling bitterness or negativity: *a jaundiced viewpoint.*

jaunt (jônt *or* jänt) *n.* A short trip or excursion; an outing. ❖ *intr.v.* **jaunt·ed, jaunt·ing, jaunts** To make a short trip or excursion.

jaun·ty (jôn′tē *or* jän′tē) *adj.* **jaun·ti·er, jaun·ti·est 1.** Having or expressing a carefree self-confident air: *a jaunty grin; a hat worn at a jaunty angle.* **2.** Lively; sprightly: *music with jaunty rhythms.* **—jaun′ti·ly** *adv.* **—jaun′ti·ness** *n.*

ja·va (jä′və *or* jăv′ə) *n. Informal* Brewed coffee.

Ja·va[1] (jä′və *or* jăv′ə) An island of Indonesia separated from Borneo by the **Java Sea,** an arm of the western Pacific Ocean. It was the center of an early civilization.

Ja·va[2] (jä′və *or* jăv′ə) A trademark for a computer programming language for developing Internet applications that can be used by different kinds of computers.

Java man *n.* Pithecanthropus.

Jav·a·nese (jăv′ə-**nēz′** *or* jăv′ə-**nēs′**) *adj.* Relating to Java or its people, language, or culture. ❖ *n., pl.* **Javanese 1.** A native or inhabitant of Java. **2.** The language spoken by the main ethnic group of Java.

jave·lin (jăv′lĭn *or* jăv′ə-lĭn) *n.* **1.** A light spear that is thrown for distance in an athletic contest. **2.** A light spear thrown with the hand and used as a weapon.

jaw (jô) *n.* **1.** Either of two structures of bone or cartilage that in most vertebrates form the framework of the mouth, help to open and close it, and hold the teeth. **2.** often **jaws** The parts of the body that form the walls of the mouth and serve to open and close it: *His jaws ached after his braces were tightened.* **3.** Any of various structures of invertebrate animals, such as the pincers of spiders or mites, that function similarly to the jaws of vertebrates. **4. jaws** Something resembling or conceived as a pair of jaws: *the jaws of a large wrench; into the jaws of defeat.* ❖ *intr.v.* **jawed, jaw·ing, jaws** *Slang* To talk in a gossipy manner; chatter. **—jaw′less** *adj.*

jaw·bone (jô′bōn′) *n.* One of the bones in which the teeth are set, especially the lower jaw.

jaw·less fish (jô′lĭs) *n.* Any of various long thin fishes that lack a jaw and paired fins. Lampreys and hagfishes are jawless fishes.

jay (jā) *n.* Any of various birds that have a loud harsh call, are usually brightly colored, and often have a crest, such as the blue jay of North America.

Jay (jā), **John** 1745–1829. American politician who served in both Continental Congresses and was the first chief justice of the US Supreme Court (1789–1795).

jay·walk (jā′wôk′) *intr.v.* **jay·walked, jay·walk·ing, jay·walks** To cross a street in violation of the traffic rules, especially by crossing in the middle of a block or when the light is red. **—jay′walk′er** *n.*

jazz (jăz) *n.* **1.** A style of music native to the United States that has strong and often complex rhythms and melodies that are made up by musicians as variations of a main melody. **2.** *Slang* Empty talk; nonsense. ◆ **jazz up** *Slang* To make more lively or engaging: *Try to jazz up your writing a bit.*

jazz·y (jăz′ē) *adj.* **jazz·i·er, jazz·i·est 1.** Resembling jazz. **2.** *Slang* Showy; flashy: *a jazzy car.*

JD *abbr.* An abbreviation of: **1.** Juris Doctor (Doctor of Law). **2.** juvenile delinquent.

jeal·ous (jĕl′əs) *adj.* **1.** Resenting another's success or advantages; envious: *jealous of the success of others.* **2.** Fearful of losing affection or position to another. **3.** Concerning or caused by feelings of envy or the fear of losing position or affection: *jealous thoughts.* **4.** Careful or watchful in guarding something: *We are jealous of our good name.* [From Middle English *jelous,* from Late Latin *zēlus,* zeal.] **—jeal′ous·ly** *adv.*

jeal·ous·y (jĕl′ə-sē) *n., pl.* **jeal·ous·ies** A jealous attitude or feeling.

jean (jēn) *n.* **1.** A strong twilled cotton, used in making uniforms and work clothes. **2. jeans** Pants made of jean or denim.

Jeanne d'Arc (zhän **därk′**) See **Joan of Arc.**

jeep (jēp) *n.* A small rugged motor vehicle with four-wheel drive, used by the US Army during and after World War II. [Probably from *GP,* the manufacturer's designation for this vehicle.]

jeer (jîr) *v.* **jeered, jeer·ing, jeers** —*intr.* To speak or shout in a mocking or scoffing way. —*tr.* To speak to or shout at in a mocking or scoffing way; taunt: *Hecklers jeered the speaker during the lecture.* ❖ *n.* A mocking or scoffing remark or shout.

Jef·fer·son (jĕf′ər-sən), **Thomas** 1743–1826. The third president of the United States (1801–1809), who was a member of the second Continental Congress and drafted the Declaration of Independence (1776). —SEE NOTE.

Jefferson City The capital of Missouri, in the central part of the state on the Missouri River. It was chosen as the capital in 1821.

Je·ho·vah (jĭ-**hō′**və) *n.* God, especially in older translations of the Old Testament.

Je·ho·vah's Witness (jĭ-**hō′**vəz) *n.* A member of a religious group preaching the imminent end of the world and opposed to war and to the authority of the government in matters of conscience.

je·june (jə-**jo͞on′**) *adj.* Not interesting; dull: *another jejune political speech full of empty promises.*

je·ju·num (jə-**jo͞o′**nəm) *n., pl.* **je·ju·na** (jə-**jo͞o′**nə) The part of the small intestine between the duodenum and the ileum.

jell (jĕl) *intr.v.* **jelled, jell·ing, jells 1.** To become firm or thicken; congeal: *The gravy jelled as it cooled.* **2.** To take shape; crystallize: *Plans for the weekend haven't jelled yet.* ❑ *These sound alike:* **jell, gel** (jellylike mixture).

jel·lied (jĕl′ēd) *adj.* **1.** Caused to become jelly or have the consistency of jelly: *a jellied sauce.* **2.** Coated or spread with jelly: *a slice of jellied toast.*

jel·ly (jĕl′ē) *n., pl.* **jel·lies 1.** A soft clear food with a springy consistency that is made by boiling fruit juice or other liquid with pectin or gelatin. **2.** A substance resembling this: *petroleum jelly.* **3.** A jellyfish. ❖ *intr.v.* **jel·lied, jel·ly·ing, jel·lies** To become thickened; turn into jelly. [From Middle English *gele,* from Latin *gelāre,* to freeze.]

javelin

Thomas Jefferson
1805 portrait by Rembrandt Peale (1778–1860)

BIOGRAPHY

Thomas Jefferson

As the principal author of the Declaration of Independence, Thomas **Jefferson** stressed self-government and individual rights, two ideas that have had long-standing importance in American government. Jefferson served as the country's third president from 1801 to 1809, during which time he secured the Louisiana Purchase from France (1803). Although he was himself a slaveholder, he played a significant role in ending the importation of slaves (1808). Politics was just one of Jefferson's many lifelong interests, which included science, architecture, philosophy, and the arts. In his retirement Jefferson founded the University of Virginia (1819).

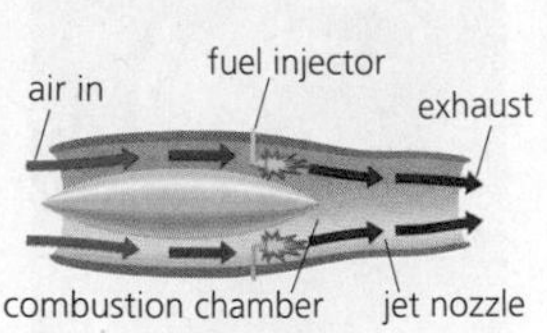

jet engine

jel·ly·bean (jĕl′ē-bēn′) *n.* A small chewy candy, shaped somewhat like a bean, with a hard sugar coating.

jel·ly·fish (jĕl′ē-fĭsh′) *n.* Any of numerous invertebrate sea animals having a soft, often umbrella-shaped body with stinging tentacles.

jel·ly·roll (jĕl′ē-rōl′) *n.* A thin sheet of sponge cake layered with jelly and then rolled up.

Jen·ner (jĕn′ər), **Edward** 1749–1823. British physician who developed a vaccine for smallpox that involved inoculating a person with the substance from cowpox lesions. —SEE NOTE AT **vaccine.**

jen·net (jĕn′ĭt) *n.* **1.** A female donkey. **2.** A small Spanish horse used for riding.

jen·ny (jĕn′ē) *n., pl.* **jen·nies 1.** The female of certain animals, especially the donkey. **2.** A spinning jenny.

jeop·ard·ize (jĕp′ər-dīz′) *tr.v.* **jeop·ard·ized, jeop·ard·iz·ing, jeop·ard·iz·es** To put at risk of loss or injury; endanger: *Not getting enough sleep can jeopardize one's health.*

jeop·ard·y (jĕp′ər-dē) *n., pl.* **jeop·ard·ies** Risk of loss or injury; danger or peril: *The active volcano put the nearby city in jeopardy.*

jer·bo·a (jər-bō′ə) *n.* Any of various small rodents of Asia and northern Africa having a long tufted tail and long hind legs used for leaping.

Jer·e·mi·ah¹ (jĕr′ə-mī′ə) A Hebrew prophet of the seventh and sixth centuries BC.

Jer·e·mi·ah² (jĕr′ə-mī′ə) *n.* A book of the Bible in which Jeremiah denounces the sins of the Israelites and prophesies the destruction of Jerusalem.

Jer·i·cho (jĕr′ĭ-kō′) An ancient city of Palestine near the northwest shore of the Dead Sea. According to the Bible, it was captured and destroyed by Joshua.

jerk¹ (jûrk) *v.* **jerked, jerk·ing, jerks** —*tr.* To move (something) with a quick pull, push, or twist: *I jerked my foot out of the cold water.* —*intr.* To move in sudden uneven motions: *The train jerked as we left the station.* ❖ *n.* **1.** A sudden abrupt motion, such as a yank or twist. **2.** A sudden and uncontrolled contraction of a muscle. **3.** *Slang* A stupid or foolish person. **4.** A lift in weightlifting in which the weight is heaved above the head from shoulder height with a sudden motion.

jerk² (jûrk) *tr.v.* **jerked, jerk·ing, jerks** To cut (meat) into strips and dry in the sun or cure with smoke. [From *jerky*, meat.]

jer·kin (jûr′kĭn) *n.* A close-fitting, hip-length jacket having no sleeves and no collar, worn over a doublet by men, especially in the 1500s.

jerk·y¹ (jûr′kē) *adj.* **jerk·i·er, jerk·i·est 1.** Making sudden starts and stops: *jerky movements.* **2.** *Slang* Silly; foolish. **—jerk′i·ly** *adv.* **—jerk′i·ness** *n.*

jerk·y² (jûr′kē) *n.* Meat, such as beef, that has been cut into strips and dried in the sun or cured with smoke. [From Quechua *ch'arki.*]

jer·ry-build (jĕr′ē-bĭld′) *tr.v.* **jer·ry-built** (jĕr′ē-bĭlt′), **jer·ry-build·ing, jer·ry-builds** To build hastily, cheaply, and poorly.

jer·sey (jûr′zē) *n., pl.* **jer·seys 1.** A soft knitted fabric of polyester, cotton, or other material, used for clothing. **2.** A garment made of this or a similar fabric. **3.** A shirt worn by an athlete, often displaying the name of the player, team, or sponsor. **4.** often **Jersey** Any of a breed of light brown cattle developed on the island of Jersey and raised for milk.

Jersey The largest of the Channel Islands in the English Channel.

Je·ru·sa·lem (jə-ro͞o′sə-ləm *or* jə-ro͞o′zə-ləm) A city lying partly in east-central Israel and partly in the Israeli-occupied West Bank. The legal status of Jerusalem, which is Israel's capital and is considered a holy city by Jews, Muslims, and Christians, remains disputed.

jes·sa·mine (jĕs′ə-mĭn) *n.* Variant of **jasmine.**

jest (jĕst) *n.* **1.** A playful mood or manner: *Their teasing was only done in jest.* **2.** A playful act or remark. ❖ *intr.v.* **jest·ed, jest·ing, jests** To act or speak playfully. [From Middle English *gest*, notable deed, tale, from Latin *gesta*, deeds, from *gerere*, to do.]

jest·er (jĕs′tər) *n.* A person who jests, especially a person employed to entertain by joking at a medieval court.

Jes·u·it (jĕzh′o͞o-ĭt *or* jĕz′o͞o-ĭt) *n.* A member of the Society of Jesus, a Roman Catholic religious order for men.

Je·sus (jē′zəs) 4? BC–AD 29? Jewish religious leader who was crucified after his teaching and reported miracle-working incurred the disfavor of the Roman government. Christians believe Jesus to be the Christ and son of God.

jet¹ (jĕt) *n.* **1.** A dense black form of coal that can be polished to a bright shine and used to make beads and other ornaments. **2.** A deep black. [From Middle English *get*, from Greek *gagātēs*, from *Gagas*, a town of Lycia, an ancient country of Asia Minor.]

jet² (jĕt) *n.* **1.** A high velocity stream of liquid or gas forced through a small opening or nozzle under pressure: *A jet of water shot out of the hose.* **2.** An outlet or nozzle through which a stream is forced: *a gas jet.* **3a.** An aircraft or other vehicle propelled by a jet engine. **b.** A jet engine. ❖ *v.* **jet·ted, jet·ting, jets** —*intr.* **1.** To travel by jet plane: *jetted from New York City to Seattle.* **2.** To move very quickly. —*tr.* To propel outward or squirt as under pressure. [From Old French *jeter*, to spout forth, from Latin *iactāre*, to throw.]

jet engine *n.* An engine that develops its thrust from a jet of exhaust gases produced by burned fuel.

jet lag *n.* The temporary disruption of body rhythms, such as sleeping and waking, that results from high-speed air travel through several time zones.

jet-pro·pelled (jĕt′prə-pĕld′) *adj.* Propelled by one or more jet engines: *a jet-propelled airplane.*

jet propulsion *n.* **1.** The driving of an aircraft by the powerful thrust developed when a jet of gas is forced out of a jet engine. **2.** Propulsion by means of any fluid that is forced out in a stream in the opposite direction.

jet·sam (jĕt′səm) *n.* Cargo and other things thrown overboard to lighten a ship in distress.

jet stream *n.* **1.** A strong wind, often reaching very high speeds, that blows from a westerly direction at altitudes of 10 to 15 miles (16 to 24 kilometers). **2.** A rapidly moving stream of liquid or gas as from a jet engine.

jet·ti·son (jĕt′ĭ-sən *or* jĕt′ĭ-zən) *tr.v.* **jet·ti·soned, jet·ti·son·ing, jet·ti·sons 1.** To cast (something) overboard, especially as a means of lightening a ship or aircraft in distress. **2.** *Informal* To discard (something) as unwanted or burdensome: *jettisoned the marketing plan.*

jet·ty (jĕt′ē) *n., pl.* **jet·ties 1.** A structure, as of stone, earth, and timbers, projecting into a body of water to affect the current or tide or to protect a harbor or shoreline. **2.** A wharf.

Jew (jo͞o) *n.* **1.** A person who is an adherent of Judaism. **2.** A member of the widely dispersed people originally descended from the ancient Hebrews and sharing an ethnic heritage based on Judaism.

jew·el (jo͞o′əl) *n.* **1.** A precious stone; a gem. **2.** A costly ornament, such as a ring or necklace, made of precious metal set with gems. **3.** A small gem or crystal used as a bearing in a watch. **4.** A person or thing that is greatly admired or valued: *The only grandchild is the jewel of the family.* ❖ *tr.v.* **jew·eled, jew·el·ing, jew·els** or **jew·elled, jew·el·ling, jew·els** To adorn with jewels. [From Middle English *jeuel*, from Anglo-Norman.]

jew·el·er (jo͞o′ə-lər) *n.* A person who makes, repairs, or sells jewelry.

jew·el·ry (jo͞o′əl-rē) *n.* Ornaments, such as bracelets or rings, made of precious metals and gems or of inexpensive or imitation materials.

ă	pat	ôr	core
ā	pay	oi	boy
âr	care	ou	out
ä	father	o͝o	took
ĕ	pet	o͝or	lure
ē	be	o͞o	boot
ĭ	pit	ŭ	cut
ī	bite	ûr	urge
îr	pier	th	thin
ŏ	pot	*th*	this
ō	toe	zh	vision
ô	paw	ə	about

Jew·ish (jo͞o′ĭsh) *adj.* Relating to the Jews or their culture or religion. **—Jew′ish·ness** *n.*

Jew·ry (jo͞o′rē) *n.* The Jewish people.

Jew's harp also **jew's harp** (jo͞oz) *n.* A small musical instrument consisting of a U-shaped frame that is held between the teeth and an attached blade of flexible metal that is plucked to produce twanging tones.

Jez·e·bel (jĕz′ə-bĕl′) Flourished about ninth century BC. Phoenician princess and queen of Israel.

jib (jĭb) *n.* A triangular sail set forward of the mast and stretching to the bow or bowsprit.

jibe¹ (jīb) *v.* **jibed, jib·ing, jibes** *—intr.* To shift a sail from one side of a boat or ship to the other when sailing before the wind. *—tr.* To cause (a sail) to shift from one side of a boat or ship to the other when sailing before the wind. ❖ *n.* The act of jibing. [Alteration of *gybe*, from obsolete Dutch *gijben*.]

❑ *These sound alike:* **jibe¹** (shift a sail), **gibe** (jeer), **jibe²** (agree).

jibe² (jīb) *intr.v.* **jibed, jib·ing, jibes** To be in accord; agree: *The account of the other witness doesn't jibe with yours.*

❑ *These sound alike:* **jibe²** (agree), **gibe** (jeer), **jibe¹** (shift a sail).

jibe³ (jīb) *n. & n.* Variant of **gibe.**

Jid·da (jĭd′ə) A city of west-central Saudi Arabia on the Red Sea west of Mecca.

jif·fy (jĭf′ē) *n., pl.* **jif·fies** *Informal* A moment; an instant: *I'll have this fixed in a jiffy.*

jig (jĭg) *n.* **1a.** Any of various lively dances in triple time. **b.** Music written for such a dance. **2.** Any of various devices used to guide a tool or hold work as it is put into a machine, such as a saw or drill. **3.** A metal fishing lure with one or more hooks, designed to bob up and down to attract fish. ❖ *intr.v.* **jigged, jig·ging, jigs 1.** To dance a jig. **2.** To move up and down or to and fro in a quick, jerky way.

jig·ger (jĭg′ər) *n.* A small cup holding 1½ ounces (44 milliliters) of liquor.

jig·gle (jĭg′əl) *tr. & intr.v.* **jig·gled, jig·gling, jig·gles** To shake or cause to shake up and down or back and forth with short quick jerks: *By jiggling the wire we got the light to work. The plane jiggled slightly as it landed on the ground.* ❖ *n.* A jiggling motion.

jig·saw (jĭg′sô′) *n.* A saw with a narrow blade that moves up and down, used for cutting curves.

jigsaw puzzle *n.* A puzzle consisting of irregularly shaped pieces of wood or cardboard that form a picture when fitted together.

ji·had (jĭ-**häd′**) *n.* **1.** In Islam, an individual's striving for spiritual perfection. **2.** A Muslim holy war or political struggle to defend the faith against unbelievers. [From Arabic *jihād*, from *jahada*, to strive.]

jil·bab (jĭl-**bäb′**) *n.* A loose, long-sleeved, full-length outer garment worn by Muslim women. [From Arabic *jilbāb*.]

jilt (jĭlt) *tr.v.* **jilt·ed, jilt·ing, jilts** To drop or cast aside (a lover or sweetheart) suddenly or without care.

Jim Crow or **jim crow** (jĭm) *n.* The practice of segregating and openly discriminating against black people, especially in the American South from the late 1800s until the mid-1900s.

jim·my (jĭm′ē) *n., pl.* **jim·mies** A short crowbar with curved ends. ❖ *tr.v.* **jim·mied, jim·my·ing, jim·mies** To pry (something) open with or as with a jimmy: *jimmy a door.*

jim·son·weed (jĭm′sən-wēd′) *n.* A tall, coarse, poisonous plant having large, trumpet-shaped white or purplish flowers and prickly seed capsules.

jin·gle (jĭng′gəl) *intr. & tr.v.* **jin·gled, jin·gling, jin·gles** To make or cause to make a tinkling or ringing metallic sound: *Coins jingled in the fare box as the passengers boarded the bus.* ❖ *n.* **1.** A tinkling or ringing sound made by small metal objects striking together: *the jingle of sleigh bells.* **2.** A catchy rhyme or verse often used in advertising slogans.

jin·go·ism (jĭng′gō-ĭz′əm) *n.* Extreme nationalism characterized by hostility to foreign countries.

jin·ni (jĭn′ē *or* jĭ-**nē′**) *n., pl.* **jinn** (jĭn) In the Koran and Muslim tradition, a spirit able to appear in either human or animal form and exercising supernatural influence over people. [From Arabic *jinnī*.]

jin·rik·sha (jĭn-**rĭk′**shô′) *n.* A small two-wheeled carriage drawn by one or two people.

jinx (jĭngks) *n.* **1.** A person or thing that is believed to bring bad luck; a hex. **2.** A condition or period of bad luck that appears to have been caused by a specific person or thing. ❖ *tr.v.* **jinxed, jinx·ing, jinx·es** To bring bad luck to. [Possibly from *jynx*, a kind of woodpecker, from Greek *iunx*.]

jit·ney (jĭt′nē) *n., pl.* **jit·neys** A small vehicle, especially a bus or van, that carries passengers for a low fare: *A jitney runs from the apartment buildings to the shopping center.*

jit·ter·bug (jĭt′ər-bŭg′) *n.* A vigorous energetic dance performed to fast jazz or swing music, popular in the 1940s. ❖ *intr.v.* **jit·ter·bugged, jit·ter·bug·ging, jit·ter·bugs** To perform this dance.

jit·ters (jĭt′ərz) *pl.n.* A fit of nervousness: *The exam gave me a case of the jitters.*

jit·ter·y (jĭt′ə-rē) *adj.* **jit·ter·i·er, jit·ter·i·est** Having or feeling nervous unease.

jiu·jit·su (jo͞o-**jĭt′**so͞o) *n.* Variant of **jujitsu.**

jive (jīv) *n.* **1.** *Slang* Nonsensical or deceptive talk. **2.** Jazz or swing music. **3.** The jargon used by jazz musicians and fans.

Joan of Arc (jōn əv ärk), Saint. French name **Jeanne d'Arc** (zhän **därk′**) 1412?–1431. French military leader who organized the resistance that forced the English to end their siege of Orléans (1429). She was later tried by the English for heresy and sorcery and burned at the stake.

job (jŏb) *n.* **1.** A position at which an activity is regularly done for pay: *Her job is doing research at a laboratory.* **2.** A task that must be done; a duty: *My job is to fix lunch; your job is to wash the dishes.* See Synonyms at **task. 3.** Something resulting from or produced by work: *You did a fine job on the report.* **4.** An operation done to improve one's appearance, or the result of such an operation: *a nose job.* ◆ **on the job** At work: *Do not surf the Internet while on the job.* [Perhaps from Middle English *gobbe*, lump.]

Job¹ (jōb) In the Bible, a man whose faith in God survived the test of repeated troubles.

Job² (jōb) *n.* A book of the Bible in which Job argues with three friends that his sufferings are not a punishment for past sins.

job·ber (jŏb′ər) *n.* **1.** A person who buys merchandise from manufacturers and sells it to retailers at a profit. **2.** A person who works by the job or by the contract.

job·less (jŏb′lĭs) *adj.* **1.** Having no job; unemployed. **2.** Relating to those who are without jobs: *jobless benefits.* ❖ *n. (used with a plural verb)* Unemployed people considered as a group. **—job′less·ness** *n.*

Jo·cas·ta (jō-**kăs′**tə) *n.* In Greek mythology, a queen of Thebes who unknowingly married her son, Oedipus.

jock (jŏk) *n.* **1.** An athlete, especially in a school setting. **2.** An athletic supporter.

jock·ey (jŏk′ē) *n., pl.* **jock·eys** A person who rides horses in races, especially as a profession. ❖ *v.* **jock·eyed, jock·ey·ing, jock·eys** *—tr.* **1.** To direct or maneuver by cleverness or skill: *She jockeyed the car into a tight parking space.* **2.** To ride (a horse) in a race. *—intr.* **1.** To ride a

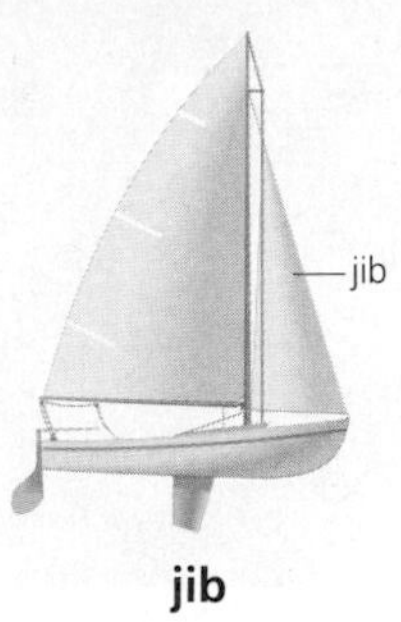

jib

Joan of Arc
detail from the 16th-century manuscript *Lives of Famous Women* by Antoine Dufour

jockey

Andrew Johnson

Lyndon B. Johnson

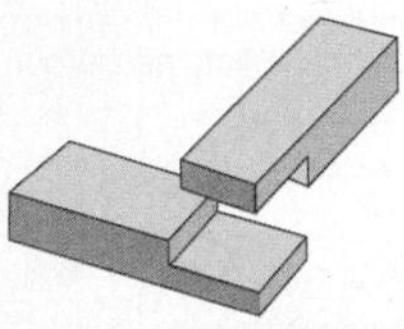

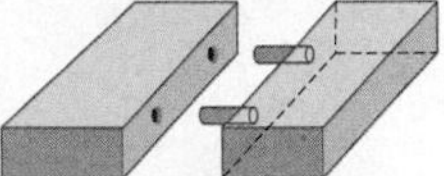

joint
three types of woodworking joints

ă	pat	ôr	core
ā	pay	oi	boy
âr	care	ou	out
ä	father	o͝o	took
ĕ	pet	o͝or	lure
ē	be	o͞o	boot
ĭ	pit	ŭ	cut
ī	bite	ûr	urge
îr	pier	th	thin
ŏ	pot	*th*	this
ō	toe	zh	vision
ô	paw	ə	about

horse as a jockey. **2.** To maneuver for a certain position or advantage: *jockeyed for a promotion.*

jock·strap (jŏk′străp′) *n.* An athletic supporter.

jo·cose (jō-kōs′) *adj.* Given to joking; merry. **—jo·cose′ly** *adv.* **—jo·cos′i·ty** (jō-kŏs′ĭ-tē) *n.*

joc·u·lar (jŏk′yə-lər) *adj.* **1.** Given to joking. **2.** Meant as a joke; humorous: *a jocular remark.* [From Latin *ioculus,* joke.] **—joc′u·lar′i·ty** (jŏk′yə-lăr′ĭ-tē) *n.* **—joc′u·lar·ly** *adv.*

joc·und (jŏk′ənd *or* jō′kənd) *adj.* Having a cheerful disposition or quality; merry; lighthearted. **—joc′und·ly** *adv.*

jodh·purs (jŏd′pərz) *pl.n.* Pants that fit loosely above the knees and tightly from the knees to the ankles, worn for horseback riding. [After *Jodhpur,* a city of western India.]

Jo·el[1] (jō′əl) A Hebrew prophet of the sixth century BC.

Jo·el[2] (jō′əl) *n.* A book of the Bible in which Joel describes a plague of locusts and warns of a coming day of judgment by God.

jo·ey (jō′ē) *n., pl.* **jo·eys** A young marsupial, especially a baby kangaroo.

jog (jŏg) *v.* **jogged, jog·ging, jogs** *—tr.* **1.** To move by shoving, bumping, or jerking; jar: *The old horse trotted along jogging me up and down.* **2.** To stir or shake up; rouse: *Let's see if I can jog your memory.* *—intr.* **1.** To run at a steady slow trot, especially for exercise. **2.** To go or travel at a slow pace: *The old car jogged along until it reached the hill.* ❖ *n.* **1.** A slight push; a nudge. **2.** A slow steady pace. **3.** A bumping or jolting motion. [Perhaps from Middle English *shoggen,* to shake, or Middle English *shokken,* to move rapidly.] **—jog′ger** *n.*

jog·gle (jŏg′əl) *tr. & intr.v.* **jog·gled, jog·gling, jog·gles** To shake a little; nudge. ❖ *n.* A shake or nudge.

Jo·han·nes·burg (jō-hăn′ĭs-bûrg′ *or* jō-hä′nĭs-bûrg′) The largest city of South Africa, in the northeast part of the country south of Pretoria. It was founded in 1886 after the discovery of gold nearby.

John[1] (jŏn) 1167?–1216. King of England (1199–1216) who was forced to sign the Magna Carta (June 15, 1215), a milestone in English freedom.

John[2] (jŏn) *n.* **1.** The fourth Gospel of the New Testament, traditionally thought to have been written by Saint John the Evangelist. **2.** Any of three books of the New Testament written in the form of letters, traditionally thought to have been written by John the Evangelist.

John, Saint. Known as "the Evangelist." Flourished first century AD. One of the 12 Apostles, traditionally considered the author of the fourth Gospel, three epistles, and the book of Revelation.

John XXIII, Saint. 1881–1963. Pope (1958–1963) noted for organizing a council to examine the Roman Catholic Church's role in the modern world.

John Bull *n.* A personification of England or the English people. [After *John Bull,* a character in *Law Is a Bottomless Pit* by John Arbuthnot.]

John Doe *n.* **1.** A made-up name used in legal proceedings to refer to an unknown or unidentified man or boy. **2.** An average or ordinary man.

John Hancock *n. Informal* A person's signature. [After John *Hancock.*]

john·ny·cake (jŏn′ē-kāk′) *n.* Thin flat cornmeal bread, often baked on a griddle.

John Paul II, Saint. 1920–2005. Pope (1978–2005) who was the first Polish-born pope. He promoted conservative Catholic teachings and sought reconciliation with other religious groups.

John·son (jŏn′sən), **Andrew** 1808–1875. The 17th president of the United States (1865–1869). His administration was marked by reconstruction policies in the South. In 1868 he was impeached but was acquitted by one vote.

Johnson, Lyndon Baines 1908–1973. The 36th president of the United States (1963–1969). He oversaw the passage of legislation that protected people against racial discrimination and that provided affordable health insurance for the elderly and financial assistance to the poor. He also faced criticism for escalating US involvement in the Vietnam War after 1964.

Johnson, Samuel 1709–1784. British writer of essays, poems, and other works, known for his acclaimed *A Dictionary of the English Language* (1755).

John the Baptist, Saint. Flourished about first century AD. Jewish prophet who according to the New Testament baptized Jesus.

join (join) *v.* **joined, join·ing, joins** *—tr.* **1.** To put or bring together; link; connect: *The George Washington Bridge joins New York and New Jersey. The children joined hands.* **2.** To put or bring into close association: *The two families were joined by marriage.* **3.** To meet and merge with; be united with: *The Missouri River joins the Mississippi near St. Louis.* **4.** To become a member of: *join the photography club.* **5.** To enter into the company of: *Can you join us for lunch?* *—intr.* **1.** To come together: *The roads join just before the bridge.* **2.** To act together; join forces: *The two groups joined together to oppose the new law.* **3.** To become a member of a group. **4.** To take part; participate: *Everyone joined in the celebration.* ❖ *n.* A joint; a junction. [From Middle English *joinen,* from Latin *iungere.*]

SYNONYMS **join, combine, unite, link, connect**
These verbs mean to put or bring together. **Join** can mean to bring separate things together physically: *We joined the pipes together and turned on the water.* **Combine** often means to mix or merge different things for a specific purpose: *I combined oil, vinegar, and herbs to make a salad dressing.* **Unite** suggests joining of separate parts into a thoroughly blended whole with its own identity: *The prince united the little kingdoms to form a large nation.* **Link** and **connect** can mean to attach firmly without taking away the special characteristics of each part: *We linked the two brackets together with screws. The tunnel under the English Channel connects Great Britain and France.*
ANTONYMS **separate, divide**

---

join·er (joi′nər) *n.* **1.** A skilled carpenter who makes woodwork, such as cabinets and doors, for houses and other buildings. **2.** *Informal* A person inclined to join many groups or organizations.

joint (joint) *n.* **1.** A place where two or more things are joined together: *a joint in a pipe.* **2.** A point at which movable body parts are connected or come together in an animal: *a knee joint; the joints in a spider's leg.* **3.** The way in which two parts are joined or the place at which two parts are held together: *A flexible joint allows the table leg to move.* **4.** The place on the stem of a plant, especially a grass, from which a leaf grows. **5.** *Slang* A cheap or disreputable gathering place. **6.** A large cut of meat for roasting. ❖ *adj.* **1.** Undertaken or shared by two or more people or parties: *a joint effort; a joint bank account.* **2.** Sharing with another or others: *joint owners.* **3.** Involving both houses of a legislature: *a joint session of Congress.* ❖ *tr.v.* **joint·ed, joint·ing, joints 1.** To connect with a joint or joints: *The plumber jointed the new pipes.* **2.** To cut (meat) apart at the joints. ◆ **out of joint 1.** Not in place at the joint; dislocated. **2.** *Informal* Out of order or unsatisfactory: *Her whole world was out of joint.*

Joint Chiefs of Staff *n.* The principal military advisory group to the president of the United States, composed of the chiefs of the Army, Navy, and Air Force and the commandant of the Marine Corps.

joint·ly (joint′lē) *adv.* Together; in common: *The business is owned jointly by three partners.*

joist (joist) *n.* Any of the parallel horizontal beams that support a floor or ceiling.

joke (jōk) *n.* **1.** Something said or done to cause laughter, especially an amusing story with a punchline. **2.** A mischievous trick; a prank. **3.** A person or thing that is an object of amusement or laughter. ❖ *intr.v.* **joked, jok·ing, jokes** To tell or play jokes. [From Latin *iocus.*]

jok·er (jō′kər) *n.* **1.** A person who tells or plays jokes. **2.** A playing card bearing the figure of a jester, used as the highest card or as any card the holder desires.

joke·ster (jōk′stər) *n.* A person who tells or plays jokes.

Jol·li·et also **Jo·li·et** (jō′lē-ĕt′ *or* jō′lē-**ĕt′**), **Louis** 1645–1700. French-Canadian explorer of the upper Mississippi Valley who descended the Mississippi River to the mouth of the Arkansas River (1673).

jol·li·ty (jŏl′ĭ-tē) *n., pl.* **jol·li·ties** Merriment or revelry.

jol·ly (jŏl′ē) *adj.* **jol·li·er, jol·li·est 1.** Full of fun and good spirits. **2.** Showing or causing happiness or mirth; cheerful. ❖ *adv. Chiefly British* Very: *That's a jolly good idea!*

Jolly Roger *n.* A black flag bearing a white skull and crossbones, formerly used on pirate ships.

jolt (jōlt) *v.* **jolt·ed, jolt·ing, jolts** —*tr.* **1.** To move or dislodge with a sudden force: *The bicycle jolted me off the seat as it bumped over some rocks.* **2.** To make suddenly active or effective: *My remark jolted her memory.* **3.** To disturb suddenly and severely: *He was jolted by the betrayal of his best friend.* —*intr.* To move in a bumpy or jerky fashion: *The bus jolted to a stop as the driver jammed on the brakes.* ❖ *n.* **1.** A sudden jerk or bump. **2.** A sudden shock or surprise: *The news of their arrival came as quite a jolt.*

Jo·nah[1] (jō′nə) In the Bible, a Hebrew prophet who was swallowed by a whale and later disgorged unharmed.

Jo·nah[2] (jō′nə) *n.* A book of the Bible that relates Jonah's eventual success in his mission to the Assyrians.

Jones (jōnz), **John Paul** 1747–1792. British-born American naval officer in the American Revolution.

Jones, Mary Harris Known as "Mother Jones." 1837–1930. Irish-born American labor leader and union organizer who in 1905 helped found the Industrial Workers of the World.

jon·quil (jŏng′kwəl *or* jŏn′kwəl) *n.* A kind of daffodil with long narrow leaves and flowers with a short cup-shaped central part.

Jop·lin (jŏp′lĭn), **Scott** 1868–1917. American pianist and composer known for his ragtime works, including "Maple Leaf Rag" (1899).

Jor·dan (jôr′dn) A country of southwest Asia in northwest Arabia east of Israel. Amman is the capital.

Jordan, Michael Jeffrey Born 1963. American basketball player who holds a National Basketball Association record for most seasons leading the league in scoring.

Jordan River A river of southwest Asia rising in Syria and Lebanon and flowing about 225 miles (360 kilometers) south to the northern end of the Dead Sea.

Jo·seph[1] (jō′zəf *or* jō′səf) In the Bible, a son of Jacob and Rachel and the ancestor of one of the tribes of Israel.

Jo·seph[2] (jō′zəf *or* jō′səf) Known as "Chief Joseph." 1840?–1904. Nez Percé leader who conducted a retreat of the Nez Percé from US forces (1877) but was forced to surrender before reaching Canada.

Joseph, Saint. Flourished about first century AD. In the Bible, the husband of Mary, mother of Jesus.

josh (jŏsh) *v.* **joshed, josh·ing, josh·es** —*tr.* To tease in a lighthearted playful way: *She joshed her brother about his strange new haircut.* —*intr.* To make or exchange jokes.

Josh·u·a[1] (jŏsh′o͞o-ə) In the Bible, a Hebrew leader who succeeded Moses as leader of Israel.

Josh·u·a[2] (jŏsh′o͞o-ə) *n.* A book of the Bible that relates the Israelites' conquest of Canaan.

jos·tle (jŏs′əl) *tr.v.* **jos·tled, jos·tling, jos·tles** To push and come into rough contact with while moving; bump: *The students jostled each other on the crowded dance floor.* ❖ *n.* A rough shove or push. **—jos′tler** *n.*

jot (jŏt) *n.* The smallest bit; an iota: *They didn't care one jot.* ❖ *tr.v.* **jot·ted, jot·ting, jots** To write down briefly and hastily: *She jotted some notes in the margin. He jotted down my address.*

joule (jo͞ol *or* joul) *n.* A unit used to measure energy, equal to the work done when a force of 1 newton acts over a distance of 1 meter. [After James Prescott *Joule* (1818–1889), British physicist.]

jounce (jouns) *intr. & tr.v.* **jounced, jounc·ing, jounc·es** To move or cause to move with bumps and jolts: *The bus jounced along the bumpy road.* ❖ *n.* A rough jolting movement.

jour·nal (jûr′nəl) *n.* **1.** A daily record of events, experiences, proceedings, or business transactions; a diary or log. **2.** A periodical containing articles on a particular subject: *a medical journal.* **3.** The part of an axle or a machine shaft that is supported by a bearing. [From Middle English, from Late Latin *diurnālis,* daily.]

jour·nal·ism (jûr′nə-lĭz′əm) *n.* The collecting, writing, editing, and presenting of news or news articles: *In her long career in journalism, she worked for newspapers, magazines, and news blogs.*

jour·nal·ist (jûr′nə-lĭst) *n.* A person employed in journalism, especially a reporter or editor.

jour·nal·is·tic (jûr′nə-lĭs′tĭk) *adj.* Relating to or characteristic of journalism or journalists.

jour·ney (jûr′nē) *n., pl.* **jour·neys 1.** A trip, especially one over a great distance: *a long journey across Europe and Asia.* **2.** The distance traveled on a journey or the time required for such a trip: *a thousand-mile journey; a three-day journey.* **3.** A process that is compared to traveling, such as a series of experiences: *her journey from teenager to adult.* ❖ *intr.v.* **jour·neyed, jour·ney·ing, jour·neys** To travel; make a trip: *We journeyed throughout India.* [From Middle English *journei,* day's travel, from Late Latin *diurnum,* day.]

jour·ney·man (jûr′nē-mən) *n.* **1.** A person who has completed an apprenticeship and works for another person. **2.** A competent but undistinguished worker.

joust (joust *or* jŭst) *n.* A combat between two armored knights on horseback armed with lances. ❖ *intr.v.* **joust·ed, joust·ing, jousts** To take part in a joust.

Jove (jōv) *n.* In Roman mythology, Jupiter.

jo·vi·al (jō′vē-əl) *adj.* Full of fun and good cheer; jolly: *a jovial host.* **—jo′vi·al′i·ty** (jō′vē-**ăl′**ĭ-tē) *n.* **—jo′vi·al·ly** *adv.*

jowl[1] (joul) *n.* **1.** The jaw, especially the lower jaw. **2.** The cheek, especially of a hog. [From Old English *ceafl.*]

jowl[2] (joul) *n.* Loosely hanging flesh on or near the lower jaw. [From Middle English *cholle.*]

joy (joi) *n.* **1.** A feeling of great happiness or delight. **2.** A source or cause of joy: *Some books are a joy to read.*

Joyce (jois), **James** 1882–1941. Irish writer whose works have greatly influenced modern fiction. His novels include *Finnegans Wake* (1939).

joy·ful (joi′fəl) *adj.* Feeling, causing, or showing joy: *a joyful celebration; a joyful shout.* See Synonyms at **glad.** **—joy′ful·ly** *adv.* **—joy′ful·ness** *n.*

joy·less (joi′lĭs) *adj.* Without cheer or joy; dismal.

Joy·ner-Ker·see (joi′nər-kûr′sē), **Jacqueline** Known as "Jackie." Born 1962. American athlete. Two-time world champion in both the heptathlon and long jump, she won five medals at the 1988 and 1992 Olympics.

joy·ous (joi′əs) *adj.* Full of joy; joyful: *a joyous occasion.* **—joy′ous·ly** *adv.* **—joy′ous·ness** *n.*

joy ride *n. Slang* A fast and reckless automobile ride, often in a stolen car.

joy·stick (joi′stĭk′) *n.* **1.** A stick or handle used to control

Mother Jones
photographed c. 1902

Joseph[2]
photographed in 1903

WRITERS CHOOSE THEIR WORDS

Tree-ear entered the city gates and stopped in midstep. How crowded it was! People, oxen, and carts **jostled** one another in the narrow streets; the houses were so close together that Tree-ear wondered how their residents could breathe.

—Linda Sue Park
A Single Shard

Juan Carlos
photographed in 2011

jug

juggler

ă	pat	ôr	core
ā	pay	oi	boy
âr	care	ou	out
ä	father	ŏŏ	took
ĕ	pet	ŏŏr	lure
ē	be	ōō	boot
ĭ	pit	ŭ	cut
ī	bite	ûr	urge
îr	pier	th	thin
ŏ	pot	*th*	this
ō	toe	zh	vision
ô	paw	ə	about

an aircraft. **2.** A manual control used to control onscreen graphics, especially in a video game.

jr. or **Jr.** *abbr.* An abbreviation of junior.

Juan Car·los (hwän **kär′**lōs) Born 1938. Spanish king. He ascended to the throne in 1975 and helped restore democracy after the death of Francisco Franco. He abdicated in 2014.

Ju·ba (**jōō′**bə) The capital of South Sudan, in the southern part of the country on the White Nile River.

ju·bi·lant (**jōō′**bə-lənt) *adj.* Full of joyful exultation; rejoicing: *A jubilant crowd celebrated their team's victory.* **—ju′bi·lant·ly** *adv.*

ju·bi·la·tion (jōō′bə-**lā′**shən) *n.* Great rejoicing: *The good news was greeted with jubilation.*

ju·bi·lee (**jōō′**bə-lē′ *or* jōō′bə-**lē′**) *n.* **1.** A special anniversary, especially a 50th anniversary, or the celebration of it. **2.** A season or occasion of joyful celebration.

Ju·dah¹ (**jōō′**də) In the Bible, a son of Jacob and Leah and the ancestor of one of the tribes of Israel.

Ju·dah² (**jōō′**də) An ancient kingdom of southern Palestine between the Mediterranean Sea and the Dead Sea. It lasted from about 931 BC until 586 BC.

Ju·da·ic (jōō-**dā′**ĭk) *adj.* Relating to or characteristic of Jews or Judaism: *Judaic traditions.*

Ju·da·ism (**jōō′**dē-ĭz′əm *or* **jōō′**dā-ĭz′əm *or* jōō-**dā′**ĭz′-əm) *n.* **1.** The religion of the Jewish people, based on belief in one God and on the teachings set forth especially in the Hebrew Scriptures and the Talmud. **2.** The cultural, religious, and social practices and beliefs of the Jews.

Ju·das (**jōō′**dəs) *n.* A person who betrays others under the appearance of friendship.

Judas Is·car·i·ot (ĭ-**skăr′**ē-ət) Died about AD 30. In the Bible, one of the 12 Apostles and the betrayer of Jesus.

Jude (jōōd) *n.* A book of the New Testament written in the form of a letter in which Saint Jude denounces false preachers.

Jude, Saint. Flourished about first century AD. In the Bible, one of the 12 Apostles.

Ju·de·a (jōō-**dē′**ə *or* jōō-**dā′**ə) An ancient region and kingdom of southern Palestine made up of present-day southern Israel and southwest Jordan.

judge (jŭj) *v.* **judged, judg·ing, judg·es** *—tr.* **1.** To form an opinion about or an evaluation of (something) after careful consideration: *The critic judged the play to be compelling drama.* **2.** To hear and decide (a case) in a court of law. **3.** To determine the winners of (a contest or issue): *The teachers judged the school spelling bee.* *—intr.* **1.** To form an opinion or evaluation. **2.** To act or decide as a judge. ❖ *n.* **1.** A person who gives an opinion about the value, quality, or outcome of something: *a good judge of character; a poor judge of painting.* **2.** A public official who hears and decides cases in a court of law. **3.** A person who decides the outcome of a dispute or the winner of a contest or competition. **4. Judges** *(used with a singular verb)* A book of the Bible containing a history of the Israelites after the death of Joshua. [From Middle English *jugen*, from Latin *iūdicāre*, from *iūdex*, judge.] **—judg′er** *n.*

judge·ship (**jŭj′**shĭp′) *n.* The position of responsibilities of a judge or the period during which a judge is in office.

judg·ment also **judge·ment** (**jŭj′**mənt) *n.* **1.** The ability to make distinctions and form opinions or evaluations: *Saving money shows good judgment.* **2.** An opinion or estimate made after careful consideration: *We await the judgment of the referee.* **3.** A decision reached in a court of law: *The high court handed down a judgment holding certain practices illegal.*

Judgment Day *n.* In Judeo-Christian and Muslim traditions, the day at the end of the world when God judges the moral worth of individual humans or the whole human race.

ju·di·cial (jōō-**dĭsh′**əl) *adj.* **1.** Relating to courts of law or the administration of justice: *the judicial branch of government.* **2.** Relating to or appropriate to the office of a judge: *judicial robes.* **3.** Decreed by a court: *a judicial decision.* **—ju·di′cial·ly** *adv.*

ju·di·ci·ar·y (jōō-**dĭsh′**ē-ĕr′ē *or* jōō-**dĭsh′**ə-rē) *n., pl.* **ju·di·ci·ar·ies 1.** The judicial branch of government. **2.** A system of courts of law and judges. **3.** The judges of these courts.

ju·di·cious (jōō-**dĭsh′**əs) *adj.* Having or showing wise and sound judgment; prudent: *Conservation involves the judicious use of resources.* **—ju·di′cious·ly** *adv.* **—ju·di′cious·ness** *n.*

ju·do (**jōō′**dō) *n.* A sport and method of physical training similar to wresting. Judo was developed in Japan in the late 1800s and was adapted from jujitsu. [From Japanese *jūdō* : *jū*, soft + *dō*, way.]

jug (jŭg) *n.* **1.** A tall, often rounded vessel with a narrow mouth, a handle, and usually a stopper or cap. **2.** The amount that a jug can hold: *We drank a jug of cider.* **3.** A small pitcher.

jug·ger·naut (**jŭg′**ər-nôt′) *n.* A force that is overwhelming or unstoppable. [From Hindi *jagannāth*, "lord of the world," title of Krishna and name of a giant wagon that used to draw a statue of Krishna in a parade and under whose wheels worshipers would throw themselves.]

jug·gle (**jŭg′**əl) *v.* **jug·gled, jug·gling, jug·gles** *—tr.* **1.** To keep (two or more objects) in the air at one time by alternately tossing and catching them. **2.** To have difficulty holding or balancing: *The tourist was juggling luggage and cameras.* **3.** To change or rearrange so as to mislead or cheat: *juggled the figures in the account books.* *—intr.* **1.** To perform as a juggler. **2.** To use trickery to deceive. [From Middle English *jogelen*, to perform tricks, from Latin *ioculārī*, to jest, from *ioculus*, joke.]

jug·gler (**jŭg′**lər) *n.* **1.** An entertainer who juggles balls or other objects. **2.** A person who uses tricks to mislead or cheat.

jug·u·lar (**jŭg′**yə-lər) *adj.* Relating to or located in the neck or throat. ❖ *n.* A jugular vein. [From Latin *iugulum*, collarbone.]

jugular vein *n.* Any of several large veins in the neck that carry blood from the head into other veins that empty into the heart.

juice (jōōs) *n.* **1.** A liquid naturally contained in plant or animal tissue, especially in plant parts such as fruits, stems, or roots. **2.** A beverage made from such a liquid, often with other ingredients added. **3.** A fluid secreted within the body: *digestive juices.* **4.** *Slang* Electric current. [From Middle English *jus*, from Latin *iūs*.]

juic·er (**jōō′**sər) *n.* An appliance used to extract juice from fruits and vegetables.

juic·y (**jōō′**sē) *adj.* **juic·i·er, juic·i·est 1.** Full of juice: *juicy berries.* **2.** Arousing interest or excitement: *He told me a juicy piece of gossip.* **3.** Rewarding or gratifying: *She was given a juicy part in the play.* **—juic′i·ly** *adv.* **—juic′i·ness** *n.*

ju·jit·su also **jiu·jit·su** (jōō-**jĭt′**sōō) *n.* An art of weaponless self-defense developed in Japan that uses techniques that exploit an opponent's weight and strength to one's own advantage.

juke·box (**jōōk′**bŏks′) *n.* A money-operated machine that plays music, usually equipped with pushbuttons for the selection of particular recordings.

ju·lep (**jōō′**lĭp) *n.* A mint julep.

Jul·ian calendar (**jōōl′**yən) *n.* The solar calendar introduced in Rome by Julius Caesar in 46 BC having a year of 365 days and a leap year of 366 days every fourth year. It has been replaced by the Gregorian calendar.

ju·li·enne (jōō′lē-**ĕn′**) *n.* A clear soup or broth containing vegetables cut into long thin strips. ❖ *adj.* Cut into long thin strips: *julienne potatoes.*

Ju·ly (jōō-**lī′**) *n.* The seventh month of the year in the

Gregorian calendar, having 31 days. [From Middle English *Juil*, from Latin *Iūlius*, after *Iūlius* Caesar, Julius Caesar.]

jum·ble (jŭm′bəl) *tr.v.* **jum·bled, jum·bling, jum·bles** To mix in a confused way; throw together carelessly: *The shirts were all jumbled together in a heap on the floor.* ❖ *n.* **1.** A confused or disordered mass: *a jumble of socks in a drawer.* **2.** A disordered state; a muddle.

jum·bo (jŭm′bō) *n., pl.* **jum·bos** An unusually large person, animal, or thing. ❖ *adj.* Very large: *jumbo shrimp; a jumbo jet.* [After *Jumbo*, a large elephant exhibited by P.T. Barnum.]

jump (jŭmp) *v.* **jumped, jump·ing, jumps** —*intr.* **1.** To rise up off the ground or a surface by pushing with the legs and feet: *The frog jumped into the pond.* **2.** To move suddenly and in one motion: *jump out of bed.* **3.** To move quickly or involuntarily, as in fear or surprise: *I jumped at the sudden noise.* **4.** To enter eagerly into an activity: *She jumped into the race for mayor.* **5.** To form an opinion or judgment hastily: *Let's not jump to conclusions.* **6.** To rise or increase suddenly: *Prices jumped over the past month.* **7.** To pass from one part to another further on; skip: *We jumped ahead to the middle chapters.* —*tr.* **1.** To leap over or across: *jumped the stream.* **2.** To leap onto: *jump a bus.* **3.** *Slang* To spring upon in or as if in attack: *The robbers jumped the unsuspecting tourists in the park.* **4.** To cause to leap: *jump a horse over a fence.* **5.** To skip; move ahead: *jump a space in typing.* **6.** To leave (a course or track): *Two subway cars jumped the tracks.* ❖ *n.* **1.** A leap or spring: *The cat made a graceful jump from the floor to the shelf.* **2.** The distance covered by a leap: *a jump of 16 feet.* **3.** Any of several track-and-field events in which contestants jump. **4.** An abrupt rise: *a jump in temperature.* **5.** A sudden involuntary movement; a jerk or start: *gave a jump in surprise.* ◆ **jump the gun** To start doing something too soon. **jump the shark** To undergo a sustained decline in quality or popularity. **jump through hoops** To make extraordinary efforts, especially in following an established procedure: *jumped through hoops to get approval for a loan.*

jump ball *n.* In basketball, a method of starting play or determining which team should have the ball, in which an official tosses the ball up between two opposing players who jump and try to tap it to a teammate.

jump·er[1] (jŭm′pər) *n.* **1.** A person or thing that jumps: *That horse is a good jumper.* **2.** A short length of wire or other electrical conductor used to make a temporary electrical connection.

jump·er[2] (jŭm′pər) *n.* **1.** A sleeveless dress worn over a blouse or sweater. **2.** A loose smock or jacket worn over other clothes to protect them. **3.** *Chiefly British* A pullover sweater. [Probably from *jump*, short coat, ultimately from Arabic *jubba*, long garment with wide open sleeves.]

jump·ing bean (jŭm′pĭng) *n.* A seed of certain Mexican plants that contains a moth larva whose movements cause the seed to jerk or roll.

jumping jack *n.* **1.** A toy figure with jointed limbs that can be made to dance by pulling an attached string. **2.** An exercise that is performed by jumping to a position with the legs spread wide and the hands touching overhead and then returning to a position with the feet together and the arms at the sides.

jump rope *n.* **1.** A rope held at each end and twirled so that one can jump over it as it touches the ground. **2.** The game or activity played with a jump rope.

jump shot *n.* A basketball shot made by a player at the highest point of a jump.

jump-start (jŭmp′stärt′) *tr.v.* **jump-start·ed, jump-start·ing, jump-starts** To start (the engine of a motor vehicle) by using a cable connected to the battery of another vehicle or by engaging the clutch when the vehicle is rolling downhill or being pushed. ❖ *n.* The act of jump-starting a motor vehicle.

jump suit *n.* **1.** A parachutist's uniform. **2.** also **jump·suit** (jŭmp′so͞ot′) A one-piece garment that consists of a shirt and attached pants.

jump·y (jŭm′pē) *adj.* **jump·i·er, jump·i·est 1.** Moving in jumps; jerky. **2.** Easily upset or excited; nervous. —**jump′i·ness** *n.*

jun·co (jŭng′kō) *n., pl.* **jun·cos** or **jun·coes** Any of various North American songbirds having a gray or brown body with white outer tail feathers.

junc·tion (jŭngk′shən) *n.* **1.** The act of joining or the condition of being joined: *The junction of the Missouri and Mississippi Rivers takes place at St. Louis.* **2.** The place at which two things join or meet: *There is a motel at the junction of the two highways.* [From Latin *iūnctiō*, from *iungere*, to join.]

junc·ture (jŭngk′chər) *n.* **1.** The act of joining or the condition of being joined. **2.** The point, line, or seam at which two things join; a joint: *Many small animals live along the juncture between meadow and woodland.* **3.** A point in time, especially a crisis or turning point: *At this juncture, a new government was formed.*

June (jo͞on) *n.* The sixth month of the year in the Gregorian calendar, having 30 days. [From Old English *Juin*, from Latin *Iūnō*, Juno.]

Ju·neau (jo͞o′nō′) The capital of Alaska, in the southeast part of the state south of Whitehorse, Yukon Territory, Canada. It was settled by gold miners in 1880.

June beetle *n.* The June bug.

June bug *n.* Any of various large brown beetles having adults that emerge in the spring and larvae that feed on roots and can damage crops.

June·teenth (jo͞on-tēnth′) *n.* June 19, an African-American holiday commemorating the date in 1865 when many slaves in Texas learned they had been freed by the Emancipation Proclamation issued earlier on January 1, 1863.

jun·gle (jŭng′gəl) *n.* **1.** An area of land having a dense growth of tropical plants. **2.** A confused or tangled mass, often the scene of intense competition or violence: *He felt totally out of place in the corporate jungle.* [From Sanskrit *jaṅgalam*, desert, wasteland.]

jungle gym *n.* A structure of crisscrossing poles and bars on which children can play and climb.

jun·ior (jo͞on′yər) *adj.* **1.** Used to distinguish a son from his father when both have the same name. **2.** Intended for or including youthful people: *the junior skating championship.* **3.** Lower in rank or shorter in length of service: *a junior partner in a law firm; the junior senator from Texas.* **4.** Relating to or for the third year of a four-year high school or college: *the junior class.* ❖ *n.* **1.** A person who is younger than another: *I am my aunt's junior by twenty-five years.* **2.** A person of lower rank or shorter service. **3.** A student in the third year at a four-year high school or college. [From Middle English, from Latin *iūnior.*]

junior college *n.* An educational institution offering a two-year course that is generally the equivalent of the first two years of a four-year undergraduate course.

junior high school *n.* A school attended between elementary and high school that includes the seventh, eighth, and sometimes ninth grades.

junior varsity *n.* A high-school or college sports team that competes on the level below varsity.

ju·ni·per (jo͞o′nə-pər) *n.* Any of various evergreen trees or shrubs having needlelike or scalelike leaves and small bluish-gray cones that resemble berries. [From Middle English, from Latin *iūniperus.*]

junk[1] (jŭngk) *n.* **1.** Material of any kind that is old, worn-out, and fit to be discarded or recycled, such as scrap metal, rags, or paper; trash. **2.** *Informal* Something

jumping jack

junk²

Jupiter

WRITERS CHOOSE THEIR WORDS

She led Anson past the farmyard and up an ascent that rose so quickly that soon they were hand in hand, helping each other clamber over the mossy boulders that **jutted** out unexpectedly.

—Gary D. Schmidt
Anson's Way

ă	pat	ôr	core
ā	pay	oi	boy
âr	care	ou	out
ä	father	o͝o	took
ĕ	pet	o͝or	lure
ē	be	o͞o	boot
ĭ	pit	ŭ	cut
ī	bite	ûr	urge
îr	pier	th	thin
ŏ	pot	*th*	this
ō	toe	zh	vision
ô	paw	ə	about

cheap or shoddy: *That cheap toaster is nothing but junk.* ❖ *tr.v.* **junked, junk·ing, junks** To discard as worn-out or useless: *He junked the old toaster after it stopped working.* [From Middle English *jonk*, an old cable or rope.]

junk² (jŭngk) *n.* A Chinese flatbottom sailing vessel with a high stern and battened sails. [From Javanese *djong.*]

jun·ket (jŭng′kĭt) *n.* **1.** A trip made by a government official at public expense. **2.** A dessert made from flavored milk and rennet.

junk food *n.* Food that is high in calories but low in nutritional value.

junk·ie (jŭng′kē) *n. Slang* **1.** A person addicted to narcotics. **2.** A person who has an unflagging interest in something; a devotee: *a video game junkie.*

junk mail *n.* Unrequested mail, such as advertisements and catalogs, sent to large numbers of people.

junk·yard (jŭngk′yärd′) *n.* A yard or other open area used to store junk, such as scrap metal or car parts.

Ju·no (jo͞o′nō) *n.* In Roman mythology, the chief goddess and the wife and sister of Jupiter, worshipped as the goddess of women, marriage, childbirth, and the moon, and as the protector of the state. She was identified with the Greek Hera.

jun·ta (ho͝on′tə *or* jŭn′tə) *n.* **1.** A group of military leaders who jointly govern a nation after seizing power. **2.** A council or small legislative body in government, especially in Central or South America.

Ju·pi·ter (jo͞o′pĭ-tər) *n.* **1.** In Roman mythology, the chief god, the patron of the Roman state, and the husband and brother of Juno. He is identified with the Greek Zeus. **2.** The fifth planet from the sun and the largest in the solar system, with a diameter about 11 times that of Earth. It turns on its axis faster than any other planet. See table at **solar system.**

Ju·ras·sic (jo͝o-răs′ĭk) *n.* The second and middle period of the Mesozoic Era, from about 200 to 146 million years ago. During the Jurassic, dinosaurs were the dominant form of land life and the earliest birds appeared. See table at **geologic time.** —**Ju·ras′sic** *adj.*

ju·ris·dic·tion (jo͝or′ĭs-**dĭk′**shən) *n.* **1.** The right of a court to hear a particular case, based on the scope of its authority: *A justice of the peace has jurisdiction in a town or village.* **2.** Authority or control; power: *Schools come under the jurisdiction of the state education department.* **3.** The range or extent of authority or control: *Cases of treason are beyond the jurisdiction of local courts.* **4.** A geographic area under a specified authority or control.

ju·ris·pru·dence (jo͝or′ĭs-**pro͞od′**ns) *n.* **1.** The science or philosophy of law. **2.** A division, type, or particular body of law: *federal jurisprudence; bankruptcy jurisprudence.*

ju·rist (**jo͝or′**ĭst) *n.* A person who is skilled in the law, especially a judge, lawyer, or legal scholar.

ju·ror (jo͝or′ər *or* **jo͝or′**ôr′) *n.* A member of a jury.

ju·ry (**jo͝or′**ē) *n., pl.* **ju·ries 1.** A body of people selected to decide a verdict in a legal case, based on the evidence presented: *the right to trial by jury.* **2.** A group of people chosen to judge contestants or award prizes, as in a competition. [From Middle English *jure*, from Latin *iūrāre*, to swear.]

just (jŭst) *adj.* **1.** Honorable and fair: *a just ruler of the people.* **2.** Morally right; righteous: *a just cause.* **3.** Properly due or deserved; merited: *just punishment.* **4.** Based on fact or good reason; well-founded: *a just appraisal of his work.* **5.** Valid according to the law; lawful: *a jury's just decision.* ❖ *adv.* (jəst *or* jĭst; jŭst *when stressed*) **1.** Exactly: *Everything went just as we had predicted.* **2.** Only a moment ago: *We've just run out of milk.* **3.** By a small amount; barely: *just made the bus; just after 6:00.* **4.** Only; merely: *It was just a dream.* **5.** Perhaps; possibly: *I just may go.* ◆ **just about** Almost; very nearly: *We are just about finished.* —**just′ly** *adv.* —**just′ness** *n.*

jus·tice (jŭs′tĭs) *n.* **1.** The quality of being just or fair: *A sense of justice forced the reporter to investigate both sides of the story.* **2.** Moral rightness in action or attitude; righteousness: *We argued for the justice of our cause.* **3.** Fair treatment in accordance with honor or the law: *We only seek justice for the accused.* **4.** The carrying out of the law or the way in which the law is carried out: *the administration of justice through local and county courts.* **5.** A judge or a justice of the peace: *a local justice; a justice of the Supreme Court.* **6.** Good reason; sound basis: *The customer was angry, and with justice.* ◆ **do justice to** To treat adequately or fairly: *I cannot do justice to her accomplishments in this brief report.*

justice of the peace *n., pl.* **justices of the peace** An official, especially one who is associated with a town or county, who has authority to try minor offenses, perform marriages, and authorize arrests.

jus·ti·fi·a·ble (jŭs′tə-fī′ə-bəl *or* jŭs′tə-**fī′**ə-bəl) *adj.* Having sufficient grounds for justification; possible to justify: *The high price of the table is justifiable when one considers the fine workmanship.* —**jus′ti·fi′a·bly** *adv.*

jus·ti·fi·ca·tion (jŭs′tə-fĭ-**kā′**shən) *n.* **1.** The act of justifying or the condition of being justified. **2.** Something that justifies; a good reason: *Illness is a justification for not finishing your report on time.*

jus·ti·fy (jŭs′tə-fī′) *tr.v.* **jus·ti·fied, jus·ti·fy·ing, jus·ti·fies 1.** To show or prove to be right, just, or valid: *His fine performance justified the director's decision of casting him in the play.* **2.** To declare innocent; clear of blame: *The jury decided that the evidence justified the defendant's actions.* **3.** To format (a paragraph, for example) so that the lines of text begin and end evenly at a straight margin.

jut (jŭt) *intr.v.* **jut·ted, jut·ting, juts** To extend sharply outward or upward; project: *The branches of that huge tree jut over the street.*

jute (jo͞ot) *n.* **1.** A strong fiber used to make rope, twine, and coarse cloth such as burlap. **2.** Either of two Asian plants that yield such fiber. [From Bengali *jhuṭo*, from Sanskrit *jūṭaḥ*, twisted hair.]

Jute *n.* A member of a Germanic people who invaded Britain in the fifth and sixth centuries AD and settled there with the Angles and Saxons, eventually forming the Anglo-Saxon peoples.

ju·ve·nile (jo͞o′və-nīl′ *or* **jo͞o′**və-nəl) *adj.* **1.** Not fully grown or developed; young: *a juvenile coyote.* **2.** Relating to or for children or young people: *the juvenile section of the library; a juvenile court.* **3.** Immature; childish: *juvenile behavior.* See Synonyms at **young.** ❖ *n.* A young person or animal. [From Latin *iuvenis.*]

juvenile delinquency *n.* Antisocial or criminal behavior by children or adolescents.

juvenile delinquent *n.* A child or adolescent guilty of antisocial or juvenile behavior.

jux·ta·pose (jŭk′stə-**pōz′**) *tr.v.* **jux·ta·posed, jux·ta·pos·ing, jux·ta·pos·es** To place side by side, especially for comparison or contrast: *We juxtaposed the two photographs of the house to see how it had changed.* —**jux′ta·po·si′tion** (jŭk′stə-pə-**zĭsh′**ən) *n.*

JV *abbr.* An abbreviation of junior varsity.

k[1] or **K** (kā) *n., pl.* **k's** or **K's** also **ks** or **Ks** The 11th letter of the English alphabet.

k[2] *abbr.* An abbreviation of karat.

K[1] The symbol for the element **potassium.**

K[2] *abbr.* An abbreviation of: **1.** kelvin. **2.** kilobyte. **3.** kindergarten. **4.** strikeout.

Kaa·ba (kä′bə) *n.* A Muslim shrine at Mecca. Muslims throughout the world turn toward this shrine when praying.

kab·ba·lah or **kab·ba·la** or **ka·ba·la** or **ca·ba·la** (**kăb′**-ə-lə *or* kə-**bä′**lə) *n.* often **Kabbalah** A form of Jewish mystical theology based on esoteric interpretations of the Hebrew Scriptures. [From Hebrew *qabbālâ*, received doctrine, tradition, from *qibbēl*, to receive.] **—kab′ba·lism** *n.* **—kab′ba·list** *n.* **—kab′ba·list′ic** *adj.*

ka·bob (kə-**bŏb′**) *n.* A variant of **kebab.**

Ka·bu·ki (kə-**boo͞′**kē) *n.* A type of popular Japanese drama, evolved from the older No theater. In Kabuki, elaborately costumed performers use stylized movements, dances, and songs to enact tragedies and comedies. [From Japanese : *ka*, singing + *bu*, dancing + *ki*, art.]

Ka·bul (kä′bo͝ol *or* kə-**bo͞ol′**) The capital of Afghanistan, in the eastern part of the country.

Kad·dish (kä′dĭsh) *n.* A Jewish prayer recited in Hebrew at daily services and by mourners after the death of a close relative.

kaf·tan (**kăf′**tăn′ *or* kăf-**tăn′**) *n.* Variant of **caftan.**

Ka·gan (**kā′**gən), **Elena** Born 1960. American jurist who was appointed an associate justice of the US Supreme Court in 2010.

Kah·lo (**kä′**lō), **Frida** 1907–1954. Mexican artist known for her surrealist self-portraits.

Kai·ser (**kī′**zər) *n.* Any of the emperors of the Holy Roman Empire (AD 962–1806), of Austria (1804–1918), or of Germany (1871–1918). [From German, from Latin *Caesar*, Caesar.]

kaiser roll *n.* A large roll with a hard crust, often used for sandwiches.

Ka·la·ha·ri (kä′lə-**här′**ē) A desert plateau region of southern Botswana, eastern Namibia, and western South Africa.

ka·la·ma·ta olive also **ca·la·ma·ta olive** (kä′lə-**mä′**tə *or* kăl′ə-**mä′**tə) *n.* A variety of olive that has a fruity flavor and a meaty texture.

kale (kāl) *n.* A plant having large, dark-green, usually wrinkled leaves that are eaten as a vegetable.

ka·lei·do·scope (kə-**lī′**də-skōp′) *n.* **1.** A tube in which mirrors reflect light from bits of loose colored glass contained at one end, causing them to appear as changing symmetrical designs when viewed from the other end as the tube is rotated. **2.** A series of changing phases or events: *American politics is a kaleidoscope of ideas.* [From Greek *kalos*, beautiful + Greek *eidos*, form + *-scope.*] **—ka·lei′do·scop′ic** (kə-lī′də-**skŏp′**ĭk) *adj.* **—ka·lei′-do·scop′i·cal·ly** *adv.*

ka·lim·ba (kə-**lĭm′**bə) *n.* An mbira.

kam·eez (kə-**mēz′**) *n.* A long loose tunic, typically extending to or below the knees and slit to the waist at the sides, worn chiefly by women in South Asia. [From Punjabi, Hindi, and Urdu *qamīz*, all ultimately from Portuguese *camisa*, shirt, from Late Latin *camisia.*]

Ka·me·ha·me·ha I (kə-mā′ə-**mā′**ə) 1758?–1819. King of the Hawaiian Islands (1795–1819) who conquered and united all the islands under his rule (1810).

ka·mi·ka·ze (kä′mĭ-**kä′**zē) *n.* A Japanese pilot in World War II trained to make a suicidal crash attack, especially upon a ship. [From Japanese : kami, divine + kaze, wind.]

Kam·pa·la (käm-**pä′**lə) The capital of Uganda, in the southern part of the country on Lake Victoria.

Kam·pu·che·a (kăm′po͞o-**chē′**ə) See **Cambodia.**

Kan·da·har (kŭn′də-**här′** *or* kän′də-**här′**) A city of southeast Afghanistan southwest of Kabul. It has long been important for its strategic location on the trade routes of Central Asia.

kan·ga·roo (kăng′gə-**roo͞′**) *n., pl.* **kangaroo** or **kan·ga·roos** Any of various Australian marsupials having short forelegs, long hind legs used for leaping, and a long strong tail. The female kangaroo carries the newborn in a pouch on the outside of her body.

kangaroo court *n.* A court that is not authorized or legal, especially one that is hastily assembled with the sole purpose of condemning a prisoner.

kangaroo rat *n.* Any of various small long-tailed rodents found in dry regions of western North America, having long hind legs used for leaping.

Kan·sas (**kăn′**zəs) A state of the central United States north of Oklahoma. It was admitted as the 34th state in 1861. Topeka is the capital and Wichita the largest city. —SEE NOTE.

Kansas City A city of western Missouri on the Missouri River west-northwest of St. Louis. It was established as a fur-trading post in the 1820s.

ka·o·lin (**kā′**ə-lĭn) *n.* A fine clay used in making ceramics.

ka·pok (**kā′**pŏk′) *n.* A silky fiber from the seedpods of a large tropical tree, used as a stuffing for pillows, mattresses, and life preservers.

kap·pa (**kăp′**ə) *n.* The tenth letter of the Greek alphabet, written Κ, κ. In English it is represented as *K, k.*

Ka·ra·chi (kə-**rä′**chē) A city of southern Pakistan on the Arabian Sea. It was developed as a trading center in the early 1700s, and it was Pakistan's capital from 1947 until 1959.

Ka·ra·ko·ram Range (kăr′ə-**kôr′**əm) A mountain range of northern Pakistan and India and southwest China. It rises to 28,251 feet (8,611 meters).

kar·a·o·ke (kâr′ē-**ō′**kē) *n.* A music entertainment system that plays previously recorded musical accompaniment to songs that a person sings live. [From Japanese : *kara*, empty + *ōke(sutora)*, orchestra.]

kar·at also **car·at** (**kăr′**ət) *n.* A unit of measure used to in-

kameez

GEOGRAPHY

Kansas The name **Kansas** comes from a Native American people, the Kansa (or Kaw). A possible translation is "people of the south wind." The plural *–s* was added to the name when referring to this people, and this form was used for the state.

kayak

keffiyeh

Helen Keller

dicate the proportion of pure gold contained in an alloy. For example, since 24 karats is pure gold, a bracelet of 12-karat gold contains 12 parts gold and 12 parts alloy.

❑ *These sound alike:* **karat, carat** (weight of gems), **caret** (proofreader's mark), **carrot** (plant).

ka·ra·te (kə-**rä′**tē) *n.* An art of self-defense developed in Japan, in which sharp blows and kicks are delivered to sensitive points on the body of an opponent. [From Japanese : *kara*, empty + *te*, hand.]

kar·ma (**kär′**mə) *n.* **1.** In Hinduism and Buddhism, the total effect of a person's actions and conduct, believed to determine that person's destiny in this life or in a future reincarnation. **2.** Fate; destiny. [From Sanskrit, deed, action that has consequences, karma.] **—kar′mic** *adj.*

Kash·mir also **Cash·mere** (**kăsh′**mîr′ *or* kăsh-**mîr′**) **1.** A historical region of northwest India and northeast Pakistan. It became part of the princely state of Jammu and Kashmir in 1846. **2.** See **Jammu and Kashmir.**

ka·ta (**kä′**tä) *n., pl.* **kata** or **ka·tas** A system of basic body positioning and movement exercises, as in karate or judo. [From Japanese, traditional form.]

Kath·man·du (kăt′măn-**do͞o′**) The capital of Nepal, in the central part of the country in the eastern Himalaya Mountains. It was founded in about 723.

ka·ty·did (**kā′**tē-dĭd′) *n.* Any of various usually green insects that have long antennae and are closely related to the grasshoppers. The males make shrill sounds by rubbing their front wings together.

Kau·ai (**kou′**ī′ *or* kou-**ī′**) An island of Hawaii northwest of Oahu.

kay·ak (**kī′**ăk′) *n.* **1.** An Inuit or Yupik boat consisting of a light wooden frame covered with watertight skins, with only a small opening for the paddler. **2.** A lightweight sports canoe of a similar design. ❖ *intr.v.* **kay·aked, kay·ak·ing, kay·aks** To travel or race in a kayak. [From Inuit and Yupik *qajaq*.]

kay·o (kā-**ō′** *or* **kā′**ō′) *n., pl.* **kay·os** A knockout in boxing. ❖ *tr.v.* **kay·oed, kay·o·ing, kay·os** To knock (someone) out in boxing.

Ka·zakh (**kä′**zăk′ *or* kə-**zăk′**) *adj.* Relating to Kazakhstan or its people, language, or culture. ❖ *n., pl.* **Ka·zakhs** or **Kazakh 1.** A native or inhabitant of Kazakhstan. **2.** The Turkic language of the Kazakhs.

Ka·zakh·stan (**kä′**zăk-stän′ *or* kə-**zăk′**stän′) A country of west-central Asia on the Caspian Sea south of Russia. It was part of the USSR from 1920 until 1991. Astana is the capital.

ka·zoo (kə-**zo͞o′**) *n., pl.* **ka·zoos** A toy musical instrument with a membrane in the mouthpiece that vibrates and produces a buzzing sound when the player hums into it.

Kb *abbr.* An abbreviation of kilobit.

KB *abbr.* An abbreviation of kilobyte.

KBO *abbr.* An abbreviation of Kuiper belt object.

kc *abbr.* An abbreviation of kilocycle.

ke·a (**kē′**ə) *n.* A brownish-green New Zealand parrot that has a powerful curved beak and eats plants, insects, and carrion.

Keats (kēts), **John** 1795–1821. British poet whose works include "Ode to a Nightingale" (1819).

ke·bab or **ke·bob** also **ka·bob** (kə-**bŏb′**) *n.* Shish kebab.

keel (kēl) *n.* **1.** A strong beam, as of wood or metal, that runs along the center line of a vessel from one end to the other. The frame of the entire vessel is built up from the keel. **2.** A ridge extending down from the bottom of the hull of a boat or ship that improves directional control and is often weighted for added stability. ◆ **keel over** To collapse or fall down: *I almost keeled over with surprise.* [From Middle English *kele*, from Old Norse *kjölr*.]

keel·boat (**kēl′**bōt′) *n.* A riverboat with a keel but without sails, used for carrying freight.

keel·haul (**kēl′**hôl′) *tr.v.* **keel·hauled, keel·haul·ing, keel·hauls 1.** To drag (a person) under the keel of a ship as punishment. **2.** To scold or criticize harshly.

keen[1] (kēn) *adj.* **keen·er, keen·est 1.** Having a sharp edge or point: *A keen knife slit the heavy canvas.* **2.** Having highly attuned senses; very sensitive: *the keen eyes of the owl.* **3.** Characterized by intellectual quickness; sharp; bright: *a keen observer of politics.* **4.** Intense or bracing: *a keen wind.* **5.** Eager; enthusiastic: *He's really keen on hunting for fossils.* [From Old English *cēne*, brave.] **—keen′ly** *adv.* **—keen′ness** *n.*

keen[2] (kēn) *n.* A crying or wailing in sorrow for the dead. ❖ *intr.v.* **keened, keen·ing, keens** To cry or wail in sorrow for the dead. [From Irish Gaelic *caoininim*, I lament, from Old Irish *coínim*.]

keep (kēp) *v.* **kept** (kĕpt), **keep·ing, keeps** *—tr.* **1.** To retain in one's possession; continue to have: *I keep my old photographs.* **2.** To hold for future use; save: *I kept some food for you.* **3.** To put in a customary place; store: *Where do you keep your bike?* **4.** To cause to continue in a certain position or condition: *Keep the boat headed for that island.* **5.** To continue or maintain (an activity, for example): *keep watch.* **6.** To take care of; provide for or manage: *keep house; keep a large family.* **7.** To raise: *We keep ducks and geese.* **8.** To make regular entries in: *keep a record; keep a diary.* **9.** To celebrate or observe: *keeping the Sabbath.* **10.** To habitually do something, such as work, during (a certain time period): *kept office hours on Tuesdays.* **11.** To be faithful to; fulfill: *keep a promise.* **12.** To prevent or restrain: *We kept the kite from hitting the tree.* **13.** To refrain from telling: *keep a secret.* **14.** To detain or delay: *I was kept after school.* *—intr.* **1.** To remain in a state or condition: *keep warm; keep in touch.* **2.** To continue or persist: *He kept on talking.* **3.** To restrain oneself: *I could not keep from laughing.* **4.** To stay fresh or unspoiled: *Fruit doesn't keep well.* ❖ *n.* **1.** The things needed to live: *There are many ways to earn one's keep.* **2.** The stronghold of a castle or fort. **3.** Care; charge: *The child was in my keep for the day.* ◆ **for keeps** Permanently: *The kitten was mine for keeps.* **keep an eye on** To watch over attentively; mind: *Please keep an eye on your brother while I go to the store.* **keep (one's) eyes open** or **keep (one's) eyes peeled** To be on the lookout: *Keep your eyes peeled for fireflies.* **keep to (oneself) 1.** To avoid other people; remain alone. **2.** To refrain from telling others: *We could not keep such good news to ourselves.* **keep up 1.** To maintain in good condition: *keep up the gardens.* **2.** To continue at the same level or pace: *The wind kept up all night.* **3.** To match others in success or lifestyle: *Our company must keep up with the competition.* **4.** To remain adequately informed: *kept up with the progress on the new project.* [From Old English *cēpan*, to observe, seize.]

SYNONYMS **keep, retain, withhold, reserve** These verbs mean to maintain something in one's possession or control. **Keep** is the most general: *They received a few offers but eventually decided to keep the house.* **Retain** means to continue to hold something, especially when in danger of losing it: *Though unhappy, I retained my sense of humor.* **Withhold** means to refuse to give or allow: *The tenants withheld their rent until the landlord repaired the boiler.* **Reserve** means to hold for future use: *Please reserve your questions for the discussion period.*

keep·er (**kē′**pər) *n.* **1.** A person who watches over or guards something; an attendant or guard. **2.** A person who takes care of or manages something: *the keeper of a small shop.* **3.** *Informal* Something that is worth keeping, especially a fish that is large enough to be legally caught.

keep·ing (**kē′**pĭng) *n.* **1.** Care; custody: *documents in the keeping of my lawyer.* See Synonyms at **care. 2.** Agree-

ă	pat	ôr	core
ā	pay	oi	boy
âr	care	ou	out
ä	father	o͝o	took
ĕ	pet	o͝or	lure
ē	be	o͞o	boot
ĭ	pit	ŭ	cut
ī	bite	ûr	urge
îr	pier	th	thin
ŏ	pot	*th*	this
ō	toe	zh	vision
ô	paw	ə	about

ment; conformity: *wearing formal clothes in keeping with the important occasion.*

keep·sake (kēp′sāk′) *n.* An object that someone keeps in memory of the person who gave it or the place it came from; a memento.

kef·fi·yeh (kə-fē′ə) *n.* A square of cloth, often embroidered, traditionally worn as a headdress by Arab men, either by winding it around the head or by folding it into a triangle, draping it over the head, and securing it with an agal. [From Arabic *kūfiya*, from *al-Kūfa*, Kufa, a city in central Iraq.]

keg (kĕg) *n.* **1.** A small barrel with a capacity of about 30 gallons (114 liters). **2.** A keg and its contents: *a keg of mackerel in brine.*

Kel·ler (kĕl′ər), **Helen Adams** 1880–1968. American writer. Blind and deaf since infancy, she learned to read, write, and speak. She lectured widely on behalf of sightless people and wrote twelve books, including *Out of the Dark* (1913).

kelp (kĕlp) *n.* Any of various brown or green seaweeds of ocean waters that can grow very long and are often found in large clusters.

Kelt (kĕlt) *n.* Variant of **Celt.**

Kelt·ic (kĕl′tĭk) *n. & adj.* Variant of **Celtic.**

kel·vin (kĕl′vĭn) *n.* A unit of absolute temperature having the same value as one Celsius degree. It is used in the Kelvin scale. See table at **measurement.** [After the First Baron *Kelvin* (1824–1907), British physicist.]

Kelvin scale *n.* A temperature scale beginning at absolute zero (−273.15°C), in which each degree is equal to one kelvin. On the Kelvin scale, water freezes at 273.15 degrees and boils at 373.15 degrees.

ken (kĕn) *n.* **1.** Range of understanding; comprehension: *Many forces of nature are beyond our ken.* **2.** Range of vision: *The powerful telescope brought many unobserved stars within our ken.* ❖ *intr.v.* **kenned** or **kent** (kĕnt), **ken·ning, kens** *Scots* To have an understanding of something. [From Middle English *kennen*, to recognize, from Old English *cennan*, to declare.]

Ken·ne·dy (kĕn′ĭ-dē), **Anthony McLeod** Born 1936. American jurist who was appointed an associate justice of the US Supreme Court in 1988.

Kennedy, Cape See Cape **Canaveral.**

Kennedy, John Fitzgerald 1917–1963. The 35th president of the United States (1961–1963). Kennedy established the Peace Corps (1961) and advocated civil rights reform. He was assassinated in Dallas, Texas.

ken·nel (kĕn′əl) *n.* **1.** A shelter for a dog or dogs. **2.** An establishment for the breeding, training, or boarding of dogs. ❖ *tr.v.* **ken·neled, ken·nel·ing, ken·nels** or **ken·nelled, ken·nel·ling, ken·nels** To place or keep in or as if in a kennel. [From Middle English *kenel*, from Latin *canis*, dog.]

kent (kĕnt) *v. Scots* A past tense and past participle of **ken.**

ken·te (kĕn′tā) *n.* **1.** A brightly patterned, hand-woven ceremonial cloth of the Ashanti. **2.** A durable machine-woven fabric similar to this fabric.

Ken·tuck·y (kən-tŭk′ē) A state of the east-central United States north of Tennessee. It was admitted as the 15th state in 1792. Frankfort is the capital and Lexington the largest city. —SEE NOTE.

Ken·ya (kĕn′yə *or* kēn′yə) A country of east-central Africa on the Indian Ocean north of Tanzania. Nairobi is the capital.

Ken·yat·ta (kĕn-yä′tə), **Jomo** 1893?–1978. Kenyan politician who was the first prime minister (1963–1974) and president (1964–1978) of independent Kenya.

ke·pi (kā′pē *or* kĕp′ē) *n., pl.* **ke·pis** A French military cap with a flat round top and a visor.

Kep·ler (kĕp′lər), **Johannes** 1571–1630. German astronomer and mathematician who was the first to accurately describe the elliptical orbits of Earth and the planets around the sun.

kept (kĕpt) *v.* Past tense and past participle of **keep.**

ker·a·tin (kĕr′ə-tĭn) *n.* A tough fibrous protein that is found in the outer layer of skin of vertebrate animals and is the main component of hair, nails, horns, claws, and feathers. [From Greek *kerās*, horn.] —SEE NOTE AT **triceratops.**

ker·chief (kûr′chĭf *or* kûr′chēf′) *n., pl.* **ker·chiefs** also **ker·chieves** (kûr′chĭvz *or* kûr′chēvz) **1.** A square scarf worn over the head or around the neck. **2.** A handkerchief.

ker·nel (kûr′nəl) *n.* **1.** A grain or seed, especially of a cereal plant such as corn or wheat. **2.** The often edible seed inside the shell of a nut. **3.** The most important or essential part; the core: *the kernel of truth in a witty saying.* [From Old English *cyrnel.*]

❑ *These sound alike:* **kernel, colonel** (officer).

ker·o·sene (kĕr′ə-sēn′ *or* kăr′ə-sēn′) *n.* A thin light-colored oil that is obtained from petroleum and used chiefly as a fuel for heating and cooking and in lamps.

kes·trel (kĕs′trəl) *n.* Any of various small falcons that have reddish-brown feathers and that hover for long periods of time when hunting.

ketch (kĕch) *n.* A two-masted fore-and-aft rigged sailing vessel with a large sail on the mainmast and a shorter mast placed aft.

ketch·up (kĕch′əp *or* kăch′əp) also **cat·sup** (kăt′səp *or* kăch′əp *or* kĕch′əp) *n.* A thick spicy sauce, usually made with tomatoes, used as a seasoning. [From Malay *kicap*, fish sauce, from Hokkein, a variety of Chinese spoken in southeastern China and Taiwan *kē-chiap* : kē *pickled fish* + chiap *sauce, juice.*]

ket·tle (kĕt′l) *n.* **1.** A metal pot, usually with a lid, for boiling liquids or for cooking. **2.** A teakettle. [From Old English *cetil*, from Latin *catīllus*, little bowl.]

ket·tle·drum (kĕt′l-drŭm′) *n.* A large drum having a bowl-shaped body of brass or copper and a parchment head that can be tuned by adjusting its tension.

key¹ (kē) *n., pl.* **keys 1.** A small piece of metal with notches or grooves that is inserted into a lock to open or close it. **2.** A device that functions like a key: *a key for opening cans; a clock key.* **3.** A keycard. **4.** Something that contributes to an accomplishment or achievement: *Your hard work has been the key to our success.* **5.** Something that solves a problem or explains a mystery: *evidence that became the key to solving the crime.* **6.** A set of answers to a test. **7.** An explanatory table, such as that explaining colors and symbols on a map. **8.** Any of the buttons or levers moved by the fingers in operating a machine or playing a musical instrument: *piano keys; the shift key on a computer keyboard.* **9.** A scale or group of musical tones related to a primary tone: *a piece written in the key of D.* **10.** The pitch of a voice or other sound. **11.** A general tone or level of intensity: *The candidate spoke in a relaxed and lower key to friends and supporters.* **12.** An area at each end of a basketball court between the baseline and the foul line and including the circle around the foul line. ❖ *adj.* Of crucial importance; significant: *key decisions.* ❖ *tr.v.* **keyed, key·ing, keys 1.** To adapt to special conditions; adjust: *Farming methods are keyed to the local weather conditions.* **2.** To enter (data) into a computer by means of a keyboard. **3.** To tune (a musical instrument) to a particular note: *Key the guitar to E flat.* **4.** To lock with a key. ◆ **key on** To pay close attention to; focus on: *We keyed on playing good defense.* **key up** To make nervous; excite: *I was too keyed up about my trip to eat.* [From Old English *cǣg.*]

❑ *These sound alike:* **key¹, cay** (island), **key²** (island), **quay** (wharf).

key² (kē) *n., pl.* **keys** A low-lying island or reef along a

John F. Kennedy
photographed in 1963

kente

GEOGRAPHY

Kentucky The name of the state of **Kentucky** probably comes from a Seneca word meaning "field, meadow." The name was first applied in 1776 to a county established by the state of Virginia and later to the new state when it was organized in 1792.

kettledrum

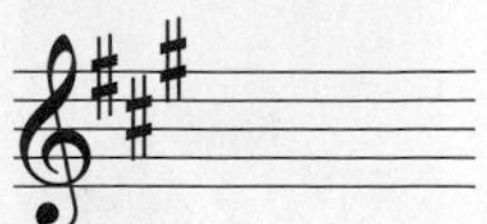
key signature
for the key of A major

keystone

ă	pat	ôr	core
ā	pay	oi	boy
âr	care	ou	out
ä	father	o͝o	took
ĕ	pet	o͝or	lure
ē	be	o͞o	boot
ĭ	pit	ŭ	cut
ī	bite	ûr	urge
îr	pier	th	thin
ŏ	pot	*th*	this
ō	toe	zh	vision
ô	paw	ə	about

coast, especially in the Gulf of Mexico. [From Spanish *cayo*.]

❑ *These sound alike:* **key²**, **cay** (island), **key¹** (lock opener), **quay** (wharf).

Key (kē), **Francis Scott** 1779–1843. American lawyer who wrote a poem in 1814 that was set to music and renamed "The Star-Spangled Banner." In 1931, it was adopted by Congress as the national anthem.

key·board (kē′bôrd′) *n.* **1.** A panel of buttons used for typing and performing other functions on a computer or typewriter. **2.** A row of levers that are pressed with the fingers to produce or alter the sound of a musical instrument, such as a piano or organ. ❖ *tr.v.* **key·board·ed, key·board·ing, key·boards** To enter (text or data) into a computer by using a keyboard. **—key′board′er** *n.*

key·card (kē′kärd′) *n.* A usually plastic card, typically bearing a magnetic strip or containing an electronic chip, used to operate a lock or other mechanism.

key fob *n.* A small, portable electronic device that remotely unlocks, activates, or deactivates a piece of equipment, such as a car, motorized door, or alarm.

key·hole (kē′hōl′) *n.* The opening in a lock into which a key fits.

key·log·ger (kē′lô′gər) *n.* A software program or hardware device that records or transmits a computer user's keystrokes. A keylogger is usually installed without the user's knowledge.

key·note (kē′nōt′) *n.* **1.** The principal tone of a musical scale or key; the tonic. **2.** The basic idea or theme, as of a speech, book, or political campaign.

keynote address *n.* An opening address, as at a political convention, that outlines the issues to be considered.

key·pad (kē′păd′) *n.* A panel of buttons or keys arranged in a grid, used to input data into a cell phone, calculator, or other electronic device.

key·punch (kē′pŭnch′) *n.* A keyboard machine formerly used to punch holes in cards for data-processing systems.

key signature *n.* The group of sharps or flats placed to the right of the clef on a staff to show the musical key of a piece.

key·stone (kē′stōn′) *n.* **1.** The central wedge-shaped stone of an arch that locks the other stones together. **2.** The essential element that supports a whole: *The keystone of their business was their downtown store.*

key·stroke (kē′strōk′) *n.* A stroke of a key, as on a computer keyboard.

Key West A city of extreme southern Florida on the island of **Key West,** the westernmost of a group of islands off Florida in the Gulf of Mexico.

key·word (kē′wûrd′) *n.* A word used to find information about that word or to find other words: *keywords at the top of a dictionary column; entered a keyword in the search engine.*

kg *abbr.* An abbreviation of kilogram.

KGB (kā′jē-**bē′**) *n.* The intelligence and internal security agency of the former Soviet Union.

khak·i (kăk′ē *or* kä′kē) *n.* **1.** A yellowish brown. **2.** A strong, heavy, khaki-colored cloth. **3. khakis a.** Pants made of this cloth. **b.** A uniform made of this cloth. [From Persian *khāk*, dust.] **—khak′i** *adj.*

khan (kän *or* kăn) *n.* **1.** A ruler, official, or important person in India and some countries of central Asia. **2.** A medieval ruler of a Mongol, Tartar, or Turkish tribe.

Khar·toum (kär-**to͞om′**) The capital of Sudan, in the east-central part of the country on the Nile River. It was founded in about 1821 as an Egyptian army camp.

Khmer (kmâr) *n., pl.* **Khmer** or **Khmers 1.** A member of a people of Cambodia. **2.** The official language of Cambodia.

Khru·shchev (**kro͞osh′**chĕf *or* **kro͞osh′**chôf), **Nikita Sergeyevich** 1894–1971. Soviet politician who served as first secretary of the Communist Party (1953–1964) and Soviet premier (1958–1964). He denounced Stalin (1956) and improved his country's image abroad, but he was deposed in 1964.

Khy·ber Pass (**kī′**bər) A narrow mountain pass on the border between eastern Afghanistan and northern Pakistan. It has long been a strategic trade and invasion route. The highest point of the pass is about 3,510 feet (1,070 meters).

kib·ble (**kĭb′**əl) *tr.v.* **kib·bled, kib·bling, kib·bles** To crush or grind (grain, for example) coarsely. ❖ *n.* A meal ground by this process and used in the form of pellets especially for pet food.

kib·butz (kĭ-**bo͝ots′** *or* kĭ-**bo͞ots′**) *n., pl.* **kib·but·zim** (kĭb′-o͝ot-**sēm′** *or* kĭb′o͞ot-**sēm′**) A collective farm or settlement in modern Israel. [From Hebrew *qibbûṣ*, gathering.]

kib·itz (**kĭb′**ĭts) *intr.v.* **kib·itzed, kib·itz·ing, kib·itz·es** *Informal* **1.** To chat; converse. **2.** To look on and offer unwanted advice. **—kib′itz·er** *n.*

kick (kĭk) *v.* **kicked, kick·ing, kicks** *—intr.* **1.** To extend the leg away from the body; strike out with the foot or feet. **2.** In sports, to score, gain ground, or begin play by kicking a ball. **3.** To propel the body in swimming by moving the legs. **4.** To recoil when fired: *The rifle kicked after he pulled the trigger. —tr.* **1.** To strike with the foot: *The mule kicked the stable door.* **2.** To propel or produce by striking with the foot: *a herd of cattle that kicked up swirls of dust.* **3.** To spring back against suddenly: *The rifle kicked her shoulder when she fired it.* **4.** In sports, to score (a goal or point) by kicking a ball. **5.** *Slang* To free oneself of; overcome: *kicking a bad habit.* ❖ *n.* **1.** A blow with the foot: *The cow gave the bucket a kick.* **2a.** The action of kicking a ball, as in a football kickoff or punt. **b.** A kicked ball: *Block that kick!* **c.** The distance covered by a kicked ball. **3.** Any of various moves in dance in which the leg is extended from the body. **4.** The recoil of a cannon or firearm. **5.** *Slang* A feeling of pleasure; a thrill: *They will get a kick out of this greeting card.* ◆ **kick around** *Informal* **1.** To treat badly; abuse. **2.** To move from place to place. **3.** To think about or discuss: *Several new ideas were kicked around at the meeting.* **kick back 1.** To recoil unexpectedly and violently: *The rifle kicked back and bruised my shoulder.* **2.** *Informal* To take it easy; relax: *kicked back at home and watched TV.* **kick in** *Informal* To contribute (one's share) to a common fund: *kick in a few dollars for the office party.* **kick off 1.** *Informal* To begin; start: *kicked off the day with a big breakfast.* **2.** In football, to begin or resume play with a kickoff. **kick out** *Slang* To throw out; dismiss: *was kicked out of the library for repeated talking.* **kick the bucket** *Slang* To die. **kick up** *Informal* To stir up (trouble): *Our cats kick up a fuss until they are fed.* [From Middle English *kiken*, perhaps of Scandinavian origin.] **—kick′er** *n.*

Kick·a·poo (**kĭk′**ə-po͞o′) *n., pl.* **Kickapoo** or **Kick·a·poos 1.** A member of a Native American people formerly living in Wisconsin and Illinois and now living in Kansas, Oklahoma, and Mexico. **2.** The Algonquian language of the Kickapoo.

kick·back (**kĭk′**băk′) *n.* **1.** A sharp reaction or recoil. **2.** *Slang* A part of a payment returned by agreement to the payer, especially in the form of a bribe.

kick·ball (**kĭk′**bôl′) *n.* A game having rules similar to baseball but played with a large ball that is rolled and kicked instead of being pitched and batted.

kick·board (**kĭk′**bôrd′) *n.* A board that floats, held on to by a swimmer so that the legs can move freely in the water while the upper part of the body remains afloat.

kick·off (**kĭk′**ôf′) *n.* **1.** In football, soccer, or rugby, a kick of a stationary ball that begins play. **2.** *Informal* A beginning: *The concert was the kickoff for the orchestra's new season.*

kick·stand (kĭk′stănd′) *n.* A metal bar that can be pushed down to hold a bicycle or motorcycle upright when it is not being ridden.

kid (kĭd) *n.* **1a.** A young goat. **b.** Leather made from the skin of a young goat; kidskin. **2.** *Informal* A child or young person. ❖ *adj.* **1.** Made of kid: *kid gloves.* **2.** *Informal* Younger than oneself: *my kid brother.* ❖ *v.* **kid·ded, kid·ding, kids** —*tr.* **1.** To make fun of; tease: *They kidded me about my mismatched socks.* **2.** To deceive, especially for fun; fool: *Are you kidding me or have you really won the lottery?* —*intr.* To engage in teasing or good-humored fooling. [From Middle English *kide*, from Old Norse *kidh.*] **—kid′der** *n.*

kid·nap (kĭd′năp′) *tr.v.* **kid·napped, kid·nap·ping, kid·naps** or **kid·naped, kid·nap·ing, kid·naps** To abduct or confine (a person) illegally by force or threat of force. **—kid′nap′per, kid′nap′er** *n.*

kid·ney (kĭd′nē) *n., pl.* **kid·neys 1.** Either of a pair of organs that are located in the rear of the abdominal cavity of vertebrate animals. They regulate the amount of water in the body and filter wastes from the blood. **2.** The kidney of certain animals, eaten as food. [From Middle English *kidenere.*]

kidney bean *n.* A type of bean having large, reddish seeds shaped somewhat like a kidney.

kid·skin (kĭd′skĭn′) *n.* Soft leather made from the skin of a young goat.

Ki·ev (kē′ĕf *or* kē′ĕv) The capital of Ukraine, in the north-central part of the country, southwest of Moscow, Russia. It is one of the oldest cities in eastern Europe and was the center of the first Russian state.

Ki·ga·li (kĭ-gä′lē *or* kē-gä′lē) The capital of Rwanda, in the central part of the country north-northeast of Bujumbura, Burundi.

Kil·i·man·ja·ro (kĭl′ə-mən-jär′ō), **Mount** The highest mountain in Africa, in northeast Tanzania near the Kenya border, rising to 19,341 feet (5,895 meters).

kill¹ (kĭl) *v.* **killed, kill·ing, kills** —*tr.* **1.** To cause the death of; deprive of life. **2.** To put an end to; destroy: *The rainy weekend killed our plans for a picnic.* **3.** To cause severe pain to; hurt intensely: *These narrow boots are killing my feet.* **4.** To pass (time) in idle activity: *kill an hour looking at magazines.* **5.** To thwart passage of; veto: *kill a congressional bill.* **6.** To cause to stop working: *kill a motor.* **7.** To delete or remove: *kill several paragraphs of a news story.* **8.** In ice hockey, to prevent a team on a power play from scoring during (a penalty). —*intr.* **1.** To cause death. **2.** To make such a strong impression as to overcome: *always dresses to kill when going to dinner parties.* ❖ *n.* **1.** An act of killing. **2.** An animal that has just been killed, especially in hunting. ◆ **kill off** To destroy totally or on a large scale: *Continued destruction of marshes could kill off several species of fish.* [From Middle English *killen.*]

kill² (kĭl) *n.* A creek. [From Dutch *kil*, from Middle Dutch *kille.*]

kill·deer (kĭl′dîr′) *n., pl.* **killdeer** or **kill·deers** A North American wading bird having two black bands across the breast and a shrill call that sounds like its name.

kill·er (kĭl′ər) *n.* **1.** A person, animal, or thing that kills. **2.** *Slang* Something that is extremely difficult to deal with or withstand: *That test was a killer!* ❖ *adj.* **1.** Causing death and destruction: *a killer tornado.* **2.** *Slang* Having a big or effective impact; formidable: *a killer smile; made killer profits.*

killer whale *n.* An orca.

kill·ing (kĭl′ĭng) *n.* **1.** The act or action of causing death. **2.** A sudden large profit: *make a killing in the stock market.*

kill·joy (kĭl′joi′) *n.* A person who spoils the fun of others.

kiln (kĭln *or* kĭl) *n.* Any of various ovens used for hardening, burning, or drying things such as grain or clay, especially an oven used for firing pottery, porcelain, or brick. [From Old English *cyln*, from Latin *culīna*, kitchen, stove.]

ki·lo (kē′lō) *n., pl.* **ki·los** A kilogram.

kilo– *pref.* A prefix that means: **1.** One thousand (10^3): *kilowatt.* **2.** 1,024 (2^{10}): *kilobyte.*

kil·o·bit (kĭl′ə-bĭt′) *n.* One thousand bits, used as a unit to measure the rate of the transmission of computer data.

kil·o·byte (kĭl′ə-bīt′) *n.* A unit of computer memory equal to 1,024 (2^{10}) bytes.

kil·o·cal·o·rie (kĭl′ə-kăl′ə-rē) *n.* The quantity of heat needed to raise the temperature of one kilogram of water one degree Celsius.

kil·o·cy·cle (kĭl′ə-sī′kəl) *n.* A kilohertz.

kil·o·gram (kĭl′ə-grăm′) *n.* The basic unit of mass or weight in the metric system equal to 1,000 grams (about 2.2 pounds). See table at **measurement.**

kil·o·hertz (kĭl′ə-hûrts′) *n.* A unit of frequency equal to 1,000 cycles per second, used to express the frequency of radio waves.

kil·o·li·ter (kĭl′ə-lē′tər) *n.* A metric unit of volume equal to 1,000 liters.

kil·o·me·ter (kĭ-lŏm′ĭ-tər *or* kĭl′ə-mē′tər) *n.* A unit of length equal to 1,000 meters (0.62 mile). See table at **measurement.**

kil·o·ton (kĭl′ə-tŭn′) *n.* **1.** A unit of weight or capacity equal to 1,000 metric tons. **2.** A unit of explosive force equal to the force with which 1,000 metric tons of TNT explode.

kil·o·watt (kĭl′ə-wŏt′) *n.* A unit of power, especially electric power, equal to 1,000 watts.

kil·o·watt-hour (kĭl′ə-wŏt-our′) *n.* A unit of energy, especially electrical energy, equivalent to one kilowatt acting for a period of one hour.

kilt (kĭlt) *n.* **1.** A knee-length pleated skirt, usually of a tartan wool, worn by men in the Scottish Highlands. **2.** A similar skirt worn by women, girls, and boys.

kil·ter (kĭl′tər) *n.* Good condition; proper form: *programs designed to bring the economy back into kilter.*

kim·chi (kĭm′chē) *n., pl.* **kim·chis** A spicy Korean dish made of salted, fermented vegetables.

ki·mo·no (kə-mō′nō) *n., pl.* **ki·mo·nos** A long loose robe with wide sleeves and a sash, traditionally worn in Japan especially for formal occasions. [From Japanese : *kiru*, to wear + *mono*, object.]

kin (kĭn) *pl.n.* **1.** A person's relatives; family: *visited my aunt and her kin.* **2.** A group of related organisms or species: *whales and their kin.* ❖ *adj.* Related; kindred: *We found out that the Wilsons are kin to us.* [From Old English *cyn.*] —SEE NOTE AT **king.**

ki·na (kē′nə) *n.* The basic monetary unit of Papua New Guinea.

ki·na·ra (kē-när′ə) *n.* A holder for one black, three red, and three green candles, used in celebrating Kwanzaa. [From Swahili, little tower, candelabrum.]

kind¹ (kīnd) *adj.* **kind·er, kind·est 1.** Having a friendly, generous, or warm-hearted nature: *It was kind of you to offer to babysit.* **2.** Showing understanding for others: *kind words.* [From Old English *gecynde*, natural.]

kind² (kīnd) *n.* A particular sort or type: *What kind of toothpaste do you use?* ◆ **in kind 1.** With produce or goods rather than with money: *paying in kind.* **2.** In the same manner or with an equivalent: *return a polite remark in kind.* **kind of** *Informal* Rather; somewhat: *I'm kind of hungry.* [From Old English *gecynd.*]

kin·der·gar·ten (kĭn′dər-gär′tn) *n.* A class for children from four to six years of age that prepares them for elementary school. [From German *Kindergarten* : *Kind*, child + *Garten*, garden.]

kind·heart·ed (kīnd′här′tĭd) *adj.* Kind, sympathetic, or

Mount Kilimanjaro

kimono

kinara

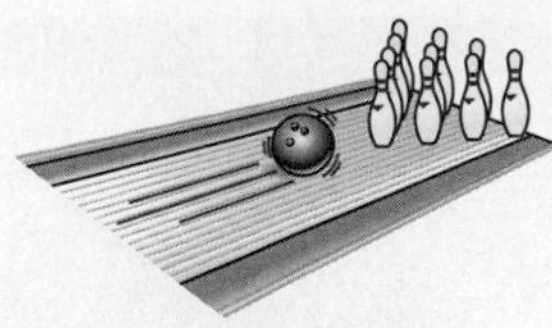

kinetic energy
The bowling ball has kinetic energy because it is moving. When it hits the pins, some of that energy will be passed on to the pins.

WORD HISTORY

king Our Modern English noun **king** comes from the Old English noun *cyning* [**kün′**ing]. The word root *cyn–* is related to the modern word **kin,** as in "kinfolk, relatives." The suffix *–ing* originally meant "son of, descended from." Thus the family names Browning and Whiting mean "son of Brown" and "descendant of White," and *cyning* meant literally "son of the people," which can be understood as "(royal) descendant of the nation."

Martin Luther King, Jr.
photographed in 1960

ă	pat	ôr	core
ā	pay	oi	boy
âr	care	ou	out
ä	father	o͝o	took
ĕ	pet	o͝or	lure
ē	be	o͞o	boot
ĭ	pit	ŭ	cut
ī	bite	ûr	urge
îr	pier	th	thin
ŏ	pot	*th*	this
ō	toe	zh	vision
ô	paw	ə	about

generous. **—kind′heart′ed·ly** *adv.* **—kind′heart′ed·ness** *n.*

kin·dle (kĭn′dl) *v.* **kin·dled, kin·dling, kin·dles** *—tr.* **1.** To build and start (a fire). **2.** To arouse; excite: *The teacher used experiments to kindle our interest in science. —intr.* **1.** To catch fire: *The paper kindled on the third match.* **2.** To become inflamed or stirred up: *Passion kindled in their hearts.* **—kin′dler** *n.*

kin·dling (kĭnd′lĭng) *n.* Sticks and other small pieces of material used to start a fire.

kind·ly (kīnd′lē) *adj.* **kind·li·er, kind·li·est 1.** Considerate and helpful; kind: *a kindly and warm-hearted friend; kindly advice.* **2.** Agreeable; pleasant: *a kindly breeze.* ❖ *adv.* **1.** Out of kindness: *She kindly offered to help.* **2.** In a kind way; cordially; warmly: *greeted them kindly.* **3.** As a matter of courtesy; please: *Kindly read the notice aloud.* **—kind′li·ness** *n.*

kind·ness (kīnd′nĭs) *n.* **1.** The quality or state of being kind; generosity. **2.** A kind act or kind treatment; a favor: *We are grateful for your many kindnesses.*

kin·dred (kĭn′drĭd) *n.* **1.** A group of related people, such as a clan. **2.** *(used with a plural verb)* A person's family or relatives. ❖ *adj.* Having a similar origin or nature: *kindred feelings.*

kin·e·mat·ics (kĭn′ə-**măt′**ĭks) *n.* *(used with a singular verb)* The branch of physics that deals with the characteristics of motion, without reference to mass or the causes of motion.

ki·net·ic (kə-**nĕt′**ĭk *or* kī-**nĕt′**ĭk) *adj.* Relating to or produced by motion. [From Greek *kīnein,* to move.]

kinetic energy *n.* The energy possessed by a body because it is in motion.

ki·net·ics (kə-**nĕt′**ĭks *or* kī-**nĕt′**ĭks) *n.* *(used with a singular verb)* The branch of physics that deals with forces and motion; dynamics.

kin·folk (kĭn′fōk′) also **kins·folk** (kĭnz′fōk′) or **kin·folks** (kĭn′fōks′) *pl.n.* A person's relatives; kindred.

king (kĭng) *n.* **1.** A man who rules a nation, usually inheriting his position for life. **2.** A person who is the most outstanding or important in a particular group or category: *That reporter is king of sportswriters.* **3.** Something that is regarded as the most powerful or important: *In the South, cotton was once king.* **4.** The most important piece in chess, able to move one square in any direction. **5.** In checkers, a piece that has reached the opponent's side of the board and is able to move both backward and forward. **6.** A playing card bearing the figure of a king and ranking next above a queen. **7. Kings** Either of the two biblical books, I Kings or II Kings, that tell the history of the kings of Israel and Judah. [From Old English *cyning.*] —SEE NOTE.

King, Coretta Scott 1927–2006. American civil rights leader noted for her work on behalf of the King Center for Nonviolent Social Change after the assassination of her husband, Martin Luther King, Jr.

King, Martin Luther, Jr. 1929–1968. American cleric whose nonviolent tactics helped form the foundation of the civil rights movement of the 1950s and 1960s. —SEE NOTE.

king·bird (kĭng′bûrd′) *n.* Any of various insect-eating songbirds of the Americas that defend their territories by chasing away other birds.

king·bolt (kĭng′bōlt′) *n.* A vertical bolt that connects the front axle to the body of a wagon or other vehicle and acts as a pivot when the vehicle turns.

king crab *n.* Any of several large crabs found along the coastal waters of Alaska, Japan, and Siberia, valued for their meat.

king·dom (kĭng′dəm) *n.* **1.** A country or other political unit that is ruled by a king or queen. **2.** An area, province, or realm: *the kingdom of the imagination.* **3.** A broad classification into which organisms are grouped, ranking above a phylum and, in some systems, below a domain. One common system of classification divides life into five kingdoms: prokaryotes (bacteria and archaea), protists, fungi, plants, and animals. See table at **taxonomy.**

king·fish·er (kĭng′fĭsh′ər) *n.* Any of various colorful birds that feed on fish and have a long bill and a crest on the head.

King James Bible *n.* An English translation of the Bible from Hebrew and Greek published in 1611 at the direction of James I for the Church of England; the Authorized Version.

king·ly (kĭng′lē) *adj.* **king·li·er, king·li·est** Relating to or fit for a king; regal; royal: *a kingly manner.* ❖ *adv.* As a king; royally. **—king′li·ness** *n.*

king·pin (kĭng′pĭn′) *n.* **1.** A headpin. **2.** The most important person or part in an organization, industry, or system. **3.** A kingbolt.

king·ship (kĭng′shĭp′) *n.* **1.** The position or power of a king. **2.** The area ruled by a king; a kingdom. **3.** The period during which a king rules; a reign.

king-size (kĭng′sīz′) or **king-sized** (kĭng′sīzd′) *adj.* **1.** Larger or longer than the usual or standard size: *king-size muffins.* **2.** Large in intensity: *a king-sized headache.*

king snake *n.* Any of various nonvenomous snakes of the Americas, having a black or brown body with white, yellow, or reddish markings. King snakes are constrictors and eat small animals and other snakes.

King·ston (kĭng′stən) The capital of Jamaica, in the southeast part of the island on the Caribbean Sea. It was founded in about 1692.

Kings·town (kĭngz′toun′) The capital of St. Vincent and the Grenadines, in the West Indies on the southwest coast of St. Vincent Island.

kink (kĭngk) *n.* **1.** A tight curl or twist, as in a hair, wire, or rope. **2.** A painful cramp or stiffness in a muscle, especially of the neck or back; a crick. **3.** A flaw or difficulty, as in a plan: *Technicians finally got the kinks out of the new computer program.* ❖ *intr. & tr.v.* **kinked, kink·ing, kinks** To form or cause to form a kink; curl or twist sharply: *When the hose kinks, water can't flow through it.*

kink·a·jou (kĭng′kə-jo͞o′) *n.* A furry tree-dwelling mammal of tropical America having a long tail that can curl around objects.

kink·y (kĭng′kē) *adj.* **kink·i·er, kink·i·est 1.** Full of kinks; tightly curled or twisted: *kinky wire; kinky hair.* **2.** Having or appealing to unconventional tastes. **—kink′i·ness** *n.*

kins·folk (kĭnz′fōk′) *pl.n.* Variant of **kinfolk.**

Kin·sha·sa (kĭn-**shä′**sə) The capital of the Democratic Republic of the Congo, in the western part of the country on the Congo River. It is named for an early village that occupied the site.

kin·ship (kĭn′shĭp′) *n.* **1.** The condition of being related by blood, marriage, or adoption; family relationship. **2.** A connection or similarity between people or things.

kins·man (kĭnz′mən) *n.* A male relative.

kins·wom·an (kĭnz′wo͝om′ən) *n.* A female relative.

ki·osk (kē′ŏsk′ *or* kē-**ŏsk′**) *n.* **1.** A small structure, usually opened in front, that is used as a newsstand, as a place for selling goods, or as a place to conduct transactions, as at a bank. **2.** A cylindrical structure on which advertisements are posted. [From Turkish *köşk,* gazebo, pavilion.]

Ki·o·wa (kī′ə-wô′ *or* **kī′**ə-wä′ *or* **kī′**ə-wā′) *n., pl.* **Kiowa** or **Ki·o·was 1.** A member of a Native American people of the southern Great Plains. **2.** The language of the Kiowa.

kip (kĭp) *n.* The basic monetary unit of Laos.

Kip·ling (kĭp′lĭng), **(Joseph) Rudyard** 1865–1936. Indian-born British writer whose major works, including

The Jungle Book (1894), are set in British-occupied India.

kip·per (kĭp′ər) *n.* A herring or salmon that has been split, salted, and smoked. ❖ *tr.v.* **kip·pered, kip·per·ing, kip·pers** To prepare (fish) by splitting, salting, and smoking.

Ki·ri·ba·ti (kēr′ə-bä′tē *or* kîr′ə-băs′) An island country of the west-central Pacific Ocean near the equator. Capital, Tarawa.

kirk (kûrk) *n. Scots* A church.

Ki·shi·nev (kĭsh′ə-nĕf′) See **Chişinău.**

kiss (kĭs) *v.* **kissed, kiss·ing, kiss·es** —*tr.* **1.** To touch with the lips as a sign of affection, greeting, or reverence. **2.** To touch lightly or gently: *Rain kissed the flowers.* **3.** To strike lightly; brush against: *I barely kissed her car with my bumper.* —*intr.* To engage in mutual touching or caressing with the lips. ❖ *n.* **1.** A touch with the lips as a token of affection, greeting, or reverence. **2.** A slight or gentle touch. **3.** A small piece of candy, especially of chocolate.

kiss·er (kĭs′ər) *n.* **1.** A person who kisses. **2.** *Slang* The mouth or face.

kit¹ (kĭt) *n.* **1a.** A set of articles or tools for a certain purpose: *a first-aid kit; a sewing kit.* **b.** A bag or other container for carrying such a set. **2.** A set of parts or materials to be assembled: *a model airplane kit.* [From Middle English *kitte*, wooden tub, probably from Middle Dutch.]

kit² (kĭt) *n.* A kitten or one of the young of certain other fur-bearing mammals, such as a fox or rabbit. [From *kitten.*]

kitch·en (kĭch′ən) *n.* A room or area where food is prepared or cooked. [From Old English *cycene*, from Late Latin *coquīna*, from *coquere*, to cook.]

kitch·en·ette (kĭch′ə-nĕt′) *n.* A small kitchen.

kitchen police *n.* **1.** Enlisted military personnel assigned to work in a kitchen. **2.** Military duty helping the cooks in a kitchen.

kite (kīt) *n.* **1.** A light frame, as of wood, covered with paper or similar material and designed to be flown in the wind at the end of a long string. **2.** Any of various graceful birds of prey having long pointed wings and often a forked tail. [From Old English *cȳta*, bird of prey.]

kite·board (kīt′bôrd′) *n.* Any of the boards, usually equipped with bindings for the feet, used in kiteboarding. ❖ *intr.v.* **kiteboard·ed, kiteboard·ing, kite·boards** To engage in kiteboarding. **—kite′board·er** *n.*

kite·board·ing (kīt′bôr′dĭng) *n.* Any of several sports, such as kitesurfing and snowkiting, in which a person, often wearing a harness, is pulled by holding a control bar that is attached to a power kite.

kite·surf·ing (kīt′bôr′dĭng) *n.* **1.** A form of kiteboarding in which a person is pulled by a power kite across water while riding a kiteboard or wakeboard. **2.** A similar sport, such as snowkiting. **—kite′surf′** *v.* **—kite′-surf′er** *n.*

kith and kin (kĭth′ ən kĭn′) *pl.n.* Friends and relatives.

kit·ten (kĭt′n) *n.* A young cat. [From Middle English *kitoun*, probably from Late Latin *cattus*, cat.]

kit·ty¹ (kĭt′ē) *n., pl.* **kit·ties** A collection of money funded by more than one person, such as the players in a card game. [Probably from *kit*, set of articles.]

kit·ty² (kĭt′ē) *n., pl.* **kit·ties** A kitten or cat. [From *kitten.*]

kit·ty-cor·nered (kĭt′ē-kôr′nərd) *adj. & adv.* Variant of **cater-cornered.**

Kitty Hawk A town of northeast North Carolina on a sandy peninsula north of Cape Hatteras. Nearby is the site of the Wright brothers' first two successful flights (December 17, 1903).

ki·wi (kē′wē) *n., pl.* **ki·wis 1.** Any of several flightless birds of New Zealand having a long slender bill, a rounded body, and brownish feathers. **2.** A kiwifruit.

ki·wi·fruit (kē′wē-fro͞ot′) *n.* **1.** A fuzzy brown fruit with sweet green pulp. **2.** The woody vine that bears this fruit, native to China and widely grown in New Zealand.

KKK *abbr.* An abbreviation of Ku Klux Klan.

Klan (klăn) *n.* The Ku Klux Klan.

Kleen·ex (klē′nĕks′) A trademark used for a soft facial tissue.

klep·to·ma·ni·a (klĕp′tə-mā′nē-ə *or* klĕp′tə-mān′-yə) *n.* An uncontrollable urge to steal, especially when there is no personal need or desire for the things stolen. **—klep′to·ma′ni·ac′** (klĕp′tə-mā′nē-ăk′) *n.*

klieg light (klēg) *n.* A powerful lamp used especially when making movies to light a scene. [After John H. *Kliegl* (1869–1959) and Anton Tiberius *Kliegl* (1872–1927), German-born American lighting experts.]

Klon·dike (klŏn′dīk′) A region of Yukon Territory, Canada, just east of Alaska and traversed by the **Klondike River,** about 100 miles (160 kilometers) long. Gold was discovered here in August 1896.

klutz (klŭts) *n. Slang* A clumsy or stupid person.

km *abbr.* An abbreviation of kilometer.

knack (năk) *n.* **1.** A special talent or skill: *The mechanic has a knack for fixing cars.* **2.** A tendency or pattern of behavior: *has a knack for saying the wrong thing.*

knack·wurst or **knock·wurst** (nŏk′wûrst′ *or* nŏk′-wo͝orst′) *n.* A short, thick, highly seasoned sausage.

knap·sack (năp′săk′) *n.* A bag made of sturdy material and having shoulder straps for carrying articles such as camping supplies on the back.

knave (nāv) *n.* **1.** A dishonest crafty man: *The knave got the advantage by trickery.* **2.** A male servant: *a kitchen knave.* **3.** A man of humble birth or position. **4.** A jack in a deck of playing cards. **—knav′ish** *adj.* **—knav′ish·ly** *adv.* —SEE NOTE AT **knit.**

❑ *These sound alike:* **knave, nave** (part of a church).

knav·er·y (nā′və-rē) *n.* Dishonest or crafty dealing.

knead (nēd) *tr.v.* **knead·ed, knead·ing, kneads 1.** To mix and work (a substance) into a pliable mass, as by folding, stretching, and pressing: *The cook kneaded the pizza dough.* **2.** To squeeze, press, or roll with the hands, as in massaging: *The coach kneaded the runner's sore leg muscles.* **3.** To make or shape by or as if by kneading. **—knead′er** *n.*

❑ *These sound alike:* **knead, need** (necessity).

knee (nē) *n.* **1a.** The joint at which the human thigh and lower leg come together. **b.** The region around this joint. **2.** A corresponding joint in the leg of another animal. **3.** Something that resembles a knee, as a point where something bends sharply. **4.** The part of a pair of pants that covers the knee. ❖ *tr.v.* **kneed, knee·ing, knees** To push or strike with the knee: *The waiter kneed the kitchen door open.* —SEE NOTE AT **knit.**

knee breeches *pl.n.* Trousers extending to or just below the knee.

knee·cap (nē′kăp′) *n.* The patella.

knee-deep (nē′dēp′) *adj.* **1.** Reaching as high as the knees: *The prairie grass was knee-deep.* **2.** Submerged to the knees: *The hikers were knee-deep in swampy water.* **3.** Deeply occupied or engaged: *I'm knee-deep in work.*

knee-high (nē′hī′) *adj.* Reaching as high as the knee: *knee-high boots.* ❖ *n.* (nē′hī′) A sock or stocking that extends to just below the knee.

kneel (nēl) *intr.v.* **knelt** (nĕlt) or **kneeled, kneel·ing, kneels** To rest or fall on one or both knees: *The tailor knelt to mark the pants for hemming.* [From Old English *cnēowlian*, from *cnēow*, knee.]

kneel·er (nē′lər) *n.* **1.** A person who kneels, as when praying. **2.** Something, such as a stool, cushion, or board, on which to kneel.

knee·pad (nē′păd′) *n.* A protective covering for the knee.

BIOGRAPHY

Martin Luther King, Jr.

When Martin Luther **King,** Jr., was a young man, discrimination against African Americans was practiced widely and openly throughout the country. In many states, especially in the South, segregation was enforced by law, resulting in separate schools, hospitals, restaurants, parks, and even toilets and drinking fountains for whites and African Americans. King studied to become a Baptist preacher and devoted his life to ending discrimination by using only nonviolent means. The many demonstrations he led included the boycott (1955–1956) of segregated city bus lines in Montgomery, Alabama, and protests in Birmingham (1963) that resulted in clashes with the police. King led more than 200,000 protesters in the 1963 March on Washington, at which he delivered his "I have a dream" speech. He became an international figure and was awarded the Nobel Peace Prize in 1964. In the mid-1960s, King's efforts expanded to address further concerns, such as poverty and the Vietnam War. In April 1968, while in Memphis, Tennessee, supporting a strike, he was shot and killed.

kitesurfing

WORD HISTORY

knit The *k* at the beginning of the word **knit** is one of those mysterious "silent letters" that make no sense and that we just have to memorize when learning to spell. Once upon a time, though, most of these "silent letters" did make sense because they weren't silent. Over 500 years ago, *knit* (and similar words like **knave, knee,** and **knight**) were pronounced with a consonant cluster (kn) at the beginning. As time passed, a (k) sound at the beginning of a word was lost in pronunciation if it was followed by an (n) sound.

WRITERS CHOOSE THEIR WORDS

When the Sillingtons first settled in Clarion County, before there was a state road parallel to the lake, they owned all the land down to the water's edge. The house itself is perched atop a **knoll,** and from the upstairs windows you get a good view of the lake.

—E.L. Konigsburg
The View From Saturday

ă	pat	ôr	core
ā	pay	oi	boy
âr	care	ou	out
ä	father	o͝o	took
ĕ	pet	o͝or	lure
ē	be	o͞o	boot
ĭ	pit	ŭ	cut
ī	bite	ûr	urge
îr	pier	th	thin
ŏ	pot	*th*	this
ō	toe	zh	vision
ô	paw	ə	about

knell (nĕl) *intr.v.* **knelled, knell·ing, knells** To ring slowly and solemnly: *The church bells knelled all day.* ❖ *n.* **1.** The sound of a bell rung slowly and solemnly, as for a funeral. **2.** A signal of disaster, death, or destruction: *Construction of a new highway sounded the knell of the farm.* [From Old English *cnyllan.*]

knelt (nĕlt) *v.* A past tense and a past participle of **kneel.**

Knes·set (knĕs′ĕt′) *n.* The parliament of Israel.

knew (no͞o) *v.* Past tense of **know.**

❑ *These sound alike:* **knew, gnu** (antelope), **new** (not old).

knick·er·bock·ers (nĭk′ər-bŏk′ərz) *pl.n.* Loose pants that are gathered in a band just below the knees.

knick·ers (nĭk′ərz) *pl.n.* **1.** Long bloomers formerly worn as underwear by women and girls. **2.** Loose pants that are gathered in with a band just below the knees.

knick·knack also **nick·nack** (nĭk′năk′) *n.* A small ornamental article; a trinket.

knife (nīf) *n., pl.* **knives** (nīvz) **1.** A tool made of a sharp blade with a handle, used for cutting, carving, or spreading. **2.** A cutting edge or blade of a tool or machine. ❖ *v.* **knifed, knif·ing, knifes** —*tr.* **1.** To stab with a knife. **2.** *Informal* To betray by underhand means. —*intr.* To cut or slash a way through something: *The shark's fin knifed through the water.* [From Old English *cnīf,* from Old Norse *knīfr.*]

knight (nīt) *n.* **1.** In the Middle Ages, a man who served a king or lord as a mounted soldier in return for the right to hold and profit from land, especially such a man raised to an order of chivalry after training as a page and squire. **2.** A man given a rank of honor by a sovereign for personal merit or service to the country. **3.** A chess piece shaped like the head of a horse that can be moved two squares horizontally and one vertically or two squares vertically and one horizontally. ❖ *tr.v.* **knight·ed, knight·ing, knights** To make (a person) a knight. [From Old English *cniht.*] **—knight′ly** *adj. & adv.* —SEE NOTE AT **knit.**

❑ *These sound alike:* **knight, night** (darkness).

knight-errant (nīt′ĕr′ənt) *n., pl.* **knights-errant** In medieval times, a knight who traveled in search of adventure.

knight·hood (nīt′ho͝od′) *n.* **1.** The rank or dignity of a knight. **2.** The behavior or qualities suitable for a knight; chivalry. **3.** Knights considered as a group.

knish (kə-**nĭsh′**) *n.* A piece of dough stuffed with potato, meat, or cheese and baked or fried.

knit (nĭt) *v.* **knit** or **knit·ted, knit·ting, knits** —*tr.* **1.** To make (a fabric or garment) by forming yarn or thread into interlocked loops either by hand with special needles or by machine: *I knit a sweater.* **2.** To join closely; unite securely: *Shared interests knitted the group together.* **3.** To draw together in wrinkles; furrow: *knit one's brows in thought.* —*intr.* **1.** To make a fabric or garment by knitting: *I would like to learn to knit.* **2.** To grow together or become joined, as a fractured bone. **3.** To come together in wrinkles or furrows, as the brows. ❖ *n.* A fabric or garment made by knitting: *a cotton knit.* [From Old English *cnyttan,* to knot.] **—knit′ter** *n.* —SEE NOTE.

❑ *These sound alike:* **knit, nit** (louse egg).

knit·ting (nĭt′ĭng) *n.* **1.** The act or process of making knitted fabric or garments: *Knitting is a useful skill.* **2.** Fabric or a garment that has been knitted or is being knitted: *I brought along my knitting.*

knitting needle *n.* A long, thin, pointed rod used in pairs or sets to knit yarn into cloth.

knit·wear (nĭt′wâr′) *n.* Knitted garments.

knives (nīvz) *n.* Plural of **knife.**

knob (nŏb) *n.* **1.** A rounded lump or mass: *a brass knob on top of a bedpost.* **2.** A rounded handle or dial: *the knob that controls the stereo's volume.* [From Middle English *knobe.*] **—knob′by** *adj.*

knock (nŏk) *v.* **knocked, knock·ing, knocks** —*tr.* **1.** To strike with a hard blow or hit: *knocked the ball out of the park.* **2.** To affect in a specified way by striking hard: *I accidentally knocked the glass of water over.* **3.** To cause to strike: *I knocked my head on the low doorway.* **4.** To produce by hitting or striking: *knocked a hole in the wall.* **5.** *Slang* To criticize; find fault with: *The critic knocked the actor's performance.* —*intr.* **1.** To strike a blow or series of blows causing a noise: *The neighbor knocked on our door.* **2.** To collide with something: *In the dark, I knocked into the table.* **3.** To make a pounding or clanking noise: *The old car's engine knocks whenever we drive up a hill.* ❖ *n.* **1.** A sharp blow or hit: *The doctor gave me a knock on the knee.* **2.** The sound of a blow on a hard surface; a rap. **3.** A pounding or clanking noise, as of an engine in need of repairs. ◆ **knock down** To break up or take apart: *We knocked down the tent and packed it in the car.* **knock off** *Informal* **1.** To cease; stop: *knock off work; knock off piano practice.* **2.** To complete, accomplish, or dispose of hastily or easily; finish: *I knocked off several letters this afternoon.* **3.** To eliminate; deduct: *Using the coupon knocked five dollars off our bill.* **knock out 1.** To make unconscious, as by a blow with the fist. **2.** To make useless or prevent from working: *The storm knocked out power in our neighborhood.* **3.** *Informal* To exhaust completely: *That long math exam really knocked me out.* [From Old English *cnocian.*]

knock·a·bout (nŏk′ə-bout′) *adj.* **1.** Rough and boisterous. **2.** Suitable for rough use. ❖ *n.* A small sailing boat with a mainsail and a jib.

knock·down (nŏk′doun′) *n.* The act or an instance of knocking down. ❖ *adj.* **1.** Powerful and overwhelming: *a knockdown punch.* **2.** Designed to be put together and taken apart quickly and easily: *knockdown furniture.*

knock·er (nŏk′ər) *n.* A metal ring, knob, or hammer hinged to a door for use in knocking.

knock-knee (nŏk′nē′) *n.* A deformity of the legs in which the knees are abnormally close together and the ankles are spread apart. **—knock′-kneed′** *adj.*

knock·out (nŏk′out′) *n.* **1.** A victory in boxing in which the loser is unable to rise from the canvas within a specified period of time. **2.** A blow that renders a person unconscious or gains such a victory. **3.** *Slang* A strikingly attractive person or thing.

knock·wurst (nŏk′wûrst′ *or* nŏk′wo͝orst′) *n.* Variant of **knackwurst.**

knoll (nōl) *n.* A small rounded hill. [From Old English *cnoll.*]

knot (nŏt) *n.* **1.** A tangle of interlacing thread, cord, hair, or similar material. **2.** A fastening made by tying material such as string, rope, or cord in a certain way: *a square knot.* **3.** A decorative bow of ribbon, fabric, or braid. **4.** A tight cluster of people or things: *a knot of spectators at the theater's entrance.* **5.** A difficult problem. **6.** A feeling of tightness in the body: *a knot in my stomach.* **7a.** A round swelling on a tree trunk where a branch grows out. **b.** The hard dark spot in a board where such a branch grew. **8.** A unit of speed equal to one nautical mile per hour, about 1.15 statute miles (1.85 kilometers) per hour, used especially by ships and aircraft. ❖ *tr.v.* **knot·ted, knot·ting, knots 1.** To tie or fasten in or with a knot: *We knotted the rope around the post.* **2.** To entangle in knots: *My hair got knotted by the wind.* [From Old English *cnotta.*]

❑ *These sound alike:* **knot, not** (in no way).

knot·hole (nŏt′hōl′) *n.* A hole in a piece of lumber where a knot has dropped out or been removed.

knot·ty (nŏt′ē) *adj.* **knot·ti·er, knot·ti·est 1.** Tied or snarled in knots: *knotty string.* **2.** Having many knots or knobs: *knotty lumber.* **3.** Difficult to understand or solve: *a knotty algebra problem.*

know (nō) *v.* **knew** (no͞o), **known** (nōn), **know·ing,**

knows —*tr.* **1.** To believe correctly and with good reason: *He knows that two plus two equals four.* **2.** To have a correct idea about: *She knows the answer to the question.* **3.** To regard as true; be sure of: *I know that the play will be a success.* **4.** To have skill in or a practical grasp of: *I know how to make lasagna.* **5.** To be acquainted or familiar with: *I know my neighbors well.* **6.** To recognize: *I know the tune, but I can't remember the words.* **7.** To have fixed in the memory: *The actors must know their lines well.* **8.** To be able to distinguish: *Does that little child know right from left?* —*intr.* **1.** To possess knowledge or understanding: *My sister knows about the history of photography.* **2.** To be aware: *I knew about their plans for the weekend.* ◆ **in the know** *Informal* In possession of special or secret information: *My job at the town hall put me in the know about local politics.* —**know′a·ble** *adj.* —**know′er** *n.*

❑ *These sound alike:* **know, no**[1] (not so), **no**[2] (not any), **No**[1] (Japanese drama).

know-how (nō′hou′) *n.* Practical knowledge; skill: *Building a house requires lots of know-how.*

know·ing (nō′ĭng) *adj.* **1.** Having knowledge or awareness: *a knowing hiker, wise in the ways of the woods.* **2.** Showing shrewdness or resourcefulness. **3.** Suggestive of inside or secret information: *a knowing glance.* —**know′ing·ly** *adv.*

know-it-all (nō′ĭt-ôl′) *n. Informal* A person who claims or pretends to know everything.

knowl·edge (nŏl′ĭj) *n.* **1.** Awareness or understanding gained through experience or study: *He has a thorough knowledge of carpentry.* **2.** The fact or state of knowing: *Knowledge of the company's bad sales record made investors cautious.*

SYNONYMS knowledge, information, learning These nouns refer to what is known, as through study or experience. **Knowledge,** the broadest term, includes facts and ideas, understanding, and the totality of what is known: *My teacher has a good, general knowledge of many different subjects.* **Information** often suggests a collection of facts and data: *I can't make a decision until I have all the information on the case.* **Learning** usually means knowledge that is gained by schooling and study: *His learning is amazing considering how young he is.*

---

knowl·edge·a·ble (nŏl′ĭ-jə-bəl) *adj.* Having or showing knowledge or intelligence; well informed: *a candidate who is knowledgeable about foreign policy.*

known (nōn) *v.* Past participle of **know.** ❖ *adj.* Proved or generally recognized: *a singer of known talent.*

Knox (nŏks), **Henry** 1750–1806. American Revolutionary soldier who helped George Washington force the British to evacuate Boston (1776).

Knox, John 1514?–1572. Scottish religious reformer and founder of Scottish Presbyterianism. He helped Protestantism become the established religion in Scotland.

knuck·le (nŭk′əl) *n.* **1.** A joint of a finger, especially one of the joints connecting a finger to the hand. **2.** The rounded mass formed by the bones in a joint of the finger: *I scraped my knuckles on the sidewalk.* **3.** A cut of meat from a leg joint: *pig's knuckles.* ❖ *tr.v.* **knuck·led, knuck·ling, knuck·les** To rub, press, or hit with the knuckles. ◆ **knuckle down** To apply oneself earnestly to a task: *We knuckled down and studied for the test.* **knuckle under** To yield to pressure; give in: *I knuckled under and agreed to go to the store.* [From Middle English *knokel.*]

knuckle ball *n.* In baseball, a slow pitch that has no spin and veers erratically, thrown by gripping the ball with the nails or knuckles near the tips of the index and middle fingers, and often the third finger.

KO (kā′ō′) *Slang tr.v.* **KO'd, KO'ing, KO's** To knock out, as in boxing. ❖ *n.* (kā-ō′ *or* kā′ō′) A knockout, as in boxing.

ko·a·la (kō ä′lə) *n.* An Australian marsupial that has dense grayish fur, large ears, and sharp claws. Koalas live in eucalyptus trees and feed chiefly on their leaves. The female koala carries her young in a pouch. [From Dharuk (Aboriginal language of southeast Australia) *gula, gulawan*ʸ.]

Koch (kôk *or* kôkн), **Robert** 1843–1910. German bacteriologist who demonstrated that specific diseases are caused by specific microorganisms. He identified the bacterial causes of anthrax, tuberculosis, and cholera.

kohl·ra·bi (kōl-rä′bē *or* kōl-răb′ē) *n., pl.* **kohl·ra·bies** A plant related to the cabbage, having a thick rounded stem that resembles a turnip and is eaten as a vegetable.

ko·la (kō′lə) *n.* Variant of **cola**[2].

Kol·ka·ta (kōl-kä′tə) A city of eastern India in the delta of the Ganges River. Formerly known as Calcutta, it was founded around 1690.

Ko·mo·do dragon (kə-mō′dō) *n.* A large monitor lizard of Indonesia measuring up to 10 feet (3 meters) long.

kook (ko͞ok) *n. Informal* A crazy or eccentric person. [Possibly from *cuckoo.*]

kook·a·bur·ra (ko͝ok′ə-bûr′ə) *n.* A large kingfisher of southern and eastern Australia, having a call that sounds like wild laughter.

kook·y (ko͞o′kē) *adj.* **kook·i·er, kook·i·est** *Slang* Strange or crazy: *a kooky idea.* —**kook′i·ness** *n.*

ko·pek (kō′pĕk) *n.* A Russian coin equal to 1⁄100 of a ruble.

Ko·ran or **Qur·'an** (kə-răn′ *or* kə-rän′) *n.* The sacred book of Islam, believed by Muslims to contain the word of Allah as revealed to the prophet Muhammad. [From Arabic *(al-)qur'ān,* (the) reading, recitation, Koran, from *qara'a,* to recite.]

Ko·re·a (kə-rē′ə) A peninsula and former country of eastern Asia between the Yellow Sea and the Sea of Japan. It is the site of an ancient civilization dating to the 12th century BC. The peninsula is now divided between North Korea and South Korea.

Ko·re·an (kə-rē′ən) *adj.* Relating to Korea or its people, language, or culture. ❖ *n.* **1.** A native or inhabitant of Korea. **2.** The language of the Koreans.

Korean War *n.* A war fought between North Korea, aided by China, and South Korea, aided by United Nations forces consisting mainly of US troops, lasting from 1950 to 1953.

ko·ru·na (kôr′ə-nä′) *n.* The basic monetary unit of the Czech Republic. [From Czech, ultimately from Latin *corōna,* crown (stamped on the coin).]

Kos·ci·uśz·ko (kôsh-cho͝osh′kō) or **Kos·ci·us·ko** (kŏs′-ē-ŭs′kō *or* kŏs′kē-ŭs′kō), **Thaddeus** 1746–1817. Polish general who aided American forces in the Revolutionary War and was a leader in Poland's struggle for independence from Russia.

ko·sher (kō′shər) *adj.* **1.** Conforming to or prepared in accordance with Jewish dietary laws. **2.** *Slang* Proper; correct: *Is it kosher to wear jeans in the office?* ❖ *tr.v.* **ko·shered, ko·sher·ing, ko·shers** To make proper or ritually pure. ◆ **keep kosher** To observe Jewish dietary laws. [From Hebrew *kāšēr,* proper.]

Ko·so·vo (kô′sə-vō′ *or* kō′sə-vō′) A republic of the western Balkan Peninsula. Formerly part of Serbia, Kosovo declared independence in 2008, but its sovereignty was not universally recognized at that time. Priština is the capital.

ko·to (kō′tō) *n., pl.* **ko·tos** A Japanese musical instrument having usually 13 silk strings stretched over a long, hollow, wooden body and played by plucking.

kow·tow (kou-tou′ *or* kou′tou′) *intr.v.* **kow·towed, kow·tow·ing, kow·tows 1.** To kneel and touch the forehead to the ground in expression of deep respect, worship, or submission. **2.** To show exaggerated respect

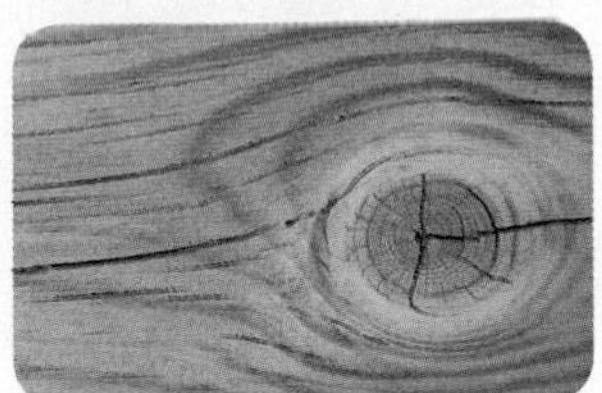

knot
knot in a board

koala

kookaburra

Krishna
Krishna (*right*) with the goddess Radha (*left*)

USAGE

kudos The word **kudos** looks like a plural noun, but historically it is a singular noun: *Kudos is* (not *are*) *due her for her fine work.* Nowadays, *kudos* is often treated as a plural: *She received many kudos for her work.* Because of this plural use, a singular form *kudo,* meaning "a compliment," has arisen. This change follows the pattern whereby the words *pea* and *cherry* were shortened from nouns ending with an (s) sound (English *pease* and French *cerise*) that were mistakenly thought to be plural. The singular *kudo* is usually viewed as incorrect in formal contexts.

kurta

ă	pat	ôr	core
ā	pay	oi	boy
âr	care	ou	out
ä	father	o͝o	took
ĕ	pet	o͝or	lure
ē	be	o͞o	boot
ĭ	pit	ŭ	cut
ī	bite	ûr	urge
îr	pier	th	thin
ŏ	pot	*th*	this
ō	toe	zh	vision
ô	paw	ə	about

or obedience; fawn: *kowtowed to the boss hoping to win favor.* ❖ *n.* The act of kneeling and touching the forehead to the ground. [From Mandarin *kòu tóu,* a kowtow : *kòu,* to knock + *tóu,* head.]

KP *n.* **1.** The assignment of working in a kitchen for one of the armed services. **2.** The soldiers or other military personnel who have such an assignement. [From *k(itchen) p(olice).*]

kph *abbr.* An abbreviation of kilometers per hour.

Kr The symbol for the element **krypton.**

kraal (krôl *or* kräl) *n.* **1.** A village of southern Africa, usually surrounded by a fence or stockade. **2.** A pen for sheep or cattle in southern Africa.

Kra·ków (**krăk′**ou *or* **krä′**kou) A city of southern Poland south-southeast of Warsaw. It was the national capital from the 1100s until 1595.

Krem·lin (**krĕm′**lĭn) *n.* **1.** The citadel of Moscow, housing the major offices of the government. **2.** The government of Russia and formerly of the Soviet Union.

krill (krĭl) *n., pl.* **krill** Small shrimplike crustaceans that are the principal food of certain whales and are also eaten by seals, fishes, and other sea animals. [From Norwegian *kril,* young fish.]

Krish·na (**krĭsh′**nə) *n.* A Hindu god worshipped as an incarnation of the god Vishnu. [From Sanskrit *Kṛṣṇaḥ,* from *kṛṣṇa-,* black.]

Kriss Krin·gle (**krĭs′ krĭng′**gəl) *n.* Santa Claus. [Alteration of German *Christkindl,* Christ child, Christmas gift.]

kro·na[1] (**krō′**nə) *n., pl.* **kro·nur** (**krō′**nər) The basic monetary unit of Iceland. [From Icelandic *króna,* ultimately from Latin *corōna,* crown (stamped on the coin).]

kro·na[2] (**krō′**nə) *n., pl.* **kro·nor** (**krō′**nôr′ *or* **krō′**nər) The basic monetary unit of Sweden. [From Swedish.]

kro·ne (**krō′**nə) *n., pl.* **kro·ner** (**krō′**nər) The basic monetary unit of Norway and Denmark. [From Norwegian and Danish.]

kryp·ton (**krĭp′**tŏn′) *n. Symbol* **Kr** A colorless, chemically inert gaseous element used chiefly in fluorescent lamps and photographic flash lamps. Atomic number 36. See **Periodic Table.** [From Greek *kruptos,* hidden (so called because of its rarity).]

KS *abbr.* An abbreviation of Kansas.

Kua·la Lum·pur (**kwä′**lə lo͝om-**po͝or′**) The capital of Malaysia, on the southwest Malay Peninsula northwest of Singapore. It was founded by tin miners in 1857.

Ku·blai Khan (ko͞o′blī **kän′**) also **Ku·bla Khan** (ko͞o′blə **kän′**) 1215–1294. Mongol emperor (1260–1294) and founder of the Mongol dynasty in China. A grandson of Genghis Khan, he established a great capital, now Beijing.

ku·dos (**ko͞o′**dōz′ *or* **ko͞o′**dōs′ *or* **ko͞o′**dŏs′) *n.* Praise, fame, or renown for exceptional achievement: *The diplomat received kudos for settling the dispute.* [From Greek *kūdos,* magical glory.] —SEE NOTE.

ku·du (**ko͞o′**do͞o) *n.* Either of two large African antelopes having a brownish or grayish coat with white vertical stripes. The male has long horns twisted in a spiral.

kud·zu (**kŭd′**zo͞o) *n.* An East Asian vine that has clusters of purple flowers and is a common weed in the southeast United States. [From Japanese *kuzu.*]

ku·fi (**ko͞o′**fē) *n., pl.* **ku·fis 1.** Any of various styles of brimless hats and caps traditionally worn by Muslim men, especially a crocheted or knit skullcap. **2.** A brimless cylindrical hat traditionally worn by West African men. [From Arabic *kūfiya,* keffiyeh.]

ku·gel (**ko͞o′**gəl) *n.* A baked pudding of noodles or potatoes, eggs, and seasonings, traditionally eaten by Jews on the Sabbath.

Kui·per belt (**kī′**pər) *n.* A disk-shaped region in the outer solar system, lying beyond the orbit of Neptune and containing thousands of small, icy celestial objects. Some of these objects enter the inner solar system as comets. [After Gerard *Kuiper* (1905–1973), Dutch-born American astronomer.]

Kuiper belt object *n.* Any of the small icy bodies orbiting the sun in the Kuiper belt, generally having a diameter less than Pluto's. Pluto is a Kuiper belt object. [After Gerard *Kuiper* (1905–1973), Dutch-born American astronomer.]

Ku Klux Klan (ko͞o′ klŭks **klăn′**) *n.* **1.** A secret society founded in the southern United States after the Civil War to restore the domination of whites over blacks through the use of terrorism. **2.** A secret organization founded in Georgia in 1915 for a similar purpose and modeled on the earlier society.

kum·quat (**kŭm′**kwŏt′) *n.* **1.** A small thin-skinned fruit somewhat like an orange but having sweet edible skin and sour pulp. **2.** Any of several trees or shrubs that bear such fruit. [From Cantonese *gam gwat,* gold orange.]

ku·na (**ko͞o′**nə) *n.* The basic monetary unit of Croatia.

kung fu (**kŭng′ fo͞o′**) *n.* Any of various Chinese martial arts using sharp blows and kicks. [From Mandarin *gōngfu,* skill, art, labor.]

Kurd (kûrd *or* ko͝ord) *n.* A member of a group of peoples speaking Iranian languages and living primarily in an extensive plateau region of southeast Turkey, northeast Iraq, and northwest Iran.

Kurd·ish (**kûr′**dĭsh *or* **ko͝or′**dĭsh) *adj.* Relating to the Kurds or their language or culture. ❖ *n.* The language of the Kurds.

kur·ta (**kûr′**tə) *n.* A loose long-sleeved shirt, often extending to the knees, worn primarily in South Asia. [From Hindi and Urdu *kurtā,* from Persian *kurta.*]

Ku·wait (ko͞o-**wāt′**) **1.** A country of the northeast Arabian Peninsula at the northwest end of the Persian Gulf. The city of Kuwait is its capital. **2.** The capital of Kuwait, in the east-central part of the country on the Persian Gulf.

kW *abbr.* An abbreviation of kilowatt.

kwa·cha (**kwä′**chə) *n.* The basic monetary unit of Malawi and Zambia.

Kwan (kwän), **Michelle** Born 1980. American figure skater who won the world championships five times and the US championships nine times between 1996 and 2006.

kwan·za (**kwän′**zə) *n.* The basic monetary unit of Angola.

Kwan·zaa also **Kwan·za** (**kwän′**zə) *n.* An African-American cultural festival, celebrated from December 26 to January 1.

kwa·shi·or·kor (kwä′shē-**ôr′**kôr′) *n.* A severe form of malnutrition, usually of children, caused by a lack of protein in the diet and characterized by protrusion of the abdomen and discoloration of the skin and hair.

kWh or **kW-hr** *abbr.* An abbreviation of kilowatt-hour.

KY *abbr.* An abbreviation of Kentucky.

kyat (chät) *n.* The basic monetary unit of Myanmar (Burma).

Kyo·to (kē-**ō′**tō *or* **kyō′**tō) A city of west-central Honshu, Japan, north-northeast of Osaka. Founded in the eighth century, Kyoto was Japan's capital from 794 until 1868.

Kyr·gyz or **Kir·ghiz** (kîr-**gēz′**) *adj.* Relating to Kyrgyzstan or its people, language, or culture. ❖ *n., pl.* **Kyrgyz** or **Kyr·gyz·es** or **Kirghiz** or **Kir·ghiz·es 1.** A native or inhabitant of Kyrgyzstan. **2.** The language of the Kyrgyz.

Kyr·gyz·stan (**kîr′**gē-stän′) A country of Central Asia bordering on southeast Kazakhstan and northwest China. It was part of the USSR from 1922 until 1991. Bishkek is the capital.

Kyu·shu (kē-**o͞o′**sho͞o *or* **kyo͞o′**sho͞o) The southernmost of the major islands of Japan, southwest of Honshu.

l[1] or **L** (ĕl) *n., pl.* **l's** or **L's** also **ls** or **Ls** The 12th letter of the English alphabet. —SEE NOTE.
l[2] *abbr.* An abbreviation of: **1.** length. **2.** liter.
L[1] also **l** The symbol for the Roman numeral 50.
L[2] *abbr.* An abbreviation of: **1.** large. **2.** left. **3.** low.
L. *abbr.* An abbreviation of: **1.** lake. **2.** Latin.
la (lä) *n.* In music, the sixth tone of a major scale.
La The symbol for the element **lanthanum.**
LA *abbr.* An abbreviation of: **1.** Los Angeles. **2.** Louisiana.
lab (lăb) *n.* A laboratory.
Lab or **lab** (lăb) *n.* A Labrador retriever.
la·bel (lā′bəl) *n.* **1.** An item, such as a small piece of paper or cloth attached to an article, that is used to identify a thing or person, or to provide other appropriate information: *the label on a can of peaches; the address label on a package.* **2.** A descriptive word or phrase: *the political labels* liberal *and* conservative. ❖ *tr.v.* **la·beled, la·bel·ing, la·bels** or **la·belled, la·bel·ling, la·bels 1.** To attach a label to: *label a package for mailing.* **2.** To identify or designate with a label; describe or classify: *The government labeled the writers dissidents.*
la·bi·al (lā′bē-əl) *adj.* **1.** Relating to the lips. **2.** Formed by closing or partly closing the lips, as the sounds *b, m,* or *w.* ❖ *n.* A labial consonant. [From Latin *labium,* lip.]
la·bor (lā′bər) *n.* **1.** Physical or mental effort; work: *the labor involved in climbing a hill.* **2.** A specific task or piece of work: *the twelve labors of Hercules.* **3.** Work for wages. **4a.** Workers considered as a group: *negotiations between labor and management.* **b.** Labor unions considered as a group. **5.** The process and effort of childbirth. ❖ *intr.v.* **la·bored, la·bor·ing, la·bors 1.** To work; toil: *Many workers labored in the fields picking lettuce.* **2.** To move slowly and with difficulty; struggle: *The long freight train labored over the mountain pass.* **3.** To suffer from a burden or disadvantage: *They are laboring under the misconception that others will cooperate.* [From Middle English *labour,* from Latin *labor.*] **—la′bor·er** *n.*
lab·o·ra·to·ry (lăb′rə-tôr′ē) *n., pl.* **lab·o·ra·to·ries 1.** A room or building equipped for scientific research or experiments. **2.** A place where medical drugs or chemicals are manufactured.
Labor Day *n.* The first Monday in September, celebrated as a holiday in honor of working people.
la·bored (lā′bərd) *adj.* Showing obvious effort; forced; strained: *labored breathing.*
la·bor-in·ten·sive (lā′bər-ĭn-tĕn′sĭv) *adj.* Requiring a large amount of labor or work, especially in comparison to the amount of money or materials that are needed: *An archaeological dig is a labor-intensive undertaking.*
la·bo·ri·ous (lə-bôr′ē-əs) *adj.* **1.** Demanding great effort; difficult: *a laborious task.* **2.** Hard-working; industrious: *Restoring artworks requires skilled and laborious workers.* **—la·bo′ri·ous·ly** *adv.* **—la·bo′ri·ous·ness** *n.*
la·bor·sav·ing (lā′bər-sā′vĭng) *adj.* Designed to save or reduce human labor: *A dishwasher is a laborsaving device.*
labor union *n.* An organization of workers formed to protect and further their mutual interests by bargaining as a group with their employers over wages, working conditions, and benefits.
la·bour (lā′bər) *n. & v. Chiefly British* Variant of **labor.**
Lab·ra·dor (lăb′rə-dôr′) The part of the province of Newfoundland and Labrador, Canada, that lies on the North American mainland, east of Quebec on the northeast portion of the **Labrador Peninsula.**
Labrador retriever *n.* A dog of a breed developed in Canada, having a short yellow, black, or brown coat and often used to retrieve game.
la·bur·num (lə-bûr′nəm) *n.* Any of several poisonous trees or shrubs that are planted for their drooping clusters of yellow flowers.
lab·y·rinth (lăb′ə-rĭnth′) *n.* **1.** A complex structure of connected passages through which it is difficult to find one's way; a maze. **2. Labyrinth** In Greek mythology, the maze built by Daedalus in Crete to confine the Minotaur. **3.** Something complicated or confusing in design or construction. **4.** The system of tubes and spaces that make up the inner ear of many vertebrate animals. [From Middle English *laberinthe,* from Greek *laburinthos.*]
lab·y·rin·thine (lăb′ə-rĭn′thĭn *or* lăb′ə-rĭn′thēn′) *adj.* Relating to or resembling a labyrinth.
lac (lăk) *n.* A resinous substance secreted by a tropical Asian scale insect and used in making shellac.
❑ *These sound alike:* **lac, lack** (deficiency).
lace (lās) *n.* **1.** A delicate fabric of fine threads woven in an open weblike pattern with fancy designs. **2.** A cord or string drawn through eyelets or around hooks to pull and tie opposite edges together, as of a shoe. ❖ *tr.v.* **laced, lac·ing, lac·es 1.** To draw together and tie the laces of: *laced her skates tightly before the game.* **2.** To weave in and out; interlace: *laced his fingers together; lace a vine onto a trellis.* **3.** To add a substance, especially alcohol or a poison, to: *laced the punch with rum.* [From Middle English *las,* from Latin *laqueus,* noose.]
lac·er·ate (lăs′ə-rāt′) *tr.v.* **lac·er·at·ed, lac·er·at·ing, lac·er·ates** To rip or tear, especially in an injury: *He fell off the bicycle and lacerated his arm.*
lac·er·a·tion (lăs′ə-rā′shən) *n.* A jagged wound or cut.
lace·wing (lās′wĭng′) *n.* Any of various insects that have two pairs of delicate wings and long antennae. Lacewing larvae feed on aphids and other garden pests.
lack (lăk) *n.* **1.** Shortage or absence: *Lack of water leads to dehydration.* **2.** A particular shortage or absence: *The lack of instructions made it hard to assemble the bookcase.* ❖ *v.* **lacked, lack·ing, lacks** *—tr.* To be without: *Some streets lack trees altogether. —intr.* To be wanting or deficient: *A diet of nothing but rice is lacking in protein.* [From Middle English *lak.*]
❑ *These sound alike:* **lack, lac** (resinous substance).

WORD HISTORY

l[1] Have you ever noticed that we pronounce the l in *hold* and *help,* but not in *half* and *talk*? Where did the *l* go? Over a period of about 200 years, from about 1500 to 1700, the sound represented by the letter *l* disappeared in the pronunciation of many words such as *should, would, calf, half, talk, walk, balm, calm,* and *palm.* But it didn't disappear completely because of people's awareness of spelling. That's why you may occasionally hear this silent *l* pronounced in certain words such as *almond, alms, balm, calm,* and *palm.*

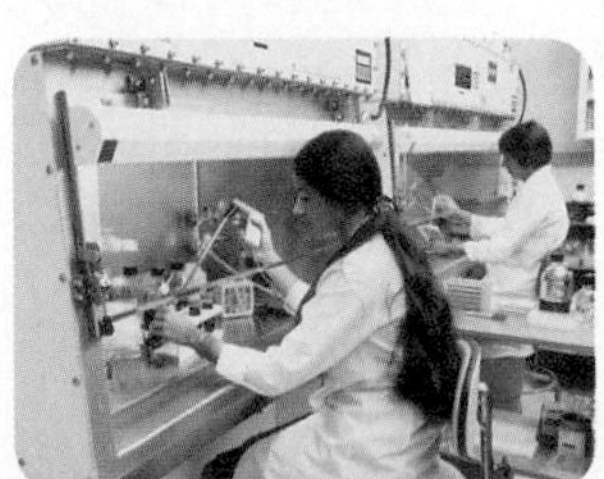

laboratory

lacrosse

lady's slipper

ă	pat	ôr	core
ā	pay	oi	boy
âr	care	ou	out
ä	father	ŏŏ	took
ĕ	pet	ŏŏr	lure
ē	be	ōō	boot
ĭ	pit	ŭ	cut
ī	bite	ûr	urge
îr	pier	th	thin
ŏ	pot	*th*	this
ō	toe	zh	vision
ô	paw	ə	about

lack·a·dai·si·cal (lăk′ə-**dā′**zĭ-kəl) *adj.* Lacking spirit or interest; listless. **—lack′a·dai′si·cal·ly** *adv.*

lack·ey (**lăk′**ē) *n., pl.* **lack·eys 1.** A male servant in uniform; a footman. **2.** A follower who behaves like a servant; a flunky.

lack·lus·ter (**lăk′**lŭs′tər) *adj.* Lacking in excellence or distinction; mediocre; dull: *a lackluster performance in the 100-yard dash.*

la·con·ic (lə-**kŏn′**ĭk) *adj.* Using few words; terse; concise: *a laconic reply.* **—la·con′i·cal·ly** *adv.*

lac·quer (**lăk′**ər) *n.* Any of various materials similar to varnish that are applied to a surface and leave a glossy finish when dry. ❖ *tr.v.* **lac·quered, lac·quer·ing, lac·quers** To coat with lacquer.

lac·ri·mal (**lăk′**rə-məl) *adj.* Relating to or producing tears: *the lacrimal glands.*

la·crosse (lə-**krôs′**) *n.* A game played on a field by two teams of ten players each, in which players use a long stick with a webbed pouch on one end to carry and pass a ball, the object being to propel the ball into the opposing team's goal. [From French *(jeu de) la crosse,* (game of) the hooked stick.]

lac·tase (**lăk′**tās′) *n.* An enzyme that breaks lactose down into simpler sugars. It is found in some yeasts and in the digestive juices of young mammals and many adult humans.

lac·tate (**lăk′**tāt′) *intr.v.* **lac·tat·ed, lac·tat·ing, lac·tates** To secrete milk.

lac·ta·tion (lăk-**tā′**shən) *n.* **1.** The production and secretion of milk by the mammary glands. **2.** The period during which the mammary glands secrete milk: *vitamins needed during lactation.*

lac·tic (**lăk′**tĭk) *adj.* Relating to or derived from milk.

lactic acid *n.* An organic acid that is produced by the bacteria that cause milk to sour or fruit to ferment and is used as a flavoring and preservative for foods. It is also produced by muscle tissue during exercise.

lac·tose (**lăk′**tōs′) *n.* A white crystalline sugar that is found in milk and has the formula $C_{12}H_{22}O_{11}$. It is used in infant foods, bakery products, and various sweets.

la·cu·na (lə-**kyōō′**nə) *n., pl.* **la·cu·nae** (lə-**kyōō′**nē) or **la·cu·nas 1.** An empty space or missing part; a gap: *The committee found a lacuna in the zoning regulations.* **2.** A space or cavity in bone or tissue.

lac·y (**lā′**sē) *adj.* **lac·i·er, lac·i·est** Relating to or resembling lace: *a lacy shawl; a lacy covering of moss and lichens on the rocks.*

lad (lăd) *n.* A boy or young man.

lad·der (**lăd′**ər) *n.* **1.** A usually portable device for climbing up or down, consisting of two long side pieces joined by equally spaced rungs or steps. **2.** A means of moving higher or lower: *He used his accomplishments as a ladder to success.* **3.** A series of levels or stages: *She's high on the corporate ladder.* [From Old English *hlǣder.*]

lad·die (**lăd′**ē) *n.* A boy or young man; a lad.

lade (lād) *v.* **lad·ed, lad·en** (**lād′**n) or **lad·ed, lad·ing, lades** *—tr.* To load or burden. *—intr.* To take on a load.

lad·en (**lād′**n) *adj.* **1.** Weighed down with a load; heavy: *a ship laden with goods from China.* **2.** Oppressed; burdened: *a company laden with debts.*

lad·ing (**lā′**dĭng) *n.* **1.** The act of loading. **2.** Cargo; freight: *a bill of lading.*

la·dle (**lād′**l) *n.* A long-handled spoon with a deep bowl used for serving liquids. ❖ *tr.v.* **la·dled, la·dling, la·dles** To lift out and pour with a ladle. [From Old English *hlædel,* from *hladan,* to draw out, lade.]

la·dy (**lā′**dē) *n., pl.* **la·dies 1.** A woman of high social standing. **2.** A woman with good manners or polite behavior. **3.** A woman, especially when spoken of in a polite way: *the lady who lives next door.* **4.** A woman who is the head of a household. **5. ladies** Used as a form of address for a group of women: *Good evening, ladies and gentlemen.* **6. Lady** *Chiefly British* A general feminine title of nobility or other high rank. [From Old English *hlǣfdige.*]

la·dy·bird (**lā′**dē-bûrd′) *n.* A ladybug.

la·dy·bug (**lā′**dē-bŭg′) *n.* Any of numerous small beetles, often reddish with black spots, that feed mostly on other insects, including aphids and other pests. [From *(Our) Lady,* the Virgin Mary (probably from its seven spots being considered a symbol of the seven sorrows of the Virgin Mary).]

lady in waiting *n., pl.* **ladies in waiting** A woman appointed to attend a queen or princess in a royal court.

la·dy·like (**lā′**dē-līk′) *adj.* Characteristic of or appropriate for a lady.

la·dy·ship also **La·dy·ship** (**lā′**dē-shĭp′) *n.* Used as a title and form of address for a woman holding the rank of lady.

la·dy's slipper (**lā′**dēz) *n.* Any of various orchids of northern regions having flowers with a large petal that resembles a slipper or shoe.

La·fa·yette (lăf′ē-**ĕt′** *or* lä′fā-**ĕt′**), Marquis de. 1757–1834. French politician who served on George Washington's staff in the American Revolution and took part in the 1789 and 1830 French revolutions.

La Flesche (lä **flĕsh′**), **Susette** Originally Inshta Theumba ("Bright Eyes"). 1854–1903. Omaha lecturer and activist whose work helped bring about more favorable US government policies toward Native Americans.

lag (lăg) *intr.v.* **lagged, lag·ging, lags 1.** To fail to keep up; straggle: *Several runners began to lag behind the main group in the race.* **2.** To weaken or diminish; slacken: *Our enthusiasm for the hike lagged as the sky clouded over.* ❖ *n.* **1.** The act or condition of lagging: *The cold weather caused a lag in interest in the field trip.* **2.** The extent or degree of lagging; a gap: *A huge lag separated the first and second place finishers in the race.* **—lag′ger** *n.*

la·ger (**lä′**gər) *n.* A type of beer of German origin that is fermented for a relatively long time at a low temperature.

lag·gard (**lăg′**ərd) *n.* A person who lags behind; a straggler. ❖ *adj.* Lagging behind; slow: *a laggard runner.*

la·goon (lə-**gōōn′**) *n.* A shallow body of water separated from the sea by sandbars or reefs. [From Latin *lacūna,* pool, hollow, from *lacus,* lake.]

La·gos (**lā′**gŏs′ *or* **lä′**gōs) The largest city of Nigeria, in the southwest part of the country on the Gulf of Guinea. It was the capital of Nigeria from 1960 until 1991.

La·hore (lə-**hôr′**) A city of northeast Pakistan near the Indian border south-southeast of Islamabad. The city is known for its splendid 16th-century architecture.

laid (lād) *v.* Past tense and past participle of **lay[1]**.

laid-back (**lād′băk′**) *adj. Informal* Casual or relaxed in atmosphere or character; easy-going.

lain (lān) *v.* Past participle of **lie[1]**.

❑ *These sound alike:* **lain, lane** (path).

lair (lâr) *n.* The den or dwelling place of a wild animal.

laird (lârd) *n. Scots* The owner of a landed estate; a lord.

lais·sez faire (lĕs′ā **fâr′**) *n.* An economic doctrine that opposes government regulation of commerce and industry beyond the minimum necessary for free enterprise to operate.

la·i·ty (**lā′**ĭ-tē) *n.* The laypeople of a religious group as distinguished from the clergy.

lake (lāk) *n.* A large inland body of fresh water or salt water. [From Old English *lacu,* from Latin *lacus.*]

Lake or **Lake of** For the names of actual lakes, see the specific proper name; for example, **Erie, Lake.**

lake dwelling *n.* A dwelling, especially a prehistoric dwelling, that rests on piles over a shallow lake. **—lake dweller** *n.*

lake trout *n.* A large North American trout that has dark coloring with pale spots and lives in lakes.

La·ko·ta (lə-**kō′**tə) *n., pl.* **Lakota** or **La·ko·tas 1.** A member of the largest group of the Sioux peoples, living in the western Great Plains. **2.** The Siouan language of the Lakota.

la·ma (lä′mə) *n.* A Tibetan Buddhist monk, especially one having religious authority in a monastery.

lamb (lăm) *n.* **1.** A young sheep. **2.** The meat of a young sheep. **3.** A sweet mild-mannered person. ❖ *intr.v.* **lambed, lamb·ing, lambs** To give birth to a lamb or lambs. [From Old English.]

Lamb (lăm), **Charles** 1775–1834. British critic who with his sister **Mary Ann Lamb** (1764–1847) wrote the children's book *Tales from Shakespeare* (1807).

lam·baste (lăm-**bāst′**) *tr.v.* **lam·bast·ed, lam·bast·ing, lam·bastes** *Informal* **1.** To thrash; beat. **2.** To scold; berate: *The two candidates lambasted each other in the debate.*

lamb·da (**lăm′**də) *n.* The eleventh letter of the Greek alphabet, written Λ, λ. In English it is represented as *L, l.*

lam·bent (**lăm′**bənt) *adj.* **1.** Flickering gently over a surface: *lambent moonlight.* **2.** Glowing softly; luminous: *lambent eyes.* **3.** Showing effortless brilliance or lightness: *a lambent mind.*

lamb·skin (**lăm′**skĭn′) *n.* **1.** The hide of a lamb, especially with its wool still on it. **2.** Leather made from the dressed hide of a lamb. **3.** Parchment made from such hide.

lame (lām) *adj.* **lam·er, lam·est 1.** Unable to walk easily or at all; disabled: *A leg injury made me lame.* **2.** Painful or stiff: *My back is lame after all that heavy lifting.* **3.** Weak and ineffectual; unsatisfactory: *Forgetfulness is a lame excuse for missing our meeting.* ❖ *tr.v.* **lamed, lam·ing, lames** To make lame; disable. **—lame′ly** *adv.* **—lame′ness** *n.*

la·mé (lă-**mā′**) *n.* A fabric in which flat metal threads, often of gold or silver, are woven with threads of fiber such as silk.

lame duck *n.* **1.** A public officeholder who has not been reelected and is filling out a term of office before the inauguration of a successor. **2.** An ineffective person; a weakling.

la·ment (lə-**mĕnt′**) *v.* **la·ment·ed, la·ment·ing, la·ments** *—tr.* **1.** To express grief for or about; mourn: *lament the death of a loved one.* **2.** To regret deeply; deplore: *lament the state of the city.* *—intr.* To express or show grief; mourn. ❖ *n.* **1.** An expression of grief: *giving way to tears and laments.* **2.** A sorrowful song or poem. [From Middle English *lamenten*, from Latin *lāmentum*, a lament.]

la·men·ta·ble (lə-**mĕn′**tə-bəl *or* **lăm′**ən-tə-bəl) *adj.* Deserving of lament or regret: *a lamentable mistake.* **—lam′en·ta·bly** *adv.*

lam·en·ta·tion (lăm′ən-**tā′**shən) *n.* **1.** The act of lamenting. **2. Lamentations** *(used with a singular verb)* A book of the Bible traditionally considered to be written by Jeremiah, in which the fall of Jerusalem is lamented.

lam·i·na (**lăm′**ə-nə) *n., pl.* **lam·i·nae** (**lăm′**ə-nē′) or **lam·i·nas 1.** A thin plate, scale, or layer. **2.** The flat wide part of a leaf; a blade.

lam·i·nate (**lăm′**ə-nāt′) *tr.v.* **lam·i·nat·ed, lam·i·nat·ing, lam·i·nates 1.** To cover with a thin sheet of material, as for preservation. **2.** To make (plywood, glass, or plastics) by joining several layers. **3.** To beat or press into a thin plate or sheet. **4.** To split into thin layers. ❖ *n.* (*also* **lăm′**ə-nĭt) Something, such as plywood, made by joining layers together. **—lam′i·na′tor** *n.*

lam·i·na·tion (lăm′ə-**nā′**shən) *n.* **1.** The act or process of laminating or the state of being laminated. **2.** A thin layer.

lamp (lămp) *n.* **1.** A device that gives off light by using oil, gas, or electricity: *When the lights went out we lit a kerosene lamp.* **2.** A device that uses light for heat or radiation: *a sun lamp.* [From Middle English *laump*, from Greek *lampas*, from *lampein*, to shine.]

lamp·black (**lămp′**blăk′) *n.* A gray or black soot that collects when substances containing carbon, such as oil or gas, burn incompletely. Lampblack is used as a pigment and in explosives and fertilizers.

lamp·light (**lămp′**līt′) *n.* The light shed by a lamp.

lamp·light·er (**lămp′**lī′tər) *n.* A person formerly employed to light gas-burning street lights.

lam·poon (lăm-**po͞on′**) *n.* A piece of writing that uses satire to make fun of a person, group, idea, or institution. ❖ *tr.v.* **lam·pooned, lam·poon·ing, lam·poons** To make fun of with a lampoon: *The comedy lampooned the manners of the upper class.*

lamp·post (**lămp′**pōst′) *n.* A post supporting a street lamp.

lam·prey (**lăm′**prē) *n., pl.* **lam·preys** Any of various fishes having a long thin body and a jawless sucking mouth. Lampreys attach to other fish and feed on their body fluids.

lamp·shade (**lămp′**shād′) *n.* A shade placed over a lamp to soften its direct light.

lance (lăns) *n.* **1.** A long wooden spear with a sharp metal head, used as a weapon, especially by knights or soldiers on horseback. **2.** An implement used for spearing fish. ❖ *tr.v.* **lanced, lanc·ing, lanc·es 1.** To pierce with a lance. **2.** To make a surgical incision in: *The doctor lanced the swelling.* [From Middle English *launce*, from Latin *lancea.*]

lance corporal *n.* An enlisted person in the US Marine Corps ranking above private first class and below corporal.

lance·let (**lăns′**lĭt) *n.* Any of various small fishlike sea animals that have a long thin body with a stiff rodlike strip of cells along the back but no skull or backbone. Lancelets are usually found buried in sand.

Lan·ce·lot (**lăn′**sə-lŏt′) *n.* In Arthurian legend, a knight of the Round Table whose love for Guinevere caused him to go to war with King Arthur.

lanc·er (**lăn′**sər) *n.* A soldier on horseback equipped with a lance.

lan·cet (**lăn′**sĭt) *n.* A surgical knife with a short, pointed, double-edged blade.

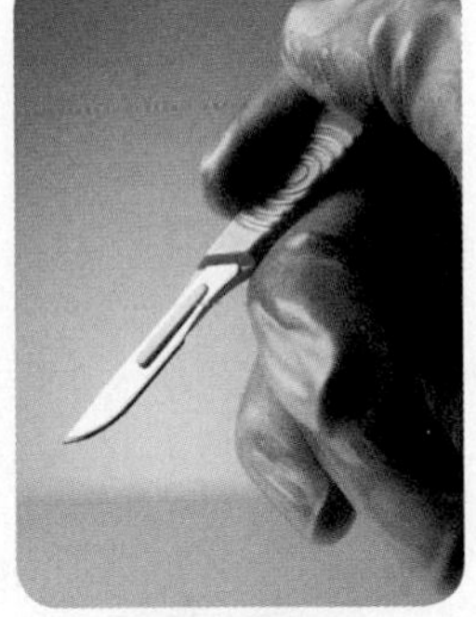

lancet

land (lănd) *n.* **1.** The part of the earth's surface not covered by water; ground: *Only one third of the earth's surface is land.* **2.** A particular part of the earth, especially a region or country. **3.** An area of ground that is publicly or privately owned, especially when not developed; landed property: *buy land in Hawaii.* **4.** Soil; earth: *Farmers plow the land.* ❖ *v.* **land·ed, land·ing, lands** *—tr.* **1.** To bring to and unload on land: *land cargo.* **2.** To set (a vehicle) down on the ground or another surface: *land a plane at New York.* **3.** *Informal* To cause to arrive in a place or condition: *Their protest landed them in court.* **4.** To catch and pull in (a fish). **5.** *Informal* To get, secure, or win: *She landed a good job.* **6.** *Informal* To deliver (a blow). *—intr.* **1.** To come to shore: *The boat landed in heavy surf.* **2.** To go or put ashore; disembark: *We landed on the dock.* **3.** To descend and settle on the ground or another surface: *The seaplane landed on the lake.* **4.** *Informal* To arrive in a place or certain condition: *The proposal landed in the file cabinet.* [From Old English.]

lan·dau (**lăn′**dô′ *or* **lăn′**dou′) *n.* **1.** A four-wheeled carriage with two passenger seats facing each other and a top that can be lowered. **2.** An automobile with a top similar to that of this carriage.

land bridge *n.* An isthmus.

land·ed (**lăn′**dĭd) *adj.* **1.** Owning land: *the landed gentry.*

lane

Dorothea Lange
photographed in 1936

2. Consisting of land in the form of property: *a landed estate.*

land·fall (lănd′fôl′) *n.* **1.** The act or an instance of sighting or reaching land after a voyage or flight. **2.** The land sighted or reached after a voyage or flight. **3.** The reaching of land by a storm or a part of a storm.

land·fill (lănd′fĭl′) *n.* **1.** A tract of land in which garbage and trash are buried between layers of dirt. **2.** A method of disposing of garbage and trash using such tracts of land.

land·form (lănd′fôrm′) *n.* A feature of the earth's surface, such as a plateau, valley, or mountain.

land grant *n.* A grant of public land made by a government for a railroad, state college, or other public use.

land·hold·er (lănd′hōl′dər) *n.* A person who owns land. **—land′hold′ing** *adj. & n.*

land·ing (lăn′dĭng) *n.* **1.** The act or process of coming to land or of coming to rest, as after a voyage or flight: *the landing of a spacecraft on the moon.* **2.** A wharf or pier: *an old boat landing.* **3.** A platform or area at the top or bottom of a set of stairs.

landing field *n.* An area of level land used by aircraft for landings and takeoffs.

landing gear *n.* The structure attached to the underside of an aircraft or a spacecraft that supports it on land or in water.

landing strip *n.* An aircraft runway without airport facilities.

land·la·dy (lănd′lā′dē) *n.* **1.** A woman who owns land or buildings rented to tenants. **2.** A woman who runs an inn or a boarding house.

land·less (lănd′lĭs) *adj.* Owning or having no land.

land·locked (lănd′lŏkt′) *adj.* **1.** Entirely or almost entirely surrounded by land: *Switzerland is a landlocked country.* **2.** Living only in inland waters: *landlocked salmon.*

land·lord (lănd′lôrd′) *n.* **1.** A person, especially a man, who owns land or buildings rented to tenants. **2.** A man who runs an inn or a boarding house.

land·lub·ber (lănd′lŭb′ər) *n.* A person unfamiliar with sailing or with life aboard a ship or boat.

land·mark (lănd′märk′) *n.* **1.** A familiar or easily recognized feature of a landscape. **2.** A fixed object that marks a boundary, as a stone or metal post. **3.** An event that is important in history: *The discovery of penicillin was a landmark in the treatment of certain diseases.* **4.** A building or place preserved for its special historical importance or interest: *Philadelphia has many early American landmarks.*

land·mass (lănd′măs′) *n.* A large area of land, such as a continent, that is wholly or mostly surrounded by water: *the landmass of Eurasia.*

land mine *n.* A small bomb or similar device buried in the ground and set to explode when stepped on or run over by a vehicle.

land·own·er (lănd′ō′nər) *n.* A person who owns land. **—land′own′ing** *adj.*

land plant *n.* Any of a large group of plants that live on land, including the vascular plants and the mosses, liverworts, and hornworts.

land·scape (lănd′skāp′) *n.* **1.** An expanse of scenery that can be seen from one place. **2.** A painting or picture showing such an expanse of scenery. ❖ *v.* **land·scaped, land·scap·ing, land·scapes** *—tr.* To change or improve the appearance of (a piece of land) by moving soil and planting trees, shrubs, or flowers. *—intr.* To change or improve grounds as a profession.

land·slide (lănd′slīd′) *n.* **1a.** The downward sliding of a relatively dry mass of earth and rock: *There were several landslides as a result of the earthquake.* **b.** The mass of soil and rock that moves in this way: *Heavy equipment was needed to clear the landslide.* **2.** A very large majority of votes resulting in victory for a candidate or political party.

land·ward (lănd′wərd) *adv. & adj.* To or toward land: *drifted landward; the landward side of the boat.*

lane (lān) *n.* **1.** A narrow path or road, often bordered by hedges, trees, fences, or walls: *a country lane; a lane between old houses.* **2.** A set course or way used by ships or aircraft: *the shipping lanes of the Atlantic.* **3.** A strip marked off on a street or highway to accommodate one line of traffic: *a highway with four lanes.* **4.** A similar strip marked off or divided from others for contestants in a race. **5.** A bowling alley. **6.** In basketball, the rectangular area marked on a court from the end line to the foul line.

❑ *These sound alike:* **lane, lain** (placed oneself flat).

Lange (lăng), **Dorothea** 1895–1965. American photographer known for her portraits of rural workers during the Great Depression.

lan·guage (lăng′gwĭj) *n.* **1a.** Communication of thoughts and feelings through a system of arbitrary signals, such as voice sounds, gestures, or written symbols. **b.** Such a system including its rules for combining its components, such as words: *Over a thousand languages are spoken in Africa.* **2.** A system of signs, symbols, rules, or gestures used to convey information: *a computer language.* **3.** The special words and expressions used by members of a group or profession: *medical language.* **4.** A particular way or style of speaking or writing: *formal language.* **5.** Words or wording, as of a legal document: *the language of a contract.* [From Middle English *langage*, from Latin *lingua*, tongue.]

language arts *pl.n.* Courses that develop the use of language skills, especially reading, spelling, and written composition.

lan·guid (lăng′gwĭd) *adj.* **1.** Lacking speed or force: *a languid wave of the hand.* **2.** Lacking spirit or energy; listless: *a languid mood.* **—lan′guid·ly** *adv.*

lan·guish (lăng′gwĭsh) *intr.v.* **lan·guished, lan·guish·ing, lan·guish·es 1.** To lose strength or vigor; grow weak: *During a long drought crops languish from lack of rain.* **2.** To suffer from miserable or depressing conditions. **3.** To remain unattended or be neglected: *legislation that languished in committee.* **4.** To become listless and depressed; pine: *languish from separation from family and friends.*

lan·guor (lăng′gər *or* lăng′ər) *n.* **1.** Lack of energy; tiredness; listlessness. **2.** A dreamy, lazy mood or quality: *the languor of a summer afternoon.* **3.** Extreme stillness or quiet. **—lan′guor·ous** *adj.*

La Ni·ña (lä nēn′yä) *n.* A periodic cooling of the ocean surface off the western coast of South America that affects Pacific and other weather patterns.

lank (lăngk) *adj.* **lank·er, lank·est 1.** Long and lean; slender: *the athlete's lank body.* **2.** Long, straight, and limp: *lank hair.* **—lank′ly** *adv.*

lank·y (lăng′kē) *adj.* **lank·i·er, lank·i·est** Tall, thin, and gawky. **—lank′i·ness** *n.*

lan·o·lin (lăn′ə-lĭn) *n.* A yellowish-white fatty substance obtained from wool and used in soaps, cosmetics, and ointments.

Lan·sing (lăn′sĭng) The capital of Michigan, in the south-central part of the state northwest of Detroit. It became the state capital in 1847.

lan·tern (lăn′tərn) *n.* **1.** A case or container that protects a light from the weather, usually designed to be carried. **2.** A room at the top of a lighthouse where the light is located. **3.** A structure built on top of a roof or dome as decoration or to let in light and air. [From Middle English, from Greek *lamptēr*, from *lampein*, to shine.]

lan·tha·nide (lăn′thə-nīd′) *n.* Any of a series of naturally

ă	pat	ôr	core
ā	pay	oi	boy
âr	care	ou	out
ä	father	o͝o	took
ĕ	pet	o͝or	lure
ē	be	o͞o	boot
ĭ	pit	ŭ	cut
ī	bite	ûr	urge
îr	pier	th	thin
ŏ	pot	*th*	this
ō	toe	zh	vision
ô	paw	ə	about

occurring metallic elements with atomic numbers ranging from 57 to 71. See **Periodic Table.**

lan·tha·num (lăn′thə-nəm) *n. Symbol* **La** A soft, silvery metallic element that is used in making glass for lenses and lights for movie and television studios. Atomic number 57. See **Periodic Table.**

lan·yard (lăn′yərd) *n.* **1.** A short rope used to secure rigging on a ship. **2.** A cord worn around the neck for carrying a knife, key, or whistle. **3.** A cord with a hook at one end, used to fire a cannon.

La·os (lous *or* lä′ōs′) A country of southeast Asia north of Cambodia. Vientiane is the capital. **—La·o′tian** (lā-ō′shən *or* **lou′**shən) *adj. & n.*

lap[1] (lăp) *n.* **1.** The flat place that is formed by the front part of the legs above the knees of a person who is sitting: *The puppy curled up in my lap.* **2.** The part of a person's clothing that covers the lap: *the lap of a skirt.* **3.** An area of responsibility, interest, or control: *The opportunity just dropped in my lap.* [From Old English *læppa,* flap.]

lap[2] (lăp) *v.* **lapped, lap·ping, laps** *—tr.* **1.** To fold, wrap, or wind over or around: *Lap the pie dough over the edge of the pan.* **2.** To extend partly over (something else); overlap: *The shingles lap one another to make the roof watertight. —intr.* **1.** To fold or wind around something. **2.** To extend over something else; overlap: *Shingles lap in straight rows.* ❖ *n.* **1a.** A part folded or extending over something else; an overlapping part: *the front lap of a jacket.* **b.** The amount that a part extends over something else: *The curtains have a lap of three inches.* **2a.** One complete length or circuit, as of a pool or track: *a race of four laps.* **b.** A part or stage, as of a journey: *The first lap of our trip across the country was from New York to Ohio.* [From Middle English *lappen,* from *lappe,* fold, flap.]

lap[3] (lăp) *v.* **lapped, lap·ping, laps** *—tr.* **1.** To take up and swallow (a liquid) by using the tongue: *The kitten lapped up the milk.* **2.** To wash or splash with a light slapping sound: *The sea lapped the shore gently. —intr.* To wash or splash against something with a light slapping sound: *Waves lapped against the dock.* ❖ *n.* The act or sound of lapping: *listened to the lap of the waves.* [From Old English *lapian.*]

La Paz (lə päz′ *or* lä päs′) The administrative capital and largest city of Bolivia, in the western part of the country southeast of Lima, Peru. It is built on the site of an Inca village and is the highest capital in the world, about 12,010 feet (3,660 meters) above sea level.

lap dog *n.* **1.** A pet dog that is small enough to be held in the lap. **2.** *Informal* A person who is eager to do what another asks, especially as a way to maintain a position of privilege or favor.

la·pel (lə-pĕl′) *n.* One of the two flaps that extend down from the collar of a coat or jacket and fold back against the chest.

lap·i·dar·y (lăp′ĭ-dĕr′ē) *n., pl.* **lap·i·dar·ies** A person who cuts, polishes, or engraves gems. ❖ *adj.* **1.** Relating to gemstones or the art of working with them. **2.** Marked by conciseness, precise, or refined expression: *a writer with a lapidary style.*

lap·is laz·u·li (lăp′ĭs lăz′ə-lē *or* lăz′yə-lē) *n.* **1.** A typically opaque, deep-blue rock that is used as a gemstone. **2.** A deep blue.

Lap·land (lăp′lănd′ *or* lăp′lənd) A region of extreme northern Europe including northern Norway, Sweden, and Finland and part of northwest Russia. It is largely within the Arctic Circle.

Lapp (lăp) *n. Often Offensive* A Sami.

lap robe *n.* A blanket or fur piece for covering the lap, legs, and feet.

lapse (lăps) *intr.v.* **lapsed, laps·ing, laps·es 1.** To fall to a lower or worse condition: *lapse into bad habits.* **2.** To pass gradually or smoothly; slip: *He lapsed into unconsciousness.* **3.** To be no longer valid or active; end or expire: *I let my membership in the club lapse.* ❖ *n.* **1.** A slip or failure, especially a minor one: *a lapse of memory.* **2.** A fall into a lower or worse condition: *a lapse into bad habits.* **3.** A period of time; an interval: *a lapse of three months between trips.* **4.** The ending of an agreement, right, privilege, or custom through neglect, disuse, or the passage of time: *the lapse of a lease.*

lap·top (lăp′tŏp′) *n.* A portable computer small enough to use on one's lap.

lar·board (lär′bərd) *n.* The port side of a ship or boat. ❖ *adj.* On the port side.

lar·ce·nous (lär′sə-nəs) *adj.* **1.** Relating to or involving larceny: *Auto theft is a larcenous crime.* **2.** Guilty of larceny.

lar·ce·ny (lär′sə-nē) *n., pl.* **lar·ce·nies** The crime of taking another's property without right or permission; theft.

larch (lärch) *n.* **1.** Any of various cone-bearing trees having clusters of needlelike leaves that are shed every year. **2.** The hard strong wood of such a tree.

lard (lärd) *n.* A solid or semisolid white substance made from pig fat and used in cooking. ❖ *tr.v.* **lard·ed, lard·ing, lards 1.** To cover or coat with lard or a similar fat. **2.** To insert strips of fat or bacon in (meat) before cooking. **3.** To enrich with additions; embellish: *She larded her lecture with jokes.*

lar·der (lär′dər) *n.* **1.** A room or cupboard where food is stored. **2.** A supply of food.

large (lärj) *adj.* **larg·er, larg·est 1.** Greater than average in size, amount, or number; big: *The blue whale is the largest mammal. He paid a large amount for that sports car.* **2.** Important; significant: *The scientists announced a large discovery of fossils.* ◆ **at large 1.** Not in confinement or captivity; at liberty: *The thief has not been found yet and is still at large.* **2.** As a whole; in general: *The economy at large is doing well.* **3.** Representing a nation, state, or district as a whole: *a councilor-at-large.* **—large′ness** *n.*

SYNONYMS large, big, enormous, great, huge These adjectives mean notably above the average in size or magnitude. *Chicago is a large city. Factory outlet stores usually offer big discounts. Computers store an enormous amount of data. They took a cruise on a great ocean liner. Everyone had huge helpings of potato salad at the picnic.*
ANTONYM small

large-heart·ed (lärj′här′tĭd) *adj.* Having a generous or sympathetic nature.

large intestine *n.* The wide lower section of the intestine that extends from the end of the small intestine to the anus. It absorbs water and eliminates the waste matter that is left after food is digested.

large·ly (lärj′lē) *adv.* For the most part; mainly: *The hills are largely covered with trees.*

large-scale (lärj′skāl′) *adj.* **1.** Large in scope or effect; extensive: *large-scale farming of huge acreages.* **2.** Drawn or made larger in size than average, especially to show detail: *a large-scale map.*

lar·gess also **lar·gesse** (lär-**zhĕs′** *or* lär-**jĕs′**) *n.* **1.** Generosity in giving gifts. **2.** Money or gifts given.

lar·go (lär′gō) *adv. & adj.* In music, in a very slow tempo.

la·ri (lä′rē) *n., pl.* **lari** The basic monetary unit of Georgia. [From Georgian.]

lar·i·at (lăr′ē-ət) *n.* A lasso. [From Spanish *la reata,* the rope : *la,* the + *reata,* rope used to control animals (from *reatar,* to tie again).]

lark[1] (lärk) *n.* **1.** Any of various songbirds found mostly in Eurasia and Africa and having a melodious song, especially the skylark. **2.** Any of several similar but unre-

lanyard

laptop

SCIENCE

laser A **laser** emits a thin, intense beam of light that can travel long distances without spreading out very much. Almost any light beam consists of many waves traveling in roughly the same direction. In laser light, the waves are all precisely in step with each other. Such light is called *coherent*. Lasers produce coherent light through a process called "stimulated emission." The laser contains a chamber in which atoms of a medium such as a gas or a crystalline solid are excited to a high energy level. When a flash of light, in the form of a wave of the correct frequency, is sent through the chamber, it makes the excited atoms emit photons, forming a beam of light that is in step with the original wave. These waves then stimulate other atoms to emit more coherent light. The chamber has mirrors at both ends, so the light travels back and forth, repeatedly stimulating emission. One of the mirrors is partially transparent, allowing the laser beam to exit from that end.

ă	pat	ôr	core
ā	pay	oi	boy
âr	care	ou	out
ä	father	o͝o	took
ĕ	pet	o͝or	lure
ē	be	o͞o	boot
ĭ	pit	ŭ	cut
ī	bite	ûr	urge
îr	pier	th	thin
ŏ	pot	*th*	this
ō	toe	zh	vision
ô	paw	ə	about

lated birds, such as the meadowlark. [From Old English *lāwerce*.]

lark² (lärk) *n.* Something done just for fun or adventure: *We went to the zoo on a lark.* ❖ *intr.v.* **larked, lark·ing, larks** To engage in fun or pranks. [Perhaps short for *skylark*, to frolic, or possibly from dialectal *lake*, play.]

lark·spur (lärk′spûr′) *n.* The delphinium.

lar·va (lär′və) *n., pl.* **lar·vae** (lär′vē) or **lar·vas 1.** The immature wormlike form of certain insects, from the time it hatches from the egg until it changes into the adult form. A caterpillar is the larva of a butterfly or moth. **2.** The immature stage of certain other animals, usually differing greatly in form from the parent. A tadpole is the larva of a frog or toad. **—lar′val** *adj.*

la·ryn·ge·al (lə-rĭn′jē-əl *or* lăr′ən-jē′əl) *adj.* Relating to, affecting, or near the larynx.

lar·yn·gi·tis (lăr′ĭn-jī′tĭs) *n.* Inflammation of the larynx, causing hoarseness and sometimes temporary loss of the voice.

lar·ynx (lăr′ĭngks) *n., pl.* **la·ryn·ges** (lə-rĭn′jēz) or **lar·ynx·es** The upper part of the windpipe, containing the vocal cords.

la·sa·gna (lə-zän′yə) *n.* **1.** Pasta in flat, very wide strips. **2.** A dish made by baking this pasta with layers of sauce and fillings such as cheese or meat.

La Salle (lə săl′), Sieur de. Title of **Robert Cavelier.** 1643–1687. French explorer in North America who claimed Louisiana for France (1682).

las·civ·i·ous (lə-sĭv′ē-əs) *adj.* **1.** Feeling or showing lust; lewd. **2.** Tending to excite lust. **—las·civ′i·ous·ly** *adv.* **—las·civ′i·ous·ness** *n.*

la·ser (lā′zər) *n.* **1.** A device that emits a very narrow and intense beam of light or other radiation of a single wavelength either continuously or in pulses. Light from lasers can be used to cut hard substances, remove diseased tissue, or transmit communications signals. **2.** The beam of light produced by one of these devices. —SEE NOTE.

laser disc *n.* An optical disc.

laser printer *n.* A printer that uses a laser to produce an image on a rotating drum before transferring the image to paper.

lash¹ (lăsh) *n.* **1.** A stroke or blow given with a whip or other flexible object. **2.** The flexible part of a whip. **3.** An eyelash. ❖ *v.* **lashed, lash·ing, lash·es** *—tr.* **1.** To strike with a whip or other flexible object. **2.** To strike with force or violence: *The storm lashed the shore with high winds.* **3.** To move or wave rapidly: *The alligator lashed its tail in the water.* **4.** To attack or criticize with harsh language: *Newspaper editorials lashed the government for incompetence.* *—intr.* **1.** To move rapidly or violently; dash: *The waves lashed against the shore.* **2.** To strike with a whip or other flexible object: *The mule's tail lashed at the flies.* **3.** To make a harsh verbal or written attack: *The president lashed out against critics of the government.* [From Middle English, probably from *lashen*, to deal a blow.]

lash² (lăsh) *tr.v.* **lashed, lash·ing, lash·es** To fasten or secure, as with a rope or cord: *The crew lashed the cargo firmly in place.* [From Middle English *lashen*, to lace, from Old French *lachier*.]

LA·SIK (lā′sĭk) *n.* Eye surgery in which the cornea is reshaped using a laser, performed to correct certain refractive disorders, such as myopia.

lass (lăs) *n.* A girl or young woman.

las·sie (lăs′ē) *n.* A lass.

las·si·tude (lăs′ĭ-to͞od′) *n.* A state or feeling of weariness, diminished energy, or listlessness: *The disease brought on a long period of lassitude and inactivity.*

las·so (lăs′ō *or* lă-so͞o′) *n., pl.* **las·sos** or **las·soes** A long rope with an adjustable loop at one end, used especially to catch horses and cattle. ❖ *tr.v.* **las·soed, las·so·ing, las·sos** or **las·soes** To catch with a lasso: *lasso a runaway calf.*

last¹ (lăst) *adj.* **1.** Being, coming, or placed after all others; final: *the last day of the school year.* **2.** Being the only one left: *my last dime.* **3.** Most recent; just passed: *last week.* **4.** Most unlikely; least expected: *The last thing you would expect is snow during the summer.* **5.** The latest possible: *We waited until the last second to get on the plane.* ❖ *adv.* **1.** After all others; at the end: *The recipe says to add the flour last.* **2.** Most recently; latest: *I last saw them when I was a child.* ❖ *n.* **1.** A person or thing that is last: *I've read every chapter but the last.* **2.** The end: *They held out until the last.* ◆ **at last** or **at long last** After a long time; finally: *At last we fell asleep.* [From Old English *lætest*, latest.] **—last′ly** *adv.*

last² (lăst) *v.* **last·ed, last·ing, lasts** *—intr.* **1.** To continue; go on: *The song lasted three minutes.* **2.** To remain in good condition; endure: *Appliances don't last like they used to.* **3.** To be enough: *The food supply should last for a long time.* *—tr.* To supply adequately; be enough for: *One loaf of bread can't last us a week.* [From Old English *lǣstan*.]

last³ (lăst) *n.* A block shaped like a human foot and used in making and repairing shoes. [From Old English *lǣste*, from *lǣst*, sole of the foot.]

last·ing (lăs′tĭng) *adj.* Continuing or remaining for a long time; enduring: *a lasting peace between nations.* **—last′ing·ly** *adv.*

Last Judgment *n.* In Christianity and certain other religious traditions, the final judgment by God of all humankind.

last minute *n.* The moment just before it is too late: *We made our preparations at the last minute before the wedding.* **—last′-min′ute** *adj.*

last straw *n.* The last in a series of annoyances or disappointments that finally leads to loss of patience, trust, or hope.

Last Supper *n.* In the Bible, the last meal of Jesus with the Apostles on the night before his crucifixion.

last word *n.* **1.** The final statement, as in a verbal argument. **2.** The power or authority to make a final decision. **3.** A convincing or authoritative statement or treatment: *This report is the last word on nutrition.* **4.** *Informal* The newest or most up-to-date style or development; the latest thing: *The model is the last word in racing bikes.*

Las Ve·gas (läs vā′gəs) The largest city of Nevada, in the southeast part of the state near the California and Arizona borders. It is a major tourist center.

lat. *abbr.* An abbreviation of latitude.

Lat. *abbr.* An abbreviation of Latin.

latch (lăch) *n.* A fastener for a door, gate, or window, usually consisting of a movable bar that fits into a notch or slot. ❖ *tr. & intr.v.* **latched, latch·ing, latch·es** To close or be closed with a latch: *Latch the door. Does the door latch securely?* ◆ **latch on to** or **latch onto** To get hold of; obtain.

latch·key (lăch′kē′) *n.* A key for unfastening a latch or lock, especially one on a door.

late (lāt) *adj.* **lat·er, lat·est 1.** Coming or happening after the expected, usual, or proper time; tardy: *I am late for my appointment.* **2.** Coming toward the end or more advanced part of a time period or series of events: *It was late in the meeting when we discussed that issue.* **3.** Of a time just past; recent: *a late model car; the late recession.* **4.** Having recently died: *The senator's late husband was a surgeon.* ❖ *adv.* **later, latest 1.** After the usual, expected, or proper time: *The train arrived late.* **2.** At the end or at an advanced stage: *Our team scored the winning run late in the game.* **3.** Recently: *as late as last week.* ◆ **of late** Recently; lately: *The trains have been running on a new schedule of late.* [From Old English *læt*.] **—late′ness** *n.*

late·com·er (lāt′kŭm′ər) *n.* A person or thing that arrives later than others or has arrived recently: *Latecomers to the show may have difficulty finding seats.*

la·teen (lə-tēn′ *or* lă-tēn′) *adj.* Being, relating to, or rigged with a triangular sail hung on a long pole attached at an angle to the top of a short mast.

Late Latin *n.* Latin from the third to the seventh century AD.

late·ly (lāt′lē) *adv.* Not long ago; recently: *The weather has been cold lately.*

la·tent (lāt′nt) *adj.* Present but not evident or active; hidden: *Many of a child's latent talents only emerge in adulthood.* **—la′ten·cy** *n.*

lat·er (lā′tər) *adj.* Comparative of **late.** More recent: *The later plays of Shakespeare.* ❖ *adv.* Comparative of **late.** At a later time or period: *That job can be done later.* ❖ *interj. Informal* Used to express goodbye.

lat·er·al (lăt′ər-əl) *adj.* Relating to, situated on, directed toward, or coming from the side: *Lateral growth on a plant branches out from the stem. A lateral pass in football is to the side of the field.* ❖ *n.* In football, a usually underhand pass that is thrown sideways or somewhat backward from the passer. ❖ *v.* **lat·er·aled, lat·er·al·ing, lat·er·als** also **lat·er·alled, lat·er·al·ling, lat·er·als** *—intr.* In football, to throw a lateral. *—tr.* In football, to throw (the ball) in a lateral. [From Middle English, from Latin *latus*, side.] **—lat′er·al·ly** *adv.*

lateral line *n.* A series of sensory pores along the head and sides of fishes and some amphibians by which water currents, vibrations, and pressure changes are detected.

lat·est (lā′tĭst) *adj.* Superlative of **late.** Most recent: *the latest popular songs.* ◆ **at the latest** No later than: *I'll visit them next week at the latest.*

la·tex (lā′tĕks′) *n.* **1.** The milky or colorless sap of certain plants, such as the rubber tree and milkweeds, that hardens when exposed to air. **2.** A material made of such sap from rubber trees, used to manufacture thin elastic products such as balloons, disposable gloves, and medical devices; natural latex. Some people are allergic to this substance. **3.** A synthetic material made from petroleum, used in paints, adhesives, and other products; synthetic latex.

lath (lăth) *n., pl.* **laths** (lă*th*z *or* lăths) **1.** A thin narrow strip of wood or metal used as a supporting structure for plaster, shingles, slates, or tiles. **2.** A quantity of laths or work made using laths. ❖ *tr.v.* **lathed, lath·ing, laths** To cover or line with laths.

lathe (lā*th*) *n.* A machine for shaping a piece of material, such as wood, by spinning the material rapidly about its axis while pressing a fixed cutting or scraping tool against it.

lath·er (lă*th*′ər) *n.* **1.** Foam formed when soap and water mix. **2.** Froth formed by heavy sweating, especially on a horse. **3.** *Informal* A condition of anxious agitation: *The students were in a lather over the proposed restrictions.* ❖ *v.* **lath·ered, lath·er·ing, lath·ers** *—tr.* To cover with lather. *—intr.* To produce or form lather: *The race caused the horse to lather heavily.*

la·ti (lä′tē′) *n.* Plural of **lats.**

Lat·in (lăt′n) *n.* **1a.** The language of the ancient Romans, later widely used in science, law, and diplomacy and in the liturgy of the Roman Catholic Church. **b.** The classical form of this language, used from about 200 BC to about 200 AD. **2a.** A member of a Latin people, especially a native or inhabitant of Latin America. **b.** A Latino or Latina. **3.** A native or inhabitant of ancient Rome. ❖ *adj.* **1.** Relating to ancient Rome or its people or culture. **2.** Relating to the Latin language. **3a.** Relating to the peoples or countries of Latin America. **b.** Relating to Latinos or their culture. **4.** Relating to the languages that developed from Latin, such as French, Italian, and Spanish.

La·ti·na (lə-tē′nə *or* lă-tē′nə *or* lä-tē′nə) *n.* A Latino woman or girl.

Latin America The countries of the Western Hemisphere south of the United States, especially those whose peoples speak Spanish, Portuguese, or French.

Latin American *n.* **1.** A native or inhabitant of Latin America. **2.** A person of Latin-American ancestry. **—Lat′in-A·mer′i·can** *adj.*

La·ti·no (lə-tē′nō *or* lă-tē′nō *or* lä-tē′nō) *n., pl.* **La·ti·nos** **1.** A Latin American. **2.** A person of Latin-American ancestry, especially one living in the United States.

lat·i·tude (lăt′ĭ-to͞od′) *n.* **1.** Distance north or south of the equator measured in degrees. A degree of latitude is about 69 statute miles or 60 nautical miles. **2.** A region of the earth indicated by its approximate latitude: *Some of the coldest temperatures on earth occur in the polar latitudes.* **3.** Freedom from confining regulations or restrictions: *The attorney general gave his staff wide latitude in investigating this case.* **—lat′i·tu′di·nal** *adj.*

la·trine (lə-trēn′) *n.* A communal toilet of the type often used in camps or military barracks.

lats (läts) *n., pl.* **la·ti** (lä′tē′) The basic monetary unit of Latvia.

lat·te (lä′tā) *n.* A caffe latte.

lat·ter (lăt′ər) *adj.* **1.** Being the second of two that are mentioned: *Apples and oranges are both tasty but I prefer the latter fruit.* **2.** Closer to the end: *November comes in the latter part of the year.* **—lat′ter·ly** *adv.*

Lat·ter-day Saint (lăt′ər-dā′) *n.* A Mormon.

lat·tice (lăt′ĭs) *n.* **1.** An open framework made of strips of wood, metal, or a similar material that cross at regular intervals. **2.** A screen, window, or grate made of such a framework. ❖ *tr.v.* **lat·ticed, lat·tic·ing, lat·tic·es** **1.** To form into a lattice: *We latticed strips of cane to make the chair seat.* **2.** To furnish with a lattice. **—lat′ticed** *adj.*

lat·tice·work (lăt′ĭs-wûrk′) *n.* **1.** A lattice or structure resembling a lattice. **2.** An open, crisscross pattern or weave.

Lat·vi·a (lăt′vē-ə) A country of northern Europe on the Baltic Sea north of Lithuania. Latvia was part of the USSR from 1940 to 1991. Riga is the capital.

Lat·vi·an (lăt′vē-ən) *adj.* Relating to Latvia or its people, language, or culture. ❖ *n.* **1.** A native or inhabitant of Latvia. **2.** The Baltic language of Latvia.

laud (lôd) *tr.v.* **laud·ed, laud·ing, lauds** To praise highly: *The principal lauded the school's graduates during commencement.*

laud·a·ble (lô′də-bəl) *adj.* Deserving praise; praiseworthy. **—laud′a·bly** *adv.*

lau·da·num (lôd′n-əm) *n.* An alcohol solution of opium, formerly used as a painkiller.

laud·a·to·ry (lô′də-tôr′ē) *adj.* Expressing praise: *laudatory remarks.*

laugh (lăf) *v.* **laughed, laugh·ing, laughs** *—intr.* To make sounds and facial movements to express certain emotions, especially happiness, amusement, scorn, or nervousness. *—tr.* To affect or influence by laughter: *We laughed our worries away.* ❖ *n.* **1.** The act or sound of laughing: *a good-natured laugh.* **2.** often **laughs** Fun; amusement: *dressed up like clowns just for laughs.* ◆ **laugh at 1.** To be amused by: *I could only laugh at how wrong I had been.* **2.** To make fun of; mock: *The umpire told them to stop laughing at the pitcher.* **laugh off** To consider or treat as ridiculously or laughably trivial: *The politician laughed off her opponent's allegation.* [From Old English *hliehhan*.]

laugh·a·ble (lăf′ə-bəl) *adj.* Causing or deserving of laughter; amusing or ridiculous. **—laugh′a·ble·ness** *n.* **—laugh′a·bly** *adv.*

laugh·ing gas (lăf′ĭng) *n.* Nitrous oxide.

laser

last[3]

lateen

latitude

lattice

launch pad
space shuttle *Atlantis* at Kennedy Space Center

laurel

ă	pat	ôr	core
ā	pay	oi	boy
âr	care	ou	out
ä	father	o͝o	took
ĕ	pet	o͝or	lure
ē	be	o͞o	boot
ĭ	pit	ŭ	cut
ī	bite	ûr	urge
îr	pier	th	thin
ŏ	pot	*th*	this
ō	toe	zh	vision
ô	paw	ə	about

laugh·ing·stock (lăf′ĭng-stŏk′) *n.* A person or thing that is made fun of; an object of ridicule.

laugh·ter (lăf′tər) *n.* The act or sound of laughing.

launch¹ (lônch *or* länch) *v.* **launched, launch·ing, launch·es** —*tr.* **1.** To throw or propel with force; hurl: *launch a spear.* **2.** To cause (a self-propelled vehicle or projectile) to go into motion: *launch a rocket.* **3.** To put (a boat or ship) into the water; set afloat. **4.** To set going or start into action: *The institute launched a new research program.* See Synonyms at **begin.** —*intr.* **1.** To set out; make a start: *He launched forth on a new career.* **2.** To enter energetically into something; plunge: *She launched into a review of the new movie.* ❖ *n.* The act of launching something, such as a rocket or spacecraft. [From Middle English *launchen,* from Latin *lanceāre,* to wield a lance.] —**launch′er** *n.*

launch² (lônch *or* länch) *n.* **1.** A large boat carried by a ship. **2.** A large, open motorboat. [Probably from Malay *lancha.*]

launch pad or **launch·ing pad** (lôn′chĭng *or* län′chĭng) *n.* The platform or base from which a rocket or space vehicle is launched.

laun·der (lôn′dər *or* län′dər) *tr.v.* **laun·dered, laun·der·ing, laun·ders 1.** To wash or wash and iron (clothes, for example). **2.** To make (illegally obtained money) appear lawfully obtained or legitimate, especially by transferring it from one legitimate account or business to another.

laun·dro·mat (lôn′drə-măt′ *or* län′drə-măt′) A self-service laundry where customers wash and dry clothes in coin-operated machines.

laun·dry (lôn′drē *or* län′drē) *n., pl.* **laun·dries 1.** Clothes and linens that have just been or will be washed: *Sort the laundry by color.* **2.** A place or business establishment where clothes and linens are washed and ironed. [From Middle English *lavendrie,* from Latin *lavandāria,* things to be washed, from *lavāre,* to wash.]

lau·re·ate (lôr′ē-ĭt) *n.* **1.** A person who has been honored for achievements, especially in the arts or sciences. **2.** A poet laureate.

lau·rel (lôr′əl) *n.* **1a.** A small shrub or tree native to the Mediterranean region, having glossy, aromatic, evergreen leaves. **b.** Any of various related shrubs or trees, such as the mountain laurel. **2.** A wreath of laurel given as a mark of honor. **3.** often **laurels** Honors and glory won for great achievement: *The soldier won laurels for her bravery.*

la·va (lä′və *or* lăv′ə) *n.* **1.** Molten rock that flows from a volcano or from a crack in the earth. **2.** The rock formed when this substance cools and hardens. [From Italian.]

lav·a·to·ry (lăv′ə-tôr′ē) *n., pl.* **lav·a·to·ries 1.** A room with a sink for washing and often a toilet; a bathroom. **2.** A sink or washbowl, especially one with running water and a drain. **3.** A flush toilet. [From Middle English *lavatorie,* basin, from Latin *lavāre,* to wash.]

lave (lāv) *tr. & intr.v.* **laved, lav·ing, laves** To wash or bathe.

lav·en·der (lăv′ən-dər) *n.* **1a.** Any of various plants having small, fragrant purplish flowers that yield an oil used in perfumes, cosmetics, and soaps. **b.** The fragrant dried flowers or leaves of these plants. **2.** A pale or light purple. [From Middle English *lavandre,* from Medieval Latin *lavendula,* perhaps from Latin *līvidus,* bluish.] —**lav′en·der** *adj.*

lav·ish (lăv′ĭsh) *adj.* **1.** Given or provided very plentifully: *a party with lavish refreshments.* **2.** Very generous or free in giving: *Be lavish with praise.* ❖ *tr.v.* **lav·ished, lav·ish·ing, lav·ish·es** To give or bestow in abundance: *The grandparents lavished affection on their grandchildren.* —**lav′ish·ly** *adv.* —**lav′ish·ness** *n.*

La·voi·sier (lä-vwä-zyā′), **Antoine Laurent** 1743–1794. French chemist who discovered that air consists of a mixture of two gases, which he called oxygen and nitrogen.

law (lô) *n.* **1.** A rule that requires or forbids certain conduct or activities, established by custom or by an authority, such as a legislature. **2.** A set or system of such rules: *Corporate law governs business.* **3.** The condition of social order created by obedience to such rules: *a breakdown of law and order.* **4.** The study of such rules: *a professor of law.* **5.** The profession of a lawyer: *practice the law.* **6.** The system of courts administering the laws of a community: *We are all equal before the law.* **7.** A person or agency responsible for enforcing the law: *a fugitive pursued by the law.* **8.** A statement or ruling that must be obeyed: *The king's word was law.* **9. Law** The body of principles held to express the will of God, especially as revealed in the Bible: *Mosaic Law.* **10.** A generally accepted rule, principle, or practice: *the laws of good health.* **11.** A statement describing how particular phenomena always behave when specific conditions exist: *the law of gravity.* [From Old English *lagu,* from Old Norse *lag, lagu,* that which is laid down.]

law-a·bid·ing (lô′ə-bī′dĭng) *adj.* Obeying the law: *law-abiding citizens.*

law·break·er (lô′brā′kər) *n.* A person or organization that breaks the law.

law·ful (lô′fəl) *adj.* **1.** Allowed by law: *lawful acts.* **2.** Established or recognized by the law: *a lawful heir.* **3.** Law-abiding: *lawful citizens.* —**law′ful·ly** *adv.* —**law′ful·ness** *n.*

law·giv·er (lô′gĭv′ər) *n.* A person who establishes a set or system of laws for a people.

law·less (lô′lĭs) *adj.* **1.** Not governed by law: *the lawless frontier.* **2.** Disregarding or violating the law: *a lawless mob.* —**law′less·ly** *adv.* —**law′less·ness** *n.*

law·mak·er (lô′mā′kər) *n.* A person who takes part in writing or passing laws; a legislator. —**law′mak′ing** *n.*

lawn¹ (lôn) *n.* A piece of ground planted with grass that is usually mowed regularly, as near a house or in a park. [From Middle English *launde,* glade, from Old French, pasture, wooded area.]

lawn² (lôn) *n.* A very fine thin fabric of cotton or linen. [From Middle English *laun,* after *Laon,* a city of northern France.]

lawn bowling *n.* A game played on a level lawn in which players roll wooden balls as close as possible to a smaller target ball.

lawn mower also **lawn·mow·er** (lôn′mō′ər) *n.* A machine that has rotating blades for cutting grass.

lawn tennis *n.* Tennis, especially as played on a grass court.

law·ren·ci·um (lô-rĕn′sē-əm) *n.* *Symbol* **Lr** A radioactive element that has been artificially produced by scientists. The half-life of its longest-lived isotope is about four hours. Atomic number 103. See **Periodic Table.** [After Ernest Orlando *Lawrence* (1901–1958), American physicist.]

law·suit (lô′so͞ot′) *n.* A suit or case brought before a court of law for settlement.

law·yer (loi′yər) *n.* A person who is trained and qualified to give legal advice to clients and represent them in a court of law; an attorney.

lax (lăks) *adj.* **lax·er, lax·est 1.** Not careful or strict; negligent: *lax about paying bills.* **2.** Not firm; loose; slack: *a lax cable.* [From Middle English, from Latin *laxus,* loose.] —**lax′ly** *adv.* —**lax′ness** *n.*

lax·a·tive (lăk′sə-tĭv) *n.* A medicine or food that stimulates bowel movements. ❖ *adj.* Stimulating bowel movements.

lax·i·ty (lăk′sĭ-tē) *n.* The quality or condition of being lax.

lay¹ (lā) *v.* **laid** (lād), **lay·ing, lays** —*tr.* **1a.** To place or put, especially on a flat surface or in a horizontal position: *I laid the baby in the crib.* **b.** To put or place in a certain condition: *They laid themselves open for trouble.* **2.** To put or set in place: *lay tiles for flooring.* **3.** To produce (an egg or eggs). **4.** To cause to settle, subside, or become calm: *The rain laid the dust.* **5.** To assign; charge: *They lay the blame on us.* **6.** To put in order; prepare: *lay the table for dinner.* **7.** To spread over a surface: *lay paint on a canvas.* **8.** To impose as a burden or punishment: *lay a fine on an offender.* **9.** To place or give (importance, for example): *lay emphasis.* **10.** To present for consideration: *lay a case before the court.* **11.** To place (a bet); wager. —*intr.* To produce an egg or eggs: *The hens stopped laying suddenly.* ❖ *n.* The way or arrangement in which something is situated or organized: *the lay of the land.* ◆ **lay aside 1.** To give up; abandon. **2.** To save for future use. **lay away 1.** To save for future use. **2.** To reserve (merchandise) until wanted or paid for. **lay by** To save for future use. **lay down 1.** To give up and surrender: *laid down their arms.* **2.** To specify: *lay down rules by which to live.* **lay in** To store for future use: *lay in supplies for a blizzard.* **lay into** *Slang* **1.** To scold harshly. **2.** To beat up physically. **lay off 1.** To dismiss or suspend from a job. **2.** *Slang* To stop doing something; quit. **lay out 1.** To arrange according to plan: *laying out the streets of a new housing development.* **2.** To spend (money). **lay over** To make a stopover in the course of a journey. **lay up 1.** To store for future needs. **2.** *Informal* To keep in bed or out of action with an illness or injury. **lay waste to** To ravage: *Rebel troops laid waste to the town.* [From Old English *lecgan.*] —SEE NOTE.

❑ *These sound alike:* **lay¹** (put), **lay²** (not of the clergy), **lay³** (poem), **lay⁴** (placed oneself flat), **lei¹** (garland), **lei²** (Romanian currency).

lay² (lā) *adj.* **1.** Relating to or involving people who are not members of the clergy: *a lay missionary.* **2.** Not of or belonging to a particular profession: *a lay observer on the scientific expedition.* [From Middle English *lai*, from Late Latin *lāicus*, from Greek *lāos*, the people.]

❑ *These sound alike:* **lay²** (not of the clergy), **lay¹** (put), **lay³** (poem), **lay⁴** (placed oneself flat), **lei¹** (garland), **lei²** (Romanian currency).

lay³ (lā) *n.* A poem or song that tells a story; a ballad. [From Middle English *lai*, from Old French.]

❑ *These sound alike:* **lay³** (poem), **lay¹** (put), **lay²** (not of the clergy), **lay⁴** (placed oneself flat), **lei¹** (garland), **lei²** (Romanian currency).

lay⁴ (lā) *v.* Past tense of **lie¹**.

❑ *These sound alike:* **lay⁴** (placed oneself flat), **lay¹** (put), **lay²** (not of the clergy), **lay³** (poem), **lei¹** (garland), **lei²** (Romanian currency).

lay·a·way (lā′ə-wā′) *n.* A payment plan in which a seller agrees to hold a piece of merchandise for a customer who has left a deposit until the full price is paid.

lay·er (lā′ər) *n.* **1.** A single thickness of material lying between others or covering a surface: *a cake with three layers.* **2.** A depth or level: *a novel with many layers of meaning.* **3.** A person who lays something: *a carpet layer.* **4.** A hen kept for laying eggs. ❖ *tr. & intr.v.* **lay·ered, lay·er·ing, lay·ers** To form, arrange, or split into layers. —**lay′er·ing** *n.*

lay·ette (lā-ĕt′) *n.* A set of clothing, bedding, and other supplies for a newborn child.

lay·man (lā′mən) *n.* **1.** A person who is not a cleric. **2.** A person who does not have the specialized knowledge or training of a member of a profession.

lay·off (lā′ôf′) *n.* **1.** A dismissal or suspension of one or more employees, especially because there is no longer enough available work or because the company is being restructured. **2.** A period of temporary inactivity.

lay·out (lā′out′) *n.* A planned arrangement of parts or areas: *the layout of a factory.*

lay·o·ver (lā′ō′vər) *n.* A short stop or break in a journey.

lay·per·son (lā′pûr′sən) *n.* **1.** A person who is not a cleric. **2.** A person who does not have the specialized knowledge or training of a member of a profession.

lay-up (lā′ŭp′) *n.* In basketball, a usually one-handed, banked shot made close to the basket after driving in.

lay·wom·an (lā′wo͝om′ən) *n.* **1.** A woman who is not a cleric. **2.** A woman who does not have the specialized knowledge or training of a member of a profession.

Laz·a·rus (lăz′ər-əs) In the New Testament, the man whom Jesus miraculously raised from the dead.

Lazarus, Emma 1849–1887. American writer whose sonnet "The New Colossus" (1883) is inscribed on the base of the Statue of Liberty.

laze (lāz) *intr.v.* **lazed, laz·ing, laz·es** To relax lazily; loaf: *lazed around all day in the sun.*

la·zy (lā′zē) *adj.* **la·zi·er, la·zi·est 1.** Not willing to work or be energetic: *a lazy person.* **2.** Causing idleness or a lack of energy: *lazy summer afternoons.* **3.** Slow-moving: *lazy clouds floating overhead.* [Probably of Low German origin.] —**la′zi·ly** *adv.* —**la′zi·ness** *n.*

lb. *abbr.* An abbreviation of pound.

lcd *abbr.* An abbreviation of least common denominator.

LCD *abbr.* An abbreviation of liquid-crystal display.

lcm *abbr.* An abbreviation of least common multiple.

lea (lē *or* lā) *n.* A stretch of grassy ground; a meadow.

❑ *These sound alike:* **lea, lee** (wind side).

leach (lēch) *tr.v.* **leached, leach·ing, leach·es 1.** To dissolve out (soluble materials) by passing a liquid through ashes, rock, or other matter: *Heavy rains leached minerals from the soil.* **2.** To pass a liquid through (a substance), dissolving the soluble materials in it: *Heavy rains leached the soil of minerals.*

❑ *These sound alike:* **leach, leech** (worm).

lead¹ (lēd) *v.* **led** (lĕd), **lead·ing, leads** —*tr.* **1.** To show the way to, as by going along or ahead; conduct: *The guide will lead us to the top of the mountain.* See Synonyms at **guide. 2.** To guide, as by the hand or an attached rope: *I led the pony out of the barn.* **3.** To serve as a route for: *The trail led us to a cabin.* **4.** To serve as a channel or passage for: *This pipe leads the water away from the house.* **5.** To cause to think or act in a certain way: *His remarks led me to conclude that he was a musician.* **6.** To be the head of; direct: *He led the group in a song.* **7.** To go at the head of; be first in: *She's still leading the race.* **8.** To live; experience: *A pilot often leads an exciting life.* —*intr.* **1.** To be first; be ahead: *Only one runner is now leading in the race.* **2.** To act as a guide: *The scouts led as the army followed.* **3.** To be or form a way, route, or passage: *The trail leads to a little stream.* **4.** To make the first play in a game or contest. **5.** To guide a partner in a dance. ❖ *n.* **1.** The front, foremost, or winning position: *Our team took the lead in the game.* **2.** The amount by which one is ahead: *a five-point lead.* **3.** A guiding indication; a clue or hint: *leads that helped solve the crime.* **4.** An example or preceding event: *They followed the committee's lead and voted against the amendment.* **5.** The main role, as in a play or movie. **6.** The opening paragraph of a news story. ◆ **lead off** To begin; start. **lead on** To draw into unwise action or mistaken opinion; deceive: *They led the investors on with false promises of oil discoveries.* **lead to** To tend toward or result in: *The discovery of oil led to the development of a city here.* **lead up to** To result in by a series of steps: *These events led up to a change in management of the company.* [From Old English *lǣdan.*]

❑ *These sound alike:* **lead¹, lede** (beginning of news story).

lead² (lĕd) *n.* **1.** *Symbol* **Pb** A soft, heavy, bluish-gray metallic element that is easily shaped, very durable, and resistant to corrosion. It is used in making radiation shielding, solder, and containers for corrosive substances. Atomic number 82. See **Periodic Table. 2.** A piece of lead or other metal attached to a length of line, used in measuring depths. **3.** A material, often made mostly

lava
eruption of Mt. Stromboli in Italy

USAGE

lay The verbs **lay** and **lie** are frequently confused. *Lay* means "to put, place, or prepare" and normally takes an object. Its past tense is *laid: He always lays his glasses down carefully. I laid* (not *lay*) *the newspaper on the table and left the room. Lie* means "to recline or be situated" and does not take an object. Its past tense is *lay: She sometimes lies on the sofa after lunch. When I lay down, I fell asleep. She was lying* (not *laying*) *on the sofa.*

Emma Lazarus

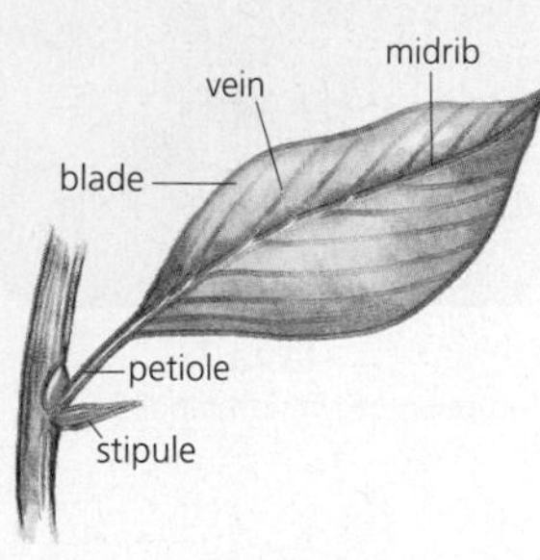

leaf

Mary and Louis Leakey

ă	pat	ôr	core
ā	pay	oi	boy
âr	care	ou	out
ä	father	o͝o	took
ĕ	pet	o͝or	lure
ē	be	o͞o	boot
ĭ	pit	ŭ	cut
ī	bite	ûr	urge
îr	pier	th	thin
ŏ	pot	*th*	this
ō	toe	zh	vision
ô	paw	ə	about

of graphite, used as the writing substance in pencils. **4.** Bullets from or for firearms; shot. ❖ *tr.v.* **lead·ed, lead·ing, leads 1.** To treat with lead or a lead compound: *leaded paint.* **2.** To cover, join, or weight with lead. [From Old English *lēad.*]

❑ *These sound alike:* **lead²**, **led** (guided).

lead·en (lĕd′n) *adj.* **1.** Made of lead: *a leaden fishing weight.* **2.** Dull dark gray: *leaden skies.* **3.** Heavy or sluggish: *leaden feet worn out from a long hike.* **4.** Gloomy; depressed: *leaden spirits.*

lead·er (lē′dər) *n.* **1.** A person who leads, guides, or has power over others. **2.** One who is ahead of others, as in a race. **3.** A short length of fishing line between the main line and the hook.

lead·er·ship (lē′dər-shĭp′) *n.* **1.** The position or office of a leader. **2.** The guidance or command of a leader or leaders: *Under the leadership of skillful diplomats, the peace conference was a success.* **3.** Ability to lead: *The mayor showed strong leadership during the crisis.* **4.** A group of leaders: *the leadership of the labor union.*

lead·ing (lē′dĭng) *adj.* **1.** Having the first or front position: *the leading swimmer in the race.* **2.** Most important; main; principal: *the leading industrial countries.*

lead·off (lēd′ôf′) *n.* **1.** An opening play or move. **2.** A person or thing that leads off. **—lead′off′** *adj.*

leaf (lēf) *n., pl.* **leaves** (lēvz) **1.** A flat, usually green structure that is attached to the stem of a plant and that functions mainly to make food for the plant through the process of photosynthesis. **2.** A sheet of paper in a book. **3a.** A very thin sheet of metal. **b.** Such sheets considered as a group: *gold leaf.* **4.** A movable or removable part of a table top. ❖ *intr.v.* **leafed, leaf·ing, leafs 1.** To produce or put forth leaves: *Most trees leafed out early this spring.* **2.** To turn through pages: *leaf through a book.* [From Old English *lēaf.*]

leaf·let (lē′flĭt) *n.* **1.** One of the separate segments of a compound leaf, as of a clover. **2.** A booklet or small pamphlet.

leaf·stalk (lēf′stôk′) *n.* The stalk by which a leaf is attached to a stem.

leaf·y (lē′fē) *adj.* **leaf·i·er, leaf·i·est 1.** Covered with or having many leaves: *leafy branches.* **2.** Consisting of leaves: *kale and other leafy vegetables.*

league¹ (lēg) *n.* **1.** An association or alliance of nations, organizations, or people working to help one another. **2.** An association of sports teams or clubs that compete chiefly with each other. **3.** A level of competition: *The ski jump was out of his league.* ❖ *intr.v.* **leagued, leagu·ing, leagues** To form an association or alliance. ◆ **in league** Joined or working together. [Alteration of Middle English *liege*, from Medieval Latin *liga*, from Latin *ligāre*, to bind.]

league² (lēg) *n.* A unit of distance, approximately equal to three miles (4.8 kilometers). [From Middle English *lege*, from Latin *leuga*, a measure of distance, of Celtic origin.]

League of Nations An organization of nations established in 1920 to promote cooperation and peace. It disbanded in 1946, and the United Nations took over many of its functions.

leagu·er (lē′gər) *n.* A person who belongs to a league.

leak (lēk) *v.* **leaked, leak·ing, leaks** *—intr.* **1.** To allow something to escape, enter, or pass through an opening or openings: *The roof leaks in a heavy rain.* **2.** To escape or pass through an opening or break: *Water leaked from the rusty pail.* **3.** To become known through a break in secrecy: *The news leaked out.* *—tr.* **1.** To let (something) escape or pass through a hole or opening: *The roof leaks water.* **2.** To disclose (secret information) without permission: *Someone leaked the jury's verdict before it was announced in court.* ❖ *n.* **1.** A hole, crack, or similar opening through which something can escape or pass: *I fixed the leak in the roof.* **2.** A disclosure of secret information. [From Middle English *leken*, probably from Middle Dutch *lēken.*]

❑ *These sound alike:* **leak, leek** (plant).

leak·age (lē′kĭj) *n.* **1.** The process, act, or an instance of leaking. **2a.** Something that escapes or enters by leaking. **b.** An amount lost as the result of leaking.

Lea·key (lē′kē) Family of British and Kenyan scientists including **Louis** (1903–1972) and **Mary** (1913–1996), who used a series of fossil discoveries in Tanzania to make the influential argument that humans evolved in Africa. Several members of their family have continued their research.

leak·y (lē′kē) *adj.* **leak·i·er, leak·i·est** Having or allowing a leak or leaks: *a leaky valve.* **—leak′i·ness** *n.*

lean¹ (lēn) *v.* **leaned, lean·ing, leans** *—intr.* **1.** To slant from an upright position: *The tree leaned in the high wind.* **2.** To rest one's weight on or against for support: *I leaned against the wall to rest.* **3.** To rely for assistance or support; depend: *Friends lean on each other for encouragement.* **4.** To have a tendency or preference: *I lean toward the challenger in this election.* *—tr.* To set or place in a slanting or supported position: *I leaned the ladder against the tree. Lean your head a bit to the right.* ❖ *n.* A slant or inclination: *The lean of the ladder makes it look as if it will fall.* [From Old English *hleonian.*]

❑ *These sound alike:* **lean¹** (slant), **lean²** (thin), **lien** (legal right).

lean² (lēn) *adj.* **lean·er, lean·est 1.** Not fat or fleshy; thin: *a lean cat.* **2.** Containing little or no fat: *lean meat.* **3.** Not productive, plentiful, or satisfying: *The long drought brought a lean harvest.* ❖ *n.* Meat with little or no fat. [From Old English *hlǣne.*] **—lean′ness** *n.*

❑ *These sound alike:* **lean²** (thin), **lean¹** (slant), **lien** (legal right).

SYNONYMS lean, thin, slender, spare, skinny, scrawny These adjectives mean having little or no excess flesh. **Lean** means lacking fat: *Leaner cuts of meat are better for your health.* **Thin** and **slender** mean having a lean body: *Mountain climbers tend to be thin and supple. The slender snake slipped easily through the thick hedge.* **Spare** often means trim with good muscle tone: *You have the spare figure of a marathon runner.* **Skinny** and **scrawny** mean unattractively thin, as if undernourished: *The boy had skinny, freckled legs with prominent knees. Judging by dog's scrawny body, we guessed it had not eaten in days.*
ANTONYM fat

---

lean·ing (lē′nĭng) *n.* An inclination, tendency, or preference.

leant (lĕnt) *v. Chiefly British* A past tense and a past participle of **lean¹**.

lean-to (lēn′to͞o′) *n., pl.* **lean-tos 1.** A shed with a sloping roof, built against a wall or the side of a building. **2.** A simple shelter, often having a roof that slopes in one direction and an open side.

leap (lēp) *v.* **leaped** or **leapt** (lĕpt *or* lēpt), **leap·ing, leaps** *—intr.* **1.** To jump or bound upward; spring: *The toad leaped from my hand.* **2.** To move suddenly from one state or subject to another: *A solution leaped into mind.* *—tr.* **1.** To jump or spring over: *The deer leap our garden fence.* **2.** To cause to jump: *leap a horse over a fence.* ❖ *n.* **1.** The act of leaping; a spring or jump. **2.** The distance covered in a jump: *a leap of ten feet.* [From Old English *hlēapan.*]

leap·frog (lēp′frôg′) *n.* A game in which one player bends over while the next in line jumps over him or her. ❖ *v.* **leap·frogged, leap·frog·ging, leap·frogs** *—tr.* To leap over in a game of leap frog. *—intr.* To move quickly to a more advanced position or state, especially when skipping an intermediate level.

leap year *n.* A year in which there are 366 days, the extra day being February 29. A year is a leap year if its number can be divided exactly by four, except years at the end of a century, which must be exactly divisible by 400.

learn (lûrn) *v.* **learned** also **learnt** (lûrnt), **learn·ing, learns** —*tr.* **1.** To gain knowledge of or skill in (something) through study or experience: *I finally learned how to sail. Is it hard to learn to speak French?* **2.** To find out: *We learned who won the election from the newspaper.* **3.** To memorize: *Learn the tune and then add the words.* —*intr.* To gain knowledge or skill: *I learned of their plans by letter.* [From Old English *leornian.*]

learn·ed (**lûr′**nĭd) *adj.* **1.** Having or showing deep knowledge; scholarly: *a learned professor.* **2.** Meant for scholars: *a learned journal.* **—learn′ed·ly** *adv.*

learn·ing (**lûr′**nĭng) *n.* **1.** Instruction; education: *Learning was a lot easier once the noise stopped.* **2.** Thorough knowledge or skill gained by study: *Fortunately I have teachers of great learning.* See Synonyms at **knowledge.**

learning disability *n.* Any of various disorders of attention, memory, or reasoning that interfere with the ability to learn.

lease (lēs) *n.* **1.** A written agreement granting use of property for a certain time in exchange for rent. **2.** The period of time specified in such an agreement. ❖ *tr.v.* **leased, leas·ing, leas·es 1.** To grant the use of (property) by lease: *The landlord leased the house to new tenants.* **2.** To acquire or hold (property) by lease: *We leased the house from the landlord.* [From Middle English *les,* from Anglo-Norman *lesser,* to lease.]

leash (lēsh) *n.* **1.** A cord, chain, or strap attached to a collar or harness and used to hold or lead a dog or other animal. **2.** A strap or cord used to keep something close to its user or in a designated location. ❖ *tr.v.* **leashed, leash·ing, leash·es** To restrain with or as if with a leash. [From Middle English *les,* from Old French *laissier,* to let go.]

least (lēst) *adj.* A superlative of **little.** Smallest in degree, size, or importance: *I made the least number of mistakes of anyone in my group.* ❖ *adv.* Superlative of **little.** To the smallest degree: *I like vanilla ice cream least.* ❖ *n.* The smallest thing or amount: *The least you could do would be to apologize.* ◆ **at least 1.** According to the lowest estimate; not less than: *I go running at least three days a week.* **2.** In any event; anyway: *You might at least call before you come over.* **in the least** At all: *I'm not in the least concerned.*

least common denominator *n.* The least common multiple of the denominators of a set of fractions.

least common multiple *n.* The smallest number that is a common multiple of two other numbers; for example, 12 is the least common multiple of 3 and 4.

least·wise (**lēst′**wīz′) *adv. Informal* In any event; at least.

leath·er (**lĕth′**ər) *n.* Material made from the cleaned and tanned hide of an animal.

leath·er·ette (lĕth′ə-**rĕt′**) *n.* Imitation leather.

leath·ern (**lĕth′**ərn) *adj.* Made of or resembling leather.

leath·er·y (**lĕth′**ə-rē) *adj.* Resembling leather: *leathery hands.*

leave¹ (lēv) *v.* **left** (lĕft), **leav·ing, leaves** —*tr.* **1.** To go out of or go away from: *She just left the room. He left town on Thursday.* **2.** To end one's association with; withdraw from: *He left our band and started another.* **3.** To go without taking; forget: *I left my umbrella on the train.* **4.** To allow to remain unused: *I left some milk in the glass.* **5.** To allow to remain in a certain condition or place: *I left the light on all night.* **6.** To give to another to do or use; entrust: *Leave the job to me.* **7.** To give by will; bequeath: *His uncle left him a piece of land.* **8.** To have as a remainder after subtraction: *12 minus 5 leaves 7.* —*intr.* To go away; depart: *We left after lunch.* ◆ **leave alone** or **let alone** To refrain from disturbing or interfering: *Leave the puzzle alone.* **leave off** To stop; cease: *Let's start the story where we left off.* **leave out** To omit: *Don't leave out the pepper from the recipe.* [From Old English *lǣfan.*]

leave² (lēv) *n.* **1.** Permission; consent: *My parents gave me leave to stay up late.* **2.** Official permission to be absent from work or duty; leave of absence. **3.** The length of such an absence. [From Old English *lēafe.*]

leave³ (lēv) *intr.v.* **leaved, leav·ing, leaves** To put forth leaves; leaf: *The trees leaved early this spring.* [From Middle English *leven,* from *lef,* leaf.]

leav·en (**lĕv′**ən) *n.* **1.** A substance, such as yeast, used to cause dough or batter to rise. **2.** An influence or element that serves to lighten or enliven the whole: *The leaven of good humor made it a friendly debate.* ❖ *tr.v.* **leav·ened, leav·en·ing, leav·ens 1.** To cause (dough or batter) to rise, as by adding yeast. **2.** To spread through so as to change or enliven. —SEE NOTE.

leav·en·ing (**lĕv′**ə-nĭng) *n.* Something that leavens; leaven.

leaves (lēvz) *n.* Plural of **leaf.**

leave-tak·ing (**lēv′**tā′kĭng) *n.* An exchange of goodbyes; a farewell.

leav·ings (**lē′**vĭngz) *pl.n.* Scraps left over; remains: *The turkey leavings were fed to the dog.*

Leav·itt (**lĕv′**ĭt), **Henrietta Swan** 1868–1921. American astronomer known for her studies of the brightness of stars and her formula for measuring distances between galaxies.

Leb·a·nese (lĕb′ə-**nēz′** *or* lĕb′ə-**nēs′**) *adj.* Relating to Lebanon or its people or culture. ❖ *n., pl.* **Lebanese** A native or inhabitant of Lebanon.

Leb·a·non (**lĕb′**ə-nən *or* **lĕb′**ə-nŏn′) A country of southwest Asia on the Mediterranean Sea north of Israel. Beirut is the capital.

lech·er (**lĕch′**ər) *n.* A man who engages in lechery.

lech·er·ous (**lĕch′**ər-əs) *adj.* Given to, characterized by, or inciting lechery. **—lech′er·ous·ly** *adv.*

lech·er·y (**lĕch′**ə-rē) *n.* Excessive interest in or indulgence in sexual activity.

lec·i·thin (**lĕs′**ə-thĭn) *n.* Any of various fatty substances containing phosphorus, present in the cell membranes of plant and animal cells. Lecithin is extracted from seeds and used commercially in foods, cosmetics, paints, and plastics.

lec·tern (**lĕk′**tərn) *n.* **1.** A desk with a slanted top for holding books from which to read scriptures during a church service. **2.** A stand that serves as a support for the notes or books of a speaker.

lec·ture (**lĕk′**chər) *n.* **1.** A prepared talk providing information about a given subject, delivered before an audience or a class. **2.** A serious lengthy warning or scolding: *The judge gave the reckless driver a lecture in court.* ❖ *v.* **lec·tured, lec·tur·ing, lec·tures** —*intr.* To deliver a lecture or lectures: *lecturing on history at the university.* —*tr.* **1.** To give a lecture to (an audience or class). **2.** To scold or warn at length. [From Middle English *lecture,* reading, from Medieval Latin *lēctūra,* from Latin *legere,* to read.] **—lec′tur·er** *n.*

led (lĕd) *v.* Past tense and past participle of **lead¹.**
❑ *These sound alike:* **led, lead²** (element).

LED (ĕl′ē-**dē′** *or* lĕd) *n.* A semiconductor diode that produces light when an electric current is applied to it. LEDs are used in light bulbs and digital displays. [From *l(ight)-e(mitting) d(iode).*]

Le·da (**lē′**də) *n.* In Greek mythology, the mother of Helen and Pollux by Zeus in the form of a swan, and of Castor and Clytemnestra by her own husband.

lede (lēd) *n.* The first sentence or introductory portion of a news story.
❑ *These sound alike:* **lede, lead¹** (guide).

WORD HISTORY

leaven The word **leaven,** meaning "an agent added to dough to make it rise," comes from the Old French word *levain.* This in turn comes from the Latin *levāmen,* "something that raises," which is formed from the Latin verb *levāre,* "to raise, lighten, relieve." From the related adjective *levis,* "light," we get **levity,** which is what we have when we lighten up. From related Latin words we also get **elevate,** "to lift or raise up," as well as **alleviate,** "to lighten, make easier, soothe."

Henrietta Swan Leavitt

lectern

Robert E. Lee
photographed in 1865

leek

ă	pat	ôr	core
ā	pay	oi	boy
âr	care	ou	out
ä	father	ŏŏ	took
ĕ	pet	ŏŏr	lure
ē	be	ōō	boot
ĭ	pit	ŭ	cut
ī	bite	ûr	urge
îr	pier	th	thin
ŏ	pot	*th*	this
ō	toe	zh	vision
ô	paw	ə	about

ledge (lĕj) *n.* **1.** A narrow shelf projecting from a wall: *a window ledge.* **2.** A cut or projection with a flat horizontal surface on the side of a cliff or rock wall.

ledg·er (lĕj′ər) *n.* An account book in which sums of money received and paid out by a business are recorded.

lee (lē) *n.* The side away from the wind; the sheltered side: *sailing along the lee of the island.* ❖ *adj.* Sheltered or away from the wind: *the lee side of a ship.* [From Old English *hlēo*, shelter, protection.]
❑ *These sound alike:* **lee, lea** (meadow).

Lee (lē), **Ann** Known as "Mother Ann." 1736–1784. British religious leader and founder (1776) of the Shakers in America.

Lee, (Nelle) Harper 1926–2016. American writer. Her novel *To Kill a Mockingbird* (1960) deals with racial injustice in the South.

Lee, Robert Edward 1807–1870. American Confederate general in the Civil War. He won victories at the Second Battle of Bull Run (1862), Fredericksburg (1862), and Chancellorsville (1863) before he surrendered to Gen. Ulysses S. Grant at Appomattox (1865).

leech (lēch) *n.* **1.** Any of various segmented worms that suck blood from other animals, including humans, and are usually found in freshwater habitats. **2.** A person who constantly attempts to gain from someone else; a parasite. [From Old English *lǣce*, physician, leech.]
❑ *These sound alike:* **leech, leach** (dissolve out).

Leeds (lēdz) A borough of north-central England northeast of Manchester. It was incorporated in 1626.

leek (lēk) *n.* A vegetable related to the onion, having a narrow white bulb and long dark-green leaves. [From Old English *lǣc*.]
❑ *These sound alike:* **leek, leak** (escape).

leer (lîr) *n.* A sly, lustful, or cunning look. ❖ *intr.v.* **leered, leer·ing, leers** To look with a leer.

leer·y (lîr′ē) *adj.* **leer·i·er, leer·i·est** Suspicious; wary: *I am very leery of schemes that promise instant riches.* **—leer′i·ly** *adv.*

lees (lēz) *pl.n.* Sediment that settles during fermentation, especially in wine; dregs.

Leeu·wen·hoek or **Leu·wen·hoek** (lā′vən-ho͝ok′), **Anton van** 1632–1723. Dutch naturalist and pioneer of microscopic research. He was the first to describe protozoa, bacteria, and spermatozoa.

lee·ward (lē′wərd *or* lo͞o′ərd) *adv. & adj.* On or toward the side to which the wind is blowing: *an island off the leeward side of the boat.* ❖ *n.* The lee side: *a whale to leeward of us.*

Lee·ward Islands (lē′wərd) **1.** The northern group of the Lesser Antilles in the West Indies, extending from the Virgin Islands southeast to Dominica. The islands were visited by Columbus in 1493. **2.** A chain of small islets of Hawaii in the central Pacific Ocean west-northwest of the main islands. The Leewards constitute a government bird sanctuary.

lee·way (lē′wā′) *n.* **1.** Extra space, time, or resources allowing freedom or safety: *We left plenty of leeway to reach the airport during rush hour.* **2.** The drift of a ship or plane to leeward of its course.

left[1] (lĕft) *adj.* **1a.** Belonging to or located on the side of the body to the west when one is facing north: *writes with her left hand.* **b.** Relating to, directed toward, or located on the left side: *the left arm of the chair.* **2.** often **Left** Belonging to the political left; leftist. ❖ *n.* **1a.** The direction or position on the left side: *The sun set on my left as I drove north.* **b.** The left side. **c.** A turn in the direction of the left hand or side. **2.** often **Left** The people and groups who advocate liberal or radical ways to change society, especially in politics, in an attempt to achieve equality or improve the life of the working classes. **3.** A punch or blow delivered with the left hand. ❖ *adv.* On or to the left. [From Middle English *lift*, from Old English *lyft*, weak, useless.]

left[2] (lĕft) *v.* Past tense and past participle of **leave**[1].

left field *n.* **1.** In baseball, the section of the outfield that is to the left, looking from home plate. **2.** The position played by the left fielder.

left fielder *n.* In baseball, the player who defends left field.

left-hand (lĕft′hănd′) *adj.* **1.** Relating to or located on the left: *the upper left-hand corner.* **2.** Relating to, designed for, or done with the left hand.

left-hand·ed (lĕft′hăn′dĭd) *adj.* **1a.** Using the left hand, as for writing or throwing, more skillfully or easily than the right hand. **b.** In sports, swinging from left to right: *a left-handed golfer.* **2a.** Done with the left hand. **b.** Designed for use by the left hand: *left-handed scissors.* **3.** Turning or moving from right to left: *a left-handed screw.* **4.** Insincere or doubtful: *a left-handed compliment.* ❖ *adv.* **1.** With the left hand. **2.** From the left to the right: *She bats left-handed.* **—left′-hand′ed·ly** *adv.* **—left′-hand′ed·ness** *n.*

left-hand·er (lĕft′hăn′dər) *n.* A person who is left-handed.

left·ist (lĕf′tĭst) *n.* A person who advocates or sympathizes with the ideas of the political left, especially a socialist or communist. ❖ *adj.* Advocating or sympathizing with ideas of the political left: *leftist publications.*

left·o·ver (lĕft′ō′vər) *adj.* Remaining unused or uneaten: *leftover fabric; leftover rice.*

left·o·vers (lĕft′ō′vərs) *pl.n.* Remaining food kept after a meal for future consumption: *had leftovers for dinner.*

left wing also **Left Wing** *n.* The liberal or radical faction of a group. **—left′-wing′** *adj.* **—left′wing′er** *n.*

left·y (lĕf′tē) *n., pl.* **left·ies** *Informal* A person who is left-handed.

leg (lĕg) *n.* **1.** A limb of a human or other animal that is used for support or for moving from place to place. **2.** The part of a garment, especially of a pair of pants, that covers the leg. **3.** A supporting part resembling a leg in shape or function: *a table leg.* **4.** Either of the sides of a right triangle that is not the hypotenuse. **5.** A stage of a journey or course: *the first leg of the trip.* ◆ **leg it** To walk or run. **on (one's) last legs** At the end of one's strength or resources; ready to collapse, fail, or die. [From Middle English, from Old Norse *leggr*.]

leg·a·cy (lĕg′ə-sē) *n., pl.* **leg·a·cies 1.** An inheritance consisting of money or property. **2.** Something passed on to those who come later in time; a heritage: *a legacy of religious freedom.*

le·gal (lē′gəl) *adj.* **1.** Relating to the law: *legal knowledge.* **2.** Established or permitted by law: *legal activities.* **3.** Relating to or characteristic of lawyers or their profession: *legal fees.* **4.** Acceptable or allowable under official rules: *the legal moves in chess.* [From Middle English, from Latin *lēgālis*, from *lēx*, law.] **—le′gal·ly** *adv.*

legal age *n.* The age at which a person assumes the legal rights and responsibilities of an adult.

le·gal·i·ty (lē-găl′ĭ-tē) *n., pl.* **le·gal·i·ties 1.** The state of being legal; lawfulness. **2.** Something required by law.

le·gal·ize (lē′gə-līz′) *tr.v.* **le·gal·ized, le·gal·iz·ing, le·gal·iz·es** To make legal. **—le′gal·i·za′tion** (lē′gə-lĭ-zā′shən) *n.*

legal tender *n.* Money that must by law be accepted in payment of a debt.

leg·ate (lĕg′ĭt) *n.* An official envoy or ambassador, especially one representing the pope.

leg·a·tee (lĕg′ə-tē′) *n.* The inheritor of a legacy.

le·ga·tion (lĭ-gā′shən) *n.* **1.** A group of diplomatic representatives in a foreign country ranking below an embassy. **2.** The building occupied by such a group.

le·ga·to (lĭ-gä′tō) *adv. & adj.* In a musical style in which notes are connected smoothly without any noticeable break between them.

leg·end (lĕj′ənd) *n.* **1a.** A story handed down from earlier times, often believed to be historically true. **b.** A group of such stories. **2.** A person or thing that is famous enough to inspire legends: *He's a legend in his own time.* **3.** An inscription on a coin, a banner, or another object. **4.** An explanatory caption under a map, chart, or illustration. [From Middle English, legende, from Medieval Latin *(lectiō) legenda,* (lesson) to be read, from Latin *legere,* to read.]

leg·en·dar·y (lĕj′ən-dĕr′ē) *adj.* **1.** Relating to or based on a legend: *legendary heroes.* **2.** Talked about or celebrated in a legend or legends: *The fox's cunning is legendary.* **3.** Very well-known; famous.

leg·er·de·main (lĕj′ər-də-**mān′**) *n.* **1.** Skill in performing tricks with the hands, especially by a magician or juggler; sleight of hand. **2.** A display of trickery.

leg·ged (lĕg′ĭd *or* lĕgd) *adj.* Having a certain kind or number of legs: *four-legged animals.*

leg·ging (lĕg′ĭng) *n.* **1.** A leg covering worn especially by soldiers and workers, often made of cloth or leather and usually extending from the waist or knee to the ankle. **2.** Tight-fitting knit pants, usually worn by women and children.

leg·gy (lĕg′ē) *adj.* **leg·gi·er, leg·gi·est 1.** Having long legs: *a tall, leggy boy.* **2.** Having long often leafless stems: *leggy petunias.*

Leg·horn (lĕg′hôrn′ *or* lĕg′ərn) *n.* Any of a breed of white chickens that produce a large number of white eggs.

leg·i·ble (lĕj′ə-bəl) *adj.* Capable of being read: *clear, legible handwriting.* **—leg′i·bil′i·ty** *n.* **—leg′i·bly** *adv.*

le·gion (lē′jən) *n.* **1.** The major unit of the ancient Roman army, consisting of at least 3,000 foot soldiers and 100 cavalry troops. **2.** A large military unit. **3.** A large group or number of people or things; a multitude: *Legions of insects settled on the fields.* **4.** often **Legion** A national organization of people who once served in the armed forces.

le·gion·ar·y (lē′jə-nĕr′ē) *adj.* Relating to or belonging to a legion. ❖ *n., pl.* **le·gion·ar·ies** A soldier of a legion.

le·gion·naire (lē′jə-**nâr′**) *n.* A member of a legion.

leg·is·late (lĕj′ĭ-slāt′) *v.* **leg·is·lat·ed, leg·is·lat·ing, leg·is·lates** *—intr.* To make or pass laws: *Only Congress is empowered to legislate. —tr.* To create or bring about by making laws: *legislate reforms in the housing code.*

leg·is·la·tion (lĕj′ĭ-**slā′**shən) *n.* **1.** The act or process of making laws: *Our Constitution gives Congress the authority of legislation.* **2.** A proposed or enacted law or group of laws: *legislation being discussed in Congress.*

leg·is·la·tive (lĕj′ĭ-slā′tĭv) *adj.* **1.** Relating to the making of laws: *legislative powers.* **2.** Relating to a legislature: *legislative decree.* **3.** Having power to make laws: *the legislative branch of government.*

leg·is·la·tor (lĕj′ĭ-slā′tər) *n.* A member of a government body that makes laws: *Senators and representatives are legislators.* [From Latin *lēgis lātor,* proposer of a law.]

leg·is·la·ture (lĕj′ĭ-slā′chər) *n.* A body of people empowered to make and change the laws of a nation or state.

le·git·i·ma·cy (lə-**jĭt′**ə-mə-sē) *n.* The quality or fact of being legitimate.

le·git·i·mate (lə-**jĭt′**ə-mĭt) *adj.* **1.** In accordance with the law; lawful: *the legitimate owner of the property.* **2.** Supported by logic or common sense; reasonable: *Some problems have more than one legitimate solution.* **3.** Authentic; genuine; real: *We have a legitimate complaint.* **4.** *Often Offensive* Born of legally married parents: *a legitimate child.* **—le·git′i·mate·ly** *adv.*

le·git·i·mize (lə-**jĭt′**ə-mīz′) *tr.v.* **le·git·i·mized, le·git·i·miz·ing, le·git·i·miz·es** To make legitimate.

leg·ume (lĕg′yōōm′ *or* lə-**gyōōm′**) *n.* **1.** Any of a group of related plants having seedpods that split along two sides. Beans, peas, clover, and alfalfa are all legumes. **2.** The pod or seed of such a plant, used as food.

le·gu·mi·nous (lə-**gyōō′**mə-nəs) *adj.* Relating to legumes.

leg warmer *n.* A knitted covering for the leg, resembling a sock without a foot.

Le Ha·vre (lə **hä′**vrə *or* lə **häv′**) A city of northern France on the English Channel west-northwest of Paris. It is a major port.

lei[1] (lā *or* **lā′**ē) *n., pl.* **leis** A garland of flowers worn around the neck as an ornament. [From Hawaiian.]

❑ *These sound alike:* **lei**[1] (garland), **lay**[1] (put), **lay**[2] (not of the clergy), **lay**[3] (poem), **lay**[4] (placed oneself flat), **lei**[2] (Romanian currency).

lei[2] (lā) *n.* Plural of **leu.**

❑ *These sound alike:* **lei**[1] (Romanian currency), **lay**[1] (put), **lay**[2] (not of the clergy), **lay**[3] (poem), **lay**[4] (placed oneself flat), **lei** (garland).

Leip·zig (**līp′**sĭg *or* **līp′**sĭk) A city of east-central Germany south-southwest of Berlin. It was originally a Slavic settlement.

lei·sure (**lē′**zhər *or* **lĕzh′**ər) *n.* Freedom from work or time-consuming tasks: *Vacation is customarily a time of leisure and relaxation.* ◆ **at (one's) leisure** When one has free time; at one's convenience: *Respond to this letter at your leisure.*

lei·sure·ly (lē′zhər-lē *or* **lĕzh′**ər-lē) *adj.* Characterized by leisure; unhurried: *a leisurely lunch.* ❖ *adv.* In an unhurried manner; slowly: *strolled leisurely toward town.* **—lei′sure·li·ness** *n.*

lek (lĕk) *n.* The basic monetary unit of Albania.

lem·ming (**lĕm′**ĭng) *n.* Any of various small stout rodents that live in northern regions and are noted for their mass migrations.

lem·on (**lĕm′**ən) *n.* **1a.** An oval yellow citrus fruit having sour juicy pulp. **b.** The spiny evergreen tree that bears such fruit. **2.** *Informal* Something that is unsatisfactory or defective: *That car is a lemon; it breaks down all the time.* [From Middle English *limon,* from Persian *līmū.*] **—lem′on·y** *adj.*

lem·on·ade (lĕm′ə-**nād′**) *n.* A drink made of lemon juice, water, and sugar.

lem·pi·ra (lĕm-**pîr′**ə) *n.* The basic monetary unit of Honduras.

le·mur (**lē′**mər) *n.* Any of various small primates of the island of Madagascar that have large eyes, soft fur, and a long tail. Lemurs live in trees and are active chiefly at night.

Len·a·pe (**lĕn′**ə-pē) *n., pl.* **Lenape** or **Len·a·pes** A Delaware Indian.

lend (lĕnd) *v.* **lent** (lĕnt), **lend·ing, lends** *—tr.* **1.** To give or allow the use of (something) with the understanding that it is to be returned: *My parents lent me the car to go to the movies.* **2.** To provide (money) temporarily on condition that the amount borrowed be returned, usually with an interest fee. **3.** To contribute; impart: *The painting lent a feeling of warmth to the room.* **4.** To make available for another's use: *The neighbors lent their help after the storm. —intr.* To make a loan. ◆ **lend a hand** To be of assistance. **lend itself to** To be suitable for: *This novel lends itself to several interpretations.* [From Old English *lǣnan.*] **—lend′er** *n.* —SEE NOTE AT **borrow.**

L'En·gle (**lĕng′**gəl), **Madeleine** 1918–2007. American writer best known for her books for children, especially the science fiction series beginning with *A Wrinkle in Time* (1962).

length (lĕngkth *or* lĕngth) *n.* **1.** The measured distance of a thing from end to end along its greatest dimension: *the length of a boat.* **2.** The extent of something: *traveled the length of the Nile River.* **3.** The amount of time

Anton van Leeuwenhoek

lei[1]

lemur

something takes; duration: *the length of the meeting.* **4.** The state, quality, or fact of being long: *The length of the journey wore us out.* **5.** The measure of something used as a unit to estimate distances: *two arm's lengths.* **6.** A piece of something, often of a standard size: *a length of wire.* **7.** often **lengths** The extent or degree to which a goal is pursued: *went to great lengths to prove his point.* ◆ **at length 1.** After some time; eventually: *At length we arrived at the dock.* **2.** In detail; fully: *spoke at length about her travels.*

Vladimir Ilich Lenin

length·en (lĕngk′thən *or* lĕng′thən) *tr. & intr.v.* **length·ened, length·en·ing, length·ens** To make or become longer: *lengthen pants legs; shadows that lengthen as sunset approaches.*

length·wise (lĕngkth′wīz′ *or* lĕngth′wīz′) *adv.* Along the direction of the length: *fold a sheet of paper lengthwise.* ❖ *adj.* In the direction of the length: *lengthwise folds in the paper.*

length·y (lĕngk′thē *or* lĕng′thē) *adj.* **length·i·er, length·i·est** Long, especially too long: *a lengthy explanation.* **—length′i·ly** *adv.* **—length′i·ness** *n.*

le·ni·ent (lē′nē-ənt *or* lēn′yənt) *adj.* Inclined to forgive; merciful; generous: *a lenient judge.* [From Latin *lēnis*, soft.] **—le′ni·ence, le′ni·en·cy** *n.*

Le·nin (lĕn′ĭn), **Vladimir Ilich** 1870–1924. Russian founder of the Bolsheviks, leader of the Russian Revolution (1917), head of the revolutionary government (1917–1921), and first head of the Soviet Union (1922–1924).

Len·in·grad (lĕn′ĭn-grăd′) See **Saint Petersburg.**

Len·ni Len·a·pe (lĕn′ē lĕn′ə-pē) *n.* A Delaware Indian.

Len·non (lĕn′ən), **John** 1940–1980. British rock musician who was a member of the Beatles. He cowrote many of the group's songs, including "A Day in the Life" (1967).

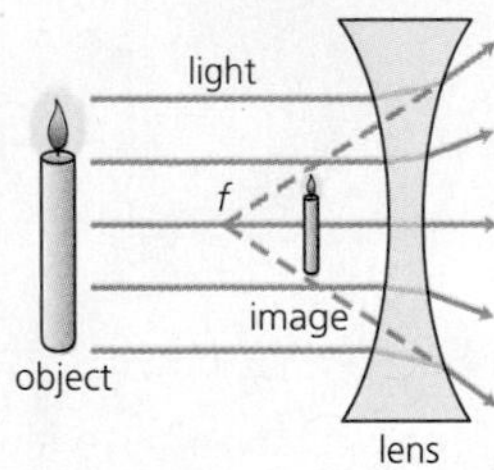

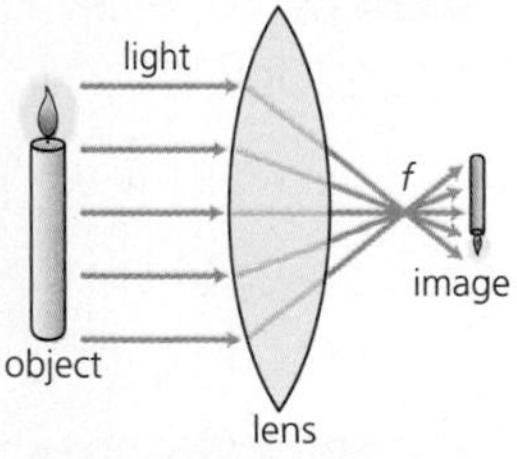

lens

light passing through a biconcave lens (*top*) and through a biconvex lens (*bottom*); *f* indicates the focal point

lens (lĕnz) *n., pl.* **lens·es 1a.** A piece of glass or plastic shaped so as to focus or spread parallel light rays that pass through it to form an image. **b.** A combination of two or more such lenses used to form an image, as in a camera or telescope. **2.** A transparent structure behind the iris of the eye that focuses light entering the eye on the retina. [From Latin *lēns*, lentil.]

lent (lĕnt) *v.* Past tense and past participle of **lend.**

Lent *n.* A 40-day period of fasting and penitence observed by many Christians, usually from Ash Wednesday until Easter, not counting Sundays. **—Lent′en** *adj.*

len·til (lĕn′təl) *n.* **1.** The round flat seed of a pod-bearing plant related to the beans and peas, eaten as a vegetable. **2.** The plant that bears such seeds.

Le·o (lē′ō) *n.* **1.** A constellation in the Northern Hemisphere near Cancer, traditionally pictured as a lion. **2.** The fifth sign of the zodiac in astrology.

Le·o·nar·do da Vin·ci (lē′ə-när′dō də vĭn′chē) 1452–1519. Italian painter, engineer, and scientist who is best known for his paintings *The Last Supper* (about 1495) and *Mona Lisa* (about 1503).

le·one (lē-ōn′) *n.* The basic monetary unit of Sierra Leone.

le·o·nine (lē′ə-nīn′) *adj.* Relating to or characteristic of a lion: *a leonine roar.*

leop·ard (lĕp′ərd) *n.* A large meat-eating wild cat of Africa and Asia, having either light-brown fur with black spots or black fur. [From Middle English, from Greek *leopardos.*]

le·o·tard (lē′ə-tärd′) *n.* A tight-fitting one-piece garment, sometimes with sleeves, worn especially by dancers and acrobats. [After Jules *Léotard* (1830–1870), French aerialist.]

lep·er (lĕp′ər) *n.* A person who has leprosy. [From Middle English *lepre*, ultimately from Greek *lepros*, scaly.]

lep·re·chaun (lĕp′rĭ-kôn′) *n.* In Irish folklore, an elflike creature who can reveal hidden treasure if caught. [From Old Irish *luchorpán*, little figure.]

lep·ro·sy (lĕp′rə-sē) *n.* An infectious disease in tropical regions caused by bacteria that damage the skin and nerves. If untreated, leprosy can result in disfigurement and blindness. **—lep′rous** (lĕp′rəs) *adj.*

les·bi·an (lĕz′bē-ən) *n.* A woman whose sexual orientation is toward women. ❖ *adj.* Relating to or being a lesbian. —SEE NOTE AT **gay.**

le·sion (lē′zhən) *n.* An abnormal structure in a bodily organ or tissue, such as a wound, sore, or tumor, caused usually by injury or disease.

Le·so·tho (lə-sō′tō *or* lə-sōō′tōō) A country of southern Africa forming an enclave within east-central South Africa. Maseru is the capital.

less (lĕs) *adj.* A comparative of **little. 1.** Smaller in amount, quantity, or degree; not so much: *less time to spare; less food to eat.* **2.** Lower in importance or rank: *No less a person than the president gave the order.* ❖ *adv.* Comparative of **little.** To a smaller extent, degree, or quantity: *The game was less enjoyable than I had hoped.* ❖ *prep.* Minus; without: *Five less three is two.* ❖ *n.* A smaller amount or quantity: *The house sold for less than we thought.* ◆ **less than** Not at all: *a less than satisfactory answer.* **much less** or **still less** Especially not: *I'm not blaming anyone, much less you.* —SEE NOTE AT **few.**

-less *suff.* A suffix that means: **1.** Without or lacking: *motherless; nameless.* **2.** Not acting in a certain way: *relentless.* **3.** Not acted on in a certain way: *dauntless.* —SEE NOTE.

les·see (lĕ-sē′) *n.* A tenant holding a lease.

less·en (lĕs′ən) *tr. & intr.v.* **less·ened, less·en·ing, less·ens** To make or become less: *a drug to lessen the pain; pain that lessened immediately.* See Synonyms at **decrease.**

❑ *These sound alike:* **lessen, lesson** (instruction).

less·er (lĕs′ər) *adj.* A comparative of **little. 1.** Smaller in amount, value, or importance: *a lesser evil; lesser gods.* **2.** Of a smaller size than other similar forms: *the lesser anteater.* ❖ *adv.* A comparative of **little.** Less. Used before a participle: *works by lesser-known authors.* ❖ *n.* A person or thing that is lower in importance, rank, size, or degree: *the lesser of two evils.*

Lesser Antilles See **Antilles.**

les·son (lĕs′ən) *n.* **1.** Something to be learned, especially an assignment or exercise in which something is studied or taught: *an algebra textbook divided into 40 lessons.* **2.** A period of time devoted to teaching or learning a certain subject: *three piano lessons a week.* **3.** An experience or example from which one can learn: *The poor grades taught me a lesson in the value of studying.* **4.** A reading from the Bible given as part of a religious service. [From Middle English *lessoun*, from Latin *lēctiō*, a reading.]

❑ *These sound alike:* **lesson, lessen** (make less).

les·sor (lĕs′ôr′ *or* lĕ-sôr′) *n.* A person who rents property to another by lease.

lest (lĕst) *conj.* **1.** For fear that: *tiptoed lest the guard should hear her.* **2.** So that something or someone will not or would not: *double-knotted his shoelaces lest they come untied.*

let¹ (lĕt) *v.* **let, let·ting, lets** *—tr.* **1a.** To grant permission to: *The crowd let the speaker continue without interruption.* **b.** To allow something to happen: *Let your hot cocoa cool a bit.* **2.** To cause to: *Let me know what happened.* **3.** Used as an auxiliary verb to express a request, command, or warning: *Let's finish the job!* **4.** Used as an auxiliary verb to express a proposal or assumption: *Let x equal 3.* **5.** To permit to move in a specified way: *Let the cat out.* **6.** To permit to escape; release: *Who let the air out of the balloon?* **7.** To rent or lease: *They let rooms to students.* *—intr.* To become rented or leased. ◆ **let down 1.** To cause to come down gradually; lower: *The crane let down the piano.* **2.** To fail to meet the expectations of; disappoint: *Don't let*

ă	pat	ôr	core
ā	pay	oi	boy
âr	care	ou	out
ä	father	ŏŏ	took
ĕ	pet	ŏŏr	lure
ē	be	ōō	boot
ĭ	pit	ŭ	cut
ī	bite	ûr	urge
îr	pier	th	thin
ŏ	pot	*th*	this
ō	toe	zh	vision
ô	paw	ə	about

me down. **let off 1.** To excuse from work or duty: *They let me off so I could go home early.* **2.** To release with little or no punishment: *They were let off with a warning.* **let on 1.** To allow to be known; admit: *Don't let on that I'm going too.* **2.** To pretend: *They let on that they had been to Europe.* **let out 1.** To come to a close; end: *School lets out next week.* **2.** To make known; reveal: *Who let that information out?* **3.** To increase the size of (a garment, for example). **let up** To slow down, diminish, or stop: *The rain finally let up.* [From Old English *lǣtan.*]

let² (lĕt) *n.* A stroke in tennis or other net games that must be repeated, especially a serve that has touched the net before falling into the proper part of the court. [From Middle English *lette,* obstacle, from Old English *lettan,* to hinder.]

–let *suff.* A suffix that means: **1.** A small one: *booklet.* **2.** Something worn on: *armlet.*

let·down (lĕt′doun′) *n.* **1.** A decrease or slowing down, as in energy or effort. **2.** A disappointment: *Losing that game was a real letdown.*

le·thal (lē′thəl) *adj.* Causing or capable of causing death: *a lethal disease; a lethal weapon.* [From Latin *lētum,* death.] **—le′thal·ly** *adv.*

le·thar·gic (lə-thär′jĭk) *adj.* Relating to, causing, or characterized by lethargy: *spend a lethargic afternoon lying on the beach.* **—le·thar′gi·cal·ly** *adv.*

leth·ar·gy (lĕth′ər-jē) *n., pl.* **leth·ar·gies 1a.** Lack of energy or vigor; sluggishness. **b.** Lack of interest or enthusiasm; apathy. **2.** An abnormal state of drowsiness, as caused by disease or drugs.

Le·to (lē′tō) *n.* In Greek mythology, a goddess who was the mother of Apollo and Artemis by Zeus.

let's (lĕts) Contraction of *let us.*

Lett (lĕt) *n.* A member of a Baltic people that make up the main population of Latvia.

let·ter (lĕt′ər) *n.* **1.** A symbol or character that is part of an alphabet, is used in the writing of a word, and usually indicates a speech sound. **2.** A written or printed message addressed to a person: *I wrote three letters to friends this week.* **3.** A document giving the person who bears it certain rights or privileges: *carried a letter of safe passage through enemy territory.* **4. letters** *(used with a singular verb)* Literature: *English letters.* **5.** The exact or literal meaning: *the letter of the law.* **6.** An emblem in the shape of the initial of a school, awarded for achievement in athletics. ❖ *tr.v.* **let·tered, let·ter·ing, let·ters** To mark or write with letters: *lettered our name on the mailbox.* ◆ **to the letter** To the last detail; exactly: *We followed the instructions to the letter.* [From Middle English *lettre,* from Latin *littera.*] **—let′ter·er** *n.*

letter carrier *n.* A mail carrier.

let·ter·head (lĕt′ər-hĕd′) *n.* **1.** A printed heading at the top of a sheet of letter paper, usually consisting of the name and address of the sender. **2.** Letter paper with such a heading.

let·ter·ing (lĕt′ər-ĭng) *n.* **1.** The act of forming letters. **2.** The letters formed, drawn, or painted, as on a sign.

let·ter-per·fect (lĕt′ər-pûr′fĭkt) *adj.* Perfect in every detail.

Let·tish (lĕt′ĭsh) *adj.* Relating to the Letts or their language or culture. ❖ *n.* The Latvian language.

let·tuce (lĕt′əs) *n.* Any of various forms of a plant cultivated for its large green or reddish leaves, used in salad. [From Middle English *letuse,* from Latin *lactūca.*]

let·up (lĕt′ŭp′) *n.* **1.** A reduction in pace, force, or intensity. **2.** A pause or stop: *no letup in the storm.*

le·u (lĕ′o͞o) *n., pl.* **lei** (lā) The basic monetary unit of Romania.

leu·cine (lo͞o′sēn′) *n.* An essential amino acid that is found in plant and animal protein.

leu·ke·mi·a (lo͞o-kē′mē-ə) *n.* Any of several cancers of the blood characterized by the uncontrolled growth in the number of white blood cells.

leu·ko·cyte also **leu·co·cyte** (lo͞o′kə-sīt′) *n.* A white blood cell.

lev (lĕf) *n., pl.* **lev·a** (lĕv′ə) The basic monetary unit of Bulgaria.

Le·vant (lə-vănt′) A region on the eastern coast of the Mediterranean Sea north of the Arabian Peninsula and south of Turkey, usually including Israel, Jordan, Lebanon, Palestine, and Syria.

lev·ee (lĕv′ē) *n.* **1.** A bank of earth or other material built up along a river to keep it from flooding. **2.** A landing place on a river. [From Old French *lever,* to raise.]
❑ *These sound alike:* **levee, levy** (collect).

lev·el (lĕv′əl) *n.* **1.** Relative position or rank on a scale: *Science gets more complex at the college level.* **2.** Position along a vertical axis; height or depth: *The divers descended to a level of 60 feet.* **3.** A story or floor of a building. **4.** A flat stretch of land. **5.** An instrument for determining whether a surface is horizontal or vertical, used especially by carpenters and masons. ❖ *adj.* **1.** Having a flat even surface: *level farmland.* **2.** Horizontal: *Is the picture on this wall level?* **3.** Steady; uniform: *a level tone of voice.* **4.** Being at the same height, rank, or position; even: *The two tabletops are level with each other.* **5.** Reasonable and careful; sensible: *a level head.* ❖ *v.* **lev·eled, lev·el·ing, lev·els** or **lev·elled, lev·el·ling, lev·els** —*tr.* **1.** To make smooth, flat, or horizontal: *level ground for a new building.* **2.** To cut, tear, or knock down to the ground: *A tornado leveled several buildings.* **3.** To place on the same level; equalize: *level differences between schools.* **4.** To aim carefully: *level a rifle at the target.* —*intr. Informal* To be frank and open: *Let's level with each other.* ◆ **(one's) level best** The best one can do. **on the level** *Informal* Without deception; honest. [From Middle English, an instrument to check that a surface is horizontal, from Latin *lībella,* balance.] **—lev′el·er, lev′el·ler** *n.* **—lev′el·ly** *adv.* **—lev′el·ness** *n.*

lev·el·head·ed (lĕv′əl-hĕd′ĭd) *adj.* Having common sense and good judgment; sensible. **—lev′el·head′ed·ness** *n.*

lev·er (lĕv′ər *or* lē′vər) *n.* **1.** A simple machine consisting of a rigid bar that pivots on a fixed point and can be used to transmit force, as in raising or moving a weight at one end by pushing down on the other. **2.** A projecting handle used to control, adjust, or operate a device or machine: *a gear shift lever.* [From Middle English, from Old French *levier,* from *lever,* to raise, from Latin *levāre.*]

lev·er·age (lĕv′ər-ĭj *or* lē′vər-ĭj) *n.* **1.** The action or mechanical advantage of a lever. **2.** An advantage in position or in power to act effectively: *Great wealth gives a person leverage in many business situations.* **3.** The use of borrowed funds, often for a risky investment. ❖ *tr.v.* **lev·er·aged, lev·er·ag·ing, lev·er·ag·es** To provide (a company, for instance) with leverage.

Le·vi (lē′vī′) In the Bible, a son of Jacob and Leah and the ancestor of one of the tribes of Israel.

le·vi·a·than (lə-vī′ə-thən) *n.* **1.** A huge sea creature mentioned in the Bible. **2.** Something of enormous size or bulk.

Le·vi's (lē′vīz′) A trademark for pants made of denim.

lev·i·tate (lĕv′ĭ-tāt′) *intr. & tr.v.* **lev·i·tat·ed, lev·i·tat·ing, lev·i·tates** To rise or cause to rise into the air and float, especially through supposed supernatural means.

Le·vite (lē′vīt′) *n.* In the Bible, a member of the tribe of Levi but not descended from Aaron and, if male, chosen to assist the Temple priests.

Le·vit·i·cus (lə-vĭt′ĭ-kəs) *n.* A book of the Bible that contains Hebrew ceremonial rituals and laws governing the priests and Levites.

leotard

WORD BUILDING

–less The suffix **–less** comes from the Old English suffix *–lēas,* from the word *lēas,* meaning "without." In Old English and Middle English, *–less* was often used to convey the negative or opposite of words ending in *–ful,* as in *careful/careless* and *fearful/fearless.* But *–less* was also used to coin words that had no counterpart ending in *–ful*: *headless, loveless, motherless.* Although *–less* normally forms adjectives by attaching to nouns, sometimes it attaches to verbs, as in *tireless,* "without tiring."

C.S. Lewis

Meriwether Lewis

ă	pat	ôr	core
ā	pay	oi	boy
âr	care	ou	out
ä	father	o͝o	took
ĕ	pet	o͝or	lure
ē	be	o͞o	boot
ĭ	pit	ŭ	cut
ī	bite	ûr	urge
îr	pier	th	thin
ŏ	pot	*th*	this
ō	toe	zh	vision
ô	paw	ə	about

lev·i·ty (lĕv′ĭ-tē) *n., pl.* **lev·i·ties** A light humorous manner or attitude; frivolity. —SEE NOTE AT **leaven.**

lev·y (lĕv′ē) *tr.v.* **lev·ied, lev·y·ing, lev·ies 1.** To impose or collect: *levy a sales tax; levy tariffs.* **2.** To draft into military service. **3.** To declare and carry on (war). ❖ *n., pl.* **lev·ies 1.** The act of levying. **2.** Money collected as a tax, tariff, or other fee. **3.** A body of troops drafted into military service. [From Middle English *levien,* from Old French *lever,* to raise.]

❑ *These sound alike:* **levy, levee** (embankment).

lewd (lo͞od) *adj.* **lewd·er, lewd·est 1.** Lustful. **2.** Obscene; indecent. **—lewd′ly** *adv.* **—lewd′ness** *n.*

Lew·is (lo͞o′ĭs), **Carl** Born 1961. American athlete who won nine Olympic gold medals in track and field, including four in the 1984 Olympics.

Lewis, C(live) S(taples) 1898–1963. British writer whose works include a series of fictional books known as *The Chronicles of Narnia* (1950–1956).

Lewis, Meriwether 1774–1809. American explorer who with William Clark led an expedition (1804–1806) from St. Louis to the mouth of the Columbia River.

lex·i·cog·ra·pher (lĕk′sĭ-kŏg′rə-phər) *n.* A person who writes, edits, or compiles a dictionary.

lex·i·cog·ra·phy (lĕk′sĭ-kŏg′rə-fē) *n.* The process or work of writing, editing, or compiling a dictionary.

lex·i·con (lĕk′sĭ-kŏn′) *n.* **1.** A dictionary, especially one giving translations of words from an ancient language. **2.** A stock of terms used in a particular subject or profession; a vocabulary.

Lex·ing·ton (lĕk′sĭng-tən) **1.** A city of north-central Kentucky east of Louisville. It is a noted center for the raising of thoroughbred horses. **2.** A town of northeast Massachusetts northwest of Boston. The Battle of Lexington (April 19, 1775) marked the beginning of the American Revolution.

Ley·den jar (līd′n) *n.* An early device for storing electric charge that consists of a jar covered inside and out with metal foil and a metal rod that touches the inner foil and passes out of the jar through an insulated stopper. The rod is used to conduct electric charge into the jar.

LF An abbreviation of: **1.** left field. **2.** low frequency.

LGBT *abbr.* An abbreviation of lesbian, gay, bisexual, transgender.

Lha·sa (lä′sə *or* lăs′ə) A city of southwest China, the capital of Tibet. Since the mid-1600s, it has been the center of Tibetan Buddhism.

Li The symbol for the element **lithium.**

li·a·bil·i·ty (lī′ə-bĭl′ĭ-tē) *n., pl.* **li·a·bil·i·ties 1.** The state of being liable. **2.** Something for which one is liable; an obligation, responsibility, or debt: *My insurance company limits my liability to $1,000 if my car is damaged.* **3.** Something that holds one back; a disadvantage: *Poor spelling is a liability for a secretary.*

li·a·ble (lī′ə-bəl) *adj.* **1.** Legally obligated or responsible: *The drivers argued about who was liable to pay for fixing the cars.* **2.** Subject; susceptible; prone: *Delicate glass is especially liable to breakage.* **3.** Likely: *liable to make mistakes.*

li·ai·son (lē′ā-zŏn′ *or* lē-ā′zŏn′) *n.* **1.** A means of communication between different groups or units of an organization, especially in the military. **2.** A person who maintains communication: *I work as the company's liaison with the people who sell our line of products.* [From Latin *ligātiō,* from *ligāre,* to bind.]

li·an·a (lē-ä′nə *or* lē-ăn′ə) *n.* A climbing tropical vine having woody stems.

li·ar (lī′ər) *n.* A person who tells lies.

li·bel (lī′bəl) *n.* **1.** A false or misleading publication or broadcast that damages a person's reputation. **2.** The act of presenting such material to the public: *charged the writer with libel.* ❖ *tr.v.* **li·beled, li·bel·ing, li·bels** or **li·belled, li·bel·ling, li·bels** To write or publish a false or damaging statement about (a person). **—li′bel·er** *n.*

li·bel·ous also **li·bel·lous** (lī′bə-ləs) *adj.* Involving or being a libel: *a libelous story in the newspaper.*

lib·er·al (lĭb′ər-əl *or* lĭb′rəl) *adj.* **1.** Tending to give generously: *a liberal contributor to the charity.* **2.** Generous in amount; ample: *a liberal helping of food.* **3.** Not strict or literal; approximate: *The movie is a liberal adaptation of the story.* **4.** Relating to the liberal arts. **5.** Open to new ideas and tolerant of the ideas and behavior of others; broad-minded: *a person with liberal attitudes.* **6.** often **Liberal** Relating to a political party that believes in the natural goodness of humans and favors civil liberties, democratic reform, and social progress. ❖ *n.* **1.** A person who is liberal. **2.** often **Liberal** A member of a liberal party. [From Middle English, noble, generous, from Latin *līber,* free.] **—lib′er·al·ly** *adv.* **—lib′er·al·ness** *n.*

liberal arts *pl.n.* College studies such as languages, history, philosophy, and science that provide general knowledge and the ability to think analytically, rather than practical or professional skills.

lib·er·al·ism (lĭb′ər-ə-lĭz′əm *or* lĭb′rə-lĭz′əm) *n.* **1.** Liberal political views and policies. **2.** Generosity; liberality: *a donor known for her liberalism in support of the arts.*

lib·er·al·i·ty (lĭb′ə-răl′ĭ-tē) *n., pl.* **lib·er·al·i·ties 1.** The quality or state of being liberal or generous. **2.** An instance of being liberal.

lib·er·al·ize (lĭb′ər-ə-līz′ *or* lĭb′rə-līz′) *tr. & intr.v.* **lib·er·al·ized, lib·er·al·iz·ing, lib·er·al·iz·es** To make or become more liberal: *liberalized some of the regulations.* **—lib′er·al·i·za′tion** (lĭb′ər-ə-lĭ-zā′shən *or* lĭb′rə-lĭ-zā′shən) *n.*

lib·er·ate (lĭb′ə-rāt′) *tr.v.* **lib·er·at·ed, lib·er·at·ing, lib·er·ates 1.** To set free, as from confinement or control: *The Emancipation Proclamation liberated many slaves.* **2.** To set free as a result of chemical combination: *liberate a gas.* [From Latin *līber,* free.] **—lib′er·a′tion** *n.* **—lib′er·a′tor** *n.*

Li·be·ri·a (lī-bîr′ē-ə) A country of western Africa on the Atlantic Ocean west of Côte d'Ivoire. It was founded in 1821 as a settlement for freed slaves from the United States. Monrovia is the capital.

lib·er·tine (lĭb′ər-tēn′) *n.* A person who lives an irresponsible immoral life; a rake. ❖ *adj.* Morally unrestrained: *a libertine existence.*

lib·er·ty (lĭb′ər-tē) *n., pl.* **lib·er·ties 1.** Freedom from imprisonment, slavery, or forced labor. **2a.** Freedom from oppressive restriction or control by a government or other power. **b.** A right to engage in certain actions without interference by a government or other power: *the liberties protected by the Bill of Rights.* **3.** The right or power to act as one chooses: *Freelance writers have great liberty in setting their work schedules.* **4.** often **liberties** An action that is unwarranted or improper: *He takes liberties with history to make his argument sound better.* **5.** A period during which a sailor is permitted to go ashore. ◆ **at liberty** Not in confinement or under constraint; free: *Am I at liberty to speak openly?* [From Middle English *liberte,* from Latin *lībertās,* from *līber,* free.]

Li·bra (lē′brə) *n.* **1.** A constellation in the Southern Hemisphere near Scorpius, traditionally pictured as a balance. **2.** The seventh sign of the zodiac in astrology.

li·brar·i·an (lī-brâr′ē-ən) *n.* A person who is specially trained to work in a library.

li·brar·y (lī′brĕr′ē) *n., pl.* **li·brar·ies 1.** A place where books, magazines, recordings, and other materials are kept in an organized arrangement so they can be easily found for reading and borrowing. **2.** A collection of books or other items containing information. **3.** A room in a private home for such a collection. [From Middle English *librarie,* from Latin *liber,* book.]

li·bret·tist (lĭ-brĕt′ĭst) *n.* The author of a libretto.

li·bret·to (lĭ-brĕt′ō) *n., pl.* **li·bret·tos** or **li·bret·ti** (lĭ-brĕt′ē) The text of a dramatic musical work, such as an opera.

Li·bre·ville (lē′brə-vĭl′) The capital of Gabon, in the northwest part of the country on the Gulf of Guinea. It was founded in 1843.

Lib·y·a (lĭb′ē-ə) A country of northern Africa on the Mediterranean Sea west of Egypt. Tripoli is the capital. —**Lib′yan** *adj. & n.*

lice (līs) *n.* Plural of **louse** (sense 1).

li·cense (lī′səns) *n.* **1a.** Official or legal permission to do or own a specified thing: *The group has license to run a daycare center.* **b.** A document, card, plate, or tag issued as proof that such permission has been granted: *The doctor's license is hung on the wall.* **2.** Freedom of action: *I took the license to stop by without calling beforehand.* ❖ *tr.v.* **li·censed, li·cens·ing, li·cens·es** To grant a license to or for: *The doctor was not licensed to practice medicine in this state.* [From Middle English *licence*, from Latin *licentia*, freedom, from *licēre*, to be permitted.]

li·censed practical nurse (lī′sənst) *n.* A nurse who has completed a practical nursing program and is licensed by a state to provide routine patient care under the direction of a registered nurse or physician.

license plate *n.* A rectangular, usually metal plate having numbers or letters or both, used to identify a vehicle that is officially registered with the government.

li·cen·tious (lī-sĕn′shəs) *adj.* Lacking moral restraint; immoral. —**li·cen′tious·ly** *adv.* —**li·cen′tious·ness** *n.*

li·chee (lē′chē) *n.* Variant of **lychee.**

li·chen (lī′kən) *n.* An organism that consists of a fungus and an alga growing in close association with each other. Lichens often live on rocks and tree bark and can also be found in extremely cold environments. [From Greek *leikhēn.*]

❑ *These sound alike:* **lichen, liken** (compare).

lick (lĭk) *tr.v.* **licked, lick·ing, licks 1a.** To pass the tongue over: *The dog licks her pups.* **b.** To lap up: *The cat licked cream from a dish.* **2.** To move or flicker like a tongue: *Flames lick the burning logs.* **3.** *Slang* To punish with a beating; thrash. **4.** *Slang* To defeat soundly: *We licked the other team.* ❖ *n.* **1.** A movement of the tongue over something: *a kitten's wet lick.* **2.** A small quantity; bit: *We couldn't find a lick of evidence.* **3.** A salt lick. **4.** A blow or hard stroke. ◆ **lick (one's) wounds** To recover from a defeat. [From Old English *liccian.*]

lic·o·rice (lĭk′ər-ĭs *or* lĭk′ər-ĭsh) *n.* **1a.** A plant having a sweet strong-tasting root used as a flavoring. **b.** The root of this plant. **2a.** A candy made from or flavored with the licorice root. **b.** A chewy candy made from sugar, corn syrup, and flavorings, often manufactured in long flexible tubes. [From Middle English *licoris*, from Greek *glukurrhiza* : *glukus*, sweet + *rhiza*, root.]

lid (lĭd) *n.* **1.** A removable cover or top for a hollow container: *the lid for a jar; the lid of a box.* **2.** An eyelid. [From Old English *hlid.*]

lie[1] (lī) *intr.v.* **lay** (lā), **lain** (lān), **ly·ing** (lī′ĭng), **lies 1.** To place oneself in a flat or resting position: *The cow lay down in the pasture.* **2.** To be in a flat or resting position: *I lay in the hammock all afternoon.* **3.** To be or rest on a surface: *Forks and spoons lay on the table.* **4.** To be located: *Many tiny islands lie off the coast.* **5.** To remain in a certain condition or position: *We let the land lie unused.* **6.** To consist or have as a basis: *The answer lay in further research.* **7.** To extend: *Our land lies between the river and the trees.* **8.** To be buried: *Here lie my grandparents.* ❖ *n.* The manner or position in which something lies, as the surface or slope of a piece of land. ◆ **lie low 1.** To keep oneself or one's plans hidden. **2.** To wait until it is the right moment to act. [From Old English *licgan.*] —SEE NOTE AT **lay**[1].

❑ *These sound alike:* **lie**[1] (be flat), **lie**[2] (falsehood), **lye** (alkaline solution).

lie[2] (lī) *n.* An untrue statement made in order to deceive someone; a falsehood. ❖ *intr.v.* **lied, ly·ing** (lī′ĭng), **lies 1.** To tell a lie or lies: *The suspect lied to the police.* **2.** To create an illusion or a false impression: *Even photographs can lie.* [From Old English *lyge.*]

❑ *These sound alike:* **lie**[2] (falsehood), **lie**[1] (be flat), **lye** (alkaline solution).

Liech·ten·stein (lĭk′tən-stīn′ *or* lĭKH′tən-shtīn′) A small principality in the Alps of central Europe between Austria and Switzerland. Vaduz is the capital.

lie detector *n.* An instrument that records changes in bodily conditions, such as blood pressure and pulse rate, that usually occur when a person is not telling the truth.

liege (lēj) *n.* **1.** A lord to whom subjects owed allegiance and services in feudal times. **2.** A person owing allegiance and services to such a lord; a vassal. ❖ *adj.* Relating to the relationship between lord and vassal: *my liege lord.*

liege·man (lēj′mən) *n.* **1.** A feudal vassal or subject. **2.** A loyal supporter, follower, or subject.

lien (lēn *or* lē′ən) *n.* A legal claim on the property of a person as payment for a debt.

❑ *These sound alike:* **lien, lean**[1] (slant), **lean**[2] (thin).

lieu (lo͞o) *n. Archaic* Place; stead. ◆ **in lieu of** In place of; instead of: *received a check in lieu of cash.*

lieu·ten·an·cy (lo͞o-tĕn′ən-sē) *n.* The duty, authority, or rank of a lieutenant.

lieu·ten·ant (lo͞o-tĕn′ənt) *n.* **1a.** A first lieutenant. **b.** A second lieutenant. **2.** An officer in the Navy ranking above an ensign and below a lieutenant commander. **3.** An officer in a police or fire department ranking next below a captain. **4.** A chief assistant; a deputy: *a staff member acting as the president's lieutenant.*

lieutenant colonel *n.* An officer in the US Army, Air Force, or Marine Corps, ranking above a major and below a colonel.

lieutenant commander *n.* An officer in the US Navy or Coast Guard ranking above a lieutenant and below a commander.

lieutenant general *n.* An officer in the US Army, Air Force, or Marine Corps, ranking above a major general and below a general.

lieutenant governor *n.* **1.** An elected official ranking just below the governor of a US state. **2.** The nonelected chief of government of a Canadian province.

lieutenant junior grade *n., pl.* **lieutenants junior grade** A lower-ranking lieutenant in the US Navy or Coast Guard, ranking just above an ensign.

life (līf) *n., pl.* **lives** (līvz) **1.** The property or quality that distinguishes living organisms from dead organisms and nonliving matter. Living organisms have the ability to grow, reproduce, and respond to their environment. **2.** The fact of being alive: *risk one's life.* **3.** The period of time between birth and death; a lifetime: *a long and interesting life.* **4.** The time during which something exists and works: *the life of a car.* **5.** Living organisms considered as a group: *plant life; marine life.* **6.** A living person: *Dozens of lives were lost in the flood.* **7.** A way of living: *the outdoor life; city life.* **8.** Liveliness; spirit: *a puppy, curious and full of life.* **9.** An account of a person's life; a biography. ◆ **bring to life 1.** To cause to regain life or consciousness. **2.** To make lively or lifelike: *A good actor brings a character to life.* **come to life** To become lively; grow excited: *She always comes to life when talking about her granddaughter.* **for life** Till the end of one's life: *They were friends for life.* **take (someone's) life** To commit murder. **true to life** Accurately representing real life: *The movie is true to life.* [From Old English *līf.*]

life·blood (līf′blŭd′) *n.* **1.** Blood regarded as necessary

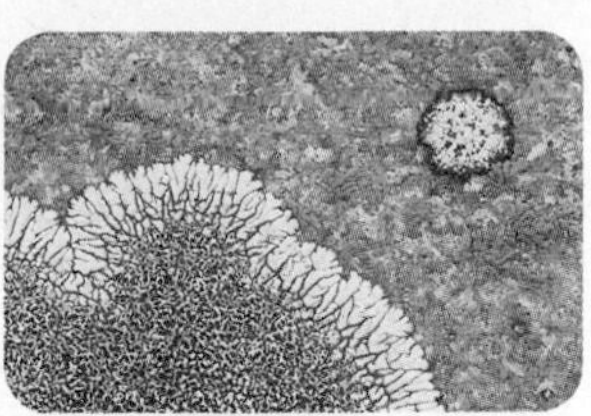
lichen

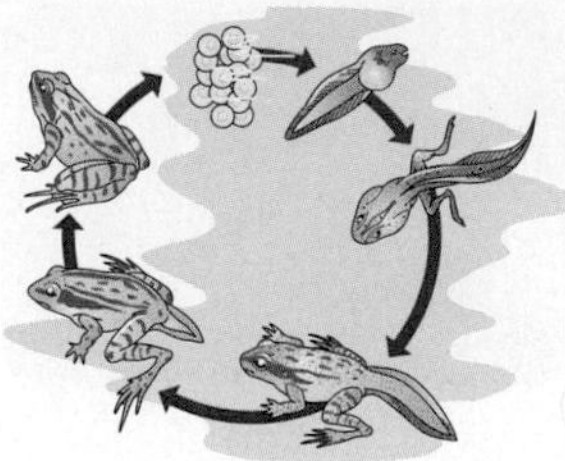

life cycle
clockwise from top: stages in the life cycle of a frog, from eggs to tadpole to adult frog

life jacket

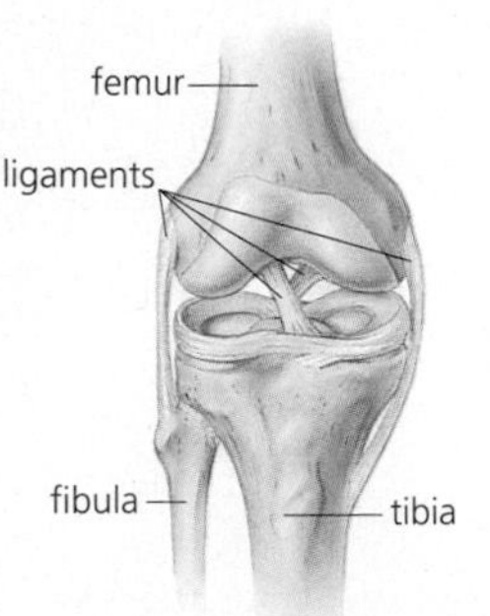

ligament

ă	pat	ôr	core
ā	pay	oi	boy
âr	care	ou	out
ä	father	o͝o	took
ĕ	pet	o͝or	lure
ē	be	o͞o	boot
ĭ	pit	ŭ	cut
ī	bite	ûr	urge
îr	pier	th	thin
ŏ	pot	*th*	this
ō	toe	zh	vision
ô	paw	ə	about

for life. **2.** An essential or vital part: *The conductor is the lifeblood of the orchestra.*

life·boat (līf′bōt′) *n.* A strong boat carried on a ship or kept along the shore, used if the ship has to be abandoned or for rescue service.

life buoy *n.* A ring made of cork or other buoyant material for keeping a person afloat.

life cycle *n.* The series of changes through which a living organism passes, from its beginning as a fertilized egg to its mature state in which offspring can be produced.

life expectancy *n.* The length of time a person is expected to live, as determined by statistical studies.

life form *n.* A kind of organism: *marine life forms; the earliest life forms.*

life·guard (līf′gärd′) *n.* An expert swimmer trained and employed to watch over other swimmers, as at a beach or swimming pool.

life insurance *n.* Insurance on a person's life, paid for by regular premiums and guaranteeing a certain sum of money to a specified person, such as a spouse or child, on the death of the holder.

life jacket *n.* A life preserver in the form of a jacket or vest.

life·less (līf′lĭs) *adj.* **1.** Having no life; dead or inanimate. **2.** Not supporting life; having no living organisms: *a lifeless planet.* **3.** Lacking spirit or vitality; dull: *a lifeless party.* —**life′less·ly** *adv.* —**life′less·ness** *n.*

life·like (līf′līk′) *adj.* Accurately representing real life: *a lifelike statue.*

life·line (līf′līn′) *n.* **1.** An anchored line thrown as a support to someone falling or drowning. **2.** A line used to raise and lower deep-sea divers. **3.** A means or route for transporting vital supplies.

life·long (līf′lông′) *adj.* Lasting over a lifetime: *a lifelong friend; a lifelong ambition.*

life preserver *n.* A device, such as a vest filled with a buoyant material, designed to keep a person afloat in the water.

life raft *n.* A usually inflatable raft used by people who have been forced into water by an emergency, such as a shipwreck or airplane crash.

life·sav·er (līf′sā′vər) *n.* **1.** A lifeguard or other person who saves the lives of others. **2.** A person or thing that provides help in a crisis or emergency: *Their call to the fire department was a lifesaver.* **3.** A life preserver shaped like a ring.

life·sav·ing (līf′sā′vĭng) *n.* The skills and methods used in saving lives, especially in keeping people from drowning.

life science *n.* Any of the sciences, such as botany, zoology, microbiology, or ecology, that deal mainly with living organisms.

life-size (līf′sīz′) also **life-sized** (līf′sīzd′) *adj.* Being of the same size as the person or object represented: *a life-size statue of a person.*

life·span or **life span** (līf′spăn′) *n.* The average or longest period of time that an organism or an object can be expected to survive or last: *exercise to increase your lifespan; the lifespan of a bridge.*

life·style (līf′stīl′) *n.* The way of life or style of living of a person or group, including diet, tastes, work, and interests.

life support *n.* The methods or equipment needed to keep someone alive who might otherwise die, either from disease or from environmental conditions that are not capable of sustaining life. —**life′-sup·port′** (līf′sə-pôrt′) *adj.*

life·time (līf′tīm′) *n.* The period of time that a person lives or a thing exists or works properly: *the average lifetime of a person; the lifetime of our car.* ❖ *adj.* Continuing for all one's life; lifelong: *a lifetime friend.*

life·work (līf′wûrk′) *n.* The chief or entire work of a person's lifetime.

lift (lĭft) *v.* **lift·ed, lift·ing, lifts** —*tr.* **1.** To raise to a higher position; elevate: *lifted her eyes; lift the suitcase from the floor.* **2.** To transport by air: *The helicopter lifted supplies to the town.* **3.** To raise or improve in condition, status, or estimation: *The news lifted everybody's spirits.* **4.** To end; stop; suspend: *lift a siege.* **5.** *Informal* To steal; pilfer: *The robber lifted a priceless painting.* **6.** To copy from something already published; plagiarize: *The reporter lifted the paragraph from a magazine article.* —*intr.* **1.** To be raised: *These windows lift easily.* **2.** To disappear by or as if by rising: *The heavy fog finally lifted.* ❖ *n.* **1.** The act of lifting or being lifted: *Give me a lift into the saddle.* **2.** A short ride in a vehicle: *Can I have a lift to the store?* **3.** The extent or height something is raised. **4.** An elevation of the spirit: *Good grades give students a big lift.* **5.** An amount or weight lifted; a load. **6.** *Chiefly British* An elevator. **7.** An upward force acting on an object, as on an airplane wing during takeoff. ◆ **lift off** To begin flight: *The rocket lifted off at dawn.* [From Middle English *liften*, from Old Norse *lypta*.]

lift·off (lĭft′ôf′) *n.* The takeoff of a rocket from its launch pad.

lig·a·ment (lĭg′ə-mənt) *n.* A sheet or band of tough fibrous tissue that connects two bones or holds an organ of the body in place.

lig·a·ture (lĭg′ə-cho͝or′ *or* lĭg′ə-chər) *n.* **1.** Something used for tying or binding, such as a thread used in surgery to tie off a bleeding vein or artery. **2.** In printing, two or three letters joined to form a single character, as *œ.* **3.** A curved line connecting a series of notes on a musical score to indicate that they are to be played or sung smoothly.

light¹ (līt) *n.* **1.** A form of radiant energy that can be perceived by the human eye. It is made up of electromagnetic waves that travel at a speed of about 186,282 miles (299,792 kilometers) per second. **2.** Radiant energy that cannot be perceived by the human eye, as infrared light and ultraviolet light. **3.** Illumination; brightness: *The fireworks produced bursts of light.* **4.** A source of light, as the sun or a lamp: *a light in the window.* **5.** Daylight: *Flowers need a lot of light to bloom.* **6.** Dawn; daybreak. **7.** A source of fire, as a match. **8.** Understanding through knowledge and information: *Research shed new light on the dinosaurs.* **9.** Public attention; general knowledge: *Reports brought to light the need for improvements in fire protection.* **10.** A famous or outstanding person: *one of the leading lights of the theater.* **11.** A way of looking at or considering a certain matter: *This puts the problem in a different light.* **12.** A light shade or color: *The lights in the photograph are too bright.* ❖ *v.* **light·ed** or **lit** (lĭt), **light·ing, lights** —*tr.* **1.** To set burning; ignite: *light a fire.* **2.** To cause to give out light; turn on: *light a lamp.* **3.** To provide, cover, or fill with light: *Let's light the room with candles.* **4.** To make lively or bright: *A smile lighted the child's face.* **5.** To guide or direct by means of a light: *A flashlight was enough to light our way along the path.* —*intr.* **1.** To start to burn; become ignited: *The oven won't light for some reason.* **2.** To become light or bright: *The neon sign lighted up after dark.* ❖ *adj.* **light·er, light·est 1.** Having light: *a nice light room to work in.* **2.** Bright; not dark: *light gray; light hair.* ◆ **in light of** Taking into consideration: *In light of the report, let's try a different approach to the problem.* [From Old English *lēoht*.]

light² (līt) *adj.* **light·er, light·est 1.** Having little weight; not heavy: *a light suitcase; a light jacket.* **2.** Having little force or impact: *a light breeze; a light blow.* **3.** Low in intensity or amount: *a light rain; a light lunch.* **4.** Not harsh or severe: *The judge gave the convict a light sentence.* **5.** Indistinct; faint: *The light print was hard to* *read.* **6.** Not serious or profound: *light comedy.* **7.** Not important; slight: *The boat suffered only light damage.* **8.** Carrying little weight or equipment: *light cavalry.* **9.** Free from care or worry: *a light heart.* **10.** Moving easily and quickly; nimble: *light on one's feet.* **11.** Appearing to be graceful and delicate: *light wood carvings; a light structure.* **12.** Requiring little effort or exertion: *light household chores.* **13.** Somewhat unsteady or faint; dizzy: *feel light in the head.* **14.** Having fewer calories; not fatty or rich: *light foods; light soft drinks.* **15.** Easily awakened or disturbed: *a light sleeper.* ❖ *adv.* **lighter, lightest** Lightly, especially with little baggage: *We always travel light.* ❖ *intr.v.* **light·ed** or **lit** (lĭt), **light·ing, lights 1.** To come to rest; land; perch: *The bird lit on the feeder.* **2.** To get down, as from a mount or vehicle; alight: *Several passengers lighted from the rear of the plane.* ◆ **light into** *Informal* To attack verbally or physically; assail. **light out** *Informal* To leave hastily; run off. [From Old English *lēoht.*]

light bulb *n.* A device consisting of a gas-filled glass tube or bulb that emits light when an electric current is supplied to it.

light·en¹ (līt′n) *v.* **light·ened, light·en·ing, light·ens** —*tr.* To make lighter in color or brighter: *He lightened the blue paint by mixing in some white.* —*intr.* **1.** To become lighter in color or brighter: *The clouds thinned and the sky lightened quickly.* **2.** To give off flashes of lightning.

light·en² (līt′n) *v.* **light·ened, light·en·ing, light·ens** —*tr.* **1.** To make less heavy; reduce the weight of: *Leaving out those books will lighten the load.* **2.** To make less troublesome or oppressive: *hire an assistant to lighten the load of work.* **3.** To gladden or cheer: *a song to lighten everyone's heart.* —*intr.* **1.** To become less in weight. **2.** To become less troublesome or oppressive. **3.** To become cheerful.

light·er¹ (lī′tər) *n.* A person or device that lights or ignites something: *a lamp lighter; a cigarette lighter.*

light·er² (lī′tər) *n.* A barge used for loading and unloading ships and for carrying cargo short distances. [From Middle English, perhaps from *lighten,* to make less heavy.]

light·face (līt′fās′) *n.* A typeface that has thin light lines. This definition is in lightface.

light-foot·ed (līt′fo͝ot′ĭd) *adj.* Moving with light and graceful steps; nimble.

light·head·ed (līt′hĕd′ĭd) *adj.* Faint or dizzy: *felt lightheaded from running.* **—light′head′ed·ly** *adv.* **—light′head′ed·ness** *n.*

light·heart·ed (līt′här′tĭd) *adj.* Carefree and cheerful: *a lighthearted attitude.* See Synonyms at **glad. —light′heart′ed·ly** *adv.* **—light′heart′ed·ness** *n.*

light·house (līt′hous′) *n.* A tower with a powerful light at the top, used to mark the entrance to a harbor or to warn ships away from dangerous waters.

light·ing (lī′tĭng) *n.* **1.** Light supplied, as for a room or an area; illumination: *right lighting for reading.* **2.** The arrangement or equipment that provides light: *installed outdoor lighting.*

light·ly (līt′lē) *adv.* **1.** With little pressure or force: *Tread lightly on the floor to avoid waking the baby.* **2.** To a small amount or degree: *The streets were lightly covered with snow.* **3a.** In a carefree manner; cheerfully: *took the setback lightly.* **b.** Without proper care or consideration: *treated his illness lightly.* **4.** With agility; nimbly: *The deer leaped lightly over the fence.*

light meter *n.* A device that measures the intensity of light, used especially in photography.

light·ness¹ (līt′nĭs) *n.* **1.** The quality or condition of being lighted; brightness. **2.** Paleness of color.

light·ness² (līt′nĭs) *n.* **1.** The property or quality of having little weight or force: *the lightness of straw.* **2.** Ease or quickness of movement; agility: *lightness of step.* **3.** Freedom from worry or trouble: *lightness of heart.* **4.** Lack of appropriate seriousness: *lightness of conduct.*

light·ning (līt′nĭng) *n.* A flash of light in the sky caused by an electrical discharge between clouds or between a cloud and the earth's surface. The flash heats the air and usually causes thunder. —SEE NOTE.

lightning bug *n.* A firefly.

lightning rod *n.* A metal rod placed high on a building to prevent damage from lightning by conducting electricity along a wire to the ground.

light·ship (līt′shĭp′) *n.* A ship with powerful lights and other warning signals, anchored in dangerous waters to alert and guide other vessels.

light·weight (līt′wāt′) *n.* **1.** A person or thing that weighs relatively little. **2a.** A boxer weighing more than 126 and not more than 135 pounds (about 57–61 kilograms). **b.** A contestant in some other sports in a similar weight class. **3.** *Informal* A person of little ability, importance, or influence: *was a real lightweight as a political commentator.* ❖ *adj.* Not heavy; weighing relatively little: *a lightweight jacket.*

light year *n.* The distance that light travels in one year, about 5.88 trillion miles (9.46 trillion kilometers).

lig·nite (lĭg′nīt′) *n.* A soft brownish-black form of coal in which the condition of the plant matter is between peat and bituminous coal; brown coal.

lik·a·ble also **like·a·ble** (lī′kə-bəl) *adj.* Easy to like; having a pleasing personality: *a pleasant likable classmate.*

like¹ (līk) *v.* **liked, lik·ing, likes** —*tr.* **1.** To be fond of: *We are old friends and like each other.* **2.** To find pleasant; enjoy: *They liked the place and decided to stay.* **3.** To feel about; regard: *How do you like your new school?* **4.** To want to have: *Would you like some gravy?* —*intr.* To have a desire or preference: *If you like, we can go home now.* ❖ *n.* Something that is liked; a preference: *my likes and dislikes.* [From Old English *līcian,* to please.]

like² (līk) *prep.* **1.** Resembling; similar to: *You look like your mother.* **2.** In the same way as: *Don't act like a clown.* **3.** In the typical manner of: *It's not like him to give up easily.* **4.** Such as: *I draw things like buildings and street scenes.* **5.** As if it is likely to be: *It looks like a good year for farmers.* **6.** Inclined to; desirous of: *I felt like going home.* ❖ *adj.* **1.** Having the same or almost the same characteristics; similar: *We made this and like repairs to the car.* **2.** Equivalent: *The company will donate a like amount to the charity.* ❖ *adv.* As if: *We worked like crazy to get the job done on time.* ❖ *n.* **1.** Something equal or similar to something else: *Owls eat mice, chipmunks, and the like.* **2.** Nearly; approximately: *a price more like fifty dollars.* ❖ *conj.* **1.** In the same way that: *To dance like she does takes lots of practice.* **2.** As if: *It looks like we'll finish on time.* [From Old English *gelīc.*]

–like *suff.* A suffix that means similar to or characteristic of: *childlike; lifelike.*

like·a·ble (lī′kə-bəl) *adj.* Variant of **likable.**

like·li·hood (līk′lē-ho͝od′) *n.* The chance of a thing happening; probability: *The likelihood of snow is very remote in July.*

like·ly (līk′lē) *adj.* **like·li·er, like·li·est 1.** Having or showing a tendency or probability: *It is likely to rain at any moment.* **2.** Seeming to be true; credible: *a likely excuse for being late.* **3.** Appropriate or suitable: *That candidate seems a likely choice for the job.* **4.** Showing promise of success; promising: *a likely way of proceeding.* ❖ *adv.* Probably: *Most likely the barn will need some repairs.*

lik·en (lī′kən) *tr.v.* **lik·ened, lik·en·ing, lik·ens** To describe as resembling something else; compare: *He likened his youth to a summer day.*

❑ *These sound alike:* **liken, lichen** (organism).

lighthouse

SCIENCE

lightning As storm clouds develop, particles with a positive electric charge gather at the top of the clouds, while particles with a negative electric charge gather at the bottom. The negatively charged particles repel the electrons of atoms in nearby objects, such as the bases of other storm clouds or tall objects on the ground. As a result, these objects take on a positive charge. The difference in charge, or *voltage,* builds until an electric current starts to flow between the objects. The current flow heats up the air so much that it glows. That glow is what we call **lightning.** Initially, a bolt of lightning carrying negative charge darts from one storm cloud to another or from a storm cloud to the ground, leaving the bottom of the cloud with a positive charge. In response, a second bolt flies in the opposite direction, to neutralize the positive charge on the bottom of the cloud. The heat generated by the lightning causes the air to expand, creating sound waves that we hear as *thunder.*

lilac

Lydia Liliuokalani

Abraham Lincoln
posthumous 1887 portrait by George P.A. Healy (1813–1894)

ă	pat	ôr	core
ā	pay	oi	boy
âr	care	ou	out
ä	father	o͝o	took
ĕ	pet	o͝or	lure
ē	be	o͞o	boot
ĭ	pit	ŭ	cut
ī	bite	ûr	urge
îr	pier	th	thin
ŏ	pot	*th*	this
ō	toe	zh	vision
ô	paw	ə	about

like·ness (līk′nĭs) *n.* **1.** Similarity or resemblance: *an amazing likeness between brothers.* **2.** A copy or picture of a person or thing: *The portrait is a perfect likeness of you.* **3.** Appearance; form: *At once the prince took on the likeness of a frog.*

like·wise (līk′wīz′) *adv.* **1.** Similarly; in like manner: *Once he saw her open her package, he did likewise.* **2.** Moreover; besides: *The Sahara Desert is hot and likewise dry.*

lik·ing (lī′kĭng) *n.* A feeling of fondness or affection; a preference: *a special liking for apples.*

li·lac (lī′lək *or* lī′lŏk *or* lī′lăk) *n.* **1.** A shrub that bears clusters of fragrant purplish or white flowers. **2.** A pale purple.

li·lan·ge·ni (lĭ-läng′gĕ-nē) *n., pl.* **em·a·lan·ge·ni** (ĕm′ə-läng-gĕn′ē) The basic monetary unit of Swaziland.

Li·li·u·o·ka·la·ni (lə-lē′ə-ō-kə-lä′nē), **Lydia Kamakaeha Paki** 1838–1917. Queen of the Hawaiian Islands (1891–1893). She was the last Hawaiian ruler to govern the islands.

Li·long·we (lĭ-lông′wā) The capital of Malawi, in the south-central part of the country. It was founded in the 1940s.

lilt (lĭlt) *n.* **1.** A cheerful lively manner of speaking. **2.** A light happy tune or song. ❖ *tr. & intr.v.* **lilt·ed, lilt·ing, lilts** To sing, play, or speak in a lively rhythmic manner: *the bird lilted its song.*

lil·y (lĭl′ē) *n., pl.* **lil·ies 1.** Any of various plants that grow from bulbs and have showy flowers shaped like trumpets. **2.** Any of various similar or related plants, such as a water lily. **3.** The flower of any of these plants.

lily of the valley *n., pl.* **lilies of the valley** A plant having a slender one-sided cluster of fragrant, bell-shaped white flowers.

lily pad *n.* One of the large, flat floating leaves of a water lily.

Li·ma (lē′mə) The capital of Peru, in the west-central part of the country near the Pacific Ocean. It was founded by Francisco Pizarro in 1535.

li·ma bean (lī′mə) *n.* **1.** The light-green kidney-shaped seed of a tropical American plant, eaten as a vegetable. **2.** The plant that bears such seeds.

limb (lĭm) *n.* **1.** A leg, arm, wing, or other paired appendage of an animal body, usually used for grasping or moving. **2.** One of the larger branches of a tree. [From Old English *lim.*]
❑ *These sound alike:* **limb, limn** (draw).

lim·ber (lĭm′bər) *adj.* Bending or moving easily; flexible: *limber muscles; a limber athlete.* ❖ *tr. & intr.v.* **lim·bered, lim·ber·ing, lim·bers** To exercise so as to make or become limber: *She stretched to limber up her muscles. He limbered up before the important game.* **—lim′ber·ness** *n.*

lim·bo[1] (lĭm′bō) *n., pl.* **lim·bos 1.** often **Limbo** In Roman Catholic belief, the abode of just or innocent souls, such as unbaptized people, kept from heaven but not condemned to Purgatory or Hell. **2.** A place or condition of neglect or oblivion: *Construction for the new pool was kept in limbo until new funds were found.* [From Middle English, from Latin *limbus*, border.]

lim·bo[2] (lĭm′bō) *n., pl.* **lim·bos** A West Indian dance in which dancers bend over backward to pass under a horizontal pole. [Probably of African origin.]

Lim·burg·er (lĭm′bûr′gər) *n.* A soft white cheese with a very strong odor.

lime[1] (līm) *n.* **1.** An oval green citrus fruit having sour juicy pulp. **2.** Any of several trees that bear such fruit. [From Arabic *līma*, probably from Persian *līmū*, lemon.]

lime[2] (līm) *n.* A European linden. [From Old English *lind.*]

lime[3] (līm) *n.* Calcium oxide. ❖ *tr.v.* **limed, lim·ing, limes** To treat with lime; apply lime to. [From Old English *līm*, birdlime.] **—lim′y** *adj.*

lime·light (līm′līt′) *n.* **1.** The center of public attention: *The president is always in the limelight.* **2.** An early type of light used in the theater, in which lime was heated to produce light.

lim·er·ick (lĭm′ər-ĭk) *n.* A humorous five-line poem that follows the rhyme scheme *aabba.* [After *Limerick*, a borough of southwest Ireland.]

lime·stone (līm′stōn′) *n.* A form of sedimentary rock that consists mainly of calcium carbonate, used as a building material and in making lime and cement.

lime·wa·ter (līm′wô′tər) *n.* A solution of calcium hydroxide and water, used in calamine lotion and sometimes as an antacid.

lim·it (lĭm′ĭt) *n.* **1.** A point or line beyond which something ends or cannot go: *the 12-mile fishing limit; the limit of my patience.* **2. limits** The boundary surrounding a certain area: *within the city limits.* **3.** The greatest amount of something allowed: *a speed limit.* ❖ *tr.v.* **lim·it·ed, lim·it·ing, lim·its** To place a limit on; confine: *Try to limit your talk to ten minutes.* [From Middle English *limite*, from Latin *līmes*, boundary.]

lim·i·ta·tion (lĭm′ĭ-tā′shən) *n.* **1.** Something that limits; a restriction: *Poor ice conditions put limitations on how fast the bobsled could go.* **2.** The act of limiting or the state of being limited.

lim·it·ed (lĭm′ĭ-tĭd) *adj.* **1.** Confined within certain limits; restricted: *a small house with limited space.* **2.** Not accomplishing the greatest achievements or possessing the best talent: *a popular but limited actor.* **3.** Traveling fast and making few stops: *a limited train.* ❖ *n.* A limited train or bus.

lim·it·less (lĭm′ĭt-lĭs) *adj.* Having no limit or boundary; unrestricted or infinite: *limitless space in the sky.*

limn (lĭm) *tr.v.* **limned, limn·ing** (lĭm′nĭng), **limns 1.** To draw or paint. **2.** To describe.
❑ *These sound alike:* **limn, limb** (body part).

lim·ou·sine (lĭm′ə-zēn′ *or* lĭm′ə-zēn′) *n.* **1.** A large, luxurious vehicle driven by a chauffeur. **2.** A van or small bus used to carry passengers especially to airports and hotels. [From French, possibly from *Limousin*, a region of France.]

limp (lĭmp) *intr.v.* **limped, limp·ing, limps 1.** To walk lamely: *After my knee injury, I limped for several days.* **2.** To move or proceed haltingly or with difficulty: *The damaged ship limped back to port.* ❖ *n.* A lame or irregular way of walking. ❖ *adj.* **limp·er, limp·est 1.** Lacking stiffness: *a limp wet towel.* **2.** Not vigorous or strong; weak: *a limp handshake.* [Probably from Old English *lemphealt* : *lemp-*, hanging loosely + *-healt*, lame, limping.] **—limp′ly** *adv.* **—limp′ness** *n.*

lim·pet (lĭm′pĭt) *n.* Any of numerous small saltwater mollusks that have a cone-shaped shell and cling to rocks.

lim·pid (lĭm′pĭd) *adj.* Perfectly clear; transparent: *limpid water.*

linch·pin (lĭnch′pĭn′) *n.* **1.** An iron pin inserted in the end of an axle to prevent a wheel from slipping off. **2.** Something that keeps different parts together and functioning: *The linchpin of the candidate's campaign was his proposal for improving the economy.* [From Middle English *linpin* : *lin*, linchpin (from Old English *lynis*) + *pin*, pin.]

Lin·coln (lĭng′kən) The capital of Nebraska, in the southeast part of the state southwest of Omaha. It was chosen as the state capital in 1867.

Lincoln, Abraham 1809–1865. The 16th president of the United States (1861–1865). He led the Union during the Civil War and issued the Emancipation Proclamation (1863), freeing all slaves in the Confederate states. —SEE NOTE.

Lind·bergh (lĭnd′bûrg′ *or* lĭn′bûrg′), **Charles Augustus** 1902–1974. American aviator who made the first solo flight across the Atlantic Ocean (May 20–21, 1927). His wife, **Anne Morrow Lindbergh** (1906–2001), accompanied him on many flights and is known for her books, including *North to the Orient* (1935).

lin·den (lĭn′dən) *n.* Any of various trees having heart-shaped leaves and clusters of fragrant yellowish flowers, often planted for shade. [From Old English *lind.*]

line¹ (līn) *n.* **1.** A geometric figure formed by a point moving in a fixed direction and in the reverse direction. A line has infinite length but no width. **2a.** A thin continuous mark, as one made on paper by a pen or pencil. **b.** Something resembling such a mark: *a brow furrowed with deep lines.* **3.** A border or boundary: *the county line; the line between courage and rashness.* **4.** A group of people or things arranged in a row: *a line of customers at the counter.* **5.** often **lines** Outline, contour, or styling: *the lines of a new car.* **6a.** A row of words printed or written across a page or column. **b.** A brief letter: *I'll drop you a line.* **7a.** A single verse of poetry. **b.** A unit of continuous text spoken by an actor. **8.** A cable, rope, cord, or wire: *a fishing line.* **9.** A course or direction; a route: *the line of flight of migrating birds.* **10.** A general method or way of doing something: *Let's continue our present line in teaching safety at school.* **11.** A series of people or things following one another in time: *the line of French kings.* **12.** Ancestry or lineage: *Her family line goes back to China.* **13a.** A system of transportation: *a bus line.* **b.** A branch of a transportation system: *all lines go through Detroit.* **c.** A railroad track. **14a.** A wire or system of wires connecting telephone or telegraph stations. **b.** A telephone connection: *Their line is busy.* **15.** A pipe, channel, or wire used to carry water, gas, or electricity from one point to another. **16.** A range of merchandise having several styles and sizes: *a line of fashionable dresses.* **17.** A person's trade or occupation: *What is your line of work?* **18.** The range of a person's ability or interests: *That sort of work is out of my line.* **19.** A connected series of musical notes: *a melodic line.* **20.** In football, the players stationed at the line of scrimmage as a play begins. **21.** The battle area or combat troops closest to the enemy: *The wounded were taken behind the lines.* **22.** *Informal* False or exaggerated talk intended to impress or deceive a listener: *Disgraced politicians often try to feed voters a line about reforming themselves.* ❖ *v.* **lined, lin·ing, lines** —*tr.* **1.** To mark or cover with lines: *line paper.* **2.** To form a line along: *Thousands of people lined the sidewalks.* **3.** To place in a line or row: *Line the children up by the door.* **4.** In baseball, to hit (a ball) hard in a straight line. —*intr.* In baseball, to hit a line drive: *The batter lined out to the shortstop.* ◆ **all along the line 1.** In every place. **2.** At every stage or moment: *Building the house has been difficult all along the line.* **in line for** Next in order for: *She's in line for a promotion.* **line up 1.** To arrange in or form a line. **2.** To organize and make ready: *We lined up support for a class in scuba diving.* **out of line 1.** Uncalled for; improper: *That remark was out of line.* **2.** Unruly and out of control. [From Old English *līne*, from Latin *līnum*, thread, linen.]

line² (līn) *tr.v.* **lined, lin·ing, lines 1.** To cover the inside surface of with a layer of material: *The tailor lined the coat with satin.* **2.** To serve as a lining for or in: *Tissue paper lined the box.* **3.** To fill plentifully: *The store shelves were lined with toys.* ◆ **line (one's) pockets** To make a profit, especially by illegitimate means. [From Middle English *linen*, from Old English *līn*, linen.]

lin·e·age (lĭn′ē-ĭj) *n.* **1.** Direct descent from a particular ancestor; ancestry. **2.** All of the descendants of a particular ancestor.

lin·e·al (lĭn′ē-əl) *adj.* **1.** Being in the direct line of descent: *Without children, the couple had no lineal descendants.* **2.** Linear. —**lin′e·al·ly** *adv.*

lin·e·a·ment (lĭn′ē-ə-mənt) *n.* A distinctive outline or feature, especially of a face.

lin·e·ar (lĭn′ē-ər) *adj.* **1.** Relating to or resembling a line, especially a straight line: *linear distance.* **2.** Consisting of or using lines: *a linear design.* **3.** Relating to length: *The meter is a unit of linear measurement.* —**lin′e·ar·ly** *adv.*

linear accelerator *n.* A device that accelerates charged subatomic particles, such as protons and electrons, in a straight line by means of alternating negative and positive impulses from electric fields. Linear accelerators are used to bring about high-speed particle collisions in order to study subatomic structures.

linear equation *n.* An algebraic equation, such as $y = 2x + 7$, in which each term is either a constant or a single variable multiplied by a constant. The graph of a linear equation with two variables is a straight line.

linear measure *n.* **1.** Measurement of length. **2.** A system of units, such as miles, feet, and inches, used for measuring length.

line·back·er (līn′băk′ər) *n.* In football, a player stationed just behind a team's defensive line.

line drive *n.* A baseball hit sharply so that it flies low and fast in a nearly straight line.

line-i·tem veto (līn′ī′təm) *n.* The right or power of a government executive to reject any of the individual provisions that make up a legislative bill.

line·man (līn′mən) *n.* **1.** A person who installs or repairs telephone, telegraph, or electric power lines. **2.** A person who inspects and repairs railroad tracks. **3.** In football, a player positioned on the line of scrimmage at the snap of the ball.

lin·en (lĭn′ən) *n.* **1a.** Thread spun from fibers of the flax plant. **b.** Cloth woven from this thread. **2.** also **linens** Articles or garments, such as sheets, tablecloths, or shirts, made of linen or a similar material, such as cotton. [From Middle English, from Old English *līnen*, made of flax, probably from Latin *līnum*, flax.]

line of force *n., pl.* **lines of force** An imaginary line in a field of electric or magnetic force that indicates the direction in which the force is acting. —SEE NOTE AT **magnetism.**

line of scrimmage *n., pl.* **lines of scrimmage** In football, either of two imaginary lines that run parallel to the goal line at either end of the ball as it rests before being snapped. Each team lines up at its own line of scrimmage for a new play.

lin·er¹ (lī′nər) *n.* **1.** A person or thing that draws lines. **2.** A commercial ship or airplane carrying passengers on a regular route. **3.** In baseball, a line drive.

lin·er² (lī′nər) *n.* **1.** A person who makes or puts in linings. **2.** Something used as a lining. **3.** A jacket for a phonograph record.

line segment *n.* The part of a line lying between two given points on the line.

lines·man (līnz′mən) *n.* **1a.** In football, an official who marks the downs and the position of the ball and watches for violations from the sidelines. **b.** In soccer and similar field games, an official who indicates when the ball has gone out of bounds. **c.** In tennis and other court games, an official whose chief duty is to call shots that fall out of bounds. **d.** In ice hockey, an official whose chief duty is to call offsides and icing. **2.** A person who installs or repairs telephone, telegraph, or electric power lines.

line spectrum *n.* A spectrum produced by a luminous gas or vapor and consisting of a series of distinct, fairly narrow lines characteristically produced by the atoms of that gas or vapor.

line·up (līn′ŭp′) *n.* **1a.** The members of a team chosen to start a game. **b.** A list of such players. **2.** A group of people lined up, as for purposes of identification: *a*

BIOGRAPHY

Abraham Lincoln

Born in a log cabin in Kentucky and raised on frontier farms, Abraham **Lincoln** knew an early life of hardship. His schooling totaled less than one year, but he taught himself by reading as many books as he could. As a lanky young man, Lincoln studied law on his own, and after serving in the Illinois state legislature and the US House of Representatives he returned to Illinois to run a private law practice. In 1854, he reentered politics in order to oppose the expansion of slavery to states west of the Mississippi. Lincoln's forceful arguments in debates with Stephen Douglas (1858) brought him to national attention and led to his election as president in 1860. Only a month after he took office, the Civil War began, plunging the country into one of its darkest times. After two years of fighting, President Lincoln issued the Emancipation Proclamation, declaring all slaves in Confederate territory to be free. His leadership and determination to preserve the Union helped it to win the Civil War, and his courage in the face of the agony of war helped the nation to survive. Lincoln lived to see the war's end in 1865, but shortly after the Confederacy surrendered, he was assassinated by John Wilkes Booth while attending a play.

line of scrimmage

Carl Linnaeus

lintel

ă	pat	ôr	core
ā	pay	oi	boy
âr	care	ou	out
ä	father	o͝o	took
ĕ	pet	o͝or	lure
ē	be	o͞o	boot
ĭ	pit	ŭ	cut
ī	bite	ûr	urge
îr	pier	th	thin
ŏ	pot	*th*	this
ō	toe	zh	vision
ô	paw	ə	about

lineup of possible suspects in the crime. **3.** A group of people, organizations, or things enlisted for a specific purpose.

–ling[1] *suff.* A suffix that means: **1.** A person connected with: *earthling.* **2.** A person or thing having a specified quality: *hireling.* **3.** A person or thing that is small, young, or inferior: *duckling.*

–ling[2] *suff.* A suffix that means in a specified way or condition: *darkling.*

lin·ger (lĭng′gər) *intr.v.* **lin·gered, lin·ger·ing, lin·gers 1.** To stay in a place or be slow in leaving it: *The children lingered in the toy shop until closing.* See Synonyms at **stay[1]**. **2.** To continue or persist: *The taste of cherries lingered in my mouth.* **3.** To consider or do something in an unhurried or leisurely fashion: *We lingered over the question for an hour.* [From Middle English *lengeren*, from Old English *lengan*, to lengthen, prolong.]

lin·ge·rie (län′zhə-**rā′**) *n.* Women's underwear.

lin·go (**lĭng′**gō) *n., pl.* **lin·goes** Language that is difficult to understand, as the jargon of a special group: *Doctors have a lingo all their own.* [From Latin *lingua*, language.]

lin·gua fran·ca (**lĭng′**gwə **frăng′**kə) *n.* A language used between people who normally speak different languages.

lin·gual (**lĭng′**gwəl) *adj.* **1.** Relating to the tongue. **2.** Produced by the tongue, as the letter *l.*

lin·gui·ne also **lin·gui·ni** (lĭng-**gwē′**nē) *n.* Pasta in long, flat, thin strands.

lin·guist (**lĭng′**gwĭst) *n.* **1.** A person who speaks several languages fluently. **2.** A specialist in linguistics. [From Latin *lingua*, language.]

lin·guis·tic (lĭng-**gwĭs′**tĭk) *adj.* Relating to language or linguistics. **—lin·guis′ti·cal·ly** *adv.*

lin·guis·tics (lĭng-**gwĭs′**tĭks) *n. (used with a singular verb)* The study of the nature and structure of language.

lin·i·ment (**lĭn′**ə-mənt) *n.* A liquid medicine rubbed on the skin to soothe pain or relieve stiffness, as from bruises or sore muscles.

lin·ing (**lī′**nĭng) *n.* **1.** An inner covering or coating: *the stomach lining; the lining in a jacket.* **2.** Material used as such a covering or coating.

link (lĭngk) *n.* **1a.** One of the rings or loops forming a chain. **b.** One of a series of connected units: *a sausage link.* **2.** Something that joins or connects: *a new rail link between the city and the airport.* **3.** An association or relationship: *The governor denied that he had links to organized crime.* **4.** A graphical item or segment of text in a webpage or other electronic document that, when clicked, causes another webpage or section of the same webpage to be displayed: *That newspaper's homepage includes links to numerous government resources.* ❖ *v.* **linked, link·ing, links** *—tr.* **1.** To connect or join with or as if with a link: *The telephone links the far corners of the globe.* See Synonyms at **join. 2a.** To make or have a link to (another webpage or electronic document): *The blog links important news stories from across the web.* **b.** To make a link in (a webpage or electronic document): *The teacher linked the class website to an online map.* *—intr.* **1.** To become connected with or as if with a link: *The two expeditions plan to link up by radio.* **2a.** To make or have a link to a webpage or electronic document: *The shocking news story was linked to by many blogs. The article linked to photos of the damage.* **b.** To follow a link in a webpage or electronic document: *With a click of the mouse, I linked to the museum's website.* [From Middle English *linke*, of Scandinavian origin; akin to Old Norse *hlekkr*.]

link·age (**lĭng′**kĭj) *n.* **1.** The act or process of linking. **2.** The state or condition of being linked. **3.** A system or arrangement of machine parts, such as rods, springs, or pivots, used to transmit power or motion.

link·ing verb (**lĭng′**kĭng) *n.* A verb that connects the subject of a sentence with a predicate noun or adjective; a copula. For example, the verbs *are* and *seem* are linking verbs in the sentences *The children are happy* and *You seem sleepy.* —SEE NOTE AT **adjective.**

links (lĭngks) *pl.n.* A golf course. [From Old English *hlinc*, ridge.]

❑ *These sound alike:* **links, lynx** (wild cat).

Lin·nae·us (lĭ-**nē′**əs *or* lĭ-**nā′**əs), **Carl** or **Carolus** 1707–1778. Swedish botanist who founded the modern classification system for plants and animals.

lin·net (**lĭn′**ĭt) *n.* A small brownish finch of Eurasia and Africa.

li·no·le·um (lĭ-**nō′**lē-əm) *n.* A sturdy washable material made in sheets by pressing a mixture of hot linseed oil, rosin, powdered cork, and coloring onto a cloth backing, used especially for covering floors.

lin·seed (**lĭn′**sēd′) *n.* The seed of the flax plant, especially when used as the source of linseed oil; flaxseed.

linseed oil *n.* A yellow oil extracted from flax seeds that thickens and hardens when exposed to air and is used in paints, varnishes, printing inks, and linoleum.

lin·sey-wool·sey (lĭn′zē-**wo͝ol′**zē) *n., pl.* **lin·sey-wool·seys** A coarse fabric of cotton or linen woven with wool.

lint (lĭnt) *n.* **1.** Clinging bits of fiber and fluff from a material: *My shirt was covered with lint from the wash.* **2.** Downy material scraped from linen cloth and used to dress wounds. [From Middle English *linet*, from Latin *līnum*, flax.]

lin·tel (**lĭn′**tl) *n.* The horizontal beam that forms the top of a door or window frame and supports the structure above it.

li·on (**lī′**ən) *n.* **1.** A large wild cat of Africa and India, having a tawny coat and a heavy mane around the neck and shoulders in the male. **2.** A cougar. **3.** A powerful or influential person. ◆ **lion's share** The greatest or best part: *One candidate got the lion's share of the media attention.* [From Middle English *lioun*, from Greek *leōn*.]

li·on·ess (**lī′**ə-nĭs) *n.* A female lion.

li·on·heart·ed (**lī′**ən-här′tĭd) *adj.* Extraordinarily courageous.

li·on·ize (**lī′**ə-nīz′) *tr.v.* **li·on·ized, li·on·iz·ing, li·on·iz·es** To treat as a celebrity: *The public lionized the popular author.*

lip (lĭp) *n.* **1.** Either of the two fleshy muscular folds of tissue that together surround the mouth. **2.** The edge or rim that surrounds an opening: *the lip of a pitcher.* **3.** Either of the two parts into which the corolla or calyx of certain plants is divided: *the lips of a snapdragon blossom.* **4.** *Slang* Disrespectful talk: *gave the teacher lip.* [From Old English *lippa*.]

lip·ase (**lĭp′**ās′ *or* **lī′**pās′) *n.* An enzyme that promotes the breakdown of fats into glycerol and fatty acids.

lip·id (**lĭp′**ĭd) *n.* Any of a large group of organic compounds, including fats, oils, waxes, and sterols, that are oily to the touch and insoluble in water. They are a source of stored energy and are a component of cell membranes.

lip-read (**lĭp′**rēd′) *intr.v.* **lip-read** (**lĭp′**rĕd′), **lip-read·ing, lip-reads** To interpret utterances by lip reading.

lip reading *n.* The skill of understanding unheard speech by interpreting movements of the lips and face of the speaker.

lip service *n.* Agreement or respect expressed in words but without sincerity or the intention of doing anything: *He paid lip service to the suggestion that we should volunteer to clean the park.*

lip·stick (**lĭp′**stĭk′) *n.* A stick of waxy coloring matter applied to the lips and enclosed in a small case.

liq·ue·fac·tion (lĭk′wə-**făk′**shən) *n.* **1.** The act or process of liquefying. **2.** The condition of being liquefied.

liq·ue·fy (**lĭk′**wə-fī′) *tr. & intr.v.* **liq·ue·fied, liq·ue·fy·**

lion
male (*left*) and female (*right*)

ing, liq·ue·fies To make or become liquid: *Butter liquefies at low heat.* **—liq′ue·fi′a·ble** *adj.* **—liq′ue·fi′er** *n.*

li·queur (lĭ-kûr′) *n.* A sweet syrupy alcoholic beverage usually served after dinner.

liq·uid (lĭk′wĭd) *n.* **1.** A substance that is neither a solid nor a gas, with molecules that move freely within the container in which it is put. The volume of a liquid usually remains unchanged or changes only slightly under pressure. **2.** A substance that people drink for nourishment or refreshment: *It's hot today, so be sure to drink plenty of liquids.* ❖ *adj.* **1.** Being a liquid: *a liquid rocket fuel.* **2.** Clear and shining like water. **3.** Flowing without abrupt breaks: *a cascade of liquid piano notes.* **4.** Existing as or readily converted into cash: *liquid assets such as savings bonds.* [From Middle English, from Latin *liquidus*, from *liquēre*, to be liquid.]

liquid air *n.* A very cold liquid formed when air is put under great pressure and cooled. It is used as a source of nitrogen and oxygen and as a refrigerant.

liq·ui·date (lĭk′wĭ-dāt′) *tr.v.* **liq·ui·dat·ed, liq·ui·dat·ing, liq·ui·dates 1.** To pay off or settle: *liquidate one's debts.* **2.** To close down (a business firm) by settling its accounts and dividing up any remaining assets. **3.** To eliminate, especially by killing. **—liq′ui·da′tion** *n.*

liquid-crystal display (lĭk′wĭd-krĭs′təl) *n.* A thin display screen that is made of an array of cells containing a liquid whose molecules align to block or transmit light in response to an electric current.

li·quid·i·ty (lĭ-kwĭd′ĭ-tē) *n.* **1.** The quality or condition of being liquid. **2.** The quality of being readily convertible to cash.

liquid measure *n.* A system of units for measuring the volume of liquids, as in pints, gallons, or liters.

liquid oxygen *n.* A very cold transparent liquid formed when oxygen is put under great pressure and cooled. It is used as a rocket fuel and in explosives.

liq·uor (lĭk′ər) *n.* An alcoholic beverage, such as whiskey or gin, made by distillation rather than by fermentation.

li·ra (lîr′ə) *n., pl.* **li·re** (lîr′ā) or **li·ras 1.** The former basic monetary unit of Italy, Malta, San Marino, and Vatican City. **2.** The basic monetary unit of Turkey.

Lis·bon (lĭz′bən) The capital of Portugal, in the western part of the country on an inlet of the Atlantic Ocean. It was devastated by a major earthquake in 1755.

lisle (līl) *n.* A fine, smooth, tightly twisted cotton thread or a fabric knitted from it, often used to make underwear, socks, and gloves.

lisp (lĭsp) *n.* A speech defect in which sounds represented by *s* and *z* are pronounced *th* as in *thin* and *then.* ❖ *intr. & tr.v.* **lisped, lisp·ing, lisps** To speak or say with a lisp.

lis·some also **lis·som** (lĭs′əm) *adj.* Moving or bending easily; lithe. **—lis′some·ly** *adv.*

list¹ (lĭst) *n.* A series of names, words, or other items written or printed one after the other: *a guest list; a shopping list.* ❖ *tr.v.* **list·ed, list·ing, lists** To make a list of; include in a list: *The hotel's guests are listed in the register.* [From Old Italian *lista*, of Germanic origin.]

list² (lĭst) *n.* A tilt to one side, as of a ship: *a ship's sudden list to starboard.* ❖ *intr. & tr.v.* **list·ed, list·ing, lists** To lean or cause to lean to one side, as a ship; heel: *The ship listed heavily in the sudden gust of wind.*

list³ (lĭst) *intr. & tr.v.* **list·ed, list·ing, lists** *Archaic* To listen to; hear.

lis·ten (lĭs′ən) *intr.v.* **lis·tened, lis·ten·ing, lis·tens 1.** To make an effort to hear something: *I listened to music on the radio.* **2.** To pay attention; heed: *No one listened to my advice.* ◆ **listen in 1.** To listen to a conversation between others; eavesdrop. **2.** To tune in and listen to a broadcast. [From Old English *hlysnan*.] **—lis′ten·er** *n.*

list·ing (lĭs′tĭng) *n.* **1.** An entry in a list or directory: *a telephone listing.* **2.** A list: *a listing of dentists.*

list·less (lĭst′lĭs) *adj.* Lacking energy or enthusiasm; lethargic: *The long days indoors left us feeling dull and listless.* **—list′less·ly** *adv.* **—list′less·ness** *n.*

list price *n.* A basic price published in a price list, often reduced by a dealer.

Liszt (lĭst), **Franz** 1811–1886. Hungarian composer and pianist whose compositions include the *Hungarian Rhapsodies* (1853).

lit¹ (lĭt) *v.* A past tense and a past participle of **light¹**.

lit² (lĭt) *v.* A past tense and a past participle of **light²**.

lit. *abbr.* An abbreviation of: **1.** liter. **2.** literature.

lit·a·ny (lĭt′n-ē) *n., pl.* **lit·a·nies 1.** A Christian liturgical prayer consisting of phrases recited by a leader alternating with responses by the congregation. **2.** A repetitive recital, series, or list: *Each negotiator recited a familiar litany of grievances and demands.*

lit·as (lĭt′äs) *n.* The basic monetary unit of Lithuania.

li·tchi (lē′chē) *n.* Variant of **lychee.**

li·ter (lē′tər) *n.* A metric unit of volume equal to 1,000 cubic centimeters, or about 1.06 liquid quarts. See table at **measurement.**

lit·er·a·cy (lĭt′ər-ə-sē) *n.* **1.** The ability to read or write. **2.** Understanding or knowledge of a particular field: *computer literacy.*

lit·er·al (lĭt′ər-əl) *adj.* **1.** Following the usual or exact meaning of a word or group of words: *The literal interpretation of a poem is often too narrow.* **2.** Corresponding word for word with the original: *a literal translation.* **3.** Not exaggerated; factual: *a literal account of events.* [From Middle English, from Latin *littera*, letter.]

lit·er·al·ly (lĭt′ər-ə-lē) *adv.* **1.** In a literal manner: *Translated literally, "carte blanche" means "blank card."* **2.** Really; actually: *Literally millions of lives were saved by the vaccine.*

lit·er·ar·y (lĭt′ə-rĕr′ē) *adj.* **1.** Relating to literature: *a literary critic.* **2.** Relating to writers or the profession of writing.

lit·er·ate (lĭt′ər-ĭt) *adj.* **1.** Able to read and write. **2.** Familiar with literature; literary. **3.** Having knowledge in a particular field: *literate in architecture.* ❖ *n.* A person who can read and write.

lit·er·a·ture (lĭt′ər-ə-cho͝or′ *or* lĭt′ər-ə-chər) *n.* **1.** A body of writing in prose or verse, especially writing having recognized artistic value: *has read much American literature of the 1900s.* **2.** The art or occupation of a literary writer. **3.** The study of literature. **4.** A body of writing on a given subject: *medical literature.* **5.** Printed material: *election campaign literature.*

lithe (līth) *adj.* **lith·er, lith·est 1.** Easily bent; supple: *lithe birch branches.* **2.** Marked by effortless grace: *a lithe dancer.* **—lithe′ly** *adv.*

lith·i·um (lĭth′ē-əm) *n. Symbol* **Li** A soft, silvery metallic element that is highly reactive and occurs in small quantities in some minerals. Lithium is the lightest of all metals and is used in batteries, alloys, ceramics, and glass for large telescopes. Atomic number 3. See **Periodic Table.**

lith·o·graph (lĭth′ə-grăf′) *n.* A print produced by lithography. ❖ *tr.v.* **lith·o·graphed, lith·o·graph·ing, lith·o·graphs** To produce by lithography. **—li·thog′ra·pher** (lĭ-thŏg′rə-fər) *n.* **—lith′o·graph′ic** *adj.*

li·thog·ra·phy (lĭ-thŏg′rə-fē) *n.* A printing process in which an image is drawn on a flat printing surface such as a metal plate and treated to hold ink. The other areas of the surface are treated to repel ink.

lith·o·sphere (lĭth′ə-sfîr′) *n.* The outer part of the earth, consisting of the crust and upper mantle. It is approximately 62 miles (100 kilometers) thick.

Lith·u·a·ni·a (lĭth′o͞o-ā′nē-ə) A country of north-central Europe on the Baltic Sea south of Latvia. It was part of the USSR from 1940 to 1991. Vilnius is the capital.

Lith·u·a·ni·an (lĭth′o͞o-ā′nē-ən) *adj.* Relating to Lithu-

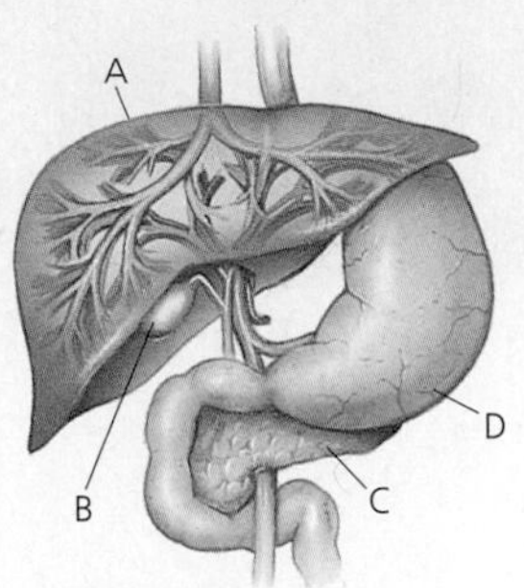

liver¹
A. liver
B. gallbladder
C. pancreas
D. stomach

liverwort

ă pat	ôr core
ā pay	oi boy
âr care	ou out
ä father	ŏŏ took
ĕ pet	ŏŏr lure
ē be	ōō boot
ĭ pit	ŭ cut
ī bite	ûr urge
îr pier	th thin
ŏ pot	*th* this
ō toe	zh vision
ô paw	ə about

ania, its people, language, or culture. ❖ *n.* **1.** A native or inhabitant of Lithuania. **2.** The Baltic language of the Lithuanians.

lit·i·gant (lĭtʹĭ-gənt) *n.* A person or group that is prosecuting or defending a lawsuit or legal action.

lit·i·gate (lĭtʹĭ-gātʹ) *intr.v.* **lit·i·gat·ed, lit·i·gat·ing, lit·i·gates** To prosecute or defend (a lawsuit or legal action).

lit·i·ga·tion (lĭtʹĭ-gāʹshən) *n.* **1.** The process of carrying on a lawsuit: *prolonged litigation over a contested will.* **2.** A lawsuit.

lit·mus (lĭtʹməs) *n.* A bluish powder, obtained from certain lichens, that changes to red with increasing acidity and to deeper blue with increasing alkalinity. [From Middle English *litmose,* of Scandinavian origin; akin to Old Norse *litmosi,* dyer's herbs : *litr,* color + *mosi,* moss.]

litmus paper *n.* Paper that has been treated with litmus, used to distinguish acid and alkaline solutions.

litmus test *n.* **1.** A test for chemical acidity or alkalinity using litmus paper. **2.** A test that uses a single issue for a decision: *using the candidates' stand on taxes as a litmus test.*

li·tre (lēʹtər) *n. Chiefly British* Variant of **liter.**

lit·ter (lĭtʹər) *n.* **1.** Carelessly scattered scraps of paper or other waste material. **2.** The group of offspring born to a mammal at a single time. **3a.** Material, such as straw or hay, spread for animals to sleep on. **b.** Loose material, especially clay, spread to absorb the urine and feces of an animal. **4.** A stretcher used to carry a sick or wounded person. **5.** A couch mounted on a framework covered with curtains and used to carry a person from place to place. **6.** Fallen leaves and other decaying organic matter that make up the top layer of a forest floor. ❖ *v.* **lit·tered, lit·ter·ing, lit·ters** —*tr.* **1.** To make untidy by discarding garbage carelessly: *The crowd littered the street with trash.* **2.** To give birth to (a litter). —*intr.* **1.** To scatter bits of trash. **2.** To give birth to a litter.

lit·ter·bug (lĭtʹər-bŭgʹ) *n. Informal* A person who litters public areas with trash.

lit·tle (lĭtʹl) *adj.* **lit·tler** or **less** (lĕs) also **les·ser** (lĕsʹər), **lit·tlest** or **least** (lēst) **1.** Small in size, quantity, or degree: *a little book; little money.* **2.** Short in duration; brief: *We have little time left.* **3.** Younger or youngest. Used especially of a sibling: *my little brother.* **4.** Unimportant; trivial: *a little problem.* ❖ *adv.* **less** also **lesser, least 1.** Not much: *He slept very little that night.* **2.** Not at all: *Little did the class realize the teacher planned a surprise test.* ❖ *n.* **1.** A small amount: *I received only a little of what they owe.* **2.** A short distance or time: *waited a little.* ◆ **a little** Somewhat; a bit: *She feels a little better now.* **little by little** By small degrees; gradually. [From Old English *lȳtel.*]

SYNONYMS **little, small, miniature, tiny** These adjectives all mean notably below average in size. *I am knitting a little blanket for the baby. The house would be too small for a large family, but it's perfect for two people. The children played with miniature model cars. The recipe calls for a tiny pinch of salt.*

Little Dipper *n.* A group of seven stars in the constellation Ursa Minor that forms the outline of a dipper.

Little League *n.* An organization of baseball and softball teams for children.

Little Rock The capital of Arkansas, in the central part of the state on the Arkansas River. It became the state capital in 1836.

lit·to·ral (lĭtʹər-əl) *adj.* On or relating to a shore, especially a seashore: *a littoral property.* ❖ *n.* **1.** A coastal region; a shore. **2.** The region or zone between the limits of high and low tides. [From Latin *lītorālis,* from *lītus,* shore.]

li·tur·gi·cal (lĭ-tûrʹjĭ-kəl) *adj.* Relating to or used in liturgy.

lit·ur·gy (lĭtʹər-jē) *n., pl.* **lit·ur·gies** An established form or set of forms for public religious worship.

liv·a·ble also **live·a·ble** (lĭvʹə-bəl) *adj.* **1.** Suitable for living in: *a very livable house.* **2.** Bearable; endurable: *a life of hardship that was barely livable.*

live¹ (lĭv) *v.* **lived, liv·ing, lives** —*intr.* **1.** To be alive; exist: *Birch trees live only in cold climates.* **2.** To continue to remain alive: *My grandmother lived to be 85.* **3.** To support oneself; subsist: *It takes hard work to live off the land.* **4.** To reside or dwell: *They live in an apartment.* **5.** To conduct one's life in a certain manner: *live happily.* —*tr.* To spend or pass (one's life): *I have lived my whole life in this town.* ◆ **live down** To overcome or reduce the shame of (a misdeed, for example) over a period of time. **live up to 1.** To live or act in accordance with: *I try to live up to my ideals.* **2.** To prove equal to: *The new car did not live up to our expectations.* **3.** To carry out; fulfill: *She lived up to her part of the bargain.* **live with** To put up with; resign oneself to: *We'll just have to live with the situation.* [From Old English *libban, lifian.*]

live² (līv) *adj.* **1.** Alive; living: *live animals in the circus.* **2.** Glowing; burning: *live coals.* **3.** Active and energetic: *a live and forceful personality.* **4.** Carrying electric current: *a live circuit.* **5.** Not yet exploded, but capable of being fired: *live ammunition.* **6.** Of current interest or importance: *a live issue.* **7.** Broadcast while actually being performed: *a live television program.* **8.** Containing living bacteria or active viruses, sometimes in a weakened form: *a live polio vaccine.* ❖ *adv.* At, during, or from the time of actual occurrence or performance: *The concert was broadcast live on television.* [Short for *alive.*]

live·li·hood (līvʹlē-hŏŏdʹ) *n.* The means of supporting life; a way of earning a living.

live·long (lĭvʹlôngʹ) *adj.* Whole; entire: *all the livelong day.*

live·ly (līvʹlē) *adj.* **live·li·er, live·li·est 1.** Full of life, energy, or activity: *a lively baby.* **2.** Full of spirit; exciting: *a lively discussion.* **3.** Tending to bounce or rebound strongly: *a lively soccer ball.* ❖ *adv.* **live·lier, live·liest** In a lively manner: *The whirling dancers stepped lively about the floor.* **—liveʹli·ness** *n.*

li·ven (līʹvən) *tr. & intr.v.* **li·vened, li·ven·ing, li·vens** To make or become lively: *Music livens up a party. The party livened up as more guests arrived.*

live oak (līv) *n.* Any of various evergreen oak trees of the southern and western United States and Mexico.

liv·er¹ (lĭvʹər) *n.* **1.** A large organ located in the abdomen of vertebrate animals. The liver secretes bile and acts in the formation of blood proteins, the breakdown of toxins, the metabolism of fats, and the storage of carbohydrates. **2.** A similar organ of invertebrate animals. **3.** The liver of certain animals, used as food. [From Old English *lifer.*]

liv·er² (lĭvʹər) *n.* A person who lives in a specified manner: *city livers.*

liv·er·ied (lĭvʹə-rēd *or* lĭvʹrēd) *adj.* Wearing livery: *a liveried footman.*

liv·er·mo·ri·um (lĭvʹər-môrʹē-əm) *n. Symbol* **Lv** A radioactive element that has been artificially produced by scientists. The half-life of its most stable isotope is about 53 milliseconds. Atomic number 116. See **Periodic Table.** [After the Lawrence *Livermore* National Laboratory.]

Liv·er·pool (lĭvʹər-pōōlʹ) A city of northwest England near the Irish Sea north of Wales.

liv·er·wort (lĭvʹər-wûrtʹ *or* lĭvʹər-wôrtʹ) *n.* Any of numerous small plants that are related to the mosses and do not bear flowers. Liverworts are leafy or flat and usually grow in damp areas.

liv·er·wurst (lĭvʹər-wûrstʹ *or* lĭvʹər-wŏŏrstʹ) *n.* A type of sausage containing mostly ground liver.

liv·er·y (lĭvʹə-rē *or* lĭvʹrē) *n., pl.* **liv·er·ies 1.** A uniform worn by servants: *a chauffeur dressed in livery.* **2.** The distinctive clothing worn by members of a specific group. **3.** The stabling and care of horses for a fee. **4.** A livery stable.

livery stable *n.* A stable that boards horses and keeps horses and carriages for hire.

lives (līvz) *n.* Plural of **life.**

live·stock (līv′stŏk′) *n.* Domestic animals that are raised for home use or for profit, especially on a farm. Cattle, horses, sheep, and pigs are livestock.

live wire (līv) *n.* **1.** A wire that is charged with an electric current. **2.** *Slang* An exciting, energetic, or imaginative person.

liv·id (lĭv′ĭd) *adj.* **1.** Discolored, as from a bruise; black-and-blue. **2.** Pale or ashen, as from shock. **3.** Extremely angry; furious. **—liv′id·ly** *adv.*

liv·ing (lĭv′ĭng) *adj.* **1.** Having life; alive: *famous living persons.* **2.** Currently existing or in use: *a living language.* **3.** Relating to the routine conduct of life: *the difficult living conditions of the arctic winter.* **4.** Enough to live on: *a living wage.* **5.** True to life: *a portrait that is the living image of my parents.* ❖ *n.* **1.** The condition of being alive: *the high cost of living.* **2.** A manner or style of life: *We prefer simple living.* **3.** A means of maintaining life; livelihood: *They make their living by fishing.*

living room *n.* A room in a household for leisure activities and entertaining guests.

liz·ard (lĭz′ərd) *n.* Any of numerous reptiles having a scaly, often slender body, a tapering tail, and usually four legs. Iguanas and chameleons are lizards. [From Middle English *lesarde*, from Latin *lacerta*.]

Lju·blja·na (lo͞o′blē-ä′nə) The capital of Slovenia, in the central part of the country west-northwest of Zagreb, Croatia.

lla·ma (lä′mə) *n.* A South American mammal related to the camel, raised for its warm wool and used for carrying loads. [From Spanish, from Quechua.]

lla·no (lä′nō *or* yä′nō) *n., pl.* **lla·nos** A broad, grassy, almost treeless plain, as in South America and the southern Great Plains of the United States.

lo (lō) *interj.* An expression used to attract attention.

❑ *These sound alike:* **lo, low¹** (not high), **low²** (bellow).

load (lōd) *n.* **1.** The weight or force supported by a structure or some part of it. **2a.** Something that is carried, as by a vehicle, person, or animal: *a load of firewood.* **b.** The quantity or amount carried: *a wagon with a full load of hay.* **3.** The amount of work required of or done by a person or machine: *The student had a heavy load of homework.* **4.** A single charge of ammunition for a gun. **5.** Something that oppresses or burdens: *That's a load off my mind.* **6.** The mechanical resistance that a machine must overcome. **7.** The power output of a generator or power plant. **8.** often **loads** *Informal* A great number or amount: *There were loads of people at the parade.* ❖ *v.* **load·ed, load·ing, loads** *—tr.* **1.** To put (something) into or onto a structure or vehicle: *load grain onto a train.* **2.** To put something into or onto (a structure or vehicle): *load a ship.* **3.** To provide or fill nearly to overflowing: *Our hosts loaded the table with food.* **4.** To weigh down; burden: *loaded the students with homework.* **5a.** To put (something necessary) into a device: *load paper into a printer; load cartridges into a rifle.* **b.** To put something necessary into (a device): *load a flashlight with new batteries.* **c.** To put (a computer program or data) into a computer's memory. *—intr.* **1.** To receive a load: *The ship loaded in port.* **2.** To put ammunition into a firearm. **3.** To be transferred into a computer's memory. ◆ **get a load of** *Slang* To look at or listen to (something considered ridiculous or impressive): *Hey, get a load of this goofy picture!* [From Old English *lād*, course, way.] **—load′er** *n.*

❑ *These sound alike:* **load, lode** (ore deposit).

load·ed (lō′dĭd) *adj.* **1.** Carrying a load. **2.** Having ammunition in place: *a loaded weapon.* **3.** Having a hidden or underlying implication: *a loaded question.* **4.** *Slang* Very wealthy.

load·star (lōd′stär′) *n.* Variant of **lodestar.**

load·stone (lōd′stōn′) *n.* Variant of **lodestone.**

loaf¹ (lōf) *n., pl.* **loaves** (lōvz) **1.** A shaped mass of bread baked in one piece. **2.** A shaped mass of food: *a meatloaf.* [From Old English *hlāf.*]

loaf² (lōf) *intr.v.* **loafed, loaf·ing, loafs** To spend time lazily or aimlessly; idle: *We loafed all morning accomplishing little.* [Probably from *loafer.*]

loaf·er (lō′fər) *n.* A person who spends time lazily or idly; an idler. [From obsolete *land-loafer*, vagabond.]

Loafer A trademark for a slip-on leather shoe resembling a moccasin but with a flat, low heel.

loam (lōm) *n.* Soil composed of sand, clay, silt, and decayed plant matter. **—loam′y** *adj.*

loan (lōn) *n.* **1.** The act of lending: *the loan of a raincoat to a friend.* **2a.** Something lent for temporary use: *The lamp is a loan from my neighbor.* **b.** A sum of money that is lent, usually with an interest fee: *took out a loan to buy a car; repaid the loan over five years.* ❖ *tr.v.* **loaned, loan·ing, loans** To lend: *Libraries loan books to the public.* —SEE NOTE AT **borrow.**

❑ *These sound alike:* **loan, lone** (solitary).

loan·word (lōn′wûrd′) *n.* A word that has been borrowed from a foreign language; for example, *encore, spaghetti,* and *sombrero* are loanwords in English.

loath (lōth *or* lō*th*) *adj.* Not willing; reluctant; averse: *They were loath to accept the offer of help from their rivals.*

loathe (lō*th*) *tr.v.* **loathed, loath·ing, loathes** To dislike greatly; detest: *I loathe cleaning the bathroom.*

loath·ing (lō′*th*ĭng) *n.* Extreme dislike; abhorrence.

loath·some (lō*th*′səm *or* lōth′səm) *adj.* Detestable; abhorrent. **—loath′some·ly** *adv.* **—loath′some·ness** *n.*

loaves (lōvz) *n.* Plural of **loaf¹.**

lob (lŏb) *tr.v.* **lobbed, lob·bing, lobs** To hit, throw, or propel (a ball) in a high arc. ❖ *n.* A ball that is lobbed.

lob·by (lŏb′ē) *n., pl.* **lob·bies 1.** An entrance hall or a waiting room at or near the entrance to a building such as a hotel or theater. **2.** A group of people who try to influence lawmakers in favor of a cause. ❖ *v.* **lob·bied, lob·by·ing, lob·bies** *—intr.* To try to influence lawmakers for or against a cause: *Industry groups often lobby against antipollution laws.* *—tr.* To seek to influence (lawmakers) in their voting: *lobbied Congress to approve the bill.*

lob·by·ist (lŏb′ē-ĭst) *n.* A person who tries to influence lawmakers for or against a cause.

lobe (lōb) *n.* A rounded part or projection, especially of a leaf or organ of the body, such as the lungs.

lobed (lōbd) *adj.* Having a lobe or lobes: *a lobed leaf.*

lo·be·li·a (lō-bē′lē-ə *or* lō-bēl′yə) *n.* Any of numerous plants having clusters of blue, red, or purplish flowers. [After Matthias de *Lobel* (1538–1616), Flemish botanist and physician.]

lob·ster (lŏb′stər) *n.* Any of various sea animals related to the crabs and shrimps, having a long hard-shelled body with five pairs of legs, the first pair of which are claws. ❖ *intr.v.* **lobstered, lobster·ing, lobsters** To catch or try to catch lobsters.

lobster pot *n.* A cage used for catching lobsters.

lo·cal (lō′kəl) *adj.* **1.** Relating to or characteristic of a particular area or place: *local governments; a local storm.* **2.** Making all stops on a route; not express: *a local train.* **3.** Affecting only one part of the body: *a local infection.* ❖ *n.* **1.** A person who lives in a certain region or neighborhood: *The locals are concerned about the town's growth.* **2.** A local branch of an organization, especially of a labor union. **3.** A train or bus that makes all stops along its

llama

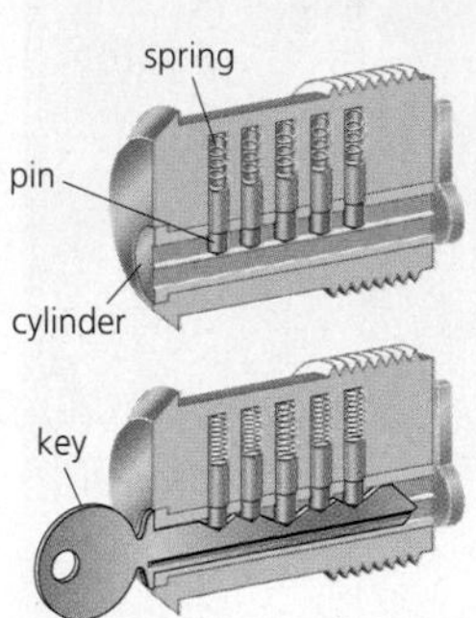

lock[1]
a pin-tumbler cylinder lock

locket
top: closed
bottom: open

route. [From Middle English, from Latin *locus*, place.] **—lo′cal·ly** *adv.*

lo·cale (lō-**kăl′**) *n.* A place, especially with reference to a particular event or circumstance: *The locale in many of Dickens's stories is London.*

lo·cal·ism (**lō′**kə-lĭz′əm) *n.* A local custom, habit, or expression.

lo·cal·i·ty (lō-**kăl′**ĭ-tē) *n., pl.* **lo·cal·i·ties** A certain neighborhood, place, or region.

lo·cal·ize (**lō′**kə-līz′) *tr. & intr.v.* **lo·cal·ized, lo·cal·iz·ing, lo·cal·iz·es** To confine or become restricted to a particular area: *The pain localized in my abdomen.*

lo·cate (**lō′**kāt′ *or* lō-**kāt′**) *v.* **lo·cat·ed, lo·cat·ing, lo·cates** *—tr.* **1.** To determine or show the position of: *locate Austria on a map.* **2.** To find by searching, inquiring, or examining: *locate information.* **3.** To place or situate: *We located the vegetables in a sunny corner of the garden. —intr.* To go and live somewhere; settle: *The family located in Iowa.*

lo·ca·tion (lō-**kā′**shən) *n.* **1.** A place where something is or could be located; a site: *a good location for a house.* **2.** The act or process of locating: *the location of water by drilling.* **3.** A site away from a movie studio where filming occurs: *shot on location in Spain.*

loch (lŏk *or* lŏкн) *n. Scots* **1.** A lake. **2.** An arm of the sea partly surrounded by land.

❑ *These sound alike:* **loch, lock[1]** (security device), **lock[2]** (hair).

lo·ci (**lō′**sī′) *n.* Plural of **locus.**

lock[1] (lŏk) *n.* **1.** A device used to fasten and secure something, such as a door or lid of a box, operated by a key, combination, or card. **2.** A section of a waterway, closed off with gates, in which a ship can be raised or lowered by pumping water in or out. **3.** A mechanism in a firearm for exploding the charge. **4.** One of several wrestling holds. **5.** A secure hold; control: *The popular candidate had a lock on the election.* ❖ *v.* **locked, lock·ing, locks** *—tr.* **1.** To fasten or secure with a lock or locks: *lock the door.* **2.** To confine by means of a lock: *The keepers locked the animals in their cages.* **3.** To fix in place so that movement is impossible: *The ship was locked in the ice.* **4.** To join or link firmly; intertwine: *The two friends locked arms and walked off. —intr.* **1.** To become tightly held, fastened, or secured: *The door locks automatically.* **2.** To become joined or intertwined: *The railroad cars locked as they came together.* [From Old English *loc*, bolt, bar.]

❑ *These sound alike:* **lock[1]** (security device), **loch** (lake), **lock[2]** (hair).

lock[2] (lŏk) *n.* **1.** A strand or curl of hair. **2. locks** The hair of the head: *the baby's red locks.* **3.** A small tuft of wool or cotton. [From Old English *locc*.]

❑ *These sound alike:* **lock[2]** (hair), **loch** (lake), **lock[1]** (security device).

lock·down (**lŏk′**doun′) *n.* A procedure or situation in which people are confined in a secure place during an emergency.

lock·er (**lŏk′**ər) *n.* **1.** A compartment, as in a gymnasium, that can be locked to keep clothes or valuables safe. **2.** A refrigerated cabinet or room for storing frozen foods. **3.** A flat trunk used for storage.

lock·et (**lŏk′**ĭt) *n.* A small ornamental metal case for a picture, a lock of hair, or another keepsake, usually worn on a chain around the neck.

lock·jaw (**lŏk′**jô′) *n.* Tetanus.

lock·out (**lŏk′**out′) *n.* The act of closing a workplace during a labor dispute in order to force employees to meet the employer's terms.

lock·smith (**lŏk′**smĭth′) *n.* A person who makes or repairs locks.

lo·co·mo·tion (lō′kə-**mō′**shən) *n.* The act or power of moving from place to place.

lo·co·mo·tive (lō′kə-**mō′**tĭv) *n.* An engine that moves on its own power and is used to pull or push railroad cars. ❖ *adj.* **1.** Able to move independently from place to place. **2.** Relating to locomotion.

lo·co·weed (**lō′**kō-wēd′) *n.* Any of several plants of western North America that cause severe illness when eaten by cattle, sheep, and other grazing animals.

lo·cus (**lō′**kəs) *n., pl.* **lo·ci** (**lō′**sī′) **1.** A locality; a place. **2.** A curve, a surface, or another figure that contains all and only the points that satisfy a given mathematical condition.

lo·cust (**lō′**kəst) *n.* **1.** Any of various grasshoppers that travel in large swarms and can do great damage to crops. **2.** Any of certain cicadas. **3.** Any of several trees having feathery leaves, drooping clusters of fragrant flowers, and long pods. [From Middle English *locuste*, from Latin *locusta*.]

lo·cu·tion (lō-**kyo͞o′**shən) *n.* **1.** A particular word, phrase, or expression. **2.** A manner or style of speaking.

lode (lōd) *n.* **1.** A deposit or vein of a metal-bearing ore: *The miners dug into a rich lode of silver.* **2.** A rich source or supply: *found a lode of important documents in the archives.*

❑ *These sound alike:* **lode, load** (weight).

lode·star also **load·star** (**lōd′**stär′) *n.* A star, such as Polaris, used as point of navigational reference.

lode·stone also **load·stone** (**lōd′**stōn′) *n.* A piece of magnetite that acts like a magnet.

lodge (lŏj) *n.* **1.** A cottage or cabin, especially a temporary house used during a vacation or for recreational activity: *a fishing lodge.* **2.** Any of various Native American dwellings, such as a wigwam or hogan. **3.** An inn. **4.** The den of certain animals, such as beavers. **5.** A branch or meeting place of a fraternal organization or secret society. ❖ *v.* **lodged, lodg·ing, lodg·es** *—tr.* **1.** To provide with a place to stay temporarily: *We can lodge many guests in our home.* **2.** To rent a room to: *We lodge local students at reasonable rates.* **3.** To fix or implant: *The surveyors lodged stakes in the ground at the corners of the property.* **4.** To present (a charge or complaint) to an appropriate official or office; register: *The angry tenant lodged a complaint with the housing agency. —intr.* **1.** To live in a place temporarily: *We lodged in an old hotel.* **2.** To live in a rented room or rooms: *He is lodging above a restaurant this year.* **3.** To be or become fixed or implanted: *The blade of the saw lodged in the wood.* [From Middle English *logge*, from Old French *loge*, of Germanic origin.]

lodg·er (**lŏj′**ər) *n.* A person who rents a room or rooms in another person's house.

lodg·ing (**lŏj′**ĭng) *n.* **1.** A temporary place to live or stay: *The vacationers sought lodging for the weekend.* **2. lodgings** A rented room or rooms.

lodg·ment also **lodge·ment** (**lŏj′**mənt) *n.* **1.** The act of lodging or the state of being lodged. **2.** Something lodged or deposited.

lo·ess (**lō′**əs *or* lĕs *or* lŭs) *n.* A yellow to gray fine-grained silt or clay, deposited as dust blown by the wind.

loft (lôft) *n.* **1.** A large, open, upper floor in a commercial building or warehouse. **2.** Such a floor used as an apartment or artist's studio. **3.** An open space under a roof; an attic or garret. **4.** A gallery or balcony, as in a church: *a choir loft.* **5.** A hayloft. ❖ *tr.v.* **loft·ed, loft·ing, lofts** To send (a ball) in a high arc.

loft·y (**lôf′**tē) *adj.* **loft·i·er, loft·i·est 1.** Of great height; towering: *lofty mountains.* **2.** Elevated in character or spirit; exalted; noble: *lofty thoughts; lofty principles.* **3.** Arrogant; haughty: *Lofty treatment of others does not win friends.* **—loft′i·ly** *adv.* **—loft′i·ness** *n.*

log[1] (lôg) *n.* **1.** A long thick segment of a tree, used for building, firewood, or lumber. **2.** A device trailed from a ship to determine its speed through the water. **3a.** An

ă	pat	ôr	core
ā	pay	oi	boy
âr	care	ou	out
ä	father	o͝o	took
ĕ	pet	o͝or	lure
ē	be	o͞o	boot
ĭ	pit	ŭ	cut
ī	bite	ûr	urge
îr	pier	th	thin
ŏ	pot	*th*	this
ō	toe	zh	vision
ô	paw	ə	about

official record of speed, progress, and important events, kept on a ship or aircraft. **b.** A journal or record. ❖ *v.* **logged, log·ging, logs** —*tr.* **1.** To cut down the trees on (a section of land). **2.** To cut (trees) into logs. **3.** To enter (something) in a logbook. **4.** To travel (a certain distance or at a certain speed): *We logged several hundred miles in our two-day journey.* —*intr.* To cut down, trim, and haul timber. ◆ **log in** or **log on** To enter into a computer the information required to begin a session. **log out** or **log off** To enter into a computer the command to end a session. [From Middle English *logge.*]

log² (lôg) *n.* A logarithm. [From *logarithm.*]

lo·gan·ber·ry (**lō′**gən-bĕr′ē) *n.* **1.** The edible dark-red fruit of a prickly plant related to the blackberry and the raspberry. **2.** The plant that bears such fruit. [After James Harvey *Logan* (1841–1928), American horticulturalist.]

log·a·rithm (**lô′**gə-rĭ*th*′əm) *n.* The power to which a base, usually 10, must be raised to produce a given number. For example, if the base is 10, then 2 is the logarithm of 100 because 100 is 10^2. **—log′a·rith′mic** (lô′gə-**rĭ*th*′**mĭk) *adj.*

log·book (**lôg′**bo͝ok′) *n.* The official record book of a ship or aircraft.

log·ger (**lô′**gər) *n.* **1.** A person who logs; a lumberjack. **2.** A tractor, crane, or other machine used for hauling or loading logs.

log·ger·head (**lô′**gər-hĕd′) *n.* A large sea turtle that has a large head with powerful jaws and feeds chiefly on sea animals such as mollusks and jellyfish. ◆ **at loggerheads** In disagreement; at odds: *The legislators were at loggerheads over the budget.*

log·gi·a (**lô′**jē-ə) *n.* A gallery or arcade along the front or side of a building that is open on at least one side.

log·ging (**lô′**gĭng) *n.* The work of cutting down trees, sawing them into logs, and moving the logs to a mill.

log·ic (**lŏj′**ĭk) *n.* **1.** The study of the principles of reasoning; the science of reasoning and of proof. **2.** Sound thinking; clear reasoning: *Their logic is undeniable when it comes to this issue.* **3.** A particular method of reasoning; a way of thinking: *By my logic, the car's starter is faulty, not the battery.* [From Middle English *logik*, from Greek *logos*, reason.]

log·i·cal (**lŏj′**ĭ-kəl) *adj.* **1.** Using or agreeing with the principles of logic: *a logical consequence.* **2.** Reasonably expected: *A small apartment is a logical choice for a single person.* **3.** Reasoning or capable of reasoning clearly and rationally: *a logical mind.* **—log′i·cal·ly** *adv.*

lo·gi·cian (lō-**jĭsh′**ən) *n.* A person who practices or is skilled in logic.

lo·gis·tic (lō-**jĭs′**tĭk) also **lo·gis·ti·cal** (lō-**jĭs′**tĭ-kəl) *adj.* Relating to logistics.

lo·gis·tics (lō-**jĭs′**tĭks *or* lə-**jĭs′**tĭks) *n.* *(used with a singular or plural verb)* **1.** The planning and carrying out of a military operation. Logistics includes the transportation, housing, and supplying of troops. **2.** The management of the details of an operation or process.

lo·go (**lō′**gō′) *n., pl.* **lo·gos** A symbol or design that identifies a brand.

log·roll·ing (**lôg′**rō′lĭng) *n.* **1.** A sport in which two people stand on a floating log, spinning it with their feet until one falls. **2.** The exchange of political favors among lawmakers who agree to vote for each other's legislation.

lo·gy (**lō′**gē) *adj.* **lo·gi·er, lo·gi·est** Sluggish; lethargic: *felt logy after eating the turkey.*

–logy *suff.* A suffix that means: **1.** Oral or written expression: *phraseology.* **2.** Science, theory, or study: *sociology.*

loin (loin) *n.* **1a.** The part of the body of a person or four-legged animal on each side of the spine between the ribs and hipbones. **b.** A cut of meat taken from this part of an animal. **2. loins a.** The region of the hips, groin, and lower abdomen. **b.** The reproductive organs.

loin·cloth (**loin′**klôth′) *n.* A strip of cloth worn around the hips and groin.

Loire (lwär) The longest river of France, rising in south-central France and flowing about 630 miles (1,015 kilometers) north and west to the Bay of Biscay.

loi·ter (**loi′**tər) *intr.v.* **loi·tered, loi·ter·ing, loi·ters 1.** To stand about idly; linger: *I loitered about the station, waiting for the train to come.* **2.** To go slowly, stopping often: *The shoppers loitered on their way past the store windows.* **—loi′ter·er** *n.*

loll (lŏl) *v.* **lolled, loll·ing, lolls** —*intr.* **1.** To move, stand, sit, or rest in a lazy way: *The bathers lolled about the side of the pool.* **2.** To hang or let hang loosely or droop: *The limp flag lolled from the pole.* —*tr.* To allow to hang or droop: *The calf lolled its tongue on the hot day.*

lol·li·pop also **lol·ly·pop** (**lŏl′**ē-pŏp′) *n.* A piece of hard candy on the end of a stick.

Lo·mé (lō-**mā′**) The capital of Togo, in the southern part of the country on the Gulf of Guinea.

lo mein (**lō′ mān′**) *n.* A Chinese dish of wheat noodles that are boiled then seasoned and stir-fried.

Lon·don (**lŭn′**dən) The capital of the United Kingdom, on the Thames River in southeast England. Its growth as an important trade center dates from 886.

London, John Griffith Pen name Jack London. 1876–1916. American writer of adventure novels, including *The Call of the Wild* (1903).

lone (lōn) *adj.* **1.** Alone; solitary: *a lone traveler on the deserted road.* **2.** Being the only one of its kind; sole: *the lone hiker to reach the summit.* **3.** Standing by itself; remote: *a lone tree on the hillside.*

❑ *These sound alike:* **lone, loan** (something lent).

lone·ly (**lōn′**lē) *adj.* **lone·li·er, lone·li·est 1.** Sad at being alone: *feeling lonely with no friends.* See Synonyms at **alone. 2.** Without others of a similar kind; solitary: *Hers was a lonely voice of protest in a culture of complacency.* **3.** Not used or visited by people; remote: *a lonely road.* **—lone′li·ness** *n.*

lone·some (**lōn′**səm) *adj.* **1.** Sad at being alone. See Synonyms at **alone. 2.** Producing a feeling of loneliness: *a lonesome voyage.* **3.** Not used or visited by people; remote: *a lonesome mountain trail.*

long¹ (lông) *adj.* **long·er, long·est 1.** Measuring a large amount from end to end; having great distance: *The Mississippi is a long river.* **2.** Having great duration: *The candidate gave a long speech.* **3.** Of a certain extent or duration: *The movie was two hours long.* **4.** Made up of many items: *a long shopping list.* **5a.** Extending beyond average or standard length: *a long chess game.* **b.** Extending or landing beyond a given boundary, limit, or goal: *Her serve was long.* **6.** Having an abundance of: *long on kindness.* **7.** Relating to the vowel sounds in words such as *mate, meet, mite, mote, moot,* and *mute.* ❖ *adv.* **longer, longest 1.** During or for a large amount of time: *Stay as long as you like.* **2.** For or throughout a specific period: *all night long.* **3.** Beyond a given boundary, limit, or goal: *Her serve went long.* **4.** At a very distant time: *That was long before you were born.* ❖ *n.* A long time: *It won't be long before we leave.* ◆ **long ago** At a time or during a period well before the present: *I read that book long ago.* **no longer** Not now as formerly: *a bankrupt company that is no longer in business.* [From Old English *lang.*]

long² (lông) *intr.v.* **longed, long·ing, longs** To have a strong desire; wish very much: *The students longed for summer vacation.* [From Old English *langian.*]

long. *abbr.* An abbreviation of longitude.

long·boat (**lông′**bōt′) *n.* The longest boat carried by a sailing ship.

long·bow (**lông′**bō′) *n.* A large bow for shooting arrows, used during the Middle Ages.

long-dis·tance (**lông′dĭs′**təns) *adj.* Covering or carried over a great distance: *a long-distance race.*

locoweed

loggerhead

long jump

loom²

long division *n.* The process of dividing one number by another in which each step of the division is written out, especially when the divisor is a large number.

lon·gev·i·ty (lŏn-jĕv′ĭ-tē) *n., pl.* **lon·gev·i·ties** Long life.

Long·fel·low (lông′fĕl′ō), **Henry Wadsworth** 1807–1882. American writer whose poems include *The Song of Hiawatha* (1855).

long·hand (lông′hănd′) *n.* Ordinary handwriting in which the words are fully written out.

long·horn (lông′hôrn′) *n.* Any of various cattle having long horns, especally a breed that originated in the region that is now Texas.

long·house or **long house** (lông′hous′) *n.* A long dwelling, especially of certain Native American, Polynesian, and Indonesian peoples, designed to house numerous families under the same roof.

long·ing (lông′ĭng) *n.* A deep yearning; a strong desire: *a longing for success.* **—long′ing·ly** *adv.*

Long Island A long narrow island of southeast New York bordered on the south by the Atlantic Ocean. **Long Island Sound,** an arm of the Atlantic, separates it from Connecticut on the north.

lon·gi·tude (lŏn′jĭ-to͞od′) *n.* Distance east or west on the earth's surface, measured in degrees from a certain meridian, usually the Prime Meridian in Greenwich, England.

lon·gi·tu·di·nal (lŏn′jĭ-**to͞od′**n-əl) *adj.* **1.** Involving length or longitude. **2.** Placed or running lengthwise: *longitudinal stripes running the length of the garter snake.* **—lon′gi·tu′di·nal·ly** *adv.*

long jump *n.* A jump for distance rather than height in an athletic contest.

long-lived (lông′līvd′ *or* lông′lĭvd′) *adj.* Having a long life; existing for a long time: *a long-lived partnership.*

long-play·ing record (lông′plā′ĭng) *n.* A phonograph record that turns at 33⅓ revolutions per minute and usually providing about 25 minutes of sound on each side.

long-range (lông′rānj′) *adj.* **1.** Involving a lengthy period; not immediate: *long-range plans.* **2.** Designed for covering great distances: *long-range transport planes.*

long·shore·man (lông′shôr′mən) *n.* A dock worker who loads and unloads ships.

long shot *n.* **1.** An entry, as in a horse race, with only a slight chance of winning. **2.** Something that is risky but rewarding if successful. ◆ **by a long shot** To any extent; at all. Usually used in negative sentences: *That's not going to happen by a long shot.*

long-stand·ing or **long·stand·ing** (lông′stăn′dĭng) *adj.* Of long duration: *a long-standing business partnership.*

long-suf·fer·ing (lông′sŭf′ər-ĭng) *adj.* Patiently enduring pain or difficulty.

long-term (lông′tûrm′) *adj.* Involving a long period of time: *a long-term investment.*

long ton *n.* A ton weighing 2,240 pounds (1,016 kilograms). See table at **measurement.**

long-wind·ed (lông′wĭn′dĭd) *adj.* Writing or talking at great length; tiresome. **—long′-wind′ed·ly** *adv.* **—long′-wind′ed·ness** *n.*

look (lo͝ok) *v.* **looked, look·ing, looks** *—intr.* **1.** To use the eyes to see; perceive by sight: *I looked at the photograph.* **2.** To turn one's gaze or attention: *Everyone looked toward the camera. You must look carefully at all of the facts.* **3.** To appear; seem: *These bananas look ripe.* **4.** To search: *I looked all over for my keys.* **5.** To face in a certain direction: *The house looks on the sea.* *—tr.* **1.** To turn one's eyes upon: *The teacher looked me in the eye.* **2.** To show by one's appearance: *He looks his age.* ❖ *n.* **1.** The action of looking; a gaze or glance: *a quick look at the map.* **2.** An expression or appearance: *The gathering clouds have a threatening look.* **3. looks** Personal appearance: *The children have their parents' good looks.* ◆ **look after** To take care of: *Someone must look after the baby.* **look a gift horse in the mouth** To be critical or suspicious of something that has been received for free. **look alive** or **look sharp** *Informal* To act or respond quickly. **look down on** To regard with contempt or scorn. **look for** To search for; seek: *a bird looking for food.* **look forward to** To think of (a future event) with pleasure and excitement. **look into** To inquire into; investigate: *The detective looked into the matter of the missing money.* **look on** or **look upon** To regard; consider: *We look on you as a model student.* **look out** To be watchful or careful; take care: *Look out for that speeding car!* **look over** To examine, often hastily: *The police looked over the scene and determined it was safe to move forward.* **look up 1.** To search for and find, as in a reference book. **2.** To visit: *look up an old friend.* **3.** To become better; improve: *Things are at last looking up.* **look up to** To admire: *I look up to my parents.* [From Old English *lōcian.*] **—look′er** *n.*

look·ing glass (lo͝ok′ĭng) *n.* A mirror.

look·out (lo͝ok′out′) *n.* **1.** The act of looking or watching: *keeping a sharp lookout.* **2.** A high place with a wide view for keeping watch. **3.** A person assigned to watch for something: *The captain sent a lookout up the mast.* **4.** A particular worry or concern: *Making sure no one gets hurt is a lifeguard's lookout.*

loom¹ (lo͞om) *intr.v.* **loomed, loom·ing, looms 1.** To come into view, often with a threatening appearance: *Storm clouds loomed over the mountains.* **2.** To seem close at hand; be about to happen: *The examination loomed before the students.* [Perhaps of Scandinavian origin.]

loom² (lo͞om) *n.* A machine or frame on which threads or yarns are woven to make cloth. [From Old English *gelōma,* tool.]

loon¹ (lo͞on) *n.* Any of several large diving birds having a dark speckled back, a pointed bill, webbed feet, and a cry that resembles a laugh. [Perhaps from Old Norse *lōmr,* diver.]

loon² (lo͞on) *n. Informal* A foolish or crazy person. [Probably from *loon* (the bird) and influenced by *lunatic.*]

loon·y (lo͞o′nē) *Informal adj.* **loon·i·er, loon·i·est 1.** Very foolish or silly: *How did you come up with that loony idea?* **2.** Crazy; mad: *He thinks he makes sense, but we think he's loony.* ❖ *n., pl.* **loon·ies** A foolish or crazy person.

loop (lo͞op) *n.* **1.** A length of rope, thread, or wire that crosses over itself, making an opening. **2.** A circular path or oval pattern that closes or nearly closes on itself: *The car followed a loop around the town.* **3.** A fastening or ornament made from a bent or crossed piece of cloth, cord, or other material: *a belt loop.* **4.** A closed electric circuit. **5.** A series of instructions in a computer program that are repeated a specified number of times or until a certain result has been achieved. **6.** A maneuver in which an aircraft flies a circular path in a vertical plane. ❖ *v.* **looped, loop·ing, loops** *—tr.* **1.** To make into a loop or loops: *loop string and tie the ends.* **2.** To fasten or join with a loop or loops: *looped together the pieces of string.* **3.** To encircle with a loop: *loop the pole with this rope.* **4.** To fly (an aircraft) in a loop or loops. *—intr.* **1.** To form a loop: *yarn that loops easily for knitting.* **2.** To move or fly in a loop. ◆ **in the loop** Part of a group that is kept informed about something. **out of the loop** Not part of a group that is kept informed about something.

loop·hole (lo͞op′hōl′) *n.* **1.** A way of avoiding or escaping a cost or legal burden that would otherwise apply. Loopholes often involve an omission or an unclear provision in a law or contract: *A loophole in the law allowed the corporation to avoid paying the new tax.* **2.** A small

ă	pat	ôr	core
ā	pay	oi	boy
âr	care	ou	out
ä	father	o͝o	took
ĕ	pet	o͝or	lure
ē	be	o͞o	boot
ĭ	pit	ŭ	cut
ī	bite	ûr	urge
îr	pier	th	thin
ŏ	pot	*th*	this
ō	toe	zh	vision
ô	paw	ə	about

hole or slit in a wall for looking or shooting through.

loose (lo͞os) *adj.* **loos·er, loos·est 1.** Not tightly fastened or secured: *a loose shoelace; loose bricks.* **2.** Free from confinement, bonds, or fetters: *The stallion was loose on the prairie.* **3.** Not tight-fitting or tightly fitted: *a loose robe.* **4.** Not tightly stretched; slack: *the loose skin of a cow's neck.* **5.** Not tightly packed; not compact: *loose gravel.* **6.** Not bound or gathered together: *loose notebook pages.* **7.** Lacking moral restraint: *loose conduct.* **8.** Not strict or exact: *a loose translation.* ❖ *adv.* In a loose manner or condition. ❖ *tr.v.* **loosed, loos·ing, loos·es 1.** To set free; release: *We loosed our dog from its leash.* **2.** To make less tight, firm, or compact. **3.** To untie, undo, or unwrap: *We loosed the ribbon from the package.* **4.** To discharge (a missile): *loose an arrow.* [From Middle English *los,* from Old Norse *lauss.*] **—loose′ly** *adv.* **—loose′ness** *n.*

loose-leaf (lo͞os′lēf′) *adj.* Having pages that can be easily removed or replaced: *a loose-leaf notebook.*

loos·en (lo͞o′sən) *v.* **loos·ened, loos·en·ing, loos·ens** —*tr.* **1.** To make looser or less tight: *loosened his tie; loosened her grip on the rope.* **2.** To make less strict or rigid; relax: *The school loosened its student dress code.* —*intr.* To become loose or looser: *The knot loosened easily.* **—loos′en·er** *n.*

loot (lo͞ot) *n.* **1.** Valuable things pillaged in time of war; spoils. **2.** Stolen goods or money. **3.** *Slang* Money. ❖ *v.* **loot·ed, loot·ing, loots** —*tr.* To take things from (a place) by force or without right; plunder: *Rioters looted the downtown stores.* —*intr.* To take goods by force or through lawless behavior. **—loot′er** *n.*

❑ *These sound alike:* **loot, lute** (musical instrument).

lop[1] (lŏp) *tr.v.* **lopped, lop·ping, lops 1.** To cut (a part) from; remove: *lopped dead branches from the tree.* **2.** To cut off a part or parts from; trim: *lopped the shrub.* [Perhaps from Middle English *loppe,* small branches and twigs.]

lop[2] (lŏp) *intr.v.* **lopped, lop·ping, lops** To hang loosely; droop: *The puppy's ears lopped.*

lope (lōp) *intr.v.* **loped, lop·ing, lopes** To run or ride with a long easy gait: *The horse loped along the trail.* ❖ *n.* A long easy gait. [From Middle English *lopen,* to leap, from Old Norse *hlaupa.*]

lop-eared (lŏp′îrd′) *adj.* Having bent or drooping ears: *a lop-eared rabbit.*

lop·sid·ed (lŏp′sī′dĭd) *adj.* **1.** Heavier or larger on one side than on the other. **2.** Leaning or sagging to one side: *a lopsided stack of books.* **3.** Characterized by a large margin of victory. **—lop′sid′ed·ly** *adv.* **—lop′sid′ed·ness** *n.*

lo·qua·cious (lō-kwā′shəs) *adj.* Very talkative; talking a great deal or too much. **—lo·qua′cious·ly** *adv.* **—lo·qua′cious·ness** *n.*

lord (lôrd) *n.* **1.** In feudal times, a man of high rank, as a king or the owner of a manor. **2. Lord** *Chiefly British* A general masculine title of nobility or other high rank. **3. Lord** God. **4.** A man with great authority or power: *a press lord who owns many newspapers.* ◆ **lord it over** To behave in a domineering manner toward: *The older students lorded it over the newcomers.* [From Old English *hlāford* : *hlāf,* bread + *weard,* guardian.]

lord·ly (lôrd′lē) *adj.* **lord·li·er, lord·li·est 1.** Characteristic of a lord: *a lordly estate; a lordly deed.* **2.** Arrogant; haughty: *a lordly and superior manner.* **—lord′li·ness** *n.*

lord·ship (lôrd′shĭp′) *n.* **1.** often **Lordship** Used as a title and form of address for a man holding the rank of lord: *your Lordship.* **2.** The rank or domain of a lord.

Lord's Prayer (lôrdz prâr) *n.* The prayer taught by Jesus to his disciples. In English it begins with the words *Our Father.*

Lord's Supper *n.* **1.** The Last Supper. **2.** The sacrament of Holy Communion.

lore (lôr) *n.* The accumulated facts, traditions, or beliefs about something, especially when passed from generation to generation by oral tradition: *sailing lore; the lore of the frontier.*

lor·ry (lôr′ē) *n., pl.* **lor·ries** *Chiefly British* A motor truck.

Los An·ge·les (lôs ăn′jə-ləs) The largest city of California, in the southern part of the state on the Pacific Ocean north-northwest of San Diego. It was founded by the Spanish in 1781 and is noted for its entertainment industry.

lose (lo͞oz) *v.* **lost** (lôst), **los·ing, los·es** —*tr.* **1.** To be unable to find; mislay: *I lost my gloves yesterday.* **2.** To be deprived of (something one has had): *We lost our peach trees during the storm. She lost her husband in the accident.* **3.** To be unable to keep control or the allegiance of: *We lost their support. Don't lose your temper.* **4.** To fail to win: *They lost the game.* **5.** To fail to use; waste: *lose a chance by hesitating.* **6.** To stray or wander from: *lose one's way.* **7.** To fail to see, hear, understand, or follow: *lose the airplane in the clouds; lose track of what was said.* **8.** To outrun or escape capture by: *The swift deer was able to lose the pursuing wolves.* **9.** To cause (someone) to be deprived of; cost: *That blunder lost him the job.* **10.** To destroy. Usually used in the passive: *All my belongings were lost in the fire.* —*intr.* **1.** To suffer loss or destruction: *Many investors lost heavily in the recession.* **2.** To be defeated: *Their team lost in overtime.* ◆ **lose it** *Slang* To lose control mentally or emotionally: *I completely lost it when I heard the bad news.* **lose out** To be unsuccessful. **lose out on** To fail to win or get; miss: *He lost out on the opportunity because he did not say he was interested.* **lose time 1.** To operate too slowly. Said of a timepiece. **2.** To delay forward progress: *We'll lose a lot of time if we go the roundabout way.* [From Old English *losian,* to perish.] **—los′er** *n.*

los·ing (lo͞o′zĭng) *adj.* **1.** Failing to win: *the losing team.* **2.** Relating to one that fails to win: *a losing season.* ❖ *n.* **1.** The act of one who loses; loss. **2.** often **losings** Something lost, such as money.

loss (lôs) *n.* **1a.** The act or an instance of losing: *a loss of memory; the loss of a game.* **b.** The state of being deprived of a person or thing: *Her loss was made easier by her cheerful outlook.* **2.** A person or thing that is lost: *Because of the accident, our car was a complete loss.* **3.** The suffering or damage caused by losing a person or thing: *The doctor's retirement is a great loss to the community.* **4. losses** Soldiers killed or wounded; casualties. ◆ **at a loss 1.** Below cost: *They sold the cherry crop at a loss.* **2.** Perplexed; puzzled: *I am at a loss to explain his behavior.*

lost (lôst) *v.* Past tense and past participle of **lose.** ❖ *adj.* **1.** Unable to find the way: *a lost tourist.* **2a.** No longer in one's possession, care, or control: *a lost fortune; a lost opportunity.* **b.** No longer known or practiced: *a lost art.* **c.** Beyond reach, communication, or influence: *lost to the world.* **3.** Not won or unlikely to be won; unsuccessful: *a lost cause.* **4.** Confused; bewildered: *At first we were lost in the advanced class.* **5.** Beyond recovery or redemption; destroyed: *lost honor; a lost soul.* **6.** Completely involved or preoccupied: *lost in thought.*

lot (lŏt) *n.* **1. a lot** or **lots** *Informal* A large amount or number: *I have a lot of work to do. We made lots of new friends.* **2.** A number of people or things considered as a group: *We packed this lot of fruit for shipment.* **3.** A piece of land: *the empty lot behind the house.* **4.** A movie studio. **5.** One of a set of objects, such as bits of paper or straw, used to determine something by chance: *They drew lots to see who would go first.* **6.** The use of lots to determine something: *We decided who would go first by lot.* **7.** The decision made in this manner. **8.** Fortune in life; luck: *It is the lot of many to struggle for a living.* [From Old English *hlot.*] —SEE NOTE.

loon[1]

lop-eared

USAGE

lot When *a lot* is the grammatical subject of a clause and is followed by a prepositional phrase beginning with *of,* it can take either a singular or a plural verb, depending on whether the object of the preposition is singular or plural: *A lot of my apartment is carpeted. A lot of people live in Los Angeles.* You will sometimes see the phrase *a lot* as in *a lot of money* spelled as one word, *alot.* This is not an acceptable spelling.

lotus

GEOGRAPHY

Louisiana In 1682, French explorers traveling in the lower Mississippi River valley claimed all the land drained by the river for France. They called this land *Louisiane*, naming it after their king, Louis XIV. The territory was immense—roughly one-third the size of the present-day United States. Over the years, as the result of various wars and treaties, this territory changed hands several times and was eventually carved up into smaller regions that became separate states. Only the lowermost part, at the end of the Mississippi River, retained the name, which got Anglicized to **Louisiana.**

ă	pat	ôr	core
ā	pay	oi	boy
âr	care	ou	out
ä	father	ŏŏ	took
ĕ	pet	ŏŏr	lure
ē	be	ōō	boot
ĭ	pit	ŭ	cut
ī	bite	ûr	urge
îr	pier	th	thin
ŏ	pot	*th*	this
ō	toe	zh	vision
ô	paw	ə	about

lo·ti (lō′tē) *n., pl.* **ma·lo·ti** (mä-lō′tē) The basic monetary unit of Lesotho. [From Sotho (a Bantu language of southern Africa) *Maloti*, a range of mountains in Lesotho.]

lo·tion (lō′shən) *n.* A liquid or cream applied to the skin to heal, soften, cleanse, or soothe.

lot·ter·y (lŏt′ə-rē) *n., pl.* **lot·ter·ies** A contest in which tickets are sold, the winning ticket or tickets being determined in a random drawing.

lo·tus (lō′təs) *n.* **1.** Any of various water plants with large floating leaves and fragrant flowers, especially an Asian species with pink flowers and a North American species with yellow flowers. **2.** In Greek mythology, a fruit that causes a dreamy idle state in those who eat it. [From Greek *lōtos.*]

loud (loud) *adj.* **loud·er, loud·est 1.** Characterized by high volume and intensity of sound: *That band plays loud music.* **2.** Producing loud sounds: *a loud trumpet.* **3.** Clamorous or insistent: *issuing loud denunciations.* **4.** Too bright; gaudy; flashy: *a loud garish suit.* ❖ *adv.* **louder, loudest** In a loud manner: *Speak louder, please.* [From Old English *hlūd.*] —**loud′ly** *adv.* —**loud′ness** *n.*

loud·mouth (loud′mouth′) *n. Informal* A person given to loud or unpleasant talk.

loud·speak·er (loud′spē′kər) *n.* A device that changes an electric signal into sound, especially one that is part of a public-address or stereophonic system.

Lou·is XIV (lo͞o′ē) 1638–1715. King of France (1643–1715) whose reign was the longest in French history and was characterized by the expansion of French influence in Europe and the establishment of overseas colonies.

Louis XVI 1754–1793. King of France (1774–1792) who was convicted of treason and executed during the French Revolution.

Lou·i·si·an·a (lo͞o-ē′zē-ăn′ə *or* lo͞o′zē-ăn′ə) A state of the southern United States on the Gulf of Mexico between Texas and Mississippi. It was admitted as the 18th state in 1812. Baton Rouge is the capital and New Orleans the largest city. —SEE NOTE.

Louisiana French *n.* French as spoken by the descendants of the French settlers of Louisiana.

Louisiana Purchase A former territory of the western United States extending from the Mississippi River to the Rocky Mountains between the Gulf of Mexico and the Canadian border. It was purchased from France on April 30, 1803, for $15 million.

Lou·is·ville (lo͞o′ē-vĭl′ *or* lo͞o′ə-vəl) A city of north-central Kentucky on the Ohio River west of Lexington.

lounge (lounj) *intr.v.* **lounged, loung·ing, loung·es 1.** To move or act in a lazy or relaxed way: *lounge in a comfortable chair.* **2.** To pass time idly: *I lounged around the house on my day off.* ❖ *n.* **1a.** A waiting room or bar in a hotel or airport terminal. **b.** An informal room for relaxing or gathering: *the new student lounge.* **2.** A long couch or sofa.

lour (lour) *v. & n.* Variant of **lower¹**.

louse (lous) *n.* **1.** *pl.* **lice** (līs) Any of numerous small wingless insects that live as parasites on the bodies of many birds and mammals, including humans. **2.** *pl.* **lous·es** *Slang* A mean or contemptible person. [From Old English *lūs.*]

lous·y (lou′zē) *adj.* **lous·i·er, lous·i·est 1.** Low in quality; inferior: *a lousy restaurant.* **2.** Mean or contemptible: *What a lousy thing to do!* **3.** Sick or unwell: *I feel lousy.* **4.** Covered or overrun with lice. —**lous′i·ly** *adv.*

lout (lout) *n.* An awkward, often boorish person; an oaf.

lou·ver (lo͞o′vər) *n.* **1.** An opening, as in a door, fitted with horizontal slats set at a slant so as to admit light and air and often to keep out rain. **2.** One of the slats used in such an opening. —**lou′vered** *adj.*

lov·a·ble also **love·a·ble** (lŭv′ə-bəl) *adj.* Having qualities that attract affection; endearing: *a lovable kitten.* —**lov′a·ble·ness** *n.* —**lov′a·bly** *adv.*

love (lŭv) *n.* **1.** A feeling of affection, concern, or devotion toward a person. **2a.** A strong liking for something: *a love of reading.* **b.** Something that is very much liked: *Gardening is her great love.* **3.** A beloved person: *He met his love when he was on vacation.* **4.** A score of zero in tennis. ❖ *tr.v.* **loved, lov·ing, loves 1.** To feel love or strong affection for: *We love our parents.* **2.** To like enthusiastically; delight in: *The audience loved the performance.* ◆ **in love** Feeling love and devotion toward someone. [From Old English *lufu.*]

love·bird (lŭv′bûrd′) *n.* Any of various small parrots that are often kept as pets and seem to show great fondness between mates.

love·less (lŭv′lĭs) *adj.* **1.** Showing or feeling no love: *a loveless tone in his voice.* **2.** Receiving no love; unloved.

love·lorn (lŭv′lôrn′) *adj.* Deprived of love or one's lover.

love·ly (lŭv′lē) *adj.* **love·li·er, love·li·est 1.** Having attractive qualities of character or appearance; beautiful or endearing: *a lovely person; a lovely house.* **2.** Pleasing or enjoyable; delightful: *We spent a lovely weekend at the lake.* —**love′li·ness** *n.*

lov·er (lŭv′ər) *n.* **1.** A person who loves another person, especially one who is involved in a romantic relationship with another. **2.** A person who is fond of or devoted to something: *a lover of jazz.*

love seat or **love·seat** (lŭv′sēt′) *n.* A small sofa that seats two people.

love·sick (lŭv′sĭk′) *adj.* Unable to act normally as a result of feeling love.

lov·ing (lŭv′ĭng) *adj.* Feeling or showing love; affectionate. —**lov′ing·ly** *adv.*

low¹ (lō) *adj.* **low·er, low·est 1.** Being a relatively small distance above a certain level, as above sea level or the surface of the earth: *a low wall.* **2.** Situated below the surrounding surfaces: *water standing in low spots.* **3.** Near to the ground or horizon: *low branches; low clouds.* **4.** Near or nearer to from a reference point: *took a low position next to the goal.* **5.** Of less than usual depth; shallow: *The river is low.* **6a.** Less than usual or expected in degree, intensity, or amount: *a low temperature; a low cost; a low level of understanding.* **b.** Inferior in rank, position, or status: *a low grade of oil.* **7.** Not very advanced in development or complexity: *the lowest forms of life.* **8.** Below the middle range of musical pitch: *the low tones of a tuba.* **9.** Not loud; soft: *Speak in a low voice.* **10.** Being at or near the worst or least desirable point: *Her career reached a low point at that company.* **11.** Inadequate in amount; almost gone: *Our supplies are low.* **12.** Immoral or contemptible; base: *a low trick.* **13.** Lacking liveliness or good spirits; discouraged or dejected: *feeling low.* **14.** Lacking strength or vigor; weak: *a patient in low condition.* **15.** Not favorable; disapproving: *She has a low opinion of his work.* **16.** Relating to a gear setting, as in a car transmission, that produces a lower vehicle speed than normal as compared with engine speed. **17.** Situated near the equator: *the low latitudes.* ❖ *adv.* **lower, lowest 1.** In or to a low position, level, or degree: *The plane flew low over the canyon.* **2.** Softly; quietly: *speak low.* ❖ *n.* **1.** A low position, level, or degree: *The price of peanuts fell to a new low.* **2.** A region of atmospheric pressure that is below normal. **3.** Low gear: *She put the car in low when driving down the steep road.* [From Middle English *loue*, from Old Norse *lāgr.*] —**low′ness** *n.*

❑ *These sound alike:* **low¹** (not high), **lo** (exclamation), **low²** (moo).

low² (lō) *n.* A deep sound made by cattle; a moo. ❖ *intr.v.* **lowed, low·ing, lows** To make such a sound; moo. [From Old English *hlōwan*, to low.]

❑ *These sound alike:* **low²** (moo), **lo** (exclamation), **low¹** (not high).

low·boy (lō′boi′) *n.* A low chest of drawers with a top that can be used as a table.

low·brow (lō′brou′) *adj.* Having tastes and preferences that are not sophisticated. **—low′brow′** *n.*

low-cal (lō′kăl′) *adj.* Having fewer calories than what is typical: *low-cal foods.*

Low Countries A region of northwest Europe made up of Belgium, the Netherlands, and Luxembourg.

low-down or **low·down** (lō′doun′) *adj.* Despicable; contemptible: *a low-down way of gaining success.* ❖ *n.* Correct information or details: *the low-down on the scandal.*

Low·ell (lō′əl), **James Russell** 1819–1891. American editor, poet, and diplomat who edited the *Atlantic Monthly* (1857–1861) and served as US minister to Spain (1877–1880) and Great Britain (1880–1885).

low·er¹ (lou′ər *or* lour) also **lour** (lour) *intr.v.* **low·ered, low·er·ing, low·ers** also **loured, lour·ing, lours 1.** To look angry or sullen; scowl. **2.** To appear dark or stormy, as the sky or weather: *The sky lowered as the hurricane approached.* ❖ *n.* A sullen or angry look. [From Middle English *louren.*]

low·er² (lō′ər) *adj.* Comparative of **low¹**. **1.** Below another in rank, position, or authority: *the lower court.* **2.** Situated below a similar or comparable thing: *a lower shelf.* **3.** Relating to or being an older division of the geologic period named. ❖ *v.* **low·ered, low·er·ing, low·ers** *—tr.* **1.** To let, bring, or move something down: *lower the flag; lower one's head.* **2.** To reduce, as in height, amount, degree, or quality: *The company lowered its prices.* **3.** To reduce in strength or intensity: *Lower your voice.* **4.** To reduce in standing or respect: *I wouldn't lower myself to do that.* *—intr.* **1.** To move down: *The helicopter lowered over the clearing.* **2.** To become less: *The temperature lowered after dusk.* ◆ **lower the boom** To act suddenly and forcefully to stop something or reprimand someone who has done something wrong: *Our teacher finally lowered the boom and punished students who came late.*

low·er·case (lō′ər-kās′) *adj.* Relating to a letter that is smaller than and often having a different shape from its capital letter, such as *v* or *i,* as contrasted with *V* and *I.* ❖ *n.* Lowercase letters.

low·er house (lō′ər) *n.* The branch of a bicameral legislature, such as the US House of Representatives, that is larger and more representative of the population.

low·er·most (lō′ər-mōst′) *adj.* Lowest.

low·est common denominator (lō′ĭst) *n.* A least common denominator.

lowest common multiple *n.* Least common multiple.

low frequency *n.* A radio-wave frequency in the range between 30 kilohertz and 300 kilohertz.

Low German *n.* **1.** The German dialects spoken in northern Germany. **2.** A group of Germanic languages, including Dutch and Flemish, spoken in the Low Countries.

low·land (lō′lənd) *n.* An area of land that is low in relation to the surrounding country. ❖ *adj.* Relating to or characteristic of a lowland.

low·land·er (lō′lən-dər) *n.* A native or inhabitant of a lowland.

low·ly (lō′lē) *adj.* **low·li·er, low·li·est 1.** Low in rank or position: *a person of lowly birth.* **2.** Meek or humble in manner: *a lowly person.* ❖ *adv.* In a meek and humble manner. **—low′li·ness** *n.*

low-pitched (lō′pĭcht′) *adj.* **1.** Low in tone: *a low-pitched voice.* **2.** Having little slope: *a low-pitched roof.*

low-pres·sure (lō′prĕsh′ər) *adj.* **1.** Having or using less than the usual pressure: *a low-pressure tire.* **2.** Having a relatively low barometric pressure: *a low-pressure system developing in the atmosphere.*

low profile *n.* Behavior or activity carried out so as not to attract attention.

low-spir·it·ed (lō′spĭr′ĭ-tĭd) *adj.* Being in low spirits; depressed; sad.

low-tech (lō′tĕk′) *adj.* Relating to low technology.

low technology *n.* Technology that does not involve highly advanced scientific methods or newly developed and specialized devices. **—low′-tech·nol′o·gy** *adj.*

low tide *n.* **1.** The tide as it reaches its lowest point. **2.** The time at which this occurs.

lox (lŏks) *n., pl.* **lox** or **lox·es** Salmon that has been cured in brine and is often smoked. [From Yiddish *laks.*]

loy·al (loi′əl) *adj.* **1.** Faithful to a person, idea, custom, or duty: *a loyal worker.* **2.** Faithful to a country or government: *a loyal citizen.* [From Latin *lēgālis,* legal.] **—loy′al·ly** *adv.*

loy·al·ist (loi′ə-lĭst) *n.* A person who remains loyal to the established government, political party, or ruler, especially during a civil war or revolution.

loy·al·ty (loi′əl-tē) *n., pl.* **loy·al·ties 1.** The condition of being loyal; faithful and loyal conduct. **2.** often **loyalties** A feeling or attitude of devoted attachment and affection: *My loyalties lie with my family.*

loz·enge (lŏz′ĭnj) *n.* **1.** A flat diamond-shaped figure. **2.** A small candy, especially one containing medicine for soothing a sore throat.

LP (ĕl′pē′) *n.* A long-playing phonograph record.

LPN *abbr.* An abbreviation of licensed practical nurse.

Lr The symbol for the element **lawrencium.**

LSD (ĕl′ĕs-dē′) *n.* A powerful drug that causes hallucinations and distorted perceptions.

LT or **Lt.** *abbr.* An abbreviation of lieutenant.

Ltd. or **ltd.** *abbr.* An abbreviation of limited.

Lu The symbol for the element **lutetium.**

Lu·an·da (lo͞o-ăn′də) The capital of Angola, in the northwest part of the country on the Atlantic Ocean. It was founded in 1575.

lu·au (lo͞o-ou′ *or* lo͞o′ou′) *n.* An elaborate Hawaiian feast with traditional foods and entertainment. —SEE NOTE AT **ukulele.**

lub·ber (lŭb′ər) *n.* **1.** A clumsy person. **2.** An inexperienced sailor; a landlubber.

lu·bri·cant (lo͞o′brĭ-kənt) *n.* A slippery substance, such as oil, grease, or graphite, used to coat the surfaces of objects that move against each other, to reduce friction and wear.

lu·bri·cate (lo͞o′brĭ-kāt′) *v.* **lu·bri·cat·ed, lu·bri·cat·ing, lu·bri·cates** *—tr.* **1.** To apply a lubricant to or to make slippery: *lubricate a bike chain.* **2.** To make easier: *tried to lubricate the relations between new classmates by playing games.* *—intr.* To act as a lubricant. **—lu′bri·ca′tion** *n.* **—lu′bri·ca′tor** *n.*

lu·cent (lo͞o′sənt) *adj.* **1.** Giving off light; luminous; bright. **2.** Translucent; clear; lucid.

lu·cid (lo͞o′sĭd) *adj.* **1.** Easily understood; clear: *a lucid explanation.* **2.** Thinking or expressing oneself clearly, especially between periods of confusion: *The feverish patient was lucid now and then.* **3.** Transparent: *lucid waters.* **—lu·cid′i·ty, lu′cid·ness** *n.* **—lu′cid·ly** *adv.*

Lu·ci·fer (lo͞o′sə-fər) *n.* In Christian tradition, an angelic being who was cast from heaven as punishment for his rebellious pride. Lucifer is traditionally identified with Satan. [From Old English, from Latin *lūcifer,* bearer of light.]

luck (lŭk) *n.* **1.** The chance happening of good or bad events; fate; fortune: *Luck favored our team with a winning season.* **2.** Good fortune; success: *beginner's luck.* ◆ **in luck** Enjoying success; fortunate. **out of luck** Lacking good fortune. **press one's luck** or **push (one's) luck** To risk one's good fortune, often by acting with too much confidence.

WRITERS CHOOSE THEIR WORDS

It was almost exactly two hours later that Jessica found herself suddenly wide awake and staring through the darkness at the **luminous** hands of her clock.

—Zilpha Keatley Snyder *The Witches of Worm*

lupine

luster

ă	pat	ôr	core
ā	pay	oi	boy
âr	care	ou	out
ä	father	ŏŏ	took
ĕ	pet	ŏŏr	lure
ē	be	ōō	boot
ĭ	pit	ŭ	cut
ī	bite	ûr	urge
îr	pier	th	thin
ŏ	pot	*th*	this
ō	toe	zh	vision
ô	paw	ə	about

luck·i·ly (lŭk′ə-lē) *adv.* With or by favorable chance; fortunately.

luck·less (lŭk′lĭs) *adj.* Having no luck; unlucky.

luck·y (lŭk′ē) *adj.* **luck·i·er, luck·i·est 1.** Marked by or having good luck; fortunate: *a lucky day; a lucky person.* **2.** Seeming to cause good luck: *a lucky penny.* **—luck′i·ness** *n.*

lu·cra·tive (lo͞o′krə-tĭv) *adj.* Producing wealth; profitable: *a lucrative business; a lucrative investment.* **—lu′cra·tive·ly** *adv.*

lu·cre (lo͞o′kər) *n.* Money or profits.

lu·di·crous (lo͞o′dĭ-krəs) *adj.* Laughable because of obvious absurdity; ridiculous. **—lu′di·crous·ly** *adv.* **—lu′di·crous·ness** *n.*

luff (lŭf) *n.* **1.** The act of sailing toward the wind. **2.** The forward edge of a fore-and-aft sail. ❖ *intr.v.* **luffed, luff·ing, luffs** To steer a sailing vessel toward the wind.

lug[1] (lŭg) *n.* **1.** A projecting part, as on a machine, used to support something: *take the nuts off the lugs to remove the tire.* **2.** A projecting part of a larger piece that helps to provide traction, as on the sole of a boot. **3.** *Slang* A clumsy fool; a blockhead. [From Middle English *lugge*, earflap, probably of Scandinavian origin.]

lug[2] (lŭg) *tr.v.* **lugged, lug·ging, lugs** To drag or haul with great difficulty: *lug boxes up to the attic.* [From Middle English *luggen*, of Scandinavian origin.]

lug·gage (lŭg′ĭj) *n.* The bags, suitcases, boxes, or trunks for carrying belongings on a trip; baggage.

lug·sail (lŭg′səl) *n.* A four-sided sail that hangs on a yard slanting across the mast.

lu·gu·bri·ous (lo͝o-go͞o′brē-əs) *adj.* Sad or mournful; sorrowful: *the lugubrious cry of wolves.* **—lu·gu′bri·ous·ly** *adv.* **—lu·gu′bri·ous·ness** *n.*

Luke (lo͝ok) *n.* The third Gospel of the New Testament, traditionally thought to have been written by Saint Luke.

Luke, Saint. Flourished first century AD. Companion of Saint Paul and traditionally considered to be the author of the third Gospel of the New Testament and the Acts of the Apostles.

luke·warm (lo͞ok′wôrm′) *adj.* **1.** Neither hot nor cold; mildly warm: *lukewarm water.* **2.** Lacking in enthusiasm; indifferent: *a lukewarm greeting.* **—luke′warm′ly** *adv.* **—luke′warm′ness** *n.*

lull (lŭl) *v.* **lulled, lull·ing, lulls** *—tr.* To cause to sleep or rest; calm; soothe: *a song to lull a baby to sleep. —intr.* To become calm: *The high winds finally lulled.* ❖ *n.* A temporary lessening of activity or noise; a calm interval: *a lull in the storm; a lull in sales.*

lull·a·by (lŭl′ə-bī′) *n., pl.* **lull·a·bies** A soothing song meant to lull a child to sleep.

lum·ba·go (lŭm-bā′gō) *n.* A pain that affects the muscles and tendons of the lower back and hips.

lum·bar (lŭm′bər *or* lŭm′bär′) *adj.* Relating to, near, or situated in the part of the back and sides between the lowest ribs and the pelvis.

❑ *These sound alike:* **lumbar, lumber[1]** (wood), **lumber[2]** (walk clumsily).

lum·ber[1] (lŭm′bər) *n.* Timber sawed into boards and planks. ❖ *intr.v.* **lum·bered, lum·ber·ing, lum·bers** To cut down and prepare lumber. [Perhaps from *lumber*, to walk clumsily.]

❑ *These sound alike:* **lumber[1]** (wood), **lumbar** (lower back), **lumber[2]** (walk clumsily).

lum·ber[2] (lŭm′bər) *intr.v.* **lum·bered, lum·ber·ing, lum·bers** To walk or move in a clumsy or noisy manner: *The truck lumbered down the bumpy road.* [From Middle English *lomeren*, possibly of Scandinavian origin.]

❑ *These sound alike:* **lumber[2]** (walk clumsily), **lumbar** (lower back), **lumber[1]** (wood).

lum·ber·jack (lŭm′bər-jăk′) *n.* A person whose work is to chop down trees and transport timber to a sawmill.

lum·ber·yard (lŭm′bər-yärd′) *n.* A business that sells lumber and other building materials from a yard.

lu·men (lo͞o′mən) *n., pl.* **lu·mens** or **lu·mi·na** (lo͞o′mə-nə) **1.** The open space within a tubular organ, such as a blood vessel or an intestine. **2.** A unit used to measure the amount of light passing through a given area per second. One lumen is equal to the amount of light that passes through a given area (shaped like a cone) that is illuminated by a light with a brightness of one candela.

lu·mi·nar·y (lo͞o′mə-nĕr′ē) *n., pl.* **lu·mi·nar·ies 1.** A celestial object that gives off light, particularly the sun or moon. **2.** A famous person, especially one noted for high achievement: *a luminary of stage and screen.*

lu·mi·nes·cence (lo͞o′mə-**nĕs′**əns) *n.* The production of light accompanied by little heat and at a temperature below that of incandescent bodies. Fluorescence and phosphorescence are examples of luminescence that can be produced by biochemical or chemical processes. **—lu′mi·nes′cent** *adj.*

lu·mi·nos·i·ty (lo͞o′mə-**nŏs′**ĭ-tē) *n., pl.* **lu·mi·nos·i·ties 1.** The condition or property of being luminous. **2.** Something luminous.

lu·mi·nous (lo͞o′mə-nəs) *adj.* **1.** Giving off its own light; shining: *the luminous firefly.* **2.** Full of light; bright: *a full luminous moon.* **3.** Easily understood; clear: *simple luminous prose.* [From Middle English, from Latin *lūmen*, light.] **—lu′mi·nous·ly** *adv.*

lump[1] (lŭmp) *n.* **1.** An irregularly shaped mass or piece: *a lump of rock.* **2.** A small cube of sugar. **3.** A swelling or bump: *A lump rose on my finger where I was stung.* ❖ *adj.* **1.** Formed into a lump or lumps: *lump sugar.* **2.** Not divided into parts; whole: *We want the entire payment in one lump sum.* ❖ *v.* **lumped, lump·ing, lumps** *—tr.* To put together; consider as a whole: *The coach lumped the fifth and sixth graders together in one gym class. —intr.* To form into a lump or lumps: *The sauce lumped because we didn't stir it.* [From Middle English *lumpe*, of Low German origin.]

lump[2] (lŭmp) *tr.v.* **lumped, lump·ing, lumps** *Informal* To endure or put up with something: *You can like my cooking or lump it.* [Perhaps from dialectal *lump*, to look sullen.]

lump·ec·to·my (lŭm-**pĕk′**tə-mē) *n., pl.* **lump·ec·to·mies** Surgical removal of a tumor from the breast, along with a small amount of surrounding tissue.

lump·y (lŭm′pē) *adj.* **lump·i·er, lump·i·est** Full of or covered with lumps: *lumpy gravy.* **—lump′i·ness** *n.*

lu·na·cy (lo͞o′nə-sē) *n., pl.* **lu·na·cies 1.** Mental derangement. **2.** Foolish or reckless conduct.

lu·nar (lo͞o′nər) *adj.* **1.** Relating to the moon: *lunar phases; a lunar crater.* **2.** Measured by the revolution of the moon around Earth: *a lunar calendar.*

lunar month *n.* An interval of about 29½ days between one new moon and the next, during which the moon makes one revolution around Earth relative to the sun.

lunar year *n.* A period of 12 lunar months, about 354⅓ days.

lu·na·tic (lo͞o′nə-tĭk) *n.* **1.** A mentally deranged person. **2.** A very foolish person. ❖ *adj.* **1.** Mentally deranged; mad. **2.** Relating to or for the mentally ill: *a lunatic asylum.* **3.** Wildly or recklessly foolish: *a lunatic idea.*

lunch (lŭnch) *n.* **1.** A meal eaten between breakfast and dinner, usually at midday. **2.** The food for this meal. ❖ *intr.v.* **lunched, lunch·ing, lunch·es** To eat lunch.

lunch·eon (lŭn′chən) *n.* Lunch, often a formal lunch.

lunch·eon·ette (lŭn′chə-**nĕt′**) *n.* A restaurant that serves light meals such as breakfast or lunch.

lunch·meat (lŭnch′mēt′) *n.* Processed meat, often molded into a loaf and sliced for use in sandwiches or salads.

lunch·room (lŭnch′ro͝om′ *or* lŭnch′ro͞om′) *n.* The cafeteria or room in a building, such as a school, where light meals are served and eaten.

lung (lŭng) *n.* **1.** Either of two spongy organs that occupy the chest cavity of air-breathing vertebrates and provide oxygen to the blood while removing carbon dioxide. **2.** A similar organ found in some invertebrate animals.

lunge (lŭnj) *n.* **1.** A sudden thrust or pass, as with a sword. **2.** A sudden forward movement: *The fielder made a lunge for the ball.* ❖ *intr.v.* **lunged, lung·ing, lung·es** To make a sudden forward movement: *The cat lunged at the bird.* —**lung′er** *n.*

lung·fish (lŭng′fĭsh′) *n.* Any of several freshwater fishes of Africa, Australia, and South America, having gills as well as a lunglike organ that enables them to breathe air and survive out of water, especially during drought conditions.

lu·pine also **lu·pin** (lo͞o′pən) *n.* Any of numerous plants having compound leaves and long spikes of variously colored flowers.

lurch[1] (lûrch) *intr.v.* **lurched, lurch·ing, lurch·es 1a.** To make an abrupt sudden movement: *The train lurched and moved away from the platform.* **b.** To move suddenly and unsteadily; stagger: *He lurched forward under the heavy load of his backpack.* **2.** To roll or pitch suddenly: *The ship lurched as the wave hit the bow.* ❖ *n.* **1.** A staggering or tottering movement. **2.** A sudden rolling or pitching: *The train gave a lurch and started out of the station.*

lurch[2] (lûrch) *n.* A condition of having lost a cribbage game by a wide margin. ◆ **in the lurch** In a difficult or embarrassing position. [Perhaps from Middle English *lurching*, a total victory at *lorche*, a kind of game.]

lure (lo͝or) *n.* **1.** A strong attraction, charm, or enticement: *the lure of fame.* **2.** A decoy used in catching animals, especially an artificial bait used to attract and catch fish. ❖ *tr.v.* **lured, lur·ing, lures** To attract or tempt, especially with a bait: *We lured the cat inside with a dish of food.*

lu·rid (lo͝or′ĭd) *adj.* **1.** Causing shock or horror: *a lurid description of a train crash.* **2.** Bright and intense in color; vivid: *The lurid flames of a distant fire lit up the night sky.* —**lu′rid·ly** *adv.* —**lu′rid·ness** *n.*

lurk (lûrk) *intr.v.* **lurked, lurk·ing, lurks 1.** To wait out of view: *The cat lurked in the grass, waiting for the mouse to approach.* **2.** To move about secretly; sneak. **3.** To exist without being seen or suspected: *Danger lurked around every corner.* —**lurk′er** *n.*

Lu·sa·ka (lo͞o-sä′kə) The capital of Zambia, in the south-central part of the country. It was founded in 1905.

lus·cious (lŭsh′əs) *adj.* **1.** Having a delicious taste or smell: *a luscious peach.* **2.** Appealing to the senses or the mind: *a luscious singing voice.* —**lus′cious·ly** *adv.*

lush (lŭsh) *adj.* **lush·er, lush·est 1.** Having or covered in thick plentiful plant growth: *a lush green lawn.* **2.** Juicy and tender: *lush pears.* **3.** Luxurious; abundant and rich: *the lush decor of a royal palace.* [From Middle English, relaxed, soft, from Latin *laxus*, loose.] —**lush′ly** *adv.* —**lush′ness** *n.*

lust (lŭst) *n.* **1.** Intense sexual desire. **2.** An overwhelming desire or craving: *a lust for power.* ❖ *intr.v.* **lust·ed, lust·ing, lusts** To have an intense or overwhelming desire: *The pirates lusted after riches.*

lus·ter (lŭs′tər) *n.* **1.** Soft reflected light; sheen; gloss: *the luster of pearls.* **2.** Radiance of light; brightness: *the luster of the warming sun.* **3.** Glory; splendor: *Her newest discoveries add luster to her name.* **4.** The shiny metallic surface that is found on pottery and china.

lust·ful (lŭst′fəl) *adj.* Full of lust; lewd. —**lust′ful·ly** *adv.* —**lust′ful·ness** *n.*

lus·tre (lŭs′tər) *n. & v. Chiefly British* Variant of **luster.**

lus·trous (lŭs′trəs) *adj.* **1.** Having luster; shining; gleaming: *a silk cloth with a lustrous sheen.* **2.** Well-known or distinguished; illustrious: *lustrous achievements.* —**lus′trous·ly** *adv.* —**lus′trous·ness** *n.*

lust·y (lŭs′tē) *adj.* **lust·i·er, lust·i·est** Full of strength and vitality; robust. —**lust′i·ly** *adv.* —**lust′i·ness** *n.*

lute (lo͞ot) *n.* A stringed instrument having a body shaped like a pear sliced lengthwise and a fingerboard that has frets. It is played by plucking.

❑ *These sound alike:* **lute, loot** (stolen goods).

lute

lu·te·ti·um (lo͞o-tē′shē-əm) *n. Symbol* **Lu** A silvery-white metallic element used in nuclear technology. Atomic number 71. See **Periodic Table.**

Lu·ther (lo͞o′thər), **Martin** 1483–1546. German theologian and leader of the Reformation. His writings on theology, reformation of liturgy, and German translation of the Bible (1534) led to the establishment of the Lutheran Church.

Lu·ther·an (lo͞o′thər-ən) *adj.* Relating to Martin Luther or the Protestant denomination founded on his teachings. ❖ *n.* A member of the Lutheran Church.

Lux·em·bourg also **Lux·em·burg** (lŭk′səm-bûrg′) **1.** A country of northwest Europe southwest of Belgium. The city of Luxembourg is the capital. **2.** The capital of Luxembourg, in the southern part of the country.

lychee

lux·u·ri·ant (lŭg-zho͝or′ē-ənt *or* lŭk-sho͝or′ē-ənt) *adj.* **1.** Growing abundantly; lush: *luxuriant vegetation.* **2.** Abundantly productive: *luxuriant fields.* **3.** Highly ornamented: *a luxuriant dining room.* —**lux·u′ri·ance** *n.* —**lux·u′ri·ant·ly** *adv.*

lux·u·ri·ate (lŭg-zho͝or′ē-āt′ *or* lŭk-sho͝or′ē-āt′) *intr.v.* **lux·u·ri·at·ed, lux·u·ri·at·ing, lux·u·ri·ates 1.** To indulge oneself in luxury: *We luxuriated by taking a room in the expensive hotel.* **2.** To take great pleasure or delight: *luxuriate in the warm sunshine.*

lux·u·ri·ous (lŭg-zho͝or′ē-əs *or* lŭk-sho͝or′ē-əs) *adj.* **1.** Fond of luxury: *a luxurious taste for expensive clothes.* **2.** Providing great pleasure or comfort, especially at great cost: *luxurious bedsheets that are made of silk.* —**lux·u′ri·ous·ly** *adv.* —**lux·u′ri·ous·ness** *n.*

lux·u·ry (lŭg′zhə-rē *or* lŭk′shə-rē) *n., pl.* **lux·u·ries 1.** Something that is not essential but gives pleasure or comfort: *Eating in a good restaurant is a luxury I can't afford these days.* **2.** A way of living that brings comfort; use of the best or most costly things: *live in luxury.* ❖ *adj.* Providing luxury: *a luxury car.*

Lv The symbol for **livermorium.**

-ly[1] *suff.* A suffix that means: **1.** Having the characteristics of; like: *sisterly.* **2.** Recurring at a specified interval of time: *hourly.*

-ly[2] *suff.* A suffix that means: **1.** In a specified manner: *gradually.* **2.** At a specified interval: *weekly.*

ly·ce·um (lī-sē′əm) *n.* **1.** A hall in which lectures and concerts are presented. **2.** An organization that sponsors educational programs and entertainment.

ly·chee (lē′chē) also **li·tchi** or **li·chee** (lē′chē) *n., pl.* **ly·chees** or **li·tchis 1.** A sweet edible fruit of a tree native to China, having leathery red skin with white pulp and a large seed. **2.** The tree that bears such fruit.

Lyd·i·a (lĭd′ē-ə) An ancient country of western Asia Minor on the Aegean Sea. It may have been the earliest kingdom to use minted coins (seventh century BC).

lye (lī) *n.* **1.** A strong alkaline solution made by allowing water to wash through wood ashes, used in making soap and in cleaning. **2.** Sodium hydroxide.

❑ *These sound alike:* **lye, lie**[1] (be flat), **lie**[2] (falsehood).

ly·ing[1] (lī′ĭng) *v.* Present participle of **lie**[1].

ly·ing[2] (lī′ĭng) *v.* Present participle of **lie**[2]. ❖ *adj.* Given to or marked by falsehood: *a lying witness.*

Lyme disease (līm) *n.* A disease caused by bacteria and usually characterized by skin rash, chills, fever, and fatigue often lasting for several weeks. It is transmitted

lynx

by deer ticks. [After *Lyme*, a town of southeast Connecticut.]

lymph (lĭmf) *n.* The clear fluid that flows through the vessels of the lymphatic system. Lymph carries waste from tissues and transports white blood cells. [From Latin *lympha*, water nymph, from Greek *numphē*.]

lym·phat·ic (lĭm-**făt′**ĭk) *adj.* Relating to or carrying lymph.

lymphatic system *n.* A network of vessels, tissues, and organs in vertebrate animals that regulates fluid balance by draining excess fluid from the tissues and returning it to the blood and that also produces and carries cells that help the body fight disease. In humans the lymphatic system includes the bone marrow, thymus, spleen, and lymph nodes.

lymph node *n.* Any of the small, bean-shaped masses of tissue found along the vessels of the lymphatic system. Lymph nodes filter foreign substances from the blood and may become swollen during infection.

lym·pho·cyte (**lĭm′**fə-sīt′) *n.* Any of various white blood cells that are formed in the lymphatic system and function as part of the body's immune system. Lymphocytes include B cells and T cells.

lym·phoid (**lĭm′**foid′) *adj.* Relating to lymph, lymphocytes, or the lymphatic system.

lynch (lĭnch) *tr.v.* **lynched, lynch·ing, lynch·es** To execute (a person), especially by hanging, without due process of law. [Probably after Charles *Lynch* (1736–1796), American militiaman and justice of the peace who held hasty, unofficial trials that resulted in whippings of Tory sympathizers in Virginia during the American Revolution.] **—lynch′er** *n.*

lynx (lĭngks) *n., pl.* **lynx** or **lynx·es** Any of several wild cats having thick soft fur, tufted ears, and a short tail.
❑ *These sound alike:* **lynx, links** (golf course).

Ly·on or **Ly·ons** (lē-ōN′) A city of east-central France on the Rhone River. It was founded in 43 BC as a Roman colony.

ly·on·naise (lī′ə-**nāz′** *or* lē′ə-**nĕz′**) *adj.* Cooked with onion: *lyonnaise potatoes.*

Ly·ra (**lī′**rə) *n.* A constellation in the Northern Hemisphere traditionally pictured as a lyre.

lyre (līr) *n.* A stringed instrument related to the harp that has two curved arms connected at the upper end by a crossbar. It is used to accompany a singer or reciter of poetry, as was commonly done in ancient Greece. [From Middle English *lire*, from Greek *lura*.]

lyre·bird (**līr′**bûrd′) *n.* An Australian bird, the male of which has a long tail that is shaped like a lyre when spread.

lyr·ic (**lĭr′**ĭk) *adj.* **1.** Relating to poetry that expresses personal feelings and thoughts. **2.** Relating to musical drama, especially opera. ❖ *n.* **1.** A lyric poem. **2.** often **lyrics** The words of a song.

lyr·i·cal (**lĭr′**ĭ-kəl) *adj.* **1.** Expressing deep personal feelings or thoughts: *a lyrical description of her youth.* **2.** Lyric.

lyr·i·cism (**lĭr′**ĭ-sĭz′əm) *n.* The quality of being lyric; lyric expression.

lyr·i·cist (**lĭr′**ĭ-sĭst) *n.* A writer of song lyrics or of lyric poetry.

ly·sine (**lī′**sēn′) *n.* An essential amino acid that is formed by the reaction of certain proteins with water.

ly·sis (**lī′**sĭs) *n., pl.* **ly·ses** (**lī′**sēz′) The destruction of a cell, as by a virus.

ly·so·some (**lī′**sə-sōm′) *n.* A structure in animal cells that contains enzymes that break down cellular waste materials and food particles or other materials from outside the cell.

lyt·ic (**lĭt′**ĭk) *adj.* Relating to lysis.

ă	pat	ôr	core
ā	pay	oi	boy
âr	care	ou	out
ä	father	o͝o	took
ĕ	pet	o͝or	lure
ē	be	o͞o	boot
ĭ	pit	ŭ	cut
ī	bite	ûr	urge
îr	pier	th	thin
ŏ	pot	*th*	this
ō	toe	zh	vision
ô	paw	ə	about

M

m¹ or **M** (ĕm) *n., pl.* **m's** or **M's** also **ms** or **Ms** The 13th letter of the English alphabet.

m² *abbr.* An abbreviation of: **1.** mass. **2.** meter (measurement). **3.** minute.

M¹ also **m** The symbol for the Roman numeral 1,000.

M² *abbr.* An abbreviation of: **1.** male. **2.** medium. **3.** Monsieur. **4.** month.

M. *abbr.* An abbreviation of master.

ma (mä *or* mô) *n. Informal* Mother.

MA *abbr.* An abbreviation of: **1.** Massachusetts. **2.** Master of Arts.

ma'am (măm) *n.* Madam.

ma·ca·bre (mə-kä′brə *or* mə-käb′) *adj.* Suggesting the horror of death or injury; gruesome: *a macabre play set during a plague.* [From Old French *(Danse) Macabre,* (dance) of death.]

mac·ad·am (mə-kăd′əm) *n.* Pavement made of layers of small stones packed together, now usually bound with asphalt or tar. [After John Loudon *McAdam* (1756–1836), Scottish civil engineer.]

mac·ad·am·ize (mə-kăd′ə-mīz′) *tr.v.* **mac·ad·am·ized, mac·ad·am·iz·ing, mac·ad·am·iz·es** To build or pave (a road) with macadam.

ma·caque (mə-kăk′ *or* mə-käk′) *n.* Any of several monkeys of Asia and northern Africa having short tails.

mac·a·ro·ni (măk′ə-rō′nē) *n.* Pasta in any of various hollow shapes, especially short curved tubes.

mac·a·roon (măk′ə-ro͞on′) *n.* A chewy cookie made with sugar, egg whites, and ground almonds or coconut.

Mac·Ar·thur (mĭk-är′thər), **Douglas** 1880–1964. American general who served as US chief of staff (1930–1935) and commanded Allied forces in the South Pacific during World War II.

Ma·cau (mə-kou′) A city and administrative region of southeast China located on **Macau Peninsula** and two offshore islands in the South China Sea west of Hong Kong. It was a Portuguese overseas province until 1999, when it returned to Chinese rule.

ma·caw (mə-kô′) *n.* Any of various large, often brightly colored parrots with a long tail and strong beak, found in Mexico and Central and South America.

Mac·beth (mək-bĕth′) Died 1057. King of Scotland (1040–1057) who gained the throne after killing King Duncan (died 1040) in battle. Legends about him are the basis of Shakespeare's *Macbeth.*

Mac·ca·bee (măk′ə-bē′) A family of Jewish patriots of the second and first centuries BC who led a successful revolt against Syrian rule in Judea.

Mac·don·ald (mĭk-dŏn′əld), Sir **John Alexander** 1815–1891. Scottish-born Canadian politician. He was instrumental in uniting the British colonies in North America into one self-governing country and served as the first prime minister of Canada (1867–1873 and 1878–1891).

mace¹ (mās) *n.* **1.** A heavy club with a spiked metal head, used as a weapon in medieval times. **2.** A ceremonial staff carried or displayed as a symbol of authority. [From Middle English, from Old French *masse.*]

mace² (mās) *n.* A spice made from the bright red covering of the seed of the nutmeg. [From Middle English *macis,* from Greek *makir,* a kind of spice.]

Mace A trademark for an aerosol spray that causes irritation to the eyes, skin, and respiratory tract, used to repel an attacker.

Mac·e·do·ni·a (măs′ĭ-dō′nē-ə) also **Mac·e·don** (măs′ĭ-dən) **1.** A historical region of southeast Europe on the Balkan Peninsula, including modern Macedonia, northern Greece, and southwest Bulgaria. It was a powerful empire in the fourth century BC. **2.** A country of the south-central Balkan Peninsula south of Serbia. It was part of Yugoslavia from 1946 until 1991. Skopje is the capital.

Mac·e·do·ni·an (măs′ĭ-dō′nē-ən) *adj.* Relating to ancient or modern Macedonia or its peoples, languages, or cultures. ❖ *n.* **1.** A native or inhabitant of ancient or modern Macedonia. **2.** The language of ancient Macedonia. **3.** The Slavic language of modern Macedonia.

mac·er·ate (măs′ə-rāt′) *v.* **mac·er·at·ed, mac·er·at·ing, mac·er·ates** —*tr.* **1.** To make soft by soaking in a liquid: *Macerate strawberries in sweetened water before serving them.* **2.** To cause (the body) to become thin. —*intr.* To become soft by soaking.

Mach also **mach** (mäk) *n.* Mach number.

ma·chet·e (mə-shĕt′ē *or* mə-chĕt′ē) *n.* A large heavy knife with a broad blade, used as a weapon and as a tool for clearing paths and cutting sugar cane. [From Spanish, probably from *maza,* mallet.]

Ma·chi·a·vel·li (măk′ē-ə-vĕl′ē), **Niccolò** 1469–1527. Italian political theorist whose book *The Prince* (1513) describes how a ruler can gain power, arguing that a ruler may be justified in taking immoral actions to maintain control.

Ma·chi·a·vel·li·an (măk′ē-ə-vĕl′ē-ən) *adj.* **1.** Relating to the political theories of Niccolò Machiavelli. **2.** Showing or being deceptive or underhanded; crafty; cunning. ❖ *n.* A person who follows Machiavelli's political principles or is given to deceptive behavior for personal advancement.

mach·i·na·tion (măk′ə-nā′shən *or* măsh′ə-nā′shən) *n.* A cunning scheme or plot to do something harmful.

ma·chine (mə-shēn′) *n.* **1.** A device of fixed and moving parts for performing tasks: *a washing machine.* **2.** A simple device that applies force or changes its direction. The gear, inclined plane, lever, and screw are all simple machines. **3.** A person who acts or performs a task mechanically without thinking. **4.** An organized group of people that controls the policies and activities of a political party in an area: *the key members of the local political machine.* **5.** A computer: *The librarian can't check out books right now because the machine is down.* **6.** An answering machine. ❖ *tr.v.* **ma·chined, ma·chin·ing, ma·**

macaque

Niccolò Machiavelli

Machu Picchu

mackerel

mackerel sky

macramé

ă	pat	ôr	core
ā	pay	oi	boy
âr	care	ou	out
ä	father	o͝o	took
ĕ	pet	o͝or	lure
ē	be	o͞o	boot
ĭ	pit	ŭ	cut
ī	bite	ûr	urge
îr	pier	th	thin
ŏ	pot	*th*	this
ō	toe	zh	vision
ô	paw	ə	about

chines To cut, shape, or finish by machine: *The workers machine metal at the factory.* [From Greek *mēkhanē*.]

machine gun *n.* A gun that fires rapidly and repeatedly when the trigger is pressed.

ma·chine-gun (mə-**shēn′**gŭn′) *tr.v.* **ma·chine-gunned, ma·chine-gun·ning, ma·chine-guns** To fire at with a machine gun.

ma·chin·er·y (mə-**shē′**nə-rē *or* mə-**shēn′**rē) *n., pl.* **ma·chin·er·ies 1.** Machines or machine parts considered as a group: *The factory is full of machinery.* **2.** The working parts of a particular machine: *The machinery of an automobile engine includes pistons and gears.* **3.** A system of people or things that operate together to keep something going: *the complex machinery of modern society.*

machine shop *n.* A workshop where machines or machine parts are made, finished, or repaired.

machine tool *n.* A power-driven tool used to cut or shape metal.

ma·chin·ist (mə-**shē′**nĭst) *n.* **1.** A person skilled in the use of machine tools to work metal. **2.** A person who makes, operates, or repairs machines.

ma·chis·mo (mä-**chēz′**mō) *n.* An exaggerated sense of manliness that places great value on strength, courage, and aggressiveness.

Mach number also **mach number** (mäk) *n.* The ratio of the speed of an object to the speed of sound in a particular surrounding medium. For example, an aircraft flying through air at twice the speed of sound has a Mach number of 2. [After Ernst *Mach* (1838–1916), Austrian physicist.]

ma·cho (**mä′**chō) *adj.* Characterized by or showing machismo: *The cowboy has a macho image.* ❖ *n., pl.* **ma·chos 1.** Machismo. **2.** A person characterized by machismo.

Ma·chu Pic·chu (**mä′**cho͞o **pēk′**cho͞o *or* **mä′**cho͞o **pē′**-cho͞o) An ancient Inca fortress city in the Andes southeast of Lima, Peru. Its extensive ruins include an elaborate system of stone terraces.

mac·in·tosh (**măk′**ĭn-tŏsh′) *n.* Variant of **mackintosh.**

Mac·ken·zie (mə-**kĕn′**zē), **Alexander** 1822–1892. Scottish-born Canadian politician. As prime minister (1873–1878) he established the Supreme Court of Canada and reformed the electoral system.

mack·er·el (**măk′**ər-əl *or* **măk′**rəl) *n., pl.* **mackerel** or **mack·er·els** Any of several silvery fishes, especially one of the northern Atlantic Ocean that has dark markings on the back and is used as food.

mackerel sky *n.* A sky covered with a series of small, pufflike clouds resembling the scales of a mackerel.

mack·i·naw (**măk′**ə-nô′) *n.* A short coat of heavy, usually plaid woolen material.

Mackinaw blanket *n.* A thick woolen blanket in solid colors or stripes, formerly used in northern and western North America.

mack·in·tosh also **mac·in·tosh** (**măk′**ĭn-tŏsh′) *n. Chiefly British* A raincoat. [After Charles *Macintosh* (1766–1843), Scottish inventor.]

mac·ra·mé (**măk′**rə-mā′) *n.* Coarse lacework made by weaving and knotting threads or cords into a pattern.

macro– *pref.* A prefix that means large: *macrophage.* —SEE NOTE AT **micro–.**

mac·ro·cosm (**măk′**rə-kŏz′əm) *n.* The entire world; the universe.

ma·cron (**mā′**krŏn′ *or* **măk′**rŏn′) *n.* **1.** A mark (¯) placed over a vowel to show that it has a long sound, as in (ā), the vowel sound in *make.* **2.** A similar mark used to indicate that a syllable is stressed in a foot of verse.

mac·ro·phage (**măk′**rə-fāj′) *n.* Any of the large cells of the immune system that engulf and destroy pathogens that enter the body.

mad (măd) *adj.* **mad·der, mad·dest 1.** Very irritated; angry: *The unfair accusation made me mad.* **2a.** Having a serious mental disorder, especially one that distorts the perception of reality. **b.** Characteristic of such illness: *mad laughter.* **3.** Mentally or emotionally agitated or distressed: *He's been going mad with jealousy.* **4.** Very foolish or unwise: *a mad idea.* **5.** Feeling or showing strong liking or enthusiasm: *He is mad about skiing.* **6.** Wildly excited or confused; frantic: *a mad scramble for the bus.* **7.** Affected by rabies; rabid: *a mad dog.* ◆ **like mad** *Informal* **1.** With great energy; rapidly: *ran like mad.* **2.** To a great extent: *It's snowing like mad.* [From Old English *gemǣdde*, from *gemād*, insane.] **—mad′ly** *adv.* **—mad′ness** *n.*

Mad·a·gas·car (măd′ə-**găs′**kər) An island country in the Indian Ocean off the southeast coast of Africa. Antananarivo is the capital.

mad·am (**măd′**əm) *n.* Used as a polite form of address for a woman: *Right this way, madam.*

Ma·dame (mə-**dăm′** *or* **măd′**əm) *n., pl.* **Mes·dames** (mā-**dăm′** *or* mā-**däm′**) Used as a courtesy title before the name of a woman, especially a married woman, in a French-speaking area: *Madame Cartier.*

mad·cap (**măd′**kăp′) *adj.* Not sensible; rash; impulsive: *a madcap idea.*

mad cow disease *n.* A fatal disease of cattle in which the tissues of the brain deteriorate, resulting in abnormal behaviors and loss of muscle control. A form of the disease is thought to be able to be spread to humans through the eating of infected meat.

mad·den (**măd′**n) *v.* **mad·dened, mad·den·ing, mad·dens** —*tr.* To make mad: *Heat and the flies maddened the horse.* —*intr.* To become mad.

mad·den·ing (**măd′**n-ĭng) *adj.* Causing great anger; infuriating: *a maddening racket outside my window.* **—mad′den·ing·ly** *adv.*

mad·der (**măd′**ər) *n.* **1.** A Eurasian plant having small yellow flowers and a fleshy red root that is the source of dye. **2.** A red dye made from the root of this plant.

made (mād) *v.* Past tense and past participle of **make.** ❖ *adj.* **1.** Constructed, shaped, or formed: *a carefully made piece.* **2.** Assured of success: *a made man.* ◆ **made for** Perfectly suited for: *Those two are made for each other.*
❑ *These sound alike:* **made, maid** (servant).

Ma·dei·ra Islands (mə-**dîr′**ə) A group of islands of Portugal in the northeast Atlantic Ocean west of Morocco. The island of **Madeira** is noted for its wine.

Mad·e·moi·selle (măd′ə-mə-**zĕl′** *or* măd-mwä-**zĕl′**) *n., pl.* **Mad·e·moi·selles** (măd′ə-mə-**zĕlz′** *or* măd-mwä-**zĕlz′**) or **Mes·de·moi·selles** (mād′mwä-**zĕl′**) Used as a courtesy title before the name of a girl or an unmarried woman in a French-speaking area: *Mademoiselle Leblanc.*

made-to-or·der (**mād′**to͞o-**ôr′**dər) *adj.* Made in accordance with particular instructions or requirements; custom-made: *a made-to-order suit.*

made-up (**mād′ŭp′**) *adj.* **1.** Not real; imaginary; invented: *made-up stories.* **2.** Covered with cosmetics or makeup: *the clown's made-up face.*

mad·house (**măd′**hous′) *n.* **1.** *Offensive* A hospital or asylum for people with mental disorders. **2.** *Informal* A place of great confusion or disorder.

Mad·i·son (**măd′**ĭ-sən) The capital of Wisconsin, in the south-central part of the state west of Milwaukee. It was settled in 1836.

Madison, Dolley Payne Todd 1768–1849. First lady of the United States (1809–1817) as the wife of President James Madison. During the British invasion of Washington, DC (1814), she carried government papers and a portrait of George Washington to safety.

Madison, James 1751–1836. The fourth president of the United States (1809–1817), whose presidency was marked by the War of 1812 with Great Britain (1812–1815).

mad·man (**măd′**măn′ *or* **măd′**mən) *n.* A man who is or appears to be mentally ill.

Ma·don·na (mə-**dŏn′**ə) *n.* The Virgin Mary, especially as depicted in religious art.

mad·ras (**măd′**rəs *or* mə-**drăs′** *or* mə-**dräs′**) *n.* A lightweight cotton cloth, usually having a plaid, striped, or checked pattern.

Ma·dras (mə-**drăs′** *or* mə-**dräs′**) See **Chennai.**

Ma·drid (mə-**drĭd′**) The capital of Spain, in the central part of the country north-northeast of Toledo. It was built on the site of a Moorish fortress captured in the 11th century.

mad·ri·gal (**măd′**rĭ-gəl) *n.* **1.** A musical composition written for two or more unaccompanied voices. **2.** A short poem about love that can be set to music.

mad·wom·an (**măd′**wo͝om′ən) *n.* A woman who is or appears to be mentally ill.

mael·strom (**māl′**strəm) *n.* **1.** A large and violent whirlpool. **2.** A violent or turbulent situation: *the maelstrom of war.* [From obsolete Dutch : *malen,* to grind + *stroom,* stream.]

maes·tro (**mīs′**trō) *n., pl.* **maes·tros** or **maes·tri** (**mīs′**trē) A master in an art, especially a conductor, composer, or music teacher.

Ma·fi·a (**mä′**fē-ə) *n.* **1.** A secret criminal organization that originated in Sicily, employs violence against people who do not cooperate with it, and operates especially in Italy and the United States. **2.** Any of various similar criminal organizations, especially when dominated by members of a single nationality.

mag·a·zine (**măg′**ə-zēn′ *or* măg′ə-**zēn′**) *n.* **1.** A publication, often issued weekly or monthly, that contains written matter, such as articles or stories, and usually pictures and advertising. **2.** A building or room in a fort or on a warship where ammunition is stored. **3.** In some firearms, a container in which cartridges are held until they pass into the chamber for firing. [From Arabic *maḫāzin,* storehouses, from *ḫazana,* to store.]

Ma·gel·lan (mə-**jĕl′**ən), **Ferdinand** 1480?–1521. Portuguese navigator who led the expedition that included the first ship to sail around the world (1519–1522).

Magellan, Strait of A channel separating South America from Tierra del Fuego and other islands south of the continent. Ferdinand Magellan sailed through the strait in October and November 1520.

Mag·el·lan·ic Clouds (măj′ə-**lăn′**ĭk) *pl.n.* Two small galaxies that are the galaxies closest to the Milky Way.

ma·gen·ta (mə-**jĕn′**tə) *n.* A bright purplish-red. [After *Magenta,* a town of northwest Italy.]

mag·got (**măg′**ət) *n.* The legless, soft-bodied, wormlike larva of any of various flies, usually found in decaying matter.

Ma·gi (**mā′**jī′) *pl.n.* In the New Testament, the three wise men of the East who traveled to Bethlehem to pay respect to the infant Jesus.

mag·ic (**măj′**ĭk) *n.* **1.** The art that claims to use supernatural powers to control natural events, effects, or forces through charms, spells, or rituals. **2.** The art or skill of using sleight of hand and other tricks to produce entertaining and baffling effects. **3.** A mysterious quality that seems to enchant; a special charm: *the magic of the woods in the fall.* ❖ *adj.* Relating to magic and its practice: *a magic trick; a magic wand.* [From Middle English *magik,* from Greek *magikē,* from *magos,* magician.]

mag·i·cal (**măj′**ĭ-kəl) *adj.* **1.** Relating to or produced by magic: *the magical appearance of a rabbit from a hat.* **2.** Enchanting; charming: *a magical performance of the play.* —**mag′i·cal·ly** *adv.*

ma·gi·cian (mə-**jĭsh′**ən) *n.* **1.** A person who uses magic; a sorcerer; a wizard. **2.** An entertainer who performs tricks of magic.

magic lantern *n.* An early kind of slide projector.

mag·is·te·ri·al (măj′ĭ-**stîr′**ē-əl) *adj.* **1.** Relating to a magistrate or a magistrate's official functions: *magisterial duties.* **2.** Having or showing authority; authoritative: *a magisterial account of the American Revolution.* **3.** Domineering; overbearing; dogmatic: *The director's magisterial attitude offended the actors.* —**mag′is·te′ri·al·ly** *adv.*

mag·is·tra·cy (**măj′**ĭs-trə-sē) *n., pl.* **mag·is·tra·cies 1.** The position, duties, or term of office of a magistrate. **2.** A body of magistrates.

mag·is·trate (**măj′**ĭ-strāt′ *or* **măj′**ĭ-strĭt) *n.* **1.** A civil official with the authority to administer the law. **2.** A judge, such as a justice of the peace, who has limited authority.

mag·ma (**măg′**mə) *n.* The molten rock material under the earth's crust that forms igneous rock when it has cooled. [From Middle English, sediment, dregs, from Greek, unguent.]

Mag·na Car·ta or **Mag·na Char·ta** (**măg′**nə **kär′**tə) *n.* A document of English political and civil liberties issued by King John in 1215. The Magna Carta guaranteed certain liberties to the people of England and limited the king's power.

mag·na cum lau·de (**mäg′**nə ko͝om **lou′**də) *adv.* With high honors. Used to show that someone has achieved academic distinction: *graduate magna cum laude.*

mag·na·nim·i·ty (măg′nə-**nĭm′**ĭ-tē) *n., pl.* **mag·na·nim·i·ties** The quality of being magnanimous; nobility.

mag·nan·i·mous (măg-**năn′**ə-məs) *adj.* Moral and dignified, especially in showing kindness or forgiveness; generous and unselfish: *a magnanimous person.* —**mag·nan′i·mous·ly** *adv.*

mag·nate (**măg′**nāt′ *or* **măg′**nĭt) *n.* A powerful and influential person, especially in business: *a real estate magnate.* [From Middle English *magnat,* from Latin *magnus,* great.]

mag·ne·sia (măg-**nē′**zhə *or* măg-**nē′**shə) *n.* Magnesium oxide. [From Medieval Latin *magnēsia,* mineral ingredient of the philosophers' stone, from Greek *Magnēsiē,* Magnesia, an ancient city of Asia Minor.]

mag·ne·si·um (măg-**nē′**zē-əm *or* măg-**nē′**zhəm) *n.* *Symbol* **Mg** A lightweight, moderately hard, silvery metallic element that burns with an intense white flame and is an essential component of chlorophyll. Atomic number 12. See **Periodic Table.**

magnesium oxide *n.* A white powdery compound, MgO, used in making electrical insulation, cosmetics, antacids, and pharmaceuticals.

mag·net (**măg′**nĭt) *n.* **1.** A stone, piece of metal, or other solid that has the property, either natural or induced, of attracting iron or steel. **2.** An electromagnet. **3.** A person, place, object, or situation that exerts a powerful attraction: *Our garden is a magnet for rabbits.* [From Middle English *magnes,* from Greek *Magnēs (lithos),* Magnesian (stone), from *Magnēsiā,* Magnesia, an ancient city of Asia Minor.]

mag·net·ic (măg-**nĕt′**ĭk) *adj.* **1.** Relating to magnetism or magnets. **2.** Having the properties of a magnet; showing magnetism. **3.** Producing, caused by, or operating by magnetism: *a magnetic compass; a magnetic recording.* **4.** Relating to the magnetic properties of the earth: *The earth's magnetic north pole is in a different place from the geographic North Pole.* **5.** Having the power to attract or charm: *a popular performer with a magnetic personality.* —**mag·net′i·cal·ly** *adv.*

magnetic disk *n.* A memory device, such as a hard disk, that is covered with a magnetic coating. Data is encoded on the disk by magnetizing extremely small iron particles that are scattered throughout the coating.

magnetic field *n.* A condition in the region of space around a magnet or an electric current, in which a magnetic force exists. —SEE NOTE AT **magnetism.**

Dolley Madison
1804 portrait by Gilbert Stuart (1755–1828)

James Madison

madras

Ferdinand Magellan

SCIENCE

magnetism The force known as **magnetism** is caused by the motion of electrons. As these tiny, negatively charged particles revolve around an atomic nucleus, they create an electric current that produces a *magnetic field*. This invisible field is made up of *lines of force* that surround and loop through the atom. The places where these lines of force come together, and where the magnetic field is strongest, are called the north and south *magnetic poles*. In some naturally occurring substances, these tiny magnetic fields are all aligned in the same direction, and the entire substance acts like a magnet—with north and south poles and a magnetic field. Other substances can be temporarily magnetized. One way to magnetize a substance, such as a coil of wire, is to run an electric current through it. Electrically produced magnets, called *electromagnets*, are found in many industrial and everyday devices, such as motors and generators.

magnolia

ă	pat	ôr	core
ā	pay	oi	boy
âr	care	ou	out
ä	father	o͝o	took
ĕ	pet	o͝or	lure
ē	be	o͞o	boot
ĭ	pit	ŭ	cut
ī	bite	ûr	urge
îr	pier	th	thin
ŏ	pot	*th*	this
ō	toe	zh	vision
ô	paw	ə	about

magnetic flux *n.* A measure of the strength of the magnetic field around a magnet or an electric current. It is based on the total number of magnetic lines of force that pass through a specific area.

magnetic needle *n.* A narrow thin piece of magnetized steel for use in a compass. It points toward the earth's magnetic poles.

magnetic north *n.* The direction in which the earth's north magnetic pole lies, to which the magnetic needle of a compass points. In most places, magnetic north differs from the true or geographic north.

magnetic pole *n.* **1.** Either of two regions of a magnet where the magnetic field is strongest. **2.** Either of two variable points on the earth's surface toward which a compass needle points. The magnetic poles differ from the geographic poles. The north magnetic pole is in the Arctic, and the south magnetic pole is in Antarctica.

magnetic resonance imaging *n.* A technique that uses a magnetic field and radio waves to produce images of structures inside the body.

magnetic tape *n.* A plastic tape coated with tiny magnetic particles for use in recording sounds or pictures.

mag·net·ism (măg**′**nĭ-tĭz′əm) *n.* **1.** The force produced by a magnetic field. **2.** The properties or effects of magnets: *Magnetism causes a compass needle to point north.* **3.** An unusual power to attract or influence: *the magnetism of the popular leader.* —SEE NOTE.

mag·net·ite (măg**′**nĭ-tīt′) *n.* A mineral composed of iron oxide that is strongly attracted by a magnet and is an important iron ore.

mag·net·ize (măg**′**nĭ-tīz′) *tr.v.* **mag·net·ized, mag·net·iz·ing, mag·net·iz·es** To make (an object) magnetic: *You can magnetize a nail by wrapping it in a wire that will carry an electric current.* **—mag′net·i·za′tion** (măg′nĭ-tĭ-**zā′**shən) *n.* **—mag′net·iz′er** *n.*

mag·ne·to (măg-**nē′**tō) *n., pl.* **mag·ne·tos** A device that produces alternating current and is used to fire spark plugs in some internal-combustion engines.

mag·ne·tron (**măg′**nĭ-trŏn′) *n.* A type of electron tube that produces microwave radiation by applying magnetic and electric fields to a stream of electrons that a heated filament emits. Magnetrons are used in radar and in microwave ovens.

magnet school *n.* A public school designed to attract students from a wide geographic area by offering specialized educational programs, often in a specific area, such as science, the humanities, or art.

mag·ni·fi·ca·tion (măg′nə-fĭ-**kā′**shən) *n.* The act, process, or degree of magnifying.

mag·nif·i·cence (măg-**nĭf′**ĭ-səns) *n.* Richness or splendor of surroundings; grand or imposing beauty: *the magnificence of the Grand Canyon.*

mag·nif·i·cent (măg-**nĭf′**ĭ-sənt) *adj.* **1.** Splendid in appearance; remarkable: *a magnificent cathedral.* See Synonyms at **grand. 2.** Outstanding of its kind; excellent: *a magnificent place for sailing.* **—mag·nif′i·cent·ly** *adv.*

mag·ni·fy (**măg′**nə-fī′) *v.* **mag·ni·fied, mag·ni·fy·ing, mag·ni·fies** —*tr.* **1.** To make (an object) appear larger than it really is: *A microscope magnifies the cell so that you can study it.* **2.** To cause to appear greater or seem more important; exaggerate: *The wind magnifies the effect of the cold.* —*intr.* To make or be capable of making an object appear larger than it really is. [From Middle English *magnifien*, to praise, from Latin *magnificāre*, from *magnificus*, magnificent.] **—mag′ni·fi′er** *n.*

mag·ni·fy·ing glass (**măg′**nə-fī′ĭng) *n.* A lens or combination of lenses that makes objects appear larger than they really are.

mag·ni·tude (**măg′**nĭ-to͞od′) *n.* **1.** Greatness, as of position, size, or significance: *finally understood the magnitude of the problem.* **2.** A measure of the total amount of energy released by an earthquake, as indicated on the Richter scale. **3.** The relative brightness of a star or other celestial object as measured on a numerical scale in which lower numbers mean greater brightness.

mag·no·lia (măg-**nōl′**yə) *n.* **1.** Any of numerous trees or shrubs having large white, pink, or yellow flowers that are often fragrant. **2.** The flower of such a tree or shrub. [After Pierre *Magnol* (1638–1715), French botanist.]

mag·pie (**măg′**pī′) *n.* **1.** Any of various usually black and white birds that have a long tail and a loud, harsh call. **2.** A person who chatters.

ma·guey (mə-**gā′** *or* **măg′**wā) *n., pl.* **ma·gueys 1.** Any of various agaves of Mexico that are harvested for their sap and for their large stiff leaves, which yield a fiber used for making rope or twine. **2.** The fiber of such a plant.

Mag·yar (**măg′**yär′ *or* **mä′**dyär′) *n.* **1.** A member of the main ethnic group of Hungary. **2.** The language of the Magyars; Hungarian. **—Mag′yar** *adj.*

ma·ha·ra·ja or **ma·ha·ra·jah** (mä′hə-**rä′**jə *or* mä′hə-**rä′**-zhə) *n.* A king or prince in India ranking above a raja. [From Sanskrit *mahārājāh*, great king.]

ma·ha·ra·ni or **ma·ha·ra·nee** (mä′hə-**rä′**nē) *n., pl.* **ma·ha·ra·nis** or **ma·ha·ra·nees 1.** The wife of a maharaja. **2.** A princess in India ranking above a rani.

ma·hat·ma (mə-**hät′**mə *or* mə-**hăt′**mə) *n.* **1.** In Hinduism, a person revered for great knowledge and love of humanity. **2. Mahatma** Used especially in Hinduism as a title of respect for a holy person.

Ma·hi·can (mə-**hē′**kən) also **Mo·hi·can** (mō-**hē′**kən *or* mə-**hē′**kən) *n., pl.* **Mahican** or **Ma·hi·cans** also **Mohican** or **Mo·hi·cans 1.** A member of a Native American people, formerly living in the upper Hudson River valley, with populations now living in Oklahoma and Wisconsin. **2.** The Algonquian language of the Mahican.

mah·jong also **mah·jongg** (**mä′zhŏng′**) *n.* A game of Chinese origin played by people using tiles bearing various designs. Each player tries to win by forming certain combinations by drawing and discarding tiles.

ma·hog·a·ny (mə-**hŏg′**ə-nē) *n., pl.* **ma·hog·a·nies 1a.** Any of various tropical American trees having hard reddish-brown wood. **b.** The wood of such a tree or a similar tree, used in making furniture and musical instruments. **2.** A reddish brown. [Perhaps of Taíno origin.]

ma·hout (mə-**hout′**) *n.* The keeper and driver of an elephant. [From Sanskrit *mahāmātraḥ*, one having great measure.]

maid (mād) *n.* **1.** A housemaid or chambermaid. **2.** A woman servant. **3.** *Archaic* An unmarried girl or woman. [From Middle English *maide*, from Old English *mægden*, maiden.]

❑ *These sound alike:* **maid, made** (created).

maid·en (**mād′**n) *n. Archaic* An unmarried girl or woman. ❖ *adj.* **1.** Relating to or suited to a maiden: *youthful maiden beauty.* **2.** Unmarried. Used of a girl or woman: *a maiden aunt.* **3.** First or earliest: *a ship's maiden voyage.*

maid·en·hair fern (**mād′**n-hâr′) *n.* Any of various ferns having thin dark stalks and delicate feathery fronds.

maid·en·hood (**mād′**n-ho͝od′) *n.* The quality or condition of being a maiden.

maiden name *n.* The surname that a girl is given at birth and that some women change when they marry.

maid in waiting *n., pl.* **maids in waiting** An unmarried woman who attends a queen or princess.

maid of honor *n., pl.* **maids of honor 1.** An unmarried woman who is the bride's chief attendant at a wedding. **2.** An unmarried noblewoman who attends a queen or princess.

maid·ser·vant (**mād′**sûr′vənt) *n.* A woman servant.

mail¹ (māl) *n.* **1a.** Letters, postcards, packages, and printed matter sent through a postal system. **b.** Such materials for a specified person or organization: *What came in* *the mail today?* **2.** often **mails** A system by which letters and other postal materials are transported. **3.** Mail or messages sent electronically; email. ❖ *tr.v.* **mailed, mail·ing, mails** To send by mail. [From Middle English *male*, bag, from Old French, of Germanic origin.]

❑ *These sound alike:* **mail[1]** (postal material), **mail[2]** (armor), **male** (man).

mail[2] (māl) *n.* Flexible armor made of connected metal rings, loops of chain, or overlapping scales, worn to protect the body in battle. [From Middle English *maille*, from Old French *maile*, from Latin *macula*, blemish, mesh.]

❑ *These sound alike:* **mail[2]** (armor), **mail[1]** (postal material), **male** (man).

mail·bag (**māl′**băg′) *n.* A large canvas sack that is used for carrying mail.

mail·box (**māl′**bŏks′) *n.* **1.** A public box for depositing outgoing mail. **2.** A private box where incoming mail is delivered. **3.** A computer file or set of files for collecting and storing email.

mail carrier *n.* A person who delivers mail or collects it from mailboxes.

mail·ing (**mā′**lĭng) *n.* Something sent by mail: *The senator sent out a mailing that explained her voting record.*

mail·man (**māl′**măn′ *or* **māl′**mən) *n.* A man who carries and delivers mail.

mail order *n.* An order for goods to be shipped through the mail.

mail·room (**māl′**ro͞om′ *or* **māl′**ro͝om′) *n.* A room where all of the mail that is sent to or from a company is handled.

mail·wom·an (**māl′**wo͝om′ən) *n.* A woman who carries and delivers mail.

maim (mām) *tr.v.* **maimed, maim·ing, maims** To disable, usually by causing the loss of the use of a limb: *Accidents maim many people each year.*

main (mān) *adj.* Most important; principal; chief: *Look for the main idea in each paragraph. The main reason I want to travel to Italy is to see the museums.* ❖ *n.* **1.** A large pipe, duct, conduit, or conductor used to carry water, oil, gas, or electricity. **2.** The open sea. ◆ **in the main** For the most part; on the whole: *Your ideas are, in the main, useful.* [From Middle English, from Old English *mægen*, strength.]

❑ *These sound alike:* **main, mane** (neck hair).

main clause *n.* The independent clause in a complex sentence. For example, in the sentence *When we reached the summit, we admired the view,* the clause *we admired the view* is the main clause.

main drag *n. Slang* The principal street of a city or town.

Maine (mān) A state of the northeast United States northeast of New Hampshire. It was admitted as the 23rd state in 1820. Augusta is the capital and Portland the largest city. —SEE NOTE.

main·frame (**mān′**frām′) *n.* A powerful computer, often serving many terminals and usually used by large, complex organizations.

main·land (**mān′**lănd′ *or* **mān′**lənd) *n.* The principal land mass of a country, territory, or continent as opposed to its islands or peninsulas: *took a ferry across the strait to the mainland.*

main·ly (**mān′**lē) *adv.* For the most part; chiefly: *Homework for history class consists mainly of reading.*

main·mast (**mān′**məst *or* **mān′**măst′) *n.* The principal mast of a sailing ship.

main·sail (**mān′**səl *or* **mān′**sāl′) *n.* The largest sail set on the mainmast of a sailing ship.

main·spring (**mān′**sprĭng′) *n.* **1.** The spring that drives a mechanism, especially a clock or watch. **2.** The most important cause or force: *A desire for justice was the mainspring of the reform movement.*

main·stay (**mān′**stā′) *n.* **1.** A main support: *Agriculture is a mainstay of the economy.* **2.** A strong rope or cable that holds in place the mainmast of a sailing vessel.

main·stream (**mān′**strēm′) *n.* The prevailing attitudes, values, and practices of a society or group: *Their ideas are outside the mainstream.* ❖ *tr.v.* **main·streamed, main·stream·ing, main·streams** To integrate (a student with special needs) into regular school classes.

main·tain (mān-**tān′**) *tr.v.* **main·tained, main·tain·ing, main·tains 1.** To keep up; carry on; continue: *The train maintains its speed on hills. She maintained good relations with her former employer.* **2.** To keep in an existing state or condition: *maintained my composure during the ordeal.* **3.** To keep in good repair: *maintain public roads.* **4.** To provide for the upkeep of; bear the expenses of: *maintain a large family.* **5.** To defend against criticism or attack: *The politician maintained his stance against new taxes.* **6.** To declare as true; affirm: *maintain one's innocence.*

main·te·nance (**mān′**tə-nəns) *n.* **1.** The act of maintaining or the condition of being maintained: *maintenance of calm during the emergency; maintenance of the traditions by the family.* **2.** The work involved in maintaining; care; upkeep: *maintenance of an old building.* **3.** Means of support or livelihood: *Wages provide maintenance.*

main·top (**mān′**tŏp′) *n.* A platform on the mainmast of a ship.

main yard *n.* The yard or pole on which the mainsail of a sailing ship is extended.

mai·tre d′ (mā′trə **dē′** *or* mā′tər **dē′**) *n., pl.* **mai·tre d′s** (mā′trə **dēz′** *or* mā′tər **dēz′**) *Informal* A headwaiter.

maize (māz) *n.* The corn plant or its edible kernels. [From Spanish *maíz*, from Arawakan *mahiz.*]

❑ *These sound alike:* **maize, maze** (labyrinth).

Maj. or **MAJ** *abbr.* An abbreviation of major (military rank).

ma·jes·tic (mə-**jĕs′**tĭk) *adj.* Impressive or beautiful in a dignified or inspiring way. See Synonyms at **grand.** —**ma·jes′ti·cal** *adj.* —**ma·jes′tic·al·ly** *adv.*

maj·es·ty (**măj′**ĭ-stē) *n., pl.* **maj·es·ties 1.** The greatness and dignity of a sovereign: *The royal couple arrived at the palace in all their majesty.* **2.** Supreme authority or power: *the majesty of the law.* **3. Majesty** Used as a title for a sovereign, such as a king or queen: *Your Majesty.* **4.** A quality of stateliness, splendor, or grandeur: *the majesty of the Rocky Mountains.* [From Middle English *mageste*, from Latin *māiestās.*]

Maj. Gen. or **MajGen** *abbr.* An abbreviation of major general.

ma·jor (**mā′**jər) *adj.* **1.** Greater than others in importance or rank: *a major American novelist.* **2.** Great in scope or effect: *a major improvement.* **3a.** Relating to or based on a major scale: *a major chord.* **b.** Relating to a musical tone that is a half step greater than a minor interval. ❖ *n.* **1.** An officer in the US Army, Air Force, or Marine Corps ranking above a captain and below a lieutenant colonel. **2.** In schools and colleges, a field of study chosen as a specialty: *My major is French.* **3.** A major scale, key, or interval: *the key of D major.* **4. majors** The major leagues of a sport, especially baseball. ❖ *intr.v.* **ma·jored, ma·jor·ing, ma·jors** To study or specialize in a particular subject: *I am majoring in Spanish.* [From Middle English *majour*, from Latin *māior.*]

Ma·jor·ca (mə-**jôr′**kə *or* mə-**yôr′**kə) An island of Spain in the western Mediterranean Sea off the east-central coast of the mainland. It is the largest of the Balearic Islands.

ma·jor-do·mo (mā′jər-**dō′**mō) *n., pl.* **ma·jor-do·mos** The head steward or butler in the household of a sovereign or great noble.

ma·jor·ette (mā′jə-**rĕt′**) *n.* **1.** A female dancer who twirls a baton, usually in a group and sometimes with a marching band. **2.** A drum majorette.

mail[2]
chain-mail tunic

GEOGRAPHY

Maine The name of the state of **Maine** comes from an older English word *main,* also written *maine,* which was used to refer to a continent or mainland. Early explorers of the region needed to distinguish between the many islands and the mainland, and the area soon became known as "the main." *Maine* was made the official name of the state when it was organized in 1820.

maintop
foremast (*left*), mainmast with maintop (*center*), and mizzenmast (*right*)

USAGE

majority When **majority** refers to a particular number of votes, it takes a singular verb: *Her majority was five votes.* When it refers to a group of people or things that are in the majority, it may take either a singular or plural verb, depending on whether the group is considered as a whole or as a set of people considered individually. So we say *The majority elects the candidate it wants,* since the election is accomplished by the group as a whole, but we say *The majority of the voters live in the city,* since living in the city is something that each voter does individually.

major scale
C major scale

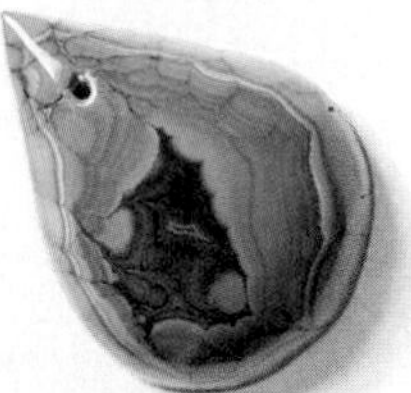

malachite

ă	pat	ôr	core
ā	pay	oi	boy
âr	care	ou	out
ä	father	o͝o	took
ĕ	pet	o͝or	lure
ē	be	o͞o	boot
ĭ	pit	ŭ	cut
ī	bite	ûr	urge
îr	pier	th	thin
ŏ	pot	*th*	this
ō	toe	zh	vision
ô	paw	ə	about

major general *n.* An officer in the US Army, Air Force, or Marine Corps ranking above a brigadier general and below a lieutenant general.

ma·jor·i·ty (mə-**jôr′**ĭ-tē) *n., pl.* **ma·jor·i·ties 1.** The greater number or part of something; a number more than half of a total: *The majority of the class did well on the test.* **2.** The amount by which a greater number of votes exceeds the remaining number of votes: *The candidate won by a majority of 5,000 votes.* **3.** A political party or group that has the greater number of members or supporters: *The party is a majority in the city.* **4.** The status of having reached the age of legal responsibility, usually 18 or 21. —SEE NOTE.

major league *n.* **1.** Either of the two principal groups of professional baseball teams in the United States. **2.** A league of principal importance in other professional sports.

ma·jor-league (**mā′**jər-**lēg′**) *adj.* **1.** Relating to a major league: *a major-league player.* **2.** *Informal* Prominent or important: *a major-league decision.* **3.** *Informal* Extreme: *You are a major-league pain in the neck.*

ma·jor-lea·guer (**mā′**jər-**lē′**gər) *n.* A member of a major-league sports team.

ma·jor·ly (**mā′**jər-lē) *adv. Slang* To a great or an intense degree; extremely: *a lecture that was majorly boring.*

Major Prophets *n.* The biblical Books of Isaiah, Jeremiah, and Ezekiel.

major scale *n.* A musical scale in which the third and fourth tones and the seventh and eighth tones are separated by half steps and all other tones are separated by whole steps.

Ma·ju·ro (mə-**jo͝or′**ō) The capital of the Marshall Islands, in the central Pacific Ocean.

make (māk) *v.* **made** (mād), **mak·ing, makes** —*tr.* **1.** To cause to exist or happen; bring about; create: *The students made noise in the hall.* **2a.** To bring into existence by shaping, changing, or putting together material: *make a dress; make a wall of stones.* **b.** To draw up; establish; enact: *make rules.* **3.** To change from one form or function into another: *made clay into bricks.* **4.** To cause to be or become: *The invitation made us happy.* **5a.** To cause to act in a specified way: *The pepper made me sneeze.* **b.** To force; compel: *His allergies made him stay home.* **6.** To prepare; fix: *make breakfast.* **7.** To carry out, perform, or engage in: *make a phone call; make war.* **8.** To reach in time: *We just made the bus.* **9.** To acquire the rank of or a place on: *made lieutenant; made the baseball team.* **10.** To gain or acquire: *make money; make friends.* **11.** To be suited for: *This area would make a good soccer field.* **12.** To develop into: *She will make a fine doctor.* **13.** To arrange or agree to: *make a date.* **14a.** To formulate or arrive at in one's mind: *make plans; make a decision.* **b.** To determine the meaning of: *What do you make of their proposal?* **15.** To form or amount to; constitute: *Two wrongs don't make a right.* **16.** To cover (a distance): *made 200 miles before sunset.* **17.** To assure the success of: *The scenery makes the movie.* —*intr.* **1.** To cause something to be in a specified manner: *The actors made ready for the play.* **2.** To go or move, as in a certain direction: *The ship made for harbor.* ❖ *n.* **1.** A style or manner in which something is made: *disliked the make of the coat.* **2.** A specific line of manufactured goods; a brand: *Three makes of small trucks are available.* **3.** The origin of a product's manufacturing: *a bicycle of French make.* ◆ **make a face** To distort the features of the face: *She made a face when they said things in poor taste.* **make away with** To carry off; steal. **make believe** To pretend. **make do** To manage; get along. **make ends meet** To make enough money to pay one's expenses. **make for** To help promote; further: *The steady breeze made for excellent sailing.* **make fun of** To mock; ridicule. **make good 1.** To carry out successfully: *He made good his escape.* **2.** To fulfill: *I will make good my promise.* **3.** To make compensation for; make up for: *He made good the loss.* **4.** To succeed: *She made good as an artist.* **make it** *Informal* To be successful. **make light of** To treat as unimportant: *He made light of his promotion.* **make much of** To treat as of great importance. **make off with** To snatch or steal. **make out 1.** To see or identify, especially with difficulty: *Can you make out that sign?* **2.** To understand: *I can't make out what she means in the letter.* **3.** To write out or fill out: *make out a tax form.* **4.** *Informal* To represent as being: *You make me out to be a liar.* **5.** To get along in a given way; fare: *How are you making out with the dance lessons?* **6.** *Informal* To kiss and caress. **make sense 1.** To be understandable: *The explanation made no sense.* **2.** To be practical or advisable: *It makes sense to go now.* **make something of** To start a fight or quarrel over. **make the best of** To accept (a bad situation) in as good a light as possible. **make the most of** To use to the greatest advantage. **make up 1.** To put together; construct or compose: *We made up a model of the new building.* **2.** To constitute; form: *A basketball team is made up of five players.* **3.** To apply cosmetics. **4.** To devise as a fiction or falsehood; invent: *make up a story.* **5.** To compensate for: *We made up the lost time by taking a short cut.* **6.** To resolve a quarrel: *They talked over the their differences and made up.* **7.** To take (an examination or course) again or at a later time. **make up (one's) mind** To come to a definite decision or opinion. [From Old English *macian.*] **—mak′a·ble, make′a·ble** *adj.*

make-be·lieve (**māk′**bĭ-lēv′) *n.* Playful imagining or acting as if one were another person or in an invented place: *Fairies exist in the land of make-believe.* ❖ *adj.* Imaginary; fictional.

mak·er (**mā′**kər) *n.* **1.** A person or thing that makes. **2. Maker** God: *prayed to their Maker.*

make·shift (**māk′**shĭft′) *adj.* Serving as a temporary substitute: *a makeshift table.* ❖ *n.* Something used or assembled as a temporary substitute: *I didn't have a chair, so I used the crate as a makeshift.*

make·up or **make-up** (**māk′**ŭp′) *n.* **1.** The way in which something is put together or arranged; construction: *What is the makeup of the police department?* **2.** The qualities or temperament that make up a personality; disposition: *It's just not in my makeup to complain.* **3.** Cosmetics applied especially to the face. **4.** A special examination given to a student who has missed or failed a previous one.

mal– *pref.* A prefix that means bad or wrongly: *malpractice; malformed.*

Mal·a·bo (**măl′**ə-bō′ *or* mä-**lä′**bō) The capital of Equatorial Guinea, on an island off the coast of Cameroon. It was founded in 1827.

Mal·a·chi[1] (**măl′**ə-kī′) A Hebrew prophet of the fifth century BC.

Mal·a·chi[2] (**măl′**ə-kī′) *n.* A book of the Bible in which Malachi warns the Jews to follow God's laws.

mal·a·chite (**măl′**ə-kīt′) *n.* A light green to dark green copper carbonate mineral. It is used as a source of copper and in making ornamental objects, jewelry, and stonework. [From Middle English *molochites*, from Greek *malakhē*, mallow.]

mal·ad·just·ed (măl′ə-**jŭs′**tĭd) *adj.* Poorly adjusted to the demands or stresses of daily living.

mal·ad·just·ment (măl′ə-**jŭst′**mənt) *n.* Inability to adjust to one's environment or one's circumstances.

mal·a·droit (măl′ə-**droit′**) *adj.* Lacking skill; awkward or inept. **—mal′a·droit′ly** *adv.*

mal·a·dy (**măl′**ə-dē) *n., pl.* **mal·a·dies 1.** A disease, disorder, or ailment. **2.** An unwholesome condition.

mal·aise (mă-**lāz′**) *n.* A general feeling of discomfort or unease.

mal·a·mute also **mal·e·mute** (măl′ə-myo͞ot′) *n.* A large dog of a breed developed in the North American Arctic as a sled dog, having erect ears, a bushy tail, and a thick coat.

ma·lar·i·a (mə-lâr′ē-ə) *n.* An infectious disease of tropical areas that is characterized by repeated episodes of chills, fever, and sweating. It is caused by a parasite that multiplies inside red blood cells and is transmitted by the bite of an infected mosquito. [From Italian *mala aria*, bad air.] **—ma·lar′i·al** *adj.*

Ma·la·wi (mə-lä′wē) A country of southeast Africa east of Zambia. Lilongwe is the capital.

Ma·lay (mə-lā′ *or* mā′lā′) *adj.* **1.** Relating to Malaysia, the Malay Peninsula, or the Malay Archipelago. **2.** Relating to a people inhabiting the Malay Peninsula and some adjacent areas. ❖ *n.* **1.** A member of this people. **2.** The language of this people. **—Ma·lay′an** (mə-lā′ən) *adj. & n.*

Mal·a·ya·lam (măl′ə-yä′ləm) *n.* A language spoken on the southwest coast of India.

Malay Archipelago An island group of southeast Asia between Australia and mainland Asia. It includes the islands of Indonesia, the Philippines, and Malaysia.

Malay Peninsula A peninsula of southeast Asia made up of southwest Thailand, western Malaysia, and the island of Singapore.

Ma·lay·sia (mə-lā′zhə *or* mə-lā′shə) A country of southeast Asia made up of the southern Malay Peninsula and the northern part of the island of Borneo. Kuala Lumpur is the capital.

Mal·colm X (măl′kəm ĕks) Originally Malcolm Little. 1925–1965. American activist who advocated separatism and black pride. In 1964 he founded the Organization of Afro-American Unity.

mal·con·tent (măl′kən-tĕnt′) *adj.* Dissatisfied with existing conditions. ❖ *n.* A dissatisfied or rebellious person.

Mal·dives (môl′dīvz *or* măl′dīvz) An island country in the Indian Ocean southwest of Sri Lanka made up of 19 groups of coral islands. Male is the capital.

male (māl) *adj.* **1a.** Relating to or characteristic of the sex that can fertilize egg cells and father offspring. **b.** Relating to or being a reproductive organ that produces male gametes: *male flower parts.* **c.** Relating to or being the gamete that is smaller and more motile than the other corresponding gamete: *male reproductive cells.* **2.** Composed of men or boys: *a male choir.* **3.** Designed to be inserted into a socket or opening: *a male plug.* ❖ *n.* **1.** A male organism. **2.** A man or boy. [From Middle English, from Latin *masculus*.] **—male′ness** *n.*

❑ *These sound alike:* **male, mail[1]** (postal material), **mail[2]** (armor).

Ma·le (mä′lē) The capital of the Maldives, in the Indian Ocean southwest of Sri Lanka.

mal·e·dic·tion (măl′ĭ-dĭk′shən) *n.* **1.** A curse: *a witch's malediction.* **2.** Slander.

mal·e·fac·tor (măl′ə-făk′tər) *n.* **1.** A person who has committed a crime; a criminal. **2.** An evildoer.

ma·lev·o·lence (mə-lĕv′ə-ləns) *n.* The wish for harm or evil to come to others; ill will; malice.

ma·lev·o·lent (mə-lĕv′ə-lənt) *adj.* Wishing harm to others; malicious. **—ma·lev′o·lent·ly** *adv.*

mal·fea·sance (măl-fē′zəns) *n.* Wrongdoing or misconduct, especially by a public official: *An official who accepts a bribe is guilty of malfeasance.*

mal·for·ma·tion (măl′fôr-mā′shən) *n.* **1.** The condition of being malformed; deformity. **2.** A body part that is malformed; a deformity.

mal·formed (măl-fôrmd′) *adj.* Having an imperfect or abnormal form: *blight that causes malformed ears of corn.*

mal·func·tion (măl-fŭngk′shən) *intr.v.* **mal·func·tioned, mal·func·tion·ing, mal·func·tions** To fail to function properly. ❖ *n.* A failure to function well: *a malfunction in the computer.* [From *mal-*, wrongly (from Latin *malus*, bad) + *function*.]

Ma·li (mä′lē) A country of western Africa west of Niger. It was a powerful empire from the 1200s to the 1500s. Bamako is the capital.

mal·ice (măl′ĭs) *n.* **1.** The desire to harm others or to see others suffer; ill will; spite. **2.** The intent to commit an unlawful act without justification or excuse. [From Middle English, from Latin *malitia*, from *malus*, bad.]

ma·li·cious (mə-lĭsh′əs) *adj.* Having, showing, or motivated by malice; deliberately harmful; spiteful: *told malicious lies.* **—ma·li′cious·ly** *adv.* **—ma·li′cious·ness** *n.*

ma·lign (mə-līn′) *tr.v.* **ma·ligned, ma·lign·ing, ma·ligns** To make evil, harmful, and often false statements about: *malign a person's reputation; maligned the other candidates in his speech.* ❖ *adj.* **1.** Evil in nature; injurious: *Poverty can be a malign influence.* **2.** Intending or threatening harm or ill will: *a malign look.* [From Middle English *malignen*, from Latin *malignus*, evil.]

ma·lig·nan·cy (mə-lĭg′nən-sē) *n., pl.* **ma·lig·nan·cies** **1.** The quality or condition of being malignant. **2.** A malignant tumor or condition.

ma·lig·nant (mə-lĭg′nənt) *adj.* **1a.** Threatening to life or health; deadly: *a malignant disease.* **b.** Tending to grow and spread throughout the body: *a malignant tumor.* **2.** Having or showing ill will; malicious: *malignant thoughts.* **—ma·lig′nant·ly** *adv.*

ma·lig·ni·ty (mə-lĭg′nĭ-tē) *n., pl.* **ma·lig·ni·ties** **1.** Intense ill will or hatred; malice. **2.** An act or feeling of great malice.

ma·lin·ger (mə-lĭng′gər) *intr.v.* **ma·lin·gered, ma·lin·ger·ing, ma·lin·gers** To pretend to be ill or injured in order to avoid work or duty. **—ma·lin′ger·er** *n.*

mall (môl) *n.* **1.** A large shopping center containing different kinds of stores and businesses. **2.** A street lined with shops and closed to vehicles. **3.** A shady public walk or promenade. [After *The Mall* in London, England, originally an alley for playing pall-mall, a kind of croquet.]

❑ *These sound alike:* **mall, maul** (hammer).

mal·lard (măl′ərd) *n., pl.* **mallard** or **mal·lards** A wild duck, the male of which has a glossy green head and a white ring around the neck. [From Middle English *malarde*, from Old French *malart*.]

mal·le·a·ble (măl′ē-ə-bəl) *adj.* **1.** Capable of being shaped or formed, as by pressure or hammering: *copper and other malleable metals.* **2.** Easily controlled or influenced: *a boss who wanted a malleable workforce.* **3.** Able to adjust to changing circumstances; adaptable. **—mal′le·a·bil′i·ty** *n.*

mal·let (măl′ĭt) *n.* **1a.** A hammer with a wooden head and a short handle, used to drive a chisel or wedge. **b.** A similar tool with a rubber, leather, or plastic head, used to strike a surface without damaging it. **2.** A long-handled hammer used to strike the ball in the games of croquet and polo. [From Middle English *mailet*, from Latin *malleus*, hammer.]

mal·le·us (măl′ē-əs) *n., pl.* **mal·le·i** (măl′ē-ī′) The largest and outermost of the three small bones in the middle ear; the hammer.

mal·low (măl′ō) *n.* Any of various plants having showy flowers that are pink, purple, or white and have five petals.

mal·nour·ished (măl-nûr′ĭsht) *adj.* Suffering from malnutrition: *emergency food shipments for the malnourished refugees.*

mal·nu·tri·tion (măl′no͞o-trĭsh′ən) *n.* Nutrition that is inadequate for the body's needs. Malnutrition can be caused by a poor diet or by the inability to digest food properly.

malamute

Malcolm X
photographed in 1964

WRITERS CHOOSE THEIR WORDS

The throne itself was of pure, unalloyed gold, and since pure, unalloyed gold is almost as **malleable** as clay, a crew of dragon goldsmiths was kept busy all the time repairing the throne where the Lord might have dented it.

—Laurence Yep
Dragonwings

mallet

USAGE

man The use of **man** to mean "a human; a man or woman" has a long history in English. Many people feel that it is unfair to women to use a word that is mainly thought of as male to represent women. Therefore, many job titles in which *man* occurs are being replaced by neutral terms. For example, *firefighter* is often used instead of *fireman, Member of Congress* instead of *Congressman,* and *chair* or *chairperson* instead of *chairman.* In addition, compounds formed with *woman,* as in *businesswoman, policewoman,* and *chairwoman,* are now used as parallel terms to the compounds formed with *man.*

manatee

mandala
Tibetan mandala

ă	pat	ôr	core
ā	pay	oi	boy
âr	care	ou	out
ä	father	o͝o	took
ĕ	pet	o͝or	lure
ē	be	o͞o	boot
ĭ	pit	ŭ	cut
ī	bite	ûr	urge
îr	pier	th	thin
ŏ	pot	*th*	this
ō	toe	zh	vision
ô	paw	ə	about

mal·oc·clu·sion (măl′ə-klo͞o′zhən) *n.* A condition in which the upper and lower teeth do not meet properly when the jaw is closed; a faulty bite.

mal·o·dor·ous (măl-ō′dər-əs) *adj.* Having a bad odor: *a malodorous swamp.* —**mal·o′dor·ous·ly** *adv.*

ma·lo·ti (mä-lō′tē) *n.* Plural of **loti.**

mal·prac·tice (măl-**prăk′**tĭs) *n.* Improper or substandard performance in providing professional services: *a doctor who had been sued by several patients for malpractice.*

malt (môlt) *n.* **1.** Barley or other grain that has been soaked in water and allowed to sprout and then dried. It is used chiefly in brewing and distilling. **2.** Malted milk. ❖ *tr.v.* **malt·ed, malt·ing, malts 1.** To make (grain) into malt. **2.** To mix or prepare with malt.

Mal·ta (**môl′**tə) An island country in the Mediterranean Sea south of Sicily made up of the island of **Malta** and two smaller islands. Valletta is the capital.

malt·ed milk (**môl′**tĭd) *n.* A drink made of milk mixed with a powder of dried milk, malted barley, and wheat flour, often with the addition of ice cream and flavoring.

Mal·tese (môl-**tēz′** *or* môl-**tēs′**) *adj.* Relating to Malta or its people, language, or culture. ❖ *n., pl.* **Maltese 1.** A native or inhabitant of Malta. **2.** The Semitic language of the Maltese. **3.** A dog of a toy breed having a long silky white coat.

Maltese cross *n.* A cross having the form of four arrowheads placed with their points toward the center of a circle.

mal·tose (**môl′**tōs′ *or* **môl′**tōz′) *n.* A sugar made by the action of various enzymes on starch. It is formed in the body during digestion.

mal·treat (măl-**trēt′**) *tr.v.* **mal·treat·ed, mal·treat·ing, mal·treats** To treat cruelly or roughly. —**mal·treat′ment** *n.*

mal·ware (**măl′**wâr′) *n.* Computer software that is designed to do harm by interfering with normal computer functions or by sending personal data about the user to unauthorized parties over the Internet. [From *mal(icious)* + *-ware.*]

ma·ma or **mam·ma** (**mä′**mə *or* mə-**mä′**) *n. Informal* Mother.

mam·bo (**mäm′**bō) *n., pl.* **mam·bos 1.** A Latin-American dance resembling the rumba. **2.** The music for this dance. ❖ *intr.v.* **mam·boed, mam·bo·ing, mam·bos** To perform this dance.

mam·mal (**măm′**əl) *n.* Any of various warm-blooded animals that have a backbone, hair or fur, and, in the females, mammary glands that produce milk for feeding their young. Cats, dogs, bats, elephants, whales, humans, and kangaroos are all mammals. —**mam·ma′li·an** (mă-**mā′**lē-ən) *adj. & n.*

mam·ma·ry gland (**măm′**ə-rē) *n.* One of the milk-producing glands in a female mammal, consisting of a system of ducts that convey the milk to an external nipple or teat.

mam·mo·gram (**măm′**ə-grăm′) *n.* **1.** An x-ray image of the human breast. **2.** The procedure performed to produce such an image.

Mam·mon (**măm′**ən) *n.* **1.** In the New Testament, riches and avarice personified as a false god. **2.** often **mammon** Riches regarded as an evil influence.

mam·moth (**măm′**əth) *n.* Any of various extinct elephants that were often very large and had long, upwardly curving tusks and thick hair. Mammoths lived throughout the Northern Hemisphere during the Ice Age. ❖ *adj.* Huge; gigantic: *a mammoth skyscraper.* [From obsolete Russian *mamont.*]

man (măn) *n., pl.* **men** (mĕn) **1.** An adult male human. **2.** A human without regard to sex or age; a person. **3.** A human or an adult human male belong to a specific occupation, group, nationality, or other category: *a milkman; a congressman; an Irishman.* **4.** Humans considered as a group; humanity: *man's quest for peace.* **5.** A male human endowed with qualities, such as strength, considered characteristic of manhood. **6.** A husband or male lover. **7.** A male servant, employee, or worker: *ten men on the job.* **8.** Any of the pieces used in board games, such as chess or checkers. ❖ *tr.v.* **manned, man·ning, mans 1.** To take one's place or post at; get ready to work or operate: *Man the oars.* **2.** To supply with men: *The captain manned the ship with a new crew of sailors.* ❖ *interj.* An expression used to show intense feeling: *Man! What fun!* ◆ **to a man** Without exception: *They supported the new labor contract to a man.* [From Old English *mann.*] —SEE NOTE.

Man, Isle of An island in the Irish Sea off the northwest coast of England. It is an autonomous possession of the British crown.

man·a·cle (**măn′**ə-kəl) *n.* often **manacles 1.** Handcuffs. **2.** Something that restricts freedom or restrains. ❖ *tr.v.* **man·a·cled, man·a·cling, man·a·cles 1.** To put manacles on: *The police officer manacled the thief.* **2.** To restrain; hamper: *manacled by my tiny office.*

man·age (**măn′**ĭj) *v.* **man·aged, man·ag·ing, man·ag·es** —*tr.* **1.** To exert control over; be in charge of; direct: *manage a restaurant; manages a staff of 20.* **2.** To direct or control the use of; handle or operate: *manage a bulldozer.* **3.** To succeed in doing or accomplishing; contrive or arrange: *Despite the bitter cold, I managed to stay warm.* —*intr.* **1.** To direct or conduct business affairs: *The book offers advice to executives on how to manage effectively.* **2.** To carry on; get along: *I don't know how we managed without your help.* [From Italian *maneggiare,* from Latin *manus,* hand.]

man·age·a·ble (**măn′**ĭ-jə-bəl) *adj.* Capable of being managed or controlled: *a manageable problem.* —**man′age·a·bil′i·ty** *n.*

man·age·ment (**măn′**ĭj-mənt) *n.* **1.** The act, manner, or practice of managing: *hotel management.* **2.** The people who manage a business or organization: *I work for the management.*

man·ag·er (**măn′**ĭ-jər) *n.* **1.** A person who manages a business or another enterprise. **2.** A person who is in charge of the business affairs of an entertainer. **3.** A person who is in charge of the training and performance of an athlete or team.

man·a·ge·ri·al (măn′ĭ-**jîr′**ē-əl) *adj.* Relating to or characteristic of a manager or management: *managerial skills.*

Ma·na·gua (mə-**näg′**wə) The capital of Nicaragua, in the western part of the country on **Lake Managua.**

Ma·na·ma (mə-**năm′**ə) The capital of Bahrain, on the Persian Gulf. It became capital in 1971.

ma·nat (mä-**nät′**) *n.* The basic monetary unit of Azerbaijan and Turkmenistan. [From Azerbaijani and Turkmen, from Russian *moneta,* coin, from Latin *monēta,* coinage.]

man-at-arms (măn′ət-**ärmz′**) *n., pl.* **men-at-arms** (mĕn′ət-**ärmz′**) A soldier, especially a heavily armed mounted soldier in the Middle Ages.

man·a·tee (**măn′**ə-tē′) *n.* Any of various large plant-eating water mammals that have flippers shaped like paddles and are found in warm coastal waters of the Atlantic Ocean.

Man·ches·ter (**măn′**chĕs′tər *or* **măn′**chĭ-stər) **1.** A city of northwest England east-northeast of Liverpool. Founded on the site of Celtic and Roman settlements, it was first chartered in 1301. **2.** The largest city of New Hampshire, in the southeast part of the state south-southeast of Concord. In the 1800s, it was an important textile center.

Man·chu (**măn′**cho͞o *or* măn-**cho͞o′**) *n., pl.* **Manchu** or **Man·chus 1.** A member of a people native to Manchuria who ruled China from 1644 to 1912. **2.** The language of the Manchu. ❖ *adj.* Relating to the Manchu or their language or culture.

Man·chu·ri·a (măn-chŏŏr′ē-ə) A historical region of northeast China bordering on modern-day Russia, Inner Mongolia, and North Korea. It was the homeland of the Manchu people who conquered China in the 1600s. —**Man·chu′ri·an** *adj. & n.*

man·da·la (mŭn′də-lə) *n.* Any of various complex geometric designs used in Hinduism and Buddhism as aids to meditation.

Man·da·lay (măn′dl-ā′ *or* măn′dl-ā′) A city of central Myanmar (Burma) north of Yangon. It was the capital of the kingdom of Burma from 1860 to 1885.

Man·dan (măn′dăn′) *n., pl.* **Mandan** or **Man·dans 1.** A member of a Native American people living in North Dakota. **2.** The Siouan language of the Mandan.

man·da·rin (măn′də-rĭn) *n.* **1.** A high public official in the Chinese Empire. **2.** A high government official or a person having great influence. **3.** A mandarin orange.

Mandarin *n.* **1.** Any of a group of related dialects of Chinese spoken mainly in the north and west of China. **2.** The official language of China, based on the Mandarin dialect spoken in and around Beijing.

mandarin orange *n.* A small sweet orange having loose skin and segments that separate easily.

man·date (măn′dāt′) *n.* **1.** The support or approval of the voters, expressed in the results of an election of their representatives. **2.** An official and authoritative command, order, or instruction, especially one issued by a higher court to a lower court. **3a.** A commission from the League of Nations giving a member nation control over the government of a territory. **b.** A territory under such control. ❖ *tr.v.* **man·dat·ed, man·dat·ing, man·dates 1.** To put (a territory) under a mandate. **2.** To make mandatory; require: *The law mandates desegregation in all schools.* [From Latin *mandāre*, to order.]

man·da·to·ry (măn′də-tôr′ē) *adj.* Required; obligatory: *A college degree is mandatory for most teaching jobs.*

Man·de·la (măn-dĕl′ə), **Nelson Rolihlahla** 1918–2013. South African president (1994–1999) and political leader. —SEE NOTE.

man·di·ble (măn′də-bəl) *n.* **1.** The lower jaw of a vertebrate animal. **2.** The upper or lower part of a bird's beak. **3.** An organ in the mouth of many invertebrate animals used for seizing and biting food, especially either of a pair of such organs in an insect or other arthropod. [From Middle English, from Late Latin *mandibula*, from Latin *mandere*, to chew.]

man·do·lin (măn′də-lĭn′ *or* măn′dl-ĭn) *n.* A musical instrument having a pear-shaped body and a neck with frets over which pairs of strings are stretched and played with a pick.

man·drake (măn′drāk′) *n.* A low-growing European plant having a forked root thought to resemble the human body. The root was once believed to have magical powers and was used in medicines.

man·drill (măn′drəl) *n.* A large monkey of west-central Africa having an olive-brown body with a brightly colored rump and face that are especially pronounced in the male.

mane (mān) *n.* **1.** A growth of long hair on the neck of certain mammals, such as a horse or a male lion. **2.** A long thick growth of hair on a person's head. [From Old English *manu.*]

❑ *These sound alike:* **mane, main** (chief).

ma·neu·ver (mə-nōō′vər) *n.* **1.** A movement or combination of movements involving skill and dexterity: *a gymnastics maneuver.* **2.** A controlled change in movement or direction of a vehicle or vessel, especially an aircraft. **3a.** A planned movement of troops or warships: *By a series of brilliant maneuvers, the general outwitted the enemy.* **b.** often **manuevers** A large-scale military exercise in which battle movements are practiced. ❖ *v.* **ma·neu·vered, ma·neu·ver·ing, ma·neu·vers** —*intr.* **1.** To make controlled changes in movement or direction: *The ship had to maneuver very carefully to avoid the icebergs.* **2.** To change tactics or approach; plan skillfully: *Our lawyer maneuvered to get the trial postponed.* **3.** To carry out a military maneuver. —*tr.* **1.** To direct skillfully by changes in course or in position: *learned to maneuver a car on an icy road.* **2.** To manage or direct, especially by trickery: *She maneuvered her opponent into taking a stand that lost him the election.* **3.** To cause (troops or warships) to carry out a military maneuver. [From Medieval Latin *manuopera*, hand work.] —**ma·neu′ver·a·bil′i·ty** *n.* —**ma·neu′ver·a·ble** *adj.*

man·ful (măn′fəl) *adj.* Having or showing characteristics traditionally associated with masculinity, such as courage or reserve. —**man′ful·ly** *adv.*

man·ga (mäng′gə) *n.* A style of comic strip or comic book originally developed in Japan, characterized by stylized, colorful art.

man·ga·nese (măng′gə-nēz′) *n. Symbol* **Mn** A grayish, brittle metallic element found in several minerals and used to increase the hardness and strength of steel and other important alloys. Atomic number 25. See **Periodic Table.**

mange (mānj) *n.* A skin disease of dogs and other mammals, caused by mites and characterized by itching and loss of hair. [From Middle English *manjeue*, from Old French *mangier*, to eat.]

man·ger (mān′jər) *n.* A trough or open box in which feed for horses or cattle is placed.

man·gle[1] (măng′gəl) *tr.v.* **man·gled, man·gling, man·gles 1.** To disfigure by crushing, hacking, or tearing: *The accident completely mangled our car.* **2.** To ruin; spoil: *The orchestra completely mangled the music.* [From Middle English *manglen*, from Old French *mangoner*, to cut to bits.]

man·gle[2] (măng′gəl) *n.* A machine that presses fabrics by running them between heated rollers. ❖ *tr.v.* **man·gled, man·gling, man·gles** To smooth or press with a mangle: *mangle sheets.* [From Dutch *mangel.*]

man·go (măng′gō) *n., pl.* **man·goes** or **man·gos 1.** A tropical fruit having a smooth rind and sweet, juicy, yellow-orange flesh. **2.** The tree that bears such fruit.

man·grove (măn′grōv′ *or* măng′grōv′) *n.* Any of various tropical trees or shrubs that can live in salt water and often form dense thickets along seacoasts. Mangroves have roots that grow from the stem and provide support. [Probably Portuguese *mangue* (from Taíno) + *grove.*]

mang·y (mān′jē) *adj.* **mang·i·er, mang·i·est 1.** Having or appearing to have mange: *a mangy stray dog.* **2.** Having many bare spots; shabby: *a mangy old coat.*

man·han·dle (măn′hăn′dl) *tr.v.* **man·han·dled, man·han·dling, man·han·dles** To handle in a rough manner: *The porters manhandled the suitcases.*

Man·hat·tan (măn-hăt′n) A borough of New York City in southeast New York, mainly on **Manhattan Island,** at the mouth of the Hudson River between Long Island and northeast New Jersey. The Dutch bought the island in 1626 from an Algonquian Indian tribe.

man·hole (măn′hōl′) *n.* A hole in a street, with a removable cover, that allows a person to reach underground sewers, pipes, or other structures for repair or inspection.

man·hood (măn′hŏŏd′) *n.* **1.** The state of being an adult male person: *He has reached manhood.* **2.** The group of qualities, such as courage and strength, thought of as appropriate to a man. **3.** Men in general: *the manhood of the country.*

man-hour (măn′our′) *n.* A unit of labor equal to one person working for one hour, used to express industrial production and costs.

ma·ni·a (mā′nē-ə *or* mān′yə) *n.* **1.** An intense enthusiasm or desire: *He has a mania for horror movies.* **2.** A

BIOGRAPHY

Nelson Mandela Although born the son of a tribal chief and educated as a lawyer, Nelson **Mandela** lived as a second-class citizen in his own country, under a system of legalized discrimination against nonwhites called *apartheid*. Mandela dedicated himself to ending apartheid, but he was frustrated by the violent tactics the South African police used to suppress the antiapartheid movement's peaceful efforts. In 1961 Mandela founded a military group to counter the police, and in 1964 he was convicted of plotting to overthrow the government. Sentenced to life in prison, he soon became a widely recognized symbol of the injustice of apartheid. Under growing international pressure to change its policies, the South African government finally repealed many apartheid laws and freed Mandela in 1990. He immediately began efforts to establish a democratic, multiracial government, for which he shared a 1993 Nobel Peace Prize. In 1994, a new constitution was adopted, and Mandela was elected president in the first elections open to all South Africans.

Nelson Mandela
photographed in 2008

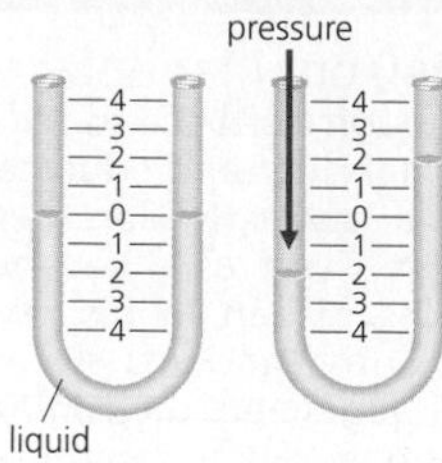

manometer

To calculate pressure in a U-tube manometer, add the sum of the readings above and below zero. The manometer on the left is at equilibrium. On the right the pressure is 4 (2 above zero and 2 below zero).

mantel

mantilla

ă	pat	ôr	core
ā	pay	oi	boy
âr	care	ou	out
ä	father	o͝o	took
ĕ	pet	o͝or	lure
ē	be	o͞o	boot
ĭ	pit	ŭ	cut
ī	bite	ûr	urge
îr	pier	th	thin
ŏ	pot	*th*	this
ō	toe	zh	vision
ô	paw	ə	about

manifestation of bipolar disorder in which a person becomes excessively active and has rapidly changing ideas. [From Middle English, madness, from Greek *maniā.*]

ma·ni·ac (mā**′**nē-ăk′) *n.* **1.** A mentally deranged person. **2.** A person who acts in a wildly irresponsible way: *Look at that maniac zooming through the red light!* **3.** A person who has extreme enthusiasm for something: *She's a soccer maniac.* **—ma′ni·ac′, ma·ni′a·cal** (mə-nī**′**ə-kəl) *adj.*

man·ic (măn**′**ĭk) *adj.* **1.** Full of or characterized by frenetic activity or wild excitement: *the manic pace of modern life in the city.* **2.** Relating to or affected by mania.

man·ic-de·pres·sive disorder (măn′ĭk-dĭ-**prĕs′**ĭv) *n.* Bipolar disorder.

man·i·cure (măn**′**ĭ-kyo͝or′) *n.* A cosmetic treatment for the fingernails, including shaping and polishing. ❖ *tr.v.* **man·i·cured, man·i·cur·ing, man·i·cures** To trim, clean, and polish (the fingernails). [From Latin *manus,* hand + Latin *cūra,* care.]

man·i·cur·ist (măn**′**ĭ-kyo͝or′ĭst) *n.* A person who gives manicures.

man·i·fest (măn**′**ə-fĕst′) *adj.* Clear and apparent; obvious: *It is strange that such a manifest hoax has fooled so many people.* ❖ *tr.v.* **man·i·fest·ed, man·i·fest·ing, man·i·fests** To reveal; show; display: *Her fidgeting manifested a desire to leave.* ❖ *n.* A list of cargo or passengers: *The ship's manifest was incomplete.* **—man′i·fest·ly** *adv.*

man·i·fes·ta·tion (măn′ə-fĕ-**stā′**shən) *n.* **1.** The act of showing, demonstrating, or proving: *a manifestation of bravery.* **2.** Something that reveals; a sign or indication: *Rust on the pipes was a manifestation of tiny leaks.*

Manifest Destiny *n.* The belief during the 1800s that the United States was both destined and morally obligated to expand throughout North America.

man·i·fes·to (măn′ə-**fĕs′**tō) *n., pl.* **man·i·fes·toes** or **man·i·fes·tos** A public declaration of principles and aims, especially of a political nature.

man·i·fold (măn**′**ə-fōld′) *adj.* **1.** Of many kinds; varied: *This work involves manifold tasks.* **2.** Having many parts, forms, or aspects: *A knowledge of many subjects demonstrates manifold intelligence.* ❖ *n.* A pipe or tube that has several openings for making multiple connections: *The exhaust manifold of an engine connects to each cylinder.*

ma·nil·a or **ma·nil·la** (mə-**nĭl′**ə) *n.* Manila paper. ❖ *adj.* Made of Manila paper.

Ma·nil·a (mə-**nĭl′**ə) The capital of the Philippines, on **Manila Bay,** an inlet of the South China Sea. It was founded in 1571.

Manila hemp *n.* The fiber obtained from the stalks of the abaca plant, used to make rope, fabric, and paper.

Manila paper *n.* A strong paper or thin cardboard with a smooth finish, usually brown or yellow in color, originally made from Manila hemp.

man·i·oc (măn**′**ē-ŏk′) *n.* Cassava.

ma·nip·u·late (mə-**nĭp′**yə-lāt′) *tr.v.* **ma·nip·u·lat·ed, ma·nip·u·lat·ing, ma·nip·u·lates 1.** To arrange, operate, or control by the hands or by mechanical means: *The pilot manipulated the airplane's controls.* **2.** To influence or manage in a clever or devious way: *He manipulated public opinion in his favor.* **—ma·nip′u·la′tive** *adj.* **—ma·nip′u·la′tor** *n.*

ma·nip·u·la·tion (mə-nĭp′yə-**lā′**shən) *n.* **1.** The act of manipulating. **2.** Clever or devious management: *the manipulation of public opinion through advertising.* [From French, from Spanish *manipulación,* from Latin *manipulus,* handful.]

Man·i·to·ba (măn′ĭ-**tō′**bə) A province of south-central Canada west of Ontario. It was admitted to the Canadian confederation in 1870. Winnipeg is the capital.

man·i·tou (măn**′**ĭ-to͞o′) *n., pl.* **man·i·tous** In Algonquian religious belief, a supernatural power that exists throughout the world and is possessed by both spirits and humans.

man·kind (măn**′**kīnd′) *n.* **1.** The human race; humankind. **2.** Men, as opposed to women, considered as a group.

man·ly (măn**′**lē) *adj.* **man·li·er, man·li·est 1.** Relating to or characteristic of men, especially when considered traditionally masculine: *manly courage.* **2.** Having well-developed or toned muscles: *a manly physique.* **—man′li·ness** *n.*

man·made or **man-made** (măn**′**mād**′**) *adj.* Made by humans rather than occurring in nature; synthetic: *man-made fibers; a manmade lake.*

man·na (măn**′**ə) *n.* **1.** In the Bible, the food miraculously provided for the Israelites in the wilderness after their flight from Egypt. **2.** Something of value that a person receives unexpectedly: *viewed the bonus as manna from heaven.*

manned (mănd) *adj.* Occupied, operated, or performed by a person: *manned spacecraft.*

man·ne·quin (măn**′**ĭ-kĭn) *n.* A life-size model of the human body, used mainly for fitting or displaying clothes. [From Middle Dutch *mannekijn,* figurine.]

man·ner (măn**′**ər) *n.* **1.** The way in which something is done or happens: *We always work in a careful manner.* See Synonyms at **method. 2.** A way of acting; behavior: *The new boss has a gruff manner.* **3. manners** Socially proper behavior; etiquette: *Did no one ever teach him manners?* **4.** Kind; sort: *We had all manner of incidents on our long trip.* ◆ **in a manner of speaking** In a way; so to speak. [From Middle English *manere,* from Old French *maniere,* from Latin *manus,* hand.]

❑ *These sound alike:* **manner, manor** (estate).

man·nered (măn**′**ərd) *adj.* **1.** Having manners of a specific kind: *ill-mannered people.* **2.** Artificial or affected: *quaint and mannered speech.*

man·ner·ism (măn**′**ə-rĭz′əm) *n.* A distinctive personal trait; a quirk: *She has a mannerism of scratching her chin when thinking.*

man·ner·ly (măn**′**ər-lē) *adj.* Having good manners; polite. ❖ *adv.* With good manners; politely.

man·nish (măn**′**ĭsh) *adj.* **1.** Relating to men; masculine. **2.** Resembling or suggestive of a man rather than a woman: *a mannish way of walking.* **—man′nish·ly** *adv.*

ma·no (mä**′**nō) *n., pl.* **ma·nos** A handheld stone or roller for grinding corn or other grains on a metate. [From Spanish, hand, mano, from Latin *manus,* hand.]

ma·noeu·vre (mə-**no͞o′**vər) *n. & v. Chiefly British* Variant of **maneuver.**

man-of-war (măn′ə-**wôr′**) *n., pl.* **men-of-war** (mĕn′ə-**wôr′**) A warship, especially a sailing ship.

ma·nom·e·ter (mă-**nŏm′**ĭ-tər) *n.* An instrument that measures the pressure of liquids and gases.

man·or (măn**′**ər) *n.* **1.** An estate including its lands. **2.** The main house on an estate. **3.** The estate of a feudal lord. [From Middle English *maner,* from Latin *manēre,* to remain.]

❑ *These sound alike:* **manor, manner** (way of acting).

ma·no·ri·al (mə-**nôr′**ē-əl) *adj.* Relating to or like a manor: *a manorial estate.*

man·pow·er (măn**′**pou′ər) *n.* **1.** The power supplied by human physical effort: *Lifting that piano requires a lot of manpower.* **2.** The people working or available for work, especially on a particular task: *Most of their manpower is now devoted to developing new products.*

man·sard roof (măn**′**särd′) *n.* A roof having two slopes on all four sides, with the lower slope much steeper than the upper. [After François *Mansart* (1598–1666), French architect.]

manse (măns) *n.* **1.** A house lived in by a Christian minister. **2.** A large stately residence; a mansion.

man·ser·vant (măn**′**sûr′vənt) *n., pl.* **men·ser·vants** (mĕn**′**sûr′vənts) A male servant.

man·sion (măn′shən) *n.* A large stately house. [From Middle English *mansioun*, from Latin *mānsiō*, a dwelling, from *manēre*, to dwell, remain.]

man·slaugh·ter (măn′slô′tər) *n.* The unlawful killing of a person without having murderous intent or under extenuating circumstances.

man·ta (măn′tə) *n.* A very large ray found in warm seas worldwide, having a long thin tail and two hornlike fins on the front of the head.

manta ray *n.* The manta.

man·tel also **man·tle** (măn′tl) *n.* **1.** An ornamental facing around a fireplace. **2.** A mantelpiece.

man·tel·piece (măn′tl-pēs′) *n.* The shelf over a fireplace.

man·til·la (măn-tē′yə *or* măn-tĭl′ə) *n.* A scarf, usually of lace, traditionally worn over the head and shoulders by women in Spain and Latin America.

man·tis (măn′tĭs) *n., pl.* **man·tis·es** or **man·tes** (măn′-tēz) Any of various large, mostly tropical insects having powerful front legs used for preying on other insects.

man·tis·sa (măn-tĭs′ə) *n.* The fractional part of a logarithm to the base ten. In the logarithm 2.749, the mantissa is .749.

man·tle (măn′tl) *n.* **1.** A loose sleeveless coat worn over outer garments; a cloak. **2.** Something that covers or conceals: *a soft mantle of snow.* **3.** The layer of the earth between the crust and the core. **4.** A sheath of threads that is used in gas lights and lanterns and gives a brilliant light when heated by a flame. **5.** The layer of soft tissue that covers the body of a mollusk, such as a clam or an oyster, and secretes the material that forms the shell. **6.** Variant of **mantel.** ❖ *tr.v.* **man·tled, man·tling, man·tles** To cover with or as if with a cloak: *Night mantled the earth.* [From Old English *mentel*, from Latin *mantellum.*]

man·tra (măn′trə) *n.* **1.** In Hinduism, a sacred word or phrase repeated when praying or meditating. **2.** A commonly repeated word or phrase: *The politician's mantra was "Better education for all."*

man·u·al (măn′yo͞o-əl) *adj.* **1.** Relating to the hands: *manual dexterity.* **2.** Used by or operated with the hands: *manual controls.* **3.** Employing human rather than mechanical energy: *manual labor.* ❖ *n.* A small book of instructions; a handbook. [From Middle English, from Latin *manuālis*, from *manus*, hand.] **—man′u·al·ly** *adv.*

manual alphabet *n.* An alphabet used for communication by hearing-impaired people in which finger positions represent letters.

man·u·fac·ture (măn′yə-făk′chər) *tr.v.* **man·u·fac·tured, man·u·fac·tur·ing, man·u·fac·tures 1.** To make or process (a product), especially with the use of machines: *a factory that manufactures cars.* **2.** To make or process (a raw material) into a finished product: *manufacture cotton to make fabric.* **3.** To make up; concoct: *manufactured a flimsy excuse.* ❖ *n.* The act or process of manufacturing products.

man·u·fac·tur·er (măn′yə-făk′chər-ər) *n.* A person or company that manufactures something, especially the owner or operator of a factory.

ma·nure (mə-no͝or′) *n.* Animal dung, especially the dung of cattle, used as fertilizer.

man·u·script (măn′yə-skrĭpt′) *n.* **1a.** A handwritten book, poem, or other document. **b.** A collection of such handwritten documents bound together. **2.** The form of a book, paper, or article as it is submitted for publication in print: *send a manuscript to a publisher.* **3.** Handwriting as opposed to printing.

Manx (măngks) *adj.* Relating to the Isle of Man or its people, language, or culture. ❖ *n., pl.* **Manx 1.** *(used with a plural verb)* The natives or inhabitants of the Isle of Man. **2.** The extinct Celtic language of the Isle of Man. **3.** A domestic cat of a tailless breed that originated on the Isle of Man.

man·y (mĕn′ē) *adj.* **more** (môr), **most** (mōst) **1.** Consisting of or amounting to a large number; numerous: *I had many friends at the party.* **2.** Being one of a large number: *Many a brave person has refused to go down these rapids.* ❖ *n. (used with a plural verb)* **1.** The majority of the people: *the will of the many.* **2.** A large number of people or things: *A good many of us were at the party.* ❖ *pron. (used with a plural verb)* A large number of people or things: *Many were invited but few came.* ◆ **as many** The same number of: *moved three times in as many years.*

man·y-sid·ed (mĕn′ē-sī′dĭd) *adj.* **1.** Having many sides: *a many-sided polygon.* **2.** Having many aspects, talents, or interests.

Mao·ism (mou′ĭz′əm) *n.* The beliefs and practices of Mao Zedong. **—Mao′ist** *adj. & n.*

Mao·ri (mou′rē) *n., pl.* **Maori** or **Mao·ris 1.** A member of a Polynesian people of New Zealand. **2.** The language of the Maori. ❖ *adj.* Relating to the Maori or their language or culture.

Mao Ze·dong (mou′ dzə′dŏng′) also **Mao Tse-tung** (mou′ tsŭ′to͝ong′) 1893–1976. Chinese Communist leader who helped found the Chinese Communist Party (1921) and served as party chairman (1943–1976) and the first head of state of the People's Republic of China (1949–1959). His regime was marked by disastrous reforms and political repression that resulted in the deaths of millions of Chinese people.

map (măp) *n.* **1.** A drawing or chart of a region of the earth, often showing political divisions such as countries and physical features such as mountains and rivers. **2.** A drawing or chart of the moon, a planet, the stars, or other features of the sky. **3.** A visual display of the arrangement of genes on a chromosome: *a genetic map of a fruit fly.* **4.** A visual representation of the arrangement of the parts of something complex, such as the pages on a website. ❖ *tr.v.* **mapped, map·ping, maps 1.** To make a map of; represent on a map. **2.** To plan in detail: *Let's map out our schedule.* **3.** To locate (a gene) on a chromosome in relation to other known genes. ◆ **put on the map** To make well-known or famous: *The new racetrack put the rural town on the map.* [From Latin *mappa*, napkin, cloth (on which maps were drawn).]

ma·ple (mā′pəl) *n.* **1.** Any of various trees or shrubs having broad leaves with deep notches and paired, winged seeds. **2.** The hard wood of a maple, often used in making furniture. **3.** The flavor of the concentrated sap of the sugar maple. [From Old English *mapul.*]

maple sugar *n.* A sugar made by boiling down maple syrup.

maple syrup *n.* **1.** A sweet syrup made from the sap of the sugar maple. **2.** Syrup made from various sugars and flavored with maple syrup or artificial maple flavoring.

map·mak·er (măp′mā′kər) *n.* A person who makes maps; a cartographer.

Ma·pu·to (mə-po͞o′tō) The capital of Mozambique, in the extreme southern part of the country on the Indian Ocean. It was founded in the late 1700s.

mar (mär) *tr.v.* **marred, mar·ring, mars 1.** To deface or damage: *marred the top of the table with a knife.* **2.** To spoil; ruin: *Rain marred their day at the beach.*

mar·a·bou (măr′ə-bo͞o′) *n.* A large African stork that scavenges for carrion and has a naked head and neck, black wings, and soft white down on the underside.

ma·ra·ca (mə-rä′kə) *n.* A Latin-American percussion instrument consisting of a hollow gourd rattle containing pebbles or dried beans. Maracas are often played in pairs.

Ma·ra·cai·bo (măr′ə-kī′bō *or* mä′rä-kī′vō) A city of northwest Venezuela at the outlet of **Lake Maracaibo,** the largest lake of South America. It was founded in 1571.

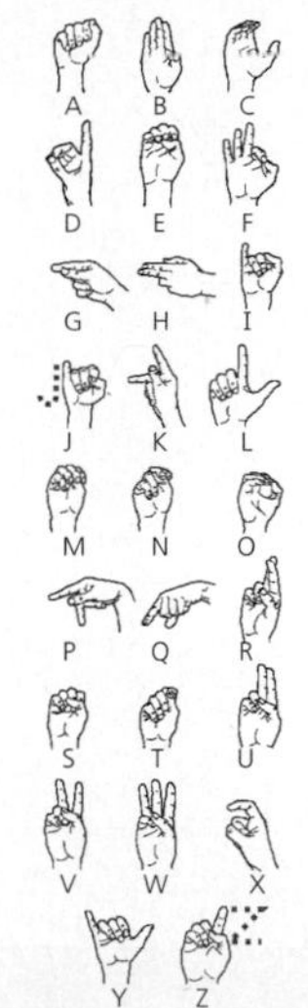

manual alphabet

Mao Zedong

maple
sugar maple

maraca

mar·a·schi·no cherry (măr′ə-**skē′**nō *or* măr′ə-**shē′**nō) *n.* A cherry preserved in a sweet red syrup, used especially in desserts and cocktails.

Ma·ra·thi (mə-**rä′**tē) *n.* The principal Indic language of west-central India.

mar·a·thon (**măr′**ə-thŏn′) *n.* **1.** A cross-country footrace of 26 miles, 385 yards (42.195 kilometers). **2.** A long-distance race other than a footrace: *a swimming marathon.* **3.** A contest of endurance: *a dance marathon.*

Mar·a·thon (**măr′**ə-thŏn′) A village and plain of ancient Greece northeast of Athens. It was the site of a major victory over the Persians in 490 BC.

ma·raud (mə-**rôd′**) *v.* **ma·raud·ed, ma·raud·ing, ma·rauds** —*intr.* To roam and raid in search of plunder. —*tr.* To raid or pillage for plunder. **—ma·raud′er** *n.*

mar·ble (**mär′**bəl) *n.* **1.** A hard rock made from the action of heat and pressure on limestone or dolomite. Some kinds of marble have irregularly colored marks due to impurities. Marble can be polished to a smooth luster and is used in buildings and statues. **2a.** A little ball made of a hard substance such as glass. **b. marbles** *(used with a singular verb)* A children's game played with such balls. ❖ *tr.v.* **mar·bled, mar·bling, mar·bles** To color and streak (paper, for example) in imitation of marble. ❖ *adj.* Made of or resembling marble: *a marble floor.* [From Middle English, from Greek *marmaros.*]

mare[2]
several maria on the moon's surface

march[1] (märch) *v.* **marched, march·ing, march·es** —*intr.* **1.** To walk steadily and rhythmically forward in step with others: *The band marched down the street during the parade.* **2.** To walk in a purposeful or determined manner; stride: *I marched up to the podium and read my speech.* **3.** To advance with a steady movement: *Time marches on.* **4.** To participate in an organized walk, as for a public cause. —*tr.* To cause to march: *The duck marched its ducklings to the edge of the lake.* ❖ *n.* **1.** The act of marching: *the army's rapid march to the fort.* **2.** A long tiring journey by foot: *a march of ten miles.* **3.** The distance covered by marching: *We were still a march of six hours from camp.* **4.** Forward movement; progress: *the dramatic march of modern science.* **5.** A musical composition in regularly accented meter that is appropriate to accompany marching. **6.** An organized walk or procession by a group of people for a specific cause or issue. [From Middle English *marchen*, from Old French *marchier*, of Germanic origin.]

Maria Theresa

march[2] (märch) *n.* A border region; a frontier. [From Middle English, from Old French *marche*, of Germanic origin.]

March *n.* The third month of the year in the Gregorian calendar, having 31 days. [From Middle English, from Latin *Mārtius (mēnsis)*, (month) of Mars.]

mar·chio·ness (**mär′**shə-nĭs *or* mär′shə-**nĕs′**) *n.* **1.** The wife or widow of a marquis. **2.** A noblewoman ranking above a countess and below a duchess.

Mar·co·ni (mär-**kō′**nē), **Guglielmo** 1874–1937. Italian physicist and inventor. In 1901 he used radio waves to transmit signals in Morse code across the Atlantic Ocean.

Mar·di Gras (**mär′**dē **grä′**) *n.* The day before Ash Wednesday, celebrated as a holiday in many places with carnivals and parades. [From French, fat Tuesday (from the feasting on Mardi Gras before fasting during Lent).]

mare[1] (mâr) *n.* An adult female horse, zebra, donkey, or other related animal. [From Middle English *mere.*]

ma·re[2] (**mä′**rā) *n., pl.* **ma·ri·a** (**mä′**rē-ə) Any of the large dark areas on the moon, Mars, or other planets. [From Latin, sea.]

Mar·gar·et of An·jou (**mär′**gə-rət *or* **mär′**grət əv ăn-**jo͞o′**) 1430?–1482. French-born queen consort of Henry VI of England (1421–1471). She wielded military and political power on behalf of her mentally ill husband for 16 years until her forces were defeated at the Battle of Tewkesbury (1471).

mar·ga·rine (**mär′**jər-ĭn) *n.* A substitute for butter made from vegetable oils and other ingredients.

mar·gin (**mär′**jĭn) *n.* **1.** An edge or border: *the margins of the forest.* See Synonyms at **border. 2.** The blank space that surrounds the written or printed area on a page. **3.** An extra amount allowed beyond what is needed: *You should allow a ten-minute margin for delays in getting to school.* **4.** A measure, quantity, or degree of difference: *We won the election by a large margin.* **5.** The difference between the cost and the selling price of something: *wanted to improve the product's margin of profitability.* [From Middle English, from Latin *margō.*]

mar·gin·al (**mär′**jə-nəl) *adj.* **1.** Written or printed in the margin: *There were marginal notes through the whole book.* **2.** Relating to, in, or on the border or edge: *the northern states marginal to Canada.* **3.** Barely acceptable: *marginal writing ability.* **4.** Making a very small profit: *a marginal business.* **—mar′gin·al·ly** *adv.*

mar·gin·al·ize (**mär′**jə-nə-līz′) *tr.v.* **mar·gin·al·ized, mar·gin·al·iz·ing, mar·gin·al·iz·es** To confine to a lower or outer limit, as in society: *policies that marginalized homeless people.*

ma·ri·a (**mä′**rē-ə) *n.* Plural of **mare[2]**.

Mar·i·an·a Islands (mâr′ē-**ăn′**ə) An island group in the western Pacific Ocean east of the Philippines. Guam, the largest island of the group, is independent of the others, which are known formally as the **Commonwealth of the Northern Mariana Islands.**

Mariana Trench A depression in the floor of the western Pacific Ocean south and east of Guam. It has a maximum depth of 35,760 feet (10,900 meters).

Ma·ri·a The·re·sa (mə-**rē′**ə tə-**rā′**sə) 1717–1780. Holy Roman empress (1745–1780), archduchess of Austria, and queen of Hungary and Bohemia (1740–1780) whose reign was marked by the War of the Austrian Succession (1740–1748) and the Seven Years' War (1756–1763).

Ma·rie An·toi·nette (mə-**rē′** ăn′twə-**nĕt′**) 1755–1793. Queen of France (1774–1793) as the wife of Louis XVI. She was convicted of treason and executed during the French Revolution.

mar·i·gold (**mâr′**ĭ-gōld′) *n.* Any of various plants of the Americas that have showy orange, yellow, or reddish flowers and are often planted in gardens.

mar·i·jua·na (măr′ə-**wä′**nə) *n.* **1.** The dried leaves or flowers of the hemp plant, which contain an illegal intoxicating drug. Certain states allow the medical use of marijuana for the treatment of nausea, loss of appetite, and other symptoms of diseases such as cancer and AIDS. **2.** The hemp plant.

ma·rim·ba (mə-**rĭm′**bə) *n.* A musical instrument somewhat like a large xylophone, having tuned wooden bars that are struck with wooden mallets.

ma·ri·na (mə-**rē′**nə) *n.* A boat basin that has docks, moorings, supplies, and repair facilities for small boats.

mar·i·nade (măr′ə-**nād′**) *n.* A mixture of oil, vinegar or wine, and spices, used for soaking meat, poultry, fish, or vegetables before cooking. ❖ *tr.v.* (**măr′**ə-nād′) **mar·i·nad·ed, mar·i·nad·ing, mar·i·nades** To marinate.

mar·i·nate (**măr′**ə-nāt′) *tr.v.* **mar·i·nat·ed, mar·i·nat·ing, mar·i·nates** To soak (meat or fish, for example) in a marinade.

ma·rine (mə-**rēn′**) *adj.* **1.** Relating to the sea: *marine biology.* **2.** Living or found in the sea: *marine life.* **3.** Relating to shipping or navigation: *a marine chart.* ❖ *n.* **1.** A soldier serving on a ship or at a naval base. **2. Marine** A member of the US Marine Corps. [From Middle English, from Latin *marīnus*, from *mare*, sea.]

Marine Corps *n.* A branch of the US armed forces whose troops are specially trained for amphibious landings and combat.

mar·i·ner (**măr′**ə-nər) *n.* A person who navigates or helps to navigate a ship.

ă	pat	ôr	core
ā	pay	oi	boy
âr	care	ou	out
ä	father	o͝o	took
ĕ	pet	o͝or	lure
ē	be	o͞o	boot
ĭ	pit	ŭ	cut
ī	bite	ûr	urge
îr	pier	th	thin
ŏ	pot	*th*	this
ō	toe	zh	vision
ô	paw	ə	about

mar·i·o·nette (măr′ē-ə-**nĕt′**) *n.* A puppet controlled from above by strings or wires attached to its limbs.

mar·i·tal (**măr′**ĭ-tl) *adj.* Relating to marriage: *marital vows.* —**mar′i·tal·ly** *adv.*

mar·i·time (**măr′**ĭ-tīm′) *adj.* **1.** Located on or near the sea: *a maritime fishing village.* **2.** Relating to shipping or navigation: *maritime law.*

Maritime Provinces The Canadian provinces of Nova Scotia, New Brunswick, and Prince Edward Island, bordering on the Atlantic Ocean.

mar·jo·ram (**mär′**jər-əm) *n.* A perennial plant related to mint, having aromatic leaves that are used as a seasoning.

mark[1] (märk) *n.* **1.** A visible trace or impression, such as a line or spot, left on a surface. **2.** A written or printed symbol used for punctuation. **3.** An indication of some quality or condition: *Taking responsibility for your own mistakes is a mark of maturity.* **4.** A lasting impression: *The Crusades left their mark on Western civilization.* **5.** Something that is aimed at; a target: *The arrow found its mark.* **6.** A label, seal, or inscription placed on an article: *The manufacturer's mark can be found on every product.* **7.** A recognized standard of quality: *Your latest work is not up to the mark.* **8.** A letter or number used to indicate the quality of a person's work: *excellent marks in arithmetic.* **9a.** The place from which racers begin and sometimes end their contest. **b.** A point reached or gained in a race: *The swimmers just passed the halfway mark.* ❖ *v.* **marked, mark·ing, marks** —*tr.* **1.** To make a mark on: *Someone had marked the important pages of the book.* **2.** To form, make, or write by a mark: *marked a square on the sidewalk.* **3.** To give evidence of; reveal: *The cool winds mark the beginning of fall.* **4.** To be a feature of; distinguish; characterize: *Her painting is marked by an unusual use of color.* **5.** To give attention to; notice: *Mark my words: they are asking for trouble.* **6.** To take note of in writing; write down: *marked the appointment on my calendar.* **7.** To determine the quality of (something) according to a grade or mark: *The teacher is marking the tests now.* **8.** To guard (an opponent), as in soccer. —*intr.* **1.** To make a visible impression: *The pen marks under water.* **2.** To give grades for school work: *I've never had a teacher that marks easily.* ◆ **mark down** To mark for sale at a lower price. **mark time 1.** To indicate or signal the rhythm or pace of a piece of music. **2.** To move the feet in a marching step without advancing. **3.** To suspend progress for the time being; wait: *The work crew marked time while the architects changed the plans.* **4.** To perform the actions of a job or task without really accomplishing anything. **mark up 1.** To cover with marks. **2.** To mark for sale at a higher price. [From Old English *mearc.*]

mark[2] (märk) *n.* A deutsche mark. [From German.]

Mark (märk) *n.* The second Gospel of the New Testament, traditionally thought to have been written by Saint Mark.

Mark, Saint. Author of the second Gospel of the New Testament and disciple of Saint Peter.

mar·ka (**mär′**kä) *n.* The basic monetary unit of Bosnia and Herzegovina.

Mark An·to·ny (**ăn′**tə-nē) or **Mark An·tho·ny** (**ăn′**thə-nē) 83?–30 BC. Roman orator, politician, and soldier. He allied himself with Cleopatra against Octavian but was defeated in 31.

mark·down (**märk′**doun′) *n.* **1.** A reduction in price. **2.** The amount by which a price is reduced.

marked (märkt) *adj.* **1.** Having a mark or marks: *Pedestrians use the marked crosswalk.* **2.** Clearly defined and evident; noticeable: *a marked difference in price.* **3.** Singled out or distinguished, as for a dire fate: *a marked man.*

mark·ed·ly (**mär′**kĭd-lē) *adv.* In a manner that is noticeable and obvious: *When one works hard, grades should improve markedly.*

mark·er (**mär′**kər) *n.* **1.** An implement, especially a pen with a felt tip, used for marking or writing: *We used markers to make posters for the science fair.* **2.** Something that marks a place, as a bookmark or tombstone. **3.** A person who marks, especially a person who gives academic grades.

mar·ket (**mär′**kĭt) *n.* **1a.** A public gathering for buying and selling goods: *The farmer took cheese to market.* **b.** A place where goods are offered for sale: *We walked by the market before going home.* **2.** A store that sells a particular type of merchandise: *a fish market.* **3.** A system of exchange in which prices are determined by people competing to buy and sell things: *She works in the bond market.* **4.** The business of buying and selling a particular product: *the international coffee market.* **5a.** A region or country where goods may be sold: *We produce computers for foreign markets.* **b.** A particular type or group of buyers: *The college market includes people 16 to 22 years old.* **6.** A desire to buy; demand: *There is always a market for our bicycles.* ❖ *tr.v.* **mar·ket·ed, mar·ket·ing, mar·kets 1.** To sell or offer for sale: *The co-op marketed vegetables from local farmers.* **2.** To try to make (a product or service) appealing to particular groups of consumers; promote by marketing. ◆ **in the market** Interested in buying: *We are in the market for a new car.* **on the market 1.** Available for buying: *There are several good brands of skis on the market.* **2.** Up for sale: *He put the family business on the market.* [From Middle English, from Latin *mercātus,* from *mercārī,* to buy.] —**mar′ket·er** *n.*

mar·ket·a·ble (**mär′**kĭ-tə-bəl) *adj.* **1.** Fit for sale, as in a market: *marketable produce.* **2.** In demand by buyers or employers: *marketable goods; marketable skills.* —**mar′ket·a·bil′i·ty** *n.*

mar·ket·ing (**mär′**kĭ-tĭng) *n.* The business activity of identifying particular groups of consumers and making a product or service appealing to them, usually including advertising, branding, and pricing.

mar·ket·place (**mär′**kĭt-plās′) *n.* **1.** A public square or other place in which a market is set up. **2.** The general process of buying and selling; business activities.

mark·ing (**mär′**kĭng) *n.* **1.** A mark or marks: *markings left along the trail.* **2.** A mark or pattern of marks on an organism: *a snake with dark markings on the head.*

marks·man (**märks′**mən) *n.* A man skilled at shooting at a target.

marks·man·ship (**märks′**mən-shĭp′) *n.* Skill at shooting a gun or another weapon.

marks·wom·an (**märks′**wo͝om′ən) *n.* A woman skilled at shooting at a target.

mark·up (**märk′**ŭp′) *n.* **1.** An increase in the price of an item for sale. **2.** An amount added to the cost of an item to figure its selling price. **3.** The collection of tags that describe the format of an electronic document.

markup language *n.* A coding system, such as HTML, used to structure and link electronic text files.

marl (märl) *n.* A kind of rock or a loose soil mixture that contains clay, carbonate of lime, and shells, used as fertilizer.

mar·lin (**mär′**lĭn) *n.* Any of several large ocean fishes that have a long spearlike upper jaw and are often caught for sport.

❑ *These sound alike:* **marlin, marline** (rope).

mar·line (**mär′**lĭn) *n.* A light rope made of two loosely twisted strands, used to finish off the ends of larger ropes to keep them from unraveling.

❑ *These sound alike:* **marline, marlin** (fish).

mar·line·spike (**mär′**lĭn-spīk′) *n.* A pointed metal tool used to separate strands of rope or wire in splicing.

mar·ma·lade (**mär′**mə-lād′) *n.* A jam made by boiling the pulp and rind of fruits.

Mar·ma·ra (**mär′**mər-ə), **Sea of** A sea of northwest

marigold

marquee

Mars

Thurgood Marshall

ă	pat	ôr	core
ā	pay	oi	boy
âr	care	ou	out
ä	father	ŏŏ	took
ĕ	pet	ŏŏr	lure
ē	be	ōō	boot
ĭ	pit	ŭ	cut
ī	bite	ûr	urge
îr	pier	th	thin
ŏ	pot	*th*	this
ō	toe	zh	vision
ô	paw	ə	about

Turkey. It is connected to the Black Sea through the Bosporus and to the Aegean Sea through the Dardanelles.

mar·mo·set (mär′mə-sĕt′ *or* mär′mə-zĕt′) *n.* Any of various very small Central and South American monkeys that have a long tail and feed on sap and gum from trees.

mar·mot (mär′mət) *n.* Any of various burrowing rodents having short legs, short ears, and a bushy tail, such as the woodchuck.

Marne (märn) A river of northeast France, about 325 miles (525 kilometers) long, flowing generally northwest to the Seine River near Paris.

ma·roon[1] (mə-ro͞on′) *tr.v.* **ma·rooned, ma·roon·ing, ma·roons 1.** To put (a person) ashore on a deserted island. **2.** To leave alone and helpless: *I was marooned with a cold while everyone else went skating.* [From Spanish *cimarrón*, wild, runaway.]

ma·roon[2] (mə-ro͞on′) *n.* A dark reddish brown to dark purplish red. [From Italian *marrone.*]

mar·quee (mär-kē′) *n.* A structure that projects over the entrance to a building, such as a theater or hotel, and often bears a signboard.

mar·quess also **mar·quis** (mär′kwĭs) *n.* A British nobleman ranking below a duke and above an earl or count.

Mar·quette (mär-kĕt′), Père **Jacques** 1637–1675. French missionary who in 1673 accompanied Louis Jolliet on an extensive exploration of several American rivers, including the Mississippi River.

mar·quis (mär-kē′) *n., pl.* **mar·quis** (mär-kēz′) **1.** A nobleman ranking below a duke and above an earl or count, especially used outside of Great Britain. **2.** (mär′kwĭs) *pl.* **mar·quis·es** (mär′kwĭ-sĭz) Variant of **marquess.**

mar·quise (mär-kēz′) *n.* A marchioness.

mar·riage (măr′ĭj) *n.* **1.** A relationship between two adults who have exchanged vows of love or commitment and are legally recognized as a family unit. **2.** The state or relationship of two adults who are married: *Theirs is a very happy marriage.* **3.** A close union: *Poetry is a marriage of beautiful sound and intense meaning.*

mar·riage·a·ble (măr′ĭ-jə-bəl) *adj.* Suitable for marriage.

mar·ried (măr′ēd) *adj.* **1.** Having a spouse: *a married woman; a married man.* **2.** Joined by marriage: *a married couple.* **3.** Relating to marriage: *married life.*

mar·row (măr′ō) *n.* **1.** Bone marrow. **2.** The essential, innermost, or most important part; the pith: *the marrow of an argument.*

mar·ry[1] (măr′ē) *v.* **mar·ried, mar·ry·ing, mar·ries** —*tr.* **1.** To join in marriage: *They have been married for 25 years.* **2.** To take as a spouse: *She married him two years ago.* **3.** To perform a marriage ceremony for: *The rabbi married the couple.* **4.** To give in marriage. —*intr.* To enter into marriage; wed: *They married in June.* [From Middle English *marien*, from Latin *marītāre*, from *marītus*, married.]

mar·ry[2] (măr′ē) *interj. Archaic* An expression used to show surprise or emphasis. [From Middle English *Marie*, the Virgin Mary, ultimately from Greek *Maria.*]

Mars (märz) *n.* **1.** In Roman mythology, the god of war, identified with the Greek Ares. **2.** The fourth planet from the sun, with a diameter about half that of Earth. Mars has seasons similar to but much longer than Earth's. See table at **solar system.**

Mar·seille also **Mar·seilles** (mär-sā′) A city of southeast France on an arm of the Mediterranean Sea east of the Rhone River. The oldest city of France, it was founded by Greeks in about 600 BC.

marsh (märsh) *n.* An area of low-lying wet land that usually has few trees and other woody plants growing in it.

mar·shal (mär′shəl) *n.* **1a.** In some countries, a military officer of the highest rank. **b.** A field marshal. **2.** In the United States: **a.** A federal or city officer who carries out court orders and performs duties similar to those of a sheriff. **b.** The head of a police or fire department. **3.** A person in charge of a ceremony or parade. ❖ *tr.v.* **mar·shaled, mar·shal·ing, mar·shals** also **mar·shalled, marshal·ling, mar·shals** To place in proper or methodical order; organize: *The research team marshaled facts to defend its theory.* [From Middle English, from Old French *mareschal*, of Germanic origin.]

❑ *These sound alike:* **marshal, martial** (of war).

Mar·shall (mär′shəl), **John** 1755–1835. American politician who served as the chief justice of the US Supreme Court (1801–1835). He helped establish the concept that the courts could declare laws unconstitutional and thus invalid.

Mar·shall, Thurgood 1908–1993. American jurist who served as an associate justice of the US Supreme Court (1967–1991), becoming the court's first African American justice. As a lawyer for the NAACP Marshall argued *Brown v. Board of Education of Topeka, Kansas* (1954) before the Supreme Court. The court's decision brought about the end of legal segregation in public schools.

Marshall Islands An island country in the central Pacific Ocean southwest of Hawaii. Majuro is the capital.

marsh gas *n.* Methane that occurs naturally in swamps.

marsh·land (märsh′lănd′) *n.* A marshy tract of land.

marsh·mal·low (märsh′mĕl′ō *or* märsh′măl′ō) *n.* **1.** A soft, usually white candy with a spongy texture. **2.** also **marsh mallow** A plant found in marshes of Europe and North America, having pink flowers and a spongy root formerly used in making marshmallow candies.

marsh marigold *n.* Any of several plants that grow in wet places and have bright-yellow flowers resembling those of the buttercup.

marsh·y (mär′shē) *adj.* **marsh·i·er, marsh·i·est** Relating to or resembling a marsh. **—marsh′i·ness** *n.*

mar·su·pi·al (mär-so͞o′pē-əl) *n.* Any of various mammals whose young continue to develop after birth in a pouch on the outside of the female's body. Kangaroos, opossums, and wombats are marsupials. ❖ *adj.* Relating to or being a marsupial. [From Greek *marsippion*, pouch.]

mart (märt) *n.* A trading center, market, or store: *a fruit and vegetable mart.*

mar·ten (mär′tn) *n., pl.* **marten** or **mar·tens 1.** Any of several mammals related to the weasel and the mink, having thick soft brown fur. **2.** The fur of such a mammal.

❑ *These sound alike:* **marten, martin** (bird).

Mar·tha's Vineyard (mär′thəz) An island of southeast Massachusetts off the southwest coast of Cape Cod. It was a whaling and fishing center in the 1700s and early 1800s.

mar·tial (mär′shəl) *adj.* **1.** Relating to or suitable for war: *martial music.* **2.** Relating to the armed forces or the military profession: *martial training.* [From Middle English *marcial*, from Latin *Mārtiālis*, from *Mārs*, Mars.]

❑ *These sound alike:* **martial, marshal** (military officer).

martial art *n.* Any of several Asian arts of combat or self-defense, including karate and judo, that are usually practiced as a sport.

martial law *n.* Temporary military rule of a civilian population, as in an emergency or during a war.

Mar·tian (mär′shən) *adj.* Relating to the planet Mars. ❖ *n.* A being that supposedly lives on the planet Mars.

mar·tin (mär′tn) *n.* Any of several swallows, especially one that has glossy blue-black feathers and a forked tail.

❑ *These sound alike:* **martin, marten** (weasel).

Mar·tin (mär′tn), **Paul, Jr.** Born 1938. Canadian businessman and politician who served as prime minister of Canada (2003–2006).

mar·ti·net (mär′tn-ĕt′) *n.* A person who believes in and demands strict obedience to rules. [After Jean *Martinet* (died 1672), French army officer.]

mar·ti·ni (mär-tē′nē) *n., pl.* **mar·ti·nis** A cocktail made of gin or vodka and dry vermouth.

Mar·ti·nique (mär′tn-ēk′) An island and French territory in the Windward Islands of the West Indies. Fort-de-France is the capital.

Martin Luther King Day *n.* The third Monday in January, observed in the United States in honor of the birthday of Martin Luther King, Jr.

mar·tyr (mär′tər) *n.* **1.** A person who chooses to suffer death or torture rather than give up religious principles. **2.** A person who suffers much or makes great sacrifices to further a belief, cause, or principle. **3.** A person who endures great suffering. ❖ *tr.v.* **mar·tyred, mar·tyr·ing, mar·tyrs 1.** To make a martyr of. **2.** To cause to suffer; torture or torment.

mar·tyr·dom (mär′tər-dəm) *n.* **1.** The condition of being a martyr. **2.** The suffering of death by a martyr. **3.** Extreme suffering.

mar·vel (mär′vəl) *n.* A person or thing that causes surprise, astonishment, or wonder: *Radio was once considered a marvel of technology.* See Synonyms at **wonder.** ❖ *intr.v.* **mar·veled, mar·vel·ing, mar·vels** also **mar·velled, mar·vel·ling, mar·vels** To be filled with surprise, astonishment, or wonder: *We marveled at the gymnast's strength and grace.* [From Middle English *merveille*, from Latin *mīrābilis*, wonderful.]

mar·vel·ous also **mar·vel·lous** (mär′və-ləs) *adj.* **1.** Causing wonder or astonishment: *a marvelous cure for the disease.* **2.** Excellent; notably superior: *a marvelous collection of rare books.* **—mar′vel·ous·ly** *adv.*

Marx (märks) Family of American comedians, including the brothers **Leonard** (1887–1961), known as "Chico"; **Arthur** (1888–1964), known as "Harpo"; **Julius** (1890–1977), known as "Groucho"; **Milton** (1892–1977), known as "Gummo"; and **Herbert** (1901–1979), known as "Zeppo." Some of their many popular Broadway shows were made into movies, including *Horse Feathers* (1932) and *Duck Soup* (1933).

Marx, Karl 1818–1883. German philosopher and revolutionary. He collaborated with Friedrich Engels on *The Communist Manifesto* (1848) and also wrote *Das Kapital* (1867–1894). His works form the foundation for many communist regimes.

Marx·ism (märk′sĭz′əm) *n.* The political, economic, and social theories of Karl Marx, which claim that struggle between the classes plays a central role in the development of societies, and which predict that all societies will eventually develop from capitalism through socialism to communism.

Marx·ist (märk′sĭst) *n.* A person who follows or believes in Marxism. ❖ *adj.* Relating to Karl Marx or Marxism.

Mar·y (mâr′ē) Flourished about first century AD. In the New Testament, the mother of Jesus. According to Christian doctrine, she conceived while still a virgin, through the action of the Holy Spirit.

Mar·y·land (mĕr′ə-lənd) A state of the eastern United States south of Pennsylvania. It was admitted as one of the original Thirteen Colonies in 1788. Annapolis is the capital and Baltimore the largest city. —SEE NOTE.

Mary Mag·da·lene (măg′də-lən *or* măg′də-lēn′) In the New Testament, a repentant woman who washed the feet of Jesus.

Mary Queen of Scots also **Mary Stu·art** (sto͞o′ərt) 1542–1587. Queen of Scotland (1542–1567). The Catholic monarch during the Scottish Reformation, she was imprisoned by Elizabeth I and executed for sedition.

mar·zi·pan (mär′zə-păn′) *n.* A very sweet confection flavored with ground almonds. It is molded into decorative shapes and often colored to look like fruit.

ma·sa (mä′sə) *n.* Dough made of dried corn that has been soaked in limewater, then rinsed and ground. Masa is used to make tortillas and tamales.

ma·sa·la (mä-sä′lä) *n.* Any of various mixtures of spices that are used in South Asian cuisine.

masc. *abbr.* An abbreviation of masculine.

mas·car·a (mă-skăr′ə) *n.* A cosmetic used to darken the eyelashes.

mas·cot (măs′kŏt′ *or* măs′kət) *n.* An animal, person, or object believed to bring good luck or used as the symbol of a sports team or other organization.

mas·cu·line (măs′kyə-lĭn) *adj.* **1.** Relating to men or boys. **2.** Marked by or possessing qualities traditionally attributed to a man: *a masculine hair style.* **3.** In grammar, relating to or belonging to the gender of nouns that refer to males or to things classified as male: *In French the word for "boat" is masculine.*

mas·cu·lin·i·ty (măs′kyə-lĭn′ĭ-tē) *n.* The quality or condition of being masculine.

ma·ser (mā′zər) *n.* **1.** Any of several devices that amplify or generate microwaves. Masers are similar to lasers but emit microwaves instead of light. **2.** A natural object or region of space that acts like a maser, as a region where stars are formed.

Mas·er·u (măz′ə-ro͞o′ *or* mä′sə-**ro͞o′**) The capital of Lesotho, in the western part. It was founded in 1869.

mash (măsh) *n.* **1.** A mixture of crushed grain and water that ferments and is used in making beer, ale, and whiskey. **2.** A mixture of crushed grain and water fed to livestock and fowl. **3.** A soft pulpy mixture. ❖ *tr.v.* **mashed, mash·ing, mash·es 1.** To convert (grain) into mash. **2.** To convert into a soft pulpy mixture: *mash potatoes.* **3.** To crush; smash: *I mashed the walnut with a hammer.* ◆ **mash up** To combine (two or more audio or video recordings) to produce a composite recording. **—mash′er** *n.*

mashed potatoes (măsht) *pl.n.* Potatoes that are boiled and mashed, often with milk and butter.

mask (măsk) *n.* **1.** A covering, often having openings for the eyes, worn over part or all of the face as a disguise: *a Halloween mask.* **2.** A protective covering for the face: *a welder's mask.* **3.** A covering for the mouth and nose: *a dust mask.* **4.** A usually rubber frame that forms a watertight seal around the eyes and nose and holds a transparent piece of plastic or glass, allowing the wearer to see underwater. **5.** A representation of a face, often made of plaster or clay. **6.** Something that disguises or conceals: *His smile was a mask to cover his true feelings.* **7.** An area of contrasting color on the face and usually across the eyes of an animal. ❖ *tr.v.* **masked, mask·ing, masks 1.** To cover with a mask: *The robbers masked their faces.* **2.** To cover in order to conceal, protect, or disguise: *She masked the baseboard with tape before painting the wall.* ❑ *These sound alike:* **mask, masque** (masquerade).

masked (măskt) *adj.* **1.** Wearing or marked with a mask: *a masked bandit; a masked monkey.* **2.** Disguised; hidden: *masked disappointment.*

mask·ing tape (măs′kĭng) *n.* A tape with adhesive on one side used for various purposes, such as to cover a surface that is not to be painted.

mas·och·ism (măs′ə-kĭz′əm) *n.* The tendency to derive pleasure from being subjected to pain or mistreatment. **—mas′o·chist** *n.*

ma·son (mā′sən) *n.* **1.** A person who builds or works with stone or brick. **2. Mason** A Freemason.

Ma·son-Dix·on Line (mā′sən-dĭk′sən) The boundary between Pennsylvania and Maryland, regarded as the dividing line between Free States and Slave States before the Civil War.

Ma·son·ic (mə-sŏn′ĭk) *adj.* Relating to Freemasons or Freemasonry.

Mason jar *n.* A glass jar with a wide mouth and an air-

GEOGRAPHY

Maryland The state of **Maryland** took its name from the colony that was chartered by King Charles I of England in 1632. It was named in honor of Queen Henrietta Maria (1609–1669), Charles's wife.

Mary Queen of Scots

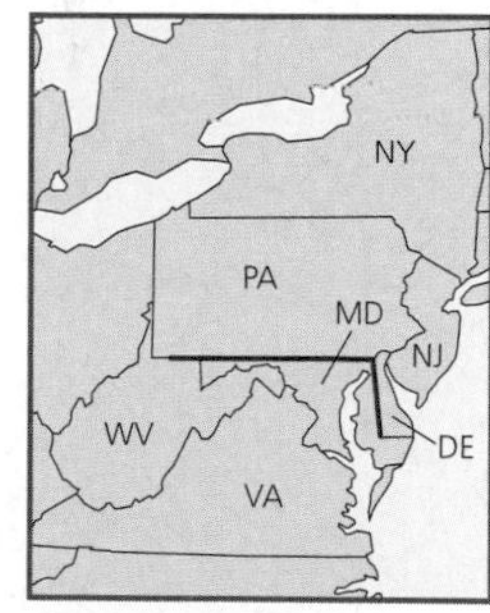

Mason-Dixon Line

GEOGRAPHY

Massachusetts The name **Massachusetts** is of Native American origin and means "at the big hills." The English explorer John Smith gave the name *Massachuset* to a New England village in the early 1600s. The English plural *-s* was added to the name when referring to a Native American people of the region, and this form was applied to the British colony and later to the newly formed state.

mast
two masts on a ketch

ă	pat	ôr	core
ā	pay	oi	boy
âr	care	ou	out
ä	father	o͝o	took
ĕ	pet	o͝or	lure
ē	be	o͞o	boot
ĭ	pit	ŭ	cut
ī	bite	ûr	urge
îr	pier	th	thin
ŏ	pot	*th*	this
ō	toe	zh	vision
ô	paw	ə	about

tight metal lid, used for canning and preserving food. [After John L. *Mason* (1832–1902), American inventor.]

ma·son·ry (mā′sən-rē) *n., pl.* **ma·son·ries 1.** The trade or skill of a mason. **2.** Work done by a mason; stonework or brickwork. **3. Masonry** Freemasonry.

masque (măsk) *n.* **1.** A dramatic entertainment performed by masked players, popular in European courts in the 1500s and 1600s. **2.** A masquerade dance or party. ❑ *These sound alike:* **masque, mask** (disguise).

mas·quer·ade (măs′kə-**rād′**) *n.* **1a.** A dance or party at which masks and fancy costumes are worn. **b.** A costume worn at such a dance or party. **2.** A disguise or false pretense. ❖ *intr.v.* **mas·quer·ad·ed, mas·quer·ad·ing, mas·quer·ades 1.** To wear a mask or disguise, as at a masquerade. **2.** To have a deceptive appearance; disguise oneself: *The undercover police officer masqueraded as a taxi driver.* **—mas′quer·ad′er** *n.*

mass (măs) *n.* **1.** A unified body of matter with no specific shape: *a mass of clay.* **2.** A large amount or number that is not specified: *A mass of people entered the stadium.* **3.** The major part; the majority: *The mass of voters supported the winning candidate.* **4.** The physical bulk or size of a solid body: *the huge mass of the ocean liner.* **5.** A measure of the amount of matter contained in a physical body. Mass is independent of gravity and therefore is different from weight. **6. masses** The common people. ❖ *tr. & intr.v.* **massed, mass·ing, mass·es** To gather into or assemble in a mass: *The army massed its troops at the country's borders. The people massed downtown to watch the parade.* ❖ *adj.* **1.** Relating to, involving, or attended by large numbers of people: *a mass demonstration.* **2.** Done on a large scale: *mass production.* [From Middle English *masse,* from Greek *māza.*] —SEE NOTE AT **force.**

Mass also **mass** *n.* **1.** The public celebration of the Eucharist in the Roman Catholic Church and some Protestant churches. **2.** A musical composition written for certain parts of the Mass. [From Middle English *messe,* from Late Latin *missa.*]

Mas·sa·chu·sett also **Mas·sa·chu·set** (măs′ə-**cho͞o′**sĭt *or* măs′ə-**cho͞o′**zĭt) *n., pl.* **Massachusett** or **Mas·sa·chu·setts** also **Massachuset** or **Mas·sa·chu·sets 1.** A member of a Native American people formerly living along the eastern coast of Massachusetts. **2.** Their extinct Algonquian language.

Mas·sa·chu·setts (măs′ə-**cho͞o′**sĭts) A state of the northeast United States north of Connecticut. It was admitted as one of the original Thirteen Colonies in 1788. Boston is the capital. —SEE NOTE.

mas·sa·cre (**măs′**ə-kər) *n.* **1.** An act of cruelly killing a large number of people. **2.** The slaughter of a large number of animals. ❖ *tr.v.* **mas·sa·cred** (**măs′**ə-kərd), **mas·sa·cring** (**măs′**ə-krĭng *or* **măs′**ə-kər-ĭng), **mas·sa·cres** To kill cruelly in large numbers; slaughter. [From Old French *macecre,* butchery.]

mas·sage (mə-**säzh′** *or* mə-**säj′**) *n.* The rubbing or kneading of muscles and joints of the body to improve blood circulation and relax muscles. ❖ *tr.v.* **mas·saged, mas·sag·ing, mas·sag·es 1.** To give a massage to. **2.** To manipulate (data, for example): *The pollsters massaged the numbers to favor their candidate.*

Mas·sa·soit (măs′ə-**soit′**) 1580?–1661. Wampanoag leader who aided the Pilgrim colonists and signed a peace treaty with them at Plymouth.

mass-en·er·gy equivalence (**măs′ĕn′**ər-jē) *n.* The principle that mass and energy can be converted into each other and that a particular quantity of mass is equivalent to a particular quantity of energy. The principle was stated mathematically by Albert Einstein as $E = mc^2$, where E is the energy in ergs, m is the mass in grams, and c is the speed of light in centimeters per second.

mas·seur (mă-**sûr′** *or* mə-**sûr′**) *n.* A man who gives massages professionally.

mas·seuse (mă-**sœz′**) *n.* A woman who gives massages professionally.

mas·sive (**măs′**ĭv) *adj.* **1.** Bulky, heavy, and solid: *a massive dining room table; a massive building.* **2.** Large in comparison with the usual amount: *a massive dose of penicillin.* **3.** Large or impressive in scope, intensity, degree, or scale: *a massive migration of birds.* **—mas′sive·ly** *adv.*

mass media *pl.n.* The various media of public communication by which information is conveyed to a large audience, such as television, radio, films, newspapers, and blogs.

mass noun *n.* A noun that refers to something that cannot be counted and thus does not take a plural form or appear with an article such as *a* or *an. Furniture, honesty,* and *wildlife* are mass nouns.

mass number *n.* The total of the neutrons and protons present in an atomic nucleus.

mass-pro·duce (măs′prə-**do͞os′**) *tr.v.* **mass-pro·duced, mass-pro·duc·ing, mass-pro·duc·es** To produce in large quantities, especially on an assembly line: *mass-produce cars.*

mass production *n.* The act or process of producing large quantities of a product, as on an assembly line.

mass transit *n.* The public transportation system of a city and the area around it. Buses, subways, and trains are forms of mass transit.

mast (măst) *n.* **1.** A tall upright pole that supports the sails and rigging of a ship or boat. **2.** A tall vertical structure, such as an antenna for radio transmission. [From Old English *mæst.*]

mas·tec·to·my (mă-**stĕk′**tə-mē) *n., pl.* **mas·tec·to·mies** Surgical removal of all or part of a breast, usually performed as a treatment for cancer.

mas·ter (**măs′**tər) *n.* **1.** A person who directs, rules, or controls others; a ruler: *Caesar was the master of the Roman Empire.* **2a.** The owner or keeper of an animal. **b.** The owner of a slave. **3.** A person in control of something: *the master of a banana plantation.* **4.** The captain of a merchant ship. **5.** An artisan who employs others, especially a person who trains apprentices. **6.** A male teacher, schoolmaster, or tutor, especially in a private school. **7.** A person of great learning, skill, or ability; an expert: *a master in metal work.* **8. Master** A person who has received a master's degree. **9. Master** Used as a title before the name of a boy not considered old enough to be addressed as Mister. ❖ *adj.* **1.** Relating to or characteristic of a master. **2.** Principal; chief: *a master bedroom.* **3.** Highly skilled; expert: *a master carpenter.* **4.** Being a part of a mechanism that controls all other parts: *a master switch.* **5.** Being the original from which copies are made: *a master recording.* ❖ *tr.v.* **mas·tered, mas·ter·ing, mas·ters 1.** To become the master of; bring under control: *master one's emotions.* **2.** To become skilled in the use of: *master a foreign language.* [From Old English *mægester,* from Latin *magister.*]

mas·ter·ful (**măs′**tər-fəl) *adj.* **1.** Acting like a master; domineering. **2.** Expert; skillful: *a masterful performance of the concerto.* **—mas′ter·ful·ly** *adv.*

mas·ter·ly (**măs′**tər-lē) *adj.* Knowledgeable and skillful like a master: *a masterly debate.* ❖ *adv.* With the skill of a master. **—mas′ter·li·ness** *n.*

mas·ter·mind (**măs′**tər-mīnd′) *n.* A person who plans or directs something. ❖ *tr.v.* **mas·ter·mind·ed, mas·ter·mind·ing, mas·ter·minds** To plan or direct (something): *mastermind the team's turnaround.*

master of ceremonies *n., pl.* **masters of ceremonies** A person who acts as the host at a formal gathering and introduces the speakers and entertainers.

mas·ter·piece (**măs′**tər-pēs′) *n.* **1.** An outstanding work;

something done with skill or brilliance: *The bridge was a masterpiece of engineering.* **2.** The greatest work of an artist or craftsperson: *This figure is the sculptor's masterpiece.*

mas·ter's degree (măs′tərz) *n.* A degree awarded by a college or university to a student who has completed at least one year of study beyond the bachelor's degree in a program. It ranks below a doctorate.

master sergeant *n.* **1.** A noncommissioned officer in the US Army and Marine Corps below sergeant major. **2.** A high-ranking noncommissioned officer in the US Air Force.

mas·ter·work (măs′tər-wûrk′) *n.* A masterpiece.

mas·ter·y (măs′tə-rē) *n., pl.* **mas·ter·ies 1.** Complete control or domination. **2.** Possession of great skill, knowledge, or technique: *her mastery of the piano.*

mast·head (măst′hĕd′) *n.* **1.** The top of a ship's mast. **2.** The listing in a newspaper, a magazine, or another publication of its owners, staff, and information about its operation.

mas·ti·cate (măs′tĭ-kāt′) *tr.v.* **mas·ti·cat·ed, mas·ti·cat·ing, mas·ti·cates** To chew (food). [From Late Latin *masticāre*, from Greek *mastikhān*, to grind the teeth.] **—mas′ti·ca′tion** *n.*

mas·tiff (măs′tĭf) *n.* A dog of a large powerful breed developed as a guard dog, having a short coat, large head, and square jaws.

mas·to·don (măs′tə-dŏn′) *n.* Any of several extinct mammals that resembled elephants and had long curved tusks. Mastodons disappeared from North America about 10,000 years ago.

mas·toid (măs′toid′) *n.* The bone in the lower part of the skull behind the ear.

mas·tur·bate (măs′tər-bāt′) *intr.v.* **mas·tur·bat·ed, mas·tur·bat·ing, mas·tur·bates** To perform an act of masturbation.

mas·tur·ba·tion (măs′tər-**bā′**shən) *n.* The act of stimulating the genitals, usually manually, to produce sexual pleasure.

mat[1] (măt) *n.* **1.** A flat piece of coarse material, often made of woven straw, hemp, or rushes, used as a floor covering or for wiping one's shoes. **2.** A small piece of material put under a dish, vase, or other object to protect or decorate the top of a table. **3.** A thick pad or mattress used on the floor for tumbling, wrestling, or acrobatics. **4.** A dense or tangled mass: *a mat of hair.* ❖ *v.* **mat·ted, mat·ting, mats** *—tr.* **1.** To tangle into a thick compact mass: *mat fibers together to make felt.* **2.** To cover with a mat or with matting: *They matted the floor of the hut.* *—intr.* To become tangled into a thick compact mass: *The cat's fur matted without brushing.* [From Old English *matte*, from Late Latin *matta.*]

mat[2] (măt) *n.* **1.** A piece of cardboard or other material placed around a picture as a frame or border between the picture and its frame. **2.** Variant of **matte.** ❖ *tr.v.* **mat·ted, mat·ting, mats** To put a mat around (a picture). ❖ *adj.* Variant of **matte.** [From French, dull.]

mat·a·dor (măt′ə-dôr′) *n.* The person who fights and kills the bull in a bullfight.

Ma·ta Ha·ri (mä′tə här′ē *or* măt′ə hăr′ē) 1876–1917. Dutch spy who apparently spied for Germany during World War I and was arrested and executed by the French.

match[1] (măch) *n.* **1a.** A person or thing exactly like another: *Find the match for this fabric.* **b.** A person or thing that is similar to or goes well with another: *This tie is a good match for your shirt.* **2.** A person or thing with equal or near equal capabilities: *The runners were a good match and ran a very close race.* **3.** A sports contest: *a wrestling match.* **4a.** A marriage or an arrangement of marriage. **b.** A person viewed as a possible partner in marriage. ❖ *v.* **matched, match·ing, match·es** *—tr.* **1.** To be alike; correspond exactly to: *This sock doesn't match that one.* **2.** To resemble or harmonize with; be suitable for: *Your shirt matches your slacks.* **3.** To fit together: *Match the edges of the seam and sew them together.* **4.** To find or provide a match for: *We could not match the color of the old paint on the door.* **5a.** To provide with an opponent or competitor: *The teacher matched one group against the other in a spelling bee.* **b.** To place in competition: *They matched wits.* **6.** To join or give in marriage. *—intr.* **1.** To be alike or equal: *Finally your socks match.* **2.** To harmonize with another: *This tie and this shirt match.* [From Old English *gemæcca*, companion, mate.]

match[2] (măch) *n.* **1.** A narrow piece of material, usually wood or cardboard, that is coated at one end with a substance that catches fire easily when scratched against a surface that is rough or that has been treated with chemicals. **2.** An easily ignited cord or wick, formerly used to fire cannons and muskets or matchlock guns. [From Middle English *mecche*, lamp wick, from Greek *muxa.*]

match·book (măch′bo͝ok′) *n.* A small cardboard folder containing safety matches and a surface for striking them.

match·box (măch′bŏks′) *n.* A box for matches that usually has a surface for striking them.

match·less (măch′lĭs) *adj.* Having no rival or equal: *his matchless ability to play the guitar.*

match·lock (măch′lŏk′) *n.* A musket in which the powder charge is ignited by a wick or match.

match·mak·er (măch′mā′kər) *n.* **1.** A person who arranges or tries to arrange marriages for others. **2.** A person who arranges athletic competitions, especially in professional boxing.

match·stick (măch′stĭk′) *n.* A short slender piece of wood from which a match is made.

match·up (măch′ŭp′) *n.* The pairing of two people or things, as for sports competition or for comparison: *The finals featured a matchup of two former champions.*

mate[1] (māt) *n.* **1.** One of a matched pair: *Where is the mate to this sock?* **2.** A spouse or romantic partner. **3.** The male or female of a pair of animals that are breeding. **4.** A close associate; a partner: *We need more help from our mates to finish the job.* **5a.** An officer on a merchant ship ranking below the master. **b.** An officer of the US Navy ranking below and assisting a warrant officer. ❖ *v.* **mat·ed, mat·ing, mates** *—tr.* **1.** To join closely; pair. **2.** To unite in marriage. **3.** To bring (a male and a female animal) together for breeding. *—intr.* To pair; breed: *Many animals mate in the spring.* [From Middle English, from Middle Low German *mate*, messmate.]

mate[2] (māt) *n.* In chess, a checkmate. ❖ *tr. & intr.v.* **mat·ed, mat·ing, mates** To checkmate or achieve a checkmate. [From Middle English *mat*, from Arabic *māt*, he has died.]

ma·te[3] (mä′tā) also **ma·té** (mä-tĕ′) *n.* **1.** A drink resembling tea, made from the dried leaves of an evergreen South American shrub related to holly. **2.** The shrub that bears such leaves. [From Quechua *mati*, calabash container.]

ma·te·ri·al (mə-tîr′ē-əl) *n.* **1.** The substance or substances from which something is or can be made: *Hemp is often used as material for ropes.* **2.** Cloth or fabric: *a length of silk material.* **3.** Something, such as an idea or information, that is used or developed to make something else: *historical material for a novel.* **4. materials** Tools or apparatus needed to perform a certain task: *building materials.* ❖ *adj.* **1.** Relating to or composed of matter: *not a ghost, but a material being.* **2.** Relating to or affecting physical well-being: *material comforts.* **3.** Relating to or concerned with the physical as opposed to the spiritual or intellectual: *I did it not for material gain but for personal satisfaction.* **4.** Important; relevant: *Is your remark material to this discussion?* [From Middle English, from Latin *māteria*, matter.]

WRITERS CHOOSE THEIR WORDS

Although pests like mice, cockroaches, and mosquitoes sometimes seem to **materialize** out of thin air, by the 18th century just about everyone agreed that they were born from parents of the same species, not from muck or swamp water.

—Louise E. Robbins
Louis Pasteur and the Hidden World of Microbes

Matterhorn

mattock

ă	pat	ôr	core
ā	pay	oi	boy
âr	care	ou	out
ä	father	o͝o	took
ĕ	pet	o͝or	lure
ē	be	o͞o	boot
ĭ	pit	ŭ	cut
ī	bite	ûr	urge
îr	pier	th	thin
ŏ	pot	*th*	this
ō	toe	zh	vision
ô	paw	ə	about

ma·te·ri·al·ism (mə-tîr′ē-ə-lĭz′əm) *n.* **1.** The philosophical doctrine that physical matter is the only reality and that everything, including the mind, thoughts, and feelings, can be explained in terms of matter. **2.** The tendency to be concerned with money and possessions rather than with spiritual or intellectual things. **—ma·te′ri·al·ist** *n.* **—ma·te′ri·al·is′tic** *adj.* **—ma·te′ri·al·is′ti·cal·ly** *adv.*

ma·te·ri·al·ize (mə-tîr′ē-ə-līz′) *intr.v.* **ma·te·ri·al·ized, ma·te·ri·al·iz·ing, ma·te·ri·al·iz·es 1.** To come into existence; become real: *Support for the project never materialized.* **2.** To appear, especially suddenly: *The mountains in the distance materialized as the fog lifted.*

ma·te·ri·al·ly (mə-tîr′ē-ə-lē) *adv.* **1.** With regard to material well-being; physically: *rich materially but unhappy.* **2.** To a significant extent or degree; considerably: *My assistant's help aided materially in carrying out this experiment.*

ma·te·ri·el or **ma·té·ri·el** (mə-tîr′ē-**ĕl′**) *n.* Equipment, apparatus, and supplies, especially those used by a military force.

ma·ter·nal (mə-**tûr′**nəl) *adj.* **1.** Relating to or characteristic of a mother or motherhood: *maternal health.* **2.** Inherited from one's mother: *a maternal trait.* **3.** Related through one's mother: *maternal aunts and uncles.* [From Latin *māter*, mother.] **—ma·ter′nal·ly** *adv.*

ma·ter·ni·ty (mə-**tûr′**nĭ-tē) *n., pl.* **ma·ter·ni·ties 1.** The state of being a mother. **2.** The feelings or characteristics that are part of being a mother; motherliness. ❖ *adj.* Relating to or effective during pregnancy, childbirth, or the first months of motherhood: *maternity care.*

math (măth) *n.* Mathematics.

math·e·mat·i·cal (măth′ə-**măt′**ĭ-kəl) *adj.* **1.** Relating to mathematics. **2.** Precise; exact: *mathematical correctness.* **—math′e·mat′i·cal·ly** *adv.*

math·e·ma·ti·cian (măth′ə-mə-**tĭsh′**ən) *n.* A person who is skilled in or who specializes in mathematics.

math·e·mat·ics (măth′ə-**măt′**ĭks) *n.* *(used with a singular verb)* The study of the measurement, properties, and relationships of quantities and sets, using numbers and symbols. Arithmetic, algebra, and geometry are branches of mathematics.

mat·i·nee or **mat·i·née** (măt′n-**ā′**) *n.* An entertainment, such as a movie or a dramatic performance, presented in the afternoon.

ma·tri·arch (**mā′**trē-ärk′) *n.* **1.** A woman who is a mother and head of a family, clan, or tribe. **2.** A respected older woman.

ma·tri·ar·chy (**mā′**trē-är′kē) *n., pl.* **ma·tri·ar·chies** A social system in which the mother is the head of the family and women have authority over men and children. **—ma′tri·ar′chal** (mā′trē-**är′**kəl) *adj.*

ma·tri·ces (**mā′**trĭ-sēz′ *or* **măt′**rĭ-sēz′) *n.* A plural of **matrix.**

mat·ri·cide (**măt′**rĭ-sīd′) *n.* **1.** The act of killing one's mother. **2.** Someone who kills his or her mother. **—mat′ri·cid′al** *adj.*

ma·tric·u·late (mə-**trĭk′**yə-lāt′) *tr. & intr.v.* **ma·tric·u·lat·ed, ma·tric·u·lat·ing, ma·tric·u·lates** To enroll or allow to enroll in a college or university. **—ma·tric′u·la′tion** *n.*

mat·ri·mo·ny (**măt′**rə-mō′nē) *n., pl.* **mat·ri·mo·nies** The act or condition of being married; marriage. **—mat′ri·mo′ni·al** *adj.*

ma·trix (**mā′**trĭks) *n., pl.* **ma·tri·ces** (**mā′**trĭ-sēz′ *or* **măt′**rĭ-sēz′) or **ma·trix·es 1.** A situation or substance within which something is contained, originates, or develops. The mineral grains of a rock in which fossils are embedded are a matrix. **2.** A regular arrangement of things, such as words or mathematical symbols, in columns and rows.

ma·tron (**mā′**trən) *n.* **1.** A married woman or widow, especially a mother who is dignified and has an established social position. **2.** A woman who acts as a supervisor or guard in a school, hospital, or prison, or other public institution. [From Middle English *matrone*, from Latin *mātrōna*, from *māter*, mother.] **—ma′tron·ly** *adv. & adj.*

matron of honor *n., pl.* **matrons of honor** A married woman who serves as chief attendant of the bride at a wedding.

matte (măt) *n.* A dull finish on something, as of paint or paper. ❖ *adj.* also **mat** Having a dull finish.

mat·ted (**măt′**ĭd) *adj.* **1.** Formed into a mass; tangled: *matted underbrush.* **2.** Covered with mats or matting: *a matted floor.*

mat·ter (**măt′**ər) *n.* **1a.** Something that occupies space, has mass, and can exist ordinarily as a solid, liquid, or gas. **b.** A specific type of substance: *organic matter.* **2.** The substance or content of something: *The matter of the book was very interesting.* See Synonyms at **subject. 3.** A subject of concern, feeling, or action: *For me, this exam is a serious matter.* **4.** Trouble; difficulty: *What's the matter with them?* **5.** A certain quantity, amount, or extent: *The highway construction lasted a matter of years.* **6.** Something written or printed or to be written or printed: *reading matter.* ❖ *intr.v.* **mat·tered, mat·ter·ing, mat·ters** To be of importance: *Our success mattered a great deal to us.* ◆ **as a matter of fact** In fact; actually. **no matter** Regardless of: *No matter where you go, I'll be thinking of you.* [From Middle English *mater*, from Latin *māteria*.]

Mat·ter·horn (**măt′**ər-hôrn′) A mountain, 14,692 feet (4,478 meters) high, in the Alps on the Italian-Swiss border.

matter of course *n.* Something that is expected; a natural or logical result.

mat·ter-of-fact (**măt′**ər-əv-**făkt′**) *adj.* **1.** Adhering strictly to the facts; literal: *a matter-of-fact description of the party.* **2.** Showing no emotion: *a matter-of-fact tone of voice.* **—mat′ter-of-fact′ly** *adv.*

Mat·thew (**măth′**yo͞o) *n.* The first Gospel of the New Testament, traditionally thought to have been written by Saint Matthew.

Matthew, Saint. Flourished about first century AD. One of the 12 Apostles, traditionally regarded as author of the first Gospel of the New Testament.

mat·ting (**măt′**ĭng) *n.* **1.** A coarse fabric of woven straw, hemp, or rushes, used especially for making mats or covering floors. **2.** Material formed into a mat: *a matting of leaves on the forest floor.*

mat·tock (**măt′**ək) *n.* A digging tool with a flat blade, used for cutting roots or breaking up soil.

mat·tress (**măt′**rĭs) *n.* A pad of heavy cloth filled with soft material or a group of springs, used on or as a bed. [From Middle English *materas*, from Arabic *maṭraḥ*, place where something is thrown, mat, cushion, from *ṭaraḥa*, to throw.]

mat·u·ra·tion (măch′ə-**rā′**shən) *n.* The process of maturing or ripening.

ma·ture (mə-**tyo͝or′** *or* mə-**cho͝or′**) *adj.* **ma·tur·er, ma·tur·est 1.** Having reached full growth or development: *a mature dragonfly.* **2.** Having the mental, emotional, or physical qualities associated with an adult: *a child who seems very mature.* **3.** Suitable or intended for adults: *a film with mature subject matter.* **4.** Worked out fully in the mind: *a mature plan of action.* **5.** Having reached the limit of its time; due: *a mature savings bond.* ❖ *v.* **ma·tured, ma·tur·ing, ma·tures** *—tr.* To bring to full development: *Working in the hospital has matured him.* *—intr.* **1.** To reach full growth or development: *The peaches matured on the tree.* **2.** To become due: *This bond matures in seven years.* [From Middle English, from Latin *mātūrus*.] **—ma·ture′ly** *adv.*

ma·tur·i·ty (mə-**tyo͝or′**ĭ-tē *or* mə-**to͝or′**ĭ-tē *or* mə-choo͝or′ĭ-tē) *n., pl.* **ma·tur·i·ties 1.** The condition of being mature; full growth or development: *Tomatoes reach maturity in late summer.* **2.** The time at which payment of a loan or bond becomes due.

mat·zo or **mat·zoh** (mät′sə) *n., pl.* **mat·zos** or **mat·zohs** (mät′səz) or **mat·zot** or **mat·zoth** (mät-sôt′) A brittle flat piece of unleavened bread, eaten especially during Passover. [From Yiddish *matse*, from Hebrew *maṣṣâ*.]

maud·lin (môd′lĭn) *adj.* Overly or foolishly sentimental. [Alteration of *(Mary) Magdalene*, who was frequently depicted as a tearful penitent.]

Mau·i (mou′ē) The second-largest island of Hawaii, situated northwest of Hawaii Island.

maul (môl) *n.* A heavy hammer or mallet, used to drive stakes, piles, or wedges. ❖ *tr.v.* **mauled, maul·ing, mauls 1.** To injure or damage by tearing or beating: *The bear cub mauled the salmon before eating it.* **2.** To handle roughly: *The package was mauled in the mail.*
❑ *These sound alike:* **maul, mall** (shopping center).

Mau·na Lo·a (mou′nə lō′ə *or* mô′nə lō′ə) An active volcano, 13,679 feet (4,169 meters) high, of south-central Hawaii Island.

maun·der (môn′dər *or* män′dər) *intr.v.* **maun·dered, maun·der·ing, maun·ders 1.** To talk in a rambling or confused way. **2.** To wander about in an aimless or confused way.

Mau·ri·ta·ni·a (môr′ĭ-tā′nē-ə) A country of northwest Africa west of Mali and bordering on the Atlantic Ocean. Nouakchott is the capital.

Mau·ri·tius (mô-rĭsh′əs *or* mô-rĭsh′ē-əs) An island country in the southwest Indian Ocean made up of the island of **Mauritius** and several smaller islands. Port Louis is the capital.

mau·so·le·um (mô′zə-lē′əm) *n.* A stately building housing a tomb or tombs.

mauve (mōv) *n.* A light rosy or grayish purple.

ma·ven (mā′vən) *n.* A person who has special knowledge or experience; an expert.

mav·er·ick (măv′ər-ĭk *or* măv′rĭk) *n.* **1.** A person who refuses to go along with the policies or views of a group. **2.** An unbranded calf or colt, traditionally belonging to the first person to brand it. [Possibly after Samuel Augustus *Maverick* (1803–1870), American cattleman who left his calves unbranded.]

maw (mô) *n.* The mouth, throat, gullet, or stomach of an animal.

mawk·ish (mô′kĭsh) *adj.* Excessively and foolishly sentimental: *a mawkish poem.* **—mawk′ish·ly** *adv.*

max (măks) *Slang n.* The maximum: *The car can seat five adults, but that's the max.* ❖ *adj.* Maximal. ❖ *adv.* Maximally: *We'll pay $250 max.* ❖ *intr.v.* **maxed, max·ing, max·es 1.** To reach one's limit, as of endurance or capability: *The weightlifter maxed out at 180 kilograms.* **2.** To reach a point from which no additional growth, improvement, or benefit is possible: *The salary for this position maxes at $65,000.*

max. *abbr.* An abbreviation of maximum.

max·il·la (măk-sĭl′ə) *n., pl.* **max·il·lae** (măk-sĭl′ē) or **max·il·las 1.** The upper jawbone in mammals or a similar bone in other vertebrates. **2.** Either of a pair of appendages behind the mandibles in insects, spiders, crabs, and other arthropods.

max·il·lar·y (măk′sə-lĕr′ē) *adj.* Relating to a maxilla. ❖ *n., pl.* **max·il·lar·ies** A maxilla bone.

max·im (măk′sĭm) *n.* A brief statement of a basic principle or rule of behavior; a proverb.

max·i·mize (măk′sə-mīz′) *tr.v.* **max·i·mized, max·i·miz·ing, max·i·miz·es** To make as great or large as possible: *Working hard will maximize your opportunities.*

max·i·mum (măk′sə-məm) *n., pl.* **max·i·mums** or **max·i·ma** (măk′sə-mə) **1.** The greatest known or greatest possible number, measure, quantity, or degree: *The temperature reached a maximum of only 10 degrees today.* **2.** An upper limit permitted by law or other authority: *The maximum speed limit on this road is 55 miles per hour.* ❖ *adj.* Having or being the greatest number, measure, quantity, or degree that is possible: *The train has a maximum speed of 120 miles per hour.* [From Latin *maximus*, greatest.]

Max·well (măks′wĕl′), **James Clerk** 1831–1879. British physicist who developed four laws of electromagnetism showing that light is composed of electromagnetic waves.

may (mā) *aux.v.* Past tense **might** (mīt) **1.** To be allowed or permitted to: *May I go outside?* **2.** Used to indicate likelihood or possibility: *It may rain today.* **3.** Used to express a desire or wish: *May your days be filled with laughter.* **4.** Used to express purpose or result in clauses starting with *so that: I tell you this so that you may understand.* [From Old English *mæg*.]

May *n.* The fifth month of the year in the Gregorian calendar, having 31 days. [From Middle English *Mai*, from Latin *Maia*, a goddess of ancient Italy.]

May, Theresa Mary Born 1956. British politician who was appointed prime minister in 2016.

Ma·ya (mä′yə) *n., pl.* **Maya** or **Ma·yas 1.** A member of an American Indian people of southeast Mexico, Guatemala, and Belize whose civilization reached its height around AD 300–900. **2.** Any of the languages spoken by the Maya.

Ma·yan (mä′yən) *n.* **1.** A Maya. **2.** A family of Indian languages spoken in Central America, especially by the Maya. ❖ *adj.* Relating to the Maya or their languages or culture.

may·be (mā′bē) *adv.* Possibly; perhaps: *Maybe we can go swimming tomorrow.* ❖ *n.* **1.** An uncertainty: *There are too many maybes with the current plans to formalize a schedule.* **2.** An uncertain reply: *I invited a dozen people; ten people are definitely coming, but two are maybes.*

may·day (mā′dā′) *interj.* An expression used internationally as a call for help, especially for planes or ships in trouble. [From French *(venez) m'aider*, (come) help me!]

May Day *n.* May 1, celebrated in some countries as a spring holiday, and in others in honor of workers.

may·flow·er (mā′flou′ər) *n.* Any of various plants that bloom in spring.

may·fly (mā′flī′) *n.* Any of various delicate insects having transparent wings and long filaments extending from the end of the body. Adult mayflies live for only a few days and do not feed.

may·hem (mā′hĕm′ *or* mā′əm) *n.* **1.** In law, the willful maiming or injuring of a person. **2.** A state of confusion or destructive disorder.

may·n't (mā′ənt *or* mānt) Contraction of *may not.*

may·on·naise (mā′ə-nāz′ *or* mā′ə-nāz′) *n.* A thick dressing made of beaten raw egg yolk, oil, lemon juice or vinegar, and seasonings.

may·or (mā′ər *or* mâr) *n.* The chief government official of a city or town. [From Middle English *maire*, from Latin *māior*, greater, superior.] **—may′or·al** *adj.*

may·or·al·ty (mā′ər-əl-tē *or* mâr′əl-tē) *n., pl.* **may·or·al·ties 1.** The position of a mayor. **2.** The term of office of a mayor.

May·pole also **may·pole** (mā′pōl′) *n.* A pole decorated with streamers, ribbons, and flowers, around which people dance on May Day.

Mays (māz), **Willie Howard, Jr.** Born 1931. American baseball player (1951–1972) who hit 660 home runs.

maze (māz) *n.* **1.** A complicated and often confusing network of pathways. **2.** A muddle or tangle: *a maze of contradictions.*
❑ *These sound alike:* **maze, maize** (corn plant).

mausoleum
Tomb of Humayun, Delhi, India

Theresa May
photographed in 2017

Willie Mays
photographed in 1956

mbira

William McKinley

USAGE

me The correct pronoun to use in sentences like *John and ______ are going home* is the nominative form, such as *I, he, she,* or *they,* not the objective form, such as *me, him, her,* or *them.* Therefore you say *John and I are going home,* not *Me and John are going home.*

ă	pat	ôr	core
ā	pay	oi	boy
âr	care	ou	out
ä	father	o͝o	took
ĕ	pet	o͝or	lure
ē	be	o͞o	boot
ĭ	pit	ŭ	cut
ī	bite	ûr	urge
îr	pier	th	thin
ŏ	pot	*th*	this
ō	toe	zh	vision
ô	paw	ə	about

ma·zur·ka (mə-zûr′kə *or* mə-zo͝or′kə) *n.* **1.** A Polish dance that resembles the polka. **2.** Music written for this dance.

Mb *abbr.* An abbreviation of megabit.

MB *abbr.* An abbreviation of: **1.** Manitoba. **2.** megabyte.

Mba·bane (əm-bä-bän′) The capital of Swaziland, in the northwest part of the country near the South African border.

mbi·ra (ĕm-bîr′ə) *n.* A musical instrument made of a hollow gourd or wooden resonator and a number of usually metal strips that vibrate when plucked. [From Bantu.]

Mbps *abbr.* An abbreviation of megabits per second.

MC (ĕm′sē′) *n.* A master of ceremonies.

Mc·Cart·ney (mə-kärt′nē), Sir **(James) Paul** Born 1942. British rock musician who was a member of the Beatles. He cowrote many of the group's songs, including "Yellow Submarine" (1966).

Mc·Clin·tock (mə-klĭn′tək *or* mə-klĭn′tŏk′), **Barbara** 1902–1992. American geneticist who proved that genes can change position on chromosomes.

Mc·Cor·mick (mə-kôr′mĭk), **Cyrus Hall** 1809–1884. American inventor and manufacturer who developed a mechanical reaper (1831).

Mc·Cul·lers (mə-kŭl′ərz), **Carson Smith** 1917–1967. American writer whose novels include *The Heart Is a Lonely Hunter* (1940) and *The Member of the Wedding* (1946).

Mc·Kin·ley (mə-kĭn′lē), **Mount** or **De·na·li** (də-nä′lē) A peak, 20,320 feet (6,194 meters) high, of south-central Alaska. It is the highest point in North America.

McKinley, William 1843–1901. The 25th president of the United States (1897–1901). His presidency was marked by the Spanish-American War (1898) and the occupation of Cuba and the Philippines.

Md The symbol for the element **mendelevium.**

MD *abbr.* An abbreviation of: **1.** Maryland. **2.** Medicinae Doctor (Doctor of Medicine). **3.** muscular dystrophy.

me (mē) *pron.* The objective form of **I**[1]. **1.** Used as the direct object of a verb: *He helped me.* **2.** Used as the indirect object of a verb: *She sent me a letter.* **3.** Used as the object of a preposition: *They brought the books to me.* —SEE NOTE.

❑ *These sound alike:* **me, mi** (musical tone).

ME *abbr.* An abbreviation of Maine.

mead[1] (mēd) *n.* An alcoholic beverage made of fermented honey and water. [From Old English *medu.*]

mead[2] (mēd) *n. Archaic* A meadow. [From Old English *mǣd.*]

Mead (mēd), **Margaret** 1901–1978. American anthropologist noted for her studies of adolescence in traditional cultures of Oceania.

mead·ow (mĕd′ō) *n.* A tract of land that is covered in grasses, especially one used as a pasture or for hay.

mead·ow·lark (mĕd′ō-lärk′) *n.* Any of several songbirds of the Americas that have a brownish back and a yellow breast with a black V-shaped marking.

mea·ger also **mea·gre** (mē′gər) *adj.* **1.** Lacking in quantity or richness; scanty: *a meager dinner.* **2.** Having little flesh; thin: *a meager face.* **—mea′ger·ly** *adv.*

meal[1] (mēl) *n.* A substance, especially grain, that has been ground. [From Old English *melu.*]

meal[2] (mēl) *n.* **1.** The food served and eaten in one sitting. **2.** The customary time for eating food: *Don't eat between meals.* [From Old English *mǣl.*]

meal·time (mēl′tīm′) *n.* The usual time for eating a meal.

meal·y (mē′lē) *adj.* **meal·i·er, meal·i·est 1.** Like meal; dry and granular: *a soft and mealy apple.* **2.** Made of or containing meal: *mealy chicken feed.* **3.** Covered with meal: *sweep the mealy floor.* **4.** Lacking color; pale: *a mealy complexion.* **—meal′i·ness** *n.*

meal·y-mouthed (mē′lē-mou*th*d′ *or* mē′lē-moutht′) *adj.* Unwilling to say directly or simply what one thinks is right or true.

mean[1] (mēn) *v.* **meant** (mĕnt), **mean·ing, means** *—tr.* **1.** To be used to convey; have the sense of; signify: *The Spanish word "frijol" means "bean."* **2.** To intend to convey or indicate: *What did you mean by that statement?* **3.** To have as a purpose or intention: *They mean no harm.* **4.** To design or intend for a certain purpose or end: *This building was meant for grain storage.* **5.** To be likely to result in; be attended by: *Dark clouds often mean a storm.* **6.** To bring about or have as a consequence: *Friction means heat.* **7.** To be of a specified importance; matter: *Your friendship means a great deal to me.* *—intr.* To have intentions of a certain kind: *She means well, despite her mistakes.* ◆ **mean business** *Informal* To be in earnest. [From Old English *mǣnan,* to tell of.]

❑ *These sound alike:* **mean**[1] (signify), **mean**[2] (unkind), **mean**[3] (middle point), **mien** (manner).

mean[2] (mēn) *adj.* **mean·er, mean·est 1.** Lacking kindness and goodwill: *The teacher was not being mean in asking you to be quiet.* **2.** Cruel; spiteful: *a mean remark made in anger.* **3.** Miserly; stingy. **4.** Low, as in quality, rank, or value; inferior: *rose from mean origins to fame and success.* **5.** *Slang* Hard to cope with; difficult: *She throws a mean curve ball.* **6.** Excellent: *He plays a mean game of chess.* [From Old English *gemǣne,* common.]

❑ *These sound alike:* **mean**[2] (unkind), **mean**[1] (signify), **mean**[3] (middle point), **mien** (manner).

mean[3] (mēn) *n.* **1.** Something that is midway between two extremes. **2.** A number or quantity that has a value that is intermediate between other numbers or quantities, especially an arithmetic mean or average. **3.** Either the second or third term of a proportion of four terms. In the proportion ⅔ = ⁴⁄₆, the means are 3 and 4. **4. means a.** Something, such as a method or course of action, by which an act or end is achieved: *a practical means of using the sun's energy to generate electricity.* **b.** Money, property, or other wealth: *a person of means.* ❖ *adj.* **1.** Occupying a middle or intermediate position between two extremes: *mean test scores.* **2.** Middling; average. ◆ **by all means** Without fail; certainly. **by any means** In any way possible; to any extent: *We must fix this problem by any means.* **by means of** With the use of; owing to: *They crossed the river by means of a raft.* **by no means** In no sense; certainly not: *By no means should you go sailing in rough weather.* [From Middle English *mene,* middle, from Latin *mediānus.*] —SEE NOTE.

❑ *These sound alike:* **mean**[3] (middle point), **mean**[1] (signify), **mean**[2] (unkind), **mien** (manner).

me·an·der (mē-ăn′dər) *intr.v.* **me·an·dered, me·an·der·ing, me·an·ders 1.** To follow a winding and turning course: *The river meanders through the valley.* **2.** To wander aimlessly and idly: *We meandered through the fields and woods.* See Synonyms at **wander.** [After the *Maeander* River in Asia Minor.]

mean·ing (mē′nĭng) *n.* **1.** Something that is meant or signified, especially by language: *The word "head" has several meanings.* **2.** Something that one wishes to communicate: *The writer's meaning was easy to understand.* **3.** A goal or purpose: *What is the meaning of all this?* ❖ *adj.* Full of meaning; expressive: *a meaning smile.* **—mean′ing·ly** *adv.*

mean·ing·ful (mē′nĭng-fəl) *adj.* Full of meaning; significant: *a meaningful discussion.* **—mean′ing·ful·ly** *adv.* **—mean′ing·ful·ness** *n.*

mean·ing·less (mē′nĭng-lĭs) *adj.* Having no meaning or significance: *a meaningless phrase.* **—mean′ing·less·ly** *adv.*

mean·ness (mēn′nĭs) *n.* **1.** The condition of being inferior or lacking in quality, character, or value. **2.** Selfishness; stinginess: *a miser's meanness.* **3.** A spiteful act.

mean sea level *n.* The average level of the ocean's surface, used as the standard for determining land elevations and ocean depths. Mean sea level is determined by measuring tide levels every hour for an extended time period and finding their arithmetical mean.

meant (mĕnt) *v.* Past tense and past participle of **mean¹**.

mean·time (mēn′tīm′) *n.* The time between one occurrence and another: *In the meantime, keep practicing your music.* ❖ *adv.* Meanwhile.

mean·while (mēn′wīl′) *n.* Meantime. ❖ *adv.* **1.** During or in the time between two events: *Meanwhile, she continued to improve her swimming stroke.* **2.** At the same time: *I'll put the food on the plates, and meanwhile, you set the table.*

mea·sles (mē′zəlz) *n.* *(used with a singular or plural verb)* **1.** A highly contagious viral disease with symptoms that include coughing, fever, and red spots on the skin. **2.** Any of several milder diseases that have symptoms similar to measles, especially German measles.

mea·sly (mēz′lē) *adj.* **mea·sli·er, mea·sli·est 1.** *Slang* Contemptibly small; meager: *A measly dollar is all they gave me.* **2.** Having measles.

meas·ur·a·ble (mĕzh′ər-ə-bəl) *adj.* Possible to be measured: *The speed of light is very fast, but it is nonetheless measurable.* **—meas′ur·a·bly** *adv.*

meas·ure (mĕzh′ər) *n.* **1.** The size or amount of something as determined by comparison with a standard: *What are the measures of that window?* **2.** A unit of measure specified by a scale, as an inch or pint. **3.** A system of such standards and units, as the metric system. **4.** Something, such as a container or ruler, used for measuring. **5.** The extent or degree of something: *There is a large measure of planning involved in putting on a play.* **6.** A standard of evaluation or basis for comparison: *A book's sales shouldn't be the only measure of its success.* **7.** Limit; bounds: *His generosity knows no measure.* **8.** often **measures** An action taken for a specified purpose or end: *It took drastic measures to clean up the harbor.* **9.** A legislative bill or act; a law. **10.** Poetic meter. **11.** The music between two bars on a staff. ❖ *v.* **meas·ured, meas·ur·ing, meas·ures** *—tr.* **1.** To find the size, amount, capacity, or degree of: *Measure this board for me.* **2.** To serve as a measure of: *The foot measures length.* **3.** To mark off or dole out by measuring: *measure off a yard of fabric.* **4.** To estimate by comparison or evaluation; appraise: *measure the importance of a problem.* **5.** To choose with care; weigh: *I measured my words before answering the question.* *—intr.* **1.** To have a measurement: *The paper measures 8 by 12 inches.* **2.** To take measurements: *Always measure accurately.* ◆ **for good measure** In addition to the required amount. **measure up** To have the necessary qualifications: *The baseball player didn't measure up and was sent to the minors.* **measure up to** To be the equal of; fulfill or meet: *Did the concert measure up to your expectations?*

meas·ured (mĕzh′ərd) *adj.* **1.** Found out by measuring: *the measured distance of almost a mile.* **2.** Regular in rhythm and number: *a measured beat.* **3.** Careful; deliberate: *measured and precise words.* **—meas′ured·ly** *adv.*

meas·ure·less (mĕzh′ər-lĭs) *adj.* Too great to be measured; immeasurable: *Infinity is measureless.*

meas·ure·ment (mĕzh′ər-mənt) *n.* **1.** The act or process of measuring: *The experiment begins with measurement of the solution's acidity.* **2.** The dimension, quantity, or capacity found by measuring and expressed in units: *The tailor took my measurements.* See table on page 592.

meat (mēt) *n.* **1.** The flesh of an animal eaten as food, especially beef, pork, or lamb, as distinguished from fish or poultry. **2.** The edible part of a nut or fruit: *chop nut meats.* **3.** The essential part of something; the gist: *the meat of the story.* **4.** *Archaic* Food: *meat and drink.* [From Old English *mete,* food.]

❑ *These sound alike:* **meat, meet¹** (come upon), **meet²** (fitting), **mete** (allot).

meat·ball (mēt′bôl′) *n.* A small ball of ground meat combined with various ingredients or seasonings and cooked.

meat·loaf (mēt′lōf′) *n.* A baked loaf of ground meat and other ingredients.

meat·y (mē′tē) *adj.* **meat·i·er, meat·i·est 1.** Full of meat; fleshy: *a large meaty turkey.* **2.** Relating to or like meat: *a meaty odor.* **3.** Rich in substance; significant: *a meaty book.* **—meat′i·ness** *n.*

mec·ca (mĕk′ə) *n.* A place regarded as a center of activity or interest: *The scientist's lab was a mecca for young chemists.*

Mec·ca (mĕk′ə) A city of western Saudi Arabia near the coast of the Red Sea. The birthplace of Muhammad, it is the holiest city of Islam and a pilgrimage site.

me·chan·ic (mĭ-kăn′ĭk) *n.* A worker skilled in making, using, or repairing machines and tools. **—me·chan′ic** *adj.*

me·chan·i·cal (mĭ-kăn′ĭ-kəl) *adj.* **1.** Relating to or involving machines or tools: *mechanical difficulties with the power saw.* **2.** Operated, produced, or performed by machine. **3.** Performed as if by a machine; showing no variety; dull: *routine mechanical tasks.* **4.** Relating to the science of mechanics. [From Middle English, from Greek *mēkhanē,* device, machine.] **—me·chan′i·cal·ly** *adv.*

mechanical drawing *n.* **1.** A drawing, as of tools or machines, done with rulers, compasses, and similar instruments. **2.** The technique or art of making such drawings; drafting.

mechanical engineering *n.* The branch of engineering that specializes in the design, production, and uses of machines.

me·chan·ics (mĭ-kăn′ĭks) *n.* **1.** *(used with a singular verb)* The branch of physics that studies the action of forces on solids, liquids, and gases at rest or in motion. **2.** *(used with a singular or plural verb)* The development, production, and use of machines or mechanical structures. **3.** *(used with a plural verb)* The technical aspects of something, such as an activity or a sport: *the mechanics of swimming.*

mech·a·nism (mĕk′ə-nĭz′əm) *n.* **1a.** A machine or mechanical device: *An egg beater is a useful mechanism.* **b.** The working parts of a machine: *an old clock's simple mechanism.* **2.** A system of parts that interact: *the mechanism of the solar system.* **3.** A process or means by which something is done or is brought into being: *A constitution is a mechanism for establishing a democratic government.*

mech·a·nis·tic (mĕk′ə-nĭs′tĭk) *adj.* **1.** Relating to mechanics as a branch of physics. **2.** Relating to the philosophy that all natural events can be explained by material causes and physical principles.

mech·a·nize (mĕk′ə-nīz′) *tr.v.* **mech·a·nized, mech·a·niz·ing, mech·a·niz·es** To equip with machinery: *mechanize a bakery.* **—mech′a·ni·za′tion** (mĕk′ə-nĭ-zā′shən) *n.*

med. *abbr.* An abbreviation of: **1.** medicine. **2.** medium.

med·al (mĕd′l) *n.* A flat piece of metal with a special design, given as an award. [From Italian *medaglia,* coin worth half a denarius, from Late Latin *mediālis,* of the middle.]

❑ *These sound alike:* **medal, meddle** (interfere).

med·al·ist (mĕd′l-ĭst) *n.* **1.** A person who has received a medal. **2.** A person who designs, makes, or collects medals.

me·dal·lion (mĭ-dăl′yən) *n.* **1.** A large medal. **2.** A round or oval ornament or design resembling a large medal. **3.** A circular portion of food, especially a cut of meat without any bones: *medallions of veal.*

med·dle (mĕd′l) *intr.v.* **med·dled, med·dling, med·dles 1.** To interfere in other people's business. **2.** To

meadowlark

USAGE

mean³ When **means** has the meaning of "financial resources," it takes a plural verb: *Her means are more than adequate for her to live there.* When *means* has the sense of "a way to an end," the word is singular when it refers to a particular method: *The best means of traveling there is by plane. Means* is plural when it refers to a group of methods: *What are the most effective means for doing this project?*

WRITERS CHOOSE THEIR WORDS

Snug in their furs, the two children ran out across the great snow-covered slope in front of the house, through the grove, and down to where a frozen river **meandered** across the park, after falling over two or three artificial cascades, now stiff and gleaming with icicles.

—Joan Aiken
The Wolves of Willoughby Chase

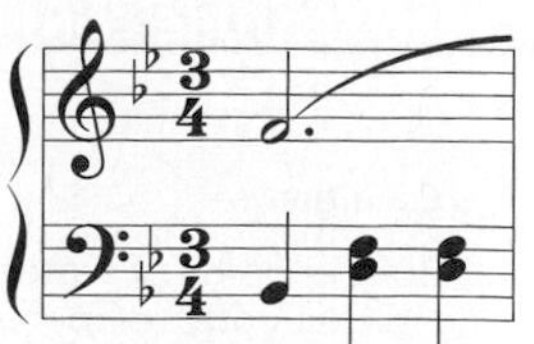
measure

Measurement

INTERNATIONAL SYSTEM

The International System (abbreviated **SI**, for Système International, the French name for the system) is an expanded and modified version of the metric system made up of seven base units from which all others in the system are derived. Larger or smaller multiples of any base unit are formed by adding a prefix to the unit and multiplying it by the appropriate factor. For example, to get a kilometer (multiplying factor = 10^3), you would multiply one meter by **1,000.** Similarly, to get a centimeter (multiplying factor = 10^{-2}), you would multiply one meter by **0.01.**

BASE UNITS			PREFIXES					
Unit	**Quantity**	**Symbol**	**Prefix**	**Symbol**	**Multiplying Factor**	**Prefix**	**Symbol**	**Multiplying Factor**
meter	length	m	tera-	T	10^{12} = 1,000,000,000,000	deci-	d	10^{-1} = 0.1
kilogram	mass	kg	giga-	G	10^{9} = 1,000,000,000	centi-	c	10^{-2} = 0.01
second	time	s	mega-	M	10^{6} = 1,000,000	milli-	m	10^{-3} = 0.001
ampere	electric current	A	kilo-	k	10^{3} = 1,000	micro-	μ	10^{-6} = 0.000,001
kelvin	temperature	K	hecto-	h	10^{2} = 100	nano-	n	10^{-9} = 0.000,000,001
mole	amount of matter	mol	deca-	da	10^{1} = 10	pico-	p	10^{-12} = 0.000,000,000,001
candela	luminous intensity	cd						

US CUSTOMARY SYSTEM

Unlike the International System of Units, the United States Customary System grew more out of customs and habits than as a planned system. For this reason it is not based on a carefully devised decimal system, but on commonly known distances and quantities. For example, the unit *foot* is based on the average length of a human foot, and the unit *gallon* is based on the quantity held by a container commonly used for holding wine.

LENGTH		LIQUID VOLUME OR CAPACITY		WEIGHT	
Unit	**Relation to Other US Customary Units**	**Unit**	**Relation to Other US Customary Units**	**Unit**	**Relation to Other US Customary Units**
inch	1/12 foot	ounce	1/16 pint	grain	1/7000 pound
foot	12 inches or ⅓ yard	gill	4 ounces	dram	1/16 ounce
yard	36 inches or 3 feet	pint	16 ounces	ounce	16 drams
rod	16½ feet or 5¼ yards	quart	2 pints or ¼ gallon	pound	16 ounces
furlong	220 yards or ⅛ mile	gallon	128 ounces or 8 pints	ton (short)	2,000 pounds
mile	5,280 feet or 1,760 yards			ton (long)	2,240 pounds

CONVERSION BETWEEN METRIC AND US CUSTOMARY SYSTEMS

The metric system is very similar to the International System, but it contains more than just the base units. For example, it includes multiples of base units, such as centimeters, decigrams, and milliseconds. It also includes a unit of volume, the liter, defined as a thousand cubic centimeters.

FROM US CUSTOMARY TO METRIC			FROM METRIC TO US CUSTOMARY		
When you know	**multiply by**	**to find**	**When you know**	**multiply by**	**to find**
inches	25.4	millimeters	millimeters	0.04	inches
	2.54	centimeters	centimeters	0.39	inches
feet	30.48	centimeters	meters	3.28	feet
yards	0.91	meters		1.09	yards
miles	1.61	kilometers	kilometers	0.62	miles
fluid ounces	29.57	milliliters	milliliters	0.03	fluid ounces
pints	0.47	liters	liters	1.06	quarts
quarts	0.95	liters		0.26	gallons
gallons	3.79	liters		2.11	pints
ounces	28.35	grams	grams	0.035	ounces
pounds	0.45	kilograms	kilograms	2.20	pounds

TEMPERATURE CONVERSION BETWEEN CELSIUS AND FAHRENHEIT

°C = (°F – 32) ÷ 1.8			°F = (°C × 1.8) + 32		
Condition	**Fahrenheit**	**Celsius**	**Condition**	**Fahrenheit**	**Celsius**
Boiling point of water	212°	100°	Freezing point of water	32°	0°
Normal body temperature	98.6°	37°	Lowest temperature Gabriel Fahrenheit could obtain mixing salt and ice	0°	–17.8°

handle something carelessly or ignorantly; tamper: *Don't meddle with my cell phone!* [From Middle English *medlen*, from Anglo-Norman *medler*, from Latin *miscēre*, to mix.] **—med′dler** *n.*

❑ *These sound alike:* **meddle, medal** (award).

med·dle·some (mĕd′l-səm) *adj.* Inclined to interfere in other people's business.

Mede (mēd) *n.* A native or inhabitant of ancient Media.

Me·de·a (mĭ-dē′ə) *n.* In Greek mythology, a princess and sorceress who helps Jason obtain the Golden Fleece.

me·di·a (mē′dē-ə) *n.* A plural of **medium.**

Me·di·a (mē′dē-ə) An ancient country of southwest Asia in present-day northwest Iran. Originally settled by an Indo-European people, it was conquered by Cyrus the Great in about 550 BC.

me·di·ae·val (mē′dē-ē′vəl *or* mĕd′ē-ē′vəl *or* mĭ-dē′vəl) *adj.* Variant of **medieval.**

me·di·al (mē′dē-əl) *adj.* **1.** Relating to or occurring in the middle: *the medial position.* **2.** Average; ordinary. **3.** In mathematics, relating to a mean or average. **—me′di·al·ly** *adv.*

me·di·an (mē′dē-ən) *adj.* **1.** Located in the middle: *a median barrier.* **2.** Relating to or constituting the middle value in a set of numbers: *median score.* ❖ *n.* **1.** Something that lies halfway between two extremes; a medium. **2.** The dividing area, either paved or landscaped, between opposing lanes of traffic on some highways. **3.** In mathematics, the middle number of a sequence having an odd number of values or the average of the two middle values if the sequence has an even number of values. For example, in the sequence 3, 4, 5, 6, 7, the median is 5; in the sequence 4, 8, 12, 16, the median is 10. **4.** In geometry: **a.** A line joining a vertex of a triangle to the midpoint of the opposite side. **b.** A line that joins the midpoints of the sides of a trapezoid that are not parallel.

me·di·ate (mē′dē-āt′) *v.* **me·di·at·ed, me·di·at·ing, me·di·ates** *—tr.* **1.** To settle (differences) by working with all sides: *mediate a dispute.* **2.** To bring about (an agreement) by working with all sides: *A negotiator mediated the new contract between the company and its workers.* *—intr.* To help the opposing sides in a dispute come to an agreement: *The teacher mediated between the two students.* [From Latin *medius*, middle.] **—me′di·a′tion** *n.*

me·di·a·tor (mē′dē-ā′tər) *n.* A person or agency that mediates in a dispute.

med·ic (mĕd′ĭk) *n.* **1.** A person in a medical corps of the armed services. **2.** A physician or surgeon. **3.** A medical student or intern.

Med·i·caid (mĕd′ĭ-kād′) *n.* A program in the United States, jointly funded by the federal government and the states, that pays hospitals and physicians for providing medical care to people whose incomes are below a certain level.

med·i·cal (mĕd′ĭ-kəl) *adj.* Relating to the study or practice of medicine: *a medical problem; medical school.* **—med′i·cal·ly** *adv.*

Med·i·care (mĕd′ĭ-kâr′) *n.* A program in the United States, funded by the federal government, that pays hospitals and physicians for medical care provided to people over 65 years old.

med·i·cate (mĕd′ĭ-kāt′) *tr.v.* **med·i·cat·ed, med·i·cat·ing, med·i·cates** **1.** To treat (a person, injury, or part of the body) with medicine. **2.** To put medicine on or in: *medicate a bandage.*

med·i·ca·tion (mĕd′ĭ-kā′shən) *n.* **1.** A substance that helps to cure a disease, heal an injury, or relieve pain; a medicine. **2.** The act or process of medicating.

Med·i·ci (mĕd′ə-chē′) Italian noble family that produced three popes and two queens of France. **Lorenzo** "the Magnificent" (1449–1492) was a patron of the arts whose clients included Michelangelo.

me·dic·i·nal (mĭ-dĭs′ə-nəl) *adj.* **1.** Relating to or having the properties of medicine: *medicinal plants.* **2.** Having an unappealing, bitter flavor. **—me·dic′i·nal·ly** *adv.*

med·i·cine (mĕd′ĭ-sĭn) *n.* **1.** The scientific study of diseases and disorders of the body and the methods of diagnosing, treating, and preventing them. **2.** The practice of this science as a profession. **3.** A drug or other substance used to treat a disease or injury. **4a.** A group of practices or beliefs, especially among Native Americans, believed to control nature, influence spiritual beings, or prevent or cure disease. **b.** Something, such as a ceremony or a sacred object, believed to have such abilities. [From Middle English, from Latin *medicus*, physician.]

medicine ball *n.* A large heavy stuffed ball used for conditioning exercises.

medicine man *n.* A male shaman, especially among Native American peoples.

medicine woman *n.* A female shaman, especially among Native American peoples.

me·di·e·val also **me·di·ae·val** (mē′dē-ē′vəl *or* mĕd′ē-ē′vəl *or* mĭ-dē′vəl) *adj.* **1.** also **Medieval a.** Relating to or characteristic of the Middle Ages. **b.** Relating to a historical period roughly coinciding with the European Middle Ages and characterized by feudal or aristocratic social structures, as in Japan or China. **2.** *Informal* Old-fashioned or lacking insight: *medieval ideas about social reform.* [From Latin *medius*, middle + Latin *aevum*, age.]

Medieval Latin *n.* Latin as used from about 700 to 1500.

Me·di·na (mĭ-dē′nə) A city of western Saudi Arabia north of Mecca. It is the site of Muhammad's tomb and is a holy site.

me·di·o·cre (mē′dē-ō′kər) *adj.* Neither good nor bad; ordinary; undistinguished: *a mediocre actor.*

me·di·oc·ri·ty (mē′dē-ŏk′rĭ-tē) *n., pl.* **me·di·oc·ri·ties** **1.** The fact or condition of being mediocre. **2.** An ordinary undistinguished quality or performance.

med·i·tate (mĕd′ĭ-tāt′) *v.* **med·i·tat·ed, med·i·tat·ing, med·i·tates** *—intr.* **1.** To train, calm, or empty the mind, often by achieving an altered state, as by focusing on a single object. **2.** To think deeply and quietly; reflect: *The counselor meditated on the problem before coming to a decision.* *—tr.* **1.** To reflect on; contemplate. **2.** To consider at length; plan: *meditated a change of jobs.* [From Latin *meditārī*.] **—med′i·ta′tor** *n.*

med·i·ta·tion (mĕd′ĭ-tā′shən) *n.* **1.** The process of meditating; contemplation: *The poet stared out the window, lost in meditation.* **2.** Deep reflection on spiritual or religious matters.

med·i·ta·tive (mĕd′ĭ-tā′tĭv) *adj.* Devoted to or characterized by meditation. **—med′i·ta′tive·ly** *adv.*

Med·i·ter·ra·ne·an (mĕd′ĭ-tə-rā′nē-ən) The region surrounding the Mediterranean Sea. Several important ancient civilizations flourished in the region, which was dominated for centuries by Phoenicia, Carthage, Greece, Rome, and the Byzantine and Ottoman empires. —SEE NOTE.

Mediterranean Sea An inland sea surrounded by Europe, Asia, and Africa. It connects with the Atlantic Ocean through the Strait of Gibraltar; with the Black Sea through the Dardanelles, the Sea of Marmara, and the Bosporus; and with the Red Sea through the Suez Canal.

me·di·um (mē′dē-əm) *n., pl.* **me·di·a** (mē′dē-ə) or **me·di·ums** **1.** A position, choice, or course of action midway between extremes: *a happy medium between hot and cold weather.* **2a.** The substance or surrounding environment in which an animal, plant, or other organism normally lives and thrives: *Some plants can grow in a salty medium.* **b.** The environment or surroundings in which a person thrives: *She's in her medium when she's on the stage.* **c.** An artificial substance in which bacteria or other microorganisms are grown for scientific purposes. **3.** A substance through which something is transmitted:

median

WORD BUILDING

Mediterranean The word **Mediterranean** is a nice, long word that is good for a spelling bee. It comes from the Latin *mediterrāneus*, from the Latin word root *medi–*, "the middle, in the middle," and *terra*, "land." The Latin phrase *mare mediterrāneum* therefore means "the sea in the middle of the land." The sea got this name because it is surrounded by southern Europe, northern Africa, and western Asia. The Latin word root *medi–* also appears in our words *medium* and *median*, while *terra* appears in *territory* and *terrain*.

meerkat

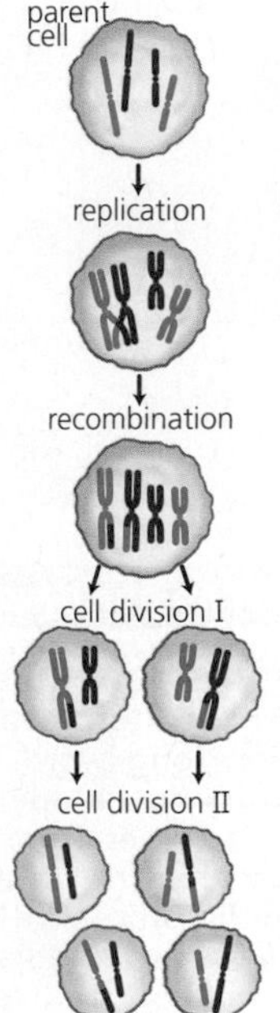

meiosis

In meiosis a parent cell replicates and recombines, divides once to create two daughter cells, then divides again creating four daughter cells, each of which has half the genetic content of the original parent cell.

ă	pat	ô	paw
ā	pay	ôr	core
âr	care	oi	boy
ä	father	ou	out
ĕ	pet	o͝o	took
ē	be	o͝or	lure
ĭ	pit	o͞o	boot
ī	bite	ŭ	cut
îr	pier	ûr	urge
ŏ	pot	th	thin
ō	toe	*th*	this
		zh	vision
		ə	about

Air is one of the media through which sound can travel. **4.** An agency by which something is accomplished, transported, or transferred: *Money is a medium of exchange.* **5.** One of the techniques, materials, or means of expression available to an artist: *That artist uses the medium of lithography.* **6.** *pl.* **media a.** A means for communicating to large numbers of people: *television, radio, and other media.* **b.** Any of various kinds of devices for storing digital data. **7. media** *(used with a singular or plural verb)* The group of journalists and others whose work involves communicating information: *The governor provided a statement to the media.* **8.** *pl.* **mediums** A person who claims to be able to communicate with the spirits of the dead. ❖ *adj.* Occurring midway between extremes; intermediate: *a new bookshelf of medium height.* [From Latin.]

medium frequency *n.* A radio-wave frequency lying in the range between 300 and 3,000 kilohertz.

med·ley (**mĕd′**lē) *n., pl.* **med·leys 1.** A mixture or variety: *a medley of events in the program.* **2.** A musical arrangement that uses a series of melodies from different sources. [From Middle English *medle,* from Anglo-Norman *medlee,* meddling.]

me·dul·la (mĭ-**dŭl′**ə *or* mĭ-**do͞o′**lə) *n., pl.* **me·dul·las** or **me·dul·lae** (mĭ-**dŭl′**ē *or* mĭ-**do͞o′**lē) **1.** The inner core of certain structures of vertebrate animals, as the marrow of bone. **2.** The medulla oblongata.

medulla ob·lon·ga·ta (ŏb′lông-**gä′**tə) *n., pl.* **medulla ob·lon·ga·tas** or **medullae ob·lon·ga·tae** (ŏb′lông-**gä′**tē) A mass of nerve tissue located at the top of the spinal cord and at the base of the brain. It controls breathing, blood pressure, heart rate, and certain other involuntary functions.

me·dus·a (mĭ-**do͞o′**sə) *n., pl.* **me·du·sas** or **me·du·sae** (mĭ-**do͞o′**sē) The dome-shaped structure of jellyfish and certain other related animals, having a mouth underneath surrounded by tentacles. [From Latin *Medūsa,* Medusa (from the Medusa's snaky locks).]

Me·dus·a (mĭ-**do͞o′**sə) *n.* In Greek mythology, the Gorgon who was killed by Perseus.

Med·ved·ev (myĕd-**vyĕd′**ĕv *or* myĭ-**dvyĕ′**dyĭf), **Dmitry Anatolyevich** Born 1965. Russian president (2008–2012) and prime minister (appointed 2012).

meek (mēk) *adj.* **meek·er, meek·est 1.** Showing patience and humility; gentle. **2.** Easily imposed upon; submissive: *Meek customers often fail to demand prompt service.* [From Middle English *meke,* of Scandinavian origin; akin to Old Norse *mjūkr,* soft.] **—meek′ly** *adv.* **—meek′ness** *n.*

meer·kat (**mîr′**kăt′) *n.* A small burrowing mammal of southern Africa, having brownish-gray fur and a long tail, which it uses for balance when it stands on its hind legs.

meer·schaum (**mîr′**shəm *or* **mîr′**shôm′) *n.* **1.** A soft claylike material that is usually white and is used as a building stone and for making tobacco pipes. **2.** A tobacco pipe with a meerschaum bowl. [From German : *Meer,* sea + *Schaum,* foam.]

meet[1] (mēt) *v.* **met** (mĕt), **meet·ing, meets** —*tr.* **1.** To come upon by chance or arrangement: *I was surprised to meet my old teacher in the park. I am supposed to meet my friends at the restaurant.* **2.** To get to know (another person) initially, especially by being introduced: *Have you met my sister?* **3.** To come together in conflict or opposition: *Our team will meet theirs in the playoffs.* **4.** To be present at the arrival of: *She is on her way to meet the train.* **5.** To come into contact with; join: *The stream meets the river at the rapids.* **6.** To come to the notice of: *There is more here than meets the eye.* **7.** To deal or cope with effectively: *We have met every problem and continued our progress.* **8.** To satisfy (a requirement, for example); fulfill: *You meet all the conditions for getting the loan.* **9.** To pay; settle: *Is there enough money to meet our expenses?* —*intr.* **1.** To come together; come face to face: *We'll meet tonight at the ice rink.* **2.** To become acquainted with one another for the first time: *My parents met on the ferry.* **3.** To come into contact; be joined: *The boards meet at the corner.* **4.** To come together as opponents: *The two teams met again last night.* **5.** To come together in a group; assemble: *The committee meets tonight.* ❖ *n.* A meeting or contest: *a track meet.* ◆ **meet (one's) Maker** To die. **meet with 1.** To experience or undergo: *The explorers met with great difficulty when crossing the mountains.* **2.** To receive: *Our plan met with their approval.* [From Old English *mētan.*]

❑ *These sound alike:* **meet**[1] (come upon), **meat** (animal flesh), **meet**[2] (fitting), **mete** (allot).

meet[2] (mēt) *Archaic adj.* Fitting; proper. [From Old English *gemǣte.*] **—meet′ly** *adv.*

❑ *These sound alike:* **meet**[2] (fitting), **meat** (animal flesh), **meet**[1] (come upon), **mete** (allot).

meet·ing (**mē′**tĭng) *n.* **1.** A coming together; an encounter: *a chance meeting of friends.* **2.** A gathering or assembly of people, usually for a business, social, or religious purpose. **3.** A point where two or more things come together; a junction: *the meeting of two railroad lines.* ◆ **meeting of the minds** Agreement; concord.

meet·ing·house (**mē′**tĭng-hous′) *n.* A building used for public meetings and especially for Quaker religious services.

meg (mĕg) *n. Informal* A megabyte.

mega– *pref.* A prefix that means: **1.** One million (10^6): *megahertz; megabit.* **2.** 1,048,576 (2^{20}): *megabyte.* **3.** Large: *megalith.* **4.** Surpassing other examples of its kind; extraordinary: *megahit.*

meg·a·bit (**mĕg′**ə-bĭt′) *n.* One million bits, used as a unit to measure the rate of the transmission of computer data.

meg·a·byte (**mĕg′**ə-bīt′) *n.* A unit of computer memory equal to 1,024 kilobytes (2^{20} bytes).

meg·a·cy·cle (**mĕg′**ə-sī′kəl) *n.* One megahertz.

meg·a·hertz (**mĕg′**ə-hûrts′) *n., pl.* **megahertz** A unit of frequency equal to one million cycles per second, used to express the frequency of radio waves.

meg·a·hit (**mĕg′**ə-hĭt′) *n.* A product or event, such as a movie or concert, that is exceedingly successful.

meg·a·lith (**mĕg′**ə-lĭth′) *n.* A very large stone used in the building of prehistoric monuments.

meg·a·lo·ma·ni·a (mĕg′ə-lō-**mā′**nē-ə *or* mĕg′ə-lō-**mān′**yə) *n.* An obsession with making oneself powerful or getting what one wants, especially on a grand scale. **—meg′a·lo·ma′ni·ac′** *n.*

meg·a·lop·o·lis (mĕg′ə-**lŏp′**ə-lĭs) *n.* A large urban region containing several large cities that border each other.

meg·a·phone (**mĕg′**ə-fōn′) *n.* A large funnel-shaped horn, used to direct and amplify the voice.

meg·a·pix·el (**mĕg′**ə-**pĭk′**səl) *n.* One million pixels.

meg·a·ton (**mĕg′**ə-tŭn′) *n.* A unit of explosive force equal to that of one million metric tons of TNT.

meg·a·watt (**mĕg′**ə-wŏt′) *n.* A unit of electrical power equal to one million watts.

Mei·ji (**mā′**jē′) See **Mutsuhito.**

mei·o·sis (mī-**ō′**sĭs) *n., pl.* **mei·o·ses** (mī-**ō′**sēz′) A form of cell division in which the number of chromosomes is reduced to half the original number, resulting in the production of reproductive cells such as gametes in animals and spores in plants and fungi. —SEE NOTE AT **cell division.**

Meit·ner (**mīt′**nər), **Lise** 1878–1968. Austrian-born Swedish physicist and pioneer in the study of nuclear fission.

meit·ner·i·um (mīt-**nûr′**ē-əm) *n. Symbol* **Mt** A radioactive element that has been artificially produced by scientists. The half-life of its longest-lived isotope is seven-tenths of a second. Atomic number 109. See **Periodic Table.**

Me·kong (mā′kông′) A river of southeast Asia flowing about 2,800 miles (4,500 kilometers) from southeast China to the South China Sea through southern Vietnam.

mel·an·cho·li·a (mĕl′ən-**kō′**lē-ə) *n.* Extreme, persistent sadness or depression.

mel·an·chol·ic (mĕl′ən-**kŏl′**ĭk) *adj.* **1.** Sad and gloomy; melancholy. **2.** Relating to or suffering from melancholia. —SEE NOTE AT **humor.**

mel·an·chol·y (**mĕl′**ən-kŏl′ē) *n.* Sadness or depression of the spirits. ❖ *adj.* **1.** Sad; gloomy. See Synonyms at **sad. 2.** Inspiring sadness; depressing: *the melancholy notes of a funeral dirge.* [From Middle English *malencolie*, from Greek *melankholiā* : *melās*, black + *kholē*, bile (from the former belief that melancholy was caused by too much black bile in the body).]

Mel·a·ne·sia (mĕl′ə-**nē′**zhə) A division of Oceania in the southwest Pacific Ocean made up of the islands northeast of Australia and south of the equator.

Mel·a·ne·sian (mĕl′ə-**nē′**zhən) *adj.* Relating to Melanesia or its peoples, languages, or cultures. ❖ *n.* **1.** A member of any of the peoples of Melanesia. **2.** The group of languages spoken in Melanesia.

mé·lange also **me·lange** (mā-**länzh′**) *n.* A mixture.

mel·a·nin (**mĕl′**ə-nĭn) *n.* A dark pigment found in most animals. In humans it occurs in the skin, hair, and eyes.

mel·a·no·ma (mĕl′ə-**nō′**mə) *n.* A dark-colored, usually malignant tumor that most often arises in the skin.

Mel·ba toast (**mĕl′**bə) *n.* Crisp, thinly sliced toast. [After Dame Nellie *Melba* (1861–1931), Australian singer.]

Mel·bourne (**mĕl′**bərn) A city of southeast Australia southwest of Canberra. It was settled in 1835.

meld[1] (mĕld) *intr. & tr.v.* **meld·ed, meld·ing, melds** To merge or cause to merge; unite; blend. ❖ *n.* A blend or a merger: *This restaurant features a meld of French and Indian cuisines.* [Possibly from a blend of *melt* and *weld.*]

meld[2] (mĕld) *v.* **meld·ed, meld·ing, melds** —*tr.* In certain card games, to declare or show (a card or combination of cards) as a means of adding points to a score. —*intr.* To meld a card or combination of cards. ❖ *n.* A combination of cards to be presented for a score. [Probably from German *melden*, to announce.]

me·lee (**mā′**lā′ *or* mā-**lā′**) *n.* A confused fight among a number of people.

Me·le·ke·ok (mə-**lā′**kā-o͝ok) The capital of Palau, on the eastern shore of an island in the northeast part of the country.

mel·lif·lu·ous (mə-**lĭf′**lo͞o-əs) *adj.* Having a pleasant and soothing sound: *a mellifluous voice.* **—mel·lif′lu·ous·ly** *adv.*

mel·lo·phone (**mĕl′**ō-fōn′) *n.* A brass musical instrument, similar to the French horn, often used in military or marching bands.

mel·low (**mĕl′**ō) *adj.* **mel·low·er, mel·low·est 1a.** Soft, sweet, or juicy; fully ripened: *a mellow peach.* **b.** Rich and full in flavor; properly aged: *mellow wine.* **2.** Rich and soft in quality: *the mellow colors of autumn.* **3.** Having or showing gentleness, wisdom, and tolerance; mature. **4.** Relaxed and unhurried; easygoing: *a mellow conversation.* ❖ *tr. & intr.v.* **mel·lowed, mel·low·ing, mel·lows** To make or become mellow: *Time often mellows youthful intolerance. Wine mellows over a period of years.* [From Middle English *melwe.*] **—mel′low·ly** *adv.*

me·lod·ic (mə-**lŏd′**ĭk) *adj.* Relating to or containing melody. **—me·lod′i·cal·ly** *adv.*

me·lo·di·ous (mə-**lō′**dē-əs) *adj.* Containing pleasant sounds; pleasant to listen to: *a melodious voice.* **—me·lo′di·ous·ly** *adv.*

mel·o·dra·ma (**mĕl′**ə-drä′mə *or* **mĕl′**ə-drăm′ə) *n.* **1.** A drama characterized by exaggerated emotions, conflicts between characters, and often a happy ending. **2.** This kind of drama: *Melodrama is common on daytime TV.* **3.** Behavior or occurrences full of exaggerated emotions.

mel·o·dra·mat·ic (mĕl′ə-drə-**măt′**ĭk) *adj.* **1.** Relating to or characteristic of melodrama: *a melodramatic ending.* **2.** Exaggerated in emotion or sentiment: *a melodramatic speech.* **—mel′o·dra·mat′i·cal·ly** *adv.*

mel·o·dy (**mĕl′**ə-dē) *n., pl.* **mel·o·dies 1a.** A succession of rhythmically arranged musical tones that forms a complete unit, often repeated several times in a song or other composition. **b.** The main part in a musical composition that has harmony. **2.** A pleasing arrangement of sounds: *The melody of a robin singing.* [From Middle English *melodie*, from Greek *melōidiā*, singing, choral song : *melos*, tune + *aoidē*, song.]

mel·on (**mĕl′**ən) *n.* **1.** Any of several large fruits, such as a cantaloupe or watermelon, that grow on a vine and have a hard rind and juicy edible flesh. **2.** Any of the vines that bear such fruit. [From Late Latin *mēlō*, from Greek *mēlopepōn* : *mēlon*, apple + from *pepōn*, gourd.]

melt (mĕlt) *v.* **melt·ed, melt·ing, melts** —*intr.* **1.** To be changed from a solid to a liquid state, especially by heating: *The ice melted in the sun.* **2.** To be taken up into a solution; dissolve: *Sugar melts in water.* **3.** To disappear gradually: *The crowd melted away after the rally.* **4.** To pass or merge into something else: *The blue melted into the green in the painting.* **5.** To become gentle in feeling: *Their hearts melted at the sight of the baby.* —*tr.* **1.** To change (a solid) to a liquid, especially by heating. **2.** To dissolve (a substance) in a solution: *The perfume consists of strong-smelling oils that are melted in alcohol.* **3.** To make gentler or milder; soften: *a look to melt the hardest heart.* ❖ *n.* A sandwich with melted cheese over the main ingredient, sometimes without the top slice of bread: *a tuna melt.* [From Old English *meltan.*] **—melt′er** *n.*

melt·down (**mĕlt′**doun′) *n.* **1.** The overheating of the core of a nuclear reactor, resulting in melting of the core and escape of radiation. **2.** *Informal* An emotional breakdown.

melt·ing point (**mĕl′**tĭng) *n.* The temperature at which a given solid becomes a liquid. The melting point of ice is 0°C.

melting pot *n.* **1.** A container in which a substance is melted; a crucible. **2.** A place where people of different cultures or races form a single culture.

Mel·ville (**mĕl′**vĭl), **Herman** 1819–1891. American writer whose experiences at sea provided the basis of his novel *Moby Dick* (1851).

mem·ber (**mĕm′**bər) *n.* **1.** A part or organ of a plant, animal, or human body, especially a leg, arm, wing, or branch. **2.** A person or thing that belongs to a group: *a member of the cat family.* **3.** A quantity that belongs to a mathematical set; an element of a set. [From Middle English *membre*, from Latin *membrum.*]

mem·ber·ship (**mĕm′**bər-shĭp′) *n.* **1.** The condition or state of being a member. **2.** The total number of members in a group: *The membership voted in a new club president.*

mem·brane (**mĕm′**brān′) *n.* **1.** A thin flexible layer of tissue that covers, lines, separates, or connects parts of a living organism. **2.** A layer that surrounds a cell or organelle, typically consisting of lipids and proteins. **3.** A thin sheet or layer of natural or artificial material.

mem·bra·nous (**mĕm′**brə-nəs) *adj.* Relating to, made of, or similar to a membrane.

meme (mēm) *n.* **1.** An electronically transmitted image usually combining a humorous caption with a photo or short video clip from another source. **2.** A unit of cultural information, such as a

Lise Meitner
photographed in the 1930s

USAGE

men When *man* and *men* are used in compounds, such as *fireman, firemen, salesman,* and *salesmen,* both *-man* and *-men* are usually pronounced (mən).

menorah

ă	pat	ôr	core
ā	pay	oi	boy
âr	care	ou	out
ä	father	ŏŏ	took
ĕ	pet	ŏŏr	lure
ē	be	ōō	boot
ĭ	pit	ŭ	cut
ī	bite	ûr	urge
îr	pier	th	thin
ŏ	pot	*th*	this
ō	toe	zh	vision
ô	paw	ə	about

cultural practice or idea, that is transmitted verbally or by repeated action from one mind to another.

me·men·to (mə-**mĕn′**tō) *n., pl.* **me·men·tos** or **me·men·toes** A reminder of the past; a keepsake: *These shells are mementos of our trip to the beach.*

mem·o (**mĕm′**ō) *n., pl.* **mem·os** A memorandum.

mem·oir (**mĕm′**wär′ *or* **mĕm′**wôr′) *n.* **1.** An account of the personal experiences of an author: *a memoir of childhood on a farm.* **2.** often **memoirs** An account of a person's own life; an autobiography: *wrote her memoirs when she turned 80.* **3.** A biography. [From Old French *memoire,* memory, from Latin, *memoria.*]

mem·o·ra·bil·i·a (mĕm′ər-ə-**bĭl′**ē-ə *or* mĕm′ər-ə-**bĭl′**yə) *pl.n.* Things from the past that are worth remembering or keeping.

mem·o·ra·ble (**mĕm′**ər-ə-bəl) *adj.* Worth being remembered or noted: *Memorable events are sometimes pictured on stamps.* **—mem′o·ra·bly** *adv.*

mem·o·ran·dum (mĕm′ə-**răn′**dəm) *n., pl.* **me·mo·ran·dums** or **me·mo·ran·da** (mĕm′ə-**răn′**də) **1.** A short note written as a reminder. **2.** A written record or communication, as in a business office. **3.** A short written statement outlining the terms of a legal or business agreement.

me·mo·ri·al (mə-**môr′**ē-əl) *n.* **1.** Something, such as a monument or holiday, established to serve as a remembrance of a person or event. **2.** A written statement of facts or a petition addressed to a government or legislature. ❖ *adj.* Serving as a remembrance of a person or event; commemorative: *memorial services; a memorial plaque.*

Memorial Day *n.* The last Monday in May, observed in the United States in honor of those members of the armed forces killed in war. Before 1971, it had been observed on May 30.

me·mo·ri·al·ize (mə-**môr′**ē-ə-līz′) *tr.v.* **me·mo·ri·al·ized, me·mo·ri·al·iz·ing, me·mo·ri·al·iz·es 1.** To honor with a memorial; commemorate. **2.** To present a memorial to; petition.

mem·o·rize (**mĕm′**ə-rīz′) *tr.v.* **mem·o·rized, mem·o·riz·ing, mem·o·riz·es** To commit to memory; learn by heart. **—mem′o·ri·za′tion** (mĕm′ə-rĭ-**zā′**shən) *n.* **—mem′o·riz′er** *n.*

mem·o·ry (**mĕm′**ə-rē) *n., pl.* **mem·o·ries 1.** The power or ability of remembering past experiences: *Thanks to a good memory, I could recall the details of what happened.* **2.** The part of the mind where knowledge is stored: *I committed the poem to memory.* **3.** Something remembered: *a pleasant memory of summer vacation.* **4.** The fact of being remembered; remembrance: *a ceremony in memory of our forebears.* **5.** The period of time covered by the ability of a group of people to remember: *the heaviest gale in living memory.* **6a.** A unit of a computer in which data is stored for later use. **b.** A computer's capacity for storing information: *How much memory does this computer have?* [From Middle English *memorie,* from Latin *memoria.*]

Mem·phis (**mĕm′**fĭs) **1.** An ancient city of Egypt south of Cairo. It was supposedly founded by the first king of united Egypt. **2.** The largest city of Tennessee, in the southwest part of the state on the Mississippi River. It was established in 1819 on the site of a fort built in 1797.

men (mĕn) *n.* Plural of **man.** —SEE NOTE.

men·ace (**mĕn′**ĭs) *n.* **1.** A threat or danger: *a reef that is a menace to passing ships.* **2.** A troublesome or annoying person. ❖ *tr.v.* **men·aced, men·ac·ing, men·ac·es** To threaten; endanger: *The erupting volcano menaced the nearby town.* [From Middle English *manace,* from Latin *mināx,* threatening.]

me·nag·er·ie (mə-**năj′**ə-rē *or* mə-**năzh′**ə-rē) *n.* **1.** A collection of wild animals kept in cages or pens on exhibition. **2.** A place where such animals are kept.

men-at-arms (mĕn′ət-**ärmz′**) *n.* Plural of **man-at-arms.**

mend (mĕnd) *v.* **mend·ed, mend·ing, mends** *—tr.* **1.** To make repairs to; fix: *mend a jacket.* **2.** To reform or correct: *The judge always warns criminals to mend their ways. —intr.* **1.** To improve in health: *The patient is mending well.* **2.** To heal: *Her ankle mended slowly.* ❖ *n.* The act of mending. ◆ **on the mend** Improving, especially in health. [From Middle English *menden,* short for *amenden,* to amend.] **—mend′er** *n.*

men·da·cious (mĕn-**dā′**shəs) *adj.* **1.** Lying; untruthful: *a mendacious person.* **2.** False; untrue: *a mendacious explanation.* [From Latin *mendāx.*] **—men·da′cious·ly** *adv.*

men·dac·i·ty (mĕn-**dăs′**ĭ-tē) *n., pl.* **men·dac·i·ties 1.** The condition of being mendacious; untruthfulness. **2.** A lie: *The witness's testimony is a complete mendacity.*

Men·del (**mĕn′**dl), **Gregor Johann** 1822–1884. Moravian botanist and founder of the science of genetics who discovered the principle of inherited characteristics.

men·de·le·vi·um (mĕn′də-**lē′**vē-əm) *n. Symbol* **Md** A radioactive metallic element that has been artificially produced by scientists. Atomic number 101. See **Periodic Table.** [After Dmitri Ivanovich *Mendeleev* (1834–1907), Russian chemist.]

Men·dels·sohn (**mĕn′**dl-sən), **Felix** 1809–1847. German pianist and composer whose works include the *Italian* (1833) and *Scottish* (1842) symphonies.

men·di·cant (**mĕn′**dĭ-kənt) *adj.* Depending on alms for a living: *a mendicant order of friars.* ❖ *n.* A beggar. [From Middle English *mendicaunt,* from Latin *mendīcāre,* to beg.] **—men′di·can·cy** *n.*

Men·e·la·us (mĕn′ə-**lā′**əs) *n.* In Greek mythology, a Spartan king who fights in the Trojan War for the return of his wife, Helen.

men·folk (**mĕn′**fōk′) or **men·folks** (**mĕn′**fōks′) *pl.n.* **1.** Men considered as a group. **2.** The members of a community or family who are men.

men·ha·den (mĕn-**hād′**n) *n., pl.* **menhaden** or **men·ha·dens** Any of several fishes of western Atlantic waters, used chiefly as bait and as a source of fish oil and fertilizer.

me·ni·al (**mē′**nē-əl *or* **mēn′**yəl) *adj.* **1.** Relating to work or a job regarded as servile; lowly: *They let me run errands and perform other menial tasks for them.* **2.** Relating to or appropriate for a servant. ❖ *n.* A servant who performs the simplest or most unpleasant tasks. **—me′ni·al·ly** *adv.*

men·in·gi·tis (mĕn′ĭn-**jī′**tĭs) *n.* Inflammation of the membranes that enclose the brain and spinal cord, usually resulting from a bacterial or viral infection.

me·ninx (**mē′**nĭngks) *n., pl.* **me·nin·ges** (mə-**nĭn′**jēz) Any of the three membranes enclosing the brain and spinal cord.

me·nis·cus (mə-**nĭs′**kəs) *n., pl.* **me·nis·ci** (mə-**nĭs′**ī *or* mə-**nĭs′**kī) or **me·nis·cus·es 1.** A crescent or crescent-shaped body, as the piece of cartilage at the knee joint. **2.** A lens that is concave on one side and convex on the other. **3.** The curved upper surface of a column of liquid. The surface is concave if the liquid adheres to the container walls and convex if it does not.

Men·non·ite (**mĕn′**ə-nīt′) *n.* A member of an Anabaptist church noted for its simplicity of living and pacifism. [After *Menno* Simons (1492–1559), Frisian religious leader.]

men-of-war (mĕn′ə-**wôr′**) *n.* Plural of **man-of-war.**

Me·nom·i·nee (mə-**nŏm′**ə-nē) *n., pl.* **Menominee** or **Menomi·nees 1.** A member of a Native American people living in northeast Wisconsin. **2.** The Algonquian language of the Menominee.

men·o·pause (**mĕn′**ə-pôz′) *n.* The time at which menstruation ceases, occurring usually between 45 and 55 years of age.

me·no·rah (mə-**nôr′**ə) *n.* A candelabrum used in Jewish religious ceremonies, especially one with nine branches used in the celebration of Hanukkah.

men·serv·ants (**mĕn′**sûr′vənts) *n.* Plural of **manservant.**

men·ses (**mĕn′**sēz) *pl.n. (used with a singular or plural verb)* Menstruation.

men·stru·al (**mĕn′**stro͞o-əl) *adj.* Relating to or involving menstruation.

menstrual period *n.* A single monthly occurrence of menstruation.

men·stru·ate (**mĕn′**stro͞o-āt′) *intr.v.* **men·stru·at·ed, men·stru·at·ing, men·stru·ates** To undergo menstruation.

men·stru·a·tion (mĕn′stro͞o-**ā′**shən) *n.* The monthly flow of blood from the uterus that begins at puberty in women and that results from the shedding of the lining of the uterus when fertilization of an egg does not take place. Certain other primates also undergo menstruation.

men·su·ra·tion (mĕn′sə-**rā′**shən *or* mĕn′shə-**rā′**shən) *n.* **1.** The act, process, or technique of measuring. **2.** The branch of mathematics that deals with finding measurements, such as lengths, areas, and volumes.

–ment *suff.* A suffix that means: **1.** Act, action, or process: *statement; government.* **2.** State of being acted upon: *amazement; involvement.* **3.** Result of an action or a process: *advancement.* **4.** Means, instrument, or agent of an action or a process: *inducement.* —SEE NOTE.

men·tal (**mĕn′**tl) *adj.* **1.** Relating to the mind: *mental capacity.* **2.** Occurring in or done by the mind: *a mental image; mental arithmetic.* **3.** *Often Offensive* Intended for the care of the mentally ill: *a mental hospital.* [From Middle English, from Latin *mēns*, mind.] **—men′tal·ly** *adv.*

mental disorder *n.* Any of various disorders or diseases, such as schizophrenia or bipolar disorder, characterized by patterns of thought and behavior that cause significant distress or disability.

mental health *n.* **1a.** A state of emotional and psychological well-being: *Rest is important for your mental health.* **b.** A person's overall emotional and psychological condition: *Her mental health was poor after she lost her job.* **2.** A field made up of various professions, such as psychiatry and social work, that deals with the promotion of psychological well-being.

mental illness *n.* A mental disorder.

men·tal·i·ty (mĕn-**tăl′**ĭ-tē) *n., pl.* **men·tal·i·ties 1.** An outlook or characteristic way of thinking: *a cautious mentality.* **2.** Mental ability or capacity; intelligence: *a studious group of scholars of high mentality.*

mental retardation *n. Often Offensive* Impaired mental development due to disease, injury, or genetic defect.

men·thol (**mĕn′**thôl′) *n.* A white crystalline compound obtained from peppermint oil and used in perfumes, as a flavoring, and as a mild anesthetic. [From German, from Latin *mentha*, mint.]

men·tion (**mĕn′**shən) *tr.v.* **men·tioned, men·tion·ing, men·tions** To speak or write about briefly; refer to: *I mentioned your idea during the conversation.* ❖ *n.* The act of referring to something briefly or casually: *He made no mention of the incident in his report.* ◆ **not to mention** In addition to; as well as: *He was depressed, not to mention worried, about losing his cell phone.*

men·tor (**mĕn′**tôr′ *or* **mĕn′**tər) *n.* **1.** A wise and trusted advisor. **2. Mentor** In Greek mythology, Odysseus's trusted counselor.

men·u (**mĕn′**yo͞o) *n.* **1.** A list of foods and drinks available or served, as at a restaurant. **2.** The foods served or available at a meal. **3.** A list of available options, especially as displayed on a screen: *used the mouse to select "paste" from the menu.* [From Old French *menut*, small, from Latin *minūtus*.]

me·ow (mē-**ou′**) *n.* The cry of a cat. ❖ *intr.v.* **me·owed, me·ow·ing, me·ows** To make the crying sound of a cat.

Meph·i·stoph·e·les (mĕf′ĭ-**stŏf′**ə-lēz′) *n.* The devil in the Faust legend to whom Faust sells his soul.

Mer·cal·li scale (mər-**kä′**lē) *n.* A scale of earthquake intensity based on observed effects and ranging from I (detectable only with instruments) to XII (causing almost total destruction). [After Giuseppe *Mercalli* (1850–1914), Italian seismologist.]

mer·can·tile (**mûr′**kən-tēl′ *or* **mûr′**kən-tīl′) *adj.* **1.** Relating to merchants or trade: *mercantile law.* **2.** Relating to mercantilism.

mer·can·til·ism (**mûr′**kən-tē-lĭz′əm) *n.* The economic system that prevailed in Europe in the 1500s and 1600s and stressed government regulation of the economy, profit from foreign trade, the founding of colonies and trade monopolies, and the storing of wealth in the form of gold and silver. **—mer′can·til·ist** *n.*

Mer·ca·tor projection (mər-**kā′**tər) *n.* A map projection made with parallel straight lines instead of curved lines for latitude and longitude. In a Mercator projection, the areas near the poles appear disproportionately large, because the lines of longitude on the globe decrease in distance from each other as they approach the poles. [After Gerhardus *Mercator* (1512–1594), Flemish cartographer.]

mer·ce·nar·y (**mûr′**sə-nĕr′ē) *adj.* **1.** Working only out of a desire for money. **2.** Hired for service in a foreign army. ❖ *n., pl.* **mer·ce·nar·ies** A soldier who is hired to serve in a foreign army.

mer·cer·ize (**mûr′**sə-rīz′) *tr.v.* **mer·cer·ized, mer·cer·iz·ing, mer·cer·iz·es** To treat (cotton thread) with sodium hydroxide, so as to shrink the fibers, add luster, and make it dye more easily. [After John *Mercer* (1791–1866), British calico printer.]

mer·chan·dise (**mûr′**chən-dīz′ *or* **mûr′**chən-dīs′) *n.* Things that may be bought or sold; commercial goods. ❖ *v.* (**mûr′**chən-dīz′) **mer·chan·dised, mer·chan·dis·ing, mer·chan·dis·es** *—tr.* **1.** To buy and sell (goods). **2.** To promote the sale of, as through advertising. *—intr.* To buy and sell goods; trade commercially. **—mer′chan·dis′er** *n.*

mer·chant (**mûr′**chənt) *n.* **1.** A person who buys and sells goods for profit. **2.** A person who runs a retail business; a shopkeeper. ❖ *adj.* **1.** Relating to trade or commerce; commercial: *a merchant establishment.* **2.** Relating to the merchant marine: *a merchant sailor.* [From Middle English *marchaunt*, from Latin *mercārī*, to trade.]

mer·chant·man (**mûr′**chənt-mən) *n.* A ship used in commerce.

merchant marine *n.* **1.** A nation's commercial or trading ships considered as a group. **2.** The personnel who serve on such ships.

mer·ci·ful (**mûr′**sĭ-fəl) *adj.* Having, showing, or feeling mercy; compassionate. **—mer′ci·ful·ly** *adv.*

mer·ci·less (**mûr′**sĭ-lĭs) *adj.* Having or showing no mercy; cruel: *a merciless tyrant.* **—mer′ci·less·ly** *adv.*

mer·cu·ri·al (mər-**kyo͝or′**ē-əl) *adj.* **1.** Clever, shrewd, or quick. **2.** Changeable; fickle: *a mercurial disposition.* **3.** Containing or caused by the action of the element mercury. **—mer·cu′ri·al·ly** *adv.*

mer·cu·ric (mər-**kyo͝or′**ĭk) *adj.* Relating to or containing mercury with a valence of 2.

mercuric chloride *n.* A poisonous white compound used as an antiseptic, in insecticides and batteries, and in photography.

mercuric sulfide *n.* A poisonous black or red compound formed by the reaction of mercury and sulfur and used as a pigment.

mer·cu·ry (**mûr′**kyə-rē) *n.* **1.** *Symbol* **Hg** A silvery-white, poisonous metallic element that is a liquid at room tem-

WORD BUILDING

–ment The suffix **–ment** forms nouns, chiefly by attaching to verbs. It can have several meanings, the most common being "an act or an instance of doing something" or "the state of being acted upon." Thus an *entertainment* can be "an act of entertaining" and *amazement* is "the state of being amazed." The suffix *–ment* can be traced back to the Latin noun suffix *–mentum.* Although its use in English dates back to the 1300s, it wasn't until the 1500s and 1600s that a great number of words were coined with *–ment.*

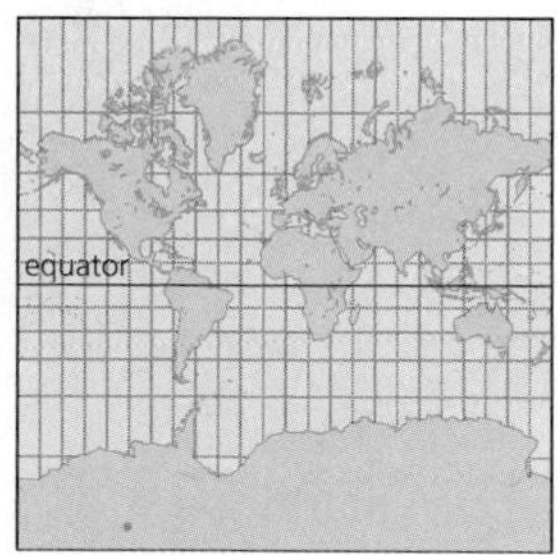

Mercator projection

Mercury

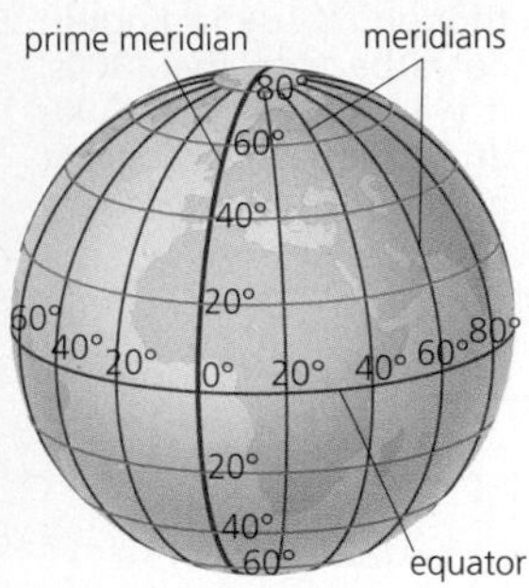

meridian

meringue
lemon meringue pie

ă	pat	ôr	core
ā	pay	oi	boy
âr	care	ou	out
ä	father	ŏŏ	took
ĕ	pet	ŏŏr	lure
ē	be	ōō	boot
ĭ	pit	ŭ	cut
ī	bite	ûr	urge
îr	pier	th	thin
ŏ	pot	*th*	this
ō	toe	zh	vision
ô	paw	ə	about

perature and is used in thermometers, barometers, and pesticides. Atomic number 80. See **Periodic Table. 2.** Temperature: *The mercury only rose to 25°F today.* [From Middle English *mercurie*, from Latin *Mercurius*, Mercury.]

Mercury *n.* **1.** In Roman mythology, the messenger of the gods and patron of travelers, thieves, and commerce, identified with the Greek Hermes. **2.** The planet nearest the sun and the smallest in the solar system, with a diameter about two fifths that of Earth. It orbits the sun once every 88 days, the shortest time for any planet. See table at **solar system.**

mer·cy (**mûr′**sē) *n., pl.* **mer·cies 1.** Kindness or compassion toward another person: *The victorious army showed great mercy toward the vanquished foe.* **2.** A tendency to be kind and forgiving. **3.** Something for which to be thankful; a blessing: *It's a mercy no one was hurt.* ◆ **at the mercy of** Without any protection against; helpless before: *Drifting in the boat, they were at the mercy of the weather.* [From Middle English *merci*, from Old French, from Latin *mercēs*, reward.]

mercy killing *n.* Euthanasia.

mere (mîr) *adj.* Superlative **mer·est** Being nothing more than what is specified: *The king at that time was a mere child.*

mere·ly (**mîr′**lē) *adv.* Only; simply: *The fact that they arrived at the party at the same time was merely a coincidence.*

me·ren·gue (mə-**rĕng′**gā) *n.* **1.** A dance in 2/4 time that originated in the Dominican Republic and Haiti having a quick tempo and characterized by a sliding step. **2.** The music for this dance.

mer·e·tri·cious (mĕr′ĭ-**trĭsh′**əs) *adj.* **1.** Attracting attention in a vulgar way. **2.** Plausible but actually false or insincere: *meretricious arguments.* **3.** Relating to prostitutes or prostitution. **—mer′e·tri′cious·ly** *adv.*

mer·gan·ser (mər-**găn′**sər) *n.* Any of various fish-eating diving ducks having a long narrow hooked bill and usually a crested head.

merge (mûrj) *v.* **merged, merg·ing, merg·es** *—tr.* To bring together so as to become one; unite: *The new management merged the two companies.* *—intr.* To come together to form one; blend together: *The two streams merge below town.* [From Latin *mergere*, to plunge, immerse.]

merg·er (**mûr′**jər) *n.* The action of merging, especially the union of two or more corporations or organizations.

me·rid·i·an (mə-**rĭd′**ē-ən) *n.* **1a.** An imaginary great circle passing through any place on the earth's surface and through the North and South Poles. **b.** Either half of such a circle from pole to pole. All the places on the same meridian have the same longitude. **2.** A similar semicircle that joins the poles of a celestial object or the poles of the celestial sphere. **3.** The highest point; the zenith: *High office is the meridian of a career in politics.*

me·ringue (mə-**răng′**) *n.* **1.** A mixture of stiffly beaten egg whites and sugar, often used as a topping for cakes or pies. **2.** A small pastry shell made of meringue.

me·ri·no (mə-**rē′**nō) *n., pl.* **me·ri·nos 1.** Any of a breed of sheep originally from Spain, having fine soft wool. **2.** Cloth or yarn made from this wool or any fine wool.

mer·it (**mĕr′**ĭt) *n.* **1.** Superior worth; excellence: *a painting of great merit.* **2.** Something deserving of praise or reward: *the merits of a good education.* **3. merits** The actual facts of a matter, whether good or bad: *School grades should reflect the merits of one's work.* ❖ *tr.v.* **mer·it·ed, mer·it·ing, mer·its** To be worthy of; deserve: *Hard work merits praise.* [From Middle English, from Latin *meritum*, something deserved, reward.]

mer·i·toc·ra·cy (mĕr′ĭ-**tŏk′**rə-sē) *n., pl.* **mer·i·toc·ra·cies** A social system in which promotions and pay are based on individual ability or achievement.

mer·i·to·ri·ous (mĕr′ĭ-**tôr′**ē-əs) *adj.* Having merit; deserving praise. **—mer′i·to′ri·ous·ly** *adv.*

Mer·kel (**mûr′**kəl), **Angela** Born 1954. German politician who became Germany's first woman chancellor in 2005.

Mer·lin (**mûr′**lĭn) *n.* In Arthurian legend, a magician who served as the royal counselor to King Arthur.

mer·maid (**mûr′**mād′) *n.* An imaginary sea creature with the head and upper body of a woman and the tail of a fish.

mer·man (**mûr′**măn′ *or* **mûr′**mən) *n.* An imaginary sea creature with the head and upper body of a man and the tail of a fish.

mer·ri·ment (**mĕr′**ĭ-mənt) *n.* Enjoyable fun and amusement.

mer·ry (**mĕr′**ē) *adj.* **mer·ri·er, mer·ri·est 1.** Full of cheerfulness, liveliness, and good feelings: *a merry and festive crowd.* **2.** Characterized by fun and liveliness; festive: *a merry celebration.* **—mer′ri·ly** *adv.*

mer·ry-go-round (**mĕr′**ē-gō-round′) *n.* A revolving circular platform having seats, usually in the form of horses, on which people ride for amusement.

mer·ry·mak·ing (**mĕr′**ē-mā′kĭng) *n.* **1.** Participation in festive activities. **2.** A festive party or celebration. **—mer′ry·mak′er** *n.*

me·sa (**mā′**sə) *n.* A high land area with a flat top and steep sides, larger than a butte and smaller than a plateau, common in the southwest United States. [From Spanish, from Latin *mēnsa*, table.]

mes·ca·line (**mĕs′**kə-lēn′ *or* **mĕs′**kə-lĭn) *n.* A hallucinogenic drug derived from certain cactuses.

mes·clun (**mĕs′**klən) *n.* A mixture of young, leafy greens used as salad.

Mes·dames (mā-**däm′** *or* mā-**dăm′**) *n.* Plural of **Madame.**

Mes·de·moi·selles (mād′mwä-**zĕl′**) *n.* A plural of **Mademoiselle.**

mesh (mĕsh) *n.* **1a.** Any of the open spaces in a net, sieve, or wire screen: *The meshes of this net are one inch square.* **b.** often **meshes** The cords, threads, or wires forming a net or screen: *the fine wire meshes of the screen.* **2.** A net or network: *a fine mesh of interlacing wires.* **3.** A fabric with an open network of interlacing threads. **4. meshes** An entanglement; a trap: *caught in the meshes of their own bad decisions.* **5.** The engagement of two sets of gear teeth. ❖ *v.* **meshed, mesh·ing, mesh·es** *—tr.* **1.** To catch in or as if in a net. **2.** To cause (gear teeth) to become engaged. *—intr.* To become engaged or interlocked: *The teeth of the gears failed to mesh.* [From Middle English, probably from Middle Dutch *maesche*.]

mesh·work (**mĕsh′**wûrk′) *n.* Meshed material: *Macramé is an art form involving meshwork.*

mes·mer·ize (**mĕz′**mə-rīz′) *tr.v.* **mes·mer·ized, mes·mer·iz·ing, mes·mer·iz·es 1.** To fascinate or enthrall: *The performance mesmerized the audience.* **2.** To hypnotize. [After Franz *Mesmer* (1734–1815), Austrian physician.]

Mes·o·a·mer·i·ca (mĕz′ō-ə-**mĕr′**ĭ-kə *or* mĕs′ō-ə-**mĕr′**ĭ-kə) A region extending south and east from central Mexico into parts of Guatemala, Belize, Honduras, and Nicaragua. It was the site of many pre-Columbian civilizations. **—Mes′o·a·mer′i·can** *adj. & n.*

mes·o·derm (**mĕz′**ə-dûrm′ *or* **mĕs′**ə-dûrm′) *n.* The middle of the three layers of cells found in the early embryo of most animals, developing into muscles, bones, cartilage, blood vessels, and the organs of the reproductive system and the urinary tract.

Mes·o·lith·ic (mĕz′ə-**lĭth′**ĭk *or* mĕs′ə-**lĭth′**ĭk) *adj.* Relating to the middle period of human culture in the Stone Age, between the Paleolithic and Neolithic Periods, beginning around 15,000 to 11,500 years ago in western Asia and southern Europe. The Mesolithic Period is characterized by the appearance of small-bladed stone tools and weapons and by the beginnings of settled communities. ❖ *n.* The Mesolithic Period.

Mes·o·po·ta·mi·a (mĕs′ə-pə-**tā′**mē-ə) An ancient region of southwest Asia between the Tigris and Euphrates Rivers in modern-day Iraq. Probably settled before 5000 BC, the area was the home of many early civilizations. **—Mes′o·po·ta′mi·an** *adj. & n.*

mes·o·sphere (**mĕz′**ə-sfîr′ *or* **mĕs′**ə-sfîr′) *n.* A layer of the atmosphere, between the stratosphere and the thermosphere, that extends from about 31 to about 50 miles (50 to 80 kilometers) above the earth's surface.

Mes·o·zo·ic (mĕz′ə-**zō′**ĭk *or* mĕs′ə-**zō′**ĭk) *n.* The era of geologic time from about 251 to 66 million years ago. The Mesozoic Era was characterized by the development of flowering plants and by the appearance and extinction of dinosaurs. See table at **geologic time. —Mes′o·zo′ic** *adj.*

mes·quite (mĕ-**skēt′**) *n.* Any of several thorny shrubs or small trees found in hot, dry regions of the Americas, having edible pods that are often used as forage for livestock. [From Nahuatl *mizquitl.*]

mess (mĕs) *n.* **1a.** An untidy or dirty condition: *The kitchen is in a mess.* **b.** A person or thing that is in such a condition: *The house is a mess.* **2.** A disorderly mass or collection of things: *Who left the mess on the kitchen table?* **3.** A confusing or troublesome situation; a muddle: *We're in a mess because we ran out of paper.* **4.** A portion or quantity of food: *caught and cooked a mess of fish.* **5a.** A meal served to a group of people, especially a military group: *The soldiers lined up for morning mess.* **b.** A group, especially a military group, that takes its meals together. **c.** A room or hall where such a group takes meals. ❖ *v.* **messed, mess·ing, mess·es** *—tr.* To make untidy or disorderly: *We took off our muddy boots so as not to mess the rug. —intr.* **1.** To use or handle something carelessly: *Who messed with the computer?* **2.** To take a meal: *The officers messed with their units.* ◆ **mess around** *Informal* To pass time aimlessly. **mess up 1.** To botch or ruin: *Losing my notes messed up my chances of doing well on the examination.* **2.** To make a mistake: *I messed up and overcooked the fish.* [From Middle English *mes,* course of a meal, from Late Latin *missus,* placed, sent, from Latin *mittere,* to place.]

mes·sage (**mĕs′**ĭj) *n.* **1.** A usually short communication sent from one person or group to another: *I found the message you left at my desk. She sent me a quick message by email.* **2.** An official statement delivered to a group: *a presidential message to Congress.* **3.** A basic theme, lesson, or moral: *a movie with a message for all of us.* ❖ *tr.v.* **mes·saged, mes·sag·ing, mes·sag·es** To send a message to: *As soon as I turned on my computer, my friends started messaging me.* [From Middle English, from Medieval Latin *missaticum,* from Latin *mittere,* to send.]

Mes·sei·gneurs (mā-sĕ-**nyœr′**) *n.* Plural of **Monseigneur.**

mes·sen·ger (**mĕs′**ən-jər) *n.* **1.** A person who carries messages or runs errands. **2.** Something that indicates what is about to happen; a forerunner. ❖ *tr.v.* **mes·sen·gered, mes·sen·ger·ing, mes·sen·gers** To send by messenger: *We messengered the documents to our lawyer.*

messenger RNA *n.* A form of RNA that carries genetic information from the DNA in the nucleus of a cell to the ribosomes in the cytoplasm, specifying the particular protein to be synthesized.

Mes·si·ah (mĭ-**sī′**ə) *n.* **1.** The expected savior and king of the Jews, foretold by the prophets of the Hebrew Scriptures. **2.** In Christianity, another name for Jesus. **3. messiah** A leader who is regarded as a savior or liberator of a people. [From Middle English *Messias,* from Aramaic *məšîḥā,* the anointed one.]

mes·si·an·ic also **Mes·si·an·ic** (mĕs′ē-**ăn′**ĭk) *adj.* **1.** Relating to a messiah. **2.** Characterized by the belief that a particular cause or movement will triumph or save the world: *messianic nationalism.*

Mes·sieurs (mā-**syœ′** *or* **mĕs′**ərz) *n.* Plural of **Monsieur.**

mess kit *n.* A compact kit containing cooking and eating utensils, used by soldiers and campers.

Messrs.[1] (**mĕs′**ərz) *n.* Plural of **Mr.**

Messrs.[2] *abbr.* An abbreviation of Messieurs.

mess·y (**mĕs′**ē) *adj.* **mess·i·er, mess·i·est 1.** In a mess; untidy: *a messy house.* **2.** Causing a mess: *the messy work of car repair.* **3.** Given to making messes; not neat or organized: *a messy roommate.* **4.** Difficult or unpleasant; complicated: *a messy situation.* **—mess′i·ly** *adv.* **—mess′i·ness** *n.*

mes·ti·za (mĕs-**tē′**zə) *n.* A woman having European and Native American ancestors.

mes·ti·zo (mĕs-**tē′**zō) *n., pl.* **mes·ti·zos** or **mes·ti·zoes** A person having European and Native American ancestors. [From Spanish, from Late Latin *mixtīcius,* mixed, from Latin *miscēre,* to mix.]

met (mĕt) *v.* Past tense and past participle of **meet**[1]**.**

met·a·bol·ic (mĕt′ə-**bŏl′**ĭk) *adj.* Relating to or resulting from metabolism. **—met′a·bol′i·cal·ly** *adv.*

me·tab·o·lism (mĭ-**tăb′**ə-lĭz′əm) *n.* **1.** The chemical processes taking place in a cell or organism that are needed to sustain life. In metabolism, some substances are broken down to yield the energy used for biological activities such as cell growth and repair, while other substances are synthesized from simple molecules. **2.** The processing of a specific substance in a cell or organism: *carbohydrate metabolism.* [From Greek *metabolē,* change : *meta-,* aside + *ballein,* to throw.]

me·tab·o·lize (mĭ-**tăb′**ə-līz′) *v.* **me·tab·o·lized, me·tab·o·liz·ing, me·tab·o·liz·es** *—tr.* To subject (a substance) to metabolism: *Humans cannot metabolize cellulose. —intr.* To undergo metabolism: *Simple sugars metabolize quickly.*

met·a·car·pal (mĕt′ə-**kär′**pəl) *adj.* Relating to the metacarpus. ❖ *n.* Any of the bones of the metacarpus.

met·a·car·pus (mĕt′ə-**kär′**pəs) *n., pl.* **met·a·car·pi** (mĕt′ə-**kär′**pī) **1.** The part of the human hand that includes the five bones between the wrist and the fingers. **2.** The corresponding part of the forefoot of a four-legged animal.

Met·a·com (**mĕt′**ə-kŏm′) Known as **Phil·ip** (**fĭl′**ĭp). Died 1676. Wampanoag leader who waged King Philip's War (1675–1676) against New England colonists.

met·al (**mĕt′**l) *n.* **1.** Any of a large group of elements, including iron, gold, copper, lead, and magnesium, that tend to lose electrons (becoming positive ions) and that conduct heat and electricity well. Metals usually have a shiny surface and can be hammered into thin sheets or drawn into wires. **2.** An alloy, such as steel or bronze, made of two or more metals. [From Middle English, from Greek *metallon.*]

❑ *These sound alike:* **metal, mettle** (courage).

met·a·lan·guage (**mĕt′**ə-lăng′gwĭj) *n.* A language or vocabulary used to describe or analyze another language.

me·tal·lic (mĭ-**tăl′**ĭk) *adj.* **1.** Relating to or having the qualities of a metal: *a metallic gleam.* **2.** Containing metal: *a metallic chemical compound.*

met·al·loid (**mĕt′**l-oid′) *n.* **1.** A nonmetallic element, such as arsenic, having properties of both a metal and a nonmetal. **2.** A nonmetallic element, such as carbon, that can form alloys with metals. ❖ *adj.* Relating to or having the property of a metalloid.

met·al·lur·gist (**mĕt′**l-ûr′jĭst) *n.* A person who specializes in metallurgy.

met·al·lur·gy (**mĕt′**l-ûr′jē) *n.* The science and technology of extracting metals from their ores, refining them for

mesa

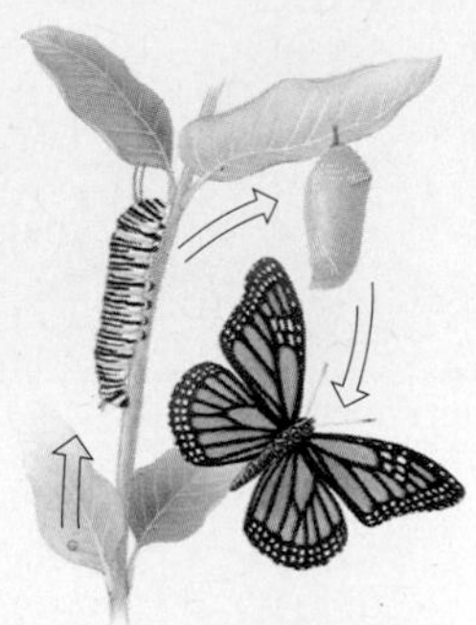

metamorphosis
development of a monarch butterfly

metate
metate (*left*) and mano (*right*)

use, and creating alloys and useful objects from metals. **—met′al·lur′gi·cal** (mĕt′l-**ûr′**jə-kəl) *adj.*

met·al·work (**mĕt′**l-wûrk′) *n.* Articles, especially decorative objects, made of metal.

met·al·work·ing (**mĕt′**l-wûr′kĭng) *n.* The act or process of making or shaping things out of metal.

met·a·mor·phic (mĕt′ə-**môr′**fĭk) *adj.* **1.** Changed by metamorphism: *metamorphic rock.* **2.** Relating to or characterized by metamorphosis: *metamorphic development of a moth.*

met·a·mor·phism (mĕt′ə-**môr′**fĭz′əm) *n.* The process by which rocks are changed in composition, texture, or internal structure by great heat or pressure.

met·a·mor·phose (mĕt′ə-**môr′**fōz′ *or* mĕt′ə-**môr′**fōs′) *v.* **met·a·mor·phosed, met·a·mor·phos·ing, met·a·mor·phos·es** *—intr.* **1.** To undergo metamorphism or metamorphosis: *Limestone metamorphoses into marble. The tadpoles will metamorphose into frogs.* **2.** To change completely in form or appearance; transform: *In the book, the teenager metamorphoses into a werewolf. —tr.* To cause to undergo metamorphism or metamorphosis.

met·a·mor·pho·sis (mĕt′ə-**môr′**fə-sĭs) *n., pl.* **met·a·mor·pho·ses** (mĕt′ə-**môr′**fə-sēz′) **1.** A marked or complete change in appearance, character, or form. **2.** Change in the form and habits of an animal during natural development after the embryonic stage. Metamorphosis occurs when caterpillars become butterflies and when tadpoles become frogs. [From Greek *metamorphōsis*, from *metamorphoun*, to transform.]

met·a·phase (**mĕt′**ə-fāz′) *n.* The stage in mitosis and meiosis during which the chromosomes group together toward the center of the cell and line up before separating.

met·a·phor (**mĕt′**ə-fôr′) *n.* **1.** A figure of speech in which a word or phrase that is ordinarily associated with one thing is applied to something else, thus making a comparison between the two. For example, when Shakespeare wrote, "All the world's a stage," he was using metaphor. **2.** Something that is meant to be viewed as a representation of something else; a symbol: *Her play is meant to be a metaphor for corporate greed.* [From Middle English *methaphor*, from Greek *metaphora* : *meta*-, across + *pherein*, to carry.]

met·a·phor·i·cal (mĕt′ə-**fôr′**ĭ-kəl) or **met·a·phor·ic** (mĕt′ə-**fôr′**ĭk) *adj.* Relating to or using metaphors: *used a metaphorical expression to describe the experience.* **—met′a·phor′i·cal·ly** *adv.*

met·a·phys·i·cal (mĕt′ə-**fĭz′**ĭ-kəl) *adj.* **1.** Relating to metaphysics. **2.** Hard to understand; highly abstract. **—met′a·phys′i·cal·ly** *adv.*

met·a·phy·si·cian (mĕt′ə-fĭ-**zĭsh′**ən) *n.* A person who specializes or is skilled in metaphysics.

met·a·phys·ics (mĕt′ə-**fĭz′**ĭks) *n.* *(used with a singular verb)* The branch of philosophy that deals with the ultimate nature of things.

me·tas·ta·sis (mĭ-**tăs′**tə-sĭs) *n., pl.* **me·tas·ta·ses** (mĭ-**tăs′**tə-sēz′) **1.** The spread of disease-causing cells, especially cancerous cells, from one location in the body to other locations. **2.** A secondary cancerous growth formed by the spread of cancerous cells from a primary growth located elsewhere in the body.

me·tas·ta·size (mə-**tăs′**tə-sīz′) *intr.v.* **me·tas·ta·sized, me·tas·ta·siz·ing, me·tas·ta·siz·es** To spread from one part of the body to another.

met·a·tag (**mĕt′**ə-tăg′) *n.* A tag in a markup language that contains descriptive information about a webpage and does not appear when the webpage is displayed in a browser.

met·a·tar·sal (mĕt′ə-**tär′**səl) *adj.* Relating to the metatarsus. ❖ *n.* Any of the bones of the metatarsus.

met·a·tar·sus (mĕt′ə-**tär′**səs) *n., pl.* **met·a·tar·si** (mĕt′ə-**tär′**sī) **1.** The part of the human foot that forms the instep and includes the five bones between the ankle and the toes. **2.** The corresponding part of the foot of a bird or the hind foot of a four-legged animal.

me·ta·te (mĭ-**tä′**tē *or* mĕ-**tä′**tē) *n.* A stone block with a shallow concave surface, used with a mano for grinding corn or other grains. [From Spanish, from Nahuatl *metlatl.*]

mete (mēt) *tr.v.* **met·ed, met·ing, metes** To distribute by or as if by measuring portions; allot: *The judge meted out a punishment to fit the crime.* [From Old English *metan.*]

❑ *These sound alike:* **mete, meat** (animal flesh), **meet**[1] (come upon), **meet**[2] (fitting).

me·te·or (**mē′**tē-ər *or* **mē′**tē-ôr′) *n.* A bright trail or streak in the night sky, formed when a meteoroid enters the atmosphere and is so heated by friction with air molecules that it glows. [From Middle English *metheour*, atmospheric phenomenon, from Greek *meteōros*, high in the air.]

me·te·or·ic (mē′tē-**ôr′**ĭk) *adj.* **1.** Relating to or produced by meteors: *a meteoric flash.* **2.** Relating to the atmosphere: *Clouds are meteoric phenomena.* **3.** Like a meteor in speed, brilliance, or briefness: *the book's meteoric surge in popularity.*

me·te·or·ite (**mē′**tē-ə-rīt′) *n.* A meteoroid that has fallen to the earth's surface from outer space without completely burning up.

me·te·or·oid (**mē′**tē-ə-roid′) *n.* A solid body that travels through space and is smaller than an asteroid and at least as large as a speck of dust.

me·te·or·ol·o·gist (mē′tē-ə-**rŏl′**ə-jĭst) *n.* **1.** A person who specializes in meteorology. **2.** A person who reports and forecasts weather conditions.

me·te·or·ol·o·gy (mē′tē-ə-**rŏl′**ə-jē) *n.* The science that deals with the atmosphere and atmospheric conditions or phenomena, especially weather and weather conditions. **—me′te·or·o·log′i·cal** (mē′tē-ər-ə-**lŏj′**ĭ-kəl) *adj.* **—me′te·or·o·log′i·cal·ly** *adv.*

me·ter[1] (**mē′**tər) *n.* **1.** The arrangement of accented and unaccented syllables in a line of poetry; poetic rhythm. **2.** The pattern of beats in a measure of music; musical rhythm. [From Middle English *metre*, from Greek *metron.*]

me·ter[2] (**mē′**tər) *n.* The basic unit of length in the metric system, equal to 39.37 inches. It was redefined in 1983 as the distance traveled by light in a vacuum in 1/299,792,458 of a second. See table at **measurement.** [From French *mètre*, from Greek *metron*, measure.]

me·ter[3] (**mē′**tər) *n.* **1.** A device used to measure and record speed, temperature, or distance, or to indicate the amount of something used, as gas or electricity. **2.** A parking meter. ❖ *tr.v.* **me·tered, me·ter·ing, me·ters** To measure with a meter: *metered the flow of water.* [From *-meter*, measuring device, from French *-mètre*, from Greek *metron*, measure.]

–meter *suff.* A suffix that means measuring device: *speedometer.*

me·ter-kil·o·gram-sec·ond (mē′tər-kĭl′ə-grăm-**sĕk′**ənd) *adj.* Relating to a system of measurement in which the meter, the kilogram, and the second are the basic units of length, mass, and time.

meth (mĕth) *n. Slang* Methamphetamine.

meth·a·done (**mĕth′**ə-dōn′) *n.* A strong synthetic narcotic drug that is less addictive than morphine or heroin. It is used as a substitute for these drugs in programs for treating addiction.

meth·am·phet·a·mine (mĕth′ăm-**fĕt′**ə-mēn′) *n.* A derivative of amphetamine that is used in crystalline form as a central nervous system stimulant, both medically and illicitly.

meth·ane (**mĕth′**ān′) *n.* A colorless, odorless, flammable gas that is the simplest of the hydrocarbons and has the

ă	pat	ôr	core
ā	pay	oi	boy
âr	care	ou	out
ä	father	o͝o	took
ĕ	pet	o͝or	lure
ē	be	o͞o	boot
ĭ	pit	ŭ	cut
ī	bite	ûr	urge
îr	pier	th	thin
ŏ	pot	*th*	this
ō	toe	zh	vision
ô	paw	ə	about

formula CH_4. It is the major constituent of natural gas and forms by the decomposition of plant or other organic compounds, as in marshes and coal mines.

meth·a·nol (mĕth′ə-nôl′ *or* mĕth′ə-nōl′) *n.* A colorless, flammable, and poisonous liquid compound having the formula CH_3OH. It is used as an antifreeze, a fuel, and a solvent.

meth·i·cil·lin (mĕth′ĭ-**sĭl′**ĭn) *n.* An antibiotic used to treat infections caused by staphylococcus bacteria that are resistant to penicillin. It is no longer in wide use.

me·thinks (mĭ-**thĭngks′**) *intr.v.* Past tense **me·thought** (mĭ-**thôt′**) *Archaic* It seems to me. —SEE NOTE.

me·thi·o·nine (mə-**thī′**ə-nēn′) *n.* An essential amino acid that is found in various proteins.

meth·od (**mĕth′**əd) *n.* **1.** A regular or orderly way of doing something: *Boiling is one method of cooking rice.* **2.** Orderly arrangement of parts or steps in order to accomplish a goal: *Lack of method in solving problems wastes time.* [From Middle English, from Greek *methodos.*]

SYNONYMS **method, system, routine, manner** These nouns refer to the procedures followed to accomplish a task or reach a goal. **Method** suggests a detailed, logically ordered plan: *He developed a method for finishing his chores in half the time.* **System** means a coordinated group of methods: *Her system of doing experiments was very efficient.* **Routine** means a habitual, often tiresome method: *My routine for cleaning the house never changes.* **Manner** means a personal or distinctive way of doing something: *They play chess in a most serious manner.*

me·thod·i·cal (mə-**thŏd′**ĭ-kəl) also **me·thod·ic** (mə-**thŏd′**ĭk) *adj.* **1.** Arranged or done in regular order; systematic: *a methodical inspection.* **2.** Characterized by orderly habits or behavior: *a methodical researcher.* **—me·thod′i·cal·ly** *adv.* **—me·thod′i·cal·ness** *n.*

Meth·od·ism (**mĕth′**ə-dĭz′əm) *n.* The beliefs and worship of the Methodists.

Meth·od·ist (**mĕth′**ə-dĭst) *n.* A member of a Protestant church founded in England in the 1700s on the teachings of John and Charles Wesley.

me·thought (mĭ-**thôt′**) *v. Archaic* Past tense of **methinks.**

Me·thu·se·lah (mə-**thōō′**zə-lə) In the Bible, a man said to have lived 969 years.

meth·yl (**mĕth′**əl) *adj.* Relating to or being the simplest hydrocarbon unit, CH_3, that is derived from methane and occurs in many important chemical compounds.

methyl alcohol *n.* Methanol.

met·i·cal (**mĕt′**ĭ-kăl′) *n., pl.* **met·i·cais** (mĕt′ĭ-**kīsh′**) The basic monetary unit of Mozambique.

me·tic·u·lous (mĭ-**tĭk′**yə-ləs) *adj.* Showing or acting with extreme concern for details. [From Latin *metīculōsus,* timid, from *metus,* fear.] **—me·tic′u·lous·ly** *adv.*

me·tre¹ (**mē′**tər) *n. Chiefly British* Variant of **meter¹.**

me·tre² (**mē′**tər) *n. Chiefly British* Variant of **meter².**

met·ric¹ (**mĕt′**rĭk) *adj.* Relating to the metric system.

met·ric² (**mĕt′**rĭk) *n.* A standard of measurement, especially one that evaluates a complex process or system.

met·ri·cal (**mĕt′**rĭ-kəl) *adj.* **1.** Relating to or composed in poetic meter. **2.** Relating to measurement. **—met′ri·cal·ly** *adv.*

met·ri·ca·tion (mĕt′rĭ-**kā′**shən) *n.* Conversion to the metric system of weights and measures.

metric system *n.* A decimal system of weights and measures based on the meter as its unit of length, the kilogram as its unit of mass, and the second as its unit of time.

metric ton *n.* A unit of mass or weight equal to 1,000 kilograms (2,205 pounds).

met·ro¹ (**mĕt′**rō) *n., pl.* **met·ros** A subway system.

met·ro² (**mĕt′**rō) *Informal adj.* Metropolitan: *metro Los Angeles.*

met·ro·nome (**mĕt′**rə-nōm′) *n.* A device that makes a series of regularly repeated clicks at adjustable intervals. It is used to provide a steady beat for practicing music.

me·trop·o·lis (mĭ-**trŏp′**ə-lĭs) *n.* **1.** A major city, especially the largest or most important city of a country, state, or region. **2.** A city regarded as at the center of a specific activity: *a great cultural metropolis.* [From Middle English *metropol,* from Greek *mētropolis,* mother-city : *mētēr,* mother + *polis,* city.]

met·ro·pol·i·tan (mĕt′rə-**pŏl′**ĭ-tən) *adj.* Relating to or characteristic of a major city: *metropolitan bus routes.* ❖ *n.* **1.** A person from a major city. **2.** A bishop who presides over a church province.

–metry *suff.* A suffix that means process or science of measurement: *photometry.*

met·tle (**mĕt′**l) *n.* The ability to meet a challenge or persevere under demanding circumstances; determination: *Adversity never fails to test someone's mettle.* [Variant of *metal.*]

❏ *These sound alike:* **mettle, metal** (element).

met·tle·some (**mĕt′**l-səm) *adj.* Full of mettle; spirited.

MeV or **mev** *abbr.* An abbreviation of million electron volts.

mew (myōō) *intr.v.* **mewed, mew·ing, mews** To make the high-pitched cry of a cat. ❖ *n.* The crying sound of a cat. [From Middle English *meuen,* of imitative origin.]

mewl (myōōl) *intr.v.* **mewled, mewl·ing, mewls** To cry softly, as a baby does; whimper.

❏ *These sound alike:* **mewl, mule¹** (animal), **mule²** (slipper).

mews (myōōz) *pl.n. (used with a singular or plural verb)* **1.** A group of buildings originally containing stables and often converted into apartments. **2.** A street or alley on which such buildings stand.

❏ *These sound alike:* **mews, muse** (consider), **Muse** (goddess).

Mex·i·can (**mĕk′**sĭ-kən) *adj.* Relating to Mexico or its people, languages, or cultures. ❖ *n.* A native or inhabitant of Mexico.

Mexican American *n.* A US citizen or resident of Mexican ancestry. **—Mex′i·can-A·mer′i·can** *adj.*

Mexican War *n.* A war (1846–1848) between the United States and Mexico that resulted in Mexico's giving up lands that now make up all or most of California, Arizona, New Mexico, Nevada, Utah, and Colorado.

Mex·i·co (**mĕk′**sĭ-kō′) A country of south-central North America south of the United States. It was originally inhabited by the Aztecs and Maya among others. Mexico was held by the Spanish from 1521 until 1821. Mexico City is the capital.

Mexico, Gulf of An arm of the Atlantic Ocean in southeast North America bordering on eastern Mexico, the southeast United States, and Cuba.

Mexico City The capital of Mexico, in the central part of the country. It was founded on the site of an ancient Aztec capital destroyed by Cortés in 1521.

me·zu·zah also **me·zu·za** (mə-**zōōz′**ə *or* mə-zōō-**zä′**) *n., pl.* **me·zu·zahs** also **me·zu·zas** (mə-**zōōz′**əz) or **me·zu·zot** (mə-zōō-**zôt′**) A small piece of parchment inscribed with biblical passages, rolled up in a container, and attached by many Jewish families to their door frames as a sign of faith. [From Hebrew *məzûzâ,* doorpost.]

mez·za·nine (**mĕz′**ə-nēn′ *or* mĕz′ə-**nēn′**) *n.* **1.** A partial story between two main stories of a building. **2.** The lowest balcony in a theater or the first few rows of the balcony.

mez·zo for·te (**mĕt′**sō **fôr′**tā′) *adv. & adj.* In music, moderately loud.

mezzo pi·a·no (pē-**ä′**nō) *adv. & adj.* In music, moderately soft.

WORD HISTORY

methinks Most people nowadays regard **methinks** as a weird way of saying "I think." Actually, in Shakespeare's day, 400 years ago, it meant "it seems to me." There were originally two separate verbs spelled *think,* one meaning "to use the mind" and the other meaning "to seem." The second one could be used in phrases like *it thinks me* or (in reverse order) *me thinks it, me thinks,* meaning "it seems to me." Since *methinks* could introduce thoughts in a similar manner to *I think,* it was easily reinterpreted as an old-fashioned equivalent of *I think.*

metronome

mezuzah

Michelangelo Buonarroti

GEOGRAPHY

Michigan The state of **Michigan** gets its name from an Ojibwa or Ottawa word meaning "big lake." The name was first applied to Lake Michigan, one of the Great Lakes. The state then took its name from the lake.

WORD BUILDING

micro– The basic meaning of the prefix **micro–** is "small." It comes from Greek *mīkros,* meaning "small." In English *micro–* has been chiefly used since the 1800s to form scientific words. It is the counterpart for the prefix *macro–* ("large") in pairs such as *microcosm/macrocosm.*

ă	pat	ôr	core
ā	pay	oi	boy
âr	care	ou	out
ä	father	ŏŏ	took
ĕ	pet	ŏŏr	lure
ē	be	ōō	boot
ĭ	pit	ŭ	cut
ī	bite	ûr	urge
îr	pier	th	thin
ŏ	pot	*th*	this
ō	toe	zh	vision
ô	paw	ə	about

mez·zo-so·pran·o (mĕt′sō-sə-**prăn′**ō *or* mĕt′sō-sə-prä′nō) *n., pl.* **mez·zo-so·pran·os 1.** A woman's singing voice of medium range, lower than a soprano and higher than a contralto. **2.** A woman having such a voice. **3.** A part written in the range of this voice.

mg *abbr.* An abbreviation of milligram.

Mg Symbol for the element **magnesium.**

mgmt. *abbr.* An abbreviation of management.

mgr. *abbr.* An abbreviation of manager.

Mgr. *abbr.* An abbreviation of: **1.** Monseigneur. **2.** Monsignor.

MHz *abbr.* An abbreviation of megahertz.

mi (mē) *n.* In music, the third tone of a major scale.
❑ *These sound alike:* **mi, me** (pronoun).

MI *abbr.* An abbreviation of Michigan.

mi. or **mi** *abbr.* An abbreviation of mile.

Mi·am·i[1] (mī-**ăm′**ē *or* mī-**ăm′**ə) *n., pl.* **Miami** or **Mi·am·is 1.** A member of a Native American people originally living in Wisconsin and now living in Indiana and Oklahoma. **2.** The variety of Illinois spoken by the Miami.

Mi·am·i[2] (mī-**ăm′**ē) A city of southeast Florida on a narrow inlet of the Atlantic Ocean. It was settled in the 1870s.

mi·as·ma (mī-**ăz′**mə *or* mē-**ăz′**mə) *n., pl.* **mi·as·mas** or **mi·as·ma·ta** (mī-**ăz′**mə-tə *or* mē-**ăz′**mə-tə) **1.** A harmful atmosphere or influence. **2.** A bad-smelling vapor arising from rotting organic matter and formerly thought to cause disease. **—mi·as′mal** *adj.*

mic (mīk) *n. Informal* A microphone.

mi·ca (**mī′**kə) *n.* A member of a group of aluminum silicate minerals that can be split easily into thin, partly transparent sheets. Mica is highly resistant to heat and is used in electric fuses and other electrical equipment. [From Latin *mīca,* grain.]

Mi·cah[1] (**mī′**kə) A Hebrew prophet of the eighth century BC.

Mi·cah[2] (**mī′**kə) *n.* A book of the Bible in which Micah predicts the destruction of Jerusalem and the coming of the Messiah.

mice (mīs) *n.* Plural of **mouse.**

Mi·chael (**mī′**kəl) *n.* The guardian archangel of the Jews in the Hebrew Scriptures. In Christian tradition, Michael led the angels in the war against Satan.

Mich·ael·mas (**mĭk′**əl-məs) *n.* September 29, on which a Christian feast in honor of the archangel Michael is observed.

Mi·chel·an·ge·lo Buo·nar·ro·ti (mī′kəl-**ăn′**jə-lō′ bwôn′ə-**rô′**tē) 1475–1564. Italian sculptor, painter, architect, and poet whose best-known works include the marble sculpture *David* (1501) and the paintings on the ceiling of the Sistine Chapel (1508–1512).

Mich·i·gan (**mĭsh′**ĭ-gən) A state of the north-central United States north of Indiana. It was admitted as the 26th state in 1837. Lansing is the capital and Detroit the largest city. —SEE NOTE.

Michigan, Lake The third largest of the Great Lakes, chiefly between Wisconsin and Michigan. It is connected at its northern end with Lake Huron.

Mic·mac (**mĭk′**măk′) *n., pl.* **Micmac** or **Mic·macs** Variant of **Mi′kmaq.**

mi·cra (**mī′**krə) *n.* A plural of **micron.**

micro– or **micr–** *pref.* A prefix that means: **1.** Small or smaller: *microcircuit.* **2.** Requiring or involving magnification or enlargement: *microscope.* **3.** One millionth: *microsecond.* —SEE NOTE.

mi·crobe (**mī′**krōb′) *n.* A microorganism, especially a bacterium that causes disease. **—mi·cro′bi·al** (mī-**krō′**-bē-al) *adj.*

mi·cro·bi·ol·o·gist (mī′krō-bī-**ŏl′**ə-jĭst) *n.* A scientist who specializes in microbiology.

mi·cro·bi·ol·o·gy (mī′krō-bī-**ŏl′**ə-jē) *n.* The branch of biology that deals with microorganisms. **—mi′cro·bi′o·log′i·cal** (mī′krō-bī′ə-**lŏj′**ĭ-kəl) *adj.*

mi·cro·chip (**mī′**crə-chĭp′) *n.* An integrated circuit.

mi·cro·cir·cuit (**mī′**krō-sûr′kĭt) *n.* An electric circuit made of miniaturized components.

mi·cro·cosm (**mī′**krə-kŏz′əm) *n.* Something regarded as a miniature representation of something else: *The problems of the family are the nation's problems in microcosm.* [From Middle English *microcosmos,* from Greek *mīkros kosmos,* little world.]

mi·cro·cred·it (**mī′**krō-krĕd′ĭt) *n.* The business or policy of making microloans to impoverished entrepreneurs.

mi·cro·fi·ber (**mī′**krō-fī′bər) *n.* A very thin synthetic fiber that can be woven or knit into cloth that looks and feels like natural-fiber cloth but is more water-repellent and easier to care for.

mi·cro·film (**mī′**krə-fĭlm′) *n.* **1.** A film on which written or printed material can be reproduced in greatly reduced size. **2.** A reproduction made on microfilm. ❖ *tr.v.* **mi·cro·filmed, mi·cro·film·ing, mi·cro·films** To reproduce on microfilm.

mi·cro·loan (**mī′**krō-lōn′) *n.* A very small, often short-term loan made to an impoverished entrepreneur, as in an underdeveloped country.

mi·cro·man·age (mī′krō-**măn′**ĭj) *tr.v.* **mi·cro·man·aged, mi·cro·man·ag·ing, mi·cro·man·ag·es** To manage (employees or projects), in such detail that it is meddlesome or irritating.

mi·cro·me·te·or·ite (mī′krō-**mē′**tē-ə-rīt′) *n.* A tiny particle of meteorite dust.

mi·crom·e·ter[1] (mī-**krŏm′**ĭ-tər) *n.* A device for measuring very small distances, angles, or objects, especially one based on the rotation of a finely threaded screw.

mi·cro·me·ter[2] (**mī′**krō-mē′tər) *n.* A unit of length equal to one millionth (10^{-6}) of a meter; a micron.

mi·cron (**mī′**krŏn′) *n., pl.* **mi·crons** or **mi·cra** (**mī′**krə) A unit of length equal to one millionth (10^{-6}) of a meter.

Mi·cro·ne·si·a (mī′krō-**nē′**zhə) A division of Oceania in the western Pacific Ocean made up of the islands east of the Philippines and north of the equator.

Micronesia, Federated States of An island country in the Caroline Islands of the western Pacific Ocean. Palikir is the capital.

Mi·cro·ne·sian (mī′krə-**nē′**zhən) *adj.* Relating to Micronesia or its peoples, languages, or cultures. ❖ *n.* **1.** A member of any of the peoples inhabiting Micronesia. **2.** A group of languages spoken in Micronesia.

mi·cro·nu·tri·ent (mī′krō-**nōō′**trē-ənt) *n.* A substance, such as a vitamin or mineral, that is essential in very small amounts for the proper growth and metabolism of a living organism.

mi·cro·or·gan·ism (mī′krō-**ôr′**gə-nĭz′əm) *n.* A microscopically small organism or virus. Bacteria, protozoans, and many fungi are microorganisms.

mi·cro·phone (**mī′**krə-fōn′) *n.* A device that converts sound waves into an electric current, usually fed into an amplifier, a recorder, or broadcast transmitter. [From Greek *mīkros,* small + Greek *phōnē,* sound.]

mi·cro·proc·es·sor (**mī′**krō-prŏs′ĕs-ər) *n.* An integrated circuit that contains the entire central processing unit of a computer on a single chip.

mi·cro·scope (**mī′**krə-skōp′) *n.* **1.** An optical instrument consisting of a lens or combination of lenses for magnifying objects that are invisible or indistinct to the unaided eye. **2.** An instrument, such as an electron microscope, that uses electrons or other means to produce magnified images.

mi·cro·scop·ic (mī′krə-**skŏp′**ĭk) *adj.* **1.** Too small to be seen by the eye alone but large enough to be seen through a microscope: *microscopic cells.* **2.** Relating to or done with a microscope: *microscopic study of a specimen.*

3. Done with great attention to detail: *a microscopic analysis of the city's budget.* —**mi′cro·scop′i·cal·ly** *adv.*

mi·cros·co·py (mī-krŏs′kə-pē) *n., pl.* **mi·cros·co·pies 1.** The study or use of microscopes. **2.** Investigation using a microscope.

mi·cro·sec·ond (mī′krō-sĕk′ənd) *n.* A unit of time equal to one millionth (10^{-6}) of a second.

mi·cro·wave (mī′krō-wāv′) *adj.* Relating to or being electromagnetic radiation between radio waves and infrared waves in the electromagnetic spectrum. Microwaves have frequencies between 300 megahertz and 300 gigahertz and wavelengths between 1 meter and 1 millimeter. ❖ *n.* **1.** A wave of microwave radiation. **2.** A microwave oven. ❖ *tr.v.* **mi·cro·waved, mi·cro·wav·ing, mi·cro·waves** To cook or heat (food) in a microwave oven.

microwave oven *n.* An oven in which microwaves are used to heat and cook food.

mid¹ (mĭd) *adj.* Middle; central. [From Old English.]

mid² (mĭd) *prep.* Amid: *mid smoke and flame.* [Alteration of *amid.*]

mid– *pref.* A prefix that means middle: *midsummer.* —SEE NOTE.

mid·air (mĭd′âr′) *n.* A point or region in the air: *a trapeze suspended in midair.* ❖ *adj.* Occurring in midair: *a midair collision.*

Mi·das (mī′dəs) *n.* In Greek mythology, a king who is given the power of turning all that he touches to gold.

Mid-At·lan·tic States (mĭd′ăt-lăn′tĭk) See **Middle Atlantic States.**

mid·brain (mĭd′brān′) *n.* The part of the brain that lies between the forebrain and the hindbrain. Its functions include control of reflex actions and eye movements.

mid·day (mĭd′dā′) *n.* The middle of the day; noon.

mid·dle (mĭd′l) *adj.* **1.** Equally distant from extremes; central: *the middle seats of the row.* **2.** Being halfway or intermediate in a sequence or series: *the middle child of three in the family.* **3.** often **Middle** Being a stage in the development of a thing, form, or period that is between earlier and later stages: *the Middle Kingdom of ancient Egypt.* ❖ *n.* **1.** An area or point equally distant from extremes; a center: *the middle of the room.* **2.** Something between a beginning and an end; an intermediate part: *A story has a beginning, a middle, and an end.* **3.** The middle part of the human body; the waist. [From Middle English *middel*, from Old English.]

middle age *n.* The time of human life between youth and old age, usually reckoned as the years between 40 and 60.

mid·dle-aged (mĭd′l-ājd′) *adj.* Relating to middle age.

Middle Ages *pl.n.* The period in European history between ancient times and the Renaissance, often dated from AD 476 to 1453.

Middle Atlantic States also **Mid-At·lan·tic States** (mĭd′ăt-lăn′tĭk) A region of the eastern United States including New York, Pennsylvania, New Jersey, and usually Delaware and Maryland.

middle C *n.* The musical tone represented by a note on the first ledger line above the bass clef.

middle class *n.* The people of a society who occupy a social and economic position between the working classes and the wealthy. The middle class usually includes professionals and highly skilled workers.

Middle Dutch *n.* The Dutch language from the middle of the 1100s through the 1400s.

middle ear *n.* The space between the eardrum and the inner ear. In humans and other mammals it contains three small bones that carry sound vibrations from the eardrum to the inner ear.

Middle East also **Mid·east** (mĭd-ēst′) An area made up of the countries of southwest Asia and northeast Africa.

Middle English *n.* The English language from about 1100 to 1500, between Old English and Modern English.

Middle Low German *n.* Low German from the middle of the 1200s through the 1400s.

mid·dle·man (mĭd′l-măn′) *n.* **1.** A trader who buys goods from producers and sells to retailers or consumers. **2.** An intermediary or a go-between.

middle school *n.* A school at a level between elementary and high school, typically including grades five or six through eight. —**mid′dle-school′** *adj.*

mid·dle·weight (mĭd′l-wāt′) *n.* **1.** A boxer weighing more than 147 and not more than 160 pounds (about 66–72 kilograms). **2.** A contestant in other sports in a similar weight class.

Middle West See **Midwest.**

mid·dling (mĭd′lĭng *or* mĭd′lĭn) *adj.* Of medium size, position, or quality; average: *a middling performance on the test.*

Mid·east (mĭd-ēst′) See **Middle East.**

mid·field (mĭd′fēld′) *n.* In sports, the section of a playing field midway between goals.

mid·field·er (mĭd′fēl′dər) *n.* A player in certain sports, such as soccer and lacrosse, positioned behind the forward line and playing both offense and defense.

midge (mĭj) *n.* Any of various very small flies, some of which form large swarms near ponds and lakes.

midg·et (mĭj′ĭt) *n.* **1.** *Offensive* A very small person of normal proportions. **2.** A small or miniature version of something.

mid·land (mĭd′lənd) *n.* The middle or interior part of a country or region.

mid·most (mĭd′mōst′) *adj.* Situated in the exact middle or nearest the middle.

mid·night (mĭd′nīt′) *n.* The middle of the night, specifically 12:00 at night.

midnight sun *n.* The sun as seen at midnight during the summer within the Arctic and Antarctic Circles.

mid·point (mĭd′point′) *n.* A point halfway between limits or endpoints.

mid·rib (mĭd′rĭb′) *n.* The central vein of a leaf.

mid·riff (mĭd′rĭf) *n.* The middle part of the human body that extends from just below the chest to the waist.

mid·sec·tion (mĭd′sĕk′shən) *n.* A middle section, especially the midriff of the human body.

mid·ship (mĭd′shĭp′) *adj.* Relating to or located in the middle of a ship.

mid·ship·man (mĭd′shĭp′mən *or* mĭd-shĭp′mən) *n.* A student training to be an officer at a naval academy.

mid·ships (mĭd′shĭps′) *adv.* Amidships.

midst (mĭdst *or* mĭtst) *n.* **1.** The middle position or part; the center: *a tree in the midst of the garden.* **2.** The condition of being surrounded by something: *trouble in the midst of good fortune.* **3.** A position near or among others: *a stranger in our midst.* ❖ *prep.* Among; amid. [From Middle English *middes*, from Old English *midde*, middle.]

mid·stream (mĭd′strēm′) *n.* **1.** The middle of a stream. **2.** The middle of a course of action or period of time: *We changed plans in midstream.*

mid·sum·mer (mĭd′sŭm′ər) *n.* **1.** The middle of the summer. **2.** The summer solstice, occurring on or about June 21 in the Northern Hemisphere. ❖ *adj.* Relating to or occurring during the middle of summer.

mid·term (mĭd′tûrm′) *n.* **1.** The middle of a school term or a political term of office. **2.** An examination given at the middle of a school term. —**mid′term′** *adj.*

mid·town (mĭd′toun′) *n.* The central part of a town or city.

mid·way (mĭd′wā′) *n.* The area of a fair, carnival, or circus where sideshows and other amusements are located. ❖ *adv.* In the middle of a distance or period of time.

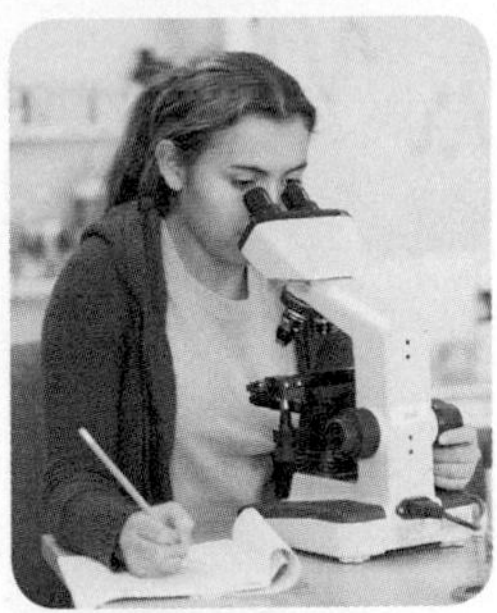

microscope

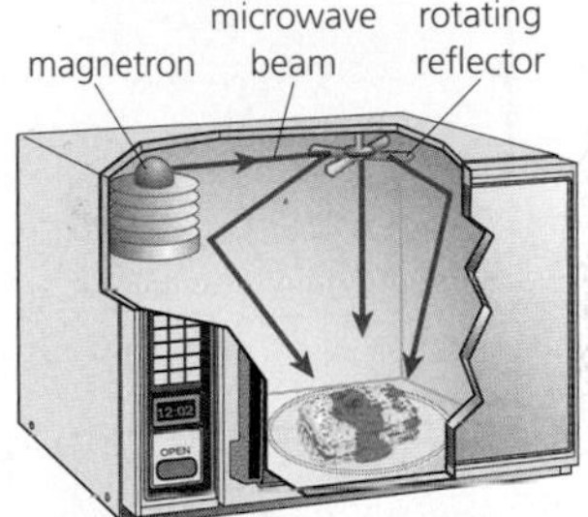

microwave oven

A magnetron, when activated by an electric current, emits a microwave beam that is then distributed throughout the oven by a rotating reflector. The microwave beams agitate water molecules in the food, generating enough heat to cook it.

WORD BUILDING

mid– The prefix **mid–**, which means "middle," is mostly added to nouns that refer to a time (*midmorning, midsummer, midyear*) or place (*midbrain, midstream, midtown*). When *mid–* is attached to a word beginning with a capital letter, it is always necessary to use a hyphen: *mid-November, Mid-Atlantic States.* The prefix *mid–* can be traced back to the Old English adjective *midd,* meaning "middle."

milkweed

Midway A United States territory made up of two small islands and a surrounding coral reef in the central Pacific Ocean northwest of Honolulu. The Battle of Midway (June 4–7, 1942) was a major victory for Allied forces during World War II.

mid·week (mĭd′wēk′) *n.* The middle of the week.

Mid·west (mĭd-wĕst′) or **Middle West** A region of the north-central United States around the Great Lakes and the upper Mississippi River valley. The area is known for its rich farmlands and highly industrialized centers.

mid·wife (mĭd′wīf′) *n., pl.* **mid·wives** (mĭd′wīvz′) A person, usually a woman, who is trained to assist women in childbirth. [From Middle English *midwif* : probably *mid*, with + *wif*, (the) woman (giving birth).] —SEE NOTE AT **with.**

mid·win·ter (mĭd′wĭn′tər) *n.* **1.** The middle of the winter. **2.** The winter solstice, occurring on or about December 22 in the Northern Hemisphere. ❖ *adj.* Relating to or occurring in the middle of the winter.

mid·year (mĭd′yîr′) *adj.* Relating to or occurring in the middle of a year: *midyear reviews.*

mien (mēn) *n.* A person's manner of behavior or appearance; bearing: *the mien of a dignified professor.*

❏ *These sound alike:* **mien, mean¹** (signify), **mean²** (unkind), **mean³** (middle point).

miff (mĭf) *tr.v.* **miffed, miff·ing, miffs** To offend or annoy: *I was miffed by their failure to do the job properly.*

might¹ (mīt) *n.* **1.** Great power or force: *the might of a great army.* **2.** Physical strength: *pushed with all my might.* See Synonyms at **strength.** [From Old English *mæct.*]

❏ *These sound alike:* **might¹** (power), **might²** (past tense of may), **mite¹** (small animal), **mite²** (small amount of money).

might² (mīt) *aux.v.* Past tense of **may. 1.** Used to indicate possibility or probability: *We might go to the beach tomorrow.* **2.** Used to express permission: *She asked if she might stay out late.* [From Old English *mæhte.*]

❏ *These sound alike:* **might²** (past tense of may), **might¹** (power), **mite¹** (small animal), **mite²** (small amount of money).

might·y (mī′tē) *adj.* **might·i·er, might·i·est 1.** Having or showing great power, strength, or skill: *a mighty hunter.* **2.** Great in size, scope, or intensity: *a mighty stone fortress.* ❖ *adv. Informal* Very; extremely: *They've been gone a mighty long time.* **—might′i·ly** *adv.* **—might′i·ness** *n.*

mi·graine (mī′grān′) *n.* A very severe headache, often accompanied by nausea, that usually affects only one side of the head and tends to recur. [From Middle English, from Greek *hēmikrāniā* : *hēmi-*, half, one side + *krānion*, head.]

mi·grant (mī′grənt) *n.* **1.** A person or animal that migrates. **2.** A farm worker who travels from one area to another in search of work. ❖ *adj.* Migratory; migrating.

mi·grate (mī′grāt′) *intr.v.* **mi·grat·ed, mi·grat·ing, mi·grates 1.** To move from one country or region and settle in another. **2.** To move regularly to a different region, especially at a particular time of the year: *Many monarch butterflies migrate from Canada to Mexico in the fall.* [From Latin *migrāre.*]

mi·gra·tion (mī-grā′shən) *n.* The act or an instance of migrating.

mi·gra·to·ry (mī′grə-tôr′ē) *adj.* **1.** Traveling from one place to another; migrating regularly: *migratory birds.* **2.** Relating to migration: *long migratory flights.*

mi·ka·do (mĭ-kä′dō) *n., pl.* **mi·ka·dos** An emperor of Japan.

mike (mīk) *Informal n.* A microphone. ❖ *tr.v.* **miked, mik·ing, mikes** To supply with or transmit through a microphone: *The assistant miked the singers before they went onstage.*

Mi'k·maq or **Mic·mac** (mĭk′măk′) *n., pl.* **Mi'kmaq** or **Mi'k·maqs** or **Micmac** or **Mic·macs 1.** A member of a Native American people living in northeast Maine and southeast Canada. **2.** The Algonquian language of the Mi'kmaq.

mil (mĭl) *n.* A unit of length equal to one thousandth (10^{-3}) of an inch (0.025 millimeter), used chiefly to measure the diameter of wires. [From Latin *mīlle*, thousand.]

❏ *These sound alike:* **mil, mill¹** (grinding machine), **mill²** (unit of money).

mi·la·dy (mĭ-lā′dē) *n.* Used as a form of address for an English noblewoman.

Mi·lan (mĭ-lăn′ *or* mĭ-län′) A city of northern Italy northeast of Genoa. It has been an important commercial, financial, cultural, and industrial center since medieval times

milch (mĭlch) *adj.* Giving milk: *a milch cow.*

mild (mīld) *adj.* **mild·er, mild·est 1.** Gentle or kind in disposition, manner, or behavior: *a mild grandparent.* **2.** Moderate in type, degree, effect, or force: *a mild reprimand; a mild soap.* **3a.** Not extreme, as in temperature: *a mild climate.* **b.** Warm and full of sunshine: *a mild day.* **—mild′ly** *adv.* **—mild′ness** *n.*

mil·dew (mĭl′do͞o′) *n.* **1.** Any of various fungi or water molds that form a white or grayish coating on surfaces, such as plant leaves, cloth, or leather, especially under damp warm conditions. **2.** The coating formed by such a fungus or water mold. ❖ *v.* **mil·dewed, mil·dew·ing, mil·dews** *—intr.* To become covered or spotted with mildew: *The leather coat mildewed in the damp closet.* *—tr.* To cause to become covered or spotted with mildew. [From Old English *mildēaw*, honeydew, nectar.]

mile (mīl) *n.* **1.** A unit of length equal to 5,280 feet or 1,760 yards (about 1,609 meters); a statute mile. See table at **measurement. 2.** A nautical mile. [From Old English *mīl*, from Latin *mīlia (passuum)*, a thousand (double paces).]

mile·age (mī′lĭj) *n.* **1.** Length or distance in miles: *The mileage between the two cities is considerable.* **2a.** Total miles covered or traveled over a given time: *We haven't put much mileage on the car in the last month.* **b.** The amount of service, use, or wear measured by miles used or traveled: *a tire that gives long mileage.* **3.** The distance a motor vehicle travels on a given amount of fuel: *a mileage of 32 miles per gallon.* **4.** An allowance of a given amount for traveling expenses at a certain rate per mile: *The company pays a mileage of 45 cents per mile when I use my car for business travel.*

mile·post (mīl′pōst′) *n.* A post along a highway that indicates the distance in miles to a certain place.

mile·stone (mīl′stōn′) *n.* **1.** A stone marker set up on a roadside to indicate the distance in miles from a given point. **2.** An important event; a turning point: *The Bill of Rights was a milestone in the history of human rights.*

mi·lieu (mĭl-yo͞o′ *or* mē-lyœ′) *n., pl.* **mi·lieus** or **mi·lieux** (mē-lyœ′) An environment or a setting: *People often feel most comfortable in their own milieu.*

mil·i·tant (mĭl′ĭ-tənt) *adj.* **1.** Fighting or making war: *militant bands of insurgents.* **2.** Aggressive or combative, especially in the service of a cause: *Militant strikers blocked the entrances to the business.* ❖ *n.* A militant person. **—mil′i·tan·cy** *n.* **—mil′i·tant·ly** *adv.*

mil·i·ta·rism (mĭl′ĭ-tə-rĭz′əm) *n.* **1.** Glorification of military spirit or ideals. **2.** A policy in which maintaining strong armed forces is of chief importance to a country or an organization. **—mil′i·ta·ris′tic** *adj.*

mil·i·ta·rist (mĭl′ĭ-tər-ĭst) *n.* A person who supports militarism.

mil·i·ta·rize (mĭl′ĭ-tə-rīz′) *tr.v.* **mil·i·ta·rized, mil·i·ta·riz·ing, mil·i·ta·riz·es 1.** To equip or train for war. **2.** To fill with militarism. **—mil′i·ta·ri·za′tion** (mĭl′ĭ-tər-ĭ-zā′shən) *n.*

ă	pat	ôr	core
ā	pay	oi	boy
âr	care	ou	out
ä	father	o͝o	took
ĕ	pet	o͝or	lure
ē	be	o͞o	boot
ĭ	pit	ŭ	cut
ī	bite	ûr	urge
îr	pier	th	thin
ŏ	pot	*th*	this
ō	toe	zh	vision
ô	paw	ə	about

mil·i·tar·y (mĭl′ĭ-tĕr′ē) *adj.* **1.** Relating to or characteristic of the army, navy, or other branches of the armed forces: *a military base; military uniforms.* **2.** Relating to war: *military history.* ❖ *n., pl.* **military** also **mil·i·tar·ies** The army, navy, or other branches of the armed forces of a country: *funding for the military; a takeover by the military.* [From Middle English *militari*, from Latin *mīles*, soldier.] **—mil′i·tar′i·ly** (mĭl′ĭ-târ′ə-lē) *adv.*

mil·i·tate (mĭl′ĭ-tāt′) *intr.v.* **mil·i·tat·ed, mil·i·tat·ing, mil·i·tates** To have force or influence; bring about an effect or change: *Carelessness militates against doing a good job.*

mi·li·tia (mə-lĭsh′ə) *n.* **1.** An army composed of citizens rather than professional soldiers. **2.** A military force that is not part of a regular army and is subject to call for service in an emergency.

mi·li·tia·man (mə-lĭsh′ə-mən) *n.* A man who is a member of a militia.

milk (mĭlk) *n.* **1a.** A white liquid produced by the mammary glands of female mammals for feeding their young. **b.** The milk of certain mammals, especially cows, used as food by humans. **2.** A liquid resembling milk: *coconut milk.* ❖ *v.* **milked, milk·ing, milks** *—tr.* **1a.** To squeeze milk from the teats or udder of (a cow, goat, or other mammal). **b.** To draw out or extract a liquid from: *milked the snake of its venom.* **2.** *Informal* To obtain money or benefits from, in order to achieve personal gain: *milk the treasury of its funds.* **3.** *Informal* **a.** To draw out or extract something from: *milked the witness for information.* **b.** To obtain the greatest possible advantage from (a situation). *—intr.* To draw milk from a cow, goat, or other animal. [From Old English *milc.*]

milk·er (mĭl′kər) *n.* **1.** A person or machine that milks animals. **2.** An animal kept to give milk, as a cow or goat.

milk·maid (mĭlk′mād′) *n.* A girl or woman who milks cows.

milk·man (mĭlk′măn′) *n.* A man who sells or delivers milk.

milk of magnesia *n.* A milky white suspension of magnesium hydroxide in water used as an antacid and a laxative.

milk·shake (mĭlk′shāk′) *n.* A beverage that is made of milk, flavoring, and usually ice cream and is blended or shaken until foamy.

milk snake *n.* Any of various king snakes often having red, black, and yellow or white bands.

milk·sop (mĭlk′sŏp′) *n.* A person who lacks courage; a weakling.

milk sugar *n.* Lactose.

milk tooth *n.* Any of the temporary teeth that first grow in the mouth of a young mammal.

milk·weed (mĭlk′wēd′) *n.* Any of numerous plants having small flowers in clusters, milky juice, and pods that split open to release seeds with downy tufts.

milk·y (mĭl′kē) *adj.* **milk·i·er, milk·i·est 1.** Resembling milk, especially in color. **2.** Consisting of or yielding milk. **—milk′i·ness** *n.*

Milky Way *n.* The galaxy containing the solar system, visible as a broad band of faint light in the night sky.

mill¹ (mĭl) *n.* **1.** A building equipped with machines for grinding grain into flour or meal. **2.** A device or machine that grinds grain. **3.** A device or machine for grinding, crushing, or pressing: *a cider mill.* **4.** A building or group of buildings equipped with machinery for processing a material of some kind: *a steel mill.* **5.** A business or institution that produces something in great numbers and without regard for standards of quality: *a diploma mill; a puppy mill.* ❖ *v.* **milled, mill·ing, mills** *—tr.* **1.** To grind or crush into powder or fine grains: *mill wheat.* **2.** To process or produce (steel, paper, or another product) in a mill. **3.** To put ridges or grooves on the edge of (a coin). *—intr.* To move around in a confused or disorderly manner: *During the fire drill the students milled about the playground.* [From Old English *mylen*, from Late Latin *molīna*, from *molere*, to grind.]

❑ *These sound alike:* **mill¹** (grinding machine), **mil** (unit of length), **mill²** (unit of money).

mill² (mĭl) *n.* A unit of money equal to one thousandth of a US dollar, or one tenth of a cent. [Short for Latin *millēsimus*, thousandth.]

❑ *These sound alike:* **mill²** (unit of money), **mil** (unit of length), **mill¹** (grinding machine).

Mill (mĭl), **John Stuart** 1806–1873. British philosopher and economist whose works include *Principles of Political Economy* (1848).

Mil·lay (mĭ-lā′), **Edna Saint Vincent** 1892–1950. American poet whose volumes include *The Harp Weaver and Other Poems* (1923).

Edna Saint Vincent Millay

mill·dam (mĭl′dăm′) *n.* A dam built across a stream to raise the water level and provide water power to turn a mill wheel.

mil·len·ni·um (mə-lĕn′ē-əm) *n., pl.* **mil·len·ni·a** (mə-lĕn′ē-ə) or **mil·len·ni·ums 1.** A span of one thousand years. **2.** A thousand-year reign of Jesus on the earth, mentioned in the book of Revelation. **3.** A period of joy, prosperity, and peace. [From Latin *mīlle*, thousand + Latin *annus*, year.] **—mil·len′ni·al** *adj.*

mill·er (mĭl′ər) *n.* **1.** A person who owns or operates a mill for grinding grain. **2.** Any of various moths whose wings and body have a powdery appearance.

mil·let (mĭl′ĭt) *n.* **1.** The small seeds of any of several cereal grasses, widely used for food, livestock feed, and birdseed. **2.** The plant that bears such seeds, often used as hay. [From Middle English *milet*, from Old French, from Latin *milium.*]

milli– *pref.* A prefix that means one thousandth: *millimeter.*

mil·li·bar (mĭl′ə-bär′) *n.* A unit of atmospheric pressure equal to one thousandth (10^{-3}) of a bar. Standard atmospheric pressure at sea level is about 1,013 millibars.

mil·li·gram (mĭl′ĭ-grăm′) *n.* A unit of mass or weight equal to one thousandth (10^{-3}) of a gram.

mil·li·li·ter (mĭl′ə-lē′tər) *n.* A metric unit of volume equal to one thousandth (10^{-3}) of a liter. See table at **measurement.**

mil·li·me·ter (mĭl′ə-mē′tər) *n.* A unit of length equal to one thousandth (10^{-3}) of a meter. See table at **measurement.**

mil·li·ner (mĭl′ə-nər) *n.* A person who makes, trims, designs, or sells women's hats.

mil·li·ner·y (mĭl′ə-nĕr′ē) *n., pl.* **mil·li·ner·ies 1.** Women's hats, including trimmings for hats. **2.** The business of making, designing, or selling women's hats.

mill·ing (mĭl′ĭng) *n.* **1.** The act or process of grinding, especially of grinding grain into flour or meal. **2.** The act or process of cutting ridges on the edges of coins. **3.** The ridges cut on the edges of coins.

mil·lion (mĭl′yən) *n., pl.* **million** or **mil·lions 1.** The number, written as 10^6 or 1 followed by six zeros, that is equal to 1,000 × 1,000. **2.** An indefinitely large number: *There are millions of things to do in a big city.* [From Middle English *milioun*, from Old French *milion*, from Latin *mīlle*, thousand.]

mil·lion·aire (mĭl′yə-**nâr′**) *n.* A person whose wealth amounts to at least a million dollars, pounds, or similar units in another currency.

mil·lionth (mĭl′yənth) *n.* **1.** The ordinal number matching the number 1,000,000 in a series. **2.** One of a million equal parts. **—mil′lionth** *adv. & adj.*

mil·li·pede (mĭl′ə-pēd′) *n.* Any of various small invertebrate animals having a cylindrical body composed of many narrow segments, most of which have two pairs of legs.

SCIENCE

mimicry Many animals, and even some plants and fungi, have evolved to imitate certain characteristics of other kinds of organisms. **Mimicry,** the name for this imitation of one species by another, is often a strategy for avoiding predation. Some harmless king snakes, for example, have a pattern of black, yellow, and red bands that is very similar to the pattern found in venomous coral snakes. This color pattern protects the king snakes; coyotes, hawks, and other predators avoid both the dangerous coral snakes and the tasty king snakes. Mimicry can be even more devious. One fungus species that infects plants causes the plant to make a structure that looks like a flower but is full of fungal spores; when an insect visits the fake flower looking for nectar, it picks up the spores and gives them a ride to another plant.

minaret
minaret of the Nuruosmaniye Mosque, Istanbul, Turkey

ă	pat	ôr	core
ā	pay	oi	boy
âr	care	ou	out
ä	father	o͝o	took
ĕ	pet	o͝or	lure
ē	be	o͞o	boot
ĭ	pit	ŭ	cut
ī	bite	ûr	urge
îr	pier	th	thin
ŏ	pot	*th*	this
ō	toe	zh	vision
ô	paw	ə	about

mil·li·sec·ond (mĭl′ĭ-sĕk′ənd) *n.* A unit of time equal to one thousandth (10^{-3}) of a second.

mill·pond (mĭl′pŏnd′) *n.* A pond formed by a milldam, used to supply water to run a mill.

mill·race (mĭl′rās′) *n.* **1.** The fast-moving stream of water that drives a mill wheel. **2.** The channel for the water that drives a mill wheel.

mill·stone (mĭl′stōn′) *n.* **1.** One of a pair of large cylindrical stones used to grind grain. **2.** An obstacle to success.

mill wheel *n.* A wheel, usually turned by moving water, that supplies the power for a mill.

mi·lord (mĭ-**lôrd′**) *n.* Used to address an English nobleman or gentleman.

milque·toast (mĭlk′tōst′) *n.* A person who is meek or timid.

milt (mĭlt) *n.* The sperm cells of male fishes, together with the milky liquid containing them.

Mil·ton (mĭl′tən), **John** 1608–1674. English poet who is best known for *Paradise Lost* (1667).

Mil·wau·kee (mĭl-**wô′**kē) The largest city of Wisconsin, in the southeast part of the state on Lake Michigan. It was a major center of German immigration during the 1800s.

mime (mīm) *n.* **1.** Acting by means of gestures and movements without speech; pantomime. **2.** An actor in pantomime. ❖ *v.* **mimed, mim·ing, mimes** —*tr.* To act out (something) with gestures and body movements. —*intr.* To act as a mimic. [From Greek *mīmos.*] **—mim′er** *n.*

mim·e·o·graph (mĭm′ē-ə-grăf′) *n.* **1.** A machine that makes copies of material that is written, drawn, or typed on a stencil. **2.** A copy made by such a machine. ❖ *tr.v.* **mim·e·o·graphed, mim·e·o·graph·ing, mim·e·o·graphs** To copy with a mimeograph.

mim·ic (mĭm′ĭk) *tr.v.* **mim·icked, mim·ick·ing, mim·ics** **1.** To copy or imitate closely, as in speech, expression, or gesture, often so as to ridicule: *That bird can mimic its owner. The boy mimicked his father's laugh.* See Synonyms at **imitate. 2.** To simulate or reproduce: *trying to mimic conditions on the surface of the moon.* **3.** To resemble by biological mimicry: *an insect mimicking a twig.* ❖ *n.* **1.** A person who imitates, especially a performer or comedian skilled in pantomime. **2.** A copy or imitation. [From Greek *mīmikos,* of mimes.]

mim·ic·ry (mĭm′ĭ-krē) *n., pl.* **mim·ic·ries 1.** The art or practice of mimicking. **2.** The resemblance of one organism to another or to an object in its surroundings, especially for concealment or protection. —SEE NOTE.

mi·mo·sa (mĭ-**mō′**sə *or* mĭ-**mō′**zə) *n.* **1.** Any of various tropical trees or shrubs having feathery leaves and clusters of small yellow, pink, or white flowers. **2.** A drink of champagne and orange juice.

min. *abbr.* An abbreviation of: **1.** minimum. **2.** minor. **3.** minute.

min·a·ret (mĭn′ə-**rĕt′**) *n.* A tall slender tower on a mosque from which a muezzin summons the people to prayer. [From Turkish *minārat,* from Arabic *manāra,* lamp.]

mince (mĭns) *v.* **minced, minc·ing, minc·es** —*tr.* **1.** To cut or chop into very small pieces. **2.** To change or make (words) less distressing, especially for the sake of politeness: *The doctor minced no words in describing the patient's condition.* —*intr.* **1.** To walk in an affected way or with very short steps. **2.** To speak in an affected way. ❖ *n.* Mincemeat. [From Middle English *mincen,* from Old French *mincier,* from Latin *minūtia,* smallness.]

mince·meat (mĭns′mēt′) *n.* A mixture of finely chopped fruit, spices, suet, and sometimes meat, used especially as a pie filling.

mind (mīnd) *n.* **1.** The part or faculty of a person by which one feels, perceives, thinks, remembers, desires, and imagines: *Use your mind to solve the problem.* **2.** A person of great intellect or intelligence: *Newton was one of the great minds of science.* **3.** Focus of thought and attention: *Sometimes it's hard to keep your mind on your work.* **4.** Remembrance; memory: *Keep our invitation in mind.* **5.** Opinion or sentiment; attitude or point of view: *It's not too late to change your mind.* **6.** Desire; purpose: *had half a mind not to go.* **7.** A healthy mental condition; sanity: *lose one's mind.* ❖ *v.* **mind·ed, mind·ing, minds** —*tr.* **1.** To pay attention to: *Mind what I'm saying.* **2.** To obey: *The children were told to mind the babysitter.* **3.** To be careful about: *Mind how you swing the hammer.* **4.** To take care of; look after: *stayed home to mind the baby.* **5.** To object to or dislike: *I don't mind mopping the floor.* —*intr.* **1.** To be troubled or concerned: *I don't mind if you borrow the car.* **2.** To behave obediently: *I hope the children mind while we're in the car.* **3.** To take notice; pay attention: *You'll slip on the ice if you don't mind.* ◆ **bring** or **call to mind** To cause (something) to be remembered or thought of: *a meal that brought to mind her childhood in the country.* **of one mind** In agreement: *We're of one mind about the proposed tunnel.* [From Old English *gemynd.*]

mind-bog·gling (mīnd′bŏg′lĭng) *adj. Informal* Overwhelming; perplexing: *was faced with a mind-boggling problem.*

mind·ed (mīn′dĭd) *adj.* **1.** Disposed; inclined: *Come over for a visit if you are so minded.* **2.** Having a specific kind of mind: *a strong-minded person.*

mind·ful (mīnd′fəl) *adj.* Attentive; heedful: *always mindful of the importance of reading.* **—mind′ful·ly** *adv.*

mind·less (mīnd′lĭs) *adj.* **1.** Lacking intelligence; foolish. **2.** Having no purpose or meaning: *a mindless act.* **—mind′less·ly** *adv.*

mind reading *n.* The supposed ability to know or discern another's thoughts through extrasensory means of communication; telepathy. **—mind reader** *n.*

mind·set or **mind-set** (mīnd′sĕt′) *n.* A particular attitude or disposition regarding a situation: *Thanks to his positive mindset, he was able to overcome the setback.*

mind's eye (mīndz) *n.* The ability of forming mental images of something that is not real or present; the imagination.

mine¹ (mīn) *n.* **1a.** A hole or passage dug in the earth to extract metals, coal, salt, or other minerals: *a gold mine.* **b.** An excavation made on the surface of the ground in which the topmost layer of earth is removed and ore and minerals are extracted from that layer. **2.** An abundant supply or source: *The Internet is a mine of information.* **3.** A tunnel dug under enemy positions or fortifications to cause them to collapse, to lay explosives, or to gain an entrance. **4.** An explosive device that can be buried in the ground or concealed in a body of water: *a land mine.* ❖ *v.* **mined, min·ing, mines** —*tr.* **1a.** To extract (ores or minerals) from the earth: *mined copper.* **b.** To dig or tunnel in (the earth) for this purpose. **2.** To place explosive mines in or under: *mine a harbor.* **3.** To analyze in detail in order to make use of: *The company mined the data collected by its website to determine who bought its products.* —*intr.* **1.** To dig in the earth to extract ore or minerals: *The company is mining for diamonds.* **2.** To work in a mine. **3.** To tunnel in the earth, especially under enemy fortifications. [From Middle English, from Old French, probably of Celtic origin.]

mine² (mīn) *pron.* *(used with a singular or plural verb)* The one or ones belonging to me: *Your car is different from mine.* ❖ *adj.* A possessive form of **I¹**. *Archaic* Used instead of *my* before a vowel or the letter *h: mine eyes; mine honor.* [From Old English *mīn.*]

mine·field (mīn′fēld′) *n.* **1.** An area in which explosive mines have been placed. **2.** A situation that has many potential hazards or dangers.

min·er (mī′nər) *n.* A person who works in a mine, especially to extract ores or minerals from the earth.

❑ *These sound alike:* **miner, minor** (under legal age).

min·er·al (mĭn′ər-əl) *n.* **1.** An inorganic solid substance found in nature that has a uniform chemical composition, a regular crystalline form, and a characteristic hardness and color. **2.** A substance, such as gold, iron ore, or stone, that is obtained by mining or quarrying. **3.** A substance that is neither animal nor vegetable. **4.** An inorganic element, such as calcium, iron, potassium, sodium, or zinc, that is essential to the nutrition of living organisms. ❖ *adj.* **1.** Relating to, resembling, or containing a mineral or minerals. **2.** Not animal or vegetable; inorganic. [From Middle English, from Medieval Latin *minerālis*, relating to mines.]

min·er·al·o·gy (mĭn′ə-rŏl′ə-jē *or* mĭn′ə-răl′ə-jē) *n.* The scientific study of minerals. **—min′er·a·log′i·cal** (mĭn′ər-ə-lŏj′ĭ-kəl) *adj.* **—min′er·al′o·gist** *n.*

mineral oil *n.* A colorless, odorless, tasteless oil distilled from petroleum and used in medicine as a laxative.

Mi·ner·va (mĭ-nûr′və) *n.* In Roman mythology, the goddess of wisdom and the arts, identified with the Greek Athena.

mine·shaft (mīn′shăft′) *n.* A vertical or sloping passageway dug in the earth for finding or mining ore.

min·e·stro·ne (mĭn′ĭ-strō′nē) *n.* A soup containing vegetables, pasta, and herbs in a meat or vegetable broth.

mine·sweep·er (mīn′swē′pər) *n.* A ship equipped for finding and destroying or removing explosive underwater mines.

min·gle (mĭng′gəl) *v.* **min·gled, min·gling, min·gles** *—tr.* To mix or combine; unite: *The poem mingled passion and wit.* *—intr.* **1.** To become mixed or united. **2.** To associate or join with others: *The guests mingled freely at the party.*

min·i (mĭn′ē) *n., pl.* **min·is** Something smaller or shorter than others of its kind. **—min′i** *adj.*

mini– *pref.* A prefix that means small: *minibike.*

min·i·a·ture (mĭn′ē-ə-chər *or* mĭn′ə-chər) *n.* **1.** A copy or reproduction on a small scale: *The architects made a miniature of the proposed building.* **2.** A very small painting or portrait. **3.** A dog of a small breed or of a variety smaller than the standard variety of its breed. ❖ *adj.* Greatly reduced in size or scale. See Synonyms at **little.** [From Italian *miniare*, to illuminate manuscripts, from Latin *minium*, red lead.]

min·i·a·tur·ize (mĭn′ē-ə-chə-rīz′ *or* mĭn′ə-chə-rīz′) *tr.v.* **min·i·a·tur·ized, min·i·a·tur·iz·ing, min·i·a·tur·iz·es** To plan or make on a very small scale.

min·i·bike (mĭn′ē-bīk′) *n.* A small motorcycle.

min·i·mal (mĭn′ə-məl) *adj.* **1.** Smallest in amount or degree; least possible: *outlined the minimal qualifications for the job.* **2.** Small in amount or degree: *prescribed a drug with minimal side effects.* **—min′i·mal·ly** *adv.*

min·i·mize (mĭn′ə-mīz′) *tr.v.* **min·i·mized, min·i·miz·ing, min·i·miz·es** **1.** To reduce to the smallest possible amount or degree: *In winter, we try to minimize the amount of heat that escapes our house.* **2.** To represent as having little importance, value, or size; depreciate. **—min′i·mi·za′tion** (mĭn′ə-mĭ-zā′shən) *n.* **—min′i·miz′er** *n.*

min·i·mum (mĭn′ə-məm) *n., pl.* **min·i·mums** or **min·i·ma** (mĭn′ə-mə) **1.** The smallest amount or degree possible: *We need a minimum of an hour to make dinner.* **2.** The lowest amount or degree reached or recorded: *The temperature's minimum yesterday was 45°.* ❖ *adj.* Representing the least possible or the lowest amount or degree. [From Latin, from *minimus*, least.]

minimum wage *n.* The lowest wage, set by law or contract, that an employer may pay an employee for a specified job.

min·ing (mī′nĭng) *n.* **1.** The work, process, or business of extracting coal, minerals, or ore from the earth. **2.** The process of placing explosive mines.

min·ion (mĭn′yən) *n.* **1.** A person who follows or serves another in a slavish or servile manner. **2.** A person who is much loved or admired; a favorite.

min·i·skirt (mĭn′ē-skûrt′) *n.* A short skirt with a hemline that falls several inches above the knee.

min·is·ter (mĭn′ĭ-stər) *n.* **1.** A person who is authorized to perform religious functions in a Christian church. **2.** A person in charge of a government department: *the minister of finance.* **3.** A diplomat ranking below an ambassador, who represents his or her government in a foreign country. ❖ *intr.v.* **min·is·tered, min·is·ter·ing, min·is·ters** To attend to another's needs; give aid or comfort: *The nurses ministered to the sick.* [From Middle English *ministre*, from Latin *minister*, servant.] **—min′is·te′ri·al** (mĭn′ĭ-stîr′ē-əl) *adj.* **—min′is·te′ri·al·ly** *adv.*

min·is·tra·tion (mĭn′ĭ-strā′shən) *n.* **1.** The act or process of serving or aiding. **2.** The act of performing the duties of a minister or cleric.

min·is·try (mĭn′ĭ-strē) *n., pl.* **min·is·tries** **1.** The position and duties of a Christian minister or cleric. **2.** The Christian clergy considered as a group. **3.** A department of government under the charge of a minister. **4.** Governmental ministers in general. **5.** The act of serving or aiding.

min·i·van (mĭn′ē-văn′) *n.* A van designed primarily for carrying passengers, often having rear seats that can be removed for loading cargo.

mink (mĭngk) *n., pl.* **mink** or **minks** **1.** Either of two meat-eating mammals of North America or Europe that live around water and have a pointed snout, short legs, and thick soft brown fur. **2.** The fur of the American mink, often used to make or trim clothing. [From Middle English, possibly of Scandinavian origin.]

Min·ne·ap·o·lis (mĭn′ē-ăp′ə-lĭs) The largest city of Minnesota, in the southeast part of the state on the Mississippi River adjacent to St. Paul. It was a leading lumbering center in the 1800s.

Min·ne·so·ta (mĭn′ĭ-sō′tə) A state of the northern United States north of Iowa and bordering on Lake Superior. It was admitted as the 32nd state in 1858. St. Paul is the capital and Minneapolis the largest city. —SEE NOTE.

min·now (mĭn′ō) *n., pl.* **minnow** or **min·nows** Any of various small freshwater fishes often used as bait. [From Middle English *meneu.*]

Mi·no·an (mĭ-nō′ən) *adj.* Relating to the Bronze Age culture that flourished in Crete from about 3000 to 1100 BC. ❖ *n.* A native or inhabitant of ancient Crete.

mi·nor (mī′nər) *adj.* **1.** Lesser or smaller in degree, size, or extent: *a minor change.* **2.** Lesser in importance or rank: *a minor role in the play.* **3.** Lesser in seriousness or danger: *a minor injury.* **4.** Not yet a legal adult: *minor children.* **5a.** Relating to or based on a minor scale: *a minor key.* **b.** Relating to a musical tone that is smaller by a half step than a major interval: *a minor third.* ❖ *n.* **1.** A person who is not yet the legal age of an adult. **2.** A secondary area of academic specialization: *graduated from college with a major in physics and a minor in philosophy.* **3.** A minor key, scale, or interval. **4. minors** The minor leagues of a sport, especially baseball. ❖ *intr.v.* **mi·nored, mi·nor·ing, mi·nors** To pursue academic studies in a minor: *She chose to minor in chemistry.* [From Middle English *minour*, from Latin.]

❑ *These sound alike:* **minor, miner** (mine worker).

Mi·nor·ca (mĭ-nôr′kə) A Spanish island in the Balearics of the western Mediterranean Sea. It was a loyalist stronghold in the Spanish Civil War.

mi·nor·i·ty (mə-nôr′ĭ-tē *or* mī-nôr′ĭ-tē) *n., pl.* **mi·nor·i·ties** **1.** The smaller in number of two groups forming a whole. **2a.** A racial, religious, political, national, or other group thought to be different from the larger group of which it is part. **b.** A group having little power or representation relative to other groups in a society.

GEOGRAPHY

Minnesota The name for the state of **Minnesota** comes from a Dakota name that was first used for the Minnesota River. The name meant "cloudy water." The state was later named after the river.

minnow

minor scale
C minor scale

mirage
heat mirage on a road

ă	pat	ôr	core
ā	pay	oi	boy
âr	care	ou	out
ä	father	o͝o	took
ĕ	pet	o͝or	lure
ē	be	o͞o	boot
ĭ	pit	ŭ	cut
ī	bite	ûr	urge
îr	pier	th	thin
ŏ	pot	*th*	this
ō	toe	zh	vision
ô	paw	ə	about

c. A member of one of these groups: *Several minorities were appointed to the committee for energy conservation.* **3.** The state or period of being younger than the age for legal adulthood.

minor league *n.* In sports, a professional league that ranks below a major league.

Minor Prophets *n.* The biblical Books of Hosea, Joel, Amos, Obadiah, Jonah, Micah, Nahum, Habakkuk, Zephaniah, Haggai, Zechariah, and Malachi.

minor scale *n.* Any of a set of musical scales having a half step instead of a whole step between the second and third tones, and sometimes one or two half steps at higher intervals.

Mi·nos (**mī′**nəs) *n.* In Greek mythology, a king of Crete who became a judge in the underworld after his death.

Min·o·taur (**mĭn′**ə-tôr′ *or* **mī′**nə-tôr′) *n.* In Greek mythology, a monster, half bull and half human, kept in the Labyrinth in Crete until Theseus killed him.

Minsk (mĭnsk) The capital of Belarus, in the central part of the country. It was ruled or occupied by various powers from the 1200s until Belarus gained independence in 1991.

min·strel (**mĭn′**strəl) *n.* **1.** A medieval musician who traveled from place to place, singing and reciting poetry. **2.** A performer in a minstrel show.

minstrel show *n.* A comic variety show of the 1800s and early 1900s, usually featuring white performers who wore black makeup on their faces.

mint[1] (mĭnt) *n.* **1.** A place where the coins of a country are made by authority of the government. **2.** A large amount, especially of money: *That painting is worth a mint.* ❖ *tr.v.* **mint·ed, mint·ing, mints 1.** To produce (money) by stamping metal; coin. **2.** To invent; make up: *The scientist minted a name for the newly discovered chemical.* ❖ *adj.* In original condition; undamaged: *an antique car in mint condition.* [From Old English *mynet,* coin, from Latin *monēta.*]

mint[2] (mĭnt) *n.* **1.** Any of various plants, such as the spearmint and peppermint, having aromatic leaves that yield an oil used as a flavoring. **2.** A candy with natural or artificial mint flavor. [From Old English *minte,* from Latin *menta.*]

mint·age (**mĭn′**tĭj) *n.* **1.** The act or process of minting coins. **2.** Coins manufactured in a mint. **3.** The fee paid to a mint by a government for which coins have been made. **4.** The impression stamped on a coin.

mint julep *n.* A drink made of bourbon, sugar, and mint leaves.

min·u·end (**mĭn′**yo͞o-ĕnd′) *n.* A number from which another is to be subtracted; for example, in the expression 100 – 23 = 77, the minuend is 100.

min·u·et (mĭn′yo͞o-**ĕt′**) *n.* **1.** A slow stately dance in 3/4 time that originated in France in the 1600s. **2.** Music for or in the rhythm of this dance.

Min·u·it (**mĭn′**yo͞o-ĭt), **Peter** 1580–1638. Dutch colonial administrator who purchased the island of Manhattan from Native Americans, supposedly for the equivalent of $24.

mi·nus (**mī′**nəs) *prep.* **1.** Reduced by the subtraction of; decreased by: *Seven minus four equals three.* **2.** *Informal* Without; lacking: *We arrived at the theater minus our tickets.* ❖ *adj.* **1.** Less than zero; negative: *a minus value.* **2.** Slightly lower or less than: *a grade of A minus.* ❖ *n.* **1.** The minus sign. **2.** A negative number or quantity: *My answer was a minus in that problem.* **3.** A disadvantage or drawback: *The lack of a baseball diamond at the camp was a minus.* [From Latin *minus,* from *minor,* less.]

min·us·cule (**mĭn′**ə-skyo͞ol′ *or* mĭ-**nŭs′**kyo͞ol′) *adj.* Very small; tiny.

minus sign *n.* The symbol –, as in 4 – 2 = 2, that is used to indicate subtraction or a negative quantity.

min·ute[1] (**mĭn′**ĭt) *n.* **1.** A unit of time equal to $\frac{1}{60}$ of an hour or 60 seconds. **2.** A unit of angular measurement that is equal to $\frac{1}{60}$ of a degree or 60 seconds. **3.** A short interval of time; a moment: *Wait a minute.* **4.** A specific point in time: *leaving this very minute.* **5. minutes** An official record of the events or discussion at a meeting of an organization. [From Middle English, from Medieval Latin *(pars) minūta (prīma),* (primary) small (part).]

mi·nute[2] (mī-**no͞ot′** *or* mĭ-**no͞ot′**) *adj.* **1.** Exceptionally small; tiny: *a minute organism.* **2.** Not worth noticing; insignificant: *a minute problem.* **3.** Marked by close examination or careful study of small details: *a minute inspection.* [From Middle English, from Latin *minūtus,* diminished, tiny.] **—mi·nute′ly** *adv.*

min·ute·man (**mĭn′**ĭt-măn′) *n.* A member of the American militia pledged to be ready to answer a call to fight on a minute's notice just before and during the Revolutionary War in the United States.

mi·nu·ti·ae (mĭ-**no͞o′**shē-ē′) *pl.n.* Small or trivial details.

minx (mĭngks) *n.* A girl or young woman who is considered bold or flirtatious.

Mi·o·cene (**mī′**ə-sēn′) *n.* The fourth epoch of the Tertiary Period, from about 23 to 5.3 million years ago. During the Miocene, grasses and grazing mammals spread. See table at **geologic time. —Mi′o·cene′** *adj.*

mir·a·cle (**mĭr′**ə-kəl) *n.* **1.** An event believed to be an act of God or of a supernatural power because it appears impossible to explain by the laws of nature. **2.** A person, thing, or event that causes great admiration, awe, or wonder: *surgical miracles.* See Synonyms at **wonder.** [From Middle English, from Latin *mīrāculum,* from *mīrārī,* to wonder at.]

miracle play *n.* A Christian religious drama of the Middle Ages that portrays miraculous events from the lives of saints and martyrs.

mi·rac·u·lous (mĭ-**răk′**yə-ləs) *adj.* **1.** Having the nature of a miracle: *a miraculous event.* **2.** Having the power to work miracles: *a miraculous drug.* **—mi·rac′u·lous·ly** *adv.*

mi·rage (mĭ-**räzh′**) *n.* An optical illusion in which nonexistent bodies of water and upside-down reflections of distant objects are seen. It is caused by distortions that occur as light passes between layers of air that are at different temperatures. [From French, from *mirer,* to look at.]

mire (mīr) *n.* **1.** An area of wet muddy ground; a bog. **2.** Deep slimy soil or mud. ❖ *v.* **mired, mir·ing, mires** —*tr.* To cause to sink or become stuck in mire. —*intr.* To sink or become stuck in mire. [From Middle English, from Old Norse *mȳrr,* bog.]

mir·ror (**mĭr′**ər) *n.* **1.** A surface that is able to reflect light, often used to form an image of an object placed in front of it. **2.** Something that reflects or gives a true picture of something else: *The city's progress is a mirror of the nation's progress.* ❖ *tr.v.* **mir·rored, mir·ror·ing, mir·rors** To reflect in or as if in a mirror: *The lake mirrored the clouds.* [From Middle English *mirour,* from Old French *mireor,* from *mirer,* to look at.]

mirror image *n.* An image that is the exact likeness of another one, but is reversed like an image in a mirror.

mirth (mûrth) *n.* Gladness and merriment, especially when expressed with laughter.

mirth·ful (**mûrth′**fəl) *adj.* Full of gladness and merriment. **—mirth′ful·ly** *adv.*

mirth·less (**mûrth′**lĭs) *adj.* Showing no merriment. **—mirth′less·ly** *adv.*

mir·y (**mīr′**ē) *adj.* **mir·i·er, mir·i·est 1.** Full of or resembling mire; swampy. **2.** Smeared with mud; muddy.

mis– *pref.* A prefix that means: **1.** Error or wrongness: *misspell.* **2.** Badness or impropriety: *misbehave.* **3.** Failure or lack of: *misfire; mistrust.* —SEE NOTE.

mis·ad·ven·ture (mĭs′əd-**vĕn′**chər) *n.* An example of misfortune; a mishap.

mis·an·thrope (mĭs′ən-thrōp′) *n.* A person who hates or distrusts humankind. [From Greek *mīsanthrōpos,* hating people : *mīsein,* to hate + *anthrōpos,* person.]

mis·an·throp·ic (mĭs′ən-**thrŏp′**ĭk) *adj.* Relating to or characteristic of a misanthrope. **—mis′an·throp′i·cal·ly** *adv.*

mis·an·thro·py (mĭs-**ăn′**thrə-pē) *n.* Hatred or distrust of humankind.

mis·ap·ply (mĭs′ə-**plī′**) *tr.v.* **mis·ap·plied, mis·ap·ply·ing, mis·ap·plies** To use or apply wrongly: *The word "horns" is often misapplied to include antlers.* **—mis·ap′pli·ca′tion** (mĭs-ăp′lĭ-**kā′**shən) *n.*

mis·ap·pre·hend (mĭs-ăp′rĭ-**hĕnd′**) *tr.v.* **mis·ap·pre·hend·ed, mis·ap·pre·hend·ing, mis·ap·pre·hends** To fail to understand correctly; misunderstand: *misapprehend an order.* **—mis·ap′pre·hen′sion** (mĭs-ăp′rĭ-**hĕn′**shən) *n.*

mis·ap·pro·pri·ate (mĭs′ə-**prō′**prē-āt′) *tr.v.* **mis·ap·pro·pri·at·ed, mis·ap·pro·pri·at·ing, mis·ap·pro·pri·ates** To take dishonestly for one's own use; embezzle: *misappropriate government funds.* **—mis′ap·pro′pri·a′tion** *n.*

mis·be·got·ten (mĭs′bĭ-**gŏt′**n) *adj.* **1.** *Offensive* Born to parents who are not married to each other. **2.** Not lawfully obtained: *misbegotten wealth.*

mis·be·have (mĭs′bĭ-**hāv′**) *v.* **mis·be·haved, mis·be·hav·ing, mis·be·haves** *—intr.* To behave badly. *—tr.* To behave or conduct (oneself) badly or inappropriately. **—mis′be·hav′ior** (mĭs′bĭ-**hāv′**yər) *n.*

misc. *abbr.* An abbreviation of miscellaneous.

mis·cal·cu·late (mĭs-**kăl′**kyə-lāt′) *tr. & intr. v.* **mis·cal·cu·lat·ed, mis·cal·cu·lat·ing, mis·cal·cu·lates** To calculate or estimate incorrectly. **—mis·cal′cu·la′tion** *n.*

mis·call (mĭs-**kôl′**) *tr.v.* **mis·called, mis·call·ing, mis·calls** To call by a wrong name.

mis·car·riage (**mĭs′**kăr′ĭj *or* mĭs-**kăr′**ĭj) *n.* **1.** The ending of a pregnancy when an embryo or fetus is expelled from the uterus before it is developed enough to survive. **2.** A failure to achieve the proper or desired result: *a miscarriage of justice.*

mis·car·ry (**mĭs′**kăr′ē *or* mĭs-**kăr′**ē) *intr.v.* **mis·car·ried, mis·car·ry·ing, mis·car·ries 1.** To have a miscarriage. **2.** To fail; go wrong: *The plan miscarried.*

mis·cast (mĭs-**kăst′**) *tr.v.* **mis·cast, mis·cast·ing, mis·casts 1.** To cast (a performer) in an unsuitable role: *The young actor was miscast in a role that required considerable experience.* **2.** To cast (a role, play, or film) in an unsuitable way: *The musical was miscast with actors who couldn't sing.*

mis·ceg·e·na·tion (mĭ-sĕj′ə-**nā′**shən *or* mĭs′ĭ-jə-**nā′**shən) *n.* Marriage or sexual relations between two people of different races, especially in historical contexts as a violation of the law.

mis·cel·la·ne·ous (mĭs′ə-**lā′**nē-əs) *adj.* **1.** Made up of a variety of different elements or ingredients: *a miscellaneous assortment of books.* **2.** Concerned with a variety of different subjects or aspects: *a website that provides miscellaneous information.* [From Latin *miscellus,* mixed.]

mis·cel·la·ny (**mĭs′**ə-lā′nē) *n., pl.* **mis·cel·la·nies** A collection of various items, parts, or ingredients.

mis·chance (mĭs-**chăns′**) *n.* An unfortunate occurrence caused by chance or luck: *If by some mischance I am late, please wait for me.*

mis·chief (**mĭs′**chĭf) *n.* **1a.** Annoying or improper behavior. **b.** Damage, injury, or trouble resulting from such behavior. **2.** A tendency to play pranks or cause trouble. [From Middle English *mischef,* from Old French *meschever,* to end badly.]

mis·chie·vous (**mĭs′**chə-vəs) *adj.* **1.** Causing mischief; naughty: *a mischievous child.* **2.** Showing a tendency to play pranks or tease: *a mischievous look on one's face.* **3.** Causing injury or damage: *a mischievous act.* **—mis′chie·vous·ly** *adv.* **—mis′chie·vous·ness** *n.*

mis·ci·ble (**mĭs′**ə-bəl) *adj.* Capable of being mixed in all proportions: *Water and alcohol are miscible.*

mis·con·ceive (mĭs′kən-**sēv′**) *tr.v.* **mis·con·ceived, mis·con·ceiv·ing, mis·con·ceives** To interpret incorrectly; misunderstand.

mis·con·cep·tion (mĭs′kən-**sĕp′**shən) *n.* A mistaken idea; a delusion.

mis·con·duct (mĭs-**kŏn′**dŭkt) *n.* Improper conduct or behavior.

mis·con·strue (mĭs′kən-**strōō′**) *tr.v.* **mis·con·strued, mis·con·stru·ing, mis·con·strues** To mistake the meaning of; misinterpret: *misconstrue someone's words.*

mis·cop·y (mĭs-**kŏp′**ē) *tr.v.* **mis·cop·ied, mis·cop·y·ing, mis·cop·ies** To copy (something) inaccurately: *miscopied her cell phone number.*

mis·count (mĭs-**kount′**) *v.* **mis·count·ed, mis·count·ing, mis·counts** *—tr.* To count (something) incorrectly. *—intr.* To make an incorrect count. ❖ *n.* (**mĭs′**kount′) An inaccurate count.

mis·cre·ant (**mĭs′**krē-ənt) *n.* A person who behaves badly, usually by breaking rules of conduct or the law.

mis·deal (mĭs-**dēl′**) *tr. & intr.v.* **mis·dealt** (mĭs-**dĕlt′**), **mis·deal·ing, mis·deals** To deal (playing cards) incorrectly. **—mis′deal′** *n.*

mis·deed (mĭs-**dēd′**) *n.* A wrong or illegal act.

mis·de·mean·or (mĭs′dĭ-**mē′**nər) *n.* A crime, such as petty theft, that is less serious than a felony and is punished less severely.

mis·di·rect (mĭs′dĭ-**rĕkt′** *or* mĭs′dī-**rĕkt′**) *tr.v.* **mis·di·rect·ed, mis·di·rect·ing, mis·di·rects 1.** To give incorrect or inaccurate instructions to: *misdirect a tourist.* **2.** To put a wrong address on (a piece of mail): *misdirect a letter.* **3.** To aim (a punch or projectile, for example) badly. **—mis′di·rec′tion** *n.*

mis·do (mĭs-**dōō′**) *tr.v.* **mis·did** (mĭs-**dĭd′**), **mis·done** (mĭs-**dŭn′**), **mis·do·ing, mis·does** (mĭs-**dŭz′**) To do wrongly or poorly; botch. **—mis·do′ing** *n.*

mi·ser (**mī′**zər) *n.* A stingy person, especially one who hoards money by living poorly. [From Latin, wretched.]

mis·er·a·ble (**mĭz′**ər-ə-bəl *or* **mĭz′**rə-bəl) *adj.* **1.** Very unhappy or uncomfortable: *I was miserable all night with a headache and high fever.* **2.** Causing discomfort or unhappiness: *miserable weather.* **3.** Wretchedly poor or inadequate: *a miserable shack.* **—mis′er·a·bly** *adv.*

mi·ser·ly (**mī′**zər-lē) *adj.* Relating to or characteristic of a miser; stingy. **—mi′ser·li·ness** *n.*

mis·er·y (**mĭz′**ə-rē) *n., pl.* **mis·er·ies 1.** Miserable conditions of life; dire poverty. **2.** Mental or emotional suffering or distress. [From Middle English *miserie,* from Latin *miseria,* from *miser,* wretched.]

mis·fire (mĭs-**fīr′**) *intr.v.* **mis·fired, mis·fir·ing, mis·fires 1.** To fail to fire or go off: *The gun misfired.* **2.** To fail to achieve the desired result; go awry: *Their plan misfired.* **—mis′fire′** *n.*

mis·fit (**mĭs′**fĭt′) *n.* A person who has adjusted poorly to his or her situation in life or does not get along well with others.

mis·for·tune (mĭs-**fôr′**chən) *n.* **1.** Bad luck or fortune. **2.** An occurrence that is unfortunate or that causes great distress: *The hurricane was a great misfortune for the fishing industry.*

mis·giv·ing (mĭs-**gĭv′**ĭng) *n.* **1.** A feeling of doubt or concern: *We had misgivings about using our savings to buy a new car.* **2.** Doubt or concern: *We left the meeting full of misgiving.*

mis·gov·ern (mĭs-**gŭv′**ərn) *tr.v.* **mis·gov·erned, mis·gov·ern·ing, mis·gov·erns** To govern or rule badly. **—mis·gov′ern·ment** *n.*

mis·guide (mĭs-**gīd′**) *tr.v.* **mis·guid·ed, mis·guid·ing,**

WORD BUILDING

mis– The basic meaning of the prefix **mis–** is "bad; badly; wrong; wrongly." Thus *misfortune* means "bad fortune" and *misbehave* means "to behave badly." Likewise, a *misdeed* is "a wrong deed" and *misdo* means "to do wrongly." *Mis–* mostly forms compounds by attaching to verbs: *mishear, misremember. Mis–* also frequently forms compounds by attaching to nouns that come from verbs: *miscalculation, mismanagement, mispronunciation.*

WRITERS CHOOSE THEIR WORDS

"Morwen?" Even muffled by the front door, Trouble's tone was clearly far too casual, and when he strolled out onto the porch Morwen felt a strong twinge of **misgiving.** Every whisker dripped the kind of deliberate unconcern that usually meant he'd been living up to his name.

—Patricia C. Wrede
Calling on Dragons

WRITERS CHOOSE THEIR WORDS

During the intelligence briefing it was called a hamlet but that was a **misnomer.** Really it was a collection of grass-and-leaf shacks along a river with no electricity, no water, no sewers, and exactly thirty-one people who spent the force of their entire lives trying to make a living out of nearby rice paddies.

—Gary Paulsen
The Car

GEOGRAPHY

Mississippi The state of **Mississippi** gets its name from the Mississippi River. Although the river was known by many different names in different regions, French explorers carried the Illinois name *Mississippi,* meaning "big river," from the northern part of the river south to the Gulf of Mexico. Eventually the entire river came to be called the Mississippi.

ă	pat	ôr	core
ā	pay	oi	boy
âr	care	ou	out
ä	father	o͝o	took
ĕ	pet	o͝or	lure
ē	be	o͞o	boot
ĭ	pit	ŭ	cut
ī	bite	ûr	urge
îr	pier	th	thin
ŏ	pot	*th*	this
ō	toe	zh	vision
ô	paw	ə	about

mis·guides To give wrong or misleading directions to; lead astray. **—mis·guid′ance** *n.*

mis·guid·ed (mĭs-**gī′**dĭd) *adj.* Acting or done out of mistaken or unrealistic opinions or beliefs: *misguided efforts.* **—mis·guid′ed·ly** *adv.*

mis·han·dle (mĭs-**hăn′**dl) *tr.v.* **mis·han·dled, mis·han·dling, mis·han·dles 1.** To handle roughly: *mishandle a parcel in the mail.* **2.** To manage badly: *mishandle money.*

mis·hap (**mĭs′**hăp′ *or* mĭs-**hăp′**) *n.* **1.** Bad luck. **2.** An unfortunate accident: *The trip was completed without mishap.*

mish·mash (**mĭsh′**măsh′) *n.* A random mixture of unrelated things; a hodgepodge.

mis·in·form (mĭs′ĭn-**fôrm′**) *tr.v.* **mis·in·formed, mis·in·form·ing, mis·in·forms** To give wrong or inaccurate information to. **—mis·in′for·ma′tion** (mĭs-ĭn′fər-**mā′**shən) *n.*

mis·in·ter·pret (mĭs′ĭn-**tûr′**prĭt) *tr.v.* **mis·in·ter·pret·ed, mis·in·ter·pret·ing, mis·in·ter·prets** To interpret or explain incorrectly: *misinterpret someone's remarks.* **—mis′in·ter′pre·ta′tion** *n.*

mis·judge (mĭs-**jŭj′**) *v.* **mis·judged, mis·judg·ing, mis·judg·es** *—tr.* To judge incorrectly: *misjudge a person.* *—intr.* To be wrong in judging something. **—mis·judg′ment** *n.*

mis·lay (mĭs-**lā′**) *tr.v.* **mis·laid** (mĭs-**lād′**), **mis·lay·ing, mis·lays 1.** To lay or put down in a place one cannot remember. **2.** To place or put down incorrectly: *They mislaid the carpet.*

mis·lead (mĭs-**lēd′**) *tr.v.* **mis·led** (mĭs-**lĕd′**), **mis·lead·ing, mis·leads 1.** To lead or guide in the wrong direction: *The sign at the traffic circle completely misled us.* **2.** To lead into error of thought or wrongdoing, especially by intentional deception.

mis·lead·ing (mĭs-**lē′**dĭng) *adj.* Tending to mislead: *misleading information.*

mis·man·age (mĭs-**măn′**ĭj) *tr.v.* **mis·man·aged, mis·man·ag·ing, mis·man·ag·es** To manage badly or ineptly. **—mis·man′age·ment** *n.*

mis·match (mĭs-**măch′**) *tr.v.* **mis·matched, mis·match·ing, mis·match·es** To match in an unsuitable way: *The two teams are mismatched.* ❖ *n.* (**mĭs′**măch′ *or* mĭs-**măch′**) An unsuitable match.

mis·no·mer (mĭs-**nō′**mər) *n.* **1.** An error in naming a person or place. **2.** A name or designation wrongly or unsuitably applied: *To call a whale "a fish" is to use a misnomer.* [From Middle English *misnoumer*, from Old French *mesnomer*, to misname.]

mi·sog·y·nist (mĭ-**sŏj′**ə-nĭst) *n.* A person who hates or mistrusts women.

mi·sog·y·ny (mĭ-**sŏj′**ə-nē) *n.* Hatred or mistrust of women.

mis·place (mĭs-**plās′**) *tr.v.* **mis·placed, mis·plac·ing, mis·plac·es 1.** To put in a wrong place. **2.** To mislay; lose: *misplace one's keys.* **3.** To place (trust, for example) in an improper or unworthy person or idea: *I fear that your confidence in me is misplaced.*

mis·placed modifier (**mĭs′**plāst′) *n.* A modifying clause or phrase that is placed in a sentence in a way that creates ambiguity or misunderstanding. For example, in *Streaking through the sky, we watched the rocket reenter the atmosphere*, the phrase *Streaking through the sky* is misplaced.

mis·play (mĭs-**plā′** *or* **mĭs′**plā′) *n.* A mistaken play in a game or sport. ❖ *tr.v.* (mĭs-**plā′**) **mis·played, mis·play·ing, mis·plays** To make a misplay of.

mis·print (mĭs-**prĭnt′**) *tr.v.* **mis·print·ed, mis·print·ing, mis·prints** To print incorrectly. ❖ *n.* (**mĭs′**prĭnt′ *or* mĭs-**prĭnt′**) An error in printing.

mis·pro·nounce (mĭs′prə-**nouns′**) *tr.v.* **mis·pro·nounced, mis·pro·nounc·ing, mis·pro·nounc·es** To pronounce incorrectly.

mis·quote (mĭs-**kwōt′**) *tr.v.* **mis·quot·ed, mis·quot·ing, mis·quotes** To quote incorrectly. **—mis′quo·ta′tion** *n.*

mis·read (mĭs-**rēd′**) *tr.v.* **mis·read** (mĭs-**rĕd′**), **mis·read·ing, mis·reads 1.** To read incorrectly: *misread a sign.* **2.** To draw the wrong conclusion from; misinterpret: *I misread your nod to mean "yes."*

mis·rep·re·sent (mĭs-rĕp′rĭ-**zĕnt′**) *tr.v.* **mis·rep·re·sent·ed, mis·rep·re·sent·ing, mis·rep·re·sents** To represent in a false or misleading manner: *The newspaper misrepresented the mayor's statements.* **—mis·rep′re·sen·ta′tion** *n.*

mis·rule (mĭs-**ro͞ol′**) *n.* Incompetent or unjust rule. ❖ *tr.v.* **mis·ruled, mis·rul·ing, mis·rules** To rule incompetently or unjustly.

miss[1] (mĭs) *v.* **missed, miss·ing, miss·es** *—tr.* **1.** To fail to hit, catch, or make contact with: *The receiver missed the pass. The ball missed the basket.* **2.** To be too late for or fail to meet: *I missed the 7:15 bus.* **3.** To fail to see or notice: *We missed the television special last night.* **4.** To fail to attend or be present for: *She has never missed a day of school.* **5.** To fail to accomplish: *He just missed winning the race.* **6.** To fail to understand or grasp: *You're missing my point.* **7.** To fail to answer correctly; get wrong: *I missed two questions on the test.* **8.** To let slip by; fail to benefit from: *We missed our chance to see our favorite actor.* **9.** To feel or regret the absence or loss of: *I miss my hometown.* **10.** To notice the absence or loss of: *After we left the theater, I missed my coat.* **11.** To avoid or escape: *If you go that way, you'll miss most of the traffic.* **12.** To lack: *The book is missing a few pages.* *—intr.* **1.** To fail to hit or make contact with something: *The ball flew toward the corner of the goal but missed.* **2.** To be unsuccessful; fail: *This is a sure-fire plan; it can't miss.* ❖ *n.* A failure to hit, succeed, or find. ◆ **miss out on** To lose a chance for: *Don't miss out on this great opportunity.* **miss the boat** *Informal* To fail to take advantage of an opportunity. **miss the mark 1.** To set a goal and fail to fulfill it. **2.** To fail to be correct or exact. [From Old English *missan.*]

miss[2] (mĭs) *n.* **1. Miss** A title of courtesy used before the last name or full name of an unmarried woman or girl. **2.** Used as a form of polite address for a young woman or girl: *I beg your pardon, miss.* **3.** An unmarried woman or girl. **4. misses** A range of clothing sizes for girls and women. [Short for *mistress.*]

mis·sal (**mĭs′**əl) *n.* A book containing all the prayers and responses necessary for celebrating the Roman Catholic Mass throughout the year. [From Middle English, from Medieval Latin *missāle*, from Late Latin *missa*, Mass.]

❑ *These sound alike:* **missal, missile** (weapon).

mis·shape (mĭs-**shāp′**) *tr.v.* **mis·shaped, mis·shaped** or **mis·shap·en** (mĭs-**shā′**pən), **mis·shap·ing, mis·shapes** To shape badly; deform.

mis·sile (**mĭs′**əl *or* **mĭs′**īl′) *n.* **1.** An object or weapon that is thrown, fired, dropped, or otherwise launched at a target. **2.** A guided missile. **3.** A ballistic missile. [From Latin *missilis*, throwable, from *mittere*, to let go, throw.]

❑ *These sound alike:* **missile, missal** (prayer book).

miss·ing (**mĭs′**ĭng) *adj.* **1.** Lost: *missing persons.* **2.** Not present; absent: *Who is missing from class today?* **3.** Lacking; wanting: *This book has 12 missing pages.*

mis·sion (**mĭsh′**ən) *n.* **1.** An assignment that a person or group of people is sent to carry out; a task: *a rescue mission.* **2.** A combat operation, especially a flight into a combat zone by military aircraft. **3.** Something that a person assumes to be the main task of his or her life: *My mission in life is to become a teacher.* **4.** A permanent diplomatic office in a foreign country. **5.** A body of people sent to a foreign land, especially by a Christian organization to spread its religion or provide educational, medical, or other assistance. **6.** An establishment of missionaries in some territory or foreign country: *Los Angeles started as a small Spanish mission.* [From Latin *missiō*, a sending, from *mittere*, to send.]

mis·sion·ar·y (mĭsh′ə-nĕr′ē) *n., pl.* **mis·sion·ar·ies** A person sent by a religious organization to make converts or do charitable work in a territory or foreign country.

Mis·sis·sip·pi (mĭs′ĭ-sĭp′ē) A state of the southeast United States west of Alabama. It was admitted as the 20th state in 1817. Jackson is the capital. —SEE NOTE.

Mis·sis·sip·pi·an (mĭs′ĭ-sĭp′ē-ən) *n.* The fifth period of the Paleozoic Era, from about 359 to 318 million years ago. During the Mississippian, shallow seas spread over many former land areas. See table at **geologic time.** —**Mis′sis·sip′pi·an** *adj.*

Mississippi River The chief river of the United States, rising in northern Minnesota and flowing about 2,300 miles (3,700 kilometers) generally southward to enter the Gulf of Mexico through a huge delta in southeast Louisiana.

mis·sive (mĭs′ĭv) *n.* A letter or message.

Mis·sou·ri[1] (mĭ-zo͝or′ē) *n., pl.* **Missouri** or **Mis·sou·ris 1.** A member of a Native American people formerly living in Missouri, with a present-day population in Oklahoma. **2.** The Siouan language of the Missouri.

Mis·sou·ri[2] (mĭ-zo͝or′ē *or* mĭ-zo͝or′ə) A state of the central United States east of Kansas. It was admitted as the 24th state in 1821. Jefferson City is the capital and St. Louis the largest city. —SEE NOTE.

Missouri River A river of the United States rising in the Rocky Mountains of southwest Montana. The longest river in the United States, it flows about 2,350 miles (3,750 kilometers) to the Mississippi River north of St. Louis, Missouri.

mis·speak (mĭs-spēk′) *tr. & intr.v.* **mis·spoke** (mĭs-spōk′), **mis·spo·ken** (mĭs-spō′kən), **mis·speak·ing, mis·speaks** To pronounce or speak incorrectly: *misspeak one's lines.*

mis·spell (mĭs-spĕl′) *tr.v.* **mis·spelled** or **mis·spelt** (mĭs-spĕlt′), **mis·spell·ing, mis·spells** To spell incorrectly.

mis·spend (mĭs-spĕnd′) *tr.v.* **mis·spent** (mĭs-spĕnt′), **mis·spend·ing, mis·spends** To spend improperly, foolishly, or wastefully; squander.

mis·state (mĭs-stāt′) *tr.v.* **mis·stat·ed, mis·stat·ing, mis·states** To state wrongly or falsely. —**mis·state′ment** *n.*

mis·step (mĭs-stĕp′) *n.* **1.** A misplaced or awkward step. **2.** A mistake in action or conduct.

mist (mĭst) *n.* **1.** A mass of tiny droplets of water in the air, close to or touching the earth. **2.** Water vapor that condenses on and clouds a surface: *mist on a windowpane.* **3.** A mass of tiny drops of a liquid, such as perfume, sprayed into the air. **4.** Something that dims or obscures; a haze. ❖ *v.* **mist·ed, mist·ing, mists** —*intr.* **1.** To be or become obscured or blurred by mist. **2.** To rain in a fine shower: *It began to mist at 4:00.* —*tr.* To conceal or cloud with or as if with mist.

mis·take (mĭ-stāk′) *n.* An error or fault resulting from poor judgment, ignorance, or carelessness. ❖ *tr.v.* **mis·took** (mĭ-sto͝ok′), **mis·tak·en** (mĭ-stā′kən), **mis·tak·ing, mis·takes 1.** To understand incorrectly; misinterpret: *mistook politeness as friendliness.* **2.** To recognize or identify incorrectly: *mistook satin for silk.* [From Middle English *mistaken*, to do wrong, from Old Norse *mistaka*, to take wrongly.]

mis·tak·en (mĭ-stā′kən) *adj.* Wrong; in error: *If I am not mistaken, you were last here a year ago.* —**mis·tak′en·ly** *adv.*

Mis·ter (mĭs′tər) *n.* **1.** Used as a courtesy title before the last name or full name of a man. **2. mister** *Informal* Used as a form of polite address for a man: *Do you need directions to town, mister?* [Alteration of *master.*]

mis·tle·toe (mĭs′əl-tō′) *n.* **1.** Any of several plants that grow as semiparasites on trees and that have leathery evergreen leaves and white berries. **2.** A sprig of certain of these plants, often used as a Christmas decoration. [From Old English *misteltān*, mistletoe twig.]

mis·took (mĭ-sto͝ok′) *v.* Past tense of **mistake.**

mis·treat (mĭs-trēt′) *tr.v.* **mis·treat·ed, mis·treat·ing, mis·treats** To treat roughly or wrongly. —**mis·treat′ment** *n.*

mis·tress (mĭs′trĭs) *n.* **1.** A woman who has a continuing romantic relationship with a man, usually a man married to someone else. **2.** A woman in a position of authority, control, or ownership, as the head of a household. **3a.** A woman who owns or keeps an animal. **b.** A woman who owns a slave. **4.** A nation or country that has dominance over others. **5. Mistress** Used formerly as a courtesy title and form of address for a woman.

mis·tri·al (mĭs′trī′əl *or* mĭs-trī′əl) *n.* A trial declared invalid because of a serious procedural error or because the jurors are unable to agree on a verdict.

mis·trust (mĭs-trŭst′) *n.* Lack of trust or confidence: *I viewed the advice on the website with mistrust.* ❖ *tr.v.* **mis·trust·ed, mis·trust·ing, mis·trusts 1.** To have no trust in; regard with suspicion: *mistrust strangers.* **2.** To doubt the truth or sincerity of: *I mistrust everything he says.* —**mis·trust′ful** *adj.* —**mis·trust′ful·ly** *adv.*

mist·y (mĭs′tē) *adj.* **mist·i·er, mist·i·est 1.** Consisting of, filled with, or covered by mist: *a misty morning.* **2.** Obscured by or as by mist; vague: *misty recollections.* **3.** Full of emotion; sentimental. —**mist′i·ly** *adv.*

mis·un·der·stand (mĭs′-ŭn-dər-stănd′) *tr.v.* **mis·un·der·stood** (mĭs′ŭn-dər-sto͝od′), **mis·un·der·stand·ing, mis·un·der·stands** To understand incorrectly or imperfectly.

mis·un·der·stand·ing (mĭs′ŭn-dər-stăn′dĭng) *n.* **1.** A failure to understand. **2.** A quarrel or disagreement.

mis·use (mĭs-yo͞oz′) *tr.v.* **mis·used, mis·us·ing, mis·us·es 1.** To use wrongly or incorrectly: *misuse a word in a sentence.* **2.** To make improper use of; abuse: *Let's not misuse our natural resources.* ❖ *n.* (mĭs-yo͞os′) Wrong or improper use: *the misuse of language.*

Mitch·ell (mĭch′əl), **Maria** 1818–1889. American astronomer and educator noted for her study of sunspots and for the discovery of a comet (1847).

mite[1] (mīt) *n.* Any of numerous very small animals that are related to ticks and spiders. Mites often live as parasites on plants or on other animals. [From Old English *mīte*, moth, worm, louse.]

❑ *These sound alike:* **mite[1]** (small animal), **might[1]** (power), **might[2]** (past tense of may), **mite[2]** (small amount of money).

mite[2] (mīt) *n.* **1.** A small amount of money, especially one given as a contribution. **2.** A coin of very small value. **3.** A very small creature or object. ◆ **a mite** *Informal* To a small degree; somewhat: *That remark was a mite unfair.* [From Middle English, from Middle Dutch and Middle Low German *mīte*, a small Flemish coin, tiny animal.]

❑ *These sound alike:* **mite[2]** (small amount of money), **might[1]** (power), **might[2]** (past tense of may), **mite[1]** (small animal).

mi·ter (mī′tər) *n.* **1.** A tall pointed hat worn by a Christian bishop as a mark of office. **2a.** A miter joint. **b.** The edge of a piece of material that has been beveled in order to make a miter joint. ❖ *tr.v.* **mi·tered, mi·ter·ing, mi·ters** To join with a miter joint.

miter box *n.* A device for guiding a handsaw, consisting of two upright sides joined at the bottom and having narrow slots for the saw.

miter joint *n.* A joint made by fitting together two beveled surfaces to form a right angle.

mit·i·gate (mĭt′ĭ-gāt′) *tr.v.* **mit·i·gat·ed, mit·i·gat·ing, mit·i·gates 1.** To make less severe or intense; moderate: *The judge mitigated the sentence.* **2.** To make alterations

GEOGRAPHY

Missouri[2] The name **Missouri** comes through French from the Illinois name for a Native American people who lived near the Missouri River. The name means "those with dugout canoes."

mistletoe

Maria Mitchell

miter

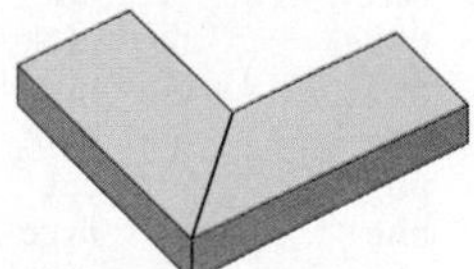
miter joint

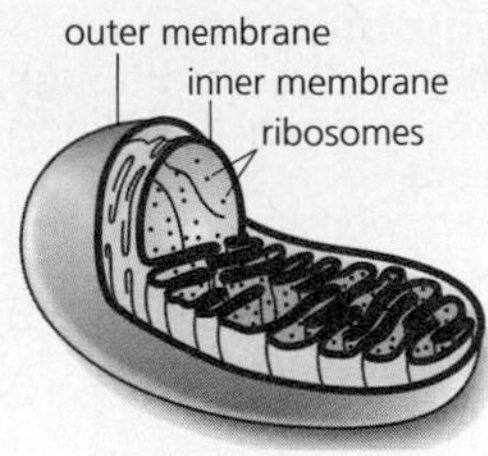

mitochondrion

PROPHASE
centrioles
chromosome
nucleus

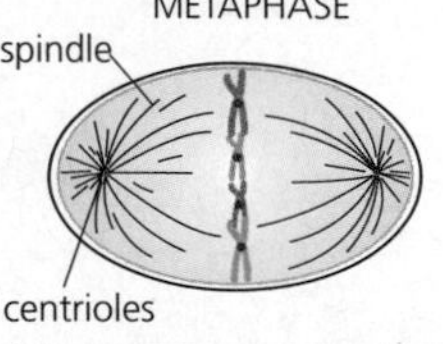

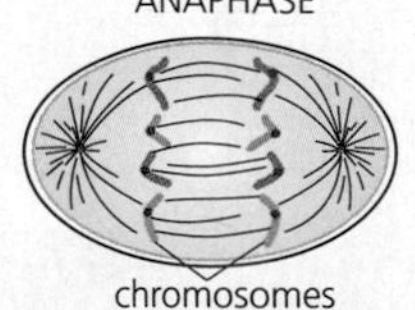

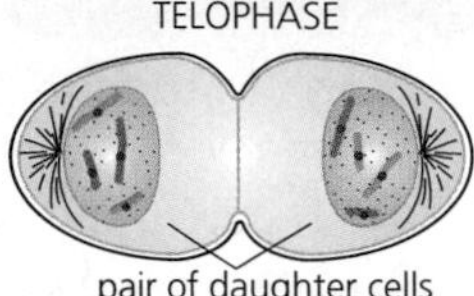

mitosis

ă	pat	ôr	core
ā	pay	oi	boy
âr	care	ou	out
ä	father	o͝o	took
ĕ	pet	o͝or	lure
ē	be	o͞o	boot
ĭ	pit	ŭ	cut
ī	bite	ûr	urge
îr	pier	th	thin
ŏ	pot	*th*	this
ō	toe	zh	vision
ô	paw	ə	about

to (land) to make it less polluted. **—mit′i·ga′tion** *n.*

mi·to·chon·dri·on (mī′tə-**kŏn′**drē-ən) *n., pl.* **mi·to·chon·dri·a** (mī′tə-**kŏn′**drē-ə) Any of certain microscopic structures found in the cytoplasm of all living cells except bacteria and archaea, containing enzymes that act in converting food to usable energy.

mi·to·sis (mī-**tō′**sĭs) *n., pl.* **mi·to·ses** (mī-**tō′**sēz) A form of cell division in which the nucleus of a cell divides, producing two new nuclei, each having the same genetic material as the original cell. —SEE NOTE AT **cell division.**

mitt (mĭt) *n.* **1.** A glove that extends over the hand but only partially covers the fingers. **2.** A large padded leather glove worn to protect the hand when catching a baseball. **3.** A mitten. **4.** *Slang* A hand or fist: *Keep your mitts off the paintings.*

mit·ten (**mĭt′**n) *n.* A covering for the hand, with a separate section for the thumb and one wide section for all four fingers. [From Middle English *mitaine*, from Old French.]

mix (mĭks) *v.* **mixed, mix·ing, mix·es** *—tr.* **1.** To combine or blend into a single mass, as by pouring, stirring, or shaking: *mix flour, water, and eggs to form dough.* **2.** To make or create by combining different ingredients: *mix cement.* **3.** To add (an ingredient or element) to something else: *mix the egg into the batter.* **4.** To combine or join: *mix joy with sorrow.* **5.** To bring into social contact: *The new league mixes boys with girls on the teams.* **6.** To combine (two or more audio tracks or channels) to produce a single audio recording. *—intr.* To become or be capable of being mixed or blended together: *Stir until the eggs mix with the flour. Oil does not mix with water.* ❖ *n.* **1.** A combination of diverse elements: *The downtown has a good mix of stores and restaurants.* **2.** A mixture, especially of ingredients packaged and sold commercially: *a brownie mix.* **3.** A recording made by combining and adjusting two or more audio tracks or channels. **4.** An animal, especially a cat or dog, resulting from the mating of two different breeds. ◆ **mix up 1.** To confuse; confound: *Your directions only mixed us up even more.* **2.** To involve, concern, or implicate: *He was mixed up in a fraudulent scheme.* [From Middle English *mixt*, mixed, from Latin *mixtus*.]

mixed (mĭkst) *adj.* **1.** Blended together into one mass: *mixed baby formula.* **2.** Composed of various elements: *a mixed reaction from the critics.* **3.** Relating to or made up of different kinds of people, as of different races or social classes: *people of mixed backgrounds.*

mixed bag *n.* A collection of dissimilar things; an assortment.

mixed martial art *n.* Any of various sports that combine techniques from different martial arts, allowing punches, throws, holds, and often kicks.

mixed metaphor *n.* A succession of metaphors whose literal meanings form a contradictory or illogical combination, thus producing an absurd effect; for example, *Lying down on the job left me out on a limb* is a mixed metaphor.

mixed number *n.* A number, such as 7⅜, consisting of a whole number and a fraction.

mix·er (**mĭk′**sər) *n.* **1.** A device that mixes or blends ingredients, especially by mechanical action: *a cement mixer.* **2.** A device used to mix two or more audio tracks or channels. **3.** An informal party where people can get to know each other.

mix·ture (**mĭks′**chər) *n.* **1.** Something made up of different ingredients, things, or kinds: *The day was a mixture of sun and clouds.* **2.** Something made up of two or more substances that are not chemically combined with each other and are capable of being separated. **3.** The act or process of mixing: *an alloy made from the mixture of two metals.*

mix-up also **mix·up** (**mĭks′**ŭp′) *n.* A state of confusion or a misunderstanding: *a mix-up over the starting time of the game.*

miz·zen (**mĭz′**ən) *n.* **1.** A fore-and-aft sail set on the mizzenmast. **2.** A mizzenmast.

miz·zen·mast or **miz·en·mast** (**mĭz′**ən-məst *or* **mĭz′**ən-măst′) *n.* The mast aft of a mainmast on a ship having three or more masts.

mks *abbr.* An abbreviation of meter-kilogram second.

mL or **ml** *abbr.* An abbreviation of milliliter.

MLB *abbr.* An abbreviation of Major League Baseball.

Mlle *abbr.* An abbreviation of Mademoiselle.

Mlles *abbr.* An abbreviation of Mesdemoiselles.

mm *abbr.* An abbreviation of millimeter.

Mme *abbr.* An abbreviation of Madame.

Mmes *abbr.* An abbreviation of Mesdames.

Mn The symbol for the element **manganese.**

MN *abbr.* An abbreviation of Minnesota.

mne·mon·ic (nĭ-**mŏn′**ĭk) *adj.* Relating to or assisting the memory. ❖ *n.* Something, such as a formula or rhyme, that helps one to remember something; for example, *i before e except after c* is a mnemonic.

Mo The symbol for the element **molybdenum.**

MO *abbr.* An abbreviation of: **1.** medical officer. **2.** Missouri. **3.** money order.

mo. *abbr.* An abbreviation of month.

mo·a (**mō′**ə) *n.* Any of various large extinct birds of New Zealand that resembled an ostrich.

moan (mōn) *n.* **1.** A low, drawn-out, mournful sound, usually of sorrow or pain. **2.** A similar sound: *the moan of the wind.* ❖ *v.* **moaned, moan·ing, moans** *—intr.* **1.** To utter a moan or moans. **2.** To make a sound resembling a moan: *The wind moaned in the chimney.* **3.** To complain, lament, or grieve: *They moaned about the lost opportunity.* *—tr.* To utter with a moan or moans: *"We can't seem to win a game," moaned the coach.*

moat (mōt) *n.* A wide deep ditch, usually filled with water, especially one surrounding a medieval town or fortress. [From Middle English *mote*, mound, moat, from Old French.]

❑ *These sound alike:* **moat, mote** (dust speck).

mob (mŏb) *n.* **1.** A large disorderly crowd. **2.** The mass of common people. **3.** often **Mob** A criminal organization, especially the Mafia operating in the United States. ❖ *tr.v.* **mobbed, mob·bing, mobs 1.** To crowd around and jostle or annoy, especially in anger or enthusiasm: *Autograph seekers mobbed the stars.* **2.** To crowd into or jam (a place): *Visitors mobbed the museum.*

mo·bile (**mō′**bəl *or* **mō′**bīl′ *or* **mō′**bēl′) *adj.* **1.** Capable of moving or being moved from place to place: *a mobile hospital; a mobile organism.* **2.** Relating to wireless communication devices, such as cell phones. **3.** Capable of moving or changing easily: *mobile features.* **4.** Fluid or flowing freely: *Mercury is a mobile metal.* **5.** Allowing relatively easy movement from one social class to another: *a mobile society.* ❖ *n.* **1.** (**mō′**bēl′) A type of sculpture consisting of parts that move, especially in response to air currents. **2.** A mobile phone. [From Middle English, from Latin *mōbilis*, from *movēre*, to move.] **—mo·bil′i·ty** (mō-**bĭl′**ĭ-tē) *n.*

Mo·bile (mō-**bēl′** *or* **mō′**bēl′) A city of southwest Alabama on **Mobile Bay,** an arm of the Gulf of Mexico. The Battle of Mobile Bay (August 1864) was a major Union naval victory in the Civil War.

mobile home *n.* A house trailer that is used as a permanent house and is usually hooked up to utilities.

mobile phone *n.* A cell phone.

mo·bi·lize (**mō′**bə-līz′) *v.* **mo·bi·lized, mo·bi·liz·ing, mo·bi·liz·es** *—tr.* **1.** To assemble or prepare for war: *mobilize troops.* **2.** To assemble or coordinate for a particular purpose or action: *mobilize public opinion to sup-*

port the campaign. —*intr.* To become prepared for war or other coordinated action. **—mo′bi·li·za′tion** (mō′bə-lĭ-**zā′**shən) *n.*

Mö·bi·us strip (**mō′**bē-əs *or* **mœ′**bē-əs) *n.* A continuous one-sided surface that can be formed by rotating one end of a rectangular strip of paper 180° and attaching it to the other end. [After August Ferdinand *Möbius* (1790–1868), German mathematician.]

mob·ster (**mŏb′**stər) *n. Informal* A member of a criminal gang.

moc·ca·sin (**mŏk′**ə-sĭn) *n.* **1.** A soft leather slipper traditionally worn by certain Native American peoples. **2.** A shoe resembling a moccasin. **3.** The water moccasin. [Of Virginia Algonquian origin.]

moccasin flower *n.* A lady's slipper orchid.

mo·cha (**mō′**kə) *n.* **1.** A rich Arabian coffee. **2.** A coffee beverage flavored with milk, sugar, and cocoa. **3.** A flavoring made of coffee mixed with chocolate. [After *Mocha*, a town of southwest Yemen.]

mock (mŏk) *v.* **mocked, mock·ing, mocks** —*tr.* **1.** To make fun of, often by imitating or depicting in an insulting way; ridicule. **2.** To treat with scorn or contempt; deride. —*intr.* To express contempt; scoff. ❖ *adj.* Simulated; false; sham: *a mock battle.* ❖ *n.* The act of mocking; mockery: *made mock of his silly behavior.* **—mock′er** *n.*

mock·er·y (**mŏk′**ə-rē) *n., pl.* **mock·er·ies 1.** Ridicule; derision. **2.** An object of ridicule. **3.** A false, offensive, or ridiculous imitation of something: *The trial was a mockery of justice.*

mock·ing·bird (**mŏk′**ĭng-bûrd′) *n.* Any of several birds of the Americas that often imitate the songs of other birds.

mock orange *n.* Any of various shrubs having fragrant white flowers resembling orange blossoms.

mock·up also **mock-up** (**mŏk′**ŭp′) *n.* A full-sized model, as of an airplane or building, used for demonstration, study, or testing.

mod (mŏd) *adj.* Stylishly up-to-date, especially in a modern unconventional way.

mod·al (**mōd′**l) *adj.* **1.** Relating to or characteristic of a mode. **2.** Relating to or expressing grammatical mood. ❖ *n.* A modal auxiliary.

modal auxiliary *n.* One of a set of English verbs, including *can, may, must, ought, shall, should, will,* and *would,* that are used with other verbs to express mood or tense.

mode (mōd) *n.* **1.** A way, manner, or style of doing: *a mode of living; a mode of travel.* **2.** The current fashion or style in dress: *a hat in the latest mode.* **3.** A given condition of functioning; a status or operation: *The spacecraft was in its recovery mode.* **4.** Any of the musical scales produced by starting, in turn, on each of the tones of a major scale and proceeding through an octave. Modes were commonly used in medieval church music. **5.** The value that occurs most frequently in a data set or series. For example, in the series 125, 140, 172, 164, 140, and 110, the mode is 140. [From Middle English, tune, from Latin *modus*, manner, tune.]

mod·el (**mŏd′**l) *n.* **1.** A small-scale reproduction or representation of something: *a model of a ship.* **2.** A style or design of something: *This car is last year's model.* **3.** A person or thing serving as an ideal example of something: *The farm is a model of efficient management.* **4.** A person hired to wear clothes in order to show them off, as in fashion shows or advertisements. **5.** A person hired to pose for an artist or photographer. **6.** In science, a description or concept of a system or set of observable events that accounts for all its known properties in a reasonable way. ❖ *v.* **mod·eled, mod·el·ing, mod·els** also **mod·elled, mod·el·ling, mod·els** —*tr.* **1.** To make or construct a model of: *The library was modeled after the Library of Congress in Washington.* **2a.** To make (something) by shaping a plastic substance: *modeled a statue from clay.* **b.** To form (a substance) into a shape: *modeled the clay into a statue.* **3.** To display (clothing, for example) to show others how it looks: *She modeled her new dress.* —*intr.* **1.** To serve or work as a model. **2.** To make a model. ❖ *adj.* **1.** Being, serving, or used as a model: *a model home.* **2.** Serving as a standard of excellence; worthy of imitation: *a model child.* [From Italian *modello*, from Latin *modus*, measure, standard.] **—mod′el·er** *n.*

mod·el·ing (**mŏd′**l-ĭng) *n.* **1.** The act or art of constructing a model out of a pliable material. **2.** The act or profession of being a model.

mo·dem (**mō′**dəm) *n.* A device that transmits and receives data using a modulated carrier wave. Modems are used to establish network and Internet connections.

mod·er·ate (**mŏd′**ər-ĭt) *adj.* **1.** Kept within reasonable limits; not excessive or extreme: *moderate prices.* **2.** Medium or average in amount or quality: *a moderate income.* **3.** Not severe; mild; temperate: *a moderate climate.* **4.** Opposed to radical or extreme views or measures, especially in politics or religion. ❖ *n.* A person who holds moderate views or opinions, especially in politics or religion. ❖ *v.* (**mŏd′**ə-rāt′) **mod·er·at·ed, mod·er·at·ing, mod·er·ates** —*tr.* **1.** To make less extreme: *moderate one's demands.* **2.** To preside over (a meeting or panel discussion). —*intr.* **1.** To become less extreme. **2.** To act as a moderator. [From Middle English *moderat*, from Latin *moderārī*, to moderate.] **—mod′er·ate·ly** *adv.*

mod·er·a·tion (mŏd′ə-**rā′**shən) *n.* **1.** The act of making more moderate: *moderation of one's demands.* **2.** The avoidance of extremes: *an advocate of political moderation.*

mod·e·ra·to (mŏd′ə-**rä′**tō) *adv. & adj.* In music, in moderate tempo.

mod·er·a·tor (**mŏd′**ə-rā′tər) *n.* **1.** The person who presides over a meeting or panel discussion. **2.** A substance, such as graphite or water, placed in a nuclear reactor to slow neutrons down to speeds at which they are likely to cause additional nuclear fission.

mod·ern (**mŏd′**ərn) *adj.* **1.** Relating to the present or the recent past: *modern history; Modern English.* **2.** Relating to a recently developed style, technique, or technology: *modern methods of farming.* **3.** Experimental; avant-garde. ❖ *n.* **1.** A person who lives in modern times. **2.** A person with modern ideas, tastes, or beliefs. [From Late Latin *modernus*.]

Modern English *n.* English since about 1500.

mod·ern·ism (**mŏd′**ər-nĭz′əm) *n.* **1.** Modern thought, character, or practice. **2.** often **Modernism** The use of innovative forms that characterizes many styles in the art and literature of the 1900s. **—mod′ern·ist** *n.*

mo·der·ni·ty (mŏ-**dûr′**nĭ-tē *or* mō-**dûr′**nĭ-tē) *n., pl.* **mo·der·ni·ties** The quality of being modern.

mod·ern·ize (**mŏd′**ər-nīz′) *v.* **mo·dern·ized, mo·dern·iz·ing, mo·dern·iz·es** —*tr.* To make modern in appearance, style, or character; update: *modernize a kitchen.* —*intr.* To become modern; accept or adopt modern ways. **—mod′ern·i·za′tion** (mŏd′ər-nĭ-**zā′**shən) *n.*

mod·est (**mŏd′**ĭst) *adj.* **1.** Having or showing a moderate estimation of one's own talents, abilities, or accomplishments. **2.** Retiring or reserved in manner; shy: *a quiet modest demeanor.* **3.** Not elaborate or showy; unpretentious: *a modest house.* **4.** Moderate in size or amount; not large: *a modest salary.* [From Latin *modestus*.] **—mod′est·ly** *adv.*

mod·es·ty (**mŏd′**ĭ-stē) *n.* **1.** The state or quality of being modest. **2.** Reserve in behavior, dress, or speech. **3.** Lack of pretentiousness; simplicity.

mod·i·cum (**mŏd′**ĭ-kəm) *n.* A small amount: *a subject in which I have only a modicum of interest.*

Möbius strip

moccasin
pair of beaded moccasins

mockingbird

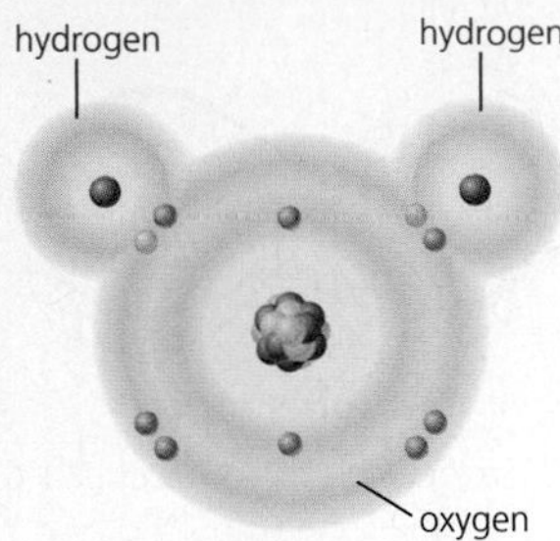

molecule
Two atoms of hydrogen and one atom of oxygen join together to form a molecule of water.

molt
molting penguin

WRITERS CHOOSE THEIR WORDS

Ralph discovered that if he made the noise fast, the motorcycle speeded up. If he slowed the sound, the motorcycle slowed down. He promptly speeded up and raced around in the rectangle of moonlight, where he made another discovery. When he ran out of breath, the **momentum** of the motorcycle carried him on until he could take another breath.

—Beverly Cleary
The Mouse and the Motorcycle

ă	pat	ôr	core
ā	pay	oi	boy
âr	care	ou	out
ä	father	ŏŏ	took
ĕ	pet	ŏŏr	lure
ē	be	ōō	boot
ĭ	pit	ŭ	cut
ī	bite	ûr	urge
îr	pier	th	thin
ŏ	pot	*th*	this
ō	toe	zh	vision
ô	paw	ə	about

mod·i·fi·ca·tion (mŏd′ə-fĭ-**kā′**shən) *n.* **1.** The action or process of modifying: *The theory is still subject to some modification.* **2.** A result of modifying; a change or adaptation: *The design was approved with certain modifications.* **3.** A small alteration, adjustment, or limitation.

mod·i·fi·er (**mŏd′**ə-fī′ər) *n.* A word, phrase, or clause that grammatically modifies another word or phrase. Adjectives and adverbs are modifiers.

mod·i·fy (**mŏd′**ə-fī′) *v.* **mod·i·fied, mod·i·fy·ing, mod·i·fies** —*tr.* **1.** To change in form or character; alter: *modify the terms of a deal.* **2.** In grammar, to add further detail about the meaning of (a word or phrase, for example). —*intr.* To be or become modified; change. [From Middle English *modifien*, from Latin *modificāre*, to measure, limit.]

mod·ish (**mō′**dĭsh) *adj.* Stylish; fashionable. **—mod′ish·ly** *adv.* **—mod′ish·ness** *n.*

mod·u·late (**mŏj′**ə-lāt′) *v.* **mod·u·lat·ed, mod·u·lat·ing, mod·u·lates** —*tr.* **1.** To change or vary the pitch, intensity, or tone of (one's voice or a musical instrument, for example). **2.** To vary the amplitude, frequency, or some other characteristic of (electromagnetic waves) in a way that makes them correspond to a signal or information that is to be transmitted. —*intr.* To pass from one musical key or tonality to another by means of a melodic or chord progression.

mod·u·la·tion (mŏj′ə-**lā′**shən) *n.* **1.** The act or process of modulating. **2.** The state of being modulated. **3.** The process by which a characteristic of electromagnetic waves, such as amplitude or frequency, is changed to make the waves correspond to a signal or information that is to be transmitted. **4.** In music, a passing or transition from one key or tonality to another.

mod·u·la·tor (**mŏj′**ə-lā′tər) *n.* A device that modulates an electromagnetic wave.

mod·ule (**mŏj′**ōōl) *n.* **1.** A standard element that is used over and over again in forming a building or structure. **2.** A self-contained unit of electronic components and circuitry that is installed as a unit. **3.** A self-contained unit of a spacecraft that is used for a particular job or set of jobs: *a lunar module.* **4.** A unit of education or instruction in which a single topic is studied for a given period of time. **—mod′u·lar** (**mŏj′**ə-lər) *adj.*

Mog·a·di·shu (mō′gə-**dē′**shōō *or* mō′gə-**dĭsh′**ōō) The capital of Somalia, on the Indian Ocean. It was settled in the ninth or tenth century.

mo·gul[1] (**mō′**gəl) *n.* A small hard mound or bump on a ski slope. [Probably of Scandinavian origin; akin to Old Norse *mūgi*, heap.]

mo·gul[2] (**mō′**gəl *or* mō-**gŭl′**) *n.* **1.** A very rich or powerful person; a magnate. **2. Mogul** Variant of **Mughal.**

mo·hair (**mō′**hâr′) *n.* **1.** The long silky hair of the Angora goat. **2.** Fabric or yarn made from this hair. [From Arabic *muḫayyar*, choice, select, from *ḫayyara*, to prefer.]

Mo·ham·med (mō-**hăm′**ĭd *or* mō-**hä′**mĭd) See **Muhammad.**

Mo·ha·ve also **Mo·ja·ve** (mō-**hä′**vē) *n., pl.* **Mohave** or **Mo·ha·ves** also **Mojave** or **Mo·ja·ves 1.** A member of a Native American people living along the lower Colorado River in California and Arizona. **2.** The Yuman language of the Mohave.

Mo·hawk (**mō′**hôk′) *n., pl.* **Mohawk** or **Mo·hawks 1.** A member of a Native American people living in upstate New York and southern Ontario. **2.** The Iroquoian language of the Mohawk.

Mo·he·gan (mō-**hē′**gən) *n., pl.* **Mohegan** or **Mo·he·gans 1.** A member of a Native American people formerly living in Connecticut, with present-day populations in Connecticut and Wisconsin. **2.** The Algonquian language of the Mohegan.

Mo·hi·can (mō-**hē′**kən *or* mə-**hē′**kən) *n.* Variant of **Mahican.**

Mohs scale (mōz) *n.* A scale used to measure the relative hardness of a mineral by its resistance to scratching by ten standard minerals ranging from talc, the softest, to diamond, the hardest. [After Friedrich *Mohs* (1773–1839), German mineralogist.]

moi·e·ty (**moi′**ĭ-tē) *n., pl.* **moi·e·ties 1.** A half. **2.** A part, portion, or share.

moi·ré (mwä-**rā′** *or* mô-**rā′**) *adj.* Having a wavy or rippled surface pattern. ❖ *n.* **1.** A wavy or rippled pattern pressed on cloth by engraved rollers. **2.** Cloth, especially silk, that has a watery rippled look.

moist (moist) *adj.* **moist·er, moist·est 1.** Slightly wet; damp: *a moist sponge.* See Synonyms at **wet. 2.** Humid or rainy: *the moist gulf air; a moist climate.* **3.** Juicy or succulent; not dried out: *Basting keeps the turkey moist in the oven.* [From Middle English *moiste*, from Latin *mūcidus*, moldy, from *mūcus*, mucus.] **—moist′ness** *n.*

mois·ten (**moi′**sən) *tr. & intr.v.* **mois·tened, mois·ten·ing, mois·tens** To make or become moist.

mois·ture (**mois′**chər) *n.* Wetness, especially that caused by water present in the air as vapor or spread thinly over a surface or surfaces.

Mo·ja·ve (mō-**hä′**vē) *n.* Variant of **Mohave.**

Mojave Desert also **Mohave Desert** An arid region of southern California southeast of the Sierra Nevada. The desert was formed by volcanic action and by materials deposited by the Colorado River.

mo·jo (**mō′**jō′) *n., pl.* **mo·jos** or **mo·joes 1.** A saying or item believed to have magical powers; a spell or charm. **2.** An ability or quality that causes one to excel or have good luck: *a pitcher who lost his mojo when he entered the major leagues.*

mo·lar (**mō′**lər) *n.* Any of the teeth located toward the back of the jaws, having broad crowns for grinding food. Humans have 12 molars.

mo·las·ses (mə-**lăs′**ĭz) *n.* A thick brown syrup produced in refining sugar.

mold[1] (mōld) *n.* **1.** A hollow container of a particular shape, used for shaping a liquid or plastic substance: *pour the batter into a mold.* **2.** Something made or shaped from a mold. **3.** General shape; form: *the round mold of a face.* **4.** Distinctive character, kind, or type: *men and women of serious mold.* ❖ *tr.v.* **mold·ed, mold·ing, molds 1.** To shape in a mold. **2.** To determine the general character of; shape in a particular way: *mold clay; mold a student's mind.* [From Middle English *molde*, from Latin *modulus*, unit of measure, from *modus*, measure.] **—mold′a·ble** *adj.* **—mold′er** *n.*

mold[2] (mōld) *n.* **1.** Any of various fungi that often form a fuzzy coating on the surface of food and other organic matter. **2.** The coating formed by such a fungus. [From Middle English *moulde.*]

Mol·da·vi·a (mŏl-**dā′**vē-ə) **1.** A historical region of eastern Romania east of Transylvania. In 1862 Moldavia united with Wallachia to form the core of modern Romania. **2.** See **Moldova.**

mold·er (**mōl′**dər) *v.* **mold·ered, mold·er·ing, mold·ers** —*intr.* To turn gradually to dust; crumble: *The ancient ruins are beginning to molder away.* —*tr.* To cause to crumble.

mold·ing (**mōl′**dĭng) *n.* **1.** The act or process of molding. **2.** Something that is molded. **3.** An ornamental strip used to decorate a surface.

Mol·do·va (mŏl-**dō′**və) Formerly **Mol·da·vi·a** (mŏl-**dā′**vē-ə). A country of eastern Europe northeast of Romania. Moldova was part of the USSR from 1924 to 1991. Chişinău is the capital.

mold·y (**mōl′**dē) *adj.* **mold·i·er, mold·i·est 1.** Covered with or containing mold: *moldy bread.* **2.** Damp and musty: *a dark moldy cupboard.* **—mold′i·ness** *n.*

mole[1] (mōl) *n.* A small, usually dark growth on the skin. [From Old English *māl.*]

mole² (mōl) *n.* **1.** Any of various small burrowing mammals having strong claws, tiny eyes, a narrow snout, and short silky fur. **2.** A spy within an organization, especially a double agent. [From Middle English *molle.*]

mole³ (mōl) *n.* In the International System, a unit that represents the amount of atoms, molecules, ions, or other elementary units in a substance, equal to the number of atoms in 0.012 kilogram of carbon-12. (That number is 6.0221×10^{23}, or Avogadro's number.) A mole of a chemical has a mass in grams numerically equal to its molecular weight. For example, carbon dioxide, CO_2, has a molecular weight of 44; therefore, one mole of it weighs 44 grams. See table at **measurement.** [From German *Mol,* from *Molekül,* molecule.]

mo·lec·u·lar (mə-lĕk′yə-lər) *adj.* Relating to, caused by, or consisting of molecules. **—mo·lec′u·lar·ly** *adv.*

molecular weight *n.* The sum of the atomic weights of the atoms contained in a molecule.

mol·e·cule (mŏl′ĭ-kyo͞ol′) *n.* **1.** A group of two or more atoms linked together by sharing electrons in a covalent bond. **2.** A small particle; a tiny bit. [From French *molécule,* from Latin *mōlēs,* mass.]

mole·hill (mōl′hĭl′) *n.* A small mound of earth dug up by a burrowing mole.

mole·skin (mōl′skĭn′) *n.* **1.** The short, soft, silky fur of a mole. **2.** A sturdy cotton cloth with a thick fine nap on one side.

mo·lest (mə-lĕst′) *tr.v.* **mo·lest·ed, mo·lest·ing, mo·lests 1.** To annoy, bother, or disturb: *Few animals dare molest a badger.* **2.** To subject to unwanted or improper sexual activity. **—mo·lest′er** *n.* **—mo′les·ta′tion** (mō′lĕ-stā′shən) *n.*

Mo·lière (mōl-yâr′) Pen name of **Jean Baptiste Poquelin.** 1622–1673. French playwright whose comedies include *Tartuffe* (1664).

mol·li·fy (mŏl′ə-fī′) *tr.v.* **mol·li·fied, mol·li·fy·ing, mol·li·fies 1.** To lessen the anger of; placate: *a new film designed to mollify critics.* **2.** To make less intense; soften or soothe: *The tender words mollified the child's distress.* **—mol′li·fi·ca′tion** (mŏl′ə-fĭ-kā′shən) *n.*

mol·lusk also **mol·lusc** (mŏl′əsk) *n.* Any of numerous soft-bodied invertebrate animals, such as snails, clams, and oysters, usually living in water and having a hard outer shell. Some mollusks, such as octopuses, squids, and slugs, have no outer shell.

Mo·loch (mō′lŏk′ *or* mŏl′ək) *n.* **1.** In the Bible, a god of some non-Hebrew peoples to whom children were sacrificed. **2.** Something that requires severe sacrifice.

Mo·lo·kai (mŏl′ə-kī′ *or* mō′lə-kī′) An island of central Hawaii between Oahu and Maui.

molt (mōlt) *v.* **molt·ed, molt·ing, molts** *—intr.* To shed an outer covering, such as skin or feathers, for replacement by a new growth: *Some snakes molt in spring. —tr.* To shed (an outer covering): *molt feathers.* ❖ *n.* The act or process of molting.

mol·ten (mōl′tən) *adj.* Made liquid by heat; melted: *molten metal.*

mo·lyb·de·num (mə-lĭb′də-nəm) *n. Symbol* **Mo** A hard, silvery-white metallic element used to toughen and harden steel. It is an essential trace element in plant metabolism. Atomic number 42. See **Periodic Table.**

mom (mŏm) *n. Informal* Mother.

mom-and-pop (mŏm′ən-pŏp′) *adj.* Relating to or being a small business that is run by the owners: *a mom-and-pop grocery store.*

mo·ment (mō′mənt) *n.* **1.** A very brief interval of time; an instant: *I'll be ready in a moment.* **2.** A certain important point in time: *the happiest moment of my life.* **3.** The present time: *I am busy at the moment.* **4.** Great significance or importance: *We were proud to witness an event of such moment.*

mo·men·ta (mō-mĕn′tə) *n.* A plural of **momentum.**

mo·men·tar·i·ly (mō′mən-târ′ə-lē) *adv.* **1.** For an instant or a moment: *I was momentarily at a loss for words.* **2.** At any moment; very soon: *The principal will see you momentarily.*

mo·men·tar·y (mō′mən-tĕr′ē) *adj.* Lasting only an instant or moment: *a momentary glance.*

mo·men·tous (mō-mĕn′təs) *adj.* Of the utmost importance or significance: *a momentous occasion.*

mo·men·tum (mō-mĕn′təm) *n., pl.* **mo·men·ta** (mō-mĕn′tə) or **mo·men·tums 1.** A measure of the motion of a moving body, equal to the body's mass multiplied by its velocity. **2.** Force or speed of motion; impetus: *The sled gained momentum as it raced down the hill.*

mom·my (mŏm′ē) *n., pl.* **mom·mies** *Informal* Mother.

Mon·a·co (mŏn′ə-kō′) A principality on the Mediterranean Sea consisting of an enclave in southeast France. The village of **Monaco,** or **Monaco-Ville,** is the capital.

mon·arch (mŏn′ərk *or* mŏn′ärk′) *n.* **1.** A ruler or sovereign, such as a king or queen, who reigns over a state, usually for life and by hereditary right. **2.** A monarch butterfly. [From Middle English *monarke,* from Greek *monarkhos.*] **—mo·nar′chic** (mə-när′kĭk) *adj.* **—mo·nar′chi·cal** *adj.*

monarch butterfly *n.* A large orange and black American butterfly noted for its long-distance migrations.

mon·ar·chism (mŏn′ər-kĭz′əm *or* mŏn′är′kĭz′əm) *n.* Belief in or support of government by a monarch.

mon·ar·chist (mŏn′ər-kĭst *or* mŏn′är′kĭst) *n.* A person who believes in or supports monarchy.

mon·ar·chy (mŏn′ər-kē *or* mŏn′är′kē) *n., pl.* **mon·ar·chies 1.** Government by a monarch. **2.** A country ruled by a monarch.

mon·as·ter·y (mŏn′ə-stĕr′ē) *n., pl.* **mon·as·ter·ies 1.** A community of monks. **2.** The building or buildings occupied by monks. **—mon′as·te′ri·al** (mŏn′ə-stîr′ē-əl *or* mŏn′ə-stĕr′ē-əl) *adj.*

mo·nas·tic (mə-năs′tĭk) *adj.* **1.** Relating to or characteristic of a monastery. **2.** Resembling life in a monastery. ❖ *n.* A monk.

mon·au·ral (mŏn-ôr′əl) *adj.* **1.** Relating to sound reception with only one ear. **2.** Using a single channel to transmit or reproduce sound; monophonic.

Mon·day (mŭn′dē *or* mŭn′dā′) *n.* The second day of the week. [From Old English *Mōnandæg,* moon's day.] **—Mon′days** *adv.*

Mo·net (mō-nā′), **Claude** 1840–1926. French painter and founder of impressionism whose works include the *Water Lilies* series (1899–1925).

mon·e·tar·y (mŏn′ĭ-tĕr′ē) *adj.* **1.** Relating to money: *the monetary value of a painting.* **2.** Relating to a nation's currency or coinage. **—mon′e·tar′i·ly** *adv.*

mon·ey (mŭn′ē) *n., pl.* **mon·eys** or **mon·ies 1.** Something, such as gold or an officially issued coin or paper note, that is legally declared to have a fixed value and to be exchangeable for all goods and services. **2.** The official coins and paper notes issued by a government and used to buy or pay for things; currency. **3.** Wealth; property and assets: *a family with plenty of money.* **4.** often **moneys, monies** Sums of money collected or stored; funds: *state tax moneys; monies set aside for research.* **5.** An amount of money sufficient for some purpose: *They lacked the money for a vacation.* **6.** Monetary profit or loss: *won big money on the lottery.*

mon·ey·bag (mŭn′ē-băg′) *n.* **1.** A bag for holding money. **2. moneybags** *(used with a singular verb) Slang* A rich and greedy person.

mon·eyed (mŭn′ēd) *adj.* **1.** Having much money; wealthy: *the large moneyed corporations.* **2.** Representing or arising from money or wealth: *the power of moneyed interests in Washington, DC.*

mon·ey·lend·er (mŭn′ē-lĕn′dər) *n.* A person whose business is lending money for a fee.

monarch butterfly

Claude Monet
1875 portrait by Pierre Auguste Renoir (1841–1919)

money order *n.* An order authorizing the payment of a specified amount of money to the bearer. Money orders can usually be bought or cashed at a bank or post office.

mon·ger (**mŭng′**gər *or* **mŏng′**gər) *n.* **1.** A dealer in a specific product or commodity: *an ironmonger.* **2.** A person who promotes something undesirable or discreditable: *a scandalmonger.*

Mon·gol (**mŏng′**gəl *or* **mŏng′**gōl′) *adj.* Relating to Mongolia or its people, language, or culture. ❖ *n.* **1.** A member of any of the traditionally nomadic peoples of Mongolia. **2.** The language of these peoples; Mongolian.

Mon·go·li·a (mŏng-**gō′**lē-ə *or* mŏng-**gōl′**yə) **1.** An ancient region of east-central Asia north of China made up of modern-day Inner Mongolia and the country of Mongolia. In the 1200s it was a great empire that eventually stretched from China to the Danube River and into Persia. **2.** Formerly **Outer Mongolia.** A country of north-central Asia between Russia and China. Ulaanbaatar is the capital.

Mon·go·li·an (mŏng-**gō′**lē-ən *or* mŏng-**gōl′**yən) *n.* **1.** A native or inhabitant of Mongolia. **2.** Any of the languages of Mongolia, related to Turkish. ❖ *adj.* Relating to Mongolia, the Mongols, or their language or culture.

mon·goose (**mŏng′**go͞os′ *or* **mŏn′**go͞os′) *n., pl.* **mon·goos·es** Any of various mammals of Asia, southern Europe, and Africa that resemble weasels and are noted for their ability to kill venomous snakes. [From Marathi *mangūs.*]

mon·grel (**mŏng′**grəl) *n.* A dog that is the result of crossing different breeds or that is of an unknown breed. [From Middle English, probably from Old English *gemang,* mixture.]

mon·ies (**mŭn′**ēz) *n.* A plural of **money.**

mon·i·tor (**mŏn′**ĭ-tər) *n.* **1.** A person who gives warnings, corrective advice, or instruction. **2.** A student who assists a teacher in routine duties such as taking attendance. **3.** A usually electronic device used to record, regulate, or control a process or activity: *a radiation monitor.* **4.** A video display or speaker used in a production studio to check audio or video quality: *The sound engineer detected a hiss on the monitor.* **5.** A device that accepts video signals from a computer and displays information on a screen. **6.** A monitor lizard. ❖ *v.* **mon·i·tored, mon·i·tor·ing, mon·i·tors** —*tr.* **1.** To keep watch over; supervise: *monitor an election.* **2.** To keep track of systematically: *monitor a patient's heartbeat.* **3.** To check the quality or content of (an electronic audio or a visual signal) by means of a receiver. —*intr.* To act as a monitor. [From Latin, from *monēre,* to warn.]

monitor lizard *n.* Any of various meat-eating, often large lizards of tropical Africa, Asia, and Australia, having a forked tongue and a long neck.

mon·i·to·ry (**mŏn′**ĭ-tôr′ē) *adj.* Giving a warning or rebuke: *a monitory glance.*

monk (mŭngk) *n.* A member of a group of men living in a monastery and bound by vows to the rules and practices of a religious order. [From Old English *munuc,* from Greek *monakhos,* alone.]

mon·key (**mŭng′**kē) *n., pl.* **mon·keys 1.** Any of various primates having long tails and hands and feet that are used for grasping. Monkeys include the baboons, macaques, and marmosets. **2.** A playful or mischievous person. ❖ *intr.v.* **mon·keyed, mon·key·ing, mon·keys** *Informal* **1.** To behave in a silly or mischievous way: *Don't monkey around during the ceremony.* **2.** To tamper or meddle with something: *Who was monkeying with my computer?*

monkey bars *pl.n.* A jungle gym.

monkey wrench *n.* **1.** A hand tool with adjustable jaws for turning nuts and bolts of various sizes. **2.** Something that disrupts: *Bad weather threw a monkey wrench into our plans.*

monorail

ă	pat	ôr	core
ā	pay	oi	boy
âr	care	ou	out
ä	father	o͝o	took
ĕ	pet	o͝or	lure
ē	be	o͞o	boot
ĭ	pit	ŭ	cut
ī	bite	ûr	urge
îr	pier	th	thin
ŏ	pot	*th*	this
ō	toe	zh	vision
ô	paw	ə	about

monk·ish (**mŭng′**kĭsh) *adj.* Relating to or characteristic of monks or monasticism.

monks·hood (**mŭngks′**ho͝od′) *n.* Aconite.

mono (**mŏn′**ō) *n. Informal* Infectious mononucleosis.

mono– or **mon–** *pref.* A prefix that means: **1.** One; only; single: *monogamy.* **2.** Containing a single atom, radical, or group: *monoxide.*

mon·o·chro·mat·ic (mŏn′ə-krō-**măt′**ĭk) *adj.* **1.** Having a single color: *a monochromatic beige rug.* **2.** Consisting of a single wavelength of light or other radiation: *monochromatic x-rays.*

mon·o·cle (**mŏn′**ə-kəl) *n.* An eyeglass, typically having a cord attached, worn in front of one eye.

mon·o·cot (**mŏn′**ə-kŏt) *n.* A monocotyledon.

mon·o·cot·y·le·don (mŏn′ə-kŏt′l-**ēd′**n) *n.* A flowering plant having a single cotyledon and usually other characteristics such as leaf veins that are parallel, flower parts in multiples of three, and a lack of woody growth. Tulips, onions, grasses, and palms are monocotyledons, while beans, roses, maples, and oaks are dicotyledons. **—mon′o·cot′y·le′don·ous** *adj.*

mo·noc·u·lar (mə-**nŏk′**yə-lər) *adj.* **1.** Relating to or having a single eye. **2.** Designed for use with only one eye: *a monocular microscope.*

mo·noe·cious (mə-**nē′**shəs) *adj.* Having separate male flowers or cones and female flowers or cones on the same plant. Oaks, pines, and corn plants are monoecious.

mo·nog·a·my (mə-**nŏg′**ə-mē) *n.* **1.** The custom or condition of being married to only one person at a time. **2.** The custom or condition of having only one sexual partner at a time. **3.** The condition of having only one mate during a breeding season or during the breeding life of a pair: *monogamy in birds.* **—mo·nog′a·mous** (mə-**nŏg′**ə-məs) *adj.*

mon·o·gram (**mŏn′**ə-grăm′) *n.* A design made up of one or more letters, usually the initials of a name. ❖ *tr.v.* **mon·o·grammed, mon·o·gram·ming, mon·o·grams** also **mon·o·gramed, mon·o·gram·ing, mon·o·grams** To mark with a monogram: *She monogrammed the sheets and towels.* [From Greek *mono-,* single + Greek *gramma,* letter.]

mon·o·graph (**mŏn′**ə-grăf′) *n.* A scholarly book or article on a specific and usually limited subject.

mon·o·lith (**mŏn′**ə-lĭth′) *n.* **1.** A large single block of stone. **2.** A memorial, monument, or other structure made from a single block of stone.

mon·o·lith·ic (mŏn′ə-**lĭth′**ĭk) *adj.* **1.** Consisting of a monolith: *a monolithic column.* **2.** Like a monolith in being massive, uniform, or unvarying: *a monolithic business empire.*

mon·o·logue (**mŏn′**ə-lôg′) *n.* **1.** A long speech delivered by an actor on the stage or a character in a story or poem. **2.** A series of jokes and stories told by a comedian while alone on the stage. **3.** A long speech made by one person in a group: *He kept talking until our conversation turned into a monologue.*

mon·o·ma·ni·a (mŏn′ə-**mā′**nē-ə *or* mŏn′ə-**mān′**yə) *n.* An intense preoccupation with one subject or idea. **—mon′o·ma′ni·ac′** (mŏn′ə-**mā′**nē-ăk′) *n.*

mo·no·mi·al (mŏ-**nō′**mē-əl) *n.* An algebraic expression consisting of a single term.

mon·o·nu·cle·o·sis (mŏn′ō-no͞o′klē-**ō′**sĭs) *n.* Infectious mononucleosis.

mon·o·phon·ic (mŏn′ə-**fŏn′**ĭk) *adj.* **1.** Having a single melodic line or part. **2.** Using a single channel to record, store, or reproduce sound: *a monophonic recording.*

mon·o·plane (**mŏn′**ə-plān′) *n.* An airplane having a single pair of wings.

mo·nop·o·list (mə-**nŏp′**ə-lĭst) *n.* A business leader who owns or promotes monopolies.

mo·nop·o·lis·tic (mə-nŏp′ə-**lĭs′**tĭk) *adj.* **1.** Maintaining a monopoly. **2.** Relating to or characteristic of a monopoly or a monopolist.

mo·nop·o·lize (mə-**nŏp′**ə-līz′) *tr.v.* **mo·nop·o·lized, mo·nop·o·liz·ing, mo·nop·o·liz·es 1.** To gain a monopoly over. **2.** To get or have sole control over: *Don't monopolize the conversation.* **—mo·nop′o·li·za′tion** (mə-nŏp′ə-lĭ-**zā′**shən) *n.* **—mo·nop′o·liz′er** *n.*

mo·nop·o·ly (mə-**nŏp′**ə-lē) *n., pl.* **mo·nop·o·lies 1a.** Complete control by one group of the means of producing or selling a product or service: *The early railroads had a near monopoly on freight and passenger transportation.* **b.** A company having such complete control: *laws to limit the power of monopolies.* **c.** A product, service, or commercial activity completely controlled by one group. **2.** The right given by a government to a person to have exclusive control of the sale and manufacture of commercial goods. **3.** Sole possession or control of something: *The US monopoly on the atomic bomb did not last long.* [From Greek *monopōlion* : *mono-*, single + *pōlein*, to sell.]

mon·o·rail (**mŏn′**ə-rāl′) *n.* **1.** A single rail serving as a track for trains that travel on it or hang from it. **2.** A railway system using a track with such a rail.

mon·o·so·di·um glu·ta·mate (mŏn′ə-**sō′**dē-əm **glo͞o′**tə-māt′) *n.* A white crystalline compound used to enhance flavor in food.

mon·o·syl·lab·ic (mŏn′ə-sĭ-**lăb′**ĭk) *adj.* **1.** Having only one syllable: *a monosyllabic word.* **2.** Consisting of or characterized by monosyllables.

mon·o·syl·la·ble (**mŏn′**ə-sĭl′ə-bəl) *n.* A word, such as *hat* or *hate*, having one syllable.

mon·o·the·ism (**mŏn′**ə-thē-ĭz′əm) *n.* The belief that there is only one God. **—mon′o·the′ist** *n.* **—mon′o·the·is′tic** *adj.*

mon·o·tone (**mŏn′**ə-tōn′) *n.* **1.** A succession of sounds or words uttered in a single tone of voice: *read the list of names in a monotone.* **2a.** A single tone repeated with different words or time values, as in chanting. **b.** A chant sung on a single tone. **3.** A tiresome repetition, as in sound, color, or style.

mo·not·o·nous (mə-**nŏt′**n-əs) *adj.* **1.** Uttered or sounded in one repeated tone; unvarying in pitch: *delivered the speech in a monotonous voice.* **2.** Never varied or enlivened; repetitiously dull: *a monotonous lecture; a monotonous diet.* **—mo·not′o·nous·ly** *adv.*

mo·not·o·ny (mə-**nŏt′**n-ē) *n., pl.* **mo·not·o·nies** Tiresome sameness or repetition.

mon·o·treme (**mŏn′**ə-trēm′) *n.* Any of various egg-laying mammals of a group that includes only the platypus and the echidnas.

mon·o·un·sat·u·rat·ed (mŏn′ō-ŭn-**săch′**ə-rā′tĭd) *adj.* Relating to an organic compound, especially an oil or fatty acid, in which there is only one double or triple bond per molecule.

mon·ox·ide (mə-**nŏk′**sīd′) *n.* An oxide in which each molecule contains a single atom of oxygen.

Mon·roe (mən-**rō′**), **James** 1758–1831. The fifth president of the United States (1817–1825), whose administration was marked by the acquisition of Florida (1819) and the Missouri Compromise (1820), in which Missouri was admitted to the union as a Slave State and Maine as a Free State in order to keep the balance of Free and Slave States in Congress even.

Monroe, Marilyn 1926–1962. American actress noted for her roles in movies, including *Some Like It Hot* (1959).

Mon·ro·vi·a (mən-**rō′**vē-ə) The capital of Liberia, in the northwest part of the country on the Atlantic Ocean. It was founded in 1822 as a haven for freed slaves.

Mon·sei·gneur (môN-sĕ-**nyœr′**) *n., pl.* **Mes·sei·gneurs** (mā-sĕ-**nyœr′**) Used as a title of honor or respect in French-speaking areas for princes or highly ranked clergy.

Mon·sieur (mə-**syœ′**) *n., pl.* **Mes·sieurs** (mā-**syœ′** *or* **mĕs′**ərz) Used as a courtesy title before the name of a man in a French-speaking area: *Monsieur Fournier.*

mon·soon (mŏn-**so͞on′**) *n.* **1.** A system of winds that influences the climate of a large area and that changes direction with the seasons, especially the wind system that produces the wet and dry seasons in southern Asia. **2.** The season during which this wind blows from the southwest, usually accompanied by heavy rains. [From Arabic *mawsim*, season.]

mon·ster (**mŏn′**stər) *n.* **1.** A dangerous or frightening creature, especially an imaginary or legendary one: *ancient stories about a monster that lives in the lake; dressed up as a monster for Halloween.* **2.** *Informal* Something that is extremely large: *a monster of a shark.* ❖ *adj. Informal* Extremely large; gigantic: *a monster wave; a song that was a monster hit.* [From Middle English *monstre*, from Latin *mōnstrum*, portent.]

mon·stros·i·ty (mŏn-**strŏs′**ĭ-tē) *n., pl.* **mon·stros·i·ties 1.** A person or thing that is monstrous. **2.** The quality or condition of being monstrous.

mon·strous (**mŏn′**strəs) *adj.* **1.** Having a frightful or hideous appearance: *a deep-sea creature with monstrous teeth.* **2.** Huge; enormous: *a monstrous iceberg.* **3.** Extremely immoral or cruel; inhuman: *a monstrous dictator.* **4.** Relating to or resembling a legendary monster: *the Cyclops and other monstrous creatures of Greek mythology.* **—mon′strous·ly** *adv.* **—mon′strous·ness** *n.*

mon·tage (mŏn-**täzh′**) *n.* **1a.** A picture made from many other pictures or designs placed next to or on top of one another. **b.** The art or process of making such a picture. **2a.** A rapid succession of different shots in a movie. **b.** The use of such a succession as a technique of making movies. [From French, from *monter*, to mount.]

Mon·ta·gnier (mŏn′tən-**yā′**), **Luc** Born 1932. French microbiologist who was one of the first to discover the virus later called HIV.

Mon·tan·a (mŏn-**tăn′**ə) A state of the northwest United States north of Wyoming. It was admitted as the 41st state in 1889. Helena is the capital and Billings the largest city. —SEE NOTE.

Montana, Joseph, Jr. Known as "Joe." Born 1956. American football player who is among the National Football League's leaders in career passing yardage. He was selected twice as the NFL's most valuable player.

mon·tane (mŏn-**tān′** *or* **mŏn′**tān′) *adj.* Relating to or characteristic of mountain areas: *animals adapted to montane forests.*

Mont Blanc See **Blanc, Mont.**

Mon·te Car·lo (**mŏn′**tē **kär′**lō) A town of Monaco on the Mediterranean Sea and the French Riviera. It is a noted resort.

Mon·te·neg·ro (mŏn′tə-**nĕg′**rō *or* mŏn′tə-**nē′**grō) A country of southeast Europe bordering on the Adriatic Sea. Podgorica is the capital.

Mon·te·rey jack (mŏn′tə-**rā′**) *n.* A mild cheese with a high moisture content.

Mon·tes·so·ri (mŏn′tĭ-**sôr′**ē), **Maria** 1870–1952. Italian physician and pioneer educator. She proposed a method of teaching young children that stresses the development of initiative and natural abilities.

Mon·te·vi·de·o (mŏn′tə-vĭ-**dā′**ō *or* mōn′tĕ-vē-**dĕ′**ō) The capital of Uruguay, in the southern part of the country on the Río de la Plata estuary.

Mon·te·zu·ma II (mŏn′tĭ-**zo͞o′**mə) 1466?–1520. Last Aztec emperor in Mexico (1502–1520), who was overthrown by the Spanish.

Mont·gom·er·y (mŏnt-**gŭm′**ə-rē *or* mŏnt-**gŭm′**rē) The capital of Alabama, in the southeast-central part of the state south-southeast of Birmingham. From February to

James Monroe

GEOGRAPHY

Montana The state of **Montana** gets its name from a Spanish or Latin word meaning "mountain." Montana became the official name of the state in 1889, when it joined the Union.

Joe Montana

Maria Montessori
photographed in the 1920s

SCIENCE

moon We earthlings usually think of our moon as *the* moon, but any planet's natural satellites are properly called moons. The earth has only one moon, but Jupiter and Saturn each have over 60. Galileo Galilei observed four of Jupiter's largest moons with a simple telescope in the early 1600s. At first he thought they were stars, but as he noted their locations night after night, he realized that they were orbiting around Jupiter. Galileo named these four moons the "Medicean stars," after his wealthy patrons, the Medici family of Florence. He identified each individual one simply by number. As more moons were discovered around Jupiter and Saturn, this numbering system became cumbersome, and astronomers decided to use the names of mythological figures instead. Jupiter's four largest moons were named Io, Europa, Ganymede, and Callisto, after lovers of the Roman god Jupiter. On a clear night, with ordinary binoculars, you can see these moons yourself.

May 1861 it served as the first capital of the Confederacy.

month (mŭnth) *n.* **1.** One of the 12 calendar divisions of the year, especially according to the Gregorian calendar, lasting about 30 days. **2.** A period extending from a date in one calendar month to the corresponding date in the following month. **3.** A lunar month. [From Old English *mōnath*.]

month·ly (**mŭnth′**lē) *adj.* **1.** Occurring, appearing, or payable every month: *a monthly meeting; monthly bills.* **2.** Continuing or lasting for a month: *average monthly rainfall.* ❖ *adv.* Every month: *a magazine published monthly.* ❖ *n., pl.* **month·lies** A periodical publication appearing once each month.

Mont·pel·ier (mŏnt-**pēl′**yər) The capital of Vermont, in the north-central part of the state, founded in 1780.

Mon·tre·al (mŏn′trē-**ôl′**) or **Mont·ré·al** (môɴ′rā-**äl′**) The largest city of Quebec, Canada, in the southern part of the province on **Montreal Island** in the St. Lawrence River. It was founded by the French in 1642.

mon·u·ment (**mŏn′**yə-mənt) *n.* **1.** A structure, such as a tower, statue, or building, erected to honor a person, group, or event. **2.** A tombstone. **3.** Something admired for its historical importance: *The Alamo is a monument of American history.* **4.** An outstanding or enduring work: *The book is a monument of scholarship.* [From Middle English, from Latin *monumentum*, from *monēre*, to remind.]

mon·u·men·tal (mŏn′yə-**mĕn′**tl) *adj.* **1.** Relating to, like, or serving as a monument: *a monumental arch.* **2.** Impressively large, sturdy, and enduring: *a monumental dam.* **3.** Of outstanding significance: *Einstein's monumental discoveries in physics.* **4.** Astounding: *monumental talent.* **—mon′u·men′tal·ly** *adv.*

moo (mo͞o) *intr.v.* **mooed, moo·ing, moos** To emit the deep bellowing sound made by a cow; low. ❖ *n., pl.* **moos** The lowing of a cow or a similar sound.

mooch (mo͞och) *v.* **mooched, mooch·ing, mooch·es** *Slang —tr.* To get or try to get by begging: *always mooching food from me. —intr.* To get or try to get something for free: *lived by mooching off friends.* **—mooch′er** *n.*

mood[1] (mo͞od) *n.* **1.** A state of mind or feeling: *I was in a good mood after the party.* **2.** An impression on the feelings or spirits of a person: *The painting has a somber mood.* **3.** Inclination; disposition: *I'm in no mood to argue.* [From Old English *mōd*.]

mood[2] (mo͞od) *n.* A set of verb forms that tells how certain the speaker is of the action expressed. In English, the indicative mood is used to make factual statements, the imperative mood to give commands, and the subjunctive mood to suggest doubt or unlikelihood. [Alteration of *mode*.]

mood·y (**mo͞o′**dē) *adj.* **mood·i·er, mood·i·est 1.** Apt to change moods often, especially having spells of anger or gloom. **2.** Gloomy; morose; glum: *his moody silence.* **—mood′i·ly** *adv.* **—mood′i·ness** *n.*

moon (mo͞on) *n.* **1.** often **Moon** The natural satellite of Earth, visible by reflected sunlight and traveling around Earth in a slightly elliptical orbit at an average distance of about 238,900 miles (384,400 kilometers). Its average diameter is 2,160 miles (3,475 kilometers) and its mass about 1/80 that of Earth. **2.** A natural satellite of a planet other than Earth: *the moons of Jupiter.* **3.** Earth's moon as seen at a particular time in its cycle of phases: *a half moon.* **4.** A month, especially a lunar month. **5.** A disk, ball, or crescent resembling the moon. ❖ *intr.v.* **mooned, moon·ing, moons** To pass time idly or aimlessly: *just mooning about.* [From Old English *mōna*.] —SEE NOTE.

moon·beam (**mo͞on′**bēm′) *n.* A ray of moonlight.

moon·calf (**mo͞on′**kăf′) *n.* A foolish person.

moon·light (**mo͞on′**līt′) *n.* The light that is reflected from the surface of the moon. ❖ *intr.v.* **moon·light·ed, moon·light·ing, moon·lights** *Informal* To work at a second job, often at night, in addition to one's regular job. **—moon′light′er** *n.*

moon·lit (**mo͞on′**lĭt′) *adj.* Lighted by the moon: *a moonlit pond.*

moon·scape (**mo͞on′**skāp′) *n.* A view or picture of the surface of the moon.

moon·shine (**mo͞on′**shīn′) *n.* **1.** Moonlight. **2.** *Informal* Foolish talk or thinking; nonsense. **3.** Whiskey that is distilled illegally. ❖ *intr.v.* **moon·shined, moon·shin·ing, moon·shines** To distill and sell liquor illegally.

moon·stone (**mo͞on′**stōn′) *n.* Any of several pearly translucent forms of feldspar that are valued as gemstones.

moon·struck (**mo͞on′**strŭk′) *adj.* **1.** Dazed with romantic love; infatuated. **2.** Mentally deranged; crazed.

moon·y (**mo͞o′**nē) *adj.* **moon·i·er, moon·i·est 1.** Relating to or suggestive of the moon or moonlight: *a moony luster.* **2.** Given to dreamy moods; absent-minded.

moor[1] (mo͝or) *v.* **moored, moor·ing, moors** *—tr.* To secure (a vessel or aircraft, for example) by means of cables, lines, or anchors. *—intr.* **1.** To secure a vessel or aircraft with lines or anchors: *We moored out in the bay.* **2.** To be secured with lines or anchors: *The sloop moored alongside the wharf.* [From Middle English *moren*, to take root.]

moor[2] (mo͝or) *n.* A broad stretch of open land, often with boggy areas and patches of low shrubs. [From Old English *mōr*.]

Moor (mo͝or) *n.* **1.** A member of a traditionally Muslim people now living in northwest Africa. **2.** One of the Muslims who invaded Spain in the 8th century and established a civilization that lasted until the late 15th century.

Moore (mo͝or *or* môr), **Marianne Craig** 1887–1972. American poet whose works are characterized by wit, irony, and unconventional meter.

moor·ing (**mo͝or′**ĭng) *n.* **1.** The act or an instance of securing a vessel or aircraft. **2.** A place at which a vessel or aircraft may be secured. **3.** often **moorings** Equipment, such as anchors, chains, or lines, for securing a vessel or aircraft: *In the storm the boat pulled free from its moorings.*

Moor·ish (**mo͝or′**ĭsh) *adj.* Relating to the Moors or their culture.

moose (mo͞os) *n., pl.* **moose** A large deer of northern regions, having a large head, high shoulders, and broad antlers in the male.

❑ *These sound alike:* **moose, mousse** (dessert).

moot (mo͞ot) *adj.* **1.** Of no practical importance; irrelevant: *Now that he's dead, the question of whether to punish him is moot.* **2.** Open to debate; arguable: *a discussion of a moot and difficult point.*

mop (mŏp) *n.* **1.** An implement for washing, dusting, or drying floors, consisting of a sponge or a bundle of yarn or rags attached to a long handle. **2.** A loosely tangled bunch or mass: *a mop of hair.* ❖ *tr.v.* **mopped, mop·ping, mops** To wash or wipe with or as if with a mop: *mopped the hallway; mopped her forehead with a towel.* ◆ **mop up 1.** To clear (an area) of remaining enemy troops after a victory. **2.** *Informal* To finish a nearly completed task. [Probably from Middle English *mappel*, ultimately from Latin *mappa*, towel, cloth.]

mope (mōp) *intr.v.* **moped, mop·ing, mopes 1.** To be gloomy or quietly resentful; sulk. **2.** To move or pass time aimlessly; dawdle: *moped around the house all day.* ❖ *n.* **1.** A person who often has gloomy moods. **2.** **mopes** Low spirits.

mo·ped (**mō′**pĕd′) *n.* A lightweight motorized bicycle that can be pedaled.

mop·pet (**mŏp′**ĭt) *n.* A young child.

mo·raine (mə-**rān′**) *n.* A mass of boulders, stones, and

ă	pat	ôr	core
ā	pay	oi	boy
âr	care	ou	out
ä	father	o͝o	took
ĕ	pet	o͝or	lure
ē	be	o͞o	boot
ĭ	pit	ŭ	cut
ī	bite	ûr	urge
îr	pier	th	thin
ŏ	pot	*th*	this
ō	toe	zh	vision
ô	paw	ə	about

other material that has been carried and deposited by a glacier.

mor·al (môr′əl) *adj.* **1.** Relating to or concerned with the judgment of right or wrong of human action and character: *moral principles.* **2.** Teaching or showing good, correct, or honorable behavior: *a moral lesson.* **3.** Being or acting in accord with standards of what is good, just, or honorable: *a moral person; a moral way of living.* **4.** Arising from the inner sense of right and wrong: *She felt she had a moral duty to help.* **5.** Psychological rather than physical or concrete: *a moral victory; gave me some moral support.* **6.** Likely but not proved: *a moral certainty.* ❖ *n.* **1.** The lesson or principle taught by a fable, story, or event. **2. morals** Rules of good or correct conduct. [From Middle English, from Latin *mōrālis*, from *mōs*, custom.]

mo·rale (mə-răl′) *n.* The state of a person's or group's spirits, as shown in confidence, cheerfulness, and willingness to work toward a goal: *The pep talk boosted our morale, and we went on to win the game.*

mor·al·ist (môr′ə-lĭst) *n.* **1.** A person who is concerned with moral principles and questions. **2.** A person who follows a system of moral principles. **3.** A person who is unduly concerned with the morals of others.

mor·al·is·tic (môr′ə-lĭs′tĭk) *adj.* **1.** Concerned with morality. **2.** Marked by a narrow-minded morality. **—mor′al·is′ti·cal·ly** *adv.*

mo·ral·i·ty (mə-răl′ĭ-tē) *n., pl.* **mo·ral·i·ties 1.** The quality of being in conformity with standards of good, right, or honorable behavior: *the questionable morality of his actions.* **2.** A set of ideas about what is right and wrong in human conduct and relationships: *religious morality.*

mor·al·ize (môr′ə-līz′) *v.* **mor·al·ized, mor·al·iz·ing, mor·al·iz·es** *—intr.* To think about or express moral judgments. *—tr.* To interpret or explain the moral meaning of; draw a moral from.

mor·al·ly (môr′ə-lē) *adv.* **1.** According to moral principles: *Is it morally right to tell a lie to keep from hurting someone's feelings?* **2.** According to accepted rules of conduct; virtuously: *live one's life morally.* **3.** According to strong conviction or likelihood: *I am morally certain that she's wrong.*

mo·rass (mə-răs′ *or* mô-răs′) *n.* **1.** An area of low soggy ground; a bog or marsh. **2.** A condition or situation that is overwhelming or confusing: *We are floundering in a morass of details.* [From Dutch *moeras*, From Old French *marois*, probably of Germanic origin.]

mor·a·to·ri·um (môr′ə-tôr′ē-əm) *n., pl.* **mor·a·to·ri·ums** or **mor·a·to·ri·a** (môr′ə-tôr′ē-ə) **1.** A stopping of some activity for the time being; a temporary ban or pause: *a moratorium on whaling.* **2.** A period of delay granted before a debt must be paid.

Mo·ra·vi·a (mə-rā′vē-ə) A region of central and eastern Czech Republic. It was settled by a Slavic people at the end of the sixth century and became part of Czechoslovakia in 1918.

Mo·ra·vi·an (mə-rā′vē-ən) *n.* A native or inhabitant of Moravia. **—Mo·ra′vi·an** *adj.*

mo·ray (môr′ā *or* mə-rā′) *n.* Any of numerous eels that have sharp teeth, are often brightly colored, and are found mostly in tropical seas. [From Portuguese *moréia*, from Greek *mūraina*.]

mor·bid (môr′bĭd) *adj.* **1.** Relating to, caused by, or having to do with disease: *morbid changes in body tissues.* **2.** Preoccupied with death, decay, or other unwholesome matters; gruesome: *a morbid imagination.* [From Latin *morbidus*, diseased, from *morbus*, disease.] **—mor′bid·ly** *adv.* **—mor′bid·ness** *n.*

mor·bid·i·ty (môr-bĭd′ĭ-tē) *n., pl.* **mor·bid·i·ties 1.** The condition of being morbid. **2.** The rate of occurrence of a disease.

mor·dant (môr′dnt) *adj.* Bitter; sarcastic: *mordant remarks.* **—mor′dan·cy** *n.* **—mor′dant·ly** *adv.*

more (môr) *adj.* Comparative of **many, much. 1a.** Greater in number: *More people came to the show tonight than ever before.* **b.** Greater in size, amount, extent, or degree: *He does more work than anybody else.* **2.** Additional; extra: *I need more time to finish making dinner.* ❖ *n.* A greater or additional quantity, number, degree, or amount: *More of our textbooks have arrived in the store.* ❖ *pron. (used with a plural verb)* A greater number of people or things: *I thought I had found all the empty bottles, but there were more in the basement.* ❖ *adv.* Comparative of **much. 1a.** To or in a greater extent or degree: *After seeing the movie again, we liked it even more.* **b.** Used to form the comparative of many adjectives and adverbs: *more difficult; more intelligently.* **2.** In addition; again: *I telephoned twice more, but got no answer.* ◆ **more and more** To a steadily increasing extent or degree: *got more and more annoyed at the noise.* **more or less 1.** About; approximately: *The trip takes six hours, more or less.* **2.** To an undetermined degree: *We were more or less in agreement.*

More (môr), Sir **Thomas** 1477?–1535. English politician and scholar who was imprisoned and beheaded for treason. His works include the essay *Utopia* (1516).

mo·rel (mə-rĕl′ *or* mô-rĕl′) *n.* Any of various edible mushrooms having a cap with irregular pits and ridges.

more·o·ver (môr-ō′vər *or* môr′ō′vər) *adv.* Beyond what has been said; besides: *We are, moreover, delighted to report that progress has been made.*

mo·res (môr′āz′ *or* môr′ēz) *pl.n.* **1.** The accepted customs and rules of behavior of a particular social group. **2.** Attitudes about proper behavior; moral conventions: *the manners and mores of suburban life.*

Mor·gan (môr′gən), **John Pierpont** 1837–1913. American financier and philanthropist noted for his control of major railroads and his consolidation of the US Steel Corporation (1901).

Morgan le Fay (lə fā′) *n.* In the legend of King Arthur, the sorceress who is Arthur's sister and enemy.

morgue (môrg) *n.* A place where the bodies of people found dead are kept until identified or claimed. [From French, from *la Morgue*, building in Paris used as a morgue.]

mor·i·bund (môr′ə-bŭnd′) *adj.* **1.** At the point of death; about to die. **2.** At the point of dying out or becoming obsolete: *a moribund tradition.*

Mor·mon (môr′mən) *n.* **1.** A member of the Mormon Church. **2.** In the Mormon Church, an ancient prophet believed to have composed a sacred history of the Americas, which was translated and published by Joseph Smith as the Book of Mormon in 1830. ❖ *adj.* Relating to the Mormons or their church. **—Mor′mon·ism** *n.*

Mormon Church *n.* A Christian church founded by Joseph Smith in 1830, having doctrines based chiefly on the Bible and the Book of Mormon. The church's headquarters have been in Salt Lake City, Utah, since 1847.

morn (môrn) *n.* The morning.

❑ *These sound alike:* **morn, mourn** (grieve).

morn·ing (môr′nĭng) *n.* **1.** The early part of the day, from midnight to noon or from sunrise to noon. **2.** The time of sunrise; dawn. **3.** The first or early part; the beginning: *the morning of a new nation.*

❑ *These sound alike:* **morning, mourning** (grieving).

morning glory *n.* Any of numerous twining vines having showy trumpet-shaped flowers that generally open in the morning and fade by evening.

morning star *n.* A planet, especially Venus, that shines brightly in the eastern sky before sunrise.

Mo·ro (môr′ō) *n., pl.* **Moro** or **Mo·ros** A member of any of the mostly Muslim Malay peoples of the southern Philippines.

mo·roc·co (mə-rŏk′ō) *n., pl.* **mo·roc·cos** A soft fine

moon

waxing crescent moon *(top)* and full moon *(bottom)*

Moorish

Great Mosque, Córdoba, Spain

moped

morel

Toni Morrison

A	B	C	D
.-	-...	-.-.	-..
E	F	G	H
.	..-.	--.	....
I	J	K	L
..	.---	-.-	.-..
M	N	O	P
--	-.	---	.--.
Q	R	S	T
--.-	.-.	...	-
U	V	W	X
..-	...-	.--	-..-
Y	Z		
-.--	--..		

Morse code
international Morse code

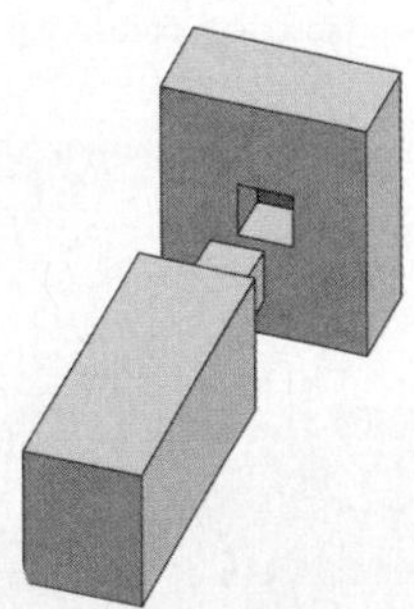

mortise

ă	pat	ôr	core
ā	pay	oi	boy
âr	care	ou	out
ä	father	o͝o	took
ĕ	pet	o͝or	lure
ē	be	o͞o	boot
ĭ	pit	ŭ	cut
ī	bite	ûr	urge
îr	pier	th	thin
ŏ	pot	*th*	this
ō	toe	zh	vision
ô	paw	ə	about

leather of goatskin, made originally in Morocco and used chiefly for binding books.

Mo·roc·co (mə-**rŏk′**ō) A country of northwest Africa on the Mediterranean Sea and the Atlantic Ocean. Rabat is the capital and Casablanca the largest city.

mo·ron (**môr′**ŏn′) *n.* A person who is considered stupid or foolish. [From Greek *mōron*, from *mōros*, stupid, foolish.] **—mo·ron′ic** (mə-**rŏn′**ĭk *or* mô-**rŏn′**ĭk) *adj.*

Mo·ro·ni (mə-**rō′**nē) The capital of the Comoros, in the Indian Ocean west of Madagascar.

mo·rose (mə-**rōs′** *or* mô-**rōs′**) *adj.* Ill-humored; gloomy. **—mo·rose′ly** *adv.* **—mo·rose′ness** *n.*

morph (môrf) *v.* **morphed, morph·ing, morphs** *—tr.* To transform (an image) by computer: *morphed the villain into a snake.* *—intr.* To be transformed: *a small computer glitch that morphed into a huge problem.*

mor·pheme (**môr′**fēm′) *n.* A unit of language that has meaning and that cannot be divided into smaller meaningful parts. For example, *fire* is a morpheme; the plural suffix *-s* in *fires* is also a morpheme.

Mor·phe·us (**môr′**fē-əs) *n.* In Greek mythology, the god of dreams.

mor·phine (**môr′**fēn′) *n.* An addictive narcotic drug extracted from opium and used in medicine as an anesthetic and sedative.

mor·phol·o·gy (môr-**fŏl′**ə-jē) *n., pl.* **mor·phol·o·gies 1.** The branch of biology that deals with the form and structure of living organisms. **2.** The form and structure of an organism. **3.** In linguistics, the study of the structure and form of words, including inflections and derivations. **—mor′pho·log′i·cal, mor′pho·log′ic** *adj.*

Mor·ris (**môr′**ĭs), **Gouverneur** 1752–1816. American political leader who helped produce the final draft of the US Constitution (1787).

Mor·ris·on (**môr′**ĭ-sən), **Toni** Born 1931. American writer whose novels, such as *Beloved* (1987), examine the experiences of African Americans.

Mor·ris·town (**môr′**ĭs-toun′) A town of northern New Jersey. The Continental Army encamped here during the winters of 1776–1777 and 1779–1780.

mor·row (**môr′**ō) *n.* **1.** The following day; the next day: *They set out on the morrow.* **2.** *Archaic* The morning.

Morse (môrs), **Samuel Finley Breese** 1791–1872. American inventor who developed a telegraphic code, which became known as Morse code.

Morse code *n.* Either of two codes used for sending messages in which letters of the alphabet and numbers are represented by combinations of short and long sounds or beams of light, known as dots and dashes. [After Samuel Finley Breese *Morse.*]

mor·sel (**môr′**səl) *n.* **1.** A small piece of food: *ate just a few morsels.* **2.** A small amount; a piece: *a morsel of gossip.*

mor·tal (**môr′**tl) *adj.* **1.** Subject to death: *All humans are mortal.* **2.** Causing or accompanying death: *a mortal wound.* **3.** Breaking a basic religious moral law and therefore seen as bringing eternal damnation: *a mortal sin.* **4.** Fought to the death: *mortal battles.* **5.** Unrelenting; deadly: *a mortal enemy.* **6.** Extreme or severe: *in mortal fear.* ❖ *n.* A human. [From Middle English, from Latin *mortālis*, from *mors*, death.] **—mor′tal·ly** *adv.*

mor·tal·i·ty (môr-**tăl′**ĭ-tē) *n., pl.* **mor·tal·i·ties 1.** The condition of being subject to death. **2.** Death, especially of large numbers: *a war accompanied by widespread civilian mortality.* **3.** The proportion of a given group of people that dies in a given period of time; death rate.

mor·tar (**môr′**tər) *n.* **1.** A bowl used to hold substances while they are crushed or ground with a pestle. **2.** A machine in which substances are ground or crushed. **3.** A building material made of sand, water, lime, and often cement, used to hold together bricks, stones, or building blocks. **4.** A muzzle-loading cannon used to fire shells in a high arc. ❖ *tr.v.* **mor·tared, mor·tar·ing, mor·tars 1.** To plaster or join with mortar. **2.** To bombard with mortar shells.

mor·tar·board (**môr′**tər-bôrd′) *n.* **1.** A square board with a handle, used for holding and carrying mortar. **2.** An academic cap with a flat square top and a tassel, worn upon graduation, for example.

mort·gage (**môr′**gĭj) *n.* **1.** A loan for the purchase of real property, such as a house, with the property itself serving as the security for the lender: *took out a mortgage from the bank.* **2.** A written agreement specifying the terms of such a loan. **3.** The money that the borrower owes to the holder of a mortgage: *a family that couldn't afford their mortgage.* ❖ *tr.v.* **mort·gaged, mort·gag·ing, mort·gag·es 1.** To pledge (property) as security for the payment of a debt. **2.** To put in jeopardy for some immediate benefit; risk: *He mortgaged his future by borrowing lots of money.* [From Middle English *morgage*, from Old French : *mort*, dead + *gage*, pledge.]

mort·ga·gee (môr′gĭ-**jē′**) *n.* The holder of a mortgage, usually a bank or other lender.

mort·ga·gor (môr′gĭ-**jôr′** *or* **môr′**gĭ-jər) also **mort·gag·er** (**môr′**gĭ-jər) *n.* A person who mortgages his or her property.

mor·tice (**môr′**tĭs) *n. & v.* Variant of **mortise.**

mor·ti·cian (môr-**tĭsh′**ən) *n.* A funeral director; an undertaker.

mor·ti·fi·ca·tion (môr′tə-fĭ-**kā′**shən) *n.* **1.** Humiliation; embarrassment. **2.** The act or practice of mortifying one's body or desires. **3.** Death or decay of a part of a living body; gangrene.

mor·ti·fy (**môr′**tə-fī′) *v.* **mor·ti·fied, mor·ti·fy·ing, mor·ti·fies** *—tr.* **1.** To cause to feel shame or embarrassment; humiliate: *I was mortified by my cousin's rudeness at the ceremony.* **2.** To discipline (one's body or physical desires) through self-denial or self-punishment, especially for religious reasons. *—intr.* To become gangrenous. [From Middle English *mortifien*, to deaden, subdue, from Latin *mortificāre*, to kill, from *mors*, death.] **—mor′ti·fi′er** *n.*

mor·tise also **mor·tice** (**môr′**tĭs) *n.* A rectangular hole in a piece of wood or other material, prepared to receive a tenon of another piece, so as to form a joint. ❖ *tr.v.* **mor·tised, mor·tis·ing, mor·tis·es** also **mor·ticed, mor·tic·ing, mor·tic·es 1.** To cut a mortise in. **2.** To join (two pieces) by means of a mortise and tenon.

mor·tu·ar·y (**môr′**cho͞o-ĕr′ē) *n., pl.* **mor·tu·ar·ies** A place where dead bodies are prepared or kept before burial or cremation.

mos. *abbr.* An abbreviation of months.

mo·sa·ic (mō-**zā′**ĭk) *n.* **1.** A picture or design made on a surface by fitting and cementing together small colored pieces, as of tile, glass, or stone. **2.** The art or process of making such pictures or designs. **3.** Something that resembles a mosaic: *a mosaic of impressions.* **4.** A viral disease of certain plants, such as tobacco or tomatoes, that causes the leaves to become spotted or wrinkled. **5.** An organism or a part having adjacent cells or tissues of different genetic types.

Mo·sa·ic (mō-**zā′**ĭk) *adj.* Relating to Moses or to the laws said to have been written by him.

mos·co·vi·um (mŏ-**skō′**vē-əm) *n. Symbol* **Mc** A radioactive element that has been artificially produced by scientists. Atomic number 115. See **Periodic Table.**

Mos·cow (**mŏs′**kou *or* **mŏs′**kō) The capital of Russia, in the western part of the country.

Mos·es (**mō′**zĭz *or* **mō′**zĭs) In the Bible, the Hebrew prophet and lawgiver who led the Israelites out of Egypt.

mo·sey (**mō′**zē) *intr.v.* **mo·seyed, mo·sey·ing, mo·seys** *Informal* **1.** To move slowly or leisurely; stroll. **2.** To get going; leave.

mosh (mŏsh) *intr.v.* **moshed, mosh·ing, mosh·es** To

knock against others intentionally while dancing at a rock concert.

Mos·lem (**mŏz′**ləm *or* **mŏs′**ləm) *n.* Variant of **Muslim.**

mosque (mŏsk) *n.* A building used as a place of Muslim worship. [From French *mosquée,* from Arabic *masjid.*]

mos·qui·to (mə-**skē′**tō) *n., pl.* **mos·qui·toes** or **mos·qui·tos** Any of numerous winged insects whose females bite and suck blood from humans and other animals. Some kinds transmit diseases such as malaria and yellow fever. [From Spanish and Portuguese, from Latin *musca,* fly.] —SEE NOTE.

moss (môs) *n.* **1.** Any of various small nonvascular plants that bear spores in a capsule and often form a dense growth on damp ground, rocks, or tree trunks. **2.** Any of several similar but unrelated plants, such as Spanish moss. [From Old English *mos,* bog.]

moss·y (**mô′**sē) *adj.* **moss·i·er, moss·i·est** Covered with or resembling moss.

most (mōst) *adj.* Superlative of **many, much. 1a.** Greatest in number: *Who won the most votes?* **b.** Largest in amount, size, or degree: *the most money.* **2.** In the greatest number of instances: *Most fish have fins.* ❖ *n.* The greatest amount or degree: *She has the most to gain.* ❖ *pron. (used with a singular or plural verb)* The greatest part or number: *Most of the apples have been picked.* ❖ *adv.* Superlative of **more, much. 1.** In the highest degree, quantity, or extent. Used with many adjectives and adverbs to form the superlative: *most honest; most impatiently.* **2.** Very: *a most impressive piece of work.* **3.** *Informal* Almost; just about: *Most everybody's here already.* ◆ **at most** or **at the most** At the maximum: *The professor spoke for ten minutes at most. We ran for two miles at the most.*

–most *suff.* A suffix that means most: *innermost.*

most·ly (**mōst′**lē) *adv.* **1.** For the most part; mainly: *The strawberry plants are mostly thriving.* **2.** Generally; usually: *We mostly try to get to bed before midnight.*

Mo·sul (mō-**so͞ol′** *or* **mō′**səl) A city of northern Iraq on the Tigris River north-northwest of Baghdad. It was an important center on the historical caravan route across northern Mesopotamia.

mote (mōt) *n.* A speck, especially of dust: *Motes drifted in the sunlight near the window.*
❑ *These sound alike:* **mote, moat** (ditch).

mo·tel (mō-**tĕl′**) *n.* A hotel for motorists, usually with rooms that open directly on a parking area. [Blend of *motor* and *hotel.*]

moth (môth) *n., pl.* **moths** (mô*th*z *or* môths) Any of numerous insects that are closely related to the butterflies but usually fly at night and have a stouter body and feathery or slender antennae. [From Old English *motthe.*]

moth·ball (**môth′**bôl′) *n.* **1.** A marble-sized ball of naphthalene, stored with clothing to repel clothes moths. **2. mothballs** A condition of long-term storage with protection against the weather: *After decades of use, the ocean liner was put into mothballs.* ❖ *tr.v.* **moth·balled, moth·ball·ing, moth·balls** To put into protective storage: *The experimental airplane was mothballed after its funding was canceled.*

moth-eat·en (**môth′**ēt′n) *adj.* **1.** Eaten away by the larvae of clothes moths: *a moth-eaten bedspread.* **2.** Old and overused: *a moth-eaten saying.*

moth·er (**mŭ*th*′**ər) *n.* **1.** A female parent or guardian of a child. **2.** A female parent of an animal. **3.** A mother superior. **4.** A woman who creates, starts, or founds something: *Susan B. Anthony was one of the mothers of the women's suffrage movement.* **5.** A source or cause: *Necessity is the mother of invention.* ❖ *adj.* **1.** Being the source or origin: *the mother church.* **2.** Native: *one's mother country.* ❖ *tr.v.* **moth·ered, moth·er·ing, moth·ers 1.** To give birth to: *She mothered two children.* **2.** To watch over or nourish: *The teacher mothered her students.* [From Old English *mōdor.*]

moth·er·board (**mŭ*th*′**ər-bôrd′) *n.* The main circuit board of a computer, usually containing the central processing unit, the main system memory, and other essential components.

Mother Goose *n.* The imaginary author of *Mother Goose's Tales,* a collection of English nursery rhymes published in the 1700s.

moth·er·hood (**mŭ*th*′**ər-ho͝od′) *n.* The condition of being a mother.

moth·er-in-law (**mŭ*th*′**ər-ĭn-lô′) *n., pl.* **moth·ers-in-law** The mother of one's wife or husband.

moth·er·land (**mŭ*th*′**ər-lănd′) *n.* **1.** A person's native land; the country of one's birth. **2.** The land of one's ancestors.

moth·er·less (**mŭ*th*′**ər-ləs′) *adj.* Having no living or known mother.

mother lode *n.* **1.** The main vein of ore in a region: *After digging for weeks, the miners finally hit the mother lode.* **2.** An abundant or rich source.

moth·er·ly (**mŭ*th*′**ər-lē) *adj.* Relating to, like, or appropriate to a mother: *motherly affection.* **—moth′er·li·ness** *n.*

moth·er-of-pearl (mŭ*th*′ər-əv-**pûrl′**) *n.* The hard, smooth, pearly layer on the inside of certain oyster shells and other seashells, used to make buttons and jewelry.

Moth·er's Day (**mŭ*th*′**ərz) *n.* The second Sunday in May, celebrated as a holiday in honor of mothers.

mother superior *n., pl.* **mothers superior** or **mother superiors** A woman in charge of a religious community of women.

mother tongue *n.* **1.** One's native language. **2.** A language from which another language develops.

mother wit *n.* Natural good judgment that does not come from schooling; common sense.

mo·tif (mō-**tēf′**) *n.* **1.** An idea or symbol that recurs in a literary or artistic work. **2.** A short passage or theme that is repeated and varied in a musical composition. **3.** A repeated figure or design in architecture or decoration: *a necktie with a floral motif.* [From French, from Old French, motive.]

mo·tile (**mōt′**l *or* **mō′**tīl′) *adj.* Moving or able to move by itself; capable of spontaneous movement. **—mo·til′i·ty** (mō-**tĭl′**ĭ-tē) *n.*

mo·tion (**mō′**shən) *n.* **1a.** The process of moving; change of position. **b.** An act of moving; a movement: *the darting motions of dragonflies.* **2.** The ability to move: *The motion in his arm returned after physical therapy.* **3.** Operation; activity: *put the engine in motion.* **4.** A formal application or request: *No state by its own mere motion can get out of the Union.* **5.** A proposal put to a vote in a group following parliamentary procedure: *I moved to adjourn the meeting, and the motion passed by voice vote.* ❖ *v.* **mo·tioned, mo·tion·ing, mo·tions** *—tr.* To direct by a wave of the hand or another gesture; to signal: *The driver stopped and motioned us to cross. —intr.* To make a gesture expressing one's wishes: *motioned for us to enter the room.* ◆ **go through the motions** To do something in a way that shows lack of purpose or interest.

mo·tion·less (**mō′**shən-lĭs) *adj.* Not moving. **—mo′tion·less·ly** *adv.*

motion picture *n.* **1.** A movie. **2. motion pictures** The movie industry.

motion sickness *n.* Nausea and dizziness caused by motion, as from traveling in a car or ship.

mo·ti·vate (**mō′**tə-vāt′) *tr.v.* **mo·ti·vat·ed, mo·ti·vat·ing, mo·ti·vates** To provide with an incentive; move to action: *Time was running out, which motivated us to play even harder.*

mo·ti·va·tion (mō′tə-**vā′**shən) *n.* **1.** The process of pro-

mosaic

mosque
Blue Mosque, Istanbul, Turkey

WORD HISTORY

mosquito How is a **mosquito** like a **musket**? Both words come from the Latin noun *musca,* "a fly" (the insect). The Latin word became *mosca* in Spanish. By adding the diminutive ending *-ito* to *mosca,* Spanish formed the word *mosquito,* meaning "little fly," which became the term for the bothersome insect we all love to hate. Latin *musca* became *mosca* in Italian also. Italian formed a diminutive noun *moschetto* (literally "little fly"), meaning "the bolt or dart fired from a catapult." Later, Italian used that word to mean "a small gun that fires lead balls" (that is, a *musket*). French borrowed this word, changing the spelling to *mousquet,* and this was borrowed into English as *musket.*

motorcycle

Lucretia Mott

mottled
immature red-shouldered hawk

ă	pat	ôr	core
ā	pay	oi	boy
âr	care	ou	out
ä	father	ŏŏ	took
ĕ	pet	ŏŏr	lure
ē	be	ōō	boot
ĭ	pit	ŭ	cut
ī	bite	ûr	urge
îr	pier	th	thin
ŏ	pot	*th*	this
ō	toe	zh	vision
ô	paw	ə	about

viding motives: *studied the motivation of people who run for public office.* **2.** The condition of being motivated, especially to perform well: *These students have a high level of motivation.* **3.** A motive or set of motives; an incentive.

mo·tive (mō′tĭv) *n.* An emotion, need, or purpose that causes a person to act in a certain way: *Our motive in writing the book was to make people aware of the issue.* ❖ *adj.* Causing or able to cause motion: *motive power supplied by a jet engine.* [From Middle English *motif,* from Late Latin *mōtīvus,* of motion, from Latin *movēre,* to move.]

mot·ley (mŏt′lē) *adj.* **1.** Made up of an odd assortment of different types: *a motley team with players of all different abilities.* **2.** Made up of many different colors: *the motley suit of a clown.* ❖ *n., pl.* **mot·leys** A costume of many colors worn by a clown or jester. [From Middle English *motle,* probably from *mot,* speck.]

mo·tor (mō′tər) *n.* **1.** A device that changes electric energy into mechanical energy. **2.** A device that produces mechanical energy from a fuel; an engine. **3.** Something, such as a machine or engine, that produces or imparts motion: *the motor of a clock.* ❖ *adj.* **1.** Propelled by an engine or motor: *a motor yacht.* **2.** Causing or producing motion: *motor power.* **3.** Relating to or intended for an engine or motor: *motor oil.* **4.** Carrying impulses from the central nervous system to the muscles: *motor nerves.* **5.** Relating to or involving muscles and their movement: *a motor reflex.* ❖ *intr.v.* **mo·tored, mo·tor·ing, mo·tors** To drive or travel in a motor vehicle. [From Middle English *motour,* one who causes motion (that is, God), from Latin *movēre,* to move.]

mo·tor·bike (mō′tər-bīk′) *n.* **1.** A lightweight motorcycle. **2.** A pedal bicycle that has an attached motor.

mo·tor·boat (mō′tər-bōt′) *n.* A boat powered by an internal-combustion engine.

mo·tor·cade (mō′tər-kād′) *n.* A procession of motor vehicles.

mo·tor·car (mō′tər-kär′) *n.* An automobile.

mo·tor·cy·cle (mō′tər-sī′kəl) *n.* A vehicle with two wheels, similar to a bicycle but larger and heavier, propelled by an internal-combustion engine. ❖ *intr.v.* **mo·tor·cy·cled, mo·tor·cy·cling, mo·tor·cy·cles** To ride a motorcycle. **—mo′tor·cy′clist** *n.*

motor home *n.* A large motor vehicle with facilities for cooking and sleeping, used as living quarters for recreational travel.

mo·tor·ist (mō′tər-ĭst) *n.* A person who drives or rides in an automobile.

mo·tor·ize (mō′tə-rīz′) *tr.v.* **mo·tor·ized, mo·tor·iz·ing, mo·tor·iz·es 1.** To equip with a motor or motors. **2.** To supply with motor-driven vehicles.

motor scooter *n.* A small, low-powered motor vehicle similar to a motorcycle but with smaller wheels, a chairlike seat, and a floorboard for the feet to rest on.

motor vehicle *n.* A self-propelled vehicle that travels on wheels but does not run on rails.

Mott (mŏt), **Lucretia Coffin** 1793–1880. American feminist and abolitionist who with Elizabeth Cady Stanton called the first convention for women's rights, held at Seneca Falls, New York (1848).

mot·tle (mŏt′l) *tr.v.* **mot·tled, mot·tling, mot·tles** To cover (a surface) with spots or streaks of different colors: *Her arms were lightly mottled with freckles.*

mot·tled (mŏt′ld) *adj.* Spotted or streaked with different colors: *a bird with mottled plumage.*

mot·to (mŏt′ō) *n., pl.* **mot·toes** or **mot·tos 1.** A phrase or statement expressing a principle, goal, or ideal: *"Don't tread on me" was the motto on the flag of the Continental Navy during the American Revolution.* **2.** A brief expression of a guiding principle; a slogan: *His motto has always been "He who hesitates is lost."* [From Italian.]

mound (mound) *n.* **1.** A pile of earth or rocks heaped up, as for protection or concealment: *the mound marking a woodchuck's hole; a burial mound.* **2.** A naturally formed area of high ground, as a small hill. **3.** A pile or mass of something: *mounds of mashed potatoes.* See Synonyms at **heap. 4.** The raised pitcher's area in the middle of a baseball diamond.

mount[1] (mount) *v.* **mount·ed, mount·ing, mounts** *—tr.* **1.** To climb; ascend: *mounted the stairs.* **2a.** To get up on: *mount a bicycle.* **b.** To provide with a riding horse. **3.** To plan and start to carry out: *mounted a campaign for literacy.* **4.** To provide (a theatrical performance) with scenery and costumes; stage. **5a.** To set in a raised position: *mounted the weathervane on the roof.* **b.** To set (guns) in position for firing. **c.** To fix securely to a support: *mount an engine in a car.* **d.** To place in a secure position for display or study: *mount a specimen on a microscope slide.* **6.** To post (a guard): *mount sentries around the encampment. —intr.* **1.** To go upward; rise: *We watched the airplane mount into the sky.* **2.** To get up on something, such as a horse. **3.** To increase; grow higher: *Expenses are mounting quickly.* ❖ *n.* **1.** A horse or another animal for riding. **2.** A frame or structure for holding or supporting something: *the mounts of a telescope.* [From Middle English *mounten,* from Old French *monter,* from Latin *mōns,* mountain.]

mount[2] (mount) *n.* A mountain. [From Old English *munt,* from Latin *mōns.*]

Mount For the names of actual mountains, see the specific proper name; for example, **Everest, Mount.**

moun·tain (moun′tən) *n.* **1.** A raised portion of the earth's surface, generally massive and rising to a great height, having more or less steep sides. **2.** A large heap or quantity: *a mountain of paperwork.* ◆ **make a mountain out of a molehill** To give too much weight or importance to a minor problem. [From Middle English *mountaine,* from Latin *montānus,* of a mountain, from *mōns,* mountain.]

mountain bike *n.* A bicycle with wide tires and horizontal handlebars, often used for cycling on unpaved trails or rugged areas. **—mountain biking** *n.*

moun·tain·eer (moun′tə-nîr′) *n.* **1.** A person who lives in a mountainous area. **2.** A person who climbs mountains for sport. ❖ *intr.v.* **moun·tain·eered, moun·tain·eer·ing, moun·tain·eers** To climb mountains for sport.

mountain goat *n.* A mammal of the northern Rocky Mountains that resembles a goat and has short black horns and thick white hair.

mountain laurel *n.* A shrub of eastern North America having poisonous evergreen leaves and clusters of pink or white flowers.

mountain lion *n.* A cougar.

moun·tain·ous (moun′tə-nəs) *adj.* **1.** Having many mountains: *a mountainous region.* **2.** Huge; massive: *mountainous snowdrifts.*

mountain range *n.* A row or group of connected mountains.

moun·tain·side (moun′tən-sīd′) *n.* The side of a mountain.

Mountain Standard Time *n.* Standard time in the seventh time zone west of Greenwich, England, used in the Rocky Mountain States of the United States, for example.

moun·tain·top (moun′tən-tŏp′) *n.* The top of a mountain.

moun·te·bank (moun′tə-băngk′) *n.* **1.** A seller of quack medicines who attracts customers with stories or tricks. **2.** A swindler; a charlatan.

Mount·ie also **Mount·y** (moun′tē) *n., pl.* **Mount·ies** *Informal* A member of the Royal Canadian Mounted Police.

mount·ing (moun′tĭng) *n.* A supporting structure or frame; a mount: *a mounting for a gem.*

Mount Ver·non (mount vûr′nən) An estate of northeast Virginia on the Potomac River near Washington, DC. It was the home of George Washington from 1752 to 1799.

mourn (môrn) *v.* **mourned, mourn·ing, mourns** —*intr.* To feel or express sorrow, especially for a person's death; grieve. —*tr.* **1.** To grieve over (a person who has died). **2.** To feel or express regret about: *mourning his lost opportunities.* [From Old English *murnan.*] —**mourn′er** *n.*

❑ *These sound alike:* **mourn, morn** (morning).

mourn·ful (môrn′fəl) *adj.* **1.** Feeling or showing grief. **2.** Causing or suggesting grief: *the mournful wail of a foghorn.* —**mourn′ful·ly** *adv.* —**mourn′ful·ness** *n.*

mourn·ing (môr′nĭng) *n.* **1.** The expression of grief and respect for a beloved person who has died: *The flag was flown at half-mast as a sign of mourning.* **2.** The condition of a person showing grief over a death or loss: *in mourning for a friend.* **3.** Traditional signs of grief for the dead, such as black clothes. **4.** The period during which a death is mourned.

❑ *These sound alike:* **mourning, morning** (daybreak).

mourning dove *n.* A grayish-brown dove of North and Central America, having a long tail and a mournful call.

mouse (mous) *n., pl.* **mice** (mīs) **1.** Any of numerous small rodents usually having a pointed snout, rounded ears, and a long narrow tail. Some kinds live in or near human dwellings. **2.** A timid person. **3.** *pl.* **mice** or **mous·es** (mous′ĭz) An input device that is moved along a flat surface to control the movement of a cursor on a computer screen. ❖ *intr.v.* (mouz) **moused, mous·ing, mous·es** To hunt for mice. [From Old English *mūs.*]

mouse·pad (mous′păd′) *n.* A flat pad that provides a surface for using a computer mouse.

mous·er (mou′zər *or* mou′sər) *n.* An animal, especially a cat, that catches mice.

mouse·trap (mous′trăp′) *n.* A trap for catching mice.

mousse (mo͞os) *n.* **1.** A chilled dessert made from whipped cream or beaten egg whites, gelatin, and flavoring. **2.** A molded dish made from meat, fish, or shellfish and whipped cream. **3.** A styling foam for hair. [From French, from Old French, moss, foam.]

❑ *These sound alike:* **mousse, moose** (deer).

mous·tache (mŭs′tăsh′ *or* mə-**stăsh′**) *n.* Variant of **mustache.**

mous·y also **mous·ey** (mou′sē *or* mou′zē) *adj.* **mous·i·er, mous·i·est 1.** Resembling a mouse, especially in color: *mousy brown hair.* **2.** Timid and shy: *a mousy person.*

mouth (mouth) *n., pl.* **mouths** (mou*th*z) **1a.** The opening of the body through which an animal takes in food. **b.** The group of organs or structures associated with this opening, such as the teeth, lips, and tongue. **c.** The opening to a cavity or canal in an organ or organism. **2.** Excessive or impudent talk: *Watch your mouth.* **3.** A natural opening, such as the opening of a cave or canyon or the part of a river that empties into a larger body of water. **4.** An opening into a container or enclosure: *the mouth of a bottle.* ❖ *tr.v.* (mou*th*) **mouthed, mouth·ing, mouths 1.** To speak or pronounce: *mouthed phrases of encouragement.* **2.** To form (words) soundlessly: *waved and mouthed "goodbye."* **3.** To hold or move around in the mouth: *The baby was mouthing her spoon.* ◆ **down in the mouth** or **down at the mouth** Discouraged; sad. **mouth off** *Slang* To speak impudently; talk back. [From Old English *mūth.*]

mouth·ful (mouth′fo͝ol′) *n.* **1.** An amount taken into the mouth at one time: *We enjoyed every mouthful of the dessert.* **2.** An important or intelligent remark: *You just said a mouthful.* **3.** A word or phrase that is long and hard to pronounce.

mouth organ *n.* **1.** A harmonica. **2.** A panpipe.

mouth·part (mouth′pärt′) *n.* Any of the parts of the mouth of an insect or a similar animal, especially a part adapted to a specific way of feeding.

mouth·piece (mouth′pēs′) *n.* **1.** The part of a device that is in or near the mouth when the device is in use: *the mouthpiece of a telephone.* **2.** A protective piece of rubber worn over the teeth, as by a football player. **3.** *Informal* A person who expresses the viewpoint of another person or of a group.

mouth-to-mouth resuscitation (mouth′tə-mouth′) *n.* A method of providing air to a person who has stopped breathing, in which the rescuer presses his or her mouth to the mouth of the victim and blows air into the victim's lungs at regular intervals.

mouth·wash (mouth′wŏsh′) *n.* A flavored, usually antiseptic liquid used to cleanse the mouth and freshen the breath.

mov·a·ble also **move·a·ble** (mo͞o′və-bəl) *adj.* **1.** Possible to move: *a movable rock.* **2.** Changing its date from year to year: *a movable holiday such as Thanksgiving.* ❖ *n.* often **movables** Furniture or other personal possessions that can be moved.

move (mo͞ov) *v.* **moved, mov·ing, moves** —*intr.* **1.** To change in position from one place or point to another: *The speaker moved to the middle of the stage.* **2.** To follow a specified course: *The earth moves around the sun.* **3.** To change one's place of residence or business: *Our family moved here last year.* **4.** To advance; progress: *Work on the house was moving slowly.* **5.** To make a formal request or proposal: *move for a court adjournment.* **6.** To be active in a particular social setting: *She moves in the highest diplomatic circles.* **7.** To take action: *If we don't move quickly, there won't be any woods left.* —*tr.* **1.** To change the place or position of: *Let's move the desk against the wall.* **2.** To cause to go from one place to another: *The police moved the crowd away from the stadium gates.* **3.** To change (a piece) to another position on a board, as in chess. **4.** To persuade or motivate: *What moved her to switch schools?* **5.** To arouse the emotions of: *That song moved me the first time I heard it.* **6.** To propose or request in a formal way, as at a meeting: *I move that we adjourn.* **7.** To empty (the bowels). ❖ *n.* **1.** The act of moving: *He made a move to open the door.* **2.** A calculated action to achieve an end: *The opponents, in a surprise move, changed their game plan.* **3a.** An act of changing the position of a piece in a board game. **b.** A player's turn to move a piece, as in checkers: *It's your move.* ◆ **get a move on** *Informal* To get started; get going. **move in** To begin to occupy a residence or place of business. **move on** To shift one's attention or emotions to other matters, often as part of recovering from a setback or difficulty: *After he didn't make the team, he moved on and tried a different sport.* **on the move 1.** Moving about from one place to another: *The taxi driver was on the move all day.* **2.** Making progress; advancing: *This area of research is really on the move.* [From Middle English *meven*, from Latin *movēre.*]

move·a·ble (mo͞o′və-bəl) *adj. & n.* Variant of **movable.**

move·ment (mo͞ov′mənt) *n.* **1.** The act or an instance of moving: *We watched the steady movement of a boat along the horizon. She snatched the ball in one quick movement.* **2.** A change in the location of military troops, ships, or aircraft. **3.** The activities of a group of people toward a specific goal: *the civil rights movement.* **4.** A tendency or trend: *a movement toward smaller cars.* **5.** A mass migration: *the westward movement of the pioneers.* **6a.** An emptying of the bowels. **b.** The waste matter removed by this action. **7.** One of the large, often separate sections of a musical composition, such as a symphony, often contrasting in tempo, rhythm, or mood with surrounding material. **8.** A mechanical device or system that produces or transmits motion: *the movement of a watch.*

mountaineer

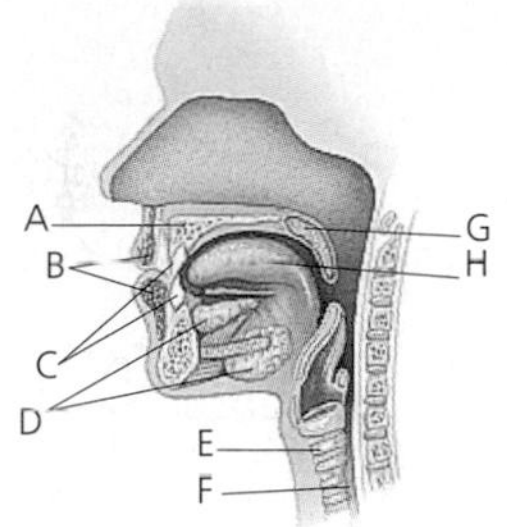

mouth
A. hard palate
B. lips
C. teeth
D. salivary glands
E. trachea
F. esophagus
G. soft palate
H. tongue

Wolfgang Amadeus Mozart

ă	pat	ôr	core
ā	pay	oi	boy
âr	care	ou	out
ä	father	o͝o	took
ĕ	pet	o͝or	lure
ē	be	o͞o	boot
ĭ	pit	ŭ	cut
ī	bite	ûr	urge
îr	pier	th	thin
ŏ	pot	*th*	this
ō	toe	zh	vision
ô	paw	ə	about

mov·er (**mo͞o′**vər) *n.* **1.** A person or thing that moves: *The railroad became a prime mover of people and products in all directions.* **2.** A person or company that is hired to move furniture and other belongings from one place to another: *The movers hoisted the piano up to the third floor.*

mov·ie (**mo͞o′**vē) *n.* **1a.** A sequence of film or video images displayed on a screen in rapid succession, creating the illusion that what is in the pictures moves as in real life. **b.** A story told in such pictures: *a movie about alien space invaders.* **2.** A showing of a movie: *He laughed during the movie. She went to the movies last night.* **3. movies** The industry that makes movies.

mov·ing (**mo͞o′**vĭng) *adj.* **1.** Changing or capable of changing position: *the moving parts of an engine.* **2.** Relating to or involving the transfer of furniture from one location to another: *a moving van.* **3.** Involving a motor vehicle in motion: *got a ticket for a moving violation.* **4.** Affecting the emotions: *a moving love story.* **—mov′ing·ly** *adv.*

moving picture *n.* A movie.

mow¹ (mou) *n.* **1.** A pile of hay or grain, especially one stored in a barn. **2.** The part of a barn where such a pile is stored. [From Old English *mūha.*]

mow² (mō) *v.* **mowed, mowed** or **mown** (mōn), **mow·ing, mows** *—tr.* **1.** To cut down (grass or grain) with a scythe or a machine such as a lawn mower: *Mow the grass before it gets too high.* **2.** To cut the grass or grain from: *mow the lawn; mow a field. —intr.* To cut down grass or other growth. ◆ **mow down** To destroy in great numbers as if cutting down, as in battle. [From Old English *māwan.*]

mow·er (**mō′**ər) *n.* **1.** A person who mows: *The mowers went out early to the fields.* **2.** A machine that mows: *a lawn mower.*

Mo·zam·bique (mō′zəm-**bēk′**) A country of southeast Africa south of Tanzania. Maputo is the capital.

Mo·zart (**mōt′**särt), **Wolfgang Amadeus** 1756–1791. Austrian composer known for his symphonies and operas, including *The Magic Flute* (1791).

moz·za·rel·la (mŏt′sə-**rĕl′**ə) *n.* A soft white Italian cheese that is often eaten melted, as on pizza.

MP *abbr.* An abbreviation of: **1.** member of Parliament. **2.** military police. **3.** mounted police.

MP3 (ĕm′pē-**thrē′**) *n.* A computer file of a song, music, or other audio information stored in a digital format for transmission over the Internet.

mpg *abbr.* An abbreviation of miles per gallon.

mph *abbr.* An abbreviation of miles per hour.

Mr. (**mĭs′**tər) *n., pl.* **Messrs.** (**mĕs′**ərz) Mister. Used as a courtesy title before the surname or full name of a man.

MRI (ĕm′är′**ī′**) *n.* **1.** An image produced by magnetic resonance imaging. **2.** The process of making such an image, especially of part of the body: *She went in for an MRI of her back.*

mRNA *abbr.* An abbreviation of messenger RNA.

Mrs. (**mĭs′**ĭz) *n., pl.* **Mmes.** (mā-**däm′** *or* mā-**dăm′**) Used as a courtesy title before the last name or full name of a married, widowed, or divorced woman.

MRSA (**mûr′**sə) *n.* A type of bacterium that is resistant to many kinds of antibiotics and can cause severe infections of the skin and other parts of the body. [From *m(ethicillin-)r(esistant)* S(taphylococcus) a(ureus).]

ms *abbr.* An abbreviation of millisecond.

MS *abbr.* An abbreviation of: **1.** Master of Science. **2.** Mississippi. **3.** multiple sclerosis.

Ms. also **Ms** (mĭz) *n., pl.* **Mses.** also **Mses** also **Mss.** also **Mss** (**mĭz′**ĭz) Used as a courtesy title before the last name or full name of a woman or girl.

Msgr. *abbr.* An abbreviation of Monseigneur.

MST *abbr.* An abbreviation of Mountain Standard Time.

Mt The symbol for the element **meitnerium.**

MT *abbr.* An abbreviation of: **1.** megaton. **2.** metric ton. **3.** Montana.

Mt. *abbr.* An abbreviation of: **1.** mount. **2.** mountain.

mu (myo͞o *or* mo͞o) *n.* The 12th letter of the Greek alphabet, written Μ, μ. In English it is represented as *M, m.*

much (mŭch) *adj.* **more** (môr), **most** (mōst) Great in quantity, degree, or extent: *much talk and little action.* ❖ *n.* **1.** A large quantity or amount: *Did you get much done?* **2.** Something remarkable or important: *In spite of all our work, the experiment did not amount to much.* ❖ *adv.* **more, most 1.** To a large extent; greatly: *We are much impressed with the results of your research.* **2.** Just about; almost: *much the same.* ◆ **as much** The same: *I enjoyed learning about the Civil War, and I said as much to the teacher when we finished the unit.* [From Old English *mycel.*]

much as *conj.* Even though; however much: *Much as I love skating, I'd rather go to the movies.*

much less *conj.* And certainly not: *I'd hate to fail a test, much less an entire class.*

mu·ci·lage (**myo͞o′**sə-lĭj) *n.* **1.** A clear brown adhesive made from the natural gum of plants. **2.** Any of various sticky gelatinous secretions produced by certain plants, algae, and bacteria.

muck (mŭk) *n.* **1.** A moist sticky mixture, as of mud and filth. **2.** Moist animal dung; manure. **3.** Dark soil containing rotting vegetable matter.

muck·rake (**mŭk′**rāk′) *intr.v.* **muck·raked, muck·rak·ing, muck·rakes** To search for and expose corruption in public affairs. [After the *muck-raker,* in *Pilgrim's Progress* by John Bunyan, who cannot look up to heaven because he is constantly raking the muck of worldly profit.] **—muck′rak′er** *n.*

mu·cous (**myo͞o′**kəs) *adj.* **1.** Relating to or like mucus. **2.** Producing or secreting mucus.

❑ *These sound alike:* **mucous, mucus** (gland secretion).

mucous membrane *n.* Any of the membranes lining the passages of the body that open onto the outside, such as those of the digestive tract and the respiratory system. Glands and cells in the mucous membranes secrete mucus, which lubricates the membranes.

mu·cus (**myo͞o′**kəs) *n.* The sticky, slippery liquid secreted by the cells and glands of the mucous membranes. Mucus lubricates and protects the mucous membranes.

❑ *These sound alike:* **mucus, mucous** (like mucus).

mud (mŭd) *n.* **1.** Wet, sticky, soft earth. **2.** Slanderous charges: *sling mud at a political opponent.*

mud·dle (**mŭd′**l) *v.* **mud·dled, mud·dling, mud·dles** *—tr.* **1.** To confuse; befuddle: *Being sleepy can muddle your thinking.* **2.** To make a mess of; bungle: *muddle a task. —intr.* To act in a confused or aimless way: *I want to do well in school this year, not just muddle along.* ❖ *n.* A jumble; a mess: *The project turned into a big muddle.* ◆ **muddle through** To keep going in a disorganized way until reaching an acceptable outcome: *The actor muddled through the rest of the scene after forgetting his lines.*

mud·dy (**mŭd′**ē) *adj.* **mud·di·er, mud·di·est 1.** Covered or soiled with mud: *a muddy field; muddy shoes.* **2.** Cloudy or dull with or as if with mud: *a muddy creek; muddy coffee.* **3.** Confused; vague: *muddy thinking.* ❖ *tr.v.* **mud·died, mud·dy·ing, mud·dies 1.** To make soiled with mud: *He muddied his boots crossing the yard.* **2.** To make cloudy or dull with or as if with mud: *soil erosion muddies the rivers.* **3.** To confuse: *remarks that only muddied the issue.* **—mud′di·ly** *adv.* **—mud′di·ness** *n.*

mud·pup·py also **mud puppy** (**mŭd′**pŭp′ē) *n., pl.* **mud·pup·pies** also **mud puppies** Any of several North American salamanders of lakes, ponds, and streams, having prominent clusters of dark red external gills.

mud·sling·ing (**mŭd′**slĭng′ĭng) *n.* The practice of making malicious charges against an opponent, especially in a political campaign. **—mud′sling′er** *n.*

mues·li (**myo͞oz′**lē) *n.* A mixture of rolled oats, nuts, and dried fruit, often used as a breakfast cereal.

mu·ez·zin (myo͞o-**ĕz′**ĭn *or* mo͞o-**ĕz′**ĭn) *n.* A crier who calls Muslims to prayer five times a day.

muff¹ (mŭf) *tr.v.* **muffed, muff·ing, muffs 1.** To perform or handle clumsily; bungle: *She played the first song well, but muffed the second. I muffed my chance for the job.* **2.** To fail to make (a catch), as in baseball.

muff² (mŭf) *n.* A tubelike cover of fur or cloth with open ends into which the hands are put for warmth. [From Medieval Latin *muffula*, mitten, perhaps of Germanic origin.]

muf·fin (**mŭf′**ĭn) *n.* **1.** A small, usually sweetened quick bread baked in a cup-shaped container. **2.** An English muffin.

muf·fle (**mŭf′**əl) *tr.v.* **muf·fled, muf·fling, muf·fles 1.** To wrap up in order to keep warm, conceal, or protect: *I muffled myself in a thick shawl.* **2a.** To make less loud or less distinct; deaden: *Heavy snow muffled the sound of the traffic.* **b.** To wrap up or pad in order to deaden the sound of: *muffle a drum.*

muf·fler (**mŭf′**lər) *n.* **1.** A scarf worn around the neck for warmth. **2.** A device that deadens noise, especially one used on an automobile engine.

muf·ti (**mŭf′**tē) *n.* Civilian clothes worn by a person who normally wears a uniform.

mug¹ (mŭg) *n.* A large heavy drinking cup, usually having a handle and often used for hot beverages. [Perhaps of Scandinavian origin.]

mug² (mŭg) *n. Informal* A person's face. ❖ *v.* **mugged, mug·ging, mugs** —*tr. Informal* To assault with the intent of robbing. —*intr.* To make faces, especially to be funny: *Everyone at the party mugged for the camera.* [Probably from *mug*, drinking cup (possibly in allusion to mugs decorated with grotesque faces).] **—mug′ger** *n.*

mug·gy (**mŭg′**ē) *adj.* **mug·gi·er, mug·gi·est** Warm and humid with little or no breeze: *a muggy day in August.* **—mug′gi·ness** *n.*

Mu·ghal (mo͞o-**gŭl′**) or **Mo·gul** (**mō′**gəl *or* mō-**gŭl′**) *n.* **1.** A member of the Muslim military force of Central Asian origin that invaded India in 1526 and established an empire there. **2.** A member of the dynasty ruling this empire until 1858. [From Urdu *muġal*, from Persian *muġul*, from Mongolian *Moṅgol*, Mongol.] **—Mu·ghal′** *adj.*

mug·wump (**mŭg′**wŭmp′) *n.* A person who acts independently, especially in politics.

Mu·ham·mad (mo͞o-**hä′**mĭd *or* mo͞o-**hăm′**ĭd) also **Mo·ham·med** (mō-**hä′**mĭd *or* mō-**hăm′**ĭd) 570?–632. Arab prophet and founder of Islam. Muslims regard him as God's messenger through whom the Koran was revealed.

mu·lat·to (mo͞o-**lăt′**ō) *n., pl.* **mu·lat·tos** or **mu·lat·toes** *Often Offensive* A person of mixed white and black ancestry, especially one having one white and one black parent.

mul·ber·ry (**mŭl′**bĕr′ē *or* **mŭl′**bə-rē) *n.* **1.** Any of several trees having irregularly shaped leaves and sweet purplish or white fruit that resemble blackberries in shape. **2.** The fruit of such a tree.

mulch (mŭlch) *n.* A protective covering, as of shredded leaves, bark, or hay, placed around growing plants to keep the soil moist, prevent the roots from freezing, and prevent weeds from growing. ❖ *tr.v.* **mulched, mulch·ing, mulch·es** To cover with mulch. [Probably from Old English *melsc*, mellow, mild.]

mule¹ (myo͞ol) *n.* **1.** The hybrid offspring of a male donkey and a female horse, having long ears and a short mane. **2.** *Informal* A stubborn person. **3.** A spinning machine that draws and twists fibers into yarn and winds the yarn at the same time. [From Old English *mūl*, from Latin *mūlus*.]

❑ *These sound alike:* **mule¹** (animal), **mewl** (whimper), **mule²** (slipper).

mule² (myo͞ol) *n.* A backless slipper or shoe, often with a closed toe. [Ultimately from Latin *mulleus (calceus)*, reddish-purple (ceremonial shoe).]

❑ *These sound alike:* **mule²** (slipper), **mewl** (whimper), **mule¹** (animal).

mule²

mul·ish (**myo͞o′**lĭsh) *adj.* Stubborn; unyielding: *a mulish disposition.* **—mul′ish·ly** *adv.* **—mul′ish·ness** *n.*

mull¹ (mŭl) *tr.v.* **mulled, mull·ing, mulls** To heat and add sugar and spices to (wine, ale, or cider).

mull² (mŭl) *tr. & intr.v.* **mulled, mull·ing, mulls** To think about; ponder: *He mulled over the idea for days.* [Probably from Middle English *mollen*, to moisten, crumble.]

mul·lein (**mŭl′**ən) *n.* Any of various plants having thick velvety leaves and tall spikes of yellow flowers.

mullein

mul·let (**mŭl′**ĭt) *n., pl.* **mullet** or **mul·lets 1.** Any of various stout gray or red saltwater or freshwater fishes often used as food. **2.** A hairstyle in which the hair is short on the top and sides of the head and is longer in back.

Mul·ro·ney (mŭl-**rō′**nē *or* mŭl-**ro͞o′**nē), **(Martin) Brian** Born 1939. Canadian prime minister (1984–1993).

multi– *pref.* A prefix that means: **1.** Many; much: *multicolored.* **2.** More than two: *multiracial.* **3.** Many times over: *multimillionaire.*

mul·ti·cel·lu·lar (mŭl′tē-**sĕl′**yə-lər) *adj.* Having or consisting of many cells: *multicellular organisms.*

mul·ti·col·ored (**mŭl′**tĭ-kŭl′ərd) also **mul·ti·col·or** (**mŭl′**tĭ-kŭl′ər) *adj.* Having many colors.

mul·ti·cul·tur·al (mŭl′tē-**kŭl′**chər-əl) *adj.* Relating to or including many cultures.

mul·ti·cul·tur·al·ism (mŭl′tē-**kŭl′**chər-ə-lĭz′əm *or* mŭl′tī-**kŭl′**chər-ə-lĭz′əm) *n.* The belief that a society should respect all the various cultures or ethnic groups of which it is composed.

mul·ti·eth·nic (mŭl′tē-**ĕth′**nĭk) *adj.* Relating to or including many ethnic groups: *a multiethnic neighborhood.*

mul·ti·far·i·ous (mŭl′tə-**fâr′**ē-əs) *adj.* Having great variety; diverse: *the multifarious occupations in a modern economy.*

mul·ti·lat·er·al (mŭl′tĭ-**lăt′**ər-əl) *adj.* **1.** Having many sides. **2.** Involving more than two nations or parties: *a multilateral trade agreement.*

mul·ti·me·di·a (mŭl′tē-**mē′**dē-ə) *pl.n. (used with a singular verb)* The combined use of several media, such as video, music, lighting, and the Internet, especially for the purpose of education or entertainment.

mul·ti·mil·lion·aire (mŭl′tē-mĭl′yə-**nâr′**) *n.* A person whose financial assets equal at least two million dollars, pounds, or similar units in another currency.

mul·ti·na·tion·al (mŭl′tē-**năsh′**ə-nəl *or* mŭl′tē-**năsh′**nəl) *adj.* **1.** Having operations or smaller divisions in more than two countries: *a multinational corporation.* **2.** Relating to or involving more than two countries: *a multinational agreement.*

mul·ti·ple (**mŭl′**tə-pəl) *adj.* Having, relating to, or consisting of more than a single element, part, or individual: *multiple images on a screen; a plan with multiple advantages.* ❖ *n.* A number that may be divided by another number with a remainder of zero; for example, 4, 6, 8, and 12 are multiples of 2.

multiple sclerosis *n.* A disease of the central nervous system that gradually destroys the sheaths around nerve fibers, leading to weakness, loss of balance and coordination, and visual disturbances.

mul·ti·pli·cand (mŭl′tə-plĭ-**kănd′**) *n.* A number that is to be multiplied by another number.

mul·ti·pli·ca·tion (mŭl′tə-plĭ-**kā′**shən) *n.* **1.** The act or

WRITERS CHOOSE THEIR WORDS

Though it was only May it was as hot as the hot height of summer. The fields with their **multitude** of restless insects stretched far and wide.

—Eleanor Estes
Ginger Pye

mummer

Murasaki Shikibu

ă	pat	ôr	core
ā	pay	oi	boy
âr	care	ou	out
ä	father	o͝o	took
ĕ	pet	o͝or	lure
ē	be	o͞o	boot
ĭ	pit	ŭ	cut
ī	bite	ûr	urge
îr	pier	th	thin
ŏ	pot	*th*	this
ō	toe	zh	vision
ô	paw	ə	about

process of multiplying. **2.** A mathematical operation performed on a pair of numbers in order to derive a third number called a product. Multiplication can be considered to be repeated addition in which one number indicates how many times the other is to be added together. For example, 3 × 4 = 4 + 4 + 4 = 4 × 3 = 3 + 3 + 3 + 3 = 12. —SEE NOTE AT **duplex.**

multiplication sign *n.* Any of three signs (×, *, or ·) placed between a pair of numbers to indicate multiplication.

mul·ti·pli·ca·tive (**mŭl′**tə-plĭ-kā′tĭv *or* mŭl′tə-**plĭk′**ə-tĭv) *adj.* Relating to or having to do with multiplication.

mul·ti·plic·i·ty (mŭl′tə-**plĭs′**ĭ-tē) *n., pl.* **mul·ti·plic·i·ties** A great number or variety: *a multiplicity of cable channels to choose from.*

mul·ti·pli·er (**mŭl′**tə-plī′ər) *n.* **1.** The number by which another number is multiplied. **2.** An instrument or device that causes an increase of a force or current.

mul·ti·ply (**mŭl′**tə-plī′) *v.* **mul·ti·plied, mul·ti·ply·ing, mul·ti·plies** —*intr.* **1.** To increase in number or amount: *Our problems kept multiplying at each stage of the project.* **2.** To produce offspring; breed: *Coyotes are multiplying in urban neighborhoods.* **3.** To perform multiplication. —*tr.* To perform multiplication on (a pair of numbers).

mul·ti·ra·cial (**mŭl′**tē-rā′shəl) *adj.* **1.** Made up of or involving various races: *a multiracial society.* **2.** Having ancestors of various races.

mul·ti·stage (**mŭl′**tĭ-stāj′) *adj.* Designed to perform a process or operation in more than one stage: *a multistage rocket.*

mul·ti·task·ing (mŭl′tē-**tăs′**kĭng) *n.* **1.** The operation of more than one process by a central processing unit at the same time. **2.** The performance of more than one task at the same time. **—mul′ti·task′** *v.*

mul·ti·tude (**mŭl′**tĭ-to͞od′) *n.* **1.** A large number: *We face a multitude of challenges.* **2.** The common people: *the concerns of the multitude.*

mul·ti·tu·di·nous (mŭl′tĭ-**to͞od′**n-əs) *adj.* Existing in great numbers; very numerous: *the multitudinous stars of our galaxy.*

mum[1] (mŭm) *adj.* Not talking; close-mouthed; silent: *They kept mum about their plans.* [From Middle English *mom,* sound made with closed lips.]

mum[2] (mŭm) *n.* A chrysanthemum. [Short for *chrysanthemum.*]

Mum·bai (**mŭm′**bī′) The largest city of India, in the west-central part of the country on the Arabian Sea southwest of Delhi. Formerly known as Bombay, it is India's main port.

mum·ble (**mŭm′**bəl) *tr. & intr.v.* **mum·bled, mum·bling, mum·bles** To utter (something) or speak in an indistinct manner, as by lowering the voice and partially closing the mouth: *He mumbled a quick apology. I can't understand you when you mumble.* ❖ *n.* A low indistinct sound or utterance: *answered the teacher in a mumble.* [From Middle English *momelen,* from Middle Dutch *mommelen.*] **—mum′bler** *n.*

mum·ble·ty-peg (**mŭm′**bəl-tē-pĕg′ *or* **mŭm′**blē-pĕg′) *n.* A game in which the players throw a knife from various positions, with the object being to make the blade stick firmly in the ground.

mum·bo jum·bo or **mum·bo-jum·bo** (**mŭm′**bō-**jŭm′**-bō) *n., pl.* **mum·bo jum·bos** or **mum·bo-jum·bos 1.** Confusing or meaningless speech or writing; gibberish. **2.** A complicated or obscure ceremony or ritual.

mum·mer (**mŭm′**ər) *n.* **1.** A masked or costumed merrymaker at a festival. **2.** A person who acts or plays in a pantomime.

mum·mer·y (**mŭm′**ə-rē) *n., pl.* **mum·mer·ies 1.** A performance by mummers. **2.** A fake or insincere show or ceremony.

mum·mi·fy (**mŭm′**ə-fī′) *v.* **mum·mi·fied, mum·mi·fy·ing, mum·mi·fies** —*tr.* To make into a mummy by embalming or by a natural process. —*intr.* To shrivel up like a mummy. **—mum′mi·fi·ca′tion** (mŭm′ə-fĭ-**kā′**shən) *n.*

mum·my[1] (**mŭm′**ē) *n., pl.* **mum·mies 1.** The body of a human or animal embalmed after death, as practiced by the ancient Egyptians and certain other cultures. **2.** A dead body shrunken or preserved by a natural process. [From Middle English *mummie,* medicinal material from embalmed corpses, from Arabic *mūmiya,* a substance used to treat wounds.]

mum·my[2] (**mŭm′**ē) *n., pl.* **mum·mies** *Informal* Mother.

mumps (mŭmps) *pl.n.* *(used with a singular or plural verb)* A contagious viral disease that causes inflammation of the salivary glands, especially those at the back of the jaw.

munch (mŭnch) *v.* **munched, munch·ing, munch·es** —*tr.* To chew (food) in a noisy steady manner: *munch popcorn.* —*intr.* To chew food noisily and steadily: *They found the cow munching away in a pasture.*

mun·dane (mŭn-**dān′** *or* **mŭn′**dān′) *adj.* **1.** Ordinary; everyday: *laundry, shopping, and other mundane tasks.* **2.** Worldly; not spiritual: *mundane interests such as politics and financial affairs.*

Mu·nich (**myo͞o′**nĭk) A city of southeast Germany near the Alps southeast of Frankfurt. It was founded in 1158 and has long been the capital of Bavaria.

mu·nic·i·pal (myo͞o-**nĭs′**ə-pəl) *adj.* Relating to a municipality: *municipal politics; the municipal airport.*

mu·nic·i·pal·i·ty (myo͞o-nĭs′ə-**păl′**ĭ-tē) *n., pl.* **mu·nic·i·pal·i·ties** A city, town, or village that is self-governing in local matters.

mu·nif·i·cent (myo͞o-**nĭf′**ĭ-sənt) *adj.* Very generous: *a munificent donor; a munificent reward.* **—mu·nif′i·cence** *n.* **—mu·nif′i·cent·ly** *adv.*

mu·ni·tions (myo͞o-**nĭsh′**ənz) *pl.n.* Supplies for warfare, especially weapons and ammunition.

Mun·ro (mən-**rō′**), **Alice** Born 1931. Canadian writer known for her vivid novels and short stories of life in rural Ontario.

mu·ral (**myo͝or′**əl) *n.* A large picture or decoration applied directly to a wall or ceiling. [From Latin *mūrus,* wall.]

mu·ral·ist (**myo͝or′**ə-lĭst) *n.* A person who designs and makes murals.

Mu·ra·sa·ki Shi·ki·bu (mo͞o′rä-**sä′**kē **shē′**kē-bo͞o′), Baroness. 978?–1031? Japanese writer whose *The Tale of Genji* greatly influenced later Japanese fiction and is among the first examples of the novel as a literary form.

mur·der (**mûr′**dər) *n.* **1.** The unlawful and deliberate killing of one person by another. **2.** *Slang* Something that is very uncomfortable, difficult, or hazardous: *These shoes are murder on my feet.* ❖ *v.* **mur·dered, mur·der·ing, mur·ders** —*tr.* **1.** To kill (a person or persons) unlawfully and with deliberate intent. **2.** To ruin; spoil: *a writer who murders the language.* —*intr.* To commit murder.

mur·der·er (**mûr′**dər-ər) *n.* A person who commits murder.

mur·der·ess (**mûr′**dər-ĭs) *n.* A woman who commits murder.

mur·der·ous (**mûr′**dər-əs) *adj.* **1.** Guilty of, capable of, or intent on murder: *a murderous mob.* **2.** Relating to murder: *murderous acts.* **3.** *Informal* Extremely difficult or hazardous: *a murderous exam; a murderous trek across the desert.*

murk also **mirk** (mûrk) *n.* Darkness; gloom: *groped his way through the murk of the night.*

murk·y (**mûr′**kē) *adj.* **murk·i·er, murk·i·est 1.** Dark or dim, as from mist: *a murky sky.* See Synonyms at **dark. 2.** Darkened, clouded, or blurry: *murky waters; murky images.* **3.** Not clearly known, understood, or expressed: *a murky future; murky writing.* **—murk′i·ness** *n.*

mur·mur (**mûr′**mər) *n.* **1.** A low continuous sound: *the murmur of the waves.* **2.** A complaint made in a low voice: *took the scolding without a murmur.* **3.** An abnormal sound made by the heart, lungs, or blood vessels. ❖ *v.* **mur·mured, mur·mur·ing, mur·murs** —*intr.* **1.** To make a low continuous sound: *The brook murmured through the forest.* **2.** To speak or complain in an undertone: *The students murmured among themselves about the new regulations.* —*tr.* To say in a low voice; utter indistinctly: *murmured his approval.*

Mus·cat (**mŭs′**kăt′ *or* **mŭs′**kət *or* məs-**kăt′**) The capital of Oman, in the northern part of the country on an inlet of the Arabian Sea.

mus·cle (**mŭs′**əl) *n.* **1.** A type of body tissue composed of fibers that are capable of contracting and relaxing to cause movement or exert force. **2.** Any of the many structures of the body that are made of such tissue and cause bodily movement: *leg muscles; the muscles of the heart.* **3.** Muscular strength; brawn: *The swim team has plenty of muscle.* **4.** *Informal* Power or authority: *a law that has no muscle.* ❖ *intr.v.* **mus·cled, mus·cling, mus·cles** *Informal* To force one's way into a place or situation where one is not wanted: *muscle in on someone else's job.* [From Middle English, from Latin *mūsculus*, little mouse.]

❑ *These sound alike:* **muscle, mussel** (mollusk).

mus·cle·bound also **mus·cle-bound** (**mŭs′**əl-bound′) *adj.* Having muscles that are overly developed and stiff, usually as a result of too much exercise.

mus·co·vite (**mŭs′**kə-vīt′) *n.* A common, usually colorless to pale gray form of mica, used as an insulator.

Muscovite *n.* A native or resident of Moscow.

mus·cu·lar (**mŭs′**kyə-lər) *adj.* **1.** Relating to or consisting of muscle: *a muscular organ.* **2.** Having strong well-developed muscles: *a muscular gymnast.* —**mus′cu·lar′i·ty** (mŭs′kyə-**lăr′**ĭ-tē) *n.* —**mus′cu·lar·ly** *adv.*

SYNONYMS **muscular, athletic, brawny, burly, sinewy** These adjectives mean strong and powerfully built. *I lift weights because I want a more muscular body. The athletic students played soccer for hours. Two brawny workers moved the grand piano. Burly men waited on the wharf to unload the ship's cargo. Professional dancers are usually lean and sinewy.*
ANTONYM **scrawny**

---

muscular dys·tro·phy (**dĭs′**trə-fē) *n.* Any of several hereditary diseases in which a person's muscles gradually deteriorate, causing progressive weakness.

mus·cu·la·ture (**mŭs′**kyə-lə-chŏŏr′) *n.* The system or arrangement of muscles in a body or a body part.

muse (myōōz) *intr.v.* **mused, mus·ing, mus·es** To consider at length; ponder; meditate: *musing over his chances in tomorrow's game.* [From Middle English *musen*, from Old French *muser*, possibly from *mus*, snout.]

❑ *These sound alike:* **muse, mews** (alley), **Muse** (goddess).

Muse *n.* **1.** In Greek mythology, one of the nine sister goddesses who preside over the arts and sciences. **2. muse a.** A guiding spirit. **b.** A source of inspiration. [From Middle English, from Greek *Mousa*.]

❑ *These sound alike:* **Muse, mews** (alley), **muse** (consider).

mu·se·um (myōō-**zē′**əm) *n.* A building in which objects of artistic, historical, or scientific interest are exhibited. [From Greek *Mouseion*, shrine of the Muses.]

mush¹ (mŭsh) *n.* **1.** A porridge made of cornmeal boiled in water or milk. **2.** A thick soft mass. **3.** *Informal* Extreme sentimentality: *That movie was just a lot of mush.* [Probably alteration of *mash*.]

mush² (mŭsh) *intr.v.* **mushed, mush·ing, mush·es** To travel over snow with a dogsled. ❖ *interj.* An expression used to command a team of sled dogs to start pulling or go faster. [Possibly alteration of French *marchons*, let's go!]

mush·room (**mŭsh′**rōōm′ *or* **mŭsh′**rŏŏm′) *n.* Any of various fungi that have a stalk topped by a fleshy often umbrella-shaped cap containing the spores. Some kinds of mushrooms are used as food, but some are poisonous. ❖ *intr.v.* **mush·roomed, mush·room·ing, mush·rooms** To grow, multiply, or spread quickly: *The city's population mushroomed during the last decade.* ❖ *adj.* **1.** Relating to or containing mushrooms: *mushroom soup.* **2.** Resembling a mushroom in shape: *a mushroom cloud.*

mush·y (**mŭsh′**ē *or* **mŏŏsh′**ē) *adj.* **mush·i·er, mush·i·est 1.** Resembling mush; soft and pulpy: *The apples were mushy and brown inside.* **2.** *Informal* Very sentimental: *a mushy love story.* —**mush′i·ly** *adv.* —**mush′i·ness** *n.*

mu·sic (**myōō′**zĭk) *n.* **1.** The art of arranging sounds in combinations by rhythm, harmony, and melody, to please or interest a listener. **2.** Vocal or instrumental sounds that have rhythm, melody, harmony, or some combination of these. **3a.** A musical composition. **b.** A group of such compositions that are related in some way: *rock music; the music of Bach.* **c.** A system of symbols or figures that represent musical sounds and rhythms: *Can you read music?* **d.** A written or printed score or part for a musical composition: *bought the music for the new hit song.* **4.** A pleasing sound or combination of sounds: *the music of the wind in the trees.* [From Middle English *musike*, from Greek *mousikē (tekhnē)*, (art) of the Muses.]

mu·si·cal (**myōō′**zĭ-kəl) *adj.* **1.** Relating to, involving, or used in producing music: *a musical instrument; musical training.* **2.** Accompanied by or set to music: *a musical play.* **3.** Devoted to or skilled in music. **4.** Pleasing to the ear; melodious: *a musical voice.* ❖ *n.* **1.** A play or movie in which songs are included along with the dialogue. **2.** A musical comedy. —**mu′si·cal·ly** *adv.*

musical comedy *n.* A comedic play or movie with songs and dialogue, usually having musical numbers and a simple plot.

mu·si·cale (myōō′zĭ-**kăl′**) *n.* A musical program performed at a party or social gathering.

mu·si·cal·i·ty (myōō′zĭ-**kăl′**ĭ-tē) *n.* **1.** The quality of being musical. **2.** Musical talent or good taste.

music box *n.* An automatic mechanical device that produces musical sounds, usually by plucking tuned pieces of thin steel.

music hall *n.* A theater for musical entertainment or vaudeville.

mu·si·cian (myōō-**zĭsh′**ən) *n.* A person who is skilled in performing or composing music.

mu·si·cian·ship (myōō-**zĭsh′**ən-shĭp′) *n.* Skill, taste, and artistry in performing or composing music.

music video *n.* A filmed or videotaped rendition of a song, often showing the musicians performing or showing images that illustrate the lyrics or the mood of the song.

musk (mŭsk) *n.* **1.** A strong-smelling substance produced by glands of the male musk deer of Asia and formerly used in making perfume. **2.** A similar substance produced by other animals, such as an otter or a civet, or made artificially. **3.** The odor of musk.

musk deer *n.* Any of several small antlerless Asian deer, the males of which have a gland that secretes musk.

mus·kel·lunge (**mŭs′**kə-lŭnj′) *n., pl.* **muskellunge** or **mus·kel·lung·es** A large North American freshwater fish that has a long snout and is often caught for sport.

mus·ket (**mŭs′**kĭt) *n.* A long-barreled gun used before the invention of the rifle. [From Italian *moschetto*, a type of crossbow, musket, from *mosca*, fly, bolt shot by a crossbow.] —SEE NOTE AT **mosquito.**

mus·ket·eer (mŭs′kĭ-**tîr′**) *n.* **1.** A soldier armed with

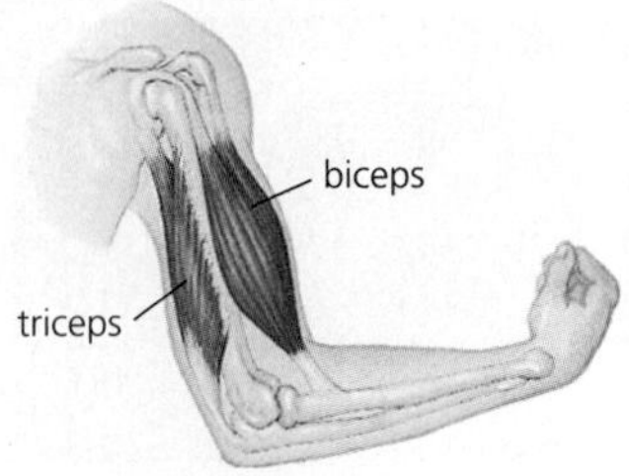

muscle
When the biceps contracts to bend the elbow, the triceps relaxes. When the triceps contracts to straighten the elbow, the biceps relaxes.

mush²

musk ox

mustang

a musket. **2.** A member of the French royal household bodyguard in the 1600s and 1700s.

mus·ket·ry (mŭs′kĭ-trē) *n.* **1.** Muskets considered as a group. **2.** The technique of firing small arms.

musk·mel·on (mŭsk′mĕl′ən) *n.* Any of several types of melon, such as the cantaloupe, having a rough rind and edible orange or green flesh with a musky odor.

Mus·ko·ge·an also **Mus·kho·ge·an** (mŭs-kō′gē-ən) *n.* A family of Native American languages of the southeast United States that includes Choctaw, Chickasaw, Creek, and Seminole. —**Mus·ko′ge·an** *adj.*

musk ox or **musk·ox** (mŭsk′ŏks′) *n.* A large oxlike mammal of northern North America and Greenland, having dark shaggy hair and curved horns and giving off a musky odor.

musk·rat (mŭs′krăt′) *n., pl.* **muskrat** or **musk·rats** **1.** A North American rodent that lives in or near water and has thick brown fur, a long scaly tail, and glands that give off a musky odor. **2.** The fur of such an animal.

musk·y (mŭs′kē) *adj.* **musk·i·er, musk·i·est** Relating to or having the heavy sweet odor of musk. —**musk′i·ness** *n.*

Mus·lim (mŭz′ləm *or* mo͝os′ləm) or **Mos·lem** (mŏz′ləm *or* mŏs′ləm) *n.* A believer in Islam. —**Mus′lim** *adj.*

mus·lin (mŭz′lĭn) *n.* A cotton cloth of plain weave, either coarse or sheer, used especially for sheets.

muss (mŭs) *tr.v.* **mussed, muss·ing, muss·es** To make untidy or messy: *The wind mussed up my hair.*

mus·sel (mŭs′əl) *n.* Any of various saltwater or freshwater mollusks having a pair of narrow, hinged, often dark-blue shells. Several kinds of saltwater mussels are used as food.

❑ *These sound alike:* **mussel, muscle** (tissue fiber).

Mus·so·li·ni (mo͞o′sə-lē′nē *or* mo͝os′ə-lē′nē), **Benito** Known as "Il Duce." 1883–1945. Italian Fascist dictator and prime minister (1922–1943) who brought Italy into World War II (1940).

mus·sy (mŭs′ē) *adj.* **muss·i·er, muss·i·est** In a state of disarray; untidy. —**muss′i·ly** *adv.*

must (mŭst) *aux.v.* **1.** To be required or obliged: *Humans must have oxygen to live.* **2.** Used to express a command or warning: *You must be careful when working on a ladder.* **3.** Used to indicate certainty or inevitability: *All good things must come to an end.* **4.** To be determined; be resolved: *If you must talk, do so quietly.* ❖ *n.* Something that is required or necessary: *A good tent is a must when you go camping.*

mus·tache also **mous·tache** (mŭs′tăsh′ *or* mə-stăsh′) *n.* The hair growing on the human upper lip, especially of a man. [From Greek *mustax*, upper lip.]

mus·ta·chio (mə-stăsh′ō *or* mə-stăsh′ē-ō′) *n., pl.* **mus·ta·chios** A mustache, especially one that is large and full.

mus·tang (mŭs′tăng′) *n.* A small, hardy wild horse of the North American plains, descended from horses brought to America by Spanish explorers and European settlers.

mus·tard (mŭs′tərd) *n.* **1.** Any of various plants of Eurasia having yellow flowers, edible leaves, and small sharp-tasting seeds. **2a.** The powdered seeds of certain of these plants. **b.** A spicy condiment made from these powdered seeds. [From Middle English, from Old French *mustarde*, from Latin *mustum*, unfermented wine.]

mus·ter (mŭs′tər) *v.* **mus·tered, mus·ter·ing, mus·ters** —*tr.* **1.** To bring together; assemble: *mustered his troops for inspection.* **2.** To bring into existence, action, or effect: *mustered enough courage to ask the boss for a raise.* —*intr.* To come together; assemble: *The troops mustered for inspection.* ❖ *n.* **1.** A gathering, especially of troops, for inspection, roll call, or some other purpose. **2.** The official roll of people in a military unit.

must·n't (mŭs′ənt) Contraction of *must not.*

must·y (mŭs′tē) *adj.* **must·i·er, must·i·est** **1.** Stale or moldy: *a musty smell from the cellar.* **2.** Overused and old-fashioned: *a musty phrase.* —**must′i·ness** *n.*

mu·ta·ble (myo͞o′tə-bəl) *adj.* **1.** Capable of or subject to change: *All things in nature are mutable.* **2.** Likely to change: *mutable weather in the mountains.* **3.** Tending to undergo genetic mutation: *mutable genes.* —**mu′ta·bil′i·ty** *n.*

mu·ta·gen (myo͞o′tə-jən) *n.* An agent, such as a chemical, ultraviolet light, or a radioactive element, that can cause or increase the frequency of mutation in an organism. —**mu′ta·gen′ic** (myo͞o′tə-jĕn′ĭk) *adj.*

mu·tant (myo͞ot′nt) *n.* An organism, cell, or gene that results from genetic mutation: *mutants that lack wings.* ❖ *adj.* Changed as a result of mutation: *a mutant gene.*

mu·tate (myo͞o′tāt) *intr. & tr.v.* **mu·tat·ed, mu·tat·ing, mu·tates** To undergo or cause to undergo change, especially by genetic mutation: *bacteria that have mutated; a chemical that mutates a gene.* [From Latin *mūtāre*, to change.]

mu·ta·tion (myo͞o-tā′shən) *n.* **1a.** A change in a gene of an organism or virus that is passed on when it reproduces or multiplies and often results in the appearance of a new or altered trait: *chemicals that can cause mutations in bacteria.* **b.** The process by which such a change occurs: *Mutation is one of the mechanisms that causes evolution.* **c.** A gene or trait that results from such a change: *Breeding flies with mutations for use in research.* **2.** A change, as in form: *a mutation in artistic styles.*

mute (myo͞ot) *adj.* **mut·er, mut·est** **1.** Unable to speak. **2.** Refraining from speech; silent: *remained mute under questioning.* **3.** Expressed without speech; unspoken: *the mute approval in his smile.* **4.** Not pronounced; silent: *the mute "h" in "hour."* ❖ *n.* **1.** *Often Offensive* A person who is incapable of speech. **2.** Any of various attachments used to soften, muffle, or alter the tone of a musical instrument. ❖ *tr.v.* **mut·ed, mut·ing, mutes** To muffle or soften the sound of: *The additional insulation in the walls muted the noise of the people living next door.* [From Middle English *muet*, from Old French, from Latin *mūtus*.] —**mute′ly** *adv.* —**mute′ness** *n.*

mu·ti·late (myo͞ot′l-āt′) *tr.v.* **mu·ti·lat·ed, mu·ti·lat·ing, mu·ti·lates** **1.** To damage by cutting off or mangling (a necessary part, such as a limb). **2.** To damage badly; ruin: *The photo was mutilated in the mail.* —**mu′ti·la′tion** *n.*

mu·ti·neer (myo͞ot′n-îr′) *n.* A person, especially a soldier or sailor, who takes part in a mutiny.

mu·ti·nous (myo͞ot′n-əs) *adj.* **1.** Relating to or being mutiny: *a mutinous act.* **2.** Engaged in or planning to engage in mutiny: *a mutinous officer.* **3.** Unruly; rebellious: *a mutinous child.* —**mu′ti·nous·ly** *adv.*

mu·ti·ny (myo͞ot′n-ē) *n., pl.* **mu·ti·nies** Open rebellion against authority, especially rebellion of sailors against officers in charge. ❖ *intr.v.* **mu·ti·nied, mu·ti·ny·ing, mu·ti·nies** To engage in mutiny; rebel. [From obsolete *mutine*, from Old French *mutin*, rebellious, from Latin *movēre*, to move.]

Mu·tsu·hi·to (mo͞o′tso͞o-hē′tō) Called **Mei·ji** (mā′jē′) 1852–1912. Emperor of Japan (1867–1912) who presided over the transformation of feudal Japan into a modern constitutional state.

mutt (mŭt) *n. Informal* A mongrel.

mut·ter (mŭt′ər) *v.* **mut·tered, mut·ter·ing, mut·ters** —*intr.* **1.** To say or speak in low unclear tones: *She muttered to herself while she worked.* **2.** To complain or grumble: *People began to mutter about the high price of food.* —*tr.* To say in low unclear tones: *He muttered something underneath his breath.* ❖ *n.* Something spoken in low unclear tones.

mut·ton (mŭt′n) *n.* The meat of a fully grown sheep.

mu·tu·al (myo͞o′cho͞o-əl) *adj.* **1.** Given and received

WRITERS CHOOSE THEIR WORDS

Alfonso looked over her shoulder for a long time, trying to **muster** enough nerve to ask her if she'd like to go bike riding tomorrow.

—Gary Soto "Broken Chain" in *Baseball in April and Other Stories*

ă	pat	ôr	core
ā	pay	oi	boy
âr	care	ou	out
ä	father	o͝o	took
ĕ	pet	o͝or	lure
ē	be	o͞o	boot
ĭ	pit	ŭ	cut
ī	bite	ûr	urge
îr	pier	th	thin
ŏ	pot	*th*	this
ō	toe	zh	vision
ô	paw	ə	about

by each toward the other; reciprocal: *mutual respect.* **2.** Having the same relationship to each other: *mutual friends.* **3.** Possessed or shared in common: *discussed our mutual problems.* [From Latin *mūtuus*, borrowed.] **—mu′tu·al·ly** *adv.*

mutual fund *n.* An investment company that continually sells new shares, invests the combined capital of its shareholders in other companies, and usually buys existing shares back at the request of the individual shareholder.

mu·tu·al·ism (myo͞o′cho͞o-ə-lĭz′əm) *n.* A relationship between two organisms of different species in which each member benefits.

muz·zle (mŭz′əl) *n.* **1.** The projecting nose and jaws of certain animals, such as a dog or horse. **2.** A device that is fitted over an animal's snout, usually used to prevent biting or eating. **3.** The front end of the barrel of a gun. ❖ *tr.v.* **muz·zled, muz·zling, muz·zles 1.** To put a muzzle on (an animal). **2.** To prevent (a person) from expressing an opinion: *tried to muzzle the opposition.* [From Middle English *mosel*, from Medieval Latin *mūsellum*, from Latin *mūsum*, snout.]

muz·zle·load·er (mŭz′əl-lō′dər) *n.* A firearm that is loaded at the muzzle. **—muz′zle·load′ing** *adj.*

MW *abbr.* An abbreviation of megawatt.

my (mī) *adj.* The possessive form of **I**[1]. **1.** Belonging or relating to me: *my pencil; my good luck to find you.* **2.** Used before various forms of address to indicate politeness or affection: *My friend, you are so right.* **3.** Used in expressions of surprise or dismay: *My word! My goodness!* ❖ *interj.* An expression used to show surprise or dismay: *My! What a mess!*

Myan·mar (myän-mär′) or **Bur·ma** (bûr′mə) A country of southeast Asia northwest of Thailand. Naypyidaw is the capital and Yangon (Rangoon) is the largest city.

my·ce·li·um (mī-sē′lē-əm) *n., pl.* **my·ce·li·a** (mī-sē′lē-ə) A mass of fine branching filaments that form the main growing structure of a fungus.

My·ce·nae (mī-sē′nē) An ancient Greek city in the northeast Peloponnesus that flourished as the center of an early Bronze Age civilization.

my·col·o·gy (mī-kŏl′ə-jē) *n., pl.* **my·col·o·gies** The scientific study of fungi. **—my·col′o·gist** *n.*

my·e·lin (mī′ə-lĭn) *n.* A whitish, fatty substance that forms a sheath around the core of many nerve fibers.

my·na or **my·nah** (mī′nə) *n.* Any of various bluish-black or dark brown Asian birds, some of which can imitate human speech. [From Hindi *mainā*.]

my·o·pi·a (mī-ō′pē-ə) *n.* A defect of the eye that makes distant objects appear blurred because their images are focused in front of the retina rather than on it; nearsightedness.

my·op·ic (mī-ŏp′ĭk) *adj.* Relating to or affected with myopia; nearsighted.

myr·i·ad (mĭr′ē-əd) *adj.* Amounting to a very large indefinite number: *the myriad fish in the ocean.* ❖ *n.* A vast number.

myrrh (mûr) *n.* An aromatic gummy substance obtained from certain African and Arabian trees and shrubs and used in perfume and incense. [From Old English *mirre*, from Greek *murrha*.]

myr·tle (mûr′tl) *n.* **1.** Any of several shrubs having evergreen leaves, white flowers, and blackish berries, often used for hedges. **2.** A trailing vine that has glossy evergreen leaves and usually blue flowers.

my·self (mī-sĕlf′) *pron.* **1.** That one that is the same as me: **a.** Used as the direct object or indirect object of a verb or as the object of a preposition, to show that the action of the verb refers back to the subject: *I injured myself. I gave myself a pep talk. I spent little of the money on myself.* **b.** Used to give emphasis: *I myself had to laugh.* **2.** My normal or healthy self: *I was sick, but I'm feeling myself again.*

mys·te·ri·ous (mĭ-stîr′ē-əs) *adj.* **1.** Difficult or impossible to understand or explain: *the mysterious disappearance of the books.* **2.** Having an air of mystery; exotic or enigmatic: *a mysterious stranger; a mysterious land that few had ever visited.* **—mys·te′ri·ous·ly** *adv.*

mys·ter·y (mĭs′tə-rē) *n., pl.* **mys·ter·ies 1.** Something that is difficult to explain or understand: *How he got into the house is a mystery.* **2.** Something that is a secret: *The teacher kept our grades a mystery.* **3.** The quality associated with the unknown or unexplained: *The old house had an air of mystery.* **4.** A piece of fiction dealing with a puzzling crime. **5.** An incident in the life of Jesus or Mary that serves as a subject for meditation by Roman Catholics. [From Middle English *misterie*, from Greek *mustērion*, secret rite, from *mustēs*, an initiate.]

mystery play *n.* A medieval play based on biblical events especially in the life of Jesus.

mys·tic (mĭs′tĭk) *adj.* Mystical. ❖ *n.* A person who practices or believes in mysticism.

mys·ti·cal (mĭs′tĭ-kəl) *adj.* **1.** Relating to mystics or mysticism and its practices: *the mystical books of the alchemists.* **2.** Strange; mysterious: *kept giving mystical answers to my questions.* **—mys′ti·cal·ly** *adv.*

mys·ti·cism (mĭs′tĭ-sĭz′əm) *n.* **1.** Belief that God or a transcendent reality can be experienced directly, especially by means of contemplation and asceticism instead of rational thought. **2.** The effort to attain such experience or the experience itself.

mys·ti·fy (mĭs′tə-fī′) *tr.v.* **mys·ti·fied, mys·ti·fy·ing, mys·ti·fies** To confuse or bewilder: *We were mystified by their response.* **—mys′ti·fi·ca′tion** (mĭs′tə-fĭ-kā′shən) *n.*

mys·tique (mĭ-stēk′) *n.* A feeling of mystery or wonder that surrounds an activity, person, or group: *the mystique of the wildlife photographer.*

myth (mĭth) *n.* **1a.** A traditional story dealing with ancestors, heroes, or supernatural beings, and usually making an attempt to explain a belief, practice, or natural phenomenon: *the myth that gods built the mountains.* **b.** Such stories considered as a group: *Greek myth.* **2.** A fictitious or imaginary story, person, or thing: *the myth of the giant fish in the lake.* **3.** A false belief that is part of an ideology: *the myth that all tax increases are bad.* [From Greek *mūthos*.]

myth·i·cal (mĭth′ĭ-kəl) also **myth·ic** (mĭth′ĭk) *adj.* **1.** Existing only in myths: *a mythical beast such as the unicorn.* **2.** Imaginary; fancied: *a mythical account of a voyage to a floating island.*

myth·o·log·i·cal (mĭth′ə-lŏj′ĭ-kəl) *adj.* **1.** Existing in myths: *a mythological animal.* **2.** Fabulous; imaginary.

my·thol·o·gy (mĭ-thŏl′ə-jē) *n., pl.* **my·thol·o·gies 1.** A body or collection of myths, especially one dealing with the origin, gods, and heroes of a specific people: *Roman mythology.* **2.** The field of scholarship that deals with the study of myths.

muzzle
of a Great Dane

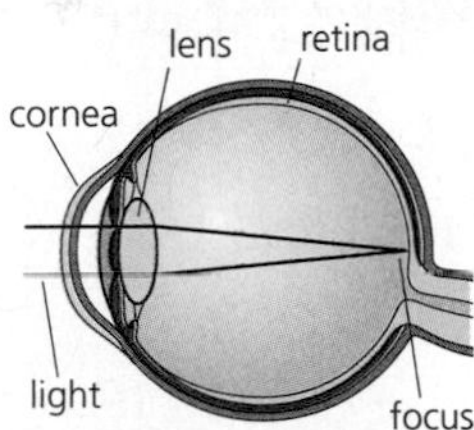

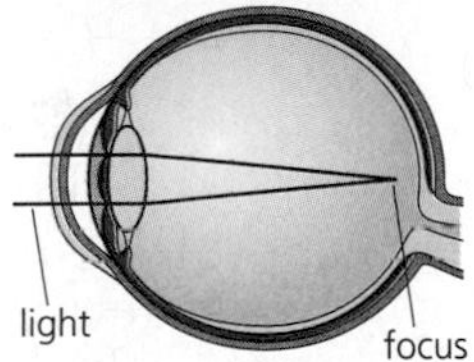

myopia
top: normal eye with light focused on the retina
bottom: myopic eye with light focused in front of the retina

nacelle

n or **N** (ĕn) *n., pl.* **n's** or **N's** also **ns** or **Ns** The 14th letter of the English alphabet.

N[1] The symbol for the element **nitrogen.**

N[2] *abbr.* An abbreviation of: **1.** needs improvement. **2.** north. **3.** northern.

n. *abbr.* An abbreviation of noun.

Na The symbol for the element **sodium.**

NA *abbr.* An abbreviation of: **1.** North America. **2.** also **n/a** not applicable.

NAACP *abbr.* An abbreviation of National Association for the Advancement of Colored People.

nab (năb) *tr.v.* **nabbed, nab·bing, nabs** *Informal* **1.** To catch in the act; arrest: *The policeman nabbed the bank robber.* **2.** To grab; snatch: *They nabbed all the tickets before we could get to the box office.*

na·bob (nā**′**bŏb′) *n.* **1.** A governor in India under the Mughal Empire. **2.** A person of wealth and prominence.

na·celle (nə-sĕl**′**) *n.* **1.** A streamlined enclosure mounted on an aircraft for housing an engine. **2.** A structure at the top of a wind turbine that houses the generator and other components.

na·cho (nä**′**chō′) *n., pl.* **na·chos** A small, usually triangular piece of tortilla, often topped with cheese or chili pepper sauce and broiled.

na·da (nä**′**də) *pron. Slang* Nothing: *"What are you doing today?" "Nada!"* [From Spanish, nothing.]

na·dir (nā**′**dər *or* nā**′**dîr′) *n.* **1.** A point on the celestial sphere directly below the observer, opposite the zenith. **2.** The lowest point: *the nadir of our troubles.*

NAFTA *abbr.* An abbreviation of North American Free Trade Agreement.

nag[1] (năg) *v.* **nagged, nag·ging, nags** *—tr.* **1.** To annoy by constant scolding, complaining, or urging. **2.** To cause continuous pain or annoyance to: *My sore neck nagged me all day. —intr.* To scold or complain constantly: *The children nagged at me all day.* ❖ *n.* A person who nags. [Probably of Scandinavian origin.] **—nag′ger** *n.*

nag[2] (năg) *n.* A horse, especially an old or worn-out horse. [From Middle English *nagge.*]

Na·ga·sa·ki (nä′gə-sä**′**kē *or* năg′ə-**săk′**ē) A city of western Kyushu, Japan, on an inlet of the East China Sea. It was rebuilt after being destroyed by the second atomic bomb used in World War II (August 9, 1945).

Na·hua·tl (nä**′**wät′l) *n., pl.* **Nahuatl** or **Na·hua·tls 1.** A member of any of various American Indian peoples of central Mexico, including the Aztecs. **2.** The Uto-Aztecan language of the Nahuatl. [From Nahuatl *náhuatl*, that which pleases the ear.] **—Na′hua′tl** *adj.*

Na·hum[1] (nā**′**həm *or* nā**′**əm) A Hebrew prophet of the 7th century BC who predicted the fall of Nineveh.

Na·hum[2] (nā**′**həm *or* nā**′**əm) *n.* A Book of the Bible that deals with the fall of Nineveh.

nai·ad (nā**′**ăd′ *or* nī**′**ăd′) *n., pl.* **nai·a·des** (nā**′**ə-dēz′ *or* nī**′**ə-dēz′) or **nai·ads 1.** In Greek mythology, one of the nymphs living in and presiding over brooks, fountains, and springs. **2.** The aquatic larva of certain insects, such as a dragonfly.

nail (nāl) *n.* **1.** A slim pointed piece of metal, often with a head, hammered into wood or other material as a fastener. **2a.** A fingernail or toenail. **b.** A claw or talon. ❖ *tr.v.* **nailed, nail·ing, nails 1.** To fasten, join, or attach with or as if with nails: *Nail the boards together.* **2.** *Slang* To seize; catch: *The police nailed the suspect in his car.* **3.** *Slang* To perform successfully or have success in: *nailed the exam.* ◆ **nail down** To discover or establish with certainty: *The reporters finally nailed down the facts of the story. We need to nail down a meeting time.*

nail·brush (nāl**′**brŭsh′) *n.* A small brush with firm bristles, used for scrubbing the hands and cleaning the fingernails and toenails.

nail file *n.* A small flat file that is used to shape the fingernails and toenails.

nail gun *n.* A device, usually powered by compressed air, that drives nails into wood or concrete.

nail polish *n.* A clear or colored cosmetic for coating fingernails or toenails.

nai·ra (nī**′**rə) *n.* The basic monetary unit of Nigeria.

Nai·ro·bi (nī-**rō′**bē) The capital of Kenya, in the south-central part of the country. It was founded in 1899.

na·ive or **na·ïve** (nī-**ēv′**) *adj.* **1.** Simple and inexperienced; guileless or unsuspecting: *He felt naive as he tried to bargain with the car salesman.* **2.** Showing a lack of experience or judgment; unsophisticated: *a naive attempt to solve a complicated problem.* **—na·ive′ly** *adv.*

na·ive·té or **na·ïve·té** (nī′ēv-**tā′** *or* nī-**ē′**vĭ-tā′) *n.* The quality of being naive; natural simplicity.

na·ked (nā**′**kĭd) *adj.* **1.** Not wearing clothing or other covering; nude. **2.** Having no vegetation or leaves: *trees with naked branches.* **3.** Not concealed, disguised, or added to: *the naked truth.* **—na′ked·ly** *adv.* **—na′ked·ness** *n.*

naked eye *n.* The eye unaided by an optical instrument, such as a telescope.

nak·fa (näk**′**fä**′**) *n.* The basic monetary unit of Eritrea.

nam·as·te (nŭm′əs-**tā′**) *interj.* An expression used especially among Hindus as a polite or respectful greeting or farewell. [From Sanskrit *namas te*, homage to you : *namaḥ*, homage + *te*, to you.]

nam·by-pam·by (năm′bē-**păm′**bē) *adj.* Sentimental, unrealistic, or indecisive.

name (nām) *n.* **1.** A word or words by which a person or thing is known or referred to. **2.** A word or group of words used to describe someone, especially as an insult: *Stop calling me names!* **3a.** General reputation: *That store has a bad name.* **b.** A distinguished reputation: *She has made a name for herself.* **4.** A famous or excellent person: *a big name in the movies.* ❖ *tr.v.* **named, nam·ing, names 1a.** To give a name to: *Have you named the baby?* **b.** To call by a name: *They named her "Best in the class."* **2.** To mention or identify by name: *Name the longest river in China.* **3.** To specify, fix, or set: *Name*

ă	pat	ôr	core
ā	pay	oi	boy
âr	care	ou	out
ä	father	ŏŏ	took
ĕ	pet	ŏŏr	lure
ē	be	ōō	boot
ĭ	pit	ŭ	cut
ī	bite	ûr	urge
îr	pier	th	thin
ŏ	pot	*th*	this
ō	toe	zh	vision
ô	paw	ə	about

the day for the party. **4.** To nominate or appoint, as to a specific duty, honor, or office: *She was named coach of the basketball team.* ◆ **in the name of 1.** By the authority of: *Open up in the name of the law!* **2.** For the reason of: *He worked tirelessly at the laboratory in the name of science.* **to (one's) name** Belonging to one: *I don't have a dollar to my name.* [From Old English *nama.*]

name·less (**nām′**lĭs) *adj.* **1.** Having or bearing no name: *nameless stars.* **2.** Unknown by name; obscure: *the nameless dead.* **3.** Not designated by name; anonymous: *a nameless benefactor.* **4.** Impossible to describe; inexpressible: *nameless horror.* **—name′less·ly** *adv.* **—name′less·ness** *n.*

name·ly (**nām′**lē) *adv.* That is to say; specifically: *First-class mail includes written matter, namely letters and postcards.*

name·sake (**nām′**sāk′) *n.* A person or thing named after another.

Na·mib·i·a (nə-**mĭb′**ē-ə) A country of southwest Africa on the Atlantic Ocean south of Angola. Windhoek is the capital.

na·na (**năn′**ə *or* **nä′**nə) *n.* **1.** A grandmother. **2.** A nanny.

Nan·jing (**nän′jĭng′**) also **Nan·king** (**năn′kĭng′**) A city of east-central China on the Yangtze River northwest of Shanghai. It was the site of a massacre by invading Japanese forces in 1937.

nan·ny (**năn′**ē) *n., pl.* **nan·nies** A person employed to take care of a child or children.

nanny goat *n.* A female goat.

nano– *pref.* A prefix that means: **1.** Extremely small or at the molecular level: *nanotechnology.* **2.** One-billionth (10^{-9}): *nanosecond.*

nan·o·bot (**năn′**ō-bŏt′) *n.* A microscopic robot built from parts that are typically 0.1 to 10 micrometers long.

nan·o·fi·ber (**năn′**ō-fī′bər) *n.* **1.** A synthetic material made of fibers that are usually carbon-based and that have a diameter of less than one micron. **2.** One of these fibers.

nan·o·me·ter (**năn′**ə-mē′tər) *n.* One billionth (10^{-9}) of a meter.

nan·o·par·ti·cle (**năn′**ō-pär′tĭ-kəl) *n.* Any of various microscopic particles, especially one consisting of a single molecule such as a fullerene, that are about a nanometer long.

nan·o·scale (**năn′**ə-skāl′) *adj.* Relating to or occurring at a size or extent so small as to be measured in nanometers.

nan·o·scop·ic (năn′ə-**skŏp′**ĭk) *adj.* Measureable on a scale that is smaller than a micron and larger than an atom.

nan·o·sec·ond (**năn′**ə-sĕk′ənd) *n.* One billionth (10^{-9}) of a second.

nan·o·struc·ture (**năn′**ō-strŭk′chər) *n.* **1.** An object whose dimensions are so small that they are measured in nanometers. **2.** The structure of such an object.

nan·o·tech (**năn′**ō-tĕk′) *n. Informal* Nanotechnology.

nan·o·tech·nol·o·gy (năn′ə-tĕk-**nŏl′**ə-jē) *n.* The science and technology of nanoscale devices and materials, such as electronic circuits, constructed using single atoms and molecules.

Nan·tuck·et (năn-**tŭk′**ĭt) An island of southeast Massachusetts south of Cape Cod. It was a whaling center until the mid-1850s.

nap[1] (năp) *n.* A brief sleep, usually during the day: *took a quick nap before dinner.* ❖ *intr.v.* **napped, nap·ping, naps 1.** To doze or sleep for a brief period: *napped while riding the bus to school.* **2.** To be unaware of danger or trouble that is just about to happen. [From Middle English *nappe,* from *nappen,* to doze, from Old English *hnappian.*] **—nap′per** *n.*

nap[2] (năp) *n.* A soft or fuzzy surface on cloth or leather. ❖ *tr.v.* **napped, nap·ping, naps** To form or raise a nap on (cloth or leather). [From Middle English *noppe,* from Middle Dutch.]

na·palm (**nā′**päm′) *n.* A mixture of gasoline and chemicals that makes a flammable jelly for use in flame throwers and bombs.

nape (nāp *or* năp) *n.* The back of the neck.

naph·tha (**năf′**thə *or* **năp′**thə) *n.* Any of several flammable liquid hydrocarbons used as solvents, as fuel, and in making various chemicals, especially those derived from petroleum, coal tar, and natural gas.

naph·tha·lene (**năf′**thə-lēn′ *or* **năp′**thə-lēn′) *n.* A white crystalline compound derived from coal tar or petroleum and used to manufacture dyes, moth repellents, explosives, and solvents.

nap·kin (**năp′**kĭn) *n.* **1.** A piece of cloth or soft paper used while eating to protect the clothes or to wipe the mouth and fingers. **2.** A sanitary napkin. [From Middle English : Old French *nape,* tablecloth + Middle English *-kin,* diminutive suffix.]

Na·ples (**nā′**pəlz) A city of south-central Italy on the **Bay of Naples,** an arm of the Tyrrhenian Sea. It was founded in about 600 BC.

na·po·le·on (nə-**pō′**lē-ən) *n.* A rectangular pastry with flaky layers separated by custard or cream. [Alteration (influenced by the name of Napoleon I), of French *napolitain,* iced pastry of layered butter cookies and jam, from *napolitain,* of Naples.]

Na·po·le·on I (nə-**pō′**lē-ən) Originally Napoleon Bonaparte. 1769–1821. Emperor of the French (1804–1814) and King of Italy (1805–1814) who was a brilliant military strategist and conquered much of Europe but was forced to abdicate (1814). After escaping from exile, he briefly regained power and was ultimately defeated at Waterloo (1815). His Napoleonic Code still forms the basis of French civil law. **—Na·po′le·on′ic** (nə-pō′lē-**ŏn′**ik) *adj.*

nar·cis·sism (**när′**sĭ-sĭz′əm) *n.* Excessive preoccupation with or admiration of oneself. [After *Narcissus.*] **—nar′cis·sist** *n.*

nar·cis·sus (när-**sĭs′**əs) *n., pl.* **nar·cis·sus·es** or **nar·cis·si** (när-**sĭs′**ī′) A daffodil, especially one having flowers with a central part that is shaped like a cup or trumpet.

Narcissus *n.* In Greek mythology, a young man who pined away in love for his own image in a pool of water and was transformed into the flower that bears his name.

nar·cot·ic (när-**kŏt′**ĭk) *n.* A drug, such as heroin, that is derived from opium or an opiumlike compound used to relieve pain. Narcotics often induce sleep, cause changes in judgment and other brain functions, and can be addictive. ❖ *adj.* Relating to narcotics. [From Middle English *narcotik,* from Greek *narkōsis,* a numbing, from *narkē,* numbness.]

Nar·ra·gan·sett (năr′ə-**găn′**sĭt) *n., pl.* **Narragansett** or **Nar·ra·gan·setts 1.** A member of a Native American people living in Rhode Island. **2.** The Algonquian language of the Narragansett.

Narragansett Bay A deep inlet of the Atlantic Ocean in eastern Rhode Island.

nar·rate (**năr′**āt′ *or* nă-**rāt′**) *tr.v.* **nar·rat·ed, nar·rat·ing, nar·rates 1.** To tell (a story, for example) in speech or writing or by means of images. **2.** To supply a running commentary for (a performance, for example). [From Latin *narrāre,* from *gnārus,* knowing.] **—nar′ra′tor** *n.*

nar·ra·tion (nă-**rā′**shən) *n.* **1.** The act of narrating. **2.** Something narrated; an account or story.

nar·ra·tive (**năr′**ə-tĭv) *n.* A narrated account; a story. ❖ *adj.* **1.** Telling a story: *narrative poems.* **2.** Relating to narration: *the narrative skill of an author.*

nar·row (**năr′**ō) *adj.* **nar·row·er, nar·row·est 1.** Small or limited in width, especially in comparison with length: *a narrow face.* **2.** Having little room: *narrow quarters.* **3.**

WRITERS CHOOSE THEIR WORDS

Thinking it over, I decided somebody else was really to blame. *Me.* I should have known what was going on months earlier. I was **naive.** I should have been more on top of things. They did it [invented a homework machine] right under my nose. I so wanted my students to be successful, and I wanted to think they were successful because of my teaching. I guess the sad truth is that I still have a lot to learn about teaching, and I can't be so trusting with students in the future.

—Dan Gutman
The Homework Machine

Napoleon I

Carry Nation

Limited in scope or variety: *a narrow selection of products.* **4.** Rigid in views and ideas; narrow-minded: *a man of narrow opinions.* **5.** Just barely successful; close: *a narrow escape.* ❖ *v.* **nar·rowed, nar·row·ing, nar·rows** —*tr.* **1.** To make narrow or narrower: *He narrowed his eyes.* **2.** To limit or restrict: *Narrow down your topic to something you can handle.* —*intr.* To become narrower: *The stream narrows at the rapids.* ❖ *n.* **1.** A part having little width, such as a mountain pass. **2. narrows** *(used with a singular or plural verb)* A narrow body of water connecting two larger ones. **—nar′row·ly** *adv.* **—nar′row·ness** *n.*

nar·row-mind·ed (năr′ō-**mīn′**dĭd) *adj.* Lacking in tolerance or sympathy. **—nar′row-mind′ed·ly** *adv.* **—nar′row-mind′ed·ness** *n.*

nar·whal (**när′**wəl) *n.* A sea mammal of northern regions that is related to the whales. Males have a single long tusk that is twisted in a spiral.

nar·y (**nâr′**ē) *adj.* Not one; no: *Nary a leaf was left on the tree.*

NASA *abbr.* An abbreviation of National Aeronautics and Space Administration.

na·sal (**nā′**zəl) *adj.* **1.** In or relating to the nose: *nasal irritation.* **2a.** Uttered so that most of the air passes through the nose rather than the mouth, as the sounds *m* or *n.* **b.** Resembling a sound uttered in such a way: *the nasal twang of a guitar.* ❖ *n.* A nasal consonant. [From Middle English *nasale,* from Latin *nāsus,* nose.] **—na′sal·ly** *adv.*

na·sal·ize (**nā′**zə-līz′) *tr. & intr.v.* **na·sal·ized, na·sal·iz·ing, na·sal·iz·es** To make nasal or produce nasal sounds. **—na′sal·i·za′tion** (nā′zə-lĭ-**zā′**shən) *n.*

nas·cent (**năs′**ənt *or* **nā′**sənt) *adj.* Coming into existence; emerging: *a nascent movement to reform campaign laws.* **—nas′cence** *n.*

Nash·ville (**năsh′**vĭl′) The capital of Tennessee, in the north-central part of the state northeast of Memphis. It was founded in 1779 and became the capital in 1843.

Nas·sau (**năs′**ô′) The capital of the Bahamas, in the Atlantic Ocean east of Miami, Florida.

nas·tur·tium (nə-**stûr′**shəm) *n.* Any of various garden plants having showy orange, yellow, or red flowers and rounded leaves. The strong-tasting leaves and flowers are edible.

nas·ty (**năs′**tē) *adj.* **nas·ti·er, nas·ti·est 1.** Disgusting; repellent: *A nasty odor rose out of the garbage can.* **2.** Unpleasant; annoying: *a nasty habit.* **3.** Malicious; spiteful; mean: *a nasty man.* **4.** Morally offensive; indecent: *a nasty word.* **5.** Unpleasant; annoying: *nasty weather.* **6.** Painful and dangerous: *a nasty cut.* **—nas′ti·ly** *adv.* **—nas′ti·ness** *n.*

na·tal (**nāt′**l) *adj.* Relating to birth: *natal care.*

Natch·ez (**năch′**ĭz) *n., pl.* **Natchez 1.** A member of a Native American people formerly living on the lower Mississippi River near the city of Natchez, Mississippi. **2.** The extinct language of the Natchez.

Na·than·ael (nə-**thăn′**yəl) See Saint **Bartholomew.**

na·tion (**nā′**shən) *n.* **1.** A group of people organized under a single government; a country. **2.** The territory occupied by such a group of people: *All across the nation new industries are developing.* **3.** The government of a country. **4a.** A people who share customs and history and often speak the same language. **b.** A federation or tribe, especially of Native Americans. [From Middle English *nacioun,* from Latin *nātiō,* from *nātus,* born, past participle of *nāscī,* to be born.]

Na·tion (**nā′**shən), **Carry Amelia Moore** 1846–1911. American temperance leader who organized a branch of the Women's Christian Temperance Union in Kansas and conducted a series of raids on saloons.

na·tion·al (**năsh′**ə-nəl *or* **năsh′**nəl) *adj.* **1.** Relating or belonging to a nation as a whole: *a national anthem; national elections.* **2.** Peculiar to or typical of the people of a nation: *national traits.* **3.** Maintained or supported by the government of a nation: *national parks.* ❖ *n.* A citizen of a particular nation: *a French national.* **—na′tion·al·ly** *adv.*

national bank *n.* **1.** A federally chartered bank in the United States, supervised by the Office of the Comptroller of the Currency, a department of the US Treasury. **2.** A bank controlled by or associated with a national government, especially a central bank.

national forest *n.* A large area of forest in which a government limits the cutting of trees and hunting.

National Guard *n.* The military reserve units of each state of the United States.

na·tion·al·ism (**năsh′**ə-nə-lĭz′əm *or* **năsh′**nə-lĭz′əm) *n.* **1.** Devotion, especially excessive or unquestioning devotion, to the interests or culture of a particular nation-state. **2.** The belief that one's own nation will benefit from acting independently, rather than in coordination with other nations.

na·tion·al·ist (**năsh′**ə-nə-lĭst *or* **năsh′**nə-lĭst) *n.* A person who believes in nationalism. ❖ *adj.* Relating to or advocating nationalism: *a nationalist party; a nationalist candidate.* **—na′tion·al·is′tic** *adj.* **—na′tion·al·is′ti·cal·ly** *adv.*

na·tion·al·i·ty (năsh′ə-**năl′**ĭ-tē *or* năsh-**năl′**ĭ-tē) *n., pl.* **na·tion·al·i·ties 1.** The status of belonging to a particular nation by origin, birth, or naturalization: *American nationality.* **2.** A people having common origins or traditions: *Many nationalities have settled in America.*

na·tion·al·ize (**năsh′**ə-nə-līz′ *or* **năsh′**nə-līz′) *tr.v.* **na·tion·al·ized, na·tion·al·iz·ing, na·tion·al·iz·es 1.** To remove from private ownership and put under the control of the government: *When did England nationalize its steel industry?* **2.** To make national, as in fame: *TV commercials are nationalizing the candidate's name.* **—na′tion·al·i·za′tion** (**năsh′**ə-nə-lĭ-**zā′**shən *or* năsh′-nə-lĭ-**zā′**shən) *n.*

national monument *n.* A natural landmark or a structure or site of historic interest maintained by a national government for public enjoyment or study.

national park *n.* A tract of land declared public property by a national government in order to preserve and develop it for recreation and study.

national seashore *n.* A recreational area along a seacoast that a national government protects and maintains for public use.

National Socialism *n.* Nazism.

na·tion-state (**nā′**shən-stāt′) *n.* A political unit consisting of an independent state in which most of the people share a common culture, history, and language: *What is now Italy was once a collection of independent nation-states.*

na·tion·wide (nā′shən-**wīd′**) *adv. & adj.* Throughout a whole nation: *The speech was broadcast nationwide. There is nationwide interest in recycling.*

na·tive (**nā′**tĭv) *adj.* **1.** Being such by birth or origin: *a native Englishman.* **2.** Being one's own because of the place of one's birth: *one's native land.* **3.** Originally living, growing, or produced in a particular place: *a plant native to Asia.* **4a.** Being a member of the original inhabitants of a particular place. **b.** Belonging to or characteristic of such inhabitants: *a native custom.* **5.** Occurring in nature in pure form or without other substances: *native copper.* **6.** Belonging to one by nature; inborn; natural: *native ability.* ❖ *n.* **1.** A person born in a particular place: *a native of New York now living in California.* **2.** One of the original inhabitants of a region. **3.** An animal or plant that originated in a particular place. [From Middle English *natif,* from Latin *nātīvus,* from *nāscī,* to be born.] **—na′tive·ly** *adv.*

Native Alaskan *n.* An Alaska Native.

Native American *n.* A member of any of the peoples

ă	pat	ôr	core
ā	pay	oi	boy
âr	care	ou	out
ä	father	ŏŏ	took
ĕ	pet	ŏŏr	lure
ē	be	ōō	boot
ĭ	pit	ŭ	cut
ī	bite	ûr	urge
îr	pier	th	thin
ŏ	pot	*th*	this
ō	toe	zh	vision
ô	paw	ə	about

living in the Western Hemisphere before the arrival of the Europeans. The ancestors of Native Americans are thought to have come to the Americas from Asia by way of the Bering Strait during the last Ice Age. —SEE NOTE.

na·tive-born (nā′tĭv-**bôrn′**) *adj.* Belonging to a place by birth.

Native Hawaiian *n.* A member or descendant of the Polynesian people that first settled the Hawaiian Islands.

na·tiv·i·ty (nə-**tĭv′**ĭ-tē *or* nā-**tĭv′**ĭ-tē) *n., pl.* **na·tiv·i·ties 1.** Birth, especially the place, condition, or circumstances of being born. **2. Nativity a.** The birth of Jesus. **b.** A representation, such as a painting, of Jesus just after birth.

natl. *abbr.* An abbreviation of national.

NATO *abbr.* An abbreviation of North Atlantic Treaty Organization.

nat·ty (**năt′**ē) *adj.* **nat·ti·er, nat·ti·est** Neat and trim; dapper: *a natty suit.* **—nat′ti·ly** *adv.* **—nat′ti·ness** *n.*

nat·u·ral (**năch′**ər-əl *or* **năch′**rəl) *adj.* **1.** Present in or produced by nature; not artificial or synthetic: *a natural pearl.* **2.** Relating to the physical world and the events that occur in it: *natural laws.* **3.** Following the usual course of nature: *a natural death.* **4a.** Having qualities or abilities that are or seem to be inborn: *a natural leader.* **b.** Present from birth; not acquired: *He has a natural curiosity for how things are put together.* **5.** Not artificial or affected; spontaneous: *a natural way of speaking.* **6.** Expected; accepted: *Their friendship is a natural consequence of their interest in art.* **7.** In music, not having or using any sharps or flats. ❖ *n.* **1a.** A person having the skills necessary for success: *You are a natural for this job.* **b.** A person suited by nature for something: *She is a natural at mathematics.* **2a.** In music, a tone that is not altered by a sharp or flat. **b.** A musical sign (♮) indicating that any sharps or flats that would otherwise affect a tone are to be canceled. **—nat′u·ral·ness** *n.*

natural food *n.* Food that contains no additives, such as preservatives or artificial coloring or flavoring.

natural gas *n.* A mixture of hydrocarbon gases, principally methane, that occurs with petroleum deposits. It is used as a fuel and in manufacturing organic compounds.

natural history *n.* The study of living things and natural objects, especially their origins, evolution, and relationships to one another.

nat·u·ral·ist (**năch′**ər-ə-lĭst *or* **năch′**rə-lĭst) *n.* A person who specializes in natural history, especially in the study of plants and animals in their natural surroundings.

nat·u·ral·ize (**năch′**ər-ə-līz′ *or* **năch′**rə-līz′) *tr.v.* **nat·u·ral·ized, nat·u·ral·iz·ing, nat·u·ral·iz·es 1.** To give full citizenship to (a person of foreign birth). **2.** To adopt (something foreign, such as a word from another language) into general use. **3.** To introduce and establish (a plant or animal) in a new environment: *Dandelions are European plants that have been naturalized in North America.* **—nat′u·ral·i·za′tion** (năch′ər-ə-lĭ-**zā′**shən *or* năch′rə-lĭ-**zā′**shən) *n.*

natural language *n.* A human written or spoken language as opposed to a computer language or invented language.

nat·u·ral·ly (**năch′**ər-ə-lē *or* **năch′**rə-lē) *adv.* **1.** In a natural manner: *behave naturally.* **2.** By nature; inherently: *Children are naturally curious.* **3.** Without a doubt; surely: *Naturally, the faster you grow, the more food you need.*

natural number *n.* A member of the set of positive integers; a whole number greater than zero.

natural resource *n.* Something, such as a forest, a mineral deposit, or fresh water, that is found in nature and is necessary or useful to humans.

natural science *n.* A science, such as biology, chemistry, or physics, that deals with the objects, occurrences, or laws of nature.

natural selection *n.* The process in nature by which organisms that are better adapted to their environment tend to survive longer and produce more offspring than organisms that are less well adapted, so that the genetic characteristics of the better-adapted individuals become more widespread in later generations. Biologists consider natural selection to be the main cause of evolution. —SEE NOTE AT **evolution.**

na·ture (**nā′**chər) *n.* **1.** The physical world and the events that occur in it. **2.** The forces and processes that produce and control events in the physical world: *the laws of nature.* **3.** The world of living things and the outdoors: *enjoying the beauties of nature.* **4.** A kind or sort: *I like games of that nature.* **5.** The essential characteristics and qualities of a thing: *the mountainous nature of the region.* **6.** The fundamental character or temperament of a person or animal: *It goes against her nature to complain.* **7.** Heredity: *behavior more influenced by nature than nurture.* [From Middle English, from Latin *nātūra*, from *nāscī*, to be born.]

na·tured (**nā′**chərd) *adj.* Having a certain kind of nature or temperament: *That child has always had a sweet-natured personality.*

naught also **nought** (nôt) *n.* Zero; the digit 0. ❖ *pron.* Nothing: *All their work was for naught.* [From Middle English, from Old English *nāwiht* : *nā*, no + *wiht*, thing.]

naugh·ty (**nô′**tē) *adj.* **naugh·ti·er, naugh·ti·est 1.** Disobedient; mischievous: *a naughty boy.* **2.** Bad or improper: *a naughty word.* [From Middle English *noughti*, evil, from *naught*, naught.] **—naugh′ti·ly** *adv.* **—naugh′ti·ness** *n.*

Na·u·ru (nä-**o͞o′**ro͞o) An island country of the central Pacific Ocean just south of the equator and west of Kiribati. Yaren is the capital.

nau·se·a (**nô′**zē-ə *or* **nô′**zhə) *n.* **1.** A feeling of sickness in the stomach, characterized by the need to vomit. **2.** Strong repugnance; disgust. [From Latin, from Greek *nautiā*, seasickness, from *nautēs*, sailor.]

nau·se·ate (**nô′**zē-āt′ *or* **nô′**zhē-āt′) *intr. & tr.v.* **nau·se·at·ed, nau·se·at·ing, nau·se·ates** To feel or cause to feel nausea.

nau·se·at·ed (**nô′**zē-ā′tĭd *or* **nô′**zhē-ā′tĭd) *adj.* Suffering from nausea: *We were nauseated after riding the rollercoaster.*

nau·seous (**nô′**shəs *or* **nô′**zē-əs) *adj.* **1.** Tending to cause nausea; sickening: *a nauseous ride on the boat through the choppy waters.* **2.** Suffering from nausea: *was nauseous from eating too many oysters.*

nau·ti·cal (**nô′**tĭ-kəl) *adj.* Relating to ships, sailors, or navigation. [From Greek *nautikos*, from *nautēs*, sailor, from *naus*, ship.] **—nau′ti·cal·ly** *adv.*

nautical mile *n.* A unit of length used in air and sea navigation, equal to 1,852 meters (about 6,076 feet).

nau·ti·lus (**nôt′**l-əs) *n., pl.* **nau·ti·lus·es** or **nau·ti·li** (**nôt′**l-ī′) **1.** Any of several tropical sea mollusks related to the squids and octopuses, having slender tentacles and a spiral shell divided into many partitions. **2.** The paper nautilus.

Nav·a·jo also **Nav·a·ho** (**năv′**ə-hō′ *or* **nä′**və-hō′) *n., pl.* **Navajo** or **Nav·a·jos** also **Navaho** or **Nav·a·hos 1.** A member of a Native American people living in New Mexico, Arizona, and Utah. **2.** The Athabascan language of the Navajo. **—Nav′a·jo′** *adj.*

na·val (**nā′**vəl) *adj.* **1.** Relating to a navy. **2.** Having a navy: *a great naval power.*

❑ *These sound alike:* **naval, navel** (bellybutton).

Na·varre (nə-**vär′**) A historical region and former kingdom of southwest Europe in the Pyrenees of northern Spain and southwest France. It was ruled by a Basque dynasty from the 9th to the 13th century.

USAGE

Native American

Many people now think of **Native American** as a more accurate and respectful term than *Indian* (or the more specific *American Indian*) when talking about the earliest inhabitants of the Americas or their descendants. Using *Native American* instead of *Indian* also avoids any confusion between these peoples and the inhabitants of India. However, *Indian* is still widely used and is not usually considered offensive. There is an important difference between these two terms when referring to the native peoples of the Arctic regions: the Eskimo, Inuit, and Aleut peoples are properly called *Native Americans,* but they are not considered to be *Indians.*

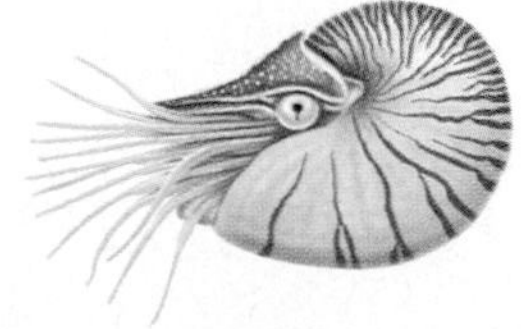

nautilus

Martina Navratilova
photographed in 2010

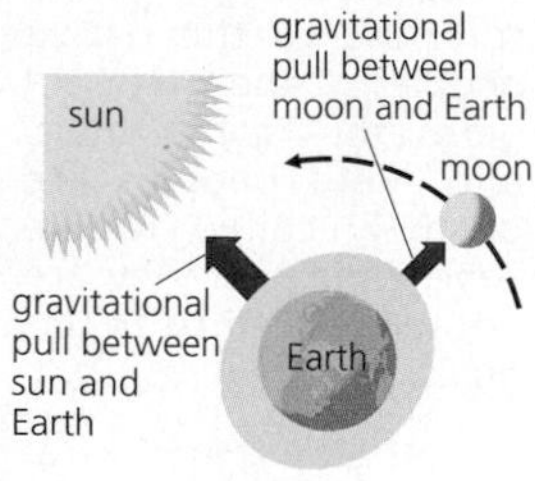

neap tide
Neap tides occur when the sun, moon, and Earth form a right angle and the gravitational pull of the sun counteracts the pull of the moon.

ă	pat	ôr	core
ā	pay	oi	boy
âr	care	ou	out
ä	father	o͝o	took
ĕ	pet	o͝or	lure
ē	be	o͞o	boot
ĭ	pit	ŭ	cut
ī	bite	ûr	urge
îr	pier	th	thin
ŏ	pot	*th*	this
ō	toe	zh	vision
ô	paw	ə	about

nave (nāv) *n.* The central part of a church flanked by the side aisles. [From Latin *nāvis*, ship (from its shape).]
❑ *These sound alike:* **nave, knave** (crafty man).

na·vel (nā′vəl) *n.* **1.** The scar left on the abdomen of mammals where the umbilical cord was attached before birth. **2.** A central point; the middle.
❑ *These sound alike:* **navel, naval** (of a navy).

navel orange *n.* A sweet seedless orange that has a structure resembling a navel at the end opposite the stem.

nav·i·ga·ble (năv′ĭ-gə-bəl) *adj.* **1.** Deep enough or wide enough for navigation. **2.** Capable of being steered: *a navigable aircraft.* **—nav′i·ga·bil′i·ty** *n.* **—nav′i·ga·bly** *adv.*

nav·i·gate (năv′ĭ-gāt′) *v.* **nav·i·gat·ed, nav·i·gat·ing, nav·i·gates** *—intr.* **1a.** To plot and control the course of a ship or aircraft. **b.** To give directions to the driver of an automobile, especially by reading a map. **c.** To determine a migratory course. Used of an animal: *How do butterflies navigate when they migrate?* **2.** To make orderly progress through something: *I navigated through the website.* *—tr.* **1.** To direct (a ship or aircraft) over a planned course. **2a.** To follow a planned course on, across, or through: *navigate a stream.* **b.** To progress through (something) in a particular order: *navigated a set of instructions.* [From Latin *nāvigāre* : *nāvis*, ship + *agere*, to drive, lead.]

nav·i·ga·tion (năv′ĭ-gā′shən) *n.* **1.** The theory and practice of navigating, especially the science of charting a course for a ship or aircraft. **2.** Travel or traffic by vessels, especially commercial shipping. **—nav′i·ga′tion·al** *adj.* **—nav′i·ga′tion·al·ly** *adv.*

nav·i·ga·tor (năv′ĭ-gā′tər) *n.* **1.** A person who plots the course of a ship or aircraft. **2.** A device that directs the course of an aircraft or missile.

Nav·ra·ti·lo·va (năv′rə-tĭ-lō′və), **Martina** Born 1956. Czech-American tennis player who won nine Wimbledon women's singles championships between 1978 and 1990.

na·vy (nā′vē) *n., pl.* **na·vies 1.** All of a nation's warships. **2.** often **Navy** A nation's entire organization for sea warfare, including vessels, personnel, and shore establishments. **3.** Navy blue. [From Middle English, from Latin *nāvigia*, ships.]

navy bean *n.* A type of bean that has small, whitish seeds.

navy blue *n.* A dark grayish blue.

navy yard *n.* A dockyard for the construction, repair, equipping, or docking of naval ships.

nay (nā) *adv.* **1.** No: *All but four senators voted nay to the treaty.* **2.** And moreover: *That act was disloyal, nay, traitorous to the country.* ❖ *n.* **1.** A vote of "no." **2.** A person who votes "no": *The nays carried it, and the bill was defeated.* [From Old Norse *nei*, no.]
❑ *These sound alike:* **nay, née** (born), **neigh** (whinny).

Nay·pyi·daw (nĕ′pyē-dô′) The capital of Myanmar (Burma), in the south-central part of the country north of Yangon (Rangoon). It was established as Myanmar's new capital in 2006.

nay·say·er (nā′sā′ər) *n.* A person who tends to oppose, deny, or take a negative view: *The naysayers at the meeting found fault with every proposal.*

Naz·a·rene (năz′ə-rēn′ *or* năz′ə-rēn′) *n.* **1.** A person who was born or lives in Nazareth. **2.** Jesus. **3.** A member of a group of early Christians who followed many Jewish practices.

Naz·a·reth (năz′ər-əth) A town of northern Israel southeast of Haifa. It is mentioned in the New Testament as the boyhood home of Jesus.

Na·zi (nät′sē *or* năt′sē) *n., pl.* **Na·zis 1.** A member of the National Socialist German Workers' Party founded in 1919 and brought to power by Adolf Hitler in 1933. **2.** An advocate or supporter of Nazism. ❖ *adj.* Relating to or typical of Nazis. [From German, short for *Nationalsozialist*, National Socialist.]

Na·zism (nät′sĭz′əm *or* năt′sĭz′əm) also **Na·zi·ism** (nät′sē-ĭz′əm *or* năt′sē-ĭz′əm) *n.* The doctrines and practices of Nazis, especially their anti-Semitism, belief in a master race, extreme nationalism, and use of military force to dominate Europe.

Nb The symbol for the element **niobium.**

NB *abbr.* An abbreviation of New Brunswick.

NC *abbr.* An abbreviation of North Carolina.

NC-17 (ĕn′sē-sĕv′ən-tēn′) A trademark used for a movie rating that allows admission to no one under the age of 18.

NCAA *abbr.* An abbreviation of National Collegiate Athletic Association.

NCO *abbr.* An abbreviation of noncommissioned officer.

Nd The symbol for the element **neodymium.**

ND *abbr.* An abbreviation of North Dakota.

N'Dja·me·na (ən-jä′mə-nə) The capital of Chad, in the southwest part of the country. It was founded in 1900.

Ne The symbol for the element **neon.**

NE *abbr.* An abbreviation of: **1.** Nebraska. **2.** New England. **3.** northeast. **4.** northeastern.

Ne·an·der·thal (nē-ăn′dər-thôl′) *n.* A species of extinct prehistoric humans characterized by short stature and a stocky body. Neanderthals lived in caves, used fire, and made stone tools. [After *Neanderthal* (Neandertal), a valley in western Germany where the first fossils were found.] **—Ne·an′der·thal′** *adj.*

Ne·a·pol·i·tan (nē′ə-pŏl′ĭ-tən) *adj.* Relating to the city of Naples, Italy. ❖ *n.* A native or resident of Naples, Italy.

neap tide (nēp) *n.* A tide that occurs when the difference between high and low tide is least. Neap tide comes twice a month, in the first and third quarters of the moon.

near (nîr) *adv.* **near·er, near·est 1.** To, at, or within a short distance or interval in space or time: *Summer vacation is drawing near.* **2.** Almost; nearly: *near exhausted by the climb.* ❖ *adj.* **nearer, nearest 1.** Close in space, time, position, or degree: *near neighbors; near equals.* **2.** Closely related by kinship or association; intimate: *near relatives.* **3a.** Almost but not actually occurring: *a near victory.* **b.** Just barely avoided: *a near tragedy.* **4.** Bearing a close resemblance: *a near likeness of her.* **5.** Closer of two or more: *the near side of the house.* **6.** Short and direct: *the nearest route to the airport.* ❖ *prep.* Close to, as in time, space, or degree: *We stayed at a little inn near London.* ❖ *v.* **neared, near·ing, nears** *—tr.* To come close or closer to: *The plane neared the runway.* *—intr.* To draw near or nearer; approach: *The holiday season nears.* [From Old English *nēar*, closer, from comparative of *nēah*, nigh, close.] **—near′ness** *n.*

near·by (nîr′bī′) *adj.* Located a short distance away; close at hand: *a nearby supermarket.* ❖ *adv.* Not far away; close by: *A brook ran nearby.*

Near East A region of southwest Asia generally defined as including Asia Minor, the Levant, and Mesopotamia and sometimes also the Arabian Peninsula, Iran, and the Nile River valley of northeast Africa.

near·ly (nîr′lē) *adv.* **1.** Almost but not quite: *That coat nearly fits.* **2.** Closely or intimately: *The two girls are nearly related.*

near·sight·ed (nîr′sī′tĭd) *adj.* Unable to see distant objects clearly; myopic. **—near′sight′ed·ly** *adv.* **—near′sight′ed·ness** *n.*

neat (nēt) *adj.* **neat·er, neat·est 1a.** Orderly and clean; tidy: *a neat room; neat handwriting.* **b.** Habitually well-organized: *a neat person.* **2.** Performed with precision and skill: *a neat, graceful takeoff.* **3.** *Slang* Wonderful; fine: *a neat party.* [From Old French, from Latin *nitidus*, elegant, gleaming.] —**neat′ly** *adv.* —**neat′ness** *n.*

neat·en (nēt′n) *tr.v.* **neat·ened, neat·en·ing, neat·ens** To put into order; make neat: *I neatened my desk at the end of the day.*

neath or **'neath** (nēth) *prep.* Beneath.

neat's-foot oil (nēts′fo͝ot′) *n.* An oil obtained from the feet and shinbones of cattle, used chiefly to finish leather. [From archaic *neat,* cow, head of cattle, from Old English.]

neb·bish (nĕb′ĭsh) *n.* A weak-willed and timid person.

Ne·bras·ka (nə-brăs′kə) A state of the central United States in the Great Plains north of Kansas. It was admitted as the 37th state in 1867. Lincoln is the capital and Omaha the largest city. —SEE NOTE.

Neb·u·chad·nez·zar II (nĕb′ə-kəd-nĕz′ər) 630?–562 BC. King of Babylonia (605–562) who destroyed Jerusalem in 586 and held the Israelites captive in Babylonia.

neb·u·la (nĕb′yə-lə) *n., pl.* **neb·u·lae** (nĕb′yə-lē′) or **neb·u·las** A thinly spread cloud of interstellar gas or dust or both, appearing as a bright or dark patch in the night sky depending on the way the light that strikes it is reflected, absorbed, or reemitted. [From Latin *nebula,* mist, cloud.] —**neb′u·lar** *adj.*

neb·u·lous (nĕb′yə-ləs) *adj.* **1.** Lacking definite form; vague; unclear. **2.** Relating to a nebula. —**neb′u·lous·ly** *adv.* —**neb′u·lous·ness** *n.*

nec·es·sar·i·ly (nĕs′ĭ-sâr′ə-lē *or* nĕs′ĭ-sĕr′ə-lē) *adv.* As a necessary result; inevitably: *Playing at home does not necessarily mean that they'll win the game.*

nec·es·sar·y (nĕs′ĭ-sĕr′ē) *adj.* **1.** Needed or required: *Getting enough sleep is necessary to stay healthy.* **2.** Following as a certain result; inevitable: *The job cuts are a necessary consequence of the economic downturn.* ❖ *n., pl.* **nec·es·sar·ies** Something needed or required. [From Latin *necessārius,* from *necesse,* necessary.]

ne·ces·si·tate (nə-sĕs′ĭ-tāt′) *tr.v.* **ne·ces·si·tat·ed, ne·ces·si·tat·ing, ne·ces·si·tates** To make necessary or unavoidable: *The poor light necessitated the use of a flash to take the picture.* —**ne·ces′si·ta′tion** *n.*

ne·ces·si·ty (nə-sĕs′ĭ-tē) *n., pl.* **ne·ces·si·ties 1.** Something needed for the existence, success, or functioning of something; a requirement: *Water is a necessity for plant growth.* **2.** The quality, condition, or fact of being necessary: *the necessity of sleep.* **3.** Something that must inevitably exist or occur: *the necessity of water freezing when cooled to 32 degrees.* **4.** Pressing or urgent need, especially that arising from poverty.

neck (nĕk) *n.* **1.** The part of the body joining the head to the shoulders or trunk. **2.** The part of a garment that fits around the neck. **3.** A narrow projection or connecting part: *the neck of a bottle.* **4.** The narrow part of a stringed instrument along which the strings extend to the pegs. ❖ *intr.v.* **necked, neck·ing, necks** *Informal* To kiss and caress. ◆ **neck and neck** So close that the lead between competitors is impossible to tell. **neck of the woods** A region or neighborhood: *It doesn't snow much in September in my neck of the woods.* **up to (one's) neck** Deeply involved or occupied fully: *I'm up to my neck in homework.* [From Old English *hnecca.*]

neck·band (nĕk′bănd′) *n.* The band around the collar of a garment.

neck·er·chief (nĕk′ər-chĭf *or* nĕk′ər-chēf′) *n.* A kerchief worn around the neck.

neck·lace (nĕk′lĭs) *n.* An ornament that goes around the neck, as a string of beads or jewels.

neck·line (nĕk′līn′) *n.* The line formed by the edge of a garment at or below the neck.

neck·tie (nĕk′tī′) *n.* A narrow band of cloth worn around the neck beneath the collar and tied in a knot or bow close to the throat.

neck·wear (nĕk′wâr′) *n.* Articles, such as neckties or scarves, worn around the neck.

nec·ro·man·cy (nĕk′rə-măn′sē) *n.* **1.** The practice of communicating with the spirits of the dead in order to predict the future. **2.** Black magic; sorcery. **3.** Magical qualities. —**nec′ro·man′cer** *n.* —**nec′ro·man′tic** *adj.*

nec·tar (nĕk′tər) *n.* **1.** A sweet liquid that is secreted by many plants, especially inside flowers, and is used by bees in making honey. **2.** In Greek mythology, the drink of the gods. **3.** A delicious drink. [From Greek *nektar,* drink of the gods.]

nec·tar·ine (nĕk′tə-rēn′) *n.* **1.** A type of peach having smooth reddish skin. **2.** The tree that bears such fruit.

née also **nee** (nā) *adj.* Born. Used to indicate the maiden name of a married woman.

❑ *These sound alike:* **née, nay** (no), **neigh** (whinny).

need (nēd) *n.* **1.** A situation in which something must be supplied in order for a certain condition to be maintained or a desired state to be achieved: *The school has a need for new computers. The crops are in need of water.* **2.** Something required or wanted: *Our needs are modest.* **3.** Necessity or obligation: *There wasn't any need for you to pay me back.* **4.** Extreme poverty or misfortune: *living in dire need.* ❖ *v.* **need·ed, need·ing, needs** —*aux.* To be required or obliged to: *You need not come today.* —*tr.* To require; have need of: *The washing machine needs repairing.* —*intr.* To be in need or want: *You will never need if you inherit a fortune.* ◆ **if need be** If necessary: *I'll go in person, if need be.* [From Middle English, from Old English *nēd.*]

❑ *These sound alike:* **need, knead** (press and shape).

need·ful (nēd′fəl) *adj.* Necessary; required. —**need′ful·ly** *adv.* —**need′ful·ness** *n.*

nee·dle (nēd′l) *n.* **1.** A slender, pointed sewing implement, made of polished steel and having an eye at one end through which a length of thread is passed and held. **2a.** A slender pointed rod used in knitting. **b.** A similar implement with a hook at one end, used in crocheting. **3.** A slender piece of a jewel or steel that transmits vibrations from the groove of a phonograph record. **4.** The pointer or indicator of a dial, gauge, or compass. **5.** A hypodermic syringe. **6.** A sharp pointed instrument used in engraving and etching. **7.** A stiff narrow leaf, as of a pine tree. ❖ *tr.v.* **nee·dled, nee·dling, nee·dles** *Informal* To goad, provoke, or tease. [From Old English *nethle.*]

nee·dle·craft (nēd′l-krăft′) *n.* The art or process of needlework.

nee·dle·point (nēd′l-point′) *n.* Embroidery on canvas done with even stitches to resemble a woven tapestry.

needless *adj.* Not needed; unnecessary: *Pronouns help a writer avoid needless repetition.* —**need′less·ly** *adv.* —**need′less·ness** *n.*

nee·dle·work (nēd′l-wûrk′) *n.* Work, such as sewing or embroidery, that is done with a needle.

need·n't (nēd′nt) Contraction of *need not.*

need·y (nē′dē) *adj.* **need·i·er, need·i·est 1.** Being in need; impoverished. **2.** Wanting or needing an excessive amount of attention or reassurance.

ne'er (nâr) *adv.* Never.

ne'er-do-well (nâr′do͞o-wĕl′) *n.* An irresponsible person who never gets anything done.

ne·far·i·ous (nə-fâr′ē-əs) *adj.* Evil; wicked: *a nefarious plot.*

ne·gate (nĭ-gāt′) *tr.v.* **ne·gat·ed, ne·gat·ing, ne·gates** **1.** To make ineffective or invalid; nullify: *This new amendment negates the former bill.* **2.** To make negative: *Sentences can be negated by using the word "not."* [From Latin *negāre.*]

ne·ga·tion (nĭ-gā′shən) *n.* **1.** The act or process of negating. **2.** A negative statement; a denial. **3.** The opposite of something regarded as positive or affirmative: *His actions are a negation of everything we believe in.*

neg·a·tive (nĕg′ə-tĭv) *adj.* **1.** Expressing or consisting

GEOGRAPHY

Nebraska The state of **Nebraska** takes its name from an Omaha word that means "flat water" or "flat river." The Omaha people used this name for the river that was later renamed the Platte (from the French word *plate,* meaning "flat"). The name *Nebraska* was used first for the territory created in 1854 and later for the state.

nebula
Orion nebula

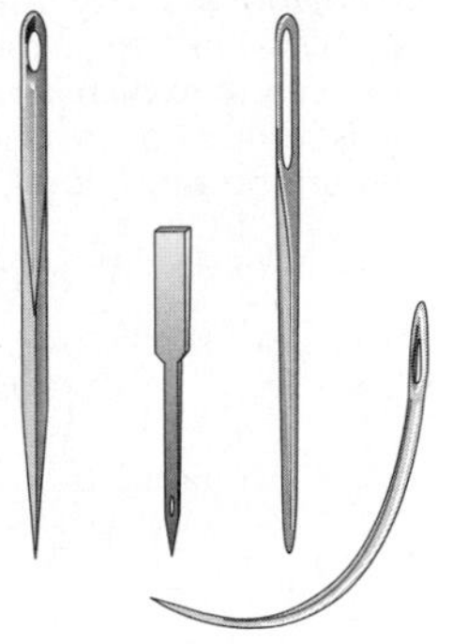

needle
left to right: sail-making, sewing machine, tapestry, and spring needles

Jawaharlal Nehru

USAGE

neither When **neither** is used as a pronoun, it takes a singular verb: *Neither of the candidates is going to speak tonight.* When *neither* is used as a conjunction, you should follow it with *nor* rather than *or: Neither rain nor snow stopped her from going for a walk every day.* In a *neither ... nor* construction, use the singular when the words used as the subject of a sentence are singular: *Neither Jennifer nor June is coming to the party.* When the words are plural, the verb is plural: *Neither the Montoyas nor the Smiths are having a party this year.* It is best to avoid sentences in which *neither* is followed by one singular and one plural.

ă	pat	ôr	core
ā	pay	oi	boy
âr	care	ou	out
ä	father	o͝o	took
ĕ	pet	o͝or	lure
ē	be	o͞o	boot
ĭ	pit	ŭ	cut
ī	bite	ûr	urge
îr	pier	th	thin
ŏ	pot	*th*	this
ō	toe	zh	vision
ô	paw	ə	about

of a negation, denial, or refusal: *a negative answer.* **2.** Indicating opposition or resistance: *a negative reaction among the people.* **3.** Unpleasant, pessimistic, or unfavorable: *a negative experience; a negative outlook; a negative review.* **4.** Not indicating the presence of a particular disease, condition, or organism: *a negative result of a blood test.* **5.** Less than zero: *Negative five can be written as –5.* **6.** Relating to or having the electric charge of an electron and therefore tending to repel electrons and attract protons. **7.** Moving away from a stimulus, such as light: *a negative tropism.* ❖ *n.* **1.** A contradiction, denial, or refusal: *answered the question with a negative.* **2.** Something that lacks positive or affirmative qualities: *There are many negatives in this proposal.* **3.** In grammar, a word or part of a word that expresses negation; for example, *no, not,* and *un-* are negatives. **4.** The side in a debate that contradicts or opposes the question being debated. **5a.** An image in which the light areas appear dark and the dark areas appear light. **b.** A film or photographic plate containing such an image. **6.** A negative number. ◆ **in the negative** In a sense or manner indicating a refusal or denial: *answered in the negative.* **—neg′a·tive·ly** *adv.* **—neg′a·tiv′i·ty** *n.*

ne·glect (nĭ-**glĕkt′**) *tr.v.* **ne·glect·ed, ne·glect·ing, ne·glects 1.** To ignore or pay no attention to; disregard: *He neglected our warnings to stay indoors.* **2.** To fail to care for or give proper attention to: *He neglects his appearance.* **3.** To fail to do, as through carelessness: *We neglected to tell the committee about the extra expenses.* ❖ *n.* **1.** The act or an example of neglecting: *You got into trouble because of your neglect of your homework.* **2.** The condition of being neglected: *The garden has fallen into neglect.* [From Latin *neglegere.*]

ne·glect·ful (nĭ-**glĕkt′**fəl) *adj.* Marked by neglect; careless; heedless: *neglectful of their responsibility.* **—ne·glect′ful·ly** *adv.*

neg·li·gee also **neg·li·gée** or **neg·li·gé** (nĕg′lĭ-**zhā′** *or* **nĕg′**lĭ-zhā′) *n.* A woman's loose dressing gown, often of soft delicate material.

neg·li·gence (**nĕg′**lĭ-jəns) *n.* Failure to act with proper care or concern in a situation.

neg·li·gent (**nĕg′**lĭ-jənt) *adj.* Guilty of neglect; lacking in proper care or concern: *a negligent worker.* **—neg′li·gent·ly** *adv.*

neg·li·gi·ble (**nĕg′**lĭ-jə-bəl) *adj.* Not worth considering; amounting to very little: *a negligible quantity.* **—neg′li·gi·bly** *adv.*

ne·go·tia·ble (nĭ-**gō′**shə-bəl *or* nĭ-**gō′**shē-ə-bəl) *adj.* **1.** Capable of being discussed in an effort to reach an agreement: *a negotiable contract.* **2.** Capable of being legally transferred from one person to another: *This certificate is negotiable when signed.* **—ne·go′tia·bil′i·ty** *n.*

ne·go·ti·ate (nĭ-**gō′**shē-āt′) *v.* **ne·go·ti·at·ed, ne·go·ti·at·ing, ne·go·ti·ates** *—intr.* To talk with others in order to reach an agreement: *We must be prepared to compromise if we are going to negotiate.* *—tr.* **1.** To arrange or settle by discussion: *They negotiated the new teachers' contract last summer.* **2.** To transfer (a promissory note, for example) to another party by means of endorsement. **3.** To succeed in going over or through: *The car negotiated a sharp turn.* [From Latin *negōtium,* business.] **—ne·go′ti·a′tor** *n.*

ne·go·ti·a·tion (nĭ-gō′shē-**ā′**shən) *n.* The act or process of negotiating: *secret negotiations between the two nations.*

Ne·gro (**nē′**grō) *Often Offensive n., pl.* **Ne·groes** A black person.

Ne·he·mi·ah[1] (nē′hə-**mī′**ə *or* nē′ə-**mī′**ə) A Jewish leader and governor of Judea in the fifth century BC when the Jews were captives in Babylon.

Ne·he·mi·ah[2] (nē′hə-**mī′**ə *or* nē′ə-**mī′**ə) *n.* A book of the Bible that relates Nehemiah's plans for rebuilding Jerusalem.

Neh·ru (**nā′**ro͞o), **Jawaharlal** 1889–1964. Indian nationalist politician who was the first prime minister of independent India (1947–1964).

neigh (nā) *n.* The long, high-pitched sound made by a horse. ❖ *intr.v.* **neighed, neigh·ing, neighs** To make the sound of a horse; whinny.
❑ *These sound alike:* **neigh, nay** (no), **née** (born).

neigh·bor (**nā′**bər) *n.* **1.** A person who lives near or next door to another. **2.** A person or thing adjacent to or near another: *Earth's nearest neighbor is the moon.* **3.** A fellow human. ❖ *tr.v.* **neigh·bored, neigh·bor·ing, neigh·bors** To be near or next to: *How many countries neighbor Thailand?* [From Middle English, from Old English *nēahgebūr* : *nēah,* near + *gebūr,* dweller.]

neigh·bor·hood (**nā′**bər-ho͝od′) *n.* **1.** A district or area with distinct characteristics. **2.** The people who live in a particular area or district: *The noise upset the entire neighborhood.* **3.** The surrounding area; the vicinity: *I just happened to be in the neighborhood.* ◆ **in the neighborhood of** Approximately: *inflation in the neighborhood of three percent a year.*

neigh·bor·ly (**nā′**bər-lē) *adj.* Having or showing the quality of a friendly neighbor: *a neighborly act of kindness.* **—neigh′bor·li·ness** *n.*

nei·ther (**nē′***th*ər *or* **nī′***th*ər) *adj.* Not either; not one nor the other: *Neither shoe fits comfortably.* ❖ *pron.* Not either one; not the one nor the other: *Neither of the shoes fits.* ❖ *conj.* **1.** Not either; not in either case. Used with *nor: They had neither seen nor heard of us.* **2.** Also not; nor: *If you won't go, neither will I.* —SEE NOTE.

nel·son (**nĕl′**sən) *n.* One of several holds in wrestling in which a wrestler slips one arm under the opponent's arm and presses the hand against the opponent's neck.

nem·a·to·cyst (**nĕm′**ə-tə-sĭst′ *or* nĭ-**măt′**ə-sĭst′) *n.* One of the stinging cells in the tentacles of a jellyfish, coral, or related animal, used to capture prey and ward off attackers.

nem·a·tode (**nĕm′**ə-tōd′) *n.* Any of numerous slender, usually very small worms, many of which are parasites that cause disease in plants and animals; a roundworm.

nem·e·sis (**nĕm′**ĭ-sĭs) *n., pl.* **nem·e·ses** (**nĕm′**ĭ-sēz′) **1a.** A source of harm or ruin: *Carelessness was your nemesis on that math exam.* **b.** Just punishment for wrongdoing. **2.** An unbeatable rival: *He met his nemesis in the tennis finals.* **3. Nemesis** In Greek mythology, the goddess of retributive justice or vengeance.

ne·ne (**nā′**nā) *n.* A rare wild goose of the Hawaiian Islands with a grayish-brown body and a black face.

neo– *pref.* A prefix that means new or recent: *Neolithic.* —SEE NOTE.

ne·o·dym·i·um (nē′ō-**dĭm′**ē-əm) *n. Symbol* **Nd** A bright, silvery metallic element used in coloring glass and in making materials with strong magnetic properties for use in computer and audio equipment. Atomic number 60. See **Periodic Table.**

Ne·o·gene (**nē′**ō-jēn′) *n.* The second and later subdivision of the Tertiary Period, from about 23 to 2.5 million years ago. During the Neogene, grasses and grazing animals evolved. See **geologic time.** **—Ne′o·gene′** *adj.*

Ne·o·lith·ic (nē′ə-**lĭth′**ĭk) *adj.* Relating to the last period of human culture in the Stone Age, beginning around 10,000 years ago in the Middle East and later in other parts of the world. It is characterized by the introduction of farming, the domestication of animals, and the development of crafts such as pottery and weaving. ❖ *n.* The Neolithic Period.

ne·ol·o·gism (nē-**ŏl′**ə-jĭz′əm) *n.* A newly coined word, phrase, or expression or a new meaning for an existing word.

ne·on (**nē′**ŏn′) *n. Symbol* **Ne** A colorless, chemically inert gaseous element found naturally in small amounts in the atmosphere. Tubes containing neon are used in electric signs or lamps, giving off a reddish-orange glow. Atomic number 10. See **Periodic Table.** [From Greek *neos*, new.]

ne·o·nate (nē′ə-nāt′) *n.* A newborn infant. **—ne′o·na′tal** (nē′ō-nāt′l) *adj.*

Ne·o·pa·gan (nē′ō-pā′gən) *adj.* Relating to Neopaganism. ❖ *n.* An adherent of Neopaganism.

Ne·o·pa·gan·ism (nē′ō-pā′gə-nĭz′əm) *n.* Any of various religious movements arising chiefly in the late 1900s that worship pagan gods or goddesses, particularly of the earth, and practice ceremonial witchcraft.

ne·o·phyte (nē′ə-fīt′) *n.* **1.** A recent convert to a belief. **2.** A beginner or novice: *He's a neophyte at politics.* [From Middle English *neophite*, from Greek *neophutos* : *neo-*, new + *phutos*, planted.]

ne·o·prene (nē′ə-prēn′) *n.* A tough synthetic rubber that is resistant to the effects of oils, solvents, heat, and weather.

Ne·pal (nə-pôl′ *or* nə-päl′) A country of South Asia in the Himalaya Mountains between India and southwest China. It was the site of a flourishing civilization by the sixth century BC. Kathmandu is the capital.

Ne·pal·ese (nĕp′ə-lēz′ *or* nĕp′ə-lēs′) *adj.* Relating to Nepal or its people, language, or culture; Nepali. ❖ *n., pl.* **Nepalese 1.** A native or inhabitant of Nepal. **2.** The Nepali language.

Ne·pal·i (nə-pô′lē *or* nə-pä′lē) *adj.* Relating to Nepal or its people, language, or culture. ❖ *n., pl.* **Ne·pa·lis 1.** A native or inhabitant of Nepal. **2.** The Indic language of Nepal, closely related to Hindi.

neph·ew (nĕf′yo͞o) *n.* A son of one's brother or sister or of the brother or sister of one's spouse. [From Middle English *neweu*, from Latin *nepōs*, grandson, nephew.]

ne·phri·tis (nə-frī′tĭs) *n., pl.* **ne·phrit·i·des** (nə-frĭt′ĭ-dēz′) or **ne·phri·tis·es** Inflammation of the kidneys.

ne·phrol·o·gy (nə-frŏl′ə-jē) *n.* The branch of medicine that deals with the diagnosis and treatment of disorders of the kidneys. **—ne·phrol′o·gist** *n.*

neph·ron (nĕf′rŏn) *n.* One of the units of the kidney that filter waste products from the blood and produce urine.

nep·o·tism (nĕp′ə-tĭz′əm) *n.* Favoritism shown by people in high office to relatives. [From Latin *nepōs*, grandson, nephew.]

Nep·tune (nĕp′to͞on′) *n.* **1.** In Roman mythology, the god of the sea, identified with the Greek Poseidon. **2.** The eighth planet from the sun and the fourth largest in the solar system, with a diameter almost four times that of Earth. It has a very active weather system with extremely long and powerful storms. See table at **solar system.**

nep·tu·ni·um (nĕp-to͞o′nē-əm) *n.* *Symbol* **Np** A silvery, radioactive metallic element that occurs in trace amounts in uranium ores. It is produced artificially by nuclear reactions. Atomic number 93. See **Periodic Table.**

nerd (nûrd) *n.* *Slang* A person who is thought to be socially awkward, especially such a person who is skilled in scientific or technical matters.

Ne·ro (nîr′ō) AD 37–68. Emperor of Rome (54–68) who was accused of setting the Great Fire of Rome (64). He committed suicide because of widespread revolts.

nerve (nûrv) *n.* **1.** Any of the bundles of fibers made up of nerve cells that carry information in the form of electrical impulses throughout the body. Nerves send sensory information to the brain and spinal cord and carry impulses to activate the muscles, organs, and glands. **2.** A sore point; a touchy subject: *She touched a nerve when she criticized my English paper.* **3a.** Courage and self-control: *Don't lose your nerve; ask for the job.* **b.** Impudence or effrontery: *He has some nerve, saying that he's better at chess than you.* **4. nerves** Any of a group of symptoms, such as trembling or restlessness, caused by the reaction of the nervous system to fear, anxiety, or stress: *an attack of nerves.* ◆ **get on (someone's) nerves** To irritate or exasperate. **strain every nerve** To make every effort. [From Latin *nervus*.]

nerve cell *n.* Any of the cells that carry information in the form of electrical impulses throughout the body. Nerve cells consist of a cell body, one or more dendrites that carry the impulses toward the cell body, and an axon, which carries the impulses away from the cell body.

nerve fiber *n.* Either of the two kinds of threadlike structures that extend from the main body of a nerve cell; an axon or a dendrite.

nerve impulse *n.* A sequence of chemical and electrical changes that move along a nerve cell when it is stimulated. Nerve impulses convey signals from the environment to the central nervous system or from the central nervous system to muscles or glands.

nerve·less (nûrv′lĭs) *adj.* **1.** Lacking strength or energy: *The pipe dropped from his nerveless fingers.* **2.** Not nervous; calm; poised: *nerveless in the face of competition.* **—nerve′less·ly** *adv.*

nerve-rack·ing or **nerve-wrack·ing** (nûrv′răk′ĭng) *adj.* Intensely distressing or irritating to the nerves: *As they announced the awards, the suspense was nerve-racking.*

nerv·ous (nûr′vəs) *adj.* **1.** Relating to or affecting the nerves or the nervous system: *a nervous disorder.* **2.** Easily agitated or distressed; high-strung or jumpy: *a nervous person.* **3.** Tending to produce anxiety or agitation: *nervous moments before takeoff.* **—nerv′ous·ly** *adv.* **—nerv′ous·ness** *n.*

nervous breakdown *n.* A collapse in mental health that usually occurs after a period of worsening symptoms and results in an inability to function normally, as in a job or at home. This term is no longer used in medicine.

nervous system *n.* **1.** The system of cells, tissues, and organs that regulates a vertebrate animal's responses to internal and external stimuli, including the brain, spinal cord, and nerves. **2.** A similar system in most invertebrate animals.

nerv·y (nûr′vē) *adj.* **nerv·i·er, nerv·i·est** Impudent or rude: *a nervy answer.* **—nerv′i·ness** *n.*

–ness *suff.* A suffix that means state, condition, or quality: *brightness.* —SEE NOTE.

nest (nĕst) *n.* **1a.** A structure or shelter made by a bird for holding its eggs and young. **b.** A similar structure or shelter in which other animals, such as insects, fish, or mammals, place their eggs or care for their young. **c.** A number of birds, insects, or other animals occupying such a structure: *a nest of hornets.* **2.** A place of lodging or shelter: *All their children have left the nest now.* **3.** A place or environment that encourages growth, especially of people or things: *streets that are a nest of criminal activity.* **4.** A set of objects of different sizes made so that each one fits into or under the one next above it in size: *a nest of tables.* ❖ *v.* **nest·ed, nest·ing, nests** —*intr.* **1.** To build or stay in a nest: *Robins nested in the willow tree.* **2.** To fit one inside another: *hollow dolls that nest inside one another.* —*tr.* **1.** To place in a nest or a protective setting: *The diamond was nested in cotton fluff.* **2.** To fit snugly together or inside one another: *nest boxes for storage.*

nest egg *n.* A sum of money saved for future use; savings.

nes·tle (nĕs′əl) *v.* **nes·tled, nes·tling, nes·tles** —*intr.* **1.** To settle down snugly and comfortably: *The cat nestled among the pillows.* **2.** To press or snuggle close: *The child nestled up to his mother.* **3.** To lie half-sheltered or partly hidden: *Farms nestle in the valley.* —*tr.* **1.** To snuggle or press close: *The baby nestled his head on my shoulder.* **2.** To place or settle as if in a nest: *I nestled the puppy in my arms.*

WORD BUILDING

neo– The prefix **neo–**, which comes from Greek, means "new or recent." The English word *neophyte*, which means "a recent convert" or "a beginner," comes from Greek *neophutos*, which meant literally "newly planted," from *neo–* + *–phutos*, "planted." Many words beginning with *neo–* do not come from Greek, but have been formed in English over the last 200 years. A number of them refer to a new or modern form of a movement or doctrine, such as *neoconservatism* or *neofascism*.

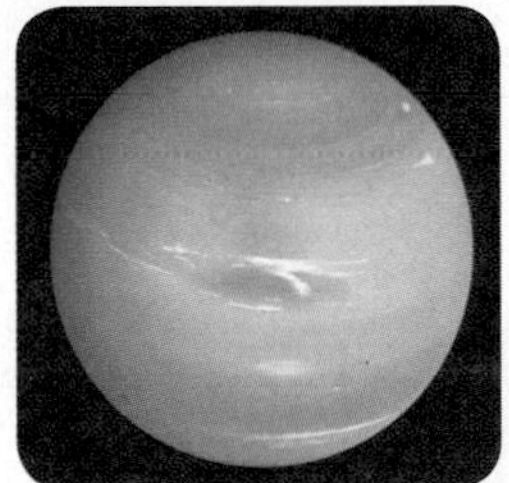

Neptune

WORD BUILDING

–ness The suffix **–ness** has had a productive life ever since Old English times. It commonly attaches to adjectives in order to form nouns meaning "the quality or state of being (whatever the adjective means)," such as *happiness* and *destructiveness*. The suffix also forms nouns from participles (themselves a kind of adjective), such as *contentedness* and *willingness*. It can also form nouns from compound adjectives, such as *kindheartedness* and *straightforwardness*. Even a phrase that is used as an adjective can have *–ness* added to it, such as *matter-of-factness*. For more information, see Note at **–ty**.

nettle

nest·ling (nĕst′lĭng *or* nĕs′lĭng) *n.* A bird that has not yet left its nest.

Nes·tor (nĕs′tər *or* nĕs′tôr′) *n.* **1.** In Greek mythology, a hero celebrated for his age and for the wisdom of his counsel among the Greeks at Troy. **2.** often **nestor** A venerable and wise old man.

net¹ (nĕt) *n.* **1.** A fabric made of threads, cords, or ropes that are woven or knotted together with holes between them. **2.** A piece of net used for a special purpose, especially: **a.** A device used to catch fish, birds, or insects. **b.** A screen or covering used as protection against insects such as mosquitoes. **c.** A piece of mesh for holding the hair in place. **d.** A fine fabric used for veils or curtains. **3a.** A barrier of mesh strung between two posts to divide a court in half, as in tennis or volleyball. **b.** The goal in soccer, hockey, or lacrosse. **c.** The cord meshwork attached to the hoop of a basket in basketball. **4a. Net** The Internet. **b.** A computer network. ❖ *tr.v.* **net·ted, net·ting, nets 1.** To catch or trap in a net: *She netted a rare butterfly.* **2.** To cover, protect, or surround with a net or network. [From Old English.]

net² (nĕt) *adj.* **1.** Remaining after all subtractions have been made: *What was your net income after expenses?* **2.** Final; ultimate: *What was the net result of your efforts?* ❖ *n.* The net amount, as of profit, income, or weight. ❖ *tr.v.* **net·ted, net·ting, nets** To bring in or yield as profit: *The cargo of spices netted a huge profit.* [From Middle English, from Latin *nitidus*, clean, elegant.]

Ne·tan·ya·hu (nĕt′n-yä′ho͞o *or* nĕ′tän-), **Benjamin** or **Binyamin** Born 1949. Israeli diplomat and politician who served as prime minister from 1996 to 1999 and began a second term in 2009.

net·book (nĕt′bo͝ok′) *n.* A portable computer that is smaller than a laptop, has less processing speed and less memory, and is used primarily for accessing the Internet.

neth·er (nĕ*th*′ər) *adj.* Located beneath or below; lower or under: *the nether regions of the earth.*

Neth·er·lands (nĕ*th*′ər-ləndz) Often called **Hol·land** (hŏl′ənd) A country of northwest Europe west of Germany on the North Sea. The kingdom of the Netherlands, proclaimed at the Congress of Vienna (1814–1815), included Belgium until 1830. Amsterdam is the constitutional capital and the largest city; The Hague is the seat of government.

Netherlands Antilles A former territory of the Netherlands in the Caribbean Sea, including Aruba, Curaçao, and Bonaire off the coast of Venezuela and several islands in the northern Windward Islands.

neth·er·most (nĕ*th*′ər-mōst′) *adj.* Lowest.

net·i·quette (nĕt′ĭ-kĕt′ *or* nĕt′ĭ-kĭt) *n.* The rules of etiquette that a person should follow when communicating over a computer network.

net·ting (nĕt′ĭng) *n.* **1.** A fabric made with open spaces between crossing strands; a net. **2.** The act or process of fishing with a net.

net·tle (nĕt′l) *n.* Any of various plants having stems and leaves covered with hairs that sting when they are touched. ❖ *tr.v.* **net·tled, net·tling, net·tles** To annoy; irritate: *I was nettled by his constant bragging.* [From Middle English, from Old English *netele*.]

net·tle·some (nĕt′l-səm) *adj.* Causing annoyance or irritation.

net·work (nĕt′wûrk′) *n.* **1.** An open fabric or structure in which cords, threads, or wires cross at regular intervals: *a network of lace.* **2.** A system or pattern made up of a number of parts, passages, lines, or routes that cross or interconnect: *a network of blood vessels.* **3.** A group of people with similar interests or concerns who communicate with each other for mutual support: *a network of parents dedicated to homeschooling.* **4a.** A chain of radio or television broadcasting stations, usually sharing a large proportion of their programs. **b.** A company that produces the programs for these stations. **5a.** A group of electric devices and connecting circuits designed to work in a specific way. **b.** A system of computers connected by telephone wires or other means in order to share information. ❖ *v.* **net·worked, net·working, net·works** —*tr.* To connect (computers) into a network. —*intr.* To interact or engage in informal communication with others for mutual assistance or support.

neu·ral (no͝or′əl) *adj.* Relating to one or more nerves or the nervous system. —**neu′ral·ly** *adv.*

neu·ri·tis (no͞o-rī′tĭs) *n.* Inflammation of a nerve.

neu·rol·o·gy (no͞o-rŏl′ə-jē) *n.* The branch of medicine that deals with the diagnosis and treatment of disorders of the nervous system. —**neu′ro·log′i·cal** (no͝or′ə-lŏj′ĭ-kəl) *adj.* —**neu·rol′o·gist** (-jĭst) *n.*

neu·ron (no͝or′ŏn′) *n.* A nerve cell. [From Greek *neuron*, sinew, string, nerve.]

neu·ro·sis (no͞o-rō′sĭs) *n., pl.* **neu·ro·ses** (no͞o-rō′sēz) A psychological state in which a person is often anxious or insecure and may or may not have a mental disorder. This term is no longer used in medicine.

neu·rot·ic (no͞o-rŏt′ĭk) *adj.* **1.** Relating to or affected by a neurosis. **2.** Overly anxious: *He's really neurotic about his grades.* ❖ *n.* A person with a neurosis, especially an overly anxious person.

neu·ro·trans·mit·ter (no͝or′ō-trănz′mĭt-ər) *n.* A chemical substance, such as acetylcholine or dopamine, that transmits impulses from one nerve cell to another.

neu·ter (no͞o′tər) *adj.* **1.** In grammar, neither masculine nor feminine in gender; for example, *it* is a neuter pronoun. **2.** Lacking or having undeveloped sex glands or sex organs. ❖ *n.* **1.** In grammar: **a.** The neuter gender. **b.** A neuter word. **2.** A neuter animal or plant. ❖ *tr.v.* **neu·tered, neu·ter·ing, neu·ters** To castrate or spay (an animal). [From Latin *neuter*, neither, neuter.]

neu·tral (no͞o′trəl) *adj.* **1a.** Not allied with, supporting, or favoring either side in a war, dispute, or contest: *a neutral nation.* **b.** Not belonging to either side in a conflict: *neutral territory.* **2.** Indicating a color, such as gray, black, or white, that lacks hue; achromatic. **3.** Without definite or distinctive characteristics: *a neutral personality.* **4.** Neither acid nor alkaline: *a neutral solution.* **5.** Having neither positive nor negative electric charge: *The neutron is a neutral particle.* ❖ *n.* **1.** A country or person that does not take part or take sides in a war or other conflict. **2.** A neutral color. **3.** A position in which a set of gears is not engaged and so no power can be transmitted: *I left the car in neutral while the mechanic checked the engine.* [From Latin *neuter*, neither, neuter.] —**neu′tral·ly** *adv.*

neu·tral·i·ty (no͞o-trăl′ĭ-tē) *n.* The condition, quality, or status of being neutral, especially a policy of taking no part in a war.

neu·tral·ize (no͞o′trə-līz′) *tr.v.* **neu·tral·ized, neu·tral·iz·ing, neu·tral·iz·es 1.** To cancel or counteract the effect of: *neutralize a poison.* **2.** To counterbalance and reduce to zero: *neutralize an electric charge.* **3.** To cause to be neither acid nor alkaline: *neutralize a solution.* —**neu′tral·i·za′tion** (no͞o′trə-lĭ-zā′shən) *n.* —**neu′tral·iz′er** *n.*

neutral zone *n.* **1.** In football, an imaginary area as wide as the length of the ball extending across the field between the lines of scrimmage. **2.** In ice hockey, the area between the two bluelines that is neither an offensive nor a defensive zone.

neu·tri·no (no͞o-trē′nō) *n., pl.* **neu·tri·nos** Any of three electrically neutral subatomic particles that have masses close to zero and that can travel nearly at the speed of light.

neu·tron (no͞o′trŏn′) *n.* An electrically neutral subatomic particle that is part of the nucleus of every element

GEOGRAPHY

Nevada The name **Nevada** was shortened from Sierra Nevada, the name of a mountain range in eastern California near what is today the Nevada border. In Spanish the word *nevada* means "snow-covered."

ă	pat	ôr	core
ā	pay	oi	boy
âr	care	ou	out
ä	father	o͝o	took
ĕ	pet	o͝or	lure
ē	be	o͞o	boot
ĭ	pit	ŭ	cut
ī	bite	ûr	urge
îr	pier	th	thin
ŏ	pot	*th*	this
ō	toe	zh	vision
ô	paw	ə	about

except hydrogen and has a mass slightly greater than that of a proton. [From *neutral*.] —SEE NOTE AT **atom.**

neutron star *n.* An extremely dense celestial object that is formed when a massive star collapses with sufficient energy to force all of its electrons into the nuclei that they orbit, where they react with protons, leaving only neutrons. Neutron stars are powerful sources of radio waves and x-rays.

Ne·vad·a (nə-văd′ə *or* nə-vä′də) A state of the western United States west of Utah. It was admitted as the 36th state in 1864. Carson City is the capital and Las Vegas the largest city. —SEE NOTE.

nev·er (nĕv′ər) *adv.* **1.** At no time; on no occasion; not ever: *I have never been here before.* **2.** Not at all; in no way: *Never fear.* ◆ **never mind 1.** Don't bother: *I had wanted help, but never mind, I'll do it myself.* **2.** Not to mention; and certainly not: *I can't tread water, never mind swim.* [From Old English *nǣfre* : *ne*, not + *ǣfre*, ever.]

nev·er·more (nĕv′ər-môr′) *adv.* Never again.

nev·er·the·less (nĕv′ər-*thə*-lĕs′) *adv.* In spite of that; still; however: *His speech was brief; nevertheless, it drew great applause.*

new (no͞o) *adj.* **new·er, new·est 1a.** Recently made, built, established, created, or formed: *Congress passed a new law.* **b.** Being or to be made, formed, or created: *The tailor laid out cloth for a new dress.* **2.** Just found, discovered, or learned: *I received new information from the government's website.* **3.** Recently obtained or acquired: *The victorious political party wasted no time in using its new political power.* **4.** Never used or worn; not old or secondhand: *Lisa received a new bicycle for her birthday.* **5.** Fresh: *I applied a new coat of paint.* **6.** Additional; further: *Industry needs new sources of energy.* **7.** Different from the previous one or ones: *Tim bought a new edition of a book.* **8.** Not previously experienced; unfamiliar; novel: *Check your dictionary for the definitions of words that are new to you.* **9.** Recently arrived or established in a place, position, or relationship: *The principal welcomed the new teachers.* **10.** Inexperienced or untrained: *He is new at this work.* **11.** Fashionable; up-to-date: *I learned a new dance at the party.* ❖ *adv.* Freshly; newly; recently: *The children played outside in the new-fallen snow.* **—new′ness** *n.*

❑ *These sound alike:* **new, gnu** (antelope), **knew** (did know).

New Amsterdam A settlement established in 1624 by the Dutch on the southern end of Manhattan Island. It was captured by the British in 1664 and renamed New York.

New·ark (no͞o′ərk) The largest city of New Jersey, in the northeast part of the state on an inlet of the Atlantic Ocean west of New York City. It was settled by Puritans in 1666.

new·bie (no͞o′bē) *n. Informal* A person who is a beginner at something.

new·born (no͞o′bôrn′) *adj.* **1.** Just born: *newborn babies.* **2.** Reborn or renewed: *newborn courage.* ❖ *n., pl.* **new·born** or **new·borns** A newborn child or animal.

New Bruns·wick (brŭnz′wĭk) A province of eastern Canada on the Gulf of St. Lawrence southeast of Quebec. New Brunswick joined Nova Scotia, Quebec, and Ontario to form the confederated Dominion of Canada in 1867. Fredericton is the capital.

new·com·er (no͞o′kŭm′ər) *n.* A person, animal, or thing that has only recently arrived in a place or situation for the first time.

New Deal *n.* The programs and policies for economic recovery and social reform introduced during the 1930s by President Franklin D. Roosevelt. **—New Dealer** *n.*

New Del·hi (dĕl′ē) The capital of India, in the north-central part of the country south of Delhi. It was constructed between 1912 and 1929 to replace Kolkata (Calcutta) as the capital.

new·el (no͞o′əl) *n.* A post that supports a handrail at the bottom of a staircase or at one of the landings. [From Middle English *nowell*, from Latin *nōdulus*, little knot.]

New England A region of the northeast United States made up of the states of Maine, New Hampshire, Vermont, Massachusetts, Connecticut, and Rhode Island.

new·fan·gled (no͞o′făng′gəld) *adj.* New and often unnecessary or undesirable: *newfangled ideas.*

New·found·land¹ (no͞o′fən-lənd) An island of the province of Newfoundland and Labrador, Canada, in the Atlantic Ocean east of the Labrador Peninsula.

New·found·land² (no͞o′fən-lənd) *n.* A large strong dog of a breed developed in Newfoundland, having a thick dark coat.

Newfoundland and Labrador A province of eastern Canada including the mainland area of Labrador, the island of Labrador, and many smaller islands. It was admitted as a province in 1949. St. John's is the capital and the largest city.

New Guin·ea (gĭn′ē) An island in the southwest Pacific Ocean north of Australia, divided between Indonesia to the west and Papua New Guinea to the east.

New Hamp·shire (hămp′shər) A state of the northeast United States between Vermont and Maine. It was admitted as one of the original Thirteen Colonies in 1788. Concord is the capital and Manchester the largest city. —SEE NOTE.

New Haven A city of southern Connecticut south-southwest of Hartford on Long Island Sound. It was settled in 1637–1638 by Puritans.

New Jer·sey (jûr′zē) A state of the eastern United States on the Atlantic Ocean east of Pennsylvania. It was admitted as one of the original Thirteen Colonies in 1787. Trenton is the capital and Newark the largest city. —SEE NOTE.

New Latin *n.* Latin as used since about 1500.

new·ly (no͞o′lē) *adv.* **1.** Not long ago; recently: *a newly acquired piece of property.* **2.** In a new or different way; freshly: *an old idea newly stated.*

new·ly·wed (no͞o′lē-wĕd′) *n.* A person recently married.

New Mex·i·co (mĕk′sĭ-kō′) A state of the southwest United States on the Mexican border east of Arizona. It was admitted as the 47th state in 1912. Sante Fe is the capital and Albuquerque the largest city. —SEE NOTE.

new moon *n.* The moon when it passes between the sun and Earth and is invisible or visible only as a thin crescent at sunset, marking the start of a lunar month.

New Neth·er·land (nĕ*th*′ər-lənd) A Dutch colony in North America along the Hudson River that was first settled in 1624 and was annexed by the English and renamed New York in 1664.

New Or·leans (no͞o ôr′lē-ənz *or* no͞o ôr′lənz *or* no͞o ôr-lēnz′ *or* no͞o ô′lənz *also* nô′lənz) The largest city of Louisiana, in the southeast part of the state on the Mississippi River. Founded in 1718, it is known for its annual Mardi Gras celebrations and as the birthplace of jazz music. In 2005, New Orleans was severely damaged by Hurricane Katrina.

news (no͞oz) *pl.n. (used with a singular verb)* **1a.** Information about recent events, especially when reported by newspapers, radio, television, and other forms of media. **b.** A presentation of such information, as on a television broadcast: *Did you watch the news last night?* **2.** New information: *The change in the bus schedule was news to me.* **3.** A fact or event that is interesting enough to be reported: *She is so famous that whatever she does is news.*

news·boy (no͞oz′boi′) *n.* A boy who sells or delivers newspapers.

GEOGRAPHY

New Hampshire The state of **New Hampshire** was named after Hampshire, a county in southern England. The English explorer Captain John Mason (1586–1635) founded and named the colony in 1629.

GEOGRAPHY

New Jersey The state of **New Jersey** gets its name from the island of Jersey in the English Channel. Jersey was the birthplace of Sir George Carteret (c. 1610–1680), who became an owner of large land holdings in the region in 1664.

GEOGRAPHY

New Mexico The name **New Mexico** is a translation of the Spanish *Nuevo Mexico,* which was used as early as the 1560s by Spanish explorers to describe the territory beyond the northern part of Mexico. In 1848, when the region became part of the United States, the English translation was adopted.

newt

BIOGRAPHY

Isaac Newton In 1665, the classes Isaac **Newton** was attending at Cambridge University were suspended for a time because of an outbreak of the plague. While he was away from school, Newton conducted his own studies, making discoveries about light and motion and beginning to develop the mathematical techniques of calculus. It was also during this time, as he told friends later, that Newton saw an apple fall from a tree and suddenly realized that the force of gravity acting on the apple was the same force that caused the moon to remain in orbit around the earth. From this realization he developed his law of universal gravitation. Newton would go on to define the nature of mass, weight, force, inertia, and acceleration. Perhaps his greatest achievement was to assert that the laws of physics are the same everywhere in the universe. This assumption underlies all modern science.

ă	pat	ôr	core
ā	pay	oi	boy
âr	care	ou	out
ä	father	o͝o	took
ĕ	pet	o͝or	lure
ē	be	o͞o	boot
ĭ	pit	ŭ	cut
ī	bite	ûr	urge
îr	pier	th	thin
ŏ	pot	*th*	this
ō	toe	zh	vision
ô	paw	ə	about

news·cast (no͞oz**′**kăst′) *n.* A radio or television program that broadcasts news reports. **—news′cast′er** *n.*

news conference *n.* A press conference.

news·girl (no͞oz**′**gûrl′) *n.* A girl who sells or delivers newspapers.

news·let·ter (no͞oz**′**lĕt′ər) *n.* A printed report giving news or information of interest to a special group.

news·mag·a·zine (no͞oz**′**măg′ə-zēn′) *n.* A magazine or television program that reports on current events and topics in the news.

news·man (no͞oz**′**măn′) *n.* A man who gathers, reports, or edits news.

news·pa·per (no͞oz**′**pā′pər) *n.* **1.** A publication, usually issued daily or weekly, containing current news, editorials, articles, and advertisements. **2.** Newsprint.

news·pa·per·man (no͞oz**′**pā′pər-măn′) *n.* **1.** A man who owns or publishes a newspaper. **2.** A man who is a newspaper reporter, writer, or editor.

news·pa·per·wom·an (no͞oz**′**pā′pər-wo͝om′ən) *n.* **1.** A woman who owns or publishes a newspaper. **2.** A woman who is a newspaper reporter, writer, or editor.

news·print (no͞oz**′**prĭnt′) *n.* Cheap thin paper made from wood pulp and used chiefly to print newspapers.

news·reel (no͞oz**′**rēl′) *n.* A short movie that gives a visual report of recent news events.

news·room (no͞oz**′**ro͞om′ *or* no͞oz**′**ro͝om′) *n.* A room, as in a newspaper office, where news stories are written and edited.

news·stand (no͞oz**′**stănd′) *n.* An open booth or stall where newspapers and magazines are sold.

news·wom·an (no͞oz**′**wo͝om′ən) *n.* A woman who gathers, reports, or edits news.

news·wor·thy (no͞oz**′**wûr′*th*ē) *adj.* **news·wor·thi·er, news·wor·thi·est** Interesting or important enough to be worth reporting to the general public: *a newsworthy event.*

news·y (no͞o**′**zē) *adj.* **news·i·er, news·i·est** *Informal* Full of news; informative: *a newsy letter.*

newt (no͞ot) *n.* Any of various small salamanders that spend part of the year on land and part of the year in the water. [From Middle English *neute*, from the phrase *(an) eute*, a newt (misunderstood as *(a) newt*), from Old English *efete*, newt.]

New Testament *n.* The second of the two main divisions of the Christian Bible, containing the Gospels and other books relating the life and teachings of Jesus and his followers.

new·ton (no͞ot**′**n) *n.* A unit used to measure force, equal to the force needed to accelerate a mass of one kilogram one meter per second per second. [After Sir Isaac *Newton.*]

New·ton (no͞ot**′**n), Sir **Isaac** 1642–1727. English mathematician and scientist. He developed the techniques of calculus and formulated a law of gravitation, a theory about the nature of light, and three laws of motion. —SEE NOTE.

New·to·ni·an (no͞o-tō**′**nē-ən) *adj.* Relating to or in accordance with the work of Sir Isaac Newton, especially in the fields of mechanics and gravitation.

New World The continents of North and South America.

New Year *n.* The first day or days of a calendar year.

New Year's Day *n.* January 1, the first day of the year, celebrated as a holiday in many countries.

New York (yôrk) **1.** A state of the northeast United States north of Pennsylvania. It was admitted as one of the original Thirteen Colonies in 1788. Albany is the capital and New York the largest city. **2.** or **New York City** A city of southern New York on **New York Bay,** an inlet of the Atlantic Ocean at the mouth of the Hudson River. It is the largest city in the United States. —SEE NOTE.

New Zea·land (zē**′**lənd) An island country in the southern Pacific Ocean southeast of Australia. Settled by the Maori by the 1200s and by the British in the 1800s, New Zealand gained its independence from Great Britain in 1931. Wellington is the capital and Auckland the largest city.

next (nĕkst) *adj.* **1.** Immediately following in time, order, or sequence: *next week; the next item on the list.* **2.** Closest or nearest in space or position: *the next town; the next room.* ❖ *adv.* **1.** In the time, order, or place immediately following: *our next oldest child.* **2.** On the first occasion after the present or previous one: *when you next wash the floor.* ◆ **next to 1.** Adjacent to: *Who is sitting next to you?* **2.** Coming immediately before or after: *She's next to last on the waiting list.* **3.** Almost; practically: *next to impossible.* [From Old English *nīehsta.*]

next door *adv.* To or in the adjacent house, building, apartment, or room: *Mike just moved next door to Tom.* ❖ *adj.* **next-door** (nĕkst**′**dôr**′**) Located or living in the adjacent house, building, apartment, or room: *our next-door neighbors.*

Nez Perce (nĕz**′** pûrs**′**) also **Nez Per·cé** (pər-sā**′**) *n., pl.* **Nez Perce** or **Nez Per·ces** (pûr**′**sĭz) also **Nez Percé** or **Nez Per·cés** (pər-sāz**′**) **1.** A member of a Native American people of the northwest United States. **2.** The Sahaptian language of the Nez Perce.

NFL *abbr.* An abbreviation of National Football League.

NG *abbr.* An abbreviation of: **1.** National Guard. **2.** no good. **3.** natural gas.

ngul·trum (əng-gŭl**′**trəm) *n.* The basic monetary unit of Bhutan.

NH *abbr.* An abbreviation of New Hampshire.

NHL *abbr.* An abbreviation of National Hockey League.

Ni The symbol for the element **nickel.**

ni·a·cin (nī**′**ə-sĭn) *n.* A vitamin belonging to the vitamin B complex that is important in carbohydrate metabolism. It is found in liver, fish, and whole-grain foods.

Ni·ag·a·ra Falls (nī-ăg**′**rə *or* nī-ăg**′**ər-ə) Waterfalls north-northwest of Buffalo, New York, consisting of the American Falls, about 850 feet (260 meters) wide, and the Horseshoe Falls, about 2,200 feet (670 meters) wide. They are located in the **Niagara River,** which flows about 35 miles (55 kilometers) north from Lake Erie to Lake Ontario along the United States–Canada border.

Nia·mey (nē-ä**′**mā) The capital of Niger, in the southwest part of the country near the border with Burkina Faso.

nib (nĭb) *n.* **1.** The point of a pen. **2.** A sharp point or tip. [From Middle English *neb*, beak, bill, from Old English.]

nib·ble (nĭb**′**əl) *v.* **nib·bled, nib·bling, nib·bles** —*tr.* **1.** To eat with small quick bites: *nibble cheese.* **2.** To bite at gently and repeatedly: *The fish nibbled the bait.* —*intr.* To take small quick bites. ❖ *n.* **1.** A small or hesitant bite. **2.** A small bite or morsel of food. [From Middle English *nebyllen.*] **—nib′bler** *n.*

Nic·a·ra·gua (nĭk′ə-rä**′**gwə) A country of Central America north of Costa Rica. Managua is the capital. **—Ni′ca·ra′guan** *adj. & n.*

nice (nīs) *adj.* **nic·er, nic·est 1.** Good; pleasant; agreeable: *The seaside hotel was a nice place to stay.* **2.** Having a pleasant appearance; attractive: *a nice dress.* **3.** Courteous and polite; considerate: *It's nice of you to help.* **4.** Morally upright; respectable. **5.** Done with skill and delicacy: *a nice bit of work.* **6a.** Requiring the ability to notice small differences: *a nice distinction.* **b.** Able to notice small differences: *a nice ear for music.* **7.** Used as an intensive with *and: The weather at the beach was nice and warm.* [From Middle English *nice*, foolish, from Old French, from Latin *nescius*, ignorant.] **—nice′ly** *adv.* **—nice′ness** *n.* —SEE NOTE.

❑ *These sound alike:* **nice, gneiss** (rock).

Nice (nēs) A city of southeast France on the Mediterranean Sea southwest of Monaco. It is the leading resort city of the French Riviera.

Ni·cene Creed (**nī′**sēn′ *or* nī-**sēn′**) *n.* A formal statement of doctrine of the Christian faith adopted at the Council of Nicaea in AD 325 and expanded in later councils.

ni·ce·ty (**nī′**sĭ-tē) *n., pl.* **ni·ce·ties 1.** Precision or accuracy; exactness: *the nicety of the computer's calculations.* **2.** A fine point, small detail, or subtle distinction: *the niceties of etiquette.* **3.** An elegant or refined feature: *the niceties of civilized life.*

niche (nĭch *or* nēsh) *n.* **1.** A recess or alcove in a wall, as for holding a statue. **2.** A cranny, hollow, or crevice, as in rock. **3.** A situation or activity specially suited to a person's abilities or character: *She finally found her niche in life.* **4.** The function or position of an organism within an ecological community. [From French, from Old French *nichier*, to nest.]

Nich·o·las (**nĭk′**ə-ləs), Saint. Fourth century AD. Bishop in Asia Minor who is often associated with Santa Claus.

nick (nĭk) *n.* A small cut, notch, or chip in a surface or edge: *a plate with a nick in it.* ❖ *tr.v.* **nicked, nick·ing, nicks** To make a small cut or notch in. ◆ **in the nick of time** Just at the critical moment; just in time. [From Middle English *nik*.]

nick·el (**nĭk′**əl) *n.* **1.** *Symbol* **Ni** A hard silvery metallic element that resists oxidation and corrosion and is used in alloys and for plating other metals. Atomic number 28. See **Periodic Table. 2.** A coin of the United States or Canada worth five cents.

nick·el·o·de·on (nĭk′ə-**lō′**dē-ən) *n.* **1.** An early movie theater that charged customers five cents to enter. **2.** A jukebox.

nickel silver *n.* A silvery, hard, malleable alloy of copper, nickel, and often zinc that resists corrosion.

Nick·laus (**nĭk′**ləs), **Jack William** Born 1940. American golfer who won 18 major international tournaments.

nick·nack (**nĭk′**năk′) *n.* Variant of **knickknack.**

nick·name (**nĭk′**nām′) *n.* **1.** A descriptive name used instead of or along with the real name of a person, place, or thing. **2.** A familiar or shortened form of a proper name: *Joseph's nickname was Joe.* ❖ *tr.v.* **nick·named, nick·nam·ing, nick·names** To give a nickname to. [From Middle English *neke name*, from the phrase *(an) eke name*, an additional name (misunderstood as *a neke name*).]

Nic·o·si·a (nĭk′ə-**sē′**ə) The capital of Cyprus, in the north-central part of the island. It was probably founded before the seventh century BC.

nic·o·tine (**nĭk′**ə-tēn′) *n.* A colorless, poisonous alkaloid that is derived from the tobacco plant and is used as an insecticide. It is the substance that makes tobacco smoking addictive.

nic·o·tin·ic acid (nĭk′ə-**tĭn′**ĭk *or* nĭk′ə-**tē′**nĭk) *n.* Niacin.

niece (nēs) *n.* A daughter of one's brother or sister or of the brother or sister of one's spouse. [From Middle English *nece*, from Latin *neptis*, granddaughter.]

nif·ty (**nĭf′**tē) *Informal adj.* **nif·ti·er, nif·ti·est** First-rate; great: *a nifty new outfit.*

Ni·ger (**nī′**jər *or* nē-**zhâr′**) A country of west-central Africa north of Nigeria. Niamey is the capital.

Ni·ge·ri·a (nī-**jîr′**ē-ə) A country of western Africa on the Gulf of Guinea. It was the site of a series of empires prior to the arrival of Europeans. Abuja is the capital and Lagos the largest city.

Niger River A river of western Africa rising in Guinea and flowing about 2,600 miles (4,180 kilometers) through Mali, Niger, and Nigeria to the Gulf of Guinea.

nig·gard (**nĭg′**ərd) *n.* A stingy person; a miser. ❖ *adj.* Stingy; miserly. [From Middle English *nigard*, stingy person, of Scandinavian origin.]

nig·gard·ly (**nĭg′**ərd-lē) *adj.* **1.** Unwilling to give, spend, or share; stingy: *niggardly in doling out the cookies.* **2.** Small or meager: *a niggardly amount.* ❖ *adv.* Stingily. —**nig′gard·li·ness** *n.*

nig·gling (**nĭg′**lĭng) *adj.* Annoying, troubling, or irritating in a petty way: *a pointless dispute over niggling details.*

nigh (nī) *adv.* **nigh·er, nigh·est 1.** Near in time, space, or relationship: *Evening drew nigh.* **2.** Nearly; almost: *talked for nigh onto two hours.* ❖ *adj.* **nigher, nighest** Being near in time, place, or relationship; close: *sick and nigh to death.* ❖ *prep.* Not far from; near.

night (nīt) *n.* **1.** The period between sunset and sunrise, especially the hours of darkness. **2.** The period between bedtime and morning: *He tossed and turned all night.* **3.** An evening or night devoted to some special purpose or event: *the opening night of a play.* **4.** Nightfall: *They worked from morning to night.* **5.** Darkness: *She ran out into the foggy night.* **6.** A time of gloom, sorrow, or ignorance: *a long night of waiting before our dreams come true.* [From Middle English, from Old English *niht*.]

❑ *These sound alike:* **night, knight** (warrior on horseback).

night blindness *n.* Inability to see normally in dim light.

night·cap (**nīt′**kăp′) *n.* **1.** A cloth cap worn in bed. **2.** A drink taken just before bedtime. **3.** The final game in a baseball double-header.

night·clothes (**nīt′**klōz′ *or* **nīt′**klōthz′) *pl.n.* Clothes, such as nightgowns and pajamas, worn in bed.

night·club (**nīt′**klŭb′) *n.* An establishment that stays open late at night and provides food, drink, and entertainment.

night crawler *n.* Any of various earthworms that come out of the ground at night.

night·fall (**nīt′**fôl′) *n.* The coming of darkness at the end of the day; dusk.

night·gown (**nīt′**goun′) *n.* A loose gown worn in bed by women and girls.

night·hawk (**nīt′**hôk′) *n.* Any of several insect-eating birds that have mottled grayish feathers and are active in the evening and at night.

night·in·gale (**nīt′**n-gāl′) *n.* A brownish bird of Eurasia and Africa, noted for the melodious song of the male at night.

Night·in·gale (**nīt′**n-gāl′ *or* **nī′**tĭng-gāl′), **Florence** 1820–1910. British nurse who is considered the founder of modern nursing.

night·life (**nīt′**līf′) *n.* Social activities or entertainment available or pursued in the evening or at night.

night-light (**nīt′**līt′) *n.* A usually small light left on all night.

night·ly (**nīt′**lē) *adj.* **1.** Relating to or occurring during the night: *The bears pay a nightly visit to the dump.* **2.** Happening or done every night: *the nightly news on TV.* —**night′ly** *adv.*

night·mare (**nīt′**mâr′) *n.* **1.** A dream that is very frightening. **2.** A very frightening experience. [From Middle English, a female demon that attacks sleeping people : *night*, night + *mare*, goblin.]

night·mar·ish (**nīt′**mâr′ĭsh) *adj.* Like something in a bad dream; frightening; appalling: *a nightmarish experience.* —**night′mar′ish·ly** *adv.*

night owl *n. Informal* A person who stays up late at night.

nights (nīts) *adv.* During the nighttime on every day or most days: *works nights at the restaurant.*

night school *n.* A school that holds classes in the evening.

night·shade (**nīt′**shād′) *n.* Any of several related plants, such as belladonna, having poisonous black or red berries and small white or purple flowers.

night shift *n.* **1.** A group of employees working during the night in a factory or business. **2.** The period of time for such work: *The night shift at the factory runs from 10 PM to 6 AM.*

GEOGRAPHY

New York The state of New York was named after the Duke of York, later King James II (1633–1701), who was granted control of the colony after England seized it from the Dutch in 1664. Under the Dutch, the colony had been known as *New Amsterdam*.

WORD HISTORY

nice The word **nice** is a great example of how a word that once meant something negative can come to mean something positive. It was borrowed into Middle English from the Old French word *nice,* which meant "silly, foolish." In Middle English, *nice* first changed to mean "foolish about clothes, fussy about looking good." A *nice* person thus wore good clothes, and a person who wore good clothes was thought of as refined; and so *nice* came to mean "refined, having good taste." People who are refined and have good taste generally cultivate good manners, and this is how *nice* finally came to mean "agreeable."

Florence Nightingale

nimbostratus

Richard Nixon

ă	pat	ôr	core
ā	pay	oi	boy
âr	care	ou	out
ä	father	o͝o	took
ĕ	pet	o͝or	lure
ē	be	o͞o	boot
ĭ	pit	ŭ	cut
ī	bite	ûr	urge
îr	pier	th	thin
ŏ	pot	*th*	this
ō	toe	zh	vision
ô	paw	ə	about

night·shirt (nīt′shûrt′) *n.* A long, loose shirt worn in bed.

night·stand (**nīt′**stănd′) *n.* A small table or stand placed at a bedside.

night·stick (**nīt′**stĭk′) *n.* A club carried by a police officer.

night table *n.* A nightstand.

night·time (**nīt′**tīm′) *n.* The time between sunset and sunrise. **—night′time′** *adj.*

night watchman *n.* One who serves as a guard at night.

ni·ho·ni·um (nē-**hō′**nē-əm, nĭ-) *n. Symbol* **Nh** A radioactive element that has been artificially produced by scientists. Atomic number 113. See **Periodic Table.**

Ni·ke (**nī′**kē) *n.* In Greek mythology, the goddess of victory.

nil (nĭl) *n.* Nothing; zero. [From Latin *nīl*, contraction of *nihil.*]

Nile (nīl) The longest river in the world, flowing about 4,150 miles (6,675 kilometers) through eastern Africa from Burundi to the Mediterranean Sea in northeast Egypt. The river has been used for irrigation in Egypt since at least 4000 BC.

nim·ble (**nĭm′**bəl) *adj.* **nim·bler, nim·blest 1.** Quick and light in movement; agile or deft: *nimble fingers.* **2.** Quick and clever in thinking or understanding: *a nimble wit.* [From Middle English *nemel*, from Old English *nǣmel*, quick to seize, and *numol*, quick at learning.] **—nim′ble·ness** *n.* **—nim′bly** *adv.*

nim·bo·strat·us (nĭm′bō-**străt′**əs *or* nĭm′bō-**strā′**təs) *n., pl.* **nim·bo·strat·i** (nĭm′bō-**străt′**ī *or* nĭm′bō-**strā′**tī) A low, gray, often dark cloud usually producing prolonged rain, sleet, or snow.

nim·bus (**nĭm′**bəs) *n., pl.* **nim·bi** (**nĭm′**bī′) or **nim·bus·es 1.** A halo or cloudy radiance glowing around the head of a god, goddess, saint, or monarch, as in a painting. **2.** A special atmosphere or aura, as of glory or romance, surrounding a person or thing. **3.** A rain cloud. [From Latin *nimbus*, cloud.]

nin·com·poop (**nĭn′**kəm-po͞op′ *or* **nĭng′**kəm-po͞op′) *n.* A stupid or silly person.

nine (nīn) *n.* **1.** The number, written 9, that is equal to 8 + 1. **2.** The ninth in a set or sequence. **3.** The first or second nine holes of an 18-hole golf course. [From Middle English, from Old English *nigon.*]

9/11 (**nīn′**ĭ-**lĕv′**ən) *n.* September 11, 2001, the date on which two hijacked airliners were flown into the towers of the World Trade Center in New York City, and another hijacked airliner was flown into a side of the Pentagon near Washington, DC. A fourth hijacked airliner crashed in open land in Pennsylvania. The attacks were organized and carried out by al-Qaeda.

nine·pins (**nīn′**pĭnz′) *n.* *(used with a singular or plural verb)* A bowling game in which nine wooden pins are the target.

nine·teen (nīn-**tēn′**) *n.* **1.** The number, written 19, that is equal to 18 + 1. **2.** The 19th in a set or sequence.

nine·teenth (nīn-**tēnth′**) *n.* **1.** The ordinal number matching the number 19 in a series. **2.** One of 19 equal parts.

nine·ti·eth (**nīn′**tē-ĭth) *n.* **1.** The ordinal number matching the number 90 in a series. **2.** One of 90 equal parts.

nine·ty (**nīn′**tē) *n., pl.* **nine·ties** The number, written 90, that is equal to 9 × 10.

Nin·e·veh (**nĭn′**ə-və) An ancient city of Assyria on the Tigris River opposite the site of present-day Mosul, Iraq. It was the capital of the Assyrian Empire and was captured and destroyed by Babylonia in 612 BC.

nin·ja (**nĭn′**jə) *n., pl.* **ninja** or **nin·jas** A professional agent in medieval Japan who was trained in the martial arts and hired for secret operations such as assassination and sabotage.

nin·ny (**nĭn′**ē) *n., pl.* **nin·nies** A fool; a simpleton.

ninth (nīnth) *n.* **1.** The ordinal number matching the number nine in a series. **2.** One of nine equal parts. **3.** A musical interval equal to an octave plus a second.

ni·o·bi·um (nī-**ō′**bē-əm) *n. Symbol* **Nb** A soft silvery metallic element used in making steel alloys and superconductors and in arc welding. Atomic number 41. See **Periodic Table.**

nip¹ (nĭp) *tr.v.* **nipped, nip·ing, nips 1.** To seize and pinch or bite: *One pony nipped the other.* **2.** To remove by pinching or snipping: *nipped off the plant leaf.* **3.** To sting or chill with the cold: *The wind nipped our ears.* **4.** To stop the growth or development of: *a plot that was nipped in the bud.* ❖ *n.* **1.** A small sharp bite, pinch, or snip. **2.** A small bit or portion removed by nipping: *nips of paper on the floor.* **3.** Sharp biting cold: *a nip in the autumn air.* **4.** A sharp biting flavor; tang. [From Middle English *nippen.*]

nip² (nĭp) *n.* A small amount of liquor. [Probably short for *nipperkin*, of Dutch or Low German origin.]

nip and tuck *adj. & adv.* So close that the advantage or lead shifts from one to another; neck and neck.

nip·per (**nĭp′**ər) *n.* **1.** often **nippers** A tool, such as pliers or pincers, used for grasping or nipping. **2.** A part, such as the large claw of a lobster, that resembles such a tool. **3.** *Chiefly British* A small boy.

nip·ple (**nĭp′**əl) *n.* **1a.** A small projecting body part near the center of the mammary gland in female humans and most other mammals that contains the outlets of the milk ducts. **b.** A corresponding but undeveloped body part in male humans and most other mammals. **2.** A soft rubber cap on a bottle from which a baby nurses.

nip·py (**nĭp′**ē) *adj.* **nip·pi·er, nip·pi·est 1.** So cold as to sting: *a nippy fall day.* **2.** Sharp or biting in taste: *nippy cheese.*

ni·qab (nə-**käb′**) *n.* A veil worn by Muslim women that covers most or all of the face, having a narrow opening or mesh covering for the eyes. [From Arabic *niqāb.*]

nir·va·na (nîr-**vä′**nə *or* nər-**vä′**nə) *n.* **1.** often **Nirvana a.** A state of wisdom that is the final goal of Buddhism, marked by a release from the attachment to the self, freedom from suffering, and the attainment of peace. **b.** A state of being that is the final goal of Hinduism, in which the soul becomes one with Brahma and frees itself from individual attachments and the eternal cycle of birth, suffering, death, and rebirth. **2.** An ideal condition of rest, harmony, or bliss. [From Sanskrit *nirvāṇam*, a blowing out, extinction.]

Ni·sei (nē-**sā′** *or* **nē′**sā′) *n., pl.* **Nisei** or **Ni·seis** A person born to parents who emigrated from Japan.

nit (nĭt) *n.* The egg of certain parasitic insects, especially a head louse. [From Middle English, from Old English *hnitu.*]

❑ *These sound alike:* **nit, knit** (loop yarn).

nit·pick (**nĭt′**pĭk′) *intr.v.* **nit·picked, nit·pick·ing, nit·picks** To be concerned with or find fault with small, unimportant details. **—nit′pick′er** *n.*

ni·trate (**nī′**trāt′ *or* **nī′**trĭt) *n.* **1.** A salt or ester of nitric acid. **2.** A fertilizer containing sodium nitrate, potassium nitrate, or ammonium nitrate.

ni·tric (**nī′**trĭk) *adj.* Derived from or containing nitrogen, especially with a higher valence than that of a comparable nitrous compound.

nitric acid *n.* A colorless to yellowish, highly corrosive acid used in making fertilizers, explosives, and rocket fuels.

nitric oxide *n.* A gas that is made when nitrogen combines with oxygen in the atmosphere, as a product of cellular metabolism, or as a result of certain chemical reactions. It can be poisonous if inhaled but carries out important physiological functions in the body, such as regulating blood flow and transmitting impulses between nerve cells.

ni·tride (nī′trīd′) *n.* A compound of nitrogen and another element, such as phosphorus or a metal, in which the nitrogen gains electrons or shares them in a way that makes it the more negative of the two elements.

ni·tri·fy (nī′trə-fī′) *tr.v.* **ni·tri·fied, ni·tri·fy·ing, ni·tri·fies 1.** To treat or combine with nitrogen or its compounds. **2.** To oxidize (an ammonium compound) into a nitrite or (a nitrite) into a nitrate, especially in soil or water by the action of nitrifying bacteria. **—ni′tri·fi·ca′tion** (nī′trə-fĭ-kā′shən) *n.*

ni·tri·fy·ing bacterium (nī′trə-fī′ĭng) *n.* Any of various bacteria in soil or water that obtain energy by converting ammonium compounds into nitrites or by converting nitrites into nitrates as part of the nitrogen cycle.

ni·trite (nī′trīt′) *n.* A salt or ester of nitrous acid, important in the nitrogen cycle.

ni·tro·cel·lu·lose (nī′trō-sĕl′yə-lōs′) *n.* A pulpy or cottony organic compound formed by treating cellulose with sulfuric acid and nitric acid. It is used in making explosives, rocket fuels, and plastics.

ni·tro·gen (nī′trə-jən) *n. Symbol* **N** A colorless, odorless gaseous element that makes up nearly four-fifths of the atmosphere by volume. Nitrogen is a necessary part of all proteins and is used in manufacturing explosives and fertilizers. Atomic number 7. See **Periodic Table.**

nitrogen cycle *n.* The circulation of nitrogen in nature, consisting of a cycle of chemical reactions in which atmospheric nitrogen is fixed in compounds in the soil, where it is taken up by plants and by animals that eat them and then returned to the soil through decomposition. The cycle is completed when nitrogen is returned to the atmosphere by the action of certain bacteria.

nitrogen fixation *n.* The conversion of atmospheric nitrogen into nitrogen compounds, such as ammonia, either by bacteria in the soil and water or by industrial processes.

ni·trog·e·nous (nī-trŏj′ə-nəs) *adj.* Containing nitrogen.

ni·tro·glyc·er·in (nī′trō-glĭs′ər-ĭn) *n.* A thick, pale-yellow, readily explosive liquid formed by treating glycerin with nitric acid and sulfuric acid. It is used in making dynamite and in medicine as a drug that dilates the blood vessels.

ni·trous (nī′trəs) *adj.* Derived from or containing nitrogen, especially with a lower valence than that of a comparable nitric compound.

nitrous oxide *n.* A colorless, sweet-smelling gas that is used as a mild anesthetic in dentistry and surgery.

nit·ty-grit·ty (nĭt′ē-grĭt′ē) *n. Informal* The specific or practical details; the heart of the matter.

nit·wit (nĭt′wĭt′) *n.* A stupid or silly person. [Possibly obsolete *nit*, stupid or ineffectual person (from *nit*, louse egg) + *wit*.]

nix (nĭks) *Slang n.* Nothing. ❖ *adv.* Not so; no: *nix on that idea.* ❖ *tr.v.* **nixed, nix·ing, nix·es** To forbid, refuse, or veto: *My parents nixed my idea of going to the mall.* [From German *nix*, zilch, informal contraction of *nichts*, nothing.]

Nix·on (nĭk′sən), **Richard Milhous** 1913–1994. The 37th president of the United States (1969–1974). He resigned from office (August 9, 1974) when Congress recommended he be impeached.

NJ *abbr.* An abbreviation of New Jersey.

NL *abbr.* An abbreviation of Newfoundland and Labrador.

NM *abbr.* An abbreviation of New Mexico.

no¹ (nō) *adv.* **1.** Not so. Used to express refusal, denial, or disagreement: *No, I'm not going.* **2.** Not at all. Often used with the comparative: *no better; no more.* **3.** Not: *Are you coming or no?* **4.** *Informal* Used to indicate agreement with a preceding statement, especially when followed by a stronger judgment supporting that statement: *"The car is getting old." "No, I know. It must be 10 years old by now."* ❖ *n., pl.* **noes** (nōz) **1.** A negative response; a denial or refusal: *The suggestion met with a chorus of noes.* **2.** A negative vote or voter. ❖ *interj.* An expression used to show strong refusal, doubt, denial, or disbelief. [From Middle English, from Old English *nā* : *ne*, not + *ā*, ever.]

❑ *These sound alike:* **no¹** (not so), **know** (have knowledge), **no²** (not any), **No¹** (Japanese drama).

no² (nō) *adj.* **1.** Not any; not one: *There are no cookies left.* **2.** Not at all; not close to being: *He's no child; he should know better.* **3.** Hardly any: *We got there in no time at all.* [From Middle English, from Old English *nān, nā* : *ne*, not + *ān*, one.]

❑ *These sound alike:* **no²** (not any), **know** (have knowledge), **no¹** (not so), **No¹** (Japanese drama).

No¹ or **Noh** (nō) *n.* The classical drama of Japan, with music and dance performed in a highly stylized manner by elaborately dressed performers on an almost bare stage. [From Japanese *nō*, talent, ability, No.]

❑ *These sound alike:* **No¹** (Japanese drama), **know** (have knowledge), **no¹** (not so), **no²** (not any).

No² The symbol for the element **nobelium.**

no. *abbr.* An abbreviation of: **1.** or **No. a.** north. **b.** northern. **2.** number.

No·ah (nō′ə) In the Bible, the man who was chosen by God to build an ark, in which he, his family, and a pair of every animal were saved from the Flood.

No·bel (nō-bĕl′), **Alfred Bernhard** 1833–1896. Swedish scientist who invented dynamite (1866).

no·bel·i·um (nō-bĕl′ē-əm) *n. Symbol* **No** A radioactive metallic element that has been artificially produced by scientists. The half-life of its longest-lived isotope is a little over three minutes. Atomic number 102. See **Periodic Table.** [After Alfred *Nobel.*]

Nobel Prize *n.* Any of six international prizes awarded annually for outstanding achievement in physics, chemistry, physiology or medicine, economics, literature, and the promotion of peace. [After Alfred *Nobel.*]

no·bil·i·ty (nō-bĭl′ĭ-tē) *n., pl.* **no·bil·i·ties 1.** A class of people distinguished by high birth and hereditary rank, and often having wealth, power, and privilege. **2.** Noble rank or status: *Congress may not grant titles of nobility.* **3.** The state or quality of being noble in character: *There is real nobility in your devoting so much time to volunteer work.*

no·ble (nō′bəl) *adj.* **no·bler, no·blest 1.** Having high or hereditary rank in society. **2.** Having or showing qualities of high moral character, as courage, generosity, or honor: *a noble spirit.* **3.** Excellent and admirable: *a noble cause.* **4.** Grand; stately; majestic: *noble mountain peaks.* **5.** Chemically inactive or inert. ❖ *n.* A member of the nobility. **—no′ble·ness** *n.* **—no′bly** *adv.*

noble gas *n.* Any of the gases (such as helium, neon, argon, and radon) that appear in the rightmost column of the periodic table and do not react chemically with other substances except under certain special conditions. See table at **Periodic Table.**

no·ble·man (nō′bəl-mən) *n.* A man of noble rank.

no·ble·wom·an (nō′bəl-wo͝om′ən) *n.* A woman of noble rank.

no·bod·y (nō′bŏd′ē *or* nō′bə-dē) *pron.* No person; not anybody: *Nobody stayed after practice was over.* ❖ *n., pl.* **no·bod·ies** A person of no importance or influence.

no-brain·er (nō′brā′nər) *n. Informal* Something, especially a choice, that is so obvious or easy as to require little or no thought.

noc·tur·nal (nŏk-tûr′nəl) *adj.* **1.** Relating to or occurring at night: *a nocturnal breeze.* **2.** Most active at night: *Owls are nocturnal birds.* [From Late Latin *nocturnālis*, from Latin *nox*, night.] **—noc·tur′nal·ly** *adv.*

noc·turne (nŏk′tûrn′) *n.* **1.** A painting of a night scene. **2.** A musical composition intended to suggest a dreamy mood.

WRITERS CHOOSE THEIR WORDS

Late one humid August night, as George lay awake listening to the usual symphony of tree frogs and crickets coming through his open bedroom window, the nightly chorus was joined by a new sound. He listened intently. What he heard made the small hairs on the back of his neck prickle. Slippered feet scuffed back and forth over the creaking floorboards of Otto's old room directly next to George's. He had gotten used to the man's **nocturnal** pacing when sleep eluded his blind uncle.

—Michael Norman and Beth Scott
Haunted Wisconsin

nocturne
Silver Moonlight, 1880, by John Atkinson Grimshaw (1836–1893)

WORD BUILDING

non– The prefix **non–**, which means "not," comes from Latin, where it was mostly used in law terms. Some of these terms were borrowed through Old French into English, which had many of them by the 1500s. But in the 1600s, the use of the prefix in English started to broaden. Today most words beginning with *non–* have nothing to do with the law. It can be added to almost any adjective, forming such words as *nonessential, nonmetallic,* and *nonproductive*. It can also be added to nouns, as in *nonentity, nonresident,* and *nonviolence*. Finally, it can be added to verbs to form adjectives like *nonskid* and *nonstop*.

WRITERS CHOOSE THEIR WORDS

I strolled around the circle, acting all **nonchalant,** looking at the opulent surroundings. "I like what you did with the place," I said, all friendly. "Nothing like a little artwork to freshen up a tomb."

—D.J. MacHale
The Soldiers of Halla

ă	pat	ôr	core
ā	pay	oi	boy
âr	care	ou	out
ä	father	ŏŏ	took
ĕ	pet	ŏŏr	lure
ē	be	ōō	boot
ĭ	pit	ŭ	cut
ī	bite	ûr	urge
îr	pier	th	thin
ŏ	pot	*th*	this
ō	toe	zh	vision
ô	paw	ə	about

nod (nŏd) *v.* **nod·ded, nod·ding, nods** *—intr.* **1.** To lower and raise the head quickly, as in agreement. **2.** To let the head fall forward when getting sleepy: *He began to nod and soon was asleep.* **3.** To be careless for a moment and make a mistake. **4.** To move up and down, sway, or droop: *flowers nodding in the breeze.* *—tr.* **a.** To lower and raise (the head) quickly, as when showing agreement, giving a greeting, or pointing something out. **b.** To express or convey by lowering and raising the head: *He nodded his approval.* ❖ *n.* A nodding movement of the head, as one used to show approval or point something out: *She gave a nod of affirmation.* ◆ **nod off** To doze for a short period of time: *nodded off during the lecture.*

nod·al (**nōd′**l) *adj.* Relating to or located at or near a node.

node (nōd) *n.* **1a.** A knob, knot, or swelling. **b.** A small mass of tissue, as a lymph node. **2.** The point on a plant stem where a leaf or stem is attached; a joint. **3.** A point or region of a vibrating or oscillating system at which the amplitude of the vibration or oscillation is zero. **4.** A terminal in a computer network. **5a.** Either of the two points at which the orbit of a planet intersects the ecliptic. **b.** Either of the two points at which the orbit of a satellite intersects the plane of orbit of a planet. [From Middle English, from Latin *nōdus*, knot.]

nod·ule (**nŏj′**ōōl) *n.* **1.** A small node, as of body tissue. **2.** A small lump or outgrowth, such as one of those formed on the roots of clover, alfalfa, or soybeans. **3.** A small lump of a mineral or a mixture of minerals.

No·ël also **No·el** (nō-**ĕl′**) *n.* **1.** Christmas. **2. noël** A Christmas carol.

no-fault (**nō′**fôlt′) *adj.* **1.** Relating to a form of automobile insurance that compensates a policy holder who is involved in an accident, regardless of who is at fault. **2.** Relating to a type of divorce that is granted without requiring proof of fault or bad conduct on the part of either spouse.

no-fly zone (**nō′flī′**) *n.* Airspace in which all aircraft or all unauthorized aircraft are forbidden to fly.

no-frills (**nō′frĭlz′**) *adj. Informal* Lacking extra or special features; basic: *bought a cheap flight on a no-frills airline.*

nog·gin (**nŏg′**ĭn) *n.* **1.** A small mug or cup. **2.** A small amount of liquid, equal to one-fourth of a pint. **3.** *Slang* The head.

no-good (**nō′**gŏŏd′) *adj.* **1.** Having no value, use, or excellence. **2.** Gross; hateful: *a no-good criminal.*

Noh (nō) *n.* Variant of **No**[1].

no-hit·ter (**nō′hĭt′**ər) *n.* In baseball, a complete game in which a pitcher does not allow the opposing team to get a hit.

noise (noiz) *n.* **1.** Sound or a sound that is loud, unpleasant, unexpected, or undesired: *You're making too much noise. I was awakened by a noise in the alley.* **2.** Sound or a sound of any kind: *The only noise was the wind in the pines.* ❖ *tr.v.* **noised, nois·ing, nois·es** To spread as a rumor or report: *He noised it about that he won a scholarship.* [From Middle English, from Old French, din, disturbance, perhaps from Latin *nausea*, seasickness.]

SYNONYMS **noise, din, racket, uproar** These nouns mean loud, confused, or disagreeable sound or sounds. **Noise** is the most general term: *There was so much noise at the party, I didn't hear my phone ring.* **Din** means a jumble of loud sounds that usually clash: *The din in the factory stops promptly at the end of the shift.* **Racket** means loud, distressing noise: *The toddlers made a racket clanging pots and pans together.* **Uproar** means disorder with loud, bewildering sound: *The uproar of the cheering crowd was deafening.*

noise·less (**noiz′**lĭs) *adj.* Having or making no noise. **—noise′less·ly** *adv.* **—noise′less·ness** *n.*

noise·mak·er (**noiz′**mā′kər) *n.* **1.** A person or thing that makes noise. **2.** A device, such as a horn or rattle, used to make noise at a party.

noi·some (**noi′**səm) *adj.* **1.** Foul, offensive, or disgusting: *a noisome odor.* **2.** Harmful or dangerous: *noisome fumes from the glue.* **—noi′some·ly** *adv.*

nois·y (**noi′**zē) *adj.* **nois·i·er, nois·i·est 1.** Making a lot of noise: *a noisy engine.* **2.** Full of, characterized by, or accompanied by noise: *noisy streets.* **—nois′i·ly** *adv.* **—nois′i·ness** *n.*

no·mad (**nō′**măd′) *n.* **1.** A member of a group of people who have no fixed home and move about from place to place seeking food, water, and grazing land for their animals. **2.** A person who roams about instead of settling in one place. [From Greek *nomas*, wandering in search of pasture, from *nomos*, pasture.] **—no·mad′ic** *adj.* **—no·mad′i·cal·ly** *adv.*

no man's land *n.* **1.** Land under dispute by two opposing parties, especially the field of battle between two opposing entrenched armies. **2.** An area of uncertainty or ambiguity.

nom de plume (nŏm′ də **plōōm′**) *n., pl.* **noms de plume** (nŏm′ də **plōōm′**) A pen name.

no·men·cla·ture (**nō′**mən-klā′chər) *n.* **1.** The system of names used in a particular profession or area of study; terminology: *meteorological nomenclature.* **2.** The system or procedure of assigning names to groups of organisms as part of a taxonomic classification: *the rules of nomenclature in botany.*

nom·i·nal (**nŏm′**ə-nəl) *adj.* **1.** In name only and not in actual fact: *The queen is the nominal ruler, but the prime minister has the real power.* **2.** So small as to be insignificant: *They charged a nominal sum for admission.* **3.** In grammar, relating to a noun or a group of words that acts like a noun. [From Latin *nōminālis*, relating to a name, relating to a noun, from Latin *nōmen*, name, noun.] **—nom′i·nal·ly** *adv.*

nom·i·nate (**nŏm′**ə-nāt′) *tr.v.* **nom·i·nat·ed, nom·i·nat·ing, nom·i·nates 1.** To propose as a candidate for election or as one to be considered for an honor or prize: *nominated him as their candidate for mayor; was nominated twice for an Academy Award.* **2.** To appoint to an office: *The president nominated a new chief of staff.* [From Latin *nōmen*, name.]

nom·i·na·tion (nŏm′ə-**nā′**shən) *n.* **1.** The act or process of nominating. **2.** The state of being nominated: *Her nomination to the court has made her famous.*

nom·i·na·tive (**nŏm′**ə-nə-tĭv) *adj.* Relating to the grammatical case of the subject of a verb and of words identified with the subject of a linking verb. For example, in the sentences *These are beautiful paintings* and *I sang the song* the words *These, paintings,* and *I* are in the nominative case. ❖ *n.* The nominative case.

nom·i·nee (nŏm′ə-**nē′**) *n.* **1.** A person proposed or selected as a candidate for an office or award: *the party's presidential nominee.* **2.** A person appointed to a position, office, or honor: *the president's nominee for FBI director.*

non– *pref.* A prefix that means not: *nonconformist.* —SEE NOTE.

non·a·gon (**nŏn′**ə-gŏn′ *or* **nō′**nə-gŏn′) *n.* A polygon with nine sides and nine angles. **—non·ag′o·nal** (nŏn-**ăg′**ə-nəl) *adj.*

non·al·co·hol·ic (nŏn′ăl-kə-**hô′**lĭk) *adj.* Containing no alcohol: *a nonalcoholic beverage.*

non·a·ligned (nŏn′ə-**līnd′**) *adj.* Not in alliance with any other nation or group of allies; neutral: *a nonaligned nation.*

nonce (nŏns) *n.* The present time or occasion. Used chiefly in the phrase *for the nonce.*

nonce word *n.* A word made up for use on one particular occasion.

non·cha·lance (nŏn′shə-läns′) *n.* The state or quality of being nonchalant: *Her nonchalance about the party made us think she didn't want to go.*

non·cha·lant (nŏn′shə-länt′) *adj.* Seeming to be carefree or casually unconcerned: *a nonchalant air.* [From Old French *nonchaloir,* to be unconcerned : *non-,* not + *chaloir,* to be of interest (from Latin *calēre,* to be warm, heat up).] **—non′cha·lant′ly** *adv.*

non·cit·i·zen (nŏn-sĭt′ĭ-zən) *n.* A person living in one country while remaining a citizen of another; a foreigner.

non·com (nŏn′kŏm′) *n. Informal* A noncommissioned officer.

non·com·bat·ant (nŏn′kəm-băt′nt *or* nŏn′kŏm′bə-tnt) *n.* **1.** A person serving in the armed forces, as a chaplain or surgeon, whose duties do not include fighting. **2.** A civilian in wartime.

non·com·mis·sioned officer (nŏn′kə-mĭsh′ənd) *n.* An enlisted member of the armed forces, as a corporal or sergeant, appointed to a rank conferring leadership over other enlisted people. Noncommissioned officers rank below commissioned officers and warrant officers.

non·com·mit·tal (nŏn′kə-mĭt′l) *adj.* Not indicating how one feels or thinks: *She gave a noncommittal answer, "We shall see."* **—non′com·mit′tal·ly** *adv.*

non·com·pli·ance (nŏn′kəm-plī′əns) *n.* Failure or refusal to comply with something, such as a doctor's orders or a law.

non com·pos men·tis (nŏn kŏm′pəs mĕn′tĭs) *adj.* Not of sound mind and therefore not legally qualified or fit to perform an act. [From Latin, *nōn compos mentis,* not in control of the mind.]

non·con·duc·tor (nŏn′kən-dŭk′tər) *n.* A substance that conducts little or no electricity, heat, or sound: *Rubber is a nonconductor of electricity.*

non·con·form·ist (nŏn′kən-fôr′mĭst) *n.* **1.** A person who does not act in accordance with or refuses to follow generally accepted customs, beliefs, or ways of doing things. **2.** often **Nonconformist** A member of a Protestant church that does not accept or follow the teachings or practices of a national church, especially the Church of England. **—non′con·form′i·ty** *n.*

non·count noun (nŏn′kount′) *n.* A mass noun.

non·de·nom·i·na·tion·al (nŏn′dĭ-nŏm′ə-nā′shə-nəl) *adj.* Not restricted to or associated with a particular religious denomination: *a nondenominational service.*

non·de·script (nŏn′dĭ-skrĭpt′) *adj.* Lacking in distinctive qualities and thus difficult to describe: *a nondescript house that looked like any other.*

none (nŭn) *pron.* **1.** Not any: *None of my friends were at the pool.* **2.** Not one; nobody: *None dared to do it.* ❖ *adv.* Not at all: *The coach was none too pleased.* [From Old English *nān* : *ne,* no, not + *ān,* one.] —SEE NOTE.
❑ *These sound alike:* **none, nun** (religious woman).

non·en·ti·ty (nŏn-ĕn′tĭ-tē) *n., pl.* **non·en·ti·ties** A person or thing of no importance or significance.

non·es·sen·tial (nŏn′ĭ-sĕn′shəl) *adj.* **1.** Having little or no importance; not essential: *nonessential supplies.* **2.** Relating to a substance that is necessary for normal functioning but not needed in the diet because the body makes it from other nutrients: *a nonessential amino acid.* ❖ *n.* Something that is not essential: *Do not take any nonessentials on the hike.*

none·the·less (nŭn′*th*ə-lĕs′) *adv.* Nevertheless.

non-Eu·clid·e·an (nŏn′yo͞o-klĭd′ē-ən) *adj.* Relating to any of several forms of modern geometry that are not based on the postulates of Euclid.

non·ex·is·tent (nŏn′ĭg-zĭs′tənt) *adj.* Not existing; entirely lacking: *planets with nonexistent atmospheres.* **—non′ex·is′tence** *n.*

non·fat (nŏn′făt′) *adj.* Lacking fat solids or having the fat content removed: *nonfat milk.*

non·fic·tion (nŏn-fĭk′shən) *n.* A category of literature, drama, film or other creative work, including essays and documentaries, whose content is based on fact and is not imagined: *I've read his novels but not his nonfiction.* **—non·fic′tion·al** *adj.*

non·flam·ma·ble (nŏn-flăm′ə-bəl) *adj.* Not easily set on fire and burned; not flammable. **—non·flam′ma·bil′i·ty** *n.*

non·flow·er·ing (nŏn-flou′ər-ĭng) *adj.* Not producing flowers.

non·in·ter·ven·tion (nŏn′ĭn-tər-vĕn′shən) *n.* Failure or refusal to intervene, especially in the affairs of another nation.

non·judg·men·tal (nŏn′jŭj-mĕn′tl) *adj.* Refraining from judgment based on one's personal standards.

non·met·al (nŏn-mĕt′l) *n.* Any of the elements, such as oxygen, carbon, nitrogen, and sulfur, that tend to gain electrons (as when forming chemical bonds) and that conduct heat and electricity poorly.

non·me·tal·lic (nŏn′mə-tăl′ĭk) *adj.* **1.** Not metallic. **2.** Relating to a nonmetal: *a nonmetallic element.*

no-no (nō′nō′) *n., pl.* **no-noes** *Informal* Something that is not acceptable or allowed: *Texting in class is a no-no.*

no-non·sense (nō-nŏn′sĕns′) *adj.* Practical, serious, and businesslike: *a no-nonsense person.*

non·pa·reil (nŏn′pə-rĕl′) *adj.* Having no equal; matchless; peerless: *a nonpareil goalie.* ❖ *n.* A person or thing that has no equal.

non·par·ti·san (nŏn-pär′tĭ-zən) *adj.* Not based on, influenced by, or supporting a political party or its interests: *nonpartisan opinions.*

non·plus (nŏn-plŭs′) *tr.v.* **non·plused, non·plus·ing, non·plus·es** also **non·plussed, non·plus·sing, non·plus·ses** To put at a loss so that one does not know what to think, say, or do; bewilder.

non·pro·duc·tive (nŏn′prə-dŭk′tĭv) *adj.* **1.** Not yielding what was expected or wanted: *a nonproductive vineyard.* **2.** Not engaged in the direct production of goods: *productive factory workers and nonproductive clerical personnel.* **—non′pro·duc′tive·ly** *adv.*

non·prof·it (nŏn-prŏf′ĭt) *adj.* Not set up or managed for the purpose of making a profit: *a nonprofit organization.* ❖ *n.* An organization, such as a charity, that does not seek to produce a profit: *donated money to local nonprofits.*

non·re·new·a·ble (nŏn′rĭ-no͞o′ə-bəl) *adj.* **1.** That cannot be renewed: *a nonrenewable prescription.* **2.** Relating to an energy source, such as oil, or a natural resource, such as a metallic ore, that cannot be replenished.

non·res·i·dent (nŏn-rĕz′ĭ-dənt) *adj.* Not making one's home at a particular place, especially not living in the same community where one works, attends school, owns property, or has official duties: *a nonresident taxpayer.* ❖ *n.* A nonresident person.

non·re·stric·tive (nŏn′rĭ-strĭk′tĭv) *adj.* In grammar, being a clause or phrase that describes a noun but does not restrict the meaning of the sentence and is set off by commas. In the sentence *The Smiths, who live in an apartment, have six cats,* the clause *who live in an apartment* is nonrestrictive.

non·sec·tar·i·an (nŏn′sĕk-târ′ē-ən) *adj.* Not limited to or associated with a particular religious denomination: *a nonsectarian college.*

non·sense (nŏn′sĕns′) *n.* **1.** Words or behavior having no sense: *The message was nonsense until we were able to read the handwriting.* **2.** Foolish or senseless talk, writing, or behavior: *Stop the nonsense and pay attention.* **3.** Something that is not important or useful: *You shouldn't waste time on this nonsense.*

non·sen·si·cal (nŏn-sĕn′sĭ-kəl) *adj.* **1.** Making no sense: *a nonsensical message.* **2.** Foolish; absurd: *a nonsensical idea.* **—non·sen′si·cal·ly** *adv.*

USAGE

none When the phrase *none of* is followed by a plural noun, you can use a singular or a plural verb, depending on your preference. So, you can say *None of the uniforms is clean,* where you emphasize that not a single uniform is clean. Or, you can say *None of the uniforms are clean,* where you emphasize that all the uniforms are dirty. Both sentences are grammatically correct. However, if the noun following *none of* is singular, the verb should be singular: *None of the equipment is worth keeping.*

USAGE

nonstandard The term **nonstandard** is used to refer to words such as *ain't* and *irregardless*. The term does not mean that such words are not used by anyone. Rather the term means that such words are not used in language that is considered standard. Nonstandard words are not used in the kind of language that is widely accepted by educated speakers as a means of communicating across a variety of regions and communities.

GEOGRAPHY

North Carolina The states **North Carolina** and **South Carolina** were one colony, called *Carolina,* until they were formally divided in 1729. The colony was originally named after Charles I of England, who granted its first charter. *Carolina* comes from the Latin name *Carolus,* which is the equivalent of *Charles.*

GEOGRAPHY

North Dakota The states of **North Dakota** and **South Dakota** take their names from the Dakota, a branch of the Sioux people who inhabited the region. The name means "friends." Both sections wished to keep the name *Dakota* when the Dakota Territory was being divided, so *North* and *South* were added to the names when they achieved statehood in 1889.

ă	pat	ôr	core
ā	pay	oi	boy
âr	care	ou	out
ä	father	o͝o	took
ĕ	pet	o͝or	lure
ē	be	o͞o	boot
ĭ	pit	ŭ	cut
ī	bite	ûr	urge
îr	pier	th	thin
ŏ	pot	*th*	this
ō	toe	zh	vision
ô	paw	ə	about

non se·qui·tur (nŏn **sĕk′**wĭ-tər) *n.* A conclusion or statement that does not follow logically from the statements that preceded it. [From Latin, *nōn sequitur,* it does not follow.]

non·stan·dard (nŏn-**stăn′**dərd) *adj.* **1.** Varying from a standard: *nonstandard lengths of boards.* **2.** Relating to a kind of language that is used by uneducated speakers and is not normally considered acceptable by educated speakers. —SEE NOTE.

non·stop (**nŏn′stŏp′**) *adj.* Made or done without any stops: *a nonstop flight from New York to Paris.* ❖ *adv.* Without making any stops: *flew nonstop to Los Angeles.*

non·un·ion (nŏn-**yo͞on′**yən) *adj.* **1.** Not belonging to a labor union: *nonunion workers.* **2.** Not recognizing or dealing with a labor union or employing union members: *a nonunion shop.*

non·vas·cu·lar plant (**nŏn′văs′**kyə-lər) *n.* Any of numerous plants, including the mosses, liverworts, and hornworts, that do not have specialized tissues for transporting water and nutrients throughout the plant.

non·ven·om·ous (nŏn-**vĕn′**ə-məs) *adj.* Not containing or transmitting venom: *nonvenomous snakes.*

non·ver·bal (nŏn-**vûr′**bəl) *adj.* Involving little or no use of words: *Gestures, signs, and symbols are forms of nonverbal communication.*

non·vi·o·lence (nŏn-**vī′**ə-ləns) *n.* The philosophy, policy, or practice of rejecting violence in favor of peaceful actions as a means of gaining one's ends. **—non·vi′o·lent** *adj.* **—non·vi′o·lent·ly** *adv.*

non·white (nŏn-**wīt′**) *n.* A person belonging to a racial group other than white; a person of color. **—non′-white′** *adj.*

non·ze·ro (nŏn-**zîr′**ō *or* nŏn-**zē′**rō) *adj.* Not equal to zero.

noo·dle[1] (**no͞od′**l) *n.* A narrow strip of dough, usually made of flour, eggs, and water and cooked in water or another liquid. [From German *Nudel.*]

noo·dle[2] (**no͞od′**l) *n. Slang* **1.** The head. **2.** A weak, foolish, or stupid person. [Probably alteration of earlier *noddle,* the head.]

nook (no͝ok) *n.* **1.** A corner, alcove, or recess, especially in a larger room: *a kitchen with a breakfast nook.* **2.** A hidden or secluded spot.

noon (no͞on) *n.* The middle of the day; twelve o'clock in the daytime. [From Old English *nōn,* canonical hour of nones, or 3 PM in the early Middle Ages, from Late Latin *nōna (hōra),* ninth (hour), nones.]

noon·day (**no͞on′**dā′) *n.* Noon. ❖ *adj.* Relating to or occurring at noon: *the noonday heat.*

no one *pron.* No person; nobody: *No one answered, so I thought you were out.*

noon·tide (**no͞on′**tīd′) *n.* Noon.

noon·time (**no͞on′**tīm′) *n.* Noon.

noose (no͞os) *n.* **1.** A loop formed in a rope by means of a slipknot so that it binds tighter as the rope is pulled. **2.** A snare or trap.

Noot·ka (**no͞ot′**kə *or* **no͝ot′**kə) *n., pl.* **Nootka** or **Noot·kas 1.** A member of a Native American people of Vancouver Island and adjacent areas of Canada and the United States. **2.** The Wakashan language of this people.

nor (nôr) *conj.* And not; or not; not either: *He has neither written nor telephoned me. These life forms are neither plants nor animals.* —SEE NOTE AT **neither.**

Nor·dic (**nôr′**dĭk) *adj.* **1.** Relating to Scandinavia or its cultures. **2.** Relating to cross-country skiing.

Nor·folk (**nôr′**fək *or* **nôr′**fôk) A city of southeast Virginia southeast of Richmond. It was founded in 1682.

norm (nôrm) *n.* **1.** A standard or pattern that is considered to be typical of a group. **2.** A pattern of behavior considered acceptable or proper. **3.** A mathematical average; mean. [From Latin *norma,* carpenter's square, rule.]

nor·mal (**nôr′**məl) *adj.* **1.** Conforming with a norm, standard, type, or pattern; typical: *normal room temperature; returned to a normal schedule.* **2.** Functioning, occurring, or being in a healthy state; not affected by disease: *normal digestion; normal liver cells.* **—nor′mal·ly** *adv.*

nor·mal·cy (**nôr′**məl-sē) *n.* Normality.

nor·mal·i·ty (nôr-**măl′**ĭ-tē) *n.* The condition of being normal.

nor·mal·ize (**nôr′**mə-līz′) *tr. & intr.v.* **nor·mal·ized, nor·mal·iz·ing, nor·mal·iz·es** To make normal or to become or return to normal: *normalized relations with a foreign government; prices normalized after the strike was settled.* **—nor′mal·i·za′tion** (nôr′mə-lĭ-**zā′**shən) *n.*

normal school *n.* A school that trains teachers, chiefly for the elementary grades.

Nor·man (**nôr′**mən) *n.* **1.** A member of a Scandinavian people who settled in northern France in the tenth century. **2.** One of the descendants of these people who invaded England in 1066. **3.** A native or inhabitant of Normandy. ❖ *adj.* Relating to Normandy, the Normans, or their language or culture.

Norman Conquest *n.* The conquest of England by the Normans under William the Conqueror in 1066.

Nor·man·dy (**nôr′**mən-dē) A historical region and former province of northwest France on the English Channel. Its beaches were the site of Allied landings on D-day (June 6, 1944) in World War II.

Norman French *n.* The dialect of Old French used in medieval Normandy.

nor·o·vi·rus (**nôr′**ō-vī′rəs) *n.* Any of a group of RNA viruses, formerly called Norwalk viruses, that cause gastroenteritis. [After *Norwalk,* Ohio, where an outbreak of gastroenteritis led to the identification of noroviruses.]

Norse (nôrs) *adj.* Relating to medieval Scandinavia, its peoples, or their languages or cultures. ❖ *n.* **1a.** *(used with a plural verb)* The people of medieval Scandinavia. **b.** The North Germanic languages, especially those of the Middle Ages. **2.** The people of Norway; the Norwegians.

Norse·man (**nôrs′**mən) *n.* A member of one of the peoples of medieval Scandinavia.

north (nôrth) *n.* **1.** The direction to the left of sunrise, directly opposite south. **2.** A region or part of the earth in this direction: *Better farmlands lie in the north of the state.* **3. North** The northern part of the United States, especially the states that supported the Union during the Civil War. ❖ *adj.* **1.** To, toward, facing, or in the north: *the north shore of Long Island.* **2.** From the north: *a north wind.* ❖ *adv.* In, from, or toward the north. [From Old English.]

North America The third-largest continent, lying northwest of South America between the Atlantic and Pacific Oceans. It includes Central America, Mexico, the islands of the Caribbean Sea, the United States, Canada, and Greenland.

north·bound (**nôrth′**bound′) *adj.* Going toward the north.

North Car·o·li·na (kăr′ə-**lī′**nə) A state of the southeast United States between Virginia and South Carolina on the Atlantic Ocean. It was admitted as one of the original Thirteen Colonies in 1789. Raleigh is the capital and Charlotte the largest city. —SEE NOTE.

North Da·ko·ta (də-**kō′**tə) A state of the north-central United States east of Montana. It was admitted as the 39th state in 1889. Bismarck is the capital and Fargo the largest city. —SEE NOTE.

north·east (nôrth-**ēst′**) *n.* **1.** The direction halfway between north and east. **2.** An area or region lying in this direction. **3. Northeast** The part of the United States including New England, New York, and sometimes Pennsylvania and New Jersey. ❖ *adj.* **1.** To, toward, facing, or in the northeast. **2.** Coming from the northeast: *northeast winds.* ❖ *adv.* In, from, or toward the northeast. **—north·east′ern** *adj.*

north·east·er (nôrth-ē′stər *or* nôr-ē′stər) *n.* A storm or gale blowing from the northeast.

north·east·er·ly (nôrth-ē′stər-lē) *adj.* **1.** Situated toward the northeast: *a house with a northeasterly view.* **2.** Coming from the northeast: *northeasterly gales.* **—north·east′er·ly** *adv.*

north·east·ward (nôrth-ēst′wərd) *adv. & adj.* Toward, to, or in the northeast: *sailed northeastward.* ❖ *n.* A direction or region to the northeast. **—north·east′wards** *adv.*

north·er (nôr′*th*ər) *n.* A storm or gale blowing from the north.

north·er·ly (nôr′*th*ər-lē) *adj.* **1.** Situated toward the north: *The compass needle points in a northerly direction.* **2.** Coming from the north: *northerly winds.* ❖ *n., pl.* **north·er·lies** A storm or wind from the north. **—north′er·ly** *adv.*

north·ern (nôr′*th*ərn) *adj.* **1.** Situated in, toward, or facing the north: *the northern border.* **2.** Coming from the north: *northern winds.* **3.** also **Northern** Relating to northern regions or the North: *a northern climate.*

north·ern·er also **North·ern·er** (nôr′*th*ər-nər) *n.* A person who lives in or comes from the north, especially the northern United States.

Northern Hemisphere *n.* **1.** The half of the earth north of the equator. **2.** The half of the celestial sphere north of the celestial equator.

Northern Ire·land (īr′lənd) A division of the United Kingdom in the northeast part of the island of Ireland. It was colonized by the British in the 1600s and remained in the United Kingdom after the establishment of the independent Republic of Ireland.

northern lights *pl.n.* The aurora borealis.

north·ern·most (nôr′*th*ərn-mōst′) *adj.* Farthest north.

Northern Spy *n.* A yellowish-red apple.

North Germanic *n.* A subdivision of the Germanic languages that includes Norwegian, Icelandic, Swedish, and Danish.

north·ing (nôr′thĭng *or* nôr′*th*ĭng) *n.* **1.** The difference in latitude between two positions as a result of northward movement. **2.** Northward movement.

North Island An island of New Zealand in the Pacific Ocean northeast of South Island. It is the smaller but more heavily populated of the country's two main islands.

North Ko·re·a (kə-rē′ə) A country of eastern Asia west of Japan on the Yellow Sea. It has been inhabited since ancient times. Pyongyang is the capital.

north·land also **North·land** (nôrth′lănd′ *or* nôrth′lənd) *n.* A region in the north of a country or area.

North·man (nôrth′mən) *n.* A Norseman.

North Pole *n.* **1.** The northern end of the earth's axis of rotation, a point in the Arctic Ocean. **2. north pole** The pole of a magnet that tends to point north.

North Sea An arm of the Atlantic Ocean between Great Britain and northwest Europe.

North Star *n.* Polaris.

North Vietnam See **Vietnam.**

north·ward (nôrth′wərd) *adv. & adj.* Toward, to, or in the north: *turned the ship's prow northward.* ❖ *n.* A direction or region to the north. **—north′wards** *adv.*

north·west (nôrth-wĕst′) *n.* **1.** The direction halfway between north and west. **2.** An area or region lying in this direction. **3. Northwest** A northwestern part of a region or country, especially the region of the United States including Washington, Oregon, and Idaho. ❖ *adj.* **1.** To, toward, facing, or in the northwest. **2.** Coming from the northwest: *northwest winds.* ❖ *adv.* In, from, or toward the northwest. **—north·west′ern** *adj.*

north·west·er (nôrth-wĕs′tər *or* nôr-wĕs′tər) *n.* A storm or gale blowing from the northwest.

north·west·er·ly (nôrth-wĕs′tər-lē) *adj.* **1.** Situated toward the northwest: *a northwesterly course.* **2.** Coming from the northwest: *northwesterly breezes.* **—north·west′er·ly** *adv.*

Northwest Passage A water route from the Atlantic Ocean to the Pacific Ocean through the Arctic Archipelago of northern Canada and along the northern coast of Alaska. It was long sought by European navigators seeking to reach India and China.

Northwest Territories A territory of northern Canada between Yukon Territory and Nunavut and including islands of the western Arctic Archipelago. It joined the Canadian confederation in 1870. Yellowknife is the capital.

Northwest Territory A historical region of the north-central United States extending from the Ohio and Mississippi Rivers to the Great Lakes. The area includes the present-day states of Ohio, Indiana, Illinois, Michigan, Wisconsin, and part of Minnesota.

north·west·ward (nôrth-wĕst′wərd) *adv. & adj.* Toward, to, or in the northwest: *flying northwestward to Alaska.* ❖ *n.* A northwestward direction or region. **—north·west′wards** *adv.*

Nor·way (nôr′wā′) A country of northern Europe west of Sweden. Oslo is the capital.

Nor·we·gian (nôr-wē′jən) *adj.* Relating to Norway or its people, language, or culture. ❖ *n.* **1.** A native or inhabitant of Norway. **2.** The Germanic language of Norway.

nos. *abbr.* An abbreviation of numbers.

nose (nōz) *n.* **1.** The part of the human face or the forward part of the head of other animals that contains the nostrils and organs of smell and forms the beginning of the respiratory tract. **2.** The sense of smell: *a dog with a good nose.* **3.** The ability to detect things, as if by smell: *a nose for gossip.* **4.** The forward end of an airplane, a rocket, a submarine, or another pointed structure. ❖ *v.* **nosed, nos·ing, nos·es** —*tr.* **1.** To touch with the nose; nuzzle: *cats nosing the stuffed animal.* **2.** To move or push with or as if with the nose: *The cow nosed the calf away from the fence.* **3.** To steer (a vehicle or one's way) ahead cautiously: *He nosed the car into the traffic.* —*intr.* **1.** To smell or sniff: *The dog was nosing around in the field.* **2.** To search or inquire persistently; snoop or pry: *The police are nosing around for information.* **3.** To move forward cautiously. ◆ **by a nose** By a narrow margin: *won the race by a nose.* **look down (one's) nose** *Informal* To consider or view with disapproval, contempt, or arrogance. **nose out 1.** To find out by or as if by smell; discover: *The dog nosed out the drugs in the luggage. The detectives nosed out the thieves' hiding place.* **2.** To defeat by a narrow margin. **on the nose** Exactly; precisely. **under (someone's) nose** In plain view. [From Middle English, from Old English *nosu.*]

nose·bleed (nōz′blēd′) *n.* An instance of bleeding from the nostrils.

nose cone *n.* The forwardmost, usually separable part of a rocket or missile that is shaped for minimum air resistance and often covered with a heat-resistant material.

nose·dive (nōz′dīv′) *n.* **1.** A very steep dive made by an airplane. **2.** A sudden drop or plunge: *The price of tea took a nosedive.* **—nose′-dive′** *v.*

nose·gay (nōz′gā′) *n.* A small bunch of flowers; a bouquet.

nos·ey (nō′zē) *adj.* Variant of **nosy.**

nosh (nŏsh) *Informal intr.v.* **noshed, nosh·ing, nosh·es** To eat a snack or light meal: *noshed on pretzels.*

nos·tal·gi·a (nŏ-stăl′jə) *n.* A bittersweet longing for the past: *an old song that filled my parents with nostalgia.*

North Pole

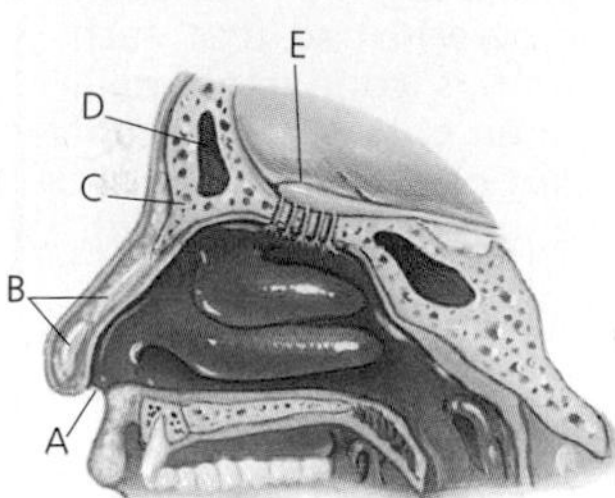

nose
A. nostril
B. cartilage
C. bone
D. frontal sinus
E. olfactory nerve

WRITERS CHOOSE THEIR WORDS

As much as I thought I had disliked the experience of our first summer together, I looked back on those weeks with what I could only describe as a fond **nostalgia.** It was a funny idea, **nostalgia.** It made me think of old people reminiscing about their youth, or an exile looking longingly back at his homeland, regardless of how oppressive it might have been.

—Cristina García
Dreams of Significant Girls

USAGE

not When you use the construction *not only ... but also,* be sure that each of its parts is parallel to the other. Rather than writing *She not only bought a new rake but also a new lawnmower,* with the *not only* being connected to a predicate and the *but also* being connected to a noun phrase, you should rewrite so that each half is connected to a predicate (... *not only bought a new rake but also bought a new lawnmower*) or so that each half is connected to a noun phrase (... *bought not only a new rake but also a new lawnmower*).

[From Greek *nostos,* a return home + Greek *algos,* pain.]

nos·tal·gic (nŏ-**stăl′**jĭk) *adj.* Full of nostalgia: *nostalgic memories.* **—nos·tal′gi·cal·ly** *adv.*

nos·tril (**nŏs′**trəl) *n.* Either of the two external openings of the nose. [From Middle English *nostrille,* from Old English *nosthyrl* : *nosu,* nose + *thyrl,* hole.] —SEE NOTE AT **pretty.**

nos·trum (**nŏs′**trəm) *n.* **1.** A medicine of doubtful effectiveness and often secret ingredients; a quack remedy. **2.** A favorite but unproved remedy for problems or evils. [From Latin *nostrum (remedium),* our (remedy).]

nos·y or **nos·ey** (**nō′**zē) *adj.* **nos·i·er, nos·i·est** *Informal* Very curious about other people's affairs; prying. **—nos′i·ly** *adv.* **—nos′i·ness** *n.*

not (nŏt) *adv.* In no way; to no degree. Used to express negation, denial, refusal, or prohibition: *I will not go. You may not have more dessert.* [From Middle English, alteration of *naught.*] —SEE NOTE.

❑ *These sound alike:* **not, knot** (tangle).

no·ta·ble (**nō′**tə-bəl) *adj.* Worthy of notice; remarkable; striking: *a notable success.* ❖ *n.* A well-known person; a prominent figure. **—no′ta·bly** *adv.*

no·ta·rize (**nō′**tə-rīz′) *tr.v.* **no·ta·rized, no·ta·riz·ing, no·ta·riz·es** To witness and certify (a document) to be authentic by adding one's signature.

no·ta·ry (**nō′**tə-rē) *n., pl.* **no·ta·ries** A notary public. [From Latin *notārius,* shorthand writer, from *nota,* mark.]

notary public *n., pl.* **notaries public** A person legally empowered to witness and certify the validity of documents by signing them.

no·tate (**nō′**tāt) *tr.v.* **no·tat·ed, no·tat·ing, no·tates** To put into notation, especially musical notation.

no·ta·tion (nō-**tā′**shən) *n.* **1.** A system of symbols or figures that represent quantities, tones, or other values: *musical notation.* **2.** The act of using such a system. **3.** A written comment or explanation: *notations in the margin of a book.* [From Latin *notāre,* to note, from *nota,* mark.]

notch (nŏch) *n.* **1.** A V-shaped cut. **2.** A narrow pass between mountains. **3.** *Informal* A level; a degree: *The defeat took him down a notch.* ❖ *tr.v.* **notched, notch·ing, notch·es 1.** To cut a notch in: *He notched each tree that he intended to fell.* **2.** To record by making notches: *notched the score on a stick.*

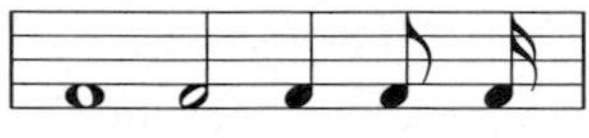

note
left to right: whole, half, quarter, eighth, and sixteenth notes

note (nōt) *n.* **1.** A brief record, especially one written down to aid the memory: *took notes during the lecture.* **2.** A short informal letter or message: *left a note for his mother on the kitchen table.* **3.** An explanation or comment on a passage in a text, usually printed at the bottom of a page or at the end of a chapter or book. **4a.** A piece of paper money; a bill. **b.** A certificate representing an amount of money, issued by a government or bank. **c.** A promissory note. **5a.** A symbol used to represent a musical tone, indicating the pitch by its position on a staff and the relative length by its shape. **b.** A musical tone. **6.** The characteristic call or cry of a bird or other animal: *heard the clear note of a cardinal.* **7.** A sign or hint that reveals a certain quality: *ended his plea on a note of hopefulness.* **8.** Importance; consequence: *Nothing of note happened.* **9.** Notice; observation: *looked out the window and took note of the weather.* ❖ *tr.v.* **not·ed, not·ing, notes 1.** To observe; notice: *We noted the shift in the wind.* **2.** To write down; make a brief record of: *She noted the birds she saw in her diary.* **3.** To make mention of; point out: *He noted that my shoelaces were untied, and I thanked him.* [From Middle English, from Old French, from Latin *nota,* mark, annotation.]

note·book (**nōt′**bo͝ok′) *n.* **1.** A book that has blank pages for writing in. **2.** A light, thin, portable computer; a laptop.

not·ed (**nō′**tĭd) ❖ *adj.* Well-known; famous: *The essay was written by a noted author.* See Synonyms at **famous.**

note·pad (**nōt′**păd′) *n.* A pad or tablet of paper: *The reporter jotted down information on her notepad.*

note·wor·thy (**nōt′**wûr′*th*ē) *adj.* **note·wor·thi·er, note·wor·thi·est** Deserving notice or attention; notable; significant: *a noteworthy invention.* **—note′wor′thi·ly** *adv.* **—note′wor′thi·ness** *n.*

noth·ing (**nŭth′**ĭng) *pron.* **1.** Not anything: *I have nothing more to say.* **2.** No part; no portion: *Nothing is left of the old house.* **3.** A person or thing of no importance: *His concern is nothing to me.* ❖ *n.* **1.** Something that has no quantitative value; zero: *a score of two to nothing.* **2.** A person or thing of no importance: *If you ask me, he's a big nothing.* ❖ *adv.* Not at all: *He looks nothing like me.* ◆ **for nothing 1.** Free of charge: *The library gave away old books for nothing.* **2.** To no avail: *My training was all for nothing since I sprained my ankle right before the race.* **3.** For no reason. **nothing doing** *Informal* Certainly not.

noth·ing·ness (**nŭth′**ĭng-nĭs) *n.* **1.** The quality or condition of being nothing; nonexistence. **2.** Empty space.

no·tice (**nō′**tĭs) *n.* **1.** Perception; observation: *The mistake escaped her notice.* **2.** Attention or consideration: *She considered no detail beneath her notice.* **3.** A written or printed announcement: *post a notice on the bulletin board.* **4.** An announcement of purpose, especially of one's intention to leave a job: *gave the boss a week's notice.* ❖ *tr.v.* **no·ticed, no·tic·ing, no·tic·es 1.** To perceive with the senses; become aware of: *noticed a coin on the ground.* See Synonyms at **see**[1]. **2.** To perceive with the mind; take note of: *noticed a flaw in my plan.* [From Latin *nōtitia,* from *nōscere,* to get to know.]

no·tice·a·ble (**nō′**tĭ-sə-bəl) *adj.* **1.** Easily observed; evident: *a noticeable change in temperature.* **2.** Worth noting; significant. **—no′tice·a·bly** *adv.*

no·ti·fi·ca·tion (nō′tə-fĭ-**kā′**shən) *n.* **1.** The act or an instance of notifying. **2.** Something, such as a letter, that makes something known: *Send me notification when you receive the book.*

no·ti·fy (**nō′**tə-fī′) *tr.v.* **no·ti·fied, no·ti·fy·ing, no·ti·fies** To give notice to; inform: *notify the police.* **—no′ti·fi′er** *n.*

no·tion (**nō′**shən) *n.* **1.** A belief or opinion: *Your notion of how math should be taught is interesting.* **2.** A mental image; an idea: *I haven't the least notion of what you mean.* See Synonyms at **idea. 3.** An impulse or whim: *She had a notion to climb the hill.* **4. notions** Small items, especially those used for sewing such as needles, buttons, and thread. [From Latin *nōtiō,* from *nōtus,* known.]

no·to·chord (**nō′**tə-kôrd′) *n.* A firm rodlike structure that extends along the length of the embryo in all vertebrates and certain related animals, such as the lancelets and the hagfishes. In most vertebrates, the notochord develops into the spinal column in the adult.

no·to·ri·e·ty (nō′tə-**rī′**ĭ-tē) *n.* The quality or condition of being notorious; bad reputation.

no·to·ri·ous (nō-**tôr′**ē-əs) *adj.* Known widely and regarded unfavorably; infamous: *a notorious swindler.* [From Latin *nōtus,* known.] **—no·to′ri·ous·ly** *adv.* **—no·to′ri·ous·ness** *n.*

Not·ting·ham (**nŏt′**ĭng-əm) A city of central England northeast of Birmingham. It was historically a center for the manufacture of textiles, lace, and hosiery.

not·with·stand·ing (nŏt′wĭth-**stăn′**dĭng *or* nŏt′wĭ*th*-**stăn′**dĭng) *prep.* In spite of: *Notwithstanding the rain, the teams played on.* ❖ *adv.* All the same; nevertheless: *They were exhausted, but proceeded notwithstanding.*

Nouak·chott (nwäk-**shŏt′**) The capital of Mauritania, in the western part of the country on the Atlantic Ocean.

nou·gat (**no͞o′**gət) *n.* A candy made from a sugar or honey paste mixed with nuts.

nought (nôt) *n. & pron.* Variant of **naught.**

ă	pat	ôr	core
ā	pay	oi	boy
âr	care	ou	out
ä	father	o͝o	took
ĕ	pet	o͝or	lure
ē	be	o͞o	boot
ĭ	pit	ŭ	cut
ī	bite	ûr	urge
îr	pier	th	thin
ŏ	pot	*th*	this
ō	toe	zh	vision
ô	paw	ə	about

noun (noun) *n.* **1.** The part of speech that is used to name a person, place, thing, quality, or action and that functions as the subject or object of a verb or as the object of a preposition. **2.** A word belonging to this part of speech. For example, in the sentence *The student asked a question,* the words *student* and *question* are nouns. [From Middle English, from Old French, from Latin *nōmen*, name.] —SEE NOTE.

nour·ish (nûr′ĭsh) *tr.v.* **nour·ished, nour·ish·ing, nour·ish·es 1.** To provide (a living thing) with the food or other substances necessary for life and growth. **2.** To promote the growth or development of; sustain: *She founded the business and nourished it with hard work.* **3.** To keep alive; harbor: *We nourished hope that the party would be a success.*

nour·ish·ment (nûr′ĭsh-mənt) *n.* **1a.** The act or process of nourishing. **b.** The condition of being nourished. **2.** Something that nourishes; food.

no·va (nō′və) *n., pl.* **no·vae** (nō′vē) or **no·vas** A white dwarf star that suddenly becomes much brighter and then gradually returns to its original brightness over a period of weeks to years. [From New Latin *(stēlla) nova*, new (star), from Latin *nova*, feminine of *novus*, new.]

No·va Sco·tia (nō′və skō′shə) A province of eastern Canada southwest of Newfoundland made up of a mainland peninsula and the adjacent Cape Breton Island. It joined the Canadian confederation in 1867. Halifax is the capital.

nov·el[1] (nŏv′əl) *n.* A long piece of written prose that tells an invented story. [Ultimately from Italian *novella*, short narrative in prose, from Latin *novellus*, new, novel, from *novus*, new.]

nov·el[2] (nŏv′əl) *adj.* Strikingly new or different: *a modern artist using a novel method of painting.* [From Middle English, from Old French, from Latin *novellus*, from *novus*, new.]

nov·el·ist (nŏv′ə-lĭst) *n.* A writer of novels.

no·vel·la (nō-vĕl′ə) *n.* A short novel.

nov·el·ty (nŏv′əl-tē) *n., pl.* **nov·el·ties 1.** The quality of being novel; newness: *We liked the new video camera until the novelty wore off.* **2.** Something new and unusual: *Edison's light bulb was at first merely an interesting novelty.* **3.** A small mass-produced article, such as a toy or trinket.

No·vem·ber (nō-vĕm′bər) *n.* The 11th month of the year in the Gregorian calendar, having 30 days. [From Middle English *Novembre*, from Old French, from Latin *November*, ninth month of the early Roman calendar, from *novem*, nine.]

no·ve·na (nō-vē′nə) *n., pl.* **no·ve·nas** or **no·ve·nae** (nō-vē′nē) In the Roman Catholic Church, a reciting of prayers or devotions for a special purpose during nine consecutive days.

nov·ice (nŏv′ĭs) *n.* **1.** A person who is new to a field or activity; a beginner. **2.** A person who has entered a religious order but has not yet taken final vows. [From Middle English, from Medieval Latin *novīcius*, from Latin *novus*, new.]

no·vi·ti·ate (nō-vĭsh′ē-ĭt *or* nō-vĭsh′ē-āt′) *n.* The period of being a novice, especially in a religious order.

No·vo·cain (nō′və-kān′) A trademark for a drug used in medicine and dentistry as a local anesthetic.

now (nou) *adv.* **1.** At the present time: *Buildings now stand where there was once a marsh.* **2.** At once; immediately: *We'd better start now.* **3.** Very recently: *He left the room just now.* **4.** At this point in the series of events; then: *The ship now began to sink.* **5.** At times: *now hot, now cold.* **6.** Nowadays: *You'll rarely see plowing with horses now.* **7.** In these circumstances; as things are: *The furnace is broken. Now we won't be able to stay.* **8.** Used to introduce a command, reproof, or request: *Now, who wants to go to the beach? Now remember to add the flour slowly.* **9.** Used to introduce an idea or a change of subject: *Now bears need more territory than most animals.* ❖ *conj.* Since; seeing that: *Now that spring is here, we can expect milder weather.* ❖ *n.* The present: *Up to now we couldn't hike on that trail.* ◆ **now and again** or **now and then** Occasionally: *I like spicy food now and again.*

now·a·days (nou′ə-dāz′) *adv.* In the present times; in these days.

no way *Informal adv.* In no way; not at all: *No way are you going into the woods alone.* ❖ *interj.* An expression used to show strong disbelief or refusal.

no·where (nō′wâr′) *adv.* **1.** Not anywhere: *The screwdriver was nowhere to be found.* **2.** To no place or result: *Until we found the screwdriver, we were getting nowhere.* ❖ *n.* **1.** A remote or unknown place, especially a wilderness: *a cabin in the middle of nowhere.* **2.** A state of nonexistence: *an idea that came out of nowhere.*

no-win (nō′wĭn′) *adj. Informal* Certain to end in failure or disappointment: *a no-win situation.*

no·wise (nō′wīz′) *adv.* In no way; not at all.

nox·ious (nŏk′shəs) *adj.* **1.** Harmful to the health of living things: *noxious chemicals.* **2.** Harmful to the mind or morals. [From Latin *noxius*, from *noxa*, damage.] **—nox′ious·ly** *adv.*

noz·zle (nŏz′əl) *n.* A projecting part with an opening, as at the end of a hose, for regulating and directing a flow of liquid or gas. [From Middle English *noselle*, socket on a candlestick, from *nose*.]

Np The symbol for the element **neptunium.**

NS *abbr.* An abbreviation of Nova Scotia.

NT *abbr.* An abbreviation of: **1.** New Testament. **2.** Northwest Territories.

nth (ĕnth) *adj.* **1.** Relating to an unspecified ordinal number: *ten to the nth power.* **2.** Highest; utmost: *delighted to the nth degree.*

nt. wt. *abbr.* An abbreviation of net weight.

nu (no͞o) *n.* The 13th letter of the Greek alphabet, written Ν, ν. It is represented in English as *N, n.*

nu·ance (no͞o′äns′) *n.* A subtle variation, as in meaning, color, or tone; a delicate shading. [From French, from Old French *nuer*, to shade, cloud, from Latin *nūbēs*, cloud.]

nub (nŭb) *n.* **1.** A lump or knob. **2.** The essence; the core: *the nub of the problem.* **—nub′by** *adj.*

nub·bin (nŭb′ĭn) *n.* A small stunted or projecting part.

nu·cle·ar (no͞o′klē-ər) *adj.* **1.** Relating to the nucleus of a cell: *a nuclear membrane.* **2.** Relating to the nuclei of atoms. **3.** Having or using energy derived from the nuclei of atoms: *a nuclear power plant.* **4.** Having atomic or hydrogen bombs: *nuclear powers.*

nuclear energy *n.* The energy that is released by the alteration of atomic nuclei, especially by fission, fusion, or radioactive decay.

nuclear family *n.* A family unit consisting of a mother and father and their children.

nuclear physics *n. (used with a singular verb)* The scientific study of the structure and reactions of atomic nuclei.

nuclear reaction *n.* A change in the structure of an atomic nucleus that results in a change in its energy or composition. Fission, fusion, and radioactive decay are nuclear reactions.

nuclear reactor *n.* A device in which a nuclear chain reaction is started and controlled, thus producing heat, which is usually used to generate electricity, and a variety of radioactive isotopes.

nu·cle·i (no͞o′klē-ī′) *n.* A plural of **nucleus.**

nu·cle·ic acid (no͞o-klē′ĭk) *n.* Any of a group of organic compounds that are found in cells and viruses and that constitute the genetic material of a particular cell or virus. The two main nucleic acids are DNA and RNA.

notebook

USAGE

noun Every noun is either a *common noun* or a *proper noun.* A *common noun* is a noun such as *book* or *student.* Such nouns can stand for one particular item, as in *I want the fifth book in the pile.* Such a noun can also stand for all items referred to by the noun: *The book is an ideal means of communication.* A common noun can also stand for an idea or an abstraction, such as *friendliness* or *truth.* A *proper noun* names someone or something that is unique and particular, such as *Abraham Lincoln* or *British Columbia.*

nozzle
garden hose nozzle

USAGE

number When the word **number** is followed by a phrase beginning with *of,* you use a singular or plural verb depending on the article that precedes *number.* You use a singular verb when *number* is preceded by the definite article *the: The number of new students is small.* You use a plural verb when *number* is preceded by the indefinite article *a: A number of students are coming to the talent show.*

ă	pat	ôr	core
ā	pay	oi	boy
âr	care	ou	out
ä	father	o͝o	took
ĕ	pet	o͝or	lure
ē	be	o͞o	boot
ĭ	pit	ŭ	cut
ī	bite	ûr	urge
îr	pier	th	thin
ŏ	pot	*th*	this
ō	toe	zh	vision
ô	paw	ə	about

nu·cle·o·lus (no͞o-**klē′**ə-ləs) *n., pl.* **nu·cle·o·li** (no͞o-**klē′**ə-lī′) A small structure within the nucleus of a cell that contains RNA and protein and is the site where ribosomes are formed.

nu·cle·on (**no͞o′**klē-ŏn′) *n.* A proton or neutron, especially as part of an atomic nucleus. **—nu′cle·on′ic** *adj.*

nu·cle·o·tide (**no͞o′**klē-ə-tīd′) *n.* Any of a group of organic compounds composed of a sugar, a phosphate, and one of several bases containing nitrogen. Nucleotides are the molecular subunits that make up DNA and RNA.

nu·cle·us (**no͞o′**klē-əs) *n., pl.* **nu·cle·i** (**no͞o′**klē-ī′) or **nu·cle·us·es 1.** A central or essential part around which other parts are grouped; a core: *the players who formed the nucleus of the team.* **2.** A basis for future growth; a starting point: *a few paintings that formed the nucleus of an art collection.* **3.** The membrane-enclosed structure in the cytoplasm of a living cell that contains the cell's DNA. Prokaryotes (bacteria and archaea) do not have nuclei. **4.** The positively charged central region of an atom, composed of protons and neutrons and containing most of the mass of the atom. **5.** A specialized mass of gray matter in the brain or spinal cord. [From Latin *nucleus*, kernel, from *nucula*, little nut, from *nux*, nut.]

nude (no͞od) *adj.* **nud·er, nud·est** Being without clothing; naked. ❖ *n.* **1.** An unclothed human figure or a representation of it. **2.** The condition of being unclothed: *in the nude.* **—nu′di·ty** (**no͞o′**dĭ-tē) *n.* **—nude′ly** *adv.*

nudge (nŭj) *tr.v.* **nudged, nudg·ing, nudg·es** To push or poke gently: *He nudged me with his elbow.* ❖ *n.* A gentle push.

nug·get (**nŭg′**ĭt) *n.* **1.** A hard lump of matter, especially of gold. **2.** A small unit or piece: *nuggets of information.*

nui·sance (**no͞o′**səns) *n.* A source of inconvenience or annoyance; a bother. [From Middle English *nusaunce*, from Old French *nuire*, to harm, from Latin *nocēre*.]

nuke (no͞ok) *Slang n.* **1.** A nuclear weapon. **2.** A plant that generates electricity by nuclear power. ❖ *tr.v.* **nuked, nuk·ing, nukes 1.** To attack with nuclear weapons. **2.** To heat or cook in a microwave oven.

Nu·ku·′a·lo·fa (no͞o′ko͞o-ə-**lô′**fə) The capital of Tonga, in the southwest Pacific Ocean.

null (nŭl) *adj.* **1.** Having no legal force; invalid: *a contract rendered null by a later agreement.* **2.** Having the quantity or value of zero; amounting to nothing. **3.** In mathematics, relating to a set that has no members. ❖ *n.* Zero; nothing. ◆ **null and void** Having no legal force or effect; not binding.

nul·li·fi·ca·tion (nŭl′ə-fĭ-**kā′**shən) *n.* **1.** The act of nullifying: *The nullification of the amendment will take time.* **2.** The state of being nullified.

nul·li·fy (**nŭl′**ə-fī′) *tr.v.* **nul·li·fied, nul·li·fy·ing, nul·li·fies 1.** To deprive of legal force; invalidate: *The Supreme Court has the right to nullify an act of Congress by finding it unconstitutional.* **2.** To counteract: *used his quickness to nullify his opponent's advantage in size.* **—nul′li·fi′er** *n.*

numb (nŭm) *adj.* **numb·er, numb·est 1.** Deprived of the power to feel or move normally: *toes numb with cold.* **2.** Showing little or no emotion; indifferent: *The customer was numb to the same old sales pitch.* ❖ *tr. & intr.v.* **numbed, numb·ing, numbs** To make or become numb: *The wind numbed our cheeks. My toes numbed with the cold.* [From Middle English *nomme*, past participle of *nimen*, to seize, from Old English *niman*.] **—numb′ly** *adv.* **—numb′ness** *n.*

num·ber (**nŭm′**bər) *n.* **1a.** A positive integer; one of a set of symbols in a fixed order that have unique meaning and that can be derived by counting. **b.** A mathematical object, such as a negative integer or a real number, that can be derived from the positive integers. **2. numbers** Arithmetic: *good at numbers.* **3.** One of a series in numerical order: *What number are you in this line?* **4.** A numeral or series of numerals assigned to a person or thing for reference or identification: *a telephone number.* **5.** A quantity determined by adding up all units or members; a total; a sum: *the number of feet in a mile.* **6.** An indefinite quantity: *The crowd was small in number.* **7. numbers** A large quantity: *There is strength in numbers.* **8.** A song or other piece of music in a program: *As an encore, the singer performed three more numbers.* **9.** In grammar, the indication by the form of a word of whether it is singular or plural: *The verb must agree in number with the subject.* **10. Numbers** *(used with a singular verb)* A book of the Bible containing two censuses of the Israelites after the Exodus from Egypt. ❖ *v.* **num·bered, num·ber·ing, num·bers** *—tr.* **1.** To assign a number to: *Number each item in the list.* **2.** To determine the number of; count: *We numbered the students in each line.* **3.** To amount to; total: *an audience numbering nearly a thousand.* **4.** To include in a certain category: *He was numbered among the better swimmers.* **5.** To mention one by one: *I'll number the advantages of the plan.* **6.** To limit in number: *The days were numbered before cold weather would set in.* *—intr.* **1.** To call off numbers; count. **2.** To amount to a group or number: *The crowd numbered in the thousands.* ◆ **without number** or **beyond number** Too many to be counted; countless. [From Middle English *nombre*, from Old French, from Latin *numerus*.] —SEE NOTE.

num·ber·less (**nŭm′**bər-lĭs) *adj.* Too many to be counted; countless.

number line *n.* A line marked with a sequence of numbers at regularly spaced points along its length.

number sign *n.* The symbol (#), used to represent the word *number.*

number system *n.* Any system of naming or representing numbers, as the decimal system.

numb·skull (**nŭm′**skŭl′) *n.* Variant of **numskull.**

nu·mer·a·ble (**no͞o′**mər-ə-bəl) *adj.* Capable of being counted; countable.

nu·mer·al (**no͞o′**mər-əl) *n.* A symbol or mark used to represent a number. [From Late Latin *numerālis*, of numbers, from Latin *numerus*, number.]

nu·mer·ate (**no͞o′**mə-rāt′) *tr.v.* **nu·mer·at·ed, nu·mer·at·ing, nu·mer·ates** To enumerate; count.

nu·mer·a·tion (no͞o′mə-**rā′**shən) *n.* **1.** The act or process of counting or numbering. **2.** A system of numbering.

nu·mer·a·tor (**no͞o′**mə-rā′tər) *n.* A number written above the line in a common fraction to indicate the number of parts of the whole. In, for example, the fraction $^2/_7$ the numerator 2 indicates that 2 of 7 equal parts of the whole are compared with the whole itself.

nu·mer·i·cal (no͞o-**mĕr′**ĭ-kəl) *adj.* **1.** Relating to a number or series of numbers: *numerical order.* **2.** Expressed or measured in numbers: *a numerical grade.* **—nu·mer′i·cal·ly** *adv.*

nu·mer·ous (**no͞o′**mər-əs) *adj.* Amounting to a large number; many: *numerous items for sale.* **—nu′mer·ous·ly** *adv.*

nu·mis·mat·ic (no͞o′mĭz-**măt′**ĭk) *adj.* Relating to coins or currency. [From Greek *nomisma*, custom, coin in circulation.]

nu·mis·mat·ics (no͞o′mĭz-**măt′**ĭks) *n. (used with a singular verb)* The study or collecting of coins, paper money, or medals.

num·skull also **numb·skull** (**nŭm′**skŭl′) *n.* A stupid person; a blockhead.

nun (nŭn) *n.* A woman who belongs to a religious order, living under vows of poverty, chastity, and obedience. [From Late Latin *nonna*, feminine of *nonnus*, tutor, monk.]

❑ *These sound alike:* **nun, none** (not any).

Nu·na·vut (**no͞o′**nə-vo͞ot′) A territory of northern

Canada including part of the mainland west of Hudson Bay and most of the Arctic Archipelago. It was formed from the eastern portion of the Northwest Territories in 1999. Iqaluit is the capital.

nun·ci·o (nŭn′sē-ō′ *or* nŏŏn′sē-ō′) *n., pl.* **nun·ci·os** A papal ambassador or representative.

nun·ner·y (nŭn′ə-rē) *n., pl.* **nun·ner·ies** A place where a group of nuns live; a convent.

nup·tial (nŭp′shəl *or* nŭp′chəl) *adj.* Relating to marriage or the wedding ceremony. ❖ *n.* often **nuptials** A wedding ceremony.

Nu·rem·berg (nŏŏr′əm-bûrg′) A city of southeast Germany north-northwest of Munich. From 1933 to 1938 it was the site of annual Nazi party congresses and later served as the location for the Allied trials of war criminals (1945–1946).

nurse (nûrs) *n.* **1.** A person who is trained to care for sick and disabled people. **2.** A person, especially a woman, employed to take care of another's children. ❖ *v.* **nursed, nurs·ing, nurs·es** —*tr.* **1.** To act as the nurse for; take care of: *nursed the patient until he could leave the hospital.* **2.** To feed (offspring) from the breast or a teat; suckle. **3.** To try to cure by special care or treatment: *She's nursed that cough for a week.* **4.** To treat or handle carefully: *He nursed his injured knee by changing his position.* **5.** To keep in the mind; harbor: *Don't nurse a grudge.* **6.** To drink slowly, as if preserving: *nursed a soda for an hour.* —*intr.* **1.** To work or act as a nurse. **2.** To be fed from the breast or a teat.

nurse·maid (nûrs′mād′) *n.* A woman employed to take care of infants or young children.

nurs·er·y (nûr′sə-rē *or* nûrs′rē) *n., pl.* **nurs·er·ies 1.** A room set apart for the use of children. **2.** A nursery school. **3.** A place where plants are raised for sale, transplantation, or experimentation.

nursery rhyme *n.* A short rhymed poem for children.

nursery school *n.* A school for children who are not old enough to attend kindergarten.

nurs·ing (nûr′sĭng) *n.* **1.** The profession of a trained nurse. **2.** The tasks performed by a nurse.

nursing home *n.* A place that provides living quarters and care for chronically ill, usually elderly patients.

nurs·ling (nûrs′lĭng) *n.* An infant or young animal that is being nursed.

nur·ture (nûr′chər) *n.* **1.** The action of raising or caring for offspring: *the nurture of an infant.* **2.** The environmental influences and conditions acting on an organism, especially in contrast to heredity: *How much of his musical ability comes from nature and how much comes from nurture?* ❖ *tr.v.* **nur·tured, nur·tur·ing, nur·tures 1.** To feed and protect; nourish: *carefully nurtured the plants in a greenhouse.* **2.** To raise or educate (a child). **3.** To help grow or develop; cultivate: *nurture a friendship.*

nut (nŭt) *n.* **1a.** An edible, oily seed enclosed in a hard shell, such as an almond, a peanut, or a walnut. **b.** In botany, a fruit having a single seed enclosed in a hard shell that does not open at maturity, such as an acorn or a hazelnut. **2.** *Slang* **a.** A crazy or eccentric person. **b.** An enthusiast; a buff: *a movie nut.* **3.** A small block of metal or wood having a threaded hole, designed to fit around and hold a bolt or screw. [From Middle English, from Old English *hnutu.*]

nut·crack·er (nŭt′krăk′ər) *n.* **1.** An implement for cracking nuts, typically consisting of two hinged metal levers between which the nut is squeezed. **2.** Either of two birds of northern Eurasia and western North America that feed chiefly on the seeds of pine cones.

nut·hatch (nŭt′hăch′) *n.* Any of several small birds that have a grayish back and a long sharp bill and are known for climbing down tree trunks headfirst.

nut·meat (nŭt′mēt′) *n.* The edible kernel of a nut.

nut·meg (nŭt′mĕg′) *n.* **1.** The hard aromatic seed of a tropical evergreen tree, used as a spice when ground or grated. **2.** The tree that bears such seeds.

nu·tri·a (nōō′trē-ə) *n.* **1.** A large rodent native to South America that lives in wetlands and has webbed feet and a long tail. **2.** The soft fur of this animal. [From Spanish *nutria,* otter, from Latin *lutra.*]

nu·tri·ent (nōō′trē-ənt) *n.* Something that nourishes, especially an ingredient in a food. ❖ *adj.* Capable of nourishing; having nutritive value.

nu·tri·ment (nōō′trə-mənt) *n.* Nourishment; food.

nu·tri·tion (nōō-trĭsh′ən) *n.* **1.** The process of nourishing or being nourished, especially the process by which a living thing takes in and uses food. **2.** The study of food and nourishment. **3.** Nourishment; diet: *Having good nutrition is important for good health.* **—nu·tri′tion·al** *adj.* **—nu·tri′tion·al·ly** *adv.*

nu·tri·tious (nōō-trĭsh′əs) *adj.* Providing nourishment; nourishing: *She ate a nutritious meal before hiking.* **—nu·tri′tious·ly** *adv.* **—nu·tri′tious·ness** *n.*

nu·tri·tive (nōō′trĭ-tĭv) *adj.* **1.** Nutritious; nourishing. **2.** Relating to nutrition.

nuts (nŭts) *Slang adj.* **1.** Crazy or irrational: *She must be nuts to think we could finish the project today.* **2.** Very enthusiastic: *He's nuts about playing the drums.* ❖ *interj.* Used to express disappointment, contempt, or refusal.

nut·shell (nŭt′shĕl′) *n.* The shell enclosing the meat of a nut. ◆ **in a nutshell** In a few words; concisely.

nut·ty (nŭt′ē) *adj.* **nut·ti·er, nut·ti·est 1.** Containing or producing nuts: *nutty cookies; nutty trees.* **2.** Having the flavor of nuts. **3.** *Slang* Crazy; silly. **—nut′ti·ly** *adv.* **—nut′ti·ness** *n.*

Nuuk (nŏŏk) The capital of Greenland, on the southwest coast of the island. It was formerly known as Godthåb.

nuz·zle (nŭz′əl) *v.* **nuz·zled, nuz·zling, nuz·zles** —*tr.* To rub or push gently with the nose or snout: *The calf nuzzled its mother.* —*intr.* To press close together; nestle. [From Middle English *noselen,* to bend down, probably from *noseling,* lying face downward, from *nose,* nose.]

NV *abbr.* An abbreviation of Nevada.

NW *abbr.* An abbreviation of: **1.** northwest. **2.** northwestern.

NWT *abbr.* An abbreviation of Northwest Territories.

NY *abbr.* An abbreviation of New York.

NYC *abbr.* An abbreviation of New York City.

ny·lon (nī′lŏn′) *n.* **1.** Any of various very strong elastic synthetic resins. **2.** Cloth or yarn made from nylon. **3.** **nylons** Stockings made of nylon. [Coined by its inventors, E.I. Du Pont de Nemours and Co., Inc.]

nymph (nĭmf) *n.* **1.** In Greek and Roman mythology, one of numerous minor goddesses dwelling in woodlands and waters and represented as beautiful young women. **2a.** The young, incompletely developed form of certain insects, such as grasshoppers, that does not pass through a pupal stage during metamorphosis. Nymphs resemble adults but are smaller and lack fully developed wings. **b.** The eight-legged immature form of certain arachnids, such as ticks and mites. [From Latin *nympha,* from Greek *numphē.*]

NZ *abbr.* An abbreviation of New Zealand.

nut

nuthatch

Annie Oakley
photographed in 1899

Barack Obama
photographed in 2009

ă	pat	ôr	core
ā	pay	oi	boy
âr	care	ou	out
ä	father	o͝o	took
ĕ	pet	o͝or	lure
ē	be	o͞o	boot
ĭ	pit	ŭ	cut
ī	bite	ûr	urge
îr	pier	th	thin
ŏ	pot	*th*	this
ō	toe	zh	vision
ô	paw	ə	about

o or **O** (ō) *n., pl.* **o's** or **O's** also **os** or **Os 1.** The 15th letter of the English alphabet. **2. O** One of the four types of blood in the ABO system. **3.** A zero.

O[1] (ō) *interj.* **1.** An expression used before the name of a person or thing being formally addressed. **2.** An expression used to show surprise or strong emotion: *O my goodness!*

❑ *These sound alike:* **O[1], oh** (exclamation), **owe** (be indebted).

O[2] The symbol for the element **oxygen.**

O[3] *abbr.* An abbreviation of: **1.** out (in baseball). **2.** outstanding.

oaf (ōf) *n.* A clumsy or stupid person. [From Old Norse *alfr*, elf, silly person.] **—oaf′ish** *adj.*

O·a·hu (ō-ä′ho͞o) An island of central Hawaii between Molokai and Kauai. It is the site of Honolulu and Pearl Harbor.

oak (ōk) *n.* **1.** Any of numerous trees or shrubs that bear acorns and often have leaves that are notched or lobed. **2.** The hard strong wood of such a tree or shrub. [From Old English *āc*.]

oak·en (ō′kən) *adj.* Made of the wood of an oak: *oaken buckets.*

Oak·ley (ōk′lē), **Annie** Originally **Phoebe Ann Moses.** 1860–1926. American sharpshooter who was the main attraction of Buffalo Bill's Wild West Show.

oa·kum (ō′kəm) *n.* Loose hemp or jute fiber used for sealing seams in wooden ships and for packing pipe joints.

oar (ôr) *n.* **1.** A long thin pole with a blade at one end, used to row or steer a boat. **2.** A person who rows a boat, especially in a race. ❖ *v.* **oared, oar·ing, oars** *—tr.* To propel by using oars: *oaring the boat down the river.* *—intr.* To move forward by rowing.

❑ *These sound alike:* **oar, o'er** (over), **or** (conjunction), **ore** (mineral).

oar·lock (ôr′lŏk′) *n.* A U-shaped or circular metal hoop on a swivel, used to hold an oar in place while rowing.

oars·man (ôrz′mən) *n.* A man who rows a boat; a rower.

oars·wom·an (ôrz′wo͝om′ən) *n.* A woman who rows a boat; a rower.

o·a·sis (ō-ā′sĭs) *n., pl.* **o·a·ses** (ō-ā′sēz) **1.** A small area in a desert that has a growth of plants because of the presence of water. **2.** A place or situation that provides comfort or refuge: *The library is an oasis in the middle of the noisy city.* [From Greek, from Egyptian *wḥ't*.]

oat (ōt) *n.* often **oats** *(used with a singular or plural verb)* **1.** The grain of a grass widely grown in cool regions, used as food for humans and livestock. **2.** The plant that bears such grain. [From Old English *āte*.]

oat·cake (ōt′kāk′) *n.* A flattened cake of baked oatmeal.

oat·en (ōt′n) *adj.* Related to, made of, or containing oats, oatmeal, or oat straw: *oaten fodder.*

oath (ōth) *n., pl.* **oaths** (ō*th*z *or* ōths) **1.** A declaration or promise to act in a certain way, calling on God, a god, or a sacred object as witness: *Each president takes an oath to uphold the Constitution.* **2.** A word or phrase that irreverently uses the name of God or something sacred; a profanity. ◆ **take an oath** To agree to a pledge of truthfulness or faithful performance. **under oath** Bound by an oath to tell the truth, as in a court of law. [From Old English *āth*.]

oat·meal (ōt′mēl′) *n.* **1.** Meal made from ground oats or from oats that have been pressed flat by rollers. **2.** A porridge made from such meal.

O·ba·di·ah[1] (ō′bə-dī′ə) A Hebrew prophet of the sixth century BC.

O·ba·di·ah[2] (ō′bə-dī′ə) *n.* A book of the Bible in which Obadiah predicts the punishment of the traditional enemies of the Israelites.

O·ba·ma (ō-bä′mə), **Barack Hussein, Jr.** Born 1961. The 44th president of the United States (2009–2017). The first African American to be elected to the US presidency, he increased government spending to address a deep recession and signed a bill expanding the availability of health insurance.

ob·bli·ga·to (ŏb′lĭ-gä′tō) *adj.* In music, not to be left out; necessary.

ob·du·ra·cy (ŏb′do͝or-ə-sē) *n.* The quality or condition of being obdurate.

ob·du·rate (ŏb′do͝o-rĭt) *adj.* **1.** Unmoved by persuasion; unyielding; stubborn: *obdurate in her refusal to go along.* **2.** Hardened against feeling or compassion; hardhearted: *an obdurate miser.* **—ob′du·rate·ly** *adv.* **—ob′du·rate·ness** *n.*

o·be·di·ence (ō-bē′dē-əns) *n.* **1.** The act of obeying rules, laws, or requests. **2.** The state of being obedient.

o·be·di·ent (ō-bē′dē-ənt) *adj.* Willing to obey: *an obedient dog.* **—o·be′di·ent·ly** *adv.*

o·bei·sance (ō-bā′səns *or* ō-bē′səns) *n.* A bow, curtsy, or other gesture of submission or respect.

ob·e·lisk (ŏb′ə-lĭsk) *n.* A tall four-sided shaft of stone that rises to a pointed top shaped like a pyramid.

o·bese (ō-bēs′) *adj.* Extremely fat; very overweight. **—o·bese′ly** *adv.* **—o·be′si·ty** (ō-bē′sĭ-tē) *n.*

o·bey (ō-bā′) *v.* **o·beyed, o·bey·ing, o·beys** *—tr.* **1.** To carry out or comply with (a request, an order, or a law): *obeying the traffic regulations.* **2.** To do what is commanded or requested by (a person or other authority): *The girl obeyed her father and picked up her toys.* *—intr.* To be obedient. [From Middle English *obeien*, from Latin *oboedīre*, to listen to.]

ob·fus·cate (ŏb′fə-skāt′) *tr.v.* **ob·fus·cat·ed, ob·fus·cat·ing, ob·fus·cates** To make (something) so confusing or murky that it is hard to understand or see: *The report was so complicated that it obfuscated the findings rather than making them clear.*

o·bi (ō′bē) *n., pl.* **o·bis** A wide sash worn with a kimono.

o·bit·u·ar·y (ō-bĭch′o͞o-ĕr′ē) *n., pl.* **o·bit·u·ar·ies** A published notice of a person's death, often with a short biography.

obj. *abbr.* An abbreviation of: **1.** object. **2.** objective.

ob·ject (ŏb′jĕkt′) *n.* **1.** Something that can be seen, touched, or perceived; a material thing. **2.** A thing being viewed, studied, or handled: *Place the object directly beneath the microscope.* **3.** A person or thing toward which emotion, thought, or action is directed: *The new baby was the object of everyone's attention.* **4.** A purpose; a goal: *The object of the project is to learn how people lived in ancient Rome.* **5a.** A noun, pronoun, or group of words acting like a noun that receives or is affected by the action of a verb. **b.** A noun, pronoun, or group of words acting like a noun that is governed by and typically follows a preposition. **6.** An item that can be selected and moved around on a computer screen. ❖ *v.* (əb-jĕkt′) **ob·ject·ed, ob·ject·ing, ob·jects** —*intr.* **1.** To express an opposing opinion or argument; protest. **2.** To be opposed; express disapproval: *We objected to the loud noise downstairs.* —*tr.* To say or offer in opposition or criticism: *We objected that they were being too loud.* [From Middle English, from Medieval Latin *obiectum*, something put forward, from Latin *obicere*, to put before.] **—ob·jec′tor** *n.*

ob·jec·tion (əb-jĕk′shən) *n.* **1.** A statement of an opposing view or argument: *You made no objection when the idea first came up.* **2.** A reason or cause for opposing or disapproving: *His only objection to buying the car was that it was too expensive.*

ob·jec·tion·a·ble (əb-jĕk′shə-nə-bəl) *adj.* Causing or apt to cause objection; offensive: *objectionable behavior.* **—ob·jec′tion·a·bly** *adv.*

ob·jec·tive (əb-jĕk′tĭv) *adj.* **1.** Real; actual: *objective facts.* **2.** Not influenced by emotion or personal prejudice; impartial: *an objective judge of the situation.* **3.** In grammar, relating to the case of a noun or pronoun that serves as the object of a verb or preposition. For example, in the sentence *She sees me, me* is in the objective case. ❖ *n.* **1.** Something worked toward; a goal; a purpose: *Our objective is to plant more trees in town.* **2.** In grammar, the objective case. **3.** The lens or system of lenses in a telescope or microscope that is closest to the object under examination. **—ob·jec′tive·ly** *adj.* **—ob·jec′tive·ness** *n.*

objective complement *n.* A noun, adjective, or pronoun that follows the direct object of certain verbs and is necessary to complete the meaning of the sentence. For example, in the sentence *We elected her governor,* the word *governor* is the objective complement.

ob·jec·tiv·i·ty (ŏb′jĕk-tĭv′ĭ-tē) *n.* The state or quality of being objective.

object lesson *n.* **1.** A lesson taught by using a material object. **2.** A real example of a moral or principle.

ob·jet d'art (ôb′zhĕ där′) *n., pl.* **ob·jets d'art** (ôb′zhĕ där′) An object valued for its artistic qualities.

ob·li·gate (ŏb′lĭ-gāt′) *tr.v.* **ob·li·gat·ed, ob·li·gat·ing, ob·li·gates** To compel or constrain by a social, legal, or moral requirement: *A doctor is obligated to help every patient.* **—ob′li·ga′tor** *n.*

ob·li·ga·tion (ŏb′lĭ-gā′shən) *n.* **1.** A legal, social, or moral requirement, duty, or promise that has the power of binding one to a certain action: *an obligation to vote.* **2.** The binding power of a law, promise, contract, or sense of duty: *the obligation of friendship.* **3.** A debt owed as payment or in return for a special service or favor: *a financial obligation; a social obligation.* **4.** The state or feeling of being obligated to another for a special service or favor: *We felt a sense of obligation toward the teacher.*

o·blig·a·to·ry (ə-blĭg′ə-tôr′ē *or* ŏb′lĭ-gə-tôr′ē) *adj.* **1.** Legally or morally binding; required or compulsory: *Attendance at school is obligatory.* **2.** Required as part of a routine course of action or cultural expectation; predictable: *The birthday party had cake, presents, and the obligatory clown.* **—o·blig′a·to′ri·ly** *adv.*

o·blige (ə-blīj′) *tr.v.* **o·bliged, o·blig·ing, o·blig·es** **1.** To force by physical, legal, social, or moral means; compel: *The weather obliged him to postpone his trip.* **2.** To make grateful or thankful: *They were obliged to her for her help.* **3.** To do a service or favor for: *The singer obliged the fans with another song.* [From Middle English *oblīgen*, from Latin *obligāre*.]

o·blig·ing (ə-blī′jĭng) *adj.* Ready to do favors for others: *The obliging youth helped his frail neighbor across the street.* **—o·blig′ing·ly** *adv.*

o·blique (ō-blēk′) *adj.* **1a.** Slanting or sloping, especially in direction. **b.** Neither parallel nor perpendicular. **2.** Indirect or evasive; not straightforward: *an oblique question.* ❖ *n.* Something, such as a line or direction, that is oblique. [From Middle English, from Latin *oblīquus*.] **—o·blique′ly** *adv.* **—o·blique′ness** *n.*

oblique angle *n.* An angle that is not a right angle or a multiple of a right angle; an acute angle or obtuse angle.

o·blit·er·ate (ə-blĭt′ə-rāt′) *tr.v.* **o·blit·er·at·ed, o·blit·er·at·ing, o·blit·er·ates** **1.** To do away with completely; destroy: *The flood obliterated the cornfield.* **2.** To cover or hide from view: *The sun obliterated the moon.* [From Latin *oblitterāre*, to erase : *ob*, over + *littera*, letter.] **—o·blit′er·a′tion** *n.* **—o·blit′er·a′tor** *n.*

o·bliv·i·on (ə-blĭv′ē-ən) *n.* **1.** The condition of being completely forgotten: *a great writer, in oblivion until the discovery of the manuscript.* **2.** The condition of being oblivious: *the oblivion of a deep sleep.*

o·bliv·i·ous (ə-blĭv′ē-əs) *adj.* Unaware or unmindful: *oblivious to her surroundings.* **—o·bliv′i·ous·ly** *adv.* **—o·bliv′i·ous·ness** *n.* —SEE NOTE.

ob·long (ŏb′lông′) *adj.* Elongated in one direction; shaped like an ellipse or a rectangle: *placed the picture in an oblong frame.* ❖ *n.* An oblong object or figure. [From Middle English, from Latin *oblongus*.]

ob·lo·quy (ŏb′lə-kwē) *n., pl.* **ob·lo·quies** **1.** Abusive language that is intended to discredit a person or thing. **2.** The ill repute or discredit suffered because of such abuse.

ob·nox·ious (ŏb-nŏk′shəs) *adj.* Very annoying or objectionable; offensive: *I moved to a different seat to avoid the obnoxious passengers on the train.* **—ob·nox′ious·ly** *adv.* **—ob·nox′ious·ness** *n.*

o·boe (ō′bō) *n.* A woodwind instrument with a thin conical shape and a mouthpiece with a double reed. It is played by pressing keys that uncover holes in its body. [From Italian, from French *hautbois* : *haut*, high + *bois*, wood.]

o·bo·ist (ō′bō-ĭst) *n.* A person who plays the oboe.

ob·scene (ŏb-sēn′) *adj.* Offensive to accepted standards of decency or modesty: *obscene language.* **—ob·scene′ly** *adv.* **—ob·scene′ness** *n.*

ob·scen·i·ty (ŏb-sĕn′ĭ-tē) *n., pl.* **ob·scen·i·ties** **1.** The condition of being obscene. **2.** Indecency or offensiveness in behavior, appearance, or expression. **3.** Something, such as a word or act, that is considered obscene.

ob·scure (əb-skyŏŏr′) *adj.* **ob·scur·er, ob·scur·est** **1.** Dark; gloomy: *an obscure hallway in the old house.* **2.** Not clearly or easily perceived; indistinct: *an obscure figure in the fog.* **3.** Not clearly or easily understood: *an obscure reference to a past incident.* **4.** Known by very few people: *an obscure poet.* ❖ *tr.v.* **ob·scured, ob·scur·ing, ob·scures** **1.** To conceal from view; hide: *Clouds obscured the stars.* **2.** To make difficult to understand: *The meaning of the message was obscured by its strange language.* [From Middle English, from Latin *obscūrus*.] **—ob·scure′ly** *adv.*

ob·scu·ri·ty (əb-skyŏŏr′ĭ-tē) *n.* **1.** The condition of having little or no light; darkness. **2.** The condition of being unknown or inconspicuous: *a great movie star, now in obscurity.* **3.** The condition of being difficult to understand: *the obscurity of the poem.*

ob·se·qui·ous (əb-sē′kwē-əs) *adj.* Overly willing to

obelisk
obelisk at Karnak Temple, Luxor, Egypt

obi

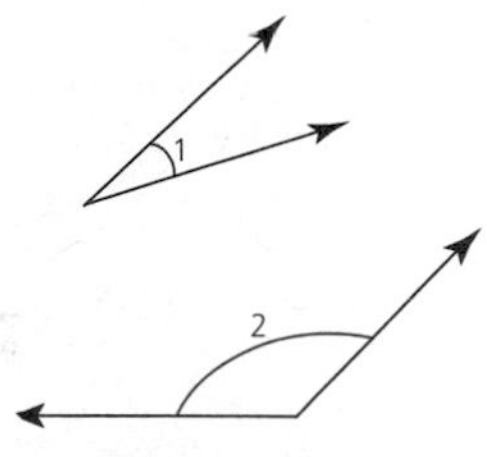

oblique angle
Angles 1 and 2 are oblique.

USAGE

oblivious While either *of* or *to* can be used acceptably with **oblivious,** *to* is more common: *He was oblivious to my presence.*

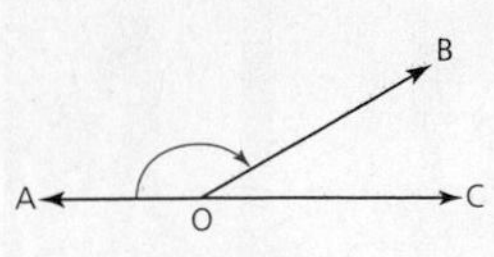

obtuse angle
Angle *AOB* is an obtuse angle.

obverse
obverse (*top*) and reverse (*bottom*) of a Polish zloty coin

ă	pat	ôr	core
ā	pay	oi	boy
âr	care	ou	out
ä	father	o͝o	took
ĕ	pet	o͝or	lure
ē	be	o͞o	boot
ĭ	pit	ŭ	cut
ī	bite	ûr	urge
îr	pier	th	thin
ŏ	pot	*th*	this
ō	toe	zh	vision
ô	paw	ə	about

serve, agree, or obey; fawning: *The director was surrounded by obsequious assistants.* **—ob·se′qui·ous·ly** *adv.* **—ob·se′qui·ous·ness** *n.*

ob·serv·a·ble (əb-zûr′və-bəl) *adj.* Possible to observe: *an observable change in light.* **—ob·serv′a·bly** *adv.*

ob·ser·vance (əb-zûr′vəns) *n.* **1.** The act of complying with a law, rule, or custom. **2.** The act of keeping or celebrating a holiday or religious festival. **3.** A customary rite or ceremony. **4.** The act of watching; observation.

ob·ser·vant (əb-zûr′vənt) *adj.* **1.** Showing keen perceptiveness; alert: *An observant neighbor noticed the broken window.* **2.** Following or observing a law, custom, or duty: *observant of the speed limit.* **—ob·ser′vant·ly** *adv.*

ob·ser·va·tion (ŏb′zər-vā′shən) *n.* **1.** The act of observing: *a tower for the observation of the countryside.* **2a.** The act of perceiving and recording something, such as a phenomenon, often with instruments. **b.** The result or record of such notation: *a meteorological observation.* **3.** A comment or remark: *She made observations about the sculpture.* **—ob′ser·va′tion·al** *adj.*

ob·ser·va·to·ry (əb-zûr′və-tôr′ē) *n., pl.* **ob·ser·va·to·ries 1.** A building or room that is designed and equipped for making observations, as in astronomy or meteorology. **2.** A structure overlooking an extensive view.

ob·serve (əb-zûrv′) *tr.v.* **ob·served, ob·serv·ing, ob·serves 1.** To be aware of; notice: *She observed a skunk crossing the road.* See Synonyms at **see**[1]. **2.** To watch attentively: *I observed how he connected the wires.* **3.** To make a scientific observation of: *observed the migration of the caribou.* **4.** To say; remark: *She observed that math was her best subject.* **5.** To adhere to or abide by: *observe the speed limit.* **6.** To keep or celebrate: *We observed Thanksgiving together.* [From Middle English *observen,* from Latin *observāre.*]

ob·serv·er (əb-zûr′vər) *n.* **1.** A person who observes: *The parade drew thousands of observers.* **2.** A person who is sent to observe and report on events without directly participating in them: *The aid organization sent an observer to the United Nations forum.*

ob·sess (əb-sĕs′) *tr.v.* **ob·sessed, ob·sess·ing, ob·sess·es** To preoccupy the mind of (someone) abnormally; haunt: *Finding someone to blame for the leak obsessed them for years.* **—ob·ses′sor** *n.*

ob·ses·sion (əb-sĕsh′ən) *n.* **1.** Recurring attention to a fixed idea or unwanted emotion. **2.** An idea, thought, or emotion that occupies the mind continually: *Collecting rocks became an obsession.* **—ob·ses′sion·al** *adj.*

ob·ses·sive (əb-sĕs′ĭv) *adj.* Related to, characteristic of, or causing an obsession: *an obsessive fear of snakes.* **—ob·ses′sive·ly** *adv.*

ob·sid·i·an (ŏb-sĭd′ē-ən) *n.* A shiny, usually black volcanic glass, formed by the rapid cooling of lava.

ob·so·les·cent (ŏb′sə-lĕs′ənt) *adj.* Passing out of use or usefulness; becoming obsolete. [From Latin *obsolēscēns,* present participle of *obsolēscere,* to fall into disuse.] **—ob′so·les′cence** *n.* **—ob′so·les′cent·ly** *adv.*

ob·so·lete (ŏb′sə-lēt′) *adj.* No longer useful, in use, or in fashion: *an obsolete word; obsolete technology.* [From Latin *obsolētus,* past participle of *obsolēscere,* to fall into disuse.] **—ob′so·lete′ly** *adv.*

ob·sta·cle (ŏb′stə-kəl) *n.* Something that holds up or stands in the way of progress toward a goal: *Being unable to read can be an obstacle to getting a job.* [From Middle English, from Latin *obstāculum,* from *obstāre,* to hinder.]

ob·ste·tri·cian (ŏb′stĭ-trĭsh′ən) *n.* A physician who specializes in obstetrics.

ob·stet·rics (ŏb-stĕt′rĭks) *n. (used with a singular verb)* The branch of medicine that deals with the care of women during pregnancy and childbirth. **—ob·stet′ric** *adj.*

ob·sti·na·cy (ŏb′stə-nə-sē) *n.* The quality or condition of being obstinate; stubbornness.

ob·sti·nate (ŏb′stə-nĭt) *adj.* **1.** Stubbornly adhering to an attitude or course of action. **2.** Difficult to control or cure: *an obstinate headache.* **—ob′sti·nate·ly** *adv.* **—ob′sti·nate·ness** *n.*

SYNONYMS obstinate, stubborn, headstrong, recalcitrant These adjectives mean determinedly unwilling to yield. **Obstinate** means unreasonably rigid and difficult to persuade: *My grandfather is obstinate about doing things in his own way.* **Stubborn** can mean unyielding in spite of pressure to change: *You are too stubborn to admit you are wrong.* **Headstrong** means stubbornly, often recklessly willful: *That headstrong boy will never follow your advice.* A person who is **recalcitrant** rebels against authority: *The federal government could hold funds from recalcitrant states that refuse to adopt the policy.*

ANTONYMS cooperative, flexible

---

ob·strep·er·ous (ŏb-strĕp′ər-əs) *adj.* Noisily defiant or unruly; boisterous. **—ob·strep′er·ous·ly** *adv.* **—ob·strep′er·ous·ness** *n.*

ob·struct (əb-strŭkt′) *tr.v.* **ob·struct·ed, ob·struct·ing, ob·structs 1.** To make impassable with obstacles; block: *The delivery truck obstructed the alley.* **2.** To interfere with so as to impede or retard; hinder: *obstructing justice.* **3.** To get in the way of so as to hide; cut off from view: *Tall buildings obstructed our view of the ocean.* [From Latin *obstruere.*] **—ob·struct′er, ob·struc′tor** *n.* **—ob·struc′tive** *adj.* **—ob·struc′tive·ly** *adv.*

ob·struc·tion (əb-strŭk′shən) *n.* **1.** Something that obstructs or gets in the way: *an obstruction in the road.* **2.** The act or action of obstructing: *the obstruction of justice.* **3.** The condition of being blocked: *an intestinal obstruction.* **4.** The act of getting in the way of another player in a sports match or race.

ob·struc·tion·ist (əb-strŭk′shə-nĭst) *n.* A person who systematically blocks or interrupts a process, especially one who uses delaying tactics to hinder the passage of legislation. **—ob·struc′tion·ism** *n.*

ob·tain (əb-tān′) *v.* **ob·tained, ob·tain·ing, ob·tains** —*tr.* To gain possession of as the result of planning or endeavor; acquire: *I obtained information for my report at the library.* —*intr.* To be in existence, in effect, or customary: *an ancient custom that still obtains.* [From Middle English *obteinen,* from Latin *obtinēre.*] **—ob·tain′a·ble** *adj.* **—ob·tain′er** *n.*

ob·trude (əb-tro͞od′) *v.* **ob·trud·ed, ob·trud·ing, ob·trudes** —*tr.* **1.** To force (ideas or opinions) upon another without invitation: *He tries to obtrude his prejudices on others.* **2.** To push forward; thrust out: *The clam obtruded its siphon.* —*intr.* To force oneself upon another: *She would not obtrude upon their privacy.* **—ob·tru′sion** (əb-tro͞o′zhən) *n.*

ob·tru·sive (əb-tro͞o′sĭv) *adj.* Tending to obtrude; brash: *obtrusive behavior.* **—ob·tru′sive·ly** *adv.*

ob·tuse (əb-to͞os′) *adj.* **ob·tus·er, ob·tus·est 1.** Slow in perception or understanding; dull: *an obtuse person.* **2.** Not sharp or pointed in form; blunt. **—ob·tuse′ly** *adv.* **—ob·tuse′ness** *n.*

obtuse angle *n.* An angle whose measure is between 90° and 180°.

ob·verse (ŏb-vûrs′ *or* ŏb′vûrs′) *adj.* Facing or turned toward the observer: *the obverse side of a clock.* ❖ *n.* (ŏb′vûrs′ *or* ŏb-vûrs′) The side or face of a coin, medal, or badge that bears the principal stamp or design. **—ob·verse′ly** *adv.* —SEE NOTE AT **divert.**

ob·vi·ate (ŏb′vē-āt′) *tr.v.* **ob·vi·at·ed, ob·vi·at·ing, ob·vi·ates** To keep from happening or make unnecessary: *I obviated the need for a plumber by fixing the leak myself.* **—ob′vi·a′tion** *n.* **—ob′vi·a′tor** *n.*

ob·vi·ous (ŏb′vē-əs) *adj.* Easily perceived or understood;

evident: *an obvious advantage.* —**ob′vi·ous·ly** *adv.*

oc·a·ri·na (ŏk′ə-**rē′**nə) *n.* A wind instrument with an oval shape, a mouthpiece, and holes that are opened and closed by the fingers.

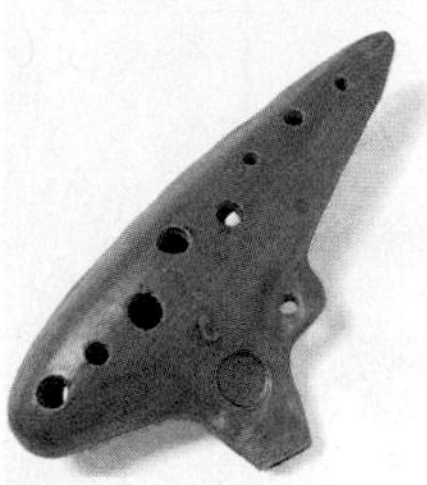
ocarina

oc·ca·sion (ə-**kā′**zhən) *n.* **1.** An event or happening, or the time of an event or happening: *On several occasions, we saw him riding a motorcycle.* **2.** An important event or happening: *Her party was quite an occasion.* **3.** A favorable or suitable time; an opportunity: *There were many occasions when we were able to go sailing.* **4.** A reason or cause: *What was the occasion for all that laughter?* ❖ *tr.v.* **oc·ca·sioned, oc·ca·sion·ing, oc·ca·sions** To be the reason for; cause: *The need to resolve the dispute occasioned the meeting.* ◆ **on occasion** From time to time; now and then: *On occasion, I like to go to the beach and watch the sunset.* [From Middle English, from Latin *occāsiō*, from *occidere*, to fall.]

oc·ca·sion·al (ə-**kā′**zhə-nəl) *adj.* **1.** Occurring or done from time to time; irregular or infrequent: *an occasional thunderstorm.* **2.** Intended for use as the need arises: *occasional chairs for a reception.* **3.** Created for a special occasion: *an occasional song.*

oc·ca·sion·al·ly (ə-**kā′**zhə-nə-lē) *adv.* From time to time; now and then: *Occasionally I go to the hospital to do volunteer work.*

oc·ci·dent (**ŏk′**sĭ-dənt) *n.* **1.** Western lands or regions; the west. **2. Occident** The countries of Europe and the Western Hemisphere. [From Middle English, from Latin *occidēns*, setting (used of the sun).]

oc·ci·den·tal or **Oc·ci·den·tal** (ŏk′sĭ-**dĕn′**tl) *adj.* Relating to the countries of the Occident or any of their peoples. ❖ *n.* A native or inhabitant of an Occidental country; a westerner.

oc·cip·i·tal (ŏk-**sĭp′**ĭ-tl) *adj.* Relating to the back of the head, especially to the occipital bone.

occipital bone *n.* The bone forming the lower back part of the skull.

occipital lobe *n.* The posterior lobe of each cerebral hemisphere, containing the main visual centers of the brain.

oc·clude (ə-**klo͞od′**) *v.* **oc·clud·ed, oc·clud·ing, oc·cludes** —*tr.* **1.** To close off or block off: *occlude a passageway.* **2.** To keep from passing: *occlude light.* **3.** To absorb or adsorb large amounts of: *metal that occludes gases.* **4.** To force (air) upward from Earth's surface, as a cold front does when it moves under a warm front. **5.** To bring (the upper and lower teeth) together in proper alignment for chewing. —*intr.* To meet properly for chewing: *The dentist said my jaws do not occlude perfectly.*

oc·clud·ed front (ə-**klo͞o′**dĭd) *n.* The front that forms when a cold front overtakes a warm front and forces the warm air upward.

oc·clu·sion (ə-**klo͞o′**zhən) *n.* **1.** The process of occluding. **2.** An obstruction in a bodily passageway, such as a blood vessel. **3.** The manner in which the teeth fit when brought together.

oc·cult (ə-**kŭlt′** *or* **ŏk′**ŭlt′) *adj.* **1.** Relating to or dealing with magical or supernatural powers. **2.** Beyond human understanding; mysterious. ❖ *n.* Occult practices or teachings.

oc·cul·ta·tion (ŏk′ŭl-**tā′**shən) *n.* The passage of a celestial object between an observer and another celestial object, blocking the more distant object from the observer's view. The passage of the moon between Earth and the sun in a solar eclipse is an example of occultation.

oc·cult·ism (ə-**kŭl′**tĭz′əm *or* **ŏk′**ŭl-tĭz′əm) *n.* A belief in or the study of occult powers and the supernatural. —**oc·cult′ist** *n.*

oc·cu·pan·cy (**ŏk′**yə-pən-sē) *n., pl.* **oc·cu·pan·cies 1.** The act of taking or holding in possession; the act of occupying. **2.** The state of being occupied or rented. **3.** The period during which a person or group stays in, rents, or uses certain premises or land.

oc·cu·pant (**ŏk′**yə-pənt) *n.* **1.** A person or thing occupying a place: *the occupants of a building.* **2.** A person who holds an office, position, or job.

oc·cu·pa·tion (ŏk′yə-**pā′**shən) *n.* **1.** A means of making a living; a profession or job. **2.** An activity that keeps one busy. **3.** The act or process of holding, possessing, or using a place: *the occupation of the cave by bears.* **4.** The conquest and control of a nation or territory by a foreign military force.

oc·cu·pa·tion·al (ŏk′yə-**pā′**shə-nəl) *adj.* Relating to or caused by engagement in a particular occupation: *occupational disease.* —**oc′cu·pa′tion·al·ly** *adv.*

occupational therapy *n.* The treatment of a physical or emotional disability through the use of specialized activities that help a person regain or develop the ability to function independently.

oc·cu·py (**ŏk′**yə-pī′) *tr.v.* **oc·cu·pied, oc·cu·py·ing, oc·cu·pies 1.** To fill; take up: *Reading occupies his free time.* **2.** To dwell in; inhabit: *They occupy a small cabin.* **3.** To hold or control (an office or position): *She occupies the office of president.* **4.** To seize possession of and maintain control over by force: *The troops occupied the city.* **5.** To employ or busy (oneself): *occupied himself with the crossword puzzle while waiting.* —**oc′cu·pi′er** *n.*

oc·cur (ə-**kûr′**) *intr.v.* **oc·curred, oc·cur·ring, oc·curs 1.** To take place; come about; happen: *A car crash occurred on Route 29 yesterday.* **2.** To be found to exist or appear: *Heavy rains occur during monsoons.* **3.** To come to mind: *That idea never occurred to me.* [From Latin *occurrere*, run against.]

oc·cur·rence (ə-**kûr′**əns) *n.* **1.** The action, fact, or condition of occurring: *the occurrence of a rainbow.* **2.** Something that happens; an incident: *a strange occurrence.*

o·cean (**ō′**shən) *n.* **1.** The mass of salt water that covers about 72 percent of the surface of the earth. **2.** Any of the principal divisions of this body of water, including the Atlantic, Pacific, Indian, and Arctic Oceans. [From Middle English *occean*, from Greek *Ōkeanos*, the god Oceanus, a great river encircling the earth.]

o·cean·ar·i·um (ō′shə-**nâr′**ē-əm) *n., pl.* **o·cean·ar·i·ums** or **o·cean·ar·i·a** (ō′shə-**nâr′**ē-ə) A large aquarium for the study or display of animals that live in the sea.

o·cean·front (**ō′**shən-frŭnt′) *n.* Land bordering an ocean: *The developer built a hotel on the oceanfront.*

o·cean·go·ing (**ō′**shən-gō′ĭng) *adj.* Being a vessel that is made or used for ocean voyages: *The Mississippi River is deep enough for oceangoing ships.*

O·ce·an·i·a (ō′shē-**ăn′**ē-ə) The islands of the southern, western, and central Pacific Ocean, including Melanesia, Micronesia, and Polynesia. The term sometimes includes Australia, New Zealand, and the Malay Archipelago.

o·ce·an·ic (ō′shē-**ăn′**ĭk) *adj.* **1.** Relating to the ocean. **2.** Living or found in the ocean, especially in the open sea rather than in coastal waters.

o·cean·og·ra·pher (ō′shə-**nŏg′**rə-fər) *n.* A scientist who specializes in oceanography.

o·cean·og·ra·phy (ō′shə-**nŏg′**rə-fē) *n.* The exploration and scientific study of the ocean.

o·cel·lus (ō-**sĕl′**əs) *n., pl.* **o·cel·li** (ō-**sĕl′**ī′) **1.** A simple eye, found in many invertebrate animals, composed of a number of sensory cells and often a single lens. **2.** A marking that resembles an eye. —**o·cel′lar** (ō-**sĕl′**ər) *adj.*

ocellus

oc·e·lot (**ŏs′**ə-lŏt′ *or* **ō′**sə-lŏt′) *n.* A wildcat that has a yellowish coat spotted with black and is found from southern Texas to Argentina.

o·cher or **o·chre** (**ō′**kər) *n.* **1.** Any of several oxides of iron that occur as minerals. Their colors are yellow, brown, and red, and they are used as pigments. **2.** A yellowish or brownish orange.

Sandra Day O'Connor
photographed in 1993

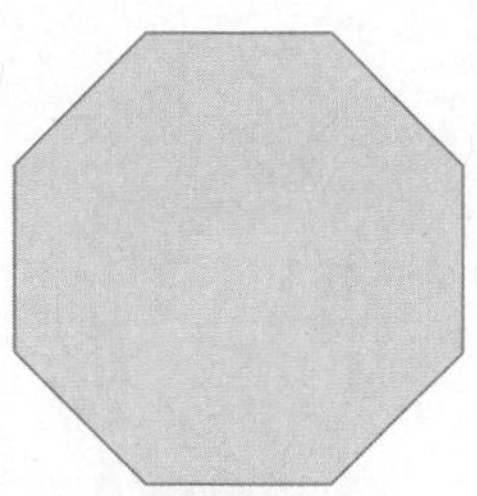

octagon

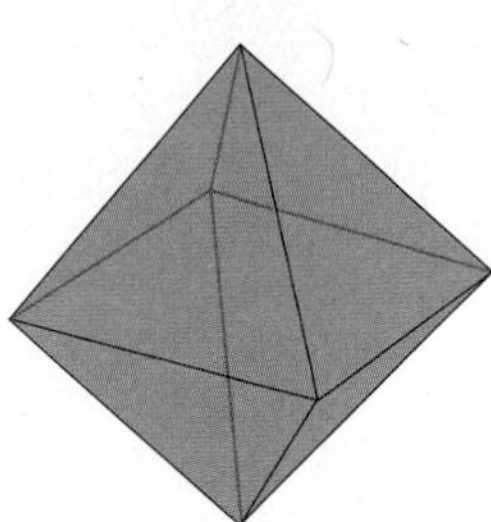

octahedron

ă	pat	ôr	core
ā	pay	oi	boy
âr	care	ou	out
ä	father	o͝o	took
ĕ	pet	o͝or	lure
ē	be	o͞o	boot
ĭ	pit	ŭ	cut
ī	bite	ûr	urge
îr	pier	th	thin
ŏ	pot	*th*	this
ō	toe	zh	vision
ô	paw	ə	about

o'clock (ə-**klŏk′**) *adv.* **1.** According to the clock: *three o'clock.* **2.** According to an imaginary clock dial, with the observer at the center and 12 o'clock considered as straight ahead horizontally or straight up vertically: *enemy planes at 10 o'clock.*

O'Con·nor (ō-**kŏn′**ər), **(Mary) Flannery** 1925–1964. American writer whose novels, including *The Violent Bear It Away* (1960), and her collections of short stories, including *A Good Man is Hard to Find* (1955), are noted for their explorations of religious faith.

O'Connor, Sandra Day Born 1930. American jurist who served as an associate justice of the US Supreme Court (1981–2006). The first woman appointed to the court, she cast the deciding votes in cases concerning controversial issues such as abortion, affirmative action, and the death penalty.

oct– or **octa–** *pref.* Variants of **octo–.**

oc·ta·gon (**ŏk′**tə-gŏn′) *n.* A polygon with eight sides and eight angles. [From Greek *oktō*, eight + Greek *-gōnos*, angled.]

oc·tag·o·nal (ŏk-**tăg′**ə-nəl) *adj.* Having eight sides and eight angles. **—oc·tag′o·nal·ly** *adv.*

oc·ta·he·dron (ŏk′tə-**hē′**drən) *n., pl.* **oc·ta·he·drons** or **oc·ta·he·dra** (ŏk′tə-**hē′**drə) A solid geometric figure having eight faces.

oc·tal (**ŏk′**təl) *adj.* Relating to or using 8 as the base of a number system.

oc·tane (**ŏk′**tān′) *n.* Any of several hydrocarbon compounds having the formula C_8H_{18} and occurring in petroleum.

octane number *n.* A number that represents the antiknock rating of gasoline, based on the percentage of a particular form of octane that is contained in the sample of gasoline.

oc·tant (**ŏk′**tənt) *n.* **1a.** One eighth of a circle; an arc of 45°. **b.** One eighth of the area of a circle; the area bounded by a pair of radii and an arc of 45° that they intercept. **2.** A navigation instrument similar to a sextant but based on an arc of 45° rather than 60°.

oc·tave (**ŏk′**tĭv *or* **ŏk′**tāv′) *n.* **1.** The interval of eight degrees between two tones of the same name, the higher of which has twice as many vibrations per second as the lower. **2.** A tone that is eight degrees above or below another tone. **3.** A series of tones included in this interval: *the lowest octave of a flute.* [From Middle English *octave*, eighth day after a feast day, from Latin *octāvus*, eighth.]

Oc·ta·vi·an (ŏk-**tā′**vē-ən) See **Augustus.**

oc·ta·vo (ŏk-**tā′**vō *or* ŏk-**tä′**vō) *n., pl.* **oc·ta·vos 1.** The page size obtained by folding a very large sheet of paper into eight leaves. **2.** A book composed of pages of this size, about 9 inches (23 centimeters) high.

oc·tet (ŏk-**tĕt′**) *n.* **1a.** A musical composition for eight voices or eight instruments. **b.** A group of eight singers or eight instrumentalists. **2.** A group of eight people or things.

octo– or **octa–** or **oct–** *pref.* A prefix that means eight: *octane.*

Oc·to·ber (ŏk-**tō′**bər) *n.* The tenth month of the year in the Gregorian calendar, having 31 days. [From Middle English *Octobre*, from Latin *Octōber*, eighth month (of the early Roman calendar), from *octō*, eight.]

oc·to·ge·nar·i·an (ŏk′tə-jə-**nâr′**ē-ən) *n.* A person between 80 and 90 years of age.

oc·to·pus (**ŏk′**tə-pəs) *n., pl.* **oc·to·pus·es** or **oc·to·pi** (**ŏk′**tə-pī′) Any of various soft-bodied sea mollusks having eight arms bearing suckers used for grasping and holding, a large head, and a mouth with a strong beak. [From Greek *oktōpous*, eight-footed : *oktō*, eight + *pous*, foot.]

oc·tup·let (ŏk-**tŭp′**lĭt) *n.* One of eight offspring born in a single birth.

oc·u·lar (**ŏk′**yə-lər) *adj.* **1.** Relating to the eye or the sense of vision. **2.** Seen by the eye; visual: *ocular evidence.* ❖ *n.* The eyepiece of a microscope, telescope, or other optical instrument. [From Late Latin *oculāris*, from Latin *oculus*, eye.]

oc·u·list (**ŏk′**yə-lĭst) *n.* **1.** An ophthalmologist. **2.** An optometrist.

oc·u·lus (**ŏk′**yə-ləs) *n., pl.* **oc·u·li** (**ŏk′**yə-lī′) **1.** A round window. **2.** A circular opening at the apex of a dome.

odd (ŏd) *adj.* **odd·er, odd·est 1.** Differing from what is ordinary or usual; peculiar; strange: *odd behavior; an odd name.* **2a.** Being one of an incomplete set or pair: *an odd shoe.* **b.** Remaining after others are grouped: *They formed two teams, leaving one odd player.* **3.** Not regular or expected: *telephoned at odd intervals.* **4.** Not exactly divisible by 2: *1, 17, and −23 are odd numbers.* **5.** More than the number indicated: *There were 20-odd guests at the party.* [From Middle English *odde*, from Old Norse *oddi*, point of land, triangle.] **—odd′ly** *adv.* **—odd′ness** *n.*

odd·ball (**ŏd′**bôl′) *Informal n.* An odd, unusual person.

odd·i·ty (**ŏd′**ĭ-tē) *n., pl.* **odd·i·ties 1.** A person or thing that is odd or strange. **2.** The condition of being odd; strangeness: *The oddity of his behavior suggested that he wasn't feeling well.*

odd job *n.* Any of various jobs not usually requiring special training.

odd man out *Informal n., pl.* **odd men out** A person who differs from the others in a group in some way.

odd·ments (**ŏd′**mənts) *pl.n.* Things that are left over; fragments; remnants.

odds (ŏdz) *pl.n.* **1.** The likelihood or probability that one thing rather than another will happen: *The odds are that it will rain tomorrow.* **2.** The ratio of the likelihood of an event's occurring to the likelihood of its not occurring: *The odds are 2 to 1 that the champion will win.* ◆ **at odds** In disagreement; in conflict: *They were at odds about what to do with the money.*

odds and ends *pl.n.* Miscellaneous items.

ode (ōd) *n.* A lyric poem that expresses in an exalted style the poet's feelings and thoughts. [From Greek *aoidē*, song.]

O·des·sa (ō-**dĕs′**ə) A city of southern Ukraine on an arm of the Black Sea. It is said to occupy the site of an ancient Greek colony that disappeared between the third and fourth centuries AD.

O·din (**ō′**dĭn) *n.* In Norse mythology, the god of wisdom and war, and the creator of the universe.

o·di·ous (**ō′**dē-əs) *adj.* **1.** Arousing or deserving hatred or strong dislike: *shocked by the criminal's odious behavior.* **2.** Extremely unpleasant; repulsive: *an odious smell.* [From Middle English, from Latin *odium*, hatred.] **—o′di·ous·ly** *adv.*

o·di·um (**ō′**dē-əm) *n.* **1.** Intense dislike; hatred. **2.** Disgrace that results from detestable conduct.

o·dom·e·ter (ō-**dŏm′**ĭ-tər) *n.* A device that indicates the distance that a vehicle has traveled. [From Greek *hodometron* : *hodos*, journey + *metron*, measure.]

o·dor (**ō′**dər) *n.* The quality of a thing that is perceived by the sense of smell: *kitchen odors.* See Synonyms at **smell.**

o·dor·if·er·ous (ō′də-**rĭf′**ər-əs) *adj.* Having or giving off an odor, especially a strong or unpleasant one: *an odoriferous bag of garbage.*

o·dor·less (**ō′**dər-lĭs) *adj.* Having no odor: *an odorless gas that was difficult to detect.*

o·dor·ous (**ō′**dər-əs) *adj.* Having a distinct or characteristic odor. **—o′dor·ous·ly** *adv.*

o·dour (**ō′**dər) *n. Chiefly British* Variant of **odor.**

O·dys·se·us (ō-**dĭs′**ē-əs) *n.* In Greek mythology, a leader of the Greeks during the Trojan War who struggled for 10 years to return home.

od·ys·sey (**ŏd′**ĭ-sē) *n., pl.* **od·ys·seys** An extended adventurous journey.

Odyssey *n.* An ancient Greek epic poem attributed to Homer, recounting the ordeals of Odysseus after the fall of Troy as he tried to return home.

Oed·i·pus (**ĕd′**ə-pəs *or* **ē′**də-pəs) *n.* In Greek mythology, the king of Thebes who unknowingly killed his father and married his mother, Jocasta.

o'er (ôr) *prep. & adv.* Over.

❑ *These sound alike:* **o'er, oar** (wooden pole), **or** (conjunction), **ore** (mineral).

of (ŭv *or* ŏv; əv *when unstressed*) *prep.* **1.** Coming from; originating at or from: *customs of the South.* **2.** Caused by; resulting from: *He died of pneumonia.* **3.** At a distance from: *one mile east of here.* **4.** So as to be separated or relieved from: *a prisoner deprived of his freedom; a patient cured of an infection.* **5.** From the total or group making up: *two of my friends; most of the cases.* **6.** Composed or made from: *shoes of the finest leather.* **7.** Associated with or adhering to: *a person of her religion.* **8.** Belonging or connected to: *the rungs of a ladder.* **9.** Possessing; having: *a person of honor.* **10.** Containing or carrying: *a bag of groceries.* **11.** Named or called: *the busy city of Chicago; the Bay of Biscay.* **12.** Centering on or directed toward: *a love of horses.* **13.** Produced by: *the fruits of our orchards.* **14.** Characterized or identified by: *a man of many accomplishments; a year of famine.* **15.** Concerning; about: *We spoke of you last night.* **16.** Set aside for: *a day of rest.* **17.** Before; until: *five minutes of two.* **18.** During: *Of recent years he has devoted himself to gardening.*

OF *abbr.* An abbreviation of outfield.

off (ôf) *adv.* **1.** Away from a place: *They drove off.* **2.** At a distance in space or time: *a mile off; a week off.* **3.** So as to be no longer on or connected: *He shaved off his beard.* **4.** So as to be no longer continuing or functioning: *Turn the lights off.* **5.** So as to be smaller, fewer, or less: *Sales are dropping off.* **6.** So as to be away from work or duty: *taking the day off.* ❖ *adj.* **1.** More distant or removed: *the off side of the barn.* **2.** Not on, attached, or connected: *Her shoes were off.* **3.** Not continuing, operating, or functioning: *The oven is off.* **4.** No longer taking place; canceled: *The dance is off.* **5.** Less or smaller: *Production is off this year.* **6.** Below standard: *His performance was off last night.* **7.** Started on the way; going: *I'm off to the movies.* **8.** In error: *off by several inches.* **9.** Away from or not engaged in work or duty: *I'm off tonight.* ❖ *prep.* **1.** So as to be removed or distant from: *The bird hopped off the branch.* **2.** Away or relieved from: *off duty.* **3.** By consuming or with the means provided by: *living off fruit; living off a pension.* **4.** Extending from: *a little alley off the main street.* **5.** Not up to the usual standard of: *off her game.* **6.** Abstaining from: *staying off tobacco.* **7.** Seaward of: *a mile off the beach.* ◆ **off and on** Stopping and starting; intermittently. [From Old English *of.*]

of·fal (**ô′**fəl) *n.* **1.** Waste parts, especially of a butchered animal. **2.** Refuse; rubbish.

❑ *These sound alike:* **offal, awful** (very bad).

off·beat (**ôf′**bēt′) *n.* A beat in a musical measure that is not normally accented. ❖ *adj.* (**ôf′bēt′**) *Slang* Not of an ordinary type; unconventional; different: *offbeat humor.*

off-brand (**ôf′**brănd′) *adj.* Relating to or being a product sold inexpensively under a relatively unfamiliar brand name and often considered inferior to better known brands.

off chance *n.* A remote or slight chance: *made other plans on the off chance it would rain.*

off-col·or (**ôf′kŭl′**ər) *adj.* **1.** Improper; in poor taste: *an off-color joke.* **2.** Not of the usual or required color: *an off-color uniform.*

of·fence (ə-**fĕns′**) *n. Chiefly British* Variant of **offense.**

of·fend (ə-**fĕnd′**) *v.* **of·fend·ed, of·fend·ing, of·fends** —*tr.* **1.** To cause anger, resentment, or annoyance in; insult or affront: *a remark that offended me.* **2.** To be displeasing to; be disagreeable to: *The smell from the chemicals offended everyone.* —*intr.* **1.** To be the cause of displeasure: *odors that offend.* **2.** To break a moral or spiritual law; sin. **3.** To break a rule or law. [From Middle English *offenden,* from Latin *offendere.*] —**of·fend′er** *n.*

of·fense (ə-**fĕns′**) *n.* **1a.** The act of causing anger, resentment, or displeasure. **b.** The state of being offended: *She took offense at the rude comment.* **2.** A violation of a moral, legal, or social code; a transgression, sin, or crime: *a punishable offense.* **3.** Something that offends: *The building was an offense to the eye.* **4.** (**ŏf′**ĕns′) The act of attacking or assaulting. **5.** (**ŏf′**ĕns′) In sports: **a.** The means or tactics used in trying to score. **b.** The players or the team trying to score.

of·fen·sive (ə-**fĕn′**sĭv) *adj.* **1.** Causing anger, displeasure, or resentment: *offensive language.* **2.** Offending the senses; unpleasant: *an offensive smell.* **3.** Relating to or designed for attack: *offensive infantry weapons.* **4.** (**ŏf′**-ĕn-sĭv) Relating to the offense of a sports team. ❖ *n.* **1.** An attack: *the third offensive of the war.* **2.** An attitude of attack: *She went on the offensive and won the debate.* —**of·fen′sive·ly** *adv.* —**of·fen′sive·ness** *n.*

of·fer (**ô′**fər) *tr.v.* **of·fered, of·fer·ing, of·fers 1.** To present for acceptance or refusal: *They offered me dessert.* **2.** To put forward for consideration; propose: *offer advice.* **3.** To present as an act of worship: *offer prayers.* **4.** To propose as payment: *offer a reward.* **5.** To make available; provide: *This apartment complex offers free parking.* **6.** To present for sale or rent: *a store offering suits at a discount.* **7.** To show readiness (to do something); volunteer: *They offered their services.* **8.** To produce; present to the public: *offered a program of music.* ❖ *n.* **1.** Something, such as a proposal, suggestion, or bid, that is offered: *an offer to teach; an offer for the car.* **2.** The act of offering: *the offer of his services.* [From Old English *offrian,* from Latin *offerre* : *ob-,* to + *ferre,* to bring.]

of·fer·ing (**ô′**fər-ĭng) *n.* **1.** The act of making an offer. **2.** Something offered, such as a contribution, gift, or religious sacrifice.

of·fer·to·ry (**ô′**fər-tôr′ē) *n., pl.* **of·fer·to·ries 1.** often **Offertory** The part of the Eucharist at which bread and wine are offered to God. **2.** often **Offertory** The music accompanying this part of the religious service. **3.** A collection of offerings at a religious service.

off-guard (**ôf′gärd′**) *adj.* Off one's guard; unprepared: *His sudden admission of guilt caught me off-guard.*

off·hand (**ôf′hănd′**) *adv.* Without preparation or forethought: *Can you say offhand when they'll call?* ❖ *adj.* Done or said without preparation or forethought: *an offhand reply.* —**off′hand′ed·ly** *adv.*

of·fice (**ô′**fĭs) *n.* **1a.** A place in which business, clerical, or professional work is done: *the principal's office.* **b.** The people working in such a place: *The office gave the boss a surprise party.* **2.** A position of authority or trust, as in a government or a corporation: *the office of president.* **3.** A public position: *She has decided to seek office.* **4.** A branch of a department of a government: *the US Patent Office.* **5.** A duty, function, or role: *He did not shirk his office.* **6.** often **offices** Something performed for another; a service or favor: *delighted by the kind offices of their friends.* **7.** A Christian religious ceremony or service, such as a rite for the dead. [From Middle English, from Latin *officium.*]

of·fice·hold·er (**ô′**fĭs-hōl′dər) *n.* A person who holds a public office.

of·fi·cer (**ô′**fĭ-sər) *n.* **1.** A person who holds an office of authority or trust in a government, corporation, club, or other institution. **2.** A person who holds a commission in the armed forces. **3.** A police officer.

of·fi·cial (ə-**fĭsh′**əl) *adj.* **1.** Relating to an office or post of authority: *official duties.* **2.** Authorized by an authority:

octopus

oculus
in the dome of the Pantheon, Rome, Italy

WORD HISTORY

often Are you one of the people who pronounce the *t* in **often**? Originally, back in the Middle Ages, everyone pronounced the *t* in this word, but in the 1400s, certain consonants became silent in English, because the words were easier to pronounce without them. Thus the *d* in *handsome* and *handkerchief* disappeared, as did the *p* in *raspberry* and the *t* in *chestnut* and *often.* As more people became educated and learned how to spell, the pronunciation of certain words became influenced by their spelling, and some sounds that had become silent, as the *t* in *often,* were sometimes pronounced again. Curiously, in other words such as *soften* and *listen,* the *t* generally remains silent.

GEOGRAPHY

Ohio The state of **Ohio** gets its name from a Seneca name meaning "beautiful river." The name was first used for the Ohio River and its largest tributary (now called the Allegheny River), and the state was later named after the river.

ă	pat	ôr	core
ā	pay	oi	boy
âr	care	ou	out
ä	father	o͝o	took
ĕ	pet	o͝or	lure
ē	be	o͞o	boot
ĭ	pit	ŭ	cut
ī	bite	ûr	urge
îr	pier	th	thin
ŏ	pot	*th*	this
ō	toe	zh	vision
ô	paw	ə	about

an official document. **3.** Holding office or performing a special duty: *an official mediator.* **4.** Formal or ceremonious: *an official banquet.* ❖ *n.* **1.** A person in a position of authority. **2.** A referee or umpire in a sports contest. **—of·fi′cial·ly** *adv.*

of·fi·ci·ant (ə-fĭsh′ē-ənt) *n.* **1.** A person who performs a religious rite. **2.** A person who presides over a religious or civil ceremony.

of·fi·ci·ate (ə-fĭsh′ē-āt′) *intr.v.* **of·fi·ci·at·ed, of·fi·ci·at·ing, of·fi·ci·ates 1.** To perform the duties of a public office: *The mayor officiates at each town meeting.* **2.** To perform the duties of a member of the clergy: *A priest officiated at their wedding.* **3.** To serve as a referee or umpire in a sports contest. **—of·fi′ci·a′tor** *n.*

of·fi·cious (ə-fĭsh′əs) *adj.* Excessively forward in offering one's services or advice to others. **—of·fi′cious·ly** *adv.* **—of·fi′cious·ness** *n.*

off·ing (ô′fĭng) *n.* The part of the sea that is distant but visible from the shore. ◆ **in the offing** In the near or immediate future; soon to come.

off-key (ôf′kē′) *adj.* Higher or lower than the correct notes of a melody. **—off′key′** *adv.*

off-lim·its (ôf-lĭm′ĭts) *adj.* Not to be entered by a certain group: *That district is off-limits to all foreigners.*

off·line (ôf′līn′) *adj.* **1.** Not connected to a computer or computer network: *offline computer terminals.* **2.** Not accessible by means of a computer or computer network: *offline medical records.* **—off′line′** *adv.*

off·load (ôf′lōd′) *tr.v.* **off·load·ed, off·load·ing, off·loads 1.** To unload (a vehicle or container). **2.** To transfer (data) to a peripheral device. **3.** *Slang* To get rid of and pass on to another: *The busy supervisor offloaded several tasks onto his employees.*

off-peak (ôf′pēk′) *adj.* Not in the period of most frequent or heaviest use: *a website that sells off-peak airplane tickets.*

off-put·ting (ôf′po͝ot′ĭng) *adj.* Tending to cause dislike or to upset; disconcerting: *I was annoyed by the clerk's off-putting remarks.*

off-road (ôf′rōd′) *adj.* Existing, occurring, or made for use off paved roads: *an off-road vehicle.*

off·screen (ôf′skrēn′) *adj.* Existing or occurring outside the frame of a movie or television screen: *the sounds of offscreen gunfire.* **—off′screen′** *adv.*

off·set (ôf′sĕt′) *n.* Something that balances, counteracts, or compensates: *The company planted trees as an offset for the woods it had cleared for a warehouse.* ❖ *tr.v.* (ôf-sĕt′) **off·set, off·set·ting, off·sets** To counterbalance or counteract; make up for: *His good passing should offset our weak defense.*

offset printing *n.* A form of printing in which an inked image is transferred from a metal or paper plate to a rotating cylinder, which in turn transfers it onto the paper.

off·shoot (ôf′sho͞ot′) *n.* **1.** A shoot that branches out from the main stem of a plant. **2.** Something that branches out or originates from a main source: *The club formed as an offshoot of the national organization.*

off·shore (ôf′shôr′) *adj.* **1.** Moving away from the shore: *an offshore breeze.* **2.** Located at a distance from the shore: *offshore rocks.* ❖ *adv.* **1.** In a direction away from shore: *The breeze was blowing offshore.* **2.** At a distance from shore: *a sea lion swimming a half mile offshore.*

off·side (ôf′sīd′) also **off·sides** (ôf′sīdz′) *adj.* **1.** In football, illegally beyond the line of scrimmage when the ball is snapped or ahead of the ball during a kickoff. **2.** In sports such as soccer and hockey, illegally ahead of the ball or puck in the attacking zone.

off-site (ôf′sīt′) *adj.* Done or located away from the site, as of a particular activity: *sent company documents to an offsite storage facility.* **—off′site′** *adv.*

off·spring (ôf′sprĭng′) *n., pl.* **offspring 1a.** A person's child or children: *Mr. Jackson is very proud of his offspring.* **b.** The young of an animal or plant: *The lion brought food to her offspring.* **2.** The result or product of something: *His design for the garden was the offspring of much research.*

off·stage (ôf′stāj′) *adj.* Taking place in an area of a stage that is invisible to the audience: *an offstage change of costume.* ❖ *adv.* Away from the area of a stage that is visible to the audience: *She walked offstage.*

off-the-cuff (ôf′*th*ə-kŭf′) *adj.* Not prepared in advance: *made some off-the-cuff remarks after finishing her speech.*

off-the-rack (ôf′*th*ə-răk′) *adj.* Relating to or being merchandise, especially clothing, made in standard sizes.

off-the-rec·ord (ôf′*th*ə-rĕk′ərd) *adj.* Not for publication or acknowledgement: *kept the mayor's off-the-record comments a secret.*

off-the-wall (ôf′*th*ə-wôl′) *adj.* **1.** Very unconventional or unusual: *off-the-wall humor.* **2.** Exhibiting bizarre behavior; crazy.

off-white (ôf′wīt′ *or* ôf′-hwīt′) *n.* A grayish or yellowish white. **—off′-white′** *adj.*

oft (ôft) *adv.* Often: *her oft-quoted poem.*

of·ten (ô′fən *or* ôf′tən) *adv.* **of·ten·er, of·ten·est** Frequently; many times. —SEE NOTE.

of·ten·times (ô′fən-tīmz′) also **oft·times** (ôf′tīmz′) *adv.* Often; frequently.

o·gan·es·son (ə-găn′ə-sŏn′, ō′gə-nĕs′ŏn, -ən) *n. Symbol* **Og** A radioactive element that has been artificially produced by scientists. Atomic number 118. See **Periodic Table.**

og·ham (ŏg′əm *or* ō′əm) *n.* **1.** An alphabetic system of inscribed notches for vowels and lines for consonants used to write Old Irish, chiefly on the edges of memorial stones, from the fifth to the early seventh century. **2.** A character used in this alphabet.

O·gla·la (ō-glä′lə) *n., pl.* **Oglala** or **O·gla·las** A member of a Native American people that is a subdivision of the Lakota, living in southwest South Dakota.

o·gle (ō′gəl *or* ô′gəl) *tr.v.* **o·gled, o·gling, o·gles** To look or stare at, especially in a desirous way. **—o′gler** *n.*

O·gle·thorpe (ō′gəl-thôrp′), **James Edward** 1696–1785. English soldier and philanthropist who secured a charter for Georgia (1732) as a refuge for unemployed debtors newly released from prison.

o·gre (ō′gər) *n.* **1.** In legends and fairy tales, a giant or monster that eats humans. **2.** A person who is especially cruel, brutish, or feared. [Probably ultimately from Latin *Orcus,* god of the underworld.]

oh (ō) *interj.* **1.** An expression used to show emotion, such as surprise, anger, or pain. **2.** An expression used to address a person directed: *Oh, waiter! Could we have a bill please?*

❏ *These sound alike:* **oh, O**[1] (exclamation), **owe** (be indebted).

OH *abbr.* An abbreviation of Ohio.

O. Henry See William Sydney **Porter.**

O·hi·o (ō-hī′ō) A state of the north-central United States west of Pennsylvania. It was admitted as the 17th state in 1803. Columbus is the capital. —SEE NOTE.

Ohio River A river formed by the confluence of the Allegheny and Monongahela Rivers in western Pennsylvania and flowing about 980 miles (1,580 kilometers) to the Mississippi River in southern Illinois.

ohm (ōm) *n.* A unit used to measure the electrical resistance of a material. One ohm is equal to the resistance of a conductor through which a current of one ampere flows when a potential difference of one volt is applied to it. [After Georg Simon *Ohm* (1789–1854), German physicist.]

ohm·me·ter (ōm′mē′tər) *n.* An instrument that measures the resistance of an electrical conductor in ohms.

Ohm's law (ōmz) *n.* A law stating that the current in an electric circuit is equal to the voltage divided by the resistance. The current increases as the voltage increases, and decreases as the resistance increases.

Oh·no (ō′nō), **Apolo Anton** Born 1982. American speedskater who earned eight medals in the 2002, 2006, and 2010 Olympics, setting a record for the most winter Olympic medals won by an American athlete.

–oid *suff.* A suffix that means like or resembling: *humanoid.* —SEE NOTE.

oil (oil) *n.* **1.** Any of numerous mineral, vegetable, or synthetic substances or animal or vegetable fats that are generally slippery, capable of being burned, liquid or easily melted, and incapable of mixing with water. **2a.** Petroleum. **b.** A substance derived from petroleum, such as a substance for lubricating machinery. **3.** Oil paint. **4.** A painting done in oil paint. ❖ *tr.v.* **oiled, oil·ing, oils** To lubricate, supply, cover, or polish with oil. [From Middle English, from Greek *elaiwon,* from *elaiwā,* olive.]

oil·can (oil′kăn′) *n.* A can for oil, especially one that has a spout to release oil drop by drop, as when lubricating machine parts.

oil·cloth (oil′klôth′) *n.* **1.** Cloth that has been coated with oil, clay, or paint to make it waterproof. **2.** A waterproof material that is made of a layer of vinyl and a layer of cotton or a synthetic fabric.

oil color *n.* Oil paint.

oil field *n.* A region of land with pockets of underground oil that can be removed.

oil of vitriol *n.* Sulfuric acid.

oil paint *n.* A paint that is made with a drying oil.

oil painting *n.* **1.** A painting done in oil paints. **2.** The art or process of painting with oil paints.

oil palm *n.* An African palm tree having fruits that resemble nuts and yield a yellowish oil used in soaps, cosmetics, foods, and other products.

oil shale *n.* A dark-brown or black shale containing hydrocarbons yielding petroleum by distillation.

oil·skin (oil′skĭn′) *n.* **1.** Cloth treated with oil so that it is waterproof. **2.** A garment made of oilskin or of a synthetic waterproof material, generally used by sailors.

oil slick *n.* A layer of oil floating on the surface of water.

oil well *n.* A hole dug or drilled in the earth in order to obtain petroleum.

oil·y (oi′lē) *adj.* **oil·i·er, oil·i·est 1.** Relating to oil: *an oily liquid.* **2.** Covered with, soaked in, or containing oil; greasy: *a pile of oily rags.* **3.** Unpleasantly smooth or ingratiating; unctuous: *oily, insincere compliments.* —**oil′i·ness** *n.*

oink (oingk) *n.* The characteristic grunting noise of a hog.

oint·ment (oint′mənt) *n.* A thick, often oily substance made to be rubbed on the skin as a medication or cosmetic; a salve. [From Middle English *oinement,* from Latin *unguentum.*]

OJ *abbr.* An abbreviation of orange juice.

O·jib·wa (ō-jĭb′wā′ *or* ō-jĭb′wə) *n., pl.* **Ojibwa** or **O·jib·was 1.** A member of a Native American people formerly inhabiting the regions around Lake Superior and now spread throughout the upper Midwest, the northern Great Plains, and southern Canada. **2.** The Algonquian language of the Ojibwa.

OK¹ or **o·kay** (ō-kā′) *Informal adj.* **1.** All right; acceptable; satisfactory: *The plan is OK with me.* **2.** Mediocre: *The food was only OK.* **3.** In proper working order: *The car's engine is OK.* **4.** Healthy or uninjured: *He fell but was OK.* ❖ *adv.* Fairly well; acceptably: *He's doing OK. The oven works OK.* ❖ *interj.* An expression used to indicate approval or agreement. ❖ *n.* Approval; acceptance; agreement: *Get your parents' OK before we start on the trip.* ❖ *tr.v.* **OK'd** or **OK'ed, OK'ing, OK's** or **o·kayed, o·kay·ing, o·kays** To approve; agree to: *The governor OK'd the plans for the construction of a new highway.* [From *o(ll) k(orrect),* slang respelling of *all correct.*]

OK² *abbr.* An abbreviation of Oklahoma.

o·ka·pi (ō kä′pē) *n., pl.* **okapi** or **o·ka·pis** An African mammal having a reddish-brown body and horizontal whitish stripes on the legs and hindquarters. The okapi is closely related to the giraffe.

o·kay (ō-kā′) *adj., adv., interj., n. & v.* Variant of **OK¹**.

O'Keeffe (ō-kēf′), **Georgia** 1887–1986. American artist known especially for her close-up paintings of flowers and for her landscapes.

O·khotsk (ō-kŏtsk′), **Sea of** An arm of the northwest Pacific Ocean north of Japan and south of northeast Russia.

O·ki·na·wa (ō′kĭ-nä′wə *or* ō′kĭ-nou′wə) An island group in the western Pacific Ocean southwest of Japan. **Okinawa,** the largest island in the group, was the scene of fierce combat in World War II between Japanese and US forces (April 1–June 21, 1945).

o·ki·na or **'o·ki·na** (ō-kē′nə) *n.* **1.** The glottal stop used in the Hawaiian language. **2.** The symbol (ʻ) used in writing to represent this glottal stop. [From Hawaiian *ʻokina,* separator.]

O·kla·ho·ma (ō′klə-hō′mə) A state of the south-central United States north of Texas. It was admitted as the 46th state in 1907. Oklahoma City is the capital. —SEE NOTE.

Oklahoma City The capital of Oklahoma, in the central part of the state. It became the capital in 1910.

o·kra (ō′krə) *n.* **1.** The narrow sticky seedpods of a tall tropical African plant, used in soups and stews and as a vegetable. **2.** The plant bearing such pods. —SEE NOTE AT **goober.**

old (ōld) *adj.* **old·er, old·est 1a.** Having lived for a long time; of great age or advanced years: *a gnarled old pine tree.* **b.** Relatively advanced in age: *her older brothers and sisters.* **2.** Of a certain age: *She's ten years old today.* **3.** Having the maturity or wisdom of age: *That boy is old for his years.* **4.** In existence for a long time; made long ago: *an old part of the city.* **5.** Showing the effects of time or long use; worn: *an old coat.* **6.** Belonging to or associated with an earlier time or period of existence: *visiting his old neighborhood.* **7.** Known for a long time and well-liked; dear: *an old friend.* **8.** often **Old** Being the earlier or earliest of two or more related things, forms, or periods: *the Old Kingdom of ancient Egypt.* **9.** Established by time or tradition: *old customs.* **10.** Used as an intensive: *You can't use any old bit with that drill.* ❖ *n.* **1.** A person or thing of a certain age: *That horse is a three-year-old.* **2.** Former times; yore: *in days of old.* [From Old English *eald.*]

old country *n.* The native country of an immigrant.

old·en (ōl′dən) *adj.* Relating to a time long past; old or ancient: *olden days.*

Old English *n.* The English language from about 450 to 1150; Anglo-Saxon.

Old Faithful A geyser in Yellowstone National Park in northwest Wyoming known for its frequent eruptions.

old-fash·ioned (ōld′făsh′ənd) *adj.* **1.** Belonging to or typical of an earlier time and no longer in style: *old-fashioned clothes.* **2.** Sticking to, preferring, or in keeping with ways or ideas of an earlier time: *strict old-fashioned grandparents.*

Old French *n.* The French language from about 800 to 1600.

Old Glory *n.* The flag of the United States.

old-growth (ōld′grōth′) *adj.* Related to or being a forest that has many old trees and has not been significantly disturbed by humans.

old hand *n.* A person who is experienced; a veteran: *an old hand at politics.*

Old High German *n.* The language of southern Germany from about 850 to 1100.

Apolo Ohno
photographed in 2010

WORD BUILDING

–oid The basic meaning of the suffix **–oid** is "like" or "resembling." Words ending in *–oid* are generally adjectives but can also be nouns. Thus *humanoid* means "having human characteristics or form" (adjective sense) or "a being having human form" (noun sense). Some nouns ending in *–oid* form adjectives by adding the suffix *–al: spheroid, spheroidal; trapezoid, trapezoidal.* The suffix *–oid* comes ultimately from the Greek noun *eidos,* meaning "shape, form."

GEOGRAPHY

Oklahoma The name **Oklahoma** comes from a Choctaw phrase that means "red people." The name *Territory of Oklahoma* was proposed by the Choctaw in 1866 as a substitute for the name *Indian Territory.* When the western section of Indian Territory was organized in 1890, it was called Oklahoma Territory, and this name was later given to the state, organized in 1907.

WORD HISTORY

Old Norse Vikings raided the coast of England in the eighth and ninth centuries, and eventually many of them ended up settling in northern England. They spoke a form of **Old Norse,** a language that was similar to Old English (also known as Anglo-Saxon), so they and local Anglo-Saxons could probably communicate with each other fairly well. As a result, many Old Norse words were borrowed into English, including many still used in Modern English, such as *bag, both, call, egg, get, lift, low, raise, sister, skin, want,* and the pronouns *they, them,* and *their.*

oleander

ă	pat	ôr	core
ā	pay	oi	boy
âr	care	ou	out
ä	father	o͝o	took
ĕ	pet	o͝or	lure
ē	be	o͞o	boot
ĭ	pit	ŭ	cut
ī	bite	ûr	urge
îr	pier	th	thin
ŏ	pot	*th*	this
ō	toe	zh	vision
ô	paw	ə	about

old·ie (ōl′dē) *n.* Something that is old, especially a song that was popular some time ago: *a radio station that played oldies.*

Old Irish *n.* The Irish language from 725 to about 950.

Old Italian *n.* The Italian language until about 1550.

old maid *n.* **1.** *Offensive* A woman, especially an older woman, who has never been married. **2.** *Informal* A person who is prim or fussy. **3.** A card game in which the player who holds a specified card at the end loses.

old man *n. Slang* **1.** One's father. **2.** One's husband.

old master *n.* **1.** An outstanding European artist, especially a painter, chiefly of the period from about 1500 to the early 1700s. **2.** A work by such an artist.

Old Norse *n.* The North Germanic language until about 1350. The Scandinavian languages are descended from Old Norse. —SEE NOTE.

Old Persian *n.* An Old Iranian language attested in cuneiform inscriptions dating from the sixth to the fifth century BC.

Old Russian *n.* The Russian language from about 1050 to the end of the 1500s.

Old Testament *n.* The first of the two main divisions of the Christian Bible, corresponding to the Hebrew Scriptures.

old-time (ōld′tīm′) *adj.* Relating to or typical of a time in the past.

old-tim·er (ōld′tī′mər) *n. Informal* **1.** An elderly person. **2.** A person who has lived in a place or engaged in a certain kind of work or activity for a long time.

old-world also **Old World** (ōld′wûrld′) *adj.* Relating to or typical of the Old World, especially in earlier times: *an old-world bird; an old-world custom.*

Old World The continents of Europe, Asia, and Africa.

o·le·an·der (ō′lē-ăn′dər *or* ō′lē-ăn′dər) *n.* A poisonous Eurasian shrub having slender evergreen leaves and showy clusters of fragrant white, pink, or red flowers.

o·le·o (ō′lē-ō′) *n., pl.* **o·le·os** Margarine.

o·le·o·res·in (ō′lē-ō-rĕz′ĭn) *n.* A naturally occurring mixture of essential oils and a resin, such as a substance extracted from pine trees.

ol·fac·to·ry (ŏl-făk′tə-rē *or* ōl-făk′tə-rē) *adj.* Relating to the sense of smell. [From Latin *olfacere*, to smell.]

olfactory nerve *n.* The nerve that carries impulses associated with smell from the nose to the brain.

ol·i·garch (ŏl′ĭ-gärk′ *or* ō′lĭ-gärk′) *n.* A member of an oligarchy.

ol·i·gar·chy (ŏl′ĭ-gär′kē *or* ō′lĭ-gär′kē) *n., pl.* **ol·i·gar·chies** **1.** A form of government in which power is exercised by a small group of people. **2.** The people forming such a group. **3.** A state governed by such a group. [From Greek *oligarkhia* : *oligos*, few + *arkhein*, to govern.] **—ol′i·gar′chic, ol′i·gar′chi·cal** *adj.*

Ol·i·go·cene (ŏl′ĭ-gō-sēn′) *n.* The third epoch of the Tertiary Period, from about 34 to 23 million years ago. During the Oligocene, modern mammals continued to develop and the first cats, dogs, and monkeys arose. See table at **geologic time. —Ol′i·go·cene′** *adj.*

ol·ive (ŏl′ĭv) *n.* **1a.** A small oval fruit having a single hard seed and usually changing in color from green to black as it ripens. Olives are eaten as food or pressed to extract olive oil. **b.** The Mediterranean tree that bears such fruit. **2.** A dull yellowish green. [From Middle English, from Greek *elaiwā*.]

olive branch *n.* **1.** A branch of an olive tree, regarded as a symbol of peace. **2.** An offer of peace.

olive drab *n.* **1.** A dull brownish or grayish olive color. **2.** Cloth of this color, often used in military uniforms.

olive green *n.* A yellowish green that is the color of green olives.

olive oil *n.* Oil pressed from olives, used in salad dressings, for cooking, as an ingredient in cosmetics, and as an emollient.

ol·la (ŏl′ə *or* ō′yä) *n.* A rounded earthenware pot, used especially for cooking or to hold water.

Ol·mec (ŏl′mĕk *or* ōl′mĕk) *n., pl.* **Olmec** or **Ol·mecs** **1.** An early Mesoamerican Indian civilization in southeast Mexico that flourished between 1300 and 400 BC and had a widespread cultural influence. **2.** A member of any of various peoples sharing the Olmec culture.

O·lym·pi·a[1] (ō-lĭm′pē-ə *or* ə-lĭm′pē-ə) A plain of southern Greece in the northwest Peleponnesus. It was the site of the ancient Olympic Games.

O·lym·pi·a[2] (ō-lĭm′pē-ə *or* ə-lĭm′pē-ə) The capital of Washington, in the western part of the state on the southern end of Puget Sound southwest of Seattle. It was settled around 1845.

O·lym·pi·ad (ō-lĭm′pē-ad′) *n.* **1.** An interval of four years between celebrations of the Olympic Games, by which the ancient Greeks reckoned dates. **2.** A celebration of the modern Olympic Games.

O·lym·pi·an (ō-lĭm′pē-ən) *adj.* **1.** In Greek mythology, relating to the greater gods and goddesses who live on Mount Olympus. **2.** Surpassing all others in scope and effect: *undertook Olympian efforts to clean the harbor.* ❖ *n.* **1.** In Greek mythology, one of the gods or goddesses who live on Mount Olympus. **2.** A contestant in the Olympic Games.

O·lym·pic (ō-lĭm′pĭk) *adj.* Relating to the Olympic Games.

Olympic Games *pl.n.* **1a.** A modern international athletic competition held every four years in a different part of the world. The Olympic Games are divided into summer and winter games that alternate every two years. **b.** *(used with a singular verb)* The set of contests that occur in one season: *an Olympic Games that was boycotted by many countries.* **2.** An ancient Greek festival of athletic competitions and contests in poetry and dancing, held every four years in Olympia.

O·lym·pics (ō-lĭm′pĭks) *n.* The Olympic Games.

O·lym·pus (ə-lĭm′pəs *or* ō-lĭm′pəs), **Mount** The highest mountain in Greece, 9,577 feet (2,919 meters) high, in the northern part of the country near the Aegean coast. In Greek myth, it is the home of the gods.

O·ma·ha[1] (ō′mə-hô′ *or* ō′mə-hä′) *n., pl.* **Omaha** or **O·ma·has** **1.** A member of a Native American people inhabiting northeast Nebraska. **2.** The Siouan language of the Omaha.

O·ma·ha[2] (ō′mə-hô′ *or* ō′mə-hä′) The largest city of Nebraska, in the eastern part of the state on the Missouri River and the Iowa border. It was founded in 1854.

O·man (ō-män′) A sultanate of the southeast Arabian Peninsula on the **Gulf of Oman,** an arm of the Arabian Sea. Muscat is the capital.

om·buds·man (ŏm′bŭdz′mən *or* ŏm′bo͝odz′mən) *n.* A man who investigates and resolves complaints, especially for a government. [From Swedish, from Old Norse *umbodhsmadhr*, deputy.]

om·buds·per·son (ŏm′bŭdz′pûr′sən *or* ŏm′bo͝odz′-pûr′sən) *n.* An ombudsman or ombudswoman.

om·buds·wom·an (ŏm′bŭdz-wo͝om′ən *or* ŏm′bo͝odz-wo͝om′ən) *n.* A woman who investigates and resolves complaints, especially for a government.

o·me·ga (ō-mĕg′ə *or* ō-mē′gə) *n.* **1.** The 24th and last letter of the Greek alphabet, written Ω, ω. In English it is represented as Ō, ō. **2.** The last of a series or group. [From Middle English, from Greek *ō mega*, large o.]

om·e·let (ŏm′ə-lĭt *or* ŏm′lĭt) *n.* A dish of beaten eggs, cooked and often folded around a filling, such as cheese.

o·men (ō′mən) *n.* A thing or event regarded as a sign of future good or bad luck. [From Latin *ōmen*.]

om·i·cron (ŏm′ĭ-krŏn′ *or* ō′mī-krŏn′) *n.* The 15th letter of the Greek alphabet, written Ο, ο. In English it is represented as O, o. [From Middle English, from Greek *ō mīkron*, small o.]

om·i·nous (ŏm′ə-nəs) *adj.* Being a sign of trouble, danger, or disaster; threatening: *ominous clouds.* **—om′i·nous·ly** *adv.* **—om′i·nous·ness** *n.*

o·mis·sion (ō-mĭsh′ən) *n.* **1.** The act of omitting something or the state of having been omitted: *the omission of several letters from a word.* **2.** Something that has been omitted: *several omissions from the guest list.*

o·mit (ō-mĭt′) *tr.v.* **o·mit·ted, o·mit·ting, o·mits 1.** To leave out; fail to include or mention: *Omit unnecessary words.* **2.** To fail to do or take advantage of; pass over; neglect: *She omitted no opportunity to tell him how proud she was of him.* [From Middle English *omitten,* from Latin *omittere.*]

omni– *pref.* A prefix that means all: *omnidirectional.* —SEE NOTE.

om·ni·bus (ŏm′nĭ-bŭs′) *n.* **1.** A bus. **2.** A printed collection of the works of one author or of writings on related subjects. ❖ *adj.* Including many different things: *an omnibus bill passed by Congress.* [From Latin *omnibus,* for everyone.]

om·ni·di·rec·tion·al (ŏm′nē-dĭ-**rĕk′**shə-nəl *or* ŏm′nē-dī-**rĕk′**shə-nəl) *adj.* Capable of transmitting or receiving signals in all directions: *an omnidirectional antenna.*

om·nip·o·tent (ŏm-**nĭp′**ə-tənt) *adj.* Having unlimited or universal power, authority, or force; all-powerful. ❖ *n.* **Omnipotent** God. **—om·nip′o·tence** *n.*

om·ni·pres·ent (ŏm′nĭ-**prĕz′**ənt) *adj.* Present or everywhere at the same time. **—om′ni·pres′ence** *n.*

om·nis·cient (ŏm-**nĭsh′**ənt) *adj.* Having total knowledge; knowing everything. ❖ *n.* **Omniscient** God. **—om·nis′cience** *n.*

om·ni·vore (**ŏm′**nə-vôr′) *n.* **1.** An organism that eats food of any kind, including animals and plants. **2.** A person who takes in everything available, as with the mind.

om·niv·o·rous (ŏm-**nĭv′**ər-əs) *adj.* **1.** Eating both plant and animal substances or products as food; eating all kinds of food: *Rats are omnivorous.* **2.** Taking in everything one can, as with the mind: *an omnivorous reader.* [From Latin *omnivorus* : *omni-*, all + *vorāre*, to devour.] **—om·niv′o·rous·ly** *adv.*

Omsk (ômsk) A city of south-central Russia on the Irtysh River. It was founded in 1716.

on (ŏn) *prep.* **1a.** Used to indicate position upon: *a plate on the table.* **b.** Used to indicate contact with or extent over: *a picture on the wall; a rash on my arm.* **c.** Used to indicate location at or along: *a house on the beach.* **d.** Used to indicate nearness to: *a city on the frontier.* **e.** Used to indicate attachment to or suspension from: *beads on a string.* **2.** Used to indicate motion or direction toward or against: *throwing the books on the floor; the march on Washington.* **3a.** Used to indicate occurrence during: *on Tuesday.* **b.** Used to indicate the occasion of: *On entering the room, she saw him.* **4a.** Used to indicate the object affected by an action: *The spotlight fell on the actress.* **b.** Used to indicate the cause or agent of a specified action: *cut his foot on a piece of broken glass; talking on the phone.* **5a.** Used to indicate source or basis: *a decision that was reached on the facts, not on opinion.* **b.** Used to indicate a source of power or energy: *The car runs on natural gas.* **6a.** Used to indicate the state or process of: *on leave; on fire.* **b.** Used to indicate the purpose of: *traveling on business.* **c.** Used to indicate a means of conveyance: *riding on a train.* **d.** Used to indicate availability by means of: *a doctor on call.* **e.** Used to indicate belonging to: *a doctor on the staff.* **f.** Used to indicate addition or repetition: *heaped error on error.* **7.** Concerning; about: *a book on carpentry.* **8.** *Informal* In one's possession: *I don't have a cent on me.* **9.** At the expense of: *This meal is on me.* ❖ *adv.* **1.** In or into a position of being attached to or covering something: *He pulled his coat on.* **2.** In the direction of something: *She was looking on when the ship came in.* **3.** Forward or ahead: *moving on to the next town.* **4.** In a continuous course: *We worked on quietly.* **5.** In or into action or operation: *Turn the television on.* **6.** In or at the present position or condition: *staying on; hang on.* ❖ *adj.* **1.** Being in operation: *The television is on.* **2.** Engaged in a given function or activity: *The dancers are on in five minutes.* **3a.** Planned; intended: *We have nothing on for the weekend.* **b.** Taking place or about to take place: *The party is on for tomorrow.* **4.** In baseball, having reached base safely; on base. ◆ **be on to** *Informal* To be aware of or have information about: *The police are on to his fraudulent tricks.* **on and off** Intermittently. **on and on** Without stopping; continuously. [From Old English *an, on.*] —SEE NOTE.

ON *abbr.* An abbreviation of Ontario.

on·board (ŏn-**bôrd′**) *adj.* Carried or used aboard a vehicle or vessel. **—on·board′** *adv.*

once (wŭns) *adv.* **1.** One time only: *once a day.* **2.** Formerly: *I was a kid once too.* **3.** At any time; ever: *If he once gets angry, he'll hold a grudge.* ❖ *n.* One single time or occurrence: *Let me go out just this once.* ❖ *conj.* As soon as; if ever; when: *Once he leaves, we can clean up.* ❖ *adj.* Having been formerly; former: *the once capital of the nation.* ◆ **at once 1.** All at one time; simultaneously. **2.** Immediately; instantly. **once and for all** Finally; conclusively. **once in a while** Now and then. **once upon a time** At some time in the past; long ago.

once-o·ver (**wŭns′**ō′vər) *n. Informal* A quick but thorough look or going over.

on·col·o·gist (ŏn-**kŏl′**ə-jĭst) *n.* A person who specializes in oncology.

on·col·o·gy (ŏn-**kŏl′**ə-jē) *n.* The branch of medicine that deals with the diagnosis and treatment of cancer.

on·com·ing (**ŏn′**kŭm′ĭng) *adj.* Coming nearer or toward a person or thing; approaching: *the oncoming storm.*

one (wŭn) *adj.* **1.** Being a single entity, unit, object, or living being: *one dog and three cats.* **2.** Characterized by unity; undivided: *We are of one mind on this question.* **3.** Being a single person or thing that is contrasted with another or others: *He was at one end of the hall, and I was at the other.* **4.** Being a particular person or thing: *late one night.* **5.** Occurring or existing indefinitely; some: *One day you will be famous.* **6.** *Informal* Used as an intensive: *That is one fine mess you've gotten us into!* **7.** Being the same in kind: *three animals of one species.* ❖ *n.* **1.** The number, written 1, that designates the first unit in a series. **2.** A single person or unit: *This is the one I like best.* **3.** A one-dollar bill. ❖ *pron.* **1.** A single person or thing: *one of my teammates.* **2.** An unspecified person; anyone: *One should be kind to one's neighbors.* ◆ **at one** In accord or unity. **one and all** Everyone. **one by one** Individually in succession. **one another** Each other: *They talk to one another every day.* [From Old English *ān.*]

❑ *These sound alike:* **one, won**[1] (Korean currency), **won**[2] (was victorious).

O·nei·da (ō-**nī′**də) *n., pl.* **Oneida** or **O·nei·das 1.** A member of a Native American people of central New York State. **2.** The Iroquoian language of the Oneida.

O'Neill (ō-**nēl′**), **Eugene Gladstone** 1888–1953. American playwright whose works include *Mourning Becomes Electra* (1931).

one-man (**wŭn′**măn′) *adj.* Consisting of, featuring, or controlled by one man: *a one-man show; a one-man band.*

one·ness (**wŭn′**nĭs) *n.* **1.** The quality or state of being one; singleness or wholeness. **2.** Sameness of character: *the oneness of the roadside landscapes.*

one-on-one (**wŭn′**ŏn-**wŭn′**) *adj.* Involving a direct exchange between two people: *a trainer who offered one-on-one instruction with gymnasts; a one-on-one chess match.* **—one′-on-one′** *adv.*

olla

early 20th-century Native American olla

WRITERS CHOOSE THEIR WORDS

While no one kept an official count, the policemen on duty that day estimated that between 1,500 and 3,000 walked across the river.

The cheerful mood of the crowd began to subside just after 9 A.M. That was when a deep, **ominous** grumbling began coming from the ice.

—Jim Murphy
Blizzard!

WORD BUILDING

omni– The prefix **omni–** means "all." It comes from the Latin word *omnis,* also meaning "all." The prefix has long been used in English to make new words. For example, by knowing this prefix means "all," you can guess that *omnipurpose* means "all-purpose." *Omni–* means the same thing as the prefix *pan–*. But *pan–* comes from Greek and is most commonly used with names of nationalities, like *Pan-American.*

USAGE

on When you use **on** as an adverb attached to a verb, it should not be joined with *to* to form the single word *onto: The speaker moved on to new subjects,* not *The speaker moved onto new subjects.*

one-per·son (wŭn′pûr′sən) *adj.* Consisting of, featuring, or controlled by one person.

one-piece (wŭn′pēs′) *adj.* Consisting of or made in a single whole piece: *a one-piece swimsuit.*

on·er·ous (ŏn′ər-əs *or* ō′nər-əs) *adj.* Troublesome or oppressive; burdensome. **—on′er·ous·ly** *adv.* **—on′er·ous·ness** *n.*

one·self (wŭn-sĕlf′) also **one's self** (wŭn sĕlf′ *or* wŭnz sĕlf′) *pron.* **1.** One's own self: *reading about oneself in the newspaper.* **2.** One's normal or healthy condition: *feeling like oneself again.*

one-sid·ed (wŭn′sī′dĭd) *adj.* **1.** Favoring one side or group; partial; biased: *a one-sided version of the disagreement.* **2.** Characterized by the domination of one competitor over another: *a one-sided match.* **3.** Existing or occurring on one side only: *a one-sided photocopy.*

one·time (wŭn′tīm′) *adj.* Former: *a onetime TV star.*

one-time (wŭn′tīm′) *adj.* Being so on a single occasion: *a one-time winner of the tournament.*

one-to-one (wŭn′tə-wŭn′) *adj.* Matching each member of a class or set with only one member of another class or set.

one-track (wŭn′trăk′) *adj.* Narrowly limited to a single idea or way of thinking: *a one-track mind.*

one-way (wŭn′wā′) *adj.* **1.** Moving or permitting movement in one direction only: *a one-way street.* **2.** Providing for travel in one direction only: *a one-way bus ticket to New York City.*

one-way mirror *n.* A mirror that is reflective on one side and transparent on the other, often used in surveillance: *The detective sat behind a one-way mirror, watching out for shoplifters.*

one-wom·an (wŭn′wo͝om′ən) *adj.* Consisting of, featuring, or controlled by one woman: *a one-woman business.*

on·go·ing (ŏn′gō′ĭng) *adj.* Going onward; continuing or progressing: *the ongoing development of the waterfront.*

on·ion (ŭn′yən) *n.* **1.** Any of several plants having long narrow leaves, usually a rounded bulb, and a strong odor and taste. **2.** The bulb of such a plant, used as a vegetable. [From Middle English *oinyon*, from Latin *uniō*.]

on·ion·skin (ŭn′yən-skĭn′) *n.* A thin, strong, translucent paper.

on·line (ŏn′līn′) *adj.* **1.** Connected to a computer or computer network. **2.** Accessible by means of a computer or computer network: *included online resources for her term paper.* **—on′line′** *adv.*

on·look·er (ŏn′lo͝ok′ər) *n.* A person who watches or looks on; a spectator or bystander.

on·ly (ōn′lē) *adj.* **1.** Alone in kind or class; sole: *our only reason for going; my only pen.* **2.** Most suitable of all; excellent or superior: *the only real contenders for the championship.* ❖ *adv.* **1.** Without anyone or anything else; alone: *We have only two sandwiches left.* **2.** Merely; just: *I only followed orders.* **3.** Exclusively; solely: *That train runs only on Sunday.* **4a.** As recently as: *He called me only last month.* **b.** In the immediate past: *I only just saw her.* ❖ *conj.* **1.** Were it not that; except that: *The climbers would have reached the summit, only the weather got bad.* **2.** With the restriction that; but: *You may climb on the rocks, only be careful.* [From Old English *ānlīc.*] —SEE NOTE.

USAGE

only Generally the adverb **only** should be used next to the word or words that it limits. Variation in the placement of *only* can change the meaning of the sentence, as the following examples show: *Dictators respect only force; they are not moved by words. Dictators only respect force; they do not worship it.*

on·o·mat·o·poe·ia (ŏn′ə-măt′ə-pē′ə) *n.* **1.** The forming of a word, such as *buzz*, that imitates the sound of the thing it refers to. **2.** The use of such words. **—on′o·mat′o·poe′ic** *adj.*

On·on·da·ga (ŏn′ən-dô′gə *or* ŏn′ən-dä′gə) *n., pl.* **Onondaga** or **On·on·da·gas 1.** A member of a Native American people of central New York State. **2.** The Iroquoian language of the Onondaga. **—On′on·da′gan** *adj.*

on·rush (ŏn′rŭsh′) *n.* A forward or onward rush or flow.

on·rush·ing (ŏn′rŭsh′ĭng) *adj.* Rushing or surging onward or forward: *the onrushing tide.*

on·screen (ŏn′skrēn′) *adj.* As shown on a movie, television, or computer screen: *a movie with an onscreen kiss.* **—on′screen′** *adv.*

on·set (ŏn′sĕt′) *n.* The beginning or start of something: *the onset of a disease.*

on·shore (ŏn′shôr′) *adj.* **1.** Moving or directed toward the shore: *an onshore breeze.* **2.** Located on the shore: *an onshore patrol.* ❖ *adv.* Toward the shore: *The wind shifted onshore.*

on·side (ŏn′sīd′) *adv. & adj.* In sports, in a position to receive the ball or puck according to the rules.

on·site (ŏn′sīt′) *adj.* Done or located at the site where something takes place: *an onsite film shoot.*

on·slaught (ŏn′slôt′) *n.* **1.** A violent attack or charge: *the enemy onslaught.* **2.** An overwhelming outpouring: *an onslaught of spam.*

On·tar·i·o (ŏn-târ′ē-ō′) A province of east-central Canada west of Quebec. It joined the Canadian confederation in 1867. Toronto is the capital.

Ontario, Lake The smallest of the Great Lakes, between southeast Ontario, Canada, and northwest New York.

on·to (ŏn′to͞o′) *prep.* **1.** On top of; to a position on or upon: *The dog jumped onto the chair.* **2.** *Informal* Aware of; knowing about: *I'm onto his tricks.* —SEE NOTE AT **on.**

o·nus (ō′nəs) *n.* A difficult responsibility or necessity.

on·ward (ŏn′wərd) *adj.* Moving or tending forward: *the onward rush of the train.* ❖ *adv.* also **on·wards** (ŏn′-wərdz) In a direction or toward a position that is ahead in space or time; forward: *The ship sailed onward through the storm.*

-onym *suff.* A suffix that means name or word: *antonym.*

on·yx (ŏn′ĭks) *n.* A type of quartz that occurs in bands of different colors, often black and white.

oo·dles (o͞od′lz) *pl.n. Informal* A great amount or large number: *oodles of fun.*

o·o·my·cete (ō′ə-mī′sēt′) *n.* A water mold. [From Greek *ōio-*, egg + Greek *mukēs*, fungus.]

oops (o͞ops) *interj.* An expression used to acknowledge a minor accident or mistake.

ooze[1] (o͞oz) *v.* **oozed, ooz·ing, ooz·es** *—intr.* **1.** To flow or leak slowly: *Blood oozed from the cut on her finger.* **2.** To disappear slowly: *His courage oozed away.* **3.** To emit a particular essence or quality: *a house that oozed with charm.* *—tr.* **1.** To give off by flowing slowly: *trees oozing sticky sap.* **2.** To emit or radiate in abundance: *a singer that oozes confidence.* [From Middle English *wosen*, from Old English *wōs*, juice.]

ooze[2] (o͞oz) *n.* Soft mud or slime, especially that covering the bottoms of oceans and lakes, composed chiefly of the remains of microscopic animals. [From Old English *wāse.*]

ooz·y[1] (o͞o′zē) *adj.* **ooz·i·er, ooz·i·est** Tending to ooze: *an oozy package of ice cream.*

ooz·y[2] (o͞o′zē) *adj.* **ooz·i·er, ooz·i·est** Resembling or containing soft mud or slime: *soft oozy ground.*

op. or **Op.** *abbr.* An abbreviation of opus.

o·pac·i·ty (ō-păs′ĭ-tē) *n., pl.* **o·pac·i·ties** The quality or condition of being opaque.

o·pal (ō′pəl) *n.* A usually transparent mineral consisting of hydrous silica. Opal can occur in almost any color, but it is often pinkish white with a milky or pearly appearance. [From Middle English *opalus*, from Greek *opallios*, probably from Sanskrit *upalaḥ*.]

o·pal·es·cent (ō′pə-lĕs′ənt) *adj.* Having the milky iridescent colors of an opal. **—o′pal·es′cence** *n.*

o·paque (ō-pāk′) *adj.* **1.** Not letting light pass through; neither transparent nor translucent: *One side of a one-way mirror is opaque, allowing people to watch other people without being seen.* **2.** Not reflecting light; not

ă	pat	ôr	core
ā	pay	oi	boy
âr	care	ou	out
ä	father	o͝o	took
ĕ	pet	o͝or	lure
ē	be	o͞o	boot
ĭ	pit	ŭ	cut
ī	bite	ûr	urge
îr	pier	th	thin
ŏ	pot	*th*	this
ō	toe	zh	vision
ô	paw	ə	about

shiny; dull: *an opaque finish on a surface.* **3.** Hard to understand; obscure: *a complicated scientific discussion that was opaque to laypeople.* [From Middle English *opake*, shady, from Latin *opācus*.] **—o·paque′ly** *adv.* **—o·paque′ness** *n.*

op. cit. *abbr.* An abbreviation of opere citato (in the book or work already referred to).

OPEC *abbr.* An abbreviation of Organization of Petroleum Exporting Countries.

o·pen (ō′pən) *adj.* **1.** Providing entrance and exit; not shut or closed: *an open door.* **2.** Providing free passage or view; not blocked or enclosed: *open country.* **3.** Having no protecting or concealing cover; exposed: *an open wound.* **4.** In sports, not closely defended by an opponent: *a pass to an open receiver.* **5a.** Not sealed or tied: *an open package.* **b.** Unfolded; spread out: *an open book.* **6.** Containing a gap across which electricity cannot pass: *an open switch.* **7.** Having spaces, gaps, or intervals: *a coarse open weave.* **8a.** Free to be used or participated in; accessible; not restricted: *an open competition.* **b.** Available or obtainable; not closed or decided: *The position is still open.* **9a.** Liable; susceptible: *The issue is open to question.* **b.** Willing or ready to consider: *I'm open to suggestions.* **10.** Free from pretense or reserve; frank: *I'll be open with you about this.* **11.** Free from prejudice or settled belief: *keeping an open mind.* **12.** Not hidden or secret: *showing open defiance.* **13.** Ready to transact business: *The store is open today.* ❖ *v.* **o·pened, o·pen·ing, o·pens** *—tr.* **1.** To make no longer shut or fastened: *opened the window.* **2.** To remove the cover or wrapping from: *open the can.* **3.** To spread apart; unfold: *opened the map.* **4a.** To begin; commence: *the topic that opens this chapter.* **b.** To begin the operation of: *They opened a new restaurant.* **5.** To make available for use: *The mayor opened the new bridge.* **6.** To make receptive, understanding, or sympathetic: *open one's heart.* *—intr.* **1.** To become open: *The door opened slowly.* **2.** To spread apart; unfold: *The tulips opened yesterday.* **3a.** To begin; commence: *The meeting opened with her report.* **b.** To begin business or operation. **4.** To have an opening; give access: *Your room opens onto a terrace.* ❖ *n.* **1.** An area of land or water that is not covered or concealed; an opening or clearing. **2.** The outdoors: *camping in the open.* **3.** A condition free of secrecy or concealment: *bring the facts into the open.* [From Old English.] **—o′pen·ly** *adv.* **—o′pen·ness** *n.*

o·pen-ac·cess (ō′pən-ăk′sĕs) *adj.* Relating to information that is freely available to the public at no cost, especially on the Internet: *an open-access journal.*

o·pen-air (ō′pən-âr′) *adj.* Outdoor: *an open-air concert.*

o·pen-and-shut (ō′pən-ən-**shŭt′**) *adj.* Presenting no difficulties; easily settled: *an open-and-shut case.*

o·pen-end·ed (ō′pən-**ĕn′**dĭd) *adj.* **1.** Not held back by definite limits, restrictions, or structure: *an open-ended contract.* **2.** Allowing for free response or discussion: *an open-ended question.*

o·pen·er (ō′pə-nər) *n.* **1.** A person or thing that opens, especially a device used to cut open cans or pry off bottle caps. **2.** The first act or event in a theatrical show or a series: *Our team won the opener.*

o·pen-eyed (ō′pən-**īd′**) *adj.* **1.** Having the eyes wide open, as in surprise. **2.** Watchful and alert.

o·pen·hand·ed (ō′pən-**hăn′**dĭd) *adj.* **1.** Done with or having the hand open: *an openhanded karate chop.* **2.** Giving freely; generous. **—o′pen·hand′ed·ly** *adv.* **—o′pen·hand′ed·ness** *n.*

o·pen·heart·ed (ō′pən-**här′**tĭd) *adj.* **1.** Frank; candid: *an openhearted discussion.* **2.** Kindly; generous. **—o′pen·heart′ed·ly** *adv.* **—o′pen·heart′ed·ness** *n.*

o·pen-hearth (ō′pən-**härth′**) *adj.* Relating to or being a furnace that produces high temperatures by preheating fuel and air, used in making high-quality steel.

open-heart surgery (ō′pən-**härt′**) *n.* Surgery performed on a heart while it is stopped and its functions are being performed by external devices.

open house *n.* **1.** A party that may be attended by all who wish to do so. **2.** An occasion in which a school or other institution is open for visiting and observation. **3.** A period during which a house for sale or rent is open to the public.

o·pen·ing (ō′pə-nĭng) *n.* **1.** The act or the process of becoming open: *the opening of the wilderness to settlers.* **2.** An open space or clearing: *an opening in the woods.* **3.** The first period or stage of something: *at the opening of the story.* **4.** The first occasion of something, especially of a play or movie. **5.** A favorable opportunity: *He finally found an opening to tell his side of the story.* **6.** An unfilled job or position; a vacancy: *an opening on the teaching staff.*

open letter *n.* A letter on a subject of general interest, addressed to an individual but intended for general readership.

o·pen-mind·ed (ō′pən-**mīn′**dĭd) *adj.* Willing to consider new ideas or the opinions of others; unprejudiced. **—o′pen-mind′ed·ly** *adv.* **—o′pen-mind′ed·ness** *n.*

open shop *n.* A policy or place of employment that does not allow an employer to discriminate against employees based on membership or nonmembership in a labor union.

o·pen-source (ō′pən-sôrs′) *adj.* Open to public participation, as in the sharing of information or the development of software: *an open-source operating system.*

o·pen·work (ō′pən-wûrk′) *n.* Ornamental or structural work, as of embroidery or metal, having many openings, usually in set patterns.

op·er·a¹ (ŏp′ər-ə *or* ŏp′rə) *n.* A theatrical performance in which the words of a play are sung with orchestral accompaniment. [From Italian, from Latin, work.]

o·pe·ra² (ō′pər-ə *or* ŏp′ər-ə) *n.* A plural of **opus.**

op·er·a·ble (ŏp′ər-ə-bəl *or* ŏp′rə-bəl) *adj.* **1.** Being such that use or operation is possible: *a damaged but operable aircraft.* **2.** Possible to put into practice; practicable: *an operable plan.* **3.** Treatable by surgery: *an operable tumor.*

opera house *n.* A theater designed chiefly for the production of operas.

op·er·ate (ŏp′ə-rāt′) *v.* **op·er·at·ed, op·er·at·ing, op·er·ates** *—intr.* **1.** To perform a function; work: *a machine that operates well.* **2.** To perform surgery. **3.** To produce an effect: *This drug operates quickly.* *—tr.* **1.** To control the functioning of; run: *operate a sewing machine.* **2.** To direct the affairs of; manage: *operate a business.* **3.** To supply with power: *a car that is operated by electricity.* [From Latin *operārī*, to work.]

op·er·at·ic (ŏp′ə-**răt′**ĭk) *adj.* Related to or like an opera: *an operatic aria.*

op·er·at·ing system (ŏp′ə-rā′tĭng) *n.* Software that is designed to control the hardware of a specific computer system in order to allow users and computer programs to make use of it.

op·er·a·tion (ŏp′ə-**rā′**shən) *n.* **1.** The act or process of operating or functioning. **2.** The condition of operating or functioning: *a machine no longer in operation.* **3.** A surgical treatment for a disease, disorder, or injury. **4.** A mathematical process or action performed in a specific way according to specific rules: *Addition is a mathematical operation.* **5.** An action undertaken by a computer resulting from a single instruction. **6.** A military action or series of actions.

op·er·a·tion·al (ŏp′ə-**rā′**shə-nəl) *adj.* **1.** Relating to an operation or a series of operations. **2.** Fit for proper functioning: *an operational aircraft.*

op·er·a·tive (ŏp′ər-ə-tĭv *or* ŏp′ə-rā′tĭv) *adj.* **1.** In effect; in force: *a law of economics that is operative in the stock*

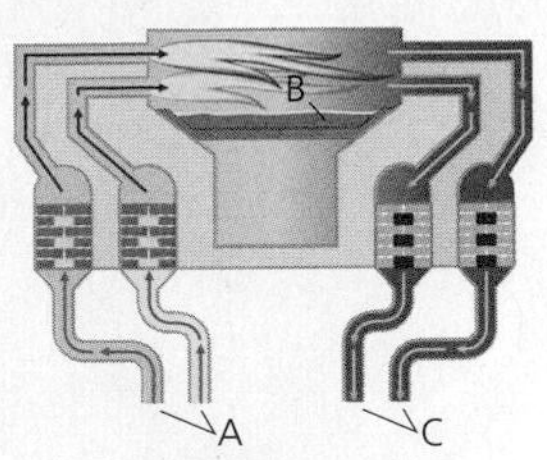

open-hearth

In an open-hearth furnace, pig iron is melted to produce steel.
A. fuel and air enter
B. molten pig iron
C. exhaust gases exit

openwork

opossum

market. **2.** Working correctly; efficient: *operative equipment.* **3.** Relating to or resulting from a surgical operation. **4.** Most important; key: *The operative word here is "low-cal."* ❖ *n.* **1.** A skilled worker. **2.** A secret agent; a spy. **3.** A private investigator.

op·er·a·tor (ŏp′ə-rā′tər) *n.* **1.** A person who operates a machine or device: *a switchboard operator.* **2.** A person who owns or manages a business or industrial process: *a mine operator.* **3.** A symbol, such as a plus sign, that represents a mathematical operation. **4.** *Informal* A person who accomplishes goals through shrewd or unfair methods.

o·per·cu·lum (ō-pûr′kyə-ləm) *n., pl.* **o·per·cu·la** (ō-pûr′kyə-lə) or **o·per·cu·lums** A lidlike structure covering an opening in an organism, such as a gill cover in fishes or a horny plate attached to the foot of a snail.

op·e·ret·ta (ŏp′ə-rĕt′ə) *n.* A musical play that is similar to an opera but is lighter and more popular in subject and style and contains spoken dialogue.

oph·thal·mol·o·gist (ŏf′thəl-mŏl′ə-jĭst *or* ŏp′thəl-mŏl′ə-jĭst) *n.* A physician who specializes in ophthalmology; an eye doctor.

oph·thal·mol·o·gy (ŏf′thəl-mŏl′ə-jē *or* ŏp′thəl-mŏl′ə-jē) *n.* The branch of medicine that deals with the diagnosis and treatment of diseases and disorders of the eye.

o·pi·ate (ō′pē-ĭt *or* ō′pē-āt′) *n.* **1.** A drug containing opium. **2.** A sedative or narcotic drug or other substance. ❖ *adj.* **1.** Containing opium. **2.** Causing sleep or sedation.

o·pine (ō-pīn′) *tr. & intr.v.* **o·pined, o·pin·ing, o·pines** To state as or express an opinion.

o·pin·ion (ə-pĭn′yən) *n.* **1.** A belief or conclusion held with confidence but not supported by positive knowledge or proof. **2.** A judgment based on special knowledge and given by an expert. **3.** A judgment or estimate of the worth or value of a person or thing: *has a high opinion of us.* **4.** The prevailing feeling or view among a group: *public opinion.* [From Middle English, from Latin *opīniō.*]

o·pin·ion·at·ed (ə-pĭn′yə-nā′tĭd) *adj.* Holding stubbornly and often unreasonably to one's own opinions: *an opinionated critic.* **—o·pin′ion·at′ed·ly** *adv.*

o·pi·oid (ō′pē-oid′) *n.* Any of various natural or synthetic compounds that affect the brain the same way opium does, having pain-relieving and narcotic effects. Morphine, methadone, and endorphins are all opioids.

o·pi·um (ō′pē-əm) *n.* A bitter addictive yellowish-brown drug prepared from the pods of a variety of poppy, and from which codeine, morphine, heroin, and other alkaloid drugs are derived.

o·pos·sum (ə-pŏs′əm *or* pŏs′əm) *n., pl.* **opossum** or **o·pos·sums** Any of various marsupials that live mostly in trees and have thick fur and a long tail. The females carry their young in a pouch. [From Virginia Algonquian.]

op·po·nent (ə-pō′nənt) *n.* A person or group that opposes another in a battle, contest, or debate. [From Latin *oppōnere,* to oppose.]

op·por·tune (ŏp′ər-to͞on′) *adj.* **1.** Suited for a particular purpose: *an opportune suggestion.* **2.** Occurring at a time that is advantageous: *an opportune moment.* [From Middle English, from Latin *ob portum (veniēns),* (coming) toward port.]

op·por·tun·ist (ŏp′ər-to͞o′nĭst) *n.* A person who takes advantage of any opportunity to achieve a goal, usually with no regard for principles of right and wrong. **—op′por·tun′ism** *n.* **—op′por·tun·is′tic** *adj.*

op·por·tu·ni·ty (ŏp′ər-to͞o′nĭ-tē) *n., pl.* **op·por·tu·ni·ties** **1.** A time or occasion that is suitable for a certain purpose; a favorable combination of circumstances. **2.** A chance for progress or advancement: *This scholarship presents you with the opportunity of a lifetime.*

op·pos·a·ble (ə-pō′zə-bəl) *adj.* Capable of moving opposite to and touching one or more other digits of the same hand or foot in a way that allows grasping: *The thumb is an opposable digit.*

op·pose (ə-pōz′) *tr.v.* **op·posed, op·pos·ing, op·pos·es** **1.** To offer resistance to or contend against: *oppose the enemy; oppose a plan.* **2.** To place in opposition; contrast: *The commentators opposed one football team to another.* ◆ **as opposed to** In contrast to: *Some runners go barefoot as opposed to wearing expensive running shoes.* [From Middle English *opposen,* to question, interrogate, from Latin *oppōnere,* to set against.] **—op·pos′er** *n.*

SYNONYMS oppose, fight, combat, resist These verbs mean to try to overcome, defeat, or turn back someone or something. **Oppose** is the most general: *They opposed the plan to shut the factory down.* **Fight** and **combat** mean to act aggressively or vigorously in opposition to something: *Citizens must work together to fight corruption in government. The development of vaccines was an important step toward combating disease.* **Resist** means to turn aside or counteract the action, effects, or force of someone or something: *The provinces united to resist the invasion.*
ANTONYM support

op·po·site (ŏp′ə-zĭt) *adj.* **1.** Placed or located directly across from something else or from each other: *the opposite sides of a house.* **2.** Moving or tending away from each other: *They went off in opposite directions.* **3.** Altogether different, as in nature or significance: *words with opposite meanings; two people with opposite views.* **4.** Being the other of a pair of things viewed in contrast or as alternatives: *the opposite sex.* ❖ *n.* A person or thing that is opposite or contrary to another: *The opposite of large is small.* ❖ *adv.* In an opposite position or positions: *He sat opposite from me.* ❖ *prep.* **1.** Across from or facing: *Park your car opposite the school.* **2.** In a complementary dramatic role to: *She played opposite him.* **—op′po·site·ly** *adv.* **—op′po·site·ness** *n.*

op·po·si·tion (ŏp′ə-zĭsh′ən) *n.* **1a.** The act of opposing: *our vigorous opposition to the law.* **b.** The condition of being in conflict: *The opposition of that country to its neighbor has a long history.* **2.** Something that serves as an opposing force or obstacle: *The old dog was the burglar's only opposition.* **3.** A position or location opposite or opposed to another. **4.** A political party or organization opposed to the group, party, or government in power. **5.** In astronomy, an arrangement in which Earth lies on or near a straight line between the sun and another planet or the moon.

op·press (ə-prĕs′) *tr.v.* **op·pressed, op·press·ing, op·press·es** **1.** To keep down by harsh and unjust treatment: *a people who were oppressed by tyranny.* **2.** To cause to feel depressed: *Grief oppressed her.* [From Middle English *oppressen,* from Latin *opprimere,* to press against.] **—op·pres′sor** *n.*

op·pres·sion (ə-prĕsh′ən) *n.* **1.** The act of oppressing or the condition of being oppressed. **2.** A feeling of being heavily weighed down, either mentally or physically.

op·pres·sive (ə-prĕs′ĭv) *adj.* **1.** Harsh and unjust; tyrannical: *The government became more oppressive after the demonstration.* **2.** Difficult to cope with: *faced an oppressive silence.* **3.** Hot and humid; sweltering: *an oppressive heat wave.* **—op·pres′sive·ly** *adv.*

op·pro·bri·ous (ə-prō′brē-əs) *adj.* **1.** Expressing reproach or scorn: *I felt shamed by her opprobrious remarks to me.* **2.** Bringing disgrace; shameful: *You should apologize for your opprobrious behavior.* **—op·pro′bri·ous·ly** *adv.*

op·pro·bri·um (ə-prō′brē-əm) *n.* Disgrace arising from shameful conduct.

ă	pat	ôr	core
ā	pay	oi	boy
âr	care	ou	out
ä	father	o͝o	took
ĕ	pet	o͝or	lure
ē	be	o͞o	boot
ĭ	pit	ŭ	cut
ī	bite	ûr	urge
îr	pier	th	thin
ŏ	pot	*th*	this
ō	toe	zh	vision
ô	paw	ə	about

opt (ŏpt) *intr.v.* **opt·ed, opt·ing, opts** To make a choice or decision: *Chris opted for pizza instead of hamburgers.*

op·tic (ŏp′tĭk) *adj.* Relating to the eye or vision. [From Middle English *optik*, from Greek *optikos*, from *optos*, visible.]

op·ti·cal (ŏp′tĭ-kəl) *adj.* **1.** Relating to sight: *an optical defect.* **2.** Designed to assist sight: *optical instruments.* **—op′ti·cal·ly** *adv.*

optical disc *n.* A plastic-coated disk on which data, as text, music, or video, is digitally stored and is read by scanning the surface with a laser.

optical fiber *n.* A flexible strand of fiber made of very pure glass or transparent plastic through which light can be transmitted for use in fiber optics.

op·ti·cian (ŏp-tĭsh′ən) *n.* A person who makes or sells lenses, eyeglasses, or other optical equipment.

optic nerve *n.* The nerve that connects the retina of the eye to the brain and carries impulses associated with vision.

op·tics (ŏp′tĭks) *n. (used with a singular verb)* The scientific study of light and vision. —SEE NOTE AT **triceratops.**

op·ti·ma (ŏp′tə-mə) *n.* A plural of **optimum.**

op·ti·mal (ŏp′tə-məl) *adj.* Most favorable or desirable; optimum: *We picked the optimal time to leave for the airport.* **—op′ti·mal·ly** *adv.*

op·ti·mism (ŏp′tə-mĭz′əm) *n.* **1.** A tendency to take a hopeful view of a situation or to expect the best possible outcome. **2.** The belief that this world is the best of all possible worlds. **3.** The belief that the universe is improving and that good will ultimately overcome evil. **—op′ti·mist** *n.* **—op′ti·mis′tic** *adj.* **—op′ti·mis′ti·cal·ly** *adv.*

op·ti·mize (ŏp′tə-mīz′) *tr.v.* **op·ti·mized, op·ti·miz·ing, op·ti·miz·es 1.** To make as perfect or effective as possible. **2.** To make (a computer program) faster and more efficient, as by rewriting the instructions. **3.** To make the most of: *The general optimized his forces.*

op·ti·mum (ŏp′tə-məm) *n., pl.* **op·ti·ma** (ŏp′tə-mə) or **op·ti·mums** The point at which the condition, degree, or amount of something is the most favorable. ❖ *adj.* Most favorable or advantageous; best: *optimum conditions for long-term investments.* [From Latin *optimum*, best.]

op·tion (ŏp′shən) *n.* **1.** The act of choosing; choice: *Her best option was to keep her day job and take classes at night.* **2.** The power or freedom to choose: *We have the option of driving or taking the train.* **3.** Something chosen or available as a choice: *a stereo system that is an option on some new cars.* See Synonyms at **choice. 4.** The right to buy or sell something within a specified time at a set price. **5.** In football, an offensive play in which a back can run with, pass, lateral, or hand off the ball. [From Latin *optiō*.]

op·tion·al (ŏp′shə-nəl) *adj.* Left to choice; not required or automatic: *Taking a history class is required in your junior year and optional in your senior year.* **—op′tion·al·ly** *adv.*

op·tom·e·trist (ŏp-tŏm′ĭ-trĭst) *n.* A person who is trained and licensed to practice optometry.

op·tom·e·try (ŏp-tŏm′ĭ-trē) *n.* The profession of examining, measuring, and treating visual defects by means of corrective lenses or other methods in which the services of a physician are not needed.

op·u·lence (ŏp′yə-ləns) *n.* **1.** Great wealth. **2.** A great amount or supply; an abundance or extravagance.

op·u·lent (ŏp′yə-lənt) *adj.* **1.** Having or showing great wealth; rich: *an opulent society.* **2.** Abundant or extravagant; luxuriant: *opulent vegetation.* **—op′u·lent·ly** *adv.*

o·pus (ō′pəs) *n., pl.* **o·pe·ra** (ō′pər-ə *or* ŏp′ər-ə) or **o·pus·es** An artistic work, especially a musical composition numbered to show the order of a composer's works.

or (ôr; ər *when unstressed*) *conj.* **1a.** Used to indicate an alternative: *hot or cold.* **b.** Used to indicate the second of two alternatives, the first being preceded by *either* or *whether: I don't know whether to laugh or cry.* **2.** Used to indicate a synonymous or equivalent expression: *acrophobia, or fear of great heights.* **3.** Used to indicate uncertainty or indefiniteness: *He's called here three or four times already.* —SEE NOTE.

❑ *These sound alike:* **or, oar** (wooden pole), **o'er** (over), **ore** (mineral).

OR *abbr.* An abbreviation of Oregon.

–or¹ *suff.* A suffix that means a person or thing that performs an action: *percolator.*

–or² *suff.* A suffix that means state, quality, or activity: *valor.*

or·a·cle (ôr′ə-kəl) *n.* **1.** A shrine, such as the shrine of Apollo at Delphi in ancient Greece, at which a god is believed to reveal the truth about something, especially what will happen in the future. **2.** A person, such as a priestess, through whom a god is believed to respond to questions of worshipers. **3.** The response to a worshiper's question given by such a person, often in the form of a mysterious statement. **4.** A person considered to be a source of wise advice or prophetic opinion.

❑ *These sound alike:* **oracle, auricle** (outer ear).

o·rac·u·lar (ô-răk′yə-lər) *adj.* **1.** Relating to an oracle or oracles: *oracular sites in ancient Greece.* **2.** Resembling an oracle, especially: **a.** Solemnly prophetic. **b.** Having a difficult or hidden meaning; mysterious. **—o·rac′u·lar·ly** *adv.*

o·ral (ôr′əl) *adj.* **1.** Spoken rather than written: *an oral examination.* **2.** Relating to the mouth: *oral hygiene.* **3.** Used in or taken through the mouth: *an oral thermometer; oral medication.* **—o′ral·ly** *adv.*

❑ *These sound alike:* **oral, aural** (of the ear).

or·ange (ôr′ĭnj) *n.* **1.** Any of several round fruits related to the grapefruit, lemon, and lime, having a reddish-yellow rind and juicy pulp divided into sections. **2.** Any of the trees that bear such fruit, having evergreen leaves and fragrant white flowers. **3.** Any of various colors between yellow and red. ❖ *adj.* **1.** Of the color orange. **2a.** Made of or from oranges: *orange juice.* **b.** Tasting or smelling like oranges. [From Middle English, ultimately from Sanskrit *nāraṅgaḥ*.]

or·ange·ade (ôr′ĭn-jād′) *n.* A drink consisting of orange juice, sugar, and water.

o·rang·u·tan (ô-răng′ə-tăn′ *or* ə-răng′ə-tăn′) *n.* Either of two large tree-dwelling apes of the islands of Borneo and Sumatra, having long arms and a reddish-brown coat. [From Malay *orang hutan* : *orang*, man + *hutan*, jungle.]

O·ran·je·stad (ō-rän′yə-stät′) The capital of Aruba, in the western part of the island.

o·rate (ô-rāt′ *or* ôr′āt′) *intr.v.* **o·rat·ed, o·rat·ing, o·rates** To speak publicly in a formal manner.

o·ra·tion (ô-rā′shən) *n.* A formal speech, usually given on a special occasion.

or·a·tor (ôr′ə-tər) *n.* **1.** A person who delivers an oration. **2.** A skilled public speaker.

or·a·tor·i·cal (ôr′ə-tôr′ĭ-kəl) *adj.* Relating to orators or oratory: *oratorical contests.* **—or′a·tor′i·cal·ly** *adv.*

or·a·to·ri·o (ôr′ə-tôr′ē-ō′) *n., pl.* **or·a·to·ri·os** A musical composition for voices and orchestra, telling a usually religious story without costumes, scenery, or dramatic action.

or·a·to·ry¹ (ôr′ə-tôr′ē) *n.* **1.** The art of public speaking. **2.** Skill or style in public speaking. [From Latin *ōrāre*, to speak, pray.]

or·a·to·ry² (ôr′ə-tôr′ē) *n., pl.* **or·a·to·ries** A place for prayer, such as a small private chapel. [From Middle English *oratorie*, from Latin *ōrāre*, to speak, pray.]

USAGE

or When you connect a series of singular elements by **or,** the verb used with them is singular: *Tom or Jack is coming.* When the elements are plural, the verb is plural: *Either the clowns or the monkeys make you laugh.* When the elements do not agree in number, it is best to find other ways to express what you are trying to say, especially in formal writing: *Either Tom is coming or his sisters are.* For more information, see Note at **either.**

orangutan

orb
12th-century gold and gemstone orb of the Holy Roman Empire

orchid

oregano

ă	pat	ôr	core
ā	pay	oi	boy
âr	care	ou	out
ä	father	o͝o	took
ĕ	pet	o͝or	lure
ē	be	o͞o	boot
ĭ	pit	ŭ	cut
ī	bite	ûr	urge
îr	pier	th	thin
ŏ	pot	*th*	this
ō	toe	zh	vision
ô	paw	ə	about

orb (ôrb) *n.* **1.** A sphere or spherical object. **2.** A celestial object such as the sun or moon. **3.** A globe surmounted by a cross, used as a ceremonial emblem of an emperor or other ruler.

or·bit (ôr′bĭt) *n.* **1a.** The path of a celestial object or artificial satellite as it travels around another object **b.** One complete revolution of such an object. **2.** The path of a body in a field of force surrounding another body; for example, the path of an electron in relation to the nucleus of an atom. **3.** Either of two depressions in the bones of the skull containing one of the eyes and its associated structures. **4.** A range of activity, influence, or control: *a matter that was not within his orbit.* ❖ *v.* **or·bit·ed, or·bit·ing, or·bits** —*tr.* To move in an orbit around: *The moon orbits Earth.* —*intr.* To move in an orbit: *the comets that orbit around the Sun.* [From Middle English *orbita*, eye socket, from Latin, orbit.] **—or′bi·tal** *adj.*

orca (ôr′kə) *n.* A black-and-white sea mammal related to the whales and dolphins that feeds mainly on fish and squid. [From Latin *ōrca*, whale.]

or·chard (ôr′chərd) *n.* **1.** An area of land devoted to the cultivation of fruit or nut trees. **2.** The trees grown on such land. [From Old English *orceard.*]

or·ches·tra (ôr′kĭ-strə) *n.* **1a.** A large group of musicians who play together on various instruments, usually including string, woodwind, brass, and percussion instruments. **b.** The instruments played by such a group of musicians. **2.** The area in a theater where the musicians sit, in front of and below the stage. **3.** The seats on the main floor of a theater. [From Greek *orkhēstrā*, the space in front of the stage in Greek theaters where the chorus performed.] **—or·ches′tral** (ôr-kĕs′trəl) *adj.*

or·ches·trate (ôr′kĭ-strāt′) *tr.v.* **or·ches·trat·ed, or·ches·trat·ing, or·ches·trates 1.** To compose or arrange (music) for performance by an orchestra. **2.** To organize in order to achieve a particular result: *orchestrated a successful political campaign.* **—or′ches·tra′tion** *n.*

or·chid (ôr′kĭd) *n.* **1.** Any of a group of mainly tropical plants having showy, unusually shaped flowers. **2.** The flower of such a plant.

or·dain (ôr-dān′) *tr.v.* **or·dained, or·dain·ing, or·dains 1.** To appoint as a minister, priest, or rabbi. **2.** To order by means of superior authority; decree. **3.** To arrange or determine beforehand; predestine: *a destiny that was ordained by fate.* **—or·dain′ment** *n.*

or·deal (ôr-dēl′) *n.* A difficult or painful experience, especially one that severely tests a person's character or endurance.

or·der (ôr′dər) *n.* **1.** A condition or arrangement of parts or elements that permits proper functioning or desired appearance: *The soda machine is out of order. Let's put the room in order.* **2.** Condition or state in general: *The old car is still in good working order.* **3.** A sequence or arrangement of things one after the other: *alphabetical order.* **4.** A condition in society marked by peaceful obedience of laws and authority: *The police restored order after the disturbance.* **5.** A command, direction, or instruction: *a court order; an order for the soldiers to retreat.* **6a.** A commission or instruction to buy, sell, or supply something: *The company ships orders free of charge.* **b.** The thing supplied, bought, or sold: *ships orders postage paid.* **7.** A portion of food in a restaurant: *an order of fried potatoes.* **8a.** The position and rank of an ordained minister or priest. **b.** often **orders** The sacrament or ceremony of admission into the priesthood or ministry. **9.** A group of people living according to a religious rule: *the Order of St. Benedict.* **10.** A social organization or club: *the Benevolent and Protective Order of Elks.* **11.** A group of people upon whom a government has conferred honor for unusual service or merit, or an emblem of such honor. **12a.** A class or kind: *Photography of that order is very rare.* **b.** Degree of quality or importance; rank: *poetry of the highest order.* **13.** Any of several styles of classical architecture distinguished by the type of column employed: *Corinthian order.* **14.** A taxonomic category of organisms that share certain characteristics, ranking above a family and below a class: *Rats, mice, squirrels, and beavers belong to the same order, the rodents.* See table at **taxonomy.** ❖ *v.* **or·dered, or·der·ing, or·ders** —*tr.* **1.** To issue a command or instruction to: *ordered the platoon to attention.* **2.** To give a command or instruction for: *ordered a review of the budget.* **3.** To give an order for; request to be supplied with: *order supplies for the camping trip.* **4.** To arrange in a sequence; put into an order: *We ordered the books according to subject.* —*intr.* To give an order; request that something be done or supplied. ◆ **in order that** With the purpose that; so that: *He proclaimed his guilt in order that he might be forgiven.* **in order to** With the intention to; so as to: *We built the shed in order to store our tools.* **in short order** With no delay; quickly. **on order** Requested but not yet delivered. **on the order of 1.** Similar to; like: *a building on the order of a pyramid.* **2.** Approximately; about: *a building costing on the order of one million dollars.* **to order** According to the buyer's wishes: *a coat made to order.* [From Middle English *ordre*, from Latin *ōrdō*.]

or·dered pair (ôr′dərd) *n.* A pair of numbers that come in a specific order and are usually written in parentheses, such as (3, 5).

or·der·ly (ôr′dər-lē) *adj.* **1.** Well arranged; neat: *an orderly kitchen.* **2.** Given to keeping things neat or well-arranged: *an orderly housekeeper.* **3.** Free from violence or disruption; peaceful: *our right to protest in an orderly manner.* ❖ *n., pl.* **or·der·lies 1.** An attendant who does nonmedical work in a hospital. **2.** A soldier assigned to a superior officer to carry messages and do other tasks. **—or′der·li·ness** *n.*

or·di·nal (ôr′dn-əl) *adj.* Relating to position in a series: *an ordinal rank of seventh.* ❖ *n.* An ordinal number.

ordinal number *n.* A number indicating position in a series. The ordinal numbers are first, second, third, and so on.

or·di·nance (ôr′dn-əns) *n.* A statute or regulation, especially one enacted by a city government.

or·di·nar·i·ly (ôr′dn-âr′ə-lē *or* ôr′dn-ĕr′ə-lē) *adv.* **1.** As a general rule; usually: *We ordinarily go shopping for groceries on Tuesday.* **2.** In the regular or usual manner: *ordinarily dressed.*

or·di·nar·y (ôr′dn-ĕr′ē) *adj.* **1.** Commonly encountered; usual: *ordinary rush-hour traffic.* **2a.** Not exceptional in quality or degree: *lived in an ordinary house.* **b.** Having no special purpose: *wore ordinary shoes, not hiking boots.* ❖ *n.* The usual or normal condition or course of events: *Nothing out of the ordinary happened all week.* [From Middle English *ordinarie*, from Latin *ōrdinārius*, from *ōrdō*, order.]

or·di·nate (ôr′dn-ĭt *or* ôr′dn-āt′) *n.* In a system of plane Cartesian coordinates, the coordinate that represents the distance from a specified point to the *x*-axis, measured parallel to the *y*-axis.

or·di·na·tion (ôr′dn-ā′shən) *n.* The act of ordaining or the state of being ordained.

ord·nance (ôrd′nəns) *n.* **1.** Military supplies, including weapons, ammunition, and maintenance equipment. **2.** The branch of a military force that acquires, stores, maintains, and issues weapons, ammunition, and combat vehicles.

Or·do·vi·cian (ôr′də-vĭsh′ən) *n.* The second period of the Paleozoic Era, from about 488 to 444 million years ago. The first fishes appeared during the Ordovician. See table at **geologic time.** **—Or′do·vi′cian** *adj.*

ore (ôr) *n.* A mineral or rock from which a valuable substance, especially a metal, can be extracted at a reasonable cost.

❑ *These sound alike:* **ore, oar** (wooden pole), **o'er** (over), **or** (alternative).

o·reg·a·no (ə-**rĕg′**ə-nō′) *n.* A perennial herb related to mint, having aromatic leaves that are used as a seasoning. [From Greek *orīganon.*]

Or·e·gon (**ôr′**ĭ-gən *or* **ôr′**ĭ-gŏn′) A state of the northwest United States north of California. It was admitted as the 33rd state in 1859. Salem is the capital and Portland the largest city. —SEE NOTE.

Oregon Trail A historical trail through the western United States from the Midwest to what is now western Oregon. It was a major path of western migration from the early 1840s until the coming of the railroad in the 1870s.

O·res·tes (ô-**rĕs′**tēz) *n.* In Greek mythology, the son of Agamemnon and Clytemnestra, who, with his sister Electra, avenged his father's murder by killing his mother and her lover.

or·gan (**ôr′**gən) *n.* **1a.** A musical instrument consisting of a set of pipes that sound tones when supplied with a flow of air controlled by a keyboard. **b.** A musical instrument, such as an electric organ, that resembles a pipe organ in tone or mechanism. **2.** A distinct part of an organism, adapted for a particular function: *the stomach and other organs of digestion.* **3.** A body or agency that is part of a larger organization: *The FBI is an organ of the Department of Justice.* **4.** A periodical published by a political party, business firm, or other group.

or·gan·elle (ôr′gə-**nĕl′**) *n.* A structure in a cell, such as a mitochondrion, chloroplast, or nucleus, that is enclosed within a membrane and serves a particular function.

organ grinder *n.* A street musician who plays a hurdy-gurdy.

or·gan·ic (ôr-**găn′**ĭk) *adj.* **1.** Involving living organisms or the products of their life processes: *decaying organic matter.* **2.** Relating to or being compounds containing carbon. **3.** Relating to or affecting an organ or organs of the body: *an organic disease.* **4a.** Using or produced with no artificial fertilizers or pesticides: *organic farming; organic vegetables.* **b.** Raised without the use of drugs, hormones, or synthetic chemicals: *organic chicken.* **5.** Made up of related parts that work together as a unit: *an organic whole.* **—or·gan′i·cal·ly** *adv.*

organic chemistry *n.* The chemistry of carbon compounds.

or·gan·ism (**ôr′**gə-nĭz′əm) *n.* **1.** An individual form of life, such as a bacterium, fungus, plant, or animal, that consists of one or many cells in which the cell parts or organs work together to carry out the processes of life, such as growth and reproduction. **2.** A group of related parts that work together as a whole: *the social organism.*

or·gan·ist (**ôr′**gə-nĭst) *n.* A musician who plays the organ.

or·gan·i·za·tion (ôr′gə-nĭ-**zā′**shən) *n.* **1.** The act of organizing: *planning the organization of a rally.* **2.** The condition of being organized: *We need to improve the organization of the supplies.* **3.** A manner of accomplishing something in an orderly or efficient way: *Your project was hampered by your lack of organization.* **4.** The way in which something is organized: *studying the organization of corporations.* **5.** A group of people united for some purpose or work: *a political organization.*

or·gan·ize (**ôr′**gə-nīz′) *v.* **or·gan·ized, or·gan·iz·ing, or·gan·iz·es** *—tr.* **1.** To put together or arrange in an orderly systematic way: *organize one's thoughts before speaking.* **2.** To form or establish in order to work together for a particular purpose: *organize a singing group.* **3a.** To cause (employees) to form or join a labor union: *organize farm workers.* **b.** To cause the employees of (a factory or industry) to form or join a labor union: *organize the shoe industry.* *—intr.* To form or join a group, especially a labor union, devoted to a particular purpose. **—or′gan·iz′er** *n.*

or·gan·ized (**ôr′**gə-nīzd′) *adj.* **1.** Functioning within a formal structure, as in the direction of activities: *organized soccer games.* **2.** Affiliated in an organization, especially a union: *organized labor.* **3.** Efficient and methodical: *an organized employee.*

or·gan·za (ôr-**găn′**zə) *n.* A sheer stiff fabric, as of silk or synthetic material, used for evening dresses or trimmings.

or·gasm (**ôr′**găz′əm) *n.* The highest point of sexual excitement.

or·gy (**ôr′**jē) *n., pl.* **or·gies** A party characterized by unrestrained behavior, especially drunkenness and sex.

o·ri·el (**ôr′**ē-əl) *n.* A bay window projecting from an upper floor, supported from below, as by a bracket.

o·ri·ent (**ôr′**ē-ənt *or* **ôr′**ē-ĕnt′) *n.* **Orient** The countries of Asia, especially of eastern Asia. ❖ *tr.v.* (**ôr′**ē-ĕnt′) **o·ri·ent·ed, o·ri·ent·ing, o·ri·ents 1.** To set or place in a position relative to the points of the compass: *orient the swimming pool north and south.* **2.** To make (someone) familiar with a new situation: *a website designed to help orient new students.* [From Middle English, from Latin *oriēns,* rising sun, east.]

O·ri·en·tal or **o·ri·en·tal** (ôr′ē-**ĕn′**tl) *adj.* Relating to the countries of the Orient or their peoples or cultures; eastern.

Oriental rug *n.* A rug made of wool that is knotted or woven by hand, produced in the Middle East and in many other parts of Asia.

o·ri·en·tate (**ôr′**ē-ĕn-tāt′) *tr.v.* **o·ri·en·tat·ed, o·ri·en·tat·ing, o·ri·en·tates** To orient.

o·ri·en·ta·tion (ôr′ē-ĕn-**tā′**shən) *n.* **1.** Location or position with respect to the points of the compass: *the orientation of a rocket in space.* **2.** Introductory instruction concerning a new situation: *attended an orientation for incoming students.* **3.** Sexual orientation.

or·i·fice (**ôr′**ə-fĭs) *n.* An opening, especially one, such as the mouth, that opens into a part of the body.

o·ri·ga·mi (ôr′ĭ-**gä′**mē) *n.* The art or process, originating in Japan, of folding paper into shapes representing flowers or birds, for example.

or·i·gin (**ôr′**ə-jĭn) *n.* **1.** The source or beginning of something: *the origin of a fire.* **2.** Ancestry: *people of Swedish origin.* **3.** The point at which the axes of a coordinate system intersect. [From Middle English *origine,* ancestry, from Latin *orīgō.*]

o·rig·i·nal (ə-**rĭj′**ə-nəl) *adj.* **1.** Existing before all others; first: *the original 13 states of the Union.* **2.** Fresh and newly created; not copied or based on something else: *an original screenplay.* **3.** Frequently producing new ideas: *an original thinker.* **4.** Being the source from which a copy or translation is made: *an original painting; a book in the original Spanish.* ❖ *n.* The first form of something from which varieties arise or are made: *Later models of the car retained many features of the original.*

o·rig·i·nal·i·ty (ə-rĭj′ə-**năl′**ĭ-tē) *n., pl.* **o·rig·i·nal·i·ties 1.** The quality of being original. **2.** The ability to act or think inventively.

o·rig·i·nal·ly (ə-**rĭj′**ə-nə-lē) *adv.* **1.** At first; in the beginning: *originally wanted to study French, but decided against it.* **2.** By origin: *originally from Oklahoma.* **3.** In a highly distinctive manner: *interpreted the piano piece most originally.*

o·rig·i·nate (ə-**rĭj′**ə-nāt′) *v.* **o·rig·i·nat·ed, o·rig·i·nat·ing, o·rig·i·nates** *—tr.* To bring into being: *Who originated the practice of grading students?* *—intr.* To come into existence; begin: *The idea of mass production originated in the United States.* **—o·rig′i·na′tor** *n.*

O·ri·no·co (ôr′ə-**nō′**kō) A river of Venezuela flowing more than 1,500 miles (2,415 kilometers), partly along

GEOGRAPHY

Oregon The state of **Oregon** takes its name from the Oregon River, the former name of the Columbia River. The origin of the river's name, however, is uncertain. It is possible that the name was created in the 1600s when a French mapmaker made a mistake in labeling that river because he miscopied an earlier map. The word that he engraved onto his map eventually came to be *Oregon* in English.

oriel

origami

oriole

oryx

Osceola

ă	pat	ôr	core
ā	pay	oi	boy
âr	care	ou	out
ä	father	ŏŏ	took
ĕ	pet	ŏŏr	lure
ē	be	ōō	boot
ĭ	pit	ŭ	cut
ī	bite	ûr	urge
îr	pier	th	thin
ŏ	pot	*th*	this
ō	toe	zh	vision
ô	paw	ə	about

the Colombia-Venezuela border, to the Atlantic Ocean.

o·ri·ole (**ôr′**ē-ōl′) *n.* Any of various songbirds that have black and yellow or black and orange feathers in the male and that often build hanging nests. [From Latin *aureolus*, golden.]

O·ri·on (ō-**rī′**ən) *n.* A constellation near the celestial equator containing several bright stars, traditionally pictured as a hunter.

or·i·son (**ôr′**ĭ-sən) *n.* A prayer.

Ork·ney Islands (**ôrk′**nē) A group of about 70 islands in the Atlantic Ocean and the North Sea off the northeast coast of Scotland. The islands became part of Scotland in 1472.

Or·lé·ans (ôr-lā-**äN′**) A city of north-central France on the Loire River south-southwest of Paris. The siege of Orléans by the English (1428–1429) was lifted by troops led by Joan of Arc.

Or·lon (**ôr′**lŏn′) A trademark for an acrylic fiber or yarn made from this fiber.

or·na·ment (**ôr′**nə-mənt) *n.* Something that adorns or makes more attractive or beautiful; a decoration. ❖ *tr.v.* (**ôr′**nə-mĕnt′) **or·na·ment·ed, or·na·ment·ing, or·na·ments** To supply or furnish with ornaments; decorate: *ornament a house for the holidays.* [From Middle English *ournement*, from Latin *ōrnāre*, to adorn.]

or·na·men·tal (ôr′nə-**mĕn′**tl) *adj.* Serving to adorn or ornament: *ornamental jewelry; ornamental plants.* ❖ *n.* Something that serves as ornamentation, especially a plant grown for its beauty: *tall grasses planted as ornamentals.*

or·na·men·ta·tion (ôr′nə-mĕn-**tā′**shən) *n.* **1.** The act of decorating or the state of being decorated. **2.** Something that ornaments or adorns; a decoration.

or·nate (ôr-**nāt′**) *adj.* Having lavish or elaborate decorations: *an ornate palace.* [From Middle English, from Latin *ōrnāre*, to embellish.] **—or·nate′ly** *adv.* **—or·nate′ness** *n.*

or·ner·y (**ôr′**nə-rē) *adj.* **or·ner·i·er, or·ner·i·est** Mean and stubborn: *an ornery old dog.*

or·ni·thol·o·gist (ôr′nə-**thŏl′**ə-jĭst) *n.* A scientist who specializes in ornithology.

or·ni·thol·o·gy (ôr′nə-**thŏl′**ə-jē) *n.* The scientific study of birds.

o·ro·tund (**ôr′**ə-tŭnd′) *adj.* **1.** Pompous; bombastic: *orotund talk.* **2.** Full in sound; strong: *an orotund voice.*

or·phan (**ôr′**fən) *n.* **1.** A child whose parents are dead. **2.** A child who has been deprived of parental care and has not been adopted. ❖ *tr.v.* **or·phaned, or·phan·ing, or·phans** To make (a child) an orphan.

or·phan·age (**ôr′**fə-nĭj) *n.* A public institution for the care and protection of children without parents.

Or·phe·us (**ôr′**fē-əs) *n.* In Greek mythology, a renowned poet and musician who nearly rescued his wife Eurydice from the underworld, but failed when he looked back at her and so broke the command of Hades.

or·tho·clase (**ôr′**thə-klās′ *or* **ôr′**thə-klāz′) *n.* A type of feldspar found in igneous rock and used in making glass, ceramics, and abrasives. Orthoclase is a silicate of potassium and aluminum and is often white or pink.

or·tho·don·tics (ôr′thə-**dŏn′**tĭks) *n.* *(used with a singular verb)* The branch of dentistry that deals with the correction of abnormal alignment of the teeth, often by the use of braces. [From Greek *orthos*, straight + Greek *odous*, tooth.] **—or′tho·don′tic** *adj.*

or·tho·don·tist (ôr′thə-**dŏn′**tĭst) *n.* A dentist who specializes in orthodontics.

or·tho·dox (**ôr′**thə-dŏks′) *adj.* **1.** Adhering to traditional or officially approved doctrines or beliefs: *orthodox theology.* **2. Orthodox a.** Relating to the Eastern Orthodox Church. **b.** Relating to Orthodox Judaism. **3.** Adhering to what is commonly accepted, customary, or traditional: *orthodox views on education.* [From Middle English *orthodoxe* : Greek *orthos*, straight, right + Greek *doxa*, opinion.]

Orthodox Church *n.* The Eastern Orthodox Church.

Orthodox Judaism *n.* The branch of Judaism that adheres to the Torah as interpreted in the Talmud.

or·tho·dox·y (**ôr′**thə-dŏk′sē) *n., pl.* **or·tho·dox·ies 1.** The quality or state of being orthodox. **2.** Adherence to traditional practice, custom, or belief.

or·thog·o·nal (ôr-**thŏg′**ə-nəl) *adj.* Relating to or containing right angles: *orthogonal lines.* [From Greek *orthos*, straight + Greek *gōniā*, angle.]

or·tho·graph·ic (ôr′thə-**grăf′**ĭk) *adj.* Relating to orthography. **—or′tho·graph′i·cal·ly** *adv.*

or·thog·ra·phy (ôr-**thŏg′**rə-fē) *n., pl.* **or·thog·ra·phies 1.** The correct spelling of words. **2.** The study of spelling. [From Greek *orthos*, straight, right + Greek *graphein*, to write.]

or·tho·pe·dics (ôr′thə-**pē′**dĭks) *n.* *(used with a singular verb)* The branch of medicine that deals with the correction or treatment, by surgery or manipulation, of disorders or injuries of the bones, joints, and associated muscles. [From Greek *orthos*, straight, right + Greek *paideia*, child-rearing.] **—or′tho·pe′dic** *adj.* **—or′tho·pe′dist** *n.*

Or·well (**ôr′**wĕl′), **George** 1903–1950. British writer whose works include *Animal Farm* (1945).

–ory *suff.* A suffix that means: **1.** Relating to: *advisory.* **2.** A place or thing used for: *reformatory.*

o·ryx (**ôr′**ĭks) *n., pl.* **oryx** or **o·ryx·es** Any of several African and Arabian antelopes having black or brown markings on the face and long, straight or slightly curved horns.

or·zo (**ôr′**zō) *n.* A pasta shaped like grains of rice, frequently used in soups. [From Italian, barley, orzo, from Latin *hordeum*.]

Os The symbol for the element **osmium.**

O·sage (**ō′**sāj′ *or* ō-**sāj′**) *n., pl.* **Osage** or **O·sag·es 1.** A member of a Native American people formerly living in Missouri and Kansas and now living in Oklahoma. **2.** The Siouan language of this people.

O·sa·ka (ō-**sä′**kə) A city of southern Honshu, Japan, on an inlet of the Pacific Ocean.

Os·ce·o·la (ŏs′ē-**ō′**lə *or* ō′sē-**ō′**lə) 1804?–1838. Seminole leader who resisted the American government's removal of his people from Florida in the 1830s.

os·cil·late (**ŏs′**ə-lāt′) *intr.v.* **os·cil·lat·ed, os·cil·lat·ing, os·cil·lates 1.** To swing back and forth with a steady rhythm: *a pendulum that oscillates.* **2.** To waver between two or more thoughts or courses of action; vacillate. **3.** To vary regularly between alternate extremes.

os·cil·la·tion (ŏs′ə-**lā′**shən) *n.* **1.** The act or process of oscillating. **2.** A single cycle of motion or variation about a central position.

os·cil·la·tor (**ŏs′**ə-lā′tər) *n.* Something that oscillates, especially a device that produces electromagnetic waves or an alternating current.

os·cil·lo·scope (ə-**sĭl′**ə-skōp′) *n.* An electronic instrument that produces a visual display on the screen of a cathode-ray tube representing oscillations of electric current and voltage.

–ose[1] *suff.* A suffix that means having or full of: *grandiose; verbose.*

–ose[2] *suff.* A suffix that means carbohydrate: *fructose.*

o·sier (**ō′**zhər) *n.* **1.** Any of several willows having long, slender, flexible twigs used in making baskets and wicker furniture. **2.** A twig of such a willow.

O·si·ris (ō-**sī′**rĭs) *n.* The ancient Egyptian god of the underworld and judge of the dead. He died and was resurrected annually.

–osis *suff.* A suffix that means: **1.** Condition; process: *osmosis.* **2.** Diseased condition: *tuberculosis.*

Os·lo (ŏz′lō *or* ŏs′lō) The capital of Norway, in the southeast part of the country. It was founded in about 1050.

os·mi·um (ŏz′mē-əm) *n. Symbol* **Os** A hard, bluish-white, extremely dense metallic element. Osmium is used to make objects that need to be durable because of heavy use, such as pen points and phonograph needles. Atomic number 76. See **Periodic Table.**

os·mo·sis (ŏz-**mō′**sĭs *or* ŏs-**mō′**sĭs) *n., pl.* **os·mo·ses** (ŏz-**mō′**sēz *or* ŏs-**mō′**sēz) **1.** The movement of a solvent through a membrane separating two solutions of different concentrations. The solvent from the side of weaker concentration moves to the side of the stronger concentration until the two concentrations are equal. **2.** The tendency of fluids to carry on this process. **3.** A gradual, often unconscious process of absorption or learning: *learned the language through osmosis.* [From *endosmose* : Greek *endo-*, within + Greek *ōsmos*, thrust, push.] **—os·mot′ic** (ŏz-**mŏt′**ĭk *or* ŏs-**mŏt′**ĭk) *adj.*

os·prey (ŏs′prē *or* ŏs′prā) *n., pl.* **os·preys** A large bird of prey having blackish and white feathers and feeding chiefly on fish. [From Middle English *osprai*, from Medieval Latin *avis praedae*, bird of prey.]

os·si·cle (ŏs′ĭ-kəl) *n.* A small bone, especially one of the three located in the middle ear that transmit sound vibrations from the eardrum to the inner ear. [From Latin *ossiculum*, diminutive of *os*, bone.]

os·si·fy (ŏs′ə-fī′) *v.* **os·si·fied, os·si·fy·ing, os·si·fies** *—intr.* **1.** To change into bone; become bony. **2.** To become rigid or conventional: *His ideas ossified as he grew older.* *—tr.* **1.** To cause to change into bone. **2.** To cause to become rigid or conventional, as in thinking. **—os′si·fi·ca′tion** (ŏs′ə-fĭ-**kā′**shən) *n.*

os·ten·si·ble (ŏ-**stĕn′**sə-bəl) *adj.* Represented or appearing as such: *His ostensible purpose was charity, but his real goal was popularity.* **—os·ten′si·bly** *adv.*

os·ten·ta·tion (ŏs′tĕn-**tā′**shən) *n.* Showy display meant to impress others. [From Middle English *ostentacione*, from Latin *ostendere*, to show.]

os·ten·ta·tious (ŏs′tĕn-**tā′**shəs) *adj.* Characterized by or given to ostentation; pretentious: *an ostentatious party.* **—os′ten·ta′tious·ly** *adv.*

os·te·o·ar·thri·tis (ŏs′tē-ō-är-**thrī′**tĭs) *n.* A disease characterized by chronic, noninflammatory degeneration of the cartilage in the joints, occurring mainly in older people.

os·te·op·a·thy (ŏs′tē-**ŏp′**ə-thē) *n.* A system of medicine that uses manipulation of bones and muscles, along with conventional medical and therapeutic procedures, to treat disease. [From Greek *osteon*, bone + English *-pathy*, treatment of disease.]

os·te·o·po·ro·sis (ŏs′tē-ō-pə-**rō′**sĭs) *n.* A disease in which the bones become porous and fragile, occurring especially in older women.

os·tler (ŏs′lər) *n.* Variant of **hostler.**

os·tra·cism (ŏs′trə-sĭz′əm) *n.* Banishment or exclusion from a group, organization, or society in general.

os·tra·cize (ŏs′trə-sīz′) *tr.v.* **os·tra·cized, os·tra·ciz·ing, os·tra·ciz·es** To banish or exclude (someone) from a group or from society. [From Greek *ostrakon*, shell, potsherd (from the potsherds used as ballots in voting for temporary banishment in ancient Greece).]

os·trich (ŏs′trĭch *or* ôs′trĭch) *n., pl.* **ostrich** or **os·trich·es** Either of two large African birds having a small head, a long neck, and long legs. Ostriches can run fast but cannot fly.

Os·wald (ŏz′wôld′), **Lee Harvey** 1939–1963. American who allegedly killed President John F. Kennedy.

OT *abbr.* An abbreviation of: **1.** Old Testament. **2.** overtime.

oth·er (ŭ*th*′ər) *adj.* **1a.** Being the remaining one of two or more: *Let me look at the other shoe.* **b.** Being the remaining ones of several: *My other friends are away on vacation.* **2.** Different: *Any other kid would have run away.* **3.** Additional; extra: *I have no other shoes.* **4.** Opposite or reverse: *Get in on the other side of the boat.* **5.** Alternate; second: *We play tennis every other day.* **6.** Just recent or past: *the other day.* ❖ *n.* **1a.** The remaining one of two or more: *One took a taxi, and the other walked home.* **b. others** The remaining ones of several: *How are the others doing now that I'm gone?* **2a.** A different person or thing: *one hurricane after the other.* **b.** An additional person or thing: *If these are only a few of the guests, how many others are you expecting?* ❖ *pron.* A different or additional person or thing: *Someone or other will apply for the job.* [From Old English *ōther.*]

other than *prep.* With the exception of; except for; besides: *Other than one sister, Amy has no close relatives.*

oth·er·wise (ŭ*th*′ər-wīz′) *adv.* **1.** In another way; differently: *He insisted that he was right, but she thought otherwise.* **2.** Under other circumstances: *Experiments make clear some things you might not understand otherwise.* **3.** In other respects: *Hitting the wrong note marred an otherwise perfect performance.* **4.** Or else: *You should follow the instructions. Otherwise, the cake won't come out right.* ❖ *adj.* Other than supposed; different: *The truth of the matter was otherwise.*

Ot·ta·wa[1] (ŏt′ə-wô) *n., pl.* **Ottawa** or **Ot·ta·was 1.** A member of a Native American people formerly living along the northern shore of Lake Huron and now living in Ontario, Michigan, and Oklahoma. **2.** The dialect of Ojibwa spoken by the Ottawa.

Ot·ta·wa[2] (ŏt′ə-wə) The capital of Canada, in southeast Ontario on the **Ottawa River** west of Montreal, Quebec. It was founded as Bytown in the 1820s and renamed Ottawa in 1855.

ot·ter (ŏt′ər) *n., pl.* **otter** or **ot·ters 1.** Any of various carnivorous mammals that resemble a weasel and live in or near water, having webbed feet and thick dark-brown fur. **2.** The fur of such a mammal. [From Old English *otor.*]

ot·to·man (ŏt′ə-mən) *n.* **1.** A sofa that has no arms or back. **2.** A cushioned footstool. [From French *ottoman*, Ottoman, Turkish, ultimately from Arabic *'uṯmān*, Osman I, founder of the Ottoman Empire.]

Ottoman *adj.* **1.** Relating to the Ottoman Empire or its peoples or cultures. **2.** Turkish. ❖ *n.* A Turk.

Ottoman Empire A vast Turkish-ruled empire of southwest Asia, northeast Africa, and southeast Europe. It was founded in the 1200s and dissolved after World War I.

Oua·ga·dou·gou (wä′gə-**dōō′**gōō) The capital of Burkina Faso, in the central part of the country. It was founded in the late 11th century.

ouch (ouch) *interj.* An expression used in response to sudden pain.

ought (ôt) *aux.v.* **1.** To be required by duty or obligation: *We ought to clean up our room.* **2.** To be required by good judgment: *You ought to wear a raincoat.* **3.** To be expected as probable or likely: *Tonight ought to be a good night for looking at stars.*
❑ *These sound alike:* **ought, aught[1]** (anything), **aught[2]** (zero).

ou·gui·ya (ōō-**gē′**yə) *n.* The basic monetary unit of Mauritania.

ounce[1] (ouns) *n.* **1a.** A unit of avoirdupois weight equal to 1/16 of a pound or 437.5 grains (28.35 grams). See table at **measurement. b.** A unit of apothecaries' weight equal to 480 grains (31.103 grams). **2.** A unit of volume or capacity used for measuring liquids, equal to 1/16 of a pint (29.57 milliliters). **3.** A tiny bit: *didn't get an ounce of respect.* [From Latin *ūncia.*]

ounce[2] (ouns) *n.* The snow leopard. [From Middle English *unce*, from Greek *lunx.*]

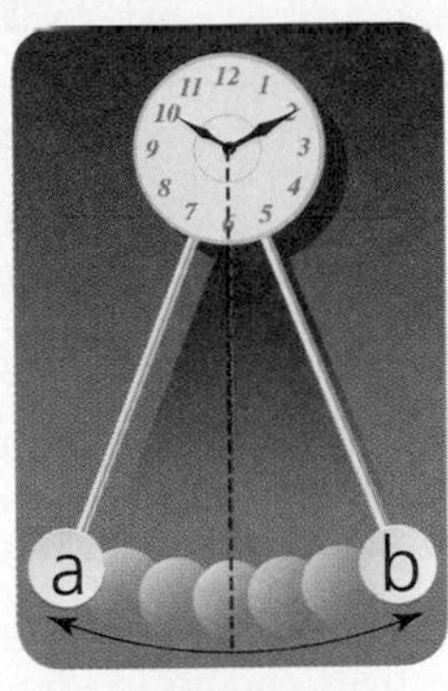

oscillation
The oscillation of the clock's pendulum takes it from point *a* to point *b* and back to *a*. The dotted red line in the middle shows the position of the pendulum at rest.

ottoman

WORD BUILDING

–ous The suffix **–ous,** which forms adjectives, has the basic meaning "having, full of, or characterized by." *Blusterous,* for example, means "full of or characterized by bluster." The suffix *–ous* can be traced back to the Latin adjective suffix *–ōsus.* Some English words ending in *–ous* that come from Latin adjectives ending in *–ōsus* are: *copious, famous, generous,* and *glorious.* Adjectives ending in *–ous* often have related nouns ending in *-ousness* or *–osity: copiousness, generosity.*

WORD BUILDING

out– There are many words in English beginning with **out–**. In words such as *outbuilding, outcast, outpour,* and *outstanding, out–* has the same meaning as the adverb *out.* So an *outcast* is "one who is cast out," and one who is *outstanding* "stands out." But in other cases *out–* takes on the sense of doing better, being greater, or going beyond, as in *outdo, outnumber,* and *outrun.* Although *out–* can attach to nouns, adjectives, or verbs to form other nouns, adjectives, or verbs, it most frequently attaches to verbs—and in fact can attach to almost any verb you please: *outbowl, outcook, outride, outsing.*

ă	pat	ôr	core
ā	pay	oi	boy
âr	care	ou	out
ä	father	ŏŏ	took
ĕ	pet	ŏŏr	lure
ē	be	ōō	boot
ĭ	pit	ŭ	cut
ī	bite	ûr	urge
îr	pier	th	thin
ŏ	pot	*th*	this
ō	toe	zh	vision
ô	paw	ə	about

our (our) *adj.* The possessive form of **we.** Relating to or belonging to us: *our friends; our house.*
❑ *These sound alike:* **our, hour** (time unit).

ours (ourz) *pron. (used with a singular or plural verb)* The one or ones belonging to us: *If your car doesn't work, take ours. Their apples are red, but ours are green.*

our·selves (our-**sĕlvz′** *or* är-**sĕlvz′**) *pron.* **1.** Those ones that are the same as us: **a.** Used as a direct object, an indirect object, or an object of a preposition to show that the action of the verb refers back to the subject: *We dressed ourselves. We made ourselves some breakfast. We brought it on ourselves.* **b.** Used to give emphasis: *We ourselves made the same discovery.* **2.** Our normal or healthy condition: *We were soon ourselves again after recovering from the flu.*

–ous *suff.* A suffix that means: **1.** Having; full of: *joyous.* **2.** Having a lower valence than the same element in a compound or ion named with an adjective ending in *-ic: ferrous.* —SEE NOTE.

oust (oust) *tr.v.* **oust·ed, oust·ing, ousts** To eject; force out: *oust an official from office.* [From Middle English *ousten,* from Latin *obstāre,* to hinder.]

oust·er (**ous′**tər) *n.* An example of ousting or being ousted: *The committee member attributed his ouster to a small group of opponents.*

out (out) *adv.* **1.** Away or forth from inside: *The cat snuck out as I came in.* **2.** Away from the center or middle: *The searchers spread out.* **3.** From a container or source: *Pour the soda out.* **4a.** Away from a usual place: *She stepped out for a minute.* **b.** Out-of-bounds: *That ball went out.* **5.** Into or in the open air; outside: *They went out to play. It's raining out.* **6a.** To depletion or extinction: *Supplies ran out.* **b.** To a finish or conclusion: *Play the game out.* **7.** Into being or view: *The moon came out.* **8.** Without inhibition; boldly: *Speak out.* **9.** Into the possession of someone else: *gave out free tickets.* **10.** Into disuse or an unfashionable status: *Bell-bottom pants went out a long time ago.* **11.** In or into a non-working condition: *The air conditioner went out.* **12.** So as to be retired in baseball: *He grounded out to the shortstop.* ❖ *adj.* **1.** No longer fashionable: *Aren't those boots out now?* **2.** Not in consideration: *Going to see that awful movie is out!* **3.** In baseball, not allowed to continue to bat or be on base; retired. **4.** Traveling or landing out-of-bounds: *That ball was out.* **5a.** Not operating or operational: *The power is out. The bridge is out.* **b.** Extinguished: *The lights are out.* **6.** Unconscious: *was out for an hour after the surgery.* **7.** No longer possessing or supplied with something: *I'd offer you coffee but we're out.* ❖ *prep.* **1.** Through; forth from: *The bird flew out the window.* **2.** Beyond or outside of: *Out this door is the garage.* ❖ *n.* **1.** A means of escape: *Her lawyer discovered an ingenious out for her.* **2.** A play in which a batter or base runner is retired in baseball. **3.** A person having no power or influence: *the outs versus the ins.* ❖ *tr.v.* **out·ed, out·ing, outs 1.** To expose as being gay, lesbian, or bisexual. **2.** To expose the secret behavior or identity of: *outed his classmate as a cheater.* [From Old English *ūt.*]

out– *pref.* A prefix that means in a way that is better or greater: *outwit.* —SEE NOTE.

out·age (**ou′**tĭj) *n.* An interruption in an operation, such as electric power.

out-and-out (**out′**n-**out′**) *adj.* Complete; utter: *an out-and-out liar.*

out·back (**out′**băk′) *n.* The remote rural part of a country, especially of Australia.

out·bid (out-**bĭd′**) *tr.v.* **out·bid, out·bid·den** (out-**bĭd′**n) or **out·bid, out·bid·ding, out·bids** To bid higher than or more competitively than: *He outbid his opponents.*

out·board (**out′**bôrd′) *adj.* **1a.** Situated outside the hull of a vessel. **b.** Being away from the center line of the hull of a ship. **2.** Situated toward or nearer the end of a wing of an aircraft. **—out′board′** *adv.*

outboard motor *n.* A removable engine mounted at the stern of a boat and linked to a propeller.

out·bound (**out′**bound′) *adj.* Outward bound; headed away: *the outbound train.*

out·box (**out′**bŏks′) *n.* **1.** An electronic folder for outgoing emails or text messages. **2.** A container for outgoing documents, located in or near one's work area.

out·break (**out′**brāk′) *n.* A sudden increase or eruption: *an outbreak of disease.*

out·build·ing (**out′**bĭl′dĭng) *n.* A building that is separate from a main building.

out·burst (**out′**bûrst′) *n.* A sudden violent display, as of activity or emotion: *an outburst of laughter.*

out·cast (**out′**kăst′) *n.* A person who has been excluded from a society or system. ❖ *adj.* Cast out; driven out; rejected.

out·class (out-**klăs′**) *tr.v.* **out·classed, out·class·ing, out·class·es** To surpass so decisively as to appear to be of a higher class: *She completely outclassed her opponents and won the competition.*

out·come (**out′**kŭm′) *n.* An end result; a consequence: *the outcome of an election.*

out·crop (**out′**krŏp′) *n.* An area of visible bedrock that is not covered with soil.

out·cry (**out′**krī′) *n., pl.* **out·cries 1.** A loud cry or clamor. **2.** A strong protest: *The rise in prices provoked a public outcry.*

out·dat·ed (out-**dā′**tĭd) *adj.* Out-of-date; old-fashioned: *outdated methods.*

out·dis·tance (out-**dĭs′**təns) *tr.v.* **out·dis·tanced, out·dis·tanc·ing, out·dis·tanc·es 1.** To outrun, as in a long-distance race. **2.** To surpass by a wide margin.

out·do (out-**dōō′**) *tr.v.* **out·did** (out-**dĭd′**), **out·done** (out-**dŭn′**), **out·do·ing, out·does** (out-**dŭz′**) To do more or better than (another): *Our team outdid theirs in everything except canoeing.*

out·door (**out′**dôr′) *adj.* Located in, done in, or suitable for the outdoors: *an outdoor game; outdoor clothing.*

out·doors (out-**dôrz′**) *adv.* In or into the open; outside: *eat outdoors.* ❖ *n.* **1.** An area outside a house or building in the open air. **2.** An area away from human settlements.

out·er (**ou′**tər) *adj.* **1.** Located on the outside; external: *outer garments; the outer wall of a fortress.* **2.** Farther from the center: *the outer limits of the universe.*

outer ear *n.* The part of the ear that is made chiefly of cartilage and includes the passage leading to the eardrum. The outer ear collects incoming sound waves and transmits them to the inner ear.

Outer Mongolia See **Mongolia** (sense 2).

out·er·most (**ou′**tər-mōst′) *adj.* Most distant from the center.

outer space *n.* The region of space beyond Earth's atmosphere.

out·field (**out′**fēld′) *n.* **1.** The playing area extending outward from a baseball diamond, divided into right, center, and left fields. **2.** The members of a baseball team playing in the outfield: *a team with a superb outfield.* **—out′field′er** *n.*

out·fit (**out′**fĭt′) *n.* **1.** A set of equipment for a particular purpose: *a diving outfit.* **2.** A set of clothing and accessories that go together: *She wore a tweed outfit.* **3.** A military unit, business organization, or other association: *an infantry outfit.* ❖ *tr.v.* **out·fit·ted, out·fit·ting, out·fits** To furnish with the necessary equipment or clothing: *outfit a ship for an expedition.* **—out′fit′ter** *n.*

out·flank (out-**flăngk′**) *tr.v.* **out·flanked, out·flank·ing, out·flanks 1.** To maneuver around and behind the flank of (an opposing force). **2.** To gain an advantage over (a competing business, for example).

out·flow (out′flō′) *n.* **1.** The act of flowing out. **2.** Something that flows out: *collect the outflow of the pipe in a barrel.* **3.** The amount flowing out.

out·fox (out-fŏks′) *tr.v.* **out·foxed, out·fox·ing, out·fox·es** To outwit; outsmart.

out·go·ing (out′gō′ĭng) *adj.* **1.** Leaving; departing: *an outgoing steamship.* **2.** To be taken out: *an outgoing order.* **3.** Friendly; sociable: *an outgoing person.*

out·grow (out-grō′) *tr.v.* **out·grew** (out-grōō′), **out·grown** (out-grōn′), **out·grow·ing, out·grows 1.** To grow too large for: *He outgrew his shoes.* **2.** To discard in the course of growing up or maturing: *She outgrew stuffed animals.* **3.** To grow larger than: *He outgrew his father.*

out·growth (out′grōth′) *n.* **1.** Something that grows out of something else: *an outgrowth on a tree branch.* **2.** A result or effect: *The choir's great performance is an outgrowth of many rehearsals.*

out·guess (out-gĕs′) *tr.v.* **out·guessed, out·guess·ing, out·guess·es** To guess or anticipate the plans or activities of.

out·house (out′hous′) *n.* **1.** A small roofed structure that has a seat with a hole or holes in it built over a pit and is used as a toilet. **2.** An outbuilding.

out·ing (ou′tĭng) *n.* An excursion or walk outdoors for pleasure.

out·land·ish (out-lăn′dĭsh) *adj.* Unconventional; strange: *outlandish clothes.*

out·last (out-lăst′) *tr.v.* **out·last·ed, out·last·ing, out·lasts** To last longer than: *Do these batteries really outlast the other brands?*

out·law (out′lô′) *n.* **1.** A person who defies the law; a declared criminal. **2.** A person who is excluded from normal legal protection, especially as a result of having committed a crime. ❖ *tr.v.* **out·lawed, out·law·ing, out·laws 1.** To declare illegal: *outlawed the sale of fireworks.* **2.** To deprive (a person) of the protection of the law. [From Old English *ūtlaga,* from Old Norse *ūtlagi.*]

out·lay (out′lā′) *n.* **1.** The act of spending money. **2.** The total amount spent: *The total outlay was $50.*

out·let (out′lĕt′) *n.* **1.** A passage or opening for letting something out: *checked the outlet for exhaust gases from the furnace.* **2.** The point where water from a lake or pond empties into a river or stream. **3.** A means of releasing energies or desires: *Music was an outlet for her desire to express herself.* **4.** A store that sells the goods of a manufacturer: *a retail outlet.* **5.** An electric receptacle, especially one that is mounted in a wall, connected to a power line, and equipped with a socket for a plug.

out·line (out′līn′) *n.* **1.** A line forming the outer edge, limit, or boundary of something. **2.** A drawing that consists of only the outer edge of an object: *She traced an outline of California from the map.* **3.** A summary, usually presenting topics under headings and subheadings: *an outline for a composition.* ❖ *tr.v.* **out·lined, out·lin·ing, out·lines 1.** To draw the outline of: *outline a picture before drawing in the details.* **2.** To give the main points of; summarize: *outline a plan.*

SYNONYMS outline, contour, profile, silhouette These nouns refer to a line that defines the boundary and shape of an object, mass, or figure: *The outline of the mountains against the sunset was a majestic sight. She could see the island's contour from the airplane. This ancient coin features the profile of a king. From the train, he saw the dark silhouette of his family waving farewell on the platform.*

---

out·live (out-lĭv′) *tr.v.* **out·lived, out·liv·ing, out·lives** To live or last longer than: *Women tend to outlive men.*

out·look (out′lo͝ok′) *n.* **1.** A point of view; an attitude: *a happy outlook on life.* **2.** The probable situation or result; the expectation: *the weather outlook for tomorrow.* **3.** A place from which something can be viewed: *a photograph taken from an outlook high in the mountains.*

out·ly·ing (out′lī′ĭng) *adj.* Relatively distant or remote from a center or middle: *factories being built in the outlying suburbs.*

out·ma·neu·ver (out′mə-no͞o′vər) *tr.v.* **out·ma·neu·vered, out·ma·neu·ver·ing, out·ma·neu·vers 1.** To overcome by more artful maneuvering. **2.** To maneuver better than: *The car outmaneuvers all others of its class.*

out·mod·ed (out-mō′dĭd) *adj.* **1.** No longer in fashion: *an outmoded style of dress.* **2.** No longer practical: *outmoded methods of production.*

out·most (out′mōst′) *adj.* Farthest out; outermost.

out·num·ber (out-nŭm′bər) *tr.v.* **out·num·bered, out·num·ber·ing, out·num·bers** To be more numerous than; exceed in number.

out of *prep.* **1a.** From within to the outside of: *got out of the car.* **b.** From a given condition: *came out of a deep sleep.* **c.** From a source, material, or cause: *made out of wood; yelled out of anger.* **2a.** Beyond the limits or range of: *The car drove out of view.* **b.** Away from what is expected or usual: *I'm out of practice.* **3.** From among: *five out of six votes.* **4.** In or into a state of being without: *We've run out of paint.* ◆ **out of it** *Informal* **1.** Not aware of or participating in a particular group, pursuit, or trend. **2.** Disoriented; not fully aware: *I was so out of it that I totally forgot about the meeting.*

out-of-bounds (out′əv-boundz′) *adv.* Beyond the designated boundaries or limits.

out-of-date (out′əv-dāt′) *adj.* Old-fashioned; outmoded.

out-of-state (out′əv-stāt′) *adj.* Relating to or being from another state: *The prestigious college attracted many out-of-state students.*

out-of-the-way (out′əv-*th*ə-wā′) *adj.* Away from areas often visited; remote: *an out-of-the-way place.*

out-of-touch (out′əv-touch′) *adj.* **1.** Unaware of the latest developments, as in current events or an area of interest. **2.** Unable to appreciate or understand the concerns or difficulties of others: *out-of-touch politicians.*

out·pa·tient (out′pā′shənt) *n.* A patient whose treatment does not require an overnight stay in a hospital or clinic. ❖ *adj.* Relating to outpatients or their care: *a center for outpatient surgery.*

out·play (out-plā′) *tr.v.* **out·played, out·play·ing, out·plays** To surpass (one's opponent) in playing a game.

out·poll (out-pōl′) *tr.v.* **out·polled, out·poll·ing, out·polls** To win more votes than: *The incumbent outpolled her rival by a wide margin.*

out·post (out′pōst′) *n.* **1a.** A detachment of troops stationed at a distance from the main unit to prevent a surprise attack. **b.** The station occupied by such troops. **2.** A remote settlement: *an outpost in the wilderness.*

out·pour·ing (out′pôr′ĭng) *n.* The act, action, or result of pouring out or producing: *the outpouring of lava; an outpouring of profanity.*

out·put (out′po͝ot′) *n.* **1.** An amount of something produced, especially during a given period of time: *the output of a mine.* **2a.** The energy, power, or work produced by a system or device: *the output of an engine; the output of a loudspeaker.* **b.** The information that a computer program produces by processing a given collection of data.

output device *n.* A device, such as a printer or speaker, that presents computer data.

out·rage (out′rāj′) *n.* **1.** An extremely vicious or wicked act. **2.** An offensive or insulting action: *an outrage to common decency.* **3.** Great anger aroused by such an act: *public outrage over the incident.* ❖ *tr.v.* **out·raged, out·rag·ing, out·rag·es 1.** To give offense to: *Such an act outrages everyone's sense of justice.* **2.** To make extremely

outcrop

WRITERS CHOOSE THEIR WORDS

Likely they had never seen a girl *not* decked out in silk and damask, *not* bathed and scrubbed raw, *not* brushed and perfumed until she gleamed and reeked of flowers. They looked at me as if I were some **outlandish** creature.

—Susan Fletcher
Shadow Spinner

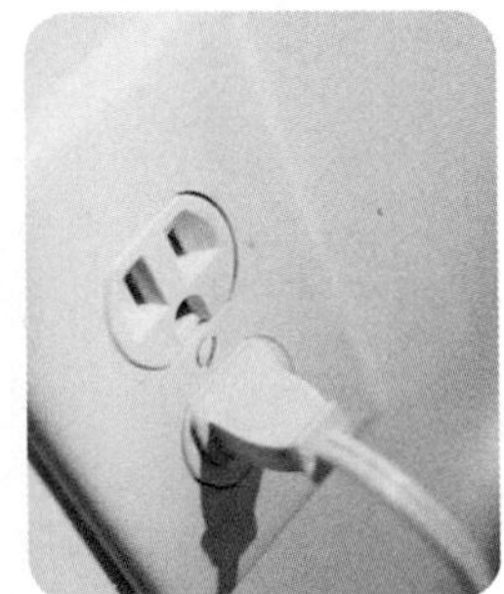

outlet

outrigger

angry or resentful: *We were outraged by his behavior.* [From Middle English, from Old French, from *outre*, beyond.]

out·ra·geous (out-rā′jəs) *adj.* **1.** Exceeding all bounds of what is right or proper; immoral or offensive: *an outrageous crime; outrageous prices.* **2.** Extremely unusual or unconventional; extraordinary: *dressed in outrageous clothing.* **—out·ra′geous·ly** *adv.*

out·ran (out-răn′) *v.* Past tense of **outrun.**

out·rank (out-răngk′) *tr.v.* **out·ranked, out·rank·ing, out·ranks** To rank above: *A colonel outranks a major.*

out·reach (out-rēch′) *tr.v.* **out·reached, out·reach·ing, out·reach·es** To exceed: *Demand for the new batteries outreached supplies.* ❖ *n.* (**out′**rēch′) A systematic attempt to provide services beyond what is ordinarily done, as to particular parts of a community.

out·rig·ger (**out′**rĭg′ər) *n.* **1.** A long thin float attached parallel to a seagoing canoe by projecting spars as a means of preventing it from capsizing. **2.** A canoe fitted with such a float.

out·right (**out′**rīt′ *or* out′rīt′) *adv.* **1.** Completely; unconditionally: *accepted her offer outright.* **2.** Without delay; on the spot: *denied the accusation outright.* ❖ *adj.* (**out′**rīt′) Complete; unconditional; out-and-out: *an outright gift; an outright lie.*

out·run (out-rŭn′) *tr.v.* **out·ran** (out-răn′), **out·run, out·run·ning, out·runs 1.** To run faster than: *outran all the opponents.* **2.** To escape from; elude: *They outran three policemen.* **3.** To go beyond; exceed: *Expenses are outrunning those of last year.*

out·sell (out-sĕl′) *tr.v.* **out·sold** (out-sōld′), **out·sell·ing, out·sells 1.** To sell faster or better than: *a new model car that has outsold all competition.* **2.** To sell more than: *That store consistently outsells the others.*

out·set (**out′**sĕt′) *n.* The beginning; the start: *The plan failed because it was flawed at the outset.*

out·shine (out-shīn′) *tr.v.* **out·shone** (out-shōn′), **out·shin·ing, out·shines 1.** To shine brighter than. **2.** To be or appear better than: *She outshines her opponents.*

out·side (out-sīd′ *or* **out′**sīd′) *n.* **1.** The outer surface; exterior: *the outside of a house.* **2.** The external or surface aspect: *On the outside, it's very attractive.* ❖ *adj.* **1.** External; outer: *an outside door.* **2.** Not belonging to or originating in a certain group: *a dispute caused by outside influences.* **3.** Being beyond the limits of one's regular occupation: *His outside interests include music and photography.* **4.** Extreme; uttermost: *The outside estimate on that car is $5,000.* **5.** Slight; remote: *an outside possibility.* **6.** In baseball, passing on the side of home plate away from a batter: *an outside pitch.* ❖ *adv.* On or to the external side: *stay outside.* ❖ *prep.* **1.** On or to the outer side of: *going outside the house.* **2.** Beyond the limits of: *going outside the country.* **3.** Except: *no information outside the figures already given.* ◆ **at the outside** At the most: *We'll be gone a week at the outside.*

outside of *prep.* **1.** Outside: *Outside of my window a bird is building a nest.* **2.** Aside from; except for: *Outside of the flat tire, that bike is in good condition.*

out·sid·er (out-sī′dər) *n.* A person who is not part of a certain group or activity: *a gate to prevent outsiders from entering.*

out·skirts (**out′**skûrts′) *pl.n.* The regions away from a central district; the surrounding areas: *on the outskirts of town.*

out·smart (out-smärt′) *tr.v.* **out·smart·ed, out·smart·ing, out·smarts** To gain the advantage over by cleverness; outwit.

out·sold (out-sōld′) *v.* Past tense and past participle of **outsell.**

out·source (**out′**sôrs′) *tr.v.* **out·sourced, out·sourc·ing, out·sourc·es** To arrange for (a job or task) to be done by another business, especially in order to save money on labor costs: *The software company outsources a number of its jobs to other companies in Asia.*

out·spo·ken (out-spō′kən) *adj.* **1.** Spoken without reserve: *outspoken remarks.* **2.** Frank and bold in speech: *an outspoken politician.* **—out·spo′ken·ly** *adv.* **—out·spo′ken·ness** *n.*

out·spread (out′sprĕd′) *adj.* Spread out; extended: *with outspread wings.*

out·stand·ing (out-stăn′dĭng *or* **out′**stăn′dĭng) *adj.* **1.** Exceptional; extraordinary: *an outstanding example of modern architecture.* **2.** Noticeable or conspicuous: *a landscape with few outstanding features.* **3.** Not settled or resolved: *outstanding debts.* **—out·stand′ing·ly** *adv.*

out·stay (out-stā′) *tr.v.* **out·stayed, out·stay·ing, out·stays 1.** To stay longer than; overstay: *The guests outstayed their welcome.* **2.** To show greater endurance than: *Our crew team outstayed the opposition.*

out·stretch (out-strĕch′) *v.* **out·stretched, out·stretch·ing, out·stretch·es** To spread or stretch out.

out·strip (out-strĭp′) *tr.v.* **out·stripped, out·strip·ping, out·strips 1.** To leave behind; outrun. **2.** To surpass: *Grain began to outstrip cattle in economic importance.*

out·take (**out′**tāk′) *n.* A shot or scene, as of a movie, that is filmed but not used in the final version.

out·ward (**out′**wərd) *adj.* **1.** Relating to, located on, or moving toward the outside or exterior: *an outward flow of gold.* **2.** Visible on the surface: *an outward appearance of calm.* ❖ *adv.* also **outwards** Away from the center. **—out′ward·ness** *n.*

out·ward·ly (**out′**wərd-lē) *adv.* **1.** On the outside. **2.** In appearance: *He seemed outwardly healthy.*

out·wear (out-wâr′) *tr.v.* **out·wore** (out-wôr′), **out·worn** (out-wôrn′), **out·wear·ing, out·wears** To wear or last longer than: *These shoes will outwear all others.*

out·weigh (out-wā′) *tr.v.* **out·weighed, out·weigh·ing, out·weighs 1.** To weigh more than: *outweighs everyone on the team.* **2.** To be of greater importance or significance than: *an objection that outweighs all others.*

out·wit (out-wĭt′) *tr.v.* **out·wit·ted, out·wit·ting, out·wits** To get the better of with cleverness or cunning; outsmart: *I won the chess game by outwitting my opponent.*

out·work (out-wûrk′) *tr.v.* **out·worked, out·work·ing, out·works** To work better or faster than: *a mason who outworks everyone else on the job.*

o·va (ō′və) *n.* Plural of **ovum.**

o·val (ō′vəl) *adj.* Having a rounded and somewhat elongated shape like that of a bird's egg: *an oval face.* ❖ *n.* An oval figure, form, or structure. [From Latin *ōvum*, egg.]

o·var·i·an (ō-vâr′ē-ən) *adj.* Relating to an ovary.

o·va·ry (ō′və-rē) *n., pl.* **o·va·ries 1.** The reproductive organ of female animals, usually one of a pair, in which egg cells and female sex hormones are produced. **2.** A plant part at the base of the pistil of a flower, which ripens into a fruit containing the seeds.

o·va·tion (ō-vā′shən) *n.* A loud and enthusiastic display of approval, usually in the form of applause. [From Latin *ovāre*, to rejoice.]

ov·en (ŭv′ən) *n.* An enclosed chamber used for baking, heating, or drying objects. [From Old English *ofen*.]

ov·en·bird (ŭv′ən-bûrd′) *n.* A small brownish North American bird that has a loud call and builds a domed nest on the ground.

o·ver (ō′vər) *prep.* **1.** Higher than; above: *a sign over the door.* **2.** Above and across: *hop over the fence.* **3.** To the other side of: *walked over the bridge.* **4.** On the other side of: *a town over the border.* **5.** Upon the surface of: *a coat of varnish over the woodwork.* **6.** Through the extent of: *read over the report.* **7.** Throughout or during: *over the years.* **8.** Through the medium of: *talked over the telephone.* **9.** So as to cover: *put a shawl over her shoul-*

ă	pat	ôr	core
ā	pay	oi	boy
âr	care	ou	out
ä	father	o͝o	took
ĕ	pet	o͝or	lure
ē	be	o͞o	boot
ĭ	pit	ŭ	cut
ī	bite	ûr	urge
îr	pier	th	thin
ŏ	pot	*th*	this
ō	toe	zh	vision
ô	paw	ə	about

ders. **10.** In excess of; more than: *over ten miles.* **11.** In superiority to: *won a victory over the rivals.* **12.** While engaged in or partaking of: *a chat over coffee.* **13.** On account of or with reference to: *an argument over methods.* ❖ *adv.* **1.** Above the top: *climbed the fence and looked over.* **2a.** Across to another or opposite side: *flying over to Europe.* **b.** Across the edge or brim: *The coffee spilled over.* **3.** To another place: *move the chair over here.* **4.** To one's home or office: *Let's invite them over.* **5.** Throughout an area: *We went all over.* **6.** To a different opinion or allegiance: *After a long talk, I won her over.* **7.** To a different person, condition, or title: *signing land over to a bank.* **8.** So as to be completely covered: *The river froze over.* **9.** From beginning to end; through: *thinking it over.* **10a.** From an upright position: *knocked the vase over.* **b.** From an upward to an inverted or reversed position: *Turn the book over.* **11a.** Once more; again: *He had to do his homework over.* **b.** In repetition: *He sang the same song ten times over.* **12.** In addition or excess: *I have a dollar left over.* ❖ *adj.* **1.** At an end: *Summer is over.* **2.** In excess: *My guess was $50 over.* ◆ **over and above** In addition to: *a special fee over and above the regular charge.* **over and over** Again and again; repeatedly. **over the top** Beyond the normal bounds; excessive. [From Old English *ofer.*]

o·ver– *pref.* A prefix that means: **1.** Above or upon in position: *overpass; overcoat.* **2.** Superiority in rank or importance: *overlord.* **3.** Into a reverse position: *overturn.* **4.** More than what is proper or usual; excessively: *overgrown; overpay.*

o·ver·a·chieve (ō′vər-ə-**chēv′**) *intr.v.* **o·ver·a·chieved, o·ver·a·chiev·ing, o·ver·a·chieves** To perform better or achieve more success than expected. **—o′ver·a·chiev′er** *n.*

o·ver·act (ō′vər-**ăkt′**) *v.* **o·ver·act·ed, o·ver·act·ing, o·ver·acts** *—tr.* To act (a part, as in a play) with unnecessary exaggeration. *—intr.* To exaggerate a part; overplay.

o·ver·ac·tive (ō′vər-**ăk′**tĭv) *adj.* Active to an excessive or abnormal degree.

o·ver·all (**ō′**vər-ôl′) *adj.* **1.** Including everything; total: *the overall cost of the project.* **2.** Viewed as a whole; general: *The overall effect is very pleasing.* ❖ *adv.* (**ō′**vər-**ôl′**) On the whole; generally: *Except for a couple of songs, it was a good concert overall.*

o·ver·alls (**ō′**vər-ôlz′) *pl.n.* Loose-fitting pants, usually of strong fabric, with a bib front and shoulder straps, often worn over regular clothing as protection from dirt.

o·ver·arm (**ō′**vər-ärm′) *adj.* Performed with the arm raised above the shoulder; overhand: *an overarm throw.*

o·ver·ate (ō′vər-**āt′**) *v.* Past tense of **overeat.**

o·ver·awe (ō′vər-**ô′**) *tr.v.* **o·ver·awed, o·ver·aw·ing, o·ver·awes** To overcome with awe.

o·ver·bal·ance (ō′vər-**băl′**əns) *v.* **o·ver·bal·anced, o·ver·bal·anc·ing, o·ver·bal·anc·es** *—tr.* To have greater weight or importance than. *—intr.* To lose one's balance.

o·ver·bear (ō′vər-**bâr′**) *tr.v.* **o·ver·bore** (ō′vər-**bôr′**), **o·ver·borne** (ō′vər-**bôrn′**), **o·ver·bear·ing, o·ver·bears** **1.** To crush or press down upon with physical force. **2.** To dominate or overcome.

o·ver·bear·ing (ō′vər-**bâr′**ĭng) *adj.* Arrogant and domineering in manner: *an overbearing person.*

o·ver·board (**ō′**vər-bôrd′) *adv.* Over the side of a boat: *He fell overboard.* ◆ **go overboard** To go to extremes, especially as a result of enthusiasm.

o·ver·book (ō′vər-**bo͝ok′**) *v.* **o·ver·booked, o·ver·book·ing, o·ver·books** *—tr.* To take more reservations for (a restaurant, for example) than there is room for: *The flight was overbooked, so some passengers had to take the next plane.* *—intr.* To take more reservations than there is room for: *Some restaurants overbook because so many customers don't show up.*

o·ver·bur·den (ō′vər-**bûr′**dn) *tr.v.* **o·ver·bur·dened, o·ver·bur·den·ing, o·ver·bur·dens** **1.** To burden with too much weight. **2.** To burden with too much work, care, or responsibility.

o·ver·came (ō′vər-**kām′**) *v.* Past tense of **overcome.**

o·ver·cast (**ō′**vər-kăst′) *adj.* **1.** Covered over, as with clouds or mist; cloudy. **2.** Gloomy; dark. ❖ *n.* A covering, as of mist or clouds.

o·ver·charge (ō′vər-**chärj′**) *tr.v.* **o·ver·charged, o·ver·charg·ing, o·ver·charg·es** **1.** To charge (someone) too high a price for something. **2.** To fill too full; overload. ❖ *n.* (**ō′**vər-chärj′) An excessive price or charge.

o·ver·coat (**ō′**vər-kōt′) *n.* A long, heavy coat for use in cold weather.

o·ver·come (ō′vər-**kŭm′**) *v.* **o·ver·came** (ō′vər-**kām′**), **o·ver·come, o·ver·com·ing, o·ver·comes** *—tr.* **1.** To defeat in a conflict or contest: *overcome a powerful team.* **2.** To get the better of; surmount: *overcome a problem.* **3.** To affect deeply; overpower: *Fear overcame him.* *—intr.* To be victorious.

o·ver·con·fi·dent (ō′vər-**kŏn′**fĭ-dənt) *adj.* Excessively confident. **—o′ver·con′fi·dence** *n.*

o·ver·crowd (ō′vər-**kroud′**) *tr.v.* **o·ver·crowd·ed, o·ver·crowd·ing, o·ver·crowds** To cause to be too crowded: *Having two games at once will overcrowd the gym.*

o·ver·de·vel·op (ō′vər-dĭ-**vĕl′**əp) *tr.v.* **o·ver·de·vel·oped, o·ver·de·vel·op·ing, o·ver·de·vel·ops** To develop to excess: *muscles overdeveloped by weightlifting.* **—o′ver·de·vel′op·ment** *n.*

o·ver·do (ō′vər-**do͞o′**) *tr.v.* **o·ver·did** (ō′vər-**dĭd′**), **o·ver·done** (ō′vər-**dŭn′**), **o·ver·do·ing, o·ver·does** (ō′vər-**dŭz′**) **1.** To do or use to excess; carry too far: *Don't overdo the workout or you will injure yourself.* **2.** To cook too long or too much.

❑ *These sound alike:* **overdo, overdue** (unpaid).

o·ver·dose (**ō′**vər-dōs′) *n.* An excessively large dose, as of medicine or a drug. ❖ *intr.v.* (ō′vər-**dōs′**) **o·ver·dosed, o·ver·dos·ing, o·ver·dos·es** To take an overdose.

o·ver·draft (**ō′**vər-drăft′) *n.* **1.** The act of overdrawing an account. **2.** The amount overdrawn.

o·ver·draw (ō′vər-**drô′**) *tr.v.* **o·ver·drew** (ō′vər-**dro͞o′**), **o·ver·drawn** (ō′vər-**drôn′**), **o·ver·draw·ing, o·ver·draws** **1.** To withdraw a sum that exceeds the available balance of (an account). **2.** To exaggerate; overstate: *I overdrew the seriousness of the problem.*

o·ver·dress (ō′vər-**drĕs′**) *tr. & intr.v.* **o·ver·dressed, o·ver·dress·ing, o·ver·dress·es** **1.** To dress in too formal or fancy a way for the occasion. **2.** To dress in clothes that are too warm for the occasion.

o·ver·drive (**ō′**vər-drīv′) *n.* **1.** A gear in a motor vehicle transmission that permits cruising at high speed with improved fuel efficiency. **2.** A state of heightened concentration or activity.

o·ver·due (ō′vər-**do͞o′**) *adj.* **1.** Unpaid after being due: *an overdue bill.* **2.** Later than scheduled or expected: *an overdue train.*

❑ *These sound alike:* **overdue, overdo** (do to excess).

o·ver·eat (ō′vər-**ēt′**) *intr.v.* **o·ver·ate** (ō′vər-**āt′**), **o·ver·eat·en** (ō′vər-**ēt′**n), **o·ver·eat·ing, o·ver·eats** To eat too much at one time.

o·ver·es·ti·mate (ō′vər-**ĕs′**tə-māt′) *tr.v.* **o·ver·es·ti·mat·ed, o·ver·es·ti·mat·ing, o·ver·es·ti·mates** **1.** To rate or estimate too highly. **2.** To value or esteem too highly. ❖ *n.* An estimate that is or proves to be too high.

o·ver·ex·pose (ō′vər-ĭk-**spōz′**) *tr.v.* **o·ver·ex·posed, o·ver·ex·pos·ing, o·ver·ex·pos·es** **1.** To expose too long or too much: *overexpose oneself to the sun.* **2.** To expose (a photographic film or plate) too long. **—o′ver·ex·po′sure** (ō′vər-ĭk-**spō′**zhər) *n.*

o·ver·flow (ō′vər-**flō′**) *v.* **o·ver·flowed, o·ver·flow·**

overalls

overhand

WRITERS CHOOSE THEIR WORDS

As displays go, it was **overkill**—too much stuff packed too closely together. But it had definitely attracted a crowd. People were staring in at the jar with eyes squinted and fingers pointed, whispering to themselves, trying to count the thousands of jelly beans.

—Brent Hartinger
Project Sweet Life

overlap
overlapping terra-cotta roof tiles

ă	pat	ôr	core
ā	pay	oi	boy
âr	care	ou	out
ä	father	o͝o	took
ĕ	pet	o͝or	lure
ē	be	o͞o	boot
ĭ	pit	ŭ	cut
ī	bite	ûr	urge
îr	pier	th	thin
ŏ	pot	*th*	this
ō	toe	zh	vision
ô	paw	ə	about

ing, o·ver·flows —*intr.* **1.** To flow or run over the top, brim, or banks. **2.** To be filled beyond capacity: *Your cup is overflowing.* —*tr.* **1.** To flow over (the top, brim, or banks): *The river overflows its banks every year.* **2.** To flow over; flood: *The river overflowed the streets.* **3.** To fill beyond capacity: *The crowd overflowed the stands.* ❖ *n.* (**ō′**vər-flō′) **1.** The act of overflowing. **2.** An amount or excess that overflows.

o·ver·grow (ō′vər-**grō′**) *v.* **o·ver·grew** (ō′vər-**gro͞o′**), **o·ver·grown** (ō′vər-**grōn′**), **o·ver·grow·ing, o·ver·grows** —*tr.* To cover over with growth: *The bushes overgrew the pathway.* —*intr.* To grow too much or larger than normal.

o·ver·growth (**ō′**vər-grōth′) *n.* A usually abundant growth over or on something: *an overgrowth of ivy.*

o·ver·hand (**ō′**vər-hănd′) also **o·ver·hand·ed** (ō′vər-**hăn′**dĭd) *adj.* Performed with the hand brought forward and down from the level of the shoulder: *an overhand stroke.* ❖ *adv.* In an overhand manner: *Throw the ball overhand.*

o·ver·hang (ō′vər-**hăng′**) *v.* **o·ver·hung** (ō′vər-**hŭng′**), **o·ver·hang·ing, o·ver·hangs** —*tr.* To project, extend, or jut out over: *A room overhangs the back porch.* —*intr.* To jut out; extend. ❖ *n.* (**ō′**vər-hăng′) Something that overhangs; a projection.

o·ver·haul (ō′vər-**hôl′** *or* **ō′**vər-hôl′) *tr.v.* **o·ver·hauled, o·ver·haul·ing, o·ver·hauls 1.** To inspect, examine, or review in order to repair or make changes: *overhaul a car's engine.* **2.** To revise or renovate extensively: *a proposal to overhaul the health care system.* ❖ *n.* (**ō′**vər-hôl′) The act or an example of overhauling: *an overhaul of the security system.*

o·ver·head (**ō′**vər-hĕd′) *adj.* Located above the level of the head: *an overhead light.* ❖ *n.* The ongoing operating expenses of a business, including rent, insurance, taxes, and electricity but excluding labor or materials. ❖ *adv.* (ō′vər-**hĕd′**) Above one's head: *birds darting overhead.*

overhead projector *n.* A machine used to project enlarged images onto a wall or screen from a transparency placed on a clear surface that is lighted from underneath.

o·ver·hear (ō′vər-**hîr′**) *tr.v.* **o·ver·heard** (ō′vər-**hûrd′**), **o·ver·hear·ing, o·ver·hears** To hear without being addressed by the speaker; hear accidentally.

o·ver·heat (ō′vər-**hēt′**) *tr. & intr.v.* **o·ver·heat·ed, o·ver·heat·ing, o·ver·heats** To make or become excessively hot: *The furnace overheated the room. The engine overheated.*

o·ver·hung (ō′vər-**hŭng′**) *v.* Past tense and past participle of **overhang.**

o·ver·joyed (ō′vər-**joid′**) *adj.* Extremely delighted.

o·ver·kill (**ō′**vər-kĭl′) *n.* **1.** Use of military force beyond the amount needed to destroy an enemy. **2.** An excess of what is necessary or appropriate: *Adding two posts to support the beam was overkill.*

o·ver·laid (ō′vər-**lād′**) *v.* Past tense and past participle of **overlay.**

o·ver·land (**ō′**vər-lănd′) *adv. & adj.* Over or across land: *He traveled overland. We made an overland journey.*

o·ver·lap (ō′vər-**lăp′**) *v.* **o·ver·lapped, o·ver·lap·ping, o·ver·laps** —*tr.* **1.** To lie over; cover part of: *The shingles overlap one another.* **2.** To have an area in common with: *The range of the moose overlaps that of the deer.* —*intr.* **1.** To lie over and partly cover something: *The scales of a fish overlap, forming a protective covering.* **2.** To have some part in common; coincide partly: *Our vacations overlap.* ❖ *n.* (**ō′**vər-lăp′) **1.** A part that overlaps. **2.** An example of overlapping.

o·ver·lay (ō′vər-**lā′**) *tr.v.* **o·ver·laid** (ō′vər-**lād′**), **o·ver·lay·ing, o·ver·lays 1.** To lay or spread over or on: *We overlaid the table with a sheet.* **2.** To cover or decorate with a surface layer: *He overlaid the wood with silver.* **3.** To create (a new telephone area code) having the same boundaries as an existing one. ❖ *n.* (**ō′**vər-lā′) **1.** Something that is laid over or covers something else. **2.** A layer or decoration, such as gold leaf or wood veneer, applied to a surface. **3.** An area code whose boundaries are the same as another area code.

o·ver·load (ō′vər-**lōd′**) *tr.v.* **o·ver·load·ed, o·ver·load·ing, o·ver·loads** To put too large a load in or on: *overload a bridge; overload an electric circuit.* ❖ *n.* (**ō′**vər-lōd′) An excessively large load.

o·ver·look (ō′vər-**lo͝ok′**) *tr.v.* **o·ver·looked, o·ver·look·ing, o·ver·looks 1a.** To look over from a higher place: *We overlooked the valley from the cliff.* **b.** To provide a view of: *The restaurant overlooks the bay.* **2.** To fail to notice or consider: *overlook an important detail.* **3.** To ignore deliberately; disregard: *I overlooked her rude remark and kept on studying.* ❖ *n.* (**ō′**vər-lo͝ok′) An elevated place that provides a view of something.

o·ver·lord (**ō′**vər-lôrd′) *n.* **1.** A lord having power over other lords. **2.** A person who dominates others.

o·ver·ly (**ō′**vər-lē) *adv.* To an excessive degree: *an overly long movie.*

o·ver·much (ō′vər-**mŭch′**) *adj.* Too much; excessive.

o·ver·night (**ō′**vər-nīt′) *adj.* **1.** Lasting for a night: *an overnight trip.* **2.** For use over a single night: *an overnight bag.* **3.** Happening as if in a single night; sudden: *an overnight success.* **4.** Mailed for guaranteed delivery on the next day. ❖ *adv.* (ō′vər-**nīt′**) **1.** During or for the length of a night: *Soak the beans overnight.* **2.** In or as if in the course of a night; suddenly: *became a sensation overnight.*

o·ver·pass (**ō′**vər-păs′) *n.* A roadway or bridge that crosses above another roadway or thoroughfare.

o·ver·pay (ō′vər-**pā′**) *v.* **o·ver·paid** (ō′vər-**pād′**), **o·ver·pay·ing, o·ver·pays** —*tr.* **1.** To pay (someone) too much. **2.** To pay an amount in excess of (a sum due). —*intr.* To pay too much. **—o′ver·pay′ment** *n.*

o·ver·pop·u·late (ō′vər-**pŏp′**yə-lāt′) *tr.v.* **o·ver·pop·u·lat·ed, o·ver·pop·u·lat·ing, o·ver·pop·u·lates** To fill (an area) with excessive population. **—o′ver·pop′u·la′tion** *n.*

o·ver·pow·er (ō′vər-**pou′**ər) *tr.v.* **o·ver·pow·ered, o·ver·pow·er·ing, o·ver·pow·ers 1.** To get the better of or conquer by superior force: *Our hitters overpowered their pitchers.* **2.** To affect strongly; overwhelm: *The heat overpowered the children, and they had to leave the beach.*

o·ver·pow·er·ing (ō′vər-**pou′**ər-ĭng) *adj.* So strong as not to be withstood.

o·ver·pro·duce (ō′vər-prə-**do͞os′**) *tr.v.* **o·ver·pro·duced, o·ver·pro·duc·ing, o·ver·pro·duc·es** To produce too much or too many of: *The factory overproduced that particular model of truck.* **—o′ver·pro·duc′tion** (ō′vər-prə-**dŭk′**shən) *n.*

o·ver·ran (ō′vər-**răn′**) *v.* Past tense of **overrun.**

o·ver·rate (ō′vər-**rāt′**) *tr.v.* **o·ver·rat·ed, o·ver·rat·ing, o·ver·rates** To rate too highly.

o·ver·reach (ō′vər-**rēch′**) *v.* **o·ver·reached, o·ver·reach·ing, o·ver·reach·es** —*tr.* **1.** To extend or reach over or beyond: *The beam overreaches the post by an inch.* **2.** To miss by reaching too far or attempting too much: *overreach a goal.* **3.** To defeat (oneself) by going too far or doing too much. —*intr.* **1.** To reach or go too far. **2.** To defeat oneself by trying too hard.

o·ver·ride (ō′vər-**rīd′**) *tr.v.* **o·ver·rode** (ō′vər-**rōd′**), **o·ver·rid·den** (ō′vər-**rĭd′**n), **o·ver·rid·ing, o·ver·rides 1.** To ride across or beyond: *The cowboys overrode the border and turned back.* **2.** To trample on (something). **3.** To prevail over; surpass: *His concern for you overrides all other considerations.* **4.** To declare null and void; set aside: *The president's veto was overridden by Congress.*

o·ver·rule (ō′vər-**ro͞ol′**) *tr.v.* **o·ver·ruled, o·ver·rul·ing, o·ver·rules 1.** To declare as invalid or as contrary to rules or law: *The judge overruled the objection of the pros-*

ecutor. **2.** To reject or render invalid a decision made by (someone).

o·ver·run (ō′vər-**rŭn′**) *tr.v.* **o·ver·ran** (ō′vər-**răn′**), **o·ver·run, o·ver·run·ning, o·ver·runs 1.** To invade and occupy: *The army overran the enemy trenches.* **2.** To spread or swarm over destructively: *Weeds overran the garden.* **3.** To occupy or move throughout in large numbers: *Tourists overran the hotel.* **4.** To overflow: *The river overran its banks.* **5.** To run or extend beyond; exceed: *The plane overran the runway.*

o·ver·seas (ō′vər-**sēz′** *or* **ō′**vər-sēz′) *adv.* Across the sea; abroad: *He was sent overseas.* ❖ *adj.* Relating to places across the sea: *an overseas flight.*

o·ver·see (ō′vər-**sē′**) *tr.v.* **o·ver·saw** (ō′vər-**sô′**), **o·ver·seen** (ō′vər-**sēn′**), **o·ver·see·ing, o·ver·sees** To watch over and direct; supervise.

o·ver·se·er (**ō′**vər-sē′ər) *n.* A person who watches over and directs workers.

o·ver·shad·ow (ō′vər-**shăd′**ō) *tr.v.* **o·ver·shad·owed, o·ver·shad·ow·ing, o·ver·shad·ows 1.** To cast a shadow over. **2.** To make insignificant in comparison: *Some writers overshadow their contemporaries.*

o·ver·shoe (**ō′**vər-shōō′) *n.* A shoe or boot worn over an ordinary shoe for protection from water, snow, or cold.

o·ver·shoot (ō′vər-**shōōt′**) *v.* **o·ver·shot** (ō′vər-**shŏt′**), **o·ver·shoot·ing, o·ver·shoots** *—tr.* **1.** To shoot or pass over or beyond: *overshoot a target.* **2.** To fly beyond or past: *The plane overshot the runway.* *—intr.* To shoot or go too far.

o·ver·shot (**ō′**vər-shŏt′) *v.* Past tense and past participle of **overshoot.** ❖ *adj.* **1.** Having an upper part that extends out past the lower part: *an overshot jaw.* **2.** Operated or turned by a stream of water that passes over its top: *an overshot water wheel.*

o·ver·sight (**ō′**vər-sīt′) *n.* **1.** An accidental omission. **2.** Watchful care or management; supervision.

o·ver·size (**ō′**vər-**sīz′**) also **o·ver·sized** (**ō′**vər-**sīzd′**) *adj.* Larger than the usual, expected, or required size: *an oversize sofa.*

o·ver·sleep (ō′vər-**slēp′**) *intr.v.* **o·ver·slept** (o′vər-**slĕpt′**), **o·ver·sleep·ing, o·ver·sleeps** To sleep longer than planned.

o·ver·state (ō′vər-**stāt′**) *tr.v.* **o·ver·stat·ed, o·ver·stat·ing, o·ver·states** To state too strongly; exaggerate: *Don't overstate the problem.* **—o′ver·state′ment** *n.*

o·ver·stay (ō′vər-**stā′**) *tr.v.* **o·ver·stayed, o·ver·stay·ing, o·ver·stays** To stay past an expected duration of: *He overstayed his welcome.*

o·ver·step (ō′vər-**stĕp′**) *tr.v.* **o·ver·stepped, o·ver·step·ping, o·ver·steps** To go beyond (a limit or bound): *She overstepped the rules.*

o·ver·stock (ō′vər-**stŏk′**) *tr.v.* **o·ver·stocked, o·ver·stock·ing, o·ver·stocks** To stock with more of (something) than is necessary or desirable. ❖ *n.* (**ō′**vər-stŏk′) An excessive supply.

o·ver·sup·ply (**ō′**vər-sə-plī′) *n., pl.* **o·ver·sup·plies** A supply in excess of what is required. ❖ *tr.v.* (ō′vər-sə-**plī′**) **o·ver·sup·plied, o·ver·sup·ply·ing, o·ver·sup·plies** To supply in excess.

o·vert (ō-**vûrt′** *or* **ō′**vûrt′) *adj.* Not concealed or hidden; open: *an overt act of war.* [From Middle English, from Old French *ovrir*, to open.] **—o·vert′ly** *adv.*

o·ver·take (ō′vər-**tāk′**) *tr.v.* **o·ver·took** (ō′vər-**tŏŏk′**), **o·ver·tak·en** (ō′vər-**tā′**kən), **o·ver·tak·ing, o·ver·takes 1.** To catch up with: *We overtook the other hikers on the mountain road.* **2.** To pass after catching up with: *The car overtook him on the last lap.* **3.** To come upon unexpectedly: *A violent storm overtook him.*

o·ver·tax (ō′vər-**tăks′**) *tr.v.* **o·ver·taxed, o·ver·tax·ing, o·ver·tax·es 1.** To impose an excessive tax or taxes on. **2.** To subject to an excessive burden or strain: *The long drive overtaxed us, and we spent a day recovering.*

o·ver·throw (ō′vər-**thrō′**) *tr.v.* **o·ver·threw** (ō′vər-**thrōō′**), **o·ver·thrown** (ō′vər-**thrōn′**), **o·ver·throw·ing, o·ver·throws 1.** To bring about the downfall or destruction of: *overthrow the government.* **2.** To throw a ball beyond (an intended mark): *She overthrew first base.* **3.** To throw over; overturn: *overthrow a table.* ❖ *n.* (**ō′**vər-thrō′) **1.** The downfall or destruction, as of a government. **2.** The act of throwing a ball beyond an intended mark.

o·ver·time (**ō′**vər-tīm′) *n.* **1.** Time worked in addition to regular working hours. **2.** Payment for this additional time worked. **3.** In sports, a period of playing time added when the regular period of play has ended in a tied score. ❖ *adv.* Beyond an established time limit, such as working hours: *work overtime.*

o·ver·tone (**ō′**vər-tōn′) *n.* **1.** Any of a series of tones whose frequency is an exact multiple of a fundamental tone. These overtones, heard along with the fundamental tone, produce the characteristic timbre of a given musical sound. **2.** An accompanying effect; a suggestion or implication: *The ambassador's remarks were full of ominous overtones.*

o·ver·took (ō′vər-**tŏŏk′**) *v.* Past tense of **overtake.**

o·ver·ture (**ō′**vər-chŏŏr′) *n.* **1a.** An instrumental composition written as an introduction to an opera, oratorio, or suite. **b.** A similar instrumental work meant to be performed as an independent concert piece. **2.** An offer or proposal indicating readiness to negotiate or establish something: *making peace overtures.*

o·ver·turn (ō′vər-**tûrn′**) *v.* **o·ver·turned, o·ver·turn·ing, o·ver·turns** *—tr.* **1.** To turn over or capsize; upset: *overturn a glass of water.* **2.** To overthrow; defeat. **3.** To legally invalidate or reverse: *The Supreme Court overturned the lower court's ruling.* *—intr.* To turn over or capsize: *The raft overturned in the rapids.*

o·ver·use (ō′vər-**yōōz′**) *tr.v.* **o·ver·used, o·ver·us·ing, o·ver·us·es** To use to excess. ❖ *n.* (ō′vər-**yōōs′**) Too much or excessive use.

o·ver·view (**ō′**vər-vyōō′) *n.* A broad comprehensive view; an overall survey.

o·ver·ween·ing (ō′vər-**wē′**nĭng) *adj.* Presumptuously arrogant; overbearing. [From Middle English *overweniing* : *over* + *wenen*, to think, suppose.]

o·ver·weight (ō′vər-**wāt′**) *adj.* Weighing more than is normal, healthy, or required.

o·ver·whelm (ō′vər-**wĕlm′**) *tr.v.* **o·ver·whelmed, o·ver·whelm·ing, o·ver·whelms 1.** To surge over and submerge; engulf: *Waves overwhelmed the dock.* **2.** To overcome completely; overpower: *The rebels overwhelmed the garrison.* **3.** To affect deeply: *Sadness overwhelmed me.* [From Middle English *overwhelmen* : *over* + *whelmen*, to overturn.]

o·ver·whelm·ing (ō′vər-**wĕl′**mĭng) *adj.* Overpowering in effect or strength: *an overwhelming majority.* **—o′ver·whelm′ing·ly** *adv.*

o·ver·work (ō′vər-**wûrk′**) *tr.v.* **o·ver·worked, o·ver·work·ing, o·ver·works** To cause to work too hard: *The manager overworks her.* ❖ *n.* (**ō′**vər-wûrk′) Too much work.

o·ver·wrought (ō′vər-**rôt′**) *adj.* **1.** Nervous or excited; very agitated. **2.** Extremely elaborate or lavish; overdone: *an overwrought prose style.*

o·vi·duct (**ō′**vĭ-dŭkt′) *n.* **1.** A tube that eggs travel through after they leave an ovary in egg-laying mammals. **2.** A fallopian tube.

o·vip·a·rous (ō-**vĭp′**ər-əs) *adj.* Producing eggs that hatch outside the body: *Birds are oviparous.*

o·vi·pos·i·tor (ō′və-**pŏz′**ĭ-tər) *n.* **1.** A tube in many female insects that extends from the end of the abdomen and is used to lay eggs. **2.** A similar organ of certain other animals, such as turtles.

o·void (**ō′**void′) *adj.* Having the shape of an egg: *an ovoid face.* ❖ *n.* Something having this shape.

overpass

SCIENCE

ozone For the earth's organisms, including people, **ozone** can be a lifesaver or a threat to health, depending on how high it is found in the atmosphere. Ozone in the lower atmosphere is a pollutant and contributes to respiratory diseases like asthma. But the ozone in the "ozone layer" of the upper atmosphere protects us by absorbing dangerous forms of ultraviolet radiation from the sun. In the 1980s, scientists discovered that the ozone had disappeared from parts of the ozone layer, especially over Antarctica, creating an "ozone hole" that allowed high levels of ultraviolet radiation to reach the earth. The destruction of the ozone was caused mostly by the release into the atmosphere of chlorofluorocarbons and other industrial chemicals. In 1987, an international treaty was signed that called for gradually phasing out the use of these chemicals.

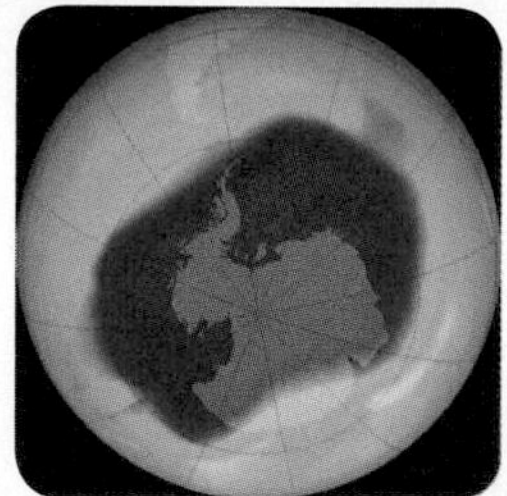

ozone hole
colorized satellite image of the atmosphere over Antarctica in 2006

ă	pat	ôr	core
ā	pay	oi	boy
âr	care	ou	out
ä	father	o͝o	took
ĕ	pet	o͝or	lure
ē	be	o͞o	boot
ĭ	pit	ŭ	cut
ī	bite	ûr	urge
îr	pier	th	thin
ŏ	pot	*th*	this
ō	toe	zh	vision
ô	paw	ə	about

o·vo·vi·vip·a·rous (ō′vō-vī-**vĭp′**ər-əs) *adj.* Producing eggs that hatch within the female's body, as in some fishes and reptiles and many invertebrate animals.

o·vu·late (**ō′**vyə-lāt′ *or* **ŏv′**yə-lāt′) *intr.v.* **o·vu·lat·ed, o·vu·lat·ing, o·vu·lates** To produce or discharge an egg cell. —**o′vu·la′tion** *n.*

o·vule (**ō′**vyo͞ol *or* **ŏv′**yo͞ol) *n.* A small structure in a plant ovary that contains the egg cell and becomes a seed after it has been fertilized.

o·vum (**ō′**vəm) *n., pl.* **o·va** (**ō′**və) A female reproductive cell; an egg.

owe (ō) *v.* **owed, ow·ing, owes** —*tr.* **1a.** To be indebted to the amount of: *He owes five dollars for the meal.* **b.** To be indebted for: *The tenants owe rent for two months.* **c.** To be in debt to: *We owe the plumber for fixing the pipe.* **2.** To be under obligation to give: *owe an apology.* **3.** To have or possess as something derived from or bestowed by; be obliged for: *She owes her good health to exercise.* —*intr.* To be in debt. [From Old English *āgan*, to possess.]

❑ *These sound alike:* **owe, O**[1] (exclamation), **oh** (expression of emotion).

Ow·ens (**ō′**ĭnz), **Jesse** 1913–1980. American athlete who won four gold medals in track and field at the 1936 Olympics.

ow·ing (**ō′**ĭng) *adj.* Still to be paid; due: *a sum that was owing.*

owing to *prep.* Because of; on account of.

owl (oul) *n.* Any of various birds of prey that are usually active at night and have a large head, large forward-facing eyes, a short hooked bill, and a flat round face. [From Old English *ūle*.]

owl·et (**ou′**lĭt) *n.* A young or small owl.

own (ōn) *adj.* Relating to or belonging to oneself or itself: *Jim's own book; my own home.* ❖ *n.* Something that belongs to one: *He built the device but the idea was my own.* ❖ *tr.v.* **owned, own·ing, owns 1.** To be legally entitled to keep, use, or sell (something): *She owns a car.* **2.** To acknowledge or admit: *I own that I've made a mistake.* ◆ **of (one's) own** Belonging completely to oneself. **on (one's) own 1.** By one's own efforts: *I planted the garden on my own.* **2.** Responsible for oneself: *He is now out of college and on his own.* **own up** To make a full confession or acknowledgment: *She owned up about the broken window.* [From Old English *āgen*.]

own·er (**ōn′**ər) *n.* Someone who owns something, especially someone who has legal title to something: *a car owner.*

own·er·ship (**ō′**nər-shĭp′) *n.* The condition of being an owner; legal right to possess a thing.

own goal *n.* A goal scored by a defender on his or her team's goal by a mistaken play, such as a misdirected pass.

ox (ŏks) *n., pl.* **ox·en** (**ŏk′**sən) **1.** A castrated adult male of domestic cattle, used for heavy work or for beef. **2.** Any of several animals that are related to or resemble domestic cattle. [From Old English *oxa*.]

ox·al·ic acid (ŏk-**săl′**ĭk) *n.* A poisonous acid found in many plants, including spinach, tomatoes, and sweet potatoes. It is used as a bleach and rust remover.

ox·bow (**ŏks′**bō′) *n.* **1.** A U-shaped piece of wood that fits under the neck of an ox, with its upper ends attached to the bar of the yoke. **2.** A U-shaped bend in a river.

ox·en (**ŏk′**sən) *n.* Plural of **ox.**

ox·ford (**ŏks′**fərd) *n.* **1.** A low shoe that laces over the instep. **2.** A tightly woven cotton cloth used primarily for men's shirts.

Ox·ford (**ŏks′**fərd) A city of south-central England on the Thames River west-northwest of London. Oxford University was founded here in the 1100s.

ox·i·da·tion (ŏk′sĭ-**dā′**shən) *n.* **1.** The chemical combination of a substance with oxygen. **2.** A chemical reaction in which the atoms of an element lose electrons, thus undergoing an increase in valence.

ox·ide (**ŏk′**sīd′) *n.* A compound of oxygen and another element or a radical. Water (H_2O) is an oxide.

ox·i·dize (**ŏk′**sĭ-dīz′) *v.* **ox·i·dized, ox·i·diz·ing, ox·i·diz·es** —*tr.* **1.** To combine with oxygen; make into an oxide. **2.** To coat with oxide: *Air oxidizes the surface of aluminum.* —*intr.* To become oxidized.

ox·i·diz·er (**ŏk′**sĭ-dī′zər) *n.* A substance that oxidizes another substance, especially one that supports the combustion of fuel; an oxidizing agent.

ox·tail (**ŏks′**tāl′) *n.* The tail of any kind of cattle, especially when used for food.

ox·y·a·cet·y·lene (ŏk′sē-ə-**sĕt′**l-ĭn *or* ŏk′sē-ə-**sĕt′**l-ēn′) *adj.* Using a mixture of oxygen and acetylene: *an oxyacetylene welding torch.*

ox·y·gen (**ŏk′**sĭ-jən) *n. Symbol* **O** An element that in its colorless and odorless gaseous form, O_2, makes up about one fifth of the atmosphere by volume. Oxygen occurs in many compounds, such as water, and is found in all living things. Atomic number 8. See **Periodic Table.** [From French *oxygène* : Greek *oxus*, sharp, acid + French *-gène*, producer.]

ox·y·gen·ate (**ŏk′**sĭ-jə-nāt′) *tr.v.* **ox·y·gen·at·ed, ox·y·gen·at·ing, ox·y·gen·ates** To combine, treat, or mix with oxygen. **—ox′y·gen·a′tion** *n.*

oxygen mask *n.* A covering that fits closely over the mouth and nose and is connected by a hose or tube to a supply of oxygen.

oxygen tent *n.* An enclosure that is placed over the head and shoulders of a patient who is having difficulty breathing to provide additional oxygen.

ox·y·he·mo·glo·bin (ŏk′sē-**hē′**mə-glō′bĭn) *n.* A bright-red chemical complex of hemoglobin and oxygen that transports oxygen from the lungs to the tissues via the blood.

ox·y·mo·ron (ŏk′sē-**môr′**ŏn′) *n., pl.* **ox·y·mo·rons** or **ox·y·mo·ra** (ŏk′sē-**môr′**ə) An expression combining terms that clash or contradict each other, as *sweet sorrow.* [From Greek *oxumōros*, pointedly foolish : *oxus*, sharp + *mōros*, dull.]

o·yez (**ō′**yĕs′ *or* **ō′**yĕz′ *or* ō′**yā′**) *interj.* An expression used three times in a row to introduce the opening of a law court. [From Middle English *oyes*, from Anglo-Norman *oyez*, hear ye.]

oys·ter (**oi′**stər) *n.* Any of several sea mollusks of shallow waters, having a rough, irregularly shaped, hinged shell. Many kinds of oysters are used as food, and some kinds produce pearls inside their shells. [From Middle English *oistre*, from Greek *ostreon*.]

oz also **oz.** *abbr.* An abbreviation of ounce.

O·zark Plateau or **O·zark Mountains** (**ō′**zärk′) An upland region of the south-central United States extending from southwest Missouri and northwest Arkansas into eastern Oklahoma.

o·zone (**ō′**zōn′) *n.* An unstable, poisonous form of gaseous oxygen, O_3, that forms naturally in the upper atmosphere and is also produced in the lower atmosphere when certain pollutants are exposed to sunlight. It is a highly reactive oxidizing agent used to deodorize air, purify water, and treat industrial wastes. [From German *Ozon*, from Greek *ozein*, to smell.] —SEE NOTE.

ozone hole *n.* A large area of the ozone layer over Antarctica that annually becomes depleted of ozone by the action of pollutants.

ozone layer *n.* A region of the atmosphere lying in the stratosphere at an altitude of 10 to 20 miles (15 to 30 kilometers), that contains a relatively high concentration of ozone. This ozone absorbs ultraviolet radiation from the sun that would otherwise be dangerous to living things.

p or **P** (pē) *n., pl.* **p's** or **P's** also **ps** or **Ps** The 16th letter of the English alphabet.

P The symbol for the element **phosphorus.**

p. *abbr.* An abbreviation of: **1.** page. **2.** participle. **3.** pint.

pa (pä) *n. Informal* Father.

Pa The symbol for the element **protactinium.**

PA *abbr.* An abbreviation of: **1.** Pennsylvania. **2.** physician assistant. **3.** also **P/A** power of attorney. **4.** public-address system.

pa'an·ga (päng′gə) *n.* The basic monetary unit of Tonga.

pace (pās) *n.* **1a.** A step made in walking; a stride. **b.** The distance spanned by such a step, specifically a unit of length equal to 30 inches (about 76 centimeters). **2a.** The rate of speed at which a person or thing walks or runs. **b.** The speed at which an activity proceeds: *the fast pace of city living.* **3.** A gait of a horse in which the feet on one side leave and return to the ground together. ❖ *v.* **paced, pac·ing, pac·es** —*tr.* **1.** To walk back and forth across: *He paced the floor impatiently.* **2.** To measure by counting the steps needed to cover a distance: *paced off the distance from the door to the stairs.* **3.** To set or regulate the speed of. —*intr.* To walk with long deliberate steps: *The tiger paced in its cage.* [From Middle English *pas,* from Old French, from Latin *passus,* stretched out.]

pace·mak·er (pās′mā′kər) *n.* **1.** A person or thing that sets the pace in a race; a pacer. **2.** An electronic device used to regulate the heartbeat.

pac·er (pā′sər) *n.* **1.** A horse trained to move at a pace. **2.** A person or thing that sets the pace in a race.

pach·y·derm (păk′ĭ-dûrm′) *n.* Any of various large thick-skinned mammals, such as an elephant, rhinoceros, or hippopotamus. [From Greek *pakhudermos,* thick-skinned : *pakhus,* thick + *derma,* skin.]

pa·cif·ic (pə-sĭf′ĭk) *adj.* **1.** Loving peace; peaceful: *a pacific people.* **2.** Peaceful in nature; serene: *a pacific scene.* [From Latin *pācificus,* from *pāx,* peace.] —**pa·cif′i·cal·ly** *adv.*

Pacific Islander *n.* A member of one of the peoples native to the islands of the southern, western, and central Pacific Ocean.

Pacific Ocean The world's largest ocean, extending from the western Americas to eastern Asia and Australia.

Pacific Standard Time *n.* Standard time as reckoned in the eighth time zone west of Greenwich, England. The west coast of the United States is in this region.

pac·i·fi·er (păs′ə-fī′ər) *n.* A rubber or plastic nipple or teething ring for a baby to suck on.

pac·i·fism (păs′ə-fĭz′əm) *n.* Opposition to war or violence as a means of solving disputes.

pac·i·fist (păs′ə-fĭst) *n.* A person who favors peace and tries to find peaceful means to solving disputes.

pac·i·fy (păs′ə-fī′) *tr.v.* **pac·i·fied, pac·i·fy·ing, pac·i·fies 1.** To quiet; calm: *pacify a baby.* **2.** To end war, fighting, or violence in (a region or country), especially by military force: *pacify the frontier.* —**pac′i·fi·ca′tion** *n.*

pack (păk) *n.* **1.** A container made to be carried on the body of a person or of an animal such as a donkey or camel, often with the things in it. **2a.** A small package containing a standard number of identical or similar items: *a pack of matches.* **b.** A set of related items: *a pack of cards.* **3a.** A group of animals that hunt together: *a pack of wolves.* **b.** A group of people, especially when massed together: *a pack of teenagers in the mall.* **4.** A large amount: *a pack of trouble.* **5.** Material, such as gauze, applied to a part of the body or inserted into a body opening or wound as treatment for an injury or disorder. ❖ *v.* **packed, pack·ing, packs** —*tr.* **1.** To put into a bag, box, or other container, as for storage, preserving, or selling: *pack groceries; pack clothes.* **2.** To fill (a container) with items: *pack a suitcase.* **3.** To press together: *He packed the sugar into the measuring cup.* **4a.** To bring together; crowd: *The ushers packed the theatergoers into the hall.* **b.** To fill up tight; cram: *The crowd packed the stadium.* **c.** To include in: *A lot of information is packed into a dictionary.* **5.** To wrap tightly for protection or to prevent leakage: *pack a valve stem.* **6.** To treat medically with a pack: *pack a wound.* **7.** *Informal* To have ready for action: *pack a pistol.* **8.** To arrange (a jury or panel, for example) so as to be favorable to one's purposes. **9.** To cause to go or leave: *pack the kids off to camp.* —*intr.* **1.** To put one's clothes or things into a box or luggage, as for traveling or storage: *I've already packed for my trip.* **2.** To become pressed together: *Brown sugar packs well for measuring.* **3.** To be capable of being stored compactly. ◆ **pack it in** *Informal* To stop work or an activity: *At 5:00, I packed it in and went home.*

pack·age (păk′ĭj) *n.* **1.** A wrapped or boxed object; a parcel. **2.** A container in which something is stored, transported, or sold. **3.** A combination of items considered, offered, or sold as a unit. ❖ *tr.v.* **pack·aged, pack·ag·ing, pack·ag·es 1.** To place in a package or make a package of. **2.** To design the wrapping or package for (a product).

package store *n.* A store that sells bottles or cans of alcoholic beverages for consumption away from its premises; a liquor store.

pack animal *n.* An animal, such as a mule, used to carry loads.

packed (păkt) *adj.* **1.** Crowded to capacity: *The concert hall was packed.* **2.** Compressed: *packed snow.* **3.** *Informal* Filled with: *an action-packed trip.*

pack·er (păk′ər) *n.* A person who packs goods, especially meat products, for transportation and sale.

pack·et (păk′ĭt) *n.* **1.** A small pouch used to distribute single portions of products in the form of liquids, powders, or small pieces: *a ketchup packet.* **2.** A small package or bundle, as of mail.

pack ice *n.* A large area of sea ice consisting of a mixture of floating ice fragments packed or squeezed together.

pack·ing (păk′ĭng) *n.* **1.** The act or process of one that packs, especially the processing and packaging of food

pack ice

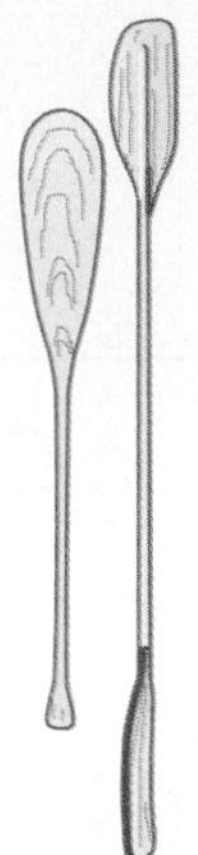

paddle[1]
left: canoe paddle
right: kayak paddle

pagoda

ă	pat	ôr	core
ā	pay	oi	boy
âr	care	ou	out
ä	father	ŏŏ	took
ĕ	pet	ŏŏr	lure
ē	be	ōō	boot
ĭ	pit	ŭ	cut
ī	bite	ûr	urge
îr	pier	th	thin
ŏ	pot	*th*	this
ō	toe	zh	vision
ô	paw	ə	about

products. **2.** A material used to prevent leakage or seepage, as around a pipe joint. **3.** Material inserted into a body opening or wound as part of a medical treatment.

pack·ing·house (păk′ĭng-hous′) *n.* **1.** A company that slaughters, processes, and packs livestock into meat and meat products. **2.** A company that processes and packs food products other than meat.

pack rat *n.* **1.** Any of various rats of North or Central America that collect a variety of small objects in their nests. **2.** *Informal* A person who collects or accumulates miscellaneous objects.

pack·sack (păk′săk′) *n.* A canvas or leather pack carried strapped to the shoulders; a knapsack.

pact (păkt) *n.* **1.** A formal agreement, as between nations; a treaty. **2.** A compact; a bargain.

pad[1] (păd) *n.* **1.** A cushion or mass of soft, firmly packed material used for stuffing, lining, or protection against injury: *chair pads; knee pads.* **2.** A piece of sports equipment made of a shaped cushioning material often attached to a hard outer surface and worn to protect against blows, collisions, or shots. **3.** A small, usually flat piece of material: *a steel-wool pad for scouring dishes.* **4.** A number of sheets of paper of the same size stacked one on top of the other and glued together at one end: *a memo pad.* **5a.** The broad floating leaf of a water lily or similar plant. **b.** The flattened fleshy stem of a cactus such as a prickly pear. **6a.** The fleshy underside of the end of a finger or toe. **b.** The fleshy part on the underside of the toes and feet of many animals. **7.** *Slang* An apartment or room. ❖ *tr.v.* **pad·ded, pad·ding, pads 1.** To line, stuff, or cover with soft, firmly packed material: *Are the shoulders of the jacket padded?* **2.** To lengthen, especially with unnecessary or false information: *pad a term paper; pad an expense account.*

pad[2] (păd) *intr.v.* **pad·ded, pad·ding, pads** To go on foot, especially with a soft, almost inaudible step: *He padded about the house barefoot.* ❖ *n.* A muffled sound of or resembling that of soft footsteps: *the soft pad of feet.* [Akin to Middle Dutch *pedden*, to tread a path.]

pad·ding (păd′ĭng) *n.* **1.** Material used to stuff, fill, protect, or line something. **2.** Unnecessary material added to a speech or written work to lengthen it.

pad·dle[1] (păd′l) *n.* **1.** A short wooden implement with a flat blade at one end, or sometimes at both ends, used without an oarlock to propel a small boat, such as a canoe or kayak. **2.** A light wooden or plastic racket used in playing table tennis and similar games. **3.** A blade or shovellike implement used for stirring or mixing. **4.** A flat appendage of certain animals, used for swimming; a flipper. ❖ *v.* **pad·dled, pad·dling, pad·dles** —*intr.* **1.** To propel a boat with a paddle or paddles. **2.** To swim by repeated short strokes of the limbs. —*tr.* **1.** To propel (a boat) with a paddle or paddles: *Paddle your own canoe.* **2.** To beat or spank with a paddle. [From Middle English *padell*, spadelike scraper for cleaning plowshares, of unknown origin.] —**pad′dler** *n.*

pad·dle[2] (păd′l) *intr.v.* **pad·dled, pad·dling, pad·dles** To splash gently or playfully in shallow water. [Perhaps akin to English *puddle* and Low German *paddlen*, to tramp about.]

pad·dle·board (păd′l-bôrd′) *n.* A surfboard or similar long narrow board that a rider propels over the water, often in a standing position by means of a long-handled paddle. ❖ *intr.v.* **pad·dle·board·ed, pad·dle·board·ing, pad·dle·boards** To propel a paddleboard.

pad·dle·fish (păd′l-fĭsh′) *n.* A large fish of the Mississippi River and its branches, having a long snout shaped like a paddle.

paddle wheel *n.* A wheel with boards or paddles around its rim, used to propel a ship.

pad·dock (păd′ək) *n.* A fenced field or area, usually near a stable, in which horses are kept, as for grazing or exercising.

pad·dy (păd′ē) *n., pl.* **pad·dies 1.** A flooded or specially watered field in which rice is grown. **2.** Rice in the husk.

pad·lock (păd′lŏk′) *n.* A detachable lock with a U-shaped bar hinged at one end, designed to be passed through a staple, link, or ring and then snapped into a hole in the body of the lock. ❖ *tr.v.* **pad·locked, pad·lock·ing, pad·locks** To lock up with or as if with a padlock.

pa·dre (pä′drā) *n.* **1.** A priest in Italy, Spain, Portugal, or Latin America. **2.** A form of address for a priest in any of these countries.

pad thai (păd′ tī′ *or* päd′ tī′) *n.* A Thai dish of stir-fried rice noodles, egg, peanuts, and other ingredients.

pae·an (pē′ən) *n.* **1.** A fervent expression of joy or praise. **2.** A hymn of thanksgiving to a god.

pa·gan (pā′gən) *n.* **1.** A person who belongs to a religion that worships more than one god, especially a person who belongs to the ancient Greek, Roman, or Celtic religion. **2.** *Offensive* **a.** A person who has no religion. **b.** A person who belongs to a religion other than Judaism, Christianity, or Islam. ❖ *adj.* Relating to pagans or paganism: *pagan gods.*

pa·gan·ism (pā′gə-nĭz′əm) *n.* **1.** Pagan beliefs or practices, such as the worship of nature deities. **2.** The condition of being a pagan.

page[1] (pāj) *n.* **1a.** A side of a sheet of paper, as in a book or newspaper. **b.** The writing or printing on one side of a sheet of paper. **2.** A webpage. **3.** A memorable event: *a new page in the course of human history.* ❖ *intr.v.* **paged, pag·ing, pag·es** To turn pages: *paging through a book.* [From Old French, from Latin *pāgina*.]

page[2] (pāj) *n.* **1.** A boy who attended a medieval knight as a first stage of training for knighthood. **2.** A person employed to run errands, carry messages, or act as a guide, as in a hotel or club. ❖ *tr.v.* **paged, pag·ing, pag·es 1.** To summon or call (a person) by name, as over a loudspeaker. **2.** To contact (someone) by sending a message to his or her pager: *The detective was paged during dinner and left the room to return the call.* [From Middle English, from Old French, of unknown origin.]

pag·eant (păj′ənt) *n.* **1.** A play or dramatic spectacle usually based on an event in history. **2a.** A procession or celebration, especially one involving costumed performers or contestants. **b.** A beauty contest.

pag·eant·ry (păj′ən-trē) *n., pl.* **pag·eant·ries 1.** Pageants and their presentation. **2.** Grand or showy display.

pag·er (pā′jər) *n.* A portable electronic device that receives text messages or alerts the person carrying it, as by beeping, that someone is trying to communicate with him or her.

pag·i·nate (păj′ə-nāt′) *tr.v.* **pag·i·nat·ed, pag·i·nat·ing, pag·i·nates** To number the pages of: *Most word-processing programs paginate documents.*

pa·go·da (pə-gō′də) *n.* **1.** A many-storied Buddhist tower, built as a memorial or shrine. **2.** A structure built in imitation of such a tower.

Pa·go Pa·go (päng′ō päng′ō *or* päng′gō päng′gō) The capital of American Samoa, in the Pacific Ocean northeast of Fiji.

paid (pād) *v.* Past tense and past participle of **pay.**

pail (pāl) *n.* **1.** A cylindrical container, open at the top and fitted with a handle; a bucket. **2a.** A pail with something in it: *carry a pail of water.* **b.** The amount that a pail holds: *pour out a pail of sand.*

❑ *These sound alike:* **pail, pale[1]** (stake), **pale[2]** (whitish).

pail·ful (pāl′fo͝ol′) *n.* The amount that a pail can hold.

pain (pān) *n.* **1.** An unpleasant feeling occurring as a result of injury or disease, usually localized in some part of the body. **2.** Mental or emotional suffering; distress. **3. pains** Trouble, care, or effort: *take great pains* *to do something right.* **4.** *Informal* A source of annoyance; a nuisance: *He's a real pain.* ❖ *tr.v.* **pained, pain·ing, pains 1.** To cause pain to (a person or animal); hurt. **2.** To cause to suffer; distress: *It pained her to see him so unhappy.* ◆ **on pain of** or **under pain of** Subject to the penalty of (a specified punishment, such as death).

❑ *These sound alike:* **pain, pane** (glass).

Paine (pān), **Thomas** 1737–1809. British-born American writer and Revolutionary leader who wrote and published works arguing in favor of the American Revolution and the French Revolution.

pain·ful (pān′fəl) *adj.* **1.** Causing or full of pain; hurtful: *a painful injury.* **2.** Causing suffering or anxiety; distressing: *a painful decision.* **—pain′ful·ly** *adv.* **—pain′ful·ness** *n.*

pain·kill·er (pān′kĭl′ər) *n.* Something, especially a drug, that relieves pain.

pain·less (pān′lĭs) *adj.* Not painful; causing no unpleasant sensations: *a painless operation.* **—pain′less·ly** *adv.* **—pain′less·ness** *n.*

pains·tak·ing (pānz′tā′kĭng) *adj.* Involving or showing great care or thoroughness; careful: *painstaking research.* **—pains′tak′ing·ly** *adv.*

paint (pānt) *n.* **1a.** A liquid mixture, usually of a finely ground solid pigment and a liquid, applied to surfaces as a protective or decorative coating. **b.** The thin layer formed when the liquid in such a mixture is applied to a surface and dries or reacts with air. **2.** A cosmetic, such as rouge, that colors. **3.** Any of a breed of muscular horse having a coat with patches of white and another color. ❖ *v.* **paint·ed, paint·ing, paints** *—tr.* **1.** To coat or decorate with paint: *paint a house.* **2.** To make (a picture) with paints. **3a.** To represent in a painting: *She painted a horse.* **b.** To describe vividly in words: *The article painted a lively picture of the festival.* **4.** To cover the surface of with a liquid medicine; swab: *paint a sore throat with antiseptic.* *—intr.* **1.** To practice the art of painting pictures. **2.** To cover something with paint. **—paint′a·ble** *adj.*

paint·ball (pānt′bôl′) *n.* **1.** A game in which players on one team seek to eliminate the players on the other team by marking them with paint that is shot in capsules from air guns. **2.** A capsule filled with paint that is shot from guns in this game.

paint·brush (pānt′brŭsh′) *n.* A brush for applying paint.

paint·ed (pān′tĭd) *adj.* **1.** Coated or decorated with paint: *a brightly painted cabinet.* **2.** Depicted in paint: *a painted portrait.*

paint·er¹ (pān′tər) *n.* A person who paints, either as an artist or worker.

pain·ter² (pān′tər) *n.* A rope attached to the bow of a boat, used for tying up. [From Middle English *peintour*, probably from Old French *pendre*, to hang, from Latin *pendēre*.]

paint·ing (pān′tĭng) *n.* **1.** The art, process, or occupation of working with paints. **2.** A picture or design in paint.

pair (pâr) *n., pl.* **pair** or **pairs 1.** A set of two members that are somehow matched or associated in function or form: *a pair of boots.* **2.** An object consisting of two joined or similar parts dependent upon each other: *a pair of binoculars.* **3a.** Two people who are married, engaged, or dating. **b.** Two people, animals, or things having something in common and considered together: *a pair of oxen.* **c.** Two mated animals. **4.** Two playing cards of the same value: *held a pair of kings.* ❖ *v.* **paired, pair·ing, pairs** *—tr.* **1.** To arrange in sets of two; couple: *Pair the questions with the correct answers.* **2.** To combine or join (one person or thing) with another to form a pair: *The camp counselors paired Olivia with Greta.* *—intr.* To form pairs or a pair: *The players paired off to practice passing.* —SEE NOTE.

❑ *These sound alike:* **pair, pare** (peel), **pear** (fruit).

pais·ley (pāz′lē) *adj.* Having a colorful pattern of curved shapes and swirls: *a paisley dress.*

Pai·ute (pī′yo͞ot′) *n., pl.* **Paiute** or **Pai·utes 1.** A member of either of two Native American peoples of the Great Basin region of the western United States. **2.** Either of the Uto-Aztecan languages of these peoples.

pa·ja·mas (pə-jä′məz *or* pə-jăm′əz) *pl.n.* A loose-fitting outfit consisting of a shirt and pants, worn for sleeping or lounging.

Pak·i·stan (păk′ĭ-stăn′ *or* pä′kĭ-stän′) A country of South Asia west of India. It was the home of the prehistoric Indus Valley civilization, which flourished until about 1500 BC. Islamabad is the capital and Karachi the largest city.

pal (păl) *Informal n.* A friend; a chum. ❖ *intr.v.* **palled, pal·ling, pals** To associate as friends. [From Romani *phral*, brother, pal, from Sanskrit *bhrātā*, brother.]

pal·ace (păl′ĭs) *n.* **1.** The official residence of a royal person. **2.** A splendid residence.

pal·an·quin (păl′ən-kēn′ *or* păl′ən-kwĭn) *n.* A covered litter, carried on poles on the shoulders of multiple bearers, formerly used in eastern, southeastern, and southern Asia.

pal·at·a·ble (păl′ə-tə-bəl) *adj.* **1.** Acceptable to the taste; agreeable enough in flavor to be eaten: *palatable food.* **2.** Acceptable to the mind or sensibilities; agreeable: *a palatable solution to the problem.* **—pal′at·a·bil′i·ty** *n.* **—pal′at·a·bly** *adv.*

pal·ate (păl′ĭt) *n.* **1.** The roof of the mouth in vertebrates, forming a complete or partial separation between the mouth cavity and the passages of the nose. **2.** The sense of taste.

❑ *These sound alike:* **palate, palette** (artist's mixing board), **pallet¹** (platform), **pallet²** (hard bed).

pa·la·tial (pə-lā′shəl) *adj.* Relating to or like a palace; spacious and magnificent: *a palatial hotel.* **—pa·la′tial·ly** *adv.*

Pa·lau (pə-lou′) An island country in the Caroline Islands of the western Pacific Ocean. Melekeok is the capital.

pa·lav·er (pə-lăv′ər) *n.* **1.** Idle chatter. **2.** Talk intended to charm or beguile. ❖ *intr.v.* **pa·lav·ered, pa·lav·er·ing, pa·lav·ers** To chatter idly.

pale¹ (pāl) *n.* **1.** A stake or pointed stick; a picket. **2.** An area enclosed by a fence or boundary. ❖ *tr.v.* **paled, pal·ing, pales** To enclose with pales; fence in. ◆ **beyond the pale** Outrageously unacceptable or unreasonable. [From Middle English *pal*, from Old French, from Latin *pālus*.]

❑ *These sound alike:* **pale¹** (stake), **pail** (bucket), **pale²** (whitish).

pale² (pāl) *adj.* **pal·er, pal·est 1.** Whitish or lighter than normal in complexion. **2.** Containing a large proportion of white; light: *a pale blue.* **3.** Not bright; dim; faint: *a pale moon.* ❖ *v.* **paled, pal·ing, pales** *—intr.* **1.** To lose normal skin coloration; turn pale. **2.** To become pale: *The sky grew red, then paled.* *—tr.* To make pale. [From Middle English, from Old French, from Latin *pallidus*.]

❑ *These sound alike:* **pale²** (whitish), **pail** (bucket), **pale¹** (stake).

Pa·le·o·cene (pā′lē-ə-sēn′) *n.* The earliest epoch of the Tertiary Period, from about 66 to 56 million years ago. During the Paleocene, placental mammals first appeared and the Rocky Mountains formed. See table at **geologic time.** **—Pa′le·o·cene′** *adj.*

Pa·le·o·gene (pā′lē-ə-jēn′) *n.* The first and earliest subdivision of the Tertiary Period, from about 66 to 23 million years ago. During the Paleogene, larger mammals and modern birds evolved. See table at **geologic time.** **—Pa′le·o·gene′** *adj.*

Pa·le·o·lith·ic (pā′lē-ə-lĭth′ĭk) *adj.* Relating to the period of Stone Age culture that began with the earliest chipped stone tools, about 2.4 million years ago. The Paleolithic

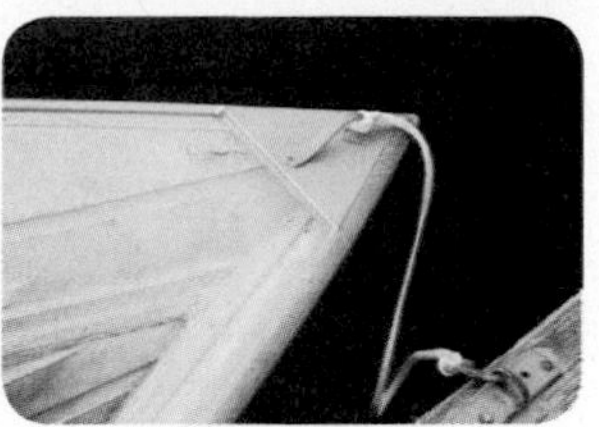

painter²

USAGE

pair The noun **pair** can be followed by a singular or plural verb. You use the singular when *pair* refers to the set taken as a whole: *This pair of shoes is on sale.* You use the plural when the two members are considered as individuals: *The pair have been working together for a year.* After a number other than one, *pair* can be either singular or plural, but the plural is now more common: *She bought six pairs* (or *pair*) *of shoes.*

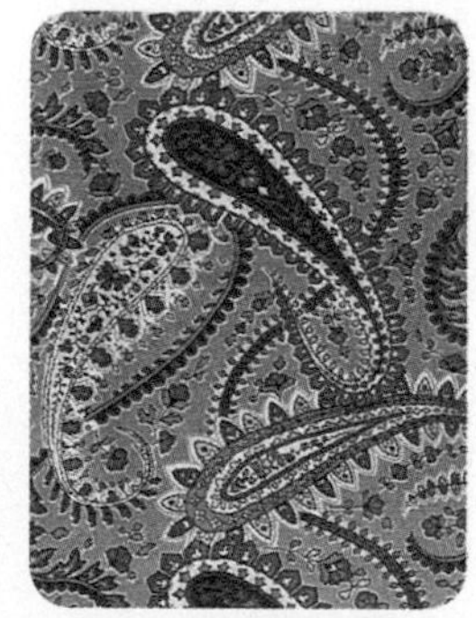

paisley

palanquin

palmate

palomino

WRITERS CHOOSE THEIR WORDS

Martha tried to call Holly again—still busy. She kept trying. A flicker of impatience shot through her. In the kitchen, she surveyed the **paltry** contents of the refrigerator, the telephone wedged between her shoulder and cocked head.

"Not much in there," said her father, crossing the room to where she stood. "I'll go shopping first thing in the morning."

—Kevin Henkes
Olive's Ocean

ă	pat	ôr	core
ā	pay	oi	boy
âr	care	ou	out
ä	father	o͝o	took
ĕ	pet	o͝or	lure
ē	be	o͞o	boot
ĭ	pit	ŭ	cut
ī	bite	ûr	urge
îr	pier	th	thin
ŏ	pot	*th*	this
ō	toe	zh	vision
ô	paw	ə	about

Period ended at different times in different parts of the world, between about 15,000 and 11,500 years ago. ❖ *n.* The Paleolithic Period.

pa·le·on·tol·o·gy (pā′lē-ŏn-**tŏl′**ə-jē) *n.* The scientific study of fossils and ancient forms of life. **—pa′le·on·tol′o·gist** *n.*

Pa·le·o·zo·ic (pā′lē-ə-**zō′**ĭk) *n.* The era of geologic time from about 542 to 251 million years ago. During the Paleozoic, marine invertebrates, fish, reptiles, and land plants first appeared. See table at **geologic time. —Pa′le·o·zo′ic** *adj.*

Pal·es·tine (**păl′**ĭ-stīn′) A historical region of southwest Asia on the eastern Mediterranean shore in roughly the same area as modern Israel and the West Bank. **—Pal′es·tin′i·an** (păl′ĭ-**stĭn′**ē-ən) *adj. & n.*

pal·ette (**păl′**ĭt) *n.* **1.** A thin board, often with a hole for the thumb, which an artist can hold while painting and on which colors are mixed. **2.** A range of colors used, as by an artist.

❑ *These sound alike:* **palette, palate** (mouth roof), **pallet[1]** (platform), **pallet[2]** (hard bed).

Pal·i·kir (**păl′**ĭ-kər) The capital of the Federated States of Micronesia, in the western Pacific Ocean.

pal·in·drome (**păl′**ĭn-drōm′) *n.* A word, phrase, verse, or sentence that reads the same backward or forward, as *Madam, I'm Adam.*

pal·ing (**pā′**lĭng) *n.* **1.** One of the pales or pickets forming a fence. **2.** A fence made of pales or pickets.

pal·i·sade (păl′ĭ-**sād′**) *n.* **1.** A fence of stakes forming a fortification. **2. palisades** A line of high cliffs, usually along a river.

palisade layer *n.* A layer of cells inside a leaf, made up of long cells that have numerous chloroplasts and are arranged perpendicular to the leaf surface.

pall[1] (pôl) *n.* **1.** A cloth covering, often of black velvet, for a coffin or tomb. **2.** A coffin, especially one being borne to a grave. **3.** A dark gloomy covering: *a pall of smog over the city.* **4.** A gloomy atmosphere: *The bad news cast a pall over the household.* [From Middle English, cloak, covering, from Old English *pæll*, from Latin *pallium*.]

❑ *These sound alike:* **pall[1]** (cloth covering), **pall[2]** (grow dull), **pawl** (hinged device).

pall[2] (pôl) *intr.v.* **palled, pall·ing, palls** To grow dull or tiresome: *a clever idea that begins to pall by the end of the movie.* [From Middle English *pallen*, to grow feeble, short for *appallen*, probably from Old French *apalir*, to grow pale, from Latin *pallidus*, pale.]

❑ *These sound alike:* **pall[2]** (grow dull), **pall[1]** (cloth covering), **pawl** (hinged device).

pal·la·di·um (pə-**lā′**dē-əm) *n. Symbol* **Pd** A soft, whitish, tarnish-resistant metallic element that occurs naturally with platinum. It is used as a catalyst and in alloys for making surgical instruments and jewelry. Atomic number 46. See **Periodic Table.**

Pal·las Athena (**păl′**əs) *n.* The goddess Athena.

pall·bear·er (**pôl′**bâr′ər) *n.* A person who helps carry the coffin at a funeral.

pal·let[1] (**păl′**ĭt) *n.* A portable platform for storing or moving cargo or freight.

❑ *These sound alike:* **pallet[1]** (platform), **palate** (mouth roof), **palette** (artist's mixing board), **pallet[2]** (hard bed).

pal·let[2] (**păl′**ĭt) *n.* A narrow hard bed or straw-filled mattress.

❑ *These sound alike:* **pallet[2]** (hard bed), **palate** (mouth roof), **palette** (artist's mixing board), **pallet[1]** (platform).

pal·li·ate (**păl′**ē-āt′) *tr.v.* **pal·li·at·ed, pal·li·at·ing, pal·li·ates 1.** To ease the effect or force of; make less severe or intense: *got a pet to palliate his loneliness.* **2.** To ease pain or other symptoms of (a disorder). **3.** To make (an offense or fault) seem less serious; help to excuse. **—pal′li·a′tion** *n.*

pal·li·a·tive (**păl′**ē-ā′tĭv *or* **păl′**ē-ə-tĭv) *adj.* **1.** Easing the effects or force of something: *He followed his rudeness with a palliative remark.* **2.** Easing the symptoms of a disorder, especially when the cause can no longer be treated. ❖ *n.* Something that palliates, such as a drug.

pal·lid (**păl′**ĭd) *adj.* Lacking healthy color; pale. **—pal′lid·ly** *adv.* **—pal′lid·ness** *n.*

pal·lor (**păl′**ər) *n.* Extreme or unnatural paleness.

palm[1] (päm) *n.* **1.** The inside surface of the hand between the wrist and the base of the fingers. **2.** A similar part of the forefoot of an animal. ❖ *tr.v.* **palmed, palm·ing, palms 1.** To conceal (an object) in the palm of the hand. **2.** To pick up secretly. **3.** In basketball, to let (the ball) rest in the palm of the hand when dribbling, in violation of the rules. ◆ **palm off** To dispose of or pass off by deception. [From Middle English, from Old French, from Latin *palma*, palm of the hand.]

palm[2] (päm) *n.* **1.** Any of various evergreen trees or shrubs of tropical and subtropical regions, usually having a branchless trunk with a crown of large leaves shaped like feathers or fans. **2.** A leaf or frond of such a tree, used as a symbol of victory, success, or joy. [From Middle English, from Old English, from Latin *palma*, palm of the hand, palm tree (from the shape of the fronds).]

pal·mate (**păl′**māt′ *or* **pä′**māt′) *adj.* **1.** Shaped somewhat like a hand with the fingers spread out: *a palmate leaf.* **2.** Having the front toes joined by a web; web-footed. **—pal′mate′ly** *adv.*

Pal·mer (**pä′**mər *or* **päl′**mər), **Arnold** 1929–2016. American golfer who was the first to win four Masters tournaments (1958, 1960, 1962, and 1964).

pal·met·to (păl-**mĕt′**ō) *n., pl.* **pal·met·tos** or **pal·met·toes** Any of several often small palms having leaves shaped like fans.

palm·ist (**pä′**mĭst) *n.* A person who practices palmistry.

palm·is·try (**pä′**mĭ-strē) *n.* The practice or art of telling fortunes from the lines, marks, and patterns on the palms of the hands.

palm oil *n.* A yellowish oil obtained from the fruits of an African palm, widely used as a cooking oil and in processed foods, soaps, and cosmetics.

Palm Sunday *n.* The Sunday before Easter, celebrated by Christians in commemoration of Jesus's entry into Jerusalem, when palm leaves were strewn before him.

pal·o·mi·no (păl′ə-**mē′**nō) *n., pl.* **pal·o·mi·nos** A horse having a light tan coat and a whitish mane and tail. [From Spanish *paloma*, dove, pigeon, from Latin *palumbēs*, pigeon.]

Pa·louse (pə-**lo͞os′**) *n., pl.* **Palouse** or **Pa·lous·es** A member of a Sahaptin-speaking Native American people living in eastern Washington.

pal·pa·ble (**păl′**pə-bəl) *adj.* **1.** Capable of being touched or felt. **2.** Easily perceived; obvious: *The excitement in the stadium was palpable.* **—pal′pa·bil′i·ty** *n.* **—pal′pa·bly** *adv.*

pal·pate (**păl′**pāt′) *tr.v.* **pal·pat·ed, pal·pat·ing, pal·pates** To examine or explore (an organ or area of the body) by touching. **—pal·pa′tion** *n.* **—pal′pa′tor** *n.*

pal·pi·tate (**păl′**pĭ-tāt′) *intr.v.* **pal·pi·tat·ed, pal·pi·tat·ing, pal·pi·tates 1.** To shake; quiver. **2.** To beat very rapidly; throb: *My pulse palpitated with fear.*

pal·pi·ta·tion (păl′pĭ-**tā′**shən) *n.* **1.** A trembling or shaking. **2.** Irregular rapid beating of the heart.

pal·sied (**pôl′**zēd) *adj.* **1.** Having symptoms of palsy. **2.** Trembling; shaking.

pal·sy (**pôl′**zē) *n., pl.* **pal·sies** Complete or partial muscle paralysis, often accompanied by trembling. ❖ *tr.v.* **pal·sied, pal·sy·ing, pal·sies** To paralyze. [From Middle

English *palasie,* from Old French *paralisie,* paralysis, from Latin *paralysis.*]

pal·try (pôl′trē) *adj.* **pal·tri·er, pal·tri·est 1.** Very small or inadequate in amount: *was paid a paltry sum for his work.* **2.** Lacking in importance or worth; insignificant: *considered the events paltry in the grand scheme of things.* **—pal′tri·ness** *n.*

Pam·pas (păm′päs *or* păm′pəz) The partly grassy, partly arid plain that covers most of central Argentina.

pam·per (păm′pər) *tr.v.* **pam·pered, pam·per·ing, pam·pers** To treat with extreme indulgence, especially in an attempt to satisfy luxurious desires.

SYNONYMS **pamper, indulge, spoil, coddle, baby** These verbs mean to make a considerable and often excessive effort to please someone. **Pamper** means to satisfy someone's appetites, tastes, or desires for luxurious things: *I pampered myself with a long hot bath.* **Indulge** means to yield to wishes or impulses, especially those that would be better left unfulfilled: *He says he wants another dessert. Don't indulge him.* **Spoil** means to indulge someone in a way that worsens his or her character: *You are spoiling that child by letting him have every toy he wants.* **Coddle** means to care for in a tender, overprotective way that can weaken character: *Don't coddle her and make her think she can't do the job all by herself.* **Baby** suggests giving someone the kind of attention one might give a baby: *My brother likes to be babied when he has the flu.*

ANTONYMS **punish, abuse**

---

pam·phlet (păm′flĭt) *n.* A short book or printed essay with a paper cover and no binding; a booklet.

pam·phlet·eer (păm′flĭ-tîr′) *n.* A writer of pamphlets, especially on political subjects.

pan[1] (păn) *n.* **1.** A wide shallow open container used for holding liquids, cooking, and other household purposes. **2.** A similar flat shallow container, such as one used to separate gold from earth or gravel by washing. ❖ *v.* **panned, pan·ning, pans** *—tr.* **1.** To wash (earth or gravel) in a pan in search of gold: *panned the debris carefully.* **2.** To cook (food) in a pan. **3.** *Informal* To review unfavorably: *The critics panned the musical.* —*intr.* To wash earth or gravel in a pan in search of gold. ◆ **pan out** To turn out well; be successful. [From Middle English, from Old English *panne,* ultimately from Latin *patina,* from Greek *patanē.*]

pan[2] (păn) *tr. & intr.v.* **panned, pan·ning, pans** To turn (a movie or television camera) to follow a moving object or scan a scene. [Short for *panoramic.*]

Pan (păn) *n.* In Greek mythology, the god of woodlands, fields, and flocks, having a human head and torso and a goat's legs, horns, and ears.

pan– *pref.* A prefix that means all: *panorama.* —SEE NOTE AT **omni–.**

pan·a·ce·a (păn′ə-sē′ə) *n.* A remedy for all diseases or woes; a cure-all.

pa·nache (pə-năsh′ *or* pə-näsh′) *n.* Dash; verve: *She trailed the cape behind her with panache.*

Pan·a·ma (păn′ə-mä′) **1.** A country of southeast Central America east of Costa Rica. Panama gained its independence from Colombia in 1903. The city of Panama is the capital. **2.** also **Panama City** The capital of Panama, in the central part of the country on the **Gulf of Panama,** an inlet of the Pacific Ocean.

Panama, Isthmus of An isthmus of Central America connecting North and South America and separating the Pacific Ocean from the Caribbean Sea.

Panama Canal A ship canal, about 51 miles (82 kilometers) long, crossing the Isthmus of Panama and connecting the Caribbean Sea with the Pacific Ocean. The canal was opened to traffic in 1914.

Panama hat *n.* A broad-brimmed hat that is hand-plaited from thin strips of the leaves of a tropical American plant.

Pan-A·mer·i·can (păn′ə-mĕr′ĭ-kən) *adj.* Relating to or including the countries of North, Central, and South America: *Pan-American conferences.*

pan·cake (păn′kāk′) *n.* A thin flat cake of batter, cooked on a hot griddle or skillet.

pan·cre·as (păng′krē-əs *or* păn′krē-əs) *n.* A long irregularly shaped gland located behind the stomach. It secretes insulin into the blood and digestive juices into the duodenum.

pan·cre·at·ic (păng′krē-ăt′ĭk *or* păn′krē-ăt′ĭk) *adj.* Relating to the pancreas: *pancreatic juice.*

pan·da (păn′də) *n.* **1.** A bear of the mountains of central China, having woolly fur with black and white markings. **2.** An arboreal mammal of northeast Asia, resembling a raccoon and having reddish fur and a long ringed tail.

pan·dem·ic (păn-dĕm′ĭk) *n.* An epidemic occurring over a wide geographic area. ❖ *adj.* Occurring over a wide geographic area. Used of a disease: *pandemic influenza.*

pan·de·mo·ni·um (păn′də-mō′nē-əm) *n.* A condition or scene of noisy confusion. [From *Pandæmonium,* the capital of Hell in *Paradise Lost,* an epic poem by John Milton : Greek *pan-,* all + Greek *daimōn,* demon + New Latin *-ium,* noun suffix.]

pan·der (păn′dər) *intr.v.* **pan·dered, pan·der·ing, pan·ders** To appeal to or satisfy the crude desires or interests of others: *His movies pander to a frustrated public's desire for a scapegoat.*

Pan·do·ra (păn-dôr′ə) *n.* In Greek mythology, the first woman, who out of curiosity opens a box that releases all the evils of human life into the world.

pane (pān) *n.* A sheet of glass or other transparent material that fills a framed section of a window or door. [From Middle English, windowpane, from Old French *pan,* piece of cloth, panel, from Latin *pannus,* cloth.]
❑ *These sound alike:* **pane, pain** (hurt).

pan·el (păn′əl) *n.* **1.** A flat piece, such as a wooden board, forming part of a surface or overlaying it: *a door with inlaid panels.* **2.** A piece of cloth sewn lengthwise into or onto a skirt or dress. **3.** A board with instruments or controls. **4.** A wooden board used as a surface for oil painting. **5.** A cartoon drawing in a sequence of cartoons that form a story. **6a.** A list or group of people chosen for jury duty. **b.** A jury. **7.** A group of people gathered together to discuss or decide something: *a panel of medical and legal experts.* ❖ *tr.v.* **pan·eled, pan·el·ing, pan·els** or **pan·elled, pan·el·ling, pan·els** To cover or decorate with panels.

pan·el·ing (păn′ə-lĭng) *n.* A building material consisting of panels covering a wall or other surface.

pan·el·ist (păn′ə-lĭst) *n.* A member of a panel.

panel truck *n.* A small delivery truck with a fully enclosed body.

pang (păng) *n.* **1.** A sudden sharp painful sensation: *hunger pangs.* **2.** A sudden sharp feeling of emotional distress: *a pang of remorse.*

Pan·gae·a (păn-jē′ə) *n.* According to the theory of plate tectonics, a continent that included all the world's landmasses in the late Paleozoic era.

pan·go·lin (păng′gə-lĭn *or* păn′gə-lĭn) *n.* Any of several African and Asian mammals having a scaly body, a long tail, and a sticky tongue with which they catch ants. [From Malay *pengguling,* roller (from its habit of rolling into a ball when frightened).]

pan·han·dle[1] (păn′hăn′dl) *intr.v.* **pan·han·dled, pan·han·dling, pan·han·dles** *Informal* To beg for money on the street or in a public area. **—pan′han′dler** *n.*

pan·han·dle[2] (păn′hăn′dl) *n.* **1.** The handle of a pan. **2.** often **Panhandle** A narrow strip of territory extending

Panama hat

pancake

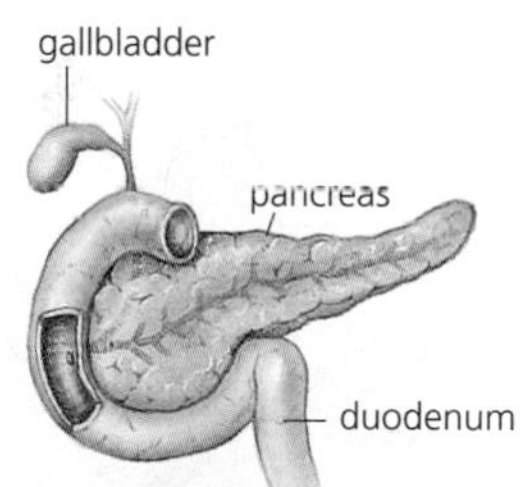

pancreas

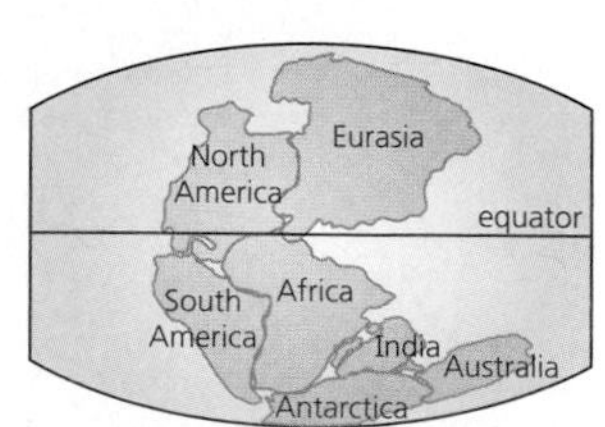

Pangaea

panicle

pannier

papaya

ă	pat	ôr	core
ā	pay	oi	boy
âr	care	ou	out
ä	father	ŏŏ	took
ĕ	pet	ŏŏr	lure
ē	be	ōō	boot
ĭ	pit	ŭ	cut
ī	bite	ûr	urge
îr	pier	th	thin
ŏ	pot	*th*	this
ō	toe	zh	vision
ô	paw	ə	about

like the handle of a pan from a broader area: *the Oklahoma Panhandle.*

pan·ic (păn′ĭk) *n.* **1.** A sudden overwhelming terror. **2.** A sudden fear of financial loss among investors. ❖ *adj.* Relating to panic: *a panic reaction.* ❖ *tr. & intr.v.* **pan·icked, pan·ick·ing, pan·ics** To cause panic in or to feel panic. See Synonyms at **frighten.** [From Greek *Pānikos*, of Pan (considered to be the source of strange noises or feelings of fear in remote or lonely places).] —**pan′ick·y** *adj.*

pan·i·cle (păn′ĭ-kəl) *n.* A loosely branched flower cluster, especially a branching raceme.

pan·ic-strick·en (păn′ĭk-strĭk′ən) *adj.* Overcome by panic; terrified.

pa·ni·ni (pə-nē′nē) *n., pl.* **panini** or **pa·ni·nis** An Italian sandwich made usually with vegetables, cheese, and grilled or cured meat. [Italian, plural (taken as a singular in English) of *panino (imbottito)*, stuffed bread, sandwich : *panino*, diminutive of *pane*, bread + *imbottire*, to stuff.]

pan·nier (păn′yər *or* păn′ē-ər) *n.* A basket or pack, especially one of a pair carried on either side of a pack animal, bicycle, or motorcycle.

pan·o·ply (păn′ə-plē) *n., pl.* **pan·o·plies 1.** A splendid display: *a panoply of flags in the parade.* **2.** The complete arms and armor of a warrior.

pan·o·ram·a (păn′ə-**răm′**ə) *n.* **1.** A view or picture of everything visible over a wide area: *a vast panorama of a mountain range.* **2.** A view or picture of a long series of events, stages, or things: *a book that presents a panorama of world history.* **3.** A wide picture depicting a scene or story that is unrolled or presented a part at a time before spectators. —**pan′o·ram′ic** *adj.* —**pan′o·ram′i·cal·ly** *adv.*

pan·pipe (păn′pīp′) *n.* often **panpipes** A musical instrument consisting of a set of tubes or reeds of different lengths bound together, played by blowing air across the tops of the tubes.

pan·sy (păn′zē) *n., pl.* **pan·sies** Any of various garden plants having flowers with rounded velvety petals of various colors. [From Middle English *pancy*, from Old French *pensee*, thought, remembrance.]

pant (pănt) *v.* **pant·ed, pant·ing, pants** —*intr.* **1.** To breathe in short quick gasps. **2.** To yearn desperately: *panted for the dawn to come.* —*tr.* To utter breathlessly: *I panted out a short response.* ❖ *n.* A short quick gasp.

Pan·ta·loon (păn′tə-lōōn′) *n.* A comic pantomime character usually portrayed as a foolish old man.

pan·ta·loons (păn′tə-**lōōnz′**) *pl.n.* Pants, especially loose baggy ones.

pan·the·ism (păn′thē-ĭz′əm) *n.* The doctrine that God is identical with the universe. —**pan′the·ist** *n.* —**pan′the·is′tic** *adj.*

pan·the·on (păn′thē-ŏn′) *n.* **1.** A temple dedicated to all of the gods. **2.** All the gods of a people: *Zeus is head of the Greek pantheon.* **3.** A group of people most highly regarded for contributions to a field or endeavor: *The pantheon of physics includes Einstein and Bohr.* [From Greek *Pantheion*, shrine of all the gods : *pan-*, all + *theos*, god.]

pan·ther (păn′thər) *n.* **1.** A large wild cat such as a leopard or jaguar, especially one having black fur. **2.** A cougar. [From Latin *panthēra*, from Greek *panthēr*.]

pant·ies (păn′tēz) *pl.n.* Short underpants for women or children.

pan·to·mime (păn′tə-mīm′) *n.* **1.** Communication by means of gesture and facial expression. **2a.** The telling of a story without words, by means of bodily movements, gestures, and facial expressions. **b.** A play or an entertainment acted in this way. ❖ *tr.v.* **pan·to·mimed, pan·to·mim·ing, pan·to·mimes** To perform or represent by gestures without speech. —**pan′to·mim′ist** *n.*

pan·try (păn′trē) *n., pl.* **pan·tries** A small room or closet, usually off a kitchen, where food, tableware, linens, and similar items are stored.

pants (pănts) *pl.n.* An outer garment that covers the body from the waist to the ankles, divided into sections to fit each leg separately.

pant·suit (pănt′sōōt′) *n.* A woman's suit having pants and a matching jacket.

pant·y·hose or **pant·y hose** (păn′tē-hōz′) *pl.n.* A one-piece undergarment consisting of stockings attached to a top that resembles underpants.

pap (păp) *n.* **1.** Soft, easily digestible food for infants or invalids. **2.** Matter designed to satisfy or entertain but lacking real value or substance: *the pap on TV every night.*

pa·pa (pä′pə *or* pə-pä′) also **pop·pa** (pä′pə) *n. Informal* Father.

pa·pa·cy (pā′pə-sē) *n., pl.* **pa·pa·cies 1.** The office or authority of the pope. **2.** The period during which a pope is in office. **3.** All of the popes or a series of popes: *the medieval papacy.* **4.** often **Papacy** The system of church government headed by the pope.

pa·pal (pā′pəl) *adj.* Relating to the pope or the office of pope: *papal history.*

pa·paw (pô′pô) *n.* Variant of **pawpaw.**

pa·pa·ya (pə-pä′yə) *n.* **1.** The large yellow fruit of a tropical American tree, having many small seeds and a sweet taste. **2.** The tree that bears such fruit. [From Spanish, of Cariban origin.]

pa·per (pā′pər) *n.* **1a.** A material produced, usually in thin sheets, from cellulose pulp derived mainly from wood, rags, and certain grasses. It is used for writing, printing, drawing, wrapping, and covering walls. **b.** A single sheet of this material. **c.** A sheet of this material with writing or printing on it. **2a.** A scholarly essay: *The professor wrote a paper on the immune system.* **b.** A report or essay assigned in school. **3a.** A document: *legal papers.* **b. papers** Documents that establish identity or give other information about the bearer. **4. papers** A collection of letters, diaries, and other personal writings. **5.** A newspaper. **6.** Wallpaper. ❖ *tr.v.* **pa·pered, pa·per·ing, pa·pers 1.** To cover or wrap in paper: *Photos of old movie stars papered the mirror.* **2.** To cover with wallpaper. ❖ *adj.* Made of or producing paper: *paper plates; a paper mill.* [From Middle English, from Old French *papier*, from Latin *papȳrus*, papyrus, from Greek *papūros*.] —**pa′per·y** *adj.*

pa·per·back (pā′pər-băk′) *n.* A book with a flexible paper binding.

pa·per·board (pā′pər-bôrd′) *n.* Cardboard; pasteboard.

pa·per·boy (pā′pər-boi′) *n.* A boy who sells or delivers newspapers.

paper clip *n.* A bent wire or plastic clip for holding sheets of paper together.

pa·per·girl (pā′pər-gûrl′) *n.* A girl who sells or delivers newspapers.

paper nautilus *n.* Any of several cephalopod mollusks with eight arms, the females of which produce a paper-thin shell-like egg case.

pa·per·weight (pā′pər-wāt′) *n.* A small heavy object for holding down loose papers.

pa·per·work (pā′pər-wûrk′) *n.* Work involving the handling of reports, letters, and forms.

pa·pier-mâ·ché also **pa·per ma·che** (pā′pər-mə-**shā′**) *n.* A material made from paper pulp mixed with glue or paste, that can be molded into various shapes when wet. ❖ *adj.* Made of this material: *a papier-mâché piñata.*

pa·pil·la (pə-pĭl′ə) *n., pl.* **pa·pil·lae** (pə-pĭl′ē) A small projection from a body surface, as one of the tiny projections on the top of the tongue.

pa·poose (pă-pōōs′) *n.* **1.** *Often Offensive* A Native American baby. **2.** A cradleboard.

pa·pri·ka (pă-**prē′**kə *or* **păp′**rĭ-kə) *n.* A usually mild powdered seasoning made from red peppers.

Pap smear (păp) *n.* A laboratory test, especially for cervical cancer, in which cells from the cervix are smeared on a slide, stained, and examined under a microscope.

Pap·u·a New Guin·ea (**păp′**yo͞o-ə no͞o **gĭn′**ē) An island country of the southwest Pacific Ocean made up of the eastern half of New Guinea, the western Solomon Islands, and adjacent islands. Port Moresby is the capital.

pa·py·rus (pə-**pī′**rəs) *n., pl.* **pa·py·rus·es** or **pa·py·ri** (pə-**pī′**rī′) **1.** A tall grasslike plant that grows in water and is native to Africa. **2.** A kind of paper made from the stems and pith of this plant. **3.** A document written on this material.

par (pär) *n.* **1.** An accepted or normal average: *below par in physical condition.* **2.** A level of equality; equal footing: *good food, but not on a par with my grandmother's.* **3.** The number of golf strokes regarded as necessary to complete a given hole or course in expert play. **4.** The value printed on the face of a stock or bond as distinguished from the current market value. ❖ *adj.* Equal to the standard; normal: *a par performance.* ◆ **par for the course** Usual; typical: *He's running real late, but that's par for the course with him.*

par. *abbr.* An abbreviation of: **1.** paragraph. **2.** parallel.

para–[1] or **par–** *pref.* A prefix that means: **1.** Alongside; near: *parathyroid gland.* **2.** Assistant: *paramedic.*

para–[2] *pref.* A prefix that means parachute: *paratrooper.*

par·a·ble (**păr′**ə-bəl) *n.* A simple story that illustrates a moral or religious lesson.

pa·rab·o·la (pə-**răb′**ə-lə) *n.* The curve formed by the set of points in a plane that are all equally distant from a given line and a given point not on the line.

par·a·bol·ic (păr′ə-**bŏl′**ĭk) *adj.* Relating to a parabola. **—par′a·bol′i·cal·ly** *adv.*

par·a·chute (**păr′**ə-sho͞ot′) *n.* **1.** A foldable device consisting of a large piece of fabric attached by cords to a harness and used to slow the fall of people or objects from great heights. **2.** A similar device used to slow speeding vehicles. ❖ *v.* **par·a·chut·ed, par·a·chut·ing, par·a·chutes** *—intr.* To descend by parachute. *—tr.* To drop (supplies, for example) by parachute. [From French : *para(sol)*, parasol + *chute*, fall.] **—par′a·chut′ist** *n.*

pa·rade (pə-**rād′**) *n.* **1.** A public procession in which assembled people or vehicles pass by spectators, often with music, costumes, and colorful display. **2a.** A formal review of marching military troops. **b.** The grounds on which such reviews are held. **3.** The people or troops participating in such a public event or military review. **4.** A line or group of moving people or things: *a parade of ants.* **5.** An ostentatious show: *making a parade of his wealth.* ❖ *v.* **pa·rad·ed, pa·rad·ing, pa·rades** *—intr.* **1.** To take part in a parade: *A company of firefighters paraded in uniform.* **2.** To display oneself proudly or vainly: *He paraded around with his new hat.* *—tr.* **1.** To exhibit ostentatiously: *paraded his children before the guests.* **2.** To assemble and guide (troops, for example) in a parade. **—pa·rad′er** *n.*

par·a·digm (**păr′**ə-dīm′) *n.* **1.** An example of how something should be done or treated; a model. **2.** A list of the inflectional forms of a word, considered as a model for determining the forms of other words like it. **3.** A set of assumptions, concepts, values, and practices, especially one shared by members of a group: *a theory that went against the dominant paradigm in physics.*

par·a·dise (**păr′**ə-dīs′ *or* **păr′**ə-dīz′) *n.* **1.** often **Paradise** The Garden of Eden. **2.** Heaven. **3.** A place of great beauty or happiness: *The park is a paradise within a noisy city.* **4.** A state of delight or happiness: *The newlyweds have been in paradise for months.* [From Middle English *paradis*, from Greek *paradeisos*, garden, enclosed park, of Iranian origin.]

par·a·dox (**păr′**ə-dŏks′) *n.* **1.** A statement that contains or implies its own contradiction and therefore has an uncertain meaning or no meaning; for example, "We destroyed the town in order to save it" is a paradox. **2.** A statement that appears contradictory but that may be true; for example, "Light is both a wave and a particle" is a paradox that can be demonstrated in experiments. **3.** A person or thing that is apparently contradictory or cannot be explained.

par·a·dox·i·cal (păr′ə-**dŏk′**sĭ-kəl) *adj.* Containing a paradox; apparently contradictory. **—par′a·dox′i·cal·ly** *adv.* **—par′a·dox′i·cal·ness** *n.*

par·af·fin (**păr′**ə-fĭn) *n.* A waxy, white or colorless, solid hydrocarbon mixture used in making candles, wax paper, lubricating materials, and sealing materials. ❖ *tr.v.* **par·af·fined, par·af·fin·ing, par·af·fins** To treat, coat, or seal with paraffin.

par·a·foil (**păr′**ə-foil′) *n.* A winglike structure made of nylon or other flexible material, used especially in kites and paragliders. When wind passes over it, it fills with air in a shape that generates lift.

par·a·glid·er (**păr′**ə-glī′dər) *n.* A narrow winglike parachute from which a rider glides while attached by a harness.

par·a·glid·ing (**păr′**ə-glī′dĭng) *n.* The sport of gliding by means of a paraglider.

par·a·gon (**păr′**ə-gŏn′) *n.* A model of excellence; a perfect example: *a paragon of honesty.*

par·a·graph (**păr′**ə-grăf′) *n.* **1.** A division of a piece of writing that begins on a new, usually indented line and that consists of one or more sentences on a single idea or aspect of the subject. **2.** A mark (¶) used to indicate where a new paragraph should begin. ❖ *tr.v.* **par·a·graphed, par·a·graph·ing, par·a·graphs** To divide (a written work) into paragraphs. [From Medieval Latin *paragraphus*, horizontal stroke marking a division in text, from Greek *paragraphos*, from *paragraphein*, to write beside : *para-*, beside + *graphein*, to write.] **—par′a·graph′ic, par′a·graph′i·cal** *adj.*

Par·a·guay (**păr′**ə-gwī′ *or* **păr′**ə-gwā′) A country of south-central South America between Brazil and Argentina. Asunción is the capital.

par·a·keet (**păr′**ə-kēt′) *n.* Any of various small parrots usually having a long pointed tail. [From French *perroquet*, probably originally a diminutive of the name *Pierre*, Peter.]

par·a·le·gal (păr′ə-**lē′**gəl) *n.* A person with specialized training who assists a lawyer.

par·al·lax (**păr′**ə-lăks′) *n.* An apparent motion of an object relative to more distant objects, caused by a change in the observer's position.

par·al·lel (**păr′**ə-lĕl′) *adj.* **1.** Having corresponding points always separated by the same distance: *a road parallel to the river.* **2.** Lying in the same plane and not intersecting: *parallel lines.* **3.** Not intersecting: *parallel planes.* **4.** Matching feature for feature; corresponding: *parallel economic developments in two countries.* **5.** Related to electric circuits in which a flowing current is split into two or more paths: *The wiring of the lights is parallel, so that if one bulb burns out, the others stay lit.* ❖ *adv.* In a parallel course or direction: *a reef running parallel to the shore.* ❖ *n.* **1.** Any of a set of parallel geometric figures, especially lines. **2.** Something closely resembling something else; a corresponding case or instance. **3.** A comparison showing close resemblance; an analogy. **4.** Any of the lines considered to encircle the earth parallel to the plane of the equator, used to represent degrees of latitude. **5.** An arrangement of an electric circuit that splits the current in two or more paths: *The lights are wired in parallel.* ❖ *tr.v.* **par·al·leled, par·al·lel·ing, par·al·lels** also **par·al·lelled, par·al·lel·ling, par·al·lels 1.** To make or place parallel: *paralleled the*

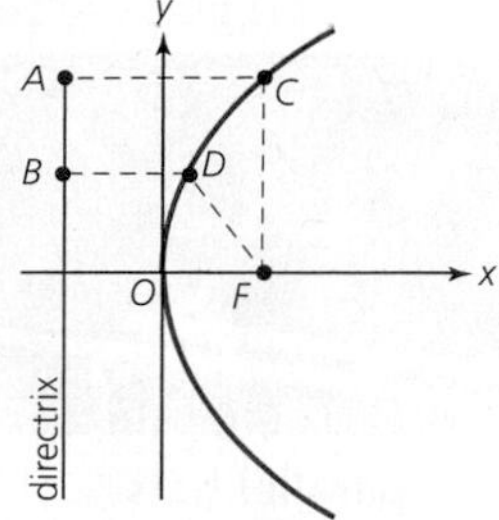

parabola

Any point on a parabola is the same distance from the directrix as it is from the focus (*F*). *AC* equals *CF* and *BD* equals *DF*.

paraglider

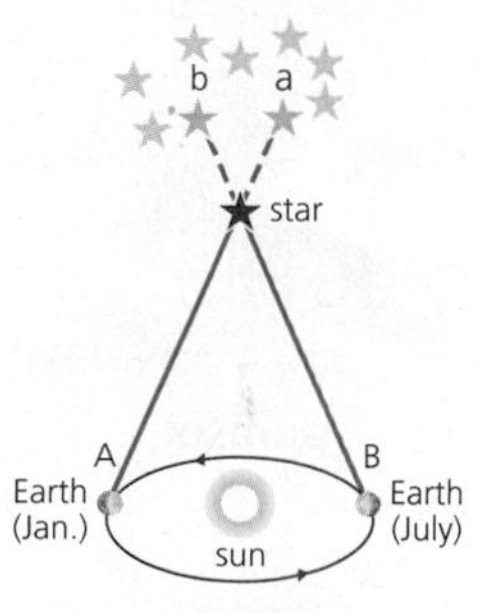

parallax

From point *A* in Earth's orbit, a nearby star (*red*) appears in position *a* among more distant stars (*yellow*). Six months later, from point *B*, the same star appears in position *b*.

parallel bars

parallelogram

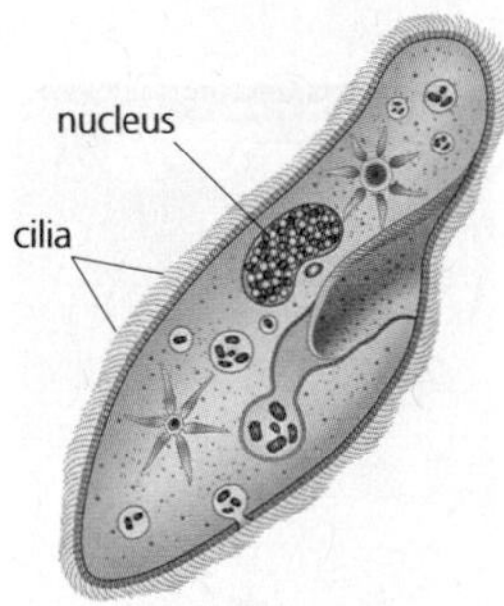

paramecium

parasol

ă	pat	ôr	core
ā	pay	oi	boy
âr	care	ou	out
ä	father	o͝o	took
ĕ	pet	o͝or	lure
ē	be	o͞o	boot
ĭ	pit	ŭ	cut
ī	bite	ûr	urge
îr	pier	th	thin
ŏ	pot	*th*	this
ō	toe	zh	vision
ô	paw	ə	about

two edges of the fabric. **2.** To be or extend parallel to: *The street paralleled a canal.* **3.** To compare; liken: *He paralleled the situation to a gathering storm.* [From Greek *parallēlos* : *para-*, beside + *allēlōn*, of one another.]

parallel bars *pl.n.* Two horizontal bars set parallel to each other at the same height, used especially for swinging maneuvers in gymnastics.

par·al·lel·e·pi·ped (păr′ə-lĕl′ə-**pī′**pĭd) *n.* A solid geometric figure having six faces, each one being a parallelogram.

par·al·lel·ism (**păr′**ə-lĕ-lĭz′əm) *n.* **1.** The quality or condition of being parallel. **2.** Similarity or correspondence.

par·al·lel·o·gram (păr′ə-**lĕl′**ə-grăm′) *n.* A plane four-sided geometric figure in which each pair of opposite sides is parallel.

pa·ral·y·sis (pə-**răl′**ĭ-sĭs) *n., pl.* **pa·ral·y·ses** (pə-**răl′**ĭ-sēz′) **1.** Partial or complete loss of the ability to move or feel sensations in a part of the body, usually resulting from damage to the nerves going to and from the part. **2.** An inability to move or function normally: *The community was paralyzed after a rash of crimes.* [From Latin, from Greek *paralusis*, from *paralūein*, to cut loose, disable.]

par·a·lyt·ic (păr′ə-**lĭt′**ĭk) *adj.* Relating to paralysis. ❖ *n.* A person affected with paralysis.

par·a·lyze (**păr′**ə-līz′) *tr.v.* **par·a·lyzed, par·a·lyz·ing, par·a·lyz·es 1.** To affect with paralysis; make unable to move or feel. **2a.** To make helpless or motionless: *paralyzed by fear.* **b.** To block the normal functioning of; bring to a standstill: *The blizzard paralyzed the city.* **—par′a·ly·za′tion** (păr′ə-lĭ-**zā′**shən) *n.*

Par·a·mar·i·bo (păr′ə-**măr′**ə-bō′) The capital of Suriname, in the northern part of the country near the Atlantic Ocean. It was founded in the 1630s.

par·a·me·ci·um (păr′ə-**mē′**sē-əm *or* păr′ə-**mē′**shē-əm) *n., pl.* **par·a·me·ci·a** (păr′ə-**mē′**sē-ə *or* păr′ə-**mē′**shē-ə) *or* **par·a·me·ci·ums** Any of various freshwater protozoans that are usually oval in shape and that move by means of cilia.

par·a·med·ic (păr′ə-**mĕd′**ĭk) *n.* A person who is trained to give emergency treatment or to assist medical professionals. **—par′a·med′i·cal** *adj.*

pa·ram·e·ter (pə-**răm′**ĭ-tər) *n.* **1.** A constant that varies in equations of the same general form, especially one whose value helps determine the shape of a specific curve or surface. **2.** A fixed limit or boundary: *We must stay within the parameters of the budget.*

par·a·mil·i·tar·y (păr′ə-**mĭl′**ĭ-tĕr′ē) *adj.* Organized or functioning like a military unit but not as part of regular military forces.

par·a·mount (**păr′**ə-mount′) *adj.* **1.** Of greatest importance or concern; primary. **2.** Supreme in rank or position; leading.

par·a·noi·a (păr′ə-**noi′**ə) *n.* **1.** A serious mental disorder marked by the delusion that one is being harassed or persecuted by others, often accompanied by an exaggerated view of one's own importance. **2.** Distrust or suspicion that is excessive or unwarranted: *The spy scandal triggered a mood of national paranoia.*

par·a·noid (**păr′**ə-noid′) *adj.* Relating to or exhibiting paranoia.

par·a·pet (**păr′**ə-pĕt′) *n.* **1.** A low wall or railing along the edge of a roof or balcony. **2.** An embankment protecting soldiers from enemy fire.

par·a·pher·na·lia (păr′ə-fər-**nāl′**yə) *pl.n.* *(used with a singular or plural verb)* The equipment used in or associated with some activity.

par·a·phrase (**păr′**ə-frāz′) *n.* A restatement in other words. ❖ *tr.v.* **par·a·phrased, par·a·phras·ing, par·a·phras·es** To restate in other words: *paraphrasing a passage to clarify its meaning.*

par·a·ple·gi·a (păr′ə-**plē′**jē-ə *or* păr′ə-**plē′**jə) *n.* Paralysis of the lower part of the body including both legs, caused by damage to the spinal cord.

par·a·ple·gic (păr′ə-**plē′**jĭk) *adj.* Relating to paraplegia. ❖ *n.* A person with paraplegia.

par·a·site (**păr′**ə-sīt′) *n.* **1.** An organism that lives and feeds on or in an organism of a different species and causes harm to its host. Lice and tapeworms are parasites. **2.** A person who takes advantage of the generosity of others without making any useful return. [From Greek *parasītos*, person who eats at someone else's table : *para-*, beside + *sītos*, grain, food.]

par·a·sit·ic (păr′ə-**sĭt′**ĭk) *adj.* **1.** Living as a parasite: *Mistletoe is a parasitic plant.* **2.** Relating to parasites: *a parasitic disease.*

par·a·sit·ism (**păr′**ə-sĭ-tĭz′əm) *n.* A relationship between two organisms of different species in which one is a parasite and the other is a host.

par·a·sit·ize (**păr′**ə-sĭ-tīz′) *tr.v.* **par·a·sit·ized, par·a·sit·iz·ing, par·a·sit·iz·es** To live on or in (a host) as a parasite: *Some kinds of ticks parasitize birds.*

par·a·sol (**păr′**ə-sôl′) *n.* A light, usually small umbrella carried as protection from the sun. [From French, from Italian *parasole* : *parare*, to shield + *sole*, sun.]

par·a·sym·pa·thet·ic nervous system (păr′ə-sĭm′pə-**thĕt′**ĭk) *n.* The part of the autonomic nervous system that generally inhibits the physiological effects of the sympathetic nervous system, as in slowing the heart, dilating blood vessels, and stimulating digestive secretions.

par·a·thy·roid (păr′ə-**thī′**roid) *n.* The parathyroid gland.

parathyroid gland *n.* Any of four small kidney-shaped glands that occur in pairs at the sides of the thyroid gland and secrete a hormone that regulates the amount of calcium and phosphorus in the body.

par·a·troop·er (**păr′**ə-tro͞o′pər) *n.* A member of an infantry unit trained and equipped to parachute from airplanes.

par·boil (**pär′**boil′) *tr.v.* **par·boiled, par·boil·ing, par·boils** To boil (food) briefly.

par·cel (**pär′**səl) *n.* **1.** Something wrapped up in a bundle; a package. **2.** A section or piece of land; a plot. **3.** A group; a bunch: *a parcel of assistants.* ❖ *tr.v.* **par·celed, par·cel·ing, par·cels** also **par·celled, par·cel·ling, par·cels** To divide into parts and distribute; allot: *parcel out work.*

parcel post *n.* The branch of the postal service that handles parcels.

parch (pärch) *v.* **parched, parch·ing, parch·es** *—tr.* **1.** To make very dry, especially by intense heat: *A south wind parched the topsoil.* **2.** To dry or roast (corn or peanuts, for example) by heating. *—intr.* To become very dry, especially from intense heat.

parch·ment (**pärch′**mənt) *n.* **1.** The skin of a sheep or goat, prepared as a material to write on. **2.** A piece of writing on a sheet or roll of this skin. **3.** Heavy paper that looks like parchment.

par·don (**pär′**dn) *tr.v.* **par·doned, par·don·ing, par·dons 1.** To release (a person) from punishment or disfavor. See Synonyms at **forgive. 2.** To let (an offense) pass without punishment. **3.** To make allowance for; excuse: *Pardon me for asking.* ❖ *n.* **1.** The act of pardoning; forgiveness. **2.** Exemption from punishment granted by an official with authority over a legal case. **3.** Polite forgiveness, as for a discourtesy, interruption, or failure to hear: *begged her pardon for being late.*

par·don·a·ble (**pär′**dn-ə-bəl) *adj.* Easily pardoned; excusable: *displayed her gold medal with pardonable pride.* **—par′don·a·bly** *adv.*

pare (pâr) *tr.v.* **pared, par·ing, pares 1.** To remove the skin or covering of with a knife: *pare potatoes.* **2.** To remove (a surface part) with a knife; trim off: *held the avocado firmly and pared away the rind.* **3.** To reduce; trim:

pared the budget to a bare minimum. [From Middle English *paren*, from Old French *parer*, from Latin *parāre*, to prepare.]

❑ *These sound alike:* **pare, pair** (two), **pear** (fruit).

par·e·gor·ic (păr′ə-**gôr′**ĭk) *n.* A medicine containing opium and camphor, used to relieve diarrhea and intestinal pain.

pa·ren·chy·ma (pə-**rĕng′**kə-mə) *n.* A simple plant tissue, composed of thin-walled cells and forming the greater part of leaves, roots, the pulp of fruit, and the pith of stems.

par·ent (**pâr′**ənt) *n.* **1a.** A person who contributes one of the two reproductive cells that join to form an embryo; a biological mother or father. **b.** A person who nurtures and raises a child. **2.** An ancestor. **3.** A guardian; a protector. **4.** An organism that produces or generates another. **—par′ent·hood′** *n.*

par·ent·age (**pâr′**ən-tĭj) *n.* Descent from parents or ancestors; lineage; origin.

pa·ren·tal (pə-**rĕn′**tl) *adj.* Relating to a parent or parents: *parental control of a child's money.* **—pa·ren′tal·ly** *adv.*

pa·ren·the·sis (pə-**rĕn′**thĭ-sĭs) *n., pl.* **par·en·the·ses** (pə-**rĕn′**thĭ-sēz′) **1.** Either or both of the upright curved lines, ( ), used to mark off additional or explanatory remarks in printing or writing. **2.** A qualifying or explanatory phrase placed within a sentence in such a way that the sentence is grammatically complete without it. **3.** A comment departing from the main topic.

par·en·thet·i·cal (păr′ən-**thĕt′**ĭ-kəl) *adj.* **1.** Contained or grammatically capable of being contained within parentheses: *a parenthetical construction at the end of a sentence.* **2.** Forming a brief explanation or digression: *a parenthetical aside during a speech.* **—par′en·thet′i·cal·ly** *adv.*

par·ent·ing (**pâr′**ən-tĭng) *n.* The rearing of a child or children, especially the care, love, and guidance given by a parent.

par·fait (pär-**fā′**) *n.* **1.** A sweet frozen dessert made with cream, eggs, and flavoring and served in a tall glass. **2.** A dessert of layers, often of ice cream with various toppings, served in a tall glass. [From French, from Old French *parfait*, perfect, from past participle of *parfaire*, to finish, perfect, from Latin *perficere*.]

pa·ri·ah (pə-**rī′**ə) *n.* A person who has been excluded from society; an outcast.

pa·ri·e·tal bone (pə-**rī′**ĭ-təl) *n.* Either of the two large bones that form the top and sides of the skull.

parietal lobe *n.* The middle portion of each cerebral hemisphere that lies beneath the parietal bone and processes sensory information from the body.

par·i·mu·tu·el (păr′ĭ-**myo͞o′**cho͞o-əl) *n.* A system of betting on races in which the winners divide the total amount bet in proportion to the amounts they bet individually.

par·ing (**pâr′**ĭng) *n.* Something, such as a skin or peeling, that has been pared off.

Par·is[1] (**păr′**ĭs) *n.* In Greek mythology, the Trojan prince whose abduction of Helen caused the Trojan War.

Par·is[2] (**păr′**ĭs) The capital of France, in the north-central part of the country on the Seine River. Paris has been the capital of France since 987.

par·ish (**păr′**ĭsh) *n.* **1a.** A division of a Roman Catholic or Anglican diocese consisting of an area with its own church. **b.** The members of such a division. **2.** An administrative district in Louisiana corresponding to a county in other states.

pa·rish·ion·er (pə-**rĭsh′**ə-nər) *n.* A member of a parish.

par·i·ty (**păr′**ĭ-tē) *n., pl.* **par·i·ties 1.** Equality, as in amount, status, value, or price: *firefighters striking for parity of pay with police officers.* **2.** A fixed relative value between two different kinds of money: *the parity between gold coins and paper currency.* **3.** A level of prices paid to farmers for their products that gives the farmers the same purchasing power they had during a chosen earlier period. **4.** The even or odd quality of an integer. If two integers are both odd or both even, they are said to have the same parity; if one is odd and one even, they have different parity.

park (pärk) *n.* **1.** A tract of land enclosed for recreational use inside a town or city. **2.** A tract of land kept in its natural state for recreational use. **3.** A fairly large or open area used for recreation or entertainment: *an amusement park.* **4.** A stadium or enclosed playing field: *a baseball park.* **5.** A place for storing or leaving vehicles: *a car park.* **6.** A position in a vehicle's transmission that disengages the gears and sets the brake in order to prevent the vehicle from moving: *put the car in park and then turned the ignition off.* ❖ *v.* **parked, park·ing, parks** *—tr.* **1.** To stop or leave (a vehicle) for a time in a certain place away from traffic. **2.** *Informal* To place or leave temporarily: *parked his lunch box on the porch while they played.* —*intr.* To park a motor vehicle: *parked in front of the restaurant.*

par·ka (**pär′**kə) *n.* A warm fur or cloth jacket with a hood.

Par·ker (**pär′**kər), **Charlie** Known as "Bird." 1920–1955. American jazz musician and composer noted for his complex saxophone solos.

park·ing (**pär′**kĭng) *n.* **1.** The act or an instance of parking a vehicle. **2.** Space in which to park vehicles or a vehicle: *I was late because I had a hard time finding parking.*

parking lot *n.* An area for parking motor vehicles.

parking meter *n.* A usually coin-operated device that authorizes the parking of a motor vehicle for a given period of time.

Par·kin·son's disease (**pär′**kĭn-sənz) *n.* A disease of the central nervous system, associated with low levels of dopamine in the brain, that causes tremors in smaller muscles and makes it difficult to move certain larger muscles. The disease usually affects older people and worsens over time. [After James *Parkinson* (1755–1824), British physician.]

Parks (pärks), **Rosa** 1913–2005. American civil rights leader. In 1955, her refusal to give up her seat on a bus to a white man in Montgomery, Alabama, resulted in a citywide bus boycott that helped launch the national civil rights movement.

park·way (**pärk′**wā′) *n.* A broad landscaped highway, often divided by a planted median strip.

par·lance (**pär′**ləns) *n.* A special kind or style of language: *in the parlance of lawyers.*

par·lay (**pär′**lā′ *or* **pär′**lē) *tr.v.* **par·layed, par·lay·ing, par·lays 1.** To bet (money) on two or more successive events at once, with the winnings of one, plus the original stake, to be automatically risked on the next. **2.** To increase (money) to a much larger amount by repeated investments: *parlayed his small capital into a fortune.* **3.** To use to great advantage or transform into something better: *parlayed a knack for mimicry into a career as an entertainer.* ❖ *n.* A bet made up of the sum of a previous wager plus its winnings.

par·ley (**pär′**lē) *n., pl.* **par·leys** A conference, especially between enemies or opponents. ❖ *intr.v.* **par·leyed, par·ley·ing, par·leys** To hold a parley; confer.

par·lia·ment (**pär′**lə-mənt) *n.* **1.** An assembly of people that makes the laws of a nation or an international organization. **2. Parliament** The national legislature of the United Kingdom, made up of the House of Commons and the House of Lords. [From Middle English *parlement*, from Old French *parler*, to talk.]

par·lia·men·tar·i·an (pär′lə-mĕn-**târ′**ē-ən) *n.* **1.** An expert in parliamentary rules and procedures. **2.** A member of a parliament.

par·lia·men·ta·ry (pär′lə-**mĕn′**tə-rē *or* pär′lə-**mĕn′**trē) *adj.* **1.** Relating to a parliament. **2.** Following the rules

parfait

parka

Rosa Parks

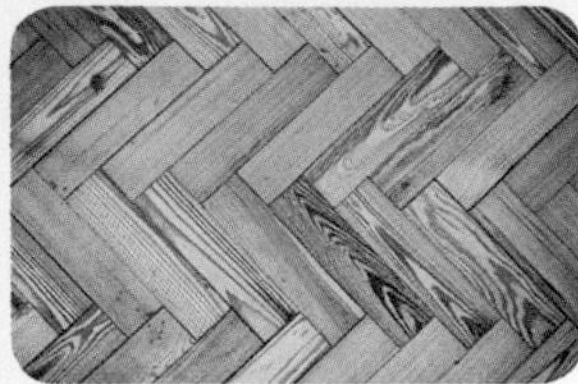

parquetry

parsley

Parthenon
Athens, Greece

ă	pat	ôr	core
ā	pay	oi	boy
âr	care	ou	out
ä	father	ŏŏ	took
ĕ	pet	ŏŏr	lure
ē	be	ōō	boot
ĭ	pit	ŭ	cut
ī	bite	ûr	urge
îr	pier	th	thin
ŏ	pot	*th*	this
ō	toe	zh	vision
ô	paw	ə	about

of procedure of a parliament: *parliamentary debate.* **3.** Having a parliament: *parliamentary government.*

par·lor (pär′lər) *n.* **1.** A room, as in a home or dormitory, for entertaining visitors. **2.** A room or separate section of a building designed for some special use: *a billiard parlor.* **3.** A small business establishment providing a service rather than selling merchandise: *a funeral parlor.* **4.** A small restaurant serving a particular product: *a pizza parlor.* [From Middle English *parlur*, from Old French, from *parler*, to talk.]

par·lour (pär′lər) *n. Chiefly British* Variant of **parlor.**

Par·me·san (pär′mə-zän′) *n.* A hard dry Italian cheese, usually served grated.

pa·ro·chi·al (pə-rō′kē-əl) *adj.* **1.** Relating to a parish: *a parochial priest.* **2.** Relating to a parochial school. **3.** Limited in range or understanding; narrow: *a parochial mind.* **—pa·ro′chi·al·ism** *n.* **—pa·ro′chi·al·ly** *adv.*

parochial school *n.* A day school supported by a religious organization.

par·o·dy (păr′ə-dē) *n., pl.* **par·o·dies 1.** A comic imitation, as of a person, literary work, or style, that exaggerates the characteristics of the original to make it seem ridiculous. **2.** Something so bad as to appear to be a mockery: *The trial was a parody of justice.* ❖ *tr.v.* **par·o·died, par·o·dy·ing, par·o·dies** To present, perform, or be a parody of: *parodied the style of editorial writers.*

pa·role (pə-rōl′) *n.* **1.** The early release of a prisoner on condition of good behavior. **2.** The period during which such a released prisoner is subject to continuing supervision. ❖ *tr.v.* **pa·roled, pa·rol·ing, pa·roles** To release on parole.

pa·rol·ee (pə-rō′lē′) *n.* A person released on parole.

par·ox·ysm (păr′ək-sĭz′əm) *n.* **1.** A sudden outburst of strong emotion: *a paroxysm of anger.* **2.** A spasm or fit; a convulsion.

par·quet (pär-kā′) *n.* **1.** Parquetry. **2.** A floor made of parquetry.

par·quet·ry (pär′kĭ-trē) *n., pl.* **par·quet·ries** Wood, often of contrasting colors, worked into a pattern or mosaic, used especially for floors.

par·ri·cide (păr′ĭ-sīd′) *n.* **1.** The act of murdering one's own father, mother, or other close relative. **2.** A person who commits parricide. **—par′ri·cid′al** (păr′ĭ-sīd′l) *adj.*

par·rot (păr′ət) *n.* **1.** Any of numerous mostly tropical birds having a short hooked bill and usually brightly colored feathers. Some kinds are kept as pets and can be taught to imitate spoken words. **2.** A person who repeats or imitates something without understanding it. ❖ *tr.v.* **par·rot·ed, par·rot·ing, par·rots** To repeat or imitate (another's words or another person), especially without understanding. [Perhaps from French *Perrot*, variant of *Pierrot*, diminutive of *Pierre*, Peter.]

par·ry (păr′ē) *tr.v.* **par·ried, par·ry·ing, par·ries 1.** To turn aside; deflect: *parry a thrust in fencing.* **2.** To avoid skillfully; evade: *parried the reporters' questions.* ❖ *n., pl.* **par·ries 1.** The act or maneuver of deflecting a blow, especially in fencing. **2.** An evasive action or answer: *met the accusation with a deft parry.*

parse (pärs) *v.* **parsed, pars·ing, pars·es** *—tr.* **1a.** To break (a sentence or phrase) down into its parts of speech with an explanation of the form and function of each word. **b.** To indicate the part of speech, form, and function of (a word in a sentence or phrase). **2.** To make sense of; comprehend: *I couldn't parse what you just said.* *—intr.* To be clearly divisible into parts of speech: *a sentence that parses easily.*

par·sec (pär′sĕk′) *n.* A unit of astronomical distance equal to 3.258 light years. [From *par(allax)* + *sec(ond).*]

Par·si (pär′sē *or* pär-sē′) *n., pl.* **Par·sis** A member of a group of Zoroastrians in India.

par·si·mo·ni·ous (pär′sə-mō′nē-əs) *adj.* **1.** Tending to spend or use as little as possible; frugal. **2.** Requiring few assumptions in order to explain something: *Science tends to favor the most parsimonious hypothesis.* **—par′si·mo′ni·ous·ly** *adv.* **—par′si·mo′ni·ous·ness** *n.*

par·si·mo·ny (pär′sə-mō′nē) *n.* **1.** Extreme reluctance to spend money or use resources; stinginess. **2.** Adoption of few assumptions in formulating a theory or interpreting data.

pars·ley (pär′slē) *n., pl.* **pars·leys** A plant having edible, fragrant, finely divided leaves used to flavor food and as a garnish. [From Middle English *perseley*, from Latin *petroselīnum*, from Greek *petroselīnon* : *petrā*, rock + *selīnon*, celery.]

pars·nip (pär′snĭp) *n.* **1.** The long whitish root of a plant related to parsley, eaten as a vegetable. **2.** The plant that has such a root.

par·son (pär′sən) *n.* **1.** A cleric in charge of a parish, especially in the Anglican Church. **2.** A member of the Christian clergy, especially a Protestant minister.

par·son·age (pär′sə-nĭj) *n.* The official residence of a parson, as provided by the church.

part (pärt) *n.* **1.** A portion, division, or segment of a whole: *arrived late and missed part of the movie; gave her a part of the orange.* **2a.** One of several equal portions that when combined make up a whole: *For the dressing we mixed two parts olive oil with one part vinegar.* **b.** A fraction: *What part of a quart is a pint?* **3.** A piece in a machine or system that can be removed or replaced; a component. **4.** often **parts** A region, area, or land: *relatives scattered in remote parts.* **5.** A role: *a small part in the play.* **6.** One of the functions or tasks that must be performed in a common effort; a duty or share: *doing one's part.* **7.** Natural ability; talent: *a man of parts.* **8a.** Music assigned to one or more musicians as part of a composition for a larger ensemble: *singing the soprano part.* **b.** A written representation of such music. **9.** The line where the hair on the head is parted. ❖ *v.* **part·ed, part·ing, parts** *—tr.* **1.** To divide into two or more parts; split: *parted the log with an axe.* **2.** To put or keep apart; come between: *They were good friends until a silly quarrel parted them.* See Synonyms at **separate. 3.** To comb (hair, for example) away from a dividing line, as on the scalp. *—intr.* **1.** To become divided or separated: *The tree trunk parted into branches higher up.* **2.** To go away or leave one another; depart or separate: *After the argument, they still parted as friends.* ❖ *adv.* In part; partially: *a part brown, part white cow.* ❖ *adj.* Not full; partial: *a part owner of the business.* ◆ **for (one's) part** So far as one is concerned: *For my part, I have no objections.* **for the most part** In most cases; chiefly. **in part** To some extent; partly. **part and parcel** A basic or essential part: *paying for moving was part and parcel of the job offer.* **part company** or **part ways** To leave one another; to separate. **part with** To give up or let go of; yield: *hated to part with her hard-earned salary.* **take part** To join in; participate: *She took part in the discussion.* [From Middle English, from Old French, from Latin *pars.*]

part. *abbr.* An abbreviation of participle.

par·take (pär-tāk′) *intr.v.* **par·took** (pär-to͝ok′), **par·tak·en** (pär-tā′kən), **par·tak·ing, par·takes 1.** To take part; participate: *partake in the festivities.* **2.** To take a portion; eat or drink a helping: *invited to partake of their dinner.* **3.** To share some of the properties of something else: *laughter that partook of a chicken's cackle.* [From Middle English *part-taker*, one who takes part.] **—par·tak′er** *n.*

par·the·no·gen·e·sis (pär′thə-nō-jĕn′ĭ-sĭs) *n.* Reproduction in which an egg develops without fertilization, as in certain insects. **—par′the·no·ge·net′ic** (pär′thə-nō-jə-nĕt′ĭk) *adj.* **—par′the·no·ge·net′i·cal·ly** *adv.*

Par·the·non (pär′thə-nŏn′) *n.* The chief temple of

the goddess Athena, built on the Acropolis at Athens, Greece, in the fifth century BC.

par·tial (pär′shəl) *adj.* **1.** Not total; incomplete: *partial success.* **2.** Favoring one side; biased. **3.** Especially attracted; particularly fond: *She's partial to detective stories.* [From Middle English *parcial,* from Old French, from Late Latin *partiālis,* from Latin *pars,* part.]

par·ti·al·i·ty (pär′shē-ăl′ĭ-tē) *n., pl.* **par·ti·al·i·ties 1.** An inclination to favor one side over another or others; a bias: *trying to judge without partiality.* **2.** A strong preference; a special fondness: *a partiality for cats.*

par·tial·ly (pär′shə-lē) *adv.* To a certain degree or extent; incompletely: *partially cooked food.*

partial product *n.* The product of the amounts represented by one digit of a multiplicand and one digit of a multiplier. For instance, in 67 × 12, the digit 6 represents 60 and the digit 1 represents 10, so 60 × 10, or 600, is a partial product. The sum of all possible partial products of two numbers is the product of those numbers.

par·tic·i·pant (pär-tĭs′ə-pənt) *n.* A person who participates: *participants in a card game.*

par·tic·i·pate (pär-tĭs′ə-pāt′) *intr.v.* **par·tic·i·pat·ed, par·tic·i·pat·ing, par·tic·i·pates** To join with others in doing something; take part: *She participated in a discussion group.* [From Latin *participāre,* from *particeps,* partaker, from *pars,* part.] —**par·tic′i·pa′tion** *n.*

par·tic·i·pa·to·ry (pär-tĭs′ə-pə-tôr′ē) *adj.* Involving active participation by individuals: *participatory democracy.*

par·ti·cip·i·al (pär′tĭ-sĭp′ē-əl) *adj.* Based on, forming, or formed from a participle: *a participial phrase; a participial adjective.*

par·ti·ci·ple (pär′tĭ-sĭp′əl) *n.* A verb form, in English usually ending in *-ing* or *-ed,* that is used with auxiliary verbs to indicate certain tenses and that can also function as an adjective. The past participle is also used to make the passive voice. [From Middle English, from Latin *participium,* from *particeps,* partaker, from *pars,* part.] —SEE NOTE.

par·ti·cle (pär′tĭ-kəl) *n.* **1.** A very small piece or part; a tiny portion or speck: *particles of dust.* **2.** A subatomic particle. **3a.** The smallest possible unit or portion: *applying every particle of strength she had left.* **b.** The least bit or degree: *hardly a particle of difference between the twins.* **4.** In grammar, any of a class of words, including many prepositions and conjunctions, that have little meaning by themselves but help to specify, connect, or limit the meanings of other words. [From Middle English, from Latin *particula,* tiny part, diminutive of *pars,* part.]

particle accelerator *n.* A device, such as a cyclotron or linear accelerator, that accelerates charged subatomic particles or nuclei to high speeds in order to collide them with other particles or targets. Particle accelerators are used to study the structures of atoms and subatomic particles.

par·ti-col·ored (pär′tē-kŭl′ərd) *adj.* Having different parts or sections colored differently; pied.

par·tic·u·lar (pər-tĭk′yə-lər) *adj.* **1.** Belonging to or associated with a specific person, group, or thing; not general: *the particular characteristics that distinguish oaks from other trees.* **2.** Distinct from others; specific; certain: *at that particular time of year.* **3.** Exceptional; special: *paying particular attention.* **4.** Providing full details: *a particular account of the incident.* **5.** Giving or demanding close attention to details; fussy: *She's very particular about how her meat is cooked.* ❖ *n.* **1.** A single item, fact, or detail: *correct in every particular.* **2. particulars** Items of information; detailed news: *reported the particulars of their voyage.* ◆ **in particular** Particularly; especially. [From Middle English, from Old French *particuler,* from Latin *particula,* small part, particle.]

par·tic·u·lar·i·ty (pər-tĭk′yə-lăr′ĭ-tē) *n., pl.* **par·tic·u·lar·i·ties 1.** The quality of being particular rather than general or universal: *the particularity of a proper noun, which names only one thing or person.* **2.** The quality of including or providing details: *the particularity of a newspaper story.* **3.** Close attention to details; fussiness. **4.** A detail; a particular.

par·tic·u·lar·ize (pər-tĭk′yə-lə-rīz′) *v.* **par·tic·u·lar·ized, par·tic·u·lar·iz·ing, par·tic·u·lar·iz·es** —*tr.* **1.** To name one by one; itemize: *an indictment that particularized the charges against him.* **2.** To make particular; individualize: *She began with mere stick figures, then particularized them by drawing in faces.* —*intr.* To give details or particulars. —**par·tic′u·lar·i·za′tion** (pər-tĭk′yə-lər-ĭ-zā′shən) *n.*

par·tic·u·lar·ly (pər-tĭk′yə-lər-lē) *adv.* **1.** To a great degree; especially: *a particularly good play.* **2.** As one specific case; specifically: *observing the constellations, particularly the Big Dipper.* **3.** With attention to particulars; in detail: *spread out the chart and studied it particularly.*

par·tic·u·late (pər-tĭk′yə-lĭt *or* pər-tĭk′yə-lāt′) *adj.* Relating to or formed of separate particles.

part·ing (pär′tĭng) *n.* **1.** The act of dividing or the state of being divided; separation: *a parting in the trail.* **2.** A departure or leave-taking. ❖ *adj.* Leaving; departing: *a parting friend.*

par·ti·san (pär′tĭ-zən) *n.* **1.** A strong supporter, as of a party, cause, person, or idea: *the president and his partisans in Congress.* **2.** A member of an organized body of fighters who attack an enemy within occupied territory; a guerilla. ❖ *adj.* **1.** Relating to a partisan or partisans: *partisan politics.* **2.** Having or showing a strong preference or bias: *too partisan to give a fair account of the battle.* [From French, from Italian *partigiano,* from *parte,* part, from Latin *pars.*]

par·ti·tion (pär-tĭsh′ən) *n.* **1.** The act or process of dividing something into parts. **2.** Something that divides or separates, as a wall dividing one room or cubicle from another. **3.** Division of a country into separate, autonomous nations. ❖ *tr.v.* **par·ti·tioned, par·ti·tion·ing, par·ti·tions 1.** To divide into separate spaces, parts, or sections: *partitioned the room with a curtain.* **2.** To form into a separate space by means of a partition: *partitioned off the dining area from the kitchen.* [From Middle English *partisoun,* from Latin *partītiō,* from Latin *partīre,* to divide, from *pars,* part.]

part·ly (pärt′lē) *adv.* To some extent but not completely: *a journey partly by boat and partly on foot.*

part·ner (pärt′nər) *n.* **1.** One of two or more people associated in some common activity, as: **a.** A member of a business partnership. **b.** Either of two people dancing together. **c.** Either of two people cooperating in a game. **2a.** A husband or wife; a spouse. **b.** A person with whom one is involved in a romantic relationship, especially a person with whom one shares a home without being married. [From Middle English *partiner,* alteration of *parcener,* joint heir, from Old French *parçon,* share, from Latin *partītiō,* partition.]

part·ner·ship (pärt′nər-shĭp′) *n.* **1.** The condition of being partners: *built the tree house in partnership with two friends.* **2.** A business contract or relationship between two or more people in which each agrees to work for a common enterprise and to share the profits or losses. **3.** A close relationship in which each member helps or cooperates with the other: *the partnership of science and industry.*

part of speech *n., pl.* **parts of speech** One of the grammatical classes into which words are placed according to how they function in a given context. Traditionally, the parts of speech in English are *noun, pronoun, verb, adjective, adverb, preposition, conjunction,* and *interjec-*

USAGE

participle You should always avoid the "dangling" **participle,** as in the sentence *Turning the corner, the view was quite different.* This sentence is constructed so that it seems that the present participle *turning* modifies the noun *view.* As you read the sentence, you might at first think that the view is turning the corner. You should rewrite such sentences: *The view was quite different when we turned the corner,* or *Turning the corner, we saw a different view.*

partridge

USAGE

pass The past tense and past participle of the verb **pass** is *passed: They passed* (or *have passed*) *our home. Past* is the corresponding adjective (*in centuries past*), adverb (*A car drove past*), preposition (*past midnight; past the crisis*), and noun (*lived in the past*).

passionflower

ă	pat	ôr	core
ā	pay	oi	boy
âr	care	ou	out
ä	father	o͝o	took
ĕ	pet	o͝or	lure
ē	be	o͞o	boot
ĭ	pit	ŭ	cut
ī	bite	ûr	urge
îr	pier	th	thin
ŏ	pot	*th*	this
ō	toe	zh	vision
ô	paw	ə	about

tion. Sometimes *article* is considered a separate part of speech.

par·took (pär-to͝ok′) *v.* Past tense of **partake.**

par·tridge (pär′trĭj) *n., pl.* **partridge** or **par·tridg·es** Any of several plump birds related to the pheasants, having brownish feathers and often hunted as game.

part-time (pärt′tīm′) *adj.* For or during only part of the usual or standard working time: *a part-time job.* **—part′-time′** *adv.*

par·tu·ri·tion (pär′tyo͞o-**rĭsh′**ən) *n.* The act or process of giving birth; childbirth.

part·way (pärt′wā′) *adv. Informal* To a certain degree or distance: *partway to town; not even partway reasonable.*

par·ty (pär′tē) *n., pl.* **par·ties 1.** A social gathering for pleasure or entertainment: *a birthday party.* **2.** A group of people participating together in some activity: *a search party.* **3.** A group organized to advance its political views and usually to nominate and support candidates for public office. **4a.** A person or group involved in a legal proceeding: *the two parties in a lawsuit.* **b.** A person or group taking part in some action or matter; a participant: *She refused to be a party to the dispute.* ❖ *intr.v.* **par·tied, par·ty·ing, par·ties** To celebrate at a party. [From Middle English *partie*, part, side, group, from Old French, from *partir*, to divide, from Latin *partīre*, from Latin *pars*, part.]

pas·cal (pă-**skăl′** *or* pä-**skäl′**) *n.* A unit used to measure pressure, equal to one newton per square meter. [After Blaise *Pascal* (1623–1662), French mathematician.]

pas·chal (păs′kəl) *adj.* Relating to Passover or Easter.

Pash·to (pŭsh′tō) *n.* The Iranian language of the Pashtuns.

Pash·tun (pŭsh′to͞on) *n.* A member of the main ethnic group of Afghanistan and parts of western Pakistan.

Pa·siph·a·ë (pə-**sĭf′**ə-ē′) *n.* In Greek mythology, the wife of Minos and the mother of the Minotaur.

pass (păs) *v.* **passed, pass·ing, pass·es** *—intr.* **1.** To go or move; proceed: *people passing from shop to shop.* **2.** To extend; run: *The river passes through our town.* **3.** To move by: *The crowd cheered as the band passed.* **4.** To go by in time: *Time seems to pass quickly when you're on vacation.* **5.** To be transferred: *Ownership of the farm passed to his niece.* **6.** To be changed from one condition to another: *Daylight passed into darkness.* **7.** To come to an end: *My anger passed.* **8.** To happen; take place: *What passed at the meeting?* **9a.** To be allowed to happen without notice or action: *She let his rude remark pass.* **b.** To decline one's turn in a game or competition. **c.** To decline an offer: *We offered him dessert, but he passed.* **10.** To undergo a course of study, an examination, or a difficulty with favorable results: *After studying hard, I passed.* **11.** To be approved: *The law passed in the Senate by a large majority.* **12.** In sports, to throw or propel a ball or puck to a teammate. *—tr.* **1.** To go by; move ahead of: *She passed the lead runner on the home stretch.* **2.** To go across; go through: *We passed the border into Virginia.* **3.** To allow to go by; spend: *He passed the winter in Vermont.* **4.** To go beyond; surpass: *The results of the experiment passed all our expectations.* **5.** To undergo (an examination, for example) with favorable results. **6.** To cause to move or go in a certain way: *I passed the bolt through the bracket and secured it.* **7a.** To transfer; circulate: *passed the news to friends.* **b.** To hand over: *Please pass the beans.* **8.** In sports, to throw or propel (a ball or puck) to a teammate. **9.** To discharge (bodily waste). **10a.** To approve or adopt: *The Senate passed the bill.* **b.** To be approved or adopted by: *The bill passed the Senate.* **11.** To pronounce; utter: *pass judgment.* ❖ *n.* **1.** A way through or around an obstacle, especially a gap in a mountain range. **2a.** A permit or ticket granting the right to come and go at will. **b.** A ticket granting free entrance or transportation. **3.** A run by a military aircraft over a target area. **4.** A situation, especially a difficult or threatening one: *His own folly brought him to this pass.* **5.** An act or statement that indicates one's romantic or sexual interest in someone else. **6.** A motion with the hand or something held in the hand: *made a pass with the sponge over the table.* **7.** In sports, an act of passing a ball or puck to a teammate. ◆ **bring to pass** To cause to happen. **come to pass** To occur. **pass away** To die. **pass for** To be accepted as or believed to be: *My mother can pass for my sister.* **pass off** To describe, offer, or sell as genuine: *passed off the rhinestones as diamonds.* **pass out** To lose consciousness. **pass over** To leave out; disregard. **pass the buck** To shift responsibility or blame to someone else. **pass up** *Informal* To let go by; refuse: *I won't pass up dessert.* —SEE NOTE.

pass·a·ble (păs′ə-bəl) *adj.* **1.** Capable of being passed or crossed: *a passable road.* **2.** Satisfactory but not outstanding; adequate: *a passable job of acting.* **—pass′a·bly** *adv.*

pas·sage (păs′ĭj) *n.* **1.** The act or process of passing: *They opened the vents to allow the passage of air.* **2.** A journey, especially by water: *a rough passage across the Atlantic.* **3.** The right to travel on something, especially a ship: *We booked passage to London.* **4.** Enactment by a legislature: *the passage of a law.* **5a.** A channel, duct, or path through or along which something may pass: *the nasal passages.* **b.** A corridor. **6.** A section of a written work or speech: *a biblical passage.* **7.** A section of a musical composition: *a passage for solo violin.*

pas·sage·way (păs′ĭj-wā′) *n.* A corridor or hallway.

pass·book (păs′bo͝ok′) *n.* A bankbook.

pas·sé (pă-**sā′**) *adj.* No longer in fashion.

pas·sen·ger (păs′ən-jər) *n.* A person riding in a vehicle who is not participating in its operation. [From Middle English *passajour*, from Old French *passageor*, from *passage*, passage.]

passenger pigeon *n.* A pigeon that was once common in North America but has been extinct since the late 1800s.

pas·ser·by (păs′ər-**bī′**) *n., pl.* **pas·sers·by** A person who happens to be passing by, especially by chance.

pas·ser·ine (păs′ə-rīn′) *adj.* Relating to a group of birds that includes more than half of all living bird species, including the songbirds. ❖ *n.* A passerine bird.

pass-fail (păs′**fāl′**) *adj.* Relating to a system of grading in which the student either passes or fails and does not receive a letter grade.

pass·ing (păs′ĭng) *adj.* **1.** Going by: *a passing car.* **2.** Not lasting long; temporary: *a passing fad.* **3.** Superficial; casual: *a passing remark.* **4.** Allowing a person to pass a test, a course of study, or something similar; satisfactory: *a passing grade.* ❖ *n.* **1.** The act of going by or the fact of having passed: *the passing of summer.* **2.** Death: *We mourned his passing.* ◆ **in passing** While going by; incidentally.

pas·sion (păsh′ən) *n.* **1.** A powerful feeling such as love, joy, or hatred. **2a.** Great enthusiasm for a certain activity or subject: *a passion for music.* **b.** The object of such enthusiasm or devotion: *Golf is his passion.* **3. Passion a.** The sufferings of Jesus on the cross following the Last Supper and including the Crucifixion. **b.** A narrative or musical setting of Jesus's sufferings.

pas·sion·ate (păsh′ə-nĭt) *adj.* **1.** Showing or expressing strong feeling: *a passionate speech.* **2.** Arising from or marked by strong feeling: *passionate involvement in a cause.* **—pas′sion·ate·ly** *adv.*

pas·sion·flow·er (păsh′ən-flou′ər) *n.* Any of various chiefly tropical vines having large showy flowers.

pas·sion·fruit (păsh′ən-fro͞ot′) *n.* The sweet edible fruit of a passionflower.

Passion play *n.* A play representing the Passion of Jesus.

pas·sive (păs′ĭv) *adj.* **1.** Acted upon but not acting in return: *He played a passive role and just went along with what the others wanted.* **2.** Accepting or submitting without objection or resistance: *a passive acceptance of one's fate.* **3.** Relating to the passive voice in grammar. ❖ *n.* **1.** The passive voice in grammar. **2.** A verb form in the passive voice. [From Middle English, from Latin *passīvus*, subject to passion or emotion, from *patī*, to experience.] **—pas′sive·ly** *adv.* **—pas′sive·ness** *n.* —SEE NOTE AT **verb.**

passive resistance *n.* Refusal to obey or cooperate with a government or other authority, especially as a form of protest against injustice.

passive smoke *n.* Secondhand smoke.

passive voice *n.* In grammar, a verb form or voice that shows that the subject receives the action expressed by the verb. In the sentence *The trees were planted in a row, were planted* is in the passive voice.

pas·siv·i·ty (pă-sĭv′ĭ-tē) *n.* The quality or condition of being passive; submissiveness.

pass·key (păs′kē′) *n.* **1.** A master key. **2.** An electronic password.

Pass·o·ver (păs′ō′vər) *n.* A Jewish holiday lasting eight days in the spring and commemorating the escape of the Jews from Egypt.

pass pattern *n.* In football, a planned course that a receiver runs in order to be in position to catch a pass.

pass·port (păs′pôrt′) *n.* **1.** An official document, generally in booklet form, that identifies a person as a citizen of a country and permits that person to travel abroad. **2.** Something that assures the achievement of something else: *Hard work is often a passport to success.*

pass·word (păs′wûrd′) *n.* A secret word, phrase, or sequence of characters that a person uses to get into a place or gain access to information.

past (păst) *adj.* **1.** Gone by; over: *That day is past.* **2.** Having existed or occurred at an earlier time; bygone: *past victories.* **3.** Just ended; just over: *in the past few days.* **4.** Having formerly been or served as: *a past vice president.* **5.** In grammar, relating to the past tense. ❖ *n.* **1.** The time before the present: *memories of the past.* **2.** A person's history, background, or former activities: *a woman with a distinguished past.* **3.** The past tense. ❖ *adv.* So as to pass by and go beyond: *He waved as he drove past.* ❖ *prep.* **1.** Beyond in time: *It is well past midnight.* **2.** Beyond in position: *My house is a mile past the river.* **3.** Beyond the power or scope of: *His behavior is past all explanation.* **4.** Beyond the number and amount of: *The child could not count past 20.* —SEE NOTE AT **pass.**

pas·ta (päs′tə) *n.* **1.** Dough made of flour, water, and sometimes eggs, molded into any of a variety of shapes and boiled. **2.** A prepared dish containing pasta as its main ingredient.

paste (pāst) *n.* **1.** A smooth sticky substance, as that made of flour and water or starch and water, used to fasten light things together. **2.** A dough of flour, water, and shortening, used in making pastry. **3.** A food that has been made soft and creamy by pounding or grinding: *almond paste.* **4.** A hard brilliant glass used in making artificial gems. ❖ *tr.v.* **past·ed, past·ing, pastes 1.** To fasten or attach with paste: *paste the broken pieces together.* **2.** To cover with something to which paste has been applied: *paste the wall with posters.* **3.** To insert (text or graphics) into a document or computer file. [From Middle English, dough, paste, from Late Latin *pasta*, from Greek, barley-porridge.]

paste·board (pāst′bôrd′) *n.* A thin firm board made of pressed wood pulp or sheets of paper pasted together.

pas·tel (pă-stĕl′) *n.* **1.** A crayon resembling a piece of chalk, used in drawing or marking. **2.** A picture drawn or painted with this type of crayon. **3.** A soft delicate color or hue. ❖ *adj.* **1.** Relating to or drawn with pastels. **2.** Pale and soft in color. [From Italian *pastello*, crayon made of pigment paste, from *pasta*, paste, from Late Latin.]

pas·tern (păs′tərn) *n.* **1.** The part of a horse's leg that is between the fetlock and the hoof. **2.** A corresponding part of the leg of a dog or other four-footed animal.

Pas·teur (păs-tûr′), **Louis** 1822–1895. French chemist who developed the process of pasteurization and several important vaccines. Pasteur was an influential proponent of the theory that germs cause communicable infectious diseases. —SEE NOTE.

pas·teur·i·za·tion (păs′chər-ĭ-zā′shən) *n.* A process in which milk, juice, or other liquids are heated to a specific temperature for a certain amount of time to kill harmful germs or prevent fermentation. [After Louis *Pasteur*.] —SEE NOTE AT **Pasteur, Louis.**

pas·teur·ize (păs′chə-rīz′) *tr.v.* **pas·teur·ized, pas·teur·iz·ing, pas·teur·iz·es** To treat (a liquid) by pasteurization.

pas·time (păs′tīm′) *n.* An activity that occupies one's spare time pleasantly.

pas·tor (păs′tər) *n.* A Christian minister or priest who is the leader of a congregation. [From Middle English *pastour*, from Latin *pāstor*, shepherd.]

pas·tor·al (păs′tər-əl *or* pă-stôr′əl) *adj.* **1.** Relating to or portraying shepherds or country life: *a pastoral scene.* **2.** Relating to a pastor or pastors: *pastoral duties.* **—pas′tor·al·ly** *adv.*

pas·tor·ate (păs′tər-ĭt) *n.* **1.** The office or term of office of a pastor. **2.** A group of pastors.

past participle *n.* A participle that expresses past or completed action or time. It is used as an adjective (as in *a finished work*), to form the passive voice (as in *The work was finished on time*), and to form the perfect tenses of the active voice (as in *I have finished the work*).

past perfect tense *n.* A verb tense that expresses action completed before a specified or implied past time. In English the past perfect tense is formed with the past participle of a verb and the auxiliary *had*, as *had learned* in the sentence *She had learned to drive before the month was over.*

pas·tra·mi (pə-strä′mē) *n., pl.* **pas·tra·mis** A seasoned smoked cut of beef, usually taken from the shoulder.

pas·try (pā′strē) *n., pl.* **pas·tries 1.** Dough of flour, water, and shortening, used for the crusts of pies, tarts, and other baked foods. **2.** A baked food, such as a tart, that is made with this dough.

past tense *n.* A verb tense used to express an action or condition that occurred in or during the past. In the sentence *I wrote a letter while you were sleeping, wrote* and *were sleeping* are in the past tense.

pas·tur·age (păs′chər-ĭj) *n.* **1.** The grass and other plants eaten by grazing animals. **2.** Land covered with grass or vegetation suitable for grazing animals.

pas·ture (păs′chər) *n.* **1.** A piece of land covered with grass and other plants eaten by grazing animals such as cattle, horses, or sheep. **2.** Grass and other plants eaten by grazing animals. ❖ *tr.v.* **pas·tured, pas·tur·ing, pas·tures** To put (animals) in a pasture to graze.

past·y[1] (pā′stē) *adj.* **past·i·er, past·i·est** Resembling paste in color or texture. [From *paste*.] **—past′i·ness** *n.*

pas·ty[2] (păs′tē) *n., pl.* **pas·ties** *Chiefly British* A seasoned meat pie. [From Middle English *pastey*, from Old French *paste*, from Late Latin *pasta*, paste.]

pat[1] (păt) *tr.v.* **pat·ted, pat·ting, pats 1.** To tap or stroke gently with the open hand, often as a sign of affection. **2.** To flatten or shape by tapping gently with the hands or a flat instrument: *pat down the curls.* ❖ *n.* **1a.** A light stroke or tap. **b.** The sound made by a stroke or tap or by light footsteps. **2.** A small piece or lump: *a pat of*

Louis Pasteur

BIOGRAPHY

Louis Pasteur In the 1860s, Louis **Pasteur** performed a series of experiments demonstrating that the fermentation of wine to vinegar was caused by microscopic organisms—germs—that infested the wine from outside, settling on it from the air and reproducing within it. These experiments contradicted the view that *fermentation* was caused by agents arising spontaneously from within the wine itself. Pasteur then carried his discovery further: If fermentation was caused by outside organisms, couldn't animal and plant diseases be caused by a similar process? Pasteur identified the organisms that caused fermentation and developed a method of killing them known as *pasteurization*. He spent the rest of his life working to isolate the germs that caused specific diseases and to find treatments to cure them.

pastoral
Summer, 1576, by Francesco Bassano the Younger (1549–1592)

patchwork

Linus Pauling
photographed in 1982

ă	pat	ôr	core
ā	pay	oi	boy
âr	care	ou	out
ä	father	o͝o	took
ĕ	pet	o͝or	lure
ē	be	o͞o	boot
ĭ	pit	ŭ	cut
ī	bite	ûr	urge
îr	pier	th	thin
ŏ	pot	*th*	this
ō	toe	zh	vision
ô	paw	ə	about

butter. ◆ **pat on the back** A word or gesture of praise or approval. [From Middle English *pat*, a blow, a stroke, probably of imitative origin.]

pat² (păt) *adj.* Ostensibly satisfactory but unconvincing because of being trite, glib, or calculated to serve a purpose: *Nobody was satisfied by the politician's pat answers to their questions.* ◆ **have down pat** To know thoroughly or perfectly: *I have the names of the state capitals down pat.* [From *pat*, tap.]

pat. *abbr.* An abbreviation of patent.

Pat·a·go·ni·a (păt′ə-**gō′**nē-ə *or* păt′ə-**gōn′**yə) A plateau region of South America in southern Argentina and Chile extending east from the Andes.

patch (păch) *n.* **1a.** A small piece of material used to cover a hole, rip, or worn place. **b.** A small piece of cloth used for patchwork. **c.** A small cloth badge attached to a garment as a decoration or an insignia. **2.** A protective pad worn over a wound or an injured eye. **3.** A small piece of land, usually with plants growing on it: *a berry patch.* **4.** A small part or area that differs from or contrasts with what surrounds it: *a patch of blue sky.* ❖ *tr.v.* **patched, patch·ing, patch·es 1.** To put a patch or patches on. **2.** To put together or mend: *They patched together the table from broken pieces.* ◆ **patch up** To settle or smooth over: *They patched up their quarrel.*

patch·work (**păch′**wûrk′) *n.* **1.** Needlework consisting of pieces of cloth of various colors sewn together, as in a quilt. **2.** A mixture of many diverse parts; a jumble: *The wallpaper is a patchwork of many colors.*

patch·y (**păch′**ē) *adj.* **patch·i·er, patch·i·est 1.** Made up of or marked by patches: *patchy pants.* **2.** Uneven in quality or performance: *patchy work.* **—patch′i·ly** *adv.* **—patch′i·ness** *n.*

pate (pāt) *n.* The human head, especially the top of the head: *a bald pate.*

pâ·té (pä-**tā′**) *n.* A meat paste. [From French, from Old French *paste*, paste, pâté.]

pa·tel·la (pə-**tĕl′**ə) *n., pl.* **pa·tel·lae** (pə-**tĕl′**ē) A flat triangular bone located at the front of the knee joint.

pat·ent (**păt′**nt) *n.* A grant made by a government that assures an inventor the sole right to make, use, and sell an invention for a stated period of time. ❖ *adj.* (*also* **pāt′**nt) Obvious; plain: *a patent falsehood.* ❖ *tr.v.* **pat·ent·ed, pat·ent·ing, pat·ents 1.** To obtain a patent on. **2.** To grant a patent to. [From Middle English *patent*, document granting a right, from Old French *(lettre) patente*, open (letter), from Latin *patēns*, open.] **—pat′ent·ly** *adv.*

pat·ent·ee (păt′n-**tē′**) *n.* A person, group, or business that has been granted a patent.

patent leather *n.* Black leather with a smooth, hard, shiny surface, used for shoes, belts, pocketbooks, and similar items.

pa·ter·nal (pə-**tûr′**nəl) *adj.* **1.** Relating to or characteristic of a father; fatherly. **2.** Received from a father: *a paternal trait in his makeup.* **3.** Related through one's father: *my paternal aunt.* **—pa·ter′nal·ly** *adv.*

pa·ter·nal·ism (pə-**tûr′**nə-lĭz′əm) *n.* The policy or practice of treating or governing people in a manner that provides for their needs but does not give them responsibility. **—pa·ter′nal·is′tic** *adj.*

pa·ter·ni·ty (pə-**tûr′**nĭ-tē) *n., pl.* **pa·ter·ni·ties 1.** The fact or condition of being a father. **2.** Ancestry or descent on a father's side.

pa·ter·nos·ter (pä′tər-**nŏs′**tər *or* pă′tər-**nŏs′**tər) *n.* The Lord's Prayer. [From Latin *pater noster*, our father (the first words of the prayer in Latin).]

path (păth) *n., pl.* **paths** (păthz *or* păths) **1.** A track or way made by footsteps: *a path in the woods.* **2.** A road or way made for a particular purpose: *shovel a path through the snow.* **3.** The route or course along which something moves: *the path of a hurricane.* **4.** A course or manner of conduct: *the path of righteousness.*

pa·thet·ic (pə-**thĕt′**ĭk) *adj.* **1.** Arousing scornful pity: *a pathetic effort at humor.* **2.** Arousing sympathy or sorrow. **—pa·thet′i·cal·ly** *adv.*

path·find·er (**păth′**fīn′dər) *n.* A person who discovers a way through or into unexplored regions.

path·o·gen (**păth′**ə-jən) *n.* Something that causes disease, especially a virus, bacterium, protozoan, or fungus.

path·o·gen·ic (păth′ə-**jĕn′**ĭk) *adj.* Capable of causing disease: *pathogenic bacteria.*

path·o·log·i·cal (păth′ə-**lŏj′**ĭ-kəl) also **path·o·log·ic** (păth′ə-**lŏj′**ĭk) *adj.* **1.** Relating to disease: *a pathological condition.* **2.** Relating to chronic behavior that is usually antisocial and manipulative, such as lying. **—path′o·log′i·cal·ly** *adv.*

pa·thol·o·gy (pă-**thŏl′**ə-jē) *n., pl.* **pa·thol·o·gies 1.** The scientific and medical study of disease and its causes, processes, and effects. **2.** The physical changes in the body and its functioning as a result of a disease or disorder. **—pa·thol′o·gist** *n.*

pa·thos (**pā′**thŏs′) *n.* A quality in a person or thing that arouses feelings of pity, sympathy, tenderness, or sorrow.

path·way (**păth′**wā′) *n.* A path.

pa·tience (**pā′**shəns) *n.* The capacity, quality, or fact of being patient.

pa·tient (**pā′**shənt) *adj.* **1.** Enduring trouble, hardship, annoyance, or delay without complaint or anger. **2.** Persevering; persistent: *the patient piecing together of evidence.* **3.** Showing or expressing patience: *a patient smile.* ❖ *n.* A person who receives medical care or treatment. **—pa′tient·ly** *adv.*

pat·i·o (**păt′**ē-ō′) *n., pl.* **pat·i·os 1.** An outdoor space for dining or recreation, next to a house or apartment. **2.** An inner courtyard open to the sky.

pat·ois (**păt′**wä′ *or* pă-**twä′**) *n., pl.* **pat·ois** (**păt′**wäz′ *or* pă-**twä′**) A regional dialect of a language, especially one used chiefly in speech rather than in writing.

pa·tri·arch (**pā′**trē-ärk′) *n.* **1.** A man who is a father and head of a family, clan, or tribe. **2.** In certain churches, a high-ranking bishop. **3.** A respected older man. **4.** In the Bible, any of the male ancestors of the Israelites.

pa·tri·ar·chal (**pā′**trē-är′kəl) *adj.* **1.** Relating to a patriarch. **2.** Ruled by a patriarch: *a patriarchal congregation.*

pa·tri·ar·chy (pā′trē-**är′**kē) *n., pl.* **pa·tri·ar·chies 1.** A social system in which the father is the head of the family. **2.** Dominance of a society by men.

pa·tri·cian (pə-**trĭsh′**ən) *n.* **1.** A member of one of the noble families of ancient Rome. **2.** A member of an aristocracy. **3.** A person of refined upbringing, manners, and tastes. **—pa·tri′cian** *adj.*

pat·ri·cide (**păt′**rĭ-sīd′) *n.* Parricide. **—pat′ri·cid′al** *adj.*

Pat·rick (**păt′**rĭk), Saint. AD 389?–461? Christian missionary and patron saint of Ireland.

pat·ri·mo·ny (**păt′**rə-mō′nē) *n., pl.* **pat·ri·mo·nies 1.** Property inherited from a father or other ancestor. **2.** An inheritance or legacy; a heritage. **—pat′ri·mo′ni·al** *adj.*

pa·tri·ot (**pā′**trē-ət) *n.* A person who loves, supports, and defends his or her country. [From Greek *patriōtēs*, person from the same country, from *patrios*, of one's fathers, from *patēr*, father.]

pa·tri·ot·ic (pā′trē-**ŏt′**ĭk) *adj.* Feeling or expressing love for one's country: *a patriotic song.* **—pa′tri·ot′i·cal·ly** *adv.*

pa·tri·ot·ism (**pā′**trē-ə-tĭz′əm) *n.* Love of and devotion to one's country.

pa·trol (pə-**trōl′**) *v.* **pa·trolled, pa·trol·ling, pa·trols** *—tr.* To walk or travel through (an area) checking for possible trouble or making inspections. *—intr.* To patrol an area: *We patrolled from midnight until dawn.* ❖ *n.* **1.** The act of patrolling: *The soldiers are out on patrol.* **2.**

A group of people, vehicles, ships, or aircraft that patrols an area. **3.** A division of a Boy Scout or Girl Scout troop, consisting of six to eight children. [From French *patrouiller*, from Old French *patouiller*, to paddle about in mud, from *pate*, paw.]

patrol car *n.* A squad car.

pa·trol·man (pə-trōl′mən) *n.* A man, such as a policeman, who patrols an assigned area.

patrol wagon *n.* A police truck used to convey prisoners.

pa·trol·wom·an (pə-trōl′wo͝om′ən) *n.* A woman, such as a policewoman, who patrols an assigned area.

pa·tron (pā′trən) *n.* **1.** A person who supports or champions something, such as an activity or institution, by giving money; a benefactor: *a patron of the arts.* **2.** A regular customer of a store, restaurant, or other business. [From Middle English, from Latin *patrōnus*, from *pater*, father.]

pa·tron·age (pā′trə-nĭj *or* păt′rə-nĭj) *n.* **1.** Support or encouragement from a patron: *dependent upon the patronage of the rich.* **2.** Support or encouragement given with an air of superiority. **3.** The trade given to a store or restaurant by its customers. **4.** Customers; clientele: *The hotel has a very exclusive patronage.* **5.** The power or act of appointing people to governmental or political positions.

pa·tron·ize (pā′trə-nīz′ *or* păt′rə-nīz′) *tr.v.* **pa·tron·ized, pa·tron·iz·ing, pa·tron·iz·es 1.** To act as a patron to; support: *patronize the arts.* **2.** To go to regularly as a customer: *patronize a store.* **3.** To treat (someone) in a condescending way; talk down to.

patron saint *n.* A saint regarded as the special guardian of a country, place, person, trade, or activity.

pa·troon (pə-tro͞on′) *n.* Under Dutch colonial rule, a landholder in New York or New Jersey who was granted land and certain rights in exchange for bringing 50 new settlers to the colony.

pat·sy (păt′sē) *n., pl.* **pat·sies** *Slang* A person who is cheated, taken unfair advantage of, or made the butt of a joke.

pat·ter[1] (păt′ər) *intr.v.* **pat·tered, pat·ter·ing, pat·ters 1.** To make a series of quick light taps: *Rain pattered on the roof.* **2.** To walk or move softly and quickly. ❖ *n.* A series of quick light tapping sounds: *heard the patter of feet on the stairs.* [From *pat*, tap.]

pat·ter[2] (păt′ər) *n.* Glib rapid speech, such as that used by a salesperson or comedian. [From Middle English *pateren*, to say prayers rapidly, from *paternoster*, the Lord's Prayer (because it would be recited rapidly and mechanically).] **—pat′ter** *v.*

pat·tern (păt′ərn) *n.* **1.** An artistic or decorative design: *a floral pattern.* **2.** A diagram, plan, or model used to make or do something: *a dress pattern.* **3.** A combination of features, actions, or events that are repeated in a recognizable arrangement: *patterns of behavior in monkeys.* **4.** A person or thing that is used as a guide or considered worth imitating. ❖ *tr.v.* **pat·terned, pat·tern·ing, pat·terns** To form or design according to a certain model: *The country's constitution is patterned after our own.*

pat·ty (păt′ē) *n., pl.* **pat·ties** A small, rounded, flattened mass of ground or minced food.

pau·ci·ty (pô′sĭ-tē) *n.* Short supply; scarcity; dearth: *a paucity of natural resources.*

Paul (pôl), Saint. AD 5?–67? Early Christian noted for his missionary work. His epistles are among the earliest and most influential sources of Christian theology.

Paul VI 1897–1978. Pope (1963–1978) noted for easing regulations on fasting and interfaith marriages.

Paul Bun·yan (pôl′ bŭn′yən) *n.* In American folklore, a giant logger who performs superhuman acts.

Pau·ling (pô′lĭng), **Linus Carl** 1901–1994. American chemist noted for his work on the structure and nature of chemical bonding and his efforts toward disarmament.

paunch (pônch *or* pänch) *n.* The belly, especially a potbelly.

paunch·y (pôn′chē *or* pän′chē) *adj.* **paunch·i·er, paunch·i·est** Having a protruding abdomen or a potbelly. **—paunch′i·ness** *n.*

pau·per (pô′pər) *n.* A very poor person, often one who lives on charity.

pause (pôz) *v.* **paused, paus·ing, paus·es** *—intr.* **1.** To stop briefly in the midst of an action or while speaking. **2.** To linger for a time: *We paused under a tree before going on.* *—tr.* To stop or suspend temporarily: *paused the music.* ❖ *n.* **1.** A brief stop or break in action or speech. **2.** Reason for hesitation: *The size of the task gives one pause.* **3.** A control mechanism on an audio or video player that halts the playing of a recording and permits playing to be easily resumed from the same point.

SYNONYMS **pause, intermission, recess, suspension** These nouns mean a temporary stop in activity. *There was a brief pause in the conversation. They served soft drinks during the play's intermission. Enjoy yourselves during winter recess. The strike caused a suspension of repair work on the highway.*

---

pa·vane (pə-vän′) *n.* **1.** A slow stately court dance of the 1500s and 1600s. **2.** A piece of music written for this dance.

pave (pāv) *tr.v.* **paved, pav·ing, paves** To cover with pavement. ◆ **pave the way** To make progress or development easier: *His experiments paved the way for new discoveries.*

pave·ment (pāv′mənt) *n.* **1.** A hard smooth surface of concrete, asphalt, brick, or a similar material, as for a road or sidewalk. **2.** The material used to make such a surface.

pa·vil·ion (pə-vĭl′yən) *n.* **1.** An ornate tent. **2.** An open structure with a roof, used at parks or fairs for amusement or shelter. **3.** One of a group of related buildings, as of a hospital. [From Middle English, from Old French *paveillon*, from Latin *pāpiliō*, butterfly, tent.]

pav·ing (pā′vĭng) *n.* **1.** The act or technique of laying pavement. **2.** Materials, such as asphalt or bricks, used for pavement.

Pav·lov (păv′lôf′ *or* păv′lôv′), **Ivan Petrovich** 1849–1936. Russian scientist who is best known for discovering psychological conditioning.

paw (pô) *n.* The foot of a mammal, especially a four-footed mammal, that has claws or nails. ❖ *tr.v.* **pawed, paw·ing, paws 1a.** To touch or strike with a paw. **b.** To scrape or beat with a paw or hoof: *The dog pawed the ground.* **2.** To handle in a clumsy or rude way.

pawl (pôl) *n.* A hinged or pivoted device that fits into a notch of a ratchet wheel, either to drive it forward or to prevent it from moving backward.

❑ *These sound alike:* **pawl, pall[1]** (cloth covering), **pall[2]** (grow dull).

pawn[1] (pôn) *tr.v.* **pawned, pawn·ing, pawns** To give or leave as security for the payment of money borrowed: *pawn jewels.* [From Middle English *paun*, pledge, security, from Old French *pan*, perhaps of Germanic origin.]

pawn[2] (pôn) *n.* **1.** A chess piece of lowest value that can move forward one square at a time or two squares on its first move and capture other pieces by moving one square diagonally forward. **2.** A person used or controlled by others. [From Middle English *poun*, from Old French *peon*, *paon*, from Medieval Latin *pedō*, foot soldier, from Latin *pēs*, foot.]

pawn·bro·ker (pôn′brō′kər) *n.* A person who lends

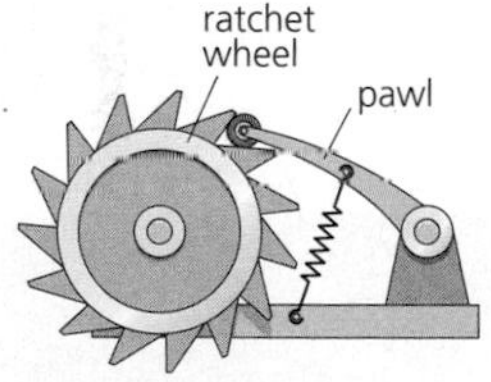

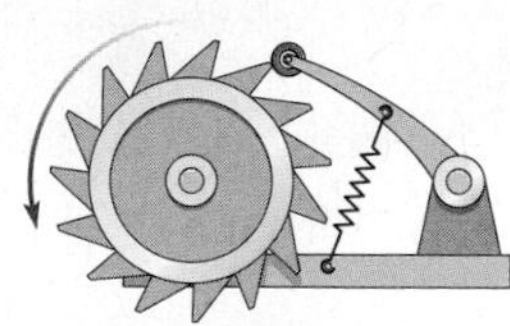

pawl
As a ratchet wheel turns, a pawl moves out of one tooth socket (*top*) and into the next.

WORD HISTORY

pea The beginning of the nursery rhyme "Pease porridge hot, pease porridge cold" preserves the original form of the word *pea*. Before about 1600, the word for the **pea** was *pease*. How did *pease* become *pea*? The story highlights an interesting kind of change that can happen in language. The older form *pease* was both a singular as well as a plural. Most often it was used in plural contexts, like *eat some pease, buy a pound of pease, pease and cabbage for dinner.* Since the word *pease* was pronounced (pēz), it sounded just like any other plural word, like *bees* or *seas,* and in fact was often spelled *peas*. This led people to think that there was a singular *pea* of which *pease* or *peas* was the plural. In this way *pea* was created, replacing *pease* as the singular.

peacock

ă	pat	ôr	core
ā	pay	oi	boy
âr	care	ou	out
ä	father	o͝o	took
ĕ	pet	o͝or	lure
ē	be	o͞o	boot
ĭ	pit	ŭ	cut
ī	bite	ûr	urge
îr	pier	th	thin
ŏ	pot	*th*	this
ō	toe	zh	vision
ô	paw	ə	about

money at interest in exchange for personal property left as security.

Paw·nee (pô-nē′) *n., pl.* **Pawnee** or **Paw·nees 1.** A member of a Native American people formerly living in Nebraska and Kansas, now living in Oklahoma. **2.** The Caddoan language of the Pawnee.

pawn·shop (pôn′shŏp′) *n.* The shop of a pawnbroker.

paw·paw or **pa·paw** (pô′pô) *n.* **1.** The fleshy fruit of a North American tree, having a taste similar to a banana. **2.** The tree that bears such fruit. [From Spanish *papaya,* papaya.]

pay (pā) *v.* **paid** (pād), **pay·ing, pays** *—tr.* **1.** To give money to in return for goods or services: *I paid her for the newspaper.* **2.** To give (money) in exchange for goods or services: *How much did you pay for the tickets?* **3.** To discharge or settle (a debt or obligation): *pay the rent.* **4.** To yield as a return: *a bond paying 8 percent interest.* **5.** To be profitable or worthwhile for: *It paid him to be careful.* **6.** To give, render, or express: *pay attention; pay a compliment.* *—intr.* **1.** To give money in exchange for goods or services. **2.** To discharge a debt or obligation. **3.** To bear a cost or penalty: *You'll pay for eating so much.* **4.** To be profitable or worthwhile: *It pays to be friendly.* ❖ *adj.* **1.** Relating to, giving, or receiving payments: *a pay raise.* **2.** Requiring payment to operate: *a pay telephone.* ❖ *n.* **1.** Money given in return for work done; wages; salary. **2.** Paid employment: *She is in the pay of our company.* ◆ **pay back 1.** To repay. **2.** To return a favor done by. **3.** To retaliate against: *paid him back for his rudeness.* **pay off 1.** To pay the full amount on (a debt). **2.** To be profitable: *an investment that pays off.* **3.** *Informal* To bribe. **pay (one's) way** To contribute one's own share; pay for oneself. **pay out 1.** To give (money) out; spend. **2.** To let out (a line or rope) by slackening. **pay up** To give all the money owed. [From Middle English *paien,* from Old French *paier,* from Late Latin *pācāre,* to appease, from Latin *pāx,* peace.]

pay·a·ble (pā′ə-bəl) *adj.* Specifying payment be made on a certain date or to a certain person: *a note payable on demand; made the check payable to me.*

pay·check (pā′chĕk′) *n.* **1.** A check issued to an employee in payment of salary or wages. **2.** Salary or wages: *The new job means a larger paycheck.*

pay·day (pā′dā′) *n.* The day on which wages are paid.

pay·ee (pā-ē′) *n.* A person to whom money is paid.

pay·er (pā′ər) *n.* **1.** A person or organization that pays. **2.** A person named responsible for paying a bill or note.

pay·load (pā′lōd′) *n.* **1.** The total weight of passengers and cargo that an aircraft carries or can carry. **2.** The total weight of the instruments, crew, and life-support systems that a spacecraft can carry. **3.** The explosive charge in the warhead of a missile or in a bomb.

pay·mas·ter (pā′măs′tər) *n.* A person in charge of paying wages and salaries.

pay·ment (pā′mənt) *n.* **1.** The act of paying: *Prompt payment of the bill will be appreciated.* **2.** An amount of money paid: *The balance is due in monthly payments.* **3.** Reward, compensation, or punishment: *To see the child healthy again is payment enough for my services.*

pay·off (pā′ôf′) *n.* **1.** Full payment of a salary or wages. **2.** The benefit gained as the result of a previous action. **3.** *Informal* A bribe.

pay·roll (pā′rōl′) *n.* **1.** A list of employees and wages due to each. **2.** The total amount of money paid to employees at a given time.

Pb The symbol for the element **lead.**

PC *abbr.* An abbreviation of: **1.** personal computer. **2.** politically correct.

p.c. *abbr.* An abbreviation of percent.

PCB (pē′sē-bē′) *n.* Any of a family of compounds containing chlorine that were formerly used in many industrial applications. PCBs were banned in the United States in 1979 because of their toxic effects on humans and other animals. [Short for *p(oly)c(hlorinated) b(iphenyl).*]

pct. *abbr.* An abbreviation of percent.

Pd The symbol for the element **palladium.**

PD *abbr.* An abbreviation of police department.

pd. *abbr.* An abbreviation of paid.

PE *abbr.* An abbreviation of: **1.** physical education. **2.** Prince Edward Island.

pea (pē) *n.* **1.** The round green seed of a climbing vine, enclosed in long green pods and eaten as a vegetable. **2.** The plant that bears such seeds. [From Middle English *pease,* from Old English *piose,* from Latin *pīsum,* from Greek *pison.*] —SEE NOTE.

peace (pēs) *n.* **1.** The absence of war or other hostilities. **2.** A treaty or agreement ending a war: *Peace was signed in 1918.* **3.** Calm; tranquility: *a little peace and quiet.* **4.** Inner calm; serenity: *peace of mind.* **5.** Public security; law and order: *He was arrested for disturbing the peace.* ◆ **at peace 1.** In a state of tranquility; serene: *She is at peace with herself.* **2.** Free from strife: *We all want to live in a world at peace.* **keep (one's) peace** or **hold (one's) peace** To be silent. [From Middle English *pes,* from Old French *pais, pes,* from Latin *pāx.*]

❑ *These sound alike:* **peace, piece** (part).

peace·a·ble (pē′sə-bəl) *adj.* **1.** Not quarrelsome, rebellious, or unruly; disposed to peace: *a peaceable disposition.* **2.** Not involving violence or war; peaceful: *a peaceable solution.* **—peace′a·bly** *adv.*

peace·ful (pēs′fəl) *adj.* **1.** Not involving war or violence: *peaceful protests.* **2.** Inclined or disposed to peace: *a peaceful nation.* **3.** Calm; tranquil: *a peaceful valley.* See Synonyms at **calm. —peace′ful·ly** *adv.* **—peace′ful·ness** *n.*

peace·keep·ing (pēs′kē′pĭng) *adj.* Relating to the preservation of peace: *a peacekeeping force sent to uphold a ceasefire.*

peace·mak·er (pēs′mā′kər) *n.* A person who makes peace, especially by settling the disputes of others.

peace pipe *n.* A calumet.

peace·time (pēs′tīm′) *n.* A time free from war.

peach (pēch) *n.* **1a.** A sweet, round, juicy fruit having downy reddish-yellow skin and a hard pit. **b.** The tree that bears such fruit. **2.** A light yellowish pink. **3.** An excellent or especially likeable person or thing.

peach·y (pē′chē) *adj.* **peach·i·er, peach·i·est 1.** Resembling a peach, especially in color or texture. **2.** Splendid; fine. **—peach′i·ness** *n.*

pea coat or **pea·coat** (pē′kōt′) *n.* A short, warm, double-breasted coat of heavy wool, traditionally worn by sailors.

pea·cock (pē′kŏk′) *n.* **1.** The male of the peafowl, having brilliant blue or green feathers and very long tail feathers that are marked with eyespots and can be spread out like a fan. **2.** A vain or showy person.

pea·fowl (pē′foul′) *n., pl.* **peafowl** or **pea·fowls** Any of several large, long-tailed birds found in Asia and Africa. [From Middle English *po, peau,* peacock, from Old English *pawa, pēa,* from Latin *pāvō.*]

pea·hen (pē′hĕn′) *n.* A female peafowl.

peak (pēk) *n.* **1a.** The pointed top of a mountain. **b.** The mountain itself. **2.** A tapering point that projects upward: *the peak of a roof.* **3.** The point of greatest development, value, or intensity: *a book written at the peak of her career.* ❖ *intr.v.* **peaked, peak·ing, peaks 1.** To be formed into a peak or peaks. **2.** To achieve the point of greatest development, value, or intensity: *Sales tend to peak just before the holidays.*

❑ *These sound alike:* **peak, peek** (glance), **pique** (resentment).

peaked[1] (pēkt *or* pē′kĭd) *adj.* Ending in a peak; pointed:

a peaked cap. [From Middle English *peked,* variant of *piked,* from *pike,* spike.]

peak·ed² (pē′kĭd) *adj.* Having a sickly appearance: *You look peaked today.* [From *peak,* to look sickly, of unknown origin.]

peal (pēl) *n.* **1.** A ringing of a set of bells. **2.** A set of bells tuned to each other. **3.** A loud burst of noise: *peals of laughter.* ❖ *tr. & intr.v.* **pealed, peal·ing, peals** To sound loudly; ring: *The bells pealed joyfully.*

❑ *These sound alike:* **peal, peel** (rind).

pea·nut (pē′nŭt′) *n.* **1a.** The oily edible seed of a plant that grows in warm regions, having yellow flowers that bend over so that the light-brown pods containing the seeds ripen underground. **b.** The seedpod of this plant. **c.** The plant that bears such pods. **2.** A peanut-shaped piece of soft, light plastic, used in cushioning items in packages during shipment. **3. peanuts** *Informal* A very small amount of money: *The intern worked for peanuts but gained much experience.*

peanut brittle *n.* A hard toffee containing peanuts.

peanut butter *n.* A paste made from ground roasted peanuts.

peanut oil *n.* The oil pressed from peanuts, used for cooking and in soaps.

pear (pâr) *n.* **1.** A sweet juicy fruit having a rounded base and a tapering stem end. **2.** The tree that bears such fruit.

❑ *These sound alike:* **pear, pair** (two), **pare** (peel).

pearl (pûrl) *n.* **1.** A smooth, slightly iridescent white or grayish rounded growth formed inside the shell of certain mollusks, especially oysters, and valued as a gem. **2.** Mother-of-pearl. **3.** Something resembling a pearl: *pearls of dew.* **4.** A person or thing that is very highly thought of: *pearls of wisdom.*

❑ *These sound alike:* **pearl, purl¹** (flow), **purl²** (knit).

pearl gray *n.* A light gray, from yellowish to light bluish gray.

Pearl Harbor An inlet of the Pacific Ocean on the southern coast of Oahu, Hawaii, west of Honolulu. It was the site of a Japanese attack on a US naval base (December 7, 1941), which caused the United States to enter World War II.

pearl·y (pûr′lē) *adj.* **pearl·i·er, pearl·i·est 1.** Resembling pearls, as in whiteness or size. **2.** Covered or decorated with pearls.

peas·ant (pĕz′ənt) *n.* A member of the class of small farmers and farm laborers.

peas·ant·ry (pĕz′ən-trē) *n.* The social class made up of peasants.

pea soup *n.* **1.** A soup made of cooked, dried peas. **2.** *Informal* Dense fog.

peat (pēt) *n.* Partially rotted plants, especially mosses, found in bogs and used as fuel and in gardening.

peat moss *n.* **1.** Sphagnum. **2.** Peat made up of moss, usually sphagnum.

peb·ble (pĕb′əl) *n.* A small stone, especially one worn smooth by erosion. ❖ *tr.v.* **peb·bled, peb·bling, peb·bles 1.** To pave or cover with pebbles. **2.** To give an irregular rough surface to (leather or paper). **—peb′bly** *adj.*

pe·can (pĭ-kän′ *or* pĭ-kăn′ *or* pē′kăn) *n.* **1.** An edible nut having a smooth oval shell. **2.** The tree that bears such nuts.

pec·ca·dil·lo (pĕk′ə-dĭl′ō) *n., pl.* **pec·ca·dil·loes** or **pec·ca·dil·los** A small sin or fault.

pec·ca·ry (pĕk′ə-rē) *n., pl.* **pec·ca·ries** Any of several tropical American mammals similar to a pig, having stiff bristles and short, straight tusks.

peck¹ (pĕk) *v.* **pecked, peck·ing, pecks** *—tr.* **1.** To strike with the beak or a pointed instrument. **2.** To make (a hole, for example) by striking repeatedly with the beak or a pointed instrument. **3.** To pick up with the beak: *The hens pecked corn off the ground. —intr.* To strike something with the beak or a pointed instrument: *The bird pecked at the dead branch.* ❖ *n.* **1a.** A stroke or light blow with the beak or a pointed instrument. **b.** A hole or mark made by such a stroke. **2.** *Informal* A light quick kiss. [From Middle English *pecken,* probably variant of *piken.*]

peck² (pĕk) *n.* **1.** A unit of dry volume or capacity equal to 8 quarts (8.8 liters). **2.** A container holding or measuring this amount. **3.** *Informal* A great deal: *a peck of trouble.* [From Middle English *pek,* from Anglo-Norman *pek,* of unknown origin.]

pec·tin (pĕk′tĭn) *n.* Any of a group of substances found in ripe fruits, such as apples, that can be made to form gels, used in preparing jellies and in certain medicines and cosmetics.

pec·to·ral (pĕk′tər-əl) *adj.* Relating to the chest or breast: *a pectoral muscle.* ❖ *n.* Any of four muscles that occur in pairs on each side of the chest.

pe·cu·liar (pĭ-kyo͞ol′yər) *adj.* **1.** Unusual or eccentric; strange: *a peculiar odor in the room.* **2.** Belonging distinctively to one person, group, or kind; unique: *a fish peculiar to this river.* **—pe·cu′liar·ly** *adv.*

pe·cu·li·ar·i·ty (pĭ-kyo͞o′lē-ăr′ĭ-tē *or* pĭ-kyo͞ol-yăr′ĭ-tē) *n., pl.* **pe·cu·li·ar·i·ties 1.** The quality or condition of being peculiar. **2.** A notable or distinctive feature or characteristic: *the peculiarities of a New York accent.* **3.** Something odd or eccentric; a quirk: *his peculiarities about money.*

pe·cu·ni·ar·y (pĭ-kyo͞o′nē-ĕr′ē) *adj.* Relating to money: *a pecuniary loss.*

ped·a·gog·ic (pĕd′ə-gŏj′ĭk) also **ped·a·gog·i·cal** (pĕd′ə-gŏj′ĭ-kəl) *adj.* Relating to teaching: *pedagogic techniques.*

ped·a·gogue (pĕd′ə-gŏg′) *n.* **1.** A schoolteacher; an educator. **2.** A person who teaches in a showy dogmatic manner.

ped·a·go·gy (pĕd′ə-gō′jē *or* pĕd′ə-gŏj′ē) *n.* The art or profession of teaching.

ped·al (pĕd′l) *n.* A lever operated by the foot, as on a machine such as an automobile or bicycle or on a musical instrument such as a piano or organ. ❖ *v.* **ped·aled, ped·al·ing, ped·als** or **ped·alled, ped·al·ling, ped·als** *—intr.* **1.** To ride a bicycle. **2.** To operate a pedal or pedals. *—tr.* To operate the pedals of: *pedaled the bike up the hill.* [From Latin *pēs,* foot.]

❑ *These sound alike:* **pedal, peddle** (sell).

ped·ant (pĕd′nt) *n.* A person who shows off his or her learning or who pays too much attention to book learning and formal rules.

pe·dan·tic (pə-dăn′tĭk) *adj.* Characterized by excessive and often showy concern for books and learning: *a pedantic mind.* **—pe·dan′ti·cal·ly** *adv.*

ped·ant·ry (pĕd′n-trē) *n., pl.* **ped·ant·ries 1.** The showy display of academic knowledge or excessive attention to details or rules. **2.** An instance of pedantic behavior.

ped·dle (pĕd′l) *tr.v.* **ped·dled, ped·dling, ped·dles 1.** To travel about selling (goods): *peddle magazines.* **2.** To spread or deal out: *Don't peddle lies.* [From *peddler.*]

❑ *These sound alike:* **peddle, pedal** (lever).

ped·dler (pĕd′lər) *n.* A person who travels about selling goods. [From Middle English *pedlere,* variant of *pedder,* perhaps from Medieval Latin *pedārius,* one who goes on foot, from Latin *pēs,* foot.]

ped·es·tal (pĕd′ĭ-stəl) *n.* **1.** A support or base, as for a column or statue. **2.** A support or foundation. **3.** A position of high regard or admiration: *Putting people on pedestals can lead to disappointment.*

pe·des·tri·an (pə-dĕs′trē-ən) *n.* A person traveling on foot, especially on city streets. ❖ *adj.* **1.** Relating to or

peahen

pear

Pearl Harbor
the sinking of the USS *Arizona* at Pearl Harbor, December 7, 1941

pediment
the US Supreme Court building

WRITERS CHOOSE THEIR WORDS

I daydreamed about money all the time now. I would buy myself clothes like the ones Hal Slater wore. They were bound to make me look less like a boy. I would become manly. I would not endure Miss Simpkins's **peevish** looks and comments about my unsuitability. I would not suffer the humiliation of having Kate pay my way. If I failed at the Academy, I could buy a ship and a crew to call me captain.

—Kenneth Oppel
Skybreaker

for pedestrians: *a pedestrian crossing.* **2.** Commonplace; ordinary: *pedestrian writing.*

pe·di·a·tri·cian (pē′dē-ə-**trĭsh′**ən) *n.* A physician who specializes in pediatrics.

pe·di·at·rics (pē′dē-**ăt′**rĭks) *n. (used with a singular verb)* The branch of medicine that deals with the care of infants and children and the treatment of their diseases. **—pe′di·at′ric** *adj.*

ped·i·cel (**pĕd′**ĭ-səl) *n.* A small plant stalk that supports a single flower.

ped·i·cure (**pĕd′**ĭ-kyo͝or′) *n.* A cosmetic treatment of the feet and toenails.

ped·i·gree (**pĕd′**ĭ-grē′) *n.* **1.** A line of ancestors; ancestry. **2.** A list or record of ancestors, especially of a purebred animal. [From Middle English *pedegrue*, from Anglo-Norman *pe de grue*, crane's foot (from the resemblance of a crane's foot to a three-line arrow that marked succession in early genealogical charts).]

ped·i·greed (**pĕd′**ĭ-grēd′) *adj.* Having a line of purebred ancestors: *pedigreed cattle.*

ped·i·ment (**pĕd′**ə-mənt) *n.* **1.** A wide triangular gable over the façade of a building in Greek architectural style. **2.** A similar piece used widely in architecture and decoration.

pe·dom·e·ter (pĭ-**dŏm′**ĭ-tər) *n.* An instrument that measures the approximate distance a person travels on foot by keeping track of the number of steps taken.

pe·dun·cle (pĭ-**dŭng′**kəl *or* **pē′**dŭng′kəl) *n.* A stalk or stem supporting a flower or an animal organ, as the eyestalk of a lobster.

peek (pēk) *intr.v.* **peeked, peek·ing, peeks 1.** To look, peer, or glance briefly, as from a place of concealment. **2.** To be partially visible; show: *Crocuses peeked through the snow.* ❖ *n.* A quick sly glance or look.

❑ *These sound alike:* **peek, peak** (mountaintop), **pique** (resentment).

peel (pēl) *n.* The skin or rind of certain fruits and vegetables, such as the orange or potato. ❖ *v.* **peeled, peel·ing, peels** *—tr.* **1.** To remove the skin or rind from: *peel a banana.* **2.** To strip away or pull off (an outer covering): *peel the bark off a tree.* *—intr.* **1.** To come off in thin strips or layers, as skin or paint. **2.** To lose or shed skin or other covering: *The house is peeling and needs to be painted.*

❑ *These sound alike:* **peel, peal** (ringing).

peel·a·ble (**pēl′**ə-bəl) *adj.* **1.** Having a peel or rind that can be peeled off: *an easily peelable orange.* **2.** Capable of being removed and reused: *peelable address labels.*

peel·ing (**pē′**lĭng) *n.* A peeled piece or strip, as of a fruit rind: *made compost from orange peelings.*

peep¹ (pēp) *n.* A weak high-pitched chirping sound, like that made by a young bird. ❖ *intr.v.* **peeped, peep·ing, peeps** To make such a sound. [Probably of imitative origin or akin to *pipe.*]

peep² (pēp) *intr.v.* **peeped, peep·ing, peeps 1.** To look from a concealed place; peek. **2.** To become visible gradually, as though emerging from a hiding place: *At dawn the sun peeped over the horizon.* ❖ *n.* A quick look or glance; a peek. [From Middle English *pepen*, to become visible gradually, perhaps alteration of *piken*, to peek, or of imitative origin.]

peep·er (**pē′**pər) *n.* **1.** A person who peeks in a sly manner. **2.** *Slang* An eye.

peep·hole (**pēp′**hōl′) *n.* A small hole or crevice through which one may look.

peer¹ (pîr) *intr.v.* **peered, peer·ing, peers 1.** To look intently, searchingly, or with difficulty: *I peered through the binoculars at the bird.* **2.** To be partially visible; show: *The moon peered from behind a cloud.* [From Middle English *peren*, probably variant of *piren*, to look closely, gaze, of unknown origin. Sense 2, from Middle English *peren*, to appear, short for *aperen*, to appear.]

❑ *These sound alike:* **peer¹** (look), **peer²** (equal), **pier** (dock).

peer² (pîr) *n.* **1.** A person who has equal standing with others, as in rank, class, or age. **2.** A man who is a member of the nobility, especially in Great Britain. [From Middle English *per*, from Old French, from Latin *pār*, equal.]

❑ *These sound alike:* **peer²** (equal), **peer¹** (look), **pier** (dock).

peer·age (**pîr′**ĭj) *n.* **1.** The rank or title of a peer or peeress. **2.** Peers and peeresses considered as a group. **3.** A book listing the peers.

peer·ess (**pîr′**ĭs) *n.* **1.** A woman who holds a noble title in her own right. **2.** The wife or widow of a peer.

peer·less (**pîr′**lĭs) *adj.* Having no equal; unmatched. **—peer′less·ly** *adv.* **—peer′less·ness** *n.*

peer pressure *n.* Pressure from one's peers to behave like them or in a way they find acceptable.

peeve (pēv) *tr.v.* **peeved, peev·ing, peeves** To annoy or make irritable. ❖ *n.* Something that annoys: *Her biggest peeve is the noisy dog next door.*

pee·vish (**pē′**vĭsh) *adj.* **1.** Easily annoyed; irritable. **2.** Showing annoyance or irritability. **—pee′vish·ly** *adv.* **—pee′vish·ness** *n.*

pee·wee (**pē′**wē) *n. Informal* A relatively or unusually small person or thing. [Probably doubling and alteration of *wee.*] **—pee′wee** *adj.*

❑ *These sound alike:* **peewee, pewee** (bird).

peg (pĕg) *n.* **1.** A cylindrical or conical pin, often of wood, used to fasten things or to plug a hole. **2.** One of the pins of a stringed musical instrument that are turned to loosen or tighten the strings so as to change their pitch. **3.** A degree, as in estimation: *My opinion of him has gone up a few pegs.* **4.** A throw in baseball. ❖ *tr.v.* **pegged, peg·ging, pegs 1.** To fasten or plug with a peg. **2.** To set or fix (a price, for example): *peg interest rates to the rate of inflation.* **3.** *Informal* To classify: *We pegged her as the math expert.* **4.** *Informal* To throw (a ball).

Peg·a·sus (**pĕg′**ə-səs) *n.* In Greek mythology, a winged horse that with a strike of the hoof caused the fountain Hippocrene to spring forth from Mount Helicon.

peg leg *n. Often Offensive* An artificial leg, especially a wooden one.

peg·ma·tite (**pĕg′**mə-tīt′) *n.* Any of various coarse-grained igneous rocks that often occur as wide veins cutting across other types of rock.

PEI *abbr.* An abbreviation of Prince Edward Island.

Pe·king (**pē′kĭng′** *or* **pā′kĭng′**) See **Beijing.**

Pe·king·ese (pē′kĭng-**ēz′** *or* pē′kĭng-**ēs′**) also **Pe·kin·ese** (pē′kə-**nēz′** *or* pē′kə-**nēs′**) *n., pl.* **Pekingese** also **Pekinese 1.** A native or inhabitant of Beijing (Peking). **2.** (pē′kə-**nēz′** *or* pē′kə-**nēs′**) A small dog of a breed originally developed in China, having long hair, large eyes, and a flat face.

Peking man *n.* An extinct type of human known from fossil remains found in China, considered to belong to the species *Homo erectus.*

pe·koe (**pē′**kō) *n.* A type of black tea, consisting of small leaves and sometimes leaf buds.

pe·lag·ic (pə-**lăj′**ĭk) *adj.* Relating to or living in the open ocean: *pelagic birds.* [From Latin *pelagicus*, from Greek *pelagos*, sea.]

pelf (pĕlf) *n.* Wealth or riches, especially when dishonestly acquired.

pel·i·can (**pĕl′**ĭ-kən) *n.* Any of various large, web-footed waterbirds of warm regions, having under the lower bill a large pouch used for holding fish.

pel·lag·ra (pə-**lăg′**rə *or* pə-**lā′**grə) *n.* A disease caused by a lack of niacin in the diet, characterized by skin eruptions, disorders of the nervous system, and mental deterioration.

ă	pat	ôr	core
ā	pay	oi	boy
âr	care	ou	out
ä	father	o͝o	took
ĕ	pet	o͝or	lure
ē	be	o͞o	boot
ĭ	pit	ŭ	cut
ī	bite	ûr	urge
îr	pier	th	thin
ŏ	pot	*th*	this
ō	toe	zh	vision
ô	paw	ə	about

pel·let (pĕl′ĭt) *n.* **1.** A small densely packed ball, as of food, wax, or medicine. **2.** A small bullet or shot.

pell-mell also **pell·mell** (pĕl′mĕl′) *adv.* In a jumbled and confused manner; helter-skelter: *The ducks flew off pell-mell.* —**pell′-mell′** *adj.*

pel·lu·cid (pə-lo͞o′sĭd) *adj.* **1.** Admitting the passage of light; transparent. **2.** Easy to understand; clear: *pellucid prose.* —**pel·lu′cid·ly** *adv.*

Pel·o·pon·ne·sus or **Pel·o·pon·ne·sos** (pĕl′ə-pə-nē′səs) A peninsula forming the southern part of Greece. It was dominated by Sparta until the fourth century BC.

pelt[1] (pĕlt) *n.* An animal skin with the fur or hair still on it. [From Middle English, from Anglo-Norman *pelet*, diminutive of *pel*, skin, from Latin *pellis*.]

pelt[2] (pĕlt) *tr.v.* **pelt·ed, pelt·ing, pelts 1.** To strike repeatedly with thrown objects: *pelted the sign with snowballs.* **2.** To hurl or throw (objects): *pelting stones at tin cans.* [From Middle English *pilten*, perhaps from Latin *pultāre*, to beat.]

pel·vic (pĕl′vĭk) *adj.* Relating to, in, or near the pelvis.

pel·vis (pĕl′vĭs) *n., pl.* **pel·vis·es** or **pel·ves** (pĕl′vēz) A basin-shaped structure formed of several different bones that rests on the lower limbs and supports the lower end of the spine.

pem·mi·can (pĕm′ĭ-kən) *n.* **1.** A food made by Native Americans from a paste of lean meat mixed with fat and berries. **2.** A similar food for use in emergencies.

pen[1] (pĕn) *n.* **1.** Any of various instruments for writing with ink, including the ballpoint pen and the fountain pen. **2.** An instrument for writing regarded as a means of expression: *The pen is mightier than the sword.* ❖ *tr.v.* **penned, pen·ning, pens** To write or compose: *penned a novel.* [From Middle English *penne*, from Latin *penna*, feather.]

pen[2] (pĕn) *n.* A small fenced-in area, especially one in which animals are kept. ❖ *tr.v.* **penned** or **pent** (pĕnt), **pen·ning, pens** To confine in a pen or other enclosure. [From Old English.]

pen[3] (pĕn) *n. Informal* A penitentiary. [Short for *penitentiary*.]

pe·nal (pē′nəl) *adj.* **1.** Relating to or prescribing punishment, as for breaking the law: *a penal colony.* **2.** Subject to punishment: *a penal offense.*

penal code *n.* A body of laws establishing the criminal offenses for a particular area.

pe·nal·ize (pē′nə-līz′ *or* pĕn′ə-līz′) *tr.v.* **pe·nal·ized, pe·nal·iz·ing, pe·nal·iz·es 1.** To subject (a person) to a penalty, especially for infringement of a law or regulation. **2.** To make (an action or condition) liable to a penalty: *Tripping is penalized in hockey.* **3.** To impose a handicap on; place at a disadvantage: *was penalized by his poor education.*

pen·al·ty (pĕn′əl-tē) *n., pl.* **pen·al·ties 1.** A punishment imposed for a violation of law. **2.** A sum established by a contract to be forfeited if the contract is breached. **3a.** In sports, a punishment or disadvantage imposed on a team or competitor for breaking a rule. **b.** An infraction of a rule; a foul: *Their center took a foolish penalty late in the game.*

penalty area *n.* **1.** An area marked on a soccer field in front of each goal within which a violation of the rules by a defending player results in a penalty kick. **2.** An area to the side of a playing field, as in lacrosse, where penalized players wait out their penalties.

penalty box *n.* An area to the side of an ice-hockey rink or a playing field where penalized players wait out their penalties.

penalty kick *n.* In soccer, a free kick on the goal awarded when the defense has committed a foul in the penalty area.

penalty killer *n.* Any of the players other than the goalie who attempt to prevent the opposing team from scoring on a power play, as in ice hockey.

penalty shot *n.* **1.** In hockey and lacrosse, an open shot that is defended only by the goalkeeper. A penalty shot is usually awarded to an offensive player who has been illegally prevented from attempting to score. **2.** In soccer, a penalty kick.

pen·ance (pĕn′əns) *n.* **1.** An act of self-denial or devotion performed voluntarily to show sorrow for a sin or other wrongdoing. **2.** In some Christian churches, a sacrament that includes contrition, confession to a priest, acceptance of punishment, and absolution.

pence (pĕns) *n. Chiefly British* A plural of **penny** (sense 2).

pen·chant (pĕn′chənt) *n.* A strong inclination; a definite liking: *a penchant for spicy cooking.*

pen·cil (pĕn′səl) *n.* **1.** A thin writing instrument consisting of a stick of graphite or some other material encased in wood or held in a mechanical holder. **2.** Something shaped or used like a pencil: *an eyebrow pencil.* ❖ *tr.v.* **pen·ciled, pen·cil·ing, pen·cils** also **pen·cilled, pen·cil·ling, pen·cils** To write or produce with a pencil. ◆ **pencil in 1.** To schedule tentatively: *penciled in a meeting for 1:00.* **2.** To schedule a tentative appointment with: *I penciled my friend in for lunch next Saturday.*

pen·dant also **pen·dent** (pĕn′dənt) *n.* A hanging ornament, such as one worn dangling from a necklace or from the ear.
❑ *These sound alike:* **pendant, pendent** (dangling).

pen·dent also **pen·dant** (pĕn′dənt) *adj.* **1.** Hanging down; dangling: *pendent vines.* **2.** Jutting; overhanging: *pendent cliffs.* **3.** Awaiting settlement; pending.
❑ *These sound alike:* **pendent, pendant** (ornament).

pend·ing (pĕn′dĭng) *adj.* **1.** Not yet decided or settled; awaiting action: *legislation pending before Congress.* **2.** Impending; about to happen. ❖ *prep.* While awaiting; until: *The bridge is closed pending an investigation of the accident.*

pen·du·lous (pĕn′jə-ləs *or* pĕn′dyə-ləs) *adj.* **1.** Hanging loosely; suspended so as to swing or sway. **2.** Wavering; undecided. —**pen′du·lous·ly** *adv.* —**pen′du·lous·ness** *n.*

pen·du·lum (pĕn′jə-ləm *or* pĕn′dyə-ləm) *n.* A mass hung from a fixed support so that it swings freely back and forth under the influence of gravity, often used to regulate the action of various devices, especially clocks. [From Latin *pendulus*, hanging, from *pendēre*, to hang.]

Pe·nel·o·pe (pə-nĕl′ə-pē) *n.* In Greek mythology, the wife of Odysseus and mother of Telemachus, celebrated for her faithfulness.

pe·ne·plain also **pe·ne·plane** (pē′nə-plān′) *n.* A large, nearly flat eroded land surface that was formerly a mountainous or hilly area.

pen·e·tra·ble (pĕn′ĭ-trə-bəl) *adj.* Capable of being penetrated: *a penetrable fort; a penetrable fabric not for winter use.* —**pen′e·tra·bil′i·ty** *n.*

pen·e·trate (pĕn′ĭ-trāt′) *v.* **pen·e·trat·ed, pen·e·trat·ing, pen·e·trates** —*tr.* **1.** To enter, pass into, or force a way into: *The needle penetrated the skin. Light penetrated the forest canopy. The soldiers penetrated enemy territory.* **2.** To enter into and permeate: *Cold penetrated my bones.* **3.** To grasp the significance of; understand: *penetrating the workings of the immune system.* —*intr.* To enter or pass into something.

pen·e·trat·ing (pĕn′ĭ-trā′tĭng) *adj.* **1.** Permeating; piercing; sharp: *penetrating cold.* **2.** Perceptive; understanding; acute: *a penetrating mind.*

pen·e·tra·tion (pĕn′ĭ-trā′shən) *n.* **1.** The act or process of penetrating. **2.** The power or ability to penetrate: *a drill with great penetration.* **3.** The ability to understand; insight.

pen·guin (pĕng′gwĭn *or* pĕn′gwĭn) *n.* Any of various flightless seabirds that live mostly in or near Antarctica and have webbed feet, narrow wings resembling flippers,

Pekingese

pelican

penguin

peninsula
satellite image of Italy and neighboring islands of Corsica, Sardinia, and Sicily

GEOGRAPHY

Pennsylvania The state of **Pennsylvania** was named after its founder, William Penn, and his father, a British admiral. It combines the name *Penn* with a form of the Latin word *silva* (also spelled *sylva*), meaning "forest."

Pentagon

ă	pat	ôr	core
ā	pay	oi	boy
âr	care	ou	out
ä	father	o͝o	took
ĕ	pet	o͝or	lure
ē	be	o͞o	boot
ĭ	pit	ŭ	cut
ī	bite	ûr	urge
îr	pier	th	thin
ŏ	pot	*th*	this
ō	toe	zh	vision
ô	paw	ə	about

and scalelike feathers that are white in front and black on the back.

pen·i·cil·lin (pĕn′ĭ-**sĭl′**ĭn) *n.* An antibiotic drug obtained from penicillium molds or synthesized in the laboratory, used to treat certain bacterial infections such as strep throat or some kinds of pneumonia.

pen·i·cil·li·um (pĕn′ĭ-**sĭl′**ē-əm) *n., pl.* **pen·i·cil·li·ums** or **pen·i·cil·li·a** (pĕn′ĭ-**sĭl′**ē-ə) Any of various bluish-green fungi that grow as molds on citrus fruits, cheeses, or bread, including several species used to produce penicillin and certain other antibiotic drugs.

pen·in·su·la (pə-**nĭn′**sə-lə) *n.* A piece of land that juts out from a larger land mass and is mostly surrounded by water. [From Latin *paene*, almost + Latin *īnsula*, island.] **—pen·in′su·lar** *adj.* —SEE NOTE AT **island.**

pe·nis (**pē′**nĭs) *n.* **1.** The sex organ of the males of mammals, reptiles, and certain birds. Most male mammals also use the penis for urination. **2.** A similar organ found in the males of certain invertebrate animals, such as insects and some snails.

pen·i·tent (**pĕn′**ĭ-tənt) *adj.* Feeling or showing sorrow for one's sins or misdeeds. ❖ *n.* A person who is penitent. **—pen′i·tence** *n.*

pen·i·ten·tial (pĕn′ĭ-**tĕn′**shəl) *adj.* **1.** Relating to or expressing sorrow for one's sins or misdeeds. **2.** Relating to penance.

pen·i·ten·tia·ry (pĕn′ĭ-**tĕn′**shə-rē) *n., pl.* **pen·i·ten·tia·ries** A prison for those convicted of serious crimes.

pen·knife (**pĕn′**nīf′) *n.* A small pocketknife.

pen·light (**pĕn′**līt′) *n.* A small flashlight that is the size and shape of a pen.

pen·man (**pĕn′**mən) *n.* **1.** An expert in penmanship. **2.** An author; a writer.

pen·man·ship (**pĕn′**mən-shĭp′) *n.* The art, skill, style, or manner of handwriting.

Penn (pĕn), **William** 1644–1718. English Quaker who founded the colony of Pennsylvania in 1681.

pen name *n.* A fictitious name used by an author.

pen·nant (**pĕn′**ənt) *n.* **1.** A long tapering flag, used on ships for signaling or identification. **2a.** A flag that serves as the emblem of the championship in professional baseball. **b.** The yearly championship in professional baseball.

pen·ne (**pĕn′**ā) *n., pl.* **penne** Pasta in small short tubes with diagonally cut ends.

pen·ni·less (**pĕn′**ē-lĭs) *adj.* Having no money or very little; very poor. **—pen′ni·less·ness** *n.*

pen·non (**pĕn′**ən) *n.* **1.** A long narrow banner borne upon a lance. **2.** A pennant, banner, or flag.

Penn·syl·va·nia (pĕn′səl-**vān′**yə *or* pĕn′səl-**vā′**nē-ə) A state of the eastern United States east of Ohio. It was admitted as one of the original Thirteen Colonies in 1787. Harrisburg is the capital and Philadelphia the largest city. **—Penn′syl·va′nian** *adj. & n.* —SEE NOTE.

Pennsylvania Dutch *n.* **1.** *(used with a plural verb)* The descendants of German and Swiss immigrants who settled in Pennsylvania in the 1600s and 1700s. **2.** The dialect of German spoken by this group. [From *Pennsylvania* + alteration of the German word meaning "German," *Deutsch* (akin to English *Dutch*).]

Penn·syl·va·nian (pĕn′səl-**vān′**yən) *n.* The sixth period of the Paleozoic Era, from about 318 to 299 million years ago. The Pennsylvanian Period is marked by the appearance of the first reptiles and widespread swamp forests. **—Penn′syl·va′nian** *adj.*

pen·ny (**pĕn′**ē) *n., pl.* **pen·nies 1.** In the United States and Canada, the coin worth one cent. **2.** *pl.* **pence** or **pen·nies a.** A coin used in Great Britain since 1971, worth 1⁄100 of a pound. **b.** A coin formerly used in Great Britain, worth 1⁄12 of a shilling or 1⁄240 of a pound. **3.** Any of various coins worth a small amount. **4.** A small sum of money: *I haven't a penny to my name.* [From Middle English *peni*, a small silver coin, from Old English *penig*.]

pen·ny·roy·al (pĕn′ē-**roi′**əl) *n.* **1.** A plant of Eurasia having small blue flowers and round leaves that yield a toxic essential oil. **2.** A strong-smelling plant of eastern North America having small bluish flowers and oblong leaves that yield a similar essential oil.

pen·ny·weight (**pĕn′**ē-wāt′) *n.* A unit of troy weight equal to 24 grains or 1⁄20 of a troy ounce (about 1.5 grams).

pen·ny-wise or **pen·ny·wise** (**pĕn′**ē-wīz′) *adj.* Careful in dealing with small sums or minor matters.

pen·ny·worth (**pĕn′**ē-wûrth′) *n.* **1.** As much as a penny will buy. **2.** A small or trifling amount. **3.** A bargain.

Pe·nob·scot (pə-**nŏb′**skət *or* pə-**nŏb′**skŏt′) *n., pl.* **Penobscot** or **Pe·nob·scots 1.** A member of a Native American people living in Maine. **2.** The Algonquian language of the Penobscot. **—Pe·nob′scot** *adj.*

pe·nol·o·gy (pē-**nŏl′**ə-jē) *n.* The theory and practice of prison management and the rehabilitation of criminals.

pen pal *n.* A friend with whom one is acquainted only by exchanging letters.

pen·sion (**pĕn′**shən) *n.* **1.** A sum of money paid regularly as a retirement benefit or by way of patronage. **2.** (pän-**syôɴ′**) A boarding house or small hotel in Europe. ❖ *tr.v.* **pen·sioned, pen·sion·ing, pen·sions 1.** To give a pension to. **2.** To retire or dismiss with a pension: *The company reduced its work force by pensioning off some older workers.* [From Middle English *pencioun*, payment, from Old French *pension*, from Latin *pēnsiō*, from *pendere*, to weigh out, pay.]

pen·sion·er (**pĕn′**shə-nər) *n.* A person who receives a pension.

pen·sive (**pĕn′**sĭv) *adj.* **1.** Engaged in deep and serious thought. **2.** Showing or expressing deep, often sad thought: *a pensive look.* **—pen′sive·ly** *adv.*

pen·stock (**pĕn′**stŏk′) *n.* **1.** A sluice or gate used to control a flow of water. **2.** A pipe used to carry water to a water wheel or turbine.

pent (pĕnt) *v.* A past tense and a past participle of **pen²**. ❖ *adj.* Penned or shut up; closely confined.

penta– or **pent–** *pref.* A prefix that means five: *pentatonic.*

pen·ta·cle (**pĕn′**tə-kəl) *n.* A pentagram.

pen·ta·gon (**pĕn′**tə-gŏn′) *n.* **1.** A polygon with five sides and five angles. **2. Pentagon** A five-sided building near Washington, DC, containing the US Department of Defense and the offices of the US Armed Forces. **—pen·tag′o·nal** (pĕn-**tăg′**ə-nəl) *adj.*

pen·ta·gram (**pĕn′**tə-grăm′) *n.* A five-pointed star, often held to have magical or mystical significance.

pen·ta·he·dron (pĕn′tə-**hē′**drən) *n., pl.* **pen·ta·he·drons** or **pen·ta·he·dra** (pĕn′tə-**hē′**drə) A solid geometric figure having five faces.

pen·tam·e·ter (pĕn-**tăm′**ĭ-tər) *n.* A line of verse made up of five metrical feet.

Pen·ta·teuch (**pĕn′**tə-to͞ok′) *n.* The first five books of the Hebrew Scriptures; the Torah.

pen·tath·lon (pĕn-**tăth′**lŏn′) *n.* An athletic contest consisting of five track and field events, usually running races at two different distances, the long jump, and the discus and javelin throws.

pen·ta·ton·ic (pĕn′tə-**tŏn′**ĭk) *adj.* Relating to or using only five musical tones: *a pentatonic scale.*

Pen·te·cost (**pĕn′**tĭ-kôst′) *n.* **1.** The seventh Sunday after Easter, observed in Christian churches in commemoration of the descent of the Holy Spirit upon the disciples. **2.** Shavuot. **—Pen′te·cos′tal** *adj.*

pent·house (**pĕnt′**hous′) *n.* An apartment or dwelling, usually with a terrace, located on the roof of a building.

pent-up (pĕnt′ŭp′) *adj.* Not given expression; repressed: *pent-up anger.*

pe·nult (pē′nŭlt′ *or* pĭ-**nŭlt′**) *n.* The next to the last syllable in a word.

pe·nul·ti·mate (pĭ-**nŭl′**tə-mĭt) *adj.* Next to last: *the penultimate chapter of the book.*

pe·num·bra (pĭ-**nŭm′**brə) *n., pl.* **pe·num·bras** or **pe·num·brae** (pĭ-**nŭm′**brē) **1.** A partial shadow between regions of complete shadow and complete illumination, especially as cast by Earth, the moon, or another body during an eclipse. **2.** The partly darkened fringe that surrounds a sunspot. [From Latin *paene*, almost + Latin *umbra*, shadow.]

pe·nu·ri·ous (pə-**nŏŏr′**ē-əs) *adj.* **1.** Extremely needy; poverty-stricken. **2.** Unwilling to spend money; stingy. **—pe·nu′ri·ous·ly** *adv.* **—pe·nu′ri·ous·ness** *n.*

pen·u·ry (**pĕn′**yə-rē) *n.* Extreme poverty.

Pe·nu·ti·an (pə-**nōō′**tē-ən *or* pə-**nōō′**shən) *n.* A family of Native American languages spoken in Pacific coastal areas from California to British Columbia.

pe·on (**pē′**ŏn′ *or* **pē′**ən) *n.* **1.** A person in a lowly position, especially one who does menial tasks. **2.** An unskilled laborer or farm worker of Latin America or the southwest United States. [From Spanish *peón*, day laborer, from Medieval Latin *pedō*, foot soldier, from Latin *pēs*, foot.]

pe·on·age (**pē′**ə-nĭj) *n.* **1.** The condition of being a peon. **2.** A system by which debtors are bound in servitude to their creditors until their debts are paid.

pe·o·ny (**pē′**ə-nē) *n., pl.* **pe·o·nies** Any of various garden plants having large pink, red, or white flowers.

peo·ple (**pē′**pəl) *n., pl.* **people 1.** Humans considered as a group: *There were all sorts of people in the waiting room.* **2.** The mass of ordinary persons; the populace: *In a democracy, political power rests with the people.* **3a.** A group of persons living in the same country under one national government: *the American people.* **b.** The citizens of a political unit: *The people of Alaska will vote tomorrow.* **4.** *pl.* **peoples** A group of persons sharing a common religion, culture, language, or condition of life: *the peoples of southwest Asia.* **5.** Family, relatives, or ancestors: *Her people are farmers.* ❖ *tr.v.* **peo·pled, peo·pling, peo·ples** To furnish with people; populate: *Many ethnic groups people the city.* —SEE NOTE.

pep (pĕp) *Informal n.* Energy; high spirits. ❖ *tr.v.* **pepped, pep·ping, peps** To bring energy or liveliness to: *The good news pepped me up.*

pep·per (**pĕp′**ər) *n.* **1a.** A black or white pungent spice made from the dried blackish berries of a tropical vine. **b.** The plant that bears such berries. **2a.** The many-seeded red, yellow, or green fruit of any of several plants, eaten as a vegetable or ground into seasonings. **b.** A plant that bears such fruit. ❖ *tr.v.* **pep·pered, pep·per·ing, pep·pers 1.** To season with pepper. **2.** To sprinkle liberally; dot. **3.** To sprinkle or spray with many small objects: *peppered the newlyweds with rice.* [From Middle English, from Old English *pipor*, from Latin *piper*, from Greek *peperi*, ultimately of Indic origin.]

pep·per·corn (**pĕp′**ər-kôrn′) *n.* A dried or preserved black, white, or green berry of the pepper vine.

pep·per·mint (**pĕp′**ər-mĭnt′) *n.* **1.** A plant having small purple or white flowers and leaves that yield an oil having a strong, pleasant taste and smell. **2.** A candy flavored with oil from this plant.

pep·per·o·ni (pĕp′ə-**rō′**nē) *n., pl.* **pep·per·o·nis** A highly spiced pork and beef sausage.

pep·per·shak·er (**pĕp′**ər-shā′kər) *n.* A container with small holes in the top for holding and sprinkling ground pepper.

pep·per·y (**pĕp′**ə-rē) *adj.* **1.** Containing pepper; hot and spicy: *a peppery stew.* **2.** Having a hot temper.

pep·sin also **pep·sine** (**pĕp′**sĭn) *n.* **1.** An enzyme that is produced in the stomach and acts as a catalyst in the digestion of protein. **2.** A substance containing this enzyme, obtained from the stomachs of hogs and calves and used to aid digestion.

pep talk *n. Informal* A speech of encouragement, as one given by a coach to a team.

pep·tic (**pĕp′**tĭk) *adj.* **1a.** Relating to or assisting digestion: *a peptic secretion.* **b.** Caused by or associated with the action of digestive juices: *a peptic ulcer.* **2.** Relating to or involving pepsin.

Pe·quot (**pē′**kwŏt′) *n., pl.* **Pequot** or **Pe·quots 1.** A member of a Native American people living in Connecticut. The Pequot and the Mohegan were the same people until the Mohegan broke away in the 1600s. **2.** The Algonquian language of the Pequot.

per (pûr) *prep.* **1.** To, for, or by each; for every: *eggs at one dollar per dozen.* **2.** According to: *changes made to the play per instructions of the author.*

per·am·bu·late (pə-**răm′**byə-lāt′) *v.* **per·am·bu·lat·ed, per·am·bu·lat·ing, per·am·bu·lates** —*tr.* **1.** To walk through. **2.** To inspect by walking through: *perambulate the plant site.* —*intr.* To walk about; stroll. **—per·am′bu·la′tion** *n.*

per·am·bu·la·tor (pə-**răm′**byə-lā′tər) *n. Chiefly British* A baby carriage.

per·cale (pər-**kāl′**) *n.* A strong closely woven cloth used to make sheets and clothing.

per cap·i·ta (pər **kăp′**ĭ-tə) *adv. & adj.* Per person: *the state's per capita income.*

per·ceive (pər-**sēv′**) *tr.v.* **per·ceived, per·ceiv·ing, per·ceives 1.** To become aware of through the senses, especially to see or hear. **2.** To achieve understanding of: *We tried to perceive their intentions by analyzing their letter.* **—per·ceiv′er** *n.*

per·cent also **per cent** (pər-**sĕnt′**) *n.* One part in a hundred. For example, 62 percent means 62 parts out of 100. ❖ *adj.* Gaining interest at a given rate or percentage: *an 8 percent savings account.* [From Latin *per centum*, by the hundred : *per*, by + *centum*, hundred.]

per·cent·age (pər-**sĕn′**tĭj) *n.* **1.** A fraction that has 100 understood as its denominator. 0.75 equals a percentage of 75. **2.** A portion or share in relation to the whole: *Teachers made up a sizable percentage of the people at the meeting.*

per·cen·tile (pər-**sĕn′**tīl′) *n.* Any of the 100 equal parts into which the range of the values of a set of data can be divided in order to show the distribution of those values. For example, a test score that is higher than 95 percent of the other scores is said to be in the 95th percentile.

per·cep·ti·ble (pər-**sĕp′**tə-bəl) *adj.* Capable of being perceived by the senses or by the mind: *a perceptible improvement in the patient's condition.* **—per·cep′ti·bil′i·ty** *n.* **—per·cep′ti·bly** *adv.*

per·cep·tion (pər-**sĕp′**shən) *n.* **1a.** The ability, act, or process of perceiving something with the senses: *the perception of a faint sound.* **b.** An instance of becoming aware of something by means of the senses: *perceptions of different odors.* **2a.** The ability, process, or state of being aware of something: *The perception of time often changes when you are having fun.* **b.** An insight or point of understanding: *What an astute perception!*

per·cep·tive (pər-**sĕp′**tĭv) *adj.* **1.** Having the ability to perceive; having keen insight: *a perceptive student of physics.* **2.** Marked by understanding and insight: *a perceptive thought.* **—per·cep′tive·ly** *adv.*

per·cep·tu·al (pər-**sĕp′**chōō-əl) *adj.* Based on or involving perception.

perch[1] (pûrch) *n.* **1.** A branch or rod that serves as a roost for a bird. **2.** A resting place or vantage point, especially one that is high up: *Lee slid down from a perch in the apple tree.* ❖ *v.* **perched, perch·ing, perch·es** —*intr.* **1.** To alight or rest on a perch: *The bird perched on a*

peony

USAGE

people When *people* is used to mean "humans," it is plural: *The people coming out of the theater were smiling.* The usual singular word referring to a human is *person.* When *people* means "a group of humans sharing a culture," it is a singular noun and its plural is *peoples: the many peoples of West Africa.*

Marguerite Perey

branch. **2.** To sit in or occupy an elevated position: *My sister perched on the arm of my chair.* —*tr.* **1.** To place on a perch: *An owl was perched in our oak tree.* **2.** To place in an elevated position: *She perched the straw hat on her head.* [From Middle English *perche*, from Old French, from Latin *pertica*, stick, pole.]

perch² (pûrch) *n., pl.* **perch** or **perch·es** Any of various mostly freshwater food fishes having spiny fins. [From Middle English *perche*, from Old French, from Latin *perca*, from Greek *perkē*.]

per·chance (pər-**chăns′**) *adv.* Perhaps; possibly.

perch·ing bird (**pûr′**chĭng) *n.* Any of a large group of birds, including the songbirds, that can grasp branches with their feet.

per·co·late (**pûr′**kə-lāt′) *v.* **per·co·lat·ed, per·co·lat·ing, per·co·lates** —*tr.* **1.** To cause (a liquid, for example) to pass through small holes or through a porous substance: *percolate oil through a filter.* **2.** To pass or ooze through: *Water percolated the sand.* —*intr.* **1.** To drain or seep through a porous material or a filter. **2.** *Informal* To become lively or active: *As she became aware of the new data, her mind began to percolate.* [From Latin *percōlāre* : *per-*, through + *cōlum*, sieve, filter.] **—per′co·la′tion** *n.*

per·co·la·tor (**pûr′**kə-lā′tər) *n.* A coffeepot in which boiling water is forced repeatedly to pass up through a center tube and filter through a basket of ground coffee.

per·cus·sion (pər-**kŭsh′**ən) *n.* **1a.** The striking together of two bodies, especially when noise is produced. **b.** A sound, vibration, or shock produced in this way. **2.** A method of medical examination in which a physician taps areas of the body and draws conclusions on the basis of the sounds produced. **3a.** The section of a band or orchestra made up of percussion instruments. **b.** Percussion instruments considered as a group.

percussion cap *n.* A thin metal cap containing an explosive substance that explodes on being struck.

percussion instrument *n.* A musical instrument, such as a drum, xylophone, piano, or maraca, in which sound is produced by one object striking another or by being scraped or shaken.

per·cus·sion·ist (pər-**kŭsh′**ə-nĭst) *n.* A person who plays percussion instruments.

per di·em (pər **dē′**əm) *adv.* Per day. ❖ *adj.* On a daily basis; daily.

per·di·tion (pər-**dĭsh′**ən) *n.* **1a.** The loss of the soul; eternal damnation. **b.** Hell. **2.** Utter loss or ruin.

per·e·grine falcon (**pĕr′**ə-grĭn) *n.* A swift-flying bird of prey with gray and white feathers, found worldwide.

per·emp·to·ry (pə-**rĕmp′**tə-rē) *adj.* **1.** Subject to no further debate or dispute; final: *a peremptory decree.* **2.** Not to be denied, refused, or opposed: *a peremptory order.* **3.** Offensively self-assured; dictatorial: *issued commands with a peremptory manner.* **—per·emp′to·ri·ly** *adv.* **—per·emp′to·ri·ness** *n.*

per·en·ni·al (pə-**rĕn′**ē-əl) *adj.* **1.** Lasting indefinitely; perpetual: *an author's perennial popularity among children.* **2.** Repeated regularly; appearing again and again: *a perennial contender for the championship.* **3.** Living for three or more years: *a perennial plant.* ❖ *n.* A perennial plant: *We planted perennials in the garden.* **—per·en′ni·al·ly** *adv.*

Pe·rey (pĕ-**rā′**), **Marguerite Catherine** 1909–1975. French physicist who discovered the element francium (1939).

per·fect (**pûr′**fĭkt) *adj.* **1a.** Lacking nothing essential to the whole; satisfying all requirements: *Our understanding of the situation is not perfect.* **b.** Completely accurate; exact: *a perfect copy.* **2.** Having no faults, flaws, or defects: *a perfect piece of marble.* **3a.** Completely suited for a particular purpose or action: *a perfect actor for the part.* **b.** Completely corresponding to a description, standard, or type: *a perfect gentleman.* **4.** Excellent and delightful in all respects: *perfect weather.* **5.** Pure; undiluted: *the perfect redness of the apple.* **6.** Complete; thorough; utter: *a perfect fool.* **7.** Having a root that is a whole number; formed by raising an integer to an integral power; for example, 25 is a perfect square, and 27 is a perfect cube. **8.** In grammar, relating to the perfect tense. ❖ *n.* **1.** The perfect tense. **2.** A verb form in the perfect tense. ❖ *tr.v.* (pər-**fĕkt′**) **per·fect·ed, per·fect·ing, per·fects** To bring to perfection or completion. [From Middle English *parfit*, from Old French, from Latin *perfectus*, past participle of *perficere*, to finish.]

SYNONYMS **perfect, faultless, flawless, impeccable** These adjectives mean without any defects or errors. *I have found the perfect solution to your problem. The lecturer argued her point with faultless logic. That museum owns the world's largest flawless gem. They spoke impeccable French after living in Paris for years.*

---

perfect game *n.* **1.** In baseball, a game, especially one pitched by a single pitcher, in which no opposing batter reaches first base. **2.** In bowling, a game in which a player bowls 12 strikes in a row.

per·fect·i·ble (pər-**fĕk′**tə-bəl) *adj.* Capable of becoming or being made perfect: *a perfectible style of writing.* **—per·fect′i·bil′i·ty** *n.*

per·fec·tion (pər-**fĕk′**shən) *n.* **1.** The quality or condition of being perfect. **2.** The act or process of perfecting. **3.** A person or thing considered to be an example of excellence.

per·fec·tion·ism (pər-**fĕk′**shə-nĭz′əm) *n.* **1.** A tendency to set extremely high standards and to be dissatisfied with anything less. **2.** A belief that humans can achieve moral or spiritual perfection. **—per·fec′tion·ist** *n.*

per·fect·ly (**pûr′**fĭkt-lē) *adv.* **1a.** In a perfect manner: *She played the piece perfectly.* **b.** To a perfect degree; precisely: *This circle is perfectly round.* **2.** Completely; wholly: *Some mushrooms are perfectly safe to eat.*

perfect number *n.* A positive integer, such as 6 or 28, that equals the sum of all of its divisors other than itself. For example, the divisors of 6, not counting 6 itself, are 1, 2, and 3. Their sum is 6.

perfect pitch *n.* The ability to identify or sing any tone heard; absolute pitch.

perfect tense *n.* In grammar, a verb tense that expresses an action completed prior to a fixed point in time. For example, *she has played* is in the present perfect tense, *she had played* is in the past perfect tense, and *she will have played* is in the future perfect tense.

per·fid·i·ous (pər-**fĭd′**ē-əs) *adj.* Disloyal; treacherous. **—per·fid′i·ous·ly** *adv.*

per·fi·dy (**pûr′**fĭ-dē) *n., pl.* **per·fi·dies** Deliberate breach of faith; treachery.

per·fo·rate (**pûr′**fə-rāt′) *tr.v.* **per·fo·rat·ed, per·fo·rat·ing, per·fo·rates 1.** To punch or bore a hole or holes in; pierce: *Perforate the top of the pie to let the steam escape.* **2.** To pierce or stamp with rows of holes to allow easy separation: *a machine that perforates sheets of postage stamps.* [From Latin *perforāre* : *per-*, through + *forāre*, to bore.]

per·fo·rat·ed (**pûr′**fə-rā′tĭd) *adj.* Pierced with holes; full of holes: *a perforated spoon.*

per·fo·ra·tion (pûr′fə-**rā′**shən) *n.* **1.** A hole or series of holes, as those between postage stamps. **2.** The act of perforating.

per·force (pər-**fôrs′**) *adv.* By force of circumstance; of necessity: *She must perforce work for wages.*

per·form (pər-**fôrm′**) *v.* **per·formed, per·form·ing, per·forms** —*tr.* **1.** To begin and carry through to completion; do; execute: *perform an experiment; perform a somersault.* **2.** To carry out or fulfill (a promise, duty, or task, for example). **3.** To present or enact before an audi-

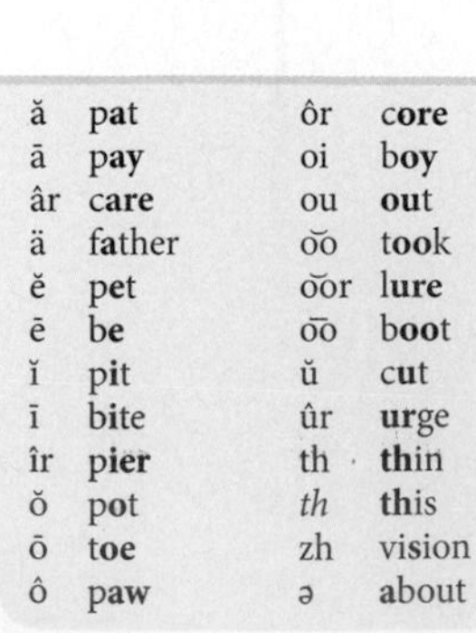

ă	pat	ôr	core
ā	pay	oi	boy
âr	care	ou	out
ä	father	ŏŏ	took
ĕ	pet	ŏŏr	lure
ē	be	ōō	boot
ĭ	pit	ŭ	cut
ī	bite	ûr	urge
îr	pier	th	thin
ŏ	pot	*th*	this
ō	toe	zh	vision
ô	paw	ə	about

ence: *perform a symphony.* —*intr.* **1.** To act or function in a specified manner: *The car performs well on curves.* **2.** To portray a role, present a musical work, or demonstrate a skill before an audience: *The juggler performed while riding a unicycle.* **—per·form′er** *n.*

per·form·ance (pər-**fôr′**məns) *n.* **1.** The act, process, or manner of performing. **2.** The way in which a person or thing functions: *Look for good steady performance when buying a car.* **3.** A public presentation of something, such as a musical or dramatic work: *The recital featured the performance of several compositions by Bach.* **4.** Something performed; an accomplishment.

per·form·ing arts (pər-**fôr′**mĭng) *pl.n.* Arts, such as dance, drama, and music, that are performed before an audience.

per·fume (**pûr′**fyo͞om′ *or* pər-**fyo͞om′**) *n.* **1.** A fragrant liquid distilled from flowers or prepared synthetically. **2.** A pleasant scent or odor. ❖ *tr.v.* (pər-**fyo͞om′**) **per·fumed, per·fum·ing, per·fumes** To fill with a fragrance or give a pleasant odor to. [From Old French *parfumer*, to perfume, from Latin *per-*, thoroughly + *fūmus*, smoke.]

per·fum·er·y (pər-**fyo͞o′**mə-rē) *n.*, *pl.* **per·fum·er·ies 1.** Perfumes considered as a group. **2.** A business that specializes in making or selling perfume. **3.** The art of making perfume.

per·func·to·ry (pər-**fŭngk′**tə-rē) *adj.* Done or acting routinely and with little interest or care: *She gave a perfunctory wave and walked away.* **—per·func′to·ri·ly** *adv.* **—per·func′to·ri·ness** *n.*

per·haps (pər-**hăps′**) *adv.* Maybe; possibly: *Perhaps he'll come with us.*

peri– *pref.* A prefix that means around, about, or enclosing: *perihelion.*

per·i·car·di·um (pĕr′ĭ-**kär′**dē-əm) *n.*, *pl.* **per·i·car·di·a** (pĕr′ĭ-**kär′**dē-ə) The membrane sac that encloses the heart.

Per·i·cles (**pĕr′**ĭ-klēz′) 495?–429 BC. Athenian leader noted for advancing democracy and for ordering the construction of the Parthenon.

per·i·gee (**pĕr′**ə-jē) *n.* The point in an orbit around Earth where a satellite is closest to Earth. [From Greek *perigeion* : *peri-*, near + *gē*, earth.]

per·i·he·li·on (pĕr′ə-**hē′**lē-ən) *n.*, *pl.* **per·i·he·li·a** (pĕr′ə-**hē′**lē-ə) The point in the orbit of a planet or other body that travels around the sun at which it is closest to the sun.

per·il (**pĕr′**əl) *n.* **1.** The condition of being in danger or at risk of harm or loss: *The drought has put the crops in peril.* **2.** Something that is dangerous or risky: *the perils of a journey in a covered wagon.*

per·il·ous (**pĕr′**ə-ləs) *adj.* Full of peril; hazardous or risky: *The spy was sent on a perilous mission.* **—per′il·ous·ly** *adv.*

pe·rim·e·ter (pə-**rĭm′**ĭ-tər) *n.* **1a.** The sum of the lengths of the segments that form the sides of a polygon. **b.** The total length of any closed curve, such as a circle or ellipse. **2.** The outer limits of an area. **3.** A fortified strip or boundary protecting a military position.

pe·ri·od (**pĭr′**ē-əd) *n.* **1.** An interval of time having a specified length or characterized by certain conditions or events: *a dormant period in the economy.* **2.** A span of time during which a specified culture, set of beliefs, or technology was predominant; a historical era: *the colonial period.* **3.** Any of various intervals of time, as the divisions of the academic day or of playing time in a game: *I have history in the fifth period.* **4.** A unit of geologic time, longer than an epoch and shorter than an era. **5.** The time it takes for a regularly recurring action or event to be repeated; a cycle. **6.** A menstrual period. **7.** A punctuation mark (.) indicating a full stop, used at the end of declarative sentences, other complete statements, and some abbreviations. [From Middle English *periode*, from Old French, from Medieval Latin *periodus*, from Greek *periodos*, a going around, cycle, period : *peri-*, around + *hodos*, way.]

pe·ri·od·ic (pĭr′ē-**ŏd′**ĭk) *adj.* **1.** Happening or repeating at regular intervals; cyclic: *the periodic motion of a pendulum.* **2.** Taking place from time to time; intermittent. **—pe′ri·od′i·cal·ly** *adv.*

pe·ri·od·i·cal (pĭr′ē-**ŏd′**ĭ-kəl) *adj.* **1.** Periodic. **2.** Relating to a publication that is issued at regular intervals of more than one day. ❖ *n.* A periodical publication, especially a magazine.

periodic table *n.* A table in which the elements are presented in order of increasing atomic number, with the elements that have similar properties usually appearing in columns. See table on pages 700–701.

per·i·pa·tet·ic (pĕr′ə-pə-**tĕt′**ĭk) *adj.* Walking about or traveling on foot from place to place: *peripatetic political candidates.*

pe·riph·er·al (pə-**rĭf′**ər-əl) *adj.* **1.** Relating to or located on the periphery: *the peripheral regions of the state.* **2.** Of minor importance or relevance. **3.** Attached to and used together with a computer, as a modem or printer: *bought a cable for connecting peripheral devices to her computer.* **—pe·riph′er·al·ly** *adv.*

peripheral nervous system *n.* The part of the vertebrate nervous system that lies outside of the brain and spinal cord.

pe·riph·er·y (pə-**rĭf′**ə-rē) *n.*, *pl.* **pe·riph·er·ies 1.** A line that forms a boundary; a perimeter. **2.** The area along a boundary.

per·i·scope (**pĕr′**ĭ-skōp′) *n.* Any of several optical instruments in which mirrors or prisms allow observation of objects that are not in a direct line of sight.

per·ish (**pĕr′**ĭsh) *intr.v.* **per·ished, per·ish·ing, per·ish·es 1.** To die or be destroyed, especially in a violent manner. **2.** To pass from existence; disappear gradually: *The dinosaurs perished from the earth.* [From Middle English *perishen*, from Old French *perir*, from Latin *perīre*, to disappear, perish : *per-*, through + Latin *īre*, to go.]

per·ish·a·ble (**pĕr′**ĭ-shə-bəl) *adj.* Liable to decay or spoil easily: *perishable fruits and vegetables.* **—per′ish·a·bly** *adv.*

per·ish·a·bles (**pĕr′**ĭ-shə-bəlz) *pl.n.* Items, especially different kinds of food, that are subject to decay or spoiling.

per·i·stal·sis (pĕr′ĭ-**stôl′**sĭs *or* pĕr′ĭ-**stăl′**sĭs) *n.*, *pl.* **per·i·stal·ses** (pĕr′ĭ-**stôl′**sēz *or* pĕr′ĭ-**stăl′**sēz) The series of muscle contractions in a tubular organ, such as an intestine, that move the material contained in it along its length.

per·i·to·ne·um (pĕr′ĭ-tn-**ē′**əm) *n.*, *pl.* **per·i·to·ne·a** (pĕr′ĭ-tn-**ē′**ə) The membrane that lines the inside of the abdomen and encloses the abdominal organs.

per·i·to·ni·tis (pĕr′ĭ-tn-**ī′**tĭs) *n.* Inflammation of the peritoneum.

per·i·wig (**pĕr′**ĭ-wĭg′) *n.* A wig, especially a peruke.

per·i·win·kle[1] (**pĕr′**ĭ-wĭng′kəl) *n.* Any of various sea snails having a thick spiral shell, especially an edible species of the North Atlantic Ocean. [Probably akin to Old English *wīnewincle* : *wine-*, of unknown meaning + Old English *wincle*, shellfish.]

per·i·win·kle[2] (**pĕr′**ĭ-wĭng′kəl) *n.* Any of several trailing plants having evergreen leaves and usually blue flowers. [From Middle English *pervinkle*, from Latin *vinca pervinca*, *vica pervica*, perhaps originally part of a magical formula relating to the plant and ultimately akin to Latin *vincīre*, to fasten, bind, or *vincere*, to win.]

per·jure (**pûr′**jər) *tr.v.* **per·jured, per·jur·ing, per·jures** To make (oneself) guilty of perjury: *The witness perjured himself.* **—per′jur·er** *n.*

per·ju·ry (**pûr′**jə-rē) *n.*, *pl.* **per·ju·ries** The crime of deliberately making a false statement while under oath.

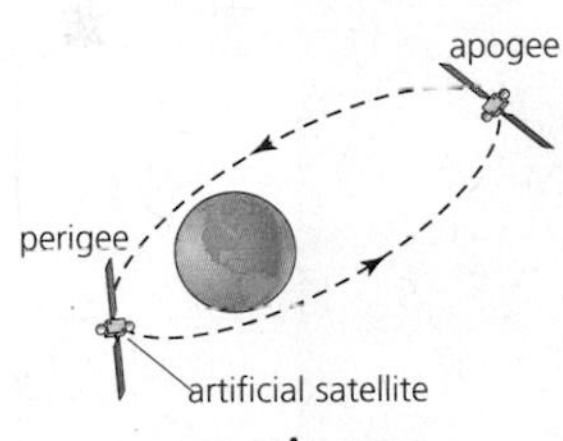

perigee

periscope
Light enters the top lens, reflects off a mirror set at a 45° angle, travels down the periscope tube, reflects off a second mirror also set at a 45° angle, and exits through the bottom lens.

Periodic Table of the Elements

The periodic table arranges the chemical elements in two ways. The first is by atomic number—the number of protons in each element's nucleus. The elements are arranged so that their atomic numbers increase as you read across each row, or **period**, from left to right. The second is by chemical family. Each column, or **group**, contains elements with similar chemical properties.

The first periodic table was designed by Dmitri Mendeleev in 1869. At that time only 63 of the elements were known. When Mendeleev made the first table, however, he knew that other elements would eventually be discovered, and he left empty spaces in his table so that the new elements could be added as they were discovered. Today's periodic table is basically the same as Mendeleev's original chart, with some improvements.

The elements of the **lanthanide series** (elements 57–71) and the **actinide series** (elements 89–103) are set apart from the rest of the periodic table because all of them have characteristics similar to those of the elements in Group 3. But since they have different atomic numbers, they are separated from the main periodic table to make it easier to read.

	Group 1	Group 2	Group 3	Group 4	Group 5	Group 6	Group 7	Group 8	Group 9
Period 1	1 H Hydrogen								
Period 2	3 Li Lithium	4 Be Beryllium							
Period 3	11 Na Sodium	12 Mg Magnesium							
Period 4	19 K Potassium	20 Ca Calcium	21 Sc Scandium	22 Ti Titanium	23 V Vanadium	24 Cr Chromium	25 Mn Manganese	26 Fe Iron	27 Co Cobalt
Period 5	37 Rb Rubidium	38 Sr Strontium	39 Y Yttrium	40 Zr Zirconium	41 Nb Niobium	42 Mo Molybdenum	43 Tc Technetium	44 Ru Ruthenium	45 Rh Rhodium
Period 6	55 Cs Cesium	56 Ba Barium	57–71 Lanthanides*	72 Hf Hafnium	73 Ta Tantalum	74 W Tungsten	75 Re Rhenium	76 Os Osmium	77 Ir Iridium
Period 7	87 Fr Francium	88 Ra Radium	89–103 Actinides**	104 Rf Rutherfordium	105 Db Dubnium	106 Sg Seaborgium	107 Bh Bohrium	108 Hs Hassium	109 Mt Meitnerium

* LANTHANIDES	57 La Lanthanum	58 Ce Cerium	59 Pr Praseodymium	60 Nd Neodymium	61 Pm Promethium	62 Sm Samarium	63 Eu Europium
** ACTINIDES	89 Ac Actinium	90 Th Thorium	91 Pa Protactinium	92 U Uranium	93 Np Neptunium	94 Pu Plutonium	95 Am Americium

ALPHABETICAL TABLE OF THE ELEMENTS

ELEMENT	SYMBOL	AT. NO.
Actinium	Ac	89
Aluminum	Al	13
Americium	Am	95
Antimony	Sb	51
Argon	Ar	18
Arsenic	As	33
Astatine	At	85
Barium	Ba	56
Berkelium	Bk	97
Beryllium	Be	4
Bismuth	Bi	83
Bohrium	Bh	107
Boron	B	5
Bromine	Br	35
Cadmium	Cd	48
Calcium	Ca	20
Californium	Cf	98
Carbon	C	6
Cerium	Ce	58
Cesium	Cs	55
Chlorine	Cl	17
Chromium	Cr	24
Cobalt	Co	27
Copernicium	Cn	112
Copper	Cu	29
Curium	Cm	96
Darmstadtium	Ds	110
Dubnium	Db	105
Dysprosium	Dy	66
Einsteinium	Es	99
Erbium	Er	68
Europium	Eu	63
Fermium	Fm	100
Flerovium	Fl	114
Fluorine	F	9
Francium	Fr	87
Gadolinium	Gd	64
Gallium	Ga	31
Germanium	Ge	32
Gold	Au	79
Hafnium	Hf	72
Hassium	Hs	108
Helium	He	2
Holmium	Ho	67
Hydrogen	H	1
Indium	In	49
Iodine	I	53
Iridium	Ir	77
Iron	Fe	26
Krypton	Kr	36
Lanthanum	La	57
Lawrencium	Lr	103
Lead	Pb	82
Lithium	Li	3
Livermorium	Lv	116
Lutetium	Lu	71
Magnesium	Mg	12
Manganese	Mn	25
Meitnerium	Mt	109
Mendelevium	Md	101

Alkali metals	Alkaline-earth metals	Transition metals	Lanthanide series	Actinide series	Other metals	Nonmetals	Noble gases

1 — atomic number
H — symbol
Hydrogen

Group 10	Group 11	Group 12	Group 13	Group 14	Group 15	Group 16	Group 17	Group 18
								2 He Helium
			5 B Boron	6 C Carbon	7 N Nitrogen	8 O Oxygen	9 F Fluorine	10 Ne Neon
			13 Al Aluminum	14 Si Silicon	15 P Phosphorus	16 S Sulfur	17 Cl Chlorine	18 Ar Argon
28 Ni Nickel	29 Cu Copper	30 Zn Zinc	31 Ga Gallium	32 Ge Germanium	33 As Arsenic	34 Se Selenium	35 Br Bromine	36 Kr Krypton
46 Pd Palladium	47 Ag Silver	48 Cd Cadmium	49 In Indium	50 Sn Tin	51 Sb Antimony	52 Te Tellurium	53 I Iodine	54 Xe Xenon
78 Pt Platinum	79 Au Gold	80 Hg Mercury	81 Tl Thallium	82 Pb Lead	83 Bi Bismuth	84 Po Polonium	85 At Astatine	86 Rn Radon
110 Ds Darmstadtium	111 Rg Roentgenium	112 Cn Copernicium	113 Nh Nihonium	114 Fl Flerovium	115 Mc Moscovium	116 Lv Livermorium	117 Ts Tennessine	118 Og Oganesson

64 Gd Gadolinium	65 Tb Terbium	66 Dy Dysprosium	67 Ho Holmium	68 Er Erbium	69 Tm Thulium	70 Yb Ytterbium	71 Lu Lutetium
96 Cm Curium	97 Bk Berkelium	98 Cf Californium	99 Es Einsteinium	100 Fm Fermium	101 Md Mendelevium	102 No Nobelium	103 Lr Lawrencium

ELEMENT	SYMBOL	AT. NO.	ELEMENT	SYMBOL	AT. NO.	ELEMENT	SYMBOL	AT. NO.	ELEMENT	SYMBOL	AT. NO.
Mercury	Hg	80	Phosphorus	P	15	Rutherfordium	Rf	104	Thallium	Tl	81
Molybdenum	Mo	42	Platinum	Pt	78	Samarium	Sm	62	Thorium	Th	90
Moscovium	Mc	115	Plutonium	Pu	94	Scandium	Sc	21	Thulium	Tm	69
Neodymium	Nd	60	Polonium	Po	84	Seaborgium	Sg	106	Tin	Sn	50
Neon	Ne	10	Potassium	K	19	Selenium	Se	34	Titanium	Ti	22
Neptunium	Np	93	Praseodymium	Pr	59	Silicon	Si	14	Tungsten	W	74
Nickel	Ni	28	Promethium	Pm	61	Silver	Ag	47	Uranium	U	92
Nihonium	Nh	113	Protactinium	Pa	91	Sodium	Na	11	Vanadium	V	23
Niobium	Nb	41	Radium	Ra	88	Strontium	Sr	38	Xenon	Xe	54
Nitrogen	N	7	Radon	Rn	86	Sulfur	S	16	Ytterbium	Yb	70
Nobelium	No	102	Rhenium	Re	75	Tantalum	Ta	73	Yttrium	Y	39
Oganesson	Og	118	Rhodium	Rh	45	Technetium	Tc	43	Zinc	Zn	30
Osmium	Os	76	Roentgenium	Rg	111	Tellurium	Te	52	Zirconium	Zr	40
Oxygen	O	8	Rubidium	Rb	37	Tennessine	Ts	117			
Palladium	Pd	46	Ruthenium	Ru	44	Terbium	Tb	65			

Frances Perkins

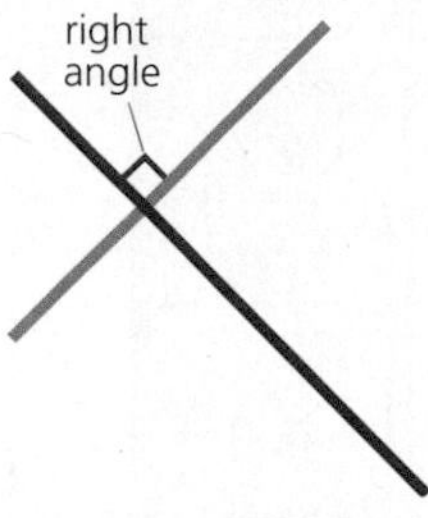

perpendicular
The purple line and the green line are perpendicular to each other.

WRITERS CHOOSE THEIR WORDS

Rowdy isn't a fast reader, but he's **persistent.** And he'll just laugh and laugh at the dumb jokes, no matter how many times he's read the same comic.

—Sherman Alexie
The Absolutely True Diary of a Part-Time Indian

ă	pat	ôr	core
ā	pay	oi	boy
âr	care	ou	out
ä	father	ŏŏ	took
ĕ	pet	ŏŏr	lure
ē	be	ōō	boot
ĭ	pit	ŭ	cut
ī	bite	ûr	urge
îr	pier	th	thin
ŏ	pot	*th*	this
ō	toe	zh	vision
ô	paw	ə	about

perk¹ (pûrk) *intr. & tr.v.* **perked, perk·ing, perks** To raise or stick up: *The dog perked its ears at the noise.* ◆ **perk up 1.** To regain or cause to regain one's good spirits or liveliness. **2.** To refresh the appearance of: *New curtains perked up the room.* [Possibly from Middle English *perken,* to perch, from *perk,* variant of *perch.*]

perk² (pûrk) *n.* A perquisite.

Per·kins (**pûr′**kĭnz), **Frances** 1882–1965. American social reformer and public official who as US secretary of labor (1933–1945) was the first woman to hold a cabinet position.

perk·y (**pûr′**kē) *adj.* **perk·i·er, perk·i·est** Lively and self-confident; cheerful. **—perk′i·ly** *adv.*

perm (pûrm) *Informal n.* A permanent.

per·ma·frost (**pûr′**mə-frôst′) *n.* A layer of permanently frozen subsoil found throughout most of the arctic regions.

per·ma·nence (**pûr′**mə-nəns) *n.* The quality or condition of being permanent.

per·ma·nent (**pûr′**mə-nənt) *adj.* Lasting or meant to last without essential change; enduring: *a permanent settlement on the frontier.* ❖ *n.* A long-lasting hairstyle usually produced by applying chemicals which straighten, curl, or wave the hair. [From Latin *permanēre,* to endure.] **—per′ma·nent·ly** *adv.*

permanent press *n.* A chemical process by which fabrics are permanently shaped and treated for resistance to wrinkles. **—per′ma·nent-press′** *adj.*

per·me·a·ble (**pûr′**mē-ə-bəl) *adj.* Capable of being passed through or permeated, especially by liquids or gases: *a permeable membrane.* **—per′me·a·bil′i·ty** *n.* **—per′me·a·bly** *adv.*

per·me·ate (**pûr′**mē-āt′) *v.* **per·me·at·ed, per·me·at·ing, per·me·ates** *—tr.* **1.** To spread or flow throughout: *The smell of baking cookies permeated the house.* **2.** To pass through the tiny openings of: *liquid permeating a membrane.* *—intr.* To spread through or penetrate something. **—per′me·a′tion** *n.*

Per·mi·an (**pûr′**mē-ən) *n.* The seventh and last period of the Paleozoic Era, from about 299 to 251 million years ago. During the Permian, conifers first arose and reptiles diversified. The Permian ended with the largest known mass extinction in the history of life. See table at **geologic time. —Per′mi·an** *adj.*

per·mis·si·ble (pər-**mĭs′**ə-bəl) *adj.* Permitted; allowable: *a permissible error.* **—per·mis′si·bly** *adv.*

per·mis·sion (pər-**mĭsh′**ən) *n.* **1.** The act of permitting. **2.** Consent, especially formal consent; authorization: *I got my mother's permission to go on the school field trip.*

per·mis·sive (pər-**mĭs′**ĭv) *adj.* Allowing freedom; tolerant or lenient: *permissive parents.* **—per·mis′sive·ly** *adv.*

per·mit (pər-**mĭt′**) *v.* **per·mit·ted, per·mit·ting, per·mits** *—tr.* **1.** To allow the doing of (something); consent to: *The town permits bicycle riding in the park.* **2.** To give consent or permission to (someone); authorize: *permitted him to explain.* **3.** To afford opportunity to; make possible: *The assembly line permitted mass production.* *—intr.* To afford opportunity; allow: *If the weather permits, we will fly.* ❖ *n.* (**pûr′**mĭt *or* pər-**mĭt′**) A document or certificate giving permission to do something. [From Middle English *permitten,* from Latin *permittere* : *per-,* through + *mittere,* to let go.]

per·mu·ta·tion (pûr′myŏŏ-**tā′**shən) *n.* **1.** A rearrangement of the elements of a group or set. For example, the permutations of the set composed of *x, y,* and *z* are *xyz, xzy, yxz, yzx, zxy, zyx.* **2.** A complete change; a transformation: *the country's permutation into a modern democracy.*

per·mute (pər-**myōōt′**) *tr.v.* **per·mut·ed, per·mut·ing, per·mutes 1.** To change the order of. **2.** To subject (a set) to permutation.

per·ni·cious (pər-**nĭsh′**əs) *adj.* **1.** Tending to cause death or serious injury; deadly: *a pernicious disease.* **2.** Causing great harm; destructive: *a pernicious habit.* **—per·ni′cious·ly** *adv.* **—per·ni′cious·ness** *n.*

per·ox·ide (pə-**rŏk′**sīd′) *n.* **1.** A compound containing the oxygen group O_2, used as an oxidizing agent or bleach. **2.** Hydrogen peroxide. ❖ *tr.v.* **per·ox·id·ed, per·ox·id·ing, per·ox·ides 1.** To treat with peroxide. **2.** To bleach (hair) with hydrogen peroxide.

per·pen·dic·u·lar (pûr′pən-**dĭk′**yə-lər) *adj.* **1.** Intersecting at or forming a right angle or right angles: *perpendicular lines.* **2.** At right angles to the horizontal; vertical. ❖ *n.* **1.** A line or plane perpendicular to a given line or plane. **2.** A vertical or nearly vertical line or plane. [From Middle English *perpendiculer,* from Latin *perpendiculum,* plumb line, from *perpendere,* to weigh carefully.]

per·pe·trate (**pûr′**pĭ-trāt′) *tr.v.* **per·pe·trat·ed, per·pe·trat·ing, per·pe·trates** To be guilty of; commit: *perpetrate a crime.* **—per′pe·tra′tion** *n.* **—per′pe·tra′tor** *n.*

per·pet·u·al (pər-**pĕch′**ōō-əl) *adj.* **1.** Lasting forever or for an indefinitely long time: *the perpetual ice of the polar regions.* **2.** Ceaselessly repeated or continuing without interruption: *perpetual nagging.* **—per·pet′u·al·ly** *adv.* **—per·pet′u·al·ness** *n.*

per·pet·u·ate (pər-**pĕch′**ōō-āt′) *tr.v.* **per·pet·u·at·ed, per·pet·u·at·ing, per·pet·u·ates 1.** To cause to continue indefinitely; make perpetual. **2.** To prolong the existence of; cause to be remembered: *perpetuate a legend.* **—per·pet′u·a′tion** *n.*

per·pe·tu·i·ty (pûr′pĭ-**tōō′**ĭ-tē) *n., pl.* **per·pe·tu·i·ties 1.** The quality or condition of being eternal. **2.** Time without end; eternity. ◆ **in perpetuity** For an indefinite period of time; forever.

per·plex (pər-**plĕks′**) *tr.v.* **per·plexed, per·plex·ing, per·plex·es 1.** To confuse or puzzle; bewilder. **2.** To make confusingly intricate; complicate.

per·plexed (pər-**plĕkst′**) *adj.* **1.** Confused or puzzled; bewildered: *a perplexed look.* **2.** Full of complexity or complications.

per·plex·i·ty (pər-**plĕk′**sĭ-tē) *n., pl.* **per·plex·i·ties 1.** The condition of being perplexed; bewilderment. **2.** The state of being intricate or complicated.

per·qui·site (**pûr′**kwĭ-zĭt) *n.* Something received in addition to a regular wage or salary, especially a benefit or something advantageous: *Free use of a car was one of the supervisor's perquisites.*

per se (pər **sā′**) *adv.* In or by itself; intrinsically.

per·se·cute (**pûr′**sĭ-kyōōt′) *tr.v.* **per·se·cut·ed, per·se·cut·ing, per·se·cutes 1.** To oppress or harass, as on the basis of race, religion, or political views. **2.** To annoy persistently; bother. **—per′se·cu′tion** (pûr′sĭ-**kyōō′**shən) *n.* **—per′se·cu′tor** *n.*

Per·se·id (**pûr′**sē-ĭd) *n.* One of a shower of meteors that appear to originate near the constellation Perseus during August.

Per·seph·o·ne (pər-**sĕf′**ə-nē) *n.* In Greek mythology, the daughter of Demeter who is carried away by Hades to become his wife and the goddess of the underworld. She is identified with the Roman Prosperpina.

Per·se·us (**pûr′**sē-əs) *n.* **1.** In Greek mythology, a son of Zeus and a mortal and the husband of Andromeda. He killed the Gorgon Medusa. **2.** A constellation in the Northern Hemisphere near Andromeda, traditionally pictured as representing Perseus.

per·se·ver·ance (pûr′sə-**vîr′**əns) *n.* The act or quality of holding to a course of action, a belief, or a purpose; steadfastness: *It took great perseverance for the Wright brothers to build an airplane.*

per·se·vere (pûr′sə-**vîr′**) *intr.v.* **per·se·vered, per·se·ver·ing, per·se·veres** To hold to or persist in a purpose, belief, or course of action, in spite of opposition or discouragement: *Despite many setbacks, they persevered in their research.* [From Middle English *perseveren*, from Latin *persevērāre*, from Latin *persevērus*, very serious.]

Per·shing (pûr′shĭng *or* pûr′zhĭng), **John Joseph** 1860–1948. American general who commanded American forces in Europe during World War I.

Per·sia (pûr′zhə *or* pûr′shə) **1.** also **Persian Empire** A vast empire of southwest Asia founded after 546 BC and conquered by Alexander the Great in 330 BC. **2.** See **Iran.**

Per·sian (pûr′zhən *or* pûr′shən) *adj.* Relating to Persia or Iran or their peoples, languages, or cultures. ❖ *n.* **1.** A native or inhabitant of Persia or Iran. **2.** The Indo-European language of Iran. **3.** A domestic cat having long silky fur and a broad round head with small ears.

Persian Gulf An arm of the Arabian Sea between the Arabian Peninsula and southwest Iran. It is an important trade route.

Persian Gulf War *n.* The Gulf War.

per·sim·mon (pər-sĭm′ən) *n.* **1.** The orange-red fruit of any of various chiefly tropical trees, having thin skin and soft sweet pulp. **2.** A tree that bears such fruit. [From Virginia Algonquian *pichamins, pushemins*, persimmons.]

per·sist (pər-sĭst′) *intr.v.* **per·sist·ed, per·sist·ing, per·sists 1.** To insist or repeat obstinately; be tenacious: *She persisted in denying her guilt.* **2.** To hold firmly and steadfastly to a purpose, state, or undertaking, despite obstacles or setbacks. **3.** To continue in existence; last: *The child's cough persisted for several weeks.* [From Latin *persistere* : *per-*, through + *sistere*, to stand.]

per·sis·tence (pər-sĭs′təns) *n.* **1.** The act of persisting. **2.** The state or quality of being persistent; perseverance. **3.** The continuance of an effect after the cause is removed: *persistence of vision.*

per·sis·tent (pər-sĭs′tənt) *adj.* **1.** Refusing to give up or let go; undaunted: *a persistent salesman.* **2.** Insistently repetitive or continuous: *the persistent ringing of the telephone.* **3.** Existing in the same state for a long period of time; enduring: *a persistent infection.* **—per·sis′tent·ly** *adv.*

per·snick·e·ty (pər-snĭk′ĭ-tē) *adj.* Excessively attentive to detail; fastidious.

per·son (pûr′sən) *n.* **1.** A living human; an individual. **2.** A human of a given characteristic: *a person of great resourcefulness.* **3.** The living body of a human: *He had two wallets on his person.* **4.** Physique and general appearance. **5.** In grammar, any of three groups of pronoun forms with corresponding verb forms that refer to the speaker (first person), the individual addressed (second person), or the individual or thing spoken of (third person). For example, in the sentence *I spoke to you about her, I* is in the first person, *you* is in the second person, and *her* is in the third person. **6.** In Christianity, any of the three separate aspects of the Trinity. ◆ **in person** In one's physical presence; personally. [From Middle English, from Old French *persone*, from Latin *persōna*, mask, role, person.] —SEE NOTE.

per·son·a·ble (pûr′sə-nə-bəl) *adj.* **1.** Having a pleasant attitude; friendly. **2.** Pleasing in appearance; attractive. **—per′son·a·bly** *adv.*

per·son·age (pûr′sə-nĭj) *n.* **1.** A character in a literary work. **2a.** A person. **b.** A person of rank or distinction.

per·son·al (pûr′sə-nəl) *adj.* **1.** Relating to a particular person; private: *the personal correspondence of the college president.* **2a.** Done, made, or performed in person: *a personal appearance.* **b.** For a particular person: *a personal favor.* **3.** Concerning a particular person and his or her private life; intimate: *a personal conversation.* **4a.** Aimed at some aspect of a person, especially in a critical or unfriendly manner: *a highly personal remark.* **b.** Tending to make remarks about or pry into another's affairs: *He always becomes personal in an argument.* **5.** Relating to the body or physical being: *personal cleanliness.* **6.** In law, relating to the person, especially the person's movable belongings: *personal property.* ❖ *n.* A personal item or notice in a newspaper.

personal computer *n.* A computer built around a microprocessor for use by an individual.

personal foul *n.* In sports, a foul that is called because of unnecessary or excessive physical contact with a player on the other team.

per·son·al·i·ty (pûr′sə-năl′ĭ-tē) *n., pl.* **per·son·al·i·ties 1.** The quality or condition of being a person. **2.** The entire group of qualities and traits, as of character or behavior, that are peculiar to each person: *He has a pleasing personality.* **3.** The qualities that make someone socially appealing: *Candidates can win more on personality than on capability.* **4.** A person of importance or renown: *television personalities.* **5.** The characteristics of a place or situation that give it distinctive character: *Colors give a room personality.*

per·son·al·ize (pûr′sə-nə-līz) *tr.v.* **per·son·al·ized, per·son·al·iz·ing, per·son·al·iz·es 1.** To make so as to meet individual needs or specifications: *The computer's operating system lets you personalize your settings.* **2.** To make personal, especially by marking as personal property. **3.** To perceive (a general remark or characterization) in a personal way.

per·son·al·ly (pûr′sə-nə-lē) *adv.* **1.** In the immediate presence of someone; in person: *I thanked her personally.* **2.** Without anyone else being involved or considered: *You will be held personally responsible if something goes wrong.* **3.** As far as oneself is concerned: *Personally, I don't mind.* **4.** As a person: *I don't know him personally.* **5.** In a personal manner: *Try not to take it personally.*

personal pronoun *n.* In grammar, a pronoun that indicates the person speaking *(I, me, we, us)*, the person spoken to *(you)*, or the person or thing spoken about *(he, she, it, they, him, her, them).*

personal watercraft *n.* **1.** A motorized recreational water vehicle usually ridden by straddling a seat. **2.** *(used with a plural verb)* Such vehicles considered as a group.

per·so·na non gra·ta (pər-sō′nə nŏn grä′tə) *adj.* Personally unacceptable or unwelcome: *After the king was overthrown, he became persona non grata and had to flee the country.*

per·son·i·fi·ca·tion (pər-sŏn′ə-fĭ-kā′shən) *n.* **1.** The act of personifying. **2.** A person or thing that typifies a certain quality or idea; an embodiment: *He is the personification of kindness.* **3.** A figure of speech in which inanimate objects or abstractions are provided with human qualities or are represented as possessing human form, as in *Flowers danced in the garden.*

per·son·i·fy (pər-sŏn′ə-fī′) *tr.v.* **per·son·i·fied, per·son·i·fy·ing, per·son·i·fies 1.** To think of or represent (an idea or inanimate object) as having human qualities or human form: *personifying justice as a blindfolded woman.* **2.** To be the embodiment or perfect example of (a certain quality or idea): *The nurse personified compassion.*

per·son·nel (pûr′sə-nĕl′) *n.* **1.** *(used with a plural verb)* The people employed by or active in an organization, business, or service. **2.** The division of an organization concerned with the selection, placement, and training of employees.

person of color *n., pl.* **people of color** also **persons of color** A person who has a racial identity other than white.

per·spec·tive (pər-spĕk′tĭv) *n.* **1a.** A view or vista: *the perspective of the city as seen from the rooftops.* **b.** A mental view or outlook: *Try to get a new perspective on the issue.* **2.** The appearance of objects from a dis-

WORD HISTORY

person Our word **person** comes via Old French from the Latin noun *persōna*. This noun originally was a term for the mask used by an actor in a play (actors in the ancient world always wore masks). It later came to refer to the actor himself or to the character being played and finally came to mean just "a person," the meaning still with us today. The older meaning "character in a play" still survives in the Latin phrase *Dramatis Personae*, "Characters of the Play," a phrase you can see at the beginning of the text of any play by Shakespeare.

personal watercraft

WRITERS CHOOSE THEIR WORDS

As we followed a few steps behind him, Charlene handed me some sheets of yellow paper and a thick, eraserless pencil. "You really want to be a reporter, then we'll let this be your first assignment. Write down everything that you consider **pertinent** to the fact that a prisoner has escaped."

—Bette Greene
Summer of My German Soldier

peruke

pestle

ă	pat	ôr	core
ā	pay	oi	boy
âr	care	ou	out
ä	father	o͝o	took
ĕ	pet	o͝or	lure
ē	be	o͞o	boot
ĭ	pit	ŭ	cut
ī	bite	ûr	urge
îr	pier	th	thin
ŏ	pot	*th*	this
ō	toe	zh	vision
ô	paw	ə	about

tance as perceived by normal binocular vision. **3.** An understanding of how aspects of a subject relate to each other and to the whole: *You have a narrow perspective of the situation.* **4.** An idea of the relative importance of something; an understanding: *I don't want to lose my perspective on the situation despite our disagreement.* **5.** The technique of representing three-dimensional objects and depth relationships on a flat surface. ❖ *adj.* Seen or represented in perspective.

per·spi·ca·cious (pûr′spĭ-**kā′**shəs) *adj.* Able to perceive, discern, or understand clearly: *a perspicacious student.* **—per′spi·ca′cious·ly** *adv.*

per·spi·cac·i·ty (pûr′spĭ-**kăs′**ĭ-tē) *n.* The ability to perceive, discern, or understand clearly.

per·spic·u·ous (pər-**spĭk′**yo͞o-əs) *adj.* Clearly expressed or presented; easy to understand: *a carefully written, perspicuous essay.* **—per·spic′u·ous·ly** *adv.*

per·spi·ra·tion (pûr′spə-**rā′**shən) *n.* **1.** The salty moisture excreted through the skin by the sweat glands; sweat. **2.** The act or process of perspiring.

per·spire (pər-**spīr′**) *intr.v.* **per·spired, per·spir·ing, per·spires** To give off perspiration.

per·suade (pər-**swād′**) *tr.v.* **per·suad·ed, per·suad·ing, per·suades** To cause (someone) to do or believe something by arguing, pleading, or reasoning; convince: *He tried to persuade them to come with us.* [From Latin *persuādēre* : *per-*, through, completely + *suādēre*, to urge.] **—per·suad′er** *n.*

per·sua·sion (pər-**swā′**zhən) *n.* **1.** The act of persuading or the state of being persuaded. **2.** The ability or power to persuade. **3a.** A strong belief: *of a certain political persuasion.* **b.** Religious belief; a religion: *people of all persuasions.*

per·sua·sive (pər-**swā′**sĭv) *adj.* Tending to or having the power to persuade. **—per·sua′sive·ly** *adv.* **—per·sua′sive·ness** *n.*

pert (pûrt) *adj.* **pert·er, pert·est 1.** High-spirited; lively: *a pert little dog.* **2.** Disrespectful or impudent: *a pert answer.* **3.** Attractive or stylish in appearance: *a pert dress.* **—pert′ly** *adv.* **—pert′ness** *n.*

per·tain (pər-**tān′**) *intr.v.* **per·tained, per·tain·ing, per·tains 1.** To have reference or relevance; relate: *a discussion pertaining to art.* **2.** To belong to as a part or accessory of: *engineering skills that pertain to aeronautics.* **3.** To be fitting or suitable: *conduct that pertains to an officer.* [From Middle English *pertenen*, from Old French *partenir*, from Latin *pertinēre* : *per-*, through, completely + *tenēre*, to hold.]

Perth (pûrth) A city of southwest Australia near the Indian Ocean. It was founded in 1829.

per·ti·na·cious (pûr′tn-**ā′**shəs) *adj.* **1.** Holding firmly to some belief, purpose, or opinion. **2.** Stubbornly persistent: *a pertinacious salesman.* **—per′ti·na′cious·ly** *adv.*

per·ti·nac·i·ty (pûr′tn-**ăs′**ĭ-tē) *n.* The quality or state of being pertinacious.

per·ti·nent (**pûr′**tn-ənt) *adj.* Clearly related to a matter at hand: *At the meeting, we were limited to discussing pertinent topics.* **—per′ti·nence** *n.*

per·turb (pər-**tûrb′**) *tr.v.* **per·turbed, per·turb·ing, per·turbs 1.** To cause (someone) to become uneasy or anxious; disturb or confuse: *He was easily perturbed over small matters.* **2.** To cause (a system) to become altered from a normal state: *volcanic eruptions that perturbed the climate.* **—per′tur·ba′tion** (pûr′tər-**bā′**shən) *n.*

per·tus·sis (pər-**tŭs′**ĭs) *n.* Whooping cough.

Pe·ru (pə-**ro͞o′**) A country of western South America north of Chile on the Pacific Ocean. It was the center of an Incan empire established beginning in the 1200s. Lima is the capital. **—Pe·ru′vi·an** (pə-**ro͞o′**vē-ən) *adj. & n.*

pe·ruke (pə-**ro͞ok′**) *n.* A large powdered wig worn by men in the 1600s and 1700s.

pe·rus·al (pə-**ro͞o′**zəl) *n.* The act or an instance of perusing; a thorough reading.

pe·ruse (pə-**ro͞oz′**) *tr.v.* **pe·rused, pe·rus·ing, pe·rus·es** To read or examine, especially with great care: *peruse a novel.*

per·vade (pər-**vād′**) *tr.v.* **per·vad·ed, per·vad·ing, per·vades** To spread or be present throughout; permeate: *The sweet scent of gardenias pervaded the house. A sense of fear pervades the novel.* [From Latin *pervādere* : *per-*, through + *vādere*, to go.]

per·va·sive (pər-**vā′**sĭv) *adj.* Tending to pervade or permeate: *a pervasive aroma.* **—per·va′sive·ly** *adv.* **—per·va′sive·ness** *n.*

per·verse (pər-**vûrs′** *or* **pûr′**vûrs′) *adj.* **1.** Morally wrong, wicked. **2.** Willfully opposing or resisting what is right, expected, or reasonable: *You're arguing just to be perverse.* **3.** Having an effect opposite to what is intended or expected. **—per·verse′ly** *adv.* **—per·verse′ness** *n.*

per·ver·sion (pər-**vûr′**zhən) *n.* **1.** The act of perverting or the state of being perverted. **2.** A sexual act or practice that is considered abnormal or deviant.

per·ver·si·ty (pər-**vûr′**sĭ-tē) *n., pl.* **per·ver·si·ties 1.** The quality of being perverse. **2.** An instance of being perverse.

per·vert (pər-**vûrt′**) *tr.v.* **per·vert·ed, per·vert·ing, per·verts 1.** To cause to turn from what is considered right, proper, or good; debase: *pervert the course of justice.* **2.** To corrupt (someone) morally. **3.** To interpret wrongly: *You have perverted the poem's meaning.* ❖ *n.* (**pûr′**vûrt′) A person who practices a sexual perversion.

per·vert·ed (pər-**vûr′**tĭd) *adj.* **1.** Turned from what is considered right and correct; misguided: *a perverted notion of the truth.* **2.** Misinterpreted; distorted: *a perverted translation of the text.* **3.** Relating to or practicing a sexual perversion.

Pe·sach (**pā′**säкн′) *n.* Passover.

pes·ky (**pĕs′**kē) *adj.* **pes·ki·er, pes·ki·est** *Informal* Troublesome; annoying: *a pesky gnat.* **—pes′ki·ly** *adv.* **—pes′ki·ness** *n.*

pe·so (**pā′**sō) *n., pl.* **pe·sos** The basic monetary unit of Argentina, Colombia, Mexico, the Philippines, and many other countries. [From Spanish, from Old Spanish, measure of weight for gold or silver, from *pēnsum*, something weighed, from *pēnsus*, past participle of *pendere*, to weigh.]

pes·si·mism (**pĕs′**ə-mĭz′əm) *n.* **1.** A tendency to stress the negative or take the gloomiest possible view. **2.** The belief that the evil in the world outweighs the good. **—pes′si·mist** *n.* **—pes′si·mis′tic** *adj.* **—pes′si·mis′ti·cal·ly** *adv.*

pest (pĕst) *n.* **1.** An annoying person or thing; a nuisance. **2.** An organism, typically an insect, that sickens or annoys humans or damages food, shelter, or other human necessities.

pes·ter (**pĕs′**tər) *tr.v.* **pes·tered, pes·ter·ing, pes·ters** To annoy persistently, as with repeated demands or questions.

pes·ti·cide (**pĕs′**tĭ-sīd′) *n.* A substance used to kill harmful animals or plants, especially insects and rodents.

pes·tif·er·ous (pĕ-**stĭf′**ər-əs) *adj.* Breeding or spreading disease: *pestiferous mounds of garbage.*

pes·ti·lence (**pĕs′**tə-ləns) *n.* A deadly epidemic disease, especially bubonic plague.

pes·ti·lent (**pĕs′**tə-lənt) *adj.* **1.** Tending to cause death; deadly; fatal: *a pestilent disease.* **2.** Causing or likely to cause epidemic disease. **3.** Harmful to law and order, morals, or society: *the pestilent threat of street crime.* **—pes′ti·len′tial** (pĕs′tə-**lĕn′**shəl) *adj.* **—pes′ti·len′tial·ly** *adv.*

pes·tle (**pĕs′**əl *or* **pĕs′**təl) *n.* A heavy tool, often with a rounded end, used for mashing substances in a mortar.

pes·to (pĕs′tō) *n.* A sauce usually made up of fresh basil, garlic, pine nuts, olive oil, and grated cheese.

pet[1] (pĕt) *n.* **1.** An animal kept for enjoyment or companionship. **2.** A person or thing of which one is especially fond; a favorite. ❖ *adj.* **1.** Kept as a pet: *a pet cat.* **2.** Being a favorite: *a pet topic.* **3.** Expressing or showing affection: *a pet name.* ❖ *tr.v.* **pet·ted, pet·ting, pets** To stroke or caress gently. [From Scottish Gaelic *peata,* tame animal, from Old Irish *petta.*]

pet[2] (pĕt) *n.* A fit of bad temper or anger. ❖ *intr.v.* **pet·ted, pet·ting, pets** To be sulky and peevish.

peta– *pref.* A prefix that means: **1.** One quadrillion (10^{15}): *petahertz.* **2.** 1,125,899,906,842,624 (2^{50}): *petabyte.*

pet·a·byte (pĕt′ə-bīt) *n.* A unit of computer memory equal to 1,024 terabytes (2^{50} bytes).

pet·a·hertz (pĕt′ə-hûrts′) *n.* A unit of frequency equal to one quadrillion hertz.

pet·al (pĕt′l) *n.* One of the often brightly colored parts of a flower that surround the reproductive organs. [From New Latin *petalum,* from Greek *petalon,* leaf.]

pe·tard (pĭ-tärd′) *n.* A small bell-shaped bomb, formerly used to blow apart a gate or wall. ◆ **be hoist with one's own petard** To be undone by one's own schemes.

pet·cock (pĕt′kŏk′) *n.* A small valve or faucet used to drain or reduce pressure, as from a boiler.

pe·ter (pē′tər) *intr.v.* **pe·tered, pe·ter·ing, pe·ters** To diminish slowly and come to an end: *Our supplies petered out.*

Pe·ter (pē′tər) *n.* Either of two books of the New Testament, traditionally attributed to the apostle Peter, in the form of letters encouraging persecuted Christians and warning against false teachers.

Peter, Saint. Died about 67 AD. The chief of the 12 Apostles, traditionally regarded as the first bishop of Rome.

Peter I Known as "Peter the Great." 1672–1725. Russian czar (1682–1725) who extended his territory around the Baltic and Caspian shores.

pet·i·ole (pĕt′ē-ōl′) *n.* A leafstalk.

pet·it also **pet·ty** (pĕt′ē) *adj.* In law, lesser in seriousness or scale.

pe·tite (pə-tēt′) *adj.* **1.** Short and slender. Used of a girl or woman. **2.** Small in size or scope; tiny.

pe·ti·tion (pə-tĭsh′ən) *n.* **1.** An entreaty, especially to a person or group in authority: *a petition for an audience.* **2.** A formal written document requesting a right or benefit from an authority: *collect signatures on a petition for a new school.* ❖ *v.* **pe·ti·tioned, pe·ti·tion·ing, pe·ti·tions** *—tr.* To address a petition to; entreat: *Hawaii first petitioned Congress for statehood in 1902.* *—intr.* To make a formal request: *The lawyer petitioned for a retrial.* **—pe·ti′tion·er** *n.*

petit larceny also **petty larceny** *n.* The theft of property whose value is below a certain specified amount.

petit point *n.* Decorative needlework done with a small diagonal stitch.

pet·rel (pĕt′rəl) *n.* Any of various usually small and darkly colored seabirds that fly close to the surface of the water.
❑ *These sound alike:* **petrel, petrol** (gasoline).

pe·tri dish (pē′trē) *n.* A shallow circular glass dish with a loose cover, used in the preparation of bacteriological cultures. [After Julius Richard *Petri* (1852–1921), German bacteriologist.]

pet·ri·fac·tion (pĕt′rə-făk′shən) also **pet·ri·fi·ca·tion** (pĕt′rə-fĭ-kā′shən) *n.* The process of turning organic materials into rock by the replacement of the organic matter with minerals.

pet·ri·fy (pĕt′rə-fī′) *tr.v.* **pet·ri·fied, pet·ri·fy·ing, pet·ri·fies 1.** To turn (wood or other organic material) into a stony mass by causing minerals to fill and finally replace its internal structure. **2.** To stun or paralyze with terror.

pet·ro·chem·i·cal (pĕt′rō-kĕm′ĭ-kəl) *n.* A chemical derived from petroleum or natural gas. **—pet′ro·chem′i·cal** *adj.*

pe·trog·ra·phy (pə-trŏg′rə-fē) *n.* The scientific description and classification of rocks.

pet·rol (pĕt′rəl) *n. Chiefly British* Gasoline.
❑ *These sound alike:* **petrol, petrel** (sea bird).

pet·ro·la·tum (pĕt′rə-lā′təm) *n.* Petroleum jelly.

pe·tro·le·um (pə-trō′lē-əm) *n.* A thick, yellow-to-black, flammable liquid mixture of hydrocarbons that occurs naturally, mainly below the surface of the earth. [From Middle English, from Medieval Latin *petrōleum* : Latin *petra,* rock + *ōleum,* oil.]

petroleum jelly *n.* A greasy, usually colorless mixture of hydrocarbons, obtained from petroleum and used in making ointments and lubricants.

pe·trol·o·gy (pə-trŏl′ə-jē) *n.* The science of the origin, composition, and structure of rocks.

pet·ti·coat (pĕt′ē-kōt′) *n.* A girl's or woman's undergarment, worn under a dress or skirt.

pet·tish (pĕt′ĭsh) *adj.* Ill-tempered; peevish. **—pet′tish·ly** *adv.* **—pet′tish·ness** *n.*

pet·ty (pĕt′ē) *adj.* **pet·ti·er, pet·ti·est 1.** Of small importance; trivial: *petty annoyances.* **2.** Showing an excessive concern with unimportant matters or minor details, especially in a narrow-minded way: *petty partisanship.* **3.** Variant of **petit.** [From Middle English *peti,* from Old French *petit.*] **—pet′ti·ly** *adv.* **—pet′ti·ness** *n.*

petty cash *n.* A small fund of money for incidental expenses, as in an office.

petty larceny *n.* Variant of **petit larceny.**

petty officer *n.* A noncommissioned officer in a nation's navy or coast guard.

pet·u·lant (pĕch′ə-lənt) *adj.* Ill-tempered; peevish: *The petulant child pouted all evening long.* **—pet′u·lance** *n.* **—pet′u·lant·ly** *adv.*

pe·tu·nia (pĭ-tōōn′yə) *n.* Any of various garden plants having funnel-shaped flowers in a variety of colors.

pew (pyōō) *n.* One of the long, fixed benches with backs used as seats in a church.

pe·wee (pē′wē) *n.* Any of various small, brown or gray, insect-eating birds of the Americas. The eastern North American pewee has a call that sounds like its name.
❑ *These sound alike:* **pewee, peewee** (small thing).

pew·ter (pyōō′tər) *n.* **1.** Any of a number of alloys of tin with varying amounts of antimony, copper, and sometimes lead, used for making kitchen utensils and tableware. **2.** Articles made of pewter.

PFC *abbr.* An abbreviation of private first class.

PG (pē′jē′) A trademark used for a movie rating that allows admission of people of all ages but suggests parental guidance in the case of children.

pg. *abbr.* An abbreviation of page.

PG-13 (pē′jē′thûr-tēn′) A trademark used for a movie rating that allows admission of people of all ages but suggests parental guidance in the case of children under the age of 13.

pH (pē′āch′) *n.* In chemistry, a numerical measure of the acidity or alkalinity of a solution equal to 7 for neutral solutions, less than 7 for acid solutions, and more than 7 for alkaline solutions.

pha·e·ton (fā′ĭ-tn) *n.* A light, four-wheeled open carriage, usually drawn by a pair of horses.

phag·o·cyte (făg′ə-sīt′) *n.* A cell, such as a white blood cell, occurring in body fluids or tissues and capable of absorbing and destroying waste or harmful material, such as bacteria that cause disease.

pha·lanx (fā′lăngks′ *or* făl′ăngks′) *n., pl.* **pha·lanx·es** or **pha·lan·ges** (fə-lăn′jēz *or* fā-lăn′jēz) **1.** A compact gathering of people: *a solid phalanx of demonstrators on the capitol steps.* **2.** In ancient Greece, a formation of

Peter I

petri dish

phaeton

Michael Phelps
photographed in 2011

USAGE

phenomenon The word **phenomena** is a plural form of **phenomenon.** It is correct to say *There are some phenomena for which scientists have no explanation.* It is incorrect to say *Only one phenomena has been studied so far.*

ă	pat	ôr	core
ā	pay	oi	boy
âr	care	ou	out
ä	father	ŏŏ	took
ĕ	pet	ŏŏr	lure
ē	be	ōō	boot
ĭ	pit	ŭ	cut
ī	bite	ûr	urge
îr	pier	th	thin
ŏ	pot	*th*	this
ō	toe	zh	vision
ô	paw	ə	about

infantry carrying overlapping shields and long spears. **3.** *pl.* **phalanges** A bone of a finger or toe.

Phan·er·o·zo·ic (făn′ər-ə-**zō′**ĭk) *n.* The period of geologic time from about 542 million years ago to the present, including the Paleozoic, Mesozoic, and Cenozoic Eras. **—Phan′er·o·zo′ic** *adj.*

phan·tasm (**făn′**tăz′əm) *n.* **1.** Something apparently seen but having no physical reality; a phantom or apparition. **2.** An unreal mental image. **—phan·tas′mal** (făn-**tăz′**məl) *adj.*

phan·tom (**făn′**təm) *n.* **1.** A ghost; an apparition. **2.** An image that appears only in the mind; an illusion. [From Middle English *fantum*, illusion, ultimately from Greek *phantasma*, from *phantos*, visible.]

phar·aoh or **Phar·aoh** (**fâr′**ō *or* **fā′**rō) *n.* A king of ancient Egypt.

phar·i·see (**făr′**ĭ-sē) *n.* **1. Pharisee** A member of an ancient Jewish sect that believed in strict observance of the Mosaic Law. **2.** A self-righteous hypocrite.

phar·ma·ceu·ti·cal (fär′mə-**sōō′**tĭ-kəl) also **phar·ma·ceu·tic** (fär′mə-**sōō′**tĭk) *adj.* Relating to pharmacy or pharmacists. ❖ *n.* A pharmaceutical preparation or product; a medicinal drug.

phar·ma·ceu·tics (fär′mə-**sōō′**tĭks) *n.* *(used with a singular verb)* The science of preparing and dispensing drugs.

phar·ma·cist (**fär′**mə-sĭst) *n.* A person who is trained in pharmacy and is licensed to practice.

phar·ma·col·o·gy (fär′mə-**kŏl′**ə-jē) *n.* The scientific study of drugs and their composition, uses, and effects.

phar·ma·cy (**fär′**mə-sē) *n., pl.* **phar·ma·cies 1.** The art of preparing and dispensing drugs. **2.** A place where drugs are sold; a drugstore.

pha·ryn·ge·al (fə-**rĭn′**jē-əl *or* făr′ĭn-**jē′**əl) *adj.* Relating to or coming from the pharynx.

phar·ynx (**făr′**ĭngks) *n., pl.* **pha·ryn·ges** (fə-**rĭn′**jēz) or **phar·ynx·es** The part of the digestive tract that consists of a short muscular tube extending from the cavities of the nose to the larynx and esophagus. [From Greek *pharunx.*]

phase (fāz) *n.* **1.** A distinct stage of development: *the next phase of our space program.* **2.** A temporary manner, attitude, or pattern of behavior: *He's just going through a phase.* **3.** An aspect; a part: *considering every phase of the problem.* **4.** One of the shapes, recurring in cycles, in which a portion of the moon or a planet is visibly illuminated. **5.** Any of the forms or states, solid, liquid, or gas, in which matter can exist, depending on temperature and pressure: *Steam and ice are phases of water.* ❖ *tr.v.* **phased, phas·ing, phas·es** To plan or carry out so as to progress in stages: *The highway construction program was carefully phased.* ◆ **phase in** To introduce, one stage at a time. **phase out** To bring or come to an end, one stage at a time. [From Greek *phasis*, appearance, phase of the moon, from *phainesthai*, to appear.]
❑ *These sound alike:* **phase, faze** (upset).

PhD *abbr.* An abbreviation of Doctor of Philosophy.

pheas·ant (**fĕz′**ənt) *n., pl.* **pheas·ants** or **pheasant** Any of various game birds having a long tail and often brightly colored feathers in the male. [From Middle English *fesaunt*, from Old French, from Latin *phāsiānus*, from Greek *phāsiānos (ornīs)*, (bird) of the Phasis River, pheasant, from *Phāsis*, the ancient name for the Rioni River in the country of Georgia.]

Phelps (fĕlps), **Michael** Born 1985. American swimmer who earned six Olympic gold medals in 2004, eight in 2008, and four more in 2012, setting records for the most gold medals won at a single Olympics and the most Olympic gold medals in a career.

phe·no·bar·bi·tal (fē′nō-**bär′**bĭ-tôl′ *or* fē′nō-**bär′**bĭ-tăl′) *n.* A white shiny crystalline compound used in medicine as a sedative and hypnotic drug.

phe·nol (**fē′**nôl′ *or* **fē′**nōl′) *n.* A poisonous, irritating, white crystalline compound that is used as a disinfectant and in making plastics and drugs.

phe·nol·phthal·ein (fē′nōl-**thăl′**ēn′ *or* fē′nōl-**thā′**lēn′) *n.* A white or pale-yellow crystalline powder used as an indicator for acid and basic solutions, in making dyes, and formerly as a laxative.

phe·nom·e·na (fĭ-**nŏm′**ə-nə) *n.* A plural of **phenomenon.**

phe·nom·e·nal (fĭ-**nŏm′**ə-nəl) *adj.* **1.** Relating to phenomena or a phenomenon. **2.** Extraordinary; outstanding: *a phenomenal memory.* **—phe·nom′e·nal·ly** *adv.*

phe·nom·e·non (fĭ-**nŏm′**ə-nŏn′) *n., pl.* **phe·nom·e·na** (fĭ-**nŏm′**ə-nə) also **phe·nom·e·nons 1.** An occurrence or fact that can be perceived by the senses or by instruments: *natural phenomena.* **2.** A remarkable or outstanding person or thing. See Synonyms at **wonder.** [From Greek *phainomenon*, from *phainesthai*, to appear.] —SEE NOTE.

phe·no·type (**fē′**nə-tīp′) *n.* The physical characteristics of an organism, as distinguished from its genetic makeup or genotype.

phen·yl (**fĕn′**əl *or* **fē′**nəl) *n.* A chemical unit that contains six carbon atoms and five hydrogen atoms in a ring and occurs as part of an organic compound or as an ion. It is structurally similar to benzene.

phen·yl·al·a·nine (fĕn′əl-**ăl′**ə-nēn′) *n.* An essential amino acid, $C_9H_{11}NO_2$, that is found in many proteins.

pher·o·mone (**fĕr′**ə-mōn′) *n.* A chemical secreted by an animal, especially an insect, that influences the behavior of other animals of the same species. Pheromones are used to attract members of the opposite sex and to mark the route to a food source.

phi (fī *or* fē) *n.* The 21st letter of the Greek alphabet, written Φ, φ. In English it is represented as *Ph, ph.*

phi·al (**fī′**əl) *n.* A vial.

Phil·a·del·phi·a (fĭl′ə-**dĕl′**fē-ə) The largest city of Pennsylvania, in the southeast part of the state southwest of Trenton, New Jersey. The First and Second Continental Congresses (1774 and 1775–1776) and the Constitutional Convention (1787) met here.

phil·an·throp·ic (fĭl′ən-**thrŏp′**ĭk) *adj.* Relating to or engaged in philanthropy; charitable. **—phil′an·throp′i·cal·ly** *adv.*

phi·lan·thro·pist (fĭ-**lăn′**thrə-pĭst) *n.* A person who is involved in promoting human welfare, as by making charitable donations.

phi·lan·thro·py (fĭ-**lăn′**thrə-pē) *n., pl.* **phi·lan·thro·pies 1a.** The desire or effort to help humankind, as by making charitable donations. **b.** Love of humankind in general. **2.** Something, such as an institution or cause, designed to promote human welfare.

phi·lat·e·ly (fĭ-**lăt′**l-ē) *n.* The collection and study of postage stamps. **—phil′a·tel′ic** (fĭl′ə-**tĕl′**ĭk) *adj.* **—phi·lat′e·list** *n.*

Phi·le·mon (fĭ-**lē′**mən *or* fī-**lē′**mən) *n.* A book of the New Testament in the form of a letter from Saint Paul to Philemon, a fellow Christian.

phil·har·mon·ic (fĭl′här-**mŏn′**ĭk) *n.* A symphony orchestra or the group of people that supports it.

Phil·ip (**fĭl′**ĭp) See **Metacom.**

Philip, Saint. Flourished first century AD. One of the 12 Apostles.

Philip II 382–336 BC. King of Macedon (359–336) who achieved a peace settlement in which all the states except Sparta participated.

Phil·ip·pines (**fĭl′**ə-pēnz′ *or* fĭl′ə-**pēnz′**) A country of eastern Asia consisting of the **Philippine Islands** in the western Pacific Ocean southeast of China. Manila is the capital. **—Phil′ip·pine′** *adj.*

Phil·is·tine (**fĭl′**ĭ-stēn′ *or* fĭ-**lĭs′**tĭn) *n.* **1.** A member of a people of ancient Palestine who were enemies of the Hebrews. **2.** A person who is smugly indifferent or hostile to art and culture. ❖ *adj.* **1.** Relating to the ancient Philistines. **2.** often **philistine** Boorish; barbarous.

phil·o·den·dron (fĭl′ə-**dĕn′**drən) *n., pl.* **phil·o·den·drons** or **phil·o·den·dra** (fĭl′ə-**dĕn′**drə) Any of various tropical American climbing plants having evergreen leaves and often grown as houseplants. [From Greek *philodendros*, fond of trees (because the plant twines around trees) : *philos*, loving + *dendron*, tree.]

phi·lol·o·gy (fĭ-**lŏl′**ə-jē) *n.* **1.** Literary study or classical scholarship. **2.** Historical linguistics. **—phi·lol′o·gist** *n.*

phi·los·o·pher (fĭ-**lŏs′**ə-fər) *n.* **1.** A student of or specialist in philosophy. **2.** A person who lives and thinks according to a particular philosophy. **3.** A person who is calm and rational under any circumstances.

phi·los·o·phers' stone (fĭ-**lŏs′**ə-fərz) *n.* In medieval alchemy, a substance that was believed to have the power of transmuting base metals into gold.

phil·o·soph·i·cal (fĭl′ə-**sŏf′**ĭ-kəl) also **phil·o·soph·ic** (fĭl′ə-**sŏf′**ĭk) *adj.* **1.** Relating to a system of philosophy: *philosophical theories.* **2.** Characteristic of a philosopher, as in calmness and wisdom: *He accepted his fate with philosophical resignation.* **—phil′o·soph′i·cal·ly** *adv.*

phi·los·o·phize (fĭ-**lŏs′**ə-fīz′) *v.* **phi·los·o·phized, phi·los·o·phiz·ing, phi·los·o·phiz·es** *—intr.* To think in a philosophical manner. *—tr.* To consider (a matter) from a philosophical standpoint.

phi·los·o·phy (fĭ-**lŏs′**ə-fē) *n., pl.* **phi·los·o·phies 1.** The study of the nature of reality, knowledge, or values, based on logical reasoning. **2.** A formal system of ideas based upon such study: *the philosophy of Plato.* **3.** A basic theory or viewpoint: *a successful philosophy of coaching.* [From Middle English *philosophie*, from Old French, from Latin *philosophia*, from Greek *philosophiā*, from *philosophos*, lover of wisdom : *philos*, loving + *sophiā*, knowledge, learning.]

phil·ter also **phil·tre** (**fĭl′**tər) *n.* A magic potion, especially a love potion.

❑ *These sound alike:* **philter, filter** (strainer).

phlegm (flĕm) *n.* Mucus produced by the mucous membranes of the respiratory tract.

phleg·mat·ic (flĕg-**măt′**ĭk) *adj.* Having or suggesting a calm sluggish temperament; unemotional. **—phleg·mat′i·cal·ly** *adv.*

phlo·em (**flō′**ĕm′) *n.* Plant tissue consisting mainly of long tubular cells through which food that is produced by photosynthesis is transported to all parts of the plant.

phlox (flŏks) *n., pl.* **phlox** or **phlox·es** Any of various plants of North America having clusters of small reddish, purple, or white flowers. [From Greek *phlox*, flame, wallflower.]

Phnom Penh (pə-**nôm′** **pĕn′** *or* **nŏm′** **pĕn′**) The capital of Cambodia, in the southern part of the country on the Mekong River. It was founded in the 1300s.

pho·bi·a (**fō′**bē-ə) *n.* An abnormal or unreasonable fear of a thing or a situation: *a phobia about riding in elevators.* [From Greek *phobos*, fear.]

phoe·be (**fē′**bē) *n.* Any of several dark-colored insect-eating birds of North America having a song that sounds like the name *Phoebe.*

Phoebe *n.* In Greek mythology, Artemis.

Phoe·bus (**fē′**bəs) *n.* **1.** In Greek mythology, Apollo. **2.** The sun.

Phoe·ni·cia (fĭ-**nĭsh′**ə *or* fĭ-**nē′**shə) An ancient country of southwest Asia along the eastern Mediterranean Sea in present-day Syria and Lebanon. The Phoenicians introduced their alphabet, which was based on symbols for sounds, to the Greeks and other peoples.

Phoe·ni·cian (fĭ-**nĭsh′**ən *or* fĭ-**nē′**shən) *adj.* Relating to ancient Phoenicia or its people, language, or culture. ❖ *n.* **1.** A native or inhabitant of ancient Phoenicia. **2.** The Semitic language of the Phoenicians.

phoe·nix (**fē′**nĭks) *n.* In Egyptian mythology, a bird that periodically consumed itself by fire and rose renewed from its own ashes.

Phoe·nix (**fē′**nĭks) The capital of Arizona, in the south-central part of the state northwest of Tucson. It was founded in the 1860s.

phone (fōn) *Informal n.* A telephone. ❖ *v.* **phoned, phon·ing, phones** *—tr.* **1.** To make a telephone connection with: *Bill phoned his parents from school.* **2.** To dial (a specific number): *Phone 411 for directory assistance.* **3.** To transmit by telephone: *The reporter phoned in her story.* *—intr.* To telephone: *He phoned to tell her that he was running late.*

–phone *suff.* A suffix that means: **1.** Sound: *homophone.* **2.** A device that receives or emits sound: *earphone.*

phone card *n.* A prepaid card or a credit card used to pay for telephone calls.

pho·neme (**fō′**nēm′) *n.* In linguistics, the smallest unit of sound that can distinguish one word from another. For example, the *m* of *mat* and the *b* of *bat* are phonemes.

pho·ne·mic (fə-**nē′**mĭk) *adj.* Relating to or indicating a phoneme or phonemes: *a phonemic sound.*

pho·net·ic (fə-**nĕt′**ĭk) *adj.* **1.** Relating to phonetics. **2.** Representing the sounds of speech with a set of symbols, each denoting a single sound: *phonetic spelling.* **—pho·net′i·cal·ly** *adv.*

pho·net·ics (fə-**nĕt′**ĭks) *n. (used with a singular verb)* The study of the sounds of speech and of their representation by symbols. **—pho′ne·ti′cian** (fō′nĭ-**tĭsh′**ən) *n.*

pho·ney (**fō′**nē) *adj. & n.* Variant of **phony.**

phon·ic (**fŏn′**ĭk) *adj.* Relating to or involving sound, especially in speech. **—phon′i·cal·ly** *adv.*

phon·ics (**fŏn′**ĭks) *n. (used with a singular verb)* Phonetics.

phono– or **phon–** *pref.* A prefix that means sound, voice, or speech: *phonograph.*

pho·no·graph (**fō′**nə-grăf′) *n.* A device that reproduces sound by means of a needle riding in the grooves of a rotating disk. **—pho′no·graph′ic** *adj.*

pho·ny also **pho·ney** (**fō′**nē) *adj.* **pho·ni·er, pho·ni·est 1.** Not genuine; fake: *a phony diamond.* **2.** Insincere, deceitful, or dishonest: *a phony smile.* ❖ *n., pl.* **pho·nies** also **pho·neys 1.** A person who is insincere or hypocritical; a fake or impostor. **2.** Something not genuine; a fake. [From earlier *fawney*, gilt brass ring used by swindlers, from Irish Gaelic *fáinne*, ring, from Old Irish.] **—pho′ni·ly** *adv.* **—pho′ni·ness** *n.*

phoo·ey (**fo͞o′**ē) *interj.* An expression used to show disappointment or contempt.

phos·phate (**fŏs′**fāt′) *n.* **1.** A salt or ester of phosphoric acid. **2.** A fertilizer containing compounds of phosphorus.

phos·pho·lip·id (fŏs′fō-**lĭp′**ĭd) *n.* Any of various molecules consisting of a lipid that contains phosphorus. Cell membranes are made of two layers of phospholipids.

phos·phor (**fŏs′**fər) *n.* **1.** A substance that can emit light after absorbing some form of radiation. **2.** Something that shows phosphorescence, as the insides of television screens.

phos·pho·res·cence (fŏs′fə-**rĕs′**əns) *n.* **1.** The process or phenomenon by which a body emits light as a result of and for some time after being exposed to radiation. **2.** The generation of light by a living thing; bioluminescence. **3.** The light that results from either of these. **—phos′pho·res′cent** *adj.*

phos·phor·ic (fŏs-**fôr′**ĭk) *adj.* Relating to or containing phosphorus, especially with a valence of 5.

philodendron

phlox

phonograph

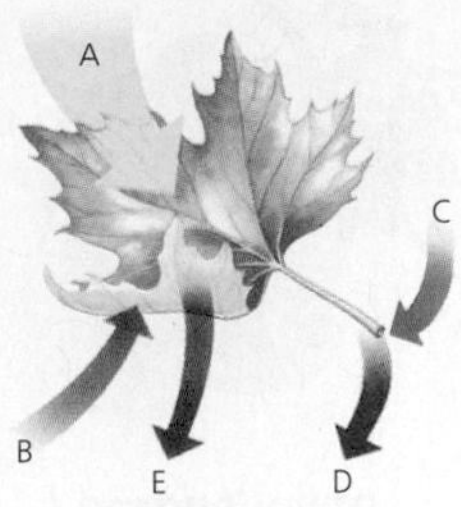

photosynthesis
A. sunlight is absorbed by chlorophyll in a leaf
B. carbon dioxide is taken in from the air
C. water is transported from the roots
D. glucose is synthesized and distributed throughout the plant
E. oxygen is released

piano¹
top: upright piano
bottom: grand piano

ă	pat	ôr	core
ā	pay	oi	boy
âr	care	ou	out
ä	father	o͝o	took
ĕ	pet	o͝or	lure
ē	be	o͞o	boot
ĭ	pit	ŭ	cut
ī	bite	ûr	urge
îr	pier	th	thin
ŏ	pot	*th*	this
ō	toe	zh	vision
ô	paw	ə	about

phosphoric acid *n.* A clear, colorless solid or syrupy liquid used in fertilizers, detergents, and drugs.

phos·pho·rous (fŏs**′**fər-əs *or* fŏs-**fôr′**əs) *adj.* Relating to or containing phosphorus, especially with a valence of 3.

phos·pho·rus (**fŏs′**fər-əs) *n. Symbol* **P** A highly reactive, poisonous nonmetallic element occurring naturally in phosphates and used in fireworks and fertilizers. Atomic number 15. See **Periodic Table.** [From Greek *phōsphoros*, bringing light, morning star : *phōs*, light + *pherein*, to bring.] **—phos·phor′ic** *adj.*

pho·to (fō**′**tō) *Informal n., pl.* **pho·tos** A photograph.

photo– or **phot–** *pref.* A prefix that means: **1.** Light: *photosynthesis.* **2.** Photographic: *photocopy.*

pho·to·cell (**fō′**tō-sĕl′) *n.* A photoelectric cell.

pho·to·cop·i·er (**fō′**tə-kŏp′ē-ər) *n.* A device for photographically reproducing written, printed, or graphic material.

pho·to·cop·y (**fō′**tə-kŏp′ē) *tr.v.* **pho·to·cop·ied, pho·to·cop·y·ing, pho·to·cop·ies** To make a photographic reproduction of (printed, written, or graphic material). ❖ *n., pl.* **pho·to·cop·ies** A photographic reproduction.

pho·to·e·lec·tric (fō′tō-ĭ-**lĕk′**trĭk) *adj.* Relating to the electrical effects caused by light. **—pho′to·e·lec′tri·cal·ly** *adv.*

photoelectric cell *n.* An electronic device that generates an electrical output when it is exposed to light. It is used to activate mechanisms that set off alarms and measure light intensity.

pho·to·gen·ic (fō′tə-**jĕn′**ĭk) *adj.* Attractive as a subject for photography: *My cousin has a very photogenic smile.* **—pho′to·gen′i·cal·ly** *adv.*

pho·to·graph (**fō′**tə-grăf′) *n.* An image formed on a light-sensitive surface, especially by a camera, and developed by chemical means to produce a positive print. ❖ *v.* **pho·to·graphed, pho·to·graph·ing, pho·to·graphs** *—tr.* To take a photograph of. *—intr.* To be a subject for photographs: *Some subjects photograph better than others.*

pho·tog·ra·pher (fə-**tŏg′**rə-fər) *n.* A person who takes photographs, especially professionally.

pho·to·graph·ic (fō′tə-**grăf′**ĭk) *adj.* **1.** Relating to or used in photography or a photograph: *a photographic lens.* **2.** Resembling a photograph, as in accuracy and detail. **3.** Capable of retaining accurate or vivid impressions: *a photographic memory.* **—pho′to·graph′i·cal·ly** *adv.*

pho·tog·ra·phy (fə-**tŏg′**rə-fē) *n.* **1.** The art or process of creating images on light-sensitive surfaces. **2.** The art, practice, or profession of making photographs. **3.** A collection of photographs or photographic works.

pho·tom·e·ter (fō-**tŏm′**ĭ-tər) *n.* An instrument used to measure and indicate some property of light, especially its intensity.

pho·tom·e·try (fō-**tŏm′**ĭ-trē) *n.* The measurement of the intensity, brightness, or other properties of light.

pho·ton (**fō′**tŏn′) *n.* The smallest unit of light or other electromagnetic energy, having no mass and no electric charge. [From Greek *phōs*, light.]

photo opportunity *n.* **1.** A short period, as at a high-level meeting, during which the news media is invited to photograph and film public figures or other people, usually without being allowed to ask questions. **2.** An event designed primarily to generate positive media coverage, as to raise awareness of a cause.

pho·to·re·cep·tor (fō′tō-rĭ-**sĕp′**tər) *n.* A cell or group of cells that senses or receives light in an animal.

pho·to·sen·si·tive (fō′tō-**sĕn′**sĭ-tĭv) *adj.* Undergoing or capable of undergoing some chemical or physical change as a result of exposure to light. **—pho′to·sen′si·tiv′i·ty** *n.*

pho·to·sphere (**fō′**tə-sfîr′) *n.* The directly visible outer layer or atmosphere of a star, especially of the sun.

pho·to·syn·the·sis (fō′tō-**sĭn′**thĭ-sĭs) *n.* The process by which green plants, algae, and certain bacteria make carbohydrates from carbon dioxide and water in the presence of chlorophyll, using light as energy. Photosynthesis normally releases oxygen as a byproduct.

pho·tot·ro·pism (fō-**tŏt′**rə-pĭz′əm *or* fō′tō-**trō′**pĭz′əm) *n.* Growth or movement of an organism, especially a plant, toward or away from light.

phrase (frāz) *n.* **1.** In grammar, a sequence of words that is meaningful but is less than a complete sentence. For example, *on the table* is a phrase. **2.** A brief, apt, and cogent expression. For example, *out of the frying pan and into the fire* is a phrase. **3.** A short section of a musical composition, typically consisting of four measures or forming part of a larger unit. ❖ *tr.v.* **phrased, phras·ing, phras·es 1.** To express orally or in writing: *He phrased his answer carefully.* **2a.** To divide (a musical passage) into phrases. **b.** To combine (notes or measures) into phrases. **—phras′al** *adj.*

phrase book *n.* A short book containing expressions in one language and their translations in another language.

phra·se·ol·o·gy (frā′zē-**ŏl′**ə-jē) *n., pl.* **phra·se·ol·o·gies 1.** A manner or style of speaking or writing: *difficult phraseology.* **2.** A set of expressions used by a particular person or group: *computer phraseology.*

phy·lum (**fī′**ləm) *n., pl.* **phy·la** (**fī′**lə) A taxonomic category of organisms that share certain characteristics, ranking above a class and below a kingdom: *Insects, lobsters, spiders, and other invertebrate animals having jointed legs belong to the same phylum, the arthropods.* See table at **taxonomy.** [From New Latin *phȳlum*, from Greek *phūlon*, class.]

phys·ic (**fĭz′**ĭk) *n.* A medicine or drug, especially a laxative.

phys·i·cal (**fĭz′**ĭ-kəl) *adj.* **1a.** Relating to the body rather than the mind or emotions: *physical fitness.* **b.** Involving vigorous bodily activity: *a physical dance performance.* **2.** Made of matter; material: *a physical object.* ❖ *n.* A physical examination. [From Middle English *phisical*, medical, from Medieval Latin *physicālis*, physical, medical, from Latin *physica*, natural science, from Greek *phusis*, nature.] **—phys′i·cal·ly** *adv.*

physical education *n.* Education in the care and development of the human body, including athletics and hygiene.

physical examination *n.* A medical examination to determine the condition of a person's health or physical fitness.

physical geography *n.* A branch of geography that deals with the natural features of the earth's surface, such as landforms, climate, winds, and ocean currents.

physical science *n.* Any of the sciences, such as physics, chemistry, astronomy, and geology, that deal mainly with nonliving matter and energy.

physical therapy *n.* The treatment of physical abnormality or injury through the use of specialized exercise, massage, manipulation of the joints, or other therapeutic methods.

phy·si·cian (fĭ-**zĭsh′**ən) *n.* A person trained and licensed to practice medicine; a medical doctor.

physician assistant *n.* A health-care worker trained and certified to provide a variety of medical services under the supervision of a physician.

phys·i·cist (**fĭz′**ĭ-sĭst) *n.* A scientist who specializes in physics.

phys·ics (**fĭz′**ĭks) *n.* **1.** *(used with a singular verb)* The science of matter and energy and the relations between them. **2.** *(used with a plural verb)* Physical study, analysis, properties, and laws: *the physics of space travel.*

phys·i·og·no·my (fĭz′ē-**ŏg′**nə-mē) *n., pl.* **phys·i·og·no·mies** A person's face or facial features, especially when regarded as revealing a person's character.

phys·i·o·log·i·cal (fĭz′ē-ə-**lŏj′**ĭ-kəl) *adj.* **1.** Relating to physiology. **2.** Involving or affecting the processes or functioning of a living thing. **—phys′i·o·log′i·cal·ly** *adv.*

phys·i·ol·o·gy (fĭz′ē-**ŏl′**ə-jē) *n.* **1.** The scientific study of the processes, activities, and functions essential to and characteristic of living organisms. **2.** The vital processes and functions of a living organism.

phys·i·o·ther·a·py (fĭz′ē-ō-**thĕr′**ə-pē) *n.* Physical therapy.

phy·sique (fĭ-**zēk′**) *n.* The body considered in terms of its proportions, muscle development, and appearance: *the physique of a dancer.*

–phyte *suff.* **1.** A plant with a specified character or habitat: *halophyte.* **2.** A plantlike organism: *saprophyte.* [From Greek *phuton*, plant, from *phuein*, to make grow.]

phy·to·plank·ton (fī′tō-**plăngk′**tən) *n.* Plankton that consists of very small plants and other photosynthetic organisms, including cyanobacteria, diatoms, and dinoflagellates.

pi (pī) *n.* **1.** (*also* pē) The 16th letter of the Greek alphabet, written Π, π. In English it is represented as *P, p.* **2.** *Symbol* **π** An irrational number equal to the circumference of a circle divided by its diameter, or approximately 3.14159.

❑ *These sound alike:* **pi, pie** (dessert).

pi·a·nis·si·mo (pē′ə-**nĭs′**ə-mō′) *adv. & adj.* In music, very softly or quietly.

pi·an·ist (pē-**ăn′**ĭst *or* **pē′**ə-nĭst) *n.* A person who plays the piano.

pi·an·o[1] (pē-**ăn′**ō) *n., pl.* **pi·an·os** A musical instrument with a manual keyboard that moves hammers that strike wire strings, producing tones. [From Italian *pianoforte* : *piano*, soft + *forte*, loud.]

pi·a·no[2] (pē-**ä′**nō *or* **pyä′**nō) *adv. & adj.* In music, softly or quietly. [From Italian, from Latin *plānus*, flat, smooth.]

pi·an·o·for·te (pē-ăn′ō-**fôr′**tā *or* pē-ăn′ō-**fôr′**tē) *n.* A piano.

pi·az·za (pē-**ăz′**ə *or* pē-**ä′**zə) *n.* **1.** A public square in an Italian town. **2.** A veranda.

pi·ca (**pī′**kə) *n.* **1.** A printer's type size equal to 12 points. **2.** The height of this type, about 1⁄16 inch, used as a unit of measure. **3.** A type size for typewriters, providing ten characters to the inch.

pic·a·dor (**pĭk′**ə-dôr′ *or* pē′kä-**dôr′**) *n., pl.* **pic·a·dors** or **pic·a·do·res** (pē′kä-**dō′**rĕs) A horseman in a bullfight who lances the bull's neck muscles so that it will tend to keep its head low for the later stages of the fight.

pic·a·resque (pĭk′ə-**rĕsk′** *or* pē′kə-**rĕsk′**) *adj.* Involving clever rogues or adventurers.

Pi·cas·so (pĭ-**kä′**sō *or* pĭ-**kăs′**ō), **Pablo** 1881–1973. Spanish artist. One of the most influential artists of the 1900s, Picasso is known especially for his many paintings and sculptures, including *Guernica* (1937).

pic·a·yune (pĭk′ə-**yo͞on′**) *adj.* **1.** Having little value or importance; paltry: *a picayune amount of change.* **2.** Small-minded; petty: *Don't be so picayune about everything!*

pic·ca·lil·li (**pĭk′**ə-lĭl′ē) *n., pl.* **pic·ca·lil·lis** A pickled relish of chopped vegetables and hot spices.

pic·co·lo (**pĭk′**ə-lō′) *n., pl.* **pic·co·los** A small flute with a range an octave above that of an ordinary flute. [From Italian *(flauto) piccolo*, small (flute).] **—pic′co·lo′ist** *n.*

pick[1] (pĭk) *v.* **picked, pick·ing, picks** *—tr.* **1.** To choose or select from a group: *pick the right person for the job.* **2.** To gather in; harvest: *pick peas.* **3a.** To remove the outer covering of; pluck: *pick a chicken clean of feathers.* **b.** To tear off bit by bit: *pick meat from the bones.* **4.** To poke and pull at with a toothpick or one's finger, for example: *pick one's teeth.* **5.** To open without using a key, as with a piece of wire: *pick a lock.* **6.** To steal the contents of: *pick someone's pocket.* **7a.** To pluck (the strings) of a musical instrument. **b.** To play (a tune or melody) in this way: *picked a tune on the guitar. —intr.* **1.** To poke and pull at something: *nervously picking at the tablecloth.* **2.** To eat small amounts of food from a meal: *He sat there, picking at his peas.* **3.** To decide or choose with care or forethought: *Such nice treats—Who gets to be the first to pick?* **4.** To find fault or make petty criticisms: *Why must she always be picking at us?* ❖ *n.* **1.** The act of selecting or choosing; choice: *had first pick of the desserts.* **2.** Something selected as the most desirable; the best or choicest part: *the pick of the crop.* **3.** In sports, an act of blocking the vision or movement of an opponent by using one's body. **4.** In football, an interception of a pass. ◆ **pick and choose** To select with great care. **pick off 1.** In baseball, to put out (a base runner standing off base) by making a quick throw to a fielder, especially from the pitcher or catcher. **2.** To intercept (a pass), as in football. **pick on** To tease or bully (someone). **pick out** To choose or select: *We picked out the juiciest berries.* **pick up 1a.** To take up (something) by hand: *pick up a book.* **b.** To collect or gather: *picked up the pieces of broken glass.* **c.** To tidy up: *He picked up the living room.* **2.** To take on (passengers or freight, for example). **3.** To acquire (knowledge) by learning or experience: *picked up Spanish quickly.* **4.** To come down with (a disease): *I picked up the flu last winter.* **5.** To gain: *The biker picked up speed as she went down the hill.* **pick up on** To notice or perceive and understand: *She picked up on my bad mood.* [From Middle English *picken*, variant of *piken*, to peck, from *pic*, point, spike, tool with a point, from Old English *pīc*.]

pick[2] (pĭk) *n.* **1.** A tool for loosening or breaking up hard surfaces, consisting of a slightly curved bar sharpened at both ends and fitted to a long handle. **2.** A pointed tool used for piercing, breaking, or picking, as an ice pick or toothpick. **3.** A small flat piece, as of plastic or bone, used to pluck the strings of an instrument; a plectrum. [From Middle English *pic*, from *pike*, sharp point.]

pick·axe or **pick·ax** (**pĭk′**ăks′) *n.* A pick, especially one having one end of the head pointed and the other with a chisel edge.

pick·er·el (**pĭk′**ər-əl *or* **pĭk′**rəl) *n., pl.* **pickerel** or **pick·er·els** Any of several slender North American freshwater fishes that have a long snout and are smaller than the pike. [From Middle English *pikerel*, young pike fish, diminutive of *pik*, pike (fish).]

pick·et (**pĭk′**ĭt) *n.* **1.** A pointed stake or spike, as one driven into the ground to support a fence, secure a tent, tether an animal, or mark a point in surveying. **2.** A person or group of people stationed outside a building to express a grievance or protest, as during a strike. **3.** A detachment of one or more troops or military vehicles placed in a position to give warning of enemy approach. ❖ *v.* **pick·et·ed, pick·et·ing, pick·ets** *—tr.* **1.** To support, enclose, secure, tether, or mark with a picket or pickets. **2.** To demonstrate against, as during a strike. **3.** To post as a picket. *—intr.* To act or serve as a picket.

picket fence *n.* A fence made of upright pointed boards that are fastened at intervals to rails that extend between posts.

pick·ing (**pĭk′**ĭng) *n.* **1.** The act of one that picks: *cotton picking.* **2. pickings a.** Leftovers or scraps: *We arrived at the picnic only in time for the pickings.* **b.** A share of spoils.

pick·le (**pĭk′**əl) *n.* **1.** A food, such as a cucumber, that has been preserved and flavored in vinegar and brine. **2.** A preparation of vinegar or brine for preserving and flavoring food. **3.** An acid or other chemical bath used to clean the surface of a metal. **4.** *Informal* A troublesome or difficult situation. ❖ *tr.v.* **pick·led, pick·ling, pick·les 1.** To preserve or flavor (food) in vinegar or a brine

Pablo Picasso
photographed in the 1950s

pickaxe

picket fence

pickup truck

WRITERS CHOOSE THEIR WORDS

Cass had spent her entire life preparing for disasters of one kind or another. Earthquakes. Hurricanes. Tornadoes. Not to mention the extinction-level events. Giant meteors. Global warming. Nuclear war. And here she was, done in by such a **piddling** thing? A mere trifle—indeed, a mere truffle. Had she trained all those years for toxic sludge only to succumb to toxic fudge?

—Pseudonymous Bosch
This Isn't What It Looks Like

piebald

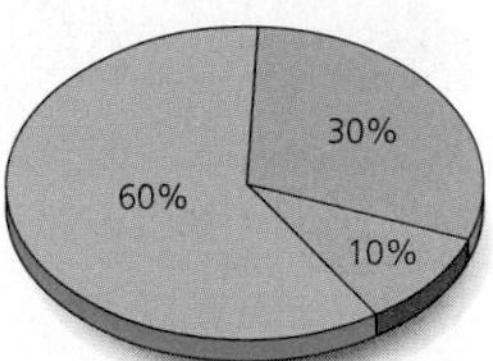

pie chart

ă	pat	ôr	core
ā	pay	oi	boy
âr	care	ou	out
ä	father	ŏŏ	took
ĕ	pet	ŏŏr	lure
ē	be	ōō	boot
ĭ	pit	ŭ	cut
ī	bite	ûr	urge
îr	pier	th	thin
ŏ	pot	*th*	this
ō	toe	zh	vision
ô	paw	ə	about

solution. **2.** To treat (metal) in a chemical bath. [From Middle English *pekill*, highly seasoned sauce, probably from Middle Dutch and Middle Low German *pēkel*, pickle, brine.]

pick·led (pĭk′əld) *adj.* Preserved in or treated with pickle: *pickled beets.*

pick·pock·et (pĭk′pŏk′ĭt) *n.* A thief who steals from someone's pockets.

pick·up (pĭk′ŭp′) *n.* **1.** The act or process of picking up, as packages, work, or freight: *The truck made a pickup at 4:00.* **2.** A person or thing that is picked up. **3.** *Informal* An improvement in condition or activity: *a pickup in attendance.* **4.** The ability to accelerate rapidly: *a car with good pickup.* **5.** The part of a phonograph that changes the variations of the record groove into an electrical signal for conversion into sound. **6.** A pickup truck.

pickup truck *n.* A light truck with an open body and low sides.

pick·y (pĭk′ē) *adj.* **pick·i·er, pick·i·est** *Informal* Excessively meticulous; fussy.

pic·nic (pĭk′nĭk) *n.* A meal eaten outdoors, as on an excursion. ❖ *intr.v.* **pic·nicked, pic·nick·ing, pic·nics** To go on or participate in a picnic. [Originally potluck of shared food, from French *pique-nique*, going Dutch, potluck : *piquer*, to pick + *nique*, nothing at all.] **—pic′nick·er** *n.*

Pict (pĭkt) *n.* One of an ancient people of northern Britain whose descendants joined with the Scots to form Scotland.

pic·to·gram (pĭk′tə-grăm′) *n.* A pictograph.

pic·to·graph (pĭk′tə-grăf′) *n.* **1.** A picture that represents a word, phrase, or idea, especially one used in early writing systems. **2.** A diagram or graph on which numerical data are represented pictorially. **—pic·tog′ra·phy** (pĭk-tŏg′rə-fē) *n.*

pic·to·ri·al (pĭk-tôr′ē-əl) *adj.* **1.** Characterized by pictures: *pictorial materials.* **2.** Represented as if in pictures; descriptive: *pictorial imagery.* **3.** Composed of or illustrated by pictures: *pictorial representations of planets.* **—pic·to′ri·al·ly** *adv.*

pic·ture (pĭk′chər) *n.* **1.** A visual representation or image that is painted, drawn, photographed, or otherwise represented on a flat surface. **2a.** A visible image, especially one on a flat surface or screen: *a picture reflected in the pond.* **b.** A vivid verbal description; an image in words. **c.** A vivid mental image. **3.** A person or thing that closely resembles another: *He is the picture of his father.* **4.** A person or thing that is a good example of a certain emotion, mood, or state of mind: *The boy was the picture of eagerness.* **5.** A combination of circumstances; the situation: *How does an education figure in the picture?* **6.** A movie. ❖ *tr.v.* **pic·tured, pic·tur·ing, pic·tures 1.** To make a representation or picture of: *A graph is a good way to picture data.* **2.** To form a mental image of; visualize; imagine: *He pictured himself flying over the town.* **3.** To describe vividly; make a verbal image of. [From Middle English, from Latin *pictūra*, from Latin *pictus*, painted, past participle of *pingere*, to paint.]

pic·tur·esque (pĭk′chə-**rĕsk′**) *adj.* **1.** Suggesting a picture; striking or interesting: *picturesque Alpine villages.* **2.** Strikingly expressive; vivid: *an essay with picturesque language.* **—pic′tur·esque′ly** *adv.* **—pic′tur·esque′ness** *n.*

picture tube *n.* A cathode-ray tube typical of older models of televisions that translates electrical signals into a visible picture on a screen.

pid·dling (pĭd′lĭng) *adj.* Of little worth or importance; trivial.

pidg·in (pĭj′ən) *n.* A simple form of speech based on a mixture of two or more languages and used for communications between groups speaking different languages.
❑ *These sound alike:* **pidgin, pigeon** (bird).

Pidgin English *n.* Any of several pidgins based on English and now spoken mostly on the Pacific islands and in West Africa.

pie (pī) *n.* A baked food composed of a pastry shell filled with fruit, meat, cheese, or other ingredients, and usually covered with a pastry crust.
❑ *These sound alike:* **pie, pi** (Greek letter).

pie·bald (pī′bôld′) *adj.* Marked with spots or patches, especially of black and white: *a piebald horse.* ❖ *n.* A piebald animal, especially a horse. [From *pie*, magpie + earlier *bald*, streaked with white (from *bald*, bald).]

piece (pēs) *n.* **1.** Something considered as a part of a larger quantity or group; a portion: *a piece of land.* **2.** A portion or part that has been separated from a whole: *a piece of pie.* **3.** An object that is one member of a set: *sixty pieces of china.* **4.** An artistic, musical, or literary work: *play a piece on the piano.* **5.** An instance, specimen, or example: *What a fine piece of work!* **6.** A coin: *a 50-cent piece.* **7.** What one has to say about something: *She said her piece at the meeting.* **8a.** In certain board games, one of the small objects used in playing. **b.** In chess, any of the figures other than a pawn; a king, queen, bishop, knight, or rook. **9.** *Slang* A firearm. **10.** *Informal* An unspecified distance: *My grandfather's farm is down the road a piece.* ❖ *tr.v.* **pieced, piec·ing, piec·es 1.** To join or unite the parts of: *pieced the puzzle together.* **2.** To mend by adding a fragment or part to: *He pieced his ragged pants.* ◆ **a piece of (one's) mind** Frank and severe criticism; censure: *The principal gave me a piece of her mind for being late again.* **of a piece** Belonging to the same class or kind. **piece by piece** In stages: *took the machine apart piece by piece.* **piece of cake** *Informal* Something that is very easy to do: *For most high school students, reciting the alphabet is a piece of cake.*
❑ *These sound alike:* **piece, peace** (tranquility).

pièce de ré·sis·tance (pyĕs də rā-zē-**stäNs′**) *n., pl.* **pièces de ré·sis·tance** (pyĕs də rā-zē-**stäNs′**) **1.** An outstanding accomplishment. **2.** The principal dish of a meal.

piece goods *pl.n.* Fabrics made and sold in standard lengths.

piece·meal (pēs′mēl′) *adv.* **1.** By a small amount at a time; in stages: *built up the collection piecemeal.* **2.** In pieces; apart: *The puzzle lay piecemeal on the floor.* ❖ *adj.* Done or made in stages: *a piecemeal accumulation.*

piece of eight *n., pl.* **pieces of eight** An old Spanish silver coin.

piece·work (pēs′wûrk′) *n.* Work paid for by the number of units produced. **—piece′work′er** *n.*

pie chart *n.* A graph in the form of a circle divided into sections like pieces of a pie.

pied (pīd) *adj.* Having patches of color; piebald: *pied cattle.*

Pied·mont (pēd′mŏnt′) **1.** A historical region of northwest Italy bordering on France and Switzerland. **2.** A plateau region of the eastern United States extending from New York to Alabama between the Appalachian Mountains and the Atlantic coastal plain.

Pied Piper *n.* A mythical hero who saved a village from an infestation of rats by playing a tune on his pipe, compelling the rats to follow him out of the town. When the town refused to pay for his services, he played his pipe again, leading all of the children out of the village as well.

pier (pîr) *n.* **1.** A platform extending from a shore over water and supported by piles or pillars, used to secure, protect, and provide access to ships or boats. **2.** A supporting structure of a bridge at the points where its spans join. **3.** Any of various other supporting structures, such as a pillar, a buttress, or the part of a wall between two windows.
❑ *These sound alike:* **pier, peer**[1] (look), **peer**[2] (equal).

pierce (pîrs) *v.* **pierced, pierc·ing, pierc·es** *—tr.* **1.**

To pass into or through (something) with or as with a sharp instrument: *Arrows pierced the target.* **2.** To make a hole or opening in; perforate: *A nail pierced the tire.* **3.** To make a way through: *explorers piercing the wilderness.* **4.** To sound sharply through: *A cry pierced the air.* —*intr.* To penetrate into or through something: *The rocket pierced through the clouds.*

Pierce (pîrs), **Franklin** 1804–1869. The 14th president of the United States (1853–1857). His presidency was marked by increasing conflict over slavery.

pierced (pîrst) *adj.* **1.** Cut through with a sharp instrument; perforated: *threw the pierced ticket in the trash.* **2.** Being a body part that has a piercing, as for jewelry: *My sister has pierced ears.* **3.** Relating to jewelry designed to be worn in a such a body part: *a pierced earring.*

pierc·ing (pîr′sĭng) *adj.* Sharp; penetrating: *piercing cold; piercing eyes.* ❖ *n.* A hole made in the skin for an earring or other piece of jewelry. **—pierc′ing·ly** *adv.*

Pierre (pîr) The capital of South Dakota, in the central part of the state on the Missouri River. It was chosen as state capital in 1889.

pi·e·ty (pī′ĭ-tē) *n., pl.* **pi·e·ties 1.** Religious devotion and reverence. **2.** The condition of being deeply respectful and obedient to parents and family: *filial piety.* —SEE NOTE.

pi·e·zo·e·lec·tric·i·ty (pē-ā′zō-ĭ-lĕk-**trĭs′**ĭ-tē *or* pī-ē′zō-ĭ-lĕk-**trĭs′**ĭ-tē) *n.* A property of certain nonconducting crystals that results in voltages being generated across them when they are subjected to mechanical stress and that causes them to change slightly in shape when voltages are applied across them. [From Greek *piezein,* to squeeze + English *electricity.*] **—pi·e′zo·e·lec′tric** *adj.*

pig (pĭg) *n.* **1.** Any of various hoofed mammals having short legs, bristly hair, and a blunt snout used for digging. Pigs are often raised for meat. **2.** *Informal* A person regarded as being like a pig, especially a greedy or messy person. **3a.** A crude block of metal, usually iron or lead, poured from a smelting furnace. **b.** A mold in which such metal is cast. ◆ **pig out** *Slang* To eat greedily; gorge oneself: *pigged out on ice cream and cake.*

pi·geon (pĭj′ən) *n.* Any of various birds having short legs, a rounded chest, and a small head, especially one common in cities and often raised for food or trained to carry messages.

❑ *These sound alike:* **pigeon, pidgin** (speech form).

pi·geon·hole (pĭj′ən-hōl′) *n.* **1.** A small compartment or recess, as in a desk, for holding papers. **2.** A small hole in which pigeons may nest. **3.** A specific, often oversimplified category. ❖ *tr.v.* **pi·geon·holed, pi·geon·hol·ing, pi·geon·holes 1.** To place in a small compartment or recess. **2.** To classify into a group; categorize: *a tendency to pigeonhole one's colleagues.*

pi·geon-toed (pĭj′ən-tōd′) *adj.* Having the toes or feet turned inward.

pig·gish (pĭg′ĭsh) *adj.* Resembling a pig, as in being greedy or stubborn: *a piggish grunt; a piggish appetite.* **—pig′gish·ly** *adv.*

pig·gy·back (pĭg′ē-băk′) *adv. & adj.* **1.** On the shoulders or back: *ride piggyback; a piggyback ride.* **2.** In or by means of truck trailers carried on railroad cars: *goods shipped piggyback.*

pig·gy bank (pĭg′ē) *n.* A child's bank for coins, shaped like a pig.

pig·head·ed (pĭg′hĕd′ĭd) *adj.* Stupidly obstinate or stubborn. **—pig′head′ed·ly** *adv.* **—pig′head′ed·ness** *n.*

pig iron *n.* Impure iron as it is drawn from a blast furnace, usually cast in oblong blocks.

pig Latin *n.* A code language formed by moving the first consonant sound of a word to the end and then adding the vowel ā, as *igpay atinlay* for *pig Latin.*

pig·let (pĭg′lĭt) *n.* A young pig.

pig·ment (pĭg′mənt) *n.* **1.** A substance or material used as coloring: *the pigments used in a paint.* **2.** A substance, such as chlorophyll or hemoglobin, that gives a characteristic color to a cell or to an organism's tissues.

pig·men·ta·tion (pĭg′mən-tā′shən) *n.* Coloring of a cell or a tissue, such as skin, fur, or leaves, by pigments.

Pig·my (pĭg′mē) *n. & adj.* Variant of **Pygmy.**

pig·pen (pĭg′pĕn′) *n.* **1.** A pen for pigs. **2.** *Informal* A dirty or very untidy place.

pig·skin (pĭg′skĭn′) *n.* **1.** The skin of a pig. **2.** Leather made from the skin of a pig. **3.** A football.

pig·sty (pĭg′stī′) *n., pl.* **pig·sties 1.** A shelter where pigs are kept. **2.** *Informal* A dirty or very untidy place.

pig·tail (pĭg′tāl′) *n.* **1.** A braid or ponytail, especially one of a pair worn one on each side of the head. **2.** A short length of wire that is used to connect other wires to each other or to an electrical device.

pi·ka (pī′kə *or* pē′kə) *n.* Any of several small mammals of mountains or grasslands of western North America and Eurasia, having rounded ears and no visible tail.

pike¹ (pīk) *n.* A long spear formerly used by infantry. [From Middle English, from Old French *pique,* from Old French *piquer,* to stab.]

pike² (pīk) *n., pl.* **pike** or **pikes** A large freshwater fish having a narrow body and a long snout, often caught for sport. [From Middle English, perhaps from Old English *pīc,* sharp point (from the shape of the fish).]

pike³ (pīk) *n.* A turnpike. [Short for *turnpike.*]

pike⁴ (pīk) *n.* A spike or sharp point, as on the tip of a spear. [From Middle English *pik,* from Old English *pīc.*]

pike⁵ (pīk) *n.* A midair position in sports such as diving and gymnastics in which the athlete bends to touch the toes or grab the calves while keeping the legs together and straight. [Probably from the resemblance of the position to the head of a pike fish.]

pik·er (pī′kər) *n. Slang* **1.** A cautious gambler. **2.** A petty or stingy person.

Pikes Peak (pīks) A mountain, 14,110 feet (4,301 meters) high, in the Rocky Mountains of central Colorado.

pike·staff (pīk′stăf′) *n.* **1.** The shaft of a pike. **2.** A walking stick tipped with a metal spike.

pi·laf or **pi·laff** (pĭ-**läf′** *or* **pē′**läf′) *n.* A seasoned dish of steamed rice, often with meat, shellfish, or vegetables.

pi·las·ter (pĭ-**lăs′**tər) *n.* A rectangular column set into a wall for decoration.

Pi·late (pī′lət), **Pontius** Flourished first century AD. Roman governor of Judea who ordered Jesus's crucifixion.

pile¹ (pīl) *n.* **1.** A mass of objects stacked or thrown together in a heap: *a pile of firewood.* See Synonyms at **heap. 2.** *Informal* **a.** A large accumulation or quantity: *a pile of complaints.* **b.** A large sum of money; a fortune: *He made his pile and retired.* ❖ *v.* **piled, pil·ing, piles** —*tr.* **1a.** To place or lay in a pile or heap: *They piled the dishes in the sink.* **b.** To load (something) with a heap or pile: *piled the table with books.* **2.** To add or increase (something) to the point of abundance or excess: *piled homework on the students.* —*intr.* **1.** To form a heap or pile. **2.** To increase or build up: *Your assignments are piling up.* **3.** To move, often in haste, in a disorderly group or mass: *Baseball fans piled out of the stadium.* [From Middle English, from Old French, from Latin *pīla,* pillar.]

pile² (pīl) *n.* A heavy beam of timber, concrete, or steel, driven into the ground as a foundation or support for a structure. [From Middle English, from Old English *pīl,* shaft, stake, from Latin *pīlum,* spear, pestle.]

pile³ (pīl) *n.* **1.** Cut or uncut loops of yarn forming the surface of certain carpets or of fabrics such as velvet and plush. **2.** Soft fine hair, fur, or wool. [From Middle English *pilus,* downy hair, from Latin, hair.]

Franklin Pierce

WORD HISTORY

piety Both **piety** and **pity** come from the same Latin word through Old French. The Latin source is the adjective *pius,* which means "faithful in one's obligations to one's family as a child, spouse, or parent," "conscientious in doing one's work," "loyal to one's community and country," "devout in one's religion," and "respectful, grateful." From *pius* was formed the word *pietās,* a noun that acquired the senses "compassion" and "kindness." *Pietās* became both *piete* and *pite* in Old French. In English *piety* and *pity* were used interchangeably until the mid-1500s, when *pity* became limited to the meaning "compassion."

pika

pilaster

pillory

piñata

pineapple

ă	pat	ôr	core
ā	pay	oi	boy
âr	care	ou	out
ä	father	o͝o	took
ĕ	pet	o͝or	lure
ē	be	o͞o	boot
ĭ	pit	ŭ	cut
ī	bite	ûr	urge
îr	pier	th	thin
ŏ	pot	*th*	this
ō	toe	zh	vision
ô	paw	ə	about

pile driver *n.* A machine that drives piles by raising a weight between guideposts and dropping it on the head of the pile.

piles (pīlz) *pl.n.* Hemorrhoids.

pile·up or **pile-up** (**pīl′**ŭp′) *n.* A serious collision usually involving several motor vehicles.

pil·fer (**pĭl′**fər) *v.* **pil·fered, pil·fer·ing, pil·fers** —*tr.* To steal (a small amount or item): *He pilfered some blackberry jam from his neighbor's cupboard.* —*intr.* To steal or filch. —**pil′fer·er** *n.*

pil·grim (**pĭl′**grəm) *n.* **1.** A religious devotee who travels to a shrine or sacred place. **2.** A person who travels, especially to a place of great personal importance. **3. Pilgrim** One of the English separatists who founded the colony of Plymouth in New England in 1620.

pil·grim·age (**pĭl′**grə-mĭj) *n.* **1.** A journey to a sacred place or shrine. **2.** A long journey with a meaningful purpose.

pil·ing (**pī′**lĭng) *n.* **1.** A heavy beam of timber, concrete, or steel driven into the ground as a foundation or support for a structure; a pile. **2.** A group of such piles or a structure made of such piles.

pill (pĭl) *n.* **1.** A small pellet or tablet of medicine, often coated, taken by swallowing whole or chewing. **2.** Something distasteful or unpleasant that must be accepted. **3.** *Slang* An ill-natured or disagreeable person.

pil·lage (**pĭl′**ĭj) *v.* **pil·laged, pil·lag·ing, pil·lag·es** —*tr.* To rob of goods by force; plunder: *The army pillaged the countryside.* —*intr.* To take booty. ❖ *n.* **1.** The act of pillaging: *the pillage of the city.* **2.** Something pillaged; spoils. —**pil′lag·er** *n.*

pil·lar (**pĭl′**ər) *n.* **1a.** A vertical structure used as a support for a building; a column. **b.** Such a structure or one similar to it used for decoration. **2.** A person occupying a central position; a mainstay: *a pillar of the community.* ❖ *tr.v.* **pil·lared, pil·lar·ing, pil·lars** To support or decorate with a pillar or pillars.

pill·box (**pĭl′**bŏks′) *n.* **1.** A small box for pills. **2.** A woman's small round hat. **3.** A small concrete structure for a machine gun or other weapon.

pill·bug (**pĭl′**bŭg′) *n.* A woodlouse, especially one that is able to roll into a tight ball.

pil·lo·ry (**pĭl′**ə-rē) *n., pl.* **pil·lo·ries** A wooden framework with holes for the head and hands, mounted on a post and formerly used to secure offenders who were subjected to public scorn as punishment. ❖ *tr.v.* **pil·lo·ried, pil·lo·ry·ing, pil·lo·ries 1.** To expose to ridicule and scorn: *He pilloried his former friends in novels.* **2.** To put in a pillory as punishment.

pil·low (**pĭl′**ō) *n.* A cloth case stuffed with soft material, such as down, feathers, or foam rubber, used to cushion the head, especially during sleep. ❖ *tr.v.* **pil·lowed, pil·low·ing, pil·lows 1.** To rest (one's head) on or as if on a pillow: *She pillowed her head on her arms.* **2.** To serve as a pillow for. [From Middle English, from Old English *pyle, pylu,* from Latin *pulvīnus.*]

pil·low·case (**pĭl′**ō-kās′) *n.* A removable cover for a pillow.

pil·low·slip (**pĭl′**ō-slĭp′) *n.* A pillowcase.

pi·lot (**pī′**lət) *n.* **1.** A person who operates an aircraft in flight. **2.** A licensed specialist who steers large ships in and out of port or through dangerous waters. **3.** A ship's helmsman. **4.** A person who guides or directs others. **5.** The part of a tool, device, or machine that leads or guides the whole. **6.** A pilot light. **7.** A television program produced as a model of a series being considered for production by a network. ❖ *tr.v.* **pi·lot·ed, pi·lot·ing, pi·lots 1.** To serve as the pilot of (a plane, for example): *piloted the boat away from the shoals.* **2.** To lead, guide, or conduct: *The tour guide piloted the students through the museum.* ❖ *adj.* Serving as a small-scale model for future work: *a pilot project.*

pi·lot·fish (**pī′**lət-fĭsh′) *n.* A small ocean fish that often swims along with sharks or other large fish.

pi·lot·house (**pī′**lət-hous′) *n.* An enclosed section on a bridge of a vessel from which the vessel is steered.

pilot light *n.* **1.** A small jet of gas kept burning to ignite a gas burner, as in a stove or water heater. **2.** A small lamp, usually red, used to indicate that an electric circuit, as in an appliance, is turned on.

Pi·ma (**pē′**mə) *n., pl.* **Pima** or **Pi·mas 1.** A member of a Native American people of south-central Arizona. **2.** The Uto-Aztecan language of the Pima.

pi·mien·to or **pi·men·to** (pĭ-**mĕn′**tō) *n., pl.* **pi·mien·tos** or **pi·men·tos** A mild-flavored red pepper, often used as a flavoring, as a stuffing for olives, or as a colorful garnish.

pim·per·nel (**pĭm′**pər-nĕl′) *n.* Any of various low-growing plants having small red, pink, or purplish flowers that close in cloudy weather.

pim·ple (**pĭm′**pəl) *n.* A small swelling on the skin, often sore and sometimes containing pus. —**pim′ply** *adj.*

pin (pĭn) *n.* **1.** A short straight stiff piece of wire with a blunt head and a sharp point, used especially for fastening. **2.** Something that resembles a pin in shape or use, as a hairpin, clothespin, or safety pin. **3.** An ornament fastened to clothing by means of a clasp. **4.** A bar or rod of wood or metal that supports or fastens things, especially by passing through or into a series of prepared holes. **5.** On a golf course, a long metal or wooden rod with a small flag at one end, inserted into a cup to indicate its location. **6.** One of the wooden clubs at which the ball is aimed in bowling. ❖ *tr.v.* **pinned, pin·ning, pins 1.** To fasten or secure with a pin or pins: *pinned the flower to her coat.* **2.** To place in a position of trusting dependence: *We pinned our hopes on him.* **3.** To win a fall from (an opponent) in wrestling: *Joe's teammates wanted him to pin the champ.* **4.** To hold fast; immobilize: *The strong current pinned the canoe against the rock.* ◆ **pin down 1.** To fix or establish clearly: *The researchers finally pinned down the cause of the accident.* **2.** To force (someone) to give firm opinions or precise information: *The school committee pinned down the superintendent on the issue of budget cuts.* **pin on** To attribute (a wrongdoing or crime): *The theft was pinned on the wrong person.*

PIN *abbr.* An abbreviation of personal identification number.

pin·a·fore (**pĭn′**ə-fôr′) *n.* A sleeveless garment similar to an apron, especially one worn as a dress or overdress.

pi·ña·ta (pĭn-**yä′**tə *or* pēn-**yä′**tə) *n.* A decorated container filled with candy and toys and suspended from the ceiling. As part of Christmas and birthday celebrations in certain Latin-American countries, blindfolded children try to break the piñata with a stick.

pin·ball (**pĭn′**bôl′) *n.* A game played on a device in which a ball rolls down a slanted surface having obstacles and targets, often with mechanical paddles that are operated by buttons to keep the ball in play.

pince-nez (**păns′nā′** *or* **pĭns′nā′**) *n., pl.* **pince-nez** (**păns′nāz′** *or* **pĭns′nāz′**) Eyeglasses that are worn on the bridge of the nose without supports that go over the ears.

pin·cer (**pĭn′**sər) *n.* **1.** often **pincers** A grasping tool having two parts hinged together to work in opposition. **2.** A jointed grasping claw, as of a lobster or scorpion.

pinch (pĭnch) *v.* **pinched, pinch·ing, pinch·es** —*tr.* **1.** To squeeze (something) between the thumb and a finger, pincers, or other edges. **2.** To cause pain or discomfort to (a part of the body) by pressing or being too tight: *These shoes pinch my toes.* **3.** To cause to be in financial distress: *Rising costs pinched the family's budget.* **4.** To nip, wither, or shrivel: *a face pinched by fear and fatigue.* **5.** *Slang* To steal: *He pinched some doughnuts from the tray.* **6.** *Slang* To arrest. —*intr.* **1.** To cause pain or discomfort by pressing or being too tight: *Do your shoes pinch at all?* **2.** To draw a thumb and a finger together on a touchscreen to cause the image to become smaller. ❖ *n.* **1.** A squeeze or other pressure caused by pressing between the thumb and a finger, pincers, or other edges: *The crab gave him a pinch on the toe.* **2.** The amount that can be held between the thumb and forefinger: *a pinch of salt.* **3.** A painful, difficult, or straitened circumstance: *the pinch of hard times.* **4.** An emergency situation: *In a pinch she can take over the work.* **5.** *Slang* A theft. **6.** *Slang* An arrest. ◆ **pinch pennies** *Informal* To be thrifty or miserly. —**pinch′er** *n.*

pinch-hit (pĭnch′hĭt′) *intr.v.* **pinch-hit, pinch-hit·ting, pinch-hits 1.** In baseball, to bat as a substitute, especially when a hit is badly needed. **2.** To substitute for another: *I'm pinch-hitting for the mechanic today.* —**pinch hit** *n.* —**pinch hitter** *n.*

pin·cush·ion (pĭn′ko͝osh′ən) *n.* A small firm cushion into which pins and needles are stuck when not in use.

pine[1] (pīn) *n.* **1.** Any of various evergreen trees that bear cones and have clusters of needle-shaped leaves. Pines are often cultivated for timber and pulp. **2.** The wood of such a tree. [From Middle English, from Old English *pīn*, from Latin *pīnus*.]

pine[2] (pīn) *intr.v.* **pined, pin·ing, pines 1.** To feel a lingering, often nostalgic desire. **2.** To lose health or waste away from longing or grief. [From Middle English *pinen*, from *pine*, suffering, from Old English *pīne*, punishment, from Latin *poena*, penalty, from Greek *poinē*.]

pin·e·al gland (pĭn′ē-əl *or* pī′nē-əl) *n.* A small gland found in the brain of many animals, involved in the regulation of hormones.

pine·ap·ple (pīn′ăp′əl) *n.* **1.** A large fleshy tropical fruit having a rough spiny skin and a tuft of narrow prickly leaves at the top. **2.** The plant that bears such fruit.

pine·cone (pīn′kōn′) *n.* The cone of a pine tree.

pine nut *n.* The edible seed of certain pine trees.

pine·wood (pīn′wo͝od′) *n.* **1.** The wood of a pine tree: *planks made of pinewood.* **2.** often **pinewoods** A forest of pines.

pine·y (pī′nē) *adj.* Variant of **piny.**

pin·feath·er (pĭn′fĕth′ər) *n.* A feather still enclosed in a narrow horny covering and just beginning to grow out from the skin.

Ping-Pong (pĭng′pông′) A trademark used for table tennis and related equipment.

pin·hole (pĭn′hōl′) *n.* A tiny puncture made by or as if by a pin.

pin·ion[1] (pĭn′yən) *n.* A bird's wing. ❖ *tr.v.* **pin·ioned, pin·ion·ing, pin·ions 1.** To restrain (a person's arms or hands, for example) by holding or fastening. **2.** To prevent (a bird) from flying by clipping or tying its wings. [From Middle English, from Old French *pignon*, from Latin *pinna*, feather.]

pin·ion[2] (pĭn′yən) *n.* A small gearwheel that engages a larger gearwheel or a rack. [From French *pignon*, from Old French *pigne*, comb, from Latin *pecten*.]

pink[1] (pĭngk) *n.* **1.** A light or pale red. **2.** Any of various plants related to the carnation, grown for their fragrant flowers. **3.** The highest or best degree: *the pink of perfection.* ❖ *adj.* **pink·er, pink·est** Light or pale red.

pink[2] (pĭngk) *tr.v.* **pinked, pink·ing, pinks 1.** To stab lightly or prick with a pointed weapon. **2.** To decorate with a pattern of small holes. **3.** To cut with pinking shears. [From Middle English *pingen, pinken*, to push, prick, from Old English *pyngan*, from Latin *pungere*.]

pink·eye (pĭngk′ī′) *n.* A severe, contagious inflammation of the mucous membrane of the eyelids and eyeballs that makes the eyes appear pink.

pink·ie also **pink·y** (pĭng′kē) *n., pl.* **pink·ies** *Informal* The little finger.

pink·ing shears (pĭng′kĭng) *pl.n.* Sewing scissors with notched blades, used to finish edges of cloth with a zigzag pattern for decoration or to prevent raveling or fraying.

pink·ish (pĭng′kĭsh) *adj.* Somewhat pink in color.

pin money *n.* Money for small expenses.

pin·na·cle (pĭn′ə-kəl) *n.* **1.** A small turret or spire on a roof. **2.** A tall pointed formation, as a mountain peak. **3.** The peak or summit of something: *at the pinnacle of his fame.*

pin·nate (pĭn′āt′) *adj.* Resembling a feather in having parts or divisions, such as leaflets, arranged along each side of a stalk. —**pin′nate′ly** *adv.*

pin·ni·ped (pĭn′ə-pĕd′) *n.* Any of various fish-eating sea mammals of a group that includes the seals and the walrus, having flippers used for swimming. [From Latin *pinna*, feather + Latin *pēs*, foot.]

pi·noch·le (pē′nŭk′əl *or* pē′nŏk′əl) *n.* A card game for two to four people, played with a deck of 48 cards having no card below a nine.

pi·ñon also **pin·yon** (pĭn′yōn′ *or* pĭn′yən) *n., pl.* **pi·ñons** or **pi·ño·nes** (pĭn-yō′nēz) also **pin·yons 1.** Any of several pine trees of northern Mexico and the southwest United States, bearing edible seeds. **2.** An edible seed of any of these trees.

pin·point (pĭn′point′) *n.* **1.** A very small or sharp point. **2.** A very small amount of something: *bright pinpoints of flame.* ❖ *tr.v.* **pin·point·ed, pin·point·ing, pin·points** To locate and identify precisely: *pinpoint the reason for the change.* ❖ *adj.* **1.** Showing care and precision: *pinpoint accuracy.* **2.** Very small; minute: *pinpoint organisms in the sea.*

pin·prick (pĭn′prĭk′) *n.* **1.** A slight puncture made by or as if by a pin. **2.** A small wound. **3.** A minor annoyance.

pin·stripe (pĭn′strīp′) *n.* **1.** A very thin stripe on a fabric. **2.** A fabric with very thin stripes.

pint (pīnt) *n.* **1.** A unit of volume or capacity used for measuring liquids, equal to 16 fluid ounces or 28.8 cubic inches (about 0.47 liter). **2.** A unit of volume or capacity used for measuring dry substances, equal to ½ quart or 34.6 cubic inches (about 0.55 liter). See table at **measurement. 3a.** A container that can hold a pint. **b.** The amount of a substance that can be held in such a container.

pin·to (pĭn′tō) *n., pl.* **pin·tos** or **pin·toes** A horse having irregular spots or markings of white and another color. ❖ *adj.* Having irregular spots or markings.

pinto bean *n.* A type of bean that has spotted seeds and is grown chiefly in the southwest United States and northern Mexico.

pin·wheel (pĭn′wēl′) *n.* **1.** A toy consisting of blades of colored paper or plastic pinned to the end of a stick so that they revolve in the wind or when blown on. **2.** A firework that forms a rotating wheel of colored flames.

pin·worm (pĭn′wûrm′) *n.* Any of various small parasitic worms that infest the lower part of the intestine in humans and other vertebrates.

pin·y also **pine·y** (pī′nē) *adj.* **pin·i·er, pin·i·est** Relating to, suggestive of, or abounding in pines.

pin·yon (pĭn′yōn′ *or* pĭn′yən) *n.* Variant of **piñon.**

pi·o·neer (pī′ə-nîr′) *n.* **1.** A person who first enters or settles a region. **2.** A person who opens up new areas of research, thought, or development. **3.** A species that is often one of the first to grow or live in an environment where there have been no living things. ❖ *tr.v.* **pi·o·neered, pi·o·neer·ing, pi·o·neers** To develop, especially as an innovation: *doctors who pioneered the use of anesthesia.*

pi·ous (pī′əs) *adj.* **1.** Having or showing religious reverence; devout: *pious worshipers; a pious silence.* **2.** Self-righteous or insincere: *a politician's pious remarks about reducing government spending.* —**pi′ous·ly** *adv.* —**pi′ous·ness** *n.*

pinnate

pinstripe

pinto

pip³
seagull eggs

pipeline
Trans-Alaska Pipeline

pipe wrench

pip¹ (pĭp) *n.* A small fruit seed, as of an orange or apple. [From Middle English *pipin*, small seed.]

pip² (pĭp) *n.* Any of the dots indicating numerical value on dice or dominoes.

pip³ (pĭp) *tr.v.* **pipped, pip·ping, pips** To break through (an eggshell) in hatching. Used mainly of birds. [Perhaps variant of *peep*, to chirp, or *peep*, to peek.]

pipe (pīp) *n.* **1a.** A tube or hollow cylinder through which a liquid or gas can be made to flow. **b.** A section or piece of such a tube. **2a.** A device for smoking, consisting of a hollow tube, as of clay or wood, with a mouthpiece at one end and a small bowl at the other. **b.** The amount of smoking material, such as tobacco, needed to fill the bowl of such a pipe. **3a.** A tubular musical instrument, especially a simple or primitive one, similar to a flute. **b.** Any of the tubes used in an organ to produce musical tones. **c. pipes** A small wind instrument consisting of a number of tuned tubes bound together. **4. pipes** A bagpipe. ❖ *v.* **piped, pip·ing, pipes** —*tr.* **1.** To transport or transmit by means of a pipe or pipes. **2.** To play (music) on a pipe or pipes. **3.** To speak or sing in a shrill tone: *The child piped a question.* **4.** To provide or connect with pipes. —*intr.* **1.** To play on a pipe. **2.** To speak shrilly; make a shrill sound. ◆ **pipe down** *Slang* To stop talking; be quiet: *Pipe down! The movie is about to start.* **pipe up** *Slang* To speak up: *If you want some pizza, pipe up before it's gone.* [From Middle English, from Old English *pīpe*, musical pipe, from Latin *pīpāre*, to chirp.]

pipe bomb *n.* An explosive device that is contained in a metal pipe.

pipe cleaner *n.* **1.** A bendable wire covered with bristles, used for cleaning the stem of a tobacco pipe. **2.** A similar flexible wire, used in making arts and crafts.

pipe fitter *n.* A person who installs and repairs piping systems.

pipe·fit·ting (pīp′fĭt′ĭng) *n.* **1.** The work or trade of installing and repairing piping systems. **2.** A section of pipe used to connect two or more pipes.

pipe·line (pīp′līn′) *n.* **1.** A long series of pipes, especially one used to carry water, petroleum, or natural gas over great distances. **2.** A direct line of communication or route of supply. ❖ *tr.v.* **pipe·lined, pipe·lin·ing, pipe·lines** To transport by or as if by a pipeline.

pipe organ *n.* A musical instrument consisting of a set of pipes that sound tones when supplied with a flow of air controlled by a keyboard.

pip·er (pī′pər) *n.* A person who plays music on a pipe or a bagpipe.

pi·pette (pī-pĕt′) *n.* A narrow tube into which small amounts of liquid are suctioned for transfer or measurement.

pipe wrench *n.* A wrench with two notched jaws, one of which is adjustable, used for gripping and turning pipes.

pip·ing (pī′pĭng) *n.* **1.** A system of pipes, such as those used in plumbing. **2.** The act of playing music on a pipe. **3.** A shrill high-pitched sound. **4.** A narrow tube of material, used as a trimming on edges or seams, as on slipcovers. ❖ *adj.* Having a high-pitched sound: *the piping notes of the flute.* ◆ **piping hot** Very hot: *piping hot biscuits.*

pip·it (pĭp′ĭt) *n.* Any of various small songbirds having brownish feathers and a streaked breast.

pip·pin (pĭp′ĭn) *n.* Any of several varieties of apple, used mainly in cooking.

pip-squeak (pĭp′skwēk′) *n. Informal* A person or thing that is small or unimportant.

pi·quant (pē′kənt *or* pē′känt′) *adj.* **1.** Pleasantly pungent or tart in taste; spicy: *a piquant sauce.* **2.** Pleasantly intriguing, provocative, or stimulating: *piquant prose.* **—pi′quan·cy** *n.* **—pi′quant·ly** *adv.*

pique (pēk) *n.* A state of vexation caused by a perceived slight or indignity; a feeling of wounded pride. ❖ *tr.v.* **piqued, piqu·ing, piques 1.** To cause to feel resentment or indignation: *Her arrogant manner piqued her neighbors.* **2.** To arouse; stir: *The unusual objects piqued his curiosity.*

❑ *These sound alike:* **pique, peak** (mountaintop), **peek** (glance).

pi·qué (pĭ-kā′ *or* pē-kā′) *n.* A tightly woven cloth with various raised patterns.

pi·ra·cy (pī′rə-sē) *n., pl.* **pi·ra·cies 1.** Robbery or other serious acts of violence committed at sea. **2.** The unauthorized use of another's invention or creation.

pi·ra·nha (pĭ-rän′yə *or* pĭ-rä′nə) *n.* Any of various tropical American freshwater fishes that have sharp teeth and are known for attacking and feeding on live animals. [From Tupí : *pirá*, fish + *ánha*, teeth.]

pi·rate (pī′rĭt) *n.* A person who robs ships at sea or plunders the land from the sea. ❖ *v.* **pi·rat·ed, pi·rat·ing, pi·rates** —*tr.* **1.** To attack and rob (a ship at sea). **2.** To publish or reproduce (another's invention or creation) without permission. —*intr.* To practice piracy.

pi·rogue (pĭ-rōg′ *or* pîr′ō) *n.* A canoe made from a hollowed tree trunk.

pir·ou·ette (pĭr′o͞o-ĕt′) *n.* In ballet, a full turn of the body on the tip of the toe or the ball of the foot. ❖ *intr.v.* **pir·ou·et·ted, pir·ou·et·ting, pir·ou·ettes** To perform a pirouette.

Pi·sa (pē′zə) A city of western Italy near the Tyrrhenian Sea. The famed Leaning Tower of Pisa is here.

Pi·sces (pī′sēz) *n.* **1.** A constellation in the equatorial region of the Northern Hemisphere, traditionally pictured as a pair of fish. **2.** The 12th sign of the zodiac in astrology.

pis·ta·chi·o (pĭ-stăsh′ē-ō′) *n., pl.* **pis·ta·chi·os 1.** The small hard-shelled nut of a tree of the Mediterranean region and western Asia, having a sweet green kernel. **2.** The tree that bears such nuts. [Ultimately from Greek *pistakion*, of Iranian origin.]

pis·til (pĭs′təl) *n.* The female reproductive organ of a flower, including the ovary, style, and stigma.

❑ *These sound alike:* **pistil, pistol** (gun).

pis·tol (pĭs′təl) *n.* A small gun designed to be held and fired with one hand.

❑ *These sound alike:* **pistol, pistil** (flower organ).

pis·ton (pĭs′tən) *n.* **1.** A solid cylinder or disk that fits snugly into a hollow cylinder and moves back and forth under the pressure of a fluid, as in many engines, or moves or compresses a fluid, as in a pump or compressor. **2.** A valve mechanism in brass instruments for changing pitch.

piston ring *n.* An adjustable metal ring that fits around a piston and closes the gap between the piston and cylinder wall.

piston rod *n.* A connecting rod that transmits power to or is powered by a piston.

pit¹ (pĭt) *n.* **1.** A natural or artificial hole or cavity in the ground. **2a.** A natural depression in the surface of a body, organ, or part: *the pit of the stomach.* **b.** A small depression in the skin left by a disease or injury; a pockmark. **3.** A concealed hole in the ground used as a trap; a pitfall. **4.** Hell. Used with *the.* **5.** The area directly in front of the stage of a theater in which the musicians sit. **6a.** A sunken area in a garage where mechanics work underneath automobiles. **b.** often **pits** The area beside an automobile racecourse where cars may be fueled and serviced during a race. **7.** An enclosed space in which animals are kept or are set to fight: *a snake pit.* ❖ *v.* **pit·ted, pit·ting, pits** —*tr.* **1.** To mark with cavities, depressions, or scars: *The moon appears to have been pitted by meteoroid impacts.* **2.** To set in competition; match: *a tournament that pits one school against another.* **3.** To place, bury, or store in a pit. —*intr.* To become marked

ă	pat	ôr	core
ā	pay	oi	boy
âr	care	ou	out
ä	father	o͝o	took
ĕ	pet	o͝or	lure
ē	be	o͞o	boot
ĭ	pit	ŭ	cut
ī	bite	ûr	urge
îr	pier	th	thin
ŏ	pot	*th*	this
ō	toe	zh	vision
ô	paw	ə	about

with pits. [From Middle English, from Old English *pytt*, from Latin *puteus*, well.]

pit² (pĭt) *n.* The single hard-shelled seed of certain fruits, such as a peach or cherry; a stone. ❖ *tr.v.* **pit·ted, pit·ting, pits** To remove the pit or pits from: *We pitted the olives for the salad.* [From Dutch.]

pi·ta (pē′tə) *n.* A round flat bread that can be opened to form a pocket for filling: *stuffed the pita with chicken salad.* [From Modern Greek.]

pit·a·pat (pĭt′ə-păt′) *intr.v.* **pit·a·pat·ted, pit·a·pat·ting, pit·a·pats 1.** To move with a series of quick tapping steps. **2.** To make a repeated tapping sound.

pitch¹ (pĭch) *n.* **1.** Any of various sticky dark thick substances obtained from coal tar, wood tar, or petroleum and used for roofing, waterproofing, and paving. **2.** Any of various natural bitumens, such as asphalt, having similar uses. **3.** A resin that is derived from the sap of a pine tree or a similar tree that bears cones. ❖ *tr.v.* **pitched, pitch·ing, pitch·es** To cover with pitch. [From Middle English *pitch*, from Old English *pic*, from Latin *pix*.]

pitch² (pĭch) *v.* **pitched, pitch·ing, pitch·es** —*tr.* **1.** To throw, usually with careful aim: *pitching horseshoes.* See Synonyms at **throw. 2.** To discard by throwing: *pitched my worn-out shoes.* **3.** In baseball: **a.** To throw (the ball) from the mound to the batter. **b.** To play (a game or part of it) as pitcher: *pitched the final game of the World Series.* **4.** To set up or establish: *pitch a tent; pitch camp.* **5.** To set at a given level or degree: *He pitched his hopes too high.* **6.** To set the musical pitch or key of: *Pitch your voice so that it harmonizes with mine.* **7.** To set at a specified downward slant: *pitched the roof at a steep angle.* —*intr.* **1.** To toss or throw something, such as a baseball or horseshoe. **2.** In baseball, to play in the position of pitcher. **3.** To plunge headlong: *He pitched over the railing.* **4.** To slope downward: *The hill pitches steeply.* **5.** To move so that the front end lifts or falls in relation to the stern or tail: *Heavy storms made the ship pitch and roll. The airplane pitched as it fought the headwind.* ❖ *n.* **1.** The act or an instance of pitching: *My pitch missed the wastebasket by a mile. The pitch of the boat made the passengers sick.* **2.** In baseball: **a.** A throw of the ball by a pitcher to a batter: *On the next pitch, the batter struck out.* **b.** A ball so thrown: *hit the pitch into left field.* **3.** A degree or level of intensity: *The dispute reached a feverish pitch.* **4.** A steep slope, as of a roof. **5.** The alternating lift and fall of the bow and stern of a ship or the nose and tail of an aircraft or spacecraft. **6a.** The quality of a sound by which it can be judged high or low, determined mostly by the frequency of the sound. **b.** The relative position of a tone in a musical scale, as determined by this quality. **c.** Any of several standards that establish the frequency of each musical tone. **7.** The distance between corresponding points on adjoining screw threads or gear teeth. **8.** The forward distance a propeller would travel in one complete revolution through an ideal medium. **9.** *Informal* A line of talk designed to persuade: *a sales pitch.* ◆ **pitch in** *Informal* **1.** To set to work vigorously. **2.** To join forces with others; help or cooperate. [From Middle English *pichen*.]

pitch-black (pĭch′blăk′) *adj.* Extremely dark; black as pitch.

pitch·blende (pĭch′blĕnd′) *n.* A black, often crusty mineral that is a principal ore of uranium.

pitch-dark (pĭch′därk′) *adj.* Extremely dark.

pitched battle (pĭcht) *n.* A fierce concentrated battle fought by opponents in close contact.

pitched roof *n.* A two-sided, sloped roof having a gable at both ends.

pitch·er¹ (pĭch′ər) *n.* **1.** A person or thing that pitches. **2.** The baseball player who pitches the ball from the mound to the batter.

pitch·er² (pĭch′ər) *n.* A container for liquids, usually having a handle and a lip or spout for pouring. [From Middle English *picher*, from Old French *pichier*, from Medieval Latin *bicārium*, drinking vessel.]

pitcher plant *n.* Any of various plants having hollow fluid-filled leaves that trap insects from which nutrients are absorbed.

pitch·fork (pĭch′fôrk′) *n.* A large fork with sharp, widely spaced prongs, used to lift and pitch hay.

pitch·out (pĭch′out′) *n.* In baseball, a pitch thrown high and away from the batter to make it easier for the catcher to throw out a base runner.

pitch pipe *n.* A small pipe that, when sounded, gives the starting pitch for a piece of music or the standard pitch for tuning an instrument.

pit·e·ous (pĭt′ē-əs) *adj.* Demanding or arousing pity. —**pit′e·ous·ly** *adv.* —**pit′e·ous·ness** *n.*

pit·fall (pĭt′fôl′) *n.* **1.** A hidden danger or unexpected difficulty: *Life is full of pitfalls.* **2.** A concealed hole in the ground for trapping animals.

pith (pĭth) *n.* **1.** The soft, spongy tissue in the center of the stems of most vascular plants. **2.** The central or essential part; the heart or essence: *the pith of her argument.*

Pith·e·can·thro·pus (pĭth′ĭ-**kăn′**thrə-pəs *or* pĭth′ĭ-kăn-**thrō′**pəs) *n.* An extinct type of human known from fossil remains found in Java, considered to belong to the species *Homo erectus.*

pith helmet *n.* A lightweight sun hat made of dried pith.

pith·y (pĭth′ē) *adj.* **pith·i·er, pith·i·est 1.** Precisely meaningful; forceful and brief: *a pithy sentence.* **2.** Full of or resembling pith: *the pithy stem of a plant.* —**pith′i·ly** *adv.* —**pith′i·ness** *n.*

pit·i·a·ble (pĭt′ē-ə-bəl) *adj.* Arousing or deserving of pity; lamentable. —**pit′i·a·bly** *adv.*

pit·i·ful (pĭt′ĭ-fəl) *adj.* **1.** Inspiring or deserving pity: *The hungry puppy was a pitiful sight.* **2.** Arousing contemptuous pity, as through ineptitude or inadequacy: *a pitiful excuse.* —**pit′i·ful·ly** *adv.* —**pit′i·ful·ness** *n.*

pit·i·less (pĭt′ĭ-lĭs) *adj.* Having no pity; merciless. —**pit′i·less·ly** *adv.* —**pit′i·less·ness** *n.*

pi·ton (pē′tŏn′) *n.* A metal spike with a loop at one end for securing a rope in mountain climbing. The pointed end is driven into rock or ice to gain support.

pit stop *n.* **1.** A stop at a pit in an automobile race for fuel or service. **2.** *Informal* A brief stop for rest, food, or fuel on a trip.

Pitt¹ (pĭt), **William** Known as "Pitt the Elder." 1708–1778. British politician who directed his country's military effort during the Seven Years' War (1756–1763).

Pitt² (pĭt), **William** Known as "Pitt the Younger." 1759–1806. British prime minister (1783–1801 and 1804–1806). He accomplished the Act of Union between Ireland and Britain (1800).

pit·tance (pĭt′ns) *n.* **1.** A meager monetary allowance or wage. **2.** A very small amount: *a pittance of bread.*

pit·ted (pĭt′ĭd) *adj.* **1.** Marked by pits; having pits in the surface: *the pitted surface of the moon.* **2.** Having the pit removed: *pitted olives.*

pit·ter-pat·ter (pĭt′ər-păt′ər) *n.* A rapid series of light tapping sounds: *the pitter-patter of little feet.*

Pitts·burgh (pĭts′bûrg′) A city of southwest Pennsylvania at the head of the Ohio River. The city grew around a fort built by the French in about 1750.

pi·tu·i·tar·y (pĭ-to͞o′ĭ-tĕr′ē) *n., pl.* **pi·tu·i·tar·ies** The pituitary gland.

pituitary gland *n.* An endocrine gland at the base of the brain in vertebrates that regulates the function of most of the body's other endocrine glands and that controls overall body growth.

pit viper *n.* Any of various venomous snakes, such as the rattlesnake or the copperhead, having a small pit

piranha

pistachio

pita

pitched roof
Alamo Square, San Francisco, California

pith helmet

SCIENCE

pixel If you look at a panel in a comic book very closely, you will see that colored or shaded areas are often made of very tiny dots. Images on computer screens are also composed of very tiny dots known as **pixels.** (*Pixel* is a shortening of *picture element.*) Each color on a computer screen is made of an arrangement of red, blue, and green pixels that adjust in intensity. Most monitors have hundreds of thousands or millions of pixels. Each pixel is lit or dimmed individually in order to create an image. Screens with the smallest pixels have the sharpest images, but they require more computer memory to store data about the color and intensity of each pixel.

Francisco Pizarro

place kick

ă	pat	ôr	core
ā	pay	oi	boy
âr	care	ou	out
ä	father	o͝o	took
ĕ	pet	o͝or	lure
ē	be	o͞o	boot
ĭ	pit	ŭ	cut
ī	bite	ûr	urge
îr	pier	th	thin
ŏ	pot	*th*	this
ō	toe	zh	vision
ô	paw	ə	about

or indentation on each side of the head that is used to sense heat.

pit·y (pĭt′ē) *n., pl.* **pit·ies 1.** Sympathy and sorrow aroused by the misfortune or suffering of another. **2.** A matter of regret: *It's a pity you can't go.* ❖ *tr.v.* **pit·ied, pit·y·ing, pit·ies** To feel pity for (someone). ◆ **have pity on** or **take pity on** To show compassion for. [From Middle English *pite,* from Old French, from Latin *pietās,* piety, compassion.] —SEE NOTE AT **piety.**

piv·ot (pĭv′ət) *n.* **1.** A short rod or shaft on which a related part rotates or swings. **2.** A person or thing on which something depends or turns; the central or crucial factor. **3.** The act or an instance of turning on or as if on a pivot. ❖ *v.* **piv·ot·ed, piv·ot·ing, piv·ots** —*tr.* **1.** To provide with a pivot or pivots. **2.** To cause to rotate, revolve, or turn. —*intr.* To turn on or as if on a pivot: *The movie pivots on the detective's refusal to believe a witness.*

piv·ot·al (pĭv′ə-tl) *adj.* **1.** Relating to or used as a pivot. **2.** Of vital or central importance: *pivotal decisions.* —**piv′ot·al·ly** *adv.*

pix·el (pĭk′səl) *n.* The most basic unit of a digital image, representing a single color or level of brightness. Pixels are arranged in rows and columns in a specific pattern to create an image. [From *picture element.*] —SEE NOTE.

pix·ie or **pix·y** (pĭk′sē) *n., pl.* **pix·ies** A creature similar to a fairy or elf, especially a mischievous playful one.

Pi·zar·ro (pĭ-zär′ō), **Francisco** 1475?–1541. Spanish explorer who conquered the Inca Empire of Peru (1531–1533).

piz·za (pēt′sə) *n.* A baked dish of Italian origin consisting of a shallow breadlike crust covered with toppings such as seasoned tomato sauce, cheese, or meat.

piz·zazz or **piz·zaz** (pĭ-zăz′) *n. Slang* Dazzling style; flamboyance; flair.

piz·ze·ri·a (pēt′sə-rē′ə) *n.* A place where pizzas are made and sold.

piz·zi·ca·to (pĭt′sĭ-kä′tō) *adj.* Played by plucking rather than bowing the strings of an instrument.

PJs or **PJ's** (pē′jāz′) *pl.n. Informal* Pajamas.

pk. *abbr.* An abbreviation of peak.

pkg. *abbr.* An abbreviation of package.

pl. *abbr.* An abbreviation of plural.

plac·ard (plăk′ärd′ *or* plăk′ərd) *n.* A sign or notice for public display. ❖ *tr.v.* **plac·ard·ed, plac·ard·ing, plac·ards** To post placards on, in, or throughout: *placard a wall.*

pla·cate (plā′kāt′ *or* plăk′āt′) *tr.v.* **pla·cat·ed, pla·cat·ing, pla·cates** To calm the anger of, especially by making concessions; appease: *placated the child with a cookie.* —**pla′cat′er** *n.* —**pla·ca′tion** (plā-kā′shən) *n.*

place (plās) *n.* **1a.** A particular area or spot with definite or indefinite boundaries. **b.** Room or space, especially adequate space: *There's place for you at the back of the room.* **2.** A city or other locality: *What place were you born in?* **3.** A dwelling; a house: *Come over to my place for supper.* **4.** A public square or a short city street: *She lives on Butler Place.* **5.** A building or area set aside for a definite purpose: *a place of worship.* **6a.** A space occupied by or allocated for a person: *two empty places near the back of the theater.* **b.** A table setting for one person: *Set an extra place for supper.* **7.** Position or rank: *My jam won first place at the fair.* **8.** The position of a person or thing as occupied by a substitute; stead: *I'm going in his place.* **9.** A particular situation or circumstance: *If you were in my place, you'd act differently.* **10.** An appropriate duty, right, or social position: *It's not my place to tell you what to do.* **11.** A job or position: *She found a place with an accounting firm.* **12.** Proper or usual position, order, context, or time: *She felt out of place in the kitchen.* **13.** A particular point that one has reached, as in a book: *mark one's place with a bookmark.* **14.** The position of a digit in relation to the other digits of a numeral. For example, in the number 1.8, the 8 is in the tenths place. ❖ *v.* **placed, plac·ing, plac·es** —*tr.* **1a.** To put in a particular spot or position; set: *place cups and saucers on the table.* **b.** To put in a particular order: *place words in alphabetical order.* **2.** To find accommodation or employment for. **3.** To rank in an order or sequence. **4.** To remember where or how (someone or something) was first encountered: *His face looks familiar, but I can't place him.* **5.** To put; let reside: *place one's trust in the government.* **6.** To apply or arrange for: *placed an order for a dozen new textbooks.* —*intr.* To arrive among the first three finishers in a race, especially to finish second. ◆ **all over the place** In or to many locations; everywhere: *Batteries are sold all over the place.* **in place 1.** In the appropriate or usual position or order: *Make sure everything is in place before we start.* **2.** In the same spot; without moving forwards or backwards: *We ran in place for ten minutes.* **in place of** Instead of. —**place′a·ble** *adj.*

❑ *These sound alike:* **place, plaice** (fish).

pla·ce·bo (plə-sē′bō) *n., pl.* **pla·ce·bos** or **pla·ce·boes 1.** A substance that has positive effects as a result of a patient's belief that it is helpful rather than as a result of a medicinal ingredient. **2.** A preparation containing no medicine, used as the control in an experiment to test the effectiveness of a drug.

place·hold·er (plās′hōl′dər) *n.* **1.** A person who holds an office or place, especially as a deputy, proxy, or appointed government official. **2.** A digit that has no value in a decimal number. **3.** A symbol that may be replaced by the name of any element in a set in a mathematical expression.

place kick *n.* In football, a kick made while the ball is held or propped up on the ground. —**place′-kick′** (plās′kĭk′) *v.*

place mat or **place·mat** (plās′măt′) *n.* A protective table mat for a single setting of dishes and flatware at meals.

place·ment (plās′mənt) *n.* **1a.** The act of placing or arranging. **b.** The state of being placed or arranged. **2.** The finding of suitable accommodation or employment for applicants.

pla·cen·ta (plə-sĕn′tə) *n., pl.* **pla·cen·tas** or **pla·cen·tae** (plə-sĕn′tē) **1.** A spongy organ that forms in the uterus of most female mammals during pregnancy and supplies oxygen and nutrients to the developing embryo or fetus through the umbilical cord. It is expelled after birth. **2.** A similar organ in some other animals, such as certain sharks and reptiles.

pla·cen·tal (plə-sĕn′tl) *adj.* **1.** Relating to the placenta. **2.** Having a placenta: *placental mammals.*

placental mammal *n.* Any of a large group of mammals in which the female bears live young that are nourished before birth by means of a placenta. All mammals except the marsupials and the monotremes are placental mammals.

plac·er (plăs′ər) *n.* A gravel or sand deposit left by a river, containing particles of valuable minerals.

place setting *n.* A set of dishes and cutlery for one person for one meal.

plac·id (plăs′ĭd) *adj.* **1.** Calm; peaceful: *the placid surface of the rural lake.* See Synonyms at **calm. 2.** Easily satisfied; complacent: *a person with a placid disposition.* —**plac′id·ly** *adv.* —**pla·cid′i·ty** (plə-sĭd′ĭ-tē), **plac′id·ness** *n.*

plack·et (plăk′ĭt) *n.* A slit in a dress, blouse, or skirt.

pla·gia·rism (plā′jə-rĭz′əm) *n.* **1.** The act of plagiarizing: *The producers of the show were guilty of plagiarism.* **2.** Something plagiarized: *His poem was a plagiarism from a magazine.* —**pla′gia·rist** *n.*

pla·gia·rize (plā′jə-rīz′) *tr.v.* **pla·gia·rized, pla·gia·riz·ing, pla·gia·riz·es 1.** To use and pass off (the ideas or writings of another) as one's own: *She plagiarized three paragraphs from a newspaper.* **2.** To make use of the passages or ideas from (another) as if they were one's own: *He plagiarized an obscure author from the 1920s.*

pla·gi·o·clase (plā′jē-ə-klās′) *n.* Any of several kinds of usually whitish feldspar found in igneous rock and consisting of aluminum silicate combined with either sodium or calcium. Plagioclase often has hairlike grooves along its crystal faces.

plague (plāg) *n.* **1.** A highly contagious, usually fatal epidemic disease, especially bubonic plague. **2.** A widespread calamity or affliction, especially one regarded as a punishment from God. **3.** A cause of annoyance; a nuisance: *The defective printer was a plague to the people working in the office.* ❖ *tr.v.* **plagued, plagu·ing, plagues 1.** To annoy; pester; harass: *Stop plaguing me with your complaints.* **2.** To cause misery or trouble in or for: *Sleeping sickness has plagued Africa for years.* [From Middle English *plage*, affliction, disease, from Latin *plāga*, blow, wound.]

plaice (plās) *n., pl.* **plaice** or **plaic·es** Any of various large flatfishes found mainly in the North Atlantic Ocean, related to the flounders and used as food. [From Middle English *plais*, from Old French, from Late Latin *platessa*, probably from Greek *platus*, broad.]

❑ *These sound alike:* **plaice, place** (area).

plaid (plăd) *n.* **1a.** Cloth with a tartan or checked pattern. **b.** A pattern of this kind. **2.** A woolen scarf of a tartan pattern worn over the left shoulder by Scottish Highlanders.

plain (plān) *adj.* **plain·er, plain·est 1.** Obvious to the mind; perfectly clear: *His meaning was quite plain.* **2.** Not elaborate or complicated; simple: *plain food.* **3.** Marked by little or no ornamentation or decoration: *a plain dress.* **4.** Open to view; clear; distinct: *The cows are in plain sight in the middle of the field.* **5.** Frank; candid; down-to-earth: *plain talk.* **6.** Lacking beauty or distinction: *a plain face.* **7.** Not pretentious; unaffected. **8.** Pure; unadulterated; natural: *plain water instead of soda water.* ❖ *n.* A large, flat, mostly treeless area of land. ❖ *adv. Informal* Clearly; simply: *plain stubborn.* [From Middle English, from Old French, from Latin *plānus*, flat, obvious.] —**plain′ly** *adv.* —**plain′ness** *n.*

❑ *These sound alike:* **plain, plane¹** (surface), **plane²** (tool).

plain·chant (plān′chănt′) *n.* A form of early unaccompanied church music; plainsong.

Plains Indian (plānz) *n.* A member of any of the Native American peoples inhabiting the Great Plains of the United States and Canada.

plains·man (plānz′mən) *n.* An inhabitant or settler of the plains, especially of the prairie regions of the United States.

plain·song (plān′sông′) *n.* **1.** Gregorian chant. **2.** A form of medieval church music that does not have a strict rhythm and is traditionally sung without accompaniment.

plain·spo·ken (plān′spō′kən) *adj.* Frank; straightforward: *a plainspoken critic.*

plaint (plānt) *n.* A complaint.

plain·tiff (plān′tĭf) *n.* The party that institutes a suit in a court of law.

plain·tive (plān′tĭv) *adj.* Expressing sorrow; mournful: *a plaintive song.* —**plain′tive·ly** *adv.*

plait (plāt *or* plăt) *n.* A braid, especially of hair. ❖ *tr.v.* **plait·ed, plait·ing, plaits 1.** To braid: *She plaited her hair.* **2.** To make by braiding: *plait straw hats.*

❑ *These sound alike:* **plait, plate** (dish).

plan (plăn) *n.* **1.** A scheme, program, or method thought out ahead of time for the accomplishment of a goal: *a plan for reorganizing the town government.* **2.** A drawing or diagram showing how to build or assemble something: *plans for a new house.* **3.** A program or policy stipulating a service or benefit: *a pension plan.* ❖ *tr.v.* **planned, plan·ning, plans 1.** To think out a scheme or program for accomplishing or attaining (something): *plan one's trip.* **2.** To have in mind; intend: *She plans to go to Canada this summer.* **3.** To design (something to be built or made): *plan a new elementary school.* —**plan′ner** *n.*

pla·nar·i·an (plə-nâr′ē-ən) *n.* Any of various small chiefly freshwater flatworms having a broad body.

plane¹ (plān) *n.* **1.** In geometry, a surface that contains all the straight lines required to connect any two points on it. **2.** A flat or level surface. **3.** A level of existence, development, or achievement: *a high moral plane.* **4.** An airplane or hydroplane. ❖ *adj.* Lying in a plane: *a plane curve.* [From Latin *plānum*, flat surface, from *plānus*, flat.]

❑ *These sound alike:* **plane¹** (surface), **plain** (clear), **plane²** (tool).

plane² (plān) *n.* A carpenter's tool with an adjustable blade for smoothing and leveling wood. ❖ *tr.v.* **planed, plan·ing, planes** To smooth or finish with a plane. [From Middle English, from Late Latin *plāna*, from *plānāre*, to plane, from Latin *plānus*, flat.]

❑ *These sound alike:* **plane²** (tool), **plain** (clear), **plane¹** (surface).

plane geometry *n.* The geometry of plane figures.

plan·er (plā′nər) *n.* A person or thing that planes, especially a machine tool used to smooth or finish the surface of wood or metal.

plan·et (plăn′ĭt) *n.* A large, nearly spherical celestial object that orbits a star, has cleared its orbit of dust and debris, does not produce its own light, and is not a satellite of another planet. [From Middle English, from Old French *planete*, from Latin *planēta*, from Greek *planētēs*, from *planāsthai*, to wander (since the planets seem to wander among the stars).] —SEE NOTE.

plan·e·tar·i·um (plăn′ĭ-târ′ē-əm) *n.* **1.** A device that projects images of celestial objects in their courses onto the ceiling of a dome. **2.** A building or room in which such a device is housed or operated.

plan·e·tar·y (plăn′ĭ-tĕr′ē) *adj.* **1.** Relating to or resembling a planet. **2.** Relating to or affecting the entire world; global: *Pollution is a planetary concern.*

plan·e·toid (plăn′ĭ-toid′) *n.* An asteroid.

plane tree *n.* Any of several trees, such as the sycamore, having ball-shaped fruit clusters and bark that flakes off in patches.

plank (plăngk) *n.* **1.** A piece of lumber cut thicker than a board. **2.** One of the principles of a political platform. **3.** A foundation; a support. ❖ *tr.v.* **planked, plank·ing, planks 1.** To furnish or cover with planks: *plank a boat.* **2.** To bake or broil and serve (fish or meat) on a board: *plank a steak.*

plank·ton (plăngk′tən) *n.* The collection of very small organisms that drift or swim weakly in great numbers in bodies of salt water or fresh water.

plant (plănt) *n.* **1a.** Any of a kingdom of organisms that manufacture their own food by photosynthesis, have cells with walls made of cellulose, and are unable to move under their own power. **b.** Any of various fungi, algae, or protists that resemble plants and were formerly classified in the plant kingdom. Scientists no longer call these organisms plants. **2a.** A factory or similar place where something is produced or processed. **b.** The buildings and equipment of an institution: *the hospital's physical plant.* **3.** A person or thing put into place to mislead or work secretly, especially a person stationed as a spy or a misleading piece of evidence. ❖ *tr.v.* **plant·ed, plant·ing, plants 1a.** To place (seeds, for example) in the ground to grow. **b.** To place seeds or young plants in (land); sow: *plant a field with corn.* **2.** To fix or set firmly: *plant one's feet on the ground.* **3.** To start; establish: *plant new colonies.* **4.** To fix firmly in the mind; implant. **5a.**

SCIENCE

planet In 1930, the astronomer Clyde Tombaugh discovered Pluto, and Pluto was classified as our solar system's ninth planet. In 2006, the International Astronomical Union (IAU) voted to change the definition of **planet.** They stated that in order for an object in space to be called a planet, it must have enough mass to form a round shape and "clear the neighborhood around its orbit." This means that a planet cannot have other objects that are in its orbit or that cross its orbit, except for smaller objects that the planet's gravity has captured, such as moons that revolve around it. Because Neptune's large mass has captured Pluto so that the two planets remain in orbits that cross, Pluto has not cleared its own orbit and was therefore deemed not to be a planet. To describe objects like Pluto, they created a new category, the *dwarf planet.* Like a planet, a dwarf planet orbits the sun, is large enough to form a nearly round shape, and does not orbit a planet (as our moon does). But a dwarf planet does not clear the neighborhood around its orbit and may cross the paths of other objects orbiting the sun. Other dwarf planets include Ceres, whose orbit is in the asteroid belt between Mars and Jupiter, and Eris, an object in the Kuiper belt beyond Pluto.

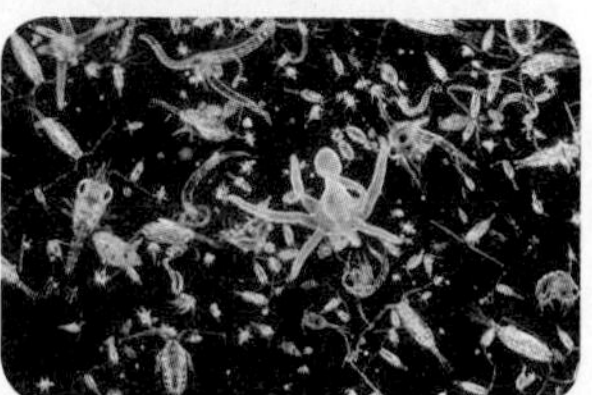
plankton

SCIENCE

plate tectonics If you look at a map of the world, you can see that the earth's continents seem to fit together like pieces of a puzzle. Geologists have also long known that rocks and fossils match up in parts of different continents. In 1915, these observations led the German meteorologist Alfred Wegener to propose the theory of *continental drift:* the continents must have been joined together in the past and then drifted apart. But no one could explain how such large landmasses could move until the 1960s, when the theory of **plate tectonics** was developed. According to this theory, continents move apart by riding piggyback on plates—huge slabs of the earth's crust and upper mantle. The movements of these plates are powered by convection currents of molten rock deep within the earth. Although the plates move only a few inches per year, over millions of years the continents are carried thousands of miles. Along their boundaries, the plates crumple, scrape, or pull apart from one another, generating volcanoes and earthquakes and creating and destroying rock on the ever-changing surface of the planet.

ă	pat	ôr	core
ā	pay	oi	boy
âr	care	ou	out
ä	father	o͝o	took
ĕ	pet	o͝or	lure
ē	be	o͞o	boot
ĭ	pit	ŭ	cut
ī	bite	ûr	urge
îr	pier	th	thin
ŏ	pot	*th*	this
ō	toe	zh	vision
ô	paw	ə	about

To place or assign (a person) so that something, such as spying, can be done in secret: *planted spies in the organization.* **b.** To place (something) so as to be found later and made known: *planted the evidence in his opponent's apartment.* [From Middle English, from Old English, from Latin *planta*, young plant, shoot.]

plan·tain¹ (plăn′tən) *n.* Any of various weedy plants having large leaves and a dense narrow cluster of small green or whitish flowers. [From Middle English *plantain*, from Old French, from Latin *plantāgō*, from *planta*, sole of the foot (from its broad leaves).]

plan·tain² (plăn′tən) *n.* **1.** A fruit that resembles a banana but has flesh that is starchier and less sweet. **2.** Any of various tropical plants that bear such fruit. [From obsolete Spanish *plántano*, variant of Spanish *plátano*, plane tree, later also plantain, banana (since both plane trees and banana plants have broad leaves), from Latin *platanus*, plane tree.]

plan·ta·tion (plăn-tā′shən) *n.* **1.** A large farm or estate on which crops are raised, often by resident workers. **2.** A group of cultivated trees or other plants or the area where they are growing.

plant·er (plăn′tər) *n.* **1.** A person or thing that plants, especially a tool or machine for planting seeds. **2.** The owner or manager of a plantation. **3.** A decorative container for a plant.

plaque (plăk) *n.* **1.** An ornamented or engraved plate, slab, or disk, used for decoration or to carry an inscription on a monument. **2.** A film of mucus and bacteria that forms on the surface of the teeth. **3.** A deposit of fatty material on the inner lining of an arterial wall, seen in atherosclerosis.

plash (plăsh) *n.* A light splash. ❖ *intr.v.* **plashed, plash·ing, plash·es** To cause a light splash.

plas·ma (plăz′mə) *n.* **1.** Blood plasma. **2.** An electrically neutral phase of matter usually formed at very high temperatures, resembling a gas but consisting of a mixture of ions, electrons, and neutral particles.

plas·mo·di·um (plăz-mō′dē-əm) *n., pl.* **plas·mo·di·a** (plăz-mō′dē-ə) A protozoan that exists as a parasite in vertebrates, especially one that causes malaria.

plas·ter (plăs′tər) *n.* **1.** A mixture of sand, lime or gypsum, and water, sometimes with fiber added, that hardens to a smooth solid and is used for covering walls and ceilings. **2.** Plaster of Paris. **3.** A pasty mixture applied to a part of the body, either as a remedy or as a cosmetic. ❖ *tr.v.* **plas·tered, plas·ter·ing, plas·ters 1.** To cover with plaster: *plaster cracks in the ceiling.* **2.** To cover as if with plaster: *The students plastered the campus with posters.* **3.** To make adhere to another surface: *plastered posters on the wall.* —**plas′ter·er** *n.*

plas·ter·board (plăs′tər-bôrd′) *n.* Drywall.

plaster of Paris *n.* Any of a group of cements made by heating gypsum to drive off part of its water of crystallization, forming, when mixed with water, a paste that hardens into a solid.

plas·tic (plăs′tĭk) *n.* Any of various synthetic materials that are made of organic polymers and can be molded, cast into various shapes, formed into sheets or films, or drawn into filaments for use as textile fibers. ❖ *adj.* **1.** Capable of being shaped or formed: *Clay is a plastic material.* **2.** Relating to shaping or modeling: *the plastic art of sculpture.* **3.** Giving form or shape to something: *the plastic forces of nature.* **4.** Made of plastic: *a plastic cup.* [From Greek *plastikos*, able to be molded, from *plassein*, to mold.] —**plas·tic′i·ty** (plă-stĭs′ĭ-tē) *n.*

plastic surgery *n.* Surgery to repair, restore, or remodel the appearance and sometimes the function of body parts.

plastic wrap *n.* Plastic that is formed into a thin, clear, flexible sheet and used as a wrapping to keep food from spoiling.

plas·tid (plăs′tĭd) *n.* Any of several structures, such as chloroplasts, that are found in the cells of plants and algae. Plastids have various functions, including the synthesis and storage of food.

Pla·ta (plä′tə), **Río de la** A wide estuary of southeast South America between Argentina and Uruguay opening on the Atlantic Ocean.

plate (plāt) *n.* **1.** A thin flat sheet or piece of metal or other material. **2.** A piece of flat metal on which something is engraved, as a name plate. **3.** A license plate. **4.** A print of a woodcut or lithograph, especially when reproduced in a book. **5.** A full-page book illustration, often in color and printed on special paper. **6.** A sheet of light-sensitive glass or metal upon which a photographic image can be recorded. **7.** A piece of metal or plastic fitted to the gums to hold false teeth in place. **8.** In baseball, home plate. **9a.** A shallow usually circular dish from which food is eaten. **b.** The contents of such a dish: *Finish your plate.* **10.** Food and service for one person at a meal: *supper at a dollar a plate.* **11.** Dishes and other household articles made of or plated with gold or silver. **12a.** An electrode, as in a storage battery or capacitor. **b.** The positive electrode of an electron tube. **13.** In plate tectonics, one of the sections of the earth's lithosphere that are constantly moving relative to one another. ❖ *tr.v.* **plat·ed, plat·ing, plates** To coat or cover with a thin layer of metal. [From Middle English, from Old French *plat*, flat, from Greek *platus*.]

❑ *These sound alike:* **plate, plait** (braid).

pla·teau (plă-tō′) *n., pl.* **pla·teaus** or **pla·teaux** (plă-tōz′) **1.** An elevated, comparatively level expanse of land. **2.** A relatively stable level or stage of growth or development: *The economy has reached a new plateau.* [From Old French *platel*, platter, from *plat*, flat.]

plate·ful (plāt′fo͝ol′) *n., pl.* **platefuls** The amount that a plate will hold.

plate glass *n.* A strong polished glass containing few defects, used for making large windows and mirrors.

plate·let (plāt′lĭt) *n.* Any of the numerous microscopic bodies, shaped like irregular disks and lacking nuclei, that are found in the blood of mammals and function in the clotting of blood.

plat·en (plăt′n) *n.* A roller or plate against which paper is held, as in a typewriter, printing press, or scanner.

plate tec·ton·ics (tĕk-tŏn′ĭks) *n.* In geology, a theory that the earth's crust is divided into a series of vast platelike sections that move relative to one another. —SEE NOTE.

plat·form (plăt′fôrm′) *n.* **1.** A floor or horizontal surface higher than an adjoining area: *a speakers' platform.* **2.** A means or opportunity for public expression: *a blog that serves as a platform for radical views.* **3.** A formal declaration of principles, as by a political party or candidate. **4.** The basic technology of a computer system's hardware and software. A platform defines how a computer is operated and determines what other kinds of software can be used.

Plath (plăth), **Sylvia** 1932–1963. American writer whose works include *Ariel* (1965), a collection of poems.

plat·ing (plā′tĭng) *n.* A thin layer or coating of metal, such as gold or silver, deposited on or applied to a surface.

plat·i·num (plăt′n-əm) *n. Symbol* **Pt** A soft, silver-white metallic element used as a catalyst and in making jewelry, electrical contacts, and dental crowns. Atomic number 78. See **Periodic Table.** [From New Latin, from obsolete Spanish *platina*, from *plata*, silver.]

plat·i·tude (plăt′ĭ-to͞od′) *n.* A trite or banal remark or statement, especially one expressed as if it were original or significant.

plat·i·tu·di·nous (plăt′ĭ-to͞od′n-əs) *adj.* **1.** Commonplace; trite: *a platitudinous remark.* **2.** Full of or inclined to use platitudes: *a platitudinous sermon.*

Pla·to (plā′tō) 427?–347? BC. Greek philosopher who presented his ideas in the form of dramatic dialogues, as in *Symposium* and *The Republic.*

Pla·ton·ic (plə-**tŏn′**ĭk) *adj.* **1.** Relating to Plato or his philosophy. **2. platonic** Friendly or affectionate without involving sexual feelings or sexual activity: *a platonic relationship.*

Pla·to·nism (**plāt′**n-ĭz′əm) *n.* The philosophy of Plato, which asserts that ideal forms are the only eternal reality and everything in the world is but a shadow or reflection of these forms.

pla·toon (plə-**to͞on′**) *n.* **1.** A unit of soldiers smaller than a company but larger than a squad, normally commanded by a lieutenant. **2.** A group of people working, traveling, or assembled together: *a platoon of firefighters.* **3.** In a football team, a group of players specially trained and sent into or withdrawn from a game as a unit.

Platte (plăt) A river, about 310 miles (500 kilometers) long, of central Nebraska formed by the confluence of the **North Platte** and **South Platte** Rivers and flowing eastward to the Missouri River.

plat·ter (**plăt′**ər) *n.* **1.** A large shallow dish or plate for serving food. **2.** A meal or course served on a platter. **3.** *Slang* A phonograph record.

plat·y·pus (**plăt′**ĭ-pəs) *n., pl.* **plat·y·pus·es** A furry egg-laying Australian mammal having webbed feet and a snout resembling a duck's bill, and living in or near water. [From Greek *platupous,* flat-footed : *platus,* flat + *pous,* foot.]

plau·dit (**plô′**dĭt) *n.* Enthusiastic expression of praise or approval: *the plaudits of the critics.*

plau·si·ble (**plô′**zə-bəl) *adj.* Believable: *a plausible excuse.* **—plau′si·bly** *adv.* **—plau′si·bil′i·ty** *n.* —SEE NOTE AT **explode.**

play (plā) *v.* **played, play·ing, plays** *—intr.* **1.** To have fun; amuse oneself: *The children went outdoors to play.* **2.** To take part in a game: *was eligible to play.* **3.** To act in jest or sport: *She looks angry, but she's just playing.* **4.** To act in a drama: *He played in last season's comedy.* **5.** To be presented for an audience: *What movie is playing tonight?* **6.** To conduct oneself in a particular way: *You're not playing fair.* **7.** To perform music: *play on a trumpet.* **8.** To be received or accepted in a certain way: *a speech that played poorly with the voters.* **9.** To move rapidly, lightly, or irregularly: *A breeze played over the lake.* *—tr.* **1a.** To engage in (a game or sport): *played tennis.* **b.** To compete against in a game or sport: *We play the Tigers tomorrow.* **c.** To occupy or work at (a position) in a game: *She plays first base.* **d.** To use or move (a card or a piece, for example) in a game or sport: *I'll play the nine of spades next.* **e.** To make (a shot or stroke), as in tennis: *played a strong backhand.* **f.** To attempt to keep or gain possession or control of: *No foul was called because he was playing the ball.* **2a.** To perform or act (a role or part) in a dramatic performance: *played Juliet on Broadway.* **b.** To assume the role of; act as: *played the peacemaker at the summit conference.* **3.** To pretend to be; mimic the activities of: *He was playing cowboy.* **4.** To bet; wager. **5.** To perform or put into effect, especially as a jest or deception: *play a joke.* **6a.** To perform on (an instrument): *play the fiddle.* **b.** To perform (a piece of music) on an instrument or instruments. **7.** To cause (a recording) to be presented in audible or visible form. **8.** To cause to move rapidly, lightly, or irregularly: *played the flashlight around the dark attic.* ❖ *n.* **1a.** A literary work written for performance on the stage. **b.** The performance of such a work: *We went to a play last night.* **2.** Activity engaged in for enjoyment or recreation: *Play is important for children and adults.* **3.** Fun or jesting. **4.** The act or manner of playing a game or sport. **5.** A manner of dealing with people: *He believes in fair play.* **6.** A move or action in a game: *It's your play.* **7.** Movement or freedom of movement: *the play of lights across a stage.* **8.** Action; use: *brought her influence into full play.* **9.** An attempt to obtain something; a bid: *a play for sympathy.* ◆ **in play** In a position to be legally played: *The ball is in play.* **out of play** Not in a position to be legally played. **play along** *Informal* To cooperate or pretend to cooperate. **play back** To replay (a recorded tape, for example). **play ball** *Slang* To cooperate. **play down** To minimize the importance of; make little of: *The economist played down the fall in stock prices.* **play on** or **play upon** To take advantage of (another's attitudes or feelings) for one's own interests: *He played on my sympathy when asking for a loan.* **play with fire** To take part in a dangerous or risky undertaking. **—play′a·ble** *adj.*

Sylvia Plath

pla·ya (**plī′**ə) *n.* An almost level area at the bottom of a desert basin, sometimes temporarily covered with water.

play·bill (**plā′**bĭl′) *n.* A poster announcing a theatrical performance.

play·boy (**plā′**boi′) *n.* A usually wealthy man who is devoted to the pursuit of leisure and romance.

play-by-play (**plā′**bī-**plā′**) *n.* A running account of the action of an event, especially a sports event, as it occurs. **—play′-by-play′** *adj.*

play·date (**plā′**dāt′) *n.* A scheduled time for a child to visit and play with another child.

play·er (**plā′**ər) *n.* **1.** A person who takes part in a game or sport. **2.** An actor. **3.** A person who plays a musical instrument. **4.** A machine that plays recorded audio or audiovisual material.

player piano *n.* A mechanical piano that uses a punched paper roll to control the keys.

play·ful (**plā′**fəl) *adj.* **1.** Full of fun and high spirits; frolicsome: *a playful cat.* **2.** Humorous; jesting: *a playful discussion.* **—play′ful·ly** *adv.* **—play′ful·ness** *n.*

play·girl (**plā′**gûrl′) *n.* A usually wealthy woman who is devoted to the pursuit of leisure and romance.

play·go·er (**plā′**gō′ər) *n.* A person who attends the theater.

play·ground (**plā′**ground′) *n.* An outdoor area for recreation and play, especially one having equipment such as seesaws and swings.

play·house (**plā′**hous′) *n.* **1.** A theater. **2.** A small house for children to play in. **3.** A child's toy house; a doll house.

play·ing card (**plā′**ĭng) *n.* A card marked with rank and suit and belonging to any of several decks used to play a wide variety of games.

play·mate (**plā′**māt′) *n.* A companion in play or recreation.

play·off (**plā′**ôf′) *n.* In sports, a game or series of games played to determine a championship or break a tie.

play·pen (**plā′**pĕn′) *n.* A portable enclosure in which a baby or a young child can be safely left to play.

play·room (**plā′**ro͞om′ *or* **plā′**ro͝om′) *n.* A room designed or set aside for play or recreation.

play·thing (**plā′**thĭng′) *n.* A thing to play with; a toy.

play·wright (**plā′**rīt′) *n.* A person who writes plays; a dramatist.

pla·za (**plä′**zə *or* **plăz′**ə) *n.* **1.** A public square or similar open area in a town or city. **2.** A shopping center. [From Spanish, from Latin *platea,* broad street.]

plea (plē) *n.* **1.** An appeal or urgent request; an entreaty: *a plea for help.* **2.** An excuse; a pretext. **3.** In law, a defendant's answer to a formal charge: *a plea of guilty.*

plea-bar·gain (**plē′**bär′gən) *intr.v.* **plea-bar·gained, plea-bar·gain·ing, plea-bar·gains** In law, to make an agreement in which a defendant pleads guilty to a charge and the prosecutor in return drops more serious charges or does not request the most severe sentence.

plead (plēd) *v.* **plead·ed** or **pled** (plĕd), **plead·ing, pleads** —*intr.* **1.** To appeal earnestly; beg: *They were pleading with him to return.* **2.** To put forward a plea in a court of law: *She pleaded guilty.* —*tr.* **1.** To put forward as a defense or excuse: *plead illness for being absent.* **2.** To argue (a case) in a court of law. [From Middle English *plaiden*, from Old French *plaidier*, from Medieval Latin *placitāre*, to appeal to the law, from Latin *placitum*, decree, opinion.] —**plead′er** *n.*

pleas·ant (plĕz′ənt) *adj.* **pleas·ant·er, pleas·ant·est 1.** Giving or affording pleasure or enjoyment; agreeable: *a pleasant climate; a pleasant aroma.* **2.** Pleasing in manner, behavior, or appearance: *a pleasant person; a pleasant disposition.* **3.** Fair and comfortable: *pleasant weather.* —**pleas′ant·ly** *adv.* —**pleas′ant·ness** *n.*

pleas·ant·ry (plĕz′ən-trē) *n., pl.* **pleas·ant·ries 1.** A humorous remark or act; a jest. **2.** A polite social remark; a civility.

pleat

please (plēz) *v.* **pleased, pleas·ing, pleas·es** —*tr.* **1.** To give (someone or something) pleasure or satisfaction: *The island pleased the sightseers.* **2.** To be the will or desire of: *May it please the court.* —*intr.* **1.** To give satisfaction or pleasure; be agreeable. **2.** To have the will or desire; wish: *do exactly as they please.* ❖ *adv.* If you are willing. Used in questions or imperative clauses to make polite requests: *Will you help me, please? Please help me.* [From Middle English *plesen*, from Old French *plaisir*, from Latin *placēre*.]

pleas·ing (plē′zĭng) *adj.* Giving pleasure or enjoyment; agreeable: *a pleasing scent.* —**pleas′ing·ly** *adv.*

pleas·ur·a·ble (plĕzh′ər-ə-bəl) *adj.* Agreeable; gratifying: *a pleasurable experience.* —**pleas′ur·a·bly** *adv.*

pleas·ure (plĕzh′ər) *n.* **1.** The state or feeling of being pleased or gratified: *She smiled with pleasure.* **2.** A source of enjoyment or delight: *Reading is his chief pleasure.* **3.** Amusement, diversion, or worldly enjoyment: *grew tired of living for pleasure.* **4.** One's preference or wish: *What is your pleasure?*

pleat (plēt) *n.* A flat fold in cloth made by doubling the material on itself and pressing or sewing it in place. ❖ *tr.v.* **pleat·ed, pleat·ing, pleats** To form pleats in; arrange in pleats: *pleat a ruffle.*

plebe (plēb) *n.* A first-year student at the US Military Academy or the US Naval Academy.

pliers

ple·be·ian (plĭ-bē′ən) *n.* **1.** One of the common people of ancient Rome. **2.** A person who is considered coarse or vulgar. —**ple·be′ian** *adj.*

pleb·i·scite (plĕb′ĭ-sīt′) *n.* A direct vote in which an entire people is allowed to approve or reject a proposal: *She was elected president by plebiscite.*

plec·trum (plĕk′trəm) *n., pl.* **plec·trums** or **plec·tra** (plĕk′trə) A small thin piece of metal, plastic, bone, or similar material, used to pluck the strings of a musical instrument such as the guitar or lute.

pled (plĕd) *v.* A past tense and a past participle of **plead.**

pledge (plĕj) *n.* **1.** A formal vow; a solemn promise: *made a pledge to do their duty.* **2a.** Something considered as security to guarantee payment of a debt or obligation: *a necklace left as a pledge for a loan.* **b.** The condition of something considered as such security: *Her jewels were left in pledge.* **3.** A token or sign: *They exchanged rings as a pledge of devotion.* **4.** Someone who has been accepted for membership in a fraternity or similar organization but has not yet been initiated. ❖ *tr.v.* **pledged, pledg·ing, pledg·es 1.** To guarantee by a solemn promise or vow: *pledged their support.* See Synonyms at **vow. 2.** To bind by a solemn promise or vow: *They pledged themselves to secrecy.* **3.** To deposit as security; pawn: *He pledged his watch for a loan.* **4a.** To promise to join (a fraternity or similar organization). **b.** To accept as a member of such an organization.

Pleis·to·cene (plī′stə-sēn′) *n.* The earlier of the two epochs of the Quaternary Period, from about 2.6 million to 12,000 years ago. During the Pleistocene, widespread glaciers formed in the Northern Hemisphere and humans first appeared. See table at **geologic time.** [From Greek *pleistos*, most + *kainos*, recent.] —**Pleis′to·cene′** *adj.*

ple·na (plē′nə *or* plĕn′ə) *n.* A plural of **plenum.**

ple·na·ry (plē′nə-rē *or* plĕn′ə-rē) *adj.* **1.** Complete in all aspects; full; absolute: *plenary powers.* **2.** Fully attended by all qualified members: *a plenary meeting of the council.*

plen·i·po·ten·ti·ar·y (plĕn′ə-pə-tĕn′shē-ĕr′ē *or* plĕn′ə-pə-tĕn′shə-rē) *adj.* Invested with full powers. ❖ *n., pl.* **plen·i·po·ten·ti·ar·ies** A diplomatic agent, such as an ambassador, having full powers to represent his or her government.

plen·i·tude (plĕn′ĭ-to͞od′) *n.* **1.** A large amount; an abundance: *There was a plenitude of vegetables that summer.* **2.** The quality of being abundant or full. —SEE NOTE AT **replete.**

plen·te·ous (plĕn′tē-əs) *adj.* Abundant; plentiful. —**plen′te·ous·ly** *adv.* —**plen′te·ous·ness** *n.*

plen·ti·ful (plĕn′tĭ-fəl) *adj.* **1.** In abundant supply; ample: *plentiful food.* **2.** Producing or yielding in abundance: *a plentiful land.* —**plen′ti·ful·ly** *adv.* —**plen′ti·ful·ness** *n.*

plen·ty (plĕn′tē) *n.* **1.** An adequate or ample amount or supply: *plenty of time.* **2.** A large amount or number; a lot: *plenty of work to do.* **3.** General abundance or prosperity: *a time of plenty.* ❖ *adj. Informal* Ample; more than enough: *There's plenty room here.* ❖ *adv. Informal* Excessively; very: *They were plenty hungry.* —SEE NOTE AT **replete.**

ple·num (plē′nəm *or* plĕn′əm) *n., pl.* **ple·nums** or **ple·na** (plē′nə *or* plĕn′ə) **1.** A meeting with all members present. **2.** An enclosure in which air or other gas is kept at a pressure greater than that outside.

ple·si·o·saur (plē′sē-ə-sôr′) *n.* Any of various extinct marine reptiles of the Mesozoic Era, having paddle-like limbs, a short tail, and sometimes a very long neck. [From Greek *plēsios*, near + *sauros*, lizard.]

pleu·ra (plo͝or′ə) *n., pl.* **pleu·rae** (plo͝or′ē) A thin membrane that envelops each lung and lines the chest cavity. —**pleu′ral** *adj.*

pleu·ri·sy (plo͝or′ĭ-sē) *n.* Inflammation of the pleura, often accompanied by fever, painful breathing and coughing, and a buildup of fluid in the chest.

Plex·i·glas (plĕk′sĭ-glăs′) A trademark for a light strong transparent plastic.

plex·us (plĕk′səs) *n., pl.* **plexus** or **plex·us·es** A network, as of nerves or blood vessels in the body.

pli·a·ble (plī′ə-bəl) *adj.* **1.** Easily bent or shaped; flexible: *pliable strips of wood.* **2.** Easily influenced or convinced: *a pliable mind.* —**pli′a·bil′i·ty, pli′a·ble·ness** *n.* —**pli′a·bly** *adv.*

pli·ant (plī′ənt) *adj.* **1.** Easily bent or shaped; pliable: *pliant materials.* **2.** Readily changing to fit conditions or to suit others: *a pliant personality.* —**pli′an·cy** *n.* —**pli′ant·ly** *adv.*

plied (plīd) *v.* Past tense and past participle of **ply².**

pli·ers (plī′ərz) *pl.n. (used with a plural verb)* A tool with two parts attached together in a manner similar to a pair of scissors, used for holding, bending, or cutting.

plies¹ (plīz) *n.* Plural of **ply¹.**

plies² (plīz) *v.* Third person singular present tense of **ply².**

plight¹ (plīt) *n.* A situation of difficulty or peril. [From Middle English *plihte*, from Anglo-Norman *plit*, fold, wrinkle, situation (influenced by Middle English *plight*, danger, risk), from Latin *plicāre*, to fold.]

plight² (plīt) *tr.v.* **plight·ed, plight·ing, plights** To promise or bind by solemn pledge. ◆ **plight (one's)**

ă	pat	ôr	core
ā	pay	oi	boy
âr	care	ou	out
ä	father	o͝o	took
ĕ	pet	o͝or	lure
ē	be	o͞o	boot
ĭ	pit	ŭ	cut
ī	bite	ûr	urge
îr	pier	th	thin
ŏ	pot	*th*	this
ō	toe	zh	vision
ô	paw	ə	about

troth **1.** To become engaged to marry. **2.** To give one's solemn oath. [From Middle English *plighten,* to put at risk, pledge (something to be forfeited), from Old English *plihtan,* from *pliht,* danger, risk.]

plinth (plĭnth) *n.* A block or slab upon which a pedestal, column, or statue is placed.

Pli·o·cene (plī′ə-sēn′) *n.* The fifth and last epoch of the Tertiary Period, from about 5.3 to 2.6 million years ago. During the Pliocene, the first distinctly modern animals appeared. See table at **geologic time.** [From Greek *pleiōn,* more + *kainos,* recent.] **—Pli′o·cene′** *adj.*

plod (plŏd) *intr.v.* **plod·ded, plod·ding, plods 1.** To walk heavily or with great effort: *They plodded wearily home through the twilight.* **2.** To work or act slowly and wearily: *He plodded through his lessons.* **—plod′der** *n.*

plop (plŏp) *v.* **plopped, plop·ping, plops** *—intr.* **1.** To fall with a sound like that of an object falling into water: *He let the dough plop down into the sink.* **2.** To let one's body drop heavily or wearily: *She plopped into the chair.* *—tr.* To place or drop so as to make a plopping sound: *He plopped the tomatoes onto the plate.* ❖ *n.* A plopping sound: *The pebble fell with a plop into the pool.*

plot (plŏt) *n.* **1a.** A small piece of ground: *a plot of good land.* **b.** A measured area of land; a lot. **2.** A ground plan, as for a building; a diagram. **3.** The series of actions or events in a novel, movie, or play. **4.** A secret plan to accomplish an often illegal purpose: *a plot against the queen.* ❖ *tr.v.* **plot·ted, plot·ting, plots 1.** To mark, note, or represent, as on a chart or map: *plotted the ship's course; plot a point on a graph.* **2.** To plan or scheme secretly or deviously: *plot revenge.* **—plot′ter** *n.*

plov·er (plŭv′ər *or* plō′vər) *n., pl.* **plover** or **plov·ers** Any of various small shorebirds having a short tail and a short bill.

plow also **plough** (plou) *n.* **1.** A farm implement consisting of a heavy blade at the end of a beam, drawn either by animals or by a motor vehicle, used for breaking up soil and cutting furrows in preparation for sowing. **2.** A device or vehicle of similar function, as a snowplow. ❖ *v.* **plowed, plow·ing, plows** also **ploughed, plough·ing, ploughs** *—tr.* **1.** To break and turn over (soil) with a plow. **2.** To make (one's way) steadily and with effort: *plowed her way through the deep snow.* **3.** To remove snow from with a snowplow: *plowed the streets after the blizzard.* *—intr.* To advance or progress steadily and with effort: *The boat plowed through the waves.* ◆ **plow into** *Informal* To strike with force: *The truck plowed into the fence.*

plow·man (plou′mən) *n.* A man who operates a plow.

plow·share (plou′shâr′) *n.* The cutting blade of a plow.

ploy (ploi) *n.* A cunning action designed to obtain advantage over an opponent.

pluck (plŭk) *v.* **plucked, pluck·ing, plucks** *—tr.* **1.** To detach by pulling with the fingers; pick: *pluck a flower.* **2.** To pull out the feathers or hair of: *pluck a chicken.* **3.** To sound (a string or strings of an instrument) by stretching and releasing, as with the fingers or a plectrum. *—intr.* To give an abrupt pull; tug: *plucked at his sleeve.* ❖ *n.* **1.** A tug; a pull. **2.** Courage and daring; spirit.

pluck·y (plŭk′ē) *adj.* **pluck·i·er, pluck·i·est** Showing spirit and courage in difficult circumstances.

plug (plŭg) *n.* **1.** A piece of wood, cork, or other material used to fill a hole. **2.** A device connected to the end of a wire or cable and fitting into a matching socket to make an electrical connection. **3.** A spark plug. **4.** A flat cake of pressed or twisted tobacco. **5.** *Informal* A favorable public mention of something, especially on television or radio: *The actor put in a plug for his new movie on his website.* ❖ *v.* **plugged, plug·ging, plugs** *—tr.* **1.** To fill (a hole) tightly with something; stop up: *plugged the leak with caulk.* **2.** *Informal* To mention favorably; promote: *plug a new brand of soap.* *—intr. Informal* To move or work doggedly and persistently: *plug away at a job.* ◆ **plug in 1.** To connect (an appliance) to an electrical outlet. **2.** To function by being connected to an electrical outlet: *a laptop computer that also plugs in.* **plug into** To connect or be connected to in the manner of an electrical appliance: *This CD player plugs into the stereo. The computer plugs into a data bank.* **—plug′ger** *n.*

plug-in (plŭg′ĭn′) *n.* A piece of computer software that increases the capabilities of another piece of software.

plum (plŭm) *n.* **1a.** The fruit of any of several small trees, having smooth usually dark purple skin, juicy flesh, and a hard pit. **b.** A tree that bears such fruit. **2.** A dark purple. **3.** Something very much wanted or envied, such as a job that pays well. [From Middle English *ploume,* from Old English *plūme.*]

❑ *These sound alike:* **plum, plumb** (weight).

plum·age (plo͞o′mĭj) *n.* The covering of feathers on a bird.

plumb (plŭm) *n.* **1.** A plumb bob. **2.** A plumb line. ❖ *adv.* **1.** Vertically; straight up and down: *a post that stands plumb.* **2.** *Informal* Directly; squarely: *fell plumb in the middle.* **3.** *Informal* Completely; utterly: *plumb wrong.* ❖ *adj.* **1.** Exactly vertical: *a plumb wall.* **2.** *Informal* Utter; sheer: *a plumb fool.* ❖ *tr.v.* **plumbed, plumb·ing, plumbs 1.** To test the depth or alignment of with or as if with a plumb. **2.** To examine closely; probe into. [From Middle English *the metal lead, lead weight,* from Old French *plom,* from Latin *plumbum.*]

❑ *These sound alike:* **plumb, plum** (fruit).

plumb bob *n.* A usually conical piece of metal attached to the end of a plumb line.

plumb·er (plŭm′ər) *n.* A person who installs and repairs pipes and plumbing.

plumb·ing (plŭm′ĭng) *n.* **1.** The pipes, fixtures, and other equipment used in a system through which a liquid or gas flows. **2.** The work or occupation of a plumber.

plumb line *n.* A line from which a weight is hung, used to measure depth, as of water, or to determine whether something is vertical.

plume (plo͞om) *n.* **1.** A feather, especially a large or showy one used for decoration. **2.** A large feather or cluster of feathers worn as an ornament or symbol of rank, as on a helmet. **3.** Something resembling a large feather: *A plume of smoke rose from the chimney.* **4.** A dispersed mass of pollutants released from a specific source. ❖ *tr.v.* **plumed, plum·ing, plumes 1.** To decorate with or as if with plumes. **2.** To congratulate (oneself): *plumed himself on his victory.* [From Middle English, from Old French, from Latin *plūma.*]

plum·met (plŭm′ĭt) *intr.v.* **plum·met·ed, plum·met·ing, plum·mets** To drop straight down; plunge: *A rock plummeted down from the cliff.*

plump[1] (plŭmp) *adj.* **plump·er, plump·est** Rounded and full in form: *a plump figure; a plump peach.* ❖ *tr. & intr.v.* **plumped, plump·ing, plumps** To make or become plump: *Chris plumped up the pillow. When I stop dieting, I really plump out.* [From Middle English *plompe,* blunt, dull, probably from Middle Dutch *plomp,* blunt, thick, perhaps of imitative origin.] **—plump′ly** *adv.* **—plump′ness** *n.*

plump[2] (plŭmp) *v.* **plumped, plump·ing, plumps** *—intr.* To drop heavily or abruptly; plop: *She plumped down on the grass.* *—tr.* To place or throw heavily or abruptly: *He plumped the books onto the table.* ❖ *n.* **1.** A heavy abrupt fall or impact. **2.** The dull sound of a heavy abrupt fall. ❖ *adv.* **1.** With a heavy or abrupt drop: *She fell down plump on the ground.* **2.** Directly; straight: *He walked plump into the pole.* [From Middle English *plumten,* to plunge, from Middle English *plumpen,* ultimately of imitative origin.]

plum pudding *n.* A sweet spiced pudding made with flour, suet, raisins, and currants.

plow
snowplow

plume
1782 self-portrait by Elizabeth Vigée-Lebrun (1755–1842)

plum·y (plo͞o′mē) *adj.* **plum·i·er, plum·i·est 1.** Consisting of or covered with feathers. **2.** Resembling a feather or plume.

plun·der (plŭn′dər) *tr.v.* **plun·dered, plun·der·ing, plun·ders** To take goods or valuables from; pillage; rob: *Pirates plundered the seaport.* ❖ *n.* **1.** The taking of property by force. **2.** Property stolen by force or by fraud; booty: *digging to hide their plunder.* **—plun′der·er** *n.*

plunge (plŭnj) *v.* **plunged, plung·ing, plung·es** *—intr.* **1.** To dive, jump, or throw oneself into a body of water: *He plunged into the lake.* **2.** To fall rapidly: *The wagon went over the cliff and plunged into the gully.* **3.** To descend steeply or sharply: *The cliff plunged into the sea.* **4.** To throw oneself wholeheartedly into an activity: *She plunged into her work.* **5.** To rush or move forward into or toward something quickly and rapidly: *animals plunging through the undergrowth.* **6.** To become suddenly lower; decrease dramatically: *Stock prices plunged.* *—tr.* **1.** To thrust, throw, or place suddenly into something: *plunged the pitchfork into the hay.* **2.** To cause to enter suddenly or violently into a situation or activity: *events that plunged the world into war.* ❖ *n.* **1.** The act of plunging: *a plunge into work.* **2.** A swim: *an early morning plunge.* **3.** A sudden decrease: *a plunge in the value of gold.* ◆ **take the plunge** *Informal* To begin an unfamiliar venture, especially after hesitating.

plung·er (plŭn′jər) *n.* **1.** A device consisting of a rubber suction cup attached to the end of a stick, used to unclog drains and pipes. **2.** A part, such as a piston, that operates with a repeated thrusting or plunging movement.

plunk (plŭngk) *v.* **plunked, plunk·ing, plunks** *—tr.* **1.** *Informal* To throw or place heavily or abruptly: *He plunked the nickel on the table.* **2.** To pluck (the strings of a musical instrument). *—intr.* **1.** To drop or sink heavily or wearily; plop: *They plunked down on the bench.* **2.** To make a short, hollow, twanging sound. ❖ *n.* **1.** A short, hollow, twanging sound. **2.** A heavy blow or hit.

plu·per·fect (plo͞o-**pûr′**fĭkt) *adj.* Relating to the past perfect tense. ❖ *n.* The past perfect tense.

plu·ral (**plo͝or′**əl) *adj.* **1.** Relating to or composed of more than one. **2.** In grammar, relating to the form of a word that designates more than one. ❖ *n.* The plural form of a word. For example, *birds* is the plural of *bird,* and *children* is the plural of *child.* [From Middle English *plurel,* from Latin *plūrālis,* from *plūs,* more.] **—plu′ral·ly** *adv.*

plu·ral·i·ty (plo͞o-**răl′**ĭ-tē) *n., pl.* **plu·ral·i·ties 1.** The condition of being plural. **2a.** In a contest of more than two candidates, the number of votes cast for the winner if this number is less than half of the total votes cast. **b.** The number by which the vote of a winning candidate is more than that of the closest opponent.

plus (plŭs) *conj.* **1.** Added to: *Two plus three equals five.* **2.** Increased by; along with: *wages plus bonuses.* ❖ *adj.* **1.** Greater than zero; positive. **2.** Indicating a positive electric charge. **3.** Added or extra: *a plus benefit.* **4.** Slightly more than: *a grade of B plus.* ❖ *n., pl.* **plus·es** or **plus·ses 1.** The plus sign. **2.** A positive number. **3.** A favorable factor or condition.

plush (plŭsh) *n.* A fabric resembling velvet but having a thicker, deeper pile. ❖ *adj.* **plush·er, plush·est 1.** Made of or covered with plush: *a plush sofa.* **2.** Luxurious; elegant: *a plush restaurant.*

plush·y (**plŭsh′**ē) *adj.* **plush·i·er, plush·i·est 1.** Resembling plush in texture. **2.** Overly luxurious: *a plushy office.*

plus sign *n.* The symbol (+), as in 3 + 2 = 5, that is used to show addition or a positive quantity.

plu·ti·no (plo͞o-**tē′**nō) *n., pl.* **plu·ti·nos** A Kuiper belt object that orbits the sun in the same time period as Pluto, making exactly two orbits for every three orbits of Neptune. [From *Plut(o)* + *-ino,* diminutive suffix.]

Plu·to (**plo͞o′**tō) *n.* **1.** In Roman mythology, the god of the dead and the ruler of the underworld, identified with the Greek Hades. **2.** A dwarf planet that until 2006 was classified as the ninth planet in our solar system. It has a diameter about one sixth that of Earth. —SEE NOTE AT **planet.**

plu·toc·ra·cy (plo͞o-**tŏk′**rə-sē) *n., pl.* **plu·toc·ra·cies 1.** Government by the wealthy. **2.** A wealthy class that controls a government. **3.** A government or state ruled by the wealthy. **—plu′to·crat′ic** *adj.*

plu·toid (**plo͞o′**toid′) *n.* A dwarf planet that orbits the sun at a greater distance on average than Neptune.

Plu·to·ni·an (plo͞o-**tō′**nē-ən) also **Plu·ton·ic** (plo͞o-**tŏn′**ĭk) *adj.* **1.** Relating to the god Pluto or to the underworld. **2.** Relating to the dwarf planet Pluto.

plu·to·ni·um (plo͞o-**tō′**nē-əm) *n. Symbol* **Pu** A naturally radioactive, silvery metallic element that occurs in trace quantities in uranium ores and is used as a source of energy in nuclear reactors. It is highly poisonous. Atomic number 94. See **Periodic Table.**

plu·vi·al (**plo͞o′**vē-əl) *adj.* **1.** Relating to rain; rainy: *During the Pleistocene Epoch, there were many pluvial periods.* **2.** Caused by rain: *a pluvial lake.*

ply[1] (plī) *n., pl.* **plies** (plīz) **1.** A layer or thickness, as of folded cloth or of wood. **2.** One of the strands twisted together to make yarn, rope, or thread: *three-ply yarn.* [From Old French *pli,* fold, from *plier,* to fold, from Latin *plicāre.*]

ply[2] (plī) *tr.v.* **plied** (plīd), **ply·ing, plies** (plīz) **1.** To use or handle (a tool); wield: *ply a broom in sweeping.* **2.** To engage in (a trade or task); perform regularly: *ply the baker's trade.* **3.** To traverse or sail over regularly: *Convoys plied the seas.* **4.** To repeatedly give something to: *plied the seals at the zoo with fish.* [From Middle English *plien,* from *applien,* to apply.]

Plym·outh (**plĭm′**əth) A town of southeast Massachusetts on **Plymouth Bay,** an inlet of the Atlantic Ocean, southeast of Boston. Founded in 1620 by Pilgrims, it was the center of **Plymouth Colony.**

ply·wood (**plī′**wo͝od′) *n.* A building material made of layers of wood glued together, usually with the grains of adjoining layers at right angles.

Pm The symbol for the element **promethium.**

PM also **PM** *abbr.* An abbreviation of post meridiem (after noon).

pneu·mat·ic (no͞o-**măt′**ĭk) *adj.* **1.** Relating to air or another gas: *pneumatic pressure.* **2.** Filled with or operated by compressed air: *a pneumatic drill.*

pneu·mo·nia (no͞o-**mōn′**yə) *n.* Any of several diseases, usually caused by bacteria or viruses, in which the lungs become inflamed. [From Greek *pneumoniā,* lung disease, from *pneumōn,* lung, variant of *pleumōn,* lung (influenced by *pneuma,* breath).]

Po The symbol for the element **polonium.**

PO *abbr.* An abbreviation of: **1.** postal order. **2.** post office.

poach[1] (pōch) *tr.v.* **poached, poach·ing, poach·es** To cook (eggs or fish, for example) in a gently boiling or simmering liquid. [From Middle English *poched,* poached eggs, from Old French *pochier,* to poach, from *poche,* pocket, bag (since the white of a poached egg encloses the yolk like a bag), of Germanic origin.] **—poach′er** *n.*

poach[2] (pōch) *tr.v.* **poached, poach·ing, poach·es 1.** To take (fish or game) illegally, especially by trespassing on another's property. **2.** To take or appropriate unfairly or illegally: *poaching another firm's best employees.* [Perhaps from French *pocher,* to put in one's pocket, or perhaps from the archaic English verb *poach,* to poke, gouge.] **—poach′er** *n.*

POC *abbr.* An abbreviation of: **1. people of color 2. person of color**

Po·ca·hon·tas (pō′kə-**hŏn′**təs) 1595?–1617. The daughter of Powhatan, who aided the English colonists at

Pocahontas

ă	pat	ôr	core
ā	pay	oi	boy
âr	care	ou	out
ä	father	o͝o	took
ĕ	pet	o͝or	lure
ē	be	o͞o	boot
ĭ	pit	ŭ	cut
ī	bite	ûr	urge
îr	pier	th	thin
ŏ	pot	*th*	this
ō	toe	zh	vision
ô	paw	ə	about

Jamestown and is said to have saved Captain John Smith from execution.

pock (pŏk) *n.* **1.** A pus-filled swelling of the skin caused by smallpox or a similar disease. **2.** A mark or scar left by such a swelling; a pockmark.

pock·et (pŏk′ĭt) *n.* **1.** A small pouch, open at the top, sewn into or onto a garment and used to hold things. **2a.** A receptacle, cavity, container, or pouch that resembles a pocket in appearance or function. **b.** The deepest part of a baseball glove, just below the web, where the ball is normally caught. **3.** A small isolated or protected area or group: *pockets of civilization along the frontier.* **4.** An air pocket. **5.** A small cavity in the earth containing ore. **6.** In football, the area behind the line of scrimmage that blockers attempt to keep clear so that the quarterback can pass the ball. ❖ *adj.* Suitable for being carried in one's pocket: *a pocket watch.* ❖ *tr.v.* **pock·et·ed, pock·et·ing, pock·ets 1.** To place in or as if in a pocket: *pocket a dime.* **2.** To take possession of dishonestly: *pocket the petty cash.* ◆ **in (one's) pocket** In one's power, influence, or possession. [From Middle English *pokete*, pouch, small bag, from Old North French *poke*, bag, sack, of Germanic origin.]

pock·et·book (pŏk′ĭt-bo͝ok′) *n.* **1.** A purse; a handbag. **2.** A container for paper money or coins that is small enough to fit into a pocket or handbag. **3.** A supply of money: *too expensive for our pocketbook.*

pock·et·ful (pŏk′ĭt-fo͝ol′) *n., pl.* **pock·et·fuls** or **pock·ets·ful** (pŏk′ĭts-fo͝ol′) The amount that a pocket will hold.

pock·et·knife (pŏk′ĭt-nīf′) *n.* A small knife with a blade or blades that fold into the handle.

pock·et-sized (pŏk′ĭt-sīzd′) or **pock·et-size** (pŏk′ĭt-sīz′) *adj.* **1.** Of a size suitable to be carried in a pocket: *a pocket-sized radio.* **2.** Small.

pocket veto *n.* An indirect veto of a bill that has been sent to the president within ten days of the end of a session of Congress, whereby the president holds on to the bill without signing it by the time the congressional session ends.

pock·mark (pŏk′märk′) *n.* A pit or scar left on the skin as a result of smallpox or a similar disease. **—pock′-marked′** *adj.*

po·co (pō′kō) *adv.* In music, to a slight degree or amount.

pod¹ (pŏd) *n.* A seed case, as of a pea, bean, or certain other plants, that splits open to release the enclosed seeds.

pod² *n.* (pŏd) A group of sea mammals, such as whales or dolphins.

–pod or **–pode** *suff.* A suffix that means a number or kind of feet: *pseudopod.*

Pod·go·ri·ca (pŏd′gə-rēt′sə) The capital of Montenegro, in the southern part near the Albanian border.

po·di·a·try (pə-dī′ə-trē) *n.* The branch of medicine that deals with the study and treatment of foot ailments. **—po·di′a·trist** *n.*

po·di·um (pō′dē-əm) *n.* An elevated platform, as for an orchestra conductor or lecturer. [From Latin, from Greek *podion*, base, from *pous*, foot.]

Poe (pō), **Edgar Allan** 1809–1849. American writer known especially for his short stories and poems, such as "The Raven" (1845).

po·em (pō′əm) *n.* A verbal composition that conveys experiences, thoughts, or feelings in a vivid and imaginative way and is characterized by the use of literary techniques such as metaphor, rhyme, and meter. [From Latin *poēma*, from Greek *poiēma*, from *poiein*, to create.]

po·et (pō′ĭt) *n.* A composer of poems.

po·et·ic (pō-ĕt′ĭk) *adj.* **1.** Relating to poetry: *poetic works.* **2.** Having a quality or style characteristic of poetry: *poetic language.*

po·et·i·cal (pō-ĕt′ĭ-kəl) *adj.* **1.** Poetic. **2.** Highly fanciful or idealized: *poetical notions about life in the country.* **—po·et′i·cal·ly** *adv.*

poetic justice *n.* The reward of someone who does good, or the punishment of someone who does evil, often in an especially appropriate or ironic manner: *It was only poetic justice that the villain's downfall should come about as a result of his own schemes.*

poet laureate *n., pl.* **poets laureate** or **poet laureates 1.** A poet appointed by the British monarch and expected to write poems celebrating occasions of national importance. **2.** A poet appointed to a similar position of honor, as in the United States.

po·et·ry (pō′ĭ-trē) *n.* **1.** The act or practice of composing poems. **2.** Poems regarded collectively: *Do you enjoy reading poetry?* **3.** A quality that suggests poetry, as in grace, beauty, or harmony.

po·go stick (pō′gō) *n.* A metal pole with footrests and a heavy spring set into the bottom end, used to propel oneself along the ground by hopping.

po·grom (pə-grŏm′ *or* pō′grəm) *n.* An organized and often officially encouraged massacre or persecution of a minority group, especially one conducted against Jews.

poi (poi) *n.* A Hawaiian food made from the root of the taro that is cooked, pounded to a paste, and often fermented. [From Hawaiian *poi.*]

poign·ant (poin′yənt) *adj.* **1.** Deeply moving; touching: *poignant memories.* **2.** Keenly distressing or painful: *poignant grief.* **—poign′an·cy** *n.* **—poign′ant·ly** *adv.*

poin·set·ti·a (poin-sĕt′ē-ə *or* poin-sĕt′ə) *n.* A tropical American plant having small yellowish flowers surrounded by showy, usually bright-red bracts that resemble petals. [After Joel Roberts *Poinsett* (1779–1851), American diplomat who sent samples of the plant to the United States while in Mexico.]

point (point) *n.* **1.** A sharp or tapered end: *the point of a pencil.* **2.** A tapering piece of land that extends into a body of water; a peninsula, cape, or promontory. **3.** A dot or period, as one used to separate the fractional and integral parts of a numeral. **4.** A geometric object having no dimensions and no property other than its location. **5.** Any of the 32 directions indicated on a mariner's compass. **6.** A position or place: *the highest point in the county.* **7.** A specified degree or condition: *the boiling point of water.* **8.** A specific moment in time: *At that point he noticed someone running away.* **9.** The important or essential part or idea: *the point of a story.* **10.** A purpose or goal: *What was the point of her visit?* **11.** A separate item or element: *Let's examine the list point by point.* **12.** A distinctive quality or characteristic: *Making friends quickly is one of his best points.* **13.** A single unit in the score of a game, contest, or test. **14.** In printing, a unit of type size equal to about 1/72 of an inch. ❖ *v.* **point·ed, point·ing, points** *—tr.* **1.** To direct or aim: *pointed the flashlight down the road.* **2.** To indicate (a direction or position): *She pointed the way to the river.* *—intr.* **1.** To direct attention toward something with a finger, narrow object, or light: *He pointed to the tree.* **2.** To be turned or directed, as in a given direction: *The compass needle pointed north.* **3.** To be an indication of something, especially of a likely event: *All signs point to an improvement in the economy.* **4.** To show the location of animals hunted as game by standing still and facing in that direction. Used of a hunting dog. ◆ **beside the point** Irrelevant to the matter at hand. **make a point of** To consider or treat (an action or activity) as indispensable: *We made a point of being on time.* **to the point** Concerning or with relevance to the matter at hand. [From Middle English, from Old French, from Latin *pūnctum.*]

point-and-click (point′ənd-klĭk′) *adj.* Being a computer application that works when a user selects it with a pointing device.

Edgar Allan Poe

pogo stick

poinsettia

point-blank (point′blăngk′) *adj.* **1.** Aimed straight at a mark or target: *a point-blank shot.* **2.** Very close to a mark or target: *at point-blank range.* **3.** Straightforward; blunt: *a point-blank answer.* ❖ *adv.* **1.** With a direct aim; straight: *He fired point-blank.* **2.** Without hesitating; bluntly: *answered point-blank.* [Perhaps partial translation of obsolete French *de point en blanc,* point-blank (literally, from the point to the white) : *point (de tir),* (firing) point + *blanc,* white.]

point·ed (poin′tĭd) *adj.* **1.** Having a sharp or tapered end or part: *pointed leaves.* **2.** Cutting; piercing: *pointed criticism.* **3.** Clearly directed or aimed, as at a particular person: *a pointed remark.* **—point′ed·ly** *adv.* **—point′ed·ness** *n.*

point·er (poin′tər) *n.* **1.** A person or thing that directs, indicates, or points, especially: **a.** A long stick or handheld laser used for indicating something, as on a map or blackboard. **b.** A marker that indicates a number on a scale, as in a clock or meter. **2.** A movable indicator, especially an arrow, on a computer screen that marks the position at which a user can execute a command, usually by clicking. **3.** Any of various breeds of dog that are trained to point at game. **4.** A piece of advice: *pointers on buying rare stamps.*

poison ivy

point·ing device (poin′tĭng) *n.* An input device, such as a mouse, used to move a cursor or pointer on a computer screen.

point·less (point′lĭs) *adj.* Having no purpose, sense, or meaning: *a pointless regulation.* **—point′less·ly** *adv.* **—point′less·ness** *n.*

point of view *n., pl.* **points of view 1.** A manner of viewing things; an attitude: *a liberal point of view.* **2.** A position from which something is observed or considered.

point·y (poin′tē) *adj.* **point·i·er, point·i·est** Having an end tapering to a point.

poise (poiz) *v.* **poised, pois·ing, pois·es** *—tr.* To balance or hold in equilibrium: *He poised the flashlight on the edge of the table. —intr.* To be balanced: *She poised on the end of the diving board.* ❖ *n.* **1.** Balance; stability; equilibrium. **2.** A calm confident manner.

polar bear

poi·son (poi′zən) *n.* **1.** A substance that causes injury, sickness, or death, especially by chemical means. **2.** Something that causes harm or destruction. ❖ *tr.v.* **poi·soned, poi·son·ing, poi·sons 1.** To kill or harm with poison. **2.** To put poison on or into: *poisoned the arrow; poisoned the drink.* **3.** To have a harmful influence on: *Jealousy poisoned their minds.* ❖ *adj.* Poisonous. **—poi′son·er** *n.*

poison ivy *n.* **1.** A shrubby or climbing plant that has leaflets in groups of three and small whitish berries and that can cause a severe itching skin rash if touched. **2.** A skin rash caused by contact with this plant.

poison oak *n.* **1.** Either of two shrubs related to and resembling poison ivy and causing a similar skin rash. **2.** Poison ivy.

poi·son·ous (poi′zə-nəs) *adj.* **1.** Containing a poison: *a poisonous mushroom.* **2.** Capable of harming by poison: *a poisonous snake.* **3.** Full of ill will; malicious: *poisonous remarks.* **—poi′son·ous·ly** *adv.* **—poi′son·ous·ness** *n.*

poison sumac *n.* A swamp shrub of the eastern United States, having compound leaves and greenish-white berries and causing an itching rash on contact with the skin.

poke[1] (pōk) *v.* **poked, pok·ing, pokes** *—tr.* **1.** To push or jab at, as with a finger or elbow: *poke someone in the ribs.* **2.** To thrust forward; push: *The otter poked its head out of the water.* **3.** To make by thrusting or jabbing: *poke a hole in the canvas.* **4.** To stir (a fire) with a poker or stick. *—intr.* **1.** To make thrusts or jabs, as with a stick. **2.** To pry or meddle; intrude: *poking into someone else's business.* **3.** To look or search in a leisurely manner: *I was just poking around the attic and came across this photograph.* **4.** To proceed in a slow or lazy manner: *The old jalopy is still poking along.* ❖ *n.* A push, thrust, or jab. ◆ **poke fun at** To make fun of; ridicule or tease. [From Middle English *poken.*]

poke[2] (pōk) *n.* A sack or bag. [From Middle English, ultimately of Germanic origin; akin to English *pouch.*]

pok·er[1] (pō′kər) *n.* A metal rod used to stir a fire. [From *poke,* to jab.]

pok·er[2] (pō′kər) *n.* Any of various card games played by two or more people who bet on the value of their hands. [Probably ultimately from German *pochen,* to knock, brag (since players would knock on the table when giving an opening bid in a German card game resembling poker).]

po·key (pō′kē) *n., pl.* **po·keys** *Slang* A jail.

pok·y also **poke·y** (pō′kē) *adj.* **pok·i·er, pok·i·est** *Informal* **1.** Not lively; dull; slow: *a poky little town.* **2.** Small and crowded: *a poky apartment.*

pol (pôl) *n. Informal* A politician.

Po·land (pō′lənd) A country of central Europe north of the Czech Republic and Slovakia on the Baltic Sea. It was unified in the 11th century, and its present boundaries date from the end of World War II. Warsaw is the capital.

po·lar (pō′lər) *adj.* **1.** Relating to, indicating, or measured in relation to a pole: *the polar region of a magnet.* **2.** Relating to the North Pole or the South Pole: *a polar expedition.* **3.** Occupying opposite extremes: *two people who are polar opposites in personality.*

polar bear *n.* A large white bear of Arctic regions.

polar cap *n.* A region around either of a planet's poles that is permanently covered with ice or other frozen material.

polar circle *n.* **1.** The Arctic Circle. **2.** The Antarctic Circle.

Po·lar·is (pə-lăr′ĭs) *n.* A bright star at the end of the handle of the Little Dipper and almost at the north celestial pole.

po·lar·i·ty (pō-lăr′ĭ-tē) *n., pl.* **po·lar·i·ties 1.** The condition of having, being aligned with, or being directed toward poles, especially magnetic or electric poles. **2.** The condition of having contrary or opposite tendencies or qualities: *political polarity.*

po·lar·ize (pō′lə-rīz′) *tr.v.* **po·lar·ized, po·lar·iz·ing, po·lar·iz·es 1.** To cause polarity in; make polar. **2.** To cause a ray of light to exhibit different properties in different directions, especially by ensuring that the light waves' vibration takes place only in one plane. **3.** To cause the positive and negative electric charges in (a physical body or system) to become separated, either wholly or in part. **4.** To cause to divide into two opposing groups: *The controversial topic polarized public opinion.* **—po′lar·i·za′tion** (pō′lər-ĭ-zā′shən) *n.*

pole[1] (pōl) *n.* **1.** Either of the points at which an axis that passes through the center of a sphere intersects the surface of the sphere. **2.** Either of the points at which the earth's axis of rotation intersects the earth's surface; the North Pole or South Pole. **3.** A point on the celestial sphere directly over the earth's North Pole or South Pole. **4.** A magnetic pole. **5.** Either of a pair of oppositely charged electric terminals. **6.** Either extremity of the main axis of a nucleus, cell, or organism. [From Middle English, from Latin *polus,* from Greek *polos,* axis, sky.]

❑ *These sound alike:* **pole**[1] (point on an axis), **pole**[2] (rod), **poll** (voting).

pole[2] (pōl) *n.* **1.** A long slender rod: *a fishing pole.* **2.** An upright post: *a telephone pole.* ❖ *tr.v.* **poled, pol·ing, poles** To push or move along by using a pole: *pole a boat down the river.* [From Middle English, from Old English *pāl,* from Latin *pālus,* stake.]

❑ *These sound alike:* **pole**[2] (rod), **pole**[1] (point on an axis), **poll** (voting).

Pole *n.* A native or inhabitant of Poland.

ă	pat	ôr	core
ā	pay	oi	boy
âr	care	ou	out
ä	father	o͝o	took
ĕ	pet	o͝or	lure
ē	be	o͞o	boot
ĭ	pit	ŭ	cut
ī	bite	ûr	urge
îr	pier	th	thin
ŏ	pot	*th*	this
ō	toe	zh	vision
ô	paw	ə	about

pole·axe or **pole·ax** (pōl′ăks′) *n.* A weapon used in the Middle Ages, consisting of a long pole ending in an axe or a combination of an axe and a hammer.

pole·cat (pōl′kăt′) *n.* **1.** Any of several Eurasian mammals related to the weasel and having mostly brown fur. **2.** A skunk.

po·lem·ic (pə-lĕm′ĭk) *n.* A controversial argument, especially an attack on a specific doctrine or belief. ❖ *adj.* also **po·lem·i·cal** (pə-lĕm′ĭ-kəl) Relating to a controversy, argument, or verbal attack. **—po·lem′i·cal·ly** *adv.*

pole·star (pōl′stär′) *n.* Polaris.

pole vault *n.* An athletic contest in which participants run forward and place one end of a long pole firmly against the ground, using the pole to swing their bodies up and over a high crossbar. **—pole′-vault′** *v.*

po·lice (pə-lēs′) *n., pl.* **police 1.** The department of government established to maintain order, enforce the law, and prevent and detect crime. **2.** *(used with a plural verb)* Police officers considered as a group. **3.** A body of people having a similar function to a police force: *campus police.* ❖ *tr.v.* **po·liced, po·lic·ing, po·lic·es** To control or keep in order, especially as part of a police force. [From French, from Old French *policie, police,* civil administration, from Late Latin *polītia,* from Greek *polīteia,* from *polis,* city.]

police dog *n.* **1.** A dog trained to aid the police. **2.** A German shepherd.

po·lice·man (pə-lēs′mən) *n.* A man who is a member of a police force.

police officer *n.* A member of a police force.

po·lice·wom·an (pə-lēs′wo͝om′ən) *n.* A woman who is a member of a police force.

pol·i·cy¹ (pŏl′ĭ-sē) *n., pl.* **pol·i·cies 1.** A plan or course of action, as of a government or a business. **2.** A guiding principle or course of action considered prudent or helpful: *Honesty is the best policy.* [From Middle English *policie,* from Old French *policie, police,* public administration, from Late Latin *polītia,* from Greek *politeia,* the state, from Greek *polis,* city.]

pol·i·cy² (pŏl′ĭ-sē) *n., pl.* **pol·i·cies** A written contract of insurance, as for medical care. [From French, from Old French *certificate,* ultimately from Greek *apodeixis,* proof.]

po·li·o (pō′lē-ō′) *n.* Poliomyelitis.

po·li·o·my·e·li·tis (pō′lē-ō-mī′ə-lī′tĭs) *n.* A contagious viral disease that mainly affects the nerve cells of the spinal cord and brain, often leading to muscle weakness and paralysis.

pol·ish (pŏl′ĭsh) *tr.v.* **pol·ished, pol·ish·ing, pol·ish·es 1.** To make smooth and shiny, as by rubbing, chemical action, or both: *polish silver.* **2.** To refine or perfect: *polish one's writing.* ❖ *n.* **1.** Smoothness and shininess of a surface or finish. **2.** A substance containing chemicals or an abrasive material for smoothing or shining a surface. **3.** A high degree of refinement; elegance of style: *Her performance shows polish.* ◆ **polish off** *Informal* To finish or dispose of quickly and easily: *polish off a meal.* **—pol′ish·er** *n.*

Po·lish (pō′lĭsh) *adj.* Relating to Poland or its people, language, or culture. ❖ *n.* The Slavic language of the Poles.

pol·ished (pŏl′ĭsht) *adj.* **1.** Made or naturally smooth and shiny: *a polished table; a polished stone.* **2.** Refined; cultured: *polished manners.* **3.** Having no errors or imperfections; flawless: *a polished performance.*

po·lite (pə-līt′) *adj.* **po·lit·er, po·lit·est 1.** Having or showing good manners; courteous: *a polite boy; a polite note.* **2.** Refined; elegant: *polite society.* [From Middle English *polit,* polished, from Latin *polīre,* to polish.] **—po·lite′ly** *adv.* **—po·lite′ness** *n.*

SYNONYMS polite, civil, courteous, genteel These adjectives mean mindful of, conforming to, or marked by good manners. **Polite** means that one is considerate of others and follows conventional social standards of good behavior: *You don't have to like all your relatives, but you must be polite to them.* **Civil** means having a minimal amount of good manners, neither polite nor rude: *He is barely civil until he has his morning coffee.* **Courteous** means polite in a gracious, dignified way: *She was courteous in declining the invitation.* **Genteel** means having refined manners and often an air of pretention: *My genteel neighbors enjoy hosting receptions in their rose garden.*

pol·i·tic (pŏl′ĭ-tĭk) *adj.* Showing good or pragmatic judgment; prudent; judicious: *a politic decision.*

po·lit·i·cal (pə-lĭt′ĭ-kəl) *adj.* **1.** Relating to the structure or affairs of government: *a political system.* **2.** Relating to or characteristic of politics or politicians: *a political party; a political campaign.* **3.** Having or influenced by the interests of a particular person or group of people: *The decision to hire him as a professor was in the college's political interests.* [From Greek *polītikos,* from *polītēs,* citizen, from *polis,* city.] **—po·lit′i·cal·ly** *adv.*

politically correct *adj.* Conforming to an established set of values or beliefs, especially in choosing words so as not to give offense when discussing race, gender, or other sensitive issues. **—political correctness** *n.*

political science *n.* The study of the processes, principles, and structure of government and political institutions.

pol·i·ti·cian (pŏl′ĭ-tĭsh′ən) *n.* **1.** A person active in politics, especially one holding a political office. **2.** A person who uses cunning and guile to achieve power or success.

pol·i·tics (pŏl′ĭ-tĭks) *n.* **1.** *(used with a singular verb)* The art or science of government or governing, as of a nation. **2.** *(used with a singular or plural verb)* The activities or affairs of a government, politician, or political party: *I avoid discussing politics at work.* **3.** *(used with a singular or plural verb)* Intrigue or maneuvering in order to gain power within a group: *He grew tired of the office politics and got another job.* **4.** *(used with a singular or plural verb)* A person's general position or attitude on political subjects: *Her politics are conservative.* —SEE NOTE.

pol·i·ty (pŏl′ĭ-tē) *n., pl.* **pol·i·ties 1.** The form of government of a nation, state, or organization. **2.** A community or society living under a certain form of government. [From Late Latin *polītia,* public administration, from Greek *polīteia,* the state, from Greek *polis,* city.]

Polk (pōk), **James Knox** 1795–1849. The 11th president of the United States (1845–1849). The Mexican War (1846–1848) occurred during his term.

pol·ka (pōl′kə *or* pō′kə) *n.* **1.** A lively dance originating in Bohemia and performed by couples. **2.** Music written for this dance. ❖ *intr.v.* **pol·kaed, pol·ka·ing, pol·kas** To dance the polka.

polka dot *n.* **1.** One of many round dots that are evenly spaced to form a pattern. **2.** A pattern or fabric with such dots.

poll (pōl) *n.* **1.** The casting and registering of votes in an election. **2.** often **polls** The place where votes are cast and counted: *went to the polls to vote for governor.* **3.** A survey of the public or of a sample of public opinion to acquire information. **4.** The head, especially the top of the head. ❖ *tr.v.* **polled, poll·ing, polls 1.** To receive (a given number of votes). **2.** To sample and record the opinions of: *polled the voters.* **3.** To cast (a vote or ballot). **4.** To cut the horns, upper branches, hair, or wool from: *He polled the sheep.*

❑ *These sound alike:* **poll, pole¹** (point on an axis), **pole²** (rod).

pol·len (pŏl′ən) *n.* Powdery grains that contain the male reproductive cells of seed plants. In flowering plants, pollen is produced in the anthers of stamens.

pole vault

USAGE

politics The word **politics** is followed by a singular verb when it refers to the art or science of governing or to political science: *Politics has been a concern of philosophers for centuries.* But in its other senses *politics* can take either a singular or plural verb. Many other nouns that end in *-ics,* such as *acoustics* and *mechanics,* are similar in this regard. Look at specific entries in the dictionary for precise information.

James Polk
1858 portrait by George Peter Alexander Healy (1813–1894)

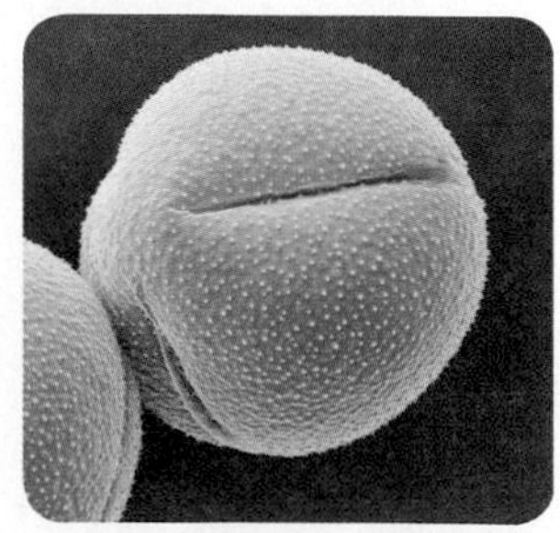

pollen
magnified pollen grain of a cactus plant

SCIENCE

pollinate A plant cannot produce seeds until it is **pollinated.** For that to happen, a pollen grain (which contains the male reproductive cell) must reach an ovule (which contains the female reproductive cell). In the case of *self-pollination,* pollination occurs within a single flower or plant; in *cross-pollination,* the pollen travels to a different plant. Pollen grains disperse by different means. Some are blown by the wind. Some are carried by birds or insects. Certain clues can help you guess what mode of pollination a plant uses. Wind-pollinated plants, like ragweed and pine trees, usually have drab-colored flowers or cones and produce large amounts of pollen. Flowers pollinated by hummingbirds are often bright red. Moths and bats visit flowers that open at night. If a flower smells like rotting flesh, it's probably fly-pollinated. The fly lands on what appears to be delicious decaying meat, unaware that the plant has lured it in to provide pollination services.

ă	pat	ôr	core
ā	pay	oi	boy
âr	care	ou	out
ä	father	o͝o	took
ĕ	pet	o͝or	lure
ē	be	o͞o	boot
ĭ	pit	ŭ	cut
ī	bite	ûr	urge
îr	pier	th	thin
ŏ	pot	*th*	this
ō	toe	zh	vision
ô	paw	ə	about

pol·li·nate (pŏl′ə-nāt′) *tr.v.* **pol·li·nat·ed, pol·li·nat·ing, pol·li·nates** To fertilize by transferring pollen to the female part of (a flower or plant). **—pol′li·na′tion** *n.* **—pol′li·na′tor** *n.* —SEE NOTE.

pol·li·wog also **pol·ly·wog** (pŏl′ē-wŏg′) *n.* A tadpole.

pol·lock or **pol·lack** (pŏl′ək) *n., pl.* **pollock** or **pol·locks** also **pollack** or **pol·lacks** Any of several ocean fishes that are closely related to the cod and are often used for food.

poll·ster (pōl′stər) *n.* A person who takes surveys of public opinion.

poll tax *n.* A fixed tax imposed on all people in a certain area, especially as a condition of voting.

pol·lut·ant (pə-lo͞ot′nt) *n.* Something that pollutes, especially a waste material that makes the environment less suitable for living things.

pol·lute (pə-lo͞ot′) *tr.v.* **pol·lut·ed, pol·lut·ing, pol·lutes 1.** To make unfit for or harmful to living organisms, especially by the addition of waste matter: *Sewage pollutes rivers.* **2.** To render morally impure; corrupt. **—pol·lut′er** *n.*

pol·lu·tion (pə-lo͞o′shən) *n.* **1.** The contamination of air, water, or soil by harmful substances. **2.** Something that pollutes.

Pol·lux (pŏl′əks) *n.* In Greek mythology, one of the twin sons of Leda, who along with his brother Castor was transformed by Zeus into the constellation Gemini.

pol·ly·wog (pŏl′ē-wŏg′) *n.* Variant of **polliwog.**

po·lo (pō′lō) *n.* A game in which two teams of three or four players on horseback use long-handled mallets to drive a ball into the opposing team's goal.

Po·lo (pō′lō), **Marco** 1254–1324. Venetian traveler who explored Asia (1271–1295) and published his account in *Travels of Marco Polo.*

pol·o·naise (pŏl′ə-**nāz′** *or* pō′lə-**nāz′**) *n.* **1.** A stately dance of Polish origin, consisting mainly of a promenade of couples. **2.** Music written for or based on the rhythms of this dance.

po·lo·ni·um (pə-lō′nē-əm) *n. Symbol* **Po** A very rare, naturally radioactive metallic element produced by the disintegration of radium. Atomic number 84. See **Periodic Table.**

polo shirt *n.* A pullover sport shirt, usually of knitted cotton, with a collar and an open neck.

pol·troon (pŏl-**tro͞on′**) *n.* An utter coward.

poly– *pref.* A prefix that means more than one; many: *polygon.*

pol·y·chaete (pŏl′ĭ-kēt′) *n.* Any of various segmented worms that live mainly in the sea and have a cluster of bristles on each side of every segment. [From Greek *polukhaitēs,* with much hair : *polu-,* poly- + *khaitē,* long hair.]

pol·y·es·ter (pŏl′ē-ĕs′tər) *n.* **1.** Any of various light, strong, weather-resistant synthetic polymers used to make plastics and fibers. **2.** A wrinkle-resistant fabric of fibers made from any of these polymers.

pol·y·eth·yl·ene (pŏl′ē-**ĕth′**ə-lēn′) *n.* A synthetic polymer produced from ethylene, used especially for containers and packaging.

po·lyg·a·mist (pə-lĭg′ə-mĭst) *n.* A person who practices polygamy.

po·lyg·a·my (pə-lĭg′ə-mē) *n.* The practice or condition of having more than one husband or wife at one time. **—po·lyg′a·mous** *adj.* **—po·lyg′a·mous·ly** *adv.*

pol·y·glot (pŏl′ē-glŏt′) *adj.* Knowing or speaking many languages. ❖ *n.* A person who speaks many languages.

pol·y·gon (pŏl′ē-gŏn′) *n.* A flat closed geometric figure bounded by three or more line segments. **—po·lyg′o·nal** (pə-lĭg′ə-nəl) *adj.*

pol·y·graph (pŏl′ē-grăf′) *n.* An instrument that simultaneously records changes in several body actions, such as blood pressure, pulse rate, and breathing rate, used in an effort to determine if a person is lying.

pol·y·he·dron (pŏl′ē-**hē′**drən) *n., pl.* **pol·y·he·drons** or **pol·y·he·dra** (pŏl′ē-**hē′**drə) A solid geometric figure bounded by polygons.

pol·y·mer (pŏl′ə-mər) *n.* Any of a large number of natural or synthetic chemical compounds of extremely high molecular weight, formed of simple molecules linked together into giant molecules. **—pol′y·mer·ize′** (pŏl′ə-mə-rīz′ *or* pə-lĭm′ə-rīz′) *v.*

pol·y·mer·ic (pŏl′ə-**mĕr′**ĭk) *adj.* Relating to a polymer or polymers.

Pol·y·ne·sia (pŏl′ə-**nē′**zhə *or* pŏl′ə-**nē′**shə) A division of Oceania including islands of the central and southern Pacific Ocean roughly between New Zealand, Hawaii, and Easter Island.

Pol·y·ne·sian (pŏl′ə-**nē′**zhən *or* pŏl′ə-**nē′**shən) *adj.* Relating to Polynesia or its peoples, languages, or cultures. ❖ *n.* **1.** A native or inhabitant of Polynesia. **2.** A group of related languages spoken in Polynesia.

pol·y·no·mi·al (pŏl′ē-**nō′**mē-əl) *n.* An algebraic expression that is the sum of two or more terms, each term consisting of a constant multiplier and one or more variables raised to powers of whole numbers.

pol·yp (pŏl′ĭp) *n.* **1.** An invertebrate water animal having a hollow, tube-shaped body with a mouth at one end surrounded by tentacles. Some organisms, like corals, live as polyps for their entire lives, while others, like jellyfish, live as polyps for only part of their lives. **2.** An abnormal growth extending from a mucous membrane.

po·lyph·o·ny (pə-lĭf′ə-nē) *n., pl.* **po·lyph·o·nies** Music with two or more melodic parts sounded together. **—pol′y·phon′ic** (pŏl′ē-**fŏn′**ĭk) *adj.*

pol·y·sty·rene (pŏl′ē-**stī′**rēn) *n.* A clear, hard, rigid synthetic polymer that is often made into a solidified foam for use as a packing material or thermal insulator.

pol·y·syl·lab·ic (pŏl′ē-sĭ-**lăb′**ĭk) *adj.* Having many syllables: *a polysyllabic word.* **—pol′y·syl·lab′i·cal·ly** *adv.*

pol·y·syl·la·ble (pŏl′ē-**sĭl′**ə-bəl) *n.* A word, such as *comfortable* or *complementary,* having many syllables.

pol·y·tech·nic (pŏl′ē-**tĕk′**nĭk) *adj.* Dealing with or offering instruction in many industrial arts and applied sciences. ❖ *n.* A school specializing in the teaching of industrial arts and applied sciences.

pol·y·the·ism (**pŏl′**ē-thē-ĭz′əm) *n.* The worship of or belief in more than one god. **—pol′y·the′ist** *n.*

pol·y·un·sat·u·rat·ed (pŏl′ē-ŭn-**săch′**ə-rā′tĭd) *adj.* Relating to an organic compound, especially a fat, in which more than one pair of carbon atoms are joined by double bonds.

pol·y·u·re·thane (pŏl′ē-**yo͝or′**ə-thān′) *n.* Any of various synthetic polymers used in making tough resistant coatings, adhesives, and electrical insulation.

po·made (pō-**mād′** *or* pŏ-**mād′**) *n.* A perfumed ointment, especially for the hair.

pome (pōm) *n.* A fruit, such as an apple, pear, or quince, having several seed chambers surrounded by an outer fleshy part.

pome·gran·ate (**pŏm′**grăn′ĭt *or* **pŏm′**ĭ-grăn′ĭt) *n.* **1.** A fruit having a tough reddish rind and many small seeds, each enclosed in juicy red flesh. **2.** The tree that bears such fruit. [From Middle English *pomme-garnate,* from Old French *pome grenate,* apple having many seeds.]

Pom·er·a·ni·an (pŏm′ə-**rā′**nē-ən) *n.* Any of a breed of small dog having a short muzzle, thick fluffy coat, and curled bushy tail.

pom·mel (**pŭm′**əl *or* **pŏm′**əl) *tr.v.* **pom·meled, pom·mel·ing, pom·mels** also **pom·melled, pom·mel·ling, pom·mels** To beat severely; pummel. ❖ *n.* **1.** The raised part at the front of a saddle. **2.** Either of the two rounded handles on top of a pommel horse. **3.** A knob on the handle of a sword.

pommel horse *n.* A piece of gymnastic equipment consisting of a padded, loaf-shaped object with two handles on top and adjustable legs.

pomp (pŏmp) *n.* Showy or stately display.

pom·pa·dour (**pŏm′**pə-dôr′) *n.* A puffed-up hairstyle in which the hair is brushed or swept up from the forehead. [After the Marquise de *Pompadour* (1721–1764), French courtier.]

pom·pa·no (**pŏm′**pə-nō′) *n., pl.* **pompano** or **pom·pa·nos** Any of several fishes of warm Atlantic waters, having a flattened silvery body and much valued as food.

Pom·pe·ii (pŏm-**pā′** *or* pŏm-**pā′**ē) An ancient city of southern Italy southeast of Naples. It was founded in the sixth or early fifth century BC and destroyed by an eruption of Mount Vesuvius in AD 79.

pom·pom (**pŏm′**pŏm′) or **pom·pon** (**pŏm′**pŏn′) *n.* **1.** A tuft or ball of material such as wool or ribbon, used as a decoration, especially on shoes, caps, or curtains. **2.** A ball of fluffy material, such as colored paper or feathers, that is waved by cheerleaders and sports fans. **3.** A small chrysanthemum or dahlia.

pom·pous (**pŏm′**pəs) *adj.* **1.** Characterized by excessive dignity and self-importance. **2.** Full of high-sounding words and phrases; bombastic: *gave a pompous speech.* —**pom′pous·ly** *adv.* —**pom·pos′i·ty** (pŏm-**pŏs′**ĭ-tē), **pom′pous·ness** *n.*

Ponce de Le·ón (**pŏns′** də **lē′**ən *or* **pŏns′** də lē-**ōn′**), **Juan** 1460–1521. Spanish explorer who set out to find the legendary Fountain of Youth but instead explored and named Florida (1513).

pon·cho (**pŏn′**chō) *n., pl.* **pon·chos 1.** A cloak with a hole in the center for the head. **2.** A similar garment used as a raincoat and having a hood.

pond (pŏnd) *n.* A still body of water smaller than a lake.

pon·der (**pŏn′**dər) *tr. & intr.v.* **pon·dered, pon·der·ing, pon·ders** To think or consider carefully and thoroughly: *He pondered the meaning of his dream. She pondered over the decision.*

pon·der·ous (**pŏn′**dər-əs) *adj.* **1.** Heavy and massive: *a ponderous dinosaur.* **2.** Dull, graceless, and difficult to read or understand: *a ponderous book.* —**pon′der·ous·ly** *adv.* —**pon′der·ous·ness** *n.*

pon·iard (**pŏn′**yərd) *n.* A dagger, especially one whose blade is triangular or square when viewed in cross section.

pons (pŏnz) *n., pl.* **pon·tes** (**pŏn′**tēz) **1.** A part of the brain stem that links the medulla oblongata and the cerebellum with upper portions of the brain. **2.** A slender tissue joining two parts of an organ. [From Latin *pōns,* bridge.]

pon·tiff (**pŏn′**tĭf) *n.* **1.** The pope. **2.** A bishop.

pon·tif·i·cal (pŏn-**tĭf′**ĭ-kəl) *adj.* **1.** Relating to, characteristic of, or suitable for a pope or bishop. **2.** Pompously dogmatic or self-important; pretentious.

pon·tif·i·cate (pŏn-**tĭf′**ĭ-kāt′) *intr.v.* **pon·tif·i·cat·ed, pon·tif·i·cat·ing, pon·tif·i·cates** To speak in a pompous dogmatic way.

pon·toon (pŏn-**to͞on′**) *n.* **1a.** A floating structure, such as a flatbottom boat, used to support a bridge. **b.** A floating structure that serves as a dock. **2.** One of the floats that supports a seaplane on water.

pontoon bridge *n.* A temporary floating bridge using pontoons for support.

po·ny (**pō′**nē) *n., pl.* **po·nies 1.** Any of several breeds of horses that are small in size when full grown. **2.** A translation of a text in a foreign language, especially one used secretly by students.

pony express *n.* A system of rapidly carrying mail by relays of ponies that operated in the western United States in 1860 and 1861.

po·ny·tail (**pō′**nē-tāl′) *n.* A gathering of hair that is fastened into a bunch close to the head so that the hair hangs down like a pony's tail.

pooch (po͞och) *n. Slang* A dog.

poo·dle (**po͞od′**l) *n.* A dog of a breed having thick curly hair and varying in size from standard to toy. [From German *Pudelhund* : Low German *pudeln,* to splash about (since poodles were bred to help waterfowl hunters) + German *Hund,* dog.]

pooh (po͞o) *interj.* An expression used to show disdain or disbelief.

pooh-pooh (**po͞o′po͞o′**) *tr.v.* **pooh-poohed, pooh-pooh·ing, pooh-poohs** *Informal* To express contempt for: *He pooh-poohed the idea.*

pool[1] (po͞ol) *n.* **1.** A small still body of water. **2.** A small collection of a liquid; a puddle: *a pool of molten steel.* **3.** A deep or still place in a stream. **4.** A swimming pool. [From Middle English, from Old English *pōl.*]

pool[2] (po͞ol) *n.* **1a.** A game of chance, resembling a lottery, in which the contestants put money into a common fund that is later paid to the winner or winners. **b.** The fund containing the money bet in a game of chance or on the outcome of an event, such as a horse race. **2.** A supply, as of vehicles or workers, available for use by a group. **3.** A game played on a six-pocket billiards table usually with 15 balls in addition to a cue ball. ❖ *tr.v.* **pooled, pool·ing, pools** To put into a common fund for use by all: *They agreed to pool their resources to finish the project quickly.* [From French *poule,* hen, pool of money (probably compared to a hen won as a prize in a contest).]

pool·room (**po͞ol′**ro͝om′ *or* **po͞ol′**ro͞om′) *n.* A commercial establishment or room for the playing of pool or billiards.

poop[1] (po͞op) *n.* A raised, enclosed structure at the stern of a ship. [From Middle English *poupe,* from Old French, from Latin *puppis.*]

poop[2] (po͞op) *tr.v.* **pooped, poop·ing, poops** *Slang* To cause to become tired or exhausted: *The long hike really pooped us out.*

poor (po͝or) *adj.* **poor·er, poor·est 1.** Having little or no money and few or no possessions. **2.** Lacking in a specified quality: *a diet poor in calcium.* **3.** Not adequate in quality; inferior. **4.** Deserving of sympathy or pity; unfortunate. ❖ *n. (used with a plural verb)* People with little or no money or possessions considered as a group. —**poor′ness** *n.*

poor·house (**po͝or′**hous′) *n.* A place where poor people are housed at public expense.

poor·ly (**po͝or′**lē) *adv.* In a poor way; badly.

pop[1] (pŏp) *v.* **popped, pop·ping, pops** —*intr.* **1.** To make a short, sharp, explosive sound. **2.** To burst open with a short, sharp, explosive sound. **3.** To appear suddenly and unexpectedly: *I just popped in to say hello. They popped by on their way into town.* **4.** To open wide suddenly: *His eyes popped with astonishment.* **5.** In baseball, to hit a short high fly ball: *She popped out to third base.* —*tr.* **1.** To cause to make a short explosive sound. **2.** To cause to burst open with a short explosive sound. **3.** To put or thrust quickly or suddenly: *He popped dinner into the microwave.* **4.** In baseball, to hit (a ball) high in the air but not far. ❖ *n.* **1.** A sudden sharp, explosive sound. **2.** A soft drink; a soda. [From Middle English *poppen,* from *pop,* a blow, stroke, of imitative origin.]

pop[2] (pŏp) *n. Informal* Father. [From *papa.*]

pop[3] (pŏp) *Informal adj.* Relating to or for the general public; popular: *pop culture.* ❖ *n.* Popular music. [Short for *popular.*]

pop. *abbr.* An abbreviation of population.

pop·corn (**pŏp′**kôrn′) *n.* **1.** A variety of corn having hard kernels that burst when heated to form white irregularly shaped puffs. **2.** The edible popped kernels of this corn.

pope or **Pope** (pōp) *n.* The bishop of Rome and head

polo

Marco Polo

pompadour
Elvis Presley photographed in the 1950s

pontoon

poplar

porcupine

porphyry

of the Roman Catholic Church. [From Middle English, from Greek *pappās*, father.]

pop fly *n.* In baseball, a short high fly ball.

pop·gun (pŏp′gŭn′) *n.* A toy gun that makes a popping noise.

pop·in·jay (pŏp′ĭn-jā′) *n.* A vain, talkative person.

pop·lar (pŏp′lər) *n.* **1.** Any of several fast-growing trees having soft light-colored wood and bearing their flowers in catkins. **2.** The wood of such a tree.

pop·lin (pŏp′lĭn) *n.* A fabric of silk, rayon, wool, or cotton with fine crosswise ridges, used in making clothing and upholstery.

pop·o·ver (pŏp′ō′vər) *n.* A light hollow muffin that expands and pops up over the rim of the pan while baking.

pop·pa (pä′pə) *n.* Variant of **papa.**

pop·py (pŏp′ē) *n., pl.* **pop·pies 1.** Any of various plants having showy, often bright-red flowers and milky sap. The small dark seeds of some kinds are used in cooking and baking. **2.** The flower of any of these plants. **3.** A vivid red to reddish orange.

pop·py·cock (pŏp′ē-kŏk′) *n. Informal* Foolish talk; nonsense.

Pop·si·cle (pŏp′sĭ-kəl *or* pŏp′sĭk′əl) A trademark used for a colored flavored ice confection with one or two sticks for a handle.

pop·u·lace (pŏp′yə-lĭs) *n.* The general public; the masses.

pop·u·lar (pŏp′yə-lər) *adj.* **1.** Enjoyed by many people: *a popular pastime.* **2.** Liked by acquaintances; having many friends or admirers: *a popular teacher.* **3.** Relating to, representing, or carried out by the people at large: *the popular vote.* **4.** Accepted or held by many people; widespread: *a popular notion.* [From Latin *populāris*, of the common people, from *populus*, the people.]

pop·u·lar·i·ty (pŏp′yə-lăr′ĭ-tē) *n.* The quality of being popular; the state of being liked by many people.

pop·u·lar·ize (pŏp′yə-lə-rīz′) *tr.v.* **pop·u·lar·ized, pop·u·lar·iz·ing, pop·u·lar·iz·es** To make popular; make known or understandable to the general public. **—pop′u·lar·i·za′tion** (pŏp′yə-lər-ĭ-zā′shən) *n.*

pop·u·lar·ly (pŏp′yə-lər-lē) *adv.* Commonly; generally: *Our friend Robert is popularly known as "Bob."*

popular vote *n.* A vote by the entire voting population rather than by specially chosen delegates. In the United States, a candidate can become president by winning the electoral vote without winning the popular vote.

pop·u·late (pŏp′yə-lāt′) *tr.v.* **pop·u·lat·ed, pop·u·lat·ing, pop·u·lates 1.** To supply with inhabitants: *populate a remote region.* **2.** To live in; inhabit.

pop·u·la·tion (pŏp′yə-lā′shən) *n.* **1a.** All of the people who live in a specified area. **b.** The total number of such people. **2.** All of the organisms of one kind that live in a particular region: *The park has a small population of wolves.* **3.** The set of individuals, items, or data from which a statistical sample is taken.

pop·u·list (pŏp′yə-lĭst) *n.* A supporter of the rights and power of ordinary people. **—pop′u·list** *adj.*

pop·u·lous (pŏp′yə-ləs) *adj.* Heavily populated; having many inhabitants.

pop-up (pŏp′ŭp′) *n.* **1.** A webpage or advertisement that opens automatically in a new window of a web browser. **2.** A pop fly. ❖ *adj.* Designed to form a three-dimensional structure when a page is opened: *a pop-up children's book.*

por·ce·lain (pôr′sə-lĭn) *n.* A hard white translucent ceramic made by baking a fine clay at a high temperature and covering it with a glaze.

porch (pôrch) *n.* **1.** A roofed platform at the entrance to a house. **2.** A gallery or room attached to the outside of a building.

por·cine (pôr′sīn′) *adj.* Resembling or typical of a pig or pigs: *a porcine snout.*

por·cu·pine (pôr′kyə-pīn′) *n.* Any of various rodents covered with long sharp spines that serve as protection.

pore[1] (pôr) *intr.v.* **pored, por·ing, pores** To read or study with great care and attention: *poring over old documents.* [From Middle English *pouren*, of unknown origin.]

❑ *These sound alike:* **pore**[1] (study), **pore**[2] (opening), **pour** (make flow).

pore[2] (pôr) *n.* A tiny opening, as in an animal's skin or on the surface of a leaf, through which liquids or gases may pass. [From Middle English, from Latin *porus*, passage, from Greek *poros*.]

❑ *These sound alike:* **pore**[2] (opening), **pore**[1] (study), **pour** (make flow).

por·gy (pôr′gē) *n., pl.* **porgy** or **por·gies** Any of various saltwater fishes found chiefly in coastal Atlantic waters and used as food.

pork (pôrk) *n.* **1.** The meat of a pig or hog used as food. **2.** Government programs or monies that primarily benefit the people in the district of the politician who gets approval for their funding.

pork·er (pôr′kər) *n.* A fattened young pig.

por·nog·ra·phy (pôr-nŏg′rə-fē) *n.* Printed or recorded words or images meant to cause sexual arousal. **—por′no·graph′ic** (pôr′nə-grăf′ĭk) *adj.*

po·ros·i·ty (pə-rŏs′ĭ-tē *or* pô-rŏs′ĭ-tē) *n., pl.* **po·ros·i·ties 1.** The condition or property of being porous. **2.** The degree to which something is porous: *a material of high porosity.*

po·rous (pôr′əs) *adj.* **1.** Full of or having pores. **2.** Easily crossed or penetrated: *a porous border.* **—po′rous·ly** *adv.* **—po′rous·ness** *n.*

por·phy·ry (pôr′fə-rē) *n., pl.* **por·phy·ries** A fine-grained igneous rock containing some relatively large crystals, especially of feldspar.

por·poise (pôr′pəs) *n., pl.* **porpoise** or **por·pois·es** Any of several sea mammals related to the whales but smaller and usually having a short blunt snout.

por·ridge (pôr′ĭj) *n.* Oatmeal or other meal boiled in water or milk until thick.

por·rin·ger (pôr′ĭn-jər) *n.* A shallow cup or bowl with a handle.

port[1] (pôrt) *n.* **1.** A place on a waterway with facilities for loading or unloading ships. **2.** A city or town with such facilities. **3.** A place that gives shelter for ships; a harbor. [From Middle English, from Latin *portus*.]

port[2] (pôrt) *n.* The left side of a ship or aircraft facing forward. ❖ *adj.* Relating to the port side: *a port cabin.* [Probably from *port*, porthole (since goods were usually loaded and unloaded from a ship's left side), or perhaps from *port*, harbor.]

port[3] (pôrt) *n.* **1.** A porthole. **2.** A place on a computer where the cable to a peripheral device, such as a modem or printer, can be connected. [From Middle English, from Latin *porta*, gate.]

port[4] (pôrt) *n.* A sweet wine that has been strengthened with brandy. [After *Oporto*, Portugal.]

por·ta·ble (pôr′tə-bəl) *adj.* Easy to carry or move: *a portable radio.*

port·age (pôr′tĭj) *n.* **1.** The carrying of boats and supplies overland between waterways. **2.** A route for such carrying. ❖ *tr. & intr.v.* **port·aged, port·ag·ing, port·ag·es** To transport or travel by portage.

por·tal (pôr′tl) *n.* **1.** A doorway, entrance, or gate, especially a large imposing one. **2.** A website used as an entry point to other websites.

Port-au-Prince (pôrt′ō-prĭns′) The capital of Haiti, in the southwest part of the country on an arm of the Caribbean Sea.

port·cul·lis (pôrt-kŭl′ĭs) *n.* A grating of iron or wooden bars or slats, suspended in the gateway of a fortified

ă	pat	ôr	core
ā	pay	oi	boy
âr	care	ou	out
ä	father	ŏŏ	took
ĕ	pet	ŏŏr	lure
ē	be	ōō	boot
ĭ	pit	ŭ	cut
ī	bite	ûr	urge
îr	pier	th	thin
ŏ	pot	*th*	this
ō	toe	zh	vision
ô	paw	ə	about

place so that it can be lowered quickly in case of attack.

por·tend (pôr-tĕnd′) *tr.v.* **por·tend·ed, por·tend·ing, por·tends** To serve as an advance indication of; presage: *an incident that portends further trouble.*

por·tent (pôr′tĕnt′) *n.* **1.** An indication of something important or disastrous that is about to occur. **2.** Great or ominous significance: *a development of great portent.*

por·ten·tous (pôr-tĕn′təs) *adj.* **1.** Being a portent; ominous: *a portentous silence.* **2.** Of great significance: *a portentous event.* **—por·ten′tous·ly** *adv.*

por·ter[1] (pôr′tər) *n.* **1.** A person hired to carry baggage, as at a station or hotel. **2.** An attendant who waits on passengers in a railroad car. **3.** A maintenance worker for a building or institution. [From Middle English *portour,* from Latin *portātor,* carrier, from *portāre,* to carry.]

por·ter[2] (pôr′tər) *n.* A dark beer resembling light stout. [Short for *porter's ale* (probably so called because it was favored by laborers in the 1700s).]

Por·ter (pôr′tər), **William Sydney** Pen name O. Henry. 1862–1910. American writer whose short stories, noted for their often surprising endings, are collected in such volumes as *Cabbages and Kings* (1904).

por·ter·house (pôr′tər-hous′) *n.* A cut of beef taken from the loin, having a T-shaped bone and a sizable tenderloin.

port·fo·li·o (pôrt-fō′lē-ō′) *n., pl.* **port·fo·li·os 1.** A portable case for holding loose papers or drawings. **2.** An assortment of works considered as evidence of skills and accomplishments. **3.** A group of investments such as stocks and bonds.

port·hole (pôrt′hōl′) *n.* **1.** A small circular window in a ship's side. **2.** An opening for a gun in a wall or parapet.

por·ti·co (pôr′tĭ-kō′) *n., pl.* **por·ti·coes** or **por·ti·cos** A porch or walkway with a roof supported by columns.

por·tion (pôr′shən) *n.* **1.** A part of a whole; a section or quantity of a larger thing: *A portion of your paycheck is withheld to pay taxes.* **2.** A part allotted to a single person or group: *Each worker received a portion of the profits.* **3.** A single helping of food: *a portion of mashed potatoes.* ❖ *tr.v.* **por·tioned, por·tion·ing, por·tions** To distribute in portions; parcel out.

Port·land (pôrt′lənd) **1.** The largest city of Maine, in the southwest part of the state on the Atlantic Ocean southwest of Augusta. It was settled in about 1632. **2.** The largest city of Oregon, in the northwest part of the state north-northeast of Salem. It was founded in 1845.

Portland cement or **portland cement** *n.* A cement made by heating a mixture of limestone and clay in a kiln and pulverizing the resulting material.

Port Lou·is (lo͞o′ĭs *or* lo͞o′ē) The capital of Mauritius, in the northwest part of the island on the Indian Ocean. It was founded in about 1735.

port·ly (pôrt′lē) *adj.* **port·li·er, port·li·est** Having a round, stout body: *a portly man.* **—port′li·ness** *n.*

Port Mores·by (môrz′bē) The capital of Papua New Guinea, on southeast New Guinea.

Port of Spain or **Port-of-Spain** (pôrt′əv-spān′) The capital of Trinidad and Tobago, on the northwest coast of Trinidad on an arm of the Atlantic Ocean.

Por·to-No·vo (pôr′tō-nō′vō) The capital of Benin, in the southeast part of the country on the Atlantic Ocean west of Lagos, Nigeria. It was probably founded in the 1500s.

por·trait (pôr′trĭt *or* pôr′trāt′) *n.* **1.** A painting, photograph, or other likeness of a person, especially one showing the face. **2.** A verbal picture or description, especially of a person.

por·trait·ist (pôr′trə-tĭst) *n.* A person who makes portraits, especially a painter or photographer.

por·trai·ture (pôr′trĭ-cho͝or′) *n.* The art of making portraits.

por·tray (pôr-trā′) *tr.v.* **por·trayed, por·tray·ing, por·trays 1.** To show by means of a picture. **2.** To describe or picture through the use of words: *the novel portrays colonial life.* **3.** To play on stage or on the screen: *portray a famous composer.*

por·tray·al (pôr-trā′əl) *n.* **1.** The act or process of portraying, representing, or acting: *a brilliant portrayal of the leading role.* **2.** A representation or description.

Por·tu·gal (pôr′chə-gəl) A country of southwest Europe on the Iberian Peninsula west of Spain. It includes the Madeira Islands and the Azores in the northern Atlantic Ocean. Lisbon is the capital.

Por·tu·guese (pôr′chə-gēz′ *or* pôr′chə-gēs′) *adj.* Relating to Portugal or its people, language, or culture. ❖ *n., pl.* **Portuguese 1.** A native or inhabitant of Portugal. **2.** The Romance language of Portugal and Brazil.

Portuguese man-of-war *n.* A colony of small invertebrate sea animals having a bluish floating bladder and many long stinging tentacles.

Port Vi·la (pôrt′ vē′lə *or* pôr vē-lä′) The capital of Vanuatu, in the southwest Pacific Ocean.

pose (pōz) *v.* **posed, pos·ing, pos·es** *—intr.* **1.** To assume or be in a certain position, as for a portrait or photograph: *The children posed in front of the fireplace.* **2.** To pretend to be someone or something that one is not: *caught posing as a detective.* —*tr.* **1.** To place in a specific position, as for a photograph: *She posed us in front of the fireplace and took several pictures.* **2.** To present, raise, or put forward: *pose a threat; pose a question.* ❖ *n.* **1.** A position assumed or taken, as for a portrait or photograph. **2.** A false appearance or attitude; a pretense: *His scholarliness is only a pose.* [From Middle English *posen,* to place, from Old French *poser,* from Late Latin *pausāre,* to rest, from Latin *pausa,* pause.]

Po·sei·don (pō-sīd′n *or* pə-sīd′n) *n.* In Greek mythology, the god of the sea, identified with the Roman Neptune.

posh (pŏsh) *adj.* **posh·er, posh·est** Luxurious and fashionable: *a posh hotel.*

pos·it (pŏz′ĭt) *tr.v.* **pos·it·ed, pos·it·ing, pos·its** To assume the existence of; postulate.

po·si·tion (pə-zĭsh′ən) *n.* **1.** A place or location: *the position of the sun in the sky.* **2.** The proper place of a person or thing: *The actors are in position to film the scene.* **3.** The way a person or thing is placed or arranged: *Try not to sit in one position too long.* **4.** An advantageous place or location: *jockeys maneuvering for position.* **5.** A situation as it relates to the surrounding circumstances: *You've put me in an awkward position.* **6.** A point of view or an attitude on a certain question: *What is your position on the proposed landfill?* **7.** A post of employment; a job: *a position in the government.* **8.** In sports, the area or station assigned to each member of a team: *defensive positions.* ❖ *tr.v.* **po·si·tioned, po·si·tion·ing, po·si·tions** To put in place or position: *position the chess pieces on the board.*

pos·i·tive (pŏz′ĭ-tĭv) *adj.* **1.** Expressing certainty, acceptance, or affirmation: *a positive answer; a positive statement.* **2.** Making, causing, or focusing on progress; constructive: *positive steps to solve the problem.* **3.** Pleasant, optimistic, or favorable: *positive qualities; a positive attitude.* **4.** Absolutely certain: *I'm positive about that.* **5a.** Greater than zero: *a positive integer.* **b.** Relating to the sign (+), used to indicate a positive number or one that is to be added. **6.** Relating to or having the electric charge of a proton and therefore tending to repel protons and attract electrons. **7.** Being a response in which a living thing moves toward a stimulus: *a positive reaction to light.* **8.** Indicating that a suspected disease, disorder, or microorganism is present: *a positive test result.* **9.** In grammar, of or being the simple uncompared degree of an adjective or adverb as opposed to the comparative or superlative degree. ❖ *n.* **1.** Something that is pleasant or constructive: *a proposal with*

portcullis
Leeds Castle, near Maidstone, England

portico
Monticello, the home of Thomas Jefferson, near Charlottesville, Virginia

Poseidon

many positives. **2a.** In grammar, the positive degree of an adjective or adverb. **b.** A word in this degree. **3.** The side in a debate that agrees with the statement being debated. **4.** A photographic image in which light and dark appear as they do in nature. **5.** A quantity greater than zero. [From Middle English *positive,* laid down, imposed, definite, from Latin *positīvus,* imposed, from *positus,* past participle of *pōnere,* to place.] **—pos′i·tive·ly** *adv.*

pos·i·tron (pŏz′ĭ-trŏn′) *n.* The antiparticle that corresponds to the electron.

poss. *abbr.* An abbreviation of possessive.

pos·se (pŏs′ē) *n.* A body of people summoned by a sheriff to aid in law enforcement.

pos·sess (pə-zĕs′) *tr.v.* **pos·sessed, pos·sess·ing, pos·sess·es 1.** To have as property; own. **2.** To control the mind or thoughts of: *Ambition possessed her.* **3.** To have as a quality, characteristic, or other attribute: *possessed great tact.* [From Middle English *possessen,* from Old French *possesser,* from Latin *possessus,* past participle of *possidēre,* to possess.] **—pos·ses′sor** *n.*

pos·sessed (pə-zĕst′) *adj.* **1.** Having or owning something: *possessed of great wealth.* **2a.** Controlled by a spirit, demon, god, or other supernatural force. **b.** Controlled by a strong inner drive: *possessed by a desire to become a musician.*

pos·ses·sion (pə-zĕsh′ən) *n.* **1.** The fact or condition of having or possessing something. **2.** Something that is owned or possessed: *leaving most of their possessions behind.* **3.** A territory subject to foreign control: *The Philippine Islands were once a possession of the United States.* **4.** The state of being dominated by or as if by evil spirits or by an obsession. **5.** In sports, control of the ball or puck by a player or team.

pos·ses·sive (pə-zĕs′ĭv) *adj.* **1.** Relating to ownership or possession. **2.** Having a desire to dominate or control. **3.** Relating to the grammatical case of a noun or pronoun that indicates possession. In the sentences *Bill's car was being repaired* and *Mary lent John her book, Bill's* and *her* are in the possessive case. ❖ *n.* **1.** The possessive case. **2.** A word in the possessive case. **—pos·ses′sive·ly** *adv.* **—pos·ses′sive·ness** *n.*

possessive adjective *n.* An adjective formed from a pronoun, indicating possession. In the sentences *This is my duty* and *The boy whose shirt was red left early,* the possessive adjectives are *my* and *whose.*

possessive pronoun *n.* One of several pronouns indicating possession and capable of substituting for noun phrases. The possessive pronouns include *mine, hers, his, ours, yours, theirs,* and *whose.*

pos·si·bil·i·ty (pŏs′ə-bĭl′ĭ-tē) *n., pl.* **pos·si·bil·i·ties 1.** The fact or condition of being possible: *the possibility of life on Mars.* **2.** Something that is possible: *His promotion now seems a possibility.* **3.** A person or thing that is capable of being chosen or winning a contest: *She seems like a strong possibility in the senatorial race.* **4. possibilities** Potential for favorable results: *The idea has tremendous possibilities.*

pos·si·ble (pŏs′ə-bəl) *adj.* **1.** Capable of happening, existing, being true, or being accomplished: *It may be possible to get there by helicopter.* **2.** Capable of being used for a certain purpose: *a possible site for the new capital.* [From Middle English *possibil,* from Latin *possibilis,* from *posse,* to be able.]

pos·si·bly (pŏs′ə-blē) *adv.* **1.** Perhaps: *He hesitated, possibly remembering his unsuccessful last attempt.* **2.** Conceivably: *Could they possibly be here already?* **3.** Under any circumstances: *I can't possibly do it.*

pos·sum (pŏs′əm) *n.* An opossum. [Short for *opossum.*]

post[1] (pōst) *n.* **1.** A piece of wood or other material set upright in the ground to serve as a marker or support. **2.** A support for a beam in the framework of a building. **3.** The starting gate at a racetrack. **4.** A terminal of a battery. **5.** A goalpost. **6.** An electronic message sent to a website: *ignored several inflammatory posts.* ❖ *tr.v.* **post·ed, post·ing, posts 1.** To put up in a prominent place for public viewing: *The winners' names will be posted on the bulletin board.* **2.** To put up signs on (property) warning against trespassing. **3.** To send (an electronic message) to a website: *posted a response to a question about car engines.* [From Middle English, from Old English, from Latin *postis.*]

post[2] (pōst) *n.* **1.** A military base: *an army post.* **2.** A local organization of military veterans. **3.** An assigned position or station, as of a guard or sentry: *a lookout post.* **4.** A position of employment, especially an appointed public office: *a high post in the government.* **5.** A place to which a person is assigned for duty: *an overseas post.* **6.** In basketball, a position usually taken by the center, near either the basket or the foul line, serving as the focus of the team's offense. **7.** A trading post. ❖ *tr.v.* **post·ed, post·ing, posts 1.** To assign to a post or station: *post a sentry.* **2.** To put forward; present: *post bail.* [From French, from Italian *posto,* past participle of *porre,* to place, from Latin *pōnere.*]

post[3] (pōst) *n.* **1.** *Chiefly British* **a.** A postal system. **b.** A delivery of mail. **c.** The mail delivered: *the morning post.* **2.** *Archaic* One of a series of stations along a mail route, furnishing fresh horses and riders. ❖ *tr.v.* **post·ed, post·ing, posts 1.** To mail (a letter). **2.** To inform of the latest news: *I try to keep posted on current events.* **3.** In bookkeeping, to transfer (figures) to a ledger. [From French *poste,* from Old French *poste,* relay station for horses, from Old Italian *posta,* feminine of Old Italian *posto,* placed.]

post– *pref.* A prefix that means: **1.** After in time; later: *postoperative.* **2.** After in position; behind: *postnasal.* —SEE NOTE.

post·age (pō′stĭj) *n.* The charge for sending something by mail.

postage stamp *n.* A small, usually adhesive label issued by a government for an amount indicated on the front. It is placed on an item of mail as evidence of the payment of postage.

post·al (pō′stəl) *adj.* Relating to the post office or mail service: *postal rates.*

postal card *n.* A card printed with the image of a postage stamp, issued by a government and used for sending messages through the mail.

postal service *n.* The public department responsible for transporting and delivering mail.

post·card (pōst′kärd′) *n.* **1.** A card printed to be sent through the mail, usually having an image on one side and space on the other side for a postage stamp, an address, and a brief message. **2.** A postal card.

post chaise *n.* A closed carriage having four wheels and drawn by horses, formerly used to transport mail and passengers.

post·date (pōst-dāt′) *tr.v.* **post·dat·ed, post·dat·ing, post·dates 1.** To put a date on (a check, for example) that is later than the actual date. **2.** To occur or exist later than: *Typewriters postdated quill pens.*

post·er (pō′stər) *n.* A large, usually printed notice or announcement, often illustrated, that is posted to advertise or publicize something.

pos·te·ri·or (pŏ-stîr′ē-ər) *adj.* **1.** Located behind a part or toward the rear of a structure. **2a.** Relating to the side of the human body in which the spine is located. **b.** Relating to the part of a nonhuman animal body that is at the opposite end from the head. **3.** Coming after in order or time; following. ❖ *n.* The buttocks.

pos·ter·i·ty (pŏ-stĕr′ĭ-tē) *n.* **1.** Future generations: *The author left a rich body of literature to posterity.* **2.** A person's descendants.

WORD BUILDING

post– The basic meaning of the prefix **post–** is "after." It comes from the Latin word *post,* meaning "behind, after." *Post–* is often used in opposition to the prefixes *ante–* and *pre–,* as in *antedate/postdate* and *prewar/postwar.* And *post–* occurs frequently in medical words, such as *postnatal* ("after birth"), *postcranial* ("behind the cranium"), and *postvertebral* ("behind the vertebrae").

postmark

ă	pat	ôr	core
ā	pay	oi	boy
âr	care	ou	out
ä	father	ŏŏ	took
ĕ	pet	ŏŏr	lure
ē	be	ōō	boot
ĭ	pit	ŭ	cut
ī	bite	ûr	urge
îr	pier	th	thin
ŏ	pot	*th*	this
ō	toe	zh	vision
ô	paw	ə	about

pos·tern (pō′stərn *or* pŏs′tərn) *n.* A small rear gate, especially one in a fort or castle.

Post Exchange A service mark used for a store on a military base that sells merchandise to military personnel and their families.

post·grad·u·ate (pōst-grăj′o͞o-ĭt *or* pōst-grăj′o͞o-āt′) *adj.* Relating to advanced study after graduation from high school or college: *postgraduate courses.* ❖ *n.* A person engaged in postgraduate study.

post·haste (pōst′hāst′) *adv.* With great speed; rapidly.

post·hu·mous (pŏs′chə-məs) *adj.* **1.** Occurring or continuing after one's death: *a posthumous award.* **2.** Published after the author's death: *a posthumous book.* **3.** Born after the death of the father: *a posthumous child.* **—post′hu·mous·ly** *adv.*

pos·til·ion also **pos·til·lion** (pō-stĭl′yən *or* pŏ-stĭl′yən) *n.* A person who rides the lead horse on the left to guide the horses drawing a coach.

Post-it (pōst′ĭt′) A trademark for a slip of notepaper with an adhesive edge that allows it to be stuck to a document and then peeled off without causing damage.

post·man (pōst′mən) *n.* A mailman.

post·mark (pōst′märk′) *n.* A mark printed over a postage stamp, especially one that cancels the stamp and records the date and place of mailing. ❖ *tr.v.* **post·marked, post·mark·ing, post·marks** To stamp with such a mark.

post·mas·ter (pōst′măs′tər) *n.* A person in charge of the operations of a post office.

post me·rid·i·em (mə-rĭd′ē-əm) *adv. & adj.* After noon. It is normally used in its abbreviated form to show time, as in 10:30 PM.

post·mis·tress (pōst′mĭs′trĭs) *n.* A woman in charge of the operations of a local post office.

post·mor·tem (pōst-môr′təm) *adj.* Occurring or done after death: *a postmortem examination of a body.* ❖ *n.* **1.** An autopsy. **2.** An analysis or review of an event that has just taken place.

post office *n.* **1.** A local office where mail is received, sorted, and delivered, and where stamps and other postal materials are sold. **2.** A postal service.

post office box *n.* A compartment at a central mailing location, in which one's incoming mail is held until one can pick it up.

post·op·er·a·tive (pōst-ŏp′ər-ə-tĭv *or* pōst-ŏp′rə-tĭv) *adj.* Happening or done after a surgical operation: *postoperative care.*

post·paid (pōst′pād′) *adj.* Having the postage paid in advance: *a postpaid reply card.*

post·par·tum (pōst-pär′təm) *adj.* Relating to the period shortly after childbirth: *postpartum recovery.*

post·pone (pōst-pōn′) *tr.v.* **post·poned, post·pon·ing, post·pones** To put off until a later time: *You may want to postpone your visit.* **—post·pone′ment** *n.*

post·script (pōst′skrĭpt′) *n.* **1.** A message added at the end of a letter, after the writer's signature. **2.** Additional information added to a manuscript, as of a book or article.

pos·tu·late (pŏs′chə-lāt′) *tr.v.* **pos·tu·lat·ed, pos·tu·lat·ing, pos·tu·lates 1.** To assume the truth or existence of (something), especially as a basis of an argument: *Aristotle postulated an "Unmoved Mover" working endlessly to keep the planets in motion.* **2.** To assume as a premise or axiom; take for granted. **3.** *Archaic* To make claim for; demand. ❖ *n.* (pŏs′chə-lĭt *or* pŏs′chə-lāt′) Something assumed without proof as being self-evident or generally accepted, especially when used as a basis for an argument. [From New Latin *postulātum*, from *postulāre*, to request.]

pos·ture (pŏs′chər) *n.* **1.** The way in which one holds or carries one's body; carriage: *A gymnast should have good posture.* **2.** A position or arrangement of the body or its parts: *a kneeling posture.* **3.** An attitude or policy with regard to something: *The government assumed a defiant posture in response to the accusations of unfair trading.* ❖ *intr.v.* **pos·tured, pos·tur·ing, pos·tures 1.** To assume an unnatural or exaggerated pose or mental attitude: *We all felt that the speaker was posturing.* **2.** To assume a pose. [From French, from Latin *positūra*, position, from *pōnere*, to place.]

post·war (pōst′wôr′) *adj.* Relating to the period after a war.

po·sy (pō′zē) *n., pl.* **po·sies** A flower or bunch of flowers.

pot (pŏt) *n.* **1.** Any of various deep rounded containers made of metal, pottery, or glass, used especially for cooking. **2.** A coffeepot. **3.** A teapot. **4.** A chamberpot. **5.** A flowerpot. **6a.** A pot with something in it: *a pot of tea.* **b.** The amount that a pot can hold: *drank a pot of coffee.* **7.** A trap for lobsters, fish, or eels, consisting of a wooden, wire, or wicker cage or basket. **8.** The total amount staked by all the players in one hand at cards: *Who won the pot?* **9.** *Informal* A fund to which the members of a group contribute for their common use. ❖ *tr.v.* **pot·ted, pot·ting, pots 1.** To plant or put in a pot: *He potted the tulip bulbs.* **2.** To preserve (food) in a pot, jar, or can. **3.** To cook in a pot. **4.** To shoot (game) for food rather than for sport: *She potted a pheasant.* [From Middle English, from Old English.]

po·ta·ble (pō′tə-bəl) *adj.* Fit to drink: *potable water.* ❖ *n.* A beverage, especially an alcoholic beverage. [From Middle English, from Late Latin *pōtābilis*, from Latin *pōtāre*, to drink.]

pot·ash (pŏt′ăsh′) *n.* Any of several chemical compounds that contain potassium, especially a strongly alkaline material obtained from wood ashes.

po·tas·si·um (pə-tăs′ē-əm) *n. Symbol* **K** A soft, highly reactive, silvery-white metallic element. It is essential for the growth of plants and animals and is used in soaps and fertilizers. Atomic number 19. See **Periodic Table.**

potassium bi·tar·trate (bī-tär′trāt′) *n.* A white crystalline powder used in baking powder and in laxatives.

potassium carbonate *n.* A strongly alkaline white powder used in making glass, enamels, and soaps.

potassium hydroxide *n.* A corrosive solid that is a strong alkali, used as a bleach and in making soaps, dyes, and batteries.

potassium nitrate *n.* A white or colorless crystalline compound used to pickle meat and in making pyrotechnics, explosives, matches, rocket propellants, and fertilizers.

po·ta·to (pə-tā′tō) *n., pl.* **po·ta·toes 1.** The starchy tuber of a widely grown plant, eaten as a vegetable. **2.** The plant that bears such tubers. **3.** The sweet potato. —SEE NOTE.

potato chip *n.* A thin slice of potato fried until crisp and then usually salted.

Pot·a·wat·o·mi (pŏt′ə-wŏt′ə-mē) *n., pl.* **Potawatomi** or **Pot·a·wat·o·mis 1.** A member of a Native American people of the upper Midwest, now living in Michigan, Kansas, Oklahoma, and Ontario. **2.** The Algonquian language of the Potawatomi.

pot·bel·ly (pŏt′bĕl′ē) *n., pl.* **pot·bel·lies** An abdomen that sags or sticks out.

potbelly stove *n.* A short rounded stove in which wood or coal is burned.

po·ten·cy (pōt′n-sē) *n., pl.* **po·ten·cies** The quality or condition of being potent.

po·tent (pōt′nt) *adj.* **1.** Possessing inner or physical strength; powerful: *a potent ruler.* **2.** Having a powerful influence on the mind or feelings; highly effective: *He made a potent argument for joining the team.* **3.** Having or capable of having strong effects on a living organism: *a potent drug.* [From Middle English, from Latin *potēns*, present participle of *posse*, to be able.]

WORD HISTORY

potato We owe both the word **potato** and the food itself to the Indians of South America. When the Spanish came to what is now Peru, they learned of this plant and its nutritious tuber. Potatoes are now so familiar all over the world that it is easy to forget that they were unknown in Europe until the 1500s and in Asia and Africa until long after that. The Spanish, in colonizing both Central and South America, adopted hundreds of words for animals and plants that were unfamiliar to them, and many of these have been passed on to English. A few other terms from the Peruvian Indians are *llama* and *puma,* while other South American Indian languages have contributed *cashew, cougar, macaw, manioc,* and *tapir.* Even more words come from native languages of Mexico, Central America, and the Caribbean, such as *avocado, barbecue, cassava, chocolate, hammock, hurricane, mangrove, tomato,* and *yucca.*

WRITERS CHOOSE THEIR WORDS

"You're *alive,* Bod. That means you have infinite **potential.** You can do anything, make anything, dream anything. If you change the world, the world will change. **Potential.** Once you're dead, it's gone. Over. You've made what you've made, dreamed your dream, written your name. You may be buried here, you may even walk. But that **potential** is finished."

—Neil Gaiman
The Graveyard Book

potential energy
top: The unstretched exercise band has no potential energy.
bottom: The effort used to stretch the exercise band is stored as potential energy. This energy causes the exercise band to snap back to its normal shape when released.

po·ten·tate (pōt′n-tāt′) *n.* A person who has the power and position to rule over others; a monarch.

po·ten·tial (pə-tĕn′shəl) *adj.* Capable of becoming or developing into something in the future: *potential buyers; potential problems.* ❖ *n.* **1.** The ability or capacity for growth, development, or future success: *Your team has the potential to win the championship.* **2.** The possibility that something might happen or result from given conditions: *The police thought the situation had the potential to turn into a riot.* **3.** The difference in voltage between two points in an electric circuit. —**po·ten′tial·ly** *adv.*

potential energy *n.* The energy that a particle or system of particles derives from position or condition rather than from motion. A raised weight, coiled spring, or charged battery has potential energy.

po·ten·ti·al·i·ty (pə-tĕn′shē-ăl′ĭ-tē) *n., pl.* **po·ten·ti·al·i·ties 1.** The state of being potential. **2.** Capacity for growth, development, or existence: *estimating a student's potentiality.* **3.** Something possessing such capacity.

po·ten·ti·om·e·ter (pə-tĕn′shē-ŏm′ĭ-tər) *n.* **1.** A specially calibrated device used to compare an unknown voltage to a standard voltage. **2.** An electrical device consisting of a resistor with three terminals that can be adjusted to control the ratios of the voltages between the terminals.

pot·ful (pŏt′fo͝ol′) *n.* **1.** The amount that a pot can hold. **2.** *Informal* A large amount: *made a potful of money on the horses.*

pot·herb (pŏt′ûrb′ *or* pŏt′hûrb′) *n.* A plant whose leaves, stems, or flowers are cooked and eaten or used as seasoning.

pot·hold·er (pŏt′hōl′dər) *n.* A small pad of fabric, silicone, or other material, used for handling hot cooking utensils.

pot·hole (pŏt′hōl′) *n.* A hole or pit, especially one in a road surface.

pot·hook (pŏt′ho͝ok′) *n.* **1.** A bent or hooked piece of iron for hanging a pot or kettle over a fire. **2.** A curved iron rod with a hooked end used for lifting hot pots, irons, or stove lids.

po·tion (pō′shən) *n.* A liquid or liquid mixture, especially one that is magical, medicinal, or poisonous. [From Middle English *pocioun,* from Old French *pocion,* from Latin *pōtiō,* a drink, from *pōtāre,* to drink.]

pot·latch (pŏt′lăch′) *n.* A ceremonial feast among certain Native American peoples of the northwest Pacific coast, in which the host gives gifts according to each guest's rank or status. Potlatch may also involve the destruction of valued items as a display of wealth. [From Nootka *p̓achitl,* to make a potlatch gift.]

pot·luck (pŏt′lŭk′) *n.* **1.** Whatever food happens to be available for a meal, especially when offered to a guest. **2.** A meal at which each guest brings food to be shared by all.

Po·to·mac River (pə-tō′mək) A river of the eastern United States rising in northeast West Virginia and flowing about 370 miles (600 kilometers) along the Virginia-Maryland border to Chesapeake Bay.

pot pie *n.* **1.** A mixture of meat or poultry and vegetables covered with a crust of pastry and baked in a deep dish. **2.** A meat or poultry stew with dumplings.

pot·pour·ri (pō′po͞o-rē′) *n., pl.* **pot·pour·ris 1.** A miscellaneous collection or assortment; a medley: *The book was a potpourri of poems, legends, and sayings.* **2.** A fragrant mixture of dried flower petals and spices used to scent the air.

pot roast *n.* A cut of beef that is browned and then cooked until tender, often with vegetables, in a covered pot.

pot·sherd (pŏt′shûrd′) *n.* A fragment of broken pottery, especially one found in an archaeological excavation.

pot·shot also **pot shot** (pŏt′shŏt′) *n.* **1.** A random or easy shot. **2.** A criticism made without careful thought and aimed at a handy target for attack: *reporters taking potshots at the mayor.*

pot·tage (pŏt′ĭj) *n.* A thick soup or stew of vegetables and sometimes meat.

pot·ted (pŏt′ĭd) *adj.* **1.** Placed in a pot: *a potted plant.* **2.** Preserved in a pot, can, or jar: *potted meat.*

pot·ter (pŏt′ər) *n.* A person who makes pottery.

Pot·ter (pŏt′ər), **Beatrix** 1866–1943. British writer and illustrator whose stories include *The Tale of Peter Rabbit* (1900) and *The Tailor of Gloucester* (1902).

pot·ter's field (pŏt′ərz) *n.* A place for the burial of unknown or impoverished people.

potter's wheel *n.* A revolving disk on which a mass of clay is shaped by hand.

pot·ter·y (pŏt′ə-rē) *n., pl.* **pot·ter·ies 1.** Objects, such as pots, vases, or dishes, shaped from moist clay and hardened by heat. **2.** The art, craft, or work of a potter. **3.** The place where a potter works.

pouch (pouch) *n.* **1.** A bag often closing with a drawstring and used for holding or carrying various things: *a mail pouch.* **2.** A sealed plastic or foil container used to package frozen or dehydrated food. **3.** A body part similar to a sac or pocket, such as the one in which a kangaroo carries its young. **4.** A puffy part, such as a fold of flesh: *pouches under the eyes.* [From Middle English *pouche,* from Old French, of Germanic origin.]

poul·tice (pōl′tĭs) *n.* A soft moist mass of bread, meal, clay, or a similar substance, usually heated, spread on cloth, and applied to an aching or inflamed part of the body. [From Middle English *pultes,* from Medieval Latin *pultēs,* thick paste, from Latin *puls,* pottage.]

poul·try (pōl′trē) *n.* Domesticated birds, such as chickens, turkeys, ducks, or geese, raised for meat or eggs.

pounce (pouns) *intr.v.* **pounced, pounc·ing, pounc·es 1.** To spring or swoop suddenly so as to seize something: *The kitten pounced on the ball.* **2.** To seize something swiftly and eagerly: *pounce on an opportunity.* ❖ *n.* The act or an instance of pouncing.

pound¹ (pound) *n.* **1a.** A unit of avoirdupois weight equal to 16 ounces (about 454 grams). See table at **measurement. b.** A unit of weight in the apothecaries' weight system equal to 12 ounces (about 373 grams). **2.** A unit of force equal to the downward force exerted by a one-pound weight where the acceleration of gravity is 32.174 feet per second per second. **3a.** The basic monetary unit of the United Kingdom. **b.** Any of several similar monetary units used in Egypt, Lebanon, Sudan, South Sudan, and Syria. **4.** The pound key on a telephone: *To be connected to an operator, press pound.* [From Middle English, from Old English *pund,* from Latin *(lībra) pondō,* (a pound) by weight.]

pound² (pound) *v.* **pound·ed, pound·ing, pounds** —*tr.* **1.** To strike or beat forcefully and repeatedly: *Pound the nail into the board.* **2.** To crush to a powder or pulp: *pounding corn into meal.* **3.** *Informal* To cause a person to learn (something) by forceful repetition: *pounded the math formulas into my head.* —*intr.* **1.** To strike vigorous repeated blows: *She pounded on the table.* **2.** To move along noisily and heavily: *They pounded up the stairs.* **3.** To pulsate rapidly and heavily; throb: *His heart pounded with excitement.* ❖ *n.* **1.** A heavy blow. **2.** The sound of a heavy blow. [From Middle English *pounen,* from Old English *pūnian.*]

pound³ (pound) *n.* **1.** A public enclosure for confining stray animals or livestock. **2.** A place where vehicles that have been impounded are held until their owners redeem them. **3.** An enclosure where trapped fish or other animals are kept alive. [From Middle English, from late Old English *pund* (found in *pundfald,* fold for livestock), of unknown origin.]

ă	pat	ôr	core
ā	pay	oi	boy
âr	care	ou	out
ä	father	o͝o	took
ĕ	pet	o͝or	lure
ē	be	o͞o	boot
ĭ	pit	ŭ	cut
ī	bite	ûr	urge
îr	pier	th	thin
ŏ	pot	*th*	this
ō	toe	zh	vision
ô	paw	ə	about

pound cake *n.* A rich yellow cake containing eggs, flour, butter, and sugar.

pound-fool·ish (**pound′fo͞o′**lĭsh) *adj.* Unwise in dealing with large sums of money or large matters.

pound key *n.* The pushbutton in the lower right corner of a telephone dialing pad, marked with a pound sign (#).

pound sign *n.* **1.** The symbol (£) for a unit of currency, especially the pound sterling. **2.** The symbol (#) for a pound as a unit of weight.

pound sterling *n.* The primary unit of British currency; the pound.

pour (pôr) *v.* **poured, pour·ing, pours** —*tr.* **1.** To cause (a fluid or loose particles) to flow or stream, as from a container: *pour the milk.* **2.** To send forth, produce, express, or utter, as if in a stream or flood: *poured money into the project; poured out his story.* —*intr.* **1a.** To flow or run freely: *Salt pours easily.* **b.** To stream or gush in or as if in a flood: *The water poured down over the rocks.* **c.** To rain hard: *It isn't sprinkling; it's pouring.* **2.** To come or go in large numbers or amounts; swarm or flood: *Fans poured into the arena.* **3.** To serve a beverage, such as tea or coffee, to a gathering: *Will you pour?* [From Middle English *pouren,* perhaps from Old French *purer,* to clean out, pulp (fruit), from Latin *pūrāre,* to purify.] —**pour′er** *n.*

❑ *These sound alike:* **pour, pore**[1] (study), **pore**[2] (opening).

pout (pout) *intr.v.* **pout·ed, pout·ing, pouts 1.** To show disappointment or displeasure; sulk. **2.** To push out the lips, especially as a sign of sullen annoyance. ❖ *n.* A sulky or sullen expression made by pushing out the lips.

pov·er·ty (**pŏv′**ər-tē) *n.* **1.** The state of being poor; lack of the means of providing material needs or comforts. **2.** Deficiency in amount; scantiness: *a poverty of imagination.* **3.** Unproductiveness; infertility: *the poverty of the rocky soil.* [From Middle English *poverte,* from Old French, from Latin *paupertās,* from *pauper,* poor.]

poverty level *n.* An income level below which a person is officially considered to be living in poverty.

pov·er·ty-strick·en (**pŏv′**ər-tē-strĭk′ən) *adj.* Suffering from poverty; very poor.

POW (pē′ō-**dŭb′**əl-yo͞o) *n.* A prisoner of war.

pow·der (**pou′**dər) *n.* **1a.** A substance in the form of a great number of very fine particles. **b.** Any of various preparations in this form, as certain medicines or cosmetics: *face powder; soap powder.* **2.** An explosive mixture, such as gunpowder. **3.** Light dry snow. ❖ *tr.v.* **pow·dered, pow·der·ing, pow·ders 1.** To reduce to powder; pulverize. **2.** To cover, dust, or sprinkle with or as if with powder: *powder cookies with sugar.* [From Middle English *poudre,* from Old French, from Latin *pulvis.*]

pow·dered sugar (**pou′**dərd) *n.* Confectioners' sugar.

powder horn *n.* An animal's horn capped at the open end, used to carry gunpowder.

powder keg *n.* **1.** A small cask for holding gunpowder or other explosives. **2.** A potentially explosive thing or situation.

powder puff *n.* A soft pad for applying powder to the skin.

powder room *n.* **1.** A women's bathroom. **2.** A bathroom for guests in a private home.

pow·der·y (**pou′**də-rē) *adj.* **1.** Composed of or similar to powder: *powdery snow.* **2.** Covered or dusted with or as if with powder: *a bee powdery with pollen.* **3.** Easily made into powder; crumbly: *a soft powdery rock.*

Pow·ell (**pou′**əl), **Colin Luther** Born 1937. American general and politician who served as chairman of the Joint Chiefs of Staff (1989–1993) and as secretary of state (2001–2005).

pow·er (**pou′**ər) *n.* **1.** The ability or capacity to act or perform effectively: *It is not in my power to help you.* **2.** often **powers** A specific ability, capability, or skill: *He has great powers of concentration.* **3.** Physical strength or force: *the power of ocean waves.* See Synonyms at **strength. 4.** Effectiveness or forcefulness: *a book of unusual power.* **5.** The ability or official capacity to exercise control; authority: *The emperor ruled with absolute power.* **6.** Control or leadership, especially of a government: *the party in power.* **7.** A source of authority or influence, especially a strong influential nation: *a world power.* **8a.** The rate at which work is done with respect to time, measured in units such as the watt or horsepower. **b.** The rate, with respect to time, at which electricity does work or creates its equivalent in heat. **c.** Relative capability for doing work in a given time: *an engine with lots of power.* **9a.** Energy that can be used for doing work, derived from such sources as wind, water, fuel, or electricity: *atomic power.* **b.** Electricity supplied to a building or community: *The power failed during the storm.* **10.** The number of times a number or expression is multiplied by itself, as shown by an exponent: *ten to the sixth power.* **11.** A number that represents the magnification of an optical instrument, such as a microscope or telescope. ❖ *adj.* **1.** Relating to political, social, or economic control: *a power struggle.* **2.** Operating with mechanical or electrical energy in place of bodily exertion: *power tools.* **3.** Relating to electricity: *power lines.* ❖ *tr.v.* **pow·ered, pow·er·ing, pow·ers** To supply with power, especially mechanical power: *The truck is powered by a gasoline engine.* [From Middle English, from Old French *pooir,* to be able, from Latin *potis,* able.]

pow·er·boat (**pou′**ər-bōt′) *n.* A motorboat.

pow·er·ful (**pou′**ər-fəl) *adj.* **1.** Having or capable of exerting power: *powerful machines; a powerful nation.* **2.** Highly effective; potent: *a powerful poison.* —**pow′er·ful·ly** *adv.*

pow·er·house (**pou′**ər-hous′) *n.* **1.** A person or thing that possesses great force or energy. **2.** A power plant.

power kite *n.* A parafoil controlled by a line or lines attached to a control bar and often a harness, flown as a source of pull in sports such as kiteboarding.

pow·er·less (**pou′**ər-lĭs) *adj.* Lacking strength, power, or authority to act or resist.

pow·er·lift·ing (**pou′**ər-lĭf′tĭng) *n.* Competitive weightlifting in which participants perform the squat, dead lift, and bench press.

power of attorney *n., pl.* **powers of attorney 1.** The legal authority to act or make decisions on another's behalf. **2.** A document granting this authority.

power plant *n.* A building or structure, including all its equipment, that generates electric energy.

power play *n.* In sports such as ice hockey, a situation in which one team has a temporary advantage because the other team has had one or more players removed from play on account of a penalty.

Pow·ha·tan[1] (pou′ə-**tăn′** *or* pou-**hăt′**n) 1550?–1618. Algonquian leader who founded the Powhatan confederacy and maintained peaceful relations with English colonists.

Pow·ha·tan[2] (pou′ə-**tăn′** *or* pou-**hăt′**n) *n., pl.* **Powhatan** or **Pow·ha·tans 1.** A member of a confederacy of Native American peoples of eastern Virginia in the 1500s and 1600s, with descendants now living chiefly in Virginia and New Jersey. **2.** The Algonquian language of the Powhatan.

pow·wow (**pou′**wou′) *n.* **1.** A council or meeting of Native Americans. **2a.** A Native American shaman. **b.** A ceremony conducted by a shaman, as in the performance of healing or hunting rituals. **3.** *Informal* A conference or gathering.

pox (pŏks) *n.* A disease, such as chickenpox or smallpox, characterized by pus-filled eruptions on the skin.

Beatrix Potter

potter's wheel

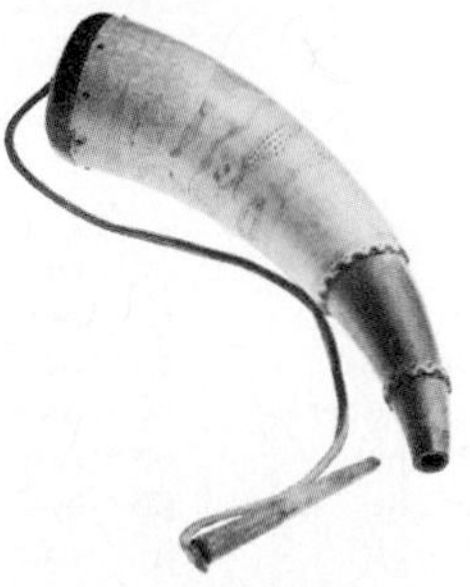

powder horn

prairie dog

praying mantis

ă	pat	ôr	core
ā	pay	oi	boy
âr	care	ou	out
ä	father	o͝o	took
ĕ	pet	o͝or	lure
ē	be	o͞o	boot
ĭ	pit	ŭ	cut
ī	bite	ûr	urge
îr	pier	th	thin
ŏ	pot	*th*	this
ō	toe	zh	vision
ô	paw	ə	about

pp. *abbr.* An abbreviation of pages.

p.p. *abbr.* An abbreviation of: **1.** parcel post. **2.** past participle. **3.** postpaid.

PQ *abbr.* An abbreviation of Quebec (postal code).

Pr The symbol for the element **praseodymium.**

PR *abbr.* An abbreviation of: **1.** public relations. **2.** Puerto Rico.

pr. *abbr.* An abbreviation of: **1.** pair. **2.** present.

prac·ti·ca·ble (**prăk′**tĭ-kə-bəl) *adj.* **1.** Capable of being done, carried out, or put into effect; possible: *a practicable solution to the problem.* **2.** Usable for a certain purpose: *a practicable ski slope.* **—prac′ti·ca·bil′i·ty** *n.* **—prac′ti·ca·bly** *adv.*

prac·ti·cal (**prăk′**tĭ-kəl) *adj.* **1.** Coming from or involving practice or action rather than theory or speculation: *gained practical experience from doing summer jobs as a teenager.* **2.** Manifested in or involving practice: *practical applications of geometry.* **3.** Capable of being used or put into effect; useful: *practical knowledge of Spanish.* **4.** Concerned with the operation or production of something useful: *Woodworking is a practical art.* **5.** Having or showing good judgment; sensible: *If we're practical, we can do the job quickly.* **6.** Being actually so in almost every respect; virtual: *The snowstorm was a practical disaster.* **—prac′ti·cal′i·ty** (prăk′tĭ-**kăl′**ĭ-tē) *n.*

practical joke *n.* A mischievous trick or prank played on a person, especially one that causes embarrassment.

prac·ti·cal·ly (**prăk′**tĭk-lē) *adv.* **1.** Almost; nearly: *The school year is practically over.* **2.** In a practical way: *They dressed practically for the long hike.*

prac·tice (**prăk′**tĭs) *tr.v.* **prac·ticed, prac·tic·ing, prac·tic·es 1.** To make a habit of; do or perform regularly: *Learn to practice self-control.* **2.** To do or work on over and over in order to gain or polish a skill: *practice the piano.* **3.** To work at, especially as a professional: *practice medicine.* **4.** To carry out in action; observe: *practice what one preaches.* ❖ *n.* **1.** A habitual or customary action or way of doing something: *makes a practice of being on time.* See Synonyms at **habit. 2a.** Experience or exercise in doing something that develops, maintains, or improves one's skill: *Practice will improve your singing.* **b.** A session of preparation or performance that a person does to acquire or polish a skill: *has soccer practice every other day.* **c.** Skill gained or maintained through repeated exercise: *Because I was out of practice, I made mistakes while playing the piano.* **3.** Action, performance, use, or effect: *Put into practice what you have learned.* **4.** Exercise of an occupation or profession: *the practice of medicine.* **5.** The business of a professional person: *She has her own law practice.* **6.** often **practices** A habitual or customary action: *The history teacher has unusual grading practices.*

prac·ticed (**prăk′**tĭst) *adj.* Skilled or expert; proficient: *a practiced archer.*

practice teacher *n.* A student teacher.

prac·tise (**prăk′**tĭs) *v. & n. Chiefly British* Variant of **practice.**

prac·ti·tion·er (prăk-**tĭsh′**ə-nər) *n.* A person who practices something, especially an occupation, profession, or technique.

prae·tor (**prē′**tər) *n.* An elected magistrate of the ancient Roman republic, ranking below a consul but having approximately the same functions.

prae·to·ri·an (prē-**tôr′**ē-ən) *adj.* **1.** Relating to a praetor. **2. Praetorian** Relating to the bodyguard of a Roman emperor. ❖ *n.* **1.** A praetor or a former praetor. **2. Praetorian** A member of the bodyguard of a Roman emperor.

prag·mat·ic (prăg-**măt′**ĭk) *adj.* **1.** Concerned or dealing with facts and actual occurrences; practical: *a pragmatic approach to solving problems.* **2.** Relating to pragmatism. [From Greek *prāgma*, deed, concrete reality, thing of consequence.] **—prag·mat′i·cal·ly** *adv.*

prag·ma·tism (**prăg′**mə-tĭz′əm) *n.* **1.** The philosophical theory that the meaning of an idea or proposition is to be judged by its practical results. **2.** A practical way of approaching or assessing situations or of solving problems.

Prague (präg) The capital of the Czech Republic, in the western part of the country south-southeast of Dresden, Germany. It was the capital of Czechoslovakia from 1918 to 1993.

Prai·a (**prī′**ə) The capital of Cape Verde, on an island in the Atlantic Ocean west of Dakar, Senegal.

prai·rie (**prâr′**ē) *n.* A wide area of flat or rolling, mostly treeless grassland, especially the large plain of central North America. [From French, meadow, from Old French *praierie*, from Latin *prāta*.]

prairie chicken *n.* Either of two plump ground-dwelling birds of western North America having mottled brown feathers.

prairie dog *n.* Any of several burrowing rodents of the plains of central North America, living in large colonies and having a call resembling a dog's bark.

prairie schooner *n.* A covered wagon.

prairie wolf *n.* A coyote.

praise (prāz) *n.* **1.** Expression of approval, admiration, or commendation: *Praise from her family meant a lot to her.* **2.** Glory, honor, and adoration as given to a deity, ruler, or hero. ❖ *tr.v.* **praised, prais·ing, prais·es 1.** To express approval of or admiration for; commend: *Everyone praised her good sense.* **2.** To extol or exalt; worship. [From Middle English, from *preisen*, to praise, from Old French *preisier*, from Late Latin *pretiāre*, to prize, from Latin *pretium*, price.] **—prais′er** *n.*

praise·wor·thy (**prāz′**wûr′*th*ē) *adj.* **praise·wor·thi·er, praise·wor·thi·est** Deserving praise; highly commendable: *a praiseworthy devotion.*

pram (prăm) *n. Chiefly British* A baby carriage. [Short for *perambulator.*]

prance (prăns) *intr.v.* **pranced, pranc·ing, pranc·es 1a.** To spring forward on the hind legs. Used of a horse. **b.** To spring forward in a manner like that of a lively horse. **2.** To walk or move with light, lively steps: *pranced onstage.* ❖ *n.* The act or an instance of prancing.

prank (prăngk) *n.* A mischievous trick or practical joke. **—prank′ish** *adj.*

prank·ster (**prăngk′**stər) *n.* A person who plays tricks or pranks.

pra·se·o·dym·i·um (prā′zē-ō-**dĭm′**ē-əm) *n. Symbol* **Pr** A soft, silvery metallic element used to color glass and ceramics yellow. Atomic number 59. See **Periodic Table.**

prate (prāt) *intr.v.* **prat·ed, prat·ing, prates** To talk foolishly and at length; chatter.

prat·tle (**prăt′**l) *intr.v.* **prat·tled, prat·tling, prat·tles** To chatter idly: *prattling about how much things cost.* ❖ *n.* Idle or meaningless chatter.

prawn (prôn) *n.* Any of various shrimps, especially one that is large or inhabits fresh water.

pray (prā) *v.* **prayed, pray·ing, prays** *—intr.* To say a prayer or prayers to God or a god, often as a request or plea. *—tr.* **1.** To utter or say a prayer or prayers (that something may happen): *The congregation prayed that the drought would end quickly.* **2.** To make a devout or earnest request for: *I pray your forgiveness.* [From Middle English *preien*, from Old French *preier*, from Latin *precārī*.]

❑ *These sound alike:* **pray, prey** (hunted animal).

prayer (prâr) *n.* **1.** A request or expression of devotion, often using a special set of words, addressed to God or a god: *The chaplain always says a prayer before eating.* **2.** The act of addressing or appealing to God or a god, as in devotion or pleading: *belief in the power of prayer.* **3. prayers** A religious service consisting mostly of prayers: *morning prayers.* **4.** An earnest wish or plea:

their prayer that everything would go smoothly. **5.** The slightest chance or hope, as for survival or success: *Without our best player, we don't have a prayer.*

prayer book *n.* A book containing religious prayers.

prayer·ful (prâr**′**fəl) *adj.* Inclined to pray frequently; devout.

pray·ing mantis (prā**′**ĭng) *n.* A European mantis that folds its front legs as though it were praying.

pre– *pref.* A prefix that means: **1.** Earlier; before: *prehistoric.* **2.** In advance: *prepay.* —SEE NOTE

preach (prēch) *v.* **preached, preach·ing, preach·es** —*tr.* **1.** To proclaim or put forth in a sermon: *preaches the gospel.* **2.** To teach or advocate and urge others to accept or follow: *Our leaders preach tolerance of others.* **3.** To deliver (a sermon): *The minister preached the morning sermon.* —*intr.* **1.** To deliver a sermon. **2.** To give religious or moral instruction, especially in a tedious manner: *a writer with an unfortunate tendency to preach.*

preach·er (prē**′**chər) *n.* A person who preaches, especially one who proclaims the gospel as an occupation.

preach·y (prē**′**chē) *adj.* **preach·i·er, preach·i·est** Inclined to or given to tedious and excessive moralizing.

pre·am·ble (prē**′**ăm′bəl) *n.* An introductory statement, especially the introduction to a formal document that serves to explain its purpose. [From Middle English, from Old French *preambule*, from Medieval Latin *praeambulum* : Latin *prae-*, in front + Latin *ambulāre*, to walk.]

pre·am·pli·fi·er (prē-**ăm′**plə-fī′ər) *n.* An electronic circuit or device designed to amplify and often otherwise process very weak signals before they are further amplified.

pre·ap·prove (prē′ə-**proov′**) *tr.v.* **pre·ap·proved, pre·ap·prov·ing, pre·ap·proves** To approve (an application, for example) at an earlier point in the approval process than is usual, sometimes before approval is even requested.

pre·ar·range (prē′ə-**rānj′**) *tr.v.* **pre·ar·ranged, pre·ar·rang·ing, pre·ar·rang·es** To arrange in advance.

Pre·cam·bri·an (prē-**kăm′**brē-ən) *n.* The span of geologic time between Hadean Time and the Cambrian Period, from about 3.8 billion to 542 million years ago. During the Precambrian, the earliest life forms appeared on the earth. See table at **geologic time.** —**Pre·cam′bri·an** *adj.*

pre·car·i·ous (prĭ-**kâr′**ē-əs) *adj.* **1.** Dangerously lacking in security or stability: *dangling in a precarious position.* **2.** Subject to chance or unknown conditions: *The economic outlook remains precarious.* [From Latin *precārius*, given as a favor, borrowed, uncertain, from *precārī*, to entreat, pray to.] —**pre·car′i·ous·ly** *adv.*

pre·cau·tion (prĭ-**kô′**shən) *n.* **1.** An action taken in advance to guard against possible danger, failure, or injury; a safeguard: *take safety precautions.* **2.** Care taken or caution shown in advance; forethought: *This safety film will emphasize the need for precaution when driving on the highway.* —**pre·cau′tion·a′ry** (prĭ-**kô′**shə-nĕr′ē) *adj.*

pre·cede (prĭ-**sēd′**) *tr.v.* **pre·ced·ed, pre·ced·ing, pre·cedes 1.** To come, exist, or occur before in time, order, position, or rank: *A short lecture will precede the movie.* **2.** To preface or introduce: *The professor preceded his lecture with some jokes.* [From Middle English *preceden*, from Latin *praecēdere* : *prae-*, before + *cēdere*, to go.]

prec·e·dence (**prĕs′**ĭ-dəns *or* prĭ-**sēd′**ns) *n.* **1.** The fact, state, or right of preceding; priority: *Business takes precedence over pleasure.* **2.** Priority claimed or received because of preeminence or superiority.

prec·e·dent (**prĕs′**ĭ-dənt) *n.* **1.** An act or instance that can serve as an example in dealing with subsequent similar instances. **2.** Convention or custom arising from practice: *The precedent has been to give an exam every six weeks.* ❖ *adj.* (prĭ-**sēd′**nt *or* **prĕs′**ĭ-dənt) Preceding.

pre·ced·ing (prĭ-**sē′**dĭng) *adj.* **1.** Existing or coming before another or others: *in preceding years; on a preceding page.* **2.** Existing or coming immediately before another or others: *the preceding year; the preceding page.*

pre·cept (**prē′**sĕpt′) *n.* A rule or principle of conduct or procedure.

pre·cep·tor (prĭ-**sĕp′**tər *or* **prē′**sĕp′tər) *n.* **1.** An instructor; a teacher. **2.** An expert or specialist who gives practical experience and training to a student.

pre·ces·sion (prē-**sĕsh′**ən) *n.* **1.** The motion of the axis of a spinning body, such as the wobbling of a spinning top, that arises when an external force acts on the axis. **2.** The motion of this kind made by the earth. **3.** The slow change from year to year in the sun's position on the celestial sphere during the equinoxes, caused by the precession of the earth's axis over a 25,800-year cycle.

pre·cinct (**prē′**sĭngkt′) *n.* **1.** A subdivision or district of a city or town patrolled by a unit of the police force. **2.** An election district of a city or town: *a canvass of the voters in his precinct.* **3. precincts** An area or enclosure with definite boundaries: *within the precincts of the university.* **4. precincts** A neighboring region; environs.

pre·cious (**prĕsh′**əs) *adj.* **1.** Of high cost or worth; valuable: *precious metals.* **2.** Highly esteemed; cherished: *thanked her for her precious advice.* **3.** Dear; beloved. ❖ *n.* A person who is dear or beloved; a darling. ❖ *adv.* Used as an intensive: *We have precious little time before the contract expires.* [From Middle English, from Old French, from Latin *pretiōsus*, from *pretium*, price.] —**pre′cious·ly** *adv.* —**pre′cious·ness** *n.*

precious stone *n.* Any of several gems, such as the diamond or the ruby, that have high economic value because of their rarity or appearance.

prec·i·pice (**prĕs′**ə-pĭs) *n.* A very steep or overhanging mass of rock, such as the face of a cliff.

pre·cip·i·tate (prĭ-**sĭp′**ĭ-tāt′) *v.* **pre·cip·i·tat·ed, pre·cip·i·tat·ing, pre·cip·i·tates** —*tr.* **1.** To cause to happen, especially suddenly or prematurely; bring on: *The revelation of the scandal precipitated the director's resignation.* **2.** To cause (water vapor) to condense from the atmosphere and fall as rain or snow. **3.** To separate chemically from a solution in the form of a solid: *We precipitated the minerals from the water by adding borax.* —*intr.* **1.** To condense and fall from the air as rain or snow. **2.** To be separated from a solution as a solid. ❖ *adj.* (prĭ-**sĭp′**ĭ-tĭt) **1.** Moving rapidly and heedlessly; speeding headlong: *the precipitate course of a tornado.* **2.** Acting or made hastily or impulsively; rash: *a precipitate decision.* **3.** Occurring suddenly and unexpectedly: *a precipitate drop in oil prices.* ❖ *n.* (prĭ-**sĭp′**ĭ-tāt′ *or* prĭ-**sĭp′**ĭ-tĭt) A solid material separated from a solution by chemical means. [From Latin *praeceps*, headlong : *prae-*, before, first + *caput*, head.]

pre·cip·i·ta·tion (prĭ-sĭp′ĭ-**tā′**shən) *n.* **1a.** A form of water, such as rain, snow, or sleet, that condenses from the atmosphere and falls to the surface of the earth. **b.** The amount of such water falling in a given area during a given period of time: *Last month's precipitation in our state was 2 inches.* **2.** Abrupt or impulsive haste. **3.** A hastening or acceleration, especially one that is sudden or unexpected. **4.** A headlong fall or rush. **5.** The production of a precipitate, as in a chemical reaction.

pre·cip·i·tous (prĭ-**sĭp′**ĭ-təs) *adj.* **1.** Similar to a precipice; extremely steep. **2.** Having several precipices: *backed away from the precipitous bluff.* —**pre·cip′i·tous·ly** *adv.* —**pre·cip′i·tous·ness** *n.*

pre·cise (prĭ-**sīs′**) *adj.* **1.** Clearly expressed or delineated; definite: *Please be precise in your instructions.* **2.** Exact in performance or execution: *threw the ball with precise aim.* **3.** Providing very specific detail: *a precise measurement.* **4.** Distinct from others; particular: *on this precise*

WORD BUILDING

pre– The basic meaning of the prefix **pre–** is "before." It comes from the Latin word *prae*, which means "before, in front." In fact, the word *prefix* itself comes from *prae* + *fīxus*, a form of the Latin verb *fīgere* ("to fasten"). *Pre–* was first used in English in combination with roots of Latin origin, as in the words *preconceive, preexist,* and *premeditate,* all of which date to the 1500s. By the 1800s and 1900s, *pre–* began being widely used with roots of English origin as well, as in the cases of *preheat* and *preset.*

precipice
Kilt Rock, Isle of Skye, Scotland

WRITERS CHOOSE THEIR WORDS

The eagle came back, seized him in his talons by the back of his coat, and swooped off. This time he flew only a short way. Very soon Bilbo was laid down, trembling with fear, on a wide shelf of rock on the mountainside. There was no path down onto it save by flying; and no path down off it except by jumping over a **precipice.**

—J.R.R. Tolkien
The Hobbit

WORD BUILDING

predict The word root *dict–* in English words comes from the past participle *dictus* of the Latin verb *dīcere,* "to say." Thus we have **predict,** "to say ahead of time, foretell" (using the prefix *pre–,* "before"), and **contradict,** "to speak against" (*contrā–,* "opposite, against"). Without any prefixes, *dict–* appears in **diction,** from the Latin noun *dictiō,* "the act of speaking."

spot. **5.** Distinct or correct in sound or meaning: *Can you give me the precise pronunciation of that word?* **6.** Strictly observing established forms and procedures: *a precise gentleman who ate breakfast at 7:15 each morning.* [From Middle English, from Latin *praecīsus,* cut short, concise, from *praecīdere,* to cut short.] **—pre·cise′ly** *adv.*

pre·ci·sion (prĭ-**sĭzh′**ən) *n.* The state or quality of being precise: *the precision of a chemist's scales.*

pre·clude (prĭ-**klo͞od′**) *tr.v.* **pre·clud·ed, pre·clud·ing, pre·cludes** To make impossible, as by action taken in advance; prevent: *High temperatures on Venus preclude any chance of life as we know it.*

pre·co·cial (prĭ-**kō′**shəl) *adj.* Hatched or born with the eyes open and the ability to move around and search for food. The young of chickens, horses, and sheep are precocial. [From Latin *praecox,* premature.]

pre·co·cious (prĭ-**kō′**shəs) *adj.* Showing particular abilities, characteristics, or interests at an unusually early age: *a mathematically precocious child.* [From Latin *praecox,* premature, from *praecoquere,* to ripen early.] **—pre·co′cious·ly** *adv.* **—pre·co′cious·ness, pre·coc′i·ty** (prĭ-**kŏs′**ĭ-tē) *n.*

pre-Co·lum·bi·an or **pre·co·lum·bi·an** (prē′kə-**lŭm′**bē-ən) *adj.* Relating to the Americas before the arrival of Columbus: *pre-Columbian empires.*

pre·con·ceived (prē′kən-**sēvd′**) *adj.* Relating to an idea that is formed in advance: *His preconceived notions about the film kept him from enjoying it.*

pre·con·cep·tion (prē′kən-**sĕp′**shən) *n.* An idea or opinion formed before adequate knowledge is available; a prejudice.

pre·con·di·tion (prē′kən-**dĭsh′**ən) *n.* A condition that must exist or be established before something can occur or be considered; a prerequisite.

pre·cur·sor (prĭ-**kûr′**sər *or* **prē′**kûr′sər) *n.* **1.** An indicator of a person or thing to come; a forerunner: *The cool breeze was a precursor of the storm.* **2.** A person or thing that precedes another: *She greeted her precursor, the former principal.* [From Middle English *precursoure,* from Latin *praecursor,* from *praecurrere,* to run before.] —SEE NOTE AT **cursive.**

pred. *abbr.* An abbreviation of predicate.

pre·date (prē-**dāt′**) *tr.v.* **pre·dat·ed, pre·dat·ing, pre·dates 1.** To mark with a date earlier than the actual one: *predate a check.* **2.** To precede in time; antedate: *The American Revolution predates the French Revolution.*

pred·a·tor (**prĕd′**ə-tər) *n.* An animal that lives by hunting other animals and eating them. [From Latin *praedātor,* from *praedārī,* to plunder, catch (prey), from *praeda,* booty, prey.]

pred·a·to·ry (**prĕd′**ə-tôr′ē) *adj.* **1.** Living by preying on other animals: *a predatory animal.* **2.** Characterized by the exploitation of others for personal gain: *predatory business practices.*

pred·e·ces·sor (**prĕd′**ĭ-sĕs′ər *or* **prē′**dĭ-sĕs′ər) *n.* **1.** A person who precedes another in time, especially in holding an office or function: *The new mayor's predecessor welcomed her.* **2.** Something that has been succeeded by another: *The new building is more spacious than its predecessor.*

pre·des·ti·na·tion (prē-dĕs′tə-**nā′**shən) *n.* **1.** The act of predestining or the condition of being predestined. **2a.** The doctrine that God has planned and ordered all events in advance. **b.** The doctrine that God has assigned every soul to eternal salvation or damnation. **3.** Fate; destiny.

pre·des·tine (prē-**dĕs′**tĭn) *tr.v.* **pre·des·tined, pre·des·tin·ing, pre·des·tines** To fix or decide beforehand, especially by divine decree: *The Greeks believed that the gods predestined the early death of heroes.*

pre·de·ter·mine (prē′dĭ-**tûr′**mĭn) *tr.v.* **pre·de·ter·mined, pre·de·ter·min·ing, pre·de·ter·mines 1.** To determine, decide, or establish in advance: *Climate predetermines the kinds of animals that can live in a region.* **2.** To influence or sway toward an action or opinion; predispose. **—pre′de·ter′mi·na′tion** *n.*

pre·dic·a·ment (prĭ-**dĭk′**ə-mənt) *n.* A situation, especially an unpleasant or troubling one, from which it is difficult to remove oneself.

pred·i·cate (**prĕd′**ĭ-kĭt) *n.* The part of a sentence or clause that expresses the action or condition of the subject and includes the verb and the objects or phrases governed by the verb, as *opened the door* in *Jane opened the door.* ❖ *adj.* Relating to the predicate of a sentence or clause. ❖ *tr.v.* (**prĕd′**ĭ-kāt′) **pred·i·cat·ed, pred·i·cat·ing, pred·i·cates** To base or establish (a statement or action, for example) on something: *She predicated her argument on the assumption that inflation would not go up.* —SEE NOTE AT **adjective.**

predicate adjective *n.* An adjective that follows a linking verb and describes the subject of the verb, as *steep* in *The path looks steep.*

predicate nominative *n.* A noun or pronoun that follows a linking verb and refers to the same person or thing as the subject of the verb, as *president* in *Roosevelt became president.*

pre·dict (prĭ-**dĭkt′**) *tr.v.* **pre·dict·ed, pre·dict·ing, pre·dicts** To tell about or make known in advance, especially on the basis of special knowledge; foretell: *predicted showers for this evening.* [From Latin *praedīcere* : *prae-,* before + *dīcere,* to say.] **—pre·dict′a·ble** *adj.* —SEE NOTE.

pre·dic·tion (prĭ-**dĭk′**shən) *n.* **1.** The act of predicting. **2.** Something that is foretold or predicted: *Her predictions came true.*

pred·i·lec·tion (prĕd′l-**ĕk′**shən *or* prēd′l-**ĕk′**shən) *n.* A special liking for something; a preference: *had a predilection for horror movies.*

pre·dis·pose (prē′dĭ-**spōz′**) *tr.v.* **pre·dis·posed, pre·dis·pos·ing, pre·dis·pos·es 1.** To incline or influence beforehand: *Her sense of humor predisposed me in her favor.* **2.** To make susceptible or liable: *conditions that predispose miners to lung disease.*

pre·dis·po·si·tion (prē′dĭs-pə-**zĭsh′**ən) *n.* The state of being predisposed; tendency, inclination, or susceptibility.

pre·dom·i·nant (prĭ-**dŏm′**ə-nənt) *adj.* **1.** Greater than all others in strength, authority, or importance; dominant: *the predominant nation.* **2.** Most common or conspicuous: *the predominant color in a design.* **—pre·dom′i·nance** *n.* **—pre·dom′i·nant·ly** *adv.*

pre·dom·i·nate (prĭ-**dŏm′**ə-nāt′) *intr.v.* **pre·dom·i·nat·ed, pre·dom·i·nat·ing, pre·dom·i·nates 1.** To have or gain power or controlling influence; prevail. **2.** To be greater than others in number or importance: *People of Italian descent predominate in this neighborhood.*

pre·em·i·nent (prē-**ĕm′**ə-nənt) *adj.* Superior to or notable above all others; outstanding: *the preeminent artist of the movement.* **—pre·em′i·nence** *n.* **—pre·em′i·nent·ly** *adv.*

pre·empt (prē-**ĕmpt′**) *tr.v.* **pre·empt·ed, pre·empt·ing, pre·empts 1.** To take the place of; displace: *The president's speech will preempt the regular shows this evening.* **2a.** To take action to prevent (an event or other action) from happening; forestall: *He resigned to preempt further investigation into his dealings.* **b.** To take action to prevent (someone else) from acting: *She got a patent to preempt others from copying her invention.* **3a.** To acquire or take for oneself before others: *got to the market early and preempted the bargains.* **b.** To gain possession of by prior right, especially to settle on (public land) so as to obtain the right to buy before others.

preen (prēn) *v.* **preened, preen·ing, preens** —*tr.* **1a.**

ă	pat	ôr	core
ā	pay	oi	boy
âr	care	ou	out
ä	father	o͝o	took
ĕ	pet	o͝or	lure
ē	be	o͞o	boot
ĭ	pit	ŭ	cut
ī	bite	ûr	urge
îr	pier	th	thin
ŏ	pot	*th*	this
ō	toe	zh	vision
ô	paw	ə	about

To smooth or clean (feathers) with the beak or bill: *The parrot preened its feathers.* **b.** To trim or clean (fur) with the tongue, as cats do. **2.** To dress or groom (oneself) with elaborate care; primp. **3.** To take self-satisfied pride in (oneself). *—intr.* **1.** To primp. **2.** To swell with pride; gloat.

pre·ex·ist (prē′ĭg-**zĭst′**) *intr.v.* **pre·ex·ist·ed, pre·ex·ist·ing, pre·ex·ists** To exist beforehand.

pref. *abbr.* An abbreviation of prefix.

pre·fab (**prē′**făb′) *Informal adj.* Prefabricated. ❖ *n.* A prefabricated house or other structure.

pre·fab·ri·cate (prē-**făb′**rĭ-kāt′) *tr.v.* **pre·fab·ri·cat·ed, pre·fab·ri·cat·ing, pre·fab·ri·cates** To build or manufacture (a building or section of a building, for example) in advance, especially in sections that can be easily shipped and assembled. **—pre′fab′ri·ca′tion** *n.*

pref·ace (**prĕf′**ĭs) *n.* **1.** An introductory essay, placed at the beginning of a book for explanation. **2.** A statement or series of remarks that introduces or explains what is to come: *a preface to a speech.* ❖ *tr.v.* **pref·aced, pref·ac·ing, pref·ac·es** To introduce or provide with a preface: *prefaced his lecture with a joke.* [From Middle English, from Latin *praefātiō* : *prae-*, before + *fārī*, to speak.] **—pref′ac·er** *n.*

pref·a·to·ry (**prĕf′**ə-tôr′ē) *adj.* Relating to or serving as an introduction; preliminary: *prefatory remarks.*

pre·fect (**prē′**fĕkt′) *n.* **1.** Any of various ancient Roman officials of high rank. **2.** Any of various modern administrative officials, such as a chief of police in Paris, France. **3.** A student monitor or officer, especially in a private school.

pre·fer (prĭ-**fûr′**) *tr.v.* **pre·ferred, pre·fer·ring, pre·fers** To choose or be in the habit of choosing as more desirable; like better: *I prefer tea to coffee.* [From Middle English *preferren*, from Old French *preferer*, from Latin *praeferre* : *prae-*, before, in front + *ferre*, to carry.] —SEE NOTE AT **pretty.**

pref·er·a·ble (**prĕf′**ər-ə-bəl) *adj.* More desirable; preferred: *I find bagels preferable to muffins.* **—pref′er·a·bly** *adv.*

pref·er·ence (**prĕf′**ər-əns) *n.* **1.** The act of preferring someone or something over another or others: *had a preference for rice over potatoes.* **2.** The state of being preferred; favor over others: *Members of the cast's family will be given preference for seating.* **3.** A person or thing preferred; one's choice: *asked for a window seat, but did not obtain her preference.* See Synonyms at **choice.**

pref·er·en·tial (prĕf′ə-**rĕn′**shəl) *adj.* Showing preference; favoring one over others: *The owner's friends always receive preferential treatment.* **—pref′er·en′tial·ly** *adv.*

pre·fer·ment (prĭ-**fûr′**mənt) *n.* The act of advancing to a higher position or office; promotion: *her preferment to an executive position.*

preferred stock (prĭ-**fûrd′**) *n.* Stock shares in a corporation that entitle the owner to be paid dividends and often assets before payments are made to the owners of common stock.

pre·fig·ure (prē-**fĭg′**yər) *tr.v.* **pre·fig·ured, pre·fig·ur·ing, pre·fig·ures 1.** To suggest, indicate, or represent by a preceding form or model; foreshadow. **2.** To imagine or picture to oneself in advance.

pre·fix (**prē′**fĭks′) *tr.v.* **pre·fixed, pre·fix·ing, pre·fix·es** To add at the beginning or front: *prefixed the title "Dr." to his name.* ❖ *n.* **1.** An affix placed at the beginning of a word to create a new word. For example, *un–* in *unable, pre–* in *preheat,* and *re–* in *replay* are prefixes. **2.** A title placed before a person's name.

pre·flight (**prē′flīt′**) *adj.* Occurring before flight.

preg·nan·cy (**prĕg′**nən-sē) *n., pl.* **preg·nan·cies 1.** The condition of being pregnant. **2.** The time during which one is pregnant.

preg·nant (**prĕg′**nənt) *adj.* **1.** Carrying developing offspring within the body. **2.** Significant; full of meaning: *a pregnant pause in the campaign speech.* **3.** Full or fraught; replete: *a situation pregnant with danger.*

pre·heat (prē-**hēt′**) *tr.v.* **pre·heat·ed, pre·heat·ing, pre·heats** To heat (an oven, for example) beforehand: *Preheat the oven to 350° before baking.*

pre·hen·sile (prē-**hĕn′**səl *or* prē-**hĕn′**sīl′) *adj.* Able to seize, grasp, or hold, especially by wrapping around an object: *a monkey's prehensile tail.*

prehensile
prehensile tail of an opossum

pre·his·tor·ic (prē′hĭ-**stôr′**ĭk) *adj.* Relating to the time before history or events were recorded in writing: *a prehistoric animal.* **—pre′his·tor′i·cal·ly** *adv.*

pre·judge (prē-**jŭj′**) *tr.v.* **pre·judged, pre·judg·ing, pre·judg·es** To judge beforehand without adequate evidence.

prej·u·dice (**prĕj′**ə-dĭs) *n.* **1.** An adverse judgment or opinion formed unfairly or before one knows the facts; a bias: *a prejudice against unfamiliar foods.* **2.** Irrational suspicion or hatred of a particular race, religion, or group. **3.** Harm or injury caused by the preconceived unfavorable conviction of another or others. ❖ *tr.v.* **prej·u·diced, prej·u·dic·ing, prej·u·dic·es 1.** To cause (someone) to judge prematurely and irrationally: *an experience that prejudiced her against dogs.* **2.** To affect harmfully by a judgment or act. [From Middle English, from Latin *praeiūdicium* : *prae-*, before + *iūdicium*, judgment.]

prej·u·di·cial (prĕj′ə-**dĭsh′**əl) *adj.* **1.** Causing injury; harmful. **2.** Causing or tending toward preconceived judgment or convictions. **—prej′u·di′cial·ly** *adv.*

prel·ate (**prĕl′**ĭt) *n.* A high-ranking member of the clergy, especially a bishop.

pre·lim·i·nar·y (prĭ-**lĭm′**ə-nĕr′ē) *adj.* Prior to or preparing for the main matter, action, or business; introductory: *preliminary sketches for a building.* ❖ *n., pl.* **pre·lim·i·nar·ies** Something that leads to or serves as preparation for a main matter, action, or business: *She began her lecture without the usual preliminaries.* [From Latin *prae-*, before + Latin *līmen*, threshold.]

prel·ude (**prĕl′**yo͞od′ *or* **prā′**lo͞od′ *or* **prē′**lo͞od′) *n.* **1.** An introductory performance, event, or action that precedes a more important one; a preliminary. **2a.** A piece or movement of music that acts as introduction to a larger work. **b.** A short composition written in a free style, especially for a keyboard instrument. [From Latin *praelūdere*, to compose a prelude (to a larger work) : *prae-*, before + *lūdere*, to play.]

pre·mar·i·tal (prē-**măr′**ĭ-tl) *adj.* Taking place or existing before marriage.

pre·ma·ture (prē′mə-**tyo͝or′** *or* prē′mə-**to͝or′** *or* prē′mə-**cho͝or′**) *adj.* **1.** Appearing or occurring before the usual time; unexpectedly early: *a premature death.* **2.** Born after too short a period of development: *a premature baby.* **—pre′ma·ture′ly** *adv.*

pre·med (**prē′mĕd′**) *Informal adj.* Premedical. ❖ *n.* **1.** A premedical student. **2.** A premedical program of study.

pre·med·i·cal (prē-**mĕd′**ĭ-kəl) *adj.* Relating to studies that prepare one for the study of medicine.

pre·med·i·tate (prē-**mĕd′**ĭ-tāt′) *tr.v.* **pre·med·i·tat·ed, pre·med·i·tat·ing, pre·med·i·tates** To plan, arrange, or plot (a crime, for example) in advance. **—pre·med′i·ta′tion** *n.*

pre·mier (prĭ-**mîr′** *or* **prē′**mîr) *adj.* **1.** First in status or importance; principal or chief. **2.** Earliest. ❖ *n.* (prĭ-**mîr′**) A prime minister or a chief administrative officer, as of a country or province. [From Middle English *primer*, from Old French *premier*, from Latin *prīmārius*, from *prīmus*, first.]

pre·miere (prĭ-**mîr′** *or* prĭ-**myâr′**) *n.* The first public performance, as of a movie or a play.

prem·ise (**prĕm′**ĭs) *n.* **1.** A proposition upon which an argument is based or from which a conclusion is drawn.

WRITERS CHOOSE THEIR WORDS

Now and then, a speed bump, or a siren, or an angry car horn made Cadel look up from his laptop. For the most part, however, he was too **preoccupied** to absorb much of the scenery, which dissolved into a kind of background blur.

—Catherine Jinks
The Genius Wars

WRITERS CHOOSE THEIR WORDS

"Yeah," Marcus agreed. "Even if he *wanted* to steal all that stuff, where was he going to put it? In a pillowcase? He's going to walk to the train station carrying a pillowcase full of clanking silverware?" We hooted with laughter at such a **preposterous** picture.

—Lois Lowry
Us and Uncle Fraud

ă	pat	ôr	core
ā	pay	oi	boy
âr	care	ou	out
ä	father	ŏŏ	took
ĕ	pet	ŏŏr	lure
ē	be	ōō	boot
ĭ	pit	ŭ	cut
ī	bite	ûr	urge
îr	pier	th	thin
ŏ	pot	*th*	this
ō	toe	zh	vision
ô	paw	ə	about

2. premises Property and the buildings on it: *The playground is part of the school premises.* ❖ *tr.v.* **prem·ised, prem·is·ing, prem·is·es** To provide a basis for; base: *a plan premised on unrealistic assumptions.*

pre·mi·um (prē**′**mē-əm) *n.* **1a.** An amount paid or required, often as an installment payment, for an insurance policy. **b.** The amount paid to obtain a loan. **c.** The amount at which a securities option is bought or sold. **2.** A sum of money or bonus paid in addition to a regular price, salary, or other amount: *Many people are willing to pay a premium to live near the ocean.* **3.** Something offered free or at a reduced price as an inducement to buy something else: *The bank offered the backpack as a premium for students opening new accounts.* **4.** An unusual or high value: *Many people place a premium on a good education.* ❖ *adj.* Of especially high quality or value: *premium gasoline.* ◆ **at a premium** More valuable than usual, as from scarcity: *Gasoline was at a premium that summer.* [From Latin *praemium*, payment, reward.]

pre·mo·lar (prē-**mō′**lər) *n.* Any of eight bicuspid teeth arranged in pairs on both sides of the upper and lower jaws between the canines and molars. **—pre·mo′lar** *adj.*

pre·mo·ni·tion (prĕm′ə-**nĭsh′**ən *or* prē′mə-**nĭsh′**ən) *n.* **1.** A presentiment of the future; a foreboding: *had a premonition of disaster.* **2.** An advance warning: *gave no premonition of her plans.* [From Latin *praemonēre*, to forewarn : *prae-*, before + *monēre*, to warn.]

pre·na·tal (prē-**nāt′**l) *adj.* Relating to the time before birth: *prenatal visits to the doctor.*

pre·oc·cu·pa·tion (prē-ŏk′yə-**pā′**shən) *n.* **1.** The state of being preoccupied; absorption of the attention or intellect. **2.** Something that preoccupies or engrosses the mind: *Increasing profits was his sole preoccupation.*

pre·oc·cu·pied (prē-**ŏk′**yə-pīd′) *adj.* Absorbed in thought; engrossed: *was preoccupied and barely touched her lunch.*

pre·oc·cu·py (prē-**ŏk′**yə-pī′) *tr.v.* **pre·oc·cu·pied, pre·oc·cu·py·ing, pre·oc·cu·pies** To hold the attention or interest of; engage deeply or completely: *questions that have preoccupied scientists for decades.*

pre·op·er·a·tive (prē-**ŏp′**ər-ə-tĭv *or* prē-**ŏp′**rə-tĭv) *adj.* Happening or done before surgery.

pre·or·dain (prē′ôr-**dān′**) *tr.v.* **pre·or·dained, pre·or·dain·ing, pre·or·dains** To appoint, decree, or ordain in advance; foreordain.

prep (prĕp) *Informal adj.* Preparatory. ❖ *n.* A preparatory school. ❖ *v.* **prepped, prep·ping, preps** *—intr.* To prepare: *students prepping for the exam.* *—tr.* **1.** To prepare (someone) for an examination or procedure. **2.** To prepare (something) for a later activity: *prepped the ingredients for the stew.*

prep. *abbr.* An abbreviation of preposition.

pre·pack·age (prē-**păk′**ĭj) *tr.v.* **pre·pack·aged, pre·pack·ag·ing, pre·pack·ag·es** To wrap or package (a product) before marketing.

pre·paid (prē-**pād′**) *v.* Past tense and past participle of **prepay.** ❖ *adj.* Paid or paid for in advance: *a prepaid vacation tour.*

prep·a·ra·tion (prĕp′ə-**rā′**shən) *n.* **1a.** The act or process of preparing: *the preparation of dinner for six people.* **b.** The condition of having been made ready beforehand; readiness: *a ship in good preparation for a voyage.* **2.** A preliminary measure necessary in getting ready for something: *final preparations for a rocket launch.* **3.** A substance or mixture prepared for a certain use: *a preparation of herbs for seasoning vegetables.*

pre·par·a·to·ry (prĭ-**pâr′**ə-tôr′ē *or* **prĕp′**ər-ə-tôr′ē) *adj.* Serving to make ready or prepare; introductory: *preparatory exercises before a race.*

preparatory school *n.* A usually private secondary school that prepares students for college.

pre·pare (prĭ-**pâr′**) *v.* **pre·pared, pre·par·ing, pre·pares** *—tr.* **1.** To make ready beforehand for some purpose, task, or event: *prepare the wood surface for painting by cleaning it.* **2.** To put together or make by combining various elements or ingredients: *prepare a book report; prepare the salad dressing.* *—intr.* To put things or oneself in readiness; get ready: *preparing to leave town.* [From Middle English *preparen*, from Old French *preparer*, from Latin *praeparāre* : *prae-*, before + *parāre*, to make ready, equip.] **—pre·par′er** *n.*

pre·par·ed·ness (prĭ-**pâr′**ĭd-nĭs) *n.* The state of being prepared, especially military readiness for combat.

pre·pay (prē-**pā′**) *tr.v.* **pre·paid, pre·pay·ing, pre·pays** To pay or pay for beforehand: *She agreed to prepay the rent.* **—pre·pay′ment** *n.*

pre·pon·der·ance (prĭ-**pŏn′**dər-əns) *n.* Superiority in weight, force, importance, or influence.

pre·pon·der·ant (prĭ-**pŏn′**dər-ənt) *adj.* Greater in weight, importance, force, or influence. **—pre·pon′der·ant·ly** *adv.*

prep·o·si·tion (prĕp′ə-**zĭsh′**ən) *n.* A word or phrase placed before a noun or pronoun that indicates the relationship between that noun or pronoun and another word. Some common English prepositions are *at, by, from, in, in regard to, of, on, to,* and *with.* **—prep′o·si′tion·al** *adj.* **—prep′o·si′tion·al·ly** *adv.*

prep·o·si·tion·al phrase (prĕp′ə-**zĭsh′**ə-nəl) *n.* A phrase that consists of a preposition and its object and acts as an adjective or adverb. For instance, the prepositional phrase *to me* acts as an adverb modifying the verb *gave* in *She gave the book to me.*

pre·pos·sess·ing (prē′pə-**zĕs′**ĭng) *adj.* Making a pleasing impression. **—pre′pos·sess′ing·ly** *adv.*

pre·pos·ter·ous (prĭ-**pŏs′**tər-əs) *adj.* Contrary to nature, reason, or common sense; absurd: *I didn't believe their preposterous excuse.* **—pre·pos′ter·ous·ly** *adv.* **—pre·pos′ter·ous·ness** *n.*

prep·py or **prep·pie** (**prĕp′**ē) *n., pl.* **prep·pies 1.** A student in a preparatory school. **2.** A person whose manner and dress are considered typical of students in traditional preparatory schools.

prep school *n. Informal* A preparatory school.

pre·puce (**prē′**pyōōs′) *n.* **1.** The foreskin of the penis. **2.** A loose fold of skin at the tip of the clitoris.

pre·quel (**prē′**kwəl) *n.* A work, such as a novel or movie, whose narrative takes place before that of a preexisting work in the same series.

pre·req·ui·site (prē-**rĕk′**wĭ-zĭt) *adj.* Required or necessary as a prior condition: *a course that is prerequisite to more advanced studies.* ❖ *n.* Something that is prerequisite.

pre·rog·a·tive (prĭ-**rŏg′**ə-tĭv) *n.* An exclusive right or privilege held by a person or group, especially a hereditary or official right.

pres. *abbr.* An abbreviation of: **1.** present. **2.** or **Pres.** president.

pres·age (**prĕs′**ĭj) *n.* **1.** A sign or warning of what is going to happen; an omen. **2.** A feeling about what is going to happen; a presentiment. ❖ *v.* **pre·sage** (prĭ-**sāj′** *or* **prĕs′**ĭj) **pre·saged, pre·sag·ing, pre·sag·es** *—tr.* **1.** To indicate or warn of in advance; portend: *A dark sky presaged the coming storm.* **2.** To foretell; prophesy: *a recession presaged by many economists.* *—intr.* To make or utter a prediction. [From Middle English, from Latin *praesāgium* : *prae-*, before + *sāgīre*, to perceive keenly.]

pres·by·ter (**prĕz′**bĭ-tər *or* **prĕs′**bĭ-tər) *n.* **1.** A priest in various hierarchical churches. **2.** An elder in a Presbyterian Church. [From Late Latin, from Greek *presbuteros*, elder, from *presbus*, old man.]

pres·by·te·ri·an (prĕz′bĭ-**tîr′**ē-ən *or* prĕs′bĭ-**tîr′**ē-ən) *n.* **Presbyterian** A member or adherent of a Presbyterian

Church. ❖ *adj.* **1.** Relating to presbyters. **2. Presbyterian** Relating to a Presbyterian Church. **—pres′by·te′ri·an·ism** *n.*

Presbyterian Church *n.* Any of various Protestant churches governed by presbyters, traditionally following Calvinist doctrine.

pre·school (**prē′skōōl′**) *adj.* Relating to the years of childhood that come before the beginning of elementary school. ❖ *n.* (**prē′**skōōl′) A nursery school.

pre·science (**prĕsh′**əns *or* **prĕsh′**ē-əns *or* **prē′**shəns) *n.* Knowledge of actions or events before they occur; foresight. **—pre′scient** *adj.*

pre·scribe (prĭ-**skrīb′**) *tr.v.* **pre·scribed, pre·scrib·ing, pre·scribes 1.** To set down as a rule or guide; impose or direct: *The government prescribes standards for the purity of food.* **2.** To order or recommend the use of (a drug, for example): *The doctor prescribed bed rest.* [From Middle English *prescriben*, from Latin *praescrībere* : *prae-*, before + *scrībere*, to write.] —SEE NOTE.

pre·scrip·tion (prĭ-**skrĭp′**shən) *n.* **1.** The act or process of prescribing. **2.** Something that is prescribed; a recommendation or rule: *prescriptions for correct usage in an English textbook.* **3a.** A written instruction from a physician indicating what treatment or medication a patient is to receive. **b.** A medicine ordered by prescription. **c.** Specifications for a set of corrective lenses, written by an ophthalmologist or optometrist.

pre·scrip·tive (prĭ-**skrĭp′**tĭv) *adj.* Relating to or giving directions, laws, or rules; stating or requiring what to do or how to do it: *prescriptive rules of spelling.* **—pre·scrip′tive·ly** *adv.*

pres·ence (**prĕz′**əns) *n.* **1.** The fact or condition of being present: *Your presence is required at the meeting.* **2.** The immediate nearness of a person or thing: *Slow oxidation of the metal in the presence of moisture causes rust.* **3.** A person's bearing: *She has great presence on the stage.* **4.** A supernatural influence felt to be nearby: *A mysterious presence frightened them away.*

presence of mind *n.* The ability to think and act calmly and efficiently, especially in an emergency.

pres·ent[1] (**prĕz′**ənt) *n.* **1.** A moment or period in time that is intermediate between past and future; now. **2a.** The present tense. **b.** A verb form in the present tense. ❖ *adj.* **1.** Being or occurring now; current: *the present situation.* **2.** Being in attendance or at hand: *The people present broke into loud applause.* **3.** Existing in something specified: *Oxygen is present in blood.* **4.** Relating to the present tense. ◆ **at present** At the present time; right now. **for the present** For the time being; temporarily. [From Middle English, from Old French, from Latin *praesēns*, present participle of *praeesse*, to be present : *prae-*, before, in front + *esse*, to be.]

pre·sent[2] (prĭ-**zĕnt′**) *tr.v.* **pre·sent·ed, pre·sent·ing, pre·sents 1a.** To make a gift or award of: *She presented the pennant to the winners.* **b.** To make a gift or award to: *The colonel presented the soldier with a medal.* **2.** To offer or display before the public: *present a drama.* **3a.** To offer for observation, examination, or consideration: *The detective presented his badge.* **b.** To provide; furnish: *The situation presents a number of problems.* **4.** To represent or depict in a certain manner: *The movie presents the outlaw as a hero.* **5a.** To introduce, especially with formal ceremony. **b.** To introduce (a young woman) to society with conventional ceremony. ❖ *n.* **1. pres·ent** (**prĕz′**ənt) Something presented; a gift. **2. pre·sent** (prĭ-**zĕnt′**) The position of a rifle or other weapon when presented. [From Middle English *presenten*, from Old French *presenter*, from Latin *praesentāre*, to show, from *praesēns*, present.]

pre·sent·a·ble (prĭ-**zĕn′**tə-bəl) *adj.* **1.** Suitable for being given, displayed, or offered: *presentable gifts.* **2.** Fit for introduction to others, especially with regard to appearance: *He made himself presentable by combing his hair.* **—pre·sent′a·bil′i·ty** *n.*

pres·en·ta·tion (prĕz′ən-**tā′**shən *or* prē′zən-**tā′**shən) *n.* **1.** The act of presenting something: *Were you there for the presentation of the awards?* **2.** Something presented before an audience, as a play or lecture.

pres·ent-day (**prĕz′**ənt-**dā′**) *adj.* Existing or occurring now; current: *present-day attitudes about education.*

pre·sen·ti·ment (prĭ-**zĕn′**tə-mənt) *n.* A sense that something is about to occur; a premonition.

pres·ent·ly (**prĕz′**ənt-lē) *adv.* **1.** In a short time; soon: *We'll be there presently.* **2.** At this time or period; now: *An expedition is presently exploring the area.*

pres·ent participle (**prĕz′**ənt) *n.* A participle that expresses present action or condition. It is formed in English by adding *-ing* to the infinitive, as *playing* in *he is playing*, and is sometimes used as an adjective, as *overwhelming* in *an overwhelming majority.*

pres·ent per·fect (**prĕz′**ənt **pûr′**fĭkt) *n.* A verb tense used to express action or condition completed at the present time. It is formed in English by combining the present tense of *have* with a past participle, as *has spoken* in *He has spoken.*

pres·ent tense (**prĕz′**ənt) *n.* A verb tense used to express action or condition in the present time, as *hits* in *She hits the ball* and *am* in *I am happy.*

pres·er·va·tion (prĕz′ər-**vā′**shən) *n.* The act of preserving or the state of being preserved.

pre·ser·va·tive (prĭ-**zûr′**və-tĭv) *adj.* Tending to preserve or capable of preserving. ❖ *n.* Something used to preserve, especially a chemical added to a food to prevent spoilage.

pre·serve (prĭ-**zûrv′**) *tr.v.* **pre·served, pre·serv·ing, pre·serves 1.** To maintain in safety, as from injury or peril; protect: *laws that help preserve wildlife.* See Synonyms at **defend. 2.** To keep in perfect or unchanged condition or form; maintain intact: *Both countries worked to preserve peaceful relations.* **3.** To protect (food) from spoilage and prepare it for future use, as by pickling or canning. ❖ *n.* **1.** often **preserves** Fruit cooked with sugar to protect against decay or fermentation: *strawberry preserves.* **2.** An area maintained for the protection of wildlife or natural resources. [From Middle English *preserven*, from Old French *preserver*, from Late Latin *praeservāre* : Latin *prae-*, before, in front + Latin *servāre*, to guard.] **—pre·serv′er** *n.*

pre·set (prē-**sĕt′**) *tr.v.* **pre·set, pre·set·ting, pre·sets** To set (an automatic control, for example) beforehand: *preset a microwave oven.*

pre·side (prĭ-**zīd′**) *intr.v.* **pre·sid·ed, pre·sid·ing, pre·sides 1.** To hold the position of authority; act as chairperson: *presided over a meeting.* **2.** To possess or exercise authority or control: *The bus driver presides behind the wheel.* [From Latin *praesidēre* : *prae-*, in front + *sedēre*, to sit.] **—pre·sid′er** *n.*

pres·i·den·cy (**prĕz′**ĭ-dən-sē) *n., pl.* **pres·i·den·cies 1.** The office, function, or term of a president. **2.** The office of a president of a republic or of the president of the United States.

pres·i·dent (**prĕz′**ĭ-dənt) *n.* **1.** The chief officer of an organization or institution, such as a club, corporation, or university. **2.** The chief executive of a republic, such as the United States.

pres·i·dent-e·lect (prĕz′ĭ-dənt-ĭ-**lĕkt′**) *n., pl.* **pres·i·dents-e·lect** A person who has been elected president but has not yet begun the term of office.

pres·i·den·tial (prĕz′ĭ-**dĕn′**shəl) *adj.* Relating to a president or presidency: *a presidential election.*

Pres·i·dents' Day (**prĕz′**ĭ-dənts) *n.* The third Monday in February, observed in the United States as a holiday in commemoration of US presidents, especially George Washington and Abraham Lincoln.

USAGE

prescribe The verbs **prescribe** and **proscribe** sound similar but have almost opposite meanings. *Prescribe* means to declare or set down as something that should be followed or undertaken. *Proscribe* means to forbid or prohibit. Something that is prescribed is to be followed, like a diet or a program of exercise. Something that is proscribed is banned or forbidden and is to be avoided.

WORD BUILDING

pressure The word root *press–* in English words and the English word **press** itself come from the past participle *pressus* of the Latin verb *premere,* "to squeeze, press." Thus we have the noun **pressure** from the Latin noun *pressūra,* "a squeezing, as of the juice from grapes or of the oil from olives." We also have the verbs **compress,** "to squeeze together" (using the prefix *com–,* "together, with"); **depress,** "to squeeze down" (*dē–,* "down"); **express,** "to press out" (*ex–,* "out, out of"); and **impress**[1], "to press on or against, drive in, imprint" (*in–*[2], "into, in").

ă	pat	ôr	core
ā	pay	oi	boy
âr	care	ou	out
ä	father	o͝o	took
ĕ	pet	o͝or	lure
ē	be	o͞o	boot
ĭ	pit	ŭ	cut
ī	bite	ûr	urge
îr	pier	th	thin
ŏ	pot	*th*	this
ō	toe	zh	vision
ô	paw	ə	about

pre·si·di·o (prĭ-sē′dē-ō′ *or* prĭ-sĭd′ē-ō′) *n.* A garrison, especially a fortress in the southwest United States built by the Spanish.

pre·sid·i·um (prĭ-sĭd′ē-əm) *n., pl.* **pre·sid·i·a** (prĭ-sĭd′ē-ə) or **pre·sid·i·ums** Any of various permanent executive committees in Communist countries having power to act for a larger governing body.

press[1] (prĕs) *v.* **pressed, press·ing, press·es** *—tr.* **1a.** To exert force or pressure against; bear down on: *an indentation where the rock pressed the ground.* **b.** To move by applying force: *press a piano key.* **2a.** To squeeze the juice or other contents from: *press grapes to make wine.* **b.** To extract (juice or other contents) by squeezing: *press juice from oranges.* **3a.** To make compact or reshape by applying steady force; compress: *press the clay into the mold.* **b.** To smooth (clothes or fabric, for example) by applying heat and pressure; iron: *Have those pants been pressed lately?* **4.** To clasp or embrace, as with affection: *I pressed her hand with gratitude.* **5.** To try hard to persuade or influence; ask or entreat insistently: *She pressed her aunt to stay for the holiday.* **6a.** To insist upon or put forward insistently: *pressed his claim.* **b.** To try to influence or persuade; pressure or entreat: *He pressed her for a reply.* **7.** To carry on or advance vigorously: *They should have pressed the attack and taken the city.* **8.** To lift (a weight) in a press: *He can press 200 pounds.* *—intr.* **1.** To exert force or pressure: *The atmosphere is pressing all around us.* **2.** To be worrisome or depressing: *The mistake was still pressing on his mind.* **3.** To advance eagerly; push forward: *The crowd pressed forward to catch a glimpse of the celebrity.* **4.** To continue a course of action, especially in spite of difficulties: *The researchers decided to press on despite the discouraging results.* **5.** To entreat someone or demand something: *He pressed for the new assignment.* **6.** To iron clothes or other material. **7.** To raise or lift a weight in a press. ❖ *n.* **1.** Any of various machines or devices used to squeeze or exert pressure on something. **2.** A printing press. **3.** A place or establishment where matter is printed. **4a.** The newspapers, magazines, broadcasts, and other media where news is reported: *The story appeared in yesterday's press.* **b.** The people, such as editors and reporters, involved in collecting, publishing, or broadcasting news: *The president met with the press and explained his policies.* **c.** Coverage in the media: *The senator got a lot of bad press because of the scandal.* **5.** A crowd or throng: *a press of people in the square.* **6.** Pressure, haste, or urgency: *In the press of business, she forgot about her lunch date.* **7.** In basketball, an aggressive defense applied over the entire court. **8.** A lift in weightlifting in which the weight is raised to shoulder level and then pushed overhead. ◆ **be hard pressed** To have difficulty in accomplishing something: *We were hard pressed to finish the project on time.* **go to press** To be submitted for printing. **pressed for time** In a hurry; under time pressure. [From Middle English *pressen,* from Old French *presser,* from Latin *pressāre.*]

press[2] (prĕs) *tr.v.* **pressed, press·ing, press·es** To force into service in the army or navy. [From Middle English *prest,* payment of wages in advance, enlistment money, from Old French *prester,* to lend, from Latin *praestāre,* to offer, supply.]

press agent *n.* A person hired to arrange advertising and publicity, as for a performer or business.

press conference *n.* An interview held for news reporters by a political figure or famous person.

press·ing (prĕs′ĭng) *adj.* Demanding immediate attention; urgent: *the pressing problems of the world.*

press secretary *n.* A person who officially manages the public affairs and the press conferences of a public figure.

pres·sure (prĕsh′ər) *n.* **1.** The act of pressing or the condition of being pressed. **2.** Continuous force applied to a gas, liquid, or solid by another gas, liquid, or solid. Pressure is expressed as the amount of force applied per unit of area. **3.** A compelling or constraining influence on the mind or will: *felt pressure from her fans to write more songs.* **4.** The condition of being subjected to physical, mental, social, or economic distress: *I am under great pressure to finish this project.* **5.** An influence acting as a source of distress or hardship: *the economic pressures on the farming community.* ❖ *tr.v.* **pres·sured, pres·sur·ing, pres·sures** To force or try to force, as by influencing or persuading: *The studio tried to pressure her into making public appearances.* —SEE NOTE.

pressure cooker *n.* An airtight metal pot that uses steam under pressure to cook food quickly.

pressure suit *n.* A garment that is worn in high-altitude aircraft or in spacecraft to compensate for low-pressure conditions.

pres·sur·ize (prĕsh′ə-rīz′) *tr.v.* **pres·sur·ized, pres·sur·iz·ing, pres·sur·iz·es 1.** To keep (a compartment, as in an aircraft) at normal atmospheric pressure. **2.** To subject (gas or liquid) to a greater pressure than normal. **—pres′sur·i·za′tion** (prĕsh′ər-ĭ-zā′shən) *n.*

pres·ti·dig·i·ta·tion (prĕs′tĭ-dĭj′ĭ-tā′shən) *n.* Performance of or skill in performing magic tricks; sleight of hand. **—pres′ti·dig′i·ta′tor** *n.*

pres·tige (prĕ-stēzh′ *or* prĕ-stēj′) *n.* The respect or esteem with which a person or thing is generally regarded. [From French, illusion, charm, ability to inspire admiration, prestige, from Latin *praestīgiae,* tricks.]

pres·ti·gious (prĕ-stē′jəs *or* prĕ-stĭj′əs) *adj.* Having prestige; esteemed: *a prestigious occupation.* **—pres·tig′ious·ly** *adv.* **—pres·tig′ious·ness** *n.*

pres·tis·si·mo (prĕ-stĭs′ə-mō′) *adv. & adj.* In music, in as fast a tempo as possible.

pres·to (prĕs′tō) *adv.* **1.** In music, in a very fast tempo. **2.** At once; right away.

pre·sum·a·bly (prĭ-zo͞o′mə-blē) *adv.* From what can reasonably be supposed: *That other girl is presumably her sister.*

pre·sume (prĭ-zo͞om′) *v.* **pre·sumed, pre·sum·ing, pre·sumes** *—tr.* **1.** To assume to be true in the absence of proof; take for granted: *I presume that she will accept the job.* **2.** To undertake without authority or permission; dare: *He presumed to make the wedding arrangements without her knowledge.* *—intr.* **1.** To take a privilege or permission for granted without making sure that it actually is granted: *He presumed on their hospitality. They said I was always welcome, but I didn't want to presume.* **2.** To take for granted that something is true; suppose. [From Middle English *presumen,* from Latin *praesūmere,* to take for granted, presume : *prae-,* before + *sūmere,* to take.] **—pre·sum′ed·ly** (prĭ-zo͞o′mĭd-lē) *adv.* **—pre·sum′er** *n.*

pre·sump·tion (prĭ-zŭmp′shən) *n.* **1.** Behavior or attitude that is arrogant or offensive. **2.** The act of presuming or accepting as true without proof: *a presumption of innocence.*

pre·sump·tive (prĭ-zŭmp′tĭv) *adj.* **1.** Based on likelihood or presumption: *an heir presumptive.* **2.** Providing a reason for belief or acceptance: *presumptive evidence.* **—pre·sump′tive·ly** *adv.*

pre·sump·tu·ous (prĭ-zŭmp′cho͞o-əs) *adj.* Going beyond what is right or proper; excessively forward: *a presumptuous attitude.*

pre·sup·pose (prē′sə-pōz′) *tr.v.* **pre·sup·posed, pre·sup·pos·ing, pre·sup·pos·es 1.** To believe or suppose in advance; take for granted: *The teacher presupposed that the students had taken algebra.* **2.** To require as a necessary prior condition: *The charred bits of wood presupposed a fire.* **—pre·sup′po·si′tion** (prē-sŭp′ə-zĭsh′ən) *n.*

pre·teen (prē′tēn′) *n.* A preadolescent boy or girl, especially one between the ages of 9 and 13. **—pre′teen′** *adj.*

pre·tend (prĭ-tĕnd′) *v.* **pre·tend·ed, pre·tend·ing, pre·tends** —*tr.* **1.** To give a false appearance of: *He pretended illness.* **2.** To make believe: *Pretend that you are on another planet.* **3.** To claim or allege insincerely or falsely: *She pretended to be an expert.* —*intr.* **1.** To act out an action or role, as in imaginative play: *children pretending in the backyard.* **2.** To claim to be a certain kind of person or to be entitled to something: *a man who pretends to expertise in music.* ❖ *adj. Informal* **1.** Make-believe or imitation: *pretend money.* **2.** Not genuine or sincere: *pretend concern.* [From Middle English *pretenden*, from Latin *praetendere* : *prae-*, in front + *tendere*, to extend.]

pre·tend·ed (prĭ-tĕn′dĭd) *adj.* **1.** Not genuine or sincere; feigned: *had only a pretended interest in the movie.* **2.** Supposed; alleged: *the pretended heir.*

pre·tend·er (prĭ-tĕn′dər) *n.* **1.** A person who pretends or alleges falsely. **2.** A person who sets forth a claim, especially a person who claims the right to a throne.

pre·tense (prē′tĕns′) *n.* **1.** A false appearance or action intended to deceive: *She made a pretense of being worried about us.* **2.** A false reason or excuse: *He left the room under the pretense of having to make a phone call.* **3.** False or extravagant display meant to impress others: *He was so modest as to be free from any hint of pretense.*

pre·ten·sion (prĭ-tĕn′shən) *n.* **1.** A claim or reason, especially a false one: *made no pretensions to being able to read Spanish.* **2.** Behavior or an act that suggests a person believes he or she is superior or deserving of merit: *quit the club because of the members' snobbery and pretension; found his pretensions obnoxious.*

pre·ten·tious (prĭ-tĕn′shəs) *adj.* **1.** Behaving as if one is important or deserving of merit when such is not the case. **2.** Extravagantly showy: *a pretentious house.* **—pre·ten′tious·ly** *adv.* **—pre·ten′tious·ness** *n.*

pret·er·ite (prĕt′ər-ĭt) *adj.* Relating to a past tense form of a verb. ❖ *n.* **1.** A preterite tense. **2.** A verb form in the preterite tense.

pre·ter·nat·u·ral (prē′tər-**năch′**ər-əl *or* prē′tər-**năch′**rəl) *adj.* **1.** Being beyond what is normal or usual. **2.** Supernatural.

pre·text (prē′tĕkst′) *n.* An excuse given to hide the real reason for something.

Pre·to·ri·a (prĭ-tôr′ē-ə) The administrative capital of South Africa, in the northeast part of the country north of Johannesburg. Founded in 1855, it became the capital of South Africa in 1910.

pret·ty (prĭt′ē) *adj.* **pret·ti·er, pret·ti·est 1.** Pleasing or appealing in a graceful or delicate way: *a pretty shell.* **2.** Clever; adroit: *a pretty maneuver.* **3.** Very bad; terrible: *in a pretty predicament.* **4.** *Informal* Large in size or extent: *a pretty fortune.* ❖ *adv.* To a fair degree; moderately: *We are in pretty good shape.* ❖ *n., pl.* **pret·ties** A person or thing that is pretty. ❖ *tr.v.* **pret·tied, pret·ty·ing, pret·ties** To make pretty: *We can pretty up the spare room for you.* ◆ **pretty much** For the most part; mostly: *We were pretty much exhausted after the hike.* [From Middle English *pratti, prettie, pritti*, clever, fine, from Old English *prættig*, cunning, clever, from *prætt*, trick.] **—pret′ti·ly** *adv.* **—pret′ti·ness** *n.* —SEE NOTE.

pret·zel (prĕt′səl) *n.* A soft or brittle glazed biscuit, usually salted on the outside and baked in the form of a loose knot or stick.

pre·vail (prĭ-vāl′) *intr.v.* **pre·vailed, pre·vail·ing, pre·vails 1.** To be greater in strength or influence; triumph: *prevailed against great odds.* **2.** To be most common or frequent; be predominant: *In this region, snow and ice prevail.* **3.** To be in force or use; be current: *an attitude that prevailed in the 1950s.* **4.** To use persuasion or inducement successfully: *The salesperson prevailed upon me to buy a spare tire.* [From Middle English *prevailen*, from Latin *praevalēre*, to be stronger : *prae-*, before, in front + *valēre*, to be strong.]

pre·vail·ing (prĭ-vā′lĭng) *adj.* **1.** Most frequent or common; predominant: *The prevailing winds come from the west.* **2.** Generally current; widespread: *the prevailing attitude.* **—pre·vail′ing·ly** *adv.*

prev·a·lent (prĕv′ə-lənt) *adj.* Widely existing or commonly occurring: *Certain diseases are more prevalent in hot humid areas.* **—prev′a·lence** *n.* **—prev′a·lent·ly** *adv.*

pre·var·i·cate (prĭ-văr′ĭ-kāt′) *intr.v.* **pre·var·i·cat·ed, pre·var·i·cat·ing, pre·var·i·cates** To stray from the truth; speak or write evasively. **—pre·var′i·ca′tion** *n.* **—pre·var′i·ca′tor** *n.*

pre·vent (prĭ-vĕnt′) *tr.v.* **pre·vent·ed, pre·vent·ing, pre·vents 1.** To keep from happening; avert: *prevent illness.* **2.** To keep (someone) from doing something; impede: *His snoring prevents me from sleeping.* [From Middle English *preventen*, to anticipate, from Latin *praevenīre*, to come before : *prae-*, before + *venīre*, to come.] **—pre·vent′a·ble, pre·vent′i·ble** *adj.*

pre·ven·ta·tive (prĭ-vĕn′tə-tĭv) *adj. & n.* Variant of **preventive.**

pre·ven·tion (prĭ-vĕn′shən) *n.* The act of preventing or impeding: *the prevention of illness.*

pre·ven·tive (prĭ-vĕn′tĭv) also **pre·ven·ta·tive** (prĭ-vĕn′tə-tĭv) *adj.* Designed to prevent or hinder: *preventive steps against accidents.* ❖ *n.* **1.** Something that prevents; an obstacle. **2.** Something that prevents or slows the course of an illness or disease.

pre·view (prē′vyo͞o′) *n.* **1.** An advance showing, as of a movie or an art exhibition, to an invited audience prior to presentation to the general public. **2.** An advance viewing, especially of scenes of a forthcoming movie. ❖ *tr.v.* **pre·viewed, pre·view·ing, pre·views** To view or exhibit in advance.

pre·vi·ous (prē′vē-əs) *adj.* **1.** Existing or occurring before something else: *on a previous occasion.* **2.** Existing or occurring immediately before something else: *the previous winter.* [From Latin *praevius*, going before : *prae-*, before + *via*, way.] **—pre′vi·ous·ly** *adv.*

pre·war (prē′wôr′) *adj.* Existing or occurring before a war.

prey (prā) *n.* **1.** An animal hunted or caught for food; quarry. **2.** The collection of animals typically hunted and eaten by a predator. **3.** A person or thing that is defenseless against attack; a victim. ❖ *intr.v.* **preyed, prey·ing, preys 1.** To hunt and kill other animals for food: *Owls prey on mice.* **2.** To take unfair advantage of other people, as by swindling. **3.** To have a harmful or troublesome effect: *Worry preyed on his mind.* [From Middle English *preie*, from Old French, from Latin *praeda*, booty, prey.]

❑ *These sound alike:* **prey, pray** (beseech).

Pri·am (prī′əm) *n.* In Greek mythology, the king of Troy and father of Cassandra, Hector, and Paris, who was killed when his city fell to the Greeks.

price (prīs) *n.* **1.** The amount of money or goods asked or given for something: *The price of the book is $5.99.* **2.** The cost, as in suffering, at which something is obtained: *The loss of privacy was one of the prices of her fame.* **3.** The cost of bribing someone: *Every man has his price.* **4.** A reward offered for the capture or killing of a person. ❖ *tr.v.* **priced, pric·ing, pric·es 1.** To establish a price for: *priced squash at 89 cents a pound.* **2.** To find out the price of: *After pricing cars for a week, we finally chose one that was within our budget.* [From Middle English *pris*, from Old French *pris*, from Latin *pretium*.]

price·less (prīs′lĭs) *adj.* **1.** Having great worth; invaluable: *priceless treasures.* **2.** Very amusing or odd: *Little children often say priceless things.*

WORD HISTORY

pretty Sometimes when certain sounds get reversed in spoken language, these reversed sounds take the place of the original ones. This is especially true in English of the (r) sound and a vowel. For example, the word **bird** was once *brid,* and the word **nostril** was once *nosthyrl,* "nose hole." The same process gives us the regional pronunciation (**pûr′**tē) for *pretty* and the pronunciation (pər-**fûr′**) for **prefer.** A similar process occurs with the (s) and (k) sounds, which is why you sometimes hear people say "ax" for **ask.**

pretzel

prickly pear
prickly pear cactus with fruit

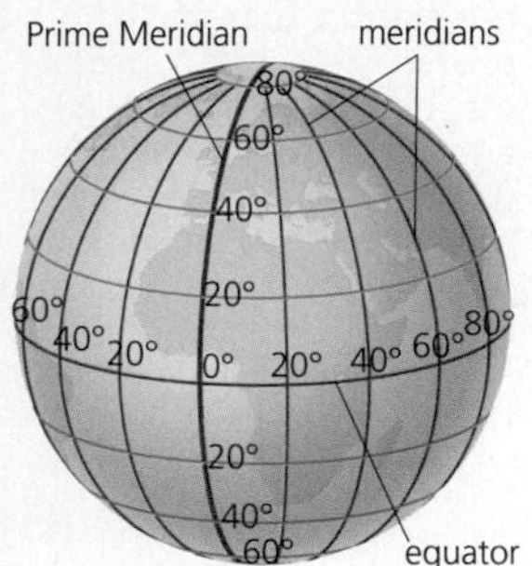

Prime Meridian

primrose

ă	pat	ôr	core
ā	pay	oi	boy
âr	care	ou	out
ä	father	ŏŏ	took
ĕ	pet	ŏŏr	lure
ē	be	ōō	boot
ĭ	pit	ŭ	cut
ī	bite	ûr	urge
îr	pier	th	thin
ŏ	pot	*th*	this
ō	toe	zh	vision
ô	paw	ə	about

prick (prĭk) *n.* **1.** The act of piercing or puncturing. **2.** The sensation of being pierced. **3.** A hole or mark left by piercing. **4.** A pointed object, such as an ice pick, goad, or thorn. ❖ *tr.v.* **pricked, prick·ing, pricks 1.** To puncture lightly: *The thorn pricked my finger.* **2.** To sting with emotional pain: *My conscience pricks me at the thought of the deed.* ◆ **prick up (one's) ears** To listen with attentive interest.

prick·er (prĭk′ər) *n.* **1.** A person or thing that pricks. **2.** A prickle or thorn.

prick·le (prĭk′əl) *n.* **1.** A small pointed structure growing from the surface of a plant. **2.** A tingling sensation. ❖ *v.* **prick·led, prick·ling, prick·les** —*tr.* **1.** To prick as if with a thorn. **2.** To cause tingling sensations: *This lotion will prickle your face.* —*intr.* To feel a tingling or pricking sensation.

prick·ly (prĭk′lē) *adj.* **prick·li·er, prick·li·est 1.** Having prickles: *a prickly cactus.* **2.** Tingling or smarting: *a prickly feeling in my foot.* **3a.** Causing trouble; vexing: *a prickly situation.* **b.** Easily irritated: *He can get prickly when criticized.* **—prick′li·ness** *n.*

prickly pear *n.* **1.** Any of various cacti that have flattened stem segments and egg-shaped, prickly, often edible fruit. **2.** The fruit of such a cactus.

pride (prīd) *n.* **1.** A sense of one's own proper dignity or worth; self-respect. **2.** Pleasure or satisfaction taken in an achievement, possession, or association: *My aunt takes a great deal of pride in her work.* **3.** A source or cause of pleasure or satisfaction; the best of a group: *The painting was the pride of his collection.* **4.** An excessively high opinion of oneself; conceit. **5.** A group of lions. ❖ *tr.v.* **prid·ed, prid·ing, prides** To indulge (oneself) in a feeling of pleasure or satisfaction: *He prided himself on his ability to fix cars.* [From Middle English, from Old English *prȳde*, from *prūd*, proud.]

pried[1] (prīd) *v.* Past tense and past participle of **pry**[1].

pried[2] (prīd) *v.* Past tense and past participle of **pry**[2].

pries[1] (prīz) *v.* Third person singular present tense of **pry**[1].

pries[2] (prīz) *v.* Third person singular present tense of **pry**[2]. ❖ *n.* Plural of **pry**[2].

priest (prēst) *n.* **1.** In certain Christian churches, a member of the clergy having the authority to administer the sacraments. **2.** In other religions, a person having the authority to conduct religious rites. [From Middle English *prest*, from Old English *prēost*, ultimately from Late Latin *presbyter*.]

priest·ess (prē′stĭs) *n.* A woman having the authority to perform and administer various rites, especially of a pagan religion.

priest·hood (prēst′ho͝od′) *n.* **1.** The office or role of a priest. **2.** The class of priests: *He entered the priesthood two years ago.*

priest·ly (prēst′lē) *adj.* **priest·li·er, priest·li·est** Relating to a priest or to the priesthood: *priestly garb.*

prig (prĭg) *n.* An arrogant, smug, or narrow-minded person, especially one with an excessive wish to appear proper. **—prig′gish** *adj.*

prim (prĭm) *adj.* **prim·mer, prim·mest** Stiffly proper or precise in manner or appearance. **—prim′ly** *adv.* **—prim′ness** *n.*

pri·ma·cy (prī′mə-sē) *n., pl.* **pri·ma·cies 1.** The condition of being first or foremost: *the lion's legendary primacy among beasts.* **2.** The office or functions of an ecclesiastical primate.

pri·ma don·na (prē′mə **dŏn′**ə) *n.* **1.** The leading woman soloist in an opera company. **2.** A conceited person who is easily upset or difficult to please.

pri·mal (prī′məl) *adj.* **1.** Being first in time; original. **2.** Of first importance; primary: *a primal necessity.*

pri·mar·i·ly (prī-**mâr′**ə-lē *or* prī-**mĕr′**ə-lē) *adv.* Chiefly; mainly: *a forest consisting primarily of hardwoods.*

pri·mar·y (prī′mĕr′ē *or* prī′mə-rē) *adj.* **1.** First in importance, rank, or quality; chief: *The primary function of a window is to let in light.* **2.** First in time or sequence; original: *the primary stages of the project.* **3.** Being a fundamental part; basic: *primary needs.* **4.** Relating to a primary school. **5.** Relating to a primary color. **6.** Relating to or being an inducting current, circuit, or coil. ❖ *n., pl.* **pri·mar·ies 1.** Something that is first in time, order, quality, or importance. **2.** A preliminary election in which registered voters select candidates for a later election. **3.** The circuit, coil, or winding of a transformer into which electricity is fed. [From Middle English, from Latin *prīmārius*, from *prīmus*, first.]

pri·mar·y-care (prī′mĕr′ē-kâr′) *adj.* Relating to medical care in which a patient regularly sees a designated doctor, who then coordinates any other necessary health services.

primary color *n.* **1.** Any of the three colors of light, red, green, and blue, from which light of any hue can be made by mixing. **2.** Any of the three colors of pigment, purplish red, greenish blue, and yellow, from which pigment of any hue can be made by mixing.

primary school *n.* A school usually including the first three or four grades of elementary school and sometimes kindergarten.

primary stress *n.* **1.** The strongest degree of stress placed on a syllable in the pronunciation of a word. **2.** A mark, such as (**′**), used to indicate such stress.

pri·mate (prī′māt′) *n.* **1.** Any of various mammals belonging to a group that includes the lemurs, monkeys, and apes including humans. Primates have large brains and can grasp objects with their hands and feet. **2.** (**prī′**mĭt *or* **prī′**māt′) A bishop of the highest rank in a province or country. [From Latin *prīmās*, of first rank, from *prīmus*, first.]

prime (prīm) *adj.* **1.** First in excellence, quality, degree, or value: *her prime accomplishments.* **2.** First in degree or rank: *my prime concern.* ❖ *n.* **1.** A period of greatest physical condition or intellectual vigor: *an athlete in the prime of her life.* **2a.** A mark (′) placed above and to the right of a letter to distinguish it from the same letter already in use: *compare the angles b and b′.* **b.** The same mark used to represent the units of feet, minutes of arc, or minutes of time: *a 10′ board; an angle of 27°13′.* **3.** A prime number. ❖ *tr.v.* **primed, prim·ing, primes 1.** To make ready or prepare, as with information: *She primed him for the contest.* **2.** To prepare for operation, as by pouring water into a pump or gasoline into a carburetor: *Prime the engine before trying to start it.* **3.** To prepare (a surface) for painting or finishing by covering with size, primer, or an undercoat. **4.** To prepare (a gun or mine) for firing by inserting a charge of gunpowder or a primer. [From Middle English, from Latin *prīmus*, first.]

Prime Meridian *n.* The zero meridian (0°), used as a reference line from which longitude east and west is measured. It passes through Greenwich, England.

prime minister *n.* **1.** A chief governmental minister appointed by a ruler. **2.** The head of the Cabinet and often also the chief executive of a parliamentary democracy.

prime number *n.* An integer greater than 1 that can only be divided without remainder by itself and 1. For example, 7, 13, and 19 are prime numbers.

prim·er[1] (prĭm′ər) *n.* **1.** An elementary textbook for teaching children to read. **2.** A book that covers the basic elements of a subject. [From Middle English, prayer book, from Medieval Latin *prīmārius*, first.]

prim·er[2] (prī′mər) *n.* **1.** A coat of paint or similar material applied to prepare a surface, as for painting. **2.** A cap or tube containing a small amount of explosive used to set off the main explosive charge of a firearm or mine.

prime time *n.* The evening hours when the largest television audience is available.

pri·me·val (prī-mē′vəl) *adj.* Relating to the distant past; ancient or original: *conditions on the primeval earth.* **—pri·me′val·ly** *adv.*

prim·i·tive (prĭm′ĭ-tĭv) *adj.* **1.** Relating to an early or original stage or state. **2.** Being in an early stage of development or evolution: *fossils of primitive mammals.* **3.** Simple or crude; not sophisticated: *a primitive form of rocket.* **4.** Relating to a usually tribal society having a relatively low level of economic and technical development. **5.** Relating to art that is made by an artist who has no formal training. [From Middle English *primitif,* from Latin *prīmitīvus,* from *prīmus,* first.] **—prim′i·tive·ly** *adv.* **—prim′i·tive·ness** *n.*

pri·mo·gen·i·ture (prī′mō-jĕn′ĭ-cho͝or′) *n.* **1.** The condition of being the firstborn child of one's parents. **2.** In some systems of law, the right of the eldest child, especially the eldest son, to inherit the entire estate of one or both parents.

pri·mor·di·al (prī-môr′dē-əl) *adj.* Relating to or belonging to the earliest ages; ancient or original: *primordial life forms; the primordial universe.* **—pri·mor′di·al·ly** *adv.*

primp (prĭmp) *v.* **primped, primp·ing, primps** *—tr.* To dress or groom with attention to detail: *She primped her hair.* *—intr.* To dress or groom oneself with elaborate care: *He primped for hours before the party.*

prim·rose (prĭm′rōz′) *n.* Any of numerous small plants grown for their clusters of variously colored flowers.

prince (prĭns) *n.* **1.** A man or boy who is a member of a royal family other than the monarch, especially a son of the monarch. **2.** A man who is a ruler of a principality. **3.** A king. **4.** A nobleman of varying rank or status. **5.** An outstanding man in a particular group or class. [From Middle English, from Latin *prīnceps.*]

prince consort *n.* The husband of a sovereign queen.

prince·dom (prĭns′dəm) *n.* **1.** The territory ruled by a prince; a principality. **2.** The rank or status of a prince.

Prince Ed·ward Island (prĭns ĕd′wərd) A province of southeast Canada consisting of **Prince Edward Island** in the southern Gulf of St. Lawrence. It joined the Canadian confederation in 1873. Charlottetown is the capital.

prince·ly (prĭns′lē) *adj.* **prince·li·er, prince·li·est** Relating to or befitting a prince: *a princely act.* **—prince′li·ness** *n.*

Prince of Wales *n.* The male heir to the British throne.

prin·cess (prĭn′sĕs′ *or* prĭn-sĕs′) *n.* **1.** A woman or girl other than the monarch who is a member of a royal family, especially a daughter of the monarch. **2.** A woman who is ruler of a principality. **3.** A queen. **4.** A noblewoman of varying rank or status. **5.** The wife of a prince. **6.** A woman regarded as having the status or qualities of a princess.

prin·ci·pal (prĭn′sə-pəl) *adj.* First or foremost in rank or importance; chief: *the principal character in the story.* ❖ *n.* **1.** A person who holds a leading position, especially the head of a school. **2.** A main participant, as in a business deal. **3a.** A sum of money originally invested, as opposed to the interest paid or accruing on it. **b.** A sum of money owed as a debt, on which interest is calculated. [From Middle English, from Latin *prīnceps,* leader, emperor.] **—prin′ci·pal·ly** *adv.* —SEE NOTE.

❑ *These sound alike:* **principal, principle** (doctrine).

prin·ci·pal·i·ty (prĭn′sə-păl′ĭ-tē) *n., pl.* **prin·ci·pal·i·ties** A territory ruled by a prince or princess.

principal parts *pl.n.* In inflected languages, the main forms of the verb from which all other forms can be derived. In English the principal parts are the present infinitive (*walk, take*), the past tense (*walked, took*), the past participle (*walked, taken*), and the present participle (*walking, taking*).

prin·ci·ple (prĭn′sə-pəl) *n.* **1.** A basic truth or statement, especially in a system of beliefs or ideas: *the principles of democracy.* **2a.** A rule or standard, especially of good behavior: *a man of proper principles.* **b.** The general set of moral or ethical standards: *She makes decisions based on principle.* **3.** A statement or set of statements describing natural phenomena or mechanical processes: *the principle of conservation of energy.* ◆ **in principle** With regard to the basics: *I agree in principle, but we'll see how the details work out.* **on principle** According to or because of principle: *I objected on principle.* [From Middle English, from Latin *prīncipium,* from *prīnceps,* leader, emperor.] —SEE NOTE AT **principal.**

❑ *These sound alike:* **principle, principal** (chief).

print (prĭnt) *n.* **1.** A mark or impression made in or on a surface by pressure: *the print of footsteps in the sand.* **2a.** Lettering produced by printing or a similar method. **b.** Matter so produced; printed material. **3.** A design or picture transferred from an engraved plate, wood block, or similar medium. **4a.** Cloth marked with a dyed pattern or design: *a cotton print.* **b.** The pattern or design on such cloth: *a paisley print.* **5.** A photographic image transferred to paper. ❖ *v.* **print·ed, print·ing, prints** *—tr.* **1.** To press (a mark or design, for example) onto or into a surface. **2.** To produce on a paper surface by means of pressed type, an electronic printer, or similar means: *The government prints money.* **3.** To offer in printed form; publish: *The newspaper refused to print the letter.* **4.** To write (something) in block letters similar to those commonly used in printed matter: *Print your name on the dotted line.* **5.** To produce (a photographic print): *Have you printed my pictures yet?* *—intr.* **1.** To produce something in printed form by means of a printing press or other reproduction process. **2.** To write block letters similar to those used in print. ◆ **in print 1.** In printed or published form: *My letter appeared in print.* **2.** Offered for sale by a publisher: *Her book has been in print now for 20 years.* **out of print** No longer offered for sale by a publisher: *That book's out of print.* **print out** To print as a function; produce printed output: *The printer is printing out a document.* [From Middle English *prent,* from Old French *preinte,* from Latin *premere,* to press.]

print·ed circuit (prĭn′tĭd) *n.* An electric circuit in which the conducting connections have been deposited in set patterns on an insulating base.

print·er (prĭn′tər) *n.* **1.** A person whose job or business is printing. **2.** A device that prints text or graphics on paper: *a laser printer.*

print·ing (prĭn′tĭng) *n.* **1.** The art, process, or business of producing printed matter on a printing press or by similar means. **2.** Printed matter. **3.** All the copies of a publication, such as a book, printed at one time: *the first printing of the dictionary.*

printing press *n.* A machine that transfers letters or images onto sheets of paper or similar material by contact with an inked surface.

print·out (prĭnt′out′) *n.* A document printed by a computer printer: *She distributed printouts of her report to the class.*

pri·on (prī′ŏn′ *or* prē′ŏn′) *n.* A microscopic particle composed of protein, thought to cause certain diseases of the nervous system such as mad cow disease.

pri·or¹ (prī′ər) *adj.* **1.** Preceding in time or order: *his prior employment.* **2.** Greater in importance or value: *a prior consideration.* [From Latin.]

pri·or² (prī′ər) *n.* The monk in charge of a priory or ranking next below an abbot in an abbey. [From Old English, from Latin *prior,* superior.]

pri·or·ess (prī′ər-ĭs) *n.* A nun in charge of a priory or ranking below an abbess in an abbey.

pri·or·i·tize (prī-ôr′ĭ-tīz′) *tr.v.* **pri·or·i·tized, pri·or·i·tiz·ing, pri·or·i·tiz·es 1.** To arrange or deal with in order of importance. **2.** To treat or consider (something) as more important than other matters: *economic policies that prioritize job creation.*

USAGE

principal The words **principal** and **principle** are often confused but do not share any meanings. *Principle* is a noun, and most of its senses refer to a basic teaching or to rules and standards: *She really sticks to her principles. Principal* is both a noun and an adjective. As a noun it generally refers to a person who has a high position or plays an important role, for example, *a principal of a school.* As an adjective *principal* means "chief" or "leading": *The principal ways to solve these problems are explained in the third chapter.*

printed circuit

prism
White light (*left*) is dispersed into a spectrum (*right*) when it passes through a prism.

WRITERS CHOOSE THEIR WORDS

Dr. Young always said that books were for reading, and if people wanted to keep them **pristine** and beautiful, they would've put them in museums instead of libraries. Personally I thought that was a pretty good way to think about things, but I put a piece of Scotch tape over the rip just in case Mrs. Finch didn't agree.

—Lisa Graff
Umbrella Summer

pri·or·i·ty (prī-ôr′ĭ-tē) *n., pl.* **pri·or·i·ties 1.** Precedence, especially in importance or urgency: *Safety is given high priority in factories.* **2.** Something considered more important than other matters: *Her major priority is finishing college.*

pri·or·y (prī′ə-rē) *n., pl.* **pri·or·ies** A monastery governed by a prior or a convent governed by a prioress.

prism (prĭz′əm) *n.* **1.** A geometric solid or polyhedron having congruent polygons lying in parallel planes as its bases and parallelograms as its sides. **2.** A solid of this type, usually with triangular bases and rectangular sides, made of glass or another transparent material and used to break light into a spectrum or to reflect images. [From Greek *prīsma*, thing sawed off, prism, from *priein*, to saw.]

pris·mat·ic (prĭz-**măt′**ĭk) *adj.* **1.** Relating to a prism. **2.** Refracting light as a prism does. **3.** Sparkling with colors, as from refracted light.

pris·on (prĭz′ən) *n.* **1.** A lawful place of confinement, especially for people convicted of serious crimes. **2.** A place or condition of confinement: *His job seemed a prison to him.*

pris·on·er (prĭz′ə-nər *or* prĭz′nər) *n.* **1.** A person held in custody, especially in a prison. **2.** A person deprived of freedom of action or expression: *He was a prisoner of his fears.*

prisoner of war *n., pl.* **prisoners of war** A person captured by or surrendering to the enemy in wartime.

pris·sy (prĭs′ē) *adj.* **pris·si·er, pris·si·est** Excessively prim and proper.

pris·tine (prĭs′tēn′ *or* prĭ-**stēn′**) *adj.* **1.** In a pure or unspoiled state: *a pristine mountain lake.* **2.** Remaining free from dirt or decay; clean or fresh: *a pristine white dress.*

prith·ee (prĭth′ē *or* prĭth′ē) *interj. Archaic* An expression used to make a polite request.

pri·va·cy (prī′və-sē) *n.* **1.** The condition of being secluded from others: *Her privacy is important to her.* **2.** Freedom from undesired intrusion: *the right of privacy.*

pri·vate (prī′vĭt) *adj.* **1.** Secluded from the sight, presence, or intrusion of others. **2.** Relating to or confined to one person: *my private opinion.* **3.** Not available for public use, control, or participation: *a private party.* **4.** Owned by a person or group of persons rather than the public or government: *private property.* **5.** Not intended to be known publicly; secret: *private negotiations.* **6.** Not holding public office: *a private citizen.* **7.** Placing a high value on personal privacy: *a very private person.* ❖ *n.* An enlisted person of the lowest rank in the Army or Marine Corps. ◆ **in private** Not in public; secretly or confidentially.

private enterprise *n.* **1.** Business activities that are not subject to government ownership or control. **2.** A privately owned business, especially one operating in a capitalist economy.

pri·va·teer (prī′və-**tîr′**) *n.* **1.** A ship that is privately owned and operated, but authorized by a government to attack and capture enemy vessels during wartime. **2.** The commander or a crew member of such a ship. ❖ *intr.v.* **pri·va·teered, pri·va·teer·ing, pri·va·teers** To sail as a privateer.

private eye *n.* A private investigator.

private first class *n., pl.* **privates first class** An enlisted soldier ranking below corporal and above private in the US Army or Marine Corps.

private investigator *n.* A person privately hired to do investigative or detective work.

private school *n.* A secondary or elementary school operated and supported by private individuals or a corporation rather than by a government.

pri·va·tion (prī-**vā′**shən) *n.* **1.** Lack of the basic necessities of life. **2.** An act, condition, or result of being deprived.

priv·et (prĭv′ĭt) *n.* Any of several shrubs having small dark-green leaves and clusters of small white flowers, often used for hedges.

priv·i·lege (prĭv′ə-lĭj *or* prĭv′lĭj) *n.* A special advantage, right, immunity, benefit, or permission granted to or enjoyed by an individual, class, or caste.

priv·i·leged (prĭv′ə-lĭjd *or* prĭv′lĭjd) *adj.* Enjoying or having privileges: *the privileged classes.*

priv·i·ly (prĭv′ə-lē) *adv.* In a private manner; privately or secretly.

priv·y (prĭv′ē) *adj.* **1.** Provided with knowledge of something private or secret: *I'm not privy to the committee's discussions.* **2.** Belonging to a person, such as the British sovereign, in a private rather than an official capacity. ❖ *n., pl.* **priv·ies** An outdoor toilet; an outhouse.

Privy Council *n.* A council of the British sovereign that consists of cabinet ministers appointed by reason of their office and others appointed for life.

prize[1] (prīz) *n.* **1.** Something offered or won as an award for superiority or victory, as in a competition or contest. **2.** Something worth having or striving for: *These tomatoes are the prize of the crop.* ❖ *adj.* **1.** Offered or given as a prize: *prize money.* **2.** Given a prize or likely to win a prize: *the prize photograph in the show.* **3.** Worthy of some prize or recognition: *We planted some prize azaleas.* ❖ *tr.v.* **prized, priz·ing, priz·es** To value highly; esteem; treasure: *I prize my grandfather's watch.* See Synonyms at **appreciate.** [From Middle English *pris*, value, price, reward.]

prize[2] (prīz) *n.* Something seized by force, especially an enemy ship and its cargo captured at sea in wartime. [From Middle English *prise*, from Old French, something taken, from Latin *prehendere*, to seize.]

prize[3] (prīz) *tr.v.* **prized, priz·ing, priz·es** To move or force with or as if with a lever; pry: *prize a fungus off a tree trunk.* [From Middle English *prise*, instrument for prying, probably from *prise*, the taking of something.]

prize·fight (prīz′fīt′) *n.* A match that is fought between professional boxers for money. **—prize′fight′er** *n.* **—prize′fight′ing** *n.*

prize·win·ning (prīz′wĭn′ĭng) *adj.* Having won a prize or deserving of a prize: *the prizewinning entry.*

pro[1] (prō) *n., pl.* **pros** An argument or consideration in favor of something: *discussed the pros and cons.* ❖ *adv.* In favor; in support: *argue pro and con.* ❖ *adj.* Supporting: *the arguments pro and con.* [From Middle English, from Latin *prō*, for.]

pro[2] (prō) *Informal n., pl.* **pros** A professional, especially in sports. ❖ *adj.* Professional: *pro football.* [Short for *professional.*]

pro–[1] *pref.* A prefix that means: **1.** Supporting or favoring: *pro-democracy.* **2.** Acting as; substituting for: *pronoun.* —SEE NOTE.

pro–[2] *pref.* A prefix that means before or earlier: *prologue.* —SEE NOTE AT **pro–**[1].

prob·a·bil·i·ty (prŏb′ə-**bĭl′**ĭ-tē) *n., pl.* **prob·a·bil·i·ties 1.** The condition of being probable; likelihood. **2.** A probable situation, condition, or event. **3.** A number expressing how likely to occur a given event is, especially a fraction expressing how many times the event will happen in a given number of trials.

prob·a·ble (prŏb′ə-bəl) *adj.* **1.** Likely to happen or be true: *the probable cost of the expedition.* **2.** Likely but not certain; plausible: *a probable explanation.* [From Middle English, from Latin *probāre*, to prove.] **—prob′a·bly** *adv.*

pro·bate (prō′bāt′) *n.* Legal establishment of the validity of a will. ❖ *tr.v.* **pro·bat·ed, pro·bat·ing, pro·bates** To establish the legal validity of (a will).

pro·ba·tion (prō-**bā′**shən) *n.* **1.** A trial period for testing a person's fitness, as for a job or membership in a club. **2.** The release of a convicted criminal on condition of

ă	pat	ôr	core
ā	pay	oi	boy
âr	care	ou	out
ä	father	ŏŏ	took
ĕ	pet	ŏŏr	lure
ē	be	ōō	boot
ĭ	pit	ŭ	cut
ī	bite	ûr	urge
îr	pier	th	thin
ŏ	pot	*th*	this
ō	toe	zh	vision
ô	paw	ə	about

good behavior: *knew he would go to prison if he violated the terms of his probation.* **3.** A trial period in which a student may try to redeem failing grades or bad conduct so as not to be suspended: *was put on probation.*

pro·ba·tion·er (prō-**bā′**shə-nər) *n.* A person on probation.

probation officer *n.* An official who supervises people who have been put on probation after being convicted of a crime.

probe (prōb) *n.* **1.** An exploratory action or expedition, or device, especially one designed to research or investigate a remote or unknown region: *an explorer's probe into the unmapped mountains.* **2.** A space probe. **3.** Any of various long slender tools used to reach into or touch something in order to examine it, especially an instrument used to explore a wound or body cavity. **4.** The act of exploring or searching with a device or instrument: *the surgeon's probe of the patient's wound.* **5.** An investigation into unfamiliar matters or questionable activities: *a Congressional probe into fraud.* ❖ *v.* **probed, prob·ing, probes** —*tr.* **1.** To explore or examine (something) with a probe. **2.** To investigate or explore: *The committee is probing the causes of the strike.* —*intr.* To conduct an investigation or search: *Have the police probed into the finances of the accused?* [From Middle English, from Late Latin *proba*, proof.]

pro·bi·ty (**prō′**bĭ-tē) *n.* Complete integrity; uprightness.

prob·lem (**prŏb′**ləm) *n.* **1.** A question to be considered, solved, or answered: *math problems; construction problems.* **2.** Something that presents difficulty or harm and needs to be dealt with: *We're having problems with the computer.* **3.** A misgiving, objection, or complaint: *I have a problem with your attitude.* ❖ *adj.* Difficult to deal with or control: *a problem child.* ◆ **no problem** *Informal* **1.** An expression used to confirm or comply with a request. **2.** An expression used to acknowledge an expression of gratitude.

prob·lem·at·ic (prŏb′lə-**măt′**ĭk) also **prob·lem·at·i·cal** (prŏb′lə-**măt′**ĭ-kəl) *adj.* Posing a problem or difficulty: *a problematic situation.*

pro·bos·cis (prō-**bŏs′**ĭs) *n., pl.* **pro·bos·cis·es** or **pro·bos·ci·des** (prō-**bŏs′**ĭ-dēz′) **1.** A long flexible snout, such as an elephant's trunk. **2.** A slender tubular mouthpart of certain insects, used for sucking food. **3.** An unusually large nose.

pro·ce·dure (prə-**sē′**jər) *n.* **1.** A manner of proceeding; a way of doing something or getting something done: *the procedure for getting a passport.* **2.** A series of steps taken to accomplish an end: *underwent a medical procedure to repair his injury.* —**pro·ce′dur·al** *adj.*

pro·ceed (prə-**sēd′**) *intr.v.* **pro·ceed·ed, pro·ceed·ing, pro·ceeds 1.** To go forward or onward, especially after an interruption; continue: *He ran some errands and then proceeded home.* **2.** To begin some action or process after doing something else: *After lunch, she proceeded to talk about the film.* ❖ *pl.n.* **pro·ceeds** (**prō′**sēdz′) The amount of money derived from a fund-raising venture. [From Middle English *proceden*, from Latin *prōcēdere* : *prō-*, forward + *cēdere*, to go.]

pro·ceed·ing (prə-**sē′**dĭng) *n.* **1.** A course of action: *a reckless proceeding.* **2. proceedings** Legal action.

proc·ess (**prŏs′**ĕs′) *n., pl.* **proc·ess·es** (**prŏs′**ĕs′ĭz *or* **prŏs′**ĭ-sēz′) **1.** A series of actions, changes, or functions bringing about a result: *the process of digestion.* **2.** A series of operations performed in the making or treatment of a product: *The metal gets coated in an electroplating process.* **3.** The course of events or passage of time: *He started playing tennis, and in the process he lost ten pounds.* **4a.** A summons ordering a defendant to appear in court. **b.** The set of actions and events that make up a judicial proceeding: *the sentencing process.* **5.** A part that extends or projects from the body or one of its organs: *A horn is a bony process that grows from the head of certain animals.* ❖ *tr.v.* **proc·essed, proc·ess·ing, proc·ess·es 1.** To put through a series of steps as part of a set procedure: *process an application.* **2.** To prepare, treat, or convert by means of a special process: *process ore to obtain minerals.* **3.** To perform operations on (computer data).

pro·ces·sion (prə-**sĕsh′**ən) *n.* **1.** A group of people, vehicles, or objects moving along in an orderly, formal manner. **2.** The movement of such a group.

pro·ces·sion·al (prə-**sĕsh′**ə-nəl) *adj.* Relating to or suitable for a procession: *She led the processional march.* ❖ *n.* **1.** A book containing the rituals observed during a religious procession. **2.** A musical piece played or sung during a procession.

proc·es·sor (**prŏs′**ĕs′ər *or* **prō′**sĕs′ər) *n.* **1.** A person or thing that processes. **2.** The central processing unit of a computer.

pro·claim (prə-**klām′**) *tr.v.* **pro·claimed, pro·claim·ing, pro·claims 1.** To announce officially and publicly; declare: *proclaim a holiday.* **2.** To indicate unmistakably; make plain: *His behavior proclaims him capable of holding the office.*

proc·la·ma·tion (prŏk′lə-**mā′**shən) *n.* **1.** The act of proclaiming. **2.** Something proclaimed, especially an official public announcement.

pro·cliv·i·ty (prō-**klĭv′**ĭ-tē) *n., pl.* **pro·cliv·i·ties** A natural inclination; a predisposition: *her proclivity for the arts.*

pro·con·sul (prō-**kŏn′**səl) *n.* In ancient Rome, a provincial administrator.

pro·cras·ti·nate (prə-**krăs′**tə-nāt′) *intr.v.* **pro·cras·ti·nat·ed, pro·cras·ti·nat·ing, pro·cras·ti·nates** To put off doing something, especially out of habitual carelessness or laziness. [From Latin *prōcrāstināre* : *prō-*, forward + *crāstinus*, of tomorrow (from *crās*, tomorrow).] —**pro·cras′ti·na′tion** *n.* —**pro·cras′ti·na′tor** *n.*

pro·cre·ate (**prō′**krē-āt′) *intr.v.* **pro·cre·at·ed, pro·cre·at·ing, pro·cre·ates** To produce offspring. —**pro′cre·a′tion** *n.*

proc·tor (**prŏk′**tər) *n.* A supervisor, especially of a school examination. ❖ *tr.v.* **proc·tored, proc·tor·ing, proc·tors** To supervise (an examination).

pro·cure (prō-**kyŏŏr′**) *tr.v.* **pro·cured, pro·cur·ing, pro·cures 1.** To get by special effort; obtain or acquire: *procured tickets for the circus.* **2.** To bring about; effect: *striving to procure a solution to the problem.* —**pro·cure′ment** *n.*

prod (prŏd) *tr.v.* **prod·ded, prod·ding, prods 1.** To jab or poke, as with a pointed object: *She prodded the cattle along.* **2.** To stir to action; urge: *continually prodded him to do his homework.* ❖ *n.* **1.** A pointed object used as a prod: *a cattle prod.* **2.** A stimulus to action. —**prod′der** *n.*

prod·i·gal (**prŏd′**ĭ-gəl) *adj.* **1.** Recklessly or extravagantly wasteful: *our prodigal consumption of natural resources.* **2.** Extravagantly generous or abundant: *prodigal praise.* ❖ *n.* An extravagant person; a spendthrift. [From Latin *prōdigere*, to drive out, squander.] —**prod′i·gal′i·ty** (prŏd′ĭ-**găl′**ĭ-tē) *n.* —**prod′i·gal·ly** *adv.*

pro·di·gious (prə-**dĭj′**əs) *adj.* **1.** Impressively large in size, force, or extent: *a prodigious sea monster.* **2.** Extraordinary: *a prodigious memory.* —**pro·di′gious·ly** *adv.*

prod·i·gy (**prŏd′**ə-jē) *n., pl.* **prod·i·gies 1.** A person with exceptional talents or powers: *a child prodigy.* **2.** An extraordinary act or event; a marvel: *geysers and rock formations that are prodigies of nature.* [From Middle English *prodige*, portent, from Latin *prōdigium*.]

pro·duce (prə-**dōōs′**) *tr.v.* **pro·duced, pro·duc·ing, pro·duc·es 1.** To bring forth (something); yield: *a plant that produces pink flowers.* **2.** To create by mental or physical effort: *produce a painting.* **3.** To manufacture:

WORD BUILDING

pro–¹ The prefix **pro–¹** comes from Latin *prō*, meaning "for." In English, *pro–¹* usually means "favoring" or "supporting," as when it is prefixed to names of nationalities: *pro-American*. In this sense, the opposite of *pro–¹* is *anti–*: *proslavery/antislavery*. Note that when *pro–¹* precedes a word beginning with a capital letter, a hyphen must be used. The prefix **pro–²** comes from Greek *pro*, meaning "before, in front." The word *prologue* comes from Greek *prologos*, from *pro–²* + *logos*, meaning "speech." In English, *pro–²* often means "before" or "earlier" and is used mainly in science terms: *prophase*.

proboscis
of a bumblebee

WORD BUILDING

produce The word root *duc–* in English words comes from the Latin verb *dūcere,* "to lead, bring, take." Thus we have **induce,** "to lead on, draw on, as by persuasion" (using the prefix *in–²,* "on, in"); **deduce,** "to draw from" (*dē–,* "from"); **educe,** "to draw out, bring out, elicit" (*ē–,* "out, out of"); **produce,** "to bring forth (as a product), lead out" (*prō–,* "forward, in front"); and **reduce,** "to lead back, pull back (in size)" (*re–,* "back").

a factory that produces parts for machines. **4.** To cause to exist; give rise to: *Industrial growth produced a new kind of business organization.* **5.** To bring forward; show; exhibit: *The magician produced a rabbit from the hat.* **6.** To supervise and finance (an artistic creation or performance): *produced a musical on Broadway.* ❖ *n.* (**prŏd′**-o͞os *or* **prō′**do͞os) Farm products, especially fruits or vegetables. [From Middle English *producen,* to extend, from Latin *prōdūcere,* to extend, bring forth : *prō-,* forth + *dūcere,* to lead.] —SEE NOTE.

pro·duc·er (prə-**do͞o′**sər) *n.* **1.** A person, organization, or thing that produces, especially one that makes something for sale: *a producer of cast iron.* **2.** A person who supervises and manages the finances, making, and public presentation of a play, film, television show, or other entertainment. **3.** An organism that produces its own food, as through photosynthesis, and constitutes the beginning of a food chain.

producer goods *pl.n.* Goods, such as raw materials or tools, that producers use to make consumer goods.

prod·uct (**prŏd′**əkt) *n.* **1.** Something produced, as by human effort or by nature: *farm products.* **2.** A direct result: *His discipline is the product of a strict education.* **3.** The result obtained when multiplication is performed.

pro·duc·tion (prə-**dŭk′**shən) *n.* **1.** The act or process of producing: *automobile production.* **2.** An item that has been produced; a product. **3a.** The act or process of producing a public show or entertainment: *During production, the script was rewritten several times.* **b.** The show or entertainment so produced: *a production of "Romeo and Juliet."* **4.** An amount produced; output or yield: *Production is down this week.*

pro·duc·tive (prə-**dŭk′**tĭv) *adj.* **1.** Producing abundantly: *productive farmlands.* **2.** Marked by abundant achievement: *a productive life.* **3.** Yielding favorable or useful results; constructive: *a productive suggestion.* **—pro·duc′tive·ly** *adv.* **—pro′duc·tiv′i·ty** (prō′dŭk-**tĭv′**ĭ-tē *or* prŏd′ək-**tĭv′**ĭ-tē) *n.*

prof·a·na·tion (prŏf′ə-**nā′**shən) *n.* The act of profaning; desecration.

pro·fane (prō-**fān′** *or* prə-**fān′**) *adj.* **1.** Showing contempt for God or sacred things; irreverent. **2.** Not religious in nature or use; secular: *both sacred and profane music.* **3.** Coarse or vulgar. ❖ *tr.v.* **pro·faned, pro·fan·ing, pro·fanes 1.** To treat or use (something sacred) in a way that shows contempt or irreverence: *profaning the name of God.* **2.** To put to an unworthy or degrading use; misuse: *profaning lovely Spanish words by mispronouncing them.* **—pro·fane′ly** *adv.* **—pro·fane′ness** *n.*

pro·fan·i·ty (prō-**făn′**ĭ-tē) *n., pl.* **pro·fan·i·ties 1a.** Abrasive, vulgar, or irreverent language. **b.** The use of profane language. **2.** The quality of being irreverent or contemptuous toward sacred things.

pro·fess (prə-**fĕs′**) *tr.v.* **pro·fessed, pro·fess·ing, pro·fess·es 1.** To declare openly; claim: *professed an interest in learning to sail.* **2.** To make a show of; pretend: *professing a sympathy that he did not really feel.* **3.** To claim knowledge of or skill in: *profess medicine.* **4.** To affirm belief in (a religion). [From Middle English *professen,* to take vows, from Latin *profitērī,* to affirm openly.]

pro·fes·sion (prə-**fĕsh′**ən) *n.* **1.** An occupation or career, especially one that requires specialized training, study, or skills: *the profession of engineering.* **2.** The group of qualified people practicing such an occupation: *members of the legal profession.* **3.** The act of professing something; an open declaration: *a profession of faith.* [From Middle English *professioun,* vow, from Latin *professiō,* public avowal, from *profitērī,* to affirm openly.]

pro·fes·sion·al (prə-**fĕsh′**ə-nəl) *adj.* **1.** Relating to or practicing a profession: *lawyers, doctors, and other professional people.* **2.** Having or showing specialized skill equal to that of a person who is specially trained in that skill: *My sixteen-year-old neighbor did a thoroughly professional repair job on the car.* **3.** Doing specified work for a living or as a career: *a professional writer.* **4.** Performed by or consisting of people receiving pay; not amateur: *professional golf.* ❖ *n.* **1.** A person who follows a profession, especially a learned profession: *We need to call in the professionals for this job.* **2.** A person who earns a living in a given profession. **3.** A person who is skilled or experienced in a certain field; a qualified expert. **—pro·fes′sion·al·ly** *adv.*

pro·fes·sor (prə-**fĕs′**ər) *n.* A teacher, especially of the highest rank, at a college or university. [From Middle English *professour,* from Latin *professor,* from *profitērī,* to profess.] **—pro·fes′sor·ship′** *n.*

pro·fes·so·ri·al (prō′fĭ-**sôr′**ē-əl *or* prŏf′ĭ-**sôr′**ē-əl) *adj.* Relating to or characteristic of a professor. **—pro′fes·so′ri·al·ly** *adv.*

prof·fer (**prŏf′**ər) *tr.v.* **prof·fered, prof·fer·ing, prof·fers** To present for acceptance; offer: *proffered her legal services to our school.* ❖ *n.* An offer: *the proffer of help.*

pro·fi·cient (prə-**fĭsh′**ənt) *adj.* Having or characterized by advanced knowledge or ability in a particular area: *proficient at playing the harmonica.* **—pro·fi′cien·cy** *n.* **—pro·fi′cient·ly** *adv.*

SYNONYMS **proficient, adept, skilled, skillful, accomplished, expert** These adjectives mean having or showing knowledge or ability, as in a branch of learning or a skill. **Proficient** suggests advanced ability gained through training: *It takes many years of study and experience to become a proficient surgeon.* **Adept** suggests being naturally good at something that one has improved through practice: *The dressmaker became adept at cutting fabric without a pattern.* **Skilled** suggests sound, thorough ability and often mastery, as in an art, craft, or trade: *Only the most skilled gymnasts are accepted for the Olympic team.* **Skillful** means skilled with a natural knack: *The tailor was especially skillful at measuring things by eye.* **Accomplished** suggests refinement because of training and practice: *The accomplished violinist played the sonata perfectly.* **Expert** applies to one with exceptional skill and command: *A virtuoso is a person who is expert in playing a musical instrument.*

pro·file (**prō′**fīl′) *n.* **1a.** A side view of an object, especially of the human head. **b.** A representation of a human head or other object seen from the side: *the profile of Lincoln on the penny.* **2.** The outline of something: *the jagged profile of the city skyline.* See Synonyms at **outline. 3.** A biographical account that describes what the person is best known for. **4a.** A set of characteristics that identify or are thought to identify a particular type of person: *The police constructed a profile of the thief and used it to track him down.* **b.** A summary or analysis of something: *a profile of the ten best restaurants.* ❖ *tr.v.* **pro·filed, pro·fil·ing, pro·files** To draw or produce a profile of. [From Italian *profilare,* to draw in outline : *pro-,* forward + *filare,* to draw a line.]

prof·it (**prŏf′**ĭt) *n.* **1.** The money made in a business venture, sale, or investment after all expenses have been met: *made a profit of five cents on every newspaper she sold.* **2.** An advantage gained from doing something; a benefit: *She saw no profit in complaining.* ❖ *v.* **prof·it·ed, prof·it·ing, prof·its** *—intr.* To gain an advantage; benefit: *profiting from the experience of others. —tr.* To be an advantage to: *It would profit you to pay closer attention to what is being said.* [From Middle English, from Latin *prōficere,* to make progress, to profit.]

❑ *These sound alike:* **profit, prophet** (person inspired by God).

prof·it·a·ble (**prŏf′**ĭ-tə-bəl) *adj.* **1.** Yielding a profit; money-making: *a profitable business.* **2.** Yielding ben-

ă	pat	ôr	core
ā	pay	oi	boy
âr	care	ou	out
ä	father	o͝o	took
ĕ	pet	o͝or	lure
ē	be	o͞o	boot
ĭ	pit	ŭ	cut
ī	bite	ûr	urge
îr	pier	th	thin
ŏ	pot	*th*	this
ō	toe	zh	vision
ô	paw	ə	about

efits; rewarding; worthwhile: *learned much that proved profitable later.*

prof·it·eer (prŏf′ĭ-**tîr′**) *n.* A person who makes excessive profits on goods in short supply. ❖ *intr.v.* **prof·it·eered, prof·it·eer·ing, prof·it·eers** To act as a profiteer.

prof·li·gate (**prŏf′**lĭ-gĭt *or* **prŏf′**lĭ-gāt′) *adj.* **1.** Given to extreme self-indulgence; dissolute. **2.** Recklessly wasteful of money or resources. ❖ *n.* A very wasteful or dissolute person. **—prof′li·ga·cy** (**prŏf′**lĭ-gə-sē) *n.* **—prof′li·gate·ly** *adv.*

pro·found (prə-**found′**) *adj.* **pro·found·er, pro·found·est 1.** Going well beyond what is apparent or superficial; insightful: *a profound remark.* **2.** Deeply felt or held; intense: *profound love of art.* **3.** Far-reaching; thoroughgoing: *a profound change in our society.* **4.** Total; absolute: *a profound silence.* **5.** Extending to or coming from a great depth; deep: *a profound chasm.* [From Middle English, from Latin *profundus* : *prō-*, before + *fundus*, bottom.] **—pro·found′ly** *adv.* **—pro·found′ness** *n.*

pro·fun·di·ty (prə-**fŭn′**dĭ-tē) *n., pl.* **pro·fun·di·ties 1.** Intellectual insight or understanding. **2.** Intensity of feeling or conviction. **3.** Great depth.

pro·fuse (prə-**fyo͞os′**) *adj.* **1.** Abundant; plentiful: *a profuse variety of foods.* **2.** Given or giving generously; extravagant; lavish: *profuse praise.* [From Middle English, from Latin *profūsus*, from *profundere*, to pour forth.] **—pro·fuse′ly** *adv.* **—pro·fuse′ness** *n.* —SEE NOTE AT **transfusion.**

pro·fu·sion (prə-**fyo͞o′**zhən) *n.* **1.** The condition of being profuse; abundance. **2.** A great quantity or amount: *a profusion of old books in the attic.*

pro·gen·i·tor (prō-**jĕn′**ĭ-tər) *n.* **1.** A direct ancestor. **2.** A person or thing that originates or sets a pattern for something.

prog·e·ny (**prŏj′**ə-nē) *n., pl.* **progeny** or **prog·e·nies 1.** A person's children or descendants: *The king's fortune was divided among his progeny.* **2.** The young of an animal or plant: *These seedlings are the progeny of that large maple tree.*

pro·ges·ter·one (prō-**jĕs′**tə-rōn′) *n.* A hormone that readies the lining of the uterus to receive a fertilized ovum.

prog·no·sis (prŏg-**nō′**sĭs) *n., pl.* **prog·no·ses** (prŏg-**nō′**sēz) **1a.** A prediction of the likely course or outcome of a disease: *His prognosis was for full recovery.* **b.** The likelihood of recovering from a disease: *a patient with a good prognosis.* **2.** A prediction or forecast: *a writer's prognosis for fall fashions.* [From Latin *prognōsis*, from Greek *progignōskein* : *pro-*, before + *gignōskein*, to know.]

prog·nos·tic (prŏg-**nŏs′**tĭk) *adj.* Relating to prognosis or prediction. ❖ *n.* **1.** A sign or symptom indicating the future course of a disease. **2.** A sign of future events; a portent.

prog·nos·ti·cate (prŏg-**nŏs′**tĭ-kāt′) *tr.v.* **prog·nos·ti·cat·ed, prog·nos·ti·cat·ing, prog·nos·ti·cates** To predict on the basis of present signs or symptoms: *prognosticate a good year for farm crops.* **—prog·nos′ti·ca′tion** *n.* **—prog·nos′ti·ca′tor** *n.*

pro·gram (**prō′**grăm′ *or* **prō′**grəm) *n.* **1.** A list of the order of events and other information for a public presentation or entertainment: *a printed program of the concert.* **2.** A public performance, presentation, or entertainment: *We presented a program of folk music.* **3.** A radio or television show. **4.** An ordered list of activities, courses, or procedures; a schedule: *a program of physical therapy for the injured athlete.* **5.** A course of academic study or extracurricular activities: *an excellent African studies program.* **6.** A system of services or projects designed to achieve a goal or meet a social need: *the space program; an after-school study program.* **7.** A set of coded instructions that enables a machine, especially a computer, to perform a desired sequence of operations. ❖ *tr.v.* **pro·grammed, pro·gram·ming, pro·grams 1.** To include in a program; schedule. **2.** To provide (a computer) with a program. **3.** To train to perform automatically in a certain way: *We have been programmed to expect TV commercials.* [From Greek *programma*, public notice : *pro-*, forth, publicly + *graphein*, to write.]

pro·gram·mer (**prō′**grăm′ər) *n.* A person who programs, especially one who writes computer programs.

pro·gram·ming (**prō′**grăm′ĭng) *n.* **1.** The designing, scheduling, or planning of a program, as in broadcasting. **2.** The writing of a computer program.

programming language *n.* An artificial language used to write instructions that can be understood and executed by a computer.

prog·ress (**prŏg′**rĕs′ *or* **prŏg′**rəs) *n.* **1.** Onward movement; advance: *made slow progress through the traffic.* **2.** Steady improvement, as of civilization or an individual: *faith in human progress.* ❖ *intr.v.* **pro·gress** (prə-**grĕs′**) **pro·gressed, pro·gress·ing, pro·gress·es 1.** To move along; advance; proceed: *Work on the new pool has progressed rapidly.* **2.** To make steady or regular improvements: *Medical technology is always progressing.* ◆ **in progress** Going on; under way. [From Middle English *progresse*, from Latin *prōgressus*, from *prōgredī*, to advance : *prō-*, forward + *gradī*, to go, walk.] —SEE NOTE.

pro·gres·sion (prə-**grĕsh′**ən) *n.* **1.** Movement; progress: *limbs adapted for progression on land.* **2.** A series of things or events; a sequence: *a progression of speakers at the rally.* **3.** A sequence of numbers, each derived from the one before by some regular rule.

pro·gres·sive (prə-**grĕs′**ĭv) *adj.* **1.** Moving forward; advancing: *the progressive motion of a wave.* **2.** Continuing steadily by small changes: *progressive erosion in the cliff.* **3.** Tending to spread or grow worse: *progressive paralysis.* **4.** Favoring or willing to consider new ideas, policies, or methods: *progressive leadership.* **5.** Increasing in rate of tax as the taxable amount increases: *The federal income tax is progressive, but sales taxes are not.* **6.** Indicating a verb form used to express an action or a condition that is in progress. Progressive verb forms in English use a present participle and a form of the verb *be;* for example, *I am sitting. He had been sitting. She will be sitting.* ❖ *n.* A person who favors or is willing to consider new ideas, policies, or methods. **—pro·gres′sive·ly** *adv.*

pro·hib·it (prō-**hĭb′**ĭt) *tr.v.* **pro·hib·it·ed, pro·hib·it·ing, pro·hib·its 1.** To forbid by law or authority: *The pool rules prohibit diving in the shallow end.* **2.** To prevent: *Shyness prohibited me from speaking in front of crowds.* [From Middle English *prohibiten*, from Latin *prohibēre* : *pro-*, in front + *habēre*, to hold.]

pro·hi·bi·tion (prō′ə-**bĭsh′**ən) *n.* **1.** The act of prohibiting or the condition of being prohibited. **2.** A law or order that prohibits something: *a prohibition on smoking.* **3a.** The forbidding by law of the manufacture, transportation, sale, and possession of alcoholic beverages. **b. Prohibition** The period from 1920 to 1933 during which a ban on the manufacture and sale of alcoholic beverages was in effect in the United States.

pro·hi·bi·tion·ist (prō′ə-**bĭsh′**ə-nĭst) *n.* A person in favor of outlawing the manufacture and sale of alcoholic beverages.

pro·hib·i·tive (prō-**hĭb′**ĭ-tĭv) *adj.* **1.** Prohibiting; forbidding. **2.** Preventing or discouraging purchase or use: *prohibitive prices.* **—pro·hib′i·tive·ly** *adv.*

proj·ect (**prŏj′**ĕkt′) *n.* **1.** An undertaking requiring systematic planning and work: *a land-irrigation project.* **2.** A special task undertaken by a student or group of students: *a science project.* **3.** A plan or proposal. **4.** A housing project. ❖ *v.* **pro·ject** (prə-**jĕkt′**) **pro·ject·ed, pro·ject·ing, pro·jects** *—tr.* **1.** To thrust forward or outward: *He projected his jaw in defiance.* **2.** To cause (an image) to appear on a surface: *projecting color slides onto*

profile

WORD BUILDING

progress The word root *gress–* in English words comes from the past participle *gressus* of the Latin verb *gradī*, "to walk." **Progress** therefore is literally "a walking forward, an advance" (using the prefix *prō–*, "forward"); to **transgress** means "to walk through or over to the other side, pass beyond a limit" (*trans–*, "across"); an **egress** is literally "a way out, an exit" (*ē–*, "out, out of"); and to **digress** means "to go off or astray" (*dī–*, a form of *dis–*, "apart"). The Latin noun derived from *gradī* is *gradus*, "a pace, step, stage in a process," the source of the English **grade.**

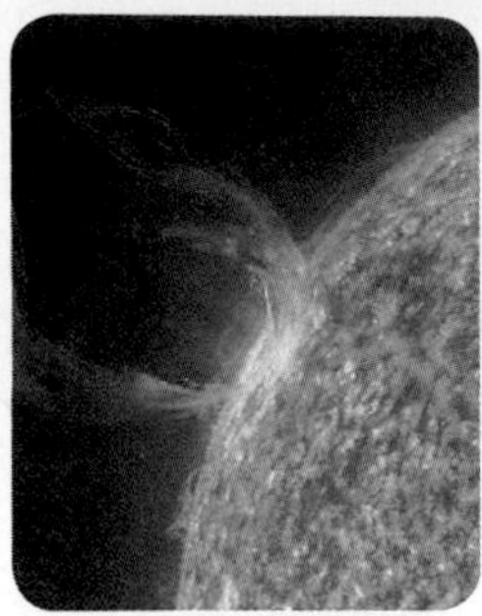

prominence
solar prominence

promontory
Thornwick Bay, near Flamborough, England

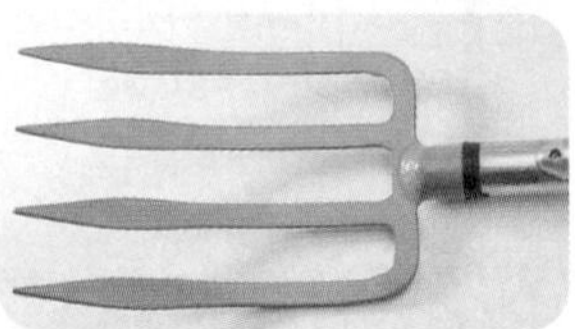

prong

a wall. **3.** To calculate, estimate, or predict (something in the future) based on present data: *project next year's costs.* **4.** To plan; intend: *projecting a new superhighway.* **5.** To direct (one's voice) so as to be heard clearly at a distance. —*intr.* **1.** To extend or jut out: *The second floor projects over the street.* **2.** To project one's voice so as to be heard clearly at a distance. [From Middle English *projecte*, from Latin *prōiectum*, projecting structure, from *prōicere*, to throw out : *prō-*, forth + *iacere*, to throw.]

pro·jec·tile (prə-**jĕk′**təl *or* prə-**jĕk′**tīl′) *n.* **1.** An object, such as a bullet or arrow, that is thrown, fired, or otherwise launched through space. **2.** A missile that can launch itself, such as a rocket. **—pro·jec′tile** *adj.*

pro·jec·tion (prə-**jĕk′**shən) *n.* **1.** The act of projecting or the condition of being projected. **2.** Something that extends outward beyond a surface: *an insect with spiny projections on its back.* **3.** An image produced by a pattern of light falling on a surface, as when a slide is projected on a screen. **4.** An estimate of what something will be in the future, based on the present trends or data: *Projections indicate that sales will be up.*

pro·jec·tion·ist (prə-**jĕk′**shə-nĭst) *n.* A person who operates a movie projector.

pro·jec·tor (prə-**jĕk′**tər) *n.* A machine that uses lenses and a source of light to project images, as of movies, onto a surface.

pro·kar·y·ote (prō-**kăr′**ē-ōt′) *n.* Any of numerous one-celled organisms that lack distinct nuclei. Bacteria and archaea are prokaryotes. **—pro·kar′y·ot′ic** (prō-kăr′-ē-**ŏt′**ĭk) *adj.*

pro·le·tar·i·an (prō′lĭ-**târ′**ē-ən) *adj.* Relating to the working class: *a proletarian revolution.* ❖ *n.* A member of the working class.

pro·le·tar·i·at (prō′lĭ-**târ′**ē-ĭt) *n.* The class of people who work for wages, especially at industrial jobs, and who do not own property; the working class. [From Latin *prōlētārius*, belonging to the lowest class of Roman citizens, from *prōlēs*, offspring (because the lowest class was seen as contributing to the state only by having children).]

pro·lif·er·ate (prə-**lĭf′**ə-rāt′) *intr.v.* **pro·lif·er·at·ed, pro·lif·er·at·ing, pro·lif·er·ates 1.** To produce new growth, offspring, cells, or particles rapidly and repeatedly; multiply at a fast rate: *Viruses proliferate in living tissue.* **2.** To increase or spread rapidly: *Fast-food restaurants have proliferated in town.* **—pro·lif′er·a′tion** *n.*

pro·lif·ic (prə-**lĭf′**ĭk) *adj.* **1.** Producing offspring or fruit in great numbers: *Rabbits are prolific animals.* **2.** Producing numerous works: *a prolific author.* [From Latin *prōlēs*, offspring.] **—pro·lif′i·cal·ly** *adv.*

pro·line (**prō′**lēn′) *n.* A nonessential amino acid that is found in most proteins.

pro·lix (prō-**lĭks′** *or* **prō′**lĭks′) *adj.* Wordy and tiresome; verbose. **—pro·lix′i·ty** *n.* **—pro·lix′ly** *adv.*

pro·logue (**prō′**lôg′) *n.* **1.** A beginning section of a play, opera, or literary work that introduces or explains what follows. **2.** An introductory act or event.

pro·long (prə-**lông′**) *tr.v.* **pro·longed, pro·long·ing, pro·longs** To lengthen in duration; protract: *a special diet for prolonging one's life.* **—pro′lon·ga′tion** (prō′-lông-**gā′**shən) *n.*

prom (prŏm) *n.* A formal dance held for a school class.

prom·e·nade (prŏm′ə-**nād′** *or* prŏm′ə-**näd′**) *n.* **1.** A leisurely walk, especially in a public place. **2.** A public place for strolling, as a park or mall. **3.** A formal dance. **4a.** A march performed by the couples in a square dance. **b.** A march by the guests at the opening of a ball. ❖ *intr.v.* **prom·e·nad·ed, prom·e·nad·ing, prom·e·nades 1.** To go on a leisurely walk; stroll. **2.** To perform a promenade at a square dance or a ball.

Pro·me·the·us (prə-**mē′**thē-əs) *n.* In Greek mythology, a Titan who stole fire from Olympus and gave it to the human race, for which Zeus chained him to a rock and sent an eagle to eat his liver, which grew back daily.

pro·me·thi·um (prə-**mē′**thē-əm) *n. Symbol* **Pm** A radioactive metallic element that has been artificially produced by scientists. Atomic number 61. See **Periodic Table.**

prom·i·nence (**prŏm′**ə-nəns) *n.* **1.** The quality or condition of being prominent; eminence or importance: *rose to a position of prominence in government.* **2.** Something that rises sharply upward or outward from its surroundings: *climbed the nearest prominence for a view of the terrain.* **3.** A slender wavy cloud of shining gas that rises from the surface of the sun.

prom·i·nent (**prŏm′**ə-nənt) *adj.* **1.** Projecting outward; bulging or jutting: *prominent brows.* **2.** Highly noticeable; conspicuous: *The new dictionary occupies a prominent place on their coffee table.* **3.** Well-known; eminent: *a prominent politician.* [From Middle English, from Latin *prōminēre*, to jut out.] **—prom′i·nent·ly** *adv.*

prom·is·cu·i·ty (prŏm′ĭ-**skyo͞o′**ĭ-tē *or* prō′mĭ-**skyo͞o′**-ĭ-tē) *n., pl.* **prom·is·cu·i·ties** The state or character of being promiscuous.

pro·mis·cu·ous (prə-**mĭs′**kyo͞o-əs) *adj.* **1.** Having sexual relations frequently with many different partners. **2.** Showing a lack of standards for making choices; indiscriminate: *a gallery with a promiscuous assortment of good and bad paintings.* **—pro·mis′cu·ous·ly** *adv.* **—pro·mis′cu·ous·ness** *n.*

prom·ise (**prŏm′**ĭs) *n.* **1.** A declaration that one will or will not do a certain thing; a vow: *kept her promise to write home once a week.* See Synonyms at **vow. 2a.** Indication of something favorable to come; grounds for expectation: *a promise of spring in the warm breeze.* **b.** Indication of future success or excellence: *a rookie pitcher who shows promise.* ❖ *v.* **prom·ised, prom·is·ing, prom·is·es** —*tr.* **1.** To declare with a promise; pledge: *I promised to come home early.* **2.** To give grounds for expecting: *clouds that promised rain.* —*intr.* To make or give a promise. [From Middle English *promis*, from Medieval Latin *prōmissa*, from Latin *prōmittere*, to send forth, promise.]

Prom·ised Land (**prŏm′**ĭst) *n.* **1.** In the Bible, the land of Canaan, promised by God to the descendants of Abraham and Sarah. **2. promised land** A place of expected or longed-for happiness: *Many people saw the state as a promised land where jobs were plentiful.*

prom·is·ing (**prŏm′**ĭ-sĭng) *adj.* Likely to develop as hoped: *a promising career.* **—prom′is·ing·ly** *adv.*

prom·is·so·ry note (**prŏm′**ĭ-sôr′ē) *n.* A written promise to pay a certain sum of money at a stated time or on demand.

prom·on·to·ry (**prŏm′**ən-tôr′ē) *n., pl.* **pro·mon·to·ries** A high ridge of land or rock jutting out into a body of water. [From Latin *prōmunturium*, probably from *prōminēre*, to jut out.]

pro·mote (prə-**mōt′**) *tr.v.* **pro·mot·ed, pro·mot·ing, pro·motes 1.** To raise to a higher rank, position, or class. **2.** To aid the progress or growth of; advance: *promoting the general welfare.* **3.** To urge the adoption or use of; advocate: *promote a measure in Congress.* **4.** To try to sell or make popular, as by advertising; publicize: *promotes a new line of products.* [From Middle English *promoten*, from Latin *prōmovēre*, to move forward.]

pro·mot·er (prə-**mō′**tər) *n.* **1.** An active supporter; an advocate: *promoters of a larger defense budget.* **2.** A person in charge of finance and publicity, as for a performer, entertainer, or production.

pro·mo·tion (prə-**mō′**shən) *n.* **1.** An advancement to a higher rank, position, or class. **2.** Encouragement; furtherance: *societies for the promotion of knowledge.* **3.** Publicity, as for a product on sale; advertising. **—pro·mo′tion·al** *adj.*

ă	pat	ôr	core
ā	pay	oi	boy
âr	care	ou	out
ä	father	o͝o	took
ĕ	pet	o͝or	lure
ē	be	o͞o	boot
ĭ	pit	ŭ	cut
ī	bite	ûr	urge
îr	pier	th	thin
ŏ	pot	*th*	this
ō	toe	zh	vision
ô	paw	ə	about

prompt (prŏmpt) *adj.* **prompt·er, prompt·est 1.** Being on time; punctual: *She is prompt in meeting deadlines.* **2.** Done or performed without delay; immediate: *He gave a prompt reply.* ❖ *tr.v.* **prompt·ed, prompt·ing, prompts 1.** To cause (someone) to act; incite: *The experience prompted her to contact her family.* **2.** To be the cause of; lead to: *The poor test scores prompted a review of teaching methods.* **3.** To assist by supplying the next word or words of a passage that has been momentarily forgotten: *prompt an actor.* ❖ *n.* **1.** A reminder or cue. **2.** A symbol that appears on a computer monitor to indicate that the computer is ready to receive input. **—prompt′er** *n.* **—prompt′ly** *adv.* **—prompt′ness** *n.*

prom·ul·gate (**prŏm′**əl-gāt′ *or* prō-**mŭl′**gāt′) *tr.v.* **prom·ul·gat·ed, prom·ul·gat·ing, prom·ul·gates 1.** To popularize or advocate: *writers who promulgated the idea of free speech.* **2.** To announce publicly and officially; proclaim: *promulgate a new constitution.* **—prom′ul·ga′tion** *n.*

pron. *abbr.* An abbreviation of: **1.** pronoun. **2.** pronunciation.

prone (prōn) *adj.* **1.** Lying with the front or face downward. **2.** Tending; inclined: *prone to make hasty judgments.* ❖ *adv.* In a prone manner: *lay prone on the bed.* **—prone′ly** *adv.* **—prone′ness** *n.*

prong (prông) *n.* One of the sharply pointed ends of a fork or other implement.

prong·horn (**prông′**hôrn′) *n., pl.* **pronghorn** or **prong·horns** A swift-running hoofed mammal of western North America, having forked horns.

pro·nom·i·nal (prō-**nŏm′**ə-nəl) *adj.* Relating to or functioning as a pronoun.

pro·noun (**prō′**noun′) *n.* **1.** The part of speech that substitutes for nouns or noun phrases. **2.** A word belonging to this part of speech, such as *she* or *who.* [From Middle English, from Latin *prōnōmen* : *prō-*, in place of + *nōmen*, noun.]

pro·nounce (prə-**nouns′**) *tr.v.* **pro·nounced, pro·nounc·ing, pro·nounc·es 1.** To articulate or produce (a word or speech sound); utter. **2.** To declare officially: *pronounced the couple to be husband and wife.* **3.** To deliver formally: *pronounce a speech.* [From Middle English *pronouncen*, to decree, from Latin *prōnūntiāre* : *prō-*, forth + *nūntius*, messenger.] **—pro·nounce′a·ble** *adj.*

pro·nounced (prə-**nounst′**) *adj.* Distinct; marked; unmistakable: *a pronounced limp.*

pro·nounce·ment (prə-**nouns′**mənt) *n.* **1.** A formal expression of opinion. **2.** An authoritative statement.

pron·to (**prŏn′**tō) *adv. Informal* Right away; immediately. [From Spanish, from Latin *prōmptus*, prompt.]

pro·nun·ci·a·tion (prə-nŭn′sē-**ā′**shən) *n.* **1.** The act or manner of pronouncing words. **2.** A way of speaking a word, especially a way that is generally understood or accepted. **3.** A written representation of the way a word is pronounced, using phonetic symbols.

proof (pro͞of) *n.* **1.** Evidence or demonstration of truth or validity: *Accident figures offer us undeniable proof of the value of using seat belts.* **2.** A demonstration of the truth of a mathematical or logical statement, based on axioms and theorems derived from these axioms. **3.** The act of testing the truth or validity of something by experiment or trial: *The burden of proof is on the prosecution.* **4a.** A trial sheet of printed material, checked against the original manuscript for errors. **b.** A trial impression of an engraved plate, stone, or block. **c.** A trial print of a photograph. **5.** The alcoholic strength of a liquor, expressed by a number that is twice the percentage by volume of alcohol present. ❖ *adj.* Fully resistant: *a tamperproof lock.*

proof·read (**pro͞of′**rēd′) *tr.v.* **proof·read** (**pro͞of′**rĕd′), **proof·read·ing, proof·reads** To read and mark corrections in (a document): *proofread the manuscript carefully.* **—proof′read′er** *n.*

prop¹ (prŏp) *n.* **1.** An object placed beneath or against a structure to keep it from falling. **2.** An object or person depended on for support or assistance. ❖ *tr.v.* **propped, prop·ping, props** To keep from falling by placing something beneath or against: *prop up a shelf with a two-by-four.* [From Middle English *proppe*, probably from Middle Dutch.]

prop² (prŏp) *n.* A movable article that is not part of a costume or scenery and is used on stage or in a movie during a dramatic performance. [Short for *property*.]

prop³ (prŏp) *n. Informal* A propeller. [Short for *propeller*.]

prop·a·gan·da (prŏp′ə-**găn′**də) *n.* **1.** The communication of a doctrine or of information reflecting particular views and interests to large numbers of people, especially by constant repetition and by withholding information that might lead to other conclusions. **2.** Material distributed for the purpose of winning people over to or turning people against a given doctrine, often without regard to truth or fairness: *wartime propaganda.*

prop·a·gan·dize (prŏp′ə-**găn′**dīz′) *v.* **prop·a·gan·dized, prop·a·gan·diz·ing, prop·a·gan·diz·es** *—tr.* To influence by or subject to propaganda: *movies that propagandized the population into supporting the war.* *—intr.* To spread propaganda. **—prop′a·gan′dist** *n.*

prop·a·gate (**prŏp′**ə-gāt′) *v.* **prop·a·gat·ed, prop·a·gat·ing, prop·a·gates** *—tr.* **1.** To cause to produce offspring or new individuals; breed: *propagate plants from cuttings.* **2.** To transmit (heat, light, or other energy) through space or a medium. **3.** To make known or accepted among many people; spread: *propagate a rumor.* *—intr.* To produce offspring. **—prop′a·ga′tion** *n.*

pro·pane (**prō′**pān′) *n.* A colorless gaseous hydrocarbon that has the formula C_3H_8. It is found in petroleum and natural gas and is widely used as a fuel.

pro·pel (prə-**pĕl′**) *tr.v.* **pro·pelled, pro·pel·ling, pro·pels** To cause to move or continue in motion: *the rearward thrust that propels a jet airplane.* [From Middle English *propellen*, from Latin *prōpellere* : *prō-*, forward + *pellere*, to drive.]

pro·pel·lant also **pro·pel·lent** (prə-**pĕl′**ənt) *n.* **1.** A fuel or an explosive charge used to propel something, especially a rocket or projectile. **2.** The compressed gas used in an aerosol container or a similar device to force out the contents.

pro·pel·ler (prə-**pĕl′**ər) *n.* A rotary device, usually driven by an engine or motor, used to propel an aircraft or boat.

pro·pen·si·ty (prə-**pĕn′**sĭ-tē) *n., pl.* **pro·pen·si·ties** A natural tendency; an inclination: *her propensity to exaggerate.* [From Latin *prōpēnsus*, inclined, from *prōpendēre*, to be inclined.]

prop·er (**prŏp′**ər) *adj.* **1.** Suitable; appropriate: *the proper tools for mending a leaky roof.* **2.** Called for by rules or conventions; correct: *the proper form for a business letter.* **3.** Strictly following the rules or conventions, especially in social behavior; seemly: *a proper gentleman.* **4.** Normally or characteristically belonging to the person or thing in question: *regained his proper frame of mind.* **5.** In the strict sense of the term: *We drove through the suburbs and entered the city proper.* [From Middle English *propre*, from Latin *proprius*.] **—prop′er·ly** *adv.* **—prop′er·ness** *n.*

proper fraction *n.* A common fraction in which the numerator is less than the denominator.

proper noun *n.* A noun that is the name of a unique person, place, or thing, such as *Abraham Lincoln, Detroit,* or *Mount Everest.* —SEE NOTE AT **noun.**

prop·er·ty (**prŏp′**ər-tē) *n., pl.* **prop·er·ties 1.** A possession or group of possessions: *He could put all his property into two suitcases.* **2.** A piece of land owned by someone: *A stream runs through our property.* **3.** An object or idea that its owner has the legal right to use: *This trademark is the legal property of its owner.* **4.** A

pronghorn

propeller
airplane propellers

characteristic quality or attribute, especially one that serves to define or describe something: *the chemical properties of a metal.* See Synonyms at **quality. 5.** A theatrical prop. [From Middle English *proprete*, from Latin *proprietās*, ownership, from *proprius*, one's own.]

pro·phase (prō′fāz′) *n.* The first stage of mitosis and meiosis, during which chromatin in the nucleus becomes more compact and forms chromosomes.

proph·e·cy (prŏf′ĭ-sē) *n., pl.* **proph·e·cies** (prŏf′ĭ-sēz) **1.** A statement by a prophet, considered as a revelation of divine will. **2.** A declaration or warning of something to come; a prediction: *prophecies that warned of financial disaster.*

proph·e·sy (prŏf′ĭ-sī′) *v.* **proph·e·sied** (prŏf′ĭ-sīd′), **proph·e·sy·ing** (prŏf′ĭ-sī′ĭng), **proph·e·sies** (prŏf′ĭ-sīz′) —*tr.* **1.** To reveal by divine inspiration: *The soothsayer prophesied that a calf must be sacrificed on the altar.* **2.** To predict (what is to happen) with certainty. —*intr.* **1.** To speak as a prophet. **2.** To predict the future.

proph·et (prŏf′ĭt) *n.* **1.** A person who is believed to speak words inspired by a god or to express the will of a god. **2.** A person who can foretell the future. **3. Prophet** In Islam, another name for Muhammad. [From Middle English *prophete*, from Greek *prophētēs* : *pro-*, forth + *phanai*, to speak.]

❑ *These sound alike:* **prophet, profit** (advantage).

pro·phet·ic (prə-fĕt′ĭk) *adj.* **1.** Relating to or characteristic of a prophet. **2.** Predicting the future: *a warning that proved prophetic.* **—pro·phet′i·cal·ly** *adv.*

pro·phy·lac·tic (prō′fə-lăk′tĭk) *adj.* Acting to prevent or defend against something, especially a disease. ❖ *n.* A prophylactic medicine, device, or action.

pro·pin·qui·ty (prə-pĭng′kwĭ-tē) *n.* **1.** Nearness; proximity. **2.** Kinship. **3.** Similarity in nature.

pro·pi·ti·ate (prō-pĭsh′ē-āt′) *tr.v.* **pro·pi·ti·at·ed, pro·pi·ti·at·ing, pro·pi·ti·ates** To soothe and win over (an angry or offended person); appease: *propitiate the gods with offerings.* **—pro·pi′ti·a′tion** *n.*

pro·pi·tious (prə-pĭsh′əs) *adj.* Favorable; suitable: *a propitious time to ask his mother for a loan.* **—pro·pi′tious·ly** *adv.* **—pro·pi′tious·ness** *n.*

pro·po·nent (prə-pō′nənt) *n.* A person who argues in support of something; an advocate: *They are proponents of socialized medicine.* [From Latin *prōpōnere*, to set forth, propose.]

pro·por·tion (prə-pôr′shən) *n.* **1.** The size, amount, or extent of one thing compared with that of another thing: *The proportion of flour to milk in the recipe is two to one.* **2.** A relationship between quantities such that if one changes the other changes as well. **3.** A pleasing or harmonious relationship between the various parts of a whole; balance or symmetry: *The new skyscraper is out of proportion to the buildings around it.* **4.** often **proportions** Size; dimensions: *a disease that reached epidemic proportions.* **5.** A relation of equality between two ratios. Four quantities, *a, b, c, d,* are said to be in proportion if $a/b = c/d$. ❖ *tr.v.* **pro·por·tioned, pro·por·tion·ing, pro·por·tions 1.** To adjust so as to achieve a particular relation between parts: *proportion the oil in the dressing properly.* **2.** To make the parts of harmonious or pleasing: *proportioned the figure nicely.*

pro·por·tion·al (prə-pôr′shə-nəl) *adj.* **1.** Corresponding in size, amount, or degree; in proportion: *The effects of the drug were proportional to the dose.* **2.** Related by a constant factor. For example, if $y = 6x$, x and y are proportional. **—pro·por′tion·al·ly** *adv.*

pro·por·tion·ate (prə-pôr′shə-nĭt) *adj.* Being in proportion; corresponding: *a promotion with a proportionate increase in responsibility.* **—pro·por′tion·ate·ly** *adv.*

pro·pos·al (prə-pō′zəl) *n.* **1.** The act of proposing; an offer: *a proposal to go fishing.* **2.** A plan or scheme offered for consideration. **3.** An offer of marriage.

pro·pose (prə-pōz′) *v.* **pro·posed, pro·pos·ing, pro·pos·es** —*tr.* **1.** To put forward for consideration or acceptance; suggest: *propose a new law.* **2.** To recommend (a person) for a position, mission, or membership; nominate. **3.** To declare an intention; intend: *She proposed to beat me at my own game.* —*intr.* To make a proposal, especially an offer of marriage. [From Middle English *proposen*, from Old French *proposer*, from Latin *prōpōnere* : *prō-*, forth + *pōnere*, to put.] —SEE NOTE AT **compose.**

prop·o·si·tion (prŏp′ə-zĭsh′ən) *n.* **1.** An offer; a proposal: *a business proposition.* **2.** A matter to be handled or dealt with; an undertaking: *Finding a cheap apartment is a difficult proposition.* **3.** A subject for discussion or analysis. **4a.** A mathematical statement, as the statement of a theorem. **b.** A statement in logic that affirms or denies something. ❖ *tr.v.* **prop·o·si·tioned, prop·o·si·tion·ing, prop·o·si·tions** *Informal* To propose a bargain to (someone), especially to propose sexual relations with.

pro·pound (prə-pound′) *tr.v.* **pro·pound·ed, pro·pound·ing, pro·pounds** To set forth; propose: *propound a theory.*

pro·pri·e·tar·y (prə-prī′ĭ-tĕr′ē) *adj.* **1.** Relating to an owner or ownership: *She has a proprietary interest in the business.* **2.** Owned by an individual or a firm under a trademark or patent: *proprietary medicines.* **—pro·pri′e·tar′i·ly** *adv.*

pro·pri·e·tor (prə-prī′ĭ-tər) *n.* **1.** A person who owns or has legal title to something. **2.** The owner and often manager of a business. **—pro·pri′e·tor·ship′** *n.*

pro·pri·e·ty (prə-prī′ĭ-tē) *n., pl.* **pro·pri·e·ties 1.** Conformity to conventional standards of behavior or morality: *The chaperone insisted on strict propriety at all times.* **2. proprieties** The rules and conventions of polite social behavior. **3.** The quality of being proper; suitability; appropriateness.

pro·pul·sion (prə-pŭl′shən) *n.* **1.** The act or process of propelling. **2.** A force that propels. [From Latin *prōpulsus*, past participle of *prōpellere*, to drive forward.]

pro·rate (prō-rāt′ *or* prō′rāt′) *tr.v.* **pro·rat·ed, pro·rat·ing, pro·rates** To divide (an expense or tax, for example) proportionately: *prorating the phone bills among the roommates.*

pro·sa·ic (prō-zā′ĭk) *adj.* **1.** Characteristic of prose rather than poetry. **2.** Straightforward; matter-of-fact. **3.** Lacking in imagination or powers of fantasy. **—pro·sa′i·cal·ly** *adv.* **—pro·sa′ic·ness** *n.*

pro·sciut·to (prō-shōō′tō) *n., pl.* **pro·sciut·tos** An aged, cured, dried, and sometimes spiced Italian ham.

pro·scribe (prō-skrīb′) *tr.v.* **pro·scribed, pro·scrib·ing, pro·scribes 1.** To forbid; prohibit. **2.** To banish; outlaw: *The queen proscribed the rebels.* [From Middle English *proscriben*, from Latin *prōscrībere*, to put up someone's name as outlawed : *prō-*, in front + *scrībere*, to write.] **—pro·scrib′er** *n.* —SEE NOTE AT **prescribe.**

pro·scrip·tion (prō-skrĭp′shən) *n.* The act of proscribing or the condition of being proscribed.

prose (prōz) *n.* Ordinary speech or writing as distinguished from verse or poetry.

pros·e·cute (prŏs′ĭ-kyōōt′) *tr.v.* **pros·e·cut·ed, pros·e·cut·ing, pros·e·cutes 1.** To initiate or conduct a legal action against (someone): *prosecuting people who break federal laws.* **2.** To pursue (an undertaking) to completion; follow to the end: *prosecuting a war.* **3.** To carry on, engage in, or practice: *prosecuting his occupation.* [From Middle English *prosecuten*, from Latin *prōsequī* : *prō-*, forward + *sequī*, to follow.]

pros·e·cu·tion (prŏs′ĭ-kyōō′shən) *n.* **1a.** The act of prosecuting a person or case in a court of law. **b.** The condition of being thus prosecuted: *risked prosecution by breaking the law.* **2.** A lawyer who initiates and conducts

ă	pat	ôr	core
ā	pay	oi	boy
âr	care	ou	out
ä	father	ŏŏ	took
ĕ	pet	ŏŏr	lure
ē	be	ōō	boot
ĭ	pit	ŭ	cut
ī	bite	ûr	urge
îr	pier	th	thin
ŏ	pot	*th*	this
ō	toe	zh	vision
ô	paw	ə	about

legal cases on behalf of a government and its citizens. **3.** The act of pursuing or performing: *the prosecution of her duties.*

pros·e·cu·tor (prŏs′ĭ-kyōō′tər) *n.* A person who initiates a legal action, especially the public official who represents the state and the people in court in prosecuting defendants accused of committing a crime.

pros·e·lyte (prŏs′ə-līt′) *n.* A new convert to a religion, party, or doctrine. [From Middle English *proselite,* from Greek *prosēlutos,* stranger, proselyte.]

pros·e·ly·tize (prŏs′ə-lĭ-tīz′) *v.* **pros·e·ly·tized, pros·e·ly·tiz·ing, pros·e·ly·tiz·es** *—intr.* To try to cause a person to change from one religion, political party, or doctrine to another. *—tr.* To convert (a person) from one religion, political party, or doctrine to another.

Pro·ser·pi·na (prō-sûr′pə-nə) also **Pro·ser·pi·ne** (prō-sûr′pə-nē) *n.* In Roman mythology, the daughter of Ceres who is carried away by Pluto to become his wife and the goddess of the underworld. She is identified with the Greek Persephone.

pro·sim·i·an (prō-sĭm′ē-ən) *n.* Any of various small primates that usually have large eyes and ears and are active at night. Lemurs and tarsiers are prosimians. [From Latin *pro-,* before + Latin *sīmius,* ape.] **—pro·sim′i·an** *adj.*

pros·o·dy (prŏs′ə-dē) *n.* The study of the form of verse, especially of its meter.

pros·pect (prŏs′pĕkt′) *n.* **1.** Something expected or foreseen; a possibility: *hurried home with the prospect of a good dinner.* **2. prospects** Chances for success: *a young woman with prospects.* **3.** A possible customer or client. **4.** A possible candidate, as for a team or position: *a football scout who looked over the college prospects.* **5.** Something presented to the eye; a scene; a view: *a lovely prospect from the tower.* ❖ *intr.v.* **pros·pect·ed, pros·pect·ing, pros·pects** To search for mineral deposits or oil. [From Middle English *prospecte,* from Latin *prōspectus,* distant view, from *prōspicere,* to look out : *prō-,* forward + *specere,* to look at.] —SEE NOTE AT **spectator.**

pro·spec·tive (prə-spĕk′tĭv) *adj.* Likely or expected to be, become, or occur: *prospective budget cuts.* **—pro·spec′tive·ly** *adv.*

pros·pec·tor (prŏs′pĕk′tər) *n.* A person who explores an area for valuable mineral deposits or oil.

pro·spec·tus (prə-spĕk′təs) *n.* **1.** A formal summary of a proposed venture or project. **2.** A printed description of a business or other venture.

pros·per (prŏs′pər) *intr.v.* **pros·pered, pros·per·ing, pros·pers** To be successful; thrive. [From Middle English *prosperen,* from Latin *prosperāre,* to render fortunate, from *prosperus,* favorable.]

pros·per·i·ty (prŏ-spĕr′ĭ-tē) *n.* The condition of being prosperous; success.

pros·per·ous (prŏs′pər-əs) *adj.* **1.** Successful; thriving: *a prosperous garden.* **2.** Economically successful; enjoying wealth or profit: *a prosperous business.* **—pros′per·ous·ly** *adv.*

pros·ta·glan·din (prŏs′tə-glăn′dĭn) *n.* Any of a group of substances that are derived from fatty acids and have a wide range of effects in the body, including the control of blood pressure, regulation of inflammation, and contraction of smooth muscle.

pros·tate (prŏs′tāt′) *n.* The prostate gland.

prostate gland *n.* A gland in male mammals surrounding the urethra at the base of the bladder. The prostate gland controls release of urine from the bladder and secretes a fluid which is a major constituent of semen.

pros·ti·tute (prŏs′tĭ-tōōt′) *n.* **1.** A person who performs sexual acts with others for pay. **2.** A person who sells his or her abilities, talent, or name for an unworthy purpose. ❖ *tr.v.* **pros·ti·tut·ed, pros·ti·tut·ing, pros·ti·tutes 1.** To offer (oneself or someone else) for sexual acts in return for pay. **2.** To sell (oneself or one's abilities) for an unworthy purpose.

pros·ti·tu·tion (prŏs′tĭ-tōō′shən) *n.* **1.** The practice or work of performing sexual acts for pay. **2.** The act of prostituting; debasement: *the prostitution of an artist's talents.*

pros·trate (prŏs′trāt′) *tr.v.* **pros·trat·ed, pros·trat·ing, pros·trates 1.** To put or throw down flat with the face down, as in submission or adoration: *prostrated himself before the mighty ruler.* **2.** To cause to lie flat: *The strong winds prostrated the saplings.* **3.** To exhaust or overcome physically or emotionally; render helpless: *a disease that prostrates its victims.* ❖ *adj.* **1.** Lying face down, as in submission: *The peasant was prostrate before the throne.* **2.** Lying flat or at full length: *Trees lay prostrate on the ground after the tornado.* **3.** Exhausted or overcome physically or emotionally; helpless: *prostrate with fever.*

pros·tra·tion (prŏ-strā′shən) *n.* **1a.** The act or process of prostrating oneself. **b.** The condition of being prostrate. **2.** Complete mental or physical exhaustion.

pro·tac·tin·i·um (prō′tăk-tĭn′ē-əm) *n. Symbol* **Pa** A rare, extremely toxic, radioactive metallic element that occurs in uranium ores. Atomic number 91. See **Periodic Table.**

pro·tag·o·nist (prō-tăg′ə-nĭst) *n.* The main character in a drama or literary work.

pro·te·an (prō′tē-ən *or* prō-tē′ən) *adj.* Taking on many different shapes or forms; highly variable: *a protean talent.* [After *Proteus,* Greek sea god who could change his shape at will.]

pro·tect (prə-tĕkt′) *tr.v.* **pro·tect·ed, pro·tect·ing, pro·tects 1.** To keep from harm, attack, injury, or damage; guard: *This apron will protect your clothes from spills.* See Synonyms at **defend. 2.** To help (domestic industry) by placing tariffs or quotas on foreign goods. **3.** In baseball, to swing at a pitch near (home plate) in order to avoid being called out on strikes. [From Middle English *protecten,* from Latin *prōtegere* : *prō-,* in front + *tegere,* to cover.]

pro·tec·tion (prə-tĕk′shən) *n.* **1a.** The act of protecting. **b.** The condition of being protected: *a hedge for protection against the wind.* **2.** A person or thing that protects: *The thin jacket was his only protection against the wind.* **3.** *Slang* Money paid to criminals who threaten violence if they are not paid.

pro·tec·tive (prə-tĕk′tĭv) *adj.* Serving to protect: *a protective coat of shellac.* **—pro·tec′tive·ly** *adv.* **—pro·tec′tive·ness** *n.*

pro·tec·tor (prə-tĕk′tər) *n.* **1.** A person who protects; a defender or guardian. **2.** Something that protects: *The catcher wears a chest protector.* **3.** A person appointed to rule during the absence or childhood of a monarch.

pro·tec·tor·ate (prə-tĕk′tər-ĭt) *n.* **1a.** A relationship of protection and partial control assumed by a strong nation over a dependent foreign country. **b.** A dependent country or region in such a relationship. **2.** The office or period of rule of the protector of a country.

pro·té·gé (prō′tə-zhā′ *or* prō′tə-zhā′) *n.* A person whose welfare, training, or career is promoted by another, more influential or experienced person.

pro·tein (prō′tēn′) *n.* One of a large class of complex organic compounds that consist of long chains of amino acids and are the basic components of all living cells. Enzymes, antibodies, and certain hormones are proteins.

pro·test (prə-tĕst′ *or* prō′tĕst′) *v.* **pro·test·ed, pro·test·ing, pro·tests** *—tr.* **1.** To express strong objections to (something), as in a formal statement or public demonstration: *Demonstrators protested the new law.* **2.** To participate in a public demonstration in opposition to (something). **3.** To declare earnestly; affirm: *protested his innocence.* *—intr.* **1.** To express strong objection. **2.** To participate in a public demonstra-

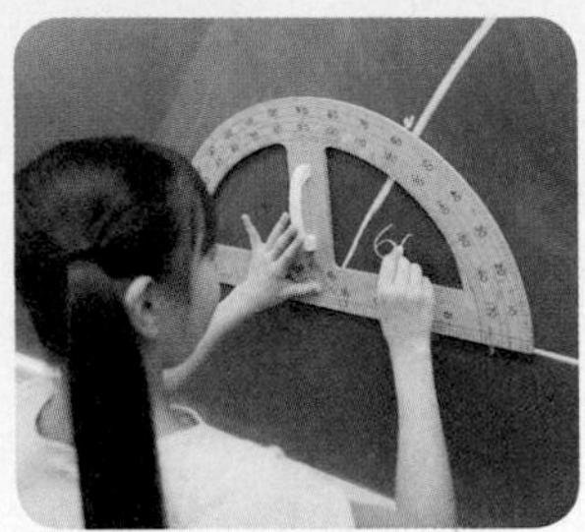

protractor

tion in opposition to something. ❖ *n.* (**prō′tĕst′**) **1.** A formal statement of disapproval or objection: *sent a protest to the mayor's office.* **2.** A public demonstration expressing disapproval about something, especially a governmental policy or practice. **3.** An act expressing disapproval or objection: *refused to buy tea in protest against the new tax.* [From Middle English *protesten*, from Latin *prōtestārī* : *prō-*, forth + *testārī*, to testify.] **—pro′test′er** *n.*

Prot·es·tant (**prŏt′**ĭ-stənt) *n.* A member of a Western Church whose principles are based on those of the Reformation. Protestants consider the Bible to be the only source of revelation and believe that salvation is possible only through faith in Jesus. ❖ *adj.* Relating to Protestantism: *a Protestant minister.* [From Latin *prōtestārī*, to protest.]

Prot·es·tant·ism (**prŏt′**ĭ-stən-tĭz′əm) *n.* **1.** Adherence to the beliefs and practices of Protestants. **2.** Protestants considered as a group.

prot·es·ta·tion (prŏt′ĭ-**stā′**shən *or* prō′tĭ-**stā′**shən) *n.* An earnest declaration; an avowal.

pro·tist (**prō′**tĭst) *n.* Any of a kingdom of usually one-celled organisms that are not plants, animals, or fungi. Protozoans, slime molds, and certain algae are protists.

pro·ti·um (**prō′**tē-əm *or* **prō′**shē-əm) *n.* The most abundant isotope of hydrogen, having one proton and no neutrons in each atom.

pro·to·col (**prō′**tə-kôl′) *n.* **1.** Ceremony and social etiquette, especially as observed by diplomats and heads of state. **2.** A record or draft of an agreement, especially one used as the basis for a later, formal document: *the protocol of an international treaty.* **3.** The plan for a course of medical treatment or for a scientific experiment. **4.** A standard procedure for regulating the transmission of data between computers.

pro·ton (**prō′**tŏn′) *n.* A stable subatomic particle with a positive electric charge that is equal in strength to the negative charge of an electron. Protons are found in the nuclei of all atoms and have 1,836 times the mass of an electron. [From Greek *prōtos*, first.] —SEE NOTE AT **atom.**

pro·to·plasm (**prō′**tə-plăz′əm) *n.* A substance resembling jelly that forms the living matter in all plant and animal cells. Protoplasm is made up of proteins, fats, and other substances suspended in water. It includes the nucleus and other organelles as well as the cytoplasm.

pro·to·star (**prō′**tə-stär′) *n.* A celestial object that is in a late stage of becoming a star. Although its core is an opaque sphere and its surface shines like a star, a protostar does not sustain nuclear fusion in its core.

pro·to·type (**prō′**tə-tīp′) *n.* An original example of something, on which later examples are based or judged: *Edison's invention factory was the prototype of modern engineering laboratories.*

pro·to·zo·an (prō′tə-**zō′**ən) *n., pl.* **pro·to·zo·ans** or **pro·to·zo·a** (prō′tə-**zō′**ə) Any of a large group of one-celled organisms that move about freely and ingest food but are not classified as animals. Protozoans are usually too small to be seen without a microscope and include the amoebas and the paramecia.

pro·tract (prō-**trăkt′**) *tr.v.* **pro·tract·ed, pro·tract·ing, pro·tracts** To draw out in time; lengthen; prolong. [From Latin *prōtrahere*, to extend, protrude (said of a body part) : *prō-*, forth + *trahere*, to drag.] **—pro·trac′tion** *n.* —SEE NOTE AT **detract.**

pro·trac·tor (prō-**trăk′**tər) *n.* A semicircular or circular instrument marked off in degrees, used for measuring and drawing angles.

pro·trude (prō-**trōōd′**) *v.* **pro·trud·ed, pro·trud·ing, pro·trudes** *—intr.* To stick out from a surface; project: *Curly hair protruded from the edges of his cap. —tr.* To push or thrust outward: *The cat protruded its nose into the hole in the wall.* [From Latin *prōtrūdere* : *prō-*, forward + *trūdere*, to thrust.]

pro·tru·sion (prō-**trōō′**zhən) *n.* **1.** The act of protruding or the condition of being protruded. **2.** A part or an object that protrudes; a projection.

pro·tu·ber·ance (prō-**tōō′**bər-əns) *n.* **1.** A protuberant part or object; a bulge or knob. **2.** The condition of being protuberant.

pro·tu·ber·ant (prō-**tōō′**bər-ənt) *adj.* Bulging or swelling outward from a surface: *slightly protuberant eyes.* **—pro·tu′ber·ant·ly** *adv.*

proud (proud) *adj.* **proud·er, proud·est 1a.** Feeling pleasure and satisfaction over something one owns, makes, does, or is a part of: *proud to be a member of the team.* **b.** Calling for or being a reason for pride: *a proud moment when she received her diploma.* **2a.** Feeling or showing justifiable self-esteem: *too proud to beg.* **b.** Filled with or showing excessive self-esteem: *a proud and haughty aristocrat.* **3.** Highly respected; honored: *a proud name.* [From Middle English, from Old English *prūd*, from Old French *prod*, valiant, from Late Latin *prōde*, advantageous.] **—proud′ly** *adv.*

prove (prōōv) *v.* **proved, proved** or **prov·en** (**prōō′**vən), **prov·ing, proves** *—tr.* **1.** To show to be true or valid by giving evidence or arguments: *proved the charge at the trial.* **2.** To demonstrate the validity of (a hypothesis or proposition). **3.** To determine the quality of by testing; try out: *proving a new car on the open road.* **4.** In law, to establish the authenticity of (a will). *—intr.* To be shown to be such; turn out: *The estimate proved too low.* [From Middle English *preven*, from Latin *probāre*, to test.] **—prov′a·ble** *adj.*

Pro·ven·çal (prō′vän-**säl′** *or* prŏv′ən-**säl′**) *adj.* Relating to Provence or its people, language, or culture. ❖ *n.* **1.** The Romance language of Provence. **2.** A native or inhabitant of Provence.

Pro·vence (prə-**väns′**) A historical region and former province of southeast France on the Mediterranean Sea. It was settled in about 600 BC by Greek colonists.

prov·en·der (**prŏv′**ən-dər) *n.* **1.** Dry food, such as hay, for livestock; feed. **2.** Food or provisions.

prov·erb (**prŏv′**ûrb′) *n.* **1.** A short saying that is in frequent use and expresses a basic truth or practical concept. **2. Proverbs** A book of the Bible that contains many proverbs and moral sayings. [From Middle English *proverbe*, from Latin *prōverbium* : *prō-*, forth + *verbum*, word.]

pro·ver·bi·al (prə-**vûr′**bē-əl) *adj.* **1.** Of the nature of a proverb or proverbs: *proverbial sayings.* **2.** Mentioned in a proverb: *slept like the proverbial baby.* **3.** Widely known and spoken of; famous: *Her skill at cards is proverbial.* **—pro·ver′bi·al·ly** *adv.*

pro·vide (prə-**vīd′**) *v.* **pro·vid·ed, pro·vid·ing, pro·vides** *—tr.* **1.** To make available; supply: *generators that provide electrical energy.* **2.** To furnish something needed or desired to: *She provided her family with food.* **3.** To have as an available feature; afford: *a filling station that provides restrooms.* **4.** To state as a stipulation or requirement: *The contract provides deadlines for completion of the work. —intr.* **1.** To take measures in preparation: *We provided against emergencies by taking extra money and clothing.* **2.** To supply means of subsistence or maintenance: *He worked hard to provide for his large family.* **3.** To make a stipulation or requirement: *He provided for a scholarship fund in his will.* [From Middle English *providen*, from Latin *prōvidēre*, to look ahead : *prō-*, forward + *vidēre*, to see.] **—pro·vid′er** *n.* —SEE NOTE.

pro·vid·ed (prə-**vī′**dĭd) *conj.* On the condition; if: *You may go, provided your homework is done.*

prov·i·dence (**prŏv′**ĭ-dəns) *n.* **1.** Care or preparation in advance; foresight. **2.** Prudent management; economy.

ă	pat	ôr	core
ā	pay	oi	boy
âr	care	ou	out
ä	father	ŏŏ	took
ĕ	pet	ŏŏr	lure
ē	be	ōō	boot
ĭ	pit	ŭ	cut
ī	bite	ûr	urge
îr	pier	th	thin
ŏ	pot	*th*	this
ō	toe	zh	vision
ô	paw	ə	about

3. The control and protection of a god; divine direction. 4. **Providence** God. —SEE NOTE AT **provide.**

Providence The capital of Rhode Island, in the northeast part of the state on Narragansett Bay. It was founded in 1636 as a refuge for religious dissenters.

prov·i·dent (prŏv′ĭ-dənt) *adj.* **1.** Providing for future needs or events. **2.** Frugal; thrifty. **—prov′i·dent·ly** *adv.* —SEE NOTE AT **provide.**

prov·i·den·tial (prŏv′ĭ-**dĕn′**shəl) *adj.* **1.** Relating to or resulting from divine providence: *the providential mission of a prophet.* **2.** Happening as if through divine intervention; very fortunate: *The providential arrival of reinforcements saved the day.* **—prov′i·den′tial·ly** *adv.*

pro·vid·ing (prə-**vī′**dĭng) *conj.* On the condition; provided: *We are going to play volleyball, providing the court is free.*

prov·ince (**prŏv′**ĭns) *n.* **1.** A political subdivision of a country or empire: *Ontario and Quebec are provinces of Canada.* **2.** In certain Christian churches, a division of territory under the jurisdiction of a metropolitan. **3. provinces** The outlying areas of a country, away from the capital or population center. **4.** The range of one's proper knowledge, functions, or responsibility; scope. **5.** A comprehensive area of knowledge, activity, or interest.

pro·vin·cial (prə-**vĭn′**shəl) *adj.* **1.** Relating to a province: *a provincial capital.* **2.** Characteristic of people from the provinces; not sophisticated or worldly: *provincial speech and dress.* **3.** Limited in perspective; narrow and self-centered: *provincial attitudes.* ❖ *n.* **1.** A person living in or coming from the provinces. **2.** A person with provincial ideas or habits. **—pro·vin′ci·al′i·ty** (prə-vĭn′shē-**ăl′**ĭ-tē) *n.* **—pro·vin′cial·ly** *adv.*

pro·vi·sion (prə-**vĭzh′**ən) *n.* **1.** The act of providing or supplying: *the provision of canteens for the day hike.* **2.** Something that is provided: *A fire escape is an important provision in a building.* **3. provisions** Stocks of food and other necessary supplies. **4.** A measure taken in preparation: *making provisions for her solo flight.* **5.** A stipulation or qualification, especially a clause in a document or agreement: *a provision of a peace treaty forbidding rearmament.* ❖ *tr.v.* **pro·vi·sioned, pro·vi·sion·ing, pro·vi·sions** To supply with provisions.

pro·vi·sion·al (prə-**vĭzh′**ə-nəl) *adj.* Serving for the time being; temporary: *a provisional government.* **—pro·vi′sion·al·ly** *adv.*

pro·vi·so (prə-**vī′**zō) *n., pl.* **pro·vi·sos** or **pro·vi·soes** A clause in a document making a qualification, condition, or restriction.

prov·o·ca·tion (prŏv′ə-**kā′**shən) *n.* **1.** The act of provoking; incitement. **2.** Something that provokes.

pro·voc·a·tive (prə-**vŏk′**ə-tĭv) *adj.* Tending to cause strong feelings or reactions: *a provocative new theory.* **—pro·voc′a·tive·ly** *adv.*

pro·voke (prə-**vōk′**) *tr.v.* **pro·voked, pro·vok·ing, pro·vokes 1.** To incite to anger or resentment: *His bullying provoked me.* **2.** To stir to action or feeling: *Conscience provoked them to speak out.* **3.** To give rise to; evoke: *The comedy provoked laughter.* **4.** To bring about deliberately; induce: *provoke a fight.* [From Middle English *provoken*, from Latin *prōvocāre*, to challenge : *prō-*, forth, out + *vocāre*, to call.] **—pro·vok′ing·ly** *adv.*

pro·vo·lo·ne (prō′və-**lō′**nē) *n.* A hard, sometimes lightly smoked Italian cheese.

pro·vost (**prō′**vōst′ *or* **prŏv′**əst) *n.* **1.** A high-ranking university administrator. **2.** The highest official in certain cathedrals. **3.** The chief magistrate of certain Scottish cities. **4.** The keeper of a prison.

prow (prou) *n.* **1.** The forward part of a ship's hull; the bow. **2.** A projecting front part, such as the nose of an aircraft.

prow·ess (**prou′**ĭs) *n.* **1.** Superior skill or ability: *She showed prowess in mathematics.* **2.** Superior strength, courage, or daring, especially in battle.

prowl (proul) *v.* **prowled, prowl·ing, prowls** *—tr.* To roam through stealthily, as if in search of prey: *Cats prowl the alleys at night.* *—intr.* To roam furtively or with predatory intent. ❖ *n.* The act or an instance of prowling: *took a prowl through the antique shops.* [From Middle English *prollen*, to move about.] **—prowl′er** *n.*

prowl car *n.* A squad car.

prox·im·i·ty (prŏk-**sĭm′**ĭ-tē) *n.* The state, quality, or fact of being near; closeness.

prox·y (**prŏk′**sē) *n., pl.* **prox·ies 1.** A person authorized to act for another; an agent. **2.** The authority to act for another: *vote by proxy.*

prude (pro͞od) *n.* A person who is overly concerned with propriety or modesty, especially in sexual matters.

pru·dence (**pro͞od′**ns) *n.* **1.** The state, quality, or fact of being prudent. **2.** Careful management; economy. —SEE NOTE AT **provide.**

pru·dent (**pro͞od′**nt) *adj.* **1.** Careful or wise in handling practical matters; sensible: *a prudent manager.* **2.** Characterized by or resulting from care or wisdom in practical matters: *a prudent investment.* [From Middle English, from Latin *prūdēns*, from *prōvidēre*, to provide for.] **—pru′dent·ly** *adv.* —SEE NOTE AT **provide.**

pru·den·tial (pro͞o-**dĕn′**shəl) *adj.* **1.** Arising from or characterized by prudence. **2.** Showing or using prudence. **—pru·den′tial·ly** *adv.*

prud·er·y (**pro͞o′**də-rē) *n., pl.* **prud·er·ies 1.** The state or quality of being prudish. **2.** An instance of prudish behavior or speech.

prud·ish (**pro͞o′**dĭsh) *adj.* Characteristic of or being a prude; priggish. **—prud′ish·ly** *adv.* **—prud′ish·ness** *n.*

prune[1] (pro͞on) *n.* A dried plum. [From Middle English *prunne*, from Latin *prūnum*, plum.]

prune[2] (pro͞on) *tr.v.* **pruned, prun·ing, prunes 1.** To cut or trim parts or branches from (a tree or shrub) to improve its growth or shape. **2.** To shorten or improve by removing unnecessary parts: *pruned my essay.* [From Middle English *proinen*, from Old French *proignier.*] **—prun′er** *n.*

Prus·sia (**prŭsh′**ə) A historical region and former kingdom of north-central Europe including present-day northern Germany and Poland. **—Prus′sian** *adj. & n.*

prus·sic acid (**prŭs′**ĭk) *n.* Hydrocyanic acid.

pry[1] (prī) *intr.v.* **pried** (prīd), **pry·ing, pries** (prīz) To look or inquire closely, curiously, or rudely: *Don't pry into her personal life. I don't mean to pry, but where were you last night?* [From Middle English *prien.*]

pry[2] (prī) *tr.v.* **pried** (prīd), **pry·ing, pries** (prīz) **1.** To raise, move, or force open with a lever: *pry the lid off a box.* **2.** To obtain or extract with difficulty: *pried answers from the child.* ❖ *n., pl.* **pries** (prīz) Something used as a lever. [From *prize*, pry.]

PS *abbr.* An abbreviation of: **1.** postscript. **2.** public school.

psalm (säm) *n.* **1.** A sacred song; a hymn. **2. Psalms** A book of the Bible containing poems that express devotion to God, sorrow for wrongdoing, and other spiritual concerns.

psalm·ist (**sä′**mĭst) *n.* A writer or composer of psalms.

Psal·ter (**sôl′**tər) *n.* A book containing the Psalms.

psal·ter·y (**sôl′**tə-rē) *n., pl.* **psal·ter·ies** An ancient stringed instrument played by plucking the strings with the fingers or a plectrum.

pseudo– or **pseud–** *pref.* A prefix that means: **1.** Falsely resembling: *pseudoscience.* **2.** Superficially resembling: *pseudopod.*

pseu·do·nym (**so͞od′**n-ĭm′) *n.* A fictitious name, especially a pen name. [From Greek *pseudōnumos*, falsely named : *pseudēs*, false + *onuma*, name.]

pseu·do·pod (**so͞o′**də-pŏd′) *n.* A temporary extension

prow

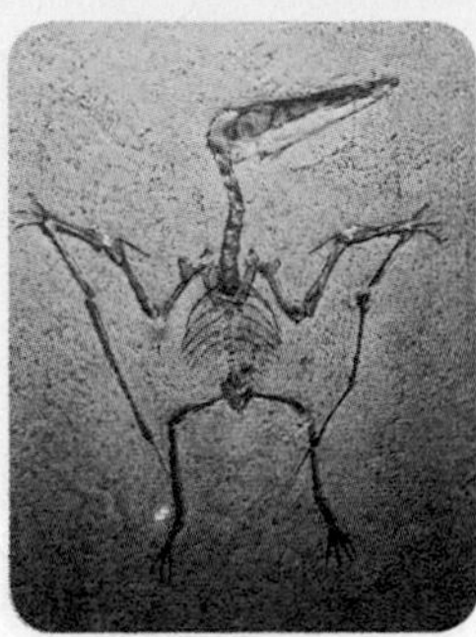

pterodactyl

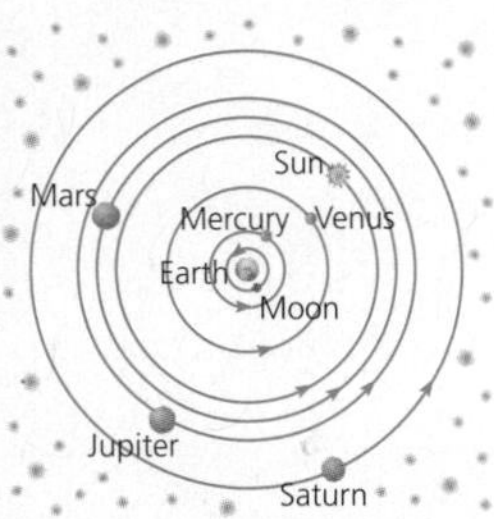

Ptolemaic system

Ptolemy[2]
initial letter from a 15th-century manuscript

ă	pat	ôr	core
ā	pay	oi	boy
âr	care	ou	out
ä	father	ŏŏ	took
ĕ	pet	ŏŏr	lure
ē	be	ōō	boot
ĭ	pit	ŭ	cut
ī	bite	ûr	urge
îr	pier	th	thin
ŏ	pot	*th*	this
ō	toe	zh	vision
ô	paw	ə	about

of the cytoplasm of a cell. Amoebas and certain other one-celled organisms use pseudopods for moving about and for surrounding and taking in food.

pseu·do·sci·ence (sōō′dō-**sī′**əns) *n.* A theory or method that is considered to be without scientific foundation.

pshaw (shô) *interj.* An expression used to show impatience, irritation, disapproval, or disbelief.

psi (sī *or* psī *or* psē) *n.* The 23rd letter of the Greek alphabet, written Ψ, ψ. In English it is represented as *Ps, ps.*

psit·ta·co·sis (sĭt′ə-**kō′**sĭs) *n.* A bacterial disease of parrots and related birds, which can be communicated to humans, producing symptoms similar to pneumonia.

pso·ri·a·sis (sə-**rī′**ə-sĭs) *n.* A chronic noncontagious skin disease that causes inflammation and white scaly patches on the skin.

PST *abbr.* An abbreviation of Pacific Standard Time.

psych (sīk) *tr.v.* **psyched, psych·ing, psyches** *Informal* **1.** To put into the right frame of mind: *The coach psyched the team up before the game.* **2.** To excite emotionally: *I'm psyched to go to the beach.* **3.** To undermine the confidence of; intimidate: *The angry looks of their huge center psyched us out.*

psy·che (**sī′**kē) *n.* **1.** The mind. **2.** The soul or spirit. [From Greek *psūkhē*, soul.]

Psy·che (**sī′**kē) *n.* In Greek mythology, a young woman who loved Eros and was united with him after Aphrodite's jealousy was overcome.

psy·che·del·ic (sī′kĭ-**dĕl′**ĭk) *adj.* Relating to or causing hallucinations or distortions of perception: *psychedelic drugs.*

psy·chi·a·trist (sĭ-**kī′**ə-trĭst *or* sī-**kī′**ə-trĭst) *n.* A physician who specializes in psychiatry.

psy·chi·a·try (sĭ-**kī′**ə-trē *or* sī-**kī′**ə-trē) *n.* The branch of medicine that deals with the study and treatment of mental disorders. [From Greek *psūkhē*, mind + Greek *iatros*, physician.] **—psy′chi·at′ric** (sī′kē-**ăt′**rĭk) *adj.*

psy·chic (**sī′**kĭk) *n.* A person who is said to be sensitive to spiritual forces or forces that have no physical explanation or who claims to have extraordinary mental powers, such as extrasensory perception or mental telepathy. ❖ *adj.* **1.** Relating to the human mind or psyche. **2a.** Sensitive to nonphysical forces or capable of extraordinary mental processes. **b.** Relating to such processes.

psycho– or **psych–** *pref.* A prefix that means the mind or mental processes: *psychoanalysis.*

psy·cho·a·nal·y·sis (sī′kō-ə-**năl′**ĭ-sĭs) *n.* A type of psychotherapy, often based on the work of Sigmund Freud, in which a patient speaks extensively about memories, current personal concerns, and dreams in order to solve problems or to increase self-understanding.

psy·cho·an·a·lyst (sī′kō-**ăn′**ə-lĭst) *n.* A person who practices psychoanalysis.

psy·cho·an·a·lyze (sī′kō-**ăn′**ə-līz′) *tr.v.* **psy·cho·an·a·lyzed, psy·cho·an·a·lyz·ing, psy·cho·an·a·lyz·es** To treat (a person) by psychoanalysis.

psy·cho·log·i·cal (sī′kə-**lŏj′**ĭ-kəl) *adj.* **1.** Relating to psychology. **2.** Relating to or derived from the mind or emotions. **3.** Capable of influencing the mind or emotions: *psychological persuasion.* **—psy′cho·log′i·cal·ly** *adv.*

psy·chol·o·gist (sī-**kŏl′**ə-jĭst) *n.* A person trained to perform psychological research, testing, and therapy.

psy·chol·o·gy (sī-**kŏl′**ə-jē) *n., pl.* **psy·chol·o·gies 1.** The branch of science that deals with the study of human behavior and mental processes, applied sometimes to the treatment of personal or mental health problems with counseling or psychotherapy. **2.** The emotional characteristics and behavior associated with an individual, group, or activity: *the psychology of war.* [From Greek *psūkhē*, mind, spirit + Greek *-logiā*, study.]

psy·cho·path (**sī′**kə-păth′) *n.* A person who engages repeatedly in criminal and antisocial behavior without remorse or empathy for those victimized. **—psy′cho·path′ic** *adj.*

psy·cho·sis (sī-**kō′**sĭs) *n., pl.* **psy·cho·ses** (sī-**kō′**sēz) A mental state marked by loss of contact with reality and often by hallucinations or delusions, seen in certain mental illnesses, such as schizophrenia.

psy·cho·so·mat·ic (sī′kō-sō-**măt′**ĭk) *adj.* **1.** Relating to a disorder having physical symptoms but originating from mental or emotional causes. **2.** Relating to the influence of the mind on the body.

psy·cho·ther·a·py (sī′kō-**thĕr′**ə-pē) *n.* A type of therapy based on the exploration of painful feelings and experiences, especially through talking, in order to resolve personal problems and treat mental and emotional disorders.

psy·chot·ic (sī-**kŏt′**ĭk) *adj.* Relating to or affected by psychosis. ❖ *n.* A person who is affected by psychosis. **—psy·chot′i·cal·ly** *adv.*

Pt The symbol for the element **platinum.**

pt. *abbr.* An abbreviation of: **1.** pint. **2.** point.

PTA *abbr.* An abbreviation of Parent Teacher Association.

ptar·mi·gan (**tär′**mĭ-gən) *n., pl.* **ptarmigan** or **ptar·mi·gans** Any of various grouses of northern regions, having feathers that are brownish in summer and white in winter and feathered legs and feet. [From Scottish Gaelic *tarmachan.*]

PT boat (pē-**tē′**) *n.* A fast maneuverable vessel used to torpedo enemy ships.

pte·rid·o·phyte (tə-**rĭd′**ə-fīt′ *or* **tĕr′**ĭ-dō-fīt′) *n.* Any of various nonflowering vascular plants that reproduce by means of spores, such as the ferns and the horsetails.

pter·o·dac·tyl (tĕr′ə-**dăk′**təl) *n.* Any of various short-tailed pterosaurs. [From Greek *pteron*, feather, wing + Greek *daktulos*, finger.]

pter·o·saur (**tĕr′**ə-sôr′) *n.* Any of various extinct flying reptiles that had wings formed by a flap of skin extending from a long slender toe on each front leg.

Ptol·e·ma·ic (tŏl′ə-**mā′**ĭk) *adj.* Relating to the astronomer Ptolemy.

Ptolemaic system *n.* The astronomical system of Ptolemy, in which Earth is at the center of the universe and all other bodies revolve around it.

Ptol·e·my[1] (**tŏl′**ə-mē) An Egyptian dynasty of Macedonian kings (323–30 BC) including **Ptolemy I** (367?–283?), who succeeded Alexander the Great as ruler of Egypt (323–285), and **Ptolemy XV** (47–30), who ruled (44–30) with his mother, Cleopatra.

Ptol·e·my[2] (**tŏl′**ə-mē) Flourished second century AD. Alexandrian astronomer who based his astronomy on the belief that all heavenly bodies revolve around Earth.

pto·maine (**tō′**mān′) *n.* Any of various nitrogen-containing substances, some of which are poisonous, that form when proteins decompose.

pty·a·lin (**tī′**ə-lĭn) *n.* An enzyme in saliva that breaks down starches into sugars.

Pu The symbol for the element **plutonium.**

pub (pŭb) *n.* A place of business that serves beer or other alcoholic drinks and often simple meals.

pu·ber·ty (**pyōō′**bər-tē) *n.* The stage in the development of a human or other mammal in which the reproductive organs become fully functional.

pu·bic (**pyōō′**bĭk) *adj.* Relating to or in the region of the pubis.

pu·bis (**pyōō′**bĭs) *n., pl.* **pu·bes** (**pyōō′**bēz) The forward portion of either of the hipbones, joining to form the front arch of the pelvis.

pub·lic (**pŭb′**lĭk) *adj.* **1.** Concerning or affecting the people or community: *public safety.* **2.** Maintained for or used by the people or community; not private: *the public library.* **3.** Capitalized in shares of stock that can be traded on the open market: *a public company.* **4.** Participated in or attended by the people or community: *a public debate.* **5.** Serving or acting on behalf of the people or community: *a public official.* **6.** Known or available to all: *made the testimony public.* ❖ *n.* **1.** The community or people as a whole: *a building open to the public.* **2.** A group of people with a common interest: *the reading public.* ◆ **in public** In such a way as to be visible to the scrutiny of the people. [From Middle English *publik*, from Latin *pūblicus*, from *populus*, people.] —SEE NOTE AT **collective noun.**

pub·lic-ad·dress system (pŭb′lĭk-ə-**drĕs′**) *n.* An electronic system using amplifiers and loudspeakers to project sound throughout a given area.

pub·li·can (pŭb′lĭ-kən) *n.* **1.** *Chiefly British* The keeper of a tavern or bar. **2.** A collector of taxes in the ancient Roman empire.

pub·li·ca·tion (pŭb′lĭ-**kā′**shən) *n.* **1.** The act or process of publishing matter in printed or electronic form. **2.** An issue of printed or electronic matter, such as a magazine, offered for sale or distribution. **3.** Communication of information to the public.

public defender *n.* An attorney employed by the government to represent indigent defendants in criminal cases.

public domain *n.* **1.** The condition of not being protected by a patent or copyright and therefore being available to the public for use without charge. **2.** Land that the state or federal government owns and controls.

public housing *n.* Housing that a government builds, operates, and owns.

pub·li·cist (**pŭb′**lĭ-sĭst) *n.* A person who publicizes, especially a press or publicity agent.

pub·lic·i·ty (pŭ-**blĭs′**ĭ-tē) *n.* **1.** Public notice or interest created by spreading information about something in the media: *The book has received widespread publicity.* **2.** The information given out to the media to attract such notice or interest: *They tried to shape the publicity to make the defendant look innocent.*

pub·li·cize (**pŭb′**lĭ-sīz′) *tr.v.* **pub·li·cized, pub·li·ciz·ing, pub·li·ciz·es** To give publicity to or draw public attention to: *publicized the concert.*

pub·lic·ly (**pŭb′**lĭk-lē) *adv.* **1.** In a public manner; openly: *They publicly acknowledged the partnership.* **2.** By or with the consent of the public: *a publicly owned water system.*

public relations *pl.n.* *(used with a singular verb)* The art or science of establishing and promoting a favorable relationship with the public.

public school *n.* **1.** A school in the United States supported by public funds and providing free education for the children of a community. **2.** A private boarding school in Great Britain for study before entering a university.

public servant *n.* A person who holds a government position.

public television *n.* Television that provides programs, especially of an educational nature, for the public and has few or no commercials.

public utility *n.* A private company subject to governmental regulation that provides an essential service or commodity, such as water, electricity, or communication to the public.

public works *pl.n.* Construction projects, such as highways or dams, financed by public funds and constructed by a government for the benefit or use of the general public.

pub·lish (**pŭb′**lĭsh) *tr.v.* **pub·lished, pub·lish·ing, pub·lish·es 1.** To prepare and issue (a book, music, or other material) for public distribution, especially for sale. **2.** To bring to public attention; announce. [From Middle English *publishen*, to make known publicly, from Latin *pūblicāre*.]

pub·lish·er (**pŭb′**lĭ-shər) *n.* A person or business that produces and distributes something, such as a book or magazine, in printed or electronic form.

Puc·ci·ni (po͞o-**chē′**nē), **Giacomo** 1858–1924. Italian operatic composer whose works include *La Bohème* (1896) and *Madame Butterfly* (1904).

puce (pyo͞os) *n.* A deep red to dark grayish purple.

puck (pŭk) *n.* A hard rubber disk used in ice hockey.

Puck *n.* A mischievous sprite in English folklore.

puck·er (**pŭk′**ər) *v.* **puck·ered, puck·er·ing, puck·ers** —*tr.* To gather into small wrinkles or folds: *puckered my lips; puckered the curtains.* —*intr.* To become gathered, contracted, and wrinkled. ❖ *n.* **1.** A wrinkle or wrinkled part, as in tightly stitched cloth. **2.** An expression on the face in which the lips are tightly pulled together and pushed outward. [Probably from *pock*, bag, sack, variant of *poke*.]

puck·ish (**pŭk′**ĭsh) *adj.* Mischievous; impish: *a puckish grin.* **—puck′ish·ly** *adv.*

pud·ding (**po͝od′**ĭng) *n.* **1.** A sweet dessert, usually containing flour or a cereal product, that has been boiled, steamed, or baked. **2.** A preparation that is like sausage, made with minced meat stuffed into a bag or skin and boiled. [From Middle English *poding*, a kind of sausage, from Old French *boudin*.]

pud·dle (**pŭd′**l) *n.* **1.** A small pool of water, especially rainwater. **2.** A small pool of a liquid. [From Middle English *podel*, from Old English *pudd*, ditch.]

pudg·y (**pŭj′**ē) *adj.* **pudg·i·er, pudg·i·est** Somewhat fat; chubby: *a pudgy face.* **—pudg′i·ness** *n.*

Pueb·lo (**pwĕb′**lō) *n., pl.* **Pueblo** or **Pueb·los 1.** A member of any of numerous Native American peoples, including the Hopi, living in villages in New Mexico and Arizona. **2. pueblo** *pl.* **pueb·los** A village or community of any of the Pueblo peoples, typically made up of adobe or stone apartment dwellings of several stories clustered around a central plaza. **—Pueb′lo** *adj.*

puer·ile (**pyo͝or′**ĭl′ *or* **pwĕr′**ĭl′) *adj.* Immature; childish.

Puer·to Ri·co (pwĕr′tə **rē′**kō *or* pôrt′ə **rē′**kō) A self-governing island of the United States in the Caribbean Sea east of Hispaniola. It was colonized by Spain in the 1500s and ceded to the United States in 1898 after the Spanish-American War. San Juan is the capital.

puff (pŭf) *n.* **1a.** A short forceful discharge or gust, as of air, smoke, or vapor. **b.** A short abrupt sound produced by such a discharge or gust. **2.** An act of drawing in and expelling the breath, as in smoking tobacco. **3.** Something that looks light and fluffy: *little puffs of white clouds.* **4.** A soft pad for applying powder or lotion. **5.** A light flaky pastry, often filled with custard or cream. **6.** A light padded bed covering. **7.** A section of full gathered fabric that balloons out as though filled with air. ❖ *v.* **puffed, puff·ing, puffs** —*intr.* **1.** To come forth in puffs: *Smoke puffed from the steamboat.* **2.** To breathe heavily and rapidly, as from fatigue: *He began to puff from the hard climb.* **3.** To take puffs on smoking material. —*tr.* **1.** To smoke (a pipe, for example). **2.** To emit or give forth in puffs: *The train puffed smoke.* **3.** To inflate or distend: *The wind puffed out the sail.* ◆ **puff up** To swell or seem to swell, as from air or pride: *puffed up and glared at the person who interrupted.* [From Middle English *puffen*, to puff, from Old English *pyffan*.]

puff adder *n.* **1.** A venomous African viper that inflates its body when disturbed and has crescent-shaped, yellowish markings. **2.** A nonvenomous hognose snake of North America.

puff·ball (**pŭf′**bôl′) *n.* **1.** Any of various ball-shaped fungi that let out a puff of spores when broken open. **2.** *Informal* The fluffy head of a dandelion that has gone to seed.

puff·er·fish (**pŭf′**ər-fĭsh′) *n.* Any of various often poi-

Giacomo Puccini

pueblo
Taos Pueblo, New Mexico

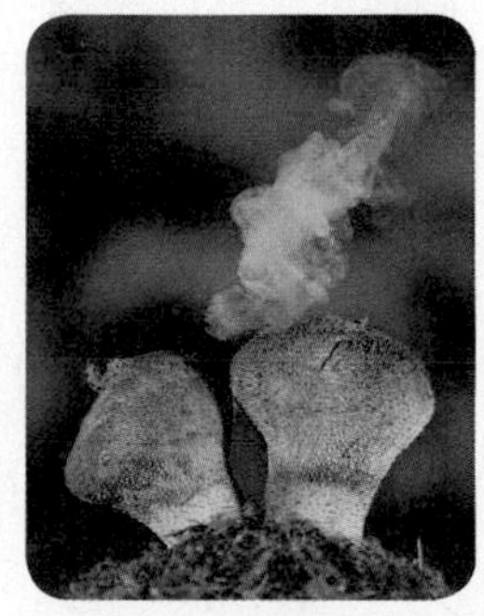

puffball

puffin

pug

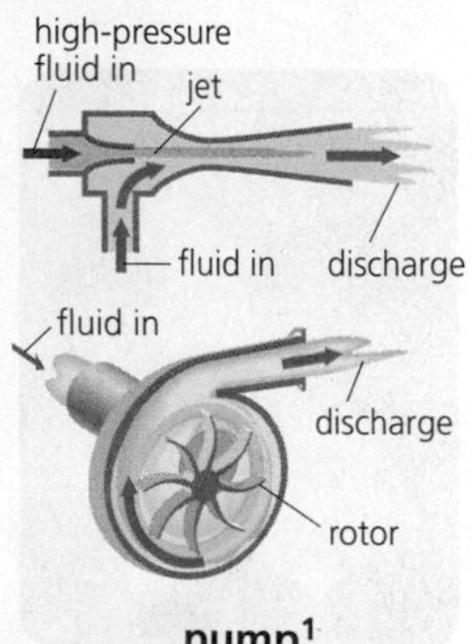

pump[1]
In a jet pump (*top*), a stream of high-pressure fluid passing through a narrow outlet creates a suction effect that draws in a second fluid. In a centrifugal pump (*bottom*), a spinning rotor forces a fluid outward, creating a partial vacuum that draws more fluid into the pump.

ă	pat	ôr	core
ā	pay	oi	boy
âr	care	ou	out
ä	father	o͝o	took
ĕ	pet	o͝or	lure
ē	be	o͞o	boot
ĭ	pit	ŭ	cut
ī	bite	ûr	urge
îr	pier	th	thin
ŏ	pot	*th*	this
ō	toe	zh	vision
ô	paw	ə	about

sonous marine fishes that puff themselves up with water or air when threatened.

puf·fin (pŭf′ĭn) *n.* Any of several black-and-white northern seabirds, having a large, brightly colored bill that is narrow from side to side.

puff·y (pŭf′ē) *adj.* **1.** Swollen: *the puffy eyes of a crying child.* **2.** Full and rounded, like a balloon filled with air: *puffy sleeves.* **—puff′i·ness** *n.*

pug (pŭg) *n.* A small short-haired dog having a short nose, wrinkled face, and curled tail.

Pu·get Sound (pyo͞o′jĭt) A deep inlet of the Pacific Ocean in western Washington.

pu·gi·lism (pyo͞o′jə-lĭz′əm) *n.* The skill, practice, and sport of fighting with the fists; boxing. **—pu′gi·list** *n.*

pug·na·cious (pŭg-nā′shəs) *adj.* Combative in nature; belligerent. [From Latin *pugnāre*, to fight, from *pugnus*, fist.] **—pug·na′cious·ly** *adv.* **—pug·nac′i·ty** (pŭg-năs′ĭ-tē) *n.*

pug nose *n.* A short nose that is somewhat flattened and turned up at the end. **—pug′-nosed′** (pŭg′nōzd′) *adj.*

puis·sance (pwĭs′əns *or* pyo͞o′ĭ-səns) *n.* Power; might. **—puis′sant** *adj.* **—puis′sant·ly** *adv.*

puke (pyo͞ok) *Slang intr. & tr.v.* **puked, puk·ing, pukes** To vomit. ❖ *n.* Vomit.

pu·la (po͞o′lä) *n.* The basic monetary unit of Botswana.

Pu·las·ki (po͞o-lăs′kē), **Casimir** 1747–1779. Polish general who aided American forces in the Revolutionary War.

pul·ing (pyo͞o′lĭng) *adj.* Whining; whimpering: *a puling infant.*

Pu·lit·zer (po͝ol′ĭt-sər *or* pyo͞o′lĭt-sər), **Joseph** 1847–1911. Hungarian-born American newspaper publisher who established and endowed the Pulitzer Prizes for journalism, literature, and music.

pull (po͝ol) *v.* **pulled, pull·ing, pulls** *—tr.* **1.** To apply force to (something) so as to cause or tend to cause motion toward the source of the force: *pulled her chair up to the table; pulled the wagon down the street.* **2.** To take from a fixed position or place; remove: *pull weeds.* **3.** To tug at; jerk: *I pulled the lever until it broke.* **4.** To rip or tear; rend: *The puppy pulled the towel into bits.* **5.** To stretch (taffy, for example) repeatedly. **6.** To injure (a muscle) by stretching or straining it too much. **7.** *Informal* To cause (people) to attend an event or performance; draw: *The play pulls large crowds.* **8.** *Slang* To draw out (a knife or gun) in readiness for use. *—intr.* **1.** To exert force in moving something toward the source of the force: *Pull harder and the window will open.* **2.** To inhale or drink deeply: *He pulled on the water bottle.* **3a.** To move in a certain direction or toward a certain goal: *pulled into the driveway; pulled even with the race leader.* **b.** To gain a position closer to an objective: *Our team has pulled within three points of the league leader.* **4.** *Informal* To express or feel great empathy or sympathy: *We're pulling for the mayor in the fall election.* ❖ *n.* **1.** The act or process of pulling: *gave the drawer a pull.* **2.** The force used in pulling: *a rope that will stand a 200-pound pull.* **3.** A sustained effort: *a long pull to the summit.* **4.** Something, such as a knob on a drawer, that is used for pulling. **5.** A deep inhalation or draft, as on a cigarette or of a beverage. **6.** *Slang* Special influence: *He has a lot of pull in his hometown.* ◆ **pull away** To move away or backward; withdraw: *I pulled away from the edge of the cliff.* **pull in** To arrive at a destination. **pull off** *Informal* To perform in spite of difficulties or obstacles; bring off: *The team pulled off an upset victory.* **pull (oneself) together** To regain one's composure. **pull out 1.** To leave or depart. **2.** To withdraw, as from a situation or commitment. **pull over** To bring a vehicle to a stop at a curb or at the side of a road: *I pulled over to look at the view.* **pull through** To come successfully through trouble or illness. **pull together** To make a joint effort: *We'll meet the deadline if we all pull together.* [From Old English *pullian*.] **—pull′er** *n.*

SYNONYMS **pull, drag, draw, tow, tug** These verbs mean to apply force to something, causing it to move toward that force. *She pulled her sled up the hill. He dragged his dog away from the cat in the tree. The weary traveler drew his chair closer to the fire. The car towed a large trailer. I tugged my desk to the other side of the room.*
ANTONYM **push**

pul·let (po͝ol′ĭt) *n.* A young hen, especially one less than a year old. [From Middle English *polet*, from Latin *pullus*, chicken.]

pul·ley (po͝ol′ē) *n., pl.* **pul·leys 1.** A simple machine consisting of a freely turning wheel with a groove around its edge through which a rope or chain can run to change the direction of the force exerted on the rope or chain. **2.** A similar wheel that drives or is driven by a belt passing around its edge.

Pull·man car (po͝ol′mən) *n.* A railroad car having private sleeping compartments or parlors. [After George Mortimer *Pullman* (1831–1897), American industrialist and inventor.]

pull·out (po͝ol′out′) *n.* **1.** A withdrawal, especially of troops. **2.** An aircraft's change from a dive to level flight. **3.** An object designed to be pulled out.

pull·o·ver (po͝ol′ō′vər) *n.* A garment, such as a sweater, that is put on by being drawn over the head.

pull-up (po͝ol′ŭp′) *n.* The act or exercise of chinning oneself on an overhead bar; a chin-up.

pul·mo·nar·y (po͝ol′mə-nĕr′ē *or* pŭl′mə-nĕr′ē) *adj.* Relating to or affecting the lungs: *a pulmonary infection.* [From Latin *pulmō*, lung.]

pulp (pŭlp) *n.* **1.** A soft, moist, shapeless mass of matter. **2.** The soft juicy or fleshy part of fruit or of certain vegetables. **3.** A moist mixture, as of ground wood and rags, used to make paper. **4.** The soft inner part of a tooth, containing blood vessels and nerve tissue. **5.** A publication, such as a magazine or book, containing lurid subject matter. ❖ *tr.v.* **pulped, pulp·ing, pulps** To reduce to pulp: *pulp logs.*

pul·pit (po͝ol′pĭt *or* pŭl′pĭt) *n.* **1.** An elevated platform, lectern, or stand used in preaching or conducting a religious service. **2.** A position, especially a public office, from which one may expound one's views to a wide audience. [From Middle English, from Latin *pulpitum*, wooden platform.]

pulp·wood (pŭlp′wo͝od′) *n.* Soft wood, such as pine, spruce, or aspen, used in making paper.

pulp·y (pŭl′pē) *adj.* Containing or resembling pulp: *a pulpy fruit.*

pul·sar (pŭl′sär′) *n.* A rotating neutron star that emits radiation, usually radio waves, in very short and regular pulses.

pul·sate (pŭl′sāt′) *intr.v.* **pul·sat·ed, pul·sat·ing, pul·sates 1.** To expand and contract rhythmically, as the heart does. **2.** To produce rhythmic sounds or other vibrations: *Music pulsated throughout the room.*

pul·sa·tion (pŭl-sā′shən) *n.* **1.** The action of pulsating. **2.** A single beat, throb, or vibration.

pulse[1] (pŭls) *n.* **1.** The rhythmical expansion and contraction of the arteries as blood is pumped through them by the beating of the heart. **2.** A regular or rhythmical beating: *the pulse of the drums.* **3.** A single beat or throb; a pulsation. **4.** A short sudden change in a normally constant quantity: *A telegraph message is sent as a series of electrical pulses.* ❖ *intr.v.* **pulsed, puls·ing, puls·es** To pulsate; beat. [From Middle English *pous*, from Latin *pulsus*, from *pellere*, to beat.]

pulse[2] (pŭls) *n.* **1.** The edible seeds of certain plants that bear pods, such as lentils. **2.** A plant that bears such seeds. [From Middle English *puls*, from Latin, pottage of meal and pulse.]

pul·ver·ize (pŭl′və-rīz′) *tr.v.* **pul·ver·ized, pul·ver·iz·ing, pul·ver·iz·es 1.** To pound, crush, or grind to powder or dust: *She pulverized the stone with a mallet.* **2.** To overwhelm or defeat utterly: *The visitors pulverized the home team.* **—pul′ver·i·za′tion** (pŭl′vər-ĭ-zā′-shən) *n.*

pu·ma (po͞o′mə) *n.* A cougar.

pum·ice (pŭm′ĭs) *n.* A porous lightweight rock of volcanic origin, used as an abrasive.

pum·mel (pŭm′əl) *tr.v.* **pum·meled, pum·mel·ing, pum·mels** also **pum·melled, pum·mel·ling, pum·mels 1.** To beat, as with the fists; pommel. **2.** To cause to undergo harm or loss: *international events that pummeled the stock market.*

pump¹ (pŭmp) *n.* A machine for raising, compressing, or transferring fluids. ❖ *v.* **pumped, pump·ing, pumps** —*tr.* **1.** To raise or cause to flow by means of a pump: *Derricks pump oil out of the ground.* **2.** To empty of liquid or gas by means of a pump: *pump out a flooded cellar.* **3.** To cause to move up and down in the manner of a pump handle: *a bicyclist pumping the pedals; a driver pumping the brakes.* **4.** To draw, deliver, or pour forth: *a reporter who pumps out a new story every day.* **5.** To put in or insert: *The teacher pumped new enthusiasm into the class.* **6.** To invest (money) repeatedly or persistently in something. **7.** To question closely: *pumped him for information.* —*intr.* To raise or move gas or liquid with a pump. ◆ **pump up 1.** To inflate with gas by means of a pump: *I pumped up my bicycle tires.* **2.** *Slang* To fill with enthusiasm, strength, and energy: *The coach's pep talk pumped up the players for the game.* [From Middle English *pumpe*.] **—pump′er** *n.*

pump² (pŭmp) *n.* A low-cut shoe without laces, straps, or other fasteners.

pum·per·nick·el (pŭm′pər-nĭk′əl) *n.* A dark bread made from whole, coarsely ground rye.

pump·kin (pŭmp′kĭn *or* pŭm′kĭn) *n.* **1.** A large round fruit having a thick orange rind and pulp often used for making pies. **2.** A plant that bears such fruit.

pun (pŭn) *n.* A play on words that involves different senses of the same word or the similar sense or sound of different words. ❖ *intr.v.* **punned, pun·ning, puns** To make a pun. **—pun′ner** *n.*

punch¹ (pŭnch) *n.* **1.** A tool for piercing: *a leather punch.* **2.** A tool for forcing a pin, bolt, or rivet in or out of a hole. **3.** A tool for stamping a design on a surface. ❖ *v.* **punched, punch·ing, punch·es** —*tr.* **1.** To make (a hole or opening), as by using a punch. **2.** To make a hole in (something), as by using a punch: *The conductor punched my train ticket.* —*intr.* To pierce something; make a hole or opening: *My foot punched through the ice.* [From Middle English *pounce*, from Latin *pungere*, to puncture.]

punch² (pŭnch) *tr.v.* **punched, punch·ing, punch·es 1a.** To hit with a sharp blow of the fist: *He punched my shoulder.* **b.** To make (a hole) by thrusting the fist: *She punched a hole in the wall.* **2.** To press quickly in order to operate: *punched the "enter" key.* **3.** To herd (cattle). ❖ *n.* **1.** A blow with the fist. **2.** Impressive or effective force: *a story with a lot of punch.* ◆ **punch in 1.** To check in formally at a job upon arrival. **2.** To enter data on a keypad or similar device. **punch out 1.** To check out formally at a job upon departure. **2.** To knock unconscious with a punch. [From Middle English *pouncen, punchen*, to thrust, prod, puncture, ultimately from Latin *pungere*, to prick.] **—punch′er** *n.*

punch³ (pŭnch) *n.* A beverage containing fruit juices and often other ingredients, such as a soft drink or carbonated water. [From Hindi *pañc*, five, probably as used in *pañcāmṛt*, a drink in a Hindu ritual using five ingredients.]

punch card *n.* A medium for feeding data into a computer, essentially a card punched with holes or notches to represent letters and numbers or with a pattern of holes to represent related data.

pun·cheon¹ (pŭn′chən) *n.* **1.** A short upright timber used in structural framing. **2.** A roughly dressed heavy timber, with one face finished flat. **3.** A tool used for punching, perforating, or stamping. [From Middle English *punchoun*, from Old French *ponçon, ponchon*, from Latin *pūnctus*, punctured.]

pun·cheon² (pŭn′chən) *n.* **1.** A cask that can hold from 72 to 120 US gallons (273 to 454 liters). **2.** The amount that a puncheon can hold. [From Middle English *punchoun*, from Old French *ponçon, ponchon*, punch, cask (probably because inspected casks were marked with a punch).]

punch·ing bag (pŭn′chĭng) *n.* **1.** A stuffed or inflated bag that is usually suspended so that it can be punched or kicked for practice or exercise. **2.** A target of frequent criticism or abuse.

punch line *n.* The climax of a joke or humorous story, producing a sudden humorous effect.

punch·y (pŭn′chē) *adj.* **punch·i·er, punch·i·est 1.** Characterized by vigor or drive. **2.** Groggy or dazed from or as if from being punched.

punc·til·i·ous (pŭngk-tĭl′ē-əs) *adj.* **1.** Attentive to the details of etiquette. **2.** Conscientious and exacting; precise. **—punc·til′i·ous·ly** *adv.*

punc·tu·al (pŭngk′cho͞o-əl) *adj.* Acting or arriving exactly on time; prompt. **—punc′tu·al′i·ty** (pŭngk′choo-ăl′ĭ-tē) *n.* **—punc′tu·al·ly** *adv.*

punc·tu·ate (pŭngk′cho͞o-āt′) *tr.v.* **punc·tu·at·ed, punc·tu·at·ing, punc·tu·ates 1.** To provide (written or printed material) with punctuation marks: *punctuate the sentence.* **2.** To interrupt periodically: *The evening silence was punctuated by the hooting of an owl.* **3.** To stress or emphasize.

punc·tu·at·ed equilibrium (pŭngk′cho͞o-ā′tĭd) *n.* The theory that evolution follows a pattern in which the formation of new species over relatively short periods of time alternates with a lack of change in those species over much longer periods of time.

punc·tu·a·tion (pŭngk′cho͞o-ā′shən) *n.* **1.** The use of standard marks in writing and printing to separate sentences and parts of sentences in order to make the meaning clear. **2.** A mark or the marks so used.

punctuation mark *n.* One of a set of marks or signs, such as the comma (,) or the period (.), used to punctuate written material.

punc·ture (pŭngk′chər) *v.* **punc·tured, punc·tur·ing, punc·tures** —*tr.* **1.** To pierce with a pointed object: *I punctured the tomato with my fork.* **2.** To cause to collapse or deflate by or as if by piercing with something sharp: *The setback punctured her ego.* —*intr.* To be pierced or punctured: *The tire punctured when it hit the curb.* ❖ *n.* **1.** The act or an instance of puncturing. **2.** A hole or depression made by something sharp, especially such a hole in a tire.

pun·dit (pŭn′dĭt) *n.* **1.** A commentator: *political pundits.* **2.** An expert or authority. [From Sanskrit *paṇḍitaḥ*, scholar.]

pun·gent (pŭn′jənt) *adj.* **1.** Sharp or acrid to the taste or smell: *a pungent sauce; pungent smoke.* **2.** Penetrating, biting, or caustic: *pungent remarks.* **—pun′gen·cy** *n.* **—pun′gent·ly** *adv.*

pun·ish (pŭn′ĭsh) *tr.v.* **pun·ished, pun·ish·ing, pun·ish·es 1.** To subject to a penalty for an offense, sin, or fault: *Society punishes criminals.* **2.** To inflict a penalty for (an offense): *punish cruelty.* **3.** To treat roughly or harshly: *Heavy surf punished the small boat.* **—pun′ish·er** *n.*

pun·ish·a·ble (pŭn′ĭ-shə-bəl) *adj.* Liable to punishment: *a crime punishable by imprisonment.*

punching bag

pun·ish·ment (pŭn′ĭsh-mənt) *n.* **1a.** An act of punishing: *the punishment of wrongdoers.* **b.** The condition of being punished. **2.** A penalty for a crime or wrongdoing: *What punishment was given for the crime?* **3.** Rough or harsh handling or treatment: *These shoes have taken a lot of punishment.*

pu·ni·tive (pyo͞o′nĭ-tĭv) *adj.* Inflicting or tending to inflict punishment: *a punitive decree.* **—pu′ni·tive·ly** *adv.*

Pun·jab (pŭn′jăb′ *or* pŭn-jăb′) A historical region of northeast Pakistan and northwest India east of the Indus River.

Pun·ja·bi (pŭn-jä′bē *or* pŭn-jăb′ē) *adj.* Relating to the Punjab or its people, language, or culture. ❖ *n., pl.* **Pun·ja·bis 1.** A native or inhabitant of the Punjab. **2.** An Indic language spoken in the Punjab.

punk (pŭngk) *n.* **1.** *Slang* **a.** An often aggressive or violent young man. **b.** An inexperienced young person. **2a.** Punk rock. **b.** A performer or follower of punk rock.

punk rock *n.* Rock music having lyrics that express emotional isolation and antisocial attitudes, usually played very fast.

pup
seal pup (*right*) with its mother (*left*)

pun·ster (pŭn′stər) *n.* A person who make puns.

punt[1] (pŭnt) *n.* A flatbottom boat with squared ends for use in shallow waters, usually propelled with a long pole. ❖ *intr.v.* **punt·ed, punt·ing, punts** To go or ride in a punt. [From Old English, from Latin *pontō*, pontoon, flatbottom boat, from *pōns*, bridge.] **—punt′er** *n.*

punt[2] (pŭnt) *n.* In football, a kick in which the ball is dropped from the hands and kicked before it touches the ground. ❖ *v.* **punt·ed, punt·ing, punts** *—tr.* To kick (a ball) by means of a punt. *—intr.* **1.** To execute a punt. **2.** *Informal* To cease doing something; give up: *Let's punt on this plan and try something else.* [Perhaps from alteration of *bunt*.] **—punt′er** *n.*

pu·ny (pyo͞o′nē) *adj.* **pu·ni·er, pu·ni·est** Small or inferior in size, strength, or significance; weak. **—pu′ni·ly** *adv.* **—pu′ni·ness** *n.*

pup (pŭp) *n.* **1.** A young dog; a puppy. **2.** One of the young of certain other animals, such as a seal or a shark. **3.** An inexperienced or conceited young person: *What did that young pup say to her?*

pu·pa (pyo͞o′pə) *n., pl.* **pu·pae** (pyo͞o′pē) or **pu·pas** An insect in the stage of development between the larva and the adult form, during which it undergoes complete transformation within a protective covering such as a cocoon.

pu·pal (pyo͞o′pəl) *adj.* Relating to or being a pupa or pupae: *during the pupal stage.*

❑ *These sound alike:* **pupal, pupil**[1] (student), **pupil**[2] (iris opening).

pu·pate (pyo͞o′pāt′) *intr.v.* **pu·pat·ed, pu·pat·ing, pu·pates** To become a pupa. **—pu·pa′tion** *n.*

pu·pil[1] (pyo͞o′pəl) *n.* A student receiving instruction from a teacher. [From Middle English *pupille*, orphan, from Latin *pūpillus*, from *pūpus*, boy.]

❑ *These sound alike:* **pupil**[1] (student), **pupal** (of a pupa), **pupil**[2] (iris opening).

pu·pil[2] (pyo͞o′pəl) *n.* The opening in the center of the iris through which light enters the eye. [From Middle English *pupille*, from Latin *pūpilla*, little doll (from the tiny image reflected in the pupil).]

❑ *These sound alike:* **pupil**[2] (iris opening), **pupal** (of a pupa), **pupil**[1] (student).

pup·pet (pŭp′ĭt) *n.* **1.** A small figure of a person or animal, fitting over the hand or fitted with strings that are moved from above. **2.** A person whose behavior is determined by the will of others: *a political puppet.*

pup·pet·eer (pŭp′ĭ-tîr′) *n.* A person who operates puppets as entertainment for others.

pup·pet·ry (pŭp′ĭ-trē) *n., pl.* **pup·pet·ries** The art of making and operating puppets.

pup·py (pŭp′ē) *n., pl.* **pup·pies** A young dog.

pup tent *n.* A small tent made of waterproof material.

pur·blind (pûr′blīnd′) *adj.* **1.** Having poor vision; nearly or partly blind. **2.** Slow in understanding or discerning; dull. **—pur′blind′ly** *adv.*

pur·chase (pûr′chĭs) *tr.v.* **pur·chased, pur·chas·ing, pur·chas·es** To obtain in exchange for money or its equivalent; buy: *I purchased a new cell phone.* ❖ *n.* **1.** Something that is bought: *The car was a wise purchase.* **2.** The act or an instance or buying: *the purchase of land.* **3.** A secure position, grasp, or hold: *He got purchase on the ledge and climbed up.* **—pur′chas·a·ble** *adj.* **—pur′chas·er** *n.*

pure (pyo͝or) *adj.* **pur·er, pur·est 1.** Having a homogeneous or uniform composition; not mixed: *pure oxygen.* **2.** Free from impurities: *pure chocolate.* **3.** Complete; utter: *pure happiness.* **4.** Having no moral failing or guilt: *a pure heart.* **5.** Having never experienced sexual intercourse; virginal. **6.** Purebred. **7.** Not concerned with or directed toward practical application; theoretical: *pure mathematics.* **—pure′ly** *adv.* **—pure′ness** *n.*

pure·bred (pyo͝or′brĕd′) *adj.* Having ancestors of the same breed or variety: *a purebred dog.* ❖ *n.* (pyo͝or′brĕd′) A purebred animal.

pu·rée (pyo͝o-rā′ *or* pyo͝or′ā) *tr.v.* **pu·réed, pu·rée·ing, pu·rées** To press (food) through a sieve or process it in a blender so that it becomes a mushy pulp. ❖ *n.* Food prepared in this way.

pur·ga·tive (pûr′gə-tĭv) *adj.* Tending to purge something, especially the bowels. ❖ *n.* A purgative substance; a laxative.

pur·ga·to·ry (pûr′gə-tôr′ē) *n., pl.* **pur·ga·to·ries 1.** In the Roman Catholic Church, a state in which souls who have died in grace are punished until they are cleansed of their sins. **2.** A place or condition of suffering, atoning for sins, or remorse. **—pur′ga·to′ri·al** (pûr′gə-tôr′ē-əl) *adj.*

purge (pûrj) *v.* **purged, purg·ing, purg·es** *—tr.* **1a.** To clear (a container or space, for example) of something unclean or unwanted: *purge a water pipe of air.* **b.** To remove or eliminate (unwanted physical matter): *purge the air from a water pipe.* **2.** To remove or eliminate (an unwanted element): *purged offensive text from the document.* **3.** To rid (a nation or a political party, for example) of people considered undesirable. **4a.** To clear (a storage device) of unwanted data. **b.** To delete (unwanted data) from a storage device. *—intr.* **1.** To cause or undergo an emptying of the bowels. **2.** To vomit or force oneself to vomit, especially as a symptom of an eating disorder. ❖ *n.* The act or process of purging.

pu·ri·fi·ca·tion (pyo͝or′ə-fĭ-kā′shən) *n.* The act or an instance of cleansing or purifying.

pu·ri·fy (pyo͝or′ə-fī′) *tr.v.* **pu·ri·fied, pu·ri·fy·ing, pu·ri·fies 1.** To rid of impurities: *purify water.* **2.** To rid of foreign or objectionable elements: *tried to purify the political party of its dissenters.* **3.** To free from moral or spiritual defilement: *rituals to purify the soul.* **—pu′ri·fi′er** *n.*

Pu·rim (po͝or′ĭm *or* po͞o-rēm′) *n.* A Jewish holiday celebrating the rescue of the Jews by Esther from a plot to massacre them.

pu·rine (pyo͝or′ēn′) *n.* Any of a group of organic compounds containing two rings consisting of five carbon and four nitrogen atoms. Purines include important components of DNA and RNA as well as caffeine and uric acid.

pur·ist (pyo͝or′ĭst) *n.* A person who practices or urges strict correctness, as in the use of words. **—pu·ris′tic** (pyo͞o-rĭs′tĭk) *adj.*

Pu·ri·tan (pyo͝or′ĭ-tn) *n.* **1.** A member of a group of Protestants in England and the American Colonies in the 1500s and 1600s who advocated reform of the Church

ă	pat	ôr	core
ā	pay	oi	boy
âr	care	ou	out
ä	father	o͝o	took
ĕ	pet	o͝or	lure
ē	be	o͞o	boot
ĭ	pit	ŭ	cut
ī	bite	ûr	urge
îr	pier	th	thin
ŏ	pot	*th*	this
ō	toe	zh	vision
ô	paw	ə	about

of England and a strict morality. **2. puritan** A person considered excessively strict in morals.

pu·ri·tan·i·cal (pyo͝or′ĭ-tăn′ĭ-kəl) *adj.* **1.** Strict in matters of religious or moral conduct: *a puritanical education.* **2. Puritanical** Relating to or characteristic of the Puritans.

Pu·ri·tan·ism (pyo͝or′ĭ-tn-ĭz′əm) *n.* **1.** The practices and doctrines of the Puritans. **2. puritanism** Moral strictness, especially in regard to social pleasures.

pu·ri·ty (pyo͝or′ĭ-tē) *n.* **1.** The quality or condition of being pure: *the purity of mountain air.* **2.** Freedom from immorality or guilt: *a life of great purity.* **3.** The degree to which something is homogeneous or uniform.

purl[1] (pûrl) *intr.v.* **purled, purl·ing, purls** To flow or ripple with a murmuring sound, as a brook does. ❖ *n.* The sound made by rippling water. [Probably of Scandinavian origin.]

❑ *These sound alike:* **purl**[1] (flow), **pearl** (gem), **purl**[2] (knit).

purl[2] (pûrl) *v.* **purled, purl·ing, purls** *—tr.* To knit (yarn) with a purl stitch. *—intr.* To do knitting with a purl stitch. ❖ *n.* Inversion of knit stitch; purl stitch.

❑ *These sound alike:* **purl**[2] (knit), **pearl** (gem), **purl**[1] (flow).

pur·loin (pər-loin′ *or* pûr′loin′) *tr.v.* **pur·loined, pur·loin·ing, pur·loins** To steal, especially in a stealthy way. **—pur·loin′er** *n.*

purl stitch *n.* An inverted knitting stitch, created by pulling a loop of yarn from the front of the fabric to the back through a previous stitch.

pur·ple (pûr′pəl) *n.* **1.** Any of a group of colors with a hue between that of blue and red. **2.** Cloth of this color, formerly worn as a symbol of royalty or high rank. ❖ *adj.* **1.** Of the color purple. **2.** Elaborate and ornate: *purple prose.* [From Old English, from Latin *purpura*, purple, from Greek *porphurā*, a shellfish yielding crimson dye, crimson.]

Purple Heart *n.* A US military decoration awarded to members of the armed services who have been wounded in action.

pur·plish (pûr′plĭsh) *adj.* Somewhat purple in color.

pur·port (pər-pôrt′) *tr.v.* **pur·port·ed, pur·port·ing, pur·ports** To have or present the often false appearance of being or intending; claim or profess: *an author who purports to have witnessed the events.* ❖ *n.* (pûr′pôrt′) **1.** Meaning that is presented, intended, or implied: *the purport of a letter.* **2.** Intention; purpose: *What was her purport in going to Alaska?* **—pur·port′ed·ly** (pər-pôr′tĭd-lē) *adv.*

pur·pose (pûr′pəs) *n.* **1.** The reason for which something exists; the point or effect of something: *The purpose of an airliner is to transport people.* **2.** The result that one intends to achieve by doing something; a motive or goal: *Her purpose in coming here is to talk to you.* **3.** Determination; resolve: *a woman of purpose.* ◆ **on purpose** Intentionally; deliberately: *did it on purpose.* [From Middle English *porpos*, from Anglo-Norman *purposer*, to intend.]

pur·pose·ful (pûr′pəs-fəl) *adj.* **1.** Having a purpose or goal: *children engaged in purposeful activities.* **2.** Determined or resolute: *entered the room with a purposeful look.* **—pur′pose·ful·ly** *adv.*

pur·pose·less (pûr′pəs-lĭs) *adj.* Lacking a purpose; aimless or meaningless. **—pur′pose·less·ly** *adv.*

pur·pose·ly (pûr′pəs-lē) *adv.* With a specific purpose; deliberately.

purr (pûr) *n.* **1.** The soft vibrant sound made by a cat. **2.** A sound similar to that made by a cat: *the purr of the car's engine.* ❖ *intr.v.* **purred, purr·ing, purrs** To make a purr.

purse (pûrs) *n.* **1.** A bag used for carrying personal items, especially by women; a handbag. **2.** A small bag or pouch, used to carry money. **3.** An available amount of money or resources: *a project funded by the public purse.* **4.** A sum of money given as a prize: *a race with a purse of $50,000.* ❖ *tr.v.* **pursed, purs·ing, purs·es** To gather or contract (the lips or brow) into wrinkles or folds; pucker: *purse one's brow in thought.* [From Old English *purs*, from Greek *bursa*, leather bag, wineskin.]

purs·er (pûr′sər) *n.* The officer in charge of money matters on board a ship or commercial aircraft.

pur·su·ance (pər-so͞o′əns) *n.* The act of putting something into effect.

pur·su·ant to (pər-so͞o′ənt) *prep.* In accordance with.

pur·sue (pər-so͞o′) *tr.v.* **pur·sued, pur·su·ing, pur·sues** **1.** To follow in an effort to overtake or capture; chase: *The hounds pursued the fox.* **2.** To strive to gain or accomplish: *pursue a college degree.* **3.** To proceed along (a course); follow: *The ship pursued a southerly course.* **4a.** To engage in; practice: *pursue a hobby.* **b.** To continue to engage in; carry on or advance: *Do you want to pursue this discussion?* **5.** To try to have a romantic relationship with (someone): *a lady who was pursued by many suitors.* **6.** To continue to torment or afflict; haunt: *Bad memories pursued him wherever he went.* [From Middle English *purseuen*, from Latin *prōsequī*, to follow after.]

pur·suit (pər-so͞ot′) *n.* **1.** The act or an instance of pursuing or chasing: *the pursuit of the suspect by the police.* **2.** The act of striving to gain or accomplish something: *the pursuit of higher education.* **3.** An activity, such as a vocation or hobby, engaged in regularly.

pu·ru·lent (pyo͝or′ə-lənt) *adj.* Containing, discharging, or causing the production of pus: *a purulent infection.* [From Middle English *purulente*, from Latin *pūrulentus*, from *pūs*, pus.]

pur·vey (pər-vā′ *or* pûr′vā′) *tr.v.* **pur·veyed, pur·vey·ing, pur·veys** **1.** To supply or sell (food, for example): *purvey provisions for an army.* **2.** To make widely known; spread widely: *ideas that are purveyed by political activists.* **—pur·vey′ance** *n.* **—pur·vey′or** *n.*

pus (pŭs) *n.* A thick yellowish-white liquid, consisting mostly of white blood cells, that forms in infected body tissues.

push (po͝osh) *v.* **pushed, push·ing, push·es** *—tr.* **1.** To apply pressure to (something), especially in order to move it: *He pushed the rock, but it wouldn't budge.* **2.** To move (something) by exerting force against it: *push a stalled car out of the intersection.* **3.** To force (one's way): *We pushed our way through the crowd.* **4.** To urge (someone) to do something or pressure (someone) for something: *They pushed her to try out for the basketball team. They pushed him for an answer.* **5.** *Informal* To promote or try to sell: *push a new brand of toothpaste.* **6.** To enlarge the area, scope, or amount of: *Pioneers pushed their farms westward. The new ad pushed sales into the millions.* **7.** *Informal* To approach in age: *He's pushing 70 but still runs a mile a day.* *—intr.* **1.** To exert pressure or force against something: *Let's all push to get the door open.* **2.** To advance despite difficulty or opposition; press forward: *The fans pushed toward the movie star.* **3.** To expend great or vigorous effort: *She pushed to finish the report on time.* ❖ *n.* **1.** The act of pushing; a shove or press: *His car needed a push to get started.* **2.** A vigorous effort: *They made a push and finished the project.* **3.** Something that provokes someone to do something; a stimulus: *What he needs is a push, and he'll finish the application.* ◆ **push around** *Informal* To treat or threaten to treat roughly; intimidate. **push off** *Informal* To set out, especially in a boat; depart. **push on** To continue or proceed along one's way. [From Middle English *pushen*, from Latin *pulsāre*, from *pellere*, to strike, push.]

push·but·ton (po͝osh′bŭt′n) *n.* also **push button** A small button that activates an electric circuit when pushed. ❖ *adj.* also **push-button** Equipped with or operated by a pushbutton: *a pushbutton telephone.*

Purple Heart

pushup

pussy willow

putt

ă	pat	ôr	core
ā	pay	oi	boy
âr	care	ou	out
ä	father	ŏŏ	took
ĕ	pet	ŏŏr	lure
ē	be	ōō	boot
ĭ	pit	ŭ	cut
ī	bite	ûr	urge
îr	pier	th	thin
ŏ	pot	*th*	this
ō	toe	zh	vision
ô	paw	ə	about

push·cart (pŏŏsh′kärt′) *n.* A light cart that is pushed by hand.

push·er (pŏŏsh′ər) *n. Slang* A person who sells drugs illegally.

push·o·ver (pŏŏsh′ō′vər) *n.* **1.** A person or group easily defeated or taken advantage of: *The team we played last week was a pushover.* **2.** Something that is easily done: *an exam that was a pushover.*

push·up (pŏŏsh′ŭp′) *n.* An exercise for strengthening arm muscles, performed by lying face down with the palms on the floor and pushing the body up and down with the arms.

push·y (pŏŏsh′ē) *adj.* **push·i·er, push·i·est** Disagreeably aggressive or forward: *a pushy sales clerk.*

pu·sil·lan·i·mous (pyōō′sə-lăn′ə-məs) *adj.* Lacking courage; cowardly. **—pu′sil·lan′i·mous·ly** *adv.*

puss[1] (pŏŏs) *n. Informal* A cat. [Probably of Germanic origin.]

puss[2] (pŏŏs) *Slang n.* **1.** The mouth. **2.** The face. [From Irish Gaelic *pus*, mouth.]

puss·y (pŏŏs′ē) *n., pl.* **puss·ies** *Informal* A cat.

puss·y·foot (pŏŏs′ē-fŏŏt′) *intr.v.* **puss·y·foot·ed, puss·y·foot·ing, puss·y·foots 1.** To move stealthily or cautiously. **2.** *Informal* To act cautiously or timidly.

pussy willow *n.* A shrub or small tree that has silky silvery catkins in early spring.

pus·tule (pŭs′chōōl *or* pŭs′tyōōl) *n.* **1.** A small inflamed swelling on the skin filled with pus. **2.** A similar swelling, as a blister.

put (pŏŏt) *v.* **put, put·ting, puts** *—tr.* **1.** To place in a specified location; set: *Where did I put my umbrella? She put the books on the table.* **2.** To cause to be in a given condition: *His friendly manner put me at ease.* **3.** To cause (someone) to undergo something; subject: *put a prisoner to death.* **4.** To assign; attribute: *He put a false interpretation on the events.* **5.** To estimate: *I put the time at 5:00.* **6.** To impose or levy: *put a tax on gasoline.* **7.** To wager (a stake); bet: *put $50 on a horse.* **8.** To hurl with an overhand pushing motion: *The athlete put the shot 30 feet.* **9.** To bring up for consideration: *I put a question to the teacher.* **10.** To express; state: *I put my opinions honestly.* **11.** To adapt: *put lyrics to music.* **12.** To apply: *We'll do all right if we put our minds to it.* *—intr.* To proceed. Used of ships: *The ship put into the harbor.* ❖ *adj.* Fixed; stationary: *Just stay put for a minute.* ◆ **put across** To state so as to be understood clearly or accepted readily: *I put across my ideas to the committee.* **put by** To save for later use: *We put by four quarts of stewed tomatoes.* **put down 1.** To write down. **2.** To end by force; repress: *put down a rebellion.* **3.** *Slang* To belittle; disparage: *Don't put down your teammates.* **4.** To attribute: *We put his bad mood down to a lack of sleep.* **5.** To kill (an animal) by euthanasia: *Our dog got so frail we finally had to put him down.* **put forth 1.** To grow: *The tree put forth leaves.* **2.** To bring to bear; exert: *put forth effort.* **3.** To offer for consideration: *put forth an idea.* **put forward** To propose for consideration: *put forward a new theory.* **put in 1.** To spend (time) at a location or job: *She put in four years with the armed services.* **2.** To plant: *We put in two rows of rhubarb this year.* **3.** To introduce into a conversation; say: *I'll put in a good word for you with your boss.* **put off 1.** To delay; postpone: *I put off taking the test until next week.* **2.** To repel or repulse, as from bad manners: *His harsh tone put me off.* **put on 1.** To clothe oneself with: *We put on evening clothes for dinner.* **2.** To apply; activate: *put on the brakes.* **3.** To assume (an expression, for example): *He put on an accent to amuse his friends.* **4.** *Slang* To tease or mislead (another): *You're putting me on!* **5.** To add: *put on weight.* **6.** To produce; perform: *put on a play.* **put (one's) finger on** To identify: *couldn't put her finger on the problem.* **put (one's) foot down** To take a firm stand: *I'm putting my foot down—you must be home by 9:00.* **put out 1.** To extinguish: *The firefighters arrived in time to put out the flames.* **2.** To inconvenience or offend: *I hope we're not putting you out by arriving on such short notice.* **3.** In baseball, to retire a runner. **put (someone) up to** To cause to commit a funny, mischievous, or malicious act: *I put her up to playing the practical joke.* **put up 1.** To erect; build. **2.** To provide (funds) in advance: *They put up money for the new show.* **3.** To provide lodgings for: *They agreed to put me up for the night.* **put up with** To endure without complaint. [From Middle English *putten*, from Old English *pȳtan*, to put out.]

put·down or **put-down** (pŏŏt′doun′) *n. Slang* A criticism, insult, or disparaging remark: *She interpreted his remarks as a putdown.*

Pu·tin (pōō′tn), **Vladimir** Born 1952. Russian politician who served as president (2000–2008) and prime minister (2008–2012) before being reelected to the presidency in 2012.

put-on (pŏŏt′ŏn′) *adj.* Feigned; pretended: *a put-on air of friendliness.* ❖ *n. Slang* Something intended to deceive, often as a joke.

pu·tre·fy (pyōō′trə-fī′) *intr. & tr.v.* **pu·tre·fied, pu·tre·fy·ing, pu·tre·fies** To decay or cause to decay and have a foul odor. **—pu′tre·fac′tion** (pyōō′trə-făk′shən) *n.*

pu·trid (pyōō′trĭd) *adj.* **1.** Decomposed and having a foul smell; rotten: *putrid meat.* **2.** Relating to, showing, or caused by putrefaction: *a putrid smell.*

putt (pŭt) *n.* A light golf stroke made on the green to get the ball into the hole. ❖ *v.* **putt·ed, putt·ing, putts** *—tr.* To hit (a golf ball) with such a stroke on the green. *—intr.* To putt a golf ball.

put·tee (pŭ-tē′ *or* pŭt′ē) *n.* often **puttees 1.** A strip of cloth wound spirally around the lower leg from the knee to the ankle. **2.** A gaiter covering the lower leg.

putt·er[1] (pŭt′ər) *n.* **1.** A short golf club used for putting. **2.** A golfer who is putting: *She's a good putter.*

put·ter[2] (pŭt′ər) *intr.v.* **put·tered, put·ter·ing, put·ters** To occupy oneself with minor or unimportant tasks: *puttering around in the garden.* [Probably alteration of *potter*, from Old English *potian*, to poke.] **—put′ter·er** *n.*

put·ty (pŭt′ē) *n., pl.* **put·ties** Any of several soft, moldable materials used especially to fill holes in woodwork or to secure panes of glass. ❖ *tr.v.* **put·tied, put·ty·ing, put·ties** To fill, cover, or fasten with putty.

puz·zle (pŭz′əl) *n.* **1.** Something, such as a game or problem, that requires careful thinking in order to be solved: *The difficult word puzzle took an hour to solve.* **2.** Something that confuses or perplexes; a mystery: *It's a puzzle to me how she can finish her homework so quickly.* ❖ *v.* **puz·zled, puz·zling, puz·zles** *—tr.* **1.** To baffle or confuse by presenting a difficult problem or matter. **2.** To clarify or solve (something confusing) by reasoning or study: *She puzzled out the algebra problem.* *—intr.* **1.** To be perplexed. **2.** To ponder over a problem in order to solve or understand it. **—puz′zler** *n.*

puz·zle·ment (pŭz′əl-mənt) *n.* The state of being confused or baffled.

PVT or **Pvt** *abbr.* An abbreviation of private.

Pyg·my also **Pig·my** (pĭg′mē) *n., pl.* **Pyg·mies** also **Pig·mies 1.** also **pygmy** A member of any of various African or Asian peoples having an average height of less than 5 feet (1.5 meters). **2. pygmy** An individual of unusually small size. ❖ *adj.* **1.** also **pygmy** Relating to the Pygmies. **2. pygmy** Much smaller than the usual or typical kind: *a pygmy hippopotamus.*

py·ja·mas (pə-jä′məz *or* pə-jăm′əz) *pl.n. Chiefly British* Variant of **pajamas.**

py·lon (pī′lŏn′) *n.* **1.** A movable, brightly colored cone or shaft of rubber that is used to signal something to be avoided, such as a hazard or work zone on a roadway.

2. *Football* A flexible, usually padded marker that stands upright at each corner of the end zone to make it easier to tell if a touchdown has been scored. **3.** A structure or tower that supports something, such as a tower supporting high-tension wires. **4.** A monumental gateway to an Egyptian temple, formed by a pair of flat-topped pyramids. [From Greek *pulōn*, gateway, from *pulē*, gate.]

py·lo·rus (pī-**lôr′**əs) *n., pl.* **py·lo·ri** (pī-**lôr′**ī′) The passage that connects the stomach to the small intestine.

Pyong·yang (**pyŭng′yäng′** *or* **pyŭng′yăng′**) The capital of North Korea, in the southwest-central part of the country. It became the capital in 1948.

py·or·rhe·a (pī′ə-**rē′**ə) *n.* An inflammation of the gums and tooth sockets that causes the teeth to become loose.

pyr·a·mid (**pĭr′**ə-mĭd) *n.* **1.** A solid geometric figure having a polygon as its base and triangular faces that meet at a common vertex. **2.** A massive ancient monument, as in Egypt, having a rectangular base and four triangular faces, usually rising to a single apex, and serving as a tomb or temple. **3.** An organization or system that has fewer elements in more important or more powerful positions than in lower ones: *the top people in the corporation's pyramid.* [From Greek *pūramis*.] **—py·ram′i·dal** (pĭ-**răm′**ĭ-dl) *adj.*

pyre (pīr) *n.* A pile of wood to be burned, especially when used to burn a corpse as part of a funeral rite.

Pyr·e·nees (**pîr′**ə-nēz′) A mountain range of southwest Europe extending along the French-Spanish border from the Bay of Biscay to the Mediterranean Sea. It rises to 11,168 feet (3,404 meters).

Py·rex (**pī′**rĕks′) A trademark for any of several types of glass that resist heat and chemicals.

pyr·i·dox·ine (pĭr′ĭ-**dŏk′**sēn *or* pĭr′ĭ-**dŏk′**sĭn) *n.* A vitamin of the B complex, found especially in grains, yeast, liver, and fish and acting in various parts of normal metabolism; vitamin B_6.

py·rim·i·dine (pī-**rĭm′**ĭ-dēn′) *n.* Any of a group of organic compounds having a single ring consisting of four carbon and two nitrogen atoms. Pyrimidines include important components of DNA and RNA.

py·rite (**pī′**rīt′) *n.* A yellow mineral composed of a sulfide of iron, used as an iron ore and in making sulfur dioxide.

py·ro·ma·ni·a (pī′rō-**mā′**nē-ə *or* pī′rō-**mān′**yə) *n.* The irresistible urge to start fires. [From Greek *pūr*, fire + Greek *maniā*, madness.] **—py′ro·ma′ni·ac′** *adj. & n.*

py·ro·tech·nic (pī′rə-**tĕk′**nĭk) *adj.* Relating to or resembling fireworks: *a pyrotechnic display.* **—py′ro·tech′ni·cal·ly** *adv.*

py·ro·tech·nics (pī′rə-**tĕk′**nĭks) *pl.n.* **1.** *(used with a singular verb)* The art of manufacturing or setting off fireworks. **2.** A fireworks display. **3.** A brilliant display: *The pyrotechnics of his speech awed the audience.*

Pyr·rhic victory (**pĭr′**ĭk) *n.* A victory that is achieved only at immense cost, as of lives or resources. [After *Pyrhhus* (319–272 BC), ancient king who defeated his enemies but had great losses.]

Py·thag·o·ras (pĭ-**thăg′**ər-əs) Flourished sixth century BC. Greek philosopher and mathematician. The Pythagorean theorem is attributed to him. **—Py·thag′o·re′an** (pĭ-thăg′ə-**rē′**ən) *adj. & n.*

Pythagorean theorem *n.* A theorem stating that the square of the length of the longest side of a right triangle is equal to the sum of the squares of the lengths of the other sides. [After *Pythagoras*.]

Pyth·i·as (**pĭth′**ē-əs) *n.* A legendary Greek man under sentence of death whose friend Damon was willing to die in his place.

py·thon (**pī′**thŏn′) *n.* Any of various very large nonvenomous snakes of Africa, Asia, and Australia that coil around and suffocate their prey. [From Latin *Pȳthōn*, mythical serpent killed by Apollo near Delphi.]

pylon

top: pylon supporting electric power transmission lines
bottom: main entrance to the Temple of Horus, Edfu, Egypt

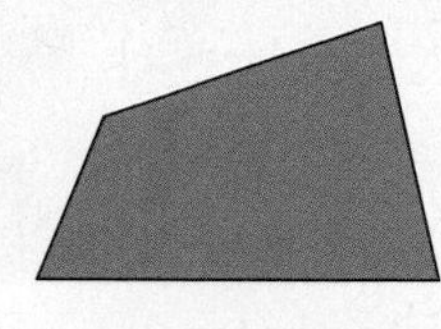

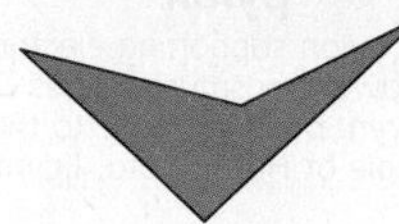

quadrilateral
two quadrilaterals

q or **Q** (kyo͞o) *n., pl.* **q's** or **Q's** also **qs** or **Qs** The 17th letter of the English alphabet.

q. *abbr.* An abbreviation of quart.

Qa·tar (**kä′**tər *or* **kŭt′**ər) A country of eastern Arabia on a peninsula in the southwest Persian Gulf. Doha is the capital.

QED *abbr.* An abbreviation of quod erat demonstrandum (which was to be demonstrated).

qt. or **qt** *abbr.* An abbreviation of quart.

quack[1] (kwăk) *n.* The sound made by a duck. ❖ *intr.v.* **quacked, quack·ing, quacks** To make such a sound. [From Middle English *quek*, of imitative origin.]

quack[2] (kwăk) *n.* **1.** An untrained person who pretends to be a physician and gives medical advice and treatment. **2.** A charlatan. ❖ *adj.* Relating to or characteristic of a quack: *a quack cure.* [Short for *quacksalver*, obsolete term for a charlatan, from Dutch.]

quack·er·y (**kwăk′**ə-rē) *n., pl.* **quack·er·ies** The practice of a quack.

quad (kwŏd) *n.* A quadrangle: *the campus quad.*

quadr– or **quadra–** Variants of **quadri–.**

quad·ran·gle (**kwŏd′**răng′gəl) *n.* **1.** A quadrilateral. **2a.** A rectangular area bordered on all sides by buildings. **b.** The buildings surrounding such an area.

quad·rant (**kwŏd′**rənt) *n.* **1a.** An arc equal to one quarter of the circumference of a circle; an arc of 90°. **b.** The region of a plane bounded by such an arc and the pair of radii that extend from its endpoints to the center of the circle of which it is a part. **c.** Any of four regions into which a plane is divided by the axes of a Cartesian coordinate system. **2.** An object, such as a machine part, shaped like a quarter of a circle. **3.** An instrument with an arc of 90°, used to measure angles, as between a celestial object and the horizon.

quad·rat·ic (kwŏ-**drăt′**ĭk) *adj.* Relating to or containing mathematical terms or expressions that are of the second degree and no higher.

quadratic equation *n.* An equation of the general form $ax^2 + bx + c = 0$, where x is the independent variable, a, b, and c are constants, and a is not equal to zero.

quad·ren·ni·al (kwŏ-**drĕn′**ē-əl) *adj.* **1.** Happening once in four years: *the quadrennial Olympic Games.* **2.** Lasting for four years. **—quad·ren′ni·al·ly** *adv.*

quadri– or **quadr–** or **quadra–** or **quadru–** *pref.* A prefix that means four: *quadrilateral.*

quad·ri·ceps (**kwŏd′**rĭ-sĕps′) *n.* The large four-part muscle at the front of the thigh that acts to extend the leg.

quad·ri·lat·er·al (kwŏd′rə-**lăt′**ər-əl) *n.* A polygon with four sides and four angles. **—quad·ri·lat′er·al** *adj.*

qua·drille (kwŏ-**drĭl′**) *n.* **1.** A square dance of French origin, performed by four couples. **2.** A piece of music written to accompany this dance.

quad·ril·lion (kwŏ-**drĭl′**yən) *n.* The number, written as 10^{15} or 1 followed by 15 zeros, that is equal to one thousand times one trillion. **—quad·ril′lionth** *n.*

quad·ri·ple·gia (kwŏd′rə-**plē′**jə) *n.* Paralysis of the body from the neck down, caused by damage to the spinal cord. **—quad′ri·ple′gic** *adj. & n.*

quadru– Variant of **quadri–.**

quad·ru·ped (**kwŏd′**rə-pĕd′) *n.* An animal having four feet, such as most reptiles and mammals.

quad·ru·ple (kwŏ-**dro͞o′**pəl *or* kwŏ-**drŭp′**əl) *adj.* **1.** Consisting of four parts or members. **2.** Four times as much in size, strength, number, or amount. ❖ *n.* A number or amount four times larger than another. ❖ *tr. & intr.v.* **quad·ru·pled, quad·ru·pling, quad·ru·ples** To multiply or be multiplied by four: *They promised to quadruple my salary. The town's population quadrupled in the 1900s.* [From Latin *quadruplus*, fourfold.]

quad·rup·let (kwŏ-**drŭp′**lĭt *or* kwŏ-**dro͞o′**plĭt) *n.* **1.** One of four offspring born in a single birth. **2.** A group or set of four of one kind.

quaff (kwŏf *or* kwăf) *tr. & intr.v.* **quaffed, quaff·ing, quaffs** To drink heartily: *quaffed the lemonade; quaffed from a spring.*

quag·mire (**kwăg′**mīr′ *or* **kwŏg′**mīr′) *n.* **1.** An area of land that is soft and muddy. **2.** An unpleasant situation that is difficult to get out of: *The peacekeeping mission turned into a quagmire.*

qua·hog (**kō′**hôg′ *or* **kwô′**hôg′ *or* **kwō′**hôg′) *n.* A clam of the Atlantic coast of North America, having a hard rounded shell and much used as food.

quail[1] (kwāl) *n., pl.* **quail** or **quails** Any of various small, plump, short-tailed birds having brownish feathers. [From Middle English, from Old French, quaille.]

quail[2] (kwāl) *intr.v.* **quailed, quail·ing, quails** To shrink back in fear; cower: *My dog looks ferocious, but he quails at the sight of a stranger.* [From Middle English *quailen*, to give way, break down, from Middle Dutch *quelen*, to suffer, be ill.]

quaint (kwānt) *adj.* **quaint·er, quaint·est** Charmingly odd, especially in an old-fashioned way: *a quaint village.* [From Middle English *queint*, clever, cunning, peculiar, from Latin *cognitus*, knowing, from *cognōscere*, to learn.] **—quaint′ly** *adv.* **—quaint′ness** *n.*

quake (kwāk) *intr.v.* **quaked, quak·ing, quakes 1.** To shake or vibrate, as from shock or lack of balance: *The ground quaked as the stampede passed.* **2.** To shiver or tremble, as from fear or cold: *His legs quaked with fear.* ❖ *n.* **1.** An instance of shaking or quivering: *a quake in one's voice.* **2.** An earthquake. [From Old English *cwacian.*]

Quak·er (**kwā′**kər) *n.* A member of the Society of Friends. **—Quak′er·ism** *n.*

qual·i·fi·ca·tion (kwŏl′ə-fĭ-**kā′**shən) *n.* **1.** The act of qualifying or the condition of being qualified: *Her qualification as a surgeon took years of hard work.* **2.** A skill or other quality that suits a person for a particular job or task: *What are the qualifications for an airline pilot?* **3.** A condition or circumstance that must be met or complied with: *He fulfilled the qualifications for registering to vote.*

ă	pat	ôr	core
ā	pay	oi	boy
âr	care	ou	out
ä	father	o͝o	took
ĕ	pet	o͝or	lure
ē	be	o͞o	boot
ĭ	pit	ŭ	cut
ī	bite	ûr	urge
îr	pier	th	thin
ŏ	pot	*th*	this
ō	toe	zh	vision
ô	paw	ə	about

4. A restriction or modification: *The group accepted the proposal without qualification.*

qual·i·fied (kwŏl′ə-fīd′) *adj.* **1.** Competent or meeting the requirements, as for a job: *a fully qualified doctor.* **2.** Limited; restricted: *an attitude of qualified optimism.* **—qual′i·fied′ly** (kwŏl′ə-fīd′lē *or* kwŏl′ə-fī′ĭd-lē) *adv.*

qual·i·fi·er (kwŏl′ə-fī′ər) *n.* **1.** A person or thing that qualifies. **2.** In grammar, a word or phrase that limits or modifies the meaning of another word or phrase; for example, an adjective is a qualifier of a noun.

qual·i·fy (kwŏl′ə-fī′) *v.* **qual·i·fied, qual·i·fy·ing, qual·i·fies** *—tr.* **1.** To make eligible or qualified, as for a position or task: *Her grades qualify her for the Honor Society.* **2.** To make less harsh or extreme; moderate: *He qualified his remarks to avoid offending anyone.* **3.** To limit the meaning of; modify: *Adjectives qualify other words.* *—intr.* To be or become qualified.

qual·i·ta·tive (kwŏl′ĭ-tā′tĭv) *adj.* Relating to quality, especially as distinguished from quantity or amount: *qualitative differences between the two bikers.* **—qual′i·ta′tive·ly** *adv.*

qualitative analysis *n.* A testing of a substance or mixture to find out what its chemical constituents are.

qual·i·ty (kwŏl′ĭ-tē) *n., pl.* **qual·i·ties 1.** A characteristic or property that distinguishes something: *the sour quality of vinegar.* **2.** A personal trait, especially a character trait: *He has many good qualities.* **3.** Excellence; superiority: *a store that sells only clothes of quality.* **4.** Degree or grade of excellence: *meat of poor quality.* ❖ *adj.* Having a high degree of excellence: *received quality healthcare.* [From Middle English *qualite*, from Latin *quālis*, of what kind.]

SYNONYMS quality, characteristic, property, attribute, feature, trait These nouns refer to what distinguishes or identifies a person or thing. **Quality** and **characteristic** are the most general: *The voice had a soft, musical quality. Name a common characteristic of mammals.* **Property** means a basic or essential quality possessed by all members of a group: *This experiment illustrates some properties of crystals.* **Attribute** and **feature** often mean a quality that a person or thing is given credit for having: *What are the attributes of a good leader? A catchy melody is one of the features of a successful song.* **Trait** means a single, clearly defined characteristic: *His jealous streak is a disturbing trait.*

---

qualm (kwŏm *or* kwôm) *n.* **1.** An uneasy feeling that an action may not be proper or right: *He had no qualms about telling lies.* **2.** A sudden disturbing feeling: *qualms of homesickness.* **3.** A sudden feeling of faintness, nausea, or sickness.

quan·da·ry (kwŏn′də-rē *or* kwŏn′drē) *n., pl.* **quan·da·ries** A condition of uncertainty or doubt; a dilemma: *in a quandary over what to do next.*

quan·ta (kwŏn′tə) *n.* Plural of **quantum.**

quan·ti·fy (kwŏn′tə-fī′) *tr.v.* **quan·ti·fied, quan·ti·fy·ing, quan·ti·fies** To determine or express the quantity of.

quan·ti·ta·tive (kwŏn′tĭ-tā′tĭv) *adj.* Relating to quantity, measurement, or number: *experiments that give quantitative proof of a theory.* **—quan′ti·ta′tive·ly** *adv.*

quantitative analysis *n.* A testing of a substance or mixture to find out the amounts and proportions of its chemical constituents.

quan·ti·ty (kwŏn′tĭ-tē) *n., pl.* **quan·ti·ties 1.** An amount or number: *The elements are found in nature in various quantities.* **2.** A considerable amount or number: *Pennsylvania was the first state to produce oil in quantity.* **3.** Something, such as a number or symbol that represents a number, on which a mathematical operation is performed. [From Middle English *quantite*, from Latin *quantus*, how great.]

quan·tum (kwŏn′təm) *n., pl.* **quan·ta** (kwŏn′tə) The smallest amount of a physical quantity that can exist on its own. A photon is a quantum of electromagnetic radiation.

quantum leap *n.* An abrupt, large increase, especially in knowledge: *The decoding of hieroglyphics led to a quantum leap in our understanding of ancient Egypt.*

quantum physics *n. (used with a singular verb)* The branch of physics that uses quantum theory to describe the properties of a physical system.

quantum theory *n.* A theory in physics based on the idea that matter behaves both as particles and as waves. According to this theory, radiant energy is transferred from one body to another in pulsations, each of which consists of a definite amount of energy called a quantum.

Qua·paw (kwô′pô) *n.* **1.** A member of a Native American people formerly living in Arkansas along the Arkansas River, now living in Oklahoma. **2.** The Siouan language of the Quapaw.

quar·an·tine (kwôr′ən-tēn′) *n.* **1a.** A period of time during which a person, animal, plant, or object thought to carry a contagious disease can be held at a port of entry and kept in isolation in an effort to prevent the disease from entering the country. **b.** A place where such people, animals, plants, or objects are held. **2.** An enforced confinement or isolation, especially one meant to keep a contagious disease from spreading. ❖ *tr.v.* **quar·an·tined, quar·an·tin·ing, quar·an·tines** To keep confined or isolated, especially as a way to keep a disease from spreading; place in quarantine. [From Old Italian *quarantina*, from *quaranta (giorni)*, forty (days), from Latin *quadrāgintā*.]

quark (kwôrk *or* kwärk) *n.* Any of a group of elementary particles supposed to be the basic units that combine in threes to make up protons and neutrons.

quar·rel (kwôr′əl) *n.* **1.** An angry argument or dispute. **2.** A reason for argument or dispute: *I have no quarrel with what you say.* ❖ *intr.v.* **quar·reled, quar·rel·ing, quar·rels** or **quar·relled, quar·rel·ling, quar·rels 1.** To engage in a quarrel; argue or dispute angrily: *The boys quarreled over the use of the tennis court.* **2.** To disagree or find fault: *quarrel with a court decision.* [From Middle English *querele*, from Latin *querēla*, complaint, from *querī*, to complain.] **—quar′rel·er, quar′rel·ler** *n.*

quar·rel·some (kwôr′əl-səm) *adj.* Tending to quarrel: *a quarrelsome family.* **—quar′rel·some·ness** *n.*

quar·ry¹ (kwôr′ē) *n., pl.* **quar·ries 1.** An animal hunted or chased. **2.** An object of pursuit. [From Middle English *quirre*, entrails of a deer given to hounds as a reward, from Latin *cor*, heart.]

quar·ry² (kwôr′ē) *n., pl.* **quar·ries** An open excavation from which stone is obtained by digging, cutting, or blasting. ❖ *tr.v.* **quar·ried, quar·ry·ing, quar·ries 1.** To obtain (stone) from a quarry. **2.** To make a quarry in: *quarry a mountain for its marble.* [From Middle English *quarre*, from Old French *quarriere*, from Latin *quadrum*, square.]

quart (kwôrt) *n.* **1.** A unit of volume or capacity used for measuring liquids, equal to two pints or 16 fluid ounces (about 0.95 liter). See table at **measurement. 2a.** A container having a capacity of one quart. **b.** The amount of a substance that can be held in such a container: *a quart of juice.*

quar·ter (kwôr′tər) *n.* **1.** One of four equal parts. **2.** A US or Canadian coin worth twenty-five cents. **3.** A period of fifteen minutes; one-fourth of an hour. **4a.** A period of three months; one-fourth of a year: *Sales picked up in the last quarter.* **b.** A school or college term lasting about three months. **5.** Any of four equal divisions of a lunar month marked by the phases of the moon. **6.** In

quail¹

quarry²
marble quarry in Carrara, Italy

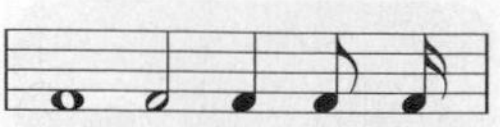

quarter note
left to right: whole, half, quarter, eighth, and sixteenth notes

quartz
cluster of amethyst crystals

quay
Venice, Italy

Queen Anne's lace

ă	pat	ôr	core
ā	pay	oi	boy
âr	care	ou	out
ä	father	o͝o	took
ĕ	pet	o͝or	lure
ē	be	o͞o	boot
ĭ	pit	ŭ	cut
ī	bite	ûr	urge
îr	pier	th	thin
ŏ	pot	*th*	this
ō	toe	zh	vision
ô	paw	ə	about

football and certain other sports, one of the four equal time periods that make up a game. **7.** One leg of a four-legged animal, including the adjacent parts: *a quarter of beef.* **8a.** One of the four main divisions of the horizon as outlined by the four major points of the compass. **b.** A region or place: *People came from every quarter.* **9.** A district or section, as of a city: *the Arab Quarter.* **10.** often **quarters** An assigned post or station, as on a ship: *a call to quarters.* **11. quarters** A place to which a person is assigned to sleep or reside: *the officers' quarters on a ship.* **12.** often **quarters** An unspecified person or group of persons: *Help arrived from unexpected quarters.* **13.** Mercy, especially when granted to a foe: *They gave no quarter to their enemies.* ❖ *adj.* **1.** Being one of four equal or equivalent parts: *received a quarter share of the inheritance.* **2.** Being equal to one-fourth of a particular unit of measure: *a quarter cup of flour.* ❖ *tr.v.* **quar·tered, quar·ter·ing, quar·ters 1.** To divide into four equal or equivalent parts: *Mother quartered an orange for us.* **2.** To furnish with housing: *The general quartered the troops in the town.* [From Middle English, from Latin *quārtārius*, from *quārtus*, fourth.]

quar·ter·back (**kwôr′**tər-băk′) *n.* In football, the offensive player behind the line of scrimmage who usually calls the signals for the plays and receives the ball when it is snapped.

quar·ter·deck (**kwôr′**tər-dĕk′) *n.* The after part of the upper deck of a ship, usually reserved for officers.

quar·ter·ly (**kwôr′**tər-lē) *adj.* Occurring or appearing at three-month intervals: *a quarterly magazine; a quarterly payment.* ❖ *n., pl.* **quar·ter·lies** A magazine published every three months. ❖ *adv.* In or by quarters: *receive dividends quarterly.*

quar·ter·mas·ter (**kwôr′**tər-măs′tər) *n.* **1.** A military officer responsible for the food, clothing, and equipment of troops. **2.** A petty officer responsible for the steering of a ship.

quarter note *n.* A musical note having one-fourth the time value of a whole note.

quarter rest *n.* A musical rest having one-fourth the time value of a whole rest.

quar·ter·staff (**kwôr′**tər-stăf′) *n., pl.* **quar·ter·staves** (**kwôr′**tər-stāvz′) A long wooden pole formerly used as a weapon.

quar·tet also **quar·tette** (kwôr-**tĕt′**) *n.* **1a.** A musical composition for four voices or four instruments. **b.** A group of four singers or four instrumentalists. **2.** A group of four people or things. [From French *quartette*, from Italian *quartetto*, from Latin *quārtus*, fourth.]

quar·to (**kwôr′**tō) *n., pl.* **quar·tos 1.** The page size obtained by folding a very large sheet of paper into four leaves. **2.** A book printed on pages of this size, about 12 inches (30 centimeters) high.

quartz (kwôrts) *n.* A hard transparent mineral composed of silicon dioxide; the most common of all minerals. It occurs as a component of rocks such as sandstone and granite, and separately in a variety of forms such as rock crystal, flint, and agate. Some crystalline forms, such as amethyst, are considered gemstones. [From German *Quarz*, of Slavic origin.]

quartz glass *n.* A type of glass made of pure silica. Quartz glass is highly transparent to ultraviolet light.

quartz·ite (**kwôrt′**sīt′) *n.* A metamorphic rock essentially made of quartz, formed by the heating and compressing of sandstone.

qua·sar (**kwā′**zär′ *or* **kwā′**sär′) *n.* An extremely distant, compact celestial object whose power output is several thousand times that of the entire Milky Way galaxy.

quash[1] (kwŏsh) *tr.v.* **quashed, quash·ing, quash·es** In law, to set aside or annul: *The judge quashed the indictment.* [From Middle English *quashen*, from Medieval Latin *quassāre*, from Latin *cassus*, empty, void.]

quash[2] (kwŏsh) *tr.v.* **quashed, quash·ing, quash·es** To put down or suppress by force: *quash a rebellion.* [From Middle English *quashen*, from Latin *quassāre*, to shatter.]

quasi– *pref.* A prefix that means resembling but not being: *quasi-science.*

Qua·ter·nar·y (**kwŏt′**ər-nĕr′ē *or* kwə-**tûr′**nə-rē) *n.* The second and last period of the Cenozoic Era, from about 2.6 million years ago to the present. Humans first appeared during the Quaternary. See table at **geologic time.** —**Qua′ter·nar′y** *adj.*

quat·rain (**kwŏt′**rān′ *or* kwŏ-**trān′**) *n.* A stanza of four lines in a poem.

qua·ver (**kwā′**vər) *intr.v.* **qua·vered, qua·ver·ing, qua·vers 1.** To shake, as from weakness; tremble; quiver. **2.** To speak in an unsteady or faltering voice. **3.** To produce a trill on a musical instrument or with the voice. ❖ *n.* **1.** A quavering sound. **2.** A trill that is sung or played on a musical instrument. —**qua′ver·y** *adj.*

quay (kē *or* kā) *n.* A wharf or reinforced bank where ships are loaded or unloaded. [From Middle English *keie*, from Old North French *cai*, of Celtic origin.]

quea·sy (**kwē′**zē) *adj.* **quea·si·er, quea·si·est 1.** Sick to one's stomach; nauseated. **2.** Easily nauseated. **3.** Causing nausea; sickening. **4.** Easily troubled or squeamish. —**quea′si·ly** *adv.* —**quea′si·ness** *n.*

Que·bec (kwĭ-**bĕk′**) or **Qué·bec** (kā-**bĕk′**) **1.** A province of eastern Canada east of Ontario. The region was claimed for France in 1663 and ceded to Great Britain in 1763. It joined the Canadian confederation in 1867. Quebec is the capital and Montreal the largest city. **2.** also **Quebec City** or **Québec City** The capital of Quebec, Canada, in the southern part of the province on the St. Lawrence River. A French colony was established here in 1608.

Que·chan (kĕch′ən *or* **kwŭt′**sän′) *n., pl.* **Quechan** or **Que·chans 1.** A member of a Native American people living along the lower Colorado River. **2.** The Yuman language of this people. [From Quechan *kʷaćán*, those who descended (from the sacred mountain of creation).]

Quech·ua (**kĕch′**wə) *n., pl.* **Quechua** or **Quech·uas 1.** A member of a South American Indian people originally having been part of the Inca Empire. **2.** The language of this people, now widely spoken from Colombia to Chile. —**Quech′uan** *adj.*

queen (kwēn) *n.* **1a.** A woman who rules a nation, usually inheriting her position for life. **b.** The wife or widow of a king. **2.** Something eminent or considered as the most outstanding in some way: *Paris is regarded as the queen of cities.* **3a.** A playing card bearing the figure of a queen. It ranks above a jack and below a king. **b.** The most powerful chess piece, able to move in any direction over any number of empty squares in a straight line. **4.** In a colony of bees, wasps, ants, or termites, a female that lays eggs. In most colonies there is only one queen, and the other females do not reproduce.

Queen Anne's lace *n.* A plant having feathery leaves and flat clusters of small white flowers. It is a wild form of the carrot.

queen·ly (**kwēn′**lē) *adj.* **queen·li·er, queen·li·est 1.** Having the status of a queen. **2.** Relating to or befitting a queen; majestic and regal. —**queen′li·ness** *n.*

queen mother *n.* A widowed queen who is the mother of the ruling monarch.

Queens (kwēnz) A borough of New York City in southeast New York on western Long Island. It was settled in 1635 and became part of New York City in 1898.

queer (kwîr) *adj.* **queer·er, queer·est 1.** Unusual; odd or unconventional: *a queer expression on his face.* **2.** Gay, lesbian, bisexual, or transgender. This term used to be used primarily as an insult, and some people still find it offensive. —**queer′ly** *adv.* —**queer′ness** *n.*

quell (kwĕl) *tr.v.* **quelled, quell·ing, quells 1.** To put down forcibly; suppress: *quell a revolt.* **2.** To allay; calm: *quell one's fears.*

quench (kwĕnch) *tr.v.* **quenched, quench·ing, quench·es 1.** To put out or extinguish (a fire, for example). **2.** To satisfy (thirst): *quenched his thirst with a can of soda.*

quer·u·lous (**kwĕr′**ə-ləs *or* **kwĕr′**yə-ləs) *adj.* **1.** Given to complaining or fretting; peevish: *a querulous person.* **2.** Expressing complaints or grievance; grumbling: *a querulous tone of voice.* **—quer′u·lous·ly** *adv.* **—quer′u·lous·ness** *n.*

que·ry (**kwîr′**ē) *n., pl.* **que·ries** A question; an inquiry. ❖ *tr.v.* **que·ried, que·ry·ing, que·ries 1.** To express doubt about; question: *querying the wisdom of his decision.* **2.** To ask questions of: *The police queried the suspect about her recent activities.* [From Latin *quaerere*, to ask, seek.]

que·sa·dil·la (kā′sə-**dē′**yə) *n.* A flour tortilla folded over a filling, then fried or toasted.

quest (kwĕst) *n.* **1.** A search, especially for something held valuable or precious: *Space exploration represents the latest quest for knowledge of the universe.* **2.** An expedition undertaken in medieval stories by a knight in order to find something or achieve a lofty purpose: *the quest for the Holy Grail.*

ques·tion (**kwĕs′**chən) *n.* **1.** A sentence, phrase, or gesture by which someone tries to get information through a reply. **2.** A subject or point open to debate; an unsettled issue: *Your point raises broad constitutional questions.* **3.** A subject that is being discussed or considered: *The chair called for a vote on the question of building a new library.* **4.** A difficult matter; a problem: *We all agree that building a new pool is only a question of money.* **5.** Uncertainty; doubt: *There is no question about his ability to do the job.* ❖ *tr.v.* **ques·tioned, ques·tion·ing, ques·tions 1.** To ask a question or questions of: *My dad questioned me about my thoughts on the election.* See Synonyms at **ask. 2.** To express doubt about; dispute: *No one questions her decisions.* ◆ **in question** Under consideration or discussion. **out of the question** Not to be considered; unthinkable or impossible. [From Middle English *questioun*, from Latin *quaestiō*, inquiry, from *quaerere*, to ask, seek.] **—ques′tion·er** *n.*

ques·tion·a·ble (**kwĕs′**chə-nə-bəl) *adj.* Open to doubt or suspicion; uncertain: *remedies of questionable value.* **—ques′tion·a·bly** *adv.*

question mark *n.* A punctuation mark (?) written at the end of a sentence or phrase to show that a question is being asked.

ques·tion·naire (kwĕs′chə-**nâr′**) *n.* A form with a series of questions, often used to gather statistical information or to sample public opinion on a certain subject.

quet·zal (kĕt-**säl′**) *n., pl.* **quetzals** or **quet·za·les** (kĕt-**sä′**lās) **1.** Any of several Central American birds having brilliant bronze-green and red feathers and in the male, long flowing tail feathers. **2.** The basic monetary unit of Guatemala.

Quet·zal·co·a·tl (kĕt-säl′kō-**ät′**l) *n.* A god of the Toltecs and Aztecs, represented as a plumed serpent.

queue (kyo͞o) *n.* **1.** A line of people awaiting their turn, as at a ticket window. **2.** A long braid of hair that hangs down the back; a pigtail. **3.** A sequence of stored data or programs waiting to be processed: *Three documents are in the printing queue.* ❖ *intr.v.* **queued, queu·ing, queues** To get in line; wait in a queue: *We'll have to queue up for tickets to the show.* [From Latin *cauda*, tail.]

❑ *These sound alike:* **queue, cue¹** (billiards stick), **cue²** (signal).

Que·zon City (**kā′**sôn′ *or* **kā′**sōn′) A city of the Philippines adjoining Manila. It was the capital of the Philippines from 1948 to 1976.

quib·ble (**kwĭb′**əl) *intr.v.* **quib·bled, quib·bling, quib·bles** To find fault or argue over for petty reasons: *quibble over details.* ❖ *n.* A minor criticism or irrelevant objection. **—quib′bler** *n.*

quiche (kēsh) *n.* A rich unsweetened custard pie often containing ingredients such as vegetables, cheese, or seafood.

quick (kwĭk) *adj.* **quick·er, quick·est 1.** Moving or acting with speed; fast: *quick on one's feet.* See Synonyms at **fast¹. 2.** Learning, thinking, or understanding with speed; bright: *a quick mind.* **3.** Perceiving or reacting with speed: *He was quick to sense that something was wrong.* **4.** Occurring or accomplished in a brief space of time: *a quick recovery.* ❖ *n.* **1.** The sensitive tender flesh under the fingernails. **2.** The most personal and sensitive aspect of the emotions: *a remark that cut me to the quick.* **3.** *(used with a plural verb)* Living people: *the quick and the dead.* ❖ *adv.* **quicker, quickest** Quickly; promptly: *Come quick!* [From Old English *cwic*, alive.] **—quick′ly** *adv.* **—quick′ness** *n.* —SEE NOTE.

quick bread *n.* A bread that is made with a leavening agent, such as baking powder, and may be baked as soon as the ingredients are mixed.

quick·en (**kwĭk′**ən) *v.* **quick·ened, quick·en·ing, quick·ens** —*tr.* **1.** To make more rapid; accelerate: *quicken one's steps.* **2.** To make keener, livelier, or more intense; stir: *Such stories quicken the imagination.* —*intr.* To become more rapid.

quick-freeze (**kwĭk′**frēz′) *tr.v.* **quick-froze** (**kwĭk′**-frōz′), **quick-fro·zen** (**kwĭk′**frō′zən), **quick-freez·ing, quick-freez·es** To freeze (food) quickly enough so that it keeps its natural flavor and nutritional value.

quick·lime (**kwĭk′**līm′) *n.* Calcium oxide; lime.

quick·sand (**kwĭk′**sănd′) *n.* Sand mixed with water, forming a soft shifting mass that yields easily to pressure and tends to engulf objects resting on its surface. [From Middle English *quyksond* : *quik*, living + *sand*, sand.] —SEE NOTE AT **quick.**

quick·sil·ver (**kwĭk′**sĭl′vər) *n.* The element mercury. [From Old English *cwic seolfor* : *cwic*, living + *seolfor*, silver.]

quick·step (**kwĭk′**stĕp′) *n.* A fast military march at the rate of 120 steps per minute.

quick-tem·pered (**kwĭk′**tĕm′pərd) *adj.* Easily angered.

quick-wit·ted (**kwĭk′**wĭt′ĭd) *adj.* Quick to think and act; mentally alert and sharp. See Synonyms at **intelligent.**

quid¹ (kwĭd) *n.* A piece of something to be chewed, as tobacco. [From Old English *cwidu*, cud.]

quid² (kwĭd) *n., pl.* **quid** or **quids** *Chiefly British* A pound sterling. [Possibly from Latin *quid*, something, what.]

qui·es·cent (kwē-**ĕs′**ənt *or* kwī-**ĕs′**ənt) *adj.* Inactive, quiet, or at rest. **—qui·es′cence** *n.*

qui·et (**kwī′**ĭt) *adj.* **qui·et·er, qui·et·est 1.** Making little or no noise; silent or almost silent: *quiet neighbors; a quiet engine.* **2.** Free of noise; hushed: *a quiet street.* **3.** Not moving; still; calm: *a quiet lake.* **4.** Tranquil; peaceful; serene: *a quiet place in the country.* **5.** Not showy or bright; subdued: *quiet colors.* **6.** Restrained in style; understated: *a quiet strength.* ❖ *n.* The quality or condition of being quiet: *the quiet of the forest in winter.* ❖ *tr. & intr.v.* **qui·et·ed, qui·et·ing, qui·ets** To make or become quiet: *The teacher quieted the class. The audience quieted down.* [From Middle English, from Latin *quiētus.*] **—qui′et·er** *n.* **—qui′et·ly** *adv.*

qui·e·tude (**kwī′**ĭ-to͞od′) *n.* Calm; tranquility.

quill (kwĭl) *n.* **1a.** A long stiff feather, usually from the tail or wing of a bird. **b.** The hollow stem of a feather. **2.** A writing pen made from a feather. **3.** One of the hollow spines of a porcupine or hedgehog.

quilt (kwĭlt) *n.* A bed covering made of two layers of cloth with a layer of batting in between, held together by decorative stitching. ❖ *v.* **quilt·ed, quilt·ing, quilts** —*tr.* To

quetzal

quiche

WORD HISTORY

quick When someone yells at you to "look alive," you know it means to "be quick." **Quick** comes from the Old English adjective *cwic* (pronounced kwĭk), which meant "alive." This sense is now obsolete except in the phrase *the quick and the dead*, which means "the living and the dead." It is also found in the word **quicksand,** which is sand that acts like it's alive. In Middle English the word *quik* developed the senses "lively, active, swift." A similar development took place in French. The French adverb *vite* means "quickly," and it comes from the Latin word *vītā*, meaning "with life." This is a form of the Latin noun *vīta*, "life," which is also the source of **vital** and **vitamin.**

quinoa
cooked quinoa

quoin

USAGE

quote The verb **quote** should be used when you are referring to the exact wording of a source: *In her speech, she quoted the proverb "A bird in the hand is worth two in the bush."* When you mention or summarize an original source, use cite: *He cited three books about architecture in his argument. To make her point, she cited the chapter in the novel in which the main character returns home.*

ă	pat	ôr	core
ā	pay	oi	boy
âr	care	ou	out
ä	father	o͝o	took
ĕ	pet	o͝or	lure
ē	be	o͞o	boot
ĭ	pit	ŭ	cut
ī	bite	ûr	urge
îr	pier	th	thin
ŏ	pot	*th*	this
ō	toe	zh	vision
ô	paw	ə	about

make into a quilt or construct like a quilt: *quilt a skirt.* —*intr.* To work on or make a quilt or quilts: *They quilt together once a week.* [From Middle English *quilte*, from Latin *culcita*, mattress.]

quilt·ing (**kwĭl′**tĭng) *n.* **1.** The process of doing quilted work. **2.** Material used to make quilts. **3.** Quilted material.

quince (kwĭns) *n.* **1.** A hard pleasant-smelling fruit similar to an apple, used chiefly for making jam or jelly. **2.** The tree that bears such fruit.

qui·nine (**kwī′**nīn′) *n.* A bitter-tasting, colorless drug derived from certain cinchona barks and used to treat malaria.

quinine water *n.* Tonic water.

qui·no·a (**kēn′**wä *or* kĭ-**nō′**ə) *n.* **1.** The small edible seeds of a plant that is native to the Andes Mountains. **2.** The plant that bears such seeds. [From Spanish *quinua, quínoa*, from Quechua *kinwa*.]

quin·tes·sence (kwĭn-**tĕs′**əns) *n.* **1.** The essence or basic element of a thing: *The quintessence of democracy is freedom of choice.* **2.** The purest or most typical example: *Her speech was the quintessence of clear thinking.*

quin·tet (kwĭn-**tĕt′**) *n.* **1a.** A musical composition for five voices or five instruments. **b.** A group of five singers or five instrumentalists. **2.** A group of five people or things. [Probably from Italian *quintetto*, from Latin *quīntus*, fifth.]

quin·tu·ple (kwĭn-**to͞o′**pəl *or* kwĭn-**tŭp′**əl) *adj.* **1.** Consisting of five parts or members. **2.** Five times as much in size, strength, number, or amount: *a quintuple increase.* ❖ *n.* A number or amount five times larger than another. ❖ *tr. & intr.v.* **quin·tu·pled, quin·tu·pling, quin·tu·ples** To multiply or be multiplied by five.

quin·tup·let (kwĭn-**tŭp′**lĭt) *n.* **1.** One of five offspring born in a single birth. **2.** A group or set of five of one kind.

quip (kwĭp) *n.* A clever or witty remark. ❖ *intr.v.* **quipped, quip·ping, quips** To make a quip or quips.

quire (kwīr) *n.* **1.** A unit consisting of 24 or sometimes 25 sheets of paper of the same size and stock; one twentieth of a ream. **2.** A collection of leaves of paper, folded one within the other, in a manuscript or book.
❑ *These sound alike:* **quire, choir** (singers).

quirk (kwûrk) *n.* **1.** A peculiarity of behavior: *Everyone has quirks.* **2.** An unpredictable event or act: *a quirk of fate.*

quirt (kwûrt) *n.* A riding whip with a short, stiff handle and a usually braided leather lash.

quis·ling (**kwĭz′**lĭng) *n.* A traitor who serves as the puppet of the enemy occupying his or her territory. [After Vidkun *Quisling* (1887–1945), head of Norway's government during the Nazi occupation (1940–1945).]

quit (kwĭt) *v.* **quit** or **quit·ted** (**kwĭt′**ĭd), **quit·ting, quits** —*tr.* **1.** To discontinue; stop; cease: *Quit bothering me!* See Synonyms at **stop. 2.** To give up; abandon or resign from: *quit one's job.* **3.** To exit (a computer application). **4.** To leave; depart from: *They decided to quit the city for the country.* —*intr.* **1.** To cease functioning or performing an action: *The motor quit when we were a few miles from home.* **2.** To give up, as in defeat. ◆ **call it quits** To give up dealing with something; abandon an activity, effort, or arrangement.

quit·claim (**kwĭt′**klām′) *n.* The transfer of a title or deed by a seller who does not make any warranty as to the legal right to the property.

quite (kwīt) *adv.* **1.** Completely; altogether: *I am not quite finished with that book.* **2.** Really; actually; truly: *I'm quite positive you're wrong.* **3.** Somewhat; rather: *We plan to leave quite soon.*

Qui·to (**kē′**tō) The capital of Ecuador, in the north-central part of the country. The city was captured by the Incas from its indigenous inhabitants in 1487 and held by the Spanish from 1534 until 1822.

quit·ter (**kwĭt′**ər) *n.* A person who gives up easily.

quiv·er¹ (**kwĭv′**ər) *intr.v.* **quiv·ered, quiv·er·ing, quiv·ers** To shake with a slight vibrating motion; tremble: *The dart quivered after it struck the board.* ❖ *n.* The act or motion of quivering. [From Middle English *quiveren*, perhaps from Old English *cwifer*, nimble.]

quiv·er² (**kwĭv′**ər) *n.* A case for holding and carrying arrows. [From Middle English, from Anglo-Norman *quiveir*, of Germanic origin.]

quix·ot·ic (kwĭk-**sŏt′**ĭk) *adj.* Idealistic but impractical: *a quixotic attempt to lower the voting age to twelve.* **—quix·ot′i·cal·ly** *adv.*

quiz (kwĭz) *n., pl.* **quiz·zes** A short oral or written test. ❖ *tr.v.* **quizzed, quiz·zing, quiz·zes 1.** To question (someone), especially closely or repeatedly. **2.** To test the knowledge of by asking questions: *quizzed the class on state capitals.* See Synonyms at **ask.**

quiz show *n.* A radio or television show in which contestants answer questions, usually for prizes.

quiz·zi·cal (**kwĭz′**ĭ-kəl) *adj.* Showing puzzlement; perplexed: *a quizzical look on his face.* **—quiz′zi·cal·ly** *adv.*

quoin (koin *or* kwoin) *n.* **1a.** An outside corner of a wall. **b.** A stone forming such a corner. **2.** A keystone.
❑ *These sound alike:* **quoin, coin** (money).

quoit (kwoit *or* koit) *n.* **1. quoits** *(used with a singular verb)* A game in which players try to toss rings around a peg. **2.** One of the rings used in this game.

quo·rum (**kwôr′**əm) *n.* The minimum number of members of a committee or organization that must be present for the valid transaction of business.

quo·ta (**kwō′**tə) *n.* **1.** An amount of something assigned, as to be done, made, or sold: *a machine shop's production quota.* **2a.** A number or percentage, especially of people, that represents an upper limit: *strict immigration quotas.* **b.** A number or percentage, especially of people, that represents a required or targeted minimum: *a system of quotas for hiring minority applicants.*

quot·a·ble (**kwō′**tə-bəl) *adj.* Suitable for or worthy of quoting. **—quot′a·bil′i·ty** *n.*

quo·ta·tion (kwō-**tā′**shən) *n.* **1.** The act of quoting: *These remarks are not for direct quotation.* **2.** A passage that is quoted: *a quotation from Shakespeare.* **3.** A statement of the price of a security or the price itself: *the latest stock market quotations.*

quotation mark *n.* Either of a pair of punctuation marks used to mark the beginning and end of a passage attributed to another person or repeated word for word. They appear in the form of double quotation marks (" ") and single quotation marks (' ').

quote (kwōt) *tr.v.* **quot·ed, quot·ing, quotes 1a.** To repeat or cite (a sentence, for example): *quote a familiar proverb.* **b.** To repeat a passage in or statement by: *quote the Bible; quote the mayor.* **2.** To cite or refer to for illustration or proof: *quoted statistics to show he was right.* **3.** To state (a price) for securities, goods, or services. ❖ *n.* **1.** *Informal* A quotation. **2.** A quotation mark. —SEE NOTE.

quoth (kwōth) *tr.v. Archaic* Said; spoke.

quo·tient (**kwō′**shənt) *n.* The number that results when one number is divided by another.

Qur·'an (kə-**răn′** *or* kə-**rän′**) *n.* Variant of **Koran.**

q.v. *abbr.* An abbreviation of quod vide (which see).

r^1 or **R** (är) *n., pl.* **r's** or **R's** also **rs** or **Rs** The 18th letter of the English alphabet.

r^2 *abbr.* An abbreviation of: **1.** radius. **2.** or **R** resistance.

R^1 A trademark for a movie rating that allows admission only to people of a certain age, usually 17 and older, unless accompanied by a parent or guardian.

R^2 *abbr.* An abbreviation of: **1.** Republican. **2.** right. **3.** roentgen. **4.** run (in baseball).

R. *abbr.* An abbreviation of: **1.** rabbi. **2.** rector. **3.** river.

Ra^1 (rä) *n.* In ancient Egyptian mythology, the sun god, the chief god represented as a man with the head of a falcon crowned with a solar disk and the sacred serpent.

Ra^2 The symbol for the element **radium.**

RA *abbr.* An abbreviation of residence assistant.

Ra·bat (rə-bät′) The capital of Morocco, on the Atlantic Ocean northeast of Casablanca. It was founded in the 1100s on the site of an earlier Muslim fortress.

rab·bi (răb′ī) *n., pl.* **rab·bis 1.** A person trained in Jewish law, ritual, and tradition, and ordained for leadership of a Jewish congregation. **2.** A scholar qualified to interpret Jewish law. [From Middle English *rabi*, from Hebrew *rabbī*, my master.]

rab·bin·i·cal (rə-bĭn′ĭ-kəl) *adj.* Made up of, related to, or characteristic of rabbis: *a rabbinical assembly.*

rab·bit (răb′ĭt) *n., pl.* **rab·bits** or **rabbit 1.** Any of various burrowing mammals having long ears, soft fur, and a short furry tail. **2.** The fur of such a mammal. [From Middle English *rabet*, young rabbit, from Middle Dutch *robbe*, rabbit.]

rabbit ears *pl.n. Informal* An indoor television antenna consisting of two adjustable rods connected to a base and swiveling apart at an angle.

rab·ble (răb′əl) *n.* **1.** A noisy unruly crowd or mob. **2.** The lowest or coarsest class of people.

rab·ble-rous·er (răb′əl-rou′zər) *n.* A leader or speaker who stirs up the emotions of the public; a demagogue.

rab·id (răb′ĭd) *adj.* **1.** Affected by or relating to rabies: *a rabid dog; a rabid bite.* **2.** Raging; uncontrollable: *rabid thirst.* **3.** Overzealous; fanatical: *a rabid baseball fan.* **—rab′id·ly** *adv.* **—rab′id·ness** *n.*

ra·bies (rā′bēz) *n.* An infectious viral disease that affects the central nervous system of mammals and is characterized by fever, agitation, and difficulty swallowing. It is transmitted by the bite of an infected animal and usually results in death if not treated. [From Latin *rabiēs*, rage.]

rac·coon (ră-ko͞on′) *n., pl.* **rac·coons** or **raccoon 1.** A North American mammal having grayish-brown fur, black face markings resembling a mask, and a bushy black-ringed tail. **2.** The fur of such a mammal. [Of Virginia Algonquian origin.]

race^1 (rās) *n.* **1.** A group of people considered to be distinct on the basis of physical characteristics that are transmitted genetically. Most biologists do not consider race to be a scientifically valid concept. **2.** A group of organisms that have similar genetically based characteristics and form a distinct type within a species or breed. [From Old Italian *razza*, race, lineage.]

race^2 (rās) *n.* **1a.** A contest of speed, as in running or riding: *a horse race.* **b. races** A series of such competitions: *go to the races.* **2.** An extended competition for supremacy: *the presidential race.* ❖ *v.* **raced, rac·ing, rac·es** *—intr.* **1.** To take part in a race. **2.** To rush at top speed; dash: *raced home.* *—tr.* **1.** To compete against in a race: *I'll race you to the house.* **2.** To enter into a race or races: *She races horses for a living.* **3.** To cause to run at high speed: *race an engine.* [From Middle English *ras*, from Old Norse *rās*, rush, running.]

race·course (rās′kôrs′) *n.* A course, such as a racetrack, laid out for racing.

race·horse (rās′hôrs′) *n.* A horse bred and trained for racing.

ra·ceme (rā-sēm′ *or* rə-sēm′) *n.* A flower cluster having stalked flowers arranged singly along a stem, as in the lily of the valley, with the flowers at the bottom opening first.

raceme

rac·er (rā′sər) *n.* **1.** A person, animal, or thing that races or takes part in a race. **2.** A vehicle used in racing. **3.** Any of various fast-moving North American snakes.

race·track (rās′trăk′) *n.* A usually oval, specially surfaced course on which races are held.

ra·cial (rā′shəl) *adj.* Relating to or based on race or races: *one's racial heritage; racial discrimination.* **—ra′cial·ly** *adv.*

racial profiling *n.* The use of suspicions based on race rather than on evidence by law enforcement officers dealing with a specific individual.

rac·ism (rā′sĭz′əm) *n.* **1.** The belief that race accounts for differences in human character or ability and that a particular race is superior to others. **2.** Discrimination or prejudice based on race. **—rac′ist** *adj. & n.*

rack^1 (răk) *n.* **1a.** A frame, stand, or bar in or on which to hang or display certain articles: *a coat rack; a magazine rack.* **b.** A triangular frame for arranging billiard balls at the start of a game. **2.** A metal bar having teeth that mesh with those of a pinion or gearwheel. **3.** An instrument of torture on which the victim's body was stretched. **4.** A pair of antlers. ❖ *tr.v.* **racked, rack·ing, racks 1.** To place (billiard balls, for example) in or on a rack. **2.** To cause great physical or mental suffering to: *Pain racked his body.* ◆ **rack up** *Informal* To accumulate or score: *rack up points.*

❑ *These sound alike:* **rack^1** (frame), **rack^2** (cut of meat), **wrack^1** (ruin), **wrack^2** (wreckage).

rack^1
top: rack of antlers
bottom: rack of billiard balls

rack^2 (răk) *n.* **1.** A rib cut of lamb or veal between the shoulder and the loin. **2.** The neck and upper spine of mutton, pork, or veal.

❑ *These sound alike:* **rack^2** (cut of meat), **rack^1** (frame), **wrack^1** (ruin), **wrack^2** (wreckage).

rack·et^1 also **rac·quet** (răk′ĭt) *n.* In sports, a device used to strike a ball or shuttlecock, consisting of an oval frame with tight interlaced strings and a handle. [From

SCIENCE

radioactivity Within the nuclei of "stable" atoms, such as those of lead, the force binding the protons and neutrons to each other individually is great enough to hold the nuclei together as a whole. In the nuclei of other atoms, especially of heavy ones such as uranium atoms, this energy is not great enough, and the nuclei are "unstable." An unstable nucleus gives off particles and energy in a process known as **radioactivity.** When enough particles and energy have been given off to create a new, stable nucleus (often the nucleus of an entirely different element), the radioactivity ceases. For example, uranium-238, a very unstable element, goes through 18 different stages of *radioactive decay* before finally turning into a stable isotope of lead—lead-206. All known elements with an atomic number greater than 83 (bismuth) are radioactive, and many isotopes of elements with lower atomic numbers are radioactive too.

ă	pat	ôr	core
ā	pay	oi	boy
âr	care	ou	out
ä	father	o͝o	took
ĕ	pet	o͝or	lure
ē	be	o͞o	boot
ĭ	pit	ŭ	cut
ī	bite	ûr	urge
îr	pier	th	thin
ŏ	pot	*th*	this
ō	toe	zh	vision
ô	paw	ə	about

Middle English *raket*, a kind of handball, from Old French *rachette*, palm of the hand, racket, from Arabic *rāḥat (al-yad)*, palm (of the hand).]

rack·et² (răk′ĭt) *n.* **1.** A loud unpleasant noise. See Synonyms at **noise. 2.** A dishonest business, especially one that obtains money through fraud or extortion. **3.** *Slang* A business or occupation.

rack·et·eer (răk′ĭ-tîr′) *n.* A person who runs or works in a criminal racket.

rac·quet (răk′ĭt) *n.* Variant of **racket¹.**

rac·quet·ball (răk′ĭt-bôl′) *n.* A game played on a four-walled court by two to four players with short rackets and a small rubber ball.

rac·y (rā′sē) *adj.* **rac·i·er, rac·i·est 1.** Slightly improper or indecent; risqué. **2.** Lively; sprightly. **—rac′i·ly** *adv.* **—rac′i·ness** *n.*

rad (răd) *n.* A unit used to measure energy absorbed by a material from radiation, equal to 100 ergs per gram of material. Many scientists now measure this energy in grays rather than in rads.

ra·dar (rā′där) *n.* **1.** A method of detecting distant objects and determining their position, speed, or other characteristics by causing radio waves to be reflected from them and analyzing the reflected waves. **2.** The equipment used in doing this. [From *ra(dio) d(etecting) a(nd) r(anging).*]

radi– *pref.* Variant of **radio–.**

ra·di·al (rā′dē-əl) *adj.* **1.** Relating to, arranged like, or directed along a radius or radii. **2.** Having parts that are arranged like radii: *the radial body of a starfish.* ❖ *n.* A radial tire. **—ra′di·al·ly** *adv.*

radial symmetry *n.* A pattern in which similar forms or features are regularly spaced around a central point.

radial tire *n.* A tire built around cords that lie approximately at right angles to the center of the tread.

ra·di·ance (rā′dē-əns) *n.* The quality or state of being radiant.

ra·di·ant (rā′dē-ənt) *adj.* **1.** Sending forth light, heat, or other radiation: *a radiant star.* **2.** Consisting of or transmitted as radiation: *radiant energy.* **3.** Filled with brightness; beaming: *a radiant smile.* **—ra′di·ant·ly** *adv.*

radiant energy *n.* Energy in the form of waves, especially electromagnetic waves. X-rays, radio waves, and visible light are all forms of radiant energy.

ra·di·ate (rā′dē-āt′) *v.* **ra·di·at·ed, ra·di·at·ing, ra·di·ates** *—intr.* **1.** To send out rays or waves. **2.** To be sent forth as radiation: *light that radiates from a star.* **3.** To extend in straight lines from a center. *—tr.* **1.** To send forth (heat, light, or other energy), especially in the form of waves. **2.** To exude; project: *radiate confidence.*

ra·di·a·tion (rā′dē-ā′shən) *n.* **1.** The act or process of radiating. **2a.** Energy in the form of electromagnetic waves or streams of particles, such as photons or electrons. Radiation is given off by nuclear reactions, as in fission, and by radioactive decay. **b.** The emission or movement of such energy through space or a medium, such as air. **3.** The use of such energy, especially x-rays, in medical diagnosis and treatment. —SEE NOTE AT **convection.**

ra·di·a·tor (rā′dē-ā′tər) *n.* **1a.** A heating device that circulates steam or hot water so as to radiate heat. **b.** A similar device that produces heat by means of an electric current. **2.** A cooling device, as in an automotive engine, through which water or other fluids circulate as a coolant.

rad·i·cal (răd′ĭ-kəl) *adj.* **1.** Going to a root or source; fundamental; thoroughgoing: *a radical reform of the tax code.* **2.** Departing markedly from the usual or customary: a radical new design. **3.** Advocating extreme or revolutionary changes, as in politics or government. ❖ *n.* **1.** A person who advocates fundamental or revolutionary changes. **2.** A root, such as $\sqrt{2}$, especially as indicated by a radical sign. **3.** An atom or a group of atoms with one unpaired electron. [From Middle English, of a root, from Latin *rādīx*, root.] **—rad′i·cal·ly** *adv.*

radical expression *n.* A mathematical expression or form in which radical signs appear.

rad·i·cal·ism (răd′ĭ-kə-lĭz′əm) *n.* The doctrines or practices of radicals.

radical sign *n.* The sign $\sqrt{}$ placed around a number, as in $\sqrt{9}$, to show that a root of the enclosed number is to be taken.

rad·i·cand (răd′ĭ-kănd′) *n.* The number or expression written under a radical sign, as 3 in $\sqrt{3}$ or $x - 5$ in $\sqrt{x-5}$.

ra·di·i (rā′dē-ī′) *n.* A plural of **radius.**

ra·di·o (rā′dē-ō) *n., pl.* **ra·di·os 1.** Electromagnetic waves having frequencies below 300 megahertz. **2a.** A device that generates such electromagnetic waves and alters them so that they carry an audio signal between points without using wires; a transmitter. **b.** A device that receives such waves and converts them back into sound waves; a receiver. **3.** The system or industry that uses radio signals to broadcast audio content, as for entertainment or news programs. **4.** The audio content created for or distributed by such a system. ❖ *tr.v.* **ra·di·oed, ra·di·o·ing, ra·di·os 1.** To send (messages) by radio. **2.** To signal or communicate with by radio.

radio– or **radi–** *pref.* A prefix that means radiation: *radiograph.*

ra·di·o·ac·tive (rā′dē-ō-ăk′tĭv) *adj.* Relating to or exhibiting radioactivity: *a radioactive element.*

radioactive decay *n.* The spontaneous transformation of a radioactive nucleus into a lighter, more stable nucleus, accompanied by the release of radiation in the form of alpha particles, beta particles, or gamma rays.

ra·di·o·ac·tiv·i·ty (rā′dē-ō-ăk-tĭv′ĭ-tē) *n.* **1.** The release of radiation by unstable atomic nuclei during radioactive decay or during a nuclear reaction such as fission. **2.** The radiation released in these processes. —SEE NOTE.

radio astronomy *n.* The branch of astronomy that deals with the study of objects in space by means of the radio waves that these objects emit.

radio beam *n.* A beam of radio signals transmitted by a beacon to guide aircraft or ships.

ra·di·o·car·bon (rā′dē-ō-kär′bən) *n.* A radioactive isotope of carbon, especially carbon-14.

radiocarbon dating *n.* A method of determining the age of organic remains based on the amount of carbon-14 in them. The carbon-14 in an organism at the time of its death decays at a steady rate, so the age of the remains can be calculated from the amount of carbon-14 that is left.

radio frequency *n.* A frequency within the range (3 hertz to 300 megahertz) at which radio waves are usually transmitted.

ra·di·o·gram (rā′dē-ō-grăm′) *n.* A message sent by wireless telegraphy.

ra·di·o·graph (rā′dē-ō-grăf′) *n.* An image produced, as on photographic film, by radiation other than visible light, especially by x-rays. ❖ *tr.v.* **ra·di·o·graphed, ra·di·o·graph·ing, ra·di·o·graphs** To make a radiograph of.

ra·di·o·i·so·tope (rā′dē-ō-ī′sə-tōp′) *n.* A radioactive isotope of a chemical element.

ra·di·ol·o·gy (rā′dē-ŏl′ə-jē) *n.* The branch of medicine that deals with the diagnosis and treatment of medical conditions through the use of images made using x-rays, ultrasonic waves, and other techniques. **—ra′di·ol′o·gist** *n.*

ra·di·om·e·ter (rā′dē-ŏm′ĭ-tər) *n.* **1.** A device used to detect and measure light and infrared radiation, consisting of a glass bulb containing a partial vacuum in which a set of vanes, each darkened on one side and shiny on the other, spin about a central axis when light strikes them. **2.** An instrument that detects electromagnetic radiation.

ra·di·o·phone (rā′dē-ō-fōn′) *n.* A radiotelephone.

ra·di·o·sonde (rā′dē-ō-sŏnd′) *n.* An instrument carried aloft, chiefly by balloon, to gather and transmit information about the weather.

ra·di·o·tel·e·phone (rā′dē-ō-**tĕl′**ə-fōn′) *n.* A telephone in which audible communication is established by radio.

radio telescope *n.* A very sensitive radio receiver, typically having an antenna fixed on a wide bowl-shaped reflector, used to detect radio waves coming from space.

radio wave *n.* An electromagnetic wave having a frequency in the range used for radio and radar.

rad·ish (răd′ĭsh) *n.* **1.** An edible, strong-tasting, red-skinned or white root, usually eaten raw. **2.** The plant that has such a root. [From Old English *rædic*, from Latin *rādīx*, root.]

ra·di·um (rā′dē-əm) *n. Symbol* **Ra** A rare, white, highly radioactive metallic element used in cancer treatment and scientific research. Atomic number 88. See **Periodic Table.** [From Latin *radius*, ray.]

ra·di·us (rā′dē-əs) *n., pl.* **ra·di·i** (rā′dē-ī′) or **ra·di·us·es 1a.** A line segment that joins the center of a circle with any point on its circumference. **b.** A line segment that joins the center of a sphere with any point on its surface. **2.** The length of such a line segment. **3.** A circular area measured by a given radius: *all houses within a radius of 50 miles.* **4a.** The shorter of the two bones of the human forearm, extending from the elbow to the thumb side of the wrist. **b.** The corresponding bone in the foreleg of other vertebrates.

ra·don (rā′dŏn) *n. Symbol* **Rn** A colorless, radioactive, chemically inert gaseous element produced by the radioactive decay of radium. Atomic number 86. See **Periodic Table.** [From *rad(ium)* + *-on*, inert gas.]

raf·fi·a (răf′ē-ə) *n.* **1.** A fiber obtained from the leaves of an African palm tree, used for baskets and mats. **2.** The tree that yields such fiber.

raf·fle (răf′əl) *n.* A lottery in which a number of people buy chances to win a prize. **—raf′fle** *v.*

raft[1] (răft) *n.* **1.** A floating platform made of planks, logs, or barrels and used for transport or by swimmers. **2.** A flatbottom inflatable craft for floating or drifting on water. ❖ *intr.v.* **raft·ed, raft·ing, rafts** To travel by raft: *rafted down the river.* [From Middle English, from Old Norse *raptr*, beam, rafter.]

raft[2] (răft) *n. Informal* A great number or amount. [Alteration of *raff*, English dialect term for rubbish.]

raft·er[1] (răf′tər) *n.* A person who travels by raft.

raf·ter[2] (răf′tər) *n.* One of the beams supporting a pitched roof. [From Old English *ræfter*, rafters, beams.]

rag[1] (răg) *n.* **1.** A scrap of cloth. **2. rags** Threadbare or tattered clothing. [From Middle English *ragge*, of Scandinavian origin.]

rag[2] (răg) *intr. & tr.v.* **ragged, rag·ging, rags** *Slang* **1.** To tease; taunt. **2.** To criticize or scold.

rag·a·muf·fin (răg′ə-mŭf′ĭn) *n.* A dirty child wearing tattered clothing.

rage (rāj) *n.* **1.** Violent anger or a fit of such anger: *flew into a rage.* See Synonyms at **anger. 2.** A fad or craze: *when torn jeans were the rage.* ❖ *intr.v.* **raged, rag·ing, rag·es 1.** To speak or act in violent anger. **2.** To move with great violence: *The storm raged outside.*

rag·ged (răg′ĭd) *adj.* **1.** Torn, frayed, or tattered: *ragged clothes.* **2.** Dressed in threadbare or tattered clothes: *a ragged scarecrow.* **3.** Jagged or uneven: *a ragged edge.* **4.** Imperfect; sloppy: *The actor gave a ragged performance.* ◆ **run (someone) ragged** To cause to be very tired or worn out; exhaust: *Their boss is a taskmaster who runs all the employees ragged.* **—rag′ged·ly** *adv.* **—rag′ged·ness** *n.*

rag·ged·y (răg′ĭ-dē) *adj.* **rag·ged·i·er, rag·ged·i·est** Worn-out or tattered; ragged.

rag·lan (răg′lən) *adj.* Having or being a sleeve that extends in one piece to the neckline of a garment. ❖ *n.* A garment with raglan sleeves. [After Fitzroy James Henry Somerset (1788–1855), First Baron *Raglan*, British field marshal.]

ra·gout (ră-**goo͞′**) *n.* A seasoned meat or fish and vegetable stew. [From French *ragoût*, from *ragoûter, ragouster*, to revive the taste.]

rag·tag (răg′tăg′) *adj.* **1.** Shaggy or unkempt; ragged. **2.** Disorderly and diverse in appearance and composition: *a ragtag gang.*

rag·time (răg′tīm′) *n.* An early form of jazz having a steady rhythm and a melody with many notes falling on the unaccented beats.

rag·weed (răg′wēd′) *n.* Any of various weedy plants having narrow clusters of small greenish flowers whose pollen is one of the chief causes of hay fever.

rah (rä) *interj.* An expression used to show approval or encouragement.

raid (rād) *n.* **1.** A sudden attack by a small armed force. **2.** A sudden and forcible entry into a place by police: *a raid on a gambling den.* ❖ *tr.v.* **raid·ed, raid·ing, raids 1.** To carry out a raid on. **2.** *Informal* To open or gain access to quickly or sneakily: *raided the refrigerator for a snack.* **—raid′er** *n.*

rail[1] (rāl) *n.* **1.** A horizontal bar supported at both ends or at close intervals, as in a fence. **2.** A fence or barrier made of such bars and supports. **3.** A steel bar used, usually as one of a pair, as a track for railroad cars or other wheeled vehicles. **4.** The railroad as a means of transportation: *travel by rail.* ❖ *tr.v.* **railed, rail·ing, rails** To enclose or supply with a rail or rails. [From Middle English *raile*, from Latin *rēgula*, straight piece of wood, ruler.]

rail[2] (rāl) *n.* Any of various brownish short-winged marsh birds. [From Middle English *rale*, from Old French *raale*.]

rail[3] (rāl) *intr.v.* **railed, rail·ing, rails** To object or criticize in bitter, harsh, or abusive language: *railed against the notion of creating another government bureaucracy.* [From Middle English *railen*, from Old Provençal *ralhar*, to chat, joke, from Late Latin *ragere*, to bray.]

rail fence *n.* A fence of split logs that are secured to stakes or laid across each other at an angle.

rail·ing (rā′lĭng) *n.* A structure having a raised rail that serves as a guard or barrier or as a handrail, as on a balcony or next to a staircase.

rail·road (rāl′rōd′) *n.* **1.** A road or path built of parallel steel rails supported by ties and used by trains and other wheeled vehicles. **2.** A system of railroad tracks, together with the stations, land, trains, and other related property under one management. ❖ *tr.v.* **rail·road·ed, rail·road·ing, rail·roads 1.** To force or rush (a person or thing) toward a particular goal or end: *Don't let them railroad you into doing more work. The committee railroaded the bill through the legislature.* **2.** To convict or punish (someone) without a fair hearing or on false evidence.

rail-split·ter (rāl′splĭt′ər) *n.* A person who splits logs, as for fences.

rail·way (rāl′wā′) *n.* **1.** A railroad, especially one operated over a limited area: *a commuter railway.* **2.** A track that acts as a pathway for equipment with wheels.

rai·ment (rā′mənt) *n.* Clothing.

rain (rān) *n.* **1a.** Water that condenses from vapor in the atmosphere and falls to the earth as drops. **b.** A fall of such water; a rainstorm or shower. **2. rains** A rainy season. **3.** A heavy or abundant fall or rush: *a rain of insults; a rain of arrows.* ❖ *v.* **rained, rain·ing, rains** —*intr.* **1.** To fall in drops from clouds: *the water that rained down on the roof.* **2.** To fall like rain: *Acorns*

radio telescope

raft[1]
whitewater rafting

raglan

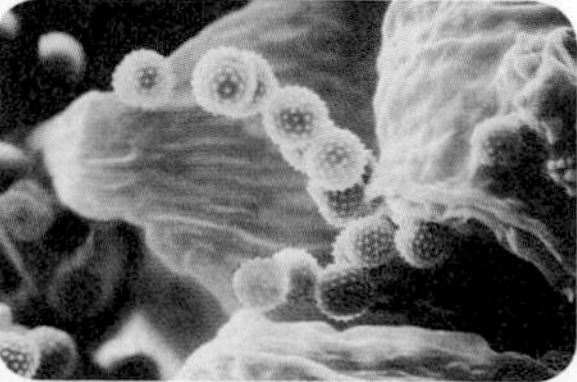
ragweed
ragweed plant *(top)* and pollen *(bottom)*

Ramesses II

rained from the oaks overhead. **3.** To release rain: *clouds that rain on the land.* —*tr.* **1.** To send down like rain: *rained balloons on the delegates at the convention.* **2.** To give or offer in great amounts: *rain gifts on someone.* ◆ **rain cats and dogs** *Informal* To rain very heavily. **rain out** To force the cancellation or postponement of (an outdoor event) because of rain: *The ball game was rained out.*

❑ *These sound alike:* **rain, reign** (rule), **rein** (strap).

rain·bow (rān′bō′) *n.* **1.** An arc-shaped spectrum of color seen in the sky opposite the sun, especially after rain, caused by the refraction of sunlight through droplets of water. The colors of the rainbow are red, orange, yellow, green, blue, indigo, and violet. **2.** A similar spectrum, as one seen in the mist of a waterfall.

rain check *n.* **1.** A ticket stub entitling the holder to admission to a future event if the scheduled event is canceled because of rain. **2.** An assurance to a customer that a sold-out sale item may be purchased later at the sale price. **3.** A promise that an unaccepted offer will be renewed in the future: *He declined our invitation to dinner but asked for a rain check.*

rain·coat (rān′kōt′) *n.* A waterproof or water-resistant coat.

rain date *n.* A second date that is scheduled for an outdoor event in case rain causes the cancellation of the first date.

rain·drop (rān′drŏp′) *n.* A drop of rain.

rain·fall (rān′fôl′) *n.* **1.** A fall of rain; a shower. **2.** The amount of water, measured in inches or other units of length, that falls over a given area during a given time in the form of rain, snow, hail, or sleet.

rain·for·est or **rain forest** (rān′fôr′ĭst) *n.* A dense evergreen forest with an annual rainfall of at least 160 inches (406 centimeters).

rain·storm (rān′stôrm′) *n.* A storm accompanied by rain.

rain·wa·ter (rān′wô′tər) *n.* Water that has fallen as rain.

rain·wear (rān′wâr′) *n.* Waterproof clothing.

rain·y (rā′nē) *adj.* **rain·i·er, rain·i·est** Characterized by, full of, or bringing rain: *a rainy afternoon; rainy weather.* **—rain′i·ness** *n.*

raise (rāz) *tr.v.* **raised, rais·ing, rais·es 1.** To move to a higher position; lift: *raise the window slightly.* **2a.** To set in an upright or erect position: *raise a flagpole.* **b.** To build; erect: *raise a barn.* **3.** To increase in size, quantity, or worth: *raise prices.* **4.** To increase in intensity, degree, strength, or pitch: *Don't raise your voice at me.* **5.** To grow or breed: *raise corn; raise livestock.* **6.** To bring up; rear: *raise children.* **7.** To accustom to something from an early age: *was raised on comic books and cartoons.* **8.** To put forward for consideration: *raise a question.* **9a.** To stir up; set in motion: *raise a fuss.* **b.** To bring about; provoke: *raise doubts.* **10.** To gather together; collect: *raise money.* ❖ *n.* An increase in wages or salary: *ask for a raise.* ◆ **raise to a power 1.** To indicate, as by an exponent, that a number or mathematical quantity is to be used a given number of times as a factor. **2a.** To calculate the value of (a number, such as 9^4, to which an exponent has been applied). **b.** To write (an algebraic expression affected by an exponent, such as $[a + b]^2$) in expanded form, such as $a^2 + 2ab + b^2$. **—rais′er** *n.*

❑ *These sound alike:* **raise, raze** (tear down).

rai·sin (rā′zĭn) *n.* **1.** A sweet dried grape. **2.** A deep brownish purple.

ra·ja or **ra·jah** (rä′jə) *n.* A prince, chief, or ruler in India or the East Indies.

rake¹ (rāk) *n.* A long-handled tool with teeth or prongs at one end, used especially to gather leaves or to loosen or smooth earth. ❖ *v.* **raked, rak·ing, rakes** —*tr.* **1.** To gather or smooth with a rake: *rake leaves; rake the lawn.* **2.** To gain in abundance: *The business suddenly began raking in the money.* **3.** To direct gunfire along the length of (a military position, for example). —*intr.* To use a rake. ◆ **rake up** To revive or bring to light; uncover: *raking up old gossip.* [From Old English *raca.*]

rake² (rāk) *n.* An immoral or dissolute man. [Short for *rakehell.*]

rake³ (rāk) *n.* Inclination from the perpendicular, as of a ship's mast.

rak·ish (rā′kĭsh) *adj.* **1.** Having a trim streamlined appearance, as a boat. **2.** Dashingly or sportingly stylish. **—rak′ish·ly** *adv.*

Ra·leigh (rô′lē *or* rä′lē) The capital of North Carolina, in the east-central part of the state northeast of Charlotte. It was selected as the capital in 1788.

ral·ly¹ (răl′ē) *v.* **ral·lied, ral·ly·ing, ral·lies** —*tr.* **1.** To call together for a common purpose: *trying to rally supporters at a demonstration.* **2.** To reassemble and restore to order: *The general rallied the troops.* **3.** To rouse or revive from inactivity or decline: *The coach will rally the team's confidence.* —*intr.* **1.** To come together for a common purpose. **2.** To recover abruptly from a setback or disadvantage: *The team rallied in the last inning to win the game.* **3.** To show a sudden improvement in health or spirits: *The patient rallied after four days of fever.* **4.** In sports, to exchange several strokes before a point is won, as in tennis. ❖ *n., pl.* **ral·lies 1.** A gathering, especially one intended to inspire enthusiasm for a cause: *a political rally.* **2.** An abrupt recovery from a setback or disadvantage. **3.** A sudden improvement in health or spirits. **4.** A rise in stock market prices and trading volume after a decline. **5.** In sports: **a.** An exchange of several strokes before a point is won, as in tennis. **b.** An automobile race that takes place on public roads. [From Old French *ralier,* to ally, bring together.]

ral·ly² (răl′ē) *v.* **ral·lied, ral·ly·ing, ral·lies** —*tr.* To tease good-humoredly. —*intr.* To engage in good-humored teasing or jesting. [From Old French *railler.*] **—ral′li·er** *n.*

ram (răm) *n.* **1.** A male sheep. **2.** A battering ram. ❖ *tr.v.* **rammed, ram·ming, rams 1.** To strike or drive against with a heavy impact: *The ship rammed an iceberg.* **2.** To force into a narrow space; jam: *rammed the clothes into a suitcase.* **3.** To force passage or acceptance of: *legislators who rammed a bill through Congress.*

RAM (răm) *n.* The main memory of a computer, in which data can be accessed by the central processing unit in any order without having to go through other data first. [From *r(andom-)a(ccess) m(emory).*]

Ram·a·dan (răm′ə-**dän′** *or* **răm′**ə-dän′) *n.* The ninth month of the Islamic year, observed with fasting from sunrise to sunset.

ram·ble (răm′bəl) *intr.v.* **ram·bled, ram·bling, ram·bles 1.** To wander aimlessly; stroll or roam: *The children rambled in the woods.* See Synonyms at **wander. 2.** To follow an irregularly winding course of motion or growth: *The brook rambled through the countryside.* **3.** To speak or write at length, often wandering off the subject: *He rambled on about his recent trip.* ❖ *n.* A leisurely stroll: *an early morning ramble.*

ram·bler (răm′blər) *n.* **1.** A person or thing that rambles. **2.** A climbing rose having many small flowers.

ram·bling (răm′blĭng) *adj.* **1.** Often or habitually roaming: *a rambling herd of buffalo.* **2.** Extending over an irregular area; sprawling: *a rambling estate.* **3.** Lengthy and tending to wander off the subject: *a rambling speech.*

ram·bunc·tious (răm-**bŭngk′**shəs) *adj.* Boisterous and disorderly.

ra·men (rä′mən) *n.* **1.** A Japanese dish of noodles in broth. **2.** A thin white noodle served in this dish.

Ram·es·ses II or **Ram·e·ses II** (răm′ĭ-sēz′) also **Ram·ses II** (răm′sēz′) Known as "Ramesses the Great." 14th–13th century BC. King of Egypt (1304–1237 BC) whose

ă	pat	ôr	core
ā	pay	oi	boy
âr	care	ou	out
ä	father	ŏŏ	took
ĕ	pet	ŏŏr	lure
ē	be	ōō	boot
ĭ	pit	ŭ	cut
ī	bite	ûr	urge
îr	pier	th	thin
ŏ	pot	*th*	this
ō	toe	zh	vision
ô	paw	ə	about

reign was marked by the building of numerous monuments.

ram·i·fi·ca·tion (răm′ə-fĭ-**kā′**shən) *n.* **1.** A resulting development; a consequence. **2.** The act or process of branching out. **3.** A branch or an arrangement of branching parts extending from a main body.

ram·i·fy (**răm′**ə-fī′) *intr. & tr.v.* **ram·i·fied, ram·i·fy·ing, ram·i·fies** To extend or cause to extend in branches or divisions; branch out or cause to branch out. [From Middle English *ramifien*, from Latin *rāmus*, branch.]

ramp (rămp) *n.* **1.** A sloping passage or roadway that leads from one level to another. **2.** A movable stairway used for entering and leaving an airplane. ◆ **ramp up** To increase gradually: *ramped up production at the factory.*

ram·page (**răm′**pāj′) *n.* A course of violent, frenzied behavior or action. ❖ *intr.v.* (*also* răm-**pāj′**) **ram·paged, ram·pag·ing, ram·pag·es** To move about wildly or violently; rage: *a mob rampaging through the streets.*

ram·pant (**răm′**pənt) *adj.* **1.** Growing or extending unchecked: *a rampant growth of weeds; rampant corruption in the city government.* **2.** Rearing up on the hind legs or on a hind leg, especially with the forelegs raised: *a rampant lion on a coat of arms.* **—ram′pant·ly** *adv.*

ram·part (**răm′**pärt′) *n.* **1.** A wall or bank raised around a fort, city, or other area for protection against attack. **2.** A means of protection or defense; a bulwark.

ram·rod (**răm′**rŏd′) *n.* **1.** A rod used to force the charge into the muzzle of a gun. **2.** A rod used to clean the barrel of a gun.

ram·shack·le (**răm′**shăk′əl) *adj.* So poorly made or maintained that disintegration is likely; rickety.

ran (răn) *v.* Past tense of **run.**

ranch (rănch) *n.* **1.** A large farm, especially in the western United States, on which large herds of cattle, sheep, or horses are raised. **2.** A large farm on which a particular crop or kind of animal is raised. ❖ *intr.v.* **ranched, ranch·ing, ranch·es** To work on or manage a ranch. [From Spanish *rancho*, small farm, ultimately from Old French *renc, reng*, row, line, of Germanic origin.]

ranch·er (**răn′**chər) *n.* A person who owns or manages a ranch.

ran·che·ro (răn-**chârʹ**ō) *n., pl.* **ran·che·ros** A rancher, especially in the southwest United States.

ranch house *n.* **1.** The house of a rancher. **2.** A one-story house with a low-pitched roof.

ran·cid (**răn′**sĭd) *adj.* **1.** Having the unpleasant smell or taste of decomposed oils or fats: *rancid butter.* **2.** Repulsive; nasty: *rancid remarks.*

ran·cor (**răng′**kər) *n.* Bitter resentment; deep-seated ill will. **—ran′cor·ous** *adj.* **—ran′cor·ous·ly** *adv.*

rand (rănd *or* ränd) *n.* The basic monetary unit of South Africa.

R & B *abbr.* An abbreviation of rhythm and blues.

R & D *abbr.* An abbreviation of research and development.

ran·dom (**răn′**dəm) *adj.* Having no specific pattern, purpose, or objective: *random noise; random movements.* ◆ **at random** Without a method or purpose; unsystematically: *Choose a card at random from the deck.* **—ran′dom·ness** *n.*

ran·dom-ac·cess memory (**răn′**dəm-**ăk′**sĕs) *n.* RAM.

ra·nee (**rä′**nē) *n.* Variant of **rani.**

rang (răng) *v.* Past tense of **ring[2].**

range (rānj) *n.* **1a.** A number or grouping of things in the same category or within specified limits: *a business offering a range of services.* **b.** An extent or amount of variation: *a wide price range.* **c.** The extent or sphere of an activity: *a matter outside the range of my responsibility.* **2.** The set of values that the dependent variable of a mathematical function can take. **3a.** The maximum or effective distance limiting operation, as of a sound, radio signal, or missile: *a radio receiver with a range of 200 miles.* **b.** The maximum distance that a ship, aircraft, or other vehicle can travel before using up its fuel. **c.** The distance between a projectile missile and its target. **4a.** A place for shooting guns at targets. **b.** A place where golf shots can be practiced. **c.** A testing area in which rockets and missiles are fired and flown. **5a.** The geographic area in which a kind of animal, plant, or other organism normally lives or grows. **b.** A large expanse of open land on which livestock wander and graze. **c.** A row or chain of mountains. **6.** A stove with spaces for cooking a number of things at the same time: *an electric range.* ❖ *intr.v.* **ranged, rang·ing, rang·es 1.** To vary between specified limits: *children whose ages ranged from four to ten.* **2.** To move through, along, or around in an area or region: *Raiders ranged up and down the coast.* **3.** To extend in a certain direction: *a ridge ranging westward from the peak.* [From Middle English *raunge*, row, rank, from Old French *rang, reng*, line, of Germanic origin.]

rang·er (**rān′**jər) *n.* **1.** A warden who maintains and protects a natural area, such as a forest. **2.** A member of an armed troop employed to patrol a specific region. **3.** A wanderer.

Ran·goon (răn-**go͞on′** *or* răng-**go͞on′**) See **Yangon.**

rang·y (**rān′**jē) *adj.* **rang·i·er, rang·i·est** Having long slender limbs: *a tall rangy young man.*

ra·ni also **ra·nee** (**rä′**nē) *n., pl.* **ra·nis** also **ra·nees 1.** The wife of a raja. **2.** A princess or queen in India or the East Indies.

rank[1] (răngk) *n.* **1.** A relative position or degree of value in a graded group: *in the top rank of his class.* **2.** A relative position in a society. **3.** An official position or grade: *an adviser with cabinet rank.* **4.** A row or line, especially of people or things side by side: *The soldiers formed ranks for inspection.* **5. ranks a.** The armed forces. **b.** Personnel, especially enlisted military personnel. **6.** A body of people classed together; numbers: *joined the ranks of factory workers.* ❖ *v.* **ranked, rank·ing, ranks** *—tr.* **1.** To place in a row or rows. **2.** To give a particular order or position to; classify: *ranked the children according to age.* *—intr.* To hold a certain rank: *ranked eighth in the class.* ◆ **pull rank** To use one's superior rank to gain an advantage. [From Middle English *rank*, line, row, from Old French *renc*, of Germanic origin.]

rank[2] (răngk) *adj.* **rank·er, rank·est 1.** Growing thickly or excessively: *rank weeds.* **2.** Strong and unpleasant in odor or taste: *a rank cigar.* **3.** Complete; absolute: *a rank amateur.* [From Old English *ranc*, strong, overbearing.] **—rank′ness** *n.*

rank and file *n.* **1.** The enlisted troops of an army. **2.** The ordinary members of a group, organization, or society, in contrast to the leaders and officers.

Ran·kin (**răng′**kĭn), **Jeannette** 1880–1973. American reformer and politician who was the first woman US representative (1917–1919 and 1941–1943).

rank·ing (**răng′**kĭng) *adj.* Of the highest rank; preeminent: *the ranking officer.* ❖ *n.* **1. rankings** A list of items in a group, such as schools or sports teams, ranked according to a rating system or a record of performance: *Our school's football team is at the bottom of the rankings.* **2.** A position in such a list: *This tennis player has a high ranking.*

ran·kle (**răng′**kəl) *v.* **ran·kled, ran·kling, ran·kles** *—intr.* To cause persistent irritation or resentment. *—tr.* To embitter; irritate: *His boasting rankles me.*

ran·sack (**răn′**săk′) *tr.v.* **ran·sacked, ran·sack·ing, ran·sacks 1.** To search thoroughly: *ransack a drawer.* **2.** To rob of valuables and leave in disarray; pillage. **—ran′sack′er** *n.*

ran·som (**răn′**səm) *n.* **1.** The release of property or a person in return for payment of a demanded price. **2.** The price or payment demanded. ❖ *tr.v.* **ran·somed,**

rampant

ranch house

Jeannette Rankin

raspberry

ratline

ă	pat	ôr	core
ā	pay	oi	boy
âr	care	ou	out
ä	father	o͝o	took
ĕ	pet	o͝or	lure
ē	be	o͞o	boot
ĭ	pit	ŭ	cut
ī	bite	ûr	urge
îr	pier	th	thin
ŏ	pot	*th*	this
ō	toe	zh	vision
ô	paw	ə	about

ran·som·ing, ran·soms 1. To obtain the release of by paying a certain price: *The king ransomed his captured knights after the battle.* 2. To release after receiving such a payment. [From Middle English *raunsoun*, from Latin *redēmptiō*, a buying back.]

rant (rănt) *intr.v.* **rant·ed, rant·ing, rants** To speak or write in an angry or violent manner: *The property owner ranted against high taxes.* ❖ *n.* A loud, violent, or extravagant speech or piece of writing. **—rant′er** *n.*

rap[1] (răp) *tr.v.* **rapped, rap·ping, raps 1.** To hit sharply and swiftly; strike: *rapped the table with his fist.* **2.** To utter sharply: *rap out a complaint.* **3.** To criticize or blame. ❖ *n.* **1.** A quick light blow or knock. **2.** A knocking or tapping sound. **3.** *Slang* A reprimand; a rebuke. **4.** *Slang* A prison sentence. ◆ **take the rap** *Slang* To accept punishment or take the blame for an offense or error. [From Middle English *rappen*, possibly of imitative origin.] **—rap′per** *n.*

❑ *These sound alike:* **rap**[1] (knock), **rap**[2] (talk), **wrap** (envelop).

rap[2] (răp) *n.* **1.** A form of popular music developed especially in urban African-American communities and characterized by spoken or chanted rhyming lyrics with a strong rhythmic accompaniment. **2.** *Slang* A talk, discussion, or conversation. ❖ *intr.v.* **rap·ped, rap·ping, raps 1.** To perform rap. **2.** To discuss freely and at length: *rapped about issues affecting teenagers.* [Possibly from *rap*, to strike.] **—rap′per** *n.*

❑ *These sound alike:* **rap**[2] (talk), **rap**[1] (knock), **wrap** (envelop).

ra·pa·cious (rə-pā′shəs) *adj.* **1.** Having or showing a great desire to acquire money or possess things; greedy. **2.** Living by killing prey, especially in large numbers: *rapacious coyotes.* **3.** Taking by force; plundering: *rapacious pirates.* **—ra·pa′cious·ly** *adv.* **—ra·pa′cious·ness, ra·pac′i·ty** (rə-păs′ĭ-tē) *n.*

rape[1] (rāp) *n.* **1.** The crime of forcing a person to have sexual intercourse or of having sexual intercourse with a person who is unable to give consent. **2.** Destruction or damaging treatment of a place: *the rape of the country by invaders.* ❖ *tr.v.* **raped, rap·ing, rapes 1.** To force (a person) to have sexual intercourse, or to have sexual intercourse with a person who is unable to give consent. **2.** To destroy or severely damage (a place): *feared that the mining companies would rape the land.* [From Middle English, from Latin *rapere*, to seize.]

rape[2] (rāp) *n.* A plant having small seeds used as a source of oil and animal feed. Certain varieties of rape yield canola oil. [From Middle English, from Latin *rāpum*, turnip.]

Raph·a·el (răf′ē-əl *or* rä′fē-ĕl′) Originally Raffaelo Sanzio. 1483–1520. Italian Renaissance painter whose works include religious subjects, portraits, and frescoes.

rap·id (răp′ĭd) *adj.* **rap·id·er, rap·id·est** Fast; swift: *rapid progress; walking with rapid strides.* See Synonyms at **fast**[1]. ❖ *n.* often **rapids** An extremely fast-moving part of a river, caused by a steep descent in the riverbed: *went over the rapids in a kayak.* **—ra·pid′i·ty** (rə-pĭd′ĭ-tē), **rap′id·ness** *n.* **—rap′id·ly** *adv.*

rapid eye movement *n.* REM.

rap·id-fire (răp′ĭd-fīr′) *adj.* **1.** Designed to fire shots in rapid succession. **2.** Marked by continuous rapid occurrence: *rapid-fire questions.*

ra·pi·er (rā′pē-ər) *n.* A light sword with a sharp point, used for thrusting.

rap·ine (răp′ĭn) *n.* The seizure of property by force; plunder.

rap·ist (rā′pĭst) *n.* A person who commits rape.

rap·port (ră-pôr′) *n.* A relationship of mutual trust and understanding.

rap·scal·lion (răp-skăl′yən) *n.* A rascal.

rapt (răpt) *adj.* **1.** Deeply moved or delighted; enchanted: *The children were listening with rapt admiration.* **2.** Deeply absorbed; preoccupied: *The painter stood at her easel, rapt in thought.*

❑ *These sound alike:* **rapt, wrapt** (enveloped).

rap·tor (răp′tər) *n.* A bird of prey, such as a hawk, eagle, or owl.

rap·ture (răp′chər) *n.* **1.** The state of being overpowered by an intense, usually joyful emotion; ecstasy. **2.** In Christianity, the sudden taking of people into the air to meet Jesus at the Second Coming. **—rap′tur·ous** *adj.*

rare[1] (râr) *adj.* **rar·er, rar·est 1.** Occurring infrequently; uncommon: *a rare disease.* **2.** Excellent; extraordinary: *a rare sense of honor.* **3.** Thin in density: *rare gases in the earth's upper atmosphere.* [From Middle English, from Latin *rārus*.] **—rare′ness** *n.*

rare[2] (râr) *adj.* **rar·er, rar·est** Cooked for just a short time so as to keep juice and redness: *rare meat.* [From Old English *hrēr*.] **—rare′ness** *n.*

rare·bit (râr′bĭt) *n.* Welsh rabbit.

rare earth *n.* **1.** An oxide of a rare-earth element. **2.** A rare-earth element.

rare-earth element (râr′ûrth′) *n.* A lanthanide.

rar·e·fy (râr′ə-fī′) *v.* **rar·e·fied, rar·e·fy·ing, rar·e·fies** —*tr.* **1.** To make thin, less compact, or less dense: *High altitudes that rarefy the air.* **2.** To purify or refine. —*intr.* To become thin, less compact, or less dense. **—rar′e·fi′a·ble** *adj.*

rare·ly (râr′lē) *adv.* Infrequently; seldom. —SEE NOTE AT **hardly.**

rar·i·ty (râr′ĭ-tē) *n., pl.* **rar·i·ties 1.** The quality or condition of being rare; infrequency of occurrence: *the rarity of four-leaf clovers.* **2.** Something that is rare: *Snow is a rarity in Florida.*

ras·cal (răs′kəl) *n.* **1.** A person who is playfully mischievous. **2.** A dishonest person; a scoundrel.

ras·cal·i·ty (răs-kăl′ĭ-tē) *n., pl.* **ras·cal·i·ties 1.** The behavior or character typical of a rascal. **2.** A mean or mischievous act.

rash[1] (răsh) *adj.* **rash·er, rash·est** Too bold or hasty; reckless: *I soon regretted my rash decision.* [From Middle English, active, unrestrained.] **—rash′ly** *adv.* **—rash′ness** *n.*

rash[2] (răsh) *n.* **1.** An outbreak of usually red bumps, blotches, or blisters on the skin, sometimes accompanied by itching or pain. **2.** An occurrence that happens many times within a brief period: *a rash of burglaries in the building.* [Possibly from Old French *raschier*, to scrape, scratch.]

rash·er (răsh′ər) *n.* **1.** A thin slice of fried or broiled bacon. **2.** A dish or an order of thin slices of fried or broiled bacon.

rash·guard also **rash guard** (răsh′gärd′) *n.* A tight-fitting stretchable shirt worn especially by surfers to protect the upper body from abrasion, as from rubbing against a surfboard.

rasp (răsp) *n.* **1.** A coarse file with sharp raised points on its surface. **2.** A harsh grating sound. ❖ *v.* **rasped, rasp·ing, rasps** —*tr.* **1.** To scrape or file using a rasp. **2.** To utter in a grating voice. **3.** To grate on (nerves or feelings). —*intr.* **1.** To make a harsh grating sound. **2.** To scrape harshly; grate.

rasp·ber·ry (răz′bĕr′ē) *n.* **1a.** A sweet, red, many-seeded fruit that grows on any of various prickly plants having long woody stems. **b.** A plant that bears such fruits. **2.** *Slang* A jeering sound made by vibrating the tongue between the lips while exhaling.

rasp·y (răs′pē) *adj.* **rasp·i·er, rasp·i·est** Grating; rough: *a raspy voice.*

Ras·ta·far·i·an (răs′tə-fâr′ē-ən) *n.* A person who believes in Rastafarianism. ❖ *adj.* Relating to Rastafarianism or Rastafarians.

Ras·ta·far·i·an·ism (räs′tə-fâr′ē-ə-nĭz′əm) *n.* A religious and political movement originating in Jamaica in the 1930s that regards Ethiopia as the Promised Land and former Ethiopian emperor Haile Selassie as savior.

rat (răt) *n.* **1.** Any of various long-tailed rodents that resemble mice but are larger. **2.** *Informal* A despicable person, especially one who informs on associates. **3.** *Slang* A person who frequently passes time at a particular place: *a mall rat; a rink rat.* ❖ *intr.v.* **rat·ted, rat·ting, rats 1.** To hunt for or catch rats. **2.** *Slang* To betray one's associates by giving information; squeal: *After the corrupt city councilman was arrested, he ratted on other councilmen involved in the scam.* [From Old English *ræt.*] **—rat′ter** *n.*

ratch·et (răch′ĭt) *n.* **1.** A mechanism made up of a pawl or hinged catch that fits into the sloping teeth of a wheel or bar, allowing motion in one direction only. **2.** The pawl, wheel, or bar on such a mechanism.

rate (rāt) *n.* **1.** A quantity measured with respect to another measured quantity. For example, the distance that is or could be traveled during a given unit of time is called a rate of speed. **2.** A measure of a part with respect to a whole; a proportion: *a national unemployment rate of 4.8 percent.* **3.** The cost or price charged per unit of a commodity or service: *postal rates.* **4.** A charge or payment calculated in relation to a particular sum or quantity: *a bank account that earns high interest rates.* ❖ *v.* **rat·ed, rat·ing, rates** *—tr.* **1.** To place in a particular grade or rank: *The teacher rated her third in her class.* **2.** To calculate the value of; appraise: *The jeweler rated the quality of the gems.* **3.** To regard or account: *The critic rated the movie excellent.* **4.** *Informal* To merit or deserve: *a restaurant that rates four stars.* *—intr.* To hold a certain rank; be valued or placed in a certain class: *This movie rates as the best of the year.* ◆ **at any rate** Whatever the case may be; in any case: *You should at any rate apologize.*

rate of exchange *n., pl.* **rates of exchange** The ratio at which the unit of currency of one country may be exchanged for that of another country.

rath·er (răth′ər) *adv.* **1.** Preferably; more willingly: *I'd rather stay home tonight.* **2.** More exactly; more accurately: *He's my friend, or rather he was.* **3.** To a certain extent; somewhat: *feeling rather sleepy.* **4.** On the contrary: *The photograph did not show the whole family, but rather only the cousins.*

rat·i·fy (răt′ə-fī′) *tr.v.* **rat·i·fied, rat·i·fy·ing, rat·i·fies** To give formal approval to; confirm: *ratify an amendment to the Constitution.* **—rat′i·fi·ca′tion** (răt′ə-fĭ-kā′shən) *n.*

rat·ing (rā′tĭng) *n.* **1.** A classification assigned according to quality, performance, skill, or specialty: *beef marked with a "choice" rating.* **2.** An evaluation of the financial status of a person or business: *a high credit rating.* **3.** A specified value, as of performance or capacity: *the insulation rating of the shingles.* **4.** An estimate of the popularity of a television or radio program, made by polling selected members of the audience.

ra·tio (rā′shō *or* rā′shē-ō′) *n., pl.* **ra·tios 1.** Relation in degree or number between two similar things. **2.** A relationship between two quantities, equivalent to the quotient of the two values. For example, if a box contains six apples and four oranges, the ratio of apples to oranges is 6 to 4, which can also be written 6:4 or 6/4 or as the decimal 1.5. [From Latin *ratiō*, calculation, from *rērī*, to reckon, consider.]

ra·tion (răsh′ən *or* rā′shən) *n.* **1.** A fixed amount, especially of food, allotted periodically: *a horse's daily ration of oats.* **2. rations** Food issued or available to members of a group: *a soldier's rations.* ❖ *tr.v.* **ra·tioned, ra·tion·ing, ra·tions 1.** To give or make available in fixed limited amounts, as during a period of scarcity: *A drought made it necessary to ration water.* See Synonyms at **distribute. 2.** To supply with allotments of food; give rations to.

ra·tion·al (răsh′ə-nəl) *adj.* **1.** Having or using the ability to reason. **2.** Consistent with or based on reason; logical: *rational behavior.* **3.** Relating to a rational number. **—ra′tion·al′i·ty** (răsh′ə-năl′ĭ-tē) *n.* **—ra′tion·al·ly** *adv.*

ra·tion·ale (răsh′ə-năl′) *n.* The fundamental reason; the basis.

ra·tion·al·ism (răsh′ə-nə-lĭz′əm) *n.* The theory that reason, rather than experience, authority, or spiritual revelation, provides the main basis for knowledge. **—ra′tion·al·ist** *n.*

ra·tion·al·ize (răsh′ə-nə-līz′) *v.* **ra·tion·al·ized, ra·tion·al·iz·ing, ra·tion·al·iz·es** *—tr.* **1.** To make rational or logical: *Attempts to rationalize spelling have failed.* **2.** To make up reasons or excuses for (one's behavior) in order to avoid responsibility or blame, usually without realizing that one is doing so. *—intr.* **1.** To think rationally. **2.** To rationalize one's behavior: *He always rationalizes instead of accepting criticism.* **—ra′tion·al·i·za′tion** (răsh′ə-nə-lĭ-zā′shən) *n.*

rational number *n.* A number that can be expressed as an integer or a quotient of integers, excluding zero as the denominator. For example, 2, 5, and −½ are rational numbers.

rat·line (răt′lĭn) *n.* Any of the small ropes fastened horizontally to the shrouds of a ship and forming a ladder for going aloft.

rat race *n.* An activity or routine that is stressful, tiring, and often competitive: *The lawyer decided to quit the rat race and move to the countryside.*

rat·tan (ră-tăn′) *n.* **1.** The stems of any of various climbing tropical palms, used to make furniture, baskets, and canes. **2.** Any of the palms that have such stems.

rat·ter (răt′ər) *n.* A dog or cat that catches or kills rats.

rat·tle (răt′l) *v.* **rat·tled, rat·tling, rat·tles** *—intr.* **1a.** To make a quick succession of short sharp sounds: *so frightened that his teeth rattled.* **b.** To move with such sounds: *The old train rattled along the track.* **2.** To talk rapidly and at length, usually without much thought: *rattled on about his relatives.* *—tr.* **1.** To shake noisily: *rattled the coins in her pocket.* **2.** To utter or perform rapidly or effortlessly: *rattle off a list of names.* **3.** *Informal* To disturb the composure or confidence of; unnerve. ❖ *n.* **1.** A quick succession of short sharp sounds: *the rattle of the rain on the roof.* **2.** A device that rattles when shaken: *a baby's rattle.* **3.** The series of dry horny rings at the end of a rattlesnake's tail that make a rattling sound when shaken.

rat·tler (răt′lər) *n.* **1.** A person or thing that rattles. **2.** A rattlesnake.

rat·tle·snake (răt′l-snāk′) *n.* Any of various venomous American snakes having at the end of the tail several dry horny rings that can be shaken rapidly to make a rattling sound.

rat·trap (răt′trăp′) *n.* **1.** A device for trapping rats. **2.** *Informal* A dwelling that is unsanitary or in great need of repair.

rat·ty (răt′ē) *adj.* **rat·ti·er, rat·ti·est 1.** Relating to or characteristic of rats. **2.** Infested with rats. **3.** Shabby or shoddy; in need of repair: *The kitchen looked ratty.*

rau·cous (rô′kəs) *adj.* **1.** Rough-sounding and harsh: *the crow's raucous cries.* **2.** Boisterous and disorderly: *a raucous party.* **—rau′cous·ly** *adv.*

raun·chy (rôn′chē *or* rän′chē) *adj.* **raun·chi·er, raun·chi·est** *Informal* **1.** Obscene, lewd, or vulgar: *isn't allowed to watch raunchy movies.* **2.** Grimy; unkempt.

rav·age (răv′ĭj) *tr.v.* **rav·aged, rav·ag·ing, rav·ag·es** To bring heavy destruction upon; devastate: *A hurricane ravaged the coast.* ❖ *n.* **1.** The act of ravaging; heavy destruction. **2. ravages** Severe damage; havoc: *the ravages of smallpox.* **—rav′ag·er** *n.*

rattan

rattlesnake

WORD BUILDING

re– The primary meaning of the prefix **re–**, which comes from Latin, is "again." *Re–* combines chiefly with verbs, as in *rearrange, recall, remake,* and *rewrite*. The prefix has been used with this meaning extensively in English since the 1600s. Sometimes it is necessary to use a hyphen with *re–* to distinguish between pairs such as *recollect* (rĕk′ə **lĕkt′**) and *re-collect* (rē′kə-**lĕkt′**) or *recreation* (rĕk′rē-**ā′**shən) and *re-creation* (rē′krē-**ā′**shən). A hyphen may also be used when *re–* precedes a word beginning with e, as in *re-enact* and *re-enter.*

rave (rāv) *intr.v.* **raved, rav·ing, raves 1.** To speak wildly without making any sense: *The delirious patient was ranting and raving all night long.* **2.** To speak with wild enthusiasm or praise: *raving about her new skis.* ❖ *n.* **1.** The act or an instance of raving. **2.** *Informal* An opinion, description, or review full of enthusiastic praise. **3.** An all-night dance party, usually featuring electronically synthesized music. ❖ *adj. Informal* Relating to or being an extravagantly enthusiastic review or opinion: *rave reviews.* [From Middle English *raven*, from Old North French *resver*, to dream, wander, rave.]

rav·el (răv′əl) *tr. & intr.v.* **rav·eled, rav·el·ing, rav·els** also **rav·elled, rav·el·ling, rav·els** To separate or become separated into single loose threads; fray: *Unhappy with her work, she raveled the edge of the sweater. The rug raveled where it was worn.* ❖ *n.* A broken or discarded thread.

ra·ven (rā′vən) *n.* A large black bird that resembles a large crow and has a deep croaking cry. ❖ *adj.* Black and shiny: *has dark eyes and raven hair.* [From Old English *hrǣfn*.]

rav·en·ing (răv′ə-nĭng) *adj.* Greedily seeking, seizing, and eating prey: *ravening wolves.*

rav·en·ous (răv′ə-nəs) *adj.* **1.** Greedily eager for food; extremely hungry: *a ravenous appetite.* **2.** Greedy for gratification: *ravenous for power.* **—rav′en·ous·ly** *adv.*

ra·vine (rə-vēn′) *n.* A deep narrow valley or gorge in the earth's surface made by running water.

rav·ing (rā′vĭng) *adj.* **1.** Talking or behaving irrationally; wild. **2.** Worthy of admiration: *a raving beauty.* ❖ *n.* Wild irrational speech.

rav·i·o·li (răv′ē-ō′lē) *n., pl.* **ravioli** or **rav·i·o·lis 1.** A small casing of pasta with any of various fillings, such as chopped meat or cheese. **2.** A dish made with ravioli.

rav·ish (răv′ĭsh) *tr.v.* **rav·ished, rav·ish·ing, rav·ish·es 1.** To rape. **2.** To overwhelm with emotion; enrapture. **3.** *Archaic* To seize and take by force. **—rav′ish·er** *n.* **—rav′ish·ment** *n.*

rav·ish·ing (răv′ĭ-shĭng) *adj.* Extremely attractive; entrancing: *a ravishing beauty.* **—rav′ish·ing·ly** *adv.*

raw (rô) *adj.* **raw·er, raw·est 1.** Uncooked: *raw meat.* **2a.** In a natural condition; not processed or refined: *raw wool.* **b.** Not finished, covered, treated, or coated: *furniture sanded down to raw wood.* **3.** Untrained and inexperienced: *raw recruits.* **4.** Badly irritated; sore: *a raw open wound.* **5.** Powerfully impressive; stark: *raw talent.* **6.** Unpleasantly damp and chilly: *raw weather.* ◆ **in the raw 1.** In a crude or unrefined state. **2.** Nude; naked. [From Old English *hrēaw*.]

raw·boned (rô′bōnd′) *adj.* Having a lean gaunt frame with prominent bones.

raw deal *n.* A transaction that is not fair or beneficial: *You got a raw deal when you paid so much for that lousy guitar.*

raw·hide (rô′hīd′) *n.* **1.** The hide of cattle or other animals before it has been tanned. **2.** A whip or rope made of such hide.

raw material *n.* **1.** An unprocessed natural product used in manufacturing. **2.** Something that is used as the basis for making something else: *These surveys are the raw material for my analysis.*

ray[1] (rā) *n.* **1.** A thin line or narrow beam of light or other radiation. **2.** A small amount; a trace: *a ray of hope.* **3.** A line or part extending from a point. **4.** A small flower having a single long, narrow lobe, such as one of those surrounding the dense disk-shaped central flower cluster of a daisy or sunflower. [From Middle English *rai*, from Latin *radius*.]

❑ *These sound alike:* **ray**[1] (beam), **ray**[2] (fish), **re**[1] (musical tone).

ray[2] (rā) *n.* Any of various ocean fishes having a horizontally flattened body, often with the fins forming extensions resembling wings, and a long narrow tail. [From Middle English *rai*, from Latin *raia*.]

❑ *These sound alike:* **ray**[2] (fish), **ray**[1] (beam), **re**[1] (musical tone).

ray·on (rā′ŏn) *n.* **1.** Any of several types of synthetic fibers made from cellulose. **2.** Fabric made from such fibers.

raze (rāz) *tr.v.* **razed, raz·ing, raz·es** To destroy or tear down completely; level: *razed old tenements.* See Synonyms at **destroy.**

❑ *These sound alike:* **raze, raise** (lift up).

ra·zor (rā′zər) *n.* **1.** An instrument with a sharp blade or set of blades, used primarily for shaving the face or other body parts. **2.** A device for holding a razorblade, with guards to prevent cutting the skin. **3.** An electric instrument with vibrating or rotating blades used for shaving. ❖ *tr.v.* **ra·zored, ra·zor·ing, ra·zors** To shave, cut, or remove with or as with a razor.

ra·zor·blade (rā′zər-blād′) *n.* A thin, rectangular piece of steel having at least one sharp edge for use in a razor.

razz (răz) *Slang tr.v.* **razzed, razz·ing, razz·es** To ridicule; heckle.

Rb The symbol for the element **rubidium.**

RBI *abbr.* An abbreviation of runs batted in.

RC *abbr.* An abbreviation of: **1.** Red Cross. **2.** Roman Catholic.

RD *abbr.* An abbreviation of rural delivery.

Rd. *abbr.* An abbreviation of road.

RDA *abbr.* An abbreviation of recommended daily allowance.

re[1] (rā) *n.* In music, the second tone of a major scale. [From Middle English, from Medieval Latin.]

❑ *These sound alike:* **re**[1] (musical tone), **ray**[1] (beam), **ray**[2] (fish).

re[2] (rē) *prep.* Concerning; in reference to. [From Latin *rē*, a form of *rēs*, thing.]

Re The symbol for the element **rhenium.**

re– *pref.* A prefix that means: **1.** Again; anew: *reassemble.* **2.** Back; backward: *react.* —SEE NOTE.

reach (rēch) *v.* **reached, reach·ing, reach·es** *—tr.* **1.** To stretch out or put forth (a body part); extend: *reached out an arm.* **2.** To touch or grasp by stretching out: *couldn't reach the shelf.* **3.** To arrive at: *reached our destination.* **4.** To go or extend as far as; get to: *The property reaches the shore.* **5.** To succeed in communicating with; get in touch with: *reached the fire department in time to save the building.* **6.** To succeed in achieving; accomplish or produce by effort: *reach a conclusion.* *—intr.* **1.** To extend or move a hand, arm, or other body part, especially when trying to touch or grasp something: *reach for a glass.* **2.** To extend in space or time: *a coat that reached to the knee; a career that reached over several decades.* ❖ *n.* **1.** The act or an instance of stretching or thrusting out: *The frog seized the butterfly with a sudden reach of its tongue.* **2.** The distance or extent to which something can reach: *the radio station's reach.* **3.** The range of a person's understanding; comprehension: *a subject beyond their reach.* [From Old English *rǣcan*.]

SYNONYMS reach, achieve, attain, gain These verbs mean to succeed in arriving at a goal or objective. **Reach** is the most general term: *After hours of debate, they finally reached a decision.* **Achieve** suggests reaching by applying one's skill or initiative: *Through their pioneering research, the team of chemists achieved international fame.* **Attain** often means to reach because of the force of one's ambitions: *After years of law school, she attained her goal of becoming a lawyer.* **Gain** suggests making considerable effort to overcome obstacles: *Slowly the new management gained the workers' confidence.*

re·act (rē-ăkt′) *intr.v.* **re·act·ed, re·act·ing, re·acts 1.** To

ă	pat	ôr	core
ā	pay	oi	boy
âr	care	ou	out
ä	father	o͝o	took
ĕ	pet	o͝or	lure
ē	be	o͞o	boot
ĭ	pit	ŭ	cut
ī	bite	ûr	urge
îr	pier	th	thin
ŏ	pot	*th*	this
ō	toe	zh	vision
ô	paw	ə	about

act in response to a stimulus or prompting: *The iris of the eye reacts to bright light.* **2.** To act in opposition to a former condition or act: *musicians who reacted against formal theory.* **3.** To undergo a reaction. —SEE NOTE.

re·ac·tant (rē-ăk′tənt) *n.* A substance participating in a chemical reaction, especially a directly reacting substance present at the start of the reaction.

re·ac·tion (rē-ăk′shən) *n.* **1.** An action or feeling that is a response to a situation or event: *The crowd's reaction to each speech was thunderous applause.* **2.** An action that results directly from or counteracts another action, especially the change in a body's motion as a result of a force applied to it. **3.** A nuclear reaction. **4a.** The process or condition of taking part in a chemical change. **b.** A chemical change. **5.** A response in an organism or in a specific tissue or organ, as to a drug or other substance. **6. reactions** The ability to respond to new or changing events or influences: *To play video games well, you have to have quick reactions.*

re·ac·tion·ar·y (rē-ăk′shə-nĕr′ē) *adj.* Opposing progress or reform; extremely conservative: *a reactionary politician.* ❖ *n., pl.* **re·ac·tion·ar·ies** An extreme conservative.

re·ac·ti·vate (rē-ăk′tə-vāt′) *tr.v.* **re·ac·ti·vat·ed, re·ac·ti·vat·ing, re·ac·ti·vates 1.** To make active again. **2.** To restore (something) to its original effectiveness or ability to function. **—re·ac′ti·va′tion** *n.*

re·ac·tive (rē-ăk′tĭv) *adj.* **1.** Tending to be responsive or to react to a stimulus. **2.** Characterized by reaction. **3.** Tending to participate in reactions.

re·ac·tor (rē-ăk′tər) *n.* **1.** A person or thing that reacts to a stimulus. **2.** A nuclear reactor.

read (rēd) *v.* **read** (rĕd), **read·ing, reads** —*tr.* **1.** To look through and take in the meaning of (written or printed characters, words, or sentences): *reading books.* **2.** To speak aloud the words of (something written or printed): *She read the poem while we listened.* **3.** To know (a language or system of notation) well enough to understand written and printed matter: *reads Chinese; reads music.* **4a.** To examine and take in the meaning of (language in a form other than written or printed words or symbols): *reads American Sign Language; reads Braille.* **b.** To take in the meaning of (a graphic representation): *reading a map.* **5.** To detect by observing closely: *read disappointment in her eyes.* **6.** To determine the intent or mood of: *I can read your mind.* **7.** To indicate or register: *The speedometer read 50 miles per hour.* **8.** To obtain (computer data) from a storage medium: *The central processing unit read the data from the disk.* —*intr.* **1.** To examine and take in the meaning of printed or written characters, as of words or music: *learning to read.* **2.** To speak aloud the words one is reading: *He reads to his children every night.* **3.** To learn by reading: *We read about the elections in the paper.* **4.** To have a certain wording: *Recite the poem exactly as it reads.* **5.** To have a certain character or quality for the reader: *Her prose reads well.* ❖ *n. Informal* Something that is or can be read: *a book that is an easy read.* ◆ **read between the lines** To find a hidden or unexpressed meaning. **read out** To read aloud. **read up** To study or learn by reading: *We've been reading up on dinosaurs lately.* [From Old English *rǣdan*, to advise.]

❑ *These sound alike:* **read, reed** (grass).

read·a·ble (rē′də-bəl) *adj.* **1.** Easily read; legible: *a readable typeface.* **2.** Pleasurable or interesting to read. **—read′a·bil′i·ty, read′a·ble·ness** *n.*

read·er (rē′dər) *n.* **1.** A person who reads. **2.** A textbook with passages for practice in reading. **3.** An anthology, especially a literary anthology. **4.** A device that reads or retrieves data, as from a storage device or credit card. **5.** An e-reader.

read·er·ship (rē′dər-shĭp′) *n.* The readers of a publication considered as a group.

read·i·ly (rĕd′ə-lē) *adv.* **1.** Without hesitation; willingly: *He readily undertook the task.* **2.** Without difficulty; easily: *paints that are readily available at a hardware store.*

read·ing (rē′dĭng) *n.* **1.** The act or activity of a person who reads. **2.** An official or public recitation of written material: *a poetry reading.* **3.** A personal interpretation: *We listened to her reading of the political situation.* **4.** Written or printed material. **5.** The data or information shown by a graduated instrument or gauge: *took a reading from the thermometer.*

re·ad·just (rē′ə-jŭst′) *tr.v.* **re·ad·just·ed, re·ad·just·ing, re·ad·justs** To adjust or arrange again: *readjust the settings on a machine.* **—re′ad·just′ment** *n.*

read-on·ly memory (rĕd′ōn′lē) *n.* ROM.

read·y (rĕd′ē) *adj.* **read·i·er, read·i·est 1.** Prepared or available for action or use: *getting ready for school; ground ready for planting.* **2.** Inclined; willing: *ready to accept any reasonable offer.* **3.** Likely or about to do something: *He seemed ready to go.* **4.** Prompt in apprehending or reacting: *a ready wit; a ready response.* **5.** Available: *ready cash.* ❖ *tr.v.* **read·ied, read·y·ing, read·ies** To cause to be ready: *readied the boat to go fishing.* ◆ **make ready** To make preparations. [From Old English *rǣde.*] **—read′i·ness** *n.*

read·y-made or **read·y·made** (rĕd′ē-mād′) *adj.* **1.** Already made, prepared, or available: *a ready-made dinner.* **2.** Handy, especially because of familiarity or preplanning: *ready-made responses to the reporters' questions.*

Rea·gan (rā′gən), **Ronald Wilson** 1911–2004. The 40th president of the United States (1981–1989). His administration was marked by economic recovery and improved relations with the Soviet Union.

re·a·gent (rē-ā′jənt) *n.* A substance used in a chemical reaction to detect, measure, or produce another substance.

real¹ (rēl) *adj.* **1.** Not imaginary, fictional, or pretended; actual: *a story about real people; concealed his real purpose and identity.* **2.** Being so in fact; not artificial or counterfeit: *a real diamond, not a fake one.* See Synonyms at **authentic. 3.** Being no less than what is stated; worthy of the name: *a real friend.* **4.** Utter or extreme: *a real mess; in real trouble.* **5.** Relating to land, buildings, or other stationary property that cannot be moved by the owner: *a tax on her real property.* **6.** Relating to a real number. ❖ *adv. Informal* Very: *I'm real sorry about that.* ◆ **for real** *Informal* Truly so in fact or actuality: *That description can't be for real.* [From Middle English, from Latin *rēs*, thing.]

❑ *These sound alike:* **real¹** (actual), **reel¹** (tape spool), **reel²** (stagger).

re·al² (rā-äl′) *n., pl.* **re·als** or **re·al·es** (rā-ä′lĕs) A silver coin formerly used in Spain and Latin America. [From Spanish *real*, royal, from Latin *rēgālis.*]

re·al³ (rā-äl′) *n., pl.* **re·ais** (rā-īsh′) The basic monetary unit of Brazil. [From Portuguese *real*, royal, from Latin *rēgālis*, royal.]

real estate (rēl) *n.* Land, the resources (such as water, trees, or minerals) on or in it, and the buildings built on it.

re·al·ism (rē′ə-lĭz′əm) *n.* **1.** A tendency to accept facts and be practical. **2.** The representation in art and literature of objects, actions, and social conditions as they actually are, without idealizing or presentation in abstract form. **—re′al·ist** *n.*

re·al·is·tic (rē′ə-lĭs′tĭk) *adj.* **1.** Tending to or expressing an awareness of facts and things as they actually are; practical: *a realistic admission of defeat.* **2.** Accurately represented, as in artistic or literary realism: *realistic characters in a play.* **—re′al·is′ti·cal·ly** *adv.*

re·al·i·ty (rē-ăl′ĭ-tē) *n., pl.* **re·al·i·ties 1.** The quality or condition of being actual or true: *Some scientists ques-*

WORD BUILDING

react The word root *act–* in English words and the word **act** itself come from the past participle *āctus* of the Latin verb *agere,* "to drive, lead, do, perform, deal with, act." Thus we have **react,** "to do in response" (using the prefix *re–,* "back, again"); **transact,** "to carry through, manage, do business" (*trans–,* "through, across"); and the adjective **exact,** which in Latin literally meant "driven out, achieved, made precise" (*ex–,* "out").

Ronald Reagan
photographed in 1985

reamer
juice reamer

tioned the reality of global warming. **2.** A person or thing that is real: *seeing their dreams become realities.* **3.** The state of things as they actually exist: *The reality of the situation is that we've spent all the money in the budget.*

reality show *n.* A television show featuring non-actors interacting or competing, often in a highly contrived situation.

re·al·i·za·tion (rē′ə-lĭ-**zā′**shən) *n.* **1.** The act of realizing or the condition of being realized: *shocked by the realization that they had run out of money.* **2.** The result of realizing: *the realization of his hopes.*

re·al·ize (**rē′**ə-līz′) *tr.v.* **re·al·ized, re·al·iz·ing, re·al·iz·es 1.** To understand completely or correctly; grasp: *He realized that the situation was serious.* **2.** To bring into reality; fulfill: *realized her ambition to succeed.* **3.** To obtain or bring in, as profit or gain: *realized a large sum on the investment.*

real-life (rēl-**līf′**) *adj.* Actually happening or having happened; not fictional: *a movie based on real-life events.*

real·ly (**rē′**lē) *adv.* **1.** In actual truth or fact: *There isn't really a lake there; it's just a mirage.* **2.** To a great degree; very much: *I'd really like to meet your parents.* **3.** Very; utterly: *That was a really great movie.* **4.** Without a doubt; indeed: *Really, I don't want more dessert.*

realm (rĕlm) *n.* **1.** A community or territory over which a sovereign rules; a kingdom. **2.** An area or field, as of knowledge or activity: *the realm of science.*

real number (rēl) *n.* A number that is a rational or irrational number.

real time (rēl) *n.* The actual time during which something occurs: *Phone calls occur in real time, whereas communication by email does not.* **—real′-time′** (**rēl′**tīm′) *adj.*

real·ty (**rēl′**tē) *n.* Real estate.

ream¹ (rēm) *n.* **1.** A standard quantity of paper of the same size and stock, now usually 500 sheets. **2.** often **reams** A very large amount. [From Middle English *rem*, from Arabic *rizma*, bundle.]

ream² (rēm) *tr.v.* **reamed, ream·ing, reams 1.** To shape, enlarge, or adjust (a hole) with or as if with a reamer: *reamed the hole in the wall after drilling it.* **2.** To squeeze the juice out of (fruit) with a reamer. [Possibly from Middle English *rimen*, to make room, from Old English *rȳman*.]

ream·er (**rē′**mər) *n.* **1.** A tool for shaping or enlarging holes. **2.** A kitchen utensil used for extracting juice from citrus fruits.

reap (rēp) *v.* **reaped, reap·ing, reaps** *—tr.* **1.** To cut for harvest, as with a scythe: *reap wheat.* **2a.** To harvest (a crop). **b.** To harvest a crop from: *reaping a field.* **3.** To gain as a result of effort: *Edison reaped fame from his many inventions.* *—intr.* To cut or harvest grain or a similar crop. [From Old English *rīpan, reopan.*]

reap·er (**rē′**pər) *n.* A person or machine that cuts down and gathers grain or a similar crop.

rear¹ (rîr) *n.* **1.** The part of something that is farthest from or opposite to the front: *the rear of the head.* **2.** The part of an army or arrangement of troops or ships that is farthest from the fighting front. **3.** *Informal* The buttocks. ❖ *adj.* Relating to, at, or located in the rear: *a rear entrance.* [From Middle English *rere*, rear of an army, short for *rerewarde*, rear guard.]

rear² (rîr) *v.* **reared, rear·ing, rears** *—tr.* **1.** To care for (children or a child) during the early stages of life; bring up. **2.** To tend (plants or animals): *rearing sheep for their wool.* **3.** To build; erect: *rear a skyscraper.* *—intr.* To rise on the hind legs, as a horse: *The frightened horse reared and neighed.* [From Old English *rǣran*, to raise.]

rear admiral *n.* A commissioned officer in the US Navy or Coast Guard, ranking above captain and below vice admiral.

rear·most (**rîr′**mōst′) *adj.* Farthest in the rear; last: *sat in the rearmost row.*

re·ar·range (rē′ə-**rānj′**) *tr.v.* **re·ar·ranged, re·ar·rang·ing, re·ar·rang·es** To change the arrangement of: *We rearranged the furniture in the living room.* **—re′ar·range′ment** *n.*

rear·view mirror (**rîr′vyōō′**) *n.* A mirror, such as one attached to a car windshield, that provides a view of what is behind.

rear·ward (**rîr′**wərd) *adv. & adj.* At, to, or toward the rear. **—rear′wards** *adv.*

rea·son (**rē′**zən) *n.* **1.** The basis or motive for an action, decision, or belief: *There are good reasons to learn how to swim.* **2.** A statement or fact that justifies or explains an action, decision, or belief: *What reason did she give for leaving so soon?* **3.** A fact or cause that explains why something exists or occurs: *The reason for the building's collapse is unknown.* **4.** The ability to think, understand, and make decisions logically and sensibly; intelligence: *Use reason to decide, not your emotions.* **5.** A normal mental state; sanity: *lost his reason.* **6.** Sound judgment; good sense: *a woman of reason.* ❖ *v.* **rea·soned, rea·son·ing, rea·sons** *—intr.* **1.** To use the ability to think logically and sensibly: *reason about the world.* **2.** To argue logically and persuasively: *The mayor tried to reason with the angry crowd.* *—tr.* To determine or conclude by logical thinking: *The doctor reasoned that the patient had a virus.* ◆ **by reason of** Because of. **within reason** Within the bounds of good sense or practicality. [From Middle English *resoun*, from Latin *ratiō*, from *rērī*, to consider, think.]

rea·son·a·ble (**rē′**zə-nə-bəl) *adj.* **1.** Capable of reasoning: *a reasonable woman.* **2.** In accordance with reason; logical: *a reasonable solution.* **3.** Not excessive or extreme; fair: *a reasonable price.* **—rea′son·a·ble·ness** *n.* **—rea′son·a·bly** *adv.*

rea·son·ing (**rē′**zə-nĭng) *n.* **1.** The use of reason, especially to form conclusions and judgments. **2.** Evidence or arguments used in thinking or argumentation.

re·as·sem·ble (rē′ə-**sĕm′**bəl) *v.* **re·as·sem·bled, re·as·sem·bling, re·as·sem·bles** *—tr.* **1.** To fit or join the parts of (something) together again. **2.** To bring or gather together again. *—intr.* To gather together again, especially in a different place.

re·as·sign (rē′ə-**sīn′**) *tr.v.* **re·as·signed, re·as·sign·ing, re·as·signs** To assign to a new position, duty, or location: *Our principal was reassigned to a different school.*

re·as·sure (rē′ə-**shŏŏr′**) *tr.v.* **re·as·sured, re·as·sur·ing, re·as·sures 1.** To restore confidence to: *I felt reassured that I was up to the job.* **2.** To assure (someone) again: *He reassured me he would call back.* **—re′as·sur′ance** *n.* **—re′as·sur′ing·ly** *adv.*

re·bar (**rē′**bär′) *n.* A rod or bar used for reinforcement in concrete or asphalt pourings.

re·bate (**rē′**bāt′) *n.* A return of part of an amount given in payment or a reduction in an amount to be paid. ❖ *tr.v.* (**rē′**bāt′ *or* rĭ-**bāt′**) **re·bat·ed, re·bat·ing, re·bates** To deduct or return (an amount).

re·bel (rĭ-**bĕl′**) *intr.v.* **re·belled, re·bel·ling, re·bels 1.** To refuse loyalty to and oppose by force an established government or a ruling authority. **2.** To resist or defy an authority or a generally accepted convention: *rebelled against wearing a tie in summer.* ❖ *n.* **reb·el** (**rĕb′**əl) **1.** A person who rebels or is in rebellion. **2. Rebel** A Confederate soldier. [From Middle English *rebellen*, from Latin *rebellāre*, from *bellum*, war.]

re·bel·lion (rĭ-**bĕl′**yən) *n.* **1a.** Open, organized, and armed resistance to an existing government. **b.** An instance of this. **2a.** Defiance toward an authority or established convention. **b.** An instance of this.

re·bel·lious (rĭ-**bĕl′**yəs) *adj.* **1.** Prone to or participating in a rebellion. **2.** Relating to or characteristic of a rebellion: *rebellious behavior.* **3.** Characterized by or expressing defiance of authority or convention: *a rebel-*

ă	pat	ôr	core
ā	pay	oi	boy
âr	care	ou	out
ä	father	ŏŏ	took
ĕ	pet	ŏŏr	lure
ē	be	ōō	boot
ĭ	pit	ŭ	cut
ī	bite	ûr	urge
îr	pier	th	thin
ŏ	pot	*th*	this
ō	toe	zh	vision
ô	paw	ə	about

lious artistic movement. **—re·bel′lious·ly** *adv.* **—re·bel′lious·ness** *n.*

re·birth (rē-**bûrth′** *or* **rē′**bûrth′) *n.* **1.** A second or new birth; reincarnation. **2.** A renaissance; a revival: *the rebirth of classical learning.*

re·boot (rē-**bo͞ot′**) *tr.v.* **re·boot·ed, re·boot·ing, re·boots** To restart (a computer).

re·born (rē-**bôrn′**) *adj.* **1.** Reincarnated. **2.** Emotionally or spiritually revived.

re·bound (**rē′bound′** *or* rĭ-**bound′**) *v.* **re·bound·ed, re·bound·ing, re·bounds** *—intr.* **1.** To spring or bounce back after hitting or colliding with something. **2.** To recover, as from a disappointment: *We rebounded after the loss to win the second game.* **3.** In basketball, to gain possession of the ball as it bounces off the backboard or rim. *—tr.* In basketball, to gain possession of (the ball) as it bounces off the backboard or rim. ❖ *n.* (**rē′**bound′) **1.** A springing or bounding back: *hit the ball on the rebound.* **2.** A quick recovery from or reaction to disappointment or depression. **3.** In basketball, the act of gaining possession of a ball as it bounces off the backboard or rim.

re·buff (rĭ-**bŭf′**) *n.* **1.** A blunt or abrupt rejection or refusal: *her rebuff of my offer.* **2.** An abrupt setback to progress or action: *a rebuff to his ambitions.* ❖ *tr.v.* **re·buffed, re·buff·ing, re·buffs 1.** To reject bluntly, often disdainfully; snub: *They rebuffed our offer to help.* **2.** To repel or drive back: *rebuffed the attack.*

re·build (rē-**bĭld′**) *tr.v.* **re·built** (rē-**bĭlt′**), **re·build·ing, re·builds** To build again; reconstruct: *rebuild a church.*

re·buke (rĭ-**byo͞ok′**) *tr.v.* **re·buked, re·buk·ing, re·bukes** To criticize sharply; reprimand. ❖ *n.* A sharp criticism or reprimand.

re·bus (**rē′**bəs) *n., pl.* **re·bus·es** A representation of words by pictures or symbols, often presented as a puzzle.

re·but (rĭ-**bŭt′**) *tr.v.* **re·but·ted, re·but·ting, re·buts** To prove or try to prove (something) false, especially by presenting opposing evidence or arguments.

re·but·tal (rĭ-**bŭt′**l) *n.* **1.** The act of rebutting something, such as an accusation. **2.** A statement made in rebutting something.

re·cal·ci·trant (rĭ-**kăl′**sĭ-trənt) *adj.* Stubbornly resistant to or defiant of authority or guidance. See Synonyms at **obstinate. —re·cal′ci·trance** *n.*

re·call (rĭ-**kôl′**) *tr.v.* **re·called, re·call·ing, re·calls 1.** To ask or order to return: *The government recalled the ambassador.* **2.** To remember; recollect: *recalling his boyhood love of horses.* **3.** To request return of (a product), as for repairs or adjustments. ❖ *n.* (*also* **rē′**kôl′) **1.** The act of recalling or summoning back, especially an official order to return. **2.** The ability to remember information or experiences. **3.** The procedure by which a public official may be removed from office by popular vote. **4.** A request by a manufacturer for the return of a defective product, as for repairs or adjustments.

re·cant (rĭ-**kănt′**) *v.* **re·cant·ed, re·cant·ing, re·cants** *—tr.* To take back or deny the validity of (a statement or belief previously held): *recanted his position on the new tax bill.* *—intr.* To make a formal denial or disavowal of a previously held statement or belief. **—re′can·ta′tion** (rē′kăn-**tā′**shən) *n.*

re·cap¹ (rē-**kăp′**) *tr.v.* **re·capped, re·cap·ping, re·caps** To replace a cap or covering on: *recapped the bottle.*

re·cap² (**rē′**kăp′) *Informal tr.v.* **re·capped, re·cap·ping, re·caps** To recapitulate: *At the end of the baseball game, the announcer recapped the highlights of the game.* ❖ *n.* A recapitulation, as of a news report.

re·ca·pit·u·late (rē′kə-**pĭch′**ə-lāt′) *v.* **re·ca·pit·u·lat·ed, re·ca·pit·u·lat·ing, re·ca·pit·u·lates** *—tr.* To repeat in shorter form; summarize or sum up. *—intr.* To make a summary. **—re′ca·pit′u·la′tion** *n.*

re·cap·ture (rē-**kăp′**chər) *n.* The act of taking again or recovering. ❖ *tr.v.* **re·cap·tured, re·cap·tur·ing, re·cap·tures 1.** To capture again: *recapture a city.* **2.** To recollect or recall vividly.

re·cast (rē-**kăst′**) *tr.v.* **re·cast, re·cast·ing, re·casts 1.** To mold again: *She recast the statue.* **2.** To rearrange, as with a new wording or form: *recast a question.*

recd. *abbr.* An abbreviation of received.

re·cede (rĭ-**sēd′**) *intr.v.* **re·ced·ed, re·ced·ing, re·cedes 1.** To move back or away from a limit, point, or mark: *The floodwaters finally receded.* **2.** To slope backward: *a man with a chin that recedes.* **3.** To become fainter or more distant: *Over the years his memory of that summer receded.*

re·ceipt (rĭ-**sēt′**) *n.* **1.** The act of receiving or the fact of being or having been received: *sent payment upon receipt of the merchandise.* **2.** often **receipts** The quantity or amount received: *box office receipts.* **3.** A written acknowledgment that a specified article, sum of money, or shipment of merchandise has been received. ❖ *tr.v.* **re·ceipt·ed, re·ceipt·ing, re·ceipts** To give or write a receipt for (money paid or goods or services delivered).

re·ceiv·a·ble (rĭ-**sē′**və-bəl) *adj.* Awaiting or requiring payment; due or collectible: *accounts receivable.*

re·ceive (rĭ-**sēv′**) *v.* **re·ceived, re·ceiv·ing, re·ceives** *—tr.* **1.** To get or acquire (something given, offered, or transmitted): *receive payment.* **2.** To hear or see (information, for example): *received good news.* **3.** To take in and convert to another form: *The antenna received a very faint radio signal.* **4.** To bear the weight of; support: *Girders received the weight of the building.* **5.** To experience or be given: *receive a fine.* **6.** To take the force or impact of (a blow, for example): *The island received the full fury of the gale.* **7.** To greet or welcome: *received us as if we were royalty.* *—intr.* **1.** To acquire or get something. **2.** To partake of Holy Communion. **3.** To convert electromagnetic signals into visible or audible signals, as in radio. **4.** In football, to catch or take possession of a kicked ball. [From Middle English *receiven,* from Latin *recipere* : *re-,* back + *capere,* to take.]

re·ceiv·er (rĭ-**sē′**vər) *n.* **1.** A person or thing that receives; a recipient. **2.** A person appointed by a court to hold the funds or property of another while a court case is being decided. **3.** The unit of a communications system, such as radio or television, that receives an incoming signal and converts it, as into a sound or light. **4.** In football, a member of the offensive team who is eligible to catch a forward pass.

re·ceiv·er·ship (rĭ-**sē′**vər-shĭp′) *n.* **1.** The office or function of a court-appointed receiver. **2.** The condition of being held by a court-appointed receiver.

re·cent (**rē′**sənt) *adj.* Belonging to or occurring in a time not long before the present. [From Middle English, from Latin *recēns.*] **—re′cent·ly** *adv.* **—re′cent·ness** *n.*

re·cep·ta·cle (rĭ-**sĕp′**tə-kəl) *n.* **1.** A container that holds items or matter. **2.** The expanded tip of a stalk or stem that bears a flower or group of flowers.

re·cep·tion (rĭ-**sĕp′**shən) *n.* **1.** The act or process of receiving or of being received. **2.** A welcome, greeting, or acceptance: *a friendly reception.* **3.** A social gathering, especially one honoring or introducing someone: *a wedding reception.* **4a.** The act or process of receiving electrical or electromagnetic signals. **b.** The quality or condition of the signals received. **5.** In football, the act or an instance of catching a forward pass. [From Middle English *recepcion,* from Latin *receptiō,* from *recipere,* to receive.]

re·cep·tion·ist (rĭ-**sĕp′**shə-nĭst) *n.* An office worker employed chiefly to receive visitors and answer the telephone.

re·cep·tive (rĭ-**sĕp′**tĭv) *adj.* Ready or willing to receive favorably: *receptive to change.* **—re·cep′tive·ly** *adv.* **—re·cep′tive·ness** *n.*

re·cep·tor (rĭ-**sĕp′**tər) *n.* **1.** A specialized cell or group

rear²

of nerve endings that senses or receives stimuli. **2.** A structure or site on a cell that is capable of combining with a hormone, antigen, globulin, or other chemical substance.

re·cess (rē′sĕs′ *or* rĭ-**sĕs′**) *n.* **1a.** A temporary halt in or stoppage of customary activity: *The judge ordered a court recess.* See Synonyms at **pause. b.** A period in the school day during which students are given time to play or relax. **2.** often **recesses** A remote, secret, or secluded place: *a bird that lives deep in the recesses of the forest.* **3.** An indentation or small hollow. ❖ *v.* **re·cessed, re·cess·ing, re·cess·es** —*tr.* **1.** To place in a recess: *The lights in the kitchen are recessed.* **2.** To suspend (an activity) for a recess: *The hearings have been recessed until tomorrow.* —*intr.* To take a recess: *The investigators recessed for lunch.*

re·ces·sion (rĭ-**sĕsh′**ən) *n.* **1.** The act of withdrawing or going back. **2.** An extended decline in business, usually viewed by economists as two or more three-month periods in a row in which the gross national product declines.

re·ces·sion·al (rĭ-**sĕsh′**ə-nəl) *n.* A piece of music played as participants exit at the end of a ceremony.

re·ces·sive (rĭ-**sĕs′**ĭv) *adj.* **1.** Tending to recede or go backward: *a recessive chin.* **2.** Relating to a gene that does not produce its characteristic effect if a dominant gene is present at the same position on the other of a pair of chromosomes. ❖ *n.* A recessive gene. **—re·ces′sive·ly** *adv.*

re·charge (rē-**chärj′**) *tr.v.* **re·charged, re·charg·ing, re·charg·es 1.** To charge (a storage battery) again. **2.** To charge the storage battery in (an electronic device) again: *recharged my cell phone.* **—re·charge′a·ble** *adj.*

rec·i·pe (**rĕs′**ə-pē′) *n.* **1.** A set of directions with a list of ingredients for making or preparing something, especially food. **2.** A formula for accomplishing a certain thing: *a recipe for success.* [From Latin, singular imperative of *recipere*, to take, receive.]

re·cip·i·ent (rĭ-**sĭp′**ē-ənt) *adj.* Receiving or able to receive. ❖ *n.* A person or thing that receives something: *the recipient of an award.*

re·cip·ro·cal (rĭ-**sĭp′**rə-kəl) *adj.* **1.** Done, given, felt, or owed in return: *a reciprocal invitation to lunch.* **2.** Felt, experienced, or done by each side with regard to the other; mutual: *reciprocal suspicion between the two leaders.* **3.** Relating to either of a pair of numbers whose product is 1. ❖ *n.* Either of a pair of numbers whose product is 1; for example, the number 3 is the reciprocal of ⅓. [From Latin *reciprocus*, alternating.] **—re·cip′ro·cal·ly** *adv.*

re·cip·ro·cate (rĭ-**sĭp′**rə-kāt′) *v.* **re·cip·ro·cat·ed, re·cip·ro·cat·ing, re·cip·ro·cates** —*tr.* **1.** To give or take mutually: *reciprocating favors.* **2.** To show or feel in return: *reciprocated her love.* —*intr.* **1.** To make a return for something given or done: *You buy lunch today, and I'll reciprocate tomorrow.* **2.** To move back and forth alternately, as a machine part: *a power saw that reciprocates.* **—re·cip′ro·ca′tion** *n.*

rec·i·proc·i·ty (rĕs′ə-**prŏs′**ĭ-tē) *n., pl.* **rec·i·proc·i·ties 1.** A reciprocal condition or relationship. **2.** A mutual exchange or interchange, especially the exchange of rights or privileges of trade between nations.

re·cit·al (rĭ-**sīt′**l) *n.* **1.** The act of reading or reciting in a public performance. **2.** A very detailed account or report of something: *the traveler's recital of his experiences.* **3.** A performance of music or dance, especially one by a solo performer.

rec·i·ta·tion (rĕs′ĭ-**tā′**shən) *n.* **1.** The act of reciting something memorized, as a poem or oration, in a public performance. **2.** The material presented in a public recitation. **3.** A spoken presentation or report of prepared lessons by a student in school.

ă	pat	ôr	core
ā	pay	oi	boy
âr	care	ou	out
ä	father	o͝o	took
ĕ	pet	o͝or	lure
ē	be	o͞o	boot
ĭ	pit	ŭ	cut
ī	bite	ûr	urge
îr	pier	th	thin
ŏ	pot	*th*	this
ō	toe	zh	vision
ô	paw	ə	about

rec·i·ta·tive[1] (**rĕs′**ĭ-tā′tĭv *or* rĭ-**sī′**tə-tĭv) *adj.* Relating to a recital or recitation.

rec·i·ta·tive[2] (rĕs′ĭ-tə-**tēv′**) *n.* **1.** A style of singing in which words are sung mostly in the rhythm of speech and with little accompaniment by instruments, used especially in opera and oratorios. **2.** A musical passage sung in this style.

re·cite (rĭ-**sīt′**) *tr.v.* **re·cit·ed, re·cit·ing, re·cites 1.** To repeat or say aloud (something prepared or memorized), especially before an audience. **2.** To tell in detail: *recited his difficulties.* [From Middle English *reciten*, from Latin *recitāre*, to read out.]

reck·less (**rĕk′**lĭs) *adj.* Lacking care or caution; careless: *reckless driving.* [From Old English *rēcelēas*.] **—reck′less·ly** *adv.* **—reck′less·ness** *n.*

reck·on (**rĕk′**ən) *v.* **reck·oned, reck·on·ing, reck·ons** —*tr.* **1.** To count or calculate; figure: *reckon time.* **2.** To consider as being; regard as: *reckon him an expert in the field.* **3.** *Informal* To think or assume: *Do you reckon we'll be through in time?* —*intr.* **1.** To make a calculation; figure. **2.** To anticipate; expect: *We didn't reckon on so many guests.* **3.** *Informal* To think or assume. ◆ **reckon with** To take into account or deal with. [From Old English *gerecenian*, to recount, arrange.]

reck·on·ing (**rĕk′**ə-nĭng) *n.* **1.** The act of counting or computing. **2.** A statement of an amount due. **3.** A settlement of accounts: *a day of reckoning.* **4.** The act or process of calculating the position of a ship or aircraft.

re·claim (rĭ-**klām′**) *tr.v.* **re·claimed, re·claim·ing, re·claims 1.** To take back: *reclaimed the throne.* **2.** To make (land) usable for growing crops or living on, as by draining, irrigating, or fertilizing: *reclaim marshlands.* **3.** To extract (useful substances) from garbage or waste products. **4.** To turn back, as from error, to a right or proper course; reform: *efforts to reclaim convicts from a life of crime.* **—re·claim′a·ble** *adj.* **—rec′la·ma′tion** (rĕk′lə-**mā′**shən) *n.*

re·cline (rĭ-**klīn′**) *intr.v.* **re·clined, re·clin·ing, re·clines** To lie back or down: *reclined on the couch.* [From Middle English *reclinen*, from Latin *reclīnāre* : *re-*, back + *-clīnāre*, to bend, lean.]

rec·luse (**rĕk′**lo͞os′ *or* rĭ-**klo͞os′**) *n.* A person who withdraws from the world to live in seclusion or solitude. ❖ *adj.* **re·cluse** (rĭ-**klo͞os′** *or* **rĕk′**lo͞os′) Withdrawn from the world; solitary. [From Middle English, from Latin *reclūsus*, shut up : *re-*, back, up + *claudere*, to close.]

re·clu·sive (rĭ-**klo͞o′**sĭv) *adj.* **1.** Seeking or preferring seclusion or isolation: *a reclusive hermit.* **2.** Providing seclusion: *a reclusive hut.*

rec·og·ni·tion (rĕk′əg-**nĭsh′**ən) *n.* **1.** The act of recognizing or the condition of being recognized. **2.** Acknowledgment or approval: *an award in recognition of excellent service.* **3.** Attention or favorable notice; praise: *world recognition for his work in physics.*

rec·og·nize (**rĕk′**əg-nīz′) *tr.v.* **rec·og·nized, rec·og·niz·ing, rec·og·niz·es 1.** To know to be something that has been perceived before: *She recognized his face from the photo.* **2.** To know or identify from past experience or knowledge: *I recognized friendliness in her smile.* **3.** To accept as valid or real: *recognize the concerns of taxpayers.* **4.** To acknowledge or approve of: *recognized his right to vote.* **5.** To accept officially the national status of (a new nation). **6.** To permit (someone) to speak at a meeting. **—rec′og·niz′a·ble** *adj.* **—rec′og·niz′a·bly** *adv.*

re·coil (rĭ-**koil′**) *intr.v.* **re·coiled, re·coil·ing, re·coils 1.** To move or jerk backward, as a gun upon firing. **2.** To shrink back in fear or dislike. **3.** To fall back; return: *Your rudeness will one day recoil upon you.* ❖ *n.* (*also* **rē′**koil′) **1.** The backward action of a firearm upon firing. **2.** The act of recoiling.

rec·ol·lect (rĕk′ə-**lĕkt′**) *tr. & intr.v.* **rec·ol·lect·ed, rec·ol·lect·ing, rec·ol·lects** To remember.

rec·ol·lec·tion (rĕk′ə-**lĕk′**shən) *n.* **1.** The act or power of recollecting. **2.** Something recollected: *I have no recollection of meeting him.*

re·com·bi·nant DNA (rē-**kŏm′**bə-nənt) *n.* DNA that has been altered through laboratory manipulation in which genes from one organism are spliced into the genetic material of an organism of a different species.

re·com·bi·na·tion (rē′kŏm-bə-**nā′**shən) *n.* The rearrangement of genetic material when segments of paired chromosomes are interchanged during meiosis. **—re′com·bine′** *v.*

rec·om·mend (rĕk′ə-**mĕnd′**) *tr.v.* **rec·om·mend·ed, rec·om·mend·ing, rec·om·mends 1.** To praise or commend to another as being worthy or desirable: *I highly recommend her for the job.* **2.** To advise or counsel (a course of action): *My teacher recommended that I should write my report about whales.* **3.** To make attractive or acceptable: *His honesty recommends him.*

rec·om·men·da·tion (rĕk′ə-mĕn-**dā′**shən) *n.* **1.** The act of recommending. **2.** Something that recommends, especially a favorable statement about someone's qualifications or character. **3.** Something, such as a course of action, that is recommended.

rec·om·pense (**rĕk′**əm-pĕns′) *tr.v.* **rec·om·pensed, rec·om·pens·ing, rec·om·pens·es 1.** To pay or reward, as for something done: *recompensed her for her services.* **2.** To treat (someone) in a certain way as a reward or punishment. **3.** To make up for: *recompense losses.* ❖ *n.* **1.** Amends made for something, such as damage or loss. **2.** Payment in return for something given or done.

rec·on·cile (**rĕk′**ən-sīl′) *tr.v.* **rec·on·ciled, rec·on·cil·ing, rec·on·ciles 1.** To restore friendship between; make friendly again: *reconcile old enemies.* **2.** To settle or resolve, as a dispute. **3.** To bring (oneself) to accept something: *reconciling herself to the loss of a ring.* **4.** To make compatible, consistent, or harmonious: *I have been trying to reconcile my way of thinking with yours.* **—rec′on·cil′i·a′tion** (rĕk′ən-sĭl′ē-**ā′**shən) *n.*

re·con·di·tion (rē′kən-**dĭsh′**ən) *tr.v.* **re·con·di·tioned, re·con·di·tion·ing, re·con·di·tions** To restore by repairing, renovating, or rebuilding.

re·con·nais·sance (rĭ-**kŏn′**ə-səns) *n.* An inspection or exploration of an area, especially one made to gather information about the presence, arrangement, or activity of military forces.

re·con·noi·ter (rē′kə-**noi′**tər *or* rĕk′ə-**noi′**tər) *v.* **re·con·noi·tered, re·con·noi·ter·ing, re·con·noi·ters** *—tr.* To make a survey or inspection of, especially to gain information. *—intr.* To make a reconnaissance.

re·con·sid·er (rē′kən-**sĭd′**ər) *tr.v.* **re·con·sid·ered, re·con·sid·er·ing, re·con·sid·ers** To consider again, especially with the possibility of making a change. **—re′con·sid′er·a′tion** *n.*

re·con·struct (rē′kən-**strŭkt′**) *tr.v.* **re·con·struct·ed, re·con·struct·ing, re·con·structs 1.** To construct again; rebuild. **2.** To determine or trace from information or clues; create again mentally: *reconstruct the events that preceded the accident.*

re·con·struc·tion (rē′kən-**strŭk′**shən) *n.* **1.** The act or result of reconstructing. **2. Reconstruction** The period (1865–1877) during which the states of the former Confederacy were occupied by federal troops and progressively readmitted to the Union.

re·con·struc·tive (rē′kən-**strŭk′**tĭv) *adj.* **1.** Relating to reconstruction. **2.** Relating to surgery that restores or corrects the structure or appearance of a body part: *a reconstructive operation on the face.*

re·cord (rĭ-**kôrd′**) *tr.v.* **re·cord·ed, re·cord·ing, re·cords 1.** To set down for preservation in writing or other permanent form: *She recorded each change of course in the logbook.* **2.** To register or indicate, especially in permanent form: *This cash register records every sale.* **3.** To render (sound or images) into permanent form for reproduction, as on a DVD or in a computer file. ❖ *n.* **rec·ord** (**rĕk′**ərd) **1.** An account usually set down in writing as a means of preserving knowledge: *a record of what happened on the trip.* **2.** Something that records past events: *a fossil record.* **3.** The known history of performance or achievement: *your high-school record.* **4.** The highest or lowest measurement known, as in a sports event or weather readings: *the record for least rainfall in a year.* **5a.** A disk designed to be played on a phonograph. **b.** A musical recording that is issued on a medium of some kind. **6.** A collection of related data treated as a unit in a computer memory. ◆ **off the record** Not for publication: *The senator told the reporters that his remarks were off the record.* **on record** Known to have been stated or to have taken a certain position: *She's on record as opposing the new law.* [From Middle English *recorden*, from Latin *recordārī*, to remember.]

re·cord·er (rĭ-**kôr′**dər) *n.* **1.** A person or thing that records. **2.** A flute with a whistlelike mouthpiece and eight holes.

re·cord·ing (rĭ-**kôr′**dĭng) *n.* **1.** Something on which sound or visual images have been recorded, as a DVD or compact disc. **2.** A recorded sound or picture.

re·count[1] (rĭ-**kount′**) *tr.v.* **re·count·ed, re·count·ing, re·counts** To tell in detail; narrate the particulars of: *The book recounts the siege of Troy.* [From Early Modern English *recounten*, from Old French *reconter* : *re-*, again + *conter*, to relate.]

re·count[2] (rĭ-**kount′**) *tr.v.* **re·count·ed, re·count·ing, re·counts** To count again: *The officials recounted the ballots.* ❖ *n.* (**rē′**kount′) A second count, especially of votes: *The losing candidate demanded a recount.* [From *re-*, again + *count*, to count.]

re·coup (rĭ-**ko͞op′**) *tr.v.* **re·couped, re·coup·ing, re·coups 1.** To receive the equivalent of (something lost); make up for: *recouped his losses when the stock market rebounded.* **2.** To pay back; compensate: *The landlord recouped the tenants for damages.* [From Middle English *recoupen*, to cut short, from Old French *recouper*, to cut back.]

re·course (**rē′**kôrs′ *or* rĭ-**kôrs′**) *n.* **1.** The act or an instance of turning or applying to a person or thing for aid or protection: *You have recourse to the courts.* **2.** A person or thing to turn to for help or protection.

re·cov·er (rĭ-**kŭv′**ər) *v.* **re·cov·ered, re·cov·er·ing, re·cov·ers** *—tr.* **1.** To get back; regain: *The police tried to recover the stolen bicycle.* **2.** To regain control over (oneself): *recovered himself sufficiently to speak in public.* **3.** To make up for; compensate for: *She recovered her losses.* *—intr.* To return to a normal or healthy condition: *recover after a long illness.* **—re·cov′er·a·ble** *adj.*

re·cov·er·y (rĭ-**kŭv′**ə-rē) *n., pl.* **re·cov·er·ies 1.** A return to a normal condition, as of health. **2.** The act of getting back or regaining.

recovery room *n.* A hospital room equipped for the care and observation of patients immediately following surgery.

re-cre·ate (rē′krē-**āt′**) *tr.v.* **re-cre·at·ed, re-cre·at·ing, re-cre·ates** To create again or anew. **—re′-cre·a′tion** *n.*

rec·re·a·tion (rĕk′rē-**ā′**shən) *n.* Refreshment of one's mind or body after work through some activity, such as a sport or game, that amuses or excites. **—rec′re·a′tion·al** *adj.* **—rec′re·a′tion·al·ly** *adv.*

rec·re·a·tion·al vehicle (rĕk′rē-**ā′**shə-nəl) *n.* A vehicle, such as a motor home, used for traveling and recreational activities.

re·crim·i·nate (rĭ-**krĭm′**ə-nāt′) *intr.v.* **re·crim·i·nat·ed, re·crim·i·nat·ing, re·crim·i·nates** To counter one accusation with another. **—re·crim′i·na′tion** *n.*

re·cruit (rĭ-**kro͞ot′**) *tr.v.* **re·cruit·ed, re·cruit·ing, re·cruits 1a.** To arrange for (someone) to join one of the armed forces. **b.** To assemble (an armed force) by such

WRITERS CHOOSE THEIR WORDS

"My counselors have commanded me to have your head cut off, and at once," he said, "because the law commands it. But I shall nevertheless ignore this order and not slay you, for the reason that this would be poor **recompense** for your having come here at great risk of your life to save my soul."

—Scott O'Dell
The Road to Damietta

WORD BUILDING

rectify The word roots *rect–* and *recti–* in English words come from the past participle *rēctus* of the Latin verb *regere,* "to make or keep straight, guide, direct, rule." Hence we have **rectify,** "to make right, remedy" (using the suffix *–fy,* "to make"); **rectangle,** "a figure with four right angles"; **rectitude,** "uprightness"; and **rectilinear,** "in a straight line." From the same Latin word root that *regere* comes from, there was also a Latin noun *rēgula,* "a rod for measuring or drawing straight lines; ruler; rule." Its adjective *rēgulāris,* "conforming to the rule, regular" is the source of our word **regular.**

recumbent

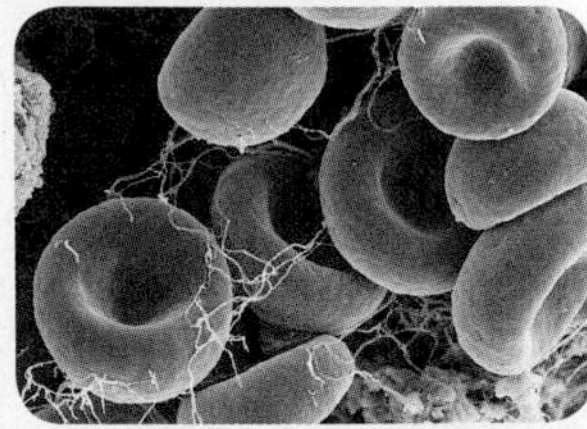

red blood cell

ă	pat	ôr	core
ā	pay	oi	boy
âr	care	ou	out
ä	father	o͝o	took
ĕ	pet	o͝or	lure
ē	be	o͞o	boot
ĭ	pit	ŭ	cut
ī	bite	ûr	urge
îr	pier	th	thin
ŏ	pot	*th*	this
ō	toe	zh	vision
ô	paw	ə	about

arranging: *recruit a new army.* **2.** To arrange for (someone) to be employed by an organization or to participate in an activity: *They recruited new editors for the magazine.* ❖ *n.* **1.** A newly enlisted member of the armed forces. **2.** A new member of any organization or body of people. **—re·cruit′er** *n.* **—re·cruit′ment** *n.*

rec·tal (rĕk′təl) *adj.* Relating to the rectum.

rec·tan·gle (rĕk′tăng′gəl) *n.* A four-sided plane figure with four right angles. [From Medieval Latin *rēctangulum,* a right triangle : Latin *rēctus,* right, straight + Latin *angulus,* angle.] —SEE NOTE AT **rectify.**

rec·tan·gu·lar (rĕk-**tăng′**gyə-lər) *adj.* **1.** Having the shape of a rectangle. **2.** Having right angles or a rectangular base, side, or sides: *a rectangular box.* **3.** Being a system of coordinates using axes that meet at right angles. **—rec·tan′gu·lar·ly** *adv.*

rec·ti·fy (rĕk′tə-fī′) *tr.v.* **rec·ti·fied, rec·ti·fy·ing, rec·ti·fies** To set right; correct: *tried to rectify my previous error.* [From Middle English *rectifien,* from Latin *rēctus,* right.] **—rec′ti·fi′er** *n.* —SEE NOTE.

rec·ti·lin·e·ar (rĕk′tə-**lĭn′**ē-ər) *adj.* Moving in, consisting of, bounded by, or characterized by a straight line or lines. **—rec′ti·lin′e·ar·ly** *adv.* —SEE NOTE AT **rectify.**

rec·ti·tude (rĕk′tĭ-to͞od′) *n.* Moral correctness. —SEE NOTE AT **rectify.**

rec·tor (rĕk′tər) *n.* **1.** In the Episcopal and Anglican churches, a cleric in charge of a parish. **2.** In the Roman Catholic Church, a priest in a church, seminary, or university who is both its spiritual head and the manager of its affairs. **3.** The principal of certain schools, colleges, or universities.

rec·to·ry (rĕk′tə-rē) *n., pl.* **rec·to·ries** The house in which a rector lives.

rec·tum (rĕk′təm) *n.* The lower end of the digestive tract, extending from the colon to the anus.

re·cum·bent (rĭ-**kŭm′**bənt) *adj.* Lying down; reclining. **—re·cum′bent·ly** *adv.*

re·cu·per·ate (rĭ-**ko͞o′**pə-rāt′) *intr.v.* **re·cu·per·at·ed, re·cu·per·at·ing, re·cu·per·ates 1.** To return to normal health or strength; recover. **2.** To recover from a financial loss. **—re·cu′per·a′tion** *n.* **—re·cu′per·a′tive** *adj.*

re·cur (rĭ-**kûr′**) *intr.v.* **re·curred, re·cur·ring, re·curs** To happen, come up, or show up again or repeatedly; return: *an area where earthquakes recur.* [From Latin *recurrere* : *re-,* back + *currere,* to run.]

re·cur·rent (rĭ-**kûr′**ənt) *adj.* Occurring or appearing again or repeatedly; returning regularly: *a recurrent dream.* **—re·cur′rence** *n.*

re·cy·cle (rē-**sī′**kəl) *tr.v.* **re·cy·cled, re·cy·cling, re·cy·cles 1.** To extract useful materials from (garbage or waste): *a plan to recycle bottles, cans, and newspapers.* **2.** To extract and reuse (useful substances found in garbage or waste): *a company that recycles rubber from used tires.* **—re·cy′cla·ble** *adj.*

red (rĕd) *n.* **1.** The color of blood or of a ripe strawberry. **2.** often **Red** A revolutionary, especially a Communist. ❖ *adj.* **red·der, red·dest 1.** Having a color resembling that of blood or a ripe strawberry. **2.** often **Red** Communist. ◆ **in the red** Operating at a loss; in debt. [From Old English *rēad.*] **—red′ness** *n.*

red blood cell *n.* Any of the cells in the blood that contain hemoglobin and give the blood its red color. Red blood cells carry oxygen from the lungs to various parts of the body. In mammals, they do not contain a nucleus. —SEE NOTE.

red-blood·ed (**rĕd′blŭd′**ĭd) *adj.* Strong and full of vigor.

red·cap (**rĕd′**kăp′) *n.* A porter, usually in a railroad station.

red card *n.* A red-colored card shown by a referee, especially in soccer, to eject a player from the game.

Red Cloud 1822–1909. Oglala leader of the resistance against the development of a trail through Wyoming and Montana by the US government (1865–1867).

red·coat (**rĕd′**kōt′) *n.* A British soldier, especially one serving during the American Revolution or the War of 1812.

Red Cross *n.* An international organization that cares for the victims of war, floods, earthquakes, and other disasters.

red·den (**rĕd′**n) *v.* **red·dened, red·den·ing, red·dens** —*tr.* To make red: *The dye reddened the gelatin.* —*intr.* **1.** To become red. **2.** To blush: *His cheeks redden when he gets embarrassed.*

red·dish (**rĕd′**ĭsh) *adj.* Somewhat red.

red dwarf *n.* A dwarf star whose mass ranges from one-tenth to one-half the mass of the sun. Because dwarf stars have a relatively cool surface temperature, they appear reddish orange in color.

re·deem (rĭ-**dēm′**) *tr.v.* **re·deemed, re·deem·ing, re·deems 1.** To recover ownership of by paying a specified sum: *redeemed his ring from the pawnbroker.* **2.** To pay off (a mortgage, for example). **3.** To turn in (coupons, for example) and receive something in exchange. **4.** To exchange (stocks or bonds, for example) for cash. **5a.** To set free; rescue. **b.** To save from sin and its consequences. **6.** To make up for: *a deed that redeemed her earlier mistake.* [From Middle English *redemen,* from Latin *redimere* : *re-, red-,* back + *emere,* to buy.] **—re·deem′a·ble** *adj.*

re·deem·er (rĭ-**dē′**mər) *n.* **1.** A person who redeems. **2. Redeemer** In Christianity, a way of referring to Jesus.

re·demp·tion (rĭ-**dĕmp′**shən) *n.* **1.** The act of redeeming: *redemption of a promissory note.* **2.** The recovery of something pawned or mortgaged; a repurchase. **3.** The act of rescuing, as by payment of ransom or by complying with demands: *redemption of hostages.* **4.** In Christianity, salvation from sin through Jesus's sacrifice.

red flag *n.* A warning signal: *His hesitation should have raised a red flag that he wasn't really interested.*

red-hand·ed (**rĕd′hăn′**dĭd) *adv. & adj.* In the act of doing something wrong: *The thief was caught red-handed with the loot.*

red·head (**rĕd′**hĕd′) *n.* A person with red hair.

red·head·ed (**rĕd′**hĕd′ĭd) *adj.* Having red hair: *a red-headed boy.*

red herring *n.* **1.** A smoked herring having a reddish color. **2.** Something that draws attention away from the subject under notice or discussion.

red-hot (**rĕd′hŏt′**) *adj.* **1.** Hot enough to glow red: *a red-hot bar of steel.* **2.** Heated, as with excitement or anger. **3.** New; very recent: *red-hot information.*

red-let·ter (**rĕd′lĕt′**ər) *adj.* Memorably happy; important: *a red-letter day.*

red light *n.* **1.** A red light that signals traffic to stop. **2.** *Informal* A command to stop.

red·line (**rĕd′**līn′) *n.* In ice hockey: **a.** The red line that crosses the center of the rink, dividing it in half. **b.** Either of two red lines that cross the rink near the end boards, on which the goal is positioned.

red·o·lent (**rĕd′**l-ənt) *adj.* **1.** Having or giving off a pleasant odor: *redolent thickets of honeysuckle.* **2.** Suggestive; reminiscent: *a campaign redolent of machine politics.* [From Middle English, from Latin *redolēre,* to smell.] **—red′o·lence** *n.* **—red′o·lent·ly** *adv.*

re·dou·ble (rē-**dŭb′**əl) *tr. & intr.v.* **re·dou·bled, re·dou·bling, re·dou·bles 1.** To make or become twice as great. **2.** To repeat, especially with greater intensity.

re·doubt·a·ble (rĭ-**dou′**tə-bəl) *adj.* **1.** Causing awe or fear. **2.** Worthy of respect or honor.

re·dound (rĭ-**dound′**) *intr.v.* **re·dound·ed, re·dound·ing, re·dounds** To have an effect or consequence: *Kind acts will redound to your credit.* [From Middle English *redounden,* from Latin *redundāre,* to overflow.]

red pepper *n.* **1.** The ripened fruit of any of several varieties of the pepper plant. **2.** Cayenne pepper.

re·dress (rĭ-drĕs′) *tr.v.* **re·dressed, re·dress·ing, re·dress·es** To set right; remedy or rectify: *The mayor agreed to redress their grievances.* ❖ *n.* (*also* rē′drĕs) **1.** The act of setting right; correction; remedy: *a redress of a wrong.* **2.** Satisfaction for wrong done; reparation.

Red Sea A long narrow sea between northeast Africa and the Arabian Peninsula. It is linked with the Arabian Sea to the south and (via the Suez Canal) with the Mediterranean Sea to the north.

red snapper *n.* Any of several food fishes of tropical and semitropical waters, having a red or reddish body.

red·start (rĕd′stärt′) *n.* **1.** A small North American songbird, the male of which has black feathers and orange patches on the wings and tail. **2.** A European songbird having grayish feathers and a rust-red breast and tail.

red state *n.* A US state in which a majority has voted for the Republican candidate in a statewide election. [From the fact that states electing Republican candidates are often red on maps in the news.]

red tape *n.* The procedures that are needed to gain bureaucratic approval for something, especially when they are too complicated and cause delay or inaction. [From the former use of red tape in binding British official documents.]

red tide *n.* A growth of plankton in the ocean that gives the water a reddish color. Toxins produced by the plankton can contaminate shellfish and kill fish.

re·duce (rĭ-do͞os′) *tr.v.* **re·duced, re·duc·ing, re·duc·es** **1.** To make less in amount, degree, or extent; diminish: *reduce the volume of the stereo.* **2.** To bring into a lower or worse condition or state: *The explosion reduced the building to rubble.* **3a.** To lower the valence of (an atom or element). **b.** To remove oxygen from chemical combination with or in (an element or compound). **4.** To change (a mathematical expression) into a simpler form without affecting its value or meaning. [From Middle English *reducen*, to bring back, bring down, from Latin *redūcere* : *re-*, back + *dūcere*, to lead.] **—re·duc′er** *n.* **—re·duc′i·ble** *adj.* —SEE NOTE AT **produce.**

re·duc·tion (rĭ-dŭk′shən) *n.* **1.** The act or process of reducing. **2.** The result of reducing: *The recovery brought about a reduction in unemployment.* **3.** The amount by which something is made smaller or less: *a reduction of 10 percent in the price of wheat.* **4.** The changing of a mathematical expression into a simpler form, as by dividing a fraction's numerator and denominator by any integral factors that they have in common.

re·dun·dan·cy (rĭ-dŭn′dən-sē) *n., pl.* **re·dun·dan·cies** The condition or an instance of being redundant.

re·dun·dant (rĭ-dŭn′dənt) *adj.* **1.** Expressing the same idea more than once, especially in different words: *a redundant paragraph in the speech.* **2.** Having a function already performed by something or someone else: *redundant machine parts; a redundant employee.* [From Latin *redundāre*, to overflow : *re-*, *red-*, back + *undāre*, to surge, from *unda*, wave.] **—re·dun′dant·ly** *adv.*

red-winged blackbird (rĕd′wĭngd′) *n.* A blackbird of North and Central America, the male of which has bright-red patches on the wings.

red·wood (rĕd′wo͝od′) *n.* **1a.** A very tall cone-bearing evergreen tree of northern California and southern Oregon, sometimes growing to a height of over 300 feet. **b.** The soft reddish-brown wood of such a tree, which is resistant to decay. **2.** A sequoia tree.

reed (rēd) *n.* **1.** Any of various tall hollow-stemmed grasses or similar plants that grow in wet places. **2a.** A flexible strip of cane or metal set in the mouthpiece of certain wind instruments to produce tones by vibrating when air passes over it. **b.** A woodwind instrument, such as an oboe or clarinet, having a reed. [From Old English *hrēod.*]

❑ *These sound alike:* **reed, read** (understand writing).

reed·y (rē′dē) *adj.* **reed·i·er, reed·i·est** **1.** Full of reeds: *a reedy marsh.* **2.** Resembling a reed: *a slim reedy girl.* **3.** Having the sound of a reed instrument: *the oboe's reedy tone.* **—reed′i·ness** *n.*

reef[1] (rēf) *n.* An irregular mass, strip, or ridge of rock or coral that rises to or close to the surface of a body of water. [From obsolete Dutch *rif*, possibly from Old Norse, ridge.]

reef[2] (rēf) *n.* A portion of a sail rolled and tied down to decrease the area of the sail that is exposed to the wind. ❖ *tr.v.* **reefed, reef·ing, reefs** To reduce the area of (a sail) by making a reef. [From Middle English *rif*, from Old Norse, ridge, reef.]

reek (rēk) *intr.v.* **reeked, reek·ing, reeks** To give off a strong or unpleasant odor: *a salad reeking of garlic.* ❖ *n.* A strong unpleasant odor. [From Old English *rēcan*, to expose to smoke.]

❑ *These sound alike:* **reek, wreak** (inflict).

reel[1] (rēl) *n.* **1.** A device that turns on a central axis and is used for winding and storing rope, film, tape, fishing line, and other flexible materials. **2.** The amount of material wound on a reel. ❖ *tr.v.* **reeled, reel·ing, reels** **1.** To wind onto a reel. **2.** To pull in (a fish) by winding on a reel: *reel in a marlin.* ◆ **reel off** To recite fluently and usually at length: *He reeled off a list of names.* [From Old English *hrēol.*]

❑ *These sound alike:* **reel**[1] (tape spool), **real**[1] (actual), **reel**[2] (stagger).

reel[2] (rēl) *v.* **reeled, reel·ing, reels** *—intr.* **1.** To be thrown off balance, as from a blow or hit. **2.** To stagger or sway: *After spinning around, she reeled across the lawn.* **3.** To go round and round in a whirling motion: *The events of the day reeled in his mind.* ❖ *n.* **1.** A staggering, swaying, or whirling movement. **2a.** Any of several fast lively folk dances. **b.** A piece of music for this dance. [From Middle English *relen*, to whirl about, probably from *reel*, spool.]

❑ *These sound alike:* **reel**[2] (stagger), **real**[1] (actual), **reel**[1] (tape spool).

re·e·lect (rē′ĭ-lĕkt′) *tr.v.* **re·e·lect·ed, re·e·lect·ing, re·e·lects** To elect again. **—re′e·lec′tion** *n.*

re·en·ter (rē-ĕn′tər) *v.* **re·en·tered, re·en·ter·ing, re·en·ters** *—tr.* **1.** To enter or come in to again: *reentered the room wearing a hat.* **2.** To become again a participant, member, or part of: *reenter civilian life after military service.* **3.** To record again on a list or ledger. *—intr.* To come in or enter again. **—re·en′trance** *n.*

re·en·try (rē-ĕn′trē) *n., pl.* **re·en·tries** **1.** The act of reentering; a second or subsequent entry. **2.** The return of a missile or spacecraft to Earth's atmosphere.

re·es·tab·lish (rē′ĭ-stăb′lĭsh) *v.* **re·es·tab·lished, re·es·tab·lish·ing, re·es·tab·lish·es** To establish again; restore. **—re′es·tab′lish·ment** *n.*

re·fec·to·ry (rĭ-fĕk′tə-rē) *n., pl.* **re·fec·to·ries** A room where meals are served, especially in a college or other institution.

re·fer (rĭ-fûr′) *v.* **re·ferred, re·fer·ring, re·fers** *—tr.* **1.** To direct to a person or organization for help or information: *refer a patient to a heart specialist.* **2.** To submit (something) to a person or group for examination or action: *refer a proposed bill to a committee.* *—intr.* **1.** To pertain; concern: *questions referring to today's lesson.* **2.** To make mention or reference: *She kept referring to our team as "the losers."* **3.** To have a meaning in relation to something else: *The word* chair *refers to a piece of furniture.* **4.** To use a book, website, or other source to get information: *refer to a dictionary.* [From Middle English *referren*, from Latin *referre* : *re-*, back + *ferre*, to carry.] —SEE NOTE AT **transfer.**

SCIENCE

red blood cell Human blood gets its distinctive red color from the abundant **red blood cells** that it contains. The red blood cells, in turn, are red because they are full of an iron-containing protein called *hemoglobin.* This protein is like a sophisticated dump truck. When hemoglobin is in the lungs it picks up oxygen molecules, which bind to the iron atoms. Blood vessels carry the hemoglobin throughout the body, where the oxygen is released for use by muscle, nerve, and other cells. The oxygen-depleted hemoglobin then returns to the lungs to pick up another load. All animals have some oxygen distribution system, but only vertebrate animals have red blood cells. Earthworms have hemoglobin that floats freely in the blood rather than being contained in cells. Certain animals do not use hemoglobin at all. Horseshoe crabs and many mollusks, such as octopuses, use a copper-containing molecule to transport oxygen, making their blood bluish instead of red.

Red Cloud

reel[1]
film reel

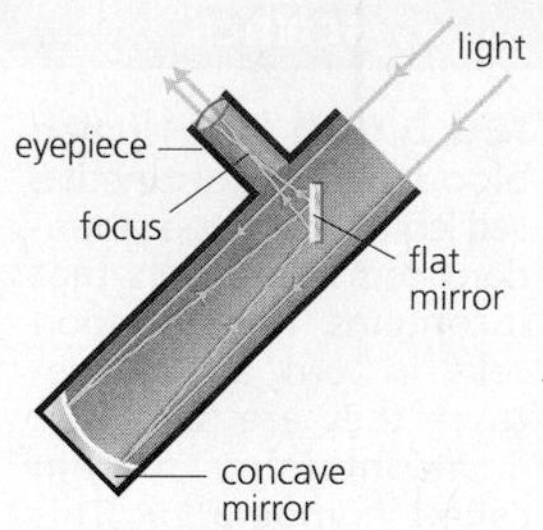

reflecting telescope
Light is gathered by reflecting off a concave mirror. It is then reflected off an angled flat mirror toward the eyepiece.

reflection
reflection of Mt. Shuksan in Picture Lake, Washington

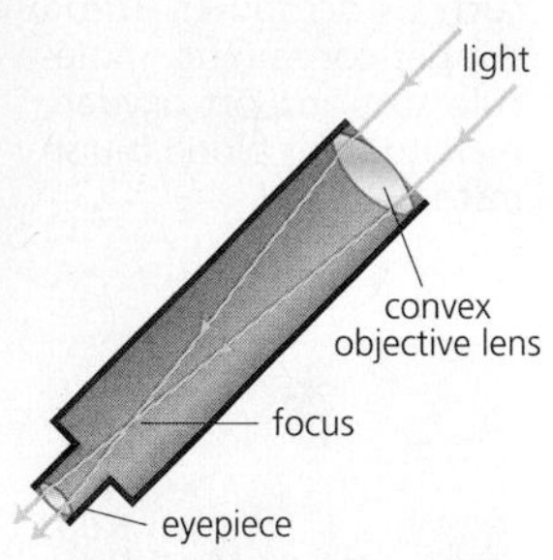

refracting telescope
Light is gathered by being refracted through a convex objective lens. It then exits through the eyepiece.

ă	pat	ôr	core
ā	pay	oi	boy
âr	care	ou	out
ä	father	o͝o	took
ĕ	pet	o͝or	lure
ē	be	o͞o	boot
ĭ	pit	ŭ	cut
ī	bite	ûr	urge
îr	pier	th	thin
ŏ	pot	*th*	this
ō	toe	zh	vision
ô	paw	ə	about

ref·e·ree (rĕf′ə-rē′) *n.* **1.** In sports, an official supervising play. **2.** A person to whom something is referred for settlement or decision; an arbitrator or arbiter. ❖ *tr. & intr.v.* **ref·e·reed, ref·e·ree·ing, ref·e·rees** To judge or act as a referee.

ref·er·ence (rĕf′ər-əns *or* rĕf′rəns) *n.* **1.** An act of referring: *Let's file that article away for future reference.* **2.** The state of being related or referred: *a reply in reference to your query.* **3.** A mention of an occurrence or situation: *He made frequent references to his trip to Europe.* **4.** A note in a book or other publication that directs the reader to another part of the book or to another source of information. **5a.** A person who is in a position to recommend another or to vouch for his or her fitness, as for a job: *May I use you as a reference?* **b.** A statement about a person's character or qualifications for something.

reference book *n.* A book, such as an encyclopedia, that provides information arranged for easy access.

ref·er·en·dum (rĕf′ə-rĕn′dəm) *n.* **1.** The practice of placing a measure directly before the voters rather than deciding it through a legislative body. **2.** Such a vote: *The referendum on the school bond issue passed.*

re·fer·ral (rĭ-fûr′əl) *n.* **1.** The act or an instance of referring: *the patient's referral to a specialist.* **2.** A person or thing that has been referred: *The doctor saw many of her own patients plus several referrals.*

re·fill (rē-fĭl′) *tr.v.* **re·filled, re·fill·ing, re·fills** To fill again: *He refilled the glass with water.* ❖ *n.* (**rē′**fĭl′) **1.** A second or subsequent filling: *held out her glass for a refill.* **2.** A product packaged to replace the used contents of a container.

re·fine (rĭ-fīn′) *tr.v.* **re·fined, re·fin·ing, re·fines 1.** To remove unwanted matter from; make pure: *refine oil; refine sugar.* **2.** To make polished or elegant: *refine one's table manners.* **—re·fin′er** *n.*

re·fined (rĭ-fīnd′) *adj.* **1.** Free from coarseness; polite or cultivated: *She is a refined person.* **2.** Made pure, as through an industrial refining process: *refined uranium.*

re·fine·ment (rĭ-fīn′mənt) *n.* **1.** The act or process of refining: *Your writing has undergone much refinement.* **2.** A small change or addition intended to improve something: *We made some refinements to the computer program.* **3.** Elegance; cultivation.

re·fin·er·y (rĭ-fī′nə-rē) *n., pl.* **re·fin·er·ies** An industrial plant for purifying a crude substance, such as petroleum or sugar.

re·fit (rē-fĭt′) *tr.v.* **re·fit·ted, re·fit·ting, re·fits** To prepare and equip for additional use.

re·flect (rĭ-flĕkt′) *v.* **re·flect·ed, re·flect·ing, re·flects** —*tr.* **1.** To throw or bend back (light, for example) from a surface. **2.** To give back or show an image of; mirror: *The shop window reflected his face.* **3.** To show as a result: *The price of a product reflects the costs of producing it.* —*intr.* **1.** To be thrown or bent back: *light reflecting from the water.* **2.** To think seriously; contemplate. ◆ **reflect on 1.** To form or express thoughts about: *We reflected on the meaning of the poem.* **2.** To give evidence of the qualities of (someone): *Keeping your room neat reflects positively on you.* [From Middle English *reflecten*, from Latin *reflectere*, to bend back : *re-*, back + *flectere*, to bend.]

re·flect·ing telescope (rĭ-flĕk′tĭng) *n.* A telescope in which light from an object is gathered and focused by a concave mirror.

re·flec·tion (rĭ-flĕk′shən) *n.* **1.** The act or process of reflecting: *the reflection of light by a mirror.* **2a.** Something, such as sound, light, or heat, that is reflected. **b.** An image formed by reflected light: *the reflection of the trees in the river.* **3a.** Serious thought; meditation: *After long reflection, he decided to audition for the play.* **b.** An idea, remark, or piece of writing resulting from this. **4.** A manifestation or result: *Her achievements are a reflection of her courage.*

re·flec·tive (rĭ-flĕk′tĭv) *adj.* **1a.** Relating to, produced by, or resulting from reflection: *the reflective properties of glass.* **b.** Tending to reflect: *a reflective surface.* **2.** Thoughtful; pensive: *a reflective mood.*

re·flec·tor (rĭ-flĕk′tər) *n.* **1.** Something, such as a surface, that reflects. **2.** A reflecting telescope.

re·flex (rē′flĕks′) *n.* **1.** An involuntary response to a stimulus. **2. reflexes** The ability to take action in response to other actions or events: *To be a goalie, you need quick reflexes.*

re·flex·ive (rĭ-flĕk′sĭv) *adj.* **1.** Relating to a reflex: *a reflexive twitch.* **2.** Being a verb that has an identical subject and direct object. For example, in the sentence *She dressed herself, she* and *herself* refer to the same person, so *dressed* is a reflexive verb. **3.** Being a pronoun used as direct object of a reflexive verb. For example, in the sentence *He blames himself, himself* is a reflexive pronoun. ❖ *n.* A reflexive verb or pronoun. **—re·flex′ive·ly** *adv.*

re·for·est (rē-fôr′ĭst) *tr.v.* **re·for·est·ed, re·for·est·ing, re·for·ests** To replant (an area) with trees. **—re′for·es·ta′tion** *n.*

re·form (rĭ-fôrm′) *v.* **re·formed, re·form·ing, re·forms** —*tr.* **1.** To improve, as by correcting errors or removing defects: *a plan to reform the health care system.* **2.** To cause to give up harmful ways: *work designed to reform criminals.* —*intr.* To become changed for the better: *He saw the foolishness of his behavior and reformed.* ❖ *n.* **1.** A change for the better; an improvement: *the reform of city government.* **2.** A movement or policy that aims at this: *prison reform.* **—re·form′er** *n.*

ref·or·ma·tion (rĕf′ər-mā′shən) *n.* **1.** The act of reforming or the condition of being reformed: *a total reformation of the public school system.* **2. Reformation** A religious movement in the 1500s in Western Europe that was aimed at reforming the Roman Catholic Church but resulted in the founding of the Protestant churches, which rejected the authority of the Pope and claimed the Bible as the only source of religious revelation.

re·for·ma·to·ry (rĭ-fôr′mə-tôr′ē) *n., pl.* **re·for·ma·to·ries** An institution for disciplining and training young lawbreakers.

Reform Judaism *n.* The branch of Judaism founded in the 1800s that does not require strict observance of religious laws and rituals.

reform school *n.* A reformatory.

re·fract (rĭ-frăkt′) *tr.v.* **re·fract·ed, re·fract·ing, re·fracts** To cause the path of (light or other radiation) to bend or deflect by refraction. [From Latin *refringere*, to break up.]

re·fract·ing telescope (rĭ-frăk′tĭng) *n.* A telescope in which light from an object is gathered and focused by lenses.

re·frac·tion (rĭ-frăk′shən) *n.* **1.** The bending or turning of a wave, such as a light or sound wave, when it passes from one medium to another of different density. **2.** The apparent change in position of a celestial object caused by the bending of light as it enters Earth's atmosphere.

re·frac·tor (rĭ-frăk′tər) *n.* **1.** Something that refracts. **2.** A refracting telescope.

re·frac·to·ry (rĭ-frăk′tə-rē) *adj.* **1.** Stubbornly resistant to authority or control: *a refractory child.* **2.** Difficult to melt or work; resistant to heat: *a refractory ore.* **3.** Not responsive to medical treatment: *a refractory disease.*

re·frain¹ (rĭ-frān′) *intr.v.* **re·frained, re·frain·ing, re·frains** To hold oneself back; forbear: *refrain from talking.* [From Middle English *refreinen*, from Latin *refrēnāre*, to restrain : *re-*, back + *frēnum*, bridle.]

re·frain² (rĭ-frān′) *n.* **1.** A phrase, verse, or group of verses repeated several times throughout the course of a song or poem, especially at the end of each stanza. **2.** The music for the refrain of a song. [From Middle

English *refrein*, from Old French *refraindre*, to repeat, from Latin *refringere*.]

re·fresh (rĭ-frĕsh′) *tr.v.* **re·freshed, re·fresh·ing, re·fresh·es 1.** To revive with or as if with food, drink, or rest: *I refreshed myself with an afternoon nap.* **2.** To make cool, clean, or damp; freshen: *An afternoon shower refreshed the lawn.* **3.** To renew, as by providing a reminder: *refresh one's memory.* **4.** To update (the information displayed on a screen). **—re·fresh′er** *n.*

re·fresh·ing (rĭ-frĕsh′ĭng) *adj.* **1.** Serving to refresh: *a refreshing breeze.* **2.** New and different in a pleasant way: *a refreshing viewpoint on art.* **—re·fresh′ing·ly** *adv.*

re·fresh·ment (rĭ-frĕsh′mənt) *n.* **1.** The act of refreshing or the condition of being refreshed. **2.** Something that refreshes. **3.** often **refreshments** A snack, light meal, or drink: *served refreshments at the party.*

re·fried beans (rē′frīd′) *pl.n.* Beans that have been cooked and then mashed and fried.

re·frig·er·ant (rĭ-frĭj′ər-ənt) *n.* A substance used to cool something by absorbing heat from it, either directly or in a refrigerator.

re·frig·er·ate (rĭ-frĭj′ə-rāt′) *tr.v.* **re·frig·er·at·ed, re·frig·er·at·ing, re·frig·er·ates 1.** To cool or chill (a substance). **2.** To preserve (food) by storing at a low temperature. [From Latin *refrīgerāre*, from *frīgus*, coldness.] **—re·frig′er·a′tion** *n.*

re·frig·er·a·tor (rĭ-frĭj′ə-rā′tər) *n.* An appliance, cabinet, or room for storing food or other substances at a low temperature.

ref·uge (rĕf′yo͞oj) *n.* **1.** Protection; shelter: *seeking refuge in the castle.* **2.** A place providing protection or shelter: *a wildlife refuge.* [From Middle English, from Latin *refugere*, to run away.]

ref·u·gee (rĕf′yo͞o-jē′) *n.* A person who flees in search of refuge, as in times of war or religious persecution.

re·ful·gent (rĭ-fo͝ol′jənt) *adj.* Shining radiantly; brilliant: *a crown refulgent with gems.* **—re·ful′gence** *n.* **—re·ful′gent·ly** *adv.*

re·fund (rĭ-fŭnd′ *or* rē′fŭnd′) *tr.v.* **re·fund·ed, re·fund·ing, re·funds** To pay back (money): *The store refunded the full price of the TV set.* ❖ *n.* (rē′fŭnd′) **1.** A repayment of funds: *She demanded a refund.* **2.** An amount repaid: *How much was your refund?* **—re·fund′a·ble** *adj.*

re·fur·bish (rē-fûr′bĭsh) *tr.v.* **re·fur·bished, re·fur·bish·ing, re·fur·bish·es** To brighten or freshen up; renovate: *refurbish a house.*

re·fus·al (rĭ-fyo͞o′zəl) *n.* **1.** The act of refusing. **2.** The opportunity or right to accept or reject something before it is offered elsewhere.

re·fuse[1] (rĭ-fyo͞oz′) *tr.v.* **re·fused, re·fus·ing, re·fus·es 1.** To indicate unwillingness (to do something). **2.** To indicate unwillingness to accept; turn down: *refuse an offer.* **3.** To indicate unwillingness to give; deny: *We were refused permission to leave early.* [From Middle English *refusen*, from Old French *refuser*.]

ref·use[2] (rĕf′yo͞os) *n.* Discarded or rejected matter; trash. [From Middle English, from Old French *refuser*, to refuse.]

ref·u·ta·tion (rĕf′yo͞o-tā′shən) *n.* **1.** The act of refuting. **2.** Something, such as an argument, that refutes someone or something.

re·fute (rĭ-fyo͞ot′) *tr.v.* **re·fut·ed, re·fut·ing, re·futes** To prove to be false or wrong: *refuted their statements.* **—re·fut′er** *n.*

re·gain (rē-gān′) *tr.v.* **re·gained, re·gain·ing, re·gains 1.** To recover possession of; get back: *regain lost territory.* **2.** To have (an ability or desirable condition) restored: *regain one's hearing; regain one's health.* **3.** To add back (body weight that has been lost). **4.** To manage to reach again: *regain the shore.*

re·gal (rē′gəl) *adj.* **1.** Relating to a king; royal: *regal power.* **2.** Befitting a king: *a regal bearing.* [From Middle English, from Latin *rēgālis*, from *rēx*, king.]

re·gale (rĭ-gāl′) *v.* **re·galed, re·gal·ing, re·gales** *—tr.* **1.** To entertain or amuse: *regaled us with their stories and jokes.* **2.** To provide a lavish feast for. *—intr.* To feast.

re·ga·lia (rĭ-gāl′yə) *pl.n.* *(used with a singular or plural verb)* **1.** The emblems and symbols of royalty, as the crown and scepter. **2.** The special symbols and costume that distinguish a certain rank, office, or order. **3.** Fine or fancy clothes; finery.

re·gard (rĭ-gärd′) *tr.v.* **re·gard·ed, re·gard·ing, re·gards 1.** To look at closely; observe: *regarded the coyotes with a fixed stare.* **2.** To consider in a particular way: *I regarded her as the brightest of my friends.* **3.** To relate to; concern: *This decision regards the future of our band.* ❖ *n.* **1.** A look or gaze: *a judge's cold regard.* **2.** Careful thought or attention: *She gives little regard to her appearance.* **3.** Esteem or affection: *showing regard for his parents.* **4. regards** Good wishes; greetings: *Send her my regards, will you?* **5.** A particular point or matter: *I can't help you in that regard.* ◆ **in regard to** or **with regard to** With respect to. —SEE NOTE.

re·gard·ful (rĭ-gärd′fəl) *adj.* **1.** Attentive; mindful: *regardful of the feelings of other people.* **2.** Respectful: *addressing her in a regardful voice.*

re·gard·ing (rĭ-gär′dĭng) *prep.* In reference to; concerning: *laws regarding sanitation.* —SEE NOTE AT **regard.**

re·gard·less (rĭ-gärd′lĭs) *adv.* In spite of everything; anyway: *She still loved him, regardless.* ◆ **regardless of 1.** In spite of: *were able to enjoy ourselves regardless of the rain.* **2.** With no attention to: *freedom for all, regardless of race or creed.* **—re·gard′less·ly** *adv.* —SEE NOTE AT **irregardless.**

re·gat·ta (rĭ-gä′tə *or* rĭ-găt′ə) *n.* A boat race or races, organized as a sporting event.

re·gen·cy (rē′jən-sē) *n., pl.* **re·gen·cies 1.** A group of regents appointed to rule a kingdom jointly. **2.** The government or period of rule of a regent.

re·gen·er·ate (rĭ-jĕn′ə-rāt′) *v.* **re·gen·er·at·ed, re·gen·er·at·ing, re·gen·er·ates** *—tr.* **1.** To replace (a lost or damaged body part) by growing new tissue: *A starfish that has lost an arm will regenerate a new one.* **2.** To give new life to; revive: *The reforms were intended to regenerate the nation's economic life.* *—intr.* To become replaced by the growth of new tissue: *A salamander's tail regenerates if it is cut off.* **—re·gen′er·a′tion** *n.* **—re·gen′er·a′tive** *adj.*

re·gent (rē′jənt) *n.* **1.** A person appointed to rule when a monarch is absent, too young, or unable to rule. **2.** A member of a board that governs an institution such as a state university.

reg·gae (rĕg′ā) *n.* Popular music of Jamaican origin having elements of Calypso and rhythm and blues, usually with an accent placed on the offbeat.

reg·i·cide (rĕj′ĭ-sīd′) *n.* **1.** The killing of a king. **2.** A person who kills a king.

re·gime also **ré·gime** (rā-zhēm′ *or* rĭ-zhēm′) *n.* **1.** A form of government: *a communist regime.* **2.** A government in power; an administration. **3.** A system of diet, exercise, or medical treatment; a regimen.

reg·i·men (rĕj′ə-mən) *n.* A system of recommended behavior, especially of diet or exercise, that is followed for its beneficial effect on one's overall health or condition.

reg·i·ment (rĕj′ə-mənt) *n.* A unit of soldiers, composed of two or more battalions. ❖ *tr.v.* (rĕj′ə-mĕnt′) **reg·i·ment·ed, reg·i·ment·ing, reg·i·ments 1.** To put into systematic order. **2.** To force to conform to a single pattern, as by rigid discipline. **—reg′i·men′tal** (rĕj′ə-mĕn′tl) *adj.* **—reg′i·men·ta′tion** *n.*

reg·i·men·tals (rĕj′ə-mĕnt′lz) *pl.n.* The uniform and insignia of a particular regiment.

Re·gi·na (rĭ-jī′nə) The capital of Saskatchewan, Canada,

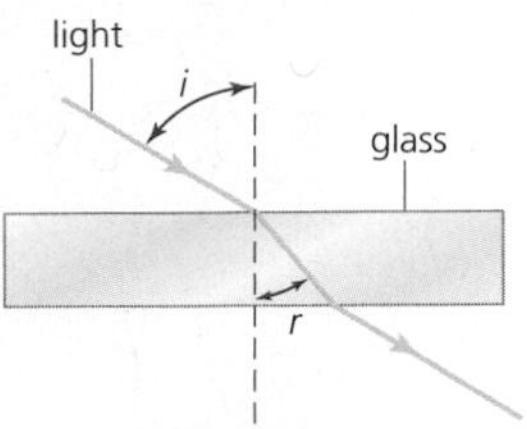

refraction
refraction of light
i: angle of incidence
r: angle of refraction

regalia

USAGE

regard Use **regard** in the singular in the phrase *in regard to: I have a few ideas in regard to use of the school's basketball courts.* You can also use *regarding, as regards,* and *with respect to* to mean "with reference to": *As regards the use of the school's basketball courts, I have a few ideas.*

in the southern part of the province west of Winnipeg, Manitoba. It was founded in 1882.

re·gion (rē′jən) *n.* **1.** A large area of a surface or space: *the upper regions of the atmosphere.* **2.** A portion of the earth's surface: *the coastal region.* **3.** A section or area of the body: *the abdominal region.* **4.** A field of interest or activity; a sphere: *all regions of the physical sciences.* [From Middle English *regioun*, from Latin *regiō*, from *regere*, to rule.]

re·gion·al (rē′jə-nəl) *adj.* **1.** Relating to a large geographic region: *a local crisis that turned into a regional disaster.* **2.** Relating to a particular region: *a regional accent.* —**re′gion·al·ly** *adv.*

reg·is·ter (rĕj′ĭ-stər) *n.* **1a.** An official record of items, names, or transactions: *a register of all real-estate properties.* **b.** A book in which such a record is kept. **2.** A person who registers: *a register of deeds.* **3.** A device that automatically records or displays a number or quantity. **4.** A device resembling a grill that can be adjusted to control the flow of heated or cooled air into a room. **5a.** The range of a voice or musical instrument from its lowest to highest tones. **b.** A part of such a range: *the low register of a contralto.* ❖ *v.* **reg·is·tered, reg·is·ter·ing, reg·is·ters** —*tr.* **1.** To record in a register: *register a birth.* **2.** To express or write down; record: *I want to register a complaint.* **3.** To indicate, as on a scale or device: *A Geiger counter registers radioactivity.* **4.** To be indicated as: *The earthquake registered 6.1 on the Richter scale.* **5.** To enroll in order to vote or attend classes. **6.** To show or make apparent: *His face registered surprise.* **7.** To cause (mail) to be officially recorded by the post office. —*intr.* **1.** To place one's name in a register: *You can register for the conference in the lobby.* **2.** To have one's name placed on a list of eligible voters. **3.** To enroll as a student. **4.** To be shown: *Recognition did not register on her face.* **5.** To make an impression: *failed to register in my memory.*

reg·is·tered nurse (rĕj′ĭ-stərd) *n.* A nurse who has graduated from a nursing school, passed a state registration examination, and been licensed to practice nursing.

reg·is·trar (rĕj′ĭ-strär′) *n.* An official, as at a university, who is responsible for keeping records.

reg·is·tra·tion (rĕj′ĭ-strā′shən) *n.* **1.** The act of registering, as of voters or students. **2.** The number of people registered: *Voter registration in our county is 11,000.* **3.** An entry in a register. **4.** A document showing proof of registration.

reg·is·try (rĕj′ĭ-strē) *n., pl.* **reg·is·tries 1.** The act of registering; registration. **2.** A ship's registered nationality: *The tanker has a Liberian registry.* **3.** A book of official records. **4.** A place where official records are kept.

re·gress (rĭ-grĕs′) *intr.v.* **re·gressed, re·gress·ing, re·gress·es** To return to a previous, usually worse or less developed state: *When I left the country, my ability to speak the language regressed.* [From Latin *regredī* : *re-*, back + *gradī*, to go.] —**re·gres′sion** (rĭ-grĕsh′ən) *n.*

re·gret (rĭ-grĕt′) *tr.v.* **re·gret·ted, re·gret·ting, re·grets** To feel sad, disappointed, or remorseful about (something that one wishes could be different): *I regret not speaking to her before she left.* ❖ *n.* **1.** A feeling of sadness, disappointment, or remorse about something that one wishes could be different. **2. regrets** A polite reply turning down an invitation: *send one's regrets.* [From Middle English *regreten*, to lament, from Old French *regreter* : *re-*, again + *greter*, to weep.] —**re·gret′ta·ble** *adj.*

re·gret·ful (rĭ-grĕt′fəl) *adj.* Full of regret; sorrowful or sorry. —**re·gret′ful·ly** *adv.* —**re·gret′ful·ness** *n.*

reg·u·lar (rĕg′yə-lər) *adj.* **1.** Customary or usual: *Our regular teacher was out sick.* **2.** Not special; ordinary: *I wore regular sneakers, not hiking boots.* **3.** Following a set pattern or arrangement in space: *studs at regular intervals in the wall.* **4.** Occurring frequently or repeatedly, especially at set intervals in time: *regular flights over the islands.* **5.** Doing the same thing or going to the same place frequently or habitually: *a regular customer.* **6.** Following an established procedure or discipline: *They followed regular procedure in cleaning the furnace.* **7.** *Informal* Friendly and likable: *He's a regular guy.* **8.** *Informal* Complete; thorough: *a regular scoundrel.* **9.** Belonging to or constituting the permanent army of a country. **10.** Having all sides equal and all angles equal: *a regular polyhedron.* **11.** In grammar, conforming to the usual pattern of inflection, derivation, or word formation: *a regular verb.* ❖ *n.* **1.** A habitual customer: *The server recognized him as one of the regulars.* **2.** A soldier belonging to a regular army. [From Middle English *reguler*, living under religious rule, from Latin *rēgula*, rod, rule.] —**reg′u·lar′i·ty** (rĕg′yə-lăr′ĭ-tē) *n.* —**reg′u·lar·ly** *adv.* —SEE NOTE AT **rectify.**

reg·u·late (rĕg′yə-lāt′) *tr.v.* **reg·u·lat·ed, reg·u·lat·ing, reg·u·lates 1.** To control or direct according to a rule or law: *power to regulate commerce.* **2.** To adjust for proper functioning: *regulate a carburetor.* **3.** To adjust or control according to a requirement: *This valve regulates the flow of water.* **4.** To put or maintain in order: *regulate one's sleeping habits.* —**reg′u·la′tor** *n.*

reg·u·la·tion (rĕg′yə-lā′shən) *n.* **1.** The act or process of regulating. **2.** The condition of being regulated: *freedom from government regulation.* **3.** A rule, order, or law by which something is regulated: *traffic regulations.* **4.** In sports, the standard playing period for a timed game, prior to overtime or a shootout.

reg·u·la·to·ry (rĕg′yə-lə-tôr′ē) *adj.* Having the ability to regulate or oversee.

re·gur·gi·tate (rē-gûr′jĭ-tāt′) *v.* **re·gur·gi·tat·ed, re·gur·gi·tat·ing, re·gur·gi·tates** To cause (partially digested food) to come back up from the stomach into the throat or mouth. —**re·gur′gi·ta′tion** *n.*

re·ha·bil·i·tate (rē′hə-bĭl′ĭ-tāt′) *tr.v.* **re·ha·bil·i·tat·ed, re·ha·bil·i·tat·ing, re·ha·bil·i·tates 1.** To restore (someone) to good health or useful life, as through training or therapy. **2.** To restore to good condition or operation: *rehabilitate a house.* **3.** To cause to be regarded again in a positive way; reestablish esteem for: *rehabilitate a forgotten poet.* **4.** To restore the former rank or privileges of: *When the dictatorship was overthrown, many people who had been imprisoned were rehabilitated.* —**re′ha·bil′i·ta′tion** *n.*

re·hash (rē-hăsh′) *tr.v.* **re·hashed, re·hash·ing, re·hash·es** To present or go over again, without anything new resulting: *John and Susan rehashed their disagreement.* ❖ *n.* (rē′hăsh′) The act or result of rehashing: *His book is a rehash of some earlier ideas.*

re·hears·al (rĭ-hûr′səl) *n.* **1.** The act or process of practicing in preparation for a performance or ceremony. **2.** A session devoted to such practice: *a wedding rehearsal.*

re·hearse (rĭ-hûrs′) *v.* **re·hearsed, re·hears·ing, re·hears·es** —*tr.* **1.** To practice (all or part of a program) in preparation for a performance: *The boys rehearsed their skit.* **2.** To train by rehearsal: *rehearse a choir.* —*intr.* To practice something, such as a speech, before presenting it publicly.

Rehn·quist (rĕn′kwĭst′), **William Hubbs** 1924–2005. American jurist who served as an associate justice of the US Supreme Court (1972–1986) and as the chief justice (1986–2005).

reign (rān) *n.* **1.** The exercise of political power by a monarch. **2.** The period during which a monarch rules. ❖ *intr.v.* **reigned, reign·ing, reigns 1.** To exercise the power of a monarch: *Queen Victoria reigned from 1837 to 1901.* **2.** To be predominant or pervasive: *A stillness reigned after the storm.* [From Middle English *regne*, from Latin *rēgnum*, from *rēx*, king.]

ă	pat	ôr	core
ā	pay	oi	boy
âr	care	ou	out
ä	father	o͝o	took
ĕ	pet	o͝or	lure
ē	be	o͞o	boot
ĭ	pit	ŭ	cut
ī	bite	ûr	urge
îr	pier	th	thin
ŏ	pot	*th*	this
ō	toe	zh	vision
ô	paw	ə	about

❑ *These sound alike:* **reign, rain** (water drops), **rein** (strap).

re·im·burse (rē′ĭm-**bûrs′**) *tr.v.* **re·im·bursed, re·im·burs·ing, re·im·burs·es** To pay back; compensate. —**re′im·burs′a·ble** *adj.* —**re′im·burse′ment** *n.*

rein (rān) *n.* **1.** Either of two long narrow straps attached to each end of the bit of a bridle and used by a rider or driver to control a horse or other animal: *held the reins tightly as the horses sped off.* **2.** A means of restraint or guidance: *the reins of government.* ❖ *tr.v.* **reined, rein·ing, reins 1.** To check or hold back by the use of reins: *reined in the horse.* **2.** To restrain or control: *The police captain reined in the detectives.* ◆ **give rein to** or **give free rein to** To release from restraints; allow to go unchecked: *She gave free rein to her feelings.* [From Middle English, from Latin *retinēre*, to retain.]

❑ *These sound alike:* **rein, rain** (water drops), **reign** (rule).

re·in·car·nate (rē′ĭn-**kär′**nāt) *v.* **re·in·car·nat·ed, re·in·car·nat·ing, re·in·car·nates** —*tr.* To cause to be reborn in another body. —*intr.* To be reborn in another body.

re·in·car·na·tion (rē′ĭn-kär-**nā′**shən) *n.* Rebirth of the soul in another body.

rein·deer (**rān′**dîr′) *n., pl.* **reindeer** or **rein·deers** A deer of the Arctic tundra and northern forest regions of Eurasia, having large spreading antlers in both the male and the female. Reindeer and caribou belong to the same species. [From Middle English *rein-der* : Old Norse *hreinn*, reindeer + Middle English *der*, animal.]

re·in·force (rē′ĭn-**fôrs′**) *tr.v.* **re·in·forced, re·in·forc·ing, re·in·forc·es 1.** To make stronger by adding extra support to; strengthen: *reinforce a bridge.* **2.** To strengthen (a military force) with additional troops or equipment. **3.** To give more force or effectiveness to; strengthen: *The news reinforced our suspicions.* —**re′in·force′a·ble** *adj.*

re·in·force·ment (rē′ĭn-**fôrs′**mənt) *n.* **1.** The act or process of reinforcing. **2.** Something that reinforces. **3. reinforcements** Additional troops or equipment sent to support a military action.

re·in·state (rē′ĭn-**stāt′**) *tr.v.* **re·in·stat·ed, re·in·stat·ing, re·in·states** To restore to a previous condition or position: *After a leave of absence, she was reinstated in her job.* —**re′in·state′ment** *n.*

re·it·er·ate (rē-**ĭt′**ə-rāt′) *tr.v.* **re·it·er·at·ed, re·it·er·at·ing, re·it·er·ates** To say over again; repeat: *The coach reiterated his instructions.* —**re·it′er·a′tion** *n.*

re·ject (rĭ-**jĕkt′**) *tr.v.* **re·ject·ed, re·ject·ing, re·jects 1.** To refuse to accept, use, or submit to: *We rejected the idea of working overtime.* **2.** To refuse to consider or grant; deny: *My mother rejected my plans for a big party.* **3.** To fail to give affection or love to (a person). **4.** To resist the introduction of (a transplanted organ or tissue); fail to accept as part of one's own body. ❖ *n.* (**rē′**jĕkt) A person or thing that has been rejected: *rejects from military service.* [From Middle English *rejecten*, from Latin *rēicere* : *re-*, back + *iacere*, to throw.] —SEE NOTE AT **inject.**

re·jec·tion (rĭ-**jĕk′**shən) *n.* **1.** The act of rejecting or the condition of being rejected: *the rejection of a manuscript by a publisher.* **2.** A notification that someone or something has been rejected: *rejections sent to college applicants.*

re·joice (rĭ-**jois′**) *v.* **re·joiced, re·joic·ing, re·joic·es** —*intr.* To feel joy; be delighted: *I rejoice in your good fortune.* —*tr.* To fill with joy; gladden.

re·join[1] (rĭ-**join′**) *tr.v.* **re·joined, re·join·ing, re·joins** To answer or reply sharply: *"I disagree!" Sammy rejoined.* [From Middle English *rejoinen*, from Old French *rejoindre.*]

re·join[2] (rē-**join′**) *tr.v.* **re·joined, re·join·ing, re·joins 1.** To join together again. **2.** To return to; reunite with: *The explorer rejoined his family.*

re·join·der (rĭ-**join′**dər) *n.* A reply, especially in disagreement: *his rejoinder to the criticism against him.*

re·ju·ve·nate (rĭ-**jo͞o′**və-nāt′) *tr.v.* **re·ju·ve·nat·ed, re·ju·ve·nat·ing, re·ju·ve·nates** To make (someone) appear or feel young or vigorous again: *Her vacation completely rejuvenated her.* [From Latin *iuvenis*, young.] —**re·ju′ve·na′tion** *n.*

re·lapse (rĭ-**lăps′**) *intr.v.* **re·lapsed, re·laps·ing, re·laps·es 1.** To fall back into a previous condition: *We relapsed into our old sloppy habits.* **2.** To become sick again after a partial recovery. ❖ *n.* (**rē′**lăps *or* rĭ-**lăps′**) A falling back into a previous condition, especially a return to illness.

re·late (rĭ-**lāt′**) *v.* **re·lat·ed, re·lat·ing, re·lates** —*tr.* **1.** To tell or narrate: *relate a story.* **2.** To bring into association; link or connect: *I related his grumpiness to a lack of sleep.* —*intr.* **1.** To have a connection with something: *a question relating to foreign policy.* **2.** To interact with other people in a meaningful way: *She relates well to her classmates.* **3.** To feel a sympathetic understanding toward someone or something: *I can relate to the problems you're facing.* [From Latin *relātus*, carried over.]

re·lat·ed (rĭ-**lā′**tĭd) *adj.* **1.** Connected; associated: *closely related topics.* **2.** Connected by kinship, marriage, or common origin. —**re·lat′ed·ness** *n.*

re·la·tion (rĭ-**lā′**shən) *n.* **1.** A connection or association between two or more things: *the relation of health and a good diet.* **2.** The connection of people by blood or marriage. **3.** A person connected to another by blood or marriage; a relative. **4. relations** The dealings or associations of people, groups, or nations: *a country's foreign relations.* **5.** The act of telling; an account: *his relation of his experiences in Alaska.*

re·la·tion·ship (rĭ-**lā′**shən-shĭp′) *n.* **1.** The condition or fact of being related; a connection or an association: *What is the relationship between diet and heart disease?* **2.** A connection or tie between people: *a business relationship.* **3.** Kinship: *What is the relationship between me and my aunt's cousin?* **4.** A romantic or sexual involvement.

rel·a·tive (**rĕl′**ə-tĭv) *adj.* **1.** Considered in comparison with something else: *the relative quiet of the suburbs.* **2.** Related or relating: *made comments relative to my work.* **3.** In grammar, referring to an antecedent, as the pronoun *who* in *the woman who plays guitar.* ❖ *n.* **1.** A person related by blood or marriage. **2.** In grammar, a relative term, especially a relative pronoun.

relative clause *n.* A subordinate clause introduced by a relative pronoun. For example, in the sentence *He who hesitates is lost,* the relative clause is *who hesitates.*

relative humidity *n.* The quotient of the amount of water vapor contained in the air at a given temperature divided by the maximum that the air could contain at that temperature.

rel·a·tive·ly (**rĕl′**ə-tĭv-lē) *adv.* In comparison with something else: *a relatively minor problem.*

relative pronoun *n.* A pronoun that introduces a relative clause and refers to an antecedent. For example, in the sentence *The house that I live in has a porch,* the relative pronoun is *that.*

rel·a·tiv·i·ty (rĕl′ə-**tĭv′**ĭ-tē) *n.* **1.** The condition of being relative. **2.** The two-part theory of space and time developed by Albert Einstein. The first part states that the observed speed of light is always constant regardless of the motion of the observer or the light source. The second part extends this theory to accelerating bodies, such as bodies in gravitational fields. Some logical consequences of relativity are that measurements of space and time depend on the motion of the observer, that mass and energy are equivalent, and that gravity can be described as the curvature of space-time by mass.

re·lax (rĭ-**lăks′**) *v.* **re·laxed, re·lax·ing, re·lax·es** —*tr.* **1.** To make less tight or tense: *relax one's muscles.* **2.** To

WRITERS CHOOSE THEIR WORDS

F'lar looked to Ramoth [the dragon] to repopulate the five empty Weyrs, even as he looked to himself and Lessa to **rejuvenate** the pride and faith of dragonriders and of Pern itself. He only hoped time enough remained to him to do what was necessary.

—Anne McCaffrey
Dragonflight

relay race
passing a baton

make less severe or strict: *relax a dress code.* **3.** To relieve of nervousness or anxiety: *Listening to jazz relaxes me.* —*intr.* **1.** To take one's ease; rest: *I relaxed on the sofa.* **2.** To become less tight or tense. **3.** To become less severe or strict. **4.** To become less nervous or anxious. [From Middle English *relaxen*, from Latin *relaxāre*, from *laxus*, loose.]

re·lax·a·tion (rē′lăk-sā′shən) *n.* **1.** The act or process of relaxing: *a relaxation of the muscles.* **2.** The condition of being relaxed: *She lay in the hammock in perfect relaxation.* **3.** Refreshment of body or mind; fun; diversion.

re·laxed (rĭ-lăkst′) *adj.* **1.** Not severe or strict. **2.** Free from strain or tension: *relaxed muscles.* **3.** Free from anxiety or nervousness: *a relaxed evening meal.*

re·lay (rē′lā) *n.* **1.** A switch that is operated by an electric current. **2.** A relay race. **3.** A crew of laborers who relieve another crew; a shift. **4.** A fresh team of animals, as for a stagecoach. ❖ *tr.v.* (rē′lā *or* rĭ-lā′) **re·layed, re·lay·ing, re·lays** To pass or send along by or as if by relay: *relay the message to the boss.*

relay race *n.* A race between two or more teams, in which each member of a team goes only a part of the total distance.

re·lease (rĭ-lēs′) *tr.v.* **re·leased, re·leas·ing, re·leas·es** **1.** To set free from confinement or bondage; liberate: *release prisoners.* **2.** To set free from something that fastens or holds back; let go: *release balloons.* **3.** To relieve, as from an obligation or debt: *an order that released Private Davis from active duty.* **4.** To make available, as to the public: *release a film.* ❖ *n.* **1.** The act or an instance of releasing, as from confinement or suffering: *release of a prisoner.* **2.** A written discharge, as from a hospital or prison. **3.** A letting go of something caught or held fast: *release of a balloon.* **4a.** The act or an instance of issuing something to the public. **b.** Something that is issued to the public: *a press release.* **5.** A device for locking or releasing a mechanism. [From Middle English *relesen*, from Latin *relaxāre*, to relax, let go.]

rel·e·gate (rĕl′ĭ-gāt′) *tr.v.* **rel·e·gat·ed, rel·e·gat·ing, rel·e·gates** To send or remove, especially to a place or condition of less importance: *a player who was relegated to the sidelines; a technology that was relegated to obsolescence.* —**rel′e·ga′tion** *n.*

re·lent (rĭ-lĕnt′) *intr.v.* **re·lent·ed, re·lent·ing, re·lents** To become more lenient, compassionate, or forgiving. —**re·lent′ing·ly** *adv.*

re·lent·less (rĭ-lĕnt′lĭs) *adj.* **1.** Mercilessly harsh; unyielding. **2.** Steady and persistent; unremitting: *a relentless wind.* —**re·lent′less·ly** *adv.* —**re·lent′less·ness** *n.*

rel·e·vant (rĕl′ə-vənt) *adj.* Related to the matter at hand; pertinent: *relevant questions.* —**rel′e·vance, rel′e·van·cy** *n.* —**rel′e·vant·ly** *adv.*

re·li·a·ble (rĭ-lī′ə-bəl) *adj.* Capable of being relied upon; dependable: *a reliable friend; a reliable car.* —**re·li′a·bil′i·ty, re·li′a·ble·ness** *n.* —**re·li′a·bly** *adv.*

re·li·ance (rĭ-lī′əns) *n.* **1.** The act of relying; dependence: *farmers' reliance on migrant workers.* **2.** Confidence; trust: *complete reliance on their friends.*

re·li·ant (rĭ-lī′ənt) *adj.* Having or showing reliance. —**re·li′ant·ly** *adv.*

rel·ic (rĕl′ĭk) *n.* **1.** An object or custom surviving from a culture or period that has disappeared: *relics of an ancient civilization.* **2.** Something that is treasured for its age or historic interest. **3.** An object of religious significance, especially something thought to be associated with a saint. [From Middle English *relik*, object of religious veneration, from Latin *reliquiae*, sacred remains, from *relinquere*, to leave behind.]

re·lief (rĭ-lēf′) *n.* **1a.** The easing of a pain, distress, or anxiety: *relief from a cold.* **b.** Something that lessens pain, distress, or anxiety: *The sight of land was a relief to the shipwrecked sailors.* **2a.** Assistance and help, as in the form of food or money, given to the needy, aged, or disaster victims. **b.** Assistance from the government because of need or poverty. **3a.** Release from a job or duty. **b.** A person who takes over the duties of another: *a sentry waiting for his relief.* **4a.** The projection of a sculptured figure from a flat background. **b.** The apparent projection of a figure in a painting or drawing. **5.** The variations in elevation of an area of the earth's surface: *a map that shows relief.* **6.** Sharpness of outline resulting from contrast: *a white sail in relief against the dark sky.* **7.** In baseball, the pitching done by a relief pitcher.

relief map *n.* A map that shows the physical features of land, as by using contour lines, colors, or shading.

relief pitcher *n.* In baseball, a pitcher who replaces another during a game.

re·lieve (rĭ-lēv′) *tr.v.* **re·lieved, re·liev·ing, re·lieves** **1.** To lessen or reduce (pain or anxiety, for example); ease. **2.** To make less unpleasant, tiresome, or boring: *We sang songs to relieve the monotony of the work.* **3.** To free from pain, anxiety, or distress: *relieve them of worries.* **4.** To release, as from a duty or position, by providing or acting as a substitute: *The second shift relieves us at six o'clock.* **5.** To give assistance or aid to: *relieve the victims of the flood.* **6.** *Informal* To rob or deprive: *Two men relieved me of my wallet.* [From Middle English *releeven*, from Latin *relevāre*, from *levāre*, to raise.] —**re·liev′a·ble** *adj.* —**re·liev′er** *n.*

re·li·gion (rĭ-lĭj′ən) *n.* **1.** Belief in and reverence for a supernatural being or beings, usually regarded as creating and governing the universe. **2.** A particular variety of such belief, especially when organized into a system of doctrine and practice: *the Hindu religion.* **3.** A set of beliefs, values, and practices based on the teachings of a spiritual leader.

re·li·gious (rĭ-lĭj′əs) *adj.* **1.** Having or showing belief in and reverence for God or a supernatural being. **2.** Relating to, concerned with, or teaching religion: *a religious book.* **3.** Very faithful; conscientious: *a religious attention to detail.* ❖ *n., pl.* **religious** A member of a monastic order, as a monk or nun. —**re·li′gious·ly** *adv.* —**re·li′gious·ness** *n.*

re·lin·quish (rĭ-lĭng′kwĭsh) *tr.v.* **re·lin·quished, re·lin·quish·ing, re·lin·quish·es** **1.** To leave; abandon: *They relinquished camp and traveled inland.* **2.** To give up, put aside, or surrender: *relinquish claim to the land.* See Synonyms at **yield. 3.** To let go; release: *relinquished my grasp on the fishing pole.* [From Middle English *relinquishen*, from Latin *relinquere* : *re-*, back + *linquere*, to leave.] —**re·lin′quish·ment** *n.*

rel·ish (rĕl′ĭsh) *n.* **1.** A spicy or savory condiment, such as chopped pickles, served with food. **2a.** Great enjoyment; pleasure; zest: *He began the task with relish.* **b.** A keen liking for something: *I have a relish for fried plantains.* **c.** Something that adds zest or pleasure: *Her wit added relish to the discussion.* See Synonyms at **zest.** ❖ *tr.v.* **rel·ished, rel·ish·ing, rel·ish·es** **1.** To take pleasure in; enjoy: *He relished going to the beach at dawn.* **2.** To be pleased with or look forward to: *I don't relish having to clean the basement.* [From Middle English *reles*, taste, from Old French *relaissier*, to leave behind.]

re·live (rē-lĭv′) *tr.v.* **re·lived, re·liv·ing, re·lives** To undergo again; live through another time: *We relived our childhood by looking through the photo album.*

re·lo·cate (rē-lō′kāt) *tr. & intr.v.* **re·lo·cat·ed, re·lo·cat·ing, re·lo·cates** To establish or become established in a new place: *The company relocated its operations overseas in order to reduce labor costs. I relocated to Cleveland after I was promoted.* —**re′lo·ca′tion** *n.*

re·luc·tant (rĭ-lŭk′tənt) *adj.* **1.** Unwilling; averse: *reluctant to leave.* **2.** Marked by unwillingness: *made a reluctant confession.* [From Latin *reluctārī*, to be reluctant.] —**re·luc′tance** *n.* —**re·luc′tant·ly** *adv.*

ă	pat	ôr	core
ā	pay	oi	boy
âr	care	ou	out
ä	father	o͝o	took
ĕ	pet	o͝or	lure
ē	be	o͞o	boot
ĭ	pit	ŭ	cut
ī	bite	ûr	urge
îr	pier	th	thin
ŏ	pot	*th*	this
ō	toe	zh	vision
ô	paw	ə	about

re·ly (rĭ-lī′) *intr.v.* **re·lied, re·ly·ing, re·lies 1.** To be dependent for support or help: *I'm relying on my parents to pay my rent.* **2.** To have trust or confidence: *We're relying on you to be a good example for the others.*

REM (rĕm) *n.* The rapid jerking movement of the eyes during certain stages of sleep when dreaming takes place. [From *r(apid) e(ye) m(ovement).*]

re·made (rē-mād′) *v.* Past tense and past participle of **remake.**

re·main (rĭ-mān′) *intr.v.* **re·mained, re·main·ing, re·mains 1.** To continue to be in the same state or condition: *This issue remains open to debate.* **2.** To continue to be in the same place; stay: *The children remained after their mother left.* See Synonyms at **stay**[1]. **3.** To be left over after the loss, removal, or destruction of others: *A few stone columns remained.* **4.** To be left as still to be dealt with: *The solution to the problem remains to be seen.* [From Middle English *remainen,* from Latin *remanēre* : *re-,* back + *manēre,* to remain.]

re·main·der (rĭ-mān′dər) *n.* **1.** The remaining part; the rest: *the remainder of the year.* **2a.** In division, the difference between the dividend and the product of the quotient and divisor. For example, 10 divided by 6 gives 1 with a remainder of 4. **b.** In subtraction, a difference.

re·mains (rĭ-mānz′) *pl.n.* **1.** All that remains after the loss, removal, or destruction of other parts: *the remains of last night's supper.* **2.** A dead body or parts of a dead body. **3.** Ancient ruins or fossils.

re·make (rē-māk′) *tr.v.* **re·made** (rē-mād′), **re·mak·ing, re·makes** To make again or new. ❖ *n.* (**rē′**māk′) **1.** The act of making again. **2.** Something made again, especially a new version of an older movie or song: *a remake of a classic movie.*

re·mand (rĭ-mănd′) *tr.v.* **re·mand·ed, re·mand·ing, re·mands 1.** To send or order back. **2.** To send back (a person) into legal custody, as to a jail or prison. **3.** To send back (a legal case) to a lower court for further proceedings. ❖ *n.* **1.** The act of remanding. **2.** The condition of being remanded: *a prisoner on remand.* **—re·mand′ment** *n.*

re·mark (rĭ-märk′) *v.* **re·marked, re·mark·ing, re·marks** *—tr.* **1.** To express as a comment: *He remarked that the book was selling well.* **2.** To notice; observe: *They remarked several changes in the town.* *—intr.* To make a comment or observation. ❖ *n.* **1.** A casual statement; a comment: *a remark about the weather.* **2.** The act of noticing or observing; mention: *a score worthy of remark.*

re·mark·a·ble (rĭ-mär′kə-bəl) *adj.* Worthy of notice, especially for being unusual or extraordinary: *The change in his personality was remarkable.* **—re·mark′a·bly** *adv.*

re·match (rē-măch′ *or* rē′măch′) *n.* A second contest between the same opponents.

Rem·brandt van Rijn or **Rem·brandt van Ryn** (rĕm′-brănt′ vän rīn′) 1606–1669. Dutch painter whose works include historical and religious scenes, group portraits, and self-portraits.

re·me·di·a·ble (rĭ-mē′dē-ə-bəl) *adj.* Possible to remedy: *remediable problems.* **—re·me′di·a·bly** *adv.*

re·me·di·al (rĭ-mē′dē-əl) *adj.* **1.** Supplying a remedy: *a remedial operation.* **2.** Intended to correct something, especially deficient skills in a subject: *taught remedial reading.* **—re·me′di·al·ly** *adv.*

rem·e·dy (rĕm′ĭ-dē) *n., pl.* **rem·e·dies 1.** Something, such as a medicine or treatment, that relieves pain, cures disease, or corrects a disorder. **2.** Something that corrects a fault, error, or wrong: *a remedy for inflation.* ❖ *tr.v.* **rem·e·died, rem·e·dy·ing, rem·e·dies 1.** To relieve or cure (a disease or disorder). **2.** To set right or correct (an error, for example).

re·mem·ber (rĭ-mĕm′bər) *v.* **re·mem·bered, re·mem·ber·ing, re·mem·bers** *—tr.* **1.** To recall to the mind; think of again: *I finally remembered the address.* **2.** To keep carefully in memory: *Remember your doctor's appointment.* **3.** To keep (someone) in mind as worthy of affection or recognition. **4.** To give (someone) a gift or tip: *remembered her nieces at Christmas.* **5.** To give greetings from (someone): *Remember me to your parents.* *—intr.* To have or use the power of memory. [From Middle English *remembren,* from Latin *rememorārī,* to remember again.]

re·mem·brance (rĭ-mĕm′brəns) *n.* **1.** The act of remembering: *the remembrance of things past.* **2.** The condition of remembering. **3.** Something remembered; a memory. **4.** Something that serves to remind; a memento or souvenir.

re·mind (rĭ-mīnd′) *tr.v.* **re·mind·ed, re·mind·ing, re·minds** To cause (someone) to remember or think of something: *Remind her to water the plants.* **—re·mind′er** *n.*

rem·i·nisce (rĕm′ə-nĭs′) *intr.v.* **rem·i·nisced, rem·i·nisc·ing, rem·i·nisc·es** To think about or tell of past experiences or events.

rem·i·nis·cence (rĕm′ə-nĭs′əns) *n.* **1.** The act or process of recalling the past: *lost in the reminiscence of childhood.* **2.** Something remembered; a memory: *pleasant reminiscences of the summer.* **3.** often **reminiscences** A narration or account of past experiences or events.

rem·i·nis·cent (rĕm′ə-nĭs′ənt) *adj.* **1.** Containing remembered events: *a reminiscent account of her childhood.* **2.** Recalling to the mind; suggestive: *a melody reminiscent of a folk song.*

re·miss (rĭ-mĭs′) *adj.* **1.** Careless in attending to duty; negligent: *She's very remiss in answering letters.* **2.** Exhibiting carelessness or slackness: *His performance of his duties was remiss.* **—re·miss′ly** *adv.*

re·mis·sion (rĭ-mĭsh′ən) *n.* **1.** Pardon or forgiveness: *the remission of sin.* **2.** Release from a debt, obligation, or penalty. **3.** A lessening of the intensity, seriousness, or destructive effect of a disease or disorder.

re·mit (rĭ-mĭt′) *v.* **re·mit·ted, re·mit·ting, re·mits** *—tr.* **1.** To send or transmit (money) in payment. **2.** To refrain from imposing (a tax or penalty, for example). **3.** To pardon; forgive: *remit sins.* **4.** To decrease; reduce: *The storm remitted its fury.* *—intr.* **1.** To transmit money. **2.** To grow less; diminish. [From Middle English *remitten,* to send back, from Latin *remittere* : *re-,* back + *mittere,* to send.] **—re·mit′ter** *n.*

re·mit·tance (rĭ-mĭt′ns) *n.* **1.** The act of sending money to someone. **2.** The money sent to someone.

re·mix (rē-mĭks′) *tr.v.* **re·mixed, re·mix·ing, re·mix·es** To recombine or reedit (audio tracks or channels from a recording) to produce a new recording. ❖ *n.* (**rē′**mĭks′) A recording produced by remixing.

rem·nant (rĕm′nənt) *n.* **1.** A portion or quantity left over; a remainder: *remnants of an old document.* **2.** A surviving trace or vestige: *the last remnants of an ancient empire.* **3.** A leftover piece of fabric remaining after the rest has been used or sold.

re·mod·el (rē-mŏd′l) *tr.v.* **re·mod·eled, re·mod·el·ing, re·mod·els** also **re·mod·elled, re·mod·el·ling, re·mod·els** To make over in structure or style; reconstruct: *remodel a kitchen.* **—re·mod′el·er, re·mod′el·ler** *n.*

re·mon·strance (rĭ-mŏn′strəns) *n.* A strong protest or objection.

re·mon·strate (rĭ-mŏn′strāt′ *or* rĕm′ən-strāt′) *intr.v.* **re·mon·strat·ed, re·mon·strat·ing, re·mon·strates** To argue or plead in opposition to something.

rem·o·ra (rĕm′ər-ə) *n.* Any of several fishes having on the head a sucking disk with which they attach themselves to sharks and other larger fish.

re·morse (rĭ-môrs′) *n.* Bitter regret or guilt for having done something wrong. [From Middle English *remors,* from Latin *remordēre,* to torment.]

re·morse·ful (rĭ-môrs′fəl) *adj.* Feeling or expressing

Rembrandt
c. 1633 self-portrait

WRITERS CHOOSE THEIR WORDS

Although men were expected to enlist, any woman who actively participated in the Civil War was an oddity if not a **renegade.** In the 1860s Americans held extremely rigid ideas about what women could and should do. Men concerned themselves with the outside world; women raised children and took care of the home.

—Anita Silvey
I'll Pass for Your Comrade: Women Soldiers in the Civil War

remorse: *a remorseful criminal; a remorseful sob.* —**re·morse′ful·ly** *adv.*

re·morse·less (rĭ-**môrs′**lĭs) *adj.* Having no pity or compassion; merciless. —**re·morse′less·ly** *adv.* —**re·morse′less·ness** *n.*

re·mote (rĭ-**mōt′**) *adj.* **re·mot·er, re·mot·est 1.** Located far away: *a remote Arctic island.* **2.** Distant in time: *the remote past.* **3.** Barely perceptible; slight: *There is a remote possibility that it will snow today.* **4.** Far removed in relevance; barely connected: *Her interests are remote from those of most people.* **5.** Distantly related by blood or marriage: *a remote cousin.* **6.** Operating or controlled from a distance: *remote sensors.* ❖ *n.* A remote-control device. [From Middle English, from Latin *remōtus*, from *removēre*, to move away.] —**re·mote′ly** *adv.*

remote control *n.* **1.** The control of an activity, process, or machine from a distance, especially by signals from a wireless device. **2.** A device used to control a machine or a piece of equipment from a distance.

re·mov·al (rĭ-**mo͞o′**vəl) *n.* **1.** The act of removing: *Removal of the piano took four men.* **2.** Relocation: *the removal of the business to New Jersey.* **3.** Dismissal, as from office or duties: *the removal of an adviser.*

re·move (rĭ-**mo͞ov′**) *v.* **re·moved, re·mov·ing, re·moves** —*tr.* **1.** To move or convey from a position or place: *remove the pie from the oven.* **2.** To take off or away: *removed my boots.* **3.** To do away with; eliminate: *remove a stain.* **4.** To dismiss from an office or position. —*intr.* To change one's place of residence or business; move. ❖ *n.* Distance or degree of separation or remoteness: *We stood at a safe remove from the demolition site.* —**re·mov′a·ble** *adj.*

re·moved (rĭ-**mo͞ovd′**) *adj.* **1.** Distant; remote. **2.** Separated in relationship by a given degree or descent: *My first cousin's child is my first cousin once removed.* —**re·mov′ed·ly** (rĭ-**mo͞o′**vĭd-lē) *adv.* —**re·mov′ed·ness** *n.*

re·mu·ner·ate (rĭ-**myo͞o′**nə-rāt′) *tr.v.* **re·mu·ner·at·ed, re·mu·ner·at·ing, re·mu·ner·ates** To pay (a person) for goods, services, or losses.

re·mu·ner·a·tion (rĭ-myo͞o′nə-**rā′**shən) *n.* **1.** An act of remunerating. **2.** Something, such as a payment, that remunerates.

re·mu·ner·a·tive (rĭ-**myo͞o′**nər-ə-tĭv) *adj.* Providing suitable profit; profitable.

Re·mus (**rē′**məs) *n.* In Roman mythology, the twin brother of Romulus.

ren·ais·sance (rĕn′ĭ-**säns′** *or* **rĕn′**ĭ-säns′) *n.* **1.** A rebirth or revival: *a renaissance of downtown business.* **2. Renaissance a.** The humanistic revival of classical art, literature, architecture, and learning in Europe. **b.** The period of this revival, roughly the 1300s through the 1500s. ❖ *adj.* **Renaissance** Relating to the Renaissance or its artistic works or styles. [From French, from Old French *renaistre*, to be born again.]

re·nal (**rē′**nəl) *adj.* Relating to the kidneys.

rend (rĕnd) *tr.v.* **rent** (rĕnt) or **rend·ed, rend·ing, rends 1.** To tear or split apart or into pieces: *The wind rent the flag.* See Synonyms at **tear¹**. **2.** To pull away forcibly; wrest: *She rent the keys from his hand.* **3.** To cause division in: *The group was rent by internal squabbles.* [From Middle English *renden*, from Old English *rendan*.]

ren·der (**rĕn′**dər) *tr.v.* **ren·dered, ren·der·ing, ren·ders 1.** To cause to become; make: *The hailstorm rendered the crop worthless.* **2.** To give or make available; provide: *render assistance.* **3.** To give in return or as what is owed: *render thanks for her thoughtfulness.* **4.** To give up; surrender; yield: *They rendered their lives in fighting the fire.* **5.** To pronounce; hand down: *render a judgment.* **6.** To represent in words or in art: *render a memory into prose; render a leaf in detail.* **7.** To convert (graphics) from an electronic file into a visual form, as on a computer monitor. **8.** To translate: *render a Latin text into English.* **9.** To perform (a musical composition, for example). **10.** To melt down or process (fat) by heating.

ren·dez·vous (**rän′**dā-vo͞o′) *n., pl.* **ren·dez·vous** (**rän′**dā-vo͞oz′) **1.** A prearranged meeting. **2.** A designated place for a meeting. ❖ *intr. & tr.v.* **ren·dez·voused** (**rän′**dā-vo͞od′), **ren·dez·vous·ing** (**rän′**dā-vo͞o′ĭng), **ren·dez·vous** (**rän′**dā-vo͞oz′) To bring or come together at a certain time and place. [From French *rendez vous*, present yourselves.]

ren·di·tion (rĕn-**dĭsh′**ən) *n.* **1.** The act of rendering. **2.** A translation: *an English rendition of a German phrase.* **3.** An interpretation or a performance of a musical composition or dramatic work.

ren·e·gade (**rĕn′**ĭ-gād′) *n.* **1.** A person who rejects a cause, allegiance, religion, or group for another. **2.** An outlaw or a rebel. ❖ *adj.* Relating to or resembling a renegade; traitorous: *a band of renegade soldiers.*

re·nege (rĭ-**nĭg′** *or* rĭ-**nĕg′**) *intr.v.* **re·neged, re·neg·ing, re·neges 1.** To fail to carry out a promise or duty: *renege on a commitment.* **2.** In card games, to fail to follow suit when possible and when required by the rules.

re·new (rĭ-**no͞o′**) *tr.v.* **re·newed, re·new·ing, re·news 1.** To make new or as if new again; restore: *renew an old building.* **2.** To take up again; resume: *renewed her study of music.* **3a.** To arrange for an extension of: *renew a prescription.* **b.** To arrange to extend the loan of: *renew a library book.* **4.** To refill the supply of; replace: *renew supplies.*

re·new·a·ble (rĭ-**no͞o′**ə-bəl) *adj.* **1.** Capable of being renewed: *a renewable membership in the club.* **2.** Capable of being replaced; replaceable: *Wood is a renewable source of energy.*

re·new·al (rĭ-**no͞o′**əl) *n.* **1.** The act of renewing or the condition of being renewed. **2.** Something renewed.

ren·net (**rĕn′**ĭt) *n.* A dried extract prepared from the lining of the fourth stomach of calves or the young of certain other animals, used in cheesemaking to curdle milk.

ren·nin (**rĕn′**ĭn) *n.* An enzyme that causes milk to curdle, extracted from rennet or produced by genetically engineered microorganisms, and used in making cheeses.

Ren·oir (**rĕn′**wär′ *or* rən-**wär′**), **Pierre Auguste** 1841–1919. French impressionist painter whose works include *Luncheon of the Boating Party* (1881).

re·nounce (rĭ-**nouns′**) *tr.v.* **re·nounced, re·nounc·ing, re·nounc·es 1.** To give up (something), especially by formal announcement: *renounces her title; renounced their claim to the land.* **2.** To decide or declare that one will no longer adhere to (a belief or position) or engage in (an activity): *renounced his political beliefs; renounced violence.* —**re·nounce′ment** *n.* —**re·nounc′er** *n.*

ren·o·vate (**rĕn′**ə-vāt′) *tr.v.* **ren·o·vat·ed, ren·o·vat·ing, ren·o·vates** To restore to an earlier condition, as by repairing or remodeling: *renovate a house.* —**ren′o·va′tion** *n.* —**ren′o·va′tor** *n.*

re·nown (rĭ-**noun′**) *n.* Widespread honor and fame.

re·nowned (rĭ-**nound′**) *adj.* Having renown; famous: *a renowned orator.* See Synonyms at **famous.**

rent¹ (rĕnt) *n.* A payment made in exchange for the use of the property of another for a period of time: *pay the monthly rent on an apartment.* ❖ *v.* **rent·ed, rent·ing, rents** —*tr.* **1.** To occupy or use (another's property) for a time in return for money: *rent an apartment; rent a bicycle.* **2.** To grant the use of (one's own property or a service) for a time in return for money: *rented our upstairs apartment to a friend.* —*intr.* To be for rent: *The apartment rented for $850 a month.* ◆ **for rent** Available for use or service in return for payment. [From Middle English *rente*, from Old French, from Latin *rendere*, to return.] —**rent′er** *n.*

rent² (rĕnt) *v.* A past tense and a past participle of **rend.** ❖ *n.* **1.** An opening made by rending: *a rent in the gar-*

ă	pat	ôr	core
ā	pay	oi	boy
âr	care	ou	out
ä	father	o͝o	took
ĕ	pet	o͝or	lure
ē	be	o͞o	boot
ĭ	pit	ŭ	cut
ī	bite	ûr	urge
îr	pier	th	thin
ŏ	pot	*th*	this
ō	toe	zh	vision
ô	paw	ə	about

ment. **2.** A breach of relations between people or groups; a split: *a rent in the family.*

rent·al (rĕn′tl) *n.* **1.** An amount paid or received as rent. **2.** A piece of property available for renting: *a summer rental.* **3.** The act of renting: *the rental of a car.*

re·nun·ci·a·tion (rĭ-nŭn′sē-ā′shən) *n.* The act or an instance of renouncing: *the renunciation of a belief.*

re·o·pen (rē-ō′pən) *tr. & intr.v.* **re·o·pened, re·o·pen·ing, re·o·pens 1.** To open or become open again: *They reopened a trail. The store will reopen after the holiday.* **2.** To take up again or be taken up again; resume: *When new evidence appeared, the police reopened the case.*

re·or·gan·ize (rē-ôr′gə-nīz′) *v.* **re·or·gan·ized, re·or·gan·iz·ing, re·or·gan·iz·es** *—tr.* To organize again or differently: *She reorganized her ideas as an outline. —intr.* To undergo or effect changes in organization: *The group is reorganizing.* **—re·or′gan·i·za′tion** (rē-ôr′gə-nĭ-zā′shən) *n.* **—re·or′gan·iz′er** *n.*

rep[1] (rĕp) *n. Informal* A representative.

rep[2] (rĕp) *n. Informal* A repetition of an exercise movement.

Rep. *abbr.* An abbreviation of: **1.** representative. **2.** republic. **3.** Republican.

re·paid (rĭ-pād′) *v.* Past tense and past participle of **repay.**

re·pair[1] (rĭ-pâr′) *tr.v.* **re·paired, re·pair·ing, re·pairs 1.** To restore to proper or useful condition after damage or injury: *repair an automobile.* **2.** To set right; remedy: *repair an oversight.* ❖ *n.* **1.** The work, act, or process of repairing: *My car is in need of repair.* **2.** often **repairs** An instance or a result of repairing: *My car is in the shop for repairs.* **3.** General condition after use or repairing: *a truck in good repair.* [From Middle English *reparen,* from Latin *reparāre* : *re-,* again + *parāre,* to put in order.] **—re·pair′a·ble** *adj.* **—re·pair′er** *n.*

re·pair[2] (rĭ-pâr′) *intr.v.* **re·paired, re·pair·ing, re·pairs** To go: *The guests repaired to the dining room.* [From Middle English *repairen,* from Late Latin *repatriāre,* to return to one's country.]

re·pair·man (rĭ-pâr′măn′) *n.* A man whose job is making repairs.

re·pair·wom·an (rĭ-pâr′wo͝om′ən) *n.* A woman whose job is making repairs.

rep·a·ra·tion (rĕp′ə-rā′shən) *n.* **1.** The act or process of making amends. **2.** Something done or paid to make amends; a compensation. **3. reparations** Compensation required from a defeated nation for damage or injury during a war. **4.** The act or process of repairing or the condition of being repaired.

rep·ar·tee (rĕp′ər-tē′ *or* rĕp′ər-tā′) *n.* **1.** A swift witty reply. **2.** Conversation marked by the exchange of witty retorts.

re·past (rĭ-păst′) *n.* A meal or the food provided or eaten at a meal.

re·pa·tri·ate (rē-pā′trē-āt′) *tr.v.* **re·pat·ri·at·ed, re·pat·ri·at·ing, re·pat·ri·ates** To restore or return to the country of birth, citizenship, or origin: *repatriated the refugees; repatriated the Egyptian artifacts.*

re·pay (rĭ-pā′) *tr.v.* **re·paid** (rĭ-pād′), **re·pay·ing, re·pays 1.** To pay back: *repaid a debt.* **2.** To give compensation for; make a return for: *repay kindness with kindness.* **3.** To make or do in return: *repay a visit.* **—re·pay′a·ble** *adj.* **—re·pay′ment** *n.*

re·peal (rĭ-pēl′) *tr.v.* **re·pealed, re·peal·ing, re·peals** To withdraw or annul officially; revoke: *repeal a law.* ❖ *n.* The act or process of repealing: *the repeal of an amendment.* [From Middle English *repelen,* from Old French *rapeler* : *re-,* back + *apeler,* to appeal.]

re·peat (rĭ-pēt′ *or* rē′pēt′) *v.* **re·peat·ed, re·peat·ing, re·peats** *—tr.* **1.** To say again: *repeat a question.* **2.** To say in duplication of what another has said: *repeat the phrase after the teacher.* **3.** To recite from memory: *repeat a poem.* **4.** To tell to someone else: *repeat gossip.* **5.** To do, experience, or produce again: *We want to repeat our past successes.* **6.** To express (oneself) in the same way or words: *He's always repeating himself. —intr.* **1.** To do or say something again. **2.** To occur or happen again: *The melody repeats during the refrain.* ❖ *n.* **1.** The act of repeating: *the repeat of a performance.* **2.** Something repeated: *This television program is a repeat.* **3a.** A section of a musical composition that is repeated. **b.** A sign consisting of a pair of vertical dots, used to mark the beginning or end of such a passage. ❖ *adj.* Relating to a person or thing that repeats: *a repeat offender; a repeat performance.* [From Middle English *repeten,* from Latin *repetere,* to seek again.] **—re·peat′er** *n.*

re·peat·ed (rĭ-pē′tĭd) *adj.* Said, done, or occurring again and again: *We heard repeated knocks at the door.* **—re·peat′ed·ly** *adv.*

re·peat·ing decimal (rĭ-pē′tĭng) *n.* A decimal that consists of or contains an endlessly repeating pattern of digits, as 0.585858 . . . .

re·pel (rĭ-pĕl′) *tr.v.* **re·pelled, re·pel·ling, re·pels 1.** To drive off, force back, or keep away: *repel an enemy attack.* **2.** To refuse; reject: *She repelled my offer of help.* **3.** To cause aversion in: *His rudeness repels me.* **4.** To be resistant to: *a fabric that repels water.* [From Middle English *repellen,* from Latin *repellere* : *re-,* back + *pellere,* to drive.]

re·pel·lent (rĭ-pĕl′ənt) *adj.* **1.** Acting or tending to repel; capable of repelling: *an odor that is repellent to dogs.* **2.** Causing aversion or disgust: *a repellent manner.* **3.** Resistant or impervious to a specified substance or influence: *a water-repellent cloth.* ❖ *n.* **1.** A substance used to drive off a pest or pests: *an insect repellent.* **2.** A substance used to treat a fabric to make it repellent, as a substance that makes cloth resistant to water.

re·pent (rĭ-pĕnt′) *v.* **re·pent·ed, re·pent·ing, re·pents** *—intr.* To feel remorse or regret for a sin or something wrong that one has done. *—tr.* To feel regret or remorse for: *repented my bad manners.* [From Middle English *repenten,* from Old French *repentir.*] **—re·pent′er** *n.*

re·pen·tance (rĭ-pĕn′təns) *n.* **1.** The act or process of repenting. **2.** Remorse or contrition for past conduct or sin.

re·pen·tant (rĭ-pĕn′tənt) *adj.* Feeling or showing repentance; penitent: *a repentant child.*

re·per·cus·sion (rē′pər-kŭsh′ən *or* rĕp′ər-kŭsh′ən) *n.* **1.** An often indirect effect, influence, or result produced by an event or action: *His decision may have alarming repercussions.* **2.** The recoil or rebounding motion of something after impact. **3.** A reflection, especially of sound.

rep·er·toire (rĕp′ər-twär′) *n.* **1.** All of the songs, plays, operas, or other works that a person or company is prepared to perform. **2.** The range or number of skills, aptitudes, or special accomplishments of a particular person or group: *Telling a joke just isn't in his repertoire.*

rep·er·to·ry (rĕp′ər-tôr′ē) *n., pl.* **rep·er·to·ries 1.** A repertoire. **2.** A theater in which a company presents works from a given repertoire.

rep·e·ti·tion (rĕp′ĭ-tĭsh′ən) *n.* **1.** The act or process of repeating or being repeated: *the repetition of a word.* **2.** A recitation or recital, especially of prepared or memorized material.

rep·e·ti·tious (rĕp′ĭ-tĭsh′əs) *adj.* Filled with repetition, especially needless or tedious repetition: *tired of their repetitious arguments.* **—rep′e·ti′tious·ly** *adv.* **—rep′e·ti′tious·ness** *n.*

re·pet·i·tive (rĭ-pĕt′ĭ-tĭv) *adj.* Given to or characterized by repetition. **—re·pet′i·tive·ly** *adv.* **—re·pet′i·tive·ness** *n.*

re·place (rĭ-plās′) *tr.v.* **re·placed, re·plac·ing, re·plac·es 1.** To put back into a former position or place: *replaced the dish in the cabinet.* **2.** To take or fill the place

WRITERS CHOOSE THEIR WORDS

The moon was full when the boys left, and full a month later when Old Tallow returned with her dogs. Many things happened in that time. The women made a new camp. They **replenished** their store of dried meat. They fished and trapped. They found a rice bay and busied themselves harvesting every grain.

—Louise Erdrich
The Porcupine Year

WORD BUILDING

replete English words that contain the word roots *ple–* or *plen–* come from Latin words meaning "full" or "to fill." Our adjective **replete,** for example, comes from the Latin verb *replēre,* "to fill up" (*re–,* "again"), and our verb and adjective **complete** come from the Latin verb *complēre,* "to fill in, fit" (*com–,* "altogether, completely"). From the related Latin adjective *plēnus,* "full," comes our word **plenty,** as well as a fancier way of saying the same thing—**plenitude.**

ă	pat	ôr	core
ā	pay	oi	boy
âr	care	ou	out
ä	father	o͝o	took
ĕ	pet	o͝or	lure
ē	be	o͞o	boot
ĭ	pit	ŭ	cut
ī	bite	ûr	urge
îr	pier	th	thin
ŏ	pot	*th*	this
ō	toe	zh	vision
ô	paw	ə	about

of: *Automobiles replaced horses.* **3.** To be or provide a substitute for: *replace a broken window.* **4.** To pay back or return; refund. **—re·place′a·ble** *adj.*

re·place·ment (rĭ-**plās′**mənt) *n.* **1.** The act or process of replacing or of being replaced: *the replacement of funds.* **2.** A person or thing that replaces: *Stay until your replacement arrives.*

re·play (rē-**plā′**) *tr.v.* **re·played, re·play·ing, re·plays** To play over again: *replay a tape.* ❖ *n.* (**rē′**plā′) **1.** The act or process of replaying. **2.** Something replayed.

re·plen·ish (rĭ-**plĕn′**ĭsh) *tr.v.* **re·plen·ished, re·plen·ish·ing, re·plen·ish·es** To supply more of (something) so as to fill a container or make a supply complete: *replenish the water in the tank.* **—re·plen′ish·er** *n.* **—re·plen′ish·ment** *n.*

re·plete (rĭ-**plēt′**) *adj.* **1.** Plentifully supplied; abounding: *a land replete with streams and forests.* **2.** Filled; gorged: *After two pieces of pie, he felt replete.* **—re·ple′tion** *n.* —SEE NOTE.

rep·li·ca (**rĕp′**lĭ-kə) *n.* **1.** A copy or reproduction of a work of art, especially one made by the original artist. **2.** A copy or reproduction, especially one on a smaller scale than the original: *a replica of an early telephone.*

rep·li·cate (**rĕp′**lĭ-kāt′) *v.* **rep·li·cat·ed, rep·li·cat·ing, rep·li·cates** *—tr.* To duplicate, copy, reproduce, or repeat: *After she published the results of her experiment, other scientists replicated her findings. —intr.* To become replicated; undergo replication: *a virus that replicates in healthy cells.*

rep·li·ca·tion (rĕp′lĭ-**kā′**shən) *n.* **1.** The act or process of duplicating or reproducing. **2.** A copy or reproduction.

re·ply (rĭ-**plī′**) *v.* **re·plied, re·ply·ing, re·plies** *—intr.* **1.** To say or give an answer: *Did you reply to his email?* **2.** To respond by an action: *We replied to their snowballs with some of our own.* See Synonyms at **answer.** *—tr.* To say or give as an answer: *She replied that she would go.* ❖ *n., pl.* **re·plies** A response in speech or writing: *Thank you for your reply to my letter of June 1.* **—re·pli′er** *n.*

re·port (rĭ-**pôrt′**) *n.* **1.** An oral or written account often presented in detail: *a news report.* **2.** Rumor; common talk: *We learned it by report.* **3.** Reputation: *a person of good report.* **4.** An explosive sound, as of a firearm being discharged. ❖ *v.* **re·port·ed, re·port·ing, re·ports** *—tr.* **1.** To make or present an account of; relate: *report the problem in a memo to the manager.* **2.** To tell or relate (that something happened): *reported that a tree had fallen in the neighborhood.* **3.** To write or provide for publication or broadcast: *report the news.* **4.** To complain about or denounce: *report them to the police. —intr.* **1.** To make a report: *Could you report on what happened?* **2.** To present oneself: *report for duty.* **3.** To be accountable: *I report directly to the president.* [From Middle English, from Latin *reportāre*, to report : *re-*, back + *portāre*, to carry.]

report card *n.* A report of a student's achievement presented at regular intervals to a parent or guardian.

re·port·ed·ly (rĭ-**pôr′**tĭd-lē) *adv.* By report; supposedly.

re·port·er (rĭ-**pôr′**tər) *n.* **1.** A person who investigates, writes, or presents news stories. **2.** A person who writes down the official account of the proceedings in a courtroom.

re·pose (rĭ-**pōz′**) *n.* **1.** The act of resting or the state of being at rest. **2.** Peace of mind; freedom from anxiety: *seeking security and repose.* **3.** Calmness; tranquility: *the repose of the lake.* ❖ *v.* **re·posed, re·pos·ing, re·pos·es** *—tr.* To lay (oneself) down to rest. *—intr.* **1.** To lie at rest; relax or sleep: *workers reposing at the end of day.* **2.** To lie supported by something: *a dish reposing on the table.* [From Late Latin *repausāre*, to cause to rest.]

re·pos·i·to·ry (rĭ-**pŏz′**ĭ-tôr′ē) *n., pl.* **re·pos·i·to·ries** A place where things may be put for safekeeping.

re·pos·sess (rē′pə-**zĕs′**) *tr.v.* **re·pos·sessed, re·pos·sess·ing, re·pos·sess·es** To retake or regain possession of: *repossess an appliance bought on credit.* **—re′pos·ses′sion** (rē′pə-**zĕsh′**ən) *n.*

rep·re·hend (rĕp′rĭ-**hĕnd′**) *tr.v.* **rep·re·hend·ed, rep·re·hend·ing, rep·re·hends** To express disapproval of; reprove: *reprehend their actions.* **—rep′re·hen′sion** (rĕp′rĭ-**hĕn′**shən) *n.*

rep·re·hen·si·ble (rĕp′rĭ-**hĕn′**sə-bəl) *adj.* Deserving rebuke or censure; worthy of blame: *a reprehensible deed.* **—rep′re·hen′si·bil′i·ty** *n.* **—rep′re·hen′si·bly** *adv.*

rep·re·sent (rĕp′rĭ-**zĕnt′**) *tr.v.* **rep·re·sent·ed, rep·re·sent·ing, rep·re·sents 1.** To stand for; symbolize: *The rose represents beauty.* **2.** To indicate or communicate by sounds or symbols: *letters represent sounds.* **3.** To portray, as in a picture; depict: *The painting represents an eagle soaring over trees.* **4.** To describe (something) as having certain characteristics: *represented a product's value falsely.* **5.** To act as the delegate or agent for, especially in a legislative body. **6.** To serve as an example of; typify: *Her feelings represent those of the majority.* **7.** To be the equivalent of: *The amount you eat plus the amount you drink represents your total intake.*

rep·re·sen·ta·tion (rĕp′rĭ-zĕn-**tā′**shən) *n.* **1.** The act of representing or the condition of being represented. **2.** Something that represents, such as a picture or symbol. **3.** The condition of serving as an official delegate or agent. **4.** The right or privilege of being represented in a governmental body: *no taxation without representation.* **5.** An account or statement of facts, conditions, or arguments: *improper representations of a product.*

rep·re·sen·ta·tion·al (rĕp′rĭ-zĕn-**tā′**shə-nəl) *adj.* Relating to representation, especially realistic graphic representation.

rep·re·sen·ta·tive (rĕp′rĭ-**zĕn′**tə-tĭv) *n.* **1.** A person or thing that serves as an example or type for others of the same class. **2.** A person who serves as a delegate or agent for another. **3.** A member of the US House of Representatives or of the lower house of a state legislature. ❖ *adj.* **1.** Representing, depicting, or portraying or able to do so. **2.** Having power to act as an official delegate or agent. **3.** Relating to government by representation. **4.** Serving as a typical example.

re·press (rĭ-**prĕs′**) *tr.v.* **re·pressed, re·press·ing, re·press·es 1.** To hold back by an act of will: *trying to repress his laughter.* **2.** To put down by force or intimidation; quell: *repress an uprising.* **3.** To force (painful memories, for example) out of the conscious mind. [From Middle English *repressen*, from Latin *reprimere* : *re-*, back, down + *premere*, to press.]

re·pres·sion (rĭ-**prĕsh′**ən) *n.* **1.** The action of repressing or the state of being repressed. **2.** The exclusion of painful desires, impulses, or fears from the conscious mind.

re·pres·sive (rĭ-**prĕs′**ĭv) *adj.* Relating to or tending to cause repression: *repressive measures.* **—re·pres′sive·ly** *adv.*

re·prieve (rĭ-**prēv′**) *tr.v.* **re·prieved, re·priev·ing, re·prieves 1.** To postpone or cancel the punishment of. **2.** To bring relief to: *The teacher reprieved the proctor from overseeing the examination.* ❖ *n.* **1.** The postponement or cancellation of a punishment. **2.** Temporary relief, as from danger.

rep·ri·mand (**rĕp′**rə-mănd′) *tr.v.* **rep·ri·mand·ed, rep·ri·mand·ing, rep·ri·mands** To criticize from a position of authority. ❖ *n.* A criticism from someone in authority. [From Latin *reprimenda (culpa)*, (fault) to be repressed, from *reprimere*, to restrain.]

re·print (**rē′**prĭnt′) *n.* A new printing, as of a book or a scholarly article, that is identical to an original. ❖ *tr.v.* (rē-**prĭnt′**) **re·print·ed, re·print·ing, re·prints** To print again. **—re·print′er** *n.*

re·pri·sal (rĭ-**prī′**zəl) *n.* Retaliation for injury or damage inflicted, often by one nation against another.

re·prise (rĭ-**prēz′**) *n.* **1.** A repetition of a melody, especially after other intervening material. **2.** A melody repeated in this way. **3.** (*often* rĭ-**prīz′**) A recurrence or resumption of an action.

re·proach (rĭ-**prōch′**) *tr.v.* **re·proached, re·proach·ing, re·proach·es** To express disapproval of, criticism of, or disappointment in (someone). ❖ *n.* **1.** Blame; rebuke. **2.** Something that implies rebuke or blame: *Their hard work was a reproach to our laziness.* **3.** Disgrace; shame.

re·proach·ful (rĭ-**prōch′**fəl) *adj.* Expressing blame or reproach: *a reproachful glance.* **—re·proach′ful·ly** *adv.*

rep·ro·bate (**rĕp′**rə-bāt′) *n.* A morally unprincipled person. ❖ *adj.* Morally unprincipled; shameless.

re·pro·duce (rē′prə-**dōōs′**) *v.* **re·pro·duced, re·pro·duc·ing, re·pro·duc·es** *—tr.* **1.** To produce again; recreate: *The researchers tried to reproduce the results of the experiment.* **2.** To make a copy, imitation, or representation of: *The old paintings are reproduced beautifully in the book.* **3.** To generate or produce (offspring): *Mules are infertile and cannot reproduce themselves.* *—intr.* **1.** To generate or produce offspring: *Mice can reproduce several times in a year.* **2.** To undergo copying: *Black-and-white photographs reproduce well.*

re·pro·duc·tion (rē′prə-**dŭk′**shən) *n.* **1.** The act of reproducing or the process of being reproduced: *the electronic reproduction of sound.* **2.** Something that is reproduced; a copy, imitation, or representation: *a reproduction of a painting.* **3.** The process by which organisms produce other organisms of the same kind.

re·pro·duc·tive (rē′prə-**dŭk′**tĭv) *adj.* Relating to reproduction.

reproductive cell *n.* A cell, such as a sperm cell or an egg cell, that unites with another to form a fertilized cell that develops into a new organism.

reproductive system *n.* The system of organs and structures involved with reproduction, especially sexual reproduction.

re·proof (rĭ-**prōōf′**) *n.* The act or an instance of reproving; a rebuke.

re·prove (rĭ-**prōōv′**) *tr.v.* **re·proved, re·prov·ing, re·proves 1.** To find fault with (someone). **2.** To express disapproval of (a fault, for example).

rep·tile (**rĕp′**tīl′ *or* **rĕp′**tĭl) *n.* Any of various cold-blooded vertebrate animals, such as snakes, turtles, and crocodiles, that are covered with scales or horny plates, lay eggs, and breathe by means of lungs. [From Middle English *reptil*, from Latin *rēptilis*, creeping.]

rep·til·i·an (rĕp-**tĭl′**ē-ən *or* rĕp-**tĭl′**yən) *adj.* **1.** Relating to reptiles: *reptilian eggs.* **2.** Resembling a reptile, especially in an unpleasant way: *cold reptilian eyes.*

re·pub·lic (rĭ-**pŭb′**lĭk) *n.* **1.** A nation whose head of state is not a monarch and in modern times is usually a president. **2.** A nation ruled by officers and representatives elected by the people. **3.** often **Republic** A specific republican government of a nation: *the Fourth Republic of France.* [From Latin *rēspūblica* : *rēs*, thing + *pūblicus*, of the people.]

re·pub·li·can (rĭ-**pŭb′**lĭ-kən) *adj.* **1.** Relating to or characteristic of a republic: *a republican form of government.* **2. Republican** Relating to the Republican Party. ❖ *n.* **1.** A person who advocates a republican form of government. **2. Republican** A member of the Republican Party.

Republican Party *n.* One of the two major political parties of the United States, organized in 1854 to oppose slavery.

re·pu·di·ate (rĭ-**pyōō′**dē-āt′) *tr.v.* **re·pu·di·at·ed, re·pu·di·at·ing, re·pu·di·ates 1.** To reject the validity or authority of; disavow: *repudiate an agreement.* **2.** To reject as unfounded, untrue, or unjust: *repudiate an accusation.* **3.** To refuse to recognize or pay: *repudiate an old debt.* **—re·pu′di·a′tion** *n.* **—re·pu′di·a′tive** *adj.*

re·pug·nance (rĭ-**pŭg′**nəns) *n.* Extreme dislike or aversion.

re·pug·nant (rĭ-**pŭg′**nənt) *adj.* Arousing disgust or aversion; offensive or repulsive: *a repugnant odor; repugnant behavior.*

re·pulse (rĭ-**pŭls′**) *tr.v.* **re·pulsed, re·puls·ing, re·puls·es 1.** To drive back; repel: *repulse the enemy attackers.* **2.** To rebuff or reject with rudeness, coldness, or denial: *She repulsed his offers to help.* ❖ *n.* **1.** The act of repulsing or the state of being repulsed. **2.** A firm rejection. [From Middle English *repulsen*, from Latin *repellere*.]

re·pul·sion (rĭ-**pŭl′**shən) *n.* **1.** The act of repulsing or the condition of being repulsed: *the repulsion of a surprise attack.* **2.** Extreme aversion.

re·pul·sive (rĭ-**pŭl′**sĭv) *adj.* **1.** Causing repugnance or aversion; disgusting: *a repulsive odor.* **2.** Tending to repel or drive off.

rep·u·ta·ble (**rĕp′**yə-tə-bəl) *adj.* Having a good reputation; honorable: *a reputable antiques dealer.* **—rep′u·ta·bly** *adv.*

rep·u·ta·tion (rĕp′yə-**tā′**shən) *n.* **1.** The general estimation in which a person is held by the public. **2.** A state of being noted for a particular characteristic: *He has a reputation for honesty.*

re·pute (rĭ-**pyōōt′**) *tr.v.* **re·put·ed, re·put·ing, re·putes** To consider; suppose: *He is reputed to be honest.* ❖ *n.* Reputation: *a man of ill repute.*

re·put·ed (rĭ-**pyōō′**tĭd) *adj.* Generally supposed to be such: *questioned the reputed leader of the movement.* **—re·put′ed·ly** *adv.*

re·quest (rĭ-**kwĕst′**) *tr.v.* **re·quest·ed, re·quest·ing, re·quests 1.** To express a desire for; ask for: *requested information about the proposal; requested to see the evidence; requested that the cab driver slow down.* **2.** To ask (a person) to do something: *I requested him to come along.* ❖ n. **1.** The act of asking: *Other sizes are available on request.* **2.** Something asked for: *We received requests for extra copies of the article.*

Req·ui·em (**rĕk′**wē-əm) *n.* **1.** In the Roman Catholic Church, a mass for a person who has died. **2.** A musical composition for such a mass.

re·quire (rĭ-**kwīr′**) *tr.v.* **re·quired, re·quir·ing, re·quires 1.** To be in need of; need: *Do you require help?* **2.** To call for as necessary; demand: *Skiing requires practice.* **3.** To impose an obligation on; order: *The school requires all students to study mathematics.*

re·quire·ment (rĭ-**kwīr′**mənt) *n.* **1.** Something that is needed; a necessity: *a person's daily food requirement.* **2.** Something demanded as a necessary condition to something else: *What are the requirements for the job?*

req·ui·site (**rĕk′**wĭ-zĭt) *adj.* Required; essential. ❖ *n.* Something that is essential; a necessity.

req·ui·si·tion (rĕk′wĭ-**zĭsh′**ən) *n.* **1.** A formal or official request or demand for something needed. **2.** The taking of something by such a request or demand. ❖ *tr.v.* **req·ui·si·tioned, req·ui·si·tion·ing, req·ui·si·tions 1.** To confiscate or demand, as for military needs. **2.** To make demands of: *requisitioned the department for additional supplies.*

re·quite (rĭ-**kwīt′**) *tr.v.* **re·quit·ed, re·quit·ing, re·quites 1.** To make return for (something done or felt) in a similar or appropriate fashion: *requite another's love.* **2.** To avenge. **—re·quit′er** *n.*

re·run (**rē′**rŭn′) *n.* A movie or television show that is replayed. ❖ *tr.v.* (rē-**rŭn′**) **re·ran** (rē-**răn′**), **re·run, re·run·ning, re·runs** To present a rerun of.

re·sale (**rē′**sāl′ *or* rē-**sāl′**) *n.* The act of selling again.

re·scind (rĭ-**sĭnd′**) *tr.v.* **re·scind·ed, re·scind·ing, re·scinds** To make void; repeal or annul. **—re·scind′a·ble** *adj.* **—re·scind′er** *n.*

res·cue (**rĕs′**kyōō) *tr.v.* **res·cued, res·cu·ing, res·cues** To set free, as from danger or imprisonment; save. ❖

WRITERS CHOOSE THEIR WORDS

"You have no cause to be alarmed, Captain. My father, though some of his ventures were undoubtedly illegal, was ... is ... a noble man. The idea of harming another creature would be **repugnant** to him."

—Eoin Colfer
Artemis Fowl: The Arctic Incident

n. An act of rescuing or saving: *A passerby came to our rescue.* [From Middle English *rescouen*, from Old French *rescourre.*] **—res′cu·er** *n.*

re·search (rĭ-sûrch′ *or* rē′sûrch′) *n.* Careful study of a given subject, field, or problem, undertaken to discover facts or principles: *I'm doing research on our town's history.* ❖ *tr.v.* **re·searched, re·search·ing, re·search·es 1.** To do research on (something); investigate: *He is researching the origins of football.* **2.** To do research for (something): *The journalist started researching her next newspaper article.* **—re·search′er** *n.*

re·sem·blance (rĭ-zĕm′bləns) *n.* The state or quality of resembling, especially similarity in appearance or in external or superficial details.

re·sem·ble (rĭ-zĕm′bəl) *tr.v.* **re·sem·bled, re·sem·bling, re·sem·bles** To have a similarity or likeness to; be like. [From Middle English *resemblen*, from Old French *resembler*, from Latin *simulāre*, to imitate.]

re·sent (rĭ-zĕnt′) *tr.v.* **re·sent·ed, re·sent·ing, re·sents** To feel angry at (something considered mean, unjust, or offensive): *resent a rude remark.* [From Old French *resentir*, to feel strongly, from Latin *sentīre*, to feel.]

re·sent·ful (rĭ-zĕnt′fəl) *adj.* Full of, characterized by, or inclined to feel resentment. **—re·sent′ful·ly** *adv.* **—re·sent′ful·ness** *n.*

re·sent·ment (rĭ-zĕnt′mənt) *n.* Anger felt as a result of something considered mean, unjust, or offensive.

res·er·va·tion (rĕz′ər-vā′shən) *n.* **1.** The act of reserving; a keeping back or withholding. **2.** Something that is kept back or withheld. **3.** A limiting qualification, condition, or exception: *accepted the offer with one reservation.* **4.** A doubt or misgiving: *has reservations about the plan.* **5.** A tract of land set apart by the federal government for a certain purpose, especially one for the use of a Native American people. **6.** An arrangement by which space, as in a hotel or on an airplane, is secured in advance.

re·serve (rĭ-zûrv′) *tr.v.* **re·served, re·serv·ing, re·serves 1.** To keep back, as for a particular purpose or later use: *reserve a tablecloth for special occasions.* See Synonyms at **keep. 2.** To order or book in advance for a specified time or date: *reserve a table in a restaurant.* **3.** To keep or retain for oneself: *I reserve the right to reply at a later date.* ❖ *n.* **1.** Something kept back or saved for future use or a special purpose: *a fuel reserve.* **2.** A tendency to talk little and keep one's feelings to oneself. **3.** A reservation of public land: *a forest reserve.* **4.** often **reserves** The part of a country's armed forces not on active duty but available in an emergency. [From Middle English *reserven*, from Latin *reservāre*, to keep back.]

re·served (rĭ-zûrvd′) *adj.* **1.** Held in reserve; kept back or set aside: *a reserved seat.* **2.** Marked by self-restraint and reticence: *a shy, reserved person.* **—re·serv′ed·ly** (rĭ-zûr′vĭd-lē) *adv.*

re·serv·ist (rĭ-zûr′vĭst) *n.* A member of a military reserve.

res·er·voir (rĕz′ər-vwär′ *or* rĕz′ər-vwôr′) *n.* **1.** A natural or artificial pond or lake used for storing water. **2.** A chamber or receptacle used for storing a fluid: *the reservoir of a fountain pen.* **3.** A large or extra supply; a reserve: *a reservoir of goodwill.*

re·side (rĭ-zīd′) *intr.v.* **re·sid·ed, re·sid·ing, re·sides 1.** To live in a place permanently or for an extended period: *She resides in Miami.* **2.** To lie or be contained: *the spirit of fellowship that resides within us.* [From Middle English *residen*, from Latin *residēre*, to remain behind, reside.] **—re·sid′er** *n.*

res·i·dence (rĕz′ĭ-dəns) *n.* **1.** The place in which a person lives; a dwelling. **2.** The act or period of residing somewhere: *He learned Spanish during his residence in Mexico.* **3.** A residency.

res·i·den·cy (rĕz′ĭ-dən-sē) *n., pl.* **res·i·den·cies** The period during which a physician receives specialized clinical training: *After she finished her residency in dermatology at the hospital, she went into private practice.*

res·i·dent (rĕz′ĭ-dənt) *n.* **1.** A person who resides in a particular place permanently or for an extended period. **2.** A physician serving a period of residency. ❖ *adj.* **1.** Living in a particular place: *a resident alien.* **2.** Living somewhere in connection with one's work: *a resident physician.* **3.** *Informal* Regularly filling a particular role as part of a group: *You'll have to ask Michelle—she's our resident art expert.*

res·i·den·tial (rĕz′ĭ-dĕn′shəl) *adj.* **1.** Relating to or having residence: *a residential college.* **2.** Suitable for or limited to residences: *a residential neighborhood.*

re·sid·u·al (rĭ-zĭj′o͞o-əl) *adj.* **1.** Remaining as a residue: *the residual solids left when a liquid evaporates.* **2.** Remaining after another part has disappeared or been taken away: *After I got better, the doctor wanted to check for any residual effects of the illness.* ❖ *n.* **1.** Something left over at the end of a process; a remainder. **2.** A payment made to a performer, writer, or director for each repeat showing of a recorded television show or commercial. **—re·sid′u·al·ly** *adv.*

res·i·due (rĕz′ĭ-do͞o′) *n.* Something that remains after a part is removed. [From Middle English, from Latin *residuus*, remaining, from *residēre*, to remain behind.]

re·sign (rĭ-zīn′) *v.* **re·signed, re·sign·ing, re·signs** *—tr.* **1.** To submit (oneself) passively; accept as inevitable: *resigned myself to a long wait.* **2.** To give up (a position, for example), especially by formal notification. *—intr.* To give up one's job or office; quit, especially by formal notification. [From Middle English *resignen*, from Latin *resignāre*, to unseal : *re-*, back, off + *signum*, mark, seal.] —SEE NOTE AT **sign.**

res·ig·na·tion (rĕz′ĭg-nā′shən) *n.* **1.** The act or an instance of resigning: *The commissioner regretted his resignation.* **2.** Acceptance of something that seems inescapable; submission: *a tone of resignation in her voice.* **3.** An oral or written statement that one is resigning a position or office.

re·signed (rĭ-zīnd′) *adj.* Feeling or marked by resignation; acquiescent: *a resigned look on his face.* **—re·sign′ed·ly** (rĭ-zī′nĭd-lē) *adv.*

re·sil·ient (rĭ-zĭl′yənt) *adj.* **1.** Capable of returning to an original shape or position, as after having been compressed. **2.** Having the ability to recover quickly, as from misfortune. [From Latin *resilīre*, to leap back.] **—re·sil′ience** *n.*

res·in (rĕz′ĭn) *n.* **1.** Any of several clear or translucent, yellowish or brownish substances that ooze from certain plants, such as many pines, and are used in varnishes and lacquers and for many other purposes. **2.** Any of various artificial substances that have similar properties and are used in making plastics. [From Middle English, from Greek *rhētīnē.*] **—res′in·ous** *adj.*

re·sist (rĭ-zĭst′) *v.* **re·sist·ed, re·sist·ing, re·sists** *—tr.* **1a.** To take action in opposition to; try to eliminate, reduce, or stop: *resisted the effort to close the school.* **b.** To take action to defeat or thwart (an invading or occupying military force). See Synonyms at **oppose. 2.** To undergo little or no change as a result of the action of; withstand: *a material that resists corrosion.* **3.** To keep from giving in or yielding to: *resist pressure; resist temptation.* *—intr.* To make an effort to resist something: *After smelling such delicious food, I just couldn't resist.* [From Middle English *resisten*, from Latin *resistere* : *re-*, back + *sistere*, to place.]

re·sis·tance (rĭ-zĭs′təns) *n.* **1.** The act, process, or capability of resisting: *The enemy offered little resistance.* **2.** A force that tends to oppose or retard motion: *an automobile body shaped to lessen wind resistance.* **3.** often **Resistance** An underground organization leading the struggle for national liberation in a country under the

ă	pat	ôr	core
ā	pay	oi	boy
âr	care	ou	out
ä	father	o͝o	took
ĕ	pet	o͝or	lure
ē	be	o͞o	boot
ĭ	pit	ŭ	cut
ī	bite	ûr	urge
îr	pier	th	thin
ŏ	pot	*th*	this
ō	toe	zh	vision
ô	paw	ə	about

control of military forces or an oppressive government. **4.** The capacity of an organism to defend itself against a disease. **5.** The opposition that an object offers to the passage of an electric current, resulting in a change of electric energy into heat.

re·sis·tant (rĭ-**zĭs′**tənt) *adj.* Resisting or capable of resisting: *a carpet that is resistant to stains.*

re·sist·less (rĭ-**zĭst′**lĭs) *adj.* **1.** Impossible to resist; irresistible. **2.** Powerless to resist; unresisting.

re·sis·tor (rĭ-**zĭs′**tər) *n.* A device used to control current in an electric circuit by providing resistance.

res·o·lute (**rĕz′**ə-lo͞ot′) *adj.* Firm or determined; unwavering: *a resolute voice.* **—res′o·lute′ly** *adv.* **—res′o·lute′ness** *n.*

res·o·lu·tion (rĕz′ə-**lo͞o′**shən) *n.* **1.** The state or quality of being resolute; firm determination: *face the future with resolution.* **2.** A firm decision to do something: *a resolution to get in shape.* **3.** A formal statement of a decision or an expression of opinion adopted by an assembly, legislature, or other organization. **4.** The act of solving or explaining a problem or puzzle. **5.** The ending or concluding of a dispute or disagreement: *Diplomats sought resolution of the conflict.* **6a.** The musical progression of a dissonant tone or chord to a consonant tone or chord. **b.** The tone or chord at which such a progression ends. **7.** The act or process of separating or reducing something into its smaller parts: *the resolution of sunlight into its spectral colors by a prism.* **8.** The clarity or fineness of detail that can be distinguished in an image.

re·solve (rĭ-**zŏlv′**) *v.* **re·solved, re·solv·ing, re·solves** *—tr.* **1.** To make a firm decision (to do something) or about (something): *He resolved to work harder. I resolved that I would do better the next time.* **2.** To cause (a person) to reach a decision: *She was resolved to make the most of a bad situation.* **3.** To find a solution to; solve: *resolve a conflict.* **4.** To remove or dispel (doubts). **5.** To change or convert: *The issue resolved itself to a single question.* **6.** To cause (a musical tone or chord) to pass from dissonance to consonance. *—intr.* To reach a decision or make a determination: *Have you resolved on a course of action?* ❖ *n.* **1.** Firmness of purpose; resolution: *work together with resolve.* **2.** A decision or resolution: *a resolve to try harder.*

res·o·nance (**rĕz′**ə-nəns) *n.* **1.** The quality or condition of being resonant: *the resonance of a speaker's voice.* **2a.** The increased response of a physical body or system to an oscillating driving force when the force oscillates at a frequency at which the body or system tends to oscillate naturally. **b.** A frequency at which such a body or system tends to oscillate naturally. **c.** The reinforcement of sounds, especially musical tones, as a result of the shape and physical properties of the structure in which they are produced.

res·o·nant (**rĕz′**ə-nənt) *adj.* **1.** Strong and deep in tone; resounding: *a resonant voice.* **2.** Continuing to sound in the ears or memory; echoing. **3.** Producing or having resonance. **—res′o·nant·ly** *adv.*

res·o·nate (**rĕz′**ə-nāt′) *intr.v.* **res·o·nat·ed, res·o·nat·ing, res·o·nates 1.** To exhibit or produce resonance. **2.** To evoke a feeling of shared emotion or belief: *an issue that resonates with voters.*

re·sort (rĭ-**zôrt′**) *intr.v.* **re·sort·ed, re·sort·ing, re·sorts 1.** To go or turn for help or as a means of achieving something: *The government resorted to censorship.* **2.** To go customarily or frequently. ❖ *n.* **1.** A place where people go for relaxation or recreation: *a ski resort.* **2.** A person or thing turned to for aid or relief: *I would ask him only as a last resort.* **3.** The act of turning to for aid or relief; recourse: *We were able to raise money without resort to borrowing.*

re·sound (rĭ-**zound′**) *intr.v.* **re·sound·ed, re·sound·ing, re·sounds 1.** To make a loud, long, or reverberating sound: *The music resounded through the hall.* **2.** To be filled with sound; reverberate: *The stadium resounded with cheers.*

re·source (**rē′**sôrs′ *or* rĭ-**sôrs′**) *n.* **1.** Something that can be used for support or help: *We have exhausted every resource at our disposal.* **2. resources** An available supply that can be drawn on when needed. **3.** Something that is a source of wealth to a country. **4.** The ability to deal with a situation effectively.

re·source·ful (rĭ-**sôrs′**fəl) *adj.* Able to act effectively or imaginatively, especially in a difficult situation: *a resourceful leader.* **—re·source′ful·ly** *adv.* **—re·source′ful·ness** *n.*

re·spect (rĭ-**spĕkt′**) *tr.v.* **re·spect·ed, re·spect·ing, re·spects 1.** To feel or show high regard for; esteem. **2.** To avoid violation of or interference with: *respect the speed limit.* ❖ *n.* **1.** A feeling of high regard; esteem: *respect for one's elders.* **2.** The condition of being regarded with honor or esteem: *She is held in respect by her colleagues.* **3.** Willingness to show consideration or appreciation. **4. respects** Polite expressions of consideration or regard: *pay one's respects to the family of the deceased.* **5.** A particular aspect or feature: *The two plans differ in one major respect.* **6.** Relation; reference: *I have a comment with respect to your question.* [From Latin *respicere*, to look back at, regard : *re-*, back + *specere*, to look at.] —SEE NOTE AT **regard.**

re·spect·a·ble (rĭ-**spĕk′**tə-bəl) *adj.* **1.** Worthy of respect or esteem: *respectable people.* **2.** Relating to or appropriate to proper behavior or conventional conduct. **—re·spect′a·bil′i·ty** *n.* **—re·spect′a·bly** *adv.*

re·spect·ful (rĭ-**spĕkt′**fəl) *adj.* Showing or marked by proper respect: *a respectful tone of voice.* **—re·spect′ful·ly** *adv.*

re·spect·ing (rĭ-**spĕk′**tĭng) *prep.* With respect to; concerning: *laws respecting personal property.*

re·spec·tive (rĭ-**spĕk′**tĭv) *adj.* Relating to each of two or more people or things; particular: *The delegates to the conference are experts in their respective fields.*

re·spec·tive·ly (rĭ-**spĕk′**tĭv-lē) *adv.* Each in the order named: *Albany, Augusta, and Atlanta are respectively the capitals of New York, Maine, and Georgia.*

res·pi·ra·tion (rĕs′pə-**rā′**shən) *n.* **1.** The act or process of inhaling and exhaling; breathing. **2.** Cellular respiration.

res·pi·ra·tor (**rĕs′**pə-rā′tər) *n.* **1.** A medical ventilator. **2.** A filter worn over the mouth or nose, or both, to protect the respiratory system.

res·pi·ra·to·ry (**rĕs′**pər-ə-tôr′ē *or* rĭ-**spīr′**ə-tôr′ē) *adj.* Relating to or affecting respiration.

respiratory system *n.* The system of organs and passages involved in the intake and exchange of oxygen and carbon dioxide between a living organism and its environment.

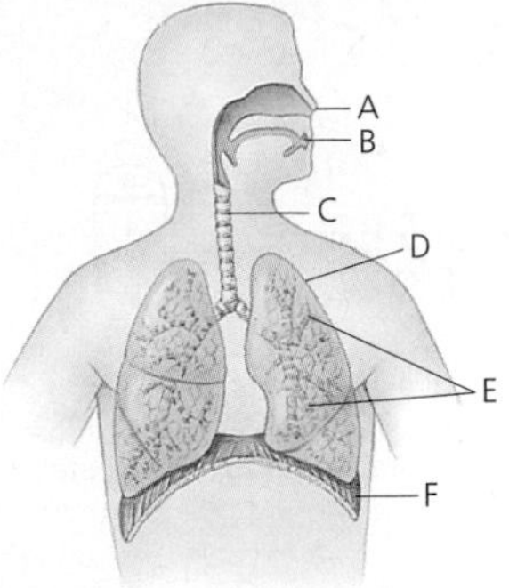

respiratory system
A. nose
B. mouth
C. trachea
D. lung
E. bronchial tubes
F. diaphragm

re·spire (rĭ-**spīr′**) *intr.v.* **re·spired, re·spir·ing, re·spires 1.** To inhale and exhale; breathe. **2.** To carry on the metabolic process of cellular respiration. [From Middle English *respiren*, from Latin *respīrāre*, to breathe in and out.]

res·pite (**rĕs′**pĭt) *n.* **1.** A usually short interval of rest or relief. **2.** In law, the temporary suspension of a death sentence; a reprieve.

re·splen·dent (rĭ-**splĕn′**dənt) *adj.* Splendid or dazzling in appearance; brilliant: *She was resplendent in her jeweled gown.* **—re·splen′dence** *n.*

re·spond (rĭ-**spŏnd′**) *v.* **re·spond·ed, re·spond·ing, re·sponds** *—intr.* **1.** To make a reply; answer: *responded to an instant message.* See Synonyms at **answer. 2.** To act in return or in answer: *Our team responded with two goals in the second half.* **3.** To react positively or favorably: *The patient responded to the treatment.* *—tr.* To say as a reply: *She responded that she would be delighted to help.* [From Middle English *responden*, from

rest[1]
rest (*center*) equivalent to the duration of an eighth note

WRITERS CHOOSE THEIR WORDS

When we got home that night, my father phoned the carpenters and the plasterers. He told them that he didn't care that it was late on a Friday night. And he didn't care that tomorrow was a Saturday. They had better be at the house first thing in the morning, ready to fix the ceiling permanently and to offer **restitution** for the property damage their carelessness had caused.

—Gary D. Schmidt
The Wednesday Wars

ă	pat	ôr	core
ā	pay	oi	boy
âr	care	ou	out
ä	father	o͝o	took
ĕ	pet	o͝or	lure
ē	be	o͞o	boot
ĭ	pit	ŭ	cut
ī	bite	ûr	urge
îr	pier	th	thin
ŏ	pot	*th*	this
ō	toe	zh	vision
ô	paw	ə	about

Latin *respondēre* : *re-*, back + *spondēre*, to promise.]

re·sponse (rĭ-**spŏns′**) *n.* **1.** The act of responding. **2.** An answer or reply: *I never received a response to my letter.* **3.** A reaction, as that of a living organism or mechanism to a stimulus or action. **4.** Something that is spoken or sung by a congregation or choir in answer to the minister or priest.

re·spon·si·bil·i·ty (rĭ-spŏn′sə-**bĭl′**ĭ-tē) *n., pl.* **re·spon·si·bil·i·ties 1.** The state, quality, or fact of being responsible: *Responsibility usually comes with age.* **2.** Something that one is responsible for; a duty or obligation: *The two cats are my responsibility.*

re·spon·si·ble (rĭ-**spŏn′**sə-bəl) *adj.* **1.** Liable to account for anything that happens or goes wrong: *As the eldest, you'll be responsible while we're away.* **2.** Having to account for one's actions; accountable: *Cabinet members are responsible to the president.* **3.** Involving important duties or obligations: *a responsible job.* **4.** Being the cause or source of something: *Viruses are responsible for many diseases.* **5.** Dependable; reliable; trustworthy: *a mature and responsible person.* **—re·spon′si·ble·ness** *n.* **—re·spon′si·bly** *adv.*

re·spon·sive (rĭ-**spŏn′**sĭv) *adj.* **1.** Answering or replying; responding. **2.** Reacting readily, as to suggestions or influences: *a responsive student.* **3.** Containing or using responses: *The minister led a responsive reading.* **—re·spon′sive·ly** *adv.* **—re·spon′sive·ness** *n.*

rest[1] (rĕst) *n.* **1.** A period of inactivity, relaxation, or sleep: *The hikers stopped for a brief rest.* **2.** Sleep or relaxation resulting from this: *Be sure to get plenty of rest.* **3.** Mental or emotional calm: *His reassurances put my mind at rest.* **4.** An absence or ending of motion: *The car slowed and came to rest.* **5.** The repose of death: *go to one's eternal rest.* **6.** The condition of being settled or resolved: *The principal's decision put the matter to rest.* **7a.** An interval of silence in a piece of music corresponding to the length of a given note. **b.** A symbol indicating such a silence. **8.** A device used as a support: *a head rest.* ❖ *v.* **rest·ed, rest·ing, rests** *—intr.* **1.** To cease motion, work, or activity: *We rested for a bit after we reached the waterfall.* **2.** To lie down, especially to sleep: *rested for an hour on the sofa.* **3.** To lie or lean on a support: *Her head rested on the pillow.* **4.** To be in or come to a motionless state: *The ball rolled across the street, finally resting against the curb.* **5.** To be located or be in a specified place: *The painting rests today in the art museum.* **6.** To be fixed or directed on something: *His gaze rested on the book.* **7.** To depend or rely: *The whole theory rests on one basic assumption.* **8.** To conclude the presentation of evidence in a legal case. *—tr.* **1.** To give rest or repose to: *I rested my eyes.* **2.** To lay or lean for ease, support, or repose: *I rested the rake against the fence.* **3.** To base or ground: *You rest your entire argument on mistaken belief.* **4.** To fix or direct (the gaze, for example). **5.** To conclude the presentation of evidence in (a legal case). [From Old English *rest, ræst.*]

❑ *These sound alike:* **rest[1]** (period of inactivity), **rest[2]** (remainder), **wrest** (pull away).

rest[2] (rĕst) *n.* **1.** The part that is left over after something has been taken away; the remainder: *pay the rest on credit.* **2.** That or those remaining: *The beginning was boring, but the rest was interesting.* [From Middle English, from Latin *restāre*, to stay behind : *re-*, back, behind + *stāre*, to stand.]

❑ *These sound alike:* **rest[2]** (remainder), **rest[1]** (period of inactivity), **wrest** (pull away).

re·start (rē-**stärt′**) *v.* **re·start·ed, re·start·ing, re·starts** *—tr.* To start again: *I restarted the engine after it had stalled.* *—intr.* To begin operation again: *The dishwasher restarted after the power was restored.*

re·state (rē-**stāt′**) *tr.v.* **re·stat·ed, re·stat·ing, re·states** To state again or in a new form. **—re·state′ment** *n.*

res·tau·rant (**rĕs′**tər-ənt *or* **rĕs′**tə-ränt′) *n.* A business establishment where meals are served to the public. [From French, restorative soup, restaurant, from *restaurer*, to restore.]

res·tau·ra·teur (rĕs′tər-ə-**tûr′**) *n.* The manager or owner of a restaurant.

rest·ful (**rĕst′**fəl) *adj.* Giving, marked by, or suggesting rest; tranquil: *a restful vacation.* **—rest′ful·ness** *n.*

res·ti·tu·tion (rĕs′tĭ-**to͞o′**shən) *n.* **1.** The act of restoring something to its rightful owner: *the restitution of his stolen passport.* **2.** Something given or done to make up for damage, loss, or injury: *sought restitution for the broken window.*

res·tive (**rĕs′**tĭv) *adj.* **1.** Impatient or restless under restriction, opposition, criticism, or delay: *The crowd gradually became restive.* **2.** Refusing to move. Used of a horse or other animal. **—res′tive·ly** *adv.* **—res′tive·ness** *n.*

rest·less (**rĕst′**lĭs) *adj.* **1.** Marked by a lack of quiet, rest, or sleep: *a restless night.* **2.** Unable to rest, relax, or be still: *a restless child.* **3.** Never still or motionless: *the restless sea.* **—rest′less·ly** *adv.* **—rest′less·ness** *n.*

res·to·ra·tion (rĕs′tə-**rā′**shən) *n.* **1a.** The action of restoring: *The damage was too great for restoration.* **b.** A particular act of restoring: *The restoration of the sculptures was expensive.* **c.** The state of being restored: *The house is now in restoration.* **2.** Something restored: *This building is a restoration of a colonial farmhouse.* **3. Restoration a.** The return of monarchy to Britain when Charles II assumed the throne in 1660. **b.** The period between this return and the Revolution of 1688.

re·stor·a·tive (rĭ-**stôr′**ə-tĭv) *adj.* **1.** Relating to restoration. **2.** Tending or having the power to restore. ❖ *n.* Something that restores.

re·store (rĭ-**stôr′**) *tr.v.* **re·stored, re·stor·ing, re·stores 1.** To bring back into existence or use; reestablish: *Such stories restore my faith in humanity.* **2.** To bring back to an original condition: *restore an old building.* **3.** To bring (someone) back to a prior position: *restore an emperor to the throne.* [From Middle English *restoren*, from Latin *restaurāre*.]

re·strain (rĭ-**strān′**) *tr.v.* **re·strained, re·strain·ing, re·strains 1.** To hold back or keep in check; control: *restrained my anger when I was insulted.* **2.** To prevent (someone) from doing something or acting in a certain way: *restrained them from going.* **3.** To fasten or secure so as to prevent or limit movement: *Passengers should be restrained by seat belts.* [From Middle English *restreinen*, from Latin *restringere*, to bind back.]

re·straint (rĭ-**strānt′**) *n.* **1.** The act of restraining: *the security guard's restraint of the shoplifter.* **2.** The condition of being restrained: *He had to be held in restraint.* **3.** Something that holds back or restrains: *a program of wage restraints.* **4.** Control or repression of feelings; constraint: *cried without restraint.*

re·strict (rĭ-**strĭkt′**) *tr.v.* **re·strict·ed, re·strict·ing, re·stricts** To keep or confine within limits: *restricted my diet to grains, fruits, and vegetables.*

re·strict·ed (rĭ-**strĭk′**tĭd) *adj.* **1.** Kept within certain limits: *a restricted number of students.* **2.** Excluding or unavailable to certain groups: *a restricted area.*

re·stric·tion (rĭ-**strĭk′**shən) *n.* **1**The action of restricting or the state of being restricted: *restriction of immigration.* **2.** Something that limits or restricts: *The students were subjected to restrictions on their personal liberties.*

re·stric·tive (rĭ-**strĭk′**tĭv) *adj.* **1.** Tending or serving to restrict: *vetoed the restrictive legislation.* **2.** Relating to restriction. **3.** In grammar, being a clause or phrase that describes a noun and restricts the meaning of the sentence. In the sentence *People who read a great deal have large vocabularies,* the clause *who read a great deal* is restrictive. **—re·stric′tive·ly** *adv.* **—re·stric′tive·ness** *n.*

rest·room (rĕst′ro͝om′ *or* rĕst′ro͞om′) *n.* A room with toilets and sinks for public use.

re·struc·ture (rē-strŭk′chər) *tr.v.* **re·struc·tured, re·struc·tur·ing, re·struc·tures 1.** To alter the makeup or pattern of. **2.** To make a basic change to (a system, for example): *restructured the company so that it would become profitable again.*

re·sult (rĭ-zŭlt′) *intr.v.* **re·sult·ed, re·sult·ing, re·sults 1.** To come about as a consequence: *Nothing resulted from his efforts.* See Synonyms at **follow. 2.** To end in a certain way: *The negotiations resulted in a new treaty.* ❖ *n.* The consequence of a particular action, operation, or course: *The book is the result of years of hard work. The result of adding 3 and 2 is 5.*

re·sul·tant (rĭ-zŭl′tənt) *adj.* Issuing or following as a result or consequence: *the resultant good feeling after signing the treaty.*

re·sume (rĭ-zo͞om′) *v.* **re·sumed, re·sum·ing, re·sumes** —*tr.* **1.** To begin or take up again after a break: *resumed our dinner.* **2.** To assume, occupy, or take again: *The former prime minister resumed power.* **3.** To take on or take back again. —*intr.* To begin again or continue after interruption: *The meeting will resume after lunch.* [From Middle English *resumen*, from Latin *resūmere* : *re-*, again, back + *sūmere*, to take.]

re·su·mé or **re·su·me** or **ré·su·mé** (rĕz′o͞o-mā′ *or* rĕz′-o͞o-mā′) *n.* **1.** An outline of one's professional history and experience, submitted when applying for a job. **2.** A summary: *a brief resumé of the week's events.*

re·sump·tion (rĭ-zŭmp′shən) *n.* The act or an instance of resuming: *a resumption of diplomatic relations.*

re·sur·gence (rĭ-sûr′jəns) *n.* **1.** A continuing after interruption; a renewal. **2.** A restoration to use, acceptance, activity, or vigor; a revival. **—re·sur′gent** *adj.*

res·ur·rect (rĕz′ə-rĕkt′) *tr.v.* **res·ur·rect·ed, res·ur·rect·ing, res·ur·rects 1.** To bring back to life; raise from the dead. **2.** To bring back into practice, notice, or use: *resurrect an old custom.*

res·ur·rec·tion (rĕz′ə-rĕk′shən) *n.* **1.** The act of bringing someone dead back to life or of being brought back to life. **2.** The act of bringing back into practice, notice, or use: *the resurrection of an ancient practice.* **3. Resurrection** In Christianity: **a.** The rising of Jesus from the dead on the third day after the Crucifixion. **b.** The restoration of the dead to life at the Last Judgment.

re·sus·ci·tate (rĭ-sŭs′ĭ-tāt′) *tr.v.* **re·sus·ci·tat·ed, re·sus·ci·tat·ing, re·sus·ci·tates 1.** To return life or consciousness to; revive. **2.** To restore to use, activity, or vigor: *a film that resuscitated the actor's career.* **—re·sus′ci·ta′tion** *n.*

re·sus·ci·ta·tor (rĭ-sŭs′ĭ-tā′tər) *n.* An apparatus that resuscitates by forcing oxygen into a person's lungs.

re·tail (rē′tāl′) *n.* The sale of commodities in small quantities to the general public. ❖ *adj.* Relating to or engaged in the sale of goods at retail. ❖ *adv.* At a retail price: *The radio costs more retail than wholesale.* ❖ *v.* **re·tailed, re·tail·ing, re·tails** —*tr.* To sell in small quantities directly to consumers. —*intr.* To sell goods at retail. **—re′tail′·er** *n.*

re·tain (rĭ-tān′) *tr.v.* **re·tained, re·tain·ing, re·tains 1.** To keep possession of; continue to have: *The new premier retained his post as minister of finance.* See Synonyms at **keep. 2.** To keep or hold in a particular place, condition, or position: *Certain plants retain moisture.* **3.** To keep in mind; remember: *Be sure to take notes since you can't possibly retain everything.* **4.** To hire (an attorney, for example) by the payment of a fee: *retain a lawyer.* **5.** To require (a student) to repeat a class or grade because the student is not doing well enough to move on. [From Middle English *reteinen*, from Latin *retinēre* : *re-*, back + *tenēre*, to hold.] —SEE NOTE AT **tenacious.**

re·tain·er[1] (rĭ-tā′nər) *n.* **1.** A person or thing that retains, as a device, frame, or groove that restrains or guides. **2.** An appliance used to hold teeth in position after orthodontic treatment. **3.** A servant or attendant, especially in a household of a person of high rank.

re·tain·er[2] (rĭ-tā′nər) *n.* **1.** The act of hiring a professional adviser, such as an attorney or consultant. **2.** The fee paid to hire a professional adviser.

re·tal·i·ate (rĭ-tăl′ē-āt′) *intr.v.* **re·tal·i·at·ed, re·tal·i·at·ing, re·tal·i·ates** To attack or injure someone in response to a hurtful action. [From Late Latin *retāliāre* : Latin *re-*, back + Latin *tāliō*, punishment in kind.] **—re·tal′i·a′tion** *n.* **—re·tal′i·a·to′ry** (rĭ-tăl′ē-ə-tôr′ē) *adj.*

re·tard (rĭ-tärd′) *tr.v.* **re·tard·ed, re·tard·ing, re·tards** To slow the progress of; delay; hold back: *The growth of the crop was retarded by the drought.* [From Middle English *retarden*, from Latin *retardāre*, from *tardus*, slow.]

re·tar·da·tion (rē′tär-dā′shən) *n.* **1a.** The act or process of delaying or holding back: *the drought's retardation of crop growth.* **b.** The condition of being delayed or held back. **2.** *Often Offensive* Impaired mental development.

re·tard·ed (rĭ-tär′dĭd) *adj.* **1.** *Often Offensive* Affected with impaired mental development. **2.** Occurring or developing later than desired or expected; delayed: *The company's growth was retarded due to poor management.*

retch (rĕch) *intr.v.* **retched, retch·ing, retch·es** To strain or make an effort to vomit.

re·ten·tion (rĭ-tĕn′shən) *n.* **1.** The act of retaining or the condition of being retained: *the retention of moisture by a cactus.* **2.** The ability to retain or remember things: *a student with remarkable powers of retention.* **3.** The practice of requiring a student to repeat a class or grade because he or she is not doing well enough to keep up with the work at the next level.

re·ten·tive (rĭ-tĕn′tĭv) *adj.* Having the quality, power, or capacity of retaining: *a retentive memory.* **—re·ten′tive·ness** *n.*

ret·i·cent (rĕt′ĭ-sənt) *adj.* Tending to say little, especially about one's thoughts and feelings: *a shy, reticent child.* **—ret′i·cence** *n.*

re·tic·u·late (rĭ-tĭk′yə-lĭt *or* rĭ-tĭk′yə-lāt′) *adj.* Resembling or forming a net or network: *reticulate veins of a leaf.* **—re·tic′u·late·ly** *adv.* **—re·tic′u·la′tion** *n.*

reticulate

ret·i·na (rĕt′n-ə) *n., pl.* **ret·i·nas** or **ret·i·nae** (rĕt′n-ē′) A light-sensitive membrane that lines the back of the inside of the eyeball and is connected to the brain by the optic nerve. [From Middle English, from Medieval Latin *rētina*, from Latin *rēte*, net.] **—ret′i·nal** *adj.*

ret·i·nol (rĕt′n-ôl′) *n.* Vitamin A.

ret·i·nue (rĕt′n-o͞o′) *n.* A group of servants or attendants accompanying a person of rank.

re·tire (rĭ-tīr′) *v.* **re·tired, re·tir·ing, re·tires** —*intr.* **1.** To give up one's work, business, or office, usually because of advancing age: *retire from teaching.* **2.** To withdraw, as for rest or seclusion: *The judge retired to her study.* **3.** To go to bed: *retire for the night.* **4.** To fall back or retreat, as from battle. —*tr.* **1.** To cause to withdraw from one's usual field of activity. **2.** To withdraw from use or active service: *retire an old battleship.* **3.** To lead (troops) away from action; withdraw. **4.** To take out of circulation: *retired the bonds.* **5.** To pay off (a debt). **6.** In baseball, to put out (a batter or a team). [From Old French *retirer*, to draw back.]

re·tired (rĭ-tīrd′) *adj.* Withdrawn from one's occupation, business, or office; having finished one's active working life.

re·tir·ee (rĭ-tīr′ē′) *n.* A person who has retired from active working life.

re·tire·ment (rĭ-tīr′mənt) *n.* **1.** Withdrawal from one's active working life. **2.** The act of retiring or the state of being retired: *the retirement of a debt.*

re·tir·ing (rĭ-tīr′ĭng) *adj.* Shy and reserved: *He had a retiring manner.*

retriever

WORD BUILDING

retro– The prefix **retro–**, meaning "backward, back," comes from the Latin prefix *retrō–*, meaning "backward, behind." The most common English words beginning with *retro–* are derived from Latin words or elements. *Retroactive* comes from *retrō–* and the verb *agere*, "to drive." *Retrograde* combines *retrō–* with the verb *gradī*, "to walk." *Retrospect* adds *retrō–* to the verb *specere*, "to look at." Since the 1800s, many scientific or technical terms have been coined with *retro–*, such as *retrorocket*.

Paul Revere
1768 portrait by John Singleton Copley (1738–1815)

ă	pat	ôr	core
ā	pay	oi	boy
âr	care	ou	out
ä	father	o͝o	took
ĕ	pet	o͝or	lure
ē	be	o͞o	boot
ĭ	pit	ŭ	cut
ī	bite	ûr	urge
îr	pier	th	thin
ŏ	pot	*th*	this
ō	toe	zh	vision
ô	paw	ə	about

re·tort¹ (rĭ-**tôrt′**) *v.* **re·tort·ed, re·tort·ing, re·torts** —*tr.* **1.** To reply, especially to answer in a quick, biting, or witty manner. See Synonyms at **answer. 2.** To present a counterargument to (an argument or accusation). —*intr.* **1.** To make a reply, especially a quick, biting, or witty one. **2.** To present a counterargument. ❖ *n.* A quick incisive reply. [From Latin *retorquēre*, to bend back.]

re·tort² (rĭ-**tôrt′** *or* **rē′**tôrt′) *n.* A closed laboratory vessel with an outlet tube, used for distillation or decomposition by heat. [From French *retorte*, from Medieval Latin *retorta*, from Latin *retorquēre*, to bend back.]

re·touch (rē-**tŭch′**) *tr.v.* **re·touched, re·touch·ing, re·touch·es 1.** To make new details or touches to for correction or improvement; touch up: *retouch a painting.* **2.** To improve or alter (a photographic negative or print), as by removing flaws or adding details.

re·trace (rē-**trās′**) *tr.v.* **re·traced, re·trac·ing, re·trac·es** To go back over: *retrace one's steps.*

re·tract (rĭ-**trăkt′**) *v.* **re·tract·ed, re·tract·ing, re·tracts** —*tr.* **1.** To take back; disavow: *He refused to retract his statement.* **2.** To pull (something) into a container or covering: *The airplane retracted its landing gear.* —*intr.* To move or be movable into a container or covering: *a knife with a blade that retracts.* **—re·tract′a·ble** *adj.* —SEE NOTE AT **detract.**

re·trac·tion (rĭ-**trăk′**shən) *n.* **1.** The act of retracting or the state of being retracted. **2.** The disavowal of a previously held statement or belief. **3.** The power of drawing back or of being drawn back.

re·tread (rē-**trĕd′**) *tr.v.* **re·tread·ed, re·tread·ing, re·treads** To fit (a worn automobile tire) with a new tread. ❖ *n.* (**rē′**trĕd′) **1.** A retreaded tire. **2.** A revision or reworking, especially one showing little creativity: *a retread of an old movie.*

re·treat (rĭ-**trēt′**) *n.* **1.** The act or process of withdrawing, especially from something dangerous or unpleasant. **2.** The signal for a military or tactical withdrawal. **3.** A place affording peace, quiet, privacy, or security: *We see our cabin as a retreat in the country.* ❖ *intr.v.* **re·treat·ed, re·treat·ing, re·treats** To fall or draw back; withdraw or retire. [From Middle English *retret*, from Latin *retrahere*, to draw back, retract.]

re·trench (rĭ-**trĕnch′**) *v.* **re·trenched, re·trench·ing, re·trench·es** —*tr.* To cut down; reduce; curtail: *retrench expenses.* —*intr.* To curtail expenses; economize.

re·tri·al (**rē′**trī′əl *or* **rē′**trīl′) *n.* A second trial, as of a court case.

ret·ri·bu·tion (rĕt′rə-**byo͞o′**shən) *n.* Punishment administered in return for a wrong committed.

re·trib·u·tive (rĭ-**trĭb′**yə-tĭv) *adj.* Involving or characterized by retribution. **—re·trib′u·tive·ly** *adv.*

re·triev·al (rĭ-**trē′**vəl) *n.* **1.** The act or process of retrieving. **2.** The retrieving of data from computer storage devices or from other resources like websites. **3.** The possibility of being retrieved or restored: *lost possessions beyond retrieval.*

re·trieve (rĭ-**trēv′**) *v.* **re·trieved, re·triev·ing, re·trieves** —*tr.* **1.** To search for, find, and get back; recover: *retrieve a coat from the closet; retrieve artifacts from a shipwreck.* **2.** To find and carry back (game or a thrown object). **3a.** To recall to mind (a memory, for example); remember. **b.** To find and read (stored data); gain access to. —*intr.* To find and bring back game or a thrown object: *a dog trained to retrieve.*

re·triev·er (rĭ-**trē′**vər) *n.* Any of several breeds of dog trained to find and bring back birds or other animals shot by hunters.

ret·ro (**rĕt′**rō) *adj.* Imitating or resembling something from the past, such as a clothing style.

retro– *pref.* A prefix that means backward or back: *retrograde.* —SEE NOTE.

ret·ro·ac·tive (rĕt′rō-**ăk′**tĭv) *adj.* Applying to a period prior to enactment: *a retroactive pay increase.* **—ret′ro·ac′tive·ly** *adv.*

ret·ro·fit (**rĕt′**rə-fĭt′) *tr.v.* **ret·ro·fit·ted** or **ret·ro·fit, ret·ro·fit·ting, ret·ro·fits** To provide (a device, vehicle, building, or system) with newly developed or previously unavailable parts or equipment: *retrofit cars with new safety features.*

ret·ro·grade (**rĕt′**rə-grād′) *adj.* **1.** Moving or tending to move backward. **2.** Opposite to the usual order; inverted or reversed.

ret·ro·gress (**rĕt′**rə-grĕs′ *or* rĕt′rə-**grĕs′**) *intr.v.* **ret·ro·gressed, ret·ro·gress·ing, ret·ro·gress·es 1.** To go or move backward. **2.** To return to an earlier, inferior, or less complex condition. **—ret′ro·gres′sion** (rĕt′rə-**grĕsh′**ən) *n.*

ret·ro·rock·et (**rĕt′**rō-rŏk′ĭt) *n.* A rocket engine used to slow, stop, or reverse the motion of an aircraft, spacecraft, missile, or other vehicle.

ret·ro·spect (**rĕt′**rə-spĕkt′) *n.* A review, survey, or contemplation of things in the past. ◆ **in retrospect** Looking backward or reviewing the past: *It's easy to see what went wrong in retrospect.*

ret·ro·spec·tive (rĕt′rə-**spĕk′**tĭv) *adj.* Looking back on or contemplating the past: *a retrospective examination of her career.* ❖ *n.* An exhibition or performance of works produced by an artist over a long period. —SEE NOTE AT **spectator.**

ret·ro·vi·rus (**rĕt′**rə-vī′rəs) *n., pl.* **ret·ro·vi·rus·es** Any of a group of RNA viruses, such as HIV, that can produce a DNA copy of their RNA once they are inside a cell. The DNA is then inserted into the genome of the infected host cell.

re·turn (rĭ-**tûrn′**) *v.* **re·turned, re·turn·ing, re·turns** —*intr.* **1.** To go or come back, as to a former condition or place: *return home.* **2.** To revert in speech, thought, or practice: *We finally returned to the discussion.* **3.** To revert to a former owner. **4.** To respond or answer. —*tr.* **1.** To send, put, or carry back. **2.** To give back, as in exchange for or response to something: *return merchandise.* **3.** To give back to the owner: *returned the book to my grandmother.* **4.** To render or deliver (an indictment or verdict). **5.** To produce or yield (interest or profit) as a payment for labor, investment, or expenditure: *Selling hot dogs returned him about 10 percent.* **6.** In sports: **a.** To hit (a tennis ball, for example) back to one's opponent in court games like tennis. **b.** To run with (the ball) after a kickoff, punt, interception, or fumble in football. ❖ *n.* **1.** The act of coming, going, bringing, or sending back: *a return to familiar places.* **2.** Something brought or sent back. **3.** A recurrence, as of an event: *the return of spring.* **4.** The profit or interest earned, as on an investment: *a 5 percent return.* **5.** A formal tax statement on the required official form: *an income tax return.* **6.** often **returns** A report on the vote in an election. **7.** The key or mechanism on a machine, such as a typewriter or computer, that positions the carriage or cursor for the beginning of a new line. **8.** In sports: **a.** The act of hitting a ball back to one's opponent, as in tennis. **b.** The ball hit in such an act. **c.** The act of returning the ball in football. ◆ **in return** In repayment or reciprocation. **—re·turn′a·ble** *adj.*

re·turn·ee (rĭ-tûr′**nē′**) *n.* A person who has returned after a long absence, as from a voyage.

re·un·ion (rē-**yo͞on′**yən) *n.* **1.** The act of reuniting or the state of being reunited. **2.** A gathering of the members of a group who have been separated: *a yearly family reunion.*

re·u·nite (rē′yo͞o-**nīt′**) *tr. & intr.v.* **re·u·nit·ed, re·u·nit·ing, re·u·nites** To bring or come together again.

re·use (rē-**yo͞oz′**) *tr.v.* **re·used, re·us·ing, re·us·es** To use again. **—re·us′a·ble** *adj.*

rev (rĕv) *Informal tr.v.* **revved, rev·ving, revs 1.** To increase the speed of (an engine or motor): *rev the engine.* **2.** To make livelier or more productive: *a plan to rev up the economy.*

Rev. *abbr.* An abbreviation of Reverend.

re·vamp (rē-vămp′) *tr.v.* **re·vamped, re·vamp·ing, re·vamps** To patch up, revise, restore, or reconstruct: *revamp a magazine's layout.*

re·veal (rĭ-vēl′) *tr.v.* **re·vealed, re·veal·ing, re·veals 1.** To make known (something concealed or secret); disclose: *reveal a secret.* **2.** To bring to view; show: *The anecdote revealed much about his character.* [From Middle English *revelen,* from Latin *revēlāre* : *re-,* back, off + *vēlāre,* to cover (from *vēlum,* veil).]

rev·eil·le (rĕv′ə-lē) *n.* **1.** The sounding of a bugle early in the morning to awaken people in a camp or garrison. **2.** This bugle call.

rev·el (rĕv′əl) *intr.v.* **rev·eled, rev·el·ing, rev·els** also **rev·elled, rev·el·ling, rev·els 1.** To take great pleasure or delight: *He revels in our lively discussions.* **2.** To engage in uproarious festivities; make merry. ❖ *n.* often **revels** A noisy festivity or celebration; merrymaking. **—rev′el·er, rev′el·ler** *n.*

rev·e·la·tion (rĕv′ə-lā′shən) *n.* **1.** The act of revealing or disclosing something. **2.** Something revealed, especially something surprising: *revelations about the senator's dealings.* **3.** In theology, a manifestation of divine will or truth. **4. Revelation** A book of the New Testament consisting of a mystical vision of the end of the world.

rev·el·ry (rĕv′əl-rē) *n., pl.* **rev·el·ries** Boisterous merrymaking.

re·venge (rĭ-vĕnj′) *n.* **1.** The act of inflicting harm or pain on someone for an injury or wrong that person has done: *At the end of the movie, the girl takes revenge on her tormentors.* **2.** Something done in retaliation, especially a defeat of a rival who has previously been victorious: *We lost to them at the start of the season, but we got our revenge in the playoffs.* ❖ *tr.v.* **re·venged, re·veng·ing, re·veng·es 1.** To inflict punishment in return for (an injury or insult): *The prince vowed to revenge his father's murder.* **2.** To seek or take vengeance for (oneself or another person). **—re·venge′ful** *adj.*

re·venge·ful (rĭ-vĕnj′fəl) *adj.* Full of or given to revenge.

rev·e·nue (rĕv′ə-no͞o) *n.* **1.** The income that a government collects for payment of public expenses. **2.** Yield from property or investment; income.

re·ver·ber·ate (rĭ-vûr′bə-rāt′) *intr.v.* **re·ver·ber·at·ed, re·ver·ber·at·ing, re·ver·ber·ates 1.** To resound in a succession of echoes. **2.** To have a prolonged or continuing effect: *major changes in policy that reverberated throughout the whole company.* **3.** To be repeatedly reflected, as sound waves, heat, or light. **—re·ver′ber·a′tion** *n.*

re·vere (rĭ-vîr′) *tr.v.* **re·vered, re·ver·ing, re·veres** To regard with respectful awe and devotion. [From Latin *reverērī.*]

Re·vere (rĭ-vîr′), **Paul** 1735–1818. American silversmith and Revolutionary hero. On April 18, 1775, he made his famous ride to warn of the British advance on Lexington and Concord, Massachusetts.

rev·er·ence (rĕv′ər-əns) *n.* **1.** A feeling of profound awe and respect and often love; veneration. **2.** An act showing respect, especially a bow or curtsy. **3. Reverence** A form of address used for certain members of the Christian clergy: *your Reverence.*

rev·er·end (rĕv′ər-ənd) *adj.* **1.** Worthy of or deserving reverence: *a reverend man.* **2. Reverend** Used as a title for certain members of the Christian clergy: *the Reverend Martin Chase.* ❖ *n. Informal* A cleric or minister. [From Middle English, from Latin *reverendus,* to be revered, from *reverērī,* to revere.]

rev·er·ent (rĕv′ər-ənt) *adj.* Marked by, feeling, or showing reverence: *a reverent hymn.* [From Middle English, from Latin *reverēns,* present participle of *reverērī,* to revere.] **—rev′er·ent·ly** *adv.*

rev·er·en·tial (rĕv′ə-rĕn′shəl) *adj.* **1.** Expressing reverence; reverent. **2.** Inspiring reverence.

rev·er·ie (rĕv′ə-rē) *n.* **1.** A state of abstracted thought; daydreaming: *lost in reverie.* **2.** A daydream.

re·ver·sal (rĭ-vûr′səl) *n.* **1.** The act or an example of reversing. **2.** A change for the worse.

re·verse (rĭ-vûrs′) *adj.* **1.** Turned backward in position, direction, or order: *looked at the reverse side of the page.* **2.** Causing backward movement: *reverse gear.* ❖ *n.* **1.** The opposite or contrary of something: *His opinion is the exact reverse of mine.* **2.** The back or rear of something: *the reverse of a page.* **3a.** A mechanism for moving backward, such as a gear in an automobile. **b.** The position or operating condition of such a mechanism: *put the car in reverse and backed out of the parking space.* **4.** A change to an opposite position, condition, or direction. **5.** A change for the worse; a setback: *the many reverses in his career.* ❖ *v.* **re·versed, re·vers·ing, re·vers·es** *—tr.* **1.** To turn around to the opposite direction: *The wind reversed the weather vane.* **2.** To turn inside out or upside down: *reverse a jacket; reverse the painting.* **3.** To exchange the positions of: *reverse the order of the numbers.* **4.** To annul (a decision or decree, for example): *The court reversed the decision.* *—intr.* To move or turn in the opposite direction. [From Middle English *revers,* from Latin *reversus,* past participle of *revertere,* to turn back.] **—re·verse′ly** *adv.* **—re·vers′er** *n.* —SEE NOTE AT **divert.**

reverse dive *n.* A dive in which the diver leaves the board facing forward and rotates the body backward.

reverse osmosis *n.* The movement of a solvent through a membrane from the side with a stronger concentration of a solution to the side with a weaker concentration. Reverse osmosis can only occur through the application of pressure to the side of stronger concentration and is used for purifying water.

re·vers·i·ble (rĭ-vûr′sə-bəl) *adj.* **1.** Capable of being reversed. **2.** Wearable with either side turned outward: *a reversible vest.* **3.** Relating to a process, such as a chemical reaction, that can be reversed such that the system that undergoes the process is returned to its original state.

re·ver·sion (rĭ-vûr′zhən) *n.* A return to a former condition, belief, or interest.

re·vert (rĭ-vûrt′) *intr.v.* **re·vert·ed, re·vert·ing, re·verts 1.** To return or go back to a former condition, belief, subject, or practice. **2.** To become the legal property of the former owner or the former owner's heirs: *According to the contract, the copyright reverts from the publisher to the author after 15 years.* —SEE NOTE AT **divert.**

re·view (rĭ-vyo͞o′) *tr.v.* **re·viewed, re·view·ing, re·views 1.** To look over, study, or examine again: *Let's review Chapter 5.* **2.** To look back on; think over: *review the day's events.* **3.** To examine so as to correct or criticize: *reviewed the data.* **4.** To write or give a critical report on (a new book or play, for example). **5.** To inspect formally (a group of soldiers or other military personnel). ❖ *n.* **1.** A reexamination or reconsideration. **2.** A studying of something covered earlier in school. **3.** An inspection or examination. **4.** A report or essay that discusses a work or a performance and attempts to judge its worth: *a book review.* **5.** A formal military inspection. **6.** A revue.

❑ *These sound alike:* **review, revue** (show).

re·view·er (rĭ-vyo͞o′ər) *n.* A person who reviews, especially one who writes reviews, as for a newspaper or magazine.

re·vile (rĭ-vīl′) *tr.v.* **re·viled, re·vil·ing, re·viles** To denounce with abusive language.

reverse

reverse (*top*) and obverse (*bottom*) of a Polish zloty coin

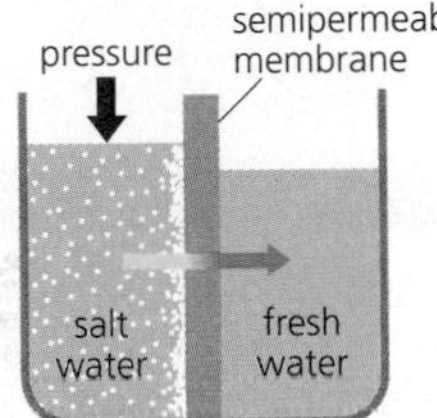

reverse osmosis

Pressure forces water across a semipermeable membrane which dissolved salts and impurities cannot pass through.

rhea

USAGE

rhetoric The word **rhetoric** was once primarily the name of an important branch of philosophy and an art deserving of serious study. The word now often refers to language that is pretentious, fancy, and insincere and does not mean much. When one politician says that another's speech is full of rhetoric, it is unlikely to be intended (or taken) as a compliment.

GEOGRAPHY

Rhode Island The state of **Rhode Island** was probably named after Rhodes, a Greek island off the coast of Turkey. It is known that a 16th-century Italian explorer compared the size of an American island that is today part of the state of Rhode Island to that of Rhodes. But the 17th-century Dutch settlers called the same island by a similar-sounding name meaning "red island," which may have also influenced its name. The state later took its name from the island.

ă	pat	ôr	core
ā	pay	oi	boy
âr	care	ou	out
ä	father	o͝o	took
ĕ	pet	o͝or	lure
ē	be	o͞o	boot
ĭ	pit	ŭ	cut
ī	bite	ûr	urge
îr	pier	th	thin
ŏ	pot	*th*	this
ō	toe	zh	vision
ô	paw	ə	about

re·vise (rĭ-vīz′) *tr.v.* **re·vised, re·vis·ing, re·vis·es 1.** To prepare a newly edited version of (a text). **2.** To reconsider and change or modify: *revise an opinion.* [From Latin *revīsere,* to look at again : *re-,* again + *vīsere,* to look at (from *vidēre,* to see).]

re·vi·sion (rĭ-vĭzh′ən) *n.* **1.** The act or process of revising. **2.** A new or revised version, as of a book or other text.

re·viv·al (rĭ-vī′vəl) *n.* **1a.** The act or an instance of reviving. **b.** The condition of being revived. **2.** A restoration to use, acceptance, activity, or vigor after a period of obscurity or inactivity. **3.** A new presentation of a previously produced play, movie, opera, or similar work. **4a.** A renewal of interest in religion. **b.** A meeting or meetings promoting such a religious renewal and often characterized by emotional preaching and public testimony.

re·vive (rĭ-vīv′) *v.* **re·vived, re·viv·ing, re·vives** —*tr.* **1.** To bring back to life or consciousness: *revive someone who has fainted.* **2.** To give new health, strength, or spirit to: *The music revived me.* **3.** To restore to use: *Congress revived the rank of full general to honor Grant.* —*intr.* **1.** To return to life or consciousness. **2.** To regain health, strength, or good spirits. **3.** To return to use, currency, or notice. **—re·viv′er** *n.*

rev·o·ca·ble (rĕv′ə-kə-bəl) *adj.* Capable of being revoked: *A driver's license is revocable if parking tickets are not paid up.*

rev·o·ca·tion (rĕv′ə-kā′shən) *n.* The act or an instance of revoking.

re·voke (rĭ-vōk′) *tr.v.* **re·voked, re·vok·ing, re·vokes** To make void by reversing, recalling, or withdrawing; cancel: *revoke an edict; revoke a license.* [From Middle English *revoken,* from Latin *revocāre* : *re-,* back + *vocāre,* to call.]

re·volt (rĭ-vōlt′) *v.* **re·volt·ed, re·volt·ing, re·volts** —*intr.* **1.** To attempt to overthrow the authority of the state; rebel. **2.** To oppose or refuse to accept something: *We revolted against her notion of what the front page should look like.* **3.** To feel disgust or repugnance. —*tr.* To fill with disgust; repel. ❖ *n.* An act of rebellion against authority; an uprising.

re·volt·ing (rĭ-vōl′tĭng) *adj.* Causing disgust; offensive: *a revolting display of bad manners.* **—re·volt′ing·ly** *adv.*

rev·o·lu·tion (rĕv′ə-lo͞o′shən) *n.* **1a.** Movement around a point in a closed path, especially as distinguished from rotation around an axis. **b.** A spinning or rotation around an axis. **c.** A single complete cycle of motion about a point in a closed path. **2.** The overthrow of one government and its replacement with another. **3.** A sudden or momentous change: *the computer revolution.*

rev·o·lu·tion·ar·y (rĕv′ə-lo͞o′shə-nĕr′ē) *adj.* **1.** Relating to or being a revolution: *revolutionary war.* **2.** Bringing about or supporting a political or social revolution: *revolutionary writings.* **3.** Characterized by or resulting in radical change: *a revolutionary new teaching idea.* ❖ *n., pl.* **rev·o·lu·tion·ar·ies** A person who takes part in or favors revolution.

rev·o·lu·tion·ist (rĕv′ə-lo͞o′shə-nĭst) *n.* A revolutionary.

rev·o·lu·tion·ize (rĕv′ə-lo͞o′shə-nīz′) *tr.v.* **rev·o·lu·tion·ized, rev·o·lu·tion·iz·ing, rev·o·lu·tion·iz·es 1.** To bring about a radical change in; alter drastically: *The automobile revolutionized travel in the United States.* **2.** To subject to a political or social revolution.

re·volve (rĭ-vŏlv′) *v.* **re·volved, re·volv·ing, re·volves 1.** To orbit a central point: *Earth revolves around the sun.* **2.** To turn on an axis; rotate. **3.** To be centered: *The book's plot revolves around a search for buried treasure.*

re·volv·er (rĭ-vŏl′vər) *n.* A pistol having a revolving cylinder with chambers for cartridges that may be fired one after another.

revolving door *n.* A door made of upright panels that rotate around a central axis.

re·vue (rĭ-vyo͞o′) *n.* A musical show consisting of skits, songs, and dances, often satirizing current events, trends, and personalities.

❑ *These sound alike:* **revue, review** (examine).

re·vul·sion (rĭ-vŭl′shən) *n.* **1.** A sudden strong change or reaction in feeling, especially a feeling of violent disgust or loathing. **2.** A turning away or withdrawal from something: *revulsion of public opinion from support of the policy.*

re·ward (rĭ-wôrd′) *n.* **1.** Something given or received in return for worthy behavior or in retribution for evil acts. **2.** Money offered or given for a special service, such as the return of a lost article or the capture of a criminal. **3.** A satisfying return or result; profit: *an investment with a handsome reward.* ❖ *tr.v.* **re·ward·ed, re·ward·ing, re·wards** To give a reward to or for: *reward her for bravery.*

re·ward·ing (rĭ-wôr′dĭng) *adj.* **1.** Offering satisfaction: *a rewarding experience.* **2.** Producing profit: *a rewarding investment.*

re·wind (rē-wīnd′) *intr.v.* **re·wound** (rē-**wound′**), **re·wind·ing, re·winds 1.** To wind again or anew: *rewound the thread on the spool.* **2.** To reverse the playing of an audio or visual recording. ❖ *n.* (**rē′**wīnd′) A control mechanism for rewinding an audio or visual recording.

re·word (rē-wûrd′) *tr.v.* **re·word·ed, re·word·ing, re·words 1.** To change the wording of: *reword a contract.* **2.** To state or express again in different words: *The speaker reworded the answer to the question.*

re·work (rē-wûrk′) *tr.v.* **re·worked, re·work·ing, re·works** To work over again; revise.

re·write (rē-rīt′) *tr.v.* **re·wrote** (rē-rōt′), **re·writ·ten** (rē-rĭt′n), **re·writ·ing, re·writes 1.** To write again, especially in a different or improved form. **2.** To put (material submitted to a newspaper or magazine) in a form suitable for publishing. **3.** To save (an edited computer file) over its most recent version in the same storage location. ❖ *n.* (**rē′**rīt′) **1.** The act or an instance of rewriting. **2.** Something rewritten. **—re·writ′er** *n.*

Rey·kja·vík (rā′kyə-vēk′ *or* **rā′**kyə-vĭk′) The capital of Iceland, in the southwest part of the island. Traditionally founded in 874, it became capital of the country in 1918.

Rf The symbol for the element **rutherfordium.**

RF *abbr.* An abbreviation of right field.

RFD *abbr.* An abbreviation of rural free delivery.

RFID *abbr.* radio frequency identification

Rg The symbol for the element **roentgenium.**

Rh The symbol for the element **rhodium.**

rhap·so·dy (răp′sə-dē) *n., pl.* **rhap·so·dies 1.** Excessively enthusiastic expression of feeling in speech or writing. **2.** A literary work written in an impassioned or exalted style. **3.** A state of elated bliss; ecstasy. **4.** A usually instrumental composition of irregular form that often incorporates improvisation.

rhe·a (rē′ə) *n.* Either of two flightless South American birds that resemble an ostrich but are smaller.

Rhea *n.* In Greek mythology, a Titan who is the sister and wife of Cronus and the mother of many of the gods and goddesses.

rhe·ni·um (rē′nē-əm) *n. Symbol* **Re** A rare, dense, silvery-white metallic element with a very high melting point that is used in electrical contacts and catalysts. Atomic number 75. See **Periodic Table.** [From Latin *Rhēnus,* the Rhine.]

rhe·o·stat (rē′ə-stăt′) *n.* A resistor whose value can be continuously varied between two extremes, used to control the flow of current in an electric circuit.

rhe·sus monkey (rē′səs) *n.* A brown to grayish monkey of Asia that is often used in biological and medical research.

rhet·o·ric (rĕt′ər-ĭk) *n.* **1.** The art or study of using language effectively and persuasively. **2.** A style of speaking or writing, especially the language of a particular subject. **3.** Elaborate, pretentious, or insincere writing or speech. —SEE NOTE.

rhe·tor·i·cal (rĭ-tôr′ĭ-kəl) *adj.* **1.** Relating to rhetoric. **2.** Concerned primarily with effect; showy. **—rhe·tor′i·cal·ly** *adv.*

rhetorical question *n.* A question to which no answer is expected, often used to make one's language more interesting, persuasive, or emphatic.

rhet·o·ri·cian (rĕt′ə-rĭsh′ən) *n.* **1.** An expert in or teacher of rhetoric. **2.** An eloquent speaker or writer.

rheu·mat·ic (ro͞o-măt′ĭk) *adj.* Relating to rheumatism.

rheumatic fever *n.* An inflammatory disease that is marked by fever and joint pain and occurs after an infection with streptococcal bacteria. It can cause permanent damage to the heart valves.

rheu·ma·tism (ro͞o′mə-tĭz′əm) *n.* Any of several disorders that primarily affect the joints, causing pain and disability.

rheu·ma·toid (ro͞o′mə-toid′) *adj.* Related to rheumatism.

rheumatoid arthritis *n.* A chronic disease in which the joints, especially of the hands and feet, become inflamed, leading to stiffness, deformity, and limited movement.

rheu·ma·tol·o·gy (ro͞o′mə-tŏl′ə-jē) *n.* The branch of medicine that deals with the diagnosis and treatment of arthritis and other disorders involving the joints, muscles, and bones. **—rheu′ma·tol′o·gist** *n.*

Rh factor (är′āch′) *n.* A substance in the red blood cells of most people that causes a person whose blood lacks this substance to produce antibodies against it during a transfusion. For a blood transfusion to be successful, both the blood of a donor and the blood of the recipient must have or must be missing the Rh factor. [From *rh(esus monkey)*, because it was first detected in the blood of this animal.]

Rhine (rīn) A river of western Europe flowing about 820 miles (1,320 kilometers) from eastern Switzerland north and northwest through Germany and the Netherlands to the North Sea.

Rhine·land (rīn′lănd′ *or* rīn′lənd) A region along the Rhine River in western Germany. It includes noted vineyards and highly industrial sections.

rhine·stone (rīn′stōn′) *n.* A colorless artificial gem of glass or paste, having facets in imitation of a diamond.

rhi·ni·tis (rī-nī′tĭs) *n.* Inflammation of the nasal mucous membranes.

rhi·no (rī′nō) *n., pl.* **rhi·nos** *Informal* A rhinoceros.

rhi·noc·er·os (rī-nŏs′ər-əs) *n., pl.* **rhinoceros** or **rhi·noc·er·os·es** Any of several large African or Asian mammals having short legs, thick tough skin, and one or two upright horns on the snout. [From Middle English *rinoceros*, from Greek *rhīnokerōs* : *rhīno-*, nose + *keras*, horn.]

rhi·zoid (rī′zoid′) *n.* A slender rootlike filament that grows from an alga, fungus, moss, liverwort, or fern, used for attachment and nourishment.

rhi·zome (rī′zōm′) *n.* A plant stem that grows under or along the ground and that sends out shoots and roots.

rho (rō) *n.* The 17th letter of the Greek alphabet, written Ρ, ρ. In English it is represented as *R, r.*

❑ *These sound alike:* **rho, roe** (fish eggs), **row¹** (continuous line), **row²** (use oars).

Rhode Island (rōd) A state of the northeast United States on the Atlantic Ocean east of Connecticut. It was admitted as one of the original Thirteen Colonies in 1790. Providence is the capital. —SEE NOTE.

Rho·de·sia (rō-dē′zhə) **1.** A former British colony in south-central Africa, consisting of modern-day Zambia and Zimbabwe. **2.** See **Zimbabwe.**

rho·di·um (rō′dē-əm) *n. Symbol* **Rh** A hard, durable, silvery-white metallic element that is resistant to acids and is used for plating silverware and jewelry. Atomic number 45. See **Periodic Table.**

rho·do·den·dron (rō′də-dĕn′drən) *n.* Any of numerous evergreen shrubs, having clusters of white, pinkish, or purplish, often bell-shaped flowers. [From Greek, oleander : *rhodon*, rose + *dendron*, tree.]

rhom·bus (rŏm′bəs) *n., pl.* **rhom·bus·es** or **rhom·bi** (rŏm′bī) A parallelogram that has four equal sides.

Rhone or **Rhône** (rōn) A river rising in south-central Switzerland and flowing about 505 miles (815 kilometers) to Lake Geneva then through eastern and southern France to the Mediterranean Sea.

rhu·barb (ro͞o′bärb′) *n.* **1a.** Any of several plants having large leaves with long thick reddish or green stalks. **b.** The edible leaf stalks of these plants, which are usually cooked and sweetened. **2.** *Informal* A noisy argument or quarrel. [From Middle English *rubarbe*, from Old French, from Late Latin *rhabarbarum* : Greek *rhā*, rhubarb + Latin *barbarus*, foreign.]

rhyme (rīm) *n.* **1.** Correspondence or repetition of the final sounds of words or of lines of verse. **2.** A poem having a regular repetition of sounds at the ends of lines. **3.** A word that has the same or similar final sound as another, as *baboon* and *harpoon.* ❖ *v.* **rhymed, rhym·ing, rhymes** *—intr.* **1.** To form a rhyme: *"Hour" rhymes with "power."* **2.** To make use of or have rhymes: *Not all poetry rhymes. —tr.* To put into a rhyme or compose with rhymes. [From Middle English *rime*, from Old French, of Germanic origin.] **—rhym′er** *n.* —SEE NOTE.

❑ *These sound alike:* **rhyme, rime** (frost).

rhyme scheme *n.* The arrangement of rhymes in a poem or stanza.

rhythm (rĭth′əm) *n.* **1.** A movement, action, or condition that recurs in a regular sequence or pattern: *the rhythm of the tides.* **2.** The pattern of sound in language, especially the regular pattern of stressed and unstressed syllables in poetry. **3.** A musical pattern formed by a series of notes or beats that are of different lengths or stresses. **4.** A particular pattern of rhythm: *a waltz rhythm.* [From Greek *rhuthmos.*]

rhythm and blues *pl.n. (used with a singular or plural verb)* A style of music developed by African Americans that combines blues and jazz and is characterized by a strong backbeat and repeated variations of musical phrases.

rhyth·mic (rĭth′mĭk) also **rhyth·mi·cal** (rĭth′mĭ-kəl) *adj.* Relating to or having rhythm. **—rhyth′mi·cal·ly** *adv.*

RI *abbr.* An abbreviation of Rhode Island.

ri·al (rē-ôl′ *or* rē-äl′) *n.* The basic monetary unit of Iran.

rib (rĭb) *n.* **1.** Any of a series of long curved bones, occurring in 12 pairs in humans, extending from the spine to or toward the breastbone and enclosing the chest cavity. **2.** A part similar to a rib and serving to shape or support: *a rib of an umbrella.* **3.** A cut of meat containing one or more ribs. **4.** One of the main veins of a leaf. **5.** A raised ridge in woven cloth or knitted material. **6.** A long, narrow architectural element projecting from a surface, especially on a vaulted ceiling. ❖ *tr.v.* **ribbed, rib·bing, ribs 1.** To support, shape, or provide with a rib or ribs. **2.** *Informal* To make fun of; tease.

rib·ald (rĭb′əld *or* rī′bôld′) *adj.* Characterized by or indulging in humor that is vulgar and lewd: *a ribald story.* **—rib′ald·ry** *n.*

rib·bon (rĭb′ən) *n.* **1.** A narrow strip or band of fabric, especially fine fabric such as satin or velvet, used for decorating, tying, or trimming. **2. ribbons** Tattered or ragged strips: *torn to ribbons.* **3.** An inked strip of cloth used for making an impression, as in a typewriter. **4.** A strip or band of colored cloth worn or displayed as the symbol of a prize or medal: *won a blue ribbon.*

rhododendron

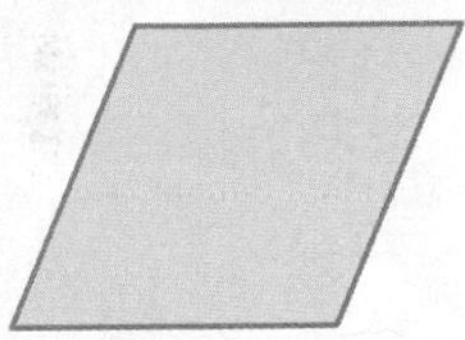

rhombus

WORD HISTORY

rhyme **Rhyme** may seem like a complicated way of writing a word that could just as well be written *rime*—and in fact *rime* was the original spelling in English. Why did people make the spelling more complicated? Part of the answer has to do with people's admiration of Greek as a language of learning: many words borrowed into English from Greek contain *rh*'s and *y*'s, so changing *ri–* to *rhy–* made the word look more like a fancy word from Greek. But another reason for the modern spelling was the influence of the word *rhythm.* This comes from the Latin word *rhythmus,* referring to harmony or rhythm in music. So our spelling *rhyme* is really a cross between Latin *rhythmus* and French *rime.*

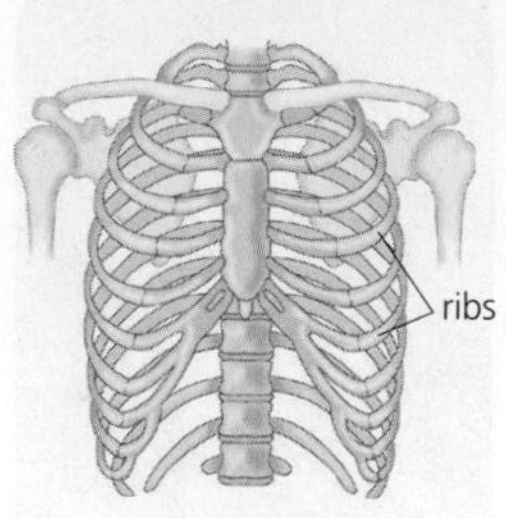

rib cage

Richelieu

Sally Ride
photographed in 1979

ă	pat	ôr	core
ā	pay	oi	boy
âr	care	ou	out
ä	father	o͝o	took
ĕ	pet	o͝or	lure
ē	be	o͞o	boot
ĭ	pit	ŭ	cut
ī	bite	ûr	urge
îr	pier	th	thin
ŏ	pot	*th*	this
ō	toe	zh	vision
ô	paw	ə	about

rib cage *n.* The enclosing structure formed by the ribs and the bones to which they are attached.

ri·bo·fla·vin (rī′bō-flā′vĭn) *n.* A vitamin belonging to the vitamin B complex that is important in carbohydrate metabolism and the maintenance of mucous membranes; vitamin B_2. It is found in milk, leafy vegetables, meat, and egg yolks.

ri·bo·nu·cle·ic acid (rī′bō-no͞o-**klē′**ĭk) *n.* RNA.

ri·bose (rī′bōs′) *n.* A simple sugar present in ribonucleic acid, riboflavin, and other nucleotides and nucleic acids.

ri·bo·some (rī′bə-sōm′) *n.* A very small structure in the cytoplasm of cells where proteins are synthesized.

rice (rīs) *n.* **1.** The starchy grain of a kind of grass widely grown in warm regions as a source of food. **2.** The plant that bears such grain.

rice paper *n.* A thin paper made chiefly from the pith of a shrub native to China.

rich (rĭch) *adj.* **rich·er, rich·est 1.** Having great material wealth: *a rich industrial nation.* **2.** Made of rare or costly materials and often with fine craftsmanship: *a rich brocade.* **3a.** Having an abundant supply; plentiful: *Milk is rich in protein.* **b.** Abundant in natural resources: *rich land.* **4.** Productive and therefore profitable: *The rich soil yielded a large harvest.* **5.** Containing a large amount of choice ingredients such as butter and sugar, and therefore heavy and sweet: *a rich dessert.* **6.** Highly varied, developed, or complex: *Folk music is a rich cultural tradition.* **7a.** Pleasantly full and mellow: *a rich tenor voice.* **b.** Warm and deep in color: *a rich brown velvet.* ❖ *n. (used with a plural verb)* Wealthy people considered as a group. —**rich′ly** *adv.* —**rich′ness** *n.*

Rich·ard I (rĭch′ərd) Known as "the Lion-Hearted." 1157–1199. King of England (1189–1199) who was a leader of the Third Crusade (1190–1192).

Ri·che·lieu (rĭsh′ə-lo͞o′), Duc de. 1585–1642. French cardinal and politician who led France during the Thirty Years' War (1618–1648).

rich·es (rĭch′ĭz) *pl.n.* **1.** Great wealth. **2.** Valuable possessions.

Rich·mond (rĭch′mənd) The capital of Virginia, in the east-central part of the state northwest of Norfolk. It was the capital of the Confederacy during the Civil War (1861–1865).

Rich·ter scale (rĭk′tər) *n.* A scale, ranging from 0 to 9, used to rate the strength or total energy of earthquakes, with each increase of one full unit representing a 10-fold increase in energy, so that an earthquake measuring 7 is ten times as powerful as one measuring 6. [After Charles Francis *Richter* (1900–1985), American seismologist.]

rick (rĭk) *n.* A stack of hay, straw, or similar material, especially when covered for protection from the weather.

rick·ets (rĭk′ĭts) *n. (used with a singular or plural verb)* A bone disease found in children that is caused by a deficiency of vitamin D and results in abnormal growth of the bones.

rick·et·y (rĭk′ĭ-tē) *adj.* **rick·et·i·er, rick·et·i·est 1.** Likely to fall apart or break; shaky: *a rickety old bridge.* **2.** Having or resembling rickets.

rick·sha or **rick·shaw** (rĭk′shô) *n.* A jinriksha.

ric·o·chet (rĭk′ə-shā′ *or* rĭk′ə-**shā′**) *intr.v.* **ric·o·cheted** (rĭk′ə-shād′), **ric·o·chet·ing** (rĭk′ə-shā′ĭng), **ric·o·chets** (rĭk′ə-shāz′) To rebound at least once from a surface: *A bullet ricocheted off the rock.* ❖ *n.* An example of such a rebound.

rid (rĭd) *tr.v.* **rid** or **rid·ded, rid·ding, rids** To free from, especially from something objectionable or unwanted: *She rid herself of her financial troubles.* ◆ **get rid of** To rid oneself of (something); discard or get free of: *Let's get rid of that broken TV.*

rid·dance (rĭd′ns) *n.* The act of ridding: *riddance of household pests.* ◆ **good riddance** An expression used to show relief that someone or something has been gotten rid of.

rid·den (rĭd′n) *v.* Past participle of **ride.** ❖ *adj.* Dominated or obsessed by: *disease-ridden; worry-ridden.*

rid·dle[1] (rĭd′l) *tr.v.* **rid·dled, rid·dling, rid·dles 1.** To pierce with numerous holes: *riddle a target with bullets.* **2.** To spread throughout: *a government riddled with corruption.* [From Middle English *ridelen,* to sift, from Old English *hriddel,* sieve.]

rid·dle[2] (rĭd′l) *n.* **1.** A question or statement requiring thought to answer or understand. **2.** Something that is difficult to understand: *It is a riddle to me why they are so excited.* [From Old English *rǣdels.*]

ride (rīd) *v.* **rode** (rōd), **rid·den** (rĭd′n), **rid·ing, rides** —*intr.* **1a.** To be carried or move, as in a vehicle or on horseback: *ride in a car.* **b.** To participate in a board sport such as snowboarding. **2.** To travel over a surface: *The car rides smoothly.* **3.** To be carried along or progress smoothly: *rode to victory on a wave of public support.* **4.** To depend: *My grade rides on the results of the test.* **5.** To continue without interference: *Let the problem ride.* —*tr.* **1a.** To sit on and move or drive: *ride a bicycle; ride a horse.* **b.** To glide or move while standing on or having one's feet attached to (a board, such as a snowboard). **2.** To travel over, along, or through: *a delivery van riding the back roads.* **3.** To be supported or carried on: *surfers riding the waves.* **4.** To take part in by riding: *a jockey riding the fourth race.* **5.** *Informal* To tease or ridicule. ❖ *n.* **1.** The act or an instance of riding, as in a vehicle or on an animal. **2.** A device, such as one at an amusement park, that one rides for pleasure or excitement. **3.** A means of transportation: *waiting for her ride to come.* ◆ **ride out** To survive or outlast: *rode out the storm.* **ride shotgun** To ride in the front passenger seat of a car or truck. [From Old English *rīdan.*]

Ride (rīd), **Sally** 1951–2012. American astronaut who in 1983 became the first American woman to enter outer space.

rid·er (rī′dər) *n.* **1.** A person who rides, especially a person who rides horses. **2.** A clause that is added to a legislative bill and that usually has little relevance to the main issue of the bill. **3.** An amendment added to a document and considered to be part of it.

ridge (rĭj) *n.* **1.** A long narrow upper section or crest: *the ridge of a wave; the ridge of a roof.* **2a.** A long narrow chain of hills or mountains, or a long narrow flat-topped strip of high land. **b.** A long mountain range on the ocean floor. **3.** A narrow, elongated zone of relatively high atmospheric pressure. **4.** A long, narrow, or crested part of the body: *the ridge of the nose.* **5.** A narrow raised strip, as in cloth or on plowed ground. ❖ *tr.v.* **ridged, ridg·ing, ridg·es** To mark with, form into, or provide with a ridge or ridges.

ridge·pole (rĭj′pōl′) *n.* **1.** A horizontal beam at the ridge of a roof to which sloping beams are attached. **2.** The horizontal pole at the top of a tent.

rid·i·cule (rĭd′ĭ-kyo͞ol′) *n.* **1.** The act of using words, gestures, images, or other products of expression to make other people laugh at or feel contempt for a person or thing: *a cartoonist's ridicule of a politician.* **2.** The words or other expressions used in this way: *a torrent of ridicule.* ❖ *tr.v.* **rid·i·culed, rid·i·cul·ing, rid·i·cules** To subject to ridicule; make fun of.

ri·dic·u·lous (rĭ-dĭk′yə-ləs) *adj.* Deserving or inspiring ridicule; absurd or silly: *a ridiculous idea.* —**ri·dic′u·lous·ly** *adv.* —**ri·dic′u·lous·ness** *n.*

rid·ing habit (rī′dĭng) *n.* The outfit typically worn by a horseback rider.

ri·el (rē-**ĕl′**) *n.* The basic monetary unit of Cambodia.

rife (rīf) *adj.* **rif·er, rif·est 1.** Widespread; prevalent: *Malaria is rife in low-lying tropical regions.* **2.** Abundant; numerous: *The article is rife with valuable insights.*

riff·raff (rĭf′răf′) *n.* **1.** People regarded as disreputable or worthless. **2.** Rubbish; trash.

ri·fle[1] (rī′fəl) *n.* A gun designed to be fired from the shoulder, with a barrel containing spiral grooves designed to cause the bullet to spin when fired. ❖ *tr.v.* **ri·fled, ri·fling, ri·fles** To cut spiral grooves within (a gun barrel, for example). [From *rifle,* to cut spiral grooves in, from Old French *rifler,* to plunder, scratch.]

ri·fle² (rī′fəl) *v.* **ri·fled, ri·fling, ri·fles** *—tr.* **1.** To search (an area, for example) thoroughly, especially using the hands in order to steal or remove something. **2.** To rob or search with the intent to rob: *rifled the travelers of their belongings.* **3.** To steal (goods). *—intr.* To search vigorously: *I rifled through my bag looking for my keys.* [From Middle English *riflen,* to plunder, from Old French *rifler,* probably of Germanic origin.]

ri·fle·man (rī′fəl-mən) *n.* **1.** A soldier equipped with a rifle. **2.** A person who shoots a rifle skillfully.

ri·fling (rī′flĭng) *n.* **1.** The process or operation of cutting spiral grooves in a rifle barrel. **2.** Grooves cut in a rifle barrel.

rift (rĭft) *n.* **1.** A fissure, crack, or opening, as in rock. **2.** A break in friendly relations: *a rift between former friends.* [From Middle English, of Scandinavian origin.]

rig (rĭg) *tr.v.* **rigged, rig·ging, rigs 1.** To provide with equipment: *rig a garage to store a boat.* **2a.** To equip (a ship) with sails, shrouds, and yards. **b.** To fit (sails or shrouds, for example) to masts and yards. **3.** To make or construct in haste or in a makeshift manner: *rig up a tent for the night.* **4.** To manipulate dishonestly for personal gain: *rig a prize fight.* ❖ *n.* **1.** The arrangement of masts, spars, and sails on a sailing vessel: *a fore-and-aft rig.* **2.** Special equipment or gear, especially equipment used for drilling oil wells: *a drilling rig.* **3.** A vehicle with one or more horses harnessed to it. **4.** A truck, tractor, or tractor-trailer.

Ri·ga (rē′gə) The capital of Latvia, in the central part of the country on an inlet of the Baltic Sea. It was founded as a trading post on a site originally inhabited by Baltic tribes.

rig·a·ma·role (rĭg′ə-mə-rōl′) *n.* Variant of **rigmarole.**

rig·ger (rĭg′ər) *n.* **1.** A person who rigs something. **2.** A ship with a specific kind of rigging: *a square rigger.*

rig·ging (rĭg′ĭng) *n.* **1.** The system of ropes, chains, and tackle used to support and control the masts, sails, and yards of a sailing vessel. **2.** The supporting material for construction work.

right (rīt) *adj.* **right·er, right·est 1.** Conforming with justice or morality: *do the right thing.* **2.** In accordance with fact, reason, or truth; correct: *the right answer.* **3.** Fitting, proper, or appropriate: *the right tool for the job.* **4.** Most favorable, desirable, or convenient: *in the right place at the right time.* **5.** Healthy; sound: *not in her right mind.* **6.** Meant to be worn or positioned on the outside, in front, or on top: *wear the jacket with the right side outward.* **7a.** Belonging to or located on the side of the body to the east when one is facing north: *kicked the ball with her right foot.* **b.** Relating to, directed toward, or located on the right side: *the right arm of the chair.* **8.** often **Right** Belonging to the political right. **9a.** Formed by or in reference to a line or plane that is perpendicular to another line or plane. **b.** Having the axis perpendicular to the base: *a right cone.* **c.** Having a right angle: *a right triangle.* ❖ *n.* **1.** That which is just, moral, or proper: *the difference between right and wrong.* **2a.** The direction or position on the right side. **b.** The right side. **c.** A turn in the direction of the right hand or side. **3.** often **Right** The people and groups who advocate conservative or reactionary measures, especially in politics. **4.** A punch or blow delivered with the right hand. **5a.** Something that a person or community has a claim to by law, tradition, or nature: *the right of free speech.* **b.** Something, especially humane treatment, claimed to be due to animals by moral principle. ❖ *adv.* **1.** Toward or on the right: *turning right.* **2.** In a straight line; directly: *came right to the door.* **3.** In the proper or desired manner; well: *The jacket doesn't fit right.* **4.** Exactly; just: *right where we were standing.* **5.** Immediately: *called right after breakfast.* **6.** Accurately; correctly: *answered the question right.* **7.** *Informal* Very: *a right nice place.* **8.** Used as an intensive: *Keep right on going.* ❖ *v.* **right·ed, right·ing, rights** *—tr.* **1.** To put in or restore to an upright or proper position: *She righted the kayak.* **2.** To set right; correct: *This new law should right unfair hiring practices.* **3.** To make reparation or amends for: *right a wrong.* *—intr.* To regain an upright or proper position. ◆ **by rights** In a just manner; properly. **right away** Immediately; at once: *I have to leave right away.* **right on** *Slang* An expression used for encouragement, support, or enthusiastic agreement. **to rights** In a satisfactory or orderly condition. **—right′ness** *n.*

❑ *These sound alike:* **right, rite** (ceremony), **write** (compose).

right angle *n.* An angle formed by the perpendicular intersection of two straight lines; an angle of 90°. **—right′-an′gled** (rīt′ăng′gəld) *adj.*

right ascension *n.* The angular distance of a star or planet on the celestial sphere from the vernal equinox, measured eastward along the celestial equator.

right-click (rīt′klĭk′) *intr.v.* **right-clicked, right-click·ing, right-clicks** To click the secondary button of a mouse having two buttons with different functions.

right·eous (rī′chəs) *adj.* Being or acting in accord with standards of what is good and just; moral or just: *a righteous parishioner; a righteous judgment.* **—right′eous·ly** *adv.* **—right′eous·ness** *n.*

right field *n.* **1.** In baseball, the part of the outfield that is to the right as viewed from home plate. **2.** The position played by the right fielder.

right fielder *n.* In baseball, the player who defends right field.

right·ful (rīt′fəl) *adj.* **1.** Right; just: *a rightful position of honor.* **2.** Having a just, proper, or legal claim: *the car's rightful owner.* **3.** Owned by a just or proper claim: *a rightful share of the money.* **—right′ful·ly** *adv.*

right-hand (rīt′hănd′) *adj.* **1.** Relating to or located on the right: *the right-hand margin.* **2.** Relating to, designed for, or done with the right hand: *a right-hand throw.* **3.** Helpful; reliable: *my right-hand assistant.*

right-hand·ed (rīt′hăn′dĭd) *adj.* **1a.** Using the right hand, as for writing or throwing, more skillfully or easily than the left hand. **b.** In sports, swinging from right to left: *a right-handed tennis player.* **2a.** Done with the right hand: *a right-handed throw.* **b.** Designed for use by the right hand: *a right-handed glove.* **3.** Turning or moving from left to right: *a screw with a right-handed thread.* ❖ *adv.* **1.** With the right hand: *draws right-handed.* **2.** From the right to the left: *bats right-handed.* **—right′-hand′ed·ly** *adv.* **—right′-hand′ed·ness** *n.*

right-hand·er (rīt′hăn′dər) *n.* A person who is right-handed.

right·ist (rī′tĭst) *n.* A person who advocates or sympathizes with the ideas of the political right. ❖ *adj.* Advocating or sympathizing with ideas of the political right.

right·ly (rīt′lē) *adv.* **1.** In a correct or proper manner: *act rightly.* **2.** With honesty; justly. **3.** *Informal* Really: *I don't rightly know.*

right-mind·ed (rīt′mīn′dĭd) *adj.* Having ideas and views based on what is right or intended to be right.

right of way *n., pl.* **rights of way** or **right of ways 1.** The right to travel over property owned by someone else. **2.** The strip of land over which structures such as highways, railroads, or power lines are built. **3.** The customary or legal right of a person, vessel, or vehicle to pass in front of another.

right-side up (rīt′sīd′) *adv.* **1.** With the top facing upward: *Keep this box right-side up.* **2.** In or into the correct position: *Turn the painting right-side up.*

rigging

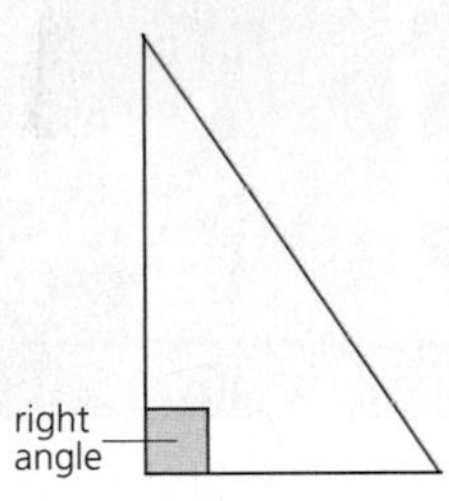

right angle

rind

ring¹

right triangle *n.* A triangle that contains a right angle.

right wing also **Right Wing** *n.* The conservative or reactionary faction of a group. **—right′-wing′** *adj.* **—right′-wing′er** *n.*

right·y (rī′tē) *n., pl.* **right·ies** *Informal* A person who is right-handed.

rig·id (rĭj′ĭd) *adj.* **1.** Not changing shape or bending; stiff; inflexible: *a rigid iron frame.* **2.** Not changing or adjusting to different conditions or problems: *a rigid thinker.* **3.** Scrupulously or severely maintained or performed; rigorous or harsh: *rigid discipline.* [From Middle English *rigide*, from Latin *rigidus*.] **—rig′id·ly** *adv.* **—rig′id·ness** *n.*

ri·gid·i·ty (rĭ-jĭd′ĭ-tē) *n.* The quality or state of being rigid; stiffness; inflexibility.

rig·ma·role (rĭg′mə-rōl′) also **rig·a·ma·role** (rĭg′ə-mə-rōl′) *n.* **1.** Confused and rambling speech; nonsense. **2.** A complicated and petty set of procedures.

rig·or (rĭg′ər) *n.* **1.** Strictness or severity, as in temperament, action, or judgment: *the rigor of the army's discipline.* **2.** A harsh or trying circumstance; a hardship: *the rigors of working on a sailing ship.* **3.** Strictness in adhering to standards or a method; exactitude: *tested the hypothesis with scientific rigor.* [From Middle English *rigour*, from Latin *rigor*.]

rigor mor·tis (môr′tĭs) *n.* Muscular stiffening following death.

rig·or·ous (rĭg′ər-əs) *adj.* **1.** Characterized by or acting with rigor: *a rigorous training program; a rigorous examination of policy.* **2.** Severe or harsh: *the rigorous climate of the desert.* **—rig′or·ous·ly** *adv.* **—rig′or·ous·ness** *n.*

rile (rīl) *tr.v.* **riled, ril·ing, riles** To anger or irritate; vex; annoy.

rill (rĭl) *n.* A small brook.

rim (rĭm) *n.* **1.** The usually curved or circular border or edge of something: *the rim of a cup.* See Synonyms at **border. 2.** The outer part of a wheel around which the tire is fitted. ❖ *tr.v.* **rimmed, rim·ming, rims 1.** To furnish with a rim. **2.** To roll around the rim of (a basket or golf cup, for example) without falling in: *His putt rimmed the cup.*

rime (rīm) *n.* A frost or coating of grains of ice, as on grass or trees. ❖ *tr.v.* **rimed, rim·ing, rimes** To cover with or as if with frost or ice. [From Old English *hrīm*.]

❑ *These sound alike:* **rime, rhyme** (poem).

rind (rīnd) *n.* A tough outer covering, skin, or coating, as of fruit or cheese.

ring¹ (rĭng) *n.* **1.** A circular object, form, line, or arrangement: *a ring of flowers.* **2.** A small circular band, often of precious metal, worn on a finger. **3.** A circular band meant to carry, encircle, or hold something: *a napkin ring.* **4. rings** A pair of circular metal bands suspended in the air and used for gymnastic exercises. **5.** An enclosed, usually circular area in which exhibitions, sports, or contests take place: *a circus ring.* **6.** A rectangular arena, set off by ropes, in which boxing matches are held. **7.** A group of people acting privately or illegally for their own gain: *a ring of thieves.* **8.** A group of atoms bound together chemically in an arrangement that can be represented as a closed geometric figure: *a benzene ring.* ❖ *v.* **ringed, ring·ing, rings** *—tr.* **1.** To surround with a ring; encircle: *Let's ring the statue with rose bushes.* **2.** To ornament or fit with a ring or rings: *ringed the centerpiece with a holly wreath.* **3.** To hem in (cattle or other animals) by riding in a circle around them. **4a.** To toss a horseshoe so that the inner curve hits (the stake). **b.** To toss a quoit over (the peg). *—intr.* To form a ring or rings: *Spectators ringed around the wrestlers.* [From Old English *hring*.]

❑ *These sound alike:* **ring¹** (circle), **ring²** (sound), **wring** (squeeze).

ring² (rĭng) *v.* **rang** (răng), **rung** (rŭng), **ring·ing, rings** *—intr.* **1.** To give forth a clear resonant sound, such as that of a bell when struck: *The doorbell rang.* **2.** To sound a bell in order to summon someone: *rang for the maid.* **3.** To hear a persistent buzzing or humming: *ears ringing from the loud music.* **4.** To be filled with talk or rumors: *The town is ringing with stories of your success.* **5.** To appear to have a certain quality: *That story rings true.* *—tr.* **1.** To cause (a bell, for example) to ring. **2.** To announce or signal by ringing: *ring the New Year in.* **3.** *Chiefly British* To call (someone) on the telephone: *Let's ring her and invite her.* ❖ *n.* **1.** The sound made by a bell or another vibrating object. **2.** A loud sound that is continued or repeated: *the ring of the whistling wind.* **3.** A telephone call: *Give me a ring from the hotel.* **4.** A suggestion of a particular quality: *His offer has a suspicious ring.* ◆ **ring a bell** *Informal* To arouse an often vague memory: *That name doesn't ring a bell with me.* **ring up 1.** To record, especially by means of a cash register. **2.** To accomplish or achieve: *rang up several victories.* [From Old English *hringan*.]

❑ *These sound alike:* **ring²** (sound), **ring¹** (circle), **wring** (squeeze).

ringed (rĭngd) *adj.* **1.** Wearing or marked with a ring or rings. **2.** Encircled or surrounded by bands or rings.

ring·er¹ (rĭng′ər) *n.* A horseshoe or quoit thrown so it encircles the peg.

ring·er² (rĭng′ər) *n.* **1.** A person who sounds a bell or chime. **2.** *Slang* A contestant entered dishonestly into a competition. **3.** *Slang* A person who bears a striking resemblance to another: *a ringer for his father.*

ring·git (rĭng′gĭt) *n.* The basic monetary unit of Malaysia.

ring·lead·er (rĭng′lē′dər) *n.* A person who leads others, especially in unlawful or improper activities.

ring·let (rĭng′lĭt) *n.* **1.** A long curl of hair. **2.** A small circle or ring.

ring·mas·ter (rĭng′măs′tər) *n.* A person who is in charge of and introduces the acts in a circus.

ring·side (rĭng′sīd′) *n.* A place providing a close view of a spectacle, especially the area immediately outside an arena or ring, as at a circus.

ring·tone (rĭng′tōn′) *n.* A digital sound file that a telephone plays to indicate an incoming call.

ring·worm (rĭng′wûrm′) *n.* Any of a number of contagious fungal infections of the skin, hair, or nails. Ringworm of the skin is marked by ring-shaped, scaly itching patches.

rink (rĭngk) *n.* **1.** An area surfaced with smooth ice for skating, often enclosed with boards. **2.** A smooth floor suited for roller-skating. **3.** An area, often having artificial grass and boards, used for indoor soccer and other sports. [From Middle English *renk*, jousting or fighting area, possibly from Old French *renc*, line, of Germanic origin.]

rin·ky-dink (rĭng′kē-dĭngk′) *Slang adj.* **1.** Old-fashioned; worn-out. **2.** Unimportant. **3.** Of cheap or poor quality.

rinse (rĭns) *tr.v.* **rinsed, rins·ing, rins·es 1.** To wash lightly with water: *rinse the dishes.* **2.** To remove (soap, for example) by washing lightly with water. ❖ *n.* **1.** The act of washing lightly. **2.** The water or other solution used in rinsing. **3.** A solution used in conditioning or coloring the hair.

Río de la Plata See **Plata, Río de la.**

Ri·o de Ja·nei·ro (rē′ō dā zhə-nâr′ō) A city of southeast Brazil on an arm of the Atlantic Ocean. It was the capital of Brazil until 1960.

Ri·o Grande (rē′ō grănd′ *or* grăn′dā *or* grăn′dē) A river rising in southwest Colorado and flowing about 1,900 miles (3,000 kilometers) through central New Mexico to southwest Texas, where it turns southeast and forms the US-Mexico border. It empties into the Gulf of Mexico.

ri·ot (rī′ət) *n.* **1.** A wild disturbance created by a large number of people. **2.** In law, a violent disturbance of the

ă	pat	ôr	core
ā	pay	oi	boy
âr	care	ou	out
ä	father	ŏŏ	took
ĕ	pet	ŏŏr	lure
ē	be	ōō	boot
ĭ	pit	ŭ	cut
ī	bite	ûr	urge
îr	pier	th	thin
ŏ	pot	*th*	this
ō	toe	zh	vision
ô	paw	ə	about

peace by three or more people assembled for a common purpose. **3.** A profuse display: *The garden was a riot of bright colors.* **4.** *Slang* An extremely funny person or thing: *That cartoon is a riot.* ❖ *intr.v.* **ri·ot·ed, ri·ot·ing, ri·ots** To take part in a riot. **—ri′ot·er** *n.*

Riot Act *n.* An English law providing that groups of 12 or more people who disturb the peace must disperse upon being read part of this act. This law was enacted in 1715 and repealed in 1973. ◆ **read the riot act** To warn or reprimand forcefully: *The teacher read the riot act to the rowdy students.*

ri·ot·ous (rī′ət-əs) *adj.* **1.** Relating to or resembling a riot: *riotous mobs.* **2.** Boisterous or unrestrained: *riotous laughter.* **—ri′ot·ous·ly** *adv.*

rip¹ (rĭp) *v.* **ripped, rip·ping, rips** *—tr.* **1a.** To cut, tear apart, or tear away roughly: *The cat's claws ripped the curtain.* See Synonyms at **tear¹**. **b.** To cause to be pulled apart, especially as an accident: *I ripped my pants when I bent over.* **2.** To split or saw (wood) along its grain. **3.** To copy (audio or audio-visual material) from a CD or DVD. **4.** To subject to strong criticism or attack: *The critic ripped the tedious movie.* *—intr.* To become torn or split apart: *My pants ripped when I bent over.* ❖ *n.* **1.** The act of ripping. **2.** A torn or split place: *Sew up the rip.* ◆ **rip into** To attack vehemently. **rip off** *Slang* **1.** To steal from; rob: *The guest ripped off the hotel by taking towels from the room.* **2.** To steal (something): *Someone must have ripped off a newspaper when the clerk wasn't looking.* **3.** To exploit, swindle, or cheat: *a liar who ripped off unsuspecting clients.* [From Middle English *rippen*, from Flemish.]

rip² (rĭp) *n.* A stretch of rough water in a river, channel, or estuary caused by waves or a tide opposing a current. [Probably from *rip*, tear.]

rip·cord (rĭp′kôrd′) *n.* A cord that is pulled to release a parachute from its pack.

rip current *n.* A strong narrow surface current that flows rapidly away from the shore, returning the water carried shoreward by waves.

ripe (rīp) *adj.* **rip·er, rip·est 1.** Fully grown and developed: *ripe fruit.* **2.** Aged and ready to be used or eaten: *a ripe cheese.* **3.** Advanced in years: *the ripe age of 85.* **4.** Fully prepared; ready: *a team ripe for its first victory.* **5.** Thoroughly matured; seasoned: *ripe judgment.* [From Old English *rīpe.*] **—ripe′ly** *adv.* **—ripe′ness** *n.*

rip·en (rī′pən) *tr. & intr.v.* **rip·ened, rip·en·ing, rip·ens** To make or become ripe or riper; mature.

rip-off (rĭp′ôf′) *n.* *Slang* **1.** A product or service that is overpriced or of poor quality. **2.** Something, such as a film or story, that is clearly imitative of or based on something else. **3.** The act of cheating, swindling, or stealing: *Their selling of those phony autographs was a rip-off.*

rip·ple (rĭp′əl) *v.* **rip·pled, rip·pling, rip·ples** *—intr.* **1.** To form or show small waves on the surface: *The curtain rippled in the wind.* **2.** To flow with such small waves on the surface: *The stream rippled through the meadow.* *—tr.* To cause to form small waves: *A breeze rippled the prairie grass.* ❖ *n.* **1.** A small wave, such as one formed on the surface of water when it is disturbed. **2.** A motion like that of a wave; an undulation: *the ripple of muscles on the running horse.* **3.** A sound like that made by rippling water: *a ripple of laughter in the audience.*

ripple effect *n.* A gradually spreading effect or influence: *The new trade agreement will have a ripple effect on the economy.*

rip-roar·ing (rĭp′rôr′ĭng) *adj.* *Informal* Noisy, lively, and exciting.

rip·saw (rĭp′sô′) *n.* A saw with coarse teeth, used for cutting wood along the grain.

rip tide *n.* A rip current.

rise (rīz) *intr.v.* **rose** (rōz), **ris·en** (rĭz′ən), **ris·ing, ris·es 1.** To assume a standing position after lying, sitting, or kneeling. **2.** To get out of bed: *rose at dawn.* **3.** To move from a lower to a higher position; ascend: *The kite rose quickly.* **4.** To increase in size, volume, or level: *The creek rose after the heavy rain.* **5.** To increase in number, amount, or value: *Prices of imports rose.* **6.** To exert oneself to deal with a matter: *rise to the challenge of an adventure.* **7.** To increase in intensity, force, or speed: *The wind has risen.* **8.** To increase in pitch or volume: *The sound of their voices rose and fell.* **9.** To become visible above the horizon: *The sun rises a little later each morning in the fall.* **10.** To slope or extend upward: *Mt. McKinley rises to 20,320 feet.* **11.** To come into existence; spring up: *Many streams rise in the snow-capped Andes.* **12.** To be erected: *New office buildings are rising all around us.* **13.** To appear at the surface of the water or the earth; emerge: *Whales must rise periodically to take in air.* **14.** To puff up; become larger: *Bread dough rises.* **15.** To attain higher status or power: *an officer who rose through the ranks.* **16.** To become apparent to the mind or senses: *Old doubts rose to challenge me.* **17.** To come back to life: *The phoenix is said to rise from its own ashes.* **18.** To rebel: *The people rose up against the tyrant.* ❖ *n.* **1.** An act of rising; upward movement. **2.** An increase in height, as of the level of water. **3.** An increase in price, worth, quantity, volume, or degree. **4.** Elevation in status or power: *her rise to stardom.* **5.** The origin or beginning: *the rise of feminism.* **6.** A gently sloping hill. [From Old English *rīsan.*]

ris·er (rī′zər) *n.* **1.** A person who rises, especially from sleep: *a late riser.* **2.** A vertical part of a stair step. **3.** A platform, often arranged with similar platforms in tiers: *The choir stood on risers on stage.*

ris·ing (rī′zĭng) *adj.* **1.** Sloping upward; ascending: *a rising road.* **2.** Developing or emerging: *a rising generation of writers.* **3.** Increasing in power or influence: *a rising nation.* **4.** About to begin a certain grade: *rising seniors.*

risk (rĭsk) *n.* **1.** The possibility of suffering harm or loss; danger: *the risk of developing heart disease.* **2.** A situation, factor, or course of action involving danger or loss: *a risk I did not want to take.* **3.** A person or thing considered with respect to the possibility of loss: *People who pay their bills are good credit risks.* ❖ *tr.v.* **risked, risk·ing, risks 1.** To expose to a chance of harm or loss; hazard: *He risked his savings in an investment scheme.* **2.** To incur the possibility of; subject oneself to the chance of: *risking an accident.* ◆ **at risk** In an unsafe state; endangered: *His bad driving puts him at risk of injury.*

risk·y (rĭs′kē) *adj.* **risk·i·er, risk·i·est** Involving risk; dangerous. **—risk′i·ness** *n.*

ri·sot·to (rĭ-sō′tō *or* rē-zōt′tō) *n., pl.* **ri·sot·tos** A dish consisting of rice cooked in broth with other ingredients, such as onions and Parmesan cheese.

ris·qué (rĭs-kā′) *adj.* Somewhat improper or indecent; suggestive.

ri·tar·dan·do (rē′tär-dän′dō) *adv. & adj.* In music, gradually slowing in tempo.

rite (rīt) *n.* **1.** The form required by custom or law for conducting a religious or other solemn ceremony: *the rite of confirmation.* **2.** A ceremonial act or series of acts: *the rites performed by various people before hunting.* **3.** The liturgy or forms of worship of a branch of the Christian church. [From Middle English, from Latin *rītus.*]

❑ *These sound alike:* **rite, right** (direction), **write** (compose).

rit·u·al (rĭch′o͞o-əl) *n.* **1.** The proper form or order of a religious or other ceremony. **2.** The set of ceremonies or rites used in a place of worship. **3.** A method or procedure faithfully followed: *Exercise was part of their daily ritual.* ❖ *adj.* Being part of a routine: *a ritual glass of milk before going to bed.* **—rit′u·al·ly** *adv.*

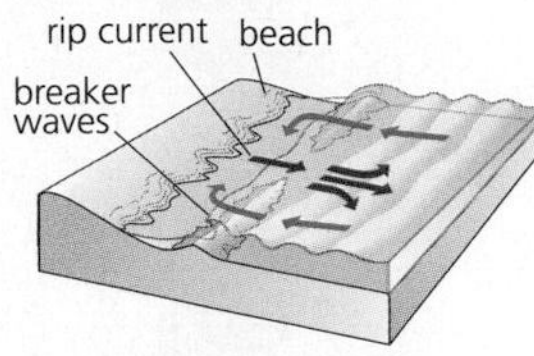

rip current

A rip current is formed when water coming ashore is channeled back to sea through a narrow passage, such as a break in a sandbar, causing an increase in the strength of the current.

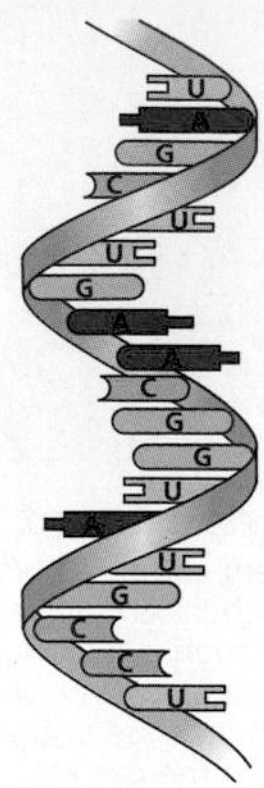

RNA
A. adenine
U. uracil
C. cytosine
G. guanine

roan

ă	pat	ôr	core
ā	pay	oi	boy
âr	care	ou	out
ä	father	o͝o	took
ĕ	pet	o͝or	lure
ē	be	o͞o	boot
ĭ	pit	ŭ	cut
ī	bite	ûr	urge
îr	pier	th	thin
ŏ	pot	*th*	this
ō	toe	zh	vision
ô	paw	ə	about

rit·u·al·ism (rĭch′o͞o-ə-lĭz′əm) *n.* **1.** The practice or observance of religious ritual. **2.** Insistence upon or adherence to ritual.

ritz·y (rĭt′sē) *adj.* **ritz·i·er, ritz·i·est** *Informal* Elegant; fancy: *ritzy hotels.*

ri·val (rī′vəl) *n.* **1.** A person who attempts to equal or outdo another; a competitor. **2.** A person or thing that equals or almost equals another: *a performance without rival.* ❖ *tr.v.* **ri·valed, ri·val·ing, ri·vals** or **ri·valled, ri·val·ling, ri·vals 1.** To compete with; attempt to equal or surpass. **2.** To be the equal of; match in excellence. [From Latin *rīvālis*, one using the same stream as another, from *rīvus*, stream.]

ri·val·ry (rī′vəl-rē) *n., pl.* **ri·val·ries** The act of trying to equal or outdo another; competition.

riv·er (rĭv′ər) *n.* **1.** A large natural stream of water that flows into an ocean, lake, or other body of water, usually fed by smaller streams that flow into it. **2.** A stream or flow resembling a river: *a river of tears.* [From Middle English *rivere*, from Latin *rīpārius*, of a bank, from *rīpa*, bank.]

riv·er·bank (rĭv′ər-băngk′) *n.* The bank of a river.

river basin *n.* The land area drained by a river and its tributaries.

riv·er·boat (rĭv′ər-bōt′) *n.* A boat suitable for use on a river.

riv·er·front (rĭv′ər-frŭnt′) *n.* The land or property along a river.

riv·et (rĭv′ĭt) *n.* A metal bolt or pin with a head on one end, used to join objects by being set through a hole in each piece and having the headless end hammered to form another head. ❖ *tr.v.* **riv·et·ed, riv·et·ing, riv·ets 1.** To fasten with a rivet: *rivet leather straps onto the suitcase.* **2.** To hold the attention of (someone) continuously: *The audience was riveted by the suspense.* **3.** To hold (one's attention) continuously: *This book riveted my attention.*

Riv·i·er·a (rĭv′ē-ĕr′ə) A narrow coastal region between the Alps and the Mediterranean Sea extending from southeast France to northwest Italy.

riv·u·let (rĭv′yə-lĭt) *n.* A small stream or brook.

Ri·yadh (rē-yäd′) The capital of Saudi Arabia, in the east-central part of the country east-northeast of Mecca. It is situated in a desert oasis.

ri·yal (rē-ôl′ *or* rē-äl′) *n.* The basic monetary unit of Qatar and Saudi Arabia.

Rn The symbol for the element **radon.**

RN *abbr.* An abbreviation of registered nurse.

RNA (är′ĕn-ā′) *n.* An acid found in all living cells and many viruses, having a composition similar to that of DNA and functioning mainly in the synthesis of proteins.

RNA virus *n.* Any of a group of viruses whose genetic material is composed of RNA, including the retroviruses.

roach (rōch) *n.* A cockroach. [From *cockroach.*]

road (rōd) *n.* **1.** An open way for the passage of vehicles, people, and animals: *the road to town; lived on Nichols Road.* **2.** A path or course: *the road to success.* **3.** A railroad. ◆ **on the road 1.** On tour, as a theatrical company. **2.** Traveling, especially as a salesperson. **3.** Wandering, as a vagabond. [From Old English *rād*, a riding, road.]

❑ *These sound alike:* **road, rode** (moved in a vehicle), **rowed** (used oars).

road·bed (rōd′bĕd′) *n.* **1a.** The foundation upon which the ties and rails of a railroad are laid. **b.** A layer of gravel or crushed rock under the ties. **2.** The foundation and surface of a road.

road·block (rōd′blŏk′) *n.* **1.** A barricade or obstruction across a road set up to prevent the passage of criminals or enemy troops. **2.** Something that prevents progress: *The lawyer hit a legal roadblock and had to rethink his strategy.*

road·ie (rō′dē) *n.* A person who loads, unloads, and sets up equipment and often performs errands for musicians on tour.

road·kill (rōd′kĭl′) *n. Informal* An animal or animals killed by a car.

road·run·ner (rōd′rŭn′ər) *n.* Either of two swift-running birds of southwest North America and Central America, having brownish streaked feathers, a long tail, and a crested head.

road·side (rōd′sīd′) *n.* The area bordering on the side of the road.

road·stead (rōd′stĕd′) *n.* An area offshore where ships can anchor safely.

road·ster (rōd′stər) *n.* **1.** An automobile having a single seat in the front for two or three people and no roof. **2.** A sports car.

road test *n.* **1.** A test of a motor vehicle under actual road conditions. **2.** A test of driving ability on the road, required of a candidate for a driver's license.

road trip *n.* A usually lengthy trip taken in a motor vehicle, especially for pleasure.

road·way (rōd′wā′) *n.* A road, especially the part over which vehicles travel.

roam (rōm) *v.* **roamed, roam·ing, roams** —*intr.* **1.** To move about without purpose or plan; wander. See Synonyms at **wander. 2.** To turn one's attention from one subject to another without much thought: *I could hear the speaker, but my thoughts were roaming.* **3.** To be directed without apparent purpose; look in an idle or casual manner: *Her eyes roamed around the room.* **4.** To use a cell phone network outside of a home service area as defined by a service plan. —*tr.* To travel over or through (an area) without a purpose or plan; wander: *Bears roam the forest.* **—roam′er** *n.*

roan (rōn) *adj.* Having a coat with reddish, brownish, or blackish hairs mixed with white or gray hairs: *a roan horse.* ❖ *n.* **1.** A roan horse or other animal. **2.** The color of a roan animal, especially a horse.

roar (rôr) *n.* **1.** The loud, deep sound made by a wild animal: *the roar of a lion.* **2.** A loud, deep cry of rage or anger. **3.** A loud, deep sound or noise: *the roar of a rocket engine.* ❖ *v.* **roared, roar·ing, roars** —*intr.* **1.** To produce or utter a roar. **2.** To laugh loudly or excitedly. **3.** To make or produce a loud, deep sound or noise: *The engines roared.* **4.** To move while making a loud noise: *The truck roared down the road.* —*tr.* To express with a loud, deep noise: *We roared our approval.* See Synonyms at **yell.** [From Old English *rārian.*]

roar·ing (rôr′ĭng) *adj.* Very lively or successful; thriving: *a roaring business.*

roast (rōst) *v.* **roast·ed, roast·ing, roasts** —*tr.* **1.** To cook with dry heat, as in an oven or near hot coals. **2.** To dry or brown by heating: *They roasted coffee beans.* **3.** To expose to great or excessive heat. **4.** In metallurgy, to heat (ores) in a furnace in order to dehydrate, purify, or oxidize. **5.** *Informal* **a.** To ridicule or criticize harshly. **b.** To honor at or subject to a roast. —*intr.* To cook food in an oven. ❖ *n.* **1.** A cut of meat for roasting. **2.** Something roasted. **3.** A facetious tribute, as at a banquet, in which the honoree is alternately praised and insulted. ❖ *adj.* Roasted: *a roast duck.* [From Middle English *rosten*, from Old French *rostir*, of Germanic origin.]

roast·er (rō′stər) *n.* **1.** A special pan or apparatus for roasting. **2.** A chicken or other animal suitable for roasting.

rob (rŏb) *tr.v.* **robbed, rob·bing, robs 1.** To take property from (a person or place) unlawfully and with the threat or use of force. **2.** To take valuables unlawfully from: *rob money from a safe.* **3.** To deprive someone unjustly or injuriously of something: *The outfielder's great catch robbed him of a home run.* **—rob′ber** *n.*

rob·ber·y (rŏb′ə-rē) *n., pl.* **rob·ber·ies** The act or crime of unlawfully taking the property of another with the threat or use of force.

robe (rōb) *n.* **1.** A long, loose, flowing outer garment. **2.** An official garment worn over other clothes on formal occasions to show office or rank: *a judge's robe.* **3.** A bathrobe or dressing gown. **4.** A blanket or covering, especially one for the lap and legs: *a lap robe.* ❖ *tr.v.* **robed, rob·ing, robes** To cover or dress in a robe or in something that functions like a robe: *fields that were robed with snow.*

Rob·erts (rŏb′ərts), **John Glover, Jr.** Born 1955. American jurist who was appointed chief justice of the US Supreme Court in 2005.

rob·in (rŏb′ĭn) *n.* **1.** A North American songbird having a rust-red breast and a dark gray back. **2.** A small European songbird having an orange breast and face and a brown back.

Robin Hood *n.* A legendary English outlaw of the 1100s, famous for his courage and practice of robbing the rich to aid the poor.

Rob·in·son (rŏb′ĭn-sən), **Jack Roosevelt** Known as "Jackie." 1919–1972. American baseball player who was the first African-American player in the major leagues in the 1900s. He had a lifetime batting average of .311.

ro·bot (rō′bŏt′) *n.* **1a.** A self-operating machine that is programmed to perform tasks on command, especially tasks that require physical movements. **b.** One of these machines designed and programmed to behave like a human being, as in science fiction. **2.** A person who works or follows orders mechanically. [From Czech, from *robota*, drudgery.]

ro·bot·ics (rō-bŏt′ĭks) *n. (used with a singular verb)* The science and study of the building and use of robots.

ro·bust (rō-bŭst′ *or* rō′bŭst′) *adj.* **1.** Full of health and strength; vigorous: *a robust rosebush with many blooms.* See Synonyms at **healthy. 2a.** Active or dynamic: *a robust workout.* **b.** Working effectively; productive: *a robust search engine.* **3.** Characterized by richness, as of flavor: *a robust blend of coffee beans.* **4.** Substantial in amount: *a robust gain in stock market prices.* [From Latin *rōbustus*, from *rōbur*, oak, strength.]

roc (rŏk) *n.* A legendary bird of prey of enormous size and strength. [From Arabic *ruḫḫ*.]

❑ *These sound alike:* **roc, rock[1]** (stone), **rock[2]** (sway).

Ro·cham·beau (rō′shăm-bō′), **Comte de** 1725–1807. French army officer who commanded French forces in the defeat of the British at Yorktown (1781) during the American Revolution.

Roch·es·ter (rŏch′ĭ-stər *or* rŏch′ĕs′tər) A city of western New York east-northeast of Buffalo near Lake Ontario. It was first settled about 1812 and grew rapidly after the opening of the Erie Canal (1825).

rock[1] (rŏk) *n.* **1.** Hard naturally occurring material that is of mineral origin; stone. **2a.** A fairly small piece of such material; a stone. **b.** A large mass of such material, as a cliff or peak. **3.** Naturally formed mineral matter that makes up a significant part of the earth's crust. **4.** Someone or something that is firm, stable, or reliable: *She was a rock during the crisis.* ◆ **on the rocks 1.** In a state of difficulty, destruction, or ruin. **2.** Without money; bankrupt. **3.** Served over ice cubes, as an alcoholic beverage. [From Middle English *rok*, from Old North French *roque*.]

❑ *These sound alike:* **rock[1]** (stone), **roc** (bird), **rock[2]** (sway).

rock[2] (rŏk) *v.* **rocked, rock·ing, rocks** *—intr.* **1.** To move back and forth or from side to side, especially gently or rhythmically. **2.** To be shaken violently: *The buildings rocked during the earthquake.* **3.** To play or dance to rock music. **4.** *Slang* To be excellent or outstanding. *—tr.* **1.** To move back and forth or from side to side, especially in order to soothe: *I rocked the baby to sleep.* **2.** To shake violently: *The earthquake rocked the villages.* **3.** To stun or upset; shock: *a scandal that rocked the town.* ❖ *n.* **1.** An act of rocking. **2.** A rhythmic swaying motion. **3.** Rock music. ◆ **rock the boat** *Slang* To disturb the balance of a situation or group. [From Old English *roccian*.]

❑ *These sound alike:* **rock[2]** (sway), **roc** (bird), **rock[1]** (stone).

rock-and-roll or **rock 'n' roll** (rŏk′ən-rōl′) *n.* Rock music.

rock bottom *n.* The lowest level or absolute bottom: *Prices have reached rock bottom.*

rock candy *n.* A hard candy made by cooling boiled sugar into large clear crystals.

rock crystal *n.* Colorless transparent quartz, used in optical instruments and as a semiprecious gemstone.

Rock·e·fel·ler (rŏk′ə-fĕl′ər) American family, including **John Davison** (1839–1937), who gained great wealth through the Standard Oil Company and spent about half of his fortune on charitable works. His grandson **Nelson Aldrich Rockefeller** (1908–1979) was governor of New York (1959–1973) and vice president of the United States (1974–1977) under Gerald Ford.

rock·er (rŏk′ər) *n.* **1.** A person or thing that rocks. **2.** A rocking chair. **3.** A rocking horse. **4.** One of the two curved pieces on which a cradle, rocking chair, or similar device rocks. **5a.** A rock song, singer, or musician. **b.** A fan of rock music. ◆ **off (one's) rocker** *Slang* Out of one's mind; crazy.

rock·et (rŏk′ĭt) *n.* **1a.** A vehicle or device propelled by one or more rocket engines. **b.** A rocket engine. **2.** A projectile weapon carrying a warhead that is propelled by rockets. **3.** A firework that is shot up into the sky. ❖ *v.* **rock·et·ed, rock·et·ing, rock·ets** *—intr.* **1.** To travel in or by means of a rocket: *rocketing to the moon.* **2.** To move with great speed: *a train that went rocketing by.* *—tr.* To transport or propel by rocket: *rocketing a satellite into orbit.*

rocket engine *n.* An engine that contains all the substances necessary for its operation and is propelled by a jet of hot gases produced by burning fuel. Since they do not rely on air for oxygen, rocket engines can be used in space.

rock·et·ry (rŏk′ĭ-trē) *n.* The science and technology of designing, building, and flying rockets.

rock·face (rŏk′fās′) *n.* A vertical surface of rock, as on a mountainside.

rock garden *n.* A rocky area in which plants are cultivated.

Rock·ies (rŏk′ēz) See **Rocky Mountains.**

rock·ing chair (rŏk′ĭng) *n.* A chair mounted on rockers or springs.

rocking horse *n.* A toy horse that is mounted on rockers or springs and is large enough for a child to ride.

rock music *n.* A form of popular music characterized by a heavily accented beat, electronic amplification, and various musical influences including blues, country, and gospel.

rock 'n' roll (rŏk′ən-rōl′) *n.* Variant of **rock-and-roll.**

rock-ribbed (rŏk′rĭbd′) *adj.* **1.** Rocky. **2.** Stern and unyielding: *a rock-ribbed conservative.*

rock salt *n.* **1.** Common salt, mainly sodium chloride, occurring in large solid masses in the earth's crust. **2.** Coarsely ground common salt.

rock·slide (rŏk′slīd′) *n.* **1.** A rapid movement of rock fragments down a slope. **2.** The mass of rock fragments resulting from such a movement.

rock·y[1] (rŏk′ē) *adj.* **rock·i·er, rock·i·est 1.** Consisting of

Jackie Robinson
photographed c. 1947

rocking chair

rococo
library of Ottobeuren Abbey, Germany

roller coaster

roller skate

ă	pat	ôr	core
ā	pay	oi	boy
âr	care	ou	out
ä	father	o͝o	took
ĕ	pet	o͝or	lure
ē	be	o͞o	boot
ĭ	pit	ŭ	cut
ī	bite	ûr	urge
îr	pier	th	thin
ŏ	pot	*th*	this
ō	toe	zh	vision
ô	paw	ə	about

or containing rocks: *rocky soil.* **2.** Resembling or suggesting rock; firm or hard. **3.** Full of obstacles or difficulties: *a rocky career.*

rock·y² (rŏk′ē) *adj.* **rock·i·er, rock·i·est 1.** Unsteady or shaky: *a rocky balance.* **2.** Appearing inclined to fail; uncertain or precarious: *a business venture that had a rocky start, but managed to succeed.*

Rock·y Mountains (rŏk′ē) also **Rock·ies** (rŏk′ēz) A major mountain system of western North America extending more than 3,000 miles (4,800 kilometers) from northwest Alaska to the Mexican border. The system, rising to 14,433 feet (4,399 meters) in central Colorado, includes numerous ranges and forms the Continental Divide.

Rocky Mountain sheep *n.* The bighorn sheep.

Rocky Mountain spotted fever *n.* An infectious disease that is marked by a rash, high fever, and muscle pains. It is caused by bacteria that are transmitted by the bite of infected ticks.

Rocky Mountain States A region of the western United States including Colorado, Idaho, Montana, Nevada, Utah, and Wyoming.

ro·co·co also **Ro·co·co** (rə-**kō′**kō *or* rō′kə-**kō′**) *n.* The ornate style of art, especially of architecture, decorative art, and music, that developed in France in the early 1700s. ❖ *adj.* Relating to the style of rococo: *a rococo chair.*

rod (rŏd) *n.* **1.** A slender, stiff, straight piece of metal, wood, or other material: *a curtain rod.* **2.** A fishing rod. **3a.** A stick or bunch of sticks used to punish a person by whipping. **b.** Punishment; correction. **4.** A scepter or staff that symbolizes power or authority. **5.** A unit of length equal to 16.5 feet (5.03 meters). **6.** Any of the elongated cells in the retina of the eye that are sensitive to dim light. **7.** Any of various rod-shaped bacteria; a bacillus. **8.** *Slang* A pistol. [From Old English *rodd.*]

rode (rōd) *v.* Past tense of **ride.**

❑ *These sound alike:* **rode, road** (passage), **rowed** (used oars).

ro·dent (**rōd′**nt) *n.* Any of various mammals that have large front teeth used for gnawing or nibbling. Mice, rats, squirrels, and beavers are rodents. [From Latin *rōdere,* to gnaw.]

ro·de·o (**rō′**dē-ō′ *or* rō-**dā′**ō) *n., pl.* **ro·de·os** A public show in which skills such as riding broncos and roping calves are displayed. [From Spanish *rodeo,* corral, from Latin *rota,* wheel.]

roe (rō) *n.* The eggs of a fish, often together with the membrane of the ovary in which they are held. [From Middle English *roughe, ro.*]

❑ *These sound alike:* **roe, rho** (Greek letter), **row¹** (continuous line), **row²** (use oars).

roent·gen (**rĕnt′**gən *or* **rŭnt′**gən) *n.* An obsolete unit used to measure the intensity of exposure to x-rays, gamma rays, and similar ionizing radiation. [After Wilhelm Konrad *Roentgen* (1845–1923), German physicist.]

roent·gen·i·um (rĕnt-**gĕn′**ē-əm *or* rĕnt-**jĕn′**ē-əm) *n.* *Symbol* **Rg** A radioactive element that has been artificially produced by scientists. Its most stable known isotope has a half-life of 3.6 seconds. Atomic number 111. See **Periodic Table.**

rog·er (**rŏj′**ər) *interj.* An expression used in radio communications to indicate that a message has been received.

rogue (rōg) *n.* **1.** A person who tricks or cheats others; a scoundrel; a rascal. **2.** A mischievous person; a scamp. ❖ *adj.* Unpredictable or operating outside of normal or desirable expectations, often with harmful results: *a rogue wave.* **—rogu′ish** *adj.*

rogues' gallery (rōgz) *n.* A collection of pictures of criminals maintained in police files and used for making identifications.

roil (roil) *tr.v.* **roiled, roil·ing, roils 1.** To make (a liquid) cloudy by stirring up sediment. **2.** To cause to be in a state of agitation or disorder: *countries that were roiled by war.*

Ro·land (**rō′**lənd) *n.* A Frankish warrior and possible nephew of Charlemagne, who in legend was killed in battle fighting Islamic warriors in the Pyrenees in 778.

role (rōl) *n.* **1.** A character or part played by a performer: *She auditioned for the role of Juliet.* **2.** The characteristic or expected social behavior of a person. [From Old French *rolle,* roll of parchment, from Latin *rota,* wheel.]

❑ *These sound alike:* **role, roll** (turn over).

role model *n.* A person who serves as a model for another person to imitate.

role-play (**rōl′**plā′) *intr.v.* **role-played, role-play·ing, role-plays** To engage in role-playing. **—role player** *n.*

role-play·ing (**rōl′**plā′ĭng) *n.* The practice of acting a certain role or assuming a kind of character, especially to appreciate other people's points of view. It is used in therapy, education, and certain games.

role-playing game *n.* A game in which players act out fantastical adventures by taking on the roles of characters. The progression of the game is sometimes determined by chance, as by the roll of dice.

roll (rōl) *v.* **rolled, roll·ing, rolls** *—intr.* **1.** To move or travel along a surface by revolving on an axis or repeatedly turning over: *The coin rolled across the sidewalk.* **2.** To move along on wheels or rollers: *The car rolled to a stop.* **3.** To travel or be carried in a vehicle: *We are rolling down the highway.* **4.** To begin to move or operate: *The presses are rolling again.* **5.** To make progress: *The campaign is rolling.* **6.** To turn over repeatedly on one's back and front: *The puppy rolled in the grass.* **7.** To take the shape of a ball or cylinder: *Yarn rolls easily.* **8.** To become flattened by applying pressure, especially with a roller: *The dough rolls out smoothly.* **9.** To move steadily or with increasing momentum: *A thick fog was rolling in.* **10.** To move or extend in gentle rises and falls: *The dunes roll to the sea.* **11.** To go by; elapse: *The years rolled by.* **12.** To move or rock from side to side: *The sailboat rolled and pitched in the storm.* **13.** To make a prolonged deep sound: *Thunder rolled in the distance.* **14.** To beat a drum with a continuous series of short blows. *—tr.* **1.** To cause to move or travel along a surface by revolving on an axis or repeatedly turning over: *roll a ball.* **2.** To move or push along on wheels or rollers: *rolled the chair under the desk.* **3.** To cause to sway or rock: *Heavy seas rolled the ship.* **4.** To cause to begin moving or operating: *roll the cameras.* **5.** To pronounce or utter with a trill: *You roll your r's in Spanish.* **6.** To beat (a drum) with a continuous series of short blows. **7.** To wrap (something) round and round upon itself: *roll up a poster.* **8.** To flatten or spread by applying pressure with a roller: *roll pastry dough.* **9a.** To envelop or enfold: *roll dirty laundry in a sheet.* **b.** To make by shaping into a ball or cylinder: *roll a cigarette.* **10.** To throw (dice) onto a surface. ❖ *n.* **1.** The act or an instance of rolling: *watched the roll of the golf ball toward the cup.* **2.** Something rolled up: *a roll of tape.* **3.** A tilting, swaying, or rocking motion: *the roll of the ship on the waves.* **4.** A gentle rise and fall in a surface: *the roll of the plains.* **5.** A piece of paper that may be or is rolled up; a scroll. **6.** A list of names of people belonging to a group: *The roll is called before a council meeting begins.* **7a.** A small rounded portion of bread. **b.** A portion of food shaped like a tube with a filling: *an egg roll.* **8.** A deep rumble: *a roll of thunder.* **9.** A succession of short sounds, such as those made by beating a drum rapidly. ◆ **on a roll** *Informal* Undergoing or experiencing sustained or increasing good fortune or success. **roll back 1.** To reduce (prices or wages, for example) to a previous lower level. **2.** To cause to turn back or retreat. **roll out 1.** To get out of bed. **2.** To initiate or produce

for the first time; introduce: *roll out a new product line.* **roll up** To arrive in a vehicle: *rolled up to the hotel in a black limousine.* [From Middle English *rollen*, from Old French *roler*, from Latin *rotula*, little wheel.]
❑ *These sound alike:* **roll, role** (part in a play).

roll call *n.* The reading aloud of a list of names of people to determine who is present.

roll·er (rō′lər) *n.* **1.** A small wheel, as on a roller skate or a caster. **2.** A cylinder used to flatten, crush, or squeeze things. **3.** A cylinder for applying paint, ink, or a similar substance onto a surface. **4.** A cylinder around which something is wound: *a window-shade roller.* **5.** A small cylinder of wire mesh or foam rubber around which hair is wound to produce a soft curl or wave. **6.** A large heavy wave that breaks along a coastline.

Rol·ler·blade (rō′lər-blād′) A trademark used for an in-line skate.

roller coaster *n.* **1.** An elevated railway with steep inclines and sharp turns that is operated as a ride, especially in an amusement park. **2.** Something that is marked by abrupt, extreme changes: *The topsy-turvy financial markets have been a real roller coaster.*

roller skate *n.* A shoe or boot with a set of wheels attached to its sole for skating on hard surfaces.

roll·er-skate (rō′lər-skāt′) *intr.v.* **roll·er-skat·ed, roll·er-skat·ing, roll·er-skates** To skate on roller skates.

roller skater *n.* A person who roller-skates.

rol·lick (rŏl′ĭk) *intr.v.* **rol·licked, rol·lick·ing, rol·licks** To behave or move in a carefree frolicsome manner.

rol·lick·ing (rŏl′ĭ-kĭng) *adj.* High-spirited and carefree; boisterous: *a rollicking song.*

roll·ing mill (rō′lĭng) *n.* **1.** A factory in which metal is rolled into sheets, bars, or other forms. **2.** A machine used for rolling metal.

rolling pin *n.* A smooth cylinder, usually with a handle at each end and often made of wood, used for rolling out dough.

rolling stock *n.* The vehicles, especially railroad cars or automobiles, owned by a company.

ro·ly-po·ly (rō′lē-pō′lē) *adj.* Short and plump; roundish in shape. ❖ *n., pl.* **ro·ly-po·lies** A pillbug.

Rom (rōm) *n., pl.* **Rom** or **Ro·ma** (rō′mə) A Romani, especially a Romani man or boy.

ROM (rŏm) *n.* Computer hardware that holds permanently stored data. After the data is installed in ROM, it cannot be added to, modified, or deleted. [From *r(ead-) o(nly) m(emory).*]

Rom. *abbr.* An abbreviation of: **1.** Roman. **2.** Romance (language family).

Ro·ma (rō′mə) *n., pl.* **Roma** *or* **Ro·mas** (rō′məz) A Romani, especially a member of a Romani people of Central and Eastern Europe.

ro·maine (rō-mān′) *n.* A type of lettuce having long crisp leaves forming a narrow head.

Ro·man (rō′mən) *adj.* **1.** Relating to ancient or modern Rome or its people or culture. **2.** Relating to or using the Roman alphabet. **3. roman** Relating to or being a style of type characterized by upright letters and vertical lines thicker than horizontal lines. **4.** Relating to the Roman Catholic Church. ❖ *n.* **1.** A native, inhabitant, or citizen of ancient or modern Rome. **2. roman** Roman print or style of type. **3. Romans** A book of the New Testament in the form of a letter from Saint Paul to the Christian church in Rome.

Roman alphabet *n.* The alphabet of ancient Rome, indirectly derived from the Greek alphabet and used in writing English and many other modern languages, especially those of Western Europe.

Roman Catholic *adj.* Relating or belonging to the Roman Catholic church. ❖ *n.* A member of the Roman Catholic church.

Roman Catholic Church *n.* The Christian church that is organized in a hierarchical structure of bishops and priests with the pope in Rome at its head.

Roman Catholicism *n.* The doctrines, practices, and organization of the Roman Catholic Church.

ro·mance (rō-măns′ *or* rō′măns′) *n.* **1.** A love affair. **2.** A strong attachment or enthusiasm for something: *a childhood romance with the sea.* **3.** A mysterious quality, as of something adventurous or heroic: *an air of romance about the old castle.* **4.** An artistic work, such as a novel or movie, that focuses on love, especially in an idealized way: *an author who writes romances.* **5.** A long narrative in prose or verse that tells of the adventures of heroes and extraordinary events, usually set in a distant time or place: *a medieval romance.* ❖ *adj.* **Romance** Relating to the Romance languages. ❖ *tr.v.* (rō-măns′) **ro·manced, ro·manc·ing, ro·manc·es** To carry on a love affair or courtship with (someone).

Romance languages *pl.n.* A group of languages that developed from Latin, including French, Italian, Portuguese, Romanian, and Spanish.

Roman Empire also called **Rome** (rōm) An empire centered in Rome that lasted from 27 BC to AD 476. At its greatest extent it included territories stretching from Britain and Germany to North Africa and the Persian Gulf.

Ro·man·esque (rō′mə-nĕsk′) *adj.* Relating to the style of architecture that flourished in Europe in the 11th and 12th centuries, characterized by thick walls and rounded vaults. ❖ *n.* The Romanesque style of architecture.

Rom·a·ni also **Rom·a·ny** (rŏm′ə-nē *or* rō′mə-nē) *n., pl.* **Romani** or **Rom·a·nis** also **Romany** or **Rom·a·nies 1.** A member of a nomadic people that originally migrated to Europe from India around the 1300s. **2.** The language of the Romani, related to Hindi. **—Rom′a·ni** *adj.*

Ro·ma·ni·a (rō-mā′nē-ə) Formerly **Ru·ma·ni·a** (ro͞o-mā′nē-ə). A country of southeast Europe with a short coastline on the Black Sea. Bucharest is the capital.

Ro·ma·ni·an (rō-mā′nē-ən) *adj.* Relating to Romania or its people, language, or culture. ❖ *n.* **1.** A native or inhabitant of Romania. **2.** The Romance language of the Romanians.

Roman numeral *n.* Any of the numerals formed with the characters I, V, X, L, C, D, and M (having the values of 1, 5, 10, 50, 100, 500, and 1,000) in the system of numeration used by the ancient Romans.

ro·man·tic (rō-măn′tĭk) *adj.* **1.** Having, showing, expressive of or conducive to feelings of love or romance: *spent a romantic evening together.* **2.** Not based on fact; imagined or idealized: *a romantic view of living in the woods.* **3.** Relating to or characteristic of romance: *a romantic story.* **4.** often **Romantic** Characteristic of romanticism in art, music, or literature: *a Romantic composer; Romantic dramas.* ❖ *n.* **1.** A romantic person. **2.** often **Romantic** A follower of romanticism. **—ro·man′ti·cal·ly** *adv.*

ro·man·ti·cism (rō-măn′tĭ-sĭz′əm) *n.* **1.** often **Romanticism** An artistic and intellectual movement that originated in Europe in the late 1700s and stressed the importance of strong emotion, rich imagination, and rebellion against social and artistic conventions. **2.** The spirit and attitudes characteristic of this movement. **—ro·man′ti·cist** *n.*

ro·man·ti·cize (rō-măn′tĭ-sīz′) *v.* **ro·man·ti·cized, ro·man·ti·ciz·ing, ro·man·ti·ciz·es** *—tr.* To view or interpret romantically. *—intr.* To think in a romantic way.

Rom·a·ny (rŏm′ə-nē *or* rō′mə-nē) *n., pl.* **Romany** or **Rom·a·nies** Variant of **Romani.**

Rome (rōm) **1.** The capital of Italy, in the west-central part of the country on the Tiber River. It was traditionally founded by Romulus in 753 BC. As capital of the Roman Empire, Rome was the largest city in the world

rolling pin

Romanesque
Notre Dame la Grande, Poitiers, France

I	1	XX	20
II	2	XL	40
III	3	L	50
IV	4	LX	60
V	5	XC	90
VI	6	C	100
VII	7	CI	101
VIII	8	D	500
IX	9	CM	900
X	10	M	1,000

Roman numeral

BIOGRAPHY

Franklin and Eleanor Roosevelt Franklin and Eleanor **Roosevelt,** distant cousins from a prominent family, formed a lasting political partnership when they married in 1905. Eleanor Roosevelt encouraged her husband to pursue a political career despite the paralysis of his legs from polio, and in 1928 Franklin Roosevelt was elected the Democratic governor of the state of New York. In 1932 he was elected president, a position to which he would be reelected three times, more than anyone else in US history. As president, Franklin initiated a group of programs collectively called the New Deal, designed to lift the country out of the depths of the Depression. As first lady, Eleanor was an influential adviser to the president and a champion for such groups as civil rights activists, youth leaders, and labor reformers. Franklin Roosevelt led the United States when the nation entered World War II in 1941, but he died suddenly in 1945 just before the war ended. Eleanor went on to serve as a delegate to the United Nations (1945–1952 and 1961–1962) and to chair the UN Commission on Human Rights (1946–1951).

from the first to the fourth century AD, but it later fell into decline, reviving only in the Middle Ages as the power of the papacy increased. **2.** See **Roman Empire.**

Ro·me·o (rō′mē-ō′) *n.* An attractive or romantic male lover.

romp (rŏmp) *intr.v.* **romped, romp·ing, romps** To play or frolic in an excited or lively manner: *dogs romping in a vacant lot.* ❖ *n.* Lively high-spirited play. **—romp′er** *n.*

Rom·u·lus (rŏm′yə-ləs) *n.* In Roman mythology, the son of Mars and legendary founder of Rome, who with his twin brother Remus was reared by a wolf.

ron·do (rŏn′dō *or* rŏn-dō′) *n., pl.* **ron·dos** A musical composition in which a principal recurring theme alternates with contrasting episodes.

rood (ro͝od) *n.* **1.** A cross or crucifix. **2.** A measure of land area equal to ¼ acre (0.10 hectare).

❑ *These sound alike:* **rood, rude** (crude).

roof (ro͞of *or* ro͝of) *n.* **1.** The exterior covering on the top of a building. **2.** The top covering of something: *the roof of a car.* **3.** The upper surface of a part of the body, such as the mouth. ❖ *tr.v.* **roofed, roof·ing, roofs** To cover with a roof. [From Old English *hrōf.*]

roof·er (ro͞o′fər *or* ro͝of′ər) *n.* A person who lays or repairs roofs.

roof·ing (ro͞o′fĭng *or* ro͝of′ĭng) *n.* Materials used in building a roof.

roof·top (ro͞of′tŏp′ *or* ro͝of′tŏp′) *n.* The outer surface of a roof.

rook[1] (ro͝ok) *n.* **1.** A black Eurasian bird that is related to the crow and nests in large colonies. **2.** A swindler or a cheat, especially at games. ❖ *tr.v.* **rooked, rook·ing, rooks** To cheat; swindle. [From Old English *hrōc.*]

rook[2] (ro͝ok) *n.* A chess piece that may move in a straight line horizontally or vertically across any number of unoccupied squares. [From Middle English *rok,* from Arabic *ruḫḫ,* from Persian.]

rook·er·y (ro͝ok′ə-rē) *n., pl.* **rook·er·ies 1.** A place where rooks roost or nest. **2.** A place where certain other birds or mammals, such as penguins or seals, gather to breed.

rook·ie (ro͝ok′ē) *n.* **1.** A first-year player, especially in a major-league sport. **2.** *Slang* A beginner; a novice.

room (ro͞om *or* ro͝om) *n.* **1.** A space that is or may be occupied: *This desk takes up too much room.* **2a.** An area of a building set off by walls or partitions. **b.** The people present in a room: *The whole room laughed.* **3. rooms** Living quarters; lodgings. **4.** Suitable opportunity or scope: *There is room for doubt.* ❖ *intr.v.* **roomed, room·ing, rooms** To occupy a rented room as a lodger: *rooming with a private family.* ◆ **room and board 1.** Meals and lodging. **2.** An amount of money charged or paid for meals and lodging. [From Old English *rūm.*]

room·er (ro͞o′mər *or* ro͝om′ər) *n.* A person who rents a room; a lodger.

❑ *These sound alike:* **roomer, rumor** (report).

room·ing house (ro͞o′mĭng *or* ro͝om′ĭng) *n.* A house where lodgers may rent rooms.

room·mate (ro͞om′māt′ *or* ro͝om′māt′) *n.* A person with whom one shares a room or apartment.

room·y (ro͞o′mē *or* ro͝om′ē) *adj.* **room·i·er, room·i·est** Having plenty of room; spacious: *a bedroom with a roomy closet.* **—room′i·ness** *n.*

Roo·se·velt (rō′zə-vĕlt′ *or* rō′zə-vəlt), **(Anna) Eleanor** 1884–1962. American diplomat and first lady of the United States (1933–1945) as the wife of Franklin D. Roosevelt. As a delegate to the United Nations (1945–1952 and 1961–1962), she helped draft the Universal Declaration of Human Rights in 1948. —SEE NOTE.

Roosevelt, Franklin Delano 1882–1945. The 32nd president of the United States (1933–1945). His administration was marked by relief programs, measures to assist recovery from the Great Depression, and US involvement in World War II. —SEE NOTE.

Roosevelt, Theodore 1858–1919. The 26th president of the United States (1901–1909). His presidency was marked by the regulation of trusts and the building of the Panama Canal.

roost (ro͞ost) *n.* **1.** A place where animals with wings, especially birds or bats, rest or sleep. **2.** A place for temporary rest or sleep. ❖ *intr.v.* **roost·ed, roost·ing, roosts 1.** To rest or sleep on a perch or in a roost. **2.** To rest or sleep.

roost·er (ro͞o′stər) *n.* A full-grown male chicken.

root[1] (ro͞ot *or* ro͝ot) *n.* **1.** A part of a plant that usually grows down into the ground and that absorbs water and minerals from the soil, stores food, and keeps the plant securely in place. **2.** A usually underground plant part similar to a root, as a tuber or rhizome. **3.** The part of an organ or body structure, as a hair or tooth, that is embedded in other tissue. **4.** A source; an origin: *the Roman roots of democracy.* **5.** The essential part; core; heart: *the root of the matter.* **6. roots** The condition of belonging to a particular culture, society, place, or environment: *We've lived here too short a time to have any roots.* **7.** A word or word element from which other words are formed, as by adding affixes. For example, *cheer* is the root of *cheerful* and *cheerless.* **8a.** A number that when multiplied by itself a given number of times produces a specified number. For example, since $2 \times 2 \times 2 \times 2 = 16$, 2 is a fourth root of 16. **b.** A solution to an equation. For example, a root of the equation $x^2 - 4 = 0$ is 2, since $2^2 - 4 = 0$. ❖ *v.* **root·ed, root·ing, roots** *—intr.* To send forth or start the growth of a root or roots: *Carrot tops will root in water.* *—tr.* **1.** To plant and fix the roots of (a plant) in soil or the ground. **2.** To establish or settle firmly: *Our love of the mountains has rooted us here.* **3a.** To dig or pull out by the roots: *rooting out tree stumps with a tractor.* **b.** To remove or get rid of: *We need to root corruption completely out of government.* [From Old English *rōt,* from Old Norse.]

❑ *These sound alike:* **root**[1] (plant part), **root**[2] (dig), **root**[3] (cheer), **route** (road).

root[2] (ro͞ot *or* ro͝ot) *v.* **root·ed, root·ing, roots** *—tr.* **1.** To dig with the snout or nose: *pigs rooting up acorns.* **2.** To reveal or make known: *a reporter who rooted out the scandal.* *—intr.* To search or rummage for something: *rooting around his desk for a pen.* [From Old English *wrōtan.*] **—root′er** *n.*

❑ *These sound alike:* **root**[2] (dig), **root**[1] (plant part), **root**[3] (cheer), **route** (road).

root[3] (ro͞ot *or* ro͝ot) *intr.v.* **root·ed, root·ing, roots 1.** To shout in encouragement, approval, or enthusiasm; cheer: *rooting for the home team.* **2.** To hope for a favorable outcome for someone: *We'll be rooting for you when you take the exam.* [Possibly alteration of *rout,* to bellow.]

❑ *These sound alike:* **root**[3] (cheer), **root**[1] (plant part), **root**[2] (dig), **route** (road).

root beer *n.* A carbonated soft drink flavored with extracts of certain plant roots and herbs and usually artificial flavorings.

root canal *n.* **1.** A passage in the root of a tooth that contains the nerve and blood vessels. **2.** A dental procedure in which the tissue from this part of the tooth is removed and replaced with filling, usually because of decay or inflammation.

root cap *n.* A thimble-shaped mass of cells that covers and protects the tip of a plant's root.

root hair *n.* A thin, hairlike outgrowth of a plant root that absorbs water and minerals from the soil.

root·less (ro͞ot′lĭs *or* ro͝ot′lĭs) *adj.* **1.** Having no roots. **2.** Not belonging to a particular place or society: *rootless refugees in a strange country.*

ă	pat	ôr	core
ā	pay	oi	boy
âr	care	ou	out
ä	father	o͝o	took
ĕ	pet	o͝or	lure
ē	be	o͞o	boot
ĭ	pit	ŭ	cut
ī	bite	ûr	urge
îr	pier	th	thin
ŏ	pot	*th*	this
ō	toe	zh	vision
ô	paw	ə	about

root·stock (rōōt′stŏk′ *or* rŏŏt′stŏk′) *n.* **1.** A root of a plant, often with part of the stem, onto which another plant is grafted. **2.** A rhizome.

rope (rōp) *n.* **1.** A flexible, heavy cord made of intertwined strands of fiber or some other material. **2.** A string of things attached or entwined together: *a rope of onions.* **3.** A sticky formation of stringy matter in a liquid. **4.** A cord with a noose on one end for hanging a person. **5.** A lasso or lariat. **6. ropes** *Informal* Specialized procedures or details: *learning the ropes.* ❖ *tr.v.* **roped, rop·ing, ropes 1.** To tie, fasten, or attach with a rope or other cord. **2.** To enclose, separate, or partition with a rope or other cord: *roped off the playing field to keep the crowd away.* **3.** To catch with a rope or lasso: *rope a calf.* **4.** *Informal* To persuade or manipulate (someone): *My brother roped his friend into driving with him to the mall.* ◆ **at the end of (one's) rope** At the end of one's patience, endurance, or resources. [From Old English *rāp.*] **—rop′er** *n.*

rop·y (rō′pē) *adj.* **rop·i·er, rop·i·est 1.** Resembling a rope or ropes. **2.** Forming sticky strings or threads, as some liquids.

Roque·fort (rōk′fərt) A trademark used for a soft, strongly flavored French cheese that has veins of blue mold.

ro·sa·ce·a (rō-zā′shē-ə) *n.* A chronic rash on the face, especially of the nose and cheeks, that appears red with acnelike pimples and is caused by enlargement of capillaries. [From Latin *rosāceus*, made of roses.]

ro·sa·ry (rō′zə-rē) *n., pl.* **ro·sa·ries 1.** A form of devotion to the Virgin Mary consisting of a series of prayers. **2.** A string of beads on which these prayers may be counted.

rose[1] (rōz) *n.* **1a.** Any of numerous shrubs or vines having prickly stems and widely cultivated for their showy, often fragrant, red, pink, white, or yellow flowers. **b.** The flower of any of these plants. **2.** A deep pink. ❖ *adj.* Deep pink. [From Old English, from Latin *rosa.*]

rose[2] (rōz) *v.* Past tense of **rise.**

ro·se·ate (rō′zē-ĭt *or* rō′zē-āt′) *adj.* **1.** Rose-colored. **2.** Cheerful or bright; optimistic: *a roseate outlook.*

Ro·seau (rō-zō′) The capital of Dominica, in the Windward Islands of the West Indies.

rose·bud (rōz′bŭd′) *n.* The bud of a rose.

rose·bush (rōz′bŏŏsh′) *n.* A shrub that bears roses.

rose-col·ored (rōz′kŭl′ərd) *adj.* **1.** Having the color rose. **2.** Cheerful or optimistic, especially to an excessive degree. ◆ **through rose-colored glasses** With an unduly cheerful, optimistic, or favorable view of things: *Romantics often see the world through rose-colored glasses.*

rose hip or **rose·hip** (rōz′hĭp′) *n.* The fruit of a rose, resembling a small apple.

rose·mar·y (rōz′mâr′ē) *n.* An evergreen shrub having small, aromatic, grayish-green leaves that are used as a seasoning in cooking.

Ro·set·ta stone (rō-zĕt′ə) *n.* A basalt tablet bearing inscriptions in Greek and Egyptian hieroglyphics and scripts. Discovered in 1799 near Rosetta, Egypt, it provided the key to deciphering Egyptian hieroglyphics.

ro·sette (rō-zĕt′) *n.* **1.** An ornament or badge of ribbon or silk that is gathered or shaped to resemble a rose and is given as an award, used to decorate clothing. **2.** A roselike marking or formation, such as one of the clusters of spots on a leopard's fur. **3.** A circular cluster of leaves that radiate from a stem at or close to the ground, as in a dandelion.

rose water *n.* A fragrant liquid made by steeping or distilling rose petals in water, used in cosmetics and cookery.

rose·wood (rōz′wŏŏd′) *n.* **1.** The hard, reddish, often fragrant wood of any of various tropical trees, used for making furniture. **2.** A tree that yields such wood.

Rosh Ha·sha·nah also **Rosh Ha·sha·na** (rôsh′ hə-**shô′**-nə *or* rôsh′ hə-**shä′**nə) *n.* The Jewish New Year, celebrated in September or October.

ros·in (rŏz′ĭn) *n.* A translucent yellowish or brownish substance obtained from the sap of pine trees. It is used to prevent slipping, as on the bows of stringed instruments, and to make varnishes, inks, soldering compounds, and adhesives. ❖ *tr.v.* **ros·ined, ros·in·ing, ros·ins** To rub or coat with rosin: *rosin a bow.*

Ross (rôs), **Betsy Griscom** 1752–1836. American patriot who, according to tradition, made the first American flag (June 1776).

ros·ter (rŏs′tər) *n.* A list, especially of the names of players on a sports team or of the personnel in a military unit.

ros·trum (rŏs′trəm) *n., pl.* **ros·trums** or **ros·tra** (rŏs′trə) An elevated platform, such as a dais or pulpit, used for public speaking.

ros·y (rō′zē) *adj.* **ros·i·er, ros·i·est 1.** Having a reddish or deep pink color: *a rosy sunset.* **2.** Bright and cheerful; optimistic: *The future looks rosy.* **—ros′i·ly** *adv.* **—ros′i·ness** *n.*

rot (rŏt) *v.* **rot·ted, rot·ting, rots** *—intr.* **1.** To break down into simple organic substances, usually by the action of bacteria or fungi: *The meat may rot if it is not refrigerated.* **2.** To become damaged or useless because of decay: *The roof of the old house had rotted away.* **3.** To deteriorate or languish: *felt he was rotting away in a boring town.* *—tr.* To cause to become rotten; decay. ❖ *n.* **1.** The process of rotting or the result of being rotted; decay. **2.** Any of several destructive plant diseases caused by fungi or bacteria. **3.** Foolish or pointless talk; nonsense. [From Old English *rotian.*]

ro·ta·ry (rō′tə-rē) *adj.* Relating to, causing, or characterized by rotation, especially around an axis: *rotary motion.* ❖ *n., pl.* **ro·ta·ries 1.** A device or machine part that rotates. **2.** A traffic circle.

ro·tate (rō′tāt) *v.* **ro·tat·ed, ro·tat·ing, ro·tates** *—intr.* **1.** To turn around on an axis or center. See Synonyms at **turn. 2.** To proceed in sequence; take turns or alternate: *The order of the classes rotates each day.* *—tr.* **1.** To cause to turn on an axis or center: *rotate a barrel.* **2.** To plant or grow (crops) in a fixed order of succession. **3.** To cause to alternate: *rotate players in a game.* [From Latin *rotāre*, from *rota*, wheel.]

ro·ta·tion (rō-tā′shən) *n.* **1a.** The act or process of turning around a center or axis: *the rotation of the earth.* **b.** A complete turn as a result of such motion. **2.** Regular change or variation in a series or sequence: *the rotation of duties in a military unit.* **3a.** In baseball, the sequence in which the starting pitchers on a team pitch in games. **b.** The pitchers used in such a sequence.

ro·ta·tor (rō′tā′tər) *n.* A person or thing that rotates.

rotator cuff *n.* A part of the shoulder that includes the tendons of four muscles that control rotation of the shoulder joint.

ro·ta·to·ry (rō′tə-tôr′ē) *adj.* **1.** Relating to, causing, or characterized by rotation: *a rotatory muscle.* **2.** Occurring or proceeding in alternation or succession.

ROTC *abbr.* An abbreviation of Reserve Officers' Training Corps.

rote (rōt) *n.* **1.** A process of memorizing by repetition, often without full understanding: *They learned the French song by rote.* **2.** Mechanical routine.
❑ *These sound alike:* **rote, wrote** (formed letters).

ro·ti·fer (rō′tə-fər) *n.* Any of various very small water organisms having at one end a ring of cilia with which they move and take in food.

ro·tis·se·rie (rō-tĭs′ə-rē) *n.* A cooking device with a rotating spit for roasting meat.

ro·tor (rō′tər) *n.* **1.** A rotating part of an electrical or a mechanical device. **2.** An assembly of airfoils that rotates, as in a helicopter.

Eleanor Roosevelt
photographed in 1952

Franklin Delano Roosevelt
photographed in 1933

Theodore Roosevelt
photographed in 1904

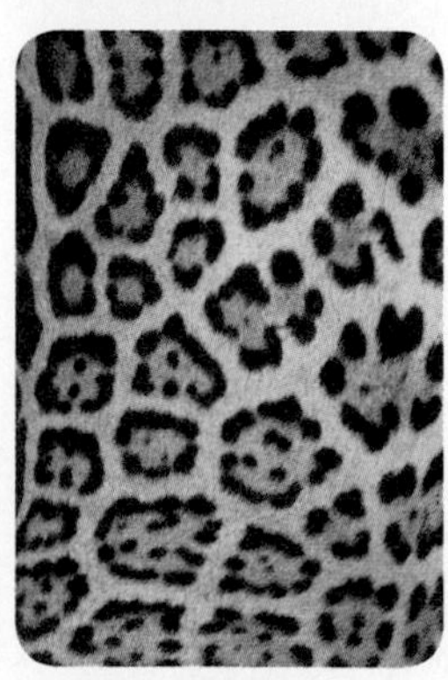

rosette
jaguar fur

rotunda
Radcliffe Camera, Oxford, England

rowel

ă	pat	ôr	core
ā	pay	oi	boy
âr	care	ou	out
ä	father	o͝o	took
ĕ	pet	o͝or	lure
ē	be	o͞o	boot
ĭ	pit	ŭ	cut
ī	bite	ûr	urge
îr	pier	th	thin
ŏ	pot	*th*	this
ō	toe	zh	vision
ô	paw	ə	about

ro·to·till·er (rō′tə-tĭl′ər) *n.* A motorized cultivator having blades that rotate to break up soil.

rot·ten (rŏt′n) *adj.* **rot·ten·er, rot·ten·est 1.** Decayed or decomposed: *rotten meat.* **2.** Having a foul odor that results from or suggests the presence of decay. **3.** Made weak or unsound by rot: *rotten floorboards.* **4.** Not honest, honorable, or decent; corrupt. **5.** Very bad; terrible: *rotten luck.* ❖ *adv.* To a very great degree: *That child is spoiled rotten.* **—rot′ten·ly** *adv.* **—rot′ten·ness** *n.*

Rot·ter·dam (rôt′ər-dăm′) A city of southwest Netherlands southeast of The Hague. It was chartered in 1328.

ro·tund (rō-tŭnd′) *adj.* Rounded in shape or figure; round or plump: *a rotund actor who played Santa Claus.* [From Latin *rotundus.*] **—ro·tun′di·ty, ro·tund′ness** *n.* **—ro·tund′ly** *adv.*

ro·tun·da (rō-tŭn′də) *n.* **1.** A circular building, especially one with a dome. **2.** A large area with a high ceiling.

rouge (ro͞ozh) *n.* **1.** A pink or red cosmetic for coloring the cheeks or lips. **2.** A reddish powder, chiefly an oxide of iron, used in polishing metal and glass. ❖ *tr.v.* **rouged, roug·ing, roug·es** To color with rouge. [From Old French *rouge*, red, from Latin *rubeus.*]

rough (rŭf) *adj.* **rough·er, rough·est 1.** Having an irregular surface; not smooth or even: *a rough bumpy road.* **2.** Coarse to the touch: *a rough, scratchy blanket.* **3.** Moving with great force or agitation; turbulent: *rough waters.* **4.** Difficult to endure or live through: *a rough winter.* **5a.** Characterized by extreme or excessive force: *In the third period, play began to get rough.* **b.** Known or reputed to be dangerous or violent: *a rough part of town.* **c.** Not gentle, polite, or refined: *rough manners.* **6.** Harsh to the ear: *a rough, raspy sound.* **7.** Being in a natural state: *a rough gem.* **8.** Not complete or fully detailed; tentative: *a rough draft.* ❖ *n.* The part of a golf hole that has longer grass than the fairway and green. ❖ *tr.v.* **roughed, rough·ing, roughs** To treat with extreme or excessive force, as in sports: *was penalized for roughing the passer.* ❖ *adv.* In a rough manner; roughly: *The engine was running rough.* ◆ **rough it** To live without the usual comforts and conveniences: *The campers roughed it in the mountains for a week.* **rough out** To prepare or describe in an unfinished form: *rough out a house plan.* [From Old English *rūh.*] **—rough′ly** *adv.* **—rough′ness** *n.*
❑ *These sound alike:* **rough, ruff** (collar).

rough·age (rŭf′ĭj) *n.* Dietary fiber: *Celery provides roughage in your diet.*

rough·en (rŭf′ən) *tr. & intr.v.* **rough·ened, rough·en·ing, rough·ens** To make or become rough.

rough·house (rŭf′hous′ *or* rŭf′houz′) *intr.v.* **rough·housed, rough·hous·ing, rough·hous·es** To engage in rowdy, uproarious behavior or play. ❖ *n.* (**rŭf′hous′**) Rowdy uproarious play or behavior.

rough·neck (rŭf′nĕk′) *n.* **1.** A rowdy or unruly person. **2.** A worker on an oil-drilling rig.

rough·shod (rŭf′shŏd′) *adj.* **1.** Shod with horseshoes having projecting nails or points to prevent slipping. **2.** Marked by brutal force. ◆ **ride roughshod over** To treat with brutal force.

rou·lette (ro͞o-lĕt′) *n.* **1.** A gambling game in which players bet on which slot on a rotating disk a ball will come to rest in. **2.** A hand tool with a toothed disk for making rows of slits or perforations. [From Old French *ruelete*, little wheel, from Latin *rota*, wheel.]

round (round) *adj.* **1a.** Having a shape that is spherical or nearly spherical; ball-shaped. **b.** Moving in or forming a circle. **c.** Shaped like a cylinder. **d.** Having a curved, nearly circular, or nearly spherical shape: *a baby's round face.* **2.** Formed with the lips assuming an oval shape: *a round vowel.* **3.** Whole or complete; full: *a round dozen.* **4.** Altered so as to be expressed as a whole number or a multiple of 10: *round numbers.* ❖ *n.* **1.** A round object: *a round of bread.* **2.** Movement around or as if in a circle; circuit: *the sun's round.* **3.** A cut of beef from the part of the thigh between the rump and the shank. **4.** A round dance. **5.** A complete course or series of events: *a round of negotiations.* **6.** often **rounds** A customary course of places visited or duties performed: *a doctor on her rounds.* **7a.** A single shot or volley from a firearm or firearms. **b.** Ammunition for a single shot. **8.** A specified period or unit of play in a game or contest. **9.** A musical composition for two or more voices in which each voice enters at a different time with the same melody. ❖ *tr.v.* **round·ed, round·ing, rounds 1.** To make round: *rounded the snow into a ball.* **2.** To make a turn about or to the other side of: *The car rounded a bend in the road.* **3.** To make full, complete, or properly balanced: *a description rounded out with details.* **4.** To adjust (a number) to be a whole number or a multiple of 10, as in representing 514 as 510. ❖ *adv.* Around: *a wheel spinning round and round.* ❖ *prep.* Around: *put the rope round the post.* ◆ **round up 1.** To seek out and bring together; gather: *round up the band members.* **2.** To herd (cattle) together from various places. [From Middle English, from Latin *rotundus.*] **—round′ness** *n.*

round·a·bout (**round′**ə-bout′) *adj.* **1.** Not going straight to the goal or conclusion; indirect: *chose a roundabout course to avoid traffic.* **2.** Evasive or vague: *a roundabout answer.* ❖ *n. Chiefly British* A traffic circle.

round dance *n.* A folk dance performed with the dancers arranged in a circle.

round·ed (roun′dĭd) *adj.* **1.** Having a curved or spherical shape: *a rounded edge.* **2.** Pronounced with the lips pursed or shaped in a round form: *a rounded vowel.*

roun·de·lay (**roun′**də-lā′) *n.* A poem or song with a regularly recurring refrain.

Round·head (**round′**hĕd′) *n.* A supporter of Parliament during the English Civil War (1642–1652) and the Commonwealth.

round·house (**round′**hous′) *n.* **1.** A circular building for housing and switching locomotives. **2.** A cabin on the quarterdeck of a ship. **3.** *Slang* A punch or swing delivered with a sweeping movement from one side.

round·ly (**round′**lē) *adv.* **1.** In the form of a circle or sphere. **2.** With full force or vigor; thoroughly: *roundly applauded.*

round robin *n.* A tournament in which each contestant is matched in turn against every other contestant.

round·ta·ble (**round′**tā′bəl) *n.* A conference or discussion with several participants.

Round Table *n.* The circular table around which King Arthur and his knights met.

round-the-clock (round′*thə*-**klŏk′**) *adj.* Lasting or continuing throughout the entire 24 hours of the day; continuous.

round·trip (**round′trĭp′**) *adj.* Relating to a trip from one place to another and then back again: *bought a roundtrip ticket to Paris.*

round·up (**round′**ŭp′) *n.* **1.** The herding of cattle or other animals together for inspection, branding, or shipping. **2.** A similar gathering together of people or things: *a roundup of suspects conducted by the police.* **3.** A summary: *a news roundup.*

round·worm (**round′**wûrm′) *n.* A nematode.

rouse (rouz) *v.* **roused, rous·ing, rous·es** *—tr.* **1.** To wake (someone) up; arouse. **2.** To cause to become active, attentive, or excited: *a sight that roused her curiosity.* *—intr.* To wake up; awaken. **—rous′er** *n.*

rous·ing (rou′zĭng) *adj.* **1.** Stirring; inspiring: *a rousing call to action.* **2.** Energetic; vigorous: *a rousing dance tune.*

Rous·seau (ro͞o-**sō′**), **Jean Jacques** 1712–1778. Swiss philosopher and writer whose works include *The Social Contract* (1762).

roust·a·bout (**rous′**tə-bout′) *n.* An unskilled laborer who moves from job to job, especially on docks or ships or in circuses or oil fields.

rout¹ (rout) *n.* **1.** A disorderly flight after a defeat: *put all the enemy forces to rout.* **2.** An overwhelming defeat. ❖ *tr.v.* **rout·ed, rout·ing, routs 1.** To put to disorderly flight; scatter. **2.** To defeat overwhelmingly; crush: *routed the opposing team.* [From Middle English *route,* gang of soldiers, from Old French, troop, defeat, from Latin *rumpere,* to break.]

rout² (rout) *v.* **rout·ed, rout·ing, routs** —*intr.* To dig with the snout; root. —*tr.* **1.** To dig up or uncover: *routing potatoes from the ground.* **2.** To drive or force out as if by digging: *rout out an informant.* [Variant of *root,* dig.]

route (ro͞ot *or* rout) *n.* **1.** A road or course for traveling from one place to another. **2.** A highway: *Route 66.* **3.** A fixed course, as of places or customers, visited regularly by a salesperson or delivery person: *a newspaper route.* **4.** A means: *the route to fame and power.* **5.** In football, a pass pattern. ❖ *tr.v.* **rout·ed, rout·ing, routes** To send or pass on by a certain route: *route the manuscript to editors.* [From Middle English, from Latin *rupta (via),* broken (road), beaten (path).]

❑ *These sound alike:* **route, root¹** (plant part), **root²** (dig), **root³** (cheer).

rout·er (**rou′**tər) *n.* A device in a computer network that handles message transfers between computers.

rou·tine (ro͞o-**tēn′**) *n.* **1.** A series of activities performed or meant to be performed regularly; a standard or usual procedure. See Synonyms at **method. 2.** A scripted piece of entertainment, especially in a nightclub or theater. **3.** A set of computer programming instructions designed to perform a specific limited task. ❖ *adj.* **1.** In accordance with standard procedure: *a routine check of passports.* **2.** Not special; ordinary: *another routine day.* **—rou·tine′ly** *adv.*

roux (ro͞o) *n., pl.* **roux** A mixture of flour and fat cooked together, used especially for thickening sauces.

❑ *These sound alike:* **roux, rue¹** (regret), **rue²** (plant).

rove (rōv) *v.* **roved, rov·ing, roves** —*intr.* To wander at random, especially over a wide area. See Synonyms at **wander.** —*tr.* To roam or wander around, over, or through: *roving the forest.* **—rov′er** *n.*

row¹ (rō) *n.* **1.** A series of people or things placed next to each other, usually in a straight line: *a row of poplar trees.* **2.** A succession without a break or gap in time: *won the title for three years in a row.* **3.** A line of adjacent seats, as in a theater. **4.** A continuous line of buildings along a street. [From Old English *rāw.*]

❑ *These sound alike:* **row¹** (series), **rho** (Greek letter), **roe** (fish eggs), **row²** (use oars).

row² (rō) *v.* **rowed, row·ing, rows** —*intr.* To propel a boat with oars. —*tr.* **1.** To propel (a boat) with oars: *rowed the boat down the stream.* **2.** To carry in a boat propelled by oars: *rowed the passengers across the lake.* [From Old English *rōwan.*] **—row′er** *n.*

❑ *These sound alike:* **row²** (use oars), **rho** (Greek letter), **roe** (fish eggs), **row¹** (series).

row³ (rou) *n.* **1.** A noisy quarrel or disturbance. **2.** A loud noise. ❖ *intr.v.* **rowed, row·ing, rows** To take part in a noisy quarrel or disturbance.

row·boat (**rō′**bōt′) *n.* A small boat propelled by oars.

row·dy (**rou′**dē) *adj.* **row·di·er, row·di·est** Rough and disorderly. ❖ *n., pl.* **row·dies** A rough disorderly person. **—row′di·ness** *n.*

row·el (**rou′**əl) *n.* A sharp-toothed wheel inserted into the end of the shank of a spur.

row house (rō) *n.* One of a series of houses situated side by side, joined by common walls, and often looking alike.

Row·ling (**rō′**lĭng), **J.K.** Pen name of Joanne Rowling. Born 1965. British writer of a popular series of books about the adventures of Harry Potter, a young wizard.

roy·al (**roi′**əl) *adj.* **1.** Relating to, belonging to, done by, or involving a king or queen, or a member of a king or queen's family: *a royal wedding; a royal edict.* **2.** Relating to or serving the government of a king or queen. **3.** Founded or authorized by a king or queen: *a royal society.* ❖ *n. Informal* A member of a monarch's family. [From Middle English *roial,* from Latin *rēgālis,* from *rēx,* king.] **—roy′al·ly** *adv.*

roy·al·ist (**roi′**ə-lĭst) *n.* **1.** A supporter of government by a king or queen; a monarchist. **2. Royalist a.** A Cavalier. **b.** An American loyal to British rule during the American Revolution; a Tory.

roy·al·ty (**roi′**əl-tē) *n., pl.* **roy·al·ties 1.** Kings, queens, and their relatives considered as a group. **2.** A person of royal rank or family: *I wish he'd quit acting like he's royalty.* **3.** The rank or power of a king or queen: *A crown is a symbol of royalty.* **4a.** A share paid to an author or composer out of the profits resulting from the sale or performance of his or her work. **b.** A share of profits paid to an inventor for the right to use his or her invention.

rpm *abbr.* An abbreviation of revolutions per minute.

RR *abbr.* An abbreviation of: **1.** railroad. **2.** rural route.

RSVP *abbr.* An abbreviation of the French phrase *répondez s'il vous plaît* ("please reply").

Rt. or **Rte.** *abbr.* An abbreviation of route.

Ru The symbol for the element **ruthenium.**

rub (rŭb) *v.* **rubbed, rub·bing, rubs** —*tr.* **1.** To press something against (a surface) and move it back and forth: *rub a window with a piece of cloth.* **2.** To cause (something) to move along a surface with pressure: *rub a cloth against a window pane; rubbed his hands on the towel.* —*intr.* **1.** To move along in contact with a surface; scrape: *The horse rubbed against the tree.* **2.** To wear away or chafe with friction: *machine parts with marks showing where they rub together.* **3.** To be removed or transferred by or as if by rubbing: *Her cheerful mood rubbed off on the rest of the group.* ❖ *n.* **1.** The act of rubbing. **2.** A difficulty; an obstacle. ◆ **rub down** To perform a brisk rubbing of the body, as in massage. **rub in** To remind someone repeatedly of (an unpleasant matter): *I know that was a stupid thing for me to do, so don't rub it in.* **rub out** To erase or obliterate by or as if by rubbing. **rub (someone) the wrong way** To annoy; irritate.

rub·ber¹ (**rŭb′**ər) *n.* **1.** A yellowish elastic material manufactured from the milky sap or latex of certain tropical plants, used in making electric insulation, elastic bands and belts, tires, and containers. **2.** Any of various synthetic materials having properties that are similar to those of this substance. **3.** A low overshoe made of rubber. **4.** In baseball, the rectangular piece of rubber that the pitcher must stay in contact with when making a pitch.

rub·ber² (**rŭb′**ər) *n.* **1.** A series of games, as in bridge or tennis, in which two out of three or three out of five must be won to end play. **2.** The deciding game in such a series.

rubber band *n.* An elastic loop of natural or synthetic rubber, used to hold objects together.

rub·ber·ize (**rŭb′**ə-rīz′) *tr.v.* **rub·ber·ized, rub·ber·iz·ing, rub·ber·iz·es** To coat or treat with rubber.

rub·ber·neck·er (**rŭb′**ər-nĕk′ər) *n. Slang* A person who looks around and gawks: *rubberneckers who caused a traffic jam.*

rubber plant *n.* **1.** Any of several tropical plants yielding sap that can be coagulated to form crude rubber. **2.** A small tree that has large, glossy, leathery leaves and is popular as a houseplant.

rubber stamp *n.* **1.** A stamp made of rubber, used to print names, dates, and other standard messages. **2.** also **rub·ber-stamp** (**rŭb′**ər-**stămp′**) A person or group that gives quick approval to a program or policy without seriously considering its merits.

J.K. Rowling
photographed in 2004

rubber plant

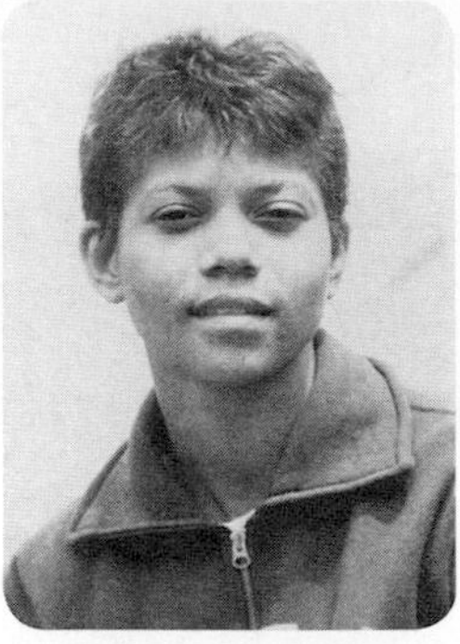

Wilma Rudolph
photographed in 1960

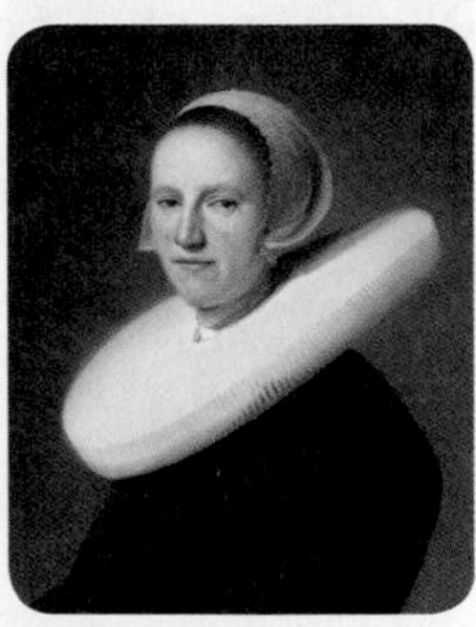

ruff
top: ruffed collar
bottom: ruffed neck feathers

ă	pat	ôr	core
ā	pay	oi	boy
âr	care	ou	out
ä	father	o͝o	took
ĕ	pet	o͝or	lure
ē	be	o͞o	boot
ĭ	pit	ŭ	cut
ī	bite	ûr	urge
îr	pier	th	thin
ŏ	pot	*th*	this
ō	toe	zh	vision
ô	paw	ə	about

rub·ber-stamp (rŭb′ər-stămp′) *tr.v.* **rub·ber-stamped, rub·ber-stamp·ing, rub·ber-stamps 1.** To mark with the imprint of a rubber stamp. **2.** To support, vote for, or approve without question or consideration.

rub·ber·y (rŭb′ə-rē) *adj.* **rub·ber·i·er, rub·ber·i·est** Relating to or resembling rubber; elastic.

rub·bing (rŭb′ĭng) *n.* An image made by placing paper over a surface with raised or indented markings and rubbing the paper with something that marks it, as chalk or charcoal.

rub·bish (rŭb′ĭsh) *n.* **1.** Useless waste material; trash: *picked up rubbish from the sidewalk.* **2.** Foolish talk or writing; nonsense.

rub·ble (rŭb′əl) *n.* A loose mass of pieces of rock or masonry broken by natural or human forces.

rub·down (rŭb′doun′) *n.* An energetic massage of the body.

ru·bel (ro͞o′bəl) *n.* The basic monetary unit of Belarus. [From Belarusian, from Old Russian *rublĭ*, cut, piece, from *rubiti*, to chop.]

ru·bel·la (ro͞o-bĕl′ə) *n.* An infectious disease that is caused by a virus and resembles measles but has less severe symptoms; German measles.

ru·bid·i·um (ro͞o-bĭd′ē-əm) *n. Symbol* **Rb** A soft, silvery metallic element that ignites spontaneously in air and reacts violently with water. Atomic number 37. See **Periodic Table.**

ru·ble (ro͞o′bəl) *n.* The basic monetary unit of Russia. [From Russian *rubl′*, from Old Russian *rublĭ*, cut, piece, from *rubiti*, to chop.]

ru·bric (ro͞o′brĭk) *n.* **1.** A class or category: *rules of behavior considered under the rubric of school safety.* **2.** A part of a manuscript or book, such as a title, heading, or initial letter, that appears in decorative red lettering or is otherwise distinguished from the rest of the text. **3.** A set of specific criteria by which an academic assignment is to be graded.

ru·by (ro͞o′bē) *n., pl.* **ru·bies 1.** A deep red translucent form of corundum that is greatly valued as a precious stone. **2.** A deep red. [From Middle English *rubi*, from Latin *rubeus*, red.]

ruck·sack (rŭk′săk′ *or* ro͝ok′săk′) *n.* A knapsack.

ruck·us (rŭk′əs) *n. Informal* A disturbance; a commotion.

rud·der (rŭd′ər) *n.* **1.** A flat structure that is hinged vertically to the stern of a ship or boat and can be turned to either side to change course. **2.** A similar structure in the tail of an aircraft, used for making horizontal changes of course.

rud·dy (rŭd′ē) *adj.* **rud·di·er, rud·di·est** Having a healthy reddish color.

rude (ro͞od) *adj.* **rud·er, rud·est 1.** Lacking courtesy; ill-mannered or insulting: *apologizing for being rude.* **2.** Being in a rough or unfinished state; crude: *a rude hut.* **3.** Relatively undeveloped; primitive: *a rude system of farming.* **4.** Sudden and jarring: *a rude shock.* **—rude′ly** *adv.* **—rude′ness** *n.*

❑ *These sound alike:* **rude, rood** (crucifix).

ru·di·men·ta·ry (ro͞o′də-**mĕn′**tə-rē *or* ro͞o′də-**mĕn′**trē) *adj.* **1.** Relating to basic principles or facts; elementary: *had only a rudimentary knowledge of economics.* **2.** Being in the earliest stages of development. **3.** Imperfectly or incompletely developed: *the rudimentary tail of a Manx cat.*

ru·di·ments (ro͞o′də-mənts) *pl.n.* **1.** Basic principles or skills: *learning the rudiments of grammar.* **2.** Things that are in an early or undeveloped form: *They had developed only the rudiments of a plan. Buds contain the rudiments of leaves.*

Ru·dolph (ro͞o′dŏlf), **Wilma Glodean** 1940–1994. American athlete who won three gold medals in track and field at the 1960 Olympics.

rue[1] (ro͞o) *tr.v.* **rued, ru·ing, rues** To feel regret, remorse, or sorrow for. ❖ *n.* Regret. [From Middle English *reuen*, from Old English *hrēowan*, to affect with grief, and *hrēowian*, to repent.]

❑ *These sound alike:* **rue**[1] (regret), **roux** (cooking mixture), **rue**[2] (plant).

rue[2] (ro͞o) *n.* Any of various Mediterranean plants having strong-smelling bitter leaves formerly used in medicine. [From Middle English *rude*, from Latin *rūta*.]

❑ *These sound alike:* **rue**[2] (plant), **roux** (cooking mixture), **rue**[1] (regret).

rue·ful (ro͞o′fəl) *adj.* Causing, feeling, or expressing sorrow or regret: *a rueful figure; a rueful admission of guilt.* **—rue′ful·ly** *adv.* **—rue′ful·ness** *n.*

ruff (rŭf) *n.* **1.** A stiffly starched frilled or pleated collar worn by men and women in the 1500s and 1600s. **2.** A projecting growth of fur or feathers around the neck of a mammal or a bird. **—ruffed** *adj.*

❑ *These sound alike:* **ruff, rough** (not smooth).

ruffed grouse (rŭft) *n.* A North American game bird having mottled brownish feathers, the male of which has a black ruff.

ruf·fi·an (rŭf′ē-ən) *n.* **1.** A tough or rowdy person. **2.** A thug or gangster.

ruf·fle (rŭf′əl) *n.* **1.** A strip of gathered or pleated cloth used for a trimming or decoration. **2.** A ruff on a bird. **3.** An irregularity or slight disturbance. ❖ *v.* **ruf·fled, ruf·fling, ruf·fles** *—tr.* **1.** To disturb the smoothness or evenness of: *The wind ruffled the boy's hair.* **2.** To upset; fluster. **3.** To cause (feathers) to stand up in tufts or projections. **4.** To pleat or gather (fabric) into a ruffle: *ruffle a strip of satin.* *—intr.* **1.** To become irregular or rough. **2.** To become flustered.

ru·fi·yaa (ro͞o′fē-yä′) *n.* The basic monetary unit of Maldives.

rug (rŭg) *n.* **1.** A piece of heavy fabric used to cover part of a floor. **2.** An animal skin used as a floor covering. **3.** *Informal* A toupee. [Of Scandinavian origin.]

rug·by or **Rug·by** (rŭg′bē) *n.* A game played with an oval ball by two teams of 15 players each on a rectangular field with goals at either end. The object is to run with the ball across the opponent's goal line or kick it through the upper portion of the goalposts. [After *Rugby*, a school in England.]

rug·ged (rŭg′ĭd) *adj.* **1.** Having a rough irregular surface: *rugged terrain.* **2.** Having wrinkles and rough features: *a rugged face.* **3.** Sturdy; hardy: *a rugged mountain guide.* **4.** Stormy; tempestuous: *a rugged winter.* **5.** Demanding great effort, ability, or endurance: *rugged conditions in the wilderness.* [From Middle English, shaggy, of Scandinavian origin.] **—rug′ged·ly** *adv.* **—rug′ged·ness** *n.*

Ruhr (ro͝or) A primarily industrial region of northwest Germany along and north of the **Ruhr River,** which flows about 145 miles (235 kilometers) westward to the Rhine River.

ru·in (ro͞o′ĭn) *n.* **1.** Total destruction or collapse: *The castle fell into ruin.* **2.** often **ruins** The remains of something that has been destroyed or has fallen into pieces from age: *Aztec ruins.* **3.** often **ruins** The state of being made worthless or extensively harmed: *Our plans are in ruins.* **4.** A cause of destruction or irreparable harm or loss: *Gambling will be his ruin.* ❖ *tr.v.* **ru·ined, ru·in·ing, ru·ins 1.** To cause (a building, for example) to be in a destroyed or collapsed state. See Synonyms at **destroy. 2.** To harm greatly; make useless or worthless: *A bad diet ruined his health.* [From Middle English *ruine*, from Latin *ruīna*.]

ru·in·a·tion (ro͞o′ə-**nā′**shən) *n.* Destruction.

ru·in·ous (ro͞o′ə-nəs) *adj.* **1.** Causing or likely to cause ruin; destructive: *a policy with ruinous consequences.* **2.** Decayed or collapsed. **—ru′in·ous·ly** *adv.*

rule (ro͞ol) *n.* **1a.** The power of governing; authority:

America under colonial rule. **b.** A period of government: *during the rule of King George III.* **2.** An official statement telling how something must be done or what may or may not be done: *the rules of tennis.* **3.** A usual or customary course of action: *I make a rule of getting up early.* **4.** A statement that tells what is true in most or all cases: *Most mammals are covered with fur, but humans are an exception to this rule.* **5.** A straightedge; a ruler. ❖ *v.* **ruled, rul·ing, rules** —*tr.* **1.** To have political control or authority over; govern: *She ruled her country wisely.* **2.** To have great influence over; dominate: *allowed his passions to rule his judgment.* **3.** To declare or decide judicially: *The Supreme Court ruled that the law was unconstitutional.* **4.** To mark (paper or another surface) with straight parallel lines. —*intr.* **1.** To be in control; exercise authority: *a monarch ruling over vast territory.* **2.** To declare a judicial decision: *How did the judge rule?* **3.** *Slang* To be excellent or superior: *That new movie rules!* ◆ **as a rule** In general; for the most part: *As a rule, I don't like sweets.* **rule out 1.** To remove from consideration; exclude: *We have ruled that option out.* **2.** To prevent from happening: *The rain ruled out the picnic.* [From Middle English *reule*, from Latin *rēgula*, rod, measure, principle.]

rul·er (ro͞oʹlər) *n.* **1.** A person, such as a king or queen, who governs a country. **2.** A straightedge for drawing straight lines and measuring length.

rul·ing (ro͞oʹlĭng) *adj.* **1.** Having control, especially political control; governing: *a ruling body; the ruling classes.* **2.** Prevailing; dominant: *a ruling passion.* ❖ *n.* An official decision.

rum (rŭm) *n.* An alcoholic liquor distilled from sugar cane or molasses. [Probably short for obsolete *rumbullion.*]

Ru·ma·ni·a (ro͞o-māʹnē-ə) See **Romania.** **—Ru·maʹni·an** *adj. & n.*

rum·ba also **rhum·ba** (rŭmʹbə *or* ro͝omʹbə) *n.* **1.** A dance of Cuban origin with complex footwork. **2.** A modern ballroom adaptation of the rumba. **3.** A piece of music for either of these dances.

rum·ble (rŭmʹbəl) *intr.v.* **rum·bled, rum·bling, rum·bles 1.** To make a deep, long, rolling sound. **2.** To move with such a sound: *A heavy truck rumbled over the wooden bridge.* ❖ *n.* **1.** A deep, long, rolling sound. **2.** *Slang* A gang fight.

rumble seat *n.* An uncovered passenger seat that opens out from the rear of a car.

ru·men (ro͞oʹmən) *n., pl.* **ru·mi·na** (ro͞oʹmə-nə) or **ru·mens** The first division of the stomach of a ruminant animal, in which food is partly digested before being regurgitated for further chewing.

ru·mi·nant (ro͞oʹmə-nənt) *n.* Any of various hoofed, usually horned mammals, such as cattle, sheep, deer, and antelopes, that have a stomach divided into four sections and that chew a cud consisting of plant food that is brought back up to the mouth from the stomach when partially digested. **—ruʹmi·nant** *adj.*

ru·mi·nate (ro͞oʹmə-nātʹ) *intr.v.* **ru·mi·nat·ed, ru·mi·nat·ing, ru·mi·nates 1.** To chew a cud, as a cow or sheep does. **2.** To think about something over and over: *I ruminated over the difficult decision.* [From Latin *rūmināre*, from *rūmen*, throat.] **—ruʹmi·naʹtion** *n.*

rum·mage (rŭmʹĭj) *v.* **rum·maged, rum·mag·ing, rum·mag·es** —*intr.* To search through the contents of a container or a mass of things: *rummaged through the drawers for a pen.* —*tr.* **1.** To search through the contents of (a container or a mass of things): *rummage a trunk for a ball glove; rummage a pile of clothes for a shirt.* **2.** To find after a search of such a container or mass: *rummaged up an old photograph.* [From Old Provençal *arumar*, to stow.]

rummage sale *n.* A sale of assorted secondhand objects: *bought a pair of skis at the church rummage sale.*

rum·my (rŭmʹē) *n.* A card game in which players try to obtain sets of three or more cards that are of the same rank or form a continuous run in a single suit.

ru·mor (ro͞oʹmər) *n.* **1.** A story or report usually spread by word of mouth that may or may not be true: *I heard a rumor that you are retiring.* **2.** Gossip; hearsay: *Rumor has it that the company will declare bankruptcy.* ❖ *tr.v.* **ru·mored, ru·mor·ing, ru·mors 1.** To spread a rumor about (someone or something): *The candidate was rumored to be dropping out of the race.* **2.** To tell a rumor (that something is the case): *It is rumored that their star player has an injury.* [From Middle English *rumour*, from Latin *rūmor.*]

❑ *These sound alike:* **rumor, roomer** (lodger).

rump (rŭmp) *n.* **1a.** The fleshy part above the hind legs of a four-footed animal. **b.** A cut of meat from this part. **2.** The human buttocks.

rum·ple (rŭmʹpəl) *v.* **rum·pled, rum·pling, rum·ples** —*tr.* To wrinkle or crease: *Don't rumple the suit.* —*intr.* To become wrinkled or creased. ❖ *n.* A wrinkle or untidy crease.

rum·pus (rŭmʹpəs) *n.* A noisy disturbance.

run (rŭn) *v.* **ran** (răn), **run, run·ning, runs** —*intr.* **1.** To move swiftly on foot so that both feet leave the ground during each stride. **2.** To retreat quickly; flee: *At the first sign of danger we ran.* **3.** To move about or roam freely: *We let the dog run in the yard.* **4a.** To go or move around quickly or hurriedly: *We ran around all morning trying to get ready for our trip.* **b.** To go when in trouble: *is always running to his lawyer.* **5.** To make a short, quick trip or visit: *I had to run to the store.* **6a.** To take part in a race by running: *run in the marathon.* **b.** To compete in a race for elected office: *She's running for governor.* **7.** To move freely, especially on wheels: *The car ran downhill.* **8.** To be in operation; work: *The engine is running.* **9.** To go back and forth, especially on a schedule: *The trains run every hour.* **10a.** To flow: *Water ran from the tap.* **b.** To melt and flow: *The icing on the cake began to run.* **c.** To give off a fluid from the body: *My nose is running.* **11.** To be wet and covered with a liquid: *His eyes ran with tears at the sad news.* **12.** To spread or dissolve, as dyes in a fabric: *colors that won't fade or run.* **13.** To extend, spread, or reach: *This road runs all the way through town. The vine runs up the wall.* **14.** To go by in time; pass: *Days ran into weeks.* **15.** To tend to persist or recur: *A talent for music runs in that family.* **16.** To take a particular form: *The report runs as follows.* **17.** To occupy or exist in a certain range: *The sizes run from small to large.* **18.** To be presented or performed for a continuous period of time: *The play ran for six months.* **19.** To pass into a specified condition: *He ran into debt.* **20.** *Informal* To leave or depart: *I'm sorry, but I have to run.* —*tr.* **1a.** To travel over on foot at a pace faster than a walk: *ran two blocks.* **b.** To cause (an animal) to travel at such a pace: *ran the horse around the racetrack for a few laps.* **2.** To cause to move quickly: *He ran his fingers over the keyboard.* **3.** To transport: *Run me into town.* **4a.** To cause to compete in a race: *ran his horse in the derby.* **b.** To nominate for elective office: *The party ran her for senator.* **5.** To cause to be in a given condition: *a boss that runs his employees ragged.* **6.** To do or carry out: *ran some errands.* **7.** To cause to function; operate: *run a machine.* **8.** In football, to try to move (the ball) forward by carrying it. **9.** To submit for consideration or review: *ran the plan by my boss.* **10.** To cause to move on a course: *ran the ship carefully through the narrows.* **11.** To smuggle: *arrested for running contraband goods.* **12.** To evade or pass through without permission: *run a roadblock; run a red light.* **13.** To cause to flow: *run water into a tub.* **14.** To cause to extend or pass: *run a rope between the trees.* **15.** To cause to crash or collide: *ran the car into a*

ruin
Sanctuary of Athena, Delphi, Greece

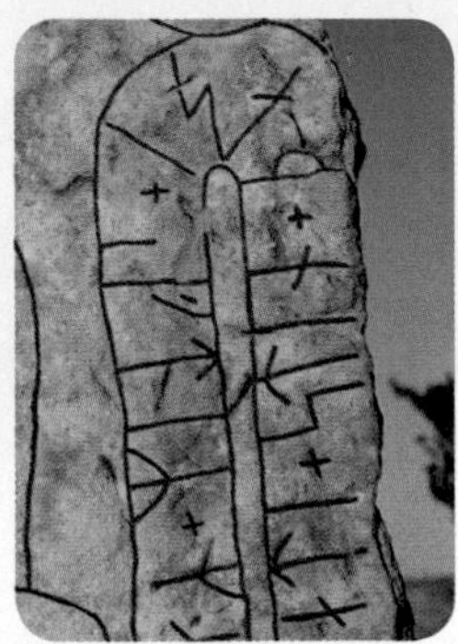

rune
detail of inscribed runes on a stone near Källby, Sweden

Mount Rushmore

ă	pat	ôr	core
ā	pay	oi	boy
âr	care	ou	out
ä	father	o͝o	took
ĕ	pet	o͝or	lure
ē	be	o͞o	boot
ĭ	pit	ŭ	cut
ī	bite	ûr	urge
îr	pier	th	thin
ŏ	pot	*th*	this
ō	toe	zh	vision
ô	paw	ə	about

pole; ran the ship aground. **16.** To present or perform for a continuous period of time: *The theater ran the popular play for many months.* **17.** To publish in a periodical: *run an advertisement.* **18.** To conduct, manage, or perform: *run an experiment; run a campaign.* **19.** To process or carry out (a computer program or command). **20.** To subject oneself or be subjected to: *run a risk.* **21.** To have (a fever): *was running a temperature of 102.* ❖ *n.* **1a.** An act of running: *exercised by going for a run.* **b.** A distance covered by or as if by running. **c.** The time it takes to cover such a distance: *It's a two minutes' run from here.* **2.** A pace faster than a walk: *She set off at a brisk run.* **3.** A quick trip or visit: *a run into town.* **4a.** A running race: *won the five-mile run.* **b.** A campaign for public office: *a run for the presidency.* **5.** In baseball, a point scored by running around all the bases and reaching home plate safely. **6.** In football, a player's attempt to move the ball forward by carrying it. **7.** Unrestricted freedom or use: *They gave us the run of the place.* **8.** An athlete's passage down a hill or across country: *The skier had two good runs today.* **9.** A scheduled or regular route: *a bus on its usual run.* **10a.** A continuous period of operation, especially of a machine or factory: *a trial run of a new engine.* **b.** The amount produced during such a period: *a run of 5,000 copies of the book.* **11.** A movement or flow. **12.** A small stream or brook. **13.** A continuous length or extent: *a long run of wire.* **14.** An outdoor enclosure for domestic animals or poultry: *a chicken run.* **15.** A length of torn or unraveled stitches in a knitted fabric: *a run in my stockings.* **16.** An unbroken series: *a run of victories.* **17.** An unbroken sequence of theatrical performances: *a long run on Broadway.* **18.** A rapid sequence of musical notes. **19.** A series of unexpected and urgent demands, as by customers: *a run on a bank.* **20.** A continuing state or condition: *a run of good luck.* **21.** A trend or tendency: *the run of events.* **22.** An execution of a specific computer program or command. ◆ **a run for (one's) money** Strong competition. **in the long run** Eventually; in the final analysis or outcome. **in the short run** In the immediate future. **on the run 1.** In rapid retreat. **2.** In hiding: *fugitives on the run.* **3.** Hurrying busily from place to place: *had lunch on the run.* **run across** To find by chance; come upon. **run after** To pursue; chase. **run along** To go away; leave. **run a temperature** To have a fever. **run away 1.** To flee; escape. **2.** To leave home. **run away with** To make off with hurriedly. **run down 1.** To stop working because of lack of force or power: *The clock finally ran down.* **2.** To chase and capture. **3.** To say mean or unpleasant things about: *You're always running down my cooking.* **4.** To go over; review: *Run down the list to make sure we didn't forget anything.* **run into 1.** To meet or find by chance: *ran into an old friend.* **2.** To encounter (something). **3.** To collide with. **run off 1.** To print, duplicate, or copy: *ran off some more copies of the paper.* **2.** To force or drive off (trespassers, for example). **run on 1.** To keep going; continue. **2.** To talk without stopping, usually about unimportant matters: *He's always running on about something.* **run out 1.** To become used up; be exhausted: *Supplies ran out.* **2.** To force to leave: *ran them out of town.* **run out of** To exhaust the supply of: *We ran out of cookies.* **run out on** To abandon; forsake: *Don't run out on your friends.* **run over 1.** To collide with, knock down, and often pass over. **2.** To read or review quickly: *I just need to run over this article.* **3.** To flow over. **4.** To go beyond a limit: *The meeting ran over.* **run short** To become scanty or insufficient in supply. **run short of** To use up so that a supply becomes insufficient or scanty. **run through 1.** To pierce, as with a sword. **2.** To use up quickly: *She ran through all her money.* **3.** To rehearse or examine quickly: *Let's run through the scene again.* **run up** To make or become greater or larger: *We ran up a huge bill at the restaurant.* [From Old English *rinnan.*]

run·a·bout (rŭn**′**ə-bout′) *n.* **1.** A small motorboat. **2.** A light aircraft. **3.** A small open automobile or carriage.

run·a·round (rŭn**′**ə-round′) *n.* Deception, usually in the form of vague excuses.

run·a·way (rŭn**′**ə-wā′) *n.* **1.** A person who has run away, as from home. **2.** Something that has escaped from control or proper confinement. **3.** *Informal* An easy victory. ❖ *adj.* **1.** Escaping or having escaped: *runaway horses.* **2.** Out of control: *a runaway car rolling down the hill.* **3.** *Informal* Easily won: *a runaway victory.*

run·down (rŭn**′**doun′) *n.* **1.** A point-by-point summary: *a rundown of the day's news.* **2.** In baseball, a play in which a runner is trapped between bases. ❖ *adj.* also **run-down** (**rŭn′doun′**) **1.** Exhausted or weak: *feeling rundown.* **2.** Old and decayed: *rundown buildings.* **3.** Unwound and not running: *a rundown clock.*

rune (ro͞on) *n.* **1.** Any of the letters of several alphabets used by ancient Germanic peoples. **2.** A similar letter in another alphabet, thought to have magical power. **—run′ic** *adj.*

rung[1] (rŭng) *n.* **1.** A rod or bar forming a step of a ladder. **2.** A crosspiece between the legs of a chair. **3.** A level or degree in a hierarchy: *The assistant manager is one rung below the manager.* [From Old English *hrung.*]

❑ *These sound alike:* **rung[1]** (rod), **rung[2]** (sounded), **wrung** (twisted).

rung[2] (rŭng) *v.* Past participle of **ring[2]**.

❑ *These sound alike:* **rung[2]** (sounded), **rung[1]** (rod), **wrung** (twisted).

run-in (rŭn**′**ĭn′) *n.* A quarrel or argument.

run·nel (rŭn**′**əl) *n.* **1.** A small stream or brook. **2.** A narrow channel or course, as for water.

run·ner (rŭn**′**ər) *n.* **1.** A person who runs, especially in a race. **2.** A messenger. **3.** A part that slides on something or on which something slides, as the blade of a skate. **4.** A long narrow carpet, as one for a hall or stairway. **5.** A long narrow tablecloth. **6.** A creeping plant stem that puts forth roots at intervals along its length, thus producing new plants.

run·ner-up (rŭn′ər-**ŭp′**) *n., pl.* **run·ners-up** A contestant that finishes a competition in second place.

run·ning (rŭn**′**ĭng) *n.* **1.** The act or an instance of running. **2.** The ability to run. **3.** The sport of someone who runs. ❖ *adj.* Continuous; ongoing: *gave us a running commentary on the game.* ❖ *adv.* Consecutively: *for four years running.* ◆ **in the running 1.** Participating in a competition. **2.** Having the possibility of winning or placing well in a competition. **out of the running 1.** Not participating in a competition. **2.** Having no possibility of winning or placing well in a competition.

running back *n.* In football, an offensive back, such as a fullback or halfback, who tries to advance the ball by running with it out of the backfield.

running board *n.* A narrow footboard extending under and beside the doors of some cars and other vehicles.

running light *n.* One of several lights on a vehicle, especially a ship, turned on at night to show position and size.

running mate *n.* The candidate for the lesser of two closely linked political offices.

run·ny (rŭn**′**ē) *adj.* **run·ni·er, run·ni·est** Inclined to run or flow: *runny icing.*

Run·ny·mede (rŭn**′**ē-mēd′) A meadow in southeast England on the Thames River west of London. King John accepted the Magna Carta here or on a nearby island in 1215.

run·off (rŭn**′**ôf′) *n.* **1.** Rainfall that is not absorbed by the soil, finally reaching streams and rivers. **2.** An extra election held to resolve a question when there was no clear majority in a prior election.

run-of-the-mill (rŭn′əv-*th*ə-**mĭl′**) *adj.* Not special or outstanding; average.

run-on sentence (rŭn′ŏn′) *n.* A sentence in which two or more main clauses are joined incorrectly, as by a comma instead of a semicolon or conjunction. For example, *I was hungry, I missed lunch* is a run-on sentence. It should read *I was hungry because I missed lunch.*

runt (rŭnt) *n.* A very small animal, especially the smallest animal in a litter.

run·way (rŭn′wā′) *n.* **1.** A strip of level, usually paved ground on which aircraft take off and land. **2.** A narrow walkway extending from a stage into an auditorium.

ru·pee (ro͞o-pē′ *or* ro͞o′pē) *n.* The basic monetary unit of India, Mauritius, Nepal, Pakistan, Seychelles, and Sri Lanka.

ru·pi·ah (ro͞o-pē′ə) *n.* The basic monetary unit of Indonesia.

rup·ture (rŭp′chər) *n.* **1.** The process or an instance of breaking open or bursting. **2.** A break in friendly relations: *a rupture in diplomatic relations.* **3.** A tear in an organ or tissue. ❖ *v.* **rup·tured, rup·tur·ing, rup·tures** —*tr.* To break open; burst. —*intr.* To undergo or suffer a rupture.

ru·ral (ro͝or′əl) *adj.* **1.** Relating to or characteristic of the country: *rural areas.* **2.** Relating to people who live in the country: *rural households.* [From Middle English, from Latin *rūs*, country.] **—ru′ral·ly** *adv.*

rural free delivery *n.* Free government delivery of mail in rural areas.

ruse (ro͞oz *or* ro͞os) *n.* A crafty trick or deception.

rush[1] (rŭsh) *v.* **rushed, rush·ing, rush·es** —*intr.* **1.** To move or act swiftly; hurry: *Fire engines rushed past us.* **2.** To flow or surge rapidly and often with noise: *Water rushed over the falls.* **3.** In football, to advance the ball by carrying it rather than passing. —*tr.* **1.** To cause to move or act with unusual haste: *Don't rush me.* **2.** To perform hastily: *rushed the throw and made an error.* **3.** To attack suddenly; charge: *rushing the barricades.* **4.** To carry or transport hastily: *rushed supplies to the camp.* **5.** In football, to run toward (a passer or kicker) in order to block or prevent a play. ❖ *n.* **1.** The act of rushing; a swift forward movement. **2.** An anxious and eager movement to or from a place in large numbers: *a rush for gold in the hills.* **3.** A flurry of hasty activity; a great hurry: *left in such a rush that she forgot her purse.* **4.** A sudden attack; a charge. **5.** In football: **a.** An attempt to advance the ball by carrying it. **b.** An act of running at a passer or kicker in order to block or prevent a play. **6.** A rapid, often noisy flow or passage: *a rush of air; a rush of words.* **7.** often **rushes** The first unedited print of a movie scene. ❖ *adj.* Performed with or requiring great haste or urgency: *a rush job.* [From Middle English *rushen*, from Latin *recūsāre*, to reject.]

rush[2] (rŭsh) *n.* **1.** Any of various tall grasslike plants that grow in wet places and have hollow or pithy stems. **2.** The stem of any of these plants, used to make chair seats or mats. [From Old English *rysc.*]

rush hour *n.* A regular period of heavy traffic, especially at the beginning or end of a workday.

Rush·more (rŭsh′môr′), **Mount** A mountain, 5,725 feet (1,745 meters) high, in western South Dakota. A monument here has massive carved likenesses of Washington, Jefferson, Lincoln, and Theodore Roosevelt.

rus·set (rŭs′ĭt) *n.* **1.** A reddish brown. **2.** A type of apple having reddish-brown skin. **3.** A type of potato having reddish-brown skin.

Rus·sia (rŭsh′ə) A country of eastern Europe and northern Asia. Founded by Slavs in the Middle Ages, Russia expanded by the 1700s into an empire stretching from the Baltic Sea to the Pacific Ocean. The empire was overthrown in 1917, and in 1922 Russia became the largest republic within the USSR. In 1991 the USSR was dismantled, and Russia again became an independent nation. Moscow is the capital.

Rus·sian (rŭsh′ən) *adj.* Relating to Russia or its people, language, or culture. ❖ *n.* **1.** A native or inhabitant of Russia. **2.** The Slavic language of the Russians.

Russian Orthodox Church *n.* The Eastern Orthodox Church that is under the leadership of the patriarch of Russia and has independent branches in other countries.

rust (rŭst) *n.* **1.** Any of the various reddish-brown oxides of iron that form on iron and many of its alloys when they are exposed to oxygen in the presence of moisture at ordinary temperatures. **2a.** Any of various plant diseases caused by fungi, characterized by reddish or brownish spots on the leaves. **b.** Any of the various fungi that cause such diseases. **3.** A reddish brown. ❖ *tr. & intr.v.* **rust·ed, rust·ing, rusts** To make or become corroded or oxidized.

rus·tic (rŭs′tĭk) *adj.* **1.** Relating to or typical of country life or country people. **2.** Lacking the refinement or elegance associated with the city: *rustic customs.* **3.** Simple or unsophisticated in a manner associated with the country: *a pleasant rustic cabin by the lake.* ❖ *n.* A person from the country.

rus·tle (rŭs′əl) *v.* **rus·tled, rus·tling, rus·tles** —*intr.* **1.** To move with soft fluttering or crackling sounds: *leaves rustled in the wind.* **2.** To steal livestock, especially cattle. —*tr.* **1.** To cause to rustle: *wind rustling the leaves.* **2.** To get quickly or briskly: *rustle up a dinner.* **3.** To steal (livestock, especially cattle). **—rus′tler** *n.*

rust·y (rŭs′tē) *adj.* **rust·i·er, rust·i·est 1.** Covered with rust; corroded. **2.** Consisting of or produced by rust: *a rusty layer on the fender.* **3.** Having a brownish-red color. **4.** Weakened because of lack of use or practice: *My juggling skills are a little rusty.* **—rust′i·ness** *n.*

rut (rŭt) *n.* **1.** A track, as in a dirt road, made by the passage of vehicles. **2.** A fixed, usually boring routine. ❖ *tr.v.* **rut·ted, rut·ting, ruts** To make ruts in.

ru·ta·ba·ga (ro͞o′tə-bā′gə *or* ro͝ot′ə-bā′gə) *n.* A plant similar to a turnip, having a yellowish root used as food. [From Swedish dialectal *rotabagge* : *rot*, root + *bagge*, bag.]

Ruth[1] (ro͞oth) In the Bible, a widow who left her homeland in order to stay with her mother-in-law, converted to Judaism, and became the great-grandmother of David.

Ruth[2] (ro͞oth) *n.* A book of the Bible that tells the story of Ruth.

Ruth, George Herman Called "Babe." 1895–1948. American baseball player. He hit 714 home runs, played in 10 World Series, and held 54 major-league records.

ru·the·ni·um (ro͞o-thē′nē-əm) *n.* *Symbol* **Ru** A hard, silvery-white metallic element that resists corrosion and is used to harden alloys of platinum and palladium. Atomic number 44. See **Periodic Table.**

Ruth·er·ford (rŭ*th*′ər-fərd *or* rŭth′ər-fərd), **Ernest** 1871–1937. New Zealand–born British physicist who was a pioneer of subatomic physics. He studied types of radiation and discovered the atomic nucleus.

ruth·er·ford·i·um (rŭ*th*′ər-fôr′dē-əm) *n.* *Symbol* **Rf** A radioactive element that has been artificially produced in trace amounts by scientists. Atomic number 104. See **Periodic Table.** [After Ernest *Rutherford.*]

ruth·less (ro͞oth′lĭs) *adj.* Showing no pity; cruel. [From Middle English *reutheles*, from *reuthe*, pity.] **—ruth′less·ly** *adv.* **—ruth′less·ness** *n.*

RV *abbr.* An abbreviation of recreational vehicle.

Rwan·da (ro͞o-än′də) A country of east-central Africa north of Burundi. Kigali is the capital.

rye (rī) *n.* **1.** The grain of a cereal grass that grows in cool climates, used for making flour and whiskey. **2.** The plant that bears such grain. **3.** Whiskey made from this grain.

❑ *These sound alike:* **rye, wry** (humorous).

rutabaga

Babe Ruth

sabot

WRITERS CHOOSE THEIR WORDS

I had no idea what Dr. Willner had said to Coach Pete, or what the coach had riding on this. It showed what a good guy Coach Pete was that he'd said nothing about it, one way or the other. He hadn't told us to lose or to make Pleasant Valley feel better, even though his job—and for all I knew, his life—might be depending on it. He'd done the legal, acceptable limit of what could be done to **sabotage** the game. He'd let the second string start and play the whole time. But even that hadn't been enough.

—Francine Prose
After

ă	pat	ôr	core
ā	pay	oi	boy
âr	care	ou	out
ä	father	o͝o	took
ĕ	pet	o͝or	lure
ē	be	o͞o	boot
ĭ	pit	ŭ	cut
ī	bite	ûr	urge
îr	pier	th	thin
ŏ	pot	*th*	this
ō	toe	zh	vision
ô	paw	ə	about

s¹ or **S** (ĕs) *n., pl.* **s's** or **S's** also **ss** or **Ss** The 19th letter of the English alphabet.

s² *abbr.* An abbreviation of second.

S¹ The symbol for the element **sulfur.**

S² *abbr.* An abbreviation of: **1.** satisfactory. **2.** south. **3.** southern. **4.** strike (in baseball).

s. *abbr.* An abbreviation of: **1.** singular. **2.** son.

–s¹ or **–es** *suff.* A suffix that forms plural nouns: *letters.*

–s² or **–es** *suff.* A suffix that forms the third person singular present tense of most verbs: *talks.*

–s³ *suff.* A suffix that forms certain adverbs, such as *nights* in *She works nights* or *unawares* in *We were caught unawares.*

–'s *suff.* A suffix that forms the possessive case of most nouns: *women's.*

's 1. Contraction of *is: She's happy.* **2.** Contraction of *has: He's been away.* **3.** Contraction of *does: What's he want?* **4.** Contraction of *us: Let's go to lunch.*

SA *abbr.* An abbreviation of: **1.** South Africa. **2.** South America.

Saar (sär *or* zär) A river, about 150 miles (245 kilometers) long, rising in northeast France and flowing north and north-northwest to western Germany.

Saar·land (**sär′**lănd′ *or* **zär′**-lănd′) or **Saar** (sär *or* zär) A region of southwest Germany in the Saar River valley on the border with France. Because of its extensive coal deposits, it was long contested between Germany and France.

Sab·bath (**săb′**əth) *n.* **1.** The seventh day of the week, Saturday, observed as the day of rest and worship in Judaism and some Christian sects. **2.** The first day of the week, Sunday, observed as the day of rest and worship in most forms of Christianity. [From Old English *sabat,* from Hebrew *šabbāt,* from *šābat,* to rest.]

sab·bat·i·cal (sə-**băt′**ĭ-kəl) *adj.* **1.** Relating to a sabbatical year. **2. Sabbatical** Relating to the Sabbath as a day of rest. ❖ *n.* A sabbatical year.

sabbatical year *n.* A leave of absence, often with pay, given to some college professors every seven years.

sa·ber (**sā′**bər) *n.* **1.** A heavy cavalry sword with a single-edged, slightly curved blade. **2.** A light flexible sword used in fencing.

sa·ber-toothed cat (**sā′**bər-to͞otht′) *n.* Any of various large extinct catlike mammals of prehistoric times, having long upper canine teeth.

Sa·bin (**sā′**bĭn), **Albert Bruce** 1906–1993. Polish-born American microbiologist and physician who developed a vaccine against polio that contained an active form of the polio virus, publicly introduced in 1962.

sa·ble (**sā′**bəl) *n.* **1a.** A mammal of northern Eurasia that is related to the minks and weasels and has soft dark fur. **b.** The highly valued fur of this mammal. **2a.** The color black. **b. sables** Black garments worn in mourning.

sa·bot (să-**bō′** *or* **săb′**ō) *n.* A shoe carved from a piece of wood, traditionally worn in some parts of Europe.

sab·o·tage (**săb′**ə-täzh′) *n.* **1.** The deliberate destruction of property or disruption of work by civilians or enemy agents in wartime. **2.** The deliberate attempt to damage, destroy, or hinder a cause or an activity. ❖ *tr.v.* **sab·o·taged, sab·o·tag·ing, sab·o·tag·es** To damage, destroy, ruin, or hinder (something) by sabotage.

sab·o·teur (săb′ə-**tûr′**) *n.* A person who commits sabotage.

sa·bre (**sā′**bər) *n. Chiefly British* Variant of **saber.**

sac (săk) *n.* A part of an organism that resembles a bag or pouch, often containing a liquid. The human bladder is a sac.

❑ *These sound alike:* **sac, sack¹** (bag), **sack²** (rob), **sack³** (wine).

Sac·a·ga·we·a (săk′ə-gə-**wē′**ə *or* sä-**kä′**gä-wē′ä) or **Sac·a·ja·we·a** (săk′ə-jə-**wē′**ə) 1787?–1812? Shoshone guide and interpreter who accompanied (1805–1806) the Lewis and Clark expedition. —SEE NOTE.

sac·cha·rin (**săk′**ər-ĭn) *n.* A white crystalline powder that tastes about 500 times sweeter than sugar and is used as a calorie-free sweetener.

❑ *These sound alike:* **saccharin, saccharine** (sweet).

sac·cha·rine (**săk′**ər-ĭn *or* **săk′**ə-rēn′) *adj.* **1.** Relating to or characteristic of sugar; sweet. **2.** Insincerely or cloyingly sweet in tone or character: *a saccharine smile.* [From Greek *sakkhar,* sugar, from Sanskrit *śarkarā.*]

❑ *These sound alike:* **saccharine, saccharin** (sweetener).

sac·er·do·tal (săs′ər-**dōt′**l *or* săk′ər-**dōt′**l) *adj.* Relating to priests or the priesthood.

sa·chem (**sā′**chəm) *n.* A chief of a Native American tribe or confederation, especially an Algonquian chief.

sa·chet (să-**shā′**) *n.* A small bag filled with a perfumed substance and used to scent clothes.

❑ *These sound alike:* **sachet, sashay** (walk casually).

sack¹ (săk) *n.* **1a.** A large bag of strong coarse material used for holding objects in bulk: *a potato sack.* **b.** A similar bag of paper or plastic: *a brown paper sack.* **c.** The amount that such a container can hold. **2.** A loose-fitting dress or jacket for women and children. **3.** *Informal* A bed, mattress, or sleeping bag. **4.** *Slang* Dismissal from a job or position: *If you show up late again, you will get the sack.* **5.** In football, an act of tackling the quarterback attempting to pass. ❖ *tr.v.* **sacked, sack·ing, sacks 1.** To put into a sack. **2.** *Slang* To fire from a job: *The bankrupt company sacked ten employees.* **3.** In football, to tackle (a quarterback attempting to pass the ball). [From Old English *sacc,* from Greek *sakkos,* of Semitic origin.]

❑ *These sound alike:* **sack¹** (bag), **sac** (body part), **sack²** (rob), **sack³** (wine).

sack² (săk) *tr.v.* **sacked, sack·ing, sacks** To rob (a captured city, for example) of its valuables; loot or plunder. ❖ *n.* The robbing, looting, or plundering of a place captured by the enemy. [Probably from French *(mettre à) sac,* (to put in) a sack.]

❑ *These sound alike:* **sack²** (rob), **sac** (body part), **sack¹** (bag), **sack³** (wine).

sack³ (săk) *n.* Any of various strong white wines from Spain and the Canary Islands, imported to England in the 1500s and 1600s. [From French *(vin) sec*, dry (wine), from Latin *siccus*, dry.]

❑ *These sound alike:* **sack³** (wine), **sac** (body part), **sack¹** (bag), **sack²** (rob).

sack·cloth (săk′klôth′) *n.* **1.** A rough coarse cloth. **2.** Garments made of sackcloth, worn as a symbol of mourning or penitence.

sack·ing (săk′ĭng) *n.* A coarse cloth, such as burlap, used for making sacks.

sa·cra (sā′krə *or* săk′rə) *n.* Plural of **sacrum.**

sac·ra·ment (săk′rə-mənt) *n.* **1.** A Christian rite believed to be a means of grace, especially: **a.** In the Eastern, Roman Catholic, and some other Western Christian churches, any of the traditional seven rites instituted by Jesus that confer grace. **b.** In most other Western Christian churches, the two rites, Baptism and the Eucharist, instituted by Jesus to confer grace. **2.** often **Sacrament a.** The Eucharist. **b.** The consecrated bread and wine of the Eucharist, or the bread alone. **—sac′ra·men′tal** (săk′rə-**mĕn′**tl) *adj.*

Sac·ra·men·to (săk′rə-**mĕn′**tō) The capital of California, in the north-central part of the state northeast of San Francisco. It became the state capital in 1854.

sa·cred (sā′krĭd) *adj.* **1.** Dedicated to or set apart for the worship of a deity: *a temple sacred to Apollo.* **2.** Worthy of religious veneration; holy. **3.** Dedicated or devoted to a single use, purpose, or person. **4.** Relating to religious practices or objects. **—sa′cred·ly** *adv.* **—sa′cred·ness** *n.*

sac·ri·fice (săk′rə-fīs′) *n.* **1a.** The act of offering something, such as an animal's life, to a deity in worship or to win favor or forgiveness. **b.** A victim offered this way. **2a.** The act of giving up something highly valued for the sake of something else considered to be of greater value. **b.** Something given up in this way. **3.** A loss of profit suffered by selling something at less than its value or cost: *forced to sell at a sacrifice.* **4.** A sacrifice bunt or sacrifice fly. ❖ *v.* **sac·ri·ficed, sac·ri·fic·ing, sac·ri·fic·es** *—tr.* **1.** To offer as a sacrifice to a deity. **2.** To give up (one thing) for another thing considered to be of greater value. **3.** To sell or give away at a loss. *—intr.* **1.** To make or offer a sacrifice. **2.** To hit a sacrifice bunt or sacrifice fly. [From Middle English, from Latin *sacrificium* : *sacer*, sacred + *facere*, to make.] **—sac′ri·fi′cial** (săk′rə-**fĭsh′**əl) *adj.*

sacrifice bunt *n.* In baseball, a bunt that allows a runner to advance a base, but results in the batter being put out.

sacrifice fly *n.* In baseball, a fly ball that allows a runner to score after it is caught by a fielder.

sac·ri·lege (săk′rə-lĭj) *n.* An act of disrespect or violence toward something sacred. **—sac′ri·le′gious** (săk′rə-**lĭj′**əs *or* săk′rə-**lē′**jəs) *adj.*

sac·ris·tan (săk′rĭ-stən) *n.* **1.** A person in charge of a sacristy. **2.** A sexton.

sac·ris·ty (săk′rĭ-stē) *n., pl.* **sac·ris·ties** A room in a church where vestments and sacred articles are kept; a vestry.

sac·ro·sanct (săk′rō-săngkt′) *adj.* Regarded as sacred and not to be violated: *the sacrosanct precincts of the temple.*

sa·crum (sā′krəm *or* săk′rəm) *n., pl.* **sa·cra** (sā′krə *or* săk′rə) A triangular bone made up of five fused vertebrae that forms the rear section of the pelvis.

sad (săd) *adj.* **sad·der, sad·dest 1.** Showing, expressing, or feeling sorrow or unhappiness: *a sad face.* **2.** Causing sorrow, gloom, or regret: *sad memories.* **3.** Deplorable or inadequate: *This place is in sad shape.* [From Old English *sæd*, sated, weary.] **—sad′ly** *adv.* **—sad′ness** *n.*

SYNONYMS sad, unhappy, melancholy, sorrowful, woebegone These adjectives mean affected with or marked by a lack of joy. **Sad** and **unhappy** are the most general terms: *I was sad when I heard that your cat ran away. He doesn't like movies that make him unhappy.* **Melancholy** means feeling a lingering or habitual sadness: *I kept telling jokes, trying to cheer up my melancholy cousin.* **Sorrowful** means experiencing a painful sadness, especially one caused by loss: *One of the mourners let out a sorrowful cry.* **Woebegone** suggests grief or wretchedness, especially as reflected in the way a person or thing appears: *The slums were filled with rows of woebegone shacks.*

ANTONYM glad

---

sad·den (săd′n) *tr. & intr.v.* **sad·dened, sad·den·ing, sad·dens** To make or become sad.

sad·dle (săd′l) *n.* **1a.** A padded leather seat for a rider, strapped onto the back of a horse or other animal. **b.** A similar padded part that fits over an animal's back and supports a pack or forms part of a harness. **2.** The seat of a bicycle, motorcycle, or similar vehicle. **3.** A cut of meat that contains part of the backbone and both loins: *a saddle of veal.* **4.** Something that resembles a saddle in shape. **5.** A saddle-shaped depression in a ridge or between two peaks. ❖ *v.* **sad·dled, sad·dling, sad·dles** *—tr.* **1.** To put a saddle onto: *saddle a pony.* **2.** To load or burden; encumber: *She was saddled with all the responsibility.* *—intr.* **1.** To saddle a horse. **2.** To get into a saddle: *Saddle up and go.* [From Old English *sadol.*]

sad·dle·bag (săd′l-băg′) *n.* **1.** One of a pair of pouches that hang across the back of a horse. **2.** A pouch that is attached behind the saddle of a bicycle or motorcycle.

saddle horse *n.* A horse bred or trained for riding.

sad·dler (săd′lər) *n.* A person who makes, repairs, or sells equipment for horses.

saddle shoe *n.* A flat casual shoe, usually white, having a band of leather in a contrasting color across the instep.

saddle soap *n.* A mild soap that contains neat's-foot oil and is used for cleaning and softening leather.

sa·dism (sā′dĭz′əm *or* săd′ĭz′əm) *n.* The tendency to derive pleasure from inflicting pain on or being mean to others. [After Count Donatien Alphonse François de *Sade* (1740–1814), French writer.] **—sa′dist** *n.* **—sa·dis′tic** (sə-dĭs′tĭk) *adj.* **—sa·dis′ti·cal·ly** *adv.*

sa·fa·ri (sə-fär′ē) *n., pl.* **sa·fa·ris** A hunting trip or journey of exploration, especially in East Africa. [From Arabic *safarīya*, journey, from *safar*, departure, journey.]

safe (sāf) *adj.* **saf·er, saf·est 1.** Free from harm; unhurt: *safe and sound.* **2.** Free from risk; sure: *a safe bet.* **3.** Providing protection or security: *a safe refuge.* **4.** In baseball, having reached a base without being put out: *The runner was safe on third.* ❖ *n.* A strong metal container in which valuables, such as money and jewels, are kept for protection. [From Middle English *sauf*, from Latin *salvus*, healthy.] **—safe′ly** *adv.*

safe-con·duct (sāf′kŏn′dŭkt) *n.* **1.** An official document or escort that assures safe passage, as through enemy territory. **2.** The protection afforded by such a document or escort.

safe-de·pos·it box (sāf′dĭ-**pŏz′**ĭt) *n.* A fireproof metal box, usually in a bank vault, for the safe storage of valuables.

safe·guard (sāf′gärd′) *n.* Something that provides protection or defense, as a safety precaution or a protective device. ❖ *tr.v.* **safe·guard·ed, safe·guard·ing, safe·guards** To protect from danger; keep safe and secure: *laws to safeguard individual rights.*

safe·keep·ing (sāf′**kē′**pĭng) *n.* The act of keeping or the condition of being kept safe; protection.

safe·ty (sāf′tē) *n., pl.* **safe·ties 1.** The condition of being

BIOGRAPHY

Sacagawea Born around 1787, **Sacagawea** was a Shoshone woman from an area near the present-day border of Idaho and Montana. In 1804, while living in what is now North Dakota, Sacagawea encountered Meriwether Lewis and William Clark and joined their expedition the following spring as an interpreter. Lewis and Clark had been commissioned by Thomas Jefferson to explore the territories along the Missouri River and west to the Pacific Ocean and to bring back information about their geography, wildlife, native peoples, and natural resources. In Sacagawea they found a native guide familiar with the region and the language of the Shoshone. She secured for the expedition not only safe routes of travel and open communication with Shoshone groups, but also the opportunity to buy horses, which they needed to complete the journey to the coast.

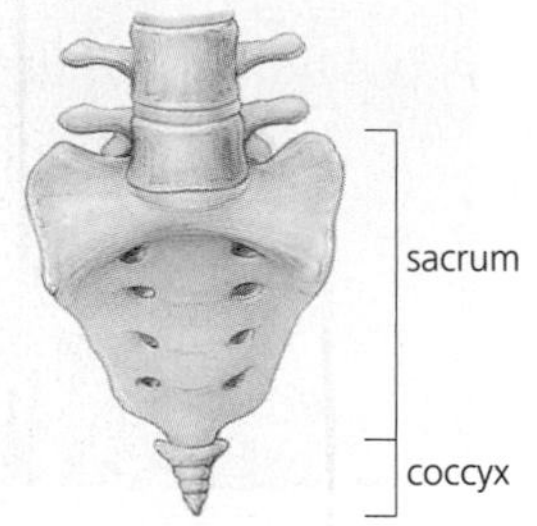

sacrum

saddle shoe

safflower

sage[2]

saguaro

ă	pat	ôr	core
ā	pay	oi	boy
âr	care	ou	out
ä	father	o͝o	took
ĕ	pet	o͝or	lure
ē	be	o͞o	boot
ĭ	pit	ŭ	cut
ī	bite	ûr	urge
îr	pier	th	thin
ŏ	pot	*th*	this
ō	toe	zh	vision
ô	paw	ə	about

safe; freedom from danger, risk, or injury. **2.** A device designed to prevent accidents, especially a lock on a gun to keep it from firing accidentally. **3.** In football: **a.** A play in which a member of the offensive team downs the ball or is tackled or forced out of bounds behind his own goal line, resulting in two points for the defensive team. **b.** A defensive back who usually plays behind the linebackers.

safety belt *n.* **1.** A seat belt. **2.** A strap or harness used to support someone working at a dangerous height.

safety glass *n.* Glass that resists shattering, especially a composite of two sheets of glass with an intermediate layer of transparent plastic.

safety match *n.* A match that will light only when it is struck on a specially prepared surface.

safety pin *n.* A pin made in the form of a clasp with a guard to cover and hold the point.

safety valve *n.* **1.** A valve in a pressurized container, such as a steam boiler, that opens if the pressure reaches a dangerous level. **2.** An outlet for the release of bottled-up energy or emotion.

saf·flow·er (săf′lou′ər) *n.* A plant having orange flowers formerly used for making dye and seeds that yield an oil used in cooking.

saf·fron (săf′rən) *n.* **1.** The dried orange-yellow stigmas from the flowers of a kind of crocus, used to flavor food and in making dye. **2.** An orange-yellow color.

sag (săg) *intr.v.* **sagged, sag·ging, sags 1.** To sink, droop, or settle from pressure or weight: *The large number of fish made the net sag.* **2.** To lose vigor, strength, or firmness: *The old mattress sagged in the middle.* **3.** To decline in amount or value: *Profits sagged.* ❖ *n.* **1.** The act or an instance of sagging or drooping: *the sag of the boards under our feet.* **2.** A sagging or sunken place: *a sag in the ceiling.* **—sag′gy** *adj.*

sa·ga (sä′gə) *n.* **1.** A long adventure story, especially one from medieval Iceland, that deals with historical or legendary heroes, families, deeds, and events. **2.** A modern story that resembles a saga.

sa·ga·cious (sə-gā′shəs) *adj.* Prudent; wise. **—sa·gac′i·ty** (sə-găs′ĭ-tē) *n.* **—sa·ga′cious·ly** *adv.* **—sa·ga′cious·ness** *n.*

sag·a·more (săg′ə-môr′) *n.* A subordinate chief among the Algonquian Indians of North America.

sage[1] (sāj) *n.* A person who is highly respected for wisdom, experience, and judgment. ❖ *adj.* **sag·er, sag·est** Having or showing wisdom and sound judgment. [From Middle English, from Old French, from Latin *sapere*, to be wise.] **—sage′ly** *adv.*

sage[2] (sāj) *n.* **1.** Any of various plants related to mint, having grayish-green aromatic leaves used as a flavoring. **2.** Sagebrush. [From Middle English *sauge*, from Latin *salvia*, from *salvus*, healthy.]

sage·brush (sāj′brŭsh′) *n.* Any of several shrubs of dry regions of the Northern Hemisphere, having aromatic silver-green leaves and clusters of small white flowers.

Sag·it·tar·i·us (săj′ĭ-târ′ē-əs) *n.* **1.** A constellation in the Southern Hemisphere near Scorpius and Capricorn, traditionally pictured as a centaur with a bow and arrow. **2.** The ninth sign of the zodiac in astrology.

sa·go (sā′gō) *n., pl.* **sa·gos** A powdery starch obtained from the pith of various Asian palm trees and cycads, used as a food thickener.

sa·gua·ro (sə-gwär′ō *or* sə-wär′ō) *n., pl.* **sa·gua·ros** A very large cactus of the southwest United States and Mexico, having upward-curving branches, white flowers, and edible red fruit.

Sa·hap·ti·an (sä-hăp′tē-ən) *n.* A Native American language family spoken in the northwest United States and including the Sahaptin and Nez Perce languages.

Sa·hap·tin (sä-hăp′tĭn) *n., pl.* **Sahaptin** or **Sa·hap·tins 1.** A member of any of various Native American peoples of Idaho, Oregon, and Washington. **2.** The Sahaptian language of the Sahaptin.

Sa·har·a (sə-hâr′ə *or* sə-hä′rə) A vast desert of northern Africa extending east from the Atlantic coast to the Red Sea south of the Atlas Mountains and the Mediterranean Sea.

sa·hib (sä′ĭb *or* sä′ēb *or* sä′hĭb) *n.* Used as a form of address for a man in South Asia, especially in colonial India. [From Arabic *ṣāḥib*, companion, master.]

said (sĕd) *v.* Past tense and past participle of **say.** ❖ *adj.* In legal use, previously named or mentioned: *The said tenant violated the lease.*

Sai·gon (sī-gŏn′) See **Ho Chi Minh City.**

sail (sāl) *n.* **1a.** A piece of fabric attached to the rigging of a vessel and used to catch the wind and cause the vessel to move over water or ice. **b.** The sails of a boat or ship. **2.** A trip in a sailing craft: *We went for a sail on the lake.* **3.** Something that resembles a sail or catches the wind like a sail, as the blade of a windmill. ❖ *v.* **sailed, sail·ing, sails** *—intr.* **1.** To move across the surface of water, especially in a sailing vessel: *The boat sails smoothly.* **2.** To travel by ship or boat: *sail around the world.* **3.** To start out on a voyage across a body of water: *The ship will sail tomorrow.* **4.** To operate a sailing craft: *learn how to sail.* **5.** To move swiftly, smoothly, or effortlessly: *She sailed through the test.* **6.** To move along through the air: *The ball sailed through the air.* *—tr.* **1.** To manage (a sailing vessel). **2.** To voyage upon or across: *sail the Pacific Ocean.* ◆ **sail into** To attack or criticize forcefully. [From Old English *segl.*]

❑ *These sound alike:* **sail, sale** (act of selling).

sail·board (sāl′bôrd′) *n.* A modified surfboard having a sail mounted on a mast that pivots on a ball joint, used in windsurfing. ❖ *intr.v.* **sail·board·ed, sail·board·ing, sail·boards** To ride a sailboard.

sail·boat (sāl′bōt′) *n.* A boat that has a sail or sails, so that it can be propelled by the wind.

sail·cloth (sāl′klôth′) *n.* A strong fabric, such as cotton canvas, suitable for making sails or tents.

sail·fish (sāl′fĭsh′) *n.* Either of two large ocean fishes having a large fin resembling a sail along the back and an upper jaw that projects into a bony pointed snout.

sail·ing (sā′lĭng) *n.* **1.** The activity of operating or riding in a sailing vessel. **2.** The skill required to operate a sailing vessel. **3.** The departure or time of departure of a ship, especially a sailing vessel.

sail·or (sā′lər) *n.* **1.** A person who is a member of a ship's crew or who serves in a navy. **2.** A person who operates a sailboat.

saint (sānt) *n.* **1a.** In certain branches of Christianity, a person who has been officially recognized as being worthy of special reverence. **b.** A person who has died and gone to heaven. **2.** A person who is revered as holy in a non-Christian religious tradition. **3.** A person who is very virtuous. ❖ *tr.v.* **saint·ed, saint·ing, saints** To name, recognize, or venerate as a saint; canonize. [From Middle English *seint*, from Latin *sānctus*, holy.]

Saint Au·gus·tine (sānt′ ô′gə-stēn′) A city of northeast Florida on the Atlantic Ocean south-southeast of Jacksonville. Founded in 1565, it is the oldest permanent European settlement in the United States.

Saint Ber·nard (bər-närd′) *n.* A large strong dog of a breed having a thick brown and white coat, developed by monks of the hospice of Saint Bernard in the Swiss Alps as a watchdog and as a rescue dog for travelers lost in the snow.

Saint Chris·to·pher-Ne·vis (krĭs′tə-fər-nē′vĭs *or* krĭs′tə-fər-nĕv′ĭs) See **Saint Kitts and Nevis.**

Saint Croix (kroi) An island of the US Virgin Islands in the West Indies east of Puerto Rico.

saint·ed (sān′tĭd) *adj.* **1.** Considered a saint; canonized. **2.** Of saintly character; holy.

Saint George's (jôr′jəz) The capital of Grenada, on the southwest coast of the island in the Windward Islands of the West Indies.

Saint He·le·na (hə-lē′nə) A volcanic island in the southern Atlantic Ocean west of Angola. Along with other islands, it forms the British dependency of **Saint Helena.** Jamestown is the capital.

Saint Hel·ens (hĕl′ənz), **Mount** A volcanic peak, 8,365 feet (2,550 meters) high, of the Cascade Range in southwest Washington. On May 18, 1980, a violent eruption reduced its height by about 1,300 feet (400 meters) and covered a large area with mud and ash.

saint·hood (sānt′ho͝od′) *n.* **1.** The status, character, or condition of being a saint. **2.** Saints considered as a group.

Saint John's 1. The capital of Antigua and Barbuda, in the Leeward Islands of the West Indies. **2.** The capital of Newfoundland, Canada, on the eastern coast of the island. Founded in 1583, it was one of the first European settlements in North America.

Saint Kitts and Ne·vis (kĭts; nē′vĭs *or* nĕv′ĭs) also **Saint Chris·to·pher-Ne·vis** (krĭs′tə-fər-nē′vĭs *or* krĭs′tə-fər-nĕv′ĭs) An island country in the Leeward Islands of the West Indies east-southeast of Puerto Rico. Basseterre is the capital.

Saint Law·rence River (lôr′əns) A river of southeast Canada flowing about 740 miles (1,200 kilometers) northeast from Lake Ontario along the Ontario–New York border and through southern Quebec to the **Gulf of Saint Lawrence,** an arm of the northwest Atlantic Ocean. The river forms part of the **Saint Lawrence Seaway,** about 2,350 miles (3,750 kilometers) long, a system of natural and artificial waterways providing passage for oceangoing ships as far west as Lake Superior.

Saint Lou·is (lo͞o′ĭs) The largest city of Missouri, in the eastern part of the state on the Mississippi River. It was founded by French fur traders in 1764.

Saint Lu·cia (lo͞o′shə *or* lo͞o-sē′ə) An island country of the West Indies in the Windward Islands south of Martinique. Castries is the capital.

saint·ly (sānt′lē) *adj.* **saint·li·er, saint·li·est** Relating to, resembling, or befitting a saint or saints. **—saint′li·ness** *n.*

Saint Patrick's Day *n.* March 17, observed by Catholics in honor of Saint Patrick, the patron saint of Ireland, and widely observed as a secular celebration of Irish heritage.

Saint Paul The capital of Minnesota, in the southeast part of the state on the Mississippi River adjacent to Minneapolis.

Saint Pe·ters·burg (pē′tərz-bûrg′) A city of northwest Russia northwest of Moscow. It was the capital of Russia from 1712 to 1918, and from 1924 to 1991 it was known as Leningrad.

Saint Thomas An island of the US Virgin Islands in the West Indies east of Puerto Rico.

Saint Valentine's Day *n.* Valentine's Day.

Saint Vincent and the Gren·a·dines (vĭn′sənt ənd *thə* grĕn′ə-dēnz′) An island country in the central Windward Islands of the West Indies. Kingstown, on the island of **St. Vincent,** is the capital.

saith (sĕth *or* sā′ĭth) *v. Archaic* A third person singular present tense of **say.**

sake[1] (sāk) *n.* **1.** Purpose; motive: *argue just for the sake of arguing.* **2.** Benefit or interest; welfare: *We bought a humidifier for the sake of the baby.* **3.** Good; advantage: *He moved to a drier climate for the sake of his health.* [From Old English *sacu*, lawsuit.]

sa·ke[2] (sä′kē) *n.* A Japanese alcoholic beverage made from fermented rice. [From Japanese *sake.*]

Sa·kha·lin (săk′ə-lēn′ *or* săk′ə-lən) An island of southeast Russia in the Sea of Okhotsk north of Hokkaido, Japan. It passed under Russian control in 1875.

sal (săl) *n.* Salt.

sa·laam (sə-läm′) *n.* **1.** A ceremonious act of deference or obeisance, especially a low bow performed while placing the right palm on the forehead. **2.** A respectful ceremonial greeting performed especially in Islamic countries. ❖ *tr. & intr.v.* **sa·laamed, sa·laam·ing, sa·laams** To greet with or perform a salaam. [From Arabic *salām*, peace, salaam.]

sal·a·ble also **sale·a·ble** (sā′lə-bəl) *adj.* Fit and suitable to sell; capable of attracting buyers. **—sal′a·bil′i·ty** *n.*

sa·la·cious (sə-lā′shəs) *adj.* **1.** Appealing to or stimulating sexual desire: *salacious reading material.* **2.** Expressing sexual desire; lustful: *a salacious wink.*

sal·ad (săl′əd) *n.* **1.** A dish consisting of raw green leafy vegetables, such as lettuce, often tossed with other ingredients and served with a dressing. **2.** The course of a meal consisting of this dish. **3.** A cold dish of chopped fruit, potatoes, eggs, or other food, usually prepared with mayonnaise. **4.** A green vegetable used in salad, especially lettuce. [From Middle English *salade*, from Latin *sāl*, salt.] —SEE NOTE AT **sauce.**

salad bar *n.* A counter in a restaurant from which customers may serve themselves a variety of salad ingredients and dressings.

salad dressing *n.* A sauce, as of mayonnaise or oil and vinegar, that is served on salad.

sal·a·man·der (săl′ə-măn′dər) *n.* **1.** Any of various small amphibians that have a long tail and smooth moist skin. **2.** In mythology, a creature resembling a lizard, believed to be capable of living in or enduring fire. [From Middle English *salamandre*, from Greek *salamandra.*]

sa·la·mi (sə-lä′mē) *n.* A highly spiced and salted sausage of pork or beef or of both these meats.

sal·a·ried (săl′ə-rēd) *adj.* Receiving or paying a salary: *a salaried employee; a salaried position.*

sal·a·ry (săl′ə-rē) *n., pl.* **sal·a·ries** A set sum of money or other compensation paid to a person on a regular basis in return for work or service. [From Middle English *salerie*, from Latin *salārium*, money given to Roman soldiers to buy salt, from *sāl*, salt.]

sale (sāl) *n.* **1.** The act of selling; an exchange of goods or services for money or other compensation. **2.** An instance of selling. **3.** An occasion when goods or services are offered for purchase at reduced prices: *a half-price sale at the store.* **4. sales a.** The business of advertising and selling goods or services. **b.** The amount of goods sold or of money brought in by selling goods. ◆ **for sale** Available in exchange for money: *Is that house for sale?* **on sale** For sale at a temporarily reduced price: *Swordfish is on sale this week at the supermarket.*

❑ *These sound alike:* **sale, sail** (fabric used to catch wind).

sale·a·ble (sā′lə-bəl) *adj.* Variant of **salable.**

Sa·lem (sā′ləm) **1.** A city of northeast Massachusetts northeast of Boston. Founded in 1626, it is noted as the site of witchcraft trials (1692). **2.** The capital of Oregon, in the northwest part of the state south-southwest of Portland. It was founded in about 1840 and became the state capital in 1859.

sales·clerk (sālz′klûrk′) *n.* A person who is employed to sell goods in a store.

sales·man (sālz′mən) *n.* A man who is employed to sell goods or services.

sales·man·ship (sālz′mən-shĭp′) *n.* Skill, ability, or persuasiveness in selling.

sales·per·son (sālz′pûr′sən) *n.* A salesman or saleswoman.

sales tax (sālz) *n.* A tax on the sale of goods, representing a fixed percentage of the purchase price and usually collected by the seller.

sales·wom·an (sālz′wo͝om′ən) *n.* A woman who is employed to sell goods or services.

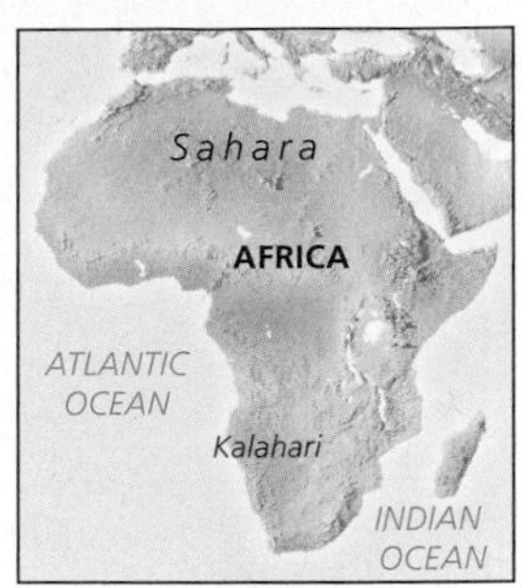

Sahara

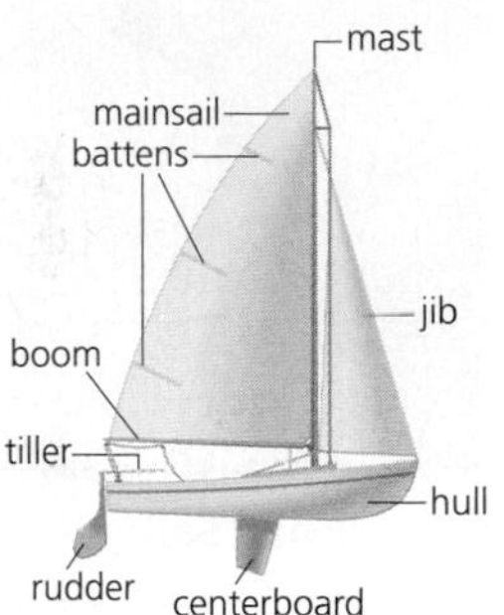

sailboat

salamander

sal·i·cyl·ic acid (săl′ĭ-sĭl′ĭk) *n.* A white, crystalline acid used to make aspirin, to treat certain skin conditions, and to preserve and flavor foods.

sa·li·ent (sā′lē-ənt *or* sāl′yənt) *adj.* **1.** Standing out and attracting attention; striking or conspicuous: *the salient points of a plan.* **2.** Projecting or jutting beyond a line or surface; protruding. ❖ *n.* **1.** The area of military defense, as a battle line, that projects closest to the enemy. **2.** A projecting angle or part. [From Latin *saliēns*, leaping, from Latin *salīre*, to leap.]

sa·line (sā′lēn′ *or* sā′līn′) *adj.* Relating to or containing salt; salty. ❖ *n.* A saline solution, especially one used in medicine and surgery. **—sa·lin′i·ty** (sə-lĭn′ĭ-tē) *n.*

Sa·lish (sā′lĭsh) *n.* **1.** A family of Native American languages of the northwest United States and British Columbia. **2.** The group of Native American peoples speaking languages of this family. **3.** The Flathead people. **—Sa′lish·an** *adj.*

sa·li·va (sə-lī′və) *n.* The watery fluid that is secreted into the mouth by the salivary glands, serving to moisten food as it is chewed and to begin the digestion of starches.

sal·i·var·y (săl′ə-vĕr′ē) *adj.* Relating to or producing saliva.

salivary gland *n.* A gland that secretes saliva, especially one of three pairs of large glands that secrete saliva into the mouth.

sal·i·vate (săl′ə-vāt′) *intr.v.* **sal·i·vat·ed, sal·i·vat·ing, sal·i·vates** To produce or secrete saliva. **—sal′i·va′tion** *n.*

Jonas Salk

Salk (sôlk), **Jonas Edward** 1914–1995. American microbiologist who developed the first effective vaccine against polio, introduced publicly in 1955.

sal·low (săl′ō) *adj.* **sal·low·er, sal·low·est** Of a sickly yellowish color or complexion.

sal·ly (săl′ē) *intr.v.* **sal·lied, sal·ly·ing, sal·lies 1.** To rush forth or leap out suddenly. **2.** To charge at and attack an enemy from a defensive position. **3.** To set out for a destination in a spirited energetic way: *I sallied forth to seek my fortune.* ❖ *n., pl.* **sal·lies 1.** A sudden rush forward; a leap. **2.** An attack from a defensive position. **3.** A quick, clever, or witty remark; a quip. **4.** A short trip or outing; a jaunt. [From Latin *salīre*, to leap.]

salm·on (săm′ən) *n., pl.* **salmon** or **salm·ons 1.** Any of various large food fishes of northern waters, having pinkish flesh and swimming from salt to fresh water to spawn. **2.** A yellowish-pink or pinkish-orange color. [From Middle English *samoun*, from Latin *salmō*.]

salsa

sal·mo·nel·la (săl′mə-nĕl′ə) *n., pl.* **sal·mo·nel·lae** (săl′mə-nĕl′ē) or **sal·mo·nel·las** or **salmonella** Any of various bacteria that cause food poisoning in humans. [After Daniel Elmer *Salmon* (1850–1914), American pathologist.]

sa·lon (sə-lŏn′ *or* săl′ŏn′) *n.* **1.** A large room for receiving and entertaining guests. **2.** A regular gathering of prominent people such as artists, writers, or politicians. **3a.** A hall or gallery in which works of art are exhibited. **b.** A public exhibition of artworks, usually by a large number of artists. **4.** A business offering a product or service related to fashion: *a beauty salon.*

sa·loon (sə-lo͞on′) *n.* **1.** A place where alcoholic drinks are sold and drunk; a bar or tavern. **2.** A large room or hall for receptions, entertainment, or exhibitions.

sal·sa (säl′sə) *n.* **1.** A spicy sauce of chopped, usually uncooked vegetables or fruit, especially tomatoes, onions, and chili peppers. **2a.** A popular form of Latin-American dance music, characterized by Cuban melodies and elements of jazz and rock. **b.** The dance that is performed to this music. —SEE NOTE AT **sauce.**

sal soda *n.* Sodium carbonate when used as a cleanser.

salt (sôlt) *n.* **1.** A colorless or white crystalline solid, chiefly sodium chloride, widely used in ground form as a food seasoning and preservative. **2.** Any of a large class of chemical compounds formed when one or more hydrogen ions of an acid are replaced by metallic ions. **3.** Something that is like salt in adding flavor or zest to something. **4.** *Informal* A sailor. ❖ *adj.* **1.** Containing or filled with salt: *a salt mine.* **2.** Having the taste or smell of salt. **3.** Preserved in salt or brine: *salt pork.* ❖ *tr.v.* **salt·ed, salt·ing, salts 1.** To season or sprinkle with salt: *Salt the stew.* **2.** To preserve (meat or fish, for example) by treating with salt. **3.** To add zest or liveliness to: *salt a lecture with jokes.* ◆ **salt away** To put aside; save. **worth (one's) salt** Efficient and capable. [From Old English *sealt*.]

salt·cel·lar (sôlt′sĕl′ər) *n.* A small dish for holding and dispensing salt.

sal·tine (sôl-tēn′) *n.* A thin crisp cracker sprinkled with salt.

Salt Lake City The capital of Utah, in the north-central part of the state near Great Salt Lake. It is the center of the Mormon Church.

salt lick *n.* A natural deposit or block of salt that animals lick.

salt·pe·ter (sôlt′pē′tər) *n.* Potassium nitrate.

salt·shak·er (sôlt′shā′kər) *n.* A container with small holes in the top for holding and sprinkling salt.

salt·wa·ter or **salt-wa·ter** (sôlt′wô′tər) *adj.* **1.** Relating to or consisting of water that contains dissolved salt: *a saltwater solution.* **2.** Living in the sea or in salt water: *saltwater fish.*

salt·y (sôl′tē) *adj.* **salt·i·er, salt·i·est 1.** Containing or seasoned with salt: *salty food.* **2.** Suggestive of the sea or sailing life. **3.** Coarse or racy: *salty humor.* **—salt′i·ness** *n.*

sa·lu·bri·ous (sə-lo͞o′brē-əs) *adj.* Good for the health; wholesome. **—sa·lu′bri·ous·ly** *adv.*

sal·u·tar·y (săl′yə-tĕr′ē) *adj.* **1.** Helpful; beneficial: *salutary advice.* **2.** Good for the health: *a salutary climate.*

sal·u·ta·tion (săl′yə-tā′shən) *n.* **1.** An expression or gesture of greeting or respect. **2.** A word or phrase of greeting used to begin a letter or message. *Dear Sir or Madam* is a salutation.

sa·lu·ta·to·ri·an (sə-lo͞o′tə-tôr′ē-ən) *n.* In some schools and colleges, the student with the second highest academic rank, who gives the opening address at graduation.

sa·lu·ta·to·ry (sə-lo͞o′tə-tôr′ē) *n., pl.* **sa·lu·ta·to·ries** An opening address, especially one delivered at graduation exercises by a salutatorian. ❖ *adj.* Having to do with or expressing a greeting or welcome.

sa·lute (sə-lo͞ot′) *n.* **1.** A gesture made as a sign of respect toward an officer or other person in the military, especially by raising the hand to the cap. **2.** A gesture of greeting or recognizing someone, such as a bow or wave: *The winning runner raised her hands as a salute to the people cheering in the stands.* **3.** An act, gesture, or display of respect: *a twenty-one gun salute.* ❖ *v.* **sa·lut·ed, sa·lut·ing, sa·lutes** —*intr.* To make a salute: *The soldiers saluted as the officers walked past.* —*tr.* To make a salute toward or out of respect for (someone): *Each crew member saluted the captain when coming on board.* [From Middle English *salut*, ultimately from Latin *salūs*, health, safety.]

Sal·va·dor (săl′və-dôr′) A city of eastern Brazil on the Atlantic Ocean north-northeast of Rio de Janeiro. It was the capital of the Portuguese possessions in the New World from 1549 until 1763.

Sal·va·do·ran (săl′və-dôr′ən) or **Sal·va·do·ri·an** (săl-və-dôr′ē-ən) *adj.* Relating to El Salvador or its people or culture. ❖ *n.* A native or inhabitant of El Salvador.

sal·vage (săl′vĭj) *n.* **1.** The rescue of a ship or its cargo from fire or shipwreck. **2.** The act of saving endangered property from loss. **3.** Goods or property saved from

ă	pat	ôr	core
ā	pay	oi	boy
âr	care	ou	out
ä	father	o͝o	took
ĕ	pet	o͝or	lure
ē	be	o͞o	boot
ĭ	pit	ŭ	cut
ī	bite	ûr	urge
îr	pier	th	thin
ŏ	pot	*th*	this
ō	toe	zh	vision
ô	paw	ə	about

destruction or disaster. ❖ *tr.v.* **sal·vaged, sal·vag·ing, sal·vag·es 1.** To save from loss or ruin. **2.** To save (discarded or damaged material) for further use. **—sal′vage·a·ble** *adj.* **—sal′vag·er** *n.*

sal·va·tion (săl-vā′shən) *n.* **1.** Preservation or deliverance from destruction, difficulty, or evil. **2.** In Christianity, the saving of the soul from sin and punishment; redemption. **3.** A person or thing that saves, rescues, or preserves: *The emergency supplies were our salvation during the hurricane.*

salve (săv *or* säv) *n.* **1.** A soothing ointment applied to wounds, burns, or sores to heal them or relieve pain. **2.** Something that soothes or heals; a balm. ❖ *tr.v.* **salved, salv·ing, salves 1.** To soothe or heal with salve. **2.** To ease or assuage: *Your praise salved their hurt feelings.*

sal·ver (săl′vər) *n.* A serving tray.

sal·vo (săl′vō) *n., pl.* **sal·vos** or **sal·voes 1a.** A simultaneous firing of weapons. **b.** The simultaneous release of a number of bombs from an aircraft. **c.** The projectiles or bombs so released. **2.** A sudden outburst, as of cheers or applause.

sal·war (săl′vär′) *n.* Loose pajamalike pants, typically having a drawstring waist and legs that narrow at the bottom, worn chiefly in South Asia. [Ultimately from Persian *šalvār*, trousers.]

Sa·mar·i·tan (sə-măr′ĭ-tn) *n.* **1.** A member of a people inhabiting Israel and the West Bank who trace their ancestry to the ancient Israelites and practice a religion related to Judaism. **2.** often **samaritan** A Good Samaritan.

sa·mar·i·um (sə-mâr′ē-əm) *n. Symbol* **Sm** A silvery or gray metallic element used to absorb neutrons in nuclear reactors. Atomic number 62. See **Periodic Table.** [After Colonel M. von *Samarski*, Russian mining official of the 1800s.]

same (sām) *adj.* **1.** Being the very one; identical: *This is the same seat I had yesterday.* **2.** Similar in kind, quality, quantity, or degree: *These books are the same size.* **3.** Being the one previously mentioned. ❖ *adv.* In the same way: *The words "sail" and "sale" are pronounced the same.* ❖ *pron.* **1.** A person or thing identical with another. **2.** A person or thing previously mentioned or described: *"Is she the one you mean?" "The same."* [From Middle English, from Old Norse *samr.*]

same·ness (sām′nĭs) *n.* **1.** The condition of being the same. **2.** A lack of variety or change; monotony.

same-sex (sām′sĕks′) *adj.* Involving or restricted to members of the same sex: *same-sex schools.*

Sa·mi (sä′mē) *n., pl.* **Sami** or **Sa·mis 1.** A member of a traditionally nomadic people living in Lapland. **2.** Any of the languages of the Sami.

Sa·mo·a (sə-mō′ə) **1.** An island group of the southern Pacific Ocean northeast of Fiji, divided between the independent nation of Samoa and the US territory of American Samoa. The islands were originally populated by Polynesians perhaps as early as 1000 BC. **2.** The independent nation constituting the western portion of the island group of Samoa. It was formerly known as Western Samoa. Apia is the capital.

Sa·mo·an (sə-mō′ən) *adj.* Relating to Samoa or its people, language, or culture. ❖ *n.* **1.** A native or inhabitant of Samoa. **2.** The Polynesian language of Samoa.

sam·o·var (săm′ə-vär′) *n.* A metal urn with a spigot, used chiefly in Russia to boil water for tea.

sam·pan (săm′păn′) *n.* A small flatbottom boat used in Asia and usually propelled by two oars.

sam·ple (săm′pəl) *n.* **1.** A part, piece, amount, or selection that is considered representative of the whole: *Could I have a sample of that fabric?* **2.** A usually short segment taken from an original recording and inserted, often repetitively, in a new recording. ❖ *tr.v.* **sam·pled, sam·pling, sam·ples 1.** To take a sample of, especially to test or examine. **2.** To use or incorporate (a part of a sound recording) in another recording. [From Middle English *saumpel*, from Latin *exemplum*, example.]

sam·pler (săm′plər) *n.* **1.** A representative selection of something: *a sampler of chocolate candies.* **2.** A piece of cloth embroidered with various designs or mottoes that serves to display fancy stitching or needlework. **3.** An electronic device that digitally records, stores, and manipulates sounds for later use in musical recordings. **4.** A person who is employed to take samples.

Samp·son (sămp′sən), **Deborah** 1760–1827. American Revolutionary soldier who fought disguised as a man (1782–1783) and was wounded twice. She was granted a full veteran's pension in 1818.

Sam·son (săm′sən) In the Bible, an Israelite judge and warrior who was betrayed to the Philistines by Delilah after she cut off his hair, the source of his strength.

Sam·u·el[1] (săm′yo͞o-əl) A Hebrew judge and prophet of the 11th century BC who anointed Saul, and later David, as king of Israel.

Sam·u·el[2] (săm′yo͞o-əl) *n.* Either of two books of the Bible that give a history of the prophet Samuel and describe the reigns of Saul and David.

sam·u·rai (săm′ə-rī′) *n., pl.* **samurai** or **sam·u·rais** A professional warrior belonging to the military aristocracy of feudal Japan. [From Japanese *warrior*, from Old Japanese *morafi*, to watch.]

San (sän) *n., pl.* **San** or **Sans 1.** A member of a traditionally nomadic hunting people of southwest Africa. **2.** Any of the languages of the San.

Sa·n'a or **Sa·na** (sä-nä′) The capital of Yemen, in the western part of the country.

San An·to·ni·o (săn ăn-tō′nē-ō′) A city of south-central Texas southwest of Austin. It was founded as a Franciscan mission in 1718.

san·a·to·ri·um (săn′ə-tôr′ē-əm) *n., pl.* **san·a·to·ri·ums** or **san·a·to·ri·a** (săn′ə-tôr′ē-ə) **1.** An institution for the treatment of chronic diseases. **2.** A health resort, especially for convalescents; a sanitarium.

sanc·ta (săngk′tə) *n.* A plural of **sanctum.**

sanc·ti·fy (săngk′tə-fī′) *tr.v.* **sanc·ti·fied, sanc·ti·fy·ing, sanc·ti·fies 1.** To make holy or sacred; purify. **2.** To give religious sanction to: *sanctify a marriage.* **3.** To set apart for sacred use.

sanc·ti·mo·ni·ous (săngk′tə-mō′nē-əs) *adj.* Having or showing an attitude of smug or hypocritical righteousness. **—sanc′ti·mo′ni·ous·ly** *adv.*

sanc·tion (săngk′shən) *n.* **1.** Authoritative permission or approval. **2.** An action taken usually by several nations acting together against a nation especially for breaking international law. ❖ *tr.v.* **sanc·tioned, sanc·tion·ing, sanc·tions 1.** To give official approval to; authorize. **2.** To penalize, especially for violating a moral principle or international law.

sanc·ti·ty (săngk′tĭ-tē) *n., pl.* **sanc·ti·ties 1.** Holiness of life; saintliness. **2.** The quality or condition of being considered holy or sacred; sacredness.

sanc·tu·ar·y (săngk′cho͞o-ĕr′ē) *n., pl.* **sanc·tu·ar·ies 1.** The holiest part of a sacred place, such as a church, temple, or mosque. **2.** A place of refuge, asylum, or protection. **3.** Immunity to arrest; asylum or protection: *They asked for sanctuary.* **4.** A reserved area in which wildlife is protected by law: *a bird sanctuary.*

sanc·tum (săngk′təm) *n., pl.* **sanc·tums** or **sanc·ta** (săngk′tə) **1.** A private place where one is free from intrusion. **2.** A sacred or holy place.

sand (sănd) *n.* **1.** Tiny particles of disintegrated rock. Sand particles are usually categorized as larger than particles of silt but smaller than gravel. **2.** often **sands** Land, such as a beach or desert, covered with this material: *crossing the desert sands.* ❖ *tr.v.* **sand·ed, sand·ing, sands 1.** To sprinkle or cover with sand: *sanded the icy*

samovar

Deborah Sampson

Carl Sandburg

sand dollar

sandpiper

ă	pat	ôr	core
ā	pay	oi	boy
âr	care	ou	out
ä	father	o͝o	took
ĕ	pet	o͝or	lure
ē	be	o͞o	boot
ĭ	pit	ŭ	cut
ī	bite	ûr	urge
îr	pier	th	thin
ŏ	pot	*th*	this
ō	toe	zh	vision
ô	paw	ə	about

sidewalk. **2.** To scrape or rub with sand or sandpaper: *sanded the board before painting it.* [From Old English.]

san·dal (săn′dl) *n.* A shoe consisting of a sole with usually leather straps that fasten it to the foot. [From Middle English, from Greek *sandalon.*]

san·dal·wood (săn′dl-wo͝od′) *n.* **1.** The aromatic wood of any of several tropical trees, used for carving decorative objects and for making perfume. **2.** Any of the trees that yield such wood.

sand·bag (sănd′băg′) *n.* A bag or sack filled with sand, often used to form protective walls.

sand·bank (sănd′băngk′) *n.* A mass of sand that forms a hillside or mound.

sand·bar (sănd′bär′) *n.* A ridge of sand formed in a river or in the water along a shore by the action of waves or currents.

sand·blast (sănd′blăst′) *tr.v.* **sand·blast·ed, sand·blast·ing, sand·blasts** To clean or etch (a glass, stone, or metal surface, for example) by means of a blast of air or steam carrying sand at high velocity. **—sand′-blast′er** *n.*

sand·box (sănd′bŏks′) *n.* A low box filled with sand for children to play in.

Sand·burg (sănd′bûrg′ *or* săn′bûrg′), **Carl** 1878–1967. American writer known for his poems celebrating American people, geography, and industry.

sand dollar *n.* A thin, flat, circular sea animal having a hard internal skeleton and living along sandy shores.

sand·er (săn′dər) *n.* **1.** A machine with a disk or belt of sandpaper, used for smoothing, polishing, or refinishing: *a floor sander.* **2.** A device, usually attached to a truck, that spreads sand on roads.

San Di·e·go (săn dē-ā′gō) A city of southern California on an inlet of the Pacific Ocean near the Mexican border.

sand·lot (sănd′lŏt′) *n.* A vacant lot used especially by children for unorganized sports and games.

sand·man (sănd′măn′) *n.* A character in fairy tales and folklore who makes children sleep by sprinkling sand in their eyes.

sand·pa·per (sănd′pā′pər) *n.* Heavy paper coated on one side with sand or other abrasive material and used for smoothing surfaces. ❖ *tr.v.* **sand·pa·pered, sand·pa·per·ing, sand·pa·pers** To rub with sandpaper.

sand·pi·per (sănd′pī′pər) *n.* Any of various small shorebirds having a slender pointed bill.

sand·stone (sănd′stōn′) *n.* A sedimentary rock formed from sand that has been compacted by pressure and is held together by a natural cement, such as silica.

sand·storm (sănd′stôrm′) *n.* A strong wind carrying clouds of sand and dust through the air.

sand·wich (sănd′wĭch *or* săn′wĭch) *n.* **1.** Two or more slices of bread with a filling, such as meat or cheese, placed between them. **2.** One slice of bread covered with a filling: *an open-faced sandwich.* **3.** Something that resembles a sandwich. ❖ *tr.v.* **sand·wiched, sand·wich·ing, sand·wich·es 1.** To make into a sandwich. **2.** To insert (one thing) between two other things tightly. **3.** To make room or time for: *sandwiched a meeting into the busy schedule.* [After John Montagu, Fourth Earl of *Sandwich* (1718–1792), British politician.]

sand·y (săn′dē) *adj.* **sand·i·er, sand·i·est 1.** Covered with, full of, or consisting of sand. **2.** Of the color of sand; light yellowish brown. **—sand′i·ness** *n.*

sane (sān) *adj.* **san·er, san·est 1.** Of sound mind; mentally healthy: *a sane person.* **2.** Having or showing good judgment; reasonable: *a sane approach to the problem.* [From Latin *sānus,* healthy.] **—sane′ly** *adv.* **—sane′-ness** *n.*

❑ *These sound alike:* **sane, seine** (fishing net).

San Fran·cis·co (săn frən-sĭs′kō) A city of northern California on a peninsula between the Pacific Ocean and **San Francisco Bay,** an inlet of the Pacific. A Spanish fortress and mission were founded here in 1776.

sang (săng) *v.* A past tense of **sing.**

san·gui·nar·y (săng′gwə-nĕr′ē) *adj.* **1.** Accompanied by bloodshed. **2.** Eager for bloodshed; bloodthirsty. **3.** Consisting of blood.

san·guine (săng′gwĭn) *adj.* **1.** Eagerly optimistic; cheerful. **2a.** Of the color of blood; red. **b.** Of a healthy reddish color; ruddy: *a sanguine complexion.* [From Middle English, from Latin *sanguineus,* from *sanguis,* blood.] **—san′guine·ly** *adv.* **—san·guin′i·ty** *n.*

san·i·tar·i·um (săn′ĭ-târ′ē-əm) *n., pl.* **san·i·tar·i·ums** or **san·i·tar·i·a** (săn′ĭ-târ′ē-ə) A sanatorium.

san·i·tar·y (săn′ĭ-tĕr′ē) *adj.* **1.** Relating to health or the protection of health. **2.** Free of germs; hygienic. [From French *sanitaire,* from Latin *sānitās,* health.] **—san′i·tar′i·ly** (săn′ĭ-târ′ə-lē) *adv.*

sanitary napkin *n.* A disposable pad of absorbent material worn to absorb menstrual flow.

san·i·ta·tion (săn′ĭ-tā′shən) *n.* **1.** The study and application of procedures and regulations that are meant to protect public health. **2.** The disposal of sewage and wastes.

san·i·tize (săn′ĭ-tīz′) *tr.v.* **san·i·tized, san·i·tiz·ing, san·i·tiz·es 1.** To make sanitary, as by cleaning. **2.** To make more acceptable by removing unpleasant or offensive features from: *a movie that was sanitized for television.*

san·i·ty (săn′ĭ-tē) *n.* **1.** Soundness of mind; good mental health. **2.** The ability to make sound or reasonable judgments.

San Jo·se (săn hō-zā′) A city of northern California southeast of San Francisco. It was founded in 1777.

San Jo·sé (sän′ hō-sĕ′) The capital of Costa Rica, in the central part of the country. It was founded in about 1736 and became the capital in 1823.

San Juan (săn **wän′** *or* sän **hwän′**) The capital of Puerto Rico, in the northeast part of the island on the Atlantic Ocean. It was founded in 1508.

sank (săngk) *v.* A past tense of **sink.**

San Ma·ri·no (săn mə-**rē′**nō) A country in the Apennines near the Adriatic Sea. It is surrounded by Italy and is the world's smallest republic. The city of **San Marino** is its capital.

sans (sănz) *prep.* Without.

San Sal·va·dor (săn **săl′**və-dôr′ *or* sän säl′vä-**dôr′**) **1.** An island of the central Bahamas in the West Indies. It is believed to be the first place in the New World visited by Christopher Columbus (October 12, 1492). **2.** The capital of El Salvador, in the west-central part of the country. It was founded in the 1500s.

San·skrit (săn′skrĭt′) *n.* An ancient Indo-European language that is the language of Hinduism and the classical literary language of India.

San·ta An·na (săn′tə ăn′ə *or* sän′tä ä′nä), **Antonio López de** 1794–1876. Mexican military and political leader who was victorious at the Alamo (1836) but was soon after defeated and captured by the Texans.

San·ta Claus (săn′tə klôz′) *n.* The personification of the spirit of Christmas, usually represented as a jolly fat old man with a white beard and red suit, who brings gifts to children on Christmas Eve. [From Middle Dutch *Sinterclaes,* St. Nicholas.]

San·ta Fe (săn′tə fā′) The capital of New Mexico, in the north-central part of the state northeast of Albuquerque. A Spanish settlement was built here in about 1609 on the site of ancient Native American ruins.

San·tee (săn-tē′) *n., pl.* **Santee** or **San·tees** A member of the eastern branch of the Sioux peoples.

San·ti·a·go (săn′tē-ä′gō *or* sän′tē-ä′gō) The capital of Chile, in the central part of the country. It was founded in 1541.

San·to Do·min·go (săn′tō də-**mĭng′**gō *or* sän′tō dō-**mĭng′**gō) The capital of the Dominican Republic, in the southeast part of the island of Hispaniola on the Caribbean Sea. It was founded in 1496.

São Pau·lo (souN **pou′**lō *or* souN **pou′**lo͞o) A city of southeast Brazil west-southwest of Rio de Janeiro. Founded in 1554, it is now the largest city in South America.

São To·mé (tə-**mā′**) The capital of São Tomé and Príncipe, on the northeast coast of **São Tomé,** the larger of the country's two main islands.

São Tomé and Prín·ci·pe (**prĭn′**sə-pə) An island country in the Gulf of Guinea off western Africa. São Tomé is the capital.

sap[1] (săp) *n.* **1.** The watery fluid that circulates through a plant, carrying food in the form of sugars to all parts of the plant. **2.** *Slang* A foolish person; a dupe. ❖ *tr.v.* **sapped, sap·ping, saps** To deplete or weaken: *The illness sapped him of his strength.* [From Old English *sæp.*]

sap[2] (săp) *n.* A covered trench or tunnel dug to a point near or within an enemy position. ❖ *tr.v.* **sapped, sap·ping, saps** To undermine the foundations of (a structure). [From Late Latin *sappa,* hoe.]

sa·pi·ent (**sā′**pē-ənt) *adj.* Having great wisdom and insight. **—sa′pi·ence** *n.* **—sa′pi·ent·ly** *adv.*

sap·ling (**săp′**lĭng) *n.* A young tree.

sap·o·dil·la (săp′ə-**dĭl′**ə) *n.* A tropical American tree whose milky sap is the source of chicle, formerly the main ingredient in chewing gum.

sa·pon·i·fi·ca·tion (sə-pŏn′ə-fĭ-**kā′**shən) *n.* The hydrolysis of an ester by an alkali, producing a free alcohol and an organic salt, especially alkaline hydrolysis of fats to make soap.

sa·pon·i·fy (sə-**pŏn′**ə-fī′) *v.* **sa·pon·i·fied, sa·pon·i·fy·ing, sa·pon·i·fies** *—tr.* **1.** To convert (an ester) by saponification. **2.** To convert (fats) into soap. *—intr.* To undergo saponification. **—sa·pon′i·fi′er** *n.*

sap·phire (**săf′**īr′) *n.* **1.** Any of several fairly pure forms of corundum, especially a blue form valued as a gem. **2.** A gem of this type. **3.** The blue color of the gem sapphire.

Sap·pho (**săf′**ō) Flourished about 600 BC. Greek poet whose work, noted for its passionate celebration of the beauty of young women and men, survives only in fragments.

sap·py (**săp′**ē) *adj.* **sap·pi·er, sap·pi·est 1.** Very sentimental: *a sappy book.* **2.** Full of sap.

sap·ro·phyte (**săp′**rə-fīt′) *n.* An organism, such as a mushroom or other fungus, that lives on and gets its nourishment from decaying organic material. **—sap′ro·phyt′ic** (săp′rə-**fĭt′**ĭk) *adj.*

sap·suck·er (**săp′**sŭk′ər) *n.* Any of various woodpeckers of North and Central America that drill holes into trees to feed on sap.

sap·wood (**săp′**wo͝od′) *n.* The outer, newly formed, usually light-colored wood of a tree, through which the sap flows.

Sar·a·cen (**săr′**ə-sən) *n.* A Muslim, especially a Muslim Arab of the time of the Crusades.

Sar·ah (**sâr′**ə) In the Bible, the wife of Abraham and mother of Isaac.

Sa·ra·je·vo (săr′ə-**yā′**vō) The capital of Bosnia and Herzegovina, in the south-central part southeast of Zagreb, Croatia.

sa·ran (sə-**răn′**) *n.* Any of various plastic resins derived from vinyl compounds and used in making transparent packaging films, bristles, pipes, and fittings, and as a textile fiber.

sar·casm (**sär′**kăz′əm) *n.* **1.** A sharply mocking, often ironic remark intended to wound. **2.** The use of such remarks.

sar·cas·tic (sär-**kăs′**tĭk) *adj.* **1.** Characterized by or expressing sarcasm: *a sarcastic remark.* **2.** Given to using sarcasm: *a sarcastic person.* **—sar·cas′ti·cal·ly** *adv.*

sar·co·ma (sär-**kō′**mə) *n., pl.* **sar·co·mas** also **sar·co·ma·ta** (sär-**kō′**mə-tə) A malignant tumor arising from connective tissue.

sar·coph·a·gus (sär-**kŏf′**ə-gəs) *n., pl.* **sar·coph·a·gi** (sär-**kŏf′**ə-jī′) or **sar·coph·a·gus·es** A stone coffin, often inscribed or ornamented with sculpture.

sar·dine (sär-**dēn′**) *n.* Any of various small herrings or similar small fishes, often canned for use as food.

Sar·din·i·a (sär-**dĭn′**ē-ə) An island of Italy in the Mediterranean Sea south of Corsica. It was settled by Phoenicians, Greeks, and Carthaginians before the sixth century BC.

sar·don·ic (sär-**dŏn′**ĭk) *adj.* Scornfully or cynically mocking; sarcastic. **—sar·don′i·cal·ly** *adv.*

Sar·gas·so Sea (sär-**găs′**ō) A part of the northern Atlantic Ocean between the West Indies and the Azores, noted for the abundance of seaweed floating on its surface.

sa·ri (**sä′**rē) *n., pl.* **sa·ris** An outer garment worn chiefly by women of India and Pakistan, consisting of a length of cloth with one end wrapped about the waist to form a long skirt and the other end draped over the shoulder. [From Hindi *sāṛī,* from Sanskrit *śaṭī.*]

Sar·ko·zy (sär-kō-**zē′**), **Nicolas** Born 1955. French politician who served as president from 2007 to 2012.

sa·rong (sə-**rông′**) *n.* A garment of brightly colored cloth worn wrapped around the waist by men and women in Malaysia, Indonesia, and the Pacific islands.

SARS (särz) *n.* Pneumonia that is caused by a virus and can lead to respiratory failure. [From *s(evere) a(cute) r(espiratory) s(yndrome).*]

sar·sa·pa·ril·la (săs′pə-**rĭl′**ə *or* särs′pə-**rĭl′**ə) *n.* **1.** Any of several tropical American plants having fragrant roots that are dried and used as a flavoring. **2.** A soft drink with natural or artificial sarsaparilla flavor.

sar·to·ri·al (sär-**tôr′**ē-əl) *adj.* Relating to a tailor, tailoring, or tailored clothing. **—sar·to′ri·al·ly** *adv.*

SASE *abbr.* An abbreviation of self-addressed stamped envelope.

sash[1] (săsh) *n.* A band or ribbon worn around the waist as part of one's clothing or over the shoulder as an ornament or symbol of rank. [From Arabic *šāš,* muslin.]

sash[2] (săsh) *n.* A frame in which the panes of a window or door are set. [Alteration of French *châssis,* frame, chassis.]

sa·shay (să-**shā′**) *intr.v.* **sa·shayed, sa·shay·ing, sa·shays** *Informal* **1.** To move or walk in an easy or casual manner. **2.** To strut or flounce in a showy manner.

❑ *These sound alike:* **sashay, sachet** (perfumed bag).

sa·shi·mi (sä-**shē′**mē) *n.* A Japanese dish consisting of thin slices of fresh raw fish.

Sas·katch·e·wan (să-**skăch′**ə-wän′) A province of south-central Canada west of Manitoba. It joined the Canadian confederation in 1905. Regina is the capital.

sass (săs) *Informal n.* Impertinent disrespectful speech; back talk. ❖ *tr.v.* **sassed, sass·ing, sass·es** To talk disrespectfully to.

sas·sa·fras (**săs′**ə-frăs′) *n.* **1.** A North American tree having irregularly shaped leaves and aromatic bark, roots, and leaves. **2.** The dried root bark of this tree, formerly used as a flavoring and in medicine.

sas·sy (**săs′**ē) *adj.* **sas·si·er, sas·si·est 1.** Rude and disrespectful; impudent. **2.** Lively and spirited; jaunty: *a sassy song.* **—sas′si·ly** *adv.*

sat (săt) *v.* Past tense and past participle of **sit.**

Sa·tan (**sāt′**n) *n.* In Jewish, Christian, and Muslim belief, a powerful spiritual being who tempts or persecutes humanity.

sandstorm
sandstorm approaching Teseney, Eritrea

Antonio López de Santa Anna

Sappho

sari

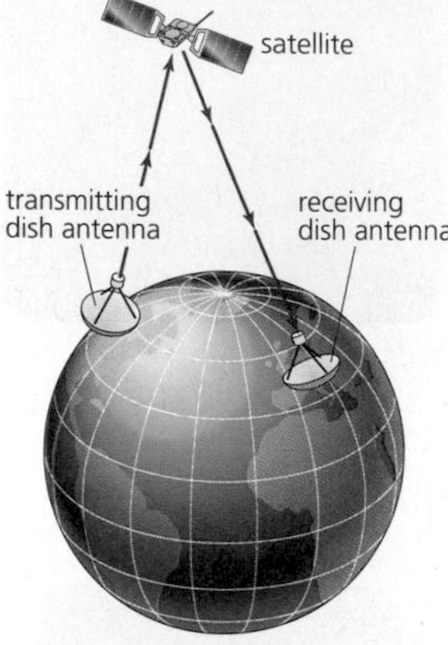

satellite
Some satellites relay information, such as television signals, between transmitting and receiving stations.

Saturn

ă	pat	ôr	core
ā	pay	oi	boy
âr	care	ou	out
ä	father	o͝o	took
ĕ	pet	o͝or	lure
ē	be	o͞o	boot
ĭ	pit	ŭ	cut
ī	bite	ûr	urge
îr	pier	th	thin
ŏ	pot	*th*	this
ō	toe	zh	vision
ô	paw	ə	about

sa·tan·ic (sə-tăn**′**ĭk *or* sā-tăn**′**ĭk) *adj.* **1.** Relating to Satan or evil. **2.** Extremely cruel or evil.

satch·el (săch**′**əl) *n.* A small bag, often having a shoulder strap, used for carrying books, clothing, and other small items.

sate (sāt) *tr.v.* **sat·ed, sat·ing, sates 1.** To satisfy (an appetite) fully. **2.** To provide (someone) with more than enough; glut.

sa·teen (să-tēn**′**) *n.* A cotton fabric with a satiny finish.

sat·el·lite (săt**′**l-īt**′**) *n.* **1.** Any of various objects launched to orbit Earth or another celestial object. **2.** A celestial object that travels in an orbit around a planet; a moon. **3.** A small unit in a system or organization that is managed or controlled by a larger, often centrally located unit.

satellite dish *n.* A dish-shaped antenna that receives or transmits satellite signals.

sa·ti·ate (sā**′**shē-āt**′**) *tr.v.* **sa·ti·at·ed, sa·ti·at·ing, sa·ti·ates 1.** To satisfy (an appetite or desire) fully; sate. **2.** To satisfy to excess.

sat·in (săt**′**n) *n.* A smooth fabric, as of silk, woven with a glossy finish on one side. ❖ *adj.* **1.** Made of or covered with satin. **2.** Glossy and smooth.

sat·in·y (săt**′**n-ē) *adj.* Smooth and glossy like satin.

sat·ire (săt**′**īr**′**) *n.* **1.** A literary work in which vice and foolishness are attacked through humor or irony. **2.** The use of humor or irony to attack or expose vice or foolishness. [From Latin *satira.*]

sa·tir·i·cal (sə-tĭr**′**ĭ-kəl) or **sa·tir·ic** (sə-tĭr**′**ĭk) *adj.* Relating to or characterized by satire: *a satirical essay.* **—sa·tir′i·cal·ly** *adv.*

sat·i·rist (săt**′**ər-ĭst) *n.* A person who uses satire, especially a writer of satirical works.

sat·i·rize (săt**′**ə-rīz**′**) *tr.v.* **sat·i·rized, sat·i·riz·ing, sat·i·riz·es** To ridicule or attack by means of satire.

sat·is·fac·tion (săt**′**ĭs-făk**′**shən) *n.* **1.** Fulfillment or gratification of desire, need, or appetite: *found no satisfaction for his craving.* **2.** Pleasure derived from such fulfillment: *She felt great satisfaction in getting the highest test score.* **3.** Something that gives fulfillment or gratification: *One of the greatest satisfactions of her life was going back to school and getting her diploma.* **4a.** Compensation for injury or loss. **b.** The opportunity to avenge a wrong.

sat·is·fac·to·ry (săt**′**ĭs-făk**′**tə-rē) *adj.* Sufficient to meet a demand or requirement; adequate: *a satisfactory grade.* **—sat′is·fac′to·ri·ly** *adv.*

sat·is·fy (săt**′**ĭs-fī**′**) *tr.v.* **sat·is·fied, sat·is·fy·ing, sat·is·fies 1.** To fulfill or gratify the need, desire, or expectation of: *The actor was satisfied with his performance.* **2.** To fulfill (a need, for example): *satisfy one's hunger.* **3.** To free from doubt or question; convince: *The firefighters were satisfied that the fire was out.* **4.** To fulfill or meet (a standard, for example): *satisfy the requirements to pass the course.* **5.** To compensate for an injury or a loss: *The judgment satisfied the injured parties.* [From Middle English *satisfien,* from Latin *satisfacere* : *satis,* sufficient + *facere,* to make.] **—sat′is·fi′er** *n.*

sat·u·rate (săch**′**ə-rāt**′**) *tr.v.* **sat·u·rat·ed, sat·u·rat·ing, sat·u·rates 1.** To soak or fill so that no more liquid may be absorbed: *Water saturated the cloth.* **2.** To fill thoroughly: *The odor of fish saturated the shop.* **3.** To cause (a substance) to unite with the greatest possible amount of another substance.

sat·u·rat·ed (săch**′**ə-rā′tĭd) *adj.* **1.** Unable to hold or contain more; full. **2.** Relating to an organic compound, especially a fatty acid, containing the maximum number of hydrogen atoms and only single bonds between the carbon atoms: *a saturated hydrocarbon.* **3.** Soaked with moisture; drenched.

saturated fat *n.* A fat containing saturated chemical compounds, found in meat and dairy products and certain plant oils, such as palm oil. Eating foods high in saturated fat can lead to cholesterol levels in the blood that are higher than normal.

sat·u·ra·tion (săch′ə-rā**′**shən) *n.* **1a.** The act or process of saturating. **b.** The condition of being saturated. **2.** The degree to which a color differs from a gray of the same brightness or lightness. **3.** A condition in which air at a given temperature contains as much water vapor as it can hold.

Sat·ur·day (săt**′**ər-dē *or* săt**′**ər-dā**′**) *n.* The seventh day of the week. **—Sat′ur·days** *adv.*

Sat·urn (săt**′**ərn) *n.* **1.** In Roman mythology, the god of agriculture. **2.** The sixth planet from the sun and the second largest in the solar system, with a diameter about ten times that of Earth. Saturn is encircled by a large, flat system of rings that are made up mostly of tiny particles of ice. See table at **solar system.**

sat·ur·na·li·a (săt′ər-nā**′**lē-ə *or* săt′ər-nāl**′**yə) *pl.n.* **Saturnalia 1.** The ancient Roman seven-day festival of Saturn, which began on December 17. **2.** *(used with a singular verb)* A time of wild celebration.

sat·ur·nine (săt**′**ər-nīn**′**) *adj.* **1.** Melancholy or sullen. **2.** Sarcastic or bitter.

sa·tyr (sā**′**tər *or* săt**′**ər) *n.* In Greek mythology, a woodland creature depicted as having the pointed ears, legs, and short horns of a goat. [From Middle English *satire,* from Greek *saturos.*]

sauce (sôs) *n.* **1.** A liquid dressing, seasoning, or topping for food. **2.** Stewed fruit: *cranberry sauce.* **3.** Something that adds zest or flavor. ❖ *tr.v.* **sauced, sauc·ing, sauc·es** To season or flavor with sauce. —SEE NOTE.

sauce·pan (sôs**′**păn**′**) *n.* A deep cooking pan with a long handle.

sau·cer (sô**′**sər) *n.* A small shallow dish for holding a cup.

sauc·y (sô**′**sē) *adj.* **sauc·i·er, sauc·i·est** Disrespectful or impertinent, often in a playful or lively way. **—sau′ci·ness** *n.* —SEE NOTE AT **sauce.**

Sau·di A·ra·bi·a (sou**′**dē ə-rā**′**bē-ə *or* sô**′**dē ə-rā**′**bē-ə) A country occupying most of the Arabian Peninsula in southwest Asia. Oil was discovered here in 1938. Riyadh is the capital.

sau·er·kraut (sour**′**krout**′**) *n.* Shredded cabbage, salted and fermented in its own juice.

Sauk (sôk) *n., pl.* **Sauk** or **Sauks 1.** A member of a Native American people of the upper Midwest, now living mainly in Oklahoma. **2.** The Algonquian language of the Sauk.

Saul (sôl) In the Bible, the first king of Israel, who defended Israel against numerous enemies.

sau·na (sô**′**nə *or* sou**′**nə) *n.* **1.** A small room or structure that provides dry heat or steam for refreshing the body. **2.** A period of time spent in a sauna.

saun·ter (sôn**′**tər) *intr.v.* **saun·tered, saun·ter·ing, saun·ters** To walk at a leisurely pace; stroll: *sauntered across the garden.* ❖ *n.* **1.** A leisurely walk. **2.** A leisurely way of walking.

sau·sage (sô**′**sĭj) *n.* Chopped and seasoned meat, usually stuffed into a prepared animal intestine or other casing and cooked or cured.

sau·té (sō-tā**′** *or* sô-tā**′**) *tr.v.* **sau·téed, sau·té·ing, sau·tés** To fry lightly in a shallow open pan. ❖ *n.* Sautéed food.

sav·age (săv**′**ĭj) *adj.* **1.** Untouched by civilization; not cultivated; wild: *savage lands.* **2.** Not civilized; barbaric: *a savage people.* **3.** Ferocious; vicious or fierce: *a savage attack.* ❖ *n.* A member of a people regarded as primitive, uncivilized, brutal, or fierce. **—sav′age·ly** *adv.* **—sav′age·ness** *n.*

sav·age·ry (săv**′**ĭj-rē) *n., pl.* **sav·age·ries 1.** The quality or condition of being savage. **2.** Savage action or behavior.

sa·van·na also **sa·van·nah** (sə-văn**′**ə) *n.* A grassland especially of warm regions, usually sparsely covered with trees.

Sa·van·nah (sə-**văn′**ə) A city of southeast Georgia near the Atlantic Ocean. It was founded in 1733.

save[1] (sāv) *v.* **saved, sav·ing, saves** —*tr.* **1.** To rescue from harm, danger, or loss: *park rangers who save lost hikers.* **2.** To prevent (someone) from dying: *The doctor operated to save the patient.* **3.** To treat with care to avoid damage or wear; safeguard: *You should wear sunglasses to save your eyesight.* **4.** To prevent the loss or waste of; conserve: *light bulbs that save energy.* **5a.** To keep for future use: *saved his earnings to buy a camera.* **b.** To spend less (money or time) than circumstances would normally require: *saved $25 at the sale; saved 15 minutes by taking a shortcut.* **6.** To spare (someone) from having to do something: *Our aunt arrived with some bread and saved us a trip to the store.* **7.** To set free from sin; redeem: *praying for God to save one's soul.* **8a.** In sports, to prevent (a goal) from being scored by an opponent. **b.** In baseball, to preserve (another pitcher's win) by protecting a lead when pitching as a relief pitcher. **9.** To copy (a file) from a computer's main memory to a disk or other storage device. —*intr.* To accumulate money for a future use: *saving for a vacation.* ❖ *n.* **1.** In sports, an act of preventing an opponent from scoring a goal. **2.** In baseball, an act of saving a win as a relief pitcher. [From Middle English *saven*, from Late Latin *salvāre*, from Latin *salvus*, safe.] —**sav′er** *n.*

save[2] (sāv) *prep.* Except; but: *All trains arrived on time save one.* ❖ *conj.* Were it not; except: *I could be a great dancer, save that I have no sense of rhythm.* [From Middle English *sauf*, from Latin *salvō*, from *salvus*, safe.]

sav·ing (sā′vĭng) *n.* **1.** Rescue from harm, danger, or loss. **2.** Avoidance of waste or expense: *the saving of energy.* **3. savings a.** Money saved: *a bank account for savings.* **b.** *(used with a singular verb)* An amount of money saved: *a coupon that offered a savings of $10.* ❖ *prep.* With the exception of: *All books were ordered, saving this one.* ❖ *conj.* Except; save.

sav·ings account (sā′vĭngz) *n.* A bank account that earns interest.

savings bank *n.* A bank that receives, invests, and pays interest on the savings of depositors.

savings bond *n.* A registered bond issued by the US government in denominations of $50 to $10,000.

sav·ior (sāv′yər) *n.* **1.** A person who saves or delivers another from danger, destruction, or loss. **2. Savior** In Christianity, a way of referring to Jesus.

sa·vor (sā′vər) *n.* **1.** A distinctive taste or smell, especially a pleasant one. **2.** A distinctive quality or sensation: *a remark with a savor of resentment.* ❖ *v.* **sa·vored, sa·vor·ing, sa·vors** —*tr.* **1.** To taste or smell, especially with pleasure: *savored each morsel of the feast.* **2.** To appreciate fully; enjoy or relish: *savored his moment of triumph.* —*intr.* **1.** To have a distinctive taste or smell: *a dish that savors of curry.* **2.** To appear to show a specific characteristic: *a reply that savored of envy.*

sa·vor·y[1] (sā′və-rē) *adj.* **1a.** Appetizing to the taste or smell: *enticed by savory aromas coming from the kitchen.* **b.** Flavorful but not sweet: *a savory meat pie.* **2.** Morally respectable; inoffensive: *His associates were anything but savory.* [From Middle English *savouri*, from Latin *sapor*, taste.]

sa·vor·y[2] (sā′və-rē) *n.* Any of several plants related to mint, having aromatic leaves used as a seasoning in cooking. [From Middle English *saverei*, from Latin *saturēia*.]

sav·vy (săv′ē) *Informal adj.* **sav·vi·er, sav·vi·est 1.** Well informed in practical matters; shrewd: *a savvy investor.* **2.** Skilled at using something: *a media-savvy celebrity.* ❖ *n.* Practical understanding; common sense: *a banker known for financial savvy.* ❖ *tr. & intr.v.* **sav·vied** (săv′ēd), **sav·vy·ing, sav·vies** (săv′ēz) To know or understand.

saw[1] (sô) *n.* Any of various hand-operated or power-driven tools having a thin metal blade or disk with a sharp-toothed edge, used for cutting wood, metal, or other hard materials. ❖ *v.* **sawed, sawed** or **sawn** (sôn), **saw·ing, saws** —*tr.* **1.** To cut or divide with a saw: *saw off a branch.* **2.** To produce or shape with a saw: *sawing curves in wood.* —*intr.* **1.** To use a saw. **2.** To be capable of being cut with a saw: *Pine wood saws easily.* [From Old English *sagu*, saw.]

saw[2] (sô) *n.* A traditional familiar saying. [From Old English *sagu*, speech.]

saw[3] (sô) *v.* Past tense of **see**[1].

saw·buck (sô′bŭk′) *n.* A sawhorse, especially one having a crossed pair of legs at each end.

saw·dust (sô′dŭst′) *n.* The small particles of wood or other material that fall from an object being sawed.

sawed-off (sôd′ôf′) *adj.* Having one end sawed off: *a sawed-off shotgun.*

saw·fish (sô′fĭsh′) *n.* Any of various large ocean fishes related to the rays and skates, having a long snout with teeth along both sides.

saw·horse (sô′hôrs′) *n.* A frame with legs, used to support a piece of wood being sawed.

saw·mill (sô′mĭl′) *n.* A place where lumber is mechanically sawed into boards.

sawn (sôn) *v.* A past participle of **saw**[1].

saw·yer (sô′yər) *n.* A person whose work is sawing wood.

sax (săks) *n.* A saxophone.

sax·i·frage (săk′sə-frĭj *or* săk′sə-frāj′) *n.* Any of numerous plants having small, loosely clustered white, yellow, or reddish flowers.

Sax·on (săk′sən) *n.* **1.** A member of a Germanic people that invaded Britain in the fifth and sixth centuries AD and together with the Angles and Jutes formed the Anglo-Saxon peoples. **2.** The West Germanic language of the ancient Saxon peoples.

sax·o·phone (săk′sə-fōn′) *n.* A wind instrument having a single-reed mouthpiece, a usually bent, flaring body made of metal, and keys operated by the player's fingers. [After *Sax*, name of a Belgian instrument-making family of the 1800s.] —**sax′o·phon′ist** *n.*

say (sā) *v.* **said** (sĕd), **say·ing, says** (sĕz) —*tr.* **1.** To utter aloud; speak: *The children said, "Good morning."* **2.** To express in words; state: *The book says that the treaty was signed in 1945.* **3.** To give expression to; show or indicate: *The clock says half past two.* **4.** To repeat or recite: *saying poetry aloud.* **5.** To suppose; assume: *Let's say that you're right.* —*intr.* To make a statement; express oneself: *The story is true, or so they said.* ❖ *n.* **1.** A turn or chance to speak: *Let each one have his or her say.* **2.** The power to influence a decision: *We haven't any say in the matter.* ❖ *adv.* **1.** Approximately: *Let's walk, say, five miles.* **2.** For example: *a tree, say a pine.* ❖ *interj.* An expression used to attract attention or express wonder: *Say, that's some car.* ◆ **that is to say** In other words. [From Old English *secgan*.] —**say′er** *n.*

say·ing (sā′ĭng) *n.* Something that is frequently said; a proverb.

say-so (sā′sō′) *n., pl.* **say-sos** *Informal* **1.** An unsupported statement or assurance: *I won't be convinced on your say-so alone.* **2.** An authoritative expression of permission or approval.

Sb The symbol for the element **antimony.**

SB *abbr.* An abbreviation of stolen base.

Sc The symbol for the element **scandium.**

SC *abbr.* An abbreviation of South Carolina.

scab (skăb) *n.* **1.** The crust discharged from and covering a healing wound. **2a.** A worker who refuses to join a

WORD HISTORY

sauce What do **sausages,** spaghetti **sauce,** potato **salad,** and spicy **salsa** have in common? The names of all four come from the Latin word *salsus,* "salty, salted." *Salsus* was also used metaphorically to mean "witty," much as our word **saucy** is used to mean "too witty for one's own good, impertinent."

savanna

saxophone

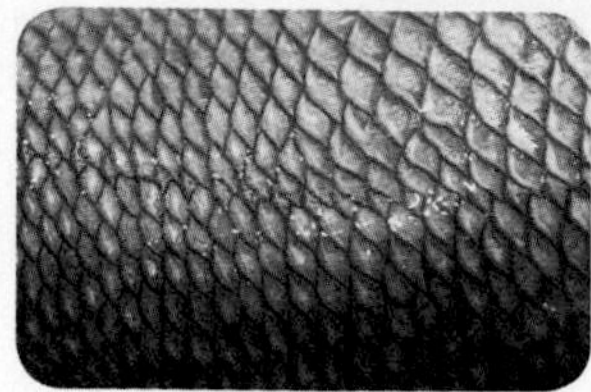

scale¹
top: fish scales
bottom: pinecone scales

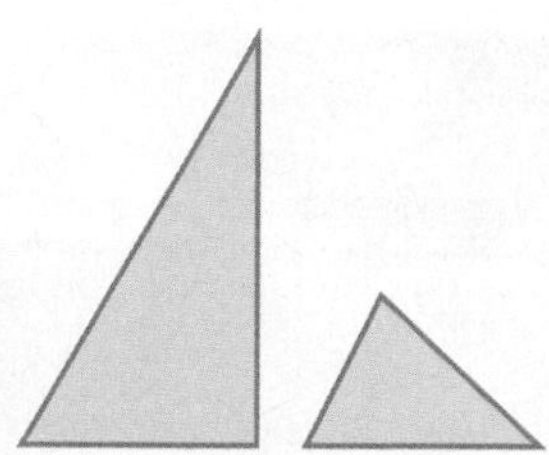

scalene
scalene triangles

scallop

ă	pat	ôr	core
ā	pay	oi	boy
âr	care	ou	out
ä	father	o͝o	took
ĕ	pet	o͝or	lure
ē	be	o͞o	boot
ĭ	pit	ŭ	cut
ī	bite	ûr	urge
îr	pier	th	thin
ŏ	pot	*th*	this
ō	toe	zh	vision
ô	paw	ə	about

labor union. **b.** A worker who takes a striker's job. **c.** An employee who works while others are on strike. ❖ *intr.v.* **scabbed, scab·bing, scabs 1.** To become covered with scabs or a scab. **2.** To work as a scab.

scab·bard (skăb′ərd) *n.* A sheath for the blade of a sword, dagger, or similar weapon.

sca·bies (skā′bēz) *n.* A contagious disease caused by small mites that burrow into the skin and cause severe itching.

scad (skăd) *n. Informal* often **scads** A large number or amount: *scads of people.*

scaf·fold (skăf′əld *or* skăf′ōld′) *n.* **1.** A temporary platform on which workers sit or stand when performing tasks at heights above the ground. **2.** A platform for the execution of condemned prisoners. **3.** A raised wooden framework or platform.

scaf·fold·ing (skăf′əl-dĭng *or* skăf′ōl′dĭng) *n.* **1.** A scaffold or system of scaffolds. **2.** The materials from which a scaffold is made.

scal·a·wag (skăl′ə-wăg′) also **scal·ly·wag** (skăl′ē-wăg′) *n.* **1.** *Informal* A shameless person; a rascal. **2.** A white Southerner who supported the federal government during Reconstruction.

scald (skôld) *tr.v.* **scald·ed, scald·ing, scalds 1.** To burn with hot liquid or steam. **2.** To treat with or subject to boiling water: *scalded and peeled the peaches.* **3.** To heat (a liquid) almost to the boiling point: *scald milk.* ❖ *n.* Injury or damage caused by scalding. [From Middle English *scalden*, from Late Latin *excaldāre*, to wash in hot water.]

scale¹ (skāl) *n.* **1a.** One of the small thin plates forming the outer covering of fishes, reptiles, and certain other animals. **b.** A similar part in other animals, such as one of the thin flat overlapping structures that cover the wings of butterflies and moths. **2.** A small, thin, often flattened plant structure, such as one of the modified leaves that cover a tree bud or one of the structures that bear the reproductive organs on the cones of a conifer. **3.** A dry thin flake or crust, as of paint, rust, or dandruff. ❖ *tr.v.* **scaled, scal·ing, scales 1.** To clear or strip of scale or scales: *scale and clean the fish.* **2.** To remove in layers: *scaled off the old paint.* [From Middle English, from Old French *escale*, of Germanic origin.]

scale² (skāl) *n.* **1a.** A system of ordered marks placed at fixed distances, used for measuring. **b.** An instrument having such a system of marks. **2a.** The proportion used to determine the relationship between the actual dimensions of something and the dimensions to which it is reduced or expanded when represented on a model, map, or drawing: *a scale of 1 inch to 50 miles.* **b.** A line with marks showing the actual dimensions of something represented on a map, plan, or drawing. **c.** The relative size or extent of something: *marketing on a large scale.* **3.** A progressive classification, as of size, amount, importance, or rank: *rated the movie on a scale of one to ten.* **4.** An ascending or descending series of musical tones following a set sequence of intervals, usually covering a range of one octave. ❖ *v.* **scaled, scal·ing, scales** —*tr.* **1.** To climb up or over: *scale a mountain.* **2.** To draw or arrange in a particular proportion or scale. **3.** To adjust or regulate according to some standard: *scaling back business to curtail spending.* —*intr.* To climb; ascend: *scaled over the wall on the obstacle course.* [From Middle English *skale*, ladder, from Latin *scālae*.]

scale³ (skāl) *n.* **1.** often **scales** An instrument or machine for weighing. **2.** Either of the pans or dishes of a balance. ❖ *v.* **scaled, scal·ing, scales** —*tr.* To weigh with scales. —*intr.* To have a given weight. [From Middle English, bowl, balance, from Old Norse *skāl*.]

scale insect *n.* Any of various small insects that feed on plant sap. Scale insects secrete a waxy substance that covers the body, and some are agricultural pests.

sca·lene (skā′lēn′ *or* skā-lēn′) *adj.* Having three unequal sides. Used of triangles.

Sca·li·a (skə-lē′ə), **Antonin** 1936–2016. American jurist who was appointed an associate justice of the US Supreme Court in 1986.

scal·lion (skăl′yən) *n.* An onion of a kind that has a small white bulb and long narrow green leaves.

scal·lop (skŏl′əp *or* skăl′əp) *n.* **1a.** Any of various soft-bodied sea mollusks having a double, hinged, fan-shaped shell with radiating fluted markings. **b.** The fleshy muscle of such an animal, used as food. **2.** A thin boneless slice of meat. **3.** One of a series of curves shaped like a scallop shell, forming a decorative border. ❖ *v.* **scal·loped, scal·lop·ing, scal·lops** —*tr.* **1.** To bake in a casserole with milk or a sauce and often with bread crumbs: *scallop potatoes.* **2.** To form scallops along the edge of (cloth, for example). —*intr.* To gather scallops for eating or sale.

scal·ly·wag (skăl′ē-wăg′) *n.* Variant of **scalawag.**

scalp (skălp) *n.* The skin that covers the top of the human head. ❖ *tr.v.* **scalped, scalp·ing, scalps 1.** To cut or tear the scalp from. **2.** *Slang* To sell (tickets, for example) at a price higher than their established value. [From Middle English, top of the head, of Scandinavian origin.]

scal·pel (skăl′pəl) *n.* A small straight knife with a thin pointed blade, used in surgery. [From Latin *scalpellum*, from *scalpere*, to scratch, cut.]

scal·y (skā′lē) *adj.* **scal·i·er, scal·i·est 1.** Covered with scales: *scaly claws.* **2.** Shedding scales or flakes: *dry scaly skin.* **—scal′i·ness** *n.*

scaly anteater *n.* The pangolin.

scam (skăm) *n. Informal* A fraudulent business scheme; a swindle. ❖ *tr.v.* **scammed, scam·ming, scams** To defraud; swindle.

scamp (skămp) *n.* **1.** A playfully mischievous person. **2.** A dishonest or scheming person; a rascal.

scam·per (skăm′pər) *intr.v.* **scam·pered, scam·per·ing, scam·pers** To run or go quickly or lightly: *The puppy scampered across the lawn.*

scan (skăn) *tr.v.* **scanned, scan·ning, scans 1.** To look at carefully or thoroughly, especially in search of something; examine: *The sailor scanned the horizon for signs of land.* **2.** To look over quickly or read hastily: *I scanned the front page of the newspaper at breakfast.* **3a.** To move a beam of electrons or energy such as light or x-rays in a regular pattern over (a surface) to produce an image: *My luggage was scanned at the airport.* **b.** To examine (a body or body part) with a CT scanner or similar device. **c.** To use a scanner to encode (text, for example) in digital format. **d.** To move a radar beam in a regular pattern over (a sector of sky) in search of a target: *scanned the sky for enemy aircraft.* **4.** To analyze (verse) to show metrical patterns. ❖ *n.* **1.** The act or an instance of scanning. **2.** An image produced by scanning.

scan·dal (skăn′dl) *n.* **1.** Something that offends the morality of the social community; a public disgrace. **2.** Malicious gossip. [From Greek *skandalon*, trap, stumbling block.]

scan·dal·ize (skăn′dl-īz′) *tr.v.* **scan·dal·ized, scan·dal·iz·ing, scan·dal·iz·es** To shock or offend the moral sensibilities of.

scan·dal·ous (skăn′dl-əs) *adj.* **1.** Causing scandal; shocking: *scandalous behavior.* **2.** Containing material damaging to reputation; defamatory: *scandalous gossip.* **—scan′dal·ous·ly** *adv.* **—scan′dal·ous·ness** *n.*

Scan·di·na·vi·a (skăn′də-nā′vē-ə) A region of northern Europe traditionally consisting of Norway, Sweden, and Denmark. Finland and Iceland are often included in the region.

Scan·di·na·vi·an (skăn′də-nā′vē-ən) *adj.* Relating to Scandinavia, its peoples, languages, or cultures. ❖ *n.* **1.** A native or inhabitant of Scandinavia. **2.** North Germanic.

scan·di·um (skăn′dē-əm) *n. Symbol* **Sc** A silvery, very lightweight metallic element that is a byproduct in the processing of certain uranium ores. Atomic number 21. See **Periodic Table.**

scan·ner (skăn′ər) *n.* **1.** A person or thing that scans. **2.** A radio receiver that continually searches frequencies and plays aloud any signal it receives. **3.** A device that converts printed images and text into a digital file that can be stored or edited.

scan·sion (skăn′shən) *n.* Analysis of verse to show metrical patterns.

scant (skănt) *adj.* **scant·er, scant·est 1.** Barely sufficient; meager; inadequate: *scant vegetation.* **2.** Falling short of an amount or measure: *a scant six miles away.* ❖ *tr.v.* **scant·ed, scant·ing, scants 1.** To give an inadequate amount to; skimp on. **2.** To neglect; treat inadequately. **—scant′ly** *adv.* **—scant′ness** *n.*

scant·y (skăn′tē) *adj.* **scant·i·er, scant·i·est 1.** Small or insufficient: *a scanty water supply.* **2.** Not covering a considerable amount of the body: *a scanty bathing suit.* **—scant′i·ly** *adv.* **—scant′i·ness** *n.*

–scape (skāp) *suff.* A suffix that means scene or view: *cityscape; landscape.*

scape·goat (skāp′gōt′) *n.* A person, group, or thing that is unjustly punished for the faults of others.

scap·u·la (skăp′yə-lə) *n., pl.* **scap·u·las** or **scap·u·lae** (skăp′yə-lē′) Either of two flat triangular bones behind the shoulders; a shoulder blade.

scar (skär) *n.* **1.** A mark left on the skin after a wound or injury has healed. **2.** A mark, as on a plant stem, where a leaf, bud, or other part was once attached. **3.** A mark or sign of damage, either physical or emotional. ❖ *v.* **scarred, scar·ring, scars** *—tr.* To mark with a scar. *—intr.* To form a scar. [From Middle English, from Greek *eskhara*, hearth, scab caused by burning.]

scar·ab (skăr′əb) *n.* **1.** Any of numerous often large broad-bodied beetles, especially one of a kind regarded as sacred by the ancient Egyptians. **2.** An ornament, sculpture, or cut gem made to look like one of these beetles, used in ancient Egypt as a symbol of the soul.

scarce (skârs) *adj.* **scarc·er, scarc·est 1.** Insufficient to meet a demand or requirement: *The pioneers' food and water were beginning to grow scarce.* **2.** Hard to find; rare: *Nickels bearing a buffalo are scarce these days.* ❖ *adv.* Scarcely; hardly. ◆ **make (oneself) scarce** *Informal* To go or stay away. **—scarce′ness** *n.*

scarce·ly (skârs′lē) *adv.* **1.** By a small margin; barely: *We scarcely made it on time.* **2.** Almost not; hardly: *I could scarcely see through the fog.* **3.** Certainly not: *They could scarcely complain after such good service.* —SEE NOTE.

scar·ci·ty (skâr′sĭ-tē) *n., pl.* **scar·ci·ties** An insufficient amount or supply; a shortage.

scare (skâr) *v.* **scared, scar·ing, scares** *—tr.* To frighten or alarm; terrify: *The dog scared the cat.* See Synonyms at **frighten.** *—intr.* To become frightened: *I don't scare easily.* ❖ *n.* A condition, sensation, or state of fear or panic. [From Middle English *skerren*, from Old Norse *skirra*, from *skjarr*, timid.]

scare·crow (skâr′krō′) *n.* A crude figure of a person set up in a field to scare birds away from crops.

scarf[1] (skärf) *n., pl.* **scarves** (skärvz) or **scarfs 1.** A rectangular or triangular piece of cloth worn around the neck, head, or shoulders. **2.** A decorative piece of cloth used to cover the top of a piece of furniture, such as a desk or table.

scarf[2] (skärf) *tr.v.* **scarfed, scarf·ing, scarfs** *Slang* To eat or drink eagerly; devour: *scarfed the pizza down.*

scar·let (skär′lĭt) *n.* A bright red to reddish orange.

scarlet fever *n.* A severe contagious bacterial disease that occurs mainly in children and is characterized by a high fever and a scarlet rash on the skin.

scarlet tanager *n.* A songbird of the Americas, the male of which has bright scarlet feathers with a black tail and wings.

scarves (skärvz) *n.* A plural of **scarf**[1].

scar·y (skâr′ē) *adj.* **scar·i·er, scar·i·est 1.** Causing fright or alarm. **2.** Easily frightened; timid. **—scar′i·ly** *adv.*

scat[1] (skăt) *intr.v.* **scat·ted, scat·ting, scats** *Informal* To go away hastily; leave at once: *I told the cat to scat.*

scat[2] (skăt) *n.* Jazz singing in which improvised, meaningless syllables are sung to a melody. ❖ *intr.v.* **scat·ted, scat·ting, scats** To sing scat.

scat[3] (skăt) *n.* Dung, especially from a wild animal.

scathe (skāth) *tr.v.* **scathed, scath·ing, scathes 1.** To harm or injure severely, especially by fire. **2.** To criticize harshly.

scath·ing (skā′thĭng) *adj.* **1.** Extremely severe; harshly critical: *a scathing verbal attack.* **2.** Harmful or painful. **—scath′ing·ly** *adv.*

scat·ter (skăt′ər) *v.* **scat·tered, scat·ter·ing, scat·ters** *—tr.* **1.** To cause to separate and go in various directions: *The wind scatters dandelion seeds.* **2.** To distribute loosely, as by sprinkling; strew: *scattering confetti during the parade.* **3.** To deflect a stream of (radiation or particles) so that they rebound in different directions. *—intr.* To separate and go in different directions; disperse.

scat·ter·brain (skăt′ər-brān′) *n.* A flighty, thoughtless, or disorganized person. **—scat′ter·brained′** *adj.*

scat·ter·ing (skăt′ər-ĭng) *n.* **1.** Something scattered, especially a small or irregular quantity or amount: *a scattering of applause.* **2.** The spreading of a beam of particles or rays over a range of directions as a result of collisions or other physical interactions.

scav·enge (skăv′ənj) *v.* **scav·enged, scav·eng·ing, scav·eng·es** *—tr.* **1.** To search through for useful material: *The cat scavenged the garbage cans for food.* **2.** To collect (something useful or edible) by searching. *—intr.* To search through refuse for useful material.

scav·en·ger (skăv′ən-jər) *n.* **1.** An animal, such as a vulture or hyena, that feeds on dead or decaying plant or animal matter. **2.** A person who searches through rubbish or discarded material for useful items.

sce·nar·i·o (sĭ-nâr′ē-ō′ *or* sĭ-när′ē-ō′) *n., pl.* **sce·nar·i·os 1.** An outline of an expected or supposed series of events: *In the worst scenario, our plan will still work.* **2.** An outline of the plot of a story or play. **3.** The text of a movie; a screenplay.

scene (sēn) *n.* **1.** A place or an area seen by a viewer; a view from a particular point: *the scene from my window.* **2.** The place where an action or event occurs: *the scene of the crime.* **3.** The place where the action of a play, movie, novel, or other narrative occurs; a setting. **4.** A part of a movie or play in which the setting is fixed and the action forms a connected unit: *The family reunion scene was the best part of the play.* **5.** A display of temper or behavior that attracts attention in public: *Don't make a scene.* ◆ **behind the scenes** Out of public view; in secret. [From Greek *skēnē*, tent, stage.]

❑ *These sound alike:* **scene, seen** (perceived with the eye).

scen·er·y (sē′nə-rē) *n., pl.* **scen·er·ies 1.** A view or views of natural features, especially in open country: *varied mountain scenery.* **2.** Backdrops, furnishings, and other items on a stage that create the setting for a theatrical production.

sce·nic (sē′nĭk *or* sĕn′ĭk) *adj.* **1.** Having or offering natural scenery, especially attractive landscapes: *a scenic route.* **2.** Relating to the stage or theatrical scenery: *scenic design.*

scent (sĕnt) *n.* **1.** A distinctive, often pleasing odor: *the scent of pine.* See Synonyms at **smell.** **2.** A perfume. **3.** The trail of a hunted animal or fugitive: *The dogs lost the deer's scent.* **4.** The sense of smell: *hunting by scent.* **5.** A hint of something; a suggestion: *a scent of excite-*

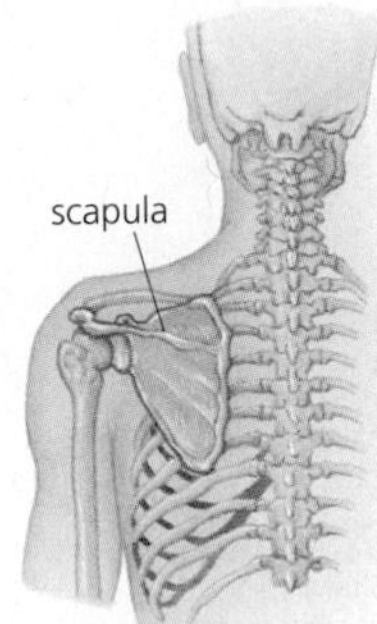

scapula

USAGE

scarcely When you follow the word **scarcely** with a clause, introduce the clause with *when* or *before* but not with *than*: *The meeting had scarcely begun when* (or *before,* but not *than*) *it was interrupted.* For more information, see Note at **hardly.**

WRITERS CHOOSE THEIR WORDS

The good food reminded Kitty of her family in Halifax—they too would be sitting down to eat after Christmas service. She was sure they'd have a goose, even if it meant a little **scarcity** in other ways.

—Donna Smyth
Loyalist Runaway

scarf[1]

schnauzer
miniature schnauzer

schooner

ment with the approach of summer. ❖ *tr.v.* **scent·ed, scent·ing, scents 1.** To perceive or identify by smelling: *wolves scenting their prey.* **2.** To suspect or detect: *scented danger.* **3.** To provide with an odor; perfume. [From Middle English *sent*, from Latin *sentīre*, to sense.]
❏ *These sound alike:* **scent, cent** (penny), **sent** (transmitted).

scep·ter (sĕp′tər) *n.* **1.** A staff held by a sovereign as a sign of authority. **2.** Ruling power or authority.

scep·tic (skĕp′tĭk) *n.* Variant of **skeptic.**

scep·ti·cal (skĕp′tĭ-kəl) *adj.* Variant of **skeptical.**

scep·ti·cism (skĕp′tĭ-sĭz′əm) *n.* Variant of **skepticism.**

sched·ule (skĕj′o͞ol *or* skĕj′o͞o-əl *or* skĕj′əl) *n.* **1.** A program of forthcoming events or appointments. **2.** A student's program of classes. **3.** A timetable of departures and arrivals: *a bus schedule.* **4.** A plan for performing work or achieving an objective: *a schedule for success.* **5.** A list of items in the form of a table or chart. ❖ *tr.v.* **sched·uled, sched·ul·ing, sched·ules 1.** To place on a schedule. **2.** To make up a schedule for. **3.** To plan or appoint for a certain time or date: *schedule the trip for next week.*

Sche·her·e·zade (shə-hĕr′ə-**zäd′**) *n.* A fictional queen who is the skilled narrator of the tales in the anonymously written *The Arabian Nights' Entertainment.*

sche·mat·ic (skē-**măt′**ĭk *or* skĭ-**măt′**ĭk) *adj.* Relating to or in the form of a scheme or diagram. **—sche·mat′i·cal·ly** *adv.*

sche·ma·tize (skē′mə-tīz′) *tr.v.* **sche·ma·tized, sche·ma·tiz·ing, sche·ma·tiz·es** To express in or reduce to a scheme.

scheme (skēm) *n.* **1.** A plan of action. **2.** An underhanded or secret plan; a plot. **3.** A chart, diagram, or outline of a plan or object. **4.** An orderly combination or arrangement: *a color scheme.* ❖ *v.* **schemed, schem·ing, schemes** *—tr.* **1.** To make up a plan or scheme for. **2.** To plot: *scheming their escape. —intr.* To make plans, especially secret and devious ones. [From Greek *skhēma*, figure, plan.] **—schem′er** *n.*

scher·zo (skĕr′tsō) *n., pl.* **scher·zos** or **scher·zi** (skĕr′-tsē) A lively movement in a musical composition, commonly in 3/4 time. [From Italian, joke.]

schism (skĭz′əm *or* sĭz′əm) *n.* **1.** A separation or division into opposing groups. **2.** A formal separation of groups within a church or other religious body.

schis·mat·ic (skĭz-**măt′**ĭk *or* sĭz-**măt′**ĭk) *adj.* Relating to or engaging in a schism. ❖ *n.* A person who encourages or engages in a schism. **—schis·mat′i·cal·ly** *adv.*

schist (shĭst) *n.* A medium-grained metamorphic rock usually composed mostly of mica or similar mineral flakes, that splits easily.

schis·to·so·mi·a·sis (shĭs′tə-sə-**mī′**ə-sĭs) *n.* Any of a group of diseases caused by parasitic worms that infest the blood of humans and other mammals. It is contracted from contaminated water and causes gradual damage to vital organs, such as the kidney and liver.

schiz·o·phre·ni·a (skĭt′sə-**frē′**nē-ə *or* skĭt′sə-**frĕn′**ē-ə) *n.* Any of a group of severe mental illnesses in which a person loses touch with reality and withdraws from others, often with disturbances in behavior and the ability to reason. [From Greek *skhizein*, to split + Greek *phrēn*, mind.]

schiz·o·phren·ic (skĭt′sə-**frĕn′**ĭk) *adj.* Relating to or affected with schizophrenia. ❖ *n.* A schizophrenic person.

schnau·zer (shnou′zər) *n.* A dog of any of three breeds originally from Germany, having a wiry grayish or black coat and a blunt muzzle.

schol·ar (skŏl′ər) *n.* **1a.** A learned person. **b.** An expert in a particular field: *a scholar of Russian history.* **2.** A pupil or student. **3.** A student who has received a particular scholarship. [From Old English *scolere*, from Latin *schola*, school.]

schol·ar·ly (skŏl′ər-lē) *adj.* Relating to or characteristic of scholars or scholarship: *scholarly research.*

schol·ar·ship (skŏl′ər-shĭp′) *n.* **1.** The methods, disciplines, and learning of a scholar. **2.** Knowledge resulting from extensive research in a particular field. **3.** A grant of financial aid awarded to a student, as for attending college.

scho·las·tic (skə-**lăs′**tĭk) *adj.* **1.** Relating to schools or education; academic: *scholastic standards; scholastic achievement.* **2.** Adhering rigidly to scholarly methods; pedantic. **—scho·las′ti·cal·ly** *adv.*

school[1] (sko͞ol) *n.* **1.** An institution for teaching and learning. **2.** A division of an educational institution, especially one for special study within a university: *a law school.* **3.** The student body of an educational institution. **4.** The building or group of buildings housing an educational institution. **5.** The instruction given at a school: *School ends early today.* **6.** The process of being educated formally: *What are your plans when you finish school?* **7.** A group of people, especially artists or writers, whose thought, work, or style shows common influences or underlying beliefs. ❖ *tr.v.* **schooled, school·ing, schools** To instruct or train: *schooling him in manners.* See Synonyms at **teach.** [From Old English *scōl*, from Latin *schola*, from Greek *skholē*.]

school[2] (sko͞ol) *n.* A large group of fish or other water animals that swim together. ❖ *intr.v.* **schooled, school·ing, schools** To form or swim in such a group. [From Middle English *scole*, from Middle Dutch *schole*.]

school board *n.* A local board that oversees public schools.

school·book (sko͞ol′bo͝ok′) *n.* A textbook or other book for use in school.

school·boy (sko͞ol′boi′) *n.* A boy attending school.

school bus *n.* A vehicle that is used for taking school children to and from school or school-related activities.

school·child also **school child** (sko͞ol′chīld′) *n.* A child attending school.

school·girl (sko͞ol′gûrl′) *n.* A girl attending school.

school·house (sko͞ol′hous′) *n.* A building used as a school.

school·ing (sko͞o′lĭng) *n.* **1.** Instruction or training given at school; formal education. **2.** Education obtained through experience or exposure: *Living on a farm has given her valuable schooling.*

school·marm (sko͞ol′märm′) *n.* A woman teacher, especially one in the 1800s or early 1900s.

school·mas·ter (sko͞ol′măs′tər) *n.* A man who is a teacher.

school·mate (sko͞ol′māt′) *n.* A companion in one's school.

school·mis·tress (sko͞ol′mĭs′trĭs) *n.* A woman who is a teacher.

school·room (sko͞ol′ro͞om′ *or* sko͞ol′ro͝om′) *n.* A classroom.

school·teach·er (sko͞ol′tē′chər) *n.* A person who teaches school below the college level.

school·work (sko͞ol′wûrk′) *n.* Lessons done at school or to be done at home.

school·yard (sko͞ol′yärd′) *n.* An open area next to a school building for play and outdoor activities.

school year *n.* The part of the year during which school is in session, typically from September to June.

schoo·ner (sko͞o′nər) *n.* A fore-and-aft-rigged sailing vessel with two or more masts, the forward mast being shorter than or as tall as the rear masts.

Schu·bert (sho͞o′bərt *or* sho͞o′bĕrt′), **Franz Peter** 1797–1828. Austrian composer of more than 600 vocal and instrumental works.

Schu·mann (sho͞o′män′ *or* sho͞o′mən), **Robert** 1810–1856. German composer whose works include symphonies and piano compositions.

ă	pat	ôr	core
ā	pay	oi	boy
âr	care	ou	out
ä	father	o͝o	took
ĕ	pet	o͝or	lure
ē	be	o͞o	boot
ĭ	pit	ŭ	cut
ī	bite	ûr	urge
îr	pier	th	thin
ŏ	pot	*th*	this
ō	toe	zh	vision
ô	paw	ə	about

schwa (shwä) *n.* A symbol (ə) used to represent a vowel sound that often occurs in unstressed syllables in English. For example, the sound of the *a* in *alone* and the *e* in *item* are represented by a schwa.

sci·at·ic (sī-ăt′ĭk) *adj.* **1.** Relating to the ischium. **2.** Relating to sciatica.

sci·at·i·ca (sī-ăt′ĭ-kə) *n.* Pain in the buttock and thigh caused by irritation of the sciatic nerve.

sciatic nerve *n.* A sensory and motor nerve that runs through the pelvis and upper leg.

sci·ence (sī′əns) *n.* **1a.** The observation, investigation, and explanation of natural phenomena: *advances in science.* **b.** Such activities applied to a particular class of natural phenomena: *the science of geology.* **2.** A method or routine that is successful or efficient from being frequently done and adjusted: *She's got packing down to a science.* [From Middle English, knowledge, learning, from Latin *scientia*, from *scīre*, to know.]

science fiction *n.* Fiction based on imaginary scientific discoveries or technological developments, often taking place in the future or on other planets.

sci·en·tif·ic (sī′ən-tĭf′ĭk) *adj.* Relating to science or using the methods of science: *scientific experiments; a scientific approach.* **—sci′en·tif′i·cal·ly** *adv.*

scientific method *n.* A method considered necessary for most scientific investigation that typically involves careful observation of phenomena, formulation of a hypothesis, experimentation to test the hypothesis, and development of a conclusion that confirms or modifies the hypothesis.

scientific name *n.* A name used by scientists, especially the taxonomic name of an organism that consists of a genus name and a second name identifying the species, such as *Homo sapiens*, the scientific name for humans.

scientific notation *n.* A method of expressing numbers in terms of a decimal number between 1 and 10 multiplied by a power of 10. The scientific notation of 10,492, for example, is 1.0492×10^4.

sci·en·tist (sī′ən-tĭst) *n.* A person who is involved in scientific investigation.

scim·i·tar (sĭm′ĭ-tər *or* sĭm′ĭ-tär′) *n.* A curved single-edged Asian sword.

scin·til·la (sĭn-tĭl′ə) *n.* A minute amount; a trace or iota: *without a scintilla of doubt.*

scin·til·late (sĭn′tl-āt′) *intr.v.* **scin·til·lat·ed, scin·til·lat·ing, scin·til·lates 1.** To throw off sparks; flash or sparkle. **2.** To be animated or brilliant: *The conversation scintillated all evening.* **—scin′til·la′tion** *n.*

sci·on (sī′ən) *n.* **1.** A descendant or heir, especially of a wealthy family. **2.** A shoot or bud that has been removed from one plant for grafting onto another.

scis·sors (sĭz′ərz) *n.* *(used with a singular or plural verb)* A cutting tool consisting of two blades, each with a ring-shaped handle, joined on a pivot that allows the cutting edges to slide past each other. [From Middle English *cisours*, from Late Latin *cīsōrium*, cutting instrument, from Latin *caedere*, to cut.]

scle·ra (sklîr′ə) *n.* The tough, white, fibrous tissue that covers all of the eyeball except the cornea.

scle·ro·sis (sklə-rō′sĭs) *n., pl.* **scle·ro·ses** (sklə-rō′sēz) **1.** A thickening or hardening of a body part, such as an artery. **2.** A disease characterized by sclerosis.

scoff (skŏf) *intr.v.* **scoffed, scoff·ing, scoffs** To express mocking contempt or derision; jeer: *They scoffed at the idea.* ❖ *n.* An expression of derision or scorn. **—scoff′er** *n.*

scoff·law (skŏf′lô′) *n.* A person who habitually violates laws, especially laws that do not involve serious criminal offenses.

scold (skōld) *tr.v.* **scold·ed, scold·ing, scolds** To express severe disapproval to; criticize harshly or angrily. ❖ *n.* A person who continually nags or criticizes. [From Middle English *scolden*, to be abusive, from *scolde*, an abusive person, probably of Scandinavian origin.] **—scold′er** *n.*

scold·ing (skōl′dĭng) *n.* A harsh or sharp criticism or reprimand.

sco·li·o·sis (skō′lē-ō′sĭs) *n.* Abnormal sideways curvature of the spine.

sconce (skŏns) *n.* A decorative wall bracket that holds candles or lights.

scone (skōn *or* skŏn) *n.* A small rich pastry that resembles a biscuit.

scoop (sko͞op) *n.* **1.** A small utensil shaped like a shovel with a short handle and a deep curved dish: *a flour scoop.* **2.** A thick-handled utensil with a round bowl, used to dispense balls of ice cream or other semisoft food. **3.** The bucket of a backhoe, dredge, or similar machine. **4.** The amount that any of these utensils, implements, or containers can hold: *ate two scoops of ice cream.* **5.** A scooping movement or action. **6.** *Informal* A news story reported ahead of a competitor. **7.** *Informal* Current information or details: *What's the scoop on the new neighbors?* ❖ *tr.v.* **scooped, scoop·ing, scoops 1.** To take up with or as if with a scoop: *scoop out the seeds; scoop up dirt.* **2.** To hollow out or form by digging: *scoop out a hole.* **3.** *Informal* To obtain and report a news story ahead of (rival newspapers, for example). [From Middle English *scope*, from Middle Dutch *schōpe*, bucket for bailing water.]

scoop·ful (sko͞op′fo͝ol′) *n.* The amount that a scoop can hold.

scoot (sko͞ot) *intr.v.* **scoot·ed, scoot·ing, scoots** To go suddenly or speedily; hurry: *They scooted off into the woods.* ◆ **scoot over** To move or slide to the side: *Scoot that chair over.*

scoot·er (sko͞o′tər) *n.* **1.** A child's vehicle consisting of a long footboard between two small end wheels, controlled by an upright steering bar attached to the front wheel. **2.** A motor scooter.

scope (skōp) *n.* **1.** The range of one's perceptions, thoughts, actions, or abilities: *broaden one's scope by reading.* **2.** Room or opportunity to function: *Give full scope to your imagination.* **3.** The area covered by an activity, a situation, or a subject: *The book was very broad in scope.* **4.** A viewing instrument such as a periscope or microscope. ❖ *tr.v.* **scoped, scop·ing, scopes** To examine or assess: *scoped out the neighborhood.* [From Greek *skopos*, target, aim.]

–scope *suff.* A suffix that means an instrument for viewing or observing: *microscope.*

scorch (skôrch) *tr.v.* **scorched, scorch·ing, scorch·es 1.** To burn the surface of. **2.** To wither or parch with intense heat: *The sun scorched the desert.* ❖ *n.* **1.** A slight or superficial burn. **2.** A discoloration caused by heat.

scorch·er (skôr′chər) *n.* *Informal* An extremely hot day.

score (skôr) *n.* **1.** The number of points made by each competitor or team in a game or contest. **2.** A record of points made in a game or contest: *The score was tied late in the game.* **3.** A result of a test or examination: *a score of 90 on a math test.* **4.** A debt or wrong that needs to be settled or revenged: *I have an old score to settle with him.* **5.** A reason or ground: *You have nothing to worry about on that score.* **6.** A group of 20 items. **7. scores** Large numbers: *scores of people.* **8a.** The written form of a musical composition. **b.** A musical composition written for a film or theater production. **9.** A notch or cut. ❖ *v.* **scored, scor·ing, scores** *—tr.* **1a.** To gain (a point or points) in a game or contest. **b.** To count or be worth as points: *That basket scored two points.* **2.** To keep a written record of the score or progress of (a game or contest). **3.** To achieve, gain, or win: *score a touchdown; scored success in the play.* **4.** To evaluate and assign a grade to: *The teacher scored the tests.* **5.** To arrange (a musical composition) for performance. **6.** To mark with

Franz Schubert

scoop
left: flour scoop
right: ice-cream scoop

scorpion

Scottish terrier

ă	pat	ôr	core
ā	pay	oi	boy
âr	care	ou	out
ä	father	o͝o	took
ĕ	pet	o͝or	lure
ē	be	o͞o	boot
ĭ	pit	ŭ	cut
ī	bite	ûr	urge
îr	pier	th	thin
ŏ	pot	*th*	this
ō	toe	zh	vision
ô	paw	ə	about

lines, notches, or cuts. —*intr.* **1.** To make a point in a game or contest. **2.** To keep the score of a game or contest. [From Old English *scoru*, twenty, from Old Norse *skor.*] —**scor′er** *n.*

score·board (skôr′bôrd′) *n.* A large board that records and indicates the score of a game for spectators.

score·card (skôr′kärd′) *n.* **1.** A printed program or card enabling a spectator to identify players and record the progress of a game. **2.** A small card used, as in golf, to record one's own performance.

score·keep·er (skôr′kē′pər) *n.* An official who records the score throughout a game or competition.

sco·ri·a (skôr′ē-ə) *n., pl.* **sco·ri·ae** (skôr′ē-ē′) **1.** Rough pieces of crusty lava containing numerous cavities that originated as gas bubbles in the hot lava. **2.** The waste left after a metal or an ore is smelted; slag.

scorn (skôrn) *n.* **1.** A strong feeling that a person or thing is inferior or unworthy; contempt or disdain. **2.** The expression of such a feeling in speech or behavior. ❖ *tr.v.* **scorned, scorn·ing, scorns 1.** To consider or treat as inferior or unworthy: *The artist was scorned by traditional thinkers.* **2.** To reject or refuse because of contempt or disdain: *scorned their offer of help.*

scorn·ful (skôrn′fəl) *adj.* Full of or expressing scorn or contempt: *a scornful laugh.* —**scorn′ful·ly** *adv.*

Scor·pi·o (skôr′pē-ō′) *n.* **1.** Variant of **Scorpius. 2.** The eighth sign of the zodiac in astrology.

scor·pi·on (skôr′pē-ən) *n.* Any of various animals related to the spiders that have large claws, a jointed body, and a tail with a venomous sting.

Scor·pi·us (skôr′pē-əs) also **Scor·pi·o** (skôr′pē-ō′) *n.* A constellation in the Southern Hemisphere near Libra and Sagittarius, traditionally pictured as a scorpion. [From Latin *scorpiō*, scorpion.]

Scot (skŏt) *n.* A native or inhabitant of Scotland.

scotch (skŏch) *tr.v.* **scotched, scotch·ing, scotch·es 1.** To put an end to; crush; stifle: *The governor scotched the rumor in his speech.* **2.** To injure so as to make harmless; wound: *The snake was scotched but not killed.*

Scotch *adj.* Scottish. ❖ *n.* **1.** *(used with a plural verb)* The people of Scotland; the Scots. **2.** The Scots language or dialect. **3.** Scotch whisky.

Scotch·man (skŏch′mən) *n.* A Scotsman.

Scotch tape A trademark used for adhesive tape.

Scotch terrier *n.* A Scottish terrier.

Scotch whisky *n.* A whiskey distilled in Scotland from malted barley.

Scotch·wom·an (skŏch′wo͝om′ən) *n.* A Scotswoman.

scot-free (skŏt′frē′) *adv.* **1.** Without having to pay. **2.** Without incurring any punishment.

Scot·land (skŏt′lənd) A country of the United Kingdom made up of the northern part of the island of Great Britain and the Hebrides, Shetland Islands, and Orkney Islands. Scotland became a part of the kingdom of Great Britain in 1707. Edinburgh is the capital and Glasgow the largest city.

Scots (skŏts) *adj.* Scottish. ❖ *n.* The language traditionally spoken in the Lowlands of Scotland, sometimes considered a variety of English.

Scots·man (skŏts′mən) *n.* A man who is a native or inhabitant of Scotland.

Scots·wom·an (skŏts′wo͝om′ən) *n.* A woman who is a native or inhabitant of Scotland.

Scott (skŏt), **Dred** 1795?–1858. American slave whose unsuccessful lawsuit against his master resulted in the Supreme Court's decision that the Missouri Compromise was unconstitutional (1857).

Scott, Sir **Walter** 1771–1832. British writer whose works include *Ivanhoe* (1819).

Scot·tie (skŏt′ē) *n.* A Scottish terrier.

Scot·tish (skŏt′ĭsh) *adj.* Relating to Scotland or its people, language, or culture. ❖ *n.* **1.** *(used with a plural verb)* The people of Scotland; the Scots. **2.** The Scots language or dialect.

Scottish Gaelic *n.* The Gaelic language traditionally spoken in the Scottish Highlands.

Scottish terrier *n.* A small dog of a breed originally from Scotland, having a dense wiry coat and a blunt muzzle.

scoun·drel (skoun′drəl) *n.* A wicked or dishonorable person; a villain. —**scoun′drel·ly** *adj.*

scour[1] (skour) *tr.v.* **scoured, scour·ing, scours 1.** To clean or polish by scrubbing vigorously: *scour a dirty pan.* **2.** To remove by scrubbing: *scour grease from a pan.* **3.** To clear (a channel or pipe) by flushing. [From Middle English *scouren*, from Late Latin *excūrāre*, to clean out.] —**scour′er** *n.*

scour[2] (skour) *v.* **scoured, scour·ing, scours** —*tr.* To search through or over thoroughly: *scoured the crime scene for clues.* —*intr.* To range or travel over or about an area, especially in a search. [From Middle English *scouren*, probably of Scandinavian origin.] —**scour′er** *n.*

scourge (skûrj) *n.* **1.** A cause of widespread suffering, as a disease or war. **2.** A means of inflicting suffering or punishment. **3.** A small whip used to inflict punishment. ❖ *tr.v.* **scourged, scourg·ing, scourg·es 1.** To cause widespread suffering to; devastate. **2.** To punish severely. **3.** To flog. —**scourg′er** *n.*

scout[1] (skout) *v.* **scout·ed, scout·ing, scouts** —*tr.* **1.** To observe or explore carefully in order to obtain information: *The soldier scouted the woods ahead.* **2.** To observe and evaluate (an athlete or entertainer, for example), as for possible hiring. —*intr.* To search: *I scouted around for my baseball glove.* ❖ *n.* **1.** A person who goes out from a main body to gather information. **2.** often **Scout** A member of the Boy Scouts or Girl Scouts. **3.** A person employed to discover and recruit people with talent. [From Middle English *scouten*, from Latin *auscultāre*, to listen.]

scout[2] (skout) *tr.v.* **scout·ed, scout·ing, scouts** To reject with scorn. [Of Scandinavian origin.]

scout·ing also **Scouting** (skou′tĭng) *n.* The activities of the Boy Scouts or Girl Scouts.

scout·mas·ter (skout′măs′tər) *n.* The adult leader of a troop of Boy Scouts.

scow (skou) *n.* A large flatbottom boat with square ends, used chiefly for transporting freight.

scowl (skoul) *intr.v.* **scowled, scowl·ing, scowls** To wrinkle or contract the brow as an expression of anger or disapproval. ❖ *n.* An angry frown. —**scowl′er** *n.*

scrab·ble (skrăb′əl) *intr.v.* **scrab·bled, scrab·bling, scrab·bles 1.** To scrape or grope about frantically with the hands: *scrabbled in the dust for the lost tool.* **2.** To move or climb with scrambling, disorderly haste: *scrabbled down the rocks to the water.* **3.** To struggle or work hard or desperately: *scrabbled for a living on the farm.*

scrag (skrăg) *n.* **1.** A bony or scrawny person or animal. **2.** A piece of lean or bony meat, especially a neck of mutton.

scrag·gly (skrăg′lē) *adj.* **scrag·gli·er, scrag·gli·est** Ragged; unkempt: *scraggly hair; scraggly undergrowth.*

scrag·gy (skrăg′ē) *adj.* **scrag·gi·er, scrag·gi·est 1.** Jagged; rough: *scraggy cliffs.* **2.** Bony and lean: *a scraggy cat.* —**scrag′gi·ly** *adv.* —**scrag′gi·ness** *n.*

scram (skrăm) *intr.v.* **scrammed, scram·ming, scrams** *Slang* To leave at once; go immediately.

scram·ble (skrăm′bəl) *v.* **scram·bled, scram·bling, scram·bles** —*intr.* **1.** To move or climb hurriedly, especially on the hands and knees: *The children scrambled over the stone wall.* **2.** To struggle or contend in order to get something: *scrambled for the best seats.* **3.** To take off with all possible haste in order to confront enemy aircraft. **4.** In football, to run with the ball when there is no open receiver. Used of a quarterback. —*tr.* **1.** To mix or gather together in a confused or disorderly manner: *scrambled the letters of a word.* **2.** To cook (beaten eggs) until firm but moist and soft. **3.** To distort or garble (an electronic signal) so that it cannot be used or understood without a special receiver. **4.** To cause (aircraft) to take off as fast as possible, especially to confront enemy aircraft. ❖ *n.* **1.** The act or an instance of scrambling. **2.** A strenuous climb or hike: *It was quite a scramble to reach the pass.* **3.** A struggle for something: *a scramble for new territory.*

scram·bler (**skrăm′**blər) *n.* An electronic device that scrambles a signal so that it can be received only with special equipment.

scrap[1] (skrăp) *n.* **1.** A small piece or bit; a fragment. **2. scraps** Leftover bits of food. **3.** Discarded waste material, especially metal suitable for reprocessing: *sold the old car as scrap.* ❖ *tr.v.* **scrapped, scrap·ping, scraps 1.** To break down into parts for disposal or salvage: *scrap an old stove.* **2.** To discard or abandon as useless; cancel: *scrap a plan.* [From Middle English *scrappe,* from Old Norse *skrap,* trifles, pieces.]

scrap[2] (skrăp) *intr.v.* **scrapped, scrap·ping, scraps** To fight, often with the fists. ❖ *n.* A fight or scuffle. [Perhaps from *scrape.*]

scrap·book (**skrăp′**bo͝ok′) *n.* A book with blank pages for mounting pictures or other mementos.

scrape (skrāp) *v.* **scraped, scrap·ing, scrapes** *—tr.* **1.** To clean, smooth, or grate by rubbing: *scrape a carrot.* **2.** To remove (material) from a surface by forceful strokes with a rough or edged instrument: *scraped ice from the windshield.* **3.** To cause to rub or move against something, often with a harsh sound: *scraped her fingernails on the wall.* **4.** To damage or injure the surface of by rubbing against something rough or sharp: *scraped my knee on the sidewalk.* **5.** To amass or produce with difficulty: *scrape together enough money for the rent.* *—intr.* **1.** To rub or move with a harsh grating noise. **2.** To survive or manage to continue by spending very little: *scraped by on a small salary.* ❖ *n.* **1.** The act of scraping. **2.** The sound of scraping. **3.** A mark or an injury caused by scraping. **4a.** An embarrassing or difficult situation. **b.** A fight.

scrap·er (**skrā′**pər) *n.* Something that scrapes, especially a tool for scraping off paint or other material.

scrap·ple (**skrăp′**əl) *n.* A mush of ground pork and cornmeal that is allowed to set and is then sliced and fried.

scrap·py[1] (**skrăp′**ē) *adj.* **scrap·pi·er, scrap·pi·est** Made up of bits and pieces; fragmentary. [From *scrap,* fragment.] **—scrap′pi·ness** *n.*

scrap·py[2] (**skrăp′**ē) *adj.* **scrap·pi·er, scrap·pi·est 1.** Quarrelsome; contentious. **2.** Full of fighting spirit. [From *scrap,* to fight.] **—scrap′pi·ness** *n.*

scratch (skrăch) *v.* **scratched, scratch·ing, scratch·es** *—tr.* **1.** To make a thin shallow cut or mark on (a surface) with a sharp instrument. **2.** To scrape or injure with the nails or claws: *The cat scratched my arm.* **3.** To rub or scrape (the skin) to relieve itching. **4a.** To write or draw something by scraping a surface: *scratched a name on a rock.* **b.** To write or mark hastily; scrawl: *scratched notes on a pad.* **5.** To strike out or cancel (a word, for example), as by drawing lines across. **6.** To withdraw from competition: *scratch a horse from a race.* **7.** To make (a living) from hard work and saving money. *—intr.* **1.** To use the nails or claws to scrape or injure: *The dog scratched at the door.* **2.** To rub or scrape the skin to relieve itching. **3.** To make a thin scraping sound: *The pencil scratched on the paper.* ❖ *n.* **1.** A mark or wound made by scratching. **2.** A sound made by scratching. ❖ *adj.* **1.** Done hurriedly or haphazardly: *a scratch outline.* **2.** Assembled at random: *a scratch team.* ◆ **from scratch** From the very beginning: *make a cake from scratch.* **scratch the surface** To make only a little progress in understanding; treat superficially: *The brief article only scratches the surface of this complicated matter.* **up to scratch** *Informal* Meeting the requirements: *The sleepy student's work was not up to scratch.* **—scratch′er** *n.*

scratch·y (**skrăch′**ē) *adj.* **scratch·i·er, scratch·i·est 1.** Rough, harsh, or irritating: *was wearing a scratchy sweater.* **2.** Making a harsh scratching sound. **—scratch′i·ly** *adv.* **—scratch′i·ness** *n.*

scrawl (skrôl) *v.* **scrawled, scrawl·ing, scrawls** *—tr.* To write hastily or carelessly: *scrawl a note on a pad.* *—intr.* To write in a sprawling irregular manner. ❖ *n.* Sprawling or unreadable handwriting. **—scrawl′er** *n.*

scraw·ny (**skrô′**nē) *adj.* **scraw·ni·er, scraw·ni·est** Thin and bony; skinny. See Synonyms at **lean**[2]. **—scraw′ni·ness** *n.*

scream (skrēm) *v.* **screamed, scream·ing, screams** *—intr.* **1.** To utter a long, loud, piercing cry, as from fear or pain. **2.** To make a loud piercing sound: *The siren screamed.* *—tr.* To utter or say in or as if in a screaming voice: *"Wait!" he screamed.* ❖ *n.* **1.** A loud piercing cry or sound. **2.** *Informal* A person or thing that is very funny. **—scream′er** *n.*

screech (skrēch) *n.* **1.** A high-pitched harsh cry; a shriek. **2.** A sound resembling this: *the screech of brakes.* ❖ *v.* **screeched, screech·ing, screech·es** *—tr.* To utter in or as if in a high-pitched harsh voice: *The children screeched an answer.* *—intr.* **1.** To cry out in a high-pitched harsh voice. **2.** To make a shrill grating sound like a screech: *The tires screeched on the wet pavement.*

screech owl

screech owl *n.* Any of various small owls having tufted ears and a wailing quavering call.

screen (skrēn) *n.* **1.** A flat movable device used to divide, conceal, or protect. **2.** Something that serves to conceal: *a screen of shrubs around the yard.* **3.** A coarse sieve. **4.** A frame covered with wire or plastic mesh, used in a window or door to keep out insects and allow air to pass in and out. **5.** A large flat white surface upon which slides or images are projected. **6.** A surface where images are electronically displayed on a device such as a television or laptop computer. **7.** The movie industry: *bring a story to the screen.* ❖ *tr.v.* **screened, screen·ing, screens 1.** To provide with a screen: *screen a porch.* **2a.** To shelter, guard, or protect: *The stone wall screened us from the wind.* **b.** To block out (something), especially as a means of protection: *lotion that screens out harmful ultraviolet rays.* **3.** To conceal from view with or as if with a screen: *Trees screened the house from the street.* See Synonyms at **hide**[1]. **4.** To separate or sift out with a sieve. **5.** To examine systematically in order to determine suitability or make an assessment: *screen job applicants; screen patients for diabetes.* **6.** To show (a movie) on a screen. **7.** In sports, to block the vision or movement of (an opponent) by using one's body. [From Middle English *screne,* from Middle Dutch *scherm,* shield, screen.]

screen·ing (**skrē′**nĭng) *n.* **1.** The mesh material used to make door or window screens. **2.** A presentation of a movie. **3.** A systematic examination or assessment, as of a medical patient or job applicant. **4. screenings** *(used with a singular or plural verb)* Refuse such as waste coal, separated out by a screen.

screen·play (**skrēn′**plā′) *n.* The script for a movie.

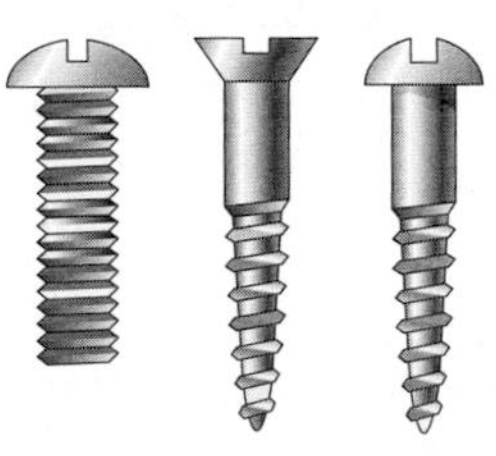

screw

left to right: round-head machine screw, flat-head wood screw, and round-head wood screw

screw (skro͞o) *n.* **1a.** A cylindrical rod having one or more helical grooves cut into its surface. **b.** The part, cut with a similar groove, into which such a rod fits. **2.** A metal pin having such grooves, fitted with a slotted head so that it can be turned by a screwdriver and used to fasten things together. **3.** A propeller, especially for a ship or motorboat. **4.** A twist or turn of or as if of a screw. ❖ *v.* **screwed, screw·ing, screws** *—tr.* **1.** To drive or tighten (a screw). **2a.** To fasten, tighten, or attach by or as if by means of a screw. **b.** To attach (a threaded cap or fitting) by twisting into place: *screw a*

scrimshaw
scrimshaw design on a whale's tooth

scroll
on a violin

scuba diving

ă	pat	ôr	core
ā	pay	oi	boy
âr	care	ou	out
ä	father	o͝o	took
ĕ	pet	o͝or	lure
ē	be	o͞o	boot
ĭ	pit	ŭ	cut
ī	bite	ûr	urge
îr	pier	th	thin
ŏ	pot	*th*	this
ō	toe	zh	vision
ô	paw	ə	about

valve onto the end of a pipe. **3.** To twist (one's face) out of normal shape. —*intr.* **1.** To turn or twist. **2.** To become attached by means of a screw. ◆ **screw up 1.** To gather or summon up: *I screwed up my courage to face the challenge.* **2.** *Slang* To make a mess of (an undertaking).

screw·ball (skro͞o′bôl′) *n.* **1.** In baseball, a pitched ball that curves in the direction opposite that of a normal curve ball. **2.** *Slang* A strange or irrational person. ❖ *adj. Slang* Strange or irrational: *That screwball idea will never work.*

screw·driv·er (skro͞o′drī′vər) *n.* A tool used to turn screws.

screw·y (skro͞o′ē) *adj.* **screw·i·er, screw·i·est** *Slang* **1.** Crazy or eccentric. **2.** Odd or inappropriate: *There's something screwy with this computer.*

scrib·ble (skrĭb′əl) *v.* **scrib·bled, scrib·bling, scrib·bles** —*tr.* To write or draw (something) hastily or carelessly: *She quickly scribbled a memo before she left.* —*intr.* To write or draw in a hurried careless way: *The bored student scribbled in his notebook.* ❖ *n.* **1.** Careless hurried writing. **2.** Meaningless marks. —**scrib′bler** *n.*

scribe (skrīb) *n.* **1.** A public clerk or secretary, especially in ancient times. **2.** A person who copies manuscripts and documents for a living. **3.** A writer or journalist. ❖ *tr.v.* **scribed, scrib·ing, scribes** To draw or mark with a scriber: *scribe a pattern; scribe metal.* [From Middle English, from Late Latin *scrība*, from Latin *scrībere*, to write.]

scrib·er (skrī′bər) *n.* A sharply pointed tool for marking lines, as on wood or metal.

scrim·mage (skrĭm′ĭj) *n.* **1.** A practice game between members of the same team. **2.** In football, the action from the time the ball is snapped until it is declared dead. ❖ *intr.v.* **scrim·maged, scrim·mag·ing, scrim·mag·es** To engage in a scrimmage.

scrimp (skrĭmp) *intr.v.* **scrimped, scrimp·ing, scrimps** To be very frugal; economize severely: *We scrimped and saved for our trip.*

scrim·shaw (skrĭm′shô′) *n., pl.* **scrimshaw** or **scrim·shaws 1.** The art of carving complex and fine designs on whale bone or whale ivory. **2.** An article made by this art.

scrip (skrĭp) *n.* A form of money issued by a local government or private organization.

script (skrĭpt) *n.* **1a.** Letters or characters written by hand; handwriting. **b.** A particular style of writing: *medieval script.* **2a.** Printer's type that resembles handwriting. **b.** Something printed with such type. **3.** The text of a play, movie, or broadcast. [From Middle English *scrite*, a piece of writing, from Latin *scrīptum*, something written.]

scrip·ture (skrĭp′chər) *n.* **1a.** A sacred writing or book. **b.** A passage from such a writing or book. **2.** often **Scripture** or **Scriptures** The sacred writings of the Bible. **3.** A statement regarded as authoritative. —**scrip′tur·al** *adj.*

scriv·en·er (skrĭv′ə-nər *or* skrĭv′nər) *n.* **1.** A scribe. **2.** A person who writes up legal documents.

scrod (skrŏd) *n.* A small cod, haddock, or similar fish, especially one used for cooking.

scroll (skrōl) *n.* **1.** A roll, as of parchment or papyrus, used especially for writing a document. **2.** An ornamental object or design that resembles a partly rolled scroll of paper. ❖ *v.* **scrolled, scroll·ing, scrolls** —*tr.* To cause (displayed text or graphics) to move up or down the screen of a computer monitor. —*intr.* To cause displayed text or graphics to move up or down the screen of a computer monitor: *scrolled down to the end of the document.*

Scrooge also **scrooge** (skro͞oj) *n.* A person who is miserly and mean-spirited. [After Ebenezer *Scrooge*, miserly main character in *A Christmas Carol* by Charles Dickens.]

scro·tum (skrō′təm) *n., pl.* **scro·ta** (skrō′tə) or **scro·tums** The external sac of skin that encloses the testes in most mammals.

scrounge (skrounj) *v.* **scrounged, scroung·ing, scroung·es** *Slang* —*tr.* **1.** To obtain by rummaging or foraging: *scrounging old books out of the attic.* **2.** To obtain (something) by begging or borrowing with no intention of returning or repaying: *scrounge a dollar from a friend.* —*intr.* To forage about; search.

scrub[1] (skrŭb) *v.* **scrubbed, scrub·bing, scrubs** —*tr.* **1.** To rub hard in order to clean. **2.** To remove (dirt or stains) by hard rubbing. **3.** To remove impurities from (a gas). **4.** *Slang* To cancel or abandon: *scrub a space flight.* —*intr.* To clean or wash something by hard rubbing. [From Middle English *shrubben*, to scratch oneself, from Middle Dutch *schrobben*, to clean by rubbing.] —**scrub′ber** *n.*

scrub[2] (skrŭb) *n.* **1.** Vegetation consisting of shrubs or small trees. **2.** In sports, a player not on the varsity or first team. [From Middle English, variant of *shrub*, shrub.]

scrub·by (skrŭb′ē) *adj.* **scrub·bi·er, scrub·bi·est 1.** Covered with or consisting of scrub or underbrush. **2.** Straggly or stunted. —**scrub′bi·ness** *n.*

scruff (skrŭf) *n.* The back of the neck or the loose skin covering it; the nape.

scruff·y (skrŭf′ē) *adj.* **scruff·i·er, scruff·i·est** Shabby; untidy: *a scruffy little house.*

scrump·tious (skrŭmp′shəs) *adj.* Very pleasing to the taste; delicious.

scru·ple (skro͞o′pəl) *n.* **1.** A feeling of uneasiness that is produced by one's conscience and tends to hinder action. **2.** A unit of apothecaries' weight equal to about 1.3 grams, or 20 grains. ❖ *intr.v.* **scru·pled, scru·pling, scru·ples** To hesitate as a result of conscience or moral principle.

scru·pu·lous (skro͞o′pyə-ləs) *adj.* **1.** Showing extreme care about details; painstaking: *a scrupulous regard for facts.* **2.** Having scruples; ethical: *a scrupulous attorney.* —**scru′pu·lous·ly** *adv.* —**scru′pu·lous·ness** *n.*

scru·ti·nize (skro͞ot′n-īz′) *tr.v.* **scru·ti·nized, scru·ti·niz·ing, scru·ti·niz·es** To observe or examine with great care. —**scru′ti·niz′er** *n.*

scru·ti·ny (skro͞ot′n-ē) *n., pl.* **scru·ti·nies** Close, careful examination or observation.

scu·ba (sko͞o′bə) *n.* A portable device including one or more tanks of compressed air, used by divers for breathing under water. [From *s(elf-)c(ontained) u(nderwater) b(reathing) a(pparatus)*.]

scuba diving *n.* The use of scuba gear when swimming underwater.

scud (skŭd) *intr.v.* **scud·ded, scud·ding, scuds** To move along swiftly and easily, especially with the wind: *The clouds scudded across the sky.*

scuff (skŭf) *v.* **scuffed, scuff·ing, scuffs** —*intr.* To scrape or drag the feet while walking. —*tr.* **1.** To scrape with the feet. **2.** To shuffle (the feet), as in embarrassment. **3.** To scrape or roughen the surface of. ❖ *n.* **1.** The act or sound of scraping. **2.** A worn or rough spot resulting from scraping.

scuf·fle (skŭf′əl) *intr.v.* **scuf·fled, scuf·fling, scuf·fles** To tussle or fight confusedly at close quarters: *The police scuffled with the thieves.* ❖ *n.* A rough disorderly struggle at close quarters. —**scuf′fler** *n.*

scull (skŭl) *n.* **1.** A long oar used at the stern of a boat and moved from side to side to propel the boat forward. **2.** One of a pair of short-handled oars used by a single rower. **3.** A small light racing boat. ❖ *tr.v.* **sculled, scull·ing, sculls** To propel (a boat) with a scull or a pair of sculls.

❑ *These sound alike:* **scull, skull** (bones of head).

scul·ler·y (skŭl′ə-rē) *n., pl.* **scul·ler·ies** A room next to the kitchen, where dishwashing and other kitchen chores are done.

scul·lion (skŭl′yən) *n.* A servant employed to do menial tasks in a kitchen.

sculpt (skŭlpt) *v.* **sculpt·ed, sculpt·ing, sculpts** —*tr.* **1.** To shape (a material) into sculpture: *sculpted the clay.* **2.** To make as or represent in sculpture: *sculpted a human figure in marble.* —*intr.* To be a sculptor; produce sculpture. [From Latin *sculpere,* to carve.]

sculp·tor (skŭlp′tər) *n.* An artist who makes sculptures.

sculp·ture (skŭlp′chər) *n.* **1.** The art or practice of shaping or making three-dimensional figures or designs, as by carving wood, chiseling stone, or casting metal. **2a.** A work of art created in this way. **b.** Such works of art considered as a group: *African sculpture.* ❖ *tr.v.* **sculp·tured, sculp·tur·ing, sculp·tures 1.** To shape (stone, metal, or wood, for example) into sculpture. **2.** To represent in sculpture: *sculpture a ballerina.* **3.** To ornament with sculpture: *sculptured the portals of the church.* **—sculp′tur·al** *adj.*

scum (skŭm) *n.* **1.** A filmy or frothy layer of matter that forms on the surface of a liquid or body of water or on a hard surface. **2.** A similar mass of waste material that rises to the surface of a molten metal. **3.** *Slang* A person or class of people regarded as worthless or contemptible. [From Middle English *scome,* from Middle Dutch *schūm.*]

scup (skŭp) *n., pl.* **scup** or **scups** A porgy of northern Atlantic waters.

scup·per (skŭp′ər) *n.* An opening in the side of a ship at deck level to allow water to run off.

scurf (skûrf) *n.* **1.** Dry skin that has flaked off, such as dandruff. **2.** A scaly crust on a surface, especially of a plant.

scur·ri·lous (skûr′ə-ləs) *adj.* **1.** Given to the use of coarse, spiteful, and abusive language. **2.** Expressed in coarse, spiteful, and abusive language: *a scurrilous attack.* **3.** Of a malicious or slanderous nature; defamatory: *published scurrilous lies about him.* **—scur′ril·ous·ly** *adv.* **—scur′ril·ous·ness** *n.*

scur·ry (skûr′ē) *intr.v.* **scur·ried, scur·ry·ing, scur·ries** To move or hurry with light quick steps; scamper.

scur·vy (skûr′vē) *n.* A disease caused by lack of vitamin C and characterized by soft bleeding gums, bleeding under the skin, and extreme weakness. ❖ *adj.* **scur·vi·er, scur·vi·est** Mean; contemptible.

scutch·eon (skŭch′ən) *n.* An escutcheon.

scut·tle[1] (skŭt′l) *n.* **1.** A small opening or hatch in a ship's deck or hull. **2.** The movable cover for such an opening. ❖ *tr.v.* **scut·tled, scut·tling, scut·tles 1.** To sink (a ship) by cutting or opening holes in the hull. **2.** *Informal* To abandon or terminate: *We scuttled our vacation plans.* [From Middle English *skottell,* from Old French *escoutille,* possibly from Spanish *escotilla.*]

scut·tle[2] (skŭt′l) *n.* A metal pail for carrying coal. [From Old English *scutel,* dish, from Latin *scutella.*]

scut·tle[3] (skŭt′l) *intr.v.* **scut·tled, scut·tling, scut·tles** To run or move with quick little steps; scurry: *The crab scuttled over the rocks.* ❖ *n.* A hurried run. [Perhaps from Middle English *scottlinge,* scampering.]

scut·tle·butt (skŭt′l-bŭt′) *n. Slang* Gossip; rumor.

Scyl·la (sĭl′ə) *n.* In Greek mythology, a female sea monster who lived in a cave opposite Charybdis and devoured sailors. ◆ **between Scylla and Charybdis** In a position where a person avoiding one danger becomes exposed to another danger.

scythe (sīth) *n.* A tool with a long curved blade and a long bent handle, used for mowing or reaping. ❖ *tr.v.* **scythed, scyth·ing, scythes** To cut with or as if with a scythe. [From Old English *sīthe,* sickle.]

Scyth·i·a (sĭth′ē-ə *or* sĭth′ē-ə) An ancient region of Eurasia extending from the mouth of the Danube River on the Black Sea to the territory east of the Aral Sea.

SD *abbr.* An abbreviation of South Dakota.

Se The symbol for the element **selenium.**

SE *abbr.* An abbreviation of: **1.** southeast. **2.** southeastern.

sea (sē) *n.* **1a.** The continuous body of salt water that covers most of the surface of the earth. **b.** A region of water within an ocean and partly enclosed by land, as the North Sea. **c.** A large body of either fresh or salt water that is completely enclosed by land, as the Caspian Sea. **2.** The condition of the ocean's surface, especially with respect to its motion or roughness: *a high sea.* **3.** A swell or wave: *choppy seas.* **4.** A vast expanse or extent: *a sea of ice.* **5.** A mare of the moon. ◆ **at sea 1.** On the sea, especially on a sea voyage. **2.** In a state of confusion; at a loss. [From Old English *sǣ.*]

❑ *These sound alike:* **sea, see[1]** (perceive with the eyes), **see[2]** (bishop's position), **si** (musical note).

sea anemone *n.* Any of numerous often colorful sea animals that live attached to an underwater surface and have a mouth surrounded by stinging tentacles.

sea·bed (sē′bĕd′) *n.* The bottom of a sea or an ocean.

sea·bird (sē′bîrd′) *n.* A bird, such as a petrel or albatross, that spends much of its time near or on the ocean, especially far from shore.

sea biscuit *n.* Hardtack.

sea·board (sē′bôrd′) *n.* Land along or near the sea.

sea·bor·gi·um (sē-bôr′gē-əm) *n. Symbol* **Sg** A radioactive element produced artificially from californium or lead. Atomic number 106. See **Periodic Table.** [After Glenn Theodore *Seaborg* (1912–1999), American chemist.]

sea breeze *n.* A cool breeze blowing inland from the sea.

sea·coast (sē′kōst′) *n.* Land along the sea.

sea cow *n.* Any of several large water mammals such as the manatee or dugong.

sea cucumber *n.* Any of various sea animals related to the starfishes and sea urchins, having a rough or spiny cucumber-shaped body and a mouth surrounded by tentacles.

sea dog *n.* A very experienced sailor.

sea·far·er (sē′fâr′ər) *n.* A sailor or mariner.

sea·far·ing (sē′fâr′ĭng) *n.* The work of a sailor. ❖ *adj.* **1.** Earning one's living at sea: *a seafaring man.* **2.** Fit to travel on the sea.

sea·food (sē′fo͞od′) *n.* Fish or shellfish from the sea eaten as food.

sea·girt (sē′gûrt′) *adj.* Surrounded by the sea.

sea·go·ing (sē′gō′ĭng) *adj.* Made or used for ocean voyages: *a seagoing barge.*

sea green *n.* A medium green or bluish green.

sea·gull also **sea gull** (sē′gŭl′) *n.* A gull, especially one that lives near coastal areas.

sea·horse or **sea horse** (sē′hôrs′) *n.* **1.** Any of several small ocean fishes having a head resembling that of a horse, a body encircled by bony ridges, and a tail that can be curled around an object. **2.** In mythology, an animal, half fish and half horse, ridden by Neptune and other sea gods.

seal[1] (sēl) *n.* **1.** A fitting or material that is used to close off an opening or connection, especially to prevent the escape or entry of a liquid or gas: *used caulk to make a seal around a window.* **2.** A design used to identify a person or thing or to show that something is authentic: *The publisher's seal appears on every title page.* **3a.** An instrument, such as a ring with an engraved design, used to stamp an impression in wax or other soft material. **b.** The impression so made. **c.** A small disk or wafer of wax, lead, or paper bearing such a mark or impression, used to show that a document or statement is genuine or valid or to fasten an envelope. **4.** A small paper sticker used to fasten or decorate an envelope. ❖ *tr.v.* **sealed, seal·ing,**

scull

sculpture

pre-Columbian sculpture at Chac Mool Beach in Cancun, Mexico

WRITERS CHOOSE THEIR WORDS

Gaily striped tents and pavilions sprang up everywhere as the workmen **scurried** about like ants. Within minutes there were racecourses and grandstands, side shows and refreshment booths, gaming fields, Ferris wheels, banners, bunting, and bedlam, almost without pause.

—Norton Juster
The Phantom Tollbooth

sea anemone

seal[1]

seal[2]

sea lion

seaplane

seals 1. To close with a seal: *sealed the envelope.* **2.** To close so that a liquid or gas cannot enter or escape: *seal a pipe joint.* **3.** To cover, secure, or fill up (an opening): *seal a tunnel with concrete.* **4.** To apply a waterproof coating to: *seal the driveway.* **5.** To affix a seal to as a mark of genuineness, authority, or legal status: *The duke signed and sealed the letter.* **6.** To establish or determine with no possibility of change: *Their fate was sealed.* ◆ **seal off** To prevent passage into and out of (an area): *The police sealed off the crime scene.* [From Middle English *sel*, from Latin *sigillum*, from *signum*, sign, seal.] —**seal′er** *n.*

seal[2] (sēl) *n.* **1.** Any of various sea mammals having a streamlined body, limbs in the form of flippers, and hair or fur that is very thick in some species. **2.** The fur of a seal. **3.** Leather made from the hide of a seal; sealskin. [From Old English *seolh.*]

sea-lane (sē′lān′) *n.* An established or frequently used sea route.

seal·ant (sē′lənt) *n.* A substance used to seal, waterproof, or coat something.

sea legs *pl.n.* The ability to adjust one's balance to the motion of a ship, especially in rough seas: *He got his sea legs after being on the ship for a couple of days.*

sea level *n.* **1.** The level of the surface of the ocean, especially the level halfway between mean high and low tide. **2.** Mean sea level.

seal·ing wax (sē′lĭng) *n.* A preparation of shellac and turpentine that is soft and fluid when hot but solid when cold, used to seal letters, jars, or batteries.

sea lion *n.* Any of several large seals, mostly of Pacific waters, having a sleek body and brownish fur.

seal·skin (sēl′skĭn′) *n.* **1.** The hide of a seal. **2.** Fur or leather from the pelt or hide of a seal.

seam (sēm) *n.* **1.** A line, ridge, or groove formed by joining two pieces of material together at their edges, as by sewing or welding. **2.** A line across a surface, as a crack or wrinkle. **3.** A thin layer or stratum, as of coal or rock. ❖ *tr.v.* **seamed, seam·ing, seams 1.** To join with or as if with a seam. **2.** To mark with a groove, wrinkle, scar, or other line. [From Old English *sēam.*] —**seam′er** *n.*

❑ *These sound alike:* **seam, seem** (appear to be).

sea·man (sē′mən) *n.* **1.** A sailor or mariner. **2.** A person in the US Navy or Coast Guard with any of three noncommissioned ranks below petty officer.

❑ *These sound alike:* **seaman, semen** (sperm).

Sea·man (sē′mən), **Elizabeth Cochrane** See Nellie **Bly.**

sea·man·ship (sē′mən-shĭp′) *n.* Skill in handling or navigating a boat or ship.

seam·stress (sēm′strĭs) *n.* A woman who sews, especially one who makes her living by sewing.

seam·y (sē′mē) *adj.* **seam·i·er, seam·i·est 1.** Unpleasant; nasty and low: *the seamy side of politics.* **2.** Having or showing a seam.

sé·ance (sā′äns′) *n.* A meeting at which people attempt to communicate with the dead.

Sea of For the names of actual seas, see the specific proper name; for example, **Japan, Sea of.**

sea otter *n.* A large otter of Pacific waters, having soft dark-brown fur.

sea·plane (sē′plān′) *n.* An airplane equipped with floats for taking off from and landing on water.

sea·port (sē′pôrt′) *n.* A harbor or town having facilities for seagoing ships.

sear (sîr) *tr.v.* **seared, sear·ing, sears 1.** To scorch or burn the surface of; char. **2.** To brown (meat) quickly using very high heat. **3.** To cause to dry up or shrivel. **4a.** To cause emotional pain or trauma to: *He was seared by their betrayal of his trust.* **b.** To cause to be felt or remembered because of emotional intensity: *Experiencing the disaster seared into his memory the desperate looks on the faces of the victims.*

❑ *These sound alike:* **sear, seer** (prophet), **sere** (withered).

search (sûrch) *v.* **searched, search·ing, search·es** —*tr.* **1.** To move around in, go through, or look through in an effort to find something: *She searched her room for her missing keys.* **2.** To examine or investigate (something) carefully; probe: *He searched his heart for the right thing to do.* **3.** To seek data matching a word, phrase, or pattern of characters in (an online database): *searched the Internet for information about ostriches; searched the document for the misspelled word "thier."* —*intr.* **1.** To search a place or space in order to find something: *searching for a lost dog.* **2.** To make a careful investigation: *searching for the right words to say.* **3.** To use a search engine or other software to find any data matching a particular pattern. ❖ *n.* **1.** The act of searching: *the search for knowledge.* **2.** The use of a search engine or other software to find any data matching a particular pattern. [From Middle English *serchen*, from Latin *circāre*, to go around.] —**search′er** *n.*

search engine *n.* **1.** A software program that searches websites for information about specified terms. **2.** A website that provides a search engine.

search·ing (sûr′chĭng) *adj.* **1.** Examining closely or thoroughly; scrutinizing: *a searching investigation of stock-market dealings.* **2.** Keenly observant: *some searching insights.* —**search′ing·ly** *adv.*

search·light (sûrch′līt′) *n.* **1.** A light equipped with a reflector to produce a bright beam in which all the rays are approximately parallel. **2.** The beam produced by such a light.

search warrant *n.* A legal order allowing a law enforcement officer to search a specified person, building, residence, or area, for evidence of a crime.

sea·shell (sē′shĕl′) *n.* The hard shell of a sea mollusk, such as a whelk or cowrie.

sea·shore (sē′shôr′) *n.* Land next to the sea.

sea·sick·ness (sē′sĭk′nĭs) *n.* Nausea or other discomfort as a result of the pitching and rolling motions of a vessel at sea. —**sea′sick′** *adj.*

sea·side (sē′sīd′) *n.* The seashore.

sea slug *n.* Any of various colorful sea mollusks that lack a shell and gills but have fringelike projections that serve as respiratory organs.

sea·son (sē′zən) *n.* **1a.** One of four natural divisions of the year—spring, summer, autumn or fall, and winter—each beginning as the sun passes through a solstice or equinox. **b.** Either of the two parts, rainy and dry, into which the year is divided in tropical climates. **2.** A period of the year devoted to or marked by a certain activity or by the appearance of something: *the baseball season; the hurricane season.* ❖ *tr.v.* **sea·soned, sea·son·ing, sea·sons 1.** To give (food) extra flavor by adding salt, pepper, spices, or other flavorings: *seasoned the pasta.* **2.** To add enjoyment or interest to: *seasoned her writing with wit.* **3.** To dry (lumber) until it is usable; cure. **4.** To accustom or harden (a person or persons) through trial and experience: *hard training to season recruits; a seasoned hunter.* ◆ **in season 1.** Available for eating fresh or for other use. **2.** Legally permitted to be caught or hunted during a specified period. **3.** At the right moment. **out of season 1.** Not available, permitted, or ready to be eaten, caught, or hunted. **2.** Not at the right moment. [From Middle English *sesoun*, from Latin *satiō*, act of sowing.]

sea·son·a·ble (sē′zə-nə-bəl) *adj.* Suitable for the time or season. —**sea′son·a·bly** *adv.* —SEE NOTE AT **seasonal.**

sea·son·al (sē′zə-nəl) *adj.* Relating to, occurring in, or varying with a particular season: *seasonal variations in temperature.* —**sea′son·al·ly** *adv.* —SEE NOTE.

sea·son·ing (sē′zə-nĭng) *n.* An ingredient that adds to the flavor of food.

ă	pat	ôr	core
ā	pay	oi	boy
âr	care	ou	out
ä	father	ŏŏ	took
ĕ	pet	ŏŏr	lure
ē	be	ōō	boot
ĭ	pit	ŭ	cut
ī	bite	ûr	urge
îr	pier	th	thin
ŏ	pot	*th*	this
ō	toe	zh	vision
ô	paw	ə	about

season ticket *n.* A ticket for a specified period of time, as for a series of performances.

sea star *n.* A starfish.

seat (sēt) *n.* **1.** Something, such as a chair or bench, that may be sat on. **2.** The part of something on which a person sits: *a bicycle seat.* **3.** A place in which a person may sit: *a ticket for a seat on the bus.* **4.** The buttocks. **5.** The part of a garment covering the buttocks: *the seat of the pants.* **6.** A part that serves as the base or support of something. **7a.** The place where something is located or based: *the seat of the treasury.* **b.** A capital or center of authority: *the county seat.* **8.** A place of residence, especially a large house on an estate. **9.** Membership in a legislature, stock exchange, or similar organization. **10.** The manner of sitting on a horse. ❖ *tr.v.* **seat·ed, seat·ing, seats 1a.** To place in or on a seat. **b.** To assist in sitting down: *The usher seated us in the front row.* **2.** To have seats for: *an auditorium that seats 5,000.* [From Middle English *sete*, probably from Old Norse *sæti*.]

seat belt *n.* A safety strap or harness designed to hold a person securely in a seat, as in a car or airplane.

Se·at·tle (sē-ăt′l) The largest city of Washington, in the west-central part of the state on Puget Sound north-northwest of Olympia. It was founded in the 1850s.

sea turtle *n.* Any of various large turtles, such as the loggerhead, that have flippers used for swimming and are found chiefly in tropical and subtropical oceans.

sea urchin *n.* Any of various sea animals having a soft body enclosed in a rounded spiny shell.

sea·ward (sē′wərd) *adv. & adj.* Toward or at the sea: *a seaward breeze.*

sea·way (sē′wā′) *n.* **1.** A sea route. **2.** An inland waterway for ocean shipping.

sea·weed (sē′wēd′) *n.* Any of various algae that live in ocean waters.

sea·wor·thy (sē′wûr′*th*ē) *adj.* **sea·wor·thi·er, sea·wor·thi·est** Fit for crossing the sea. **—sea′wor′thi·ness** *n.*

se·ba·ceous (sĭ-bā′shəs) *adj.* Relating to or secreting a fatty or oily substance.

sebaceous gland *n.* Any of the tiny glands in the skin of humans and other mammals that secrete an oily material into the hair follicles.

sec *abbr.* An abbreviation of secant.

sec. *abbr.* An abbreviation of second.

se·cant (sē′kănt′) *n.* **1.** A straight line or ray that intersects a curve, especially a circle, at two or more points. **2.** In a right triangle, the ratio of the length of a hypotenuse to the side adjacent to an acute angle.

se·cede (sĭ-sēd′) *intr.v.* **se·ced·ed, se·ced·ing, se·cedes** To withdraw formally from membership in a state, union, or other political organization: *states that seceded from the Union before the Civil War.* [From Latin *sēcēdere*, to withdraw : *sē-*, apart + *cēdere*, to go.]

se·ces·sion (sĭ-sĕsh′ən) *n.* **1.** The act of seceding. **2.** often **Secession** The withdrawal of 11 southern states from the Union in 1860–1861, which brought on the US Civil War. **—se·ces′sion·ism** *n.* **—se·ces′sion·ist** *n.*

se·clude (sĭ-klo͞od′) *tr.v.* **se·clud·ed, se·clud·ing, se·cludes** To set or keep apart, as from social contact with others: *secluded himself from the world.* [From Middle English *secluden*, to shut off, from Latin *sēclūdere* : *sē-*, apart + *claudere*, to shut.]

se·clud·ed (sĭ-klo͞o′dĭd) *adj.* **1.** Removed or distant from others; alone: *a secluded life.* **2.** Screened or hidden from view: *a secluded pool.* **—se·clud′ed·ness** *n.*

se·clu·sion (sĭ-klo͞o′zhən) *n.* **1.** The act of secluding: *The judge ordered the seclusion of the jury.* **2.** The condition of being secluded; solitude: *the seclusion of the desert.*

sec·ond[1] (sĕk′ənd) *n.* **1.** A unit of time equal to 1⁄60 of a minute. See table at **measurement**. **2.** A short period of time; a moment: *I'll be with you in a second.* **3.** A unit of angular measure equal to 1⁄60 of a minute of arc. [From Middle English *seconde*, from Medieval Latin *(pars minūta) secunda*, second (small part).]

sec·ond[2] (sĕk′ənd) *adj.* **1.** Coming next after the first in order, place, rank, time, or quality: *the second floor.* **2.** Alternate; other: *every second year.* **3.** Inferior to another: *an accomplishment second only to yours.* **4a.** Having a lower pitch or range: *the second sopranos of a choir.* **b.** Singing or playing a part having a lower range: *the second violins of an orchestra.* **5.** Relating to the transmission gear used to produce speeds next higher than those of first in a motor vehicle. ❖ *n.* **1.** The ordinal number matching the number two in a series. **2.** often **seconds** A piece of merchandise of inferior quality: *The socks on sale are seconds.* **3.** An attendant of a contestant in a duel or boxing match. **4a.** The interval between two adjacent tones of a musical scale. **b.** The second tone in a musical scale. **5.** The transmission gear used to produce speeds next highest to those of first in a motor vehicle: *put the truck in second as they drove up the hill.* ❖ *tr.v.* **sec·ond·ed, sec·ond·ing, sec·onds 1.** To endorse (a motion or nomination) as a means of bringing it to a vote. **2.** To support or promote: *I wholeheartedly second her idea.* ❖ *adv.* **1.** In the second order, place, or rank: *finished second in the race.* **2.** But for one other; save one: *the second largest seaport.* [From Middle English, from Latin *secundus*, following.] **—sec′ond·er** *n.*

sec·ond·ar·y (sĕk′ən-dĕr′ē) *adj.* **1.** Second or lower in rank or importance; not primary: *Your concerns are secondary to the immediate problem.* **2.** Not immediate or direct: *secondary sources of information.* **3.** Following what comes first in time or sequence: *a secondary delivery.* **4.** Relating to a secondary school. **5.** Relating to a secondary color. **6.** Having a current or voltage induced by the magnetic field of a current flowing in another coil: *the secondary coil of a transformer.* ❖ *n., pl.* **sec·ond·ar·ies 1.** The coil or circuit through which a secondary current flows. **2.** In football, the defensive backfield. **—sec′ond·dar′i·ly** (sĕk′ən-dâr′ə-lē) *adv.*

secondary color *n.* A color produced by mixing two primary colors in equal proportions.

secondary school *n.* A school for instruction between elementary school and college.

secondary sex characteristic *n.* Any of the physical traits that appear as an organism becomes sexually mature but are not directly involved in the act of reproducing. They include breast development and the growth of facial hair in humans.

secondary stress *n.* **1.** In a word with more than one stressed syllable, the stress that is weaker than the primary one. **2.** A mark, such as (′), used to indicate this stress.

second base *n.* **1.** In baseball, the base that is across the diamond from home plate, touched second by a runner. **2.** The position played by a second baseman.

second baseman *n.* The baseball player defending the area near second base.

second class *n.* **1.** The group ranking next below the first, highest, or best group in a system of classification. **2.** Travel accommodations ranking next below first class, as on a train or airplane. ❖ *adv.* By means of second-class travel accommodations: *traveled second class.*

sec·ond-class (sĕk′ənd-klăs′) *adj.* **1.** Of secondary status. **2.** Relating to travel accommodations ranking next below first class. **3.** Considered or treated as inferior in status, rights, or privileges in comparison with some others: *second-class citizens.*

Second Coming *n.* In Christianity, the return of Jesus as judge for the Last Judgment.

sec·ond-de·gree burn (sĕk′ənd-dĭ-grē′) *n.* A burn that blisters the skin.

sea slug

USAGE

seasonal Use the word **seasonal** to refer to what depends on or is controlled by the season of the year: *There is a seasonal increase in employment when the tourists arrive each summer.* The closely related word **seasonable** applies to what is appropriate to the season (*seasonable clothing*).

secretary bird

sedan

ă	pat	ôr	core
ā	pay	oi	boy
âr	care	ou	out
ä	father	o͝o	took
ĕ	pet	o͝or	lure
ē	be	o͞o	boot
ĭ	pit	ŭ	cut
ī	bite	ûr	urge
îr	pier	th	thin
ŏ	pot	*th*	this
ō	toe	zh	vision
ô	paw	ə	about

sec·ond-guess (sĕk′ənd-gĕs′) *tr.v.* **sec·ond-guessed, sec·ond-guess·ing, sec·ond-guess·es 1.** To criticize or correct (a person or thing) after an outcome is known. **2.** To guess or try to anticipate the plans or activities of; outguess.

sec·ond·hand (sĕk′ənd-hănd′) *adj.* **1.** Previously used by another; not new: *a secondhand coat.* **2.** Dealing in previously used goods: *a secondhand store.* **3.** Obtained or derived from another; not original; borrowed: *secondhand knowledge.* ❖ *adv.* **1.** In an arrangement in which something sold or given was previously owned: *bought the coat secondhand.* **2.** In a manner that is one step removed from the original source or action: *news gathered secondhand.*

second hand[1] *n.* The hand of a clock or watch that indicates the seconds.

second hand[2] *n.* An intermediary person or source: *heard the news at second hand.*

secondhand smoke *n.* Tobacco smoke that is inhaled by nonsmokers.

second lieutenant *n.* An officer holding the lowest commissioned rank in the US Army, Air Force, or Marine Corps.

sec·ond·ly (sĕk′ənd-lē) *adv.* In the second place; second: *Firstly, I don't like the color, and secondly, it costs too much.*

second nature *n.* A behavior or characteristic that was originally learned, but that comes to seem natural through long practice.

second person *n.* **1.** A group of words or word forms, such as verbs and pronouns, that designate the person being addressed. *You* and *your* are pronouns in the second person. **2.** The style of writing in which forms in the second person are used: *a story told in the second person.*

sec·ond-rate (sĕk′ənd-rāt′) *adj.* Inferior in quality; mediocre.

Second World War *n.* World War II.

se·cre·cy (sē′krĭ-sē) *n., pl.* **se·cre·cies 1.** The condition of being secret or hidden; concealment: *work done in secrecy.* **2.** The practice of keeping secrets: *They pledged her to secrecy.*

se·cret (sē′krĭt) *adj.* **1.** Kept hidden from general knowledge or view: *secret plans.* **2.** Working in a hidden or confidential manner: *secret agents.* **3.** Not much visited; secluded: *a secret hiding place.* **4.** Beyond ordinary understanding; mysterious: *God's secret ways.* ❖ *n.* **1.** Something kept hidden or known only to oneself or to a few. **2.** Something beyond understanding or explanation: *the secret of the homing pigeon's instinct.* **3.** A method or formula for accomplishing something: *the secret of making good pizza sauce.* ◆ **in secret 1.** Without others knowing. **2.** Privately. [From Middle English, from Latin *sēcrētus*, secret, from *sēcernere*, to set aside : *sē-*, apart + *cernere*, to separate.] **—se′cret·ly** *adv.*

sec·re·tar·i·at (sĕk′rĭ-târ′ē-ĭt) *n.* **1.** The department managed by a governmental secretary, especially for an international organization such as the United Nations. **2.** The headquarters of such a department.

sec·re·tar·y (sĕk′rĭ-tĕr′ē) *n., pl.* **sec·re·tar·ies 1.** A person employed to do clerical work, such as typing, filing, and taking messages. **2.** An officer who takes minutes of meetings, answers correspondence, and keeps records, as for a company. **3.** The head of a governmental department: *the secretary of state.* **4.** A desk with a small bookcase on top. [From Middle English *secretarie*, someone entrusted with secrets, from Latin *sēcrētus*, secret.] **—sec′re·tar′i·al** (sĕk′rĭ-târ′ē-əl) *adj.*

secretary bird *n.* A large African bird having long legs, gray and black feathers, and a crest of long quills at the back of the head.

sec·re·tar·y-gen·er·al (sĕk′rĭ-tĕr′ē-jĕn′ər-əl) *n., pl.* **sec·re·tar·ies-gen·er·al** A principal executive officer, as of a political party or governmental body such as the United Nations.

se·crete[1] (sĭ-krēt′) *tr.v.* **se·cret·ed, se·cret·ing, se·cretes** To produce and release (a substance) from a cell or gland. [From French *sécrétion*, separation, from Latin *sēcernere*, to put aside.]

se·crete[2] (sĭ-krēt′) *tr.v.* **se·cret·ed, se·cret·ing, se·cretes** To conceal in a hiding place; hide. See Synonyms at **hide**[1]. [Probably from *secret*.]

se·cre·tion (sĭ-krē′shən) *n.* **1.** The act or process of secreting a substance, especially one that is not a waste product, from a cell or gland. **2.** A substance, such as tears or a hormone, that is secreted.

se·cre·tive (sē′krĭ-tĭv *or* sĭ-krē′tĭv) *adj.* Practicing or inclined to secrecy. **—se′cre·tive·ly** *adv.* **—se′cre·tive·ness** *n.*

se·cre·to·ry (sĭ-krē′tə-rē) *adj.* Relating to or performing secretion.

secret police *n.* A police force operating in secret and often using terrorism to crush political opposition to the government.

secret service *n.* **1.** The gathering of information done in secret by a government; intelligence work. **2. Secret Service** A branch of the US Treasury Department whose work includes the protection of the president.

sect (sĕkt) *n.* **1.** A group of people forming a distinct unit within a larger group. **2.** A religious group, especially one that has separated from a larger group.

sect. *abbr.* An abbreviation of section.

sec·tar·i·an (sĕk-târ′ē-ən) *adj.* **1.** Relating to or characteristic of a sect. **2.** Narrow-minded; partisan or parochial. **—sec·tar′i·an·ism** *n.*

sec·tion (sĕk′shən) *n.* **1.** One of several parts that make up something; a piece: *a section of grapefruit.* **2.** A distinct part of a written work: *the sports section of a newspaper.* **3.** A distinct area of a town, country, or city: *the residential section of town.* **4.** One of the large divisions of the seating area of a theater or stadium. **5.** The act or process of cutting or separating, especially the separation of tissue in surgery. **6.** A picture or diagram showing the internal structure of a solid object as it would appear if the object were cut by an intersecting plane; a cross section. **7.** A group of musical instruments or voices considered as a unit: *the woodwind section of the orchestra.* ❖ *tr.v.* **sec·tioned, sec·tion·ing, sec·tions 1.** To separate into parts: *sectioned the orange.* **2.** To cut or separate (tissue) surgically. [From Middle English *seccioun*, from Latin *sectiō*, a cutting, from *secāre*, to cut.]

sec·tion·al (sĕk′shə-nəl) *adj.* **1.** Relating to or characteristic of a particular district. **2.** Composed of or divided into sections: *sectional furniture.* **—sec′tion·al·ly** *adv.*

sec·tion·al·ism (sĕk′shə-nə-lĭz′əm) *n.* Excessive devotion to local interests and customs. **—sec′tion·al·ist** *adj. & n.*

sec·tor (sĕk′tər) *n.* **1.** A division of something: *the manufacturing sector of the economy.* **2.** The part of a circle bound by two radii and the arc between them. **3.** A particular military area or zone of action. [From Latin *sector*, one that cuts, from *secāre*, to cut.]

sec·u·lar (sĕk′yə-lər) *adj.* **1.** Worldly rather than spiritual: *secular interests.* **2.** Not related to religion or a religious organization: *a concert of secular music.* **3.** Not bound by monastic rules: *the secular clergy.* [From Middle English *seculer*, from Latin *saeculum*, generation, age.]

sec·u·lar·ize (sĕk′yə-lə-rīz′) *tr.v.* **sec·u·lar·ized, sec·u·lar·iz·ing, sec·u·lar·iz·es 1.** To draw (someone) away from religious orientation; make worldly. **2.** To lift the monastic restrictions from (a member of the clergy). **—sec′u·lar·i·za′tion** (sĕk′yə-lər-ĭ-zā′shən) *n.*

se·cure (sĭ-kyo͝or′) *adj.* **se·cur·er, se·cur·est 1.** Free from danger or attack: *a secure castle.* **2.** Free from risk of loss; safe: *The jewels are secure in the vault.* **3.** Free from fear, anxiety, or doubt: *feeling secure at home.* **4.** Not likely to fail or give way: *a secure foothold.* **5.** Firmly fastened: *The antenna is secure.* **6.** Assured; certain: *a secure peace.* ❖ *tr.v.* **se·cured, se·cur·ing, se·cures 1.** To guard from danger or risk of loss: *secured the city against attack.* **2.** To cause to remain firmly in position or place; fasten: *secure the ship's hatches.* **3.** To make certain; ensure: *a constitution designed to secure our freedom.* **4.** To guarantee or make sure with a pledge: *deposited collateral to secure the loan.* **5.** To get possession of; acquire: *secure a job.* **6.** To bring about; effect: *secured their release from prison.* [From Latin *sēcūrus* : *sē-*, without + *cūra*, care.] **—se·cure′ly** *adv.*

se·cu·ri·ty (sĭ-**kyo͝or′**ĭ-tē) *n., pl.* **se·cu·ri·ties 1.** Freedom from risk or danger; safety. **2.** A person, act, or thing that gives or assures safety or confidence. **3.** Something that is deposited or is given to guarantee the fulfillment of an obligation: *an extra month's rent given as security.* **4.** A stock or bond.

secy. *abbr.* An abbreviation of secretary.

se·dan (sĭ-**dăn′**) *n.* **1.** A closed automobile having two or four doors and a front and rear seat. **2.** An enclosed chair for one person, carried on poles by two other people.

se·date¹ (sĭ-**dāt′**) *adj.* Calm and dignified; composed. [From Latin *sēdāre*, to settle, calm.] **—se·date′ly** *adv.* **—se·date′ness** *n.*

se·date² (sĭ-**dāt′**) *tr.v.* **se·dat·ed, se·dat·ing, se·dates** To administer a sedative to. [From *sedation*, a calming, from Latin *sēdāre*, to settle, calm.]

se·da·tion (sĭ-**dā′**shən) *n.* **1.** The act or process of calming by administration of a sedative. **2.** The condition brought on by a sedative.

sed·a·tive (**sĕd′**ə-tĭv) *adj.* Having a soothing, calming, or quieting effect. ❖ *n.* A sedative medicine or drug.

sed·en·tar·y (**sĕd′**n-tĕr′ē) *adj.* **1.** Marked by or requiring much sitting: *sedentary work.* **2.** Accustomed to sitting or to taking little exercise. **3.** Living in one place; not migratory: *a sedentary insect species.* **—sed′en·tar′i·ly** (sĕd′n-**târ′**ə-lē) *adv.*

Se·der (**sā′**dər) *n., pl.* **Se·ders** or **Se·dar·im** (sĭ-**där′**ĭm *or* sĕ-dä-**rĭm′**) In Judaism, the feast commemorating the departure of the Jews from Egypt, held on the first two nights of Passover. [From Hebrew *sēder*, order, arrangement.]

sedge (sĕj) *n.* Any of numerous plants that grow chiefly in wet places and resemble grasses.

sed·i·ment (**sĕd′**ə-mənt) *n.* **1.** Finely divided solid matter that falls to the bottom of a liquid. **2.** Silt, sand, stones, and other matter carried and deposited by water, wind, or ice. [From Latin *sedimentum*, act of settling, from *sedēre*, to sit, settle.]

sed·i·men·ta·ry (sĕd′ə-**mĕn′**tə-rē *or* sĕd′ə-**mĕn′**trē) *adj.* **1.** Relating to, resembling, or derived from sediment. **2.** Relating to rocks formed from sediment deposited in water.

sed·i·men·ta·tion (sĕd′ə-mən-**tā′**shən) *n.* The act or process of depositing sediment.

se·di·tion (sĭ-**dĭsh′**ən) *n.* Conduct or language that causes others to rebel against the authority of the government.

se·di·tious (sĭ-**dĭsh′**əs) *adj.* Relating to or engaged in sedition. **—se·di′tious·ly** *adv.*

se·duce (sĭ-**do͞os′**) *tr.v.* **se·duced, se·duc·ing, se·duc·es 1.** To attract or lead (someone) away from proper behavior or thinking. **2.** To persuade (someone) to engage in sexual activity, as by flirting. **—se·duc′er** *n.*

se·duc·tion (sĭ-**dŭk′**shən) *n.* **1.** The act of seducing or the condition of being seduced. **2.** Something that seduces; a temptation.

se·duc·tive (sĭ-**dŭk′**tĭv) *adj.* Tending to seduce; alluring; enticing. **—se·duc′tive·ly** *adv.* **—se·duc′tive·ness** *n.*

sed·u·lous (**sĕj′**ə-ləs) *adj.* Constant in effort or work; diligent; industrious. **—sed′u·lous·ly** *adv.* **—sed′u·lous·ness** *n.*

see¹ (sē) *v.* **saw** (sô), **seen** (sēn), **see·ing, sees** *—tr.* **1.** To perceive with the eye: *He saw a dog.* **2.** To detect by visual technology: *The security camera saw the thief as he left.* **3.** To attend as a spectator; view: *We saw a good movie last night.* **4.** To understand; comprehend: *I see what you mean.* **5.** To regard; consider to be: *We see her as a world leader.* **6.** To find out or ascertain, often by moving: *Please see who is at the door.* **7.** To have a mental picture of; grasp mentally: *They could still see their hometown as it once was.* **8.** To imagine; believe possible: *We can see him as an architect.* **9.** To foresee: *I can see great things in your future.* **10.** To know through actual experience; undergo: *We had seen hard times.* **11.** To be marked by or bring forth: *The 1930s saw the development of antibiotics.* **12.** To refer to; read: *See the footnote on the next page.* **13a.** To spend time with often or regularly, as in dating: *They've been seeing each other for two years.* **b.** To visit socially: *May I see you tonight?* **c.** To visit for consultation: *He saw a lawyer.* **14.** To receive or admit: *The doctor will see you now.* **15.** To escort; attend: *See her to the bus station.* **16.** To make sure; take care: *Always see that the door is locked.* *—intr.* **1.** To be able to perceive with the eye: *Can you see from there?* **2.** To understand; comprehend: *As you can see, life in those days was hard.* **3.** To consider: *Let's see, what movie should we go to?* ◆ **see about 1.** To attend to: *We'll see about fixing the light later on.* **2.** To investigate: *Could you see about hotels in the area?* **see after** To take care of: *Please see after your brother while I go to the store.* **see off** To take leave of (someone): *saw the guests off at the station.* **see out** To escort (a guest) to the door: *Will you please see Ms. Smith out?* **see red** *Informal* To be extremely angry: *Our teacher saw red when we came to class late.* **see through 1.** To understand the true character or nature of: *She saw through his sales pitch.* **2.** To work on (a project) until completion: *I want to see the project through to the end.* **see to** To attend to: *See to the chores, please.* [From Old English *sēon*.]

❑ *These sound alike:* **see¹** (perceive with the eyes), **see²** (bishop's position), **sea** (body of salt water), **si** (musical note).

SYNONYMS see, notice, observe, view These verbs mean to be visually aware of something. **See** is the most general term: *Did you see the lunar eclipse last night?* **Observe** can mean to look carefully and closely: *We observed a change in the color of the water as it got deeper.* **Notice** can mean to observe closely and form a rather detailed impression: *He didn't notice that frost had formed on the window.* **View** can mean to examine with a particular purpose in mind or in a special way: *The jury wished to view the evidence again.*

---

see² (sē) *n.* The position, authority, or jurisdiction of a bishop. [From Middle English *se*, from Old French, from Latin *sēdēs*, seat.]

❑ *These sound alike:* **see²** (bishop's position), **see¹** (perceive with the eyes), **sea** (body of salt water), **si** (musical note).

seed (sēd) *n., pl.* **seeds** or **seed 1.** A part of a flowering plant that develops from a fertilized ovule and contains an embryo and the food it will need to grow into a new plant. **2.** Seeds considered as a group: *a farmer buying seed.* **3.** A source or beginning: *This treaty holds the seeds of a lasting peace.* ❖ *tr.v.* **seed·ed, seed·ing, seeds 1.** To plant seeds in; sow: *seeded four acres of land.* **2.** To remove the seeds from (fruit). **3.** To sprinkle (a cloud or clouds) with particles, as of silver iodide or dry ice,

sedge

seersucker

WORD BUILDING

segment The word root *seg–,* which is a variant of *sec–,* in English words comes from the Latin verb *secāre,* "to sever, cut, slice." **Segment** comes from the Latin noun *segmentum,* "a piece removed by cutting off, a section." The past participle of *secāre* is *sectus,* from which we get **bisect,** "cut in half" (using the prefix *bi–*[1] "twice, in two") and **intersect,** "cut between or among" (*inter–,* "between.") An **insect** is literally "a creature that has been cut into pieces," that is, it has three body segments (*in–*[2], "in, into").

ă	pat	ôr	core
ā	pay	oi	boy
âr	care	ou	out
ä	father	o͝o	took
ĕ	pet	o͝or	lure
ē	be	o͞o	boot
ĭ	pit	ŭ	cut
ī	bite	ûr	urge
îr	pier	th	thin
ŏ	pot	*th*	this
ō	toe	zh	vision
ô	paw	ə	about

to cause it to disperse or produce rain. ◆ **go to seed 1.** To pass into the seed-bearing stage: *harvesting the lettuce before it goes to seed.* **2.** To deteriorate or become rundown: *The town went to seed after the factory closed.*

❑ *These sound alike:* **seed, cede** (give up).

seed coat *n.* The often thick or hard outer coat of a seed.

seed·er (sē′dər) *n.* **1.** A machine or tool used for planting seeds. **2.** A machine or tool used to remove seeds from fruit.

seed leaf *n.* A cotyledon.

seed·ling (sēd′lĭng) *n.* A young plant, especially one that grows from a seed, rather than from a cutting, for example.

seed pearl *n.* A very small pearl.

seed plant *n.* Any of numerous plants that bear seeds. The seed plants include the gymnosperms, such as pines and spruces, and the flowering plants.

seed·pod (sēd′pŏd′) *n.* A seed case, as of a pea, bean, or certain other plants, that splits open to release the enclosed seeds.

seed·y (sē′dē) *adj.* **seed·i·er, seed·i·est 1.** Having many seeds: *Raspberries are seedy.* **2.** Shabby and disreputable: *a seedy hotel.* **—seed′i·ness** *n.*

seek (sēk) *tr.v.* **sought** (sôt), **seek·ing, seeks 1.** To try to locate or discover; search for: *The elephants sought a new source of water.* **2.** To try to obtain: *seek a college education.* **3.** To make an attempt; try: *seek to learn a foreign language.* **—seek′er** *n.*

seem (sēm) *intr.v.* **seemed, seem·ing, seems 1.** To give the impression of being in a certain way; appear to be: *The cat seems sick.* **2.** To appear to exist, be true, or be obvious: *There seems to be only one solution. It seems that he was unable to do the dishes.* **3.** To appear to oneself. Used especially to weaken the force of a statement that is expressed in an infinitive phrase: *I seem to be making the matter more complicated than it should be.*

❑ *These sound alike:* **seem, seam** (line formed by joining).

seem·ing (sē′mĭng) *adj.* Having an appearance that may or may not be real; apparent: *his seeming friendliness.* **—seem′ing·ly** *adv.*

seem·ly (sēm′lē) *adj.* **seem·li·er, seem·li·est** Conforming to accepted standards of conduct and good taste; proper: *seemly behavior.*

seen (sēn) *v.* Past participle of **see**[1].

❑ *These sound alike:* **seen, scene** (place).

seep (sēp) *intr.v.* **seeped, seep·ing, seeps** To pass slowly through small openings: *Cold air seeped in through the cracks around the window.*

seep·age (sē′pĭj) *n.* **1.** The act or process of seeping; leakage. **2.** Material that has seeped.

seer (sîr) *n.* **1.** A person who sees: *a seer of sights.* **2.** A person who foresees or foretells events.

❑ *These sound alike:* **seer, sear** (scorch), **sere** (withered).

seer·suck·er (sîr′sŭk′ər) *n.* A light thin fabric, generally of cotton or rayon, having a crinkled surface and a usually striped pattern. [From Persian *shīroshakar* : *shīr,* milk + *o,* and + *shakar,* sugar.]

see·saw (sē′sô′) *n.* A long plank balanced on a central support so that with a person riding on either end, one goes up as the other goes down. ❖ *intr.v.* **see·sawed, see·saw·ing, see·saws 1.** To ride on a seesaw. **2.** To move back and forth or up and down.

seethe (sē*th*) *intr.v.* **seethed, seeth·ing, seethes 1.** To churn and foam as if boiling. **2.** To be in a state of turmoil or ferment: *The town seethed with excitement.* **3.** To be violently agitated: *She seethed with anger.* [From Old English *sēothan.*]

seg·ment (sĕg′mənt) *n.* **1.** A part into which something is or can be divided; a section or division: *the various segments of American society.* **2a.** The portion of a line between any two of its points. **b.** The region bounded by an arc of a circle and the chord that connects the endpoints of the arc. **c.** The portion of a sphere included between a pair of parallel planes that intersect it or are tangent to it. ❖ *tr. & intr.v.* (sĕg-**mĕnt′**) **seg·ment·ed, seg·ment·ing, seg·ments** To divide or become divided into segments. [From Latin *segmentum,* from *secāre,* to cut.] —SEE NOTE.

seg·men·tal (sĕg-**mĕn′**tl) *adj.* **1.** Relating to segments. **2.** Divided or organized into segments. **—seg·ment′-tal·ly** *adv.*

seg·men·ta·tion (sĕg′mən-**tā′**shən) *n.* **1.** Division into segments. **2.** The early divisions of a cell into many cells; cleavage.

seg·re·gate (sĕg′rĭ-gāt′) *tr.v.* **seg·re·gat·ed, seg·re·gat·ing, seg·re·gates 1.** To separate or isolate from others or from a main body or group: *segregate the sick children from the others.* **2.** To cause (people or institutions, for example) to be separated on the basis of race, sex, religion, or another factor.

seg·re·ga·tion (sĕg′rĭ-**gā′**shən) *n.* **1.** The act or process of segregating or the condition of being segregated. **2.** The policy or practice of separating people of different races, classes, or ethnic groups, as in schools or housing, especially as a form of discrimination.

seg·re·ga·tion·ist (sĕg′rĭ-**gā′**shə-nĭst) *n.* A person who advocates racial segregation. **—seg′re·ga′tion·ist** *adj.*

se·gue (sĕg′wā′) *intr.v.* **se·gued, se·gue·ing, se·gues** To move smoothly and without hesitation from one state, condition, situation, or element to another. ❖ *n.* An act or instance of segueing.

seine (sān) *n.* A large fishing net with weights at the lower edge and floats at the top. ❖ *tr. & intr.v.* **seined, sein·ing, seines** To fish or catch with a seine. [From Old English *segne,* from Greek *sagēnē.*]

❑ *These sound alike:* **seine, sane** (of sound mind).

Seine (sĕn *or* sān) A river of northern France flowing about 480 miles (770 kilometers) generally northwest to an inlet of the English Channel near Le Havre.

seis·mic (sīz′mĭk) *adj.* Subject to or caused by an earthquake or earthquakes: *a seismic disturbance.* [From Greek *seismos,* earthquake.]

seismo– or **seism–** *pref.* A prefix that means earthquake: *seismology.*

seis·mo·graph (sīz′mə-grăf′) *n.* An instrument that detects and records movement in the earth's crust.

seis·mol·o·gy (sīz-**mŏl′**ə-jē) *n.* The scientific study of earthquakes and other movements of the earth's crust. **—seis·mol′o·gist** *n.*

seize (sēz) *v.* **seized, seiz·ing, seiz·es** *—tr.* **1.** To grasp suddenly and forcibly; take or grab: *The police officer seized his arm.* **2.** To take by force; capture or conquer: *The kidnappers seized the prince. The invaders seized the city.* **3.** To take possession of by force: *The agents seized the contraband.* **4.** To comprehend: *seize an idea and develop it.* **5.** To make use of (an opportunity, for example): *seize the opportunity to leave.* **6.** To have a sudden effect on; overwhelm: *Stage fright seized the boy.* *—intr.* **1.** To eagerly make use of something: *seized upon her idea.* **2.** To come to a halt or freeze, especially when moving parts stop functioning and lock in place: *The icy cold has made the machine seize up. His muscles seized up after the long workout.* ◆ **seize on** To focus one's attention on: *Critics seized on the president's hesitation to take action.*

sei·zure (sē′zhər) *n.* **1.** The act or an instance of seizing or the condition of being seized: *the seizure of smuggled goods.* **2.** An instance of abnormal, especially excessive electrical activity in the brain, causing symptoms such as involuntary muscle movements and the loss of awareness or the ability to pay attention.

sel·dom (sĕl′dəm) *adv.* Not often; rarely: *A woodchuck seldom strays far from its burrow.*

se·lect (sĭ-**lĕkt′**) *tr.v.* **se·lect·ed, se·lect·ing, se·lects** To take as a choice from among several; pick out: *select the ripest pears.* ❖ *adj.* **1.** Carefully picked out or chosen: *a select group of students.* **2.** Of special quality; choice: *a select product.* [From Latin *sēligere* : *sē-*, apart + *legere*, to choose.] **—se·lec′tor** *n.*

se·lec·tion (sĭ-**lĕk′**shən) *n.* **1a.** The act of selecting something. See Synonyms at **choice. b.** A person or thing selected, such as a literary or musical text chosen for reading or performance. **2.** A range or carefully chosen group of people or things: *a selection of online resources.* **3.** Natural selection or artificial selection.

se·lec·tive (sĭ-**lĕk′**tĭv) *adj.* **1.** Characterized by selection, especially of what is considered best, most suitable, or deliberately incomplete: *the agency's selective disclosure of information.* **2.** Careful in selecting; choosy: *He is very selective in his taste in music.* **—se·lec′tive·ly** *adv.* **—se·lec′tiv′i·ty** (sĭ-lĕk′**tĭv′**ĭ-tē) *n.*

selective service *n.* A system for calling up people for compulsory military service.

se·lect·man (sĭ-**lĕkt′**măn′) *n.* One of a board of town officers chosen in New England communities to manage local affairs.

se·lect·wom·an (sĭ-**lĕkt′**wo͝om′ən) *n.* A woman who is one of a board of town officers chosen in New England communities to manage local affairs.

Se·le·ne (sə-**lē′**nē) *n.* In Greek mythology, the goddess of the moon.

se·le·ni·um (sĭ-**lē′**nē-əm) *n. Symbol* **Se** A nonmetallic element that can exist as a red powder, a black glassy material, or a gray crystal and is used in photoelectric cells. Atomic number 34. See **Periodic Table.**

self (sĕlf) *n., pl.* **selves** (sĕlvz) **1.** The total or essential being of a person apart from everyone else; the individual: *one's own self.* **2.** The qualities that distinguish one person from another; individuality: *back to his old cheerful self.* **3.** One's own interests, welfare, or advantage: *thinking of self alone.*

self– *pref.* A prefix that means: **1.** Oneself or itself: *self-evident.* **2.** Automatic or automatically: *self-winding.*

self-ad·dressed (sĕlf′ə-**drĕst′**) *adj.* Addressed to oneself: *a self-addressed stamped envelope.*

self-ap·point·ed (sĕlf′ə-**poin′**tĭd) *adj.* Designated or chosen by oneself rather than by due authority: *a self-appointed expert.*

self-as·sured (sĕlf′ə-**sho͝ord′**) *adj.* Having or showing confidence and sureness. **—self′-as·sur′ance** *n.*

self-cen·tered (**sĕlf′sĕn′**tərd) *adj.* Concerned only with one's own needs and interests; selfish. **—self′-cen′tered·ness** *n.*

self-con·fi·dence (**sĕlf′kŏn′**fĭ-dəns) *n.* Confidence in oneself or one's abilities. **—self′-con′fi·dent** *adj.*

self-con·scious (**sĕlf′kŏn′**shəs) *adj.* **1.** Excessively conscious of one's appearance or manner; socially ill at ease: *a self-conscious person.* **2.** Not natural; stilted: *a self-conscious laugh.* **—self′-con′scious·ly** *adv.* **—self′-con′scious·ness** *n.*

self-con·tained (sĕlf′kən-**tānd′**) *adj.* **1.** Not dependent on others; independent; self-sufficient: *The island was economically self-contained.* **2.** Keeping to oneself; reserved.

self-con·trol (sĕlf′kən-**trōl′**) *n.* Control of one's emotions and behavior by one's own will. **—self′-con·trolled′** *adj.*

self-de·fense (sĕlf′dĭ-**fĕns′**) *n.* Defense of oneself against attack, especially as allowed by law when the attacker presents an immediate or imminent threat to one's own life or safety.

self-de·ni·al (sĕlf′dĭ-**nī′**əl) *n.* Sacrifice of one's own desires or interests.

self-de·struct (sĕlf′dĭ-**strŭkt′**) *intr.v.* **self-de·struct·ed, self-de·struct·ing, self-de·struct·s** To harm or destroy oneself or itself: *a missile that self-destructs.* **—self′-de·struc′tion** *n.*

self-de·ter·mi·na·tion (sĕlf′dĭ-tûr′mə-**nā′**shən) *n.* **1.** Determination of one's own fate or course of action without being forced; free will. **2.** Freedom of the people of a given area to determine their own political status.

self-dis·ci·pline (**sĕlf′dĭs′**ə-plĭn) *n.* Training and control of oneself and one's conduct, usually for personal improvement.

self-ed·u·cat·ed (**sĕlf′ĕj′**ə-kā′tĭd) *adj.* Educated by one's own efforts, without formal instruction.

self-ef·fac·ing (sĕlf′ĭ-**fā′**sĭng) *adj.* Modestly or shyly keeping oneself in the background.

self-em·ployed (sĕlf′ĕm-**ploid′**) *adj.* Earning one's living by working for oneself, rather than for an employer.

self-es·teem (sĕlf′ĭ-**stēm′**) *n.* Pride in oneself; self-respect.

self-ev·i·dent (**sĕlf′ĕv′**ĭ-dənt) *adj.* Requiring no proof or explanation.

self-ex·plan·a·to·ry (sĕlf′ĭk-**splăn′**ə-tôr′ē) *adj.* Requiring no explanation; obvious.

self-ex·pres·sion (sĕlf′ĭk-**sprĕsh′**ən) *n.* Expression of one's own personality, feelings, or ideas, as through speech or art.

self-ful·fill·ing (sĕlf′fo͝ol-**fĭl′**ĭng) *adj.* Achieving fulfillment as a result of having been expected or foretold: *a self-fulfilling prophecy.*

self-gov·ern·ing (**sĕlf′gŭv′**ər-nĭng) *adj.* **1.** Exercising control or rule over oneself or itself. **2.** Having the right or power of self-government; independent.

self-gov·ern·ment (**sĕlf′gŭv′**ərn-mənt) *n.* **1.** Political independence. **2.** Representative government; democracy.

self-help (**sĕlf′hĕlp′**) *n.* The act or an instance of helping or improving oneself.

self-identify (sĕlf′ĭ-**dĕn′**tə-fī′) *intr.v.* **self-i·den·ti·fied, self-i·den·ti·fy·ing, self-i·den·ti·fies** To believe or assert that one belongs to a certain group or class: *voters who self-identify as progressive.*

self·ie (**sĕl′**fē) *n.* A picture that one takes of oneself, especially in a casual setting: *texted a selfie to my friends.*

self-im·por·tance (sĕlf′ĭm-**pôr′**tns) *n.* An excessively high opinion of one's own importance or position; conceit. **—self′-im·por′tant** *adj.*

self-im·prove·ment (sĕlf′ĭm-**pro͞ov′**mənt) *n.* Improvement of one's condition through one's own efforts.

self-in·ter·est (**sĕlf′ĭn′**trĭst *or* **sĕlf′ĭn′**tər-ĭst) *n.* **1.** Selfish regard for one's personal advantage or interest. **2.** Personal advantage or interest.

self·ish (**sĕl′**fĭsh) *adj.* **1.** Concerned mainly with oneself and having little concern for others: *a selfish person.* **2.** Showing an excessive concern with oneself and little concern for others: *a selfish act.* **—self′ish·ly** *adv.* **—self′ish·ness** *n.*

self·less (**sĕlf′**lĭs) *adj.* Having, showing, or based on no concern for oneself; unselfish: *a selfless act of charity.* **—self′less·ly** *adv.* **—self′less·ness** *n.*

self-made (**sĕlf′mād′**) *adj.* Having achieved success by one's own efforts: *a self-made woman.*

self-pol·li·na·tion (sĕlf′pŏl′ə-**nā′**shən) *n.* The transfer of pollen from the anther to the stigma of the same flower or to the stigma of another flower of the same plant. **—self′-pol′li·nate′** *v.* —SEE NOTE AT **pollinate.**

self-por·trait (**sĕlf′pôr′**trĭt *or* **sĕlf′pôr′**trāt′) *n.* A portrait of oneself made by oneself.

self-pos·ses·sion (sĕlf′pə-**zĕsh′**ən) *n.* Calm and self-assured command of one's feelings and behavior; presence of mind; poise. **—self′-pos·sessed′** *adj.*

self-pres·er·va·tion (sĕlf′prĕz′ər-**vā′**shən) *n.* **1.** Protection of oneself from harm or destruction. **2.** The instinct for survival.

seismograph

self-portrait
c. 1891 self-portrait by Paul Gauguin

selvage

semaphore

self-pro·pelled (sĕlf′prə-**pĕld′**) *adj.* Containing its own means of propulsion: *a self-propelled golf cart.*

self-re·gard (sĕlf′rĭ-**gärd′**) *n.* **1.** Consideration of one's self or one's interests. **2.** Self-respect.

self-re·li·ance (sĕlf′rĭ-**lī′**əns) *n.* Reliance on one's own capabilities or resources. **—self′-re·li′ant** *adj.*

self-re·spect (sĕlf′rĭ-**spĕkt′**) *n.* Appropriate or due respect for oneself, one's character, and one's behavior. **—self′-re·spect′ing** *adj.*

self-re·straint (sĕlf′rĭ-**strānt′**) *n.* Restraint of one's emotions, desires, or inclinations; self-control.

self-right·eous (**sĕlf′rī′**chəs) *adj.* Smugly sure of one's righteousness. **—self′-right′eous·ly** *adv.* **—self′-right′eous·ness** *n.*

self-sac·ri·fice (**sĕlf′săk′**rə-fīs′) *n.* Sacrifice of one's own interests or well-being for the sake of others or for a cause. **—self′-sac′ri·fic′ing** *adj.*

self·same (**sĕlf′**sām′) *adj.* Exactly identical; being the very same: *eating the selfsame cherries he had picked the day before.*

self-sat·is·fac·tion (sĕlf′săt′ĭs-**făk′**shən) *n.* Smug satisfaction with oneself or one's accomplishments. **—self′-sat′is·fied′** (**sĕlf′săt′**ĭs-fīd′) *adj.*

self-seek·ing (**sĕlf′sē′**kĭng) *adj.* Seeking only one's own interests or goals; selfish. ❖ *n.* Determined pursuit of one's own interests or goals.

self-ser·vice (**sĕlf′sûr′**vĭs) *adj.* Being a business or service in which customers help themselves: *a self-service laundry.*

self-serv·ing (**sĕlf′sûr′**vĭng) *adj.* Serving one's own interests or showing concern only for one's own interests: *a speech full of self-serving remarks.*

self-styled (**sĕlf′stīld′**) *adj.* As characterized by oneself, often without justification: *a self-styled artist.*

self-suf·fi·cient (sĕlf′sə-**fĭsh′**ənt) *adj.* Able to provide for oneself without help; independent. **—self′-suf·fi′cien·cy** *n.*

self-taught (**sĕlf′tôt′**) *adj.* Having taught oneself without formal training or the help of others.

self-will (**sĕlf′wĭl′**) *n.* Willfulness, especially in satisfying one's own desires or maintaining one's own opinions; stubbornness. **—self′-willed′** *adj.*

self-wind·ing (**sĕlf′wīn′**dĭng) *adj.* Designed so that manual winding is unnecessary: *a self-winding watch.*

sell (sĕl) *v.* **sold** (sōld), **sell·ing, sells** *—tr.* **1.** To exchange or deliver for money or its equivalent: *I sold my old bike to a friend.* **2.** To offer for sale: *This store sells health foods.* **3.** To surrender in exchange for something: *sell one's integrity for a glamorous career.* **4.** To be purchased in (a certain quantity); have sales of: *His memoir sold over a million copies.* **5.** To promote: *Advertising sells many products.* **6.** To persuade (a person) to recognize the worth or desirability of something: *She finally sold her husband on the idea of moving to the country.* *—intr.* To be sold or to be on sale: *That new skateboard is selling at a good price.* ❖ *n. Informal* Something that is being sold or promoted: *This book was an easy sell. Their program to raise taxes will be a difficult sell.* ◆ **sell off** To get rid of by selling, often at reduced prices. **sell out 1.** To be entirely sold: *The tickets have already sold out.* **2.** *Informal* To betray one's cause or colleagues. [From Old English *sellan,* to give, sell.]

❑ *These sound alike:* **sell, cell** (confining room).

sell·er (**sĕl′**ər) *n.* **1.** A person who sells; a vendor. **2.** An item that sells well or poorly: *This dress has been a very good seller.*

❑ *These sound alike:* **seller, cellar** (basement).

sell·out (**sĕl′**out′) *n.* **1.** The act of selling out. **2.** An event for which all tickets are sold. **3.** *Slang* A person who has betrayed a principle or a cause.

selt·zer (**sĕlt′**sər) *n.* **1.** A naturally bubbly mineral water. **2.** Carbonated water. [From German *Selterser (Wasser),* (water) of Selters, a village of central Germany.]

sel·vage (**sĕl′**vĭj) *n.* **1.** The edge of a fabric, especially one that is woven or knit in such a way that it will not ravel, fray, or curl. **2.** An ornamental fringe at either end of an Oriental rug.

selves (sĕlvz) *n.* Plural of **self.**

se·man·tic (sĭ-**măn′**tĭk) *adj.* **1.** Concerned with meaning, especially in language: *a semantic change.* **2.** Relating to semantics. [From Greek *sēmantos,* marked, significant, from *sēma,* sign.]

se·man·ti·cist (sĭ-**măn′**tĭ-sĭst) *n.* A person who specializes in semantics.

se·man·tics (sĭ-**măn′**tĭks) *n.* *(used with a singular or plural verb)* The study or science of meaning in language.

sem·a·phore (**sĕm′**ə-fôr′) *n.* **1.** A visual signaling device with flags, lights, or mechanically moving arms, as on a railroad. **2.** A system for signaling that uses an alphabetic code based on positions of the arms. [From Greek *sēma,* sign + Greek *-phoros,* carrying.]

sem·blance (**sĕm′**bləns) *n.* **1.** The appearance of something, whether it is really present or not; show: *keeping up a semblance of dignity.* **2.** A representation; a likeness: *cupped his hands together in the semblance of a heart.*

se·men (**sē′**mən) *n.* A whitish fluid produced by the male reproductive organs that carries sperm cells.

❑ *These sound alike:* **semen, seaman** (sailor).

se·mes·ter (sə-**mĕs′**tər) *n.* One of two divisions of 15 to 18 weeks each of a school year. [From Latin *(cursus) sēmēstris,* (course) of six months : *sē,* six + *mēnsis,* month.]

semi– *pref.* A prefix that means: **1.** Half: *semicircle.* **2.** Partial or partially: *semiconscious.* **3.** Occurring twice during: *semimonthly.* —SEE NOTE.

sem·i·an·nu·al (sĕm′ē-**ăn′**yo͞o-əl) *adj.* Occurring or issued twice a year: *semiannual payments; a semiannual magazine.* **—sem′i·an′nu·al·ly** *adv.*

sem·i·ar·id (sĕm′ē-**ăr′**ĭd) *adj.* Characterized by light annual rainfall and sustaining only short grasses and shrubs: *a semiarid region.*

sem·i·au·to·mat·ic (sĕm′ē-ô′tə-**măt′**ĭk) *adj.* **1.** Partially automatic. **2.** Ejecting a shell and loading the next round of ammunition automatically but requiring a trigger squeeze for each shot. ❖ *n.* A semiautomatic firearm.

sem·i·cir·cle (**sĕm′**ĭ-sûr′kəl) *n.* An arc of 180 degrees; a half circle. **—sem′i·cir′cu·lar** (sĕm′ĭ-**sûr′**kyə-lər) *adj.*

semicircular canal *n.* Any of three tubular looped structures of the inner ear that act together in maintaining the sense of balance.

sem·i·co·lon (**sĕm′**ĭ-kō′lən) *n.* A punctuation mark (;) used to connect main clauses and indicating a closer relationship between them than a period does.

sem·i·con·duc·tor (sĕm′ē-kən-**dŭk′**tər) *n.* Any of various solid crystalline substances, such as silicon or germanium, that conduct electricity more easily than insulators but less easily than conductors.

sem·i·con·scious (sĕm′ē-**kŏn′**shəs) *adj.* Partially conscious. **—sem′i·con′scious·ly** *adv.* **—sem′i·con′scious·ness** *n.*

sem·i·fi·nal (**sĕm′**ē-fī′nəl *or* sĕm′ī-**fī′**nəl) *n.* A match, competition, or examination that precedes the final one. **—sem′i·fi′nal** *adj.* **—sem′i·fi′nal·ist** *n.*

sem·i·month·ly (sĕm′ē-**mŭnth′**lē) *adj.* Occurring or issued twice a month: *semimonthly visits.* ❖ *n., pl.* **sem·i·month·lies** A semimonthly publication. ❖ *adv.* Twice a month: *We meet semimonthly.* —SEE NOTE AT **biweekly.**

sem·i·nal (**sĕm′**ə-nəl) *adj.* **1.** Relating to or containing semen or sperm cells: *seminal fluid.* **2.** Highly original and influential, and providing a basis for further development: *seminal ideas.*

ă	pat	ôr	core
ā	pay	oi	boy
âr	care	ou	out
ä	father	o͝o	took
ĕ	pet	o͝or	lure
ē	be	o͞o	boot
ĭ	pit	ŭ	cut
ī	bite	ûr	urge
îr	pier	th	thin
ŏ	pot	*th*	this
ō	toe	zh	vision
ô	paw	ə	about

sem·i·nar (sĕm′ə-när′) *n.* **1.** A course of study for a small group of students in a college or graduate school, often requiring research to be done under the guidance of a professor. **2.** A group of students in such a course. **3.** A meeting of such a group. [From Latin *sēminārium*, seed plot.]

sem·i·nar·i·an (sĕm′ə-**nâr′**ē-ən) *n.* A student at a seminary.

sem·i·nar·y (**sĕm′**ə-nĕr′ē) *n., pl.* **sem·i·nar·ies 1.** A school for the training of clergy. **2.** A school of higher education, especially a private school for girls.

Sem·i·nole (**sĕm′**ə-nōl′) *n., pl.* **Seminole** or **Sem·i·noles 1.** A member of a Native American people made up of mostly Creek groups who moved to Florida in the 1700s and 1800s, many of whom were forcibly moved to Oklahoma. **2.** Either of the Muskogean languages of the Seminole.

sem·i·pre·cious stone (sĕm′ē-**prĕsh′**əs) *n.* A gem, such as topaz, amethyst, or jade, that has commercial value but is not as rare or expensive as a precious stone.

sem·i·pro·fes·sion·al (sĕm′ē-prə-**fĕsh′**ə-nəl) *adj.* **1.** Taking part in a sport for pay, but not as a full-time occupation: *a semiprofessional baseball player.* **2.** Composed of such players: *a semiprofessional team.*

sem·i·skilled (sĕm′ē-**skĭld′**) *adj.* **1.** Having some skills but not enough to do specialized work. **2.** Requiring limited skills: *a semiskilled job.*

sem·i·sol·id (sĕm′ē-**sŏl′**ĭd) *adj.* Intermediate in properties, especially in rigidity, between solids and liquids. ❖ *n.* (**sĕm′**ē-sŏl′ĭd) A semisolid substance, such as a stiff dough or firm gelatin.

Sem·ite (**sĕm′**īt′) *n.* A member of a people presently or formerly speaking a Semitic language, such as the ancient Babylonians, Hebrews, and Phoenicians or the modern Arabs and Jews.

Se·mit·ic (sə-**mĭt′**ĭk) *adj.* **1.** Relating to a division of the Afro-Asiatic languages that includes Hebrew and Arabic. **2.** Relating to the Semites or their languages or cultures. ❖ *n.* The Semitic languages.

sem·i·tone (**sĕm′**ē-tōn′) *n.* A half step in a musical scale.

sem·i·trail·er (**sĕm′**ē-trā′lər) *n.* A trailer with a set or sets of wheels at the rear only, the forward portion being supported by the truck tractor or towing vehicle.

sem·i·trop·i·cal (sĕm′ē-**trŏp′**ĭ-kəl) *adj.* Partly tropical; subtropical.

sem·i·week·ly (sĕm′ē-**wēk′**lē) *adj.* Occurring or issued twice a week. ❖ *adv.* Twice a week. —SEE NOTE AT **biweekly.**

Sen. *abbr.* An abbreviation of: **1.** senate. **2.** senator. **3.** or **sen.** senior.

sen·ate (**sĕn′**ĭt) *n.* **1. Senate** The upper house of the US Congress, to which two members are elected by the people of each state for a six-year term. **2.** often **Senate** The upper house of the legislature in many states of the United States. **3. Senate** The upper house of the national legislature of Canada, France, and some other countries. **4.** The governing council of the ancient Roman republic and later of the Roman Empire. **5.** A governing or advisory council of some colleges and universities. [From Middle English *senat*, from Latin *senātus*, from *senex*, old, an elder.]

sen·a·tor (**sĕn′**ə-tər) *n.* A member of a senate.

sen·a·to·ri·al (sĕn′ə-**tôr′**ē-əl) *adj.* **1.** Concerning or appropriate to a senator. **2.** Made up of senators: *a senatorial advisory group.*

send (sĕnd) *v.* **sent** (sĕnt), **send·ing, sends** —*tr.* **1.** To cause to be conveyed to a place: *We sent supplies to the disaster area by airlift.* **2.** To dispatch, as by mail or telegraph; transmit: *Send an email to me. Send my regards to all.* **3.** To direct to go to a place: *sent me to the store to buy milk.* **4.** To enable to go to a place, as by providing money: *She worked hard to send herself to college.* **5.** To direct (a person) to a source of information: *The teacher sent us to the library.* **6.** To give off (light or heat, for example); emit: *The beacon sends a bright light.* **7.** To hit so as to direct with force: *The batter sent the ball to left field.* **8.** To put into a given condition or kind of behavior: *The long delay sent the train passengers into a rage.* —*intr.* **1.** To cause someone to do an errand or to convey a message: *He sent out for pizza.* **2.** To convey a request or an order, especially by mail: *send away for a catalogue.* ◆ **send for** To request to come by means of a message or messenger; summon. **send in 1.** To cause (something) to arrive or to be delivered to a recipient. **2.** To put (a player) into or back into a game or contest. **3.** To cause (someone) to arrive in or become involved in a particular place or situation: *send in the troops.* [From Old English *sendan.*] —**send′er** *n.*

send·off (**sĕnd′**ôf′) *n.* A demonstration of affection and good wishes for the beginning of a new undertaking.

Sen·e·ca (**sĕn′**ĭ-kə) *n., pl.* **Seneca** or **Sen·e·cas 1.** A member of a Native American people living in western New York State and southeast Ontario. **2.** The Iroquoian language of the Seneca.

Seneca Falls A village of west-central New York east-southeast of Rochester. The first women's rights convention was held here in 1848.

Sen·e·gal (sĕn′ĭ-**gôl′** *or* sĕn′ĭ-**gäl′**) A country of western Africa on the Atlantic Ocean south of Mauritania. Dakar is the capital.

se·nile (**sē′**nīl′ *or* **sĕn′**īl′) *adj.* **1.** Relating to or having decreased mental function, as when memory is impaired because of old age. **2.** Being a disease or condition whose cause is mainly older age: *senile cataracts.* [From Latin *senīlis*, from *senex*, old.] —**se·nil′i·ty** (sĭ-**nĭl′**ĭ-tē) *n.*

sen·ior (**sēn′**yər) *adj.* **1.** Being the older of two, especially the older of two people having the same name, as father and son. **2.** Relating to senior citizens. **3.** Being in a higher position, rank, or grade than one's peers: *a senior editor.* **4.** Relating to the fourth and last year of a high school or college: *the senior class.* ❖ *n.* **1.** A person who is older than another: *My brother is my senior by four years.* **2.** A senior citizen. **3.** A person in a higher position, rank, or grade than another. **4.** A student in the fourth and last year of a high school or college. [From Middle English, from Latin, older, from *senex*, old.]

senior citizen *n.* A relatively old person, especially one who has retired.

senior high school *n.* A high school usually including the 9th, 10th, 11th, and 12th grades.

sen·ior·i·ty (sēn-**yôr′**ĭ-tē) *n.* **1.** The condition of being older or of higher rank. **2.** Priority over others, especially because of greater length of service.

sen·na (**sĕn′**ə) *n.* **1.** Any of various plants having yellow flowers and leaves with many leaflets. **2.** A preparation of the dried leaves of one of these plants, used as a laxative. [From Arabic *sanā.*]

se·ñor (sān-**yôr′** *or* sĕ-**nyôr′**) *n., pl.* **se·ño·res** (sān-**yôr′**-ās *or* sĕ-**nyō′**rĕs) **1.** Used as a courtesy title for a man in a Spanish-speaking region. **2.** A Spanish or Spanish-speaking man. [From Spanish, from Latin *senior*, senior.]

se·ño·ra (sān-**yôr′**ə *or* sĕ-**nyō′**rä) *n.* **1.** Used as a courtesy title for a woman in a Spanish-speaking region. **2.** A Spanish or Spanish-speaking woman.

se·ño·ri·ta (sān′yə-**rē′**tə *or* sĕ′nyō-**rē′**tä) *n.* **1.** Used as a courtesy title for a girl or young woman in a Spanish-speaking region. **2.** A Spanish or Spanish-speaking unmarried woman or girl.

sen·sa·tion (sĕn-**sā′**shən) *n.* **1a.** A feeling or an awareness that results from the stimulation of a sense organ or from some condition of the body: *the sensation of heat.* **b.** The ability to perceive or feel: *a loss of sensation in the fingers due to frostbite.* **2a.** A condition of lively public interest and excitement: *News of the first artificial*

WORD BUILDING

semi– The prefix **semi–** means "half" or "partially." In general it combines with adjectives: *semiattached, semidry, semisweet. Semi–* also combines, less commonly, with nouns: *semidarkness, semidesert, semidome. Semi–* can be compared with the prefixes **hemi–** and **demi–**. All three have basically the same meaning, but *semi–* and *demi–* come from Latin, while *hemi–* comes from Greek. *Hemi–* and *demi–* are not as common as *semi–*. *Hemi–* is found mostly in scientific words, like *hemisphere,* and *demi–* is limited to a few scattered words like *demigod* and *demitasse.* For more information, see Note at **biweekly.**

sentry box

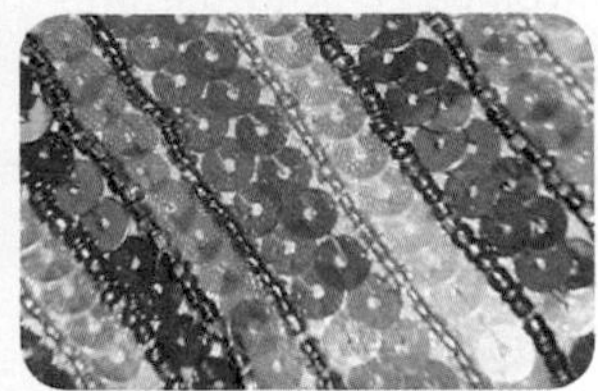
sequin

ă	pat	ôr	core
ā	pay	oi	boy
âr	care	ou	out
ä	father	o͝o	took
ĕ	pet	o͝or	lure
ē	be	o͞o	boot
ĭ	pit	ŭ	cut
ī	bite	ûr	urge
îr	pier	th	thin
ŏ	pot	*th*	this
ō	toe	zh	vision
ô	paw	ə	about

satellite caused a sensation. **b.** A person, event, or object that arouses lively interest, excitement, or admiration: *The band's new singer is a sensation.*

sen·sa·tion·al (sĕn-sā**′**shə-nəl) *adj.* **1.** Relating to sensation or the senses. **2.** Arousing great interest or excitement, especially by shocking: *a sensational television report.* **3.** Extraordinary; outstanding: *a sensational dinner.* **—sen·sa′tion·al·ly** *adv.*

sen·sa·tion·al·ism (sĕn-sā**′**shə-nə-lĭz′əm) *n.* The deliberate use of sensational subject matter or highly dramatic style, especially in writing, journalism, or politics.

sense (sĕns) *n.* **1a.** Any of the functions or abilities by which a living thing can perceive or feel its environment or be certain of its own internal conditions: *the sense of smell.* **b.** A perception or feeling due to stimulation of one or more of these functions or abilities: *have a sense of being hungry.* **2.** An ability to understand or appreciate something: *a sense of humor.* **3.** A vague feeling about something; an impression: *I have a sense that our team's going to win.* **4.** often **senses** Good judgment; practical intelligence: *She had the sense to make a reservation. Come to your senses!* **5a.** Speech, thought, or reasoning that is sound and practical: *Talk sense!* **b.** Something reasonable: *saw no sense in hurrying.* **6a.** A meaning conveyed by speech or writing: *tried to understand the sense of the poem's last line.* **b.** One of the meanings of a word or phrase: *Words sometimes have many different senses.* **7.** Consensus: *The sense of the group was that we should go ahead.* ❖ *tr.v.* **sensed, sens·ing, sens·es 1.** To become aware of through the senses; perceive: *We sensed a change in the weather.* **2.** To understand; grasp: *He sensed that his career was over.* **3.** To detect automatically: *A Geiger counter senses radioactivity.* [From Middle English, from Latin *sēnsus*, the faculty of perceiving, from *sentīre*, to feel.]

sense·less (sĕns**′**lĭs) *adj.* **1.** Lacking meaning or sense: *senseless drivel.* **2.** Lacking good judgment; foolish. **3.** *Informal* Unconscious, as from a blow to the head: *knocked senseless.* **—sense′less·ly** *adv.*

sense organ *n.* An organ or a structure of the body, such as an eye or ear, that is specially developed to receive sensory stimuli.

sen·si·bil·i·ty (sĕn′sə-bĭl**′**ĭ-tē) *n., pl.* **sen·si·bil·i·ties 1.** The ability to perceive with the senses: *It was so cold that I thought I had lost sensibility in my toes.* **2.** The ability to be sensitive to and appreciate feelings or beauty in the mind: *her acute sensibility to the feelings of others.*

sen·si·ble (sĕn**′**sə-bəl) *adj.* **1.** Showing or in accordance with good judgment; reasonable: *a sensible person; a sensible decision.* **2.** Perceptible by the senses or the mind: *a sensible difference of temperature.* **—sen′si·ble·ness** *n.* **—sen′si·bly** *adv.*

sen·si·tive (sĕn**′**sĭ-tĭv) *adj.* **1.** Capable of perceiving with a sense or senses: *Bats are sensitive to sounds that we cannot hear.* **2.** Responsive to or affected by an external condition or stimulus: *Photographic film is sensitive to light.* **3.** Designed to indicate or measure small changes of condition: *a sensitive thermometer.* **4.** Easily irritated: *sensitive skin.* **5.** Responsive to the feelings, attitudes, or circumstances of others: *a sensitive and sympathetic listener.* **6.** Easily hurt, upset, or offended: *He was sensitive about his poor performance in the race.* **7.** Requiring careful or discreet handling; delicate: *a matter too sensitive to be discussed.* **—sen′si·tive·ly** *adv.* **—sen′si·tiv′i·ty** *n.*

sensitive plant *n.* Any of various plants having leaflets that fold together or droop when touched.

sen·si·tize (sĕn**′**sĭ-tīz′) *tr. & intr.v.* **sen·si·tized, sen·si·tiz·ing, sen·si·tiz·es** To make or become sensitive or more sensitive.

sen·sor (sĕn**′**sər *or* sĕn**′**sôr′) *n.* A device, such as a photocell or thermocouple, that responds to a particular type of change in its condition or environment.

sen·so·ry (sĕn**′**sə-rē) *adj.* **1.** Relating to the senses or sensation. **2.** Carrying impulses from sense organs to the central nervous system: *sensory nerves.*

sen·su·al (sĕn**′**sho͞o-əl) *adj.* **1.** Relating to or giving pleasure to the body; physically gratifying: *the sensual experience of a warm bath.* **2.** Sexually attractive. **3.** Given to or preoccupied with gratification of the senses. **—sen′su·al′i·ty** (sĕn′sho͞o-ăl**′**ĭ-tē) *n.* **—sen′su·al·ly** *adv.*

sen·su·ous (sĕn**′**sho͞o-əs) *adj.* **1.** Relating to or derived from the senses: *both a sensuous and an intellectual response to the music.* **2.** Sexually attractive. **3.** Relating to or affecting the senses; sensory: *direct, sensuous experience of the world.* **—sen′su·ous·ly** *adv.*

sent (sĕnt) *v.* Past tense and past participle of **send.**
❑ *These sound alike:* **sent, cent** (penny), **scent** (smell).

sen·tence (sĕn**′**təns) *n.* **1.** An independent grammatical unit that has a subject that is either expressed or implied and a predicate containing at least one finite verb. For example, *It's almost midnight* and *Stop!* are sentences. **2.** The penalty imposed by a court of law or other authority upon someone found guilty of a crime or other offense: *a sentence of four years in prison for theft.* ❖ *tr.v.* **sen·tenced, sen·tenc·ing, sen·tenc·es** To impose a sentence on (a criminal defendant found guilty, for example). [From Middle English, opinion, from Latin *sententia*, from *sentīre*, to feel.]

sen·ten·tious (sĕn-tĕn**′**shəs) *adj.* **1.** Brief and pointed in meaning or expression; pithy. **2.** Full of or given to using aphorisms, especially in a pompously moralizing way. **—sen·ten′tious·ly** *adv.*

sen·ti·ment (sĕn**′**tə-mənt) *n.* **1a.** A thought, view, or attitude, especially one based mainly on emotion instead of reason: *an article expressing the writer's anti-American sentiments.* **b.** Such thoughts, views, or feelings considered as a group: *a speech full of patriotic sentiment.* **2a.** A feeling or emotion, especially a tender or romantic one: *Does she return his sentiments?* **b.** Tender, romantic, or sentimental emotion: *The movie's ending was too full of sentiment for me.* See Synonyms at **feeling.** [From Middle English *sentement*, from Latin *sentīre*, to feel.]

sen·ti·men·tal (sĕn′tə-mĕn**′**tl) *adj.* **1.** Having, showing, or caused by affectionate and tender emotion: *We have sentimental ties to this town.* **2.** Having, showing, or caused by strong or extravagant affection or sadness: *read us a sentimental story.* **—sen′ti·men′tal·ly** *adv.*

sen·ti·men·tal·ism (sĕn′tə-mĕn**′**tl-ĭz′əm) *n.* A tendency to be sentimental. **—sen′ti·men′tal·ist** *n.*

sen·ti·men·tal·i·ty (sĕn′tə-mĕn-tăl**′**ĭ-tē) *n., pl.* **sen·ti·men·tal·i·ties** The quality or condition of being sentimental, especially excessively so.

sen·ti·nel (sĕn**′**tə-nəl) *n.* A guard; a sentry. [Probably from Old Italian *sentina*, vigilance, from *sentire*, to watch.]

sen·try (sĕn**′**trē) *n., pl.* **sen·tries** A guard, especially a soldier posted at a given spot to prevent the passage of unauthorized people. [Perhaps alteration of obsolete *sentrinel*, variant of *sentinel*.]

sentry box *n.* A small shelter for a posted sentry.

Seoul (sōl) The capital of South Korea, in the northwest part of the country. Historically the capital of Korea, it became the capital of South Korea in 1948.

se·pal (sē**′**pəl) *n.* One of the usually green leaflike structures that make up the outermost part of a flower. Sepals often enclose and protect the bud. [From New Latin *sepalum*.]

sep·a·ra·ble (sĕp**′**ər-ə-bəl *or* sĕp**′**rə-bəl) *adj.* Capable of being separated.

sep·a·rate (sĕp**′**ə-rāt′) *v.* **sep·a·rat·ed, sep·a·rat·ing, sep·a·rates** *—tr.* **1.** To put or keep apart: *separated the rolls in the pan.* **2.** To keep apart by occupying a position between: *The English Channel separates England from France.* **3.** To place in different categories; sort: *separating the list of words into nouns and verbs.* **4.** To make a distinction between; distinguish: *It was hard to separate facts from opinion in the editorial.* **5.** To divide into parts: *Draw a line that separates a square into two triangles.* **6.** To end a relationship with; part: *He was separated from his wife.* **7.** To remove from a mixture; extract: *We separated the coarse sand in a sieve.* —*intr.* **1.** To come apart; become detached: *The lining has separated from the coat.* **2.** To withdraw; leave: *The state separated from the Union.* **3.** To part company: *We set out together, then separated at Nashville.* **4.** To stop living together as a couple. **5.** To become removed from a mixture: *The oil separated from the peanut butter.* ❖ *adj.* (**sĕp′**ər-ĭt *or* **sĕp′**rĭt) **1.** Not touching or adjoined; detached: *a house with a separate garage.* **2.** Distinct from others; individual or independent: *This cable is made of many separate fibers. Children's books are in a separate section of the library.* [From Middle English *separaten*, from Latin *sēparāre* : *sē-*, apart + *parāre*, to prepare.] **—sep′a·rate·ly** *adv.*

SYNONYMS **separate, divide, part, sever** These verbs mean to cause to become disconnected or disunited. **Separate** means to put apart or to keep apart: *A mountain range separates France and Spain.* **Divide** means to separate by cutting, splitting, or branching into parts: *We divided the pizza into six pieces.* **Part** often means to separate closely associated people or things: *A difference of opinion parted the old friends.* **Sever** often means to divide or cut off something abruptly and dramatically: *The United States severed diplomatic relations with Cuba in 1961.*

---

sep·a·ra·tion (sĕp′ə-**rā′**shən) *n.* **1a.** The act or process of separating: *the separation of cream from milk.* **b.** The condition of being separated: *her separation from the rest of the runners.* **2.** An intervening space; a gap: *a separation between electrical circuits.* **3.** The condition of two married people who are no longer living together as a couple.

sep·a·ra·tist (**sĕp′**ər-ə-tĭst *or* **sĕp′**rə-tĭst) *n.* **1.** A person who advocates the withdrawal of a group from a larger group, as from a political union or an established church. **2.** A person who advocates cultural, ethnic, or racial separation.

sep·a·ra·tor (**sĕp′**ə-rā′tər) *n.* A person or thing that separates, such as a device for separating cream from milk.

se·pi·a (**sē′**pē-ə) *n.* **1.** A dark-brown ink or coloring material originally prepared from the liquid secreted by cuttlefish. **2.** A dark brown. [From Middle English, cuttlefish, from Greek *sēpiā*.]

sep·pu·ku (**sĕp′**o͞o-ko͞o *or* sĕ-**po͞o′**ko͞o) *n.* Hara-kiri.

sep·sis (**sĕp′**sĭs) *n.* Infection of the blood by disease-causing microorganisms, especially bacteria. [From Greek *sēpsis*, putrefaction, from *sēpein*, to make rotten.]

sep·ta (**sĕp′**tə) *n.* Plural of **septum.**

Sep·tem·ber (sĕp-**tĕm′**bər) *n.* The ninth month of the year in the Gregorian calendar, having 30 days. [From Middle English *Septembre*, from Latin *September*, seventh month of the early Roman calendar, from *septem*, seven.]

sep·tet (sĕp-**tĕt′**) *n.* **1a.** A musical composition for seven voices or seven instruments. **b.** A group of seven singers or seven instrumentalists. **2.** A group of seven people or things.

sep·tic (**sĕp′**tĭk) *adj.* Relating to or caused by the presence of disease-causing microorganisms or their toxins in the blood: *septic shock.* [From Greek *sēptikos*, putrefying, from *sēpein*, to make rotten.]

sep·ti·ce·mi·a (sĕp′tĭ-**sē′**mē-ə) *n.* Blood poisoning.

septic tank *n.* A tank in which sewage is decomposed by bacteria.

sep·tum (**sĕp′**təm) *n., pl.* **sep·ta** (**sĕp′**tə) A thin partition or membrane between two cavities or soft masses of tissue in an organism.

sep·tup·let (sĕp-**tŭp′**lĭt) *n.* One of seven offspring born in a single birth.

sep·ul·cher (**sĕp′**əl-kər) *n.* A burial vault.

se·pul·chral (sə-**pŭl′**krəl *or* sə-**po͝ol′**krəl) *adj.* **1.** Relating to a sepulcher: *sepulchral inscriptions.* **2.** Suggestive of the grave; funereal.

se·quel (**sē′**kwəl) *n.* **1.** Something that follows as a continuation, especially a literary, dramatic, or cinematic work whose story continues that of a work that already exists. **2.** A result; an outcome. [From Middle English *sequele*, from Latin *sequēla*, from *sequī*, to follow.]

se·quence (**sē′**kwəns) *n.* **1.** A following of one thing after another; succession: *the sequence of cause and effect.* **2.** The order in which things or events occur or are arranged: *following the sequence of steps outlined in the manual.* **3.** A related or continuous series: *a sequence of incidents that led to civil war.* **4.** The order of subunits that make up a chemical compound, especially the order of nucleotides in a nucleic acid or of amino acids in a protein. ❖ *tr.v.* **se·quenced, se·quenc·ing, se·quenc·es 1.** To determine the order of subunits in a chemical compound, especially a nucleic acid or a protein molecule: *a new technique for sequencing DNA.* **2.** To organize or arrange in a sequence: *the best way to sequence the activities.* **—se·quen′tial** (sĭ-**kwĕn′**shəl) *adj.*

se·ques·ter (sĭ-**kwĕs′**tər) *tr.v.* **se·ques·tered, se·ques·ter·ing, se·ques·ters 1.** To cause to withdraw to a private or out-of-the-way place; seclude: *He sequestered himself in his room to think over what had happened.* **2.** To remove or isolate (a chemical, often a gas) from an environment: *plants that sequester toxins from wetlands.* **3.** To take possession of (property) until a legal claim is settled. **—se′ques·tra′tion** (sē′kwĭ-**strā′**shən) *n.*

se·quin (**sē′**kwĭn) *n.* A small shiny disk or spangle, often sewn on cloth or clothes for decoration. **—se′quined** *adj.*

se·quoi·a (sĭ-**kwoi′**ə) *n.* **1.** A very large cone-bearing evergreen tree of the mountains of California. **2.** A redwood tree. [After *Sequoya.*]

Se·quoy·a or **Se·quoy·ah** (sĭ-**kwoi′**ə) 1770?–1843. Cherokee scholar who developed a writing system for the Cherokee language. —SEE NOTE.

se·ra (**sîr′**ə) *n.* A plural of **serum.**

se·ra·glio (sə-**răl′**yō) *n., pl.* **se·ra·glios 1.** A large harem. **2.** A sultan's palace. [Ultimately from Persian *sarāy*, inn.]

se·ra·pe (sə-**rä′**pē) *n.* A long, often brightly colored shawl resembling a blanket, worn especially by Mexican men.

ser·aph (**sĕr′**əf) *n., pl.* **ser·a·phim** (**sĕr′**ə-fĭm) or **ser·aphs** An angel of high rank. **—se·raph′ic** (sə-**răf′**ĭk) *adj.*

Serb (sûrb) *n.* A native or inhabitant of Serbia.

Ser·bi·a (**sûr′**bē-ə) A country of southeast Europe. It was part of Yugoslavia from 1946 until 2006. Belgrade is the capital.

Ser·bi·an (**sûr′**bē-ən) *adj.* Relating to Serbia or its people, language, or culture. ❖ *n.* **1.** A Serb. **2.** The Slavic language of Serbia, written in the Cyrillic alphabet and closely related to Croatian.

Ser·bo-Cro·a·tian (sûr′bō-krō-**ā′**shən) *n.* The closely related Slavic languages of Croatia, Bosnia and Herzegovina, Montenegro, and Serbia when considered as a single language. **—Ser′bo-Cro·a′tion** *adj.*

sere (sîr) *adj.* Withered. [From Old English *sēar.*]

❑ *These sound alike:* **sere, sear** (scorch), **seer** (prophet).

ser·e·nade (sĕr′ə-**nād′** *or* **sĕr′**ə-nād′) *n.* A musical per-

Sequoya

BIOGRAPHY

Sequoya While growing up in what is now Tennessee, **Sequoya** was fascinated by the writing systems of English and other languages, and in 1809 he began his work on creating an alphabet for the Cherokee language. He settled on an alphabet with 86 symbols, one for each syllable in the spoken language, using characters he adapted from the English, Greek, and Hebrew alphabets. By 1821 Sequoya had completed this alphabet and gotten it approved by the Cherokee chieftains. As a result of Sequoya's alphabet, the *Cherokee Phoenix*, a weekly newspaper printed in Cherokee and English, began in 1828, and books started to appear in Cherokee. In 1828 Sequoya moved west to Indian Territory (later Oklahoma) and became a teacher in Indian schools.

WRITERS CHOOSE THEIR WORDS

Surely her mother must know what people were saying, must be aware of the smugly vicious gossip. Surely it must hurt her as it did Meg. But if it did she gave no outward sign. Nothing ruffled the **serenity** of her expression.

—Madeleine L'Engle
A Wrinkle in Time

serrate

ă	pat	ôr	core
ā	pay	oi	boy
âr	care	ou	out
ä	father	o͝o	took
ĕ	pet	o͝or	lure
ē	be	o͞o	boot
ĭ	pit	ŭ	cut
ī	bite	ûr	urge
îr	pier	th	thin
ŏ	pot	*th*	this
ō	toe	zh	vision
ô	paw	ə	about

formance given to honor or express love for someone, often by one person. ❖ *tr.v.* **ser·e·nad·ed, ser·e·nad·ing, ser·e·nades** To perform a serenade for (someone). [From Latin *serēnus*, serene.]

ser·en·dip·i·ty (sĕr′ən-dĭp′ĭ-tē) *n.* A fortunate discovery made by accident.

se·rene (sə-rēn′) *adj.* **1.** Content or composed; untroubled: *She remained serene throughout the ordeal.* **2.** Unaffected by disturbance; calm or peaceful: *a serene forest.* See Synonyms at **calm. 3.** Unclouded; clear and bright: *serene skies.* **4.** often **Serene** Used as part of a title and form of address for certain members of royalty: *Her Serene Majesty.* [From Middle English, from Latin *serēnus.*] **—se·rene′ly** *adv.*

se·ren·i·ty (sə-rĕn′ĭ-tē) *n.* The quality of being serene.

serf (sûrf) *n.* A member of the lowest class in a feudal society. Serfs were bound to the land owned by a lord and performed labor in return for certain rights. [From French, from Latin *servus*, slave.] **—serf′dom** *n.*

❑ *These sound alike:* **serf, surf** (waves).

serge (sûrj) *n.* A strong wool cloth often used for suits.

❑ *These sound alike:* **serge, surge** (rush).

ser·geant (sär′jənt) *n.* **1.** A noncommissioned officer in the US Army, Air Force, or Marine Corps holding any of several ranks just below lieutenant. **2.** A police officer ranking just below a captain, lieutenant, or inspector. [From Middle English *sergeaunt*, servant, soldier, from Late Latin *serviēns*, public official, from Latin *servīre*, to serve.]

sergeant at arms *n., pl.* **sergeants at arms** An officer whose job is to keep order at the meetings of a legislature, club, or other group.

sergeant major *n., pl.* **sergeants major** or **sergeant majors** A noncommissioned officer of the highest rank in the US Army or Marine Corps.

se·ri·al (sîr′ē-əl) *adj.* **1.** Arranged in or forming a series. **2.** Presented in installments: *a serial television drama.* ❖ *n.* A story or play presented in installments. **—se′ri·al·ly** *adv.*

❑ *These sound alike:* **serial, cereal** (grain).

se·ri·al·ize (sîr′ē-ə-līz′) *tr.v.* **se·ri·al·ized, se·ri·al·iz·ing, se·ri·al·iz·es** To write or publish in installments: *serialize a novel in a magazine.*

serial number *n.* A number that is one of a series and is used for identification, as of a machine: *the serial number of a car.*

se·ries (sîr′ēz) *n., pl.* **series 1.** A number of similar things or events that occur in a row or follow one another in time; a succession: *a series of tracks in the snow.* **2.** An arrangement in an electric circuit in which the current passes through a number of devices in a single path. **3.** A group of rock formations that were deposited in the same geologic period or epoch. [From Latin *seriēs*, from *serere*, to join.]

ser·ine (sĕr′ēn′) *n.* A nonessential amino acid that is found in many proteins.

se·ri·ous (sîr′ē-əs) *adj.* **1.** Careful in thought, full of concern, or restrained and dignified in manner: *He became serious when he was asked about the economy.* **2a.** Requiring or carried out with much thought or consideration: *She undertook a serious study of the policy.* **b.** Deeply interested or involved: *a serious musician.* **3.** Concerned with important rather than trivial matters: *a serious discussion.* **4.** Not joking: *I'm serious—get moving.* **5.** Worthy of concern or anxiety; not easily dealt with, answered, or solved: *a serious situation; a serious problem.* **—se′ri·ous·ly** *adv.* **—se′ri·ous·ness** *n.*

ser·mon (sûr′mən) *n.* **1.** A talk on a religious subject or text, especially one delivered as part of a service. **2.** A solemn, lengthy, and boring talk.

ser·mon·ize (sûr′mə-nīz′) *v.* **ser·mon·ized, ser·mon·iz·ing, ser·mon·iz·es** *—tr.* To deliver a sermon to (someone). *—intr.* To deliver or speak as though delivering a sermon. **—ser′mon·iz′er** *n.*

Sermon on the Mount *n.* In the New Testament, a sermon delivered by Jesus including the Beatitudes, the Lord's Prayer, and various ethical teachings.

se·ro·to·nin (sĕr′ə-tō′nĭn) *n.* A neurotransmitter that is formed from tryptophan and is found in humans and some other mammals, especially in the brain and stomach.

se·rous (sîr′əs) *adj.* Relating to, resembling, containing, or producing serum.

ser·pent (sûr′pənt) *n.* **1.** A snake. **2.** often **Serpent** In the Bible, the creature that tempted Eve to eat the forbidden fruit from the Tree of Knowledge. **3.** A sly or treacherous person. [From Middle English, from Latin *serpēns*, from *serpere*, to creep.]

ser·pen·tine (sûr′pən-tēn′ *or* sûr′pən-tīn′) *adj.* Resembling or typical of a serpent, as in form or movement: *serpentine movements; a serpentine river.*

ser·rate (sĕr′āt′) or **ser·rat·ed** (sĕr′ā′tĭd *or* sə-rā′tĭd) *adj.* Having an edge with notched projections resembling teeth, as a saw: *a serrate leaf.*

se·rum (sîr′əm) *n., pl.* **se·rums** or **se·ra** (sîr′ə) **1.** Blood plasma, especially blood plasma from which factors that cause clotting of the blood have been removed. **2.** Blood serum extracted from an animal that has immunity to a particular disease. It contains antibodies and can be used to transfer immunity to another individual by means of injection. **3.** A watery body fluid.

ser·vant (sûr′vənt) *n.* **1.** A person, such as a butler, cook, or housekeeper, who works for wages in the household of someone else. **2.** A person publicly employed to perform services for others: *Presidents often declare that they are servants of the people.* **3.** A person who expresses submission, debt, or deep respect to another: *your humble servant.*

serve (sûrv) *v.* **served, serv·ing, serves** *—tr.* **1.** To work for (someone) as a servant: *The steward serves the king.* **2a.** To prepare and offer (food): *serve dinner.* **b.** To provide food for (someone): *serving the children first.* **3.** To provide goods and services for (customers), as in a store or restaurant; wait on. **4.** To assist or promote the interests of; aid: *serving the national interest.* **5a.** To work through or complete (a period of service): *served 12 years in the Senate.* **b.** To spend (a period of time) in prison: *served four years for armed robbery.* **6.** To fight or undergo military service for: *served her country in the army.* **7.** To give homage and obedience to: *served God.* **8.** To be used profitably by: *a port that serves a wide region.* **9.** To fulfill (a task or function): *The old car served its purpose.* **10a.** To present (a summons to appear in court or another document issued by a court) to a person. **b.** To present such a summons to (someone). **11.** To put (a ball or shuttlecock) in play by hitting it, as in tennis or badminton. **12.** To assist a priest during (Mass). *—intr.* **1.** To work as a servant. **2.** To do a term of duty: *He served in the Air Force during the war.* **3.** To act in a given capacity: *serve as a clerk.* **4.** To be of use; function: *Let this serve as a reminder.* ❖ *n.* **1.** The act or right of serving in many court games. **2.** The ball served in a court game: *could not return the serve and lost the point.* ◆ **serve (someone) right** To be deserved under the circumstances. [From Middle English *serven*, from Latin *servīre*, from *servus*, slave.]

serv·er (sûr′vər) *n.* **1.** A person who serves food and drink. **2.** Something, such as a tray or a bowl, used in serving food or drink. **3.** A person who assists a priest at Mass. **4.** A file server.

ser·vice (sûr′vĭs) *n.* **1a.** Employment or work done for someone else, usually for pay: *the chef who has always been in their service; a lawyer who gave the firm many years of service.* **b.** An act or a kind of work done for someone else, especially for pay: *an office that provides medical services; a business that provides full catering service.* **2a.** A branch of the government and its employees: *the diplomatic service.* **b.** The armed forces or a branch of the armed forces: *When did she join the service?* **3a.** Help; assistance: *Can I be of service?* **b.** An act of assistance; a favor: *He did us a valuable service.* **4a.** The act or manner of serving food or fulfilling the demands of customers: *a hotel with poor service.* **b.** A set of dishes and table utensils for serving and eating food: *a service for eight people.* **5a.** Installation, maintenance, or repairs provided by a dealer or manufacturer. **b.** The provision to the public of something, especially a utility: *a town without sewer service.* **c.** The system or equipment used to provide something to the public: *The electrical service was damaged in the storm.* **6.** A religious ceremony; a rite: *a church service.* **7.** The presentation of a legal writ or summons to the person named. **8.** The act, manner, or right of serving in many court games; serve. ❖ *tr.v.* **ser·viced, ser·vic·ing, ser·vic·es 1.** To maintain or repair: *The mechanic serviced my car.* **2.** To provide services to: *Our business services the entire city.* ❖ *adj.* **1.** Relating to the armed forces: *a service medal.* **2.** Reserved for the use of employees and messengers rather than the general public: *a service entrance.* **3.** Relating to or for the maintenance and repair of products sold: *a service guarantee.* **4.** Concerned with the serving of customers: *a service manager of a department store.*

ser·vice·a·ble (sûr′vĭ-sə-bəl) *adj.* **1.** Ready or fit for service; usable. **2.** Wearing well; sturdy; durable: *serviceable work boots.* **—ser′vice·a·bil′i·ty** *n.* **—ser′vice·a·bly** *adv.*

service line *n.* A line, as on a tennis or handball court, marking the area into which or from which serves must be directed.

ser·vice·man (sûr′vĭs-măn′) *n.* **1.** A man who is a member of the armed forces. **2.** also **service man** A man whose job is to maintain and repair equipment.

service station *n.* A gas station, especially one that services and repairs motor vehicles.

ser·vice·wom·an (sûr′vĭs-wo͝om′ən) *n.* **1.** A woman who is a member of the armed forces. **2.** also **service woman** A woman whose job is to maintain and repair equipment.

ser·vile (sûr′vəl *or* sûr′vīl′) *adj.* **1.** Submissive; slavish. **2.** Appropriate to slaves or servants: *servile tasks.* **—ser′vile·ly** *adv.* **—ser·vil′i·ty** (sər-vĭl′ĭ-tē) *n.*

serv·ing (sûr′vĭng) *n.* A single portion of food or drink; a helping.

ser·vi·tude (sûr′vĭ-to͞od′) *n.* **1.** The condition of being a slave or serf. **2.** Forced labor imposed as a punishment.

ses·a·me (sĕs′ə-mē) *n.* **1.** The small flat seeds of a tropical Asian plant, used as food and as a source of oil. **2.** The plant that bears such seeds. [From Middle English *sisamie*, from Greek *sēsamē*.]

ses·sile (sĕs′īl′ *or* sĕs′əl) *adj.* **1.** Fixed to one spot: *sponges and other sessile marine animals.* **2.** Attached by the base instead of by a stem: *sessile leaves.*

ses·sion (sĕsh′ən) *n.* **1.** A meeting or series of meetings of a judicial or legislative body. **2.** A period of time during the day or year when a school holds classes: *a summer session.* **3.** A meeting of a school class, club, or other group assembled to do or discuss something of common interest: *a recording session; a gossip session.* [From Middle English *sessioun*, from Latin *sessiō*, act of sitting, from *sedēre*, to sit.]

set¹ (sĕt) *v.* **set, set·ting, sets** *—tr.* **1.** To put in a specified position; place: *set the book on the table.* **2.** To put in a specified condition: *setting him at liberty; set the wagon in motion.* **3.** To incite to hostile feeling or action: *a dispute that set the neighbors against each other.* **4.** To place in a firm or unmoving position: *set the post in a bed of concrete.* **5.** To restore (a broken or dislocated bone) to a proper or normal state. **6.** To adjust for proper functioning: *setting a mouse trap.* **7.** To adjust (an instrument, tool, or other device) so that some desired condition of operation is established: *set the television to channel eight.* **8.** To arrange tableware on (a table) or at (a place) in preparation for a meal. **9.** To arrange (hair) in a certain style, as by rolling it up with clips and curlers. **10a.** To arrange (type) into words, lines, and columns in preparation for printing. **b.** To arrange (matter to be printed) into type. **11a.** To compose (music) to fit a text. **b.** To write (words) to fit a melody. **12.** To represent as happening in a certain place or at a certain time: *setting her story in Detroit.* **13.** To fix at a given amount: *The judge set bail for the defendant at $50,000.* **14.** To establish: *setting an example; set a password.* **15.** To decide on; appoint or designate: *They set June 9 as the day of the wedding.* **16.** To assign (someone) to a given task or station: *set us to work.* **17a.** To place or fix (a jewel or an ornament, for example) in a setting: *set a diamond in a crown.* **b.** To decorate or stud, as jewels mounted in a setting: *set a bracelet with rubies.* *—intr.* **1.** To disappear behind the horizon: *The sun sets in the west.* **2.** To sit on eggs in order to hatch them: *The hens were setting.* **3.** To point toward game by holding a fixed position, as hunting dogs do. ❖ *adj.* **1.** Fixed and established: *a set purpose.* **2.** Unwilling to change: *She is very set in her ways.* **3.** Determined; intent: *He's dead set against it.* ❖ *n.* **1.** The act or process of setting. **2.** The manner in which something is set: *the set of his cap.* **3.** The arrangement of hair in a certain style, as by rolling it up with clips and curlers. ◆ **set about** To begin or start: *She quickly set about solving the problem.* **set apart 1.** To reserve for a specific use: *He set those shoes apart for the dance.* **2.** To make noticeable: *characteristics that set them apart.* **set aside** To separate and reserve for a special purpose: *I set aside money for a new hat.* **set back 1.** To slow down the progress of; hinder: *Injuries have set the team back.* **2.** *Informal* To cost (someone an amount of money): *I bet that new snowboard set you back a lot.* **set down 1.** To cause to sit; seat: *He set his child down beside him.* **2.** To put in writing; record: *set down my thoughts in a diary.* **3a.** To regard; consider: *We set him down as a fraud.* **b.** To assign to a cause; attribute: *Just set the mistake down to inexperience.* **set fire to** To cause to ignite and burn. **set forth 1.** To present for consideration; propose: *set forth a plan.* **2.** To express in words: *She set forth her idea very convincingly.* **set in** To begin to happen or be apparent: *A storm was just setting in.* **set off 1a.** To give rise to; cause to occur: *set off a chemical reaction.* **b.** To cause to explode: *set off fireworks.* **2.** To direct attention to by contrast; accentuate: *set off a passage by highlighting it.* **3.** To start on a journey. **set on fire** To cause to ignite and burn. **set out 1.** To start a journey. **2.** To begin an earnest attempt; undertake: *set out to solve the problem.* **3.** To arrange, lay out, or display: *set out his plans for the garden.* **set sail** To begin a voyage on water. **set the pace 1.** To go at a speed that other competitors attempt to match or surpass. **2.** To behave or perform in a way that others try to match. **set the stage for** To provide the underlying basis for: *The dispute set the stage for a legal battle.* **set to** To begin working energetically; start in. **set up 1.** To place in an upright position. **2.** To assemble or erect: *set up a stereo system.* **3.** To establish; found: *set up a business.* **4.** To establish in business by providing money, equipment, or other backing: *set them up in a small store.* **5.** *Informal* To put (someone else) into a difficult situation by deceit or trickery: *Don't set me up when you're the one responsible.* **6.** In sports, to make a pass to (a teammate), creating a scoring opportunity. **set upon** To attack violently. [From Old English *settan*.] —SEE NOTE.

set² (sĕt) *n.* **1.** A group of matching or related things that

sesame

sessile

USAGE

set¹ In most cases the verb **set** takes a direct object: *He set the table.* **Sit** generally does not take an object: *She sat at the table.* There are some exceptions: *The sun sets* (not *sits*). *A hen sets* (or *sits*) *on her eggs.*

Mother Seton

William Seward

have the same use or purpose or that form a unit: *a set of china.* **2.** A group of people having a common interest: *the younger set.* **3a.** The scenery constructed for a theatrical performance: *The stagehands changed sets between the scenes.* **b.** The enclosure in which a movie is filmed: *The actors assembled on the set.* **4.** The collection of parts or apparatus that makes up a radio or television receiver. **5.** In mathematics, a collection of distinct elements that have something in common: *the set of all positive integers.* **6.** In tennis and other sports, a group of games that forms one unit or part of a match. [From Middle English *sette,* from Medieval Latin *secta,* retinue, from Latin *sequī,* to follow.]

set·back (sĕt′băk′) *n.* A sudden check or reverse in progress; a change from better to worse.

Se·ton (sēt′n), Saint **Elizabeth Ann Bayley** Known as "Mother Seton." 1774–1821. American religious leader who converted to Catholicism and founded a religious order, the Sisters of Charity (1809).

set·tee (sĕ-tē′) *n.* A small or medium-sized sofa.

set·ter (sĕt′ər) *n.* **1.** A person or thing that sets: *a setter of traps.* **2.** A dog of any of several breeds having long hair and originally bred for use in hunting. Setters indicate the location of game animals by holding still and facing in that direction, sometimes in a crouch.

set theory *n.* The mathematical study of the properties of sets.

set·ting (sĕt′ĭng) *n.* **1.** The way in which something, such as an automatic control, is set. **2a.** A surrounding area; environment: *animals in a natural setting.* **b.** The time, place, and circumstances in which a narrative, drama, or film takes place: *The novel's setting was New York City in the 1920s.* **3.** A framework or border, as of precious metal, in which a jewel is firmly fixed: *a turquoise stone in a silver setting.* **4.** Music composed or arranged so that a particular poem or other text can be sung to it: *a musical setting for a psalm.* **5.** A set of eggs in a hen's nest.

set·tle (sĕt′l) *v.* **set·tled, set·tling, set·tles** —*tr.* **1.** To end or resolve (a dispute, for example) by making a decision or coming to an agreement. **2.** To decide (a lawsuit) by mutual agreement of the parties rather than by the court. **3.** To put into order; arrange or fix as desired: *settle the matter with the bank.* **4.** To put securely into a desired position or place: *She settled herself by the fire.* **5.** To establish as a resident or residents: *settled her family in Utah.* **6.** To establish residence in (a region): *pioneers who settled Nebraska.* **7.** To restore calmness or comfort to: *The music settled her nerves.* **8a.** To make compensation for (a claim). **b.** To pay (a debt). —*intr.* **1.** To stop moving and come to rest in one place: *The ball settled in the grass near the green.* **2.** To descend or sink gradually: *Dust settled on the road.* **3.** To establish one's home in: *The family settled in Toronto.* **4.** To reach a decision: *We finally settled on a solution to the problem.* **5.** To come to an agreement, especially to resolve a lawsuit out of court. ❖ *n.* A long wooden bench with a low back. ◆ **settle down 1.** To begin living a stable and orderly life. **2.** To become less nervous or restless. **settle for** To accept in spite of incomplete satisfaction: *It's not what I wanted, but I guess I'll settle for it.* [From Old English *setlan,* to seat, from *setl,* seat.]

set·tle·ment (sĕt′l-mənt) *n.* **1a.** An arrangement or agreement reached, as in business proceedings or negotiating a dispute: *a peace settlement.* **b.** The resolution of a lawsuit or dispute by mutual agreement. **2a.** The establishment of a person or group of people, as in a business or region. **b.** A newly colonized region. **c.** A small community. **3a.** The transfer of property to provide for a person's future needs. **b.** Property thus transferred. **4.** A center providing community services in a poor area.

set·tler (sĕt′lər) *n.* A person who settles in a new region.

set-to (sĕt′to͞o′) *n., pl.* **set-tos** A brief but usually heated contest or conflict.

set·up (sĕt′ŭp′) *n.* **1.** The way in which something is organized or planned. **2.** *Informal* A deceptive scheme, such as a fraud or hoax. **3.** In sports, a play or pass that creates a scoring opportunity.

sev·en (sĕv′ən) *n.* **1.** The number, written 7, that is equal to 6 + 1. **2.** The seventh in a set or series. [From Old English *seofon.*]

seven seas also **Seven Seas** *pl.n.* All the oceans of the world.

sev·en·teen (sĕv′ən-tēn′) *n.* **1.** The number, written 17, that is equal to 16 + 1. **2.** The 17th in a set or sequence. [From Old English *seofontīne.*]

sev·en·teenth (sĕv′ən-tēnth′) *n.* **1.** The ordinal number matching the number 17 in a series. **2.** One of 17 equal parts.

sev·enth (sĕv′ənth) *n.* **1.** The ordinal number matching the number seven in a series. **2.** One of seven equal parts. **3a.** The interval covering six tones in a musical scale. **b.** The seventh tone of a musical scale.

Sev·enth-day Adventist (sĕv′ənth-dā′) *n.* A member of a group of Adventists who observe the Sabbath on Saturday.

sev·en·ti·eth (sĕv′ən-tē-ĭth) *n.* **1.** The ordinal number matching the number 70 in a series. **2.** One of 70 equal parts.

sev·en·ty (sĕv′ən-tē) *n., pl.* **sev·en·ties** The number, written 70, that is equal to 7 × 10. [From Middle English *seventi,* from Old English *hundseofontig.*]

sev·er (sĕv′ər) *tr.v.* **sev·ered, sev·er·ing, sev·ers 1.** To cut or break off from a whole: *sever a limb from a tree.* **2.** To divide into parts; interrupt: *severed the army's supply lines.* **3.** To break up (a relationship, for example); dissolve. See Synonyms at **separate.** [From Middle English *severen,* from Latin *sēparāre,* to separate.]

sev·er·al (sĕv′ər-əl *or* sĕv′rəl) *adj.* **1.** Being of a number more than two or three but not many: *several miles away.* **2.** Distinct; various: *They parted and went their several ways.* ❖ *pron. (used with a plural verb)* An indefinite but small number; some or a few: *He saw several of his classmates.* [From Middle English, separate, from Medieval Latin *sēparālis,* from Latin *sēparāre,* to separate.] —**sev′er·al·ly** *adv.*

sev·er·ance (sĕv′ər-əns *or* sĕv′rəns) *n.* **1a.** The act or process of severing: *the severance of political ties.* **b.** The condition of being severed. **2.** Separation; partition.

severance pay *n.* Extra pay given an employee who has been laid off.

se·vere (sə-vîr′) *adj.* **se·ver·er, se·ver·est 1.** Unsparing or harsh; strict: *a severe law.* **2.** Grim or stern in manner or appearance: *a severe voice.* **3.** Extremely plain: *severe clothes.* **4.** Causing great distress; sharp: *a severe pain.* **5.** Very serious; extreme: *severe damage.* **6.** Very difficult; trying: *a severe test of our friendship.* [From Latin *sevērus.*] —**se·vere′ly** *adv.* —**se·vere′ness** *n.*

se·ver·i·ty (sə-vĕr′ĭ-tē) *n., pl.* **se·ver·i·ties 1.** The state or quality of being severe. **2.** The act or an instance of severe behavior, especially punishment.

Se·ville (sə-vĭl′) A city of southwest Spain southwest of Córdoba. It was the chief port of the Spanish empire until the early 1700s.

sew (sō) *v.* **sewed, sewn** (sōn) or **sewed, sew·ing, sews** —*tr.* **1.** To make, repair, or fashion by stitching, as with a needle and thread or a sewing machine: *sew a dress; sew a button onto a cuff.* **2.** To furnish with stitches for the purpose of closing, fastening, or attaching: *sew an incision closed.* —*intr.* To work with a needle and thread or a sewing machine: *Tailors sew for a living.* ◆ **sew up** *Informal* To complete successfully: *Our team sewed up the championship.* [From Old English *seowian.*] —**sew′er** *n.*

❑ *These sound alike:* **sew, so¹** (thus), **so²** (musical note), **sow¹** (plant seeds).

ă	pat	ôr	core
ā	pay	oi	boy
âr	care	ou	out
ä	father	o͝o	took
ĕ	pet	o͝or	lure
ē	be	o͞o	boot
ĭ	pit	ŭ	cut
ī	bite	ûr	urge
îr	pier	th	thin
ŏ	pot	*th*	this
ō	toe	zh	vision
ô	paw	ə	about

sew·age (so͞o′ĭj) *n.* Liquid and solid waste carried off in sewers or drains.

Sew·ard (so͞o′ərd), **William Henry** 1801–1872. American politician who arranged the purchase of Alaska from Russia (1867).

sew·er[1] (so͞o′ər) *n.* An underground pipe or channel built to carry off sewage or rainwater. [From Middle English *seuer*, from Anglo-Norman *sewere*.]

sew·er[2] (sō′ər) *n.* A person or thing that sews: *a sewer of fine clothing.*

sew·er·age (so͞o′ər-ĭj) *n.* **1.** A system of sewers. **2.** The removal of waste materials by a system of sewers. **3.** Sewage.

sew·ing (sō′ĭng) *n.* **1.** The act, occupation, or hobby of a person who sews. **2.** The article on which a person is working with needle and thread.

sewing machine *n.* A machine for sewing.

sewn (sōn) *v.* A past participle of **sew**.

sex (sĕks) *n.* **1.** Either of two divisions, male and female, into which most organisms are grouped according to their functions in the process of reproduction. **2.** The fact or condition of existing in these two divisions, especially the collection of characteristics that distinguish female and male: *the evolution of sex in plants; a study that takes sex into account.* **3.** Sexual intercourse.

sex cell *n.* A reproductive cell.

sex chromosome *n.* Either of a pair of chromosomes, usually called X and Y, that determine the sex of an individual and are found in most animals. In humans, females have two X chromosomes and males have one X and one Y chromosome.

sex hormone *n.* A hormone that regulates the sexual development of an organism and is needed for reproduction. Testosterone and estrogen are sex hormones.

sex·ism (sĕk′sĭz′əm) *n.* Discrimination that is based on gender, especially discrimination against women. **—sex′ist** *adj. & n.*

sex-linked (sĕks′lĭngkt′) *adj.* **1.** Carried by a sex chromosome, especially an X chromosome: *a sex-linked gene.* **2.** Determined by a gene or genes carried on a sex chromosome: *Colorblindness is a sex-linked trait.*

sex·tant (sĕk′stənt) *n.* A navigation instrument used to measure the altitude between the plane of the horizon and a celestial object.

sex·tet (sĕk-stĕt′) *n.* **1a.** A musical composition for six voices or six instruments. **b.** A group of six singers or six instrumentalists. **2.** A group of six people or things. [From Latin *sextus*, sixth.]

sex·ton (sĕk′stən) *n.* A person employed to take care of a church and its property and sometimes to ring bells and dig graves.

Sex·ton (sĕk′stən), **Anne** 1928–1974. American poet whose works include the collection *Live or Die* (1966).

sex·tup·let (sĕk-stŭp′lĭt) *n.* One of six offspring born in a single birth.

sex·u·al (sĕk′sho͞o-əl) *adj.* **1.** Relating to, involving, or characteristic of sex or sexuality, or the sex organs and their functions: *sexual development.* **2.** Relating to the sexes or to gender: *sexual politics.* **3.** Relating to or involving the union of male and female reproductive cells: *sexual reproduction.* **—sex′u·al·ly** *adv.*

sexual harassment *n.* Inappropriate behavior of a sexual nature, such as offensive remarks.

sexual intercourse *n.* Intimate physical contact between humans, usually involving insertion of the penis into the vagina.

sex·u·al·i·ty (sĕk′sho͞o-ăl′ĭ-tē) *n.* **1.** The quality of being sexual, especially sexual orientation and behavior. **2.** The condition of being characterized and distinguished by sex.

sexually transmitted disease *n.* Any of several diseases, such as syphilis and gonorrhea, that are transmitted by sexual contact.

sexually transmitted infection *n.* A sexually transmitted disease.

sexual orientation *n.* Sexual interest and attraction toward people of the same or opposite sex or toward people of either sex.

Sey·chelles (sā-shĕl′ *or* sā-shĕlz′) An island country in the western Indian Ocean north of Madagascar. Victoria is the capital.

Sg The symbol for the element **seaborgium.**

SGML (ĕs′jē-ĕm-ĕl′) *n.* A markup language that is used to lay out the structure of a computer document.

Sgt. or **SGT** *abbr.* An abbreviation of sergeant.

sh (sh) *interj.* An expression used to urge silence.

shab·by (shăb′ē) *adj.* **shab·bi·er, shab·bi·est 1.** Worn-out, frayed, and faded; threadbare: *shabby clothes.* **2.** Dressed in threadbare clothes. **3.** Dilapidated; deteriorated: *shabby houses.* **4.** Despicable or unfair; mean: *shabby treatment.* [From obsolete *shab*, scab, from Old English *sceabb*.] **—shab′bi·ly** *adv.* **—shab′bi·ness** *n.*

shack (shăk) *n.* A small crudely built cabin.

shack·le (shăk′əl) *n.* **1.** A metal ring usually connected to a chain and fastened or locked around the wrist or ankle of a prisoner or captive. **2.** often **shackles** A restraint or check on action or progress: *the shackles of ignorance.* ❖ *tr.v.* **shack·led, shack·ling, shack·les 1.** To put a shackle or shackles on: *shackle a prisoner.* **2.** To confine, restrain, or hamper.

shad (shăd) *n., pl.* **shad** or **shads** Any of several edible ocean fishes that swim up rivers to spawn. Shad are closely related to herring.

shade (shād) *n.* **1.** Light that has been diminished in strength by partial blocking or deflection of its rays; partial darkness. **2.** Cover or shelter from the sun or its rays: *sat in the shade under the tree.* **3.** The degree to which a color is mixed with black or less than fully lighted: *shades of gray.* **4.** Any of various devices used to reduce light or heat, as that from the sun: *a window shade.* **5.** A slight difference; a nuance: *a shade of meaning.* **6.** A small amount; a trace: *a shade under forty miles.* **7. shades** Sunglasses. **8.** A spirit; a ghost. **9. shades** Reminders; echoes: *shades of 1776.* ❖ *tr.v.* **shad·ed, shad·ing, shades 1.** To screen from light or heat: *Trees shaded the street.* **2.** To represent or produce degrees of shade or shadow in: *shade a drawing.* [From Old English *sceadu*.]

shad·ing (shā′dĭng) *n.* **1.** A screening against light or heat. **2.** The lines or other marks used in a drawing, engraving, or painting to represent gradations of color or darkness. **3.** A small change or difference.

shad·ow (shăd′ō) *n.* **1.** A dark area or shape made by an object blocking rays of light. **2.** The darkness or diminished light caused by the blocking of a light source: *The sun crossed in front of the house, leaving the backyard in shadow.* **3. shadows** The darkness following sunset: *evening shadows.* **4.** A darkened area of skin under the eye: *shadows under his eyes for lack of sleep.* **5.** The first signs of the growth of beard that makes the skin look darker: *a five-o'clock shadow.* **6.** A darker area in a picture or photograph. **7.** A feeling or cause of gloom or unhappiness: *The argument cast a shadow on their friendship.* **8.** A nearby or neighboring area: *grew up in the shadow of the ballpark.* **9.** A dominating presence or influence: *felt like he worked in his boss's shadow.* **10.** A phantom; a ghost. **11.** An imperfect imitation or inferior version: *He's a shadow of the leader he once was.* **12.** A person, such as a detective or spy, who follows another in secret. **13.** A faint indication; a premonition: *shadows of future events.* **14.** A slight trace: *beyond a shadow of a doubt.* ❖ *tr.v.* **shad·owed, shad·ow·ing, shad·ows 1.** To cast a shadow on; shade: *Her face was shadowed by her hat.* **2.** To follow (someone), especially in secret; trail. [From Middle English *shadwe*,

sextant

Anne Sexton
photographed in 1967

shagbark hickory

shako
worn by a member of the French Republican Guard

ă	pat	ôr	core
ā	pay	oi	boy
âr	care	ou	out
ä	father	o͝o	took
ĕ	pet	o͝or	lure
ē	be	o͞o	boot
ĭ	pit	ŭ	cut
ī	bite	ûr	urge
îr	pier	th	thin
ŏ	pot	*th*	this
ō	toe	zh	vision
ô	paw	ə	about

from Old English *sceaduwe*, form of *sceadu*, shade.]

shad·ow·y (shăd′ō-ē) *adj.* **shad·ow·i·er, shad·ow·i·est** **1.** Full of or dark with shadows: *shadowy woods.* See Synonyms at **dark. 2.** Vague; indistinct: *shadowy ideas.* **3.** Little known or understood; mysterious: *a newspaper article about the politician's shadowy past.*

shad·y (shā′dē) *adj.* **shad·i·er, shad·i·est 1.** Full of shade; shaded: *a shady street.* See Synonyms at **dark. 2.** Casting shade: *shady trees.* **3.** Of doubtful character or honesty; questionable: *a shady deal.* **—shad′i·ly** *adv.* **—shad′i·ness** *n.*

shaft (shăft) *n.* **1a.** The long narrow body of a spear or arrow. **b.** A spear or arrow. **2.** The handle of any of various tools or implements: *the shaft of a hammer.* **3.** One of the two parallel poles between which an animal drawing a vehicle is hitched. **4.** A long, generally cylindrical bar, especially one that turns and transmits power, as the drive shaft of an engine. **5.** The stiff central part of a feather. **6.** The section of a column between the capital and the base. **7.** A ray or beam of light. **8.** A long, narrow, often vertical passage or conduit: *a mine shaft; an elevator shaft.* [From Old English *sceaft*.]

shag (shăg) *n.* **1.** A tangle or mass, especially of rough matted hair. **2a.** A coarse long nap, as on a woolen cloth. **b.** Cloth having such a nap.

shag·bark hickory (shăg′bärk′) *n.* A North American hickory tree having shaggy bark and edible hard-shelled nuts.

shag·gy (shăg′ē) *adj.* **shag·gi·er, shag·gi·est 1.** Having, covered with, or resembling long rough hair or wool: *a shaggy dog.* **2.** Bushy or matted: *shaggy hair.*

shah (shä) *n.* Used formerly as a title for the king of Iran. [From Persian *shāh*.]

shake (shāk) *v.* **shook** (sho͝ok), **shak·en** (shā′kən), **shak·ing, shakes** —*tr.* **1.** To move or cause to move to and fro with jerky movements: *shake a tambourine.* **2.** To brandish or wave, especially in anger: *shake one's fist.* **3.** To cause to tremble, vibrate, or rock: *The earthquake shook the ground.* **4.** To remove or dislodge by jerky movements: *shake snow from the boots.* **5.** To cause to lose stability or strength, as of conviction: *Nothing could shake him from his belief.* **6.** To make uneasy; disturb; agitate: *The bad news shook her.* **7.** To clasp (hands) in greeting or leave-taking or as a sign of agreement. —*intr.* **1.** To move to and fro in short, irregular, often jerky movements: *The trees shook in the wind.* **2.** To tremble, as from cold or in anger. **3.** To shake hands: *If you agree, let's shake on it.* ❖ *n.* **1.** An act of shaking: *a shake of the head.* **2.** A trembling or vibrating movement. **3.** A beverage mixed by shaking, especially a milkshake. **4. shakes** *Informal* Uncontrollable trembling. ◆ **shake off** To free oneself of; get rid of: *We shook off our fears.* **shake up 1.** To upset or cause to be concerned: *We were shaken up by the news that our teacher was leaving.* **2.** To subject to a drastic rearrangement or reorganization: *The new director decided to shake up the entire organization.* [From Old English *sceacan*.]

shak·er (shā′kər) *n.* **1.** A person or thing that shakes. **2.** A container used for shaking: *a pepper shaker.* **3. Shaker** A member of a Christian group originating in England in 1747, and practicing communal living and celibacy.

Shake·speare (shāk′spîr), **William** 1564–1616. English poet and playwright whose plays include historical works, comedies, and tragedies, such as *Hamlet.* **—Shake·spear′e·an, Shake·spear′i·an** *adj.*

shake·up (shāk′ŭp′) *n.* A drastic reorganization: *a shakeup of government personnel.*

shak·o (shăk′ō *or* shā′kō) *n., pl.* **shak·os** or **shak·oes** A military cap with a visor in front and an upright plume on top.

shak·y (shā′kē) *adj.* **shak·i·er, shak·i·est 1.** Trembling or quivering: *a shaky voice.* **2.** Unsteady or unsound: *a shaky old dock.* **3.** Not to be depended on; wavering or doubtful: *a shaky alliance.* **—shak′i·ly** *adv.*

shale (shāl) *n.* Any of various easily split sedimentary rocks made up of layers of claylike, fine-grained sediments.

shall (shăl) *aux.v.* past tense **should** (sho͝od) **1.** Used to express future action or condition: *I shall return tomorrow.* **2.** Used to express an order, promise, requirement, or obligation: *You shall pay for your misdeeds.* **3.** Used to express determination: *I shall go if I want to.* —SEE NOTE.

shal·lop (shăl′əp) *n.* **1.** A large heavy boat, usually having two masts and carrying fore-and-aft sails or lugsails. **2.** A small open boat fitted with oars or sails or both.

shal·lot (shăl′ət) *n.* **1.** The mild-flavored bulb of a variety of onion. **2.** The plant that bears this bulb.

shal·low (shăl′ō) *adj.* **shal·low·er, shal·low·est 1.** Measuring little from the bottom to the top or surface; not deep: *a shallow lake; a shallow pan.* **2.** Lacking depth of thought, feeling, or knowledge; superficial: *shallow ideas.* **3.** Being in the part of a baseball field that is closer to home plate. **4.** Marked by inhaling much less air than normal; weak: *shallow breathing* ❖ *n.* often **shallows** A shallow part of a body of water: *went swimming in the shallows.* [From Middle English *shalou*.] **—shal′low·ly** *adv.* **—shal′low·ness** *n.*

sha·lom (shä-lōm′) *interj.* An expression used as a traditional Jewish greeting or farewell. [From Hebrew *šālôm*, peace.]

shalt (shălt) *aux.v. Archaic* A second person singular present tense of **shall.**

sham (shăm) *n.* Something false that is deceitfully passed off as genuine: *The antique turned out to be a sham.* ❖ *adj.* Fake; not genuine: *sham diamonds.* ❖ *tr.v.* **shammed, sham·ming, shams** To pretend to have or feel; feign: *shamming ignorance.* [Possibly from *shame*.]

sha·man (shä′mən *or* shā′mən) *n., pl.* **sha·mans** A member of certain societies who acts as an intermediary between the visible world and an invisible spirit world and who heals people and foretells or controls events. [Ultimately from Sanskrit *śramaṇaḥ*, a Buddhist monk.]

sham·ble (shăm′bəl) *intr.v.* **sham·bled, sham·bling, sham·bles** To walk in an awkward or lazy way, dragging the feet; shuffle. ❖ *n.* An awkward shuffling walk.

sham·bles (shăm′bəlz) *pl.n. (used with a singular verb)* A scene or condition of great disorder or destruction.

shame (shām) *n.* **1.** A painful emotion caused by the awareness of having done something wrong or foolish. **2.** The capacity for such an emotion: *Have you no shame?* **3.** A source of disgrace or embarrassment: *It's a shame that none of you offered to help the strangers.* **4.** A condition of disgrace or dishonor: *Your actions have brought shame on the entire family.* **5.** A regrettable or unfortunate situation: *It would be a shame to miss the circus.* ❖ *tr.v.* **shamed, sham·ing, shames 1.** To cause to feel shame: *She was shamed by what the others said because it was true.* **2.** To cause (someone) to do something by arousing a feeling of shame or guilt: *He was shamed into making an apology.* **3.** To bring disgrace upon: *behavior that shamed their good name.* ◆ **put to shame 1.** To fill with shame; disgrace. **2.** To outdo thoroughly; surpass: *Her batting record put the rest of us to shame.* [From Old English *sceamu*.]

shame·faced (shām′fāst′) *adj.* Feeling or indicative of shame. **—shame′fac′ed·ly** *adv.*

shame·ful (shām′fəl) *adj.* Deserving or causing shame; disgraceful: *shameful behavior.* **—shame′ful·ly** *adv.*

shame·less (shām′lĭs) *adj.* **1.** Feeling no shame: *a shameless liar.* **2.** Marked by a lack of shame: *a shameless lie.* **—shame′less·ly** *adv.*

sham·poo (shăm-po͞o′) *n., pl.* **sham·poos 1.** Any of various preparations of soap or detergent used to wash the hair and scalp. **2.** Any of various cleaning agents for rugs, upholstery, or cars. **3.** The act or process of washing the hair or cleaning something with shampoo. ❖ *tr. & intr.v.* **sham·pooed, sham·poo·ing, sham·poos** To wash or be washed with shampoo. [From Hindi *cāmpō*, imperative of *cāmpnā*, to press, massage.]

sham·rock (**shăm′**rŏk′) *n.* **1.** A plant having compound leaves with three small leaflets, especially a clover. **2.** An image of one of these plants or leaves, used as a national emblem of Ireland. [From Irish Gaelic *seamróg*, diminutive of *seamar*, clover.]

shang·hai (shăng-**hī′** *or* **shăng′**hī′) *tr.v.* **shang·haied, shang·hai·ing, shang·hais 1.** To kidnap (a person), especially by making the person unconscious with a drug or liquor, for forced service aboard a ship. **2.** To force (a person) to do something by deceitful or dishonest means.

Shang·hai (shăng-**hī′**) The largest city in China, in the eastern part of the country at the mouth of the Yangtze River on the East China Sea.

shank (shăngk) *n.* **1a.** The part of the human leg between the knee and ankle. **b.** A corresponding part of the leg in other vertebrate animals. **2.** A long narrow part of an object: *the shank of an anchor.* **3.** A cut of meat from the leg of a steer, calf, sheep, or lamb.

shan't (shănt) Contraction of *shall not.*

shan·ty (**shăn′**tē) *n., pl.* **shan·ties** A roughly built or ramshackle cabin; a shack.

❑ *These sound alike:* **shanty, chantey** (song).

shape (shāp) *n.* **1.** The outward appearance of a thing; form. **2.** Something distinguished from its surroundings by its outline: *dark shapes on the horizon that might have been houses.* **3.** The outline of a person's body; the figure. **4a.** A definite distinctive form: *Our discussion took the shape of an argument.* **b.** A desirable form: *a fabric that holds its shape.* **5.** A form or condition in which something may exist or appear: *a god in the shape of a swan.* **6.** A device for giving or determining form; a mold or pattern. **7.** Proper condition for action, effectiveness, or use: *an athlete out of shape.* ❖ *tr.v.* **shaped, shap·ing, shapes 1.** To give a certain shape or form to: *shape clay into bowls.* **2.** To change to a particular shape or form; mold: *shape a sculpture out of ice.* **3.** To modify; adapt: *shaped their plans to fit ours.* **4.** To direct the course of: *shaping a child's education.* ◆ **shape up** *Informal* **1.** To turn out; develop: *I wondered how the game was shaping up.* **2.** To improve so as to meet a standard. [From Old English *gesceap*, a creation.]

shape·less (**shāp′**lĭs) *adj.* **1.** Having no definite shape; formless: *a shapeless cloud.* **2.** Lacking a pleasing shape; not shapely: *a shapeless figure.* **—shape′less·ly** *adv.*

shape·ly (**shāp′**lē) *adj.* **shape·li·er, shape·li·est** Having a shape that is pleasing to look at; well-proportioned. **—shape′li·ness** *n.*

shard (shärd) *n.* A broken piece or fragment, as of pottery or glass.

share[1] (shâr) *n.* **1.** A part belonging to, distributed, contributed by, or owned by a person or group; a portion: *The pirates argued over their shares of the treasure.* **2.** A fair or full portion: *did her share to make the play a success.* **3.** One of the equal parts into which the capital stock of a company is divided: *bought 200 shares of the company's stock.* ❖ *v.* **shared, shar·ing, shares** *—tr.* **1.** To participate in, use, enjoy, or experience in common with other people or in turns: *sharing the responsibility; share a room.* **2.** To disclose or present to others: *He shared his adventure with the class.* **3.** To divide and distribute: *shared his estate among his children.* *—intr.* **1.** To participate: *We shared in applauding the suggestion.* **2.** To allow someone to use or enjoy something that one has. [From Old English *scearu*, division.] **—shar′er** *n.*

share[2] (shâr) *n.* A plowshare. [From Old English *scēar.*]

share·crop·per (**shâr′**krŏp′ər) *n.* A tenant farmer who pays a share of the crops as rent to the landowner.

share·hold·er (**shâr′**hōl′dər) *n.* A person who owns a share or shares in the stock of a company.

shark (shärk) *n.* **1.** Any of numerous ocean fishes that have tough skin and a skeleton made of cartilage rather than bone. Most sharks are carnivorous. **2.** A person who takes advantage of the misfortune of others for personal gain.

sharp (shärp) *adj.* **sharp·er, sharp·est 1.** Having a thin edge or fine point for cutting or piercing: *a sharp razor.* **2.** Having an edge or point: *sharp rocks.* **3.** Clear and distinct: *a sharp image.* **4.** Abrupt; not gradual: *a sharp drop to the sea.* **5.** Intelligent; smart: *a sharp student.* **6.** Acute: *the sharp eyes of a falcon.* **7.** Watchful; alert: *keep a sharp lookout.* **8.** Crafty or deceitful, especially in business dealings: *sharp selling practices.* **9.** Cold and cutting: *a sharp wind.* **10.** Harsh or biting in tone or character: *a sharp tongue.* **11.** Fierce or impetuous; violent: *a sharp blow.* **12.** Felt suddenly and intensely: *a sharp pain.* **13.** Sudden and shrill: *a sharp whistle.* **14.** Having a strong odor and flavor: *a sharp cheese.* **15a.** Higher in musical pitch than is correct: *a sharp note.* **b.** Higher in pitch by a half step than a corresponding natural tone or key: *a C sharp.* **16.** *Informal* Stylish or attractive: *a sharp dresser.* ❖ *adv.* **sharper, sharpest 1.** In a sharp manner. **2.** Promptly; exactly: *at 3:00 sharp.* **3.** Above the correct pitch: *to sing sharp.* ❖ *n.* **1.** A musical note or tone that is a half step higher than a corresponding natural tone or key. **2.** A sign (♯) used to indicate that a note is to be raised by a half step. ❖ *intr.v.* **sharped, sharp·ing, sharps** To sing or play sharp. [From Old English *scearp.*] **—sharp′ly** *adv.* **—sharp′ness** *n.*

sharp·en (**shär′**pən) *tr. & intr.v.* **sharp·ened, sharp·en·ing, sharp·ens** To make or become sharp or sharper. **—sharp′en·er** *n.*

sharp·shoot·er (**shärp′**sho͞o′tər) *n.* A person who is highly skilled at shooting a gun.

Shatt al Ar·ab or **Shatt-al-Ar·ab** (shăt′ äl **ăr′**əb) A river channel, about 120 miles (195 kilometers) long, of southeast Iraq formed by the junction of the Tigris and Euphrates Rivers and flowing southeast to the Persian Gulf.

shat·ter (**shăt′**ər) *v.* **shat·tered, shat·ter·ing, shat·ters** *—tr.* **1.** To cause to break suddenly into pieces, as with a violent blow; smash. See Synonyms at **break. 2.** To damage or destroy; ruin: *shattered his hopes.* *—intr.* To break into pieces; smash or burst: *The glass shattered when it hit the floor.*

shave (shāv) *v.* **shaved, shaved** or **shav·en** (**shā′**vən), **shav·ing, shaves** *—tr.* **1a.** To remove hair from, especially with a razor: *shave a man's face.* **b.** To cut (the beard or hair) at the surface of the skin with a razor. **2.** To cut thin slices from: *shaving a board.* **3.** To cut or scrape into small pieces; shred: *shave chocolate.* **4.** To touch gently in passing; graze. *—intr.* To remove the beard or other body hair with a razor or shaver: *Tom shaves every morning.* ❖ *n.* The act, process, or result of shaving: *a smooth shave.* ◆ **close shave** A narrow escape.

shav·er (**shā′**vər) *n.* **1.** A person who shaves. **2.** A device for shaving, especially an electric razor. **3.** *Informal* A young boy; a lad.

shav·ing (**shā′**vĭng) *n.* **1.** A thin slice or sliver, as of wood or metal, that is shaved off. **2.** The action of a person that shaves.

Sha·vu·ot (shə-**vo͞o′**ōt′ *or* shə-**vo͞o′**əs) *n.* A Jewish festival that commemorates God's revelation of the Torah on Mount Sinai.

shawl (shôl) *n.* A large piece of cloth worn as a covering for the shoulders, neck, or head.

Shaw·nee (shô-**nē′**) *n., pl.* **Shawnee** or **Shaw·nees 1.**

USAGE

shall Americans predominantly use the word **will** instead of **shall** whether speaking in the first, second, or third persons: *I, we* (or *you* or *he, she, it, they*) *will be leaving soon.* On those few occasions when we use *shall,* we tend to reserve it for polite invitations and requests, such as *Shall we go? Shall* has also been used to convey moral seriousness, as in *We shall overcome.*

WRITERS CHOOSE THEIR WORDS

"Have any of you done a bit of schoolwork all fall?" [Mom] asked. "You too, Matt. Have you?"

Well, of course not. We tried to look **shamefaced.** Bad us for not doing algebra when the world is coming to an end.

—Susan Beth Pfeffer
Life As We Knew It

shawl

sheaf
of wheat

A member of a Native American people formerly living in the east-central United States and now living in Oklahoma. **2.** The Algonquian language of the Shawnee.

shay (shā) *n. Informal* A chaise.

she (shē) *pron.* **1.** The female person or animal previously mentioned: *Nancy left, but she will be back. Our cat likes fish, but she won't eat chicken.* **2.** Something previously mentioned that is traditionally regarded as female: *I like your boat; she's really sleek.* ❖ *n.* A female animal or person: *Is the cat a he or a she?* —SEE NOTE AT **me.**

sheaf (shēf) *n., pl.* **sheaves** (shēvz) **1.** A bundle of cut stalks of grain or similar plants bound with straw or twine. **2.** A collection of things held or bound together.

shear (shîr) *tr.v.* **sheared, sheared** or **shorn** (shôrn), **shear·ing, shears 1.** To remove (fleece or hair) by clipping with a sharp instrument. **2.** To remove the fleece or hair from: *shearing a ram.* **3.** To cut with or as if with shears: *shearing a hedge.* **4.** To deprive; divest: *sheared of all privileges.* ❖ *n.* often **shears** A pair of scissors or a similar cutting tool. [From Old English *sceran.*] **—shear′er** *n.*

❑ *These sound alike:* **shear, sheer[1]** (swerve), **sheer[2]** (thin).

shear·ling (**shîr′**lĭng) *n.* **1.** A young sheep that has been sheared once. **2.** The tanned skin of a sheared sheep or lamb, with the short wool still attached. **3.** A synthetic material that resembles shearling.

sheath (shēth) *n., pl.* **sheaths** (shē*thz or* shēths) **1.** A case into which the blade of a knife or sword fits. **2.** Any of various similar coverings. **3.** A tubular structure that surrounds a plant or animal part, such as the base of a grass leaf or the tissue that encloses a muscle or nerve fiber. **4.** A close-fitting dress.

sheathe (shē*th*) *tr.v.* **sheathed, sheath·ing, sheathes 1.** To insert into or provide with a sheath: *sheathe a sword.* **2.** To provide with a protective covering: *sheathe electric wires with rubber.*

sheath·ing (**shē′***th*ĭng) *n.* **1.** A layer of boards or other materials applied to the frame of a building to strengthen and protect it from weather. **2.** A protective covering on the underwater part of a ship's hull.

sheave (shēv) *tr.v.* **sheaved, sheav·ing, sheaves** To gather and bind (grain) into a sheaf.

sheaves (shēvz) *n.* Plural of **sheaf.**

She·ba (**shē′**bə) An ancient country of southern Arabia in present-day Yemen.

shed[1] (shĕd) *tr.v.* **shed, shed·ding, sheds 1.** To have (a growth or covering) be disconnected or fall off by a natural process: *a tree shedding its leaves; a snake shedding its skin; a dog shedding its hair.* **2.** To rid oneself of: *My dad shed 10 pounds by exercising.* **3.** To send forth; give off: *The moon shed a pale light on the pond.* **4.** To repel: *This coat sheds water.* **5.** To produce and release (tears). ◆ **shed blood** To wound or kill. [From Old English *scēadan*, to divide, separate.] **—shed′der** *n.*

shed[2] (shĕd) *n.* A small structure for storage or shelter: *a tool shed.* [From Early Modern English *shadde*, perhaps variant of Middle English *shade*, shade.]

she'd (shēd) Contraction of *she had* or *she would.*

sheen (shēn) *n.* Glistening brightness; luster.

sheep (shēp) *n., pl.* **sheep 1.** A domesticated hoofed mammal having a thick fleecy coat, widely raised for its meat, wool, and skin. **2.** Any of various wild hoofed mammals related to and resembling the domestic sheep, such as the bighorn sheep. **3.** A person who is easily led or influenced.

sheep·dog also **sheep dog** (**shēp′**dôg′) *n.* A dog trained to guard and herd sheep.

sheep·fold (**shēp′**fōld′) *n.* A pen for sheep.

sheep·herd·er (**shēp′**hûr′dər) *n.* A person who herds sheep; a shepherd.

sheep·ish (**shē′**pĭsh) *adj.* **1.** Embarrassed, as by being aware of a fault: *a sheepish grin.* **2.** Meek or stupid. **—sheep′ish·ly** *adv.* **—sheep′ish·ness** *n.*

sheep·skin (**shēp′**skĭn′) *n.* **1.** The skin of a sheep, either with the fleece left on or in the form of leather or parchment. **2.** *Informal* A diploma.

sheer[1] (shîr) *intr. & tr.v.* **sheered, sheer·ing, sheers** To swerve or cause to swerve from a course. [Probably partly from Low German *scheren*, to move to and from (said of boats), and partly from Dutch *scheren*, to withdraw.]

❑ *These sound alike:* **sheer[1]** (swerve), **shear** (cut), **sheer[2]** (thin).

sheer[2] (shîr) *adj.* **sheer·er, sheer·est 1.** Thin, fine, and translucent: *sheer curtains.* **2.** Complete; utter: *dropped from sheer exhaustion.* **3.** Almost perpendicular; steep: *sheer cliffs.* [Partly from Middle English *shire*, bright, clear (from Old English *scīr*), partly from Middle English *skire*, bright, clean, and partly from Middle English *skere, shere*, blameless, free from sin (from Old Norse *skærr*).]

❑ *These sound alike:* **sheer[2]** (thin), **shear** (cut), **sheer[1]** (swerve).

sheet[1] (shēt) *n.* **1.** A large piece of cloth, used as a bed covering, especially in pairs, one under and one over the sleeper. **2.** A broad, thin, usually rectangular piece of material, such as paper, metal, or glass. **3.** A broad continuous expanse of material covering a surface: *a sheet of ice.* ❖ *tr.v.* **sheet·ed, sheet·ing, sheets** To cover or provide with sheets, especially bed sheets. [From Old English *scēte.*]

sheet[2] (shēt) *n.* A rope attached to one or both of the lower corners of a sail to move or extend it. [From Middle English *shete*, from Old English *scēat(line)*, sheet (line), from *scēata*, corner of a sail.]

sheet·ing (**shē′**tĭng) *n.* Material, such as metal or cloth, formed into or used to form sheets.

sheet lightning *n.* Lightning that appears as a broad sheet of light across a part of the sky, caused by reflection of a distant flash of lightning by clouds.

sheet metal *n.* Metal that has been rolled into a sheet.

sheet music *n.* Music printed on unbound sheets of paper.

Shef·field (**shĕf′**ēld′) A city of north-central England east of Manchester. The highly industrialized city has long specialized in the production of cutlery and steel.

sheikh also **sheik** (shēk *or* shāk) *n.* **1.** In Islam, a man respected for his piety or religious learning. **2.** The leader of an Arab family or village. [From Arabic *šayḫ*, old man, chief.]

❑ *These sound alike:* **sheikh, chic** (fashionable).

shek·el (**shĕk′**əl) *n.* **1.** An ancient Hebrew unit of weight equal to about half an ounce. **2.** An ancient Hebrew coin weighing this amount in silver or gold. **3.** Variant of **sheqel.**

shelf (shĕlf) *n., pl.* **shelves** (shĕlvz) **1.** A flat, usually rectangular piece of wood, metal, or glass, fastened at right angles to a wall or other vertical surface and used to hold or store objects. **2.** An object resembling a shelf, such as a flat ledge of rock jutting out from a cliff. **3.** A reef, sandbar, or shoal.

shelf life *n.* The length of time a product may be stored, as on a supermarket shelf, and remain suitable for use or consumption.

shell (shĕl) *n.* **1a.** The usually hard outer covering of certain animals, such as insects, turtles, and most mollusks and crustaceans. **b.** A similar hard outer covering on a nut or seed. **c.** A similar outer covering on certain eggs, such as those of birds and reptiles; an eggshell. **d.** The material of which any of such coverings is made. **2.** An outer covering or framework resembling or having the form of a shell: *a pastry shell for a pie.* **3.** A thin, usually

ă	pat	ôr	core
ā	pay	oi	boy
âr	care	ou	out
ä	father	ŏŏ	took
ĕ	pet	ŏŏr	lure
ē	be	ōō	boot
ĭ	pit	ŭ	cut
ī	bite	ûr	urge
îr	pier	th	thin
ŏ	pot	*th*	this
ō	toe	zh	vision
ô	paw	ə	about

waterproof or windproof outer garment for the upper body. **4.** A long narrow boat used in rowing races. **5a.** A projectile or piece of ammunition, especially the hollow tube containing explosives used to propel a projectile. **b.** A cartridge for a shotgun. **6.** Any of the regions in which electrons are concentrated around the nucleus of an atom. Different atoms have different numbers of shells, ranging from one to seven, arranged in layers around the nucleus. **7.** An attitude or way of behaving that hides a person's true feelings: *After a few days at the new school, he began to come out of his shell.* ❖ *v.* **shelled, shell·ing, shells** —*tr.* **1.** To remove the shells of; shuck: *shell peas for dinner.* **2.** To fire shells at; bombard: *shell a fortress.* —*intr.* To search for or gather shells, as along a beach. ◆ **shell out** *Informal* To hand over; pay: *had to shell out $50 for the food.* **—shelled** *adj.*

she'll (shēl) Contraction of *she will.*

shel·lac (shə-**lăk′**) *n.* **1.** A purified lac in the form of yellow or orange flakes, often bleached white and used in varnishes, paints, and sealing wax and formerly in making phonograph records. **2.** A solution of flakes of this material in alcohol, making a thin varnish used for finishing wood surfaces and as a sealer. ❖ *tr.v.* **shel·lacked, shel·lack·ing, shel·lacs 1.** To apply shellac to (a wooden surface, for example). **2.** *Slang* To defeat decisively.

Shel·ley (**shĕl′**ē), **Mary Wollstonecraft Godwin** 1797–1851. British writer best known for the Gothic novel *Frankenstein* (1818).

Shelley, Percy Bysshe 1792–1822. British poet whose works include "To a Skylark" (1820).

shell·fish (**shĕl′**fĭsh′) *n.* Any of various edible invertebrate animals that live in water and have a shell, especially mollusks such as clams and oysters and crustaceans such as lobsters, crabs, and shrimp.

shell shock *n.* A condition of stress caused by usually prolonged exposure to military combat.

shel·ter (**shĕl′**tər) *n.* **1.** Something that provides cover or protection: *used an abandoned shack as a shelter for the night.* **2.** An institution providing temporary housing and sometimes counseling for people, such as the homeless, runaways, or victims of domestic violence. **3.** An institution that cares for unwanted or stray animals and tries to find owners for them. ❖ *v.* **shel·tered, shel·ter·ing, shel·ters** —*tr.* To provide cover or protection for: *trees that sheltered the cows.* —*intr.* To take cover or refuge: *cows sheltering under the trees.*

shelve (shĕlv) *tr.v.* **shelved, shelv·ing, shelves 1.** To place or arrange on a shelf or shelves. **2.** To put aside as though on a shelf; postpone: *shelved the trip because we couldn't afford it.*

shelves (shĕlvz) *n.* Plural of **shelf.**

shelv·ing (**shĕl′**vĭng) *n.* **1.** Shelves considered as a group. **2.** Material for shelves.

Shen·an·do·ah Valley (shĕn′ən-**dō′**ə) A valley of northern Virginia between the Allegheny Mountains and the Blue Ridge. The valley was an important gateway to the frontier.

she·nan·i·gans (shə-**năn′**ĭ-gənz) *pl.n. Informal* **1.** Playful acts or pranks. **2.** Deceitful acts or remarks.

shep·herd (**shĕp′**ərd) *n.* **1.** A person who herds, guards, and tends sheep. **2.** A person who cares for and guides a group of people, such as a minister or teacher. ❖ *tr.v.* **shep·herd·ed, shep·herd·ing, shep·herds** To herd, guard, tend, or guide in the manner of a shepherd. See Synonyms at **guide.**

shep·herd·ess (**shĕp′**ər-dĭs) *n.* A woman or girl who herds, guards, and tends sheep.

sheq·el also **shek·el** (**shĕk′**əl) *n., pl.* **sheq·al·im** (**shĕk′**ə-lĭm) also **shekels** The basic monetary unit of Israel.

sher·bet (**shûr′**bĭt) *n.* A frozen dessert made of fruit juice or fruit purée, usually with sugar and milk or cream.

sher·iff (**shĕr′**ĭf) *n.* A public officer in the United States who is responsible for certain law enforcement and legal duties, such as making arrests and serving processes, usually for a particular county. [From Old English *scīrgerēfa* : *scīr*, shire + *gerēfa*, officer.]

Sher·man (**shûr′**mən), **William Tecumseh** 1820–1891. American Union general who as commander of Union troops in the West led the destructive "March to the Sea" (1864), which effectively cut the Confederacy in two.

sher·ry (**shĕr′**ē) *n., pl.* **sher·ries** An amber-colored dry or sweet Spanish wine.

Sher·wood Forest (**shûr′**wo͝od′) A former royal forest of central England known in legend as the home of Robin Hood and his followers.

she's (shēz) Contraction of *she is* or *she has.*

Shet·land Islands (**shĕt′**lənd) A group of islands of northern Scotland in the Atlantic Ocean northeast of the Orkney Islands. The islands became part of Scotland in 1472.

Shetland pony *n.* A small, sturdy, long-maned pony of a breed originally from the Shetland Islands.

Shetland pony

Shetland sheepdog *n.* A herding dog of a breed developed in the Shetland Islands, having a long rough coat and resembling a small collie.

SHF *abbr.* An abbreviation of super high frequency.

shib·bo·leth (**shĭb′**ə-lĭth) *n.* **1.** A custom, use of language, or other characteristic that serves to identify the members of a certain group. **2.** A slogan, saying, or theme repeated by the supporters of a certain party or cause.

shied (shīd) *v.* Past tense and past participle of **shy¹** and **shy².**

shield (shēld) *n.* **1.** A piece of armor carried on the arm for protection against arrows, swords, and similar weapons. **2.** A person or thing that provides protection: *raised her arm as a shield against the glare.* **3.** A concrete or lead structure built around a nuclear reactor to prevent radiation from escaping. **4.** An emblem or a badge: *a police shield.* ❖ *tr.v.* **shield·ed, shield·ing, shields** To protect from being attacked or exposed to danger. See Synonyms at **defend.**

shi·er (**shī′**ər) *adj.* A comparative of **shy¹.**

shies (shīz) *v.* Third person singular present tense of **shy¹** and **shy².**

shi·est (**shī′**ĭst) *adj.* A superlative of **shy¹.**

shift (shĭft) *v.* **shift·ed, shift·ing, shifts** —*tr.* **1.** To exchange (one thing) for another of the same class: *shifted game plans.* **2.** To move from one place or position to another; transfer. **3.** To change (gears), as in driving a car. —*intr.* **1.** To change position, direction, place, or form. **2.** To provide for one's needs; get along: *I can shift for myself.* **3.** To shift gears, as when driving a car. **4.** To use a shift key. ❖ *n.* **1.** A change from one person or setup to another; a substitution. **2a.** A group of workers on duty at the same time, as at a factory. **b.** The period during which such a group works: *the 9-to-5 shift.* **3.** A change in direction, attitude, judgment, or emphasis: *a shift in the wind; a shift toward greater tolerance.* **4.** A change in position. **5.** A change in the position of the spectral lines from a celestial object, either toward red or toward blue. **6a.** A loosely fitting dress that hangs straight from the shoulders. **b.** A woman's slip or chemise. **7.** A means to an end; a strategy.

shift key *n.* **1.** A key on a typewriter that, when pressed, allows uppercase letters and certain symbols to be typed. **2.** A similar key on a computer keyboard that, when pressed, allows uppercase letters and certain special characters to be typed or changes the function of another key when both are pressed at the same time.

shift·less (**shĭft′**lĭs) *adj.* Lacking ambition or purpose; lazy. **—shift′less·ly** *adv.*

shift·y (**shĭf′**tē) *adj.* **shift·i·er, shift·i·est 1.** Evasive or

WORD BUILDING

–ship The suffix **–ship** has a long history in English. It goes back to the Old English suffix *–scipe,* which was attached frequently to adjectives and nouns to indicate a particular state or condition: *hardship, friendship.* In Modern English the suffix has been added only to nouns and usually indicates a state or condition (*authorship, kinship, partnership, relationship*), the qualities belonging to a class of people (*craftsmanship, horsemanship, sportsmanship*), or rank or office (*ambassadorship*).

WORD HISTORY

shirt The nouns **shirt** and **skirt** are related to the adjective *short. Shirt* comes from the Old English word *scyrte,* which in Middle English referred to an undergarment worn on the upper part of the body. In Old Norse, which was closely related to Old English, the word *skyrta* meant "a short shirt, knee-length shirt or tunic, nightshirt." This Old Norse "skirt" kept getting longer and lower and wound up being used for a short garment below the waist, while the English word continued to refer to a short garment above the waist.

ă	pat	ôr	core
ā	pay	oi	boy
âr	care	ou	out
ä	father	o͝o	took
ĕ	pet	o͝or	lure
ē	be	o͞o	boot
ĭ	pit	ŭ	cut
ī	bite	ûr	urge
îr	pier	th	thin
ŏ	pot	*th*	this
ō	toe	zh	vision
ô	paw	ə	about

untrustworthy; deceitful. **2.** Changing direction frequently: *shifty winds.* **—shift′i·ly** *adv.*

shih tzu (shē′ dzo͞o′) *n.* A dog of a breed developed in China, having a long flowing coat, short legs, a square muzzle, and a tail that curls over the back. [From Mandarin *shīzi (gǒu),* lion (dog).]

shi·i·ta·ke (shē-tä′kē *or* shĭ-tä′kē) *n., pl.* **shiitake** A mushroom native to East Asia, having an edible golden or dark brown cap. [From Japanese : *shii,* the tree on whose dead logs the mushroom is often cultivated + *take,* mushroom.]

Shi·ite or **Shi′·ite** (shē′īt′) *n.* A member of a branch of Islam that regards Ali and his descendants as the true successors of Muhammad.

shil·in (shĭl′ĭn) *n.* The basic monetary unit of Somalia.

shil·le·lagh (shə-lā′lē) *n.* A hard wooden club or cudgel.

shil·ling (shĭl′ĭng) *n.* **1.** A coin used in the United Kingdom worth one twentieth of a pound or 5 pence. **2.** The basic monetary unit of Kenya, Tanzania, and Uganda.

shil·ly-shal·ly (shĭl′ē-shăl′ē) *intr.v.* **shil·ly-shal·lied, shil·ly-shal·ly·ing, shil·ly-shal·lies** To waste time or delay.

shim·mer (shĭm′ər) *intr.v.* **shim·mered, shim·mer·ing, shim·mers 1.** To shine with a subdued flickering light. **2.** To be reflected as a subdued, flickering light: *The moon shimmered on the pond's surface.* ❖ *n.* A flickering light; a glimmer.

shim·my (shĭm′ē) *n., pl.* **shim·mies 1.** Abnormal vibration or wobbling, as of the wheels of an automobile. **2.** A dance popular in the 1920s, characterized by rapid shaking of the body. ❖ *intr.v.* **shim·mied, shim·my·ing, shim·mies 1.** To vibrate or wobble abnormally. **2.** To shake the body, as in dancing the shimmy.

shin (shĭn) *n.* **1.** The front part of the human leg below the knee and above the ankle. **2.** A corresponding part of the leg in other vertebrate animals. **3.** The shinbone. ❖ *v.* **shinned, shin·ning, shins** *—tr.* To climb (a rope or pole, for example) by gripping and pulling with hands and legs: *shinning a tree. —intr.* To climb something by shinning it.

shin·bone (shĭn′bōn′) *n.* The tibia.

shin·dig (shĭn′dĭg′) *n.* A large party, often with dancing.

shine (shīn) *v.* **shone** (shōn) or **shined, shin·ing, shines** *—intr.* **1.** To emit light: *The sun shone on the mountains.* **2.** To reflect light; gleam: *We polished the table until it shone.* **3.** To distinguish oneself in an activity; excel: *Our band shines when we play the songs we know best.* **4.** To be apparent: *Delight shone in his eyes. —tr.* **1.** To aim the beam or glow of (a light). **2.** *past tense and past participle* **shined** To make glossy or bright by polishing. ❖ *n.* **1.** Brightness from a source of light; radiance. **2.** Brightness from reflected light. **3.** A shoeshine. **4.** Excellence in quality or appearance; splendor. **5.** Fair weather: *We'll have a picnic, rain or shine.* ◆ **take a shine to** *Informal* To like spontaneously.

shin·er (shī′nər) *n.* **1.** A person or thing that shines. **2.** *Slang* A black eye. **3.** Any of various small silvery fishes.

shin·gle[1] (shĭng′gəl) *n.* **1.** A thin oblong piece of wood or other material laid in overlapping rows to cover the roof or sides of a building. **2.** A small signboard, as one hung outside the office of a professional: *The dentist hung out her shingle.* ❖ *tr.v.* **shin·gled, shin·gling, shin·gles** To cover (a roof or wall) with shingles. [From Middle English, from Old English *scindel,* from Late Latin *scindula.*]

shin·gle[2] (shĭng′gəl) *n.* **1.** Beach gravel consisting of large smooth pebbles. **2.** A stretch of shore or beach covered with such gravel. [From Middle English.]

shin·gles (shĭng′gəlz) *pl.n. (used with a singular or plural verb)* A painful viral infection marked by skin eruptions along a nerve path, usually only on one side of the body. [From Middle English, from Medieval Latin *cingulus,* belt, girdle.]

shin·ny[1] (shĭn′ē) *n., pl.* **shin·nies 1.** Ice, street, or field hockey that is played informally with curved sticks and a ball, can, or similar object. **2.** A curved stick used in this game. [Probably from the phrase *shin ye,* a call used in the game.]

shin·ny[2] (shĭn′ē) *intr.v.* **shin·nied, shin·ny·ing, shin·nies** To climb by shinning: *shinny up a pole.* [From *shin.*]

shin splints also **shin·splints** (shĭn′splĭnts′) *pl.n. (used with a singular or plural verb)* Pain or soreness in the shin caused by excessive running or jumping.

Shin·to (shĭn′tō) *n.* The traditional religion of the Japanese, marked by worship of nature spirits and ancestors and by a lack of formal dogma. **—Shin′to·ism** *n.* **—Shin′to·ist** *adj. & n.*

shin·y (shī′nē) *adj.* **shin·i·er, shin·i·est 1.** Sending forth light; bright: *shiny stars.* **2.** Bright from reflecting light; glistening: *a shiny brass knocker.* **3.** Glossy from being rubbed or worn smooth: *shiny red apples.* **—shin′i·ness** *n.*

ship (shĭp) *n.* **1a.** A large vessel for traveling over deep water. **b.** A sailing vessel with three or more square-rigged masts. **2.** An aircraft or spacecraft. **3.** A ship's crew: *Most of the ship was on deck.* ❖ *tr.v.* **shipped, ship·ping, ships 1.** To send or transport: *shipping goods by truck.* **2.** To take (water) in over the side of a boat: *We're shipping a lot of water.* ◆ **ship out 1.** To leave, as for a distant place. **2.** To send, as to a distant place.

–ship *suff.* A suffix that means: **1.** Condition or quality: *friendship.* **2.** Rank or office: *professorship.* **3.** Art, skill, or craft: *penmanship.* **4.** A collective body: *readership.* —SEE NOTE.

ship biscuit *n.* Hardtack.

ship·board (shĭp′bôrd′) *n.* The condition of being aboard a ship: *The supplies are on shipboard.* ❖ *adj.* Existing or occurring on board a ship.

ship·build·ing (shĭp′bĭl′dĭng) *n.* The art or business of building or designing ships. **—ship′build′er** *n.*

ship·load (shĭp′lōd′) *n.* The amount that a ship can carry.

ship·mas·ter (shĭp′măs′tər) *n.* The officer in command of a merchant ship.

ship·mate (shĭp′māt′) *n.* A sailor serving on the same ship as another; a fellow sailor.

ship·ment (shĭp′mənt) *n.* **1.** The act or an instance of shipping goods: *iron ore for shipment abroad.* **2.** A quantity of goods shipped together: *a new shipment of automobiles.*

ship·per (shĭp′ər) *n.* A person or company engaged in the business of transporting or receiving goods.

ship·ping (shĭp′ĭng) *n.* **1.** The act or business of transporting goods. **2.** The body of ships belonging to one port, industry, or country.

ship·shape (shĭp′shāp′) *adj.* Orderly and neat; tidy: *I made sure my room was shipshape before my friends came over.*

ship·worm (shĭp′wûrm′) *n.* Any of various marine mollusks that resemble worms and bore into wood, often doing extensive damage to ships and wharves.

ship·wreck (shĭp′rĕk′) *n.* **1.** The destruction of a ship, as by storm or collision. **2.** A wrecked ship. ❖ *tr.v.* **ship·wrecked, ship·wreck·ing, ship·wrecks 1.** To cause (a ship) to be destroyed. **2.** To cause (a person) to suffer shipwreck.

ship·yard (shĭp′yärd′) *n.* A yard in which ships are built or repaired.

shire (shīr) *n.* A former division of Great Britain equivalent to a county.

shirk (shûrk) *tr.v.* **shirked, shirk·ing, shirks** To avoid or neglect (a task or duty). **—shirk′er** *n.*

shirr (shûr) *tr.v.* **shirred, shirr·ing, shirrs 1.** To gather (cloth) into decorative rows by parallel stitching. **2.** To bake (eggs) until set.

shirt (shûrt) *n.* **1.** A garment for the upper part of the body, generally having a collar and sleeves. **2.** An undershirt. **3.** A nightshirt. —SEE NOTE.

shirt·ing (**shûr′**tĭng) *n.* Cloth for making shirts.

shirt·waist (**shûrt′**wāst′) *n.* A tailored blouse.

shi·sha (**shē′**shə) *n.* The South Asian handicraft of embroidering fabric with small mirrors. [From Hindi *śīśā* and Urdu *šīšā*, glass, mirror, from Persian *šīša*.]

shish ke·bab (**shĭsh′** kə-bŏb′) *n.* A dish consisting of pieces of seasoned meat and sometimes vegetables roasted on skewers.

Shi·va (**shē′**və) also **Si·va** (**shē′**və *or* **sē′**və) *n.* One of the principal Hindu gods, worshiped as the destroyer and restorer of worlds and in numerous other forms.

shiv·er[1] (**shĭv′**ər) *intr.v.* **shiv·ered, shiv·er·ing, shiv·ers** To shake or tremble, as from cold or fear. ❖ *n.* An instance of shivering. [From Middle English *chiveren.*]

shiv·er[2] (**shĭv′**ər) *intr. & tr.v.* **shiv·ered, shiv·er·ing, shiv·ers** To break or cause to break into fragments or splinters; shatter. ❖ *n.* A fragment or sliver. [From Middle English *shiveren*, from *shivere*, splinter.]

shiv·er·y (**shĭv′**ə-rē) *adj.* **1.** Trembling, as from cold or fear. **2.** Causing shivers; chilling.

Sho·ah (**shō′**ə) *n.* The mass murder of European Jews and other groups by the Nazis during World War II.

shoal[1] (shōl) *n.* **1.** A shallow place in a body of water. **2.** A sandbank or sandbar at the bottom of a body of water. ❖ *adj.* Shallow: *places where the water is shoal.* [From Middle English *shold*, from Old English *sceald*, shallow.]

shoal[2] (shōl) *n.* A large school of fish or other water animals. [Probably from Middle Low German or Middle Dutch *schōle.*]

shoat (shōt) *n.* A young pig.

shock[1] (shŏk) *n.* **1.** A violent collision, impact, or explosion, or the force resulting from this: *The shock of the explosion blew out the house's windows.* **2.** Something that suddenly causes emotional distress: *The news of his death was a shock to all of us.* **3.** A sudden feeling of distress: *The shock of the news has not yet worn off.* **4.** A massive, acute physical reaction usually to injury, infection, or allergy, marked by loss of blood pressure and decreased blood flow to body tissues. **5.** The sensation and muscular spasm caused by the passage of an electric current through the body or a body part. ❖ *tr.v.* **shocked, shock·ing, shocks 1.** To surprise and disturb greatly: *We were shocked when he was accused of cheating.* **2.** To offend. **3.** To cause a state of shock in (a person or animal). **4.** To subject (a person or animal) to an electric shock. [From French *choquer*, to collide with.] —**shock′er** *n.*

shock[2] (shŏk) *n.* **1.** A pile of sheaves of grain stacked upright in a field to dry. **2.** A thick heavy mass: *a shock of hair.* ❖ *tr.v.* **shocked, shock·ing, shocks** To gather (grain) into shocks. [From Middle English *shok.*]

shock absorber *n.* A device used to absorb the energy and reduce the force of mechanical shocks, as on a car to make the ride smoother or less jarring.

shock·ing (**shŏk′**ĭng) *adj.* **1.** Highly disturbing emotionally. **2.** Highly offensive; distasteful or indecent. —**shock′ing·ly** *adv.*

shock troops *pl.n.* Soldiers trained to lead attacks.

shock wave *n.* A wave formed by the sudden compression of the medium through which the wave moves. Shock waves can be caused by explosions or objects moving at supersonic speeds.

shod (shŏd) *v.* Past tense and a past participle of **shoe.**

shod·dy (**shŏd′**ē) *adj.* **shod·di·er, shod·di·est 1.** Made or done in an inferior manner: *shoddy workmanship.* **2.** Dishonest or contemptible: *shoddy politicians.*

shoe (shōō) *n.* **1.** An outer covering for the human foot, especially one of a pair having a rigid sole and heel and a flexible upper part. **2.** A horseshoe. **3.** The part of a brake that presses against a wheel or drum to slow its motion. **4. shoes** *Informal* Position or situation: *I wouldn't want to be in your shoes.* ❖ *tr.v.* **shod** (shŏd), **shoe·ing, shoes** To furnish or fit with shoes. [From Old English *scōh.*]

❑ *These sound alike:* **shoe, shoo** (scare away).

shoe·horn (**shōō′**hôrn′) *n.* A curved implement, often of plastic or metal, used at the heel to help put on a shoe.

shoe·lace (**shōō′**lās′) *n.* A string or cord used for lacing and fastening shoes.

shoe·mak·er (**shōō′**mā′kər) *n.* A person who makes or repairs shoes.

shoe·string (**shōō′**strĭng′) *n.* A shoelace. ❖ *adj.* Consisting of a small amount of money: *a shoestring budget.* ◆ **on a shoestring** With a small amount of money: *The company started out on a shoestring.*

shoe·tree (**shōō′**trē′) *n.* A form inserted into a shoe to preserve its shape.

sho·far (**shō′**fär′ *or* **shō′**fər) *n.* A trumpet made of a ram's horn, sounded in synagogues during Rosh Hashanah and at the end of Yom Kippur. [From Hebrew *šôpār.*]

sho·gun (**shō′**gən) *n.* Any of the military commanders who ruled Japan until 1867.

shone (shōn) *v.* A past tense and a past participle of **shine.**

❑ *These sound alike:* **shone, shown** (displayed).

shoo (shōō) *interj.* An expression used to scare away animals or birds. ❖ *tr.v.* **shooed, shoo·ing, shoos** To drive or scare away by or as if by crying "shoo."

❑ *These sound alike:* **shoo, shoe** (foot covering).

shook (shŏŏk) *v.* Past tense of **shake.**

shoot (shōōt) *v.* **shot** (shŏt), **shoot·ing, shoots** —*tr.* **1a.** To hit, wound, or kill with a bullet or other missile fired from a weapon. **b.** To fire (a gun, bow, or similar weapon). **c.** To fire (a bullet, arrow, or other missile) from a weapon. **2.** To propel or launch with great force: *shoot a rocket toward the moon.* **3.** To propel in a rapid stream or flow: *a volcano shooting lava.* **4.** To pass swiftly through: *shooting the narrows in a sailboat.* **5.** To record an image or images on a photosensitive surface: *shooting lots of pictures at the dance; shot the scene in one take.* **6a.** To throw or propel (a ball or puck, for example) in a specific direction or toward the goal. **b.** To score (a basket, point, or goal) in this way. **7.** To play (a round of golf or craps, for example). —*intr.* **1.** To fire a bullet or other missile from a weapon. **2.** To appear or spurt suddenly: *Water shot out of the fountain. The sun shot through a break in the clouds.* **3.** To move quickly; dart: *A subway shot past on the far track.* **4.** To be felt moving through or along the body: *A shiver shot through my body.* **5.** To engage in hunting or the firing of weapons, especially for sport. **6.** To germinate or put forth new growth: *The beans shot up fast.* **7a.** To take pictures; photograph. **b.** To film a scene in a movie. **8.** To propel a ball or other object in a specific direction or toward the goal. ❖ *n.* **1.** A young plant or a plant part, such as a stem or leaf, that has just begun to sprout or grow. **2.** A session in which something is photographed, filmed, or videotaped: *a photo shoot.* **3.** An organized hunt: *a turkey shoot.* ❖ *interj.* An expression used to show surprise, annoyance, or disappointment. ◆ **shoot down 1.** To bring down (an aircraft, for example) by hitting and damaging with gunfire or a missile. **2.** *Informal* To ruin the hopes of; disappoint. **3.** *Informal* To put an end to; defeat: *shot down the proposal.* **shoot for** or **shoot at** *Informal* To strive or aim for; have as a goal. **shoot off** To cause to explode; set off: *shooting off fireworks.* **shoot up 1.** *Informal* To grow or get taller rapidly. **2.** To increase dramatically in amount. [From Old English *scēotan.*] —**shoot′er** *n.*

❑ *These sound alike:* **shoot, chute** (inclined trough).

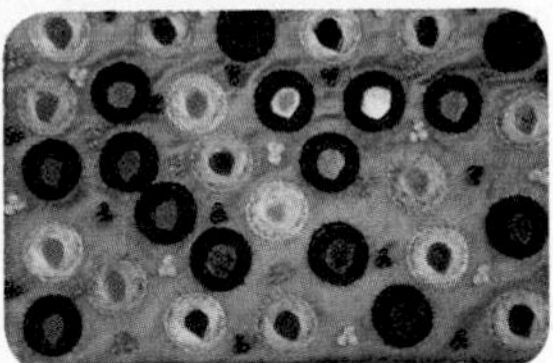
shisha

Shiva
13th-century Indian bronze statue

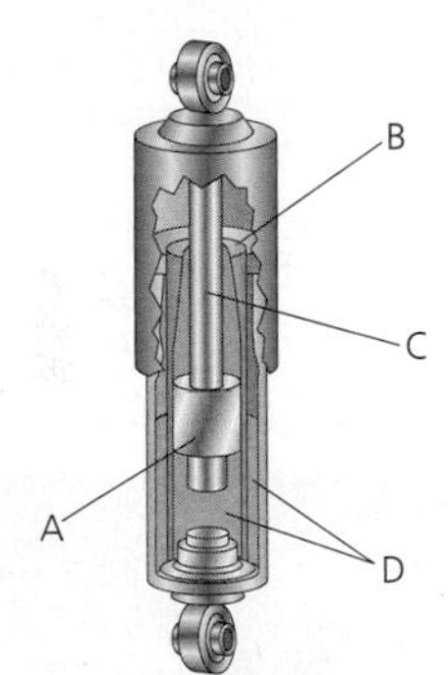

shock absorber
A. piston
B. cylinder
C. piston rod
D. oil

shofar

shoot·ing star (sho͞o′tĭng) *n.* A meteor.

shoot·out (sho͞ot′out′) *n.* **1.** A fight or battle involving firearms. **2.** In sports such as soccer and hockey, a means of resolving a tie game in which selected players from each side alternately take individual shots on goal defended only by a goalie.

shop (shŏp) *n.* **1a.** A small retail store. **b.** A specialty department in a large store. **2.** A workshop or studio, as of an artist. **3.** A place where certain goods are made or repaired. **4a.** A schoolroom equipped with machinery and tools for instruction in industrial arts. **b.** A course of study in an industrial art. ❖ *intr.v.* **shopped, shop·ping, shops** To visit stores to look at or buy things. ◆ **shop around 1.** To go from store to store in search of merchandise or bargains. **2.** To look for something, such as a better job. **talk shop** To talk about one's work. [From Old English *scoppa*, work shed.] **—shop′per** *n.*

shop·keep·er (shŏp′kē′pər) *n.* A person who owns or manages a shop.

shop·lift (shŏp′lĭft′) *v.* **shop·lift·ed, shop·lift·ing, shop·lifts** *—intr.* To steal merchandise from a store. *—tr.* To steal from a store.

shop·ping center (shŏp′ĭng) *n.* A group of stores and often restaurants and other businesses having a common parking lot.

shop·talk (shŏp′tôk′) *n.* **1.** Talk or conversation concerning one's business. **2.** The jargon used in a specific business or field.

shop·worn (shŏp′wôrn′) *adj.* Soiled, faded, frayed, or otherwise damaged from being displayed in a store.

shore[1] (shôr) *n.* **1.** The land along the edge of a body of water. **2.** often **shores** Land within national or other boundaries: *immigrants who came to these shores.* [From Old English *scora.*]

shore[2] (shôr) *tr.v.* **shored, shor·ing, shores** To support by or as if by a prop: *shore up a sagging floor.* ❖ *n.* A beam or timber propped against a structure to provide support. [From Middle English *shoren*, from *shore*, a prop.]

shore·bird also **shore bird** (shôr′bûrd′) *n.* Any of various birds, such as a sandpiper or plover, that live on the shores of coastal or inland waters.

shore·line (shôr′līn′) *n.* The edge of a body of water.

shorn (shôrn) *v.* A past participle of **shear.**

short (shôrt) *adj.* **short·er, short·est 1a.** Having little length; not long: *a short fuse.* **b.** Having little height; not tall: *a short building.* **2.** Covering a relatively small distance: *a short walk; a short toss.* **3.** Lasting a brief time: *a short vacation; a short speech.* **4.** Lacking in length or amount: *The ladder is 2 feet short.* **5.** Having an inadequate or insufficient supply: *I'm short of money.* **6.** Relating to the vowel sounds in words such as *pat, pet, pit, pot, putt,* and *put.* **7.** Rudely brief; abrupt: *He was very short with the salesclerk.* **8.** Easily provoked: *a short temper.* **9.** Containing a large amount of shortening; flaky: *a short pie crust.* ❖ *adv.* **shorter, shortest 1.** Abruptly; quickly: *stopped short.* **2.** Before a given point or goal: *The arrow fell short of the target.* ❖ *n.* **1.** A short movie. **2.** A short circuit. ❖ *v.* **short·ed, short·ing, shorts** *—tr.* To cause a short circuit in. *—intr.* To short-circuit. ◆ **for short** As an abbreviation: *His name is Joseph, but he's called "Joe" for short.* **in short** In summary; briefly. **short for** An abbreviation of: *"Jo" is short for "Joanna."* **short of 1.** Less than: *Nothing short of winning satisfies her.* **2.** Other than; without resorting to: *Nothing short of a siren would have caught their attention.* [From Old English *sceort.*] **—short′ness** *n.*

short·age (shôr′tĭj) *n.* A lack in the amount needed; deficiency: *a food shortage.*

short·bread (shôrt′brĕd′) *n.* A cookie made of flour, sugar, and much butter or other shortening.

short·cake (shôrt′kāk′) *n.* A dessert consisting of a biscuit or cake served with fruit and topped with cream.

short·change (shôrt′chānj′) *tr.v.* **short·changed, short·chang·ing, short·chang·es 1.** To give (someone) less change than is due. **2.** To swindle, cheat, or trick. **—short′chang′er** *n.*

short circuit *n.* A path in an electric circuit through which the current tends to flow rather than along the intended path. A short circuit can damage the circuit by overheating.

short-cir·cuit (shôrt′sûr′kĭt) *v.* **short-cir·cuit·ed, short-cir·cuit·ing, short-cir·cuits** *—tr.* To cause to have a short circuit. *—intr.* To become affected with a short circuit.

short·com·ing (shôrt′kŭm′ĭng) *n.* An inadequacy; a flaw.

short·cut (shôrt′kŭt′) *n.* **1.** A route that is quicker or more direct than the one usually taken. **2.** A means of saving effort or time.

short division *n.* The process of dividing one number by another without writing down all the steps, especially when the divisor is a single digit.

short·en (shôr′tn) *v.* **short·ened, short·en·ing, short·ens** *—tr.* **1.** To make short or shorter: *shortened her vacation by one day; shortened the strip of paper by cutting it.* **2.** To add shortening to (dough). *—intr.* To become short or shorter.

short·en·ing (shôr′tn-ĭng *or* shôrt′nĭng) *n.* A fat, such as butter, lard, or vegetable oil, used to make cake or pastry rich and flaky.

short·fall (shôrt′fôl′) *n.* **1.** A failure to attain a specified amount or level; a shortage. **2.** The amount by which a supply falls short of expectation, need, or demand.

short·hand (shôrt′hănd′) *n.* A system of rapid handwriting using symbols to represent words, phrases, and letters.

short-hand·ed (shôrt′hăn′dĭd) *adj.* Lacking the usual or necessary number of employees, players, workers, or assistants.

short·horn (shôrt′hôrn′) *n.* Any of a breed of cattle having short curved horns or no horns.

short-lived (shôrt′līvd′ *or* shôrt′lĭvd′) *adj.* Living or lasting only a short time: *short-lived joy.*

short·ly (shôrt′lē) *adv.* **1.** In a short time; soon: *We will leave shortly.* **2.** In a few words; briefly: *To put it shortly, we've got to finish now or not at all.* **3.** In a curt or abrupt manner: *"Why shouldn't I?" Charles demanded rather shortly.*

short-range (shôrt′rānj′) *adj.* **1.** Made for use over short distances: *short-range airlines.* **2.** Relating to the near future: *short-range goals.*

shorts (shôrts) *pl.n.* Short pants with legs that extend to the knee or above: *wore a pair of jogging shorts.*

short shrift *n.* **1.** Brief or hasty consideration: *I gave short shrift to the invitation.* **2.** Quick work; rapid settlement: *The debater made short shrift of her opponent's arguments.* **3.** A short delay before punishment, death, or some other harsh fate.

short·sight·ed (shôrt′sī′tĭd) *adj.* **1.** Nearsighted; lacking clear vision of distant objects. **2.** Lacking foresight: *The land policy was shortsighted in its neglect of the peasants.* **—short′sight′ed·ly** *adv.* **—short′sight′ed·ness** *n.*

short·stop (shôrt′stŏp′) *n.* The baseball player defending the area between second base and the third baseman.

short story *n.* A short piece of prose fiction.

short-tem·pered (shôrt′tĕm′pərd) *adj.* Easily losing one's temper; quickly angered.

short ton *n.* A unit of weight equal to 2,000 pounds (907.2 kilograms). See table at **measurement.**

short wave *n.* A radio wave having a wavelength between about 10 and 200 meters.

short-wind·ed (shôrt′wĭn′dĭd) *adj.* **1.** Breathing with

shot put

ă	pat	ôr	core
ā	pay	oi	boy
âr	care	ou	out
ä	father	o͝o	took
ĕ	pet	o͝or	lure
ē	be	o͞o	boot
ĭ	pit	ŭ	cut
ī	bite	ûr	urge
îr	pier	th	thin
ŏ	pot	*th*	this
ō	toe	zh	vision
ô	paw	ə	about

quick labored breaths. **2.** Likely to have difficulty in breathing, especially after physical stress.

Sho·sho·ne (shō-shō′nē) *n., pl.* **Shoshone** or **Sho·sho·nes 1.** A member of any of several Native American peoples living mostly in Idaho, Nevada, and Wyoming. **2.** Any of the Uto-Aztecan languages of these peoples. **—Sho·sho′ne·an** *adj.*

shot[1] (shŏt) *n.* **1.** The discharge of a gun or similar weapon: *a rifle shot.* **2.** The distance over which something is shot. **3.** An attempt to hit something with a projectile: *took a shot at the bear.* **4.** An attempt to score in a game such as soccer. **5.** A throw, drive, or stroke, as of a ball or puck, toward a goal or target: *a nice shot onto the green.* **6.** *Informal* A chance; a try: *had a shot at a good job.* **7a.** A solid projectile, such as a ball or bullet, designed to be fired from a firearm or cannon: *A blast of shot ripped through the door.* **b.** *pl.* **shot** Such projectiles considered as a group. **8.** A person who shoots, considered with regard to his or her accuracy: *He is the best shot on the hockey team.* **9a.** A photograph. **b.** A single continuous recording made with a movie camera. **10.** A hypodermic injection: *a shot of penicillin.* **11.** A drink of liquor, especially a measure of about 1½ ounces (44 milliliters). **12.** The heavy metal ball used in the shot put. ◆ **like a shot** Very quickly. **shot in the dark** *Informal* A wild guess. [From Old English *sceot.*]

shot[2] (shŏt) *v.* Past tense and past participle of **shoot.** ❖ *adj.* **1.** Interspersed with a particular quality: *an essay shot through with factual errors.* **2.** Worn out; ruined: *This mattress is totally shot.*

shot·gun (shŏt′gŭn′) *n.* **1.** A gun with a smooth bore that fires shot at close range. **2.** In football, an offensive formation in which the quarterback receives the snap several yards behind the line of scrimmage. **3.** A house in which several rooms join in a straight line from the front to the back, especially in the southern United States. ❖ *interj.* An expression used to claim the front passenger seat of a vehicle before a trip has started. ◆ **ride shotgun** To sit in the front passenger seat of a vehicle during a trip.

shot put *n.* **1.** An athletic event in which participants put a heavy metal ball as far as possible. **2.** The ball used in this competition. **—shot′-put′ter** (shŏt′po͝ot′ər) *n.*

should (sho͝od) *aux.v.* Past tense of **shall. 1.** Used to express obligation or duty: *You should send her a note.* **2.** Used to express probability or expectation: *They should arrive at noon.* **3.** Used to express condition as opposed to present fact: *If they should call while I'm out, tell them I'll be right back.* —SEE NOTE.

shoul·der (shōl′dər) *n.* **1a.** The part of the human body between the neck and upper arm. **b.** The joint that connects the arm with the trunk. **c.** The corresponding part of the body of other animals. **2.** often **shoulders** The area of the back from one shoulder to the other: *a boy with broad shoulders.* **3.** The part of a garment that covers the shoulder. **4.** A sloping or jutting side of something: *the shoulder of a mountain; the shoulder of a vase.* **5.** The edge or border running on either side of a roadway. ❖ *tr.v.* **shoul·dered, shoul·der·ing, shoul·ders 1.** To place on the shoulder or shoulders for carrying: *The porters shouldered their loads.* **2.** To take on; bear; assume: *shouldering the blame for the others.* **3.** To push or apply force to with the shoulders: *shouldered the person in front out of the way.* ◆ **shoulder to shoulder 1.** Side by side. **2.** In close cooperation. [From Old English *sculdor.*]

shoulder blade *n.* Either of the two large flat bones that form the rear of the shoulder; the scapula.

should·n't (sho͝od′nt) Contraction of *should not.*

shouldst (sho͝odst) *aux.v. Archaic* Second person singular past tense of **shall.**

shout (shout) *n.* A loud cry. ❖ *tr. & intr.v.* **shout·ed, shout·ing, shouts** To say with or utter a shout: *shouted orders; shouted at the umpire.* See Synonyms at **yell.** ◆ **shout down** To silence by shouting loudly. [From Middle English *shoute,* perhaps from Old Norse *skūta,* a taunt.] **—shout′er** *n.*

shove (shŭv) *v.* **shoved, shov·ing, shoves** *—tr.* **1.** To push forward or along: *shoved the table against the wall.* **2.** To put (something) roughly in a place: *shoved the keys into his pocket.* *—intr.* **1.** To push a person or thing along. **2.** To move forward roughly, often by shoving someone: *shoved past the security guard into his seat.* ❖ *n.* The act of shoving; a push. [From Old English *scūfan.*] **—shov′er** *n.*

shov·el (shŭv′əl) *n.* **1.** A tool with a handle and a wide scoop or blade for digging and moving material, such as dirt or snow. **2.** A large mechanical machine used for heavy digging. **3.** The amount that a shovel can hold: *put a shovel of coal into the furnace.* ❖ *v.* **shov·eled, shov·el·ing, shov·els** also **shov·elled, shov·el·ling, shov·els** *—tr.* **1.** To move or remove with a shovel: *shovel snow.* **2.** To clear or make with a shovel: *shovel the walk; shovel a path.* **3.** To place, throw, or move as if with a shovel: *shovel food into his mouth.* *—intr.* To dig or work with a shovel. [From Old English *scofl.*]

shov·el·ful (shŭv′əl-fo͝ol′) *n.* The amount that a shovel can hold.

show (shō) *v.* **showed, shown** (shōn) or **showed, show·ing, shows** *—tr.* **1a.** To cause or allow to be seen; display: *She showed them her new computer programs. The dog showed his teeth.* **b.** To present in public exhibition, for sale, or in competition: *show goods in a store.* **2.** To point out: *showed him the way to his seat.* **3.** To indicate or reveal: *His expression showed interest.* **4.** To conduct; guide: *She showed us around the village.* **5.** To demonstrate by reasoning or example: *She showed that her hypothesis was correct. He showed us how to cook squash.* **6.** To grant or allow: *They showed no mercy in their treatment of the prisoners.* *—intr.* **1.** To be or become visible: *Worry began to show on his face.* **2.** To become revealed: *Your intelligence shows in your selection of books.* **3.** *Slang* To appear at an event or appointment: *We gave a party, but our friends didn't show.* **4.** To finish third or better in a horserace or dog race. ❖ *n.* **1.** A display: *a show of power.* **2.** A trace or indication: *no show of his former might.* **3.** An insincere display; a pretense: *put on quite a show of prestige.* **4a.** A striking appearance or display; a spectacle: *the fiery show of a volcanic eruption.* **b.** A pompous or ostentatious display: *They rented the limousine just to make a show.* **5a.** A public exhibition or entertainment: *a puppet show.* **b.** A usually competitive exhibition of domestic animals. **6a.** A radio or television program. **b.** A movie. **7.** *Informal* An undertaking: *She ran the whole show.* ◆ **get the show on the road** *Slang* To get started. **show off** To display or behave in a proud or showy manner: *He keeps trying to show off in his new sports car.* **show up 1.** To be clearly visible. **2.** To put in an appearance; arrive: *I waited half an hour, but they never showed up.* **3.** *Informal* To surpass, as in ability or intelligence: *Their team really showed us up.* [From Old English *scēawian,* to look at, display.] **—show′er** *n.*

show bill *n.* An advertising poster.

show·boat (shō′bōt′) *n.* A river steamboat with a troupe of performers and a theater aboard for the performance of plays.

show business *n.* The entertainment industry.

show·case (shō′kās′) *n.* **1.** A display case, as in a store or museum. **2.** A setting in which something may be displayed to advantage.

show·down (shō′doun′) *n.* An event, especially a confrontation, that forces an issue to a conclusion.

show·er (shou′ər) *n.* **1a.** A brief fall of rain, snow, hail, or

USAGE

should Sometimes people write *could of, should of,* and *would of* when what they should write are the contractions *could've, should've,* and *would've.* When writing school papers, it is probably best to spell out *have* in these cases: *They could have avoided the conflict with better communication.*

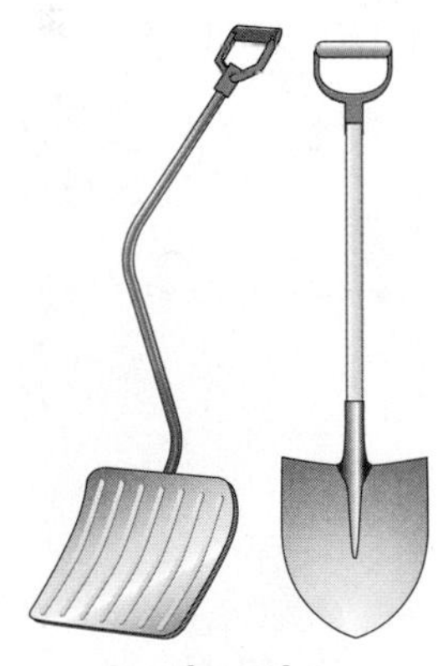

shovel
left: snow shovel
right: garden shovel

shrike

shrine
a Buddhist shrine at the Royal Palace, Luang Prabang, Laos

shuffleboard

sleet. **b.** A fall of a group of objects, especially from the sky: *a meteor shower.* **2.** An abundant flow or outpouring: *a shower of praise.* **3a.** A bath in which the water is sprayed on the bather, especially from overhead. **b.** The stall or tub in which such a bath is taken. **4.** A party held to honor and present gifts to someone: *a bridal shower.* ❖ *v.* **show·ered, show·er·ing, show·ers** —*tr.* **1.** To throw or cause to fall in a shower: *showered confetti on the parade.* **2.** To bestow or pour forth abundantly: *showered presents on the child.* —*intr.* **1.** To wash oneself in a shower. **2.** To fall or pour down in a shower. [From Old English *scūr.*]

shower bath *n.* A bath in which the water is sprayed on the bather.

show·ing (shō′ĭng) *n.* **1.** The act of presenting or displaying. **2.** Performance, as in a competition or test of skill: *a good showing.* **3.** A presentation of evidence, facts, or figures.

show·man (shō′mən) *n.* **1.** A person who produces shows. **2.** A man having a flair for dramatic behavior. **—show′man·ship′** *n.*

shown (shōn) *v.* A past participle of **show.**
❑ *These sound alike:* **shown, shone** (put forth light).

show·off (shō′ôf′) *n.* A person who seeks attention by showing off.

show·piece (shō′pēs′) *n.* Something shown, especially as an outstanding example of its kind.

show room *n.* A room in which merchandise is displayed.

show·y (shō′ē) *adj.* **show·i·er, show·i·est 1.** Attracting attention; striking: *a plant with showy flowers.* **2.** Marked by or given to striking display; flashy: *made a showy catch in the outfield.* **—show′i·ly** *adv.* **—show′i·ness** *n.*

shrank (shrăngk) *v.* A past tense of **shrink.**

shrap·nel (shrăp′nəl) *n., pl.* **shrapnel 1.** Fragments from an exploded artillery shell, mine, or bomb. **2.** An artillery shell of the 1800s filled with metal balls and designed to explode in the air over enemy troops. [After Henry *Shrapnel* (1761–1842), British army officer.]

shred (shrĕd) *n.* **1.** A long irregular strip that is cut or torn from something: *shreds of cloth.* **2.** A small amount; a bit: *not a shred of evidence.* ❖ *v.* **shred·ded** or **shred, shred·ding, shreds** —*tr.* **1.** To cut or tear into small strips: *shred cabbage.* **2.** To use a mechanical shredder to shred (paper documents, for example). —*intr.* To make a series of quick turns on a wave or snow, for example, when riding a board such as a surfboard or snowboard. [From Old English *scrēade.*]

shrew (shro͞o) *n.* **1.** Any of various small mammals that resemble a mouse and have a narrow pointed snout. **2.** A scolding woman. [From Old English *scrēawa.*]

shrewd (shro͞od) *adj.* **shrewd·er, shrewd·est 1.** Clever, sharp, and practical: *a shrewd person.* **2.** Tricky and artful. [From Middle English *shreued,* wicked.] **—shrewd′ly** *adv.* **—shrewd′ness** *n.*

shrew·ish (shro͞o′ĭsh) *adj.* Ill-tempered; nagging. **—shrew′ish·ly** *adv.* **—shrew′ish·ness** *n.*

shriek (shrēk) *n.* A shrill, often frantic cry: *shrieks of laughter; the shriek of a fire engine.* ❖ *v.* **shrieked, shriek·ing, shrieks** —*intr.* To utter a shriek: *The children shrieked in play.* —*tr.* To say with a shriek: *shriek a warning.* [From Middle English *skriken,* to shriek, of Scandinavian origin.] **—shriek′er** *n.*

shrike (shrīk) *n.* Any of various usually grayish songbirds that have a short hooked bill and prey on insects and small vertebrates, which they impale on thorns.

shrill (shrĭl) *adj.* **shrill·er, shrill·est** High-pitched and piercing: *a shrill whistle.* ❖ *tr. & intr.v.* **shrilled, shrill·ing, shrills** To utter with or make a shrill sound or cry: *He shrilled his complaint. The wind shrilled outside.* [From Middle English *shrille.*] **—shril′ly** *adv.* **—shrill′ness** *n.*

shrimp (shrĭmp) *n., pl.* **shrimp** or **shrimps 1.** Any of various small primarily marine animals that have a thin shell, are related to the lobsters and crayfish, and are often used as food. **2.** *Slang* A small or unimportant person. ❖ *intr.v.* **shrimped, shrimp·ing, shrimps** To catch or try to catch shrimp. [From Middle English *shrimpe,* possibly of Low German origin.]

shrine (shrīn) *n.* **1.** A receptacle for sacred relics. **2.** The tomb of a saint or other venerated person. **3.** A site or object that is hallowed or revered for its history or associations. [From Old English *scrīn,* box, from Latin *scrīnium,* case for books or papers.]

shrink (shrĭngk) *v.* **shrank** (shrăngk) or **shrunk** (shrŭngk), **shrunk** or **shrunk·en** (shrŭng′kən), **shrink·ing, shrinks** —*intr.* **1.** To become reduced in size, amount, or value; become smaller. **2.** To draw back; recoil: *They shrank from giving up their favorite dessert.* —*tr.* To cause to shrink. ❖ *n.* **1a.** The act of shrinking. **b.** Shrinkage. **2.** *Slang* Someone who practices psychotherapy, especially a psychologist or psychiatrist. [From Old English *scrincan,* to shrivel up.] **—shrink′a·ble** *adj.* **—shrink′er** *n.*

shrink·age (shrĭng′kĭj) *n.* **1.** The process of shrinking; constriction in size. **2.** The amount by which something shrinks. **3.** A reduction in value; depreciation.

shrive (shrīv) *tr.v.* **shrove** (shrōv) or **shrived, shriv·en** (shrĭv′ən) or **shrived, shriv·ing, shrives** To hear the confession of and give absolution to (a penitent person). **—shriv′er** *n.*

shriv·el (shrĭv′əl) *intr. & tr.v.* **shriv·eled, shriv·el·ing, shriv·els** or **shriv·elled, shriv·el·ling, shriv·els** To become or make shrunken or wrinkled: *Leaves fall and shrivel. Heat shriveled the grapes into raisins.*

shroud (shroud) *n.* **1.** A cloth used to wrap a body for burial. **2.** Something that conceals, protects, or hides: *a shroud of silence.* **3.** One of the set of ropes or cables that supports the mast of a vessel. ❖ *tr.v.* **shroud·ed, shroud·ing, shrouds 1.** To wrap (a corpse) in a shroud. **2.** To conceal; screen; hide.

shrove (shrōv) *v.* A past tense of **shrive.**

Shrove Tuesday *n.* The day before Ash Wednesday.

shrub (shrŭb) *n.* A woody plant that is smaller than a tree and generally has several separate stems rather than a single trunk; a bush.

shrub·ber·y (shrŭb′ə-rē) *n., pl.* **shrub·ber·ies** A group of shrubs.

shrub·by (shrŭb′ē) *adj.* **shrub·bi·er, shrub·bi·est** Consisting of or covered with shrubs: *a shrubby dogwood; shrubby wetlands.* **—shrub′bi·ness** *n.*

shrug (shrŭg) *v.* **shrugged, shrug·ging, shrugs** —*tr.* To raise (the shoulders), especially to show doubt, disdain, or indifference. —*intr.* To shrug the shoulders. ❖ *n.* **1.** The gesture of raising the shoulders to show doubt, disdain, or indifference. **2.** A very short woman's jacket or sweater, having long or short sleeves and usually worn open down the front. ◆ **shrug off 1.** To consider as being of little importance: *She shrugged off the home run and continued pitching.* **2.** To get rid of: *I can't seem to shrug off this cold.*

shrunk (shrŭngk) *v.* A past tense and a past participle of **shrink.**

shrunk·en (shrŭng′kən) *v.* A past participle of **shrink.**

shuck (shŭk) *n.* An outer covering, such as a corn husk, a pea pod, or an oyster shell. ❖ *tr.v.* **shucked, shuck·ing, shucks 1.** To remove the husk or shell from: *shuck corn; shuck oysters.* **2.** *Informal* To remove or strip (clothing or a similar outer covering): *shucked his shirt and jumped in the pond.* ❖ *interj.* **shucks** (shŭks) An expression used to show disappointment or annoyance. **—shuck′er** *n.*

shud·der (shŭd′ər) *intr.v.* **shud·dered, shud·der·ing, shud·ders** To tremble or shiver, as from fear or horror. ❖ *n.* A shiver, as from fear or horror.

ă	pat	ôr	core
ā	pay	oi	boy
âr	care	ou	out
ä	father	o͝o	took
ĕ	pet	o͝or	lure
ē	be	o͞o	boot
ĭ	pit	ŭ	cut
ī	bite	ûr	urge
îr	pier	th	thin
ŏ	pot	*th*	this
ō	toe	zh	vision
ô	paw	ə	about

shuf·fle (shŭf′əl) *v.* **shuf·fled, shuf·fling, shuf·fles** —*intr.* **1.** To move with short sliding steps, without or barely lifting the feet: *shuffled across the road.* **2.** To present, play, or display music or video files in random order. —*tr.* **1.** To slide (the feet) along the floor or ground. **2.** To shift about from one place to another: *shuffled the papers around.* **3.** To mix together (playing cards, for example) so as to make a random order of arrangement. ❖ *n.* **1.** A short sliding step or movement. **2.** The feature on a music or video player that plays music or other files in a random order. **3.** The mixing of cards, dominoes, or tiles.

shuf·fle·board (shŭf′əl-bôrd′) *n.* A game in which the players use pronged sticks to slide disks along a flat surface that has marked scoring areas.

shul (sho͝ol *or* sho͞ol) *n.* A synagogue.

shun (shŭn) *tr.v.* **shunned, shun·ning, shuns 1.** To avoid using, accepting, or engaging in: *shun someone's advice.* **2.** To refuse to accept socially: *His friends shunned him after he lied to them.* **—shun′ner** *n.*

shunt (shŭnt) *n.* **1.** The act or process of turning aside or moving to an alternate course. **2.** A railroad switch. **3.** A low-resistance connection between two points in an electric circuit that forms an alternative path for a portion of the current. **4.** A passage between two body parts that is constructed during surgery to divert the flow of a fluid, such as blood, from one part to another. ❖ *tr.v.* **shunt·ed, shunt·ing, shunts 1.** To move aside or onto an alternate course: *shunt traffic around a bottleneck.* **2.** To avoid by putting aside or ignoring: *problems we should not shunt aside.* **3.** To switch (a railroad car or train) from one track to another. **4.** To provide or divert (electric current) by means of a shunt. **5.** To divert the flow of (a body fluid) by means of a shunt **—shunt′er** *n.*

shush (shŭsh) *interj.* An expression used to demand silence. ❖ *tr.v.* **shushed, shush·ing, shush·es** To demand silence from by saying "shush": *She shushed the children.*

shut (shŭt) *v.* **shut, shut·ting, shuts** —*tr.* **1.** To move (a door or lid, for example) so as to block passage through an opening; close. **2.** To block entrance to or exit from; close: *shut the garage.* **3.** To fasten with a lock or latch. **4.** To lock up or confine: *She shut herself up in her room to prepare the surprise.* **5.** To exclude from a closed space: *shut the cat out of the house.* **6.** To fold up or bring together the parts of: *shut the book.* **7.** To cause to stop operating: *School was shut for vacation.* —*intr.* **1.** To move or be moved so as to block passage; close: *a door that shuts by itself.* **2.** To stop operating, especially automatically: *The light shuts off at dawn.* ◆ **shut off 1.** To stop the flow or passage of; cut off: *Be sure to shut off the water when you finish washing.* **2.** To close off; isolate: *During their camping trip they were completely shut off from everybody.* **shut up 1.** To cause (someone) to stop speaking; silence. **2.** To stop speaking.

shut·down (shŭt′doun′) *n.* A stoppage of operation, as of a factory.

shut-in (shŭt′ĭn′) *n.* A person confined indoors because of illness or disability. ❖ *adj.* (shŭt-ĭn′) Confined to a house or hospital, as by illness.

shut·out (shŭt′out′) *n.* A game in which one side does not score.

shut·ter (shŭt′ər) *n.* **1.** A hinged cover or screen for a window, usually fitted with slanted slats. **2.** A device that opens and shuts the lens opening of a camera to expose a plate, film, or sensor.

shut·tle (shŭt′l) *n.* **1.** A vehicle that takes short frequent trips over an established route: *We took the shuttle to the airport.* **2.** A device used in weaving to carry the woof threads back and forth between the warp threads. **3.** A device for holding the thread on a sewing machine. ❖ *tr. & intr.v.* **shut·tled, shut·tling, shut·tles** To move or cause to move back and forth, especially by a shuttle.

shut·tle·cock (shŭt′l-kok′) *n.* The object hit back and forth over the net in badminton, made up of a conical array of feathers or a conical plastic mesh attached to a small rounded end of cork or rubber.

shy[1] (shī) *adj.* **shi·er** (shī′ər), **shi·est** (shī′ĭst) or **shy·er** or **shy·est 1.** Easily startled; timid: *a shy deer.* **2.** Avoiding contact or familiarity with others; reserved: *a shy person.* **3.** Distrustful; wary: *shy of strangers.* **4.** Short; lacking: *He is three inches shy of six feet.* ❖ *intr.v.* **shied** (shīd), **shy·ing, shies** (shīz) **1.** To move suddenly or draw back, as if startled or afraid: *The horse shied at the sound.* **2.** To avoid engaging in, treating, or discussing something: *shied away from teaching the controversial subject.* [From Old English *scēoh.*] **—shy′ly** *adv.* **—shy′ness** *n.*

shy[2] (shī) *tr.v.* **shied** (shīd), **shy·ing, shies** (shīz) To throw (something) with a swift motion; fling.

shy·ster (shī′stər) *n. Slang* An unethical or unscrupulous lawyer or politician.

si (sē) *n.* The seventh tone of a major scale; ti.
❑ *These sound alike:* **si, sea** (ocean), **see**[1] (perceive with the eyes), **see**[2] (bishop's position).

Si The symbol for the element **silicon.**

SI *abbr.* An abbreviation of Système International [d'Unités] (International System [of Units]).

Si·am (sī-ăm′) See **Thailand. —Si′a·mese′** *n. & adj.*

Si·a·mese cat (sī′ə-mēz′) *n.* A cat of an Asian breed having blue eyes and short whitish, tan, or gray fur with darker ears, face, tail, and feet.

Siamese twin *n.* A conjoined twin. Scientists no longer use this term. [After Chang and Eng Bunker (1811–1874), joined Chinese twins born in *Siam* (Thailand).]

Si·be·ri·a (sī-bîr′ē-ə) A region of central and eastern Russia stretching from the Ural Mountains to the Pacific Ocean. The area was annexed by Russia during the 1500s and 1600s and began to be developed for its mineral resources in the early 1900s.

Si·be·ri·an husky (sī-bîr′ē-ən) *n.* A dog of a breed developed in Siberia, having a large build and thick fur.

sib·i·lant (sĭb′ə-lənt) *adj.* Producing or characterized by a hissing sound. ❖ *n.* A speech sound that suggests hissing. For example, the sounds (s), (sh), (z), and (zh) are sibilants. **—sib′i·lance** *n.* **—sib′i·lant·ly** *adv.*

sib·ling (sĭb′lĭng) *n.* One of two or more people having one or both parents in common; a brother or a sister.

sib·yl (sĭb′əl) *n.* **1.** One of a number of women who were regarded as prophets by the ancient Greeks and Romans. **2.** A woman who is a prophet.

sic[1] (sĭk) *adv.* Thus; so. Used to indicate that a quotation that contains an error or unusual spelling has been kept in its original form or is written that way intentionally. [From Latin *sīc.*]
❑ *These sound alike:* **sic**[1] (thus), **sic**[2] (attack), **sick**[1] (ill).

sic[2] also **sick** (sĭk) *tr.v.* **sicced, sic·cing, sics** also **sicked, sick·ing, sicks 1.** To set upon; attack. **2.** To urge to attack: *He sicced his dog on the burglar.* [Dialectal variant of *seek.*]
❑ *These sound alike:* **sic**[2] (attack), **sic**[1] (thus), **sick**[1] (ill).

Si·ci·ly (sĭs′ə-lē) An island of southern Italy in the Mediterranean Sea west of the southern end of the Italian peninsula. It became part of Italy in 1860.

sick[1] (sĭk) *adj.* **sick·er, sick·est 1a.** Suffering from or affected with a physical illness; ill. **b.** Nauseated; queasy: *Riding over the rough road made her sick.* **c.** For or relating to sick people: *sick wards.* **2a.** Mentally ill. **b.** Morbid or unwholesome: *a sick sense of humor.* **3.** Not dependable; unsound: *a sick economy.* **4a.** Deeply distressed; upset: *sick at heart.* **b.** Disgusted; revolted. **c.** Weary;

shutter

shuttlecock

Siberian husky

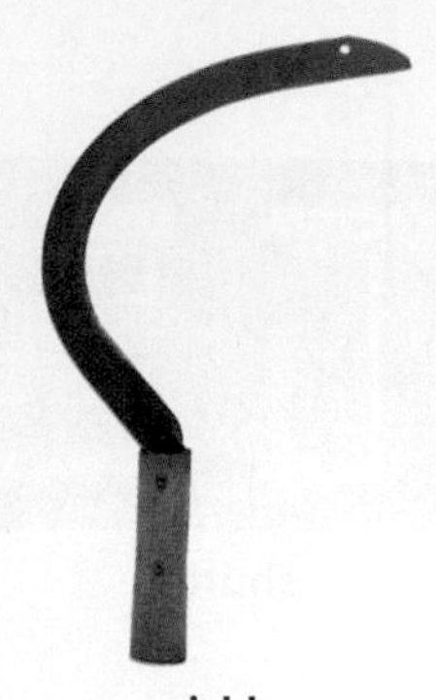

sickle

tired: *sick of work.* ◆ **sick and tired** Thoroughly weary, discouraged, or bored. [From Old English *sēoc.*]

❑ *These sound alike:* **sick**[1] (ill), **sic**[1] (thus), **sic**[2] (attack).

sick[2] (sĭk) *v.* Variant of **sic**[2].

sick·bay (sĭk**′**bā′) *n.* **1.** The hospital of a ship. **2.** A place where the sick or injured are treated.

sick·bed (sĭk**′**bĕd′) *n.* A sick person's bed.

sick·en (sĭk**′**ən) *tr. & intr.v.* **sick·ened, sick·en·ing, sick·ens** To make or become sick.

sick·en·ing (sĭk**′**ə-nĭng) *adj.* **1.** Revolting or disgusting: *a sickening smell.* **2.** Causing sickness.

sick·le (sĭk**′**əl) *n.* A tool for cutting grain or tall grass, consisting of a semicircular blade attached to a short handle. [From Old English *sicol,* from Latin *sēcula.*]

sick leave *n.* A leave of absence given to a worker because of illness.

sickle cell anemia *n.* A hereditary disease characterized by red blood cells that are sickle-shaped instead of round because of an abnormality in the hemoglobin.

sick·ly (sĭk**′**lē) *adj.* **sick·li·er, sick·li·est 1.** Tending to become sick easily; having delicate health. **2.** Caused by or associated with sickness: *a sickly appearance.* **—sick′li·ness** *n.*

sick·ness (sĭk**′**nĭs) *n.* **1.** The condition of being sick; illness. **2.** A particular disease, disorder, or illness. **3.** Nausea.

sid·dur (sĭd**′**ər *or* sĭd**′**o͝or′) *n., pl.* **sid·du·rim** (sĭ-do͝or**′**ĭm *or* sĭ′do͞o-**rĭm′**) A Jewish prayer book for everyday use.

side (sīd) *n.* **1a.** A line segment that forms part of the boundary of a polygon: *A square has four sides.* **b.** A flat surface that forms part of the boundary of a polyhedron; a face. **2.** A surface of an object, especially one joining a top and a bottom: *the side of the jar.* **3.** Either of two surfaces of a flat object, such as a piece of paper. **4a.** Either of two halves into which an object is divided by a vertical axis. **b.** Either the right or left half of the trunk of the body of a human or other animal: *poked him in the side; a side of beef.* **5.** The space immediately next to a person or thing: *walking at her side; drove onto the side of the road.* **6.** An area separated from another by an intervening object: *this side of the river.* **7.** One of two or more opposing individuals, groups, teams, or sets of opinions: *Our side won the game.* **8.** A distinct aspect or quality of something: *the spiritual side of love.* **9.** Line of descent: *I have two aunts on my mother's side.* ❖ *adj.* **1.** Located on or to the side: *a side door.* **2.** From or to one side; oblique: *a side view.* **3.** Incidental; minor: *a little side trip.* **4.** In addition to the main part: *a side order of French fries.* ❖ *intr.v.* **sid·ed, sid·ing, sides** To be on a particular side in a dispute: *She's always siding with her brother and against her sister.* ◆ **on the side 1.** In addition to the main portion: *We'll have some broccoli on the side.* **2.** In addition to the main occupation or activity: *He works as a doctor and plays violin on the side.* **side by side** Next to each other; close together. [From Old English *sīde.*]

sideburns

side·arm (sīd**′**ärm′) *adj.* In sports, thrown with or characterized by a sweep of the arm between shoulder and hip height: *a sidearm curve ball.* **—side′arm** *adv.*

side arm *n.* A small weapon, such as a pistol, carried at the side or waist.

side·board (sīd**′**bôrd′) *n.* A piece of dining room furniture containing drawers and shelves for linens and tableware.

side·burns (sīd**′**bûrnz′) *pl.n.* Growths of hair on the sides of a man's face in front of the ears, especially when worn with the rest of the beard shaved off. [Alteration of *burnsides,* after General Ambrose *Burnside* (1824–1881), American army officer.]

sid·ed (sī**′**dĭd) *adj.* Having a specified number or kind of sides: *a three-sided figure.*

side effect *n.* A usually undesirable secondary effect, especially of a drug or therapy.

side·kick (sīd**′**kĭk′) *n. Slang* A close companion or comrade.

side·light (sīd**′**līt′) *n.* **1.** A light coming from the side. **2.** Either of two lights, red to port, green to starboard, shown by ships at night. **3.** A piece of incidental information.

side·line (sīd**′**līn′) *n.* **1.** A boundary line along either of the two sides of a playing area, such as a soccer field. **2. sidelines** The space immediately outside these lines. **3.** A secondary or subsidiary line of merchandise. **4.** An activity pursued in addition to one's regular occupation.

side·long (sīd**′**lông′) *adj.* Directed to one side: *a sidelong glance.* ❖ *adv.* Toward the side: *glancing sidelong.*

si·de·re·al (sī-dîr**′**ē-əl) *adj.* Relating to or measured by the stars: *sidereal time.*

side·sad·dle (sīd**′**săd′l) *n.* A saddle designed so that a rider may sit with both legs on the same side of the horse. ❖ *adv.* On a sidesaddle: *riding sidesaddle.*

side·show (sīd**′**shō′) *n.* A small show offered as part of a larger one, as at a circus.

side·step (sīd**′**stĕp′) *v.* **side·stepped, side·step·ping, side·steps** *—intr.* **1.** To step aside: *sidestepped to make room for the runner.* **2.** To dodge an issue or a responsibility. *—tr.* **1.** To step out of the way of or aside: *The quarterback sidestepped the tackler.* **2.** To evade (an issue or a responsibility). **—side′step′per** *n.*

side·stroke (sīd**′**strōk′) *n.* A swimming stroke in which a person swims on one side and thrusts one arm forward while pushing the other backward and performing a scissors kick.

side·swipe (sīd**′**swīp′) *tr.v.* **side·swiped, side·swip·ing, side·swipes** To strike (a vehicle, for example) along the side in passing: *The car sideswiped the truck as it started to turn.* ❖ *n.* A glancing blow on or along the side.

side·track (sīd**′**trăk′) *tr.v.* **side·tracked, side·track·ing, side·tracks 1.** To divert from a main issue or course. **2.** To switch (a train or railroad car) from a main track onto a siding. ❖ *n.* A railroad siding.

side·walk (sīd**′**wôk′) *n.* A paved walkway along the side of a road.

side·wall (sīd**′**wôl′) *n.* **1.** A wall that forms the side of something. **2.** A side surface of an automobile tire.

side·ways (sīd**′**wāz′) also **side·way** (sīd**′**wā′) *adv. & adj.* **1.** Toward one side: *turn sideways; a sideways glance.* **2.** From one side: *sideways pressure.* **3.** With one side forward: *crabs moving sideways; a sideways view.*

side·wind·er (sīd**′**wīn′dər) *n.* A rattlesnake of the southwest United States and Mexico that moves by looping its body with a sideways motion and has a hornlike scaly projection above each eye.

sid·ing (sī**′**dĭng) *n.* **1.** Material, such as boards or shingles, used for covering the outside walls of a frame building. **2.** A short section of railroad track connected by switches with a main track.

si·dle (sīd**′**l) *intr.v.* **si·dled, si·dling, si·dles 1.** To move sideways. **2.** To move forward in a quiet or sly manner.

siege (sēj) *n.* The surrounding and blockading of a town or fortress by an army attempting to capture it.

si·en·na (sē-ĕn**′**ə) *n.* **1.** A special clay, containing oxides of iron and manganese, used as a pigment in making paints. **2.** A yellowish or reddish brown.

si·er·ra (sē-ĕr**′**ə) *n.* A rugged range of mountains having a jagged outline when seen from a distance. [From Spanish *sierra,* saw, sierra, from Latin *serra,* saw.]

Si·er·ra Le·one (sē-ĕr**′**ə lē-ōn**′**) A country of western Africa on the Atlantic Ocean south of Guinea. Freetown is the capital.

Sierra Nevada A mountain range of eastern California extending southeast about 400 miles (650 kilometers) from northeast California just west of the Nevada

ă	pat	ôr	core
ā	pay	oi	boy
âr	care	ou	out
ä	father	o͝o	took
ĕ	pet	o͝or	lure
ē	be	o͞o	boot
ĭ	pit	ŭ	cut
ī	bite	ûr	urge
îr	pier	th	thin
ŏ	pot	*th*	this
ō	toe	zh	vision
ô	paw	ə	about

border. It rises to 14,491 feet (4,417 meters) at Mount Whitney.

si·es·ta (sē-ĕs′tə) *n.* A rest or nap after the midday meal.

sieve (sĭv) *n.* A utensil made of mesh or having small holes, used to strain solids from liquids or to separate fine particles of loose matter from coarse ones. ❖ *tr.v.* **sieved, siev·ing, sieves** To pass (something) through a sieve.

sie·vert (sē′vərt) *n.* A unit for measuring the amount of radiation that will produce an effect on an organism, used to measure harmful levels of radiation. [After Rolf Maximilian *Sievert* (1896–1966), Swedish radiologist.]

sift (sĭft) *v.* **sift·ed, sift·ing, sifts** —*tr.* **1.** To put through a sieve or other straining device to separate fine from coarse particles: *Sift a cup of flour.* **2.** To examine carefully: *sift the evidence.* —*intr.* To make a careful examination: *sifted through the data.* **—sift′er** *n.*

sigh (sī) *v.* **sighed, sigh·ing, sighs** —*intr.* **1.** To exhale a long deep breath while making a sound, as of weariness, sorrow, or relief. **2.** To make a similar sound: *trees sighing in the wind.* **3.** To feel longing or grief; mourn. —*tr.* To express with or as if with a sigh: *"Oh well," he sighed.* ❖ *n.* The act or sound of sighing. **—sigh′er** *n.*

sight (sīt) *n.* **1.** The ability to see. **2.** The range that can be seen; the field of vision: *out of our sight.* **3.** The act or fact of seeing: *The sight of land thrilled the sailors.* **4.** Something seen or worth seeing: *the sights of Rome.* **5.** A view; a glimpse: *catch sight of her.* **6.** *Informal* An unpleasant sight; an unsightly scene, person, or object: *We were a sight after crossing the swamp.* **7.** Mental perception or consideration: *lost sight of our goals.* **8a.** A device used to help in aiming, as on a firearm or telescope. **b.** An aim or observation made with the aid of such a device. ❖ *tr.v.* **sight·ed, sight·ing, sights 1.** To see or observe: *sight land.* **2.** To observe with the help of a sight: *sight a target.* **3.** To adjust the sights of (a firearm). [From Old English *gesiht,* something seen.]

❑ *These sound alike:* **sight, cite** (quote), **site** (place).

sight·ed (sī′tĭd) *adj.* **1.** Having the ability to see. **2.** Having eyesight of a specified kind: *keen-sighted.*

sight·less (sīt′lĭs) *adj.* Unable to see with the eyes; blind.

sight·ly (sīt′lē) *adj.* **sight·li·er, sight·li·est** Pleasing to see; handsome. **—sight′li·ness** *n.*

sight-read (sīt′rēd′) *v.* **sight-read** (sīt′rĕd′), **sight-read·ing, sight-reads** —*tr.* To read or perform (music, for example) without prior preparation. —*intr.* To read or perform something without having seen or studied it.

sight·see·ing (sīt′sē′ĭng) *n.* The act or pastime of touring places of interest. **—sight′see′ing** *adj.* **—sight′-se′er** *n.*

sig·ma (sĭg′mə) *n.* The 18th letter of the Greek alphabet, written Σ, σ. In English it is represented as *S, s.*

sign (sīn) *n.* **1a.** Something that suggests a fact, quality, or condition not immediately evident; an indication: *A high temperature is a sign of an infection.* **b.** An event or incident regarded as foretelling something: *People once thought that eclipses were signs of coming disaster.* **2.** An act or gesture that conveys an idea, a desire, information, or a command: *gave the go-ahead sign.* **3.** A board, poster, or placard bearing lettering or symbols and conveying information: *a street sign.* **4.** A mark, figure, or character that represents a word, phrase, or operation, as in mathematics or musical notation. **5.** One of the 12 divisions of the zodiac, each named for a constellation and represented by a symbol. ❖ *v.* **signed, sign·ing, signs** —*tr.* **1.** To affix one's signature to: *sign a document.* **2.** To write (one's signature): *Sign your name.* **3.** To approve or guarantee (a document) by affixing one's signature. **4.** To hire by getting a signature on a contract: *signed three new players.* **5.** To give up entitlement to (property, for example) by signature: *signed over her house to her daughter.* **6.** To express by sign language: *signed the lecture to a hearing-impaired audience.* —*intr.* **1.** To make a sign; signal. **2.** To use sign language. ◆ **sign in** To record the arrival of (another or oneself) by signing a register. **sign off 1.** To announce the end of a communication or broadcast. **2.** To express approval formally: *Has the principal signed off on that purchase?* **sign out** To record the departure of (another or oneself) by signing a register. **sign up** To agree to be a participant or recipient by signing one's name; enlist: *I signed up for art classes.* [From Middle English *signe,* from Latin *signum.*] **—sign′er** *n.* —SEE NOTE.

❑ *These sound alike:* **sign, sine** (function of an acute angle).

sig·nal (sĭg′nəl) *n.* **1a.** A sign, gesture, or device that conveys information: *a traffic signal; finger signals to the pitcher.* **b.** A message conveyed by such means. **2.** A development that is the cause of action: *The announcement of the peace treaty was the signal for rejoicing.* **3.** A varying electric current or radio wave that represents sound or images. **4.** The sound, image, or message transmitted or received, as in radio or television. ❖ *adj.* Out of the ordinary; remarkable: *a signal victory.* ❖ *v.* **sig·naled, sig·nal·ing, sig·nals** or **sig·nalled, sig·nal·ling, sig·nals** —*tr.* **1.** To make a signal to: *They signaled the engineer to start.* **2.** To make known or relate by signals: *A period signals the end of a sentence.* **3.** To cause an effect in (a cell) by the release of a chemical. —*intr.* To make a signal or signals. **—sig′nal·er** *n.* —SEE NOTE AT **sign.**

sig·nal·ize (sĭg′nə-līz′) *tr.v.* **sig·nal·ized, sig·nal·iz·ing, sig·nal·iz·es 1.** To make well-known or conspicuous. **2.** To point out in detail. **—sig′nal·i·za′tion** (sĭg′nə-lĭ-zā′shən) *n.*

sig·nal·ly (sĭg′nə-lē) *adv.* To a remarkable degree; notably: *We defeated them signally.*

sig·na·ture (sĭg′nə-chər) *n.* **1.** One's name as written by oneself. **2.** The act of signing. **3.** A distinctive characteristic indicating identity: *humor is her signature.*

sign·board (sīn′bôrd′) *n.* A board bearing a sign.

sig·net (sĭg′nĭt) *n.* A seal, especially one used to stamp documents officially. [From Middle English, from Old French, small sign.]

❑ *These sound alike:* **signet, cygnet** (swan).

sig·nif·i·cance (sĭg-nĭf′ĭ-kəns) *n.* **1.** The state and quality of being significant; importance: *a development of great significance.* **2.** The sense of something; meaning.

sig·nif·i·cant (sĭg-nĭf′ĭ-kənt) *adj.* **1.** Having a meaning; meaningful: *a significant detail.* **2.** Full of hidden meaning: *a significant glance.* **3.** Having or likely to have a major effect; important: *a significant historical event.* **—sig·nif′i·cant·ly** *adv.*

significant digits *pl.n.* The digits of a number resulting from a measurement, starting at the first digit that is not a zero and extending to the right to include all digits that are not placeholders. For example, 102.3 has four significant digits, and 0.26 has two significant digits. The number of significant digits indicates the precision of the measurement.

significant figures *pl.n.* Significant digits.

sig·ni·fy (sĭg′nə-fī′) *v.* **sig·ni·fied, sig·ni·fy·ing, sig·ni·fies** —*tr.* **1.** To be a sign or an indication of; represent or mean: *What does this monument signify?* **2.** To make known: *Peter signified that he wanted to leave early.* —*intr.* To have meaning or importance. [From Middle English *signifien,* from Latin *significāre.*]

sign language *n.* A language that uses a system of hand movements and other body movements as the means of communication, especially among deaf people or between deaf and hearing people.

sign of the cross *n.* In Christianity, a sign made by tracing the outline of a cross with the right hand as an act of devotion or in giving a blessing.

si·gnor (sēn-yôr′) *n., pl.* **si·gno·ri** (sēn-yôr′ē) also **si·**

sieve

WORD BUILDING

sign The Latin root *sign–* ("mark, seal") appears in a large number of English words. The English noun **sign** comes from the Latin noun *signum,* "an indication or symbol." The English verb **sign** is derived from the Latin verb *signāre,* "to put one's mark or name on." **Signal** comes from the Latin *signāle,* "a sign or token of recognition." **Assign** comes from the Latin verb *assignāre,* "to mark something or someone for a purpose" (using the prefix *as–,* a form of *ad–,* "to, toward"). **Resign** comes from the Latin verb *resignāre,* "to unseal, cancel, give up" (*re–,* "back again, back over to").

signpost

silhouette
profile portrait of author Arthur Conan Doyle

silk
jockey silks

ă	pat	ôr	core
ā	pay	oi	boy
âr	care	ou	out
ä	father	o͝o	took
ĕ	pet	o͝or	lure
ē	be	o͞o	boot
ĭ	pit	ŭ	cut
ī	bite	ûr	urge
îr	pier	th	thin
ŏ	pot	*th*	this
ō	toe	zh	vision
ô	paw	ə	about

gnors Used as a title of courtesy for a man in an Italian-speaking area.

si·gno·ra (sēn-yôr′ə) *n., pl.* **si·gno·re** (sēn-yôr′ā) or **si·gno·ras** Used as a title of courtesy for a married woman in an Italian-speaking area.

si·gno·re (sēn-yôr′ā) *n., pl.* **si·gno·ri** (sēn-yô′rē) Used as a title of courtesy for a man in an Italian-speaking area.

si·gno·ri·na (sēn′yə-rē′nə) *n., pl.* **si·gno·ri·ne** (sēn′yə-rē′nā) or **si·gno·ri·nas** Used as a title of courtesy for an unmarried woman in an Italian-speaking area.

sign·post (sīn′pōst′) *n.* **1.** A post supporting a sign or signs with information or directions. **2.** An indication, sign, or guide.

Sikh (sēk) *n.* A member of a religion that was founded in India in the 1500s, believing in one God and combining elements of Hinduism and Islam.

si·lage (sī′lĭj) *n.* Animal feed consisting of green plants that have fermented in a silo.

si·lence (sī′ləns) *n.* **1.** The quality or condition of being still and silent. **2.** The absence of sound; stillness. **3.** A period of time without speech or noise. **4.** Refusal or failure to speak out. ❖ *tr.v.* **si·lenced, si·lenc·ing, si·lenc·es 1.** To make silent or bring to silence; quiet: *The teacher's stern look silenced the children.* **2.** To stop, prevent, or cut short the expression of; suppress: *The government tried to silence all criticism.*

si·lenc·er (sī′lən-sər) *n.* A device attached to the muzzle of a firearm to muffle the sound it makes when fired.

si·lent (sī′lənt) *adj.* **1.** Having no sound or noise; quiet: *the silent night.* **2.** Refraining from speech; saying nothing: *remained respectfully silent.* **3.** Not disposed to speak; not talkative. **4.** Not voiced or expressed; unspoken: *a silent admission of guilt.* **5.** Having no spoken dialogue and usually no soundtrack: *a silent movie.* **6.** Not pronounced or sounded, as the *k* in *knee* or the *e* in *make.* **7.** Inactive: *a silent volcano.* [From Middle English, from Latin *silēre,* to be silent.] **—si′lent·ly** *adv.*

Si·le·sia (sī-lē′zhə *or* sī-lē′shə) A region of central Europe primarily in southwest Poland and northern Czech Republic. It was settled by Slavic peoples in about AD 500.

sil·hou·ette (sĭl′o͞o-ĕt′) *n.* **1.** A drawing consisting of the outline of something, especially a human profile, filled in with a solid color. **2.** An outline of something that appears dark against a light background. See Synonyms at **outline.** ❖ *tr.v.* **sil·hou·et·ted, sil·hou·et·ting, sil·hou·ettes** To cause to be seen as a silhouette. [After Étienne de *Silhouette* (1709–1767), French finance minister.]

sil·i·ca (sĭl′ĭ-kə) *n.* Silicon dioxide, SiO_2, a compound that occurs widely in the mineral quartz, is the chief component of much sand, and is used in making glass, concrete, and other materials.

sil·i·cate (sĭl′ĭ-kāt′ *or* sĭl′ĭ-kĭt) *n.* Any of a large class of chemical compounds composed of silicon, oxygen, and at least one metal, found widely in rocks and forming the principal substance of bricks.

sil·i·con (sĭl′ĭ-kən *or* sĭl′ĭ-kŏn′) *n. Symbol* **Si** A nonmetallic element that occurs in both gray crystalline and brown amorphous forms and is used in glass, semiconductors, concrete, and ceramics. Atomic number 14. See **Periodic Table.**

silicon carbide *n.* A bluish-black crystalline compound of silicon and carbon, SiC, used as an abrasive.

sil·i·cone (sĭl′ĭ-kōn′) *n.* Any of a class of polymers based on the unit R_2SiO, in which R is an organic radical. They are used in making adhesives, lubricants, protective coatings, and synthetic rubber.

silk (sĭlk) *n.* **1.** A fine glossy fiber produced by a silkworm to form its cocoon. **2.** Thread or fabric made from this fiber. **3.** A garment made from this fabric. **4.** A fine silky material, such as the tuft at the end of an ear of corn. **5. silks** The brightly colored garments that identify a jockey or harness driver in a horse race. [From Old English *sioloc,* from Greek *Sēres,* a people of eastern Asia, perhaps China.]

silk·en (sĭl′kən) *adj.* **1.** Made of silk: *a silken scarf.* **2.** Having the look or feel of silk; smooth and glossy: *silken hair.*

silk·worm (sĭlk′wûrm′) *n.* Any of various caterpillars that produce silk cocoons, especially the caterpillar of a moth native to Asia that spins a cocoon of fine glossy fiber used to make silk fabric and thread.

silk·y (sĭl′kē) *adj.* **silk·i·er, silk·i·est 1.** Soft, smooth, and glossy like silk: *silky fur.* **2.** Pleasantly agreeable: *a silky voice.* **—silk′i·ly** *adv.* **—silk′i·ness** *n.*

sill (sĭl) *n.* A horizontal piece that holds up the vertical part of a frame, especially the piece that forms the base of a window. [From Old English *syll,* threshold.]

sil·ly (sĭl′ē) *adj.* **sil·li·er, sil·li·est 1.** Showing lack of good sense or reason; stupid: *silly mistakes.* **2.** Lacking seriousness; playful: *a silly game.* **3.** Partly conscious or dazed, as from a blow. **—sil′li·ness** *n.*

si·lo (sī′lō) *n., pl.* **si·los 1.** A container, often a tall cylindrical structure, in which silage is produced and stored. **2.** An underground shelter for a missile, usually equipped to launch the missile or to raise it to a launching position.

silt (sĭlt) *n.* A material consisting of mineral particles smaller than those of sand and larger than those of clay, often found at the bottom of bodies of water. ❖ *tr. & intr.v.* **silt·ed, silt·ing, silts** To fill or become filled with silt: *The flow of water had silted up the channel. A pond will silt up after a time.* [From Middle English *sylt,* probably of Scandinavian origin.]

Si·lu·ri·an (sĭ-lo͝or′ē-ən *or* sī-lo͝or′ē-ən) *n.* The third period of the Paleozoic Era, from about 444 to 416 million years ago. During the Silurian, jawed fishes first appeared and the first land plants and invertebrate land animals arose. See table at **geologic time. —Si·lu′ri·an** *adj.*

sil·ver (sĭl′vər) *n.* **1.** *Symbol* **Ag** A soft, shiny, white metallic element that is superior to any other metal in its ability to conduct heat and electricity. Atomic number 47. See **Periodic Table. 2.** This metal used as money or a commodity. **3.** Coins made of this metal. **4.** Tableware or other household articles made of or plated with this metal. **5.** A medal made of silver, awarded for second place in a competition. **6.** A light, shiny, or metallic gray. ❖ *adj.* **1.** Made of or containing silver. **2.** Having a light gray color like that of the metal silver: *silver hair.* ❖ *tr.v.* **sil·vered, sil·ver·ing, sil·vers** To cover or plate with silver or something that resembles silver. [From Old English *seolfor,* probably ultimately from Akkadian (ancient Semitic language spoken in Mesopotamia) *ṣarpu,* refined silver, from *ṣarāpu,* to refine.]

sil·ver·fish (sĭl′vər-fĭsh′) *n.* **1.** A silvery wingless insect that feeds on and can damage materials containing starch, such as book bindings, wallpaper, and clothing. **2.** Any of various silvery fishes, such as the tarpon.

silver lining *n.* A hopeful aspect of a bad situation.

silver nitrate *n.* A poisonous, clear, crystalline compound of silver, nitrogen, and oxygen that darkens when exposed to light, used in photography and silver plating and as an external antiseptic.

silver plate *n.* **1.** A coating or plating of silver. **2.** Tableware made of or plated with silver.

sil·ver·smith (sĭl′vər-smĭth′) *n.* A person who makes, repairs, or replates articles of silver.

sil·ver-tongued (sĭl′vər-tŭngd′) *adj.* Having the power to speak smoothly and persuasively; eloquent.

sil·ver·ware (sĭl′vər-wâr′) *n.* Metal eating and serving utensils, especially ones made of or plated with silver.

sil·ver·y (sĭl′və-rē) *adj.* **1.** Containing or coated with silver. **2.** Resembling silver in color or appearance: *sil-*

very fish. **3.** Having a clear ringing sound: *a silvery voice.*

sim·i·an (sĭm′ē-ən) *adj.* **1.** Relating to monkeys or apes including humans: *humans and other simian primates.* **2.** Relating to monkeys or apes excluding humans: *simian viruses that can infect humans.* ❖ *n.* **1.** A monkey or an ape: *differences between simians and prosimians.* **2.** A monkey or a nonhuman ape: *genes shared by humans and simians.*

sim·i·lar (sĭm′ə-lər) *adj.* **1.** Related in appearance or nature; alike though not exactly the same: *a wild cat similar to but smaller than a lion.* **2.** Having corresponding angles equal and corresponding line segments proportional in length: *similar triangles.* [From Latin *similis,* like.] —**sim′i·lar·ly** *adv.*

sim·i·lar·i·ty (sĭm′ə-lăr′ĭ-tē) *n., pl.* **sim·i·lar·i·ties 1.** The quality or condition of being similar. **2.** A corresponding feature or property: *a similarity of style.*

sim·i·le (sĭm′ə-lē) *n.* A figure of speech in which unlike things are compared, often in a phrase introduced by *like* or *as.* For example, *She runs like a gazelle* and *That house is as big as a ship* are similes.

si·mil·i·tude (sĭ-mĭl′ĭ-to͞od′) *n.* Similarity; resemblance; likeness.

sim·mer (sĭm′ər) *v.* **sim·mered, sim·mer·ing, sim·mers** —*intr.* To be cooked gently or just at the boiling point. —*tr.* To cook gently or just at the boiling point: *simmered the sauce.* ❖ *n.* The condition or process of simmering. ◆ **simmer down** To become calm after excitement or anger. [From Middle English *simpren.*]

Si·mon Ze·lo·tes (sī′mən zē-lō′tēz) or **Simon the Canaanite** Flourished first century AD. One of the 12 Apostles.

si·moom (sĭ-mo͞om′) also **si·moon** (sĭ-mo͞on′) *n.* A hot, dry wind carrying much sand, that occurs in the Sahara and Arabian deserts.

sim·per (sĭm′pər) *intr.v.* **sim·pered, sim·per·ing, sim·pers** To smile in a coy or self-conscious manner. ❖ *n.* A coy or self-conscious smile.

sim·ple (sĭm′pəl) *adj.* **sim·pler, sim·plest 1.** Having or composed of a single part or unit; not compound. **2.** Not involved or complicated; easy: *a simple explanation.* See Synonyms at **easy. 3.** Having no additions or qualifications; mere: *a simple "yes" or "no."* **4.** Not showy, elaborate, or luxurious; plain: *a simple wedding dress; simple everyday words.* **5.** Not vain, showy, or deceitful. **6.** Having or showing little intelligence, education, or experience: *a simple man who is easily cheated.* **7.** Humble or lowly in condition or rank: *a simple woodcutter.* [From Middle English, from Latin *simplus.*]

simple fraction *n.* A fraction in which both the numerator and denominator are whole numbers.

simple fracture *n.* A bone fracture that causes little or no damage to the surrounding tissues.

simple machine *n.* A simple device, such as a lever or pulley, that changes the magnitude or direction of an applied force.

sim·ple-mind·ed (sĭm′pəl-mīn′dĭd) *adj.* Lacking in understanding or sophistication: *terrified the simple-minded folk into believing their houses were haunted.* —**sim′ple-mind′ed·ly** *adv.*

simple sentence *n.* A sentence consisting of one independent clause with no subordinate clauses, as *The two boys played chess.*

sim·ple·ton (sĭm′pəl-tən) *n.* A person who lacks common sense or intelligence.

sim·plic·i·ty (sĭm-plĭs′ĭ-tē) *n., pl.* **sim·plic·i·ties 1.** The property, condition, or quality of being simple; absence of complexity or difficulty. **2.** Absence of luxury or showiness; plainness. **3.** Absence of vanity or deceitfulness; sincerity: *childlike simplicity.* **4.** Lack of good sense or intelligence; foolishness.

sim·pli·fy (sĭm′plə-fī′) *tr.v.* **sim·pli·fied, sim·pli·fy·ing, sim·pli·fies** To make simple or simpler. —**sim′pli·fi·ca′tion** (sĭm′plə-fĭ-kā′shən) *n.* —**sim′pli·fi′er** *n.*

sim·ply (sĭm′plē) *adv.* **1.** In a simple manner; plainly: *They live very simply.* **2.** Clearly: *She explained it quite simply.* **3.** Merely; only; just: *We knew him simply as Joe.* **4.** Absolutely; altogether: *The meal was simply delicious.*

sim·u·late (sĭm′yə-lāt′) *tr.v.* **sim·u·lat·ed, sim·u·lat·ing, sim·u·lates 1.** To present the appearance or other characteristics of; imitate: *a device that simulates space flight.* See Synonyms at **imitate. 2.** To make a pretense of; pretend; feign: *simulated interest.* [From Latin *similis,* like.] —**sim′u·la′tor** *n.*

sim·u·la·tion (sĭm′yə-lā′shən) *n.* **1.** The act or process of simulating. **2.** An imitation or a false appearance: *a simulation of conditions on the moon.*

si·mul·cast (sī′məl-kăst′) *tr.v.* **si·mul·cast·ed, si·mul·cast·ing, si·mul·casts** To broadcast (a program) simultaneously from two or more locations or using two or more media: *simulcast the game on radio and television.* ❖ *n.* A simulcasted broadcast.

si·mul·ta·ne·ous (sī′məl-tā′nē-əs) *adj.* Happening, existing, or done at the same time. —**si′mul·ta′ne·ous·ly** *adv.*

sin¹ (sĭn) *n.* **1.** The act of breaking a religious or moral law, especially when done deliberately. **2.** An act considered shameful or wrong. ❖ *intr.v.* **sinned, sin·ning, sins 1.** To violate a religious or moral law. **2.** To commit an offense; do wrong. [From Old English *synn.*] —**sin′ner** *n.*

sin² *abbr.* An abbreviation of sine.

Si·nai (sī′nī′), **Mount** A mountain, about 7,500 feet (2,285 meters) high, of the southern Sinai Peninsula. It is traditionally claimed to be the peak on which Moses received the Ten Commandments.

Sinai Peninsula A peninsula linking southwest Asia with northeast Africa at the northern end of the Red Sea.

since (sĭns) *adv.* **1.** From then until now, or between then and now: *He left town and hasn't been here since.* **2.** Before now; ago: *long since forgotten.* ❖ *prep.* From (a given time): *They've been friends since childhood.* ❖ *conj.* **1.** After the time when: *He hasn't spoken since he sat down.* **2.** Continuously from the time when: *She's lived in this town since she was little.* **3.** Because; inasmuch as: *Since you're not interested, I won't tell you about it.*

sin·cere (sĭn-sîr′) *adj.* **sin·cer·er, sin·cer·est** Not feigning or hypocritical; genuine: *sincere friends; a sincere apology.* —**sin·cere′ly** *adv.*

sin·cer·i·ty (sĭn-sĕr′ĭ-tē) *n.* The quality or condition of being sincere; genuineness or honesty.

Sin·clair (sĭn-klâr′ *or* sĭng-klâr′), **Upton Beall** 1878–1968. American writer and reformer whose novels include *The Jungle* (1906).

sine (sīn) *n.* In a right triangle, a function of an acute angle equal to the length of the side opposite the angle divided by the length of the hypotenuse.

❑ *These sound alike:* **sine, sign** (indication).

si·ne·cure (sī′nĭ-kyo͝or′ *or* sĭn′ĭ-kyo͝or′) *n.* A position that requires little or no work yet provides a salary. [From Medieval Latin *(beneficium) sine cūrā,* (church appointment) without care (of souls).]

sin·ew (sĭn′yo͞o) *n.* A tendon. [From Old English *seonu.*]

sin·ew·y (sĭn′yo͞o-ē) *adj.* **1.** Consisting of or resembling sinew. **2.** Lean and muscular. See Synonyms at **muscular. 3.** Strong; vigorous.

sin·ful (sĭn′fəl) *adj.* Characterized by or full of sin; wicked. —**sin′ful·ly** *adv.* —**sin′ful·ness** *n.*

sing (sĭng) *v.* **sang** (săng) or **sung** (sŭng), **sung, sing·ing, sings** —*intr.* **1.** To utter a series of words or sounds in musical tones. **2.** To perform songs or other vocal selections. **3.** To produce musical sounds: *birds that sing in tropical forests.* **4.** To make a high-pitched whining, humming, or whistling sound: *The teakettle sang.* **5.**

silo

Sinai Peninsula
satellite image

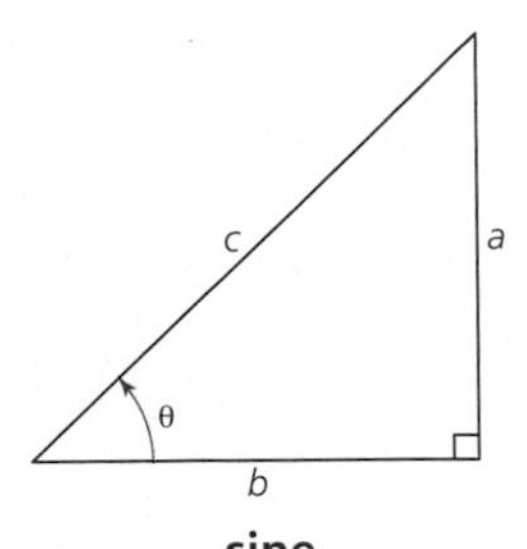

sine
sin θ = a/c

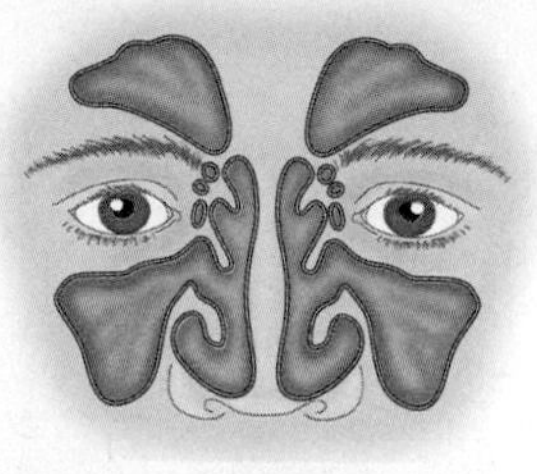

sinus

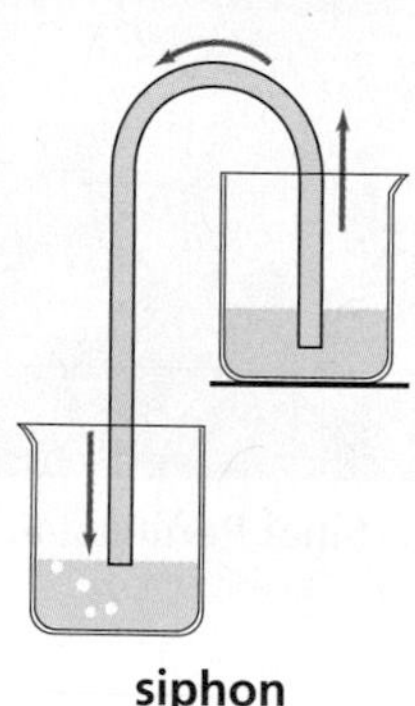

siphon

ă	pat	ôr	core
ā	pay	oi	boy
âr	care	ou	out
ä	father	o͝o	took
ĕ	pet	o͝or	lure
ē	be	o͞o	boot
ĭ	pit	ŭ	cut
ī	bite	ûr	urge
îr	pier	th	thin
ŏ	pot	*th*	this
ō	toe	zh	vision
ô	paw	ə	about

To tell or proclaim something in song or verse: *poets singing of Greece's glory.* —*tr.* **1.** To produce the musical sound of: *sang a love song.* **2.** To bring to a specified condition by singing: *sang the baby to sleep.* **3.** To tell or proclaim (something), especially in song or verse: *sang her praises.* ◆ **sing out** To call out loudly. [From Old English *singan.*]

sing. *abbr.* An abbreviation of singular.

Sin·ga·pore (sĭng**′**gə-pôr′ *or* sĭng**′**ə-pôr′) A country of southeast Asia made up of **Singapore Island** and adjacent smaller islands at the southern end of the Malay Peninsula. The city of **Singapore** is the capital.

singe (sĭnj) *tr.v.* **singed, singe·ing, sing·es 1.** To burn slightly; scorch. **2.** To burn the ends of: *singed his hair.* **3.** To burn off the feathers or bristles of by holding briefly to a flame. ❖ *n.* A slight burn. [From Old English *sengan.*]

sing·er (sĭng**′**ər) *n.* A person who sings, especially one who has had special training or sings professionally.

Sin·gha·lese (sĭng′gə-**lēz′** *or* sĭng′gə-**lēs′**) *n. & adj.* Variant of **Sinhalese.**

sin·gle (sĭng**′**gəl) *adj.* **1.** Not accompanied by another or others; alone: *only a single diner at the lunch counter.* **2.** Consisting of one thing, part, or section: *a single layer.* **3.** Not divided; unbroken: *a single slab of ice.* **4.** Separate from others; individual: *Every single person will receive a gift.* **5.** Intended or designed for use by one person: *a single bed.* **6.** Not married or involved in a romantic relationship. **7.** Having only one row of petals: *the single flowers of a tulip.* ❖ *n.* **1.** An accommodation for one person, as a room in a hotel. **2.** In baseball, a hit that allows the batter to reach first base. **3.** often **singles** A tennis or badminton match between two players. **4.** Someone who is not married or involved in a romantic relationship. **5.** A one-dollar bill. **6a.** A phonograph record with one song on each side. **b.** A song on one of these sides. **c.** A song that is released for radio broadcast: *The group has had many hit singles.* ❖ *v.* **sin·gled, sin·gling, sin·gles** —*tr.* To choose or distinguish from others: *He singled out two students for praise.* —*intr.* In baseball, to hit a single. [From Middle English *sengle,* from Latin *singulus.*]

sin·gle-breast·ed (sĭng′gəl-**brĕs′**tĭd) *adj.* Closing with a narrow overlap and fastened down the front with a single row of buttons: *He wore a single-breasted jacket.*

single file *n.* A line of people, animals, or things standing or moving one behind the other.

sin·gle-hand·ed (sĭng**′**gəl-**hăn′**dĭd) *adj.* **1.** Working or done without help; unassisted. **2.** Having or using only one hand. —**sin′gle-hand′ed·ly** *adv.*

sin·gle-mind·ed (sĭng**′**gəl-**mīn′**dĭd) *adj.* **1.** Having one purpose or opinion: *a single-minded approach to tax reform.* **2.** Steadfast; not wavering: *the single-minded pursuit of a dream.* —**sin′gle-mind′ed·ly** *adv.* —**sin′gle-mind′ed·ness** *n.*

sin·gly (sĭng**′**glē) *adv.* **1.** Without the company or help of others; alone. **2.** One by one; individually: *materials used singly or in combinations.*

sing·song (sĭng**′**sông′) *n.* **1.** Verse or song having a mechanical regularity of rhythm and rhyme. **2.** A manner of speaking marked by a tediously repetitive rising and falling of sound. ❖ *adj.* Having a tediously repetitive rhythm or manner of speaking.

sin·gu·lar (sĭng**′**gyə-lər) *adj.* **1.** Being only one; individual. **2.** Being the only one of a kind; unique. **3a.** Relating to a noun, pronoun, or adjective that refers to a single person or thing or a group considered as a unit. For example, *I* and *he* are singular pronouns and *house* is a singular noun. **b.** Relating to a verb expressing the action or state of a single subject. **4.** Deviating from the usual or expected; remarkable. **5.** Very strange; peculiar: *singular arrivals and departures at midnight.* ❖ *n.* The form taken by a word indicating one person or thing. —**sin′gu·lar·ly** *adv.*

sin·gu·lar·i·ty (sĭng′gyə-**lăr′**ĭ-tē) *n., pl.* **sin·gu·lar·i·ties 1.** The quality or condition of being singular. **2.** A distinguishing trait; a peculiarity. **3.** Something uncommon or unusual.

Sin·ha·lese (sĭn′hə-**lēz′** *or* sĭn′hə-**lēs′**) also **Sin·gha·lese** (sĭng′gə-**lēz′** *or* sĭng′gə-**lēs′**) *n., pl.* **Sinhalese** also **Singhalese 1.** A member of a people constituting the major portion of the population of Sri Lanka. **2.** The Indic language of the Sinhalese that is the chief language of Sri Lanka. ❖ *adj.* Relating to Sri Lanka, the Sinhalese, or their language or culture.

sin·is·ter (sĭn**′**ĭ-stər) *adj.* **1.** Suggesting or threatening evil: *a sinister smile.* **2.** Promising trouble; ominous: *sinister storm clouds.* [From Middle English *sinistre,* false, from Latin *sinister,* on the left, unlucky.] —**sin′is·ter·ly** *adv.*

sink (sĭngk) *v.* **sank** (săngk) or **sunk** (sŭngk), **sunk, sink·ing, sinks** —*intr.* **1.** To descend into or through a liquid; submerge: *The anchor sank to the bottom.* **2.** To move to a lower level, especially slowly or in stages: *He sank into the chair.* **3.** To appear to move downward, as the sun or moon in setting. **4.** To pass into a specified condition: *She sank into a deep sleep.* **5.** To worsen in condition or quality: *The business sank into bankruptcy.* **6.** To diminish or become weaker, as in strength, vitality, or value: *His voice sank to a faint whisper. Farm prices sank steadily.* **7.** To penetrate: *Rainfall could barely sink into the sodden earth.* **8.** To become felt or understood: *Let the meaning sink in.* —*tr.* **1.** To cause to descend beneath the surface: *Heavy storms can sink ships.* **2.** To cause to drop or lower: *sank the ladle into the soup.* **3.** To force or drive into a surface: *sank the fence post into the soil; sank my teeth into a hamburger.* **4.** To dig or drill (a mine or well) in the earth. **5.** To bring to a worse condition or quality: *Poor management sank the project in confusion.* **6.** To make weaker, quieter, or less forceful. **7.** To invest: *He sank a small fortune into real estate.* **8.** In basketball and golf, to place (a ball) into a hole or basket. ❖ *n.* **1.** A water basin having a drainpipe and usually a piped supply of water. **2.** A low land area in a rock formation where water collects. **3.** A sinkhole. ◆ **sink or swim** *Informal* To fail or succeed without alternative. [From Old English *sincan.*] —**sink′a·ble** *adj.*

❑ *These sound alike:* **sink, sync** (synchronization).

sink·er (sĭng**′**kər) *n.* A person or thing that sinks, as a weight used for sinking fishing lines or nets.

sink·hole (sĭngk**′**hōl′) *n.* A natural depression in a land surface joining with an underground passage or cavern.

sin·ner (sĭn**′**ər) *n.* A person who sins or does wrong.

Si·no-Ti·bet·an (sī′nō-tĭ-**bĕt′**n) *n.* A family of languages that includes Chinese, Tibetan, Burmese, and several other languages of Asia.

sin·u·os·i·ty (sĭn′yo͞o-**ŏs′**ĭ-tē) *n., pl.* **sin·u·os·i·ties 1.** The quality or condition of being sinuous. **2.** A bending or curving shape or movement.

sin·u·ous (sĭn**′**yo͞o-əs) *adj.* Having many curves or turns; winding. —**sin′u·ous·ly** *adv.* —**sin′u·ous·ness** *n.*

si·nus (sī**′**nəs) *n.* Any of several air-filled cavities in the bones of the skull, especially one that connects with the nose.

si·nus·i·tis (sī′nə-**sī′**tĭs) *n.* Inflammation of the sinuses or a sinus, especially in the region near the nose.

Siou·an (so͞o**′**ən) *n.* A large family of Native American languages spoken from Lake Michigan to the Rocky Mountains and southward to Arkansas as well as in South Carolina. —**Siou′an** *adj.*

Sioux (so͞o) *n., pl.* **Sioux** (so͞o *or* so͞oz) **1.** A member of any of a group of Native American peoples living in the west and north-central United States and parts of Canada. **2.** Any of the Siouan languages of these peoples.

Sioux Falls The largest city of South Dakota, in the southeast part of the state. It was first founded in about 1856.

sip (sĭp) *v.* **sipped, sip·ping, sips** *—tr.* To drink in small quantities. *—intr.* To drink something in sips. ❖ *n.* **1.** The act of sipping: *smiled after his first sip.* **2.** A small quantity of liquid sipped: *took a sip of coffee.*

si·phon also **sy·phon** (sī′fən) *n.* **1.** A tube that carries a liquid from a higher level up and over a barrier and then down to a lower level, with the flow maintained by gravity and atmospheric pressure as long as the tube remains filled. **2.** A tubular part of an animal such as a clam, through which water is taken in or expelled. ❖ *tr.v.* **si·phoned, si·phon·ing, si·phons 1.** To draw off or transfer (a liquid) through a siphon. **2.** To take or transfer (something), often secretly: *siphoned money from the bank account.* [From Middle English, from Greek *sīphōn*.]

sir (sûr) *n.* **1.** Used as a polite form of address for a man. **2. Sir** A title of honor used before the given name or the full name of a knight or baronet. [From Middle English, variant of *sire*, sire.]

sire (sīr) *n.* **1.** A father or forefather. **2.** The father of an animal, especially a domesticated animal such as a horse. **3.** *Archaic* A form of address for a superior, especially for a king. ❖ *tr.v.* **sired, sir·ing, sires** To be the father or male ancestor of. [From Middle English, from Latin *senior*, older.]

si·ren (sī′rən) *n.* A mechanical or electronic device that makes a loud wailing sound as a warning signal.

Siren *n.* **1.** In Greek mythology, one of a group of sea nymphs whose sweet singing lured sailors to destruction on the rocks surrounding their island. **2. siren** A woman regarded as beautiful and captivating.

Sir·i·us (sĭr′ē-əs) *n.* The brightest star in the night sky, located in the Southern Hemisphere near the constellation Orion.

sir·loin (sûr′loin′) *n.* A cut of meat, especially beef, from the upper part of the loin. —SEE NOTE.

si·roc·co (sə-rŏk′ō) *n., pl.* **si·roc·cos** A hot, humid south or southeast wind of southern Italy, Sicily, and the Mediterranean islands, originating in the Sahara as a dry dusty wind but becoming moist as it passes over the Mediterranean.

sis (sĭs) *n. Informal* Sister.

si·sal (sī′səl) *n.* **1.** A stiff fiber that is obtained from the leaves of a tropical agave and is used for making rope and twine. **2.** The plant that yields such a fiber.

sis·sy (sĭs′ē) *n., pl.* **sis·sies 1.** A person regarded as timid or cowardly. **2.** *Offensive* A boy or man regarded as effeminate.

sis·ter (sĭs′tər) *n.* **1.** A girl or woman having the same parents or parent as someone else. A stepsister. **2.** A fellow woman or girl. **3.** A fellow female member of a group, such as a profession or sorority. **4a. Sister** A member of a Christian religious order of women; a nun. **b.** A fellow female member of a Christian church. [From Old English *sweostor* and Old Norse *systir*.]

sis·ter·hood (sĭs′tər-ho͝od′) *n.* **1.** The relationship of being a sister or sisters. **2.** The quality of being sisterly. **3.** A group of women united by a common purpose or by vows, especially a religious order of women.

sis·ter-in-law (sĭs′tər-ĭn-lô′) *n., pl.* **sis·ters-in-law 1.** The sister of one's spouse. **2.** The wife of one's sibling. **3.** The wife of the sibling of one's spouse.

sis·ter·ly (sĭs′tər-lē) *adj.* Characteristic of or suitable to sisters or a sister: *took a sisterly interest in her education.* **—sis′ter·li·ness** *n.*

sit (sĭt) *v.* **sat** (săt), **sit·ting, sits** *—intr.* **1.** To rest with the body upright and supported on the buttocks: *He sat on the bench.* **2.** To perch: *The robin sat on the branch.* **3.** To cover eggs so that they will hatch; brood. **4.** To be situated or located; lie: *The farmhouse sits on a hill.* **5.** To lie or rest: *dishes sitting on the shelf.* **6.** To pose for an artist or photographer. **7.** To occupy a seat as a member of a body of officials: *sit in Congress.* **8.** To be in session: *Normally the Supreme Court does not sit in the summer.* **9.** To affect one with or as if with a burden; weigh: *Responsibility sat heavily on the president.* **10.** To be agreeable to one; please: *The idea did not sit well with us.* **11.** To fit, fall, or drape in a specified manner: *The jacket sits perfectly on you.* **12.** To keep watch or take care of a child; babysit. *—tr.* **1.** To cause to sit; seat: *The ushers sat the guests in the pews.* **2.** To provide seating for: *This restaurant sits forty people.* ◆ **sit down** To take a seat. **sit in 1.** To be present as a visitor or listener rather than as a full participant: *Since he was just sitting in on the course, he didn't have to do any homework.* **2.** To act as a substitute: *sat in for the regular commentator.* **3.** To participate in a sit-in. **sit out** To refrain from taking part in: *sit out a dance.* **sit pretty** *Informal* To be in a very favorable position. **sit tight** *Informal* To be patient and wait. **sit up 1.** To rise from lying down to a sitting position. **2.** To sit with the spine erect. **3.** To become suddenly alert. [From Old English *sittan*.] **—sit′ter** *n.* —SEE NOTE AT **set¹**.

si·tar (sĭ-tär′) *n.* A stringed instrument of India made of seasoned gourds and teak and having a track of movable frets with 6 or 7 metal playing strings above and 11 or more resonating strings below. [From Hindi *sitār*, from Persian : *si*, three + *tār*, string.]

sit·com (sĭt′kŏm′) *n. Informal* A situation comedy.

sit-down strike (sĭt′doun′) *n.* A protest in which workers stop working and refuse to leave their place of employment until their demands are considered or met.

site (sīt) *n.* **1.** The place where something was, is, or will be located: *a good site for a park.* **2.** The place or setting of an event: *the site of a historic battle.* **3.** A website.
❑ *These sound alike:* **site, cite** (quote), **sight** (perception).

sit-in (sĭt′ĭn′) *n.* A demonstration in which people protesting against certain conditions sit down in a strategic place and refuse to move until their demands are considered or met.

sit·ter (sĭt′ər) *n.* **1.** A person who cares for children when the parents are not home; a babysitter. **2.** A person who poses or models for an artist.

sit·ting (sĭt′ĭng) *n.* **1.** The act or position of one that sits. **2.** A period during which one is seated and occupied with a single activity, such as posing for an artist or reading a book. **3.** A session, as of a legislature or court.

Sit·ting Bull (sĭt′ĭng bo͝ol′) 1834?–1890. Hunkpapa leader who guided his people to victory at the Battle of the Little Bighorn (1876).

sitting duck *n. Informal* An easy target or victim.

sitting room *n.* A living room.

sit·u·ate (sĭch′o͞o-āt′) *tr.v.* **sit·u·at·ed, sit·u·at·ing, sit·u·ates** To place in a certain spot or position; locate.

sit·u·a·tion (sĭch′o͞o-ā′shən) *n.* **1.** A combination of circumstances at a given moment; state of affairs. **2.** A person's position or status with respect to specified conditions: *a favorable economic situation.* **3.** The place in which something is situated; location. **4.** A position of employment.

situation comedy *n.* A humorous television or radio series in which the comedy arises from the interactions between a regular cast of characters.

sit-up (sĭt′ŭp′) *n.* An exercise in which a person lying on his or her back rises to a sitting position using the abdominal muscles and then lies down again without moving the legs.

Si·va (shē′və *or* sē′və) *n.* Variant of **Shiva.**

six (sĭks) *n.* **1.** The number, written 6, that is equal to 5 + 1. **2.** The sixth in a set or sequence.

Six Nations *pl.n.* The Iroquois confederacy after it was joined by the Tuscarora in 1722.

WORD HISTORY

sirloin Some of you may know the story of how King Henry VIII dubbed the upper, choice loin of beef *Sir Loin* because it was so good. The story is old (it goes back to 1655, at least) but not true. The original spelling in Middle English is *surloin* (probably pronounced about the same as it is now), and it came from the Old French word *surloigne,* "(the meat) above the loin." The Old French word *sur* came from the Latin word *super,* "above, beyond, in addition." We see *sur* in *surcharge,* "an additional charge," and **surname,** "an additional name, a name added on to one's given name." The modern spelling of **sirloin** therefore should have been "surloin," if it had not been for that story about King Henry; the variant spelling *sirloin* was supported by the story.

Sitting Bull
photographed c. 1881

sit-up

skateboard

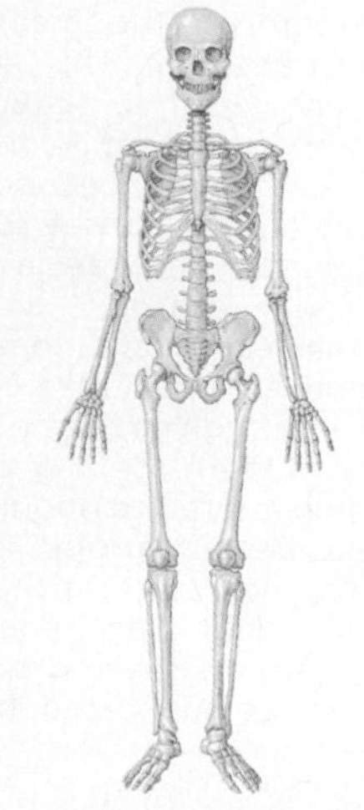

skeleton
top: human skeleton
bottom: architectural skeleton

ă	pat	ôr	core
ā	pay	oi	boy
âr	care	ou	out
ä	father	o͝o	took
ĕ	pet	o͝or	lure
ē	be	o͞o	boot
ĭ	pit	ŭ	cut
ī	bite	ûr	urge
îr	pier	th	thin
ŏ	pot	*th*	this
ō	toe	zh	vision
ô	paw	ə	about

six·pence (sĭks′pəns) *n. Chiefly British* A coin formerly used in Britain and worth six pennies.

six-shoot·er (sĭks′sho͞o′tər) *n. Informal* A revolver that can be fired six times before it has to be reloaded.

six·teen (sĭk-stēn′) *n.* **1.** The number, written 16, that is equal to 15 + 1. **2.** The 16th in a set or sequence.

six·teenth (sĭk-stēnth′) *n.* **1.** The ordinal number matching the number 16 in a series. **2.** One of 16 equal parts.

sixteenth note *n.* A musical note having one sixteenth the time value of a whole note.

sixth (sĭksth) *n.* **1.** The ordinal number matching the number six in a series. **2.** One of six equal parts. **3a.** The interval covering six tones in a musical scale. **b.** The sixth tone in a musical scale.

sixth sense *n.* A power of perception or intuition seemingly independent of the five senses.

six·ti·eth (sĭk′stē-ĭth) *n.* **1.** The ordinal number matching the number 60 in a series. **2.** One of 60 equal parts.

six·ty (sĭks′tē) *n., pl.* **six·ties** The number, written 60, that is equal to 6 × 10.

six·ty-fourth note (sĭks′tē-fôrth′) *n.* A musical note having one sixty-fourth the time value of a whole note.

siz·a·ble also **size·a·ble** (sī′zə-bəl) *adj.* Of considerable size; fairly large. **—siz′a·ble·ness** *n.* **—siz′a·bly** *adv.*

size¹ (sīz) *n.* **1.** The physical dimensions, proportions, or extent of an object. **2.** Any of a series of standard dimensions with which certain objects, such as clothing, are manufactured. **3.** Considerable extent, amount, or dimensions: *We had no difficulties of any size.* **4.** The actual state of affairs; the true situation: *We had succeeded—that was the size of it.* ❖ *tr.v.* **sized, siz·ing, siz·es 1.** To arrange, classify, or distribute according to size. **2.** To make, cut, or shape to a required size: *sized material for tents.* ◆ **size up** To make an estimate, opinion, or judgment of: *She sized up her opponent.* [From Middle English *sise*, from Old French *assise*, court session, law.]

size² (sīz) *n.* Any of several gelatinous or sticky substances made from glue, wax, or clay and used as a filler or glaze for porous materials such as paper, cloth, or wall surfaces. ❖ *tr.v.* **sized, siz·ing, siz·es** To treat or coat with size or a similar substance. [From Middle English *sise*, probably from Old French *sise*, a setting.]

size·a·ble (sī′zə-bəl) *adj.* Variant of **sizable.**

sized (sīzd) *adj.* Having a particular or specified size: *a medium-sized car.*

siz·ing (sī′zĭng) *n.* **1.** A substance used as a filler or glaze; size. **2.** The treatment of fabric or another surface with size.

siz·zle (sĭz′əl) *intr.v.* **siz·zled, siz·zling, siz·zles 1.** To make the hissing sound characteristic of frying fat. **2.** To be very hot: *a summer day that sizzled.* ❖ *n.* A hissing sound.

SJ *abbr.* An abbreviation of Society of Jesus.

SK *abbr.* An abbreviation of Saskatchewan.

ska (skä) *n.* A style of popular music of Jamaican origin that is played quickly and has a strongly accented offbeat.

skate¹ (skāt) *n.* **1.** An ice skate. **2.** A roller skate. ❖ *intr.v.* **skat·ed, skat·ing, skates 1.** To move on skates. **2.** To move smoothly or easily: *skated along on his reputation.* **3.** To ride or perform stunts on a skateboard. [From Dutch *schaats*, from Old North French *escache*, stilt.] **—skat′er** *n.*

skate² (skāt) *n.* Any of various ocean fishes related to the rays, having a broad flat body with winglike fins and laying eggs in hard cases. [From Middle English *scate*, from Old Norse *skata*.]

skate·board (skāt′bôrd′) *n.* A short narrow board having a set of four wheels mounted under it and usually ridden in a standing or crouched position. ❖ *intr.v.* **skate·board·ed, skate·board·ing, skate·boards** To ride on a skateboard. **—skate′board′er** *n.* **—skate′board′ing** *n.*

skeet (skēt) *n.* A form of trapshooting in which clay targets are used to simulate birds in flight. [Alteration of *shoot*.]

skein (skān) *n.* **1.** A length of thread or yarn wound in a long loose coil. **2.** Something resembling this: *Skeins of mist floated above the lake.*

skel·e·tal (skĕl′ĭ-tl) *adj.* **1.** Relating to, forming, characteristic of, or attached to a skeleton: *skeletal anatomy; skeletal muscles.* **2.** Very thin; bony: *skeletal stray dogs.* **3.** Extremely basic or simplified: *a skeletal summary.*

skel·e·ton (skĕl′ĭ-tn) *n.* **1a.** The internal structure, usually composed of bone and cartilage, that supports and protects the soft organs of a vertebrate. **b.** The hard protective covering or supporting structure of many invertebrates, such as crustaceans and insects. **2.** A supporting structure or framework, as of a building. **3.** An outline or sketch: *the skeleton of a research paper.* **4.** A very thin person or animal. [From Greek *skeletos*, dried up.]

skeleton key *n.* A key with a large part of the bit filed off so that it can open many different locks.

skep·tic also **scep·tic** (skĕp′tĭk) *n.* **1.** A person who habitually questions or doubts the truth of generally accepted beliefs or conclusions. **2.** A person inclined to skepticism in religious matters.

skep·ti·cal also **scep·ti·cal** (skĕp′tĭ-kəl) *adj.* Relating to or characterized by skepticism; doubting or disbelieving: *a skeptical attitude.* **—skep′ti·cal·ly** *adv.*

skep·ti·cism also **scep·ti·cism** (skĕp′tĭ-sĭz′əm) *n.* **1.** A doubting or questioning attitude or state of mind. **2.** Doubt or disbelief of religious doctrines.

sketch (skĕch) *n.* **1.** A rough preliminary drawing or painting: *a sketch of the park.* **2.** A brief composition or outline: *a biographical sketch.* **3.** A brief, light, or informal story or play. ❖ *v.* **sketched, sketch·ing, sketch·es** *—tr.* To make a sketch of: *sketch his face.* *—intr.* To make a sketch: *She loves to sketch in the park.* **—sketch′er** *n.*

sketch·book (skĕch′bo͝ok′) *n.* **1.** A pad of paper used for sketching. **2.** A book of literary sketches.

sketch·y (skĕch′ē) *adj.* **sketch·i·er, sketch·i·est 1.** Lacking in substance or completeness: *sketchy information.* **2.** *Informal* Of questionable trustworthiness or safety: *a sketchy character; a sketchy neighborhood.* **—sketch′i·ly** *adv.* **—sketch′i·ness** *n.*

skew (skyo͞o) *tr.v.* **skewed, skew·ing, skews 1.** To turn or place at an angle; slant. **2.** To distort in meaning or effect; give a bias to: *The article was skewed in favor of the proposal.* ❖ *adj.* Turned or placed to one side.

skew·er (skyo͞o′ər) *n.* A long pin of wood or metal, used to hold or suspend food during cooking. ❖ *tr.v.* **skew·ered, skew·er·ing, skew·ers** To pierce with a skewer or other pointed object.

ski (skē) *n., pl.* **skis 1.** One of a pair of long, narrow, flat runners of plastic, metal, or wood that are fastened to a boot or shoe for gliding or traveling over snow. **2.** A water ski. ❖ *v.* **skied, ski·ing, skis** *—intr.* To glide or travel on skis. *—tr.* To travel over on skis: *She skied a new trail.* [From Old Norse *skīdh*, stick, snowshoe.] **—ski′er** *n.*

skid (skĭd) *n.* **1.** The act of slipping or sliding over a surface, especially sideways: *The car went into a skid on the slippery pavement.* **2.** A plank or log used as a support or track for sliding or rolling heavy objects. **3.** A runner forming part of the landing gear of an aircraft, such as a helicopter. **4.** A shoe or wedge that applies pressure to a wheel to keep it from turning. ❖ *intr.v.* **skid·ded, skid·ding, skids** To slip or slide over a slippery surface, especially sideways. See Synonyms at **slide.**

skies (skīz) *n.* Plural of **sky.**

skiff (skĭf) *n.* A flatbottom boat with a pointed bow and a square stern, propelled by oars, sail, or motor.

ski jump *n.* **1.** A course or slanted surface leading to a sharp drop, used for making jumps on skis. **2.** A jump made by a person on skis.

ski lift *n.* An apparatus that transports skiers to the top of a ski trail or mountain, usually consisting of a moving cable with attached bars, chairs, or gondolas.

skill (skĭl) *n.* **1.** Ability resulting from training or experience. **2.** A developed ability: *He has excellent writing skills.* **3.** An art, trade, or technique, especially one requiring use of the hands or body: *a carpenter's skills.* [From Middle English *skil,* from Old Norse, discernment.]

skilled (skĭld) *adj.* **1.** Having or showing skill: *a skilled hunter.* See Synonyms at **proficient. 2.** Requiring specialized ability or training: *a skilled occupation.*

skil·let (skĭl′ĭt) *n.* A frying pan. [From Middle English *skelett,* from Latin *scutella,* plate.]

skill·ful (skĭl′fəl) *adj.* **1.** Having or using considerable skill: *a skillful cook.* See Synonyms at **proficient. 2.** Characterized by or requiring skill: *skillful violin playing.* **—skill′ful·ly** *adv.* **—skill′ful·ness** *n.*

skim (skĭm) *v.* **skimmed, skim·ming, skims** *—tr.* **1a.** To remove (floating matter) from a liquid: *skim cream off the top of the milk.* **b.** To remove floating matter from (a liquid): *skim milk.* **2.** To throw so as to bounce or slide: *skim stones over the pond.* **3.** To glide or pass quickly and lightly over or along (a surface): *skimmed the surface of the water.* **4.** To read, glance at, or consider superficially: *skim a book. —intr.* **1.** To move or glide lightly and quickly over a surface: *The sailboat skimmed across the lake.* **2.** To give a quick and superficial reading or consideration.

skim·mer (skĭm′ər) *n.* **1.** A person or thing that skims, especially a flat utensil used for skimming liquids. **2.** Any of several seabirds having long narrow wings and a long bill with a longer lower mandible used to skim the surface of the water for small fish and other food.

skim milk *n.* Milk from which the cream has been removed.

skimp (skĭmp) *intr.v.* **skimped, skimp·ing, skimps** To spend less money or use less of a supply of something than one would otherwise out of a need or desire to be thrifty: *The recession forced many businesses to skimp on advertising.*

skimp·y (skĭm′pē) *adj.* **skimp·i·er, skimp·i·est 1.** Inadequate, as in size or amount; scanty: *a skimpy meal.* **2.** Not covering a considerable amount of the body: *a skimpy bathing suit.* **—skimp′i·ly** *adv.* **—skimp′i·ness** *n.*

skin (skĭn) *n.* **1.** The membranous tissue that forms the outer covering of the body of an animal. **2.** A hide or pelt removed from the body of an animal: *a tent made of buffalo skins.* **3.** An outer layer, covering, or coating: *the skin of an apple.* **4.** A container for liquids that is made from an animal's skin. **5.** A drumhead. ❖ *tr.v.* **skinned, skin·ning, skins 1.** To remove the skin from: *skin a sheep.* **2.** To injure by scraping: *fell and skinned her knee.* ◆ **by the skin of (one's) teeth** By the smallest margin; just barely. **get under (someone's) skin** To irritate or stimulate; provoke.

skin-deep (skĭn′dēp′) *adj.* Superficial; shallow: *an acquaintanceship that was only skin-deep.*

skin-dive (skĭn′dīv′) *intr.v.* **skin-dived, skin-div·ing, skin-dives** To engage in skin diving.

skin diving *n.* The sport of underwater swimming in which the swimmer is equipped with flippers and a face mask and usually a snorkel rather than scuba gear. **—skin diver** *n.*

skin·flint (skĭn′flĭnt′) *n.* A miser.

skink (skĭngk) *n.* Any of numerous lizards having a smooth shiny body and short legs.

skin·ner (skĭn′ər) *n.* **1.** A person who strips, dresses, or sells animal skins. **2.** A mule driver.

skin·ny (skĭn′ē) *adj.* **skin·ni·er, skin·ni·est** Very thin or narrow: *skinny legs; a skinny island.* See Synonyms at **lean**[2]. **—skin′ni·ness** *n.*

skin·tight (skĭn′tīt′) *adj.* Fitting or clinging closely to the skin.

skip (skĭp) *v.* **skipped, skip·ping, skips** *—intr.* **1a.** To move by hopping on one foot and then the other: *skipped across the room.* **b.** To leap lightly about. **2.** To bounce over or be deflected from a surface: *The stone I threw skipped over the water six times.* **3.** To pass quickly from point to point: *skipping through the list hurriedly.* **4.** To be promoted in school beyond the next class or grade. **5.** *Informal* To leave hastily. *—tr.* **1.** To leap or jump lightly over: *skip rope.* **2a.** To pass over without mentioning; omit: *skipped the unimportant details.* **b.** To miss or omit (one in a series): *My heart skipped a beat.* **3.** To cause to bounce over a surface; skim. **4.** To be promoted beyond (the next class or grade). **5.** To leave hastily: *skip town.* **6.** To fail to attend: *skipped class.* ❖ *n.* **1.** A gait in which hops and steps alternate. **2.** The act of passing over something; an omission. [From Middle English *skippen.*]

skip·per[1] (skĭp′ər) *n.* The captain of a ship. [From Middle English, from Middle Dutch, from *scip,* ship.]

skip·per[2] (skĭp′ər) *n.* **1.** A person or thing that skips. **2.** Any of numerous butterflies that have a stout hairy body and dart as they fly.

skir·mish (skûr′mĭsh) *n.* **1.** A minor battle between small bodies of troops. **2.** A minor conflict. ❖ *intr.v.* **skir·mished, skir·mish·ing, skir·mish·es** To engage in a minor battle or dispute.

skirt (skûrt) *n.* **1.** A garment that hangs from the waist and is worn especially by women and girls. **2.** The part of a garment, such as a dress or coat, that hangs from the waist down. **3.** Something that hangs like a skirt, as a cloth covering the legs of a piece of furniture. **4.** A border, margin, or outer edge: *The sheep grazed at the skirt of the hill.* ❖ *v.* **skirt·ed, skirt·ing, skirts** *—tr.* **1.** To form the border of, lie along, or surround: *The road skirted the park.* **2.** To pass around rather than across or through: *We skirted the marshes.* **3.** To evade (a topic or issue, for example) in a roundabout way. *—intr.* To lie along, move along, or be an edge or border. —SEE NOTE AT **shirt.**

skit (skĭt) *n.* A short, usually humorous theatrical sketch.

skit·ter (skĭt′ər) *v.* **skit·tered, skit·ter·ing, skit·ters** *—intr.* To move rapidly across a surface with many short hops or skips. *—tr.* To cause to skitter.

skit·tish (skĭt′ĭsh) *adj.* **1.** Excitable or nervous: *a skittish colt.* **2.** Shy; bashful. **—skit′tish·ly** *adv.*

skit·tles (skĭt′lz) *n. (used with a singular verb)* A British form of the game ninepins.

Skop·je (skôp′yā′ *or* skŏp′yĕ) The capital of Macedonia, in the northern part southwest of Sofia, Bulgaria.

skul·dug·ger·y (skŭl-dŭg′ə-rē) *n.* Variant of **skullduggery.**

skulk (skŭlk) *intr.v.* **skulked, skulk·ing, skulks 1.** To lurk: *The spy skulked in the shadows.* **2.** To move about stealthily: *The cat skulked around the barn.*

skull (skŭl) *n.* The framework of bone or cartilage that supports and protects the brain and sense organs of vertebrates; the cranium. [From Middle English *sculle,* probably of Scandinavian origin.]

❑ *These sound alike:* **skull, scull** (oar).

skull and crossbones *n.* A representation of a human skull above two long crossed bones, used traditionally as a symbol of death or as a warning of the danger of death.

skull·cap (skŭl′kăp′) *n.* A small, close-fitting, brimless cap.

skull·dug·ger·y or **skul·dug·ger·y** (skŭl-dŭg′ə-rē) *n.,*

ski lift

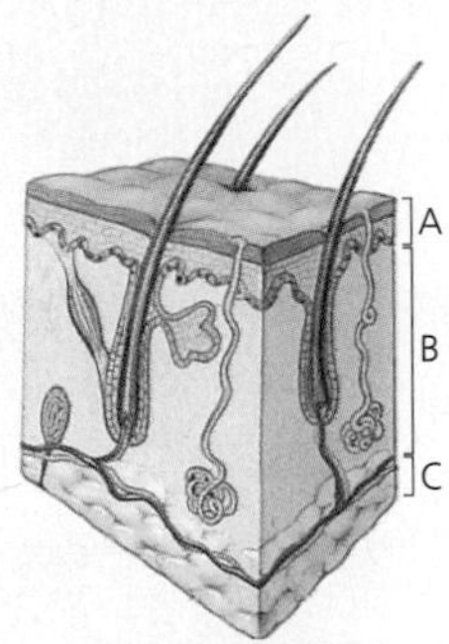

skin

cross section of human skin
A. epidermis
B. dermis
C. subcutaneous tissue

skin diving

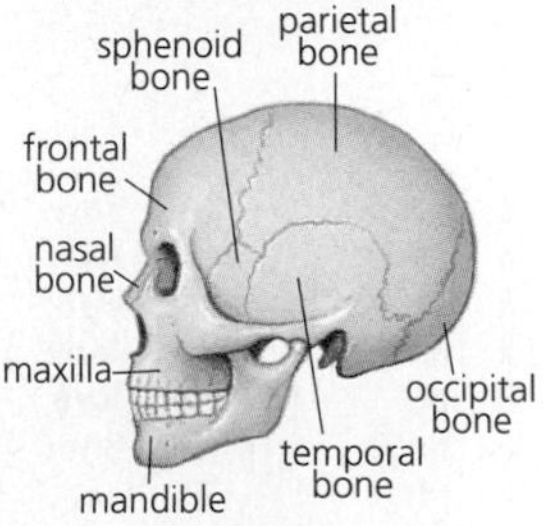

skull

lateral view of an adult human skull

pl. **skull·dug·ger·ies** or **skul·dug·ger·ies** Crafty deception or trickery.

skunk

skunk (skŭngk) *n.* **1.** Any of several small mammals that have black and white fur and a bushy tail and can spray a foul-smelling liquid from glands near the base of the tail. **2.** *Slang* An annoying or despicable person. ❖ *tr.v.* **skunked, skunk·ing, skunks** *Slang* To defeat overwhelmingly, especially by keeping from scoring.

sky (skī) *n., pl.* **skies** (skīz) **1.** The atmosphere, as seen from a given point on the earth's surface. **2.** often **skies** The appearance of the upper atmosphere, especially with respect to weather: *threatening skies.* [From Middle English *ski*, from Old Norse *ský*, cloud.]

sky blue *n.* A light to medium blue.

sky·dive (skī′dīv′) *intr.v.* **sky·dived, sky·div·ing, sky·dives** To jump and fall freely from an airplane, performing various maneuvers before opening a parachute. **—sky′div′er** *n.* **—sky′div′ing** *n.*

sky-high (skī′hī′) *adv.* **1.** To a very high level: *garbage piled sky-high.* **2.** In a lavish or enthusiastic manner: *The critics praised the movie sky-high.* **3.** To pieces or in pieces; apart: *The explosive blew the old bridge sky-high.* ❖ *adj.* Exorbitantly high: *sky-high prices.*

sky·lark (skī′lärk′) *n.* A brownish songbird of Eurasia and northern Africa that sings while in flight.

skylight

sky·light (skī′līt′) *n.* An overhead window that admits daylight.

sky·line (skī′līn′) *n.* **1.** The line along which the earth and sky appear to meet; the horizon. **2.** The outline of a mountain range or group of buildings seen against the sky.

sky·rock·et (skī′rŏk′ĭt) *n.* A firework that ascends high into the air, where it explodes in a cascade of flares and sparks. ❖ *intr. & tr.v.* **sky·rock·et·ed, sky·rock·et·ing, sky·rock·ets** To rise or cause to rise rapidly or suddenly: *Prices skyrocketed.*

sky·scrap·er (skī′skrā′pər) *n.* A very tall building.

sky·ward (skī′wərd) *adv. & adj.* Toward the sky: *turn skyward.* **—sky′wards** *adv.*

sky·writ·ing (skī′rī′tĭng) *n.* **1.** The process of writing in the sky by releasing a visible vapor from an airplane as it performs aerobatic maneuvers. **2.** The letters or words so formed. **—sky′write′** *v.* **—sky′writ′er** *n.*

slab (slăb) *n.* A broad, flat, thick piece of something, as of stone or cheese.

slack (slăk) *adj.* **slack·er, slack·est 1.** Not tense or taut; loose: *a slack rope.* **2.** Slow; dull; sluggish: *a slack pace.* **3.** Not busy: *the slack moments of the day.* **4.** Careless; negligent: *a slack performance.* ❖ *v.* **slacked, slack·ing, slacks** *—tr.* To make slower or looser; slacken. *—intr.* **1.** To be or become slack. **2.** To avoid work. ❖ *n.* **1.** A loose part of something: *take up some of the slack in the rope.* **2.** A period of little activity. **3. slacks** Casual pants that are not part of a suit. ◆ **slack off** To decrease in activity or diligence. [From Old English *slæc.*] **—slack′ness** *n.*

slack·en (slăk′ən) *tr. & intr.v.* **slack·ened, slack·en·ing, slack·ens 1.** To make or become less taut or firm: *I slackened the leash to let the dog run. The boat's sail slackened as the wind died.* **2.** To make or become slower; slow down: *The dogs slackened their pace. The plane's air speed slackened.* **3.** To make or become less vigorous or intense: *High rates slackened the demand for loans. Business slackened.*

slack·er (slăk′ər) *n.* A person who tries to avoid work or responsibility.

slag (slăg) *n.* **1.** The glassy refuse that remains after a metal has been removed from an ore by smelting. **2.** Angular porous fragments of solidified lava from a volcano; scoria.

slain (slān) *v.* Past participle of **slay.**

slake (slāk) *tr.v.* **slaked, slak·ing, slakes 1.** To satisfy (a craving): *slaked her thirst.* **2.** To lessen the force of; moderate: *slaking his anger.* **3.** To combine (lime) chemically with water, either directly or by exposure to moist air.

sla·lom (slä′ləm) *n.* **1.** The act of moving or racing in a zigzag course, as on skis. **2.** A race along such a course, laid out with markers such as flags. [From Norwegian *slalåm* : *slad*, sloping + *låm*, path.]

slam[1] (slăm) *v.* **slammed, slam·ming, slams** *—tr.* **1.** To shut forcefully and with a loud noise: *slam a door.* **2.** To throw, move, or strike forcefully and loudly: *slammed down the telephone receiver.* *—intr.* **1.** To close or swing into place forcefully and with a loud noise: *The door slammed in the wind.* **2.** To hit something with force; crash: *The meteorite slammed into the side of a hill.* ❖ *n.* **1.** An act of slamming. **2.** The noise of a forceful impact; a bang. [Perhaps of Scandinavian origin.]

slam[2] (slăm) *n.* In certain card games, such as bridge, the winning of all the tricks or all but one during the play of one hand.

slam dunk *n.* In basketball, a dramatic forceful dunk. **—slam′-dunk′** *v.*

slan·der (slăn′dər) *n.* **1.** False and malicious spoken statements that damage someone's reputation. **2.** A false and malicious statement or report about someone. ❖ *tr.v.* **slan·dered, slan·der·ing, slan·ders** To utter a slander about (someone). **—slan′der·er** *n.*

slan·der·ous (slăn′dər-əs) *adj.* Making or containing false and damaging charges about someone: *a slanderous speech.* **—slan′der·ous·ly** *adv.*

slang (slăng) *n.* **1.** A kind of language occurring most often in casual speech, consisting of made-up words and figures of speech that are deliberately used in place of standard terms to add vividness, humor, irreverence, or other effect. For example, slang terms include *cool* meaning "excellent" and *split* meaning "to leave." **2.** Language peculiar to a certain group of people; jargon: *surfers' slang.* **—slang′y** *adj.*

slant (slănt) *v.* **slant·ed, slant·ing, slants** *—intr.* To have or go in a direction other than horizontal or vertical; slope: *My handwriting slants to the right.* *—tr.* **1.** To give a direction other than horizontal or vertical to; cause to slope. **2.** To present (news or information, for example) in a way that conforms with a particular opinion; bias. ❖ *n.* **1.** A sloping line, plane, direction, or course. **2.** A personal point of view or opinion. **3.** A bias.

slant·wise (slănt′wīz′) *adv.* At a slant or slope; obliquely. ❖ *adj.* Slanting; oblique.

slap (slăp) *v.* **slapped, slap·ping, slaps** *—tr.* **1.** To strike with a flat object, such as the palm of the hand: *Grandpa slapped his knee and chuckled.* **2.** To cause to strike with a sound of a flat object striking something: *slapped the book against the desk.* **3.** To put or place quickly or carelessly: *slapped a price tag on the package.* **4.** To subject (someone) to a legal obligation: *hauled him into court and slapped him with a hefty fine.* *—intr.* To strike or beat with a sound like that of an open hand striking something: *waves slapping against the canoe.* ❖ *n.* **1a.** A sharp blow with the open hand or some other flat object. **b.** The sound made by such a blow. **2.** An injury or sharp insult: *a slap to one's pride.* [From Middle English *slappen*, to strike with the back of the hand.]

slap·dash (slăp′dăsh′) *adj.* Characterized by haste or carelessness: *slapdash work.* ❖ *adv.* In a reckless haphazard manner.

slap·stick (slăp′stĭk′) *n.* A form of comedy marked by chases, collisions, and crude practical jokes.

slash (slăsh) *v.* **slashed, slash·ing, slash·es** *—tr.* **1.** To cut or form with forceful sweeping strokes: *We slashed a path through the jungle.* **2.** To lash with sweeping strokes. **3.** To make a gash or gashes in: *slashed the screen with a knife.* **4.** To cut a decorative slit or slits in (a garment or fabric). **5.** To reduce greatly: *slash prices for a sale.* *—intr.* **1.** To make forceful sweeping strokes,

ă	pat	ôr	core
ā	pay	oi	boy
âr	care	ou	out
ä	father	ŏŏ	took
ĕ	pet	ŏŏr	lure
ē	be	ōō	boot
ĭ	pit	ŭ	cut
ī	bite	ûr	urge
îr	pier	th	thin
ŏ	pot	*th*	this
ō	toe	zh	vision
ô	paw	ə	about

as with a sharp instrument. **2.** To cut one's way with such strokes: *slashed through the thick jungle growth.* ❖ *n.* **1.** A forceful sweeping stroke made with a sharp instrument. **2.** A long cut or opening made by such a stroke. **3.** A decorative slit in a fabric or garment. **4.** A sharp reduction: *making slashes in the national budget.* **5.** A diagonal mark (/) used in writing and printing to separate alternatives, as in *and/or,* or to mean "per" as in *miles/hour.*

slat (slăt) *n.* A narrow strip of metal or wood, as in a Venetian blind.

slate (slāt) *n.* **1.** A fine-grained metamorphic rock that splits into thin layers with smooth surfaces. **2a.** A piece of such rock cut for use as a roofing material or as a writing surface. **b.** A writing tablet made of this or a similar material. **3.** A dark bluish gray. **4.** A record of past performance or activity: *start over with a clean slate.* **5.** A list of the candidates of a political party running for office. ❖ *tr.v.* **slat·ed, slat·ing, slates 1.** To cover (a roof, for example) with slates. **2.** To put on a list of candidates. **3.** To schedule or designate: *slated the appointment for Tuesday.*

slath·er (slăth′ər) *tr.v.* **slath·ered, slath·er·ing, slath·ers** *Informal* **1.** To spread thickly: *slather cream cheese on a bagel.* **2.** To cover with something in large amounts: *slather a bagel with cream cheese.*

slat·tern (slăt′ərn) *n.* An untidy, dirty woman. **—slat′tern·ly** *adj.*

slat·y (slā′tē) *adj.* **slat·i·er, slat·i·est 1.** Composed of or resembling slate. **2.** Having the color of slate.

slaugh·ter (slô′tər) *n.* **1.** The killing of animals especially for food. **2.** The killing of a large number of people; a massacre. ❖ *tr.v.* **slaugh·tered, slaugh·ter·ing, slaugh·ters 1.** To kill (an animal) especially for food. **2.** To kill (people) brutally or in large numbers. **—slaugh′ter·er** *n.*

slaugh·ter·house (slô′tər-hous′) *n.* **1.** A place where animals are butchered. **2.** A scene of massacre or carnage.

Slav (släv) *n.* A member of one of the Slavic-speaking peoples of eastern Europe.

slave (slāv) *n.* **1.** A person who is owned by and forced to work for someone else. **2.** A person controlled by a specified person or influence: *a slave to his appetites.* ❖ *intr.v.* **slaved, slav·ing, slaves** To work very hard; toil. [From Middle English *sclave,* from Old French *esclave,* from Medieval Latin *Sclāvus,* a Slav.]

slave driver *n.* **1.** An overseer of slaves at work. **2.** An extremely demanding employer or supervisor.

slave·hold·er (slāv′hōl′dər) *n.* A person who owns slaves.

slav·er[1] (slăv′ər) *intr.v.* **slav·ered, slav·er·ing, slav·ers** To let saliva dribble from the mouth; drool. ❖ *n.* Saliva drooling from the mouth. [From Middle English *slaveren,* probably from Old Norse *slafra.*]

slav·er[2] (slā′vər) *n.* **1.** A person who sells and trades slaves. **2.** A ship engaged in slave traffic.

slav·er·y (slā′və-rē *or* slāv′rē) *n., pl.* **slav·er·ies 1.** The condition of being a slave. **2.** The practice of owning slaves. **3.** Hard work or subjection like that of a slave. **4.** The condition of being subject or addicted to a specified influence.

Slave State *n.* Any of the 15 states of the Union in which slavery was legal before the Civil War.

Slav·ic (slä′vĭk) *adj.* **1.** Relating to the Slavs. **2.** Relating to the Slavic languages. ❖ *n.* A branch of the Indo-European language family that includes Russian, Polish, Bulgarian, and other languages of central and eastern Europe.

slav·ish (slā′vĭsh) *adj.* **1.** Characteristic of a slave; servile or submissive: *slavish devotion.* **2.** Showing no originality; blindly imitative: *a slavish copy of another artist's work.* **—slav′ish·ly** *adv.* **—slav′ish·ness** *n.*

Sla·vo·ni·a (slə-vō′nē-ə) A historical region of northern Croatia bordering on Bosnia, Serbia, and Hungary.

slaw (slô) *n.* Coleslaw.

slay (slā) *tr.v.* **slew** (slo͞o), **slain** (slān), **slay·ing, slays 1.** To kill violently. **2.** *past tense and past participle often* **slayed** *Slang* To overwhelm, as with laughter or love: *Those old jokes still slay me.* **—slay′er** *n.*
❑ *These sound alike:* **slay, sleigh** (sledge).

slea·zy (slē′zē) *adj.* **slea·zi·er, slea·zi·est 1.** Shabby, dirty, and tawdry: *a sleazy tavern.* **2.** Disreputable or dishonest; corrupt: *a sleazy character.* **—slea′zi·ly** *adv.* **—slea′zi·ness** *n.*

sled (slĕd) *n.* **1.** A vehicle mounted on runners, used for carrying people or loads over snow and ice. **2.** A light vehicle, often having runners, used by children for coasting over snow and ice. ❖ *v.* **sled·ded, sled·ding, sleds** *—tr.* To carry on a sled. *—intr.* To ride on a sled. [From Middle English *sledde,* from Middle Dutch.]

sled dog *n.* A dog, such as a Siberian husky, used to pull a dogsled.

sledge (slĕj) *n.* A vehicle on runners, drawn by work animals such as horses or reindeer and used for transporting loads across snow, ice, or rough ground. [From Dutch dialectal *sleedse.*]

sledge·ham·mer (slĕj′hăm′ər) *n.* A long heavy hammer, often wielded with both hands, used for driving posts and other heavy work. ❖ *tr.v.* **sledge·ham·mered, sledge·ham·mer·ing, sledge·ham·mers** To strike, as with a sledgehammer.

sleek (slēk) *adj.* **sleek·er, sleek·est 1.** Smooth and glossy: *the sleek coat of a horse.* **2.** In good health and having smooth or glossy hair, fur, or skin: *a sleek pig ready for the market.* **3.** Slender or streamlined in appearance: *a sleek racing car.* [Variant of *slick.*] **—sleek′ly** *adv.* **—sleek′ness** *n.*

sleep (slēp) *n.* **1.** A natural condition of rest, occurring periodically in many animals, that is characterized by unconsciousness and a decrease in body movement. **2.** A period of this form of rest: *a good night's sleep.* **3.** A similar condition of inactivity, such as hibernation or unconsciousness. **4.** A crust of dried tears or mucus around the eye. ❖ *v.* **slept** (slĕpt), **sleep·ing, sleeps** *—intr.* **1.** To be in the state of sleep or to fall asleep. **2.** To be inactive or inattentive: *The sudden question caught me sleeping.* *—tr.* **1.** To pass or get rid of by sleeping: *slept away the afternoon.* **2.** To provide with beds: *This cabin sleeps four.* ◆ **sleep on** *Informal* To consider (something) overnight before deciding. **sleep over** To spend the night as a guest in another's home. **sleep with** To have sexual relations with. [From Old English *slǣp.*]

sleep·er (slē′pər) *n.* **1.** A person or animal that sleeps: *a sound sleeper.* **2.** A sleeping car on a train. **3.** Something, such as a movie, play, or contestant, that becomes unexpectedly popular or successful. **4.** A spy or saboteur who is sent to an enemy country to live as a citizen of that country until instructed to take action upon receiving a special signal. **5.** A horizontal beam on or near the ground that supports weight.

sleep·ing bag (slē′pĭng) *n.* A large warmly lined bag in which a person may sleep, especially outdoors.

sleeping car *n.* A railroad car with bunks or sleeping compartments for overnight passengers.

sleeping sickness *n.* An often fatal infectious disease occurring in sub-Saharan Africa. It is caused by parasitic protozoans that are transmitted by the bite of tsetse flies and is marked by fever, extreme sluggishness, and coma.

sleep·less (slēp′lĭs) *adj.* **1.** Unable to sleep; restless or insomniac. **2.** Marked by a lack of sleep; wakeful: *sleepless nights.* **3.** Never resting; always alert or active. **—sleep′less·ly** *adv.* **—sleep′less·ness** *n.*

sleep·o·ver (slēp′ō′vər) *n.* An instance of a child spending the night at another child's house.

slalom

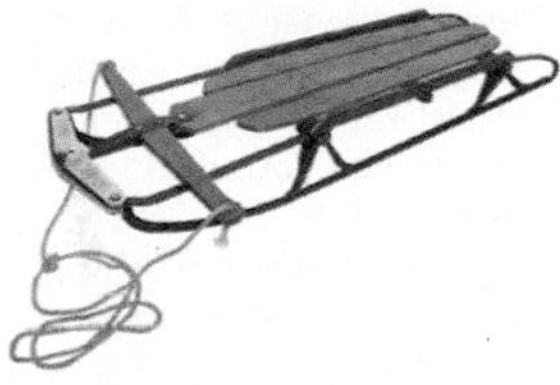
sled

sleigh

WRITERS CHOOSE THEIR WORDS

He heard a noise behind him. It was only a small noise but it sounded loud in that immense silence. It froze him dead-still where he stood for a second. Then he **slewed** round his neck and looked.

At the bottom of the cliff a little on his left was a low, dark hole—the entrance to a cave perhaps. And out of this two thin wisps of smoke were coming.

—C.S. Lewis
The Voyage of the Dawn Treader

ă	pat	ôr	core
ā	pay	oi	boy
âr	care	ou	out
ä	father	o͝o	took
ĕ	pet	o͝or	lure
ē	be	o͞o	boot
ĭ	pit	ŭ	cut
ī	bite	ûr	urge
îr	pier	th	thin
ŏ	pot	*th*	this
ō	toe	zh	vision
ô	paw	ə	about

sleep·walk·ing (slēp′wô′kĭng) *n.* The act or an instance of walking about while asleep or in a condition resembling sleep. **—sleep′walk′er** *n.*

sleep·y (slē′pē) *adj.* **sleep·i·er, sleep·i·est 1.** Ready for or needing sleep. **2.** Dulled or sluggish from sleep: *sleepy eyes.* **3.** Quiet; inactive: *a sleepy town.* **—sleep′i·ly** *adv.* **—sleep′i·ness** *n.*

sleep·y·head (slē′pē-hĕd′) *n. Informal* A person who needs sleep or who is groggy from sleep.

sleet (slēt) *n.* Small ice pellets formed by the freezing of raindrops or of melted snowflakes. ❖ *intr.v.* **sleet·ed, sleet·ing, sleets** To fall as sleet.

sleeve (slēv) *n.* **1.** The part of a garment that covers all or part of the arm. **2.** A case or covering into which an object or device fits: *a record sleeve.* ❖ *tr.v.* **sleeved, sleev·ing, sleeves** To furnish or fit with a sleeve or sleeves. ◆ **up (one's) sleeve** Hidden but ready to be used: *I still have a few tricks up my sleeve.*

sleigh (slā) *n.* A light vehicle mounted on runners for use on snow or ice, having one or more seats and usually drawn by a horse. ❖ *intr.v.* **sleighed, sleigh·ing, sleighs** To ride in or drive a sleigh. [From Middle Dutch *slēde.*]

❑ *These sound alike:* **sleigh, slay** (kill).

sleight (slīt) *n.* **1.** Quickness or skillfulness; dexterity. **2.** A clever or skillful trick or deception.

sleight of hand *n., pl.* **sleights of hand** A trick or set of tricks performed by a juggler or magician so quickly and skillfully that one cannot see how it is done.

slen·der (slĕn′dər) *adj.* **slen·der·er, slen·der·est 1.** Having little width as compared to length or height; long and thin: *a slender church spire.* See Synonyms at **lean**[2]. **2.** Small in amount or extent: *a slender chance of winning.* **—slen′der·ly** *adv.* **—slen′der·ness** *n.*

slept (slĕpt) *v.* Past tense and past participle of **sleep.**

sleuth (slo͞oth) *n.* A detective. ❖ *v.* **sleuthed, sleuth·ing, sleuths** *—tr.* To track or follow. *—intr.* To act as a detective.

slew[1] (slo͞o) *n. Informal* A large amount or number: *caught a whole slew of fish.* [From Irish Gaelic *sluagh,* multitude.]

❑ *These sound alike:* **slew**[1] (large amount), **slew**[2] (killed), **slew**[4] (turn), **slough**[1] (a hollow).

slew[2] (slo͞o) *v.* Past tense of **slay.**

❑ *These sound alike:* **slew**[2] (killed), **slew**[1] (large amount), **slew**[4] (turn), **slough**[1] (hollow).

slew[3] (slo͞o) *n.* Variant of **slough**[1].

slew[4] also **slue** (slo͞o) *intr. & tr.v.* **slewed, slew·ing, slews** also **slued, slu·ing, slues 1.** To turn or cause to turn on an axis; rotate or spin. **2.** To turn or slide, or cause to turn or slide sharply; veer or skid.

❑ *These sound alike:* **slew**[4] (turn), **slew**[1] (large amount), **slew**[2] (killed), **slough**[1] (hollow).

slice (slīs) *n.* **1a.** A thin broad piece cut from a larger object: *a slice of bread.* **b.** An often wedge-shaped piece cut from a larger, usually circular object: *a slice of pizza.* **2.** A share or portion: *a slice of the profits.* **3a.** The path of a ball that curves to the right when hit by a righthander or to the left when hit by a lefthander. **b.** A ball that follows such a path. ❖ *v.* **sliced, slic·ing, slic·es** *—tr.* **1.** To cut into slices: *slice a loaf of bread.* **2.** To cut from a larger piece: *slicing off a piece of salami.* **3.** To divide into portions. **4.** To hit (a ball) with a slice. *—intr.* **1.** To move like a knife: *The airplane sliced through the clouds.* **2.** To hit a ball with a slice. [From Middle English *sclice,* from Old French *esclicier,* to splinter, of Germanic origin.] **—slic′er** *n.*

slick (slĭk) *adj.* **slick·er, slick·est 1.** Smooth, glossy, and slippery: *slick ice.* **2.** Acting or done with skill and ease; deft; adroit: *a slick tennis shot.* **3.** Shrewd; crafty: *a slick business deal.* **4.** Attractive at first, but really shallow or insincere; glib: *a slick writing style.* ❖ *n.* **1.** A smooth or slippery surface or area. **2.** A spread-out floating mass, especially of oil. ❖ *tr.v.* **slicked, slick·ing, slicks** To make smooth, glossy, or oily: *slicked back his hair with water.* [From Middle English *slike.*]

slick·er (slĭk′ər) *n.* **1.** A long waterproof coat, usually made of oilskin. **2.** A raincoat made of a glossy or shiny material. **3.** *Informal* A person with stylish clothing and fancy manners: *a city slicker.*

slide (slīd) *v.* **slid** (slĭd), **slid·ing, slides** *—intr.* **1.** To move smoothly over a surface while maintaining continuous contact: *During recess, we slid down the snowpile.* **2.** To move or pass quietly: *I slid past the door to his office.* **3.** To lose a secure footing; slip: *slid on the ice and fell.* **4.** In baseball, to drop down, as on one's back, and skid into a base to avoid being tagged out. **5.** To go unacted upon: *Let the matter slide.* **6.** To move downward or into a less favorable position: *Prices began to slide.* *—tr.* To cause to slip or slide: *Slide that box over here.* ❖ *n.* **1.** A sliding action or movement: *her slide into third base.* **2.** A smooth, usually inclined track or chute for sliding, especially a playground apparatus built for sliding down. **3.** A part that operates by sliding, such as the movable U-shaped section of tube on a trombone. **4.** An image formed on a transparent piece of material for projection on a screen. **5.** A small glass plate on which things are placed or mounted for examination by microscope. **6.** A fall of a mass of rock, earth, or snow down a slope; an avalanche or landslide. [From Old English *slīdan.*]

SYNONYMS **slide, glide, skid, coast** These verbs mean to move smoothly and continuously, often over a slippery surface. **Slide** suggests rapid, easy movement without loss of contact with the surface: *A tear slid down my cheek.* **Glide** means to move in a smooth, free-flowing, seemingly effortless way: *A submarine glided silently through the water.* **Skid** means to slide uncontrollably, often in a sideways direction: *The car skidded on a patch of ice.* **Coast** often means to slide downward, especially as a result of gravity: *We coasted down the hill on our sleds.*

---

slide rule *n.* A device that consists of two scaled rules arranged to slide along each other, having scales that correspond to the logarithms of numbers, allowing its use in performing multiplication, division, and more complex mathematical operations. Slide rules have now been largely replaced by computers and electronic calculators.

sli·er (slī′ər) *adj.* A comparative of **sly.**

sli·est (slī′ĭst) *adj.* A superlative of **sly.**

slight (slīt) *adj.* **slight·er, slight·est 1.** Small in size, amount, or degree: *a slight change in temperature.* **2.** Small and slender in build or construction; delicate. **3.** Of little importance; trifling: *a slight misunderstanding.* **4.** Lacking in strength or substance: *There was slight evidence he was right.* ❖ *tr.v.* **slight·ed, slight·ing, slights 1.** To treat as of small importance; underestimate. **2.** To snub or insult. **3.** To neglect: *Don't slight your schoolwork.* ❖ *n.* An act of slighting, especially an insult to one's pride or self-esteem. **—slight′ness** *n.*

slight·ing (slī′tĭng) *adj.* Constituting or conveying a slight; disrespectful; discourteous. **—slight′ing·ly** *adv.*

slight·ly (slīt′lē) *adv.* **1.** To a small degree or extent; somewhat. **2.** Slenderly; delicately: *slightly built.*

slim (slĭm) *adj.* **slim·mer, slim·mest 1.** Small in thickness as compared to height; slender; thin: *a slim person.* **2.** Small in quantity or amount; scant: *a slim chance of success.* ❖ *intr. & tr.v.* **slimmed, slim·ming, slims 1.** To become or make slim. **2.** To lose or cause to lose weight, as by diet or exercise. [From Middle Dutch *slimp,* bad, crooked.]

slime (slīm) *n.* **1.** A thick, sticky, slippery substance. **2.** A slippery mucous substance secreted by certain animals, such as fish or slugs.

slime mold *n.* Any of various organisms that are found on decaying organic matter and exist either as single cells resembling amoebas or as a slimy mass that produces stalked bodies containing spores.

slim·y (slī′mē) *adj.* **slim·i·er, slim·i·est 1.** Consisting of or resembling slime: *slimy ooze.* **2.** Covered with or secreting slime: *a slimy eel.* **3.** Vile or disgusting: *a slimy hypocrite.* **—slim′i·ness** *n.*

sling (slĭng) *n.* **1a.** A looped rope, strap, or chain for hoisting or supporting something. **b.** An adjustable strap for carrying a rifle over the shoulder. **c.** A band of cloth suspended from the neck to support an injured arm or hand. **2a.** A weapon made from a looped strap in which a stone is whirled and then let fly. **b.** A slingshot. ❖ *tr.v.* **slung** (slŭng), **sling·ing, slings 1.** To raise, lower, or move (a load) in a sling. **2.** To place or carry in a sling. **3.** To hurl with or as if with a sling. **4.** To place so as to hang loosely: *We slung the hammock between two trees.*

sling·shot (slĭng′shŏt′) *n.* A Y-shaped stick with an elastic strap attached to the prongs, used for shooting small stones.

slink (slĭngk) *intr.v.* **slunk** (slŭngk) also **slinked, slink·ing, slinks** To move in a quiet sneaky way.

slip¹ (slĭp) *v.* **slipped, slip·ping, slips** *—intr.* **1.** To move smoothly, easily, and quietly: *The spy slipped past the guards.* **2.** To slide and lose one's balance or foothold: *I slipped on the ice.* **3.** To slide out of place; shift position: *The beams supporting the mine's roof were beginning to slip.* **4.** To put on or remove a piece of clothing smoothly or quietly: *slipped into his new jacket; slipped out of his wet clothes.* **5.** To escape from a hold, grip, or restraint: *slipped out of the wrestler's hold.* **6.** To fall into fault or error: *slipped up and had to recalculate the figures.* **7a.** To change gradually, easily, or unnoticed: *The economy is slipping into a recession.* **b.** To elapse quickly or without notice: *The summer is slipping by.* **8.** To decline from a former standard or level; fall: *The senator's popularity has slipped.* *—tr.* **1.** To place or insert smoothly and quietly: *slip a rope over a branch; slip a note under the door.* **2.** To put on or remove (clothing) easily or quickly: *slipped off her shoes.* **3.** To get loose or free from: *The cat slipped my grasp.* ❖ *n.* **1.** The act or an instance of slipping or sliding, especially in losing one's balance. **2.** An error or oversight; a mistake. **3.** A docking place for a ship between two piers. **4a.** A woman's undergarment that hangs from the waist like a skirt. **b.** A woman's undergarment that hangs from shoulder straps like a gown. **5.** A pillowcase. ◆ **give (someone) the slip** *Slang* To escape the pursuit of (someone). **let slip** To say unintentionally or thoughtlessly. [From Middle English *slippen*, probably of Middle Low German or Middle Dutch origin.]

slip² (slĭp) *n.* **1.** A part of a plant cut or broken off for planting or grafting; a cutting. **2.** A small piece or strip, especially of paper: *a sales slip.* **3.** A slender youthful person: *a slip of a girl.* [Probably from Middle Low German or Middle Dutch *slippe*.]

slip·cov·er (slĭp′kŭv′ər) *n.* A removable cover of cloth or plastic that fits over a piece of upholstered furniture, such as a sofa.

slip·knot (slĭp′nŏt′) *n.* **1.** A knot made with a loop so that it can slip easily along the rope around which it is tied. **2.** A knot made so that it can be untied by pulling one free end of the rope.

slip-on (slĭp′ŏn′) *n.* A piece of clothing, such as a glove or shoe, that is easily slipped on and off.

slip·page (slĭp′ĭj) *n.* **1.** The act or an instance of slipping. **2.** The amount that something has slipped: *a slippage of 20 points in the stock market.*

slip·per (slĭp′ər) *n.* A low shoe that can be slipped on and off easily, usually worn indoors.

slip·per·y (slĭp′ə-rē) *adj.* **slip·per·i·er, slip·per·i·est 1.** Causing or tending to cause slipping, as a surface that is oily or wet. **2.** Not trustworthy; elusive or tricky: *a slippery character.* **—slip′per·i·ness** *n.*

slip·shod (slĭp′shŏd′) *adj.* **1.** Carelessly done or arranged: *a slipshod plan.* **2.** Careless or negligent: *a slipshod housekeeper.*

slip-up (slĭp′ŭp′) *n.* A mistake or oversight.

slit (slĭt) *n.* A long, straight, narrow cut or opening: *slits between the boards of a fence.* ❖ *tr.v.* **slit, slit·ting, slits 1.** To cut a slit or slits in. **2.** To cut lengthwise into strips; split. **—slit′ter** *n.*

slith·er (slĭth′ər) *intr.v.* **slith·ered, slith·er·ing, slith·ers 1.** To glide or slide like a snake. **2.** To slip and slide, as on a loose or uneven surface.

sliv·er (slĭv′ər) *n.* **1.** A slender piece cut, split, or broken off, as of wood or glass; a splinter. **2.** A small narrow portion of something: *a sliver of light through the crack in the wall.*

slob (slŏb) *n. Informal* A dirty, crude, and slovenly person.

slob·ber (slŏb′ər) *intr.v.* **slob·bered, slob·ber·ing, slob·bers 1.** To let saliva or liquid dribble from the mouth; drool. **2.** To express emotion in a foolishly sentimental way; gush. ❖ *n.* **1.** Saliva or liquid spilled from the mouth. **2.** Foolishly sentimental speech or writing. **—slob′ber·y** *adj.*

sloe (slō) *n.* **1.** A tart bluish-black fruit similar to a plum. **2.** The thorny Eurasian shrub that bears these fruits. **3.** Any of several North American shrubs that bear similar fruit. [From Old English *slā*, blackthorn fruit.]

❑ *These sound alike:* **sloe, slow** (not quick).

slog (slŏg) *v.* **slogged, slog·ging, slogs** *—intr.* **1.** To walk with a slow heavy gait; plod. **2.** To work very hard for long hours. *—tr.* To make (one's way) slowly, heavily, and with great effort: *The hikers slogged their way through the heavy snow.* ❖ *n.* **1.** A long session of hard work. **2.** A long exhausting march or hike. **—slog′ger** *n.*

slo·gan (slō′gən) *n.* **1.** A phrase expressing the aims or nature of an enterprise, organization, or political candidate; a motto. **2.** A phrase used repeatedly to advertise a commercial product or service. [From Scottish Gaelic *sluagh-ghairm*, battle cry.]

sloop (slo͞op) *n.* A single-masted, fore-and-aft-rigged sailing vessel.

slop (slŏp) *n.* **1.** Watery mud or a similar substance. **2.** Spilled or splashed liquid. **3.** Unappetizing watery food. **4.** often **slops** Waste food fed to animals. **5.** Overly gushy writing or speech. ❖ *v.* **slopped, slop·ping, slops** *—intr.* **1.** To be spilled or splashed: *Soup slopped over the edge of the bowl.* **2.** To walk heavily or messily, as through mud or puddles. *—tr.* **1.** To spill (liquid). **2.** To feed slops to (animals).

slope (slōp) *v.* **sloped, slop·ing, slopes** *—intr.* To incline upward or downward; be slanted. *—tr.* To cause to slope. ❖ *n.* **1.** An inclined line, plane, surface, direction, or position. **2.** A stretch of ground forming a natural or artificial incline: *ski slopes.* **3a.** A deviation from the horizontal plane or direction. **b.** The amount or measure of such a deviation: *a slope of 20 degrees.*

slop·py (slŏp′ē) *adj.* **slop·pi·er, slop·pi·est 1.** Messy; untidy: *a sloppy room.* **2.** Carelessly done; full of oversights or mistakes: *a sloppy research paper.* **3.** *Informal* Overly sentimental; gushy: *a sloppy greeting card.* **4.** Covered or spattered with watery mud or slush; muddy. **5.** Watery and disagreeable: *a sloppy stew.* **—slop′pi·ly** *adv.* **—slop′pi·ness** *n.*

slosh (slŏsh) *v.* **sloshed, slosh·ing, slosh·es** *—tr.* To spill or splash (a liquid). *—intr.* To flounder or splash in water or another liquid.

slot (slŏt) *n.* **1.** A narrow groove or opening: *a mail slot.* **2.** An assigned place, position, or time: *a new slot for the TV program on Tuesday night.* ❖ *tr.v.* **slot·ted, slot·ting,**

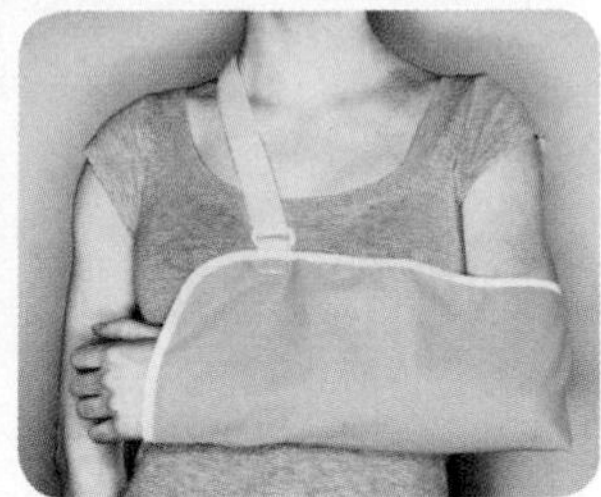

sling

slipknot

WRITERS CHOOSE THEIR WORDS

Oh, the stars were bright and beautiful and there was a **sliver** of silver moon coming up in the east. When the whaleboat rocked down on that side the silver **sliver** would suddenly rise up, like a slice in the sky; and then the whaleboat would rock back and it would disappear again.

—James Lincoln Collier and Christopher Collier
War Comes to Willy Freeman

sloop

sloth

slots **1.** To cut or make a slot or slots in. **2.** To assign to a slot: *The TV station slotted the game for prime time.*

sloth (slôth *or* slōth) *n.* **1.** Dislike and avoidance of work; laziness. **2.** Any of various slow-moving tropical American mammals that live in trees and hang upside-down from branches by their claws.

sloth·ful (slôth′fəl *or* slōth′fəl) *adj.* Sluggishly idle; lazy. —**sloth′ful·ly** *adv.* —**sloth′ful·ness** *n.*

slot machine *n.* A vending or gambling machine operated by inserting coins into a slot.

slouch (slouch) *intr.v.* **slouched, slouch·ing, slouch·es** To sit, stand, or walk with an awkward, drooping, bent posture. ❖ *n.* **1.** An awkward, drooping, overly relaxed posture or gait. **2.** *Slang* A lazy or incompetent person. —**slouch′y** *adj.*

slough¹ (slo͞o *or* slou) also **slew** (slo͞o) *n.* **1.** A hollow or depression in the ground, usually filled with mud or mire. **2.** A stagnant swamp, bog, or marsh. [From Old English *slōh.*]

❑ *These sound alike:* **slough¹, slew¹** (large amount), **slew²** (killed), **slew⁴** (turn).

slough² (slŭf) *n.* **1.** The dead outer skin shed by a reptile or amphibian. **2.** An outer layer or covering that is shed. ❖ *tr. & intr.v.* **sloughed, slough·ing, sloughs** To cast off or come off; shed: *The snake sloughed its old skin. The scab on his knee sloughed off.* [From Middle English.]

Slo·vak (slō′väk′ *or* slō′văk′) *adj.* Relating to Slovakia or its people, language, or culture. ❖ *n.* **1.** A native or inhabitant of Slovakia. **2.** The Slavic language of the Slovaks.

Slo·va·ki·a (slō-vä′kē-ə *or* slō-văk′ē-ə) A country of central Europe north of Hungary. It was part of Czechoslovakia from 1918 until 1993. Bratislava is the capital. —**Slo·va′ki·an** *n. & adj.*

slov·en (slŭv′ən) *n.* A person who is careless in personal appearance or work.

Slo·vene (slō′vēn′) also **Slo·ve·ni·an** (slō-vē′nē-ən) *adj.* Relating to Slovenia or its people, language, or culture. ❖ *n.* **1.** A native or inhabitant of Slovenia. **2.** The Slavic language of Slovenia.

Slo·ve·ni·a (slō-vē′nē-ə) A country of central Europe north of Croatia. Slovenia became part of Yugoslavia in 1918 and declared its independence in 1991. Ljubljana is the capital.

slov·en·ly (slŭv′ən-lē) *adj.* **1.** Untidy, as in dress or appearance: *slovenly garments.* **2.** Careless: *slovenly work.* —**slov′en·li·ness** *n.*

slow (slō) *adj.* **slow·er, slow·est 1.** Not moving, acting, or capable of moving or acting quickly; proceeding at a low speed: *a slow train.* **2.** Taking or requiring a long time or more time than usual: *a slow dinner.* **3.** Not suitable or made for rapid movement: *a slow track.* **4.** Behind the correct time: *My watch is slow.* **5.** Not quick or willing: *We were slow to volunteer for such a boring job.* **6.** Sluggish; inactive: *Business is slow.* **7.** Not having or showing mental quickness: *a slow learner.* **8.** Lacking excitement or interest; boring: *a slow party.* ❖ *adv.* **slower, slowest 1.** In a slow manner; not quickly or rapidly. **2.** So as to fall behind the correct time or rate: *This watch runs slow.* ❖ *tr. & intr.v.* **slowed, slow·ing, slows** To make or become slow or slower: *The wind slowed the car. The pace of the runners slowed.* [From Old English *slāw.*] —**slow′ly** *adv.* —**slow′ness** *n.*

❑ *These sound alike:* **slow, sloe** (fruit).

slow·down (slō′doun′) *n.* The act or process of slowing down, especially an intentional slowing down of production by labor or management.

slow motion *n.* The playing of a film or video recording at a slower rate than it was originally filmed or recorded at.

slow·poke (slō′pōk′) *n. Informal* A person who works, acts, or moves slowly.

sludge (slŭj) *n.* **1.** Semisolid material, as that formed from the treatment of sewage. **2.** Mire, mud, or ooze covering the ground or forming a deposit, as on a river bed. **3.** Finely broken or half-formed ice on a body of water. —**sludg′y** *adj.*

slue (slo͞o) *v.* Variant of **slew⁴.**

slug¹ (slŭg) *n.* **1.** Any of various slow-moving land mollusks that are related to the snails but have no shell. **2.** *Informal* A lazy idle person; a sluggard. **3a.** A bullet. **b.** A small metal disk for use in a vending or gambling machine, especially one used illegally. **4.** An amount of liquid swallowed in one gulp; a swig. [From Middle English *slugge*, sluggard, probably of Scandinavian origin.]

slug² (slŭg) *tr.v.* **slugged, slug·ging, slugs** To strike hard, especially with the fist or a bat. ❖ *n.* A hard blow, as with the fist or a baseball bat. [Possibly from *slug*, bullet.] —**slug′ger** *n.*

slug·gard (slŭg′ərd) *n.* A lazy idle person.

slug·gish (slŭg′ĭsh) *adj.* **1.** Showing little activity or movement; slow: *a sluggish stream.* **2.** Lacking alertness, vigor, or energy: *a sluggish response.* —**slug′gish·ly** *adv.* —**slug′gish·ness** *n.*

sluice (slo͞os) *n.* **1a.** An artificial channel for conducting water, with a gate to regulate the flow. **b.** The gate used in such a channel; a floodgate. **2.** A body of water confined and controlled by such a gate. **3.** A long inclined trough, as for moving logs or separating gold ore. ❖ *tr.v.* **sluiced, sluic·ing, sluic·es 1.** To flood or drench with a sudden flow of water. **2.** To draw off or let out by a sluice. **3.** To wash with water flowing from a sluice: *sluice sand for gold.*

slum (slŭm) *n.* An overcrowded urban area marked by squalor and poor housing conditions.

slum·ber (slŭm′bər) *intr.v.* **slum·bered, slum·ber·ing, slum·bers 1.** To sleep or doze. **2.** To be calm or inactive: *The city slumbers.* ❖ *n.* **1.** Sleep. **2.** A state of inactivity or dormancy. —**slum′ber·er** *n.* —**slum′ber·ous, slum′brous** *adj.*

slump (slŭmp) *intr.v.* **slumped, slump·ing, slumps 1.** To fall or sink heavily; collapse: *She slumped onto the sofa.* **2.** To droop or slouch: *The new recruits slumped outside their barracks.* **3.** To decline or sink suddenly: *Business slumped badly during the spring.* **4.** To perform poorly or inadequately: *The team has been slumping all month.* ❖ *n.* **1.** A sudden decline: *a stock market slump.* **2.** A drooping or slouching posture. **3.** An extended period of poor performance, especially in a sport: *a slump in his batting average.*

slung (slŭng) *v.* Past tense and past participle of **sling.**

slunk (slŭngk) *v.* A past tense and a past participle of **slink.**

slur (slûr) *tr.v.* **slurred, slur·ring, slurs 1.** To pronounce carelessly or indistinctly: *slur words.* **2.** To speak badly of; disparage. **3.** To sing or play (a series of musical tones) smoothly and without a break. ❖ *n.* **1.** A discourteous or disparaging remark: *The reporter apologized for writing slurs about the mayor.* **2.** A slurred sound. **3a.** A curved line connecting a series of notes on a musical score to indicate that they are to be played or sung smoothly. **b.** A passage played or sung in this manner.

slurp (slûrp) *tr. & intr.v.* **slurped, slurp·ing, slurps** To eat or drink noisily. ❖ *n.* A sucking noise made when eating or drinking.

slush (slŭsh) *n.* **1.** Partially melted snow or ice. **2.** Soft mud; mire. **3.** Sentimental speech or writing. —**slush′i·ness** *n.* —**slush′y** *adj.*

slush fund *n.* A fund raised for undesignated purposes.

sly (slī) *adj.* **sli·er** (slī′ər), **sli·est** (slī′ĭst) also **sly·er, sly·est 1.** Clever or cunning. **2.** Secretive or dishonest: *a sly trick.* **3.** Playfully mischievous; roguish: *a sly wink.* ◆ **on the sly** In a way intended to escape notice; secretly: *had another job on the sly.* —**sly′ness** *n.*

ă	pat	ôr	core
ā	pay	oi	boy
âr	care	ou	out
ä	father	o͝o	took
ĕ	pet	o͝or	lure
ē	be	o͞o	boot
ĭ	pit	ŭ	cut
ī	bite	ûr	urge
îr	pier	th	thin
ŏ	pot	*th*	this
ō	toe	zh	vision
ô	paw	ə	about

Sm The symbol for the element **samarium.**

smack[1] (smăk) *v.* **smacked, smack·ing, smacks** —*tr.* **1.** To press together and open (the lips) quickly and noisily, as in eating. **2.** To kiss noisily. **3.** To slap or strike with a loud sound. —*intr.* **1.** To make or give a smack. **2.** To collide loudly and sharply: *The notebook smacked against the floor.* ❖ *n.* **1.** The sound made by smacking the lips. **2.** A noisy kiss. **3.** A sharp blow or loud slap. ❖ *adv.* **1.** With a smack: *She flopped smack on her back.* **2.** Directly: *We're smack in the middle of a slump.*

smack[2] (smăk) *n.* **1.** A distinctive flavor or taste. **2.** A suggestion or trace. ❖ *intr.v.* **smacked, smack·ing, smacks 1.** To have a distinctive flavor or taste. **2.** To give an indication or suggestion: *This plan does not smack of success.* [From Old English *smæc.*]

small (smôl) *adj.* **small·er, small·est 1.** Being below the average in size, number, quantity, or extent; little: *a small car; a small business.* See Synonyms at **little. 2.** Limited in importance; trivial: *a small matter.* **3.** Carrying on an activity in a limited way: *a small farmer.* **4.** Not fully grown; very young: *a small child.* **5.** Narrow in outlook; petty: *a small mind.* **6.** Soft; low: *a small voice.* **7.** Lowercase: *type the password in small letters.* ❖ *n.* Something that is smaller or narrower than the rest: *the small of the back.* **—small′ish** *adj.* **—small′ness** *n.*

small arms *pl.n.* Firearms that can be carried in the hand.

small change *n.* **1.** Coins of low denomination. **2.** Something of little value or significance.

small fry *pl.n. Informal* Young or small children.

small intestine *n.* The part of the digestive tract in which digestion is completed and nutrients are absorbed by the blood, extending from the outlet of the stomach to the beginning of the large intestine. The human small intestine consists of the duodenum, the jejunum, and the ileum.

small-mind·ed (smôl′mīn′dĭd) *adj.* **1.** Having a narrow or selfish attitude. **2.** Characterized by pettiness or selfishness. **—small′-mind′ed·ly** *adv.* **—small′-mind′ed·ness** *n.*

small·pox (smôl′pŏks′) *n.* A serious, highly infectious, often fatal viral disease having symptoms that include fever and aches followed by the eruption of pimples that blister and develop into pockmarks. Vaccination campaigns eradicated smallpox worldwide by 1979, and the virus now exists only as a laboratory specimen.

small talk *n.* Casual or trivial conversation.

smart (smärt) *adj.* **smart·er, smart·est 1.** Intelligent, clever, or bright: *a smart student.* See Synonyms at **intelligent. 2.** Shrewd in dealing with others: *a smart business person.* **3.** Rudely flippant; impertinent: *That's enough of your smart talk!* **4.** Quick or energetic in movement: *a smart pace.* **5.** Fashionable; elegant: *a smart new coat.* **6.** Capable of making adjustments that resemble human decisions, especially in response to changing circumstances: *smart toys that respond to children's commands.* ❖ *intr.v.* **smart·ed, smart·ing, smarts** To cause or feel a sharp stinging pain: *My leg began to smart from the hornet's sting.* ❖ *n.* A stinging mental or physical pain. [From Old English *smeart*, stinging, causing pain.] **—smart′ly** *adv.* **—smart′ness** *n.*

smart al·eck (ăl′ĭk) *n. Informal* A person who makes impudent displays of knowledge. [Perhaps after *Aleck* Hoag, American confidence man and thief of the 1800s.]

smart bomb *n.* A bomb that can be guided by radio waves or a laser beam to its target.

smart·en (smär′tn) *v.* **smart·ened, smart·en·ing, smart·ens** —*tr.* **1.** To improve in appearance; spruce up. **2.** To make quicker: *smarten the pace.* —*intr.* To make oneself smart or smarter.

smart·phone (smärt′fōn′) *n.* A cell phone having a touchscreen or alphabetic keypad and many of the features of a personal computer.

smash (smăsh) *v.* **smashed, smash·ing, smash·es** —*tr.* **1.** To break (something) into pieces noisily and violently; shatter: *The ball smashed the window.* **2.** To knock or strike (something) forcefully: *The police smashed the door in.* **3.** To cause to come into forceful contact with something: *He smashed his bike into the fence.* **4.** To destroy or defeat completely: *The troops smashed the rebellion.* —*intr.* **1.** To break into pieces: *The vase smashed on the floor.* **2.** To strike or collide noisily and violently: *The car smashed into the guard rail.* ❖ *n.* **1.** The act or sound of smashing. **2.** A collision; a crash. **3.** A forceful overhand stroke, as in tennis. **4.** *Informal* A total success: *The show was a smash.* **—smash′er** *n.*

smash·ing (smăsh′ĭng) *adj. Informal* Unusually impressive or fine; wonderful: *a smashing time at the party.*

smash·up (smăsh′ŭp′) *n.* **1.** A total collapse; a failure. **2.** A serious collision between vehicles.

smat·ter·ing (smăt′ər-ĭng) *n.* A small, scattered amount, especially of knowledge: *He knows a smattering of Latin.*

smear (smîr) *v.* **smeared, smear·ing, smears** —*tr.* **1.** To spread with a sticky, greasy, or dirty substance: *smeared the wall with plaster.* **2.** To apply by spreading onto a surface: *I smeared lotion on my arms.* **3.** To blacken or destroy the reputation of: *The ad campaign smeared the candidate.* —*intr.* To spread across a surface, especially in an undesired way: *The ink smeared when I touched the paper.* ❖ *n.* **1.** A mark made by smearing. **2.** A substance placed on a slide for microscopic study. **3.** An attempt to destroy someone's reputation; slander.

smell (smĕl) *v.* **smelled** or **smelt** (smĕlt), **smell·ing, smells** —*tr.* To detect or notice the odor of (something) by means of the nerves located in the nose: *smell smoke.* —*intr.* **1a.** To have or give off an odor. **b.** To have or give off an unpleasant odor; stink. **2.** To use the sense of smell; detect the scent of something. ❖ *n.* **1.** The sense by which odors are perceived; the ability to smell. **2.** The quality that permits something to be perceived by the sense of smell; odor. **3.** The act or an instance of smelling. **4.** A distinctive quality; an aura or feeling: *This plan has a smell of success.*

SYNONYMS smell, aroma, scent, odor These nouns mean a quality that can be detected by sense organs in the nose. *The smell of gas in the hall alarmed us. The aroma of frying onions made me hungry. The scent of pine needles filled the cabin. The freshly painted room had a peculiar odor.*

---

smell·ing salts (smĕl′ĭng) *pl.n. (used with a singular or plural verb)* Any of several preparations based on ammonia, sniffed to relieve faintness and dizziness.

smell·y (smĕl′ē) *adj.* **smell·i·er, smell·i·est** *Informal* Having an unpleasant or offensive odor.

smelt[1] (smĕlt) *v.* **smelt·ed, smelt·ing, smelts** —*tr.* To melt or fuse (ores) in order to extract the metals they contain. —*intr.* To undergo such melting or fusing, as an ore does. [From Dutch or Low German *smelten.*]

smelt[2] (smĕlt) *n., pl.* **smelts** or **smelt** Any of various small, silvery, saltwater or freshwater fishes used as food. [From Old English.]

smelt[3] (smĕlt) *v.* A past tense and a past participle of **smell.**

smelt·er (smĕl′tər) *n.* **1a.** An apparatus or device for smelting ore. **b.** An establishment for smelting. **2.** A person whose work is smelting.

smid·gen also **smid·geon** (smĭj′ən) *n.* A very small quantity; a bit: *Add a smidgen of nutmeg.*

smile (smīl) *n.* A facial expression formed by an upward curving of the corners of the mouth and indicating pleasure, amusement, or derision. ❖ *v.* **smiled, smil·ing, smiles** —*intr.* **1.** To have or form a smile. **2.** To express favor or approval: *The committee smiled on our*

Bessie Smith
photographed in 1936

Joseph Smith

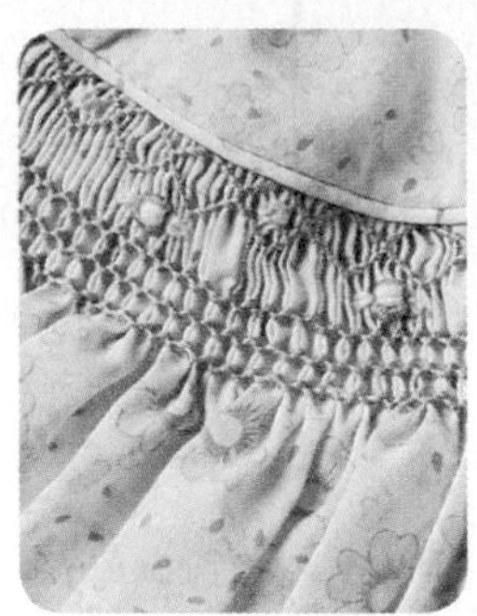

smocking

proposal. —*tr.* To express with a smile: *He smiled his agreement.* **—smil′er** *n.*

smil·ey (smī′lē) *n., pl.* **smil·eys** An emoticon, especially one indicating a smiling face [:-)].

smirch (smûrch) *tr.v.* **smirched, smirch·ing, smirch·es 1.** To soil, stain, or dirty. **2.** To dishonor or disgrace: *smirch the family's reputation.* ❖ *n.* Something that smirches; a blot or stain.

smirk (smûrk) *intr.v.* **smirked, smirk·ing, smirks** To smile in an annoyingly smug manner. ❖ *n.* A smile made in such a way. **—smirk′er** *n.*

smite (smīt) *tr.v.* **smote** (smōt), **smit·ten** (**smĭt′**n) or **smote, smit·ing, smites 1.** To hit with a heavy blow: *The sword smote the shield.* **2.** To attack, damage, or destroy by or as if by blows. **3.** To affect or afflict suddenly: *He was smitten with remorse.* **—smit′er** *n.*

smith (smĭth) *n.* A person who forges and shapes metal: *a blacksmith.*

Smith (smĭth), **Adam** 1723–1790. British political economist and philosopher. In *Wealth of Nations* (1776) he argued that economic markets should be allowed to operate without government regulations or with only minor restrictions.

Smith, Bessie 1894?–1937. American singer and songwriter who became a leading blues performer in the 1920s.

Smith, John 1580?–1631. English colonist whose accounts of his explorations in Virginia and New England aided later explorers and colonists.

Smith, Joseph 1805–1844. American religious leader who founded (1830) the Church of Jesus Christ of Latter-day Saints.

smith·er·eens (smĭ*th*′ə-**rēnz′**) *pl.n. Informal* Splintered pieces; bits: *The vase smashed to smithereens.*

smith·y (smĭth′ē *or* smĭ*th*′ē) *n., pl.* **smith·ies** The shop of a blacksmith; a forge.

smit·ten (smĭt′n) *v.* A past participle of **smite.**

smock (smŏk) *n.* A long loose garment resembling a coat, worn over other clothes to protect them while working. ❖ *tr.v.* **smocked, smock·ing, smocks 1.** To clothe in a smock. **2.** To decorate with smocking.

smock·ing (**smŏk′**ĭng) *n.* Needlework decoration consisting of small regularly spaced gathers stitched into a honeycomb pattern.

smog (smŏg) *n.* **1.** Fog that has become polluted with smoke, especially smoke from burning coal. **2.** A form of air pollution produced when sunlight reacts with hydrocarbons and nitrogen compounds released into the atmosphere, especially from automobile exhaust. Smog appears as a brownish haze and can irritate the eyes and lungs. [From *sm(oke)* + *(f)og.*] **—smog′gy** *adj.*

smoke (smōk) *n.* **1.** A mixture of gases and small suspended particles of soot or other solids, resulting from the burning of materials such as wood or coal. **2.** The act of smoking tobacco. **3.** *Informal* A cigarette or other form of tobacco that is smoked. ❖ *v.* **smoked, smok·ing, smokes** —*intr.* **1.** To inhale and exhale smoke from a cigarette, cigar, or pipe. **2.** To emit smoke: *I turned off the power when the motor began to smoke.* —*tr.* **1.** To inhale and exhale smoke from (a cigarette, cigar, or pipe). **2.** To preserve (meat or fish) by exposing to wood smoke. **3.** To expose to smoke or fumigate: *smoked the wasps' nest.* ◆ **smoke out** To force (someone or something) out of a place of hiding, especially by using smoke.

smoke detector *n.* An alarm device that automatically detects the presence of smoke.

smoke·house (**smōk′**hous′) *n.* An enclosure in which meat or fish is cured by exposing it to smoke.

smoke·less (**smōk′**lĭs) *adj.* Producing or giving off little or no smoke.

smok·er (**smō′**kər) *n.* **1.** A person who smokes tobacco. **2.** A device, such as a stove, that emits smoke.

smoke screen or **smoke·screen** (**smōk′**skrēn′) *n.* **1.** A mass of artificial smoke used to conceal military operations from an enemy. **2.** An action or statement used to conceal actual plans or intentions.

smoke·stack (**smōk′**stăk′) *n.* A large chimney or vertical pipe through which smoke and waste gases and vapors are discharged.

smok·y (**smō′**kē) *adj.* **smok·i·er, smok·i·est 1.** Producing or giving off a large amount of smoke: *needed to fix the smoky furnace.* **2.** Mixed or filled with smoke: *smoky air.* **3.** Resembling smoke in smell, taste, or appearance. **—smok′i·ness** *n.*

smol·der also **smoul·der** (**smōl′**dər) *intr.v.* **smol·dered, smol·der·ing, smol·ders** also **smoul·dered, smoul·der·ing, smoul·ders 1.** To burn with little smoke and no flame. **2.** To show signs of repressed anger or hatred: *He sat, still smoldering from the insult.* **3.** To exist in a restrained state: *Revolution smoldered among the common people.*

smooth (smo͞o*th*) *adj.* **smooth·er, smooth·est 1.** Having a surface free from irregularities; not rough; even: *the smooth surface of the polished stone.* **2.** Free from hair, whiskers, or stubble: *the smooth skin of the boy's face.* **3.** Having a fine consistency or texture: *the smooth side of the fabric.* **4.** Having an even or gentle motion or movement: *a smooth ride.* **5.** Having no obstructions or difficulties: *a smooth operation.* **6.** Serene; mild: *a smooth manner.* **7.** Flattering; ingratiating: *a smooth talker.* ❖ *tr.v.* **smoothed, smooth·ing, smoothes 1.** To make (something) smooth: *smooth out the wrinkles in a dress.* **2.** To make calm; soothe: *He smoothed over our disagreement.* **3.** To cause to appear less severe than is the case: *tried to smooth over my faults.* **—smooth′ly** *adv.* **—smooth′ness** *n.*

smooth·bore also **smooth bore** (**smo͞o*th*′bôr′**) *n.* A firearm having no rifling inside its bore.

smooth·ie (**smo͞o′***th*ē) *n.* A drink that is made by blending fruit or sometimes vegetables with juice, milk, or yogurt until smooth.

s'more (smôr) *n.* often **s'mores** A dessert or snack made of marshmallows, usually toasted over a campfire, and thin slabs of chocolate, which are then sandwiched together between graham crackers. [Contraction of *some more.*]

smor·gas·bord (**smôr′**gəs-bôrd′) *n.* **1.** A buffet meal with a variety of dishes. **2.** A varied collection: *an exhibit that was a smorgasbord of Renaissance art.* [From Swedish *smörgåsbord* : *smörgås,* bread and butter + *bord,* table.]

smote (smōt) *v.* Past tense and a past participle of **smite.**

smoth·er (**smŭ*th*′**ər) *v.* **smoth·ered, smoth·er·ing, smoth·ers** —*tr.* **1.** To cause (someone) to die from lack of oxygen; suffocate. **2.** To cause (a fire) to go out because of lack of oxygen. **3.** To cover thickly: *smother the hotdog with onions.* **4.** To conceal or hide: *smothered the facts.* **5.** To lavish too much attention on (someone). —*intr.* **1.** To suffocate. **2.** To be concealed or hidden.

smoul·der (**smōl′**dər) *v.* Variant of **smolder.**

smudge (smŭj) *v.* **smudged, smudg·ing, smudg·es** —*tr.* **1.** To smear or blur: *He touched the wet paint and smudged it.* **2.** To fill (an orchard or an inhabited area) with dense smoke from a smudge pot in order to prevent damage from frost or to repel insects. —*intr.* To become smudged: *mascara that smudges easily.* ❖ *n.* **1.** A blotch or smear. **2.** A smoky fire used to protect against frost or to repel insects. **—smudg′y** *adj.*

smudge pot *n.* A container in which oil or another smoky fuel is burned to repel insects or to protect an orchard from frost.

smug (smŭg) *adj.* **smug·ger, smug·gest** Satisfied or contented while having little concern for others: *had a smug sense of well-being.* **—smug′ly** *adv.* **—smug′ness** *n.*

ă	pat	ôr	core
ā	pay	oi	boy
âr	care	ou	out
ä	father	o͝o	took
ĕ	pet	o͝or	lure
ē	be	o͞o	boot
ĭ	pit	ŭ	cut
ī	bite	ûr	urge
îr	pier	th	thin
ŏ	pot	*th*	this
ō	toe	zh	vision
ô	paw	ə	about

smug·gle (smŭg′əl) *v.* **smug·gled, smug·gling, smug·gles** —*tr.* **1.** To import or export illegally or without paying custom charges: *smuggling drugs over the border.* **2.** To bring in or take out by stealth: *smuggled his puppy into the classroom.* —*intr.* To engage in smuggling. —**smug′gler** *n.*

smut (smŭt) *n.* **1.** Obscene material, such as books or movies. **2a.** Any of various plant diseases caused by fungi and resulting in the formation of black powdery masses on the affected plant parts. **b.** Any of the various fungi that cause such diseases. —**smut′ty** *adj.*

Smyr·na (smûr′nə) See **Izmir.**

Sn The symbol for the element **tin.**

snack (snăk) *n.* **1.** A quick light meal. **2.** Something eaten between meals. ❖ *intr.v.* **snacked, snack·ing, snacks** To eat a snack.

snaf·fle (snăf′əl) *n.* A bit for a horse, consisting of two bars joined at the center, as by a joint.

snag (snăg) *n.* **1.** A sharp, rough, or jagged projection. **2a.** A dead or partly dead tree that is still standing. **b.** A tree or part of a tree that sticks out above the surface in a body of water. **3.** A break, pull, or tear in fabric. **4.** An unforeseen or hidden obstacle: *Their travel plans have hit some snags.* ❖ *v.* **snagged, snag·ging, snags** —*tr.* **1.** To tear, damage, or destroy by a snag: *snagged her stocking.* **2.** *Informal* To catch or obtain quickly or unexpectedly: *snagged a fly ball; snagged a pair of tickets to the concert.* —*intr.* To be damaged or caught by a snag: *His sweater snagged on a tree branch.*

snail (snāl) *n.* **1.** Any of numerous slow-moving mollusks that have a coiled spiral shell. Some snails live on land, and some live in the water. **2.** A slow-moving, lazy, or sluggish person. [From Old English *snægl.*]

snail mail *n. Informal* Mail delivered by a postal system, as distinct from email.

snake (snāk) *n.* **1.** Any of numerous reptiles having a long narrow body and no legs. Some snakes have venom that they inject through their fangs. **2.** A sneaky or untrustworthy person. **3.** A long flexible wire or cable used for cleaning drains. [From Old English *snaca.*]

snake in the grass *n., pl.* **snakes in the grass** A person who is sneaky or untrustworthy.

snake·root (snāk′ro͞ot′ *or* snāk′ro͝ot′) *n.* Any of various plants having roots believed to cure the bite of a snake.

snake·skin (snāk′skĭn′) *n.* The skin of a snake, especially when prepared as leather.

snak·y (snā′kē) *adj.* **snak·i·er, snak·i·est 1.** Relating to or characteristic of snakes. **2.** Having the form or movement of a snake; serpentine. **3.** Treacherous; sly. —**snak′i·ly** *adv.* —**snak′i·ness** *n.*

snap (snăp) *v.* **snapped, snap·ping, snaps** —*intr.* **1.** To make a sharp cracking sound: *The burning log snapped in the fireplace.* **2.** To break suddenly with a sharp sound: *The twigs snapped underfoot.* **3.** To break under pressure or tension: *The rope snapped.* **4.** To suffer a physical or mental breakdown, especially while under stress. **5.** To bite, seize, or grasp at suddenly and eagerly: *The dog snapped at the bone.* **6.** To speak abruptly or sharply: *She snapped at him.* **7.** To open or close with a sharp sound: *The lid snapped shut.* **8.** To move swiftly and smartly: *The soldiers snapped to attention.* —*tr.* **1.** To break with a sharp sound. **2.** To bite or snatch at with the teeth. **3.** To cause to make a cracking sound: *snap one's fingers.* **4.** To close or shut with a sharp sound: *snap the lid on the jar.* **5.** To utter sharply or abruptly. **6.** To take (a photograph). **7.** In football, to put (the ball) in play by passing it from the line of scrimmage to a player in the backfield. ❖ *n.* **1.** A sharp cracking sound. **2.** A sudden breaking of something under strain. **3.** A fastener that closes and opens with a snapping sound. **4.** A thin crisp cookie. **5.** A brief spell of cold weather. **6.** *Informal* An easy task. **7.** A snapshot. ❖ *adj.* **1.** Made or done on the spur of the moment: *a snap decision.* **2.** *Informal* Simple; easy. ◆ **snap up** To acquire quickly: *snapped up the tickets.*

snap·drag·on (snăp′drăg′ən) *n.* Any of several garden plants having clusters of variously colored flowers whose petals are divided into an upper lip and a lower lip.

snap·per (snăp′ər) *n.* **1.** A person or thing that snaps. **2.** Any of numerous tropical and semitropical ocean fishes, many of which are used as food. **3.** A snapping turtle.

snap·ping turtle (snăp′ĭng) *n.* Any of several large American freshwater turtles having a rough shell and powerful hooked jaws that close with a snap.

snap·pish (snăp′ĭsh) *adj.* **1.** Likely to snap or bite, as a dog. **2.** Sharp in speech; irritable; curt. —**snap′pish·ly** *adv.* —**snap′pish·ness** *n.*

snap·py (snăp′ē) *adj.* **snap·pi·er, snap·pi·est 1.** *Informal* Lively; brisk: *a snappy rhythm.* **2.** *Informal* Smart or chic in appearance: *a snappy dresser.* **3.** Irritable; snappish: *snappy because of lack of sleep.* —**snap′pi·ly** *adv.* —**snap′pi·ness** *n.*

snap·shot (snăp′shŏt′) *n.* A photograph taken with a small handheld camera.

snare[1] (snâr) *n.* **1.** A trapping device, usually consisting of a noose, used for capturing birds and small animals. **2.** Something that entangles unsuspecting people: *The agents bought stolen goods as part of a snare to catch thieves.* ❖ *tr.v.* **snared, snar·ing, snares** To trap with or as if with a snare: *snare a rabbit; snare a thief.* [From Old English *snearu.*]

snare[2] (snâr) *n.* **1.** Any of the wires or cords stretched across the lower drumhead of a snare drum so as to vibrate against it when the drum is struck. **2.** A snare drum. [Probably from Middle Dutch *snāre,* string.]

snare drum *n.* A small double-headed drum having a snare or snares stretched across the lower head to make the tone rattling and sharp.

snark·y (snär′kē) *adj.* **snark·i·er, snark·i·est** *Slang* **1.** Rudely sarcastic or disrespectful; snide. **2.** Irritable or short-tempered. —**snark** *n.*

snarl[1] (snärl) *v.* **snarled, snarl·ing, snarls** —*intr.* **1.** To growl angrily or threateningly while baring the teeth. **2.** To speak angrily or threateningly. —*tr.* To utter with anger or hostility: *snarled an answer.* ❖ *n.* **1.** An angry or threatening growl, often made with bared teeth. **2.** A sound or tone of voice resembling this: *He made his demands in a grumpy snarl.* [Perhaps from Dutch *snarren,* to snarl.]

snarl[2] (snärl) *n.* **1.** A tangled mass, as of hair or yarn. **2.** A confused, complicated, or tangled situation: *a traffic snarl.* ❖ *v.* **snarled, snarl·ing, snarls** —*intr.* To become tangled: *My fishing line snarled as I made a cast.* —*tr.* **1.** To tangle: *The kitten snarled the wool.* **2.** To confuse: *Snow snarled the morning commute.* [From Middle English *snarle,* trap, probably from *snare.*]

snatch (snăch) *v.* **snatched, snatch·ing, snatch·es** —*tr.* **1.** To grasp or grab hastily or eagerly: *snatch an apple off the tree.* **2.** To take unlawfully: *snatch a purse.* —*intr.* To make grasping motions: *snatched at the rope.* ❖ *n.* **1.** The act of snatching. **2.** A small amount; a fragment: *a snatch of dialogue.* —**snatch′er** *n.*

sneak (snēk) *v.* **sneaked** also **snuck** (snŭk), **sneak·ing, sneaks** —*intr.* **1.** To go or move in a quiet stealthy way: *She sneaked onto one of the boats.* **2.** To behave in a cowardly underhanded manner: *Don't sneak around.* —*tr.* To move, give, or take in a quiet stealthy manner: *sneaked the photo into his pocket; sneak a peek at the present.* ❖ *n.* **1.** A cowardly or underhanded person. **2.** A quiet stealthy movement or action. —SEE NOTE.

sneak·er (snē′kər) *n.* A shoe for athletic use or casual wear, usually made of a flexible material with a soft rubber sole.

sneak·ing (snē′kĭng) *adj.* **1.** Acting in a stealthy furtive way. **2.** Not known or expressed: *a sneaking ambition to*

snaffle

snapdragon

snare drum

USAGE

sneak The word **sneak** has two past tense and past participle forms: *sneaked* and *snuck.* Both forms are acceptable, but because *snuck* was originally only used in certain regions, it has a more informal feel than *sneaked* does.

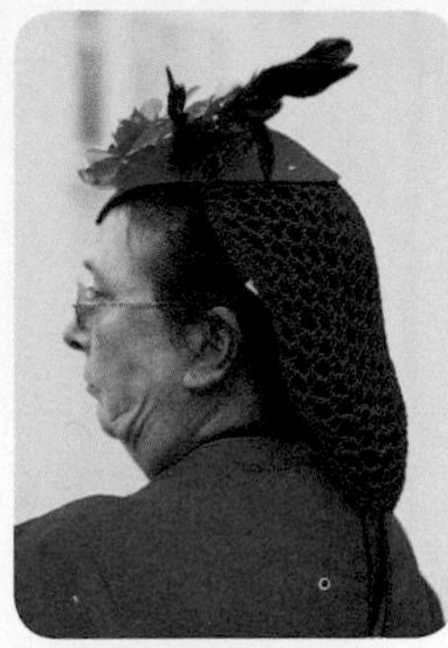

snood
hair net snood *(top)* and turkey snood *(bottom)*

snorkel

ă	pat	ôr	core
ā	pay	oi	boy
âr	care	ou	out
ä	father	ŏŏ	took
ĕ	pet	ŏŏr	lure
ē	be	ōō	boot
ĭ	pit	ŭ	cut
ī	bite	ûr	urge
îr	pier	th	thin
ŏ	pot	*th*	this
ō	toe	zh	vision
ô	paw	ə	about

take over. **3.** Gradually growing or persistent: *a sneaking suspicion.* **—sneak′ing·ly** *adv.*

sneak·y (snē′kē) *adj.* **sneak·i·er, sneak·i·est** Like a sneak; sly; furtive: *A sneaky cat ate my favorite goldfish.* **—sneak′i·ly** *adv.* **—sneak′i·ness** *n.*

sneer (snîr) *n.* **1.** A scornful facial expression made by raising one corner of the upper lip slightly. **2.** A scornful expression, sound, or statement. ❖ *v.* **sneered, sneer·ing, sneers** *—tr.* To utter with a sneer. *—intr.* To show contempt or scorn with a sneer. [From Middle English *sneren,* to mock, from Old English *fnǣran,* to breathe heavily.] **—sneer′er** *n.*

sneeze (snēz) *intr.v.* **sneezed, sneez·ing, sneez·es** To force air from the nose and mouth in an involuntary convulsive action that results from irritation of the mucous membranes of the nose. ❖ *n.* The act or the sound of sneezing. [From Old English *fnēosan.*] **—sneez′er** *n.*

snick·er (snĭk′ər) *intr.v.* **snick·ered, snick·er·ing, snick·ers** To utter a snide, partly stifled laugh. ❖ *n.* A snide, partly stifled laugh.

snide (snīd) *adj.* **snid·er, snid·est** Sarcastic, disparaging, or cruel: *a snide remark.* **—snide′ly** *adv.*

sniff (snĭf) *v.* **sniffed, sniff·ing, sniffs** *—intr.* **1.** To inhale a short audible breath through the nose, as in smelling something: *He sniffed at the jar.* **2.** To regard something with contempt or scorn: *She sniffed at those who knew less than she.* *—tr.* **1.** To inhale (something) through the nose: *sniffed the cold air.* **2.** To smell, as in enjoyment or investigation: *sniffed the roses.* **3.** To perceive or detect by or as if by sniffing: *The dog sniffed the bear's trail.* ❖ *n.* **1.** The act or the sound of sniffing. **2.** Something noticed or detected by or as if by sniffing: *a sniff of perfume; a sniff of scandal.*

snif·fle (snĭf′əl) *intr.v.* **snif·fled, snif·fling, snif·fles** To inhale briefly or repeatedly through a runny nose, as when one has a cold. ❖ *n.* **1.** The act or sound of sniffling. **2. sniffles** A condition, such as a cold, that makes a person sniffle.

snig·ger (snĭg′ər) *n.* A snicker. **—snig′ger** *v.*

snip (snĭp) *tr.v.* **snipped, snip·ping, snips** To cut or clip (something) with short quick strokes. ❖ *n.* **1.** A small piece cut or clipped off: *snips of hair lay on the floor of the barbershop.* **2.** An instance of snipping or the sound so produced. **3. snips** *(used with a singular or plural verb)* Hand shears used to cut sheet metal. **—snip·per** *n.*

snipe (snīp) *n., pl.* **snipe** or **snipes** Any of various brownish shorebirds having a long bill. ❖ *intr.v.* **sniped, snip·ing, snipes 1.** To shoot at others from a hiding place. **2.** To make petty or snide remarks to or about someone.

snip·er (snī′pər) *n.* A person who shoots at others from a hiding place.

snip·pet (snĭp′ĭt) *n.* A tidbit or morsel.

snip·py (snĭp′ē) *adj.* **snip·pi·er, snip·pi·est** *Informal* **1.** Curt and sharp-tempered: *a snippy retort.* **2.** Fragmentary.

snitch (snĭch) *Slang v.* **snitched, snitch·ing, snitch·es** *—intr.* To tell on someone; turn informer: *snitched on his brother.* *—tr.* To steal (something of little value): *snitched candy from the store.* ❖ *n.* **1.** A thief. **2.** An informer. **—snitch′er** *n.*

sniv·el (snĭv′əl) *intr.v.* **sniv·eled, sniv·el·ing, sniv·els** or **sniv·elled, sniv·el·ling, sniv·els 1.** To sniffle. **2.** To complain or whine tearfully. **—sniv′el·er, sniv′el·ler** *n.*

snob (snŏb) *n.* **1.** Someone who looks down on or snubs people he or she considers as being of a lower social class. **2.** Someone who feels undue pride in his or her perceived superiority in taste or intellect: *a musical snob.*

snob·ber·y (snŏb′ə-rē) *n., pl.* **snob·ber·ies** Snobbish behavior.

snob·bish (snŏb′ĭsh) *adj.* Befitting or characteristic of a snob; pretentious: *a snobbish attitude.* **—snob′bish·ly** *adv.* **—snob′bish·ness** *n.*

snood (snŏŏd) *n.* **1.** A net cap worn on the head to keep the hair in place. **2.** A fleshy wrinkled fold of skin that hangs down over a turkey's beak.

snoop (snōōp) *intr.v.* **snooped, snoop·ing, snoops** To look, pry, or search in a sneaky manner. ❖ *n.* A person who snoops. **—snoop′er** *n.*

snoop·y (snōō′pē) *adj.* **snoop·i·er, snoop·i·est** Likely to snoop; nosy: *He avoided his snoopy neighbors.*

snoot·y (snōō′tē) *adj.* **snoot·i·er, snoot·i·est** *Informal* **1.** Snobbishly aloof; haughty. **2.** High-class; exclusive. **—snoot′i·ly** *adv.* **—snoot′i·ness** *n.*

snooze (snōōz) *intr.v.* **snoozed, snooz·ing, snooz·es** To take a light nap; doze. ❖ *n.* A light nap.

snore (snôr) *intr.v.* **snored, snor·ing, snores** To breathe during sleep with harsh snorting noises caused by vibration of the soft palate. ❖ *n.* The act or the sound of snoring. [From Middle English *snoren,* to snort, from Old English *fnora,* sneezing.] **—snor′er** *n.*

snor·kel (snôr′kəl) *n.* **1.** A breathing apparatus used by swimmers and skin divers, consisting of a long tube curved at one end and held in the mouth. **2.** A retractable tube that can be extended from a submarine, allowing it to draw in fresh air and expel waste gases while submerged. ❖ *intr.v.* **snor·keled, snor·kel·ing, snor·kels** To swim using a snorkel. [From German *Schnorchel.*]

snort (snôrt) *n.* **1.** A rough noisy sound made by breathing forcefully through the nostrils, as that made by a horse or pig. **2.** A sound resembling this: *the snort of a steam engine.* ❖ *v.* **snort·ed, snort·ing, snorts** *—intr.* **1.** To breathe noisily and forcefully through the nostrils: *The frightened horses reared and snorted.* **2.** To make a sound resembling noisy breathing. **3.** To make a noise expressive of ridicule, disbelief, or contempt. *—tr.* To express with a snort: *She snorted her disapproval.*

snout (snout) *n.* **1.** The projecting nose, jaws, or front part of the head of an animal. **2.** A spout or nozzle shaped like such a projection. [From Middle English.] **—snout′ed** *adj.*

snow (snō) *n.* **1.** Crystals of ice that form from water vapor in the atmosphere and fall to the earth. **2.** A falling of snow; a snowstorm. **3.** Specks of light that appear on a television screen as a result of weak reception of the video signal. ❖ *v.* **snowed, snow·ing, snows** *—intr.* To fall to the earth as snow. *—tr.* To isolate, block, or cover with or as if with snow: *We were snowed in.* ◆ **snow under** To overwhelm: *I was snowed under with work.* [From Old English *snāw.*]

snow·ball (snō′bôl′) *n.* **1.** A mass of soft wet snow packed into a ball that can be thrown. **2.** Any of several shrubs having large rounded clusters of white flowers. ❖ *intr.v.* **snow·balled, snow·ball·ing, snow·balls** To grow rapidly in significance, importance, or size: *The small protests snowballed into a full-scale revolution.*

snow·bird (snō′bûrd′) *n.* **1.** Any of several birds, such as the junco, common in snowy regions. **2.** One who moves from a cold to a warm place in the winter.

snow blindness *n.* A usually temporary loss of vision and irritation of the eyes caused by exposure of the eyes to bright sunlight reflected from snow or ice.

snow·blow·er (snō′blō′ər) *n.* A machine that clears snow from a surface by collecting it in an auger and projecting it through a chute.

snow·board (snō′bôrd′) *n.* A narrow board equipped with bindings, ridden in a standing or crouching position down snow-covered slopes. ❖ *intr.v.* **snow·board·ed, snow·board·ing, snow·boards** To ride on a snowboard. **—snow′board′er** *n.*

snow·bound (snō′bound′) *adj.* Confined to one place because of heavy snow: *snowbound travelers.*

snow bunting *n.* A small bird of northern regions that has mostly white feathers in the winter.

snow·cap (snō′kăp′) *n.* A cap of snow, as on a mountaintop. **—snow′capped′** *adj.*

snow·drift (snō′drĭft′) *n.* A large mass of snow that has been piled up by the wind.

snow·drop (snō′drŏp′) *n.* Any of several plants having drooping white flowers that bloom in early spring.

snow·fall (snō′fôl′) *n.* **1.** A falling of snow. **2.** The amount of snow in a given area over a given period of time.

snow·flake (snō′flāk′) *n.* A single crystal or flake of snow.

snow·kit·ing (snō′kī′tĭng) *n.* The sport of being pulled across snow or ice by a power kite while riding a snowboard or wearing skis. **—snow′kite′** *v.* **—snow·kit′er** *n.*

snow leopard *n.* A large wild cat of the mountains of Central and South Asia, having long, thick, whitish fur with dark spots.

snow line *n.* **1.** The boundary marking the lowest altitude at which a given area is currently or permanently covered with snow, as on a mountain. **2.** The varying boundary marking the lowest latitude around the polar regions at which there is snow cover.

snow·man (snō′măn′) *n.* A figure of a person made from packed and shaped snow, usually formed by piling large snowballs on top of each other.

snow·mo·bile (snō′mō-bēl′) *n.* A small motorized vehicle for traveling on snow. It has skilike runners in front and tanklike treads and is ridden by straddling a seat.

snow·plow (snō′plou′) *n.* **1.** A vehicle or machine equipped with a flat or slightly curved surface used to remove snow, as from roads and railroad tracks. **2.** A skiing maneuver for stopping or slowing in which the tips of the skis are angled together.

snow·shoe (snō′sho͞o′) *n.* An oblong frame, usually strung with interlaced strips or a tightly stretched membrane, strapped to the foot to enable walking on deep snow. ❖ *intr.v.* **snow·shoed, snow·shoe·ing, snow·shoes** To walk or travel on snowshoes.

snowshoe hare *n.* A hare of northern North America, having large furry feet and fur that is white in winter and brown in summer.

snow·skate (snō′skāt′) *n.* A board resembling a small snowboard without bindings, ridden in a standing or crouching position down snow-covered slopes or ramps and often used to perform stunts. ❖ *intr.v.* **snow·skat·ed, snow·skat·ing, snow·skates** To use a snowskate. **—snow′skat′er** *n.*

snow·storm (snō′stôrm′) *n.* A storm with heavy snowfall and high winds.

snow·y (snō′ē) *adj.* **snow·i·er, snow·i·est 1a.** Full of or covered with snow. **b.** Subject to snowfall. **2.** Resembling snow; white: *snowy petals.*

snub (snŭb) *tr.v.* **snubbed, snub·bing, snubs 1.** To treat with scorn or contempt. **2a.** To check the movement of (a rope or cable) by securing it to a post or cleat. **b.** To secure (a boat) in this manner. ❖ *n.* **1.** A deliberate slight; scornful treatment. **2.** A sudden securing or checking of a rope.

snub-nosed (snŭb′nōzd′) *adj.* **1.** Having a short turned-up nose. **2.** Having an extremely short barrel: *a snub-nosed pistol.*

snuck (snŭk) *v.* A past tense and a past participle of **sneak.**

snuff¹ (snŭf) *v.* **snuffed, snuff·ing, snuffs** *—tr.* **1.** To inhale (something) through the nose; sniff. **2.** To examine (something) by smelling; sniff at. *—intr.* To sniff; inhale. [From Middle English *snoffen*, to sniffle, probably from *snoffe*, burned part of a candle.]

snuff² (snŭf) *tr.v.* **snuffed, snuff·ing, snuffs 1.** To put out; extinguish: *snuff out a candle.* **2.** To put an end to; destroy. **3.** To cut off the charred portion of (a candlewick). [From Middle English *snoffen.*]

snuff³ (snŭf) *n.* A preparation of finely pulverized or shredded tobacco that can be drawn up into the nostrils by inhaling or placed in the mouth between the lower lip and the gum. ◆ **up to snuff** Up to standard; adequate. [From Dutch *snuffen*, to sniff.]

snuff·box (snŭf′bŏks′) *n.* A small box used for carrying snuff.

snuf·fle (snŭf′əl) *v.* **snuf·fled, snuf·fling, snuf·fles** *—intr.* To breathe noisily through the nose; sniffle. *—tr.* To utter in a sniffling tone. ❖ *n.* The act or sound of snuffling.

snug (snŭg) *adj.* **snug·ger, snug·gest 1.** Pleasant and comfortable; cozy: *a snug apartment.* **2.** Close-fitting: *a snug sweater.* **3.** Secure; safe: *a snug hideout; a snug living.* **—snug′ly** *adv.*

snug·gle (snŭg′əl) *intr. & tr.v.* **snug·gled, snug·gling, snug·gles 1.** To lie or press close together; cuddle. **2.** To curl up closely or comfortably; nestle: *snuggle up under the covers.*

so¹ (sō) *adv.* **1.** In such a manner: *Why must you complain so?* **2.** To such an extent: *I'm so happy that I could cry.* **3.** To a great extent: *The idea is so obvious.* **4.** Consequently; as a result: *He refused to study for the exam and so nearly failed.* **5.** Approximately that amount or number; thereabouts: *The student fare is only $10 or so.* **6.** In the same way; also; likewise: *She likes the book and so do I.* **7.** Apparently: *So you think you've got troubles?* **8.** In truth; indeed: *"You aren't telling the truth." "I am so."* ❖ *adj.* **1.** True; factual: *I wouldn't have told you this if it weren't so.* **2.** Having the quality previously mentioned: *He got sick last week and has been so ever since.* ❖ *conj.* **1.** With the result or consequence that: *He failed to show up, so we went without him.* **2.** In order that: *I stayed so I could see you.* ❖ *interj.* An expression used to show surprise or comprehension: *So, you finished on time after all.* ◆ **and so on** or **and so forth** And similarly; and continuing in a like manner. **so as to** In order to: *Go early so as to be sure to get a good seat.* **so that 1.** With the purpose that: *I stopped so that you could catch up.* **2.** With the result or consequence that: *The draw bridge got stuck, so that the boats could not pass.* **so what** An expression used to express contempt or lack of interest. [From Old English *swā.*] —SEE NOTE.

❑ *These sound alike:* **so¹** (thus), **sew** (stitch), **so²** (musical note), **sow¹** (plant seed).

so² (sō) *n.* Variant of **sol¹.**

❑ *These sound alike:* **so²** (musical note), **sew** (stitch), **so¹** (thus), **sow¹** (plant seed).

SO *abbr.* An abbreviation of strikeout.

so. or **So.** *abbr.* An abbreviation of: **1.** south. **2.** southern.

soak (sōk) *v.* **soaked, soak·ing, soaks** *—tr.* **1.** To immerse in a liquid: *Soak the beans in water until soft.* **2.** To make thoroughly wet or saturated: *Soak the flowers with the hose.* **3.** To absorb (liquid, for example): *Sponges soak up moisture.* **4.** *Slang* To overcharge (someone) for something. *—intr.* **1.** To be immersed in a liquid: *The beans are soaking in water.* **2.** To seep into or permeate something: *Water is soaking into the soil.* **3.** To be taken into the mind: *She paused to let her words soak in.* ❖ *n.* The act or process of soaking: *a soak in the bathtub.* [From Old English *socian.*]

so-and-so (sō′ən-sō′) *pron.* An unnamed or unspecified person or thing: *always complaining to so-and-so about something.* ❖ *n., pl.* **so-and-sos** *Informal* Someone who is regarded as despicable: *that no-good so-and so!*

soap (sōp) *n.* **1.** A cleansing agent, manufactured in the form of bars, granules, flakes, or liquid, consisting of a mixture of the sodium or potassium salts of fatty acids that occur in natural fats and oils. **2.** A soap opera: *I watch my favorite soaps every day.* ❖ *tr.v.* **soaped, soap·ing, soaps** To treat or cover with or as if with soap. [From Old English *sāpe.*]

snowboard

snowkiting

snowshoe

USAGE

so¹ You can use either the word **so¹** or the phrase *so that* when you introduce a clause giving the reason for or purpose of an action: *He stayed so* (or *so that*) *he could hear the band's second set.* You can also use *so* or *so that* to introduce clauses that state a result or consequence: *The bridge was still closed, so* (or *so that*) *the drive took an hour.*

WRITERS CHOOSE THEIR WORDS

I was attempting my prayers in contemplative silence, as is my preferred custom of years, when I came upon one of the steerage passengers, on his hands and knees by the First-Class gates, and most violently ill from the sea. This is a curious and noteworthy character, his behaviour oftentimes odd. Though badly afflicted with a deformed foot, he is fond of walking the ship by night, and is known among the men by the **sobriquet** of "The Ghost."

—Joseph O'Connor
Star of the Sea

soccer

ă	pat	ôr	core
ā	pay	oi	boy
âr	care	ou	out
ä	father	ŏŏ	took
ĕ	pet	ŏŏr	lure
ē	be	ōō	boot
ĭ	pit	ŭ	cut
ī	bite	ûr	urge
îr	pier	th	thin
ŏ	pot	*th*	this
ō	toe	zh	vision
ô	paw	ə	about

soap·box (sōp′bŏks′) *n.* **1.** A carton in which soap is packed. **2.** A temporary platform used while making an unprepared public speech.

soap opera *n.* A drama, typically performed as a serial on daytime radio or television and characterized by sentimentality and melodrama.

soap·stone (sōp′stōn′) *n.* A soft metamorphic rock composed mostly of the mineral talc.

soap·suds (sōp′sŭdz′) *pl.n.* Suds from soapy water.

soap·y (sō′pē) *adj.* **soap·i·er, soap·i·est 1.** Covered or filled with soap: *soapy water.* **2.** Resembling soap: *a soapy texture.* **—soap′i·ness** *n.*

soar (sôr) *intr.v.* **soared, soar·ing, soars 1.** To rise, fly, or glide high, especially by using rising air currents and moving with little apparent effort, as eagles and hawks do. **2.** To rise suddenly, especially above what is normal: *The cost of living soared.*

❑ *These sound alike:* **soar, sore** (painful).

sob (sŏb) *v.* **sobbed, sob·bing, sobs** *—intr.* **1.** To weep aloud with gasps and sniffles; cry uncontrollably. See Synonyms at **cry. 2.** To utter with gasps and sniffles. *—tr.* **1.** To utter with sobs. **2.** To put or bring (oneself) to a specific state or condition by sobbing: *sob oneself to sleep.* ❖ *n.* The act or sound of sobbing. [From Middle English *sobben*, perhaps of Low German origin.]

so·ba (sō′bə) *n.* A kind of noodle made with buckwheat flour, used in Japanese cooking. [From Japanese, short for earlier *sobamugi* : *soba*, edge (in reference to three-cornered shape of the buckwheat seed) + *mugi*, barley.]

so·ber (sō′bər) *adj.* **so·ber·er, so·ber·est 1.** Not intoxicated or affected by the use of alcoholic beverages or drugs. **2.** Serious or grave: *a sober temperament.* **3.** Lacking frivolity or exaggeration: *a sober assessment of the situation.* **4.** Plain or subdued: *sober clothing.* ❖ *tr. & intr.v.* **so·bered, so·ber·ing, so·bers** To make or become sober: *The news sobered us to the difficulties we could face.* [From Middle English, from Latin *sōbrius.*] **—so′ber·ly** *adv.* **—so′ber·ness** *n.*

so·bri·e·ty (sə-brī′ĭ-tē) *n.* The state or condition of being sober.

so·bri·quet (sō′brĭ-kā′ *or* sō′brĭ-kĕt′) *n.* A nickname.

so-called (sō′kôld′) *adj.* **1.** Commonly called. **2.** Incorrectly termed: *a so-called musician.*

soc·cer (sŏk′ər) *n.* A game played with a round ball by two teams of 11 players each on a rectangular field with net goals at either end. The object is to put the ball into the opponents' goal without touching the ball with the arms or hands. [Alteration of *assoc.*, from *assoc(iation football).*]

so·cia·ble (sō′shə-bəl) *adj.* **1.** Liking company; friendly: *a sociable person.* **2.** Involving pleasant conversation: *Dinner is often the most sociable meal of the day.* **—so′cia·bil′i·ty, so′cia·ble·ness** *n.* **—so′cia·bly** *adv.*

so·cial (sō′shəl) *adj.* **1.** Relating to human society and how it is organized: *The family is a social structure.* **2.** Relating to rank or status in society: *social position.* **3.** Relating to matters affecting human welfare: *a state's social programs.* **4.** Relating to or being animals, especially insects, that live together in organized groups: *Ants, bees, and termites are social insects.* **5.** Relating to friendship and friendly relations: *She has an active social life.* **6.** Sociable or companionable: *a very social person.* ❖ *n.* An informal social gathering: *a church social.* [From Middle English *sociale*, domestic, from Latin *socius*, companion.]

so·cial·ism (sō′shə-lĭz′əm) *n.* **1.** A social system in which the government or the whole community owns the means of production, such as land and factories, and controls the distribution of goods and services. **2.** A theory or political movement supporting such a system.

so·cial·ist (sō′shə-lĭst) *n.* **1.** A person who believes in or advocates socialism. **2.** often **Socialist** A member of a party or group that advocates socialism. ❖ *adj.* Relating to socialism.

so·cial·is·tic (sō′shə-lĭs′tĭk) *adj.* Relating to, advocating, or tending toward socialism. **—so′cial·is′ti·cal·ly** *adv.*

so·cial·ite (sō′shə-līt′) *n.* A person who is prominent in fashionable society.

so·cial·ize (sō′shə-līz′) *v.* **so·cial·ized, so·cial·iz·ing, so·cial·iz·es** *—tr.* **1.** To place under government or group ownership or control: *a proposal to socialize the medical system.* **2.** To make fit for companionship with others. *—intr.* To take part in social activities. **—so′cial·i·za′tion** (sō′shə-lĭ-zā′shən) *n.*

so·cial·ly (sō′shə-lē) *adv.* **1.** In a social manner: *He is socially successful.* **2.** With regard to society: *socially important government policies.* **3.** By society: *socially acceptable behavior.*

social science *n.* Any of various scholarly or scientific fields that deal with the study of human society and of individual relationships within it, especially sociology, psychology, anthropology, economics, political science, and history. **—social scientist** *n.*

Social Security *n.* A US government program that provides financial assistance to the elderly, unemployed, or disabled, financed by a tax on employers and employees.

social service *n.* A service, such as free school lunches or an afterschool program, that a government provides, especially for disadvantaged citizens.

social studies *pl.n. (used with a singular or plural verb)* A course of study that includes geography, history, government, and sociology, taught in elementary and secondary schools.

social work *n.* Organized work and social services intended to improve the social condition of a community, and especially of the disadvantaged, by providing psychological counseling, guidance, and assistance. **—social worker** *n.*

so·ci·e·tal (sə-sī′ĭ-tl) *adj.* Relating to the structure, organization, or functioning of society.

so·ci·e·ty (sə-sī′ĭ-tē) *n., pl.* **so·ci·e·ties 1.** A group of people sharing a distinctive common culture. **2.** An organization or association of people sharing common interests or activities: *an archaeological society.* **3.** The rich, privileged, and fashionable social class. **4.** Companionship or company: *enjoying the society of friends.* **5.** A group of living things, usually of the same kind, living and functioning together: *a society of bees forming a single hive.*

Society Islands An island group in the southern Pacific Ocean east of Samoa. The islands became a French protectorate in 1843.

Society of Friends *n.* A Christian group, founded in the mid-1600s in England, that is opposed to war, oathtaking, and rituals; the Quakers.

Society of Jesus *n.* A Roman Catholic order of regular clergy, founded in 1534 by St. Ignatius of Loyola (1491–1556), that is committed to education, scholarship, and missionary work; the Jesuits.

so·ci·ol·o·gy (sō′sē-ŏl′ə-jē *or* sō′shē-ŏl′ə-jē) *n.* The study of human social behavior and its origins, development, organizations, and institutions. **—so′ci·o·log′i·cal** (sō′sē-ə-lŏj′ĭ-kəl *or* sō′shē-ə-lŏj′ĭ-kəl) *adj.* **—so′ci·ol′o·gist** *n.*

sock[1] (sŏk) *n.* A short stocking reaching a point between the ankle and the knee. [From Old English *socc*, a light shoe, from Latin *soccus.*]

sock[2] (sŏk) *tr.v.* **socked, sock·ing, socks** To hit forcefully: *socked the ball out of the park.* ❖ *n.* A punch.

sock·et (sŏk′ĭt) *n.* **1.** An opening or cavity into which an inserted part is designed to fit: *a light bulb socket.* **2a.** A hollow part in a bone into which a projection from another bone fits, as at a joint. **b.** A hollow part or hole into which a body part, such as an eye, fits.

socket wrench *n.* A wrench with interchangeable sockets to fit over various nuts and bolts.

Soc·ra·tes (sŏk′rə tēz′) 470?–399 BC. Greek philosopher whose views on politics, knowledge, logic, and morality greatly influenced Western thought.

sod (sŏd) *n.* **1.** A piece of grass and soil held together by matted roots; turf. **2.** The ground, especially when covered by grass. ❖ *tr.v.* **sod·ded, sod·ding, sods** To cover with sod.

so·da (sō′də) *n.* **1a.** Soft drinks or a soft drink: *drinks too much soda; ordered three sodas.* **b.** Carbonated water. **2.** An ice-cream soda.

soda fountain *n.* A counter equipped for preparing and serving soft drinks, ice cream, or sandwiches.

so·dal·i·ty (sō-dăl′ĭ-tē) *n., pl.* **so·dal·i·ties** An association, especially a devotional or charitable society in the Roman Catholic Church.

soda pop *n.* Soft drinks or a soft drink.

soda water *n.* **1.** Carbonated water. **2.** A solution of water, sodium bicarbonate, and acid.

sod·den (sŏd′n) *adj.* **1.** Thoroughly soaked; saturated: *sodden land.* **2.** Soggy and heavy from improper cooking. **3.** Stupid or dull, especially from drink. **—sod′den·ly** *adv.* **—sod′den·ness** *n.*

so·di·um (sō′dē-əm) *n. Symbol* **Na** A soft, lightweight, silvery-white metallic element that reacts explosively with water and is naturally abundant in combined forms, especially in common salt. Atomic number 11. See **Periodic Table.**

sodium benzoate *n.* The sodium salt of benzoic acid, used as a food preservative and antiseptic.

sodium bicarbonate *n.* Baking soda.

sodium carbonate *n.* A white powdery salt of sodium used in preparing other compounds of sodium and in making glass, detergents, soaps, and other industrial products.

sodium chloride *n.* A colorless crystalline salt of sodium, NaCl, used in making chemicals and as a preservative and seasoning for foods; common salt.

sodium fluoride *n.* A colorless crystalline salt, NaF, used in the fluoridation of water to prevent tooth decay and as an insecticide and a disinfectant.

sodium hydroxide *n.* A strongly alkaline compound of sodium, NaOH, used in making chemicals and soaps, and in refining petroleum; lye.

sodium nitrate *n.* A white crystalline compound, $NaNO_3$, used in solid rocket propellants, in the manufacture of explosives, and as a fertilizer.

sodium vapor lamp *n.* An electric lamp containing a small amount of sodium, neon, and argon, used in generating yellow light for lighting streets and highways.

Sod·om (sŏd′əm) A city of ancient Palestine that in the Bible was destroyed along with Gomorrah because of its wickedness.

so·fa (sō′fə) *n.* A long upholstered seat typically with a back and arms.

so far as *conj.* In so far as: *So far as I'm concerned, the project is finished.*

So·fi·a (sō′fē-ə *or* sō-fē′ə) The capital of Bulgaria, in the west-central part of the country. It became the capital in 1879.

soft (sôft) *adj.* **soft·er, soft·est 1.** Not hard or firm; easily molded or cut: *a soft squishy melon; soft snow.* **2.** Smooth or fine to the touch: *the soft fur of a kitten.* **3.** Not loud or harsh; quiet: *a soft voice.* **4.** Not brilliant or glaring; subdued: *a soft pink.* **5.** Mild; balmy: *a soft breeze.* **6.** Out of condition; flabby: *got soft while recovering from an injury.* **7.** *Informal* Requiring little effort; easy: *a soft job.* **8.** Tender or affectionate: *soft feelings.* **9.** Not stern; lenient: *The coach is never soft on his players.* **10.** Weak in character: *a secret agent who was soft and cracked under pressure.* **11.** *Informal* Simple-minded; foolish: *soft in the head.* **12.** Containing relatively little dissolved mineral matter: *soft water.* **13.** Being the sound of *c* in *certain* or *g* in *general,* rather than in *cat* and *go.* ❖ *adv.* In a soft manner; gently. **—soft′ly** *adv.* **—soft′ness** *n.*

soft·ball (sôft′bôl′) *n.* **1.** A game similar to baseball but played with a larger softer ball that is pitched underhand. **2.** The ball used in this game.

soft-boiled (sôft′boild′) *adj.* Boiled in the shell to a soft consistency. Used of an egg.

soft coal *n.* Bituminous coal.

soft drink *n.* A carbonated nonalcoholic beverage, usually commercially prepared and sold in cans or bottles.

soft·en (sô′fən) *tr. & intr.v.* **soft·ened, soft·en·ing, soft·ens** To make or become soft or softer. **—soft′en·er** *n.*

soft·heart·ed (sôft′här′tĭd) *adj.* Easily moved to a tender emotion, such as sympathy or pity. **—soft′heart′ed·ly** *adv.* **—soft′heart′ed·ness** *n.*

soft palate *n.* The movable fold that hangs from the back of the hard palate and closes off the nasal cavity from the mouth during swallowing and sucking.

soft serve *n.* Any of several soft, creamy frozen desserts, such as ice cream or frozen yogurt, dispensed from a machine at the point of sale. **—soft′-serve′** *adj.*

soft-shoe (sôft′sho͞o′) *n.* Tap dancing performed in shoes with soft soles and no metal taps.

soft-spo·ken (sôft′spō′kən) *adj.* Speaking with a soft or gentle voice.

soft spot *n.* **1.** A tender or sentimental feeling: *has a soft spot for puppies.* **2.** A weak or vulnerable point.

soft·ware (sôft′wâr′) *n.* The programs, routines, and symbolic languages that control the operation of a computer.

soft·wood (sôft′wo͝od′) *n.* **1.** Any of various cone-bearing trees, such as a pine, fir, or cedar. **2.** The wood of such a tree, which is usually softer than that of a hardwood.

soft·y or **soft·ie** (sôf′tē) *n., pl.* **soft·ies** *Informal* A weak or sentimental person.

sog·gy (sŏg′ē) *adj.* **sog·gi·er, sog·gi·est 1.** Saturated with moisture; soaked: *soggy bread.* **2.** Hot and humid. **—sog′gi·ly** *adv.* **—sog′gi·ness** *n.*

soil¹ (soil) *n.* **1.** The loose top layer of the earth's surface, a mixture of rock and mineral particles with organic matter, suitable for the growth of plant life. **2.** A particular kind of earth or ground: *sandy soil.* **3.** Country; region: *native soil.* [From Middle English, from Latin *solium,* seat.]

soil² (soil) *v.* **soiled, soil·ing, soils** *—tr.* **1.** To make dirty. **2.** To disgrace; tarnish: *soil one's reputation. —intr.* To become dirty or tarnished: *a fabric that soils easily.* [From Middle English *soillen,* from Old French *souiller.*]

so·journ (sō′jûrn′ *or* sō-jûrn′) *intr.v.* **so·journed, so·journ·ing, so·journs** To stay for a time; reside temporarily: *Thoreau sojourned at Walden pond.* ❖ *n.* A temporary stay. **—so′journ′er** *n.*

sol¹ (sōl) also **so** (sō) *n.* In music, the fifth tone of a major scale. [From Middle English, from Medieval Latin.]

❑ *These sound alike:* **sol¹** (musical syllable), **sol²** (currency), **sole¹** (foot part), **sole²** (only), **sole³** (fish), **soul** (spirit).

sol² (sōl) *n., pl.* **so·les** (sō′lĕs) The basic monetary unit of Peru. [From Spanish, sun (from the drawing on the coin), from Latin, sōl.]

❑ *These sound alike:* **sol²** (currency), **sol¹** (musical note), **sole¹** (foot part), **sole²** (only), **sole³** (fish), **soul** (spirit).

sol·ace (sŏl′ĭs) *n.* **1.** Comfort in distress, sorrow, or misery. **2.** Something that gives such comfort or con-

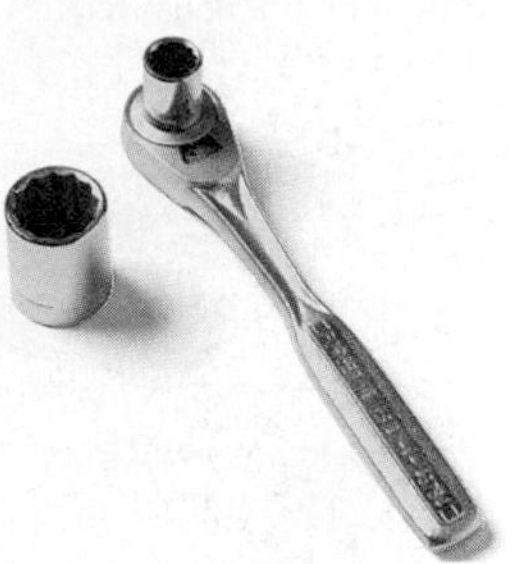

socket wrench

soft serve

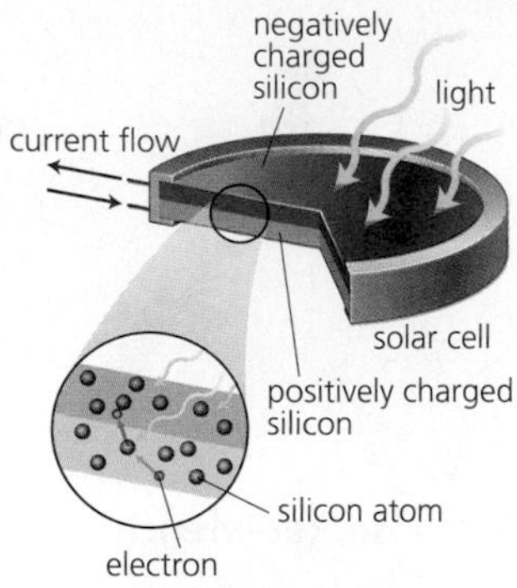

solar cell

Light energy makes electrons break away from silicon atoms, creating an electrical current.

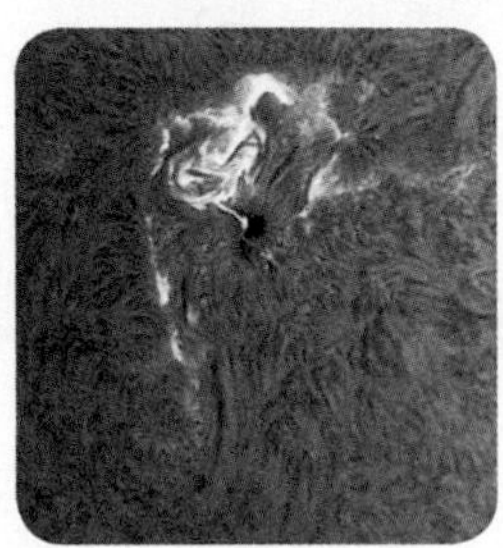

solar flare

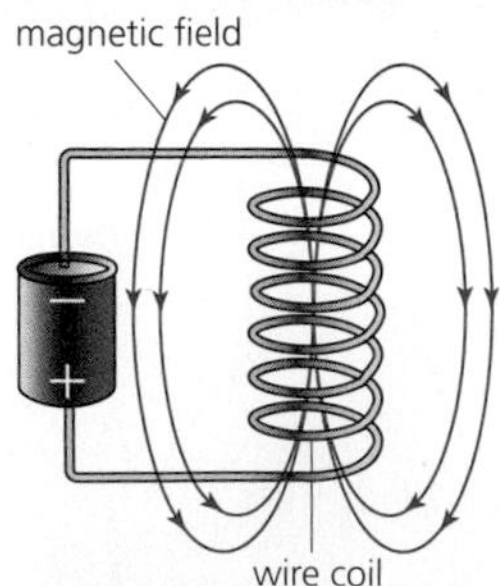

solenoid

ă	pat	ôr	core
ā	pay	oi	boy
âr	care	ou	out
ä	father	ŏŏ	took
ĕ	pet	ŏŏr	lure
ē	be	ōō	boot
ĭ	pit	ŭ	cut
ī	bite	ûr	urge
îr	pier	th	thin
ŏ	pot	*th*	this
ō	toe	zh	vision
ô	paw	ə	about

solation. ❖ *tr.v.* **sol·aced, sol·ac·ing, sol·ac·es** To provide solace; comfort.

so·lar (sō′lər) *adj.* **1.** Relating to or emitted by the sun: *solar radiation.* **2.** Using or operating by energy from the sun: *a solar heating system.* **3.** Measured with respect to the sun: *solar time.* [From Latin *sōlāris*, from *sōl*, sun.]

solar cell *n.* A semiconductor device that generates an electrical current when it is exposed to solar radiation.

solar flare *n.* A sudden eruption of magnetic energy on or near the surface of the sun, usually associated with sunspots.

solar furnace *n.* A device equipped with a large reflector that focuses the sun's rays, producing temperatures as high as 7,200°F (approximately 4,000°C).

so·lar·i·um (sō-lâr′ē-əm) *n., pl.* **so·lar·i·a** (sō-lâr′ē-ə) or **so·lar·i·ums** A room or glassed-in porch that is exposed to the sun.

solar panel *n.* **1.** A set of connected solar cells. **2.** A panel containing tubes full of circulating fluid, often placed on a rooftop to absorb solar energy for use in heating.

solar plexus *n.* **1.** The large network of nerves and nerve tissue located in the abdomen behind the stomach, having branches that supply nerves to the abdominal organs. **2.** The pit of the stomach.

solar system *n.* **1.** The sun together with the eight planets and their moons and all other bodies that orbit the sun, including asteroids and comets. **2.** A system of planets or other bodies orbiting a star. —SEE NOTE.

solar wind (wĭnd) *n.* A stream of high-speed, charged atomic particles flowing outward from the sun's corona.

solar year *n.* The period of time required for Earth to make one complete revolution around the sun, from one vernal equinox to the next. The solar year is 365 days, 5 hours, 48 minutes, and 46 seconds.

sold (sōld) *v.* Past tense and past participle of **sell.**

sol·der (sŏd′ər) *n.* Any of various alloys, mainly of tin and lead, that melt at low temperatures and are applied in the molten state to metal parts in order to join them. ❖ *tr. & intr.v.* **sol·dered, sol·der·ing, sol·ders** To join, mend, or unite with solder: *soldering the wires together.* [From Middle English *souder*, from Latin *solidāre*, to make solid.]

sol·dier (sōl′jər) *n.* **1.** A person who serves in an army. **2.** An enlisted person or noncommissioned officer. **3.** A dedicated and militant follower. **4.** A form of certain ants and termites, having a large head and powerful jaws used as fighting weapons. ❖ *intr.v.* **sol·diered, sol·dier·ing, sol·diers** To be or serve as a soldier. ◆ **soldier on** To continue or persist with determination, as in working: *She soldiered on in spite of all her setbacks.* [From Middle English *soudiour*, mercenary, from Late Latin *solidus*, gold coin.]

sol·dier·ly (sōl′jər-lē) *adj.* Relating to or befitting a soldier: *soldierly courage.*

soldier of fortune *n., pl.* **soldiers of fortune** A person willing to serve in any army or undertake risky tasks for personal gain or love of adventure.

sole[1] (sōl) *n.* **1.** The bottom surface of the foot. **2.** The bottom surface of a shoe or boot, often excluding the heel. ❖ *tr.v.* **soled, sol·ing, soles** To put a sole on (a shoe or boot): *The cobbler soled the shoes.* [From Middle English, from Latin *solea*, sandal, from Latin *solum*, bottom, sole of the foot.]

❑ *These sound alike:* **sole**[1] (foot part), **sol**[1] (musical note), **sol**[2] (currency), **sole**[2] (only), **sole**[3] (fish), **soul** (spirit).

sole[2] (sōl) *adj.* **1.** Being the only one; single; only: *Her sole purpose in coming is to see you.* **2.** Belonging or relating exclusively to one person or group: *She took sole command of the ship.* [From Middle English, from Latin *sōlus.*]

❑ *These sound alike:* **sole**[2] (only), **sol**[1] (musical note), **sol**[2] (currency), **sole**[1] (foot part), **sole**[3] (fish), **soul** (spirit).

sole[3] (sōl) *n., pl.* **sole** or **soles** Any of various flatfishes used as food. [From Middle English, from Latin *solea*, sandal, flatfish.]

❑ *These sound alike:* **sole**[3] (fish), **sol**[1] (musical note), **sol**[2] (currency), **sole**[1] (foot part), **sole**[2] (only), **soul** (spirit).

sol·e·cism (sŏl′ĭ-sĭz′əm *or* sō′lĭ-sĭz′əm) *n.* **1.** A nonstandard use of language or grammar. **2.** A violation of etiquette.

sole·ly (sōl′lē *or* sō′lē) *adv.* Entirely; exclusively: *solely responsible.*

sol·emn (sŏl′əm) *adj.* **1.** Serious and dignified; formal: *a solemn occasion.* **2.** Restrained or serious in appearance or behavior: *No one was smiling. The room was full of solemn looks.* **3.** Made or done with deep sincerity or religious belief: *a solemn oath.* **—sol′emn·ly** *adv.* **—sol′emn·ness** *n.*

so·lem·ni·ty (sə-lĕm′nĭ-tē) *n.* The quality or condition of being solemn; seriousness.

sol·em·nize (sŏl′əm-nīz′) *tr.v.* **sol·em·nized, sol·em·niz·ing, sol·em·niz·es 1.** To celebrate or observe with dignity and gravity: *solemnize the occasion.* **2.** To perform with formal ceremony: *solemnize a marriage.* **3.** To make serious or grave. **—sol′em·ni·za′tion** (sŏl′-əm-nĭ-zā′shən) *n.*

so·le·noid (sō′lə-noid′) *n.* A coil of wire that acts as a magnet when an electric current passes through it. A solenoid often has a movable iron rod that is pulled into the coil when current flows through the wire, thus allowing the entire device to act as a switch.

so·les (sō′lās) *n.* Plural of **sol**[2].

so·lic·it (sə-lĭs′ĭt) *v.* **so·lic·it·ed, so·lic·it·ing, so·lic·its** —*tr.* **1.** To seek to obtain: *solicit votes.* **2.** To ask or petition (someone) persistently; entreat: *solicited all his neighbors for donations.* —*intr.* To ask or petition for something desired. **—so·lic′i·ta′tion** *n.*

so·lic·i·tor (sə-lĭs′ĭ-tər) *n.* **1.** A person who solicits, especially one who seeks contributions or business. **2.** The chief law officer for a city, town, or government department. **3.** *Chiefly British* A lawyer who is not a member of the bar and who may be heard only in the lower courts.

so·lic·i·tous (sə-lĭs′ĭ-təs) *adj.* **1.** Anxious and concerned; attentive: *a solicitous parent.* **2.** Full of desire; eager: *solicitous to move ahead.* **—so·lic′i·tous·ly** *adv.* **—so·lic′i·tous·ness** *n.*

so·lic·i·tude (sə-lĭs′ĭ-to͞od′) *n.* The state of being solicitous; care or concern, as for another person.

sol·id (sŏl′ĭd) *adj.* **sol·id·er, sol·id·est 1.** Having a definite shape and volume; not liquid or gaseous. **2.** Relating to three-dimensional geometric figures. **3.** Firm or compact in substance: *a solid wall.* **4.** Not hollowed out: *a solid block of ice.* **5.** Being the same substance or color throughout: *solid gold.* **6.** Having no breaks; continuous: *a solid line of people.* **7.** Acting together; unanimous: *a solid voting bloc.* **8.** Of good quality or substance; well-made: *a solid foundation.* **9.** Substantial; hearty: *a solid breakfast.* **10.** Upstanding and dependable: *a solid citizen.* ❖ *n.* **1.** A substance having a definite shape and volume; one that is neither a liquid nor a gas. **2.** A geometric figure that has three dimensions. [From Middle English *solide*, from Latin *solidus.*] **—sol′id·ly** *adv.* **—sol′id·ness** *n.*

sol·i·dar·i·ty (sŏl′ĭ-dăr′ĭ-tē) *n.* Unity of purpose, interest, or sympathy.

solid geometry *n.* The branch of mathematics that deals with three-dimensional figures and surfaces.

so·lid·i·fy (sə-lĭd′ə-fī′) *tr. & intr.v.* **so·lid·i·fied, so·lid·i·fy·ing, so·lid·i·fies** To make or become solid.

so·lid·i·ty (sə-lĭd′ĭ-tē) *n.* **1.** The condition or property

The Solar System

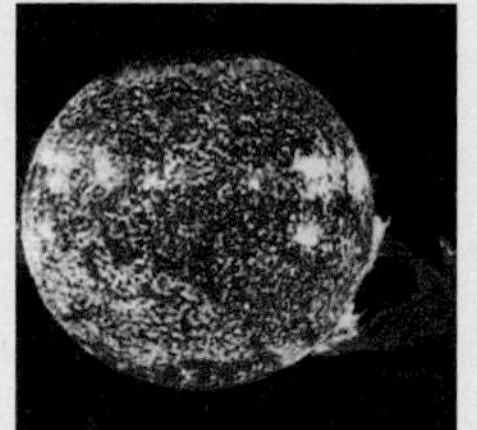
SUN

MERCURY

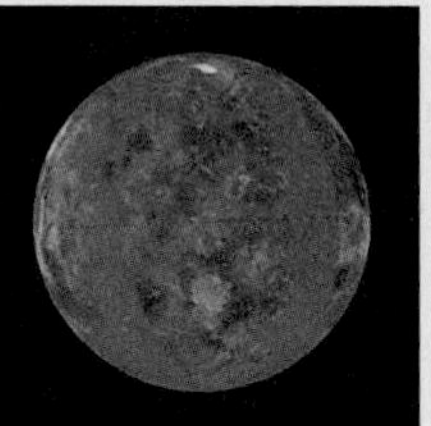
VENUS

EARTH

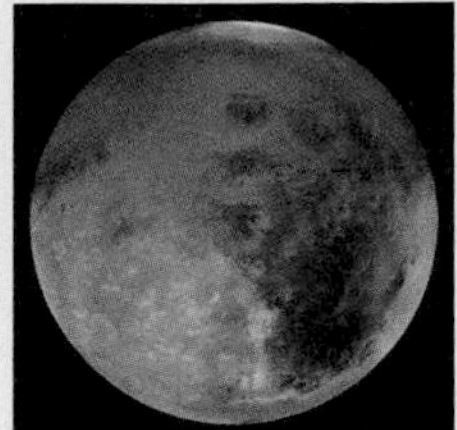
MARS

JUPITER

SATURN

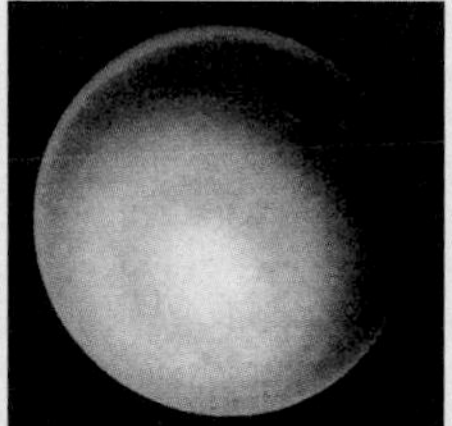
URANUS

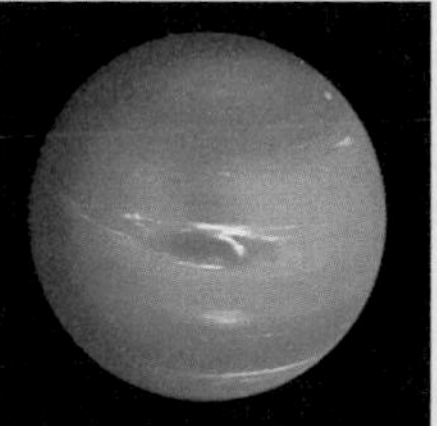
NEPTUNE

PHYSICAL PROPERTIES OF THE PLANETS

Listed below are the planets that have been identified in our solar system. The **orbital period** is the amount of time it takes for a planet to make one complete revolution around the sun. This is usually measured in relation to the fixed stars. The orbital period of Earth is exactly one year. The **rotational period** is the amount of time it takes for a body to make one complete rotation about its own axis, usually also measured relative to the stars. Earth rotates about its axis in about one day. Earth rotates from west to east, counterclockwise when seen from above the North Pole. If one of the other planets rotates about its axis clockwise from east to west (the manner opposite to that of Earth), the rotation is called **retrograde** and a minus sign (–) appears in front of the number of days in the planet's rotational period. Pluto was considered to be a planet until 2006, when the International Astronomical Union created the category of *dwarf planet*. Pluto, along with other celestial objects including Eris and Ceres, was placed in this category.

PLANET	DIAMETER (AT EQUATOR)		MASS	ORBITAL PERIOD	ROTATIONAL PERIOD	AVERAGE SURFACE TEMPERATURE		AVERAGE DISTANCE FROM SUN (in millions)	
	miles	kilometers	$\times 10^{24}$ kilograms	years	days	degrees Fahrenheit	degrees Celsius	miles	kilometers
Mercury	3,032	4,880	0.330	0.24	58.65	333	167	36.0	57.9
Venus	7,521	12,104	4.87	0.61	–243.02	867	464	67.2	108.2
Earth	7,926	12,756	5.97	1.00	0.997	59	15	93.0	149.6
Mars	4,220	6,792	0.64	1.88	1.03	–81	–65	141.6	227.9
Jupiter	88,846	142,984	1,898.1	11.86	0.41	–162	–110	483.8	778.6
Saturn	74,898	120,536	568.32	29.42	0.45	–218	–140	890.7	1,433.5
Uranus	31,763	51,118	86.81	83.75	–0.72	–323	–195	1,784.9	2,872.5
Neptune	30,775	49,528	102.41	163.71	0.67	–330	–200	2,793.1	4,495.1

PHYSICAL PROPERTIES OF THE SUN

Because the sun is not a solid body like Earth, its rotational period is not the same everywhere on its surface. Its outer layers rotate at different rates in different places, taking a longer time at the poles. The sun's core, on the other hand, does rotate as a solid body.

	DIAMETER		MASS	ROTATIONAL PERIOD (OUTER LAYERS)		TEMPERATURE		
	miles	kilometers	×	days			degrees Fahrenheit	degrees Celsius
Sun	865,000	1,392,000	1,988,500	*Equator:*	25.4	*Surface:*	10,924	6,051
				Poles:	36	*Core:*	28,278,500	15,710,000

WRITERS CHOOSE THEIR WORDS

She could, in the presence of her cello teacher, Mr. Porch, summon up the most glorious notes; pure, in fact, surprising even Minna. She played beautifully for Mr. Porch, mostly because she wanted to make him smile, as **somber** as he sometimes was.

—Patricia MacLachlan
The Facts and Fictions of Minna Pratt

sombrero

USAGE

soon When you use *no sooner* as a comparative adverb, follow it with *than,* not *when,* as in *No sooner had she left than he called.*

ă	pat	ôr	core
ā	pay	oi	boy
âr	care	ou	out
ä	father	ŏŏ	took
ĕ	pet	ŏŏr	lure
ē	be	ōō	boot
ĭ	pit	ŭ	cut
ī	bite	ûr	urge
îr	pier	th	thin
ŏ	pot	*th*	this
ō	toe	zh	vision
ô	paw	ə	about

of being solid. **2.** Soundness of mind, character, or finances.

sol·id-state (sŏl′ĭd-stāt′) *adj.* **1.** Relating to the physical properties of crystalline solids: *solid-state physics.* **2.** Based on or using transistors or related semiconductor devices: *a solid-state radio receiver.*

so·lil·o·quy (sə-lĭl′ə-kwē) *n., pl.* **so·lil·o·quies** A passage, especially in a play, in which a character reveals his or her thoughts when alone or unaware of the presence of other characters.

sol·i·taire (sŏl′ĭ-târ′) *n.* **1.** Any of a number of card games played by one person. **2.** A diamond or other gemstone set alone, as in a ring.

sol·i·tar·y (sŏl′ĭ-tĕr′ē) *adj.* **1.** Existing or living alone: *a solitary traveler on the mountain trail.* **2.** Happening, done, or made alone: *spent a solitary evening surfing the Internet.* See Synonyms at **alone. 3.** Remote; secluded: *solitary places.*

sol·i·tude (sŏl′ĭ-to͞od′) *n.* The state or quality of being alone or remote from others; isolation.

so·lo (sō′lō) *n., pl.* **so·los 1.** A musical composition or passage for a single voice or instrument, with or without accompaniment. **2.** A performance by a single singer or instrumentalist. ❖ *adj.* **1.** Composed, arranged for, or performed by a single voice or instrument. **2.** Made or done by a single individual: *a solo ascent of Mt. Everest.* ❖ *adv.* Alone or without accompaniment: *Lacking a pianist, he had to perform solo.* ❖ *intr.v.* **so·loed, so·lo·ing, so·los 1.** To perform a solo. **2.** To fly an airplane without an instructor or companion. [From Italian, from Latin *sōlus,* alone.]

so·lo·ist (sō′lō-ĭst) *n.* A person who performs a solo.

Sol·o·mon (sŏl′ə-mən) Flourished about tenth century BC. King of Israel famous for his wisdom.

Solomon Islands An island country in the western Pacific Ocean east of New Guinea. Honiara is the capital.

so long *interj. Informal* An expression used to say goodbye.

so long as *conj.* **1.** During the time that; while: *We'll stay so long as you need us.* **2.** Because of the fact that; since: *So long as you're offering, I accept.* **3.** On the condition that: *You can borrow the car so long as you finish your homework.*

sol·stice (sŏl′stĭs *or* sōl′stĭs) *n.* Either of the times of year when the sun is farthest north or south of the celestial equator. In the Northern Hemisphere, the summer solstice occurs about June 21 and the winter solstice occurs about December 21.

sol·u·bil·i·ty (sŏl′yə-bĭl′ĭ-tē) *n., pl.* **sol·u·bil·i·ties 1.** The quality or condition of being soluble. **2.** The amount of a substance that is soluble in a particular liquid, especially water.

sol·u·ble (sŏl′yə-bəl) *adj.* **1.** Capable of being dissolved: *a soluble compound.* **2.** Capable of being solved or explained: *a soluble mystery.*

sol·ute (sŏl′yo͞ot *or* sō′lo͞ot) *n.* A substance that is dissolved in another substance.

so·lu·tion (sə-lo͞o′shən) *n.* **1.** The method or procedure used in solving an equation or problem. **2.** An answer to a problem. **3.** A mixture in which particles of one or more substances are distributed so uniformly throughout another substance that they are invisible and will not settle out from the mixture even if left undisturbed: *a solution of salt in water.* **4.** The act or process of forming such a mixture. **5.** The condition or property of being dissolved.

solv·a·ble (sŏl′və-bəl) *adj.* Capable of being solved: *a solvable riddle.*

solve (sŏlv) *v.* **solved, solv·ing, solves** —*tr.* To find an answer or solution to (a problem or equation, for example). —*intr.* To solve an equation: *solve for x.*

sol·vent (sŏl′vənt) *adj.* **1.** Capable of meeting financial obligations: *a solvent business.* **2.** Capable of dissolving another substance. ❖ *n.* **1.** A substance in which another substance is dissolved. **2.** A liquid that is capable of dissolving another substance. —**sol′ven·cy** *n.*

som (sōm) *n.* The basic monetary unit of Kyrgyzstan and Uzbekistan. [From Kyrgyz *som* and Uzbek *so'm,* number, count.]

So·ma·li·a (sō-mä′lē-ə) A country of extreme eastern Africa on the Gulf of Aden and the Indian Ocean. Mogadishu is the capital.

so·mat·ic (sō-măt′ĭk) *adj.* **1.** Relating to the body, especially as distinguished from the mind: *Anxiety can have somatic causes.* **2.** Relating to body cells as distinguished from reproductive cells. [From Greek *sōma,* body.]

somatic cell *n.* Any of the cells of an organism that are not germ cells.

som·ber (sŏm′bər) *adj.* **1.** Dark; gloomy: *a somber color.* **2.** Melancholy; dismal: *a somber mood.* **3.** Serious; grave: *a somber spokesperson.* [From Late Latin *subumbrāre,* to cast a shadow.] —**som′ber·ly** *adv.* —**som′ber·ness** *n.*

som·bre·ro (sŏm-brâr′ō) *n., pl.* **som·bre·ros** A large straw or felt hat with a broad brim and tall crown, worn especially in Mexico and the southwest United States. [From Spanish, perhaps from *sombra,* shade, probably from Late Latin *subumbrāre,* to cast a shadow.]

some (sŭm) *adj.* **1.** Being an unspecified number or quantity: *some people; some sugar.* **2.** Being an unspecified portion of a whole or group: *He likes some modern art but not all.* **3.** Being a considerable number or quantity: *I have been taking piano lessons for some years now.* **4.** Unknown or unspecified by name: *Some student was just here and left you this note.* **5.** *Informal* Considerable; remarkable: *Mary's some skier.* ❖ *pron.* **1.** An indefinite or unspecified number or portion: *We took some of the books to the library.* **2.** An indefinite additional quantity: *From here to the lake is 100 miles and then some.* ❖ *adv.* **1.** Approximately; about: *Some 40 people were at the party.* **2.** *Informal* Somewhat: *He's improved some but not much.* [From Old English *sum.*]

❑ *These sound alike:* **some, sum** (amount).

–some[1] *suff.* A suffix that means characterized by a specified quality, condition, or action: *bothersome.*

–some[2] *suff.* A suffix that means a group of a specified number of members: *threesome.*

some·bod·y (sŭm′bŏd′ē *or* sŭm′bŭd′ē *or* sŭm′bə-dē) *pron.* An unspecified or unknown person; someone: *Somebody's been here, but who?* ❖ *n., pl.* **some·bod·ies** A person of importance: *He really thinks he's somebody.*

some·day (sŭm′dā′) *adv.* At some time in the future: *I'd like to go to Japan someday.*

some·how (sŭm′hou′) *adv.* In a way that is not specified or understood: *I couldn't remember the formula, but somehow I got the right answer.*

some·one (sŭm′wŭn′) *pron.* An unspecified or unknown person; somebody: *Someone called, but she didn't leave her name.*

some·place (sŭm′plās′) *adv.* Somewhere: *I don't like it here, so let's go someplace else.* ❖ *pron.* An unknown or unspecified place; somewhere: *Do you know someplace that we can get pizza?*

som·er·sault (sŭm′ər-sôlt′) *n.* An acrobatic stunt in which the body rolls forward or backward in a complete revolution with the knees bent and the feet coming over the head. ❖ *intr.v.* **som·er·sault·ed, som·er·sault·ing, som·er·saults** To perform a somersault: *Children were somersaulting on the grass.*

some·thing (sŭm′thĭng) *pron.* An unspecified or unknown thing, amount, or extent: *Something's wrong, but I'm not sure what it is. I know something about European history.* ❖ *n.* A remarkable or important thing or person: *That concert was really something.* ❖ *adv.* Somewhat: *She looks something like her mother.* ◆ **something of** To a moderate extent: *He's something of a computer expert.*

some·time (sŭm′tīm′) *adv.* At an indefinite or unstated time in the future: *I'll see you sometime around six.* ❖ *adj.* Former: *our sometime king.*

some·times (sŭm′tīmz′) *adv.* Now and then: *I see them sometimes but not often.*

some·way (sŭm′wā′) also **some·ways** (sŭm′wāz′) *adv.* In some way or other; somehow: *Don't worry—I'll fix up some dinner someway.*

some·what (sŭm′wŏt′ *or* sŭm′wŭt′ *or* sŭm′wət) *adv.* To a moderate extent or degree; rather: *He resembles his brother somewhat.* ❖ *pron.* Something: *The news was somewhat of a surprise.*

some·where (sŭm′wâr′) *adv.* **1.** At, in, or to a place not specified or known: *I found this turtle somewhere near the edge of the swamp.* **2.** To a place or state of further development or progress: *Good writers make sure that their essays lead somewhere and end with a definite point.* **3.** Approximately; roughly: *somewhere about halfway through.* ❖ *n.* An unknown or unspecified place: *I wish I had somewhere to park my bike.*

som·nam·bu·lism (sŏm-năm′byə-lĭz′əm) *n.* Sleepwalking. **—som·nam′bu·list** *n.* **—som·nam′bu·lis′tic** *adj.*

som·no·lence (sŏm′nə-ləns) *n.* A state of drowsiness; sleepiness.

som·no·lent (sŏm′nə-lənt) *adj.* **1.** Drowsy; sleepy. **2.** Causing or tending to cause sleepiness: *the somnolent sound of rain.* **—som′no·lent·ly** *adv.*

so·mo·ni (sô-mô-nē′) *n.* The basic monetary unit of Tajikistan. [After Ismoil *Somoni* (died 907), founder of the Persian dynasty considered to be the first Tajik state.]

son (sŭn) *n.* **1.** A person's male child. **2.** A male descendant: *sons of Abraham.* **3.** A man or boy regarded as if in a relationship of child to parent: *sons of freedom.* **4. Son** In Christianity, Jesus, regarded as the son of God. **5.** Used as a familiar form of address for a young man. [From Old English *sunu.*]

❑ *These sound alike:* **son, sun** (planet).

so·nar (sō′när′) *n.* **1.** A system that uses reflected sound waves to detect and locate underwater objects. **2.** An apparatus using such a system, as for detecting submarines. [From *so(und) n(avigation) a(nd) r(anging).*]

so·na·ta (sə-nä′tə) *n.* A composition for one or more solo instruments, one of which is usually a keyboard instrument, usually consisting of three or four movements that vary in key, mood, and tempo.

song (sông) *n.* **1.** A brief musical composition that is meant to be sung. **2.** The act or art of singing. **3.** A distinctive or characteristic sound made by an animal, such as a bird. **4a.** Poetry; verse. **b.** A lyric poem or ballad. ◆ **for a song** *Informal* At a low price: *bought the old books for a song.*

song·bird (sông′bûrd′) *n.* Any of a large group of birds that are able to produce and learn complicated songs or calls. Cardinals and crows are songbirds.

Song of Solomon *n.* The Song of Songs.

Song of Songs *n.* A book of the Bible consisting of a dramatic and emotional love poem, traditionally attributed to Solomon.

song·writ·er (sông′rī′tər) *n.* A person who writes lyrics or composes tunes for songs.

son·ic (sŏn′ĭk) *adj.* **1.** Relating to sound, especially audible sound. **2.** Having a speed equal to that of sound in air, about 760 miles (1,220 kilometers) per hour at sea level.

sonic barrier *n.* The sudden sharp increase in drag exerted by the atmosphere on an aircraft approaching the speed of sound.

sonic boom *n.* The shock wave caused by an aircraft traveling at a supersonic speed, sometimes causing damage to structures on the ground and often audible as a loud explosive sound.

son-in-law (sŭn′ĭn-lô′) *n., pl.* **sons-in-law** The husband of one's child.

son·net (sŏn′ĭt) *n.* A 14-line poem usually having one of several conventional rhyme schemes.

son·net·eer (sŏn′ĭ-tîr′) *n.* A composer of sonnets.

son·ny (sŭn′ē) *n., pl.* **son·nies** Used as a familiar form of address for a boy or young man.

❑ *These sound alike:* **sonny, sunny** (cheerful).

so·nor·i·ty (sə-nôr′ĭ-tē) *n., pl.* **so·nor·i·ties 1.** The quality or property of being sonorous; resonance. **2.** A sound, especially one used in music or speech: *The work is a masterful study in orchestral sonorities.*

son·o·rous (sŏn′ər-əs *or* sə-nôr′əs) *adj.* **1.** Having or producing sound, especially full, deep, or rich sound. **2.** Impressive in style of speech: *sonorous prose.* **—son′o·rous·ly** *adv.* **—son′o·rous·ness** *n.*

soon (so͞on) *adv.* **soon·er, soon·est 1.** In the near future: *Soon you'll have to leave.* **2.** Before the usual or appointed time; early: *He got there not an instant too soon.* **3.** Promptly or speedily: *Phone your mother as soon as we get into the house.* **4.** Gladly; willingly: *I'd as soon leave right now.* ◆ **sooner or later** At some time; eventually. [From Old English *sōna,* immediately.] —SEE NOTE.

soot (so͝ot *or* so͞ot) *n.* A fine black powdery substance consisting chiefly of carbon, produced when wood, coal, or hydrocarbon fuels burn incompletely. [From Old English *sōt.*]

sooth (so͞oth) *Archaic adj.* Real; true. ❖ *n.* Truth; reality. —SEE NOTE AT **soothe.**

soothe (so͞oth) *tr.v.* **soothed, sooth·ing, soothes 1.** To calm or give comfort to (a person or a person's feelings): *sang a lullaby to soothe the baby.* **2.** To ease or relieve (pain or a painful body part): *The massage soothed his aching back.* **—sooth′er** *n.* —SEE NOTE.

sooth·ing (so͞o′thĭng) *adj.* Tending to soothe; bringing relief or comfort: *soothing words.* **—sooth′ing·ly** *adv.*

sooth·say·er (so͞oth′sā′ər) *n.* A person who claims to be able to predict the future; a seer. —SEE NOTE AT **soothe.**

sooth·say·ing (so͞oth′sā′ĭng) *n.* **1.** The art or practice of foretelling events. **2.** A prediction; a prophecy.

soot·y (so͝ot′ē *or* so͞o′tē) *adj.* **soot·i·er, soot·i·est 1.** Covered with or as if with soot. **2.** Relating to or producing soot. **3.** Blackish or dusky in color.

sop (sŏp) *tr.v.* **sopped, sop·ping, sops 1.** To dip, soak, or drench in a liquid: *sop the bread in the beaten eggs.* **2.** To take up by absorption; soak up: *sop up water with a towel.* ❖ *n.* **1.** A piece of food soaked or dipped in a liquid. **2.** Something yielded to placate or soothe a person.

soph·ist (sŏf′ĭst) *n.* **1.** A person skilled in elaborate and often deceptive methods of argumentation. **2. Sophist** One of a group of ancient Greek philosophers who speculated on theology, metaphysics, and the sciences.

so·phis·ti·cate (sə-fĭs′tĭ-kāt′) *tr.v.* **so·phis·ti·cat·ed, so·phis·ti·cat·ing, so·phis·ti·cates 1.** To make less natural; cause to become less naive and more worldly: *Travel tends to sophisticate a person.* **2.** To make more complex or complicated; refine: *sophisticate the communications system.* ❖ *n.* (sə-fĭs′tĭ-kĭt) A sophisticated person. **—so·phis′ti·ca′tion** *n.*

so·phis·ti·cat·ed (sə-fĭs′tĭ-kā′tĭd) *adj.* **1.** Having acquired worldly knowledge or refinement. **2.** Elaborate, complex, or complicated: *sophisticated technology.* **3.** Suitable for or appealing to the tastes of sophisticates: *a sophisticated play.*

soph·is·try (sŏf′ĭ-strē) *n., pl.* **soph·is·tries 1.** Argumentation that is seemingly valid but actually false or misleading. **2.** An attractive but misleading or false argument.

Soph·o·cles (sŏf′ə-klēz′) 496?–406 BC. Greek dramatist whose plays include *Oedipus Rex.*

WORD HISTORY

soothe Our word **soothe** did not always mean what it means today; its oldest meaning was "to confirm something as true." From this it developed to mean "to reassure someone that something is true, to humor," which led to the modern meaning of "to calm (someone) down." It is derived from the noun *sooth,* a rare word nowadays but common in older English; it meant "truth." This noun is still around as the first part of our word **soothsayer.** Literally, then, a soothsayer was a "truth teller," not a person who soothes another's feelings.

Sophocles

sorghum

sorus
sori on a fern frond

soufflé

soph·o·more (sŏf′ə-môr′ *or* sŏf′môr′) *n.* **1.** A second-year student in a US college. **2.** A tenth-grade student in a US high school.

soph·o·mor·ic (sŏf′ə-môr′ĭk) *adj.* Immature and foolish: *a sophomoric prank.*

sop·o·rif·ic (sŏp′ə-rĭf′ĭk *or* sō′pə-rĭf′ĭk) *adj.* Inducing or tending to induce sleep. ❖ *n.* A drug or other substance that induces sleep.

sop·ping (sŏp′ĭng) *adj.* Thoroughly soaked; drenched. ❖ *adv.* Extremely; very: *sopping wet.*

sop·py (sŏp′ē) *adj.* **sop·pi·er, sop·pi·est 1.** Soaked; sopping. **2.** Rainy. **3.** *Slang* Sentimental.

so·pran·o (sə-prăn′ō *or* sə-prä′nō) *n., pl.* **so·pran·os 1.** A highest singing voice of a woman or young boy. **2.** A singer whose voice lies within this range. **3.** An instrument whose sound falls within this range. **4.** A part written in this range.

sor·cer·er (sôr′sər-ər) *n.* Someone who practices sorcery; a wizard.

sor·cer·ess (sôr′sər-ĭs) *n.* A woman who practices sorcery.

sor·cer·y (sôr′sə-rē) *n.* The use of magic or supernatural powers, especially through the aid of spirits.

sor·did (sôr′dĭd) *adj.* **1.** Morally degraded; base: *a sordid motive.* **2.** Filthy or squalid: *moved away from a sordid neighborhood.* **—sor′did·ly** *adv.* **—sor′did·ness** *n.*

sore (sôr) *adj.* **sor·er, sor·est 1.** Painful to the touch; tender: *His sore leg made him walk with a limp.* **2.** Feeling physical pain; hurting: *sore all over.* **3.** Causing misery, sorrow, or distress; grievous: *in sore need.* **4.** Causing embarrassment or irritation: *a sore subject.* **5.** *Informal* Angry; offended. ❖ *n.* An open skin wound or ulcer. ❖ *adv. Archaic* Extremely: *sore afraid.* [From Old English *sār.*] **—sore′ness** *n.*

❑ *These sound alike:* **sore, soar** (rise).

sore·ly (sôr′lē) *adv.* **1.** Painfully; grievously: *She was sorely distressed.* **2.** Extremely; greatly: *sorely needed expertise.*

sor·ghum (sôr′gəm) *n.* **1.** A grass native to sub-Saharan Africa, grown for its edible grain, as feed for animals, and as a source of syrup. **2.** Syrup made from the juice of this plant.

so·ri (sôr′ī) *n.* Plural of **sorus.**

so·ror·i·ty (sə-rôr′ĭ-tē) *n., pl.* **so·ror·i·ties 1.** A chiefly social organization of women students at a college or university. **2.** An association of women.

sor·rel¹ (sôr′əl) *n.* Any of several plants having sour-tasting leaves sometimes used in salads. [From Middle English, from Old French *surele,* from *sur,* sour, of Germanic origin.]

sor·rel² (sôr′əl) *n.* **1.** A brownish orange to light brown. **2.** A sorrel-colored horse or other animal. [From Middle English *sorel,* from Old French *sor,* red-brown, of Germanic origin.]

sor·row (sŏr′ō) *n.* **1.** Mental pain or suffering caused by loss, injury, or despair. **2.** Something that causes sadness or grief; a misfortune. **3.** The expression of sadness or grief: *He looked at them with sorrow.* ❖ *intr.v.* **sor·rowed, sor·row·ing, sor·rows** To feel or express sorrow. [From Old English *sorg.*] **—sor′row·er** *n.*

sor·row·ful (sŏr′ō-fəl) *adj.* Causing, feeling, or expressing sorrow: *a sorrowful event; a sorrowful voice.* See Synonyms at **sad. —sor′row·ful·ly** *adv.* **—sor′row·ful·ness** *n.*

sor·ry (sŏr′ē) *adj.* **sor·ri·er, sor·ri·est 1.** Feeling or expressing sympathy, pity, or regret. **2.** Worthless or inferior; poor; paltry: *a sorry excuse.* **3.** Causing sorrow or grief; grievous; sad: *a sorry development.* [From Old English *sārig,* sad, from *sār,* sore.] **—sor′ri·ly** *adv.*

sort (sôrt) *n.* **1.** A group or collection of similar people or things; a class; a kind: *What sort of machine is it?* **2.** The character or nature of something; type; quality: *a person of an interesting sort.* ❖ *tr.v.* **sort·ed, sort·ing, sorts 1.** To arrange according to class, kind, or size; classify: *sorted the blocks by color.* **2.** To separate (one kind) from the rest: *She sorted out the nails of the largest size.* ◆ **of sorts** or **of a sort** Of a mediocre or inferior kind: *a democracy of a sort.* **out of sorts 1.** Slightly ill. **2.** Irritable; cross. **sort of** *Informal* Somewhat; rather: *They were sort of interested in the question.* **—sort′er** *n.*

sor·tie (sôr′tē *or* sôr-tē′) *n.* **1.** An armed attack made from a place surrounded by enemy forces. **2.** A flight of an aircraft on a combat mission. [From French, from *sortir,* to go out.]

so·rus (sôr′əs) *n., pl.* **so·ri** (sôr′ī) A cluster of spore-forming structures on the underside of a fern frond. Each frond usually has numerous sori.

SOS (ĕs′ō-ĕs′) *n.* **1.** The letters represented by the Morse code signal · · · – – – · · ·, used as an international distress signal by ships and aircraft. **2.** A signal for help.

so-so (sō′sō′) *adj.* Neither very good nor very bad; just passable: *a so-so party.* ❖ *adv.* Indifferently; tolerably; passably: *performed so-so.*

sot (sŏt) *n.* A drunkard.

So·to·may·or (sō′tō-mī-ôr′), **Sonia Maria** Born 1954. American jurist who was appointed an associate justice of the US Supreme Court in 2009, becoming the court's first Hispanic justice.

sou (so͞o) *n.* A coin formerly used in France and worth a small amount.

souf·flé (so͞o-flā′) *n.* A light, fluffy baked dish made of eggs combined with other ingredients. [From French, from *souffler,* to puff up.]

sough (sou *or* sŭf) *intr.v.* **soughed, sough·ing, soughs** To make a soft murmuring or rustling sound. ❖ *n.* A soft murmuring or rustling sound, as of the wind or a gentle surf.

sought (sôt) *v.* Past tense and past participle of **seek.**

soul (sōl) *n.* **1.** A nonphysical part of humans regarded in many religions as immortal, separable from the body, and capable of experiencing thoughts and emotions. **2.** A spirit; a ghost. **3.** A human: *not a soul in sight.* **4.** The central or vital part of something: *The soul of that business is its sales force.* **5.** A strong, deeply felt emotion conveyed by a speaker or artist. **6.** The emotional strength or spiritual vitality sometimes described as deriving from black and especially African-American culture. **7.** Soul music. [From Old English *sāwol.*]

❑ *These sound alike:* **soul, sol¹** (musical note), **sol²** (currency), **sole¹** (foot part), **sole²** (only), **sole³** (fish).

soul·ful (sōl′fəl) *adj.* Full of or expressing a deep feeling. **—soul′ful·ly** *adv.* **—soul′ful·ness** *n.*

soul·less (sōl′lĭs) *adj.* **1.** Lacking sensitivity or the capacity for deep feeling. **2.** Not expressing authentic feeling or individuality: *soulless pop music; a soulless workplace.* **—soul′less·ly** *adv.*

soul music *n.* A style of popular music developed by African Americans, combining elements of gospel music and rhythm and blues.

sound¹ (sound) *n.* **1.** A type of wave motion that travels through gases, liquids, and elastic solids as variations of pressure and density and is detectable by human ears in air when the waves have a frequency between about 20 and 20,000 hertz. **2a.** The sensation produced in the organs of hearing by waves of this type. **b.** Sensations of this type considered as a group. **3.** A distinctive noise: *the sound of laughter.* **4.** The distance over which something can be heard; earshot: *within the sound of my voice.* **5.** A noise made as part of human speech: *the sound of y in "try."* **6.** A mental impression; import; implication: *He did not like the sound of the invitation.* **7.** Recorded material, as for a movie: *a video with very low-quality sound.* ❖ *v.* **sound·ed, sound·ing, sounds** *—intr.* **1.**

ă	pat	ôr	core
ā	pay	oi	boy
âr	care	ou	out
ä	father	o͝o	took
ĕ	pet	o͝or	lure
ē	be	o͞o	boot
ĭ	pit	ŭ	cut
ī	bite	ûr	urge
îr	pier	th	thin
ŏ	pot	*th*	this
ō	toe	zh	vision
ô	paw	ə	about

To make a sound: *The whistle sounded.* **2.** To produce a certain audible effect: *Two words that sound alike.* **3.** To seem to be: *The news sounds good.* —*tr.* To summon, announce, or signal by a sound: *sound a warning.* ◆ **sound off** To express one's views vigorously: *sounding off about the unexpected test.* [From Middle English *soun*, from Latin *sonus*.] —SEE NOTE.

sound² (sound) *adj.* **sound·er, sound·est 1.** Free from defect, decay, or damage; in good condition: *The bridge is sound.* **2.** Free from disease or injury. See Synonyms at **healthy. 3.** Solid and firm: *a sound foundation.* **4.** Financially secure: *a sound economy.* **5.** Logical and correct: *sound reasoning.* **6.** Complete or thorough. **7.** Deep and unbroken: *a sound sleep.* **8.** Legally valid; good: *sound title.* ❖ *adv.* Thoroughly; deeply: *sound asleep.* [From Old English *gesund.*] **—sound′ly** *adv.* **—sound′ness** *n.*

sound³ (sound) *n.* **1.** A long body of water, wider than a strait or channel, connecting larger bodies of water. **2.** A long wide inlet of the ocean. [From Old English *sund*, swimming, sea.]

sound⁴ (sound) *v.* **sound·ed, sound·ing, sounds** —*tr.* **1.** To measure the depth of (water), especially by means of a weighted line. **2.** To try to learn (someone's) attitudes or opinions: *I want to sound her out on this before we begin.* —*intr.* **1.** To measure depth: *sounding with a long pole.* **2.** To dive swiftly downward: *The whale sounded and did not reappear.* [From Middle English *sounden*, from Old French *sonder*, from *sonde*, sounding line.]

sound barrier *n.* The sonic barrier.

sound box *n.* A hollow chamber in the body of a musical instrument, such as a violin, that intensifies the resonance of the tone.

sound·er (soun′dər) *n.* A person or device that measures the depth of water.

sound·ing (soun′dĭng) *n.* **1.** The act or process of making measurements of depth, especially of a body of water. **2.** A measured depth of water. **3.** An investigation, as of the atmosphere, to obtain information.

sounding board *n.* **1.** A thin board forming the upper portion of the resonant chamber of a musical instrument, such as a violin or piano, and serving to increase resonance. **2.** A structure placed over or behind a podium or platform to reflect music or a speaker's voice to the audience. **3.** A person or group whose reactions to an idea or opinion serve as a measure of its effectiveness or acceptability. **4.** A device or means serving to spread or popularize an idea or point of view: *using the press as a sounding board.*

sound·less (sound′lĭs) *adj.* Having or making no sound. **—sound′less·ly** *adv.*

sound·proof (sound′pro͞of′) *adj.* Designed or treated to allow no audible sound to pass through or enter: *a soundproof room.* **—sound′proof′** *v.*

sound·track (sound′trăk′) *n.* **1.** The audio portion of a film or video recording. **2.** The music that accompanies a movie. **3.** A recording of such music available for purchase.

sound wave *n.* A series of vibrations carried through a material, such as air or water, by which sounds are transmitted. —SEE NOTE AT **sound¹.**

soup (so͞op) *n.* **1.** A liquid food prepared from meat, fish, or vegetable stock, usually with other ingredients added. **2.** Something whose appearance or characteristics are like soup, such as dense fog or a muddled situation. [From Middle English *soupe*, from Old French, of Germanic origin.]

soup kitchen *n.* A place where food is offered free or at a very low cost to the needy.

soup·y (so͞o′pē) *adj.* **soup·i·er, soup·i·est 1.** Having the consistency or appearance of soup. **2.** *Informal* Foggy. **3.** *Informal* Sentimental.

sour (sour) *adj.* **sour·er, sour·est 1.** Having an acid taste; sharp, tart, or tangy: *sour lemonade.* **2.** Spoiled; rancid: *The milk became sour.* **3.** Bad-tempered; cross; peevish: *a sour temper.* **4.** Worse than expected or than usual; bad: *His career went sour.* ❖ *n.* **1.** The sensation of a sharp acid taste. **2.** A thing that is sour. ❖ *tr. & intr.v.* **soured, sour·ing, sours** To make or become sour. [From Old English *sūr.*] **—sour′ly** *adv.* **—sour′ness** *n.*

source (sôrs) *n.* **1.** A place or thing from which something comes; a point of origin: *used the sea as a source of food.* **2.** The beginning of a stream or river. **3.** A person or thing that supplies information: *Who is your source for that story?* [From Middle English *sours*, from Old French *sourse*, from Latin *surgere*, to rise.]

sour cream *n.* Cream that has been soured by the action of bacteria, used as an ingredient in foods or as a topping.

sour·dough (sour′dō′) *n.* **1.** Sour fermented dough used as a leaven for bread. **2.** An early settler or prospector, especially in Alaska and northwest Canada in the late 1800s.

sour grapes *pl.n.* The act of denying that something is desirable after learning that it cannot be had.

sour·sop (sour′sŏp′) *n.* **1.** The spiny fruit of a tropical American evergreen tree, having tart edible pulp. **2.** The tree that bears such fruit.

Sou·sa (so͞o′zə *or* so͞o′sə), **John Philip** 1854–1932. American composer who wrote marches such as *Stars and Stripes Forever* (1897).

sou·sa·phone (so͞o′zə-fōn′) *n.* A large brass wind instrument similar to a tuba, designed for use in marching bands. [After John Philip *Sousa.*]

souse (sous) *tr.v.* **soused, sous·ing, sous·es 1.** To plunge into a liquid. **2.** To make soaking wet; drench. **3.** To steep in a brine or other liquid, as in pickling. **4.** *Slang* To make drunk. ❖ *n.* **1.** Something pickled in brine, especially the feet or ears of a pig. **2.** The brine used in pickling. **3.** *Slang* A drunkard.

south (south) *n.* **1.** The direction to the right of sunrise, directly opposite north. **2.** often **South** A region or part of the earth in this direction. **3. South** The southern part of the United States, especially the states that fought for the Confederacy in the Civil War. ❖ *adj.* **1.** To, toward, facing, or in the south: *the south side of the mountain.* **2.** From the south: *a dry south wind.* ❖ *adv.* In, from, or toward the south: *He pointed south. We hiked south.* [From Old English *sūth.*]

South Africa A country of southern Africa on the Atlantic and Indian Oceans. Pretoria is the administrative capital, Cape Town is the legislative capital, and Bloemfontein is the judicial capital. **—South African** *adj. & n.*

South America The fourth-largest continent, lying southeast of North America between the Atlantic and Pacific Oceans.

South Asia A region of southern Asia consisting of Bangladesh, Bhutan, India, the Maldives, Nepal, Pakistan, and Sri Lanka.

south·bound (south′bound′) *adj.* Going toward the south.

South Car·o·li·na (kăr′ə-lī′nə) A state of the southeast United States on the Atlantic Ocean northeast of Georgia. It was admitted as one of the original Thirteen Colonies in 1788. Columbia is the capital. —SEE NOTE AT **North Carolina.**

South China Sea An arm of the western Pacific Ocean bounded by southeast China, Taiwan, the Philippines, Borneo, and Vietnam.

South Da·ko·ta (də-kō′tə) A state of the north-central United States north of Nebraska. It was admitted as the 40th state in 1889. Pierre is the capital and Sioux Falls the largest city. —SEE NOTE AT **North Dakota.**

south·east (south-ēst′) *n.* **1.** The direction halfway between east and south. **2.** An area or region lying in this

SCIENCE

sound¹ The form of energy called **sound** is produced when matter moves or vibrates. The vibrations are transferred to another medium, usually the air, and travel through the medium as *sound waves.* You hear a sound when its vibrations reach your eardrum and cause it to vibrate. The pitch of a sound is directly related to the frequency of its waves' vibrations. Humans can hear sounds with frequencies of 20 to 20,000 hertz. One hertz is equal to one vibration per second. Other animals can detect sounds that are inaudible to us. Bats and dolphins, for instance, can hear high-frequency sounds of over 100,000 hertz, while elephants communicate with very low-frequency sounds. The loudness, or intensity, of sound is measured in *decibels.* For each increase of 10 decibels, the sound wave has 10 times as much energy—a sound of 20 decibels is twice as loud as one of 10 decibels but has 10 times the energy. A moderate conversation has a loudness of about 60 decibels. Prolonged exposure to levels above 85 decibels, the sound of a lawnmower, can lead to hearing loss.

soursop

South Pole

WORD HISTORY

soy Most people know that soy sauce is made from **soy** or **soya** and comes from the Far East, but from where in the Far East? The answer is Japan, at least as far as the English word is concerned. The Japanese, however, first learned of soy sauce from the Chinese. The Chinese name for the sauce, *jiàng yóu,* appears in Japanese as *shō-yu.* This form gave rise to the Dutch *soja,* which in turn was adopted into English as *soy* in the late 1600s, when the only Westerners allowed to trade in Japan were the Dutch.

soybean

ă	pat	ôr	core
ā	pay	oi	boy
âr	care	ou	out
ä	father	ŏŏ	took
ĕ	pet	ŏŏr	lure
ē	be	ōō	boot
ĭ	pit	ŭ	cut
ī	bite	ûr	urge
îr	pier	th	thin
ŏ	pot	*th*	this
ō	toe	zh	vision
ô	paw	ə	about

direction. **3. Southeast** A part of the southeast United States generally including Alabama, Georgia, South Carolina, and Florida. ❖ *adj.* **1.** To, toward, facing, or in the southeast: *the southeast corner.* **2.** Coming from the southeast: *a southeast wind.* ❖ *adv.* In, from, or toward the southeast: *walking southeast.* —**south·east′ern** *adj.*

Southeast Asia A region of Asia bounded roughly by the Indian subcontinent on the west, China on the north, and the Pacific Ocean on the east. It includes Indochina, the Malay Peninsula, the Malay Archipelago, and sometimes the Philippines.

south·east·er (south-ē′stər) *n.* A storm or gale blowing from the southeast.

south·east·er·ly (south-ē′stər-lē) *adj.* **1.** Situated toward the southeast: *a southeasterly direction.* **2.** Coming from the southeast: *a southeasterly breeze.* —**south·east′er·ly** *adv.*

south·east·ward (south-ēst′wərd) *adv. & adj.* To, toward, or in the southeast: *journeyed southeastward.* ❖ *n.* A direction or region to the southeast. —**south·east′wards** *adv.*

south·er (sou′*th*ər) *n.* A storm or gale blowing from the south.

south·er·ly (sŭ*th*′ər-lē) *adj.* **1.** Situated toward the south: *a southerly direction.* **2.** Coming from the south: *a southerly wind.* ❖ *n., pl.* **south·er·lies** A storm or wind from the south. —**south′er·ly** *adv.*

south·ern (sŭ*th*′ərn) *adj.* **1.** Situated in, toward, or facing the south: *the southern side of the mountain.* **2.** Coming from the south: *a southern breeze.* **3.** often **Southern** Relating to southern regions or the South: *a southern climate.*

Southern Cross *n.* A cross-shaped constellation in the Southern Hemisphere.

south·ern·er also **South·ern·er** (sŭ*th*′ər-nər) *n.* A person who lives in or comes from the south, especially the southern United States.

Southern Hemisphere *n.* **1.** The half of the earth south of the equator. **2.** The half of the celestial sphere south of the celestial equator.

southern lights *pl.n.* The aurora australis.

south·ern·most (sŭ*th*′ərn-mōst′) *adj.* Farthest south.

Southern Ocean or **Antarctic Ocean** The waters surrounding Antarctica, the southern extensions of the Atlantic, Pacific, and Indian Oceans.

south·ing (sou′*th*ĭng) *n.* **1.** The difference in latitude between two positions as a result of southward movement. **2.** Southward movement.

South Island An island of New Zealand southwest of North Island. It is the larger but less heavily populated of the country's two main islands.

South Korea A country of eastern Asia west of Japan on the Yellow Sea. It was part of the ancient country of Korea. Seoul is the capital.

south·land or **South·land** (south′lănd′) *n.* A region in the south of a country or area.

south·paw (south′pô′) *n. Slang* A left-handed person, especially a left-handed baseball pitcher.

South Pole *n.* **1.** The southern end of earth's axis of rotation, a point in Antarctica. **2. south pole** The pole of a magnet that tends to point south.

South Sea Islands The islands of the southern Pacific Ocean, roughly including the same islands as Oceania.

South Seas The oceans south of the equator, especially the southern Pacific Ocean.

South Sudan A country of northeast Africa south of Sudan. It gained its independence from Sudan in 2011. Juba is the capital.

South Vietnam See **Vietnam.**

south·ward (south′wərd) *adv. & adj.* Toward, to, or in the south: *went on a hike southward.* ❖ *n.* A direction or region to the south. —**south′wards** *adv.*

south·west (south-wĕst′) *n.* **1.** The direction halfway between south and west. **2.** An area or region lying in this direction. **3. Southwest** A region of the southwest United States generally considered to include New Mexico, Arizona, Texas, California, and Nevada and sometimes Utah and Colorado. ❖ *adj.* **1.** To, toward, facing, or in the southwest. **2.** Coming from the southwest. ❖ *adv.* In, from, or toward the southwest: *facing southwest.* —**south·west′ern** *adj.*

south·west·er (south-wĕs′tər) also **sou′·west·er** (sou-wĕs′tər) *n.* **1.** A storm or gale blowing from the southwest. **2.** A waterproof hat with a broad brim in back to protect the neck.

south·west·er·ly (south-wĕs′tər-lē) *adj.* **1.** Situated toward the southwest: *a southwesterly march.* **2.** Coming from the southwest: *a southwesterly wind.*

south·west·ward (south-wĕst′wərd) *adv. & adj.* Toward, to, or in the southwest: *sailing southwestward.* ❖ *n.* A southwestward direction or region.

sou·ve·nir (sōō′və-nîr′ *or* sōō′və-nîr′) *n.* A token kept as a remembrance, as of a place or occasion; a memento.

sou′·west·er (sou-wĕs′tər) *n.* Variant of **southwester.**

sov·er·eign (sŏv′ər-ĭn *or* sŏv′rĭn) *n.* **1.** A person or group of people with supreme authority over a state, especially a king or queen. **2.** A gold coin formerly used in Great Britain. ❖ *adj.* **1.** Independent; self-governing: *sovereign states.* **2.** Having supreme rank or power: *a sovereign leader.* **3.** Highest; supreme: *sovereign wisdom.* [From Middle English *soverain*, from Old French, from Latin *super*, above.]

sov·er·eign·ty (sŏv′ər-ĭn-tē *or* sŏv′rĭn-tē) *n., pl.* **sov·er·eign·ties** **1.** Supremacy of authority or rule: *sovereignty over a territory.* **2.** Royal rank, authority, or power: *They did not dispute his sovereignty.* **3.** Freedom from foreign control; independence: *Each state values its sovereignty.*

So·vi·et (sō′vē-ĕt′ *or* sō′vē-ĭt) *adj.* Relating to the former Soviet Union. ❖ *n.* **1. soviet** One of the local, regional, or national elected legislatures in the former Soviet Union. **2.** A native or inhabitant of the former Soviet Union.

Soviet Union See **Union of Soviet Socialist Republics.**

sow[1] (sō) *v.* **sowed, sown** (sōn) or **sowed, sow·ing, sows** —*tr.* **1.** To scatter or plant (seed) on or in the ground for growing: *Have they sown the grass seed yet?* **2.** To plant or scatter seed in or on: *She sowed the field with barley.* **3.** To propagate; spread: *sow rumors.* —*intr.* To scatter or plant seed: *The farmers will be sowing for a few more days.* [From Old English *sāwan.*]

❑ *These sound alike:* **sow**[1], **sew** (stitch), **so**[1] (thus), **so**[2] (musical note).

sow[2] (sou) *n.* **1.** An adult female pig. **2.** The adult female of certain other animals, such as a bear. [From Old English *sugu.*]

sow·bug or **sow bug** (sou′bŭg′) *n.* A woodlouse.

So·we·to (sə-wĕt′tō *or* sə-wā′tō) A former district of racially segregated townships on the southwestern outskirts of Johannesburg, South Africa.

sown (sōn) *v.* A past participle of **sow**[1].

sox (sŏks) *Informal n.* Socks.

soy (soi) *n.* **1.** The soybean. **2.** Soy sauce. —SEE NOTE.

soy·a (soi′ə) *n. Chiefly British* Soy. —SEE NOTE AT **soy.**

soy·bean (soi′bēn′) *n.* **1.** A seed of a widely cultivated plant native to East Asia. Soybeans are used for food, as a source of oil, and as animal feed. **2.** The plant that bears such seeds.

soy·milk (soi′mĭlk′) *n.* A milk substitute made from soybeans.

soy sauce *n.* A salty brown liquid made by fermenting soybeans in brine and used to flavor food.

spa (spä) *n.* **1.** A resort providing therapeutic baths. **2.** A resort area having mineral springs. **3.** A business offering various treatments, such as massages or facials, for health or cosmetic improvement.

space (spās) *n.* **1a.** A set of points that satisfies some set of geometric rules: *a space of five dimensions.* **b.** The familiar three-dimensional region or field of everyday experience. **2a.** The expanse in which the solar system, stars, and galaxies exist; the universe. **b.** The part of the universe beyond Earth's atmosphere: *when the rocket reached space.* **3.** A blank or empty area: *spaces between his teeth; words separated from each other by a space; furniture to fill the space along the wall.* **4.** An area provided for a particular purpose: *a parking space.* **5a.** A period or interval of time: *applied heat for a space of two minutes.* **b.** A little while: *Let's rest for a space.* **6.** Sufficient freedom to develop or explore one's needs, interests, and individuality: *Please give me the space to make my own decision.* ❖ *tr.v.* **spaced, spac·ing, spac·es 1.** To arrange or organize with spaces between: *Carefully space the words on the poster.* **2.** To separate or keep apart: *The two buildings are spaced far from each other.* [From Middle English, from Latin *spatium.*]

space bar *n.* A bar at the bottom of a computer or typewriter keyboard that, when pressed, introduces a space into text, as between words.

space capsule A compartment that can be separated from the rest of a spacecraft, especially one designed to accommodate a crew.

space·craft (spās′krăft′) *n., pl.* **spacecraft** A vehicle designed for space travel.

space flight *n.* Flight beyond the atmosphere of Earth.

space probe *n.* A spacecraft carrying instruments designed for use in exploring the physical properties of outer space or of celestial objects other than Earth.

space·ship (spās′shĭp′) *n.* A spacecraft.

space shuttle *n.* A reusable space vehicle designed to transport astronauts between Earth and space.

space station *n.* A large satellite equipped to support a human crew and designed to remain in orbit around Earth for a long period of time.

space suit *n.* A protective pressurized suit designed to allow the wearer to move about freely in space.

space-time (spās′tīm′) *n.* The four dimensions in which all objects are located and all events occur, viewed as a single and continuous framework for existence. Space-time consists of length, width, and depth, plus the dimension of time.

space walk *n.* An excursion by an astronaut outside a spacecraft in space. **—space walker** *n.*

spac·ing (spā′sĭng) *n.* **1.** The act or result of arranging things so that they are separated by spaces. **2.** The spaces or a space between things.

spa·cious (spā′shəs) *adj.* **1.** Having much space; roomy; extensive: *a spacious room.* **2.** Vast in range or scope: *too spacious a subject for a short lecture.* **—spa′cious·ly** *adv.* **—spa′cious·ness** *n.*

spade¹ (spād) *n.* **1.** A digging tool with a thick handle and a flat heavy blade that can be pressed into the ground with the foot. **2.** Any of various similar tools, such as a gardener's trowel. ❖ *tr.v.* **spad·ed, spad·ing, spades** To dig with a spade: *spade the garden.* [From Old English *spadu.*]

spade² (spād) *n.* **1.** A black leaf-shaped figure on a playing card. **2.** A playing card with this figure. **3.** also **spades** *(used with a singular or plural verb)* The suit of cards having this figure as its symbol. [From Italian *spada*, from Greek *spathē*, broad blade.]

spa·dix (spā′dĭks) *n., pl.* **spa·di·ces** (spā′dĭ-sēz′) A fleshy spike bearing tiny flowers, often surrounded by a part resembling a leaf or petal, as in the jack-in-the-pulpit.

spa·ghet·ti (spə-gĕt′ē) *n.* Pasta in long, often thick strands.

Spain (spān) A country of southwest Europe on the Iberian Peninsula. Long fragmented into various kingdoms, it was united in 1492 under Ferdinand of Aragon and Isabella of Castile. Madrid is the capital.

spake (spāk) *v. Archaic* A past tense of **speak.**

spam (spăm) *n.* Unrequested and unwanted email, usually of a commercial nature. ❖ *tr.v.* **spammed, spam·ming, spams** To send spam to.

spam·bot (spăm′bŏt′) *n.* A bot that sends out junk email.

span¹ (spăn) *n.* **1.** The distance between two points or ends, as of a bridge. **2.** A section of a bridge between two vertical supports. **3.** The distance from the tip of the thumb to the tip of the little finger when the hand is fully extended, formerly used as a unit of measure equal to about nine inches (23 centimeters). **4.** A period of time: *a span of four hours.* ❖ *tr.v.* **spanned, span·ning, spans 1.** To extend across in space or time: *a career that spans 30 years.* **2.** To encircle or cover with the hand or hands. [From Old English *spann*, hand's breadth.]

span² (spăn) *n.* A pair of animals matched in size, strength, or color and driven as a team: *a span of oxen.* [From Dutch *spannen*, to harness.]

span·dex (spăn′dĕks) *n.* A fiber or fabric made of a polymer containing polyurethane, used in elastic clothing.

span·gle (spăng′gəl) *n.* **1.** A small piece of sparkling metal or plastic sewn especially on clothes for decoration. **2.** A small sparkling object, drop, or spot: *spangles of sunlight.* ❖ *v.* **span·gled, span·gling, span·gles** *—tr.* To decorate with or as if with spangles. *—intr.* To sparkle in the manner of spangles.

Span·iard (spăn′yərd) *n.* A native or inhabitant of Spain.

span·iel (spăn′yəl) *n.* A small to medium-sized dog of any of several breeds having drooping ears, short legs, and a silky wavy coat.

Span·ish (spăn′ĭsh) *adj.* Relating to Spain or its people, language, or culture. ❖ *n.* **1.** The Romance language of the largest part of Spain and most of Central and South America. **2.** *(used with a plural verb)* The people of Spain.

Spanish America The former Spanish possessions in the New World, including most of South and Central America, Mexico, Cuba, Puerto Rico, the Dominican Republic, and other small islands in the Caribbean Sea.

Spanish American also **Span·ish-A·mer·i·can** (spăn′ĭsh-ə-mĕr′ĭ-kən) *adj.* **Spanish-American 1.** Relating to Spanish America or its peoples or cultures. **2.** Relating to Spain and America, especially the United States. ❖ *n.* **1.** A native or inhabitant of Spanish America. **2.** A US citizen or resident of Hispanic ancestry.

Spanish Main 1. The coastal region of mainland Spanish America in the 1500s and 1600s. **2.** The section of the Caribbean Sea crossed by Spanish ships in colonial times.

Spanish moss *n.* A plant of the southeast United States and tropical America that grows on trees and hangs down in long grayish masses.

spank (spăngk) *tr.v.* **spanked, spank·ing, spanks** To slap on the buttocks with a flat object or the open hand. ❖ *n.* A slap on the buttocks.

spank·ing (spăng′kĭng) *adj.* **1.** *Informal* Exceptional; remarkable. **2.** Bright; fast: *a spanking pace.* **3.** Brisk and fresh: *a spanking breeze.* ❖ *adv.* Used as an intensive: *a spanking new kitchen.* ❖ *n.* A series of slaps on the buttocks, given as punishment.

span·ner (spăn′ər) *n. Chiefly British* A wrench.

spar¹ (spär) *n.* **1.** A pole, such as a mast, boom, yard, or bowsprit, used on a sailing vessel. **2.** A usually metal pole used as part of a crane or derrick. [From Middle English *sparre*, rafter.]

spar² (spär) *intr.v.* **sparred, spar·ring, spars 1.** To fight

space shuttle
space shuttle *Atlantis*

space walk

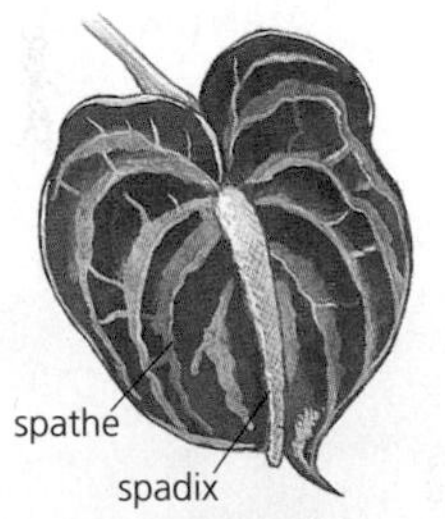

spadix

Spanish moss

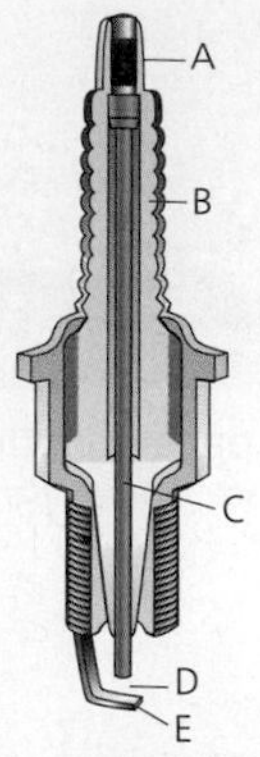

spark plug
A. terminal
B. ceramic insulation
C. center electrode
D. gap
E. ground electrode

sparrow

spat³

ă	pat	ôr	core
ā	pay	oi	boy
âr	care	ou	out
ä	father	o͝o	took
ĕ	pet	o͝or	lure
ē	be	o͞o	boot
ĭ	pit	ŭ	cut
ī	bite	ûr	urge
îr	pier	th	thin
ŏ	pot	*th*	this
ō	toe	zh	vision
ô	paw	ə	about

with an opponent in a short bout or practice session, as in boxing or the martial arts. **2.** To exchange words in a quarrel or an argument. [From Middle English *sparren*, to thrust or strike rapidly.]

spare (spâr) *tr.v.* **spared, spar·ing, spares 1.** To refrain from destroying or harming: *The construction crew spared the trees.* **2.** To refrain from denouncing or distressing; treat leniently or with consideration: *The coach did not spare his players' feelings after such a poor showing.* **3.** To allow (someone) to avoid experiencing or doing (something): *I spared you the trouble of returning the books.* **4.** To hold back or avoid: *We spared no expense for the party.* **5.** To use in small amounts: *Don't spare the pepper.* **6.** To give or grant out of one's resources: *Can you spare ten minutes?* ❖ *adj.* **spar·er, spar·est 1a.** Kept in reserve: *a spare tire.* **b.** Being in excess of what is needed; extra: *spare cash.* **c.** Free for other use: *spare time.* **2a.** Not abundant; meager: *a spare breakfast.* **b.** Thin or lean. See Synonyms at **lean²**. ❖ *n.* **1.** A replacement, such as a tire, reserved for future need. **2.** In bowling, the act of knocking down all ten pins with two rolls of the ball. ◆ **to spare** In addition to what is needed: *We have ice cream to spare.* **—spare′ly** *adv.* **—spare′ness** *n.*

spare·ribs (spâr′rĭbz′) *pl.n.* Pork ribs with most of the meat trimmed off.

spar·ing (spâr′ĭng) *adj.* Thrifty; frugal. **—spar′ing·ly** *adv.* **—spar′ing·ness** *n.*

spark (spärk) *n.* **1.** A glowing particle, such as one thrown off or left over from a fire or one caused by friction. **2a.** A flash of light, especially one produced by electric discharge. **b.** A short pulse of electric current. **3.** Something small that starts or remains of something; a seed or trace: *the spark of rebellion; no spark of interest in continuing the club.* ❖ *v.* **sparked, spark·ing, sparks** *—intr.* To give off sparks. *—tr.* To set in motion or rouse to action: *His speech sparked a controversy.*

spar·kle (spär′kəl) *intr.v.* **spar·kled, spar·kling, spar·kles 1.** To give off sparks. **2.** To give off or reflect flashes of light; glitter. **3.** To be brilliant in performance: *She sparkled on the piano.* **4.** To be lively: *The conversation sparkled at the dinner table.* **5.** To release bubbles of gas; effervesce. ❖ *n.* **1.** A small spark or glowing particle. **2.** Liveliness; vivacity. **3.** The releasing of bubbles of gas; effervescence.

spar·kler (spär′klər) *n.* **1.** A person or thing that sparkles. **2.** A firework that burns slowly and produces a shower of sparks.

spark plug *n.* A device that fits into the combustion chamber of an internal-combustion engine and produces an electric spark to ignite the fuel mixture.

spar·row (spăr′ō) *n.* **1.** Any of various small brownish or grayish seed-eating birds of North America. **2.** Any of several similar birds native to Eurasia and Africa, such as the house sparrow. [From Old English *spearwa*.]

sparrow hawk *n.* **1.** A small North American falcon that hovers when hunting; a kestrel. **2.** A Eurasian hawk similar to this hawk.

sparse (spärs) *adj.* **spars·er, spars·est** Not dense or crowded: *sparse vegetation.* **—sparse′ly** *adv.* **—sparse′ness** *n.* **—spar′si·ty** (spär′sĭ-tē) *n.*

Spar·ta (spär′tə) A city-state of ancient Greece in the southeast Peloponnesus. It was noted for its militarism and reached the height of its power in the sixth century BC.

Spar·tan (spär′tn) *adj.* **1.** Relating to Sparta or its people. **2.** also **spartan** Simple, frugal, or self-disciplined: *Spartan furnishings; a spartan lifestyle.* ❖ *n.* **1.** A citizen of Sparta. **2.** A person of Spartan character.

spasm (spăz′əm) *n.* **1.** A sudden involuntary contraction of a muscle or group of muscles. **2.** A sudden burst of energy, activity, or emotion. [From Middle English *spasme*, from Greek *spasmos*, from *spān*, to pull.]

spas·mod·ic (spăz-mŏd′ĭk) *adj.* **1.** Relating to, affected by, or resembling a spasm. **2.** Happening intermittently; fitful: *spasmodic attempts to change jobs.* **3.** Given to sudden outbursts of energy or feeling; excitable.

spas·tic (spăs′tĭk) *adj.* **1.** Relating to or marked by spasms. **2.** Affected with spastic paralysis. ❖ *n.* A person affected with spastic paralysis.

spastic paralysis *n.* Paralysis caused by damage to the central nervous system, characterized by muscle spasms and exaggerated reflexes of the tendons.

spat¹ (spăt) *v.* A past tense and a past participle of **spit¹**.

spat² (spăt) *n., pl.* **spat** or **spats** A larva of an oyster or similar shellfish that has settled by attaching to a surface. [From Anglo-Norman.]

spat³ (spăt) *n.* A cloth or leather covering for the ankle and the top part of the shoe, fastening under the shoe with a strap. [Short for *spatterdash* : from *spatter* + *dash*, to splash.]

spat⁴ (spăt) *n.* A brief quarrel. ❖ *intr.v.* **spat·ted, spat·ting, spats** To engage in a brief quarrel.

spate (spāt) *n.* **1.** A sudden flood, rush, or outpouring: *a spate of words.* **2.** *Chiefly British* A flash flood.

spathe (spā*th*) *n.* A plant part that resembles a leaf or petal and surrounds a fleshy flower spike, as in the jack-in-the-pulpit.

spa·tial (spā′shəl) *adj.* Relating to or involving space. **—spa′tial·ly** *adv.*

spat·ter (spăt′ər) *v.* **spat·tered, spat·ter·ing, spat·ters** *—tr.* **1.** To cover with spots or drops of a liquid or wet substance: *The passing car spattered my pants with mud.* **2.** To scatter in drops or small splashes: *She spattered paint on the paper.* *—intr.* To fall or land in drops or splashes: *Mud from the passing car spattered on my shoes.* ❖ *n.* **1.** A drop, splash, or small amount: *spatters of grease on the stove.* **2.** A sound that is made by something spattering: *the spatter of raindrops.*

spat·u·la (spăch′ə-lə) *n.* A tool with a broad, flat, flexible blade, used to mix, spread, or lift material, such as food or paint. [From Latin *spatula*, flat piece of wood, splint, from *spatha*, broadsword.]

spav·in (spăv′ĭn) *n.* A disease of the hock joint of horses, causing stiffness and lameness.

spawn (spôn) *n.* **1.** The eggs of animals, such as fishes, amphibians, and most mollusks, that release their eggs into water. **2.** Offspring produced in large numbers. ❖ *v.* **spawned, spawn·ing, spawns** *—intr.* To lay eggs; produce spawn: *Salmon swim up streams to spawn.* *—tr.* To give rise to; bring about: *an act that spawned a revolution; tornadoes spawned by the storm.*

spay (spā) *tr.v.* **spayed, spay·ing, spays** To remove the ovaries of (a female animal).

SPCA *abbr.* An abbreviation of Society for the Prevention of Cruelty to Animals.

speak (spēk) *v.* **spoke** (spōk), **spo·ken** (spō′kən), **speak·ing, speaks** *—intr.* **1.** To utter words; talk: *They spoke about the weather.* **2.** To express thoughts or feelings: *He spoke of his desire to travel.* **3.** To be on speaking terms: *They haven't spoken for years.* **4.** To deliver an address or a lecture: *She's speaking tonight at the rally.* **5.** To give an indication: *His manners spoke of a good upbringing.* *—tr.* **1.** To pronounce; utter: *He spoke kind words.* **2.** To converse in or be able to converse in (a language): *She speaks Chinese.* **3.** To express in words; tell: *speak the truth.* **4.** To communicate without words: *His eyes spoke volumes.* ◆ **so to speak** In a manner of speaking; as it were. **speak out** To talk freely and fearlessly, as about a public issue. **speak up 1.** To speak loud enough to be heard. **2.** To speak without fear or hesitation: *afraid to speak up at the meeting.* [From Old English *sprecan*.]

speak·eas·y (spēk′ē′zē) *n., pl.* **speak·eas·ies** A place for the illegal sale of alcoholic drinks, especially during Prohibition in the United States.

speak·er (spē′kər) *n.* **1.** A person who speaks: *speakers of Swahili.* **2.** A spokesperson. **3.** A person who delivers a speech in public. **4.** often **Speaker** The presiding officer of a legislative body. **5.** A loudspeaker.

speak·ing (spē′kĭng) *adj.* **1.** Capable of or involving speech: *a speaking voice.* **2.** Highly expressive: *speaking eyes.* ◆ **on speaking terms** Friendly enough to exchange superficial remarks: *We're on speaking terms with our neighbors.*

spear[1] (spîr) *n.* **1.** A weapon consisting of a long shaft with a sharply pointed head. **2.** A device with a sharp point and barbs for spearing fish. ❖ *tr.v.* **speared, spear·ing, spears** To pierce, as with a spear. [From Old English *spere.*]

spear[2] (spîr) *n.* A slender stalk, as of asparagus. [Alteration of *spire,* tapering point.]

spear·fish (spîr′fĭsh′) *intr.v.* **spear·fished, spear·fish·ing, spear·fish·es** To fish with a spear or spear gun.

spear gun *n.* A device that shoots a short spear under water, used to spear fish.

spear·head (spîr′hĕd′) *n.* **1.** The head of a spear. **2.** The front forces in a military campaign. **3.** The driving force in an endeavor. ❖ *tr.v.* **spear·head·ed, spear·head·ing, spear·heads** To lead: *spearheaded the effort to develop solar energy.*

spear·mint (spîr′mĭnt′) *n.* A kind of mint that yields an oil used as flavoring.

spe·cial (spĕsh′əl) *adj.* **1.** Surpassing what is common or usual; exceptional: *a special occasion.* **2.** Distinct among others of a kind: *a special camera.* **3.** Peculiar to a specific person or thing: *special interests.* **4.** Having a specific function or application: *special training.* **5.** Particularly dear and esteemed: *special friends.* **6.** Additional; extra: *a special flight.* ❖ *n.* **1.** Something arranged or designed for a particular service or occasion. **2.** A featured attraction, such as a reduced price: *a special on peaches.* **3.** A single television production that features a specific work, topic, or performer. —**spe′cial·ly** *adv.*

special delivery *n.* The delivery of a piece of mail, for an additional charge, by special messenger rather than by scheduled delivery.

special education *n.* Instruction designed for students whose needs cannot be met by standard classroom education.

special effect *n.* A visual effect added to a film, for example, to create an illusion: *a science-fiction movie with incredible special effects.*

special interest *n.* A group or organization attempting to influence legislators in favor of a particular interest or issue.

spe·cial·ist (spĕsh′ə-lĭst) *n.* A person whose work is restricted to a particular activity or to a particular branch of study or research, such as a doctor who practices a particular branch of medicine.

spe·cial·ize (spĕsh′ə-līz′) *intr.v.* **spe·cial·ized, spe·cial·iz·ing, spe·cial·iz·es 1.** To concentrate one's energy or attention on a special study, activity, or product: *specialized in underwater photography; a shop that specializes in sports clothes.* **2.** To adapt during the process of evolution to a particular environment, function, or way of life: *Some types of worm have specialized in parasitizing only one species of animal.* —**spe′cial·i·za′tion** (spĕsh′ə-lĭ-**zā′**shən) *n.*

spe·cial·ized (spĕsh′ə-līz′) *adj.* **1.** Requiring or having detailed training or expertise in a particular field: *Art restoration is a very specialized field.* **2.** Designed for a specific purpose or use: *a specialized computer application.* **3.** Adapted during the process of evolution to a particular environment, function, or way of life: *a bird with a specialized beak for eating seeds.*

special needs *pl.n.* Requirements for care or services beyond what is common or usual, especially on account of a physical disability or learning disorder: *a teacher of children with special needs.* —**spe′cial-needs′** (spĕsh′-əl-**nēdz′**) *adj.*

spe·cial·ty (spĕsh′əl-tē) *n., pl.* **spe·cial·ties 1.** A special pursuit, occupation, talent, or skill: *His specialty is portrait painting.* **2.** An item or product of a distinctive kind or of particular superiority: *The restaurant's specialty is pastry.*

spe·ci·a·tion (spē′shē-**ā′**shən) *n.* The formation of new biological species through the process of evolution. —**spe′ci·ate′** *v.*

spe·cie (spē′shē *or* spē′sē) *n.* Coined money.

spe·cies (spē′shēz *or* spē′sēz) *n., pl.* **species 1.** A taxonomic category of closely related organisms that are very similar to each other and are usually capable of interbreeding and producing fertile offspring. The species is the fundamental category of taxonomic classification, ranking below a genus. Every species has a unique scientific name with two parts, such as *Homo sapiens.* See table at **taxonomy. 2.** A type, kind, or sort: *That species of error is hard to detect.*

spe·cif·ic (spĭ-sĭf′ĭk) *adj.* **1.** Stating or stated clearly and in detail: *Be specific about what you want.* **2.** Relating to a biological species: *In the scientific name* Homo sapiens, Homo *is the generic name, and* sapiens *is the specific name.* **3.** Special, distinctive, or unique: *a specific trait.* **4.** Intended for or acting on one particular thing: *a specific remedy for the infection.* ❖ *n.* **1.** Something designed for a particular use or purpose, especially a remedy intended for a particular disorder. **2. specifics** Details; particulars: *Tell me what happened and give me the specifics.* —**spe·cif′i·cal·ly** *adv.*

spec·i·fi·ca·tion (spĕs′ə-fĭ-**kā′**shən) *n.* **1.** The act of specifying. **2a. specifications** A statement giving an exact description, as of a product or a structure to be constructed. **b.** A single item that has been specified.

specific gravity *n.* A measure of a substance's density, equal to the ratio of the density of the substance to that of water, if the substance is a liquid or solid, or to that of air, if the substance is a gas.

specific heat *n.* **1.** The ratio of the amount of heat needed to raise the temperature of a unit mass of a substance by one unit to the amount of heat needed to raise the temperature of a unit mass of a reference substance, usually water, by the same amount. **2.** The amount of heat, measured in calories, needed to raise the temperature of one gram of a substance by one degree Centigrade.

spec·i·fy (spĕs′ə-fī′) *tr.v.* **spec·i·fied, spec·i·fy·ing, spec·i·fies 1.** To state clearly or in detail: *specified the amount needed; specified that they would come.* **2.** To include in a specification.

spec·i·men (spĕs′ə-mən) *n.* **1.** An organism, part of an organism, or fossil that has been collected and usually preserved, especially for display or scientific research. **2.** A sample, as of blood, tissue, or urine, used for analysis or testing. **3.** An individual, item, or part representative of a class or whole: *The painting is a good specimen of portraits from that era.*

spe·cious (spē′shəs) *adj.* Seemingly fair, sound, or true, but actually false: *specious reasoning.*

speck (spĕk) *n.* **1.** A small spot, mark, or discoloration: *brown specks on the paper.* **2.** A small amount; a bit: *a speck of dust.* ❖ *tr.v.* **specked, speck·ing, specks** To mark with specks: *Her jeans were specked with mud.*

speck·le (spĕk′əl) *n.* A small spot, especially a spot of color that differs from the background.

speck·led (spĕk′əld) *adj.* Covered with speckles: *speckled trout.*

spec·ta·cle (spĕk′tə-kəl) *n.* **1.** Something that can be seen, especially a remarkable or impressive sight: *The meteor shower was quite a spectacle.* **2.** A public performance or display, especially on a grand scale. **3.** A

spatula

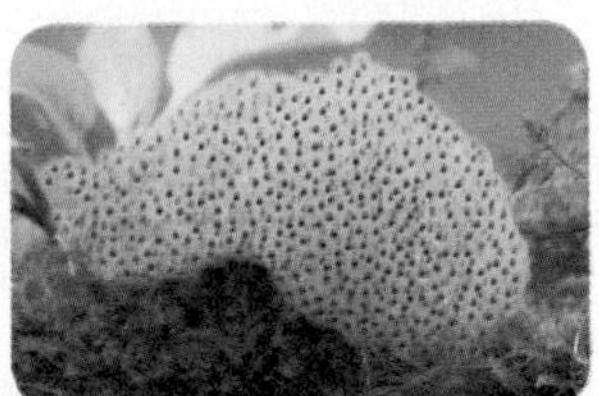

spawn
of a frog

speckled
killdeer eggs

WORD BUILDING

spectator The word root *spec–* in English words comes from the Latin verb *specere,* "to look at, observe." A **spectator,** therefore, is literally "a watcher." To **inspect** means "to look into, inquire into" (using the prefix *in–²*, "in, into"); **introspection** is literally "a mental look within oneself" (*intrō–,* "inside"); a **retrospective** means "a review, a backward look at the past" (*retrō–,* "backward"); and a **prospect** is literally "something seen ahead of one or presented to one, a view" (*pro–¹*, "in front of, before").

spectrum

speedskating

ă	pat	ôr	core
ā	pay	oi	boy
âr	care	ou	out
ä	father	o͝o	took
ĕ	pet	o͝or	lure
ē	be	o͞o	boot
ĭ	pit	ŭ	cut
ī	bite	ûr	urge
îr	pier	th	thin
ŏ	pot	*th*	this
ō	toe	zh	vision
ô	paw	ə	about

regrettable display: *He got angry and made a spectacle of himself.* **4. spectacles** A pair of eyeglasses.

spec·tac·u·lar (spĕk-**tăk′**yə-lər) *adj.* Of the nature of a spectacle; impressive or sensational: *a spectacular view.* **—spec·tac′u·lar·ly** *adv.*

spec·ta·tor (**spĕk′**tā′tər) *n.* An observer of an event, especially a sports contest. [From Latin *spectāre,* to watch.] —SEE NOTE.

spec·ter (**spĕk′**tər) *n.* **1.** A ghost; a phantom. **2.** A haunting or disturbing prospect: *the terrible specter of nuclear war.*

spec·tra (**spĕk′**trə) *n.* A plural of **spectrum.**

spec·tral (**spĕk′**trəl) *adj.* **1.** Relating to a specter; ghostly. **2.** Relating to a spectrum. **—spec′tral·ly** *adv.*

spec·trom·e·ter (spĕk-**trŏm′**ĭ-tər) *n.* **1.** A spectroscope equipped with devices for measuring the wavelengths of the radiation observed by it. **2.** An instrument used to measure the index of refraction of a substance. **—spec·trom′e·try** *n.*

spec·tro·scope (**spĕk′**trə-skōp′) *n.* Any of various instruments used to resolve radiation into spectra and to make observations or recordings.

spec·trum (**spĕk′**trəm) *n., pl.* **spec·tra** (**spĕk′**trə) or **spec·trums 1a.** A band of colors seen when white light is broken up according to wavelengths, as when passing through a prism or striking drops of water. **b.** The electromagnetic spectrum. **2.** A broad range of related qualities, ideas, or activities: *a wide spectrum of ideas.* [From Latin *spectrum,* appearance, from *specere,* to look at.]

spec·u·late (**spĕk′**yə-lāt′) *v.* **spec·u·lat·ed, spec·u·lat·ing, spec·u·lates** *—tr.* To consider as a possibility based on limited evidence: *speculated that there were mineral deposits in the rocks.* *—intr.* **1.** To make a guess based on limited evidence. **2.** To buy or sell something that involves a risk on the chance of making a profit: *speculating on the stock exchange.* [From Latin *speculārī,* to observe, from *specula,* watchtower.]

spec·u·la·tion (spĕk′yə-**lā′**shən) *n.* **1a.** The act of thinking about or discussing a subject based on limited evidence. **b.** A conclusion, idea, or opinion reached by guessing. **2a.** A business deal involving speculation. **b.** Involvement in such business deals.

spec·u·la·tive (**spĕk′**yə-lə-tĭv *or* **spĕk′**yə-lā′tĭv) *adj.* **1.** Relating to or based on mental speculation. **2.** Given to making guesses. **3.** Engaging in or involving financial speculation. **—spec′u·la·tive·ly** *adv.* **—spec′u·la·tive·ness** *n.*

spec·u·la·tor (**spĕk′**yə-lā′tər) *n.* A person who speculates.

sped (spĕd) *v.* A past tense and a past participle of **speed.**

speech (spēch) *n.* **1.** The act of speaking. **2.** The ability to speak. **3.** Something spoken; an utterance. **4.** Communication by speaking; conversation. **5.** A talk or address. **6.** The manner in which a person speaks. **7.** The language or dialect of a nation or region: *American speech.* [From Old English *sprǣc.*]

speech·less (**spēch′**lĭs) *adj.* **1.** Unable to speak. **2.** Temporarily unable to speak, as through astonishment. **3.** Not speaking; silent. **4.** Not expressed or not expressible in words: *speechless admiration.* **—speech′less·ly** *adv.* **—speech′less·ness** *n.*

speech therapy *n.* The treatment of speech disorders, especially through use of exercises and audio-visual aids that develop new speech habits.

speed (spēd) *n.* **1.** The rate at which an object changes position, especially the distance an object travels divided by the time of travel. **2.** Swiftness of action. **3.** The condition or act of moving rapidly; swiftness: *He finished the race with a show of speed.* **4.** A transmission gear or set of gears in a motor vehicle. **5a.** A number that expresses the sensitivity to light of a photographic film, plate, or paper. **b.** The capacity of a lens to admit light at a particular aperture. **c.** The length of time the shutter of a camera is open to admit light. **6.** *Archaic* Prosperity; luck. ❖ *v.* **sped** (spĕd) or **speed·ed, speed·ing, speeds** *—tr.* **1.** To cause to go or move rapidly. **2.** To increase the speed or rate of; accelerate: *speed up a mechanism.* **3.** To wish Godspeed to. *—intr.* **1.** To go or move quickly. **2.** To drive at a speed that exceeds a legal limit. **3.** To pass quickly: *The days sped by.* **4.** To move, work, or happen at a faster rate: *The phonograph speeded up.* ◆ **up to speed 1a.** Operating at maximum speed. **b.** Producing something or performing at an acceptable rate or level. **2.** *Informal* Fully informed: *brought me up to speed on the issue.* [From Old English *spēd,* success, swiftness.]

speed·boat (**spēd′**bōt′) *n.* A fast motorboat.

speed·er (**spē′**dər) *n.* A person or thing that speeds, especially a driver who exceeds a legal or safe speed.

speed·om·e·ter (spĭ-**dŏm′**ĭ-tər) *n.* An instrument that indicates speed.

speed-read·ing (**spēd′**rē′dĭng) *n.* A method of reading rapidly by skipping unimportant words in a text and by understanding groups of words at a time.

speed·skat·ing or **speed skating** (**spēd′**skā′tĭng) *n.* Competitive racing on specialized ice skates, usually around an oval course. **—speed′skat′er** *n.*

speed·up (**spēd′**ŭp′) *n.* **1.** An increase in speed; acceleration. **2.** Acceleration of production without increase in pay.

speed·way (**spēd′**wā′) *n.* **1.** A course for automobile or motorcycle racing. **2.** A road designed for high-speed traffic; an expressway.

speed·y (**spē′**dē) *adj.* **speed·i·er, speed·i·est 1.** Swift; quick: *a speedy runner.* **2.** Done without delay; prompt: *a speedy reply.* **—speed′i·ly** *adv.* **—speed′i·ness** *n.*

spe·le·ol·o·gy (spē′lē-**ŏl′**ə-jē) *n.* The study and exploration of caves. **—spe′le·ol′o·gist** *n.*

spell¹ (spĕl) *v.* **spelled** or **spelt** (spĕlt), **spell·ing, spells** *—tr.* **1.** To name or write in order the letters forming (a word or part of a word). **2.** To be the letters of; form (a word or part of a word): *These letters spell "animal."* **3.** To add up to; signify: *Her efforts spelled success.* *—intr.* To form a word or words by letters: *learned to spell.* ◆ **spell out** To make perfectly clear and understandable: *spelled out the instructions for us.* [From Middle English *spellen,* from Old French *espeller,* of Germanic origin.]

spell² (spĕl) *n.* **1.** A word or group of words believed to have magic power. **2.** The condition of being bewitched or enchanted; a trance. **3.** Fascination; charm: *the spell of a tropical island.* [From Old English, discourse.]

spell³ (spĕl) *n.* **1.** A short indefinite period of time: *Let's visit for a spell.* **2.** *Informal* A period of weather of a particular kind: *a cold spell.* **3.** A period of work; a shift: *a spell at the plane's controls.* **4.** *Informal* A period or fit of illness: *a coughing spell.* ❖ *tr.v.* **spelled, spell·ing, spells** To relieve (someone) from work temporarily by taking a turn. [From Middle English *spelan,* to spare, from Old English *spelian,* to represent, substitute for.]

spell·bind (**spĕl′**bīnd′) *tr.v.* **spell·bound** (**spĕl′**bound′), **spell·bind·ing, spell·binds 1.** To hold under a magic spell. **2.** To fascinate (someone), as if by means of a spell: *We were spellbound by the explorer's tale.*

spell·bound (**spĕl′**bound′) *adj.* Held as if under a spell; entranced; fascinated.

spell checker *n.* An application in a word processing program that checks for spelling errors in documents. **—spell check** *v.*

spell·er (**spĕl′**ər) *n.* **1.** A person who spells words: *good spellers.* **2.** A textbook with exercises that teach spelling.

spell·ing (**spĕl′**ĭng) *n.* **1.** The forming of words with letters in an accepted order. **2.** The way in which a word is spelled.

spelling bee *n.* A spelling contest in which participants drop out when they fail to spell a given word correctly.

spelt (spĕlt) *v.* A past tense and a past participle of **spell**[1].

spe·lunk·er (spĭ-**lŭng′**kər *or* **spē′**lŭng′kər) *n.* A person who explores caves chiefly as a hobby; a caver. **—spe′lunk′ing** *n.*

spend (spĕnd) *tr.v.* **spent** (spĕnt), **spend·ing, spends 1.** To pay out (money), especially to buy something: *I spent five dollars on lunch.* **2.** To pass (time) in a specified place or manner: *spent my vacation hiking.* **—spend′er** *n.*

spend·thrift (**spĕnd′**thrĭft′) *n.* A person who spends money wastefully or foolishly. ❖ *adj.* Wasteful; extravagant.

Spen·ser (**spĕn′**sər), **Edmund** 1552?–1599. English poet known chiefly for his epic romance *The Faerie Queene* (1590–1596).

spent (spĕnt) *v.* Past tense and past participle of **spend.** ❖ *adj.* **1.** Used up; consumed: *spent mineral resources.* **2.** Having no more energy, force, or strength: *a spent horse.*

sperm (spûrm) *n., pl.* **sperm** or **sperms 1.** A sperm cell. **2.** Semen.

sper·ma·ce·ti (spûr′mə-**sē′**tē *or* spûr′mə-**sĕt′**ē) *n., pl.* **sper·ma·ce·tis** A white waxy substance obtained from the head of the sperm whale and formerly used in making candles, ointments, and cosmetics.

sper·mat·o·phyte (spər **măt′**ə-fīt′ *or* **spûr′**mə-tə-fīt′) *n.* A seed plant.

sper·mat·o·zo·on (spər-măt′ə-**zō′**ŏn′ *or* spûr′mə-tə-**zō′**ŏn′) *n., pl.* **sper·mat·o·zo·a** (spər-măt′ə-**zō′**ə *or* spûr′mə-tə-**zō′**ə) A male reproductive cell of humans and most other animals, capable of uniting with an egg in the process of sexual reproduction. Each spermatozoon has a long tail that whips back and forth to produce movement.

sperm cell *n.* **1.** A male reproductive cell in animals; a spermatozoon. **2.** A male reproductive cell in plants and most algae.

sperm oil *n.* A yellow waxy oil obtained from the sperm whale, formerly used as an industrial lubricant.

sperm whale *n.* A very large whale having a long, narrow, toothed lower jaw and a massive head that contains spermaceti and sperm oil.

spew (spyo͞o) *v.* **spewed, spew·ing, spews** *—tr.* **1.** To send out or force out in large amounts: *volcanoes spewing out lava.* **2.** To vomit or cast out through the mouth. *—intr.* **1.** To flow or gush forth: *water spewed out.* **2.** To vomit.

sphag·num (**sfăg′**nəm) *n.* Any of various mosses that grow in bogs and decompose to form a type of peat.

sphe·noid bone (**sfē′**noid′) *n.* A bone with projections resembling wings, situated at the base of the skull.

sphere (sfîr) *n.* **1.** A three-dimensional geometric surface having all of its points the same distance from a given point. **2.** An object or figure having this shape. **3.** In ancient and medieval astronomy, one of the concentric, transparent, revolving globes thought to have Earth as a center and to contain the sun, moon, planets, and stars. **4.** An area or extent of interest, influence, or activity: *Poland was once in the sphere of the Soviet Union.* [From Middle English *spere,* from Greek *sphaira.*]

spher·i·cal (**sfîr′**ĭ-kəl *or* **sfĕr′**ĭ-kəl) *adj.* Relating to or having the shape of a sphere. **—spher′i·cal·ly** *adv.*

spher·oid (**sfîr′**oid′ *or* **sfĕr′**oid′) *n.* **1.** A three-dimensional geometric surface generated by rotating an ellipse on or about one of its axes. **2.** A figure or object having such a shape.

sphinc·ter (**sfĭngk′**tər) *n.* A circular muscle that usually remains contracted and keeps the opening of a body passage closed, relaxing as required by normal functioning.

sphinx (sfĭngks) *n.* **1.** *pl.* **sphinx·es** or **sphin·ges** (**sfĭn′**jēz′) **a.** In Egyptian mythology, a figure having the body of a lion and the head of a man, ram, or hawk. **b.** often **Sphinx** In Greek mythology, a winged creature having the body of a lion and the head of a woman that killed anyone who could not answer its riddle. **2.** *pl.* **sphinxes** A puzzling or mysterious person.

sphyg·mo·ma·nom·e·ter (sfĭg′mō-mə-**nŏm′**ĭ-tər) *n.* An instrument used to measure blood pressure, consisting of a pressure gauge attached to a soft inflatable cuff that wraps around the upper arm.

spice (spīs) *n.* **1.** Any of various aromatic plant parts, especially seeds or bark, that are used to flavor food. Pepper, cinnamon, and cumin are spices. **2.** Something that adds zest or interest: *The tie game added spice to the tournament.* ❖ *tr.v.* **spiced, spic·ing, spic·es 1.** To flavor with spices. **2.** To add zest or interest to: *The essay is boring; you need to spice it up.* [From Middle English, from Late Latin *speciēs,* wares, spices.]

spick-and-span (spĭk′ən-**spăn′**) *adj.* Neat and clean; spotless.

spic·ule (**spĭk′**yo͞ol) *n.* A small structure or part resembling a needle, as one of the mineral structures supporting the soft tissue of certain invertebrates, especially sponges.

spic·y (**spī′**sē) *adj.* **spic·i·er, spic·i·est 1.** Having the flavor, smell, or quality of spice: *spicy pumpkin pie.* **2.** Lively; high-spirited. **3.** Slightly scandalous: *spicy stories.* **—spic′i·ly** *adv.* **—spic′i·ness** *n.*

spi·der (**spī′**dər) *n.* Any of numerous small invertebrate animals that have eight legs and a body divided into two parts and that usually spin webs to trap insects. Spiders are sometimes confused with insects but belong to a different group, the arachnids, which also includes the scorpions, mites, and ticks. [From Old English *spīthra.*]

spider monkey *n.* Any of several tropical American monkeys having long arms and legs and a long tail that can wrap around tree branches and other objects.

spider web *n.* The silky web that a spider spins to catch its prey.

spi·der·y (**spī′**də-rē) *adj.* **1.** Resembling a spider in form, characteristics, or behavior: *the robot's spidery legs.* **2.** Resembling a spider's web in delicacy; very fine: *spidery handwriting.*

spied (spīd) *v.* Past tense and past participle of **spy.**

spies (spīz) *n.* Plural of **spy.** ❖ *v.* Third person singular present tense of **spy.**

spiff·y (**spĭf′**ē) *adj.* **spiff·i·er, spiff·i·est** *Informal* Stylish in appearance or dress.

spig·ot (**spĭg′**ət) *n.* **1.** A faucet. **2.** A wooden faucet used to stop or regulate flow from the opening of a barrel.

spike[1] (spīk) *n.* **1a.** A long, thick, sharp-pointed piece of wood or metal. **b.** A long heavy nail. **2.** A sharp-pointed projection along the top of a fence or wall. **3.** One of a number of sharp metal projections set in the soles of athletic shoes for grip. **4a.** A sharp rise followed by a sharp decline, as in a graph. **b.** A sharp momentary increase in voltage or electric current. **c.** A sudden steep increase in prices. **5.** The act of driving a volleyball at a sharp angle into the opponent's court. **6.** The act of throwing a football down against the ground after a successful play. ❖ *tr.v.* **spiked, spik·ing, spikes 1.** To fasten or provide with a spike or spikes: *spiked the rails to the railroad ties.* **2.** To shape into spikes: *spiked his hair with styling wax.* **3.** To pierce or injure with a spike. **4.** To put an end to; thwart; block: *spiked the rumor.* **5a.** To hit (a volleyball) in a spike. **b.** To throw (a football) down in a spike. **6.** *Informal* To add alcoholic liquor to: *spiked the punch.* [From Middle English, from Old Norse *spīk.*]

spike[2] (spīk) *n.* **1.** An ear of grain. **2.** A long cluster of flowers lacking or nearly lacking stalks. [From Middle English, from Latin *spīca.*]

spike heel *n.* A very thin high heel on a woman's shoe.

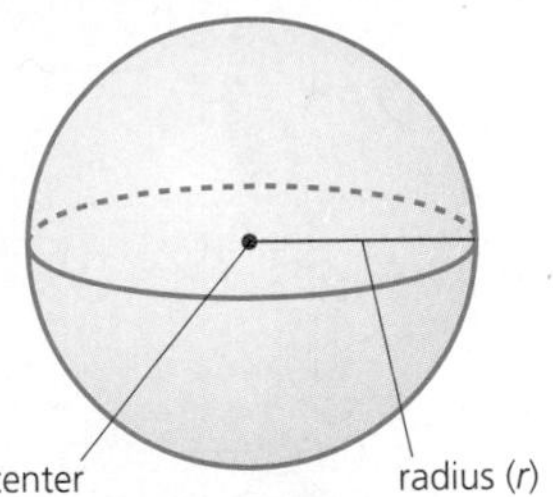

sphere

The volume (V) of a sphere can be calculated using the following equation: $V = \frac{4}{3}\pi r^3$.

sphinx

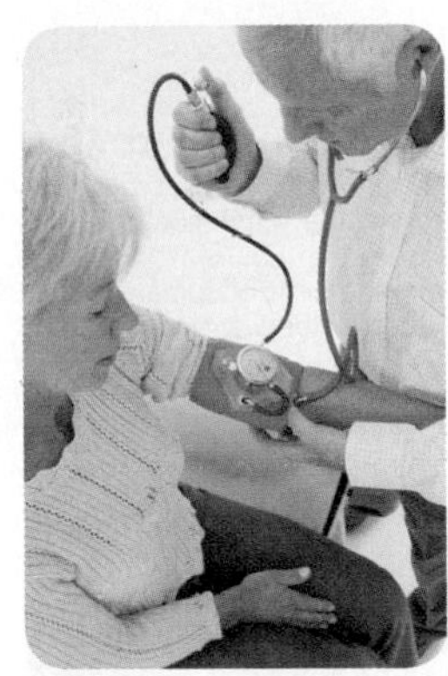

sphygmomanometer

spike[1]

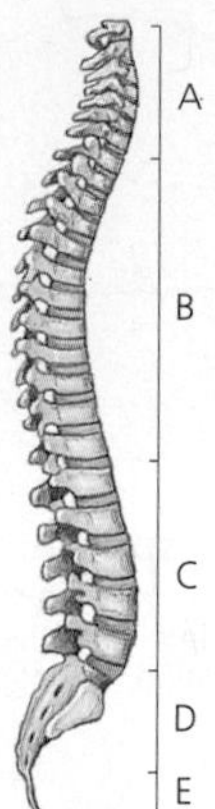

spinal column
right lateral view of an adult human spinal column
A. cervical vertebrae
B. thoracic vertebrae
C. lumbar vertebrae
D. sacrum
E. coccyx

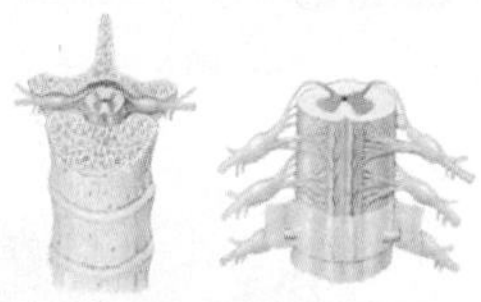

spinal cord
left: segment of vertebral column showing the spinal cord within the column
right: segment of spinal cord with nerve fibers arising from it

spinnaker

ă	pat	ôr	core
ā	pay	oi	boy
âr	care	ou	out
ä	father	o͝o	took
ĕ	pet	o͝or	lure
ē	be	o͞o	boot
ĭ	pit	ŭ	cut
ī	bite	ûr	urge
îr	pier	th	thin
ŏ	pot	*th*	this
ō	toe	zh	vision
ô	paw	ə	about

spike·nard (spīk′närd′) *n.* **1.** A fragrant plant from which a pleasant-smelling ointment was made in ancient times. **2.** The ointment made from this plant. **3.** A North American plant having small greenish flowers and an aromatic root.

spik·y (spī′kē) *adj.* **spik·i·er, spik·i·est** Having projecting sharp points: *The bird had a spiky tail.* **—spik′i·ness** *n.*

spill[1] (spĭl) *v.* **spilled** or **spilt** (spĭlt), **spill·ing, spills** *—tr.* **1.** To cause or allow to run or fall out of a container: *spilled water from the bucket.* **2.** To scatter (objects): *spilled the nails on the desk.* **3.** To shed (blood). **4.** To cause to fall; throw: *the bronco that spilled every rider.* **5.** *Informal* To divulge; make known: *spill the news.* *—intr.* **1.** To run or fall out of a container: *milk spilling over the top of the glass.* **2.** To spread beyond limits: *Fans spilled onto the playing field.* ❖ *n.* **1.** An act of spilling: *pollution caused by oil spills.* **2.** The amount spilled. **3.** A fall, as from a horse. [From Old English *spillan*, to kill.]

spill[2] (spĭl) *n.* **1.** A piece of wood or rolled paper used to light a fire. **2.** A small peg, especially one used as a plug. [From Middle English *spil.*]

spill·age (spĭl′ĭj) *n.* **1.** The act of spilling. **2.** An amount spilled: *The spillage from the tanker has spread two miles.*

spill·way (spĭl′wā′) *n.* A channel for an overflow of water, as from a reservoir.

spilt (spĭlt) *v.* A past tense and a past participle of **spill**[1].

spin (spĭn) *v.* **spun** (spŭn), **spin·ning, spins** *—intr.* **1.** To rotate or turn rapidly: *wheels spinning.* See Synonyms at **turn. 2.** To seem to be whirling, as from dizziness; reel: *his head was spinning.* **3.** To make thread or yarn by drawing out and twisting fibers. **4.** To form a web or cocoon by secreting a sticky filament, as spiders and certain insects do. *—tr.* **1.** To cause to turn or rotate rapidly: *He spun the top.* **2a.** To draw out and twist (fibers) into thread. **b.** To make (thread or yarn) by drawing out and twisting fibers: *spinning yarn on a spindle.* **3.** To form (a web or cocoon). **4.** To relate; tell: *spin tales of the sea.* **5.** To provide a slanted interpretation of (an event, for example), especially to sway public opinion. ❖ *n.* **1.** The act of spinning. **2.** A rapid rotating motion. **3.** *Informal* A short drive in a vehicle. [From Old English *spinnan.*]

spi·na bif·i·da (spī′nə **bĭf′**ĭ-də) *n.* A congenital defect in which the spinal column is not fully closed, resulting in bulging out of part of the spinal cord and possible nerve damage. [From New Latin *spīna bifida*, spine split in two.]

spin·ach (spĭn′ĭch) *n.* A plant having dark green leaves that are eaten as a vegetable.

spi·nal (spī′nəl) *adj.* **1.** Relating to the spine or spinal cord. **2.** Resembling a spine or similar part. ❖ *n.* An injection of an anesthetic into the spinal canal.

spinal canal *n.* The passage formed by successive openings in the bones of the spinal column, containing the spinal cord and the membranes that enclose it.

spinal column *n.* In vertebrate animals, the series of jointed bones enclosing the spinal cord and forming the main support of the torso; the spine.

spinal cord *n.* The part of the central nervous system that extends from the brain along the length of the spinal canal, branching to form smaller nerves that serve the various parts of the body.

spin·dle (spĭn′dl) *n.* **1a.** A rod or pin, tapered at one end and usually weighted at the other, on which fibers are spun by hand into thread and then wound. **b.** A similar rod or pin on a spinning wheel or machine. **2.** A spike on which papers are stuck to keep them in place. **3.** A machine part that rotates or serves as an axis on which other parts rotate. **4.** The cellular structure along which the chromosomes are distributed during cell division. ❖ *tr.v.* **spin·dled, spin·dling, spin·dles** To punch a hole or holes in: *Do not fold, spindle, or mutilate this card.* [From Old English *spinel.*]

spin·dling (spĭnd′lĭng) *adj.* Spindly.

spin·dly (spĭnd′lē) *adj.* **spin·dli·er, spin·dli·est** Slender and elongated, especially in a way that suggests weakness.

spin·drift (spĭn′drĭft′) *n.* Windblown sea spray.

spine (spīn) *n.* **1.** The spinal column of a vertebrate animal; the backbone. **2.** A sharp-pointed projecting plant or animal part, such as a thorn or quill. **3.** The supporting part at the back of a book, to which the covers are hinged. [From Middle English, from Latin *spīna.*]

spine·less (spīn′lĭs) *adj.* **1.** Lacking courage or willpower: *Don't be spineless; stand up for your rights.* **2.** Having no spines: *a spineless cactus.* **3.** Lacking a spinal column; invertebrate. **—spine′less·ness** *n.*

spin·et (spĭn′ĭt) *n.* **1.** A small, compact, upright piano. **2.** A small harpsichord having a single keyboard.

spin·na·ker (spĭn′ə-kər) *n.* A large triangular sail attached only at the corners, used when sailing in the same direction as the wind.

spin·ner (spĭn′ər) *n.* **1.** A person or thing that spins: *a spinner of yarn.* **2.** A device consisting of a dial and an arrow that is spun to indicate the next move in some board games. **3.** A fishing lure that spins rapidly.

spin·ner·et (spĭn′ə-**rĕt′**) *n.* **1.** One of the small organs from which a spider or silk-producing insect larva secretes the silk that it uses to spin a web or cocoon. **2.** A device for making rayon, nylon, and other synthetic fibers, consisting of a plate pierced with holes through which plastic material is forced out in the form of fine threads.

spin·ning jenny (spĭn′ĭng) *n.* An early form of spinning machine having several spindles.

spinning wheel *n.* A device for spinning fibers into thread or yarn, consisting of a hand-operated or foot-operated wheel and one spindle.

spin·off or **spin-off** (spĭn′ôf′) *n.* **1.** Something, such as a product, that is derived from something larger and more or less unrelated; a byproduct. **2.** Something derived from an earlier work, such as a television show based around a popular minor character from another show.

spi·no·saur·us (spī′nō-**sôr′**əs) *n.* A very large meat-eating dinosaur of the Cretaceous Period, having a long narrow snout and long spines on the back that may have formed a sail-like structure. [From Latin *spīna*, thorn + Greek *sauros*, lizard.]

spin·ster (spĭn′stər) *n.* *Often Offensive* A woman who has remained single beyond the traditional age for marrying.

spin·y (spī′nē) *adj.* **spin·i·er, spin·i·est** Bearing or covered with spines, thorns, or similar sharp projections: *spiny shrubs; a spiny hedgehog.*

spir·a·cle (spĭr′ə-kəl *or* spī′rə-kəl) *n.* An opening through which certain animals breathe, as the blowhole of a whale or one of the openings in the exoskeleton of an insect.

spi·ral (spī′rəl) *n.* **1.** A curve that winds around a fixed center at a distance that constantly increases or decreases. **2.** A helix. **3.** An object or a figure having the shape of a spiral: *A spiral of smoke came from the chimney.* **4.** A course or path that takes the form of a spiral. ❖ *intr.v.* **spi·raled, spi·ral·ing, spi·rals** also **spi·ralled, spi·ral·ling, spi·rals 1.** To take a spiral form or course: *Smoke spiraled from the chimney.* **2.** To rise or fall with steady acceleration: *Costs are spiraling.* [From Latin *spīra*, coil.]

spire[1] (spīr) *n.* A top part that tapers upward: *a church spire; a cluster of flowers arranged in a spire.* [From Old English *spīr.*]

spire[2] (spīr) *n.* **1.** A spiral. **2.** A single turn of a spiral. [From Greek *speira*, coil.]

spi·ril·lum (spī-rĭl′əm) *n., pl.* **spi·ril·la** (spī-rĭl′ə) Any of various bacteria that are shaped like a spiral.

spir·it (spĭr′ĭt) *n.* **1.** The force thought to give the body life. **2.** The soul, believed to depart from the body at death. **3. Spirit** The Holy Spirit. **4.** A supernatural being such as a ghost, demon, or fairy. **5.** The part of a human associated with the mind, will, and feelings: *Though they can't be here, they're with us in spirit.* **6.** One's essential nature: *her sweet and gentle spirit.* **7.** A quality that distinguishes a person, movement, or epoch: *the daring spirit of the early aviators.* **8. spirits** A mood or emotional state: *in high spirits.* **9.** A particular mood marked by vigor, courage, or liveliness: *Their team showed a lot of spirit.* **10.** Strong loyalty or dedication: *school spirit.* **11.** A prevailing mood or attitude: *a spirit of rebellion in the land.* **12.** The real meaning, sense, or intent of something: *the spirit of the law.* **13.** often **spirits** An alcohol solution of a volatile substance. **14. spirits** An alcoholic beverage. ❖ *tr.v.* **spir·it·ed, spir·it·ing, spir·its** To carry off mysteriously or secretly: *Someone spirited the papers away.* [From Middle English, from Latin *spīritus*, breath, from *spīrāre*, to breathe.]

spir·it·ed (spĭr′ĭ-tĭd) *adj.* **1.** Full of or marked by life, vigor, or courage: *a spirited defense of her rights.* **2.** Having a specified mood or nature: *high-spirited.*

spir·it·less (spĭr′ĭt-lĭs) *adj.* Lacking energy or enthusiasm; listless. **—spir′it·less·ly** *adv.* **—spir′it·less·ness** *n.*

spir·i·tu·al (spĭr′ĭ-cho͞o-əl) *adj.* **1.** Relating to or having the nature of spirit; not physical or material. **2.** Relating to or affecting the soul: *spiritual welfare.* **3.** Relating to religion; sacred: *spiritual practices.* ❖ *n.* A religious folk song of African-American origin or a song composed in imitation of such a song. **—spir′i·tu·al·ly** *adv.*

spir·i·tu·al·ism (spĭr′ĭ-cho͞o-ə lĭz′əm) *n.* **1.** The belief that the dead communicate with the living, as through a medium. **2.** A philosophy, doctrine, or religion emphasizing the spiritual aspect of being. **—spir′i·tu·al·ist** *n.*

spir·i·tu·al·i·ty (spĭr′ĭ-cho͞o-ăl′ĭ-tē) *n., pl.* **spir·i·tu·al·i·ties 1.** The state, quality, or fact of being spiritual. **2.** A religious belief or manner of pursuing a religious life.

spi·ro·chete (spī′rə-kēt′) *n.* Any of various bacteria having a slender, flexible, twisted form. Several diseases, including syphilis and Lyme disease, are caused by spirochetes.

spi·ro·gy·ra (spī′rə-jī′rə) *n.* Any of various freshwater green algae having chloroplasts in spirally twisted bands.

spit[1] (spĭt) *n.* **1.** Saliva, especially when ejected from the mouth. **2.** The act of ejecting something from the mouth. ❖ *v.* **spat** (spăt) or **spit, spit·ting, spits** —*tr.* **1.** To eject (something) from the mouth: *spat out grape seeds.* **2.** To utter in a violent manner: *spat out an oath.* —*intr.* **1.** To eject something from the mouth. **2.** To make a hissing or sputtering noise, as a cat does. **3.** To rain or snow in light, scattered drops or flakes. ◆ **spit up** To vomit. [From Middle English, from Old English *spittan*, to spit.]

spit[2] (spĭt) *n.* **1.** A slender pointed rod on which meat is speared and roasted. **2.** A narrow point of land extending into a body of water. ❖ *tr.v.* **spit·ted, spit·ting, spits** To place on or as if on a spit. [From Old English *spitu*.]

spit·ball (spĭt′bôl′) *n.* **1.** A piece of paper chewed and shaped into a lump for use as a projectile. **2.** In baseball, an illegal pitch in which a substance, such as saliva or grease, is put on the ball before it is thrown.

spite (spīt) *n.* Bad feeling toward another person characterized by the wish to hurt or humiliate that person: *spread the rumor out of spite.* ❖ *tr.v.* **spit·ed, spit·ing, spites** To act in a deliberately hurtful way in opposing the wishes or desires of (someone): *stayed out late to spite her overly strict parents.* ◆ **in spite of** Not stopped by; regardless of: *They went on in spite of their fears.*

spite·ful (spīt′fəl) *adj.* Filled with, caused by, or showing spite; malicious. **—spite′ful·ly** *adv.* **—spite′ful·ness** *n.*

spit·fire (spĭt′fīr′) *n.* A quick-tempered or very excitable person.

spit·ting image (spĭt′ĭng) *n.* A perfect likeness or counterpart.

spit·tle (spĭt′l) *n.* **1.** Spit; saliva. **2.** The frothy liquid secreted by the immature forms of certain insects.

spit·toon (spĭ-to͞on′) *n.* A bowl-shaped receptacle into which tobacco chewers spit.

spitz (spĭts) *n.* A dog of any of several breeds originating in northern regions, having a long, thick, usually white coat, pointed ears, and a tail curled over the back.

splash (splăsh) *v.* **splashed, splash·ing, splash·es** —*tr.* **1.** To dash or scatter (a liquid) about in flying masses. **2.** To dash liquid upon; wet or soil with flying masses of liquid. —*intr.* **1.** To cause a liquid to fly in scattered masses. **2.** To fall into or move through liquid so as to make it fly: *splashing in the ocean.* **3.** To spill or fly about in scattered masses. ❖ *n.* **1.** The act or sound of splashing. **2.** A flying mass of liquid. **3.** A marking produced by or as if by scattered liquid: *splashes of color.* **4.** A strong but often short-lived impression; a stir: *made a splash with her new novel.* ◆ **splash down** To land in water. Used of a spacecraft or missile. **—splash′er** *n.*

splash·down (splăsh′doun′) *n.* The landing of a missile or spacecraft in water.

splash·y (splăsh′ē) *adj.* **splash·i·er, splash·i·est 1.** Making or liable to make splashes. **2.** Covered with splashes of color. **3.** Showy; ostentatious: *a splashy wedding reception.*

splat·ter (splăt′ər) *v.* **splat·tered, splat·ter·ing, splat·ters** —*tr.* To spatter (something), especially so as to soil with splashes of liquid. —*intr.* To move or fall so as to cause heavy splashes: *The grease from the pan splattered onto my apron.* ❖ *n.* A splash of liquid.

splay (splā) *tr.v.* **splayed, splay·ing, splays** To spread out or apart: *The dog rolled on its back and splayed its legs.*

spleen (splēn) *n.* **1.** An organ that is located in the left side of the human body near the stomach and is composed of a mass of lymph nodes and blood vessels. It stores and filters blood, destroys old blood cells, and produces white blood cells. **2.** A similar organ found in other vertebrates. **3.** Ill temper; anger: *an outburst that was caused by spleen.*

splen·did (splĕn′dĭd) *adj.* **1.** Brilliant with light or color: *a splendid lighting display.* **2.** Grand; magnificent: *splendid costumes.* **3.** Excellent; praiseworthy: *a splendid record.* **—splen′did·ly** *adv.* **—splen′did·ness** *n.*

splen·dor (splĕn′dər) *n.* **1.** Great light or luster; brilliance. **2.** Magnificent appearance or display; grandeur. **3.** Distinction; fame; glory.

splice (splīs) *tr.v.* **spliced, splic·ing, splic·es 1a.** To join (ropes, for example) by weaving together strands. **b.** To join (two pieces of film, for example) at the ends. **2.** To join (pieces of wood) by overlapping them and binding the ends together. **3.** To join together or insert (segments of DNA or RNA) so as to form new genetic combinations or alter a genetic structure. ❖ *n.* A joining made by splicing. [From Middle Dutch *splissen*.] **—splic′er** *n.*

splint (splĭnt) *n.* **1.** A device made of rigid material, used to prevent motion of a joint or of the ends of a fractured bone. **2.** A thin flexible strip of wood, as one used in making baskets. [From Middle English *splent*.]

splin·ter (splĭn′tər) *n.* A sharp slender piece, as of wood, bone, or glass, split or broken off from a main body. ❖ *v.* **splin·tered, splin·ter·ing, splin·ters** —*intr.* To split or break into sharp slender pieces. —*tr.* To cause to splinter. See Synonyms at **break.** [From Middle English, from Middle Dutch.]

split (splĭt) *v.* **split, split·ting, splits** —*tr.* **1a.** To divide from end to end or along the grain: *a machine that splits logs.* **b.** To cause to be split unintentionally: *I almost split my pants laughing.* See Synonyms at **tear**[1]. **2.** To separate (people or groups); disunite: *issues that split the*

spiral
spiral pattern on a snail shell

spire[1]

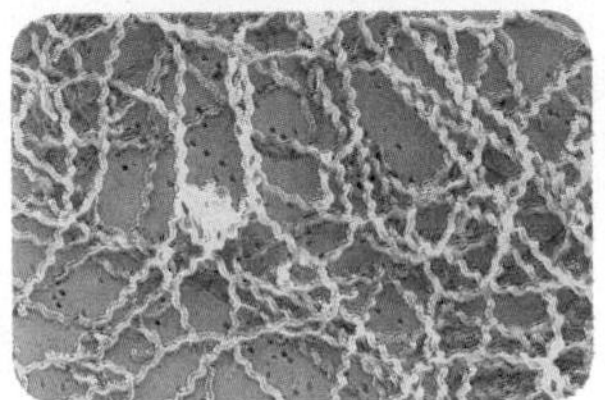

spirochete

spitz

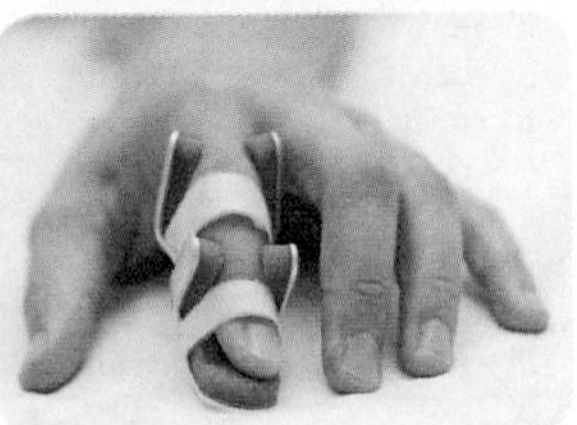

splint

USAGE

split infinitive When one or more words appear between *to* and an infinitive verb, this causes a **split infinitive**: *She wanted to briefly visit the museum before going home.* Some grammar books insist that the split infinitive is improper and should be avoided. Writers are told to move the intervening adverb elsewhere in the sentence: *She wanted to visit the museum briefly before going home.* But sometimes using a split infinitive sounds better and is actually necessary. In *We expect attendance to more than double in a year,* the phrase *more than* is necessary to the meaning of the verb phrase and cannot be displaced.

split-level

spoke[1]

ă	pat	ôr	core
ā	pay	oi	boy
âr	care	ou	out
ä	father	o͝o	took
ĕ	pet	o͝or	lure
ē	be	o͞o	boot
ĭ	pit	ŭ	cut
ī	bite	ûr	urge
îr	pier	th	thin
ŏ	pot	*th*	this
ō	toe	zh	vision
ô	paw	ə	about

party. **3.** To divide and share: *Let's split the reward.* **4.** To mark (a vote or ballot) in favor of candidates from different parties: *split the ticket.* —*intr.* To become separated into parts, especially lengthwise: *The pants split along the seam.* ❖ *n.* **1.** The act or result of splitting: *a split in the board.* **2.** A division within a group; a breach; a rupture: *a split in the party.* **3.** often **splits** An acrobatic feat in which the legs are stretched out in opposite directions at right angles to the trunk. **4.** In bowling, an arrangement of two or more pins left standing after some pins between them have been knocked down. **5.** *Sports* The recorded time for an interval or segment of a race. ❖ *adj.* **1.** Divided or separated. **2.** Cracked lengthwise; cleft. ◆ **split hairs** To see or make trivial distinctions; quibble. **split up 1.** To be divided into groups: *Let's split up so we can search both places.* **2.** To stop being friends or romantic partners: *They split up after an argument.* [From Middle Dutch *splitten.*] **—split′ter** *n.*

split infinitive *n.* An infinitive verb form with a word or words placed between *to* and the verb; for example, *to suddenly remember* is a split infinitive. —SEE NOTE.

split-lev·el (splĭt′lĕv′əl) *adj.* Having the floor levels of adjoining rooms separated by about half a story: *a split-level ranch house.*

split second *n.* An instant; a flash: *I'll be there in a split second.*

split·ting (splĭt′ĭng) *adj.* Very severe and painful, as a headache.

splotch (splŏch) *n.* An irregularly shaped stain, spot, or discolored area. ❖ *tr.v.* **splotched, splotch·ing, splotch·es** To mark with a splotch or splotches. **—splotch′y** *adj.*

splurge (splûrj) *intr.v.* **splurged, splurg·ing, splurg·es** To spend money extravagantly or wastefully, as on luxuries. ❖ *n.* An act of spending extravagantly.

splut·ter (splŭt′ər) *v.* **splut·tered, splut·ter·ing, splut·ters** —*intr.* **1.** To make repeated spitting sounds, especially as the result of being at a loss for words. **2.** To speak in a hurried or confused way, as when angry. —*tr.* To utter or express in a hurried or confused way: *spluttered out the wrong answer in his haste.* ❖ *n.* A spluttering noise. **—splut′ter·er** *n.*

spoil (spoil) *v.* **spoiled** or **spoilt** (spoilt), **spoil·ing, spoils** —*tr.* **1.** To damage, as in value or quality; flaw or ruin: *Rain spoiled our picnic.* **2.** To harm the character of (a child, for example) by being too indulgent or lenient. See Synonyms at **pamper.** —*intr.* To become unfit for use or consumption, as from decay: *Milk spoils quickly if it is not kept cold.* ❖ *n.* **1. spoils** Goods or property seized or robbed, especially after a military victory. **2. spoils** Benefits gained by a victor, especially political appointments or jobs that a winning candidate or party has control over after an election. ◆ **spoil for** To be eager for: *spoiling for a fight.* **—spoil′er** *n.*

spoil·age (spoi′lĭj) *n.* **1a.** The process of becoming spoiled. **b.** The condition of being spoiled. **2a.** Something that has been spoiled. **b.** The degree to which something has been spoiled.

spoils system *n.* The post-election practice of rewarding loyal supporters of the winning candidates or party with political jobs or appointments.

spoilt (spoilt) *v.* A past tense and a past participle of **spoil.**

spoke[1] (spōk) *n.* **1.** One of the rods or braces that connect the rim of a wheel to its hub. **2.** One of the handles that project from the rim of a ship's wheel. ❖ *tr.v.* **spoked, spok·ing, spokes** To equip with spokes. [From Old English *spāca.*]

spoke[2] (spōk) *v.* **1.** Past tense of **speak. 2.** *Archaic* A past participle of **speak.**

spo·ken (spō′kən) *v.* Past participle of **speak.** ❖ *adj.* **1.** Uttered; expressed orally: *spoken dialogue in an opera.* **2.** Speaking or using speech in a specified manner or voice: *a soft-spoken man.* ◆ **spoken for** Requested, reserved, or claimed beforehand: *Is that piece of pie spoken for?*

spoke·shave (spōk′shāv′) *n.* A tool having a blade set between two handles, used for trimming and smoothing rounded surfaces.

spokes·man (spōks′mən) *n.* A man who speaks on behalf of another or others.

spokes·per·son (spōks′pûr′sən) *n.* A spokesman or spokeswoman.

spokes·wom·an (spōks′wo͝om′ən) *n.* A woman who speaks on behalf of another or others.

spon·dee (spŏn′dē′) *n.* In poetry, a metrical foot consisting of two stressed syllables.

sponge (spŭnj) *n.* **1.** Any of numerous invertebrate water animals that have a fibrous supporting framework and that feed on small organisms filtered from the water. Sponges often form large colonies attached to an underwater surface. **2a.** The soft, porous, absorbent skeleton of certain of these animals, used for bathing or cleaning. **b.** A piece of porous absorbent plastic or other material, used for similar purposes. **3.** A gauze pad used to absorb blood and other fluids, as in surgery or in dressing a wound. **4.** A person who lives by relying on the generosity of others. ❖ *v.* **sponged, spong·ing, spong·es** —*tr.* **1.** To wash, wipe, or moisten with a sponge or cloth: *She sponged her face with a wet washcloth. Sponge the water off the table.* **2.** *Informal* To get (something) without paying for it: *She sponged a free meal from the cook at the cafeteria.* —*intr.* To live by relying on the generosity of others: *sponged off his friends until he found a job.* [From Old English, from Greek *spongos.*]

sponge cake *n.* A light porous cake made with flour, sugar, and eggs and containing no shortening.

spong·y (spŭn′jē) *adj.* **spong·i·er, spong·i·est** Resembling a sponge; soft, porous, and elastic: *a spongy bed of moss.* **—spong′i·ness** *n.*

spon·sor (spŏn′sər) *n.* **1.** A person who assumes responsibility for another person or group during a period of instruction or training. **2.** A person who supports a candidate for admission to an organization. **3.** A legislator who proposes and works for passage of a bill. **4.** A person who presents a candidate for baptism or confirmation; a godparent. **5.** A person, group, or business that financially supports a project, an event, or a program: *Most television shows have several corporate sponsors.* ❖ *tr.v.* **spon·sored, spon·sor·ing, spon·sors** To act as a sponsor for. [From Late Latin *spōnsor,* godparent, from Latin *spondēre,* to pledge.] **—spon′sor·ship′** *n.*

spon·ta·ne·i·ty (spŏn′tə-nē′ĭ-tē *or* spŏn′tə-nā′ĭ-tē) *n., pl.* **spon·ta·ne·i·ties** The quality or condition of being spontaneous.

spon·ta·ne·ous (spŏn-tā′nē-əs) *adj.* **1.** Happening or arising without apparent outside cause. **2.** Arising from a natural inclination or impulse; unplanned: *spontaneous cheers.* [From Late Latin *spontāneus,* of one's own accord, from Latin *sponte.*] **—spon·ta′ne·ous·ly** *adv.*

spontaneous combustion *n.* The bursting into flame of organic matter, such as a pile of oily rags or damp hay, as a result of heat generated by slow oxidation.

spoof (spo͞of) *n.* **1.** An imitation of something that pokes fun at it; a parody: *a spoof of grand opera.* **2.** A joke or hoax. ❖ *tr.v.* **spoofed, spoof·ing, spoofs 1.** To deceive or trick. **2.** To do a spoof of; satirize.

spook (spo͞ok) *Informal n.* A ghost. ❖ *v.* **spooked, spook·ing, spooks** —*tr.* **1.** To haunt. **2.** To startle and cause nervous activity in; frighten. —*intr.* To become frightened and nervous: *The horse spooked at the sound of thunder.*

spook·y (spo͞o′kē) *adj.* **spook·i·er, spook·i·est** *Informal* Ghostly; eerie. **—spook′i·ness** *n.*

spool (spo͞ol) *n.* **1.** A cylinder upon which thread, wire, tape, or a similar material is wound. **2.** The amount of something wound on such a cylinder: *Sewing the coat used up a whole spool of thread.* ❖ *tr.v.* **spooled, spool·ing, spools** To wind on or unwind from a spool: *spool thread.*

spoon (spo͞on) *n.* **1.** A utensil consisting of a small shallow bowl at the end of a handle, used in preparing, serving, or eating food. **2.** Something similar to this utensil in shape or function, as a curved metal fishing lure. ❖ *v.* **spooned, spoon·ing, spoons** —*tr.* To lift, scoop up, or move with a spoon. —*intr. Informal* To snuggle with another person while lying side by side facing the same direction. [From Old English *spōn*, chip of wood.]

spoon·bill (spo͞on′bĭl′) *n.* Any of several wading birds having long legs and a long flat bill with a broad rounded tip.

spoon-feed (spo͞on′fēd′) *tr.v.* **spoon-fed** (spo͞on′fĕd′), **spoon-feed·ing, spoon-feeds 1.** To feed with a spoon. **2.** To discourage from independent thought or action, as by overindulgence: *The professor spoon-fed her students, who never questioned what she said.* **3.** To provide (knowledge or information) in an oversimplified way.

spoon·ful (spo͞on′fo͝ol′) *n., pl.* **spoon·fuls** The amount that a spoon holds.

spoor (spo͝or) *n.* The track or trail of an animal, especially a wild animal.

spo·rad·ic (spə-**răd′**ĭk) *adj.* Occurring at irregular intervals; having no pattern or order: *sporadic applause.* —**spo·rad′i·cal·ly** *adv.*

spo·ran·gi·um (spə-**răn′**jē-əm) *n., pl.* **spo·ran·gi·a** (spə-**răn′**jē-ə) A plant part in which spores are formed, as in ferns, fungi, mosses, and algae.

spore (spôr) *n.* **1.** A small, usually single-celled reproductive body that is capable of growing into a new organism without uniting with another cell. Spores are produced by fungi, algae, protozoans, and plants such as mosses and ferns that do not bear seeds. **2.** A one-celled body in seed-bearing plants that develops either into the sac containing the egg cell or into a grain of pollen. **3.** A thick-walled cell formed by certain bacteria and fungi, such as an endospore. [From Greek *sporā*, seed.]

spore case *n.* A sporangium.

spo·ro·phyte (**spôr′**ə-fīt′) *n.* In plants and most algae, the individual organism or generation of organisms that produces spores. The life cycle of such an organism involves an alternation between the sporophyte and the gametophyte.

spor·ran (**spôr′**ən) *n.* A leather or fur pouch worn at the front of the kilt in the traditional dress of men of the Scottish Highlands.

sport (spôrt) *n.* **1a.** A physical activity that is governed by a set of rules and often done in competition: *My favorite sport is soccer.* **b.** often **sports** Such activities considered as a group. **2.** An active pastime; a form of recreation. **3.** Light mockery; jest; fun: *They made sport of my new hat.* **4.** A person judged by the manner of accepting the rules of a game or a difficult situation: *a good sport.* **5.** *Informal* A person who lives a jolly, extravagant life. ❖ *v.* **sport·ed, sport·ing, sports** —*intr.* **1.** To play or frolic. **2.** To joke or trifle. —*tr.* To wear, display, or show off: *He sported a bright red necktie.* ❖ *adj.* or **sports 1.** Relating to or appropriate for sports. **2.** Suitable for outdoor or informal wear: *a sports shirt.* [From Middle English *sporte*, short for *disporte*, from Old French *desporter*, to divert.]

sport·ing (**spôr′**tĭng) *adj.* **1.** Used in or appropriate for sports: *sporting goods.* **2.** Marked by sportsmanship. **3.** Relating to or associated with gambling. —**sport′ing·ly** *adv.*

sporting chance *n. Informal* A fair chance for success.

spor·tive (**spôr′**tĭv) *adj.* Playful; frolicsome. —**spor′tive·ly** *adv.* —**spor′tive·ness** *n.*

sports car *n.* An automobile equipped for racing and designed to be driven at high speeds with precise control.

sports coat *n.* A man's jacket that is similar to a suit jacket but is designed for less formal occasions.

sports jacket *n.* A sports coat.

sports·man (**spôrts′**mən) *n.* **1.** A man who is active in sports. **2.** A person whose conduct and attitude exhibit sportsmanship. —**sports′man·like′** *adj.*

sports·man·like (**spôrts′**mən-līk′) *n.* Acting with or exhibiting sportsmanship.

sports·man·ship (**spôrts′**mən-shĭp′) *n.* The attitude and conduct suitable to a person who participates in sports, especially fair play, courtesy, and grace in losing.

sports·wear (**spôrts′**wâr′) *n.* Clothes designed for comfort and casual wear.

sports·wom·an (**spôrts′**wo͝om′ən) *n.* **1.** A woman who is active in sports. **2.** A woman whose conduct and attitude exhibit sportsmanship.

sport utility vehicle *n.* An SUV.

sport·y (**spôr′**tē) *adj.* **sport·i·er, sport·i·est 1.** Appropriate to sports or participation in sports. **2.** Flashy, especially in dress.

spot (spŏt) *n.* **1.** A mark on a surface differing sharply in color from its surroundings, especially a stain or blot: *spots on the tablecloth.* **2.** A position; a location: *a good spot for watching birds.* **3.** *Informal* A situation, especially a difficult one. **4.** A flaw or defect in one's reputation. **5.** A short presentation or commercial on television or radio. **6.** *Informal* A spotlight. ❖ *v.* **spot·ted, spot·ting, spots** —*tr.* **1.** To cause to become marked or soiled with spots: *Soot spotted the curtains.* **2.** To place in a particular location; situate. **3.** To detect or recognize: *spotted him on the subway.* **4.** To give a handicap or favorable scoring margin to: *spotted her opponent six points.* **5.** To act as a spotter for (a gymnast, for example). **6.** *Informal* To lend: *Can you spot me $5 until I get my allowance?* —*intr.* To become marked or soiled with spots. ❖ *adj.* **1.** Made, paid, or delivered immediately: *spot cash; a spot sale.* **2.** Presented between major television or radio programs: *a spot announcement.* ◆ **on the spot 1.** Without delay; at once. **2.** At the scene of action. **3.** In a difficult position. [From Middle English.]

spot check *n.* A random or limited inspection or investigation.

spot-check (**spŏt′**chĕk′) *tr. & intr.v.* **spot-checked, spot-check·ing, spot-checks** To subject to or make a spot check.

spot·less (**spŏt′**lĭs) *adj.* **1.** Perfectly clean: *spotless sheets.* **2.** Free from flaw or imperfection; impeccable: *a spotless reputation.* —**spot′less·ly** *adv.*

spot·light (**spŏt′**līt′) *n.* **1.** A strong beam of light that illuminates only a small area, often used to draw attention to an actor on a stage. **2.** A lamp that produces such a light. **3.** Public attention or prominence: *She was in the spotlight after winning the race.* ❖ *tr.v.* **spot·light·ed** or **spot·lit** (**spŏt′**lĭt), **spot·light·ing, spot·lights 1.** To shine a spotlight on. **2.** To focus attention on.

spot·ted (**spŏt′**ĭd) *adj.* Marked with spots.

spot·ter (**spŏt′**ər) *n.* **1.** A person, such as a military lookout, who looks for, locates, and reports something. **2.** A person who is responsible for watching and guarding a performer during practice to prevent injury, as in weightlifting.

spot·ty (**spŏt′**ē) *adj.* **spot·ti·er, spot·ti·est 1.** Having or marked with spots; spotted. **2.** Lacking consistency; uneven in quality or occurrence: *spotty cellphone service.* —**spot′ti·ly** *adv.* —**spot′ti·ness** *n.*

spouse (spous *or* spouz) *n.* A marriage partner; one's husband or wife.

spout (spout) *v.* **spout·ed, spout·ing, spouts** —*intr.*

sponge

spool

sporran

spotter

spray[2]
spray brooch

springbok

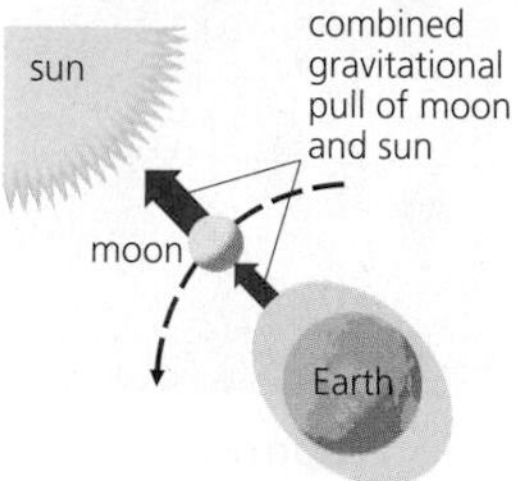

spring tide
Spring tides occur when the sun and moon are directly in line with Earth and their gravitational pulls reinforce each other.

ă	pat	ôr	core
ā	pay	oi	boy
âr	care	ou	out
ä	father	ŏŏ	took
ĕ	pet	ŏŏr	lure
ē	be	ōō	boot
ĭ	pit	ŭ	cut
ī	bite	ûr	urge
îr	pier	th	thin
ŏ	pot	*th*	this
ō	toe	zh	vision
ô	paw	ə	about

1. To gush forth in a rapid stream or in spurts: *lava spouting up from a volcano.* **2.** To give off a liquid or other substance continuously or in spurts: *whales spouting offshore.* **3.** *Informal* To speak in a wordy, dull, and pompous manner. —*tr.* **1.** To cause to flow or spurt out. **2.** To utter pompously and tediously. ❖ *n.* **1.** A tube, mouth, or pipe through which liquid is released or discharged: *the spout of a coffeepot.* **2.** A continuous stream of liquid. **3.** The burst of spray from the blowhole of a whale. [From Middle English *spouten.*] **—spout′er** *n.*

sprain (sprān) *n.* An injury caused by a painful twisting or tearing of the ligaments of a joint. ❖ *tr.v.* **sprained, sprain·ing, sprains** To cause a sprain to (a joint or muscle).

sprang (sprăng) *v.* A past tense of **spring.**

sprat (sprăt) *n.* **1.** A small edible ocean fish of the northeast Atlantic Ocean and the Mediterranean Sea that is eaten fresh or smoked and is often canned as a sardine. **2.** Any of various other similar fishes, such as a small herring.

sprawl (sprôl) *intr.v.* **sprawled, sprawl·ing, sprawls 1.** To sit or lie with the body and limbs spread out awkwardly. **2.** To spread out in a straggling or disordered fashion. ❖ *n.* **1.** A sprawling posture or condition. **2.** Uncontrolled real estate development on the outskirts of a city. [From Middle English *spraulen,* from Old English *sprēawlian,* to writhe.]

spray[1] (sprā) *n.* **1.** Water or other liquid moving in a mass of finely dispersed droplets or mist. **2.** A fine stream of droplets shot from a pressurized container. **3.** A pressurized container that shoots such a stream. **4.** Any of a large number of commercial products, including paints, insecticides, and cosmetics, that are dispensed from containers in this manner. ❖ *v.* **sprayed, spray·ing, sprays** —*tr.* **1.** To scatter (a liquid) in the form of a spray. **2.** To apply a spray to (a surface). —*intr.* To shoot sprays of liquid. [From obsolete *spray,* to sprinkle, from Middle Dutch *sprayen.*] **—spray′er** *n.*

spray[2] (sprā) *n.* **1.** A small branch bearing flowers, leaves, or berries. **2.** An ornament that resembles such a branch. [From Middle English *sprai.*]

spread (sprĕd) *v.* **spread, spread·ing, spreads** —*tr.* **1.** To open to a full or fuller extent or width; unfold: *spread out a tablecloth; a bird spreading its wings.* **2.** To widen the gap between; move farther apart: *spread her fingers wide.* **3a.** To distribute over a surface in a layer; apply: *spread varnish on the table.* **b.** To cover with a layer: *spread bread with jelly.* **4.** To distribute widely: *storms that spread destruction.* **5.** To arrange over an area or over a period of time: *spread the cards on the table; spread the payments over six months.* **6.** To cause to become widely known or seen: *spread the news.* **7a.** To prepare (a table) for a meal; set. **b.** To arrange (food) on a table. —*intr.* **1.** To become extended or enlarged: *The table spread out to accommodate more people.* **2.** To become distributed or widely dispersed: *The news spread quickly.* **3.** To cover a surface in a layer: *The paint spreads nicely.* **4.** To become separated. ❖ *n.* **1a.** The act of spreading. **b.** Dissemination or flow, as of news: *the spread of information.* **2.** An open area of land; an expanse. **3a.** The extent or limit to which something can be spread or unfolded: *wings with a six-foot spread.* **b.** Range or scope: *a wide spread of development.* **4.** A cloth covering for a bed, table, or other piece of furniture. **5.** *Informal* An abundant meal laid out on a table. **6.** A soft food that can be spread on bread or crackers. **7.** The difference, as between two figures or totals. **8.** Two facing pages, as of a newspaper or magazine. **9.** A number of points offered to make equal the chances of winning in a wager on a competition, usually between sports teams. **—spread′a·bil′i·ty** *n.* **—spread′a·ble** *adj.*

spread-ea·gle (sprĕd′ē′gəl) *adj.* Placed with the arms and legs stretched out. ❖ *tr.v.* **spread-ea·gled, spread-ea·gling, spread-ea·gles** To place with the arms and legs stretched out, especially as a form of punishment.

spread·er (sprĕd′ər) *n.* **1.** Something that spreads, such as a butter knife. **2.** A farm or garden tool for scattering fertilizer or seed.

spread·sheet (sprĕd′shēt′) *n.* **1.** A computer application for displaying and manipulating data in rows and columns. **2.** A piece of paper containing a grid of rectangles in rows and columns for recording financial data.

spree (sprē) *n.* **1.** A sudden indulgence in an activity, especially drinking or spending: *a shopping spree.* **2.** A carefree lively outing.

spri·er (sprī′ər) *adj.* A comparative of **spry.**

spri·est (sprī′ĭst) *adj.* A superlative of **spry.**

sprig (sprĭg) *n.* **1.** A small twig or shoot of a plant. **2.** A design or decoration in this shape.

spright·ly (sprīt′lē) *adj.* **spright·li·er, spright·li·est** Full of vitality and spirit; brisk. **—spright′li·ness** *n.*

spring (sprĭng) *v.* **sprang** (sprăng) or **sprung** (sprŭng), **sprung, spring·ing, springs** —*intr.* **1.** To move upward or forward in a single quick motion or a series of such motions; leap: *springing up from her chair.* **2.** To appear or come into being suddenly: *The mushroom sprang up overnight.* **3.** To issue or emerge suddenly: *A thought springs to mind.* **4.** To move suddenly, especially because of being resilient or moved by a spring: *The door sprang shut.* **5.** To move out of place; come loose, as a machine part. —*tr.* **1.** To cause to move, leap, or come forth suddenly: *The dog sprang the rabbit.* **2.** To have as a sudden condition: *The pipe sprang a leak.* **3.** To cause to operate or close suddenly: *spring a trap.* **4.** To present or produce unexpectedly: *spring a surprise party.* **5.** *Slang* To cause (someone) to escape or be released from prison or other confinement. ❖ *n.* **1.** An elastic device, such as a coil of wire, that returns to its original shape after being compressed or extended. **2.** The quality or condition of being elastic: *a mattress with a lot of spring.* **3.** The act of springing, especially a leap or jump. **4.** A small stream of water flowing naturally from the earth. **5.** The season of the year occurring between winter and summer. In the Northern Hemisphere, it lasts from the vernal equinox to the summer solstice, or in ordinary usage, from March until June. In the Southern Hemisphere, it lasts from September until December. **6.** A source, origin, or beginning. ❖ *adj.* Occurring in or appropriate to the season of spring: *spring showers.* [From Old English *springan.*]

spring·board (sprĭng′bôrd′) *n.* **1.** A flexible board, secured at one end and mounted on a fulcrum, used by gymnasts to gain momentum in leaping or tumbling. **2.** A diving board. **3.** Something that helps to launch a career or activity: *athletic fame as a springboard for a career in politics.*

spring·bok (sprĭng′bŏk′) *n., pl.* **springbok** or **spring·boks** A small brown and white African antelope that can leap high into the air.

spring fever *n.* A feeling of restlessness, excitement, or laziness, brought on by the coming of spring.

Spring·field (sprĭng′fēld′) The capital of Illinois, in the central part of the state. It was home to Abraham Lincoln for many years.

spring peeper *n.* A small brownish tree frog of eastern North America that makes a shrill, high-pitched call in early spring.

spring tide *n.* The tide in which the difference between high and low tides is greatest, occurring at or near a new moon or full moon when the sun, the moon, and Earth are aligned.

spring·time (sprĭng′tīm′) *n.* The season of spring.

spring·y (sprĭng′ē) *adj.* **spring·i·er, spring·i·est** Capable of springing back; elastic: *has a springy footstep.* **—spring′i·ly** *adv.* **—spring′i·ness** *n.*

sprin·kle (sprĭng′kəl) *v.* **sprin·kled, sprin·kling, sprin·kles** *tr.* **1.** To scatter in drops or small particles: *sprinkle sand on the ice.* **2.** To scatter drops or particles upon: *sprinkle the roses with water.* —*intr.* To rain or fall in small or infrequent drops. ❖ *n.* **1.** A small amount. **2.** A light rainfall; a drizzle. **3.** The act of sprinkling. [From Middle English *sprenklen*, perhaps of Middle Dutch or Middle Low German origin.]

sprin·kler (sprĭng′klər) *n.* **1.** One of the outlets in a sprinkler system. **2.** A device, attached to the end of a hose, for sprinkling water on a lawn.

sprinkler system *n.* A system for extinguishing fires, consisting of pipes that release water automatically when the temperature reaches a certain level.

sprin·kling (sprĭng′klĭng) *n.* A small amount of something, especially when sparsely distributed.

sprint (sprĭnt) *v.* **sprint·ed, sprint·ing, sprints** —*intr.* To move rapidly or at top speed for a brief period, as in running or swimming. —*tr.* To move over (a distance) rapidly or at top speed for a brief period: *sprinted 100 meters.* ❖ *n.* The act or an instance of sprinting, especially a short race at top speed. **—sprint′er** *n.*

sprit (sprĭt) *n.* A pole extending diagonally across a fore-and-aft sail from the lower part of the mast to the peak of the sail.

sprite (sprīt) *n.* A small or elusive supernatural being; an elf or pixie. [From Middle English *sprit*, from Latin *spīritus*, spirit.]

sprit·sail (sprĭt′səl *or* sprĭt′sāl′) *n.* A sail extended by a spar running diagonally to the sail's peak.

sprock·et (sprŏk′ĭt) *n.* A wheel having evenly-spaced teeth around its rim that fit into the links of a chain.

sprout (sprout) *v.* **sprout·ed, sprout·ing, sprouts** —*intr.* **1.** To begin to grow; produce or appear as a bud, shoot, or new growth: *The newly planted corn sprouted after the rain.* **2.** To emerge or develop rapidly: *New businesses sprouted up across the state.* —*tr.* To cause to come forth and grow: *The abandoned farmland again sprouted buckwheat and clover.* ❖ *n.* **1.** A young plant growth, such as a bud or shoot. **2. sprouts a.** The young shoots of plants such as alfalfa and soy, usually eaten raw. **b.** Brussels sprouts. [From Middle English *sprouten*.]

spruce¹ (sprōōs) *n.* **1.** Any of various evergreen trees having short needles, drooping cones, and soft wood often used for paper pulp. **2.** The wood of such a tree. [From Middle English *Spruce*, Prussia, from Medieval Latin *Prussia*.]

spruce² (sprōōs) *adj.* **spruc·er, spruc·est** Neat, fashionable, or fresh in appearance: *looked spruce in his new suit.* ❖ *tr.v.* **spruced, spruc·ing, spruc·es** To make neat, fashionable, or fresh in appearance: *We spruced up the house with a new coat of paint.* [Perhaps from obsolete *spruce leather*, Prussian leather, from Middle English *Spruce*, Prussia.]

sprung (sprŭng) *v.* A past tense and the past participle of **spring.**

spry (sprī) *adj.* **spri·er** (sprī′ər), **spri·est** (sprī′ĭst) or **spry·er, spry·est** Active, lively, or nimble. **—spry′ly** *adv.* **—spry′ness** *n.*

spud (spŭd) *n.* **1.** *Informal* A potato. **2.** A sharp tool resembling a spade, used for rooting or digging out weeds.

spume (spyōōm) *n.* Foam or froth on a liquid, as on the sea. ❖ *intr.v.* **spumed, spum·ing, spumes** To froth or foam.

spu·mo·ni or **spu·mo·ne** (spōō-mō′nē) *n.* An Italian ice cream having layers of different colors and flavors and often containing fruit and nuts.

spun (spŭn) *v.* Past tense and past participle of **spin.**

spunk (spŭngk) *n.* *Informal* Spirit; courage.

spunk·y (spŭng′kē) *adj.* **spunk·i·er, spunk·i·est** *Informal* Spirited; plucky. **—spunk′i·ly** *adv.* **—spunk′i·ness** *n.*

spun sugar *n.* Cotton candy.

spur (spûr) *n.* **1.** A short spike or sharp-toothed wheel that attaches to the heel of a rider's boot and is used to urge the horse forward. **2.** Something that urges one to action; an incentive; a stimulus: *Ambition was the spur for her great achievements.* **3.** A pointed projecting part, as on the back of a rooster's leg or on some flowers. **4.** A relatively short ridge that projects from the side of a mountain or mountain range. **5.** A short side track that connects with the main track of a railroad system. ❖ *tr.v.* **spurred, spur·ring, spurs 1.** To urge (a horse) on by the use of spurs: *The rider spurred the horse to a gallop.* **2.** To move to action; incite; stimulate: *The reward spurred us on.* ◆ **on the spur of the moment** Without planning; suddenly; impulsively. [From Old English *spura*.]

spu·ri·ous (spyŏŏr′ē-əs) *adj.* Lacking authenticity; false; not genuine: *rejected the spurious claims.* **—spu′ri·ous·ly** *adv.* **—spu′ri·ous·ness** *n.*

spurn (spûrn) *v.* **spurned, spurn·ing, spurns** —*tr.* To reject or refuse with disdain; scorn. —*intr.* To reject something contemptuously.

spurred (spûrd) *adj.* **1.** Wearing spurs. **2.** Having a spur or spurs: *spurred flowers.*

spurt (spûrt) *n.* **1.** A sudden and forcible gush or jet. **2.** A sudden short burst, as of energy, activity, or growth. ❖ *v.* **spurt·ed, spurt·ing, spurts** —*intr.* **1.** To gush forth suddenly in a stream or jet. **2.** To show a brief intense effort or a sudden increase in activity or speed: *The team spurted late in the season.* —*tr.* To force in a sudden jet or squirt.

Sput·nik (spŏŏt′nĭk *or* spŭt′nĭk) *n.* Any of the first artificial satellites put into orbit around Earth by the Soviet Union, starting in 1957.

sput·ter (spŭt′ər) *v.* **sput·tered, sput·ter·ing, sput·ters** —*intr.* **1.** To spit out or spray small particles of saliva or food from the mouth in noisy bursts. **2.** To make sporadic spitting or coughing noises: *The engine sputtered and died.* **3.** To spit out words or sounds in an excited or confused manner. —*tr.* **1.** To eject in short bursts with spitting or coughing sounds. **2.** To utter in an excited or confused manner. ❖ *n.* **1.** The act or sound of sputtering. **2.** The particles spit out during sputtering. **3.** Excited or confused speech. **—sput′ter·er** *n.*

spu·tum (spyōō′təm) *n., pl.* **spu·ta** (spyōō′tə) Matter that is spit out; spit; spittle.

spy (spī) *n., pl.* **spies** (spīz) **1.** An agent employed by a state or company to obtain secret information about another state or a competitor. **2.** A person who secretly keeps watch on another or others. ❖ *v.* **spied** (spīd), **spy·ing, spies** (spīz) —*intr.* **1.** To act or work as a spy: *The secret agents were spying for the enemy.* **2.** To watch or observe someone or something secretly: *Have you been spying on your neighbors?* —*tr.* **1.** To watch or observe secretly: *was sent to spy out the enemy camp.* **2.** To catch sight of; see: *I spied a turtle on a log.* [From Middle English *spie*, from Old French *espier*, to watch, of Germanic origin.]

spy·glass (spī′glăs′) *n.* **1.** A small telescope. **2. spyglasses** Binoculars.

spy·ware (spī′wâr′) *n.* **1.** Software that secretly gathers information about a person or organization. **2.** Software that is designed to take control of a computer's operation without the knowledge of its user.

sq. or **Sq.** *abbr.* An abbreviation of square.

squab (skwŏb) *n.* A young pigeon.

squab·ble (skwŏb′əl) *intr.v.* **squab·bled, squab·bling, squab·bles** To engage in an argument, usually over a trivial matter; bicker: *squabbling over the morning paper.* ❖ *n.* A noisy quarrel. [Probably of Scandinavian origin.] **—squab′bler** *n.*

squad (skwŏd) *n.* **1.** A small organized group of people who work for a common goal or cause. **2.** A small unit of

sprocket

WRITERS CHOOSE THEIR WORDS

Aunt Abigail was not looking at her at all, but she now stopped short in one of her rushes to the table, set down the butter-plate she was carrying, and said "There!" as though she had forgotten something. She stooped—it was perfectly amazing how **spry** she was—and pulled out from under the stove a half-grown kitten, very sleepy, yawning and stretching, and blinking its eyes.

—Dorothy Canfield Fisher
Understood Betsy

spumoni

square knot

square-rigged

squat

police officers or military personnel. **3.** An athletic team.

squad car *n.* A police patrol car connected by radio with headquarters.

squad·ron (skwŏd′rən) *n.* Any of various military units, as of soldiers, planes, or ships.

squal·id (skwŏl′ĭd) *adj.* **1.** Having a dirty or wretched appearance: *squalid buildings.* **2.** Sordid; morally repulsive: *leading a squalid existence.* **—squal′id·ly** *adv.* **—squal′id·ness** *n.*

squall[1] (skwôl) *n.* A loud, harsh cry. ❖ *intr.v.* **squalled, squall·ing, squalls** To scream or cry harshly and loudly. [Probably of Scandinavian origin.]

squall[2] (skwôl) *n.* A brief, sudden, and violent windstorm, often accompanied by rain or snow. ❖ *intr.v.* **squalled, squall·ing, squalls** To blow strongly for a short time. [Probably of Scandinavian origin.] **—squall′y** *adj.*

squal·or (skwŏl′ər) *n.* The quality or condition of being squalid.

squa·mous (skwā′məs) also **squa·mose** (skwā′mōs′) *adj.* **1.** Covered with or formed of scales; scaly. **2.** Resembling a scale or scales: *squamous cells.*

squan·der (skwŏn′dər) *tr.v.* **squan·dered, squan·der·ing, squan·ders 1.** To use or spend wastefully or extravagantly: *squander money.* **2.** To fail to take advantage of: *The team squandered their early lead and ended up losing the game.*

Squan·to (skwŏn′tō) Died 1622. Wampanoag who taught the Massachusetts colonists agricultural techniques and acted as an interpreter.

square (skwâr) *n.* **1.** A rectangle having four equal sides. **2.** Something having this shape. **3.** An L-shaped or T-shaped instrument or tool, used for drawing or testing right angles. **4.** The product that results when a number or quantity is multiplied by itself. For example, the square of 5 is 25. **5.** An open, usually four-sided area at the intersection of two or more streets. **6.** *Slang* A person considered dull, conventional, and out of touch with current trends. ❖ *adj.* **squar·er, squar·est 1.** Having four equal sides and four right angles. **2.** Forming a right angle: *a board with square corners.* **3.** Similar to a square in form: *a square field.* **4.** Being or relating to units that express the measure of area: *square miles.* **5.** Honest; direct: *a square answer.* **6.** Just; equitable: *a square deal.* **7.** *Slang* Dull and conventional: ❖ *adv.* **1.** In a square shape or form. **2.** Directly; straight: *ran square into the wall.* ❖ *v.* **squared, squar·ing, squares** *—tr.* **1.** To cut or form into a square or rectangular shape: *square a board.* **2.** To test (a joint, for example) to ensure that its parts meet at right angles. **3.** To multiply (a number, quantity, or expression) by itself. **4.** To find a square whose area is equal to (the area of a given figure): *squaring the circle.* **5.** To bring into agreement or conformity: *We must square his story with ours.* **6.** To settle; bring into balance: *square an account.* *—intr.* **1.** To be at right angles. **2.** To agree or conform: *That story doesn't square with the facts.* ◆ **square away** To put away or in order. **square off** To assume a fighting stance; prepare to fight. [From Middle English, from Old French *esquarre.*] **—square′ly** *adv.* **—square′ness** *n.*

square dance *n.* **1.** A dance in which sets of four couples form squares. **2.** Any of various similar group dances.

square-dance (skwâr′dăns′) *intr.v.* **square-danced, square-danc·ing, square-danc·es** To perform a square dance.

square knot *n.* A common knot whose loose ends lie parallel to the fixed strands.

square measure *n.* A system for expressing surface area by means of units, such as square feet and square meters, that are the squares of linear units.

square-rigged (skwâr′rĭgd′) *adj.* Fitted primarily with square sails: *a square-rigged ship.*

square-rig·ger (skwâr′rĭg′ər) *n.* A square-rigged vessel.

square root *n.* A divisor of a number that when squared gives the number. For example, 6 is the square root of 36 (written $\sqrt{36}$) because $6 \times 6 = 36$.

squash[1] (skwŏsh) *n., pl.* **squash** or **squash·es 1.** Any of various types of fruit, such as the zucchini or pumpkin, that grow on vines or shrubby plants and are eaten as a vegetable. **2.** A vine that bears such fruit. [From alteration of Narragansett *askútasquash.*]

squash[2] (skwŏsh) *v.* **squashed, squash·ing, squash·es** *—tr.* **1.** To beat or flatten into a pulp; crush: *squashed the peach on the pavement.* **2.** To suppress; quash: *squash a revolt.* *—intr.* **1.** To become crushed or flattened: *The tomato squashed when it hit the floor.* **2.** To move with a sloshing or splashing sound: *squashed through the slush.* ❖ *n.* **1.** The act or sound of squashing. **2.** A crowd. **3.** In sports, a game played in a walled court in which the players hit a hard rubber ball with long-handled rackets. [From Middle English *squachen,* from Old French *esquasser.*]

squash·y (skwŏsh′ē) *adj.* **squash·i·er, squash·i·est 1.** Easily squashed. **2.** Overripe and soft; pulpy. **3.** Boggy; marshy. **—squash′i·ly** *adv.*

squat (skwŏt) *v.* **squat·ted, squat·ting, squats** *—intr.* **1.** To sit in a crouching position with the knees bent and the buttocks on or near the heels: *squat down to watch an ant.* **2.** To take up residence on unoccupied land or in an unoccupied building without legal claim to ownership. *—tr.* **1.** To put (oneself) into a crouching position. **2.** To occupy (a building, for example) as a squatter. ❖ *adj.* **squat·ter, squat·test** Short and thick; low and broad: *a squat shape.* ❖ *n.* **1.** The act of squatting. **2.** A squatting position. **3.** A lift in weightlifting in which one stands with a weighted barbell on one's shoulders, squats down, and then straightens the legs to resume a standing position.

squat·ter (skwŏt′ər) *n.* A person who takes up residence on land or in a building without legal claim to ownership.

squaw (skwô) *n.* *Offensive* A Native American woman. [From Massachusett *squa,* younger woman.]

squawk (skwôk) *intr.v.* **squawked, squawk·ing, squawks 1.** To utter a harsh scream; screech. **2.** *Informal* To complain or protest loudly and angrily. ❖ *n.* **1.** A loud harsh screech: *the squawk of an automobile horn.* **2.** *Informal* A loud angry complaint or protest. **—squawk′er** *n.*

squeak (skwēk) *v.* **squeaked, squeak·ing, squeaks** *—intr.* To make a short, high-pitched cry or sound. *—tr.* To utter (something) in a thin, high-pitched voice. ❖ *n.* A thin, high-pitched cry or sound. ◆ **squeak by** or **squeak through** To manage barely to pass, win, or survive: *He just squeaked by in his final exams.* [From Middle English *squeken,* perhaps of Scandinavian origin.]

squeak·y (skwē′kē) *adj.* **squeak·i·er, squeak·i·est** Having or making squeaking tones: *a squeaky door; squeaky shoes.*

squeal (skwēl) *v.* **squealed, squeal·ing, squeals** *—intr.* **1.** To make a loud shrill cry or sound: *The bus squealed as it stopped.* **2.** *Slang* To become an informer; betray another by giving away information. *—tr.* To utter or produce with a squeal. ❖ *n.* A loud shrill cry or sound. **—squeal′er** *n.*

squea·mish (skwē′mĭsh) *adj.* **1.** Easily nauseated or sickened. **2.** Easily shocked or disgusted. **—squea′mish·ly** *adv.* **—squea′mish·ness** *n.*

squee·gee (skwē′jē) *n.* A tool having a rubber blade that is drawn across a surface to remove water from it, as in washing windows.

squeeze (skwēz) *v.* **squeezed, squeez·ing, squeez·es** *—tr.* **1.** To press hard on or together; compress: *The baby squeezed the rubber toy.* **2.** To press gently, as in

ă	pat	ôr	core
ā	pay	oi	boy
âr	care	ou	out
ä	father	o͝o	took
ĕ	pet	o͝or	lure
ē	be	o͞o	boot
ĭ	pit	ŭ	cut
ī	bite	ûr	urge
îr	pier	th	thin
ŏ	pot	*th*	this
ō	toe	zh	vision
ô	paw	ə	about

affection or sympathy: *squeezed her mother's hand.* **3.** To exert pressure on, as by way of extracting liquid: *squeeze an orange.* **4.** To extract by applying pressure: *squeeze juice from a lemon.* **5.** To extract by intimidation or coercion: *squeezed a confession out of the suspect.* **6.** To crowd; cram: *She squeezed her books onto the crowded shelf.* —*intr.* **1.** To exert pressure. **2.** To give way under pressure. **3.** To force one's way: *squeeze through a crowd.* ❖ *n.* **1.** An act or instance of squeezing: *gave his hand a squeeze.* **2.** *Informal* Pressure exerted to obtain something: *They put the squeeze on him and he confessed.* **—squeez′a·ble** *adj.* **—squeez′er** *n.*

squeeze play *n.* In baseball, a play in which the batter bunts so that a runner on third base may score.

squelch (skwĕlch) *v.* **squelched, squelch·ing, squelch·es** —*tr.* **1.** To subdue forcefully: *squelched a revolt.* **2.** To inhibit or suppress: *squelched a rumor; squelched my anger.* —*intr.* To make a splashing squishing sound, as when walking in mud. ❖ *n.* A squishing sound.

squib (skwĭb) *n.* **1a.** A small firecracker. **b.** A broken firecracker that burns but does not explode. **2.** A brief witty literary work, such as a lampoon.

squid (skwĭd) *n., pl.* **squids** or **squid** Any of various soft-bodied sea mollusks related to the octopuses and cuttlefish, having a long body, eight arms and two tentacles surrounding the mouth, and a pair of triangular or rounded fins.

squig·gle (skwĭg′əl) *n.* A small wiggly mark or scrawl.

squint (skwĭnt) *intr.v.* **squint·ed, squint·ing, squints** To look with the eyes partly closed, as in bright sunlight or in an attempt to see something more clearly. ❖ *n.* The act or an instance of squinting.

squire (skwīr) *n.* **1.** A man who attends or escorts a woman. **2.** An English country gentleman. **3.** A judge or other local dignitary. **4.** A young man of noble birth serving as a knight's attendant. ❖ *tr.v.* **squired, squir·ing, squires** To attend as a squire; escort. [From Middle English *squier*, esquire, from Old French *esquier.*]

squirm (skwûrm) *intr.v.* **squirmed, squirm·ing, squirms** **1.** To twist about in a wriggling motion; writhe. **2.** To feel or exhibit signs of humiliation or embarrassment. ❖ *n.* The act of squirming or a squirming movement.

squir·rel (skwûr′əl) *n.* **1.** Any of various rodents that live in trees and have gray or reddish-brown fur and a bushy tail. **2.** Any of various similar rodents, such as a ground squirrel. **3.** The fur of such a rodent. ❖ *tr.v.* **squir·reled, squir·rel·ing, squir·rels** or **squir·relled, squir·rel·ling, squir·rels** To hide or store: *squirreled away her money.* [From Middle English *squirel*, from Greek *skiouros* : *skiā*, shadow + *ourā*, tail.]

squirt (skwûrt) *v.* **squirt·ed, squirt·ing, squirts** —*intr.* **1.** To come out in a thin forceful stream or jet; spurt. **2.** To eject liquid in a jet. —*tr.* **1.** To eject (liquid) in a thin stream through a narrow opening. **2.** To wet with a spurt of liquid. ❖ *n.* **1.** The act of squirting. **2a.** A device used to squirt. **b.** The stream squirted. **3.** *Slang* **a.** A small or young person. **b.** An insignificant or contemptible person. **—squirt′er** *n.*

squish (skwĭsh) *v.* **squished, squish·ing, squish·es** —*tr.* To squash or squeeze together: *squish a ripe tomato.* —*intr.* To make a noise like that of soft mud being walked on. ❖ *n.* A squishing sound.

Sr The symbol for the element **strontium.**

Sr. *abbr.* An abbreviation of: **1.** or **sr.** senior. **2.** señor. **3.** sister (religious title).

Sra. *abbr.* An abbreviation of señora.

Sri Lan·ka (srē läng′kə *or* shrē läng′kə) An island country in the Indian Ocean off southeast India. It was formerly known as Ceylon, and Colombo is the capital.

SS[1] (ĕs′ĕs′) *n.* An elite military unit of the Nazi party that served as Hitler's personal guard and as a special security force.

SS[2] *abbr.* An abbreviation of: **1.** shortstop. **2.** Social Security. **3.** steamship.

SSN *abbr.* An abbreviation of Social Security number.

St. *abbr.* An abbreviation of: **1.** saint **2.** street

stab (stăb) *v.* **stabbed, stab·bing, stabs** —*tr.* **1.** To pierce or wound with a pointed object: *stabbed the fish with a spear.* **2.** To plunge (a pointed object) into something: *stabbed a fork into the meat.* —*intr.* To thrust with a pointed object: *stabbed at the air with his finger.* ❖ *n.* **1.** A thrust made with a pointed object. **2.** An attempt; a try: *He thought he would take a stab at painting for a living.* [From Middle English *stabben.*] **—stab′ber** *n.*

sta·bil·i·ty (stə-bĭl′ĭ-tē) *n., pl.* **sta·bil·i·ties** **1.** The condition or property of being stable. **2.** The ability of an object, such as a ship, to stay upright or return to an upright position after being tilted.

sta·bi·lize (stā′bə-līz′) *v.* **sta·bi·lized, sta·bi·liz·ing, sta·bi·liz·es** —*tr.* **1.** To make stable. **2.** To maintain the stability of (a plane or ship, for example) by means of a stabilizer. **3.** To fix the level of; keep from fluctuating: *stabilize interest rates.* —*intr.* To become stable. **—sta′bi·li·za′tion** (stā′bə-lĭ-zā′shən) *n.*

sta·bi·liz·er (stā′bə-lī′zər) *n.* **1.** Something that stabilizes. **2.** A device, such as a fin controlled by a gyroscope, used to keep a ship steady in heavy seas. **3.** A fixed airfoil used to keep an aircraft steady in flight.

sta·ble[1] (stā′bəl) *adj.* **sta·bler, sta·blest** **1a.** Not likely to change position; firm: *a stable foundation of a house.* **b.** Not likely to change, as in condition: *a stable economy.* **2.** Not likely to be affected or overthrown: *a stable government.* **3.** Firm or steady, as in purpose or character. **4.** Mentally or emotionally sound; sane or rational. **5.** Not known to decay; existing for an indefinitely long time, as an atomic particle. **6.** Not easily decomposed, as a chemical compound. [From Middle English, from Latin *stabilis.*] **—sta′bly** *adv.*

sta·ble[2] (stā′bəl) *n.* **1a.** A building for the shelter of horses or other domestic animals. **b.** The animals inhabiting such a building. **2.** All of the racehorses belonging to a single owner. **3.** A group under common management: *a stable of prizefighters.* ❖ *tr.v.* **sta·bled, sta·bling, sta·bles** To put or keep (an animal) in a stable: *stable a horse at the end of the day.* [From Middle English, from Latin *stabulum*, standing place.]

stac·ca·to (stə-kä′tō) *adv. & adj.* **1.** In a musical style in which tones are short and unconnected. **2.** Marked by abrupt, disconnected sounds: *gave orders in a staccato voice.*

stack (stăk) *n.* **1.** A large, usually conical pile of straw or food. **2.** An orderly pile, especially one arranged in layers: *a stack of firewood.* See Synonyms at **heap. 3.** A chimney or vertical exhaust pipe. **4a.** often **stacks** An extensive arrangement of shelves. **b. stacks** The part of a library where books are stored on such shelves: *You'll find that novel in the stacks.* **5.** *Informal* A large quantity: *a stack of work to do.* ❖ *tr.v.* **stacked, stack·ing, stacks** **1.** To arrange in a stack: *stacking hay; stack the books neatly.* **2a.** To prearrange the order of (a deck of cards) so as to increase one's chance of winning. **b.** To prearrange or fix unfairly: *stacked the jury with sympathetic jurors.* ◆ **stack up** *Informal* To measure up or equal: *Our team stacks up well against the competition.* [From Middle English *stak*, from Old Norse *stakkr.*]

sta·di·um (stā′dē-əm) *n., pl.* **sta·di·ums** or **sta·di·a** (stā′dē-ə) **1.** A large, usually open structure for sports events with tiered seating for spectators. **2.** A course for foot races in ancient Greece, usually semicircular and surrounded with tiers of seats. **3.** An ancient Greek measure of distance equal to about 607 feet (185 meters). [From Greek *stadion.*]

staff (stăf) *n., pl.* **staffs** or **staves** (stāvz) **1a.** A long stick or cane used as an aid in walking or as a weapon.

squid

squirrel

stained glass

stalactite

Joseph Stalin

ă	pat	ôr	core
ā	pay	oi	boy
âr	care	ou	out
ä	father	o͝o	took
ĕ	pet	o͝or	lure
ē	be	o͞o	boot
ĭ	pit	ŭ	cut
ī	bite	ûr	urge
îr	pier	th	thin
ŏ	pot	*th*	this
ō	toe	zh	vision
ô	paw	ə	about

b. A rod carried as a symbol of authority. **c.** A pole on which a flag is displayed. **2.** *pl.* **staffs** A long measuring stick, as used in surveying. **3.** *pl.* **staffs a.** A group of assistants who serve a person of authority: *the senator's campaign staff.* **b.** A group of military officers who assist and advise a commander. **c.** An organized group of employees working together on a project or enterprise: *the hospital's nursing staff.* **4.** The set of five horizontal lines and the spaces between them on which musical notes are written. ❖ *tr.v.* **staffed, staff·ing, staffs** To provide with assistants or employees. [From Old English *stæf.*]

staff·er (stăf′ər) *n.* A member of a staff: *White House staffers.*

stag (stăg) *n.* **1.** The adult male of various deer. **2.** A person who attends a social gathering unaccompanied by a partner, especially a man unaccompanied by a woman. ❖ *adj.* Relating to or for men only: *a stag party.*

stage (stāj) *n.* **1.** A raised and level platform, especially one in a theater on which actors and other entertainers perform. **2.** The acting profession or the world of theater: *Rebecca moved to New York to pursue the stage.* **3.** The scene or setting of an event or of a series of events: *The stage was set for a summit conference.* **4.** Part of a journey. **5.** A stagecoach. **6.** A level, degree, or period of time in the course of a process; a step in development: *a disease in its early stages.* **7.** Any of a series of rocket propulsion units, each of which fires after the preceding one has finished burning and been cast away. ❖ *tr.v.* **staged, stag·ing, stag·es 1.** To produce or direct (a theatrical performance). **2.** To arrange and carry out: *students staging a protest march.* **3.** To exhibit or present on or as if on a stage: *stage a boxing match.*

stage·coach (stāj′kōch′) *n.* A four-wheeled, horse-drawn vehicle formerly used to transport mail and passengers over a regular route.

stage·hand (stāj′hănd′) *n.* A worker who shifts scenery, adjusts lighting, and performs other tasks in a theatrical production.

stag·ger (stăg′ər) *v.* **stag·gered, stag·ger·ing, stag·gers** *—intr.* To move or stand unsteadily, as if carrying a great weight; totter. *—tr.* **1.** To cause to totter or sway. **2.** To overwhelm with emotion or astonishment. **3.** To arrange in parallel horizontal rows that form zigzags when viewed vertically: *stagger theater seats.* **4.** To arrange or schedule in overlapping time periods: *The terms of US senators are staggered, so that only one-third are elected every two years.* ❖ *n.* **1.** An act of staggering; a tottering motion or walk. **2.** A staggered pattern, arrangement, or order. **3. staggers** *(used with a singular verb)* Any of various diseases of horses, cattle, or other domestic animals, marked by a staggering gait and frequent falling.

stag·ger·ing (stăg′ər-ĭng) *adj.* Causing great astonishment, amazement, or dismay: *a staggering achievement.* **—stag′ger·ing·ly** *adv.*

stag·nant (stăg′nənt) *adj.* **1.** Not flowing or moving, and often foul-smelling or stale: *stagnant water.* **2.** Not changing or growing; inactive: *a stagnant industry.* **—stag′nan·cy** *n.* **—stag′nant·ly** *adv.*

stag·nate (stăg′nāt′) *intr.v.* **stag·nat·ed, stag·nat·ing, stag·nates** To be or become stagnant. **—stag·na′tion** *n.*

staid (stād) *adj.* **1.** Characterized by sedateness and often a strait-laced sense of propriety. **2.** Fixed; unchanging. **—staid′ly** *adv.* **—staid′ness** *n.*

stain (stān) *tr.v.* **stained, stain·ing, stains 1.** To discolor, soil, or spot. **2.** To taint or tarnish (someone's reputation, for example). **3.** To color (wood, for example) with a dye or tint mixed with a penetrating liquid. **4.** To treat (microscopic specimens) with chemicals or dyes that make certain features visible through a microscope. ❖ *n.* **1.** A discolored or soiled spot or smudge. **2.** A blemish on one's character or reputation. **3.** A liquid preparation applied especially to wood in order to color it. **4.** A solution used for staining microscopic specimens. **—stain′er** *n.*

stained glass (stānd) *n.* Decorative glass consisting of multiple pieces in various colors held together with strips of lead, used especially for windows.

stain·less (stān′lĭs) *adj.* **1.** Free of stains or blemishes: *a stainless reputation.* **2.** Resisting stain or corrosion: *stainless alloys.*

stainless steel *n.* Any of various steel alloys that contain enough chromium to be resistant to rusting and corrosion.

stair (stâr) *n.* **1.** often **stairs** A series or flight of steps; a staircase. **2.** One of a flight of steps. [From Old English *stǣger.*]

❑ *These sound alike:* **stair, stare** (gaze).

stair·case (stâr′kās′) *n.* A flight of steps and its supporting structure.

stair·way (stâr′wā′) *n.* A staircase.

stair·well (stâr′wĕl′) *n.* A vertical shaft containing a staircase.

stake (stāk) *n.* **1.** A piece of wood or metal pointed on one end and driven into the ground as a marker, fence pole, or tent support. **2a.** A post to which a condemned person is bound for execution by burning. **b.** Execution by burning. **3a.** often **stakes** The amount of money or the property risked in a bet or gambling game. **b.** The prize awarded to a contest winner. **c.** often **stakes** A race, especially a horse race, offering a prize to the winner. **4.** A share or an interest: *We all have a stake in completing this project on time.* ❖ *tr.v.* **staked, stak·ing, stakes 1.** To mark the location or boundaries of with or as if with stakes: *stake out a piece of land.* **2.** To fasten, secure, or support with a stake or stakes: *stake a plant.* **3.** To gamble or risk: *stake two dollars on the game.* **4.** To provide with the capital for or finance: *The bank will stake the new company.* ◆ **at stake** At risk; in jeopardy. **stake out** To keep close watch over a person or thing: *The police staked out the jewelry store.* [From Old English *staca.*]

❑ *These sound alike:* **stake, steak** (meat).

stake·out (stāk′out′) *n.* The watching of an area, building, or person, especially by the police.

sta·lac·tite (stə-lăk′tīt′) *n.* An icicle-shaped mineral deposit projecting downward from the roof of a cave or cavern, formed by dripping mineral water. [From Greek *stalaktos,* dripping, from *stalassein,* to drip.]

sta·lag·mite (stə-lăg′mīt′) *n.* A conical mineral deposit built up from the floor of a cave or cavern, formed by dripping mineral water. [From Greek *stalagma,* a drop, from *stalassein,* to drip.]

stale (stāl) *adj.* **stal·er, stal·est 1.** Having lost freshness or flavor: *stale bread.* **2.** Lacking originality; overused: *stale jokes.* **3.** Weakened by inactivity or boredom: *Some athletes work out on holidays, for fear of getting stale.*

stale·mate (stāl′māt′) *n.* **1.** A situation in which further action is blocked; a deadlock: *The peace talks have reached a stalemate.* **2.** A position in chess that results in a draw because the only piece that can be moved is the king and every move the king can make puts the king in check. ❖ *tr.v.* **stale·mat·ed, stale·mat·ing, stale·mates** To bring into a stalemate; deadlock.

Sta·lin (stä′lĭn), **Joseph** 1879–1953. Soviet politician. As general secretary of the Communist Party (1922–1953) and premier (1941–1953) of the Soviet Union, he oversaw the growth of industry and Soviet involvement in World War II. His rule is infamous for extreme political repression, which resulted in the deaths of millions of people.

Sta·lin·grad (stä′lĭn-grăd′) See **Volgograd.**

Sta·lin·ism (stä′lə-nĭz′əm) *n.* The authoritarian exercise of state power associated with Stalin and characterized by repression of political opponents. **—Sta′lin·ist** *adj. & n.*

stalk[1] (stôk) *n.* **1.** The main stem of a plant or a slender plant part supporting a leaf, flower, or other structure. **2.** A slender or elongated support or structure, such as one that holds up an organ or another body part. [From Middle English, probably from *stale,* upright of a ladder, post, handle, from Old English *stalu.*]

stalk[2] (stôk) *v.* **stalked, stalk·ing, stalks** *—tr.* **1.** To pursue or track (prey) stealthily: *The lions stalked the zebra from the tall grass.* **2.** To follow or observe (a person) persistently, especially out of obsession or derangement. *—intr.* To walk in a stiff, haughty, or angry manner: *He stalked past me in stony silence.* [From Middle English *stalken,* from Old English *stealcian,* to move stealthily.] **—stalk′er** *n.*

stall[1] (stôl) *n.* **1.** A compartment for a domestic animal in a barn or stable. **2.** A small booth or stand used for selling or displaying goods, as at a fair. **3.** A small compartment or booth: *a shower stall.* **4.** A pew in a church. **5.** A space marked off, as in a garage, for parking a motor vehicle. **6.** A sudden unintended loss of power or effectiveness in an engine. **7.** A condition in which an aircraft experiences a sudden loss of lift and a tendency to drop. ❖ *v.* **stalled, stall·ing, stalls** *—tr.* **1.** To put or lodge (an animal) in a stall. **2.** To slow down or halt the progress of; bring to a standstill: *Opponents of the bill have stalled it in Congress.* **3.** To cause (an engine or motor) to stop running. **4.** To cause (an aircraft) to go into a stall. *—intr.* **1.** To live or be lodged in a stall. **2.** To come to a standstill: *The project stalled because of a lack of money.* **3.** To stop operating because of mechanical failure. **4.** To lose forward flying speed, causing a stall. Used of an aircraft. [From Old English *steall,* standing place.]

stall[2] (stôl) *n.* A tactic used to mislead or delay. ❖ *v.* **stalled, stall·ing, stalls** *—tr.* To use delaying tactics against: *If you can stall him, we can get his present wrapped before he gets home.* *—intr.* To use delaying tactics: *stalling for time.* [From Middle English *stal,* decoy, from Anglo-Norman *estale,* of Germanic origin.]

stal·lion (stăl′yən) *n.* An adult male horse that has not been castrated, especially one kept for breeding, or an adult male of a similar animal, such as a zebra.

stal·wart (stôl′wərt) *adj.* **1.** Not easily deterred or defeated; brave and resolute: *stalwart defenders of their country.* **2.** Physically strong; sturdy; robust: *a stalwart oak.* ❖ *n.* One who steadfastly supports an organization or cause. **—stal′wart·ly** *adv.* **—stal′wart·ness** *n.*

sta·men (stā′mən) *n.* The male reproductive organ of a flower, usually consisting of a slender stalk with a pollen-bearing part at its tip.

stam·i·na (stăm′ə-nə) *n.* The ability to continue an activity for a long time; endurance. [From Latin *stāmina,* plural of *stāmen,* thread, thread of life spun by the Fates.]

stam·mer (stăm′ər) *v.* **stam·mered, stam·mer·ing, stam·mers** *—intr.* To speak with involuntary pauses or repetitions, as from nervousness or confusion. *—tr.* To say or utter with involuntary pauses or repetitions. ❖ *n.* A manner of speaking marked by stammering. **—stam′mer·er** *n.*

stamp (stămp) *v.* **stamped, stamp·ing, stamps** *—tr.* **1a.** To bring down (the foot) forcefully: *We stamped our feet to shake off the snow.* **b.** To bring the foot down onto (an object or surface) forcefully. **2.** To extinguish or destroy by or as if by trampling underfoot: *stamp out a fire.* **3.** To imprint or impress with a seal: *The border guard stamped our passports.* **4.** To put a postage stamp on: *Don't forget to stamp the letter before mailing it.* **5.** To shape or cut out by forcing into or against a mold, form, or die: *a factory that stamps metal parts.* **6.** To impress deeply or permanently: *an image stamped in her memory.* **7.** To make, characterize, or reveal: *His accent stamped him as a foreigner.* *—intr.* **1.** To thrust the foot forcefully downward. **2.** To walk with heavy forceful steps. ❖ *n.* **1.** The act of stamping. **2.** A device used to impress, shape, or cut out something to which it is applied. **3.** The impression or shape formed by such a device. **4a.** A postage stamp. **b.** A similar piece of gummed paper issued for a specific purpose: *a trading stamp.* **5.** A characteristic mark; a clear indication: *His work bears the stamp of genius.* **6.** Characteristic nature or quality: *a person of her stamp.* [From Middle English *stampen,* possibly from Old English *stempan,* to pound in a mortar.]

WRITERS CHOOSE THEIR WORDS

She decided that beginning today she would give up riding the school bus and would build up her **stamina** by running to and from school.

—Dorothy Perkyns *Last Days in Africville*

stam·pede (stăm-pēd′) *n.* **1.** A sudden violent rush of frightened animals, as of a herd of cattle. **2.** A sudden headlong rush or flight of a crowd of people. ❖ *v.* **stam·ped·ed, stam·ped·ing, stam·pedes** *—tr.* To cause (animals or people) to stampede. *—intr.* To flee in a sudden rush. [From Spanish *estampida,* from Provençal *estampir,* to stamp, of Germanic origin.]

stance (stăns) *n.* **1.** The position or manner in which a person or animal stands, especially the position taken by an athlete about to go into action: *the erect stance of a diver.* **2.** An attitude or point of view regarding some issue: *a judge with a tough stance toward repeating offenders.*

stanch[1] (stônch *or* stänch *or* stănch) also **staunch** (stônch *or* stänch) *tr.v.* **stanched, stanch·ing, stanch·es** also **staunched, staunch·ing, staunch·es 1.** To stop or check the flow of (blood or tears, for example). **2.** To stop or check the flow of blood from (a wound). [From Middle English *staunchen,* from Old French *estanchier.*]

stanch[2] (stônch *or* stänch *or* stănch) *adj.* Variant of **staunch[1]**.

stan·chion (stăn′chən *or* stăn′shən) *n.* An upright pole, post, or support.

stanchion

stand (stănd) *v.* **stood** (stŏŏd), **stand·ing, stands** *—intr.* **1.** To rise to an upright position on the feet: *I stood up from my chair to answer the telephone.* **2.** To maintain an upright position on the feet or on a base or support: *Stand straight. The rocket stood on a launching pad.* **3.** To be located or situated: *The building stands at the corner.* **4.** To measure a certain height when in an upright position: *stood six feet tall.* **5.** To be at a specified level, position, or rank: *stand 12th in line.* **6.** To remain motionless or undisturbed: *Let the mixture stand overnight.* **7.** To remain in effect or existence: *Exceptions are made, but the rule still stands.* **8.** To hold a specified position or attitude: *How do you stand on the issue?* **9.** To be in a specified state or condition: *My client stands accused of a serious crime.* **10.** To be in a position of possible gain or loss: *She stands to make a fortune.* *—tr.* **1.** To cause to stand; place upright: *Stand the books on the shelf.* **2.** To resist successfully; withstand: *a metal that can stand high temperatures.* **3.** To tolerate; endure: *I can't stand all of this noise.* **4.** To submit to or undergo: *stand trial.* **5.** *Informal* To bear the expense of; pay for: *I'll stand you a dinner to celebrate.* ❖ *n.* **1.** A place reserved for the stopping or parking of certain vehicles: *a taxi stand.* **2.** A booth, stall, or counter for the display of goods for sale: *a flower stand.* **3.** A small rack, prop, or receptacle for holding something: *an umbrella stand.* **4.** A raised structure on which someone can sit or stand and be clearly seen: *a witness stand.* **5. stands** The seating area at a playing field or stadium. **6.** A stop on a performance tour: *a one-show stand.* **7.** A desperate or final effort at defense or resistance, as in battle: *made their stand at the river.* **8.** A position or opinion that one is prepared to defend: *took a stand against bullying.* **9.** A group or growth of tall plants or trees: *a stand of pine trees.* ◆ **stand a chance** To have a chance or hope for gaining or accomplishing something. **stand bail for** To provide bail for (a person under arrest). **stand by 1.** To be ready or available to act: *We stood by in case anything went wrong.* **2.** To remain uninvolved; refrain from acting: *They stood by and let him get away.* **3.** To remain loyal to; aid or support: *Will her friends stand by her in her hour of need?* **4.** To keep or maintain: *I stand by my promise to you.* **stand down 1.** To leave a witness stand at a trial. **2.** To withdraw, as from a political contest. **3.** To end a state of readiness or alert: *ordered the national guard to stand down.* **stand for 1.** To represent; symbolize: *The rose in the poem stands for beauty.* **2.** To advocate or support: *We stand for freedom of the press.* **3.** To put up with; tolerate: *He won't stand for another delay.* **stand in** To act as a stand-in. **stand off** To stay at a distance; remain apart or aloof. **stand on** To demand observance of: *standing on his constitutional rights.* **stand out 1.** To protrude; project. **2.** To be distinctive or prominent; attract attention: *Brightly colored clothing stands out in a crowd.* **stand up 1.** To remain valid, sound, or durable: *His claim will not stand up in court.* **2.** *Informal* To fail to keep a date with. **stand up for** To side with; defend; be loyal to: *The others made fun of him, but she stood up for him.* **stand up to** To confront fearlessly; face up to: *He is mean, and we must stand up to him.* [From Old English *standan.*]

Elizabeth Cady Stanton
photographed in the late 1880s

stan·dard (stăn′dərd) *adj.* **1.** Serving as a standard of measurement, value, or quality: *a standard unit of volume.* **2.** Conforming to a standard, as in size, weight, or quality: *bolts of standard length and thickness.* **3.** Normal; familiar; usual: *a standard excuse.* **4.** Widely accepted as reliable or excellent: *a standard reference work.* **5.** Conforming to a model of usage in language admired by educated speakers for more formal situations. ❖ *n.* **1a.** A widely known and accepted measure used as a basis for a system of measures. **b.** A physical object from which such a measure can be determined under a given set of conditions. **2.** A rule or model used to judge the quality, value, or rightness of something: *moral standards.* **3.** A level of quality, value, or achievement that is required or aimed for: *an artist who sets high standards for herself.* **4.** The commodity or commodities used to back a monetary system: *the gold standard.* **5.** A flag or banner, especially one used as the emblem of a nation, military unit, or city. **6.** A musical composition that is often used in repertoires: *plays jazz standards.* [From Middle English, from Old French *estandard*, rallying place, of Germanic origin.]

standard candle *n.* A candela.

Standard English *n.* The variety of English that is most widely accepted as the model for the speech and writing of educated speakers across different regions.

standard gauge *n.* **1.** A railroad track having a width of 56.5 inches (143.5 centimeters). **2.** A railroad or railroad car built to this specification.

stan·dard·ize (stăn′dər-dīz′) *tr.v.* **stan·dard·ized, stan·dard·iz·ing, stan·dard·iz·es** To cause to conform to a standard: *decided to standardize the old electrical fixtures.* **—stan′dard·i·za′tion** (stăn′dər-dĭ-zā′shən) *n.*

standard time *n.* The time in any of the 24 time zones into which the earth is divided, computed from the position of the sun at the central meridian of each zone.

stand·by (stănd′bī′) *n., pl.* **stand·bys 1.** A person or thing that can always by depended on, as in an emergency. **2.** A person or thing kept ready and available for service as a substitute. **3.** A favorite or frequent choice.

stand·ee (stăn-dē′) *n.* A person who stands because no seats are available, as on a bus or in a theater.

stand-in (stănd′ĭn′) *n.* **1.** A substitute. **2.** A person who takes the place of another performer while the lights and camera are adjusted or during dangerous action.

stand·ing (stăn′dĭng) *n.* **1.** Status with respect to rank, reputation, or position, as in society, a profession, or a sport. **2.** High reputation; esteem: *a person of standing in the community.* **3.** Persistence in time; duration: *a friend of long standing.* **4. standings** A listing of individual competitors or of teams in a league according to their record of performance. ❖ *adj.* **1.** Remaining upright; erect: *standing timber.* **2.** Performed or done from an upright position: *a standing jump.* **3.** Remaining in effect or existence; permanent: *a standing invitation; a standing army.* **4.** Not flowing or circulating; stagnant: *several feet of standing water.*

Stan·dish (stăn′dĭsh′), **Miles** or **Myles** 1584?–1656. English colonist in America who was a military and political leader in the difficult early years of Plymouth Colony.

stand·off (stănd′ôf′) *n.* **1.** A situation in which one force neutralizes or counterbalances another. **2.** A tie or draw, as in a contest.

stand·off·ish (stănd-ô′fĭsh) *adj.* Showing reluctance to interact with others; aloof.

stand·pipe (stănd′pīp′) *n.* A large vertical pipe into which water is pumped in order to produce a desired pressure.

stand·point (stănd′point′) *n.* A position from which things are considered or judged; a point of view.

stand·still (stănd′stĭl′) *n.* A halt; a stop: *Work came to a standstill.*

stank (stăngk) *v.* A past tense of **stink.**

stan·nic (stăn′ĭk) *adj.* Relating to or containing tin, especially with a valence of 4. [From Late Latin *stannum*, tin.]

stan·nous (stăn′əs) *adj.* Relating to or containing tin, especially with a valence of 2.

Stan·ton (stăn′tən), **Elizabeth Cady** 1815–1902. American reformer and suffragist who with Lucretia Mott called the first women's rights convention, held in Seneca Falls, New York (1848). In 1869 she helped found the National Woman Suffrage Association. —SEE NOTE AT Susan Brownell **Anthony.**

stan·za (stăn′zə) *n.* One of the divisions of a poem or song, composed of two or more lines usually following a set pattern of meter and rhyme. [From Italian *stanza*, stopping place.]

sta·pes (stā′pēz) *n., pl.* **stapes** or **sta·pe·des** (stā′pĭ-dēz′) The innermost of the three small bones of the middle ear; the stirrup.

staph·y·lo·coc·cus (stăf′ə-lō-**kŏk′**əs) *n., pl.* **staph·y·lo·coc·ci** (stăf′ə-lō-**kŏk′**sī *or* stăf′ə-lō-**kŏk′**ī) Any of various bacteria that are normally found on the skin and mucous membranes, some of which can cause infections in humans.

sta·ple¹ (stā′pəl) *n.* **1.** A major product grown or produced in a region: *Rice and rubber are the staples of this Asian country.* **2.** A basic food item, such as flour or rice. **3.** A raw material. **4.** A basic or principal element or feature: *the classics that are the staples of every good library.* **5.** The fiber of cotton, wool, or flax, graded as to length or fineness. ❖ *adj.* **1.** Produced or stacked in large quantities to meet a steady demand: *Wheat is a staple crop.* **2.** Principal; main. [From Middle English *staple*, official market for purchase of export goods, from Anglo-Norman *estaple.*]

sta·ple² (stā′pəl) *n.* **1.** A thin piece of wire shaped as three sides of a square so that it can be driven into thin or soft material, such as paper, and bent to function as a fastener. **2.** A similarly shaped or U-shaped metal loop with pointed ends, driven into a surface to hold a hook or bolt or to hold wiring in place. ❖ *tr.v.* **sta·pled, sta·pling, sta·ples** To secure or fasten by means of a staple or staples. [From Old English *stapol*, post, pillar.]

stapler (stā′plər) *n.* A device used to fasten papers or other materials together by means of staples.

star (stär) *n.* **1.** A celestial object that produces its own light, consisting of a mass of gas held together by its

ă	pat	ôr	core
ā	pay	oi	boy
âr	care	ou	out
ä	father	o͝o	took
ĕ	pet	o͝or	lure
ē	be	o͞o	boot
ĭ	pit	ŭ	cut
ī	bite	ûr	urge
îr	pier	th	thin
ŏ	pot	*th*	this
ō	toe	zh	vision
ô	paw	ə	about

own gravity and generating energy by nuclear fusion in its core. **2.** Any of the celestial objects visible at night from Earth as relatively stationary, usually twinkling points of light. **3. stars a.** The celestial objects, regarded as determining and influencing human events. **b.** The future; destiny: *Fame was just not in his stars.* **4.** Something resembling a star, especially a design with several points radiating from a center. **5a.** An asterisk (*). **b.** The star key on a telephone: *For customer service, press star.* **6a.** An actor who plays a leading role in a movie, drama, or other performance. **b.** An outstanding and widely admired performer, as in movies or sports. ❖ *adj.* **1.** Outstanding or famous, especially in performing something: *a star researcher; a star figure skater.* **2.** Relating to a star or stars. ❖ *v.* **starred, star·ring, stars** —*tr.* **1.** To ornament with stars. **2.** To award or mark with a star for excellence. **3.** To present or feature (a performer) in a leading role: *a television series starring a famous actor.* —*intr.* **1.** To play the leading role in a theatrical or film production: *She's now starring in a Broadway show.* **2.** To perform excellently: *starred as the goaltender.*

star·board (stär′bərd) *n.* The right-hand side of a ship or aircraft as one faces forward. ❖ *adj.* On the right-hand side as one faces forward: *the starboard bow.* ❖ *adv.* To or toward the right-hand side as one faces forward. [From Old English *stēorbord* : *stēor-*, steering + *bord*, side.]

starch (stärch) *n.* **1.** A carbohydrate that is the chief form of stored energy in plants, especially grains and tubers, and that forms a white, tasteless powder when purified. It is an important nutrient and is also used in the production of adhesives, paper, and textiles. **2. starches** Foods having a high content of starch, as rice, beans, and potatoes. **3.** Any of various substances, such as natural starch, used to stiffen fabrics. **4.** Stiff behavior. ❖ *tr.v.* **starched, starch·ing, starch·es** To stiffen with starch. [From Middle English *sterche*, substance used to stiffen cloth, from *sterchen*, to stiffen.]

starch·y (stär′chē) *adj.* **starch·i·er, starch·i·est 1a.** Containing starch. **b.** Stiffened with starch, as a fabric. **2.** Relating to or resembling starch. **3.** Stiff; formal.

star-crossed (stär′krôst′) *adj.* Opposed by fate; ill-fated.

star·dom (stär′dəm) *n.* The status of a performer or an entertainer acknowledged as a star.

stare (stâr) *v.* **stared, star·ing, stares** —*intr.* To look steadily and directly, often with a wide-eyed gaze. —*tr.* To look at steadily and directly: *stared him in the eyes.* ❖ *n.* An intent gaze. ◆ **stare in the face** To be evident but unnoticed by (someone): *I didn't know what to do, but the answer was staring me in the face all along.* [From Old English *starian.*]

❑ *These sound alike:* **stare, stair** (step).

star·fish (stär′fĭsh′) *n.* Any of various sea animals having a thick, often spiny body with five arms extending from a central disk.

star·gaze (stär′gāz′) *intr.v.* **star·gazed, star·gaz·ing, star·gaz·es 1.** To gaze at the stars. **2.** To daydream.

stark (stärk) *adj.* **stark·er, stark·est 1.** Bare or blunt; unadorned: *the stark landscape of the moon.* **2.** Clearly distinguished or delineated: *in stark contrast.* **3.** Harsh; grim: *a stark future.* ❖ *adv.* Utterly; completely: *stark raving mad.* [From Old English *stearc*, stiff, strong.] **—stark′ly** *adv.* **—stark′ness** *n.*

star key *n.* The pushbutton in the lower left corner of a telephone dialing pad, marked with an asterisk.

star·let (stär′lĭt) *n.* A young film actress publicized as a future star.

star·light (stär′līt′) *n.* The light that reaches Earth from the stars.

star·ling (stär′lĭng) *n.* Any of various birds having a short tail, pointed wings, and dark glossy feathers, especially a species native to Eurasia that is common in North America.

star·lit (stär′lĭt′) *adj.* Illuminated by starlight.

star·ry (stär′ē) *adj.* **star·ri·er, star·ri·est 1.** Full of stars; starlit: *a starry night.* **2.** Shining like stars: *starry eyes.* **—star′ri·ness** *n.*

star·ry-eyed (stär′ē-īd′) *adj.* Full of youthful hope and confidence; naively optimistic.

Stars and Stripes *n. (used with a singular or plural verb)* The flag of the United States.

Star-Span·gled Banner (stär′spăng′gəld) *n.* The flag of the United States.

start (stärt) *v.* **start·ed, start·ing, starts** —*intr.* **1.** To begin a movement, activity, or undertaking: *Once we start in, we'll get a feel for the project.* See Synonyms at **begin. 2.** To move on the initial part of a journey: *We had started for the airport when I realized I'd forgotten my ID.* **3.** To come into operation or being; have a beginning: *School starts in September.* **4.** To have as an initial part or job: *He started as an assistant.* **5.** To move suddenly and involuntarily; startle: *The horse started at the loud noise.* **6.** In sports, to be in the first lineup of a game: *You're on the team, but do you start?* —*tr.* **1.** To begin or commence (something): *start a new job; start reading a book; start to dance.* **2.** To set into motion, operation, or activity: *She started the car.* **3.** To begin to attend: *start school.* **4.** To found; establish: *start a business.* **5.** To help or tend in an early stage of development: *start seedlings.* **6.** To rouse (game) from a resting or hiding place; flush. **7a.** To enter (a participant) into a game: *The coach decided not to start the injured goalie.* **b.** To play in the initial lineup of (a game): *He started the game but got injured.* ❖ *n.* **1.** A beginning: *I made a start on digging the garden.* **2.** A place or time at which a person or thing begins: *At the start of our trip we were cheerful.* **3.** A sudden or involuntary movement of the body; a startled reaction: *awoke with a start.* **4.** A position of advantage over rivals, as in a race: *They entered the competition, but we have a big start over them.* **5.** An act of beginning a race: *We worked on our starts in practice.* **6.** An opportunity to pursue a career or course of action: *She got her start by acting in commercials.* [From Middle English *sterten*, to move or leap suddenly.]

start·er (stär′tər) *n.* **1.** A device, usually an electric motor, that turns an internal-combustion engine through several revolutions to make it start. **2.** A person who signals the start of a race. **3a.** A contestant at the beginning of a race. **b.** A player who is a member of the starting lineup of a sports team. **4.** The first in a series, especially the first course of a meal; an appetizer.

star·tle (stär′tl) *v.* **star·tled, star·tling, star·tles** —*tr.* **1.** To cause to make a sudden involuntary movement or start: *A thud on the roof startled us.* **2.** To alarm, frighten, or surprise suddenly: *The ambassador's angry reaction startled our allies.* —*intr.* To become alarmed, frightened, or surprised. ❖ *n.* A sudden mild shock; a start. [From Old English *steartlian*, to kick.]

start-up or **start·up** (stärt′ŭp′) *n.* **1.** The act of setting into operation or motion. **2.** A business that has recently begun operation.

star·va·tion (stär-vā′shən) *n.* **1.** The act or process of starving. **2.** The condition of being starved.

starve (stärv) *v.* **starved, starv·ing, starves** —*intr.* **1.** To suffer or die from prolonged lack of food. **2.** To suffer because of a lack of something necessary: *a puppy starving for attention.* —*tr.* **1.** To cause to starve. **2.** To force to a specified state by starving: *The invading troops starved the town into submission.* [From Old English *steorfan*, to die.]

starve·ling (stärv′lĭng) *n.* A person or an animal that is starving or being starved. ❖ *adj.* **1.** Starving. **2.** Poor in quality; inadequate.

starfish

stationary
stationary exercise bicycle

stash (stăsh) *Slang tr.v.* **stashed, stash·ing, stash·es** To hide or store in a secret place: *stashing her comic books under her mattress.* ❖ *n.* **1.** A secret place where something is hidden or stored. **2.** Something, such as money, that has been hidden or stored.

state (stāt) *n.* **1.** A condition or mode of being: *a state of confusion.* **2.** A stage or form in development: *the fetal state.* **3.** A mental or emotional disposition; a mood: *in a calm rational state.* **4.** *Informal* A condition of excitement, confusion, or disorder: *got into a state over the preparations for the party.* **5.** The physical phase, form, composition, or structure of a substance: *Ice is water in the solid state.* **6.** A grand and formal style; pomp: *a queen riding in state.* **7a.** A body of people living under a single independent government; a nation: *the state of Israel.* **b.** The political organization or government of such a body of people. **c.** The territory of such a government. **8.** The power or scope of authority of a government: *the separation of church and state.* **9.** One of the political and geographic subdivisions of a country such as the United States of America. ❖ *adj.* **1.** Owned and operated by a state: *state universities.* **2.** Relating to a nation or a political and geographic subdivision of a nation: *state security.* ❖ *tr.v.* **stat·ed, stat·ing, states** To express in words; declare: *stating a problem.* [From Middle English *stat,* from Latin *status.*]

state·hood (stāt′hŏŏd′) *n.* The condition of being a state, especially a state of the United States.

state·house also **state house** (stāt′hous′) *n.* A building in which a state legislature meets; a state capitol.

state·less (stāt′lĭs) *adj.* Not being a citizen of any state or nation.

state·ly (stāt′lē) *adj.* **state·li·er, state·li·est 1.** Impressive in size or proportions; majestic: *stately mansions.* See Synonyms at **grand. 2.** Marked by a graceful dignity or formality: *a stately procession.* **—state′li·ness** *n.*

state·ment (stāt′mənt) *n.* **1.** The act of stating or declaring. **2.** Something stated or declared: *a statement of purpose.* **3.** A written summary of a financial account: *a monthly bank statement.*

Stat·en Island (stăt′n) A borough of New York City made up of **Staten Island** in southeast New York southwest of Manhattan Island. It was permanently settled in the mid-1600s and became part of New York City in 1898.

state of the art *n.* The highest level of development, as of a device, technique, or scientific field, achieved at a particular time: *the state of the art in computer hardware.* **—state′-of-the-art′** *adj.*

state·room (stāt′ro͞om′ *or* stāt′ro͝om′) *n.* A private room with sleeping accommodations on a ship or train.

state·side (stāt′sīd′) *adj.* Relating to or in the continental United States: *Soldiers undergo stateside training before being shipped abroad.* ❖ *adv. Informal* To or toward the continental United States.

states·man (stāts′mən) *n.* A man who is a leader in national or international affairs. **—states′man·ship′** *n.*

states' rights also **States' rights** (stāts) *pl.n.* **1.** The rights and powers of the state governments, especially those not granted to the federal government by the Constitution of the United States. **2.** A political belief in limiting the powers of the federal government and defending or extending those of the individual states.

states·wom·an (stāts′wo͝om′ən) *n.* A woman who is a leader in national or international affairs.

stat·ic (stăt′ĭk) *adj.* **1a.** Having no motion; being at rest. **b.** Fixed; stationary. **2.** Relating to bodies at rest or forces that balance each other. **3.** Relating to stationary electric charges; electrostatic. ❖ *n.* Distortion or interruption of a broadcast signal, such as crackling in a receiver or specks on a television screen, produced when static electricity or electricity in the atmosphere disturbs signal reception.

static electricity *n.* **1.** An electric charge accumulated on an insulated body. **2.** An electric discharge resulting from the accumulation of such a charge.

stat·ics (stăt′ĭks) *n. (used with a singular or plural verb)* The branch of physics that deals with balanced forces on and within stationary objects.

sta·tion (stā′shən) *n.* **1.** A place or location where a person or thing stands or is assigned to stand; a post: *a guard station.* **2.** A place, building, or establishment from which a service is provided or certain activities are directed: *a fire station.* **3.** A stopping place along a route, especially a stop for taking on passengers or refueling: *a bus station.* **4.** An establishment equipped to transmit radio or television signals, or the programming transmitted by such an establishment: *What station are you watching?* **5.** An establishment set up for the purpose of study or observation: *a radar station.* **6.** Social position; rank: *content with his station in life.* ❖ *tr.v.* **sta·tioned, sta·tion·ing, sta·tions** To assign to a position; post. [From Middle English *stacioun,* from Latin *statiō.*]

sta·tion·ar·y (stā′shə-nĕr′ē) *adj.* **1.** Not moving. **2.** Not capable of being moved; fixed: *a stationary bridge.* **3.** Unchanging: *a stationary sound.* [From Middle English *stacionarie,* from Medieval Latin *statiōnārius,* from Latin *statiō,* station.]

❑ *These sound alike:* **stationary, stationery** (paper).

sta·tion·er (stā′shə-nər) *n.* A person who sells stationery.

sta·tion·er·y (stā′shə-nĕr′ē) *n.* **1.** Writing paper and envelopes. **2.** Writing materials and office supplies, including pens and paper. [From Middle English *stacioner,* bookseller, from Medieval Latin *statiōnārius,* shopkeeper.]

❑ *These sound alike:* **stationery, stationary** (not moving).

station house *n.* A police or fire station.

sta·tion·mas·ter (stā′shən-măs′tər) *n.* A person in charge of a railroad or bus station.

station wagon *n.* An automobile having a large interior with a third row of seats or a luggage platform and a door or tailgate at the back.

sta·tis·tic (stə-tĭs′tĭk) *n.* A piece of numerical information.

sta·tis·ti·cal (stə-tĭs′tĭ-kəl) *adj.* Relating to or employing statistics. **—sta·tis′ti·cal·ly** *adv.*

stat·is·ti·cian (stăt′ĭ-stĭsh′ən) *n.* A person who specializes in statistics.

sta·tis·tics (stə-tĭs′tĭks) *n.* **1.** *(used with a singular verb)* The branch of mathematics that deals with the collection, organization, analysis, and interpretation of numerical data. **2.** *(used with a plural verb)* A collection or set of numerical data.

sta·tor (stā′tər) *n.* The stationary part of a machine, such as an electric motor or generator, around or within which the rotor rotates.

stat·u·ar·y (stăch′o͞o-ĕr′ē) *n., pl.* **stat·u·ar·ies 1.** Statues considered as a group: *American war memorial statuary.* **2.** The art of making statues. ❖ *adj.* Relating to or suitable for a statue.

stat·ue (stăch′o͞o) *n.* A form or likeness sculpted, cast, modeled, or carved in a material such as stone, clay, metal, or wood. [From Middle English, from Latin *statua,* from *statuere,* to set up.]

stat·u·esque (stăch′o͞o-ĕsk′) *adj.* Suggestive of a statue, as in size, proportions, or dignity; stately.

stat·u·ette (stăch′o͞o-ĕt′) *n.* A small statue.

stat·ure (stăch′ər) *n.* **1.** The natural height of a person or animal in an upright position. **2.** A level of development or achievement: *chess players of equal stature.*

stat·us (stăt′əs *or* stā′təs) *n.* **1.** Social position relative to that of others; rank or standing: *seeking to improve the status of the homeless.* **2.** High standing; prestige; *seeking*

ă	pat	ôr	core
ā	pay	oi	boy
âr	care	ou	out
ä	father	o͝o	took
ĕ	pet	o͝or	lure
ē	be	o͞o	boot
ĭ	pit	ŭ	cut
ī	bite	ûr	urge
îr	pier	th	thin
ŏ	pot	*th*	this
ō	toe	zh	vision
ô	paw	ə	about

status by buying an expensive car. **3.** The legal condition of a person or thing: *marital status.* **4.** A state of affairs; a situation: *the status of a bill in Congress.*

status quo (kwō) *n.* The existing state of affairs.

stat·ute (stăch′o͞ot) *n.* **1.** A law enacted by a legislative body. **2.** A decree or edict, as by a ruler.

statute mile *n.* A unit of length equal to 5,280 feet or 1,760 yards (1,609 meters); a mile. See table at **measurement.**

stat·u·to·ry (stăch′ə-tôr′ē) *adj.* Relating to, defined by, or regulated by statute.

staunch[1] (stônch *or* stänch) also **stanch** (stônch *or* stänch *or* stănch) *adj.* **staunch·er** also **stanch·er, staunch·est** also **stanch·est 1.** Firm and steadfast; loyal: *a staunch ally.* **2.** Strongly made or built: *staunch roots; staunch boards.* [From Middle English *staunche,* from Old French *estanchier,* to stanch.] **—staunch′ly** *adv.* **—staunch′ness** *n.*

staunch[2] (stônch *or* stänch) *v.* Variant of **stanch**[1].

stave (stāv) *n.* **1.** A strip of wood forming a part of the side of a barrel, tub, or similar structure. **2.** A rung of a ladder or chair. **3.** A heavy stick or pole; a staff. **4.** A musical staff. ❖ *tr.v.* **staved** or **stove** (stōv), **stav·ing, staves** To crush or smash inward, often by making a hole: *The rocks staved in the side of the boat.* ◆ **stave off** To keep or hold off; repel: *stave off the threat of disaster.*

staves (stāvz) *n.* A plural of **staff.**

stay[1] (stā) *v.* **stayed, stay·ing, stays** *—intr.* **1.** To continue to be in the same place: *I stayed after the others had left.* **2.** To continue to be in a specified place or condition: *stayed home; stay awake.* **3.** To remain or reside as a guest: *stay at a hotel.* **4.** To endure; persist: *We voted to stay with the original plan.* *—tr.* **1.** To remain during: *stayed the week with my grandparents.* **2.** To postpone; delay: *stay a prisoner's execution.* **3.** To satisfy or moderate temporarily: *stayed her appetite with an orange.* ❖ *n.* **1.** A brief period of residence or visiting: *a stay at the inn.* **2.** An order postponing something, such as an execution or a legal action. ◆ **stay up** To remain awake past one's usual bedtime; not go to bed. [From Middle English *steien,* from Latin *stāre.*]

SYNONYMS stay, remain, wait, linger These verbs mean to continue to be in a given place. **Stay** is the most general: *We stayed at home all evening.* **Remain** often means to continue or to be left after others have gone: *One person should remain on watch at night.* **Wait** means to stay in readiness, anticipation, or expectation: *I was waiting for you in the car.* **Linger** means to be slow in leaving: *I lingered, enjoying the starry night after the fireworks had ended.*

stay[2] (stā) *tr.v.* **stayed, stay·ing, stays** To support, brace, or prop up. ❖ *n.* **1.** A support or brace. **2.** A strip of bone, plastic, or metal used to stiffen a garment or part, such as a corset or a shirt collar. **3. stays** A corset. [From Middle English *staien,* from Old French *estaie,* a support, of Germanic origin.]

stay[3] (stā) *n.* **1.** A heavy rope or cable, usually of wire, used to brace or support a mast or spar. **2.** A rope used to steady, guide, or brace. ❖ *tr. & intr.v.* **stayed, stay·ing, stays** To put (a ship) on the opposite tack or to come about. [From Old English *stæg.*]

stay·ing power (stā′ĭng) *n.* The ability to endure or last.

stay·sail (stā′səl *or* stā′sāl′) *n.* A triangular sail hoisted on a stay.

STD *abbr.* An abbreviation of sexually transmitted disease.

stead (stĕd) *n.* **1.** The place, position, or function that belongs to or is usually occupied by another: *Zeus overthrew his father and ruled the world in his stead.* **2.** Advantage; service; purpose: *Knowing how to use a computer stood me in good stead.*

stead·fast (stĕd′făst′) *adj.* **1.** Firmly loyal or constant; faithful: *a steadfast friend.* **2.** Fixed or unchanging: *a steadfast rule.* **—stead′fast′ly** *adv.* **—stead′fast′ness** *n.*

stead·y (stĕd′ē) *adj.* **stead·i·er, stead·i·est 1.** Firm in position or place; fixed: *a steady grip on the wheel.* **2.** Not wavering or faltering: *spoke with a steady voice; kept his gaze steady on the target.* **3.** Free or almost free from change or variation; constant; uniform: *a steady wind; a steady income.* **4.** Not easily excited or disturbed; composed: *steady nerves.* **5.** Reliable; dependable: *steady workers.* ❖ *v.* **stead·ied, stead·y·ing, stead·ies** ❖ *tr. & intr.v.* To make or become steady; stabilize: *news that steadied the financial markets.* **—stead′i·ly** *adv.* **—stead′i·ness** *n.*

steady state theory *n.* A theory of the universe stating that the average density of matter in the universe is constant and that new matter is continuously being created as the universe expands. This theory has been rejected by most scientists.

steak (stāk) *n.* A slice of meat, typically beef, usually broiled or fried. [From Middle English *steke,* from Old Norse *steik.*]

❑ *These sound alike:* **steak, stake** (post).

steal (stēl) *v.* **stole** (stōl), **sto·len** (stō′lən), **steal·ing, steals** *—tr.* **1.** To take (someone else's property) without right or permission. **2.** To present or use (someone else's ideas or words) as one's own. **3.** To get or take secretly or artfully: *steal a look at a diary; steal an hour to play video games; steal the puck from an opponent.* **4.** To give (a kiss) that is unexpected or unnoticed. **5.** In baseball, to advance safely to (another base) by running to the base during the delivery of a pitch. *—intr.* **1.** To commit theft. **2.** To move secretly or stealthily: *He stole into the kitchen to grab a cookie.* **3.** To pass gradually or without notice: *The hours stole by as we talked.* **4.** In baseball, to steal a base. ❖ *n.* **1.** The act of stealing; theft. **2.** In baseball, a stolen base. **3.** In sports, an act of gaining possession of a ball or puck from an opponent. **4.** *Informal* Something acquired at a very low price; a bargain. ◆ **steal the show** To be the center of attention in a performance or other event. **—steal′er** *n.*

❑ *These sound alike:* **steal, steel** (metal).

stealth (stĕlth) *n.* **1.** The act of moving or proceeding in a quiet secretive way so as to avoid notice: *The leopard uses stealth to catch its prey.* **2.** The quality or characteristic of being furtive or secretive.

stealth·y (stĕl′thē) *adj.* **stealth·i·er, stealth·i·est** Quiet, secretive, and cautious, so as to avoid notice: *stealthy steps.* **—stealth′i·ly** *adv.* **—stealth′i·ness** *n.*

steam (stēm) *n.* **1a.** Hot water vapor produced usually by boiling liquid water. **b.** The mist that forms when hot water vapor cools and condenses into tiny droplets. **2.** Power generated by the expansion of boiling water as it changes to vapor. **3.** The energy needed to accomplish something: *Our plan to put in a garden ran out of steam.* ❖ *v.* **steamed, steam·ing, steams** *—intr.* **1.** To produce or emit steam: *Is the kettle steaming?* **2.** To become or rise up as steam: *Water vapor steamed from the vent.* **3.** To become misted or covered with steam: *The bathroom mirror steams up when the shower is used.* **4.** To move by means of steam power: *The ship steamed into the harbor.* **5.** *Informal* To become very angry; fume: *She was steaming over the insult.* *—tr.* To expose to steam, as in cooking: *steamed the carrots.* [From Old English *stēam.*]

steam·boat (stēm′bōt′) *n.* A steamship, especially one used on rivers and inland waterways.

steam engine *n.* An engine in which the energy of hot steam is converted into mechanical power, especially one in which the steam expands in a closed cylinder and drives a piston.

stave

steamroller

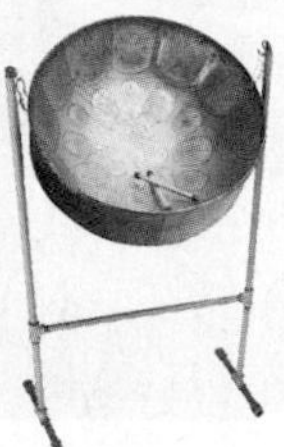

steel drum

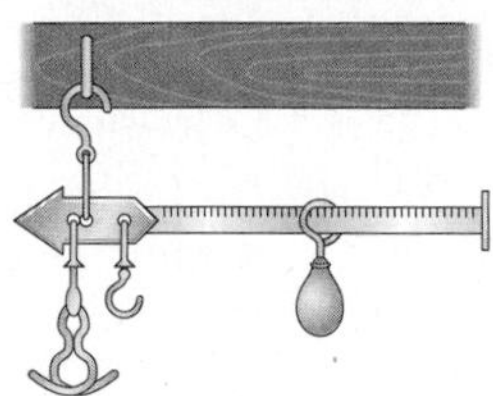

steelyard

ă	pat	ôr	core
ā	pay	oi	boy
âr	care	ou	out
ä	father	ŏŏ	took
ĕ	pet	ŏŏr	lure
ē	be	ōō	boot
ĭ	pit	ŭ	cut
ī	bite	ûr	urge
îr	pier	th	thin
ŏ	pot	*th*	this
ō	toe	zh	vision
ô	paw	ə	about

steam·er (stē′mər) *n.* **1.** A steamship. **2.** A vehicle, machine, or engine driven by steam. **3.** A container in which something is steamed: *a rice steamer.* **4.** A kind of clam that is usually cooked by steaming.

steam·fit·ter (stēm′fĭt′ər) *n.* A person who installs and repairs heating, ventilating, and air-conditioning systems.

steam·roll (stēm′rōl′) *tr. & intr.v.* **steam·rolled, steam·roll·ing, steam·rolls** To steamroller.

steam·roll·er (stēm′rō′lər) *n.* **1.** A vehicle equipped with a heavy roller for smoothing road surfaces. Steamrollers were once powered by steam engines, but most are now powered by internal-combustion engines. **2.** A crushing or overpowering force. ❖ *v.* **steam·roll·ered, steam·roll·er·ing, steam·roll·ers** —*tr.* **1.** To smooth or level (a road) with a steamroller. **2.** To defeat thoroughly; overwhelm or crush. **3.** To force or intimidate (someone) into doing or accepting something. **4.** To cause (a legislative bill, for example) to advance or be approved without adequate consideration. —*intr.* To move or proceed with an overwhelming force: *The team steamrollered over every opponent.*

steam·ship (stēm′shĭp′) *n.* A large vessel propelled by one or more steam-driven engines.

steam shovel *n.* A large steam-driven machine for digging.

steam·y (stē′mē) *adj.* **steam·i·er, steam·i·est 1.** Filled with or emitting steam: *a steamy kitchen.* **2.** Hot and humid: *a steamy August afternoon.* **—steam′i·ness** *n.*

ste·a·tite (stē′ə-tīt′) *n.* Soapstone.

steed (stēd) *n.* **1.** A horse, especially a spirited one used for riding. **2.** Another animal, such as a camel, used for riding.

steel (stēl) *n.* **1.** Any of various hard strong alloys of iron and carbon, often with other metals added to give certain desired properties, widely used as a structural material. **2.** Something, such as a sword, that is made of steel. **3.** A quality suggestive of this alloy; hardness or strength: *nerves of steel.* ❖ *adj.* **1.** Made with, relating to, or consisting of steel: *steel beams; the steel industry.* **2.** Very firm or strong. ❖ *tr.v.* **steeled, steel·ing, steels 1.** To cover, plate, edge, or point with steel. **2.** To strengthen; brace: *steel oneself against disappointment.* [From Old English *stȳle.*]

❑ *These sound alike:* **steel, steal** (take without right).

steel drum *n.* A metal percussion instrument that originated in Trinidad, made from an oil barrel and having a concave arrangement of flattened areas that produce different tones when struck.

steel gray *n.* A dark to purplish gray.

steel wool *n.* A matted or woven mass of fine steel fibers, used for cleaning, smoothing, or polishing.

steel·work (stēl′wûrk′) *n.* **1.** Something made of steel. **2. steelworks** *(used with a singular verb)* A plant where steel is made; a foundry. **—steel′work′er** *n.*

steel·y (stē′lē) *adj.* **steel·i·er, steel·i·est 1.** Made of steel. **2.** Resembling steel, as in color or hardness: *fixed me with a steely gaze.* **—steel′i·ness** *n.*

steel·yard (stēl′yärd′) *n.* A weighing device made of a horizontal bar marked off in units of weight, with a hook at the shorter end for holding the object to be weighed and a sliding counterweight at the other end that indicates the correct weight when the bar is balanced.

steep[1] (stēp) *adj.* **steep·er, steep·est 1.** Rising or falling abruptly; sharply sloped: *a steep hill.* **2.** Very high; excessive: *a steep price to pay.* [From Old English *stēap.*] **—steep′ly** *adv.* **—steep′ness** *n.*

steep[2] (stēp) *v.* **steeped, steep·ing, steeps** —*tr.* **1.** To soak in a liquid: *steep a tea bag in boiling water; steeped the cloth in red dye.* **2.** To involve or preoccupy thoroughly; immerse: *As a child, she steeped herself in adventure stories.* —*intr.* To undergo soaking in a liquid: *Let the tea steep five minutes.* ❖ *n.* The act or process of steeping. [From Middle English *stepen,* perhaps of Old English origin.]

steep·en (stē′pən) *tr. & intr.v.* **steep·ened, steep·en·ing, steep·ens** To make or become steep or steeper.

stee·ple (stē′pəl) *n.* A tall tower, usually topped by a spire, that rises from the roof of a church or other building.

stee·ple·chase (stē′pəl-chās′) *n.* A horse race across open country or over an obstacle course.

stee·ple·jack (stē′pəl-jăk′) *n.* A person who builds or maintains steeples or other high structures.

steer[1] (stîr) *v.* **steered, steer·ing, steers** —*tr.* **1.** To direct the course of (an automobile, for example): *She steered the car toward the garage.* **2.** To set and follow (a course): *We steered a course around the rocks.* **3.** To guide or maneuver (a person) into a place or course of action: *I steered the tourists toward downtown.* See Synonyms at **guide.** —*intr.* **1.** To guide a vehicle or vessel. **2.** To follow a set course. **3.** To be guided: *This car steers easily.* ❖ *n.* A piece of advice; a tip: *gave me a bum steer about the movie.* ◆ **steer clear of** To stay away from; avoid. [From Old English *stēran.*]

steer[2] (stîr) *n.* A young male of domestic cattle, castrated before reaching maturity and raised for beef. [From Old English *stēor.*]

steer·age (stîr′ĭj) *n.* **1.** The act or practice of steering a boat or a ship. **2.** The section of a passenger ship, originally near the rudder, providing the cheapest accommodations.

steer·ing wheel (stîr′ĭng) *n.* A wheel that controls steering, as on a boat or in an automobile.

steers·man (stîrz′mən) *n.* A person who steers a ship.

steg·o·saur·us (stĕg′ə-sôr′əs) *n.* A plant-eating dinosaur of the Jurassic Period, having a small head, a double row of large upright plates along the back, and sharp spikes on the tail. [From Greek *stegos,* roof + Greek *saurus,* lizard.]

stein (stīn) *n.* A large, often decorative beer mug.

Stein (stīn), **Gertrude** 1874–1946. American writer known for her experimental novels, poetry, essays, and plays. Her works include *The Autobiography of Alice B. Toklas* (1933).

Stein·beck (stīn′bĕk′), **John Ernst** 1902–1968. American writer known for his short stories and novels, including *The Grapes of Wrath* (1939).

stel·lar (stĕl′ər) *adj.* **1.** Relating to or consisting of stars. **2.** Relating to a star performer: *a stellar cast for the play.* **3.** Outstanding; prominent: *stellar achievements.* [From Latin *stēlla,* star.]

stem[1] (stĕm) *n.* **1a.** The main, often long or slender supporting part of a plant, usually growing above the ground. **b.** A slender plant part attached to or supporting a leaf, fruit, or flower; a stalk. **2.** A connecting or supporting part resembling such a plant part: *the stem of a pipe; the stem of a goblet.* **3.** The small shaft by which a watch is wound. **4.** The curving upright beam at the fore of a ship or boat. **5.** The main part of a word, to which affixes may be added to form various inflections or derivative words. ❖ *v.* **stemmed, stem·ming, stems** —*intr.* **1.** To derive; originate; spring: *His problems stem from his lack of focus.* **2.** To make progress against (a tide or current). —*tr.* To remove the stem of: *stem and pit cherries for a pie.* ◆ **from stem to stern** From one end to another. [From Old English *stefn, stemn.*]

stem[2] (stĕm) *tr.v.* **stemmed, stem·ming, stems 1.** To stop or hold back by or as if by damming; stanch. **2.** To plug or fill (a hole, for example). [From Middle English *stemmen,* from Old Norse *stemma.*]

STEM (stĕm) *abbr.* An abbreviation of **science, technology, engineering, and mathematics.**

stem cell *n.* A cell that has no specialized function but can give rise to a cell with a specialized function, such as a blood cell. Stem cells are present in embryos and in various tissues of adult organisms.

stemmed (stĕmd) *adj.* **1.** Having a stem or a specific type of stem: *a stemmed goblet; a prickly-stemmed plant.* **2.** Having the stems removed.

stench (stĕnch) *n.* A strong unpleasant smell; a stink.

sten·cil (**stĕn′**səl) *n.* **1.** A sheet, as of plastic or cardboard, in which letters or figures have been cut so that when ink or paint is applied to the sheet the patterns will appear on the surface beneath. **2.** The lettering or pattern produced with such a sheet. ❖ *tr.v.* **sten·ciled, sten·cil·ing, sten·cils** or **sten·cilled, sten·cil·ling, sten·cils 1.** To mark with a stencil. **2.** To produce by means of a stencil.

ste·nog·ra·pher (stə-**nŏg′**rə-fər) *n.* A person who is skilled in stenography, especially one employed to take and transcribe dictation or testimony.

ste·nog·ra·phy (stə-**nŏg′**rə-fē) *n.* The art or process of writing in shorthand.

sten·to·ri·an (stĕn-**tôr′**ē-ən) *adj.* Very loud and powerful: *a stentorian voice.* [After *Stentor,* a loud-voiced Greek herald in the *Iliad.*]

step (stĕp) *n.* **1.** The single complete movement of raising one foot and putting it down in another spot, as in walking. **2a.** A manner of walking; a gait: *moving with a light step.* **b.** A fixed rhythm or pace, as in dancing or marching: *keep step to the music.* **3.** The sound of someone walking: *heard his step in the corridor.* **4.** A footprint: *steps in the sand.* **5a.** The distance covered by moving one foot ahead of the other. **b.** A short walking distance: *The bus stop is just a step from my front door.* **c. steps** A course; a path: *turned her steps toward home.* **6.** One of a series of movements of the feet used in a dance. **7a.** A rest for the foot in ascending or descending, as a stair or a rung of a ladder. **b. steps** Stairs. **8a.** One of a series of actions or measures taken to achieve a goal: *taking steps to preserve the wildlife of a region.* **b.** A stage in a process or action. **9.** A grade or rank in a scale: *a step up in the corporation.* **10.** The difference in pitch between two successive tones of a musical scale. ❖ *v.* **stepped, step·ping, steps** —*intr.* **1.** To put or press the foot: *Don't step on the grass.* **2.** To shift or move slightly by taking a step: *Please step back.* **3.** To move with the feet in a certain manner: *step lively.* —*tr.* **1.** To put or set (the foot) down: *step foot on land.* **2.** To measure (a distance) by pacing: *step off ten yards on the field.* **3.** To place (a ship's mast) into position on a ship. ◆ **step aside** To resign from a post or duty, especially when being replaced. **step by step** By degrees. **step down 1.** To resign from a high post. **2.** To reduce, especially in stages: *stepping down our use of water.* **step in** To enter into an activity or a situation, especially to intervene: *Finally, the teacher stepped in and stopped the argument.* **step on it** *Informal* To go faster; hurry. **step out 1.** To walk briskly. **2.** To go outside for a short time. **step up 1.** To increase, especially in stages: *step up production.* **2.** To come forward: *step up and be counted.* [From Old English *stæpe.*]

❑ *These sound alike:* **step, steppe** (plain).

step– *pref.* A prefix that means related through the remarriage of a parent rather than by blood: *stepbrother.*

step·broth·er (**stĕp′**brŭ*th′*ər) *n.* A son of one's stepparent.

step·child (**stĕp′**chīld′) *n.* A child of one's wife or husband by an earlier marriage or relationship.

step·daugh·ter (**stĕp′**dô′tər) *n.* A daughter of one's husband or wife by an earlier marriage or relationship.

step·fa·ther (**stĕp′**fä′*th*ər) *n.* A man who is a stepparent.

step·lad·der (**stĕp′**lăd′ər) *n.* A portable ladder with a hinged supporting frame and usually topped with a small platform.

step·moth·er (**stĕp′**mŭ*th′*ər) *n.* A woman who is a stepparent.

step·par·ent (**stĕp′**pâr′ənt) *n.* A person who has married one's parent after the death of or divorce from the other parent.

steppe (stĕp) *n.* A vast semiarid, grass-covered plain as found in southeast Europe, Siberia, and central North America. [From Russian *step′.*]

❑ *These sound alike:* **steppe, step** (foot movement).

step·ping·stone (**stĕp′**ĭng-stōn′) *n.* **1.** A stone that provides a place to step, as in crossing a stream. **2.** A step or means toward the achievement of a goal.

step·sis·ter (**stĕp′**sĭs′tər) *n.* A daughter of one's stepparent.

step·son (**stĕp′**sŭn′) *n.* A son of one's husband or wife by an earlier marriage or relationship.

–ster *suff.* A suffix that means: **1.** Someone who does, performs, or takes part in something: *gangster.* **2.** Someone who has a certain quality: *youngster.*

ster·e·o (**stĕr′**ē-ō′) *n., pl.* **ster·e·os 1.** A stereophonic system of sound reproduction. **2.** Stereophonic sound: *a performance reproduced in stereo.* ❖ *adj.* **1.** Stereophonic. **2.** Stereoscopic.

ster·e·o·phon·ic (stĕr′ē-ə-**fŏn′**ĭk) *adj.* Using two or more separate channels to record, store, or reproduce sound so that the reproduced sound seems more natural in coming from more than one direction. **—ster′e·o·phon′i·cal·ly** *adv.*

ster·e·o·scope (**stĕr′**ē-ə-skōp′) *n.* An optical instrument through which two slightly different views of the same scene are presented, one to each eye, giving a three-dimensional illusion.

ster·e·o·scop·ic (stĕr′ē-ə-**skŏp′**ĭk) *adj.* **1.** Relating to vision that sees objects in three dimensions. **2.** Relating to a stereoscope.

ster·e·o·type (**stĕr′**ē-ə-tīp′) *n.* A conventional or oversimplified idea or image: *the stereotype of the meek librarian.* ❖ *tr.v.* **ster·e·o·typed, ster·e·o·typ·ing, ster·e·o·types** To make a stereotype of: *a movie that stereotypes farmers as unsophisticated yokels.* **—ster′e·o·typ′er** *n.*

ster·ile (**stĕr′**əl or **stĕr′**īl′) *adj.* **1.** Not able to produce offspring, seeds, or fruit. **2.** Producing little or no plant life; barren: *a desolate sterile region.* **3.** Free from living microorganisms, especially those that cause disease: *a sterile bandage.* **4.** Not productive or effective; fruitless: *a sterile discussion.* **5.** Lacking imagination, creativity, or vitality: *a sterile re-creation of the colonial period.* **—ster′ile·ly** *adv.* **—ste·ril′i·ty** (stə-**rĭl′**ĭ-tē) *n.*

ster·il·i·za·tion (stĕr′ə-lĭ-**zā′**shən) *n.* **1.** The act or procedure of sterilizing. **2.** The condition of being sterile or sterilized.

ster·il·ize (**stĕr′**ə-līz′) *tr.v.* **ster·il·ized, ster·il·iz·ing, ster·il·iz·es** To make sterile, especially to rid of live microorganisms or deprive of the ability to produce offspring. **—ster′il·iz′er** *n.*

ster·ling (**stûr′**lĭng) *n.* **1.** British money. **2a.** Sterling silver. **b.** Articles, such as tableware, made from sterling silver. ❖ *adj.* **1.** Consisting of or relating to British money: *ten pounds sterling.* **2.** Made of sterling silver: *sterling knives.* **3.** Of the highest quality; very fine: *She has sterling qualifications.*

sterling silver *n.* **1.** An alloy containing 92.5 percent silver with copper or another metal. **2.** Objects made of this alloy.

stern[1] (stûrn) *adj.* **stern·er, stern·est 1.** Hard, harsh, or severe in manner or character: *a stern look of reproach.* **2.** Firm or unyielding; uncompromising: *stern resistance.* **3.** Grim or gloomy in appearance or outlook: *a stern fate.* [From Old English *styrne.*] **—stern′ly** *adv.* **—stern′ness** *n.*

stern[2] (stûrn) *n.* The rear part of a ship or boat. [From Middle English *sterne,* perhaps of Scandinavian origin.]

ster·num (**stûr′**nəm) *n., pl.* **ster·nums** or **ster·na** (**stûr′**nə) A long flat bone located in the center of the chest,

steeple

stein

Gertrude Stein
photographed in 1935

stencil
stencil (*left*) and painted pattern

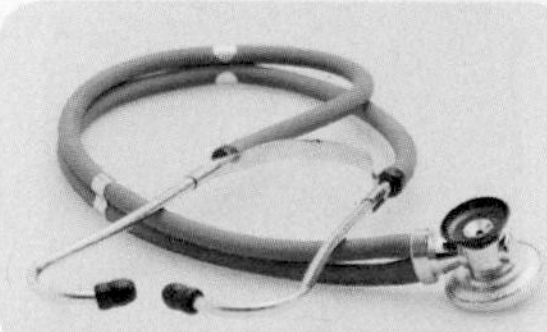
stethoscope

Robert Louis Stevenson

stile

stiletto heel

ă	pat	ôr	core
ā	pay	oi	boy
âr	care	ou	out
ä	father	o͝o	took
ĕ	pet	o͝or	lure
ē	be	o͞o	boot
ĭ	pit	ŭ	cut
ī	bite	ûr	urge
îr	pier	th	thin
ŏ	pot	*th*	this
ō	toe	zh	vision
ô	paw	ə	about

serving as a support for the collarbones and ribs; the breastbone.

stern·wheel·er (stûrn′wē′lər) *n.* A steamboat propelled by a paddle wheel at the stern.

ster·oid (stĕr′oid′ *or* stîr′oid′) *n.* **1.** Any of a large class of naturally occurring fat-soluble organic compounds based on a structure having 17 carbon atoms arranged in four rings. Steroids include sterols, certain forms of vitamins, and many hormones, including the sex hormones. **2.** Any of various synthetic hormones that have the basic structure of a steroid and are used especially in medicine. Some athletes take certain steroids illegally to increase their muscle mass. **—ste·roi′dal** (stĕ-**roid′**l *or* stĭ-**roid′**l) *adj.*

ster·ol (stîr′ôl′ *or* stĕr′ôl′) *n.* Any of various steroid alcohols, such as cholesterol, found in fatty tissues of plants and animals.

steth·o·scope (stĕth′ə-skōp′) *n.* Any of various instruments used to listen to sounds, such as the heartbeat, made within the body.

Steu·ben (sto͞o′bən), Baron **Friedrich Wilhelm von** 1730–1794. Prussian-born American Revolutionary military leader who trained General George Washington's troops.

ste·ve·dore (stē′vĭ-dôr′) *n.* A person whose job is the loading and unloading of ships.

Ste·ven·son (stē′vən-sən), **Robert Louis Balfour** 1850–1894. British writer whose novels include *The Strange Case of Dr. Jekyll and Mr. Hyde* (1886).

ste·vi·a (stē′vē-ə *or* stĕv′ē-ə) *n.* **1.** A plant native to central South America having leaves that contain a sweet-tasting compound. **2.** A sweetener made from the leaves of this plant.

stew (sto͞o) *v.* **stewed, stew·ing, stews** *—tr.* To cook (food) by simmering or boiling slowly: *stewing a chicken. —intr.* **1.** To undergo cooking by simmering or boiling slowly. **2.** *Informal* To suffer from intense heat; swelter. **3.** *Informal* To worry or be angry. ❖ *n.* **1.** A dish cooked by stewing, especially a mixture of meat or fish and vegetables in stock. **2.** *Informal* Mental agitation: *in a stew over her lost keys.*

stew·ard (sto͞o′ərd) *n.* **1.** A person who manages another's property, finances, or other affairs. **2.** A person in charge of the household affairs of a large estate, club, hotel, or resort. **3.** An attendant on a ship or airplane. [From Old English *stigweard, stīward* : *stig, stī*, hall + *weard*, keeper.] **—stew′ard·ship′** *n.*

stew·ard·ess (sto͞o′ər-dĭs) *n.* A woman who is a flight attendant.

stewed (sto͞od) *adj.* Cooked by stewing: *stewed tomatoes.*

STI *abbr.* An abbreviation of sexually transmitted infection.

stick (stĭk) *n.* **1.** A long slender piece of wood, such as a branch cut or fallen from a tree. **2.** A piece of wood that is used for fuel, cut for lumber, or shaped for a specific purpose: *a walking stick; a hockey stick.* **3.** Something that is long and thin: *a stick of dynamite; a stick of gum.* **4.** The control lever that operates the elevators and ailerons of an airplane. **5.** A poke or thrust with a pointed object. **6a. sticks** *Informal* A remote area; the backwoods. **b.** A city or town regarded as dull or unsophisticated. ❖ *v.* **stuck** (stŭk), **stick·ing, sticks** *—tr.* **1.** To pierce or prick with a pointed instrument or object: *sticking her finger on a thorn.* **2.** To push or thrust (something pointed) into or through a surface: *stuck the knife in the board.* **3.** To kill by piercing. **4.** To fasten or attach, as with a pin or nail: *stick a note on the door with a thumbtack.* **5.** To fasten or attach with an adhesive material, such as glue or tape: *stick a ticket on a car window.* **6.** To put, thrust, or push: *stuck a flower in his buttonhole; sticking her head out the window.* **7.** To detain or delay: *We were stuck in traffic for an hour.* **8.** *Informal* To put blame or responsibility on; burden: *stuck me with the bill. —intr.* **1.** To be or become fixed or embedded in place by having the point thrust in: *The arrow stuck in the tree.* **2.** To become attached or fastened: *Mud stuck to my shoes.* **3.** To be in close association; cling: *Let's stick together or we'll get lost in this crowd.* **4a.** To remain faithful or loyal: *stick by a friend in trouble.* **b.** To continue; persist: *I stuck with the lessons until the end.* **5.** To become fixed, blocked, checked, or obstructed: *The drawer stuck and would not open.* **6.** To extend; project: *hair sticking up on his head.* **7.** In boxing, to throw a jab. ◆ **stick around** *Informal* To remain; linger. **stick out** To be prominent or obvious: *That hat sticks out in a crowd.* **stick up** To rob, especially at gunpoint. **stick up for** To defend or support. [From Old English *sticca.*]

stick·ball (stĭk′bôl′) *n.* A form of baseball played with a rubber ball and a stick, such as a broom handle.

stick·er (stĭk′ər) *n.* **1.** An adhesive label, seal, or sign. **2.** A thorn, prickle, or barb.

sticker price *n.* The list price for a product or service, such as an automobile.

sticker shock *n.* Surprised disappointment on learning that something costs much more than expected.

stick·ing point (stĭk′ĭng) *n.* Something, such as an issue or situation, that causes or can cause an impasse.

stick·le·back (stĭk′əl-băk′) *n.* Any of various small freshwater and marine fishes having spiny dorsal fins.

stick·ler (stĭk′lər) *n.* **1.** One who strictly insists on something: *Our new teacher is a stickler for promptness.* **2.** Something, such as a problem, that is puzzling or difficult.

stick·pin (stĭk′pĭn′) *n.* A decorative pin used to hold a necktie in place.

stick·up (stĭk′ŭp′) *n. Slang* A robbery, especially at gunpoint.

stick·y (stĭk′ē) *adj.* **stick·i·er, stick·i·est 1.** Having the property of sticking to a surface; adhesive: *sticky paste; sticky candy.* **2.** Hot and humid; muggy. **3.** *Informal* Difficult or unpleasant: *a sticky situation.* **—stick′i·ly** *adv.* **—stick′i·ness** *n.*

sties[1] (stīz) *n.* Plural of **sty**[1].

sties[2] (stīz) *n.* Plural of **sty**[2].

stiff (stĭf) *adj.* **stiff·er, stiff·est 1.** Difficult to bend; not flexible or pliant: *a stiff new pair of shoes.* **2.** Not moving or operating easily or freely: *a stiff joint; a stiff doorknob.* **3.** Not liquid, loose, or fluid; thick: *a stiff mixture.* **4.** Rigidly formal; not easy or graceful: *a stiff writing style.* **5.** Moving with or having a strong steady force: *a stiff breeze.* **6.** Firm, as in purpose; resolute: *stiff opposition.* **7.** Difficult or laborious: *a stiff entrance requirement.* **8.** Harsh; severe: *stiff penalties.* **9.** Strong or potent: *a stiff dose of medicine.* **10.** Excessively high: *stiff prices.* ❖ *adv.* **1.** In a stiff manner: *frozen stiff.* **2.** To a complete extent; totally: *bored stiff.* ❖ *n. Slang* **1.** A corpse. **2.** An inhibited, dull, and overly formal person. **3.** A person: *those lucky stiffs.* [From Old English *stīf.*] **—stiff′ly** *adv.* **—stiff′ness** *n.*

stiff·en (stĭf′ən) *tr. & intr.v.* **stiff·ened, stiff·en·ing, stiff·ens** To make or become stiff or stiffer. **—stiff′en·er** *n.*

stiff-necked (stĭf′nĕkt′) *adj.* Stubborn and arrogant.

sti·fle (stī′fəl) *tr.v.* **sti·fled, sti·fling, sti·fles 1.** To interrupt or cut off (the voice, for example). **2.** To keep in or hold back; suppress or stop: *stifled my indignation.* **3.** To kill by depriving of air or oxygen; smother.

sti·fling (stī′flĭng) *adj.* Very hot or stuffy, almost to the point of being suffocating: *a stifling room.*

stig·ma (stĭg′mə) *n., pl.* **stig·ma·ta** (stĭg-mä′tə) *or* **stig·mas 1.** An attitude of shame or disgrace that is associated with something: *There should be no stigma attached to doing strenuous physical work.* **2. stigmata** Marks or sores that correspond to the crucifixion wounds of Jesus, sometimes appearing on the bodies of people in a state of religious ecstasy. **3.** The sticky tip of a flower pistil, on which pollen grains are deposited during pollination. [From Middle English *stigme*, from Greek *stigma*, tattoo mark.]

stig·ma·tize (stĭg′mə-tīz′) *tr.v.* **stig·ma·tized, stig·ma·tiz·ing, stig·ma·tiz·es** To characterize as shameful or dishonorable: *commercials that stigmatize smoking.* **—stig′ma·ti·za′tion** (stĭg′mə-tĭ-zā′shən) *n.*

stile (stīl) *n.* **1.** A set of steps for crossing a fence or wall. **2.** A turnstile.
❏ *These sound alike:* **stile, style** (manner).

sti·let·to (stĭ-lĕt′ō) *n., pl.* **sti·let·tos** or **sti·let·toes 1.** A small dagger with a slender tapering blade. **2.** A small sharp-pointed instrument used for making eyelet holes in needlework. **3.** A shoe that has a stiletto heel. [From Italian, diminutive of *stilo*, dagger, from Latin *stilus*, stylus, spike.]

stiletto heel *n.* A high heel on a woman's shoe that is thinner than a spike heel.

still¹ (stĭl) *adj.* **still·er, still·est 1.** Not moving; motionless: *still water.* **2.** Relating to a single or static photograph, as distinguished from a movie. **3.** Silent; quiet: *He was still for a moment and then started talking again.* **4.** Not carbonated: *still wine.* ❖ *n.* **1.** Silence; quiet; calm: *the still of the night.* **2.** A still photograph. ❖ *adv.* **1.** Without movement: *Please stand still.* **2.** Up to or at the time indicated; yet: *The book will still be here tomorrow.* **3.** In increasing amount or degree: *I've got still more good news for you.* **4.** In addition; besides: *had still another helping.* **5.** Nevertheless; all the same: *a painful but still necessary decision.* ❖ *v.* **stilled, still·ing, stills** *—tr.* **1.** To make still or tranquil. **2.** To make calm; allay: *stilled their fears.* *—intr.* To become still. [From Old English *stille.*]

still² (stĭl) *n.* **1.** An apparatus for distilling liquids, especially alcohols. **2.** A distillery. [From Middle English *stillen*, to distill.]

still·born (stĭl′bôrn′) *adj.* Dead at birth.

still life *n., pl.* **still lifes 1.** Representation of inanimate objects, such as flowers or fruit, in painting or photography. **2.** A painting, picture, or photograph of inanimate objects. **—still′-life′** *adj.*

still·ness (stĭl′nĭs) *n.* The state or an instance of being quiet or calm.

stilt (stĭlt) *n.* **1.** Either of a pair of long slender poles, each with a raised footrest, that enables the user to walk elevated above the ground. **2.** Any of various tall posts or pillars used as supports, as for a building or dock. **3.** Any of various wading birds having long legs, black and white feathers, and a long bill. [From Middle English *stilte.*]

stilt·ed (stĭl′tĭd) *adj.* Stiffly or artificially formal; pompous: *stilted conversation.*

stim·u·lant (stĭm′yə-lənt) *n.* **1.** Something, especially a medicine or drug, that temporarily speeds up or excites the function of the body or one of its systems or parts. **2.** A stimulus or an incentive.

stim·u·late (stĭm′yə-lāt′) *tr.v.* **stim·u·lat·ed, stim·u·lat·ing, stim·u·lates 1.** To rouse to activity or increased action; stir or excite: *music that stimulates the imagination.* **2.** To increase temporarily the activity of (a body organ or part): *Caffeine stimulates the nervous system.* **3.** To excite or invigorate (a person, for example) with a stimulant. **—stim′u·la′tion** *n.*

stim·u·lus (stĭm′yə-ləs) *n., pl.* **stim·u·li** (stĭm′yə-lī′) **1.** Something causing or regarded as causing a response: *Many hope the road repairs will be a stimulus to the state's economy.* **2.** Something that causes a response in an organism or body part, especially a sense organ. **3.** Government spending designed to increase economic activity. [From Latin *stimulus*, goad.]

sting (stĭng) *v.* **stung** (stŭng), **sting·ing, stings** *—tr.* **1.** To pierce or wound painfully with a sharp-pointed structure or organ, as that of certain insects. **2.** To cause to feel a sharp pain: *Smoke began to sting her eyes.* **3.** To cause to suffer emotionally or feel keen unhappiness: *The angry words stung him bitterly.* *—intr.* **1.** To have or use a stinger: *Do all bees sting?* **2.** To cause or feel a sharp pain: *The dentist said that the needle would sting a little.* ❖ *n.* **1.** The act of stinging. **2.** A wound or pain caused by stinging. **3.** A hurtful quality or power: *felt the sting of rejection.* **4.** A sharp, piercing organ or part, often ejecting venom, such as the modified ovipositor of a wasp or the spine of certain fishes. [From Old English *stingan.*] **—sting′ing·ly** *adv.*

sting·er (stĭng′ər) *n.* Something that stings, such as the sharp stinging organ of a bee, wasp, or scorpion.

sting·ray (stĭng′rā′) *n.* Any of various rays having a broad flattened body and a long whiplike tail with one or more venomous spines.

stin·gy (stĭn′jē) *adj.* **stin·gi·er, stin·gi·est** Giving or spending reluctantly: *He was never stingy with his donations to charity.* **—stin′gi·ly** *adv.* **—stin′gi·ness** *n.*

stink (stĭngk) *v.* **stank** (stăngk) or **stunk** (stŭngk), **stunk, stink·ing, stinks** *—intr.* **1.** To give off a strong foul odor. **2.** To be highly offensive. **3.** *Slang* To be of extremely poor quality: *This movie stinks.* *—tr.* To cause to stink: *The wet dog stunk up the room.* ❖ *n.* **1.** A strong offensive odor. **2.** A display of protest or concern; fuss: *The mayor's unethical actions caused quite a stink.*

stint (stĭnt) *v.* **stint·ed, stint·ing, stints** *—tr.* To restrict or limit, as in amount or number; be sparing with. *—intr.* To be frugal: *Don't stint on food.* ❖ *n.* **1.** A length of time spent at a job or fulfilling a duty: *a two-year stint in the military.* **2.** A limitation or restriction: *working without stint.*

sti·pend (stī′pĕnd′) *n.* A fixed or regular payment, such as a salary or allowance.

stip·ple (stĭp′əl) *tr.v.* **stip·pled, stip·pling, stip·ples 1.** To draw, engrave, or paint in dots or short strokes. **2.** To dot, fleck, or speckle: *a trout that is stippled with spots.* ❖ *n.* **1.** A method of drawing, engraving, or painting using dots or short strokes. **2.** The effect produced by stippling.

stip·u·late (stĭp′yə-lāt′) *tr.v.* **stip·u·lat·ed, stip·u·lat·ing, stip·u·lates** To specify or demand, especially as a condition of an agreement: *The contract stipulates that the job must be finished in six months.*

stip·u·la·tion (stĭp′yə-lā′shən) *n.* **1.** The act of stipulating. **2.** Something stipulated, especially a term or condition in an agreement.

stip·ule (stĭp′yo͞ol) *n.* One of the usually small paired parts resembling leaves at the base of a leafstalk in certain plants.

stir (stûr) *v.* **stirred, stir·ring, stirs** *—tr.* **1.** To pass an implement through (a liquid, for example), usually in circular motions, to mix or cool the contents: *She stirred the soup.* **2.** To mix or add by using an implement in this way: *He stirred flour into the sauce.* **3.** To cause to move or change position: *The wind stirred the bird's feathers.* **4.** To rouse, as from sleep or indifference: *The speaker stirred us to volunteer.* **5.** To incite or provoke deliberately: *stir up trouble.* **6.** To excite strong feelings in: *The music stirred her heart.* *—intr.* **1.** To change position slightly: *The dog stirred in its sleep.* **2.** To move about actively: *Who's that stirring in the hall?* ❖ *n.* **1.** A stirring or mixing movement: *gave the soup a stir.* **2.** An excited reaction: *News of the unexpected victory caused quite a stir.* [From Old English *styrian*, to agitate.] **—stir′rer** *n.*

stir·ring (stûr′ĭng) *adj.* Arousing strong feelings or excitement: *a stirring march.* **—stir′ring·ly** *adv.*

still life
A Still Life of Fruit, 1862, by Carl Vilhelm Balsgaard (1812–1893)

stilt
structural stilts (*top*) and a black-winged stilt (*bottom*)

stingray

stipple

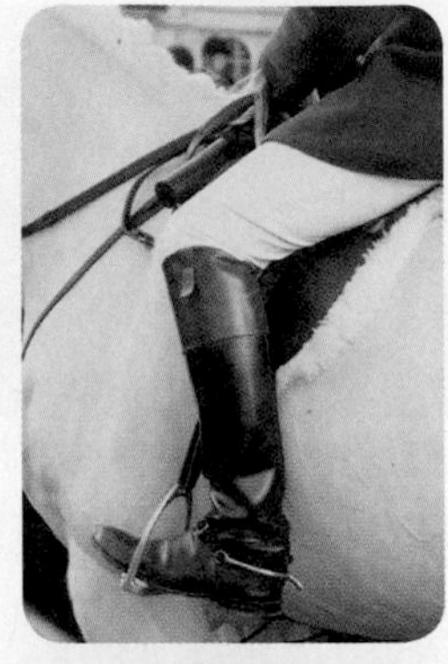

stirrup
English-style *(top)* and western-style *(bottom)* stirrups

stole[1]

ă	pat	ôr	core
ā	pay	oi	boy
âr	care	ou	out
ä	father	o͝o	took
ĕ	pet	o͝or	lure
ē	be	o͞o	boot
ĭ	pit	ŭ	cut
ī	bite	ûr	urge
îr	pier	th	thin
ŏ	pot	*th*	this
ō	toe	zh	vision
ô	paw	ə	about

stir·rup (stûr′əp *or* stĭr′əp) *n.* **1.** A loop or ring with a flat base, hung by a strap from either side of a horse's saddle to support the rider's foot. **2.** The stapes. [From Old English *stīgrāp* : *stīgan*, to mount + *rāp*, rope.]

stitch (stĭch) *n.* **1a.** A single complete movement of a threaded needle, as in sewing fabric or closing a wound during surgery. **b.** A single loop of yarn or thread around a knitting needle or crochet hook. **c.** A link, loop, or knot made in this way. **2.** A method or style of arranging thread or yarn in sewing, knitting, or crocheting: *a purl stitch.* **3.** *Informal* An article of clothing: *a baby without a stitch on.* **4.** A sudden sharp pain, especially in the side. **5.** The least part; a bit: *didn't do a stitch of work.* ❖ *v.* **stitched, stitch·ing, stitch·es** —*tr.* To fasten, join, or ornament with stitches: *stitch on a pocket; stitch a sampler.* —*intr.* To make stitches; sew.

stoat (stōt) *n., pl.* **stoat** or **stoats** The ermine. [From Middle English *stote*.]

stock (stŏk) *n.* **1.** A supply accumulated for future use; a store: *grain stocks.* **2.** The total merchandise kept on hand by a merchant or commercial establishment. **3.** All the animals kept or raised on a farm; livestock. **4.** A population of wild animals, especially of a kind of animal that is harvested commercially: *concern about depleted fish stocks.* **5.** The main stem or trunk of a plant, especially one used for grafting. **6.** A line or group of ancestors from which certain people, animals, or plants are descended. **7.** The raw material out of which something is made. **8.** Broth from boiled meat, fish, or vegetables, used in making soup, gravy, or sauces. **9.** A supporting structure, block, or frame, such as one around a ship during construction. **10.** The rear metal, wooden, or plastic handle or part of a firearm. **11a.** A document or agreement providing a person with partial ownership in a corporation, such as a claim to a portion of the corporation's money and property. Stocks are issued and traded in units called shares. **b.** A number of shares owned by a stockholder: *I have stock in that company.* **12. stocks** A device consisting of a heavy wooden frame with holes for the ankles and often the wrists, formerly used to punish offenders. **13.** A theatrical activity, especially one outside a main theatrical center: *playing in summer stock.* **14.** Any of several garden plants having long showy clusters of fragrant flowers. ❖ *v.* **stocked, stock·ing, stocks** —*tr.* **1.** To provide with a stock of something: *stock a pond with trout.* **2.** To keep for future sale or use: *We stock canned goods.* —*intr.* To gather or lay in a supply of something: *stock up on canned foods.* ❖ *adj.* **1.** Kept regularly available for sale or use: *Bread is a stock item.* **2.** Commonplace; not original: *a stock answer.* ◆ **in stock** Available for sale or use; on hand. **out of stock** Not available for sale or use. [From Old English *stocc*, tree trunk.]

stock·ade (stŏ-**kād′**) *n.* **1.** A defensive barrier made of strong upright posts driven into the ground. **2.** A fenced or enclosed area, such as a jail on a military base.

stock·bro·ker (**stŏk′**brō′kər) *n.* A person who buys or sells stocks, bonds, and other securities for a client and receives a commission in return; a broker.

stock car *n.* **1.** An automobile of standard make modified for racing. **2.** A railroad car for carrying livestock.

stock company *n.* **1.** A company or corporation whose capital is divided into shares. **2.** A permanent theatrical company that performs a fixed group of plays, usually at a single theater.

stock exchange *n.* A place or network in which stocks, bonds, or other securities are bought and sold.

stock·hold·er (**stŏk′**hōl′dər) *n.* A person who owns a share or shares of stock in a company.

Stock·holm (**stŏk′**hōlm′ *or* **stŏk′**hōm′) The capital and largest city of Sweden, in the eastern part of the country on the Baltic Sea. It was founded in the mid-1200s.

stock·ing (**stŏk′**ĭng) *n.* A close-fitting covering for the foot and leg, usually knitted using fine yarn or thread. ◆ **in (one's) stocking feet** With socks and no shoes on one's feet.

stocking cap *n.* A close-fitting knitted cap, often having a long tapering tail with a tassel attached.

stock·man (**stŏk′**mən) *n.* **1.** A man who owns or raises livestock. **2.** A man who is employed in a stockroom or warehouse.

stock market *n.* **1.** A stock exchange. **2.** A market in which stocks are bought and sold, usually in a particular country or economic region: *the US stock market.* **3.** The business transacted in such a market: *The stock market was very active all day.* **4.** The buyers and sellers of stocks: *The stock market has been jittery awaiting the latest employment figures.* **5.** The price or value of the stocks traded in a market: *a rising stock market.*

stock·pile (**stŏk′**pīl′) *n.* A supply of material stored for future use. ❖ *tr.v.* **stock·piled, stock·pil·ing, stock·piles** To accumulate and store for future use: *stockpile supplies.*

stock·room also **stock room** (**stŏk′**ro͞om′ *or* **stŏk′**-ro͝om′) *n.* A room in which a store of goods or materials is kept.

stock-still (**stŏk′stĭl′**) *adv.* Without motion; completely still: *He stood stock-still, not making a sound.*

stock·y (**stŏk′**ē) *adj.* **stock·i·er, stock·i·est** Solidly built; squat and thick: *a stocky boy.* **—stock′i·ness** *n.*

stock·yard (**stŏk′**yärd′) *n.* A large enclosed yard in which livestock, such as cattle or pigs, are kept until slaughtered, sold, or shipped elsewhere.

stodg·y (**stŏj′**ē) *adj.* **stodg·i·er, stodg·i·est 1.** Dull, unimaginative, and commonplace: *a stodgy person.* **2.** Heavy and indigestible: *stodgy food.* **3.** Solidly built; stocky. **—stodg′i·ly** *adv.* **—stodg′i·ness** *n.*

sto·gie (**stō′**gē) *n.* A cheap cigar.

sto·ic (**stō′**ĭk) *n.* **1.** A person who is seemingly indifferent to both pleasure and pain. **2. Stoic** A member of an ancient school of philosophy believing that God determined everything for the best and advocating the calm acceptance of all occurrences. ❖ *adj.* also **sto·i·cal** (**stō′**-ĭ-kəl) Seemingly indifferent to or unaffected by pleasure or pain. **—sto′i·cal·ly** *adv.*

sto·i·cism (**stō′**ĭ-sĭz′əm) *n.* **1.** Indifference to pain or pleasure; impassiveness. **2. Stoicism** The doctrines or philosophy of the Stoics.

stoke (stōk) *tr.v.* **stoked, stok·ing, stokes** To feed fuel to and tend (a fire or furnace).

stoke·hole (**stōk′**hōl′) *n.* The space about the opening in a furnace or boiler.

stok·er (**stō′**kər) *n.* **1.** A person employed to feed fuel to and tend a furnace, as on a steam locomotive. **2.** A mechanical device for feeding coal to a furnace.

stole[1] (stōl) *n.* **1.** A long narrow scarf, usually of embroidered silk or linen, worn by deacons, priests, and bishops while officiating. **2.** A tapered ornamental garment worn over both shoulders, especially by members of choirs. **3.** A long scarf of cloth or fur worn by women about the shoulders: *a mink stole.* [From Old English, from Greek *stolē*, robe.]

stole[2] (stōl) *v.* Past tense of **steal.**

sto·len (**stō′**lən) *v.* Past participle of **steal.**

stol·id (**stŏl′**ĭd) *adj.* **stol·id·er, stol·id·est** Having or showing little movement or emotion; impassive: *a stolid soldier.* **—sto·lid′i·ty** (stŏ-**lĭd′**ĭ-tē) *n.* **—stol′id·ly** *adv.*

sto·lon (**stō′**lŏn′ *or* **stō′**lən) *n.* A plant stem that grows along the ground and produces roots and shoots at the nodes; a runner.

sto·ma (**stō′**mə) *n., pl.* **sto·ma·ta** (**stō′**mə-tə) or **sto·mas** One of the tiny openings in the outer surface of a plant leaf or stem, through which gases and water vapor pass. —SEE NOTE AT **transpiration.**

stom·ach (stŭm′ək) *n.* **1a.** The enlarged portion of the digestive tract, located in vertebrates between the esophagus and the small intestine and serving as one of the main organs of digestion. **b.** A similar part of the digestive system of many invertebrates. **2.** The part of the body that contains the stomach; the abdomen or belly. **3.** A desire or an inclination, especially for something difficult or unpleasant: *He doesn't have the stomach for a fight.* ❖ *tr.v.* **stom·ached, stom·ach·ing, stom·achs** To bear, tolerate, or endure: *You shouldn't be a surgeon if you can't stomach the sight of blood.* [From Middle English *stomak*, from Greek *stomakhos*, gullet, from *stoma*, mouth.]

stom·ach·ache (stŭm′ək-āk′) *n.* Pain in the stomach or abdomen.

sto·ma·ta (stō′mə-tə) *n.* A plural of **stoma.**

stomp (stŏmp) *v.* **stomped, stomp·ing, stomps** —*tr.* To tread or trample heavily or violently on. —*intr.* To tread or trample heavily or violently: *He stomped in frustration.*

stone (stōn) *n.* **1.** Hard or compacted mineral matter; rock. **2.** A small piece of rock. **3.** A piece of rock cut or shaped for a particular purpose, as a tombstone or milestone. **4.** A gem or precious stone. **5.** A seed with a hard covering, as of a cherry or plum; a pit. **6.** A hard mass of mineral matter that collects in a hollow organ of the body, such as a kidney; a calculus. **7.** A unit of weight in Great Britain, equal to 14 pounds (6.4 kilograms). ❖ *adj.* Relating to or made from stone: *a stone wall.* ❖ *adv.* Completely; utterly: *stone cold; standing stone still.* ❖ *tr.v.* **stoned, ston·ing, stones 1.** To throw stones at. **2.** To remove the stones or pits from. [From Old English *stān.*]

Stone (stōn), **Lucy** 1818–1893. American feminist and reformer who was a founder of the American Woman Suffrage Association (1869).

Stone Age *n.* The earliest known period of human culture, characterized by the use of stone tools. It is divided into the Paleolithic, Mesolithic, and Neolithic Periods.

stone-blind (stōn′blīnd′) *adj.* Completely blind.

stone·cut·ter (stōn′kŭt′ər) *n.* **1.** A person who cuts or carves stone. **2.** A machine used to finish the surface of stone.

stone-deaf (stōn′dĕf′) *adj.* Completely deaf.

Stone·henge (stōn′hĕnj′) A group of standing stones on a plateau in southern England. The monument dates to about 2200–1800 BC, and the arrangement of the stones suggests that Stonehenge was used as a religious center and also as an astronomical observatory.

stone·ma·son (stōn′mā′sən) *n.* A person who prepares and lays stones in building.

stone's throw (stōnz) *n.* A short distance.

stone·wall (stōn′wôl′) *Informal v.* **stone·walled, stone·wall·ing, stone·walls** —*intr.* **1.** To delay or stall. **2.** To refuse to answer or cooperate: *The witness tried to stonewall as long as possible.* —*tr.* To refuse to answer or cooperate with; resist or rebuff: *The official stonewalled the investigating committee.*

stone·ware (stōn′wâr′) *n.* A heavy nonporous pottery, fired at a high temperature.

stone·work (stōn′wûrk′) *n.* **1.** The technique or process of building or making things from stone: *a mason skilled in stonework.* **2.** Work made of stone. **—stone′work′er** *n.*

ston·y (stō′nē) *adj.* **ston·i·er, ston·i·est 1.** Covered with or full of stones: *stony soil.* **2.** Resembling stone, as in hardness. **3.** Hardhearted and unfeeling: *a stony gaze.* **—ston′i·ly** *adv.* **—ston′i·ness** *n.*

stood (stŏŏd) *v.* Past tense and past participle of **stand.**

stooge (stōōj) *n.* **1.** A person who allows himself or herself to be used for another's profit or advantage; a puppet. **2.** The partner in a comedy team that sets up the jokes for the other comedian to make.

stool (stōōl) *n.* **1.** A single seat having no back or arms and supported on legs or a pedestal. **2.** A low bench or support for the feet or knees in sitting or kneeling. **3.** A low portable platform for standing on. **4a.** A toilet seat. **b.** Fecal matter.

stool pigeon *n.* **1.** *Slang* A person who acts as a decoy or an informer, especially for the police. **2.** A pigeon used as a decoy.

stoop¹ (stōōp) *v.* **stooped, stoop·ing, stoops** —*intr.* **1.** To bend forward and down from the waist or middle of the back: *stooping to pick up the newspaper.* **2.** To walk or stand with the head and upper back bent forward. **3.** To lower or debase oneself: *He wouldn't stoop to such behavior.* —*tr.* **1.** To bend (the head and body) forward and down. **2.** To debase; humble. ❖ *n.* **1.** The act of stooping. **2.** A forward bending of the head and body, especially when habitual: *walk with a stoop.* [From Old English *stūpian.*]

❑ *These sound alike:* **stoop¹** (bend forward), **stoop²** (small porch), **stoup** (church basin).

stoop² (stōōp) *n.* A small porch, staircase, or platform leading to the entrance of a house or building. [From Dutch *stoep*, front veranda.]

❑ *These sound alike:* **stoop²** (small porch), **stoop¹** (bend forward), **stoup** (church basin).

stop (stŏp) *v.* **stopped, stop·ping, stops** —*tr.* **1.** To close or block (an opening) by covering, plugging up, or filling in: *stop up the drain.* **2.** To prevent the flow or passage of: *stop traffic; stopped water from leaking out of the bottle.* **3.** To cause to halt or cease moving, progressing, or operating: *The officer stopped the car.* **4.** To bring to an end; cease: *stop running.* **5.** To order a bank to withhold payment of: *stopped the check.* **6a.** To press down (a string on a stringed instrument) to produce a tone of a desired pitch. **b.** To close (a hole on a woodwind instrument) to produce a tone of a desired pitch. —*intr.* **1.** To cease moving, progressing, acting, or operating; come to a halt: *The clock stopped during the night.* **2.** To interrupt one's course or journey for a brief visit or stay: *stop at the store on the way home.* ❖ *n.* **1.** The act of stopping or the condition of being stopped; a halt. **2.** A stay or visit: *We made a stop at Austin.* **3.** A place at which a person or thing stops: *a bus stop.* **4.** A device or means that stops, blocks, or regulates movement. **5.** The aperture of a lens, as on a camera. **6a.** A tuned set of pipes, as on an organ. **b.** A knob, lever, or key that controls such a series of pipes.

SYNONYMS **stop, cease, halt, quit** These verbs mean to bring or come to an end. *We stopped at the corner and looked both ways before crossing the street. The siren ceased abruptly. We halted at the border. They quit riding at sundown.*

---

stop·gap (stŏp′găp′) *n.* A temporary substitute or expedient.

stop·light (stŏp′līt′) *n.* A traffic light.

stop·o·ver (stŏp′ō′vər) *n.* **1.** A brief stay or visit, as in the course of a journey. **2.** A place visited briefly.

stop·page (stŏp′ĭj) *n.* The act of stopping or the condition of being stopped; a halt.

stoppage time *n.* In soccer, playing time added by the referee after the regular period of play has ended in order to compensate for stoppages in play caused by injuries, substitutions, or other interruptions.

stop·per (stŏp′ər) *n.* **1.** A device, such as a cork or plug, that is inserted into an opening to close it. **2.** In baseball, a relief pitcher. **3.** In soccer, a lone defensive player positioned in the middle of the field nearest to the goalie. ❖ *tr.v.* **stop·pered, stop·per·ing, stop·pers** To close with or as if with a stopper.

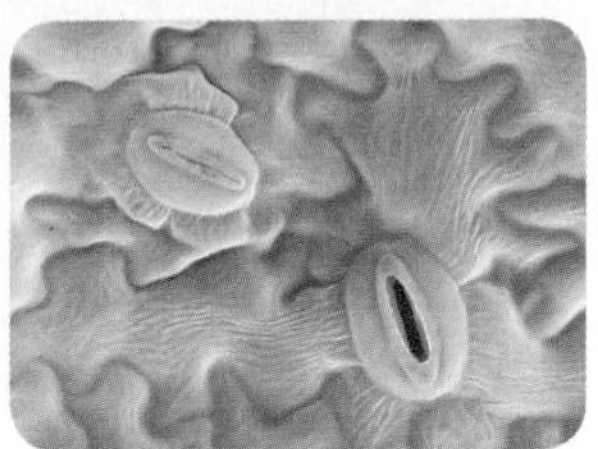

stoma
of a lavender leaf

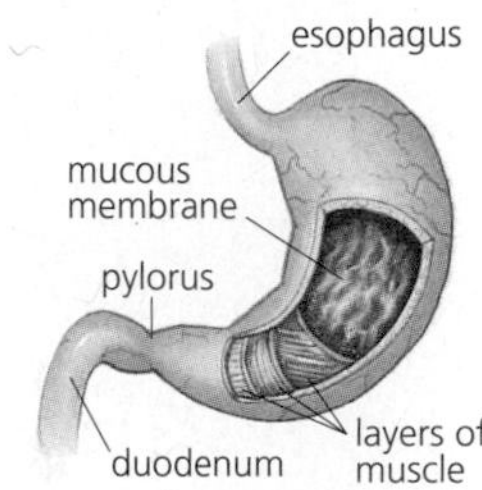

stomach
an adult human stomach

Stonehenge
aerial photograph

stoneware

stoop²

stopwatch

stork

ă	pat	ôr	core
ā	pay	oi	boy
âr	care	ou	out
ä	father	o͝o	took
ĕ	pet	o͝or	lure
ē	be	o͞o	boot
ĭ	pit	ŭ	cut
ī	bite	ûr	urge
îr	pier	th	thin
ŏ	pot	*th*	this
ō	toe	zh	vision
ô	paw	ə	about

stop·watch (stŏp′wŏch′) *n.* A watch that can be instantly started and stopped by pushing a button, used for measuring exact intervals of time.

stor·age (stôr′ĭj) *n.* **1.** The act of storing or the state of being stored: *goods in storage.* **2.** A space for storing: *We have storage in the attic.* **3.** The price charged for storing goods: *How much is storage per month?*

storage battery *n.* A group of rechargeable electric cells acting as a unit.

storage device *n.* A hardware device, such as a hard disk, used to record and store computer data.

store (stôr) *n.* **1.** A place where merchandise is offered for sale; a shop. **2.** A stock or supply reserved for future use. **3. stores** Supplies, especially of food, clothing, or arms. **4.** A great quantity or number; an abundance: *a store of knowledge.* ❖ *tr.v.* **stored, stor·ing, stores 1.** To put away for future use: *Squirrels store acorns for winter.* **2.** To copy (data) into computer memory or onto a storage device. ◆ **in store 1.** Forthcoming: *A great opportunity was in store for her.* **2.** In reserve; stored. [From Middle English *stor,* supply, from Latin *īnstaurāre,* to restore.]

store·house (stôr′hous′) *n.* **1.** A place or building in which goods are stored; a warehouse. **2.** An abundant source or supply: *a storehouse of knowledge.*

store·keep·er (stôr′kē′pər) *n.* A person who runs a retail shop or store.

store·room (stôr′ro͞om′ *or* **stôr′**ro͝om′) *n.* A room in which things are stored.

sto·rey (stôr′ē) *n. Chiefly British* Variant of **story[2]**.

sto·ried[1] (stôr′ēd) *adj.* Famous in story or history: *the storied ruins of Pompeii.* [From Middle English *portraying historical subjects.*]

sto·ried[2] (stôr′ēd) *adj.* Having or consisting of a certain number of stories: *a five-storied house.* [From *story,* a story in a building.]

stork (stôrk) *n.* Any of various large wading birds having long legs and a long straight bill.

storm (stôrm) *n.* **1.** A disturbance of the atmosphere involving strong winds and usually rain, snow, or other precipitation, often with thunder and lightning. **2.** A violent disturbance or upheaval, as in political, social, or domestic affairs. **3.** A strong or violent outburst, as of emotion or excitement. **4.** A heavy shower of objects, such as bullets or missiles. **5.** A violent sudden attack on a fortified place. ❖ *v.* **stormed, storm·ing, storms** —*intr.* **1.** To be stormy; blow forcefully and often rain, snow, hail, or sleet: *It stormed for an hour yesterday.* **2.** To be very angry; rant and rage. **3.** To move or rush about angrily: *He stormed into the room.* —*tr.* To assault or capture by a violent sudden attack: *storm the gates.* [From Old English.]

storm cellar *n.* An underground shelter in or adjacent to a house, used for protection from severe windstorms.

storm center *n.* **1.** The central area of a storm, especially the point of lowest barometric pressure within a storm. **2.** A center of trouble, disturbance, or argument.

storm door *n.* An outer or additional door added for protection against stormy weather.

storm sewer *n.* A sewer for carrying off rainwater.

storm surge *n.* An unusual rise in the water level along the seashore from onshore storm winds.

storm window *n.* A secondary window set outside of the usual window to protect against the wind and cold.

storm·y (stôr′mē) *adj.* **storm·i·er, storm·i·est 1.** Subject to, affected by, or characterized by storms: *stormy weather.* **2.** Characterized by violent emotions, passions, speech, or actions: *a stormy meeting.* **—storm′i·ly** *adv.* **—storm′i·ness** *n.*

sto·ry[1] (stôr′ē) *n., pl.* **sto·ries 1.** An account of an event or a series of events, either true or fictitious. **2.** A fictional prose or verse narrative; a tale. **3.** A short story. **4.** A news article or broadcast: *The reporter covered three stories today.* **5.** A lie: *Don't tell stories.* **6.** A statement, report, or allegation of facts: *He's sticking by his story, but I don't believe him.* [From Middle English *storie,* from Latin *historia.*]

sto·ry[2] (stôr′ē) *n., pl.* **sto·ries** A complete horizontal division of a building, consisting of an area between two levels or floors. [From Middle English *storie,* from Medieval Latin *historia,* picture, story.]

sto·ry·book (stôr′ē-bo͝ok′) *n.* A book containing a collection of stories, usually for children. ❖ *adj.* Occurring in or resembling the style or content of a storybook: *a storybook romance.*

sto·ry·tell·er (stôr′ē-tĕl′ər) *n.* **1.** A person who tells or writes stories. **2.** *Informal* A liar.

stoup (sto͞op) *n.* A basin for holy water in a church.
❏ *These sound alike:* **stoup, stoop[1]** (bend forward), **stoop[2]** (small porch).

stout (stout) *adj.* **stout·er, stout·est 1.** Bulky in figure; heavyset: *a stout man.* **2.** Strong in body or structure; sturdy: *the stout back of a donkey.* **3.** Determined, bold, or brave: *a stout heart.* ❖ *n.* A very dark beer. **—stout′ly** *adv.* **—stout′ness** *n.*

stout·heart·ed (stout′här′tĭd) *adj.* Brave; courageous. **—stout′heart′ed·ly** *adv.*

stove[1] (stōv) *n.* An apparatus that furnishes heat for warmth or cooking, using fuel or electricity as a source of power. [From Middle English *steue,* heated room, probably from Middle Low German or Middle Dutch.]

stove[2] (stōv) *v.* A past tense and a past participle of **stave.**

stove·pipe (stōv′pīp′) *n.* **1.** A metal pipe used to carry smoke or fumes from a stove to a chimney. **2.** A man's tall silk hat.

stove·top (stōv′tŏp′) *n.* The top surface of a stove, especially when used for cooking. ❖ *adj.* Used, prepared, or done on the top of a cooking stove: *a stovetop casserole; stovetop cooking.*

stow (stō) *tr.v.* **stowed, stow·ing, stows** To place or store, especially snugly or securely: *stowed her equipment in the locker.* ◆ **stow away** To hide oneself aboard a ship or other vehicle in order to obtain free transportation.

stow·a·way (stō′ə-wā′) *n.* A person who hides aboard a ship or other vehicle in order to obtain free passage.

Stowe (stō), **Harriet (Elizabeth) Beecher** 1811–1896. American writer whose antislavery novel *Uncle Tom's Cabin* (1852) advanced the cause of abolition.

strad·dle (străd′l) *tr.v.* **strad·dled, strad·dling, strad·dles 1.** To sit or stand with a leg on each side of: *She straddled the horse.* **2.** To appear to favor both sides of: *straddle a political issue.* **—strad′dler** *n.*

strafe (strāf) *tr.v.* **strafed, straf·ing, strafes** To attack (troops, for example) with machine-gun fire from low-flying aircraft.

strag·gle (străg′əl) *intr.v.* **strag·gled, strag·gling, strag·gles 1.** To move or lag behind others: *The calves straggled after the cows on the path.* **2.** To move or proceed in a scattered or irregular group: *caribou straggling north to the tundra.* **—strag′gler** *n.*

straight (strāt) *adj.* **straight·er, straight·est 1.** Extending continuously in the same direction without curving: *a straight line.* **2.** Having no waves or bends: *straight hair.* **3.** Erect; upright: *a straight back.* **4.** Relating to a midair position, as in diving, in which the body is kept rigid without bending at the hips or knees. **5.** Perfectly horizontal or vertical; level. **6.** Direct and candid: *do some straight talking.* **7.** Neatly or properly arranged; orderly: *He can't keep his desk straight.* **8.** Not interrupted; consecutive: *ended the season with six straight wins.* **9.** Not deviating politically: *a straight party line.* **10.** Not mixed with anything else; undiluted. **11.** Conforming to socially accepted values; conventional. **12.** Heterosexual. ❖ *adv.* **1.** In a straight line; directly: *The* *arrow flew straight at the target.* **2.** In an erect posture; upright: *stand straight.* **3.** Without detour or delay: *went straight home.* **4.** Candidly: *Tell me straight.* **5.** Without stopping; continuously: *It snowed for five days straight.* ❖ *n.* In poker, a series of five cards of different suits in numerical order. [From Middle English *streit*, from past participle of *strecchen*, to stretch.] **—straight′ly** *adv.* **—straight′ness** *n.*

❑ *These sound alike:* **straight, strait** (channel).

straight angle *n.* An angle of 180 degrees.

straight·a·way (strāt′ə-wā′) *adj.* Extending in a straight line or course without a curve or turn. ❖ *n.* A straight road, course, or track. ❖ *adv.* (strāt′ə-**wā′**) At once; immediately.

straight·edge (strāt′ĕj′) *n.* A stiff, flat, rectangular bar, as of wood or metal, with a straight edge for drawing or testing straight lines.

straight·en (strāt′n) *tr. & intr.v.* **straight·ened, straight·en·ing, straight·ens** To make or become straight or straighter: *straighten hair; straighten up a room.*

straight·for·ward (strāt-**fôr′**wərd) *adj.* **1.** Not evasive; honest and frank: *a straightforward reply.* **2.** Free from complications or uncertainties: *a straightforward approach to a problem.* **—straight·for′ward·ly** *adv.* **—straight·for′ward·ness** *n.*

straight·jack·et (strāt′jăk′ĭt) *n.* Variant of **straitjacket.**

straight-laced (strāt′lāst′) *adj.* Variant of **strait-laced.**

straight man *n.* The partner in a comedy team who feeds lines to the other comedian, who then makes witty replies.

straight·way (strāt′wā′) *adv.* **1.** In a direct course. **2.** Without delay; at once.

strain¹ (strān) *v.* **strained, strain·ing, strains** *—tr.* **1.** To pull, draw, or stretch tight: *The weight of the pulley strains the rope.* **2.** To exert or tax to the utmost; strive hard: *strained my eyes to read the sign.* **3.** To injure or impair by overuse or overexertion: *strain a muscle.* **4.** To force or stretch beyond a proper or legitimate limit: *strain a point.* **5.** To pass through a strainer; filter. *—intr.* **1.** To make violent or steady efforts: *strained to reach the finish line.* **2.** To pull forcibly or violently: *The dog strained at its leash.* **3.** To stretch or exert one's muscles or nerves to the utmost. ❖ *n.* **1.** A pressure, stress, or force: *felt a strain on the line.* **2.** An injury resulting from excessive effort or twisting: *a muscle strain.* **3.** Great pressure or demands on one's mind, body, or resources: *felt the strain of extra homework.* [From Middle English *streinen*, from Latin *stringere*, to bind.]

strain² (strān) *n.* **1.** A group of organisms of the same species, not usually considered a separate breed or variety. **2.** The collective descendants of a common ancestor; a race, stock, line, or breed. **3.** A kind or sort. **4.** An inborn or inherited tendency. **5.** The tone, tenor, or substance of something: *spoke in an academic strain.* **6.** often **strains** A piece, passage, or sound of music: *the strains of the waltz.* [From Old English *strēon*, gain.]

strained (strānd) *adj.* **1.** Passed through a strainer: *strained peaches.* **2.** Done with or marked by excessive effort; forced: *strained humor.* **3.** Under severe stress; on the point of collapse: *strained relations between the two countries.* **4.** Twisted; wrenched: *a strained ankle.*

strain·er (strā′nər) *n.* A device with many small holes, used for separating liquids from solids.

strait (strāt) *n.* often **straits 1.** A narrow channel that connects two larger bodies of water. **2.** A position of difficulty, perplexity, distress, or need: *He was in desperate straits for money.* [From Middle English *streit*, from Latin *strictus*, narrow.]

❑ *These sound alike:* **strait, straight** (erect).

strait·ened (strā′tənd) *adj.* Difficult to endure or deal with, especially because of a lack of money: *found himself in straitened circumstances.*

strait·jack·et also **straight·jack·et** (strāt′jăk′ĭt) *n.* **1.** A long-sleeved garment of strong material used to bind the arms tightly against the body as a means of restraining a violent patient or prisoner. **2.** Something that restricts, hinders, or confines.

strait-laced or **straight-laced** (strāt′lāst′) *adj.* Excessively strict in behavior, morality, or opinions.

Strait of For the names of actual straits, see the specific proper name; for example, **Magellan, Strait of.**

strand¹ (strănd) *n.* A beach or other strip of land bordering a body of water. ❖ *tr.v.* **strand·ed, strand·ing, strands 1.** To trap on the shore or in shallow water: *The tide stranded the whales.* **2.** To leave in a difficult or helpless position. [From Old English.]

strand² (strănd) *n.* **1.** A complex of fibers or filaments that have been twisted together to form a rope, cord, yarn, or cable. **2.** A single filament, such as a fiber or thread, of a woven or braided material. **3.** Something that is plaited or twisted into a ropelike structure: *a strand of DNA; a strand of pearls.* [From Early Modern English *strond*.]

strange (strānj) *adj.* **strang·er, strang·est 1.** Previously unknown; unfamiliar: *a strange fish of tropical waters.* **2.** Not of one's own particular locality, environment, or kind: *a strange language.* **3.** Out of the ordinary; unusual or striking: *a strange feeling.* **4.** Reserved in manner; distant: *became strange to me after our quarrel.* [From Middle English *straunge*, from Latin *extrāneus*, foreign.] **—strange′ly** *adv.* **—strange′ness** *n.*

strang·er (strān′jər) *n.* **1.** A person who is neither a friend nor an acquaintance. **2.** A foreigner, newcomer, or outsider.

stran·gle (străng′gəl) *tr.v.* **stran·gled, stran·gling, stran·gles 1.** To kill by squeezing the throat to obstruct the airway. **2.** To suppress or stifle: *strangle a cry.* **3.** To restrict or limit the growth or action of: *strangle the enemy's supply lines.* **—stran′gler** *n.*

stran·gu·la·tion (străng′gyə-**lā′**shən) *n.* The act of strangling or the state of being strangled.

strap (străp) *n.* **1.** A long narrow strip of leather or other pliant material, used to hold things down, bind things together, or keep things in place: *the straps of an evening gown.* **2.** A narrow band formed into a loop for grasping with the hand: *pulled the suitcase along by its strap.* ❖ *tr.v.* **strapped, strap·ping, straps** To fasten or secure with a strap: *strapped an air tank to the diver's back.*

strap·ping (străp′ĭng) *adj.* Having a sturdy muscular physique; robust.

stra·ta (strā′tə *or* străt′ə) *n.* A plural of **stratum.**

strat·a·gem (străt′ə-jəm) *n.* **1.** A scheme or maneuver designed to achieve an objective, as in surprising an enemy or deceiving someone. **2.** The use of such schemes or maneuvers.

stra·te·gic (strə-**tē′**jĭk) *adj.* **1.** Relating to strategy: *the strategic importance of the Panama Canal.* **2.** Essential in relation to a plan of action: *strategic locations.* **—stra·te′gi·cal·ly** *adv.*

strat·e·gist (străt′ə-jĭst) *n.* A person who is skilled in strategy.

strat·e·gy (străt′ə-jē) *n., pl.* **strat·e·gies 1.** The use of planning to achieve one's goals, especially in a large enterprise such as war: *relied on strategy rather than brute force.* **2.** A plan of action intended to achieve a specific goal within a larger enterprise: *devised a new strategy for winning the election.* [From Greek *stratēgos*, commanding officer, general.]

Strat·ford-on-Av·on (străt′fərd-ŏn-**ā′**vən) also **Strat·ford-up·on-Av·on** (străt′fərd-ə-pŏn-**ā′**vən) A town of central England south-southeast of Birmingham. William Shakespeare was born and died here.

strat·i (străt′ī *or* strā′tī) *n.* Plural of **stratus.**

Harriet Beecher Stowe
1853 portrait by Alanson Fisher (1807–1884)

stratification
cliff in Red Rock Canyon State Park, near Cantil, California

Johann Strauss
1888 portrait of Johann Strauss the Younger by August Eisenmenger (1830–1907)

ă pat	ôr core
ā pay	oi boy
âr care	ou out
ä father	o͝o took
ĕ pet	o͝or lure
ē be	o͞o boot
ĭ pit	ŭ cut
ī bite	ûr urge
îr pier	th thin
ŏ pot	*th* this
ō toe	zh vision
ô paw	ə about

strat·i·fi·ca·tion (străt′ə-fĭ-kā′shən) *n.* **1.** Formation or deposition of layers, as of rock or sediments. **2.** The condition of being stratified. **3.** A layered arrangement.

strat·i·fy (străt′ə-fī′) *v.* **strat·i·fied, strat·i·fy·ing, strat·i·fies** —*tr.* To form, arrange, or deposit in layers. —*intr.* To become layered; form strata.

strat·o·cu·mu·lus (străt′ō-**kyo͞om′**yə-ləs) *n., pl.* **strat·o·cu·mu·li** (străt′ō-**kyo͞om′**yə-lī′) A low-lying cloud formation occurring in extensive horizontal layers with distinct rounded tops.

strat·o·sphere (străt′ə-sfîr′) *n.* The layer of the earth's atmosphere that lies above the troposphere and below the mesosphere.

stra·tum (strā′təm *or* străt′əm) *n., pl.* **stra·ta** (strā′tə *or* străt′ə) or **stra·tums 1.** A horizontal layer of material, especially one of several parallel layers arranged one on top of another. **2.** A bed or layer of rock whose composition is more or less the same throughout. **3.** A level of society composed of people with similar social, cultural, or economic status.

strat·us (străt′əs *or* strā′təs) *n., pl.* **stra·ti** (străt′ī *or* strā′tī) A low-altitude cloud formation consisting of a horizontal layer of gray clouds.

Strauss (strous *or* shtrous), **Johann** Known as "the Elder." 1804–1849. Austrian violinist and composer. His son **Johann** (1825–1899), known as "the Younger," is best known for his waltzes, such as "The Blue Danube" (1867).

Strauss, Richard 1864–1949. German composer whose works include the opera *Salome* (1905).

Stra·vin·sky (strə-vĭn′skē), **Igor Fyodorovich** 1882–1971. Russian-born composer whose works include the ballet *The Rite of Spring* (1913).

straw (strô) *n.* **1a.** Stalks of wheat, oats, or other grain from which the seeds have been removed by threshing, used as bedding and food for animals, as stuffing or padding, and for making such items as hats and baskets. **b.** A single stalk of such grain. **2.** A slender tube used to suck up liquids. **3.** Something of minimal value or importance: *not worth a straw.* [From Old English *strēaw.*]

straw·ber·ry (strô′bĕr′ē) *n.* **1.** A sweet, red, fleshy fruit of any of various plants, having many small seeds on the surface. **2.** A low-growing plant that bears such fruit.

straw man *n.* **1.** A distortion or misrepresentation of an opponent's views, used to make the views appear unreasonable and to avoid addressing the opponent's real arguments. **2.** A person who is set up as a cover or front for a questionable enterprise.

straw vote *n.* An unofficial vote or poll indicating the trend of opinion.

stray (strā) *intr.v.* **strayed, stray·ing, strays 1.** To wander about or roam, especially beyond established limits: *The woodchuck seldom strays far from its burrow.* **2.** To follow a winding course; meander. **3.** To become diverted from a subject: *Don't stray from the topic.* ❖ *n.* A person or an animal that has strayed and is lost. ❖ *adj.* **1.** Strayed or having strayed; lost: *a stray cat.* **2.** Scattered or separate: *stray shafts of sunlight.*

streak (strēk) *n.* **1.** A line, mark, smear, or band different in color or texture from its surroundings. **2.** An inherent, often contrasting quality: *a mean streak.* **3.** A ray or flash of light: *a streak of lightning.* **4.** The characteristic color of a mineral after it has been ground into a powder. **5.** *Informal* A brief run or stretch, as of luck: *a winning streak.* ❖ *v.* **streaked, streak·ing, streaks** —*tr.* To mark with a streak: *Dog tracks streaked the floor.* —*intr.* **1.** To form a streak or streaks. **2.** To move at high speed; rush: *Lightning streaked across the sky.*

streak·y (strē′kē) *adj.* **streak·i·er, streak·i·est 1.** Marked with, characterized by, or occurring in streaks. **2.** Variable or uneven in character or quality. —**streak′i·ly** *adv.* —**streak′i·ness** *n.*

stream (strēm) *n.* **1a.** A body of running water that flows in a more or less regular course, as a brook or small river. **b.** A steady current in such a body of water. **2.** A steady flow or succession of something: *a stream of electrons; a stream of questions.* ❖ *v.* **streamed, stream·ing, streams** —*intr.* **1.** To flow in or as if in a stream: *Water streamed into the reservoir.* **2.** To pour forth or give off a stream; flow: *His eyes streamed with tears.* **3.** To move or travel in large numbers. —*tr.* **1.** To give off or discharge (a body fluid, for example). **2.** To transmit (audio or video content) in real time, especially over the Internet. [From Old English *strēam.*]

stream·er (strē′mər) *n.* **1.** A long narrow flag or banner. **2.** A long narrow strip of material used for ornament or decoration: *a hall decked with streamers of crepe paper.*

stream·let (strēm′lĭt) *n.* A small stream.

stream·line (strēm′līn′) *tr.v.* **stream·lined, stream·lin·ing, stream·lines 1.** To construct or design so as to offer the least resistance to the flow of a fluid. **2.** To improve the efficiency of, often by simplification: *streamline a computer design; streamline a factory process.*

stream·lined (strēm′līnd′) *adj.* **1.** Having smooth curves that offer little resistance to the flow of a fluid: *a car with a streamlined body.* **2.** Effectively organized or simplified: *a streamlined procedure.*

street (strēt) *n.* **1a.** A public way or road in a city or town: *met on the corner of Harrison Street and Fifth Street.* **b.** A public way or road along with its houses and buildings: *lived on Elm Street.* **2.** The people living or working in or along a street: *The whole street came out to watch the parade.* ❖ *adj.* **1.** Taking place in the street: *a street performance.* **2.** Living or making a living on the streets: *a street vendor.* **3.** Crude; vulgar: *street language.* **4.** Appropriate for wear or use in public: *street clothes.*

street·car (strēt′kär′) *n.* A vehicle running on rails and providing public transportation with frequent stops, especially on the streets of a city.

street hockey *n.* A variation of ice hockey played on pavement, often with a ball instead of a puck.

street-smart (strēt′smärt′) *adj.* Having or displaying street smarts.

street smarts *n.* Skills for living in an often hostile urban environment.

street·wise (strēt′wīz′) *adj.* Street-smart.

strength (strĕngkth *or* strĕngth) *n.* **1.** The state or quality of being physically strong: *the strength needed to lift a box.* **2.** The power to resist force, stress, or attack: *the strength of steel.* **3.** Concentration or effectiveness, as of a solution or drug. **4.** Intensity, as of sound or light: *the strength of the signal.* **5.** The capacity to persuade others; persuasiveness: *the strength of an argument.* **6.** The ability to deal with difficulty or to maintain a moral or intellectual position firmly: *Does he have the strength to overcome such a setback?* **7.** A valuable quality; an asset: *Religion is his strength.* **8.** The number of people making up a normal or ideal organization: *a team at full strength.* ◆ **on the strength of** On the basis of: *gave her an "A" on the strength of her essay.* [From Old English *strengthu.*]

SYNONYMS **strength, power, might, force** These nouns mean the capacity to act or work effectively. **Strength** means great physical, mental, or moral energy: *She gathered her strength and moved the boulder out of the way.* **Power** means the ability to do something and especially to produce an effect: *Using her full legal power, the judge ordered the strikers to go back to work.* **Might** often means great power: *It took all his might to lift the end of the piano.* **Force** often means the application of strength or power: *The mayor threatened to use force to remove the demonstrators from the lobby.*

strength·en (strĕngk′thən *or* strĕng′thən) *tr. & intr.v.* **strength·ened, strength·en·ing, strength·ens** To make or become strong or stronger.

stren·u·ous (strĕn′yo͞o-əs) *adj.* **1.** Requiring great effort or energy: *engaged in strenuous exercise.* **2.** Vigorously active; energetic: *strenuous efforts.* [From Latin *strēnuus.*] **—stren′u·ous·ly** *adv.*

strep (strĕp) *adj.* Streptococcal. ❖ *n.* Strep throat.

strep throat *n.* An infection of the throat caused by certain streptococci and marked by fever, pain, and swollen lymph nodes in the neck.

strep·to·coc·cal (strĕp′tə-**kŏk′**əl) *adj.* Relating to or caused by a streptococcus.

strep·to·coc·cus (strĕp′tə-**kŏk′**əs) *n., pl.* **strep·to·coc·ci** (strĕp′tə-**kŏk′**sī *or* strĕp′tə-**kŏk′**ī) Any of several rounded bacteria that form pairs or chains and cause various diseases in humans.

strep·to·my·cin (strĕp′tə-**mī′**sĭn) *n.* An antibiotic drug produced by certain bacteria and used to treat tuberculosis and other bacterial infections.

stress (strĕs) *n.* **1.** Importance, significance, or emphasis placed on something: *The report puts a lot of stress on safety procedures.* **2a.** The relative force given to a sound or syllable in a spoken word or phrase: *In the word "historical," the main stress is on the second syllable.* **b.** A stress mark. **3.** The relative force of sound given to a syllable or word according to a metrical pattern. **4.** A musical accent, such as one beat of a measure. **5.** A force that tends to strain or deform something: *The stress of all the weight caused the shelf to warp.* **6.** A condition of extreme difficulty or strain: *an economy under great stress.* **7.** A condition of psychological strain, usually in response to difficult or unpleasant events, that can cause symptoms such as high blood pressure, insomnia, and irritability. **8.** Something that causes such a condition: *couldn't stand the stresses of her job.* ❖ *tr.v.* **stressed, stress·ing, stress·es 1.** To give importance or emphasis to: *Our dentist stressed oral hygiene as a way of preventing disease.* **2.** To put sound, musical, or metrical stress on: *The rhythm stresses the third of four beats.* **3.** To subject to physical or mental pressure, tension, or strain: *The weight of the bathtub stressed the floor boards.* ◆ **stress out** *Informal* To feel or cause to feel anxious or upset because of a difficult or unpleasant situation: *I am stressing out because of the deadline. The project's deadline is stressing me out.*

stress mark *n.* **1.** A mark showing that a syllable in a word is accented or stressed when the word is pronounced. **2.** A mark indicating rhythmical stress in a line of poetry.

stretch (strĕch) *v.* **stretched, stretch·ing, stretch·es** *—tr.* **1.** To lengthen, widen, or distend: *stretch a rubber band.* **2.** To cause to extend from one place to another or across a given space: *Stretch the canvas over the frame.* **3.** To make taut; tighten: *stretched the plastic wrap.* **4.** To reach or put forth; extend: *stretch out her hand.* **5.** To extend (oneself) when lying down: *stretched herself out on the couch.* **6.** To cause to last longer than otherwise would be possible, especially by economizing: *stretch one's paycheck.* **7.** To increase the quantity of by adding ingredients or by dilution: *stretched the soup by watering it down.* **8.** To interpret or regard (something) in a way that is beyond or contrary to the usual or proper limits: *stretch the meaning of the law.* **9.** To wrench or strain (a muscle, for example). *—intr.* **1.** To become lengthened, widened, or distended: *The cover stretches to fit over the opening.* **2.** To extend or reach over a distance or area or in a given direction: *The wheat field stretched to the north.* **3.** To lie down at full length: *stretched out on the bed.* **4.** To extend one's muscles or limbs, as after sleep or before exercise. ❖ *n.* **1.** The act of stretching or the state of being stretched: *did some stretches to loosen up my back; felt the stretch in my back as I bent down.* **2.** The extent to which something can be stretched; elasticity: *a fabric with a lot of stretch.* **3.** Something that is difficult or barely possible to accomplish: *He is trying out for the lead role, but that has to be a stretch for him.* **4a.** A continuous or unbroken length, area, or expanse: *a stretch of open ground.* **b.** A straight section of a course or track leading to the finish line. **5.** A continuous period of time: *slept for a short stretch.* **6.** In baseball, a series of movements in which the pitcher raises both hands and then lowers them, pausing briefly before throwing. It is used instead of a wind-up, especially when runners are on base. ❖ *adj.* Made of an elastic material that stretches easily: *stretch pants.* ◆ **stretch (one's) legs** To go for a walk, especially after a lengthy period of sitting. [From Old English *streccan.*]

stretch·er (strĕch′ər) *n.* **1.** A movable bed or cot on which a person can be carried in a lying position. **2.** Any of various devices for stretching or shaping, as a wooden frame for canvas.

strew (stro͞o) *tr.v.* **strewed, strewn** (stro͞on) or **strewed, strew·ing, strews 1.** To spread here and there; scatter: *strewed the papers on the floor.* **2.** To cover (an area or a surface) with scattered or sprinkled things: *The beach was strewn with debris.*

stri·ate (strī′āt′) also **stri·at·ed** (strī′ā′tĭd) *adj.* Marked with striations; striped, grooved, or ridged.

stri·a·tion (strī-**ā′**shən) *n.* **1a.** A thin line or band, especially one of several that are parallel or close together. **b.** One of a number of parallel lines or grooves on the surface of a rock, formed when pieces of rock frozen into the base of a glacier moved across the rock and scratched it. **2.** The state of being marked with stripes, bands, grooves, or ridges.

strick·en (strĭk′ən) *v.* A past participle of **strike.** ❖ *adj.* **1.** Struck or wounded, as by a projectile. **2.** Affected by something overwhelming, such as disease, trouble, or painful emotion.

strict (strĭkt) *adj.* **strict·er, strict·est 1.** Demanding or imposing a rigid discipline: *a strict teacher.* **2.** Rigidly conforming to established rule, principle, or condition: *a strict Catholic.* **3.** Precise; exact: *in strict accordance with the law.* **4.** Carefully maintained or observed: *strict silence.* [From Middle English *stricte,* narrow, small, from Latin *strictus,* tight, strict, past participle of *stringere,* to draw tight.] **—strict′ly** *adv.* **—strict′ness** *n.*

stric·ture (strĭk′chər) *n.* **1.** A restraint, limit, or restriction. **2.** An abnormal narrowing of a duct or passage of the body. **3.** An adverse remark or criticism; a censure.

stride (strīd) *v.* **strode** (strōd), **strid·den** (strĭd′n), **strid·ing, strides** *—intr.* **1.** To walk vigorously with long steps. **2.** To take a single long step, as in passing over an obstruction. *—tr.* **1.** To walk with long steps on, along, or over. **2.** To step over or across. ❖ *n.* **1.** The act of striding. **2.** A single long step. **3.** The distance traveled in such a step. **4.** A step forward: *new strides in the field of medicine.* ◆ **take in stride** To cope with calmly, without interrupting one's normal routine: *took the postponement of the recital in stride.* [From Old English *strīdan.*]

stri·dent (strīd′nt) *adj.* Loud, harsh, grating, or shrill: *a strident voice.* **—stri′den·cy** *n.*

strife (strīf) *n.* Heated, often violent conflict or disagreement.

strike (strīk) *v.* **struck** (strŭk), **struck** or **strick·en** (strĭk′ən), **strik·ing, strikes** *—tr.* **1.** To hit with the hand, an implement, or a weapon: *struck the stake with a sledgehammer.* **2.** To inflict (a blow): *strike a blow at injustice.* **3a.** To collide with or crash into: *She struck the desk with her knee.* **b.** To cause to come into violent or forceful contact: *He struck his knee on the table leg.* **4.** To make a military attack on; assault. **5.** To afflict suddenly, as with a disease or impairment: *He was suddenly stricken with weakness in one arm.* **6.** To produce or play

streetcar

string bean

strip mine

ă	pat	ôr	core
ā	pay	oi	boy
âr	care	ou	out
ä	father	ŏŏ	took
ĕ	pet	ŏŏr	lure
ē	be	ōō	boot
ĭ	pit	ŭ	cut
ī	bite	ûr	urge
îr	pier	th	thin
ŏ	pot	*th*	this
ō	toe	zh	vision
ô	paw	ə	about

by hitting some device, as a key on a piano: *struck the opening chords of the sonata.* **7.** To indicate with a sound: *The clock struck five.* **8.** To ignite by friction: *strike a match.* **9.** To impress strongly or anew: *struck her as a good idea.* **10.** To come upon; reach; discover: *strike gold.* **11.** To make or conclude: *strike a bargain.* **12.** To dismantle or pack up: *The stagehands struck the sets. The hikers struck camp.* **13.** To arrange oneself in; assume: *strike a pose.* —*intr.* **1.** To deal a blow or blows; hit: *struck at the lock until it broke.* **2.** To aim a stroke or blow; try to hit: *struck at the mosquito, but missed.* **3.** To make contact suddenly and violently; collide: *The two railroad cars struck with a loud boom.* **4.** To begin an attack: *The army struck at dawn.* **5.** To set out or proceed, especially in a new direction: *They struck off into the woods.* **6.** To indicate the time with a sound: *The clock struck at noon.* **7.** To discover something suddenly or unexpectedly: *struck on an idea.* **8.** To engage in a strike against an employer. ❖ *n.* **1.** An attack, especially a military air attack. **2.** The stopping of work by employees in an attempt to force an employer to meet certain demands. **3.** In baseball, a pitched ball that is counted against the batter, typically one swung at and missed or one allowed to cross home plate and judged to have passed through the strike zone. **4.** In bowling, the knocking down of all ten pins with one roll of the ball. ◆ **on strike** Refusing to work in an attempt to force an employer to meet a demand: *on strike for better wages.* **strike down 1.** To cause to fall by a blow. **2.** To render ineffective; cancel: *The court struck down the judgment.* **strike out 1.** To set out energetically: *decided to strike out for the mountains on foot.* **2a.** In baseball, to pitch three strikes to (a batter), putting the batter out. **b.** In baseball, to be struck out. **3.** To fail in an endeavor: *I auditioned for a part in the play, but I struck out.* **strike up** To initiate or begin: *struck up a friendship with the new student.* [From Old English *strīcan*, to stroke, rub.]

strike·bound (**strīk′**bound′) *adj.* Closed, immobilized, or slowed down by a strike.

strike·break·er (**strīk′**brā′kər) *n.* A person who works for an employer while the employer's workers are on strike.

strike·out (**strīk′**out′) *n.* In baseball, an example of striking out a batter or of a batter being struck out.

strik·er (**strī′**kər) *n.* **1.** An employee on strike against an employer. **2.** A person or thing that strikes. **3.** A forward on a soccer team.

strike zone *n.* In baseball, the area over home plate through which a pitch must pass in order to count as a strike rather than a ball, roughly between the batter's knees and mid chest.

strik·ing (**strī′**kĭng) *adj.* Capturing the attention and making a vivid visual or mental impression. —**strik′·ing·ly** *adv.*

string (strĭng) *n.* **1a.** Material made of drawn-out, twisted fiber, used for fastening, tying, or lacing: *a ball of string.* **b.** A strand or cord of such material: *used a string to tie the package.* **2.** Something resembling a string or appearing as a long, thin line: *a string of corn silk.* **3.** A set of things threaded together: *a string of beads.* **4.** A series or sequence of items: *a string of letters in a secret code; a string of victories.* **5a.** A cord stretched across a musical instrument and struck, plucked, or bowed to produce tones. **b.** also **strings** Stringed instruments or their players considered as a group. **6.** *Informal* A limiting or hidden condition. Also used in the plural: *a gift with no strings attached.* **7.** In sports, a group of players constituting a ranked team within a team: *plays first string.* ❖ *tr.v.* **strung** (strŭng), **string·ing, strings 1.** To fit or furnish with a string or strings: *string a piano.* **2.** To connect by running a string or cord through; thread: *string beads.* **3.** To arrange in a line or series: *strung the words into a sentence.* **4.** To fasten, tie, or hang with a string or strings: *strung balloons from the ceiling.* **5.** To stretch out or extend: *strung the cable across the stream.* ◆ **string along** *Informal* **1.** To go along with something; agree: *We're stringing along with his plan, hoping it will work.* **2.** To fool, cheat, or deceive: *They made many promises but were just stringing us along.* [From Old English *streng.*]

string bean *n.* **1.** A long, narrow green bean pod eaten as a vegetable. **2.** The bushy or climbing plant that bears such pods.

stringed instrument (strĭngd) *n.* A musical instrument, such as a guitar or violin, played by plucking, bowing, or striking tightly stretched strings.

strin·gent (**strĭn′**jənt) *adj.* Rigorous; severe: *stringent restrictions.* —**strin′gent·ly** *adv.*

string·er (**strĭng′**ər) *n.* **1a.** A long heavy bar or timber that connects or supports parts of a structure. **b.** A board along the side of a staircase supporting or covering the ends of the steps. **2.** A part-time reporter for the news media. **3.** A member of a string or squad on a sports team: *a second stringer.*

string quartet *n.* **1.** A group of four musicians playing stringed instruments, usually two violins, a viola, and a cello. **2.** A composition for such a group.

string·y (**strĭng′**ē) *adj.* **string·i·er, string·i·est 1.** Resembling, made of, or having strings: *stringy hair.* **2.** Slender and sinewy: *a stringy piece of meat.* —**string′i·ness** *n.*

strip[1] (strĭp) *tr.v.* **stripped, strip·ping, strips 1.** To remove clothing or covering from: *stripped the beds.* **2.** To remove or take off (clothing or covering): *stripped off his shirt.* **3.** To clear of a natural covering or growth; make bare: *strip a tree of its bark.* **4.** To rob of wealth or property; plunder: *The invaders stripped the countryside.* **5.** To damage or break the threads of (a screw, for example) or the teeth of (a gear). [From Middle English *strepen*, from Old English *bestrȳpan*, to plunder.]

strip[2] (strĭp) *n.* **1.** A long narrow piece or area of approximately even width: *a strip of paper; a strip of desert.* **2.** A comic strip. **3.** An airstrip. [Perhaps from Middle English *stripe* or Middle Low German *strippe*, strap, thong.]

stripe (strīp) *n.* **1.** A long narrow band that differs, as in color or texture, from the area on either side: *a zebra's stripes.* **2.** A strip of cloth or braid worn on a uniform to show rank, awards received, or length of service: *a sergeant's stripes.* **3.** Sort; kind: *film directors of a bold new stripe.* ❖ *tr.v.* **striped, strip·ing, stripes** To mark with a stripe or stripes.

strip·ling (**strĭp′**lĭng) *n.* An adolescent boy or young man.

strip mall *n.* A building containing a row of shops and businesses that open onto the same parking lot.

strip mine *n.* An open mine, especially a coal mine, whose seams or outcrops run close to ground level and are exposed by removing the overlying soil and rocks. —**strip′-mine′** *v.*

strive (strīv) *intr.v.* **strove** (strōv), **striv·en** (**strĭv′**ən) or **strived, striv·ing, strives 1.** To exert much effort or energy: *strove to improve his writing skills.* **2.** To struggle or fight forcefully; contend: *The pioneers strove against great odds.*

strobe (strōb) *n.* A strobe light.

strobe light *n.* A lamp that produces very short, intense flashes of light in rapid succession. [From Greek *strobos*, spinning.]

strode (strōd) *v.* Past tense of **stride.**

stroke[1] (strōk) *n.* **1.** The act or an instance of striking, as with the hand or a weapon; a blow: *a stroke of the sword.* **2a.** The striking of a bell or gong. **b.** The sound so produced. **c.** The time so indicated: *at the stroke of midnight.* **3.** A sudden action, event, or process having a strong impact or effect: *a stroke of lightning.* **4a.** A sudden severe attack, as of paralysis or sunstroke. **b.** A sudden loss of brain function caused by a blockage or rupture of a blood vessel to the brain, marked by loss of muscle control, loss of sensation or consciousness, dizziness, or slurred speech. **5.** An inspired or effective idea or act: *a stroke of genius.* **6.** A single uninterrupted movement, especially when repeated or in a back-and-forth motion. **7.** Any of a series of movements of a piston from one end of the limit of its motion to another. **8.** A single completed movement of the limbs and body, as in swimming or rowing. **9.** A movement of the upper body and arms for the purpose of striking a ball, as in golf or tennis. **10.** A single mark made by a writing or marking implement, such as a pen. ❖ *tr.v.* **stroked, strok·ing, strokes 1.** To hit or propel (a ball, for example) with a smooth swinging motion. **2.** To set the pace for (a rowing crew). [From Middle English.]

stroke[2] (strōk) *tr.v.* **stroked, strok·ing, strokes** To rub lightly, with or as if with the hand or something held in the hand; caress: *stroked the cat's head.* ❖ *n.* A light caressing movement, as of the hand. [From Old English *strācian.*]

stroll (strōl) *v.* **strolled, stroll·ing, strolls** —*intr.* To walk or wander at a leisurely pace: *People strolled about the park.* —*tr.* To walk along or through at a leisurely pace: *stroll the beach.* ❖ *n.* A leisurely walk.

stroll·er (strō′lər) *n.* **1.** A person who strolls. **2.** A light wheeled carriage often having a retractable hood, used for transporting small children.

strong (strông) *adj.* **strong·er, strong·est 1.** Exerting or capable of exerting great physical force: *It took a strong push to move the stalled car. The ox is a strong animal.* **2.** In good or sound health; robust: *a strong constitution.* **3.** Having force of character, will, morality, or intelligence: *a strong personality.* **4.** Capable of enduring force or wear; not easily broken: *strong furniture.* **5.** Intense in degree or quality: *strong feelings; a strong wind.* **6.** Very active and increasing in value: *a strong economy.* **7.** Extreme; drastic: *strong measures.* **8.** Persuasive; cogent: *a strong argument.* **9.** Concentrated: *a strong vinegar.* **10.** Highly active chemically: *a strong acid.* **11.** Having a specified number of units or members: *Five hundred strong, they marched forward.* **12.** Of a color having a high degree of saturation; vivid. **13.** Stressed or accented in pronunciation or poetic meter. Used of a word or syllable. [From Old English *strang.*] —**strong′ly** *adv.*

strong·box (strông′bŏks′) *n.* A stoutly made box or safe for storing valuables.

strong·hold (strông′hōld′) *n.* **1.** A fortress or fortified place. **2.** A place of survival or refuge. **3.** An area dominated or occupied by a special group.

stron·ti·um (strŏn′chē-əm *or* strŏn′tē-əm) *n. Symbol* **Sr** A soft, silvery metallic element that reacts easily with air and is used in making alloys, fireworks, and signal flares. Atomic number 38. See **Periodic Table.**

strontium-90 *n.* A radioactive isotope of strontium with a mass number of 90 and a half-life of 28 years that occurs in the fallout from nuclear explosions. It poses a health hazard to humans because it can be absorbed by the body.

strop (strŏp) *n.* A flexible strip of leather or canvas used for sharpening a razor. ❖ *tr.v.* **stropped, strop·ping, strops** To sharpen (a razor) on a strop.

stro·phe (strō′fē) *n.* A stanza of a poem.

strove (strōv) *v.* Past tense of **strive.**

struck (strŭk) *v.* Past tense and a past participle of **strike.**

struc·tur·al (strŭk′chər-əl) *adj.* **1.** Relating to, characterized by, or having structure. **2.** Used in or necessary to construction: *structural steel.* —**struc′tur·al·ly** *adv.*

structural formula *n.* A chemical formula that shows how the atoms making up a compound are arranged within the molecule.

struc·ture (strŭk′chər) *n.* **1.** Something made up of a number of parts that are held together or put together in a particular way. **2.** The way in which parts are arranged or put together to form a whole. **3.** Something constructed, such as a building or bridge: *They completed work on the structure last May.* **4.** A plant or animal part or organ: *A paramecium moves by means of tiny hairlike structures called cilia.* ❖ *tr.v.* **struc·tured, struc·tur·ing, struc·tures** To give form or arrangement to: *I structured my day around my dance lessons.* [From Middle English *structure,* building materials, from Latin *strūctūra,* structure, from *struere,* to construct.]

strug·gle (strŭg′əl) *intr.v.* **strug·gled, strug·gling, strug·gles 1.** To exert muscular energy, as against a physical force or mass: *We struggled to control the fire.* **2a.** To make a strenuous effort; strive: *struggled to stay awake.* **b.** To be strenuously engaged; wrestle: *struggled all night with the math homework.* **3.** To compete or contend: *Passengers struggled for room on the subway.* ❖ *n.* **1.** The act of struggling. **2.** Strenuous effort or striving: *the struggle for survival.* **3.** Combat; battle or strife: *hand-to-hand struggles; a legal struggle.* [From Middle English *strogelen.*] —**strug′gler** *n.*

strum (strŭm) *v.* **strummed, strum·ming, strums** —*tr.* To play (a stringed instrument or music on a stringed instrument) by stroking or brushing the strings. —*intr.* To strum a stringed instrument or a tune on such an instrument. ❖ *n.* The act or sound of strumming.

strung (strŭng) *v.* Past tense and past participle of **string.**

strut (strŭt) *n.* **1.** A vain or showy way of walking. **2.** A bar or rod used to brace a mechanical structure against forces applied from the side. ❖ *v.* **strut·ted, strut·ting, struts** —*intr.* To walk in a vain or showy way; swagger. —*tr.* **1.** To display in order to impress others. **2.** To brace or support with a strut or struts.

strych·nine (strĭk′nīn′ *or* strĭk′nĭn) *n.* A very poisonous white crystalline compound obtained from certain plants, used as a poison for rats and other pests.

stub (stŭb) *n.* **1.** The usually short end remaining after something bigger has been used up: *the stub of a pencil.* **2a.** The part of a check or receipt retained as a record. **b.** The part of a ticket returned as a voucher of payment. ❖ *tr.v.* **stubbed, stub·bing, stubs** To strike (one's toe or foot) against something.

stub·ble (stŭb′əl) *n.* **1.** The short stiff stalks of grain or hay left after a crop has been harvested. **2.** Something resembling this, especially a short stiff growth of hair that eventually appears after shaving.

stub·born (stŭb′ərn) *adj.* **stub·born·er, stub·born·est 1.** Refusing to change one's mind or course of action despite pressure to do so: *a stubborn child.* See Synonyms at **obstinate. 2.** Continuously enduring; persistent: *a stubborn idea.* **3.** Difficult to treat or deal with: *A stubborn stain ruined the tablecloth.* —**stub′born·ly** *adv.* —**stub′born·ness** *n.*

stub·by (stŭb′ē) *adj.* **stub·bi·er, stub·bi·est 1.** Short, broad, and stocky: *stubby legs.* **2.** Full of stubs: *stubby grass.* —**stub′bi·ness** *n.*

stuc·co (stŭk′ō) *n., pl.* **stuc·coes** or **stuc·cos** A durable finish for walls, usually of plaster or cement.

stuck (stŭk) *v.* Past tense and past participle of **stick.**

stuck-up (stŭk′ŭp′) *adj. Informal* Snobbish; conceited.

stud[1] (stŭd) *n.* **1.** An upright post in the framework of a wall for supporting lath, drywall, or similar material. **2.** Any of various projecting pins or pegs, as in machinery. **3.** A removable button used to fasten and ornament, as on a dress shirt. ❖ *tr.v.* **stud·ded, stud·ding, studs 1.** To provide with or construct with studs or a stud. **2.** To set with objects that project or stand out from the surface: *stud a bracelet with turquoise.* **3.** To be dotted about on; strew: *Daisies studded the meadow.* [From Old English *studu.*]

stroller

stupa
Golden Temple at Dambulla, Sri Lanka

ă	pat	ôr	core
ā	pay	oi	boy
âr	care	ou	out
ä	father	ŏŏ	took
ĕ	pet	ŏŏr	lure
ē	be	ōō	boot
ĭ	pit	ŭ	cut
ī	bite	ûr	urge
îr	pier	th	thin
ŏ	pot	*th*	this
ō	toe	zh	vision
ô	paw	ə	about

stud² (stŭd) *n.* **1.** A male animal, especially a stallion, kept for breeding. **2.** A group of horses or other animals kept for breeding. **3.** *Slang* A usually young man regarded as attractive and well-built. [From Old English *stōd*, a place for breeding horses.]

stu·dent (**stōōd′**nt) *n.* **1.** A person who is enrolled in or attends classes at a school, college, or university. **2.** A person who studies something: *a student of languages.*

student teacher *n.* A college student who teaches in a classroom under a teacher's supervision as part of a degree in education.

stud·ied (**stŭd′**ēd) *adj.* **1.** Carefully contrived; deliberate: *a studied pose.* **2.** Learned; knowledgeable.

stu·di·o (**stōō′**dē-ō) *n., pl.* **stu·di·os 1.** An artist's workroom. **2.** A photographer's place of business. **3.** A place where an art is taught or studied: *a ceramics studio.* **4.** A room or building for movie, television, or radio productions. **5.** A room or building where musical recordings are produced. **6.** A company that produces movies. **7.** A studio apartment.

studio apartment *n.* A small apartment usually consisting of one main living space, a small kitchen, and a bathroom.

stu·di·ous (**stōō′**dē-əs) *adj.* **1.** Devoted to study: *a studious life.* **2.** Marked by steady attention and effort; assiduous: *a studious avoidance of anything silly.* **—stu′di·ous·ly** *adv.* **—stu′di·ous·ness** *n.*

stud·y (**stŭd′**ē) *n., pl.* **stud·ies 1.** The effort to acquire knowledge, especially by reading or observation: *The study of the disease has led to several treatments.* **2.** An act or effort made in the pursuit of knowledge: *devoted most of his time to his studies.* **3.** Attentive observation or examination: *a new drug that is under study.* **4.** A branch of knowledge; a subject: *technical studies.* **5.** A work on a particular subject: *published a study of bird behavior.* **6.** A musical composition written or played as an exercise; an etude. **7.** An artist's preliminary sketch. **8.** A room intended for or equipped for studying. ❖ *v.* **stud·ied, stud·y·ing, stud·ies** *—tr.* **1.** To apply one's mind to gaining knowledge and understanding of (a subject): *study French.* **2.** To read or look at carefully: *studied the map.* **3.** To try to memorize: *Have you studied your lines for the play?* **4.** To take (a course) at a school: *He studies law at night.* **5.** To investigate: *She studied the behavior of bees.* *—intr.* **1.** To apply oneself to learning, especially by reading: *How long did you study for the test?* **2.** To pursue a course of study: *studied in London.*

stuff (stŭf) *n.* **1.** The material out of which something is made or formed; substance. **2.** The basic elements of something; essence: *the stuff of which fear is made.* **3.** *Informal* Unspecified material or articles: *venders selling stuff on the street.* **4.** *Slang* Specific talk or actions: *Don't give me that stuff about being tired.* **5.** Special capability: *They showed their stuff on the debate team.* ❖ *tr.v.* **stuffed, stuff·ing, stuffs 1a.** To pack tightly: *stuffed the Christmas stockings.* **b.** To block a passage; obstruct: *stuffed the hole in the window with a rag.* **2.** To fill with an appropriate stuffing: *stuff a pillow.* **3.** To cram with food: *He stuffed himself at dinner.*

stuffed shirt *n.* *Informal* A stiff or pompous person.

stuff·ing (**stŭf′**ĭng) *n.* **1.** Padding put in things made of or covered with cloth, as upholstered furniture or cushions: *a doll with the stuffing coming out.* **2.** Food put into the cavity of a piece of meat or a vegetable that has been hollowed out.

stuff·y (**stŭf′**ē) *adj.* **stuff·i·er, stuff·i·est 1.** Lacking sufficient ventilation; close: *an overheated stuffy room.* **2.** Having blocked breathing passages: *a stuffy nose.* **3.** Dull and boring: *a stuffy party.* **—stuff′i·ly** *adv.* **—stuff′i·ness** *n.*

stul·ti·fy (**stŭl′**tə-fī′) *tr.v.* **stul·ti·fied, stul·ti·fy·ing, stul·ti·fies 1.** To cause (someone) to lose interest or feel dull: *a speaking tone that stultified the audience.* **2.** To make useless or ineffectual: *customs that stultify free thought.* **—stul′ti·fi·ca′tion** (stŭl′tə-fĭ-**kā′**shən) *n.*

stum·ble (**stŭm′**bəl) *intr.v.* **stum·bled, stum·bling, stum·bles 1a.** To trip and almost fall: *The horse stumbled.* **b.** To move unsteadily or falteringly: *He stumbled out of bed.* **2.** To make a mistake; blunder: *Do you stumble over words?* **3.** To come upon accidentally or unexpectedly: *They stumbled upon the clue.* ❖ *n.* **1.** The act of stumbling; a fall. **2.** A mistake or blunder. **—stum′bler** *n.*

stum·bling block (**stŭm′**blĭng) *n.* An obstacle or impediment.

stump (stŭmp) *n.* **1.** The part of a tree trunk left protruding from the ground after the tree has fallen or been cut down. **2.** A short or broken part left after the main part has been cut away, broken off, or worn down: *a stump of a tail.* **3.** A place or occasion used for making political speeches. ❖ *v.* **stumped, stump·ing, stumps** *—tr.* **1.** To clear stumps from: *stump a field.* **2.** To puzzle or baffle completely: *The last question on the test stumped everyone.* *—intr.* To go about making political speeches, especially as part of a campaign: *The candidate has been stumping throughout the state.* [From Middle English *stumpe*, possibly from Middle Low German *stump*.] **—stump′y** *adj.*

stump speech *n.* A speech given by a candidate as part of a political campaign, especially in different places.

stun (stŭn) *tr.v.* **stunned, stun·ning, stuns 1.** To daze or render senseless, as by a blow or a loud noise. **2.** To shock or stupefy, as with the emotional impact of an experience: *The scandal stunned the neighborhood.* [From Middle English *stonen*, from Old French *estoner* : Latin *ex-*, out + Latin *tonāre*, to thunder.]

stung (stŭng) *v.* Past tense and past participle of **sting.**

stunk (stŭngk) *v.* A past tense and the past participle of **stink.**

stun·ning (**stŭn′**ĭng) *adj.* **1.** Causing or capable of causing emotional shock or loss of consciousness. **2.** Strikingly attractive: *a stunning suit.* **3.** Impressive or surprising: *a stunning performance.* **—stun′ning·ly** *adv.*

stunt¹ (stŭnt) *tr.v.* **stunt·ed, stunt·ing, stunts 1.** To stop or slow (growth or development): *Poor soil can stunt the growth of plants.* **2.** To stop or slow the growth or development of: *The trees on the ridge were stunted by the strong winds. Bad luck stunted her ambitions.* [From Middle English, foolish, short-witted, from Old English.]

stunt² (stŭnt) *n.* **1.** A feat displaying unusual strength, skill, or daring. **2.** Something done to attract attention or publicity: *The protest was just a publicity stunt to get media attention for the new movie.*

stu·pa (**stōō′**pə) *n.* A dome-shaped Buddhist shrine or monument.

stu·pe·fy (**stōō′**pə-fī′) *tr.v.* **stu·pe·fied, stu·pe·fy·ing, stu·pe·fies 1.** To dull the senses or consciousness of: *The dull routine stupefied them.* **2.** To amaze; astonish: *a record-breaking time that stupefied the sports world.* **—stu′pe·fac′tion** (stōō′pə-**făk′**shən) *n.*

stu·pen·dous (stōō-**pĕn′**dəs) *adj.* **1.** Of astonishing force, volume, degree, or excellence; marvelous: *stupendous risks.* **2.** Amazingly large; huge: *stupendous temple ruins.* **—stu·pen′dous·ly** *adv.*

stu·pid (**stōō′**pĭd) *adj.* **stu·pid·er, stu·pid·est 1.** Slow to learn or understand. **2.** Marked by a lack of intelligence or care; senseless: *He gave a stupid answer. Skating on thin ice is a stupid thing to do.* **3.** Pointless; worthless: *a stupid task.* [From Latin *stupidus*, from *stupēre*, to be stunned.] **—stu′pid·ly** *adv.*

stu·pid·i·ty (stōō-**pĭd′**ĭ-tē) *n., pl.* **stu·pid·i·ties 1.** The quality or condition of being stupid. **2.** A stupid act, remark, or idea.

stu·por (stōō′pər) *n.* A state of reduced sensibility or consciousness; a daze.

stur·dy (stûr′dē) *adj.* **stur·di·er, stur·di·est 1.** Having or showing rugged physical strength. **2.** Substantially made or built; stout: *sturdy canvas.* **3.** Marked by determination; firm: *sturdy opposition to the plan.* **—stur′di·ly** *adv.* **—stur′di·ness** *n.*

stur·geon (stûr′jən) *n.* Any of various large edible freshwater or saltwater fishes having hard bony scales on the body. Their roe is a source of caviar. [From Middle English *sturgeoun*, from Old French *estourgeon*, of Germanic origin.]

stut·ter (stŭt′ər) *intr. & tr.v.* **stut·tered, stut·ter·ing, stut·ters** To speak or utter with constant hesitations or repetitions of sounds. ❖ *n.* The act or habit of stuttering. **—stut′ter·er** *n.*

Stuy·ve·sant (stī′vĭ-sənt), **Peter** 1612?–1672. Dutch colonial administrator who was forced in 1664 to surrender the colony of New York (then New Netherland) to England.

sty[1] (stī) *n., pl.* **sties** (stīz) **1.** An enclosure for pigs. **2.** A very dirty or untidy place. [From Old English *stig.*]

sty[2] (stī) *n., pl.* **sties** (stīz) An oil-producing gland that has become inflamed in one of the eyelids. [From Middle English *stīanīe, styanye* : from Old English *stīgend*, rising up + Middle English *eie*, eye.]

style (stīl) *n.* **1.** The manner in which something is expressed or performed: *a style of speech; a writing style.* **2.** The combination of features that characterize a person, group, school, or era: *music in the baroque style.* **3.** Sort; kind; type: *a style of furniture.* **4.** A comfortable and elegant mode of existence: *living in style.* **5a.** A particular fashion, especially of dressing: *the styles of the 1980s.* **b.** The fashion of the moment: *Dresses of various lengths are in style.* **6.** A quality of individuality expressed in one's actions and tastes: *She does things with style.* **7.** The slender stalk of a flower pistil, rising from the ovary and tipped by the stigma. ❖ *tr.v.* **styled, styl·ing, styles** To arrange, design, or fashion in a special way. [From Middle English *stile*, from Latin *stilus*, stylus.]

❑ *These sound alike:* **style, stile** (turnstile).

sty·li (stī′lī) *n.* A plural of **stylus.**

styl·ish (stī′lĭsh) *adj.* Conforming to the current style; fashionable: *wore a stylish outfit to the party.* **—styl′ish·ly** *adv.* **—styl′ish·ness** *n.*

styl·ist (stī′lĭst) *n.* **1.** A person who cuts or styles hair. **2.** A writer or speaker who cultivates an artful literary style. **3.** A designer of or an expert on styles in decorating, dress, or beauty.

sty·lis·tic (stī-lĭs′tĭk) *adj.* Relating to style, especially literary style.

styl·ize (stī′līz′) *tr.v.* **styl·ized, styl·iz·ing, styl·iz·es** To represent in a particular style, especially a nonrealistic style.

sty·lus (stī′ləs) *n., pl.* **sty·lus·es** or **sty·li** (stī′lī) **1.** A sharp pointed instrument used for writing, marking, or engraving. **2.** A phonograph needle.

sty·mie (stī′mē) *tr.v.* **sty·mied** (stī′mēd), **sty·mie·ing** (stī′mē-ĭng), **sty·mies** (stī′mēz) To block or thwart: *The setback stymied their hopes.*

styp·tic (stĭp′tĭk) *adj.* Contracting the blood vessels so as to stop bleeding; astringent. ❖ *n.* A styptic drug or substance.

sty·rene (stī′rēn′) *n.* A colorless oily liquid hydrocarbon from which polystyrene is made.

Sty·ro·foam (stī′rə-fōm′) A trademark for a resilient spongelike polystyrene foam.

Styx (stĭks) *n.* In Greek mythology, the river across which the souls of the dead are ferried.

sua·sion (swā′zhən) *n.* Persuasion: *moral suasion.*

suave (swäv) *adj.* **suav·er, suav·est** Smoothly agreeable and courteous: *a portrait of a suave, well-dressed gentleman.* [From Latin *suāvis*, delightful, sweet.] **—suave′ly** *adv.* **—suav′i·ty, suave′ness** *n.*

sub[1] (sŭb) *n. Informal* **1.** A submarine. **2.** A submarine sandwich.

sub[2] (sŭb) *Informal n.* A substitute. ❖ *intr.v.* **subbed, sub·bing, subs** To act as a substitute.

sub– *pref.* A prefix that means: **1.** Under; beneath: *submarine.* **2.** A subordinate or secondary part: *subplot; subdivision.* **3.** Less than completely or normally; almost: *subtropical.* —SEE NOTE.

sub·a·tom·ic (sŭb′ə-tŏm′ĭk) *adj.* **1.** Relating to particles that are smaller than an atom. **2.** Having dimensions or participating in reactions characteristic of the parts of the atom.

subatomic particle *n.* One of the basic units of which atoms are made. Protons, neutrons, and electrons are subatomic particles.

sub·com·mit·tee (sŭb′kə-mĭt′ē) *n.* A subordinate committee composed of members appointed from a main committee.

sub·com·pact (sŭb-kŏm′păkt′) *n.* An automobile smaller than a compact.

sub·con·scious (sŭb-kŏn′shəs) *adj.* Not wholly conscious; partially or imperfectly conscious. ❖ *n.* The unconscious. **—sub·con′scious·ly** *adv.*

sub·con·ti·nent (sŭb′kŏn′tə-nənt *or* sŭb-kŏn′tə-nənt) *n.* A large landmass, such as India, that is part of a continent but is considered as an independent entity.

sub·cu·ta·ne·ous (sŭb′kyōō-tā′nē-əs) *adj.* Located or placed just beneath the skin. **—sub′cu·ta′ne·ous·ly** *adv.*

sub·di·vide (sŭb′dĭ-vīd′ *or* sŭb′dĭ-vīd′) *v.* **sub·di·vid·ed, sub·di·vid·ing, sub·di·vides** *—tr.* To divide into smaller parts, especially to divide (land) into lots. *—intr.* To form into subdivisions.

sub·di·vi·sion (sŭb′dĭ-vĭzh′ən *or* sŭb′dĭ-vĭzh′ən) *n.* **1.** The act or process of subdividing. **2.** A subdivided part. **3.** An area of real estate subdivided into individual lots.

sub·dom·i·nant (sŭb-dŏm′ə-nənt) *n.* The fourth tone of a musical scale, next below the dominant. ❖ *adj.* Less than dominant; ranking below one that is dominant: *the subdominant male in a pride of lions.*

sub·due (səb-dōō′) *tr.v.* **sub·dued, sub·du·ing, sub·dues 1.** To conquer; vanquish. **2.** To quiet or bring under control by physical force or persuasion: *subdue the wild horse.* **3.** To make less intense; tone down: *Hearing that you weren't going subdued my excitement about the party.*

sub·head (sŭb′hĕd′) or **sub·head·ing** (sŭb′hĕd′ĭng) *n.* **1.** The heading or title of a subdivision of a printed subject. **2.** A subordinate heading or title.

sub·hu·man (sŭb-hyōō′mən) *adj.* **1.** Considered to be less advanced evolutionarily than humans: *subhuman primates.* **2.** Regarded as not being fully human.

sub·ject (sŭb′jĭkt) *adj.* **1.** Under the power or authority of another: *subject to the jurisdiction of a government.* **2.** Prone; disposed: *Are you subject to colds?* **3.** Likely to incur or receive; exposed: *a statement subject to misinterpretation.* **4.** Contingent or dependent: *The project was subject to approval by the board.* ❖ *n.* **1.** A person who owes allegiance to a government or ruler: *a subject of the throne.* **2a.** A person or thing about which something is said or done: *a subject of discussion.* **b.** Something that is treated in a work of art. **3.** A theme of a musical composition. **4.** A course or area of study: *Her favorite subject is math.* **5.** An individual used as the object of medical or scientific study: *the subjects of an experiment.* **6.** The part of a sentence or clause that identifies who or what does the action or what is described by the predicate. The subject is usually a noun, pronoun, or noun phrase. ❖ *tr.v.* (səb-jĕkt′) **sub·ject·ed, sub·ject·ing, sub·jects 1.**

sturgeon

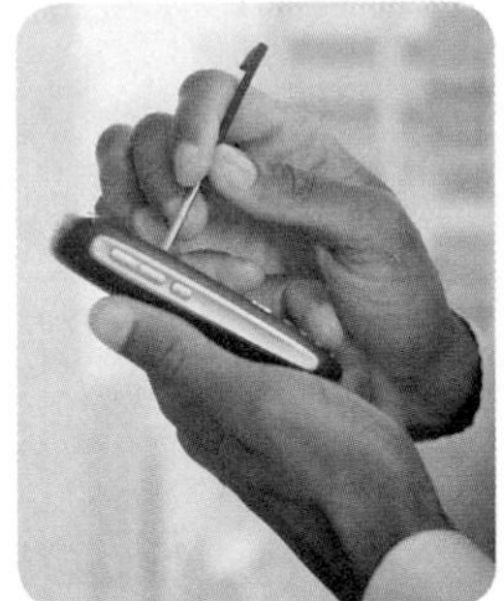

stylus

WORD BUILDING

sub– The prefix **sub–** can be traced back to the Latin preposition *sub*, meaning "under." Some words beginning with *sub–* that came into English from Latin include *submerge, suburb,* and *subvert.* When *sub–* is used to form words in English, it can mean "under" (*submarine, subsoil, subway*), "subordinate" (*subcommittee, subplot, subset*), or "less than completely" (*subhuman, substandard*). *Sub–* can form compounds by combining with verbs as well as with adjectives and nouns, as in *subdivide, sublease,* and *sublet.*

To bring under control or authority: *The ancient Romans subjected many peoples.* **2.** To cause to undergo or experience: *subjected me to many tests.* **—sub·jec′tion** *n.*

SYNONYMS **subject, matter, topic, theme** These nouns mean the principal idea or point of a speech, piece of writing, or work of art. **Subject** is the most general: *Many paintings of the 1700s have historical subjects.* **Matter** often means the material that is the object of thought: *This will be an interesting matter for you to discuss.* **Topic** means a subject of discussion, argument, or conversation: *The hospital is giving a series of lectures on the topic of nutrition.* **Theme** often means a subject, idea, point of view, or perception that is developed in a work of art: *The theme of this poem is the healing power of love.*

---

sub·jec·tive (səb-**jĕk′**tĭv) *adj.* **1.** Coming from or taking place within the mind rather than the external world. **2.** Particular to a given person; personal: *a subjective experience.* **3.** In grammar, relating to the nominative case.

subject matter *n.* That which is being considered, discussed, or depicted, as in a written work.

sub·ju·gate (**sŭb′**jə-gāt′) *tr.v.* **sub·ju·gat·ed, sub·ju·gat·ing, sub·ju·gates** To bring under control; conquer. [From Middle English *subjugaten*, from Latin *subiugāre* : *sub-*, under + *iugum*, yoke.] **—sub′ju·ga′tion** *n.*

sub·junc·tive (səb-**jŭngk′**tĭv) *adj.* Relating to the mood of a verb used to express an uncertainty, a wish, or an unlikely condition. For example, in the sentence *If I were you, I would go,* the word *were* is a subjunctive form. ❖ *n.* **1.** The subjunctive mood. **2.** A subjunctive construction.

sub·lease (**sŭb′lēs′**) *tr.v.* **sub·leased, sub·leas·ing, sub·leas·es 1.** To sublet (property) from someone. **2.** To sublet (property) to someone. ❖ *n.* A lease of property granted by a person who already rents the property.

sub·let (**sŭb′lĕt′**) *tr.v.* **sub·let, sub·let·ting, sub·lets 1.** To rent (property one holds by lease) to someone else. **2.** To rent (property from someone who has a lease on it). ❖ *n.* (**sŭb′**lĕt′) Property, especially an apartment, rented by a tenant to someone else.

sub·li·ma·tion (sŭb′lə-**mā′**shən) *n.* The act or process of changing directly from solid to gas without becoming a liquid.

sub·lime (sə-**blīm′**) *adj.* **1.** Characterized by nobility; majestic. **2.** Not to be excelled; supreme. **3.** Inspiring awe; impressive: *a sublime performance.* ❖ *intr.v.* **sub·limed, sub·lim·ing, sub·limes** To undergo the process of sublimation. **—sub·lime′ly** *adv.*

sub·ma·chine gun (sŭb′mə-**shēn′**) *n.* A lightweight automatic gun fired from the shoulder or the hip.

sub·ma·rine (**sŭb′**mə-rēn′ *or* sŭb′mə-**rēn′**) *n.* **1.** A ship that can operate underwater. **2.** A submarine sandwich. ❖ *adj.* Beneath the surface of the sea; undersea: *a submarine volcano.*

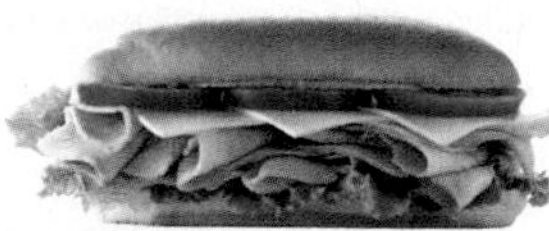
submarine sandwich

submarine sandwich *n.* A large sandwich consisting of a long roll filled with layers of ingredients such as meat, cheese, tomatoes, lettuce, and condiments.

sub·merge (səb-**mûrj′**) *v.* **sub·merged, sub·merg·ing, sub·merg·es** *—tr.* **1.** To place under water: *submerged the dish.* **2.** To cover with water: *The flood submerged the island.* *—intr.* To go under water. [From Latin *submergere* : *sub-*, under + *mergere*, to plunge.]

sub·merse (səb-**mûrs′**) *tr.v.* **sub·mersed, sub·mers·ing, sub·mers·es** To submerge. **—sub·mer′sion** (səb-**mûr′**zhən *or* səb-**mûr′**shən) *n.*

sub·mis·sion (səb-**mĭsh′**ən) *n.* **1.** The act of submitting to the power of another. **2.** The condition of being submissive or compliant: *forced into submission.* **3a.** The act of submitting something for consideration: *the submission of a manuscript to a publisher.* **b.** Something submitted for consideration: *received a number of submissions in the mail.*

sub·mis·sive (səb-**mĭs′**ĭv) *adj.* Inclined or willing to submit: *a submissive personality.*

sub·mit (səb-**mĭt′**) *v.* **sub·mit·ted, sub·mit·ting, sub·mits** *—tr.* **1.** To yield or surrender (oneself) to the will or authority of another: *They submitted themselves to his judgment.* **2.** To subject to a condition or process. **3.** To commit (something) to the consideration of another: *We submitted our ideas to our boss.* **4.** To offer as a proposition or contention: *I submit that the terms of the contract are unreasonable.* *—intr.* To yield; surrender; acquiesce: *He submitted to their demands.* [From Middle English *submitten*, from Latin *submittere*, to set under : *sub-*, under + *mittere*, to cause to go.] **—sub·mit′tal** *n.*

sub·or·der (**sŭb′**ôr′dər) *n.* A category in taxonomy that ranks between an order and a family.

sub·or·di·nate (sə-**bôr′**dn-ĭt) *adj.* **1.** Belonging to a lower or inferior rank; secondary: *a subordinate position.* **2.** Subject to the authority or control of another. ❖ *n.* A person or thing that is subordinate: *He is courteous to his subordinates.* ❖ *tr.v.* (sə-**bôr′**dn-āt′) **sub·or·di·nat·ed, sub·or·di·nat·ing, sub·or·di·nates** To put in a lower or inferior rank or class: *subordinate a court to a higher one.* **—sub·or′di·nate·ly** *adv.* **—sub·or′di·na′tion** *n.*

subordinate clause *n.* A clause that cannot stand alone as a full sentence. For example, *when I saw him* in the sentence *When I saw him, he was feeling fine* is a subordinate clause.

sub·or·di·nat·ing conjunction (sə-**bôr′**dn-ā′tĭng) *n.* A conjunction such as *after, because, if,* or *where,* that introduces a subordinate clause.

sub·orn (sə-**bôrn′**) *tr.v.* **sub·orned, sub·orn·ing, sub·orns 1a.** To induce (a person) to commit an unlawful or evil act. **b.** To induce (a person) to give false testimony. **2.** To induce someone to give (false testimony). **—sub′or·na′tion** (sŭb′ôr-**nā′**shən) *n.* **—sub·orn′er** *n.*

sub·poe·na (sə-**pē′**nə) *n.* An order issued by a court or other governmental body, requiring a person to appear and give testimony or to release certain evidence. ❖ *tr.v.* **sub·poe·naed, sub·poe·na·ing, sub·poe·nas 1.** To summon (a person) with such an order. **2.** To demand (a piece of evidence) by means of such an order. [From Middle English *sub pena*, from Medieval Latin *sub poenā*, under a penalty : Latin *sub*, under + Latin *poena*, penalty.]

sub-Sa·har·an (sŭb′sə-**hâr′**ən *or* sŭb′sə-**här′**ən) *adj.* Relating to or situated in the region of Africa south of the Sahara desert.

sub·scribe (səb-**scrīb′**) *v.* **sub·scribed, sub·scrib·ing, sub·scribes** *—intr.* **1.** To make an agreement to receive a certain service or a scheduled series of things over a period of time in exchange for money: *subscribe to a concert series; subscribe to an online newspaper.* **2.** To promise to pay or contribute money: *subscribe to a charity.* **3.** To feel or express hearty approval: *I subscribe to your opinion.* *—tr.* To sign (one's name) at the end of a document. [From Middle English *subscriben*, from Latin *subscrībere* : *sub-*, under + *scrībere*, to write.] **—sub·scrib′er** *n.*

sub·script (**sŭb′**skrĭpt′) *n.* A symbol or character written directly beneath or next to and slightly below another symbol or character, as in a mathematical expression or chemical formula. **—sub′script′** *adj.*

sub·scrip·tion (səb-**skrĭp′**shən) *n.* **1.** An agreement to receive a service or a scheduled series of things over a period of time in exchange for money: *a subscription to the ballet; a subscription to antivirus software.* **2.** The signing of one's name, as to a legal document.

sub·se·quent (**sŭb′**sĭ-kwĕnt′) *adj.* Following in time or order; succeeding: *heavy rains and subsequent floods.* **—sub′se·quence** *n.* **—sub′se·quent′ly** *adv.*

ă	pat	ôr	core
ā	pay	oi	boy
âr	care	ou	out
ä	father	o͝o	took
ĕ	pet	o͝or	lure
ē	be	o͞o	boot
ĭ	pit	ŭ	cut
ī	bite	ûr	urge
îr	pier	th	thin
ŏ	pot	*th*	this
ō	toe	zh	vision
ô	paw	ə	about

sub·serve (səb-sûrv′) *tr.v.* **sub·served, sub·serv·ing, sub·serves** To be useful to (a purpose or an end).

sub·ser·vi·ent (səb-sûr′vē-ənt) *adj.* **1.** Subordinate in capacity or function. **2.** Inclined or willing to submit to others; obsequious. **—sub·ser′vi·ence** *n.*

sub·set (sŭb′sĕt′) *n.* A set that has all of its members contained in another set. For example, if *A* is a set and *B* is a set and every member of *A* is a member of *B*, then *A* is a subset of *B*.

sub·side (səb-sīd′) *intr.v.* **sub·sid·ed, sub·sid·ing, sub·sides 1.** To sink to a lower or normal level: *The floodwaters subsided.* **2.** To become less agitated or active; abate: *The wind finally subsided.* [From Latin *subsīdere* : *sub-*, under, down + *sīdere*, to settle.]

sub·sid·i·ar·y (səb-sĭd′ē-ĕr′ē) *adj.* **1.** Serving to assist or supplement; auxiliary: *subsidiary roads.* **2.** Secondary in importance; subordinate: *a subsidiary aim of the project.* ❖ *n., pl.* **sub·sid·i·ar·ies 1.** Something that is subsidiary to another. **2.** A company having more than half of its stock owned by another company.

sub·si·dize (sŭb′sĭ-dīz′) *tr.v.* **sub·si·dized, sub·si·diz·ing, sub·si·diz·es** To assist or support with a subsidy: *The committee appropriated funds to subsidize the investigation.* **—sub′si·diz′er** *n.*

sub·si·dy (sŭb′sĭ-dē) *n., pl.* **sub·si·dies** A payment or grant of money made to help support an enterprise regarded as in the public interest: *government subsidies to farmers.*

sub·sist (səb-sĭst′) *intr.v.* **sub·sist·ed, sub·sist·ing, sub·sists 1.** To exist; be. **2.** To continue or remain in existence. **3.** To maintain life; live: *Horses can subsist on grass.*

sub·sis·tence (səb-sĭs′təns) *n.* **1.** The act or state of subsisting. **2.** A means of subsisting.

sub·soil (sŭb′soil′) *n.* The layer of earth below the topsoil.

sub·son·ic (sŭb-sŏn′ĭk) *adj.* Having a speed less than that of sound.

sub·spe·cies (sŭb′spē′shēz *or* sŭb′spē′sēz) *n., pl.* **subspecies** A subdivision of a species of organisms having distinctive characteristics, usually located in a specific geographic region.

sub·stance (sŭb′stəns) *n.* **1a.** That which has mass and occupies space; matter. **b.** A material of a particular kind or composition. **2.** The essence of what is said or written; the gist: *the substance of the report.* **3.** That which is solid or real; reality as opposed to appearance: *a dream without substance.* **4.** Density; body: *Air has little substance.* **5.** Material possessions; wealth: *a person of substance.* [From Middle English *substaunce*, from Latin *substāre*, to be present : *sub-*, under + *stāre*, to stand.]

substance abuse *n.* Excessive or inappropriate use of a drug, especially one that is illegal, addictive, or physically harmful.

sub·stan·dard (sŭb-stăn′dərd) *adj.* Failing to meet a standard; below standard: *a substandard job performance.*

sub·stan·tial (səb-stăn′shəl) *adj.* **1.** Considerable in importance, value, degree, amount, or extent: *making substantial progress.* **2.** Solidly built; strong: *substantial houses.* **3.** Ample; sustaining: *a substantial meal.* **4.** Possessing wealth or property; well-to-do. **5.** Relating to or having substance; material. **6.** Not imaginary; true; real. **—sub·stan′tial·ly** *adv.*

sub·stan·ti·ate (səb-stăn′shē-āt′) *tr.v.* **sub·stan·ti·at·ed, sub·stan·ti·at·ing, sub·stan·ti·ates** To support with proof or evidence; verify: *substantiate a claim.*

sub·stan·tive (sŭb′stən-tĭv) *adj.* **1.** Substantial; considerable: *This article needs substantive changes before it can be published.* **2.** Not apparent or imaginary; real: *Is the accusation supported by any substantive evidence?* ❖ *n.* In grammar, a word or a group of words functioning as a noun.

sub·sti·tute (sŭb′stĭ-to͞ot′) *n.* A person or thing that takes the place of another; a replacement. ❖ *v.* **sub·sti·tut·ed, sub·sti·tut·ing, sub·sti·tutes** —*tr.* To put or use (a person or thing) in place of another: *substitute walnuts for pecans in the recipe.* —*intr.* To take the place of another: *I substituted for him in the game.* [From Middle English, from Latin *substituere*, to substitute : *sub-*, in place of + *statuere*, to cause to stand.] **—sub′sti·tu′tion** *n.*

sub·stra·tum (sŭb′strā′təm *or* sŭb′străt′əm) *n., pl.* **sub·stra·ta** (sŭb′strā′tə *or* sŭb′străt′ə) or **sub·stra·tums 1a.** An underlying layer. **b.** A layer of earth beneath the topsoil; subsoil. **2.** The foundation or groundwork for something. **3.** The material upon which another material is coated or fabricated.

sub·ter·fuge (sŭb′tər-fyo͞oj′) *n.* **1.** A deceptive plan or trick: *The meeting was a subterfuge to get him out of his office while it was searched.* **2.** The use of deception to attain a goal: *tried to get her to sign the contract by subterfuge.*

sub·ter·ra·ne·an (sŭb′tə-**rā′**nē-ən) *adj.* Located or operating beneath the earth's surface; underground.

sub·ti·tle (sŭb′tīt′l) *n.* **1.** A secondary and usually explanatory title, as of a literary work. **2.** A printed translation of the dialogue of a foreign-language film or video, shown at the bottom of the screen.

sub·tle (sŭt′l) *adj.* **sub·tler, sub·tlest 1.** So slight as to be difficult to detect or analyze; elusive: *subtle changes.* **2.** Difficult to understand; complicated: *a subtle problem.* **3.** Able to make fine distinctions; keen: *a subtle mind.* [From Middle English *sotil*, from Latin *subtīlis*.] **—sub′tle·ness** *n.* **—sub′tly** *adv.*

sub·tle·ty (sŭt′l-tē) *n., pl.* **sub·tle·ties 1.** The state or quality of being subtle: *the subtlety of his plan.* **2.** Something subtle, especially a nicety of thought or a fine distinction.

sub·to·tal (sŭb′tōt′l) *n.* The total of part of a set of numbers. ❖ *tr.v.* **sub·to·taled, sub·to·tal·ing, sub·to·tals** also **sub·to·talled, sub·to·tal·ling, sub·to·tals** To total (a subset of a set of numbers).

sub·tract (səb-trăkt′) *v.* **sub·tract·ed, sub·tract·ing, sub·tracts** —*tr.* To take away; deduct: *subtract five from seven.* —*intr.* To perform the arithmetic operation of subtraction.

sub·trac·tion (səb-**trăk′**shən) *n.* **1.** The act or process of subtracting; deduction. **2.** The mathematical operation of finding the difference between two numbers.

sub·trac·tive (səb-**trăk′**tĭv) *adj.* **1.** Marked by or involving subtraction. **2.** Being any of the primary colors of pigment that can be mixed to make pigment of any hue.

sub·tra·hend (sŭb′trə-hĕnd′) *n.* A number that is to be subtracted from another number; for example, in the equation 8 − 5 = 3, the subtrahend is 5.

sub·trop·i·cal (sŭb-**trŏp′**ĭ-kəl) *adj.* Relating to or being the regions bordering on the tropics.

sub·trop·ics (sŭb-**trŏp′**ĭks) *pl.n.* Subtropical regions.

sub·urb (sŭb′ûrb′) *n.* **1.** A usually residential area or community outside or near a city. **2. suburbs** The usually residential region around a major city. [From Middle English *suburbe*, from Latin *suburbium* : *sub-*, near + *urbs*, city.]

sub·ur·ban (sə-**bûr′**bən) *adj.* **1.** Relating to or characteristic of a suburb: *a suburban area.* **2.** Located or residing in a suburb: *a suburban school.*

sub·ur·ban·ite (sə-**bûr′**bə-nīt′) *n.* A person who lives in a suburb.

sub·ur·bi·a (sə-**bûr′**bē-ə) *n.* **1.** The suburbs. **2.** Suburbanites considered as a group.

sub·ver·sion (səb-**vûr′**zhən *or* səb-**vûr′**shən) *n.* **1.** The act or an instance of subverting. **2.** The condition of being subverted.

sub·ver·sive (səb-**vûr′**sĭv) *adj.* Intended or serving to

WRITERS CHOOSE THEIR WORDS

The camp was a good one, and they stayed more days than Maroo could count, living on fish, hares, and the green food they found in the woods. Full summer came. The bitter winds **subsided;** there were no more snow showers, and the last patches of snow melted away.

—Ann Turnbull
Maroo of the Winter Caves

subway

succulent

ă	pat	ôr	core
ā	pay	oi	boy
âr	care	ou	out
ä	father	ŏŏ	took
ĕ	pet	ŏŏr	lure
ē	be	ōō	boot
ĭ	pit	ŭ	cut
ī	bite	ûr	urge
îr	pier	th	thin
ŏ	pot	*th*	this
ō	toe	zh	vision
ô	paw	ə	about

subvert a government or institution: *subversive plots.*

sub·vert (səb-vûrt′) *tr.v.* **sub·vert·ed, sub·vert·ing, sub·verts** To overthrow or weaken (a government or institution). [From Middle English *subverten*, from Latin *subvertere* : *sub-*, under + *vertere*, to turn.]

sub·way (sŭb′wā′) *n.* **1a.** An underground urban railroad, usually operated by electricity. **b.** A passage for such a railroad. **2.** An underground tunnel or passage, as for pedestrians.

suc·ceed (sək-sēd′) *v.* **suc·ceed·ed, suc·ceed·ing, suc·ceeds** —*intr.* **1.** To replace another in an office or position: *She succeeded to the throne.* **2.** To accomplish something desired or attempted: *He succeeded in repairing the watch.* —*tr.* **1.** To come after in time or order; follow. See Synonyms at **follow. 2.** To come after and take the place of: *Reagan succeeded Carter as president.* [From Middle English *succeden*, from Latin *succēdere* : *sub-*, near + *cēdere*, to go.] **—suc·ceed′er** *n.*

suc·cess (sək-sĕs′) *n.* **1.** The achievement of something desired, planned, or attempted: *the success of the experiment.* **2.** The gaining of fame or prosperity: *an athlete spoiled by success.* **3.** A person or thing that is successful: *The project was a big success.*

suc·cess·ful (sək-sĕs′fəl) *adj.* **1.** Having a favorable outcome: *a successful attempt.* **2.** Having gained something desired or intended. **3.** Having achieved wealth or fame: *She is a successful actor.* **—suc·cess′ful·ly** *adv.*

suc·ces·sion (sək-sĕsh′ən) *n.* **1.** The act or process of following in order or sequence: *the succession of events.* **2.** A group of people or things arranged or following in order; a sequence: *We heard a succession of sharp sounds.* **3.** The gradual replacement of one type of ecological community, especially of plants, by another. **4.** The sequence or right of one person after another to succeed to a title, throne, or position: *a war over the succession to the Spanish throne.*

suc·ces·sive (sək-sĕs′ĭv) *adj.* Following in uninterrupted order; consecutive: *three successive years of drought.* **—suc·ces′sive·ly** *adv.*

suc·ces·sor (sək-sĕs′ər) *n.* A person or thing that succeeds another.

suc·cinct (sək-sĭngkt′) *adj.* **suc·cinct·er, suc·cinct·est** Characterized by clear precise expression in few words; concise and terse: *gave a succinct explanation.* **—suc·cinct′ly** *adv.* **—suc·cinct′ness** *n.*

suc·cor (sŭk′ər) *n.* Assistance in time of distress; relief. ❖ *tr.v.* **suc·cored, suc·cor·ing, suc·cors** To give assistance to in time of distress, difficulty, or want.

❑ *These sound alike:* **succor, sucker** (dupe).

suc·co·tash (sŭk′ə-tăsh′) *n.* A stew consisting of kernels of corn, lima beans, and tomatoes. [From Narragansett *msíckquatash*, boiled whole-kernel corn.]

Suc·coth (sōō-kôt′ *or* sŏŏk′əs) *n.* Variant of **Sukkot.**

suc·cu·lent (sŭk′yə-lənt) *adj.* **1.** Full of juice; juicy: *succulent berries.* **2.** Having thick, fleshy, water-storing leaves or stems: *a succulent plant.* ❖ *n.* A succulent plant, such as a cactus. **—suc′cu·lence** *n.*

suc·cumb (sə-kŭm′) *intr.v.* **suc·cumbed, suc·cumb·ing, suc·cumbs 1.** To submit to something overpowering or overwhelming; give up or give in: *succumb to the pressures of one's friends.* **2.** To die.

such (sŭch) *adj.* **1.** Of this kind or a similar kind: *an eye specialist, one of many such doctors in the hospital.* **2.** Of a degree or quality indicated: *Their happiness was such that they were in tears.* **3.** Of so extreme a degree or quality: *We never dreamed of such wealth.* ❖ *adv.* **1.** To so extreme a degree; so: *She is such a good friend.* **2.** Very; especially: *He has done such good work lately.* ❖ *pron.* **1.** Such a person or persons or thing or things: *We expected problems, and such occurred.* **2.** A person or thing implied or indicated: *Such are the fortunes of love.* **3.** Similar things or people; the like: *pins, needles, and such.* ◆ **such as** For example. [From Old English *swylc.*]

suck (sŭk) *v.* **sucked, suck·ing, sucks** —*tr.* **1.** To draw (liquid) into the mouth by moving the tongue and lips. **2.** To draw in (something) by lowering the pressure inside: *a vacuum cleaner sucking up dirt.* **3.** To hold or move inside the mouth, especially while creating suction: *suck a cough drop.* —*intr.* To suckle. ❖ *n.* The act or sound of sucking.

suck·er (sŭk′ər) *n.* **1.** A part by which an organism clings to something by suction: *Leeches have two suckers, one in the front and one in the back.* **2.** Any of various freshwater fishes of North America and Asia, having a thick-lipped mouth used for feeding by suction. **3.** A shoot growing from the base of a tree or shrub. **4.** A lollipop. **5.** *Informal* A person who is easily fooled.

❑ *These sound alike:* **sucker, succor** (help).

suck·le (sŭk′əl) *v.* **suck·led, suck·ling, suck·les** —*tr.* To provide milk from the breast or a teat; nurse: *Mammals suckle their young.* —*intr.* To suck at a breast or teat: *The lambs are suckling.*

suck·ling (sŭk′lĭng) *n.* A young animal that is still being nursed by its mother. ❖ *adj.* Not yet weaned: *a suckling pig.*

Su·cre (sōō′krā) The constitutional capital of Bolivia, in the south-central part of the country southeast of La Paz.

su·crose (sōō′krōs′) *n.* A crystalline sugar having the formula $C_{12}H_{22}O_{11}$, found in many plants, especially sugar cane, sugar beets, and sugar maple, and widely used as a sweetener.

suc·tion (sŭk′shən) *n.* A force that causes a fluid or solid to be drawn into a space because of a difference in pressures. ❖ *adj.* Creating, using, or done by suction: *a suction pump.* ❖ *tr.v.* **suc·tioned, suc·tion·ing, suc·tions** To draw away or remove (something) by means of suction: *used a vacuum cleaner to suction up wood shavings from the floor.*

Su·dan (sōō-dăn′) **1.** A region of northern Africa south of the Sahara and north of the equator. It extends across the continent from the Atlantic coast to Ethiopia. **2.** A country of northeast Africa south of Egypt. In 2011, citizens of the southern part voted to form a separate nation. Khartoum is the capital.

sud·den (sŭd′n) *adj.* **1.** Happening without warning; unforeseen: *a sudden storm.* **2.** Hasty; abrupt: *a sudden change of mind.* ◆ **all of a sudden** Very quickly and unexpectedly; suddenly. [From Middle English *sodein*, from Latin *subitāneus*, from *subīre*, to approach stealthily.] **—sud′den·ly** *adv.* **—sud′den·ness** *n.*

sudden death *n.* Extra play added to determine the winner of a tied game, with the victory awarded to the first to score.

suds (sŭdz) *pl.n.* A foam or lather, especially of soapy water. **—sud′sy** *adj.*

sue (sōō) *v.* **sued, su·ing, sues** —*tr.* To bring legal action against (a person) in order to satisfy a claim or grievance. —*intr.* **1.** To institute legal proceedings: *He sued for his right to the property.* **2.** To make an appeal or entreaty: *sue for peace.* [From Middle English *seuen*, from Latin *sequī*, to follow.]

suede also **suède** (swād) *n.* **1.** Leather with a soft velvety nap. **2.** Cloth made to resemble suede. [From French *Suède*, Sweden.]

su·et (sōō′ĭt) *n.* The hard fatty tissue around the kidneys of cattle and sheep, used in cooking, for making tallow, and as bird feed.

Su·ez Canal (sōō-ĕz′ *or* sōō′ĕz′) A ship canal, about 100 miles (160 kilometers) long, linking the Red Sea with the Mediterranean Sea across the **Isthmus of Suez,** a narrow neck of land between northeast Africa and southwest Asia. It was opened in 1869.

suf·fer (sŭf′ər) *v.* **suf·fered, suf·fer·ing, suf·fers** —*intr.*

1. To feel or endure pain or distress: *suffer from disease.* **2.** To have a specified shortcoming or weakness: *The film suffered from a poor sound track.* **3.** To undergo a loss, setback, or decline in effectiveness; become worse: *When morale is bad, the team's performance suffers.* —*tr.* **1.** To undergo or be subjected to (something painful, injurious, or unpleasant): *suffer a heart attack; suffer a defeat.* **2.** To endure or bear; tolerate: *She does not suffer fools easily.* **—suf′fer·er** *n.* —SEE NOTE AT **transfer.**

suf·fer·ance (sŭf′ər-əns *or* sŭf′rəns) *n.* Consent or permission implied or given by failure to prohibit.

suf·fer·ing (sŭf′ər-ĭng *or* sŭf′rĭng) *n.* **1.** The condition of a person or thing that suffers. **2.** An instance of pain or distress.

suf·fice (sə-fīs′) *v.* **suf·ficed, suf·fic·ing, suf·fic·es** —*intr.* **1.** To meet present needs; be sufficient: *The food will suffice until next week.* **2.** To be capable or competent: *No words can suffice to convey my gratitude.* —*tr.* To be sufficient or adequate for: *enough water to suffice them for three days.*

suf·fi·cien·cy (sə-fĭsh′ən-sē) *n., pl.* **suf·fi·cien·cies 1.** The quality or condition of being sufficient. **2.** An adequate amount or quantity.

suf·fi·cient (sə-fĭsh′ənt) *adj.* As much as is needed; enough; adequate: *Are these really sufficient reasons for going?* **—suf·fi′cient·ly** *adv.*

suf·fix (sŭf′ĭks) *n.* In grammar, an affix added to the end of a word serving to form a new word or indicate a grammatical function; for example, *-ness* in *gentleness* and *-es* in *boxes* are suffixes. ❖ *tr.v.* **suf·fixed, suf·fix·ing, suf·fix·es** To add as a suffix.

suf·fo·cate (sŭf′ə-kāt′) *v.* **suf·fo·cat·ed, suf·fo·cat·ing, suf·fo·cates** —*tr.* **1.** To stop the breathing of; kill by depriving of oxygen. **2.** To cause discomfort to by cutting off a supply of air. **3.** To suppress the development or creativity of; stifle: *The new doctor sometimes felt suffocated in the backward town.* —*intr.* **1.** To die from a lack of oxygen. **2.** To feel discomfort from a lack of fresh air: *We were suffocating in the hot room.* **3.** To become or feel oppressed or stifled. **—suf′fo·ca′tion** *n.*

suf·frage (sŭf′rĭj) *n.* The right to vote.

suf·fra·gette (sŭf′rə-jĕt′) *n.* A woman advocating women's right to vote, especially in the United Kingdom in the late 1800s or early 1900s.

suf·fra·gist (sŭf′rə-jĭst) *n.* A person who advocates extending voting rights, especially to women.

suf·fuse (sə-fyo͞oz′) *tr.v.* **suf·fused, suf·fus·ing, suf·fus·es** To spread through or over, as with liquid, color, or light: *A greenish haze suffused the woods.*

sug·ar (sho͝og′ər) *n.* **1.** A sweet crystalline or powdered solid, consisting of sucrose obtained mainly from sugarcane or sugar beets and used especially in foods to improve taste. **2.** Any of a class of crystalline carbohydrates, such as sucrose, glucose, or lactose, that dissolve in water and have a characteristic sweet taste. **3.** Sucrose. ❖ *tr.v.* **sug·ared, sug·ar·ing, sug·ars** To coat or sweeten with sugar. [From Middle English *sugre,* from Sanskrit *śarkarā,* grit, ground sugar.]

sugar beet *n.* **1.** A type of beet having whitish roots from which sugar is obtained. **2.** The root of one of these plants.

sug·ar·cane or **sugar cane** (sho͝og′ər-kān′) *n.* A tall grass grown in warm regions, having thick stems containing sweet sap that is the chief commercial source of sugar.

sug·ar·coat (sho͝og′ər-kōt′) *tr.v.* **sug·ar·coat·ed, sug·ar·coat·ing, sug·ar·coats 1.** To cause to seem more appealing: *The governor sugarcoated the budget cuts by promising to cut taxes.* **2.** To coat with sugar: *The manufacturer sugarcoats the pills to make them easier to take.*

sug·ar·less (sho͝og′ər-lĭs) *adj.* **1.** Sweetened with a substance that is not a kind of sugar: *sugarless gum sweetened with aspartame.* **2.** Not sweet: *a bitter, sugarless substance.*

sugar loaf *n.* **1.** Sugar packed into the shape of a rounded cone. **2.** A mountain or hill shaped like a rounded cone.

sugar maple *n.* An eastern North American maple tree having sap that is the source of maple syrup and maple sugar.

sug·ar·plum (sho͝og′ər-plŭm′) *n.* A small round piece of sugary candy.

sug·ar·y (sho͝og′ə-rē) *adj.* **sug·ar·i·er, sug·ar·i·est 1.** Containing, resembling, or tasting like sugar. **2.** Excessively kind or sentimental: *sugary compliments.*

sug·gest (səg-jĕst′ *or* sə-jĕst′) *tr.v.* **sug·gest·ed, sug·gest·ing, sug·gests 1.** To offer for consideration or action: *I suggest that we take a walk.* **2.** To express or say indirectly: *Are you suggesting I lied to you?* **3.** To make evident indirectly; imply: *a silence that suggests disapproval.* **4.** To bring or call to mind by association; evoke: *a cloud that suggests a dragon.*

sug·gest·i·ble (səg-jĕs′tə-bəl *or* sə-jĕs′tə-bəl) *adj.* Easily influenced by suggestions.

sug·ges·tion (səg-jĕs′chən *or* sə-jĕs′chən) *n.* **1.** The act of suggesting. **2.** Something suggested: *Let's follow her suggestion.* **3.** A trace; a touch: *turn back at the first suggestion of rain.*

sug·ges·tive (səg-jĕs′tĭv *or* sə-jĕs′tĭv) *adj.* **1.** Tending to bring something to mind: *These ruins are suggestive of a highly developed civilization.* **2.** Giving a suggestion: *a suggestive message in an advertisement.* **3.** Tending to imply something improper or indecent: *suggestive song lyrics.* **—sug·ges′tive·ly** *adv.*

su·i·cid·al (so͞o′ĭ-sīd′l) *adj.* **1.** Considering or intending to commit suicide. **2.** Relating to suicide: *suicidal thoughts.* **3.** Very likely to result in death or great harm to oneself: *a suicidal plan to climb the mountain alone.*

su·i·cide (so͞o′ĭ-sīd′) *n.* **1.** The act or an instance of intentionally killing oneself. **2.** A person who commits suicide. **3.** The destruction or ruin of one's own interests: *Refusing to follow company policy would be professional suicide.* [From Latin *suī,* of oneself + Latin *caedere,* to kill.]

suit (so͞ot) *n.* **1.** A set of matching outer garments designed to be worn together, especially a jacket with pants or a skirt. **2.** An outfit worn for a special activity or purpose: *a gym suit.* **3.** One of the four sets marked with identifying symbols (spades, clubs, hearts, or diamonds) in a deck of playing cards. **4.** A court action to recover a right or claim; a lawsuit. ❖ *tr.v.* **suit·ed, suit·ing, suits 1.** To meet the requirements of: *The house suited them.* **2a.** To be appropriate or acceptable for: *The song suited the occasion.* **b.** To make appropriate; adapt: *They suited the play to their audience.* **3.** To please; satisfy: *This choice suits me just fine.*

suit·a·ble (so͞o′tə-bəl) *adj.* Appropriate to a given purpose or occasion: *suitable shelter; packed suitable clothes for the trip.* **—suit′a·bil′i·ty** *n.* **—suit′a·bly** *adv.*

suit·case (so͞ot′kās′) *n.* A usually rectangular piece of luggage for carrying clothing.

suite (swēt) *n.* **1.** A series of connected rooms used as a living unit. **2.** (*also* so͞ot) A set of matching furniture. **3.** A staff of attendants; a retinue. **4.** An instrumental composition consisting of a succession of dances in the same or related keys or of a series of varying movements. ❑ *These sound alike:* **suite, sweet** (sugary).

suit·or (so͞o′tər) *n.* **1.** A man who is courting a woman. **2.** A person who sues in court.

su·ki·ya·ki (so͞o′kē-yä′kē) *n.* A Japanese dish of sliced meat, bean curd, and vegetables fried together. [From Japanese : *suki,* strip + *yaku,* to roast.]

Suk·kot or **Suc·coth** (so͞o-kôt′ *or* so͝ok′əs) *n.* A Jewish harvest festival celebrated in the autumn and commemorating the huts in which the Israelites lived during their 40 years in the wilderness.

suffragist
suffragists picketing outside the White House, Washington, DC, in 1917

sulky

sumac

sumo

ă	pat	ôr	core
ā	pay	oi	boy
âr	care	ou	out
ä	father	o͝o	took
ĕ	pet	o͝or	lure
ē	be	o͞o	boot
ĭ	pit	ŭ	cut
ī	bite	ûr	urge
îr	pier	th	thin
ŏ	pot	*th*	this
ō	toe	zh	vision
ô	paw	ə	about

Su·la·we·si (so͞o′lä-**wā′**sē) also **Cel·e·bes** (**sĕl′**ə-bēz′ *or* sə-**lē′**bēz′) An irregularly shaped island of central Indonesia on the equator east of Borneo. The island is noted for its rare species of animals.

sul·fate (**sŭl′**fāt′) *n.* A compound, especially a salt, formed when sulfuric acid reacts with another substance. Epsom salt is a sulfate of magnesium. Gypsum is a sulfate of calcium.

sul·fide (**sŭl′**fīd′) *n.* A compound of sulfur having a valence of 2 with another element.

sul·fite (**sŭl′**fīt′) *n.* A salt or ester of sulfurous acid.

sul·fur also **sul·phur** (**sŭl′**fər) *n. Symbol* **S** A pale yellow nonmetallic element that is used in vulcanizing rubber and in making gunpowder, fertilizer, and medicines. Atomic number 16. See **Periodic Table.** [From Middle English *sulphur*, from Latin *sulfur*.]

sulfur dioxide *n.* A colorless, extremely irritating gas or liquid having the formula SO_2, used in many industrial processes, especially the manufacture of sulfuric acid.

sul·fu·ric (sŭl-**fyo͝or′**ĭk) *adj.* Relating to or containing sulfur, especially with a valence of 6.

sulfuric acid *n.* A strong acid having the formula H_2SO_4. Sulfuric acid combines easily with water, which makes it a good drying agent. It is the most widely used acid in industry.

sul·fur·ous also **sul·phur·ous** (**sŭl′**fər-əs) *adj.* Relating to or containing sulfur, especially with a valence of 4.

sulk (sŭlk) *intr.v.* **sulked, sulk·ing, sulks** To be sullenly silent or withdrawn. ❖ *n.* A mood or display of sullen silence or withdrawal.

sulk·y (**sŭl′**kē) *adj.* **sulk·i·er, sulk·i·est** Sullenly silent or withdrawn. ❖ *n., pl.* **sulk·ies** A light two-wheeled vehicle with room only for a driver and pulled by a single horse, especially in harness racing. [Perhaps from obsolete *sulke*, sluggish, perhaps from Old English *āseolcan*, to become sluggish.]

sul·len (**sŭl′**ən) *adj.* **sul·len·er, sul·len·est** Showing a brooding ill humor or resentment; morose: *a sullen disposition.* **—sul′len·ly** *adv.* **—sul′len·ness** *n.*

sul·ly (**sŭl′**ē) *tr.v.* **sul·lied, sul·ly·ing, sul·lies** To bring shame or dishonor upon: *sullied his reputation.*

sul·phur (**sŭl′**fər) *n.* Variant of **sulfur.**

sul·phur·ous (**sŭl′**fər-əs) *adj.* Variant of **sulfurous.**

sul·tan (**sŭl′**tən) *n.* A ruler of a Muslim country, especially of the former Ottoman Empire. [From Arabic *sulṭān*.]

sul·tan·a (sŭl-**tăn′**ə) *n.* **1.** The wife, mother, sister, or daughter of a sultan. **2.** A usually yellow seedless raisin.

sul·tan·ate (**sŭl′**tə-nāt′) *n.* **1.** The office, power, or reign of a sultan. **2.** A country ruled by a sultan.

sul·try (**sŭl′**trē) *adj.* **sul·tri·er, sul·tri·est** Very hot and humid: *a sultry summer day.*

sum (sŭm) *n.* **1.** A number obtained as a result of adding numbers. For example, 5 is the sum of 2 + 3. **2.** The whole amount, quantity, or number: *the sum of our knowledge.* **3.** An amount of money: *the sum of $10,000.* **4.** An arithmetic problem: *He's good at sums.* **5.** A summary: *That is my view, in sum.* ❖ *tr.v.* **summed, sum·ming, sums** To add (numbers). ◆ **sum up** To present (material) in a condensed form; summarize: *summed up the lecture in one paragraph.* [From Middle English *summe*, from Latin *summa*, from *summus*, highest.]

❑ *These sound alike:* **sum, some** (a few).

su·mac (**so͞o′**măk *or* **sho͞o′**măk) *n.* Any of various shrubs or small trees having feathery leaves and usually red, hairy fruit. Some kinds, such as the poison sumac, can cause an itching rash when touched.

Su·ma·tra (so͝o-**mä′**trə) An island of western Indonesia in the Indian Ocean south of the Malay Peninsula. It was an important stopping point on the trading route between China and India.

Su·mer (**so͞o′**mər) An ancient country of southern Mesopotamia in present-day southern Iraq. The Sumerians are believed to have invented cuneiform writing.

Su·me·ri·an (so͞o-**mîr′**ē-ən *or* so͞o-**mĕr′**ē-ən) *adj.* Relating to ancient Sumer or its people, language, or culture. ❖ *n.* **1.** A member of an ancient people whose civilization in Mesopotamia flourished around 3000 BC. **2.** The language of the Sumerians.

sum·ma cum lau·de (**so͝om′**ə ko͝om **lou′**də) *adv. & adj.* With the greatest academic honor: *She graduated summa cum laude from college.*

sum·mar·i·ly (sə-**mĕr′**ə-lē) *adv.* Speedily and without ceremony: *The dishonest cashier was summarily fired.*

sum·ma·rize (**sŭm′**ə-rīz′) *tr.v.* **sum·ma·rized, sum·ma·riz·ing, sum·ma·riz·es** To make a summary of; restate briefly: *summarized his views.* **—sum′ma·ri·za′tion** (sŭm′ər-ĭ-**zā′**shən) *n.*

sum·ma·ry (**sŭm′**ə-rē) *n., pl.* **sum·ma·ries** A brief statement mentioning the main points of something: *a summary of our findings.* ❖ *adj.* **1.** Presented in condensed form; brief. **2.** Done speedily and without ceremony: *a summary rejection of a proposal.*

❑ *These sound alike:* **summary, summery** (like summer).

sum·ma·tion (sə-**mā′**shən) *n.* **1a.** The act or process of adding; addition. **b.** A number obtained by adding; a sum. **2.** A concluding part of an argument containing a summary of the main points, especially in a court of law.

sum·mer (**sŭm′**ər) *n.* **1.** The warmest season of the year, occurring between spring and fall. In the Northern Hemisphere, it lasts from June until September. In the Southern Hemisphere, it lasts from December until March. **2.** The season extending from the summer solstice to the autumnal equinox. ❖ *intr.v.* **sum·mered, sum·mer·ing, sum·mers** To stay in a place for the summer: *They summered at a beach resort.* ❖ *adj.* Occurring in or appropriate to the summer: *a summer wedding; summer clothing.* [From Old English *sumor*.]

sum·mer·house (**sŭm′**ər-hous′) *n.* A small roofed structure in a park or garden, used for a shady place to rest.

summer school *n.* A session of school held during the summer vacation.

summer solstice *n.* **1.** In the Northern Hemisphere, the solstice that occurs on or about June 21, marking the beginning of summer. **2.** In the Southern Hemisphere, the solstice that occurs on or about December 21.

summer squash *n.* Any of several kinds of squash, such as the zucchini, that are eaten before the rind hardens.

sum·mer·time (**sŭm′**ər-tīm′) *n.* The summer season.

sum·mer·y (**sŭm′**ə-rē) *adj.* Relating to, intended for, or suggesting summer: *summery weather.*

❑ *These sound alike:* **summery, summary** (brief).

sum·mit (**sŭm′**ĭt) *n.* **1.** The highest point or part; the top, especially of a mountain. **2.** A conference or meeting of high-level leaders, usually called to construct a program of action. [From Middle English *somet*, from Old French *sommette*, from Latin *summus*, highest.]

sum·mon (**sŭm′**ən) *tr.v.* **sum·moned, sum·mon·ing, sum·mons 1.** To call together; convene: *summon a meeting of the delegates.* **2.** To send for; request to appear: *summoned a doctor to help the injured man.* **3.** To bring to mind or remember: *I summoned up an image of the house I grew up in.* **4.** To bring into existence, action, or effect; muster: *I summoned up my willpower not to laugh.* [From Middle English *somonden*, from Latin *summonēre*, to remind privately, hint to : *sub-*, secretly + *monēre*, to warn.]

sum·mons (**sŭm′**ənz) *n., pl.* **sum·mons·es 1.** A document ordering a defendant, witness, or juror to appear in court. **2.** A call or an order to appear or do something. ❖ *tr.v.* **sum·monsed, sum·mons·ing, sum·monsed** To order (someone) to appear in court by issuing a summons.

su·mo (so͞o′mō) *n.* A Japanese form of men's wrestling in which a competitor loses if forced from the ring or if he touches the ground other than with the soles of his feet.

sump (sŭmp) *n.* A pit or low-lying place that collects liquids.

sump·tu·ous (sŭmp′cho͞o-əs) *adj.* Of a size or splendor suggesting great expense; lavish: *a sumptuous feast.* [From Middle English, from Latin *sūmptus*, expense.] **—sump′tu·ous·ly** *adv.*

sun (sŭn) *n.* **1.** often **Sun** The star around which Earth and all of the planets and other bodies of the solar system orbit and that supplies the energy that sustains life on Earth. It has a diameter of about 865,000 miles (1,392,000 kilometers), a mass about 335,000 times that of Earth, and an average distance from Earth of about 93 million miles (150 million kilometers). See table at **solar system. 2.** A star that is the center of a system of planets. **3.** The radiation given off by the sun, especially infrared light, visible light, and ultraviolet light. ❖ *v.* **sunned, sun·ning, suns** *—tr.* To expose to the sun, as for warming, drying, or tanning. *—intr.* To bask in the sun; sunbathe. [From Old English *sunne.*]
❑ *These sound alike:* **sun, son** (male offspring).

sun·bathe (sŭn′bāth′) *intr.v.* **sun·bathed, sun·bath·ing, sun·bathes** To expose the body to the sun.

sun·beam (sŭn′bēm′) *n.* A ray of sunlight.

sun·block (sŭn′blŏk′) *n.* A chemical preparation that is applied to the skin to protect it from the ultraviolet rays of the sun.

sun·bon·net (sŭn′bŏn′ĭt) *n.* A woman's bonnet having a wide brim and a flap at the back to protect the neck from the sun.

sun·burn (sŭn′bûrn′) *n.* An inflammation or blistering of the skin caused by overexposure to the ultraviolet rays in sunlight. ❖ *tr.v.* **sun·burned** or **sun·burnt** (sŭn′-bûrnt′), **sun·burn·ing, sun·burns** To cause (someone) to have a sunburn.

sun·dae (sŭn′dē *or* sŭn′dā′) *n.* A dish of ice cream with toppings such as syrup, fruit, and nuts.

Sun·day (sŭn′dē *or* sŭn′dā′) *n.* The first day of the week. [From Old English *sunnandæg.*] **—Sun′days** *adv.*

Sunday school *n.* A school, usually associated with a church or synagogue, that provides religious education on Sundays.

sun·der (sŭn′dər) *v.* **sun·dered, sun·der·ing, sun·ders** *—tr.* To force or break apart: *A misunderstanding sundered their friendship. —intr.* To break into parts; come apart. [From Old English *sundrian.*]

sun·di·al (sŭn′dī′əl) *n.* An instrument that indicates the time of day by the shadow cast by a central pointer on a dial.

sun·down (sŭn′doun′) *n.* The time of sunset.

sun·dries (sŭn′drēz) *pl.n.* Miscellaneous articles; various things.

sun·dry (sŭn′drē) *adj.* Various; miscellaneous: *a drawer full of pens, paper clips, and sundry items.* [From Old English *syndrig*, separate.]

sun·fish (sŭn′fĭsh′) *n.* **1.** Any of various small North American freshwater fishes having a flat, often brightly colored body. **2.** Any of several large ocean fishes having a rounded short-tailed body.

sun·flow·er (sŭn′flou′ər) *n.* Any of several tall plants having large flower heads with yellow rays and dark centers and bearing edible seeds that are rich in oil.

sung (sŭng) *v.* A past tense and the past participle of **sing.**

sun·glass·es (sŭn′glăs′ĭz) *pl.n.* Eyeglasses having dark or partly reflective lenses to protect the eyes from the sun's glare.

sunk (sŭngk) *v.* A past tense and the past participle of **sink.**

sunk·en (sŭng′kən) *adj.* **1.** Fallen in or depressed: *sunken cheeks.* **2.** Situated beneath the surface of the water or ground; submerged: *a sunken reef.* **3.** Below the surrounding level: *a sunken bathtub.*

sun·lamp or **sun lamp** (sŭn′lămp′) *n.* **1.** A lamp that gives off radiation similar to that of sunlight, used in therapeutic and cosmetic treatments. **2.** A very bright lamp equipped with a reflector, used in photography.

sun·light (sŭn′līt′) *n.* The light of the sun.

sun·lit (sŭn′lĭt′) *adj.* Illuminated by the sun: *a sunlit prairie.*

Sun·na (so͝on′ə) *n.* The proper way of life in Islam, based on the teachings and practices of Muhammad and on the guidance of the Koran.

Sun·ni (so͝on′ē) *n.* The branch of Islam that accepts the first four caliphs as the rightful successors of Muhammad. **—Sun′ni** *adj.*

sun·ny (sŭn′ē) *adj.* **sun·ni·er, sun·ni·est 1.** Full of sunshine: *a sunny day.* **2.** Cheerful: *a sunny mood.*
❑ *These sound alike:* **sunny, sonny** (little boy).

sun·rise (sŭn′rīz′) *n.* **1.** The daily first appearance of the sun above the eastern horizon. **2.** The time at which this occurs.

sun·screen (sŭn′skrēn′) *n.* A cream or lotion used to protect the skin from the damaging ultraviolet rays of the sun.

sun·set (sŭn′sĕt′) *n.* **1.** The daily disappearance of the sun below the western horizon. **2.** The time at which this occurs.

sun·shade (sŭn′shād′) *n.* Something, such as an awning, used as protection from the sun.

sun·shine (sŭn′shīn′) *n.* **1.** The light of the sun; sunlight. **2.** Happiness or cheerfulness.

sun·spot (sŭn′spŏt′) *n.* Any of the dark spots that appear on the surface of the sun and that are associated with strong magnetic fields.

sun·stroke (sŭn′strōk′) *n.* Heat stroke caused by overexposure to the sun, characterized by a rise in body temperature that can lead to convulsions and coma.

sun·tan (sŭn′tăn′) *n.* A darkening of the skin resulting from exposure to the ultraviolet rays in sunlight. **—sun′tanned′** *adj.*

sun·up (sŭn′ŭp′) *n.* The time of sunrise.

Sun Yat-sen (so͝on′ yät′sĕn′) 1866–1925. Chinese politician who was influential in the overthrow of the last Chinese dynasty and served as the provisional president of the Republic of China (1911–1912).

sup¹ (sŭp) *tr. & intr.v.* **supped, sup·ping, sups** To eat or drink by taking small amounts. ❖ *n.* A small swallow or mouthful of liquid; a sip. [From Middle English *soupen*, from Old English *sūpan.*]

sup² (sŭp) *intr.v.* **supped, sup·ping, sups** To eat supper. [From Middle English *soupen*, from Old French *soupe*, soup.]

su·per (so͞o′pər) *Informal n.* A superintendent in a building. ❖ *adj.* **1.** Very large, great, or extreme: *a super skyscraper.* **2.** Excellent: *a super party.*

super– *pref.* A prefix that means: **1.** Above; over; upon: *superimpose.* **2.** Superior in size, quality, number, or degree: *superhuman.* **3.** Exceeding a standard or norm: *supersonic.* **4.** Excessive in degree or intensity: *supersensitive.*

su·per·a·bun·dant (so͞o′pər-ə-bŭn′dənt) *adj.* More than sufficient; excessive: *superabundant zeal.* **—su′per·a·bun′dance** *n.*

su·per·an·nu·at·ed (so͞o′pər-ăn′yo͞o-ā′tĭd) *adj.* **1.** Retired or ineffective because of advanced age. **2.** Outdated; obsolete: *superannuated laws.*

su·perb (so͞o-pûrb′) *adj.* **1.** Of unusually high quality; excellent: *a superb meal.* **2.** Majestic; imposing: *a superb view.* [From Latin *superbus*, arrogant, superior.] **—su·perb′ly** *adv.*

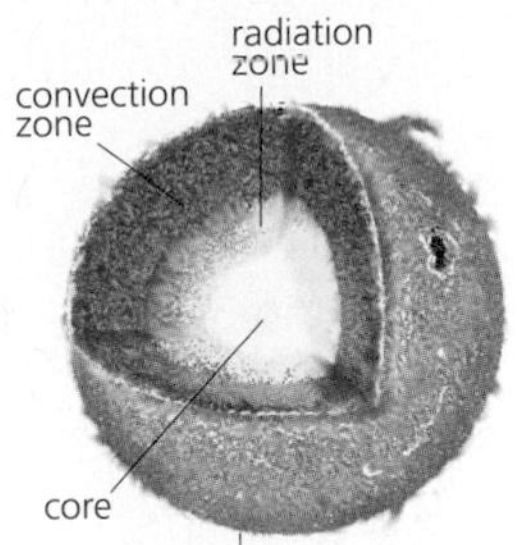

sun

sundial

sunflower

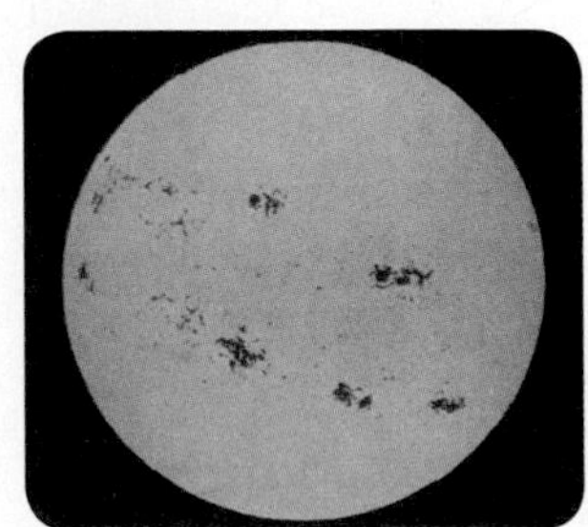
sunspot

su·per·charge (so͞o′pər-chärj′) *tr.v.* **su·per·charged, su·per·charg·ing, su·per·charg·es** To increase the power of (an internal-combustion engine) with a supercharger.

su·per·charg·er (**so͞o′**pər-chär′jər) *n.* A device that forces air under high pressure into the cylinders of an internal-combustion engine, thereby increasing power.

su·per·cil·i·ous (so͞o′pər-**sĭl′**ē-əs) *adj.* Feeling or showing arrogant disdain; haughty: *a supercilious smile.* [From Latin *supercilium*, eyebrow, pride : *super-*, above + *cilium*, lower eyelid.] **—su′per·cil′i·ous·ly** *adv.*

su·per·com·put·er (**so͞o′**pər-kəm-pyo͞o′tər) *n.* A mainframe computer that is among the largest, fastest, or most powerful of those available at a given time.

su·per·con·duc·tiv·i·ty (so͞o′pər-kŏn′dŭk-**tĭv′**ĭ-tē) *n.* The flow of electric current without resistance in certain metals, alloys, and ceramics at temperatures ranging from absolute zero to about 100 kelvin.

su·per·con·duc·tor (**so͞o′**pər-kən-dŭk′tər) *n.* A substance that at a very low temperature conducts electric current without resistance.

su·per·con·ti·nent (**so͞o′**pər-kŏn′tə-nənt) *n.* A large continent that is thought to have split into smaller continents in the geologic past.

su·per·cool (so͞o′pər-**ko͞ol′**) *tr.v.* **su·per·cooled, su·per·cool·ing, su·per·cools 1.** To cool (a liquid) below its freezing point without causing solidification. **2.** To cool (a gas) below its boiling point without causing condensation.

su·per·e·rog·a·to·ry (so͞o′pər-ĭ-**rŏg′**ə-tôr′ē) *adj.* **1.** Performed or observed beyond the required or expected degree. **2.** Unnecessary; superfluous.

su·per·fi·cial (so͞o′pər-**fĭsh′**əl) *adj.* **1.** Relating to, affecting, or being on or near the surface: *a superficial wound.* **2.** Concerned only with what is apparent or obvious; shallow: *a superficial person.* **3.** Not extensive or important; minor or insignificant: *superficial changes to the script.* [From Middle English, from Latin *superficiēs*, surface.] **—su′per·fi′ci·al′i·ty** (so͞o′pər-fĭsh′ē-**ăl′**ĭ-tē) *n.* **—su′per·fi′cial·ly** *adv.*

su·per·fine (so͞o′pər-**fīn′**) *adj.* **1.** Of exceptional quality; excellent. **2.** Excessively delicate or refined: *a superfine distinction.* **3.** Having extremely fine texture: *superfine sandpaper.*

su·per·flu·i·ty (so͞o′pər-**flo͞o′**ĭ-tē) *n., pl.* **su·per·flu·i·ties 1.** The quality or condition of being superfluous. **2.** Something superfluous.

su·per·flu·ous (so͞o-**pûr′**flo͞o-əs) *adj.* Being beyond what is required or sufficient: *Many items on the budget are superfluous.* **—su·per′flu·ous·ly** *adv.*

su·per·heat (so͞o′pər-**hēt′**) *tr.v.* **su·per·heat·ed, su·per·heat·ing, su·per·heats 1.** To heat excessively; overheat. **2.** To heat (steam or other vapor) that is already at its boiling point for a given pressure. **3.** To heat (a liquid) above its boiling point without causing vaporization. ❖ *n.* (**so͞o′**pər-hēt′) The heat that something absorbs when superheated.

su·per·high frequency (**so͞o′**pər-hī′) *n.* A radio-wave frequency between 3,000 and 30,000 megahertz.

su·per·high·way (so͞o′pər-**hī′**wā′) *n.* An expressway.

su·per·hu·man (so͞o′pər-**hyo͞o′**mən) *adj.* **1.** Beyond what is human; divine or supernatural: *superhuman beings.* **2.** Beyond ordinary or normal human ability or power.

su·per·im·pose (so͞o′pər-ĭm-**pōz′**) *tr.v.* **su·per·im·posed, su·per·im·pos·ing, su·per·im·pos·es** To lay or place (something) over or upon something else.

su·per·in·tend (so͞o′pər-ĭn-**tĕnd′** *or* so͞o′prĭn-**tĕnd′**) *tr.v.* **su·per·in·tend·ed, su·per·in·tend·ing, su·per·in·tends** To have charge of; oversee; supervise. **—su′per·in·ten′dence** *n.*

su·per·in·ten·dent (so͞o′pər-ĭn-**tĕn′**dənt *or* so͞o′prĭn-**tĕn′**dənt) *n.* **1.** A person who supervises or is in charge of something. **2.** A janitor or custodian, as in an apartment building.

su·pe·ri·or (so͞o-**pîr′**ē-ər) *adj.* **1.** Higher than another in rank, station, or authority: *a superior court; a superior officer.* **2.** Higher in quality or nature: *a superior product.* **3.** Excellent; extraordinary. **4.** Larger or more numerous than another: *an army defeated by the enemy's superior numbers.* **5.** Morally or socially better than others: *What makes him feel so superior?* ❖ *n.* **1.** A person who surpasses another in rank or quality. **2.** The head of religious community, such as a monastery or convent. [From Middle English, from Latin, from *super*, over.]

Superior, Lake The largest and westernmost of the Great Lakes, between the north-central United States and southern Ontario, Canada.

su·pe·ri·or·i·ty (so͞o-pîr′ē-**ôr′**ĭ-tē) *n.* The fact or quality of being superior.

su·per·la·tive (so͞o-**pûr′**lə-tĭv) *adj.* **1.** Of the highest order, quality, or degree: *a superlative specimen.* **2.** In grammar, relating to the extreme degree of comparison of an adjective or adverb, as in *best, brightest,* or *most comfortable.* ❖ *n.* **1.** In grammar, the superlative degree of an adjective or adverb. **2.** An adjective or adverb expressing the superlative degree. *Brightest* is the superlative of the adjective *bright,* and *most brightly* is the superlative of the adverb *brightly.* **—su·per′la·tive·ly** *adv.* **—su·per′la·tive·ness** *n.*

su·per·man (**so͞o′**pər-măn′) *n.* A man with superhuman powers.

su·per·mar·ket (**so͞o′**pər-mär′kĭt) *n.* A large self-service retail store that sells food and other household supplies.

su·per·nat·u·ral (so͞o′pər-**năch′**ər-əl) *adj.* **1.** Relating to existence outside the natural world; spiritual or divine. **2.** Relating to actions or events regarded as violating the laws of nature. ❖ *n.* Supernatural phenomena and beings: *belief in the supernatural.*

su·per·no·va (so͞o′pər-**nō′**və) *n., pl.* **su·per·no·vae** (so͞o′pər-**nō′**vē) or **su·per·no·vas** A massive star that explodes, brightening suddenly and releasing an enormous burst of energy for a short time.

su·per·nu·mer·ar·y (so͞o′pər-**no͞o′**mə-rĕr′ē) *adj.* Exceeding a fixed or required number; extra. ❖ *n., pl.* **su·per·nu·mer·ar·ies 1.** A person or thing that is in excess of the regular or required number. **2.** An actor who has no speaking part in a play or movie: *She was a supernumerary in the crowd scene.*

su·per·pow·er (**so͞o′**pər-pou′ər) *n.* A country that has great military power and often economic and cultural influence over other countries around the world.

su·per·sat·u·rate (so͞o′pər-**săch′**ə-rāt′) *tr.v.* **su·per·sat·u·rat·ed, su·per·sat·u·rat·ing, su·per·sat·u·rates 1.** To cause (a chemical solution) to be more concentrated than is normally possible under given conditions. **2.** To cause (a vapor) to remain gaseous under conditions where condensation would normally occur.

su·per·script (**so͞o′**pər-skrĭpt′) *n.* A character written or printed just above and to one side of another character. For example, in the equation $e = mc^2$, the superscript is 2. **—su′per·script′** *adj.*

su·per·sede (so͞o′pər-**sēd′**) *tr.v.* **su·per·sed·ed, su·per·sed·ing, su·per·sedes** To take the place of; replace or supplant: *Electric light bulbs superseded candles and kerosene lamps as the major source of indoor light.*

su·per·son·ic (so͞o′pər-**sŏn′**ĭk) *adj.* Relating to, traveling at, or caused by a speed greater than the speed of sound in a given medium, especially air.

supersonic transport *n.* An aircraft designed to carry passengers or cargo at supersonic speeds.

su·per·star (**so͞o′**pər-stär′) *n.* A widely acclaimed performer, as in films, music, or sports.

su·per·sti·tion (so͞o′pər-**stĭsh′**ən) *n.* **1.** A belief that

ă	pat	ôr	core
ā	pay	oi	boy
âr	care	ou	out
ä	father	o͝o	took
ĕ	pet	o͝or	lure
ē	be	o͞o	boot
ĭ	pit	ŭ	cut
ī	bite	ûr	urge
îr	pier	th	thin
ŏ	pot	*th*	this
ō	toe	zh	vision
ô	paw	ə	about

some object, action, or circumstance not logically related to a course of events influences its outcome: *the superstition that four-leafed clovers bring good luck.* **2.** An action or practice that is based on faith in magic or chance: *the superstition of knocking on wood to avoid bad luck.*

su·per·sti·tious (so͞o′pər-**stĭsh′**əs) *adj.* **1.** Inclined to believe in superstition: *a superstitious person.* **2.** Relating to superstition: *a superstitious fear of Friday the 13th.* **—su′per·sti′tious·ly** *adv.* **—su′per·sti′tious·ness** *n.*

su·per·struc·ture (**so͞o′**pər-strŭk′chər) *n.* **1.** The part of a building that is above the foundation. **2.** The parts of a ship that are above the main deck.

su·per·tank·er (**so͞o′**pər-tăng′kər) *n.* A very large ship used for transporting oil and other liquids in large quantities.

su·per·vene (so͞o′pər-**vēn′**) *intr.v.* **su·per·vened, su·per·ven·ing, su·per·venes 1.** To come or occur as something additional or unexpected. **2.** To follow immediately after; ensue.

su·per·vise (**so͞o′**pər-vīz′) *tr.v.* **su·per·vised, su·per·vis·ing, su·per·vis·es** To direct, oversee, and manage: *She supervises a staff of chemists. Who supervises your work?* [From Medieval Latin *supervīsus*, past participle of *supervidēre* : Latin *super-*, over + Latin *vidēre*, to see.]

su·per·vi·sion (so͞o′pər-**vĭzh′**ən) *n.* The act or process of supervising; control; direction.

su·per·vi·sor (**so͞o′**pər-vī′zər) *n.* A person who supervises.

su·per·vi·so·ry (so͞o′pər-**vī′**zə-rē) *adj.* Relating to supervision or a supervisor: *She works in a supervisory capacity.*

su·perwom·an (**so͞o′**pər-wo͝om′ən) *n.* A woman with more than human powers.

su·pine (**so͞o′**pīn′) *adj.* **1.** Lying on the back or having the face upward. **2.** Not inclined to act; lethargic; passive.

sup·per (**sŭp′**ər) *n.* **1.** An evening meal, especially dinner when eaten in the evening. **2.** A social gathering at which supper is served. [From Middle English *sopere*, from Old French *souper*, to sup.]

sup·plant (sə-**plănt′**) *tr.v.* **sup·plant·ed, sup·plant·ing, sup·plants** To take the place of; supersede: *Computers have supplanted the typewriter.*

sup·ple (**sŭp′**əl) *adj.* **sup·pler, sup·plest 1.** Easily bent or folded: *a wallet made of supple leather.* **2.** Moving easily; agile; limber: *a supple body.* **3.** Yielding or changing easily; adaptable: *a supple mind.* [From Middle English *souple*, from Latin *supplex*, suppliant.] **—sup′ple·ly** *adv.* **—sup′ple·ness** *n.*

sup·ple·ment (**sŭp′**lə-mənt) *n.* **1.** Something added to complete a thing, make up for a deficiency, or extend or strengthen the whole: *This book is a supplement to the regular required reading.* **2.** A section added to a newspaper, book, or document to give further information. **3.** A supplementary angle. ❖ *tr.v.* (**sŭp′**lə-mĕnt′) **sup·ple·ment·ed, sup·ple·ment·ing, sup·ple·ments** To provide a supplement to: *The teacher supplemented our reading with films.*

sup·ple·men·ta·ry (sŭp′lə-**mĕn′**tə-rē *or* sŭp′lə-**mĕn′**trē) *adj.* Added or serving as a supplement; additional: *supplementary information.*

supplementary angle *n.* One of a pair of angles whose sum is 180 degrees.

sup·pli·ant (**sŭp′**lē-ənt) *adj.* Asking humbly and earnestly; beseeching: *a suppliant beggar.* ❖ *n.* A supplicant.

sup·pli·cant (**sŭp′**lĭ-kənt) *n.* A person who supplicates. ❖ *adj.* Supplicating.

sup·pli·cate (**sŭp′**lĭ-kāt′) *tr.v.* **sup·pli·cat·ed, sup·pli·cat·ing, sup·pli·cates 1.** To ask for humbly or earnestly, as by praying. **2.** To make an earnest appeal to; beseech: *supplicated his captors for mercy.* **—sup′pli·ca′tion** *n.*

sup·ply (sə-**plī′**) *tr.v.* **sup·plied, sup·ply·ing, sup·plies 1.** To make available for use; provide: *Most hotels supply towels for their guests.* **2.** To furnish or equip with something: *supply the players with uniforms.* **3.** To fill sufficiently; satisfy: *supply a need.* ❖ *n., pl.* **sup·plies 1.** The act of supplying: *The funds covered transport and supply of the explorers.* **2.** An amount available or adequate for a given use; stock: *Our supply of milk is low.* **3.** often **supplies** Materials or provisions stored and dispensed when needed: *paint, brushes, and other art supplies.* [From Middle English *supplien*, from Latin *supplēre*, to fill up : *sub-*, from below + *plēre*, to fill.] **—sup·pli′er** *n.*

sup·port (sə-**pôrt′**) *tr.v.* **sup·port·ed, sup·port·ing, sup·ports 1.** To bear the weight of, especially from below; keep from falling, sinking, or slipping: *beams that support the floor joists; supported the baby's head with his hand.* **2.** To be capable of bearing; withstand: *This elevator won't support more than 300 pounds.* **3.** To provide for by supplying with money or other necessities: *She supports two children.* **4.** To give confidence, comfort, or strength to: *supported his friend during a crisis.* **5.** To provide evidence for; show to be true: *The experiment supports his theory.* **6.** To approve or argue for; favor: *support a political candidate; support gun control laws.* **7.** To act in a secondary or subordinate role to (a leading performer). ❖ *n.* **1.** The act, process, or fact of supporting: *The pillars provide support for the roof.* **2.** A person or thing that supports: *The bridge has four main supports.* **3.** The provision of money or the necessities of life: *a letter asking for financial support.* [From Middle English *supporten*, from Latin *supportāre*, to carry : *sub-*, from below + *portāre*, to carry.]

sup·port·a·ble (sə-**pôr′**tə-bəl) *adj.* Bearable; endurable. **—sup·port′a·bly** *adv.*

sup·port·er (sə-**pôr′**tər) *n.* **1.** A person or thing that supports. **2.** A person who promotes or favors someone or something; an advocate: *the candidate's loyal supporters.* **3.** An athletic supporter.

sup·por·tive (sə-**pôr′**tĭv) *adj.* Providing support or assistance.

sup·pose (sə-**pōz′**) *tr.v.* **sup·posed, sup·pos·ing, sup·pos·es 1.** To assume to be true or real for the sake of an argument or illustration: *Suppose we were rich.* **2.** To believe, especially on uncertain grounds: *I suppose you've already had lunch.* **3.** To consider as a suggestion: *Suppose we stop and rest a minute.* [From Middle English *supposen*, from Old French *supposer*, from Latin *suppōnere*, to put under.]

sup·posed (sə-**pōzd′**) *adj.* **1.** (*also* sə-**pō′**zĭd) Presumed to be true or real; reputed: *the supposed model for a fictional character.* **2.** (*often* sə-**pōst′**) **a.** Intended or imagined: *a medicine that is supposed to relieve pain.* **b.** Required: *He's supposed to be at school.* **c.** Permitted: *We are not supposed to be here at night.* **d.** Believed; expected: *You're supposed to be my friend.* **—sup·pos′ed·ly** (sə-**pō′**zĭd-lē) *adv.*

sup·po·si·tion (sŭp′ə-**zĭsh′**ən) *n.* **1.** The act of supposing: *an argument based on supposition, not fact.* **2.** Something supposed; an assumption: *made plans based on the supposition of good weather.*

sup·pos·i·to·ry (sə-**pŏz′**ĭ-tôr′ē) *n., pl.* **sup·pos·i·to·ries** A medication prepared in a solid form, designed to be inserted into a body cavity other than the mouth, especially in the rectum or vagina.

sup·press (sə-**prĕs′**) *tr.v.* **sup·pressed, sup·press·ing, sup·press·es 1.** To put an end to forcibly; subdue; crush: *suppress a rebellion.* **2.** To restrict or forbid the activities of: *The government was accused of suppressing the opposition party.* **3.** To keep from being revealed or published: *suppress news of the leader's illness.* **4.** To keep back, restrain; check: *suppress a laugh.* [From Middle

supertanker

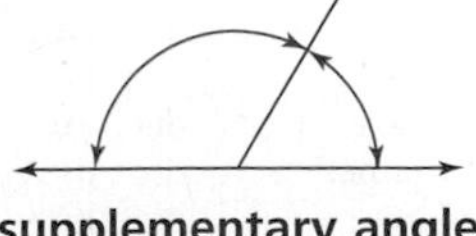

supplementary angle
Each of the two angles shown is a supplementary angle to the other one.

English *suppresen,* from Latin *supprimere* : *sub-,* down + *premere,* to press.]

sup·pres·sion (sə-prĕsh′ən) *n.* **1.** The act of suppressing. **2.** The condition of being suppressed.

sup·pu·rate (sŭp′yə-rāt′) *intr.v.* **sup·pu·rat·ed, sup·pu·rat·ing, sup·pu·rates** To form or fill with pus: *The infected wound suppurated.* **—sup′pu·ra′tion** *n.*

su·prem·a·cy (so͝o-prĕm′ə-sē) *n., pl.* **su·prem·a·cies 1.** The quality or condition of being supreme: *a struggle for supremacy between two colonial powers.* **2.** Supreme power or authority.

su·preme (so͝o-prēm′) *adj.* **1.** Greatest in power, authority, or rank; dominant over others: *a supreme commander.* **2.** Greatest in importance, degree, significance, character, or achievement: *supreme intelligence.* **3.** Ultimate; final: *the supreme sacrifice.* **—su·preme′ly** *adv.*

Supreme Being *n.* God.

Supreme Court *n.* **1.** The highest federal court in the United States, consisting of nine justices and having legal authority over all other courts in the nation. **2. supreme court** The highest court in most states within the United States.

Supreme Soviet *n.* The legislature of the former Soviet Union, consisting of two houses, one whose members were elected from the population as a whole and another whose members were elected by the national republics of the Soviet Union.

Supt. *abbr.* An abbreviation of superintendent.

sur·cease (sûr′sēs′ *or* sər-sēs′) *tr. & intr.v.* **sur·ceased, sur·ceas·ing, sur·ceas·es** To bring or come to an end; stop. ❖ *n.* Cessation: *He talked without surcease.*

sur·charge (sûr′chärj′) *n.* **1.** An additional sum added to the usual amount or cost. **2.** An additional or excessive burden; an overload: *words carrying a surcharge of emotion.* ❖ *tr.v.* **sur·charged, sur·charg·ing, sur·charg·es 1.** To charge (a person) an additional sum. **2.** To overload or overburden: *clouds that are surcharged with rain; a person who is surcharged with guilt.* —SEE NOTE AT **sirloin.**

surfing

sur·coat (sûr′kōt′) *n.* **1.** A loose outer coat or gown. **2.** A tunic worn in the Middle Ages by a knight over his armor.

sure (sho͝or *or* shûr) *adj.* **sur·er, sur·est 1.** Confident, as of something awaited or expected: *I'm sure the package will come today.* **2.** Impossible to doubt or dispute; certain: *sure proof of her innocence.* **3.** Bound or destined to happen: *a sure victory for the team.* **4.** Steady; unwavering; firm: *a sure hold on the suitcase.* **5.** Dependable; reliable: *The surest way of seeing that something gets done right is to do it yourself.* **6.** Careful to do something: *Be sure to brush your teeth.* ❖ *adv. Informal* Surely; certainly. ◆ **for sure** *Informal* Certainly; unquestionably: *We'll win today for sure.* **make sure** To make certain; establish something without doubt: *I think the movie starts at 5:00, but I'll call to make sure.* **to be sure** Indeed; certainly. [From Middle English *seur,* from Latin *sēcūrus.*] **—sure′ness** *n.*

sure-fire (sho͝or′fīr′) *adj. Informal* Bound to be successful or perform as expected: *a sure-fire solution to the problem.*

sure-foot·ed or **sure·foot·ed** (sho͝or′fo͝ot′ĭd) *adj.* **1.** Not likely to stumble or fall: *a sure-footed mule.* **2.** Confident and capable. **—sure′foot′ed·ness** *n.*

sure·ly (sho͝or′lē) *adv.* **1.** Certainly; without doubt: *Surely you can't be serious.* **2.** Without fail: *Slowly but surely spring returns.*

sure thing *n.* An outcome that is assured; a certainty. ❖ *interj. Informal* Of course; certainly: *Are you coming? Sure thing!*

sur·e·ty (sho͝or′ĭ-tē) *n., pl.* **sur·e·ties 1.** The condition of being sure, especially of oneself; self-assurance. **2.** Something beyond a doubt; a certainty. **3.** A formal promise or pledge to take responsibility in case of loss or damage; a security. **4.** A person who agrees to be responsible if another does not pay a debt or fulfill a promise.

surf (sûrf) *n.* The waves of the sea as they break upon a shore or reef. ❖ *v.* **surfed, surf·ing, surfs** *—intr.* **1.** To ride on a surfboard. **2.** *Informal* To look at a variety of things casually, especially while browsing the Internet or television channels. *—tr.* **1.** To ride on or along (a wave) on a surfboard. **2.** *Informal* To browse (the Internet or television channels, for example).

❑ *These sound alike:* **surf, serf** (slave).

sur·face (sûr′fəs) *n.* **1a.** The outermost layer or boundary of an object: *the surface of a plate; the surface of the moon.* **b.** A material layer that makes up such a boundary. **2.** The outward or superficial appearance: *On the surface, the house looked new.* **3a.** A portion of space that has length and breadth but no thickness. **b.** The boundary of a three-dimensional geometric figure. ❖ *v.* **sur·faced, sur·fac·ing, sur·fac·es** *—tr.* To provide with a surface or apply a surface to: *surfaced the driveway with asphalt.* *—intr.* **1.** To rise to the surface, as of a body of water. **2.** To emerge after being hidden: *She knew the lost book would surface when she cleaned her room.* [From French : *sur-,* above + *face,* face.]

surface tension *n.* A property of liquids that makes their surfaces behave as if they were covered by a thin, elastic film. Surface tension is caused by the uneven attraction that molecules at or near the surface of a liquid have for each other.

surf·board (sûrf′bôrd′) *n.* A long narrow board used for surfing. **—surf′board′** *v.*

sur·feit (sûr′fĭt) *tr.v.* **sur·feit·ed, sur·feit·ing, sur·feits** To feed or supply to excess; satiate. ❖ *n.* **1a.** Indulgence in something, such as food, to excess. **b.** A result of such overindulgence; a feeling of fullness or disgust. **2.** An excessive amount.

surf·er (sûr′fər) *n.* A person who surfs.

surf·ing (sûr′fĭng) *n.* The sport of riding waves, especially while standing or lying on a surfboard.

surge (sûrj) *intr.v.* **surged, surg·ing, surg·es 1.** To rise and move in a billowing or swelling manner. **2.** To roll or be tossed about on waves, as a boat. **3.** To move like advancing waves: *The crowd surged forward.* **4.** To increase suddenly: *Excitement surged through his veins.* ❖ *n.* **1.** A powerful wave or swell of water. **2.** A heavy swelling motion like that of great waves. **3a.** A sudden onrush or increase: *a surge of excitement.* **b.** A sudden increase or change in electric current or voltage. [From Latin *surgere,* to rise.]

❑ *These sound alike:* **surge, serge** (cloth).

sur·geon (sûr′jən) *n.* A doctor specializing in surgery.

Surgeon General *n., pl.* **Surgeons General 1.** The chief medical officer in the US Public Health Service. **2.** The chief medical officer of the US Army, Navy, or Air Force.

surge protector *n.* A device that protects equipment plugged into it from a surge in electric current.

sur·ger·y (sûr′jə-rē) *n., pl.* **sur·ger·ies 1.** The branch of medicine that deals with the diagnosis and treatment of injuries, deformities, or diseases by examining, removing, or repairing the affected part or parts after cutting into the body. **2.** A surgical operation or procedure, especially one involving the removal or replacement of a diseased organ or tissue. **3.** An operating room or a laboratory of a surgeon or surgical staff: *He's in surgery right now.* [From Middle English *cirurgie,* from Greek *kheirourgiā* : *kheir,* hand + *ourgos,* working.]

sur·gi·cal (sûr′jĭ-kəl) *adj.* **1.** Relating to or characteristic of surgeons or surgery: *surgical instruments.* **2.** Extremely accurate; precise: *surgical air strikes.* **—sur′gi·cal·ly** *adv.*

Su·ri·na·me (so͝o′rə-nä′mə) A country of northeast

ă	pat	ôr	core
ā	pay	oi	boy
âr	care	ou	out
ä	father	o͝o	took
ĕ	pet	o͝or	lure
ē	be	o͞o	boot
ĭ	pit	ŭ	cut
ī	bite	ûr	urge
îr	pier	th	thin
ŏ	pot	*th*	this
ō	toe	zh	vision
ô	paw	ə	about

South America on the Atlantic Ocean west of French Guiana. Paramaribo is the capital.

sur·ly (sûr′lē) *adj.* **sur·li·er, sur·li·est** Ill-humored; gruff; sullen. —**sur′li·ness** *n.*

sur·mise (sər-**mīz′**) *tr.v.* **sur·mised, sur·mis·ing, sur·mis·es** To conclude or infer (something) on slight evidence; suppose: *Astronomers surmise that there may be life elsewhere in the universe.* ❖ *n.* An idea or opinion based on slight evidence; a guess.

sur·mount (sər-**mount′**) *tr.v.* **sur·mount·ed, sur·mount·ing, sur·mounts 1.** To climb up and over: *surmount a hill.* **2.** To overcome; triumph over: *surmount a weakness.* **3.** To be placed or located above; top: *A weathervane surmounted the steeple.*

sur·name (**sûr′**nām′) *n.* A name shared in common to identify the members of a family. —SEE NOTE AT **sirloin.**

sur·pass (sər-**păs′**) *tr.v.* **sur·passed, sur·pass·ing, sur·pass·es 1.** To be better than (someone) in an accomplishment or ability: *surpassed her classmates in academic honors.* **2.** To be or go beyond, as in degree or quality; exceed: *The success of the program surpassed their expectations.*

sur·pass·ing (sər-**păs′**ĭng) *adj.* Excellent; exceeding: *surpassing skill as a painter.*

sur·plice (**sûr′**plĭs) *n.* A loose-fitting white garment with full flowing sleeves, worn over a cleric's cassock in certain churches.

sur·plus (**sûr′**pləs *or* **sûr′**plŭs′) *adj.* Being more than or in excess of what is needed or required: *Surplus grain is usually sold abroad or stored.* ❖ *n.* An amount or quantity in excess of what is needed. [From Middle English, from Medieval Latin *superplūs* : Latin *super-*, over + Latin *plūs*, more.]

sur·prise (sər-**prīz′**) *tr.v.* **sur·prised, sur·pris·ing, sur·pris·es 1.** To cause to feel wonder, astonishment, or amazement, as at something unexpected: *Thinking I was sick at home, she was surprised to see me at school.* **2.** To come upon suddenly or find unexpectedly; catch unawares: *She surprised me late at night as I was getting another piece of pie.* **3.** To attack or capture suddenly and without warning: *The police surprised the suspects in a raid on their hideout.* ❖ *n.* **1.** The act of surprising or the condition of being surprised: *Imagine our surprise on finding that the test had been canceled.* **2.** Something, such as an attack, a gift, or an event, that surprises. [From Middle English *surprisen*, to overcome, from Old French *surprendre*, to surprise : *sur-*, over + *prendre*, to take.] —**sur·pris′ing·ly** *adv.*

SYNONYMS surprise, astonish, amaze, astound These verbs mean to affect a person strongly as being unexpected or unusual. **Surprise** means to fill with often sudden wonder or disbelief: *I surprised my friend with an unexpected party.* **Astonish** means to overwhelm with surprise: *The sight of such an enormous crowd astonished us.* **Amaze** means to affect with great wonder: *The violinist's skill amazed the audience.* **Astound** means to shock with surprise: *They were astounded by the waiter's rudeness.*

---

sur·real (sə-**rēl′**) *adj.* **1.** Having qualities attributed to or associated with surrealism. **2.** Having an oddly dreamlike quality. —**sur·real′ly** *adv.*

sur·re·al·ism (sə-**rē′**ə-lĭz′əm) *n.* **1.** A literary and artistic movement of the 1900s attempting to depict dreams and other products of the unconscious mind. **2.** Literature or art produced in this style. —**sur·re′al·ist** *adj. & n.*

sur·re·al·is·tic (sə-rē′ə-**lĭs′**tĭk) *adj.* **1.** Relating to surrealism. **2.** Having a dreamlike or unreal quality. —**sur·re′al·is′ti·cal·ly** *adv.*

sur·ren·der (sə-**rĕn′**dər) *v.* **sur·ren·dered, sur·ren·der·ing, sur·ren·ders** —*tr.* **1.** To give up or hand over (something) to another on demand or under pressure: *surrendered his passport to the official; surrendered the coast to the invading army.* See Synonyms at **yield. 2.** To give over (oneself) entirely to something such as an emotion, influence, or effort. —*intr.* To submit to the power of another or a group, especially after resisting; give up: *The general expected the enemy to surrender as soon as they saw they were outnumbered.* ❖ *n.* The act or an instance of surrendering: *Lee's surrender to Grant took place on April 9, 1865.* [From Middle English *surrendren*, from Old French *surrendre* : *sur-*, over + *rendre*, to deliver.]

sur·rep·ti·tious (sûr′əp-**tĭsh′**əs) *adj.* Obtained, done, or made in secret; stealthy: *a surreptitious glance at the clock on the wall.* —**sur′rep·ti′tious·ly** *adv.* —**sur′rep·ti′tious·ness** *n.*

sur·rey (**sûr′**ē) *n., pl.* **sur·reys** A four-wheeled horse-drawn carriage having two to four seats.

surrey

sur·ro·gate (**sûr′**ə-gĭt *or* **sûr′**ə-gāt′) *n.* **1.** A person or thing that takes the place of another; a substitute. **2.** A judge in some states having jurisdiction over the probate of wills and settlement of estates. ❖ *adj.* Substitute: *a surrogate parent.*

surrogate mother *n.* A woman who carries and gives birth to a child for someone else. The child develops either from her own egg or from another woman's fertilized egg that has been implanted in her uterus.

sur·round (sə-**round′**) *tr.v.* **sur·round·ed, sur·round·ing, sur·rounds 1.** To extend on all sides of; encircle: *the field of gravitation surrounding the earth; the hills that surround the rural town.* **2.** To shut in or enclose on all sides so as to prevent escape or outside communication. [From Middle English *surrounden*, to inundate, from Late Latin *superundāre* : Latin *super-*, over + Latin *unda*, wave.]

sur·round·ings (sə-**roun′**dĭngz) *pl.n.* The things and circumstances that affect and surround one; environment.

sur·tax (**sûr′**tăks′) *n.* An additional tax.

sur·veil·lance (sər-**vā′**ləns) *n.* **1.** Close observation of a person or group, especially one under suspicion. **2.** The act of observing or the condition of being observed.

sur·vey (sər-**vā′** *or* **sûr′**vā′) *v.* **sur·veyed, sur·vey·ing, sur·veys** —*tr.* **1.** To look over the parts or features of; view broadly: *surveyed the neighborhood from a rooftop.* **2.** To inspect or examine carefully: *surveyed the damage done by the storm.* **3.** To determine the area, boundaries, or elevation of (land or features of the earth's surface) by measuring angles and distances and using geometry and trigonometry. **4.** To gather data from (people) or about (people's attitudes or opinions) by asking a series of questions: *surveyed students on their opinions about homework.* —*intr.* To make a survey. ❖ *n.* (**sûr′**vā′) *pl.* **sur·veys 1.** A general view or investigation of something: *The discussion will begin with a survey of contemporary rock music.* **2.** A gathering of data, such as opinions, from a relatively small group that represents a larger group: *conducted a survey of 1,000 Americans.* **3a.** The act or process of surveying a piece of land. **b.** A map or report of what has been surveyed. [From Middle English *surveien*, from Medieval Latin *supervidēre* : Latin *super-*, over + Latin *vidēre*, to look.]

sur·vey·ing (sər-**vā′**ĭng) *n.* The measurement of features on the earth's surface, especially for use in mapmaking and locating property boundaries.

sur·vey·or (sər-**vā′**ər) *n.* A person whose work is surveying land.

sur·viv·al (sər-**vī′**vəl) *n.* **1a.** The act or process of surviving. **b.** The fact of having survived. **2.** A person or thing that has survived: *a custom that is a survival of an ancient tradition.*

sur·vive (sər-**vīv′**) *v.* **sur·vived, sur·viv·ing, sur·vives**

sushi

suspension bridge
Golden Gate Bridge, San Francisco, California

WRITERS CHOOSE THEIR WORDS

The front door of Tito's building opened, and a stocky man filled it. He put his thumbs in his belt and looked from side to side. Then he hunched his shoulders twice and came down the stairs. Jamal watched him **swagger** down the street.

—Walter Dean Myers
Scorpions

ă	pat	ôr	core
ā	pay	oi	boy
âr	care	ou	out
ä	father	o͝o	took
ĕ	pet	o͝or	lure
ē	be	o͞o	boot
ĭ	pit	ŭ	cut
ī	bite	ûr	urge
îr	pier	th	thin
ŏ	pot	*th*	this
ō	toe	zh	vision
ô	paw	ə	about

—*intr.* **1.** To stay alive or in existence: *trying to survive in the woods; a folktale that has survived for centuries.* **2.** To carry on despite hardships or trauma; persevere. —*tr.* **1.** To live longer than; outlive: *The late Mr. Smith was survived by his wife and three children.* **2.** To live or persist through: *The plants survived the frost.* [From Middle English *surviven*, from Latin *supervīvere* : *super-*, over + *vīvere*, to live.]

sur·vi·vor (sər-vī**′**vər) *n.* **1.** A person who has survived an accident or disaster that caused the death of others. **2.** A living descendant, relative, or heir of a person who has died. **3.** Someone who has the ability to cope with and recover from great difficulties: *They had to move out of their house, but they are survivors and will make the best of it.*

sus·cep·ti·bil·i·ty (sə-sĕp′tə-**bĭl′**ĭ-tē) *n., pl.* **sus·cep·ti·bil·i·ties 1.** The quality or condition of being susceptible. **2.** The capacity to be affected by deep emotions or strong feelings; sensitivity. **3. susceptiblilities** Feelings; sensibilities.

sus·cep·ti·ble (sə-**sĕp′**tə-bəl) *adj.* **1.** Easily influenced or affected: *Is he susceptible to persuasion? I am susceptible to colds.* **2.** Especially sensitive; highly impressionable: *a susceptible child.* **3.** Permitting an action to be performed; capable of undergoing a specified action: *a poem susceptible to several interpretations.*

su·shi (**so͞o′**shē) *n.* Small portions of cold cooked rice wrapped in seaweed and topped or wrapped with slices of raw or cooked fish, egg, or vegetables.

sus·pect (**sŭs′**pĕkt′) *adj.* Open to or viewed with suspicion: *suspect motives; a suspect policy.* ❖ *n.* A person who is suspected, especially of having committed a crime. ❖ *tr.v.* (sə-**spĕkt′**) **sus·pect·ed, sus·pect·ing, sus·pects 1.** To consider to be true or probable without being sure; imagine: *The early Greeks were the first to suspect that the earth is round.* **2.** To have doubts about; distrust: *We suspected his intentions.* **3.** To consider (someone) guilty without proof: *The police suspect her of fraud.* [From Middle English *suspect*, from Latin *suspectāre* : *sub-*, from below + *specere*, to look at.]

sus·pend (sə-**spĕnd′**) *tr.v.* **sus·pend·ed, sus·pend·ing, sus·pends 1.** To bar temporarily from a position, membership, or privilege, usually as a punishment: *suspend a student from school.* **2.** To cause to stop for a period; interrupt: *suspended her work to have lunch.* **3.** To put off for the time being; postpone: *suspend judgment until all the facts are known.* **4.** To render temporarily ineffective: *suspended his driver's license.* **5.** To hang so as to allow free movement: *suspended a swing from the tree.* **6.** To support or keep from falling without apparent attachment; cause to float: *For an instant the acrobat seemed to suspend himself in midair.* [From Middle English *suspenden*, from Latin *suspendere* : *sub-*, from below + *pendere*, to hang.]

sus·pend·ers (sə-**spĕn′**dərz) *pl.n. (used with a plural verb)* A pair of straps worn over the shoulders to hold up one's pants.

sus·pense (sə-**spĕns′**) *n.* **1.** Excitement, worry, or fear resulting from an uncertain or mysterious situation. **2.** The state or quality of being undecided or uncertain.

sus·pen·sion (sə-**spĕn′**shən) *n.* **1.** The act of suspending or the condition of being suspended: *a suspension of the rules.* See Synonyms at **pause. 2.** A temporary ban that prohibits someone from fulfilling a particular task or duty, especially attending school. **3.** A mixture in which small particles of a substance are dispersed throughout a gas or liquid and are large enough to be seen. If left undisturbed, the particles are likely to settle to the bottom. Muddy water is a suspension. **4.** The combination of springs, shock absorbers, and other devices that are connected to the wheels of a vehicle and reduce the intensity of the shocks transmitted to the vehicle's body.

suspension bridge *n.* A bridge in which the roadway is hung from cables anchored at both ends and supported at intervals by towers.

sus·pi·cion (sə-**spĭsh′**ən) *n.* **1.** The act of suspecting something on little evidence or without proof: *She had a strong suspicion that she was being double-crossed.* **2.** The condition of being suspected, especially of wrongdoing: *held under suspicion of theft.* **3.** The state or feeling of having no confidence or certainty about something; distrust: *looked with suspicion on the claims made on the website.*

sus·pi·cious (sə-**spĭsh′**əs) *adj.* **1.** Arousing suspicion; causing distrust: *suspicious behavior.* **2.** Tending to suspect; distrustful: *She was suspicious of anything out of the ordinary.* **3.** Expressing suspicion: *a suspicious glance.* **—sus·pi′cious·ly** *adv.*

Sus·que·han·na River (sŭs′kwə-**hăn′**ə) A river of the northeast United States rising in central New York and flowing about 445 miles (715 kilometers) south to Chesapeake Bay.

sus·tain (sə-**stān′**) *tr.v.* **sus·tained, sus·tain·ing, sus·tains 1.** To keep in existence; maintain: *sustain an effort; sustain a note for four beats.* **2.** To keep alive; supply with needed nourishment: *the grasses that sustain antelope.* **3.** To support the spirits of; encourage: *His kind words sustained them through the crisis.* **4.** To support from below; keep from falling or sinking: *strong beams that sustain the weight of the roof.* **5.** To experience or suffer: *sustained minor injuries in the accident.* **6.** To affirm the validity of; uphold: *The judge sustained the prosecutor's objection.* ❖ *n.* The ability of a musical instrument to continue sounding a single note. [From Middle English *sustenen*, from Latin *sustinēre* : *sub-*, from below + *tenēre*, to hold.] **—sus·tain′er** *n.*

sus·tain·a·ble (sə-**stā′**nə-bəl) *adj.* **1.** Capable of being sustained: *The runner's pace was not sustainable throughout the race.* **2.** Using methods, as in growing crops, that do not harm the environment despite being used over long periods of time: *Sustainable farming systems prevent erosion of the soil.*

sus·te·nance (**sŭs′**tə-nəns) *n.* **1.** The act of sustaining or the condition of being sustained. **2.** The support of life, as with food and other necessities. **3.** Something that supports life, especially food.

su·ture (**so͞o′**chər) *n.* **1.** The process of joining two surfaces or edges together along a line by sewing. **2a.** The fine thread or other material used in surgery to close a wound or join tissues. **b.** A stitch used in surgery. **3.** The line where bones connect in an immovable joint: *the sutures of the skull.* ❖ *tr.v.* **su·tured, su·tur·ing, su·tures** To join by means of sutures, as in surgery. [From Middle English, from Latin *sūtūra*, from *suere*, to sew.]

SUV (ĕs′yo͞o′**vē′**) *n.* A large four-wheel-drive vehicle designed for off-road travel. [From *sport utility vehicle*.]

Su·va (**so͞o′**və) The capital of Fiji, in the South Pacific Ocean.

su·ze·rain (**so͞o′**zər-ən *or* **so͞o′**zə-rān′) *n.* **1.** A nation that controls the foreign affairs of another nation but allows it to govern its domestic affairs. **2.** In feudal times, a lord to whom vassals gave service in return for use of land.

su·ze·rain·ty (**so͞o′**zər-ən-tē *or* **so͞o′**zə-rān′tē) *n., pl.* **su·ze·rain·ties** The power of or the area controlled by a suzerain.

svelte (svĕlt) *adj.* **svelt·er, svelt·est** Slender or graceful in figure or outline; slim. [From French, from Italian *svelto*.]

SW *abbr.* An abbreviation of: **1.** southwest. **2.** southwestern.

swab also **swob** (swŏb) *n.* **1.** A small piece of cotton, sponge, or other absorbent material attached to the end of a stick or wire and used for cleansing, applying medicine, or collecting a sample of a substance. **2.** A mop used for cleaning floors or decks. ❖ *tr.v.* **swabbed, swab·bing, swabs** also **swobbed, swob·bing, swobs 1.** To use a swab on: *swab the skin with antiseptic.* **2.** To clean with a swab: *swab the decks.* **—swab′ber** *n.*

swad·dle (swŏd′l) *tr.v.* **swad·dled, swad·dling, swad·dles 1.** To wrap or envelop, as in bandages. **2.** To wrap (an infant) in swaddling clothes. ❖ *n.* A band or cloth used for swaddling.

swad·dling clothes (swŏd′lĭng) *pl.n.* Long narrow strips of cloth wrapped around a newborn infant to hold its legs and arms still.

swag (swăg) *n.* **1a.** An ornamental drapery that hangs in a curve between two points. **b.** A decorative carved, painted, or molded representation of such a drapery. **2.** A promotional item, especially one given for free. **3.** *Slang* Stolen property; loot.

swag·ger (swăg′ər) *intr.v.* **swag·gered, swag·ger·ing, swag·gers** To walk or conduct oneself in an arrogant or insolent manner. ❖ *n.* A swaggering manner of moving or behaving.

Swa·hi·li (swä-hē′lē) *n., pl.* **Swahili** or **Swa·hi·lis 1.** A Bantu language widely used on the coast and islands of eastern Africa from Somalia to Mozambique and an official language of Tanzania. **2.** An inhabitant of coastal eastern Africa for whom Swahili is the mother tongue. [From Arabic *sawāḥilī*, belonging to the coasts.]

swain (swān) *n. Archaic* **1.** A country lad, especially a shepherd. **2.** A young male suitor or lover.

swal·low[1] (swŏl′ō) *v.* **swal·lowed, swal·low·ing, swal·lows** *—tr.* **1.** To move (food or drink) from the mouth through the throat and esophagus into the stomach by muscular action. **2.** To put up with (something unpleasant); tolerate: *swallow an insult.* **3.** To refrain from expressing; suppress: *swallow one's pride.* **4.** To consume as if by ingestion; devour: *a building that was swallowed by fire.* **5.** *Slang* To believe without question: *She swallowed their story about why they were late.* **6.** To take back; retract: *swallow one's words.* *—intr.* To perform the act of swallowing. ❖ *n.* **1.** The act of swallowing. **2.** An amount swallowed. [From Old English *swelgan.*]

swal·low[2] (swŏl′ō) *n.* Any of various small swift-flying birds having narrow pointed wings, a forked or notched tail, and a large mouth for catching flying insects. [From Old English *swealwe.*]

swal·low·tail (swŏl′ō-tāl′) *n.* **1.** A deeply forked tail, like that of a swallow. **2.** Any of various large, often colorful butterflies having an extension at the end of each hind wing. The two extensions together resemble the forked tail of a swallow. **3.** A tailcoat. **—swal′low-tailed′** *adj.*

swam (swăm) *v.* Past tense of **swim.**

swa·mi (swä′mē) *n., pl.* **swa·mis** A Hindu religious teacher.

swamp (swŏmp) *n.* A wetland area, especially one in which trees or shrubs grow. ❖ *v.* **swamped, swamp·ing, swamps** *—tr.* **1.** To drench in or cover with water: *The road is swamped with rainwater.* **2.** To overwhelm or burden with too much of something: *We are swamped with work.* **3.** To fill (a boat) with water to the point of sinking. *—intr.* To become full of water or sink. [Perhaps of Low German origin.] **—swamp′y** *adj.*

swamp·land (swŏmp′lănd′) *n.* Land of swampy consistency or having many swamps on it.

swan (swŏn) *n.* Any of various large waterbirds having webbed feet, a long slender neck, and usually white feathers. [From Old English.]

swan dive *n.* A forward dive performed with the legs straight together, the back arched, and the arms stretched out from the sides.

swank (swăngk) *adj.* **swank·er, swank·est** Very fashionable or elegant; grand: *a swank hotel.* ❖ *n.* **1.** Elegance. **2.** An excessive display of style or arrogance in behavior; swagger.

swank·y (swăng′kē) *adj.* **swank·i·er, swank·i·est** Very fashionable or elegant; swank. **—swank′i·ly** *adv.* **—swank′i·ness** *n.*

swan song *n.* A farewell or last appearance, work, or action, as by an actor, writer, or athlete before death or retirement.

swap (swŏp) *tr. & intr.v.* **swapped, swap·ping, swaps** To trade (one thing) for another; exchange. ❖ *n.* An exchange of one thing for another. **—swap′per** *n.*

sward (swôrd) *n.* Ground covered with short, thickly growing grass.

swarm[1] (swôrm) *n.* **1.** A large number of insects or other small organisms, especially when in motion: *a swarm of mosquitoes.* **2.** A group of bees, wasps, or ants, when migrating with a queen to establish a new colony. **3.** A group of people or things, especially when moving or occurring in a group: *a swarm of reporters; swarms of tornadoes.* ❖ *v.* **swarmed, swarm·ing, swarms** *—intr.* **1.** To move in or form a swarm, as bees or other insects: *Ants usually swarm in the spring.* **2.** To move or gather in large numbers: *Fans swarmed onto the playing field after the game.* **3.** To be filled or overrun: *The stream is swarming with fish.* *—tr.* To fill with a crowd: *Thousands of fans swarmed the stadium.* [From Old English *swearm.*]

swarm[2] (swôrm) *tr. & intr.v.* **swarmed, swarm·ing, swarms** To climb by gripping with the arms and legs.

swarth·y (swôr′thē) *adj.* **swarth·i·er, swarth·i·est** Having a dark color or complexion: *the sailor's swarthy skin.* **—swarth′i·ly** *adv.* **—swarth′i·ness** *n.*

swash (swŏsh) *n.* **1.** A splash of liquid. **2.** The sound of such a splash. ❖ *v.* **swashed, swash·ing, swash·es** *—intr.* To strike, move, or wash with a splashing sound: *water swashing around his feet.* *—tr.* **1.** To splash (a liquid). **2.** To splash a liquid against.

swash·buck·ler (swŏsh′bŭk′lər) *n.* **1.** A sword-wielding adventurer. **2.** A dramatic or literary work that is full of swordplay and romantic adventure. **—swash′buck′ling** *adj. & n.*

swas·ti·ka (swŏs′tĭ-kə) *n.* **1.** An ancient religious symbol and symbol of good fortune in the shape of a cross having two bars of equal length intersecting in the middle at right angles, with the ends of the arms also bent at right angles. **2.** Such a symbol with a clockwise bend to the arms, used as the emblem of the Nazi party and the symbol of Nazi Germany. [From Sanskrit *svastikaḥ*, sign of good luck, from *svasti*, well-being.]

swat (swŏt) *tr.v.* **swat·ted, swat·ting, swats** To deal a sharp blow to; slap. ❖ *n.* A quick blow; a slap. **—swat′ter** *n.*

swatch (swŏch) *n.* A small sample strip of cloth or other material.

swath (swŏth) *n.* **1.** A path cut through tall grass or grain, as by a scythe or lawnmower. **2.** The mown grass or grain lying on such a path. **3.** A strip or path, often when made by removing something: *the hurricane's swath of destruction.* ◆ **cut a swath** To create a great stir, impression, or display. [From Old English *swæth*, track.]

swathe (swŏth *or* swāth) *tr.v.* **swathed, swath·ing, swathes 1.** To wrap or bind with or as if with strips of cloth: *His right ankle was swathed in bandages.* **2.** To cover or wrap with something that envelops or encloses: *The actress was swathed in a long black cape.* ❖ *n.* A bandage, binding, or other wrapping.

sway (swā) *v.* **swayed, sway·ing, sways** *—intr.* **1.** To move back and forth or from side to side: *trees swaying in the wind.* **2.** To lean or bend to one side; veer: *She swayed and put out a hand to steady herself.* *—tr.* **1.** To cause to move back and forth or from side to side. **2.** To cause to lean or bend to one side: *The heavy load made the ship sway to the right.* **3.** To have influence on

swallowtail

swan

WRITERS CHOOSE THEIR WORDS

As if to emphasize his thoughts the mosquitos—with the fire gone and protective smoke no longer saving him—came back in thick, nostril-clogging **swarms.**

—Gary Paulsen
Hatchet

swastika
Hindu symbol of good luck

or control over: *issues most likely to sway voters.* ❖ *n.* **1.** The act of moving from side to side with a swinging motion. **2.** Power; influence: *when the liberals held sway.* [From Middle English *sweien*, probably of Scandinavian origin.]

sway·back (swā′băk′) *n.* An abnormal inward or downward curve of the spine. **—sway′backed′** *adj.*

Swa·zi·land (swä′zē-lănd′) A country of southeast Africa between South Africa and Mozambique. Mbabane is the capital.

swear (swâr) *v.* **swore** (swôr), **sworn** (swôrn), **swear·ing, swears** *—tr.* **1.** To make a solemn statement or promise (that one will do something, especially that one will tell the truth), often while calling on a sacred person or thing to confirm the honesty of one's remarks: *He swore that he would return. She swore to do her duty.* See Synonyms at **vow. 2.** To compel or require (someone) to promise to do something by means of an oath: *swore them to secrecy.* **3.** To administer a legal oath to: *All the witnesses have been sworn. —intr.* **1.** To swear that one will do something. **2.** To use obscene or blasphemous language. ❖ *n.* A swearword. ◆ **swear by 1.** To have great reliance on or confidence in: *He swears by his personal physician.* **2.** To have reliable knowledge of; be sure of: *I think she left early, but I couldn't swear by it.* **3.** To take an oath by. **swear in** To administer a legal or official oath to: *swear in the new mayor.* **swear off** *Informal* To pledge to renounce or give up: *swore off sweets.* [From Old English *swerian.*] **—swear′er** *n.*

swear·word (swâr′wûrd′) *n.* An obscene or blasphemous word.

sweat (swĕt) *v.* **sweat·ed** or **sweat, sweat·ing, sweats** *—intr.* **1.** To give off a salty liquid through pores in the skin; perspire. **2.** To give off a liquid in droplets, as moisture from certain cheeses or sap from a tree. **3.** To collect moisture in small drops from the air, as a cold water pipe. **4.** *Informal* To work long and hard: *We were sweating for hours out in the garden.* **5.** *Informal* To fret or worry: *He sweated over his debts. —tr.* **1.** To give off (moisture) through a porous surface, such as skin. **2.** To make wet by perspiration: *His shirt was sweated through.* **3.** *Informal* To fret or worry about: *Don't sweat the details.* ❖ *n.* **1.** The salty liquid given off by the sweat glands of the skin. **2.** Water that condenses on a surface and forms small drops. **3.** The process or condition of sweating: *worked up a sweat.* **4.** Strenuous exhaustive labor; drudgery: *It took a lot of sweat to move that furniture.* ◆ **no sweat** *Slang* Easily done or handled. **sweat blood** *Informal* To work extremely hard. **sweat out** *Slang* To endure anxiously: *sweat out an examination.*

sweat·er (swĕt′ər) *n.* A knitted or crocheted jacket or pullover.

sweat gland *n.* Any of the tiny tubular glands that are found in the skin of humans and that give off sweat through pores.

sweat·pants (swĕt′pănts′) *pl.n.* Cotton jersey pants usually having a drawstring or elasticized waistband, worn especially for exercising.

sweat·shirt (swĕt′shûrt′) *n.* A long-sleeved pullover or hooded jacket usually made of heavy cotton jersey and having a fleeced backing.

sweat·shop (swĕt′shŏp′) *n.* A shop or factory where employees work long hours for low wages under poor conditions.

sweat·y (swĕt′ē) *adj.* **sweat·i·er, sweat·i·est 1.** Covered with, wet with, or smelling of sweat. **2.** Causing sweat. **—sweat′i·ly** *adv.*

Swede *n.* A native or inhabitant of Sweden.

Swe·den (swēd′n) A country of northern Europe east of Norway. Stockholm is the capital.

Swed·ish (swē′dĭsh) *adj.* Relating to Sweden or its people, culture, or language. ❖ *n.* The Germanic language of Sweden and parts of Finland.

sweep (swēp) *v.* **swept** (swĕpt), **sweep·ing, sweeps** *—tr.* **1.** To clean or clear with a broom or brush: *swept the hallway.* **2.** To clear away with a broom or brush: *sweep snow from the steps.* **3.** To clear (a space or path) with a broom or brush. **4.** To move, remove, or convey by force: *floodwaters sweeping away everything in their path.* **5.** To remove or carry off with a swift brushing motion: *The dealer swept the cards off the table.* **6.** To search thoroughly: *The counselor swept the dormitory during the fire drill.* **7.** To touch or brush lightly: *branches sweeping the river's surface.* **8.** To pass over or through a surface or medium with a continuous movement: *The conductor swept her baton through the air.* **9.** To drag the bottom of (a body of water). **10.** To win all the games in (a series) or all stages in (a contest): *swept the playoffs. —intr.* **1.** To clean or clear a surface, as with a broom. **2.** To move swiftly with a strong steady force: *The wind swept over the plain.* **3.** To move swiftly and majestically: *The dancer swept through the crowd.* **4.** To trail, as a long garment. **5.** To extend gracefully, especially in a curve: *wildflowers sweeping down the slopes.* **6.** To extend in a wide range: *Searchlights swept through the sky.* ❖ *n.* **1.** A clearing out or removal with a broom or brush. **2.** A thorough search of an area: *a sweep of the building by the police.* **3.** A wide curving motion: *the sweep of the oars.* **4.** The range or scope covered by sweeping: *the sweep of a flashlight beam.* **5.** A broad reach or extent: *a sweep of glistening snow.* **6.** A curve or contour: *the sweep of her hair.* **7.** In football, an end run in which a lineman leaves the line of scrimmage and blocks for the ball carrier. **8.** A person who sweeps, especially a chimney sweep. **9.** Victory in all games of a series or all stages of a contest. **10.** A long oar used to propel a boat. **11.** A long pole attached to a pivot and used to raise and lower a bucket in a well. [From Middle English *swepen*, from Old English *swēop*, past tense of *swāpan.*] **—sweep′er** *n.*

sweep·ing (swē′pĭng) *adj.* **1.** Having wide-ranging influence or effect: *sweeping changes.* **2.** Moving in or as if in a long curve: *sweeping gestures.* **3.** Overwhelming; complete: *a sweeping victory.* ❖ *n.* **1.** The action or work of a person who sweeps. **2. sweepings** Things swept up. **—sweep′ing·ly** *adv.*

sweep·stakes (swēp′stāks′) *pl.n. (used with a singular or plural verb)* **1.** A lottery in which the participants' contributions form a fund that is awarded as a prize to one or several winners. **2.** An event or contest, especially a horse race, whose result determines the winner of such a lottery. **3.** The prize won in such a lottery.

sweet (swēt) *adj.* **sweet·er, sweet·est 1.** Having the taste of sugar or a substance containing or resembling sugar, such as honey. **2.** Containing or made with sugar: *a sweet wine.* **3.** Pleasing to the senses, feelings, or mind; agreeable: *a sweet melody.* **4.** Having a pleasing disposition; lovable: *a sweet child.* **5.** Not salted: *sweet butter.* **6.** Not spoiled; fresh: *milk that is still sweet.* **7.** *Informal* Remarkable; outstanding. ❖ *n.* **1.** Sweet taste or quality; sweetness. **2. sweets** Foods, such as candy or pastries that are high in sugar content. **3.** *Chiefly British* A sweet dish, such as pudding, served as a dessert. **4.** A dear or beloved person. [From Old English *swēte.*] **—sweet′ly** *adv.* **—sweet′ness** *n.*

❑ *These sound alike:* **sweet, suite** (series of rooms).

sweet·bread (swēt′brĕd′) *n.* The thymus gland or pancreas of an animal, especially a calf or lamb, used for food.

sweet·bri·er also **sweet·bri·ar** (swēt′brī′ər) *n.* A wild rose having prickly stems, fragrant leaves, and fragrant pink flowers.

sweet corn *n.* A type of corn having kernels that are

sweetbrier

sweet William

ă	pat	ôr	core
ā	pay	oi	boy
âr	care	ou	out
ä	father	o͝o	took
ĕ	pet	o͝or	lure
ē	be	o͞o	boot
ĭ	pit	ŭ	cut
ī	bite	ûr	urge
îr	pier	th	thin
ŏ	pot	*th*	this
ō	toe	zh	vision
ô	paw	ə	about

sweet and juicy when young, commonly cooked and eaten as food.

sweet·en (swēt′n) *v.* **sweet·ened, sweet·en·ing, sweet·ens** —*tr.* **1.** To make sweet or sweeter by adding sugar or another sweet substance: *sweetened his coffee.* **2.** To make more pleasant or agreeable: *sweeten a job offer with added benefits.* —*intr.* To become sweet.

sweet·en·er (swēt′n-ər) *n.* A substance, such as sugar or aspartame, that sweetens.

sweet·en·ing (swēt′n-ĭng) *n.* **1.** The act or process of making sweet. **2.** A sweetener.

sweet·heart (swēt′härt′) *n.* **1.** A person whom one loves. **2.** *Informal* A sweet, lovable person.

sweet·ie (swē′tē) *n. Informal* Sweetheart; dear.

sweet·meat (swēt′mēt′) *n.* A piece of candy or other sweet delicacy.

sweet pea *n.* A climbing plant related to the pea, having fragrant, variously colored flowers.

sweet potato *n.* **1.** The thick, sweet, yellowish or orange root of a tropical American vine, cooked and eaten as a vegetable. **2.** The vine that has such a root.

sweet tooth *n. Informal* A fondness or desire for sweets.

sweet William *n.* A garden plant having dense clusters of flowers in various combinations of red, pink, and white.

swell (swĕl) *v.* **swelled, swelled** or **swol·len** (swō′lən), **swell·ing, swells** —*intr.* **1.** To increase in size or volume as a result of internal pressure; expand: *The balloon swelled as I filled it with helium.* **2.** To increase in force, size, number, or degree: *Membership in the club swelled.* **3.** To increase in loudness or intensity, as a sound. **4.** To bulge out, as a sail. **5a.** To rise in billows, as clouds. **b.** To rise in swells, as the sea. **6a.** To be or become filled with pride, arrogance, or anger. **b.** To rise from within: *Pride swelled within me.* —*tr.* **1.** To cause to increase in volume, size, number, degree, or intensity: *The new students swelled our class.* **2.** To fill with emotion: *Joy swelled her heart.* ❖ *n.* **1.** A gentle rise or curve in a surface: *a landscape of swells and dips.* **2.** A long wave that moves continuously through the water without breaking. **3.** A gradual increase in amount or intensity: *a swell of enthusiasm for the new movie.* **4.** *Informal* A person who is fashionably dressed or of high social position. ❖ *adj.* **swell·er, swell·est** *Informal* Fine; excellent: *had a swell time.* [From Old English *swellan.*]

swell·ing (swĕl′ĭng) *n.* **1.** The condition of being swollen or expanded. **2.** Something swollen, especially a part of the body that has become abnormally swollen, as through disease or injury.

swel·ter (swĕl′tər) *intr.v.* **swel·tered, swel·ter·ing, swel·ters** To suffer from oppressive heat: *We sweltered in the stuffy room.* ❖ *n.* A condition of oppressive heat: *sat on the porch in the afternoon swelter.* [From Middle English *swelteren*, from *swelten*, to faint from heat, from Old English *sweltan*, to perish.]

swel·ter·ing (swĕl′tər-ĭng) *adj.* **1.** Oppressively hot and humid. **2.** Suffering from heat.

swept (swĕpt) *v.* Past tense and past participle of **sweep.**

swept·back (swĕpt′băk′) *adj.* Extending sharply rearward from the points of attachment: *sweptback airplane wings.*

swerve (swûrv) *tr. & intr.v.* **swerved, swerv·ing, swerves** To turn aside or be turned aside suddenly from a straight course: *I swerved my bike to avoid the tree. The bus swerved into the passing lane.* ❖ *n.* The act of swerving.

swift (swĭft) *adj.* **swift·er, swift·est 1.** Moving or capable of moving with great speed; fast. See Synonyms at **fast**[1]. **2.** Coming, occurring, or accomplished quickly: *a swift response.* ❖ *adv.* Quickly: *swift-flowing streams.* ❖ *n.* Any of various small, dark, fast-flying birds that have long pointed wings and a short forked tail and that eat flying insects. [From Old English.] —**swift′ly** *adv.* —**swift′ness** *n.*

Swift (swĭft), **Jonathan** 1667–1745. Irish-born English writer whose works include *Gulliver's Travels* (1726).

swig (swĭg) *Informal n.* A large swallow, as of liquor; a gulp. ❖ *tr. & intr.v.* **swigged, swig·ging, swigs** To drink (liquid) or engage in drinking liquid in large gulps.

swill (swĭl) *v.* **swilled, swill·ing, swills** —*tr.* **1.** To drink eagerly or greedily. **2.** To feed (animals) with swill. —*intr.* To eat or drink eagerly or greedily. ❖ *n.* **1.** A mixture of liquid and solid food given to animals, especially pigs. **2.** Liquor or other alcohol of poor quality. **3.** A swig or gulp. [From Old English *swilian.*]

swim (swĭm) *v.* **swam** (swăm), **swum** (swŭm), **swim·ming, swims** —*intr.* **1.** To move through water by means of the limbs, fins, or tail. **2.** To float on water or another liquid: *leaves swimming on the lake.* **3.** To be covered or flooded with or as if with a liquid: *The French fries swam in ketchup.* **4.** To experience a floating or giddy sensation; be dizzy: *a thought that made his head swim.* **5.** To appear to spin or reel: *The room swam before my eyes.* —*tr.* **1.** To move through or across (a body of water) by swimming. **2.** To perform (a swimming stroke). ❖ *n.* **1a.** The act of swimming: *went to the pool for a swim before lunch.* **b.** The period of time spent swimming. **2.** A state of dizziness. ❖ *adj.* Relating to or used for swimming: *a swim mask.* [From Old English *swimman.*] —**swim′mer** *n.* —**swim′ming** *adj. & n.*

swim bladder *n.* A gas-filled sac in many fishes that functions to maintain buoyancy and, in some species, to aid in respiration or to produce sound.

swim·mer·et (swĭm′ə-rĕt′) *n.* One of the paired appendages along the abdomen of a shrimp, lobster, or related animal, used for swimming and in females for carrying eggs.

swim·ming·ly (swĭm′ĭng-lē) *adv.* With great ease and success: *School is going swimmingly.*

swimming pool *n.* A structure that is filled with water and used for swimming.

swim·suit (swĭm′so͞ot′) *n.* A garment worn while swimming; a bathing suit.

swin·dle (swĭn′dl) *tr.v.* **swin·dled, swin·dling, swin·dles 1.** To cheat or defraud of money or property. **2.** To obtain by cheating or fraud: *swindled money from gullible people.* ❖ *n.* The act or an instance of swindling; a fraud. —**swin′dler** *n.*

swine (swīn) *n., pl.* **swine 1.** Any of various mammals, especially the domesticated pig, that have a stout body with thick skin, a short neck, and a movable snout. **2.** A person regarded as contemptible or despicable.

swine·herd (swīn′hûrd′) *n.* A person who tends swine.

swing (swĭng) *v.* **swung** (swŭng), **swing·ing, swings** —*intr.* **1.** To move back and forth when suspended from above: *a pendulum swinging from the ceiling.* **2.** To move back and forth on a hinge or around an axis: *a gate swinging in the wind.* **3.** To try to hit something with a sweeping motion of the arm or arms: *swing at the ball.* **4.** To move laterally or in a curve: *The car swung over to the curb.* **5.** To ride on a swing. **6.** *Slang* To be put to death by hanging. **7.** To have an exciting rhythmic quality, like that of swing music: *a song that swings.* **8.** *Slang* To be lively, trendy, and exciting: *a nightclub that really swings.* —*tr.* **1.** To cause to move back and forth, as on a swing: *She swung her arms as she walked.* **2.** To cause to move in a broad arc or curve: *swing a bat.* **3.** To lift or hoist with a sweeping motion: *swung the pouch over his shoulder.* **4.** *Informal* To manage or arrange successfully: *swing a deal.* ❖ *n.* **1.** The act of swinging, especially a back-and-forth movement, as of a pendulum. **2.** A sweep or stroke of something that swings. **3.** The manner in which a person or thing swings something, such as a baseball bat: *a golfer with a smooth swing.* **4.** A shift from one attitude or condition to an-

sweptback
airplane with sweptback wings

Jonathan Swift
1718 portrait by Charles Jervas (1675?–1739)

Swiss chard

swordtail

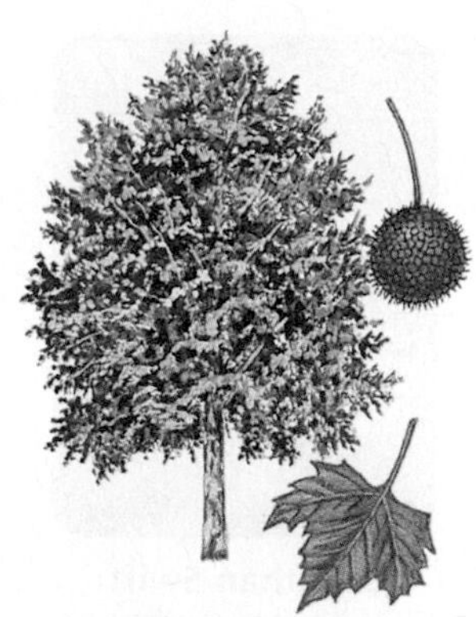
sycamore
American sycamore

ă	pat	ôr	core
ā	pay	oi	boy
âr	care	ou	out
ä	father	o͝o	took
ĕ	pet	o͝or	lure
ē	be	o͞o	boot
ĭ	pit	ŭ	cut
ī	bite	ûr	urge
îr	pier	th	thin
ŏ	pot	*th*	this
ō	toe	zh	vision
ô	paw	ə	about

other: *a swing toward conservatism.* **5.** A seat suspended from above, on which one may ride back and forth for recreation. **6a.** A type of popular dance music developed about 1935 and based on jazz but using a larger band and less improvisation. **b.** The rhythmic quality characteristic of this music. ◆ **in full swing** At the highest level of activity or operation. [From Old English *swingan*, to flog, swing.] **—swing′er** *n.*

swin·ish (swī′nĭsh) *adj.* **1.** Resembling or befitting swine. **2.** Bestial or brutish.

swipe (swīp) *n.* A sweeping blow or stroke. ❖ *v.* **swiped, swip·ing, swipes** *—tr.* **1.** To hit with a sweeping blow. **2.** To pass (a swipe card) through an electronic reader. **3.** *Informal* To steal. *—intr.* To make a sweeping stroke.

swipe card *n.* A plastic card with a magnetic strip containing encoded data that is passed through an electronic device, used especially to make electronic transactions and to provide access to restricted areas.

swirl (swûrl) *v.* **swirled, swirl·ing, swirls** *—intr.* To move with a twisting whirling motion: *The dancers swirled around the room.* See Synonyms at **turn.** *—tr.* To cause to move with a twisting or whirling motion. ❖ *n.* **1.** The motion of whirling or twisting. **2.** Something that swirls, coils, or whirls. [From Middle English *swirlen*, probably of Low German or Scandinavian origin.]

swish (swĭsh) *v.* **swished, swish·ing, swish·es** *—intr.* **1.** To make a hissing or rustling sound: *Her skirt swished as she walked.* **2.** To move with such a sound: *We swished through the tall grass.* *—tr.* To cause to make a swishing sound or movement: *The wind swished the curtains.* ❖ *n.* **1.** A sharp hissing or rustling sound. **2.** A movement making such a sound. **3.** In basketball, a shot that goes through the net of the basket without hitting the backboard or rim.

Swiss (swĭs) *adj.* Relating to Switzerland or its people or culture. ❖ *n., pl.* **Swiss** A native or inhabitant of Switzerland.

Swiss chard *n.* A variety of beet having large succulent leaves that are eaten as a vegetable.

Swiss cheese *n.* A firm whitish cheese with many large holes and a nutty flavor.

switch (swĭch) *n.* **1.** An exchange or a swap, especially one done secretly. **2.** A shift, as of attention or opinion. **3.** A device used to open or close an electric circuit or to make a connection to another circuit. **4.** A device consisting of two sections of railroad track and various movable parts, used to transfer a train from one track to another. **5.** A slender flexible rod, stick, or twig, especially one used for whipping. **6.** A thick strand of real or artificial hair worn as part of a hairdo. ❖ *v.* **switched, switch·ing, switch·es** *—tr.* **1.** To exchange: *We switched seats.* **2.** To shift, transfer, or change: *switch the conversation to a more interesting topic.* **3.** To control (an electric current) by operating a switch. **4.** To cause (an electrical device) to begin or cease operation by controlling the current to it with a switch: *Switch on the lights.* **5.** To move (a train) from one railroad track to another. **6.** To whip with or as if with a switch. **7.** To jerk or swish abruptly or sharply: *The cat switched its tail.* *—intr.* **1.** To make or undergo a shift or exchange. **2.** To swish sharply from side to side. [Probably of Low German or Flemish origin.] **—switch′er** *n.*

switch·blade (swĭch′blăd′) *n.* A pocketknife with a blade that is quickly pushed open by a spring when a button on the handle is pressed.

switch·board (swĭch′bôrd′) *n.* One or more panels containing switches and other equipment for controlling electric circuits.

switch hitter *n.* In baseball, a player who can bat either right-handed or left-handed.

switch·man (swĭch′mən) *n.* A man who operates railroad switches.

Swit·zer·land (swĭt′sər-lənd) A country of west-central Europe north of Italy. Switzerland maintained a policy of neutrality through both World Wars. Bern is the capital and Zurich the largest city.

swiv·el (swĭv′əl) *n.* A device that joins two parts in a way that allows one part to turn without turning the other. ❖ *tr. & intr.v.* **swiv·eled, swiv·el·ing, swiv·els** or **swiv·elled, swiv·el·ling, swiv·els** To turn or rotate, as on a swivel. [From Middle English.]

swivel chair *n.* A chair that swivels on its base.

swob (swŏb) *n. & v.* Variant of **swab.**

swol·len (swō′lən) *v.* A past participle of **swell.** ❖ *adj.* **1.** Expanded by or as if by internal pressure. **2.** Overblown; exaggerated: *swollen praise.*

swoon (swo͞on) *intr.v.* **swooned, swoon·ing, swoons** To faint. ❖ *n.* A fainting spell; a faint.

swoop (swo͞op) *v.* **swooped, swoop·ing, swoops** *—intr.* To move with a sudden sweeping motion, as toward prey: *The owl swooped down and caught the mouse.* *—tr.* To snatch or take with a sudden sweeping motion: *The hawk swooped up the rabbit.* ❖ *n.* The act or an instance of swooping. [From Old English *swāpan*, to sweep, swing.]

swoosh (swo͝osh *or* swo͞osh) *v.* **swooshed, swoosh·ing, swoosh·es** *—intr.* To move with or make a rushing sound. *—tr.* To cause to move with or make a rushing or swirling sound.

sword (sôrd) *n.* **1.** A hand weapon consisting of a long pointed blade set in a handle or hilt. **2.** Military power or the use of force, as in war. [From Old English *sweord.*]

sword·fish (sôrd′fĭsh′) *n.* A large ocean fish having a long pointed upper jaw that projects forward like a sword.

sword·play (sôrd′plā′) *n.* The act or art of using a sword, as in fencing.

swords·man (sôrdz′mən) *n.* A man who is skilled in the use of swords. **—swords′man·ship′** *n.*

sword·tail (sôrd′tāl′) *n.* A small tropical freshwater fish that has a long swordlike extension of the tail fin in the male and is often kept in home aquariums.

swore (swôr) *v.* Past tense of **swear.**

sworn (swôrn) *v.* Past participle of **swear.**

swum (swŭm) *v.* Past participle of **swim.**

swung (swŭng) *v.* Past tense and past participle of **swing.**

syc·a·more (sĭk′ə-môr′) *n.* **1.** Any of various trees having leaves resembling those of a maple, ball-shaped seed clusters, and bark that flakes off in large patches. **2.** A kind of maple tree native to Eurasia. **3.** A kind of fig tree native to Africa and southwest Asia, having clusters of figs on short leafless twigs. [From Middle English *sicamour*, a kind of fig tree, from Greek *sūkomoros.*]

syc·o·phant (sĭk′ə-fənt *or* sī′kə-fənt) *n.* A person who attempts to win favor or advancement by flattering influential people.

Syd·ney (sĭd′nē) The largest city of Australia, in the southeast part of the country northeast of Canberra.

syl·la·bi (sĭl′ə-bī′) *n.* A plural of **syllabus.**

syl·lab·ic (sĭ-lăb′ĭk) *adj.* **1.** Relating to a syllable or syllables. **2.** Pronounced with every syllable distinct. **3.** Relating to a consonant that forms a syllable without a vowel, such as the (l) sound in *riddle* (**rĭd′**l). ❖ *n.* A syllabic sound.

syl·lab·i·fy (sĭ-lăb′ĭ-fī′) or **syl·lab·i·cate** (sĭ-lăb′ĭ-kāt′) *tr.v.* **syl·lab·i·fied, syl·lab·i·fy·ing, syl·lab·i·fies** or **syl·lab·i·cat·ed, syl·lab·i·cat·ing, syl·lab·i·cates** To form or divide into syllables. **—syl·lab′i·fi·ca′tion, syl·lab′i·ca′tion** *n.*

syl·la·ble (sĭl′ə-bəl) *n.* A single uninterrupted sound forming part of a word or in some cases an entire word. [From Middle English *sillable*, from Greek *sullabē.*]

syl·la·bus (sĭl′ə-bəs) *n., pl.* **syl·la·bus·es** or **syl·la·bi**

(sĭl′ə-bī′) An outline, summary, or plan, especially of a scheduled course of study.

syl·lo·gism (sĭl′ə-jĭz′əm) *n.* **1.** A form of reasoning in which two propositions, one called the major premise and the other called the minor premise, are stated, followed by a conclusion that is logically derived from them. An example of a syllogism is *All horses have tails* (major premise); *Big Red is a horse* (minor premise); *therefore Big Red has a tail* (conclusion). **2.** Reasoning from the general to the specific; deduction.

sylph (sĭlf) *n.* **1.** In legend and folklore, a spirit of the air. **2.** A slim graceful woman or girl.

syl·van (sĭl′vən) *adj.* **1.** Relating to or characteristic of woodlands or forests: *sylvan life.* **2.** Located in or inhabiting a wood or forest. **3.** Having many trees; wooded: *sylvan slopes.*

sym·bi·o·sis (sĭm′bē-ō′sĭs *or* sĭm′bī-ō′sĭs) *n., pl.* **sym·bi·o·ses** (sĭm′bē-ō′sēz *or* sĭm′bī-ō′sēz) A close association between two or more different organisms of different species, often but not necessarily benefiting each member. Three different kinds of symbioses are commensalism, mutualism, and parasitism.

sym·bi·ot·ic (sĭm′bē-ŏt′ĭk *or* sĭm′bī-ŏt′ĭk) *adj.* Relating to or characterized by symbiosis. **—sym′bi·ot′i·cal·ly** *adv.*

sym·bol (sĭm′bəl) *n.* **1.** Something that stands for something else, as by association, resemblance, or convention: *The lamb is a symbol of innocence.* **2.** A printed or written sign used to represent an operation, element, quantity, quality, or relation, as in mathematics or music. [From Middle English *simbal*, creed, from Greek *sumbolon*, token for identification (by comparison with a counterpart) : *sun-*, together + *ballein*, to throw.]

❑ *These sound alike:* **symbol, cymbal** (musical instrument).

sym·bol·ic (sĭm-bŏl′ĭk) also **sym·bol·i·cal** (sĭm-bŏl′ĭ-kəl) *adj.* **1.** Relating to or expressed by means of a symbol or symbols. **2.** Serving as a symbol. **3.** Using symbolism, as a work of art. **—sym·bol′i·cal·ly** *adv.*

sym·bol·ism (sĭm′bə-lĭz′əm) *n.* **1a.** The practice of representing things by means of symbols. **b.** The attachment of symbolic meaning or significance to objects, events, or relationships. **2.** A system of symbols or representation. **3.** A symbolic meaning or representation.

sym·bol·ize (sĭm′bə-līz′) *v.* **sym·bol·ized, sym·bol·iz·ing, sym·bol·iz·es** *—tr.* To serve as a symbol of: *The poet uses rain to symbolize grief.* *—intr.* To use symbols.

sym·met·ri·cal (sĭ-mĕt′rĭ-kəl) also **sym·met·ric** (sĭ-mĕt′rĭk) *adj.* Relating to or having symmetry.

sym·me·try (sĭm′ĭ-trē) *n., pl.* **sym·me·tries 1.** An exact matching of form and arrangement of parts on opposite sides of a boundary, such as a plane or line, or around a point or axis. **2.** A relationship in which there is a characteristic correspondence, equivalence, or identity between parts. [From Greek *summetros*, of like measure : *sun-*, together + *metron*, measure.]

sym·pa·thet·ic (sĭm′pə-thĕt′ĭk) *adj.* **1.** Feeling, expressing, or resulting from sympathy: *a sympathetic person; a sympathetic glance.* **2.** Easy to identify with and care about: *a gloomy novel without a single sympathetic character.* **3.** In agreement; favorable; inclined: *They were sympathetic to the plan.* **—sym′pa·thet′i·cal·ly** *adv.*

sympathetic nervous system *n.* The part of the autonomic nervous system that, in general, inhibits the physiological effects of the parasympathetic nervous system, especially under stressful conditions, as in speeding up the heart, contracting blood vessels, and reducing digestive secretions.

sym·pa·thize (sĭm′pə-thīz′) *intr.v.* **sym·pa·thized, sym·pa·thiz·ing, sym·pa·thiz·es 1.** To feel or express sympathy or compassion for another. **2.** To share or understand the feelings or ideas of another: *We sympathized with her intentions.* **—sym′pa·thiz′er** *n.*

sym·pa·thy (sĭm′pə-thē) *n., pl.* **sym·pa·thies 1.** A feeling or expression of pity or sorrow for the distress of another; compassion: *Even the referee felt sympathy for the losing team.* **2.** Mutual understanding or affection between people: *There was a natural sympathy between the two friends.* **3.** Agreement with or support for an opinion or position: *I am in sympathy with their beliefs.* [From Greek *sumpathēs*, affected by like feelings : *sun-*, together + *pathos*, emotion.]

sym·phon·ic (sĭm-fŏn′ĭk) *adj.* Relating to or having the character or form of a symphony.

symphonic poem *n.* A tone poem.

sym·pho·ny (sĭm′fə-nē) *n., pl.* **sym·pho·nies 1.** An extended musical composition for orchestra, usually consisting of at least three movements. **2a.** A symphony orchestra. **b.** A performance by a symphony orchestra: *attended the symphony last night.*

symphony orchestra *n.* A large orchestra composed of string, wind, and percussion sections.

sym·po·si·um (sĭm-pō′zē-əm) *n., pl.* **sym·po·si·ums** or **sym·po·si·a** (sĭm-pō′zē-ə) **1.** A meeting or conference for discussion of a topic. **2.** A collection of writings on a particular topic. [From Greek *sumposion*, drinking party : *sun-*, together + *posis*, drinking.]

symp·tom (sĭm′təm *or* sĭmp′təm) *n.* **1.** A sign or indication of a disorder or disease, usually a noticeable change in how a person feels or looks. **2.** An indication or characteristic sign of the existence of something else: *The scarcity of birds was a symptom of broader problems in the environment.* [From Greek *sumptōma*, from *sumpiptein*, to coincide.]

syn. *abbr.* An abbreviation of synonym.

syn·a·gogue also **syn·a·gog** (sĭn′ə-gŏg′) *n.* **1.** A building or place of meeting for worship and religious instruction in the Jewish faith. **2.** A congregation of Jews for the purpose of worship or religious study. [From Middle English *sinagoge*, from Greek *sunagōgē*, from *sunagein*, to bring together.]

syn·apse (sĭn′ăps′ *or* sĭ-năps′) *n.* The point at which a nerve impulse passes from one nerve cell to another nerve cell or to a muscle cell or gland cell. **—syn·ap′tic** (sĭ-năp′tĭk) *adj.* —SEE NOTE

sync or **synch** (sĭngk) *Informal n.* **1.** Synchronization. **2.** Harmony; accord: *in sync with today's fashions.*

❑ *These sound alike:* **sync, sink** (go under water).

syn·chro·nize (sĭng′krə-nīz′ *or* sĭn′krə-nīz′) *v.* **syn·chro·nized, syn·chro·niz·ing, syn·chro·niz·es** *—intr.* **1.** To occur at the same time; be simultaneous. **2.** To operate at the same rate and time. *—tr.* To cause to occur or operate at the same rate and time: *Let's synchronize our watches.* **—syn′chro·ni·za′tion** (sĭng′krə-nĭ-zā′shən) *n.*

syn·chro·nous (sĭng′krə-nəs *or* sĭn′krə-nəs) *adj.* **1.** Occurring or existing at the same time. **2.** Moving or operating at the same rate and together in time. **3.** Having identical periods or identical periods and phases, as two waves, satellites, or pendulums.

syn·chro·tron (sĭng′krə-trŏn′ *or* sĭn′krə-trŏn′) *n.* A machine in which charged subatomic particles are accelerated to high energies by electric fields. The particles are held in a circular path by an increasing magnetic field.

syn·cline (sĭn′klīn′) *n.* A fold of rock layers that slope upward on both sides from a low point.

syn·co·pate (sĭng′kə-pāt′ *or* sĭn′kə-pāt′) *tr.v.* **syn·co·pat·ed, syn·co·pat·ing, syn·co·pates 1.** To change (a musical rhythm) by syncopation. **2.** To shorten (a word) by syncope.

syn·co·pa·tion (sĭng′kə-pā′shən *or* sĭn′kə-pā′shən) *n.* **1.** In music, a shift of accent in a passage or a composition that occurs when a normally weak beat is stressed. **2.** Something, such as a rhythm, that is syncopated. **3.** Syncope.

SCIENCE

synapse You pick up a snowball and feel coldness. You see a puppy and reach out to pat it. How do sensations travel from your hand to your brain and vice versa? Ancient Roman and Islamic physicians knew that sensations moved along long thin fibrous nerve cells (neurons), but they didn't know how that movement happened. It wasn't until the late 1700s that scientists identified the cause: electrical impulses were speeding from one end of a nerve cell to the other. The next puzzle was to figure out how that impulse was communicated across the **synapse,** that is, the gap between neurons. Many years and many experiments later, we know that the signals are relayed by chemicals called *neurotransmitters* that are released by a neuron, diffuse across the synapse, and are received by another neuron or other cell. Understanding synaptic transmission has led to better understanding of diseases that affect the nervous system, such as Parkinson's disease and epilepsy, and to the development of many new drugs.

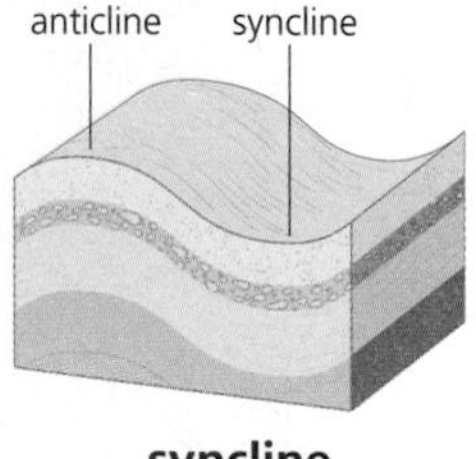

syncline

syncopation
from Mozart's Symphony No. 25

syn·co·pe (sĭng′kə-pē *or* sĭn′kə-pē) *n.* **1.** The shortening of a word by omission of a sound, letter, or syllable from the middle of a word; for example, *bos'n* for *boatswain.* **2.** A brief loss of consciousness caused by a temporary deficiency of oxygen in the brain; a blackout.

syn·di·cate (sĭn′dĭ-kĭt) *n.* **1.** An association of people or firms formed to promote a common interest or carry out a business enterprise. **2.** A loose affiliation of gangsters in control of organized criminal activities. **3.** An agency that sells articles or photographs for simultaneous publication in a number of newspapers or periodicals. ❖ *v.* (sĭn′dĭ-kāt′) **syn·di·cat·ed, syn·di·cat·ing, syn·di·cates** —*tr.* **1.** To organize into or manage as a syndicate. **2.** To sell (an article, for example) through a syndicate for publication. —*intr.* To join together in a syndicate.

syn·drome (sĭn′drōm′) *n.* A group of symptoms that collectively indicate a disease, psychological disorder, or other abnormal condition. [From Greek *sundromos,* running together.]

syn·fu·el (sĭn′fyo͞o′əl) *n.* A liquid or gaseous fuel derived from coal, shale, or tar sand, or obtained by fermentation of certain substances, such as grain.

syn·od (sĭn′əd) *n.* A council or assembly of churches or church officials.

syn·o·nym (sĭn′ə-nĭm′) *n.* A word having the same or almost the same meaning as that of another word. For example, the words *wide* and *broad* are synonyms.

syn·on·y·mous (sĭ-nŏn′ə-məs) *adj.* Having the same or a similar meaning: *synonymous words.*

syn·on·y·my (sĭ-nŏn′ə-mē) *n., pl.* **syn·on·y·mies 1.** The quality of being synonymous. **2.** The study or classification of synonyms.

syn·op·sis (sĭ-nŏp′sĭs) *n., pl.* **syn·op·ses** (sĭ-nŏp′sēz) A brief summary or outline of a subject or written work: *a synopsis of a play.*

syn·op·size (sĭ-nŏp′sīz′) *tr.v.* **syn·op·sized, syn·op·siz·ing, syn·op·siz·es** To make a synopsis of; summarize.

syn·tac·tic (sĭn-tăk′tĭk) or **syn·tac·ti·cal** (sĭn-tăk′tĭ-kəl) *adj.* Relating or conforming to the rules or patterns of syntax. —**syn·tac′ti·cal·ly** *adv.*

syn·tax (sĭn′tăks′) *n.* The way in which words are put together to form phrases and sentences.

syn·the·sis (sĭn′thĭ-sĭs) *n., pl.* **syn·the·ses** (sĭn′thĭ-sēz′) **1.** The combination of separate parts into a single unit or whole. **2.** The single unit or whole formed in this way. **3.** The formation of a chemical compound by combining simpler compounds or elements. [From Greek *sunthesis,* from *suntithenai,* to put together.]

syn·the·size (sĭn′thĭ-sīz′) *tr.v.* **syn·the·sized, syn·the·siz·ing, syn·the·siz·es** To produce by a process of synthesis: *synthesize an antibiotic.*

syn·the·siz·er (sĭn′thĭ-sī′zər) *n.* **1.** A person or thing that synthesizes. **2.** An electronic musical instrument that can be made to produce a wide range of musical sounds, including sounds that imitate those of conventional instruments.

syn·thet·ic (sĭn-thĕt′ĭk) *adj.* **1.** Relating to or involving synthesis. **2.** Produced by synthesis; not of natural origin: *synthetic rubber; synthetic fabrics.* ❖ *n.* A synthetic chemical compound or material. —**syn·thet′i·cal·ly** *adv.*

syph·i·lis (sĭf′ə-lĭs) *n.* A sexually transmitted disease caused by a bacterial infection that is often characterized in its early stages by sores on the genitals. If untreated, skin ulcers develop, followed by often fatal infection of major organs of the body.

sy·phon (sī′fən) *n. & v.* Variant of **siphon.**

Syr·i·a (sîr′ē-ə) A country of southwest Asia on the eastern Mediterranean coast west of Iraq. Damascus is the capital.

sy·ringe (sə-rĭnj′ *or* sîr′ĭnj) *n.* **1.** A medical instrument used to inject fluids into the body or draw fluids from the body. **2.** A hypodermic syringe. [From Middle English *siringe,* from Greek *sūrinx,* shepherd's pipe.]

syr·inx (sîr′ĭngks) *n., pl.* **sy·rin·ges** (sə-rĭn′jēz *or* sə-rĭng′gēz) or **syr·inx·es 1.** The vocal organ of a bird, situated at or near the division of the trachea into the right and left bronchi. **2.** The panpipe.

syr·up (sĭr′əp *or* sûr′əp) *n.* **1.** A thick, sweet, sticky liquid, consisting of sugar, water, and flavoring or medicine. **2.** A thick, sugary liquid made by boiling down plant sap, juice, or grain extracts. [From Middle English *sirup,* from Arabic *šarāb.*] —**syr′up·y** *adj.*

sys·tem (sĭs′təm) *n.* **1.** A group of elements or parts that interact to form a complex whole, especially: **a.** An organism as a whole, especially with regard to its vital processes or functions: *The animal's entire system seems to be affected by the disease.* **b.** A group of related organs or parts in the body: *the digestive system; the skeletal system.* **c.** A set of mechanical or electrical parts that work together: *the heating system of a building.* **d.** A network of pathways or channels, as for travel or communications: *a highway system.* **2.** An organized set of related principles or rules: *a philosophical system.* See Synonyms at **method. 3.** A social, economic, or political organizational form: *a system of government.* [From Greek *sustēma* : *sun-,* together + *histanai,* set up, establish.]

sys·tem·at·ic (sĭs′tə-măt′ĭk) also **sys·tem·at·i·cal** (sĭs′tə-măt′ĭ-kəl) *adj.* **1.** Characterized by, based on, or forming a system. **2.** Working or done in a step-by-step manner: *a systematic researcher; a systematic review.*

sys·tem·a·tize (sĭs′tə-mə-tīz′) *tr.v.* **sys·tem·a·tized, sys·tem·a·tiz·ing, sys·tem·a·tiz·es** To form or organize into a system: *systematized the procedures for admitting students.*

sys·tem·ic (sĭ-stĕm′ĭk *or* sĭ-stē′mĭk) *adj.* **1.** Relating to an entire system: *The recession is not limited to one area of the economy, but is systemic.* **2.** Relating to or affecting the entire body: *a systemic infection.*

sys·to·le (sĭs′tə-lē) *n.* The phase of a heartbeat in which the chambers of the heart, especially the ventricles, contract and drive the blood through the aorta and the blood vessels leading to the lungs. —**sys·tol′ic** (sĭ-stŏl′ĭk) *adj.*

ă	pat	ôr	core
ā	pay	oi	boy
âr	care	ou	out
ä	father	o͝o	took
ĕ	pet	o͝or	lure
ē	be	o͞o	boot
ĭ	pit	ŭ	cut
ī	bite	ûr	urge
îr	pier	th	thin
ŏ	pot	*th*	this
ō	toe	zh	vision
ô	paw	ə	about

t or **T** (tē) *n., pl.* **t's** or **T's** also **ts** or **Ts** The 20th letter of the English alphabet. ◆ **to a T** Perfectly; precisely: *The jacket fit me to a T.*

T *abbr.* An abbreviation of temperature.

Ta The symbol for the element **tantalum.**

tab[1] (tăb) *n.* **1.** A projection, flap, or short strip attached to an object to aid in opening, handling, or identifying it. **2.** A small, usually decorative flap or tongue on a garment. **3.** A small auxiliary control surface attached to a larger one, as on an aircraft.

tab[2] (tăb) *n.* **1.** *Informal* A bill or check, as for a meal in a restaurant: *I'll pay the tab.* **2.** A key on a computer or typewriter keyboard for formatting, especially indenting, text. ◆ **keep tabs on** To watch or observe carefully: *kept tabs on the children during the trip to the museum.* [Short for *tablet* or *tabulation.*]

tab·ard (tăb′ərd) *n.* **1.** A sleeveless or short-sleeved tunic worn by a knight over his armor and embroidered with his coat of arms. **2.** A similar garment worn by a herald and bearing his lord's coat of arms.

Ta·bas·co (tə-băs′kō) A trademark used for a spicy sauce made from a strong-flavored red pepper.

tab·bou·leh or **ta·bou·li** (tə-bo͞o′lē) *n.* A salad of crushed wheat grains, scallions, tomatoes, mint, and parsley.

tab·by (tăb′ē) *n., pl.* **tab·bies** A domestic cat having fur with stripes or with swirls of darker color on a lighter background.

tab·er·na·cle (tăb′ər-năk′əl) *n.* **1.** often **Tabernacle** The portable sanctuary in which the Jews housed the Ark of the Covenant during their wanderings through the desert. **2.** often **Tabernacle** A case or box on a church altar containing the consecrated host and wine of the Eucharist. **3.** A place of worship.

ta·ble (tā′bəl) *n.* **1.** A piece of furniture supported by one or more legs and having a flat top surface on which objects can be placed. **2.** The objects laid out on a table for a meal: *Would you please clear the table?* **3.** The food and drink served at a meal: *sets a fine table.* **4.** The people assembled at a table, especially for a meal: *The entire table burst into laughter.* **5.** An orderly presentation of data, especially one in which the data are arranged in columns and rows in an essentially rectangular form. ❖ *tr.v.* **ta·bled, ta·bling, ta·bles** To postpone consideration of; shelve: *table a piece of legislation.* ◆ **under the table** In secret: *The business deal was done under the table.* [From Middle English, from Latin *tabula,* board.]

tab·leau (tăb′lō′ *or* tă-blō′) *n., pl.* **tab·leaux** or **tab·leaus** (tăb′lōz′ *or* tă-blōz′) **1.** A vivid graphic description. **2.** A silent part of a scene when all the performers onstage freeze in position and then resume action as before.

ta·ble·cloth (tā′bəl-klôth′) *n.* A cloth to cover a table, especially during a meal.

ta·ble·land (tā′bəl-lănd′) *n.* A flat elevated region; a plateau or mesa.

table linen *n.* Tablecloths and napkins.

table salt *n.* A refined mixture of salts, chiefly sodium chloride, used in granular form in cooking and as a seasoning.

ta·ble·spoon (tā′bəl-spo͞on′) *n.* **1.** A large spoon used for serving food. **2.** A household cooking measure equal to 3 teaspoons or ½ fluid ounce (about 15 milliliters).

ta·ble·spoon·ful (tā′bəl-spo͞on-fo͝ol′) *n.* The amount that a tablespoon can hold.

tab·let (tăb′lĭt) *n.* **1.** A slab or plaque, as of stone, with a surface bearing an inscription. **2.** A pad of writing paper fastened together along one edge. **3.** A lightweight, portable computer with a touchscreen. **4.** A small flat pellet of medicine to be taken orally.

table tennis *n.* A game similar to tennis, played on a table with paddles and a small hollow plastic ball.

ta·ble·ware (tā′bəl-wâr′) *n.* The dishes, glassware, and silverware used in setting a table for a meal.

tab·loid (tăb′loid′) *n.* A newspaper of small size, especially one focusing on crime stories, scandals, rumors, or gossip.

ta·boo (tə-bo͞o′ *or* tă-bo͞o′) *n., pl.* **ta·boos 1.** A ban or inhibition resulting from social custom or tradition. **2.** A prohibition preventing certain things considered sacred from being used, approached, or mentioned. **3.** A word or act prohibited for cultural reasons. ❖ *adj.* Excluded or forbidden from use, approach, or mention: *a taboo subject.* [From Tongan *tabu,* under prohibition.]

ta·bor (tā′bər) *n.* A small drum, traditionally played with one hand while playing a pipe with the other.

ta·bou·li (tə-bo͞o′lē) *n.* Variant of **tabbouleh.**

tab·u·lar (tăb′yə-lər) *adj.* **1.** Having a plane surface; flat: *a tabular crystal.* **2.** Organized or presented in the form of a table or list: *tabular data.* **3.** Calculated from information given in a mathematical table, as of square roots or sines and cosines.

tab·u·late (tăb′yə-lāt′) *tr.v.* **tab·u·lat·ed, tab·u·lat·ing, tab·u·lates 1.** To arrange in tabular form; condense and list. **2.** To cut or form with a plane surface. —**tab′u·la′tion** *n.*

tab·u·la·tor (tăb′yə-lā′tər) *n.* A person or thing that tabulates, especially a machine that reads, sorts, and prints out data from punch cards.

ta·chom·e·ter (tə-kŏm′ĭ-tər) *n.* An instrument that measures the rotations per minute of a rotating shaft. [From Greek *takhos,* speed.]

tac·it (tăs′ĭt) *adj.* Implied from actions; not spoken or written: *a tacit agreement.*

tac·i·turn (tăs′ĭ-tûrn′) *adj.* Not inclined to talk much; untalkative.

tack (tăk) *n.* **1.** A short light nail with a sharp point and a flat head. **2.** The lower forward corner of a fore-and-aft sail. **3a.** The direction of a ship in relation to the position of its sails: *the starboard tack.* **b.** In sailing, the act of changing from one position or direction to another. **4.** A course of action or an approach, especially when differing from a previous one: *try a new tack.* **5.** A large

tabby

tackle

taco

tae kwon do

loose stitch used to hold edges together temporarily or to mark places on a fabric. ❖ *v.* **tacked, tack·ing, tacks** —*tr.* **1.** To fasten or attach with or as if with a tack. **2.** To sew with a loose temporary stitch: *Tack the facing to the seams.* **3.** To add as an extra item: *tack two dollars onto the bill.* **4.** To change the course of (a boat or ship) by turning toward and past the direction of the wind. —*intr.* **1.** To change the direction of a sailing vessel by turning toward and past the direction of the wind. **2.** To change one's course of action. [From Middle English *tak*, probably of Germanic origin.]

tack·le (tăk′əl) *n.* **1.** The equipment used in a particular activity, especially in fishing; gear. **2.** (*also* **tā′**kəl) **a.** A system of ropes and pulleys for raising and lowering rigging and for applying tension. **b.** A rope and its pulley. **3a.** The act of stopping an opposing player carrying the ball, especially by forcing the player to the ground, as in football or rugby. **b.** In football, an offensive lineman positioned between a guard and an end, or a defensive lineman positioned next to an end, closer to the ball. **c.** The act of trying to take the ball away from an opponent, as in soccer or field hockey. ❖ *tr.v.* **tack·led, tack·ling, tack·les 1.** To undertake (a job) or deal with (a problem). **2.** To stop (an opposing player carrying the ball), especially by forcing the player to the ground. **3.** To try to take (the ball) from an opponent, as in soccer. —**tack′ler** *n.*

tack·y[1] (tăk′ē) *adj.* **tack·i·er, tack·i·est** Slightly adhesive or gummy to the touch; sticky: *a tacky surface.* [From *tack*, small nail.]

tack·y[2] (tăk′ē) *adj.* **tack·i·er, tack·i·est** *Informal* **1.** Lacking style or good taste: *tacky clothes.* **2.** Distasteful or offensive: *That was a tacky thing to say.* [From obsolete English *tackey*, an inferior horse.]

ta·co (tä′kō) *n., pl.* **ta·cos** A corn tortilla folded around a filling such as ground meat or cheese. [From Spanish, plug, wad of bank notes.]

tac·o·nite (tăk′ə-nīt′) *n.* A low-grade iron ore consisting mainly of quartz, magnetite, and hematite.

tact (tăkt) *n.* The ability to speak or act without offending others.

tact·ful (tăkt′fəl) *adj.* Having or showing tact; considerate and discreet: *a tactful person.* —**tact′ful·ly** *adv.* —**tact′ful·ness** *n.*

tac·tic (tăk′tĭk) *n.* A plan or measure for achieving a goal; a maneuver: *a successful tactic for passing legislation.*

tac·ti·cal (tăk′tĭ-kəl) *adj.* **1.** Relating to or using tactics: *a tactical maneuver.* **2.** Characterized by ingenuity or skill: *a tactical decision.*

tac·tics (tăk′tĭks) *n.* (*used with a singular verb*) The art of deploying and directing troops, ships, and aircraft against an enemy. [From Greek *taktikē (tekhnē)*, (art) of deploying forces in war, from *tassein*, to arrange.]

tac·tile (tăk′təl *or* tăk′tīl′) *adj.* **1.** Capable of being felt by the sense of touch; tangible. **2.** Used for feeling: *tactile organs such as antennae.*

tact·less (tăkt′lĭs) *adj.* Lacking or showing a lack of tact; inconsiderate or indiscreet. —**tact′less·ly** *adv.*

tad (tăd) *n. Informal* **1.** A small amount or degree. **2.** A small boy. ◆ **a tad** To a small degree; somewhat: *acting a tad silly.*

tad·pole (tăd′pōl′) *n.* The aquatic larva of a frog or toad, having gills, a long tail, and in early stages, no legs. As it grows into an adult, legs and lungs develop and the tail gradually disappears. [From Middle English *taddepol* : *tadde, tode*, toad + *pol*, head.]

tae kwon do (tī′ kwŏn′ dō′) *n.* A Korean martial art that emphasizes powerful kicks. [Korean *t'aekwŏndo* : *t'ae-*, to trample + *kwŏn*, fist + *-do*, way.]

taf·fe·ta (tăf′ĭ-tə) *n.* A crisp smooth fabric with a slight sheen used especially for women's garments. [From Middle English *taffata*, from Persian *tāftah*, silk of linen cloth, from *tāftan*, to twist, spin.]

taf·fy (tăf′ē) *n.* A sweet chewy candy made by boiling a flavored syrup until it is very thick and then pulling it until it is glossy and holds its shape.

Taft (tăft), **William Howard** 1857–1930. The 27th president of the United States (1909–1913), who worked to increase the regulation of trusts. He later served as the chief justice of the US Supreme Court (1921–1930).

tag[1] (tăg) *n.* **1.** A strip, as of paper, metal, or leather, attached to something or worn by someone for the purpose of identifying, classifying, or labeling: *a name tag; a price tag.* **2.** The plastic or metal tip at the end of a shoelace. **3.** A name or descriptive term applied to someone or something. **4.** A piece of graffiti identifying the graffiti writer by an assumed name or symbol. **5.** A saying or quotation used as ornamentation in speech or writing. **6.** A sequence of letters in a markup language that specifies how to format a computer document. For example, <i> indicates that following text should be made italic. ❖ *v.* **tagged, tag·ging, tags** —*tr.* **1.** To place a tag on: *tagged each item for sale.* **2.** To recognize or identify with a tag: *She tagged the teacher as a stickler.* **3.** To write a graffiti tag on (a surface). **4.** To put a ticket on (a vehicle) for a traffic or parking violation. —*intr.* To follow after; accompany: *My little sister always wants to tag along.* [From Middle English, dangling piece of cloth on a garment, possibly of Scandinavian origin.]

tag[2] (tăg) *n.* **1.** A children's game in which one player pursues the others until he or she is able to touch one of them, who then in turn becomes the pursuer. **2.** In baseball, the act of tagging a base runner. ❖ *tr.v.* **tagged, tag·ging, tags 1.** To touch (another player) in a game of tag. **2.** In baseball, to touch (a base runner) with the ball in order to put the runner out. ◆ **tag up** In baseball, to return to a base before running to the next base after a fielder has caught a fly ball. [Perhaps variant of Scots *tig*, touch, tap.]

Ta·ga·log (tə-gä′lôg) *n., pl.* **Tagalog** or **Ta·ga·logs 1.** A member of a people native to the Philippines. **2.** The language of this people.

Ta·hi·ti (tə-hē′tē) An island of the southern Pacific Ocean in the Society Islands. It was first settled by Polynesians in prehistoric times.

Ta·hi·tian (tə-hē′shən) *adj.* Relating to Tahiti or its people, language, or culture. ❖ *n.* **1.** A native or inhabitant of Tahiti. **2.** The Polynesian language of Tahiti.

tai chi (tī′ chē′) *n.* A Chinese martial art and system of physical exercises, often practiced as a way of meditating or improving well-being.

tai·ga (tī′gə) *n.* A coniferous forest region of Eurasia and North America, located just south of the tundra.

tail (tāl) *n.* **1.** The hindmost part of an animal when it extends beyond the main part of the body. **2.** The hindmost or rear part, especially: **a.** The rear end of a vehicle, especially an automobile. **b.** The rear portion of the fuselage of an aircraft. **3.** A long thin structure, often extending from a main structure, especially: **a.** A long thin part on some kites that hangs down from the main part and provides stability. **b.** The long glowing stream of gas and dust that is forced from the head of a comet when it is close to the sun. **4.** The lowest part of a garment such as a shirt or coat. **5. tails a.** A formal evening costume typically worn by men. **b.** A tailcoat. **6.** A ponytail or pigtail. **7. tails** The side of a coin not having the principal design: *heads or tails.* **8.** The trail of a person or animal in flight: *on the criminal's tail.* **9.** A person assigned to follow and report on someone else: *The police put a tail on the suspect.* ❖ *v.* **tailed, tail·ing, tails** —*tr.* To follow and observe: *The detective tailed the suspect.* —*intr.* To veer from a straight course: *The golf shot tailed off and missed the green.*

❑ *These sound alike:* **tail, tale** (story).

tail·coat (tāl′kōt′) *n.* A man's black coat worn for formal

ă	pat	ôr	core
ā	pay	oi	boy
âr	care	ou	out
ä	father	ŏŏ	took
ĕ	pet	ŏŏr	lure
ē	be	ōō	boot
ĭ	pit	ŭ	cut
ī	bite	ûr	urge
îr	pier	th	thin
ŏ	pot	*th*	this
ō	toe	zh	vision
ô	paw	ə	about

daytime occasions, divided in back into two long tapered ends.

tail end *n.* **1.** The hindmost part. **2.** The very end: *the tail end of the day.*

tail·gate (tāl′gāt′) *n.* A hinged board or panel at the rear of a vehicle, such as a pickup truck, that can be lowered for loading and unloading. ❖ *v.* **tail·gat·ed, tail·gat·ing, tail·gates** *—tr.* To drive too closely behind (another vehicle). *—intr.* To follow another vehicle too closely. ❖ *adj.* Relating to a picnic that is served next to a parked vehicle.

tail·light (tāl′līt′) *n.* A red light mounted on the rear of a vehicle to make it visible in the dark.

tai·lor (tā′lər) *n.* A person who makes, mends, and alters garments such as suits, coats, and dresses. ❖ *tr.v.* **tai·lored, tai·lor·ing, tai·lors 1.** To make (clothing), especially to specific requirements or measurements. **2.** To make or adapt for a particular purpose: *tailored his speech to his audience.* [From Middle English *taillour,* from Anglo-Norman, from Old French *taillier,* to cut.] **—tai′lored** *adj.*

tail·pipe (tāl′pīp′) *n.* The pipe through which exhaust gases from an engine are discharged.

tail·spin (tāl′spĭn′) *n.* The rapid descent of an aircraft in a steep spiral spin.

tailwind (tāl′wĭnd′) *n.* A wind blowing in the same direction as that of the course of a vehicle.

Ta·í·no (tä-ē′nō) also **Tai·no** (tī′nō) *n., pl.* **Taíno** or **Taínos** also **Taino** or **Tai·nos 1.** A member of an Arawak people of the West Indies whose culture was destroyed under Spanish colonization in the early 1500s. **2.** The language of this people.

taint (tānt) *tr.v.* **taint·ed, taint·ing, taints 1.** To affect slightly with something bad or undesirable: *a reputation that was tainted by rumors of unlawful activity.* **2.** To contaminate with an infectious agent, toxin, or undesirable substance: *drinking water that is tainted with parasites.* **3.** To affect with decay or rot; spoil: *The fish was tainted.* ❖ *n.* An undesirable or corrupting influence or association: *a career that was ended by the taint of scandal.* [Partly from obsolete *taynt,* to color, dye (from Anglo-Norman *teindre,* from Latin *tingere*), and partly from Middle English *teinten,* to convict (from Old French *ataindre,* to attain, touch upon).]

Tai·pei also **Tai·peh** (tī′pā′ *or* tī′bā′) The capital and largest city of Taiwan, in the northern part of the country. It was founded in the 1700s.

Tai·wan (tī′wän′) Officially **Republic of Chi·na** (chī′-nə) A country off the southeast coast of China made up of the island of **Taiwan** (formerly called Formosa) and smaller islands. Taiwan separated from mainland China in 1949. Taipei is the capital.

Ta·jik·i·stan (tä-jĭk′ĭ-stăn′ *or* tä-jĭk′ĭ-stän′) A country of south-central Asia east of Uzbekistan. It was part of the USSR from 1922 until 1991. Dushanbe is the capital.

ta·ka (tä′kə) *n.* The basic monetary unit of Bangladesh.

take (tāk) *v.* **took** (to͝ok), **tak·en** (tā′kən), **tak·ing, takes** *—tr.* **1.** To get into one's possession by means of the hands; grasp: *Take your partner's hand. Take the book and look at it.* **2.** To carry, convey, lead, or cause to go along to another place: *Take the umbrella with you. The bus took us to the museum. Are you taking the dog on your walk?* **3.** To capture physically; seize: *take an enemy fortress.* **4.** To kill, snare, or trap (fish or game, for example): *Poachers have taken some animals from the reserve.* **5.** To remove from a place: *took the dishes out of the sink.* **6.** To acquire in a game or competition; win: *took the crown in horse racing.* **7.** To select and offer to buy: *I'll take a vanilla milkshake.* **8a.** To put (food or drink, for example) into the body; eat or drink: *took a little soup for dinner.* **b.** To draw in; inhale: *took a deep breath.* **9.** To be struck by: *The ship took a torpedo in the bow.* **10.** To affect in a particular way: *Your action took me by surprise.* **11.** To charm or captivate: *The kids were really taken with the puppy.* **12.** To claim for oneself: *take all the credit.* **13.** To be subjected to; experience or endure: *The car took a beating on that long drive.* **14.** To have as a feeling; feel or perceive: *take pride in one's work; take offense at a rude remark.* **15.** To undertake, make, or perform: *take a walk; take a decision.* **16.** To have (a perception) through one of the senses: *I took a look at the display case.* **17.** To apply oneself to the study of: *take art lessons; take Spanish.* **18.** To require the use of: *It takes a lot of money to live in this town. This camera takes 35-millimeter film.* **19.** To use for safety or protection: *We took shelter in a cave.* **20.** To use or require (time): *Mowing the grass takes an hour. He took three days to record the song.* **21.** To require or have as a fitting or proper accompaniment: *a verb that takes a direct object.* **22.** To use (something) as a means of transportation: *take a train to Boston.* **23.** To choose and then follow (a particular route or direction): *Take a right at the next corner.* **24.** To wear or fit comfortably into (a garment size): *For shirts, he takes a medium.* **25.** To assume occupancy of: *take a seat.* **26.** To obtain, as through measurement or a specified procedure: *took the patient's temperature.* **27.** To create by writing: *take notes.* **28.** To create or make (a photograph): *took a picture of the boat.* **29.** To accept or deal with (something): *You must take the bad with the good. He does not take criticism well.* **30.** To regard or believe as true: *I'll take your word.* **31.** To follow (advice or a suggestion, for example): *I took your advice and studied for the exam.* **32.** To accept or adopt as one's own: *take a stand on an issue; take an interest in a hobby.* **33.** To allow to come in; give access or admission to: *The boat took a lot of water but remained afloat. We can't take more than 100 guests.* **34.** In baseball, to refrain from swinging at (a pitch). **35.** To subtract: *take 15 from 30.* *—intr.* **1.** To start growing; root or germinate: *Have the seeds taken?* **2.** To have the intended effect; operate or work: *The skin graft took.* ❖ *n.* **1.** A quantity collected at one time, especially the amount of profit or receipts taken by a business: *counted today's take.* **2a.** A scene filmed or televised without stopping the camera. **b.** A recording made in a single session. **3.** An interpretation or assessment, as of an event: *What is your take on the scandal?* ◆ **take advantage of 1.** To put to good use; avail oneself of: *take advantage of the sale.* **2.** To use unfairly and selfishly; exploit: *They took advantage of our friendship just to get a ride to the movies.* **take after** To resemble in appearance, temperament, or character: *He takes after his grandfather.* **take apart** To divide into parts; disassemble: *We had to take the chair apart to refinish it.* **take back** To retract (something stated or written): *I took back my promise when I saw I had been cheated.* **take care** To be careful: *Take care when you cross the street.* **take care of** To assume responsibility for the maintenance, support, or treatment of: *I'm taking care of the puppy now.* **take effect 1.** To become operative, as under law or regulation: *The new rules are to take effect today.* **2.** To produce a desired effect: *The antibiotic finally took effect.* **take for 1.** To regard as: *Many take him for a genius.* **2.** To consider mistakenly: *The teacher took me for my sister.* **take for granted 1.** To assume to be true, real, or forthcoming: *took it for granted that he would pass the test.* **2.** To underestimate the value of: *volunteers who felt they were being taken for granted.* **take hold 1.** To seize, as by grasping. **2.** To become established: *The new shrubs took hold on the hill.* **take in 1.** To receive (an amount of money) for a business or activity: *We took in $5,000 in donations.* **2.** To grant admittance to; receive as a guest or employee. **3.** To reduce in size; make smaller or shorter: *He had to take in the slacks before he could wear them.* **4.** To understand: *We took in the lecture despite its complexity.* **5.** To

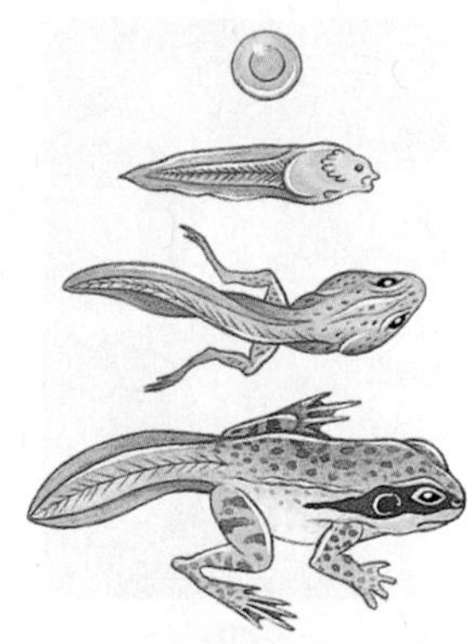

tadpole
egg and three stages of a tadpole metamorphosing into a frog

William Taft
1911 portrait by Anders Zorn (1860–1920)

tallit

talon
talons of an eagle

tamarind

ă pat	ôr core
ā pay	oi boy
âr care	ou out
ä father	o͝o took
ĕ pet	o͝or lure
ē be	o͞o boot
ĭ pit	ŭ cut
ī bite	ûr urge
îr pier	th thin
ŏ pot	*th* this
ō toe	zh vision
ô paw	ə about

look at thoroughly; view: *We took in the scenery.* **6.** To deceive: *I was taken in by a swindler.* **take into account** To consider: *Taking into account how little time he had to recover, he played well.* **take off 1.** To remove, as clothing: *took off our coats in the hallway.* **2.** To go off; leave: *She took off early from practice.* **3.** To rise in flight: *A flock of geese took off from the pond.* **4.** To spend (time) away from work. **take offense** To become angered, resentful, or displeased: *I took offense at his comment.* **take on 1.** To undertake or begin to handle: *took on some extra duties while a coworker was out.* **2.** To hire; engage: *take on an assistant.* **3.** To oppose in competition: *offered to take on any opponent.* **take (one's) time** To act slowly or at one's leisure. **take out 1.** To extract; remove: *had to have two teeth taken out.* **2.** *Informal* To escort, as a date. **3.** To express (a pent-up emotion): *took out his anger on the recruits.* **take over** To assume the control or management of (a company, for example). **take place** To happen; occur: *When did the event take place?* **take sick** or **take ill** To become sick. **take sides** To associate with and support a particular faction, group, cause, or person. **take to 1.** To go to, as for safety: *took to the hills.* **2.** To become fond of or attached to: *The new kitten really took to me.* **take up 1.** To absorb: *roots taking up water.* **2.** To develop an interest in or engage in: *decided to take up stamp collecting.* **3.** To use up or occupy: *The job took up all of her time. The bed takes up half the room.* **take up with** *Informal* To begin to associate with; consort with. [From Old English *tacan*, from Old Norse *taka*.] —**tak′er** *n.* —SEE NOTE AT **bring.**

take·off (tāk′ôf′) *n.* **1.** The act or process of rising in flight. Used of an airplane or rocket. **2.** *Informal* An amusing imitation, parody, or caricature.

take·out (tāk′out′) *adj.* Intended to be eaten off the premises: *takeout pizza.*

take·o·ver (tāk′ō′vər) *n.* The act or an instance of assuming control or management of something, especially the seizure of power.

talc (tălk) *n.* A fine-grained white, greenish, or gray mineral that is a silicate of magnesium and has a soft soapy texture. It is used in face powder and talcum powder, for coating paper, and as a filler in paints and plastics. [From French, from Arabic *ṭalq*, from Persian *talk*.]

tal·cum powder (tăl′kəm) *n.* A fine, often perfumed powder made from purified talc for use on the skin.

tale (tāl) *n.* **1.** Something told or related; a recital of events or happenings: *told us a tale of suspense.* **2.** A narrative of real or imaginary events; a story. **3.** A falsehood or lie: *Don't tell tales.* [From Old English *talu*.]
❑ *These sound alike:* **tale, tail** (hindmost part).

tal·ent (tăl′ənt) *n.* **1a.** A natural ability, as for artistic accomplishment. **b.** A person or group of people with such ability: *a great literary talent.* **2a.** An ancient unit of weight in the Middle East, Greece, and Rome. **b.** An ancient unit of currency based on this weight. [From Middle English, inclination, disposition, from Greek *talanton*, sum of money.]

tal·ent·ed (tăl′ən-tĭd) *adj.* Having talent; gifted: *a talented painter.*

ta·li (tā′lī′) *n.* Plural of **talus**[1].

Ta·li·ban (tăl′ə-băn′) *n.* A fundamentalist Muslim group of Afghanistan and western Pakistan, known for its military and paramilitary activities.

tal·is·man (tăl′ĭs-mən) *n., pl.* **tal·is·mans** An object marked with magic signs and believed to give supernatural powers or protection to its bearer.

talk (tôk) *v.* **talked, talk·ing, talks** —*intr.* **1.** To converse by means of spoken language: *We talked for hours.* **2.** To utter or pronounce words: *The baby can talk.* **3.** To imitate the sounds of human speech: *The parrot talks.* **4.** To express one's thoughts or emotions by means of a spoken language: *talked about the issue.* **5.** To convey one's thoughts in a way other than by spoken words: *talk with one's hands.* **6.** To express one's thoughts in writing: *In this book, the author talks about geology.* **7.** To spread rumors; gossip: *If you do that, people will talk.* **8.** To consult or confer with someone: *I talked with the doctor.* **9.** To reveal information concerning oneself or others, especially under pressure: *Has the prisoner talked?* —*tr.* **1.** To utter or pronounce (words): *The two-year-old is talking sentences now.* **2.** To speak of or discuss (something) or give expression to in words: *talk music; talk treason.* **3.** To speak or know how to speak in (a language or idiom): *talked French with the flight crew.* **4.** To gain, influence, or bring into a specified state by talking: *talked me into coming.* ❖ *n.* **1.** An exchange of ideas or opinions; a conversation. **2.** A speech or lecture. **3.** Hearsay, rumor, or speculation. **4.** A subject of conversation: *a musical that is the talk of the town.* **5.** Empty speech or unnecessary discussion: *all talk and no action.* **6.** A particular manner of speech: *baby talk.* ◆ **talk back** To make a rude reply. **talk down** To address someone in a condescending manner: *The speaker talked down to the young audience.* **talk over** To consider thoroughly in conversation; discuss: *We talked over the problem and decided what to do.* **talk sense** To speak rationally and coherently. [From Middle English *talken*.]

talk·a·tive (tô′kə-tĭv) *adj.* Tending to talk a great deal. —**talk′a·tive·ly** *adv.* —**talk′a·tive·ness** *n.*

talk·ing-to (tô′kĭng-to͞o′) *n., pl.* **talk·ing-tos** *Informal* A scolding.

tall (tôl) *adj.* **tall·er, tall·est 1.** Having greater than ordinary height: *a tall tree.* **2.** Having a specified height: *a plant three feet tall.* **3.** *Informal* Imaginary; fanciful or boastful: *a tall tale.* **4.** Impressively great or difficult: *a tall order to fill.* ❖ *adv.* **taller, tallest** With proud bearing; straight: *stand tall.* [From Middle English *tal*, brave, quick, from Old English *getæl*, swift.] —**tall′ness** *n.*

Tal·la·has·see (tăl′ə-**hăs′**ē) The capital of Florida, in the northwest part of the state west of Jacksonville. It was originally a Native American village.

Tal·linn (tăl′ĭn *or* tä′lĭn) The capital of Estonia, in the northwest part of the country on the Gulf of Finland opposite Helsinki, Finland.

tal·lit (tä-lēt′) *n., pl.* **tal·lits** or **tal·li·tot** (tä-lē′tôt) A shawl with ritually knotted tassels at each of four corners traditionally worn by Jewish men and boys, especially at morning prayer.

tal·low (tăl′ō) *n.* A mixture of fats obtained from animals such as cattle or sheep and used to make soaps and lubricants. In the past, candles were made from tallow. [From Middle English *talou*.]

tal·ly (tăl′ē) *n., pl.* **tal·lies 1.** A reckoning or score. **2.** A stick on which notches are made to keep a count or score. ❖ *v.* **tal·lied, tal·ly·ing, tal·lies** —*tr.* To reckon or record a mark: *tallied up our bill.* —*intr.* **1.** To be alike; correspond or agree: *The two accounts tallied in every detail.* **2.** To score a point or goal in a game or contest: *The midfielder tallied again in the third period.*

tal·ly·ho (tăl′ē-**hō′**) *interj.* An expression used to urge hounds on during fox hunting.

Tal·mud (täl′mo͝od *or* tăl′məd) *n.* The collection of ancient theological and legal writings that constitutes the basis of religious authority in Orthodox Judaism. [From Hebrew *talmūd*, learning, instruction.]

tal·on (tăl′ən) *n.* A claw of an animal, especially a bird of prey.

ta·lus[1] (tā′ləs) *n., pl.* **ta·li** (tā′lī′) **1.** The bone that forms a joint with the tibia and fibula, making up the main bone of the ankle. **2.** The ankle. [From Latin *tālus*, ankle.]

ta·lus[2] (tā′ləs) *n., pl.* **ta·lus·es** A sloping mass of rock debris at the base of a cliff. [From Latin *talūtium*, gold-bearing outcrop.]

tam (tăm) *n.* A tam-o'-shanter.

ta·ma·le (tə-**mä′**lē) *n.* A Mexican dish made of fried chopped meat and crushed peppers wrapped in cornhusks and steamed.
❑ *These sound alike:* **tamale, tomalley** (lobster liver).

tam·a·rack (**tăm′**ə-răk′) *n.* A North American larch tree.

tam·a·rind (**tăm′**ə-rĭnd′) *n.* **1.** The pulp from the seedpods of a tropical tree, having a pleasant sour taste and used as food and flavoring. **2.** The tree that bears such pods. [From Middle English *tamarinde*, from Arabic *tamr hindī* : *tamr*, dates + *hindī*, of India.]

tam·a·risk (**tăm′**ə-rĭsk′) *n.* Any of numerous shrubs or small trees native to Africa and Eurasia and also found in western North America, having small leaves and clusters of small pinkish flowers.

tam·bour (**tăm′**bo͝or′ *or* tăm-**bo͝or′**) *n.* **1.** A drum or drummer. **2.** A small embroidery frame consisting of two hoops that fit one inside the other and between which fabric is stretched.

tam·bou·rine (tăm′bə-**rēn′**) *n.* **1.** A percussion instrument consisting of a small drumhead with small metal disks fitted into the rim that jingle when the instrument is struck or shaken. **2.** A similar instrument without a drumhead.

tame (tām) *adj.* **tam·er, tam·est 1.** In a domesticated state: *Cattle are tame animals.* **2.** Unafraid; not timid: *The squirrel was very tame and took a nut from my hand.* **3.** Unexciting or uninteresting; dull: *After the rapids, this stretch of the river seems very tame.* ❖ *tr.v.* **tamed, tam·ing, tames 1.** To make tame; domesticate: *tame a wild horse.* **2.** To subdue or curb: *taming his fears.* **—tame′ly** *adv.* **—tame′ness** *n.* **—tam′er** *n.*

Tam·il (**tăm′**əl *or* **tŭm′**əl *or* **tä′**məl) *n., pl.* **Tamil** or **Tam·ils 1.** A member of a people of southern India and northern Sri Lanka. **2.** The language of the Tamil.

tam-o′-shan·ter (**tăm′**ə-shăn′tər) *n.* A tight-fitting Scottish cap, sometimes having a pompom, feather, or tassel in the center. [After the hero of *"Tam o' Shanter,"* a poem by Robert Burns.]

tamp (tămp) *tr.v.* **tamped, tamp·ing, tamps 1.** To pack down tightly: *tamp the gravel.* **2.** To pack clay, sand, or dirt into (a hole) above an explosive.

Tam·pa (**tăm′**pə) A city of west-central Florida on **Tampa Bay,** an inlet of the Gulf of Mexico. It was established as a fort in 1824.

tam·per (**tăm′**pər) *intr.v.* **tam·pered, tam·per·ing, tam·pers 1.** To interfere in a harmful manner: *caught tampering with the switches.* **2.** To engage in secret or improper dealings, as in an effort to influence: *tamper with the jury.* **—tam′per·er** *n.*

tam·pon (**tăm′**pŏn′) *n.* An elongated piece of material inserted into the vagina to absorb the blood released during menstruation.

tan[1] (tăn) *v.* **tanned, tan·ning, tans** *—tr.* **1.** To convert (an animal hide) into leather by causing it to undergo a chemical process that stabilizes the proteins, making it more resistant to decay. **2.** To make (a person or a person's skin) darker by exposure to the sun. *—intr.* To become darker from exposure to the sun. ❖ *n.* **1.** A light or moderate yellowish brown to brownish orange. **2.** A suntan. **3.** Tannin or a solution made from it. ❖ *adj.* **tan·ner, tan·nest 1.** Light or moderate yellowish-brown to brownish-orange. **2.** Having a suntan. [From Middle English *tannen*, to tan, from Medieval Latin *tannum*, tanbark.]

tan[2] *abbr.* An abbreviation of tangent.

tan·a·ger (**tăn′**ĭ-jər) *n.* Any of various songbirds of the Americas that often have brightly colored feathers in the male.

Ta·nakh (tä-**näKH′**) *n.* The Hebrew Scriptures.

tan·dem (**tăn′**dəm) *n.* **1.** An arrangement of two or more people or things placed one behind the other: *The clowns rode unicycles in tandem.* **2.** A tandem bicycle. ❖ *adv.* One behind the other: *riding tandem.* [From Latin, at last, at length.]

tandem bicycle *n.* A bicycle built for two or more people sitting one behind the other.

tang (tăng) *n.* **1.** A sharp distinctive flavor, taste, or odor, as that of orange juice. **2.** A trace or hint of something. **3.** A sharp point, tongue, or prong. **4.** A projection by which a tool such as a file, chisel, or knife is attached to its handle.

tan·ge·lo (**tăn′**jə-lō′) *n., pl.* **tan·ge·los** A citrus fruit that is a cross between a grapefruit and a tangerine.

tan·gent (**tăn′**jənt) *n.* **1.** A line, curve, or surface touching but not intersecting another. **2.** In a right triangle, a function of an acute angle equal to the length of the side opposite the angle divided by the length of the side adjacent to the angle. **3.** A sudden digression or change of course: *go off on a tangent.* ❖ *adj.* Making contact at a point or along a line; touching but not intersecting. [From Latin *(līnea) tangēns*, touching (line), from *tangere*, to touch.]

tan·gen·tial (tăn-**jĕn′**shəl) *adj.* **1.** Relating to or moving along in the direction of a tangent. **2.** Only superficially relevant to the matter at hand. **—tan·gen′tial·ly** *adv.*

tan·ger·ine (tăn′jə-**rēn′** *or* **tăn′**jə-rēn′) *n.* A type of mandarin orange having deep orange skin that peels easily.

tan·gi·ble (**tăn′**jə-bəl) *adj.* **1.** Capable of being felt with the sense of touch: *a tangible vibration.* **2.** Capable of being touched: *a tangible product like steel.* **3.** Capable of being treated as fact; real or concrete: *tangible evidence.* **4.** Capable of being understood or realized: *a tangible benefit.* **—tan′gi·bly** *adv.*

Tan·gier (tăn-**jîr′**) also **Tan·giers** (tăn-**jîrz′**) A city of northern Morocco at the western end of the Strait of Gibraltar. It was founded by the ancient Phoenicians.

tan·gle (**tăng′**gəl) *v.* **tan·gled, tan·gling, tan·gles** *—tr.* **1.** To mix together or intertwine in a confused mass; snarl: *A bad cast tangled my fishing line.* **2.** To catch or hold as if in a net; entrap: *He was tangled up in the scandal.* *—intr.* **1.** To be or become entangled. **2.** *Informal* To enter into an argument, dispute, or conflict: *We tangled over the wording of our editorial.* ❖ *n.* **1.** A confused snarled mass: *a tangle of vines.* **2.** A confused state or condition. **3.** *Informal* An argument.

tan·go (**tăng′**gō) *n., pl.* **tan·gos 1.** A Latin American ballroom dance in 2/4 or 4/4 time. **2.** The music for this dance. ❖ *intr.v.* **tan·goed, tan·go·ing, tan·gos** To perform this dance.

tang·y (**tăng′**ē) *adj.* Having a sharp distinctive flavor, taste, or odor: *a tangy cheese.*

tank (tăngk) *n.* **1a.** A large, often metallic container for holding or storing fluids or gases: *a gasoline tank.* **b.** The amount that such a container can hold: *Buy a tank of gas.* **2.** A large, usually glass-walled container in which live fish, reptiles, or other animals are kept. **3.** An enclosed, heavily armored combat vehicle mounted with a cannon and guns and moving on treads. ❖ *intr.v.* **tanked, tank·ing, tanks** *Slang* To decline suddenly and sharply: *When the company announced that its sales would not meet expectations, its stock tanked.*

tank·ard (**tăng′**kərd) *n.* A large drinking cup having a single handle and often a hinged cover.

tank·er (**tăng′**kər) *n.* A ship, truck, or plane equipped to transport liquids, such as oil, in bulk.

tan·ki·ni (tăng-**kē′**nē) *n., pl.* **tan·ki·nis** A two-piece women's swimsuit having a tank top and a bikini bottom. [Blend of *tank top* + *bikini.*]

tank top *n.* A sleeveless, tight-fitting, usually knit shirt with shoulder straps.

tan·ner (**tăn′**ər) *n.* A person who tans hides.

tan·ner·y (**tăn′**ə-rē) *n., pl.* **tan·ner·ies** A place where hides are tanned.

tan·nic (**tăn′**ĭk) *adj.* Relating to or obtained from tannin.

tanager

tandem bicycle

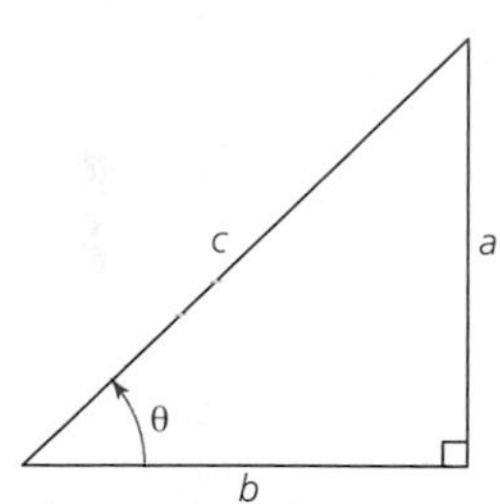

tangent
tan θ = a/b

tank top

tapa

tarantula

ă	pat	ôr	core
ā	pay	oi	boy
âr	care	ou	out
ä	father	o͝o	took
ĕ	pet	o͝or	lure
ē	be	o͞o	boot
ĭ	pit	ŭ	cut
ī	bite	ûr	urge
îr	pier	th	thin
ŏ	pot	*th*	this
ō	toe	zh	vision
ô	paw	ə	about

tannic acid *n.* A yellowish to light-brown tannin obtained from certain plants and used in tanning hides, in dyeing, and in making beer and wine.

tan·nin (tăn′ĭn) *n.* **1.** Any of various plant compounds that bind with proteins and promote the tanning of leather. **2.** Any of various other substances that promote the tanning of leather.

tan·ning (tăn′ĭng) *n.* **1.** The art or process of making leather from animal hides. **2.** Darkening of the skin by exposure to the ultraviolet rays in sunlight.

tan·sy (tăn′zē) *n., pl.* **tan·sies** Any of several strong-smelling plants having feathery leaves and broad clusters of yellow flowers.

tan·ta·lite (tăn′tə-līt′) *n.* A black to red-brown mineral that contains tantalum and some niobium and is used as an ore for both.

tan·ta·lize (tăn′tə-līz′) *tr.v.* **tan·ta·lized, tan·ta·liz·ing, tan·ta·liz·es** To excite (someone) by presenting something desirable while keeping it out of reach.

tan·ta·lum (tăn′tə-ləm) *n. Symbol* **Ta** A hard, heavy, gray metallic element that is very resistant to corrosion at lower temperatures. It is used in electronic devices, nuclear reactor parts, and surgical instruments. Atomic number 73. See **Periodic Table.**

tan·ta·mount (tăn′tə-mount′) *adj.* Equivalent in effect or value: *a rule tantamount to a dictatorship.*

tan·trum (tăn′trəm) *n.* A fit of bad temper: *The child threw a tantrum when he was told to go to bed.*

Tan·za·ni·a (tăn′zə-**nē′**ə) A country of east-central Africa on the Indian Ocean south of Kenya. Dodoma is the capital and Dar es Salaam the largest city.

Tao (dou *or* tou) *n.* **1.** In Taoism, the basic, eternal principle of the universe. **2.** In Confucianism, the right manner of human activity and virtuous conduct.

Tao·ism (**tou′**ĭz′əm *or* **dou′**ĭz′əm) *n.* A Chinese system of religion and philosophy that emphasizes living simply and in harmony with nature and is based on the teachings of Lao-tzu, a legendary sixth-century BC philosopher.

tap[1] (tăp) *v.* **tapped, tap·ping, taps** —*tr.* **1.** To strike gently with a light blow or blows: *tap him on the shoulder.* **2.** To give a light rap with: *tap a pencil on the desk.* **3.** To produce with a succession of light blows: *tap out a rhythm.* **4.** To repair or reinforce (shoe heels or toes) by putting on a tap or taps. —*intr.* **1.** To deliver a gentle light blow or blows. **2.** To walk making light clicks. ❖ *n.* **1a.** A gentle blow. **b.** The sound made by such a blow. **2a.** A layer of leather or other material used to repair and reinforce the worn heel or toe of a shoe. **b.** A metal plate attached to the toe or heel of a shoe, as for tap-dancing. [From Middle English *tappen*, possibly from Old French *taper*.]

tap[2] (tăp) *n.* **1a.** A valve and spout used to regulate the flow of a fluid at the end of a pipe. **b.** A plug for a hole in a cask from which a liquid is drained or poured out. **2.** A tool for cutting a screw thread into the inner wall of a drilled hole. **3.** A wiretap. ❖ *tr.v.* **tapped, tap·ping, taps 1.** To furnish with a spigot or tap. **2.** To pierce in order to draw off liquid: *tap a maple tree.* **3.** To draw (liquid) from a vessel or container: *tap a barrel.* **4.** To make a connection with, as to divert part of a flow: *tap an electric circuit.* **5.** To wiretap (a telephone). ◆ **on tap** Ready to be drawn; in a tapped cask. [From Old English *tæppa*.]

ta·pa (tä′pə *or* tăp′ə) *n.* **1.** The fibrous inner bark of a kind of mulberry tree. **2.** A cloth made in the islands of the Pacific Ocean by pounding this bark.

tap dance *n.* A dance in which the dancer sounds out and elaborates the rhythm by striking the floor with taps that are attached to the heels and toes of his or her shoes. **—tap′-dance′** *v.* **—tap dancer** *n.*

tape (tāp) *n.* **1.** A narrow strip of strong woven fabric, as that used in sewing. **2.** A continuous narrow, flexible strip of cloth, metal, paper, or plastic, as adhesive tape, magnetic tape, or ticker tape. **3.** A string or strip stretched across the finish line of a race to be broken by the winner. **4a.** A length, reel, or cassette of magnetic tape. **b.** A recording made on magnetic tape: *We listened to a tape of a speech from 1972.* ❖ *tr.v.* **taped, tap·ing, tapes 1.** To fasten, wrap, or bind with tape: *tape a bow on a package; tape a sprained wrist.* **2.** To measure with a tape measure. **3.** To record (sounds or pictures) on magnetic tape. [From Middle English, from Old English *tæppe*.]

tape deck *n.* A tape recorder and player having no built-in amplifiers or speakers, used as a component in an audio system.

tape measure *n.* A tape of cloth, paper, or metal marked off in a scale, as of inches or centimeters, used for taking measurements.

ta·per (tā′pər) *n.* **1.** A small or slender candle. **2.** A gradual decrease in thickness or width of an elongated object: *the taper of a cone.* ❖ *v.* **ta·pered, ta·per·ing, ta·pers** —*intr.* **1.** To become gradually thinner toward one end: *a candle tapering to a point.* **2.** To diminish or lessen gradually: *The storm tapered off.* —*tr.* **1.** To make thinner or narrower at one end: *tapered the board to fit the slot.* **2.** To make smaller gradually.

❑ *These sound alike:* **taper, tapir** (animal).

tape-re·cord (tāp′rĭ-kôrd′) *tr.v.* **tape-re·cord·ed, tape-re·cord·ing, tape-re·cords** To record on magnetic tape.

tape recorder *n.* A mechanical device for recording on magnetic tape and usually for playing back the recorded material.

tape recording *n.* **1.** A magnetic tape on which sound or visual images have been recorded. **2.** The act of recording on magnetic tape.

tap·es·try (tăp′ĭ-strē) *n., pl.* **tap·es·tries** A heavy cloth woven with rich, often many-colored designs and scenes, usually hung on walls for decoration and sometimes used to cover furniture.

tape·worm (tāp′wûrm′) *n.* Any of various long flatworms that live as parasites in the intestines of humans and other animals.

tap·i·o·ca (tăp′ē-**ō′**kə) *n.* A starch made from cassava roots, used in puddings and as a thickener in cooking.

ta·pir (tā′pər *or* tə-**pîr′**) *n.* Any of several tropical American or Asian mammals having a stocky body, short legs, and a long fleshy snout.

❑ *These sound alike:* **tapir, taper** (candle).

tap·root (**tăp′**ro͞ot′ *or* **tăp′**ro͝ot′) *n.* The main, often thick root of a plant, growing straight downward from the stem.

taps (tăps) *pl.n. (used with a singular or plural verb)* A bugle call or drum signal sounded at night, as at a military camp, as an order to put out lights and also sounded at funerals and memorial services.

tar[1] (tär) *n.* A thick oily dark mixture consisting mainly of hydrocarbons, made by heating wood, coal, or other organic materials in the absence of oxygen. ❖ *tr.v.* **tarred, tar·ring, tars** To coat with tar. ◆ **tar and feather** To punish (a person) by covering with tar and feathers. [From Old English *teru*.]

tar[2] (tär) *n. Informal* A sailor. [Possibly short for *tarpaulin*.]

tar·an·tel·la (tăr′ən-**tĕl′**ə) *n.* **1.** A lively whirling dance of southern Italy. **2.** The music for this dance. [From Italian, after *Taranto*, Italy.]

ta·ran·tu·la (tə-**răn′**chə-lə) *n.* Any of various large, hairy, mostly tropical spiders capable of inflicting a bite that is painful but usually not dangerous to humans. [From Medieval Latin, from Old Italian *tarantola*, after *Taranto*, Italy.]

Ta·ra·wa (tə-**rä′**wə *or* **tăr′**ə-wä′) The capital of Kiribati, on an atoll in the western Pacific Ocean.

tar·dy (tär′dē) *adj.* **tar·di·er, tar·di·est 1.** Occurring, arriving, acting, or done later than expected: *a tardy guest.* **2.** Moving slowly; sluggish: *tardy acceptance of new ideas.* **—tar′di·ly** *adv.* **—tar′di·ness** *n.*

tare[1] (târ) *n.* Any of several weedy plants that grow in grain fields. [From Middle English.]

❑ *These sound alike:* **tare[1]** (weed), **tare[2]** (weight), **tear[1]** (rend).

tare[2] (târ) *n.* The weight of a container or wrapper that is subtracted from the gross weight to obtain the net weight. [From Middle English, from Old French, from Arabic *ṭarḥa*, that which is thrown away, subtraction.]

❑ *These sound alike:* **tare[2]** (weight), **tare[1]** (weed), **tear[1]** (rend).

tar·get (tär′gĭt) *n.* **1.** An object that is shot at to test accuracy in rifle or archery practice. **2.** Something aimed or fired at: *The target of the snowball was a trash can.* **3.** An object of criticism or attack: *the target of her satire.* **4.** A desired goal or aim: *the target of the research program.*

tar·iff (tăr′ĭf) *n.* **1.** A list or system of duties imposed by a government on imported or exported goods. **2.** A duty or duties imposed in this way: *a tariff on wool.* **3.** A schedule of prices or fees.

tar·nish (tär′nĭsh) *v.* **tar·nished, tar·nish·ing, tar·nish·es** *—tr.* **1.** To dull the luster of; discolor: *Being in the ground for so long had tarnished the old coins.* **2.** To detract from or spoil: *The scandal tarnished his reputation.* *—intr.* **1.** To lose luster; become discolored: *The silver cup tarnished as it sat on the shelf.* **2.** To diminish or become tainted. ❖ *n.* **1.** The condition of being tarnished. **2.** Discoloration of a metal surface, as from oxidation.

ta·ro (tär′ō *or* tăr′ō) *n., pl.* **ta·ros 1.** A tropical plant having broad leaves and a large starchy underground stem used as food. **2.** The large underground stem of this plant, similar to a potato.

tarp (tärp) *n.* A tarpaulin.

tar·pa·per (tär′pā′pər) *n.* Heavy paper coated or saturated with tar, used as a waterproof protective material in building.

tar·pau·lin (tär-pô′lĭn *or* tär′pə-lĭn) *n.* **1.** Material, such as waterproof canvas, used to cover and protect things from moisture. **2.** A sheet of this material: *put a tarpaulin over the boat.*

tar·pon (tär′pən) *n., pl.* **tarpon** or **tar·pons** Any of several large silvery fishes often caught for sport.

tar·ra·gon (tăr′ə-gŏn′) *n.* A perennial plant native to Eurasia, having aromatic leaves that are used as a seasoning.

tar·ry[1] (tăr′ē) *intr.v.* **tar·ried, tar·ry·ing, tar·ries 1.** To delay or be late in coming, going, or doing: *tarry on the way to school.* **2.** To remain or stay temporarily: *tarried after the show to chat with friends.* [From Middle English *tarien.*]

tar·ry[2] (tär′ē) *adj.* **tar·ri·er, tar·ri·est** Relating to, resembling, or covered with tar: *a tarry substance.*

tar·sal (tär′səl) *adj.* Relating to or near the ankle.

tar·si·er (tär′sē-ər *or* tär′sē-ā′) *n.* Any of several insect-eating primates of Southeast Asia that have large eyes, long fingers and toes, and a long tail.

tar·sus (tär′səs) *n., pl.* **tar·si** (tär′sī) **1.** The section of the vertebrate foot located between the leg and the metatarsus. **2.** The bones making up this section, especially the seven small bones of the human ankle.

tart[1] (tärt) *adj.* **tart·er, tart·est 1.** Having a sharp pungent taste; sour: *tart cranberries.* **2.** Sharp or bitter in tone or meaning; biting: *a tart answer.* [From Old English *teart*, sharp, severe.] **—tart′ly** *adv.* **—tart′ness** *n.*

tart[2] (tärt) *n.* A small, shallow pastry shell with a sweet or savory filling and no crust on top. [From Middle English *tarte*, perhaps from Late Latin *torta*, a kind of bread.]

tar·tan (tär′tn) *n.* **1.** Any of a number of fabric patterns consisting of stripes in different colors and widths crossed at right angles against a solid background, each forming a distinctive design worn by the members of a Scottish clan. **2.** A twilled wool fabric or garment having such a pattern.

tar·tar (tär′tər) *n.* **1.** A hard yellowish deposit that collects on the teeth, consisting of food particles and secretions held together by insoluble salts such as calcium carbonate. **2.** A reddish acid substance, chiefly a potassium salt of tartaric acid, found in the juice of grapes and deposited on the sides of casks during winemaking.

Tar·tar (tär′tər) *n.* A Tatar, especially one of those who invaded western Asia and eastern Europe in the Middle Ages. **—Tar′tar** *adj.*

tar·tar·ic acid (tär-tăr′ĭk) *n.* Any of four organic acids used in tanning, to make cream of tartar, and in various foods, beverages, and chemicals.

tartar sauce *n.* Mayonnaise mixed with chopped pickles and other ingredients, used as a condiment for seafood.

Tar·ta·rus (tär′tər-əs) *n.* In Greek mythology, the regions below Hades where the gods confine the Titans.

Tash·kent (tăsh-**kĕnt′**) The capital of Uzbekistan, in the eastern part of the country north of Dushanbe, Tajikistan. It is one of the oldest cities of central Asia.

task (tăsk) *n.* **1.** A piece of work assigned or done as part of one's duties. **2.** A difficult or tedious undertaking: *the task of building a nation.* ❖ *tr.v.* **tasked, task·ing, tasks 1.** To assign a task to or impose a task on: *She tasked us with cleaning out the attic.* **2.** To subject to strain or hardship: *The history project tasked his ability to organize information.*

SYNONYMS task, job, chore, assignment These nouns mean a piece of work that one must do. A **task** is a well-defined responsibility that is sometimes burdensome and is usually required by someone else: *The receptionist's main task is to answer the telephones.* **Job** often suggests a specific short-term piece of work: *We spent the day doing odd jobs around the house.* **Chore** often means a minor, routine, or odd job: *I have to finish my chores before I can go out.* **Assignment** usually means a task given to a person by an authority: *For tonight's assignment, read the first chapter.*

---

task·bar (tăsk′bär′) *n.* A row of buttons on a computer screen that represent programs that are running.

task force *n.* A temporary grouping of forces and resources for a specific goal: *a military task force.*

task·mas·ter (tăsk′măs′tər) *n.* A person who regularly assigns tasks, especially difficult or burdensome ones.

Tas·ma·ni·a (tăz-**mā′**nē-ə) An island of southeast Australia in the Indian Ocean south of Melbourne. It joined Australia in 1901.

Tas·ma·ni·an devil (tăz-**mā′**nē-ən) *n.* A meat-eating marsupial of Tasmania, having black fur and a long tail.

tas·sel (tăs′əl) *n.* **1.** A bunch of loose threads or cords bound at one end and hanging free at the other, used as an ornament on curtains and clothing, for example. **2.** Something resembling such an ornament, especially the pollen-bearing flower cluster of a corn plant. ❖ *tr.v.* **tas·seled, tas·sel·ing, tas·sels** or **tas·selled, tas·sel·ling, tas·sels** To decorate or fringe with tassels.

taste (tāst) *v.* **tast·ed, tast·ing, tastes** *—tr.* **1.** To distinguish the flavor of (something) by taking it into the mouth. **2.** To eat or drink a small quantity of: *I've already eaten, so I'll just taste the salmon.* **3.** To partake of, especially for the first time; experience: *tasted freedom and loved it.* *—intr.* To have a distinct flavor: *The stew tastes salty.* ❖ *n.* **1.** The sense that responds to the chemical makeup of substances in contact with the taste buds. **2.** A basic sensation produced by this sense, such as

tarpaulin
covering a haystack

tarragon

Tasmanian devil

tassel

sweetness, saltiness, sourness, or bitterness. **3.** A sensation combining these basic sensations with sensations of smell and texture; flavor. **4.** A distinctive feeling or reaction: *an experience that left a bad taste in my mouth.* **5.** A small quantity eaten or tasted: *Have a taste of this pie.* **6.** A limited or first experience; a sample: *got a taste of fame and did not like it.* **7.** A personal preference or liking: *a taste for mysteries.* **8.** The ability to recognize and appreciate what is beautiful, excellent, or appropriate: *good taste in clothes.* **9.** The sense of what is proper, seemly, or least likely to offend in a given social situation: *a remark made in bad taste.* [From Middle English *tasten*, to touch, taste, from Old French *taster*.]

taste bud *n.* Any of numerous rounded structures on the surface of the tongue that contain cells producing nerve impulses corresponding to sweet, sour, salty, or bitter stimuli.

taste·ful (tāst′fəl) *adj.* Having, showing, or being in keeping with good taste: *a tasteful reply.* **—taste′ful·ly** *adv.* **—taste′ful·ness** *n.*

taste·less (tāst′lĭs) *adj.* **1.** Lacking in flavor: *a tasteless dish.* **2.** Having or showing poor taste: *a tasteless remark.* **—taste′less·ly** *adv.* **—taste′less·ness** *n.*

tast·y (tā′stē) *adj.* **tast·i·er, tast·i·est** Having a pleasing flavor: *a tasty meal.* **—tast′i·ly** *adv.* **—tast′i·ness** *n.*

tat (tăt) *intr. & tr.v.* **tat·ted, tat·ting, tats** To do tatting or to produce (something) by tatting.

Ta·tar (tä′tər) *n.* **1.** A member of a group of Turkic peoples mostly living in west-central Russia and parts of Siberia and central Asia. **2.** Any of the Turkic languages of the Tatars.

tat·ter (tăt′ər) *n.* **1.** A torn and hanging piece of cloth; a shred. **2. tatters** Torn and ragged clothing; rags. ❖ *tr. & intr.v.* **tat·tered, tat·ter·ing, tat·ters** To make or become ragged.

tat·tered (tăt′ərd) *adj.* **1.** Torn into shreds; ragged: *tattered clothes.* **2.** Dressed in ragged clothes: *a tattered ragamuffin.* **3.** Shabby or dilapidated.

tat·ting (tăt′ĭng) *n.* **1.** Lace made by looping and knotting a single strand of heavy thread on a small hand shuttle. **2.** The act or art of making such lace.

tat·tle (tăt′l) *intr.v.* **tat·tled, tat·tling, tat·tles** To report someone's misbehavior, especially to a person in authority: *The boy tattled on his sister.* **—tat′tler** *n.*

tat·tle·tale (tăt′l-tāl′) *n.* A person who tattles on others.

tat·too[1] (tă-to͞o′) *n., pl.* **tat·toos 1.** A signal sounded on a drum or bugle to summon soldiers or sailors to their quarters at night. **2.** A display of military exercises. **3.** A continuous even drumming or rapping. [From Dutch *taptoe*, tap-shut (closing time for taverns), tattoo : *tap*, spigot, tap + *toe*, shut.]

tat·too[2] (tă-to͞o′) *n., pl.* **tat·toos** A design made on the skin, especially by pricking the skin with a sharp implement and inserting dye or by making small cuts that cause scars. ❖ *tr.v.* **tat·tooed, tat·too·ing, tat·toos** To mark (the skin) with a tattoo. [From Tahitian *tatau*.]

tau (tou *or* tô) *n.* The 19th letter of the Greek alphabet, written Τ, τ. In English it is represented as *T, t.*

taught (tôt) *v.* Past tense and past participle of **teach.**
❑ *These sound alike:* **taught, taut** (tense).

taunt (tônt) *tr.v.* **taunt·ed, taunt·ing, taunts** To tease (someone), especially in a brazen or insulting manner. ❖ *n.* A mocking remark directed at someone.

taupe (tōp) *n.* A brownish gray.

Tau·rus (tôr′əs) *n.* **1.** A constellation in the Northern Hemisphere, traditionally pictured as a bull. **2.** The second sign of the zodiac in astrology.

taut (tôt) *adj.* **taut·er, taut·est 1.** Pulled or drawn tight: *a taut rope.* **2.** Strained; tense: *taut nerves.* **3.** Neatly or efficiently arranged: *a taut ship; a taut movie script.* **—taut′ly** *adv.* **—taut′ness** *n.*
❑ *These sound alike:* **taut, taught** (instructed).

tau·tol·o·gy (tô-tŏl′ə-jē) *n., pl.* **tau·tol·o·gies 1.** Needless repetition of the same information in different words; redundancy. **2.** A statement made up of simpler statements that is logically true whether the simpler statements are true or false; for example, the statement *Either it will rain tomorrow or it will not rain tomorrow* is a tautology.

tav·ern (tăv′ərn) *n.* **1.** A place of business that serves alcoholic beverages and often basic meals. **2.** An inn for travelers. [From Middle English *taverne*, from Latin *taberna*, hut, tavern.]

taw (tô) *n.* **1.** A large fancy marble used for shooting. **2.** The line from which a player shoots in marbles.

taw·dry (tô′drē) *adj.* **taw·dri·er, taw·dri·est 1.** Cheap and gaudy in nature or appearance. **2.** Shameful or indecent: *tawdry secrets.* [From *tawdry lace*, lace necktie, alteration of *Saint Audrey's lace* (sold at the annual Saint Audrey's fair, Ely, England), after *Saint Audrey* (Saint Etheldreda), queen of Northumbria, who died in 679 of a throat tumor, supposedly because she delighted in fancy necklaces as a young woman.] **—taw′dri·ness** *n.*

taw·ny (tô′nē) *n.* A light brown to brownish orange. **—taw′ny** *adj.*

tax (tăks) *n.* **1.** A contribution for the support of a government required of people, groups, or businesses within the domain of that government. **2.** A burdensome or excessive demand; a strain: *The extra orders are a tax on our system of production.* ❖ *tr.v.* **taxed, tax·ing, tax·es 1.** To place a tax on (income, property, or goods). **2.** To require a tax from: *tax the people.* **3.** To make difficult or excessive demands upon: *Don't tax my patience.* [From Middle English, from *taxen*, to tax, from Latin *taxāre*, to touch, reproach, reckon.]

tax·a·ble (tăk′sə-bəl) *adj.* Subject to taxation: *taxable income.*

tax·a·tion (tăk-sā′shən) *n.* The act or practice of imposing taxes: *no taxation without representation.*

tax·i (tăk′sē) *n., pl.* **tax·is** or **tax·ies** A taxicab. ❖ *v.* **tax·ied** (tăk′sēd), **tax·i·ing** or **tax·y·ing, tax·ies** or **tax·is** (tăk′sēz) *—intr.* **1.** To be transported by taxi. **2.** To move slowly over the surface of the ground or water before takeoff or after landing: *The airplane taxied to the runway.* *—tr.* To cause (an aircraft) to taxi.

tax·i·cab (tăk′sē-kăb′) *n.* An automobile that carries passengers for a fare, usually calculated on a meter.

tax·i·der·my (tăk′sĭ-dûr′mē) *n.* The art or process of preparing, stuffing, and mounting the skins of animals for exhibition in a lifelike form. **—tax′i·der′mist** *n.*

tax·on·o·my (tăk-sŏn′ə-mē) *n., pl.* **tax·on·o·mies** The science of classifying and naming organisms based on shared characteristics and natural relationships. [From French *taxonomie* : Greek *taxis*, arrangement + Greek *-nomiā*, system of rules.] **—tax′o·nom′ic** (tăk′sə-nŏm′ĭk) *adj.*

tax·pay·er (tăks′pā′ər) *n.* A person who pays or is required to pay taxes.

Tay·lor (tā′lər), **Zachary** 1784–1850. The 12th president of the United States (1849–1850). His presidency was marked by debate over whether new territories should be admitted to the union as Free or Slave States.

Zachary Taylor
1848 portrait by James Reid Lambdin (1807–1889)

Tb The symbol for the element **terbium.**

TB *abbr.* An abbreviation of tuberculosis.

Tbi·li·si (tə-bə-lē′sē) The capital of Georgia, in the southeast part of the country north of Yerevan, Armenia.

tbs. or **tbsp.** *abbr.* An abbreviation of tablespoon.

Tc The symbol for the element **technetium.**

T cell *n.* Any of the lymphocytes that mature in the thymus and have several functions in the immune system. T cells destroy infected cells and cancer cells and also regulate the function of B cells.

ă	pat	ôr	core
ā	pay	oi	boy
âr	care	ou	out
ä	father	o͝o	took
ĕ	pet	o͝or	lure
ē	be	o͞o	boot
ĭ	pit	ŭ	cut
ī	bite	ûr	urge
îr	pier	th	thin
ŏ	pot	*th*	this
ō	toe	zh	vision
ô	paw	ə	about

Taxonomy

Taxonomy is the scientific classification of life. Traditionally it is based on the system first developed by the Swedish botanist Carl Linnaeus in the 1700s. In the Linnaean system, organisms are divided into groups with Greek or Latin names. As scientists learn more about how organisms are related to each other, these classifications change. Most modern biologists divide life into three **domains**: archaea, bacteria, and eukaryotes. The eukaryotes are usually divided into four **kingdoms**: protists, fungi, plants, and animals. Another system divides life into five kingdoms, grouping the archaea and bacteria together into the kingdom Prokaryota (the prokaryotes).

DOMAIN	KINGDOM	TYPES OF ORGANISMS
Archaea	*	one-celled organisms without a nucleus that often live in extreme environments
Bacteria	*	one-celled organisms without a nucleus that live in soil, water, and other organisms
Eukaryota	**Protista**	one-celled organisms such as amoebas, euglenas, and some parasites; also many algae
	Fungi	mushrooms, yeasts, and molds
	Plantae	plants and (in some classifications) green algae
	Animalia	multicellular animals, including sponges, snails, insects, fishes, amphibians, reptiles, birds, and mammals

* In the three-domain system, the level of kingdom is usually not used for archaea or bacteria (phylum is the highest rank recognized).

Below the kingdom are six major lower levels. From highest to lowest these are **phylum** (or **division** in the plant kingdom), **class, order, family, genus,** and **species.** These categories indicate how closely or distantly organisms are related to each other, based on structural and genetic similarities.

The chart below compares the classification of four organisms in the animal kingdom: the black horsefly, eastern newt, blue whale, and house mouse.

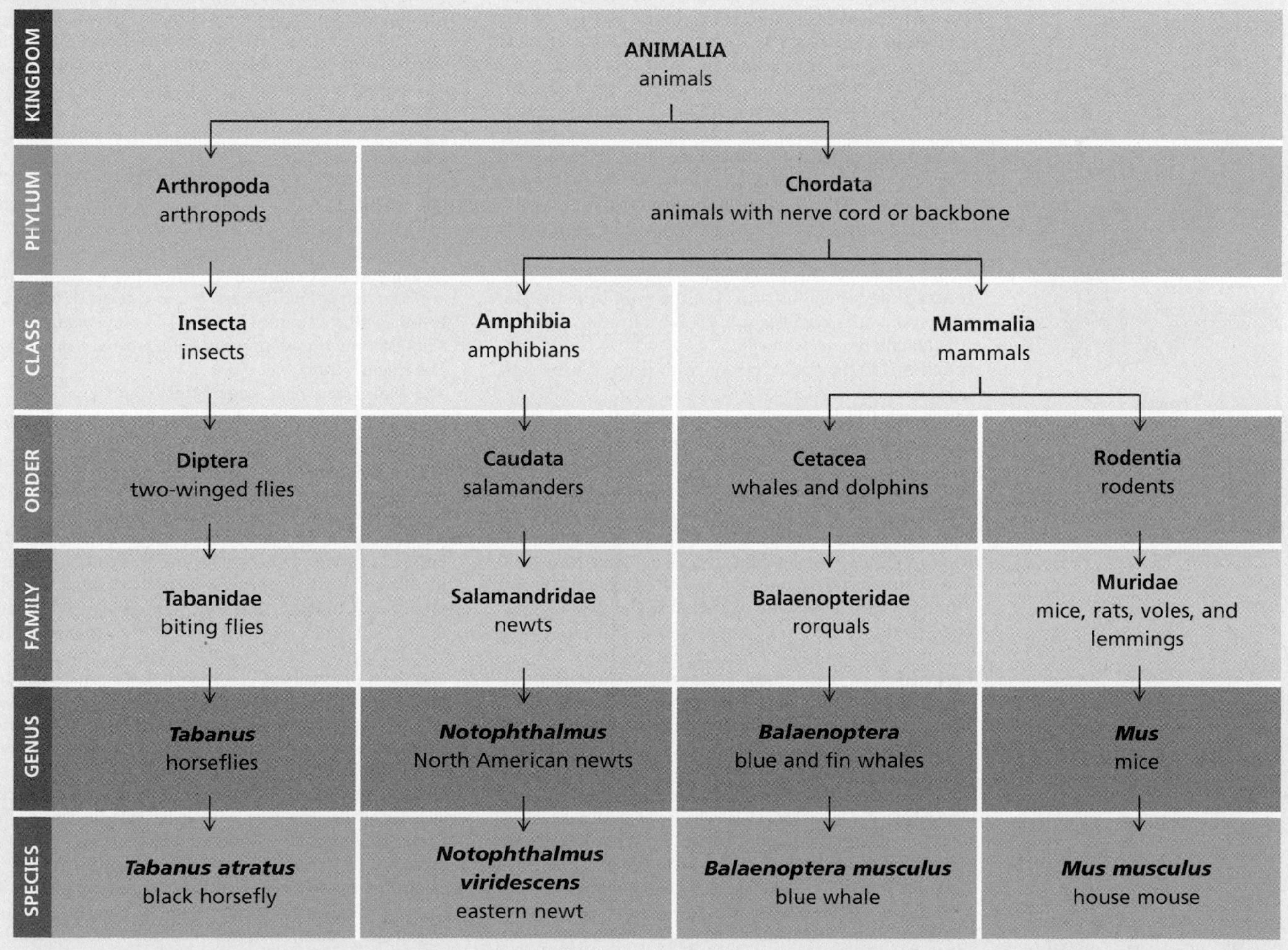

Peter Tchaikovsky

teakettle

team

ă	pat	ôr	core
ā	pay	oi	boy
âr	care	ou	out
ä	father	o͝o	took
ĕ	pet	o͝or	lure
ē	be	o͞o	boot
ĭ	pit	ŭ	cut
ī	bite	ûr	urge
îr	pier	th	thin
ŏ	pot	*th*	this
ō	toe	zh	vision
ô	paw	ə	about

Tchai·kov·sky (chī-**kôf′**skē), **Peter Ilich** 1840–1893. Russian composer whose works include symphonies and ballets, such as *The Nutcracker* (1892).

TCP/IP (tē′sē-pē′ ī′pē′) *n.* A protocol that allows computers to transmit data over networks. TCP/IP is the basis for standard Internet protocols.

TD *abbr.* An abbreviation of touchdown.

Te The symbol for the element **tellurium.**

tea (tē) *n.* **1a.** The young dried leaves of an eastern Asian evergreen shrub or small tree having fragrant white flowers and glossy leaves. **b.** The shrub or small tree that bears such leaves. **2.** An aromatic beverage made by steeping tea leaves in hot water. **3.** Any of various beverages made by steeping various parts of certain other plants, such as peppermint leaves. **4.** *Chiefly British* **a.** A light afternoon meal consisting usually of sandwiches and cakes served with tea. **b.** An afternoon reception or gathering at which tea is served.

❑ *These sound alike:* **tea, tee** (peg for a golf ball), **ti** (musical tone).

teach (tēch) *v.* **taught** (tôt), **teach·ing, teach·es** *—tr.* **1.** To give knowledge or skill to: *He teaches children.* **2.** To provide knowledge of; give instruction about: *She teaches math.* **3.** To advocate or preach: *teach religious tolerance.* **4.** To carry on instruction on a regular basis in: *taught third grade.* *—intr.* To give instruction or be employed as a teacher: *How long has he been teaching?* [From Old English *tǣcan.*]

SYNONYMS **teach, train, instruct, educate, school** These verbs mean to pass on knowledge or skill. **Teach** is the most general: *Your sister can teach you how to ride a bicycle.* **Train** means to teach particular skills intended to fit a person for a certain role, such as a job: *It is the manager's responsibility to train all new employees.* **Instruct** usually means to provide knowledge in an organized way: *The manual instructs you how to assemble the bookshelf.* **Educate** often means to instruct in a formal way: *They wanted their children to be educated in the very best schools.* **School** often means to teach with a hard, demanding process: *The violinist has been schooled to practice certain exercises every day.*

teach·a·ble (tē′chə-bəl) *adj.* **1.** Capable of being taught: *Geometry is a teachable subject.* **2.** Able and willing to be taught: *teachable students.*

teach·er (tē′chər) *n.* A person who teaches, especially one hired to teach.

teach·ing (tē′chĭng) *n.* **1.** The act, practice, occupation, or profession of a teacher. **2.** Something taught, especially a precept or doctrine: *the teachings of Confucius.*

tea·cup (tē′kŭp′) *n.* A small cup for drinking tea.

tea·house (tē′hous′) *n.* A public establishment serving tea and light refreshments.

teak (tēk) *n.* **1.** A tall Asian tree having large leaves and hard, strong, heavy wood. **2.** The dark or yellowish-brown wood of such a tree, used for furniture and shipbuilding.

tea·ket·tle (tē′kĕt′l) *n.* A covered kettle with a spout and handle, used for boiling water, as for tea.

teal (tēl) *n., pl.* **teal** or **teals 1.** Any of several small freshwater ducks, often having brightly marked feathers. **2.** A moderate or dark bluish green to greenish blue. [From Middle English *tele.*]

team (tēm) *n.* **1.** A group on the same side, as in a game. **2.** Two or more people organized to work together: *a team of scientists.* **3.** Two or more animals used to pull a vehicle or farm implement: *a team of horses.* ❖ *v.* **teamed, team·ing, teams** *—tr.* To harness or join together so as to form a team. *—intr.* To form a team or association: *We teamed up to clean the beach.* [From Old English *tēam*, team of draft animals.] —SEE NOTE AT **collective noun.**

❑ *These sound alike:* **team, teem** (abound).

team·mate (tēm′māt′) *n.* A member of one's own team.

team·ster (tēm′stər) *n.* **1.** A truck driver. **2.** A person who drives a team of draft animals.

team·work (tēm′wûrk′) *n.* Cooperative effort by members of a group or team to achieve a common goal.

tea·pot (tē′pŏt′) *n.* A covered pot with a handle and spout, used for brewing and pouring tea.

tear[1] (târ) *v.* **tore** (tôr), **torn** (tôrn), **tear·ing, tears** *—tr.* **1a.** To pull apart or into pieces by force; rend: *Tear the paper in half.* **b.** To cause to be pulled apart, especially as an accident: *I tore my pants while climbing a tree.* **c.** To cause a cut or wound in (the skin, for example). **2.** To make (an opening) by ripping, especially as an accident: *tore a hole in my sock.* **3.** To separate or detach forcefully: *tore the pipe from the wall.* **4.** To divide or disrupt emotionally: *He is torn between duty and loyalty to his friends.* *—intr.* **1.** To become torn: *Heavy denim does not tear easily.* **2.** To move with great speed; rush headlong: *He went tearing into town.* ❖ *n.* **1.** The act of tearing. **2.** The result of tearing; a rip or rent. ◆ **tear down** To demolish: *They had to tear down what was left of the building after the fire.* **tear into 1.** To attack with great energy: *tore into her opponent.* **2.** To begin to do something with great energy: *tore into the food.* **tear up** To tear to pieces: *Tear up the letter when you've read it.* [From Old English *teran.*]

❑ *These sound alike:* **tear**[1], **tare**[1] (weed), **tare**[2] (weight).

SYNONYMS **tear, rip, rend, split** These verbs mean to pull apart or separate by force. **Tear** means to pull something apart or into pieces: *He tore the napkin into bits.* **Rip** suggests ripping by force or in a rough manner: *Carpenters ripped up the old floorboards.* **Rend** is a formal word that refers to violent tearing or wrenching apart: *The mourners rent their clothing in grief.* **Split** means to cut or break something into parts or layers, especially along its entire length: *They split the logs with an axe to make firewood.*

tear[2] (tîr) *n.* **1.** A drop of the clear salty liquid secreted by glands of the eyes. **2. tears a.** This clear liquid, spilling from the eyes and wetting the cheeks, especially as an expression of emotion. **b.** The act of weeping: *harsh criticism that left me in tears.* ❖ *intr.v.* **teared, tear·ing, tears** To fill with tears: *Chopping the onion made my eyes tear. His eyes teared up when he heard the news.* [From Old English *tēar.*]

❑ *These sound alike:* **tear**[2], **tier** (row).

tear·drop (tîr′drŏp′) *n.* **1.** A tear. **2.** An object shaped like a tear.

tear·ful (tîr′fəl) *adj.* **1.** Filled with or accompanied by tears: *a tearful farewell.* **2.** So piteous as to bring forth tears: *a tearful movie.* **—tear′ful·ly** *adv.*

tear gas (tîr) *n.* Any of various chemicals that when dispersed as a gas or a mist irritate the eyes and cause blinding tears. It is used especially by police to control riots.

tease (tēz) *v.* **teased, teas·ing, teas·es** *—tr.* **1.** To make fun of (someone); mock playfully. **2.** To annoy or pester; vex: *teasing the cat by pulling its tail.* **3.** To disentangle and dress the fibers of: *tease wool.* **4.** To raise a nap (on cloth), as with a teasel. **5.** To brush or comb (the hair) toward the scalp for a full airy effect. *—intr.* To annoy or make fun of persistently: *Quit teasing!* ❖ *n.* A person or a remark that teases.

tea·sel (tē′zəl) *n.* **1.** Any of several plants having prickly stems and flowers surrounded by stiff bracts. **2.** The flower head of such a plant, used to brush the surface of fabrics so as to form a nap.

tea·spoon (tē′spo͞on′) *n.* **1.** The common small spoon used especially for stirring coffee or tea and for consuming desserts. **2.** A household cooking measure equal to ⅓ tablespoon (about 5 milliliters).

tea·spoon·ful (tē′spo͞on-fo͝ol′) *n.* The amount that a teaspoon can hold.

teat (tēt *or* tĭt) *n.* The part of a mammary gland of a female human or other mammal through which milk is taken; a nipple.

tech. *abbr.* An abbreviation of technical.

tech·ne·ti·um (tĕk-**nē′**shē-əm) *n. Symbol* **Tc** A silvery-gray, radioactive metallic element that is used as a tracer in various medical applications. Atomic number 43. See **Periodic Table.**

tech·ni·cal (**tĕk′**nĭ-kəl) *adj.* **1.** Relating to or derived from technique: *technical ability.* **2.** Used in or peculiar to a particular subject; specialized: *technical language.* **3.** Relating to or involving the practical, mechanical, or industrial arts or the applied sciences: *a technical school.* **4.** Relating to technology: *technical assistance overseas.* **5.** According to a principle or rule: *a technical foul.* **6.** Strictly or narrowly defined: *a victory only in the technical sense.* [From Greek *tekhnikos,* of art, from *tekhnē,* art.] **—tech′ni·cal·ly** *adv.*

tech·ni·cal·i·ty (tĕk′nĭ-**kăl′**ĭ-tē) *n., pl.* **tech·ni·cal·i·ties** **1.** The quality or condition of being technical. **2.** Something meaningful or relevant only to a specialist: *caught on a legal technicality.*

tech·ni·cian (tĕk-**nĭsh′**ən) *n.* A person who is skilled in a certain technical field or process: *a dental technician.*

Tech·ni·col·or (**tĕk′**nĭ-kŭl′ər) A trademark used for a method of making movies in color.

tech·nique (tĕk-**nēk′**) *n.* **1.** A procedure or method for accomplishing a complicated task, as in a science or an art. **2.** Skill in handling such procedures or methods: *As a pianist, she has superb technique.* [From Greek *tekhnikos,* technical.]

tech·no·log·i·cal (tĕk′nə-**lŏj′**ĭ-kəl) *adj.* Relating to or resulting from technology: *technological developments.* **—tech′no·log′i·cal·ly** *adv.*

tech·nol·o·gist (tĕk-**nŏl′**ə-jĭst) *n.* A specialist in technology.

tech·nol·o·gy (tĕk-**nŏl′**ə-jē) *n., pl.* **tech·nol·o·gies** **1.** The use of scientific knowledge to solve practical problems, especially in industry and commerce. **2.** The methods and materials used to solve practical problems: *aerospace technology.* **3.** Electronic or digital products and systems considered as a group: *office technology.*

Te·cum·seh (tĭ-**kŭm′**sə) 1768–1813. Shawnee leader who attempted to establish a confederacy of Native Americans against white settlement in the Northwest Territory.

ted·dy bear (**tĕd′**ē) *n.* A child's toy bear, usually stuffed with soft material. [After *Teddy,* nickname of Theodore Roosevelt, who was depicted in a cartoon sparing the life of a bear cub.]

Te De·um (tā′ **dā′**əm) *n.* A hymn of praise to God sung as part of a liturgy.

te·di·ous (**tē′**dē-əs) *adj.* Extremely boring, long, or slow: *a tedious lecture.* See Synonyms at **boring. —te′di·ous·ly** *adv.*

te·di·um (**tē′**dē-əm) *n.* The quality or condition of being tedious; boredom. [From Latin *taedium,* from *taedēre,* to weary.]

tee (tē) *n.* **1.** A small peg stuck in the ground to support a golf ball for a shot. **2.** A raised area from which a golfer hits the first shot toward a hole. ❖ *tr.v.* **teed, tee·ing, tees** To place (a golf ball) on a tee. ◆ **tee off 1.** To drive a golf ball from a tee. **2.** *Slang* To make (someone) angry or irritated.

❑ *These sound alike:* **tee, tea** (drink), **ti** (musical tone).

teem (tēm) *intr.v.* **teemed, teem·ing, teems** To be full of things; swarm or abound: *The pond water teemed with microbes.* [From Old English *tīeman, tēman.*]

❑ *These sound alike:* **teem, team** (group).

teen (tēn) *n.* **1. teens a.** The numbers 13 through 19. **b.** The 13th through 19th items in a series or scale, as years of a century or degrees of temperature: *a temperature in the upper teens.* **2.** A teenager.

teen·age (**tēn′**āj′) *adj.* Relating to or for those aged 13 through 19.

teen·ag·er (**tēn′**ā′jər) *n.* A person between the ages of 13 and 19.

tee·ny (**tē′**nē) also **teen·sy** (**tēn′**sē) *adj.* **tee·ni·er, tee·ni·est** also **teen·si·er, teen·si·est** *Informal* Tiny.

tee·pee (**tē′**pē) *n.* Variant of **tepee.**

tee shirt *n.* Variant of **T-shirt.**

tee·ter (**tē′**tər) *intr.v.* **tee·tered, tee·ter·ing, tee·ters 1.** To move or sway unsteadily; totter: *I teetered as I crossed the deck of the moving ship.* **2.** To be dangerously close to failure or ruin: *The bank teetered on the edge of collapse.* ❖ *n.* A seesaw.

tee·ter-tot·ter (**tē′**tər-tŏt′ər) *n.* A seesaw.

teeth (tēth) *n.* Plural of **tooth.**

teethe (tēth) *intr.v.* **teethed, teeth·ing, teethes** To have teeth coming through the gums: *The baby is fussy because he's teething.*

tee·to·tal·er or **tee·to·tal·ler** (**tē′**tōt′l-ər) *n.* A person who does not drink any alcohol.

Tef·lon (**tĕf′**lŏn′) A trademark for a durable plastic based on compounds of carbon and fluorine, used to coat cooking utensils and to prevent sticking of machine parts.

Te·gu·ci·gal·pa (tē-go͞o′sē-**gäl′**pä) The capital of Honduras, in the south-central part of the country. It was founded in the late 1500s.

Teh·ran or **Te·he·ran** (tĕ-**răn′** *or* tĕ-**rän′**) The capital of Iran, in the north-central part of the country south of the Caspian Sea. It became capital in 1788.

tek·tite (**tĕk′**tīt′) *n.* Any of numerous dark-brown to green glassy objects, usually small and round, composed of silica and various oxides. They are thought to have resulted from impacts of large meteorites with the earth's surface.

Tel A·viv–Ya·fo (tĕl′ ə-**vēv′**yä′fō) or **Tel A·viv–Jaf·fa** (tĕl′ ə-**vēv′jăf′**ə *or* tĕl′ ə-**vēv′**y**ăf′**ə) A city of west-central Israel on the Mediterranean Sea west-northwest of Jerusalem. Tel Aviv was founded in 1909 by settlers from the ancient city of Jaffa. The communities merged in 1950.

tele– *pref.* A prefix that means: **1.** Distance; distant: *telemetry.* **2.** Telegraph or telephone: *telegram.* **3.** Television: *telecast.*

tel·e·cast (**tĕl′**ĭ-kăst′) *tr.v.* **tel·e·cast** or **tel·e·cast·ed, tel·e·cast·ing, tel·e·casts** To broadcast (a program or programs) by television. ❖ *n.* A television broadcast.

tel·e·com·mu·ni·ca·tion (tĕl′ĭ-kə-myo͞o′nĭ-**kā′**shən) *n.* often **telecommunications** *(used with a singular verb)* The science and technology of communicating over long distances, as by telephone, radio, television, computer networks, or other electronic means.

tel·e·com·mute (**tĕl′**ĭ-kə-myo͞ot′) *intr.v.* **tel·e·com·mut·ed, tel·e·com·mut·ing, tel·e·com·mutes** To work at home using a computer connected to the network of one's employer.

tel·e·gram (**tĕl′**ĭ-grăm′) *n.* A message transmitted by telegraph.

tel·e·graph (**tĕl′**ĭ-grăf′) *n.* **1.** A communications system in which a message in the form of electric impulses is sent, either by wire or radio, to a receiving station. **2.** A message sent by such a system; a telegram. ❖ *tr.v.* **tel·e·graphed, tel·e·graph·ing, tel·e·graphs 1.** To transmit (a message) by telegraph: *telegraphed our congratulations.* **2.** To send or convey a message to (someone) by telegraph.

tel·e·graph·ic (tĕl′ĭ-**grăf′**ĭk) *adj.* **1.** Relating to or sent by

teasel

WRITERS CHOOSE THEIR WORDS

Father Ignatius—bored to distraction with the **tedious** little Roux boy's **tedious** little sins, and anxious to get back to his beehives—had trained Pepper at least to get to the point quickly. "I won't waste your time, boy, if you don't waste mine," he had in fact said.

—Geraldine McCaughrean *The Death-Defying Pepper Roux*

tee

telegraph. **2.** Brief; concise: *a telegraphic style of writing.*

te·leg·ra·phy (tə-lĕg′rə-fē) *n.* Communication by means of telegraph.

Te·lem·a·chus (tə-lĕm′ə-kəs) *n.* In Greek mythology, the son of Odysseus and Penelope, who helped his father kill Penelope's suitors.

tel·e·mar·ket·ing (tĕl′ə-mär′kĭ-tĭng) *n.* The marketing of goods or services by telephone.

tel·e·me·ter (tĕl′ə-mē′tər *or* tə-lĕm′ĭ-tər) *n.* A measuring, transmitting, and receiving device used in telemetry.

te·lem·e·try (tə-lĕm′ĭ-trē) *n.* The automatic measurement and transmission of data from a distant source to a receiving station.

te·lep·a·thy (tə-lĕp′ə-thē) *n.* The supposed process of communicating thoughts directly from one mind to another without using sound, sight, or any other physical sense. **—tel′e·path′ic** (tĕl′ə-păth′ĭk) *adj.*

tel·e·phone (tĕl′ə-fōn′) *n.* An instrument for transmitting speech or other sounds over a distance by converting the sounds into signals that are sent to a similar instrument that converts them back into sounds. ❖ *tr.v.* **tel·e·phoned, tel·e·phon·ing, tel·e·phones 1.** To call or communicate with (a person) by telephone. **2.** To transmit (a message or information) by telephone. **3.** To make a telephone call to (a specific number): *Telephone 911 in an emergency.* [From Greek *tēle*, far off + Greek *phonos*, sound.]

telephone book *n.* A listing of the names of telephone subscribers with their numbers and addresses.

tel·e·phon·ic (tĕl′ə-fŏn′ĭk) *adj.* **1.** Relating to telephones. **2.** Transmitted by or conveyed by telephone.

te·leph·o·ny (tə-lĕf′ə-nē) *n.* **1.** The transmission of sound between distant points, especially by radio or telephone. **2.** The technology and manufacture of telephone equipment.

tel·e·pho·to·graph (tĕl′ə-fō′tə-grăf′) *n.* **1.** A photograph made with a telephoto lens. **2.** A photograph transmitted and reproduced by telephotography.

tel·e·pho·tog·ra·phy (tĕl′ə-fə-tŏg′rə-fē) *n.* **1.** The photographing of distant objects using a telephoto lens on a camera. **2.** The transmission of photographs, pictures, and charts over a distance.

tel·e·pho·to lens (tĕl′ə-fō′tō) *n.* A camera lens that produces a large image of a distant object.

Tel·e·Promp·Ter (tĕl′ə-prŏmp′tər) A trademark used for a device that shows an actor or speaker a script that is unseen by a television audience.

tel·e·scope (tĕl′ĭ-skōp′) *n.* **1.** A device that uses an arrangement of lenses, mirrors, or both to collect visible light, allowing observation or photographic recording of distant objects. **2.** Any of various devices, such as a radio telescope, used to collect and analyze electromagnetic radiation other than light coming from distant sources. ❖ *intr.v.* **tel·e·scoped, tel·e·scop·ing, tel·e·scopes** To slide inward or outward in overlapping sections, as the tubular sections of a hand telescope do: *a tripod with legs that telescope to the desired length.* [From Greek *tēleskopos*, far-seeing : *tēle-*, far off + *skopos*, watcher.]

tel·e·scop·ic (tĕl′ĭ-skŏp′ĭk) *adj.* **1.** Relating to a telescope. **2.** Seen or obtained by means of a telescope: *telescopic data.* **3.** Visible only by means of a telescope: *telescopic features on the moon's surface.* **4.** Capable of sliding inward or outward in overlapping sections: *a telescopic antenna.*

tel·e·thon (tĕl′ə-thŏn′) *n.* A lengthy television program to raise funds for a charity.

tel·e·vise (tĕl′ə-vīz′) *tr.v.* **tel·e·vised, tel·e·vis·ing, tel·e·vis·es** To broadcast by television: *Four channels televised the presidential debate.*

tel·e·vi·sion (tĕl′ə-vĭzh′ən) *n.* **1.** The transmission and reception of video content by means of electromagnetic waves through the air or directly by cable. **2.** An electronic device for viewing television programs and movies, consisting of a screen and speakers: *Don't sit too close to the television.* **3.** The industry of producing and broadcasting television programs.

tell (tĕl) *v.* **told** (tōld), **tell·ing, tells** *—tr.* **1.** To express in words; say: *Have you told the truth? Did you tell them that you were sick?* **2.** To give an account of; describe or relate: *tell a story.* **3.** To make known; indicate or inform: *Who told my secret? She told me about your situation.* **4.** To discover by observation; perceive or identify: *We could tell that she was upset.* **5.** To command; order: *told us to stand in line.* *—intr.* **1.** To give an account or description of something: *The legend tells of a hidden treasure.* **2.** To reveal secrets; inform: *You shouldn't tell on your friends.* ◆ **tell time** To determine the time of day indicated by the positions of the hands on a clock. [From Old English *tellan*.]

tell·er (tĕl′ər) *n.* **1.** A person who tells: *a teller of tall tales.* **2.** A bank employee who receives and pays out money. **3.** A person who counts votes in a legislative assembly.

tell·ing (tĕl′ĭng) *adj.* Revealing something important or meaningful; significant: *a telling moment in the debate; a description with telling details.* **—tell′ing·ly** *adv.*

tell·tale (tĕl′tāl′) *n.* A person or thing that reveals information. ❖ *adj.* Serving to indicate or reveal: *a telltale sign.*

tel·lu·ride (tĕl′yə-rīd′) *n.* A chemical compound of tellurium and another element or radical.

tel·lu·ri·um (tĕ-lo͝or′ē-əm) *n.* *Symbol* **Te** A brittle, silvery-white nonmetallic element that is used to improve the alloys of various metals. Atomic number 52. See **Periodic Table.**

tel·o·phase (tĕl′ə-fāz′ *or* tē′lə-fāz′) *n.* The final phase of mitosis and meiosis, in which the chromosomes of the daughter cells are grouped in new nuclei.

te·mer·i·ty (tə-mĕr′ĭ-tē) *n.* Excessive boldness or daring; audacity: *had the temerity to demand an apology from her boss.*

temp (tĕmp) *Informal n.* A temporary worker, as in an office. ❖ *intr.v.* **temped, temp·ing, temps** To work as a temporary worker: *Many college students temp during the summer.* [Short for *temporary worker*.]

temp. *abbr.* An abbreviation of temperature.

tem·per (tĕm′pər) *tr.v.* **tem·pered, tem·per·ing, tem·pers 1.** To moderate: *tempering justice with mercy.* **2.** To bring (a substance) to a desired physical condition by mixing with something else or treating in some special way: *tempered the paint with oil.* **3.** To harden or strengthen (metal or glass) by applying heat or by heating and cooling. ❖ *n.* **1.** A state of mind or emotions; a disposition: *an even temper.* **2.** Calmness of mind or emotions; composure: *Don't lose your temper.* **3.** A tendency to become angry or irritable: *has a quick temper.* **4a.** The condition of being tempered. **b.** The degree of hardness and elasticity of a metal, especially steel, achieved by tempering.

tem·per·a (tĕm′pər-ə) *n.* **1.** A type of paint made by mixing pigment with a substance such as egg yolk that is soluble in water. **2.** Painting done with this type of paint.

tem·per·a·ment (tĕm′prə-mənt *or* tĕm′pər-ə-mənt) *n.* The manner of thinking, behaving, or reacting characteristic of a specific person: *a nervous temperament.*

tem·per·a·men·tal (tĕm′prə-mĕn′tl *or* tĕm′pər-ə-mĕn′tl) *adj.* **1.** Relating to or caused by temperament. **2.** Excessively sensitive, irritable, or moody: *a temperamental person.*

tem·per·ance (tĕm′pər-əns *or* tĕm′prəns) *n.* **1.** Moderation and self-restraint, as in behavior or expression. **2.** Restraint in the use of or abstinence from alcoholic beverages.

tem·per·ate (tĕm′pər-ĭt *or* tĕm′prĭt) *adj.* **1.** Exercising moderation and self-restraint. **2.** Moderate in degree or

SCIENCE

temperature What is the difference between **temperature** and **heat**? Think of a teacup and a large pot, both filled with water. If both start at the same temperature, it takes more energy to boil the water in the pot than the water in the cup. The heat contained in a an object such as a quantity of water depends on its *mass*—that is, on the amount of matter in the object. Since there is more water in the pot than in the cup, there is more total heat energy in the pot of water than in the cup of water. Temperature, however, does not depend on the mass of the water but on the speed of the particles in that mass. When a material receives more heat energy, the atoms in the material move faster and faster. For this reason a pot of boiling water and a cup of boiling water can have the same temperature (100° C) even though they contain a different amount of heat.

ă	pat	ôr	core
ā	pay	oi	boy
âr	care	ou	out
ä	father	o͝o	took
ĕ	pet	o͝or	lure
ē	be	o͞o	boot
ĭ	pit	ŭ	cut
ī	bite	ûr	urge
îr	pier	th	thin
ŏ	pot	*th*	this
ō	toe	zh	vision
ô	paw	ə	about

quality; restrained: *a temperate response to the provocation.* **3.** Characterized by moderate temperatures, weather, or climate.

Temperate Zone Either of two intermediate latitude zones of the earth, the **North Temperate Zone,** between the Arctic Circle and the Tropic of Cancer, or the **South Temperate Zone,** between the Antarctic Circle and the Tropic of Capricorn.

tem·per·a·ture (tĕm′pər-ə-cho͝or′ *or* tĕm′prə-cho͝or′) *n.* **1a.** The relative hotness or coldness of a body or an environment. **b.** A numerical measure of hotness or coldness on a standard scale, such as the Fahrenheit, Celsius, or Kelvin scale. **2.** An abnormally high body temperature that is caused by a disease or disorder; a fever. —SEE NOTE.

tem·pered (tĕm′pərd) *adj.* **1.** Having a specified temper or disposition: *a sweet-tempered child.* **2.** Strengthened, hardened, or toughened by tempering: *a tempered steel blade.*

tem·pest (tĕm′pĭst) *n.* **1.** A violent windstorm, often accompanied by rain, snow, or hail. **2.** A violent commotion or tumult; an uproar.

tem·pes·tu·ous (tĕm-pĕs′cho͞o-əs) *adj.* **1.** Relating to or resembling a tempest: *tempestuous winds.* **2.** Tumultuous; noisy: *a tempestuous meeting of angry parents in the neighborhood.* **—tem·pes′tu·ous·ly** *adv.*

tem·pi (tĕm′pē) *n.* A plural of **tempo.**

tem·plate (tĕm′plĭt) *n.* A pattern or gauge, such as a metal plate cut to a desired shape, used as a guide in making something accurately, as in carpentry.

tem·ple[1] (tĕm′pəl) *n.* **1.** A building dedicated to religious ceremonies or worship: *a Hindu temple; the temple of Athena.* **2.** A synagogue, especially of a Reform congregation. **3. Temple** Either of two successive buildings in ancient Jerusalem serving as the primary center for Jewish worship. [From Middle English, from Old English *tempel,* from Latin *templum.*]

tem·ple[2] (tĕm′pəl) *n.* Either of the flat regions at the sides of the head next to the forehead. [From Middle English, from Latin *tempus.*]

tem·po (tĕm′pō) *n., pl.* **tem·pos** or **tem·pi** (tĕm′pē) **1.** The speed at which a piece of music is or should be played, often indicated by a composer on the written score. **2.** A characteristic rate or rhythm of something; a pace: *the tempo of life in a city.*

tem·po·ral[1] (tĕm′pər-əl *or* tĕm′prəl) *adj.* **1.** Relating to or limited by time: *temporal and spatial dimensions.* **2.** Relating to worldly affairs, especially as distinguished from spiritual concerns: *land and other temporal possessions of the church.* **3.** Lasting only for a time; not eternal: *this temporal existence.* [From Middle English, from Latin *temporālis,* from *tempus,* time.] **—tem′po·ral·ly** *adv.*

tem·po·ral[2] (tĕm′pər-əl *or* tĕm′prəl) *adj.* Relating to or near the temples of the skull. [From Latin *tempora,* temples.]

temporal bone *n.* Either of a pair of bones forming the sides and part of the base of the skull.

temporal lobe *n.* The portion of each cerebral hemisphere located in front of the occipital lobe, containing the speech and language centers of the brain.

tem·po·rar·y (tĕm′pə-rĕr′ē) *adj.* Lasting, used, serving, or enjoyed for a limited time only; not permanent: *a temporary job.* ❖ *n., pl.* **tem·po·rar·ies** An employee who works for a limited time only: *Her position is being filled for now by a temporary.*

tem·po·rize (tĕm′pə-rīz′) *intr.v.* **tem·po·rized, tem·po·riz·ing, tem·po·riz·es** To compromise or act evasively in order to gain time, avoid an argument, or postpone a decision. **—tem′po·ri·za′tion** (tĕm′pər-ĭ-zā′shən) *n.* **—tem′po·riz′er** *n.*

tempt (tĕmpt) *tr.v.* **tempt·ed, tempt·ing, tempts 1.** To try to get (someone) to do wrong, especially by a promise of reward. **2.** To be inviting or attractive to: *Your offer tempts me.* **3.** To provoke or risk provoking: *Do not tempt fate.* [From Middle English *tempten,* from Latin *temptāre,* to feel, try.]

temp·ta·tion (tĕmp-tā′shən) *n.* **1.** The act of tempting or the condition of being tempted. **2.** Something tempting or enticing: *The restaurant's desserts were a real temptation for us.*

tempt·ing (tĕmp′tĭng) *adj.* Having strong appeal; enticing: *a tempting offer.*

tem·pu·ra (tĕm′po͝o-rə *or* tĕm-po͝or′ə) *n.* A Japanese dish of vegetables and shrimp or other seafood dipped in batter and fried.

ten (tĕn) *n.* **1.** The number, written 10, that is equal to 9 + 1. **2.** The tenth in a set or sequence. **3.** A ten-dollar bill.

ten·a·ble (tĕn′ə-bəl) *adj.* Defensible or logical: *His theory is tenable.* **—ten′a·bly** *adv.*

te·na·cious (tə-nā′shəs) *adj.* **1.** Holding or tending to hold firmly to something, such as a point of view: *a man tenacious in his convictions.* **2.** Persistent or enduring; stubborn: *stayed home with a tenacious cold.* **3.** Tending to retain; retentive: *a tenacious memory.* **—te·nac′i·ty** (tə-năs′ĭ-tē) *n.* —SEE NOTE.

ten·an·cy (tĕn′ən-sē) *n., pl.* **ten·an·cies 1.** Possession or occupancy of lands, buildings, or other property, as by lease or rent. **2.** The period of a tenant's occupancy or possession.

ten·ant (tĕn′ənt) *n.* **1.** A person who pays rent to use or occupy land, a building, or other property owned by another. **2.** A dweller in a place; an occupant. —SEE NOTE AT **tenacious.**

tenant farmer *n.* A person who lives on and farms land owned by another and pays rent in cash or with a share of the produce.

Ten Commandments *pl.n.* In the Bible, the ten laws given to Moses by God.

tend[1] (tĕnd) *intr.v.* **tend·ed, tend·ing, tends 1.** To have a tendency: *I tend to get carsick on long trips.* **2.** To be disposed or inclined: *She tends toward conservativism in economic matters.* **3.** To move or extend in a certain direction: *Our course tended toward the north.* [From Middle English *tenden,* from Latin *tendere.*]

tend[2] (tĕnd) *v.* **tend·ed, tend·ing, tends** —*tr.* **1.** To have the care of; look after: *tend a sick child.* **2.** To manage the activities and transactions of: *tend a sales counter.* —*intr.* **1.** To be an attendant or servant. **2.** To apply one's attention; attend: *tend to one's own business.* [From Middle English *tenden,* short for *attenden,* to wait on.]

ten·den·cy (tĕn′dən-sē) *n., pl.* **ten·den·cies 1.** A leaning or inclination to think, act, or behave in a certain way: *He has a tendency to write long sentences.* **2.** A characteristic likelihood: *Linen has a tendency to wrinkle.* **3.** Prevailing movement in a given direction: *the northward tendency of the Gulf Stream.*

ten·der[1] (tĕn′dər) *adj.* **ten·der·er, ten·der·est 1.** Easily crushed or bruised; fragile: *tender flowers.* **2.** Easily chewed or cut: *a tender steak.* **3.** Young and vulnerable: *of tender age.* **4a.** Easily hurt; sensitive: *tender skin.* **b.** Painful; sore: *a tender tooth.* **5.** Gentle and loving: *a tender heart; a tender glance.* [From Middle English, from Latin *tener.*]

ten·der[2] (tĕn′dər) *tr.v.* **ten·dered, ten·der·ing, ten·ders** To offer formally: *tender a letter of resignation.* ❖ *n.* **1.** A formal offer or bid. **2.** Something, especially money, offered in payment: *Those IOUs are not legal tender.* [From Latin *tendere,* to hold forth, extend.]

tend·er[3] (tĕn′dər) *n.* A person who tends something: *a furnace tender.*

ten·der·foot (tĕn′dər-fo͝ot′) *n., pl.* **ten·der·foots** or **ten·der·feet** (tĕn′dər-fēt′) **1.** A newcomer not yet hardened to rough outdoor life. **2.** An inexperienced person; a beginner.

temple[1]
Todaiji Temple, Nara, Japan

WORD BUILDING

tenacious The word root *ten–* in English words comes from the Latin verb *tenēre,* "to hold." The English word **tenacious,** for example, comes from *tenēre* by way of the Latin adjective *tenāc–,* "holding fast, persistent." The Latin word root *ten–* often has the form *tain–* in French, and English has words from both forms. A **tenant** is one "holding land from a lord or holding something on lease." **Retain** is "to keep back, keep possession of" (*re–,* "back").

GEOGRAPHY

Tennessee The name of **Tennessee** comes from the name of a Cherokee town in the area. The English applied it to the Tennessee River, and the name was later used for the state.

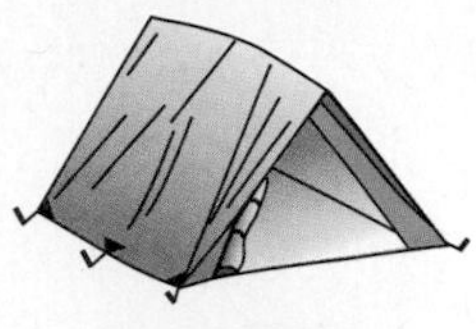

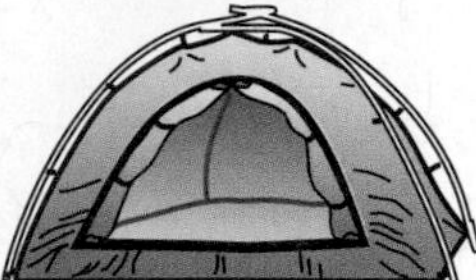

tent
top: A-frame tent
bottom: pop-up tent

tentacle

tepee

ă	pat	ôr	core
ā	pay	oi	boy
âr	care	ou	out
ä	father	o͝o	took
ĕ	pet	o͝or	lure
ē	be	o͞o	boot
ĭ	pit	ŭ	cut
ī	bite	ûr	urge
îr	pier	th	thin
ŏ	pot	*th*	this
ō	toe	zh	vision
ô	paw	ə	about

ten·der·heart·ed (tĕn′dər-här′tĭd) *adj.* Easily moved by another's distress; compassionate.

ten·der·ize (tĕn′də-rīz′) *tr.v.* **ten·der·ized, ten·der·iz·ing, ten·der·iz·es** To make (meat) tender, as by marinating or pounding.

ten·der·iz·er (tĕn′də-rī′zər) *n.* **1.** A substance applied to meat to make it tender. **2.** A mallet used to make meat tender.

ten·der·loin (tĕn′dər-loin′) *n.* The most tender part, as of a loin of beef.

ten·don (tĕn′dən) *n.* A band of tough fibrous tissue that connects a muscle to a bone. [From Greek *tenōn* (influenced by Latin *tendere*, to stretch).]

ten·dril (tĕn′drəl) *n.* **1.** A twisting, slender structure by which a plant, such as a grape or cucumber, twines around and often climbs an object. **2.** Something, such as a ringlet of hair, that is long, slender, and curling.

ten·e·ment (tĕn′ə-mənt) *n.* **1.** A building for people to live in, especially one that is rented to tenants. **2.** An apartment house that is poorly maintained and often overcrowded.

ten·et (tĕn′ĭt) *n.* An opinion, doctrine, or principle held as being true by a person or organization.

ten-gal·lon hat (tĕn′găl′ən) *n.* A cowboy hat.

ten·ge (tĕn-gĕ′) *n.* The basic monetary unit of Kazakhstan.

Ten·nes·see (tĕn′ĭ-sē′ *or* tĕn′ĭ-sē′) A state of the southeast United States west of North Carolina. It was admitted as the 16th state in 1796. Nashville is the capital and Memphis the largest city. —SEE NOTE.

ten·nes·sine (tĕn′ə-sēn′) *n. Symbol* **Ts** A radioactive element that has been artificially produced by scientists. Atomic number 117. See **Periodic Table.**

ten·nis (tĕn′ĭs) *n.* A game played with rackets and a light ball by two players or two pairs of players on a rectangular court, as of grass or clay, divided by a net.

tennis shoe *n.* A sneaker.

Ten·ny·son (tĕn′ĭ-sən), **Alfred** Known as Alfred, Lord Tennyson. 1809–1892. British poet whose works include "The Charge of the Light Brigade" (1854).

ten·on (tĕn′ən) *n.* A projection on the end of a piece of wood designed to fit into a mortise to make a joint.

ten·or (tĕn′ər) *n.* **1.** The general course or character of something: *The tenor of the negotiations was friendly and respectful.* **2.** The general meaning; gist; drift: *She was polite, but the tenor of her remarks was negative.* **3a.** The highest natural adult male voice. **b.** A singer whose voice lies within this range. **c.** An instrument whose sound falls within this range. **d.** A part written in this range.

ten·pin (tĕn′pĭn′) *n.* **1.** One of the bottle-shaped pins used in bowling. **2. tenpins** *(used with a singular verb)* Bowling.

tense[1] (tĕns) *adj.* **tens·er, tens·est 1.** Taut; tightly stretched: *tense muscles.* **2.** Characterized by nervous tension or suspense: *a tense situation.* ❖ *tr. & intr.v.* **tensed, tens·ing, tens·es** To make or become tense: *tensed his body; felt my neck muscles tense up.* [From Latin *tēnsus*, past participle of *tendere*, to stretch.]

tense[2] (tĕns) *n.* **1.** Any of the inflected forms of a verb that indicate the time, such as past or present, and continuance or completion of the action or state. **2.** A set of tense forms indicating a particular time: *the future tense.* [From Middle English, from Latin *tempus*.]

ten·sile (tĕn′səl *or* tĕn′sīl′) *adj.* **1.** Relating to tension. **2.** Capable of being stretched or extended.

tensile strength *n.* The measure of the largest force that can be applied to a material before it breaks apart.

ten·sion (tĕn′shən) *n.* **1a.** The act or process of stretching something tight. **b.** The condition of being so stretched; tautness. **2a.** A force that tends to stretch or elongate something. **b.** A measure of such a force: *a tension of 50 pounds.* **3.** Mental, emotional, or nervous strain: *working under great tension.* **4.** Unfriendliness or hostility between people or groups: *tension among the teammates.* **5.** A difference of electrical potential; voltage.

ten·sor (tĕn′sər *or* tĕn′sôr′) *n.* A muscle that stretches or tightens a body part.

tent (tĕnt) *n.* A portable shelter made of fabric or other material stretched over a supporting framework of poles. [From Middle English, from Old French *tente*, from Latin *tendere*, to stretch out.]

ten·ta·cle (tĕn′tə-kəl) *n.* **1.** One of the narrow, flexible, unjointed parts extending from the body of certain animals, such as a jellyfish or sea anemone, that are used for feeling, grasping, or moving. **2.** Something resembling a tentacle, especially in the ability to extend its influence or control: *The company started out in agriculture but has now spread its tentacles into many other industries.*

ten·ta·tive (tĕn′tə-tĭv) *adj.* **1.** Not fully worked out, concluded, or agreed on: *a tentative production schedule.* **2.** Uncertain; hesitant: *a tentative reply.*

tent caterpillar *n.* Any of several destructive caterpillars that live in colonies and eat the leaves of trees in which they construct silken tentlike webs.

ten·ter (tĕn′tər) *n.* A frame on which cloth is stretched while it dries to keep it from shrinking.

ten·ter·hook (tĕn′tər-ho͝ok′) *n.* A hooked nail used to fasten cloth on a tenter. ◆ **on tenterhooks** In a state of uneasiness, suspense, or anxiety: *I was on tenterhooks waiting to hear who won.*

tenth (tĕnth) *n.* **1.** The ordinal number matching the number ten in a series. **2.** One of ten equal parts.

ten·u·ous (tĕn′yo͞o-əs) *adj.* **1.** Having little substance; flimsy: *the tenuous character of his ideas.* **2.** Long and thin; slender: *a tenuous nylon rope.* [From Latin *tenuis*, thin.] **—ten′u·ous·ly** *adv.*

ten·ure (tĕn′yər *or* tĕn′yo͝or′) *n.* **1.** The holding of something, such as an office or position: *The board revoked her tenure as department head.* **2.** The period of holding something: *He had a long tenure as president of the society.* **3.** The status of holding one's position on a permanent basis: *She attained tenure as a history professor.*

te·pee also **tee·pee** (tē′pē) *n.* A portable dwelling of certain Native American peoples, consisting of a conical framework of poles covered with skins or bark. [From Sioux *t^hípi*, dwelling.]

tep·id (tĕp′ĭd) *adj.* **1.** Moderately warm; lukewarm: *tepid water.* **2.** Lacking enthusiasm; halfhearted: *tepid praise.*

te·qui·la (tə-kē′lə) *n.* An alcoholic liquor distilled from the juice of an agave plant.

tera– *pref.* A prefix that means: **1.** One trillion (10^{12}): *terahertz.* **2.** 1,099,511,627,776 (2^{40}): *terabyte.*

ter·a·byte (tĕr′ə-bīt′) *n.* A unit of computer memory equal to 1,024 gigabytes (2^{40} bytes).

ter·a·hertz (tĕr′ə-hûrts′) *n.* A unit of frequency equal to one trillion hertz.

ter·bi·um (tûr′bē-əm) *n. Symbol* **Tb** A soft, silvery-gray metallic element used in color television tubes and x-ray machines. Atomic number 65. See **Periodic Table.**

Teresa of Calcutta (tə-rē′sə *or* tə-rē′zə), Saint. 1910–1997. Albanian-born Indian nun noted for her charity work among India's poor.

term (tûrm) *n.* **1.** A limited or established period of time that something is supposed to last, as a school or court session, tenure in public office, or a prison sentence. **2.** A point in time at which something ends; a termination: *a lease approaching its term.* **3a.** A word or group of words having a particular meaning: *a medical term.* **b. terms** Language of a certain kind; chosen words: *He spoke in no uncertain terms.* **4.** often **terms** An element of an agreement; a condition: *peace terms.* **5. terms** The relation between two people or groups: *We're on good terms with the neighbors.* **6a.** Each of the quantities or expressions that form the parts of a ratio or the numerator and denominator of a fraction. **b.** Any of the quantities in an equation that are connected to other quantities by a plus sign or minus sign. ❖ *tr.v.* **termed, term·ing, terms** To call by a particular term or name; designate. ◆ **in terms of 1.** As measured or indicated by: *distances expressed in terms of miles.* **2.** In relation to; with reference to: *Although the food was good, the party was a failure in terms of dancing.* [From Middle English *terme*, from Latin *terminus*, boundary.]

ter·mi·nal (tûr**′**mə-nəl) *adj.* **1.** Relating to, situated at, or forming a limit, end, or boundary. **2.** Causing, ending in, or approaching death; fatal: *a terminal disease.* ❖ *n.* **1.** A point or part that forms the end. **2.** A point at which another conductor can be connected to an electric device or component. **3a.** A building in an airport where travelers board and get off airplanes. **b.** An end of a railroad or other transportation line, or a station at such an end. **4.** A device, often having a keyboard and a screen, by which one can read, enter, or manipulate information in a computer system.

ter·mi·nate (tûr**′**mə-nāt′) *v.* **ter·mi·nat·ed, ter·mi·nat·ing, ter·mi·nates** —*tr.* **1.** To bring to an end or halt: *terminate an employee's contract.* **2.** To occur at or form the end of; conclude: *A sonata terminated the concert.* —*intr.* **1.** To come to an end: *The lecture terminated in a question and answer period.* **2.** To have as an end or result: *The negotiations terminated in a new peace treaty.* **—ter′mi·na′tion** *n.*

ter·mi·nol·o·gy (tûr′mə-**nŏl′**ə-jē) *n., pl.* **ter·mi·nol·o·gies** The group of technical terms used in a particular subject, trade, science, or art.

ter·mi·nus (tûr**′**mə-nəs) *n., pl.* **ter·mi·nus·es** or **ter·mi·ni** (tûr**′**mə-nī′) **1.** The final point; the end. **2.** An endpoint on a transportation line or the town in which it is located.

ter·mite (tûr**′**mīt′) *n.* Any of numerous pale-colored, usually soft-bodied insects that live in large complex colonies. Many kinds of termites feed on wood, often damaging or destroying wooden structures. [From Late Latin *termes*, wood-eating worm.]

term limits *pl.n.* A restriction on the number of terms an official may serve.

tern (tûrn) *n.* Any of various seabirds that resemble the gulls but are generally smaller and have a forked tail. [Of Scandinavian origin.]

❑ *These sound alike:* **tern, turn** (rotate).

Terr. *abbr.* An abbreviation of territory.

ter·race (tĕr**′**ĭs) *n.* **1.** A porch or walkway bordered by colonnades. **2.** A platform extending outdoors from a floor of a house or apartment building. **3.** An open, often paved area adjacent to a house; a patio. **4.** A raised bank of earth having vertical or sloping sides and a flat top. **5.** A row of buildings erected on raised ground or on a sloping site. **6.** A residential street, especially along the top or slope of a hill: *Turn left on Maple Terrace.* ❖ *tr.v.* **ter·raced, ter·rac·ing, ter·rac·es** To form into a terrace or terraces: *terraced the hillside.*

ter·ra cot·ta (tĕr**′**ə kŏt**′**ə) *n.* **1.** A hard, waterproof ceramic clay used in pottery and building construction. **2.** Ceramic wares made of this material.

terra fir·ma (fûr**′**mə) *n.* Solid ground; dry land: *back on terra firma after our long ocean voyage.*

ter·rain (tə-**rān′**) *n.* **1.** An area of land; a region. **2.** The surface features of an area of land: *The trail led us over some rough terrain.*

ter·ra·pin (tĕr**′**ə-pĭn) *n.* The diamondback terrapin.

ter·rar·i·um (tə-**râr′**ē-əm) *n., pl.* **ter·rar·i·ums** or **ter·rar·i·a** (tə-**râr′**ē-ə) A small container for growing plants and sometimes keeping small animals, such as turtles or lizards. [From Latin *terra*, earth.]

ter·res·tri·al (tə-**rĕs′**trē-əl) *adj.* **1.** Relating to the earth or its inhabitants: *The craters of the moon look like some terrestrial craters.* **2.** Living or growing on land or on or in the ground: *terrestrial mammals.* **3.** Transmitted from structures on the earth and not involving satellites: *terrestrial radio.*

ter·ri·ble (tĕr**′**ə-bəl) *adj.* **1.** Causing great alarm or fear; dreadful: *a terrible storm.* **2.** Extreme in extent or degree; intense: *the terrible heat in the tropics.* **3.** Unpleasant; disagreeable: *We had a terrible time at the party.* **4.** Very bad: *a terrible movie.* [From Middle English, from Latin *terribilis*, from *terrēre*, to frighten.] **—ter′ri·bly** *adv.*

ter·ri·er (tĕr**′**ē-ər) *n.* A usually small active dog of any of several breeds originally developed for hunting small burrowing animals.

ter·rif·ic (tə-**rĭf′**ĭk) *adj.* **1.** Very good or fine: *a terrific party.* **2.** Awesome; astounding: *a train moving at a terrific speed.* **3.** Intensely strong, especially in an unpleasant way: *a terrific storm; a terrific headache.* **—ter·rif′i·cal·ly** *adv.*

ter·ri·fy (tĕr**′**ə-fī′) *tr.v.* **ter·ri·fied, ter·ri·fy·ing, ter·ri·fies** To fill with terror; make deeply afraid: *Heights terrify me.* See Synonyms at **frighten.**

ter·ri·to·ri·al (tĕr′ĭ-**tôr′**ē-əl) *adj.* **1.** Relating to the geographic area under a given jurisdiction. **2.** Relating or restricted to a particular territory; regional.

territorial waters *pl.n.* Inland and coastal waters under the jurisdiction of a nation or state.

ter·ri·to·ry (tĕr**′**ĭ-tôr′ē) *n., pl.* **ter·ri·to·ries 1.** An area of land; a region. **2.** The land and waters under the jurisdiction of a government. **3.** also **Territory a.** A political subdivision of a country, especially one that is not a state but has its own legislature. **b.** A geographic region that is dependent on an external government. **4.** An area for which a person is responsible as a representative or agent: *Utah is his territory for sales.* **5.** An area, such as a nesting ground, in which an animal lives and from which it keeps out intruders, especially of the same species. **6.** In sports, the area of a field defended by a team. [From Middle English *territorie*, from Latin *territōrium*, from *terra*, earth.]

ter·ror (tĕr**′**ər) *n.* **1.** Intense overpowering fear. **2.** A cause of intense fear: *Outlaws were the terror of the ranchers.* **3.** Violence committed or threatened by a group, especially against civilians, in the pursuit of political goals. [From Middle English *terroure*, from Latin *terror*, from *terrēre*, to frighten.]

ter·ror·ism (tĕr**′**ə-rĭz′əm) *n.* The use of violence or the threat of violence, especially against civilians, in the pursuit of political goals. **—ter′ror·ist** *adj. & n.*

ter·ror·ize (tĕr**′**ə-rīz′) *tr.v.* **ter·ror·ized, ter·ror·iz·ing, ter·ror·iz·es 1.** To fill or overpower with terror. **2.** To force (someone) into action by causing fear.

ter·ry (tĕr**′**ē) *n.* A pile fabric, usually of cotton, with uncut loops on one or both sides, used for towels and bathrobes.

terse (tûrs) *adj.* **ters·er, ters·est** Brief and to the point; concise: *a terse reply.* **—terse′ly** *adv.* **—terse′ness** *n.*

ter·ti·ar·y (tûr**′**shē-ĕr′ē) *adj.* Third in place, order, degree, or rank.

Tertiary *n.* The first and earlier period of the Cenozoic Era, from about 66 to 2.6 million years ago. Most modern classes of plants and animals first appeared during the Tertiary. See table at **geologic time. —Tertiary** *adj.*

test (tĕst) *n.* **1.** A means of determining the presence, quality, or truth of something; a trial: *a vision test; a test of an athlete's endurance.* **2.** A series of questions, problems, or physical responses designed to determine knowledge, intelligence, or ability. **3.** A basis for evaluation or judgment: *This slope will provide a good test of our skiing skills.* **4.** A physical or chemical reaction for determining the properties or presence of a particular substance or class of substances, such as disease germs

Mother Teresa
photographed in 1980

termite

terrace
terraced rice paddies

terra cotta

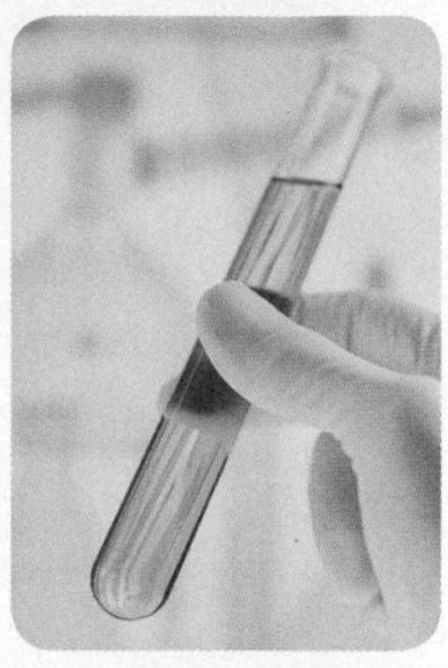

test tube

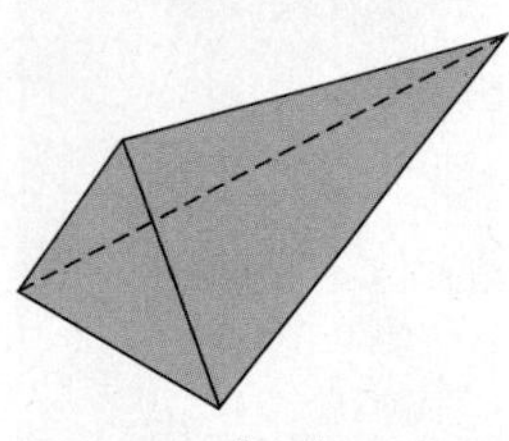

tetrahedron

GEOGRAPHY

Texas The name **Texas** comes from a Caddo word meaning "friend" or "ally" that the Spaniards applied to the area in eastern Texas where the Caddo lived. The state later took its name from this area.

ă	pat	ôr	core
ā	pay	oi	boy
âr	care	ou	out
ä	father	o͝o	took
ĕ	pet	o͝or	lure
ē	be	o͞o	boot
ĭ	pit	ŭ	cut
ī	bite	ûr	urge
îr	pier	th	thin
ŏ	pot	*th*	this
ō	toe	zh	vision
ô	paw	ə	about

of a particular type. ❖ *v.* **test·ed, test·ing, tests** *—tr.* To subject to a test: *tested the pen by scribbling on scrap paper; testing job applicants; tested the water sample for bacteria.* *—intr.* **1.** To undergo a test, especially with an indicated result: *The ore tested high in uranium content.* **2.** To exhibit a given characteristic when subjected to a test: *tested positive for strep throat.* **—test′er** *n.*

tes·ta·ment (tĕs′tə-mənt) *n.* **1.** Something that serves as tangible proof or evidence. **2.** A statement of belief; a credo. **3.** A document providing for the disposing of a person's property after death; a will. **4. Testament** Either of the two main divisions of the Christian Bible.

tes·tate (tĕs′tāt′) *adj.* Having made a legally valid will before death.

tes·ta·tor (tĕs′tā′tər *or* tĕ-**stā′**tər) *n.* A deceased person who has left a legally valid will.

test ban *n.* An agreement between nations to halt testing of nuclear weapons.

test-drive (**tĕst′**drīv′) *tr.v.* **test-drove** (**tĕst′**drōv′), **test-driv·en** (**tĕst′**drĭv′ən), **test-driv·ing, test-drives** To drive (a motor vehicle) to test its performance and condition.

tes·tes (**tĕs′**tēz) *n.* Plural of **testis.**

tes·ti·cle (**tĕs′**tĭ-kəl) *n.* A testis, especially one contained within a scrotum.

tes·ti·fy (**tĕs′**tə-fī′) *v.* **test·i·fied, test·i·fy·ing, test·i·fies** *—intr.* **1.** To give testimony in a legal case or before a deliberative body: *Two witnesses testified against him in court.* **2.** To express or declare a strong belief. *—tr.* **1.** To declare publicly; make known. **2.** To state or affirm as testimony in a legal case or before a deliberative body: *testified in court that she saw the defendant.* [From Middle English *testifien*, from Latin *testificārī*, from *testis*, witness.]

tes·ti·mo·ni·al (tĕs′tə-**mō′**nē-əl) *n.* **1.** A statement in support of a particular fact, truth, or claim. **2.** A written affirmation of the quality of another's character or worth; a recommendation. **3.** Something given as a tribute for a person's achievement.

tes·ti·mo·ny (**tĕs′**tə-mō′nē) *n., pl.* **tes·ti·mo·nies 1.** A declaration by a witness under oath. **2.** Evidence in support of a fact or assertion; proof.

tes·tis (**tĕs′**tĭs) *n., pl.* **tes·tes** (**tĕs′**tēz) The reproductive organ of male animals, usually one of a pair, in which sperm and the male sex hormones are produced.

tes·tos·ter·one (tĕs-**tŏs′**tə-rōn′) *n.* A hormone produced primarily in the testes and responsible for the development of male secondary sex characteristics.

test pilot *n.* A pilot who flies new or experimental aircraft in order to test them.

test tube *n.* A cylindrical tube of clear glass, usually open at one end and rounded at the other, used in laboratory tests and experiments.

test-tube baby (**tĕst′**to͞ob′) *n.* A baby developed from an egg that was fertilized outside the body and then placed in the uterus of the biological or surrogate mother.

tes·ty (**tĕs′**tē) *adj.* **tes·ti·er, tes·ti·est** Irritable, impatient, or exasperated: *I was testy after being stuck in traffic.* **—tes′ti·ly** *adv.* **—tes′ti·ness** *n.*

tet·a·nus (**tĕt′**n-əs) *n.* A serious, often fatal disease caused by bacteria that generally enter the body through a deep wound. The main symptoms are muscular rigidity and muscular spasms, especially in the muscles of the neck and jaw.

tête-à-tête (tāt′ə-**tāt′** *or* tĕt′ə-**tĕt′**) *n.* A private conversation between two people.

teth·er (**tĕth′**ər) *n.* **1.** A rope or chain that is secured to keep an animal within a small area. **2.** A similar ropelike restraint used as a safety measure, especially for young children and astronauts. **3.** The range or scope of one's resources or abilities: *an overworked intern at the end of his tether* ❖ *tr.v.* **teth·ered, teth·er·ing, teth·ers** To fasten or restrict with or as if with a tether. [From Middle English *teder*, from Old Norse *tjōdhr*.]

Te·ton (**tē′**tŏn′) *n., pl.* **Teton** or **Te·tons** A Lakota.

tet·ra (**tĕt′**rə) *n.* Any of numerous small, brightly colored tropical freshwater fishes that are often kept in home aquariums.

tet·ra·he·dron (tĕt′rə-**hē′**drən) *n., pl.* **tet·ra·he·drons** or **tet·ra·he·dra** (tĕt′rə-**hē′**drə) A solid geometric figure having four triangular faces.

te·tram·e·ter (tĕ-**trăm′**ĭ-tər) *n.* A line of verse made up of four metrical feet.

tet·rarch (**tĕt′**rärk′ *or* **tē′**trärk′) *n.* **1.** A governor of one of the four divisions of a country or province, especially in the Roman Empire. **2.** A subordinate ruler.

Teu·ton (**to͞ot′**n) *n.* **1.** A member of an ancient people who lived in Denmark and northern Germany until about 100 BC. **2.** A German.

Teu·ton·ic (to͞o-**tŏn′**ĭk) *adj.* **1.** Relating to the ancient Teutons. **2.** Germanic.

Tex·as (**tĕk′**səs) A state of the south-central United States south of Oklahoma. It was admitted as the 28th state in 1845. Austin is the capital and Houston the largest city. —SEE NOTE.

Tex-Mex (**tĕks′mĕks′**) *adj.* Characterized by a blend of Mexican and southwest US cultural elements: *Tex-Mex music; Tex-Mex food.* [From *Tex(as)* + *Mexi(can)*.]

text (tĕkst) *n.* **1.** The original wording or words of something written or printed. **2.** The main body of a printed work as distinguished from a preface, footnote, or illustration. **3.** Words treated as data by a computer. **4.** A passage of a written work, especially the Bible, used as the starting point of a sermon or discussion. **5.** A subject; a topic: *the text of a discussion.* **6.** A textbook. ❖ *v.* **text·ed, text·ing, texts** *—tr.* **1.** To send a text message to: *She texted me when she arrived at the airport.* **2.** To communicate by text message: *He texted that he would be late.* *—intr.* To send text messages: *Our teacher doesn't allow us to text during class.* [From Middle English, from Latin *textus*, structure, context, body of a passage, from *texere*, to weave, fabricate.]

text·book (**tĕkst′**bo͝ok′) *n.* A book used in schools or colleges for the formal study of a subject.

tex·tile (**tĕks′**tīl′ *or* **tĕks′**təl) *n.* **1.** A cloth or fabric, especially when woven or knitted. **2.** Fiber or yarn for weaving or knitting into cloth. [From Latin *textilis*, woven, from *texere*, to weave.]

text message *n.* A usually short message that is sent electronically, especially from one phone to another.

text messaging *n.* **1.** The process by which text messages are transmitted. **2.** The service provided by a telecommunications company for transmitting text messages.

tex·tu·al (**tĕks′**cho͞o-əl) *adj.* Relating to or conforming to a text. **—tex′tu·al·ly** *adv.*

tex·ture (**tĕks′**chər) *n.* **1.** The structure of the interwoven threads or strands of a fabric: *Burlap has a coarse texture.* **2.** The appearance and feel of a surface: *The plaster gives the wall a rough texture.* **3.** The characteristic composition or structure of a substance or object: *soil with a sandy texture.*

Th The symbol for the element **thorium.**

–th or **–eth** *suff.* A suffix that forms ordinal numbers: *hundredth.*

Thai (tī) *adj.* Relating to Thailand or its people, language, or culture. ❖ *n., pl.* **Thai** or **Thais 1.** A native or inhabitant of Thailand. **2.** The official language of Thailand.

Thai·land (**tī′**lănd′ *or* **tī′**lənd) Formerly **Si·am** (sī-**ăm′**). A country of southeast Asia on the **Gulf of Thailand,** an arm of the South China Sea. Bangkok is the capital.

thal·a·mus (**thăl′**ə-məs) *n., pl.* **thal·a·mi** (**thăl′**ə-mī′) A large rounded mass of gray nerve tissue located under the cerebrum, to which it relays sensory stimuli.

thal·li·um (thăl′ē-əm) *n. Symbol* **Tl** A soft, very poisonous metallic element used in making glass that is highly refractive and has a low melting point. It was formerly used in making rodent and ant poisons. Atomic number 81. See **Periodic Table.**

Thames (tĕmz) A river of southern England flowing about 210 miles (340 kilometers) eastward to the North Sea.

than (thăn *or* thən) *conj.* **1.** Used to introduce the second element or clause of an unequal comparison: *She's a better skier than I am.* **2.** Used to introduce the second element after certain words indicating difference: *He draws differently than she does.* ❖ *prep.* In comparison with: *We admire no one more than him.*

thane (thān) *n.* **1.** In Anglo-Saxon England, a freeman granted land by the king in return for military service. **2.** A feudal lord or baron in Scotland.

thank (thăngk) *tr.v.* **thanked, thank·ing, thanks 1.** To express gratitude to: *We thanked her for the kind offer.* **2.** To hold responsible; credit: *We can thank the parade for this traffic jam.* [From Old English *thancian.*]

thank·ful (thăngk′fəl) *adj.* Showing or feeling gratitude; grateful: *responded with a thankful smile.* **—thank′ful·ly** *adv.* **—thank′ful·ness** *n.*

thank·less (thăngk′lĭs) *adj.* **1.** Not feeling or showing gratitude; ungrateful. **2.** Not likely to be appreciated: *a thankless task.*

thanks (thăngks) *pl.n.* **1.** An expression of gratitude: *wrote a note of thanks to my grandparents for their gift.* **2.** Grateful feelings or thoughts; gratitude: *a heart full of thanks for our escape.* ❖ *interj.* An expression used to show gratitude. ◆ **thanks to** On account of; because of: *I was able to finish my chores, thanks to your help.*

thanks·giv·ing (thăngks-gĭv′ĭng) *n.* **1.** An act of giving thanks; an expression of gratitude, especially to God. **2. Thanksgiving** A holiday for giving thanks, celebrated in the United States on the fourth Thursday of November and in Canada on the second Monday of October.

that (thăt *or* thət) *pron., pl.* **those** (thōz) **1.** Used to refer to the one mentioned or understood: *What kind of soup is that?* **2.** Used to refer to the event, action, or time just mentioned: *We went to dinner. After that, we saw a movie.* **3.** Used to indicate the farther or less immediate one: *That is for sale; this is not.* **4. those** Used to indicate an unspecified number of people: *those who refused to join.* **5.** Used as a relative pronoun to introduce a clause, especially a restrictive clause: *the car that has the flat tire.* **6.** In, on, by, or with which: *each summer that the concerts are performed.* ❖ *adj., pl.* **those 1.** Being the one singled out, implied, or understood: *that place; those mountains.* **2.** Being the one further removed or less obvious: *That route is shorter than this one.* ❖ *adv.* **1.** To such an extent or degree: *Is your problem that complicated?* **2.** To a high degree; very: *I can't outrun my older brother; I'm a very fast runner, but I'm not that fast.* ❖ *conj.* **1.** Used to introduce a subordinate clause stating a result, wish, purpose, reason, or cause: *We hope that you will enjoy the book.* **2a.** Used to introduce a subordinate clause modifying an adverb or adverbial expression: *The dogs will go anywhere that they are welcome.* **b.** Used to introduce a subordinate clause that is joined to an adjective or a noun as a complement: *I was sure that she was right. He has a feeling that interest rates will rise soon.* **3.** Used to introduce a noun clause that is usually the subject or object of a verb or predicate nominative: *That you will finish the assignment is not up for debate.* ◆ **that is** To explain more clearly; in other words: *on the first floor, that is, the floor at street level.* [From Old English *thæt.*] —SEE NOTE.

thatch (thăch) *n.* Plant stalks or leaves, such as straw, reeds, or palm fronds, used for roofing. ❖ *tr.v.* **thatched, thatch·ing, thatch·es** To cover with thatch: *thatch a cottage.* [From Old English *thæc.*]

Thatch·er (thăch′ər), **Margaret Hilda** 1925–2013. British politician who served as prime minister (1979–1990).

thaw (thô) *v.* **thawed, thaw·ing, thaws** *—intr.* **1.** To change from a frozen solid to a liquid by gradual warming; melt. **2.** To lose stiffness or numbness by being warmed: *I sat by the fire until my feet thawed.* **3.** To become warm enough for snow and ice to melt: *It often thaws in January.* **4.** To become less formal or reserved: *Relations between the countries began to thaw.* *—tr.* To cause to thaw: *I thawed the chicken before preparing it for dinner.* ❖ *n.* **1.** The process of thawing. **2.** A period of warm weather during which snow and ice melt.

the[1] (thē *before a vowel,* thə *before a consonant*) *def.art.* **1.** Used before nouns or noun phrases that refer to specified people or things: *The pen that I was looking for was under the newspaper.* **2.** Used before a noun to stress its importance or prominence: *Last night's party was the event of the year.* **3.** Used to indicate uniqueness: *the moon; the Prince of Wales.* **4.** Used before a singular noun to make it general: *The whooping crane is an endangered species.* **5.** Used before a proper name, as of a monument or ship: *the Alamo.* **6.** Used before an adjective to make it function as a noun and signify a class: *the rich and the powerful.* **7.** Used before a noun, meaning "per" or "each": *She can have my entire stock at one dollar the box.* **8.** Used before a present participle, signifying the action in the abstract: *the weaving of rugs.* [From Old English, alteration of *se,* masculine demonstrative pronoun.]

the[2] (thē *before a vowel,* thə *before a consonant*) *adv.* **1.** To that extent; by that much: *the sooner the better.* **2.** Beyond any other: *Of all my cousins, I like you the best.* [From Old English *thȳ, thē.*]

the·a·ter or **the·a·tre** (thē′ə-tər) *n.* **1.** A building, room, or outdoor structure for presenting plays, films, or other dramatic performances. **2.** Dramatic literature or its performance; drama: *the theater of Shakespeare.* **3.** A place that is the setting for dramatic events. **4.** A large geographic area in which military operations are coordinated: *the European theater during World War II.* [From Middle English *theatre,* from Greek *theātron,* from *theāsthai,* to watch.]

the·at·ri·cal (thē-ăt′rĭ-kəl) *adj.* **1.** Relating to or suitable for the theater. **2.** Marked by self-display or exaggerated behavior; affectedly dramatic: *had a theatrical way of saying goodbye.* **—the·at′ri·cal·ly** *adv.*

Thebes (thēbz) **1.** An ancient city on the Nile River in present-day central Egypt. It flourished from the mid-22nd to the 18th century BC. The tomb of Tutankhamen is nearby. **2.** An ancient city of east-central Greece northwest of Athens.

thee (thē) *pron.* The objective case of **thou.**

theft (thĕft) *n.* **1.** The unlawful taking of something that belongs to another: *The homeowner took steps to prevent theft.* **2.** An instance of this: *There were several car thefts in our neighborhood last week.*

their (thâr) *adj.* The possessive form of **they.** Belonging to or relating to them: *Pittsburgh is their hometown.* [From Middle English, from Old Norse *theira,* theirs.]

❑ *These sound alike:* **their, there** (at that place), **they're** (they are).

theirs (thârz) *pron. (used with a singular or plural verb)* The one or ones belonging to them: *If your car is not working, use theirs.*

them (thĕm *or* thəm) *pron.* The objective case of **they. 1.** Used as the direct object of a verb: *I helped them fix a flat tire.* **2.** Used as the indirect object of a verb: *I paid them a visit.* **3.** Used as the object of a preposition: *I saved the best seats for them.* [From Middle English *theim,* from Old Norse *theim* and Old English *thǣm.*] —SEE NOTE AT **me.**

USAGE

that Use **that** to introduce a restrictive relative clause, which identifies the noun being talked about: *The house that Jack built has been torn down.* In this sentence the clause *that Jack built* identifies which house was torn down. Use **which** with a nonrestrictive relative clause, which gives additional information about something that has already been identified: *The students in science class have been complaining about the textbook, which is hard to follow.* By the time we get to *which* in this sentence, we already know that the textbook is the one used in science. The fact that the textbook is hard to follow is additional information.

thatch
thatched roof

USAGE

there When you use **there** before a verb such as *be, seem,* or *appear,* make sure that the verb agrees in number with the following subject: *There is a great pizza place across the street. There are beautiful wildflowers in the meadow.*

WORD BUILDING

thermo– The prefix **thermo–** comes from the Greek word *thermos,* meaning "warm, hot." When used to form words in English, *thermo–* generally refers to heat, as in *thermodynamic,* or sometimes to thermoelectricity, as in *thermocouple.* Most of the words that begin with *thermo–,* such as *thermostat* and *thermosphere,* only came into being in the 1800s and 1900s. Sometimes before a vowel *thermo–* becomes *therm–,* as in *thermion,* "an ion emitted by heat."

ă	pat	ôr	core
ā	pay	oi	boy
âr	care	ou	out
ä	father	o͝o	took
ĕ	pet	o͝or	lure
ē	be	o͞o	boot
ĭ	pit	ŭ	cut
ī	bite	ûr	urge
îr	pier	th	thin
ŏ	pot	*th*	this
ō	toe	zh	vision
ô	paw	ə	about

the·mat·ic (thĭ-**măt′**ĭk) *adj.* Relating to or being a theme or themes. **—the·mat′i·cal·ly** *adv.*

theme (thēm) *n.* **1.** A topic of discussion or discourse. See Synonyms at **subject. 2.** An implicit or recurring idea; a motif: *a party with a tropical island theme.* **3.** A short composition assigned to a student as a writing exercise. **4.** The principal melody in a musical composition. [From Middle English *teme,* from Greek *thema.*]

them·selves (*th*ĕm-**sĕlvz′** *or* *th*əm-**sĕlvz′**) *pron.* **1.** The ones that are the same as them: **a.** Used as the direct or indirect object of a verb or as the object of a preposition, to show that the action of the verb refers back to the subject: *They prepared themselves for the trip. The travelers gave themselves plenty of time. They saved the best for themselves.* **b.** Used to give emphasis: *The cooks themselves will eat in the kitchen.* **2.** Their normal or healthy selves: *After getting over their jet lag, they're themselves again.*

then (*th*ĕn) *adv.* **1.** At that time: *We were younger then. Come at noon; I'll be ready then.* **2.** Next in time, space, or order; immediately afterward: *We'll get ice cream, and then we'll go home.* **3.** Moreover; besides: *It costs $20, and then there's the sales tax to pay.* **4a.** In that case: *If you want to go, then go.* **b.** Therefore; consequently: *If x equals 11 and y equals 3, then xy equals 33.* ❖ *n.* That time or moment: *From then on, we were close friends.* ❖ *adj.* Being so at the time: *the then president.* ◆ **and then some** *Informal* With considerably more in addition: *I made enough to serve all the guests and then some.* **then again** From another standpoint; on the other hand: *I want to go to camp this summer. Then again, I'll really miss my parents.* [From Old English *thenne.*]

thence (*th*ĕns *or* thĕns) *adv.* From there on: *We flew to Chicago and thence to St. Louis.*

thence·forth (*th*ĕns-**fôrth′** *or* thĕns-**fôrth′**) *adv.* From that time forward; thereafter: *Thenceforth she became steadily more conservative.*

thence·for·ward (*th*ĕns-**fôr′**wərd *or* thĕns-**fôr′**wərd) *adv.* **1.** Thenceforth. **2.** From that time or place on.

the·oc·ra·cy (thē-**ŏk′**rə-sē) *n., pl.* **the·oc·ra·cies 1.** Government ruled by or subject to religious authority. **2.** A country or state governed in this way.

the·o·crat·ic (thē′ə-**krăt′**ĭk) *adj.* Relating to or based on theocracy: *a theocratic ruler.*

the·o·lo·gi·an (thē′ə-**lō′**jən) *n.* A person who is learned in theology.

the·o·log·i·cal (thē′ə-**lŏj′**ĭ-kəl) *adj.* Relating to theology.

the·ol·o·gy (thē-**ŏl′**ə-jē) *n., pl.* **the·ol·o·gies 1.** The study of the nature of God and religious truth; rational inquiry into religious questions. **2.** A system or school of opinions concerning God and religious questions: *Lutheran theology; Sunni theology.* [From Middle English *theologie,* from Greek *theologiā* : *theos,* god + *-logiā,* study.]

the·o·rem (**thē′**ər-əm *or* **thîr′**əm) *n.* **1.** An idea that has been demonstrated as true or is assumed to be able to be demonstrated as true. **2.** A mathematical statement whose truth can be proved on the basis of a given set of axioms or assumptions.

the·o·ret·i·cal (thē′ə-**rĕt′**ĭ-kəl) also **the·o·ret·ic** (thē′ə-**rĕt′**ĭk) *adj.* **1.** Based on or relating to theory. **2.** Restricted to theory; not practical: *theoretical physics.* **—the′o·ret′i·cal·ly** *adv.*

the·o·re·ti·cian (thē′ər-ĭ-**tĭsh′**ən *or* thîr′ĭ-**tĭsh′**ən) *n.* A person who formulates, studies, or is expert in the theory of a science or an art.

the·o·rist (**thē′**ər-ĭst *or* **thîr′**ĭst) *n.* A person who formulates a theory; a theoretician.

the·o·rize (**thē′**ə-rīz′ *or* **thîr′**īz) *intr.v.* **the·o·rized, the·o·riz·ing, the·o·riz·es** To formulate a theory or theories; speculate.

the·o·ry (**thē′**ə-rē *or* **thîr′**ē) *n., pl.* **the·o·ries 1.** A set of statements or principles devised to explain a group of facts or phenomena. Most theories that are accepted by scientists have been tested by experiments and can be used to make predictions about natural phenomena. **2.** The branch of a science or art consisting of its explanations, accepted principles, and methods of analysis: *music theory.* **3.** A belief that guides action or assists comprehension or judgment: *We went fishing on the theory that the rain would cause the fish to bite.* **4.** An assumption based on limited information or knowledge; a guess: *I have a theory about why he's so grumpy.* [From Greek *theōriā.*]

ther·a·peu·tic (thĕr′ə-**pyo͞o′**tĭk) *adj.* Having the capability of healing or curing: *therapeutic exercises.* **—ther′a·peu′ti·cal·ly** *adv.*

ther·a·peu·tics (thĕr′ə-**pyo͞o′**tĭks) *n.* *(used with a singular verb)* The medical treatment of disease.

ther·a·pist (**thĕr′**ə-pĭst) *n.* A person who specializes in a particular kind of therapy.

ther·a·py (**thĕr′**ə-pē) *n., pl.* **ther·a·pies 1.** Treatment of illness, injury, or disability. **2.** Psychotherapy. **3.** Healing power or quality: *the therapy of fresh air and exercise.* [From Greek *therapeia.*]

there (*th*âr) *adv.* **1.** At or in that place: *Set the package over there.* **2.** To, into, or toward that place: *How long did it take to get there?* **3.** At that stage, moment, or point: *Stop there before you make any more mistakes.* **4.** In that matter: *I can't agree with you there.* ❖ *pron.* **1.** Used to introduce a clause or sentence: *There are different kinds of pepper. There must be another exit.* **2.** Used to indicate a person in direct address: *Hello there.* ❖ *n.* That place or point: *I'll never know how we got out of there.* ❖ *interj.* An expression used to show feelings such as satisfaction, sympathy, relief, or anger: *There, there, you'll be fine.* [From Old English *thǣr.*] —SEE NOTE.

❑ *These sound alike:* **there, their** (belonging to them), **they're** (they are).

there·a·bouts (*th*âr′ə-**bouts′**) *adv.* **1.** Near that place; about there: *somewhere in the Rockies or thereabouts.* **2.** About that number, amount, or time: *at 8:00 or thereabouts.*

there·af·ter (*th*âr-**ăf′**tər) *adv.* From a specified time onward; from then on: *Thereafter, people were glad to come to our concerts.*

there·at (*th*âr-**ăt′**) *adv.* **1.** At that place; there. **2.** At the event; on account of that: *I replied sharply, and thereat the man kept quiet.*

there·by (*th*âr-**bī′**) *adv.* By that means; because of that: *We put down the storm windows to keep out drafts and thereby conserve heat.*

there·fore (***th*âr′**fôr′) *adv.* For that reason or cause; consequently: *Fungi lack chlorophyll and are therefore dependent upon other plants and animals for their food.*

there·from (*th*âr-**frŭm′** *or* *th*âr-**frŏm′**) *adv.* From that place, time, or thing.

there·in (*th*âr-**ĭn′**) *adv.* **1.** In that place, time, or thing: *the house and everything therein.* **2.** In that respect: *He was never elected president; therein lay his great frustration.*

there·of (*th*âr-**ŭv′** *or* *th*âr-**ŏv′**) *adv.* Relating to or concerning this, that, or it: *born in the United States and subject to the jurisdiction thereof.*

there·on (*th*âr-**ŏn′**) *adv.* On or upon this, that, or it.

there·to (*th*âr-**to͞o′**) *adv.* To that, this, or it: *She got a house with furnishings in addition thereto.*

there·to·fore (***th*âr′**tə-fôr′) *adv.* Until that time; before that: *a house where none had been theretofore.*

there·un·der (*th*âr-**ŭn′**dər) *adv.* Under this, that, or it: *the floor planks and all stowed thereunder.*

there·un·to (*th*âr′ŭn-**to͞o′**) *adv.* *Archaic* To that, this, or it; thereto.

there·up·on (*th*âr′ə-**pŏn′**) *adv.* After that; directly following that: *He criticized the judge and was thereupon summoned to court.*

there·with (thâr-**wĭth′** *or* thâr-**wĭth′**) *adv.* With this, that, or it: *She got a microscope, and therewith her fate was sealed—she had to become a scientist.*

ther·mal (**thûr′**məl) *adj.* **1.** Relating to, using, producing, or caused by heat. **2.** Intended or designed to help retain body heat: *thermal underwear.* ❖ *n.* A current of warm air that rises because it is less dense than the air around it. [From Greek *thermē*, heat.] **—ther′mal·ly** *adv.*

therm·i·on (**thûr′**mī′ən) *n.* An electrically charged particle, especially an electron, that is emitted by a conducting material at high temperatures.

thermo– or **therm–** *pref.* A prefix that means heat: *thermometer.* —SEE NOTE.

ther·mo·cou·ple (**thûr′**mə-kŭp′əl) *n.* A thermoelectric device used to measure temperatures, especially high temperatures, accurately. It usually consists of a junction of dissimilar metals across which a voltage that varies with temperature is produced. Thermocouples are used as thermometers, to generate electricity, and to make refrigeration devices.

ther·mo·dy·nam·ic (thûr′mō-dī-**năm′**ĭk) *adj.* **1.** Relating to thermodynamics. **2.** Relating to or operating by mechanical power derived from heat.

ther·mo·dy·nam·ics (thûr′mō-dī-**năm′**ĭks) *n.* *(used with a singular verb)* The part of physics that deals with the relationships between heat and other forms of energy.

ther·mo·e·lec·tric (thûr′mō-ĭ-**lĕk′**trĭk) *adj.* Relating to or having to do with electricity that is generated by the action of heat.

ther·mo·e·lec·tric·i·ty (thûr′mō-ĭ-lĕk-**trĭs′**ĭ-tē *or* thûr′-mō-ē′lĕk-**trĭs′**ĭ-tē) *n.* Electricity generated by a flow of heat, as in a thermocouple.

ther·mo·graph (**thûr′**mə-grăf′) *n.* A thermometer that records the temperatures it measures.

ther·mom·e·ter (thər-**mŏm′**ĭ-tər) *n.* An instrument that measures temperature, such as one that consists of a glass tube in which a liquid expands or contracts as the temperature increases or decreases.

ther·mo·nu·cle·ar (thûr′mō **no͞o′**klē-ər) *adj.* **1.** Relating to or derived from the fusion of atomic nuclei at high temperatures or the energy produced in this way. **2.** Relating to weapons based on nuclear fusion, especially as distinguished from those based on nuclear fission.

ther·mo·plas·tic (thûr′mə-**plăs′**tĭk) *adj.* Soft and pliable when heated but hard when cooled. ❖ *n.* A thermoplastic material.

Ther·mop·y·lae (thər-**mŏp′**ə-lē) A narrow pass of east-central Greece. A small force of Spartan defenders was annihilated by the Persians here in 480 BC.

ther·mos (**thûr′**məs) *n.* A vacuum bottle used to keep beverages hot or cold.

ther·mo·sphere (**thûr′**mə-sfîr′) *n.* The outermost layer of the atmosphere, lying outside the mesosphere, having temperatures that increase steadily with altitude.

ther·mo·stat (**thûr′**mə-stăt′) *n.* A device that automatically controls a piece of heating or cooling equipment in such a way as to keep the temperature nearly constant.

the·sau·rus (thĭ-**sôr′**əs) *n., pl.* **the·sau·rus·es** or **the·sau·ri** (thĭ-**sôr′**ī′) **1.** A book of synonyms, often including antonyms. **2.** A book that lists all the words relating to a general idea or to a specific subject, such as medicine or music. [From Greek *thēsauros*, treasury.]

these (*th*ēz) *pron. & adj.* Plural of **this.**

The·se·us (**thē′**sē-əs) *n.* In Greek mythology, the king of Athens who slew the Minotaur.

the·sis (**thē′**sĭs) *n., pl.* **the·ses** (**thē′**sēz) **1.** A statement put forth for consideration, especially when supported by an argument. **2.** A long essay resulting from original research written especially by a candidate for an academic degree. [From Greek, from *tithenai*, to put.]

thes·pi·an (**thĕs′**pē-ən) *adj.* Relating to drama; dramatic. ❖ *n.* An actor or actress.

the·ta (**thā′**tə *or* **thē′**tə) *n.* The eighth letter of the Greek alphabet, written Θ, θ. In English it is represented as *Th, th.*

thew (thyo͞o) *n.* often **thews 1.** Muscular power or strength. **2.** A well-developed sinew or muscle.

they (*th*ā) *pron.* **1.** The people, animals, or things previously mentioned: *Emily and Dylan worked here last summer, but now they are back in school.* **2.** People considered as a group: *He's as smart as they come.* [From Middle English *thei*, from Old Norse *their.*] —SEE NOTE.

they'd (*th*ād) Contraction of *they had* or *they would.*

they'll (*th*āl) Contraction of *they will.*

they're (*th*âr) Contraction of *they are.*

❑ *These sound alike:* **they're, their** (belonging to them), **there** (at that place).

they've (*th*āv) Contraction of *they have.*

thi·a·mine (**thī′**ə-mĭn *or* **thī′**ə-mēn′) *n.* A vitamin belonging to the vitamin B complex that is essential for carbohydrate metabolism and normal functioning of the nervous system; vitamin B_1. It is found in whole grains, legumes, yeast, and meat.

thick (thĭk) *adj.* **thick·er, thick·est 1.** Relatively great in depth or in extent from one surface to the opposite; not thin: *a thick board.* **2.** Measuring in this dimension: *a board two inches thick.* **3.** Heavy in form or build; thickset: *a thick neck.* **4.** Flowing slowly; heavy or viscous: *thick oil.* **5.** Dense or concentrated: *thick fog; a thick forest.* **6.** Very noticeable; pronounced; heavy: *speaking with a thick accent.* **7.** *Informal* Lacking mental agility; stupid. **8.** *Informal* Very friendly: *Those two are thick friends.* ❖ *adv.* So as to be thick; thickly: *Slice it thick.* ❖ *n.* **1.** The thickest part. **2.** The most active or intense part: *in the thick of the battle.* ◆ **thick and thin** Good and bad times: *promised to be there to help through thick and thin.* [From Old English *thicce.*] **—thick′ly** *adv.*

thick·en (**thĭk′**ən) *tr. & intr.v.* **thick·ened, thick·en·ing, thick·ens 1.** To make or become thick or thicker: *We thickened the gravy. The fog thickened.* **2.** To make or become more intricate or complex. **—thick′en·er** *n.*

thick·en·ing (**thĭk′**ə-nĭng) *n.* **1.** The act or process of making or becoming thick. **2.** A substance, such as corn starch, used to thicken a liquid.

thick·et (**thĭk′**ĭt) *n.* A dense growth of shrubs or underbrush. [From Old English *thiccet*, from *thicce*, thick.]

thick·set (**thĭk′sĕt′**) *adj.* **1.** Having a solid stocky form or body; stout: *a thickset man.* **2.** Placed or positioned closely together: *thickset rose bushes.*

thick-skinned (**thĭk′skĭnd′**) *adj.* **1.** Having a thick skin or rind. **2.** Not easily offended, as by criticism or insult.

thief (thēf) *n., pl.* **thieves** (thēvz) One who commits the act or crime of theft. [From Old English *thēof.*]

thieve (thēv) *tr. & intr.v.* **thieved, thiev·ing, thieves** To take (something) by theft or commit theft.

thigh (thī) *n.* **1.** The part of the human leg between the hip and the knee. **2.** A similar part in other vertebrate animals.

thigh·bone (**thī′**bōn′) *n.* The femur.

thim·ble (**thĭm′**bəl) *n.* A small cup, usually of metal or plastic, worn for protection on the finger that pushes the needle in sewing. [From Old English *thȳmel*, leather finger covering, from *thūma*, thumb.]

Thim·phu (**thĭm′**po͞o′ *or* **tĭm′**po͞o′) The capital of Bhutan, in the western part of the country in the eastern Himalaya Mountains.

thin (thĭn) *adj.* **thin·ner, thin·nest 1a.** Relatively small in extent from one surface to the opposite; not thick: *a thin board.* **b.** Not great in diameter or cross section; fine: *thin wire.* **2.** Lean or slender in form or build: *a*

USAGE

they In order to avoid using **he** in reference to any person (who could be either male or female), people sometimes use **they** to refer to a singular noun or pronoun. We often hear sentences like *Someone left their book* and *Why not call a classmate and ask them for the assignment?* These uses of *they* violate the traditional grammatical rule of number agreement, since *they* is supposed to refer only to plural nouns and pronouns. In formal writing, it is best to avoid this problem when you can by not using *they* (as in *Someone left a book*) or by revising to use only plural nouns and pronouns (as in *Why not call some of your classmates and ask them for the assignment?*). For more information, see Note at **me.**

WRITERS CHOOSE THEIR WORDS

[The Otters] talk too much, eat too much, drink too much, sleep too much, swim too much, chew too much betel nut, and they are without any question the rudest creatures in the world. But it's an equal-opportunity impoliteness, the Otters all lay into one another without discrimination, and as a result they have all grown so **thick-skinned** that nobody minds what anyone else says.

—Salman Rushdie
Luka and the Fire of Life

thimble

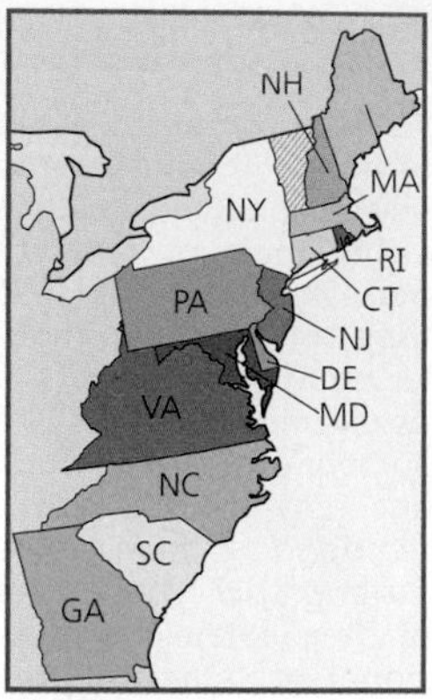

Thirteen Colonies

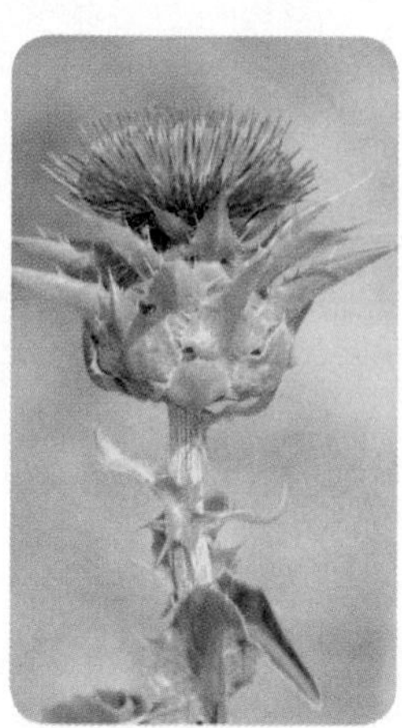

thistle

ă	pat	ôr	core
ā	pay	oi	boy
âr	care	ou	out
ä	father	o͝o	took
ĕ	pet	o͝or	lure
ē	be	o͞o	boot
ĭ	pit	ŭ	cut
ī	bite	ûr	urge
îr	pier	th	thin
ŏ	pot	*th*	this
ō	toe	zh	vision
ô	paw	ə	about

thin man. See Synonyms at **lean**[2]. **3.** Not dense or concentrated; sparse: *hair that was thin on top.* **4a.** Flowing with relative ease; not viscous: *a thin oil.* **b.** Watery: *thin soup.* **5.** Lacking substance or force; flimsy: *a thin excuse.* **6.** Lacking in strength or resonance, as a sound or tone: *The old piano had a thin sound.* ❖ *adv.* So as to be thin; thinly: *Slice the bread thin.* ❖ *tr. & intr.v.* **thinned, thin·ning, thins** To make or become thin or thinner: *I thinned the gravy. Wait until the crowd thins out.* [From Old English *thynne.*] **—thin′ly** *adv.* **—thin′ness** *n.*

thine (*th*īn) *pron. (used with a singular or plural verb)* The one or ones belonging to thee. ❖ *adj. Archaic* A possessive form of **thou.** Used instead of *thy* before an initial vowel or *h*: *Know thine enemy.*

thing (thĭng) *n.* **1.** An object or entity that is not or cannot be named specifically: *What is this thing for? I can't see a thing in the dark.* **2.** A person, pet, or other animal: *That baby is the sweetest thing!* **3.** An article of clothing: *I can't wear that thing to the dance!* **4. things** Personal possessions; belongings: *Have you packed your things for the weekend?* **5.** An act, deed, or work: *Mowing their lawn was a nice thing to do.* **6.** The result of work or activity: *He's always drawing things.* **7.** A thought or utterance: *What a rotten thing to say!* **8.** A matter of concern: *many things on my mind.* **9.** A goal or objective: *In golf, the thing is to make the fewest strokes possible.* **10.** A turn of events; a circumstance: *The flood was a terrible thing.* **11. things** The general state of affairs; conditions: *Things are really looking up.* **12.** *Informal* The latest fashion or fad: *Long sweaters are the thing this fall.* **13.** *Slang* An activity uniquely suitable or satisfying to one: *doing his own thing.* ◆ **first thing** *Informal* Right away; before anything else: *We'll get the kitten vaccinated first thing.* [From Old English *thing,* assembly.]

think (thĭngk) *v.* **thought** (thôt), **think·ing, thinks** *—tr.* **1.** To have or form in the mind: *Think what we could do with a new computer.* **2a.** To reason about or reflect on; ponder: *Think how complex language is. Think the matter through.* **b.** To decide by reasoning: *thinking what to do.* **3.** To judge or regard; look upon: *I think it only fair.* **4.** To believe; suppose: *He always thought he was right.* **5.** To devise; invent: *She thought up a plan to improve the library.* *—intr.* **1.** To use the power of reason, as by conceiving ideas or making judgments: *I was very tired, so it was difficult to think.* **2.** To weigh or consider an idea: *They are thinking about moving.* **3a.** To bring a thought to mind by imagination or invention: *No one before had thought of bifocal glasses.* **b.** To recall a thought or image to mind: *She thought of her childhood when she saw the movie.* **4.** To believe; suppose: *It's later than you think.* **5.** To have care or consideration: *Think first of the ones you love.* ◆ **think better of** To change one's mind about; reconsider. **think twice** To consider something carefully. [From Old English *thencan.*]

think tank *n.* A group or institution organized for intensive research and solving of problems in such areas as technology and political strategy.

thin·ner (thĭn′ər) *n.* A liquid, such as turpentine, that is mixed with a paint or varnish to make it flow more easily as it is applied.

thin-skinned (thĭn′skĭnd′) *adj.* **1.** Having a thin rind or skin. **2.** Easily offended, as by criticism or insult.

third (thûrd) *n.* **1.** The ordinal number matching the number three in a series. **2.** One of three equal parts. **3a.** The interval covering three tones in a musical scale. **b.** The third tone in a musical scale. **4.** The transmission gear used to produce speeds next higher than those of second in a motor vehicle. [From Old English *thridda.*]

third base *n.* **1.** In baseball, the base that must be touched last by a runner before reaching home plate, located to the left as one looks toward the pitcher from home plate. **2.** The position played by a third baseman.

third baseman *n.* The baseball player defending the area near third base.

third class *n.* Accommodations, as on a ship or train, that are of the third and usually lowest order of luxury and price. **—third′-class′** *adj.*

third-de·gree burn (thûrd′dĭ-grē′) *n.* A severe burn in which the outer layer of skin is destroyed and sensitive nerve endings are exposed.

third dimension *n.* **1.** The quality of depth or thickness in an object or a space. **2.** The quality of seeming real or lifelike. **—third′-di·men′sion·al** *adj.*

third person *n.* **1.** A group of words or word forms, such as verbs and pronouns, that designate a person or thing other than the speaker or the one spoken to or the writer and the one reading what has been written. *She* and *them* are pronouns in the third person. **2.** The style of writing in which forms in the third person are used: *a story written in the third person.*

Third World *n.* The developing nations of Africa, Asia, and Latin America.

thirst (thûrst) *n.* **1a.** A sensation of dryness in the mouth and throat related to a need or desire to drink. **b.** The desire to drink. **2.** An insistent desire; a craving: *a thirst for adventure.* ❖ *intr.v.* **thirst·ed, thirst·ing, thirsts** **1.** To feel a need to drink. **2.** To have a strong craving; yearn: *thirsting for knowledge.* [From Old English *thurst.*]

thirst·y (thûr′stē) *adj.* **thirst·i·er, thirst·i·est** **1.** Desiring to drink: *Salty foods make one thirsty.* **2.** Arid; parched: *fields thirsty for rain.* **3.** Having a strong desire: *thirsty for knowledge.*

thir·teen (thûr-tēn′) *n.* **1.** The number, written 13, that is equal to 12 + 1. **2.** The 13th in a set or sequence.

Thirteen Colonies The 13 British colonies in North America that became the original states of the United States, including New Hampshire, Massachusetts, Rhode Island, Connecticut, New York, New Jersey, Pennsylvania, Delaware, Maryland, Virginia, North Carolina, South Carolina, and Georgia.

thir·teenth (thûr-tēnth′) *n.* **1.** The ordinal number matching the number 13 in a series. **2.** One of 13 equal parts.

thir·ti·eth (thûr′tē-ĭth) *n.* **1.** The ordinal number matching the number 30 in a series. **2.** One of 30 equal parts.

thir·ty (thûr′tē) *n., pl.* **thir·ties** The number, written 30, that is equal to 3 × 10.

thir·ty-sec·ond note (thûr′tē-sĕk′ənd) *n.* A musical note having the time value of 1⁄32 of a whole note.

this (*th*ĭs) *pron., pl.* **these** (*th*ēz) **1.** Used to refer to the person or thing present, nearby, or just mentioned: *This is my friend Anna. This is my house.* **2.** Used to refer to what is about to be said: *This will really make you laugh.* **3.** Used to refer to the present occasion or time: *Taylor has stayed out later than this.* **4.** Used to indicate the nearer or the more immediate one: *That little scene was nothing compared to this.* ❖ *adj., pl.* **these** **1.** Being just mentioned or present in space, time, or thought: *We left early this morning.* **2.** Being nearer or more immediate: *Walk on this side of the street, not that side.* **3.** Being about to be stated or described: *Just wait until you hear this story.* ❖ *adv.* To this extent; so: *I never stayed up this late before.* [From Old English.]

this·tle (thĭs′əl) *n.* Any of numerous plants having prickly leaves and flower heads that have prickly bracts and are often purplish. [From Old English *thistel.*]

thith·er (thĭ*th*′ər *or* thĭth′ər) *adv.* To or toward that place; in that direction; there: *running hither and thither.*

thobe (thōb) *n.* **1.** An ankle-length, long-sleeved, gownlike garment worn chiefly by men of the Arabian Peninsula. **2.** A similar, often embroidered women's garment, usually worn for formal occasions. [From Arabic *ṯawb.*]

thole pin (thōl) *n.* A peg set in pairs in the gunwales of a boat to serve as an oarlock. [From Old English *thol*.]

Thom·as (tŏm′əs), Saint. Flourished first century AD. One of the 12 Apostles, who doubted that Jesus had risen from the dead until he saw the wounds.

Thomas, Clarence Born 1948. American jurist who was appointed an associate justice of the US Supreme Court in 1991.

Thomas, Dylan Marlais 1914–1953. British writer known especially for his poetry. He also wrote essays, short fiction, and radio dramas.

thong (thông) *n.* **1.** A narrow strip, as of leather, used for binding or lashing. **2.** A whip of plaited leather or cord. **3.** A sandal held on the foot by a strip that passes between the toes. **4.** A garment for the lower body consisting of a narrow strip of fabric that passes between the thighs and is supported by a waistband.

Thor (thôr) *n.* In Norse mythology, the god of thunder.

tho·rac·ic (thə-răs′ĭk) *adj.* Relating to, in, or near the thorax.

thoracic duct *n.* The main duct of the lymphatic system, rising along the spinal column and joining a vein near the heart.

tho·rax (thôr′ăks′) *n., pl.* **tho·rax·es** or **tho·ra·ces** (thôr′ə-sēz′) **1.** The part of the human body between the neck and the diaphragm, enclosed partly by the ribs; the chest. **2.** A similar part in other vertebrates. **3.** The middle region of the body of certain arthropods, including the insects and most crustaceans, lying between the head and the abdomen.

Tho·reau (thə-rō′ *or* thôr′ō), **Henry David** 1817–1862. American writer whose works include *Walden* (1854).

tho·ri·um (thôr′ē-əm) *n. Symbol* **Th** A silvery-white, radioactive metallic element used in magnesium alloys and as a source of energy in nuclear reactors. Atomic number 90. See **Periodic Table.**

thorn (thôrn) *n.* **1.** A sharp, usually woody structure growing from the stem of a plant. **2.** Any of various plants that bear such structures. **3.** A person or thing that causes irritation, annoyance, or discomfort: *a critic who has been a thorn in the mayor's side for years.* [From Old English.]

thorn·y (thôr′nē) *adj.* **thorn·i·er, thorn·i·est 1.** Full of or covered with thorns or other sharp structures: *thorny branches.* **2.** Controversial or problematic: *They argued about several thorny issues during the meeting.*

thor·ough (thûr′ō) *adj.* **1.** Complete in all respects: *a thorough search.* **2.** Painstakingly accurate or careful: *a thorough worker.* **3.** Absolute; utter: *a thorough success.* [From Old English *thuruh*, from end to end, through.] **—thor′ough·ly** *adv.* **—thor′ough·ness** *n.*

thor·ough·bred (thûr′ō-brĕd′) *n.* **1.** A purebred or pedigreed animal, especially a horse. **2. Thoroughbred** Any of a breed of horse, bred chiefly for racing, originating from crosses between Arabian stallions and English mares.

thor·ough·fare (thûr′ō-fâr′) *n.* **1.** A main road or public highway. **2.** A heavily traveled passage, such as a strait or channel.

thor·ough·go·ing (thûr′ō-gō′ĭng) *adj.* Very thorough; complete: *a thoroughgoing overhaul of the company's management.*

those (thōz) *pron. & adj.* Plural of **that.**

thou (thou) *pron.* Used to address one person, especially a familiar person in literary or religious writing. [From Old English *thū*.] —SEE NOTE AT **y'all.**

though (thō) *conj.* **1.** Despite the fact that; although: *He walked to work even though it was raining.* **2.** Even if: *Though our chances of winning are slim, I think we should play.* ❖ *adv.* However; nevertheless: *It's not going to snow; it may rain, though.*

thought (thôt) *v.* Past tense and past participle of **think.** ❖ *n.* **1.** The act or process of thinking: *spending hours in thought.* **2.** A product of thinking; an idea: *Let me have your thoughts on this subject.* See Synonyms at **idea. 3.** The intellectual activity or the ideas of a particular time or group: *ancient Greek thought.* **4.** Consideration; attention: *giving serious thought to the matter.* **5.** Intention; purpose: *She had no thought of hurting his feelings.*

thought·ful (thôt′fəl) *adj.* **1.** Occupied with thought; contemplative: *was thoughtful for a minute.* **2.** Showing or marked by careful thought: *a thoughtful paper.* **3.** Having or showing concern for others; considerate: *Bringing a gift was a thoughtful gesture.* **—thought′ful·ly** *adv.* **—thought′ful·ness** *n.*

thought·less (thôt′lĭs) *adj.* **1.** Characterized by or showing lack of thought or care; careless: *a thoughtless error.* **2.** Inconsiderate of others' feelings: *a thoughtless remark.* **—thought′less·ly** *adv.* **—thought′less·ness** *n.*

thou·sand (thou′zənd) *n.* The number, written as 1,000 or 10^3, that is equal to 10 × 100. [From Old English *thūsend*.]

thou·sandth (thou′zəndth *or* thou′zənth) *n.* **1.** The ordinal number matching the number 1,000 in a series. **2.** One of 1,000 equal parts.

thrash (thrăsh) *v.* **thrashed, thrash·ing, thrash·es** —*tr.* **1.** To strike or beat, especially with a flail or a stick. **2.** To swing or strike in a manner suggesting the action of a flail: *The alligator thrashed its tail.* **3.** To defeat utterly: *The team thrashed its opponent and won by a wide margin.* —*intr.* To move wildly or violently: *The fish was thrashing as the girl reeled it in.*

thrash·er (thrăsh′ər) *n.* Any of various songbirds of the Americas having a long tail, a long curved beak, and usually a brown head and back.

thrash·ing (thrăsh′ĭng) *n.* A severe beating.

thread (thrĕd) *n.* **1a.** Fine thin cord made of two or more strands of fiber twisted together and used in sewing and weaving cloth. **b.** A piece of such cord. **2.** Something that resembles a thread in thinness or fineness: *a thread of smoke coming out of the chimney.* **3.** Something that suggests the continuousness of such a strand: *He lost the thread of his argument.* **4.** A helical or spiral ridge on a screw, nut, or bolt. ❖ *v.* **thread·ed, thread·ing, threads** —*tr.* **1a.** To pass one end of a thread through the eye of (a needle, for example). **b.** To pass (something) through in the manner of thread: *thread the film through the projector.* **2.** To pass a thread, tape, or film into or through (a device): *thread the sewing machine; thread a film projector.* **3.** To connect by running a thread through; string: *thread beads.* **4.** To cut a thread onto (a screw, nut, or bolt). **5.** To make (one's way) cautiously through something: *pedestrians threading their way through a crowd.* **6.** To remove (body hair) by using a looped thread that has been wound tightly in the middle. —*intr.* **1.** To make one's way cautiously. **2.** To proceed in a winding course. [From Old English *thrǣd*.] **—thread′er** *n.*

thread·bare (thrĕd′bâr′) *adj.* **1.** Having the nap worn down so that the threads show through; shabby or frayed: *a threadbare rug.* **2.** Wearing old shabby clothing. **3.** Overused to the point of being no longer effective; trite: *threadbare excuses.*

thread·y (thrĕd′ē) *adj.* **thread·i·er, thread·i·est 1.** Consisting of or resembling thread. **2.** Lacking fullness of tone; thin: *a thready voice.*

threat (thrĕt) *n.* **1.** An expression of an intention to inflict pain, injury, or punishment. **2.** An indication of impending danger or harm: *The night air held a threat of frost.* **3.** Something, such as a person, thing, or idea, regarded as a possible danger. [From Old English *thrēat*, oppression.]

threat·en (thrĕt′n) *v.* **threat·ened, threat·en·ing, threat·ens** —*tr.* **1.** To express a threat against (someone). **2.** To be a source of danger to; menace: *Land-*

thobe

thong

thrasher

three-piece suit

slides threatened the mountain village.* **3.** To give signs or warning of; portend: *Dark skies threaten rain.* **4.** To announce the possibility of, in or as in a threat: *They are always threatening to move to the suburbs.* **5.** To cause (someone) to feel that his or her power or self-esteem is in danger of being lessened: *He felt threatened by his colleague's promotion.* —*intr.* **1.** To express or use threats. **2.** To indicate danger or harm.

three (thrē) *n.* **1.** The number, written 3, that is equal to 2 + 1. **2.** The third in a set or sequence. [From Old English *thrī.*]

3-D or **3D** also **three-D** (**thrē′dē′**) *adj.* Three-dimensional. ❖ *n.* A three-dimensional medium, display, or performance, especially a cinematic or graphic medium in three dimensions: *They shot the movie in 3-D.*

three-di·men·sion·al (thrē′dĭ-**mĕn′**shə-nəl) *adj.* **1.** Relating to, having, or existing in three dimensions. **2.** Relating to or producing visual images in which there is an illusion of depth and perspective: *a three-dimensional image projected with light from a laser.*

three-piece suit (**thrē′pēs′**) *n.* A suit that consists of a jacket, pants, and vest.

three·score (**thrē′skôr′**) *n.* Three times twenty; sixty.

three·some (**thrē′**səm) *n.* **1.** A group of three people or things. **2.** An activity, especially a golf match, that involves three people.

thren·o·dy (**thrĕn′**ə-dē) *n., pl.* **thren·o·dies** A poem or song of mourning or lamentation.

thre·o·nine (**thrē′**ə-nēn′) *n.* An essential amino acid that is formed by the reaction of certain proteins with water.

thresh (thrĕsh) *v.* **threshed, thresh·ing, thresh·es** —*tr.* **a.** To separate the seeds from (the stalks and husks of grain-bearing plants): *threshing rice by beating it; using a combine to thresh wheat.* **b.** To separate (grains or seeds) in this manner: *a machine for threshing grain.* —*intr.* To separate grains or seeds from stalks and husks.

thresh·er (**thrĕsh′**ər) *n.* **1.** A person or thing, especially a machine, that threshes. **2.** Any of various large sharks having a tail with a long upper lobe with which they strike the surface of the water.

thresh·old (**thrĕsh′**ōld′ *or* **thrĕsh′**hōld′) *n.* **1.** The piece of wood or stone placed beneath a door; a doorsill. **2.** The place or point of beginning; the outset: *Science is on the threshold of a better understanding of the atmosphere.* **3.** The lowest level or intensity at which a stimulus can be perceived or can produce a given effect: *a sound at the threshold of hearing.*

threw (thro͞o) *v.* Past tense of **throw.**

❑ *These sound alike:* **threw, through** (in and out of).

thrice (thrīs) *adv.* Three times: *She was thrice named class president.*

thrift (thrĭft) *n.* Wisdom in the management of money and other resources; frugality. [From Middle English *thrift*, prosperity, perhaps from Old Norse, from *thrīfask*, to thrive.]

thrift·y (**thrĭf′**tē) *adj.* **thrift·i·er, thrift·i·est** Practicing thrift; economical and frugal. —**thrift′i·ly** *adv.* —**thrift′i·ness** *n.*

thrill (thrĭl) *tr.v.* **thrilled, thrill·ing, thrills** To cause to feel a sudden intense sensation, as of joy, fear, or excitement: *She was thrilled to learn that she had won the contest.* ❖ *n.* **1.** A quivering or trembling caused by sudden excitement or emotion. **2.** A source or cause of excitement or emotion: *the thrill of riding a roller coaster.*

thrill·er (**thrĭl′**ər) *n.* Something that thrills, especially an exciting or suspenseful book, story, or movie.

thrive (thrīv) *intr.v.* **thrived** or **throve** (thrōv), **thrived** or **thriv·en** (**thrĭv′**ən), **thriv·ing, thrives 1.** To grow vigorously; flourish: *Some plants thrive in sandy soil.* **2.** To make steady progress; prosper: *The town thrived and grew larger.* [From Middle English *thriven*, from Old Norse *thrīfask.*]

throat (thrōt) *n.* **1a.** The front portion of the neck. **b.** The part of the digestive tract that forms a passage between the rear of the mouth and the esophagus and includes the pharynx and the larynx. **2.** A narrow passage or part suggesting the human throat: *the throat of a bottle.* [From Middle English *throte.*]

throat·y (**thrō′**tē) *adj.* **throat·i·er, throat·i·est** Uttered or sounding as if uttered deep in the throat; guttural, hoarse, or husky: *a throaty growl.* —**throat′i·ly** *adv.* —**throat′i·ness** *n.*

throb (thrŏb) *intr.v.* **throbbed, throb·bing, throbs 1.** To beat rapidly or violently; pound: *His heart was throbbing with excitement.* **2.** To feel a pulsating pain: *My toe was throbbing after I stubbed it.* **3.** To vibrate or sound with a slow steady rhythm: *hearing the boat's engines throbbing all night.* ❖ *n.* The act of throbbing; a beating or vibration.

throe (thrō) *n.* **1.** A severe pang or spasm of pain, as in childbirth. **2. throes** A condition of great struggle or trouble: *a country in the throes of an economic depression.*

throm·bin (**thrŏm′**bĭn) *n.* An enzyme in the blood that aids blood clotting by reacting with fibrinogen to form fibrin.

throm·bo·sis (thrŏm-**bō′**sĭs) *n., pl.* **throm·bo·ses** (thrŏm-**bō′**sēz) The formation or presence of a thrombus.

throm·bus (**thrŏm′**bəs) *n., pl.* **throm·bi** (**thrŏm′**bī) A blood clot that forms in a blood vessel or a chamber of the heart and obstructs the circulation.

throne (thrōn) *n.* **1.** The chair occupied by a monarch or an honored person on ceremonial occasions. **2.** The power, rank, or authority of a monarch; sovereignty: *succeed to the throne.* [From Middle English *trone*, from Greek *thronos.*]

❑ *These sound alike:* **throne, thrown** (propelled through the air).

throng (thrông) *n.* A large group of people or things gathered or crowded closely together. ❖ *v.* **thronged, throng·ing, throngs** —*tr.* To crowd into; fill: *People thronged the platforms of the subway station.* —*intr.* To gather, press, or move in a throng: *People thronged to the new restaurant.* [From Old English *gethrang.*]

throt·tle (**thrŏt′**l) *n.* **1.** A valve that regulates the flow of a fluid, such as the valve in an internal-combustion engine that controls the flow of fuel to the combustion chamber. **2.** A pedal or lever that controls such a valve. ❖ *tr.v.* **throt·tled, throt·tling, throt·tles 1.** To control (an engine, its fuel, or working fluid) with or as if with a throttle. **2.** To suppress: *The dictator tried to throttle the press.* **3.** To strangle (a person); choke.

through (thro͞o) *prep.* **1.** In one side and out the opposite or another side of: *going through the door.* **2.** Among or between; in the midst of: *a walk through the flowers.* **3.** By way of: *He entered through a side door.* **4.** By means of: *getting an apartment through an agency.* **5.** Here and there in; around: *a tour through France.* **6.** From the beginning to the end of: *staying up through the night.* **7.** At or near the end of: *We are through our testing period.* **8.** Up to and including: *a play that runs through December; a volume that covers A through D.* **9.** Past and without stopping for: *driving through a red light.* **10.** Because of; on account of: *We succeeded through hard work.* ❖ *adv.* **1.** From one end or side to another or an opposite end or side: *I opened the window and climbed through.* **2.** From beginning to end; completely: *I glanced at the article but haven't read it through.* **3.** Thoroughly: *We got soaked through in the rain.* **4.** Over the total distance; all the way: *We drove straight through to Boston.* **5.** To the end or conclusion: *I mean to see this matter through.* ❖ *adj.* **1.** Allowing continuous passage without obstruction: *a through street.* **2.** Going all the way to the end without stopping: *This is a through flight.* **3.** Passing from

WRITERS CHOOSE THEIR WORDS

In an open space a spear-throw from the foot of the steps a crowd was already gathered, jostling round the makeshift arena and **thronging** the steep slopes of the Vallum on either side; shadowy in the autumn dusk save for the glow of a brazier here and there among them, and the splashing yellow light of one big lantern in their midst. Justin made his way toward it, shouldering through the noisy, shifting **throng.**

—Rosemary Sutcliff
The Silver Branch

ă	pat	ôr	core
ā	pay	oi	boy
âr	care	ou	out
ä	father	o͝o	took
ĕ	pet	o͝or	lure
ē	be	o͞o	boot
ĭ	pit	ŭ	cut
ī	bite	ûr	urge
îr	pier	th	thin
ŏ	pot	*th*	this
ō	toe	zh	vision
ô	paw	ə	about

one end or side to another: *a through beam.* **4.** Finished; done: *Are you through with your homework?* **5.** Having no more use, value, or potential; washed-up: *If he injures that knee again, he's through as a basketball player.* **6.** Having no further dealings or connection: *Jane and I are through.* [From Old English *thurh.*]

❑ *These sound alike:* **through, threw** (propelled).

through·out (thrōō-**out'**) *prep.* In, to, through, or during every part of: *throughout the country; throughout the night.* ❖ *adv.* **1.** In or through all parts; everywhere: *The house is beautiful throughout.* **2.** During the entire time or extent: *She was questioned for two hours and remained calm throughout.*

through·way (**thrōō'**wā') *n.* Variant of **thruway.**

throve (thrōv) *v.* A past tense of **thrive.**

throw (thrō) *v.* **threw** (thrōō), **thrown** (thrōn), **throw·ing, throws** —*tr.* **1.** To propel through the air with a motion of the hand or arm: *throw a ball.* **2.** To propel or discharge into the air by any means: *The erupting volcano threw ash into the air.* **3.** To cause to move with great force or speed; propel or displace: *The tide threw cargo from the sunken ship onto the shore.* **4.** To cause to fall off: *The horse threw its rider.* **5.** *Informal* To perplex or cause confusion in; disconcert: *Don't let his friendly manner throw you.* **6.** To put on or off quickly or carelessly: *threw a jacket on and ran out the door.* **7.** To put suddenly or forcefully into a given condition, position, or activity: *new regulations that threw the players into confusion.* **8.** To form on a potter's wheel: *throw a vase.* **9a.** To roll (dice). **b.** To roll (a particular combination) with dice. **c.** To discard or play (a card). **10.** To send forth; project: *She threw me an encouraging look.* **11.** To cause (one's voice) to seem to come from a source other than oneself. **12.** To cause to fall on or over something; cast: *The rising sun threw shadows across the lawn. We threw sheets over the furniture before we painted the ceiling.* **13.** To arrange or give: *throw a party.* **14.** To move (a switch or control lever) in order to activate or deactivate a device. **15.** *Informal* To lose (a fight, for example) purposely. —*intr.* To cast, fling, or hurl something. ❖ *n.* **1.** The act or an instance of throwing. **2.** The distance to which something can be thrown. **3a.** A roll or cast of dice. **b.** The combination of numbers so obtained. **4.** A scarf, shawl, or light coverlet. ◆ **throw away 1.** To discard as useless: *threw away the empty box.* **2.** To fail to take advantage of: *threw away a chance to make a fortune.* **throw in 1.** To add (an extra thing or amount) with no additional charge. **2.** To engage (a clutch, for example). **throw off 1.** To cast out; rid oneself of. **2.** To give off; emit: *The blanket threw off an unusual odor.* **throw out 1.** To reject or discard: *Threw out yesterday's paper.* **2.** To disengage (a clutch, for example). **3.** In baseball, to put out (a base runner) by throwing the ball to the player guarding the base to which the base runner is moving. **throw up** To vomit. [From Old English *thrāwan.*] —**throw'er** *n.*

SYNONYMS throw, hurl, fling, pitch, toss These verbs mean to propel something through the air with a motion of the hand or arm. **Throw** is the most general: *The lifeguard threw a life preserver to the struggling swimmer.* **Hurl** and **fling** mean to throw with great force: *In Greek mythology, Zeus hurls lightning bolts from Olympus as if they were spears. The paper carrier flung the newspaper onto the porch.* **Pitch** often means to throw with careful aim: *He pitched the wad of paper into the wastebasket.* **Toss** usually means to throw lightly or casually: *She tossed the day's mail onto the desk.*

---

throw·back (**thrō'**băk') *n.* One that has characteristics of an earlier time: *a song that is a throwback to the disco era.*

thrown (thrōn) *v.* Past participle of **throw.**

❑ *These sound alike:* **thrown, throne** (monarch's chair).

throw rug *n.* A small rug used to cover part of a floor.

thru (thrōō) *prep. & adv. & adj. Informal* Through.

thrum (thrŭm) *v.* **thrummed, thrum·ming, thrums** —*tr.* To play (a stringed instrument) in an idle or monotonous way. —*intr.* To strum idly on a stringed instrument. ❖ *n.* The sound made by thrumming.

thrush[1] (thrŭsh) *n.* Any of numerous songbirds usually having a brownish back and a spotted breast and noted for their clear melodious song. [From Old English *thrysce.*]

thrush[2] (thrŭsh) *n.* An infection caused by a fungus that produces white spots on the mouth, throat, and tongue. [Probably of Scandinavian origin.]

thrust (thrŭst) *v.* **thrust, thrust·ing, thrusts** —*tr.* **1.** To push or drive quickly and forcibly: *thrust a pole into the ground.* **2.** To issue or extend: *thrust out his fingers.* **3.** To force into a specified condition or situation: *She was thrust into a position of responsibility.* —*intr.* **1.** To push something into or at something else: *The knight thrust at the dragon.* **2.** To grow or extend upwards: *towers thrusting into the sky.* ❖ *n.* **1.** A forceful shove, push, or stab. **2.** The force that tends to move an object, especially the force that moves an airplane or rocket by reaction to the rearward ejection of exhaust gases from an engine. **3.** The essence or main point: *the thrust of the governor's proposal.*

thru·way also **through·way** (**thrōō'**wā') *n.* An expressway.

thud (thŭd) *n.* **1.** A dull sound, as that of a heavy object striking a solid surface. **2.** A blow or fall causing such a sound. ❖ *intr.v.* **thud·ded, thud·ding, thuds** To make a heavy dull sound.

thug (thŭg) *n.* A habitually violent person, especially one who shows criminal behavior.

thu·li·um (**thōō'**lē-əm) *n. Symbol* **Tm** A soft, silvery-gray metallic element used in small, portable x-ray machines. Atomic number 69. See **Periodic Table.**

thumb (thŭm) *n.* **1.** The short thick first digit of the human hand, which can be moved so that it is opposite each of the other fingers. **2.** A similar digit in other animals, especially monkeys, apes, and other primates. **3.** The part of a glove or mitten that covers the thumb. ❖ *v.* **thumbed, thumb·ing, thumbs** —*intr.* **1.** To scan written matter by turning pages with the thumb: *thumbed through the magazine.* **2.** *Informal* To hitchhike. —*tr. Informal* To ask for (a ride) from a passing automobile by signaling with the thumb. ◆ **all thumbs** Clumsy with one's hands. **under (one's) thumb** Under the control or influence of someone. [From Old English *thūma.*]

thumb·nail (**thŭm'**nāl') *n.* **1.** The nail of the thumb. **2.** An image on a computer screen that is reduced in size. Clicking on the thumbnail causes the image to become larger. ❖ *adj.* **1.** Relating to or being the size of a thumbnail: *a thumbnail image.* **2.** Brief; cursory: *a thumbnail biography.*

thumb·screw (**thŭm'**skrōō') *n.* **1.** A screw made so that it can be turned with the thumb and fingers. **2.** An instrument of torture formerly used to compress the thumb.

thumbs-down (thŭmz'**doun'**) *n.* An act, instance, or sign of disapproval.

thumbs-up (thŭmbz'**ŭp'**) *n.* An act, instance, or sign of approval.

thumb·tack (**thŭm'**tăk') *n.* A tack with a smooth rounded head that can be pressed into place with the thumb.

thump (thŭmp) *n.* **1.** A blow with a blunt object. **2.** The muffled sound produced by or as if by such a blow; a thud. ❖ *v.* **thumped, thump·ing, thumps** —*tr.* **1.** To beat so as to produce a thump or thumps: *thumped the desk with her fist.* **2.** To move or cause to strike with a

thyme

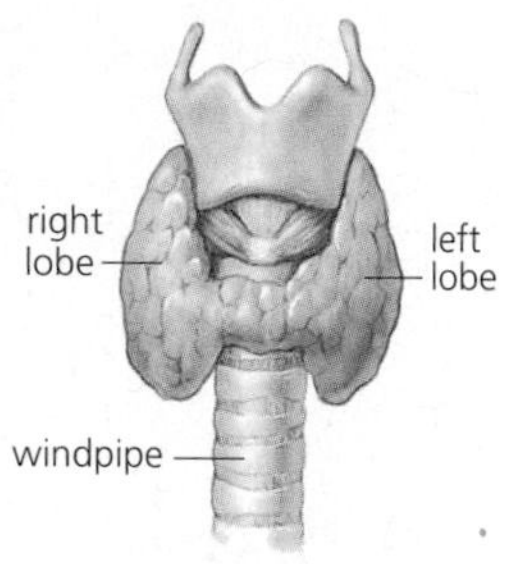

thyroid gland

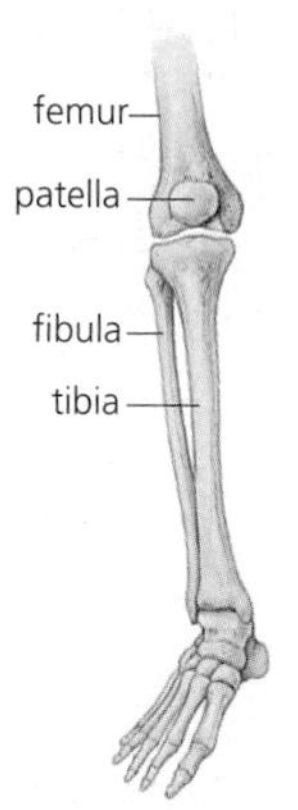

tibia

ă	pat	ôr	core
ā	pay	oi	boy
âr	care	ou	out
ä	father	o͝o	took
ĕ	pet	o͝or	lure
ē	be	o͞o	boot
ĭ	pit	ŭ	cut
ī	bite	ûr	urge
îr	pier	th	thin
ŏ	pot	*th*	this
ō	toe	zh	vision
ô	paw	ə	about

thump or thumps: *thumped the book on the table.* —*intr.* **1.** To hit or fall in such a way as to produce a thump: *The book thumped on the floor.* **2.** To move or collide with a thump or thumps: *She thumped up the stairs.* **3.** To beat or throb audibly: *His heart thumped with fear.*

thun·der (**thŭn′**dər) *n.* **1.** The crashing or booming sound that accompanies a stroke of lightning. **2.** A sound that resembles or suggests thunder: *the thunder of applause.* ❖ *v.* **thun·dered, thun·der·ing, thun·ders** —*intr.* **1.** To produce thunder: *It stormed and thundered.* **2.** To produce sounds like thunder: *guns thundering in the distance.* **3.** To move while making a loud noise: *The express train thundered past us.* —*tr.* To utter loudly or threateningly: *The captain thundered orders to the sailors.* [From Old English *thunor.*] —SEE NOTE AT **lightning.**

thun·der·bolt (**thŭn′**dər-bōlt′) *n.* A stroke of lightning accompanied by thunder.

thun·der·boom·er (**thŭn′**dər-bo͞o′mər) *n. Informal* A thunderstorm.

thun·der·clap (**thŭn′**dər-klăp′) *n.* A single sharp crash of thunder.

thun·der·cloud (**thŭn′**dər-kloud′) *n.* A large dark cloud carrying an electric charge and producing lightning and thunder; a cumulonimbus cloud.

thun·der·head (**thŭn′**dər-hĕd′) *n.* The swollen upper portion of a thundercloud, usually associated with the development of a thunderstorm.

thun·der·ous (**thŭn′**dər-əs) *adj.* **1.** Producing thunder or a similar sound **2.** Loud and unrestrained in a way that suggests thunder: *thunderous applause.* **—thun′der·ous·ly** *adv.*

thun·der·show·er (**thŭn′**dər-shou′ər) *n.* A short, often heavy rainstorm accompanied by thunder and lightning.

thun·der·snow (**thŭn′**dər-snō′) *n.* **1.** A violent storm of thunder and lightning that is accompanied by snow instead of rain. **2.** The snow produced by such a storm.

thun·der·storm (**thŭn′**dər-stôrm′) *n.* A storm of heavy rain accompanied by lightning and thunder and sometimes hail.

thun·der·struck (**thŭn′**dər-strŭk′) *adj.* Amazed; astonished: *He stood thunderstruck at the sidelines watching the team's defeat.*

Thurs·day (**thûrz′**dē *or* **thûrz′**dā′) *n.* The fifth day of the week. [From Old English *thūresdæg*, alteration of *thunres dæg*, Thor's day.] **—Thurs′days** *adv.*

thus (*th*ŭs) *adv.* **1.** In this manner: *Lay the pieces out thus.* **2.** To a stated degree or extent; so: *I haven't looked at your work thus far.* **3.** Consequently; therefore.

thwack (thwăk) *tr.v.* **thwacked, thwack·ing, thwacks** To strike or hit with a flat object; whack. ❖ *n.* A hard blow with a flat object.

thwart (thwôrt) *tr.v.* **thwart·ed, thwart·ing, thwarts** **1.** To prevent from taking place; frustrate; block: *They thwarted his plans.* **2.** To oppose and defeat the efforts, plans, or ambitions of (someone). ❖ *n.* A seat across a boat on which a rower may sit.

thy (*th*ī) *adj.* The possessive form of **thou.**

thyme (tīm) *n.* Any of several perennial plants related to mint, having small aromatic leaves used as a seasoning. [From Middle English *time*, from Greek *thumon.*]

❑ *These sound alike:* **thyme, time** (moment).

thy·mine (**thī′**mēn′) *n.* A base that is a component of DNA.

thy·mus (**thī′**məs) *n., pl.* **thy·mus·es** **1.** A ductless glandular organ located behind the top of the breastbone, having a role in building resistance to disease. It reaches maximum development in early childhood and is absent or very small in adults. **2.** A similar structure in other vertebrate animals.

thy·roid (**thī′**roid′) *n.* The thyroid gland.

thyroid cartilage *n.* The largest cartilage of the larynx, having two broad projections that join in front to form the Adam's apple.

thyroid gland *n.* An endocrine gland having two lobes, located in front of and to either side of the windpipe in humans. It is found in all vertebrates and produces several hormones, including thyroxine, that regulate body metabolism and the amount of calcium in the blood.

thy·rox·ine (thī-**rŏk′**sēn′ *or* thī-**rŏk′**sĭn) also **thy·rox·in** (thī-**rŏk′**sĭn) *n.* A hormone that contains iodine, produced by the thyroid gland and acting to regulate body metabolism. It is also produced synthetically for the treatment of thyroid disorders.

thy·self (*th*ī-**sĕlf′**) *pron. Archaic* Yourself.

ti (tē) *n.* In music, the seventh tone of a major scale.

❑ *These sound alike:* **ti, tea** (drink), **tee** (peg for a golf ball).

Ti The symbol for the element **titanium.**

ti·ar·a (tē-**ăr′**ə *or* tē-**är′**ə) *n.* **1.** An ornament that looks like a small crown, often is set with jewels, and is worn on the head by women on formal occasions. **2.** The tall three-tiered crown historically worn by the pope.

Ti·ber (**tī′**bər) A river of central Italy flowing about 252 miles (406 kilometers) south and southwest through Rome to the Tyrrhenian Sea.

Ti·bet (tə-**bĕt′**) An autonomous region of western China on a high plateau north of the Himalaya Mountains. Lhasa is the capital.

Ti·bet·an (tĭ-**bĕt′**n) *adj.* Relating to Tibet or its people, language, or culture. ❖ *n.* **1a.** A native or inhabitant of Tibet. **b.** A member of a Buddhist people who make up the largest ethnic group in Tibet. **2.** The language of the Tibetans.

tib·i·a (**tĭb′**ē-ə) *n., pl.* **tib·i·ae** (**tĭb′**ē-ē′) or **tib·i·as** **1.** The inner and larger of the two bones of the human leg between the knee and the ankle; the shinbone. **2.** A similar bone in other vertebrate animals.

tic (tĭk) *n.* A recurring spasmodic contraction or twitching of a set of muscles, usually in the face or limbs.

❑ *These sound alike:* **tic, tick[1]** (clicking sound), **tick[2]** (animal), **tick[3]** (cloth case).

tick[1] (tĭk) *n.* **1.** A light sharp clicking sound made repeatedly by a machine, such as a clock. **2.** A light mark used to check off or call attention to an item. ❖ *v.* **ticked, tick·ing, ticks** —*intr.* **1.** To produce recurring clicking sounds. **2.** To function characteristically: *What makes him tick?* —*tr.* To count, record, or check off with a tick: *a clock ticking the hours; tick off each name.* [From Middle English *tik*, light tap.]

❑ *These sound alike:* **tick[1]** (clicking sound), **tic** (muscle contraction), **tick[2]** (animal), **tick[3]** (cloth case).

tick[2] (tĭk) *n.* Any of various small bloodsucking animals that are parasites on humans and other vertebrate animals and transmit certain diseases, such as Lyme disease. Ticks are arachnids, not insects. [From Middle English *tik.*]

❑ *These sound alike:* **tick[2]** (animal), **tic** (muscle contraction), **tick[1]** (clicking sound), **tick[3]** (cloth case).

tick[3] (tĭk) *n.* The sturdy cloth case of a mattress or pillow that encloses the stuffing. [From Middle English *tike*, probably from Middle Dutch *tīke*, ultimately from Latin *thēca*, receptacle.]

❑ *These sound alike:* **tick[3]** (cloth case), **tic** (muscle contraction), **tick[1]** (clicking sound), **tick[2]** (animal).

tick·er (**tĭk′**ər) *n.* **1.** A telegraphic instrument that receives news reports and prints them on paper tape. **2.** Any of various devices that receive and record similar information, such as stock-market quotations, by electronic means. **3.** *Slang* The heart.

ticker tape *n.* The strip of paper on which a telegraphic ticker prints.

tick·et (**tĭk′**ĭt) *n.* **1.** A paper slip or card that entitles the holder to a specified service or right: *a bus ticket; a theater ticket.* **2.** An e-ticket. **3.** A tag attached to and giving information about merchandise; a label. **4.** A list of candidates endorsed by a political party or group in an election. **5.** A legal notice that is given to a person charged with a violation of law, especially a minor violation: *I got a ticket for speeding.* ❖ *tr.v.* **tick·et·ed, tick·et·ing, tick·ets 1.** To provide with a ticket for admission or passage. **2.** To attach a tag to; label. **3.** To mark or intend for a specified use: *cars ticketed for shipment.* **4.** To serve (a person) with a notice of legal violation: *The police officer ticketed the motorist who had been driving too fast.* [From Old French *estiquet*, post serving as a target in certain sports, notice, label, from *estiquier*, to stick.]

tick·ing (tĭk′ĭng) *n.* A strong, tightly woven cloth of cotton or linen used to make pillow and mattress coverings.

tick·le (tĭk′əl) *v.* **tick·led, tick·ling, tick·les** —*tr.* **1.** To touch (the body) lightly, causing laughter or twitching movements. **2.** To delight or amuse; please. —*intr.* To feel or cause a tingling sensation. ❖ *n.* The act or sensation of tickling. ◆ **tickled pink** *Informal* Very pleased; delighted: *I was tickled pink by the compliment.* **—tick′ler** *n.*

tick·lish (tĭk′lĭsh) *adj.* **1.** Sensitive to tickling: *a ticklish child.* **2.** Easily offended or upset; touchy. **3.** Requiring skillful or tactful handling: *a ticklish problem.*

Ti·con·der·o·ga (tī′-kŏn-də-**rō′**gə) A village of northeast New York at the southern end of Lake Champlain. A French fort built here in 1755 was taken by the British in 1759 and named Fort Ticonderoga.

tic-tac-toe also **tick-tack-toe** (tĭk′tăk′**tō′**) *n.* A game played by two people, each trying to make a line of three X's or three O's in a square figure with nine spaces. [Probably imitative of the sounds of the original children's game, in which players brought pencils down on a numbered slate with their eyes shut.]

tid·al (tīd′l) *adj.* Relating to or affected by tides: *tidal marshes.*

tidal flat *n.* A flat area along the coast that is underwater at high tide and uncovered at low tide.

tidal pool *n.* A pool of water remaining after a tide has retreated.

tidal wave *n.* **1.** The swell or crest of the surface of ocean water at high tide. **2.** A storm surge. **3.** *Informal* A tsunami.

tid·bit (tĭd′bĭt′) *n.* A choice morsel, as of food or gossip.

tid·dly·winks (tĭd′lē-wĭngks′) *pl.n.* *(used with a singular verb)* A game in which the players try to pop small disks into a cup by pressing them on the edge with a larger disk.

tide (tīd) *n.* **1a.** The regular rise and fall in the surface level of the earth's oceans, seas, and bays caused by the gravitational attraction of the moon and sun. **b.** A particular occurrence of such a variation: *will walk along the beach at the next low tide.* **c.** The water that moves when such a variation occurs. **2a.** Something that fluctuates like the waters of the tide: *a rising tide of anger among the voters.* **b.** A large amount or number moving or occurring in a mass: *a tide of angry letters.* **3.** A time or season: *eveningtide; Christmastide.* **4.** A favorable occasion; an opportunity. ◆ **tide over** To support through a difficult period: *lent me $100 to tide me over until payday.* [From Old English *tīd*, division of time.]

tide·land (tīd′lănd′) *n.* Land along a coast that is under water at high tide.

tide·wa·ter (tīd′wô′tər) *n.* **1.** Water that flows onto the land when the tide is very high. **2.** Water, especially water in streams or rivers, that is affected by tides. **3.** Low coastal land drained by streams that are affected by tides.

tid·ings (tī′dĭngz) *pl.n.* News; information: *tidings of great joy.* [From Middle English, from Old Norse *tīdhendi*, events.]

ti·dy (tī′dē) *adj.* **ti·di·er, ti·di·est 1.** Orderly and clean in appearance: *a tidy room.* **2.** *Informal* Substantial; considerable: *a tidy sum of money.* ❖ *tr. & intr.v.* **ti·died, ti·dy·ing, ti·dies** To put in order; make neat: *Tidy up your room. We tidied up after dinner.* [From Middle English *tidi*, in season, healthy, from *tide*, time.] **—ti′di·ly** *adv.* **—ti′di·ness** *n.*

tie (tī) *v.* **tied, ty·ing** (tī′ĭng), **ties** —*tr.* **1.** To fasten or secure with or as if with a cord, rope, or strap: *tie up a parcel; tie a dog to a fence.* **2.** To fasten by drawing together the parts of (something) and knotting with strings or laces: *bending to tie her shoes.* **3.** To make by fastening ends or parts: *tie a knot.* **4.** To put a knot or bow in: *tie a necktie; tie a scarf.* **5a.** To equal (an opponent or a score, for example) in a contest: *He tied the pole-vaulting record last year.* **b.** To equal a score in (a contest): *tied the game with minutes remaining.* **6.** To bring together in a relationship; connect or unite: *people who are tied by marriage or family.* **7.** To join (successive musical tones of the same pitch) so that there is no break between them. —*intr.* **1.** To be fastened or attached: *an apron that ties in back.* **2.** To achieve equal scores in a contest. ❖ *n.* **1.** A cord, string, rope, or other means by which something is tied. **2.** A necktie. **3.** Something that connects or unites; a bond: *the ties of friendship; family ties.* **4.** An equality of scores, votes, or performances in a contest: *The game ended in a tie.* **5.** A beam or rod that joins parts of a structure and gives support. **6.** One of the timbers or slabs of concrete laid across a railroad bed to support the rails. **7.** A curved line above or below two musical notes of the same pitch, indicating that they are to be played or sung with no break. ◆ **tie in 1.** To bring into or have a close relation with; connect or coordinate: *Your story ties in with what she told me.* **2.** To include as part of a tie-in for a promotional offer: *Their marketing campaign ties the movie in with a brand of car.* **tie the knot** *Informal* **1.** To get married. **2.** To perform a marriage ceremony. **tie up 1.** To secure or be secured to a shore or pier; dock. **2.** To block or stop: *an accident that tied up traffic.* **3.** To keep busy; engage: *I will be tied up in meetings all day.* **4.** To place or invest (money) so that it cannot be used freely: *tied up her money in a new house.* [From Old English *tīgan.*]

tie·break·er (tī′brā′kər) *n.* An additional contest or period of play designed to establish a winner among tied contestants. **—tie′break′ing** *adj.*

tie clip *n.* An ornamental pin or clip that holds the ends of a necktie to the front of a shirt.

tie-dye (tī′dī′) *tr.v.* **tie-dyed, tie-dye·ing, tie-dyes** To dye (a fabric) after tying parts of the fabric so that they will not absorb the dye, giving the fabric a streaked or mottled look.

tie-in (tī′ĭn′) *n.* **1.** A connection or association: *the tie-in between economic hardship and civil strife.* **2.** A product or event that is based on an existing character, setting, or object from a book, movie, or similar source from popular culture: *That special ice-cream flavor is a tie-in to a popular children's book series.*

tier (tîr) *n.* One of a series of rows placed one above another: *a stadium with four tiers of seats; a wedding cake with three tiers.*

❑ *These sound alike:* **tier, tear**[2] (eye drop).

tiered (tîrd) *adj.* Arranged or formed in tiers: *tiered balconies; a three-tiered wedding cake.*

Ti·er·ra del Fue·go (tē-ĕr′ə dĕl fwā′gō) A group of islands off southern South America separated from the mainland by the Strait of Magellan. The main island, also called **Tierra del Fuego,** is divided between Chile and Argentina.

tie-up (tī′ŭp′) *n.* A temporary stoppage, as of work or traffic: *The strike caused a work tie-up at the factory.*

tic-tac-toe

tide

high tide *(top)* and low tide *(bottom)* at the Bay of Fundy, Canada

tie-dye

tiger

tiger-eye
tiger-eye beads

tiger moth

ă	pat	ô r	core
ā	pay	oi	boy
âr	care	ou	out
ä	father	o͝o	took
ĕ	pet	o͝or	lure
ē	be	o͞o	boot
ĭ	pit	ŭ	cut
ī	bite	ûr	urge
îr	pier	th	thin
ŏ	pot	*th*	this
ō	toe	zh	vision
ô	paw	ə	about

tiff (tĭf) *n.* **1.** An argument about a trivial matter; a quarrel. **2.** An instance of being annoyed or irritated.

ti·ger (tīʹgər) *n.* **1.** A very large wild cat of Asia, having tawny fur with crosswise black stripes. **2.** An enthusiastic, fierce, or aggressive person. [From Old English *tigras*, tigers, from Greek *tigris*, tiger.]

ti·ger-eye (tīʹgər-īʹ) also **ti·ger's-eye** (tīʹgərz-īʹ) *n.* A yellow-brown gemstone.

tiger lily *n.* A tall lily with black-spotted orange flowers.

tiger moth *n.* Any of numerous often brightly colored moths having wings marked with spots or stripes.

tight (tīt) *adj.* **tight·er, tight·est 1.** Fastened, held, or closed securely: *a tight knot; a tight lid.* **2.** Stretched or drawn out to the fullest extent: *a tight rope.* **3.** Of such close construction as to be impermeable, especially by water or air: *a tight roof.* **4.** Leaving little empty space between; compact: *planes flying in tight formation.* **5.** Leaving little time to spare; full: *a tight schedule.* **6.** Fitting close or too close to some part of the body; snug: *The tight shoes hurt his feet.* **7.** Constricted: *a tight feeling in the chest.* **8.** Reluctant to give or spend money; stingy. **9a.** Difficult to obtain: *Money was tight.* **b.** Affected by scarcity: *a tight money market.* **10.** Difficult to deal with or get out of: *in a tight spot.* **11.** Closely contested; close: *a tight race; a tight game.* ❖ *adv.* **tighter, tightest 1.** Firmly; securely: *Screw the lid on tight.* **2.** Soundly: *sleep tight.* [From Middle English, dense, of Scandinavian origin.] **—tightʹly** *adv.* **—tightʹness** *n.*

tight·en (tītʹn) *tr. & intr.v.* **tight·ened, tight·en·ing, tight·ens** To make or become tight or tighter.

tight·fist·ed (tītʹfĭsʹtĭd) *adj.* Stingy.

tight·lipped also **tight-lipped** (tītʹlĭptʹ) *adj.* **1.** Having the lips pressed together. **2.** Reluctant to speak; close-mouthed: *He was tightlipped about the meeting.*

tight·rope (tītʹrōpʹ) *n.* A tightly stretched rope or wire, on which acrobats perform high above the ground.

tights (tīts) *pl.n.* **1.** A snug stretchable garment covering the body from the waist down, designed for general wear by women and girls. **2.** A similar garment designed for athletics, worn especially by dancers and acrobats.

tight·wad (tītʹwŏdʹ) *n. Slang* A stingy person; a miser.

Ti·gris (tīʹgrĭs) A river rising in eastern Turkey and flowing about 1,150 miles (1,850 kilometers) southeast through Iraq to the Euphrates River.

ti·la·pi·a (tə-läʹpē-ə) *n.* Any of various freshwater fishes that are native to Africa and the Middle East and are raised worldwide for food.

til·de (tĭlʹdə) *n.* A diacritical mark (~) placed over letters in some languages to indicate nasal sounds, as in the word *cañon* (Spanish for "canyon") or *pão* (Portuguese for "bread").

tile (tīl) *n.* **1.** A thin flat slab of baked clay, plastic, concrete, or other hard material, laid in rows as a covering for floors, walls, and roofs. **2.** A short length of clay or concrete pipe, used in sewers and drains. **3.** A block of concrete or fired clay used for building walls. **4.** Tiles considered as a group: *bought tile for the kitchen floor.* **5.** A marked playing piece used in certain games. ❖ *tr.v.* **tiled, til·ing, tiles** To cover or provide with tiles.

til·ing (tīʹlĭng) *n.* **1.** The laying of tiles. **2.** Tiles considered as a group. **3.** A tiled surface.

till[1] (tĭl) *tr.v.* **tilled, till·ing, tills** To prepare (land) for the raising of crops, as by plowing and harrowing; cultivate. [From Old English *tilian.*] **—tillʹa·ble** *adj.*

till[2] (tĭl) *prep.* Until: *I won't see you till tomorrow.* ❖ *conj.* Until: *I can't help you till you tell me what's wrong.* [From Old English *til*, from Old Norse.]

till[3] (tĭl) *n.* A drawer or compartment for money, as in a cash register. [From Middle English *tille.*]

till[4] (tĭl) *n.* A mass of material deposited by a glacier; a mixture containing clay, sand, gravel, and boulders.

till·age (tĭlʹĭj) *n.* **1.** The cultivation of land. **2.** Tilled land.

till·er[1] (tĭlʹər) *n.* A person who tills land.

til·ler[2] (tĭlʹər) *n.* A lever used to turn a boat's rudder. [From Middle English *teler, tiler*, stock of a crossbow, tiller, from Latin *tēla*, woven fabric, loom.]

tilt (tĭlt) *v.* **tilt·ed, tilt·ing, tilts** *—tr.* **1.** To cause to slope, as by raising one end; incline; tip: *The children tilted the barrel to empty it.* **2.** To cause to be advantageous to one party rather than another: *a policy that tilted the balance of trade in their favor.* **3.** To aim or thrust (a lance) in a joust. *—intr.* **1.** To slope; incline. **2.** To favor one side over another in a dispute: *her political views tilt to the right.* **3.** To be advantageous to one side over another, as in a dispute. **4a.** To joust. **b.** To engage in combat; fight: *tilting at injustices.* ❖ *n.* **1.** A slant; a slope. **2.** A tendency to favor one side in a dispute: *a tilt toward conservative rulings.* **3.** A joust. **4.** A combat, especially a verbal duel. ◆ **at full tilt** *Informal* At full speed. [From Middle English *tilten*, to cause to fall, perhaps of Scandinavian origin.]

tim·ber (tĭmʹbər) *n.* **1.** Trees or wooded land considered as a source of wood. **2.** Wood for building; lumber. **3.** A beam or shaped piece of wood, as one used in forming a ship's frame. **4.** Personal quality; character: *a man of heroic timber.* ❖ *tr.v.* **tim·bered, tim·ber·ing, tim·bers** To support or frame with timbers. [From Old English, building, trees for building.]

❑ *These sound alike:* **timber, timbre** (sound quality).

tim·bered (tĭmʹbərd) *adj.* **1.** Covered with trees; wooded: *a timbered slope.* **2.** Made of or framed by timbers, especially exposed timbers: *a timbered barn.*

timber hitch *n.* A knot used to fasten a rope around a log, pole, or spar that is to be towed or hoisted.

tim·ber·line (tĭmʹbər-līnʹ) *n.* **1.** The elevation in a mountainous region above which trees do not grow. **2.** The northern or southern latitude beyond which trees do not grow.

timber wolf *n.* The gray wolf.

tim·bre (tămʹbər *or* tĭmʹbər) *n.* **1.** The combination of qualities of a sound that distinguishes it from other sounds of the same pitch and volume. **2.** Distinctive character: *the timbre of the painter's work.*

❑ *These sound alike:* **timbre, timber** (trees).

tim·brel (tĭmʹbrəl) *n.* An ancient musical instrument similar to the tambourine.

Tim·buk·tu (tĭmʹbŭk-**to͞oʹ** *or* tĭm-**bŭkʹ**to͞o) A city of central Mali northeast of Bamako. Founded in the 11th century, it became a center of Islamic learning by the 14th century.

time (tīm) *n.* **1a.** A continuous measurable quantity, ordinarily distinct from space, in which events occur in an order that does not seem to be reversible, proceeding from the past through the present to the future. **b.** An interval bounded by two points of this quantity, as by the beginning and end of an event: *the time it takes to go from one place to another.* **c.** A number, as of years, days, or minutes, representing such an interval. **d.** A similar number representing a given point, such as the present, reckoned in hours and minutes: *The time was 5:15.* **e.** A system by which such intervals are measured or such numbers are reckoned: *standard time; solar time.* **2.** The characteristic beat of a musical rhythm: *three-quarter time.* **3a.** A moment or period designated for a given activity: *harvest time; time for bed.* **b.** A period at one's disposal: *Do you have time for dinner?* **4a.** often **times** An interval, especially a span of years, marked by similar events, conditions, or phenomena; an era: *Victorian times; a time of famine.* **b. times** The present with respect to prevailing conditions and trends: *changed with the times.* **5a.** An appointed or fated moment, especially of death or giving birth: *She died before her time.* **b.** A person's experience during a specific period or occasion: *had a good time at the party.* **6a.** The customary period of work of an employee: *working full time.* **b.** The hourly pay rate: *She gets double time on weekends.* **7a.** One of several instances: *I let the phone ring three times.* **b. times** Used to indicate the number of instances by which something is multiplied or divided: *This building is three times taller than that one.* ❖ *adj.* Relating to or measuring time. ❖ *tr.v.* **timed, tim·ing, times 1.** To set the time at which (something) happens or is to happen. **2.** To regulate or adjust so that an action occurs or force is applied at the correct time: *time a leap carefully; time an automobile engine.* **3.** To record or register the speed or duration of: *We timed the game at two hours even.* **4.** To speculate based on the anticipated short-term performance of (a market): *time the stock market.* ◆ **against time** With a quickly approaching time limit: *working against time.* **any time** Used to acknowledge an expression of gratitude. **at one time 1.** Simultaneously. **2.** At a period or moment in the past: *At one time they were classmates.* **at the same time** However; nonetheless. **at times** On occasion; sometimes. **behind the times** Out-of-date; old-fashioned. **for the time being** Temporarily. **from time to time** Once in a while; at intervals. **high time** Long overdue: *It's high time that you went to bed.* **in good time 1.** In a reasonable length of time. **2.** Quickly. **in no time** Almost instantly; immediately. **in time 1.** Before a time limit expires: *They had to hurry to arrive in time for the movie.* **2.** In the end; eventually: *In time you will see that she is right.* **3.** In the proper musical tempo. **on time 1.** According to schedule; punctually. **2.** By paying in installments: *buy a car on time.* **time after time** Again and again; repeatedly. **time and again** Again and again; repeatedly. [From Old English *tīma.*]

❑ *These sound alike:* **time, thyme** (plant).

time bomb *n.* **1.** A bomb that can be set to explode at a certain time. **2.** An existing condition or an incident that seems likely to happen that threatens a disastrous outcome: *That volcano is a ticking time bomb waiting to go off.*

time·card (tīm′kärd′) *n.* A card or electronic record that indicates an employee's starting and quitting times each work day.

time clock *n.* A clock that records the starting and quitting times of employees.

time frame *n.* A period during which something takes place or is expected to take place.

time-hon·ored (tīm′ŏn′ərd) *adj.* Honored or adhered to because of age or age-old observance: *time-honored customs.*

time·keep·er (tīm′kē′pər) *n.* A person who keeps track of time, as in a sports event.

time-lapse (tīm′lăps′) *adj.* Relating to, using, or being a technique that photographs a naturally slow process, such as plant growth, at intervals. Continuous play of the sequence of pictures gives an accelerated view of the process.

time·less (tīm′lĭs) *adj.* **1.** Independent of time; eternal: *the timeless struggle between good and evil.* **2.** Seemingly unaffected by time; ageless: *a timeless village on the coast.* **—time′less·ness** *n.*

time·line (tīm′līn′) *n.* **1.** A timetable. **2.** A chronology, especially a representation of key events within a particular historical period.

time·ly (tīm′lē) *adj.* **time·li·er, time·li·est** Occurring at a suitable or opportune time; well-timed: *a timely remark.*

time machine *n.* A fictional or hypothetical device allowing a person to travel into the past or future.

time-out or **time out** (tīm′out′) *n.* **1.** In sports, a brief period in a game for rest, consultation, or substitution, during which play is stopped. **2.** A punishment for children in which they are separated from others for a brief period.

time·piece (tīm′pēs′) *n.* An instrument, such as a watch or clock, that measures, records, or indicates time.

tim·er (tī′mər) *n.* **1.** A person or thing that measures time; a timekeeper. **2.** A timepiece, especially one used to measure intervals of time. **3.** A switch that controls another mechanism at set times.

times (tīmz) *prep.* Multiplied by: *Eight times three equals twenty-four.*

time·sav·ing (tīm′sā′vĭng) *adj.* Serving to save time through an efficient method or a shorter route; expeditious. **—time′sav′er** *n.*

time·scale (tīm′skāl′) *n.* **1.** A period of time seen in relation to a process or a series of phenomena: *the existence of a planet measured against a cosmic timescale.* **2.** A schedule or arrangement of events or commitments: *The two nations agreed to a timescale for disarmament.*

time signature *n.* A musical sign placed on a staff to indicate the meter. This sign is usually a fraction in which the numerator represents the number of beats per measure and the denominator represents the kind of note getting one beat.

times sign *n.* The symbol ×, as in 4 × 2 = 8, that is used to indicate multiplication.

time·ta·ble (tīm′tā′bəl) *n.* A schedule listing the times at which certain events are expected to occur, as the arrival and departure of trains at a station.

time-test·ed (tīm′tĕs′tĭd) *adj.* Proved effective over a long period of time: *a time-tested recipe.*

time trial *n.* A competitive event in which participants are timed in order to select those who qualify for another event.

time·worn (tīm′wôrn′) *adj.* **1.** Showing the effects of being used too much; worn out by overuse over time: *The timeworn path became muddy whenever it rained.* **2.** Used too often; trite: *a timeworn joke.*

time zone *n.* Any of the areas into which the earth is divided for purposes of keeping standard time. The standard time is usually one hour earlier in each successive zone to the west and one hour later in each successive zone to the east. For example, New York is in the Eastern Time Zone and Chicago is in the Central Time Zone, so when it is noon in New York, it is 11:00 AM in Chicago.

tim·id (tĭm′ĭd) *adj.* **tim·id·er, tim·id·est** Easily frightened; hesitant and fearful. **—ti·mid′i·ty** *n.* **—tim′id·ly** *adv.*

tim·ing (tī′mĭng) *n.* **1.** The regulation of occurrence, pace, or coordination to achieve the most desirable effects, as in music, theater, or sports. **2.** The coordination of the sparking of the spark plugs with the movement of the pistons in an internal-combustion engine.

Ti·mor (tē′môr *or* tē-**môr′**) An island of the western Pacific Ocean in the Malay Archipelago east of Java, divided between Indonesia and East Timor.

tim·or·ous (tĭm′ər-əs) *adj.* Easily frightened; timid. **—tim′or·ous·ly** *adv.* **—tim′or·ous·ness** *n.*

tim·o·thy (tĭm′ə-thē) *n., pl.* **tim·o·thies** Any of several grasses having long, narrow, dense flower clusters, widely grown for hay. [Probably after *Timothy* Hanson, American farmer of the 1700s.]

Timothy *n.* Either of two books of the New Testament in the form of letters from Saint Paul to Timothy, one of his followers.

tim·pa·ni also **tym·pa·ni** (tĭm′pə-nē) *pl.n. (used with a singular or plural verb)* A set of kettledrums.

tin (tĭn) *n.* **1.** *Symbol* **Sn** A soft, silvery metallic element that is used to coat other metals to prevent corrosion and is a part of numerous alloys, such as pewter and bronze. Atomic number 50. See **Periodic Table. 2.** Tin plate. **3.** A can or container made of tin plate: *a tin of sardines.* ❖ *tr.v.* **tinned, tin·ning, tins 1.** To plate or

timber hitch

time signature

top: 2/4 time indicates two beats per measure
bottom: 3/4 time indicates three beats per measure

WRITERS CHOOSE THEIR WORDS

At first, Lynet had been hesitant before Morgan's awe-inspiring presence, but it was not in Lynet's nature to be **timorous** for long. Besides, Lynet soon learned that Terence was right: beneath Morgan's grand facade, she was capable of warm feelings and even generosity toward those she liked, and it soon became clear to Lynet that *she* was one of that select few.

—Gerald Morris
The Savage Damsel and the Dwarf

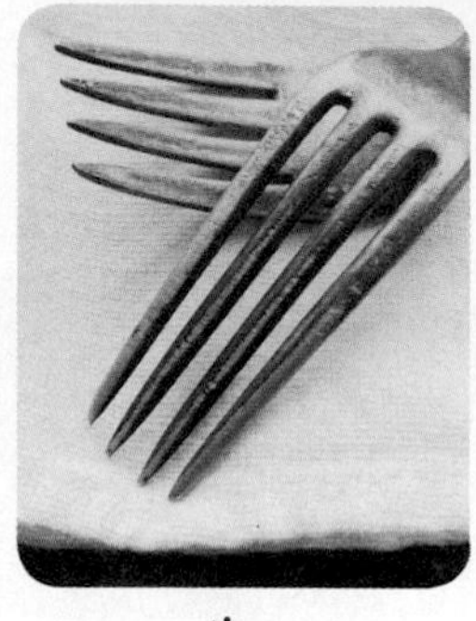

tine

tiramisu

coat with tin. **2.** To preserve or pack in tins; can. ❖ *adj.* Relating to or made of tin. [From Old English.]

tin can *n.* A cylindrical container made of thin steel coated on the inside with tin or a similar material that resists rust, used for preserving food.

tinc·ture (tĭngk**′**chər) *n.* An alcohol solution of a medicine: *tincture of iodine.*

tin·der (tĭn**′**dər) *n.* Material that catches fire easily, used to kindle fires: *We use dry twigs as tinder.*

tin·der·box (tĭn**′**dər-bŏks′) *n.* **1.** A metal box for holding tinder. **2.** A potentially dangerous or explosive situation.

tine (tīn) *n.* **1.** A narrow, pointed part on a fork, pitchfork, or similar implement. **2.** A branch of a deer's antlers.

tin·foil also **tin foil** (tĭn**′**foil′) *n.* A thin pliable sheet of aluminum or a tin-lead alloy, used as a protective wrapping, as for foods.

ting (tĭng) *n.* A light metallic sound, as of a small bell. ❖ *intr.v.* **tinged** (tĭngd), **ting·ing, tings** To give forth a light metallic sound.

tinge (tĭnj) *tr.v.* **tinged** (tĭnjd), **tinge·ing** or **ting·ing** (tĭn**′**jĭng), **ting·es 1.** To color slightly; tint: *The sunset tinged the sky with red.* **2.** To affect slightly, as with a contrasting quality. ❖ *n.* A small amount of color or some other property or quality: *a tinge of sadness in her remarks.* [From Middle English *tingen*, from Latin *tingere.*]

tin·gle (tĭng**′**gəl) *v.* **tin·gled, tin·gling, tin·gles** *—intr.* To have a prickling stinging sensation, as from cold or excitement. *—tr.* To cause to tingle. ❖ *n.* A prickling or stinging sensation.

tin·ker (tĭng**′**kər) *n.* **1.** A person who travels about fixing metal household utensils. **2.** A person who enjoys experimenting with and repairing machine parts. ❖ *intr.v.* **tin·kered, tin·ker·ing, tin·kers 1.** To work as a tinker. **2.** To make unskilled or experimental efforts at repair.

tin·kle (tĭng**′**kəl) *intr. & tr.v.* **tin·kled, tin·kling, tin·kles** To make or cause to make light metallic sounds, as of a small bell. ❖ *n.* A light clear metallic sound.

tin·ny (tĭn**′**ē) *adj.* **tin·ni·er, tin·ni·est 1.** Relating to or containing tin. **2.** Tasting or smelling of tin: *tinny canned food.* **3.** Having a thin metallic sound: *a tinny voice.*

tin plate *n.* Thin sheet iron or steel coated with tin to prevent rusting.

tin-plate (tĭn**′**plāt′) *tr.v.* **tin-plat·ed, tin-plat·ing, tin-plates** To coat with tin, as by dipping or electroplating.

tin·sel (tĭn**′**səl) *n.* Very thin sheets, strips, or threads of a glittering material used as a decoration.

tin·smith (tĭn**′**smĭth′) *n.* A person who works with light metal, such as tin.

tint (tĭnt) *n.* **1.** A shade of a color, especially a pale or delicate variation. **2.** A gradation of color made by adding white. **3.** A barely detectable amount or degree; a trace: *a tint of envy in his voice.* ❖ *tr.v.* **tint·ed, tint·ing, tints** To give a tint to; color: *tint hair.* [From Latin *tīnctus*, dyeing.] **—tint′er** *n.*

tin·tin·nab·u·la·tion (tĭn′tĭ-năb′yə-**lā′**shən) *n.* The ringing or sounding of bells.

ti·ny (tī**′**nē) *adj.* **ti·ni·er, ti·ni·est** Very small: *The glass shattered into tiny pieces.* See Synonyms at **little.**

tip^{1} (tĭp) *n.* **1.** The end of an object with a point or projection: *a house on the tip of the island; asparagus tips.* **2.** A piece meant to be fitted to the end of something: *the barbed tip of a harpoon.* ❖ *tr.v.* **tipped, tip·ping, tips 1.** To furnish with a tip: *tipped the Christmas ornaments with a metal hook.* **2.** To decorate or cover the tip of: *tipped the strawberries with a dab of chocolate.* **3.** To remove the tip of: *tip artichokes.* [From Middle English.]

tip^{2} (tĭp) *v.* **tipped, tip·ping, tips** *—tr.* **1.** To push or knock over; overturn or topple: *The wind tipped the vase over.* **2.** To move to a slanting position; tilt: *She tipped the rearview mirror downward.* **3.** To touch or raise (one's hat) in greeting. *—intr.* **1.** To topple over; overturn: *The garbage can tipped over because of the wind.* **2.** To become tilted; slant: *The old cabinet tips toward the wall.* [From Middle English *tippen.*]

tip^{3} (tĭp) *v.* **tipped, tip·ping, tips** *—tr.* **1.** To strike gently; tap. **2a.** In baseball, to hit (a pitched ball) with the side of the bat so that it glances off. **b.** To tap or deflect (a ball or puck, for example), especially in scoring. *—intr.* To deflect or glance off. Used of a ball or puck. [From Middle English *tippe*, a tap, perhaps of Low German origin.]

tip^{4} (tĭp) *n.* **1.** A small sum of money given to someone for performing a service; a gratuity: *We gave our waiter a tip of 20 percent of the bill.* **2.** Useful information; a helpful hint: *a book with tips on car repair.* ❖ *v.* **tipped, tip·ping, tips** *—tr.* **1a.** To give a tip to: *tipped the waiter generously.* **b.** To give as a tip: *tipped $5.* **2.** To provide with useful information: *tipped the police about the robbery.* *—intr.* To give tips or a tip: *a diner who tips generously.* **—tip′per** *n.*

tip-off^{1} (tĭp**′**ôf′) *n.* *Informal* **1.** A piece of secret, advance, or exclusive information. **2.** Something that signals a previously unknown fact or probability: *Her smile was a tip-off that the test had gone well.* [From *tip*, light blow, tap.]

tip-off^{2} (tĭp**′**ôf′) *n.* In basketball, an act of starting play at the beginning of a period with a jump ball. [From *tip*, light blow, tap + *(kick)off.*]

tip·pet (tĭp**′**ĭt) *n.* **1.** A scarf, cape, or other covering for the shoulders with long ends that hang down in front. **2.** A long hanging part, as of a sleeve, hood, or cape. **3.** A long stole worn by members of the Anglican clergy.

tip·ple (tĭp**′**əl) *tr. & intr.v.* **tip·pled, tip·pling, tip·ples** To drink (alcoholic liquor) or engage in such drinking, especially habitually or to excess. **—tip′pler** *n.*

tip·sy (tĭp**′**sē) *adj.* **tip·si·er, tip·si·est 1.** Slightly drunk. **2.** Unsteady or crooked. **—tip′si·ly** *adv.*

tip·toe (tĭp**′**tō′) *intr.v.* **tip·toed, tip·toe·ing, tip·toes** To walk or move quietly on one's toes. ❖ *n.* The tip of a toe. ❖ *adv.* **1.** On one's toes: *The young girl stood tiptoe in order to see over the counter.* **2.** Stealthily; warily.

tip·top (tĭp**′**tŏp′) *n.* The highest point; the summit: *hiked to the tiptop of the peak.* ❖ *adj.* Excellent; first-rate: *feeling in tiptop shape.*

ti·rade (tī**′**rād′ *or* tī-**rād′**) *n.* A long, angry or violent speech, usually denouncing or criticizing something or someone; a diatribe.

tir·a·mi·su (tîr′ə-**mē′**so͞o *or* tîr′ə-mē-**so͞o′**) *n.* A dessert of cake soaked with a liquid such as coffee or rum and layered with a cheese filling.

Ti·ra·në (tə-**rä′**nə) The capital of Albania, in the west-central part of the country. It became capital in 1920.

tire^{1} (tīr) *v.* **tired, tir·ing, tires** *—intr.* **1.** To lose strength or energy; grow weary: *When you're sick, you tend to tire easily.* **2.** To become bored; lose interest: *The audience tired after the first 10 minutes of the movie.* *—tr.* **1.** To diminish the strength or energy; fatigue: *The long walk tired me.* **2.** To exhaust the interest or patience of; bore: *His long speech tired the listeners.* [From Old English *tēorian.*]

tire^{2} (tīr) *n.* **1.** A covering for a wheel, usually made of rubber reinforced with cords of nylon, fiberglass, or other material and filled with compressed air. Tires are used to absorb shocks and provide traction. **2.** A hoop of metal or rubber fitted around a wheel. [From Middle English *tire*, iron rim of a wheel, probably from *tir*, attire.]

tired (tīrd) *adj.* **1a.** Exhausted; fatigued: *a tired athlete.* **b.** Impatient; bored: *a tired audience.* **2.** Overused; hackneyed; trite: *a tired joke.*

tire iron *n.* A tool consisting of a metal bar having one end shaped like a chisel and the other end often in the

ă	pat	ôr	core
ā	pay	oi	boy
âr	care	ou	out
ä	father	o͝o	took
ĕ	pet	o͝or	lure
ē	be	o͞o	boot
ĭ	pit	ŭ	cut
ī	bite	ûr	urge
îr	pier	th	thin
ŏ	pot	*th*	this
ō	toe	zh	vision
ô	paw	ə	about

form of a socket wrench, used for changing tires on metal rims.

tire·less (tīr′lĭs) *adj.* Not tiring easily; indefatigable: *a tireless worker.* **—tire′less·ly** *adv.*

tire·some (tīr′səm) *adj.* Causing fatigue or boredom, especially from being unvarying or overly long; wearisome: *a tiresome job; a long tiresome speech.* See Synonyms at **boring.** **—tire′some·ly** *adv.*

'tis (tĭz) Contraction of *it is.*

tis·sue (tĭsh′o͞o *or* tĭsh′yo͞o) *n.* **1.** A group of animal or plant cells that are similar in form and function and often make up a particular organ or part: *connective tissue.* **2.** Tissue paper. **3.** A piece of soft absorbent paper used as toilet paper, a handkerchief, or a towel.

tissue paper *n.* Light thin paper used for wrapping, packing, or protecting breakable objects.

tit (tĭt) *n.* Any of various small insectivorous songbirds of Eurasia and Africa. [Short for *titmouse.*]

Ti·tan (tīt′n) *n.* **1.** In Greek mythology, one of a family of giants who were overthrown and supplanted by the family of Zeus. **2. titan** A person of great size, strength, or importance. [From Middle English, a name for the sun, from Greek.]

ti·tan·ic[1] (tī-tăn′ĭk) *adj.* Having great size, strength, or importance: *a titanic struggle; a titanic mistake.*

ti·tan·ic[2] (tī-tăn′ĭk *or* tĭ-tăn′ĭk) *adj.* Relating to or containing titanium, especially with a valence of 4.

ti·ta·ni·um (tī-tā′nē-əm *or* tĭ-tā′nē-əm) *n. Symbol* **Ti** A shiny, white metallic element that is strong, lightweight, and highly resistant to corrosion. Atomic number 22. See **Periodic Table.**

tit for tat *n.* Repayment in kind, as for an injury; retaliation.

tithe (tīth) *n.* **1.** A tenth part of one's annual income, especially for the financial support of a church or clergy. **2.** A tenth part. ❖ *tr.v.* **tithed, tith·ing, tithes 1.** To pay or give one tenth of (one's annual income). **2.** To levy a tithe on.

tit·il·late (tĭt′l-āt′) *tr.v.* **tit·il·lat·ed, tit·il·lat·ing, tit·il·lates** To excite or stimulate (another) in a pleasurable way: *an author expert in titillating the reader.* **—tit′il·la′tion** *n.*

ti·tle (tīt′l) *n.* **1a.** An identifying name given to a book, painting, musical composition, or other work. **b.** A general or descriptive heading, as of a book chapter. **2.** A word attached to a person's name as a mark of distinction showing rank, office, or noble birth, or used as a sign of respect. **3a.** The legal right or claim to ownership or possession. **b.** The document, such as a deed, that serves as evidence of such a legal right: *receiving title to their house.* **4.** A championship in sports. ❖ *tr.v.* **ti·tled, ti·tling, ti·tles** To give a title to.

ti·tled (tīt′ld) *adj.* Having a title, especially a noble title.

tit·mouse (tĭt′mous′) *n., pl.* **tit·mice** (tĭt′mīs′) Any of various small grayish birds of woodland areas, especially several North American species that have a tuft of feathers on the head. [From Middle English *titmose* : *tit-*, probably from Old Norse *tittr*, small peak, titmouse + *mose*, titmouse, from Old English *māse.*]

tit·ter (tĭt′ər) *intr.v.* **tit·tered, tit·ter·ing, tit·ters** To laugh in a restrained nervous way; giggle. ❖ *n.* A nervous giggle. **—tit′ter·er** *n.*

tit·tle (tĭt′l) *n.* **1.** A small diacritic mark, such as an accent, vowel mark, or dot over an *i.* **2.** The tiniest bit.

tit·u·lar (tĭch′ə-lər) *adj.* **1.** Relating to, constituting, or bearing a title: *the titular role in a play.* **2.** Existing in name only; nominal: *the titular ruler of a country.*

tiz·zy (tĭz′ē) *n., pl.* **tiz·zies** *Informal* A state of nervous excitement or confusion; a dither.

Tl The symbol for the element **thallium.**

TLC *abbr.* An abbreviation of tender loving care.

Tlin·git (tlĭng′gĭt *or* tlĭng′kĭt *or* klĭng′kĭt) *n., pl.* **Tlingit** or **Tlin·gits 1.** A member of a Native American people living in southeast Alaska. **2.** The language of the Tlingit.

Tm The symbol for the element **thulium.**

TN *abbr.* An abbreviation of Tennessee.

TNT (tē′ĕn-tē′) *n.* A yellow crystalline compound used mainly as an explosive. [From *t(ri)n(itro)t(oluene).*]

to (to͞o; tə *when unstressed*) *prep.* **1.** In the direction of; so as to reach: *a trip to Chicago.* **2.** Towards: *He turned to me.* **3.** Reaching as far as: *The water was clear to the bottom.* **4.** Toward or reaching a certain state: *the governor's rise to power.* **5.** In contact with: *Their faces were pressed to the window.* **6.** In front of: *We stood face to face.* **7.** For the attention, benefit, or possession of: *Tell it to me.* **8.** For the purpose of; for: *We went out to lunch.* **9.** Used to indicate belonging or appropriateness: *Where is the top to this jar?* **10.** Concerning or regarding: *Did you get an answer to your letter?* **11.** In a relationship with: *The brook runs parallel to the road.* **12.** With the resulting condition of: *torn to shreds.* **13.** As an accompaniment of: *singing to an old tune.* **14.** Composing or constituting; in: *two pints to a quart.* **15.** In accord with: *That's not really to my liking.* **16.** As compared with: *This book is superior to her others.* **17.** Before: *The time is ten to five.* **18.** Up till; until: *works from nine to five.* **19.** In honor of: *a toast to our visitors.* **20a.** Used before a verb to indicate the infinitive: *I'd like to go.* **b.** Used alone when the infinitive is understood: *Go if you want to.* ❖ *adv.* **1.** In a shut position: *slammed the door to.* **2.** Into consciousness: *The patient came to.* **3.** Into a state of action or attentiveness: *They sat down for lunch and everybody fell to.*

❑ *These sound alike:* **to, too** (also), **two** (number).

toad (tōd) *n.* Any of various frogs that have rough, dry skin and live mostly on land when full grown.

❑ *These sound alike:* **toad, toed** (having toes), **towed** (pulled).

toad·stool (tōd′sto͞ol′) *n.* A mushroom considered unfit for eating, especially a poisonous one.

toad·y (tō′dē) *n., pl.* **toad·ies** A person who flatters others for the sake of gain; a sycophant. ❖ *tr. & intr.v.* **toad·ied, toad·y·ing, toad·ies** To be a toady or behave like a toady: *shamelessly toadying to his boss.*

to and fro *adv.* Back and forth: *I'm always running to and fro.*

toast[1] (tōst) *v.* **toast·ed, toast·ing, toasts** *—tr.* **1.** To heat and brown (bread, for example) by exposure to radiant heat. **2.** To warm thoroughly, as before a fire: *toast one's feet by the fireplace.* *—intr.* To become toasted. ❖ *n.* Sliced bread that is heated and browned. [From Middle English *tosten*, from Old French *toster.*]

toast[2] (tōst) *n.* **1a.** The act of raising a glass and drinking in honor of or to the health of a person or thing. **b.** A person or thing honored in this way. **2.** A person who receives much attention or acclaim: *The star of the play became the toast of London.* ❖ *v.* **toast·ed, toast·ing, toasts** *—tr.* To drink in honor of or to the health of: *The guests toasted the newly married couple.* *—intr.* To propose or drink a toast. [Perhaps from the use of spiced toast to flavor drinks.]

toast·er (tō′stər) *n.* A device that toasts slices of bread by means of electrically heated wire coils.

toast·mas·ter (tōst′măs′tər) *n.* A person who proposes the toasts and introduces the speakers at a banquet.

to·bac·co (tə-băk′ō) *n., pl.* **to·bac·cos** or **to·bac·coes 1.** The leaves of a tropical American plant, processed for use in cigarettes, cigars, or snuff or for smoking in pipes. **2.** The plant that bears such leaves. **3.** Any of several related plants. **4.** Products, such as cigarettes, cigars, or snuff, made from tobacco. **5.** The habit of smoking tobacco: *He gave up tobacco years ago.*

to·bac·co·nist (tə-băk′ə-nĭst) *n.* A person who sells tobacco and smoking supplies.

titmouse

toboggan

toga

USAGE

together You can use *together with* following the subject of a sentence or clause to introduce an addition: *The king, together with two aides, is expected in an hour.* Notice that the addition does not change the number of the verb (*is*) that follows the original subject (*the king*). The same is true of the words or phrases *along with, besides,* and *in addition to.*

ă	pat	ôr	core
ā	pay	oi	boy
âr	care	ou	out
ä	father	o͝o	took
ĕ	pet	o͝or	lure
ē	be	o͞o	boot
ĭ	pit	ŭ	cut
ī	bite	ûr	urge
îr	pier	th	thin
ŏ	pot	*th*	this
ō	toe	zh	vision
ô	paw	ə	about

To·ba·go (tə-**bā′**gō) An island of Trinidad and Tobago in the southeast West Indies northeast of Trinidad.

to·bog·gan (tə-**bŏg′**ən) *n.* A long narrow sled without runners, made of thin boards curved upward at the front end. ❖ *intr.v.* **to·bog·ganed, to·bog·gan·ing, to·bog·gans** To ride on a toboggan.

toc·ca·ta (tə-**kä′**tə) *n.* A musical composition, usually for the organ or another keyboard instrument, in a free style with elaborate passages.

toc·sin (**tŏk′**sĭn) *n.* **1a.** An alarm sounded on a bell. **b.** A bell used to sound an alarm. **2.** A warning; an omen.

to·day (tə-**dā′**) *n.* **1.** The present day: *the schedule for today.* **2.** The present age or period: *the composers of today.* ❖ *adv.* **1.** During or on the present day: *He will arrive today.* **2.** During or at the present time: *Today more vitamins are sold than ever before.*

tod·dle (**tŏd′**l) *intr.v.* **tod·dled, tod·dling, tod·dles** To walk with short unsteady steps, as a small child does. ❖ *n.* An unsteady gait.

tod·dler (**tŏd′**lər) *n.* A young child who is just learning how to walk.

to-do (tə-**do͞o′**) *n., pl.* **to-dos** (tə-**do͞oz′**) *Informal* An excited reaction; a fuss or commotion.

toe (tō) *n.* **1.** One of the narrow extensions of the foot of a human or other vertebrate animal. **2.** The part of a sock, stocking, shoe, or boot that fits over the toes. ❖ *v.* **toed, toe·ing, toes** —*tr.* To touch, kick, or reach with the toes. —*intr.* To walk, stand, or move with the toes pointed in a specified direction: *She toes out.* ◆ **on (one's) toes** Ready to act; alert. **step on (someone's) toes** or **tread on (someone's) toes** To hurt or offend the feelings of.

❑ *These sound alike:* **toe, tow¹** (pull), **tow²** (flax).

toed (tōd) *adj.* Having toes, especially a certain kind or number of toes: *a long-toed bird; a two-toed sloth.*

❑ *These sound alike:* **toed, toad** (animal), **towed** (pulled).

toe·nail (**tō′**nāl′) *n.* **1.** A nail on a toe. **2.** A nail driven at an oblique angle, as in joining a vertical beam to a horizontal beam. ❖ *tr.v.* **toe·nailed, toe·nail·ing, toe·nails** To join or secure (beams) with nails driven at an oblique angle.

tof·fee (**tô′**fē) *n.* A hard chewy candy made of brown sugar or molasses and butter.

to·fu (**tō′**fo͞o) *n.* A usually soft white food that is made from soybeans and has a high protein content.

to·ga (**tō′**gə) *n.* **1.** A loose one-piece outer garment worn in public by citizens of ancient Rome. **2.** A robe of office; a professional or ceremonial gown.

to·geth·er (tə-**gĕ*th*′**ər) *adv.* **1.** In or into a single group, mass, or place: *Many people were crowded together.* **2.** In or into contact: *rubbing one's hands together.* **3.** In association with or in relationship to another: *My cats get along together.* **4.** By cooperative effort: *We built the deck together.* **5.** Simultaneously: *The bells rang out together.* **6.** *Informal* Into an effective condition to do something: *Get yourself together.* —**to·geth′er·ness** *n.* —SEE NOTE.

tog·gle (**tŏg′**əl) *n.* A pin, rod, or bolt fitted or inserted into a loop in a rope, chain, or strap to prevent slipping, to tighten, or to hold something. ❖ *v.* **tog·gled, tog·gling, tog·gles** —*tr.* To furnish or fasten with a toggle. —*intr.* To switch between electronic, mechanical, or computer-related options, as with a keystroke or by flipping a switch.

toggle bolt *n.* A fastener consisting of a threaded bolt and toggle, used to attach objects to thin walls.

toggle joint *n.* A joint consisting of two arms attached by a pivot shaped like an elbow that allows force to be applied to the ends of the levers as the joint is expanded.

toggle switch *n.* An electrical switch that is opened and closed by a toggle joint that is loaded with a spring, with one of the levers projecting outward so that it can be moved by a finger.

To·go (**tō′**gō′) A country of western Africa on the Gulf of Guinea west of Benin. Lomé is the capital.

tö·grög (**tœ′**grœg) *n.* The basic monetary unit of Mongolia. [From Mongolian.]

togs (tŏgz) *pl.n.* Clothing: *gardening togs.*

toil (toil) *intr.v.* **toiled, toil·ing, toils 1.** To labor continuously; work strenuously: *We toiled all day at mowing the lawn.* **2.** To proceed with difficulty: *toiling up a steep hill.* ❖ *n.* Exhausting labor or effort. [From Middle English *toilen,* from Latin *tudiculāre,* to stir up, from *tudicula,* a machine for bruising olives.] —**toil′er** *n.*

toi·let (**toi′**lĭt) *n.* **1.** A fixture for urination and defecation, consisting of a bowl fitted with a hinged seat and having a flushing device. **2.** A room or booth containing such a fixture. **3.** The act or process of grooming or dressing oneself; toilette.

toilet paper *n.* Thin absorbent paper, usually in rolls, used to clean oneself after defecation or urination.

toi·let·ry (**toi′**lĭ-trē) *n., pl.* **toi·let·ries** An article, such as toothpaste or a hairbrush, used in dressing or grooming oneself.

toi·lette (twä-**lĕt′**) *n.* **1.** The act or process of dressing or grooming oneself. **2.** A person's dress or style of dress.

toil·some (**toil′**səm) *adj.* Characterized by or requiring toil.

to·ken (**tō′**kən) *n.* **1.** Something that serves as an indication or representation of something else; a sign: *A white flag is a token of surrender.* **2.** Something that signifies or gives proof of authority, validity, or identity: *The crown is a token of royal status.* **3.** A person considered as a representative of a social group, especially a single individual or one of a small number of employees hired primarily to prevent an employer of being accused of discrimination. **4.** A keepsake; a souvenir: *This ring was a token of our wedding anniversary.* **5.** A piece of stamped metal used as a substitute for currency: *subway tokens.* ❖ *tr.v.* **to·kened, to·ken·ing, to·kens** To symbolize or serve as a warning of. ❖ *adj.* **1.** Done as an indication or pledge: *a token payment.* **2.** Minimal or merely symbolic: *token resistance to the new leader.* ◆ **by the same token** In like manner; similarly. **in token of** As an indication of: *a ring given in token of love.*

to·ken·ism (**tō′**kə-nĭz′əm) *n.* The policy of making only a superficial effort or symbolic gesture toward the accomplishment of a goal, such as racial integration.

To·ky·o (**tō′**kē-ō′ *or* **tō′**kyō) The capital of Japan, in east-central Honshu on **Tokyo Bay,** an inlet of the Pacific Ocean.

told (tōld) *v.* Past tense and past participle of **tell.**

To·le·do (tə-**lē′**dō *or* tō-**lĕ′**thō) A city of central Spain south-southwest of Madrid. As a Moorish capital (712–1085) it was a center of Arab and Hebrew learning.

tol·er·a·ble (**tŏl′**ər-ə-bəl) *adj.* **1.** Able to be tolerated; endurable: *tolerable food.* **2.** Acceptable but not superior; passable; adequate: *in tolerable health.* —**tol′er·a·bly** *adv.*

tol·er·ance (**tŏl′**ər-əns) *n.* **1.** The capacity for or the practice of recognizing and respecting the beliefs or practices of others. **2.** The capacity to endure hardship or pain. **3.** The amount that something is allowed to vary from the value intended: *The bolt was made to a tolerance of .001 inch.* **4.** Lessening in the physiological response to a drug that occurs after continued use, resulting in the need for larger doses to produce a given response.

tol·er·ant (**tŏl′**ər-ənt) *adj.* **1.** Inclined to tolerate the beliefs or practices of others. **2.** Able to withstand or endure an adverse environmental condition: *plants tolerant of extreme heat.*

tol·er·ate (**tŏl′**ə-rāt′) *tr.v.* **tol·er·at·ed, tol·er·at·ing, tol·er·ates 1.** To allow without prohibiting or opposing;

permit. **2.** To recognize and respect (the beliefs, rights, or practices of others). **3.** To put up with; endure: *He tolerated their insults for weeks before filing a complaint.* **4.** To have a tolerance for (a drug or poison). [From Latin *tolerāre.*]

tol·er·a·tion (tŏl′ə-rā′shən) *n.* **1.** Tolerance of the actions or beliefs of others. **2.** Official recognition of the rights of individuals or groups who hold different views than the majority of the population, especially in matters of religion.

Tol·kien (tōl′kēn′), **J(ohn) R(onald) R(euel)** 1892–1973. British writer of the fantasies *The Hobbit* (1937) and *The Lord of the Rings* (1954–1955).

toll[1] (tōl) *n.* **1.** A fixed charge or tax for a privilege, especially for passage across a bridge or along a road. **2.** A charge for a service, as a telephone call to another country. **3.** An amount or extent of loss or destruction, as of life, health, or property: *The hurricane took a heavy toll along the coast.* [From Old English, from Latin *telōnēum*, tollbooth, from Greek *telos*, tax.]

toll[2] (tōl) *v.* **tolled, toll·ing, tolls** —*tr.* **1.** To sound (a bell) slowly at regular intervals: *tolling the church bells.* **2.** To announce or summon by tolling: *The bell tolled the hour. The church bells tolled the monks to Vespers.* —*intr.* To sound in slowly repeated single tones. ❖ *n.* **1.** The act of tolling. **2.** The sound of a bell being struck. [From Middle English *tollen*, to ring an alarm, perhaps from *tollen*, to entice, pull, variant of *tillen*.]

toll·booth (tōl′bo͞oth′) *n.* A booth where a toll is collected.

toll·gate (tōl′gāt′) *n.* A gate barring passage of vehicles to a road, tunnel, or bridge until a toll is paid.

Tol·stoy (tōl′stoi *or* tŏl′stoi), Count **Leo** 1828–1910. Russian writer and philosopher whose novels include *War and Peace* (1869).

Tol·tec (tōl′tĕk′ *or* tŏl′tĕk′) *n., pl.* **Toltec** or **Tol·tecs** A member of an ancient Nahuatl-speaking people of central and southern Mexico. **—Tol·tec′an** *adj.*

tol·u·ene (tŏl′yo͞o-ēn′) *n.* A colorless liquid related to benzene that burns easily and is composed of carbon and hydrogen. It is used in making fuels, dyes, explosives, and other industrial chemicals.

tom (tŏm) *n.* The male of various animals, especially a male cat or turkey.

tom·a·hawk (tŏm′ə-hôk′) *n.* A light axe formerly used as a weapon and tool by certain Native American peoples. [From Virginia Algonquian *tamahaac.*]

to·mal·ley (tə-măl′ē *or* tŏm′ăl′ē) *n., pl.* **to·mal·leys** The soft, greenish liver of cooked lobster.
❑ *These sound alike:* **tomalley, tamale** (Mexican dish).

to·ma·to (tə-mā′tō *or* tə-mä′tō) *n., pl.* **to·ma·toes 1.** The fleshy, usually reddish fruit of a widely cultivated South American plant, eaten raw or cooked as a vegetable. **2.** The plant that bears such fruit. [Alteration of Spanish *tomate*, from Nahuatl *tomatl.*]

tomb (to͞om) *n.* **1.** A place of burial; a grave. **2.** A vault or chamber for the burial of the dead.

tom·boy (tŏm′boi′) *n.* A girl who behaves in a way that is perceived to be stereotypically boyish or masculine.

tomb·stone (to͞om′stōn′) *n.* A gravestone.

tom·cat (tŏm′kăt′) *n.* A male cat.

tome (tōm) *n.* **1.** One of the books in a work of several volumes. **2.** A book, especially a large or scholarly one.

tom·fool·er·y (tŏm-fo͞o′lə-rē) *n.* Foolish behavior; silliness; nonsense.

to·mor·row (tə-môr′ō) *n.* **1.** The day following today. **2.** The future: *space flights of tomorrow.* ❖ *adv.* On or for the day following today: *I will return your book tomorrow.*

tom-tom (tŏm′tŏm′) *n.* Any of various small-headed drums, usually tall and narrow, that are beaten with the hands. [From Hindi *ṭamṭam*, probably of imitative origin.]

ton (tŭn) *n.* **1a.** A unit of weight equal to 2,000 pounds; a short ton. **b.** A unit of weight equal to 2,240 pounds; a long ton. **c.** A metric ton. See table at **measurement. 2.** *Informal* **a.** A very large quantity of something: *buying tons of books.* **b.** Used adverbially with *a* or in the plural to mean "to a great extent" or "frequently": *felt a ton better; has been exercising tons lately.*
❑ *These sound alike:* **ton, tun** (cask).

ton·al (tō′nəl) *adj.* Relating to tones, a tone, or tonality. **—ton′al·ly** *adv.*

to·nal·i·ty (tō-năl′ĭ-tē) *n., pl.* **to·nal·i·ties 1.** A system or arrangement of musical tones with respect to a tonic. **2.** The arrangement of all of the tones and chords of a musical composition with respect to a tonic.

tone (tōn) *n.* **1a.** A sound that has a distinct pitch, quality, and duration; a note. **b.** The interval of a major second in a musical scale; a whole step. **2a.** The quality or character of sound. **b.** The characteristic quality or timbre of a particular instrument or voice. **3a.** A color or shade of color. **b.** Quality of color. **4a.** The tension that normally remains in a muscle when it is at rest. **b.** Normal firmness of body tissue or an organ. **5.** A manner of expression in speech or writing: *an angry tone of voice.* **6.** A general quality or atmosphere: *the tone of the debate; a quiet tone of elegance in the room.* ❖ *v.* **toned, ton·ing, tones** —*tr.* **1.** To give a particular tone or inflection to. **2.** To soften or change the color of (a painting or photograph, for example). **3.** To make firmer or stronger: *exercises that tone up the body.* —*intr.* To harmonize in color. ◆ **tone down** To make less vivid, harsh, or violent; moderate. [From Middle English *ton*, from Greek *tonos*, a stretching.]

tone-deaf (tōn′dĕf′) *adj.* **1.** Unable to distinguish differences in musical pitch. **2.** Unable to appreciate or understand the concerns or difficulties of others; out-of-touch.

tone poem *n.* A piece of music based on a story or ideal and usually consisting of a single movement for a symphony orchestra.

ton·er (tō′nər) *n.* **1.** A powdery ink used dry or suspended in a liquid to produce a document using a photocopier or laser printer. **2.** A lotion used to refresh the skin.

Ton·ga (tŏng′gə) A country in the southwest Pacific Ocean east of Fiji made up of about 150 islands, of which about 36 are inhabited. Nuku'alofa is the capital.

Ton·gan (tŏng′gən *or* tŏng′ən) *adj.* Relating to Tonga or its people, language, or culture. ❖ *n.* **1.** A native or inhabitant of Tonga. **2.** The Polynesian language of Tonga.

tongs (tôngz) *pl.n. (used with a singular or plural verb)* A device consisting of two arms joined at or near one end by a pivot or hinge, used for holding, lifting, or grasping objects.

tongue (tŭng) *n.* **1.** The fleshy muscular organ, attached in most vertebrates to the floor of the mouth, that is the main organ of taste, aids in chewing and swallowing, and, in humans, is used in forming speech sounds. **2.** A similar part in an invertebrate animal. **3.** The tongue of an animal, such as a cow, used as food. **4.** A strip that projects from the edge of a board and fits into a matching groove on another board. **5.** Something that resembles a tongue in shape or function, as the flap of material under the laces or buckles of a shoe. **6.** A spoken language: *Her native tongue is Swedish.* **7.** The power of speech or the ability to express oneself: *I do not have the tongue to tell you what I really think.* **8.** A manner of speech: *He has a sharp tongue.* **9.** The part of a bell that hangs inside and strikes the walls to create the ringing noise. ❖ *tr.v.* **tongued, tongu·ing, tongues** To separate (notes played on a brass or wind instrument) by shutting off the stream of air with the tongue. ◆ **hold**

Leo Tolstoy

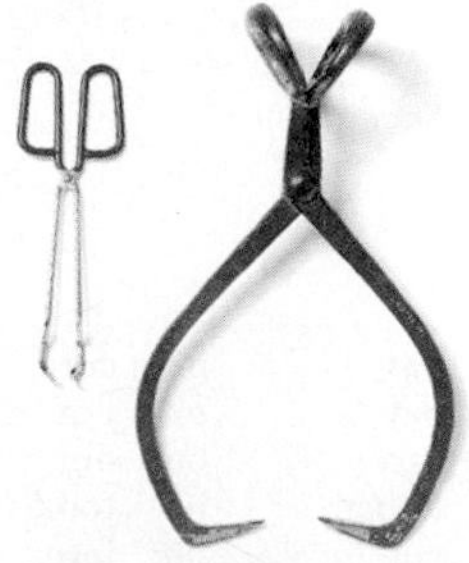
tongs
left: kitchen tongs
right: ice tongs

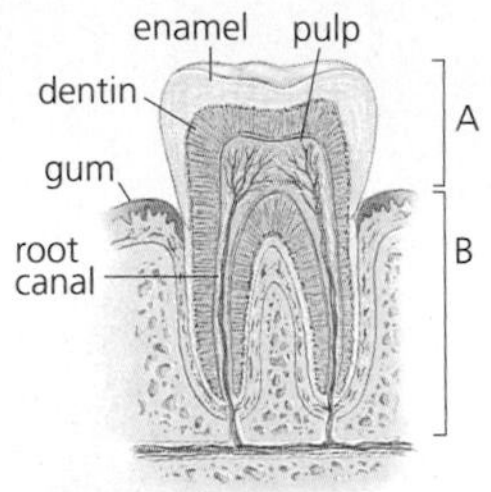

tooth
cross section of a molar
A. crown
B. root

topiary

(one's) tongue To be or keep silent. **on the tip of one's tongue** On the verge of being recalled or spoken. **tongue in cheek** or **with tongue in cheek** Ironically or jokingly: *expressed her interest with tongue in cheek.* [From Old English *tunge.*]

tongue-tied (tŭng′tīd′) *adj.* Speechless or confused in expression, as from shyness or embarrassment.

tongue twister *n.* **1.** A word or group of words that is difficult to speak rapidly. **2.** Something that is difficult to pronounce.

ton·ic (tŏn′ĭk) *n.* **1.** A medication or other agent that is supposed to restore or improve health or well-being. **2.** The first note of a musical scale; the keynote. **3.** Tonic water. ❖ *adj.* In music, of or based on the keynote.

tonic water *n.* A carbonated beverage flavored with quinine.

to·night (tə-**nīt′**) *adv.* On or during the present or coming night: *I'll see you tonight at 10:00.* ❖ *n.* This night or the night of this day: *Tonight is a very special occasion.*

Ton·kin (**tŏn′kĭn′** *or* **tŏng′kĭn′**) A historical region of southeast Asia on the **Gulf of Tonkin,** an arm of the South China Sea, now forming most of northern Vietnam.

ton·nage (**tŭn′**ĭj) *n.* **1.** The number of tons of water a ship displaces when afloat. **2.** The capacity of a merchant ship in units of 100 cubic feet. **3.** A charge per ton on cargo. **4.** The total shipping of a country or port, figured in tons. **5.** Weight measured in tons.

ton·sil·lec·to·my (tŏn′sə-**lĕk′**tə-mē) *n., pl.* **ton·sil·lec·to·mies** The removal of a tonsil or tonsils by means of surgery.

ton·sil·li·tis (tŏn′sə-**lī′**tĭs) *n.* Inflammation of the tonsils or a tonsil.

ton·sils (**tŏn′**səlz) *pl.n.* The two oval-shaped tissues that are located at the back of the throat, thought to help protect the body from respiratory infections.

ton·so·ri·al (tŏn-**sôr′**ē-əl) *adj.* Relating to a barber or barbering.

ton·sure (**tŏn′**shər) *n.* **1.** The act of shaving the head or part of the head, especially as a preliminary to becoming a priest or a member of a monastic order. **2.** The part of a monk's or priest's head so shaven. ❖ *tr.v.* **ton·sured, ton·sur·ing, ton·sures** To shave the head of.

too (to͞o) *adv.* **1.** In addition; also: *I can play the piano too.* **2.** More than enough; excessively: *You worry too much.* **3.** Very; extremely: *I'm only too happy to be of service.* **4.** *Informal* Indeed; so: *You will too do it!*

❑ *These sound alike:* **too, to** (toward), **two** (number).

took (to͝ok) *v.* Past tense of **take.**

tool (to͞ol) *n.* **1.** A device, especially a mechanical one held in the hand, used to do work or perform a task. **2a.** A machine, such as a lathe, used to make machine parts and other objects. **b.** The part of such a machine that cuts or shapes. **3.** Something used in the performance of an operation; an instrument: *the necessary fiscal and monetary tools to stop inflation.* **4.** Something regarded as necessary to the carrying out of one's occupation: *Words are the tools of her trade.* **5.** A person used to carry out the designs of another; a dupe. ❖ *v.* **tooled, tool·ing, tools** —*tr.* To form, work, or decorate with a tool. —*intr.* To work with a tool. ◆ **tool up** To provide an industry or factory with machinery and tools for a particular job.

❑ *These sound alike:* **tool, tulle** (fabric).

tool·bar (**to͞ol′**bär′) *n.* A row of icons on a computer screen for activating commands or functions.

tool·box (**to͞ol′**bŏks′) *n.* A case for carrying or storing tools.

toot (to͞ot) *v.* **toot·ed, toot·ing, toots** —*intr.* **1.** To sound a horn or whistle in short blasts. **2.** To make a sound resembling that of a horn or whistle blown in short blasts. —*tr.* To blow or sound (a horn or whistle). ❖ *n.* A blast, as of a horn.

tooth (to͞oth) *n., pl.* **teeth** (tēth) **1.** Any of a set of hard bony structures set in sockets around the jaws of most vertebrate animals, used to grasp, hold, and chew and as weapons of attack and defense. **2.** A similar hard structure in an invertebrate animal. **3.** A projecting part resembling a tooth in shape or function, as on a gearwheel, saw, or comb. **4.** A small, notched projection along a margin, especially of a leaf. ◆ **to the teeth** Lacking nothing; completely: *armed to the teeth.* [From Old English *tōth.*]

tooth·ache (**to͞oth′**āk′) *n.* An aching pain in or near a tooth.

tooth·brush (**to͞oth′**brŭsh′) *n.* A brush used for cleaning the teeth.

toothed (to͞otht *or* to͞o*th*d) *adj.* Having teeth, especially a certain number or type: *sharp-toothed jaws; a plastic-toothed comb; a toothed whale.*

tooth·paste (**to͞oth′**pāst′) *n.* A paste used to clean the teeth.

tooth·pick (**to͞oth′**pĭk′) *n.* A small piece of wood or other material for removing food particles from between the teeth.

tooth·pow·der (**to͞oth′**pou′dər) *n.* A powder used to clean the teeth.

tooth·some (**to͞oth′**səm) *adj.* **1.** Delicious; savory: *a toothsome pie.* **2.** Pleasant; attractive.

top¹ (tŏp) *n.* **1.** The uppermost part, point, surface, or end: *read the words at the top of the page; luggage on the top of the car.* **2.** Something, such as a lid or cap, that covers or forms an uppermost part: *the top of a trash can.* **3.** A garment worn on the upper half of the body. **4a.** The highest rank or position: *He is at the top of the company.* **b.** The highest degree, point, or pitch; the acme: *singing at the top of her powers.* **5.** The earliest part or beginning: *Please play the piece again, from the top.* **6.** The first half of an inning in baseball. ❖ *adj.* **1.** Situated at the top: *the top drawer.* **2.** Of the highest degree, amount, or quality: *in top form; the top ten books of the 1900s.* ❖ *tr.v.* **topped, top·ping, tops 1.** To furnish with, form, or serve as a top: *top a cake with frosting.* **2.** To reach the top of: *We topped the hill and started to climb down.* **3.** To exceed or surpass: *He just topped the old record.* **4.** To be at the head of: *She tops her class.* ◆ **off the top of (one's) head** *Informal* Without preparation or previous thought: *I don't have any figures, but I can give you an estimate off the top of my head.* **on top of** *Informal* **1.** In control of: *It's a touchy situation, but she's on top of it.* **2.** Fully informed about: *a blogger who is always on top of the latest news.* **3.** In addition to; besides: *two papers due next week and an exam on top of that.* **top off** To fill up (a container), especially when it is almost full to begin with. **top out** To cease rising: *interest rates topped out at 10 percent.* [From Old English.]

top² (tŏp) *n.* A toy having one end tapered to a point, allowing it to be spun, as by suddenly pulling a string wound around it. [From Old English.]

to·paz (**tō′**păz′) *n.* **1.** A colorless, blue, yellow, brown, or pink mineral consisting largely of aluminum silicate and valued as a gem. **2.** Any of various yellow gemstones, especially a yellow variety of sapphire or corundum. **3.** A light yellow variety of quartz.

top·coat (**tŏp′**kōt′) *n.* A lightweight overcoat.

To·pe·ka (tə-**pē′**kə) The capital of Kansas, in the northeast part of the state west of Kansas City. It was founded in 1854.

top·gal·lant (tə-**găl′**ənt *or* tŏp-**găl′**ənt) *adj.* Relating to the mast above the topmast or its sails or rigging.

top hat *n.* A man's hat having a narrow brim and a tall crown shaped like a cylinder.

top-heav·y (**tŏp′**hĕv′ē) *adj.* **top-heav·i·er, top-heav·**

ă	pat	ôr	core
ā	pay	oi	boy
âr	care	ou	out
ä	father	o͝o	took
ĕ	pet	o͝or	lure
ē	be	o͞o	boot
ĭ	pit	ŭ	cut
ī	bite	ûr	urge
îr	pier	th	thin
ŏ	pot	*th*	this
ō	toe	zh	vision
ô	paw	ə	about

i·est Having too much weight at the top and therefore likely to topple.

to·pi·ar·y (tō′pē-ĕr′ē) *adj.* Relating to or characterized by the clipping of live shrubs or trees into decorative shapes, as of animals. ❖ *n., pl.* **to·pi·ar·ies 1.** Topiary work or art. **2.** A shrub or tree clipped into a decorative shape.

top·ic (tŏp′ĭk) *n.* **1.** The subject of a speech or piece of writing: *The topic of this article is medical research.* See Synonyms at **subject. 2.** A subject of discussion or conversation. [From Greek *topos,* place.]

top·i·cal (tŏp′ĭ-kəl) *adj.* **1.** Being of current interest or relevance: *topical news items; ecology and other topical issues.* **2.** Relating to, applied to, or affecting a particular part of the body: *topical application of an ointment.* **3.** Relating to or arranged by a particular topic of topics: *a topical concordance of Shakespeare's plays.* **—top′i·cal·ly** *adv.*

topic sentence *n.* The sentence within a paragraph or discourse that states the main thought, often placed at the beginning.

top·knot (tŏp′nŏt′) *n.* A crest or knot of hair or feathers on the crown of the head.

top·most (tŏp′mōst′) *adj.* Highest; uppermost.

top-notch or **top·notch** (tŏp′nŏch′) *adj. Informal* First-rate; excellent: *We ate a top-notch dinner at a fancy restaurant.*

to·pog·ra·pher (tə-pŏg′rə-fər) *n.* A person who is skilled in topography.

to·pog·ra·phy (tə-pŏg′rə-fē) *n., pl.* **to·pog·ra·phies 1.** The detailed description or drawing of the physical features of a place or region. **2.** The physical features of a place or region. **—top·o·graph·ic** (tŏp′ə-grăf′ĭk), **top·o·graph·i·cal** (tŏp′ə-grăf′ĭ-kəl) *adj.*

to·pol·o·gy (tə-pŏl′ə-jē) *n., pl.* **to·pol·o·gies** The mathematical study of geometric properties that are not normally affected by changes in the size or shape of geometric figures. In topology, a donut and a coffee cup with a handle are equivalent shapes, because each has a single hole. **—top′o·log′i·cal** (tŏp′ə-lŏj′ĭ-kəl) *adj.* **—top′o·log′i·cal·ly** *adv.*

top·ping (tŏp′ĭng) *n.* A sauce, frosting, or garnish for food.

top·ple (tŏp′əl) *v.* **top·pled, top·pling, top·ples** *—tr.* **1.** To push or knock over: *bumped the table and toppled the lamp.* **2.** To bring about the downfall or ending of: *protests that toppled the corrupt government. —intr.* To totter and fall: *Poorly constructed buildings toppled in the earthquake.*

tops (tŏps) *adj. Slang* First-rate; excellent.

top·sail (tŏp′səl *or* tŏp′sāl′) *n.* A square sail set above the lowest sail on the mast of a square-rigged ship.

top-se·cret (tŏp′sē′krĭt) *adj.* **1.** Containing or relating to information of the highest level of national security classification: *top-secret documents; a top-secret mission.* **2.** Known or accessible only to authorized personnel.

top·soil (tŏp′soil′) *n.* The layer of soil at the surface of the ground.

top·sy-tur·vy (tŏp′sē-tûr′vē) *adv.* **1.** Upside-down. **2.** In a state of utter disorder or confusion: *turned the room topsy-turvy looking for the keys.* ❖ *adj.* **top·sy-tur·vi·er, top·sy-tur·vi·est** Confused; disordered: *a topsy-turvy political situation.*

toque (tōk) *n.* **1.** Any of several styles of usually brimless hats, especially a tall white hat with a pleated crown, traditionally worn by chefs. **2.** A close-fitting knitted cap having no brim or a brim that is folded up; a tuque.

To·rah also **to·rah** (tôr′ə *or* tô-rä′) *n.* **1a.** The first five books of the Hebrew Scriptures. **b.** A scroll on which these books are written, used in a synagogue during services. **2.** The body of Jewish religious law and learning including both sacred literature and oral tradition. [From Hebrew *tôrâ,* law, instruction, from *hôrâ,* to throw, direct, teach.]

torch (tôrch) *n.* **1a.** A portable light produced by the flame of a stick of wood or of a flammable material wound about the end of a stick of wood. **b.** *Chiefly British* A flashlight. **2.** Something that serves to enlighten, guide, or illuminate: *passing the torch of learning to the new generation.* **3.** A portable device that burns a fuel, usually a gas, to produce a flame hot enough for welding, soldering, brazing, or cutting metals. [From Middle English *torche,* from Latin *torqua,* from *torquēre,* to twist.]

tore (tôr) *v.* Past tense of **tear[1].**

tor·e·a·dor (tôr′ē-ə-dôr′) *n.* A bullfighter.

tor·ment (tôr′mĕnt′) *n.* **1.** Great physical pain or mental anguish: *the torment of a toothache; the torments of jealousy.* **2.** A source of harassment, annoyance, or pain: *That dog is the torment of its owners.* ❖ *tr.v.* (tôr-**mĕnt′** *or* **tôr′**mĕnt′) **tor·ment·ed, tor·ment·ing, tor·ments 1.** To cause to undergo great pain or anguish. **2.** To annoy, pester, or harass: *Stop tormenting me with silly questions.* [From Middle English, from Latin *tormentum,* from *torquēre,* to twist.] **—tor·men′tor** *n.*

torn (tôrn) *v.* Past participle of **tear[1].**

tor·na·do (tôr-nā′dō) *n., pl.* **tor·na·does** or **tor·na·dos 1.** A violently whirling column of air that measures from a few yards to more than a mile wide and rotates with wind speeds up to around 300 miles (485 kilometers) per hour. Tornadoes usually form at the bottom of a funnel-shaped extension of a thundercloud. **2.** A whirlwind or hurricane. [From Spanish *tronada,* thunderstorm, from Latin *tonāre,* to thunder.]

To·ron·to (tə-rŏn′tō) The capital of Ontario, Canada, in the southern part of the province on Lake Ontario. It was founded as York in 1793 and renamed Toronto in 1834. Toronto is Canada's largest city.

tor·pe·do (tôr-pē′dō) *n., pl.* **tor·pe·does** A cylindrical, self-propelled underwater projectile launched from an airplane, ship, or submarine and designed to explode against or near a target. ❖ *tr.v.* **tor·pe·doed, tor·pe·do·ing, tor·pe·does 1.** To attack, strike, or sink with a torpedo. **2.** To destroy; wreck: *The surprise appearance of the police torpedoed the robbers' plans.* [From Latin *torpēdō,* numbness.]

tor·pid (tôr′pĭd) *adj.* **1.** Sluggish, lethargic, or not active: *The marching band failed to energize the torpid crowd.* **2.** Conducive to sluggishness or inactivity, especially due to heat and humidity: *a torpid summer evening.* **3.** Dormant; hibernating. [From Latin *torpidus,* numb, paralyzed.]

tor·por (tôr′pər) *n.* **1.** A state of mental or physical inactivity; lethargy: *The smell of dinner aroused him out of his torpor.* **2.** The dormant, inactive state of a hibernating animal: *the low body temperature of an animal in torpor.*

torque (tôrk) *n.* A force that causes an object to rotate about an axis or puts twisting stress on an object.

tor·rent (tôr′ənt) *n.* **1.** A swift-flowing stream. **2.** A heavy downpour; a deluge: *rain falling in torrents.* **3.** A heavy uncontrolled outpouring: *a torrent of insults.*

tor·ren·tial (tô-rĕn′shəl *or* tə-rĕn′shəl) *adj.* Caused by or resembling a torrent: *torrential rain.*

tor·rid (tôr′ĭd) *adj.* **tor·rid·er, tor·rid·est 1.** Very dry and hot: *torrid weather.* **2.** Passionate; ardent: *a torrid romance.* [From Latin *torridus,* from *torrēre,* to punch.] **—tor′rid·ly** *adv.*

tor·sion (tôr′shən) *n.* **1a.** The act or process of twisting or turning. **b.** The condition of being twisted or turned. **2.** The stress that an object undergoes when one of its ends is twisted out of line with the other end.

tor·so (tôr′sō) *n., pl.* **tor·sos** The human body except for the head and limbs; the trunk.

tort (tôrt) *n.* In law, a wrong that does not violate a con-

toque

tornado

WRITERS CHOOSE THEIR WORDS

Though it was past ten o'clock at night, the sky still clung to and retained some lingering skirts of light from the departed day; and the sullen heats of the **torrid** afternoon broke up and rolled away at the dispersing touch of the cool fingers of the short midsummer night.

—Kenneth Grahame
The Wind in the Willows

toucan

tract but nonetheless harms someone toward whom one has a legal duty. A person who is injured as a result of such a wrong may seek compensation in a civil suit.

❑ *These sound alike:* **tort, torte** (cake).

torte (tôrt *or* **tôr′**tə) *n.* A rich cake made with many eggs and nuts.

❑ *These sound alike:* **torte, tort** (wrongful act).

tor·til·la (tôr-**tē′**yə) *n.* A round, flat Mexican bread made from cornmeal or wheat flour and water and baked on a hot surface.

tor·toise (**tôr′**tĭs) *n.* Any of various turtles that live on land.

tor·toise·shell (**tôr′**tĭs-shĕl′) *n.* **1a.** The mottled, horny, brownish outer covering of the shell of certain sea turtles, formerly used to make combs, jewelry, and other items. **b.** A synthetic imitation of natural tortoiseshell. **2.** A domestic cat having a coat with irregular patches of different colors, usually black and reddish-orange.

tor·tu·ous (**tôr′**cho͞o-əs) *adj.* **1.** Winding; twisting: *a tortuous road.* **2.** Not straightforward; devious: *a tortuous argument.* [From Middle English, from Latin *tortus*, a twisting, from *torquēre*, to twist.] **—tor′tu·ous·ly** *adv.*

tor·ture (**tôr′**chər) *n.* **1.** Infliction of severe physical pain in order to punish someone or force someone to do something or provide information. **2.** Excruciating physical or mental pain. ❖ *tr.v.* **tor·tured, tor·tur·ing, tor·tures 1.** To subject to torture. **2.** To bring great physical or mental pain upon (another): *He is tortured by anxiety.* [From Middle English, from Late Latin *tortūra*, from Latin *torquēre*, to twist.] **—tor′tur·er** *n.*

tor·tur·ous (**tôr′**chər-əs) *adj.* **1.** Relating to or causing torture. **2.** Twisted; strained.

To·ry (**tôr′**ē) *n., pl.* **To·ries 1.** A member of a British political party founded in 1689 that was the rival of the Whigs and has been known as the Conservative Party since 1832. **2.** An American who favored the British during the American Revolution. **3.** often **tory** A political conservative.

toss (tôs) *v.* **tossed, toss·ing, toss·es** *—tr.* **1.** To throw lightly or casually: *toss a ball to a teammate.* See Synonyms at **throw. 2.** To throw upward: *The bull tossed him over the fence.* **3.** To cause to move from side to side or up and down: *Heavy seas tossed the ship.* **4.** To move or lift (the head) with a sudden movement. **5.** To mix (food) lightly so as to cover with dressing or sauce: *toss a salad.* **6.** To flip (a coin) to decide something. **7.** To throw away; discard: *tossed the empty can in the trash. —intr.* **1.** To be thrown here and there; be flung to and fro. **2.** To move about restlessly; twist and turn: *I tossed in my sleep all night.* ❖ *n.* **1.** The act of tossing or the condition of being tossed. **2.** A rapid upward movement, as of the head.

toss·up (**tôs′**ŭp′) *n. Informal* An even chance or choice: *It's a tossup as to who will win.*

tot (tŏt) *n.* **1.** A small child. **2.** A small amount, as of liquor.

to·tal (**tōt′**l) *n.* **1.** An amount obtained by addition; a sum. **2.** The whole amount of something; the entirety: *The storm damaged the total of the housing units.* ❖ *adj.* **1.** Relating to or constituting the whole amount; entirety: *the total population of the state.* **2.** Complete; absolute; utter: *a total eclipse.* ❖ *v.* **to·taled, to·tal·ing, to·tals** or **to·talled, to·tal·ling, to·tals** *—tr.* **1.** To find the sum of; add up: *totaling expenses.* **2.** To equal a total of; amount to: *Your bill totals $25.* **3.** To demolish completely; wreck: *He totaled his new car in the accident. —intr.* To add up; amount: *It totals to three dollars.* [From Middle English, from Latin *tōtus*.] **—to′tal·ly** *adv.*

to·tal·i·tar·i·an (tō-tăl′ĭ-**târ′**ē-ən) *adj.* Relating to a form of government in which one political party exercises absolute control over society and uses falsehood and violence to silence opposition. ❖ *n.* A person who supports or practices such a form of government. **—to·tal′i·tar′i·an·ism** *n.*

to·tal·i·ty (tō-**tăl′**ĭ-tē) *n., pl.* **to·tal·i·ties 1.** The quality or state of being total. **2.** A total amount; a sum.

tote (tōt) *tr.v.* **tot·ed, tot·ing, totes** *Informal* To haul; carry: *toted my gear to the car.*

tote bag *n.* A large handbag or shopping bag, usually with double handles and an open top.

to·tem (**tō′**təm) *n.* **1.** An animal, plant, or natural object that serves among certain peoples as the emblem of a clan or family and is sometimes claimed by the members as an ancestor, founder, or guardian. **2.** A representation of such an object. [From Ojibwa *nindoodem*, my totem.] **—to·tem′ic** *adj.*

totem pole *n.* A post carved and painted with a series of family or clan crests or with figures representing mythic beings and put up before a dwelling, as among certain Native American peoples of the northwest Pacific coast.

tot·ter (**tŏt′**ər) *intr.v.* **tot·tered, tot·ter·ing, tot·ters 1.** To sway as if about to fall: *A pile of books tottered at the edge of the table.* **2.** To walk unsteadily; stagger: *The baby tottered and fell down.*

tou·can (**to͞o′**kăn′ *or* to͞o-**kăn′**) *n.* Any of various tropical American birds having brightly colored feathers and a very large bill. [From Tupí *tucano*, type of bird.]

touch (tŭch) *v.* **touched, touch·ing, touch·es** *—tr.* **1.** To cause a part of the body, especially the hand or fingers, to come in contact with (something), especially so as to feel: *I touched the soft sweater.* **2.** To bring something into contact with: *She touched the snake with a stick.* **3.** To press or push lightly; tap: *He touched the screen with his finger.* **4.** To eat or drink; taste: *You haven't touched your food.* **5.** To disturb or move by handling: *Just don't touch anything in my room!* **6.** To meet without going beyond; adjoin: *the line where their property touches ours.* **7.** To affect the emotions of: *The ending of the movie touched him deeply.* **8.** To match in quality; equal: *None of her teammates can touch her ability at passing.* **9.** To color slightly; tinge: *a white petal touched with pink. —intr.* To be or come into contact: *Don't let the live wires touch.* ❖ *n.* **1.** The act or an instance of touching, especially a light push or tap: *set the alarm with the touch of a button.* **2.** The sense by which external objects or forces are perceived through contact with the body. **3.** A sensation experienced in touching something with a characteristic texture: *felt the touch of snowflakes on her face.* **4.** A small change or addition, or the effect achieved by it: *Candlelight provided just the right touch.* **5a.** A suggestion, hint, or tinge: *a touch of jealousy.* **b.** A mild attack: *a touch of the flu.* **c.** A small amount; a dash: *a touch of paprika.* **6.** A facility; a knack: *a touch for carpentry.* **7.** The state of being in contact or communication: *kept in touch with several classmates.* ◆ **in touch 1.** Aware of the latest developments: *He's in touch with the newest trends in fashion.* **2.** Able to be contacted, as by telephone or email: *Although she's on vacation, she'll be in touch with the office daily.* **out of touch 1.** Unaware of the latest developments: *He doesn't read the news, so he's out of touch with current events.* **2.** Unable to be contacted, as by telephone or email: *I'll be out of touch while I'm flying over the Pacific Ocean.* **touch down** To make contact with the ground; land: *The plane touched down smoothly.* **touch off 1.** To cause to explode: *touch off the fireworks.* **2.** To trigger; initiate: *The scandal touched off a public uproar.* **touch up** To improve by making minor corrections, changes, or additions: *I touched up the painting before submitting it.* [From Middle English *touchen*, from Old French *touchier*.]

touch-and-go (**tŭch′**ən-**gō′**) *adj.* Dangerous and uncertain in nature or outcome; precarious.

ă	pat	ôr	core
ā	pay	oi	boy
âr	care	ou	out
ä	father	o͝o	took
ĕ	pet	o͝or	lure
ē	be	o͞o	boot
ĭ	pit	ŭ	cut
ī	bite	ûr	urge
îr	pier	th	thin
ŏ	pot	*th*	this
ō	toe	zh	vision
ô	[illegible]	ə	about

touch·back (tŭch′băk′) *n.* In football, an instance of downing the ball behind one's goal line after the ball has been kicked or passed over the line by an opponent. The team with the ball resumes play on its own 20-yard line.

touch·down (tŭch′doun′) *n.* **1.** In football, the act of having possession of the ball on or across the opponent's goal line for a score of six points. **2.** The contact or moment of contact of an aircraft or spacecraft with the surface on which it lands.

touched (tŭcht) *adj.* **1.** Emotionally affected; moved. **2.** Somewhat demented or mentally unbalanced.

touch football *n.* A variety of football played without protective clothing in which players tag rather than tackle the ball carrier.

touch·ing (tŭch′ĭng) *adj.* Causing a sympathetic reaction; moving: *a touching speech.* ❖ *prep.* Concerning; about: *I have heard nothing touching his departure.* **—touch′ing·ly** *adv.*

touch·line (tŭch′līn′) *n.* In soccer and rugby, either of the sidelines bordering the playing field.

touch-me-not (tŭch′mē-nŏt′) *n.* The sensitive plant.

touch·pad (tŭch′păd′) *n.* A pointing device consisting of a soft pad sensitized to finger movement or pressure and used especially on laptop computers as an alternative to a mouse.

touch·screen (tŭch′skrēn′) *n.* A monitor screen that is responsive to pressure, as from a finger.

touch·stone (tŭch′stōn′) *n.* **1.** A hard black stone, such as jasper or basalt, formerly used to test a sample of silver or gold. The streak left by rubbing the sample on the touchstone was compared with the streak left by a standard alloy. **2.** An excellent quality or example used for testing the value or genuineness of something; a standard.

touch·tone (tŭch′tōn′) *adj.* Relating to a telephone having buttons that, when pushed, produce tones of differing pitches that correspond to the numbers on the buttons.

touch·y (tŭch′ē) *adj.* **touch·i·er, touch·i·est 1.** Tending to take offense easily; oversensitive. **2.** Requiring special tact or skill; delicate: *a touchy operation.*

tough (tŭf) *adj.* **tough·er, tough·est 1.** Able to withstand heavy strain or load without tearing or breaking; strong and resilient: *a tough fabric.* **2.** Difficult to cut or chew: *a tough steak.* **3.** Physically hardy; rugged: *a tough goalie.* **4.** Strong-minded; resolute: *a tough man to convince.* **5.** Aggressive; pugnacious: *tough criminals.* **6.** Demanding or troubling; difficult: *a tough lesson.* **7.** *Slang* Too bad; unfortunate: *a tough break.* ❖ *n.* A thug or hoodlum. [From Old English *tōh.*] **—tough′ly** *adv.* **—tough′ness** *n.*

❑ *These sound alike:* **tough, tuff** (rock).

tough·en (tŭf′ən) *tr. & intr.v.* **tough·ened, tough·en·ing, tough·ens** To make or become tough.

tou·pee (tōō-pā′) *n.* A small wig or hairpiece worn to cover a bald spot.

tour (tŏŏr) *n.* **1.** A trip with visits to many places of interest for business, pleasure, or instruction: *a tour of Europe.* **2.** A brief trip to or through a place for the purpose of seeing it: *a tour of the printing plant.* **3.** A journey to fulfill a round of engagements in several places: *a concert tour.* **4.** A period of duty at a single place or job. ❖ *intr. & tr.v.* **toured, tour·ing, tours** To go on a tour or make a tour of: *touring through Spain; touring Canada.* [From Middle English, a turn, from Latin *tornus*, lathe.]

tour de force (tōōr′ də fôrs′) *n., pl.* **tours de force** (tōōr′ də fôrs′) A feat requiring great skill or strength, often deliberately undertaken for its difficulty.

tour·ism (tŏŏr′ĭz′əm) *n.* **1.** The practice of traveling for pleasure. **2.** The business of providing tours and services for travelers.

tour·ist (tŏŏr′ĭst) *n.* A person who travels for pleasure.

tour·ma·line (tŏŏr′mə-lĭn *or* tŏŏr′mə-lēn′) *n.* A complex crystalline silicate mineral containing aluminum, boron, and other elements. It is used in electronic instruments and in certain varieties as a gemstone.

tour·na·ment (tŏŏr′nə-mənt *or* tûr′nə-mənt) *n.* **1.** A contest made up of a series of games or trials: *a tennis tournament.* **2.** A medieval jousting match.

tour·ne·dos (tŏŏr′nə-dō′) *n., pl.* **tour·ne·dos** (tŏŏr′nə-dō′ *or* tŏŏr′nə-dōz′) A cut of beef from the tenderloin, often bound in bacon or suet for cooking.

tour·ney (tŏŏr′nē *or* tûr′nē) *n., pl.* **tour·neys** A tournament.

tour·ni·quet (tŏŏr′nĭ-kĭt *or* tûr′nĭ-kĭt) *n.* A device, such as a tightly encircling bandage, used to stop temporarily the flow of blood in a large artery in one of the limbs.

tou·sle (tou′zəl *or* tou′səl) *tr.v.* **tou·sled, tou·sling, tou·sles** To disarrange or rumple; dishevel.

Tous·saint L'Ou·ver·ture (tōō-săN′ lōō-vĕr-tür′), **François Dominique** 1743?–1803. Haitian military and political leader who led a successful slave revolt (1791–1793), establishing the first black-led government in the Americas. —SEE NOTE.

tout (tout) *tr.v.* **tout·ed, tout·ing, touts** To promote or praise energetically; publicize: *touting the proposal at the town meeting.*

tow¹ (tō) *tr.v.* **towed, tow·ing, tows** To draw or pull along behind by a chain or line: *tow a car.* See Synonyms at **pull.** ❖ *n.* The act or an instance of towing: *trying to get a tow from a police truck.* ◆ **in tow 1.** In a condition of being towed: *a car with a trailer in tow.* **2.** As a companion or follower: *came to dinner with a friend in tow.* [From Old English *togian.*]

❑ *These sound alike:* **tow¹** (pull), **toe** (foot part), **tow²** (flax).

tow² (tō) *n.* Coarse broken flax or hemp fibers that are ready for spinning. [From Middle English *tou*, possibly from Old English *tow-*, spinning.]

❑ *These sound alike:* **tow²** (flax), **toe** (foot part), **tow¹** (pull).

to·ward (tôrd *or* tə-wôrd′) also **to·wards** (tôrdz) *prep.* **1.** In the direction of: *driving toward the river.* **2.** In a position facing: *She had her back toward me.* **3.** Somewhat before in time: *It started raining toward dawn.* **4.** In relation to; regarding: *a positive attitude toward the future.* **5.** In furtherance or partial fulfillment of: *a payment toward the house.* **6.** With a view to: *efforts toward peace.*

tow·el (tou′əl) *n.* A piece of absorbent cloth or paper used for wiping or drying. ❖ *tr.v.* **tow·eled, tow·el·ing, tow·els** or **tow·elled, tow·el·ling, tow·els** To wipe or rub dry with a towel. [From Middle English *touail*, from Old French *toaille*, of Germanic origin.]

tow·er (tou′ər) *n.* **1.** A building or part of a building that is high in proportion to its width and length. **2.** A tall slender structure used for observation, signaling, or pumping: *a control tower.* **3.** A person who embodies a virtue such as strength or firmness: *His father is a tower of strength.* ❖ *intr.v.* **tow·ered, tow·er·ing, tow·ers** To rise to a conspicuous height: *skyscrapers towering over New York.* [From Old English *tour*, from Latin *turris.*]

tow·er·ing (tou′ər-ĭng) *adj.* **1.** Of imposing height; very tall: *towering peaks.* **2.** Outstanding; preeminent. **3.** Intense; extreme: *in a towering rage.*

tow·head (tō′hĕd′) *n.* A person having white-blond hair resembling tow. **—tow′head′ed** *adj.*

tow·hee (tō′hē *or* tō-hē′) *n.* **1.** A songbird of eastern North America having black, white, and rust-colored feathers in the male. **2.** Any of several similar birds found in western North America.

town (toun) *n.* **1a.** An area in which people live that is larger than a village and smaller than a city. **b.** An area that is a political unit governed by a town meeting, especially in New England. **c.** *Informal* A city: *Chicago is*

BIOGRAPHY

Toussaint L'Ouverture

François Dominique **Toussaint L'Ouverture** was born into slavery in the French colony of Saint Domingue (now Haiti). When the colony's slaves revolted in 1791, Toussaint helped to turn the unplanned rebellion into an organized revolution against the slave owners. The French government, unable to contain the revolt, agreed to ban slavery altogether, and General Toussaint established himself as governor of the colony and set up a semi-independent government. Still hoping for full independence, Toussaint put forth a constitution for Haiti in 1801. The French leader Napoleon, seeking to reestablish slavery, sent a large invasion force to the colony in 1802. Toussaint was arrested and sent to France, where he died in prison, but the French invasion force was decisively defeated by the Haitian army in 1803, and Haiti declared full independence in 1804.

tow¹

tracery
Cathedral of Notre-Dame, Paris, France

track and field
track and field events

a big town. **d.** The residents of a town: *The whole town came out to watch the parade.* **2.** The commercial center or district of an area: *She goes into town every Tuesday.* [From Old English *tūn*, enclosed place, village.]

town crier *n.* A person formerly employed to walk about the streets of a town shouting public announcements.

town hall *n.* The building that contains the offices of the public officials of a town and that houses the town council and courts.

town·ship (**toun′**shĭp′) *n.* **1.** A subdivision of a county in most Northeastern and Midwestern US states. **2.** A unit of land area used in surveying, equal to 36 square miles (93 square kilometers).

towns·peo·ple (**tounz′**pē′pəl) *pl.n.* The inhabitants or citizens of a town or city.

tow·path (**tō′**păth′) *n.* A path along a canal or river used by animals towing boats.

tox·e·mi·a (tŏk-**sē′**mē-ə) *n.* A condition in which the blood contains toxins, either produced by body cells at a local source of infection or by the growth of microorganisms.

tox·ic (**tŏk′**sĭk) *adj.* **1.** Capable of causing injury or death, especially by the action of a biological or chemical toxin; poisonous: *toxic jellyfish stings; toxic industrial wastes.* **2.** Relating to or caused by a toxin or other poison: *toxic hepatitis.* **3.** Relating to a debt for which the borrower is in default and the value of the collateral has fallen so much that its sale would not cover the loan amount. **4.** Causing social tension or unpleasantness: *a toxic personality.* [From Greek *toxikon*, poison for arrows, from *toxon*, bow.]

tox·ic·i·ty (tŏk-**sĭs′**ĭ-tē) *n., pl.* **tox·ic·i·ties 1.** The condition or property of being toxic. **2.** The degree to which a substance is toxic.

tox·i·col·o·gy (tŏk′sĭ-**kŏl′**ə-jē) *n.* The scientific and medical study of poisons, their effects and detection, and the treatment of poisoning. **—tox′i·col′o·gist** *n.*

tox·in (**tŏk′**sĭn) *n.* **1.** A poisonous substance, especially a protein, that is produced by living cells or organisms and is capable of causing disease when introduced into the body. Toxins often stimulate the body to produce antitoxins that can neutralize them. **2.** A toxic substance that does not have a biological origin, such as a chemical pollutant.

toy (toi) *n.* **1.** An object for a child to play with. **2.** Something of little importance; a trifle. **3.** A dog of a very small breed or of a variety smaller than the standard variety of its breed. ❖ *intr.v.* **toyed, toy·ing, toys** To amuse oneself idly; trifle: *talking on the phone and toying with a pencil.*

Tpk. *abbr.* An abbreviation of turnpike.

tr. *abbr.* An abbreviation of: **1.** transitive. **2.** translation.

trace¹ (trās) *n.* **1.** A visible mark made or left by the passage of a person, thing, or animal. **2.** A barely perceivable indication; a touch. **3a.** An extremely small amount. **b.** Something, such as an element or chemical compound, that is present in a substance or mixture in very small amounts. **4.** A line drawn on a graph to represent a continuous set of values of a variable: *the trace made by a seismograph.* ❖ *v.* **traced, trac·ing, trac·es** *—tr.* **1.** To follow the course or trail of: *trace a lost letter.* **2.** To follow the history or development of: *trace the beginnings of the Industrial Revolution.* **3.** To locate or discover by searching or researching evidence. **4.** To draw or sketch (a figure). **5.** To form (letters) with special care. **6.** To copy by following lines seen through a sheet of transparent paper. *—intr.* **1.** To make one's way along a trail or course. **2.** To have origins; be traceable. [From Middle English, from Old French *tracier*, to make one's way.] **—trace′a·ble** *adj.*

trace² (trās) *n.* One of two side straps or chains connecting a harnessed draft animal to a vehicle. [From Middle English *trais*, from Old French, from Latin *tractus*, a hauling.]

trac·er (**trā′**sər) *n.* **1a.** A person employed to locate missing people or goods. **b.** A search organized to locate missing people or goods. **2.** A bullet that leaves a luminous or smoky trail. **3.** An identifiable substance, such as a dye or radioactive isotope, that can be followed through the course of a mechanical, chemical, or biological process, providing information about the process or the distribution of the substances involved in it.

trac·er·y (**trā′**sə-rē) *n., pl.* **trac·er·ies** Ornamental work of interlaced and branching lines.

tra·che·a (**trā′**kē-ə) *n., pl.* **tra·che·ae** (**trā′**kē-ē′) or **tra·che·as** A thin-walled tube of cartilage and membrane leading from the larynx to the bronchi and carrying air to the lungs; the windpipe.

tra·che·ot·o·my (trā′kē-**ŏt′**ə-mē) *n., pl.* **tra·che·ot·o·mies** The procedure of cutting into the trachea through the neck, as to make an artificial opening for breathing.

tra·cho·ma (trə-**kō′**mə) *n.* A contagious disease caused by bacteria that results in severe inflammation of the membranes that line the eyelid and cover the eyeball.

track (trăk) *n.* **1.** A mark or trail of marks left by something that has passed: *tire tracks.* **2.** A pathway or course over which something moves: *a bicycle track in the park.* **3.** A course of action or way of proceeding: *on the right track.* **4.** Awareness of something occurring or passing: *Keep track of the score.* **5.** A rail or set of parallel rails on which a train or trolley runs: *railroad tracks.* **6.** A groove or ridge that holds or guides a moving part or device: *The curtain had come off its track.* **7.** Either of the continuous metal belts with which vehicles such as bulldozers and tanks move over the ground. **8.** A racetrack. **9.** Track and field. **10.** A path or band on a film or magnetic tape on which sound, images, or other information is recorded. **11.** A selection from a sound recording: *the title track of the album.* **12.** One of the separate sound recordings that are combined to produce a stereophonic sound reproduction: *the vocal track of a song.* ❖ *tr.v.* **tracked, track·ing, tracks 1.** To follow the footprints or trail of: *They tracked the animal through the woods.* **2.** To carry on the feet and deposit as tracks: *Don't track mud on the floor.* **3.** To observe or monitor the course of: *Radar is used to track weather balloons.* **4.** To watch the progress of; follow: *She tracked the performance of their best pitcher.* ◆ **track down** To pursue until found or captured: *The hounds tracked down the fox. I finally tracked down a copy of the book I wanted.* [From Middle English *trak*, from Old French *trac*, perhaps of Germanic origin.] **—track′er** *n.*

track and field *n.* Athletic events performed on a running track and the field associated with it. **—track′-and-field′** *adj.*

track·ball (**trăk′**bôl′) *n.* A ball mounted in an input device and rotated to control a pointer on a computer screen.

track·ing station (**trăk′**ĭng) *n.* A facility containing instruments for observing and maintaining contact with an artificial satellite or spacecraft.

track meet *n.* A track-and-field competition between two or more teams.

track record *n.* *Informal* A record of actual performance or accomplishment.

tract¹ (trăkt) *n.* **1.** An expanse of land or water. **2a.** A system of body organs and tissues that together perform a specialized function: *the digestive tract.* **b.** A bundle of nerve fibers that begin and end at the same place and have the same function. [From Middle English, period of time, from Latin *tractus*, course, space, period of time, from *trahere*, to draw.]

tract² (trăkt) *n.* A leaflet or pamphlet containing a declaration, especially one put out by a religious or political

ă	pat	ôr	core
ā	pay	oi	boy
âr	care	ou	out
ä	father	o͝o	took
ĕ	pet	o͝or	lure
ē	be	o͞o	boot
ĭ	pit	ŭ	cut
ī	bite	ûr	urge
îr	pier	th	thin
ŏ	pot	*th*	this
ō	toe	zh	vision
ô	paw	ə	about

group. [From Middle English *tracte*, treatise, probably short for Latin *tractātus*, from *tractāre*, to discuss.]

trac·ta·ble (trăk′tə-bəl) *adj.* **1.** Easily managed or controlled; governable: *a tractable child.* **2.** Easily worked; malleable: *tractable metals.* **—trac′ta·bly** *adv.*

trac·tion (trăk′shən) *n.* **1.** The act of drawing or pulling, especially the drawing of a vehicle or load over a surface. **2.** The condition of being drawn or pulled. **3.** Pulling power, as of a draft animal or an engine. **4.** The friction that prevents a wheel from slipping or skidding over the surface on which it runs. **5a.** A pulling force applied to a part of the body, as to correct a broken or dislocated bone. **b.** The condition of having such force applied: *a leg in traction.* [From Latin *tractus*, past participle of *trahere*, to pull, draw.] —SEE NOTE AT **detract.**

trac·tor (trăk′tər) *n.* **1.** A vehicle powered by a gasoline or diesel engine, equipped with large tires that have deep treads, and used especially for pulling farming equipment or machinery. **2.** A truck having a cab and no body, used for pulling large vehicles such as trailers and vans. [From Latin *tractus*, past participle of *trahere*, to draw.] —SEE NOTE AT **detract.**

trade (trād) *n.* **1.** The business of buying and selling goods; commerce. **2.** A branch or kind of business: *the building and construction trades.* **3.** An exchange of one thing for another, as by bartering: *Everyone brings something to market for sale or trade.* **4.** An occupation, especially one requiring special skill with the hands; a craft: *the tailor's trade.* **5.** often **trades** The trade winds. ❖ *v.* **trad·ed, trad·ing, trades** *—intr.* **1.** To engage in buying, selling, or bartering: *He traded for furs along the Oregon coast.* **2.** To exchange one thing for another. **3.** To shop regularly: *He trades at the local grocery store.* *—tr.* **1.** To exchange or swap: *trade books with a friend.* **2.** To buy and sell (stocks, for example). ◆ **trade in** To surrender or sell (an old or used item), using the proceeds as partial payment on a new purchase. [From Middle English, course, from Middle Low German.]

trade-in (trād′ĭn′) *n.* Something accepted as partial payment for a new purchase.

trade·mark (trād′märk′) *n.* A name or symbol that is used to identify a product or service, especially an officially registered name or symbol that is protected against use by others. ❖ *tr.v.* **trade·marked, trade·mark·ing, trade·marks 1.** To label (a product) with a trademark. **2.** To register as a trademark.

trade name *n.* A name under which a product or service is marketed or under which a business operates.

trade·off (trād′ôf′) *n.* An exchange of one thing in return for another, especially a giving up of something desirable for something else regarded as more desirable.

trad·er (trā′dər) *n.* **1.** A person who trades; a dealer. **2.** A ship employed in foreign trade.

trade school *n.* A school that offers training in skilled trades; a vocational school.

trades·man (trādz′mən) *n.* **1.** A man who practices a manual trade. **2.** A man engaged in retail trade.

trades·per·son (trādz′pûr′sən) *n.* **1.** A person who practices a manual trade. **2.** A person engaged in retail trade.

trades·wom·an (trādz′wo͝om′ən) *n.* **1.** A woman who practices a manual trade. **2.** A woman who is a merchant.

trade union *n.* A labor union.

trade wind *n.* often **trade winds** Any of a consistent system of winds over most of the tropics, blowing from the northeast in the Northern Hemisphere and from the southeast in the Southern Hemisphere.

trad·ing post (trā′dĭng) *n.* A station or store in a sparsely settled area established by traders for bartering.

tra·di·tion (trə-dĭsh′ən) *n.* **1.** The passing down of elements of a culture from generation to generation, especially orally: *cultural practices that are preserved by tradition.* **2.** A custom or usage handed down from generation to generation: *the traditions of Tibetan Buddhism.* **3.** A set of such customs or usages: *We follow our family tradition and have a reunion each fall.* [From Middle English *tradicioun*, from Latin *trāditiō*, from *trādere*, to hand over : *trāns-*, over + *dare*, to give.]

tra·di·tion·al (trə-dĭsh′ə-nəl) *adj.* Relating to or in accord with tradition. **—tra·di′tion·al·ly** *adv.*

Tra·fal·gar (trə-făl′gər), **Cape** A cape on the southwest coast of Spain northwest of the Strait of Gibraltar. The British navy defeated the French and Spanish here in 1805.

traf·fic (trăf′ĭk) *n.* **1.** The movement of vehicles, people, or messages along routes of transportation or communication: *analyzed patterns of traffic at the dangerous intersection; laid fiber-optic cables that handle Internet traffic.* **2.** The amount, as of vehicles, people, or aircraft, in movement: *Traffic is heavy during rush hour.* **3a.** The commercial exchange of goods; trade. **b.** Illegal or improper commercial activity: *traffic in drugs.* ❖ *intr.v.* **traf·ficked, traf·fick·ing, traf·fics** To carry on trade or other dealings. **—traf′fick·er** *n.*

traffic circle *n.* A circular intersection of roads around which traffic moves in one direction.

traffic light *n.* A road signal for directing traffic by means of colored lights.

tra·ge·di·an (trə-jē′dē-ən) *n.* **1.** A writer of tragedies. **2.** An actor who performs tragic roles in the theater.

tra·ge·di·enne (trə-jē′dē-ĕn′) *n.* A woman who performs tragic roles in the theater.

trag·e·dy (trăj′ĭ-dē) *n., pl.* **trag·e·dies 1.** A serious play or literary work that ends with great misfortune or ruin for the main character or characters, especially as a result of some personal flaw or weakness. **2.** The branch of literature including such works. **3.** A disastrous event; a calamity. [From Middle English *tragedie*, from Greek *tragōidiā*, *tragos*, goat, *aoidē*, song.]

trag·ic (trăj′ĭk) *adj.* **1.** Relating to dramatic tragedy. **2.** Writing or performing tragedy. **3.** Bringing or involving death, grief, or destruction: *a tragic accident.* **—trag′i·cal·ly** *adv.*

trag·i·com·e·dy (trăj′ĭ-kŏm′ĭ-dē) *n.* A film, television show, or play that has qualities of both tragedy and comedy.

trail (trāl) *v.* **trailed, trail·ing, trails** *—tr.* **1.** To allow to drag or stream behind, as along the ground: *a child trailing a toy dog.* **2.** To drag (the body, for example) wearily. **3.** To follow the traces or scent of, as in hunting; track: *hounds trailing a bear.* **4.** To follow behind: *The great ship was trailed by a dozen small boats.* **5.** To lag behind: *Our team trailed the visiting team by a score of 14 to 7.* *—intr.* **1.** To drag or be dragged along, brushing the ground: *Her long skirt was trailing on the floor.* **2.** To extend, grow, or droop loosely over a surface. **3.** To drift in a thin stream: *smoke trailing from a dying fire.* **4.** To become gradually fainter: *Her voice trailed off.* **5.** To walk or proceed with dragging steps: *trailed along in glum silence.* **6.** To be behind in competition; lag: *The home team trailed by 10 points.* ❖ *n.* **1.** A path or beaten track, as through woods or wilderness. **2.** A designated course through one or more bodies of water, as for recreational boaters. **3.** A mark or trace left by a moving body: *The car left a trail of dust.* **4.** The scent of a person or animal: *hounds following the trail of a bear.* **5.** Something that is drawn along or follows behind; a train: *The mayor came down the street followed by a trail of reporters.* **6.** Something that hangs loose and long. [From Middle English *trailen*, probably from Old French *trailler*, to hunt without a foreknown course.]

trail bike *n.* A dirt bike or a mountain bike.

trail·blaz·er (trāl′blā′zər) *n.* **1.** A person who blazes

trackball

tractor
tractor pulling a plow

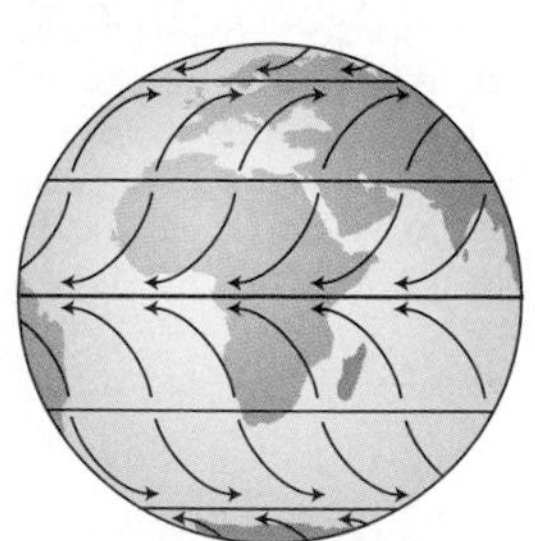
trade wind
As warm, moist air rises along the equator, surface air moves in to take its place, creating trade winds.

WORD BUILDING

trans– The prefix **trans–** comes from the Latin prefix *trāns–*, from the Latin preposition *trāns,* "across, beyond, through." Many of the most common English words beginning with *trans–* are derived from Latin words or elements, such as *transfer, transfuse, translate, transmit, transpire,* and *transport.* Another large group of words has *trans–* in combination with English adjectives, as in *transatlantic, transcontinental, transoceanic, transpacific,* and *transpolar,* with the meaning "across" or "through" a particular geographic element.

WORD BUILDING

transfer The word root *fer–* in English words comes from the Latin verb *ferre,* "to carry, bear." **Transfer** literally means "to carry across," and therefore "to carry from place to place" (using the Latin prefix *trāns–*, across); **confer** is "to bring with oneself (to someone)," and therefore "to give, bestow" (*com–*, "with"); **defer** is "to bring away," and therefore "to carry elsewhere, put off" (*dē–*, "down, away"); **refer** is "to carry back to an earlier condition" (*re–*, "back, again"); and **suffer** is "to carry (oneself) under," and therefore "to undergo, experience, experience something bad" (*suf–*, a form of *sub–*, "under").

ă	pat	ôr	core
ā	pay	oi	boy
âr	care	ou	out
ä	father	ŏŏ	took
ĕ	pet	ŏŏr	lure
ē	be	ōō	boot
ĭ	pit	ŭ	cut
ī	bite	ûr	urge
îr	pier	th	thin
ŏ	pot	*th*	this
ō	toe	zh	vision
ô	paw	ə	about

a trail. **2.** An innovative leader in a field; a pioneer.

trail·er (trā′lər) *n.* **1.** A vehicle that has no motor and that is pulled behind a car, truck, or other vehicle to carry or move something. **2.** A furnished vehicle that can be hauled by a car or truck and used when parked as a home or office. **3.** A short filmed advertisement for a movie; a preview. **—trail′er·a·ble** *adj.*

train (trān) *n.* **1a.** A series of connected railroad cars pulled or pushed by one or more locomotives. **b.** An underground railroad in a city; a subway. **2.** A long line of moving people, animals, or vehicles: *a wagon train.* **3.** A part of a gown that trails behind the wearer. **4.** A staff of followers; a retinue: *people in the king's train.* **5.** An orderly succession of related events or thoughts; a sequence: *The ring of the telephone interrupted my train of thought.* **6.** A set of linked mechanical parts: *a train of gears.* ❖ *v.* **trained, train·ing, trains** *—tr.* **1.** To instruct or show a certain way of acting or behaving: *training a child to be polite.* **2.** To make proficient with specialized instruction and practice. See Synonyms at **teach. 3.** To prepare physically, as with regular exercise: *coaches training the players for the championship game.* **4.** To cause (a plant or one's hair) to take a desired course or shape. *—intr.* To give or undergo a course of training: *trained daily for the marathon.* [From Middle English, a drawing out, from Old French, from *trainer,* to drag.]

train·ee (trā-nē′) *n.* A person who is being trained.

train·er (trā′nər) *n.* A person who trains, especially one who coaches athletes, racehorses, or show animals.

train·ing (trā′nĭng) *n.* **1.** The process or routine of one who trains. **2.** The state of being trained.

train·load (trān′lōd′) *n.* The number of occupants or the amount of material that a passenger or freight train can hold.

train·man (trān′mən) *n.* A member of the operating crew on a railroad train, especially the brakeman.

traipse (trāps) *intr.v.* **traipsed, traips·ing, traips·es** To walk or wander about. [Possibly from Old French *trespasser,* to trespass.]

trait (trāt) *n.* **1.** A distinctive feature, as of a person's character. See Synonyms at **quality. 2.** A physical or behavioral feature of an organism: *the evolution of certain floral traits.*

trai·tor (trā′tər) *n.* A person who betrays one's country, a cause, or a trust, especially one who commits treason. [From Middle English *traitour,* from Latin *trāditor,* from *trādere,* to betray.]

trai·tor·ous (trā′tər-əs) *adj.* **1.** Having the character of a traitor; disloyal: *traitorous behavior.* **2.** Constituting treason: *a traitorous act.*

tra·jec·to·ry (trə-jĕk′tə-rē) *n., pl.* **tra·jec·to·ries** The path of a moving body or particle. [From Latin *trāiectus,* past participle of *trāicere,* to throw across.]

tram (trăm) *n.* **1.** *Chiefly British* A streetcar. **2.** An open wagon or car run on tracks in a coal mine.

tram·mel (trăm′əl) *n.* **1.** A shackle used to teach a horse to amble. **2.** Something that restricts activity or free movement; a restraint. ❖ *tr.v.* **tram·meled, tram·mel·ing, tram·mels** or **tram·melled, tram·mel·ling, tram·mels** To hinder the activity or free movement of.

tramp (trămp) *v.* **tramped, tramp·ing, tramps** *—intr.* To walk with a firm heavy step: *tramp up the stairs. —tr.* **1.** To traverse on foot: *tramp the fields in search of wild berries.* **2.** To tread down; trample: *tramp down snow.* ❖ *n.* **1.** A heavy footfall. **2.** A walking trip; a hike: *a long tramp through the woods.* **3.** A person who travels aimlessly about as a vagrant. **4.** A cargo vessel that has no regular schedule but takes on freight whenever hired to do so.

tram·ple (trăm′pəl) *v.* **tram·pled, tram·pling, tram·ples** *—tr.* To tread heavily so as to crush, bruise, or destroy: *The dog trampled the flowers in the garden. —intr.* To treat harshly, as if tramping upon: *He is always trampling on her feelings.* ❖ *n.* The action or sound of trampling. **—tram′pler** *n.*

tram·po·line (trăm′pə-lēn′) *n.* A sheet of taut fabric attached with springs to a metal frame and used for gymnastic springing and tumbling. [From Italian *tràmpoli,* stilts, of Germanic origin.]

trance (trăns) *n.* **1.** A condition of altered consciousness during which voluntary movement is lost, produced by hypnotism, drugs, or catalepsy. **2.** A dazed condition, as between sleeping and waking. **3.** A condition in which little or no attention is paid to one's surroundings, as in daydreaming or deep thought. [From Middle English *traunce,* from Latin *trānsīre,* to go over or across.]

tran·quil (trăng′kwəl *or* trăn′kwəl) *adj.* **1.** Free from commotion or disturbance: *a tranquil lake.* **2.** Free from anxiety, tension, or restlessness: *leading a tranquil life.* See Synonyms at **calm.** [From Middle English, from Latin *tranquillus.*] **—tran′quil·ly** *adv.*

tran·quil·i·ty or **tran·quil·li·ty** (trăng-**kwĭl′**ĭ-tē *or* trăn-**kwĭl′**ĭ-tē) *n.* The quality or condition of being tranquil; serenity.

tran·quil·ize (trăng′kwə-līz′ *or* trăn′kwə-līz′) *tr. & intr.v.* **tran·quil·ized, tran·quil·iz·ing, tran·quil·iz·es** To make or become tranquil or calm.

tran·quil·iz·er (trăng′kwə-līz′ər *or* trăn′kwə-līz′ər) *n.* Any of various drugs used to relieve tension or anxiety.

trans (trănz) *adj.* Transgender.

trans– *pref.* A prefix that means: **1.** Across; beyond: *transpolar.* **2.** Through: *transcontinental.* **3.** Change; transfer: *transliterate.* —SEE NOTE.

trans·act (trăn-**săkt′** *or* trăn-**zăkt′**) *v.* **trans·act·ed, trans·act·ing, trans·acts** *—tr.* To do, carry out, or conduct (business or affairs). *—intr.* To conduct business. —SEE NOTE AT **react.**

trans·ac·tion (trăn-**săk′**shən *or* trăn-**zăk′**shən) *n.* **1.** The act of transacting or the fact of being transacted: *the transaction of business.* **2.** Something transacted, especially a business agreement or exchange: *cash transactions only.*

trans·at·lan·tic (trăns′ət-**lăn′**tĭk *or* trănz′ət-**lăn′**tĭk) *adj.* **1.** Situated on or coming from the other side of the Atlantic Ocean: *transatlantic military bases.* **2.** Spanning or crossing the Atlantic Ocean: *a transatlantic flight.*

tran·scend (trăn-**sĕnd′**) *tr.v.* **tran·scend·ed, tran·scend·ing, tran·scends 1.** To pass beyond the limits of: *an experience that transcends human understanding.* **2.** To be greater than, as in quality or power; surpass: *a composition that transcends all his previous ones.* [From Middle English *transcenden,* from Latin *trānscendere* : *trāns-*, over + *scandere,* to climb.]

tran·scen·dent (trăn-**sĕn′**dənt) *adj.* Surpassing others; preeminent or supreme: *a scientist of transcendent genius.*

tran·scen·den·tal (trăn′sĕn-**dĕn′**tl) *adj.* Beyond common thought or experience; mystical or supernatural. **—tran′scen·den′tal·ly** *adv.*

trans·con·ti·nen·tal (trăns′kŏn-tə-**nĕn′**tl) *adj.* Spanning or crossing a continent: *a transcontinental railroad line.*

tran·scribe (trăn-**skrīb′**) *tr.v.* **tran·scribed, tran·scrib·ing, tran·scribes 1.** To write or type a copy of: *transcribe a dictated letter.* **2.** To adapt or arrange (a musical composition). **3.** To represent (speech sounds) using phonetic symbols. **4.** To transfer (information) from one computer recording and storing system to another. [From Latin *trānscrībere* : *trāns-*, over + *scrībere,* to write.]

tran·script (trăn′skrĭpt′) *n.* **1.** Something transcribed, especially a written, typed, or printed copy: *a transcript of a radio interview.* **2.** A record of a student's academic performance issued by a school.

tran·scrip·tion (trăn-**skrĭp′**shən) *n.* **1.** The act or process of transcribing. **2.** An adaptation of a musical composition. **3.** A representation of speech sounds in phonetic symbols. **4.** The process in a cell by which genetic material is copied from a strand of DNA to a strand of messenger RNA.

tran·sept (trăn′sĕpt′) *n.* Either of the two lateral arms of a church built in the shape of a cross.

trans fatty acid *n.* An unsaturated fatty acid produced when vegetable oils are converted to solid fats. Trans fatty acids were once commonly used in margarines, shortenings, and fried foods, but they have been found to increase the risk of heart disease and have mostly been replaced with other ingredients in food products. Also called *trans fat.*

trans·fer (trăns-**fûr′** *or* **trăns′**fər) *v.* **trans·ferred, trans·fer·ring, trans·fers** —*tr.* **1.** To move or cause to pass from one place, person, or thing to another: *Bees transfer pollen from one flower to another.* **2.** To shift the ownership of (property) to another. **3.** To move (a design, for example) from one surface to another, as by impression: *Trace the design, then transfer it to the leather.* —*intr.* **1.** To move oneself from one location or job to another. **2.** To change from one public conveyance to another: *transferred to another bus.* ❖ *n.* (**trăns′**fər) **1.** also **trans·fer·al** (trăns-**fûr′**əl) The conveyance or removal of something from one place, person, or thing to another: *the transfer of land by purchase.* **2.** A person or thing that transfers or is transferred, as a student who changes schools. **3.** A design conveyed by contact from one surface to another. **4a.** A ticket entitling a passenger to change from one public conveyance to another as part of one trip. **b.** A place where such a change is made. [From Middle English *transferren,* from Latin *trānsferre* : *trāns-,* across + *ferre,* to carry.] —SEE NOTE.

trans·fer·a·ble (trăns-**fûr′**ə-bəl) *adj.* Capable of being transferred: *a ticket that is not transferable to others.*

trans·fer·ence (trăns-**fûr′**əns *or* **trăns′**fər-əns) *n.* **1.** The act or process of transferring. **2.** The fact of being transferred.

transfer RNA *n.* A form of RNA that delivers amino acids to the ribosomes during protein synthesis.

trans·fig·u·ra·tion (trăns-fĭg′yə-**rā′**shən) *n.* **1.** A marked change in form or appearance, especially one that exalts or glorifies. **2. Transfiguration** In the New Testament, the sudden radiant change in Jesus's appearance that took place in the presence of the Apostles.

trans·fig·ure (trăns-**fĭg′**yər) *tr.v.* **trans·fig·ured, trans·fig·ur·ing, trans·fig·ures 1.** To change the form or appearance of; transform. **2.** To glorify or exalt.

trans·fix (trăns-**fĭks′**) *tr.v.* **trans·fixed, trans·fix·ing, trans·fix·es 1.** To render motionless, as with terror: *The sight of the approaching tornado transfixed him.* **2.** To pierce or impale with a pointed weapon or object.

trans·form (trăns-**fôrm′**) *tr.v.* **trans·formed, trans·form·ing, trans·forms 1.** To change markedly the form or appearance of. **2.** To change the nature, function, or condition of; convert: *A steam engine transforms heat into energy.* **3.** To perform a mathematical transformation on.

trans·for·ma·tion (trăns′fər-**mā′**shən) *n.* **1.** The act or an instance of transforming. **2.** The state of being transformed. **3.** A marked change, as in appearance, usually for the better. **4a.** The conversion of an algebraic expression to another expression of a different form. **b.** The replacement of the variables in an algebraic expression or equation by their values in terms of another set of variables. **—trans′for·ma′tion·al** *adj.*

trans·form·er (trăns-**fôr′**mər) *n.* A device used to transfer electrical energy from one circuit to another, often with a change of voltage or current.

trans·fuse (trăns-**fyo͞oz′**) *tr.v.* **trans·fused, trans·fus·ing, trans·fus·es 1.** To pour (something) out of one vessel into another. **2.** To cause to be instilled or imparted. **3.** To diffuse through; permeate: *The glade was transfused with sunlight.* **4.** To give a transfusion of or to: *transfuse blood; transfuse a patient.* [From Middle English *transfusen,* to transmit, from Latin *trānsfundere,* to transfuse : *trāns-,* across + *fundere,* to pour.]

trans·fu·sion (trăns-**fyo͞o′**zhən) *n.* **1.** The act or process of transfusing. **2.** The transfer of blood from one person to another. —SEE NOTE.

trans·gen·der (trăns-**jĕn′**dər *or* trănz-**jĕn′**dər) *adj.* Relating to or being a person whose gender identity does not conform to that typically associated with the sex to which they were assigned at birth.

trans·gen·ic (trăns-**jĕn′**ĭk *or* trănz-**jĕn′**ĭk) *adj.* **1.** Relating to or being an organism whose genome has been altered by the transfer of a gene or genes from another species or breed: *transgenic mice; transgenic corn.* **2.** Relating to the study of transgenic organisms: *transgenic research.* ❖ *n.* A transgenic organism: *labeling transgenics.*

trans·gress (trăns-**grĕs′** *or* trănz-**grĕs′**) *v.* **trans·gressed, trans·gress·ing, trans·gress·es** —*tr.* **1.** To go beyond or over (a limit or boundary): *His conduct transgressed the boundaries of politeness.* **2.** To act in violation of (a law, for example). —*intr.* To commit an offense by violating a law, principle, or duty. [From Middle English *transgressen,* from Latin *trānsgredī,* to step across.] **—trans·gres′sor** *n.* —SEE NOTE AT **progress.**

trans·gres·sion (trăns-**grĕsh′**ən *or* trănz-**grĕsh′**ən) *n.* A violation of a law, principle, or duty.

tran·si·ent (**trăn′**zē-ənt *or* **trăn′**zhənt *or* **trăn′**shənt) *adj.* **1.** Passing away with time; transitory: *transient happiness.* **2.** Remaining in a place only a brief time: *a transient guest at a hotel.* ❖ *n.* A person or thing that is transient, especially a person making a brief stay at a hotel or boarding house. [From Latin *trānsiēns,* present participle of *trānsīre,* to go over.] **—tran′si·ence, tran′si·en·cy** *n.*

tran·sis·tor (trăn-**zĭs′**tər *or* trăn-**sĭs′**tər) *n.* **1.** A semiconductor device having at least three electrical contacts and used for amplification and switching. **2.** Any of various devices serving the same purpose but employing a different technology: *an optical transistor.* **3.** A radio equipped with transistors.

tran·sis·tor·ized (trăn-**zĭs′**tə-rīzd′ *or* trăn-**sĭs′**tə-rīzd′) *adj.* Equipped with transistors: *a transistorized circuit.*

tran·sit (**trăn′**sĭt *or* **trăn′**zĭt) *n.* **1.** The act of passing over, across, or through; passage. **2a.** The moving of people or goods from one place to another, especially on a local public transportation system. **b.** The vehicles or system of vehicles used for such moving of people or goods: *I take public transit to work each morning.* **3a.** The passage of a celestial object across the meridian of an observer. **b.** The passage of a celestial object or its shadow across the disk of a larger celestial object. **4.** A surveying instrument consisting of a telescope provided with scales for measuring horizontal and vertical angles. ❖ *tr.v.* **tran·sit·ed, tran·sit·ing, tran·sits** To pass over, across, or through.

tran·si·tion (trăn-**zĭsh′**ən *or* trăn-**sĭsh′**ən) *n.* **1.** Change from one form, state, style, or place to another. **2.** Change from one subject or section to another in a piece of writing: *Your report needs a transition from your analysis of the data to your conclusion.* **—tran·si′tion·al** *adj.*

tran·si·tive (**trăn′**sĭ-tĭv *or* **trăn′**zĭ-tĭv) *adj.* Relating to a verb that requires a direct object to complete its meaning. In the sentence *I bought a book,* the verb *bought* is transitive. **—tran′si·tive·ly** *adv.* —SEE NOTE AT **verb.**

transitive property *n.* The property of a relationship between three elements such that if the relationship holds between the first and second elements and between the second and third elements, it must also hold between the first and third elements. For example, being greater than something else is a transitive relationship,

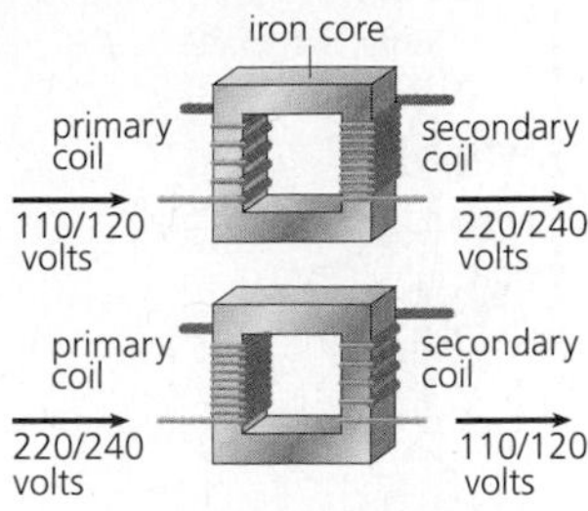

transformer

Change in voltage is directly related to the number of turns of the wire. At top, outgoing voltage is doubled because the secondary coil has twice as many turns as the primary coil. At bottom, voltage is halved.

WORD BUILDING

transfusion The word root *fus–* in English words comes from the Latin word *fūsus,* the past participle of the verb *fundere,* "to pour." A **transfusion,** then, is literally "a pouring out of one thing into another" (using the Latin prefix *trāns–,* "across, change in"). **Diffuse** means "widespread, scattered," literally "poured out all over the place" (*dif–,* a form of *dis–,* "apart, in different directions"). To **infuse** means "to pour into, fill" (*in–,* "in, into"). And **profuse** means "generous, abundant," literally "poured forth freely" (*pro–,* "forth").

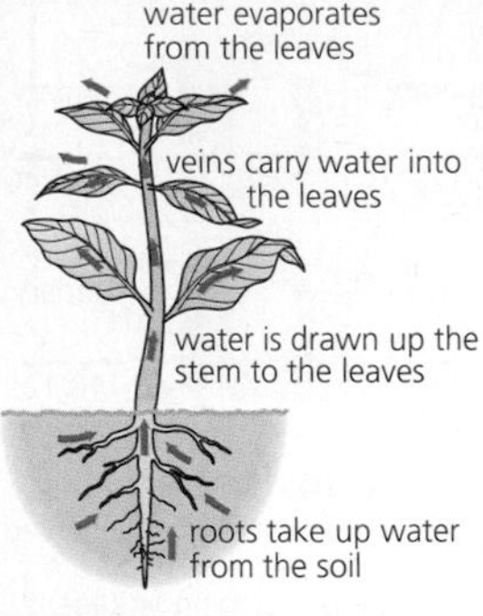

transpiration

SCIENCE

transpiration For a plant to carry out photosynthesis, it has to take in carbon dioxide from the atmosphere and release oxygen. This gas exchange takes place through tiny openings in the leaves, called *stomata.* A consequence of this process is that water vapor, coming from the moist surfaces of the cells inside the plant, is released through the stomata. This loss of water vapor is called **transpiration.** Plants need much more water than animals do because they are constantly losing so much through their leaves. It is estimated that ten percent of the water vapor in the atmosphere comes from transpiration. Plants can control this process to some extent, though; during dry periods, stomata close tightly to reduce the amount of water vapor that escapes.

ă	pat	ôr	core
ā	pay	oi	boy
âr	care	ou	out
ä	father	o͝o	took
ĕ	pet	o͝or	lure
ē	be	o͞o	boot
ĭ	pit	ŭ	cut
ī	bite	ûr	urge
îr	pier	th	thin
ŏ	pot	*th*	this
ō	toe	zh	vision
ô	paw	ə	about

because if 12 is greater than 6 and 6 is greater than 3, then 12 must be greater than 3.

tran·si·to·ry (trăn′sĭ-tôr′ē *or* trăn′zĭ-tôr′ē) *adj.* Existing or lasting only briefly; short-lived: *transitory happiness.*

trans·late (trăns′lāt′ *or* trănz′lāt′) *v.* **trans·lat·ed, trans·lat·ing, trans·lates** —*tr.* **1.** To express in another language: *translate a book.* **2.** To put into simpler terms; explain or interpret: *It is difficult to see how you could translate his silence.* —*intr.* **1a.** To make a translation. **b.** To work as a translator. **2.** To be capable of being expressed in another language: *Her poetry translates well.* [From Middle English *translaten,* from Latin *trānslātus,* past participle of *trānsferre,* to transfer.]

trans·la·tion (trăns-lā′shən *or* trănz-lā′shən) *n.* **1.** The act or process of translating. **2.** A translated version of a text: *translations from the French.* **3.** The process by which messenger RNA directs the amino acid sequence of a growing protein during protein synthesis.

trans·la·tor (trăns′lā′tər *or* trănz′lā′tər) *n.* A person who translates, especially a person employed to render written works into another language.

trans·lit·er·ate (trăns-lĭt′ə-rāt′ *or* trănz-lĭt′ə-rāt′) *tr.v.* **trans·lit·er·at·ed, trans·lit·er·at·ing, trans·lit·er·ates** To represent (letters or words) in the corresponding characters of another alphabet. —**trans·lit′er·a′tion** *n.*

trans·lu·cent (trăns-lo͞o′sənt *or* trănz-lo͞o′sənt) *adj.* Transmitting light, but scattering it enough so that images become blurred or are indistinct. —**trans·lu′cence, trans·lu′cen·cy** *n.*

trans man *n.* A transgender person who identifies as a man.

trans·mi·gra·tion (trăns′mī-grā′shən *or* trănz′mī-grā′shən) *n.* In theology, the passing of a soul at death into another body; reincarnation.

trans·mis·sion (trăns-mĭsh′ən *or* trănz-mĭsh′ən) *n.* **1.** The act or process of transmitting: *the transmission of news; the transmission of a disease.* **2.** Something, such as a message, that is transmitted. **3.** An assembly of gears and associated parts by which power is transmitted from an engine to an axle in a motor vehicle.

trans·mit (trăns-mĭt′ *or* trănz-mĭt′) *tr.v.* **trans·mit·ted, trans·mit·ting, trans·mits 1.** To send from one person, place, or thing to another: *transmit a message.* **2.** To cause to spread: *transmit an infection.* **3.** To pass on (a trait or traits) by biological inheritance. **4.** To send out (a signal), as by wire or radio. **5.** To cause or allow (energy or a disturbance) to travel or spread, as through a medium: *Glass transmits light.* **6.** To carry (power, force, or energy) from one part of a machine to another. [From Middle English *transmitten,* from Latin *trānsmittere* : *trāns-,* across + *mittere,* to send.]

trans·mit·tal (trăns-mĭt′l *or* trănz-mĭt′l) *n.* The act or process of transmitting; a transmission.

trans·mit·ter (trăns-mĭt′ər *or* trănz-mĭt′ər) *n.* **1.** A person or thing that transmits. **2.** A device used in a communications system to send forth information, especially: **a.** A switching device that opens and closes a telegraph circuit. **b.** The part of a telephone that changes sounds into electrical impulses that are sent over wires. **c.** A device that generates a radio signal, modulates it with information, often a voice or music signal, and radiates it by means of an antenna.

trans·mu·ta·tion (trăns′myo͞o-tā′shən *or* trănz′myo͞o-tā′shən) *n.* In physics, the changing of one element into another by one or more nuclear reactions.

trans·mute (trăns-myo͞ot′ *or* trănz-myo͞ot′) *tr.v.* **trans·mut·ed, trans·mut·ing, trans·mutes** To change from one form, nature, state, or substance into another; transform: *Socialism transmuted the political life of the country.* [From Middle English *transmuten,* from Latin *trānsmūtāre* : *trāns-,* over + *mūtāre,* to change.]

trans-Nep·tu·ni·an object (trăns′nĕp-to͞o′nē-ən *or* trănz′nĕp-to͞o′nē-ən) *n.* A celestial object that orbits the sun at a greater distance on average than Neptune. Pluto and Eris are trans-Neptunian objects.

trans·o·ce·an·ic (trăns′ō-shē-ăn′ĭk *or* trănz′ō-shē-ăn′ĭk) *adj.* **1.** Situated beyond or on the other side of the ocean. **2.** Spanning or crossing the ocean: *transoceanic navigation.*

tran·som (trăn′səm) *n.* **1a.** A horizontal crosspiece over a door. **b.** A small hinged window above a door or another window. **2.** A horizontal dividing piece in a window.

tran·son·ic (trăn-sŏn′ĭk) *adj.* Relating to conditions of flight or airflow at speeds near the speed of sound.

trans·pa·cif·ic (trăns′pə-sĭf′ĭk *or* trănz′pə-sĭf′ĭk) *adj.* **1.** Situated on or coming from the other side of the Pacific Ocean. **2.** Spanning or crossing the Pacific Ocean: *a transpacific journey.*

trans·par·en·cy (trăns-pâr′ən-sē) *n., pl.* **trans·par·en·cies 1.** The condition or state of being transparent. **2.** A transparent object, especially a photographic slide.

trans·par·ent (trăns-pâr′ənt) *adj.* **1.** Capable of transmitting light so that objects and images are clearly visible, as if there were nothing between the observer and the light source. **2.** Allowing electromagnetic radiation of a specified frequency, such as x-rays, light, or radio waves, to pass with little or no interference. **3.** So fine in texture that it can be seen through; sheer: *a transparent fabric.* **4.** Easily seen through or detected: *transparent lies.* **5.** Accessible to the public; not hidden: *transparent financial records.* [From Middle English, from Medieval Latin *trānspārēre,* to show through.] —**trans·par′ent·ly** *adv.*

tran·spi·ra·tion (trăn′spə-rā′shən) *n.* **1.** The fact or process of transpiring. **2.** The process of giving off water vapor through small openings in a plant part, such as a leaf. —SEE NOTE.

tran·spire (trăn-spīr′) *intr.v.* **tran·spired, tran·spir·ing, tran·spires 1.** To become known; come to light: *It soon transpired that he was a spy.* **2.** To happen; take place: *The events transpired on a hot summer night.* **3.** To carry out transpiration: *Plants transpire more when the air is dry.* [From Medieval Latin *trānspīrāre* : Latin *trāns-,* across + Latin *spīrāre,* to breathe.]

trans·plant (trăns-plănt′) *v.* **trans·plant·ed, trans·plant·ing, trans·plants** —*tr.* **1.** To uproot and replant (a growing plant). **2.** To transfer to and establish in a new place: *The early colonists transplanted their customs to the New World.* **3.** To transfer (tissue or an organ) from one body or body part to another. —*intr.* To be capable of being transplanted. ❖ *n.* (**trăns′**plănt′) **1.** The act or process of transplanting. **2.** Something that is transplanted. **3.** An operation in which tissue or an organ is transplanted: *The doctor performed a heart transplant.* —**trans·plant′a·ble** *adj.* —**trans′plan·ta′tion** *n.*

trans·po·lar (trăns-pō′lər) *adj.* Extending across or crossing either of the polar regions: *a transpolar flight.*

trans·port (trăns-pôrt′) *tr.v.* **trans·port·ed, trans·port·ing, trans·ports 1.** To move or carry from one place to another; convey: *transport cargo; transport passengers.* **2.** To move to strong emotion; enrapture: *She was transported with joy.* ❖ *n.* (**trăns′**pôrt′) **1.** An act of transporting: *goods lost in transport.* **2.** A ship or aircraft used to transport troops or military equipment. **3.** A vehicle, such as an aircraft, used to transport passengers, mail, or freight. **4a.** The system of transporting passengers or goods in a particular country or area: *public transport.* **b.** The vehicles, such as buses and trains, used in such a system. [From Middle English *transporten,* from Latin *trānsportāre* : *trāns-,* across + *portāre,* to carry.]

trans·por·ta·tion (trăns′pər-tā′shən) *n.* **1.** The act or an instance of transporting: *the transportation of mail.* **2.** A means of transport; a conveyance: *Planes are fast transportation.* **3.** The business of conveying passengers or goods: *a company engaged in transportation.*

trans·pose (trăns-**pōz′**) *tr.v.* **trans·posed, trans·pos·ing, trans·pos·es 1.** To reverse or transfer the order or place of; interchange: *transpose the letters of a word.* **2.** To move (an algebraic term) from one side of an equation to the other by adding or subtracting that term to or from both sides. **3.** To write or perform (a musical composition) in a key other than the original or given key. **—trans′po·si′tion** (trăns′pə-**zĭsh′**ən) *n.*

trans·ra·cial (trăns-**rā′**shəl *or* trănz-**rā′**shəl) *adj.* Involving two or more races: *a transracial adoption.*

trans·ship (trăns-**shĭp′**) *tr. & intr.v.* **trans·shipped, trans·ship·ping, trans·ships** To transfer or be transferred from one conveyance to another for reshipment. **—trans·ship′ment** *n.*

tran·sub·stan·ti·a·tion (trăn′səb-stăn′shē-**ā′**shən) *n.* **1.** Conversion of one substance into another. **2.** In many Christian churches, the doctrine holding that the bread and wine of the Eucharist are transformed into the body and blood of Jesus.

trans·u·ran·ic (trăns′yo͝o-**răn′**ĭk *or* trănz′yo͝o-**răn′**ĭk) *adj.* Having an atomic number greater than 92, the atomic number of uranium.

trans·ver·sal (trăns-**vûr′**səl *or* trănz-**vûr′**səl) *n.* A line that intersects a system of lines.

trans·verse (trăns-**vûrs′** *or* trănz-**vûrs′** *or* **trăns′**vûrs′ *or* **trănz′**vûrs′) *adj.* Situated or lying across; crosswise: *a transverse beam.* ❖ *n.* Something, such as a part or beam, that is transverse. **—trans·verse′ly** *adv.* —SEE NOTE AT **divert.**

trans woman *n.* A transgender person who identifies as a woman.

Tran·syl·va·nia (trăn′sĭl-**vān′**yə *or* trăn′sĭl-**vā′**nē-ə) A historical region of western Romania. Formerly under Hungarian rule, Transylvania became part of Romania in the early 1900s.

trap (trăp) *n.* **1.** A device for catching and holding animals, as a concealed pit or a clamp that springs shut suddenly. **2.** A scheme or plan for catching or tricking an unsuspecting person. **3a.** A device for separating and collecting solids or other materials from the liquid that flows through a drain. **b.** A device for keeping a drain sealed against a backward flow of foul gases, especially a U-shaped or S-shaped bend in a pipe that remains full of liquid. **4.** A device that hurls clay pigeons into the air to be shot at in trapshooting. **5.** A sandy depression in a golf course that stops a ball from going any farther and is hard to hit out of. **6. traps** Percussion instruments, such as snare drums and cymbals, especially in a jazz band. **7.** In soccer, the act of trapping the ball. **8.** In football, a play in which the ball carrier advances through a hole in the defensive line created by allowing a defensive lineman to run into the backfield. **9.** *Slang* The human mouth. ❖ *v.* **trapped, trap·ping, traps** *—tr.* **1.** To catch in a trap; ensnare. **2.** To prevent from escaping or getting free: *The firefighters were briefly trapped in the attic.* **3.** To deceive or trick by means of a scheme or plan: *The investigator trapped him by getting him to brag about the stolen goods.* **4.** In sports, to catch (a ball) immediately after it has hit the ground. **5.** In soccer, to get control of (a moving ball) by using the foot, leg, or another part of the body. *—intr.* To trap animals, especially for their fur. [From Old English *træppe.*]

trap·door (**trăp′**dôr′) *n.* A hinged or sliding door in a floor, roof, or ceiling.

tra·peze (tră-**pēz′**) *n.* A short horizontal bar hung from two parallel ropes, used for gymnastics exercises or for acrobatic stunts. [From Greek *trapezion*, small table.]

tra·pe·zi·um (trə-**pē′**zē-əm) *n., pl.* **tra·pe·zi·ums** or **tra·pe·zi·a** (trə-**pē′**zē-ə) A quadrilateral having no parallel sides.

trap·e·zoid (**trăp′**ĭ-zoid′) *n.* A quadrilateral having two parallel sides. **—trap′e·zoi′dal** *adj.*

trap·per (**trăp′**ər) *n.* A person who traps animals for their fur.

trap·ping (**trăp′**ĭng) *n.* **1.** often **trappings** An ornamental covering or harness for a horse. **2. trappings** Articles of dress or adornment, especially accessories: *They enjoyed their fancy car and all the trappings of success.*

trap·shoot·ing (**trăp′**sho͞o′tĭng) *n.* The sport of shooting at clay pigeons that are hurled into the air by a machine.

trash (trăsh) *n.* **1.** Worthless or discarded material or objects; refuse or rubbish. **2.** A place or container where rubbish is thrown away: *threw the rotten apple in the trash.* **3.** Something considered worthless or of inferior quality, such as a piece of writing. **4.** A person or group of people regarded as worthless or contemptible. **5.** *Slang* Insulting or unpleasant language directed at another person. ❖ *tr.v.*. **trashed, trash·ing, trash·es** *Slang* **1.** To throw away; discard. **2.** To wreck or destroy: *Those hoodlums trashed our house.* **3.** To subject to scathing criticism: *The newspaper trashed the new movie.*

trash·y (**trăsh′**ē) *adj.* **trash·i·er, trash·i·est 1.** Resembling or containing trash. **2.** In very poor taste or of very poor quality: *a trashy movie.* **—trash′i·ness** *n.*

trau·ma (**trô′**mə *or* **trou′**mə) *n., pl.* **trau·mas** or **trau·ma·ta** (**trô′**mə-tə *or* **trou′**mə-tə) **1.** A serious wound or injury, as from violence or an accident. **2.** An emotional shock that causes lasting damage to one's mental or emotional health. [From Greek.] **—trau·mat′·ic** (trô-**măt′**ĭk *or* trou-**măt′**ĭk) *adj.* **—trau·mat′i·cal·ly** *adv.*

trau·ma·tize (**trô′**mə-tīz′ *or* **trou′**mə-tīz′) *tr.v.* **trau·ma·tized, trau·ma·tiz·ing, trau·ma·tiz·es** To subject to a trauma.

tra·vail (trə-**vāl′** *or* **trăv′**āl′) *n.* **1.** Work, especially when arduous or involving painful exertion; toil. **2.** Tribulation or agony. ❖ *intr.v.* **tra·vailed, tra·vail·ing, tra·vails** To work strenuously; toil. [From Middle English, from Late Latin *tripālium*, instrument of torture.]

trav·el (**trăv′**əl) *v.* **trav·eled, trav·el·ing, trav·els** or **trav·elled, trav·el·ling, trav·els** *—intr.* **1.** To go from one place to another, as on a trip; journey: *travel through Mexico.* **2.** To be transmitted, as light or sound; move or pass: *How fast does sound travel through water?* **3.** To keep or be in company: *She travels in wealthy circles.* **4.** In basketball, to move illegally while holding the ball, usually by taking more than two steps between dribbles or by moving a foot that has been established as a pivot. *—tr.* To pass or journey over or through; traverse: *travel the countries of Africa.* ❖ *n.* **1.** The act or process of traveling: *Travel is slow in the mountains.* **2. travels** A series of journeys. [From Middle English *travailen*, to toil, from Old French *travailler*, to toil, travail.]

travel agency *n.* A business that arranges transportation, accommodations, and sightseeing for travelers. **—travel agent** *n.*

trav·eled (**trăv′**əld) *adj.* **1.** Having made journeys; experienced in travel. **2.** Frequented by travelers: *a heavily traveled road.*

trav·el·er or **trav·el·ler** (**trăv′**əl-ər *or* **trăv′**lər) *n.* A person who travels or has traveled, as to distant places.

trav·el·er's check (**trăv′**əl-ərz *or* **trăv′**lərz) *n.* A check or draft purchased in various denominations from a bank or other financial institution and signed by a traveler upon purchase and again later in the presence of the person cashing it.

trav·el·ing salesman (**trăv′**ə-lĭng *or* **trăv′**lĭng) *n.* A salesman who travels in a given territory.

trav·e·logue also **trav·e·log** (**trăv′**ə-lôg′) *n.* **1.** A lecture about travel, often accompanied by a film, a video, or slides. **2.** A narrated film or video about travels.

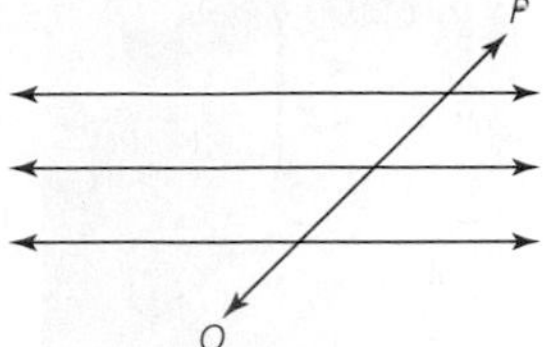

transversal
Line *PQ* is a transversal.

trap

trapeze

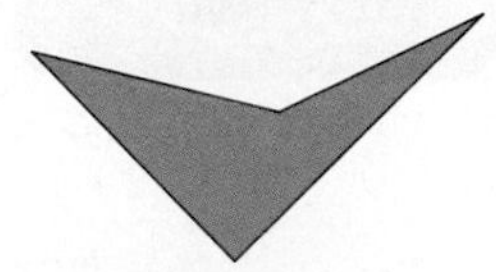

trapezium

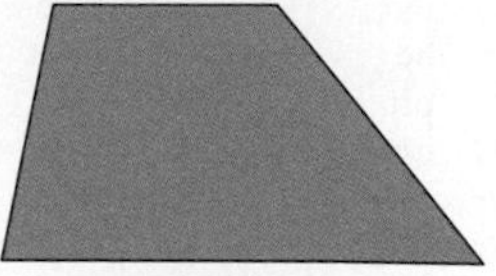

trapezoid

tread

treadmill

treble clef

tree frog

ă	pat	ôr	core
ā	pay	oi	boy
âr	care	ou	out
ä	father	ŏŏ	took
ĕ	pet	ŏŏr	lure
ē	be	ōō	boot
ĭ	pit	ŭ	cut
ī	bite	ûr	urge
îr	pier	th	thin
ŏ	pot	*th*	this
ō	toe	zh	vision
ô	paw	ə	about

tra·verse (trə-vûrs′ *or* trăv′ərs) *v.* **tra·versed, tra·vers·ing, tra·vers·es** —*tr.* **1.** To travel or pass across, over, or through: *traversed the desert safely.* **2.** To ski diagonally across (a slope). **3.** To move to and fro over: *Searchlights traversed the sky.* **4.** To extend across; cross: *A bridge traversed the mountain stream.* —*intr.* To move to the side or back and forth. ❖ *n.* **trav·erse** (trăv′ərs *or* trə-vûrs′) **1.** A passing over, across, or through. **2.** Something lying across something else, such as a beam or a rung of a ladder. ❖ *adj.* **trav·erse** (trăv′ərs *or* trə-vûrs′) Lying or extending across: *a traverse curtain rod.* [From Middle English *traversen*, from Late Latin *trānsversāre*.]

trav·es·ty (trăv′ĭ-stē) *n., pl.* **trav·es·ties 1.** A grotesque likeness. **2.** A grotesque imitation, such as a parody of a literary work.

tra·vois (trə-voi′) *n., pl.* **tra·vois** (trə-voiz′) A frame slung between trailing poles and pulled by a dog or horse, formerly used by Plains Indians to transport goods and belongings.

trawl (trôl) *n.* **1.** A large tapered fishing net that is towed along the sea bottom. **2.** A long fishing line towed by a boat and supporting many smaller lines bearing baited hooks. ❖ *v.* **trawled, trawl·ing, trawls** —*tr.* To catch (fish) with a trawl. —*intr.* To fish with a trawl.

trawl·er (trô′lər) *n.* **1.** A boat used for trawling. **2.** A person who trawls.

tray (trā) *n.* A flat shallow receptacle with a raised edge or rim, used for carrying, holding, or displaying articles.

treach·er·ous (trĕch′ər-əs) *adj.* **1.** Characterized by betrayal of confidence or trust: *a treacherous friend.* **2.** Marked by unforeseen hazards; dangerous: *a beach with a treacherous surf.*

treach·er·y (trĕch′ə-rē) *n., pl.* **treach·er·ies 1.** Willful betrayal of confidence, fidelity, or trust; perfidy. **2.** An act of such willful betrayal.

trea·cle (trē′kəl) *n. Chiefly British* Molasses.

tread (trĕd) *v.* **trod** (trŏd) or **tread·ed, trod·den** (trŏd′n) or **trod** or **treaded, tread·ing, treads** —*tr.* **1.** To walk on, over, or along: *people treading the sidewalks on their way to work.* **2.** To stamp or trample: *They threshed the rice by treading it on a hard earthen floor.* **3.** To make (a path or trail) by walking or trampling. **4.** To perform or execute by walking or dancing: *tread a measure of the minuet.* —*intr.* **1.** To go on foot; walk. **2.** To set down the foot; step. **3.** To press, crush, or injure something by trampling: *Don't tread on the grass.* ❖ *n.* **1a.** The act, manner, or sound of treading: *the swift tread of a horse.* **b.** An instance of treading; a step. **c.** A mark that is made by treading, as in snow. **2.** The upper horizontal part of a step in a staircase. **3.** The part of a wheel or tire that makes contact with the road or rails. **4.** The pattern of grooves or raised ridges on a tire. **5.** The part of a shoe sole that touches the ground. **6.** Either of the continuous, notched belts with which bulldozers, tanks, and some tractors move over the ground. ◆ **tread water 1.** To keep the head above water while in an upright position by pumping the legs. **2.** To expend effort but make little or no progress toward achieving a goal. [From Old English *tredan*.]

tread·le (trĕd′l) *n.* A pedal or lever operated by the foot to drive a wheel, as in a sewing machine or potter's wheel. ❖ *intr.v.* **tread·led, tread·ling, tread·les** To operate a treadle.

tread·mill (trĕd′mĭl′) *n.* **1.** An exercise device consisting of a continuous moving belt on which a person can walk or run while remaining in one place. **2.** A wheel on whose inner or outer circumference a person or animal treads, used to power machinery. **3.** A monotonous routine or set of tasks.

trea·son (trē′zən) *n.* Betrayal of one's country, especially by committing hostile acts against it or aiding its enemies in committing such acts. [From Middle English *treisoun*, from Latin *trāditiō*, a handing over.]

trea·son·a·ble (trē′zə-nə-bəl) *adj.* Treasonous: *his treasonable actions.*

trea·son·ous (trē′zə-nəs) *adj.* Relating to, constituting, or involving treason; treasonable.

treas·ure (trĕzh′ər) *n.* **1.** Accumulated or stored wealth in the form of money or valuables such as jewels. **2.** A person or thing considered especially precious or valuable. ❖ *tr.v.* **treas·ured, treas·ur·ing, treas·ures** To value highly; cherish: *He treasures the gold watch his colleagues gave him.* See Synonyms at **appreciate.** [From Middle English *tresour*, from Greek *thēsauros*.]

treas·ur·er (trĕzh′ər-ər) *n.* A person having charge of funds or revenues, especially the chief financial officer of a government, corporation, or association.

treas·ure-trove (trĕzh′ər-trōv′) *n.* **1.** Treasure found hidden. **2.** A discovery of great value.

treas·ur·y (trĕzh′ə-rē) *n., pl.* **treas·ur·ies 1.** A place in which treasure is kept. **2a.** A place in which private or public funds are received, kept, managed, and given or paid out. **b.** Such funds or revenues. **3.** A collection of literary or artistic treasures: *a treasury of good music.* **4. Treasury** The department of a government in charge of collecting, managing, and paying out public funds.

Treasury bill *n.* A US Treasury bond that is sold at a discount from its face value and reaches face value in one year or less.

treat (trēt) *v.* **treat·ed, treat·ing, treats** —*tr.* **1.** To act or behave in a specified manner toward: *We will treat you fairly.* **2.** To regard or handle in a certain way: *treated the matter seriously.* **3.** To deal with in speech, writing, or art: *The essay treats the subject with humor.* **4.** To provide food, entertainment, or gifts at one's own expense: *Did you say you'd treat us today?* **5.** To subject to a physical or chemical process or action in order to change in some way: *treating cloth with bleach.* **6.** To give medical care to (a person) or for (a disease). —*intr.* **1.** To deal with a subject or topic in writing or speech: *The book treats of the early experimenters in science.* **2.** To pay for another's entertainment, food, or drink. ❖ *n.* **1.** A meal, entertainment, or something similar that is paid for by someone else: *Let this lunch be my treat.* **2.** A source of special delight or pleasure: *What a treat it was to visit the museum!* [From Middle English *treten*, from Latin *tractāre*, from *trahere*, to draw.]

treat·a·ble (trē′tə-bəl) *adj.* Possible to treat; responsive to treatment: *a treatable disorder.*

trea·tise (trē′tĭs) *n.* A systematic, usually extensive written discourse on a subject.

treat·ment (trēt′mənt) *n.* **1.** The act, manner, or method of handling or dealing with a person or thing: *equal treatment under the law.* **2a.** The use of a substance or procedure, such as a drug, surgery, or exercise, to cure or improve a disease or medical condition. **b.** The substance or procedure so used.

trea·ty (trē′tē) *n., pl.* **trea·ties 1.** A formal agreement between two or more nations. **2.** A document containing such an agreement.

treb·le (trĕb′əl) *adj.* **1.** Triple. **2.** Relating to or having the highest musical part, voice, or range. ❖ *n.* The highest musical voice, part, instrument, or range. ❖ *tr. & intr.v.* **treb·led, treb·ling, treb·les** To make or become triple.

treble clef *n.* A symbol on a musical staff indicating that the note on the second line from the bottom of the staff is G above middle C.

tree (trē) *n.* **1.** A tall woody plant usually having a single main trunk and a distinct crown. **2.** Something that resembles a tree in form, especially a diagram or arrangement that has branches showing relationships of hierarchy or lineage. ❖ *tr.v.* **treed, tree·ing, trees** To force up a tree: *The dogs treed a raccoon.* ◆ **up a tree** *Informal* In a situation of great difficulty or perplexity; helpless. [From Old English *trēow*.]

tree fern *n.* Any of various treelike ferns having a woody stem and large feathery fronds.

tree frog or **tree·frog** (trē′frôg′) *n.* Any of various small frogs that live in trees and have toes with sticky pads used for clinging to tree trunks, branches, and leaves.

tree·house (trē′hous′) *n.* A structure built in the limbs of a tree and usually used for recreation.

tree line or **tree·line** (trē′līn′) *n.* The timberline.

tree of heaven *n.* A rapidly growing tree native to China that has compound leaves and strong-smelling yellowish-green flowers and is often planted along city streets.

Tree of Knowledge *n.* In the Bible, the tree in the Garden of Eden whose forbidden fruit Adam and Eve tasted.

tree·top (trē′tŏp′) *n.* The uppermost part of a tree.

tre·foil (trē′foil′ *or* trĕf′oil′) *n.* **1.** Any of various plants, such as a clover, having compound leaves with three leaflets. **2.** An ornament, symbol, or architectural form having three divisions like those of a clover leaf. [From Middle English, from Latin *trifolium* : *tri-*, three + *folium*, leaf.]

trek (trĕk) *intr.v.* **trekked, trek·king, treks 1.** To make a slow or arduous journey: *trekked across the Arctic tundra.* **2.** To journey on foot, especially to hike. ❖ *n.* A journey, especially a long and difficult one.

trel·lis (trĕl′ĭs) *n.* A lattice used for training creeping plants.

trem·a·tode (trĕm′ə-tōd′) *n.* Any of numerous flatworms that are parasites in animals and use suckers or hooks to attach to their hosts.

trem·ble (trĕm′bəl) *intr.v.* **trem·bled, trem·bling, trem·bles 1.** To shake involuntarily, as from excitement, weakness, or anger. **2.** To feel fear or anxiety: *I tremble to think what has happened.* **3.** To vibrate or quiver: *leaves trembling in the breeze.* ❖ *n.* The act of trembling; a shudder. [From Middle English *tremblen*, from Old French *trembler*, from Latin *tremulus*, trembling.]

tre·men·dous (trĭ-mĕn′dəs) *adj.* **1a.** Extremely large in amount, extent, or degree; enormous: *traveling at a tremendous speed.* **b.** Very great in scope or importance: *tremendous influence.* **2.** Remarkable; wonderful: *a tremendous party.* [From Latin *tremendus*, causing dread, from *tremere*, to tremble.] **—tre·men′dous·ly** *adv.*

trem·o·lo (trĕm′ə-lō′) *n., pl.* **trem·o·los 1.** A tremulous effect produced by rapid repetition of a single musical tone or by rapid alternation of two musical tones. **2.** Vibrato, especially in singing.

trem·or (trĕm′ər) *n.* **1.** A shaking or vibrating movement, as of the earth. **2.** An involuntary shaking of muscles, as in the hands.

trem·u·lous (trĕm′yə-ləs) *adj.* **1a.** Marked by quivering, trembling, or shaking: *tremulous hands.* **b.** Marked by a rapid varying between pitches or tones: *a tremulous voice.* **2.** Timid; fearful: *He was tremulous in the presence of the queen.*

trench (trĕnch) *n.* **1.** A deep furrow or ditch. **2.** A long ditch used for concealing or protecting soldiers in warfare. **3.** A long deep valley on the ocean floor. ❖ *tr.v.* **trenched, trench·ing, trench·es** To cut a trench in: *trench a field.* [From Middle English, from Old French, from *trenchier*, to cut.]

trench·ant (trĕn′chənt) *adj.* **1.** Forceful and clear; penetrating: *a trenchant argument.* **2.** Cutting; caustic: *trenchant criticism.* **—trench′ant·ly** *adv.*

trench coat *n.* A belted raincoat in a military style, having straps on the shoulders and deep pockets.

trench·er (trĕn′chər) *n.* A wooden board or platter on which food is served or carved.

trench foot *n.* Frostbite of the feet, often affecting soldiers who must stand in cold water for long periods of time.

trench mouth *n.* A painful infection of the mouth and throat caused by certain bacteria and marked by ulcers, bleeding, and bad breath.

trend (trĕnd) *n.* **1.** A general tendency or course of events: *a warming trend after a cold spell.* **2.** Current style; vogue: *the latest trend in fashion.* ❖ *intr.v.* **trend·ed, trend·ing, trends** To show a general tendency; tend: *In the 1950s, jazz trended away from big bands to small groups of musicians.* [From Middle English *trenden*, to revolve, from Old English *trendan*.]

trend·y (trĕn′dē) *adj.* **trend·i·er, trend·i·est** *Informal* In accord with the latest fad or fashion: *trendy clothes.*

Tren·ton (trĕn′tən) The capital of New Jersey, in the west-central part of the state northeast of Philadelphia. It was settled in about 1679 by Quakers.

tre·pan (trĭ-păn′) *n.* A tool used in mining for boring shafts in rock. ❖ *tr.v.* **tre·panned, tre·pan·ning, tre·pans** To bore (a shaft) through rock with a trepan. **—trep′a·na′tion** (trĕp′ə-nā′shən) *n.*

trep·i·da·tion (trĕp′ĭ-dā′shən) *n.* A state of alarm or dread; apprehension: *We approached the rapids with trepidation.*

tres·pass (trĕs′pəs *or* trĕs′păs′) *intr.v.* **tres·passed, tres·pass·ing, tres·pass·es 1.** To invade the property or rights of another without consent, especially to enter another's land wrongfully. **2.** To commit an unlawful act against the person, rights, or property of another: *trespass on someone's privacy.* **3.** To commit an offense or a sin; err or transgress. ❖ *n.* (trĕs′păs′ *or* trĕs′pəs) **1.** An illegal act committed against the person, rights, or property of another, especially the illegal entry onto another's land. **2.** A transgression of a moral law or duty; a sin. [From Middle English *trespassen*, from Old French *trespasser* : *tres-*, over + *passer*, to pass.] **—tres′pass·er** *n.*

tress (trĕs) *n.* A long lock or ringlet of hair.

tres·tle (trĕs′əl) *n.* **1.** A horizontal beam or bar extending between two pairs of legs that spread outward at an angle, used as a support. **2.** A framework made up of slanted supports and horizontal crosspieces used to hold up a bridge. [From Middle English *trestel*, from Latin *trānstrum*, beam.]

T. rex (tē′ rĕks′) *n.* A very large meat-eating dinosaur, *Tyrannosaurus rex*, having a large head, sharp teeth, and short front legs.

tri– *pref.* A prefix that means three: *tripartite.*

tri·ad (trī′ăd′) *n.* **1.** A group of three. **2.** In music, a chord of three tones, especially a chord that consists of a tone and the third and fifth tones above it.

tri·al (trī′əl *or* trīl) *n.* **1a.** A proceeding in which opposing sides in a dispute present evidence and make arguments on the application of the law before a judge or jury: *The case is expected to go to trial.* **b.** An instance of such a proceeding: *the trial of Socrates.* **2a.** The act or process of testing and trying by use and experience: *the trial of a new aircraft.* **b.** An instance of such testing, especially as part of a series of tests or experiments: *a clinical trial of a new drug.* **3.** An effort or attempt: *He succeeded on his second trial.* **4.** Something, such as an annoying person or a state of anguish, that tries one's patience, endurance, or belief: *The lack of water was a trial to the hikers.* ◆ **on trial** In the process of being tried, as in a court of law.

tri·an·gle (trī′ăng′gəl) *n.* **1.** A closed plane geometric figure formed by three points not in a straight line connected by three line segments; a polygon with three sides. **2.** Something shaped like such a figure. **3.** Any of various flat objects having the outline of a triangle and used as guides in drawing or drafting. **4.** A percussion instrument consisting of a bar of metal in the shape of a triangle that is left open at one angle. —SEE NOTE AT **triceratops.**

tri·an·gu·lar (trī-ăng′gyə-lər) *adj.* **1.** Relating to or shaped like a triangle. **2.** Having a base that is a triangle: *a triangular prism.*

trefoil

trench coat

trestle
trestle bridge over the Sheyenne River, near Luverne, North Dakota

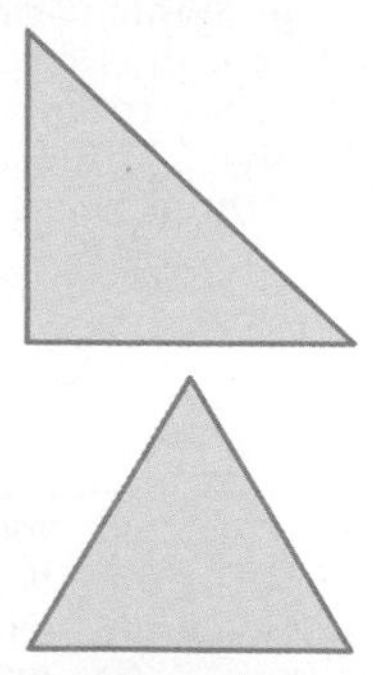

triangle
top: right triangle
bottom: equilateral triangle

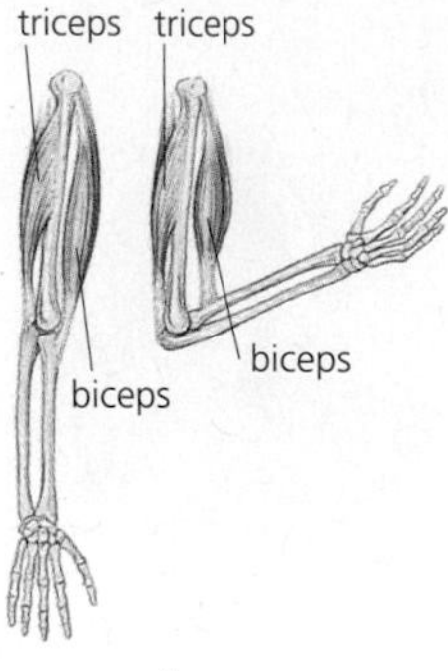

triceps

WORD HISTORY

triceratops The name of the dinosaur known as the **triceratops** is made out of three Greek roots. The first part, *tri–*, means "three," and appears in other English words, such as **triangle** and **tripod.** The *–cerat–* part is from the Greek word for "horn," *keras*. This Greek word was also used to name the hard protein that horns and hair are made of, **keratin.** The *–ops* at the end of the dinosaur's name means "face," and is related to other Greek words meaning "eye" and "to see." These words are the source of such English terms as **optics** and **autopsy** (which once meant "personal inspection"). So the triceratops is simply a dinosaur having "three horns on the face."

ă	pat	ôr	core
ā	pay	oi	boy
âr	care	ou	out
ä	father	o͝o	took
ĕ	pet	o͝or	lure
ē	be	o͞o	boot
ĭ	pit	ŭ	cut
ī	bite	ûr	urge
îr	pier	th	thin
ŏ	pot	*th*	this
ō	toe	zh	vision
ô	paw	ə	about

tri·an·gu·late (trī-ăng**′**gyə-lāt′) *tr.v.* **tri·an·gu·lat·ed, tri·an·gu·lat·ing, tri·an·gu·lates 1.** To divide into triangles. **2.** To survey by means of triangulation. **3.** To make triangular. **4.** To measure by using trigonometry.

tri·an·gu·la·tion (trī-ăng′gyə-**lā′**shən) *n.* **1.** A method used in surveying in which a region is divided into a set of triangular elements based on a line of known length, so that an accurate determination of distances and directions can be made by using trigonometry. **2.** The set of triangles laid out for this purpose. **3.** The location of an unknown point, as in navigation, by means of trigonometry.

Tri·as·sic (trī-**ăs′**ĭk) *n.* The earliest period of the Mesozoic Era, from about 251 to 200 million years ago. During the Triassic, land life diversified, dinosaurs arose, and the earliest mammals appeared. See table at **geologic time.** —**Tri·as′sic** *adj.*

tri·ath·lon (trī-**ăth′**lŏn′) *n.* An athletic competition consisting of three successive events, usually swimming, bicycling, and running.

trib·al (**trī′**bəl) *adj.* Relating to or characteristic of a tribe: *tribal customs.*

tribe (trīb) *n.* **1.** A unit of social organization consisting of a number of families, clans, or other groups who share a common ancestry and culture. A tribe does not usually have a formalized or permanent leadership. **2.** A group of related organisms usually containing several genera. **3.** Any of the 12 divisions of ancient Israel. [From Middle English, from Latin *tribus*, division of the Roman people.]

trib·u·la·tion (trĭb′yə-**lā′**shən) *n.* **1.** Great affliction or distress; suffering: *a time of great tribulation.* **2.** An experience that tests one's endurance, patience, or faith; a trial. [From Middle English *tribulacioun*, from Latin *trībulāre*, to oppress.]

tri·bu·nal (trī-**byo͞o′**nəl *or* trĭ-**byo͞o′**nəl) *n.* **1.** A court of law. **2.** A committee or board appointed to judge or settle a particular matter or dispute. **3.** Something that has the power to judge or determine: *the tribunal of public opinion.*

trib·une (**trĭb′**yo͞on′ *or* trĭ-**byo͞on′**) *n.* **1.** An official of ancient Rome chosen by the common people to protect their rights. **2.** A protector or champion of the people. [From Middle English, from Latin *tribūnus*, from *tribus*, tribe.]

trib·u·tar·y (**trĭb′**yə-tĕr′ē) *n., pl.* **trib·u·tar·ies 1.** A stream that flows into a larger river or stream. **2.** A ruler or nation that pays tribute. ❖ *adj.* **1.** Making additions or yielding supplies; contributory. **2.** Paying tribute: *a tributary colony.*

trib·ute (**trĭb′**yo͞ot) *n.* **1.** A gift, payment, or other acknowledgment of gratitude, respect, or admiration: *The plaque on the wall is a tribute to the coach's generosity.* **2a.** A sum of money paid by one ruler or nation to another as acknowledgment of submission or as the price for protection by that nation. **b.** A forced payment or contribution. [From Middle English *tribut*, from Latin *tribūtum*, from *tribuere*, to pay, distribute.]

trice (trīs) *n.* A very short period of time; an instant: *I'll do it for you in a trice.*

tri·ceps (**trī′**sĕps′) *n., pl.* **triceps** A large muscle that runs along the back of the upper arm, having three points of origin and serving to extend the forearm.

tri·cer·a·tops (trī-**sĕr′**ə-tŏps′) *n.* A large plant-eating dinosaur having three sharp horns on its head and a bony plate covering the back of the neck. —SEE NOTE.

tri·chi·na (trĭ-**kī′**nə) *n., pl.* **tri·chi·nae** (trĭ-**kī′**nē) or **tri·chi·nas** A very small parasitic worm that lives in the intestines and muscles of pigs and other mammals and that causes trichinosis. [From Greek *trikhinos*, hairy.]

trich·i·no·sis (trĭk′ə-**nō′**sĭs) *n.* A disease that results from eating incompletely cooked pork containing trichinae, marked by intestinal disorders, fever, and pain.

trick (trĭk) *n.* **1.** An act or procedure intended to achieve an end by deceptive means: *He used a trick to get other people to do his work for him.* **2.** A mischievous action; a prank: *a college student who liked to play tricks on his roommates.* **3a.** A special skill; a knack: *There's a trick to making a good soufflé.* **b.** A way of doing something particular to a certain field or activity: *the tricks of the trade.* **4.** A deception or optical illusion: *This landscape can play tricks on the eyes.* **5.** A feat of magic or sleight of hand: *showed us a card trick.* **6.** A skillful or clever act designed to amuse: *Can your dog do tricks?* **7.** A mean, stupid, or childish act: *That was a dirty trick.* **8.** All of the cards played in a single round of a card game. ❖ *tr.v.* **tricked, trick·ing, tricks** To cheat or deceive: *She tricked me into believing she could play the piano.* ❖ *adj.* **1.** Relating to or involving tricks: *trick photography.* **2.** Capable of doing tricks: *a trick dog.* **3.** Used to play tricks: *a trick deck of cards.* **4.** Weak and liable to give way: *a trick knee.* ◆ **do the trick** To bring about the desired result: *If you are thirsty, this orange juice will do the trick.* **not miss a trick** To be extremely alert, especially to other people's deceptions: *The teacher was known for not missing a trick.* [From Middle English *trik*, from Old North French *trikier*, to deceive, probably from Latin *trīcae*, tricks.]

trick·er·y (**trĭk′**ə-rē) *n., pl.* **trick·er·ies** The practice or use of tricks; deception: *He got the money by trickery.*

trick·le (**trĭk′**əl) *v.* **trick·led, trick·ling, trick·les** —*intr.* **1.** To flow or fall in drops or in a thin stream: *Sand trickled through his fingers.* **2.** To move or proceed slowly or bit by bit: *The audience trickled in before curtain time.* —*tr.* To cause to trickle: *trickled the syrup on the waffle.* ❖ *n.* **1.** The act or condition of trickling. **2.** A slow, small, or irregular quantity that moves, proceeds, or occurs intermittently: *a trickle of water from the roof; a trickle of orders in the mail.*

trick·ster (**trĭk′**stər) *n.* A person who plays tricks.

trick·y (**trĭk′**ē) *adj.* **trick·i·er, trick·i·est 1.** Given to or characterized by trickery. **2.** Requiring caution or skill: *a tricky situation.*

tri·col·or (**trī′**kŭl′ər) *n.* **1.** A flag with three colors. **2.** also **Tricolor** The French flag, having bands of red, white, and blue. ❖ *adj.* Having three colors.

tri·corn also **tri·corne** (**trī′**kôrn′) *n.* A hat that has the brim turned up on three sides. ❖ *adj.* Having three corners, horns, or projections. [From French *tricorne*, from Latin *tricornis*, three-horned : *tri-*, tri- + *cornū*, horn.]

tri·cot (**trē′**kō) *n.* A lightweight knit fabric, often of nylon, used especially for underwear.

tri·cus·pid (trī-**kŭs′**pĭd) *n.* A tooth having three points. ❖ *adj.* Having three points, as a tooth.

tri·cy·cle (**trī′**sĭk′əl *or* **trī′**sĭ-kəl) *n.* A vehicle used especially by small children, having three wheels and moved by pedals.

tri·dent (**trīd′**nt) *n.* **1.** A long three-pronged fork or weapon, especially a spear. **2.** In Greek and Roman mythology, the three-pronged spear carried by Poseidon or Neptune. [From Middle English, from Latin *tridēns* : *tri-*, three + *dēns*, tooth.]

tried (trīd) *v.* Past tense and past participle of **try.** ❖ *adj.* Thoroughly tested and proved to be good or trustworthy: *a tried recipe.*

tri·en·ni·al (trī-**ĕn′**ē-əl) *adj.* **1.** Occurring every third year. **2.** Lasting three years. ❖ *n.* **1.** A third anniversary. **2.** A ceremony or celebration occurring every three years.

tries (trīz) *v.* Third person singular present tense of **try.** ❖ *n.* Plural of **try.**

tri·fle (**trī′**fəl) *n.* **1.** Something of little importance or value. **2.** A small amount; a little. **3.** A dessert of cake soaked in brandy or another sweet liquid and topped with jam, custard, and whipped cream. ❖ *intr.v.* **tri·fled, tri·fling, tri·fles** To treat something flippantly or without seriousness; play or toy: *Don't trifle with me!* ◆ **a trifle** Very little; somewhat: *I had just a trifle too much to eat.*

tri·fling (trī′flĭng) *adj.* Of slight worth or importance: *a trifling sum.* —**tri′fling·ly** *adv.*

trig·ger (trĭg′ər) *n.* The lever pressed by the finger to discharge a gun. ❖ *tr.v.* **trig·gered, trig·ger·ing, trig·gers** To start; set off: *His thoughtless remark triggered an argument.* [From Dutch *trekker*, from Middle Dutch *trecken*, to pull.]

trig·o·no·met·ric function (trĭg′ə-nə-mĕt′rĭk) *n.* A function of an angle, as the sine, cosine, or tangent, whose value is expressed as a ratio of two of the sides of a right triangle in which the angle is included.

trig·o·nom·e·try (trĭg′ə-nŏm′ĭ-trē) *n.* The study of the properties and uses of trigonometric functions. [From Greek *trigōnon*, triangle + Greek *-metriā*, measuring.]

trill (trĭl) *n.* **1.** A fluttering or tremulous sound, as that made by certain birds; a warble. **2.** The rapid alternation of two musical tones that are either a half or a whole tone apart. **3.** A rapid vibration of one organ of speech against another, as of the tip of the tongue against the ridge behind the upper front teeth. ❖ *v.* **trilled, trill·ing, trills** —*tr.* **1.** To sound, sing, or play with a trill. **2.** To make (a sound) with a trill: *In Spanish you trill the r's.* —*intr.* To produce or give forth a trill.

tril·lion (trĭl′yən) *n.* The number, written as 10^{12} or 1 followed by 12 zeros, that is equal to one thousand times one billion. [From French : *tri-*, third power + *million*, million.] —**tril′lionth** *n.*

tril·li·um (trĭl′ē-əm) *n.* Any of various plants having three leaves grouped together and a single flower with three petals.

tri·lo·bite (trī′lə-bīt′) *n.* Any of numerous extinct sea animals that had a body with a hard outer covering divided by grooves into three lengthwise sections. Trilobites lived during the Paleozoic Era and are often found as fossils.

tril·o·gy (trĭl′ə-jē) *n., pl.* **tril·o·gies** A group of three related dramatic or literary works.

trim (trĭm) *tr.v.* **trimmed, trim·ming, trims 1.** To make neat, even, or tidy by clipping, smoothing, or pruning: *trimmed the hedges.* **2.** To remove or reduce by cutting: *trim the crust off the bread; trim a budget.* **3.** To decorate, ornament, or embellish: *trim a Christmas tree.* **4.** In sailing, to adjust (the sails and yards) so that they receive the wind properly: *trimmed sail and steered the ship past the sandbar.* ❖ *n.* **1.** A cutting or clipping to make neat: *My hair needs a trim.* **2.** Proper shape, order, or condition: *in good trim for the game.* **3.** Ornamentation on the surface of something, as braid on clothing or moldings on windows. **4a.** The readiness of a ship for sailing. **b.** The balance of a ship. **5.** The position of an aircraft when compared to how it flies parallel to the ground. ❖ *adj.* **trim·mer, trim·mest 1.** In good or neat order: *He looked very trim in his new suit.* **2.** In good physical condition; fit; slim: *a trim figure.* **3.** Having lines, edges, or forms of neat and pleasing simplicity: *a trim schooner.* [From Middle English *trimmen*, to make firm, from Old English *trum*, strong.] —**trim′ly** *adv.* —**trim′mer** *n.* —**trim′ness** *n.*

tri·mes·ter (trī-mĕs′tər *or* trī′mĕs′tər) *n.* **1.** A period or term of three months. **2.** One of three terms making up an academic year at some schools and colleges.

trim·ming (trĭm′ĭng) *n.* **1.** The act of trimming. **2.** Something added as decoration; an ornament: *fur trimming on a coat.* **3. trimmings** Accessories; extras: *roast turkey with all the trimmings.* **4. trimmings** Scraps or material removed when something is trimmed.

Trin·i·dad (trĭn′ĭ-dăd′) An island of Trinidad and Tobago in the Atlantic Ocean off northeast Venezuela. It was visited by Columbus in 1498. —**Trin′i·dad′i·an** *adj. & n.*

Trinidad and Tobago An island country of the southeast West Indies off northeast Venezuela. Port of Spain, on the island of Trinidad, is the capital.

tri·ni·tro·tol·u·ene (trī-nī′trō-tŏl′yo͞o-ēn′) *n.* TNT.

trin·i·ty (trĭn′ĭ-tē) *n., pl.* **trin·i·ties 1.** A group made up of three closely related members. **2. Trinity** In most Christian faiths, the union of the three divine persons, the Father, Son, and Holy Spirit, in one God. [From Middle English *trinite*, from Latin *trīnitās*, from *trīnus*, triple.]

trin·ket (trĭng′kĭt) *n.* A small ornament, such as a piece of jewelry.

tri·no·mi·al (trī-nō′mē-əl) *adj.* Consisting of or relating to three names or terms: *a trinomial expression in math.* ❖ *n.* A polynomial that is composed of three terms, such as $x^2 + 4x - 3$.

tri·o (trē′ō) *n., pl.* **tri·os 1a.** A musical composition for three voices or three instruments. **b.** A group of three singers or three instrumentalists. **c.** The middle section of a minuet or scherzo, a march, or one of various dances. **2.** A group of three people or things.

tri·ode (trī′ōd′) *n.* An electron tube having three electrodes, usually an anode, a cathode, and a grid that controls the flow of current between the anode and cathode.

tri·ox·ide (trī-ŏk′sīd′) *n.* An oxide that contains three atoms of oxygen per molecule.

trip (trĭp) *n.* **1.** A going from one place to another; a journey: *a trip from Cleveland to Pittsburgh.* **2.** A stumble or fall. **3.** A maneuver causing someone to stumble or fall. **4.** A mistake or blunder. **5.** A device, such as a catch for triggering a mechanism. **6.** *Slang* An intense or exciting experience: *a power trip.* ❖ *v.* **tripped, trip·ping, trips** —*intr.* **1.** To stumble: *He tripped over a root and fell.* **2.** To move nimbly with light rapid steps; skip: *The children tripped happily over the bridge.* **3.** To be released, as a tooth on an escapement wheel in a watch. **4.** To make a mistake: *I tripped up on the last test question.* **5.** To make a trip. —*tr.* **1.** To cause to stumble or fall. **2.** To catch or trap in an error or inconsistency: *The police tripped up the suspect during questioning.* **3.** To release (a catch, trigger, or switch), thereby setting something in operation.

tri·par·tite (trī-pär′tīt) *adj.* **1.** Composed of or divided into three parts. **2.** Relating to or executed by three parties: *a tripartite agreement.*

tripe (trīp) *n.* **1.** The rubbery lining of the stomach of cattle or sheep, used as food. **2.** *Informal* Something with no value; rubbish: *the tripe in a gossip magazine.*

tri·ple (trĭp′əl) *adj.* **1.** Consisting of three parts or members. **2.** Three times as much in size, strength, number, or amount. **3.** Consisting of three beats to a musical measure. ❖ *n.* **1.** A number or amount three times as great as another. **2.** A group or set of three; a triad. **3.** In baseball, a hit that enables the batter to reach third base safely. ❖ *v.* **tri·pled, tri·pling, tri·ples** —*tr.* To make three times as great in number or amount. —*intr.* **1.** To become three times as great in number or amount: *Prices tripled in 20 years.* **2.** In baseball, to hit a triple.

triple jump *n.* A distance jump in an athletic contest consisting of a hop landing on the takeoff foot, a stride landing on the other foot, and a jump landing on both feet.

triple play *n.* In baseball, a defensive play in which three outs are made during a single turn at bat.

trip·let (trĭp′lĭt) *n.* **1.** A group or set of three of one kind. **2.** One of three offspring born in a single birth. **3.** A group of three musical notes having the time value of two notes of the same kind.

triple time *n.* In music, a meter in which each measure contains three beats.

trident

trillium

trilobite

tripod

triptych

trivet

ă	pat	ôr	core
ā	pay	oi	boy
âr	care	ou	out
ä	father	o͝o	took
ĕ	pet	o͝or	lure
ē	be	o͞o	boot
ĭ	pit	ŭ	cut
ī	bite	ûr	urge
îr	pier	th	thin
ŏ	pot	*th*	this
ō	toe	zh	vision
ô	paw	ə	about

trip·li·cate (trĭp′lĭ-kĭt) *n.* One of a set of three identical objects or copies. ❖ *tr.v.* (trĭp′lĭ-kāt′) **trip·li·cat·ed, trip·li·cat·ing, trip·li·cates 1.** To make threefold; triple. **2.** To make three identical copies of.

tri·pod (trī′pŏd′) *n.* An adjustable stand with three legs, as one used to support a camera. —SEE NOTE AT **triceratops.**

Trip·o·li (trĭp′ə-lē) The capital of Libya, in the northwest part of the country on the Mediterranean Sea.

trip·tych (trĭp′tĭk) *n.* A painting or carving consisting of three panels hinged together.

tri·sect (trī′sĕkt′ *or* trī-**sĕkt′**) *tr.v.* **tri·sect·ed, tri·sect·ing, tri·sects** To divide into three equal parts. **—tri·sec′tion** *n.*

Tris·tan (trĭs′tən *or* trĭs′tän′) or **Tris·tram** (trĭs′trəm) *n.* In Arthurian legend, a knight who falls in love with the Irish princess Iseult.

trite (trīt) *adj.* **trit·er, trit·est** Not evoking interest because of overuse or repetition: *deleted the trite expressions.* **—trite′ly** *adv.* **—trite′ness** *n.*

trit·i·um (trĭt′ē-əm *or* trĭsh′ē-əm) *n.* A rare radioactive isotope of hydrogen having a nucleus that consists of a proton and two neutrons. It is made artificially and is used as a tracer and in nuclear weapons.

tri·ton (trīt′n) *n.* Any of various mollusks of tropical oceans, having a large, pointed, spiral shell.

Tri·ton (trīt′n) *n.* In Greek mythology, a god of the sea portrayed as having the head and trunk of a man and the tail of a fish.

tri·umph (trī′əmf) *n.* **1.** The fact of being victorious; success: *Her political campaign ended in triumph.* **2.** A noteworthy or spectacular success: *The bridge is a triumph of engineering.* **3.** Exultation or rejoicing over success or victory: *a cry of triumph.* ❖ *intr.v.* **tri·umphed, tri·umph·ing, tri·umphs 1.** To be victorious or successful; win: *triumph over adversity.* **2.** To rejoice over a success or victory; exult: *The players were triumphing after their team's win.* [From Middle English *triumphe*, from Latin *triumphus*, triumph.]

tri·um·phal (trī-**ŭm′**fəl) *adj.* Relating to, of the nature of, or celebrating a triumph: *a triumphal march.*

tri·um·phant (trī-**ŭm′**fənt) *adj.* **1.** Rejoicing over success or victory: *the team's triumphant return home.* **2.** Victorious; successful: *a triumphant political campaign.*

tri·um·vir (trī-**ŭm′**vər) *n., pl.* **tri·um·virs** or **tri·um·vi·ri** (trī-**ŭm′**və-rī′) One of three men sharing civil authority in ancient Rome.

tri·um·vi·rate (trī-**ŭm′**vər-ĭt) *n.* **1.** Government by triumvirs. **2.** The office or term of a triumvir. **3.** An association or group of three: *a triumvirate of business leaders.*

tri·va·lent (trī-**vā′**lənt) *adj.* In chemistry, having valence 3.

triv·et (trĭv′ĭt) *n.* **1.** A metal stand with short feet, placed under a hot dish on a table. **2.** A three-legged metal stand for holding a kettle or pot in a hearth.

triv·i·a (trĭv′ē-ə) *pl.n.* *(used with a singular or plural verb)* **1.** Insignificant or inessential matters; trifles. **2.** Miscellaneous facts, especially as the subject of questions in games and quizzes.

triv·i·al (trĭv′ē-əl) *adj.* **1.** Of little significance or value; trifling: *trivial matters.* **2.** Concerned with or involving unimportant matters: *a trivial remark.* **—triv′i·al′i·ty** (trĭv′ē-**ăl′**ĭ-tē) *n.* **—triv′i·al·ly** *adv.*

tRNA *abbr.* An abbreviation of transfer RNA.

tro·che (trō′kē) *n.* A small, circular medicinal lozenge.
❑ *These sound alike:* **troche, trochee** (metrical foot in poetry).

tro·chee (trō′kē) *n.* In poetry, a metrical foot consisting of a stressed syllable followed by an unstressed syllable.
❑ *These sound alike:* **trochee, troche** (lozenge).

trod (trŏd) *v.* A past tense and past participle of **tread.**

trod·den (trŏd′n) *v.* A past participle of **tread.**

trog·lo·dyte (trŏg′lə-dīt′) *n.* A member of a fabulous or prehistoric people that lived in caves, dens, or holes.

Tro·jan (trō′jən) *adj.* Relating to ancient Troy or its inhabitants. ❖ *n.* A native or inhabitant of ancient Troy.

Trojan horse *n.* **1.** In Greek mythology, the hollow wooden horse in which Greeks hid and gained entrance to Troy during the Trojan War. **2.** A subversive group or device placed within enemy ranks.

Trojan War *n.* In Greek mythology, the ten-year war waged against Troy by the Greeks, caused by the carrying off of Helen by Paris.

troll[1] (trōl) *v.* **trolled, troll·ing, trolls** *—tr.* **1.** To fish for or in by trailing a line from behind a slowly moving boat: *troll bass; troll a bay.* **2.** To sing in succession the parts of (a round, for example). **3.** To visit (one or more websites) in hope of finding something useful or interesting. *—intr.* **1.** To fish by trailing a line, as from a moving boat. **2.** To sing heartily or gaily. **3.** To post inflammatory or otherwise unwanted material on an electronic forum, especially anonymously. ❖ *n.* A person who makes inflammatory posts on an electronic forum. [From Middle English *trollen*, to wander about, from Old French *troller*, of Germanic origin.]

troll[2] (trōl) *n.* A creature of Scandinavian folklore, variously described as a friendly or mischievous dwarf or as a giant, that lives in caves, in the hills, or under bridges. [From Old Norse.]

trol·ley (trŏl′ē) *n., pl.* **trol·leys 1.** A streetcar. **2.** A device that makes contact with an overhead wire, third rail, or underground conductor and supplies current to an electrically powered vehicle. **3.** A carriage or basket that hangs from wheels that run on an overhead track.

trolley bus *n.* An electric bus that runs without tracks and is powered by electricity from an overhead wire.

trolley car *n.* A streetcar.

trom·bone (trŏm-**bōn′** *or* trəm-**bōn′**) *n.* A brass instrument consisting of a long, looped cylindrical tube, a movable U-shaped slide for producing different pitches, and a flaring bell. [From Italian, from *tromba*, trumpet, of Germanic origin.]

troop (tro͞op) *n.* **1.** A group of soldiers. **2. troops** Military units; soldiers. **3.** A unit of Boy Scouts or Girl Scouts under the guidance of an adult leader. **4.** A group or company of people, animals, or things: *a troop of students on a field trip.* ❖ *intr.v.* **trooped, troop·ing, troops** To move or go as a group: *children trooping home from school.* [From Old French *trope.*]
❑ *These sound alike:* **troop, troupe** (group of actors).

troop·er (tro͞o′pər) *n.* **1a.** A member of a unit of cavalry. **b.** A cavalry horse. **2.** A mounted police officer. **3.** A state police officer.

troop·ship (tro͞op′shĭp′) *n.* A ship designed for transporting troops.

tro·phy (trō′fē) *n., pl.* **tro·phies 1.** A prize or memento received as a symbol of victory, especially in sports. **2.** A specimen or part, such as the antlers of a deer, preserved as a token of a successful hunt. **3.** A memento, as of one's personal achievements. [From Latin *trophaeum*, monument to victory.]

trop·ic (trŏp′ĭk) *n.* **1.** Either of two parallels of latitude on the earth, the Tropic of Cancer or the Tropic of Capricorn, at 23° 27′ north and south of the equator, representing the points farthest north and south at which the sun can shine directly overhead. **2. tropics** or **Tropics** The region of the earth between these parallels, characterized by warm temperatures with little seasonal variation. **3.** The corresponding lines on the celestial sphere that mark the limits of the apparent north-to-south motion of the sun. ❖ *adj.* Relating to the tropics; tropical. [From Middle English *tropik*, from Greek *tropikos*, of turning, from *tropē*, a turning.]

trop·i·cal (trŏp′ĭ-kəl) *adj.* **1.** Relating to, occurring in, or characteristic of the tropics. **2.** Hot and humid; torrid. **—trop′i·cal·ly** *adv.*

Tropic of Cancer *n.* The parallel of latitude 23°27' north of the equator, forming the northern boundary of the tropics.

Tropic of Capricorn *n.* The parallel of latitude 23°27' south of the equator, forming the southern boundary of the tropics.

tro·pism (trō′pĭz′əm) *n.* Growth or movement of an organism toward or away from an external stimulus, such as light, heat, or gravity.

tro·po·pause (trō′pə-pôz′ *or* trŏp′ə-pôz′) *n.* The boundary between the upper troposphere and the lower stratosphere, varying in altitude from approximately 5 miles (8 kilometers) at the poles to 11 miles (18 kilometers) at the equator.

tro·po·sphere (trō′pə-sfîr′ *or* trŏp′ə-sfîr′) *n.* The lowest region of the atmosphere, bounded by the surface of the earth and the tropopause and characterized by temperatures that decrease with increasing altitude. Weather and most cloud formations occur in the troposphere.

trot (trŏt) *n.* **1.** A running gait of a horse or other four-footed animal in which diagonal pairs of legs move forward together. **2.** A gait of a person, faster than a walk; a jog: *a trot around the playing field.* **3.** A word-for-word translation of a work in a foreign language, sometimes used secretly in preparing a class assignment; a pony. ❖ *v.* **trot·ted, trot·ting, trots** *—intr.* **1.** To go or move at a trot: *The horses trotted down the road.* **2.** To proceed rapidly; hurry: *trotted up and down the stairs doing chores.* —*tr.* To cause to trot: *She trotted her pony around the ring.* ◆ **trot out** *Informal* To bring out and show for inspection or admiration: *The trainer trotted out the show dogs one by one.* [From Middle English, from Old French *troter*, to trot, of Germanic origin.]

troth (trôth *or* trōth) *n.* **1.** Betrothal. **2.** A person's pledged faithfulness.

Trot·sky (trŏt′skē), **Leon** 1879–1940. Russian revolutionary who was a leader of the Bolshevik Revolution (1917). He was later expelled from the Communist Party (1927) and banished (1929) for his opposition to Stalin.

trot·ter (trŏt′ər) *n.* **1.** A horse that trots, especially one trained for harness racing. **2.** *Informal* A foot, especially the foot of a pig or sheep prepared as food.

trou·ba·dour (tro͞o′bə-dôr′ *or* tro͞o′bə-do͝or′) *n.* A poet of the 1100s and 1200s in southern France, northern Italy, and northern Spain, who composed and sang songs and poems, often about love.

trou·ble (trŭb′əl) *n.* **1.** A state of distress, affliction, danger, or need: *The ship was in trouble and signaled for help.* **2.** A cause or source of distress, disturbance, or difficulty: *Minding the baby won't be any trouble.* **3.** An effort, especially one that causes inconvenience or bother: *They went to a lot of trouble on our account.* **4.** A condition of pain, disease, or malfunction: *stomach trouble.* ❖ *v.* **troub·led, troub·ling, troub·les** *—tr.* **1.** To afflict with pain or discomfort: *My stomach is troubling me.* **2.** To cause to be anxious or worried: *I am troubled by your lack of interest.* **3.** To inconvenience; bother: *May I trouble you for the time?* **4.** To agitate; stir up: *A stiff wind troubled the lake.* —*intr.* To take pains: *Don't trouble to see me off.* [From Middle English, from Old French *troubler*, to trouble, from Late Latin *turbidāre*.]

trou·bled (trŭb′əld) *adj.* Having emotional or mental problems that interfere with daily life: *a troubled teenager.*

trou·ble·mak·er (trŭb′əl-mā′kər) *n.* A person or thing that stirs up trouble or strife. **—trou′ble·mak′ing** *n.* & *adj.*

trou·ble·shoot·er (trŭb′əl-sho͞o′tər) *n.* A person whose job is to locate and eliminate sources of trouble.

trou·ble·some (trŭb′əl-səm) *adj.* Characterized by or causing trouble or anxiety: *a troublesome car; a troublesome situation.*

trough (trôf) *n.* **1.** A long, narrow, generally shallow receptacle, especially one for holding water or feed for animals. **2.** A gutter under the eaves of a roof for carrying off rainwater. **3.** A long narrow depression, as between waves or ridges. **4.** An extended region of low atmospheric pressure, often associated with a front. [From Old English *trog*.]

trounce (trouns) *tr.v.* **trounced, trounc·ing, trounc·es** **1.** To thrash; beat. **2.** To defeat decisively: *trounced the opposing field hockey team.*

troupe (tro͞op) *n.* A company or group of actors, singers, dancers, or other performers. [From French *troupe*, troop.]

❑ *These sound alike:* **troupe, troop** (group of soldiers).

trou·sers (trou′zərz) *pl.n.* Pants.

trous·seau (tro͞o′sō *or* tro͞o-sō′) *n., pl.* **trous·seaux** (tro͞o′sōz *or* tro͞o-sōz′) or **trous·seaus** The possessions, such as clothing and linens, that a woman assembles for her marriage.

trout (trout) *n., pl.* **trout** or **trouts** Any of various chiefly freshwater fishes usually having a speckled body and valued as food. [From Old English *trūht*, from Late Latin *trūcta*.]

trow·el (trou′əl) *n.* **1.** A hand tool with a flat blade for spreading or smoothing such substances as mortar and cement. **2.** A tool with a scoop-shaped blade used for digging, as in setting plants.

troy (troi) *adj.* Measured or expressed in troy weight.

Troy (troi) also **Il·i·um** (ĭl′ē-əm) An ancient city of northwest Asia Minor. It is the legendary site of the Trojan War.

troy weight *n.* A system of weights in which the grain is the same as in the avoirdupois system, one ounce equals 480 grains, and one pound equals 12 ounces.

tru·an·cy (tro͞o′ən-sē) *n., pl.* **tru·an·cies** **1.** The absence of a child from school without permission. **2.** The neglect of work or duty.

tru·ant (tro͞o′ənt) *n.* **1.** A person who is absent without permission. **2.** A person who shirks work or duty. ❖ *adj.* **1.** Absent without permission, especially from school: *a truant pupil.* **2.** Idle, lazy, or neglectful: *a truant worker.*

truant officer *n.* An official who investigates unauthorized absences from school.

truce (tro͞os) *n.* A temporary stopping of fighting by mutual agreement.

truck[1] (trŭk) *n.* **1.** Any of various heavy motor vehicles designed for carrying or pulling loads. **2.** A two-wheeled barrow used for moving heavy objects by hand. **3.** A wheeled, sometimes motorized platform for conveying loads in a warehouse or freight yard. **4.** One of the swiveling frames of wheels under each end of a railroad car or trolley car. ❖ *v.* **trucked, truck·ing, trucks** *—tr.* To transport (goods) by truck. *—intr.* **1.** To carry goods by truck. **2.** To drive a truck. [Short for *truckle* or from Latin *trochus*, iron hoop (from Greek *trokhos*, wheel).]

truck[2] (trŭk) *n.* **1.** Vegetables and fruit raised to be sold in a market. **2.** *Informal* Dealings: *He is too high and mighty to have any truck with us.* [From Old North French *troquer*, to barter.]

truck cap *n.* An enclosed unit usually having windows and a rear hatch, mounted in or over the bed of a pickup truck.

truck·er (trŭk′ər) *n.* A person who drives a truck.

truck farm *n.* A farm producing vegetables and fruit to be sold in a market.

truck·le (trŭk′əl) *n.* A small wheel or roller. [From Middle English *trokel*, pulley, from Latin *trochlea*, system of pulleys.]

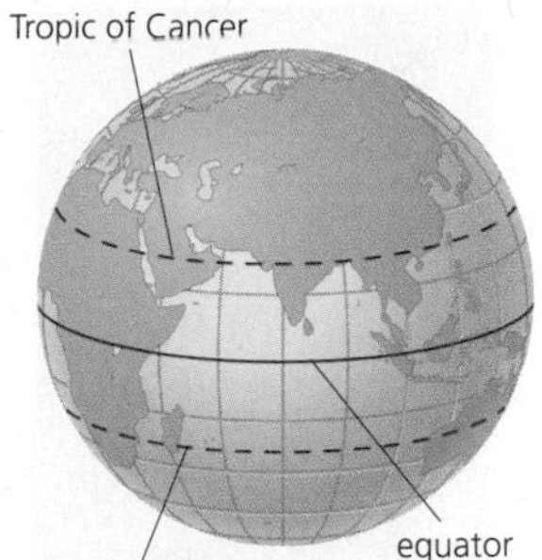

tropic

Leon Trotsky
photographed in the 1920s

trough
feeding trough

trowel
masonry trowels

Harry S. Truman
photographed c. 1947

Donald Trump
photographed in 2017

Sojourner Truth

USAGE

try The phrase *try and,* as in *Could you try and make less noise,* is informal and is best used in conversation. When writing, use the phrase *try to* instead: *We should try to practice as much as we can.*

ă	pat	ôr	core
ā	pay	oi	boy
âr	care	ou	out
ä	father	o͝o	took
ĕ	pet	o͝or	lure
ē	be	o͞o	boot
ĭ	pit	ŭ	cut
ī	bite	ûr	urge
îr	pier	th	thin
ŏ	pot	*th*	this
ō	toe	zh	vision
ô	paw	ə	about

truck·load (trŭk′lōd′) *n.* The amount of cargo that a truck can hold.

truc·u·lent (trŭk′yə-lənt) *adj.* **1.** Ready or willing to fight; belligerent. **2.** Showing or expressing bitter opposition: *a truculent glance.* **3.** Violent or cruel: *truculent warriors.* [From Latin *truculentus*, from *trux*, fierce.] **—truc′u·lent·ly** *adv.*

Tru·deau (tro͞o-dō′), **Justin** Born 1971. Canadian prime minister (took office 2015).

Tru·deau, Pierre Elliot 1919–2000. Canadian prime minister (1968–1979 and 1980–1984).

trudge (trŭj) *intr.v.* **trudged, trudg·ing, trudg·es** To walk in a laborious heavy-footed way; plod.

true (tro͞o) *adj.* **tru·er, tru·est 1.** Consistent with fact or reality; not false or erroneous: *Is what the advertisement says true? We tried to determine the true cost of owning such an old car.* **2.** Not imitation or counterfeit; real or genuine: *true gold.* See Synonyms at **authentic. 3.** Having the characteristics of a certain group or type; typical: *The horseshoe crab is not a true crab.* **4a.** Faithful; loyal: *Be true to your friends.* **b.** Faithful to one's spouse or romantic partner. **5.** Sincerely felt or expressed; unfeigned: *true sorrow.* **6.** Rightful; legitimate: *the true heir to the land.* **7a.** Accurately shaped, fitted, or placed: *Are the car's wheels true?* **b.** Determined with reference to the earth's axis, not the magnetic poles: *true north.* ❖ *adv.* **1.** In accord with reality, fact, or truthfulness: *She speaks true.* **2.** Without swerving from a course; exactly: *I'll sail the ship straight and true.* ❖ *tr.v.* **trued, tru·ing** or **true·ing, trues** To adjust or fit (something) so as to make it balanced, level, or square: *true the edges of a seam.* [From Old English *trēowe*, firm, trustworthy.]

true-blue (tro͞o′blo͞o′) *adj.* Loyal or faithful; staunch: *my true-blue friend.*

truf·fle (trŭf′əl) *n.* **1.** Any of various fleshy blackish or light-brown fungi that grow underground and are regarded as a food delicacy. **2.** A round, soft candy made of chocolate, butter or cream, sugar, and various flavorings, often coated with cocoa powder.

tru·ism (tro͞o′ĭz′əm) *n.* A statement that is obviously true or that is often presented as true.

tru·ly (tro͞o′lē) *adv.* **1.** Sincerely; genuinely: *I am truly sorry.* **2.** Truthfully; accurately: *The newspaper reported the story truly.* **3.** Indeed: *The view from the hilltop is truly magnificent.*

Tru·man (tro͞o′mən), **Harry S.** 1884–1972. The 33rd president of the United States (1945–1953). He authorized the use of the atomic bomb against Japan (1945) and ordered US involvement in the Korean War (1950–1953).

trump (trŭmp) *n.* often **trumps** In card games, a suit declared to outrank all other suits during the play of a hand. ❖ *v.* **trumped, trump·ing, trumps** *—tr.* **1.** To take (a card or trick) with a trump. **2.** To get the better of (a competitor) by using a crucial, often hidden resource. *—intr.* To play a trump. ◆ **trump up** To devise fraudulently: *The dictator trumped up charges against his opponents.*

Trump (trŭmp), **Donald John** Born 1946. The 45th president of the United States (took office 2017). Before running for office, he was a businessperson.

trump·er·y (trŭm′pə-rē) *n., pl.* **trump·er·ies 1.** Showy but worthless finery. **2.** Nonsense; rubbish.

trum·pet (trŭm′pĭt) *n.* **1.** A high-pitched brass instrument consisting of a long metal tube, looped once and having a mouthpiece at one end and a flaring bell at the other. Modern trumpets are equipped with three valves for producing variations in pitch. **2.** Something shaped like a trumpet: *the yellow trumpets of the daffodils.* **3.** A resounding call, as that of the elephant. ❖ *v.* **trum·pet·ed, trum·pet·ing, trum·pets** *—intr.* **1.** To play a trumpet. **2.** To make a loud resounding sound like that of a trumpet: *Elephants trumpeted in the distance. —tr.* To shout or announce loudly. [From Middle English *trompet*, from Old French *trompette*, from *trompe*, horn, from Old High German *trumpa*.] **—trum′pet·er** *n.*

trumpet creeper *n.* A woody vine of the United States having reddish-orange flowers shaped like trumpets.

trun·cate (trŭng′kāt′) *tr.v.* **trun·cat·ed, trun·cat·ing, trun·cates** To cut short: *He truncated his speech in order to maintain the audience's attention.* ❖ *adj.* Appearing to end abruptly, as a leaf of a tulip tree.

trun·cheon (trŭn′chən) *n.* A short stick carried by police officers; a billy club.

trun·dle (trŭn′dl) *v.* **trun·dled, trun·dling, trun·dles** *—tr.* **1.** To push or propel on wheels or rollers: *trundling a wheelbarrow.* **2.** To carry or cause to move, especially in a vehicle: *My father trundled us off to school in the minivan. —intr.* To move along by rolling or spinning: *The bus trundled down the road.* **—trun′dler** *n.*

trundle bed *n.* **1.** A low bed on casters that can be rolled under another bed when not in use. **2.** A set of two beds, one of which can be rolled under the other.

trunk (trŭngk) *n.* **1.** The woody main stem of a tree. **2.** The main part of the body, not including the arms, legs, and head. **3.** A long flexible snout, especially of an elephant, used for grasping and holding. **4.** A main body, not including parts that branch off: *the trunk of a nerve.* **5.** A covered compartment of an automobile, used for luggage or storage. **6.** A large box or case with a lid that clasps shut, used as luggage or for storage. **7. trunks** Men's shorts worn for swimming or athletics. [From Middle English *trunke*, from Latin *truncus*.]

truss (trŭs) *n.* **1.** A device worn to support a hernia so that it will not enlarge or spread. **2.** A framework, as of beams or bars, used to support a roof, bridge, or other structure. ❖ *tr.v.* **trussed, truss·ing, truss·es 1.** To tie up securely; bind. **2.** To bind the wings and legs of (a fowl) before cooking. **3.** To support or brace with a truss.

trust (trŭst) *n.* **1.** Firm belief in the integrity, ability, or character of a person or thing; confidence or reliance: *taking it on trust that our friend is telling the truth.* **2.** The condition and resulting obligation of having confidence placed in one: *violated a public trust.* **3.** Custody; care: *The children are in my trust.* See Synonyms at **care. 4.** Reliance on something in the future; hope: *We have trust that the future will be better.* **5.** Reliance on the intention and ability of a purchaser to pay in the future; credit: *goods bought on trust.* **6.** In law, a relationship in which one party holds a title to property while another party is entitled to receive the benefits of that property. **7.** The property under such control. **8.** A combination of business firms and corporations, joined for the purpose of reducing competition and controlling prices. ❖ *v.* **trust·ed, trust·ing, trusts** *—tr.* **1.** To have or place confidence in; depend on: *Trust me.* **2.** To expect with assurance; assume: *I trust that you will be on time.* **3.** To believe: *I trust what you say.* **4.** To grant discretion to confidently: *Can I trust them with the boat? —intr.* **1.** To have or place confidence; depend: *Trust in me.* **2.** To be confident; hope. ◆ **in trust** In the possession or care of a trustee. [From Middle English, perhaps from Old Norse *traust*, confidence.]

trus·tee (trŭ-stē′) *n.* **1.** A person or firm that has legal control of property for another person's benefit. **2.** A member of a group or board that manages the affairs of an institution.

trus·tee·ship (trŭ-stē′shĭp′) *n.* **1.** The position or function of a trustee. **2a.** Administration of a territory by a country or countries so commissioned by the United Nations. **b.** A trust territory.

trust·ful (trŭst′fəl) *adj.* Inclined to believe or confide readily; full of trust: *a child's trustful eyes; a trustful person.* **—trust′ful·ly** *adv.* **—trust′ful·ness** *n.*

trust fund *n.* A collection of property, especially money, stocks, and bonds, held by one party (such as a parent) for the benefit of another (such as a child).

trust territory *n.* A colony or territory placed under the administration of one or more countries by the United Nations.

trust·wor·thy (trŭst′wûr′*th*ē) *adj.* **trust·wor·thi·er, trust·wor·thi·est** Warranting trust; reliable: *a trustworthy assistant.*

trust·y (trŭs′tē) *adj.* **trust·i·er, trust·i·est** Reliable; trustworthy.

truth (tro͞oth) *n., pl.* **truths** (tro͞o*th*z *or* tro͞oths) **1.** Accordance with fact or actuality: *a story with an appearance of truth.* **2.** A statement proven to be or accepted as true: *scientific truths.* **3.** Sincerity; integrity: *There was no truth in his speech.* **4.** Reality; actuality: *The truth is that we will win no matter what they try to do.* [From Old English *trēowth*, loyalty.]

Truth (tro͞oth), **Sojourner** 1797?–1883. American abolitionist and feminist. After she escaped from slavery in 1827, she lectured widely against slavery and for the rights of women.

truth·ful (tro͞oth′fəl) *adj.* **1.** Consistently telling the truth; honest: *a truthful person.* **2.** Corresponding to reality; true: *a truthful account of the events.* **—truth′ful·ly** *adv.* **—truth′ful·ness** *n.*

try (trī) *v.* **tried** (trīd), **try·ing, tries** (trīz) *—tr.* **1.** To make an effort (to do or accomplish something); attempt: *Try to understand.* **2.** To taste, sample, or otherwise test in order to determine something, such as quality: *Let's try the pasta dish.* **3a.** To conduct the trial of (a legal claim): *to try a criminal case.* **b.** To put (an accused person) on trial in a court. **4.** To subject to great strain or hardship; tax: *a task that tried his strength.* **5.** To melt (fat, for example) to separate out impurities; render. *—intr.* To make an effort; strive. ❖ *n., pl.* **tries** (trīz) An attempt; an effort. ◆ **try on** To put on (a garment) to test its fit: *tried on the pants in the dressing room.* **try (one's) hand** To attempt to do something for the first time: *thought he would try his hand at making an omelet.* **try out 1.** To undergo a competitive qualifying test, as for a job or athletic team: *I wanted to try out for the basketball team.* **2.** To test or use experimentally: *tried out her new snowshoes.* [From Middle English *trien*, from Old French *trier*, to pick out.] —SEE NOTE.

try·ing (trī′ĭng) *adj.* Causing strain, hardship, or distress: *trying circumstances.*

try·out (trī′out′) *n.* A test to evaluate or find out qualifications of applicants, as for a theatrical role or athletic team.

try·pan·o·some (trĭ-păn′ə-sōm′) *n.* Any of various parasitic protozoans that are carried into the bloodstream of humans and other animals by the bite of certain insects and that can cause serious diseases such as sleeping sickness.

tryp·sin (trĭp′sĭn) *n.* An enzyme that is produced in the pancreas and that aids digestion by breaking down proteins.

tryp·to·phan (trĭp′tə-făn′) *n.* An essential amino acid that is formed from proteins during digestion.

try square *n.* A carpenter's tool consisting of a straightedge set at right angles to a straight bar, used for measuring and marking square work.

tryst (trĭst) *n.* **1.** An agreement between lovers to meet at a certain time and place. **2.** The meeting or meeting place so arranged.

tsar (zär *or* tsär) *n.* Variant of **czar** (sense 1).

tset·se fly (tsĕ′tsē *or* tsē′tsē) *n.* Any of several blood-sucking African flies that carry and transmit by their bite the protozoans that cause sleeping sickness.

T-shirt also **tee shirt** (tē′shûrt′) *n.* A short-sleeved collarless shirt or undershirt.

tsp. *abbr.* An abbreviation of teaspoon.

T-square (tē′skwâr′) *n.* A ruler with a short crosspiece at one end, used for drawing parallel lines.

tsu·na·mi (tso͞o-nä′mē) *n., pl.* **tsu·na·mis** or **tsunami** A very large ocean wave that is caused by an underwater earthquake or volcanic eruption and often causes extreme destruction when it strikes land. [From Japanese : *tsu*, harbor + *nami*, wave.]

tu·a·ta·ra (to͞o′ə-tär′ə) *n., pl.* **tuatara** or **tu·a·ta·ras** A reptile of New Zealand that resembles a lizard and is the only living member of a group that flourished during the time of the dinosaurs. [From Maori *tuatara* : *tua*, back + *tara*, spine.]

tub (tŭb) *n.* **1.** An open, flatbottom, usually round container, used for washing, packing, or storing. **2.** The amount that such a container can hold. **3.** A bathtub. [From Middle English, from Middle Dutch or Middle Low German *tubbe*.]

tu·ba (to͞o′bə) *n.* A large brass instrument having a bass range and several valves to change its pitch. [From Latin *tuba*, trumpet.]

tub·by (tŭb′ē) *adj.* **tub·bi·er, tub·bi·est 1.** Having a rounded shape: *a tubby fishing boat.* **2.** *Informal* Short and fat.

tube (to͞ob) *n.* **1.** A hollow cylinder, especially one that conveys a fluid or functions as a passage. **2.** An organ of the body having the shape or function of a tube: *the bronchial tubes.* **3.** A small flexible container with a screw cap at one end, used for holding toothpaste or a similar substance that can be squeezed out. **4.** The part of a wind instrument that extends from the mouthpiece to the end that is open to the air. **5.** *Chiefly British* A subway. **6a.** An inner tube. **b.** An inflated circular tube or cushion that is used to float on water or to glide over snow. **7.** A vacuum tube or an electron tube. **8.** *Informal* Television: *watched the tube for an hour.* ◆ **down the tube** or **down the tubes** *Informal* Into a state of failure or ruin: *In an instant, all my hard work went down the tube.* [From Latin *tubus*.]

tube foot *n.* One of the numerous fluid-filled muscular tubes on the outer surface of an echinoderm, such as a starfish or sea urchin, used for locomotion, feeding, and respiration.

tu·ber (to͞o′bər) *n.* A swollen, fleshy, usually underground outgrowth of the stem of a plant, such as a potato, bearing buds from which new plants grow. [From Latin *tūber*, lump.]

tu·ber·cle (to͞o′bər-kəl) *n.* **1.** A small swelling, as on the roots of certain plants or on skin or a bone. **2.** A swelling of this kind caused by tuberculosis.

tu·ber·cu·lar (to͞o-bûr′kyə-lər) *adj.* **1.** Relating to or covered with tubercles. **2.** Relating to or affected with tuberculosis. ❖ *n.* A person having tuberculosis.

tu·ber·cu·late (to͞o-bûr′kyə-lĭt′) *adj.* Tubercular.

tu·ber·cu·lin (to͞o-bûr′kyə-lĭn) *n.* A liquid derived from cultures of the bacteria that cause tuberculosis, used in testing for the disease.

tu·ber·cu·lo·sis (to͞o-bûr′kyə-lō′sĭs) *n.* A contagious disease caused by bacteria and characterized by abnormal growths in the tissues of the body, especially the lungs. It is most often transmitted by breathing contaminated air.

tu·ber·cu·lous (to͞o-bûr′kyə-ləs) *adj.* Having or caused by tuberculosis or tubercles.

tube·rose (to͞ob′rōz′) *n.* A Mexican plant having a tuberous root and highly fragrant white flowers.

tu·ber·ous (to͞o′bər-əs) *adj.* Producing, consisting of, or resembling a tuber: *tuberous roots.*

tub·ing (to͞o′bĭng) *n.* **1.** Tubes considered as a group. **2.** A system of tubes. **3.** A piece or length of tube.

Tub·man (tŭb′mən), **Harriet** 1820?–1913. American abolitionist who escaped from slavery in 1849 and became the most famous conductor on the Underground Railroad, leading more than 300 slaves to freedom. —SEE NOTE.

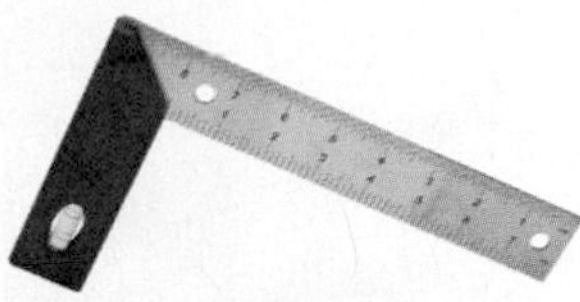

try square

Harriet Tubman

BIOGRAPHY

Harriet Tubman Born and raised a slave on a Maryland plantation, Harriet **Tubman** was the most famous and successful of conductors on the Underground Railroad, leading over 300 slaves to freedom in the North and Canada. In the 12 years after she left her family and escaped to freedom in the North, Tubman returned at least 19 times to lead other slaves along similar routes, successfully evading bounty hunters seeking the often huge rewards for her capture. At the outbreak of the Civil War, the Union commissioned Tubman to work among the wounded soldiers in the South as a nurse, scout, and spy. In this position, Tubman was able to gain information about rebel supplies and sources of ammunition, which proved valuable in several Union raids on coastal areas in the Carolinas.

tundra
Thelon Wildlife Sanctuary, Northwest Territories, Canada

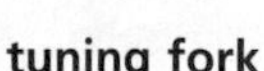

tuning fork

tuque

ă	pat	ôr	core
ā	pay	oi	boy
âr	care	ou	out
ä	father	o͝o	took
ĕ	pet	o͝or	lure
ē	be	o͞o	boot
ĭ	pit	ŭ	cut
ī	bite	ûr	urge
îr	pier	th	thin
ŏ	pot	*th*	this
ō	toe	zh	vision
ô	paw	ə	about

tu·bu·lar (to͞o′byə-lər) *adj.* **1.** Shaped like a tube: *tubular flowers.* **2.** Made of or being tubes or a tube: *a tubular frame.*

tu·bule (to͞o′byo͞ol) *n.* A very small tube or tubular structure.

tuck (tŭk) *v.* **tucked, tuck·ing, tucks** —*tr.* **1.** To thrust or fold the edge of in order to secure or confine: *He tucked the shirt into his pants.* **2.** To cover or wrap snugly: *tucked in the baby and turned off the light.* **3.** To make a fold or folds in. **4a.** To put in an out-of-the-way and snug place: *a cabin tucked among the pines.* **b.** To store in a safe spot; save: *tuck away a bit of lace.* —*intr.* To make tucks. ❖ *n.* **1.** The act of tucking. **2.** A flattened pleat or fold, especially a narrow one stitched in place. **3a.** A midair position in some sports, such as diving, in which the knees are bent and the thighs are drawn close to the chest, with the hands often clasped around the shins. **b.** A position in skiing in which the skier squats while holding the poles parallel to the ground and under the arms. [From Middle English *tuken*, possibly from Middle Low German or Middle Dutch *tocken, tucken.*]

tuck·er[1] (tŭk′ər) *n.* **1.** A person or thing that tucks, especially an attachment on a sewing machine for making tucks. **2.** A piece of lace, linen, or other material formerly worn by women around the neck and shoulders.

tuck·er[2] (tŭk′ər) *tr.v.* **tuck·ered, tuck·er·ing, tuck·ers** *Informal* To make weary; exhaust: *The long climb up the hill tuckered him out.* [Perhaps from *tuck.*]

Tuc·son (to͞o′sŏn′) A city of southeast Arizona south-southeast of Phoenix. A Spanish mission was founded nearby in 1700, and the present city was first settled in 1776.

Tu·dor (to͞o′dər) *adj.* **1.** Relating to the royal house of Tudor, which ruled England from 1485 to 1603. **2.** Characteristic of the period of this royal house, especially in architectural style.

Tues·day (to͞oz′dē *or* to͞oz′dā′) *n.* The third day of the week. [From Old English *Tīwesdæg*, day of Tiu (the god of war).] **—Tues′days** *adv.*

tu·fa (to͞o′fə) *n.* A soft brittle sedimentary rock made up of calcium carbonate and usually formed by the evaporation of water, especially at the mouth of a hot spring or on a drying lake bed.

tuff (tŭf) *n.* A rock made up of particles of volcanic ash, varying in size from fine sand to coarse gravel.
❑ *These sound alike:* **tuff, tough** (rugged).

tuft (tŭft) *n.* A short cluster of strands, as of hair, grass, or yarn, attached at the base or growing close together. ❖ *tr.v.* **tuft·ed, tuft·ing, tufts 1.** To decorate or supply with a tuft or tufts. **2.** To pass threads through the layers of (a quilt, a mattress, or upholstery), securing the thread ends with a knot or button.

tug (tŭg) *v.* **tugged, tug·ging, tugs** —*tr.* **1.** To pull at vigorously or repeatedly: *The puppy was tugging the leash.* See Synonyms at **pull. 2.** To move by pulling with great effort or exertion; drag: *I tugged a chair across the room.* **3.** To tow by a tugboat. —*intr.* To pull something vigorously or repeatedly: *tugged at the coat's zipper.* ❖ *n.* **1.** A strong pull or pulling force. **2.** A tugboat. [From Middle English *tuggen*, from Old English *tēon.*]

tug·boat (tŭg′bōt′) *n.* A small powerful boat designed for towing or pushing larger vessels.

tug of war *n., pl.* **tugs of war** A contest in which two teams tug on opposite ends of a rope, each trying to pull the other across a dividing line.

tu·i·tion (to͞o-ĭsh′ən) *n.* **1.** A fee for instruction, especially at a college or private school. **2.** Instruction; teaching: *The beginner was under the experienced musician's tuition.*

tu·la·re·mi·a (to͞o′lə-rē′mē-ə) *n.* An infectious disease of rodents and other small mammals, caused by bacteria and transmitted to humans through the bite of various insects or contact with infected animals.

tu·lip (to͞o′lĭp) *n.* Any of several plants that grow from a bulb and are widely cultivated for their showy, variously colored, cup-shaped flowers. [From Ottoman Turkish *tülbend*, muslin, gauze, turban.]

tulle (to͞ol) *n.* A fine, often starched net used especially for veils, gowns, and tutus.
❑ *These sound alike:* **tulle, tool** (device).

Tul·sa (tŭl′sə) A city of northeast Oklahoma northeast of Oklahoma City.

tum·ble (tŭm′bəl) *v.* **tum·bled, tum·bling, tum·bles** —*intr.* **1.** To pitch headlong; fall: *He tumbled on the ice.* **2.** To fall, roll, or move end over end: *The kittens tumbled over each other.* **3.** To spill, roll out, or come out in confusion or disorder: *Schoolchildren tumbled out of the bus.* **4.** To perform acrobatic maneuvers, such as somersaults, rolls, or twists. **5.** To lose a position, status, or power: *The team tumbled from first to last place.* **6.** To decrease suddenly or dramatically: *Prices tumbled.* —*tr.* To put, spill, or toss haphazardly: *tumbling logs out of a truck.* ❖ *n.* **1.** An act of tumbling; a fall: *took a tumble on the stairs.* **2.** A sudden or dramatic decrease: *a tumble in rents.* [From Middle English *tumblen*, from Old English *tumbian*, to dance about.]

tum·ble·down (tŭm′bəl-doun′) *adj.* Being in such bad repair as to seem in danger of collapsing; very rickety: *a tumbledown shack.*

tum·bler (tŭm′blər) *n.* **1.** An acrobat or gymnast who tumbles. **2.** A drinking glass having no handle or stem. **3.** The part in a lock that releases the bolt when turned by a key. **4.** The drum of a clothes dryer.

tum·ble·weed (tŭm′bəl-wēd′) *n.* Any of various densely branched plants that break off from the roots at the end of the growing season and are rolled about by the wind.

tum·bling (tŭm′blĭng) *n.* Gymnastics, such as somersaults and rolls, performed without specialized equipment.

tum·brel or **tum·bril** (tŭm′brəl) *n.* **1.** A two-wheeled cart, especially a farmer's cart that can be tilted to dump a load. **2.** A cart used to carry condemned prisoners to their execution, as during the French Revolution.

tu·mes·cence (to͞o-mĕs′əns) *n.* **1.** A swelling or enlarging. **2.** A swollen condition.

tu·mes·cent (to͞o-mĕs′ənt) *adj.* Swollen or becoming swollen.

tu·mid (to͞o′mĭd) *adj.* Swollen or distended.

tum·my (tŭm′ē) *n., pl.* **tum·mies** *Informal* **1.** The stomach. **2.** The abdomen.

tu·mor (to͞o′mər) *n.* An abnormal growth of tissue resulting from uncontrolled cell growth. [From Middle English *tumour*, from Latin *tumor*, a swelling, from *tumēre*, to swell.]

tu·mult (to͞o′mŭlt′) *n.* **1.** A great noise, as of a crowd: *had to shout over the tumult in the cafeteria.* **2.** A disorderly commotion or disturbance. **3.** Agitation of the mind or emotions.

tu·mul·tu·ous (to͞o-mŭl′cho͞o-əs) *adj.* Characterized by tumult; noisy and disorderly: *a tumultuous crowd.*

tun (tŭn) *n.* **1.** A large cask for liquids, especially wine. **2.** A measure of liquid capacity, especially one equal to approximately 252 gallons (955 liters).
❑ *These sound alike:* **tun, ton** (weight unit).

tu·na[1] (to͞o′nə) *n., pl.* **tuna** or **tu·nas 1a.** Any of various often large ocean fishes that have a streamlined body and small scales. Several kinds of tuna are important sources of canned fish. **b.** Any of several related food fishes, such as the bonito. **2.** The edible flesh of a tuna, often canned or processed. [From Spanish *atún*, from Arabic *at-tūn*, from Latin *thunnus.*]

tu·na[2] (to͞o′nə) *n.* The edible red fruit of any of several prickly pear cacti. [From Taíno.]

tun·a·ble also **tune·a·ble** (to͞o′nə-bəl) *adj.* Capable of being tuned: *a tunable wind instrument.*

tun·dra (tŭn′drə) *n.* A cold treeless area of arctic regions, having permanently frozen subsoil and only low-growing mosses, lichens, and stunted shrubs as plant life.

tune (to͞on) *n.* **1.** A melody, especially a simple and easily remembered one: *She whistled a tune while she walked down the street.* **2.** The state of being in correct musical pitch: *sang out of tune.* **3.** Agreement or harmony: *ideas in tune with the times.* ❖ *tr.v.* **tuned, tun·ing, tunes 1.** To put in proper musical pitch: *tune a guitar.* **2.** To adjust (an engine, for example) for top performance. **3.** To adjust (a radio, for example) to a desired frequency. ◆ **to the tune of** To the sum or extent of: *paid extra for the tickets to the tune of 20 dollars each.* **tune in** To adjust an electronic receiver to receive signals at a particular frequency or to receive a desired program. **tune out** To adjust an electronic receiver so as not to receive a particular signal. [From Middle English, from Anglo-French *tun, tuen,* tone.]

tune·ful (to͞on′fəl) *adj.* Full of tune; melodious. **—tune′ful·ly** *adv.*

tun·er (to͞o′nər) *n.* **1.** A person or thing that tunes: *a piano tuner.* **2.** A device for tuning, especially an electronic circuit or device used to select signals at a specific radio frequency for amplification and conversion to sound.

tune-up (to͞on′ŭp′) *n.* An adjustment, as of a motor or engine, made to improve working order or efficiency.

tung oil (tŭng) *n.* A yellowish or brownish oil extracted from the seeds of an Asian tree and used as a drying agent in paints and varnishes and for waterproofing.

tung·sten (tŭng′stən) *n. Symbol* **W** A hard, gray to white metallic element that is very resistant to corrosion and high temperatures. It is used to make light-bulb filaments and to increase the hardness and strength of steel. Atomic number 74. See **Periodic Table.**

tu·nic (to͞o′nĭk) *n.* **1.** A loose-fitting, knee-length garment worn in ancient Greece and Rome. **2.** A long, plain military jacket, usually having a high stiff collar. **3.** A long loose-fitting garment extending to the thighs or longer.

tu·ni·cate (to͞o′nĭ-kĭt) *n.* Any of various sea animals having a cylindrical or roundish body enclosed in a tough outer covering. Tunicates often live in colonies attached to a surface. [From Latin *tunicāre,* to clothe with a tunic, from *tunica,* tunic.]

tun·ing fork (to͞o′nĭng) *n.* A small two-pronged metal device that when struck produces a tone of fixed pitch that is used as a reference, as in tuning musical instruments.

Tu·nis (to͞o′nĭs) The capital of Tunisia, in the northern part of the country on an inlet of the Mediterranean Sea.

Tu·ni·sia (to͞o-nē′zhə *or* to͞o-nē′shə) A country of northern Africa on the Mediterranean Sea between Algeria and Libya. Tunis is the capital. **—Tu·ni′sian** *adj. & n.*

tun·nel (tŭn′əl) *n.* **1.** An underground or underwater passage. **2.** A passage through or under a mountain or other barrier. ❖ *v.* **tun·neled, tun·nel·ing, tun·nels** or **tun·nelled, tun·nel·ling, tun·nels** *—tr.* **1.** To make a tunnel under or through: *tunneling the granite.* **2.** To produce, shape, or dig in the form of a tunnel: *tunnel a passage under a wall.* *—intr.* To make a tunnel: *tunneled under the harbor.*

tun·ny (tŭn′ē) *n., pl.* **tunny** or **tun·nies** A tuna.

tu·pe·lo (to͞o′pə-lō′) *n., pl.* **tu·pe·los 1.** Any of several trees having small, often bluish-black fruits and soft light wood. **2.** The wood of such a tree.

Tu·pí (to͞o-pē′) or **Tu·pi** (to͞o′pē *or* to͞o-pē′) *n., pl.* **Tupí** or **Tupís** also **Tupi** or **Tu·pis 1.** A member of a group of South American Indian peoples living along the coast of Brazil, in the Amazon River valley, and in Paraguay. **2.** The language of the Tupí. **—Tu′pi·an** *adj.*

tuque (to͞ok) *n.* A close-fitting knitted cap having no brim or a brim that is folded up.

tur·ban (tûr′bən) *n.* **1.** A headdress consisting of a long piece of cloth wound around a small cap or directly around the head, traditionally worn in North Africa, the Near East, and Central and South Asia. **2.** A similar headdress or hat. [From French *turbant,* from Ottoman Turkish *tülbend,* muslin, gauze.]

tur·bid (tûr′bĭd) *adj.* **1.** Having sediment or foreign particles stirred up or suspended: *turbid water.* **2.** Heavy, dark, or dense: *turbid smoke.* **3.** In a state of turmoil; muddled: *turbid feelings.* **—tur′bid·ness, tur·bid′i·ty** *n.*

tur·bine (tûr′bĭn *or* tûr′bīn′) *n.* Any of various machines in which the kinetic energy of a moving fluid is converted to rotary motion as the fluid pushes against a series of vanes or paddles arranged about the circumference of one or more wheels.

tur·bo·charg·er (tûr′bō-chär′jər) *n.* A device that uses the exhaust gas of an internal-combustion engine to drive a turbine that in turn drives a supercharger attached to the engine.

tur·bo·jet (tûr′bō-jĕt′) *n.* **1.** A jet engine in which the exhaust gas operates a turbine that in turn drives a compressor that forces air into the intake of the engine. **2.** An aircraft powered by an engine or engines of this type.

tur·bo·prop (tûr′bō-prŏp′) *n.* **1.** A turbojet engine that drives an external propeller as well as producing jet propulsion. **2.** An aircraft powered by an engine or engines of this type.

tur·bot (tûr′bət) *n., pl.* **turbot** or **tur·bots** A flatfish of coastal waters of Europe and North Africa that has a brown knobby upper side and is used as food.

tur·bu·lence (tûr′byə-ləns) *n.* **1.** The state or quality of being turbulent. **2.** Turbulent flow. **3.** An eddying motion of the atmosphere that interrupts the flow of wind.

tur·bu·lent (tûr′byə-lənt) *adj.* **1.** Moving rapidly or violently: *turbulent waters.* **2.** Characterized by disorder, commotion, or unrest: *a turbulent period in history.* [From Middle English, from Latin *turbulentus,* from *turba,* turmoil.]

turbulent flow *n.* Movement of a fluid in which the pressure and velocity in any small region of the fluid fluctuate at random.

tu·reen (to͞o-rēn′) *n.* A broad deep dish with a cover, used for serving soups or stews at the table.

turf (tûrf) *n., pl.* **turfs** also **turves** (tûrvz) **1a.** A surface layer of earth containing a dense growth of grass and its matted roots; sod. **b.** An artificial substitute for such a grassy layer, as on a playing field. **2.** A piece cut from a layer of earth or sod. **3.** Peat, especially in the form of cut pieces, that is burned for fuel. **4.** *Informal* **a.** A geographical area or territory under someone's authority or influence. **b.** A range of authority or influence: *The mathematics department is his turf.* **5a.** A racetrack. **b.** The sport or business of horse racing. [From Old English.]

tur·gid (tûr′jĭd) *adj.* **1.** Excessively ornate or complex in style or language: *The description runs on for 20 turgid pages.* **2.** Swollen or distended, as by a fluid or inner pressure. **—tur·gid′i·ty** *n.* **—tur′gid·ly** *adv.*

Turk (tûrk) *n.* **1.** A native or inhabitant of Turkey or the Ottoman Empire. **2.** A member of a Turkic-speaking people.

tur·key (tûr′kē) *n., pl.* **tur·keys 1.** A large, brownish North American bird having a bare head and neck with fleshy wattles. It is widely domesticated as a source of food. **2.** The meat of a turkey.

Tur·key (tûr′kē) A country of southwest Asia and southeast Europe between the Mediterranean Sea and the Black Sea. It was the center of the Ottoman Empire. Ankara is the capital and Istanbul the largest city.

Turk·ic (tûr′kĭk) *n.* A group of languages that includes

turban

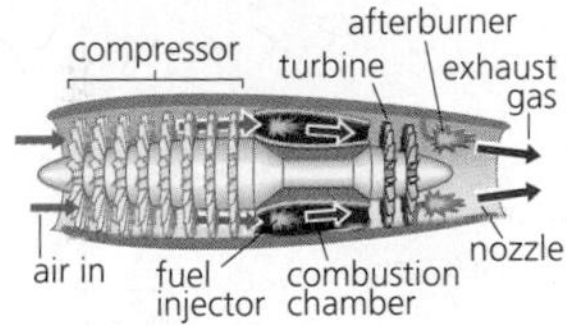

turbojet

tureen

turkey
female *(left)* and male *(right)*

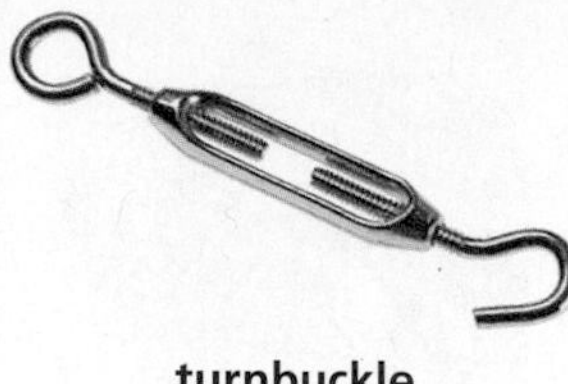

turnbuckle

turquoise
a nugget *(left)* and in a sterling silver pendant *(right)*

turret
on the Tower of Belem, Lisbon, Portugal

ă	pat	ôr	core
ā	pay	oi	boy
âr	care	ou	out
ä	father	o͝o	took
ĕ	pet	o͝or	lure
ē	be	o͞o	boot
ĭ	pit	ŭ	cut
ī	bite	ûr	urge
îr	pier	th	thin
ŏ	pot	*th*	this
ō	toe	zh	vision
ô	paw	ə	about

Turkish. ❖ *adj.* Relating to Turkic or the Turkic-speaking peoples.

Turk·ish (tûr′kĭsh) *adj.* Relating to Turkey or its people, language, or culture. ❖ *n.* The language of the Turks, used mainly in Turkey and Cyprus.

Turk·men (tûrk′mĕn *or* **tûrk′**mən) *adj.* Relating to Turkmenistan or its people, language, or culture. ❖ *n., pl.* **Turkmen** or **Turk·mens 1.** A native or inhabitant of Turkmenistan. **2.** The Turkic language of the Turkmen.

Turk·men·i·stan (tûrk′mĕn-ĭ-**stăn′** *or* tûrk′mĕn-ĭ-**stän′**) A country of west-central Asia on the Caspian Sea south of Uzbekistan. It was once part of ancient Persia. Turkmenistan was part of the USSR from 1925 to 1991. Ashgabat is the capital and the largest city.

tur·mer·ic (**tûr′**mər-ĭk *or* **to͞o′**mər-ĭk) *n.* **1.** A yellowish powder obtained from the rhizome of an Indian plant, used as a seasoning, especially in curries, and as a dye. **2.** The plant that yields such powder. [From Middle English *termerite*, akin to French *terre mérite*, turmeric : Latin *terra*, earth + Latin *merita*, deserving.]

tur·moil (**tûr′**moil′) *n.* A state of extreme confusion or agitation; commotion or tumult: *a country in turmoil over labor strikes.*

turn (tûrn) *v.* **turned, turn·ing, turns** —*tr.* **1.** To cause to move around an axis or a center; cause to rotate or revolve. **2.** To cause to move around in order to achieve a result, such as opening or loosening: *turn the key; turn a screw.* **3.** To alter or control the functioning of (a mechanical device, for example) by a rotating or similar movement: *turn the iron to a hotter setting.* **4.** To perform or accomplish by rotating or revolving: *turn a somersault.* **5.** To change the position of so that the underside becomes the upper side: *turn a page.* **6.** To give a rounded form to (wood, for example) by rotating against a cutting tool. **7.** To change the position of (something) by moving in an arc of a circle; pivot: *turned his chair toward the speaker.* **8a.** To fold, bend, or twist (something). **b.** To change the position or arrangement of (something) by folding, bending, or twisting: *turned the hat inside out.* **c.** To injure by twisting: *turn an ankle.* **d.** To upset or make nauseated: *That story turns my stomach.* **9.** To change the direction or course of: *turn the car to the left.* **10.** To make a course around or about: *turn a corner.* **11.** To present in a specified direction by rotating or pivoting: *turn one's face to the wall.* **12.** To aim or focus; train: *turn one's gaze to the sky.* **13.** To cause to act or go against; make opposed: *News of the scandal turned public opinion against the candidate.* **14.** To send or let go: *turned the dogs loose.* **15.** To cause to change; transform: *Autumn turns the green leaves golden.* **16.** To make use of: *turn a bad situation to one's advantage.* **17.** To get by buying and selling: *turn a fair profit.* —*intr.* **1.** To move around an axis or a center; rotate or revolve: *How fast is the wheel turning?* **2.** To have a sensation of revolving or whirling, especially as a result of dizziness or giddiness. **3.** To change position from side to side or back and forth: *I tossed and turned all night.* **4.** To progress through pages so as to arrive at a given place: *Please turn to page 361.* **5.** To direct one's way or course: *The truck turned into the service station.* **6.** To change or reverse one's way, course, or direction: *Too tired to go farther, we turned and went home.* **7.** To become hostile or opposed: *The peasants turned against the cruel king.* **8.** To direct one's attention, interest, or thought toward or away from something: *Let's turn to another subject. In later life the scientist turned to painting.* **9.** To have recourse to a person or thing for help, support, or information: *You can always turn to your parents.* **10a.** To change so as to be; become: *His hair turned gray. The night turned into day.* **b.** To reach and pass (a certain age, for example): *My niece has turned three.* **11.** To become sour: *The milk has turned.* **12.** To change color: *The leaves have turned.* ❖ *n.* **1.** The act of turning or the condition of being turned; rotation or revolution. **2.** A change of direction, motion, or position: *Make a left turn at the corner.* **3.** A curve, as in a road or path: *a sharp turn in the road.* **4.** A departure or change, as in a trend: *a strange turn of events.* **5.** One of a series of opportunities that occur in succession or in scheduled order: *waiting for her turn at bat.* **6.** A distinctive, graceful, or artistic expression or arrangement: *a lovely turn of phrase.* **7.** A movement or development in a particular direction: *a turn for the worse.* **8.** A deed or an action having a good or bad effect on another: *She did me a good turn.* **9.** A single wind or convolution, as of wire on a spool. ◆ **at every turn** In every place; at every moment. **in turn** In the proper order or sequence. **out of turn** Not in the proper order or sequence. **turn away** To send away; dismiss: *turned away the canvassers who came to the door.* **turn back 1.** To reverse one's direction of motion: *stopped on the road and had to turn back.* **2.** To fold down: *turned back the covers before getting into bed.* **turn down 1.** To lessen the speed, volume, intensity, or flow of: *I turned down the radio.* **2.** To reject or refuse, as a person, piece of advice, or suggestion: *was turned down for the job.* **3.** To fold or be capable of folding down: *turn down the bed.* **turn in 1.** To hand in; give over: *She turned in her keys at the end of the lease.* **2.** To inform on or deliver: *One of his classmates found out he was cheating and turned him in.* **3.** *Informal* To go to bed: *She was tired and so decided to turn in.* **turn off 1.** To stop the operation, activity, or flow of; shut off: *Turn off the TV.* **2.** *Slang* To affect with dislike, displeasure, or revulsion: *Brussels sprouts really turn me off.* **turn on 1.** To cause to begin the operation, activity, or flow of: *Turn on the porch light.* **2.** To begin to display or use: *a politician who knows how to turn on the charm.* **3.** *Slang* To cause to become interested or excited: *That teacher really turned her on to science.* **turn (one's) back on** To abandon or reject. **turn out 1.** To shut off: *turned out the lights.* **2.** To arrive or assemble, as for a public event or entertainment: *A good crowd turned out for the picnic.* **3.** To end up; result: *The cake turned out beautifully.* **4.** To evict; expel: *They were turned out of the apartment when the lease was up.* **turn over 1.** To change the position of so that the bottom is on top or the top is on bottom. **2.** To shift one's position or shift the position of by rolling from one side to the other. **3.** To think about; consider: *turning over the lecture in my mind.* **4.** To transfer to another; surrender: *turned over the keys to a more experienced driver.* **turn over a new leaf** To change one's conduct or attitude for the better. **turn up 1.** To increase the speed, volume, intensity, or flow of: *Turn up the radio so we can hear the news.* **2.** To find: *Our investigation turned up several clues.* **3.** To be found: *A stray kitten turned up on our doorstep one morning.* **4.** To make an appearance; arrive: *He turned up just in time for supper.* [From Old English *turnian, tyrnan*, from Latin *tornāre*, to turn in a lathe.]

❑ *These sound alike:* **turn, tern** (sea bird).

SYNONYMS turn, rotate, spin, whirl, swirl These verbs mean to move or cause to move in a circle. **Turn** is the most general: *The boy in front of me turned and stared at my desk.* **Rotate** means to move around an axis or center: *The top rotated with decreasing speed and finally fell over.* **Spin** means to rotate rapidly, often within a narrow space: *The sheets were spinning in the clothes dryer.* **Whirl** means to rotate or turn rapidly or forcefully: *During the blizzard, snowflakes whirled down from the sky.* **Swirl** often means to move rapidly in a circle: *Floodwaters swirled wildly under the bridge.*

turn·a·round (**tûrn′**ə-round′) *n.* **1.** A space, as in a driveway, permitting the turning around of a vehicle. **2.** A dramatic change in fortune or performance, especially for the better: *Stock prices fell in the morning but rallied in an afternoon turnaround.* **3.** A dramatic change in opinion, behavior, or allegiance: *The new recipe caused me to do a complete turnaround in my opinion of asparagus.*

turn·buck·le (tûrn′bŭk′əl) *n.* A device for adjusting the tension of a rope or cable, consisting of a center section with holes into which rods attached to the ends of the rope or cable can be screwed to increase the tension.

turn·coat (tûrn′kōt′) *n.* A person who goes over to the opposite party; a traitor.

Tur·ner (tûr′nər), **Nat** 1800–1831. American slave leader who led a rebellion in Virginia during which about 50 whites were killed (1831). He was captured and executed.

tur·nip (tûr′nĭp) *n.* **1.** A plant having a large whitish root and edible leaves. **2.** The root of this plant, eaten as a vegetable.

turn·key (tûrn′kē′) *n., pl.* **turn·keys** The keeper of the keys in a prison; a jailer.

turn·off (tûrn′ôf′) *n.* A branch of a road or path leading away from a main thoroughfare, especially an exit on a highway.

turn·out (tûrn′out′) *n.* **1.** The number of people who participate in a particular event or activity: *a great turnout for the picnic; low voter turnout for the election.* **2.** A number of things produced; output: *The factory increased its turnout.* **3.** The act or an instance of turning out: *her quick turnout of another novel.*

turn·o·ver (tûrn′ō′vər) *n.* **1.** The act or fact of turning over: *preventing the turnover of vehicles in accidents.* **2.** An abrupt change or transfer: *a peaceful turnover of power after the dictator was deposed.* **3.** A small pastry made by spreading a filling on half of a piece of dough, folding the other half on top, and sealing the edges. **4.** The number of times a particular stock of goods is sold and restocked during a given period. **5.** The amount of business transacted during a given period. **6.** The number of workers that have left a workplace or industry and been replaced in a given period of time, or the rate at which this happens. **7.** In sports, a loss of possession of the ball to the opposing team, as by a misplay or a violation of the rules.

turn·pike (tûrn′pīk′) *n.* A toll road, especially an expressway with tollgates.

turn·stile (tûrn′stīl′) *n.* A device that limits or counts the number of people moving from one area to another by causing each person to pass through individually. It consists of a vertical frame with bars that project from it and revolve or with panels that retract to allow passage.

turn·ta·ble (tûrn′tā′bəl) *n.* **1a.** The rotating circular platform of a phonograph on which the record is placed. **b.** A phonograph without amplifiers or loudspeakers. **2.** A circular platform equipped with a railway track and capable of rotating, used for turning locomotives. **3.** A rotating platform or disk, such as a lazy Susan.

tur·pen·tine (tûr′pən-tīn′) *n.* **1.** A thin, easily vaporized oil composed of carbon and hydrogen. It is distilled from the wood or resin of certain pine trees and used as a paint thinner, solvent, and liniment. **2.** The sticky mixture of resin and oil from which this oil is distilled.

tur·pi·tude (tûr′pĭ-to͞od′) *n.* Baseness; depravity.

tur·quoise (tûr′kwoiz′ *or* tûr′koiz′) *n.* **1.** A bluish-green mineral containing aluminum and copper, valued in certain of its forms as a gem. **2.** A light to brilliant bluish green. [From Middle English *turkeis*, from Old French *(pierre) turqueise*, Turkish (stone), turquoise.] —**tur′quoise′** *adj.*

tur·ret (tûr′ĭt) *n.* **1.** A small tower or tower-shaped projection on a building. **2.** A low, usually rotating structure containing guns, as on a tank or warship. **3.** An attachment for a lathe consisting of a rotating cylinder holding various cutting tools. [From Middle English *touret*, from Old French *torete*, from *tor*, tower.]

tur·tle (tûr′tl) *n.* Any of various reptiles living either in water or on land and having a bony or leathery shell into which the head, legs, and tail can be pulled for protection. [Perhaps from French *tortue*, from Old French.]

tur·tle·dove or **turtle dove** (tûr′tl-dŭv′) *n.* A small dove of Eurasia and Africa, having a white-edged tail and a soft purring voice.

tur·tle·neck (tûr′tl-nĕk′) *n.* **1.** A high, tubular, often rolled-down collar that fits closely around the neck. **2.** A garment, such as a sweater, having such a collar.

turves (tûrvz) *n.* A plural of **turf.**

Tus·ca·ro·ra (tŭs′kə-**rôr′**ə) *n., pl.* **Tuscarora** or **Tus·ca·ro·ras** **1.** A member of a Native American people formerly living in North Carolina and now living in western New York and southeast Ontario. The Tuscarora joined the Iroquois confederacy in 1722. **2.** The Iroquoian language of the Tuscarora.

tusk (tŭsk) *n.* A long pointed tooth, usually one of a pair, projecting outside of the mouth of certain animals, such as an elephant, walrus, or boar. [From Old English *tūx, tūsc*, canine tooth.]

tus·sle (tŭs′əl) *intr.v.* **tus·sled, tus·sling, tus·sles** To fight roughly; scuffle. ❖ *n.* A rough or vigorous fight; a scuffle.

tus·sock (tŭs′ək) *n.* A clump or tuft, as of growing grass.

Tut·ankh·a·mun or **Tut·ankh·a·men** (to͞ot′äng-**kä′**-mən) Flourished about 1350 BC. King of Egypt (1355–1346 BC). His tomb was found almost intact in 1922, inspiring worldwide interest of ancient Egypt.

tu·te·lage (to͞ot′l-ĭj) *n.* **1.** The activity or capacity of a guardian; guardianship. **2.** The act or capacity of a tutor; instruction. **3.** The state of being under the direction of a guardian or tutor.

tu·tor (to͞o′tər) *n.* **1.** A private instructor. **2.** In law, the guardian of a minor. ❖ *tr.v.* **tu·tored, tu·tor·ing, tu·tors** To act as tutor to; instruct or teach privately: *tutored the boy in math.* [From Middle English *tutour*, from Latin *tutor*, from *tuērī*, to guard.]

tu·to·ri·al (to͞o-**tôr′**ē-əl) *adj.* Relating to a tutor or private instructor. ❖ *n.* A book, class, or computer program that provides instruction in a particular area: *watched the tutorial to learn how to use the software system.*

Tut·si (to͞ot′sē) *n., pl.* **Tut·si** or **Tut·sis** A member of a Bantu-speaking people of Rwanda and Burundi.

tut·ti-frut·ti (to͞o′tē-fro͞o′tē) *n., pl.* **tut·ti-frut·tis** A confection, especially ice cream, containing a variety of chopped and usually candied fruits. [From Italian : *tutti*, all + *frutti*, fruits.]

Tu·tu (to͞o′to͞o), **Desmond** Born 1931. South African archbishop who was a leader in the antiapartheid struggle.

Tu·va·lu (to͞o-vä′lo͞o *or* to͞o′və-lo͞o′) An island country of the western Pacific Ocean north of Fiji. It gained its independence from Great Britain in 1978. Funafuti is the capital.

tux (tŭks) *n. Informal* A tuxedo.

tux·e·do (tŭk-sē′dō) *n., pl.* **tux·e·dos** or **tux·e·does** A man's formal suit, including a jacket without tails, pants, a bow tie, and often a cummerbund.

TV (tē′vē′) *n.* Television.

TVA *abbr.* An abbreviation of Tennessee Valley Authority.

TV dinner *n.* A frozen prepared meal that only needs to be heated before serving.

twad·dle (twŏd′l) *intr.v.* **twad·dled, twad·dling, twad·dles** To talk foolishly. ❖ *n.* Foolish, trivial, or idle talk.

twain (twān) *n. & adj. & pron.* Two.

Twain (twān), **Mark** See Samuel Langhorne **Clemens.**

twang (twăng) *v.* **twanged, twang·ing, twangs** —*intr.*

turtleneck

tusk
on an African elephant

Desmond Tutu

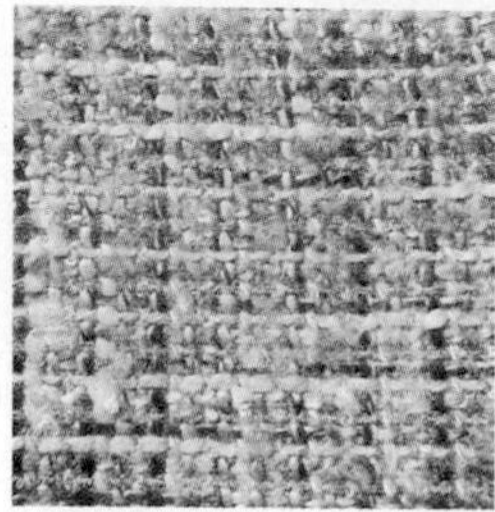
tweed

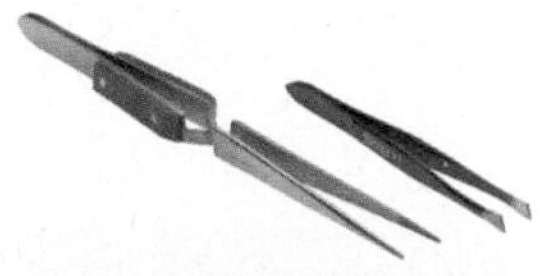
tweezers
left: jeweler's tweezers
right: eyebrow tweezers

To emit a sharp vibrating sound, as the string of a musical instrument does when plucked. —*tr.* **1.** To cause to make a sharp vibrating sound. **2.** To utter with a strongly nasal tone of voice. ❖ *n.* **1.** A sharp vibrating sound, as that of a plucked string. **2.** A strongly nasal tone of voice.

'twas (twŭz *or* twŏz; twəz *when unstressed*) Contraction of *it was.*

tweak (twēk) *tr.v.* **tweaked, tweak·ing, tweaks 1.** To pinch, pluck, or twist sharply: *He tweaked her nose playfully.* **2.** To make fun of; tease. **3.** To adjust; fine-tune: *tweaked the radio dial to get better reception.* ❖ *n.* **1.** A sharp twisting pinch. **2.** A teasing remark.

tweed (twēd) *n.* **1.** A coarse woolen fabric made in a twill weave and used chiefly for casual suits and coats. **2. tweeds** Clothes made of this fabric.

tweet (twēt) *n.* **1.** A weak chirping sound, as of a small bird. **2.** A message posted on Twitter. Tweets are limited to 140 characters. ❖ *intr.v.* **tweet·ed, tweet·ing, tweets 1.** To utter a weak chirping sound. **2.** To post a message on Twitter.

tweet·er (twē′tər) *n.* A small loudspeaker designed to reproduce high-pitched sounds in a high-fidelity sound system.

tweez·ers (twē′zərz) *pl.n. (used with a singular or plural verb)* Small pincers used for plucking or handling small objects.

twelfth (twĕlfth) *n.* **1.** The ordinal number matching the number 12 in a series. **2.** One of 12 equal parts.

twelve (twĕlv) *n.* **1.** The number, written 12, that is equal to 11 + 1. **2.** The 12th in a set or sequence. [From Old English *twelf.*]

twelve·month (twĕlv′mŭnth′) *n.* A year.

twen·ti·eth (twĕn′tē-ĭth *or* twŭn′tē-ĭth) *n.* **1.** The ordinal number matching the number 20 in a series. **2.** One of 20 equal parts.

twen·ty (twĕn′tē *or* twŭn′tē) *n., pl.* **twen·ties 1.** The number, written 20, that is equal to 2 × 10. **2.** The 20th in a set or sequence. **3.** A twenty-dollar bill. [From Old English *twēntig.*]

twen·ty-one (twĕn′tē-wŭn′ *or* twŭn′tē-wŭn′) *n.* The game of blackjack.

twerp (twûrp) *n. Slang* A silly and contemptible person.

Twi (chwē *or* chē) *n.* A language spoken in Ghana.

twice (twīs) *adv.* **1.** In two cases or on two occasions; two times: *He saw the movie twice.* **2.** In doubled degree or amount: *She works twice as hard as her colleagues.*

twice-told (twīs′tōld′) *adj.* Very familiar because of repeated telling.

twid·dle (twĭd′l) *v.* **twid·dled, twid·dling, twid·dles** —*tr.* To turn over or around idly or lightly; fiddle with. —*intr.* To trifle with something. ❖ *n.* The act or an instance of twiddling. ◆ **twiddle (one's) thumbs** To do little or nothing; be idle.

twig (twĭg) *n.* A small branch or young shoot of a tree or shrub. [From Old English *twigge.*]

twi·light (twī′līt′) *n.* **1.** The diffused light from the sky during the early evening or early morning when the sun is below the horizon. **2.** The interval of time during which the sun is just below the horizon; the period between sunset and night. **3.** A period or condition of decline following growth, glory, or success: *a man in the twilight of his life.*

twill (twĭl) *n.* **1.** A fabric having diagonal parallel ribs. **2.** A weave that produces diagonal ribs on the surface of a fabric. ❖ *tr.v.* **twilled, twill·ing, twills** To weave (cloth) so as to produce diagonal ribs.

twin (twĭn) *n.* **1.** One of two offspring born in a single birth: *She always dresses differently from her twin.* **2.** One of two identical or similar people, animals, or things; a counterpart: *Where is the twin to this sock?* ❖ *adj.* **1.** Being two or one of two offspring born at the same birth: *her twin sister; twin lambs.* **2.** Being two or one of two identical or similar people, animals, or things: *a twin bed; twin cities.* [From Old English *twinn,* twofold.]

twin bed *n.* One of a matching pair of single beds.

twine (twīn) *v.* **twined, twin·ing, twines** —*tr.* **1.** To twist together (threads or fibers, for example); intertwine. **2.** To form by twisting or interlacing: *twine a garland.* **3.** To encircle or coil about: *A vine twined the fence.* —*intr.* **1.** To become twisted, interlaced, or interwoven. **2.** To go in a winding course: *a stream twining through the valley.* ❖ *n.* A strong cord or string made of threads twisted together. [From Middle English *twinen,* from Old English *twīn,* double thread.]

twinge (twĭnj) *n.* **1.** A sudden and sharp physical pain. **2.** A mental or emotional pain. ❖ *intr.v.* **twinged, twing·ing, twing·es** To feel a twinge.

twin·kle (twĭng′kəl) *intr.v.* **twin·kled, twin·kling, twin·kles 1.** To shine with slight intermittent gleams; sparkle: *stars twinkling in the sky.* **2.** To be bright or sparkling, as with merriment or delight: *Her eyes twinkle.* ❖ *n.* **1.** A slight intermittent gleam of light; a glimmer. **2.** A sparkle of merriment or delight in the eye. **3.** A brief interval; a twinkling. [From Old English *twinclian.*]

twin·kling (twĭng′klĭng) *n.* **1.** The act of blinking. **2.** A blink or twinkle. **3.** The time that it takes to blink; an instant: *was gone in the twinkling of an eye.*

twirl (twûrl) *tr. & intr.v.* **twirled, twirl·ing, twirls** To rotate or revolve briskly: *twirl a baton; pinwheels twirling in the wind.* ❖ *n.* The act of twirling or the condition of being twirled; a sharp quick spin or whirl. **—twirl′er** *n.*

twist (twĭst) *v.* **twist·ed, twist·ing, twists** —*tr.* **1a.** To wind together (threads, for example) so as to produce a single strand. **b.** To form in this manner: *twist a length of rope.* **2.** To wind or coil (rope, for example) about something. **3.** To cause to rotate or turn in another direction: *They twisted their heads around at the sound.* **4.** To form into a spiral, as by turning the ends in opposite directions: *twisting wire into a loop.* **5a.** To turn or open by turning: *twisted off the bottle cap.* **b.** To pull, break, or snap by turning: *twist off a dead branch.* **6.** To injure by wrenching; sprain: *twist one's ankle.* **7.** To alter or distort the intended meaning of: *The prosecutor twisted the words of the witness.* —*intr.* **1.** To be or become twisted. **2.** To move or progress in a winding course; meander: *The river twisted toward the sea.* **3.** To squirm; writhe: *twist with pain.* ❖ *n.* **1.** Something twisted or formed by twisting, as a length of yarn or cord. **2.** A sliver of citrus peel twisted over or dropped into a beverage for flavoring. **3.** A spin, twirl, or rotation. **4.** A change in direction; a turn: *a sharp twist in the path.* **5.** An unexpected change in a process or a departure from a pattern: *a story with a twist.* [From Middle English *twisten,* from *twist,* a divided object, fork, rope, from Old English *-twist,* rope.] **—twist′a·ble** *adj.*

twist·er (twĭs′tər) *n. Informal* A tornado.

twit (twĭt) *n. Slang* A foolishly annoying person.

twitch (twĭch) *v.* **twitched, twitch·ing, twitch·es** —*intr.* To move with a jerk or spasm. —*tr.* To pull, jerk, or move sharply: *The bird twitched its tail.* ❖ *n.* **1.** A sudden involuntary or spasmodic movement, as of a muscle. **2.** A sudden pull; a tug.

twit·ter (twĭt′ər) *v.* **twit·tered, twit·ter·ing, twit·ters** —*intr.* **1.** To utter a series of light chirping sounds, made by certain birds. **2.** To speak rapidly and softly. —*tr.* To utter or say with a twitter. ❖ *n.* **1.** The light chirping sound made by certain birds. **2.** A similar sound, especially light speech or laughter. **3.** A state of agitation or excitement. [From Middle English *twiteren,* of imitative origin.]

Twit·ter (twĭt′ər) A trademark for an online social networking service that limits posts to 140 characters.

two (to͞o) *n.* **1.** The number, written 2, that is equal to 1

ă	pat	ôr	core
ā	pay	oi	boy
âr	care	ou	out
ä	father	o͝o	took
ĕ	pet	o͝or	lure
ē	be	o͞o	boot
ĭ	pit	ŭ	cut
ī	bite	ûr	urge
îr	pier	th	thin
ŏ	pot	*th*	this
ō	toe	zh	vision
ô	paw	ə	about

+ 1. **2.** The second in a set or sequence. **3.** A two-dollar bill. [From Old English *twā*.]
❑ *These sound alike:* **two, to** (toward), **too** (also).

two-bit (to͞o′bĭt′) *adj.* **1.** *Informal* Costing or worth 25 cents. **2.** *Slang* Worth very little; petty or insignificant.

two-by-four (to͞o′bī-fôr′) *adj.* Measuring two units by four units, especially inches. ❖ *n.* A length of lumber that is 2 inches thick and 4 inches wide.

two-faced (to͞o′fāst′) *adj.* **1.** Having two faces or surfaces. **2.** Hypocritical or double-dealing; deceitful.

two-ply (to͞o′plī′) *adj.* **1.** Made of two interwoven layers. **2.** Consisting of two thicknesses or strands: *two-ply yarn.*

two·some (to͞o′səm) *n.* **1.** Two people or things together; a pair or couple. **2.** An activity involving two people, such as a round of golf.

two-step (to͞o′stĕp′) *n.* A ballroom dance in 2/4 time, characterized by long sliding steps.

two-time (to͞o′tīm′) *tr.v.* **two-timed, two-tim·ing, two-times** *Slang* **1.** To be unfaithful to (a spouse or lover). **2.** To deceive; double-cross.

two-way (to͞o′wā′) *adj.* **1a.** Affording passage in two directions: *a two-way street.* **b.** Moving in two directions: *two-way traffic.* **2.** Permitting communication in two directions: *a two-way radio.*

TX *abbr.* An abbreviation of Texas.

–ty *suff.* A suffix that means condition or quality: *loyalty.* —SEE NOTE.

ty·coon (tī-ko͞on′) *n.* A wealthy and powerful person in business or industry. [From Japanese *taikun*, title of a shogun.]

ty·ing (tī′ĭng) *v.* Present participle of **tie.**

tyke (tīk) *n.* A small child.

Ty·ler (tī′lər), **John** 1790–1862. The tenth president of the United States (1841–1845), whose administration was marked by the annexation of Texas (1845).

tym·pa·ni (tĭm′pə-nē) *pl.n.* Variant of **timpani.**

tym·pan·ic membrane (tĭm-păn′ĭk) *n.* The eardrum.

tym·pa·num (tĭm′pə-nəm) *n., pl.* **tym·pa·na** (tĭm′pə-nə) or **tym·pa·nums 1.** The middle ear. **2.** The eardrum.

type (tīp) *n.* **1.** A number of people or things having in common traits or characteristics that set them apart as a distinct class. **2.** A person or thing having the characteristics of a group or class: *the type of hero popular in Victorian novels.* **3.** An example or model having the ideal features of a group or class: *He was the perfect type of coach.* **4.** *Informal* A person regarded as a good example of a particular profession or social group: *I was sitting in the restaurant when a bunch of gangster types walked in.* **5a.** In printing, a small block of metal or wood with a raised letter or character on the upper end that leaves a printed impression when inked and pressed on paper. **b.** Such pieces considered as a group. **c.** Printed or typewritten characters; print. ❖ *v.* **typed, typ·ing, types** —*tr.* **1.** To write (something) with a typewriter. **2.** To classify according to a particular type or class: *type the rock samples by studying each; type an actor as a villain.* —*intr.* To write with a typewriter; typewrite. [From Latin *typus*, image, from Greek *tupos*, impression.]

type·face (tīp′fās′) *n.* **1.** In printing, the surface of a block of type that makes the impression. **2.** The impression made by this surface. **3.** The size or style of the letters on blocks of type.

type·script (tīp′skrĭpt′) *n.* A typewritten copy, as of a manuscript.

type·set (tīp′sĕt′) *tr.v.* **type·set, type·set·ting, type·sets** In printing, to set (written material) into type.

type·set·ter (tīp′sĕt′ər) *n.* A person who sets type; a compositor.

type·write (tīp′rīt′) *intr. & tr.v.* **type·wrote** (tīp′rōt′), **type·writ·ten** (tīp′rĭt′n), **type·writ·ing, type·writes** To engage in writing or to write (something) with a typewriter; type.

type·writ·er (tīp′rī′tər) *n.* A writing machine that produces characters similar to print by means of a hand-operated keyboard that moves a set of raised blocks, which strike the paper through an inked ribbon.

ty·phoid (tī′foid′) *n.* Typhoid fever.

typhoid fever *n.* An infectious, often fatal disease caused by bacteria transmitted in contaminated food or water. Its symptoms include high fever, intestinal bleeding, and rose-colored spots on the skin.

ty·phoon (tī-fo͞on′) *n.* A hurricane occurring in the western Pacific Ocean.

ty·phus (tī′fəs) *n.* Any of several forms of an infectious disease caused by bacteria, especially those transmitted by fleas, lice, or mites, and characterized generally by sustained high fever, delirium, and red rashes.

typ·i·cal (tĭp′ĭ-kəl) *adj.* **1.** Showing the traits or characteristics that identify a kind, group, or category: *a typical college campus.* **2.** Conforming with what usually happens: *The bus is late again? That's so typical!* **—typ′i·cal·ly** *adv.*

typ·i·fy (tĭp′ə-fī′) *tr.v.* **typ·i·fied, typ·i·fy·ing, typ·i·fies** To serve as a typical example of.

typ·ist (tī′pĭst) *n.* A person who operates a typewriter.

ty·pog·ra·pher (tī-pŏg′rə-fər) *n.* A person who sets written material into type; a printer or compositor.

ty·pog·ra·phy (tī-pŏg′rə-fē) *n., pl.* **ty·pog·ra·phies 1.** The art and technique of printing with movable type. **2.** The arrangement and appearance of printed matter. **—ty′po·graph′i·cal** (tī′pə-grăf′ĭ-kəl) *adj.*

ty·ran·ni·cal (tĭ-răn′ĭ-kəl *or* tī-răn′ĭ-kəl) *adj.* Relating to or characteristic of a tyrant or tyranny. **—ty·ran′ni·cal·ly** *adv.*

tyr·an·nize (tĭr′ə-nīz′) *v.* **tyr·an·nized, tyr·an·niz·ing, tyr·an·niz·es** —*tr.* To treat or govern tyrannically. —*intr.* **1.** To exercise absolute power. **2.** To rule as a tyrant.

Ty·ran·no·saur·us rex (tĭ-răn′ə-sôr′əs rĕks′) *n.* A very large meat-eating dinosaur having a large head, sharp teeth, and short front legs.

tyr·an·ny (tĭr′ə-nē) *n., pl.* **tyr·an·nies 1.** Absolute power, especially when exercised unjustly or cruelly. **2.** A government in which a single ruler has absolute power. **3.** The office, authority, or jurisdiction of an absolute ruler.

ty·rant (tī′rənt) *n.* **1.** An extremely oppressive, unjust, or cruel ruler. **2.** An absolute ruler who governs without legal restrictions, especially one who seized power illegally. **3.** A person who uses authority in a harsh or cruel manner: *My boss is a tyrant.* [From Middle English *tiraunt*, from Greek *turannos*.]

Tyre (tīr) An ancient Phoenician city on the eastern Mediterranean Sea in present-day southern Lebanon. It was the capital of Phoenicia after the 11th century BC.

ty·ro (tī′rō) *n., pl.* **ty·ros** A beginner in learning something.

ty·ro·sine (tī′rə-sēn′) *n.* A nonessential amino acid that is formed by the reaction of certain proteins with water.

Tyr·rhe·ni·an Sea (tə-rē′nē-ən) An arm of the Mediterranean Sea between the Italian peninsula and the islands of Corsica, Sardinia, and Sicily.

tzar (zär *or* tsär) *n.* Variant of **czar** (sense 1).

WORD BUILDING

–ty The suffix **–ty** forms nouns from adjectives. The word *subtlety,* for example, means "the quality or state of being subtle." In the same way are formed *certainty, frailty, loyalty,* and *royalty.* Another form of the same suffix is **–ity,** which is more common nowadays; we see it for example in *electricity, technicality, peculiarity,* and *similarity.* The suffixes *–ty* and *–ity* mean about the same thing as the suffix **–ness;** but whereas *–ness* is native English and is mostly added to native English adjectives, *–ty* and *–ity* come from Latin and are usually added to adjectives of Latin origin.

John Tyler
1859 portrait by George Peter Alexander Healy (1813–1894)

WORD HISTORY

ukulele The word **ukulele** is one of a small number of Hawaiian words that have been borrowed into English. Other common borrowings are **aloha** (a greeting or farewell) and **luau** (an outdoor picnic usually featuring a whole barbecued pig).

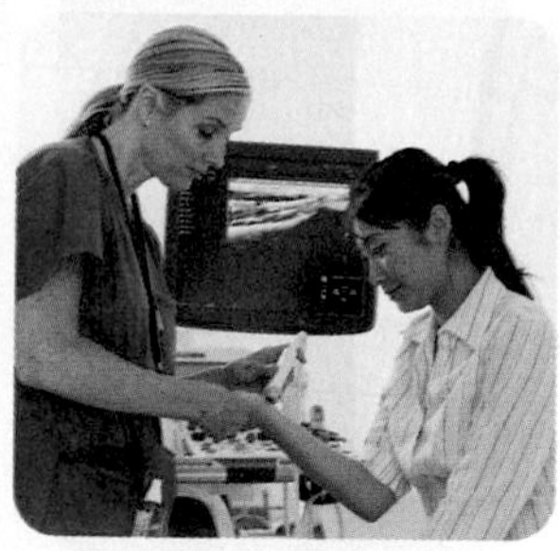

ultrasound
ultrasound of a wrist

ă	pat	ôr	core
ā	pay	oi	boy
âr	care	ou	out
ä	father	o͝o	took
ĕ	pet	o͝or	lure
ē	be	o͞o	boot
ĭ	pit	ŭ	cut
ī	bite	ûr	urge
îr	pier	th	thin
ŏ	pot	*th*	this
ō	toe	zh	vision
ô	paw	ə	about

u or **U** (yo͞o) *n., pl.* **u's** or **U's** also **us** or **Us** The 21st letter of the English alphabet.

U[1] The symbol for the element **uranium.**

U[2] *abbr.* An abbreviation of unsatisfactory.

u·biq·ui·tous (yo͞o-**bĭk′**wĭ-təs) *adj.* Being or seeming to be everywhere at the same time: *a ubiquitous bird throughout South Dakota.* [From Latin *ubīque,* everywhere.] —**u·biq′ui·tous·ly** *adv.*

u·biq·ui·ty (yo͞o-**bĭk′**wĭ-tē) *n.* Existence or apparent existence everywhere at the same time: *the ubiquity of television in modern society.*

ud·der (**ŭd′**ər) *n.* A bag-shaped part of a cow, sheep, or goat in which milk is formed and stored and from which it is taken in suckling or milking.

UFO (yo͞o′ĕf-**ō′**) *n.* An unidentified flying object.

U·gan·da (yo͞o-**găn′**də) A country of east-central Africa west of Kenya. Kampala is the capital.

ugh (ŭg *or* ŭKH) *interj.* An expression used to show disgust or horror.

ug·ly (**ŭg′**lē) *adj.* **ug·li·er, ug·li·est 1.** Displeasing to the senses, especially to the eye or ear: *an ugly building; an ugly sound.* **2.** Repulsive or offensive: *You should apologize for those ugly remarks you made.* **3.** Disagreeable; unpleasant: *an ugly temper.* [From Middle English *ugli,* frightful, repulsive, from Old Norse *uggligr,* from *uggr,* fear.] —**ug′li·ly** *adv.* —**ug′li·ness** *n.*

uh (ŭ) *interj.* An expression used to show hesitation or uncertainty.

UHF *abbr.* An abbreviation of ultrahigh frequency.

uh-huh (ŭN′**hŭN′**) *interj. Informal* An expression used to show agreement.

uh-oh (**ŭ′**ō′) *interj. Informal* An expression used to show alarm, foreboding, or dismay.

uh-uh (**ŭN′**ŭN′ *or* ŭN′**ŭN′**) *interj. Informal* An expression used to show disagreement.

UK *abbr.* An abbreviation of United Kingdom.

U·kraine (yo͞o-**krān′**) A country of eastern Europe bordering on the Black Sea west of Russia. It was part of the USSR from 1922 to 1991. Kiev is the capital.

U·krain·i·an (yo͞o-**krā′**nē-ən) *adj.* Relating to Ukraine or its people, language, or culture. ❖ *n.* **1.** A native or inhabitant of the Ukraine. **2.** The Slavic language of the Ukrainians.

u·ku·le·le (yo͞o′kə-**lā′**lē) *n.* A small four-stringed guitar, first popular in Hawaii. [From Hawaiian *ʻukulele.*] —SEE NOTE.

U·laan·baa·tar (o͞o′län-**bä′**tär′) or **U·lan Ba·tor** (o͞o′-län-**bä′**tôr′) The capital of Mongolia, in the north-central part of the country. It was founded in 1639.

ul·cer (**ŭl′**sər) *n.* An open sore on the skin or a mucous membrane of the body, such as the lining of the stomach or duodenum. [From Middle English, from Latin *ulcus.*]

ul·cer·ate (**ŭl′**sə-rāt′) *tr. & intr.v.* **ul·cer·at·ed, ul·cer·at·ing, ul·cer·ates** To affect or become affected with an ulcer.

ul·cer·a·tion (ŭl′sə-**rā′**shən) *n.* **1.** Development of an ulcer. **2.** An ulcer or an ulcerous condition.

ul·cer·ous (**ŭl′**sər-əs) *adj.* Relating to or affected with an ulcer or ulcers.

ul·na (**ŭl′**nə) *n., pl.* **ul·nas** or **ul·nae** (**ŭl′**nē) **1.** The bone that in humans extends from the elbow to the wrist on the side of the arm opposite to the thumb. **2.** The corresponding bone in the foreleg of other vertebrates. [From Latin *ulna,* elbow, forearm.] —**ul′nar** *adj.*

u·lo (**o͞o′**lō) *n.* Variant of **ulu.**

Ul·ster (**ŭl′**stər) A historical region and ancient kingdom of northern Ireland. It is now divided between Ireland and Northern Ireland.

ul·te·ri·or (ŭl-**tîr′**ē-ər) *adj.* **1.** Lying beyond what is evident or admitted, especially when intentionally concealed: *ulterior motives.* **2.** Lying beyond or outside the area of immediate interest: *the ulterior parts of the island.* —**ul·te′ri·or·ly** *adv.*

ul·ti·mate (**ŭl′**tə-mĭt) *adj.* **1.** Final; last: *the ultimate stop on the rail line.* **2.** Basic; fundamental: *ultimate truths.* **3.** Greatest possible in size or significance: *the ultimate act of courage.* ❖ *n.* The greatest extreme; the maximum: *the ultimate in laptop computers.* [From Latin *ultimus.*] —**ul′ti·mate·ly** *adv.*

ul·ti·ma·tum (ŭl′tə-**mā′**təm) *n., pl.* **ul·ti·ma·tums** or **ul·ti·ma·ta** (ŭl′tə-**mā′**tə) A final statement of terms that expresses or implies the threat of serious penalties if the terms are not accepted.

ultra– *pref.* A prefix that means beyond the range, limit, or normal degree of: *ultrasonic; ultraviolet; ultramodern.*

ul·tra·high frequency (ŭl′trə-**hī′**) *n.* A band of radio frequencies from 300 to 3,000 megahertz.

ul·tra·ma·rine (ŭl′trə-mə-**rēn′**) *n.* **1.** A blue pigment made from a powder of the mineral lapis lazuli. **2.** A bright or strong blue to purplish blue. ❖ *adj.* Having the color ultramarine. [From Medieval Latin *ultrāmarīnus,* from beyond the sea.]

ul·tra·mod·ern (ŭl′trə-**mŏd′**ərn) *adj.* Very modern in ideas or style; completely up-to-date.

ul·tra·son·ic (ŭl′trə-**sŏn′**ĭk) *adj.* Consisting of or using sound that is too high in frequency to be heard by humans: *ultrasonic waves.*

ul·tra·son·ics (ŭl′trə-**sŏn′**ĭks) *n. (used with a singular verb)* The scientific study and practical application of ultrasonic sounds.

ul·tra·sound (**ŭl′**trə-sound′) *n.* **1.** Ultrasonic sound. **2a.** The medical use of ultrasonic waves, especially to produce images of internal structures of the body or to observe a developing fetus. **b.** An image produced by this technique.

ul·tra·vi·o·let (ŭl′trə-**vī′**ə-lĭt) *adj.* Relating to electromagnetic radiation having wavelengths shorter than those of visible light but longer than those of x-rays. ❖ *n.* Ultraviolet light or the ultraviolet part of the spectrum.

u·lu (**o͞o′**lo͞o) or **u·lo** (**o͞o′**lō) *n., pl.* **u·lus** or **u·los** An Inuit or Yupik knife having an arched blade fixed to a central handle, used especially for skinning, chopping, and carving.

U·lys·ses (yo͞o-lĭs′ēz′) *n.* Odysseus.

um·bel (ŭm′bəl) *n.* A flat or rounded flower cluster in which the individual flower stalks arise from about the same point on the stem. [From Latin *umbella*, parasol.]

um·ber (ŭm′bər) *n.* **1.** A natural brown earth containing oxides of iron and manganese, used as a pigment. **2.** A dark reddish brown. ❖ *adj.* Dark reddish-brown.

um·bil·i·cal (ŭm-bĭl′ĭ-kəl) *adj.* Relating to a navel or an umbilical cord: *an umbilical hernia.*

umbilical cord *n.* The flexible cord-shaped structure connecting a fetus at the abdomen with the placenta, containing blood vessels that supply oxygen and nutrients to the fetus and remove its wastes.

um·bil·i·cus (ŭm-bĭl′ĭ-kəs) *n., pl.* **um·bil·i·ci** (ŭm-bĭl′ĭ-sī′) The navel.

um·bra (ŭm′brə) *n., pl.* **um·bras** or **um·brae** (ŭm′brē) **1.** A dark area, especially the darkest part of a shadow. **2a.** The completely dark portion of the shadow cast by Earth, the moon, or another body during an eclipse. **b.** The darkest region of a sunspot. [From Latin, shadow.] **—um′bral** *adj.*

um·brage (ŭm′brĭj) *n.* Offense; resentment: *Don't take umbrage at my question.*

um·brel·la (ŭm-brĕl′ə) *n.* A device for protection from the rain or sun, consisting of a collapsible, usually circular piece of cloth or other material mounted on a rod. [From Latin *umbella*, parasol.]

u·mi·ak (o͞o′mē-ăk′) *n.* A large open Inuit or Yupik boat made of skins stretched on a wooden frame.

ump (ŭmp) *n. Informal* An umpire.

um·pire (ŭm′pīr′) *n.* **1.** A person appointed to rule on plays, especially in baseball. **2.** A person empowered to settle a dispute. ❖ *v.* **um·pired, um·pir·ing, um·pires** *—tr.* To act as an umpire for: *umpire a game. —intr.* To be or act as an umpire. [From Middle English *noumpere*, mediator, altered to *(an) oumpere*, from the phrase *(a) noumpere*, from Old French *nonper* : *non-*, not + *per*, equal, even, paired.] —SEE NOTE AT **apron.**

ump·teen (ŭmp′tēn′) *adj. Informal* Being of a large but unspecified number: *I have umpteen reasons for not wanting to go.* **—ump′teenth′** *adj.*

UN *abbr.* An abbreviation of United Nations.

un–[1] *pref.* A prefix that means: **1.** Not: *unattached.* **2.** Contrary to: *unrest.* —SEE NOTE.

un–[2] *pref.* A prefix that means: **1.** To reverse or undo an action: *unbar.* **2.** To deprive of or remove a thing: *unburden.* **3.** To release, free, or remove from: *untie.* **4.** Used as an intensive: *unloose.* —SEE NOTE AT **un–**[1]**.**

un·a·bashed (ŭn′ə-băsht′) *adj.* **1.** Not embarrassed or ashamed: *an unabashed fan of soap operas.* **2.** Not concealed or disguised: *unabashed disgust.* **—un′a·bash′ed·ly** (ŭn′ə-băsh′ĭd-lē) *adv.*

un·a·ble (ŭn-ā′bəl) *adj.* **1.** Lacking the necessary power, authority, or means to do something: *He was unable to go to the party.* **2.** Lacking mental or physical capability or efficiency: *With a sprained ankle, she was unable to walk to school.*

un·a·bridged (ŭn′ə-brĭjd′) *adj.* Not condensed or shortened: *an unabridged book.*

un·ac·cent·ed (ŭn-ăk′sĕn-tĭd) *adj.* Having weak stress or no stress: *an unaccented syllable.*

un·ac·com·pa·nied (ŭn′ə-kŭm′pə-nēd) *adj.* **1.** Being without a companion: *unaccompanied children on a flight.* **2.** Performed or designed to be performed without accompaniment; solo: *a composition for unaccompanied flute.*

un·ac·count·a·ble (ŭn′ə-koun′tə-bəl) *adj.* **1.** Impossible to explain: *an unaccountable absence from class.* **2.** Not accountable to a higher authority; not responsible: *unaccountable for his actions.* **—un′ac·count′a·bly** *adv.*

un·ac·cus·tomed (ŭn′ə-kŭs′təmd) *adj.* **1.** Not common or usual: *treated me with unaccustomed politeness.* **2.** Not habituated or accustomed: *unaccustomed to the cold.*

un·ac·quaint·ed (ŭn′ə-kwān′tĭd) *adj.* **1.** Not familiar or acquainted with another person. **2.** Not informed or knowledgeable: *The newly hired employees are still unacquainted with the necessary procedures.*

un·ad·dressed (ŭn-ə-drĕst′) *adj.* **1.** Not brought up for discussion or solution: *Numerous questions about the landfill remained unaddressed.* **2.** Not containing the required address: *unaddressed letters.*

un·a·dorned (ŭn′ə-dôrnd′) *adj.* Lacking adornment or embellishment; simple or plain: *an unadorned book cover.*

un·a·dul·ter·at·ed (ŭn′ə-dŭl′tə-rā′tĭd) *adj.* **1.** Not mixed or diluted; pure. **2.** Thorough; utter: *unadulterated joy.*

un·af·fect·ed (ŭn′ə-fĕk′tĭd) *adj.* **1.** Not changed, modified, or affected: *Our plans were unaffected by the rain.* **2.** Marked by a lack of affectation; sincere. **—un′af·fect′ed·ly** *adv.*

un-A·mer·i·can (ŭn′ə-mĕr′ĭ-kən) *adj.* Considered to be contrary to the institutions or principles of the United States.

u·na·nim·i·ty (yo͞o′nə-nĭm′ĭ-tē) *n.* The condition of being unanimous; complete agreement.

u·nan·i·mous (yo͞o-năn′ə-məs) *adj.* **1.** Sharing the same opinion: *Critics were unanimous in praising the play.* **2.** Based on or characterized by complete agreement: *a unanimous vote.* [From Latin *ūnanimus* : *ūnus*, one + *animus*, mind.] **—u·nan′i·mous·ly** *adv.*

un·an·tic·i·pat·ed (ŭn′ăn-tĭs′ə-pā′tĭd) *adj.* **1.** Not foreseen or anticipated: *Unanticipated problems delayed the opening of the new freeway.* **2.** Not having been expected; unexpected: *unanticipated guests.*

un·ap·peal·ing (ŭn′ə-pē′lĭng) *adj.* Not appealing to the senses, as in taste or aroma: *didn't eat the unappealing stew.*

un·ap·pre·ci·at·ed (ŭn′ə-prē′shē-ā′tĭd) *adj.* Not recognized or valued, as for quality or worth: *His work maintaining the baseball field went unappreciated until he moved away.*

un·ap·proach·a·ble (ŭn′ə-prō′chə-bəl) *adj.* **1.** Not friendly; aloof: *an unapproachable boss.* **2.** Not easily reached; not accessible: *The hermit lived in an unapproachable cabin in the woods.*

un·armed (ŭn-ärmd′) *adj.* Having no weapons.

un·a·shamed (ŭn′ə-shāmd′) *adj.* **1.** Feeling or showing no remorse, shame, or embarrassment: *He was unashamed even after his friends complained about his behavior.* **2.** Not restrained or limited by a sense of shame: *living in unashamed luxury.*

un·as·sist·ed (ŭn′ə-sĭs′tĭd) *adj.* **1.** Not having assistance or help. **2.** In sports, relating to or being a play that is performed by only one player.

un·as·sum·ing (ŭn′ə-so͞o′mĭng) *adj.* Not boastful or pretentious; modest.

un·at·tached (ŭn′ə-tăcht′) *adj.* **1.** Not attached or joined to something else: *an unattached garage.* **2.** Not engaged, married, or involved in a serious romantic relationship.

un·a·vail·ing (ŭn′ə-vā′lĭng) *adj.* Not effective; unsuccessful: *my unavailing efforts to apologize.*

un·a·void·a·ble (ŭn′ə-voi′də-bəl) *adj.* Impossible to avoid; inevitable: *an unavoidable discussion.* **—un′a·void′a·bly** *adv.*

un·a·ware (ŭn′ə-wâr′) *adj.* Not aware: *She was unaware of his presence.*

un·a·wares (ŭn′ə-wârz′) *adv.* By surprise; unexpectedly: *I caught them unawares.*

un·bal·anced (ŭn-băl′ənst) *adj.* **1.** Not in balance or in proper balance: *an unbalanced scale.* **2.** Not treating all

umbel

WORD BUILDING

un–[1] The prefix **un–**[1] has the basic meaning "not." Thus *unhappy* means "not happy." *Un–*[1] chiefly attaches to adjectives, as in *unclean, uneven, unripe, unable, unequal,* and *unsafe.* It also attaches to adjectives made of participles, as in *unfeeling, unflinching, unfinished,* and *unsaid.* Less frequently *un–*[1] attaches to nouns: *unbelief, unconcern, unrest.* Another prefix, **un–**[2], sounds the same as *un–*[1] but is not related to it. Whereas *un–*[1] forms adjectives and nouns, *un–*[2] forms verbs and expresses removal, reversal, or deprivation: **undress, unravel, unnerve.** For more information, see Note at **in–**[1].

WRITERS CHOOSE THEIR WORDS

I've found it doesn't pay to lie to Paul. He has an **uncanny** ability to discover the truth on his own.

Not, of course, that it means what I tell him is the strictest truth. I just don't practice a policy of full disclosure where Paul Slater is concerned. It seems safer that way.

—Meg Cabot
Twilight

sides fairly or with due importance: *unbalanced reporting of the political campaign.* **3.** Mentally or emotionally disturbed: *an unbalanced mind.* **4.** Not balanced financially; having debits and credits that do not correspond to each other.

un·bar (ŭn-**bär′**) *tr.v.* **un·barred, un·bar·ring, un·bars** To remove the bars from; open: *unbar a window.*

un·bear·a·ble (ŭn-**bâr′**ə-bəl) *adj.* So unpleasant or painful as to be intolerable: *The hikers looked for shelter from the unbearable heat.* **—un·bear′a·bly** *adv.*

un·beat·a·ble (ŭn-**bē′**tə-bəl) *adj.* Impossible to surpass or defeat: *a team that was unbeatable.*

un·beat·en (ŭn-**bēt′**n) *adj.* **1.** Never defeated: *an unbeaten swim team.* **2.** Not beaten or trampled down: *an unbeaten path through the woods.* **3.** Not beaten or pounded, as in cooking: *unbeaten eggs.*

un·be·com·ing (ŭn′bĭ-**kŭm′**ĭng) *adj.* **1.** Not attractive or flattering: *unbecoming clothes.* **2.** Not suitable or proper: *unbecoming behavior.*

un·be·known (ŭn′bĭ-**nōn′**) *adj.* Unknown: *a problem unbeknown to us.*

un·be·knownst (ŭn′bĭ-**nōnst′**) *adj.* Unknown. ❖ *adv.* Without the knowledge of someone: *Our cousin had come to town, unbeknownst to us.*

un·be·lief (ŭn′bĭ-**lēf′**) *n.* Lack of belief or faith, especially in religious matters.

un·be·liev·a·ble (ŭn′bĭ-**lē′**və-bəl) *adj.* **1.** Not to be believed; incredible: *told an unbelievable tale.* **2.** Astonishing, extraordinary, or extreme: *complained about the waiter's unbelievable rudeness.* **—un′be·liev′a·bly** *adv.*

un·be·liev·er (ŭn′bĭ-**lē′**vər) *n.* A person who lacks belief or faith, especially in a particular religion.

un·bend (ŭn-**bĕnd′**) *v.* **un·bent** (ŭn-**bĕnt′**), **un·bend·ing, un·bends** *—tr.* To straighten (something crooked or bent): *unbend a paper clip.* *—intr.* To become straight: *muscles bending and unbending.*

un·bend·ing (ŭn-**bĕn′**dĭng) *adj.* Not flexible; uncompromising: *an unbending will.*

un·bi·ased (ŭn-**bī′**əst) *adj.* Without bias or prejudice; impartial: *A judge must be unbiased.*

un·bid·den (ŭn-**bĭd′**n) *adj.* Not asked or invited: *unbidden guests.*

un·bind (ŭn-**bīnd′**) *tr.v.* **un·bound** (ŭn-**bound′**), **un·bind·ing, un·binds 1.** To set free from bonds; release: *unbind the prisoner.* **2.** To untie or unfasten: *unbind the boat's painter from around the wooden piling.*

un·bolt (ŭn-**bōlt′**) *tr.v.* **un·bolt·ed, un·bolt·ing, un·bolts** To draw back the bolts of; unlock: *unbolt a door.*

un·born (ŭn-**bôrn′**) *adj.* **1.** Not yet born: *an unborn child.* **2.** Not yet in existence: *unborn scientific theories.*

un·bound (ŭn-**bound′**) *v.* Past tense and past participle of **unbind.** ❖ *adj.* **1.** Not having a binding: *an unbound book.* **2.** Freed from bonds or restraints.

un·bound·ed (ŭn-**boun′**dĭd) *adj.* **1.** Having no boundaries or limits: *unbounded space.* **2.** Not kept within bounds; unrestrained: *unbounded joy.*

un·break·a·ble (ŭn-**brā′**kə-bəl) *adj.* Impossible to break; able to withstand rough usage: *unbreakable bulletproof glass.* **—un·break′a·bly** *adv.*

un·bri·dled (ŭn-**brīd′**ld) *adj.* **1.** Unrestrained; uncontrolled: *moments of unbridled joy.* **2.** Not fitted with a bridle.

un·bro·ken (ŭn-**brō′**kən) *adj.* **1.** Not broken; whole; intact. **2.** Not violated: *an unbroken promise.* **3.** Uninterrupted: *unbroken silence.* **4.** Not tamed or broken: *an unbroken pony.*

un·buck·le (ŭn-**bŭk′**əl) *tr.v.* **un·buck·led, un·buck·ling, un·buck·les** To loosen or undo the buckle or buckles of.

un·but·ton (ŭn-**bŭt′**n) *tr.v.* **un·but·toned, un·but·ton·ing, un·but·tons** To unfasten the buttons of: *Unbutton your coat.*

un·called-for (ŭn-**kôld′**fôr′) *adj.* Unwanted, inappropriate, or undeserved: *an uncalled-for remark.*

un·can·ny (ŭn-**kăn′**ē) *adj.* **un·can·ni·er, un·can·ni·est 1.** Arousing wonder and fear, as if supernatural; eerie: *an uncanny light coming out of the ruins.* **2.** So keen and perceptive as to seem supernatural: *uncanny wisdom.* **—un·can′ni·ly** *adv.*

un·car·ing (ŭn-**kâr′**ĭng) *adj.* Lacking concern or sympathy: *It is impossible for an uncaring person to be a good teacher.*

un·ceas·ing (ŭn-**sē′**sĭng) *adj.* Not stopping; continuous: *unceasing activity.* **—un·ceas′ing·ly** *adv.*

un·cer·e·mo·ni·ous (ŭn-sĕr′ə-**mō′**nē-əs) *adj.* Without appropriate courtesy or formality: *an unceremonious departure.*

un·cer·tain (ŭn-**sûr′**tn) *adj.* **1.** Not known or established; questionable: *The results of the experiment are uncertain.* **2.** Not definite; undecided: *uncertain plans.* **3.** Not having sure knowledge: *He is uncertain of what happened.* **4.** Subject to change: *uncertain weather.* **—un·cer′tain·ly** *adv.*

un·cer·tain·ty (ŭn-**sûr′**tn-tē) *n., pl.* **un·cer·tain·ties 1.** The condition of being uncertain; doubt. **2.** Something that is uncertain: *the uncertainties of life.*

un·chang·ing (ŭn-**chān′**jĭng) *adj.* Remaining the same; showing or undergoing no change: *an unchanging attitude of resentment.*

un·char·i·ta·ble (ŭn-**chăr′**ĭ-tə-bəl) *adj.* **1.** Not generous. **2.** Unfair or unkind: *uncharitable remarks.*

un·chart·ed (ŭn-**chär′**tĭd) *adj.* **1.** Not recorded on a map. **2.** Unknown: *The nation's future is yet uncharted.*

un·chris·tian (ŭn-**krĭs′**chən) *adj.* **1.** Not Christian in religion. **2.** Not in accordance with the spirit or principles of Christianity.

un·cial (**ŭn′**shəl *or* **ŭn′**sē-əl) *adj.* Relating to a script with rounded capital letters found especially in Greek and Latin manuscripts of the fourth to the eighth century AD. ❖ *n.* **1.** A style of writing characterized by rounded capital letters. **2.** A capital letter written in this style. [From Latin *ūnciālis*, inch-high, from *ūncia*, a twelfth part, inch.]

UNCIAL

uncial

un·civ·i·lized (ŭn-**sĭv′**ə-līzd′) *adj.* Not civilized; barbaric.

un·clad (ŭn-**klăd′**) *adj.* Not wearing clothes; naked.

un·cle (**ŭng′**kəl) *n.* **1.** The brother of one's mother or father. **2.** The husband of a sibling of one's father or mother. ◆ **cry uncle** or **say uncle** *Informal* To indicate a willingness to give up a fight or surrender. [From Middle English, from Latin *avunculus*, maternal uncle.]

un·clean (ŭn-**klēn′**) *adj.* **un·clean·er, un·clean·est 1.** Not clean; dirty. **2.** Morally impure. **—un·clean′ness** *n.*

un·clean·ly (ŭn-**klĕn′**lē) *adj.* **un·clean·li·er, un·clean·li·est** Unclean. ❖ *adv.* (ŭn-**klēn′**lē) In an unclean manner. **—un·clean′li·ness** (ŭn-**klĕn′**lē-nĭs) *n.*

un·clear (ŭn-**klîr′**) *adj.* **un·clear·er, un·clear·est 1.** Not clear or explicit: *The directions to the zoo were unclear, and we got lost.* **2.** Confused or doubtful: *I was unclear as to what I was supposed to do next.*

Uncle Sam (**săm**) *n.* The government of the United States, often personified as a tall thin man having a white beard and wearing a blue tailcoat, red-and-white-striped pants, and a tall hat with a band of stars.

un·clog (ŭn-**klŏg′**) *tr.v.* **un·clogged, un·clog·ging, un·clogs** To clear a blockage from (a drain, for example).

un·clothe (ŭn-**klōth′**) *tr.v.* **un·clothed, un·cloth·ing, un·clothes** To remove the clothing or cover from.

un·coil (ŭn-**koil′**) *tr. & intr.v.* **un·coiled, un·coil·ing, un·coils** To unwind or become unwound: *Uncoil the hose. The snake uncoiled.*

un·com·fort·a·ble (ŭn-**kŭm′**fər-tə-bəl *or* ŭn-**kŭmf′**tə-bəl *or* ŭn-**kŭmf′**tər-bəl) *adj.* **1.** Experiencing physical discomfort. **2.** Ill at ease; uneasy: *I'm uncomfortable with*

ă	pat	ôr	core
ā	pay	oi	boy
âr	care	ou	out
ä	father	o͝o	took
ĕ	pet	o͝or	lure
ē	be	o͞o	boot
ĭ	pit	ŭ	cut
ī	bite	ûr	urge
îr	pier	th	thin
ŏ	pot	*th*	this
ō	toe	zh	vision
ô	paw	ə	about

the committee's decision. **3.** Causing discomfort: *an uncomfortable chair.* **—un·com′fort·a·bly** *adv.*

un·com·mit·ted (ŭn′kə-**mĭt′**ĭd) *adj.* Not pledged to a specific cause or course of action: *uncommitted delegates at the convention.*

un·com·mon (ŭn-**kŏm′**ən) *adj.* **un·com·mon·er, un·com·mon·est** Not common; rare; unusual: *words used in uncommon ways.* **—un·com′mon·ly** *adv.*

un·com·pro·mis·ing (ŭn-**kŏm′**prə-mī′zĭng) *adj.* Not willing to make compromises; inflexible: *took an uncompromising stance during negotiations.*

un·con·cern (ŭn′kən-**sûrn′**) *n.* Lack of worry, interest, or concern: *From the beginning he viewed the assignment with unconcern.*

un·con·cerned (ŭn′kən-**sûrnd′**) *adj.* **1.** Not interested; indifferent: *a practical thinker unconcerned with abstract questions.* **2.** Not worried or anxious: *a foolhardy sailor unconcerned about the coming storm.* **—un′con·cern′ed·ly** (ŭn′kən-**sûr′**nĭd-lē) *adv.*

un·con·di·tion·al (ŭn′kən-**dĭsh′**ə-nəl) *adj.* Without conditions or limitations; absolute: *unconditional surrender.* **—un′con·di′tion·al·ly** *adv.*

un·con·quer·a·ble (ŭn-**kŏng′**kər-ə-bəl) *adj.* Impossible to overcome or defeat: *an unconquerable spirit of heroism.*

un·con·scion·a·ble (ŭn-**kŏn′**shə-nə-bəl) *adj.* **1.** Deserving of moral condemnation: *committed an unconscionable act.* **2.** Beyond reason; excessive: *an unconscionable price.* **—un·con′scion·a·bly** *adv.*

un·con·scious (ŭn-**kŏn′**shəs) *adj.* **1.** Temporarily lacking consciousness: *The patient was still unconscious from the anesthesia.* **2.** Lacking awareness: *He was unconscious of their wishes.* **3.** Occurring without one's awareness or conscious thought: *unconscious fears.* **4.** Not done on purpose; accidental: *an unconscious insult.* ❖ *n.* The part of the mind that contains desires, fears, or memories that are not subject to conscious awareness or control. **—un·con′scious·ly** *adv.* **—un·con′scious·ness** *n.*

un·con·sid·ered (ŭn′kən-**sĭd′**ərd) *adj.* Done without reason or consideration; rash: *an unconsidered remark.*

un·con·sti·tu·tion·al (ŭn′kŏn-stĭ-**too͞′**shə-nəl) *adj.* Conflicting with the principles set forth in the constitution of a nation or state. **—un′con·sti·tu′tion·al·ly** *adv.* **—un′con·sti·tu′tion·al′i·ty** (ŭn′kŏn-stĭ-too͞′shə-**năl′**ĭ-tē) *n.*

un·con·trol·la·ble (ŭn′kən-**trō′**lə-bəl) *adj.* Impossible to control or govern: *an uncontrollable urge to laugh.* **—un′con·trol′la·bly** *adv.*

un·con·trolled (ŭn′kən-**trōld′**) *adj.* Not under control or restraint: *an uncontrolled drug; uncontrolled anger.*

un·con·ven·tion·al (ŭn′kən-**vĕn′**shə-nəl) *adj.* Not conforming to convention or accepted social norms; out of the ordinary: *unconventional forms of art.* **—un′con·ven′tion·al′i·ty** (ŭn′kən-vĕn′shə-**năl′**ĭ-tē) *n.* **—un′con·ven′tion·al·ly** *adv.*

un·co·or·di·nat·ed (ŭn′kō-**ôr′**dn-ā′tĭd) *adj.* **1.** Having poor physical coordination; clumsy or unathletic. **2.** Lacking planning, method, or organization: *The banquet was so uncoordinated that some people never got to eat.*

un·cork (ŭn-**kôrk′**) *tr.v.* **un·corked, un·cork·ing, un·corks** To remove the cork from (a bottle, for example).

un·count·ed (ŭn-**koun′**tĭd) *adj.* **1.** Not counted: *The uncounted money is in the safe.* **2.** Not capable of being counted; innumerable: *uncounted millions calling for change.*

un·cou·ple (ŭn-**kŭp′**əl) *v.* **un·cou·pled, un·cou·pling, un·cou·ples** *—tr.* To disconnect: *uncouple railroad cars.* *—intr.* To come or break loose.

un·couth (ŭn-**ko͞oth′**) *adj.* Not refined or well-mannered; crude: *uncouth behavior.* [From Old English *uncūth*, unknown : *un-*, not + *cūth*, known, knowing.]

un·cov·er (ŭn-**kŭv′**ər) *v.* **un·cov·ered, un·cov·er·ing, un·cov·ers** *—tr.* **1.** To remove a cover from: *uncovered a jar.* **2.** To reveal or disclose: *uncover a plot.* *—intr.* To take off one's hat, as in respect: *Etiquette required courtiers to uncover in the king's presence.*

un·cross (ŭn-**krôs′**) *tr.v.* **un·crossed, un·cross·ing, un·cross·es** To move (one's legs, for example) from a crossed position.

unc·tion (**ŭngk′**shən) *n.* **1.** The act of anointing as part of a religious, ceremonial, or healing ritual. **2.** An ointment or oil; a salve. **3.** Something that serves to soothe. [From Middle English *unctioun*, from Latin *ūnctiō*, from *unguere*, to anoint.]

unc·tu·ous (**ŭngk′**cho͞o-əs) *adj.* **1.** Insincerely ingratiating: *an unctuous sales pitch.* **2.** Oily; greasy. **—unc′tu·ous·ly** *adv.*

un·cul·ti·vat·ed (ŭn-**kŭl′**tə-vā′tĭd) *adj.* **1.** Not prepared for growing crops: *uncultivated land.* **2.** Not refined or cultured: *an uncultivated boor.*

un·cut (ŭn-**kŭt′**) *adj.* **1.** Not cut, trimmed, or sliced: *uncut hair; uncut bread.* **2.** Not ground or polished: *an uncut gem.* **3.** Not abridged or shortened: *an uncut novel.*

un·daunt·ed (ŭn-**dôn′**tĭd *or* ŭn-**dän′**tĭd) *adj.* Not discouraged; resolutely courageous. **—un·daunt′ed·ly** *adv.*

un·de·cid·ed (ŭn′dĭ-**sī′**dĭd) *adj.* **1.** Not yet settled; open: *plans still undecided.* **2.** Having reached no decision: *undecided whether to hire new workers.*

un·de·clared (ŭn′dĭ-**klârd′**) *adj.* **1.** Not formally declared: *an undeclared war.* **2.** Not having formally revealed something about oneself: *an undeclared candidate for governor.*

un·de·ni·a·ble (ŭn′dĭ-**nī′**ə-bəl) *adj.* Difficult or impossible to deny: *undeniable facts.* **—un′de·ni′a·bly** *adv.*

un·der (**ŭn′**dər) *prep.* **1.** In a lower position or place than: *a cat under the table.* **2.** Beneath the surface of: *under the ground.* **3.** Beneath the guise of: *under a false name.* **4.** Less than; smaller than: *under 20 years of age.* **5.** Less than the required amount or degree of: *under voting age.* **6.** Subject to the authority, rule, or control of: *under a dictatorship.* **7.** Undergoing or receiving the effects of: *under the care of a physician.* **8.** Subject to the obligation of: *under contract.* **9.** Within the group or classification of: *books listed under the category of biology.* **10.** In the process of: *The proposal is under discussion.* **11.** In view of; because of: *Under these conditions, it would be wiser to postpone your trip.* ❖ *adv.* In or into a place below or beneath: *The frog put its head under and swam off.* ❖ *adj.* Located lower than or beneath something else: *the under parts of a machine.* [From Old English.]

under– *pref.* A prefix that means: **1.** Beneath or below in position: *underground.* **2.** Inferior in rank or importance: *undersecretary.* **3.** Less in degree, rate, or quantity than normal or proper: *underestimate.* —SEE NOTE.

un·der·a·chiev·er (ŭn′dər-ə-**chē′**vər) *n.* A person who achieves less than is ordinarily expected for a person having the same intelligence or ability.

un·der·age (ŭn′dər-**āj′**) *adj.* Below the customary or required age, as for voting.

un·der·arm (**ŭn′**dər-ärm′) *adj.* **1.** Located, placed, or used under the arm. **2.** Performed with the hand brought forward and up from below the level of the shoulder; underhand. ❖ *n.* The armpit. **—un′der·arm′** *adv.*

un·der·bel·ly (**ŭn′**dər-bĕl′ē) *n.* **1.** The underside of an animal's body. **2.** A weak or vulnerable part: *The underbelly of his argument is that it runs counter to the facts.*

un·der·bid (ŭn′dər-**bĭd′**) *v.* **un·der·bid, un·der·bid·ding, un·der·bids** *—tr.* To bid lower than (a competitor). *—intr.* To bid less than the value of one's hand in bridge.

un·der·bite (**ŭn′**dər-bīt′) *n.* A condition of the teeth in which the lower teeth protrude beyond the upper teeth.

un·der·brush (**ŭn′**dər-brŭsh′) *n.* Small trees, shrubs, or similar plants growing thickly beneath taller trees.

Uncle Sam
World War I US Army recruitment poster by James Montgomery Flagg (1877–1960)

WRITERS CHOOSE THEIR WORDS

It was the sight of Spiller perhaps which had shaken Homily, confirming her worst premonitions—**uncouth,** unwashed, dishonest, and ill-bred, that's what she summed him up to be, everything she most detested and feared.

—Mary Norton
The Borrowers Afield

WORD BUILDING

under– The prefix **under–** has essentially the same meaning as the preposition *under.* For example, in words such as *underbelly, undercurrent, underlie,* and *undershirt, under–* denotes a position beneath or below. *Under–* also frequently conveys incompleteness or falling below a certain standard. Some examples are *undercharge, underdeveloped, underestimate,* and *underfeed.* Note that in this sense words beginning with *under–* often have counterparts beginning with *over–: overcharge, overestimate.*

underpass

un·der·car·riage (ŭn′dər-kăr′ĭj) *n.* **1.** A supporting framework or structure, as for the body of a car. **2.** The landing gear of an aircraft.

un·der·charge (ŭn′dər-**chärj′**) *tr.v.* **un·der·charged, un·der·charg·ing, un·der·charg·es** To charge (a customer, for example) too little.

un·der·class·man (ŭn′dər-**klăs′**mən) *n.* A student in the freshman or sophomore class at a high school or college.

un·der·clothes (**ŭn′**dər-klōz′ *or* **ŭn′**dər-klō*th*z′) *pl.n.* Clothes worn next to the skin, beneath one's outer clothing.

un·der·cloth·ing (**ŭn′**dər-klō′*th*ĭng) *n.* Underwear.

un·der·coat (**ŭn′**dər-kōt′) *n.* **1.** A covering of short hair lying underneath the longer outer hair of an animal's coat. **2.** A coat of material applied to a surface to seal it or otherwise prepare it for a final coat, as of paint.

un·der·cov·er (ŭn′dər-**kŭv′**ər) *adj.* **1.** Performed or occurring in secret: *an undercover investigation.* **2.** Engaged in spying or secret investigations: *undercover FBI agents.*

un·der·cur·rent (**ŭn′**dər-kûr′ənt) *n.* **1.** A current, as of air or water, flowing beneath a surface or another current. **2.** A partly hidden tendency, force, or influence that is often contrary to what is obvious.

un·der·cut (ŭn′dər-**kŭt′**) *tr.v.* **un·der·cut, un·der·cut·ting, un·der·cuts 1.** To make a cut under or below (something) so as to leave an overhanging projection. **2.** To diminish or destroy the effectiveness of; undermine: *The scandal undercut the senator's influence.* **3.** To sell or work for less money than (a competitor). ❖ *n.* (**ŭn′**dər-kŭt′) **1.** A cut made in the lower part of something. **2.** A notch cut in a tree to direct its fall.

un·der·de·vel·oped (ŭn′dər-dĭ-**vĕl′**əpt) *adj.* **1.** Not fully developed, as a living thing or one of its parts: *underdeveloped flowers.* **2.** Having a low level of economic development and technology in comparison to other societies: *an underdeveloped nation.*

un·der·dog (**ŭn′**dər-dôg′) *n.* A person or thing that is expected to lose a contest or struggle, as in sports or politics.

un·der·done (ŭn′dər-**dŭn′**) *adj.* Not sufficiently cooked.

un·der·em·ployed (ŭn′dər-ĕm-**ploid′**) *adj.* **1.** Employed in a part-time job when one needs or desires a full-time job. **2.** Employed at a job that requires less skill or training than one possesses.

un·der·es·ti·mate (ŭn′dər-**ĕs′**tə-māt′) *tr.v.* **un·der·es·ti·mat·ed, un·der·es·ti·mat·ing, un·der·es·ti·mates** To make too low an estimate of the value, amount, or quality of: *We underestimated how long it would take to build the shed. Don't underestimate their defense.* ❖ *n.* (ŭn′dər-**ĕs′**tə-mĭt) An estimate that is or proves to be too low.

un·der·ex·pose (ŭn′dər-ĭk-**spōz′**) *tr.v.* **un·der·ex·posed, un·der·ex·pos·ing, un·der·ex·pos·es** To expose (film) to light for too short a time to produce an image with good contrast. **—un′der·ex·po′sure** (ŭn′dər-ĭk-**spō′**zhər) *n.*

un·der·feed (ŭn′dər-**fēd′**) *tr.v.* **un·der·fed** (ŭn′dər-**fĕd′**), **un·der·feed·ing, un·der·feeds** To feed insufficiently.

un·der·foot (ŭn′dər-**fo͝ot′**) *adv.* **1.** Below or under the foot or feet. **2.** In the way: *too many toys underfoot.*

un·der·gar·ment (**ŭn′**dər-gär′mənt) *n.* A garment worn under outer garments, especially one worn next to the skin.

un·der·go (ŭn′dər-**gō′**) *tr.v.* **un·der·went** (ŭn′dər-**wĕnt′**), **un·der·gone** (ŭn′dər-**gôn′**), **un·der·go·ing, un·der·goes** (ŭn′dər-**gōz′**) **1.** To experience: *Many insects undergo several changes in body form during their development.* **2.** To endure; suffer through: *undergo hardship.*

un·der·grad·u·ate (ŭn′dər-**grăj′**o͞o-ĭt) *n.* A student who has entered a college or university but has not yet received a bachelor's or similar degree. ❖ *adj.* Relating to undergraduates: *undergraduate courses.*

un·der·ground (**ŭn′**dər-ground′) *adj.* **1.** Located or occurring below the surface of the earth: *an underground passage.* **2.** Acting or done in secret; hidden: *underground resistance to the tyrant.* **3.** Relating to an avant-garde or experimental movement or its films, publications, or art: *the underground press.* ❖ *n.* **1.** A secret organization working against a government in power. **2.** *Chiefly British* A subway system. ❖ *adv.* (ŭn′dər-**ground′**) **1.** Below the surface of the earth: *miners digging underground.* **2.** In secret: *spies working underground.*

Underground Railroad *n.* A secret system that helped fugitive slaves reach freedom in the free states and in Canada before slavery was abolished in the United States. —SEE NOTE AT Harriet **Tubman.**

un·der·growth (**ŭn′**dər-grōth′) *n.* Low-growing plants, shrubs, and young trees growing under the trees in a forest.

un·der·hand (**ŭn′**dər-hănd′) *adj.* **1.** In sports, performed with the hand brought forward and up from below the level of the shoulder: *an underhand throw.* **2.** Underhanded.

un·der·hand·ed (ŭn′dər-**hăn′**dĭd) *adj.* Done deceptively, slyly, or secretly: *used underhanded dealings to win the election.*

un·der·lie (ŭn′dər-**lī′**) *tr.v.* **un·der·lay** (ŭn′dər-**lā′**), **un·der·lain** (ŭn′dər-**lān′**), **un·der·ly·ing, un·der·lies 1.** To be located under or below: *Roman roads underlie many modern European highways.* **2.** To be the basis for; account for: *These things underlie her decision.*

un·der·line (**ŭn′**dər-līn′ *or* ŭn′dər-**līn′**) *tr.v.* **un·der·lined, un·der·lin·ing, un·der·lines 1.** To draw a line under; underscore. **2.** To stress or emphasize: *He underlined their desire to cooperate.*

un·der·ling (**ŭn′**dər-lĭng) *n.* A person of lesser rank or authority than another; a subordinate.

un·der·ly·ing (**ŭn′**dər-lī′ĭng) *adj.* **1.** Located under or beneath something: *the underlying bedrock of the Sierras.* **2.** Basic; fundamental: *underlying values.* **3.** Present but not obvious; implied: *an underlying meaning.*

un·der·mine (ŭn′dər-**mīn′**) *tr.v.* **un·der·mined, un·der·min·ing, un·der·mines 1.** To remove material supporting the base or foundation of: *flood waters undermining the foundation of a house.* **2.** To weaken or impair by damaging the basis of: *bad habits that undermined his health.*

un·der·most (**ŭn′**dər-mōst′) *adj.* Lowest in position, rank, or place. ❖ *adv.* In or to the lowest place.

un·der·neath (ŭn′dər-**nēth′**) *adv.* In or to a place beneath; below. ❖ *prep.* Beneath; below; under: *put a coaster underneath a glass.* ❖ *n.* The part or side below or under; the underside. [From Old English *underneothan* : *under*, under + *neothan*, below.]

un·der·nour·ished (ŭn′dər-**nûr′**ĭsht) *adj.* Lacking sufficient nourishment for proper health and growth.

un·der·pants (**ŭn′**dər-pănts′) *pl.n.* A lower undergarment, typically having short legs or no legs, worn next to the skin under other clothing.

un·der·pass (**ŭn′**dər-păs′) *n.* A passage underneath something, especially a part of a road that passes under another road or a railroad.

un·der·pin·ning (**ŭn′**dər-pĭn′ĭng) *n.* **1.** Material used to support a structure, such as a wall. **2.** often **underpinnings** A support or foundation.

un·der·priv·i·leged (ŭn′dər-**prĭv′**ə-lĭjd) *adj.* Lacking advantages or opportunities enjoyed by other members of one's society.

un·der·rate (ŭn′dər-**rāt′**) *tr.v.* **un·der·rat·ed, un·der·rat·ing, un·der·rates** To judge or rate too low; underestimate.

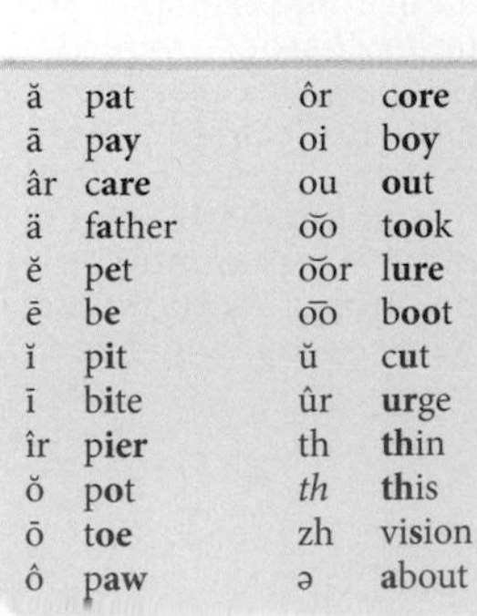

ă	pat	ôr	core
ā	pay	oi	boy
âr	care	ou	out
ä	father	o͝o	took
ĕ	pet	o͝or	lure
ē	be	o͞o	boot
ĭ	pit	ŭ	cut
ī	bite	ûr	urge
îr	pier	th	thin
ŏ	pot	*th*	this
ō	toe	zh	vision
ô	paw	ə	about

un·der·rep·re·sent·ed (ŭn′dər-rĕp′rĭ-**zĕn′**tĭd) *adj.* Not sufficiently represented: *New district boundaries are required because some neighborhoods are underrepresented in the city council.*

un·der·score (**ŭn′**dər-skôr′) *tr.v.* **un·der·scored, un·der·scor·ing, un·der·scores 1.** To underline. **2.** To emphasize; stress.

un·der·sea (**ŭn′**dər-sē′) *adj.* Existing, done, used, or operating beneath the surface of the sea: *undersea life; undersea exploration.* ❖ *adv.* **undersea** (ŭn′dər-**sē′**) also **un·der·seas** (ŭn′dər-**sēz′**) Beneath the surface of the sea.

un·der·sec·re·tar·y (ŭn′dər-**sĕk′**rə-tĕr′ē) *n.* An official directly subordinate to a cabinet member.

un·der·sell (ŭn′dər-**sĕl′**) *tr.v.* **un·der·sold** (ŭn′dər-**sōld′**), **un·der·sell·ing, un·der·sells 1.** To sell for a lower price than (another seller). **2.** To sell (a product) at a price less than the actual value.

un·der·shirt (**ŭn′**dər-shûrt′) *n.* An undergarment worn next to the skin under a shirt.

un·der·shoot (ŭn′dər-**sho͞ot′**) *tr.v.* **un·der·shot** (ŭn′dər-**shŏt′**), **un·der·shoot·ing, un·der·shoots 1.** To shoot a missile so that it falls short of (a target). **2.** To land or begin to land an aircraft short of (a landing area).

un·der·shot (**ŭn′**dər-shŏt′) *adj.* **1.** Driven by water passing from below: *an undershot water wheel.* **2.** Having the lower jaw or teeth projecting beyond the upper.

un·der·side (**ŭn′**dər-sīd′) *n.* The side or surface that is underneath; the bottom side.

un·der·signed (**ŭn′**dər-sīnd′) *adj.* Having signed at the end of a document: *the undersigned persons.* ❖ *n., pl.* **undersigned** A person whose name appears at the end of a document.

un·der·sized (ŭn′dər-**sīzd′**) also **un·der·size** (ŭn′dər-**sīz′**) *adj.* Smaller than the usual, expected, or required size: *an undersized garment.*

un·der·sold (ŭn′dər-**sōld′**) *v.* Past tense and past participle of **undersell.**

un·der·stand (ŭn′dər-**stănd′**) *v.* **un·der·stood** (ŭn′dər-**sto͝od′**), **un·der·stand·ing, un·der·stands** —*tr.* **1.** To become aware of the nature and significance of; know or comprehend: *Do you understand how soap works?* **2.** To become aware of the meaning intended or expressed by (a person or remark, for example): *She speaks Russian and can understand your new neighbors.* **3.** To know well by long experience or close contact with: *That teacher understands kids.* **4.** To be tolerant or sympathetic toward: *I don't agree, but I can still understand your point.* **5.** To draw as a conclusion; infer: *Am I to understand that you are staying for the weekend?* **6.** To accept as an agreed fact: *Are the terms of our agreement understood?* **7.** To supply or add (words, for example) mentally: *The subject of an imperative verb is understood.* —*intr.* **1.** To have knowledge or understanding: *I will keep explaining until you understand.* **2.** To have sympathy or tolerance: *You are very upset. I understand.* [From Old English *understandan.*] —**un′der·stand′a·ble** *adj.* —**un′der·stand′a·bly** *adv.*

un·der·stand·ing (ŭn′dər-**stăn′**dĭng) *n.* **1.** The ability to think clearly and intelligently; intelligence: *a person of great understanding.* **2.** The awareness or condition of a person who understands something; knowledge or comprehension: *How much understanding do you have of algebra?* **3.** Individual judgment; opinion: *In my understanding, this plan makes sense.* **4.** An agreement between two or more people or groups: *My neighbors and I have an understanding to keep the noise down.* **5.** A reconciliation of differences; a state of agreement: *After long negotiations they finally reached an understanding.* **6.** A disposition to appreciate or share the thoughts or feelings of others: *His feelings are hurt. Show some understanding!* ❖ *adj.* Compassionate; sympathetic: *a kind and understanding friend.*

un·der·state (ŭn′dər-**stāt′**) *tr.v.* **un·der·stat·ed, un·der·stat·ing, un·der·states 1.** To state in a way that minimizes the extent, size, or amount of: *They have understated the problem in order to avoid punishment.* **2.** To express with little emphasis, especially for an ironic effect.

un·der·state·ment (ŭn′dər-**stāt′**mənt *or* **ŭn′**dər-stāt′-mənt) *n.* **1.** A statement that minimizes the extent, size, or amount of something. **2.** Lack of emphasis in expression, especially for rhetorical effect: *He often uses understatement, as in saying "not bad" to mean "very good."*

un·der·stood (ŭn′dər-**sto͝od′**) *v.* Past tense and past participle of **understand.** ❖ *adj.* **1.** Agreed upon: *We recalled that the understood fee is 50 dollars.* **2.** Not expressed but implied: *"You" is the understood subject in the sentence "Get going."*

un·der·stud·y (**ŭn′**dər-stŭd′ē) *n., pl.* **un·der·stud·ies** An actor trained to substitute for the regular actor. ❖ *tr.v.* **un·der·stud·ied, un·der·stud·y·ing, un·der·stud·ies 1.** To study or know (a role) so as to be able to substitute for the regular actor. **2.** To act as an understudy to (an actor).

un·der·take (ŭn′dər-**tāk′**) *tr.v.* **un·der·took** (ŭn′dər-**to͝ok′**), **un·der·tak·en, un·der·tak·ing, un·der·takes 1.** To take upon oneself; decide or agree to do: *undertake a difficult job.* **2.** To agree or promise: *She undertook to inspect the building.*

un·der·tak·er (**ŭn′**dər-tā′kər) *n.* A funeral director.

un·der·tak·ing (**ŭn′**dər-tā′kĭng) *n.* **1.** A task or assignment undertaken; a venture. **2.** The occupation of a funeral director.

un·der·tone (**ŭn′**dər-tōn′) *n.* **1.** An underlying or implied sense or meaning. **2.** A speech tone of low pitch or volume.

un·der·took (ŭn′dər-**to͝ok′**) *v.* Past tense of **undertake.**

un·der·tow (**ŭn′**dər-tō′) *n.* An underwater current flowing strongly away from shore, usually caused as water from breaking waves flows back to sea.

un·der·val·ue (ŭn′dər-**văl′**yo͞o) *tr.v.* **un·der·val·ued, un·der·val·u·ing, un·der·val·ues 1.** To value at less than real worth: *Houses are undervalued in this neighborhood.* **2.** To have too little regard for: *Don't undervalue his abilities.*

un·der·wa·ter (**ŭn′**dər-wô′tər) *adj.* Used, done, or existing under the surface of water. —**un′der·wa′ter** *adv.*

un·der·way (ŭn′dər-**wā′**) *adv.* **1.** In motion or operation. **2.** In progress.

un·der·wear (**ŭn′**dər-wâr′) *n.* **1.** Underpants. **2.** Underclothes.

un·der·weight (**ŭn′**dər-wāt′) *adj.* Weighing less than is normal, healthy, or required.

un·der·went (ŭn′dər-**wĕnt′**) *v.* Past tense of **undergo.**

un·der·world (**ŭn′**dər-wûrld′) *n.* **1.** In various religious traditions, the world of the dead, located beneath the world of the living. **2.** The part of society engaged in crime and vice.

un·der·write (**ŭn′**dər-rīt′) *tr.v.* **un·der·wrote** (**ŭn′**dər-rōt′), **un·der·writ·ten** (**ŭn′**dər-rĭt′n), **un·der·writ·ing, un·der·writes 1.** To assume financial responsibility for: *underwrite a theatrical production.* **2.** To supply with funding, especially as a sponsor: *underwrite a public television show.* **3.** To sign (an insurance policy), thus guaranteeing payment in the event of losses or damage. **4.** To agree to buy (the stock in a new enterprise not yet sold publicly) at a fixed time and price. **5.** To write underneath or below, especially to endorse (a document). —**un′der·writ′er** *n.*

un·de·sir·a·ble (ŭn′dĭ-**zīr′**ə-bəl) *adj.* Not desirable; not wanted. ❖ *n.* A person who is not wanted or whose behavior is objectionable. —**un′de·sir′a·bil′i·ty** *n.* —**un′de·sir′a·bly** *adv.*

un·dies (**ŭn′**dēz) *pl.n. Informal* Underwear.

WRITERS CHOOSE THEIR WORDS

"You were asleep," said Dinah.

"I resent that," said Mr. Parker. "I strongly resent it. I bitterly and deeply resent it. I resent it from the depths of my being. I am not **unduly** sensitive, but—"

"You were **unduly** sleepy," said Dorinda unkindly.

—Eric Linklater
The Wind on the Moon

WORD BUILDING

uni– The basic meaning of the prefix **uni–** is "one." It comes from the Latin prefix *ūni–*, from the word *ūnus*, meaning "one." Many English words beginning with *uni–* were formed in Latin. The word *unicorn*, for example, comes from *ūni–* + *cornū*, meaning "horn," and refers to a one-horned animal. *Uniform* comes from *ūni–* + *fōrma*, "shape," and means "always the same" or literally "one shape." And *unison*, which comes from *ūni–* + *sonus*, "sound," means literally "one sound." The majority of new words with *uni–*, such as *unicellular, unicycle, unilateral*, and *univalent*, are from the 1800s. *Uni–* can be compared to the prefix *mono–*, which is from Greek.

ă	pat	ôr	core
ā	pay	oi	boy
âr	care	ou	out
ä	father	o͝o	took
ĕ	pet	o͝or	lure
ē	be	o͞o	boot
ĭ	pit	ŭ	cut
ī	bite	ûr	urge
îr	pier	th	thin
ŏ	pot	*th*	this
ō	toe	zh	vision
ô	paw	ə	about

un·dig·ni·fied (ŭn-dĭg′nə-fīd′) *adj.* Lacking in or harmful to dignity: *undignified behavior.*

un·do (ŭn-do͞o′) *tr.v.* **un·did** (ŭn-dĭd′), **un·done** (ŭn-dŭn′), **un·do·ing** (ŭn-do͞o′ĭng), **un·does** (ŭn-dŭz′) **1.** To do away with or reverse the result or effect of (a previous action): *trying to undo mistakes.* **2.** To untie, unfasten, or loosen: *undo a knot.* **3.** To open; unwrap: *undo a package.* **4.** To cause the ruin or downfall of.

❑ *These sound alike:* **undo, undue** (excessive).

un·doc·u·ment·ed (ŭn-dŏk′yə-mĕn′tĭd) *adj.* **1.** Not supported by written evidence: *The lawyer had to withdraw the undocumented accusations.* **2.** Not having the needed documents, as for permission to live or work in a foreign country: *undocumented workers.*

un·do·ing (ŭn-do͞o′ĭng) *n.* **1.** The act of unfastening or loosening. **2.** Ruin; destruction. **3.** A cause of ruin; a downfall: *Greed was his undoing.* **4.** The act of reversing or canceling something.

un·doubt·ed (ŭn-**dou′**tĭd) *adj.* Not doubted or questioned; accepted: *undoubted talent.* **—un·doubt′ed·ly** *adv.*

un·dress (ŭn-drĕs′) *v.* **un·dressed, un·dress·ing, un·dress·es** *—tr.* To remove the clothing of; disrobe. *—intr.* To take off one's clothing. ❖ *n.* Partial or complete nakedness: *in a state of undress.*

un·due (ŭn-do͞o′) *adj.* **1.** Beyond what is normal or appropriate; excessive: *an undue amount of noise.* **2.** Not proper or legal: *undue powers.* **3.** Not yet payable or due: *an undue loan.*

❑ *These sound alike:* **undue, undo** (reverse).

un·du·late (**ŭn′**jə-lāt′) *v.* **un·du·lat·ed, un·du·lat·ing, un·du·lates** *—intr.* **1.** To move in waves or with a smooth wavy motion: *wheat undulating in the breeze.* **2.** To have a wavy appearance or form. *—tr.* **1.** To cause to move in waves: *The wind undulated the wheat.* **2.** To give a wavy appearance or form to: *The hills undulate the land for miles.* [From Late Latin *undula*, small wave.]

un·du·la·tion (ŭn′jə-**lā′**shən) *n.* **1.** A regular rising and falling or movement from side to side; movement in waves. **2.** A wavy form, outline, or appearance. **3.** One of a series of waves or parts of waves.

un·du·ly (ŭn-do͞o′lē) *adv.* Excessively; immoderately: *unduly fearful.*

un·dy·ing (ŭn-dī′ĭng) *adj.* Endless; everlasting: *undying gratitude.*

un·earned (ŭn-**ûrnd′**) *adj.* **1.** Not gained by work: *unearned income.* **2.** Not deserved: *unearned praise.* **3.** Not yet earned: *unearned interest.*

un·earth (ŭn-**ûrth′**) *tr.v.* **un·earthed, un·earth·ing, un·earths 1.** To bring up out of the earth; dig up: *unearthing pottery.* **2.** To bring to public notice; uncover: *unearthing evidence about the crime.*

un·earth·ly (ŭn-**ûrth′**lē) *adj.* **un·earth·li·er, un·earth·li·est 1.** Not of the earth or this world; supernatural: *unearthly creatures such as pixies and elves.* **2.** Unnaturally strange and frightening: *an unearthly scream.* **3.** Not customary or reasonable; absurd: *gets up at an unearthly hour.* **—un·earth′li·ness** *n.*

un·eas·y (ŭn-ē′zē) *adj.* **un·eas·i·er, un·eas·i·est 1.** Lacking a sense of security: *The farmers were uneasy until the crops were harvested.* **2.** Awkward or unsure in manner: *The dog is uneasy with strangers.* **—un·eas′i·ly** *adv.* **—un·eas′i·ness** *n.*

un·ed·u·cat·ed (ŭn-ĕj′ə-kā′tĭd) *adj.* Lacking education, especially formal schooling; not educated.

un·em·ployed (ŭn′ĕm-**ploid′**) *adj.* **1.** Out of work; jobless. **2.** Not being used; idle: *an unemployed lathe.* ❖ *pl.n.* People who are out of work.

un·em·ploy·ment (ŭn′ĕm-**ploi′**mənt) *n.* **1.** The condition of being unemployed. **2.** The percentage or number of people who are involuntarily unemployed: *Unemployment rose dramatically during the Great Depression.* **3.** Insurance providing benefits to one who is unemployed: *lost her job and had to go on unemployment.*

un·e·qual (ŭn-ē′kwəl) *adj.* **1.** Not the same in any measurable way; not equal: *unequal numbers.* **2.** Not the same in rank or social position. **3.** Having opponents that are unevenly matched: *an unequal race.* **4.** Not having the required ability; not adequate: *unequal to the task.* **5.** Not fair: *unequal distribution of income.*

un·e·qualed also **un·e·qualled** (ŭn-ē′kwəld) *adj.* Not matched by others of its kind; exceptional.

un·e·quiv·o·cal (ŭn′ĭ-**kwĭv′**ə-kəl) *adj.* Admitting of no doubt; clear: *an unequivocal success.* **—un′e·quiv′o·cal·ly** *adv.*

un·err·ing (ŭn-**ĕr′**ĭng *or* ŭn-**ûr′**ĭng) *adj.* Making no mistakes; consistently accurate. **—un·err′ing·ly** *adv.*

UNESCO *abbr.* An abbreviation of United Nations Educational, Scientific, and Cultural Organization.

un·e·ven (ŭn-ē′vən) *adj.* **un·e·ven·er, un·e·ven·est 1.** Not equal, as in size, length, or quality. **2.** Having opponents that are poorly matched: *an uneven contest.* **3.** Not uniform or consistent; varying, as in quality or form: *an uneven performance; a lamp giving very uneven light.* **4.** Not level or smooth: *the uneven surface of a cobblestone road.* **5.** Not straight or parallel: *a book with uneven margins.* **—un·e′ven·ly** *adv.* **—un·e′ven·ness** *n.*

un·e·vent·ful (ŭn′ĭ-**vĕnt′**fəl) *adj.* Having no significant events. **—un′e·vent′ful·ly** *adv.*

un·ex·cep·tion·a·ble (ŭn′ĭk-**sĕp′**shə-nə-bəl) *adj.* Beyond any reasonable objection; irreproachable.

un·ex·cep·tion·al (ŭn′ĭk-**sĕp′**shə-nəl) *adj.* Not varying from what is usual or expected. **—un′ex·cep′tion·al·ly** *adv.*

un·ex·pect·ed (ŭn′ĭk-**spĕk′**tĭd) *adj.* Not expected; coming without warning. **—un′ex·pect′ed·ly** *adv.*

un·fail·ing (ŭn-fā′lĭng) *adj.* **1.** Not running out; inexhaustible: *a source of unfailing amusement.* **2.** Constant; reliable: *an unfailing friend.* **—un·fail′ing·ly** *adv.*

un·fair (ŭn-**fâr′**) *adj.* **un·fair·er, un·fair·est 1.** Not fair, right, or just: *unfair laws.* **2.** Not kind or considerate: *It was unfair of me to laugh when he felt so sad.* **—un·fair′ly** *adv.* **—un·fair′ness** *n.*

un·faith·ful (ŭn-**fāth′**fəl) *adj.* **1.** Not faithful; disloyal. **2.** Breaking trust in a marriage or relationship by having sexual relations with someone other than one's spouse or partner in the relationship. **3.** Not reflecting the fact or original source; inaccurate: *an unfaithful account of what happened.* **—un·faith′ful·ness** *n.*

un·fa·mil·iar (ŭn′fə-**mĭl′**yər) *adj.* **1.** Not acquainted: *unfamiliar with that subject.* **2.** Not within one's knowledge; strange: *an unfamiliar face.* **—un′fa·mil·iar′i·ty** (ŭn′fə-mĭl-**yăr′**ĭ-tē) *n.* **—un′fa·mil′iar·ly** *adv.*

un·fas·ten (ŭn-**făs′**ən) *v.* **un·fas·tened, un·fas·ten·ing, un·fas·tens** *—tr.* To separate the connected parts of; open: *unfastened the belt.* *—intr.* To become opened or untied: *The buckle unfastens easily.*

un·fa·vor·a·ble (ŭn-**fā′**vər-ə-bəl *or* ŭn-**fāv′**rə-bəl) *adj.* **1.** Likely to be a hindrance; disadvantageous: *unfavorable winds.* **2.** Opposed; adverse: *unfavorable criticism.* **—un·fa′vor·a·bly** *adv.*

un·feel·ing (ŭn-**fē′**lĭng) *adj.* **1.** Having no sensation; numb. **2.** Not sympathetic; callous.

un·feigned (ŭn′**fānd′**) *adj.* Not feigned; genuine or sincere.

un·fet·ter (ŭn-**fĕt′**ər) *tr.v.* **un·fet·tered, un·fet·ter·ing, un·fet·ters** To set free or keep free from restrictions or bonds.

un·fin·ished (ŭn-**fĭn′**ĭsht) *adj.* **1.** Not finished; incomplete: *unfinished business.* **2.** Not processed in a specific way; natural: *unfinished furniture.*

un·fit (ŭn-**fĭt′**) *adj.* **1.** Not suitable or adapted for a given purpose; inappropriate: *a paint that is unfit for use on* *metal.* **2.** Performing below a standard; incompetent or unqualified: *an unfit teacher.* **3.** Not in good health.

un·flap·pa·ble (ŭn-flăp′ə-bəl) *adj.* Not easily upset or excited; calm: *an unflappable clerk who handled many requests at once.* **—un·flap′pa·bil′i·ty** *n.*

un·fledged (ŭn-flĕjd′) *adj.* **1.** Not yet able to fly because the feathers are not fully developed: *an unfledged bird.* **2.** Inexperienced; immature: *an unfledged actor.*

un·flinch·ing (ŭn-flĭn′chĭng) *adj.* Not showing fear or indecision; steadfast: *an unflinching determination to find out all the facts.* **—un·flinch′ing·ly** *adv.*

un·fold (ŭn-fōld′) *v.* **un·fold·ed, un·fold·ing, un·folds** *—tr.* **1.** To open or spread out: *unfolded the map.* **2.** To reveal gradually; make known: *unfolding the details of her plans.* *—intr.* **1.** To become spread out or open: *The flower unfolded during the day.* **2.** To develop: *Their rivalry unfolded over the summer.* **3.** To be revealed gradually: *The truth unfolded as the investigation proceeded.*

un·fore·seen (ŭn′fər-**sēn′** *or* ŭn′fôr-**sēn′**) *adj.* Not felt or realized beforehand; unexpected.

un·for·get·ta·ble (ŭn′fər-**gĕt′**ə-bəl) *adj.* Permanently impressed on one's memory; memorable: *an unforgettable experience.* **—un′for·get′ta·bly** *adv.*

un·for·mat·ted (ŭn-**fôr′**măt′ĭd) *adj.* **1.** Not being in or having a proper format: *an unformatted document.* **2.** Relating to a data storage device that is not formatted into sectors, thus not allowing data to be stored: *an unformatted disk.*

un·formed (ŭn **fôrmd′**) *adj.* **1.** Having no definite shape or form. **2.** Not yet developed: *unformed ideas.*

un·for·tu·nate (ŭn-**fôr′**chə-nĭt) *adj.* **1.** Having bad luck; unlucky. **2.** Marked by, bringing, or causing misfortune: *an unfortunate turn of events.* **3.** Regrettable or inappropriate: *an unfortunate remark.* ❖ *n.* A person who has bad luck. **—un·for′tu·nate·ly** *adv.*

un·found·ed (ŭn-**foun′**dĭd) *adj.* Having no basis in fact; groundless: *unfounded accusations.*

un·friend (ŭn-**frĕnd′**) *tr.v.* **un·friend·ed, un·friend·ing, un·friends** To remove (someone) as a friend on a social networking website.

un·friend·ly (ŭn-**frĕnd′**lē) *adj.* **un·friend·li·er, un·friend·li·est 1.** Not friendly. **2.** Hostile or confrontational: *an unfriendly nation.* **3.** Not easy to use or learn to use: *a camera with an unfriendly design.* **—un·friend′li·ness** *n.*

un·furl (ŭn-**fûrl′**) *tr. & intr.v.* **un·furled, un·furl·ing, un·furls** To open or spread out or become open or spread out; unroll: *The guard unfurled the flag. The flags unfurled in the breeze.*

un·gain·ly (ŭn-**gān′**lē) *adj.* **un·gain·li·er, un·gain·li·est** Lacking grace or ease of movement; awkward; clumsy. [From *un-*, not + obsolete English *gainli*, proper (from Old Norse *gegn*, direct).] **—un·gain′li·ness** *n.*

un·god·ly (ŭn-**gŏd′**lē) *adj.* **un·god·li·er, un·god·li·est 1.** Not revering God; impious. **2.** Sinful; wicked. **3.** Outrageous: *waking him up at that ungodly hour.*

un·gov·ern·a·ble (ŭn-**gŭv′**ər-nə-bəl) *adj.* Incapable of being governed or controlled: *an ungovernable mob.*

un·gra·cious (ŭn-**grā′**shəs) *adj.* Impolite; discourteous; rude.

un·gram·mat·i·cal (ŭn′grə-**măt′**ĭ-kəl) *adj.* Not in accord with the rules of grammar.

un·grate·ful (ŭn-**grāt′**fəl) *adj.* **1.** Not feeling or expressing thanks. **2.** Disagreeable; unpleasant: *an ungrateful task.* **—un·grate′ful·ly** *adv.*

un·guard·ed (ŭn-**gär′**dĭd) *adj.* **1.** Lacking a guard or defense: *an unguarded gate.* **2.** Having or showing no caution or thought; careless: *The question caught the mayor during an unguarded moment.*

un·guent (**ŭng′**gwənt) *n.* A salve for soothing or healing; an ointment. [From Middle English, from Latin *unguentum*.]

un·gu·late (**ŭng′**gyə-lĭt *or* **ŭng′**gyə-lāt′) *n.* A hoofed animal, such as a horse, cow, deer, or antelope. [From Latin *ungula*, hoof.]

un·hand (ŭn-**hănd′**) *tr.v.* **un·hand·ed, un·hand·ing, un·hands** To remove one's hands from; let go of: *unhand me.*

un·hap·py (ŭn-**hăp′**ē) *adj.* **un·hap·pi·er, un·hap·pi·est 1.** Not happy; sad: *feeling unhappy.* See Synonyms at **sad. 2.** Not satisfied; displeased: *She's unhappy with her performance.* **3.** Not bringing good fortune; unlucky: *In an unhappy moment he made a wrong decision.* **4.** Not suitable; inappropriate: *an unhappy choice of words.* **—un·hap′pi·ly** *adv.* **—un·hap′pi·ness** *n.*

un·health·y (ŭn-**hĕl′**thē) *adj.* **un·health·i·er, un·health·i·est 1.** Being in a state of poor health; ill; sick. **2.** Being a sign or symptom of poor health: *a pale unhealthy appearance.* **3.** Causing or tending to cause poor health; not wholesome: *an unhealthy diet.* **4.** Harmful to character or morality: *an unhealthy influence on her younger sister.* **5.** Risky; dangerous: *an unhealthy situation.*

un·heard-of (ŭn-**hûrd′**ŭv′) *adj.* Not previously known or done; without an earlier example: *living in unheard-of luxury.*

un·hinge (ŭn-**hĭnj′**) *tr.v.* **un·hinged, un·hing·ing, un·hing·es 1.** To remove from hinges: *unhinged the door.* **2.** To separate or disconnect: *a disagreement that unhinged the business deal.* **3.** To confuse, upset, or derange: *The conductor was unhinged by the poor performance of the choir.*

un·ho·ly (ŭn-**hō′**lē) *adj.* **un·ho·li·er, un·ho·li·est 1.** Wicked; immoral. **2.** Not holy or sacred. **3.** Dreadful; outrageous: *an unholy mess.*

un·hook (ŭn-**ho͝ok′**) *tr.v.* **un·hooked, un·hook·ing, un·hooks 1.** To release or remove from a hook: *unhooked the porch screen.* **2.** To unfasten the hooks of: *unhook a dress.*

un·horse (ŭn-**hôrs′**) *tr.v.* **un·horsed, un·hors·ing, un·hors·es** To cause (a rider) to fall from a horse.

uni– *pref.* A prefix that means one or single: *unilateral.* —SEE NOTE.

u·ni·cam·er·al (yo͞o′nĭ-**kăm′**ər-əl) *adj.* Having or consisting of a single legislative chamber: *a unicameral parliament.*

UNICEF *abbr.* An abbreviation of United Nations Children's Fund.

u·ni·cel·lu·lar (yo͞o′nĭ-**sĕl′**yə-lər) *adj.* Having or consisting of a single cell; one-celled: *unicellular microorganisms.*

u·ni·corn (**yo͞o′**nĭ-kôrn′) *n.* A legendary animal resembling a horse and having a single long horn projecting from its forehead. [From Middle English *unicorne*, from Latin *ūnicornis*, having one horn : *ūnus*, one + *cornū*, horn.]

u·ni·cy·cle (**yo͞o′**nĭ-sī′kəl) *n.* A vehicle consisting of a frame mounted over a single wheel and usually propelled by pedals.

un·i·den·ti·fied flying object (ŭn′ī-**dĕn′**tə-fīd′) *n.* A flying object of an unknown nature, especially one suspected to have been sent by extraterrestrial beings.

u·ni·form (**yo͞o′**nə-fôrm′) *adj.* **1.** Always the same; not changing or varying: *planks of uniform length.* **2.** Being the same as or consistent with another or others: *rows of uniform brick houses.* ❖ *n.* A suit of clothing intended to identify the people who wear it as members of a specific group. [From Latin *ūnifōrmis* : *ūni-*, one + *fōrma*, shape.] **—u′ni·formed′** *adj.* **—u′ni·for′mi·ty** *n.* **—u′ni·form′ly** *adv.*

u·ni·fy (**yo͞o′**nə-fī′) *tr. & intr.v.* **u·ni·fied, u·ni·fy·ing, u·ni·fies** To make into or become a unit; unite. **—u′ni·fi·ca′tion** (yo͞o′nə-fĭ-**kā′**shən) *n.*

unicorn
a ship's figurehead

unicycle

uniform

u·ni·lat·er·al (yo͞o′nə-**lăt′**ər-əl) *adj.* **1.** On or affecting only one side: *unilateral hearing loss.* **2.** Done or undertaken by only one side: *unilateral disarmament.* **—u′ni·lat′er·al·ly** *adv.*

un·im·peach·a·ble (ŭn′ĭm-**pē′**chə-bəl) *adj.* **1.** Difficult or impossible to impeach. **2.** Beyond reproach; blameless: *unimpeachable behavior.* **3.** Beyond doubt or question; unquestionable: *unimpeachable honesty.*

un·im·por·tant (ŭn′ĭm-**pôr′**tnt) *adj.* Not important; insignificant or petty: *ignored the unimportant comments.* **—un′im·por′tance** *n.*

un·in·hab·it·ed (ŭn′ĭn-**hăb′**ĭ-tĭd) *adj.* Not inhabited; having no residents.

un·in·hib·it·ed (ŭn′ĭn-**hĭb′**ĭ-tĭd) *adj.* Free from social or moral restraints; unselfconscious: *uninhibited laughter.*

un·in·stall (ŭn′ĭn-**stôl′**) *tr.v.* **un·in·stalled, un·in·stall·ing, un·in·stalls** To remove completely from a computer system: *uninstalled the obsolete software.*

un·in·sured (ŭn′ĭn-**sho͝ord′**) *adj.* Not covered by insurance: *The emergency room accepted uninsured patients.*

un·in·tel·li·gent (ŭn′ĭn-**tĕl′**ə-jənt) *adj.* Lacking in intelligence. **—un′in·tel′li·gent·ly** *adv.*

un·in·tel·li·gi·ble (ŭn′ĭn-**tĕl′**ĭ-jə-bəl) *adj.* Difficult or impossible to understand: *unintelligible gibberish.* **—un′in·tel′li·gi·bil′i·ty** *n.* **—un′in·tel′li·gi·bly** *adv.*

un·in·ten·tion·al (ŭn′ĭn-**tĕn′**shə-nəl) *adj.* Not done or said on purpose. **—un′in·ten′tion·al·ly** *adv.*

un·in·ter·est·ed (ŭn-**ĭn′**trĭ-stĭd *or* ŭn-**ĭn′**tə-rĕs′tĭd) *adj.* Not interested in something; having no interest.

un·in·vit·ed (ŭn′ĭn-**vī′**tĭd) *adj.* Not invited or welcome.

un·ion (**yo͞on′**yən) *n.* **1a.** The act of uniting or the state of being united: *union of the two colleges into one.* **b.** A combination formed by uniting, especially a number of people or groups joined together for a purpose: *plans for the union of all colonies under one government.* **2.** A mathematical set having the property that each of its elements is also an element of two or more given sets. **3.** A partnership in marriage: *a happy union.* **4.** A labor union. **5.** A device used for joining parts, such as pipes or rods. **6.** A design on or part of a flag that symbolizes the union of two or more independent states or regions. For example, the blue part with stars is the union of the US flag. **7. Union** The United States of America, especially during the Civil War. ❖ *adj.* **1. Union** Relating to or loyal to the United States of America during the Civil War. **2.** Relating to a labor union. [From Middle English *unioun*, from Late Latin *ūniō*, from Latin *ūnus*, one.]

un·ion·ist (**yo͞on′**yə-nĭst) *n.* **1.** A person who believes in or supports labor unions. **2.** A member of a labor union. **3. Unionist** A person who was loyal to the federal government during the Civil War.

un·ion·ize (**yo͞on′**yə-nīz′) *tr.v.* **un·ion·ized, un·ion·iz·ing, un·ion·iz·es** To organize into or cause to join a labor union: *unionize factory workers.* **—un′ion·i·za′tion** (yo͞on′yə-nĭ-**zā′**shən) *n.*

Union Jack *n.* The flag of the United Kingdom.

Union of So·vi·et Socialist Republics (**sō′**vē-ĕt′ *or* **sō′**vē-ĭt) Commonly called **Soviet Union.** A former country of eastern Europe and northern Asia with coastlines on the Baltic and Black Seas and the Arctic and Pacific Oceans. It was established in December 1922. In 1991 most of the member republics declared their independence, and the USSR was officially dissolved. Moscow was the capital.

union shop *n.* A business or industrial establishment whose employees are required to be or become members of a labor union.

u·nique (yo͞o-**nēk′**) *adj.* **1.** Being the only one of its kind: *the unique manuscript of a medieval poem.* **2.** Characteristic only of a particular category, condition, or locality: *a weather pattern that is unique to coastal areas.* **3.** Remarkable; extraordinary: *a unique opportunity to buy a house.* [From Latin *ūnicus.*] **—u·nique′ly** *adv.* **—u·nique′ness** *n.*

u·ni·sex (**yo͞o′**nĭ-sĕks′) *adj.* Suitable for both males and females: *unisex clothes.*

u·ni·son (**yo͞o′**nĭ-sən *or* **yo͞o′**nĭ-zən) *n.* **1.** In music, the combination of two or more tones of the same pitch at the same time. **2.** Agreement; harmony. ◆ **in unison 1.** In complete agreement; harmonizing exactly. **2.** At the same time; at once.

u·nit (**yo͞o′**nĭt) *n.* **1.** A thing, person, group, or structure regarded as a part of a whole: *adding an extra unit to a bookcase.* **2.** A single group regarded as a distinct part within a larger group: *an army unit.* **3.** A mechanical part or piece of equipment: *an air-conditioning unit.* **4.** A precisely defined quantity used as a standard for measuring quantities of the same kind: *The meter is a unit of distance.* **5a.** The number located just to the left of the decimal point in the Arabic numeral system. **b.** The lowest positive whole number; 1: *to count in units, tens, and hundreds.* **6.** A section of a course of study focusing on one subject: *a unit on Native Americans.* [From *unity.*]

U·ni·tar·i·an (yo͞o′nĭ-**târ′**ē-ən) *n.* **1.** A person who believes in Unitarian Universalism. **2.** A Christian who does not believe in the Trinity or the divinity of Jesus, but who believes that God is a single being. **—U′ni·tar′i·an** *adj.* **—U′ni·tar′i·an·ism** *n.*

Unitarian U·ni·ver·sal·ism (yo͞o′nə-**vûr′**sə-lĭz′əm) *n.* A religious association of Christian origin that has no official creed and that considers God to be a single being and salvation to be granted to everyone. **—Unitarian Universalist** *adj. & n.*

u·nite (yo͞o-**nīt′**) *v.* **u·nit·ed, u·nit·ing, u·nites** *—tr.* **1.** To bring together or join so as to form a whole: *The chemist united the substances to form a new compound.* See Synonyms at **join. 2.** To join together or bring into close association for a common purpose: *a treaty to unite all nations in the fight against disease.* **3.** To join (a couple) in matrimony. *—intr.* **1.** To become joined or combined into a unit: *The two firms united to form a large business.* **2.** To join and act together for a common purpose: *Let's unite and stop pollution.* [From Middle English *uniten*, from Latin *ūnus*, one.]

u·nit·ed (yo͞o-**nī′**tĭd) *adj.* **1.** Combined into one. **2.** Concerned with or resulting from joint action: *a united effort to preserve the meadow.* **3.** Being in harmony; agreed: *On that point we are united.*

United Arab E·mir·ates (ĭ-**mîr′**ĭts *or* ĕm**′**ər-ĭts) A country of eastern Arabia on the Persian Gulf. Abu Dhabi is the capital.

United Kingdom or **United Kingdom of Great Britain and Northern Ireland** Commonly called **Great Britain** or **Britain.** A country of western Europe made up of England, Scotland, Wales, and Northern Ireland. It reached the height of its power in the 1800s. London is the capital.

United Nations An international organization composed of most of the countries of the world. It was founded in 1945.

United States or **United States of America** A country of central and northwest North America with coastlines on the Atlantic and Pacific Oceans. It includes the states of Alaska and Hawaii and various island territories in the Caribbean Sea and Pacific Ocean. The original Thirteen Colonies declared their independence from Great Britain in 1776. Washington, DC is the capital and New York the largest city.

United States Virgin Islands A United States territory constituting the southwest group of the Virgin Islands. Charlotte Amalie is the capital.

unit pricing *n.* The pricing of goods on the basis of cost per unit of measure.

ă	pat	ôr	core
ā	pay	oi	boy
âr	care	ou	out
ä	father	o͝o	took
ĕ	pet	o͝or	lure
ē	be	o͞o	boot
ĭ	pit	ŭ	cut
ī	bite	ûr	urge
îr	pier	th	thin
ŏ	pot	*th*	this
ō	toe	zh	vision
ô	paw	ə	about

u·ni·ty (yo͞o′nĭ-tē) *n., pl.* **u·ni·ties 1.** The state or quality of being one or united into a whole: *an issue that threatened the unity of the nation.* **2.** Accord; harmony: *Are the members of the committee in unity on this matter?* **3.** The combination or arrangement of parts, as in a work of art or literature, into a complete whole. **4.** The number 1. [From Middle English *unite*, from Latin *ūnus*, one.]

u·ni·va·lent (yo͞o′nĭ-vā′lənt) *adj.* In chemistry, having valence 1.

u·ni·ver·sal (yo͞o′nə-vûr′səl) *adj.* **1.** Relating to or affecting the entire universe: *universal laws of physics.* **2.** Including, relating to, or affecting all members of a class or group: *universal vaccination.* **3.** Done or shared by all members of a class or group: *a discovery that met with universal acclaim.* **4.** Adapted or adjustable to many sizes or mechanical uses: *a universal wrench.* **—u′ni·ver·sal′i·ty** (yo͞o′nə-vər-săl′ĭ-tē) *n.* **—u′ni·ver′sal·ly** *adv.*

universal joint *n.* A joint or coupling that transmits rotary motion from one point to another that is not in line with it.

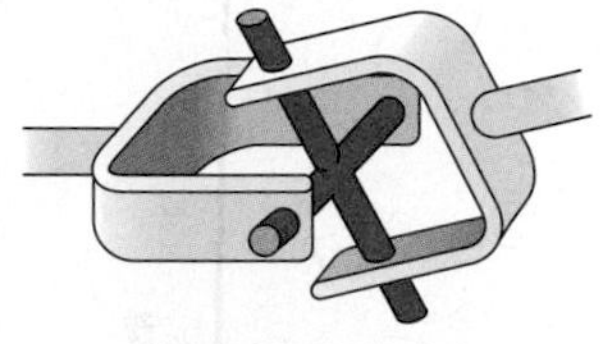
universal joint

Universal Product Code *n.* A number and barcode that identify an individual consumer product, often used for tracking inventory.

u·ni·verse (yo͞o′nə-vûrs′) *n.* **1.** All matter and energy considered as a whole, including Earth, the galaxies, and the contents of space between the galaxies; the cosmos. **2.** In mathematics, a set that contains all the objects and sets under discussion as elements or subsets. [From Middle English, from Latin *ūniversus*, whole : *ūnus*, one + *versus*, turned.]

u·ni·ver·si·ty (yo͞o′nə-vûr′sĭ-tē) *n., pl.* **u·ni·ver·si·ties** An institution of higher learning that includes one or more colleges and typically a graduate school and professional schools.

un·just (ŭn-jŭst′) *adj.* Not just or fair; unfair. **—un·just′ly** *adv.*

un·kempt (ŭn-kĕmpt′) *adj.* **1.** Not combed: *unkempt hair.* **2.** Not neat or tidy; messy: *unkempt clothes.* [From Middle English *unkemd* : *un-*, not + *kembed*, combed (from Old English *cemban*, to comb).]

un·kind (ŭn-kīnd′) *adj.* **un·kind·er, un·kind·est** Not kind or sympathetic. **—un·kind′ly** *adv.* **—un·kind′ness** *n.*

un·know·a·ble (ŭn-nō′ə-bəl) *adj.* Impossible to know; beyond human understanding.

un·known (ŭn-nōn′) *adj.* **1.** Not known or familiar; strange: *a town unknown to us.* **2.** Not identified or ascertained: *an unknown quantity.* **3.** Not widely known: *an unknown painter.* ❖ *n.* A person or thing that is unknown.

un·lace (ŭn-lās′) *tr.v.* **un·laced, un·lac·ing, un·lac·es** To loosen or undo the laces of.

un·latch (ŭn-lăch′) *tr.v.* **un·latched, un·latch·ing, un·latch·es** To unfasten or open by releasing a latch: *unlatched the door.*

un·law·ful (ŭn-lô′fəl) *adj.* Being in violation of the law; illegal. **—un·law′ful·ly** *adv.*

un·lead·ed (ŭn-lĕd′ĭd) *adj.* Not containing lead or lead compounds: *unleaded gasoline.*

un·learn (ŭn-lûrn′) *tr.v.* **un·learned** also **un·learnt** (ŭn-lûrnt′), **un·learn·ing, un·learns 1.** To put (something learned) out of the mind; forget. **2.** To stop practicing (a habit): *tried to unlearn his habit of biting his nails.*

un·learn·ed (ŭn-lûr′nĭd) *adj.* **1.** Not educated; ignorant or illiterate. **2.** Not known or acquired by training or studying: *an unlearned sense of balance.*

un·leash (ŭn-lēsh′) *tr.v.* **un·leashed, un·leash·ing, un·leash·es 1.** To release from a leash: *unleashed the guard dogs.* **2.** To set free from restraints: *unleashed his anger.*

un·leav·ened (ŭn-lĕv′ənd) *adj.* Made without yeast or other leaven: *unleavened bread.*

un·less (ŭn-lĕs′) *conj.* Except on the condition that: *You can't write the report unless you do the research first.* [From Middle English *unlesse* : *on*, on + *lesse*, less.]

un·let·tered (ŭn-lĕt′ərd) *adj.* **1.** Lacking knowledge that comes from reading books. **2.** Not able to read and write; illiterate.

un·like (ŭn-līk′) *adj.* **1.** Not alike; different: *For twins, they are very unlike.* **2.** Not equal, as in amount: *unlike sums.* ❖ *prep.* **1.** Different from; not like: *That band has a sound unlike any other.* **2.** Not typical of: *It is unlike him not to call if he cannot come.*

un·like·ly (ŭn-līk′lē) *adj.* **un·like·li·er, un·like·li·est 1.** Not likely; improbable: *an unlikely story.* **2.** Likely to fail; unpromising: *an unlikely business venture.*

un·lim·it·ed (ŭn-lĭm′ĭ-tĭd) *adj.* Having no limits or bounds: *unlimited possibilities.*

un·list·ed (ŭn-lĭs′tĭd) *adj.* Not appearing on a list: *an unlisted telephone number.*

un·load (ŭn-lōd′) *tr.v.* **un·load·ed, un·load·ing, un·loads 1a.** To remove the load or cargo from: *unload a truck.* **b.** To remove (cargo): *unload furniture from the van.* **2.** To give expression to (one's troubles or feelings). **3.** To remove the charge from (a firearm). **4.** To dispose of, especially by selling in large quantities; dump: *unloading textiles at low prices.*

un·lock (ŭn-lŏk′) *tr.v.* **un·locked, un·lock·ing, un·locks 1.** To undo (a lock), as by turning a key or executing a combination. **2.** To undo the lock of: *unlock the trunk.* **3.** To set free; release: *The news unlocked a torrent of emotion.* **4.** To solve, disclose, or reveal: *unlock a mystery.*

un·loose (ŭn-lo͞os′) *tr.v.* **un·loosed, un·loos·ing, un·loos·es 1.** To unfasten: *unloosed the leash from the dog's neck.* **2.** To set free; release.

un·loos·en (ŭn-lo͞o′sən) *tr.v.* **un·loos·ened, un·loos·en·ing, un·loos·ens** To unloose.

un·luck·y (ŭn-lŭk′ē) *adj.* **un·luck·i·er, un·luck·i·est 1.** Marked by or having bad luck: *an unlucky occurrence; an unlucky person.* **2.** Seeming to cause bad luck: *an unlucky number.* **—un·luck′i·ly** *adv.*

un·made (ŭn-mād′) *adj.* Not made: *an unmade bed.*

un·man·age·a·ble (ŭn-măn′ĭ-jə-bəl) *adj.* Difficult or impossible to manage or control: *an unmanageable amount of work.*

un·manned (ŭn-mănd′) *adj.* Lacking a crew or designed to operate without a crew: *an unmanned spacecraft.*

un·man·ner·ly (ŭn-măn′ər-lē) *adj.* Having bad manners; impolite: *unmannerly behavior.*

un·mar·ried (ŭn-măr′ēd) *adj.* Not married.

un·mask (ŭn-măsk′) *v.* **un·masked, un·mask·ing, un·masks** *—tr.* **1.** To remove a mask from. **2.** To disclose the true nature of; reveal: *finally unmasked his resentment.* *—intr.* To remove one's mask.

un·men·tion·a·ble (ŭn-mĕn′shə-nə-bəl) *adj.* Not fit to be mentioned or discussed. ❖ *n.* **1.** A person or thing that is not to be mentioned. **2. unmentionables** Underclothes.

un·mer·ci·ful (ŭn-mûr′sĭ-fəl) *adj.* **1.** Having or showing no mercy; merciless. **2.** Excessive; extreme: *unmerciful heat.* **—un·mer′ci·ful·ly** *adv.*

un·mind·ful (ŭn-mīnd′fəl) *adj.* Not giving enough care or attention; careless: *unmindful of the time.* **—un·mind′ful·ly** *adv.*

un·mis·tak·a·ble (ŭn′mĭ-stā′kə-bəl) *adj.* Impossible to mistake: *the unmistakable sound of a hyena.* **—un′mis·tak′a·bly** *adv.*

un·mit·i·gat·ed (ŭn-mĭt′ĭ-gā′tĭd) *adj.* **1.** Not diminished in intensity; without relief: *unmitigated heat.* **2.** Absolute; without exception: *an unmitigated lie.*

un·moved (ŭn-mo͞ovd′) *adj.* Emotionally unaffected: *parents unmoved by their teenager's pleas for more money.*

un·nat·u·ral (ŭn-**năch′**ər-əl) *adj.* **1.** Not in accordance with what usually occurs in nature; abnormal or unusual: *a tree with an unnatural shape.* **2.** Not included in nature; artifical: *hair dyed an unnatural color.* **3.** Against natural feelings; inhuman: *unnatural cruelty.* **4.** Strained, stiff, or affected; artificial: *an unnatural manner.* **—un·nat′u·ral·ly** *adv.*

un·nec·es·sar·y (ŭn-**nĕs′**ĭ-sĕr′ē) *adj.* Not necessary; needless: *cut unnecessary items from the budget.* **—un·nec′es·sar′i·ly** (ŭn-nĕs′ĭ-**sâr′**ə-lē) *adv.*

un·nerve (ŭn-**nûrv′**) *tr.v.* **un·nerved, un·nerv·ing, un·nerves** To cause to lose courage or firmness of purpose: *The heated argument unnerved him.*

un·ob·served (ŭn′əb-**zûrvd′**) *adj.* **1.** Not seen or noticed: *We crept up the walkway unobserved.* **2.** Not monitored for scientific study: *unobserved asteroids.* **3.** Not kept or complied with: *unobserved regulations; an unobserved holiday.*

un·ob·tru·sive (ŭn′əb-**trōō′**sĭv) *adj.* Not undesirably blatant or noticeable; inconspicuous: *quiet, unobtrusive music that played at the supermarket.* **—un′ob·tru′sive·ly** *adv.*

un·oc·cu·pied (ŭn-**ŏk′**yə-pīd′) *adj.* **1.** Not occupied or being used; vacant: *unoccupied seats.* **2.** Not busy; idle: *unoccupied workers.*

un·of·fi·cial (ŭn′ə-**fĭsh′**əl) *adj.* Not official: *The unofficial reports turned out to be incorrect.* **—un′of·fi′cial·ly** *adv.*

un·op·posed (ŭn′ə-**pōzd′**) *adj.* Not challenged by another: *The candidate was unopposed.*

un·or·gan·ized (ŭn-**ôr′**gə-nīzd′) *adj.* **1.** Lacking order, system, or unity; disorganized: *tried to straighten out my unorganized files.* **2.** Not represented by a labor union.

un·or·tho·dox (ŭn-**ôr′**thə-dŏks′) *adj.* Breaking with tradition or convention; not orthodox: *an unorthodox approach to a problem.*

un·pack (ŭn-**păk′**) *v.* **un·packed, un·pack·ing, un·packs** *—tr.* **1.** To remove the contents of (a suitcase, for example): *unpacked my knapsack.* **2.** To remove from a container or from packaging: *unpack groceries.* *—intr.* To remove objects from a container: *I unpacked as soon as I got to my hotel room.*

un·paid (ŭn-**pād′**) *adj.* **1.** Not yet paid: *an unpaid bill.* **2.** Receiving no pay; not salaried: *an unpaid volunteer.*

un·par·al·leled (ŭn-**păr′**ə-lĕld′) *adj.* Without parallel or match; unequaled: *unparalleled beauty.*

un·pleas·ant (ŭn-**plĕz′**ənt) *adj.* Not pleasing; disagreeable: *The garbage gave off an unpleasant odor.* **—un·pleas′ant·ly** *adv.*

un·plug (ŭn-**plŭg′**) *v.* **un·plugged, un·plug·ging, un·plugs** *—tr.* **1.** To remove a plug from. **2.** To disconnect (an electric appliance) by removing a plug from an outlet: *unplugged the toaster.* *—intr.* To become unplugged.

un·plugged (ŭn-**plŭgd′**) *adj.* Involving the performance of music using acoustic instruments, sometimes amplified through microphones: *an unplugged concert.*

un·pol·ished (ŭn-**pŏl′**ĭsht) *adj.* **1.** Not smooth and shiny: *unpolished shoes.* **2.** Not made perfect; not refined: *an unpolished performance.* **3.** Not having refined or perfected one's skill at something: *an unpolished singer.* **4.** Lacking good manners.

un·pop·u·lar (ŭn-**pŏp′**yə-lər) *adj.* Lacking general approval or acceptance: *an unpopular tax policy.*

un·prac·ticed (ŭn-**prăk′**tĭst) *adj.* **1.** Not yet tested or tried: *unpracticed methods.* **2.** Lacking experience; unskilled: *unpracticed volunteers.*

un·prec·e·dent·ed (ŭn-**prĕs′**ĭ-dĕn′tĭd) *adj.* Having no previous example: *an unprecedented demand for housing.*

un·pre·dict·a·ble (ŭn′prĭ-**dĭk′**tə-bəl) *adj.* Difficult to foretell or foresee: *The outcome of a game of chance is unpredictable.* **—un′pre·dict′a·bly** *adv.*

un·pre·pared (ŭn′prĭ-**pârd′**) *adj.* **1.** Having made no preparations: *unprepared for school.* **2.** Done without preparation; impromptu: *an unprepared speech.*

un·pre·pos·sess·ing (ŭn′prē-pə-**zĕs′**ĭng) *adj.* Failing to impress favorably; nondescript: *an unprepossessing motel like any other.*

un·pre·ten·tious (ŭn′prĭ-**tĕn′**shəs) *adj.* **1.** Lacking pretension or affectation; modest: *an unpretentious diner that served hearty meals.* **2.** Not elaborate; simple: *an unpretentious bungalow.*

un·prin·ci·pled (ŭn-**prĭn′**sə-pəld) *adj.* Lacking principles or moral scruples; immoral: *an unprincipled treasurer who stole money from the company.*

un·print·a·ble (ŭn-**prĭn′**tə-bəl) *adj.* Not fit to be printed, especially because of being offensive or indecent: *an unprintable story.*

un·pro·fes·sion·al (ŭn′prə-**fĕsh′**ə-nəl) *adj.* **1.** Not a member of a professional group. **2.** Not meeting the standards of a profession: *unprofessional behavior.*

un·prof·it·a·ble (ŭn-**prŏf′**ĭ-tə-bəl) *adj.* **1.** Bringing in no profit: *an unprofitable business.* **2.** Serving no useful purpose: *got into an unprofitable argument.* **—un·prof′it·a·bly** *adv.*

un·pro·nounce·a·ble (ŭn′prə-**noun′**sə-bəl) *adj.* Hard or impossible to pronounce correctly: *an unpronounceable last name.*

un·qual·i·fied (ŭn-**kwŏl′**ə-fīd′) *adj.* **1.** Without the necessary or required qualifications. **2.** Without reservation; complete: *an unqualified success.*

un·ques·tion·a·ble (ŭn-**kwĕs′**chə-nə-bəl) *adj.* Beyond question or doubt; certain: *a soldier of unquestionable valor.* **—un·ques′tion·a·bly** *adv.*

un·rav·el (ŭn-**răv′**əl) *v.* **un·rav·eled, un·rav·el·ing, un·rav·els** or **un·rav·elled, un·rav·el·ling, un·rav·els** *—tr.* **1a.** To undo the entangled, knitted, or woven threads of: *unraveled the sweater.* **b.** To separate (entangled, knitted, or woven threads). **2.** To clarify the elements of (a mystery or problem): *The detective unraveled the mystery.* **3.** To cause to fail or become ruined or unfulfilled: *Their plans to open a restaurant became unraveled.* *—intr.* **1.** To become unraveled: *The seam unraveled.* **2.** To fail or become ruined or unfulfilled: *His life unraveled after the stock market crash.*

un·read (ŭn-**rĕd′**) *adj.* **1.** Not read, studied, or examined: *an unread book.* **2.** Having read little; lacking in knowledge acquired by reading.

un·read·y (ŭn-**rĕd′**ē) *adj.* **un·read·i·er, un·read·i·est** **1.** Not ready or prepared: *The new recruits were unready for battle.* **2.** Slow to see or respond.

un·real (ŭn-**rēl′**) *adj.* **1.** Not real; imaginary. **2.** *Slang* So remarkable as to be hard to believe. **3.** Surreal.

un·re·al·is·tic (ŭn′rē-ə-**lĭs′**tĭk) *adj.* Unreasonably idealistic: *unrealistic expectations.* **—un′re·al·is′ti·cal·ly** *adv.*

un·rea·son·a·ble (ŭn-**rē′**zə-nə-bəl) *adj.* **1.** Not subject to or based on reason: *an unreasonable attitude.* **2.** Exceeding reasonable limits; immoderate: *an unreasonable amount.* **—un·rea′son·a·bly** *adv.*

un·re·gen·er·ate (ŭn′rĭ-**jĕn′**ər-ĭt) *adj.* **1.** Not spiritually renewed or reformed; not repentant: *an unregenerate sinner.* **2.** Not reconciled to change; stubborn: *an unregenerate conservative.*

un·re·lent·ing (ŭn′rĭ-**lĕn′**tĭng) *adj.* **1.** Not yielding, as in resolution; inflexible: *an unrelenting opponent.* **2.** Not diminishing in intensity: *a storm with unrelenting fury.*

un·re·li·a·ble (ŭn′rĭ-**lī′**ə-bəl) *adj.* Characterized by or showing a lack of reliability: *The jury did not believe the unreliable witness.* **—un′re·li′a·bil′i·ty** *n.* **—un′re·li′a·bly** *adv.*

un·re·mit·ting (ŭn′rĭ-**mĭt′**ĭng) *adj.* Not letting up; persistent: *an unremitting struggle for survival.* **—un′re·mit′ting·ly** *adv.*

un·re·pent·ant (ŭn′rĭ-**pĕn′**tənt) *adj.* Having or showing

WRITERS CHOOSE THEIR WORDS

The trees on each side of them swayed as the **unrelenting** wind and rain bent them against their will. The road seemed pitch-black beneath the tree canopy. Then there was a brilliant flash of lightning and a clap of thunder so loud that it sounded as if a cannon had gone off overhead.

—Lauren Brooke
Coming Home

ă	pat	ôr	core
ā	pay	oi	boy
âr	care	ou	out
ä	father	ŏŏ	took
ĕ	pet	ŏŏr	lure
ē	be	ōō	boot
ĭ	pit	ŭ	cut
ī	bite	ûr	urge
îr	pier	th	thin
ŏ	pot	*th*	this
ō	toe	zh	vision
ô	paw	ə	about

no remorse: *The unrepentant criminal was denied parole.*

un·re·quit·ed (ŭn′rĭ-**kwī′**tĭd) *adj.* Not given, rewarded, or felt in return: *unrequited love.*

un·re·served (ŭn′rĭ-**zûrvd′**) *adj.* **1.** Not held for a particular person: *an unreserved seat.* **2.** Given freely or generously: *unreserved praise.* **3.** Showing no reserve; unrestrained: *unreserved laughter.*

un·rest (ŭn-**rĕst′** *or* **ŭn′**rĕst′) *n.* **1.** An uneasy or troubled condition: *voter unrest over the scandal.* **2.** A condition of social disturbance, often involving demonstrations or rioting: *widespread unrest that threatened the dictator's grasp on power.*

un·re·strained (ŭn′rĭ-**strānd′**) *adj.* **1.** Not controlled or held in check; immoderate: *unrestrained spread of weeds; an unrestrained appetite.* **2.** Not constrained or reserved: *unrestrained laughter.*

un·ripe (ŭn-**rīp′**) *adj.* **un·rip·er, un·rip·est 1.** Not ripe; immature: *Unripe bananas are green.* **2.** Not fully prepared or ready: *The time is yet unripe for such a plan.*

un·ri·valed or **un·ri·valled** (ŭn-**rī′**vəld) *adj.* Having no rival or equal; incomparable: *the unrivaled champion.*

un·ruf·fled (ŭn-**rŭf′**əld) *adj.* **1.** Not agitated; calm: *He was unruffled after the coach's reprimand.* **2.** Regular and smooth, as the surface of water.

un·ru·ly (ŭn-**ro͞o′**lē) *adj.* **un·ru·li·er, un·ru·li·est 1.** Difficult or impossible to discipline or control: *The unruly mob stormed through the barricades.* **2.** Difficult to keep in place: *tried to comb his unruly hair.*

un·sad·dle (ŭn-**săd′**l) *tr.v.* **un·sad·dled, un·sad·dling, un·sad·dles 1.** To remove the saddle from. **2.** To throw (a rider) from a saddle. Used of a horse.

un·safe (ŭn-**sāf′**) *adj.* **un·saf·er, un·saf·est** Not safe; dangerous: *It is unsafe to drive without buckling your seat belt.*

un·said (ŭn-**sĕd′**) *adj.* Not said, especially not uttered out loud: *angry thoughts left unsaid.*

un·san·i·tar·y (ŭn-**săn′**ĭ-tĕr′ē) *adj.* Not sanitary: *The beach was closed due to unsanitary conditions.*

un·sat·is·fac·to·ry (ŭn-săt′ĭs-**făk′**tə-rē) *adj.* Not satisfactory; inadequate: *unsatisfactory living conditions.*

un·sat·u·rat·ed (ŭn-**săch′**ə-rā′tĭd) *adj.* **1.** Indicating a chemical compound in which two or more of the carbon atoms are joined by a double or triple bond and therefore can be combined with additional atoms or radicals. **2.** Capable of dissolving more of a solute: *an unsaturated solution.*

unsaturated fat *n.* A fat containing unsaturated chemical compounds, derived from plants and some animal sources, especially fish. Eating foods high in unsaturated fats can reduce the amount of cholesterol in the blood.

un·sa·vor·y (ŭn-**sā′**və-rē) *adj.* **1.** Unpleasant to the taste or smell; not savory: *an unsavory meal.* **2.** Distasteful or disagreeable: *an unsavory situation.* **3.** Morally offensive: *an unsavory character.*

un·scathed (ŭn-**skā*th*d′**) *adj.* Not harmed or injured: *Fortunately, we survived the hurricane unscathed.*

un·sci·en·tif·ic (ŭn′sī-ən-**tĭf′**ĭk) *adj.* **1.** Not according to the principles of science. **2.** Not knowledgeable about science.

un·scram·ble (ŭn-**skrăm′**bəl) *tr.v.* **un·scram·bled, un·scram·bling, un·scram·bles 1.** To straighten out or disentangle (a jumble or tangle); resolve. **2.** To restore (a scrambled message) to intelligible form: *She unscrambled the coded message.*

un·screw (ŭn-**skro͞o′**) *v.* **un·screwed, un·screw·ing, un·screws** —*tr.* **1.** To remove the screws from: *unscrewed the hinges.* **2.** To loosen, adjust, or remove by turning: *unscrewed the lid off the jar.* —*intr.* To become or allow to become unscrewed: *This lid unscrews easily.*

un·scru·pu·lous (ŭn-**skro͞o′**pyə-ləs) *adj.* Without scruples or principles; not honorable: *The unscrupulous lawyer was disbarred.* —**un·scru′pu·lous·ly** *adv.* —**un·scru′pu·lous·ness** *n.*

un·seal (ŭn-**sēl′**) *tr.v.* **un·sealed, un·seal·ing, un·seals** To break open or remove the seal of; open: *I unsealed the envelope and removed the letter.*

un·sea·son·a·ble (ŭn-**sē′**zə-nə-bəl) *adj.* Occurring or done out of season; not suitable for or characteristic of the season: *unseasonable weather.*

un·sea·soned (ŭn-**sē′**zənd) *adj.* **1.** Inexperienced: *unseasoned campers.* **2.** Not ripe or mature: *unseasoned wood.* **3.** Having no added seasoning: *unseasoned meat.*

un·seat (ŭn-**sēt′**) *tr.v.* **un·seat·ed, un·seat·ing, un·seats 1.** To remove from a seat, especially from a saddle. **2.** To remove from or force out of a position or office: *unseated the senator in the election.*

un·seem·ly (ŭn-**sēm′**lē) *adj.* **un·seem·li·er, un·seem·li·est** Not in good taste; improper. —**un·seem′ly** *adv.*

un·seen (ŭn-**sēn′**) *adj.* **1.** Not seen or noticed; invisible: *an unseen but dangerous flaw.* **2.** Not previously read: *an unseen translation.*

un·self·ish (ŭn-**sĕl′**fĭsh) *adj.* Not selfish; generous: *an unselfish contribution to charity.* —**un·self′ish·ly** *adv.* —**un·self′ish·ness** *n.*

un·set·tle (ŭn-**sĕt′**l) *tr.v.* **un·set·tled, un·set·tling, un·set·tles 1.** To move from a settled condition; disrupt: *strikes unsettling the economy.* **2.** To make uneasy; disturb: *The news unsettled him.*

un·set·tled (ŭn-**sĕt′**ld) *adj.* **1.** Not in a state of order or calmness; disturbed: *unsettled times.* **2.** Uncertain; variable: *unsettled weather.* **3.** Not determined or resolved: *an unsettled legal case.* **4.** Not paid: *unsettled accounts.* **5.** Uninhabited or not occupied by settlers: *a vast unsettled region.*

un·shack·le (ŭn-**shăk′**əl) *tr.v.* **un·shack·led, un·shack·ling, un·shack·les 1.** To remove the shackles from. **2.** To free; liberate: *unshackled him from traditional ways of thinking.*

un·shak·a·ble (ŭn-**shā′**kə-bəl) *adj.* Not capable of being shaken; firm: *a woman of unshakable convictions.* —**un·shak′a·bly** *adv.*

un·shod (ŭn-**shŏd′**) *adj.* Not having or wearing shoes or a shoe: *an unshod horse.*

un·sight·ly (ŭn-**sīt′**lē) *adj.* **un·sight·li·er, un·sight·li·est** Not pleasant to look at; unattractive. —**un·sight′li·ness** *n.*

un·skilled (ŭn-**skĭld′**) *adj.* **1.** Lacking technical training or skill: *unskilled workers.* **2.** Requiring no special training or skills: *unskilled work.*

un·so·phis·ti·cat·ed (ŭn′sə-**fĭs′**tĭ-kā′tĭd) *adj.* Not sophisticated; naive.

un·sound (ŭn-**sound′**) *adj.* **1.** Not dependably strong or solid: *a house with unsound foundations.* **2.** Not physically or mentally healthy. **3.** Not logical; fallacious: *an unsound argument.*

un·speak·a·ble (ŭn-**spē′**kə-bəl) *adj.* **1.** Beyond description; indescribable: *unspeakable anxiety.* **2.** Bad beyond description; totally objectionable: *unspeakable wickedness.* **3.** Not to be spoken: *an unspeakable word.* —**un·speak′a·bly** *adv.*

un·spoiled (ŭn-**spoild′**) *adj.* Not spoiled; pristine: *a rural, unspoiled landscape.*

un·spo·ken (ŭn-**spō′**kən) *adj.* **1.** Not expressed in words; unsaid: *an unspoken wish.* **2.** Understood without the need for words: *an unspoken agreement.*

un·sta·ble (ŭn-**stā′**bəl) *adj.* **un·sta·bler, un·sta·blest 1.** Having a strong tendency to change: *unstable prices.* **2.** Not firm; unsteady: *an unstable ladder.* **3.** Lacking control of one's emotions; characterized by unpredictable behavior. **4.** Tending to decompose easily, as a chemical compound. **5a.** Decaying after a relatively short time, as an atomic particle. **b.** Radioactive.

WRITERS CHOOSE THEIR WORDS

All day, the elders behaved unnaturally in her presence. No unintended slights, quick nods, easy smiles, teasing remarks or harsh words. They were so kind, *too* kind. Bandit felt as if she had sprouted a second head, and they were all determined to ignore politely the **unsightly** growth.

—Bette Bao Lord
In the Year of the Boar and Jackie Robinson

un·stead·y (ŭn-stĕd′ē) *adj.* **un·stead·i·er, un·stead·i·est 1.** Not steady: *an unsteady chair.* **2.** Wavering; uneven; unstable; *an unsteady voice; partially recovered from her illness but is still unsteady.* **—un·stead′i·ly** *adv.* **—un·stead′i·ness** *n.*

un·stop (ŭn-stŏp′) *tr.v.* **un·stopped, un·stop·ping, un·stops 1.** To remove the stopper from: *unstop a bottle.* **2.** To remove an obstruction from; open: *unstop a drain.*

un·stop·pa·ble (ŭn-stŏp′ə-bəl) *adj.* Impossible or hard to stop: *unstoppable floodwaters.*

un·stressed (ŭn-strĕst′) *adj.* **1.** Not accented or stressed: *an unstressed syllable.* **2.** Not exposed or subjected to stress.

un·strung (ŭn-strŭng′) *adj.* **1.** Having a string or strings loosened or removed. **2.** *Informal* Emotionally upset.

un·stud·ied (ŭn-stŭd′ēd) *adj.* Not contrived for effect; natural: *unstudied grace.*

un·sub·stan·tial (ŭn′səb-stăn′shəl) *adj.* **1.** Lacking material substance; insubstantial. **2.** Lacking a factual basis: *unsubstantial hopes.*

un·suc·cess·ful (ŭn′sək-sĕs′fəl) *adj.* Not succeeding; without success: *an unsuccessful plan; an unsuccessful person.* **—un′suc·cess′ful·ly** *adv.*

un·suit·a·ble (ŭn-so͞o′tə-bəl) *adj.* Not appropriate: *an unsuitable outfit for a wedding.* **—un·suit′a·bil′i·ty** *n.* **—un·suit′a·bly** *adv.*

un·sung (ŭn-sŭng′) *adj.* **1.** Not honored or praised; uncelebrated: *an unsung hero.* **2.** Not sung.

un·sure (ŭn-sho͝or′ *or* ŭn-shûr′) *adj.* **1.** Lacking confidence: *The unsure skater performed nervously.* **2.** Uncertain of the facts: *Terry was unsure whether Albany was the capital of New York.* **—un·sure′ly** *adv.*

un·sus·pect·ed (ŭn′sə-spĕk′tĭd) *adj.* **1.** Not under suspicion. **2.** Not known; unexpected: *Unsuspected wealth lay hidden there.*

un·sus·pect·ing (ŭn′sə-spĕk′tĭng) *adj.* Not suspicious; trusting: *an unsuspecting child.* **—un′sus·pect′ing·ly** *adv.*

un·tan·gle (ŭn-tăng′gəl) *tr.v.* **un·tan·gled, un·tan·gling, un·tan·gles 1.** To free from a tangle; disentangle: *untangle a fishing line.* **2.** To settle; clarify; resolve: *untangle a problem.*

un·tapped (ŭn-tăpt′) *adj.* **1.** Not tapped: *an untapped keg.* **2.** Not utilized: *untapped resources.*

un·taught (ŭn-tôt′) *adj.* **1.** Not instructed; ignorant. **2.** Not acquired by instruction; natural: *untaught musical skill.*

un·ten·a·ble (ŭn-tĕn′ə-bəl) *adj.* Not capable of being defended or maintained: *an untenable position.* **—un·ten′a·bly** *adv.*

un·think·a·ble (ŭn-thĭng′kə-bəl) *adj.* Impossible to imagine; inconceivable. **—un·think′a·bly** *adv.*

un·think·ing (ŭn′thĭng′kĭng) *adj.* **1.** Heedless or thoughtless: *an unthinking remark.* **2.** Showing lack of thought: *an unthinking conviction.*

un·ti·dy (ŭn-tī′dē) *adj.* **un·ti·di·er, un·ti·di·est** Not tidy and neat; sloppy. **—un·ti′di·ly** *adv.* **—un·ti′di·ness** *n.*

un·tie (ŭn-tī′) *v.* **un·tied, un·ty·ing, un·ties** *—tr.* **1.** To undo or loosen (a knot): *untie a tangled line.* **2.** To free from something that binds or restrains: *untie a package.* *—intr.* To become untied: *shoelaces that untie easily.*

un·til (ŭn-tĭl′) *prep.* **1.** Up to the time of: *They danced until dawn.* **2.** Before (a specified time): *You can't have the bike until tomorrow.* ❖ *conj.* **1.** Up to the time that: *We worked until it got dark.* **2.** Before: *Don't leave until we talk.* **3.** To the point or extent that: *He talked until he was worn out.* [From Middle English.]

un·time·ly (ŭn-tīm′lē) *adj.* **un·time·li·er, un·time·li·est 1.** Occurring at an inappropriate or unsuitable time: *an untimely visit.* **2.** Occurring too soon; premature: *an untimely death.*

un·tir·ing (ŭn-tīr′ĭng) *adj.* Not tiring or ceasing; persistent: *untiring efforts.* **—un·tir′ing·ly** *adv.*

un·to (ŭn′to͞o) *prep.* **1.** To. **2.** Until.

un·told (ŭn-tōld′) *adj.* **1.** Not told or revealed: *untold secrets.* **2.** Without limit; beyond description: *untold millions.*

un·touch·a·ble (ŭn-tŭch′ə-bəl) *adj.* **1.** Not permitted to be touched: *an untouchable idol.* **2.** Not capable of being touched or reached: *an untouchable tennis serve.* **3.** Beyond the reach of criticism or attack: *His work has been untouchable.* ❖ *n.* **Untouchable** *Often Offensive* A Dalit.

un·to·ward (ŭn-tôrd′) *adj.* **1.** Improper; unseemly: *untoward behavior.* **2.** Unfavorable or adverse: *untoward circumstances.*

un·tried (ŭn-trīd′) *adj.* **1.** Not tried, tested, or proved. **2.** Not tried in court; without a trial.

un·true (ŭn-tro͞o′) *adj.* **un·tru·er, un·tru·est 1.** Not true; false. **2.** Not faithful; disloyal.

un·truth (ŭn-tro͞oth′) *n.* **1.** Something untrue; a lie. **2.** The condition of being false.

un·used (ŭn-yo͞ozd′) *adj.* **1.** Not used or never having been used. **2.** (*also* ŭn-yo͞ost′) Not accustomed: *He is unused to working so late.*

un·u·su·al (ŭn-yo͞o′zho͞o-əl) *adj.* Not usual, common, or ordinary: *an unusual amount of snow; an unusual outfit.* **—un·u′su·al·ly** *adv.* **—un·u′su·al·ness** *n.*

un·ut·ter·a·ble (ŭn-ŭt′ər-ə-bəl) *adj.* Inexpressible or indescribable: *an unutterable word; unutterable beauty.* **—un·ut′ter·a·bly** *adv.*

un·veil (ŭn-vāl′) *tr.v.* **un·veiled, un·veil·ing, un·veils 1.** To remove a veil or covering from: *unveil a statue.* **2.** To reveal: *unveil secrets.*

un·voiced (ŭn-voist′) *adj.* **1.** Not uttered or expressed. **2.** Uttered without vibrating the vocal cords; voiceless: *an unvoiced consonant.*

un·war·rant·ed (ŭn-wôr′ən-tĭd *or* ŭn-wŏr′ən-tĭd) *adj.* Having no justification; groundless: *an unwarranted judgment lacking basis in fact.*

un·war·y (ŭn-wâr′ē) *adj.* **un·war·i·er, un·war·i·est** Not alert to danger; careless: *an unwary swimmer who got caught in a rip current.*

un·well (ŭn-wĕl′) *adj.* Being in poor health; ill: *Jason stayed home because he's feeling unwell.*

un·whole·some (ŭn-hōl′səm) *adj.* **1.** Not healthful or healthy: *unwholesome foods.* **2.** Offensive or loathsome: *unwholesome behavior.*

un·wield·y (ŭn-wēl′dē) *adj.* **un·wield·i·er, un·wield·i·est** Difficult to carry or handle because of shape or size: *an unwieldy package.*

un·will·ing (ŭn-wĭl′ĭng) *adj.* **1.** Not willing; hesitant or loath: *unwilling to face facts.* **2.** Done reluctantly: *unwilling help.* **—un·will′ing·ly** *adv.* **—un·will′ing·ness** *n.*

un·wind (ŭn-wīnd′) *v.* **un·wound** (ŭn-**wound**′), **un·wind·ing, un·winds** *—tr.* To unroll: *unwind cable.* *—intr.* **1.** To become unrolled. **2.** To become free of anxiety, worry, or tension: *went to the park to unwind.*

un·wise (ŭn-wīz′) *adj.* **un·wis·er, un·wis·est** Showing lack of wisdom; foolish: *an unwise decision.* **—un·wise′ly** *adv.*

un·wit·ting (ŭn-wĭt′ĭng) *adj.* **1.** Not knowing; unaware: *an unwitting victim of fraud.* **2.** Not intended; unintentional: *an unwitting remark.*

un·world·ly (ŭn-wûrld′lē) *adj.* **un·world·li·er, un·world·li·est 1.** Having or showing little understanding of the ways of the world; naive. **2.** Not of this world; spiritual or supernatural.

un·wor·thy (ŭn-wûr′*th*ē) *adj.* **un·wor·thi·er, un·wor·thi·est 1.** Not deserving: *a play unworthy of the award.* **2.** Not suiting or befitting: *a remark unworthy of her.* **—un·wor′thi·ness** *n.*

un·wound (ŭn-**wound**′) *v.* Past tense and past participle of **unwind.**

ă	pat	ôr	core
ā	pay	oi	boy
âr	care	ou	out
ä	father	o͝o	took
ĕ	pet	o͝or	lure
ē	be	o͞o	boot
ĭ	pit	ŭ	cut
ī	bite	ûr	urge
îr	pier	th	thin
ŏ	pot	*th*	this
ō	toe	zh	vision
ô	paw	ə	about

un·wrap (ŭn-răp′) *v.* **un·wrapped, un·wrap·ping, un·wraps** ❖ *tr.v.* To remove the wrapping from: *unwrap a gift.* ❖ *intr.v.* To have the wrapping removed.

un·writ·ten (ŭn-rĭt′n) *adj.* **1.** Not written or recorded. **2.** Having authority based on custom or tradition rather than doctrine: *an unwritten law.*

un·yield·ing (ŭn-yēl′dĭng) *adj.* **1.** Not giving way to pressure; hard or inflexible: *an unyielding steel beam.* **2.** Incapable of being changed: *an unyielding commitment to success.* **3.** Not willing to change: *an unyielding champion of civil rights.*

un·zip (ŭn-zĭp′) *tr. & intr.v.* **un·zipped, un·zip·ping, un·zips** To open or unfasten by means of a zipper or become unfastened or open in this way.

up (ŭp) *adv.* **1.** In or to a higher position: *looking up.* **2.** In or to an upright position: *She helped me up.* **3a.** Above a surface: *come up for air.* **b.** So as to detach or unearth: *pulling up weeds.* **c.** Above the horizon: *The sun came up.* **4.** Into view or existence: *write up a report.* **5.** Into consideration: *You never brought this up before.* **6.** In or toward a position conventionally regarded as higher, as on a map: *going up to Canada.* **7.** To or at a higher price: *Fares are going up again.* **8.** So as to advance, increase, or improve: *His hopes keep going up.* **9.** With or to a greater intensity, pitch, or volume: *Turn the radio up.* **10.** Into a state of excitement or turbulence: *A great wind came up.* **11.** Completely; entirely: *ate it all up.* **12.** Used as an intensive with certain verbs: *cleaning up the room.* **13.** Apart; into pieces: *tore the paper up.* ❖ *adj.* **1.** Being above an earlier position or level: *My grades are up.* **2.** Being out of bed: *Are you up yet?* **3.** Raised; lifted: *a switch in the up position.* **4.** Moving or directed upward: *an up elevator.* **5.** Excited or cheerful: *Our spirits were up.* **6.** Actively functioning: *The computers are up.* **7.** *Informal* Going on; happening: *What's up?* **8.** Being considered: *a contract up for renewal.* **9.** Finished; over: *Time's up!* **10.** *Informal* Well-informed or prepared: *I'm not up on sports.* **11.** Being ahead of or at a numerical advantage over an opponent: *up two holes in a golf match; up one player during the power play.* **12.** At bat in baseball: *You're up!* ❖ *prep.* **1.** To or toward a higher point on: *up the mountain.* **2.** Toward or at a point farther along: *up the road.* **3.** In a direction toward the source of: *up the Hudson.* ❖ *n.* **1.** An upward slope; a rise. **2.** *Slang* A feeling of excitement. ❖ *v.* **upped, up·ping, ups** *—tr.* To increase: *upping prices.* *—intr. Informal* To act suddenly or unexpectedly: *We voted his proposal down, so he up and left the meeting.* ◆ **up against** Confronted with; facing: *up against a strong opponent.* **up to 1.** Occupied with, especially devising or scheming: *up to more tricks.* **2.** Able to do or deal with: *It was hard, but she proved up to it.* **3.** Dependent on: *Winning the game is up to us.* **4a.** To the point of; as far as or until: *I'm up to page 100 in my new book. We played right up to dinnertime.* **b.** As many, as much, or as long as: *holds up to five gallons; has up to two hours for the test.* [From Old English *ūp.*]

up-and-com·ing (ŭp′ən-kŭm′ĭng) *adj.* Showing signs of future success: *an up-and-coming neighborhood.*

up·beat (ŭp′bēt′) *n.* **1.** An unaccented beat that occurs before the first beat of a measure. **2.** The upward stroke made by a conductor to indicate the beat that leads into a new measure. ❖ *adj.* Optimistic or cheerful: *The president was in an upbeat mood about the nation's economy.*

up·braid (ŭp-brād′) *tr.v.* **up·braid·ed, up·braid·ing, up·braids** To scold; reproach. [From Old English *ūpbrēdan*, to bring forward as a ground for censure : *ūp-*, up + *bregdan*, to turn, lay hold of.]

up·bring·ing (ŭp′brĭng′ĭng) *n.* The care and training received during childhood.

UPC *abbr.* An abbreviation of Universal Product Code.

up·coun·try (ŭp′kŭn′trē) *n.* The interior of a country. ❖ *adj.* Located in or coming from the upcountry: *their home in upcountry Maine.* ❖ *adv.* (*also* ŭp-kŭn′trē) In, to, or toward the upcountry: *traveling upcountry.*

up·date (ŭp-dāt′) *tr.v.* **up·dat·ed, up·dat·ing, up·dates** To bring up to date: *update a map to show recent boundary changes.* ❖ *n.* (ŭp′dāt′) **1.** The act or an instance of bringing up to date. **2.** An updated version of something: *read the latest update about computer viruses.*

up·draft (ŭp′drăft′) *n.* A current of air that flows upward.

up·end (ŭp-ĕnd′) *v.* **up·end·ed, up·end·ing, up·ends** *—tr.* To set or turn on one end: *upend a boat.* *—intr.* To become upended.

up·front or **up-front** (ŭp′frŭnt′) *adj.* Straightforward and direct; frank: *The mechanic was upfront about the cost of repairs.* ❖ *adv.* **up front** In advance; beforehand: *demanded to be paid upfront.*

up·grade (ŭp′grād′) *tr.v.* **up·grad·ed, up·grad·ing, up·grades 1.** To raise to a higher grade or standard: *The school upgraded its library by replacing outdated books.* **2.** To replace (a software program, for example) with an enhanced or improved version. ❖ *n.* **1.** The act or an instance of upgrading. **2.** An enhanced or improved software program or hardware device. **3.** An upward incline.

up·heav·al (ŭp-hē′vəl) *n.* **1.** A sudden and violent disturbance. **2.** A lifting or upward movement of the earth's crust.

up·hill (ŭp′hĭl′) *adj.* **1.** Going up a hill or slope: *an uphill street.* **2.** Marked by difficulty or strong resistance: *It was an uphill struggle to finish the project on time.* ❖ *adv.* (ŭp′hĭl′) To or toward higher ground: *going uphill.* ❖ *n.* An upward slope or incline.

up·hold (ŭp-hōld′) *tr.v.* **up·held** (ŭp-hĕld′), **up·hold·ing, up·holds 1.** To raise: *uphold a banner.* **2.** To prevent from falling; support: *The pillars uphold the roof.* **3.** To maintain or affirm: *upheld her political opinions.*

up·hol·ster (ŭp-hōl′stər *or* ə-pōl′stər) *tr.v.* **up·hol·stered, up·hol·ster·ing, up·hol·sters** To supply (furniture) with stuffing, springs, cushions, and a fabric covering. [From *upholsterer*, from Middle English *upholdester*, from *upholden*, to maintain.] **—up·hol′ster·er** *n.*

up·hol·ster·y (ŭp-hōl′stə-rē *or* ə-pōl′stə-rē) *n.* **1.** The materials used in upholstering. **2.** The craft, trade, or business of upholstering.

up·keep (ŭp′kēp′) *n.* **1.** Maintenance in proper operation, condition, and repair. **2.** The cost of such maintenance.

up·land (ŭp′lənd) *n.* **1.** Land of high elevation, especially when level. **2.** Land in the interior of a country.

up·lift (ŭp-lĭft′) *tr.v.* **up·lift·ed, up·lift·ing, up·lifts 1.** To raise; elevate. **2.** To raise to a higher social, moral, or intellectual level. ❖ *n.* (ŭp′lĭft′) **1.** The act, process, or result of lifting up. **2.** An effort or movement to raise social, moral, or intellectual standards. **3.** A geologic upheaval.

up·load (ŭp′lōd′) *tr.v.* **up·load·ed, up·load·ing, up·loads** To transfer (data or programs) to a central computer or website from another computer: *uploaded files onto the company's server.* ❖ *n.* **1.** A file that is uploaded. **2.** An instance of uploading data or a program.

up·on (ə-pŏn′) *prep.* On: *We stopped and sat down upon a flat rock.*

up·per (ŭp′ər) *adj.* **1.** Higher in place, position, or rank: *the upper floors of a building; the upper classes of society.* **2.** Situated on higher ground: *upper regions.* **3.** Relating to or being a more recent division of the geologic period named. ❖ *n.* The part of a shoe or boot above the sole.

up·per·case (ŭp′ər-kās′) *adj.* Written or printed in capital letters: *an uppercase A.* ❖ *n.* Uppercase letters: *The ransom note was written in uppercase.*

upper class *n.* The highest social and economic class in a society. **—up′per-class′** *adj.*

up·per·class·man (ŭp′ər-klăs′mən) *n.* A student in the junior or senior class at a high school or college.

up·per·cut (ŭp′ər-kŭt′) *n.* In boxing, a swinging blow directed upward, as to an opponent's chin.

upper hand *n.* A position of control or advantage.

upper house *n.* The branch of a bicameral legislature, such as the US Senate, that is smaller and less representative of the population.

up·per·most (ŭp′ər-mōst′) *adv. & adj.* In the highest place, position, or rank: *the uppermost rung of a ladder; finished uppermost in the standings.*

Upper Vol·ta (vŏl′tə *or* vōl′tə) See **Burkina Faso.**

up·pi·ty (ŭp′ĭ-tē) *adj. Informal* **1.** Haughty or presumptuous, especially for one's rank or social standing: *uppity know-it-alls who think they're better than everyone else.* **2.** Not complacent or deferential; strongly self-assertive: *had to get uppity to reach his goals.*

up·raise (ŭp-rāz′) *tr.v.* **up·raised, up·rais·ing, up·rais·es** To raise or lift up; elevate.

up·right (ŭp′rīt′) *adj.* **1.** In a vertical position; erect: *an upright post.* **2.** Morally respectable; honorable: *an upright person.* ❖ *adv.* Vertically. ❖ *n.* **1.** Something, such as a goalpost, that stands upright. **2.** An upright piano.

upright piano

upright piano *n.* A piano in which the strings are mounted vertically in a rectangular case with the keyboard at a right angle to the case.

up·ris·ing (ŭp′rī′zĭng) *n.* A popular revolt against a government or its policies; a rebellion.

up·roar (ŭp′rôr′) *n.* **1.** A condition of noisy excitement and confusion; a tumult. See Synonyms at **noise. 2.** A protest or controversy that people feel very strongly about: *The mayor's sexist remark caused an uproar.*

up·roar·i·ous (ŭp-rôr′ē-əs) *adj.* **1.** Caused or accompanied by an uproar. **2.** Loud and full; boisterous: *uproarious laughter.* **3.** Extremely funny: *an uproarious comedy.* **—up·roar′i·ous·ly** *adv.*

up·root (ŭp-ro͞ot′ *or* ŭp-ro͝ot′) *tr.v.* **up·root·ed, up·root·ing, up·roots 1.** To tear or remove (a plant and its roots) from the ground. **2.** To destroy or get rid of completely; do away with: *It's not easy to uproot old customs.* **3.** To force to leave a familiar or native place: *The government uprooted many people to build the highway.*

up·set (ŭp-sĕt′) *tr.v.* **up·set, up·set·ting, up·sets 1.** To cause to overturn; tip over: *upset a vase of flowers.* **2.** To disturb the functioning, order, or course of: *The move to the new building upset our schedule of deliveries.* **3.** To cause to feel sick: *The spicy meal upset his stomach.* **4.** To distress mentally or emotionally: *The bad news upset me.* **5.** (ŭp′sĕt′) To defeat unexpectedly (an opponent favored to win). ❖ *n.* (ŭp′sĕt′) **1.** The act of upsetting or the condition of being upset: *Who is responsible for the upset of our plans?* **2.** A game or contest in which the favorite is defeated. ❖ *adj.* **1.** Overturned: *an upset boat.* **2.** Showing symptoms of indigestion: *an upset stomach.* **3.** Mentally or emotionally disturbed: *felt upset by the news.* [From Middle English *upsetten,* to set up.]

up·shift (ŭp′shĭft′) *intr.v.* **up·shift·ed, up·shift·ing, up·shifts** To shift a motor vehicle into a higher gear. **—up′shift′** *n.*

up·shot (ŭp′shŏt′) *n.* **1.** The final result; outcome. **2.** The central idea or point; the gist: *The upshot of my story is that you should always be prepared.*

up·side (ŭp′sīd′) *n.* **1.** The upper side or portion. **2.** An advantageous aspect: *the upsides and downsides of home ownership.*

up·side down (ŭp′sīd′) *adv.* **1.** So that the upper or proper side is down: *Turn your cards upside down.* **2.** In great disorder: *The room had been turned upside down.*

up·si·lon (ŭp′sə-lŏn′ *or* yo͞op′sə-lŏn′) *n.* The 20th letter of the Greek alphabet, written Υ, υ. In English it is represented as *U, u,* or often also as *Y, y.*

up·slope (ŭp′slōp′) *n.* An upward slope. ❖ *adv. & adj.* At or in the direction of a higher point on a slope.

up·stage (ŭp′stāj′) *adv.* On, at, to, or toward the rear of a stage. ❖ *adj.* Relating to the rear of a stage. ❖ *tr.v.* (ŭp-stāj′) **up·staged, up·stag·ing, up·stag·es 1.** To distract an audience's attention from (another performer) by moving upstage, thereby forcing the other performer to face away from the audience. **2.** To steal attention or praise from: *He upstaged his rivals by announcing his discovery first.*

up·stairs (ŭp′stârz′) *adv.* **1.** Up the stairs: *plodded upstairs.* **2.** To or on a higher floor: *slept upstairs.* ❖ *adj.* (ŭp′stârz′) Located on a higher floor: *an upstairs bedroom.* ❖ *n.* (ŭp′stârz′) *(used with a singular verb)* The part of a building above the ground floor.

up·stand·ing (ŭp-stăn′dĭng *or* ŭp′stăn′dĭng) *adj.* **1.** Standing erect or upright. **2.** Morally upright; honest: *a fine upstanding woman.*

up·start (ŭp′stärt′) *n.* A person who has suddenly gained wealth or a high position, especially one who becomes arrogant because of success. ❖ *adj.* Suddenly raised to an important position: *an upstart company.*

up·state (ŭp′stāt′) *adv. & adj.* To, from, or in the northerly part of a state in the United States: *traveling upstate; upstate New York.* ❖ *n.* The northerly part of a state: *a politician from upstate.*

up·stream (ŭp′strēm′) *adv. & adj.* In a direction opposite to the current of a stream: *fish swimming upstream; upstream waters.*

up·surge (ŭp′sûrj′) *n.* A rapid or abrupt rise.

up·swing (ŭp′swĭng′) *n.* **1.** An upward swing: *the upswing of a golf stroke.* **2.** An upward trend: *an upswing in home sales.*

up·take (ŭp′tāk′) *n.* **1.** A passage for drawing up smoke or air. **2.** Understanding; comprehension: *quick on the uptake.* **3.** The act of taking in or absorbing something, such as a substance, by a living organism: *nitrogen uptake.*

up·tight (ŭp′tīt′) *adj. Slang* **1.** Rigidly conventional, especially in manners, opinions, and tastes: *a stuffy, uptight private school.* **2.** Tense or nervous: *was uptight about flying in an airplane.*

up-to-date (ŭp′tə-dāt′) *adj.* Reflecting or informed of the latest information, changes, improvements, or style: *up-to-date technology.*

up·town (ŭp′toun′) *n.* The upper part of a town or city. ❖ *adv.* (ŭp′toun′) To, toward, or in the upper part of a town or city: *move uptown.* ❖ *adj.* Relating to or located uptown: *an uptown store.*

up·turn (ŭp′tûrn′) *v.* **up·turned, up·turn·ing, up·turns** *—tr.* To turn up or over: *upturn the soil. —intr.* To turn over or up. ❖ *n.* An upward movement, curve, or trend, as in business.

up·ward (ŭp′wərd) *adv.* or **up·wards** (ŭp′wərdz) In, to, or toward a higher place, level, or position: *The hawk flew upward and out of sight.* ❖ *adj.* Directed toward a higher place or position: *upward movement.* ◆ **upward of** or **upwards of** More than; in excess of: *Upward of 500 people attended the concert.*

Ur (ûr *or* o͝or) A city of ancient Sumer in southern Mesopotamia on a site in present-day southeast Iraq. It was one of the oldest cities in Mesopotamia.

u·ra·cil (yo͝or′ə-sĭl) *n.* A base that is a component of RNA.

U·ral Mountains (yo͝or′əl) A range of western Russia forming the traditional boundary between Europe and Asia and extending about 1,470 miles (2,365 kilometers) from the Arctic Ocean southward to Kazakhstan.

Ural River A river of western Russia and western Kazakhstan rising in the southern Ural Mountains and flowing about 1,510 miles (2,430 kilometers) to the Caspian Sea.

u·ra·ni·um (yo͝o-rā′nē-əm) *n. Symbol* **U** A dense, toxic, silvery-white metallic element that is radioactive and easily oxidized. Uranium is the main source of nuclear energy. Atomic number 92. See **Periodic Table.** [After *Uranus.*]

ă	pat	ôr	core
ā	pay	oi	boy
âr	care	ou	out
ä	father	o͝o	took
ĕ	pet	o͝or	lure
ē	be	o͞o	boot
ĭ	pit	ŭ	cut
ī	bite	ûr	urge
îr	pier	th	thin
ŏ	pot	*th*	this
ō	toe	zh	vision
ô	paw	ə	about

uranium-235 *n.* The isotope of uranium that has a mass number of 235 and a half-life of 704 million years. Uranium-235 undergoes nuclear fission when it collides with neutrons, and it is capable of sustaining a chain reaction that can become explosive.

uranium-238 *n.* The most common isotope of uranium, having a mass number of 238 and a half-life of 4.47 billion years. It is capable of fission only under very special conditions but can capture neutrons to form plutonium-239, which is capable of fission.

U·ra·nus (yo͝or′ə-nəs *or* yo͞o-rā′nəs) *n.* **1.** In Greek mythology, the earliest supreme god, the son of Gaea and the father of the Titans. **2.** The seventh planet from the sun and the third largest in the solar system, with a diameter about four times that of Earth. Uranus is composed mainly of hydrogen and helium gases and is encircled by a system of thin rings. See table at **solar system.**

ur·ban (ûr′bən) *adj.* **1.** Relating to or located in a city: *urban traffic; urban dwellers; urban housing.* **2.** Characteristic of the city or city life: *urban pollution.* [From Latin *urbs*, city.]

ur·bane (ûr-bān′) *adj.* **ur·ban·er, ur·ban·est** Polite, refined, and often elegant in manner. **—ur·bane′ly** *adv.*

urban renewal *n.* The rebuilding of impoverished urban neighborhoods by major renovation or reconstruction of housing and public works.

ur·chin (ûr′chĭn) *n.* **1.** A playful or mischievous child. **2.** A sea urchin. [From Middle English *irchoun*, hedgehog, from Latin *ērĭcius*.]

Ur·du (o͝or′do͞o *or* ûr′do͞o) *n.* An Indic language that is the official written language of Pakistan and is also widely used in India.

–ure *suff.* A suffix that means: **1.** Act or process: *erasure.* **2.** Function or office: *legislature.*

u·re·a (yo͞o-rē′ə) *n.* A chemical compound that occurs in the urine of mammals and is also produced synthetically for use in fertilizers and medicine. It is the chief form in which nitrogen is excreted in mammals and certain other animals.

u·re·ter (yo͞o-rē′tər *or* yo͝or′ĭ-tər) *n.* The long narrow duct that carries urine from the kidney to the urinary bladder.

u·re·thra (yo͞o-rē′thrə) *n., pl.* **u·re·thras** or **u·re·thrae** (yo͞o-rē′thrē) The duct from which urine is discharged in most mammals and through which semen is discharged in males.

urge (ûrj) *tr.v.* **urged, urg·ing, urg·es 1.** To push, force, or drive onward; impel. **2.** To entreat earnestly and repeatedly; exhort: *The coach urged us to stay in shape over summer vacation.* **3.** To advocate earnestly the doing, consideration, or approval of: *urge the passage of new crime laws.* ❖ *n.* An impulse that prompts action or effort: *resisted the urge to laugh.* [From Latin *urgēre*.]

ur·gen·cy (ûr′jən-sē) *n., pl.* **ur·gen·cies** The quality or condition of being urgent: *the urgency of the political situation.*

ur·gent (ûr′jənt) *adj.* **1.** Calling for immediate action or attention; pressing: *an urgent situation.* **2.** Conveying a sense of pressing importance or necessity: *an urgent tone of voice.* **—ur′gent·ly** *adv.*

u·ric acid (yo͝or′ĭk) *n.* A waste product that is the chief form in which nitrogen is excreted in the urine of birds, insects, and most reptiles. It is present in small amounts in the urine of mammals.

u·ri·nal (yo͝or′ə-nəl) *n.* **1.** An upright wall fixture used by men and boys for urinating. **2.** A portable receptacle for urine.

u·ri·nal·y·sis (yo͝or′ə-năl′ĭ-sĭs) *n., pl.* **u·ri·nal·y·ses** (yo͝or′ə-năl′ĭ-sēz′) The chemical analysis of urine, used to diagnose disease or to detect the presence of a specific substance, such as a drug.

u·ri·nar·y (yo͝or′ə-nĕr′ē) *adj.* **1.** Relating to urine or its production, function, or excretion. **2.** Relating to the organs that produce and discharge urine.

urinary tract *n.* The system of organs involved in the formation and excretion of urine in vertebrate animals. In humans it consists mainly of the kidneys, ureters, bladder, and urethra.

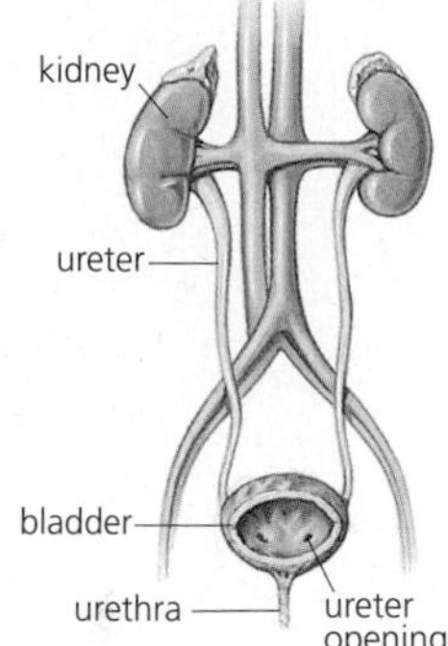

urinary tract
adult human urinary tract

u·ri·nate (yo͝or′ə-nāt′) *intr.v.* **u·ri·nat·ed, u·ri·nat·ing, u·ri·nates** To discharge urine. **—u′ri·na′tion** *n.*

u·rine (yo͝or′ĭn) *n.* A fluid containing body wastes extracted from the blood by the kidneys. In humans, urine is stored in the urinary bladder and discharged from the body through the urethra.

URL (yo͞o′är-ĕl′) *n.* An Internet address (for example, *http://www.whitehouse.gov/blog*), usually consisting of the protocol used to access the site (*http*), the domain name (*www.whitehouse.gov*), and optionally the path to a file (*blog*).

urn (ûrn) *n.* **1.** A vase, usually having a footed base or pedestal. **2.** A receptacle for cremated ashes. **3.** A metal container with a spigot, used for serving warm beverages. [From Middle English *urne*, from Latin *urna*.]
❑ *These sound alike:* **urn, earn** (gain by work).

Ur·sa Major (ûr′sə) *n.* A constellation near the north celestial pole, traditionally pictured as a large bear. Seven of its stars form the Big Dipper.

Ursa Minor *n.* A constellation that includes the star Polaris, traditionally pictured as a small bear. Seven of its stars form the Little Dipper.

U·ru·guay (yo͝or′ə-gwī′ *or* yo͝or′ə-gwā′) A country of southeast South America on the Atlantic Ocean and the Río de la Plata. Montevideo is the capital.

us (ŭs) *pron.* The objective case of **we. 1.** Used as the direct object of a verb: *The movie impressed us greatly.* **2.** Used as the indirect object of a verb: *She gave us free tickets to the show.* **3.** Used as the object of a preposition: *Tom sent his regards to us.* [From Old English *ūs*.] —SEE NOTE AT **we.**

US *abbr.* An abbreviation of United States.

USA *abbr.* An abbreviation of: **1.** United States Army. **2.** United States of America.

us·a·ble also **use·a·ble** (yo͞o′zə-bəl) *adj.* **1.** Capable of being used: *separating usable ore from waste.* **2.** In a fit condition for use: *This little room is usable as an office.*

USAF *abbr.* An abbreviation of United States Air Force.

us·age (yo͞o′sĭj *or* yo͞o′zĭj) *n.* **1.** The act or manner of using something: *a gauge that measures water usage.* **2.** A usual or accepted practice. **3.** The way in which words or phrases are used, spoken, or written: *contemporary English usage.*

USB *n. Computers* A standard for the design of cables, plugs, and other parts that transfer data between digital devices. Devices such as mice and flash drives are often powered by their USB connection. USB is short for **universal serial bus.**

USCG *abbr.* An abbreviation of United States Coast Guard.

US Customary System *n.* The main system of weights and measures used in the United States and a few other countries, based on the yard as a unit of length, the pound as a unit of weight, the gallon as a unit of liquid volume, and the bushel as a unit of dry volume.

use (yo͞oz) *v.* **used, us·ing, us·es** *—tr.* **1.** To bring or put into service; employ for some purpose: *I used a whisk to beat the eggs.* **2.** To avail oneself of; practice: *Use caution when driving at night.* **3.** To achieve a goal by means of; exploit: *He used his connections to get a job in the mayor's office.* *—intr.* (yo͞os) Used in the past tense followed by *to* to indicate a former state, practice, or custom: *I used to go there often.* ❖ *n.* (yo͞os) **1.** The act of using: *the use of a pencil for writing.* **2.** The condition or fact of being used: *The telephone is in use right now.* **3.** The manner of using; usage: *the proper use of power tools.* **4a.** The

USAGE

use We use the past tense of **use** followed by *to* and a verb to show a past condition or a past practice: *We used to go to the park on Saturdays.* But because it is impossible to hear the *d* in *used to*, it's easy to forget and leave the *d* out. It is incorrect to write *We use to play chess.* However, when you use *did* to make the past tense of *use*, you must leave out the *d*: *Didn't she use to be his friend?*

permission or privilege of using something: *I have the use of the car on Sundays.* **b.** The power or ability of using something: *lost the use of one arm.* **5.** The need or occasion to use: *Do you have any use for this book?* **6.** The quality of being suitable or adaptable to an end; usefulness: *old pieces of equipment of no practical use.* ◆ **use up** To consume completely: *We used up the peanut butter yesterday.* [From Middle English *usen,* from Latin *ūtī.*] —SEE NOTE.

use·a·ble (yōō′zə-bəl) *adj.* Variant of **usable.**

used (yōōzd) *adj.* **1.** Not new; secondhand. **2.** (*also* yōōst) Accustomed; habituated: *getting used to the cold weather; was used to taking a swim in the morning.*

use·ful (yōōs′fəl) *adj.* Capable of being used for some purpose; being of use or service: *a useful map.* **—use′ful·ly** *adv.* **—use′ful·ness** *n.*

use·less (yōōs′lĭs) *adj.* **1.** Being or having no use: *a useless new gadget.* **2.** Unable to function or assist: *When it comes to protecting the house, the dog is useless.* **—use′less·ly** *adv.* **—use′less·ness** *n.*

us·er (yōō′zər) *n.* **1.** A person or thing that uses: *a user of public transportation.* **2.** A person who uses a computer, computer program, or online service.

us·er-friend·ly (yōō′zər-frĕnd′lē) *adj.* Easy to use or learn to use: *a user-friendly software program; a user-friendly income tax form.*

us·er·name (yōō′zər-nām′) *n.* A sequence of characters used as identification when logging on to a computer system.

ush·er (ŭsh′ər) *n.* **1.** A person employed to escort people to their seats, as in a theater. **2.** A man who attends a bridal party at a wedding. ❖ *v.* **ush·ered, ush·er·ing, ush·ers** *—tr.* **1.** To serve as an usher to; escort. See Synonyms at **guide. 2.** To precede and introduce: *usher in a new era. —intr.* To work as an usher: *ushered at the concert.* [From Middle English, doorkeeper, from Latin *ōstiārius,* from *ōstium,* door.]

USMC *abbr.* An abbreviation of United States Marine Corps.

USN *abbr.* An abbreviation of United States Navy.

USS *abbr.* An abbreviation of: **1.** United States Senate. **2.** United States Ship.

USSR *abbr.* An abbreviation of Union of Soviet Socialist Republics.

u·su·al (yōō′zhōō-əl) *adj.* **1.** Commonly encountered, experienced, or observed; ordinary: *the usual traffic jams during rush hour.* **2.** Regularly or customarily used: *the usual expressions of thanks.* **3.** In conformity with regular practice or procedure: *Come at the usual time.* ◆ **as usual** As commonly or habitually happens: *She jogged that morning as usual.* [From Middle English, from Latin *ūsus,* use.] **—u′su·al·ly** *adv.*

u·su·rer (yōō′zhər-ər) *n.* A person who lends money at interest, especially at an excessively high or unlawfully high rate.

u·surp (yōō-sûrp′ *or* yōō-zûrp′) *tr.v.* **u·surped, u·surp·ing, u·surps** To seize and hold (the power or rights of another, for example) by force and without legal authority: *usurp a throne.* **—u′sur·pa′tion** *n.* **—u·surp′er** *n.*

u·su·ry (yōō′zhə-rē) *n., pl.* **u·su·ries 1.** The practice of lending money at interest, especially at an excessively high or unlawfully high rate. **2.** An excessively or unlawfully high rate of interest.

UT *abbr.* An abbreviation of Utah.

U·tah (yōō′tô′ *or* yōō′tä′) A state of the western United States north of Arizona. It was admitted as the 45th state in 1896. Salt Lake City is the capital and the largest city. —SEE NOTE.

UTC (yōō′tē′sē′) *n.* Coordinated universal time.

Ute (yōōt) *n., pl.* **Ute** or **Utes 1.** A member of a Native American people living in Utah and along the border of Colorado and New Mexico. **2.** The Uto-Aztecan language of the Ute.

u·ten·sil (yōō-tĕn′səl) *n.* An instrument, implement, or container, especially one used to prepare or eat food. [From Middle English, from Latin *ūtēnsilis,* fit for use, from *ūtī,* to use.]

u·ter·us (yōō′tər-əs) *n., pl.* **u·ter·i** (yōō′tə-rī′) or **u·ter·us·es** A hollow muscular organ of female mammals, in which a fertilized egg implants and develops; the womb.

U·ther Pen·dra·gon (yōō′thər pĕn-drăg′ən) *n.* In Arthurian legend, a king of Britain and the father of King Arthur.

u·til·i·ty (yōō-tĭl′ĭ-tē) *n., pl.* **u·til·i·ties 1.** The quality of being useful; usefulness. **2.** A commodity or service, such as electricity, water, or public transportation, that is provided by a public utility.

utility knife *n.* A knife with a small blade that can often be retracted into the handle when not in use.

u·til·ize (yōōt′l-īz′) *tr.v.* **u·til·ized, u·til·iz·ing, u·til·iz·es** To put to use, especially to make effective use of: *utilizing the stream's water to run the mill.* **—u′ti·li·za′tion** (yōōt′l-ĭ-zā′shən) *n.* **—u′til·iz′er** *n.*

ut·most (ŭt′mōst′) *adj.* Of the highest or greatest degree, amount, or intensity: *matters of the utmost importance.* ❖ *n.* The greatest possible degree, amount, or extent; the maximum.

U·to-Az·tec·an (yōō′tō-ăz′tĕk′ən) *n.* **1.** A large family of North and Central American languages that includes Ute and Hopi. **2.** A member of a people speaking a Uto-Aztecan language. **—U′to-Az′tec′an** *adj.*

u·to·pi·a (yōō-tō′pē-ə) *n.* often **Utopia 1.** A place of ideal perfection, especially in moral behavior and in social and political life. **2.** A work of fiction describing such a place. **—u·to′pi·an** *adj. & n.*

ut·ter¹ (ŭt′ər) *tr.v.* **ut·tered, ut·ter·ing, ut·ters 1.** To give forth with the voice: *utter a sigh.* **2.** To pronounce or speak; say: *utter a word.* [From Middle English *outren,* partly from Middle Low German *uteren* and partly alteration of Middle English *outen,* to disclose.]

ut·ter² (ŭt′ər) *adj.* Complete; absolute: *utter darkness.* [From Old English *ūtera,* outer.] **—ut′ter·ly** *adv.*

ut·ter·ance (ŭt′ər-əns) *n.* **1.** The act of uttering: *She found his continued utterance of old jokes quite irritating.* **2.** Something uttered or expressed; a statement.

ut·ter·ly (ŭt′ər-lē) *adv.* Completely; absolutely.

U-turn (yōō′tûrn′) *n.* A turn, as by a vehicle, completely reversing the direction of travel.

UV *abbr.* An abbreviation of ultraviolet.

UV index (yōō′vē′) *n.* A scale ranging from zero to ten that is used to estimate the risk for sunburn in midday sunlight. It takes into account conditions such as cloud cover and ozone in the atmosphere.

u·vu·la (yōō′vyə-lə) *n.* The small cone-shaped mass of fleshy tissue that hangs from the end of the soft palate above the base of the tongue. [From Middle English, from Medieval Latin *ūvula,* swollen uvula, diminutive of Latin *ūva,* grape, swollen uvula (from its shape).] **—u′vu·lar** *adj.*

Uz·bek (ōōz′bĕk′) *adj.* Relating to Uzbekistan or its people, language, or culture. ❖ *n., pl.* **Uz·beks** or **Uzbek 1.** A native or inhabitant of Uzbekistan. **2.** The Turkic language of the Uzbeks.

Uz·bek·i·stan (ōōz-bĕk′ĭ-stăn′ *or* ōōz-bĕk′ĭ-stän′) A country of west-central Asia north of Turkmenistan. Uzbekistan was part of the USSR from 1924 to 1991. Tashkent is the capital.

GEOGRAPHY

Utah The name for the state of **Utah** comes from the name of a Native American people of the region called the Ute. The name was also used for a lake and river south of the Great Salt Lake. The name of the river and the lake was adopted for the state in 1850.

ă	pat	ôr	core
ā	pay	oi	boy
âr	care	ou	out
ä	father	ŏŏ	took
ĕ	pet	ŏŏr	lure
ē	be	ōō	boot
ĭ	pit	ŭ	cut
ī	bite	ûr	urge
îr	pier	th	thin
ŏ	pot	*th*	this
ō	toe	zh	vision
ô	paw	ə	about

v or **V** (vē) *n., pl.* **v's** or **V's** also **vs** or **Vs** The 22nd letter of the English alphabet.

V[1] **1.** The symbol for the element **vanadium. 2.** also **v** The symbol for the Roman numeral 5.

V[2] *abbr.* An abbreviation of: **1.** velocity. **2.** victory. **3.** volt. **4.** volume. **5.** vowel.

v. *abbr.* An abbreviation of: **1.** verb. **2.** verse. **3.** version. **4.** versus. **5.** volume (book).

VA *abbr.* An abbreviation of Virginia.

va·can·cy (vā′kən-sē) *n., pl.* **va·can·cies 1.** The condition of being vacant or unoccupied. **2.** A position, office, or space that is unfilled or unoccupied. **3.** Emptiness of mind.

va·cant (vā′kənt) *adj.* **1.** Containing nothing; empty. See Synonyms at **empty. 2.** Not occupied or put to use: *vacant seats; vacant lands.* **3.** Expressionless; blank: *a vacant stare.* [From Middle English *vacaunt*, from Latin *vacāre*, to be empty.] **—va′cant·ly** *adv.*

va·cate (vā′kāt′ *or* vā-**kāt′**) *tr. & intr.v.* **va·cat·ed, va·cat·ing, va·cates** To cease to occupy or hold: *vacate an apartment; vacated when their lease expired.*

va·ca·tion (vā-**kā′**shən) *n.* **1.** A period of time devoted to rest or relaxation, especially one with pay granted to an employee. **2.** A holiday. ❖ *intr.v.* **va·ca·tioned, va·ca·tion·ing, va·ca·tions** To take or spend a vacation: *He vacationed on the island.* **—va·ca′tion·er** *n.*

vac·ci·nate (văk′sə-nāt′) *tr.v.* **vac·ci·nat·ed, vac·ci·nat·ing, vac·ci·nates** To inoculate (a person or animal) with a vaccine in order to give immunity against an infectious disease.

vac·ci·na·tion (văk′sə-**nā′**shən) *n.* **1.** Inoculation with a vaccine in order to give immunity against an infectious disease. **2.** A scar left on the skin where such an inoculation was made.

vac·cine (văk-**sēn′** *or* **văk′**sēn′) *n.* A preparation that is administered to stimulate the body's production of antibodies against a disease, usually containing weakened or killed disease-causing bacteria or viruses. Vaccines are normally administered as injections or in a form that can be swallowed. [From Latin *vaccīnus*, of cows, from *vacca*, cow.] —SEE NOTE.

vac·il·late (văs′ə-lāt′) *intr.v.* **vac·il·lat·ed, vac·il·lat·ing, vac·il·lates 1.** To be unable to choose between different courses of action or opinions; waver: *She vacillated about whether to leave.* **2.** To change between one state and another; fluctuate: *vacillate between hope and despair.* [From Latin *vacillāre*, to waver.] **—vac′il·la′tion** *n.*

va·cu·i·ty (vă-**kyo͞o′**ĭ-tē) *n., pl.* **va·cu·i·ties 1.** Total absence of matter; emptiness. **2.** An empty space; a vacuum. **3.** Absence of meaningful occupation; idleness. **4.** The quality or fact of lacking something specified: *a vacuity of emotions.*

vac·u·ole (**văk′**yo͞o-ōl′) *n.* A small cavity in the cytoplasm of most cells, especially plant cells, surrounded by a membrane and containing water and dissolved substances such as sugars, enzymes, and amino acids. **—vac′u·o′lar** (văk′yo͞o-**ō′**lər) *adj.*

vac·u·ous (**văk′**yo͞o-əs) *adj.* Lacking intelligence; stupid: *a vacuous remark.* **—vac′u·ous·ly** *adv.*

vac·uum (**văk′**yo͞om *or* **văk′**yo͞o-əm) *n.* **1a.** The absence of matter. **b.** A space that is empty of matter. **c.** A space containing a gas at a very low pressure. **2.** A vacuum cleaner. ❖ *tr. & intr.v.* **vac·uumed, vac·uum·ing, vac·uums** To clean with or use a vacuum cleaner. [From Latin, from *vacuus*, empty.]

vacuum bottle *n.* A bottle or flask having a vacuum between its inner and outer walls, designed to minimize the transfer of heat between the inside and the outside and thus keep the contents at a desired temperature.

vacuum cleaner *n.* An electrical appliance that draws up dirt by suction.

vac·uum-packed (**văk′**yo͞om-păkt′) *adj.* **1.** Packed in an airtight container. **2.** Sealed under low pressure or in a partial vacuum.

vacuum tube *n.* An electron tube from which all or most of the gas has been removed, permitting electrons to move with low interaction with any remaining gas molecules.

Va·duz (vä-**do͞ots′** *or* fä-**do͞ots′**) The capital of Liechtenstein, in the western part of the country on the Rhine River.

vag·a·bond (**văg′**ə-bŏnd′) *n.* A person who moves from place to place without a permanent home and often without a regular means of support. ❖ *adj.* Relating to or characteristic of a wanderer; nomadic: *leading a vagabond life.*

va·ga·ry (**vā′**gə-rē *or* və-**gâr′**ē) *n., pl.* **va·ga·ries 1.** An unpredictable development or change of circumstances: *the vagaries of mountain weather.* **2.** An extravagant or erratic notion or action.

va·gi·na (və-**jī′**nə) *n.* The passage leading from the uterus to the outside of the body in female mammals.

vag·i·nal (**văj′**ə-nəl) *adj.* Relating to the vagina.

va·grant (**vā′**grənt) *n.* A person who wanders from place to place and has no permanent home or means of livelihood. ❖ *adj.* Wandering from place to place and lacking any means of support. **—va′gran·cy** *n.*

vague (vāg) *adj.* **vagu·er, vagu·est 1.** Not clear in meaning or expression: *a vague statement; a vague promise.* See Synonyms at **ambiguous. 2.** Not thinking or expressing oneself clearly or precisely: *The senator was vague to avoid being asked questions.* **3.** Lacking definite shape, form, or character: *The vague outline of a ship appeared on the horizon.* **4.** Indistinctly felt, perceived, understood, or recalled; hazy: *a vague sense of fear.* [From Latin *vagus*, wandering.] **—vague′ly** *adv.* **—vague′ness** *n.*

va·gus nerve (**vā′**gəs) *n.* A cranial nerve that passes from the brain to the face, trunk, and abdomen. It controls the muscles of the tongue and larynx, stimulates digestion, and regulates the heartbeat. [From New Latin *(nervus) vagus*, wandering (nerve).]

SCIENCE

vaccine For centuries, smallpox was a leading cause of death all over the world. If victims survived, they often had terrible scars. Nowadays, smallpox no longer exists outside the laboratory; it was eradicated in 1977, following a massive campaign. That campaign involved vaccinating millions of people using a technique first developed by Edward Jenner, an English surgeon, in the late 1700s. Jenner observed that people who got cowpox, a mild disease contracted from milking infected cows, did not get smallpox. He then tried an experiment; he took liquid from the cowpox sores of a milkmaid and injected a young boy with it. Jenner later exposed the boy to smallpox, and the boy remained healthy. The injected material became known as a **vaccine,** after the Latin name for cowpox: *variolae vaccinae* ("smallpox of a cow").

valance
window valances

valley

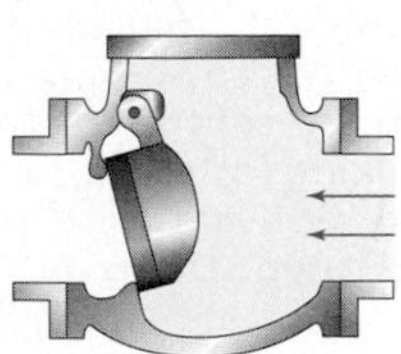

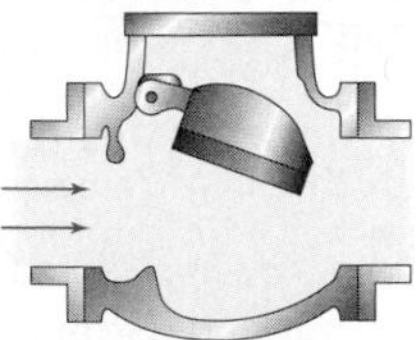

valve
top: closed valve
bottom: open valve

ă	pat	ôr	core
ā	pay	oi	boy
âr	care	ou	out
ä	father	o͝o	took
ĕ	pet	o͝or	lure
ē	be	o͞o	boot
ĭ	pit	ŭ	cut
ī	bite	ûr	urge
îr	pier	th	thin
ŏ	pot	*th*	this
ō	toe	zh	vision
ô	paw	ə	about

vain (vān) *adj.* **vain·er, vain·est 1.** Not yielding the desired outcome; fruitless: *a vain effort to regain her balance.* **2.** Lacking substance or worth; hollow: *vain promises.* **3.** Showing undue preoccupation with one's appearance or accomplishments; conceited: *He was a vain and disagreeable fellow.* ◆ **in vain 1.** To no avail; without success: *We tried in vain to open the window.* **2.** In an irreverent or disrespectful manner: *One of the Ten Commandments forbids taking God's name in vain.* [From Middle English *vein*, from Latin *vānus*, empty.] **—vain′ly** *adv.*

❑ *These sound alike:* **vain, vane** (weathervane), **vein** (blood vessel).

vain·glo·ri·ous (vān-glôr′ē-əs) *adj.* Characterized by or showing excessive pride or vanity; boastful: *being vainglorious about his athletic record.*

vain·glo·ry (vān′glôr′ē *or* vān-glôr′ē) *n.* Excessive or unwarranted pride in one's accomplishments or qualities.

val·ance (văl′əns *or* vā′ləns) *n.* **1.** An ornamental drapery hung across a top edge, as of a bed, table, or canopy. **2.** A short drapery, decorative board, or metal strip extending across the top of a window to conceal structural fixtures.

vale (vāl) *n.* A valley; a dale.

❑ *These sound alike:* **vale, veil** (mesh fabric).

val·e·dic·to·ri·an (văl′ĭ-dĭk-tôr′ē-ən) *n.* The student with the highest academic rank in a class, who delivers the valedictory at graduation.

val·e·dic·to·ry (văl′ĭ-dĭk′tə-rē) *n., pl.* **val·e·dic·to·ries** A closing or farewell statement or address, especially one delivered at graduation exercises. ❖ *adj.* Relating to or expressing a farewell: *a valedictory speech.*

va·lence (vā′ləns) *n.* **1.** The capability of an atom or a group of atoms to combine with other atoms or groups of atoms, determined by the number of electrons that an atom can lose, add, or share. **2.** A whole number, often one of several for a given element, that represents this capability. An element with a valence of 1, for example, can donate or accept one electron.

Va·len·ci·a (və-lĕn′shē-ə *or* və-lĕn′chə *or* və-lĕn′sē-ə) A city of eastern Spain on the Mediterranean coast. It was the capital of a medieval kingdom.

val·en·tine (văl′ən-tīn′) *n.* **1.** A sentimental card sent to a sweetheart, friend, or family member on Valentine's Day. **2.** A person singled out as one's sweetheart on Valentine's Day.

Val·en·tine (văl′ən-tīn′), Saint. Flourished third century AD. Roman Christian who according to tradition was martyred.

Val·en·tine's Day (văl′ən-tīnz′) *n.* February 14, celebrated in many countries by the exchange of valentines, love tokens, or sweets.

val·et (vă-lā′) *n.* **1.** A man's male servant, who takes care of his clothes and performs other personal services. **2.** An employee, as in a hotel, who performs various personal services for guests or passengers. **3.** A person who parks and retrieves cars for patrons of restaurants, theaters, and other businesses.

Val·hal·la (văl-hăl′ə) *n.* In Norse mythology, the hall in which Odin received the souls of slain heroes. [From Old Norse *Valhöll* : *valr*, the slain in battle + *höll*, hall.]

val·iant (văl′yənt) *adj.* Possessing or exhibiting valor; brave: *a valiant knight; a valiant effort.* See Synonyms at **brave. —val′iant·ly** *adv.*

val·id (văl′ĭd) *adj.* **1.** Well-grounded; just: *a valid objection.* **2.** Having legal force: *a valid passport.* [From Latin *validus*, strong.] **—va·lid′i·ty** (və-lĭd′ĭ-tē) *n.*

val·i·date (văl′ĭ-dāt′) *tr.v.* **val·i·dat·ed, val·i·dat·ing, val·i·dates 1.** To establish the soundness, accuracy, or legitimacy of: *validate a theory.* **2.** To make or declare legally valid: *validate a contract.*

val·ine (văl′ēn′) *n.* An essential amino acid that is formed by the reaction of certain proteins with water.

va·lise (və-lēs′) *n.* A small piece of hand luggage.

Val·kyr·ie (văl-kîr′ē *or* văl′kə-rē) *n.* In Norse mythology, one of Odin's women attendants who conducted the souls of the slain warriors to Valhalla. [From Old Norse *Valkyrja*, chooser of the slain.]

Val·let·ta (və-lĕt′ə) The capital of Malta, on the northeast coast of the main island.

val·ley (văl′ē) *n., pl.* **val·leys 1.** A long narrow region of low land between ranges of mountains, hills, or other uplands, often having a river or stream running along the bottom. **2.** A large region of land drained or irrigated by a river system: *the Connecticut River valley.* [From Middle English *valei*, from Latin *vallēs*.]

Valley Forge A village of southeast Pennsylvania northwest of Philadelphia. The Continental Army camped here during the winter of 1777–1778.

val·or (văl′ər) *n.* Courage and boldness, as in combat; bravery.

val·or·ous (văl′ər-əs) *adj.* Showing or having great personal bravery; valiant: *valorous deeds.*

val·our (văl′ər) *n. Chiefly British* Variant of **valor.**

val·u·a·ble (văl′yo͞o-ə-bəl *or* văl′yə-bəl) *adj.* **1.** Having high monetary or material value for use or exchange: *bought a valuable piece of jewelry.* **2.** Of great importance, use, or service: *acquire valuable information.* **3.** Having admirable or esteemed qualities: *a valuable friend.* ❖ *n.* A valuable personal possession, such as a piece of jewelry: *kept the valuables in the safe.*

val·u·a·tion (văl′yo͞o-ā′shən) *n.* **1.** The act or process of assessing value or price; an appraisal: *valuation of imported merchandise.* **2.** Assessed value or price.

val·ue (văl′yo͞o) *n.* **1.** The amount, as of goods, services, or money, that is considered a fair equivalent for something else: *walking shoes that will give you good value for your money.* **2.** Monetary or material worth: *the rising value of a rare stamp.* **3.** Worth in usefulness or importance to the possessor; utility or merit: *the value of a good education.* **4.** often **values** A principle, standard, or quality considered worthwhile or desirable: *traditional values such as honesty and hard work.* **5.** A quantity or number expressed by an algebraic term. **6.** The relative duration of a musical note or rest. ❖ *tr.v.* **val·ued, val·u·ing, val·ues 1.** To determine or estimate the worth or value of; appraise: *value a piece of jewelry at $5,000.* **2.** To consider of great worth or importance; prize: *My boss valued my contribution to the project.* See Synonyms at **appreciate. 3.** To rate according to worth or desirability: *Don't we all value health above money?* [From Middle English, from Old French *valoir*, to be worth.]

valve (vălv) *n.* **1a.** Any of various mechanical devices that control the flow of liquids, gases, or loose material through pipes or channels by blocking and uncovering openings. **b.** The movable part or element of such a device. **c.** A device in a brass wind instrument that can be opened or closed to change the pitch by altering the length of the air column in the tube. **2.** A structure located in a hollow organ or passage, such as the heart or a vein, that prevents the backward flow of a body fluid. **3.** One of the paired hinged shells of certain mollusks, such as clams and oysters. [From Middle English, half of a folding door, from Latin *valva*.]

va·moose (vă-mo͞os′) *intr.v.* **va·moosed, va·moos·ing, va·moos·es** *Slang* To leave hastily. [From Spanish *vamos*, let us go.]

vamp (vămp) *n.* The upper part of a shoe or boot covering the instep and sometimes extending over the toes. ❖ *tr.v.* **vamped, vamp·ing, vamps** To provide (a shoe) with a new vamp.

vam·pire (văm′pīr′) *n.* **1.** In popular folklore, an undead being in human form that survives by sucking the blood of living people, especially at night. **2.** A person who takes advantage of others, especially for personal gain. **3.** A vampire bat. [From German *Vampir*, of Slavic origin.]

vampire bat *n.* Any of various tropical or subtropical American bats that bite mammals and birds to feed on their blood.

van (văn) *n.* **1.** An enclosed motor vehicle having rear or side doors and side panels, used especially for transporting people. **2.** A covered or enclosed truck or wagon used for transporting goods or livestock. [Short for *caravan*.]

va·na·di·um (və-**nā′**dē-əm) *n.* *Symbol* **V** A soft, bright white metallic element used especially in making various strong varieties of steel. Atomic number 23. See **Periodic Table.**

Van Al·len belt (văn **ăl′**ən) *n.* Either of two zones of high-energy, electrically charged particles trapped in the earth's magnetic field and surrounding the planet. [After James Alfred *Van Allen* (1914–2006), American physicist.]

Van Bu·ren (văn **byo͝or′**ən), **Martin** 1782–1862. The eighth president of the United States (1837–1841).

Van·cou·ver (văn-**ko͞o′**vər) The largest city of British Columbia, Canada, in the southwest part of the province on an inlet of the Pacific Ocean opposite **Vancouver Island.**

van·dal (**văn′**dl) *n.* A person who willfully or maliciously defaces or destroys the property of another.

Vandal *n.* A member of a Germanic people that overran Gaul, Spain, northern Africa, and Rome in the fourth and fifth centuries AD.

van·dal·ism (**văn′**dl-ĭz′əm) *n.* Willful or malicious damage to or destruction of another's property.

van·dal·ize (**văn′**dl-īz′) *tr.v.* **van·dal·ized, van·dal·iz·ing, van·dal·iz·es** To destroy or damage (another's property) willfully or maliciously.

Vandyke beard (văn **dīk′**) *n.* A short pointed beard, especially one worn with the cheeks shaven and a mustache. [After Sir Anthony *Vandyke* (1599–1641), Flemish painter who painted portraits of himself and the king of England wearing such a beard.]

vane (vān) *n.* **1.** A weathervane. **2.** Any of several usually rigid blades mounted around an axis and moved by or used to direct the motion of a fluid. **3.** The thin flat part of a feather, extending from each side of a main shaft or quill. **4.** One of the stabilizing fins attached to the tail of a bomb or other missile.

❑ *These sound alike:* **vane, vain** (proud), **vein** (blood vessel).

van Gogh (văn **gō′**), **Vincent** 1853–1890. Dutch painter whose works include numerous self-portraits, a series of sunflower paintings (1888), and *Starry Night* (1889).

van·guard (**văn′**gärd) *n.* **1.** The front or leading position in an army or fleet. **2.** The foremost or leading position in a trend or movement.

va·nil·la (və-**nĭl′**ə) *n.* **1.** A tropical American orchid that is widely grown for its seedpods, which yield an aromatic substance used especially as a flavoring. **2.** The long seedpods of this plant. **3.** A flavoring extract made from the cured seedpods of this plant or produced artificially. ❖ *adj.* **1.** Flavored with vanilla: *vanilla ice cream.* **2.** Scented with or smelling like vanilla: *vanilla perfume.*

va·nil·lin (və-**nĭl′**ĭn *or* **văn′**ə-lĭn) *n.* A white or yellow crystalline compound, found in vanilla beans and certain balsams and resins or produced artificially and used in perfumes, flavorings, and medicines.

van·ish (**văn′**ĭsh) *intr.v.* **van·ished, van·ish·ing, van·ish·es 1.** To pass out of sight, especially quickly; disappear: *The sun vanished behind a cloud.* See Synonyms at **disappear. 2.** To pass out of existence: *The dinosaurs vanished from the earth.*

van·ish·ing point (**văn′**ĭ-shĭng) *n.* In a drawing or painting, the point at which real or imaginary lines drawn in perspective meet or seem to meet.

van·i·ty (**văn′**ĭ-tē) *n., pl.* **van·i·ties 1.** Excessive pride; conceit. **2.** Worthlessness, pointlessness, or futility: *the vanity of trying to hold back the forces of change.* **3.** A vanity case. **4.** A dressing table.

vanity case *n.* A small handbag or case used for carrying cosmetics or toiletries.

van·quish (**văng′**kwĭsh *or* **văn′**kwĭsh) *tr.v.* **van·quished, van·quish·ing, van·quish·es 1.** To defeat or conquer in battle; subjugate: *vanquished the invading forces.* **2.** To defeat in a conflict, contest, or competition. **3.** To overcome or subdue (an emotion, for example); suppress. **—van′quish·er** *n.*

van·tage (**văn′**tĭj) *n.* **1.** An advantage in a competition. **2.** A position, condition, or opportunity that provides superiority or an advantage. **3.** A position that affords a broad view or perspective.

Va·nu·a·tu (vä′no͞o-**ä′**to͞o) An island country of the southern Pacific Ocean east of northern Australia. Port Vila is the capital.

vape (vāp) *intr.v.* **vaped, vap·ing, vapes** To inhale and exhale vapor, especially vapor containing nicotine, from an electronic device.

vap·id (**văp′**ĭd) *adj.* **1.** Lacking liveliness, animation, or interest; dull: *He engaged in a vapid conversation about the weather.* **2.** Lacking intellectual depth or substance; superficial or vacuous: *She changed from a smart, considerate child to a silly, vapid teenager.* **3.** Lacking taste, zest, or flavor; flat: *a restaurant with cheap and vapid food.* **—vap′id·ly** *adv.*

va·por (**vā′**pər) *n.* **1.** A faintly visible mass of fine particles of matter in the air, as mist, fumes, or smoke. **2a.** The gaseous state of a substance that is solid or liquid at normal temperatures. **b.** A mixture of a vapor and air, as the fuel mixture of an internal-combustion engine.

va·por·ize (**vā′**pə-rīz′) *tr. & intr.v.* **va·por·ized, va·por·iz·ing, va·por·iz·es** To convert or be converted into vapor. **—va′por·i·za′tion** (vā′pər-ĭ-**zā′**shən) *n.*

va·por·iz·er (**vā′**pə-rī′zər) *n.* A device that converts a substance into vapor, especially a device used to vaporize medicine for inhalation.

va·por·ous (**vā′**pər-əs) *adj.* **1.** Relating to or like vapor. **2.** Producing vapors; volatile. **3.** Insubstantial or vague: *vaporous rumors.* **—va′por·ous·ly** *adv.*

va·pour (**vā′**pər) *n.* *Chiefly British* Variant of **vapor.**

va·que·ro (vä-**kâr′**ō) *n., pl.* **va·que·ros** A cowboy.

var. *abbr.* An abbreviation of: **1.** variable. **2.** variant. **3.** various.

var·i·a·ble (**vâr′**ē-ə-bəl) *adj.* **1.** Subject to variation; changeable: *a variable climate.* **2.** Capable of assuming any of a set of two or more values, as a mathematical function or symbol; not fixed in value. ❖ *n.* **1.** Something that varies or is prone to variation. **2.** A variable mathematical quantity or a symbol that represents it. **—var′i·a·bil′i·ty, var′i·a·ble·ness** *n.* **—var′i·a·bly** *adv.*

var·i·ance (**vâr′**ē-əns) *n.* **1.** The state or quality of being variable: *considerable variance in temperature across the region.* **2a.** Difference or inconsistency: *Your behavior is at variance with your beliefs.* **b.** The state or fact of being in disagreement or in conflict: *I am at variance with her over who should pay for the damage.* **3.** An exception to a rule, granted by an authority on the basis of hardship or practicality: *had to get a variance to add a room to the historic house.*

var·i·ant (**vâr′**ē-ənt) *adj.* **1.** Differing from others of the same kind or from a standard: *a variant form of a disease; a book in variant editions.* **2.** Having or exhibiting variation; varying: *words with variant spellings.* ❖ *n.* Something that differs from others of the same kind or

Martin Van Buren
1858 portrait by George Peter Alexander Healy (1813–1894)

Vandyke beard
detail of a portrait by Anthony Vandyke (1599–1641)

Vincent van Gogh
1888 self-portrait

vanishing point

variegated
variegated leaves of coleus plants

USAGE

various The word **various** is sometimes used incorrectly as a pronoun, as in *The coach spoke to various of the team members*. The same thought can be expressed correctly by using *various* as an adjective: *The coach spoke to various team members.*

WRITERS CHOOSE THEIR WORDS

Early explorers put it down on their maps as the "Great American Desert" and described it in woeful tales as the loneliest region on earth. The caprock [region] seemed to them as **vast** as the sea and more terrible, with no beginning and no end and only misery to write home about.

—L.J. Hunt
The Abernathy Boys

ă	pat	ôr	core
ā	pay	oi	boy
âr	care	ou	out
ä	father	ŏŏ	took
ĕ	pet	ŏŏr	lure
ē	be	ōō	boot
ĭ	pit	ŭ	cut
ī	bite	ûr	urge
îr	pier	th	thin
ŏ	pot	*th*	this
ō	toe	zh	vision
ô	paw	ə	about

from a standard, such as a different spelling or pronunciation of a word.

var·i·a·tion (vâr′ē-**ā′**shən) *n.* **1.** The act, fact, or process of varying. **2.** The extent or degree to which something varies: *temperature variations of more than 50 degrees Fahrenheit.* **3.** Something that is slightly different from another of the same type. **4.** A mathematical function that relates values of a variable to values of other variables. **5.** An altered version of a melody, characterized by ornamentation or changes in harmony, rhythm, or key.

var·i·cel·la (văr′ĭ-**sĕl′**ə) *n.* Chickenpox.

var·i·col·ored (**vâr′**ĭ-kŭl′ərd) *adj.* Having a variety of colors; variegated.

var·i·cose (**văr′**ĭ-kōs′) *adj.* Abnormally swollen or knotted: *varicose veins.*

var·ied (**vâr′**ēd) *adj.* Having or consisting of various forms or types; diverse: *a varied assortment of candy.* **—var′ied·ly** *adv.*

var·i·e·gat·ed (**vâr′**ē-ĭ-gā′tĭd) *adj.* Having streaks, marks, or patches of a different color or colors: *butterflies with variegated wings.*

va·ri·e·ty (və-**rī′**ĭ-tē) *n., pl.* **va·ri·e·ties 1.** The quality or condition of being various or varied; diversity: *We added some variety to the menu.* **2.** A number or collection of varied things, usually within the same general grouping; an assortment: *a variety of snacks on the table.* **3.** Something that is distinguished from others of the same kind by a specific characteristic: *regional varieties of Spanish.* **4.** A subdivision of a species consisting of a group of individuals that differ from other members of the species in certain minor characteristics: *Broccoli, cabbage, and kale are varieties of the same species.*

variety show *n.* A theatrical performance consisting of a series of unrelated acts, such as songs, dances, and comic skits.

variety store *n.* A retail store carrying a large variety of usually inexpensive merchandise.

var·i·ous (**vâr′**ē-əs) *adj.* **1a.** Of diverse kinds: *I am unable to go for various reasons.* **b.** Unlike; different: *flowers as various as the rose, the daisy, and the carnation.* **2.** Being more than one; several: *He spoke to various members of the club.* **—var′i·ous·ly** *adv.* —SEE NOTE.

var·let (**vär′**lĭt) *n.* **1.** An attendant or servant. **2.** A rascal; a knave.

var·mint (**vär′**mĭnt) *n. Informal* A person or thing that is considered undesirable, obnoxious, or troublesome. [Variant of *vermin.*]

var·nish (**vär′**nĭsh) *n.* **1.** A liquid that contains a solvent and a binder and is applied to a surface to produce a hard, transparent finish after evaporation and curing. **2.** The smooth coating or gloss that results from the application of this liquid: *Wear dulled the floor's varnish.* **3.** Something resembling or suggesting a coat of varnish; outward appearance; gloss: *hiding his temper under a varnish of good manners.* ❖ *tr.v.* **var·nished, var·nish·ing, var·nish·es 1.** To cover with varnish: *varnish a cabinet.* **2.** To give a superficial or deceptive appearance to: *tried to varnish over her lack of experience on her application.*

var·si·ty (**vär′**sĭ-tē) *n., pl.* **var·si·ties** The principal team representing a university, school, or college in sports, games, or other competitions.

var·y (**vâr′**ē) *v.* **var·ied, var·y·ing, var·ies** —*intr.* **1.** To undergo or show change: *The temperature varied throughout the day.* **2.** To be different from others of the same kind: *policies that vary from school to school.* —*tr.* **1.** To make changes in or cause to change; modify or alter: *I varied the speed of the drill to get it to work better.* **2.** To give variety to; make diverse: *vary one's diet.* [From Middle English *varien*, from Latin *variāre*, from *varius*, various.]

vas·cu·lar (**văs′**kyə-lər) *adj.* Relating to or containing cells or vessels that transport or circulate liquids such as blood, lymph, or water within an animal or plant.

vascular plant *n.* Any of numerous plants, including the seed plants and the ferns, that have well-developed vascular tissues consisting of phloem to transport sugars and other organic nutrients and xylem to transport water and minerals.

vas def·er·ens (**văs′ dĕf′**ə-rĕnz′) *n., pl.* **va·sa def·er·en·ti·a** (**vā′**zə dĕf′ə-**rĕn′**shē-ə) The duct through which sperm passes from a testis to the urethra.

vase (vās *or* vāz *or* väz) *n.* An open container, often of glass or porcelain, used for holding flowers for ornamentation. [From Latin *vās*, vessel.]

va·sec·to·my (və-**sĕk′**tə-mē) *n., pl.* **va·sec·to·mies** Surgical removal of all or part of the vas deferens, usually as a means of sterilization.

Vas·e·line (**văs′**ə-lēn′ *or* văs′ə-**lēn′**) A trademark used for a brand of petroleum jelly.

vas·sal (**văs′**əl) *n.* **1.** A person who held land from a feudal lord and received protection in return for homage and allegiance. **2.** A person who is a subordinate or dependent.

vas·sal·age (**văs′**ə-lĭj) *n.* **1.** The condition of being a vassal. **2.** The service, homage, and fealty required of a vassal. **3.** A position of subordination or subjection.

vast (văst) *adj.* **vast·er, vast·est 1.** Very great in size, extent, or quantity: *sold her collection for a vast sum.* **2.** Very great in scope or import: *a vast difference between the two policies.* [From Latin *vāstus.*] **—vast′ly** *adv.* **—vast′ness** *n.*

vat (văt) *n.* A large vessel, such as a tub or barrel, used to hold or store liquids.

Vat·i·can (**văt′**ĭ-kən) *n.* **1.** The official residence of the pope in Vatican City. **2.** The papal government; the papacy.

Vatican City An independent papal state on the Tiber River within Rome, Italy. It was created by a treaty in 1929.

va·tu (**vä′**tōō) *n.* The basic monetary unit of Vanuatu.

vaude·ville (**vôd′**vĭl′) *n.* Stage entertainment offering a variety of short acts such as singing and dancing routines and juggling performances.

Vaughan (vôn), **Sarah** 1924–1990. American jazz singer known for her complex phrasing and her virtuosity.

vault[1] (vôlt) *n.* **1.** An arched structure that forms a ceiling or roof. **2.** A room, such as a cellar, with arched walls and ceiling, especially when underground. **3.** A room or compartment for the safekeeping of valuables. **4.** A burial chamber, especially when underground. ❖ *tr.v.* **vault·ed, vault·ing, vaults** To build or cover with a vault. [From Middle English *vaute*, from Latin *volūtus*, past participle of *volvere*, to roll.]

vault[2] (vôlt) *tr. & intr.v.* **vault·ed, vault·ing, vaults** To jump or leap over, especially with the aid of a support such as the hands or a pole. ❖ *n.* **1.** The act of vaulting; a leap. **2.** A piece of gymnastic equipment with an upholstered body used especially for vaulting. [From Old Italian *voltare*, from Latin *volvere*, to turn, roll.] **—vault′er** *n.*

vaunt·ed (**vôn′**tĭd) *adj.* Excessively praised or boasted of: *The critic was not impressed by the vaunted special effects of the movie.*

vb. *abbr.* An abbreviation of verb.

V-chip (**vē′**chĭp′) *n.* A computer chip that is installed in a television to allow the viewer to prevent the display of programs with violent or sexual content.

VCR *abbr.* An abbreviation for videocassette recorder.

veal (vēl) *n.* The meat of a calf. [From Middle English *vel*, from Latin *vitellus*, from *vitulus*, calf.]

vec·tor (**vĕk′**tər) *n.* **1.** In mathematics and physical science, a quantity, such as velocity or change of position, that must be identified by its direction as well as by its measure. **2.** An organism, such as a mosquito or tick, that carries disease-causing microorganisms from one host to another [From Latin, carrier, from *vehere*, to carry.]

veer (vîr) *v.* **veered, veer·ing, veers** —*intr.* **1.** To turn aside from a course or established direction; swerve: *The plane veered east to avoid the oncoming storm.* **2.** To deviate from a purpose, behavior, or previous pattern: *His mood veered from cheerful to cranky.* —*tr.* To alter the direction of; turn: *He veered the car sharply to the left.* [From French *virer.*]

veg (vĕj) *intr.v.* **vegged, veg·ging, veg·ges** *Informal* To engage in relaxing or passive activities: *vegged out for a few hours in front of the TV.*

Ve·ga (vē**′**gə *or* vā**′**gə) *n.* The brightest star in the constellation Lyra.

ve·gan (vē**′**gən) *n.* A vegetarian who eats plant products only.

veg·e·ta·ble (vĕj**′**tə-bəl *or* vĕj**′**ĭ-tə-bəl) *n.* **1a.** A plant part, usually a root, leaf, or stem, that is used as food. Some seeds and fruits, such as beans, peas, and squash, are also called vegetables. **b.** A plant from which such parts are harvested. **2.** A plant or fungus, as opposed to an animal: *animal, mineral, or vegetable?*

vegetable oil *n.* Any of various oils obtained from plants and used in cooking, food products, and industry.

veg·e·tar·i·an (vĕj′ĭ-târ**′**ē-ən) *n.* A person whose diet does not include the flesh of animals and is mainly composed of plant parts (such as leaves, roots, fruits, nuts, and seeds), along with mushrooms and sometimes eggs and dairy products. ❖ *adj.* **1.** Relating to vegetarians or vegetarianism: *a vegetarian restaurant.* **2.** Consisting primarily or wholly of vegetables or plants: *a vegetarian meal.*

veg·e·tar·i·an·ism (vĕj′ĭ-târ**′**ē-ə-nĭz′əm) *n.* The practice of consuming a vegetarian diet.

veg·e·tate (vĕj**′**ĭ-tāt′) *v.* **veg·e·tat·ed, veg·e·tat·ing, veg·e·tates** —*intr.* To be physically inactive and mentally dull: *We vegetated in front of the TV during the storm.* —*tr.* To grow over or cover with vegetation: *dunes that were vegetated.*

veg·e·ta·tion (vĕj′ĭ-tā**′**shən) *n.* **1.** The plants of an area or region; plant life. **2.** The act or process of vegetating.

veg·e·ta·tive (vĕj**′**ĭ-tā′tĭv) *adj.* **1.** Relating to plant life: *vegetative cover.* **2a.** Relating to or characterized by the biological processes of growth and nutrition rather than reproduction. **b.** Relating to asexual rather than sexual reproduction.

ve·he·ment (vē**′**ə-mənt) *adj.* Marked by forcefulness of expression or intensity of emotion or conviction; fervent: *a vehement critic of his foreign policy.* **—ve′he·mence** *n.* **—ve′he·ment·ly** *adv.*

ve·hi·cle (vē**′**ĭ-kəl) *n.* **1a.** A device or structure for transporting people or things. **b.** A self-propelled conveyance that runs on tires; a motor vehicle. **2.** A medium through which something is transmitted, expressed, or accomplished: *Oral tales are an important vehicle of culture.* **3.** A play, role, or piece of music used to display the special abilities of a performer or group of performers. **4.** A substance, such as oil, into which pigments are mixed in making paint. [From Latin *vehiculum*, from *vehere*, to carry.]

ve·hic·u·lar (vē-hĭk**′**yə-lər) *adj.* **1.** Relating to or intended for vehicles, especially motor vehicles: *vehicular traffic; vehicular regulations.* **2.** Serving as a vehicle.

veil (vāl) *n.* **1.** A length of cloth worn over the head, shoulders, and often the face, especially by women. **2.** The part of a nun's headdress that frames the face and falls over the shoulders. **3.** Any of various cloth head coverings worn by Muslim women. **4.** Something that covers or conceals like a veil, curtain, or cloak: *a veil of secrecy.* ❖ *tr.v.* **veiled, veil·ing, veils 1.** To cover with or as if with a veil: *veil one's face.* **2.** To conceal or disguise.

❑ *These sound alike:* **veil, vale** (valley).

vein (vān) *n.* **1.** Any of a branching system of blood vessels through which blood returns to the heart from the cells, tissues, and organs of the body. **2.** One of the thickened ribs that form a supporting network in the wing of an insect. **3.** One of the strands of vascular tissue that form the conducting and supporting framework in a leaf. **4.** A long, regularly shaped deposit of an ore or a mineral in the earth: *a vein of copper ore; a vein of coal.* **5.** A long wavy strip of a different shade or color, such as in marble or wood. **6.** A particular turn of mind: *He spoke in a light playful vein.* [From Middle English *veine*, from Latin *vēna.*]

❑ *These sound alike:* **vein, vain** (proud), **vane** (weathervane).

ve·lar (vē**′**lər) *adj.* **1.** Relating to or involving the soft palate. **2.** Formed with the back of the tongue on or near the soft palate, as the *g* in *gut.*

Vel·cro (vĕl**′**krō) A trademark used for a fastening tape consisting of two strips of nylon, one of which has a surface of tiny loops, the other of which has a surface of tiny hooks that fasten to the loops.

veld also **veldt** (vĕlt *or* fĕlt) *n.* An open grazing area of southern Africa.

vel·lum (vĕl**′**əm) *n.* **1.** A fine parchment made from the skins of calf, lamb, or kid and used for the pages and binding of books. **2.** A heavy paper that looks like this parchment.

ve·loc·i·rap·tor (və-lŏs**′**ə-răp′tər) *n.* A small meat-eating dinosaur having short front legs, sharp curved claws, and a long flat snout with sharp teeth. [From Latin *vēlōx*, fast + Latin *raptor*, one who seizes.]

ve·loc·i·ty (və-lŏs**′**ĭ-tē) *n.*, *pl.* **ve·loc·i·ties 1.** The rate at which an object moves in a specified direction. **2.** Speed.

ve·lour (və-lo͝or**′**) *n.* A closely napped fabric resembling velvet, used chiefly for clothing and upholstery.

vel·vet (vĕl**′**vĭt) *n.* A soft fabric having a smooth dense pile on one side and a plain underside.

vel·vet·een (vĕl′vĭ-tēn**′**) *n.* A cotton pile fabric resembling velvet.

vel·vet·y (vĕl**′**vĭ-tē) *adj.* **vel·vet·i·er, vel·vet·i·est** Having the soft smooth texture of velvet.

ve·na ca·va (vē**′**nə kā**′**və) *n.*, *pl.* **ve·nae ca·vae** (vē**′**nē kā**′**vē) Either of two large veins that return blood to the right atrium of the heart.

ve·nal (vē**′**nəl) *adj.* **1.** Willing to be bribed; mercenary: *a venal police officer.* **2.** Marked by corrupt dealings, especially bribery: *a venal administration.* [From Latin *vēnum*, sale.]

ve·na·tion (vē-nā**′**shən *or* vĕ-nā**′**shən) *n.* **1.** Distribution or arrangement of a system of veins, as in a leaf blade or the wing of an insect. **2.** The veins of such a system considered as a group.

vend (vĕnd) *tr.v.* **vend·ed, vend·ing, vends** To offer or have available for sale.

vend·er (vĕn**′**dər) *n.* Variant of **vendor.**

ven·det·ta (vĕn-dĕt**′**ə) *n.* A feud between two families that occurs when one family member kills a member of the other family, leading to retaliatory acts of violence.

vend·ing machine (vĕn**′**dĭng) *n.* A self-service machine that dispenses merchandise after payment is made.

ven·dor or **vend·er** (vĕn**′**dər) *n.* **1.** A person or business that sells or vends something: *a popcorn vendor; a vendor of software products on the Web.* **2.** A vending machine.

ve·neer (və-nîr**′**) *n.* **1.** A thin surface layer, as of finely grained wood, glued to a base of inferior material: *a pine*

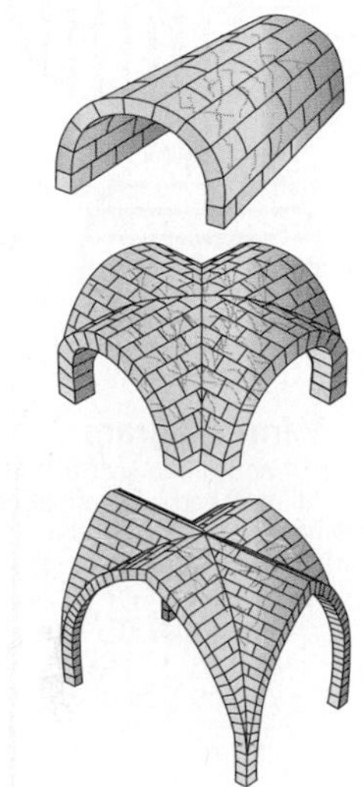

vault¹
top to bottom: barrel, groin, and rib vaults

venation
veins in a leaf

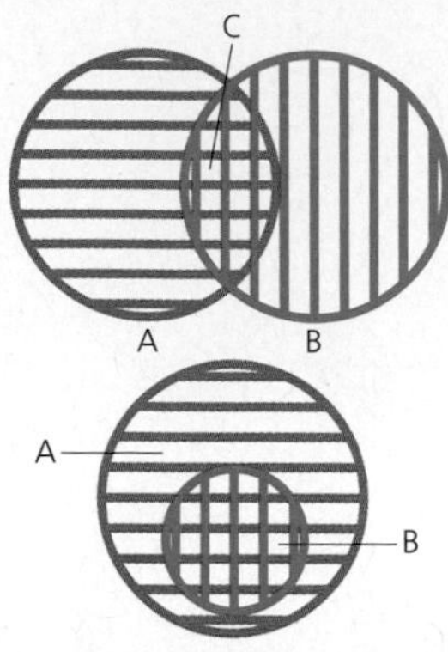

Venn diagram

top: Sets *A* and *B* intersect to form set *C*. All members of *C* are also members of both *A* and *B*. *bottom*: Set *B* is a subset of set *A*. All members of *B* are also members of *A*.

veranda

ă	pat	ôr	core
ā	pay	oi	boy
âr	care	ou	out
ä	father	o͝o	took
ĕ	pet	o͝or	lure
ē	be	o͞o	boot
ĭ	pit	ŭ	cut
ī	bite	ûr	urge
îr	pier	th	thin
ŏ	pot	*th*	this
ō	toe	zh	vision
ô	paw	ə	about

cabinet with a mahogany veneer. **2.** Any of the thin layers glued together to make plywood. **3.** A deceptive superficial show; a façade: *a veneer of friendliness.* ❖ *tr.v.* **ve·neered, ve·neer·ing, ve·neers 1.** To overlay (a surface) with a thin layer of better or finer material. **2.** To conceal, especially something common or crude, with a deceptively attractive outward show.

ven·er·a·ble (vĕn**′**ər-ə-bəl) *adj.* **1.** Worthy of respect or reverence by virtue of age, dignity, character, or position: *a venerable senator.* **2.** Deserving of reverence, especially for historic or religious associations: *venerable relics of a saint.* **—ven′er·a·bly** *adv.*

ven·er·ate (vĕn**′**ə-rāt′) *tr.v.* **ven·er·at·ed, ven·er·at·ing, ven·er·ates** To regard with respect, reverence, or heartfelt deference. **—ven′er·a′tion** *n.*

ve·ne·re·al disease (və-nîr**′**ē-əl) *n.* A sexually transmitted disease.

ve·ne·tian blind or **Ve·ne·tian blind** (və-nē**′**shən) *n.* A window blind consisting of a number of thin horizontal adjustable slats that overlap when closed.

Ven·e·zue·la (vĕn′ə-zwā**′**lə) A country of northern South America on the Caribbean Sea northeast of Colombia. Caracas is the capital.

ven·geance (vĕn**′**jəns) *n.* Infliction of harm or pain in return for a wrong committed; retribution. ◆ **with a vengeance** With great violence or force: *The snowstorm hit with a vengeance.*

venge·ful (vĕnj**′**fəl) *adj.* **1.** Desiring or seeking vengeance: *a story about a vengeful ghost.* **2.** Arising from or characterized by a desire for revenge: *vengeful anger.* **—venge′ful·ly** *adv.*

ve·ni·al (vē**′**nē-əl *or* vēn**′**yəl) *adj.* Easily excused or forgiven; minor or pardonable. [From Middle English, from Latin *venia*, forgiveness.]

Ven·ice (vĕn**′**ĭs) A city of northeast Italy on islets within a lagoon in the **Gulf of Venice,** a wide inlet of the northern Adriatic Sea. It was founded in the sixth century AD. **—Ve·ne′tian** (və-nē**′**shən) *adj. & n.*

ven·i·son (vĕn**′**ĭ-sən *or* vĕn**′**ĭ-zən) *n.* The flesh of a deer used as food.

Venn diagram (vĕn) *n.* A diagram that uses circles to represent sets. Relations between the sets can be indicated by the arrangement of the circles, as for example by drawing one circle within another to indicate that the first set is a subset of a second set. [After John *Venn* (1834–1923), British logician.]

ven·om (vĕn**′**əm) *n.* **1.** A poisonous substance that is secreted by certain snakes, spiders, scorpions, and insects, and can be transmitted to prey or to attackers by a bite or sting. **2.** Malice; spite. [From Middle English *venim*, from Latin *venēnum*, poison.]

ven·om·ous (vĕn**′**ə-məs) *adj.* **1.** Secreting and transmitting venom: *a venomous snake.* **2.** Full of or containing venom: *a venomous substance.* **3.** Malicious; spiteful: *a venomous look.* **—ven′om·ous·ly** *adv.* **—ven′om·ous·ness** *n.*

ve·nous (vē**′**nəs) *adj.* **1.** Relating to or contained in the veins of the body: *venous blood.* **2.** Having veins, as a leaf or the wings of an insect.

vent[1] (vĕnt) *n.* **1.** Forceful expression or release of pent-up thoughts or feelings: *give vent to one's anger.* **2.** An opening through which a liquid, gas, or vapor can pass or escape. ❖ *tr.v.* **vent·ed, vent·ing, vents 1.** To express (thoughts or feelings) especially forcefully: *venting their grievances.* **2.** To release or discharge (steam, for example) through an opening. **3.** To provide with a vent. [Partly from French *vent* and partly alteration of French *évent* (from Old French *esventer*, to let out air).]

vent[2] (vĕnt) *n.* A slit in a garment, as in the back seam of a jacket. [From Middle English, from Old French *fente*, slit.]

ven·ti·late (vĕn**′**tl-āt′) *tr.v.* **ven·ti·lat·ed, ven·ti·lat·ing, ven·ti·lates 1.** To admit fresh air into (a mine, for example) to replace stale or noxious air. **2.** To provide with a vent, as for airing. **3.** To expose to public discussion or examination; air: *We ventilated our misgivings.* **—ven′ti·la′tion** *n.*

ven·ti·la·tor (vĕn**′**tl-ā′tər) *n.* **1.** A device that circulates fresh air and expels stale or foul air. **2.** A machine that supplies oxygen or a mixture of oxygen and air, used in artificial respiration to control or assist breathing.

ven·tral (vĕn**′**trəl) *adj.* Relating to or located on the front or the underside of the body of a human or another animal: *the ventral scales of a snake.*

ven·tri·cle (vĕn**′**trĭ-kəl) *n.* A cavity or chamber in an organ, especially either of the chambers of the heart that contract to pump blood into arteries. **—ven·tric′u·lar** (vĕn-trĭk**′**yə-lər) *adj.*

ven·tril·o·quism (vĕn-trĭl**′**ə-kwĭz′əm) *n.* The art of projecting one's voice so that it seems to come from another source, such as from a wooden figure. [From Latin *ventriloquus*, speaking from the belly.] **—ven·tril′o·quist** *n.*

ven·ture (vĕn**′**chər) *n.* **1.** An undertaking that is dangerous, daring, or of uncertain outcome. **2.** A business enterprise involving some financial risk. ❖ *v.* **ven·tured, ven·tur·ing, ven·tures** *—tr.* **1.** To expose to danger or risk: *venturing all his capital on a deal.* **2.** To brave the dangers of: *ventured the high seas in a light boat.* **3.** To dare to say; express at the risk of denial, criticism, or censure: *venture an opinion.* *—intr.* **1.** To take a risk; dare. **2.** To proceed despite possible danger or risk: *ventured into the mountains.*

ven·ture·some (vĕn**′**chər-səm) *adj.* **1.** Given to venturing or taking risks; daring: *venturesome investors.* **2.** Involving risk or danger; hazardous: *a venturesome expedition up Mount Everest.*

ven·tu·ri (vĕn-to͝or**′**ē) *n., pl.* **ven·tu·ris** A short tube having a narrow section through which a fluid moving through the tube must pass at a higher velocity than at other points. The fluid in the narrow section exerts less pressure than that in the wider parts, allowing the use of the tube as an air speed indicator, as an atomizer, and in rockets. [After Giovanni Battista *Venturi* (1746–1822), Italian physicist.]

ven·ue (vĕn**′**yo͞o) *n.* **1.** The place where something happens: *What's the venue for the band's next concert?* **2.** The court or jurisdiction where a trial is held.

Ve·nus (vē**′**nəs) *n.* **1.** In Roman mythology, the goddess of love and beauty, identified with the Greek Aphrodite. **2.** The second planet from the sun, with a diameter about 400 miles less than that of Earth. It is the brightest object in the night sky aside from the moon. See table at **solar system.**

Venus flytrap *n.* A plant having leaves that are edged with bristles and that can close and trap insects, which are then digested and absorbed by the plant.

ve·ra·cious (və-rā**′**shəs) *adj.* **1.** Honest; truthful: *a veracious person.* **2.** Accurate; true: *a veracious description of the accident.* **—ve·ra′cious·ly** *adv.*

ve·rac·i·ty (və-răs**′**ĭ-tē) *n., pl.* **ve·rac·i·ties 1.** Adherence to the truth; honesty: *doubting the veracity of the witnesses.* **2.** Accuracy; truthfulness: *checking the veracity of his report.*

ve·ran·da or **ve·ran·dah** (və-răn**′**də) *n.* A usually roofed porch or balcony extending along the outside of a building.

verb (vûrb) *n.* **1.** The part of speech that expresses existence, action, or occurrence. **2.** A word belonging to this part of speech, such as *be, run,* or *happen.* **3.** A phrase, such as *has been thinking,* that is used as a verb. [From Middle English *verbe*, from Latin *verbum*, word, verb.] —SEE NOTE.

ver·bal (vûr**′**bəl) *adj.* **1.** Relating to or associated with words: *verbal aptitude tests.* **2.** Expressed in spoken rather than written words; oral: *a verbal agreement.* **3.** Word for word; literal: *a verbal translation.* **4.** Relating to, having the nature or function of, or derived from a verb: *verbal constructions.* **5.** Used to form verbs: *a verbal suffix.* ❖ *n.* A noun or adjective derived from a verb. **—ver′bal·ly** *adv.*

ver·bal·ize (vûr′bə-līz′) *v.* **ver·bal·ized, ver·bal·iz·ing, ver·bal·iz·es** *—tr.* To express in words: *verbalized his fears.* *—intr.* To express oneself in words.

ver·ba·tim (vər-bā′tĭm) *adj.* Using exactly the same words; corresponding word for word: *a verbatim quotation.* ❖ *adv.* Word for word; in the same words: *He repeated the speech verbatim.*

ver·be·na (vər-bē′nə) *n.* Any of various plants grown for their clusters of variously colored, often fragrant flowers

ver·bi·age (vûr′bē-ĭj *or* vûr′bĭj) *n.* An excess of words for the purpose; wordiness.

ver·bose (vər-bōs′) *adj.* Using or containing more words than necessary; wordy. **—ver·bose′ly** *adv.* **—ver·bos′i·ty** (vər-bŏs′ĭ-tē) *n.*

ver·dant (vûr′dnt) *adj.* **1.** Green with growing plants: *verdant meadows.* **2.** Green in hue: *verdant leaves.*

Ver·di (vâr′dē), **Giuseppe** 1813–1901. Italian composer whose operas include *Aïda* (1871) and *Otello* (1887).

ver·dict (vûr′dĭkt) *n.* **1.** The decision of the jury after the trial of a case. **2.** An expressed conclusion; a judgment or opinion.

ver·di·gris (vûr′dĭ-grēs′) *n.* **1.** A blue or green copper acetate, used as a pigment and as a poison for insects and fungi. **2.** A greenish coating or crust of copper salts that forms on copper, brass, or bronze that is exposed to air or sea water for a long time.

ver·dure (vûr′jər) *n.* **1.** The lush green color of healthy growing plants. **2.** A growth of green plants.

verge (vûrj) *n.* **1.** An edge or margin; a border: *on the verge of the city's industrial section.* **2.** The point beyond which an action, state, or condition is likely to begin or occur: *on the verge of tears.* ❖ *intr.v.* **verged, verg·ing, verg·es** To approach the nature or condition of something specified; come close: *enthusiasm verging on fanaticism.*

Ver·gil (vûr′jəl) See **Virgil.**

ver·i·fi·ca·tion (vĕr′ə-fĭ-kā′shən) *n.* The act of verifying or the state of being verified.

ver·i·fy (vĕr′ə-fī′) *tr.v.* **ver·i·fied, ver·i·fy·ing, ver·i·fies** To demonstrate the truth or accuracy of by presentation of evidence: *Astronomers have verified certain findings of the ancient Greeks.* [From Middle English *verifien,* from Latin *vērus,* true.]

ver·i·ly (vĕr′ə-lē) *adv.* In fact; in truth.

ver·i·si·mil·i·tude (vĕr′ə-sĭ-mĭl′ĭ-to͞od′) *n.* The quality of appearing to be real or true.

ver·i·ta·ble (vĕr′ĭ-tə-bəl) *adj.* Being truly so called; real or genuine: *a veritable success.*

ver·i·ty (vĕr′ĭ-tē) *n., pl.* **ver·i·ties 1.** The quality or condition of being real, factual, or true: *the verity of his description.* **2.** Something, such as a principle or statement, that is true: *The obedient child lived by the verity that parents know best.*

ver·mi·cel·li (vûr′mĭ-chĕl′ē *or* vûr′mĭ-sĕl′ē) *n.* Pasta in long, very thin strands.

ver·mi·form (vûr′mə-fôrm′) *adj.* Having the shape of a worm.

vermiform appendix *n.* The tubular projection attached to the large intestine near its junction with the small intestine; the appendix.

ver·mil·ion also **ver·mil·lion** (vər-mĭl′yən) *n.* **1.** A vivid red to reddish orange. **2.** Red mercuric sulfide used as a pigment. ❖ *adj.* Of a vivid red to reddish orange.

ver·min (vûr′mĭn) *n., pl.* **vermin** Various small animals, such as rats or cockroaches, that are destructive, annoying, or injurious to health. [From Middle English, from Latin *vermis,* worm.]

ver·min·ous (vûr′mə-nəs) *adj.* **1.** Infested with vermin: *a verminous mattress.* **2.** Relating to or caused by vermin: *verminous pneumonia.*

Ver·mont (vər-mŏnt′) A state of the northeast United States west of New Hampshire. It was admitted as the 14th state in 1791. Montpelier is the capital and Burlington the largest city. —SEE NOTE.

ver·mouth (vər-mo͞oth′) *n.* A sweet or dry wine flavored with aromatic herbs and used chiefly in mixed drinks.

ver·nac·u·lar (vər-năk′yə-lər) *n.* **1.** The ordinary spoken language of a country or locality as distinct from the literary language. **2.** The specialized vocabulary of a particular trade or profession: *the medical vernacular.* ❖ *adj.* **1.** Native to or commonly spoken by the members of a country or region. **2.** Using the native language of a region, especially as distinct from the literary language: *a vernacular poet.* **3.** Designating the common, nonscientific name of a biological species: *The vernacular name of* Quercus alba *is "white oak."*

ver·nal (vûr′nəl) *adj.* Relating to or occurring in the spring. [From Latin *vērnus,* from *vēr,* spring.] **—ver′nal·ly** *adv.*

vernal equinox *n.* The equinox that occurs on March 20 or 21, when the sun crosses the celestial equator while moving in a northeasterly direction, marking the beginning of spring in the Northern Hemisphere and autumn in the Southern Hemisphere.

ver·ni·er (vûr′nē-ər) *n.* **1.** A small auxiliary scale attached parallel to a main scale and arranged to indicate fractional parts of the smallest divisions of the main scale. **2.** An auxiliary device that allows fine adjustments or measurements to be made on or with an instrument or device. [After Pierre *Vernier* (1580?–1637), French mathematician.]

vernier caliper *n.* A measuring device consisting of a caliper equipped with a vernier scale.

Ver·sailles (vər-sī′ *or* vĕr-sī′) A city of north-central France west-southwest of Paris. It is best known for its magnificent palace, built by Louis XIV.

ver·sa·tile (vûr′sə-təl *or* vûr′sə-tīl′) *adj.* **1.** Capable of doing many things well: *It takes a versatile athlete to do well in the decathlon.* **2.** Having varied uses or functions: *a versatile piece of machinery.* **3.** Variable or inconstant; changeable: *a versatile temperament.* **—ver′sa·til′i·ty** (vûr′sə-tĭl′ĭ-tē) *n.*

verse (vûrs) *n.* **1.** One line of poetry. **2.** A stanza of a long poem or hymn. **3.** The art or work of a poet; poetry. **4.** A specific type of poetic writing: *free verse.* **5.** One of the numbered subdivisions of a chapter of the Bible.

versed (vûrst) *adj.* Acquainted through study or experience; skilled or knowledgeable: *versed in foreign languages.*

ver·si·fy (vûr′sə-fī′) *v.* **ver·si·fied, ver·si·fy·ing, ver·si·fies** *—tr.* **1.** To change from prose into metrical form. **2.** To treat or tell in verse. *—intr.* To write verses.

ver·sion (vûr′zhən) *n.* **1.** A description or account from a specific point of view: *his version of the accident disagreed with mine.* **2.** A translation of a written work: *the King James version of the Bible.* **3.** A form or variation of an earlier or original type: *a reworked version of the Ford Model T.* **4.** An adaptation of a work of art or literature into another medium or style: *a movie version of a play.*

ver·sus (vûr′səs *or* vûr′səz) *prep.* **1.** In conflict or competition with; against: *the plaintiff versus the defendant; Michigan versus Ohio State.* **2.** As an alternative to or in contrast with: *studying to be a chemist versus working on a farm.*

vert. *abbr.* An abbreviation of vertical.

ver·te·bra (vûr′tə-brə) *n., pl.* **ver·te·brae** (vûr′tə-brā′)

USAGE

verb Many **verbs** can be used transitively with an object as well as intransitively without an object. Using the verb *write* as an example, we can either say *I wrote the message carefully* with the object *message,* or we can say *I wrote carefully* without an object. Verbs can also be used both in the active voice *(Williams hit the ball hard to left field)* and in the passive voice *(The ball was hit hard to left field by Williams).*

verbena

GEOGRAPHY

Vermont The name for the state of **Vermont** comes from a combination of two French words that together mean "green mountain." Probably this name refers to the mountain range known as the Green Mountains, which extends through the whole state.

Andreas Vesalius
portrait by Tintoretto (1518–1594)

Amerigo Vespucci

ă	pat	ôr	core
ā	pay	oi	boy
âr	care	ou	out
ä	father	o͝o	took
ĕ	pet	o͝or	lure
ē	be	o͞o	boot
ĭ	pit	ŭ	cut
ī	bite	ûr	urge
îr	pier	th	thin
ŏ	pot	*th*	this
ō	toe	zh	vision
ô	paw	ə	about

or **ver·te·bras** Any of the bones or segments of cartilage forming the spinal column.

ver·te·bral (vûr**ʹ**tə-brəl) *adj.* Relating to or consisting of a vertebra or vertebrae: *a vertebral fracture; the vertebral column.*

ver·te·brate (vûr**ʹ**tə-brĭt *or* vûr**ʹ**tə-brāt′) *adj.* **1.** Having a backbone: *vertebrate animals.* **2.** Relating to vertebrates: *the vertebrate brain; vertebrate biology.* ❖ *n.* Any of a large group of animals having a backbone, including the fishes, amphibians, reptiles, birds, and mammals.

ver·tex (vûr**ʹ**tĕks′) *n., pl.* **ver·ti·ces** (vûr**ʹ**tĭ-sēz′) or **ver·tex·es 1.** The highest point of something; the apex or summit. **2a.** The point at which the sides of an angle intersect. **b.** The point of a triangle, cone, or pyramid that is opposite to and farthest away from its base. **c.** A point of a polyhedron at which three or more edges intersect. **d.** The point on a parabola or hyperbola where the line curves the most.

ver·ti·cal (vûr**ʹ**tĭ-kəl) *adj.* **1.** Being or situated at right angles to the horizon; directly upright. **2.** Situated at the vertex or highest point; directly overhead. ❖ *n.* **1.** Something, such as a line or plane, that is vertical. **2.** A vertical position: *a post that leans slightly from the vertical.* [From Late Latin *verticālis*, overhead, from Latin *vertex*, highest point, vertex.] **—ver**ʹ**ti·cal·ly** *adv.*

vertical angle *n.* Either of two angles formed by two intersecting lines and lying on opposite sides of the point of intersection.

vertical file *n.* A collection of resource materials, such as clippings from periodicals and photographs, arranged in a library or an archive for easy reference.

ver·ti·ces (vûr**ʹ**tĭ-sēz′) *n.* A plural of **vertex.**

ver·ti·go (vûr**ʹ**tĭ-gō′) *n., pl.* **ver·ti·goes** or **ver·ti·gos 1.** The sensation of dizziness. **2.** A confused, disoriented state of mind.

verve (vûrv) *n.* **1.** Energy and enthusiasm in the expression of ideas, especially in the fine arts: *His novels lack verve.* **2.** Liveliness or vitality; animation.

ver·y (vĕr**ʹ**ē) *adv.* **1.** In a high degree; extremely: *feeling very happy.* **2.** Truly; absolutely: *the very best advice.* ❖ *adj.* **ver·i·er, ver·i·est 1.** Being without qualification or restriction; absolute; utter: *the very end of the day.* **2.** Being the same; identical: *wearing the very clothes he had on while committing the crime.* **3.** Being particularly suitable or appropriate: *The chair was the very thing we needed to make the room feel cozy.* **4.** Used to emphasize the importance of the thing being described: *The very mountains shook.*

very high frequency *n.* A radio-wave frequency lying in the band between 30 and 300 megahertz.

very low frequency *n.* A radio-wave frequency lying in the band between 3 and 30 kilohertz.

Ve·sa·li·us (vĭ-sā**ʹ**lē-əs), **Andreas** 1514–1564. Flemish anatomist and surgeon who is considered the founder of modern anatomy. His major work, *On the Structure of the Human Body* (1543), was based on his own dissection of cadavers.

ves·i·cle (vĕs**ʹ**ĭ-kəl) *n.* **1.** A small structure in a cell in which materials such as enzymes are transported or stored. **2.** A small bladder or sac, especially one that contains a body fluid.

ve·sic·u·lar (vĕ-**sĭk**ʹyə-lər) *adj.* **1.** Relating to a vesicle or vesicles. **2.** Composed of or containing vesicles.

ves·per (vĕs**ʹ**pər) *n.* **1.** A bell that summons worshipers to vespers. **2. Vesper** The evening star, especially Venus.

ves·pers also **Ves·pers** (vĕs**ʹ**pərz) *pl.n. (used with a singular or plural verb)* **1a.** The sixth of the seven canonical hours. **b.** A Christian worship service held in the late afternoon or evening. **2.** Evensong.

Ves·puc·ci (vĕs-**po͞o**ʹchē *or* vĕs-**pyo͞o**ʹchē), **Amerigo** 1454–1512. Italian navigator and explorer of the South American coast. America was named in his honor.

ves·sel (vĕs**ʹ**əl) *n.* **1.** A hollow utensil, such as a bowl, pitcher, jar, or tank, used especially as a container for liquids. **2.** A ship, large boat, or similar craft. **3.** A narrow tubular body part through which a fluid flows or circulates: *Veins and arteries are blood vessels.* **4.** One of the tubular water-conducting structures that make up the xylem of a flowering plant, consisting of a series of dead cells attached end to end and connected by holes.

vest (vĕst) *n.* **1.** A sleeveless garment, often having buttons down the front, worn usually over a shirt or blouse and sometimes as part of a three-piece suit. **2.** A sleeveless protective garment extending to the waist: *a bulletproof vest.* **3.** *Chiefly British* An undershirt. ❖ *tr.v.* **vest·ed, vest·ing, vests 1.** To place (authority or power, for example) in the control of a person or group: *Their constitution vests ultimate power in the sovereign.* **2.** To give power or authority to: *vesting the president with executive powers.* **3.** To dress, as in religious robes or vestments. [From Latin *vestis*, garment.]

Ves·ta (vĕs**ʹ**tə) *n.* In Roman mythology, the goddess of the hearth.

vest·ed (vĕs**ʹ**tĭd) *adj.* Legally settled, fixed, or absolute; being without contingency: *a vested right to the throne.*

ves·ti·bule (vĕs**ʹ**tə-byo͞ol′) *n.* **1.** A small entrance hall or lobby. **2.** An enclosed area at the end of a railroad passenger car. **3.** A chamber, opening, or channel of the body that serves as an entrance to another chamber or cavity.

ves·tige (vĕs**ʹ**tĭj) *n.* **1.** A visible trace or sign of something that once existed: *barely a vestige of color left in the faded curtains.* **2.** An organ or structure that was present and functioning in an earlier form of an organism and that remains, usually greatly reduced in size, in later forms as a nonfunctioning part. [From Latin *vestīgium.*]

ves·tig·i·al (vĕ-**stĭj**ʹē-əl) *adj.* Relating to or being a vestige: *a vestigial doorway; vestigial wings.*

vest·ment (vĕst**ʹ**mənt) *n.* A garment, especially a robe, gown, or other article of dress, worn as an indication of office or state or by a cleric at a religious service.

ves·try (vĕs**ʹ**trē) *n., pl.* **ves·tries 1.** A room in a church where vestments and sacred objects are stored. **2.** A meeting room in a church. **3.** A committee that manages the temporal affairs of a parish.

ves·try·man (vĕs**ʹ**trē-mən) *n.* A man who is a member of a vestry.

ves·try·wom·an (vĕs**ʹ**trē-wo͝om′ən) *n.* A woman who is a member of a vestry.

Ve·su·vi·us (vĭ-**so͞o**ʹvē-əs), **Mount** A volcano, 4,200 feet (1,280 meters) high, of southern Italy. A violent eruption in AD 79 destroyed the nearby city of Pompeii.

vet[1] (vĕt) *n. Informal* A veterinarian.

vet[2] (vĕt) *n. Informal* A veteran.

vetch (vĕch) *n.* Any of various twining plants having feathery leaves and usually purplish flowers.

vet·er·an (vĕt**ʹ**ər-ən *or* vĕt**ʹ**rən) *n.* **1.** A person who has served in the armed forces: *a veteran of the Korean War.* **2.** A person who is long experienced or practiced in a profession or activity. [From Latin *veterānus*, from *vetus*, old.]

Vet·er·ans Day (vĕt**ʹ**ər-ənz *or* vĕt**ʹ**rənz) *n.* November 11, observed in honor of veterans of the armed services and in commemoration of the armistice ending World War I in 1918.

vet·er·i·nar·i·an (vĕt′ər-ə-**nâr**ʹē-ən *or* vĕt′rə-**nâr**ʹē-ən) *n.* A person specially trained and qualified to give medical treatment to animals.

vet·er·i·nar·y (vĕt**ʹ**ər-ə-nĕr′ē *or* vĕt**ʹ**rə-nĕr′ē) *adj.* Relating to the medical treatment, diseases, or injuries of animals: *a veterinary college.*

ve·to (vē**ʹ**tō) *n., pl.* **ve·toes 1a.** The constitutional power of the chief executive of a state or nation to prevent or delay the enactment of legislation passed by the legislature: *The president has the veto and will use it.* **b.** An instance in which this right is exercised: *the governor's veto of the bill.* **2.** A prohibition or rejection of a proposed or intended act: *Her plans to host a sleepover were met with a parental veto.* ❖ *tr.v.* **ve·toed, ve·to·ing, ve·toes 1.** To prevent (a legislative bill) from becoming law by exercising the power of veto. **2.** To forbid, prohibit, or decide against: *The board vetoed all wage increases.* [From Latin *vetō*, I forbid.]

vex (vĕks) *tr.v.* **vexed, vex·ing, vex·es 1.** To irritate, bother, or frustrate: *was vexed at having to carry a heavy backpack.* **2.** To cause perplexity in; baffle: *The complexity of the software program vexed him.* **3.** To cause difficulty or trouble to: *renewed fighting that vexed the diplomats' efforts to secure a cease-fire.*

vex·a·tion (vĕk-**sā′**shən) *n.* **1.** The condition of being vexed; annoyance: *frowned in vexation.* **2.** A source of irritation or annoyance: *could no longer bear the vexations of the job.*

VHF *abbr.* An abbreviation of very high frequency.

VHS (vē′āch-**ĕs′**) A trademark for a videotape format.

vi·a (**vī′**ə *or* **vē′**ə) *prep.* **1.** By way of: *going to Washington via New York City.* **2.** By means of: *sent the picture via email.*

vi·a·ble (**vī′**ə-bəl) *adj.* **1.** Capable of success or continuing effectiveness: *a viable plan.* **2.** Capable of continuing to live, grow, or develop: *viable seeds; a prematurely born but viable infant.* **—vi′a·bil′i·ty** *n.*

vi·a·duct (**vī′**ə-dŭkt′) *n.* A series of spans or arches used to carry a road or railroad over a wide valley or other roads or railroads. [From Latin *via*, road + *(aque)duct*.]

vi·al (**vī′**əl) *n.* A small glass container, usually having a closure, used especially for liquids.

❑ *These sound alike:* **vial, viol** (stringed instrument).

vi·and (**vī′**ənd) *n.* **1.** An item of food. **2. viands** Provisions; victuals.

vi·brant (**vī′**brənt) *adj.* **1.** Pulsing or throbbing with energy or activity. **2.** Vigorous, lively, and vital. **3.** Showing or marked by rapid rhythmic movement; vibrating.

vi·brate (**vī′**brāt′) *v.* **vi·brat·ed, vi·brat·ing, vi·brates** —*intr.* **1.** To move back and forth or to and fro, especially rhythmically and rapidly. **2.** To produce a sound; resonate. —*tr.* To cause to move back and forth rapidly. ❖ *n.* A setting on a cell phone that causes the phone to shake rapidly without producing a ringtone when a call or message is received. [From Latin *vibrāre*.] **—vi′bra·to′ry** (**vī′**brə-tôr′ē) *adj.*

vi·bra·tion (vī-**brā′**shən) *n.* **1a.** The act of vibrating. **b.** The condition of being vibrated. **2.** A rapid motion of a particle or an elastic solid back and forth in a straight line on both sides of a center position. **—vi·bra′tion·al** *adj.*

vi·bra·to (və-**brä′**tō) *n., pl.* **vi·bra·tos** A tremulous or pulsating effect produced in an instrumental or vocal tone by small rapid variations in pitch.

vi·bra·tor (**vī′**brā′tər) *n.* Something that vibrates, especially an electrical device used for massage.

vi·bur·num (vī-**bûr′**nəm) *n.* Any of various shrubs or small trees having rounded clusters of small white or pink flowers.

vic·ar (**vĭk′**ər) *n.* **1.** A salaried priest in charge of a parish. **2.** In the Roman Catholic Church, a priest who acts for or represents another member of the clergy, especially one of higher rank.

vic·ar·age (**vĭk′**ər-ĭj) *n.* **1.** The residence of a vicar. **2.** The office or duties of a vicar.

vi·car·i·ous (vī-**kâr′**ē-əs) *adj.* **1.** Experienced or felt by identifying with or by imaginary participation in the life of another person: *the vicarious thrills provided by reading an adventure story.* **2.** Endured or done by one person substituting for another: *vicarious punishment.* **—vi·car′i·ous·ly** *adv.*

vice[1] (vīs) *n.* **1.** A practice or habit that is considered to be evil, degrading, or immoral. **2.** Wicked or evil conduct or habits; corruption. **3.** A slight personal failing; a foible. [From Middle English, from Latin *vitium*.]

❑ *These sound alike:* **vice**[1] (wickedness), **vise** (tool).

vice[2] (vīs) *n. & v.* Variant of **vise.**

vice admiral *n.* A commissioned officer in the US Navy or Coast Guard, ranking above rear admiral and below admiral.

vice presidency or **vice-pres·i·den·cy** (vīs-**prĕz′**ĭ-dən-sē) *n.* The office of a vice president or the period during which a vice president is in office.

vice president or **vice-pres·i·dent** (**vīs′prĕz′**ĭ-dənt) *n.* An officer ranking next below a president and having authority to take the president's place in case of absence, illness, or death.

vice·roy (**vīs′**roi′) *n.* **1.** A person who is the governor of a country, province, or colony, ruling as the representative of a sovereign. **2.** An orange and black North American butterfly that resembles but is smaller than the monarch butterfly.

vi·ce ver·sa (vī′sə **vûr′**sə *or* vīs′ **vûr′**sə) *adv.* With the order or meaning reversed; conversely: *studying how hormones affect behavior, and vice versa.*

vi·chys·soise (vĭsh′ē-**swäz′**) *n.* A creamy potato soup flavored with leeks or onions and usually served cold.

vi·cin·i·ty (vĭ-**sĭn′**ĭ-tē) *n., pl.* **vi·cin·i·ties 1.** The state of being near in space or relationship; proximity. **2.** A nearby or surrounding region or place. **3.** An approximate degree or amount: *houses priced in the vicinity of $300,000.*

vi·cious (**vĭsh′**əs) *adj.* **1.** Deliberately hurtful; spiteful or malicious: *vicious gossip.* **2.** Disposed to or marked by violent or destructive behavior: *a vicious dog.* **3.** Severe or intense; fierce: *a vicious storm.* **—vi′cious·ly** *adv.*

vicious circle *n.* **1.** A situation in which the apparent solution of one problem creates a new problem and increases the difficulty of solving the original problem. **2.** A type of faulty reasoning in which the premise is used to prove the conclusion and the conclusion used to prove the premise.

vi·cis·si·tude (vĭ-**sĭs′**ĭ-to͞od′) *n.* **1.** A change or variation. **2.** A usually unforeseen change in circumstance or experience that affects one's life, especially in a trying way.

vic·tim (**vĭk′**tĭm) *n.* **1.** A person who is harmed or killed by another or by an act, agency, or condition: *the victim of a burglar; the victims of an epidemic.* **2.** A living creature killed as a religious sacrifice. **3.** A person who is tricked, swindled, or taken advantage of: *the victim of a hoax.* [From Latin *victima*.]

vic·tim·ize (**vĭk′**tə-mīz′) *tr.v.* **vic·tim·ized, vic·tim·iz·ing, vic·tim·iz·es** To make a victim of.

vic·tor (**vĭk′**tər) *n.* The winner in a fight, battle, contest, or struggle.

vic·to·ri·a (vĭk-**tôr′**ē-ə) *n.* A low, light, four-wheeled carriage for two, with a folding top and a raised seat in front for the driver. [After Queen *Victoria*.]

Vic·to·ri·a[1] (vĭk-**tôr′**ē-ə) 1819–1901. Queen of Great Britain and Ireland (1837–1901) and empress of India (1876–1901). Her reign was marked by the expansion of the British Empire and industrial growth.

Vic·to·ri·a[2] (vĭk-**tôr′**ē-ə) **1.** The capital of British Columbia, Canada, on southeast Vancouver Island. It was founded in 1843 and became the capital in the late 1860s. **2.** The capital of Hong Kong, on the northwest coast of Hong Kong Island. **3.** The capital of Seychelles, on the Indian Ocean north-northeast of Madagascar.

Victoria, Lake A lake of east-central Africa bordered by Uganda, Kenya, and Tanzania.

Vic·to·ri·an (vĭk-**tôr′**ē-ən) *adj.* **1.** Relating to or belonging to the period of the reign of Queen Victoria: *a Victorian novel.* **2.** Relating to or displaying the standards

Mount Vesuvius
engraving depicting the eruption of Mount Vesuvius in AD 79

viaduct

Victoria[1]
1859 portrait in her coronation regalia, by Franz Xaver Winterhalter (1805–1873)

Élisabeth Vigée-Lebrun
1800 self-portrait

WRITERS CHOOSE THEIR WORDS

"You are not paid to be idle," the captain often declared, and he, setting an example, was never slack in *his* duty. Even at our teas, he was **vigilant**—again, so like my father—and patiently examined me as to what I had seen, heard, or even thought—always ready with quick and wise correction.

—Avi
The True Confessions of Charlotte Doyle

ă	pat	ôr	core
ā	pay	oi	boy
âr	care	ou	out
ä	father	o͝o	took
ĕ	pet	o͝or	lure
ē	be	o͞o	boot
ĭ	pit	ŭ	cut
ī	bite	ûr	urge
îr	pier	th	thin
ŏ	pot	*th*	this
ō	toe	zh	vision
ô	paw	ə	about

or ideals of morality regarded as typical of the time of Queen Victoria. **—Vic·to′ri·an·ism** *n.*

vic·to·ri·ous (vĭk-**tôr′**ē-əs) *adj.* **1.** Being the winner in a contest or struggle: *the victorious team.* **2.** Characteristic of or expressing a sense of victory or fulfillment: *a victorious cheer.* **—vic·to′ri·ous·ly** *adv.*

vic·to·ry (**vĭk′**tə-rē) *n., pl.* **vic·to·ries 1.** A defeat of an enemy or opponent: *The soccer team savored its victory over their rivals.* **2.** A success in a struggle against difficulties or an obstacle: *Acting in the play was a victory over his greatest fear.* **3.** The state or fact of having defeated an opponent or of having achieved success: *Soldiers marched into the city in victory.* [From Middle English *victorie,* from Latin *victōria,* from *victor,* victor.]

vict·ual (**vĭt′**l) *n.* **1.** Food fit for human consumption. **2. victuals** Food supplies; provisions. [From Middle English *vitali,* from Late Latin *vīctuālia,* from Latin *vīctus,* nourishment.]

vi·cu·ña also **vi·cu·na** (vĭ-**ko͞o′**nyə *or* vī-**ko͞o′**nyə *or* vī-**ko͞o′**nə) *n.* **1.** A mammal of the Andes mountains of South America, related to the llama and having fine silky wool. **2a.** The wool of this mammal. **b.** Fabric made from this wool. [From Spanish, from Quechua *wikuña.*]

vid·e·o (**vĭd′**ē-ō′) *n., pl.* **vid·e·os 1.** A sequence of images processed electronically into an analog or digital format and displayed on a screen with sufficient rapidity as to create the illusion of motion and continuity. **2.** A movie recorded electronically. **3.** A music video.

vid·e·o·cas·sette (vĭd′ē-ō-kə-**sĕt′**) *n.* A cassette containing blank or prerecorded videotape.

vid·e·o·disc also **vid·e·o·disk** (**vĭd′**ē-ō-dĭsk′) *n.* A disc on which sounds and images, such as of a movie, are recorded.

video display *n.* A device, such as a computer screen, that gives information in visual form.

video game *n.* An electronic game played by manipulating moving figures on a display screen, often designed for play on a special gaming console rather than a personal computer.

vid·e·o·tape (**vĭd′**ē-ō-tāp′) *n.* A relatively wide magnetic tape used to record visual images and associated sound for later playback or broadcasting. ❖ *tr.v.* **vid·e·o·taped, vid·e·o·tap·ing, vid·e·o·tapes** To record on videotape: *videotape a wedding.*

vie (vī) *intr.v.* **vied, vy·ing** (**vī′**ĭng), **vies** To strive for victory or superiority; contend.

Vi·en·na (vē-**ĕn′**ə) The capital of Austria, in the northeast part of the country on the Danube River. Originally a Celtic settlement, it became the official residence of the house of Habsburg in 1278 and a leading cultural center in the 1700s.

Vien·tiane (vyĕn-**tyän′**) The capital of Laos, in the north-central part of the country on the Mekong River and the border of Thailand.

Vi·et·cong also **Vi·et Cong** (vē-ĕt′**kŏng′**) *n., pl.* **Vietcong** also **Viet Cong** A Vietnamese belonging to or supporting the National Liberation Front of the former country of South Vietnam.

Vi·et·nam (vē-ĕt′**näm′** *or* vē′ĭt-**näm′**) A country of southeast Asia in eastern Indochina on the South China Sea. It was divided between the countries of **North Vietnam** and **South Vietnam** after 1954. Vietnam was reunited in July 1976 after the end of the Vietnam War (1959–1975). Hanoi is the capital and Ho Chi Minh City the largest city.

Vi·et·nam·ese (vē-ĕt′nə-**mēz′** *or* vē-ĕt′nə-**mēs′**) *adj.* Relating to Vietnam or its people, language, or culture. ❖ *n., pl.* **Vietnamese 1.** A native or inhabitant of Vietnam. **2.** The language of Vietnam.

Vietnam War *n.* A war (1954–1975) in which the United States supported South Vietnam against Communist North Vietnam. After North Vietnam won the war, the country was united under Communist rule.

view (vyo͞o) *n.* **1a.** An examination using the eyes; a look or inspection: *picked up the rock for a closer view.* **b.** Range or field of sight: *The airplane disappeared from view.* **2a.** A scene that can be looked at from a particular position; a vista: *the view from the top of the mountain.* **b.** A way of showing or seeing something, as from a particular position or angle: *a side view of the house.* **3.** An opinion; a personal perception: *her views on education.* **4.** An aim; an intention: *These laws were made with the view of providing equal rights for all.* ❖ *tr.v.* **viewed, view·ing, views 1a.** To look at, examine, or inspect: *viewed the stars through the telescope.* **b.** To watch (a program, for example) on television. **2.** To survey or study mentally; consider: *When you view all their suggestions, you have to feel encouraged.* **3.** To think of (something) in a particular way; regard: *doesn't view herself as a success; viewed their efforts unfavorably.* See Synonyms at **see**[1]. ◆ **in view of** Taking into account; in consideration of. **on view** Placed so as to be seen; exhibited: *The photographs will be on view through next month.* [From Middle English *veue,* from Anglo-Norman, from Latin *vidēre,* to see.]

view·er (**vyo͞o′**ər) *n.* **1.** A person who views something, especially an onlooker or spectator. **2.** Any of various devices used to magnify photographic images so that they are easily visible.

view·find·er (**vyo͞o′**fīn′dər) *n.* A device on a camera that indicates what will appear in the field of view of the lens.

view·point (**vyo͞o′**point′) *n.* A position from which something is observed or considered; a point of view.

Vi·gée-Le·brun (vē-**zhā′**lə-**brœɴ′**), **(Marie Louise) Élisabeth** 1755–1842. French painter noted for her portraits, especially those of Marie Antoinette and the royal family of France.

vig·il (**vĭj′**əl) *n.* **1.** A watch kept during normal sleeping hours: *a vigil at the bedside of her sick friend.* **2.** The act or a period of observing; surveillance. **3.** The eve of a religious festival observed by staying awake as a devotional exercise. **4. vigils** Services held on the eve of a religious festival. [From Middle English *vigile,* from Latin *vigilia,* wakefulness, watch.]

vig·i·lance (**vĭj′**ə-ləns) *n.* Alert watchfulness.

vig·i·lant (**vĭj′**ə-lənt) *adj.* On the alert; watchful. **—vig′i·lant·ly** *adv.*

vig·i·lan·te (vĭj′ə-**lăn′**tē) *n.* A person who is not a member of law enforcement but who pursues and punishes those who are suspected of breaking the law.

vi·gnette (vĭn-**yĕt′**) *n.* **1.** A decorative design near the beginning or end of a chapter or book or along the border of the page. **2.** A picture that shades off into the surrounding color at the edges. **3.** A short literary sketch or scene from a movie.

vig·or (**vĭg′**ər) *n.* **1.** Physical or mental energy or strength. **2.** The capacity for growth and survival, as of plants or animals. **3.** Strong feeling; enthusiasm or intensity: *The opposing party, with great vigor, claimed the disputed votes for their candidate.* [From Middle English *vigour,* from Latin *vigor,* from *vigēre,* to be lively.]

vig·or·ous (**vĭg′**ər-əs) *adj.* **1.** Strong and healthy; robust: *a nest of vigorous young birds.* **2.** Marked by or done with force and energy: *vigorous exercise.* **—vig′or·ous·ly** *adv.*

vig·our (**vĭg′**ər) *n. Chiefly British* Variant of **vigor.**

Vi·king (**vī′**kĭng) *n.* One of a seafaring Scandinavian people who raided the coasts of northern and western Europe from the eighth through the tenth century.

vile (vīl) *adj.* **vil·er, vil·est 1.** Hateful; disgusting: *vile language.* **2.** Unpleasant or objectionable: *vile weather.* **3.** Miserable; base; wretched. [From Middle English, from Latin *vīlis,* cheap, worthless.] **—vile′ly** *adv.* **—vile′ness** *n.*

vil·i·fy (vĭl′ə-fī′) *tr.v.* **vil·i·fied, vil·i·fy·ing, vil·i·fies** To attack the reputation of (a person or thing) with strong or abusive criticism. **—vil′i·fi·ca′tion** (vĭl′ə-fĭ-**kā′**shən) *n.* **—vil′i·fi′er** *n.*

vil·la (vĭl′ə) *n.* A large and luxurious country house of a rich person.

Vil·la (vē′ə *or* bē′yä), **Francisco** Known as "Pancho." 1878?–1923. Mexican revolutionary leader who ran unsuccessfully for the presidency after the Mexican Revolution (1910).

vil·lage (vĭl′ĭj) *n.* **1.** A small group of homes and other buildings in a rural area, forming a community smaller than a town. **2.** The inhabitants of a village: *The entire village welcomed the newcomers.* [From Middle English, from Latin *vīllāticum*, farmstead.]

vil·lag·er (vĭl′ə-jər) *n.* A person who lives in a village.

vil·lain (vĭl′ən) *n.* **1.** A wicked or very bad person; a scoundrel. **2.** A dramatic or fictional character who is typically at odds with the hero. **3.** (*also* **vĭl′ān′** *or* vĭ-**lān′**) Variant of **villein. 4.** Something said to be the cause of particular trouble. [From Middle English *vilein*, feudal serf, from Old French, from Latin *vīlla*, country house.]

❑ *These sound alike:* **villain, villein** (serf).

vil·lain·ous (vĭl′ə-nəs) *adj.* Appropriate to or characteristic of a villain. **—vil′lain·ous·ly** *adv.*

vil·lain·y (vĭl′ə-nē) *n., pl.* **vil·lain·ies 1.** Villainous conduct or action. **2.** A villainous act.

vil·lein also **vil·lain** (vĭl′ən *or* **vĭl′**ān′ *or* vĭ-**lān′**) *n.* One of a class of feudal serfs who held the legal status of freemen in their dealings with all people except their lords.

❑ *These sound alike:* **villein, villain** (scoundrel).

vil·lus (vĭl′əs) *n., pl.* **vil·li** (vĭl′ī) A small projection on the surface of a mucous membrane, especially that of the small intestine.

Vil·ni·us (vĭl′nē-əs) or **Vil·na** (vĭl′nə) The capital of Lithuania, in the southeast part of the country. It was founded in 1323.

vim (vĭm) *n.* Liveliness and energy; enthusiasm.

vin·ai·grette (vĭn′ĭ-**grĕt′**) *n.* A sauce or dressing of vinegar or lemon juice and oil, often flavored with seasonings.

vin·di·cate (vĭn′dĭ-kāt′) *tr.v.* **vin·di·cat·ed, vin·di·cat·ing, vin·di·cates 1.** To clear of accusation, blame, suspicion, or doubt with supporting proof: *He vindicated himself of the charges.* **2.** To defend or maintain (one's rights, for example). **3.** To justify or support: *vindicate one's claim.*

vin·dic·tive (vĭn-**dĭk′**tĭv) *adj.* Having or showing a desire for revenge; vengeful. **—vin·dic′tive·ly** *adv.* **—vin·dic′tive·ness** *n.*

vine (vīn) *n.* **1a.** A plant having a stem that climbs on, creeps along, twines around, or clings to something for support. **b.** The stem of such a plant. **2.** A grapevine. [From Middle English, from Latin *vīnea*.]

vin·e·gar (vĭn′ĭ-gər) *n.* A sour liquid containing acetic acid, produced by fermenting an alcohol-containing liquid such as wine and used to flavor or preserve food.

vin·e·gar·y (vĭn′ĭ-gə-rē *or* **vĭn′**ĭ-grē) *adj.* **1.** Having the taste, smell, or nature of vinegar. **2.** Unpleasant.

vine·yard (vĭn′yərd) *n.* A tract of land where grapes are grown.

vin·tage (vĭn′tĭj) *n.* **1.** The grapes or wine produced by a particular vineyard or district in a single season. **2.** The year or place in which a wine is bottled. **3.** *Informal* A year or period of origin: *drives a car of 1950 vintage.* ❖ *adj.* **1.** Relating to a vintage. **2.** Characterized by excellence and maturity; classic. **3.** Of the best or most characteristic: *played songs that were vintage John Lennon.*

vint·ner (vĭnt′nər) *n.* A person who makes or sells wine.

vi·nyl (vī′nəl) *n.* **1.** The chemical radical CH_2CH, derived from ethylene and having a valence of 1. **2.** Any of various chemical compounds, typically highly reactive, that contain this radical, used in making plastics. **3.** Any of various plastics, typically tough, flexible, and shiny, often used in upholstery and clothing. **4.** Phonograph records considered as a group.

vi·ol (vī′əl) *n.* Any of a family of stringed instruments, chiefly of the 1500s and 1600s, having a flat back and usually six strings and played with a curved bow.

❑ *These sound alike:* **viol, vial** (glass container).

vi·o·la (vē-ō′lə) *n.* A musical instrument of the violin family, slightly larger than a violin, tuned a fifth lower, and having a deeper tone. **—vi·o′list** *n.*

vi·o·late (vī′ə-lāt′) *tr.v.* **vi·o·lat·ed, vi·o·lat·ing, vi·o·lates 1.** To disregard or act in a manner that does not conform to (a law or promise, for example). **2.** To do harm to (something sacred or highly respected); desecrate or defile: *violate a shrine.* **3.** To assault (a person) sexually. **4.** To disturb rudely or interrupt.

vi·o·la·tion (vī′ə-**lā′**shən) *n.* The act or an instance of violating or the condition of being violated: *the violation of a truce; a traffic violation.*

vi·o·lence (vī′ə-ləns) *n.* **1.** Action or behavior in which physical force is exerted for the purpose of causing damage or injury: *the violence of the rioters.* **2.** Great force or intensity: *the violence of a hurricane.* **3.** Extreme or powerful emotion or expression: *was frightened by the violence of his speeches.*

vi·o·lent (vī′ə-lənt) *adj.* **1.** Causing or intending to cause damage, injury, or death, often when involving great force: *a violent attack; violent blows.* **2.** Characterized by or displaying physical violence: *a man with a violent past; a violent movie.* **3.** Caused by unexpected force or injury rather than by natural causes: *a violent death.* **4.** Very forceful or intense: *a violent storm.* **5.** Having or showing great emotion, especially anger: *a violent outburst.* [From Middle English, from Latin *violentus*, from *vīs*, force.] **—vi′o·lent·ly** *adv.*

vi·o·let (vī′ə-lĭt) *n.* **1.** Any of various low-growing plants having flowers that are usually bluish-purple but are sometimes yellow or white. **2.** A bluish purple. [From Middle English, from Old French *violete*, from Latin *viola*.]

vi·o·lin (vī′ə-**lĭn′**) *n.* A stringed instrument held horizontally at the shoulder and played with a bow, having four strings tuned at intervals of a fifth and an unfretted fingerboard. [From Italian *violino*, small viola.] **—vi′o·lin′ist** *n.*

vi·o·lon·cel·lo (vē′ə-lən-**chĕl′**ō) *n., pl.* **vi·o·lon·cel·los** A cello. **—vi′o·lon·cel′list** *n.*

VIP (vē′ī-**pē′**) *n. Informal* A person of great importance. [From *v(ery) i(mportant) p(erson).*]

vi·per (vī′pər) *n.* **1.** Any of various venomous snakes chiefly of Eurasia and Africa, having a thick heavy body and a single pair of long hollow fangs. **2.** A wicked or hateful person. [From Middle English *vipera*, from Latin *vīpera*, snake.]

vi·per·ous (vī′pər-əs) *adj.* **1.** Suggestive of or relating to a viper: *viperous snakes.* **2.** Wicked; hateful: *a viperous traitor.*

vi·ra·go (və-rä′gō *or* və-**rā′**gō) *n., pl.* **vi·ra·goes** or **vi·ra·gos 1.** A woman regarded as noisy, scolding, or bossy. **2.** A large, strong, courageous woman.

vi·ral (vī′rəl) *adj.* **1.** Relating to or caused by a virus: *viral diseases.* **2.** Relating to the spread of information, ideas, or trends by means of social networks rather than conventional mass media: *a viral video.*

vir·e·o (vîr′ē-ō′) *n., pl.* **vir·e·os** Any of various small insect-eating grayish or greenish songbirds.

Vir·gil also **Ver·gil** (vûr′jəl) 70–19 BC. Roman poet who composed the *Aeneid*, an epic that tells of the wanderings of Aeneas after the sack of Troy.

Pancho Villa
photographed c. 1913

violin

GEOGRAPHY

Virginia The name **Virginia** is a Latin term that was given to the territory in 1584 by Queen Elizabeth I of England, who was known as "the Virgin Queen" because she never married. In 1863, after Virginia seceded from the United States during the Civil War, the western portion of the state voted to remain in the Union, forming the state of **West Virginia.**

Virginia creeper

vise

ă	pat	ôr	core
ā	pay	oi	boy
âr	care	ou	out
ä	father	o͝o	took
ĕ	pet	o͝or	lure
ē	be	o͞o	boot
ĭ	pit	ŭ	cut
ī	bite	ûr	urge
îr	pier	th	thin
ŏ	pot	*th*	this
ō	toe	zh	vision
ô	paw	ə	about

vir·gin (vûr′jĭn) *n.* **1.** A person who has not experienced sexual intercourse. **2. Virgin** The Virgin Mary. ❖ *adj.* **1.** Relating to or being a virgin; chaste. **2.** Being in a pure and natural state; untouched: *virgin snow.* **3.** Unused, uncultivated, or unexplored: *virgin forests.*

vir·gin·al (vûr′jə-nəl) *adj.* Relating to or appropriate to a virgin; chaste.

Vir·gin·ia (vər-jĭn′yə) A state of the eastern United States on the Atlantic Ocean north of North Carolina. It was admitted as one of the original Thirteen Colonies in 1788. Richmond is the capital and Virginia Beach the largest city. —SEE NOTE.

Virginia Algonquian *n.* The extinct Eastern Algonquian language of eastern Virginia.

Virginia Beach A city of Virginia in the southeast part of the state on the Atlantic Ocean east of Norfolk. It is a popular resort.

Virginia creeper *n.* A North American climbing vine having leaves with five leaflets and bluish-black berries.

Virginia reel *n.* An American dance in which two lines of couples face each other and perform various steps together to instructions called out by a leader.

Virgin Islands A group of islands of the northeast West Indies east of Puerto Rico. They are divided into the British Virgin Islands to the northeast and the United States Virgin Islands to the southwest.

vir·gin·i·ty (vər-jĭn′ĭ-tē) *n., pl.* **vir·gin·i·ties 1.** The quality or condition of being a virgin. **2.** The state of being pure or untouched.

Virgin Mary See **Mary.**

Vir·go (vûr′gō) *n.* **1.** A constellation near the celestial equator, traditionally pictured as a young woman. **2.** The sixth sign of the zodiac in astrology.

vir·ile (vîr′əl *or* vîr′īl′) *adj.* **1.** Relating to or having the characteristics of a strong or robust man, especially in being able to have sexual intercourse. **2.** Energetic or forceful: *a virile performance of the song.* **—vi·ril′i·ty** (və-rĭl′ĭ-tē) *n.* —SEE NOTE AT **werewolf.**

vi·rol·o·gy (vī-rŏl′ə-jē) *n.* The study of viruses and viral diseases. **—vi·rol′o·gist** *n.*

vir·tu·al (vûr′cho͞o-əl) *adj.* **1.** Existing in effect though not in actual fact, form, or name: *the virtual extinction of the buffalo.* **2.** Relating to or simulated by a computer or computer network: *virtual conversations in a chatroom.*

virtual image *n.* An image, such as one seen in a mirror, from which rays of reflected or refracted light appear to split apart from each other.

vir·tu·al·ly (vûr′cho͞o-ə-lē) *adv.* **1.** In fact or to all purposes; practically: *The city was virtually paralyzed by the blizzard.* **2.** Almost but not quite; nearly: *Virtually every household has a TV these days.*

virtual reality *n.* A computer simulation of a system, situation, or environment that enables a user to perform actions within the system and shows the effects of the actions in real time.

vir·tue (vûr′cho͞o) *n.* **1a.** Moral excellence and righteousness; goodness. **b.** A particular example or kind of moral excellence: *the virtue of patience.* **2.** A particularly effective, good, or beneficial quality; an advantage: *a plan with the virtue of being practical.* **3.** Effective force or power; ability to produce a definite result: *believing in the virtue of vitamins to fight colds.* ◆ **by virtue of** or **in virtue of** On the grounds or basis of; by reason of: *She is considered a great writer by virtue of her powerful prose style.* —SEE NOTE AT **werewolf.**

vir·tu·os·i·ty (vûr′cho͞o-ŏs′ĭ-tē) *n., pl.* **vir·tu·os·i·ties** Great technical skill or captivating personal style, especially as exhibited in the arts.

vir·tu·o·so (vûr′cho͞o-ō′sō *or* vûr′cho͞o-ō′zō) *n., pl.* **vir·tu·o·sos** or **vir·tu·o·si** (vûr′cho͞o-ō′sē) **1.** A musical performer of great excellence, technique, or ability. **2.** A person of great skill or technique: *a chef who was a virtuoso in the kitchen.* ❖ *adj.* Exhibiting the ability, technique, or personal style of a virtuoso: *a virtuoso performance.*

vir·tu·ous (vûr′cho͞o-əs) *adj.* Having or showing virtue, especially moral excellence: *virtuous conduct.* **—vir′tu·ous·ly** *adv.*

vir·u·lent (vîr′yə-lənt *or* vîr′ə-lənt) *adj.* **1.** Extremely infectious, malignant, or poisonous, as a disease or toxin: *a virulent strain of flu.* **2.** Extremely hostile or malicious: *virulent criticism.* **—vir′u·lence, vir′u·len·cy** *n.*

vi·rus (vī′rəs) *n., pl.* **vi·rus·es 1.** Any of various agents that infect living organisms, often causing disease. Viruses consist of a single or double strand of RNA or DNA surrounded by an outer coat made of protein. Because viruses can only multiply when they are inside a living cell, they are usually not considered living organisms. **2.** A computer program that can replicate itself and that spreads by inserting copies of itself into other files or programs which users later transfer to other computers. [From Latin *vīrus,* poison.]

vi·sa (vē′zə) *n.* An official authorization added to a passport, permitting entry into and travel within a particular country or region.

vis·age (vĭz′ĭj) *n.* **1.** The face or facial expression of a person. **2.** Appearance; aspect: *the green visage of spring.*

vis·cer·a (vĭs′ər-ə) *pl.n.* The soft internal organs of the body, especially those contained within the abdomen and thorax.

vis·cer·al (vĭs′ər-əl) *adj.* **1.** Relating to, situated in, or affecting the viscera. **2.** Being or arising from impulse or sudden emotion rather than from thought or deliberation: *an immediate, visceral reaction to an insult.* **—vis′cer·al·ly** *adv.*

vis·cid (vĭs′ĭd) *adj.* Thick and sticky; resembling glue. Used of a fluid. **—vis′cid·ly** *adv.*

vis·cos·i·ty (vĭ-skŏs′ĭ-tē) *n., pl.* **vis·cos·i·ties 1.** The condition or property of being viscous. **2.** The degree to which a fluid resists flow when pressure is applied to it.

vis·count (vī′kount′) *n.* A nobleman ranking below an earl or count and above a baron.

vis·count·ess (vī′koun′tĭs) *n.* **1.** The wife or widow of a viscount. **2.** A noblewoman holding the rank of viscount in her own right.

vis·cous (vĭs′kəs) *adj.* **1.** Tending to resist flow when pressure is applied, as a fluid; having a high viscosity. **2.** Sticky. **—vis′cous·ly** *adv.*

vise also **vice** (vīs) *n.* A heavy clamp, usually mounted on a workbench and operated by a screw or lever, used in carpentry or metalworking to hold a piece in position. [From Middle English *vis,* screwlike device, from Latin *vītis,* vine.]

❑ *These sound alike:* **vise, vice[1]** (wickedness).

Vish·nu (vĭsh′no͞o) *n.* One of the principal Hindu gods, worshiped as a protector and preserver of worlds.

vis·i·bil·i·ty (vĭz′ə-bĭl′ĭ-tē) *n., pl.* **vis·i·bil·i·ties 1.** The fact or degree of being visible. **2.** The greatest distance over which it is possible to see without aid from instruments under given weather conditions. **3.** The capability of being easily observed.

vis·i·ble (vĭz′ə-bəl) *adj.* **1.** Possible to see; perceptible to the eye: *a visible change of expression on her face.* **2.** Easily noticed; clear; apparent: *no visible solution to the problem.* **—vis′i·bly** *adv.*

visible light *n.* See **light[1]** (sense 1).

Vis·i·goth (vĭz′ĭ-gŏth′) *n.* A member of the western Goths that invaded the Roman Empire in the fourth century AD and settled in France and Spain.

vi·sion (vĭzh′ən) *n.* **1.** The sense of sight; eyesight. **2.** Unusual discernment; intelligent foresight: *a leader of vision.* **3.** A mental image produced by the imagination: *having visions of warm summer days.* **4.** The mystical experience of seeing something that is not in fact present to the eye or is supernatural. **5.** A person or thing of great beauty: *The mountains were a vision of newly fallen snow.* [From Middle English *visioun*, from Latin *visiō*, from *vidēre*, to see.]

vi·sion·ar·y (vĭzh′ə-nĕr′ē) *adj.* **1.** Characterized by vision or foresight. **2.** Not practicable; existing only in the imagination: *visionary schemes for getting rich.* **3.** Marked by or given to apparitions, prophecies, or revelations. ❖ *n., pl.* **vi·sion·ar·ies 1.** A person given to impractical ideas; a dreamer. **2.** A person who has visions; a seer.

vis·it (vĭz′ĭt) *v.* **vis·it·ed, vis·it·ing, vis·its** *—tr.* **1.** To go to see for reasons of business, duty, or pleasure: *visit a dentist; visit one's family.* **2.** To stay with as a guest: *visiting his former classmate in California.* **3.** To go to see or spend time at (a place) with a certain intent: *visiting Chicago over the weekend.* **4.** To access (a website). **5.** To afflict or assail: *A plague visited the village.* *—intr.* **1.** To make a visit. **2.** *Informal* To converse or chat: *I hope you'll be able to stay and visit.* ❖ *n.* The act or an instance of visiting a person or place. [From Middle English *visiten*, from Latin *vīsitāre*.]

vis·i·tant (vĭz′ĭ-tənt) *n.* **1.** A visitor; a guest. **2.** A ghost or other supernatural being. ❖ *adj.* Visiting.

vis·i·ta·tion (vĭz′ĭ-tā′shən) *n.* **1.** The act or an instance of visiting, especially an official visit for the purpose of inspection or examination. **2.** The time set aside for a parent to be with a child who is in the custody of another person. **3. Visitation** In the Roman Catholic Church, the visit of the Virgin Mary to her cousin Elizabeth. It is commemorated on May 31. **4.** An inflicting of punishment or a dispensation of comfort regarded as being ordained by God.

vis·i·tor (vĭz′ĭ-tər) *n.* A person who visits.

vi·sor (vī′zər) *n.* **1.** A piece projecting from the front of a cap or headband to shade and protect the eyes. **2.** A transparent piece on the front of a safety helmet, designed to protect the face and eyes. **3.** A shield against glare attached above the windshield of an automobile. **4.** The front piece of the helmet of a suit of armor that protects the face and eyes while allowing the wearer to see through a narrow opening.

vis·ta (vĭs′tə) *n.* **1a.** A distant view, especially one seen through an opening, as between buildings or trees. **b.** A passage or avenue that provides such a view. **2.** A broad mental view or awareness of a series of events or subjects: *a scientific discovery that opens up new vistas of human improvement.* [From Italian, something seen.]

vi·su·al (vĭzh′o͞o-əl) *adj.* **1.** Relating to the sense of sight. **2.** Seen or able to be seen by the eye; visible: *a design with a dramatic visual effect.* **3.** Done or performed by means of sight alone: *visual navigation.* **4.** Relating to a method of instruction involving sight: *visual instruction; visual aids.* **5.** Relating to artwork, such as painting or sculpture, that appeals primarily to the sense of sight.

vi·su·al·ize (vĭzh′o͞o-ə-līz′) *v.* **vi·su·al·ized, vi·su·al·iz·ing, vi·su·al·iz·es** *—tr.* To form a mental image or vision of: *Try to visualize what our new house will look like.* *—intr.* To form a mental image. **—vi′su·al·i·za′tion** (vĭzh′o͞o-ə-lĭ-zā′shən) *n.*

vi·su·al·ly impaired (vĭzh′o͞o-ə-lē) *adj.* **1.** Having a weakened ability to see; partially sighted. **2.** Completely unable to see; blind. ❖ *n.* *(used with a plural verb)* People who have impaired vision or who are blind.

vi·tal (vīt′l) *adj.* **1.** Relating to or characteristic of life: *vital processes; vital signs.* **2.** Necessary to the continuation of life; life-sustaining: *vital organs; vital functions.* **3.** Full of life or energy; animated. **4.** Having great importance; essential: *Irrigation is vital to successful farming.* [From Middle English, from Latin *vīta*, life.] **—vi′tal·ly** *adv.* —SEE NOTE AT **quick.**

vi·tal·i·ty (vī-tăl′ĭ-tē) *n., pl.* **vi·tal·i·ties 1.** The capacity to live, grow, or develop. **2.** Physical or intellectual vigor; energy or liveliness. **3.** The capacity to endure: *the vitality of an old tradition.*

vi·tal·ize (vīt′l-īz′) *tr.v.* **vi·tal·ized, vi·tal·iz·ing, vi·tal·iz·es** To make more lively; invigorate: *The candidate's supporters were vitalized by polls showing her to be in the lead.* **—vi′tal·i·za′tion** (vīt′l-ĭ-zā′shən) *n.*

vi·tals (vīt′lz) *pl.n.* **1.** The vital body organs. **2.** The essential parts of something. **3.** The vital signs.

vital signs *pl.n.* Body temperature, heart rate, respiratory rate, and blood pressure, as measured to assess health.

vi·ta·min (vī′tə-mĭn) *n.* **1.** Any of various complex organic compounds that are needed in small amounts for normal growth and activity of the body. Bacteria and plants make them themselves, and animals obtain them chiefly from their food. **2.** A preparation containing one or more vitamins, often taken as a dietary supplement. [From Latin *vīta*, life + *amine*, a type of organic compound.] —SEE NOTE.

vitamin A *n.* A vitamin important for normal vision, tissue growth, and healthy skin. It is found in fish-liver oils, milk, leafy green vegetables, and yellow or orange vegetables and fruits.

vitamin B *n.* The vitamin B complex.

vitamin B1 *n.* Thiamine.

vitamin B2 *n.* Riboflavin.

vitamin B6 *n.* Pyridoxine.

vitamin B12 *n.* A vitamin of the B complex that contains cobalt. It is found in liver, seafood, and yeast and is used to treat anemia.

vitamin B complex *n.* Any of a group of related vitamins including thiamine, riboflavin, niacin, folic acid, and vitamin B_{12}. These vitamins are important for normal cell growth and metabolism.

vitamin C *n.* A vitamin important for healthy skin, teeth, bones, and blood vessels. It is found especially in citrus fruits, tomatoes, potatoes, and green vegetables.

vitamin D *n.* Any of a group of vitamins necessary for normal bone growth. Vitamin D is found in milk, fish, and eggs and can be produced in the skin on exposure to sunlight.

vitamin E *n.* A vitamin important for normal cell growth and function. It is found in vegetable oils, nuts, seeds, and certain fruits.

vitamin K *n.* Any of a group of vitamins important for normal clotting of the blood. Vitamin K is found chiefly in leafy green vegetables. Smaller amounts are found in vegetable oils and liver.

vi·ti·ate (vĭsh′ē-āt′) *tr.v.* **vi·ti·at·ed, vi·ti·at·ing, vi·ti·ates 1.** To reduce the value or quality of; impair or spoil. **2.** To make ineffective or worthless; invalidate: *vitiate a contract.* **—vi′ti·a′tion** *n.*

vit·i·cul·ture (vĭt′ĭ-kŭl′chər) *n.* The cultivation of grapes, especially for use in making wine.

vit·re·ous (vĭt′rē-əs) *adj.* **1.** Relating to, resembling, or having the nature of glass; glassy. **2.** Relating to the vitreous humor. [From Latin *vitrum*, glass.]

vitreous humor *n.* The jelly-like substance that fills the eyeball between the retina and the lens.

vit·ri·fy (vĭt′rə-fī′) *v.* **vit·ri·fied, vit·ri·fy·ing, vit·ri·fies** *—tr.* To change or make into glass or a similar substance, especially through melting by heat. *—intr.* To become vitreous.

vit·ri·ol (vĭt′rē-ōl′) *n.* **1.** Sulfuric acid. **2.** Any of various salts of sulfuric acid, such as ferrous sulfate, zinc sulfate, or copper sulfate. **3.** Bitterly abusive feeling or expression.

vit·ri·ol·ic (vĭt′rē-ŏl′ĭk) *adj.* **1.** Relating to, similar to, or derived from vitriol. **2.** Bitterly scathing; caustic: *a vitriolic remark.*

vi·tu·per·ate (vī-to͞o′pə-rāt′) *v.* **vi·tu·per·at·ed, vi·tu·**

Vishnu

visor

SCIENCE

vitamin Our bodies cannot function properly unless we have an adequate supply of **vitamins.** This link between vitamins and good health was made in the early 1900s by the Polish biochemist Casimir Funk. Funk was studying *beriberi,* a disease that damages nerves, when he discovered an organic compound that prevented this illness. He named the compound *vitamine* or "life amine." That compound is now known as *thiamine,* but the word *vitamin* came to be used for all similar compounds, even though most of them do not include a type of chemical called an *amine.* Today we know that vitamins help prevent a variety of illnesses. But because our bodies cannot produce these compounds, we must get them from the foods we eat or from supplements.

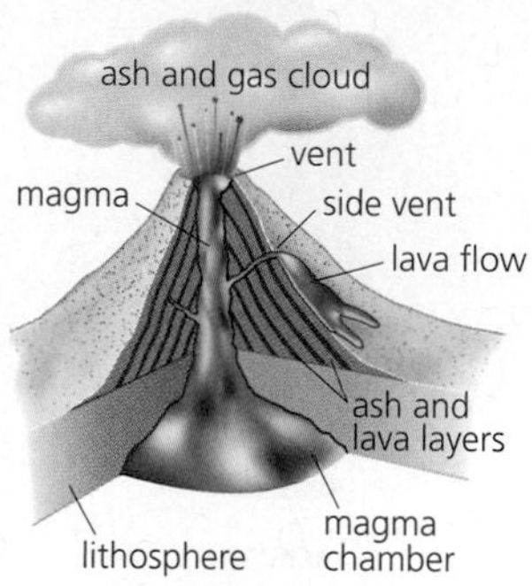

volcano

vole

volleyball

ă	pat	ôr	core
ā	pay	oi	boy
âr	care	ou	out
ä	father	o͝o	took
ĕ	pet	o͝or	lure
ē	be	o͞o	boot
ĭ	pit	ŭ	cut
ī	bite	ûr	urge
îr	pier	th	thin
ŏ	pot	*th*	this
ō	toe	zh	vision
ô	paw	ə	about

per·at·ing, vi·tu·per·ates —*tr.* To criticize harshly or angrily. —*intr.* To use harshly critical language; rail.

vi·tu·per·a·tion (vī-to͞o′pə-**rā′**shən) *n.* **1.** The act or an instance of criticizing harshly or abusively. **2.** Harshly critical language.

vi·tu·per·a·tive (vī-**to͞o′**pər-ə-tĭv) *adj.* Using, containing, or marked by harshly critical or irate language. —**vi·tu′per·a·tive·ly** *adv.*

vi·va (**vē′**və) *interj.* An expression used to show approval or applause.

vi·va·cious (vĭ-**vā′**shəs *or* vī-**vā′**shəs) *adj.* Full of animation and spirit; lively: *a vivacious host.* —**vi·va′cious·ly** *adv.* —**vi·vac′i·ty** (vĭ-**văs′**ĭ-tē *or* vī-**văs′**ĭ-tē) *n.*

viv·id (**vĭv′**ĭd) *adj.* **viv·id·er, viv·id·est 1.** Perceived as bright and distinct; brilliant: *a vivid star.* **2.** Having intensely bright color or colors: *a vivid tapestry; a vivid blue.* **3a.** Presented in a clear and striking manner; heard, seen, or felt as if real: *a vivid description.* **b.** Perceived or felt with the freshness of immediate experience: *a vivid recollection.* **4.** Active in forming lifelike images: *a vivid imagination.* [From Latin *vīvidus*, from *vīvere*, to live.] —**viv′id·ly** *adv.* —**viv′id·ness** *n.*

viv·i·fy (**vĭv′**ə-fī′) *tr.v.* **viv·i·fied, viv·i·fy·ing, viv·i·fies 1.** To give or bring life to; animate. **2.** To make more lively or intense; enliven.

vi·vip·a·rous (vī-**vĭp′**ər-əs) *adj.* Giving birth to living young that develop within the mother's body rather than hatching from eggs. Most mammals are viviparous.

viv·i·sect (**vĭv′**ĭ-sĕkt′) *tr.v.* **viv·i·sect·ed, viv·i·sect·ing, viv·i·sects** To perform vivisection on (an animal).

viv·i·sec·tion (vĭv′ĭ-**sĕk′**shən *or* **vĭv′**ĭ-sĕk′shən) *n.* The act or practice of cutting into or dissecting a living animal for the purpose of scientific research.

vix·en (**vĭk′**sən) *n.* **1.** A female fox. **2.** A woman regarded as sharp-tempered or quarrelsome. [From Middle English *fixen*, from Old English *fyxe.*]

viz. *abbr.* An abbreviation of videlicet (namely).

vi·zier (vĭ-**zîr′** *or* **vĭz′**yər) *n.* A high official in a Muslim government, especially in the Ottoman Empire. [From Arabic *wazīr*, minister.]

VJ *abbr.* An abbreviation of video jockey.

Vla·di·vos·tok (vlăd′ə-və-**stŏk′** *or* vlăd′ə-**vŏs′**tŏk′) A city of extreme southeast Russia on an arm of the Sea of Japan. It grew rapidly after the completion of the Trans-Siberian Railroad in the early 1900s.

vlog (vlŏg) *n.* A blog whose content primarily consists of videos. [From *v(ideo)* + *b(log).*]

V-neck (**vē′**nĕk′) *n.* A V-shaped neckline, as of a sweater.

vo·cab·u·lar·y (vō-**kăb′**yə-lĕr′ē) *n., pl.* **vo·cab·u·lar·ies 1.** All the words of a language. **2.** The sum of words used by or understood by a particular person or group: *a writer who uses a very rich vocabulary; the vocabulary of law.* **3.** A list of words and phrases, usually arranged alphabetically and defined or translated; a lexicon or glossary. [From Latin *vocābulum*, name.]

vo·cal (**vō′**kəl) *adj.* **1.** Relating to the production of sound through the mouth: *vocal quality; vocal organs.* **2.** Relating to or performed by singing: *vocal music.* **3.** Tending to speak often and freely; outspoken: *He is very vocal in his opposition to new taxes.* ❖ *n.* A part or melody that is sung in a musical performance or recording: *The drummer does the lead vocal on that song.* [From Middle English, from Latin *vōx*, voice.] —**vo′cal·ly** *adv.*

vocal cords *pl.n.* A pair of muscular bands or folds in the larynx that vibrate when air from the lungs is forced between them, thereby producing the sound of the voice.

vo·cal·ic (vō-**kăl′**ĭk) *adj.* **1.** Containing or consisting of vowels. **2.** Relating to or having the nature of a vowel.

vo·cal·ist (**vō′**kə-lĭst) *n.* A singer: *Six vocalists performed at the concert.*

vo·cal·ize (**vō′**kə-līz′) *v.* **vo·cal·ized, vo·cal·iz·ing, vo·cal·iz·es** —*tr.* **1.** To produce by using the vocal organs. **2.** To give voice to; articulate: *vocalize a popular opinion.* —*intr.* **1.** To use the vocal organs to produce sounds: *birds that vocalize in flight.* **2.** To sing. —**vo′cal·i·za′tion** (vō′kə-lĭ-**zā′**shən) *n.* —**vo′cal·iz′er** *n.*

vo·ca·tion (vō-**kā′**shən) *n.* **1.** A profession or occupation, especially one for which a person is particularly suited or qualified: *plans to make medicine her vocation.* **2.** An inclination for a certain kind of work: *a vocation for medicine.* **3.** A calling of an individual by God, especially for a religious career. —**vo·ca′tion·al** *adj.*

vocational school *n.* A school that offers instruction and training in skilled trades such as mechanics, plumbing, carpentry, and construction; a trade school.

vo·cif·er·ous (vō-**sĭf′**ər-əs) *adj.* Making, given to, or marked by a noisy and insistent outcry: *a vociferous crowd; vociferous protests.* —**vo·cif′er·ous·ly** *adv.*

vod·ka (**vŏd′**kə) *n.* An alcoholic liquor originally distilled from fermented wheat mash, but now also made from a mash of rye, corn, or potatoes.

vogue (vōg) *n.* **1.** The current fashion or style. **2.** Popular acceptance; popularity: *His novels enjoyed a great vogue in the 1930s.*

voice (vois) *n.* **1a.** The sound produced by the vocal organs of a vertebrate, especially a human. **b.** The ability to produce such sounds: *He caught a bad cold and lost his voice.* **2.** The condition or quality of a person's vocal sound: *a baritone in excellent voice; had a hoarse voice from coughing.* **3.** A singer. **4.** One of the individual melodic parts in a musical composition: *a fugue for four voices.* **5.** Expression or utterance, as of feelings or thoughts: *give voice to one's feelings.* **6.** The right or opportunity to express a choice or opinion: *The children had no voice in deciding where to spend their vacation.* **7.** A sound resembling or likened to a vocal sound or utterance: *the voice of the wind.* **8.** In grammar, a property of a verb that indicates the relation between the subject and the action expressed by the verb. English has two voices, active and passive. ❖ *tr.v.* **voiced, voic·ing, voic·es 1.** To give voice to; utter: *had a chance to voice her feelings.* **2.** To pronounce with vibration of the vocal cords. **3.** To provide the voice for (a cartoon character, for example). ◆ **with one voice** In complete agreement; unanimously: *Our group rejected the contract with one voice.* [From Middle English, from Latin *vōx.*]

voice box *n.* The larynx.

voiced (voist) *adj.* **1.** Having a voice or a specified kind of voice: *a soft-voiced person.* **2.** Uttered with vibration of the vocal cords, as the sounds (b) and (d).

voice·less (**vois′**lĭs) *adj.* **1.** Having no voice; mute. **2.** Uttered without vibration of the vocal cords, as the sounds (p) and (t).

voice·mail or **voice mail** (**vois′**māl′) *n.* **1.** Any of various systems for answering telephone calls and recording and saving messages. **2.** A recorded message left by a caller on a voicemail system.

voice-o·ver or **voice·o·ver** (**vois′**ō′vər) *n.* Narration or dialogue, such as in a movie or documentary, spoken by an unseen narrator or an onscreen character not seen speaking: *a character whose thoughts were revealed in a voice-over.*

void (void) *adj.* **1.** Containing no matter; empty. See Synonyms at **empty. 2.** Not occupied; unfilled: *a throne that was void.* **3.** Completely lacking; devoid: *void of all fear.* **4.** Having no legal force or validity: *declare a contract void.* ❖ *n.* An empty space; a vacuum: *the void of outer space.* ❖ *tr.v.* **void·ed, void·ing, voids 1.** To take out (the contents of something); empty. **2.** To excrete (body wastes). **3.** To leave; vacate. **4.** To make null; invalidate: *void an old passport.* [From Middle English, from Latin *vacīvus*, variant of *vacuus*, from *vacāre*, to be empty.]

voile (voil) *n.* A light sheer fabric of cotton, rayon, wool, or silk, used especially for making curtains and dresses.

vol. *abbr.* An abbreviation of volume.

vol·a·tile (vŏl**′**ə-tl *or* **vŏl′**ə-tīl′) *adj.* **1.** Changing to vapor easily or readily at normal temperatures and pressures. **2.** Changeable, especially: **a.** Inconstant; fickle: *the volatile preferences of the public.* **b.** Tending to erupt into violent action; explosive: *a volatile political situation.* [From Latin *volātilis*, flying, from *volāre*, to fly.] **—vol′a·til′i·ty** (vŏl′ə-**tĭl′**ĭ-tē) *n.*

vol·can·ic (vŏl-**kăn′**ĭk) *adj.* **1.** Relating to, resembling, or caused by a volcano or volcanoes. **2.** Produced or thrown from a volcano. **3.** Powerfully explosive: *a volcanic temper.*

vol·ca·no (vŏl-**kā′**nō) *n., pl.* **vol·ca·noes** or **vol·ca·nos** **1.** An opening in the earth's crust from which lava, ash, and hot gases flow or are ejected during an eruption. **2.** A usually cone-shaped mountain formed from the materials issuing from such an opening. [From Italian, from Latin *Volcānus*, the god Vulcan.]

vole (vōl) *n.* Any of various small rodents having a short muzzle and small ears.

Vol·ga (**vŏl′**gə *or* **vōl′**gə) A river of western Russia rising northwest of Moscow and flowing about 2,300 miles (3,700 kilometers) generally east and south to the Caspian Sea. It is the longest river of Europe.

Vol·go·grad (**vŏl′**gə-grăd′ *or* **vōl′**gə-grăd′) A city of southwest Russia on the Volga River. Known as Stalingrad from 1925 to 1961, it was besieged and severely damaged during World War II.

vo·li·tion (və-**lish′**ən) *n.* The act of making a conscious choice or decision: *He left of his own volition.*

vol·ley (**vŏl′**ē) *n., pl.* **vol·leys** **1a.** A simultaneous discharge of a number of bullets or other projectiles: *The fort's cannons responded to the attack with a volley.* **b.** The projectiles so discharged. **2.** A group of remarks, expressions, or actions directed toward a certain recipient or audience: *a volley of questions.* **3a.** An exchange of strokes in a court game, such as volleyball, ending when one side fails to make a good return and resulting in a point or the loss of service. **b.** A stroke, kick, or other strike of the ball made before the ball touches the ground. ❖ *v.* **vol·leyed, vol·ley·ing, vol·leys** *—tr.* **1.** To discharge (projectiles) in a volley. **2.** In sports, to strike (a tennis ball, for example) before it touches the ground. *—intr.* **1.** To be discharged in a volley. **2.** In sports, to make a volley, as in tennis.

vol·ley·ball (**vŏl′**ē-bôl′) *n.* **1.** A game played by two teams on a rectangular court divided by a high net, in which a ball is hit back and forth over the net with the hands. **2.** The round ball used in this game.

volt (vōlt) *n.* A unit used to measure electromotive force. One volt is equal to the force that carries one ampere of current through a conductor that has a resistance of one ohm. [After Count Alessandro *Volta* (1745–1827), Italian physicist.]

volt·age (**vōl′**tĭj) *n.* Electromotive force expressed in volts. A current of high voltage is used in transmitting electric power over long distances.

vol·ta·ic (vōl-**tā′**ĭk) *adj.* **1.** Indicating electricity that is produced as a result of chemical action. **2.** Producing electricity by chemical action: *a voltaic cell.* [After Count Alessandro *Volta* (1745–1827), Italian physicist.]

Vol·taire (vōl-**târ′** *or* vŏl-**târ′**) Pen name of François Marie Arouet. 1694–1778. French philosopher and writer whose works include *Candide* (1759).

volt·am·me·ter (**vōlt′**ăm′mē′tər) *n.* An instrument for measuring electrical current or potential.

volt·me·ter (**vōlt′**mē′tər) *n.* An instrument, such as a galvanometer, used for measuring the difference in voltage between two points in an electric circuit.

vol·u·ble (**vŏl′**yə-bəl) *adj.* Marked by a ready flow of speech; fluent. **—vol′u·bil′i·ty** *n.* **—vol′u·bly** *adv.*

vol·ume (**vŏl′**yo͞om *or* **vŏl′**yəm) *n.* **1a.** A collection of written or printed sheets bound together; a book. **b.** One book of a set: *an encyclopedia published in 16 volumes.* **2.** The amount of space occupied by a three-dimensional object or region of space: *the volume of a cube; a container having a standard volume.* **3a.** The force or intensity of a sound; loudness. **b.** A control for regulating loudness: *Don't touch the volume!* **4.** Quantity; amount: *a large volume of mail.* [From Middle English, from Latin *volūmen*, roll of writing, from *volvere*, to roll.]

vol·u·met·ric (vŏl′yo͞o-**mĕt′**rĭk) *adj.* Relating to measurement by volume. **—vol′u·met′ri·cal·ly** *adv.*

vo·lu·mi·nous (və-**lo͞o′**mə-nəs) *adj.* **1.** Having great volume or size: *a voluminous trunk.* **2.** Filling or capable of filling a large volume or many volumes: *a voluminous court record.* **3.** Speaking or writing in great amounts or at great length: *a voluminous talker.*

vol·un·tar·y (**vŏl′**ən-tĕr′ē) *adj.* **1.** Done or undertaken of one's own free will: *a voluntary decision to leave the job.* **2.** Acting or done willingly and without expectation of reward: *voluntary community work.* **3.** Normally controlled by or subject to individual will: *a voluntary muscle.* **4.** Capable of making choices; having free will. **5.** Supported by contributions and donations rather than by government assistance: *voluntary hospitals.* **—vol′un·tar′i·ly** (vŏl′ən-**târ′**ə-lē) *adv.*

vol·un·teer (vŏl′ən-**tîr′**) *n.* A person who performs or offers to perform a service voluntarily. ❖ *adj.* Being, consisting of, or done by volunteers: *volunteer firefighters.* ❖ *v.* **vol·un·teered, vol·un·teer·ing, vol·un·teers** *—tr.* To give or offer to give voluntarily: *volunteered to give blood.* *—intr.* **1.** To perform or offer to perform a service of one's own free will. **2.** To do charitable or helpful work without pay. [From Latin *voluntārius*, voluntary, from *velle*, to wish.]

vo·lup·tu·ous (və-**lŭp′**cho͞o-əs) *adj.* Marked by, giving, or suggesting sensual pleasure and luxury.

vol·vox (**vŏl′**vŏks′) *n.* Any of various freshwater green algae that form hollow, spherical, many-celled colonies.

vom·it (**vŏm′**ĭt) *v.* **vom·it·ed, vom·it·ing, vom·its** *—intr.* To eject or discharge part or all of the contents of the stomach through the mouth, usually in a series of involuntary spasms. *—tr.* To eject (the contents of the stomach) through the mouth. ❖ *n.* Matter discharged from the stomach by vomiting.

voo·doo (**vo͞o′**do͞o) *n., pl.* **voo·doos** A religion practiced chiefly in Caribbean countries, especially Haiti, derived from West African religions and Roman Catholicism, in which a supreme God rules a large group of divine beings who communicate with believers in dreams and trances. [From Louisiana French *voudou*, of West African origin.]

voo·doo·ism (**vo͞o′**do͞o-ĭz′əm) *n.* **1.** The practice and beliefs of voodoo. **2.** The practice of sorcery or witchcraft.

vo·ra·cious (və-**rā′**shəs) *adj.* **1.** Eating or eager to eat great amounts of food; ravenous: *a voracious person.* **2.** Having or marked by a strong desire for an activity or occupation: *a voracious reader.*

vor·tex (**vôr′**tĕks′) *n., pl.* **vor·tex·es** or **vor·ti·ces** (**vôr′**tĭ-sēz′) **1.** A whirling mass of water or air that sucks everything near it toward its center. **2.** A destructive place or situation regarded as drawing into its center all that surrounds it: *a vortex of despair.*

vo·ta·ry (**vō′**tə-rē) *n., pl.* **vo·ta·ries** **1.** A person bound by vows to a life of religious worship or service. **2.** A person who is devoted, as to a particular hobby or pastime; an enthusiast.

vote (vōt) *n.* **1a.** A formal expression of one's choice for a candidate for office or for a proposed idea, such as a law: *Let's decide the matter by vote.* **b.** The means by which such choice is made known, such as a raised hand or marked ballot: *Have you collected all the votes?* **2.** The

Voltaire

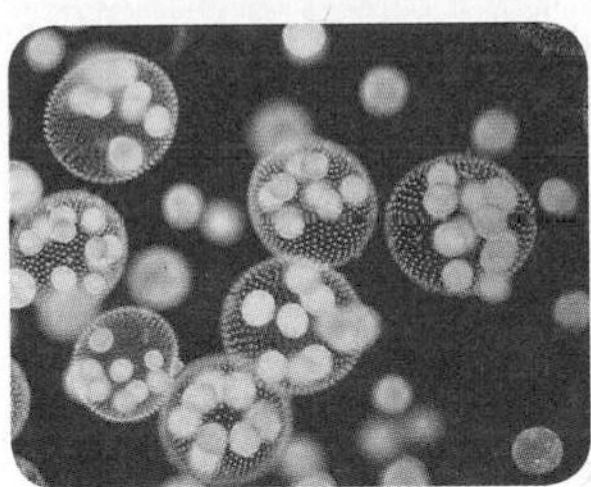

volvox

vortex

number of votes cast in an election or in an effort to resolve an issue: *a heavy vote in favor of the bill.* **3.** A group of voters alike in some way: *wooing the Republican vote.* **4.** The right to participate as a voter: *women who campaigned for the vote.* ❖ *v.* **vot·ed, vot·ing, votes** —*intr.* To express one's choice for a candidate or for the resolution of an issue; cast a vote: *voted against the measure.* —*tr.* **1.** To express one's choice for (something) by vote: *I voted "yes" in the referendum.* **2.** To determine the outcome regarding (a candidate or issue) by voting in a specified way: *vote in a new mayor; voted out their representative; vote down the amendment.* **3.** To bring into existence or make available by vote: *vote new funds for the program.* **4.** *Informal* To state as a preference or opinion: *I vote that we go there now.* [From Latin *vōtum*, vow, from *vovēre*, to vow.]

vot·er (vō′tər) *n.* A person who votes or has the right to vote.

vot·ing machine (vō′tĭng) *n.* A machine that mechanically records and counts votes.

vo·tive (vō′tĭv) *adj.* Given or dedicated in fulfillment of a vow or pledge: *a votive offering.*

vouch (vouch) *intr.v.* **vouched, vouch·ing, vouch·es** To give or serve as a guarantee; supply assurance or supporting evidence: *I can vouch for her honesty.*

vouch·er (vou′chər) *n.* **1.** A receipt, signed statement, or similar paper that serves as proof or record that something has been paid for, given, or sold. **2.** A written authorization or certificate, especially one that can be exchanged for cash or services or that represents credit for money that will be owed later.

vouch·safe (vouch-sāf′ *or* **vouch′**sāf′) *tr.v.* **vouch·safed, vouch·saf·ing, vouch·safes** To condescend to grant or give (a reply or privilege, for example); deign.

vow (vou) *n.* A solemn promise or earnest pledge, especially to live or act in a specified way: *a vow to use his knowledge only for good; take the vows of a nun.* ❖ *tr.v.* **vowed, vow·ing, vows** To promise or pledge solemnly: *She vowed that she would return home a success.* [From Middle English *vou*, from Latin *vōtum*.]

SYNONYMS **vow, promise, pledge, swear** These verbs mean to declare solemnly that one will follow a particular course of action. *The protesters vowed to remain true to their cause. I promise to write back soon. The new deputies pledged to uphold the law. The gangster swore to get revenge on the people who had crossed him.*

vow·el (vou′əl) *n.* **1.** A speech sound, such as (ē) or (ĭ), created by the relatively free passage of the breath through the larynx and mouth, usually forming the most prominent or central part of a syllable. **2.** A letter such as *a, e, i, o, u,* and sometimes *y,* that represents such a sound.

voy·age (voi′ĭj) *n.* **1.** A long journey to a foreign or distant place, especially by sea. **2.** often **voyages** The events of a voyage of discovery or exploration considered as material for a narrative. ❖ *intr.v.* **voy·aged, voy·ag·ing, voy·ag·es** To make a voyage. **—voy′ag·er** *n.*

VP *abbr.* An abbreviation of vice president.

vs. *abbr.* An abbreviation of versus.

VT *abbr.* An abbreviation of Vermont.

Vul·can (vŭl′kən) *n.* In Roman mythology, the god of fire and metalworking, identified with the Greek Hephaestus.

vul·ca·nite (vŭl′kə-nīt′) *n.* A hard rubber produced by vulcanization.

vul·ca·nize (vŭl′kə-nīz′) *tr.v.* **vul·ca·nized, vul·ca·niz·ing, vul·ca·niz·es** To give (rubber or sometimes other materials) greater strength, resistance, and elasticity by combining with sulfur or other additives in the presence of heat and pressure. **—vul′ca·ni·za′tion** (vŭl′kə-nĭ-zā′shən) *n.*

vul·gar (vŭl′gər) *adj.* **1.** Lacking good taste, refinement, or elegance; crude; coarse: *vulgar jokes; a vulgar display of wealth.* **2.** Spoken by or expressed in the language of the common people; vernacular: *"Liverleaf" is the vulgar name for a plant known to botanists as hepatica.* **3.** Associated with the great masses of people; common. **—vul′gar·ly** *adv.*

vul·gar·ism (vŭl′gə-rĭz′əm) *n.* **1.** A crude, indecent word or phrase; an obscenity. **2.** A word or expression used chiefly by uneducated people.

vul·gar·i·ty (vŭl-găr′ĭ-tē) *n., pl.* **vul·gar·i·ties 1.** The quality or condition of being vulgar. **2.** Something, such as an act or expression, that offends good taste or propriety.

vul·gar·ize (vŭl′gə-rīz′) *tr.v.* **vul·gar·ized, vul·gar·iz·ing, vul·gar·iz·es 1.** To make vulgar; cheapen: *vulgarize a novel with a TV movie.* **2.** To popularize; make generally known. **—vul′gar·i·za′tion** (vŭl′gər-ĭ-zā′shən) *n.* **—vul′gar·i′zer** *n.*

Vulgar Latin *n.* The common speech of the ancient Romans, the ancestor of the Romance languages.

Vul·gate (vŭl′gāt′ *or* **vŭl′**gĭt) *n.* The Latin version of the Bible used in the Roman Catholic Church.

vul·ner·a·ble (vŭl′nər-ə-bəl) *adj.* **1.** Easily harmed or injured: *Baby birds are helpless and vulnerable.* **2.** Open to danger and attack; unprotected: *The retreat of the army had left the outlying territories vulnerable.* **—vul′ner·a·bil′i·ty** *n.* **—vul′ner·a·bly** *adv.*

vul·pine (vŭl′pīn′) *adj.* **1.** Relating to or resembling a fox. **2.** Cunning; clever.

vul·ture (vŭl′chər) *n.* **1.** Any of various large birds that have dark feathers and a bare head and neck and that feed on the flesh of dead animals. **2.** A greedy, grasping, or ruthless person. [From Middle English, from Latin *vultur*.]

vul·va (vŭl′və) *n.* The external genital organs in female mammals.

vy·ing (vī′ĭng) *v.* Present participle of **vie.**

WRITERS CHOOSE THEIR WORDS

The last major pieces of construction in both castle and town defense were the gatehouses. Because these were the most **vulnerable** parts of the walls, they were designed and built with great care.

—David Macaulay
Castle

vulture

ă	pat	ôr	core
ā	pay	oi	boy
âr	care	ou	out
ä	father	o͝o	took
ĕ	pet	o͝or	lure
ē	be	o͞o	boot
ĭ	pit	ŭ	cut
ī	bite	ûr	urge
îr	pier	th	thin
ŏ	pot	*th*	this
ō	toe	zh	vision
ô	paw	ə	about

w[1] or **W** (dŭb′əl-yo͞o *or* dŭb′əl-yo͞o) *n., pl.* **w's** or **W's** also **ws** or **Ws** The 23rd letter of the English alphabet.

w[2] *abbr.* An abbreviation of width.

W[1] The symbol for the element **tungsten.**

W[2] *abbr.* An abbreviation of: **1.** watt. **2.** week. **3.** west. **4.** western.

w/ *abbr.* An abbreviation of with.

WA *abbr.* An abbreviation of Washington.

wack·y (wăk′ē) *adj.* **wack·i·er, wack·i·est** *Slang* **1.** Eccentric or irrational. **2.** Crazy; silly: *showed up in a wacky outfit.*

wad (wŏd) *n.* **1.** A small mass of soft material, often folded or rolled, used for padding, stuffing, or packing. **2.** A compressed ball, roll, or lump, as of tobacco or gum. **3.** A soft plug or disk used to hold an explosive charge in place in a cartridge or firearm. **4.** *Informal* A large roll of paper money: *a wad of $20 bills.* ❖ *tr.v.* **wad·ded, wad·ding, wads 1.** To squeeze, roll, crumple, or crush into a compact mass: *wad up a sheet of paper.* **2.** To insert a wad into (a firearm).

wad·ding (wŏd′ĭng) *n.* **1.** A wad or wads. **2.** A soft layer of cotton or wool used for padding or stuffing.

wad·dle (wŏd′l) *intr.v.* **wad·dled, wad·dling, wad·dles** To walk with short steps that tilt the body from side to side. ❖ *n.* A swaying walk.

wade (wād) *v.* **wad·ed, wad·ing, wades** *—intr.* To walk in or through water or another substance that makes normal movement difficult. *—tr.* To cross by wading: *The river was too deep to wade.*

wad·ers (wā′dərz) *pl.n.* Waterproof hip boots or pants worn while fishing.

wa·di (wä′dē) *n., pl.* **wa·dis** also **wa·dies** A gully or streambed in northern Africa and southwest Asia that remains dry except during the rainy season.

wad·ing bird (wā′dĭng) *n.* A long-legged bird, such as a crane or stork, that walks about in shallow water, especially in search of food.

wa·fer (wā′fər) *n.* **1.** A small, thin, crisp cake, biscuit, or candy. **2.** A small thin disk of unleavened bread used in the Eucharist.

waf·fle[1] (wŏf′əl) *n.* A light crisp cake with an indented surface, made by baking batter in a waffle iron. [From Dutch *wafel.*]

waf·fle[2] (wŏf′əl) *intr.v.* **waf·fled, waf·fling, waf·fles** *Informal* **1.** To be unable to make a decision; waver: *He waffled over whether to ask for extra credit.* **2.** To speak, write, or act evasively. [Probably from obsolete *waff,* to yelp.]

waffle iron *n.* An appliance having hinged indented plates that press a grid pattern into waffle batter as it bakes.

waft (wäft *or* wăft) *v.* **waft·ed, waft·ing, wafts** *—intr.* To float easily and gently, as on the air; drift: *The smell of the ocean wafted in when she opened the door. —tr.* To cause to go or move gently through the air or over water: *The breeze wafted the fog through the fields.* ❖ *n.* **1.** Something, such as a scent or sound, carried lightly through the air: *a waft of perfume.* **2.** A light breeze; a rush of air.

wag[1] (wăg) *v.* **wagged, wag·ging, wags** *—intr.* To move, swing, or wave repeatedly back and forth or up and down: *The puppy's tail wagged as we walked in. —tr.* To move (a body part) from side to side or up and down, as in playfulness: *The puppy wagged its tail eagerly.* ❖ *n.* The act or motion of wagging. [From Middle English *waggen.*]

wag[2] (wăg) *n.* A witty humorous person; a wit. [Perhaps from *wag,* to move back and forth.]

wage (wāj) *n.* **1.** A regular payment, usually on an hourly, daily, or weekly basis, made by an employer to an employee, usually for manual or unskilled work. **2. wages** *(used with a singular or plural verb)* A suitable return or recompense: *The wages of idleness is poverty.* ❖ *tr.v.* **waged, wag·ing, wag·es** To engage in (a war or campaign, for example). [From Middle English, from Old North French, of Germanic origin.]

wage earner *n.* A person who works for wages, especially one whose earnings support or help support a household.

wa·ger (wā′jər) *n.* A bet. ❖ *tr. & intr.v.* **wa·gered, wa·ger·ing, wa·gers** To bet or make a bet.

wag·gish (wăg′ĭsh) *adj.* Resembling a wag; jocular or witty: *a waggish columnist.*

wag·gle (wăg′əl) *intr. & tr.v.* **wag·gled, wag·gling, wag·gles** To move or cause to move with short quick motions; wag or wiggle.

Wag·ner (väg′nər), **Richard** 1813–1883. German composer whose works include *Der Ring des Nibelungen* (1853–1874), a series of four operas based on Germanic legend.

wag·on (wăg′ən) *n.* **1.** A child's low four-wheeled cart hauled by a long handle that controls the direction of the front wheels. **2a.** A four-wheeled, usually horse-drawn vehicle with a large rectangular body, used to transport loads. **b.** A roomy motor vehicle used for a similar purpose. **3.** A station wagon. **4.** A police patrol wagon. [From Middle Dutch *wagen.*]

wag·on·er (wăg′ə-nər) *n.* A person who drives a wagon.

wagon train *n.* A line or train of wagons traveling cross-country.

waif (wāf) *n.* **1.** A lost or homeless person or animal, especially an orphaned or abandoned child. **2.** A person, especially a young woman, who is thin or gaunt.

wail (wāl) *intr.v.* **wailed, wail·ing, wails 1.** To make a long, loud, high-pitched cry, as in grief, sorrow, or fear. See Synonyms at **cry. 2.** To make a prolonged sound suggesting a cry: *The wind wailed through the trees.* ❖ *n.* A long high-pitched cry or sound: *the lonesome wail of a train whistle.*

❑ *These sound alike:* **wail, wale** (mark on the skin), **whale** (sea mammal).

WRITERS CHOOSE THEIR WORDS

"You can live your life or you can watch it," he'd say every time one of our expeditions got slowed down because TJ wanted to take a picture of something, a statue, a duck **waddling** down the middle of the road, a little kid who'd just dropped his ice-cream cone on his lap.

—Frances O'Roark Dowell
Shooting the Moon

waffle[1]

WRITERS CHOOSE THEIR WORDS

The smell of soup **wafted** in Despereaux's direction. He put his nose up in the air. His whiskers trembled.

—Kate DiCamillo
The Tale of Despereaux

USAGE

wake[1] Although **wake, waken, awake,** and **awaken** have similar meanings, there are some differences in use. Only *wake* is used in the sense "to be awake," as in expressions such as *every waking hour. Wake* is more common than *waken* when used with *up,* while *awake* and *awaken* are never used with *up: She woke up* (rarely *wakened up;* never *awakened up* or *awoke up*). In figurative contexts, *awake* and *awaken* are the more common forms: *The sheriff finally awoke to the danger. The smell of the lilacs awakened old memories.*

wake[2]

ă	pat	ôr	core
ā	pay	oi	boy
âr	care	ou	out
ä	father	o͝o	took
ĕ	pet	o͝or	lure
ē	be	o͞o	boot
ĭ	pit	ŭ	cut
ī	bite	ûr	urge
îr	pier	th	thin
ŏ	pot	*th*	this
ō	toe	zh	vision
ô	paw	ə	about

wain·scot·ing (wān′skə-tĭng *or* wān′skō′tĭng) *n.* **1.** The lower part of an inside wall when finished in a material different from that of the upper part. **2.** The material, usually wood, used for this part of a wall.

waist (wāst) *n.* **1.** The part of the human body between the bottom of the rib cage and the pelvis. **2.** The part of a garment that fits around the waist or that covers the upper body from the neck or shoulders to the waist. **3.** The slender part of the abdomen of various insects, such as wasps, ants, and some flies.
❑ *These sound alike:* **waist, waste** (squander).

waist·band (wāst′bănd′) *n.* A band of material encircling and fitting the waist of a garment, such as pants.

waist·coat (wĕs′kĭt *or* wāst′kōt′) *n. Chiefly British* A vest.

waist·line (wāst′līn′) *n.* **1.** A line thought of as encircling the body at the waist. **2.** The point or line at which the skirt and bodice of a dress join.

wait (wāt) *v.* **wait·ed, wait·ing, waits** —*intr.* **1.** To remain or rest in expectation: *waiting for the guests to arrive.* See Synonyms at **stay**[1]. **2.** To pause or stay in one place until another catches up: *Wait for me!* **3.** To remain temporarily neglected, unattended to, or postponed: *Dinner will have to wait.* **4.** To work serving tables, as in a restaurant or a private home. —*tr.* **1.** To remain or stay in expectation of; await: *Wait your turn.* **2.** To be waiter or waitress at: *wait tables.* ❖ *n.* The act of waiting or a period of time spent in waiting: *a short wait.* ◆ **wait on** or **wait upon 1.** To serve the needs of; be in attendance on. **2.** To await: *They're waiting on my decision.* **wait up 1.** To postpone going to bed in anticipation of something or someone: *Let's wait up to watch the late show.* **2.** *Informal* To stop or pause so that another can catch up: *They got too far ahead, so I yelled to them to wait up.* [From Middle English *waiten,* from Old North French *waitier,* to watch, of Germanic origin.]
❑ *These sound alike:* **wait, weight** (gravity force).

wait·er (wā′tər) *n.* A man who serves at a table, such as in a restaurant.

wait·ing (wā′tĭng) *n.* The act of remaining inactive or stationary. ◆ **in waiting** In attendance, especially at a royal court.

waiting list *n.* A list of people waiting, as for an appointment or a table at a restaurant.

waiting room *n.* A room, as in a railroad station or doctor's office, for the use of people waiting.

wait·ress (wā′trĭs) *n.* A woman who serves at a table, such as in a restaurant.

waive (wāv) *tr.v.* **waived, waiv·ing, waives 1.** To give up (a right or claim, for example) by one's own choice: *waive a jury trial.* **2.** To set aside, cancel, or postpone: *Let's waive the formalities and start the discussion.*
❑ *These sound alike:* **waive, wave** (swell).

waiv·er (wā′vər) *n.* **1.** The intentional giving up of a right, claim, or privilege. **2.** A written agreement to give up such a right, claim, or privilege.
❑ *These sound alike:* **waiver, waver** (vacillate).

Wa·kash·an (wä-kăsh′ən *or* wô′kə-shăn′) *n.* A family of Native American languages spoken by the peoples of Washington and British Columbia.

wake[1] (wāk) *v.* **woke** (wōk) or **waked** (wākt), **waked** or **wok·en** (wō′kən), **wak·ing, wakes** —*intr.* **1.** To cease to sleep; become awake: *I woke before 6:00.* **2.** To remain awake: *Whether he sleeps or wakes, he hugs his teddy bear.* —*tr.* To rouse from sleep or stir, especially from an inactive condition: *Wake me at noon.* ❖ *n.* A watch or vigil kept over the body of a dead person before the burial. [From Middle English *wakien, waken,* from Old English *wacan,* to wake up, and *wacian,* to be awake, keep watch.] —SEE NOTE.

wake[2] (wāk) *n.* **1.** The visible track of waves, ripples, or foam left behind something moving through water: *the wake of a ship.* **2.** The course, track, or condition left behind something that has passed: *The hurricane left destruction in its wake.* [Possibly from Middle Low German *wake,* hole in the ice, of Scandinavian origin.]

wake·board (wāk′bôrd′) *n.* A short, very broad water ski ridden in the manner of a surfboard by a person towed by a motorboat. **—wake′board′er** *n.* **—wake′board′ing** *n.*

wake·ful (wāk′fəl) *adj.* **1.** Not sleeping or not able to sleep. **2.** Without sleep; sleepless: *a wakeful night.*

wak·en (wā′kən) *v.* **wak·ened, wak·en·ing, wak·ens** —*tr.* **1.** To rouse from sleep; awake: *The noise wakened me.* **2.** To stir from an inactive state. —*intr.* To become awake; wake up: *I plan to waken at 6:00 tomorrow.*

wale (wāl) *n.* **1.** A mark raised on the skin, as by a lash or blow; a welt. **2.** One of the parallel ribs or ridges in the surface of a fabric such as corduroy. ❖ *tr.v.* **waled, wal·ing, wales** To raise marks on (the skin), especially by whipping.
❑ *These sound alike:* **wale, wail** (cry), **whale** (sea mammal).

Wales (wālz) A principality of the United Kingdom west of England on the island of Great Britain. Cardiff is the capital.

Wa·le·sa (wä-lĕn′sə *or* vä-wĕn′sä), **Lech** Born 1943. Polish labor leader who launched the first independent trade union in communist Poland and served as the first democratically elected president of Poland (1990–1995).

walk (wôk) *v.* **walked, walk·ing, walks** —*intr.* **1.** To move over a surface by taking steps with the feet at a pace slower than a run: *The baby is just learning to walk.* **2.** To go or travel on foot: *I walked to school.* **3.** To go on foot for pleasure or exercise; stroll: *walk in the park.* **4.** To move in a way that resembles or suggests walking: *an astronaut walking in space.* **5.** *Slang* **a.** To go out on strike. **b.** To be acquitted: *It couldn't be proved that he had committed the crime, so he walked.* **6.** In baseball, to go to first base after the pitcher has thrown four balls. —*tr.* **1.** To go or pass over, on, or through by walking: *walking the historic section of the city.* **2.** To cause to walk or go at a walk: *walk a horse uphill.* **3.** To accompany in walking; escort on foot: *We walked her to the bus stop.* **4.** In baseball, to allow (a batter) to go to first base by pitching four balls. ❖ *n.* **1.** The gait of a human or two-footed animal in which the feet are lifted alternately with one part of a foot always on the ground. **2.** The gait of a four-footed animal in which at least two feet are always touching the ground. **3.** A stroll or journey on foot. **4.** A pathway or sidewalk on which to walk: *shovel snow off the walk.* **5.** An act, way, or speed of walking: *a waddling walk; a brisk walk.* **6.** A route particularly suitable for walking: *The path by the river is a nice walk.* **7.** In baseball, a base on balls. ◆ **walk away from** To survive (an accident, for example) with little or no injury. **walk off with** or **walk away with 1.** To win: *walked away with five prizes at the fair.* **2.** To steal. **walk on air** To feel very happy; be overjoyed: *I was walking on air after I heard the good news.* **walk out** To leave suddenly, often as a signal of disapproval. **walk out on** To desert or abandon. **walk over** *Informal* To treat badly or contemptuously. **walk through** To guide (someone) through (a process) one step at a time: *walked the new employees through the necessary paperwork.*

walk·er (wô′kər) *n.* **1.** A person who walks, especially a contestant in a footrace. **2.** A frame used to support someone while walking, such as an infant learning to walk or a person recovering from an injury.

walk·ie-talk·ie (wô′kē-tô′kē) *n., pl.* **walk·ie-talk·ies** A portable battery-powered two-way radio, usually used for short-range communications.

walk·ing stick (wô′kĭng) *n.* **1.** A cane or stick, used as an aid in walking. **2.** Any of numerous slow-moving insects having a slender brown or green body that resembles a stick or twig.

walk-on (wôk′ŏn′) *n.* **1.** A minor role in a dramatic production, usually without speaking lines. **2.** A performer playing such a role. **3.** A collegiate athlete who has not been recruited and has no athletic scholarship. **—walk′-on′** *adj.*

walk·out (wôk′out′) *n.* **1.** A labor strike. **2.** The act of leaving or quitting a meeting, company, or organization, especially as a sign of protest.

walk·up (wôk′ŭp′) *n.* **1.** An apartment house or building with no elevator. **2.** An apartment or office in a building with no elevator: *lives in a fourth-floor walkup.*

walk·way (wôk′wā′) *n.* A passage or path for walking.

wall (wôl) *n.* **1.** An upright structure of building material that serves to enclose an area or to separate two areas from each other. **2.** Something that is like a wall in appearance, function, or construction: *the wall of the stomach.* **3.** Something that is like a wall, as in hiding or dividing something: *a wall of fog; a wall of secrecy.* ❖ *tr.v.* **walled, wall·ing, walls 1.** To enclose, surround, or fortify with or as if with a wall. **2.** To divide or separate with or as if with a wall: *walled off half the room.* **3.** To confine or seal behind a wall: *hid the treasure by walling it up in the dungeon.* ◆ **off the wall** *Slang* **1.** Extremely unconventional; strange: *His outfit is really off the wall.* **2.** Without foundation; ridiculous: *That explanation is really off the wall.* **up the wall** *Slang* Into a state of extreme frustration, anger, or distress: *My little brother is driving me up the wall.* [From Old English *weall*, from Latin *vallus*, stake.]

wal·la·by (wŏl′ə-bē) *n., pl.* **wal·la·bies** or **wallaby** Any of various Australian marsupials that resemble kangaroos but are generally smaller.

Wal·lace (wŏl′ĭs), **Alfred Russel** 1823–1913. British naturalist who developed a concept of evolution similar to that of Charles Darwin. He traveled in the Amazon region and the Malay Archipelago collecting specimens and wrote *The Geographical Distribution of Animals* (1876).

Wal·la·chi·a also **Wa·la·chi·a** (wŏ-lā′kē-ə) A historical region of southeast Romania north of the Danube River. It was united in 1862 with Moldavia to form the core of modern Romania.

wall·board (wôl′bôrd′) *n.* Drywall.

wal·let (wŏl′ĭt) *n.* A small flat folding case for holding money, ID cards, and other flat items.

wall·eye (wôl′ī′) *n.* **1.** An eye that is directed out to one side rather than being aligned with the other eye. **2.** *pl.* **walleye** or **wall·eyes** A North American freshwater fish that has large silvery eyes and is caught for food.

wall·eyed (wôl′īd′) *adj.* Having a walleye.

wall·flow·er (wôl′flou′ər) *n.* **1.** Any of various plants having fragrant yellow, orange, or brownish flowers. **2.** A person who does not take part in the activities of a social event because of shyness or unpopularity.

wal·lop (wŏl′əp) *Informal tr.v.* **wal·loped, wal·lop·ing, wal·lops 1.** To beat forcefully or defeat thoroughly: *They walloped their opponents.* **2.** To strike with a hard blow: *walloped the ball into the outfield.* ❖ *n.* A hard blow or the ability to strike such a blow.

wal·low (wŏl′ō) *intr.v.* **wal·lowed, wal·low·ing, wal·lows 1.** To roll the body about or lie relaxed in water or mud: *The pig wallowed playfully in the mud.* **2.** To indulge oneself to a great degree in something: *The king wallowed in luxury.* **3.** To move with difficulty in a clumsy or rolling manner; flounder. ❖ *n.* **1.** The act or an instance of wallowing. **2.** A pool of water or mud where animals go to wallow.

wall·pa·per (wôl′pā′pər) *n.* Paper often colored and printed with designs and pasted to a wall as a decorative covering. ❖ *tr.v.* **wall·pa·pered, wall·pa·per·ing, wall·pa·pers** To cover with wallpaper.

Wall Street *n.* The financial industry of the United States, mainly consisting of businesses involved in the trading of stocks, bonds, and other investments.

wall-to-wall (wôl′tə-wôl′) *adj.* **1.** Completely covering a floor: *wall-to-wall carpeting.* **2.** Present or spreading throughout an entire area: *wall-to-wall people at the party.*

wal·nut (wôl′nŭt′) *n.* **1.** An edible nut having a hard rough shell. **2.** Any of several trees that bear such nuts. **3.** The hard, dark brown wood of any of these trees.

wal·rus (wôl′rəs) *n., pl.* **walrus** or **wal·rus·es** A large sea mammal of Arctic regions, related to the seals and sea lions and having tough wrinkled skin and large tusks. [From Dutch, of Scandinavian origin.]

waltz (wôlts) *n.* **1.** A ballroom dance in triple time with a strong accent on the first beat. **2.** A piece of music for this dance. ❖ *intr.v.* **waltzed, waltz·ing, waltz·es** To dance the waltz.

Wam·pa·no·ag (wäm′pə-nō′ăg) *n., pl.* **Wampanoag** or **Wam·pa·no·ags 1.** A member of a Native American people of eastern Rhode Island and southeast Massachusetts. **2.** The Algonquian language of the Wampanoag, a variety of Massachusett.

wam·pum (wŏm′pəm) *n.* **1.** Small beads made from polished shells and strung together into strands or belts, formerly used by certain Native American peoples as money or jewelry or in ceremonies. **2.** *Informal* Money. [From Massachusett *wampumpeag.*]

wan (wŏn) *adj.* **wan·ner, wan·nest 1.** Unnaturally pale, as from physical or emotional distress: *a wan face.* **2.** Suggesting weariness, illness, or unhappiness: *a wan smile.* **—wan′ly** *adv.*

wand (wŏnd) *n.* **1.** A thin supple rod, twig, or stick. **2.** A slender rod carried as a symbol of office; a scepter. **3.** A conductor's baton. **4.** A stick or baton used by a magician, conjurer, or diviner.

wan·der (wŏn′dər) *v.* **wan·dered, wan·der·ing, wan·ders** *—intr.* **1.** To move about without a destination or purpose. **2.** To go by an indirect route or stroll in a leisurely way: *We wandered toward town.* **3.** To follow an irregular winding or rambling course: *The brook wandered through the pasture.* **4.** To turn the attention from one subject to another without being clear or coherent: *I had a point to make, but my mind started wandering.* **5.** To be directed without an object or in various directions: *Her eyes wandered to the balcony.* —*tr.* To wander across or through: *wander the backwoods.* **—wan′der·er** *n.*

SYNONYMS wander, ramble, roam, rove, meander These verbs mean to move about at random or without destination or purpose. **Wander** and **ramble** both mean to move about without a fixed course or goal: *He wandered from room to room looking for something interesting to do. After breakfast we can ramble through the hills.* **Roam** and **rove** suggest wandering with freedom of movement, especially over a wide area: *Herds of bison once roamed across the Great Plains. In the early 1700s, pirates roved over the Caribbean.* **Meander** suggests wandering leisurely and sometimes aimlessly over an irregular or winding course: *She meandered down to the beach slowly, watching the waves hit the shore.*

wan·der·lust (wŏn′dər-lŭst′) *n.* A very strong desire to travel.

wane (wān) *intr.v.* **waned, wan·ing, wanes 1.** To decrease gradually in size, number, strength, or intensity: *Interest in the subject waned.* **2.** To show a progressively smaller lighted surface, as the moon does in passing from full to new. **3.** To approach an end: *The old year was waning.* ❖ *n.* **1.** The period during which the moon

walking stick

walrus

WRITERS CHOOSE THEIR WORDS

Artemis said, "You think you want [to be a goddess], but you do not. Look at us, Iris, lingering past the time when our powers were full. We **wane and wane.** Now we are like the moon in its tiniest sliver."

—Sarah Deming
Iris, Messenger

warbler

war bonnet

WORD BUILDING

–ward The basic meaning of the suffix **–ward** is "having a particular direction or location." Its use dates back to Old English. Thus *inward* means "directed or located inside." Other examples are *outward, forward, backward, upward, downward, earthward, homeward,* and *northward.* The suffix *–ward* forms adjectives and adverbs. Adverbs ending in *–ward* can also end in *–wards.* Thus *I stepped backward* and *I stepped backwards* are both correct. Only the *–ward* form is used as an adjective: *an outward appearance; a backward glance.*

ă	pat	ôr	core
ā	pay	oi	boy
âr	care	ou	out
ä	father	ŏŏ	took
ĕ	pet	ŏŏr	lure
ē	be	ōō	boot
ĭ	pit	ŭ	cut
ī	bite	ûr	urge
îr	pier	th	thin
ŏ	pot	*th*	this
ō	toe	zh	vision
ô	paw	ə	about

wanes. **2.** A time or phase of gradual decrease. ◆ **on the wane** In a period of decline or decrease.

wan·gle (wăng′gəl) *tr. & intr.v.* **wan·gled, wan·gling, wan·gles** *Informal* To obtain or achieve by cleverness or deceit: *wangle an invitation to the exclusive party.*

Wan·kel engine (väng′kəl *or* wăng′kəl) *n.* An internal-combustion engine in which a turning triangular rotor carries out the functions performed by the pistons of a conventional engine, resulting in lighter weight and fewer moving parts. [After Felix *Wankel* (1902–1988), German engineer.]

wan·na·be (wŏn′ə-bē′) *Informal n.* **1.** A person who aspires to a role or position. **2.** A person who imitates the behavior or dress of an admired person or group.

want (wŏnt) *v.* **want·ed, want·ing, wants** *—tr.* **1.** To have a strong feeling to have (something); wish (to possess or do something); desire greatly: *He wants a guitar. My parents want me to wash the car. They wanted to play outdoors.* See Synonyms at **desire. 2a.** To request the presence or help of: *I am wanted by my office.* **b.** To seek with the intent to capture or arrest as a lawbreaker: *The fugitive is wanted by the police.* **3.** To have an inclination toward; like: *Say what you want, but I still think it's too expensive.* **4.** *Informal* To be obliged: *You'll want to be careful if you're out at night.* —*intr.* To be disposed; wish: *Stop by if you want.* ❖ *n.* **1.** The condition or quality of lacking something usual or necessary: *We stayed home for want of anything better to do.* **2.** Pressing need; destitution: *lives in want.* **3.** Something desired: *has many wants.* ◆ **want out** *Slang* To desire to leave or disengage from something: *The cat wants out. The author wanted out of the contract.* [From Middle English *wanten,* to be lacking, from Old Norse *vanta.*]

want ad *n. Informal* A classified advertisement.

wan·ton (wŏn′tən) *adj.* **1.** Unnecessarily cruel; merciless: *wanton killing.* **2.** Marked by a disregard for morals or justice; unjust: *wanton destruction.* **3.** Unrestrained; excessive: *wanton luxury.* **4.** Lewd or indecent. **—wan′ton·ly** *adv.* **—wan′ton·ness** *n.*

wap·i·ti (wŏp′ĭ-tē) *n., pl.* **wapiti** or **wap·i·tis** The elk.

war (wôr) *n.* **1.** A state of open armed conflict carried on between nations, states, or parties: *The two countries are at war.* **2.** A specific instance or period of such conflict: *There have been several brief wars in the region.* **3.** The techniques or procedures of war; military science: *studied war.* **4.** A serious determined struggle or attack on something considered injurious: *a war on poverty.* ❖ *intr.v.* **warred, war·ring, wars 1.** To wage or carry on warfare. **2.** To struggle, contend, or fight: *political factions warring against one other in the media.* [From Middle English *werre,* from Old North French, of Germanic origin.]

War Between the States *n.* The Civil War.

war·ble (wôr′bəl) *tr. & intr.v.* **war·bled, war·bling, war·bles** To sing with trills, runs, or other melodic sounds. ❖ *n.* The act or an instance of singing with trills, runs, or quavers.

war·bler (wôr′blər) *n.* Any of various small songbirds that eat insects. Many warblers of the Americas have brightly colored feathers.

war bonnet *n.* A ceremonial headdress used by some Plains Indians, often having a trailing extension decorated with feathers.

war crime *n.* Any of various crimes, such as genocide, committed during a war and considered in violation of the conventions of warfare.

ward (wôrd) *n.* **1a.** A large hospital room usually shared by six or more patients. **b.** A section of a hospital devoted to the care of a particular group of patients: *a maternity ward.* **2.** An administrative division of a city or town, especially an election district. **3.** A person, especially a minor, placed under the care or protection of a guardian or court. ❖ *tr.v.* **ward·ed, ward·ing, wards** To guard; protect. ◆ **ward off** To turn aside; repel: *I warded off the insects by building a fire.* [From Old English *weard,* action of guarding.]

–ward or **–wards** *suff.* A suffix that means: **1.** In a specified direction in time or space: *downward.* **2.** Toward a specified place or position: *homeward.* —SEE NOTE.

war·den (wôr′dn) *n.* **1.** An official in charge of a prison. **2.** An official who enforces certain laws, such as hunting or fire regulations: *a game warden.*

ward·er (wôr′dər) *n.* A guard, porter, or watcher of a gate or tower.

ward·robe (wôr′drōb′) *n.* **1.** A cabinet, closet, or small room for holding clothes. **2.** Articles of clothing considered as a group, especially all the pieces of clothing belonging to one person.

–wards *suff.* Variant of **–ward.**

ware (wâr) *n.* An article for sale: *people displaying their wares in the market.*

❑ *These sound alike:* **ware, wear** (have on), **where** (at what place).

–ware *suff.* **1.** Articles of the same general kind, material, or use: *silverware.* **2.** Software: *malware.*

ware·house (wâr′hous′) *n.* A place in which goods or articles of merchandise are stored; a storehouse.

war·fare (wôr′fâr′) *n.* **1.** The waging of war against an enemy; armed conflict. **2.** A special type or method of military operation: *guerrilla warfare.* **3.** A state of disharmony or conflict; strife.

war·head (wôr′hĕd′) *n.* A part of a bomb, missile, or torpedo that is in front and contains the explosive or damaging material, such as a nuclear bomb or a chemical agent.

war·horse (wôr′hôrs′) *n.* **1.** A horse used in combat. **2.** *Informal* A person who has been through many battles, struggles, or fights.

war·like (wôr′līk′) *adj.* **1.** Belligerent; hostile: *a warlike people.* **2.** Relating to war; martial. **3.** Threatening or indicating war: *a warlike call to arms.*

war·lock (wôr′lŏk′) *n.* A man claiming or believed to practice sorcery or witchcraft. [From Old English *wǣrloga,* oath-breaker : *wǣr,* pledge + *-loga,* liar.]

war·lord (wôr′lôrd′) *n.* A military leader who has control over a region.

warm (wôrm) *adj.* **warm·er, warm·est 1.** Moderately hot; neither cool nor very hot: *warm weather; warm air.* **2.** Giving off or keeping in heat: *the warm sun; a warm sweater.* **3.** Having or causing a feeling of unusually high body heat, such as from exercise or hard work. **4.** Enthusiastic, friendly, cordial, or sincere: *a warm smile; warm greetings.* **5.** Characterized by liveliness, excitement, or disagreement; heated: *a warm debate.* ❖ *tr. & intr.v.* **warmed, warm·ing, warms** To make or become warm or warmer; heat up. ◆ **warm up 1.** To prepare for an athletic event by exercising, stretching, or practicing for a short time beforehand. **2.** To make or become ready for an event or operation: *warmed up for her speech by practicing the opening lines.* [From Old English *wearm.*] **—warm′ly** *adv.* **—warm′ness** *n.*

warm-blood·ed (wôrm′blŭd′ĭd) *adj.* Having a warm body temperature that does not vary much and is maintained by heat generated internally. Birds and mammals are warm-blooded. **—warm′-blood′ed·ness** *n.*

warm front *n.* A front along which an advancing mass of warm air rises over a mass of cold air.

warm-heart·ed (wôrm′här′tĭd) *adj.* Marked by or acting with kindness or sympathy.

warm·ing pan (wôr′mĭng) *n.* A covered metal pan on a long handle, filled with hot coals and used to warm a bed.

war·mon·ger (wôr′mŭng′gər *or* wôr′mŏng′gər) *n.* A person who advocates or tries to stir up war.

warmth (wôrmth) *n.* **1.** The state or quality of being warm; moderate heat. **2.** The sensation of moderate heat. **3.** Friendliness, kindness, or affection: *a person of great warmth.* **4.** Excitement or intensity, especially of emotion: *warmth of feeling.*

warm-up or **warm·up** (wôrm′ŭp′) *n.* **1.** The act or procedure of warming up. **2.** A period spent in warming up.

warn (wôrn) *tr.v.* **warned, warn·ing, warns 1.** To make (someone) aware in advance of something, especially of possible danger or misfortune: *warned the sailors of bad weather.* **2.** To give (someone) advice, especially about what to do; caution or counsel: *We warned them to be careful.* [From Old English *warnian.*]

❑ *These sound alike:* **warn, worn** (damaged by wear).

warn·ing (wôr′nĭng) *n.* **1.** A sign, indication, notice, or threat of coming danger or difficulty: *The dog's low growl was a warning.* **2.** Advice to beware or to stop a given course of action: *a word of warning to runners about the hot weather.* **3.** Something that serves as a cautionary example: *The accident should be a warning to all bikers.*

warp (wôrp) *v.* **warped, warp·ing, warps** —*tr.* **1.** To turn or twist (wood, for example) out of shape. **2.** To cause (something) to be changed from a normal, proper, or healthy state: *The fear of losing his fortune warped his personality.* **3.** To move (a ship) by hauling on a line that is fastened to a piling, anchor, or pier. —*intr.* **1.** To become bent or twisted out of shape: *Left in the damp basement, the boards warped.* **2.** To become changed from what is normal, proper, or healthy. **3.** To move a ship by hauling on a line that is fastened to a piling, anchor, or pier. ❖ *n.* **1.** A bend or twist, especially in a piece of wood. **2.** A change from what is normal, proper, or healthy. **3.** The threads that run lengthwise in a woven fabric, crossed at right angles to the woof. [From Old English *weorpan,* to throw away.]

war·path (wôr′păth′) *n.* A course that leads to battle or warfare.

war·rant (wôr′ənt) *n.* **1.** An official written order authorizing something, such as an arrest, search, or seizure: *a search warrant.* **2.** Justification for an action or opinion; grounds: *What warrant does he have for feeling this way?* **3.** A guarantee or proof: *Casting her in the leading role was a warrant of the movie's success.* **4.** Authorization or certification; sanction: *The school board gave the teachers its warrant to try new methods.* ❖ *tr.v.* **war·rant·ed, war·rant·ing, war·rants 1.** To guarantee: *warrant a product.* **2.** To call for, justify, or merit: *There is enough evidence to warrant a trial.*

warrant officer *n.* A military officer, usually a technician, having a rank between a noncommissioned officer and a commissioned officer.

war·ran·ty (wôr′ən-tē) *n., pl.* **war·ran·ties 1.** A guarantee that a refund, repair, or replacement will be made if a product or service proves defective or unsatisfactory to the purchaser, usually within a given time period. **2.** Official guarantee, authorization, or justification. [From Middle English *warantie,* from Old North French, from *warantir,* to guarantee.]

war·ren (wôr′ən) *n.* **1.** An area where rabbits live in burrows. **2.** *Chiefly British* An enclosure for small game animals. **3.** A crowded or mazelike area where it is easy to become lost: *a warren of narrow, dark alleys and side streets.*

war·ri·or (wôr′ē-ər) *n.* A person who is or has been in battle.

War·saw (wôr′sô′) The capital of Poland, in the east-central part of the country southeast of Gdansk. Founded in the 1200s, it became the capital in 1596.

wart (wôrt) *n.* **1.** A hard rough lump growing on the skin, caused by a virus. **2.** A similar growth, especially on a plant.

wart·hog also **wart hog** (wôrt′hôg′) *n.* Either of two wild African hogs having two pairs of curved tusks and growths resembling warts on the face.

war·time (wôr′tīm′) *n.* A period during which a war is in progress.

war·y (wâr′ē) *adj.* **war·i·er, war·i·est 1.** On guard; watchful: *We were wary of mistakes in our experiment.* **2.** Characterized by caution: *a wary look.*

was (wŭz *or* wŏz; wəz *when unstressed*) *v.* First and third person singular past tense of **be.**

wa·sa·bi (wə-sä′bē *or* wä′sə-bē) *n.* A pungent green Japanese horseradish, usually used as a condiment.

wash (wŏsh) *v.* **washed, wash·ing, wash·es** —*tr.* **1.** To clean by using water or another liquid and often soap or detergent: *wash dishes.* **2.** To soak, rinse out, and remove (dirt or stain) with water or other liquid: *wash dirt out of the jeans.* **3.** To flow over and wet with water: *Waves wash the sandy shores.* **4.** To carry, erode, remove, or destroy by the action of moving water: *Heavy rains washed the topsoil away.* **5.** To cover (a painting, for example) with a watery layer of paint or other coloring. **6.** To pour or shake water through (gravel, sand, or crushed ore) to separate out valuable material: *wash gravel for gold.* —*intr.* **1.** To clean something in or by means of water or other liquid. **2.** To undergo washing without fading or other damage: *Cotton washes well.* **3.** To flow, sweep, or beat with a lapping sound: *Waves washed over the rocks.* ❖ *n.* **1.** The act or process of washing or cleansing. **2.** A batch of articles washed or intended for washing. **3a.** A liquid preparation used in cleansing or coating something, such as mouthwash or whitewash. **b.** A thin coating, such as of watercolor or whitewash. **4.** A turbulent flow of air or water caused by the passage or action of a boat, aircraft, oar, or propeller. ◆ **come out in the wash** *Slang* To be revealed eventually. **wash down** To drink a liquid directly after eating (solid food): *washed down the chips with some juice.* **wash (one's) hands of** To refuse to accept responsibility for: *I washed my hands of the problem.* **wash out 1.** To remove or be removed by washing: *That stain will wash out easily.* **2.** To carry away or ruin by a powerful current of water: *The flood washed out the bridge.* **wash up** To wash one's hands. [From Old English *wacsan, wæscan.*]

wash·a·ble (wŏsh′ə-bəl) *adj.* Capable of being washed without fading or other damage: *a washable skirt.*

wash-and-wear (wŏsh′ən-wâr′) *adj.* Treated so as to be easily washed and to require little or no ironing: *a wash-and-wear shirt.*

wash·ba·sin (wŏsh′bā′sən) *n.* A washbowl.

wash·board (wŏsh′bôrd′) *n.* **1.** A board having a ridged surface on which clothes can be rubbed in laundering. **2.** Such a board used as a percussion instrument.

wash·bowl (wŏsh′bōl′) *n.* A basin that can be filled with water for use in washing oneself; a washbasin.

wash·cloth (wŏsh′klôth′) *n.* A small cloth of absorbent material used for washing the face or body.

washed-out (wŏsht′out′) *adj.* **1.** Carried away by moving water: *a washed-out road.* **2.** Lacking color or intensity; faded. **3.** Exhausted or tired-looking.

washed-up (wŏsht′ŭp′) *adj.* No longer successful or needed; finished: *a washed-up comedian.*

wash·er (wŏsh′ər) *n.* **1.** A person who washes: *a washer of windows.* **2.** An appliance, especially a washing machine, used for washing. **3.** A flat disk, usually of metal or rubber, that is placed beneath a nut or bolt to make the connection more secure or distribute pressure or that is placed between parts to space the parts properly or prevent leakage in a joint.

wash·ing (wŏsh′ĭng) *n.* **1.** The act or process of one that

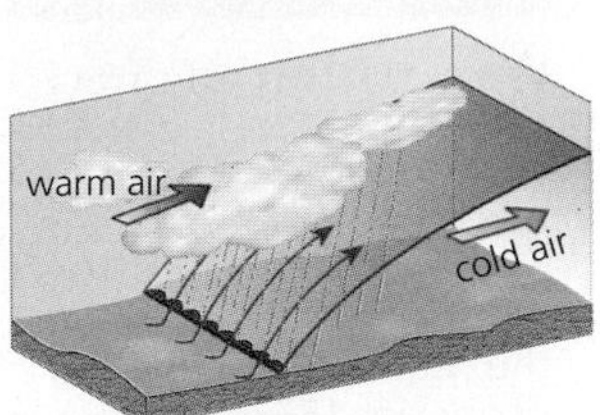

warm front

warthog

GEOGRAPHY

Washington The state of **Washington** is named after George Washington, the first president of the United States. The name was given when the region was still a territory, in 1853. It is the only state that is named after a US president.

BIOGRAPHY

George Washington
At the start of the American Revolution in 1775, the Continental Congress chose Virginia plantation owner George **Washington** as the commander of the Continental Army. An experienced soldier from the French and Indian War, Washington molded a collection of untrained civilians into an organized army. Washington's leadership and dedication held the American effort together long enough to force the British to surrender in 1781. He presided over the Constitutional Convention in 1787, guiding the delegates to forge an agreement that would unite the 13 states. In 1789, Washington was unanimously elected by the Electoral College as the first president. He served two terms and established the president's role as the strong center of the US government. In his farewell address in 1796, Washington warned against the divisiveness of political parties.

ă	pat	ôr	core
ā	pay	oi	boy
âr	care	ou	out
ä	father	o͝o	took
ĕ	pet	o͝or	lure
ē	be	o͞o	boot
ĭ	pit	ŭ	cut
ī	bite	ûr	urge
îr	pier	th	thin
ŏ	pot	*th*	this
ō	toe	zh	vision
ô	paw	ə	about

washes. **2.** A batch of clothes or linens washed or intended to be washed at one time.

washing machine *n.* A usually automatic machine for washing clothes and linens.

washing soda *n.* A form of sodium carbonate used as a general cleanser.

Wash·ing·ton (wŏsh**′**ĭng-tən) **1.** A state of the northwest United States on the Pacific Ocean north of Oregon. It was admitted as the 42nd state in 1889. Olympia is the capital and Seattle the largest city. **2.** The capital of the United States, on the Potomac River between Virginia and Maryland and having the same boundaries as the District of Columbia. It became the capital in 1800. —SEE NOTE.

Washington, Booker T(aliaferro) 1856–1915. American educator. Born into slavery, he acquired an education after emancipation and became the principal of the Tuskegee Institute, an industrial college for African Americans, which flourished under his tutelage (1881–1915).

Washington, George 1732–1799. American military leader and the first president of the United States (1789–1797). Washington served as commander of the American forces in the Revolutionary War (1775–1783). —SEE NOTE.

Washington, Martha Dandridge Custis 1731–1802. First lady of the United States (1789–1797) as the wife of President George Washington.

Wash·ing·ton's Birthday (wŏsh**′**ĭng-tənz) *n.* The third Monday in February, observed in the United States in commemoration of the birthday of George Washington, formerly observed on February 22.

wash·out (wŏsh**′**out′) *n.* **1.** Erosion of a relatively soft surface, such as an embankment, by a sudden gush of water. **2.** An event or action that fails, is canceled, or ends prematurely, often because of rainy weather.

wash·rag (wŏsh**′**răg′) *n.* A washcloth.

wash·room (wŏsh**′**ro͞om′ *or* wŏsh**′**ro͝om′) *n.* A bathroom, especially one in a public place.

wash·stand (wŏsh**′**stănd′) *n.* **1.** A stand used to hold a basin and pitcher of water for washing. **2.** A bathroom sink.

wash·tub (wŏsh**′**tŭb′) *n.* A tub used for washing clothes.

was·n't (wŭz**′**ənt *or* wŏz**′**ənt) Contraction of *was not.*

wasp (wŏsp) *n.* Any of numerous insects having a body with a narrow midsection and two pairs of wings and often capable of giving a painful sting. [From Old English *wæps, wæsp.*]

WASP or **Wasp** *n.* A white Protestant of Anglo-Saxon ancestry, especially one in the upper social class of American society.

wasp·ish (wŏs**′**pĭsh) *adj.* **1.** Relating to or typical of a wasp. **2.** Easily irritated or annoyed; snappish. **—wasp′ish·ly** *adv.* **—wasp′ish·ness** *n.*

was·sail (wŏs**′**əl *or* wŏ-sāl**′**) *n.* **1.** A toast given in drinking to someone's health or as an expression of goodwill on festive occasions. **2.** The drink used in such toasting, commonly spiced ale or wine. **3.** A festivity with much drinking. ❖ *tr.v.* **was·sailed, was·sail·ing, was·sails** To drink to the health of; toast.

wast (wŏst; wəst *when unstressed*) *v. Archaic* A second person singular past tense of **be.**

waste (wāst) *v.* **wast·ed, wast·ing, wastes** *—tr.* **1.** To spend, consume, use, or expend foolishly or needlessly; squander: *waste food by leaving it out to spoil; wasted energy by leaving the heat on all night.* **2.** To cause to lose strength, energy, or vigor: *Disease wasted his body.* **3.** To fail to take advantage of or use for profit; lose: *wasted my chance.* **4.** To destroy completely. *—intr.* **1.** To lose energy, strength, weight, or vigor: *wasting away with hunger.* **2.** To pass without being put to use: *Time is wasting.* ❖ *n.* **1.** The act or an instance of wasting or the condition of being wasted: *a waste of resources.* **2.** An area, region, or land that is uninhabited or uncultivated; a desert or wilderness. **3.** A worthless or useless byproduct, as from a manufacturing process: *industrial wastes.* **4.** Garbage; trash. **5.** The material that remains after food has been digested and that is eliminated from the body. ◆ **waste (one's) breath** To gain or accomplish nothing by speaking: *Don't waste your breath arguing; the decision's been made.* [From Middle English *wasten,* from Latin *vāstāre,* to make empty.]

❑ *These sound alike:* **waste, waist** (body part).

waste·bas·ket (wāst**′**băs′kĭt) *n.* An open container for throwing away trash.

waste·ful (wāst**′**fəl) *adj.* Characterized by or inclined to waste; extravagant: *wasteful use of resources.* **—waste′ful·ly** *adv.* **—waste′ful·ness** *n.*

waste·land (wāst**′**lănd′) *n.* Land that is desolate, barren, or ravaged.

waste·pa·per (wāst**′**pā′pər) *n.* Discarded paper.

wast·ing (wā**′**stĭng) *adj.* **1.** Gradually deteriorating; declining. **2.** Sapping the energy, strength, or substance of the body: *a wasting disease.*

wast·rel (wā**′**strəl) *n.* A person who wastes, especially one who wastes money. [From *wast(e)* + *-rel* (as in *scoundrel*).]

watch (wŏch) *v.* **watched, watch·ing, watch·es** *—intr.* **1.** To look or observe closely or attentively: *Passers-by stopped to watch as the parade went by.* **2.** To look and wait expectantly or in anticipation: *watch for an opportunity.* **3.** To stay awake at night while serving as a guard, sentinel, or watcher. *—tr.* **1.** To look steadily; observe carefully: *watched the pianist's hands as she played.* **2.** To guard or keep surveillance on: *watched the house to see who came and went.* **3.** To tend or take care of (animals or a child, for example). ❖ *n.* **1.** The act or process of keeping awake or mentally alert, especially for the purpose of guarding. **2.** The act of closely observing or the condition of being closely observed; surveillance. **3.** A person or group of people serving to guard or protect. **4.** The post or period of duty of a guard, sentinel, or watcher. **5.** A period of wakefulness, especially one observed as a religious vigil. **6.** A small portable timepiece, especially one worn on the wrist or carried in the pocket. ◆ **watch it** To be careful. **watch (one's) step 1.** To act or proceed with care and caution. **2.** To behave as it is demanded, required, or appropriate. **watch out** To be careful or on the alert; take care. **watch over** To be in charge of; superintend. [From Old English *wæccan,* to watch, be awake.]

watch·dog (wŏch**′**dôg′) *n.* **1.** A dog trained to protect people or property. **2.** A person or group who guards or protects against waste, loss, or illegal practices.

watch·er (wŏch**′**ər) *n.* A person or thing that watches or observes: *a watcher of local politics.*

watch·ful (wŏch**′**fəl) *adj.* Closely observant or alert. **—watch′ful·ly** *adv.* **—watch′ful·ness** *n.*

watch·mak·er (wŏch**′**mā′kər) *n.* A person who makes or repairs watches. **—watch′mak′ing** *n.*

watch·man (wŏch**′**mən) *n.* A man employed to stand guard or keep watch.

watch·tow·er (wŏch**′**tou′ər) *n.* An observation tower on which a guard or lookout keeps watch.

watch·word (wŏch**′**wûrd′) *n.* **1.** A secret word or phrase that one uses to identify oneself as friendly or accepted; a password. **2.** A motto used as a call for support; a rallying cry.

wa·ter (wô**′**tər) *n.* **1.** A compound of hydrogen and oxygen having the formula H_2O. It occurs as a liquid that covers about three-quarters of the earth's surface, as a solid in the form of ice, and as a gas in the form of steam or water vapor. Water freezes at 32°F (0°C) and boils at 212°F (100°C). **2.** A body of water such as a sea, lake, river, or stream. **3. waters** A particular stretch of sea or ocean, especially that of a state or country. **4.** A supply of water: *Turn off the water when you're through.* **5.** Any of various forms of water: *waste water; sparkling water.* **6.** often **waters** Mineral water. **7.** Any of various watery substances or secretions occurring in or discharged from the body, such as sweat, saliva, or urine. ❖ *v.* **wa·tered, wa·ter·ing, wa·ters** —*tr.* **1.** To sprinkle, moisten, or supply with water: *water the garden.* **2.** To give drinking water to: *water the horses.* **3.** To mix or dilute with water: *water the wine.* —*intr.* **1.** To produce or discharge fluid, as from the eyes. **2.** To salivate in anticipation of food: *My mouth watered when I smelled the fresh bread.* ◆ **water down** To reduce the strength or effectiveness of: *had to water down the sweet syrup.* **water under the bridge** A past occurrence, especially something unfortunate, that cannot be undone or made right. [From Old English *wæter.*]

wa·ter·bird also **water bird** (wô′tər-bûrd′) *n.* A swimming or wading bird.

wa·ter·board·ing (wô′tər-bôr′dĭng) *n.* An interrogation technique, widely considered a form of torture, in which a person is restrained, usually by being strapped to a board with the feet higher than the head, and immersed in or doused with water to the point of drowning. **—wa′ter·board′** *v.*

wa·ter·borne (wô′tər-bôrn′) *adj.* **1.** Floating on or supported by water; afloat. **2.** Transported by water.

wa·ter·buck (wô′tər-bŭk′) *n., pl.* **waterbuck** or **wa·ter·bucks** A large African antelope that lives near water and has a shaggy coat and curved, ridged horns in the male.

water buffalo *n.* A domesticated Asian buffalo that has large spreading horns and is used especially for pulling or carrying loads.

water bug *n.* **1.** Any of various insects that live in water or wet places. **2.** A large cockroach.

water chestnut *n.* **1a.** A tropical Asian grasslike plant that grows in water and has a crisp edible underground stem that resembles a bulb. **b.** The underground stem of this plant, used as food. **2.** A floating water plant of Asia and Africa that has a nutlike fruit and occurs widely as an aquatic weed.

water closet *n.* A room or booth containing a toilet and often a sink.

wa·ter·col·or (wô′tər-kŭl′ər) *n.* **1.** A paint in which water instead of oil is mixed with the coloring material before use. **2.** A work done in this paint. **3.** The art of using watercolors.

water cooler *n.* A device for cooling and dispensing drinking water.

wa·ter·course (wô′tər-kôrs′) *n.* A natural or artificial channel through which water flows.

wa·ter·craft (wô′tər-krăft′) *n.* **1.** A boat or ship. **2.** *(used with a plural verb)* Water vehicles considered as a group. **3.** Skill in water-related sports.

wa·ter·cress (wô′tər-krĕs′) *n.* A plant that grows in freshwater ponds and streams and has strong-tasting leaves used in salads and as a garnish.

wa·ter·fall (wô′tər-fôl′) *n.* A natural stream of water descending from a height.

wa·ter·fowl (wô′tər-foul′) *n.* A waterbird, especially a swimming bird such as a duck.

wa·ter·front (wô′tər-frŭnt′) *n.* **1.** Land that borders a body of water. **2.** The part of a town or city that borders the water, especially a wharf district where ships dock.

water gap *n.* A valley cutting across a mountain ridge through which a stream flows.

wa·ter·ing can (wô′tər-ĭng) *n.* A vessel, usually having a long spout with a perforated nozzle, used to water plants.

watering hole *n.* A small natural depression in which water collects, especially a pool where animals come to drink.

watering pot *n.* A watering can.

water lily or **wa·ter·lil·y** (wô′tər-lĭl′ē) *n.* Any of various water plants having broad floating leaves and showy, variously colored flowers.

water line *n.* **1.** The line on the hull of a ship to which the surface of the water rises. **2.** A mark or stain, such as one left on a seawall, indicating the level to which water has risen or may rise.

wa·ter·logged (wô′tər-lôgd′) *adj.* **1.** Heavy and slow-moving because it is full of water: *a waterlogged ship.* **2.** Soaked or saturated with water: *a waterlogged field.*

Wa·ter·loo (wô′tər-lo͞o′) A town of central Belgium near Brussels. Napoleon met his final defeat in the Battle of Waterloo (June 18, 1815).

water main *n.* A principal pipe in a system of pipes for conveying water.

wa·ter·mark (wô′tər-märk′) *n.* **1a.** A mark showing the height to which water has risen. **b.** A line indicating the heights of high and low tide. **2.** A design impressed on paper during manufacture and visible when the paper is held up to light. **3.** Information encoded in the data portion of an image, video, or audio file that identifies the copyright owner or a licensed user.

wa·ter·mel·on (wô′tər-mĕl′ən) *n.* **1.** An often large melon having a hard, green rind and sweet, watery, pink or reddish flesh. **2.** The vine that bears such fruit.

water mill *n.* A mill with machinery that is driven by water.

water moccasin *n.* A venomous snake of swampy regions of the southeast United States.

water mold *n.* Any of various funguslike microorganisms that live in moist environments and parasitize other organisms. Water molds cause some serious plant diseases.

water of crystallization *n.* Water combined with other substances to form a crystal and capable of being removed by sufficient heat.

water polo *n.* A water sport played by two teams of swimmers who try to throw a ball into the opponents' goal.

wa·ter·pow·er (wô′tər-pou′ər) *n.* The energy produced by falling or running water that is used for driving machinery or generating electricity.

wa·ter·proof (wô′tər-pro͞of′) *adj.* **1.** Capable of keeping water from coming through. **2.** Made of or treated with a substance to prevent penetration by water. ❖ *n.* **1.** A waterproof material or fabric. **2.** *Chiefly British* A raincoat. ❖ *tr.v.* **wa·ter·proofed, wa·ter·proof·ing, wa·ter·proofs** To make waterproof.

water rat *n.* **1.** Any of various rodents that live near water and resemble the muskrat but are smaller and have a round tail. **2.** The muskrat.

wa·ter-re·pel·lent (wô′tər-rĭ-pĕl′ənt) *adj.* Resistant to penetration by water but not entirely waterproof.

water scooter *n.* **1.** A personal watercraft. **2.** A handheld, battery-operated device that spins a propeller to pull a swimmer through the water.

wa·ter·shed (wô′tər-shĕd′) *n.* **1.** The region draining into a river, river system, or other body of water. **2.** A ridge forming the boundary between regions whose water drains into two different systems of rivers. **3.** A turning point in a course of events.

water ski *n.* A broad ski often used in pairs for skiing on water while being towed by a motorboat. **—wa′ter-ski′** *v.*

water snake *n.* Any of various nonvenomous snakes living in or near freshwater streams and ponds.

wa·ter·spout (wô′tər-spout′) *n.* A tornado or less violent whirlwind occurring over water, consisting of a funnel-shaped column of air and water droplets.

George Washington

WRITERS CHOOSE THEIR WORDS

Grandfather had been cross all day. "What a miserable exchange," he complained. "All my birds leaving and my **wastrel** son and his wretched wife descending upon me. . . . I won't have them here. They can pitch a tent outside."

—Gloria Whelan
Listening for Lions

watercolor

water polo

water ski

wattle[2]

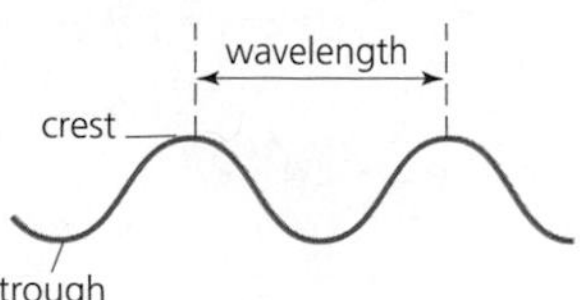

wavelength

ă	pat	ôr	core
ā	pay	oi	boy
âr	care	ou	out
ä	father	o͝o	took
ĕ	pet	o͝or	lure
ē	be	o͞o	boot
ĭ	pit	ŭ	cut
ī	bite	ûr	urge
îr	pier	th	thin
ŏ	pot	*th*	this
ō	toe	zh	vision
ô	paw	ə	about

water table *n.* The level below which the ground is completely saturated with water.

wa·ter·tight (wô′tər-tīt′) *adj.* **1.** So tightly made that no water can enter or escape. **2.** Having no flaws or loopholes: *a watertight excuse.*

water tower *n.* A standpipe or elevated tank used as a reservoir or for maintaining equal pressure in a water system.

water vapor *n.* Water in its gaseous state, especially in the atmosphere and at a temperature below the boiling point.

wa·ter·way (wô′tər-wā′) *n.* A navigable body of water, such as a river, canal, or channel.

water wheel *n.* A wheel propelled by running or falling water and used to power machinery.

water wings *pl.n.* A pair of inflatable bags that fit under a person's arms and keep that person afloat.

wa·ter·works (wô′tər-wûrks′) *pl.n.* **1.** *(used with a singular or plural verb)* The water system, including reservoirs, tanks, buildings, pumps, and pipes, that supplies water to a city or town. **2.** *(used with a singular verb)* A single unit, such as a pumping station, within such a system.

wa·ter·y (wô′tə-rē) *adj.* **wa·ter·i·er, wa·ter·i·est 1.** Filled with, consisting of, or soaked with water: *watery soil.* **2.** Containing too much water; diluted: *watery soup.* **3.** Resembling water, as in paleness, thinness, or liquidity: *a watery blue sky.*

Wat·son (wŏt′sən), **James Dewey** Born 1928. American biologist who with Francis Crick identified the structure of DNA.

watt (wŏt) *n.* A unit used to measure power, equal to one joule of work per second or about 1/746 horsepower. In electricity, a watt is equal to the amount of current (in amperes) multiplied by the amount of potential (in volts). [After James *Watt.*]

Watt (wŏt), **James** 1736–1819. British engineer and inventor whose improvements to the steam engine made possible its use in industry and transportation.

watt·age (wŏt′ĭj) *n.* An amount of power, especially electrical power, expressed in watts or kilowatts.

watt-hour (wŏt′our′) *n.* A unit of energy, especially electrical energy, equal to the work done by one watt acting for one hour and equivalent to 3,600 joules.

wat·tle[1] (wŏt′l) *n.* A structure of poles intertwined with twigs, reeds, or branches, used for walls, fences, and roofs. [From Old English *watel.*]

wat·tle[2] (wŏt′l) *n.* A fleshy, wrinkled, often brightly colored fold of skin usually hanging from the neck or throat of certain animals, especially birds such as chickens or turkeys.

wave (wāv) *v.* **waved, wav·ing, waves** —*intr.* **1.** To move freely back and forth or up and down in the air: *The reeds waved in the breeze.* **2.** To make a signal with an up-and-down or back-and-forth movement of the hand: *She waved and called out "Goodbye!"* —*tr.* **1.** To cause to move back and forth or up and down: *She waved a flag at the parade.* **2.** To move or swing as in giving a signal: *waved our hands wildly.* **3.** To signal or express by waving the hand or an object held in the hand: *waved good-bye.* **4.** To arrange into curves, curls, or swirls: *wave hair.* ❖ *n.* **1.** A ridge or swell that moves along the surface of a body of water. **2.** A moving curve or succession of curves in or on a surface; an undulation: *waves of wheat across the plain.* **3.** A disturbance or vibration, such as a sound wave, that passes through a medium or through space. **4.** A movement up and down or back and forth: *a wave of the hand.* **5.** A curve or arrangement of curves, as in hair: *a soft wave.* **6.** A widespread persistent weather condition: *a heat wave.* [From Old English *wafian.*]

❑ *These sound alike:* **wave, waive** (give up).

wave·length (wāv′lĕngkth′ *or* wāv′lĕngth′) *n.* The distance between one peak or crest of a wave and the next peak or crest. ◆ **on the same wavelength** *Informal* In complete accord; in harmony: *We were on the same wavelength when discussing the class trip.*

wave·let (wāv′lĭt) *n.* A small wave; a ripple.

wa·ver (wā′vər) *intr.v.* **wa·vered, wa·ver·ing, wa·vers 1.** To move unsteadily back and forth: *The flowers wavered in the wind.* **2.** To act in a hesitant or indecisive way; vacillate: *We wavered over the purchase of a new couch.* **3.** To become unsteady or unsure; falter: *His resolve began to waver.* **4.** To change or fluctuate: *The weather wavered between sunny and overcast.* **5.** To tremble or flicker, as sound or light. [From Middle English *waveren.*] —**wa′ver·er** *n.*

❑ *These sound alike:* **waver, waiver** (relinquishment).

wav·y (wā′vē) *adj.* **wav·i·er, wav·i·est 1.** Full of or rising in waves: *wavy hair; a wavy sea.* **2.** Having curves that resemble waves: *a wavy line.* —**wav′i·ness** *n.*

wax[1] (wăks) *n.* **1.** Any of various solid or soft sticky substances that melt or soften easily when heated. They are insoluble in water but soluble in most organic liquids. **2.** A waxy substance produced by bees; beeswax. **3.** A waxy substance produced by certain glands in the canal of the external ear. **4.** A solid plastic or very thick liquid material such as paraffin. **5.** A preparation containing wax used for polishing floors and other surfaces. ❖ *tr.v.* **waxed, wax·ing, wax·es** To coat, treat, or polish with wax: *wax a floor; wax a car.* [From Old English *weax.*]

wax[2] (wăks) *intr.v.* **waxed, wax·ing, wax·es 1.** To increase gradually in size, number, strength, or intensity: *Civilizations have waxed and waned over the centuries.* **2.** To show a progressively larger lighted surface, as the moon does in passing from new to full. [From Old English *weaxan.*]

wax bean *n.* A kind of string bean having yellow pods.

waxed paper (wăkst) *n.* Wax paper.

wax·en (wăk′sən) *adj.* **1.** Made of or covered with wax: *a waxen image.* **2.** Pale or smooth as wax: *a waxen face.*

wax myrtle *n.* Any of several evergreen shrubs, especially a species of the southeast United States that has small berries with a waxy coating.

wax paper *n.* Paper that has been made moistureproof by treatment with wax, used in cooking and storing foods.

wax·wing (wăks′wĭng′) *n.* Any of several crested, grayish-brown birds usually having waxy red tips on the wing feathers, such as the cedar waxwing.

wax·work (wăks′wûrk′) *n.* **1.** The art of modeling in wax. **2.** A figure made of wax, especially a life-size wax likeness of a famous person.

wax·y (wăk′sē) *adj.* **wax·i·er, wax·i·est 1.** Resembling wax in appearance or texture; pale, pliable, or smooth and lustrous: *a flower with waxy petals.* **2.** Full of, consisting of, or covered with wax.

way (wā) *n.* **1a.** A road, path, or highway affording passage from one place to another. **b.** An opening affording passage: *This door is the only way into the attic.* **2.** Space or opportunity to proceed: *cleared the way for the parade; opened the way to peace.* **3.** A course used in going from one place to another: *the shortest way home.* **4.** Progress or travel along a certain route or in a specific direction: *on his way north.* **5.** often **ways** *(used with a singular verb) Informal* Distance: *It is a long ways from here to Moscow.* **6.** A course of conduct or action: *the easy way out.* **7.** A manner or method of doing: *Isn't there any way to stop the leak?* **8.** A usual or habitual manner of being, living, or acting: *the American way of life.* **9.** An individual or personal manner of behaving, acting, or doing: *Have it your own way.* **10.** A specific direction: *He glanced my way.* **11.** An aspect, detail, or feature: *Our jobs are in no way comparable.* **12.** An ability or skill: *has a way with words.* **13.** A state or condition: *He is in a bad way financially.* **14.** A neighborhood or area: *Drop in when you're out our way.* ❖ *adv. Informal* **1.** By a great distance or to a great degree; far: *way off base; way over budget.* **2.** *Slang* Very; extremely: *That new skateboard is way cool.* **3.** From this place; away: *Go way.* ◆ **all the way** From beginning to end; completely: *She drove all the way from Chicago to Omaha.* **by the way** Incidentally: *By the way, I'm going on vacation next week.* **by way of** Through; via: *We walked to school by way of the park.* **go out of one's way** To do something that is inconvenient and beyond what is required: *went out of their way to put me up for the night.* **in the way** In a position that obstructs, hinders, or interferes: *There's nothing in the way of this project now.* **no way** *Informal* Under no circumstances; certainly not: *No way am I jumping into that water!* **on (one's) way** In the process of coming, going, or traveling: *It's getting dark, so I'll be on my way.* **on the way** On the route of a journey: *stopped at a diner on the way.* **out of the way** In a position that does not obstruct, hinder, or interfere: *Tell them to keep out of the way while I fix the sink.* **under way 1.** In motion or operation. **2.** In ongoing development; in progress. [From Old English *weg.*]

❑ *These sound alike:* **way, weigh** (measure weight), **whey** (watery part of milk).

way·far·er (wā′fâr′ər) *n.* A person who travels, especially on foot.

way·far·ing (wā′fâr′ĭng) *n.* Traveling, especially on foot.

way·lay (wā′lā′) *tr.v.* **way·laid** (wā′lād′), **way·lay·ing, way·lays 1.** To lie in wait for and attack from ambush. **2.** To interrupt the course or progress of: *travelers waylaid by a storm; an athlete waylaid by an injury.*

way-out (wā′out′) *adj. Slang* Very unconventional, unusual, or strange: *way-out clothes; way-out ideas.*

–ways *suff.* A suffix that means in a specified way, manner, direction, or position: *sideways.*

way·side (wā′sīd′) *n.* The side or edge of a road, way, path, or highway.

way station *n.* A station between principal stations on a route, as of a railroad.

way·ward (wā′wərd) *adj.* **1.** Stubborn or disobedient; willful or uncontrollable: *a wayward child.* **2.** Tending not to follow a procedure or method; unpredictable.

we (wē) *pron.* **1.** The person who is speaking or writing together with another or others: *We want to go swimming.* **2.** The person who is speaking or writing in an official capacity, especially a monarch or an editor of a magazine or newspaper. [From Old English *wē.*] —SEE NOTE.

❑ *These sound alike:* **we, wee** (tiny).

weak (wēk) *adj.* **weak·er, weak·est 1.** Having or showing little physical strength: *too weak to lift the box.* **2.** Having or showing little energy or poor health: *was very weak after the illness.* **3.** Having or resulting from little force of character, will, morality, or intelligence: *a weak personality.* **4.** Likely to fail under pressure, stress, or strain; lacking resistance: *a weak link in a chain.* **5.** Not having the proper or necessary concentration or effectiveness: *weak coffee; weak eyesight.* **6.** Lacking intensity: *weak sunlight.* **7.** Not very active and declining in value: *a weak housing market.* **8.** Lacking persuasiveness; unconvincing: *a weak argument.* **9.** Unstressed or unaccented in pronunciation or poetic meter. Used of a word or syllable. [From Middle English *weik*, from Old Norse *veikr*, not rigid, pliant.]

❑ *These sound alike:* **weak, week** (seven days).

weak·en (wē′kən) *tr. & intr.v.* **weak·ened, weak·en·ing, weak·ens** To make or become weak or weaker.

weak·fish (wēk′fĭsh′) *n.* A food fish of North American Atlantic waters.

weak·ling (wēk′lĭng) *n.* A person or thing having a weak body or character.

weak·ly (wēk′lē) *adj.* **weak·li·er, weak·li·est** Delicate in constitution; frail or sickly. ❖ *adv.* With little physical force or strength.

❑ *These sound alike:* **weakly, weekly** (every week).

weak-mind·ed (wēk′mīn′dĭd) *adj.* **1.** Having or showing a lack of judgment or conviction. **2.** Foolish; silly.

weak·ness (wēk′nĭs) *n.* **1.** The condition or quality of being weak: *physical weakness.* **2.** A personal defect or failing: *Concentrate on overcoming your weaknesses.* **3a.** A special fondness or liking: *a weakness for good talkers.* **b.** Something that one desires and cannot resist: *Ice cream is his weakness.*

weal[1] (wēl) *n.* **1.** Prosperity; happiness. **2.** The welfare of the community; the general good: *the public weal.* [From Old English *wela.*]

❑ *These sound alike:* **weal**[1] (prosperity), **weal**[2] (welt), **we'll** (we will), **wheal** (swelling), **wheel** (circular frame).

weal[2] (wēl) *n.* A ridge on the flesh raised by a blow; a welt. [Alteration of *wale.*]

❑ *These sound alike:* **weal**[2] (welt), **weal**[1] (prosperity), **we'll** (we will), **wheal** (swelling), **wheel** (circular frame).

wealth (wĕlth) *n.* **1.** A great quantity of money or valuable resources; riches. **2.** The state of being rich; affluence. **3.** A great amount; an abundance: *a wealth of information.*

wealth·y (wĕl′thē) *adj.* **wealth·i·er, wealth·i·est 1.** Having wealth; rich: *a wealthy family.* **2.** Well supplied; abundant: *a region wealthy in wildlife.* ❖ *n. (used with a plural verb)* Wealthy people considered as a group: *spent a lot of time socializing with the wealthy.* **—wealth′i·ly** *adv.* **—wealth′i·ness** *n.*

wean (wēn) *tr.v.* **weaned, wean·ing, weans 1.** To accustom (a young mammal) to take nourishment other than by suckling. **2.** To detach from something to which one is strongly habituated or devoted: *weaned herself from sweets.*

weap·on (wĕp′ən) *n.* **1.** An instrument of attack or defense in combat, as a gun, missile, or sword. **2.** A means used to defend against or defeat another: *Logic was her best weapon.* [From Old English *wǣpen.*]

weap·on·ize (wĕp′ə-nīz′) *tr.v.* **weap·on·ized, weap·on·iz·ing, weap·on·iz·es 1.** To supply with weapons or position weapons in: *weaponize outer space with lasers.* **2.** To produce or refine (a poisonous substance, for example) for use as a weapon.

weap·on·ry (wĕp′ən-rē) *n.* **1.** Weapons considered as a group. **2.** The design and production of weapons.

wear (wâr) *v.* **wore** (wôr), **worn** (wôrn), **wear·ing, wears** *—tr.* **1.** To carry or have on one's person as covering, adornment, or protection. **2.** To display in one's appearance: *wore a smile.* **3.** To bear, carry, or maintain in a certain way: *She wears her hair long.* **4.** To fly or display (colors). Used of a ship, jockey, or knight. **5a.** To damage, diminish, erode, or use up by long or hard use, friction, or exposure: *The wind and rain wore away the top layer of rock.* **b.** To produce by constant friction, pressure, or erosion: *wore a hole in the old shoes.* **6.** To fatigue, weary, or exhaust: *Your questions wear my patience.* *—intr.* **1.** To last under continual or hard use: *That fabric wears well.* **2.** To break down or diminish through use or friction: *The rear tires began to wear.* **3.** To pass gradually or tediously: *The December day wore on toward night.* ❖ *n.* **1.** The act of wearing or the state of being worn; use: *clothes for evening wear.* **2.** Clothing: *men's wear.* **3.** Damage resulting from use or age: *The rug shows evidence of wear.* **4.** The ability to withstand use; lasting quality: *The suit has plenty of wear left.* ◆ **wear down** To break down or exhaust by relentless pressure

wax bean

USAGE

we The pronoun **we** is correct when used as the subject of a sentence, even when it is paired with a noun: *We* (not *Us*) *students are making a video of the concert.* But when the pronoun is the object of a preposition, only *us* is correct: *For us students to make a video of the concert, we need to get permission.*

WRITERS CHOOSE THEIR WORDS

"Was finishing school so **wearisome** that you had to run away?" he asked.

"Very **wearisome,** and see what it's done to me. I can no longer break a set of dishes by accident. Now I can balance all of them on my head and stroll through Frell without dropping a single one."

—Gail Carson Levine
Ella Enchanted

weathercock

weathering

or resistance: *The child's continual pleading finally wore her parents down.* **wear off** To diminish gradually in effect: *My mouth hurt after the anesthetic wore off.* **wear out 1.** To make or become unusable through long or heavy use: *wore out a pair of hockey skates.* **2.** To exhaust; tire: *Raking the leaves wore me out.* **wear thin** To become less convincing, acceptable, or popular, as through repeated use: *Oversleeping is an excuse that has worn thin.* [From Old English *werian.*] **—wear′er** *n.*

❑ *These sound alike:* **wear, ware** (goods), **where** (at what place).

wea·ri·some (wîr′ē-səm) *adj.* Tiresome or tedious.

wea·ry (wîr′ē) *adj.* **wea·ri·er, wea·ri·est 1.** Physically or mentally tired. **2.** Showing or caused by tiredness: *a weary sigh.* **3.** Having one's interest, patience, or indulgence worn out: *I am weary of your complaints.* ❖ *tr. & intr.v.* **wea·ried** (wîr′ēd), **wea·ry·ing, wea·ries** (wîr′ēz) To make or become weary; tire. [From Old English *wērig.*] **—wea′ri·ly** *adv.* **—wea′ri·ness** *n.*

wea·sel (wē′zəl) *n.* **1.** Any of various mammals having a long narrow body, short legs, and a long tail, and feeding on small animals and birds. **2.** A cunning, sneaky, or treacherous person. ❖ *intr.v.* **wea·seled, wea·sel·ing, wea·sels** also **wea·selled, wea·sel·ling, wea·sels** To be evasive in the use of words; equivocate. ◆ **weasel out** *Informal* To back out of a situation or commitment in a sneaky or cowardly manner: *weaseled out of helping us clean up after the dance.*

weath·er (wĕth′ər) *n.* **1.** The condition or activity of the atmosphere at a given time and place, especially as described by variables such as temperature, humidity, wind velocity, and barometric pressure. **2.** Bad, rough, or stormy atmospheric conditions. ❖ *v.* **weath·ered, weath·er·ing, weath·ers** *—tr.* **1.** To expose to the action of the weather, as for drying, seasoning, or coloring: *weather lumber.* **2.** To affect or change, as in color or condition, by exposure: *Many voyages weathered the ship's hull.* **3.** To pass through (something) safely; survive: *weather a storm.* *—intr.* **1.** To show the effects of exposure to the elements. **2.** To withstand the effects of weather. ◆ **under the weather** Somewhat ill. [From Old English *weder.*]

❑ *These sound alike:* **weather, wether** (sheep), **whether** (if).

weath·er-beat·en (wĕth′ər-bēt′n) *adj.* Worn by exposure to the weather: *a weather-beaten house.*

weath·er·cock (wĕth′ər-kŏk′) *n.* A weathervane, especially one in the form of a rooster.

weath·er·glass (wĕth′ər-glăs′) *n.* An instrument, such as a barometer, that indicates change in atmospheric conditions.

weath·er·ing (wĕth′ər-ĭng) *n.* Any of the chemical or mechanical processes by which objects exposed to the weather are worn or broken down.

weath·er·proof (wĕth′ər-pro͞of′) *adj.* Capable of withstanding exposure to weather without damage. ❖ *tr.v.* **weath·er·proofed, weath·er·proof·ing, weath·er·proofs** To make weatherproof.

weather station *n.* A place where meteorological data are gathered, recorded, and released.

weath·er-strip (wĕth′ər-strĭp′) *tr.v.* **weath·er-stripped, weath·er-strip·ping, weath·er-strips** To fit or equip with weather stripping.

weather stripping *n.* Material in narrow strips, such as metal or plastic, installed around doors and windows to keep out cold or hot air.

weath·er·vane (wĕth′ər-vān′) *n.* A device for indicating wind direction.

weave (wēv) *v.* **wove** (wōv), **wo·ven** (wō′vən), **weav·ing, weaves** *—tr.* **1.** To make (cloth) on a loom by interlacing the threads of the woof and the warp. **2.** To interlace (threads, for example) into a fabric: *weave straw into a mat.* **3.** To make by interlacing or interweaving strands or strips of material: *weave a basket.* **4.** To combine into a whole made up of related parts: *She wove the separate incidents into a story.* **5.** To make or create by joining separate elements in an intricate way: *weave a captivating tale.* **6.** To spin (a web, for example). **7.** *Past tense* **weaved** To make (a path or way) by winding in and out or from side to side: *The taxi weaved its way through the traffic.* *—intr.* **1.** To engage in weaving; make cloth. **2.** *Past tense* **weaved** To move in a winding course or sway from side to side. ❖ *n.* The pattern or method of weaving a fabric: *a twill weave; a loose weave.* [From Old English *wefan.*] **—weav′er** *n.*

❑ *These sound alike:* **weave, we've** (we have).

weav·er·bird (wē′vər-bûrd′) *n.* Any of various chiefly tropical African or Asian songbirds that make nests of interwoven leaves and twigs.

web (wĕb) *n.* **1.** A structure of fine silky strands woven by spiders or by certain insect larvae. **2.** A woven fabric, especially one on or just removed from a loom. **3.** A latticed or woven structure: *A web of palm branches formed the roof of the hut.* **4.** Something intricately contrived, especially something that ensnares or entangles: *a web of deceit.* **5.** A fold of skin or thin tissue connecting the toes of certain water birds or other animals. **6.** A piece of leather or leather mesh that fills the space between the thumb and forefinger of a baseball glove. **7.** often **Web** The World Wide Web ❖ *tr.v.* **webbed, web·bing, webs** To provide with a web or webs. [From Old English.]

webbed (wĕbd) *adj.* **1.** Having the toes connected by a fold of skin or tissue: *the webbed foot of a seagull.* **2.** Formed by or provided with a web.

web·bing (wĕb′ĭng) *n.* A strong closely woven fabric used especially for seat belts and harnesses or in upholstery.

web·cam (wĕb′kăm′) *n.* A digital camera that can download images to a computer for transmission over the Internet or other network.

web-foot·ed (wĕb′fo͝ot′ĭd) *adj.* Having feet with webbed toes.

web·log (wĕb′lôg′) *n.* A blog.

web·mas·ter (wĕb′măs′tər) *n.* A person who designs, develops, markets, or maintains websites.

web·page or **Web page** (wĕb′pāj′) *n.* A document on the World Wide Web, often linked to other Web documents.

web·site or **Web site** (wĕb′sīt′) *n.* A set of webpages linked together so as to form a single unit, prepared as a collection of information by a person or organization.

Web·ster (wĕb′stər), **Daniel** 1782–1852. American politician who served numerous terms as a US representative, senator, and secretary of state between 1813 and 1850. Known for his support of a strong federal government and his opposition to slavery, he sought compromise to avoid civil war in 1850.

Webster, Noah 1758–1843. American dictionary maker whose major work, *An American Dictionary of the English Language,* was published in 1828.

wed (wĕd) *v.* **wed·ded, wed** or **wed·ded, wed·ding, weds** *—tr.* **1.** To take as a spouse; marry. **2.** To unite in marriage: *The minister wedded the young couple.* **3.** To cause to adhere devotedly or stubbornly: *argued against people who were wedded to the idea that the world was flat.* *—intr.* To take a spouse; marry.

we'd (wēd) Contraction of *we had* or *we would.*

❑ *These sound alike:* **we'd, weed**[1] (plant), **weed**[2] (token of mourning).

wed·ding (wĕd′ĭng) *n.* **1.** The act of marrying. **2.** The ceremony or celebration of a marriage. **3.** The anniversary of a marriage: *a golden wedding.*

wedge (wĕj) *n.* **1.** A piece of material, such as metal or

ă	pat	ôr	core
ā	pay	oi	boy
âr	care	ou	out
ä	father	o͝o	took
ĕ	pet	o͝or	lure
ē	be	o͞o	boot
ĭ	pit	ŭ	cut
ī	bite	ûr	urge
îr	pier	th	thin
ŏ	pot	*th*	this
ō	toe	zh	vision
ô	paw	ə	about

wood, tapered in a triangular shape and designed to be inserted into a crack or crevice and used for splitting, tightening, securing, or levering. **2.** Something shaped like a wedge: *a wedge of pie.* **3.** Something that intrudes and causes division or disruption: *Distrust drove a wedge between us.* **4.** A shoe having a solid, wedge-shaped heel that extends to the instep or toe. ❖ *v.* **wedged, wedg·ing, wedg·es** —*tr.* **1.** To split or force apart with or as if with a wedge: *wedge open a log; wedge apart the opposition.* **2.** To fix in place or tighten with a wedge: *wedged the window so it fit tightly.* —*intr.* To become lodged or jammed. [From Old English *wecg.*]

wed·lock (wĕd′lŏk′) *n.* The state of being married; matrimony.

Wednes·day (wĕnz′dē *or* wĕnz′dā′) *n.* The fourth day of the week. [From Old English *Wōdensdæg,* day of Woden (the chief god in Anglo-Saxon mythology).] —**Wednes′days** *adv.*

wee (wē) *adj.* **we·er, we·est** Very small; tiny: *a wee boy.* ◆ **wee hours** The early hours of the morning right after midnight: *We stayed up and talked into the wee hours.*

❑ *These sound alike:* **wee, we** (you and I).

weed¹ (wēd) *n.* A plant considered undesirable, especially one that grows where it is not wanted and often spreads quickly. ❖ *tr. & intr.v.* **weed·ed, weed·ing, weeds** To rid of or remove weeds. [From Old English *wēod,* grass, weed.]

❑ *These sound alike:* **weed¹** (plant), **we'd** (we had), **weed²** (token of mourning).

weed² (wēd) *n.* **1.** A token of mourning, such as a black band worn on the sleeve. **2. weeds** The black mourning clothes of a widow. [From Old English *wǣd,* garment.]

❑ *These sound alike:* **weed²** (token of mourning), **we'd** (we had), **weed¹** (plant).

weed·er (wē′dər) *n.* A person, tool, or device that removes weeds.

weed·y (wē′dē) *adj.* **weed·i·er, weed·i·est** **1.** Full of or consisting of weeds: *weedy ground; a weedy field.* **2.** Resembling, characteristic of, or being a weed: *a weedy plant.*

week (wēk) *n.* **1.** A seven-day calendar period, especially one that begins on a Sunday and continues through Saturday. **2.** A period of seven days: *had a week of rain.* **3.** The part of a calendar week devoted to work, school, or business. [From Old English *wicu.*]

❑ *These sound alike:* **week, weak** (feeble).

week·day (wēk′dā′) *n.* Any day of the week except Saturday and Sunday. —**week′days′** *adv.*

week·end (wēk′ĕnd′) *n.* The last part of the week, normally spent away from work or school, especially the period from Friday evening through Sunday evening. —**week′ends′** *adv.*

week·ly (wēk′lē) *adv.* **1.** Once a week or every week: *She visits us weekly.* **2.** By the week: *I am paid weekly.* ❖ *adj.* **1.** Relating to a week. **2.** Done, happening, or coming once a week or every week: *a weekly trip.* **3.** Computed by the week: *weekly earnings.* ❖ *n., pl.* **week·lies** A newspaper or magazine issued once a week.

❑ *These sound alike:* **weekly, weakly** (frail).

ween·ie (wē′nē) *n. Informal* A wiener.

weep (wēp) *v.* **wept** (wĕpt), **weep·ing, weeps** —*intr.* **1.** To express emotion, such as grief or sadness, by shedding tears. See Synonyms at **cry. 2.** To mourn or grieve: *wept for the dead.* **3.** To emit or run with drops of liquid: *The seams of the tent started to weep.* —*tr.* To shed (tears) as an expression of emotion; cry.

weep·ing (wē′pĭng) *adj.* **1.** Shedding tears; tearful. **2.** Dropping rain: *weeping clouds.* **3.** Having drooping branches: *a weeping cherry tree.*

weeping willow *n.* A willow tree with long, slender, drooping branches, often planted in gardens and parks.

wee·vil (wē′vəl) *n.* Any of numerous beetles that have a long downward-curving snout and that do great damage to plants and plant products.

weft (wĕft) *n.* The threads running crosswise in weaving; the woof.

We·ge·ner (vā′gə-nər), **Alfred Lothar** 1880–1930. German physicist, meteorologist, and explorer who introduced the theory of continental drift in 1915.

weigh (wā) *v.* **weighed, weigh·ing, weighs** —*tr.* **1.** To determine the weight of, as with a scale: *The grocer weighed the carrots on the scale.* **2.** To consider carefully by balancing in the mind; ponder: *weighed possible alternatives.* **3.** To choose carefully or deliberately: *He weighed his words when answering the question.* —*intr.* **1.** To be of a specified weight: *The newborn baby weighed seven pounds.* **2.** To have consequence or influence: *That factor weighed heavily in the decision.* **3.** To cause to bend heavily by or as if by added weight: *Wet snow weighed upon the branches.* **4.** To burden or oppress: *His guilty conscience weighed on him.* ◆ **weigh down 1.** To cause to bend down with added weight. **2.** To burden or oppress: *I'm weighed down with responsibility right now.* **weigh in 1.** To be weighed at a weigh-in: *The wrestlers weighed in before the competition.* **2.** To have one's baggage weighed, as at an airport. **3.** To be of a specified weight: *That new atlas weighs in at five pounds.* **4.** *Slang* To join in a discussion; utter a remark. [From Old English *wegan.*]

❑ *These sound alike:* **weigh, way** (path), **whey** (watery part of milk).

weigh-in (wā′ĭn′) *n.* An official weighing of the participants in an athletic contest, such as in a wrestling match, to make sure that they weigh within the required range for the event.

weight (wāt) *n.* **1.** The heaviness of something, such as an object or person: *The car has a weight of 2,800 pounds. The child's body weight is normal.* **2.** The force with which an object near the earth or another celestial object is attracted toward the center of the body by gravity. **3a.** A unit used as a measure of gravitational force: *a table of weights and measures.* **b.** A system of such measures: *avoirdupois weight; troy weight.* **4.** An object whose principal function is to exert a downward force by means of the action of gravity upon it, such as a paperweight or dumbbell. **5.** An object having a particular weight, used as a standard in weighing: *place a two-pound weight on the scale.* **6.** A heavy object, such as a dumbbell, lifted for exercise or in athletic competition. **7.** A load or burden; oppressiveness: *feeling a heavy weight of worry.* **8.** Influence or importance: *Her opinion has a lot of weight in the medical community.* ❖ *tr.v.* **weight·ed, weight·ing, weights 1.** To make heavy or heavier with a weight or weights. **2.** To load down, burden, or oppress. ◆ **gain weight** or **put on weight** To increase the weight of the body: *He has recovered from his long illness and gained weight.* **lose weight** To decrease the weight of the body: *I was on a diet and lost weight.*

❑ *These sound alike:* **weight, wait** (remain).

weight·less (wāt′lĭs) *adj.* **1.** Having little or no weight. **2.** Not experiencing the effects of gravity. —**weight′less·ness** *n.*

weight·lift·ing (wāt′lĭf′tĭng) *n.* The lifting of heavy weights, especially a barbell, as an exercise or in athletic competition.

weight·y (wā′tē) *adj.* **weight·i·er, weight·i·est 1.** Having considerable weight; heavy: *a weighty package.* **2.** Burdensome; oppressive: *weighty responsibilities.* **3.** Very serious or important: *a weighty matter.*

weir (wîr) *n.* **1.** A fence or barrier placed in a stream to catch or hold fish. **2.** A dam placed across a river or canal. [From Old English *wer.*]

❑ *These sound alike:* **weir, we're** (we are).

wedge

weeping willow

weevil

Duke of Wellington

BIOGRAPHY

Ida B. Wells Born during the Civil War to parents who were slaves in Mississippi, Ida B. **Wells** spent her life working tirelessly against racial discrimination. In 1889, after several years of teaching students in rural Tennessee, Wells became part owner of *Free Speech,* a radical Memphis newspaper she used as a forum for denouncing lynching. Wells's fiery editorials soon gained her recognition and notoriety. While she was on a lecture tour in the North, an angry mob burned her offices. Wells then mounted an international crusade against lynching, taking her lectures to England to gain support. Wells went on to help found the NAACP in 1909 and to found on her own the Negro Fellowship League in Chicago in 1910.

ă	pat	ôr	core
ā	pay	oi	boy
âr	care	ou	out
ä	father	o͝o	took
ĕ	pet	o͝or	lure
ē	be	o͞o	boot
ĭ	pit	ŭ	cut
ī	bite	ûr	urge
îr	pier	th	thin
ŏ	pot	*th*	this
ō	toe	zh	vision
ô	paw	ə	about

weird (wîrd) *adj.* **weird·er, weird·est** Strikingly odd or unusual, especially in an unsettling way; strange. [From Middle English *werd,* controlling fate, from Old English *wyrd,* fate.] **—weird′ly** *adv.* **—weird′ness** *n.*

weird·o (wîr′dō) *n., pl.* **weird·oes** *Slang* A very strange or eccentric person.

welch (wĕlch) *v.* Variant of **welsh.**

wel·come (wĕl′kəm) *adj.* **1.** Received with pleasure and friendliness into one's company or home: *a welcome guest.* **2.** Giving pleasure or satisfaction: *a welcome break from hard work.* **3.** Warmly or willingly permitted or invited: *You are welcome to join us.* ❖ *n.* **1.** A friendly greeting or reception. **2.** A reception upon arrival: *gave the stranger an unfriendly welcome.* ❖ *tr.v.* **wel·comed, wel·com·ing, wel·comes 1.** To greet, receive, or entertain (another or others) cordially or hospitably. **2.** To receive or accept gladly: *We would welcome a little privacy.* ❖ *interj.* An expression used to greet a visitor or recent arrival. ◆ **you're welcome** An expression used to acknowledge a statement of gratitude.

weld (wĕld) *v.* **weld·ed, weld·ing, welds** *—tr.* **1.** To join (pieces of metal) by heating them until the edges run together or until the edges are soft enough to be hammered or pressed together. **2.** To bring into close association or union: *A lifelong love of music welded their partnership.* *—intr.* To undergo welding or be capable of being welded: *an alloy that welds easily.* ❖ *n.* The joint formed when metal parts are united by welding. **—weld′er** *n.*

wel·fare (wĕl′fâr′) *n.* **1.** Health, happiness, and good fortune; well-being: *The government should promote the general welfare.* **2.** Financial or other aid provided, especially by the government, to people in need. ◆ **on welfare** Receiving regular assistance from the government or private agencies because of need. [From Middle English *wel faren,* to fare well.]

welfare state *n.* A social system in which the state assumes primary responsibility for the welfare of its citizens, as in health care, education, employment, and social security.

well[1] (wĕl) *n.* **1.** A deep hole or shaft dug or drilled into the earth to obtain water, oil, gas, sulfur, or brine. **2.** A container or reservoir, such as an inkwell, used to hold a liquid. **3.** A spring or fountain serving as a natural source of water. **4.** A source to be drawn upon: *The dictionary is a well of information.* **5.** A vertical opening that passes through the floors of a building, as for ventilation. ❖ *intr.v.* **welled, well·ing, wells** To rise to the surface, ready to flow: *Tears welled in his eyes.* [From Old English *welle.*]

well[2] (wĕl) *adv.* **bet·ter** (bĕt′ər), **best** (bĕst) **1.** In a good or proper manner: *The children behaved very well on the trip.* **2.** Skillfully or proficiently: *She plays the piano well.* **3.** Satisfactorily or sufficiently: *Did you sleep well?* **4.** Successfully or effectively: *gets along well with others.* **5.** In a favorable or approving manner: *They spoke well of you.* **6.** Thoroughly; completely: *Blend the ingredients well.* **7.** Perfectly; clearly: *How well do you remember the trip?* **8.** To a considerable degree or extent: *It was well after sunset.* **9.** In a close or familiar manner: *I knew him well.* **10.** With care or attention: *Listen well to what I say.* **11.** With reason or propriety; reasonably: *We cannot well refuse their hospitality.* ❖ *adj.* **better, best 1.** In a satisfactory condition; right or proper: *All is well.* **2a.** In good health; not sick. **b.** Cured or healed. See Synonyms at **healthy.** ❖ *interj.* **1.** An expression used to show surprise or relief. **2.** An expression used to introduce a remark or fill a pause during conversation: *Well, no one's perfect.* ◆ **as well 1.** In addition; also: *took another class as well.* **2.** With equal effect: *I might as well go.* [From Old English *wel.*]

we'll (wēl) Contraction of *we will.*

❑ *These sound alike:* **we'll, weal**[1] (prosperity), **weal**[2] (welt), **wheal** (swelling), **wheel** (circular frame).

well-ap·point·ed (wĕl′ə-poin′tĭd) *adj.* Having a full array of suitable equipment or furnishings.

well-bal·anced (wĕl′băl′ənst) *adj.* **1.** Evenly proportioned, balanced, or regulated: *had a well-balanced diet.* **2.** Mentally or emotionally stable: *raising a well-balanced child.*

well-be·ing (wĕl′bē′ĭng) *n.* The state of being healthy, happy, or prosperous; welfare.

well·born (wĕl′bôrn′) *adj.* Born to a genteel or aristocratic family.

well-bred (wĕl′brĕd′) *adj.* **1.** Raised to be well-mannered and refined. **2.** Born to parents considered to be of good stock. Used of animals.

well-de·fined (wĕl′dĭ-fīnd′) *adj.* Having definite and distinct lines or features.

well-done (wĕl′dŭn′) *adj.* Cooked all the way through: *a well-done steak.*

well-fa·vored (wĕl′fā′vərd) *adj.* Handsome; attractive.

well-fed (wĕl′fĕd′) *adj.* **1.** Adequately or properly nourished. **2.** Overfed; fat.

well-fixed (wĕl′fĭkst′) *adj. Informal* Financially secure; well-to-do.

well-found·ed (wĕl′foun′dĭd) *adj.* Based on sound judgment, reasoning, or evidence.

well-groomed (wĕl′gro͞omd′) *adj.* **1.** Neat and clean in dress and appearance: *well-groomed girls and boys.* **2.** Carefully combed and cared for: *sleek, well-groomed horses.*

well-ground·ed (wĕl′groun′dĭd) *adj.* **1.** Familiar with the most important aspect of a subject: *He's well-grounded in physics but not in chemistry.* **2.** Having a sound basis; well-founded.

well·head (wĕl′hĕd′) *n.* **1.** The source of a well or stream. **2.** A structure built over a well.

well-heeled (wĕl′hēld′) *adj.* Having plenty of money; prosperous.

Wel·ling·ton (wĕl′ĭng-tən) The capital of New Zealand, on extreme southern North Island. It was founded in 1840.

Wellington, First Duke of. 1769–1852. British general and politician whose troops defeated Napoleon at Waterloo (1815).

well-known (wĕl′nōn′) *adj.* **1.** Renowned; famous: *a well-known author.* **2.** Widely or generally known: *well-known facts.*

well-man·nered (wĕl′măn′ərd) *adj.* Polite; courteous.

well-mean·ing (wĕl′mē′nĭng) *adj.* Having or showing good intentions: *well-meaning advice.*

well-nigh (wĕl′nī′) *adv.* Nearly; almost: *well-nigh impossible.*

well-off (wĕl′ôf′) *adj.* Wealthy or prosperous.

well-read (wĕl′rĕd′) *adj.* Knowledgeable through extensive reading.

well-round·ed (wĕl′roun′dĭd) *adj.* **1.** Knowing or interested in a wide range or variety of subjects: *a well-rounded person.* **2.** Consisting of a wide range of subjects: *a well-rounded education.*

Wells (wĕlz), **Ida Bell** 1862–1931. American journalist who led an international campaign against lynching and founded the Negro Fellowship League in 1910. —SEE NOTE.

well-spo·ken (wĕl′spō′kən) *adj.* **1.** Chosen or expressed with aptness or propriety: *well-spoken words.* **2.** Courteous in speech: *a well-spoken young man.*

well·spring (wĕl′sprĭng′) *n.* **1.** The source of a stream or spring. **2.** A source: *She's a wellspring of ideas.*

well-thought-of (wĕl-**thôt′**ŭv′ *or* wĕl-**thôt′**ŏv′) *adj.* Regarded with respect; esteemed.

well-timed (wĕl′tīmd′) *adj.* Occurring or done at an opportune time: *a well-timed remark.*

well-to-do (wĕl′tə-dōō′) *adj.* Prosperous; affluent; well-off: *The mayor came from a well-to-do family.*
well-wish·er (wĕl′wĭsh′ər) *n.* A person who extends good wishes to another.
well-worn (wĕl′wôrn′) *adj.* **1.** Showing signs of much use or wear: *a well-worn suitcase.* **2.** Repeated too often; trite or hackneyed: *a well-worn phrase.*
welsh (wĕlsh *or* wĕlch) also **welch** (wĕlch) *intr.v.* **welshed, welsh·ing, welsh·es** also **welched, welch·ing, welch·es** *Informal* To cheat a person by not paying a debt or bet.
Welsh (wĕlsh) *adj.* Relating to Wales or its people, language, or culture. ❖ *n.* **1.** *(used with a plural verb)* The people of Wales. **2.** The Celtic language of Wales. [From Old English *Wælisc*, from *Wealh*, Welshman, Celt.]
Welsh cor·gi (kôr′gē) *n., pl.* **Welsh cor·gis** A dog of either of two breeds that originated in Wales, having a long body, short legs, and a head like that of a fox.
Welsh·man (wĕlsh′mən) *n.* A man who is a native or inhabitant of Wales.
Welsh rabbit *n.* A dish made of melted cheese, milk or cream, and sometimes ale, served hot over toast or crackers.
Welsh rare·bit (râr′bĭt) *n.* Welsh rabbit.
Welsh·wom·an (wĕlsh′wo͝om′ən) *n.* A woman who is a native or inhabitant of Wales.
welt (wĕlt) *n.* **1.** A ridge or bump raised on the skin by a blow or sometimes by an allergic reaction. **2.** A strip, as of leather or other material, that is stitched into a shoe between the upper and the sole. [From Middle English *welte.*]
wel·ter (wĕl′tər) *n.* **1.** A confused mass; a jumble: *a welter of papers and magazines on the table.* **2.** Confusion; turmoil. ❖ *intr.v.* **wel·tered, wel·ter·ing, wel·ters 1.** To wallow, roll, or toss about, as in mud or high seas. **2.** To lie soaked in a liquid.
wel·ter·weight (wĕl′tər-wāt′) *n.* A professional boxer who weighs more than 135 and not more than 147 pounds (about 61 66 kilograms).
Wel·ty (wĕl′tē), **Eudora** 1909–2001. American writer known for her stories and novels detailing rural Southern life. Her works include *The Optimist's Daughter* (1972).
wen (wĕn) *n.* A cyst containing oily secretions from the skin. ❑ *These sound alike:* **wen, when** (at what time).
wench (wĕnch) *n. Archaic* **1.** A young woman or girl. **2.** A woman servant.
wend (wĕnd) *tr.v.* **wend·ed, wend·ing, wends** To proceed on or along (one's way); go: *People wended their way home after the fireworks.* [From Old English *wendan.*]
went (wĕnt) *v.* Past tense of **go.**
wept (wĕpt) *v.* Past tense and past participle of **weep.**
were (wûr) *v.* **1.** Second person singular and plural past tense of **be. 2.** First and third person plural past tense of **be. 3.** Past subjunctive of **be.** ❑ *These sound alike:* **were, whir** (buzz).
we're (wîr) Contraction of *we are.* ❑ *These sound alike:* **we're, weir** (dam).
were·n't (wûrnt *or* wûr′ənt) Contraction of *were not.*
were·wolf (wâr′wo͝olf′ *or* wîr′wo͝olf′ *or* wûr′wo͝olf′) *n.* In folklore, a person who is transformed into a wolf or capable of assuming the form of a wolf. [From Old English *werewulf*: *wer*, man + *wulf*, wolf.] —SEE NOTE.
wert (wûrt) *v. Archaic* A second person singular past tense of **be.**
Wes·ley (wĕs′lē *or* wĕz′lē), **John** 1703–1791. English clergyman who was the leader of the early Methodist movement. His brother **Charles** (1707–1788) wrote many hymns.
west (wĕst) *n.* **1.** The direction in which the sun is seen to set, directly opposite east: *a wind blowing from the west.* **2.** often **West a.** A region or part of a country in this direction: *the west of Colombia.* **b.** The region of the United States west of the Mississippi River. **c.** The western part of the earth, especially Europe and the Western Hemisphere. ❖ *adj.* **1.** To, toward, facing, or in the west: *the west bank of the river.* **2.** From the west: *a west wind.* ❖ *adv.* In, from, or toward the west: *a river flowing west.* [From Old English.]
West Africa A region of western Africa between the Sahara Desert and the Gulf of Guinea. **—West African** *adj. & n.*
West Bank A disputed territory in historic Palestine west of the Jordan River, occupied by Israel in 1967.
West Berlin See **Berlin.**
west·bound (wĕst′bound′) *adj.* Going toward the west.
west·er·ly (wĕs′tər-lē) *adj.* **1.** Situated toward the west: *a westerly direction.* **2.** Coming from the west: *westerly winds.* ❖ *n., pl.* **west·er·lies** A storm or wind from the west.
west·ern (wĕs′tərn) *adj.* **1.** Situated in, facing, or toward the west: *the western sky.* **2.** Coming from the west: *a western wind.* **3.** often **Western** Relating to western regions or the West. **4. Western** Relating to those Christian churches that use or used Latin as their liturgical language. ❖ *n.* often **Western** A novel, film, television program, or other dramatic work about the American West, especially of the late 1800s.
west·ern·er also **West·ern·er** (wĕs′tər-nər) *n.* **1.** A native or inhabitant of a western region. **2.** A native or inhabitant of Europe or of a country such as the United States or Australia that was largely settled by Europeans.
Western Hemisphere The half of the earth made up of North America, Central America, and South America.
west·ern·ize (wĕs′tər-nīz′) *tr.v.* **west·ern·ized, west·ern·iz·ing, west·ern·iz·es** To cause to adopt the customs of Western civilization.
west·ern·most (wĕs′tərn-mōst′) *adj.* Farthest west.
Western Sahara A disputed region of northwest Africa on the Atlantic coast. The region was claimed by Spain in 1884 and ceded to Morocco and Mauritania in 1976, but resistance by nationalist guerrillas left Western Sahara's fate undecided.
Western Samoa See **Samoa.**
West Germanic *n.* A subdivision of the Germanic languages that includes German, Dutch, Yiddish, and English. **—West Germanic** *adj.*
West Germany See **Germany.**
West In·dies (ĭn′dēz) A group of islands between southeast North America and northern South America, including the Greater Antilles, the Lesser Antilles, and the Bahama Islands.
West Nile virus *n.* A virus that is transmitted by the bite of a mosquito and usually causes a mild fever but can result in severe, sometimes fatal disease characterized by high fever, headache, and confusion. [After the *West Nile* District of Uganda, where the virus was first isolated in 1937.]
West Point A US military installation in southeast New York on the western bank of the Hudson River north of New York City. The US Military Academy is located at West Point.
West Vir·gin·ia (vər-jĭn′yə) A state of the east-central United States west of Virginia. It was admitted as the 35th state in 1863. Charleston is the capital and the largest city. —SEE NOTE AT **Virginia.**
west·ward (wĕst′wərd) *adv. & adj.* Toward, to, or in the west: *sailed westward.* ❖ *n.* A direction or region to the west. **—west′wards** *adv.*
wet (wĕt) *adj.* **wet·ter, wet·test 1.** Covered or soaked with a liquid, such as water: *wet clothes.* **2.** Not yet dry or hardened: *wet paint; wet plaster.* **3.** Rainy, humid, or foggy: *a wet day; a wet climate.* ❖ *n.* **1.** Something

Ida B. Wells

WRITERS CHOOSE THEIR WORDS

Harry nods at the owner and takes Elizabeth's elbow; they **wend** their way around old furniture to the side wall, where paintings in curlicue frames hang in uneven lines.

—Patricia Reilly Giff
Storyteller

WORD HISTORY

werewolf The *were–* of **werewolf** is one of the last survivals of a word for "man" that used to be much more common. A *werewolf* is therefore a "man-wolf." Old English *wer,* "man," is related to the Latin word *vir,* "man." This Latin word is the basis of our words **virile,** "manly," and **virtue,** which used to mean "manliness, courage," but now means "moral excellence."

wetsuit

Phillis Wheatley

WRITERS CHOOSE THEIR WORDS

"I am a servant," Hwyll said, composedly. He stood, turned, and winked at Gawaine. "And I never argue where I can **wheedle**."

—Jane Yolen
Sword of the Rightful King

ă pat	ôr core
ā pay	oi boy
âr care	ou out
ä father	o͝o took
ĕ pet	o͝or lure
ē be	o͞o boot
ĭ pit	ŭ cut
ī bite	ûr urge
îr pier	th thin
ŏ pot	*th* this
ō toe	zh vision
ô paw	ə about

that wets; moisture: *tires spinning on the wet.* **2.** Rainy or snowy weather: *Don't stand out in the wet.* ❖ *tr. & intr.v.* **wet** or **wet·ted, wet·ting, wets** To make or become wet. [From Old English *wǣt.*] —**wet′ly** *adv.* —**wet′ness** *n.*

❑ *These sound alike:* **wet, whet** (make keen).

SYNONYMS **wet, moist, damp, humid** These adjectives mean covered with or filled with liquid. **Wet** is the most general: *I hung the wet towels on the clothesline.* **Moist** means slightly wet: *Please wipe the table with a moist sponge.* **Damp** means moist and often also unpleasantly sticky: *The damp cellar had a moldy smell.* **Humid** refers to a disagreeably high degree of water vapor in the atmosphere: *The hot, humid weather made us want to jump in the pond.*

wet blanket *n. Informal* A person or thing that discourages enjoyment or enthusiasm.

wet cell *n.* A primary electric cell having its electrolyte in the form of a liquid rather than in the form of a paste as in a dry cell.

weth·er (wĕ*th*′ər) *n.* A castrated male sheep or goat.
❑ *These sound alike:* **wether, weather** (state of the atmosphere), **whether** (if).

wet·land (wĕt′lănd′) *n.* A lowland area, such as a marsh or swamp, that is saturated with moisture.

wet·suit or **wet suit** (wĕt′so͞ot′) *n.* A tight-fitting, usually rubber garment designed to keep the body warm in water, used especially in scuba diving and water sports.

we've (wēv) Contraction of *we have.*
❑ *These sound alike:* **we've, weave** (make cloth).

whack (wăk) *tr. & intr.v.* **whacked, whack·ing, whacks** To strike with a sharp blow; slap. ❖ *n.* **1.** A sharp swift blow. **2.** The loud sound made by a sharp swift blow. ◆ **out of whack** *Informal* Out of order; not functioning correctly: *I woke up late because my alarm clock is out of whack.*

whale (wāl) *n.* Any of various often very large sea mammals that resemble fish in form but breathe air. [From Old English *hwæl.*]
❑ *These sound alike:* **whale, wail** (cry), **wale** (mark on the skin).

whale·boat (wāl′bōt′) *n.* A long fast-moving rowboat formerly used in the pursuit and harpooning of whales.

whale·bone (wāl′bōn′) *n.* **1.** A flexible horny substance forming plates or strips in the upper jaw of certain kinds of whales; baleen. **2.** An object made of this material.

whal·er (wā′lər) *n.* **1.** A person who hunts whales. **2.** A ship or boat used in whaling.

whal·ing (wā′lĭng) *n.* The business or practice of hunting and killing whales for their meat, oil, and bone.

wharf (wôrf) *n., pl.* **wharves** (wôrvz) or **wharfs** A pier where ships may tie up and load or unload.

Whar·ton (wôr′tn *or* hwôr′tn), **Edith Newbold Jones** 1862–1937. American writer whose works include *The House of Mirth* (1905).

what (wŏt *or* wŭt; wət *when unstressed*) *pron.* **1a.** Which thing or which particular one of many: *What are you having for dinner? What did she say?* **b.** Which kind, character, or designation: *What are these objects?* **2a.** That which; the thing that: *Listen to what I tell you.* **b.** Whatever thing that: *come what may.* **3.** *Informal* Something: *I'll tell you what.* ❖ *adj.* **1.** Which one or ones of several or many: *What movie did you see?* **2.** Whatever: *They soon repaired what damage had been done.* **3.** How great; how astonishing: *What a fool!* ❖ *adv.* How much; in what respect; how: *What does it matter?* ❖ *interj.* An expression used to show surprise, disbelief, or other strong and sudden excitement. ◆ **what if** What would occur if; suppose that: *What if everyone who registered to vote went to the polls?* **what it takes** The necessary expertise or qualities needed for success: *If you've got what it takes, you'll do well at this job.* [From Old English *hwæt.*]

what·ev·er (wŏt-ĕv′ər *or* wŭt-ĕv′ər) *pron.* **1.** Everything or anything that: *Please do whatever you can to help.* **2.** What amount that; the whole of what: *You may have whatever is left over.* **3.** No matter what: *Whatever you do, come early.* **4.** Which thing or things; what: *Whatever do you mean?* ❖ *adj.* **1.** Of any number or kind; any: *Whatever needs you may have, feel free to call on us.* **2.** All of; the whole of: *He used whatever strength he had left to finish the job.* **3.** Of any kind at all: *He was left with nothing whatever.* ❖ *interj. Informal* An expression used to show indifference to or scorn for something, such as a remark or suggestion: *We're having pizza tonight.—Whatever. I don't care.*

what·not (wŏt′nŏt′ *or* wŭt′nŏt′) *n.* A set of open shelves for holding ornaments. ❖ *pron.* Any of various additional or unspecified things or items: *Remember to pick up your gear and whatnot.*

what·so·ev·er (wŏt′sō-ĕv′ər *or* wŭt′sō-ĕv′ər) *pron.* Whatever. ❖ *adj.* Whatever: *They have no power whatsoever.*

wheal (wēl) *n.* A small swelling on the skin, as from an insect bite, that usually itches or burns.
❑ *These sound alike:* **wheal, weal**[1] (prosperity), **weal**[2] (welt), **we'll** (we will), **wheel** (circular frame).

wheat (wēt) *n.* **1.** The grain of any of several grasses that are native to the Mediterranean region and southwest Asia but grown in many parts of the world as an important source of food. The grain is usually ground into flour. **2.** Any of the plants that produce such grain. [From Old English *hwǣte.*]

wheat·en (wēt′n) *adj.* Relating to or made from wheat.

wheat germ *n.* The embryos of wheat kernels, rich in vitamins and used as a food supplement, as animal feed, and as a source of oil.

Wheat·ley (wēt′lē), **Phillis** 1753?–1784. African-born American poet considered the first widely recognized black writer in North America.

whee·dle (wēd′l) *v.* **whee·dled, whee·dling, whee·dles** —*tr.* **1.** To persuade or try to persuade by flattery or deceit; cajole. **2.** To get by flattering or deceit: *He wheedled a promise out of me.* —*intr.* To use flattery or deceit to achieve one's ends.

wheel (wēl) *n.* **1.** A solid disk or a rigid circular frame attached to a hub by spokes, designed to turn around an axle passed through its center. **2.** Something resembling a wheel or having a wheel for its main part, such as a steering wheel or a potter's wheel. **3. wheels** Forces that provide energy, movement, or direction: *the wheels of commerce.* **4. wheels** *Slang* A motor vehicle. **5.** *Slang* A very powerful or influential person: *He's a big wheel in business.* ❖ *v.* **wheeled, wheel·ing, wheels** —*tr.* **1.** To move, roll, or transport on wheels: *Put the books on the cart and wheel them to the library.* **2.** To cause to turn around or as if around a central axis; rotate or revolve. —*intr.* **1.** To turn around or as if around a central axis; revolve or rotate. **2.** To turn or whirl around in place; pivot: *The bull wheeled and charged.* **3.** To fly in a curving or circular course: *A hawk wheeled over the meadow.* ◆ **at the wheel** or **behind the wheel** Operating the steering mechanism of a vehicle; driving. [From Old English *hwēol.*]
❑ *These sound alike:* **wheel, weal**[1] (prosperity), **weal**[2] (welt), **we'll** (we will), **wheal** (swelling).

wheel·bar·row (wēl′băr′ō) *n.* A vehicle having one or two wheels, with handles at the rear, used to move small loads.

wheel·base (wēl′bās′) *n.* The distance from the center of the front wheel to that of the rear wheel in a motor vehicle.

wheel·chair (wēl′châr′) *n.* A chair mounted on large

wheels, used primarily by people who cannot walk or have difficulty walking.

wheeled (wēld) *adj.* Having wheels or a wheel: *a three-wheeled cart.*

wheel·er (wē′lər) *n.* **1.** A person or thing that wheels. **2.** A thing that moves on or is equipped with wheels or a wheel: *My younger brother can now ride a two-wheeler.*

wheel·er-deal·er (wē′lər-dē′lər) *n. Informal* A person who is shrewd, aggressive, or unscrupulous, especially in business.

wheel·house (wēl′hous′) *n.* A pilothouse. ◆ **in (one's) wheelhouse** In the area of one's greatest striking power: *a fastball that was right in the batter's wheelhouse.*

wheel·wright (wēl′rīt′) *n.* A person who builds and repairs wheels.

wheeze (wēz) *intr.v.* **wheezed, wheez·ing, wheez·es 1.** To breathe with difficulty, producing a hoarse whistling sound. **2.** To make a sound resembling laborious breathing: *The steam engine chugged and wheezed.* ❖ *n.* A wheezing sound. [From Middle English *whesen*, probably from Old Norse *hvæsa*, to hiss.]

wheez·y (wē′zē) *adj.* **wheez·i·er, wheez·i·est 1.** Given to wheezing. **2.** Making a wheezing sound: *a wheezy old car.*

whelk (wĕlk) *n.* Any of various large sea snails having a pointed spiral shell. [From Old English *weoloc.*]

whelm (wĕlm) *tr.v.* **whelmed, whelm·ing, whelms** *Archaic* **1.** To cover with water; submerge. **2.** To overwhelm.

whelp (wĕlp) *n.* **1.** A puppy or similar young animal. **2.** A young person; a child. ❖ *intr.v.* **whelped, whelp·ing, whelps** To give birth. Used of dogs and similar animals, such as wolves.

when (wĕn) *adv.* At what time: *When did you leave?* ❖ *conj.* **1.** At the time that: *in April, when the snow melts.* **2.** As soon as: *I'll call you when I get there.* **3.** Whenever: *When the wind blows, the windows rattle.* **4.** During the time at which; while: *When I was out, she stopped by for a visit.* **5.** Whereas; although: *He's always reading comic books when he should be studying.* **6.** Considering that; since: *How are you going to make the team when you won't practice?* ❖ *pron.* What or which time: *Since when has this been going on?* ❖ *n.* The time or date: *We knew the when but not the where of it.* [From Old English *hwenne.*] —SEE NOTE.

❑ *These sound alike:* **when, wen** (cyst).

whence (wĕns) *adv.* **1.** From where; from what place: *Whence came the traveler?* **2.** From what origin or source: *Whence comes this splendid feast?* ❖ *conj.* **1.** Out of which place; from or out of which. **2.** By reason of which; from which: *The dog was white, whence the name Snowflake.*

when·ev·er (wĕn-ĕv′ər) *adv.* **1.** At whatever time. **2.** When: *Whenever is she coming?* ❖ *conj.* **1.** At whatever time that: *We can start whenever you're ready.* **2.** Every time that: *I smile whenever I think back on that day.*

when·so·ev·er (wĕn′sō-ĕv′ər) *adv.* At whatever time at all; whenever. ❖ *conj.* Whenever.

where (wâr) *adv.* **1a.** At or in what place: *Where is the telephone?* **b.** In what situation or position: *Where would we be without your help?* **2.** From what place or source: *Where did you get that idea?* **3.** To what place or end: *Where does this road lead?* ❖ *conj.* **1.** At, to, or in a place which: *She lives where the climate is mild. Let's go where it's quiet.* **2.** At, to, or in a situation in which: *I want to know where you expect your project to be next week.* **3.** Wherever: *Where there's smoke, there's fire.* ❖ *n.* **1.** The place or occasion: *We know the when but not the where of it.* **2.** What place, source, or cause: *Where are you from?* [From Old English *hwǣr.*]

❑ *These sound alike:* **where, ware** (goods), **wear** (have on).

where·a·bouts (wâr′ə-bouts′) *adv.* About where; in, at, or near what location: *Whereabouts do you live?* ❖ *n. (used with a singular or plural verb)* The approximate location of someone or something: *His whereabouts are unknown.*

where·as (wâr-ăz′) *conj.* **1.** It being the fact that; inasmuch as: *Whereas you have worked hard to help us, so too will we work hard to help you.* **2.** While on the contrary: *We thought the dinner was tonight, whereas it was last night.*

where·at (wâr-ăt′) *conj.* **1.** Toward or at which. **2.** As a result or consequence of; whereupon.

where·by (wâr-bī′) *conj.* In accordance with which; by or through which: *I had a plan whereby we could take two hours off our traveling time.*

where·fore (wâr′fôr′) *adv.* For what purpose or reason; why: *Wherefore should we fear?* ❖ *n.* A purpose or cause: *I don't know all the whys and wherefores of the decision.*

where·in (wâr-ĭn′) *adv.* In what way; how: *Wherein have I offended?*

where·of (wâr-ŏv′ *or* wâr-ŭv′) *conj.* **1.** Of what: *I know whereof I speak.* **2.** Of which: *folk songs whereof many were handed down orally.*

where·on (wâr-ŏn′) *adv. Archaic* On which or what.

where·to (wâr′to͞o′) *adv.* To what place; toward what end: *Whereto are we heading?* ❖ *conj.* To which.

where·up·on (wâr′ə-pŏn′) *conj.* **1.** On which: *the old maple, whereupon we used to build a tree house every summer.* **2.** Closely following which: *The metal cools until it hardens, whereupon it is removed from the sand.*

wher·ev·er (wâr-ĕv′ər) *adv.* **1.** In or to whatever place or situation: *I touched up the wall with paint wherever it was needed.* **2.** Where: *Wherever have you been so long?* ❖ *conj.* In or to whatever place or situation: *My thoughts are with you wherever you go.*

where·with (wâr′wĭth′ *or* wâr′wĭth′) *pron.* The thing or things with which. ❖ *conj.* By means of which.

where·with·al (wâr′wĭth-ôl′ *or* wâr′wĭth-ôl′) *n.* The necessary means, especially financial means: *We haven't the wherewithal to build a new pool.*

whet (wĕt) *tr.v.* **whet·ted, whet·ting, whets 1.** To sharpen (a knife, for example); hone. **2.** To make more keen; stimulate: *The cooking odors whetted my appetite.* [From Old English *hwettan.*]

❑ *These sound alike:* **whet, wet** (damp).

wheth·er (wĕth′ər) *conj.* **1.** Used in indirect questions to introduce one of two alternatives: *We should find out whether the museum is open.* **2.** Used to introduce alternative possibilities: *Whether she wins or whether she loses, this will be her last tournament.* **3.** Either: *He passed the test, whether by skill or luck.*

❑ *These sound alike:* **whether, weather** (state of the atmosphere), **wether** (sheep).

whet·stone (wĕt′stōn′) *n.* A hard fine-grained stone used for sharpening tools.

whew (hwyo͞o *or* hwo͞o) *interj.* An expression used to show strong emotion, such as relief or amazement.

whey (wā) *n.* The watery part of milk that separates from the curds, as in the process of making cheese. [From Old English *hwæg.*]

❑ *These sound alike:* **whey, way** (path), **weigh** (measure weight).

which (wĭch) *pron.* **1.** What particular one or ones: *Which is your house?* **2.** The one or ones previously mentioned or implied: *My house, which is near the ocean, stays cool in summer. The nets with which they catch fish need to be repaired.* **3.** Whatever one or ones; whichever: *Choose which of these you want to take with you.* **4.** A thing or circumstance that: *She left early, which was smart.* ❖ *adj.* **1.** What particular one or ones of a number of things or people: *Which part of town do you mean?* **2.** Any one or

wheelbarrow

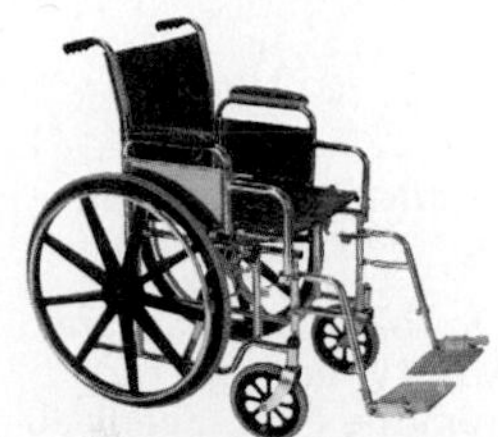

wheelchair
conventional *(top)* and racing *(bottom)*

USAGE

when Sometimes when you are trying to explain what something is, it is tempting to use **when** after a form of the verb *to be: A dilemma is when you do not know what to do.* Many people feel this use of *when* is clumsy, and it is better to rewrite such sentences using *in which: A dilemma is a situation in which you do not know what to do.*

whetstone

whippet

WRITERS CHOOSE THEIR WORDS

In that moment there was a **whir** and a click from the floor, clearly audible above the whispers rustling around them. Five hungry pairs of eyes focused instantly on the slot beside the blinking light. And out of the slot rolled a tiny ball, not a cylinder; a tiny ball hardly big enough for one small bite.

—William Sleator
House of Stairs

whisk

ă	pat	ôr	core
ā	pay	oi	boy
âr	care	ou	out
ä	father	o͝o	took
ĕ	pet	o͝or	lure
ē	be	o͞o	boot
ĭ	pit	ŭ	cut
ī	bite	ûr	urge
îr	pier	th	thin
ŏ	pot	*th*	this
ō	toe	zh	vision
ô	paw	ə	about

any number of; whichever: *Use which door you please.* **3.** Being the one or ones previously mentioned or implied: *It started to rain, at which point we ran.* [From Old English *hwilc.*] —SEE NOTE AT **that, when.**

which·ev·er (wĭch-ĕv′ər) *pron.* Whatever one or ones. ❖ *adj.* Being any one or any number of a group: *Read whichever books you please.*

whiff (wĭf) *n.* **1.** A brief passing odor carried in the air: *a whiff of popcorn.* **2.** An inhalation, as of air or smoke: *Take a whiff of this perfume.* **3.** A slight gentle gust of air; a waft. ❖ *intr.v.* **whiffed, whiff·ing, whiffs 1.** To be carried in brief gusts; waft: *smoke whiffing from the chimney.* **2.** In sports, to swing at and miss a ball or puck. **3.** In baseball, to strike out. Used of a batter.

whif·fle·tree (wĭf′əl-trē′) *n.* The crossbar to which the traces of a harness are attached, permitting a draft animal to pull a vehicle or implement.

Whig (wĭg) *n.* **1.** A member of a British political party of the 1700s and 1800s that was opposed to the Tories. **2.** A supporter of the war against England during the American Revolution. **3.** An American political party of the 1800s formed to oppose the Democratic party and favoring high tariffs and a loose interpretation of the Constitution.

while (wīl) *n.* **1.** A period of time: *stay for a while; singing all the while.* **2.** The time, effort, or trouble taken in doing something: *It will be worth your while to pay attention.* ❖ *conj.* **1.** As long as; during the time that: *It was great while it lasted.* **2.** In spite of the fact that; although: *While that guitar may look nice, it's not a very good instrument.* **3.** But; however: *The soles of the shoes are leather, while the uppers are canvas.* ❖ *tr.v.* **whiled, whil·ing, whiles** To spend (time) idly or pleasantly. [From Old English *hwīl.*]

❑ *These sound alike:* **while, wile** (trick).

whilst (wīlst) *conj. Chiefly British* While.

whim (wĭm) *n.* A sudden idea; a fancy.

whim·per (wĭm′pər) *v.* **whim·pered, whim·per·ing, whim·pers** —*intr.* To cry or sob with soft broken sounds. —*tr.* To utter in a whimper. ❖ *n.* A low, broken, sobbing sound.

whim·si·cal (wĭm′zĭ-kəl) *adj.* **1.** Marked by, arising from, or subject to whimsy: *a whimsical notion.* **2.** Playful or fanciful, especially in a humorous way: *a book with whimsical illustrations.* **—whim′si·cal·ly** *adv.*

whim·sy (wĭm′zē) *n., pl.* **whim·sies 1.** An odd or fanciful idea; a whim. **2.** Quaint, fanciful, or playful humor.

whine (wīn) *v.* **whined, whin·ing, whines** —*intr.* **1.** To make a mournful high-pitched sound, as in pain or complaint. **2.** To complain or protest in a childish or annoying way. —*tr.* To utter with a whine. ❖ *n.* **1.** The act of whining. **2.** A whining sound or complaint. [From Middle English *whinen,* from Old English *hwīnan,* to make a whizzing sound.]

❑ *These sound alike:* **whine, wine** (drink).

whin·ny (wĭn′ē) *intr.v.* **whin·nied, whin·ny·ing, whin·nies** To neigh, especially in a gentle manner. ❖ *n., pl.* **whin·nies** The sound made in whinnying; a neigh.

whip (wĭp) *v.* **whipped, whip·ping, whips** —*tr.* **1.** To strike with a strap or rod; lash: *whipped the horse with the reins.* **2.** To strike or affect in a manner similar to lashing: *Icy winds whipped my face.* **3.** To beat (cream or eggs, for example) into a froth or foam. **4.** To arouse or excite, especially with words: *The politician whipped the audience into a rage.* **5.** To move, pull, snatch, or remove suddenly: *She whipped her notebook out of her bag.* **6.** *Informal* To defeat; outdo: *You can't whip our team.* —*intr.* **1.** To move in a sudden quick manner; dart: *I watched her whip around the corner.* **2.** To move in a manner similar to a whip; thrash or snap about: *In the storm, branches whipped against the windows.* ❖ *n.* **1.** A flexible rod or thong attached to a handle, used for driving animals on or for striking or beating someone as punishment. **2.** Something that looks, bends, or lashes about like a whip. **3.** A member of a legislature selected by his or her political party to enforce party discipline: *the majority whip in the Senate.* **4.** A dessert made of sugar, whipped cream or stiffly beaten egg whites, and often fruit: *prune whip.* **5.** A lashing motion, stroke, or blow. ◆ **whip up 1.** To arouse or generate: *The mayor tried to whip up support for new construction projects.* **2.** *Informal* To prepare quickly: *We whipped up some sandwiches.* [From Middle English *whippen.*]

whip·lash (wĭp′lăsh′) *n.* **1.** The lash of a whip. **2.** An injury to the neck or spine caused by a sudden backward or forward jerk of the head.

whip·per·snap·per (wĭp′ər-snăp′ər) *n.* An unimportant and pretentious person.

whip·pet (wĭp′ĭt) *n.* Any of a breed of slender swift-running dog resembling the greyhound but smaller.

whip·poor·will (wĭp′ər-wĭl′ *or* wĭp′ər-wĭl′) *n.* A spotted brown North American bird that is active at night and has a call that sounds like its name.

whir (wûr) *intr.v.* **whirred, whir·ring, whirs** To produce a vibrating or buzzing sound or move while making such a sound: *The fan whirred in the window. A bee whirred past my ear.* ❖ *n.* A sound of buzzing or vibration.

❑ *These sound alike:* **whir, were** (existed).

whirl (wûrl) *v.* **whirled, whirl·ing, whirls** —*intr.* **1.** To revolve rapidly about a center or axis: *The propeller whirled faster and faster.* See Synonyms at **turn. 2.** To move while rotating or turning about: *The dancer whirled on stage.* **3.** To turn suddenly, changing direction: *whirled around to face me.* **4.** To have a spinning sensation; reel: *My head is whirling from the news.* —*tr.* **1.** To cause to rotate or turn rapidly: *whirl a baton.* **2.** To cause to move with a spinning motion: *The wind whirled the leaves.* ❖ *n.* **1.** The act of rotating or revolving rapidly. **2.** Something, such as a cloud of dust, that whirls or is whirled. **3.** A state of confusion; a tumult. **4.** A swift succession or round of events: *the social whirl.* **5.** *Informal* A short trip or ride: *Let's go for a whirl in the car.* **6.** *Informal* A brief or experimental try: *I've never skied before, but I'll give it a whirl.*

whirl·i·gig (wûr′lĭ-gĭg′) *n.* **1.** Any of various spinning toys. **2.** A merry-go-round. **3.** Something that is always whirling.

whirl·pool (wûrl′po͞ol′) *n.* **1.** A rapidly rotating current of water or other liquid, such as one produced by the meeting of two tides; an eddy. **2.** Something, such as a situation, that is confusing or tumultuous and is easy to be drawn into or difficult to get out of: *was sucked into a whirlpool of despair.* **3.** A bathtub or pool having jets of warm water that can be directed at a body part.

whirl·wind (wûrl′wĭnd′) *n.* **1.** A rapidly rotating column of air. **2.** A tumultuous confused rush.

whirl·y·bird (wûr′lē-bûrd′) *n. Informal* A helicopter.

whirr (wûr) *v. & n. Chiefly British* Variant of **whir.**

whisk (wĭsk) *v.* **whisked, whisk·ing, whisks** —*tr.* **1.** To cause to move with quick, light, sweeping motions: *whisking the crumbs off the table.* **2.** To whip (eggs or cream). —*intr.* To move lightly, nimbly, and rapidly. ❖ *n.* **1.** A quick, light, sweeping motion: *the whisk of a cow's tail.* **2.** A whiskbroom. **3.** A kitchen utensil, usually in the form of stiff, thin wire loops attached to a handle, used for whipping foodstuffs.

whisk·broom (wĭsk′bro͞om′ *or* wĭsk′bro͝om′) *n.* A small short-handled broom used especially to brush clothes.

whisk·er (wĭs′kər) *n.* **1a. whiskers** The hair on the cheeks and chin. **b.** A single hair of a beard or mustache. **2.** One of the bristles or long hairs growing near the mouth of certain animals, such as cats, rats, or rabbits.

whis·key also **whis·ky** (wĭs′kē) *n., pl.* **whis·keys** also

whis·kies An alcoholic liquor distilled from grain, such as corn, rye, or barley. [From Scottish Gaelic *uisge beatha*, water of life, whiskey.]

whis·per (wĭsʹpər) *n.* **1.** Soft speech produced without full voice. **2.** Something uttered very softly. **3.** A low rustling sound: *the whisper of wind in the trees.* ❖ *v.* **whis·pered, whis·per·ing, whis·pers** —*intr.* **1.** To speak softly. **2.** To make a soft rustling sound: *wind whispering in the leaves.* —*tr.* **1.** To utter very softly. **2.** To say or tell privately or secretly. [From Middle English *whisperen*, to whisper, from Old English *hwisprian*.]

whist (wĭst) *n.* A card game played by two teams of two players each that was a forerunner of bridge.

whis·tle (wĭsʹəl) *v.* **whis·tled, whis·tling, whis·tles** —*intr.* **1.** To make a clear musical sound by forcing air through the teeth or through an opening in the lips. **2.** To produce a clear, shrill, sharp musical sound by passing air over or through an opening: *The tea kettle whistled on the stove.* **3.** To make a shrill sharp cry: *The birds whistled in the trees.* **4.** To move swiftly so as to make a high-pitched sound: *The wind whistled through the trees.* —*tr.* **1.** To produce by whistling: *whistle a tune.* **2.** To summon, direct, or signal by whistling: *whistle down a cab.* ❖ *n.* **1.** A small wind instrument for making whistling sounds by means of the breath. **2.** A device for making whistling sounds by means of forced air or steam. **3.** A sound produced by whistling. **4.** A whistling sound, as of an animal or projectile. ◆ **blow the whistle** *Slang* To expose wrongdoing in the hope of bringing it to a halt. [From Old English *hwistlian*.]

Whis·tler (wĭsʹlər), **James Abbott McNeill** 1834–1903. American painter whose works include a portrait of his mother, entitled *Arrangement in Grey and Black* (1871).

whit (wĭt) *n.* The least or smallest bit: *doesn't care a whit.* [From Old English *wiht*, amount.]

white (wīt) *n.* **1.** The color of maximum lightness, as of milk, for example. **2.** The white or nearly white part, such as the albumen of an egg or the part of an eyeball around the iris. **3.** A thing that is white or nearly white, such as a white dye or a white variety of flower. **4. whites** White pants or a white outfit of a special nature: *tennis whites.* **5.** also **White** A member of a racial group of people having light skin, especially a person of European and sometimes Middle Eastern or North African origin. **6.** often **White** A political conservative or reactionary, especially one opposing the Bolsheviks in the Russian civil war. ❖ *adj.* **whit·er, whit·est 1.** Being of the color white, as new snow. **2.** Approaching the color white, as: **a.** Weakly colored; almost colorless; pale: *white wine.* **b.** Pale gray; silvery and lustrous: *white hair.* **3.** also **White** Belonging to a racial group having light skin, especially when of European and sometimes Middle Eastern or North African origin. **4.** Accompanied by or covered in snow: *a white Christmas.* **5.** Incandescent: *white flames.* **6.** With milk added. Used of tea or coffee. **7.** often **White** Politically conservative or reactionary, especially relating to the opposition of the Bolsheviks in the Russian civil war. ❖ *tr.v.* **whit·ed, whit·ing, whites** To create or leave blank spaces in (printed or illustrated matter): *whited the mistake out with correction fluid.* [From Old English *hwīt*.] —**whiteʹness** *n.*

white ant *n.* A termite.

white blood cell *n.* Any of the whitish or colorless cells in the blood that help protect the body against infections. There are several kinds of white blood cells, including the lymphocytes.

white·board (wītʹbôrdʹ) *n.* A panel covered with white, glossy plastic for writing on with erasable markers.

white·cap (wītʹkăpʹ) *n.* A wave with a crest of foam.

white-col·lar (wītʹkŏlʹər) *adj.* Relating to workers whose work usually does not involve manual labor.

white corpuscle *n.* A white blood cell.

white dwarf *n.* A celestial object that is formed when a star of low mass collapses. White dwarf stars are extremely dense but lack the mass to reach the denser states of a neutron star or black hole.

white elephant *n.* **1.** A rare whitish or light-gray form of the Asian elephant, often considered sacred in parts of South and Southeast Asia. **2.** A possession that provides few benefits and is an inconvenience or a financial burden to maintain.

white·fish (wītʹfĭshʹ) *n.* Any of various silvery freshwater fishes used as food.

white flag *n.* A white cloth or flag used to signal surrender or truce.

white gold *n.* An alloy of gold and nickel, sometimes also containing palladium or zinc, having a pale color like that of platinum.

white·head (wītʹhĕdʹ) *n.* A small white or yellowish lump in the skin caused by the buildup of fluid in a sebaceous gland.

white heat *n.* The temperature or physical condition of a white-hot substance.

White·horse (wītʹhôrsʹ) The capital of Yukon Territory, Canada, in the southern part of the territory on the Yukon River. It has been the capital since 1953.

white-hot (wītʹhŏtʹ) *adj.* So hot as to glow with a bright white light.

White House *n.* **1.** The executive mansion of the president of the United States. **2.** The executive branch of the US government: *The White House issued a bulletin.*

white lie *n.* A lie concerning a trivial matter, often told to prevent someone's feelings from being hurt.

white matter *n.* Whitish nerve tissue, especially of the brain and spinal cord, consisting chiefly of myelin-covered nerve fibers.

whit·en (wītʹn) *tr. & intr.v.* **whit·ened, whit·en·ing, whit·ens** To make or become white or whiter, especially by bleaching. —**whitʹen·er** *n.*

white night *n.* A night without full darkness, especially during the summer near the Arctic Circle.

white noise *n.* Acoustical or electrical noise in which the intensity is the same at all frequencies within a given band over time.

white oak *n.* An oak tree of eastern North America having leaves with rounded tips and hard, light-colored wood.

white·out (wītʹoutʹ) *n.* **1.** A polar weather condition in which the light reflected from the snow blends into the light reflected from the clouds, making any shadows and the horizon invisible and making it impossible to see where one is going. **2.** A usually white fluid that dries quickly and is dabbed on printed or written matter to cover mistakes.

white pepper *n.* A pungent spice consisting of whole or ground dried peppercorns from which the outer layer has been removed.

white pine *n.* **1.** A timber tree of eastern North America, having needles in clusters of five and durable wood that is easily worked. **2.** Any of several similar pine trees.

white sauce *n.* A sauce made with butter, flour, and milk, cream, or stock, used as a base for other sauces.

white·smith (wītʹsmĭthʹ) *n.* A person who works with light-colored metals, such as tin or another metal plated with tin, or who finishes and polishes metals. —SEE NOTE AT **blacksmith.**

white-tailed deer (wītʹtāldʹ) *n.* A common North American deer having a tail that is white on the underside.

white tie *n.* **1.** A white bow tie worn with a tailcoat. **2.** A style of evening dress that includes a white bow tie and a tailcoat for men and an evening gown for women.

whisker

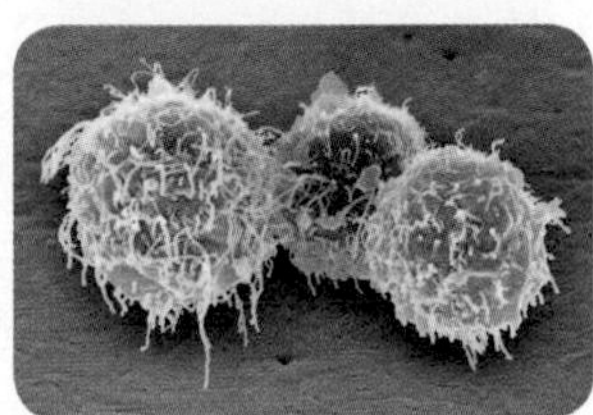

white blood cell

White House

white-tailed deer

whitewall tire

BIOGRAPHY

Walt Whitman Born on Long Island and raised in Brooklyn, Walt **Whitman** was a poet of the people. Largely self-educated, Whitman read widely and spent much time carefully observing the endless variety of people in New York City. In 1855 Whitman published *Leaves of Grass,* a volume of 12 poems that celebrated the people, democracy, and land of America. Although these poems may seem patriotic today, at the time Whitman was denounced for their unconventional style and content. Over the years Whitman expanded *Leaves of Grass* into a volume that included almost 400 poems by 1891. Whitman has since become known as one of the most original and influential of American poets.

ă	pat	ôr	core
ā	pay	oi	boy
âr	care	ou	out
ä	father	o͝o	took
ĕ	pet	o͝or	lure
ē	be	o͞o	boot
ĭ	pit	ŭ	cut
ī	bite	ûr	urge
îr	pier	th	thin
ŏ	pot	*th*	this
ō	toe	zh	vision
ô	paw	ə	about

white·wall tire (wīt′wôl′) *n.* An automobile tire having a white sidewall.

white·wash (wīt′wŏsh′) *n.* **1.** A mixture of lime and water, often with whiting, size, or glue, that is used to whiten walls, fences, and other structures. **2.** Concealment or glossing over of flaws or failures. ❖ *tr.v.* **white·washed, white·wash·ing, white·wash·es 1.** To paint or coat with whitewash. **2.** To conceal or gloss over (a flaw, for example).

white·wa·ter also **white water** (wīt′wô′tər) *n.* Turbulent or frothy water, as in rapids or surf.

whith·er (*w*ĭ*th*′ər) *adv.* To what place, result, or condition: *Whither are we going?*

❑ *These sound alike:* **whither, wither** (shrivel).

whit·ing¹ (wī′tĭng) *n.* A pure white grade of chalk that has been ground and washed for use in paints, ink, and putty. [From Middle English, from *whiten,* to whiten.]

whit·ing² (wī′tĭng) *n., pl.* **whiting** or **whit·ings 1.** A food fish of European Atlantic waters, related to the cod. **2.** Any of several silvery ocean fishes of North American coastal waters valued as food. [From Middle English, from Middle Dutch *wijting.*]

whit·ish (wī′tĭsh) *adj.* Somewhat white.

Whit·man (wĭt′mən), **Walt** 1819–1892. American poet whose *Leaves of Grass* (first published in 1855) celebrates the connections between human life and nature and the greatness of democracy and the United States. —SEE NOTE.

Whit·ney (wĭt′nē), **Eli** 1765–1825. American inventor and manufacturer who invented the cotton gin (1793), revolutionizing the cotton industry.

Whitney, Mount A peak, 14,491 feet (4,417 meters) high, in the Sierra Nevada of east-central California. It is the highest elevation in the continental United States.

Whit·sun·day (wĭt′sən-dē *or* wĭt′sən-dā′) *n.* Pentecost.

Whit·sun·tide (wĭt′sən-tīd′) *n.* The week beginning on Whitsunday, especially the first three days of this week.

whit·tle (wĭt′l) *v.* **whit·tled, whit·tling, whit·tles** —*tr.* **1.** To cut small bits or pare shavings from (a piece of wood). **2.** To fashion or shape in this way: *whittle a toy boat.* **3.** To reduce or eliminate gradually: *He whittled down his debt by making regular payments.* —*intr.* To cut or shape wood with a knife. **—whit′tler** *n.*

whiz also **whizz** (wĭz) *v.* **whizzed, whiz·zing, whiz·zes** —*intr.* **1.** To make a whirring or hissing sound, as of an object speeding through air. **2.** To do something quickly: *whizzed through her exams.* **3.** To pass quickly: *The days whizzed by.* —*tr.* To throw or spin rapidly: *whizzed the ball to me.* ❖ *n., pl.* **whiz·zes 1.** A whirring or hissing sound. **2.** *Informal* A person who is thought to be very skilled or gifted: *She's a whiz at math.*

who (ho͞o) *pron.* **1.** What or which person or persons: *Who is calling?* **2.** Used as a relative pronoun to introduce a clause referring to a person: *The boy who came yesterday is now gone.* [From Old English *hwā.*] —SEE NOTE.

whoa (wō) *interj.* **1.** An expression used as a command to stop, as to a horse. **2.** An expression used to express surprise, amazement, or great pleasure.

who'd (ho͞od) Contraction of *who would.*

who·dun·it (ho͞o-dŭn′ĭt) *n. Informal* A story dealing with a crime and its solution.

who·ev·er (ho͞o-ĕv′ər) *pron.* **1.** Whatever person or persons: *Whoever comes should be welcomed into the house.* **2.** Who: *Whoever could have dreamed of such a thing?*

whole (hōl) *adj.* **1.** Containing all component parts; complete: *I have the whole boxed set of the DVDs of that TV show.* **2.** Not divided or disjoined; in one unit: *a whole acre of land.* **3.** Constituting the full amount, extent, or duration: *The baby slept the whole trip home.* **4.** Sound; healthy: *It took a while for him to feel whole again after his lengthy illness.* ❖ *n.* **1.** A number, group, set, or thing lacking no part or element; a complete thing. **2.** An entity or system made up of interrelated parts: *the universe as a whole made up of the sun, planets, satellites, and other celestial objects.* ❖ *adv. Informal* Entirely; wholly: *a whole new idea.* ◆ **as a whole** All parts or aspects considered; altogether. **on the whole** Considering everything: *The damage doesn't look too bad, on the whole.* [From Old English *hāl.*]

❑ *These sound alike:* **whole, hole** (opening).

whole·heart·ed (hōl′här′tĭd) *adj.* Marked by full devotion or commitment; sincere: *wholehearted cooperation.* **—whole′heart′ed·ly** *adv.* **—whole′heart′ed·ness** *n.*

whole language *n.* A method of teaching people to read through the recognition of words in everyday situations.

whole note *n.* A musical note having the value of four beats in common time.

whole number *n.* **1.** A member of the set of positive integers and zero. **2.** A positive integer. **3.** An integer.

whole rest *n.* A musical rest having the value of four beats in common time.

whole·sale (hōl′sāl′) *n.* The sale of goods in large quantities, especially to a retailer. ❖ *adj.* **1.** Relating to or engaged in the sale of goods in large quantities for resale: *a wholesale dealer; wholesale prices.* **2.** Sold in large bulk or quantity, usually at a lower cost: *wholesale merchandise.* **3.** Made or accomplished extensively and indiscriminately: *wholesale destruction.* ❖ *adv.* In large bulk or quantity: *sell wholesale.* **—whole′sal′er** *n.*

whole·some (hōl′səm) *adj.* **whole·som·er, whole·som·est 1.** Conducive to or indicative of good health or well-being: *simple, wholesome food; a wholesome complexion.* **2.** Conducive to or promoting moral well-being: *wholesome entertainment.* **—whole′some·ly** *adv.* **—whole′some·ness** *n.*

whole step *n.* The interval of a major second in a musical scale. There is a whole step between C and D.

whole-wheat (hōl′wēt′) *adj.* **1.** Made from the entire grain of wheat, including the bran: *whole-wheat flour.* **2.** Made with whole-wheat flour.

who'll (ho͞ol) Contraction of *who will.*

whol·ly (hō′lē) *adv.* Entirely; completely.

❑ *These sound alike:* **wholly, holy** (sacred).

whom (ho͞om) *pron.* The objective case of **who.** —SEE NOTE AT **who.**

whom·ev·er (ho͞om-ĕv′ər) *pron.* The objective case of **whoever.**

whom·so·ev·er (ho͞om′sō-ĕv′ər) *pron.* The objective case of **whosoever.**

whoop (wo͞op *or* ho͞op) *n.* **1.** A loud cry of exultation or excitement. **2.** A hooting cry, as of a bird. **3.** The gasp characteristic of whooping cough. ❖ *v.* **whooped, whoop·ing, whoops** —*intr.* **1.** To utter a loud shout or hooting cry. **2.** To make the gasp characteristic of whooping cough. —*tr.* To utter with a whoop: *The fans whooped their delight.*

whoop·ing cough (ho͞o′pĭng *or* ho͝op′ĭng) *n.* A bacterial infection of the lungs and respiratory passages that causes spasms of coughing alternating with gasps.

whooping crane *n.* A large long-legged North American bird having mostly white feathers and a shrill trumpeting cry. It is now very rare and is in danger of becoming extinct.

whoops (wo͝ops *or* wo͞ops) *interj.* An expression used to show apology or mild surprise.

whop·per (wŏp′ər) *n. Slang* **1.** Something exceptionally big or remarkable. **2.** A gross untruth; a big lie.

whore (hôr) *n.* A prostitute.

❑ *These sound alike:* **whore, hoar** (frost).

whorl (wôrl *or* wûrl) *n.* **1.** A form that coils or spirals; a curl or swirl. **2.** An arrangement of three or more leaves, petals, or other plant parts arising from a single point. **3.**

One of the turns of a spiral shell. **4.** One of the circular ridges or convolutions of a fingerprint.

who's (ho͞oz) Contraction of *who is* or *who has.*
❑ *These sound alike:* **who's, whose** (possessive of who).

whose (ho͞oz) *adj.* **1.** The possessive form of **who. 2.** The possessive form of **which.** —SEE NOTE.
❑ *These sound alike:* **whose, who's** (who is).

who·so·ev·er (ho͞o′sō-ĕv′ər) *pron.* Whoever.

why (wī) *adv.* For what purpose, reason, or cause: *Why is the door shut?* ❖ *conj.* **1.** The reason, cause, or purpose for which: *I know why you're here.* **2.** On account of which; for which: *The reason why I went swimming yesterday was that it was very hot.* ❖ *n., pl.* **whys** A cause or reason: *studying the whys of unemployment.* ❖ *interj.* An expression used to show mild surprise, indignation, or impatience: *Why, I'm delighted to help!* [From Old English *hwȳ.*]

WI *abbr.* An abbreviation of Wisconsin.

Wic·ca (wĭk′ə) *n.* A Neopagan nature religion typically centering on a mother goddess or a goddess-god pair and the practice of ceremonial witchcraft. **—Wic′can** *adj. & n.*

Wich·i·ta[1] (wĭch′ĭ-tô′) *n., pl.* **Wichita** or **Wich·i·tas 1.** A member of a Native American confederacy formerly living in Kansas, now living in southwest Oklahoma. **2.** The Caddoan language of the Wichita.

Wich·i·ta[2] (wĭch′ĭ-tô′) The largest city of Kansas, in the south-central part of the state southwest of Kansas City. It was founded in the 1860s on the site of an earlier Wichita village.

wick (wĭk) *n.* A cord or strand of loosely woven fibers, as in a candle or oil lamp, that draws up fuel to the flame by capillary action. [From Old English *wēoce.*]

wick·ed (wĭk′ĭd) *adj.* **wick·ed·er, wick·ed·est 1.** Evil or immoral. **2.** Playfully malicious or mischievous: *played a wicked prank.* **3.** Severe and distressing: *has a wicked cough.* **—wick′ed·ly** *adv.* **—wick′ed·ness** *n.*

wick·er (wĭk′ər) *n.* **1.** Flexible twigs or strips of plastic that are interwoven and used especially for making baskets or furniture. **2.** Baskets, furniture, or other items made of this material. [From Middle English *wiker,* of Scandinavian origin.]

wick·et (wĭk′ĭt) *n.* **1.** A small gate or door, especially one built into or near a larger one. **2.** A small window or opening. **3.** In cricket, either of the two sets of three stakes, topped by a crossbar, that forms the target of the bowler. **4.** In croquet, any of the wire arches through which each player tries to hit a ball.

wick·i·up (wĭk′ē-ŭp′) *n.* A frame hut covered with matting, as of bark or brush, used by nomadic Native Americans of North America.

wide (wīd) *adj.* **wid·er, wid·est 1.** Extending over a large area from side to side; broad: *a wide street.* **2.** Having a specified extent from side to side: *a ribbon two inches wide.* **3.** Having great range or extent; including much or many: *a wide selection of dresses.* **4.** Fully open or extended: *look with wide eyes.* **5.** Being at a distance from a desired goal or point: *a shot wide of the mark.* ❖ *adv.* **wider, widest 1.** Over a great distance; extensively: *traveling far and wide.* **2.** To the full extent; completely: *The door was wide open.* **3.** Toward the side of or at a distance from a given boundary, limit, or goal: *shoot wide.* [From Old English *wīd.*] **—wide′ly** *adv.* **—wide′ness** *n.*

wide-a·wake (wīd′ə-wāk′) *adj.* **1.** Completely awake. **2.** Alert; watchful: *a wide-awake sentry.*

wide-eyed (wīd′īd′) *adj.* **1.** Having the eyes completely open. **2.** Innocent; naive.

wid·en (wīd′n) *tr. & intr.v.* **wid·ened, wid·en·ing, wid·ens** To make or become wide or wider.

wide·spread (wīd′sprĕd′) *adj.* **1.** Spread or scattered over a considerable extent: *widespread damage from last month's storm.* **2.** Occurring or accepted widely: *widespread agreement on the new proposal.*

wid·geon (wĭj′ən) *n.* Variant of **wigeon.**

wid·ow (wĭd′ō) *n.* A woman whose spouse has died and who has not remarried. ❖ *tr.v.* **wid·owed, wid·ow·ing, wid·ows** To make a widow or widower of.

wid·ow·er (wĭd′ō-ər) *n.* A man whose spouse has died and who has not remarried.

wid·ow's peak (wĭd′ōz) *n.* A V-shaped point formed by the hair near the top of the human forehead.

widow's walk *n.* A rooftop platform surrounded with a railing and originally built on coastal houses to observe ships at sea.

width (wĭdth *or* wĭth *or* wĭtth) *n.* **1.** The state, quality, or fact of being wide. **2.** The measurement of the extent of something from side to side: *a room ten feet in width.* **3.** A piece of material measured along the crosswise grain; a piece of fabric measured from selvage to selvage.

wield (wēld) *tr.v.* **wield·ed, wield·ing, wields 1.** To handle (a weapon or tool, for example), especially with skill and ease. **2.** To exercise (power or influence, for example) effectively.

wie·ner (wē′nər) *n.* **1.** Wienerwurst. **2.** A hot dog.

wie·ner·wurst (wē′nər-wûrst′ *or* wē′nər-wo͝orst′) *n.* A smoked pork or beef sausage similar to a frankfurter.

Wie·sel (vē′səl), **Elie(zer)** 1928–2016. Romanian-born writer and lecturer. A survivor of Nazi concentration camps, he dedicated his life to preserving the memory of the Holocaust.

wife (wīf) *n., pl.* **wives** (wīvz) A woman joined to another person in marriage; a female spouse. —SEE NOTE AT **husband.**

wife·ly (wīf′lē) *adj.* Relating to or befitting a wife.

Wi-Fi (wī′fī′) A trademark for the certification of products that meet certain standards for transmitting data over wireless networks.

wig (wĭg) *n.* An artificial covering of synthetic or natural hair worn on the head for adornment, as a way to hide baldness, or as part of a costume. [Short for *periwig.*]

wi·geon also **wid·geon** (wĭj′ən) *n., pl.* **wigeon** also **widgeon** or **wi·geons** also **wid·geons** Either of two wild ducks having brownish feathers, a white belly, and in the male a light-colored patch on the head.

wig·gle (wĭg′əl) *intr. & tr.v.* **wig·gled, wig·gling, wig·gles** To move or cause to move with short irregular motions from side to side: *She wiggled her toes. The dog's ears wiggled.* ❖ *n.* A wiggling movement or course. **—wig′gly** *adj.*

wig·gler (wĭg′lər) *n.* **1.** A person or thing that wiggles. **2.** The larva of a mosquito.

wig·wam (wĭg′wŏm′) *n.* A Native American dwelling commonly having an arched or conical framework covered with bark, hides, or mats.

wik·i (wĭk′ē) *n.* A collaborative website whose content can be edited by anyone who has access to it.

wild (wīld) *adj.* **wild·er, wild·est 1.** Growing, living, or occurring in a natural state; not cultivated, kept, or tamed by people: *wild plants; wild honey.* **2.** Not lived in or cultivated by people: *wild unsettled country.* **3.** Uncivilized or barbarous. **4.** Lacking discipline or control; unruly: *a wild young boy.* **5.** Full of or suggestive of strong uncontrolled feeling: *wild with joy; wild laughter.* **6.** Very strange or unlikely; outlandish: *a wild idea.* **7.** Far from the intended mark or target: *a wild throw.* **8.** In card games, having a value determined by the cardholder's choice: *playing poker with deuces wild.* ❖ *n.* **1.** A natural or undomesticated state: *Have you ever seen moose in the wild?* **2.** often **wilds** A region that is mostly uninhabited or uncultivated: *the wilds of northern Canada.* [From Old English *wilde.*] **—wild′ly** *adv.* **—wild′ness** *n.*

USAGE

who The word **who** is used for the subject of a sentence or clause, much like the pronouns *I* and *he*: *The actor who played Hamlet was there.* In this sentence *who* is the subject of *played Hamlet.* The word **whom** is used as the object of a verb. In the sentence *The student whom the teacher called on had no answer, whom* is the object of *called on. Whom* is also used as the object of a preposition: *To whom are you sending invitations?*

USAGE

whose Although *who* refers only to people, **whose** can refer to people or things. Thus, you can say *The cabinet, whose decoration is very ornate, is filled with china* as well as *The carpenter, whose skill in decoration is remarkable, built the cabinet.*

wicket
ball approaching a cricket wicket

Elie Wiesel

Oscar Wilde

Woodrow Wilson

WRITERS CHOOSE THEIR WORDS

So I'm right about the booby trap, but it's clearly more complex than I had imagined. I was right about the girl, too. How **wily** is she to have discovered this path into the food and to be able to replicate it so neatly?

—Suzanne Collins
The Hunger Games

ă	pat	ôr	core
ā	pay	oi	boy
âr	care	ou	out
ä	father	o͝o	took
ĕ	pet	o͝or	lure
ē	be	o͞o	boot
ĭ	pit	ŭ	cut
ī	bite	ûr	urge
îr	pier	th	thin
ŏ	pot	*th*	this
ō	toe	zh	vision
ô	paw	ə	about

wild boar *n.* A wild pig native to Eurasia and northern Africa, having dark dense bristles.

wild·cat (wīld′kăt′) *n.* **1.** Any of various small to medium-sized feline mammals, such as a lynx or a bobcat. **2.** A quick-tempered or fierce person. ❖ *adj.* **1.** Risky or unsound, especially financially. **2.** Relating to an oil or natural-gas well drilled in an area not known to be productive. **3.** Carried on without official permission or sanction: *a wildcat strike.*

Wilde (wīld), **Oscar Fingal O'Flahertie Wills** 1854–1900. Irish writer known for his plays, including *The Importance of Being Earnest* (1895), and his novel *The Picture of Dorian Gray* (1891).

wil·de·beest (wĭl′də-bēst′) *n., pl.* **wil·de·beests** or **wil·debeest** A gnu.

Wil·der (wīl′dər), **Laura Ingalls** 1867–1957. American writer whose books, such as *Little House on the Prairie* (1935), were based on her life on the American frontier.

Wilder, Thornton Niven 1897–1975. American writer whose works include novels and the play *Our Town* (1938).

wil·der·ness (wĭl′dər-nĭs) *n.* An unsettled uncultivated region.

wild·fire (wīld′fīr′) *n.* **1.** A raging rapidly spreading fire. **2.** Something that acts very quickly and intensely. **3.** Lightning that occurs without audible thunder.

wild·flow·er (wīld′flou′ər) *n.* **1.** A flowering plant that grows in a natural environment and has not been specially bred or cultivated. **2.** The flower of such a plant.

wild·fowl (wīld′foul′) *n.* A wild game bird, such as a duck, partridge, or quail.

wild-goose chase (wīld′go͞os′) *n.* A futile pursuit or search.

wild·life (wīld′līf′) *n.* Animals that have not been domesticated or tamed and are living in a natural environment.

wild pitch *n.* In baseball, an erratic pitch that the catcher cannot catch and that enables a base runner to advance.

wild rice *n.* **1.** The edible brownish grain of a tall North American grass that grows in water. **2.** The plant that bears such grain.

Wild West *n.* The western United States during the period of its settlement, especially with reference to its lawlessness.

wild·wood (wīld′wo͝od′) *n.* A forest or wooded area in its natural state.

wile (wīl) *n.* **1.** A trick or strategy that is deceitful, cunning, or clever. **2.** A disarming or seductive manner, device, or procedure. ❖ *tr.v.* **wiled, wil·ing, wiles 1.** To entice; lure: *wiled him into betraying his friends.* **2.** To pass (time) agreeably: *wile away a Sunday afternoon.* [From Middle English, from Old Norse *vēl*, trick, or of Low German origin.]
❑ *These sound alike:* **wile, while** (period of time).

wil·ful (wĭl′fəl) *adj.* Variant of **willful.**

Wil·helm II (vĭl′hĕlm) also **Wil·liam II** (wĭl′yəm) 1859–1941. Kaiser of Germany and king of Prussia (1888–1918). He was forced to abdicate at the end of World War I.

will¹ (wĭl) *n.* **1.** The power by which one deliberately chooses or decides upon a course of action: *the freedom of will.* **2.** Diligent purposefulness; determination: *the will to succeed.* **3.** A desire, purpose, or determination, especially of one in authority: *What is your will in this matter?* **4.** Bearing or attitude toward others; disposition: *a man of good will.* **5.** A legal declaration of how a person wishes his or her possessions to be disposed of after death. ❖ *v.* **willed, will·ing, wills** —*tr.* **1.** To decide on; choose or determine: *He can finish the race if he wills it.* **2.** To influence or induce by sheer force of will: *The coach seemed to will us to make a comeback.* **3.** To grant in a legal will; bequeath. —*intr.* **1.** To exercise the will. **2.** To make a choice; choose. [From Old English *willa.*]

will² (wĭl) *aux.v.* Past tense **would** (wo͝od) **1.** Used to indicate future action or condition: *They will return later.* **2.** Used to indicate likelihood or certainty: *You will regret this.* **3.** Used to indicate willingness: *Will you help me with this package?* **4.** Used to indicate requirement or command: *You will report to me afterward.* **5.** Used to indicate intention: *I will too if I feel like it.* **6.** Used to indicate customary or habitual action: *People will talk.* **7.** Used to indicate capacity or ability: *This metal will not crack.* **8.** Used to indicate probability or expectation: *That will be Matt calling to say he is going to be late.* ❖ *tr. & intr.v.* To wish; desire: *Do what you will. Sit here if you will.* [From Old English *willan.*] —SEE NOTE AT **shall.**

Wil·lem·stad (vĭl′əm-stät′) The capital of Curaçao, on the southern coast.

will·ful also **wil·ful** (wĭl′fəl) *adj.* **1.** Said or done on purpose; deliberate: *a willful waste of money.* **2.** Stubbornly bent on having one's own way: *a willful child.* **—will′ful·ly** *adv.* **—will′ful·ness** *n.*

Wil·liam I (wĭl′yəm) Known as "William the Conqueror." 1027?–1087. King of England (1066–1087) and duke of Normandy (1035–1087) who led the Norman invasion of England (1066).

William II See **Wilhelm II.**

Wil·liams (wĭl′yəmz) Family of American tennis players including **Venus** (born 1980) and **Serena** (born 1981), each of whom has won numerous individual Grand Slam titles, while as a team the pair has won 12 Grand Slam doubles titles.

Wil·liams, Roger 1603?–1683. English cleric who founded Providence, Rhode Island (1636), after being expelled from Massachusetts for his criticism of Puritanism.

Williams, Tennessee 1911–1983. American playwright whose works often concern family tensions. They include *The Glass Menagerie* (1944).

Williams, William Carlos 1883–1963. American poet whose verse is marked by a spare style and vivid observations of everyday occurrences and scenes.

Wil·liams·burg (wĭl′yəmz-bûrg′) A city of southeast Virginia southeast of Richmond. It was settled in about 1632 and was the capital of Virginia from 1699 to 1779. The city is now home to a restored colonial village.

William the Conqueror See **William I.**

will·ing (wĭl′ĭng) *adj.* **1.** Disposed or inclined; prepared: *I'm willing to accept your apology.* **2.** Acting or ready to act gladly: *a willing worker.* **3.** Done, given, or accepted voluntarily or ungrudgingly. **—will′ing·ly** *adv.* **—will′ing·ness** *n.*

will-o'-the-wisp (wĭl′ə-*thə*-wĭsp′) *n.* **1.** A phosphorescent light that flits over swampy ground at night, possibly caused by spontaneous combustion of gases given off by rotting organic matter. **2.** A delusive or misleading hope.

wil·low (wĭl′ō) *n.* Any of various trees or shrubs having slender flexible twigs, narrow leaves, and strong lightweight wood.

wil·low·y (wĭl′ō-ē) *adj.* **wil·low·i·er, wil·low·i·est 1.** Planted with or abounding in willows: *a willowy grove.* **2.** Suggestive of a willow, especially in flexibility, slenderness, or gracefulness.

will·pow·er or **will pow·er** (wĭl′pou′ər) *n.* The strength of will to carry out one's decisions, wishes, or plans.

wil·ly-nil·ly (wĭl′ē-nĭl′ē) *adv.* **1.** Whether desired or not: *He must do what we've asked, willy-nilly.* **2.** Without order or plan; haphazardly: *She threw her belongings into her bag willy-nilly.*

Wil·ming·ton (wĭl′mĭng-tən) The largest city of Delaware, in the northeast part of the state southwest of Philadelphia, Pennsylvania. It was founded in 1638.

Wil·son (wĭl′sən), **(Thomas) Woodrow** 1856–1924.

The 28th president of the United States (1913–1921), whose administration was marked by World War I and the introduction of Prohibition.

wilt¹ (wĭlt) *v.* **wilt·ed, wilt·ing, wilts** *—intr.* **1.** To become limp or flaccid; droop: *plants wilting in the dry heat.* **2.** To feel or show the effects of exhaustion: *We wilted after the long hike in the dunes.* *—tr.* **1.** To cause to droop or lose freshness: *The hot air from the heat vent wilted the flowers.* **2.** To deprive of energy or vigor; fatigue or exhaust. [Possibly alteration of dialectal *welk,* from Middle English *welken.*]

wilt² (wĭlt) *aux.v. Archaic* A second person singular present tense of **will²**.

wi·ly (wīʹlē) *adj.* **wi·li·er, wi·li·est** Full of wiles; cunning: *a wily fox.*

wimp (wĭmp) *n. Slang* A weak or timid person.

wim·ple (wĭmʹpəl) *n.* A piece of cloth wound around the head, framing the face, worn by women in medieval times and as part of the habit of certain orders of nuns.

win (wĭn) *v.* **won** (wŭn), **win·ning, wins** *—intr.* **1.** To achieve victory or finish first in a competition. **2.** To achieve success in an effort or venture. *—tr.* **1.** To achieve victory or finish first in (a race, for example). **2.** To receive as a prize or reward for performance: *won a blue ribbon.* **3.** To obtain or earn: *My father won his livelihood as an engineer.* **4.** To take in battle; capture: *won the old fort.* **5.** To succeed in gaining the favor or support of; prevail on: *Her speech won over the audience.* **6.** To gain the affection and loyalty of: *The new student won many friends.* ❖ *n.* A victory, especially in a competition. ◆ **win out** To succeed or prevail. [From Old English *winnan,* to fight, strive.]

wince (wĭns) *intr.v.* **winced, winc·ing, winc·es** To shrink or start involuntarily, as in pain, embarrassment, or distress: *She winced as the doctor pricked her finger to draw blood.* ❖ *n.* A shrinking or startled movement or gesture.

winch (wĭnch) *n.* A machine for pulling or lifting, consisting of a drum around which is wound a rope, cable, or chain attached to the load being moved.

wind¹ (wĭnd) *n.* **1.** A current of air, especially a natural one that moves along or parallel to the ground. **2.** A movement of air produced artificially, as by bellows or a fan. **3.** A natural current of air carrying sound or an odor: *The hounds got wind of the bear.* **4.** An influence, tendency, or destructive force: *the winds of change; the winds of war.* **5.** Breath, especially normal or adequate breathing: *had the wind knocked out of him.* **6.** Gas produced in the stomach or intestines during digestion. **7. winds a.** The brass and woodwinds sections of a band or orchestra. **b.** Wind instruments or their players considered as a group. **c.** Woodwinds. **8.** Rumor or information: *There will be trouble if wind of this gets out.* **9.** Speech or writing empty of meaning; verbiage. ❖ *tr.v.* **wind·ed, wind·ing, winds 1.** To cause to be out of or short of breath: *The long hill winded the runners.* **2.** To allow (a horse, for example) to rest so as to recover breath. ◆ **in the wind** Likely to occur; in the offing. [From Old English.]

wind² (wīnd) *v.* **wound** (wound), **wind·ing, winds** *—tr.* **1a.** To wrap (something) around itself or around something else: *She wound the string into a ball. I wound the line around the pole.* **b.** To wrap or encircle (something) in a series of coils: *wound the spool with thread.* **2a.** To go along (a curving or twisting course). **b.** To proceed on (one's way) in a coiling or spiraling course: *The brook winds its way through the forest.* **3.** To turn (a crank, for example) in a series of circular motions: *Wind the crank and then release it.* **4.** To coil the spring of (a mechanism) by turning a stem or cord, for example. *—intr.* **1.** To move in or have a curving or twisting course: *The river winds through the hills.* **2.** To be coiled or spiraled: *The vine wound around the trellis.* **3.** To be twisted or whorled into curved forms. ❖ *n.* A single turn, twist, or curve. ◆ **wind down 1.** To diminish or cause to diminish gradually in energy, intensity, or scope: *Tourism really winds down at this time of year.* **2.** To relax; unwind. **wind up 1.** To come or bring to an end: *Hunting season is winding up. We wound up the school year with a picnic.* **2.** To arrive in a place or situation after or because of a course of action: *My watch was running slow, so I wound up being late.* **3.** In baseball, to swing back the arm and raise the foot in preparation for pitching the ball. [From Old English *windan.*] **—windʹer** *n.*

wind·bag (wĭndʹbăgʹ) *n.* **1.** The flexible air-filled chamber of a bagpipe or similar instrument. **2.** *Slang* A person who talks a lot but does not say anything important or interesting.

wind·blown (wĭndʹblōnʹ) *adj.* Blown or dispersed by the wind: *windblown pollen.*

wind·break (wĭndʹbrākʹ) *n.* A row of trees, a hedge, or a fence that serves to lessen the force of or provide shelter from the wind.

Wind·break·er (wĭndʹbrāʹkər) A trademark used for a wind-resistant outer jacket with close-fitting waistband and cuffs.

wind·burn (wĭndʹbûrnʹ) *n.* An irritation or chafing of the skin caused by long exposure to the wind.

wind-chill factor (wĭndʹchĭlʹ) *n.* The temperature of windless air that would have the same effect on exposed human skin as a given combination of wind speed and air temperature.

wind·fall (wĭndʹfôlʹ) *n.* **1.** A sudden unexpected piece of good fortune. **2.** Something, such as a ripened fruit, that has been blown down by the wind. ❖ *adj.* Relating to a windfall: *windfall profits.*

wind farm (wĭnd) *n.* An arrangement of windmills or wind turbines that generate electricity.

Wind·hoek (vĭntʹho͝okʹ) The capital of Namibia, in the central part of the country.

wind·ing (wīnʹdĭng) *n.* **1.** Something wound about a center or an object. **2.** One complete turn of something wound. **3.** A curve or bend, as of a stream or road. ❖ *adj.* **1.** Turning or twisting: *a winding stream.* **2.** Spiral: *a winding staircase.*

wind instrument (wĭnd) *n.* **1.** A musical instrument in which sound is produced by a current of air, especially the breath, and which is not a keyboard instrument. Woodwind instruments, brass instruments, and the harmonica are types of wind instruments. **2.** A woodwind instrument, as opposed to a brass instrument.

wind·jam·mer (wĭndʹjămʹər) *n.* A large sailing ship.

wind·lass (wĭndʹləs) *n.* Any of various hauling or lifting devices similar to a winch.

wind·mill (wĭndʹmĭlʹ) *n.* A machine that gets power from a wheel of adjustable blades or slats turned by the wind.

win·dow (wĭnʹdō) *n.* **1.** An opening constructed in a wall, door, or roof to admit light or air, usually framed and fitted with one or more panes of glass. **2.** A pane of glass enclosed in such a framework; a windowpane. **3.** An opening or transparent part that resembles a window in function or appearance: *an envelope with a window.* **4.** A period of time during which an activity can or must take place: *a window of opportunity for preserving an unspoiled region.* **5.** A rectangular area on a computer screen in which information can be viewed independently from other such areas. [From Middle English *windou,* from Old Norse *vindauga* : *vindr,* air, wind + *auga,* eye.]

window box *n.* A long narrow box for growing plants, placed on or hung from a windowsill or ledge.

win·dow-dress·ing also **window dressing** (wĭnʹdō-drĕsʹĭng) *n.* **1.** Decorative exhibition of goods for sale in

wimple

winch

windmill

window box

windsock

Windsor chair

windsurfing

ă	pat	ôr	core
ā	pay	oi	boy
âr	care	ou	out
ä	father	o͝o	took
ĕ	pet	o͝or	lure
ē	be	o͞o	boot
ĭ	pit	ŭ	cut
ī	bite	ûr	urge
îr	pier	th	thin
ŏ	pot	*th*	this
ō	toe	zh	vision
ô	paw	ə	about

store windows. **2.** A means of improving appearances or creating a falsely favorable impression.

win·dow·pane (wĭn′dō-pān′) *n.* A piece of glass filling a window or a section of a window.

win·dow-shop (wĭn′dō-shŏp′) *intr.v.* **win·dow-shopped, win·dow-shop·ping, win·dow-shops** To look at merchandise in store windows without making purchases.

win·dow·sill (wĭn′dō-sĭl′) *n.* The horizontal member at the base of a window frame or opening.

wind·pipe (wĭnd′pīp′) *n.* A thin-walled tube of cartilage and membrane leading from the larynx to the bronchi and carrying air to the lungs; the trachea.

wind·row (wĭnd′rō′) *n.* **1.** A long row of cut hay or grain left to dry in a field before being bundled. **2.** A row, as of leaves or snow, heaped up by the wind.

wind·shield (wĭnd′shēld′) *n.* A pane of usually curved glass or other transparent material mounted in the front of a vehicle to protect passengers from the wind.

wind·sock (wĭnd′sŏk′) *n.* A large cone-shaped bag that is open at both ends and attached to a stand by a pivot to indicate the direction of the wind.

Wind·sor[1] (wĭn′zər) Ruling house of Great Britain that was founded in 1917 by George V and includes his descendants Edward VIII, George VI, and Elizabeth II.

Windsor[2], Duke of. See **Edward VIII.**

Windsor chair *n.* A wooden chair having a high rounded back of spokes and legs sloping outward.

wind·storm (wĭnd′stôrm′) *n.* A storm with high winds or violent gusts but little or no rain.

wind·surf (wĭnd′sûrf′) *intr.v.* **wind·surfed, wind·surf·ing, wind·surfs** To engage in windsurfing.

wind·surf·ing (wĭnd′sûr′fĭng) *n.* The sport of sailing while standing on a sailboard.

wind tunnel (wĭnd) *n.* A chamber through which wind can be forced at controlled speeds so its effect on an object, such as an aircraft, can be studied.

wind turbine (wĭnd) *n.* A turbine powered by the wind.

wind-up or **wind·up** (wĭnd′ŭp′) *n.* **1.** The act of bringing something to an end. **2.** A concluding part; a conclusion. **3.** In baseball, the movement of a pitcher, including the swinging back of the arm and raising of the forward foot, prior to pitching the ball.

wind·ward (wĭnd′wərd) *adj.* Relating to or moving toward the quarter from which the wind blows: *a windward tide; the windward quarter.* ❖ *adv.* In a direction from which the wind blows; against the wind. ❖ *n.* The direction from which the wind blows.

Windward Islands An island group of the southeast West Indies, including the southern group of the Lesser Antilles from Martinique south to Grenada.

wind·y (wĭn′dē) *adj.* **wind·i·er, wind·i·est 1.** Characterized by or having much wind: *a windy winter month.* **2.** Open to the wind; unsheltered: *the windy beach.* **3a.** Given to prolonged talk: *a windy speaker.* **b.** Lacking substance; empty: *a windy speech.*

wine (wīn) *n.* **1.** An alcoholic beverage made of the fermented juice of grapes. **2.** An alcoholic beverage made of the fermented juice of other fruits or plants: *dandelion wine.* **3.** The color of red wine. ❖ *tr.v.* **wined, win·ing, wines** To provide or entertain with wines. [From Old English *wīn*, from Latin *vīnum*.]

❑ *These sound alike:* **wine, whine** (complain).

wine cellar *n.* A place for storing wine.

wine·press (wīn′prĕs′) *n.* A vat in which the juice is pressed from grapes.

win·er·y (wī′nə-rē) *n., pl.* **win·er·ies** An establishment where wine is made.

wing (wĭng) *n.* **1.** One of a pair of specialized parts used for flying, as in birds, bats, or insects. **2.** An extending part resembling a wing, such as one of the thin projections on certain plant seeds. **3.** A part extending from the side of an aircraft whose principal purpose is to provide a force that holds the craft aloft. **4. wings** One of the areas that extend on either side of a stage and are concealed from the audience. **5.** A structure attached to and connected with the side of a building. **6.** A group affiliated with or subordinate to an older or larger organization. **7.** A unit of military aircraft or aviators. **8.** In certain sports such as hockey, either of two players in forward positions near the sides of the playing area. ❖ *v.* **winged, wing·ing, wings** —*intr.* To move swiftly through the air or on wings: *birds winging southward.* —*tr.* **1.** To throw (a ball, for example). **2.** To wound slightly, as in the wing or arm. ◆ **in the wings 1.** In the stage wings, unseen by the audience. **2.** Close by in the background; available at short notice. **on the wing** In flight; flying. **under (one's) wing** Under one's protection; in one's care. **wing it** *Informal* To say or do something without preparation, forethought, or sufficient experience; improvise. [From Middle English *winge*, of Scandinavian origin.]

wing case *n.* An elytron.

winged (wĭngd *or* **wĭng′**ĭd) *adj.* **1.** Having wings or parts resembling wings: *winged insects; the winged seeds of a maple.* **2.** Moving on or as if on wings; flying.

wing·er (wĭng′gər) *n.* A player who plays wing, as in hockey or soccer.

wing·less (wĭng′lĭs) *adj.* Having no wings or only undeveloped wings.

wing·nut or **wing nut** (wĭng′nŭt′) *n.* **1.** A nut with projections for enabling the thumb and forefinger to turn it. **2.** *Slang* A crazy or eccentric person.

wing·span (wĭng′spăn′) *n.* **1.** The distance between the tips of the wings on an aircraft. **2.** Wingspread.

wing·spread (wĭng′sprĕd′) *n.* The distance between the tips of the wings, as of a bird or insect, when fully extended.

wink (wĭngk) *v.* **winked, wink·ing, winks** —*intr.* **1.** To close and open the eyelid of one eye deliberately, as to convey a message, signal, or suggestion. **2.** To shine fitfully; twinkle: *A lighthouse winked in the far distance.* —*tr.* **1.** To close and open (an eye or the eyes) rapidly. **2.** To signal or express by winking: *winked his agreement.* ❖ *n.* **1a.** An act of winking. **b.** The very brief time required for a wink; an instant. **2.** A gleam or twinkle. **3.** *Informal* A brief period of sleep. ◆ **wink at** To pretend not to see. [From Old English *wincian*.]

win·ner (wĭn′ər) *n.* A person or thing that wins, especially a victor in sports or a notably successful person.

win·ning (wĭn′ĭng) *adj.* **1.** Relating to the act of winning: *pulled the winning card.* **2.** Successful; victorious: *the winning team.* **3.** Attractive; charming: *a winning personality.* ❖ *n.* **1.** The action of one that wins. **2.** often **winnings** Something won, especially money: *took her winnings to the bank.* **—win′ning·ly** *adv.*

Win·ni·peg (wĭn′ə-pĕg′) The capital of Manitoba, Canada, in the southeast part of the province east of Regina, Saskatchewan.

win·now (wĭn′ō) *tr.v.* **win·nowed, win·now·ing, win·nows 1.** To separate the chaff from (grain) by means of a current of air. **2.** To separate or get rid of (an undesirable part); sort or eliminate: *She winnowed out the old clothes from her closet.* **3.** To sort or select (a desirable part); extract: *He winnowed the important points from the long story.* **—win′now·er** *n.*

win·some (wĭn′səm) *adj.* Charming, often in a childlike or naive way.

win·ter (wĭn′tər) *n.* **1.** The coldest season of the year, occurring between fall and spring. In the Northern Hemisphere, it lasts from December until March. In the Southern Hemisphere, it lasts from June to September. **2.** The season extending from the winter solstice to the vernal equinox. ❖ *intr.v.* **win·tered, win·ter·ing, win·ters** To stay in a place for the winter: *people who winter in Florida.* ❖ *adj.* Occurring in or appropriate to the season of winter: *a howling winter storm; warm winter clothes.* [From Old English.]

win·ter·green (wĭn′tər-grēn′) *n.* **1.** A low-growing plant having spicy-smelling evergreen leaves and edible red berries. **2.** An oil or flavoring obtained from this plant.

win·ter·ize (wĭn′tə-rīz′) *tr.v.* **win·ter·ized, win·ter·iz·ing, win·ter·iz·es** To prepare or equip (a car or house, for example) for winter weather.

winter solstice *n.* **1.** In the Northern Hemisphere, the solstice that occurs on or about December 21, marking the beginning of winter. **2.** In the Southern Hemisphere, the solstice that occurs on or about June 21.

winter squash *n.* Any of several kinds of squash, such as the acorn squash, that have a thick rind and can be stored for long periods.

win·ter·time (wĭn′tər-tīm′) *n.* The winter season.

Win·throp (wĭn′thrəp), **John** 1588–1649. English colonial administrator who served several terms as governor of Massachusetts Bay Colony between 1630 and 1649.

win·try (wĭn′trē) also **win·ter·y** (wĭn′tə-rē) *adj.* **win·tri·er, win·tri·est** also **win·ter·i·er, win·ter·i·est 1.** Belonging to or characteristic of winter; cold: *wintry weather.* **2.** Suggestive of winter, as in coldness: *a wintry tone of voice.*

wintry mix *n.* A mix of such forms of precipitation as rain, freezing rain, sleet, and snow.

win-win (wĭn′wĭn′) *adj.* Relating to or being a situation in which the outcome benefits each of two groups: *a win-win proposition for the buyer and the seller.*

wipe (wīp) *tr.v.* **wiped, wip·ing, wipes 1.** To rub, as with a cloth or paper, in order to clean or dry: *wipe the dishes with a towel.* **2.** To remove by or as if by rubbing: *wiping the tears away.* **3.** To spread or apply by or as if by wiping: *wiped furniture polish over the table.* ❖ *n.* **1.** The act or an instance of wiping: *giving the table a wipe with a clean cloth.* **2.** Something used for wiping, such as a disposable cloth or towel. ◆ **wipe out 1.** To destroy or be destroyed completely. **2.** To lose one's balance and fall or jump off, as from a surfboard. [From Old English *wīpian.*] **—wip′er** *n.*

wire (wīr) *n.* **1.** A usually flexible strand or rod of metal, used for structural support, especially in concrete, and for conducting electricity, when it is covered in rubber or plastic insulation. **2.** A cable made of such strands joined or twisted together. **3a.** A telegraph service. **b.** A telegram. **4.** *Slang* A hidden microphone, as on a person's body or in a building: *The spy wore a wire.* ❖ *tr.v.* **wired, wir·ing, wires 1.** To equip with a system of electrical wires: *wire a house.* **2.** To join, connect, or attach with a wire or wires: *wired the TV to the computer.* **3.** To send by telegraph: *wire congratulations.* **4.** To send a telegram to (someone). ◆ **down to the wire** *Informal* At the very end, as in a race. **under the wire 1.** At the finish line of a race. **2.** *Informal* At the last moment. [From Old English *wīr.*]

wire·haired (wīr′hârd′) *adj.* Having a coat of stiff wiry hair: *a wirehaired fox terrier.*

wire·less (wīr′lĭs) *adj.* **1.** Having no wires. **2.** Relating to communication by transmitting electromagnetic signals through the air: *a wireless network.* **3.** *Chiefly British* Relating to radio communication. ❖ *n.* **1.** A radio telegraph or radio telephone system. **2.** *Chiefly British* A radio.

wire·line (wīr′līn′) *adj.* Relating to the transmission of electromagnetic signals through wires: *a wireline network.*

wire·tap (wīr′tăp′) *n.* **1.** An act of secretly listening to or recording a person's telephone or Internet conversations, often as part of a police investigation. **2.** A device that is connected to a communications circuit in a concealed fashion in order to enable a wiretap. ❖ *tr.v.* **wire·tapped, wire·tap·ping, wire·taps 1.** To listen to or record in secret (a conversation carried on over a telephone line or other communications channel), often as part of a police investigation. **2.** To connect a wiretap to (a telephone circuit, for example). **3.** To monitor (a telephone circuit) by means of a wiretap.

wire·worm (wīr′wûrm′) *n.* A yellowish hard-bodied larva of certain beetles that feeds on the roots and seedlings of many crop plants.

wir·ing (wīr′ĭng) *n.* **1.** The act of attaching, connecting, or installing electric wires. **2.** A system of electric wires.

wir·y (wīr′ē) *adj.* **wir·i·er, wir·i·est 1.** Relating to wire. **2.** Resembling wire in form or quality, especially in stiffness: *wiry hair.* **3.** Sinewy and lean: *an athlete with a wiry physique.* **—wir′i·ness** *n.*

Wis·con·sin (wĭs-kŏn′sĭn) A state of the north-central United States north of Illinois. It was admitted as the 30th state in 1848. Madison is the capital and Milwaukee the largest city. —SEE NOTE.

wis·dom (wĭz′dəm) *n.* **1.** The ability to discern or judge what is true, right, or lasting; insight. **2.** Common sense; good judgment. **3.** The sum of learning through the ages; knowledge.

wisdom tooth *n.* One of four molars, the last on each side of both jaws in humans, usually appearing in young adulthood.

wise[1] (wīz) *adj.* **wis·er, wis·est 1.** Having or showing wisdom or good sense; judicious or prudent: *a wise leader; a wise decision.* **2.** Shrewd; crafty: *a wise move.* **3.** Provided with information; informed: *I'm wise to your tricks.* **4.** *Slang* Rude and disrespectful; impudent. [From Old English *wīs.*] **—wise′ly** *adv.*

wise[2] (wīz) *n.* Method or manner of doing: *In no wise would that be fair.* [From Old English *wīse.*]

–wise *suff.* A suffix that means in a specified manner, position, or direction: *clockwise.* —SEE NOTE.

wise·a·cre (wīz′ā′kər) *n. Slang* A person who is conceited or shows off in a disagreeable way. [Alteration by folk etymology of Middle Dutch *wijsseggher,* soothsayer, ultimately from Old High German *wīzag,* knowledgeable.]

wise·crack (wīz′krăk′) *Informal n.* A joking or sarcastic remark. ❖ *intr.v.* **wise·cracked, wise·crack·ing, wise·cracks** To make or utter a wisecrack.

wise guy *n. Slang* A smart aleck.

wish (wĭsh) *n.* **1.** A feeling that one would like to have or do something or to see something happen; a desire or longing for a specific thing. **2.** An expression of desire for something, especially for someone's happiness or success: *Give them my best wishes.* **3.** Something desired or longed for: *He got his wish.* ❖ *v.* **wished, wish·ing, wish·es** *—tr.* **1.** To long for; want: *They wish to see you. I wish that I could speak Spanish fluently.* See Synonyms at **desire. 2.** To feel or express a desire for: *I wished them good luck.* **3.** To order, entreat, or request: *I wish you to go.* **4.** To desire (something bad) to happen to someone: *I would not wish such an illness on anyone.* *—intr.* **1.** To have or feel a desire: *He wished for a skateboard.* **2.** To express a wish. [From Middle English *wish,* from *wishen,* to wish, from Old English *wȳscan.*] **—wish′er** *n.*

wish·bone (wĭsh′bōn′) *n.* The forked bone in front of the breastbone in most birds.

wish·ful (wĭsh′fəl) *adj.* Having or expressing a wish or longing: *wishful eyes.* **—wish′ful·ly** *adv.*

wish·y-wash·y (wĭsh′ē-wŏsh′ē) *adj.* **wish·y-wash·i·er, wish·y-wash·i·est** *Informal* **1a.** Unable to make a decision: *a wishy-washy camp counselor who couldn't decide what to do.* **b.** Lacking in purpose; ineffective: *a wishy-washy response.* **2.** Thin or watery, as tea or soup.

wisp (wĭsp) *n.* **1.** A small bunch or bundle, as of hair,

wind turbine

GEOGRAPHY

Wisconsin The name **Wisconsin** comes from an Algonquian language and was originally applied to the Wisconsin River. The name later passed to the territory and the state. Unfortunately, we do not know exactly what the word *Wisconsin* means.

USAGE

–wise The suffix **–wise** forms adverbs when it attaches to adjectives or nouns. It comes from an Old English suffix *–wīse,* which meant "in a particular direction or manner." Thus *clockwise* means "in the direction that a clock goes," and *likewise* means "in like manner, similarly." For the last 50 years or so, *–wise* has also meant "with respect to," as in *saleswise,* "with respect to sales," and *taxwise,* "with respect to taxes." This usage is considered to be awkward, however, and should be avoided, especially in writing.

wisteria

WRITERS CHOOSE THEIR WORDS

We didn't play many duets because I knew only Western music and Grandma knew only Chinese tunes. I could never forget the **wistful** look on her face when she heard me playing my new flute, and I wondered why she had given it up.

—Lensey Namioka
April and the Dragon Lady

witch hazel

ă	pat	ôr	core
ā	pay	oi	boy
âr	care	ou	out
ä	father	o͝o	took
ĕ	pet	o͝or	lure
ē	be	o͞o	boot
ĭ	pit	ŭ	cut
ī	bite	ûr	urge
îr	pier	th	thin
ŏ	pot	*th*	this
ō	toe	zh	vision
ô	paw	ə	about

straw, or grass. **2.** A person or thing that is thin, frail, or slight. **3.** A faint streak, as of smoke or clouds.

wist (wĭst) *v.* Past tense and past participle of **wit²**.

wis·ter·i·a (wĭ-stîr′ē-ə) also **wis·tar·i·a** (wĭ-stâr′ē-ə) *n.* Any of several climbing woody vines having drooping clusters of showy purplish or white flowers. [After Caspar *Wistar* (1761–1818), American physician.]

wist·ful (wĭst′fəl) *adj.* Full of or expressing sad yearning: *a somber, wistful poem.* **—wist′ful·ly** *adv.* **—wist′ful·ness** *n.*

wit¹ (wĭt) *n.* **1a.** The ability to make clever and humorous remarks. **b.** A person having this ability: *a writer who was a great wit.* **2. wits a.** Resourcefulness; ingenuity: *We had to use our wits to find our way back to camp.* **b.** Sound mental faculties; sanity: *I was scared out of my wits.* ◆ **at (one's) wits' end** At the limit of one's mental resources; utterly at a loss. [From Old English.]

wit² (wĭt) *v.* **wist** (wĭst), **wit·ting** (wĭt′ĭng) *first and third person singular present tense* **wot** (wŏt) ❖ *tr. & intr.v. Archaic* To learn or know. ◆ **to wit** That is to say; namely. [From Old English *witan.*]

witch (wĭch) *n.* **1.** A person, especially a woman, who is believed to have supernatural powers and practice sorcery. **2.** A follower of Wicca. **3.** *Offensive* An old woman considered to be ugly or frightening. [From Old English *wicche.*]

witch·craft (wĭch′krăft′) *n.* The use of charms, spells, or rituals in the belief that they can call on supernatural powers to influence natural events or forces.

witch doctor *n.* In certain traditional cultures, especially in Africa, a person believed to be able to cure sickness by means of magic or the ability to drive away evil spirits.

witch hazel *n.* **1.** Any of several North American shrubs having yellow flowers that bloom in late fall or winter. **2.** A spicy-smelling liquid made from the bark and leaves of this shrub and rubbed on the skin, especially to relieve soreness.

witch-hunt (wĭch′hŭnt′) *n.* An investigation carried out supposedly to uncover disloyalty or subversive activities, but actually used to harass people with dissenting opinions or gain publicity for the investigators.

with (wĭ*th* or wĭth) *prep.* **1.** In the company of; accompanying: *Did you go with her?* **2.** Next to; alongside of: *I sat with my friends.* **3.** Having as a possession, attribute, or characteristic: *arrived with good news; just sat there with his mouth open.* **4a.** In a manner characterized by: *performed with skill.* **b.** In the performance, use, or operation of: *had trouble with the car.* **5.** In the charge or keeping of: *left the cat with the neighbors.* **6.** In the opinion or estimation of: *if it's all right with you.* **7.** Of the same opinion or belief as: *He is with us on that issue.* **8.** In the same group or mixture as; among: *planted onions with the carrots.* **9.** In the membership or employment of: *plays with a band.* **10a.** By the means or agency of: *eat with a fork.* **b.** By the presence or use of: *a pillow stuffed with feathers.* **11.** In spite of: *With all her experience, she could not get a job.* **12.** In the same direction as: *sail with the wind.* **13.** At the same time as: *gets up with the birds.* **14.** In regard or relation to: *We are pleased with her decision. I spoke with her yesterday.* **15.** Having received: *He went with his parents' permission.* **16a.** And; plus: *My books, with my brother's, make a sizable library.* **b.** Having as a part; including: *comes to $29.95 with postage and handling.* **17.** As a result or consequence of: *sick with the flu.* **18.** So as to be touching or joined to: *linked arms with their partners.* **19.** In proportion to: *fine Italian wines that improve with age.* **20.** According to the experience or practice of: *With me, rushing through a job is always a mistake.* [From Old English, with, against, from.] —SEE NOTE.

with·al (wĭ*th*-ôl′ or wĭth-ôl′) *adv.* Besides; as well: *gentle and soothing withal.*

with·draw (wĭ*th*-drô′ or wĭth-drô′) *v.* **with·drew** (wĭ*th*-dro͞o′ or wĭth-dro͞o′), **with·drawn** (wĭ*th*-drôn′ or wĭth-drôn′), **with·draw·ing, with·draws** —*tr.* **1.** To take back or away; remove: *withdraw funds from the bank.* **2.** To remove from participation or consideration: *withdrew her application.* —*intr.* **1.** To move or draw back; retire: *The dinner guests withdrew to the den.* **2.** To remove oneself from active participation: *He withdrew from the tournament.*

with·draw·al (wĭ*th*-drô′əl or wĭth-drô′əl) *n.* **1.** The act or process of withdrawing. **2.** A removal of something that has been deposited: *a withdrawal from a bank account.* **3a.** Discontinuation of the use of an addictive substance. **b.** The physiological and mental readjustment that accompanies such discontinuation.

with·drawn (wĭ*th*-drôn′ or wĭth-drôn′) *v.* Past participle of **withdraw.** ❖ *adj.* Socially retiring; shy: *a withdrawn person.*

with·drew (wĭ*th*-dro͞o′ or wĭth-dro͞o′) *v.* Past tense of **withdraw.**

with·er (wĭ*th*′ər) *v.* **with·ered, with·er·ing, with·ers** —*intr.* **1.** To dry up or shrivel from lack of moisture: *The flowers withered in the vase.* **2.** To lose vitality or force; become diminished: *The proposed tax on energy use withered away and was never adopted.* —*tr.* **1.** To cause to shrivel or fade. **2.** To render speechless or incapable of action; stun: *The principal withered the noisy student with a glance.* [From Middle English *widderen*, perhaps variant of *wederen*, to weather, from *weder*, weather.]

❑ *These sound alike:* **wither, whither** (to where).

with·ers (wĭ*th*′ərz) *pl.n.* The highest part of the back of a horse or other four-footed animal, located between the shoulder blades.

with·hold (wĭth-hōld′ or wĭ*th*-hōld′) *tr.v.* **with·held** (wĭth-hĕld′ or wĭ*th*-hĕld′), **with·hold·ing, with·holds** **1.** To refrain from giving, granting, or permitting: *Let's withhold judgment until we know the whole story.* See Synonyms at **keep. 2.** To keep in check; restrain: *withhold the applause until the end of the act.* **3.** To deduct (withholding tax) from an employee's wages or salary.

with·hold·ing tax (wĭth-hōl′dĭng or wĭ*th*-hōl′dĭng) *n.* A portion of an employee's wages or salary withheld by an employer as an advance payment of the employee's income tax.

with·in (wĭ*th*-ĭn′ or wĭth-ĭn′) *prep.* **1.** In the inner part or parts of; inside: *within the body.* **2.** Inside the limits or extent of in distance or time: *We are within ten miles of home. They arrived within an hour of us.* **3.** Not exceeding the fixed limits of; not beyond: *You must learn to live within your income.* **4.** Indicating a range to be covered or an amount needed before something can happen: *Our team has pulled within two points of the league leader.* ❖ *adv.* In or into the inner part; inside: *We stayed within.*

with·out (wĭ*th*-out′ or wĭth-out′) *adv.* On the outside: *The structure is sturdy within and without.* ❖ *prep.* **1.** Not having; lacking: *without a car to get home.* **2.** Not accompanied by; in the absence of: *no smoke without fire.*

with·stand (wĭth-stănd′ or wĭ*th*-stănd′) *tr.v.* **with·stood** (wĭth-sto͝od′ or wĭ*th*-sto͝od′), **with·stand·ing, with·stands** **1.** To resist or oppose with determined effort: *The troops withstood the attack.* **2.** To be undamaged or unaffected by: *The house withstood the storm.* —SEE NOTE AT **with.**

wit·less (wĭt′lĭs) *adj.* Lacking intelligence or wit; foolish.

wit·ness (wĭt′nĭs) *n.* **1.** A person who can give a firsthand account of something seen, heard, or experienced: *a witness of the accident.* **2a.** A person who is called to testify before a court of law. **b.** A person who is called on to be present at a transaction in order to attest to what takes place: *a witness at a wedding.* **c.** A person who signs his or her name to a document to attest to its authenticity. **3.** Something that serves as evidence; a sign.

4. One who publicly affirms religious faith. ❖ *tr.v.* **wit·nessed, wit·ness·ing, wit·ness·es 1.** To see or know by personal experience: *witness a volcanic eruption.* **2.** To provide or serve as evidence of: *The child's laughter witnessed her delight.* **3.** To sign (a document) as witness to its legality or authenticity: *witness a will.* [From Old English, from *wit*, knowledge.]

wit·ti·cism (wĭt′ĭ-sĭz′əm) *n.* A witty remark.

wit·ting (wĭt′ĭng) *adj.* **1.** Aware or conscious of something: *a witting bystander to the crime.* **2.** Done intentionally; deliberate: *a witting insult.* ❖ *v.* Present participle of **wit[2]**. **—wit′ting·ly** *adv.*

wit·ty (wĭt′ē) *adj.* **wit·ti·er, wit·ti·est 1.** Having or showing wit in expression, especially in speech or writing: *a witty person.* **2.** Characterized by or having the nature of wit; funny or jocular: *a witty saying.* **—wit′ti·ly** *adv.* **—wit′ti·ness** *n.*

wives (wīvz) *n.* Plural of **wife.**

wiz·ard (wĭz′ərd) *n.* **1.** A sorcerer or magician. **2.** A skilled or clever person: *a wizard at mathematics.* [From Middle English *wisard.*]

wiz·ard·ry (wĭz′ər-drē) *n.* The art, skill, or practice of a wizard; sorcery.

wiz·ened (wĭz′ənd) *adj.* Shriveled; withered.

w/o *abbr.* An abbreviation of without.

wob·ble (wŏb′əl) *v.* **wob·bled, wob·bling, wob·bles** *—intr.* To move unsteadily from side to side: *The old table wobbles. —tr.* To cause to wobble. ❖ *n.* The act or an instance of wobbling; unsteady motion: *The top spun with a wobble.*

wob·bly (wŏb′lē) *adj.* **wob·bli·er, wob·bli·est** Tending to wobble; unsteady.

Wo·den (wōd′n) *n.* An Anglo-Saxon god identified with Odin.

woe (wō) *n.* **1.** Sorrow or grief; misery: *yearning for company in her woe.* **2.** A misfortune or difficulty: *What is the cause of their financial woes?* ❖ *interj.* An expression used to show sorrow or dismay. ◆ **woe is me** Used to lament one's situation or fate. [From Old English *wā.*]

woe·be·gone (wō′bĭ-gôn′) *adj.* Feeling, showing, or expressing deep sorrow, grief, or wretchedness. See Synonyms at **sad.**

woe·ful (wō′fəl) *adj.* **1.** Affected by or full of woe; mournful. **2.** Causing, involving, or expressing woe. **3.** Deplorably bad: *woeful wrongs.* **—woe′ful·ly** *adv.*

wok (wŏk) *n.* A metal pan with a rounded bottom, used in Asian cooking for frying and steaming. [From Cantonese.]

woke (wōk) *v.* A past tense of **wake[1]**.

wok·en (wō′kən) *v.* A past participle of **wake[1]**.

wolf (wo͝olf) *n., pl.* **wolves** (wo͝olvz) **1a.** Any of several meat-eating mammals related to the dog and living chiefly in northern regions. **b.** The fur of such a mammal. **2.** A person who is regarded as fierce, cruel, or dangerous. ❖ *tr.v.* **wolfed, wolf·ing, wolfs** To eat hungrily or greedily: *wolfed down the hamburger.* ◆ **wolf in sheep's clothing** A person who pretends to be friendly while actually intending harm. [From Old English *wulf.*]

Wolfe (wo͝olf), **James** 1727–1759. British general in Canada who defeated the French at Quebec (1759).

wolf·hound (wo͝olf′hound′) *n.* Any of various large dogs, such as the borzoi, originally bred to hunt wolves or other large game.

wolf·ram (wo͝ol′frəm) *n.* Tungsten.

wolfs·bane (wo͝olfs′bān′) *n.* Aconite.

Woll·stone·craft (wo͝ol′stən-krăft′), **Mary** 1759–1797. British writer and reformer noted for *A Vindication of the Rights of Woman* (1792).

Wo·lof (wō′lŏf′) *n.* **1.** A member of a West African people living in coastal Senegal. **2.** The language of this people.

wol·ver·ine (wo͝ol′və-rēn′ *or* wo͝ol′və-rēn′) *n.* A meat-eating mammal of northern regions, related to the weasel and having thick dark fur and a bushy tail.

wolves (wo͝olvz) *n.* Plural of **wolf.**

wom·an (wo͝om′ən) *n., pl.* **wom·en** (wĭm′ĭn) **1.** An adult female human. **2.** Women considered as a group; womankind. **3.** A wife or female lover. **4.** A female servant, employee, or worker. ◆ **to a woman** Without exception among a group of women: *They favored the proposal to a woman.* [From Old English *wīfman* : *wīf*, woman + *man*, person.] —SEE NOTE AT **man.**

wom·an·hood (wo͝om′ən-ho͝od′) *n.* **1.** The condition of being an adult female person. **2.** The qualities considered appropriate to or representative of women. **3.** Women considered as a group.

wom·an·ish (wo͝om′ə-nĭsh) *adj.* Characteristic of or natural to a woman, especially when considered inferior to a man.

wom·an·kind (wo͝om′ən-kīnd′) *n.* Women considered as a group.

wom·an·ly (wo͝om′ən-lē) *adj.* **wom·an·li·er, wom·an·li·est** Relating to or characteristic of women, often in showing qualities traditionally attributed to women. **—wom′an·li·ness** *n.*

womb (wo͞om) *n.* **1.** The uterus. **2.** A place where something is generated or begun.

wom·bat (wŏm′băt′) *n.* Any of several Australian marsupials that resemble a small bear and feed mainly on grass, leaves, and roots.

wom·en (wĭm′ĭn) *n.* Plural of **woman.**

wom·en·folk (wĭm′ĭn-fōk′) also **wom·en·folks** (wĭm′ĭn-fōks′) *pl.n.* **1.** Women considered as a group. **2.** The women of a community or family.

won[1] (wôn) *n., pl.* **won** The basic monetary unit of North Korea and South Korea.

❑ *These sound alike:* **won[1]** (Korean currency), **won[2]** (was victorious), **one** (single).

won[2] (wŭn) *v.* Past tense and past participle of **win.**

❑ *These sound alike:* **won[2]** (was victorious), **one** (single), **won[1]** (Korean currency).

won·der (wŭn′dər) *n.* **1.** The emotion aroused by something awe-inspiring, astounding, or surprising: *gazed with wonder at the northern lights.* **2.** A person or thing that arouses awe, surprise, or admiration; a marvel: *Given how old your dog is, it's a wonder he can still run so fast!* **3.** An extraordinary or remarkable act or achievement: *That teacher has worked wonders with these students.* **4.** An event that cannot be explained by the laws of nature; a miracle. ❖ *v.* **won·dered, won·der·ing, won·ders** *—intr.* **1.** To have a feeling of awe or admiration; marvel: *They wondered at the sight of the canyon.* **2.** To be filled with curiosity or doubt: *He wondered about the future. —tr.* To feel curiosity or be in doubt about: *I wonder what she is doing.* ◆ **do wonders** To have a beneficial effect: *This medicine will do wonders for you.*

SYNONYMS wonder, marvel, miracle, phenomenon These nouns mean something that causes amazement or admiration in others. *The Egyptian pyramids are ancient wonders of architecture. This book discusses great inventions and other marvels of technology. The artificial heart is a miracle of medical science. She is a tennis phenomenon who has won many trophies.*

---

won·der·ful (wŭn′dər-fəl) *adj.* **1.** Admirable or very good; excellent: *a wonderful idea.* **2.** Capable of causing wonder; astonishing: *A soaring eagle is a wonderful sight.* **—won′der·ful·ly** *adv.*

won·der·land (wŭn′dər-lănd′) *n.* **1.** A marvelous imaginary realm. **2.** A marvelous real place or scene.

WORD HISTORY

with When you fight **with** someone, are you fighting on his or her side or against him or her? We are often confused by that usage of the word *with* since we nearly always take it to mean "in the company of, alongside of." But in Old English, *with* meant "against," a meaning it can still have in the phrase *fight with.* The meaning is also still there in the verb **withstand,** "to stand up against, resist." How did *with* come to mean "together"? Basically, the original sense "against" broadened to include "up close against, up close," a sense that is easily extended to include "up close together, together with, in the company of." As *with* changed in meaning, it replaced the Old and Middle English preposition *mid,* "together with," which survives in the word **midwife,** "a woman who is *with* the woman in childbirth."

wok

wombat

wonton

woodchuck

Victoria Woodhull

ă	pat	ôr	core
ā	pay	oi	boy
âr	care	ou	out
ä	father	o͝o	took
ĕ	pet	o͝or	lure
ē	be	o͞o	boot
ĭ	pit	ŭ	cut
ī	bite	ûr	urge
îr	pier	th	thin
ŏ	pot	*th*	this
ō	toe	zh	vision
ô	paw	ə	about

won·der·ment (wŭn′dər-mənt) *n.* **1.** Astonishment, awe, or puzzlement. **2.** Something that produces wonder; a marvel.

won·drous (wŭn′drəs) *adj.* Remarkable or extraordinary; wonderful. **—won′drous·ly** *adv.*

wont (wônt *or* wōnt *or* wŭnt) *adj.* Accustomed, apt, or used: *He was wont to go for long walks on the heath.* ❖ *n.* Customary practice; usage: *jogged every morning, as was her wont.*

won't (wōnt) Contraction of *will not.*

wont·ed (wôn′tĭd *or* wōn′tĭd *or* wŭn′tĭd) *adj.* Accustomed; usual: *He took his wonted meal of toast and tea.*

won·ton also **won ton** (wŏn′tŏn′) *n.* A small dumpling typically filled with spiced ground meat.

woo (wo͞o) *tr.v.* **wooed, woo·ing, woos 1.** To seek the affection of (someone, especially a woman) with intent of getting married or beginning a romance. **2.** To gain the favor of (someone) or move (someone) to do something by persuasion or incentives: *These ads try to woo customers away from their usual brand.* **—woo′er** *n.*

wood (wo͝od) *n.* **1a.** The tough fibrous substance beneath the bark of trees and shrubs. **b.** This substance when cut and dried, used especially for building material and fuel. **2.** often **woods** A dense growth of trees and other plants; a forest. **3.** Any of a series of golf clubs designed for hitting long shots, having a broad head made of wood, metal, or graphite. [From Old English *wudu.*]
❑ *These sound alike:* **wood, would** (past tense of will).

wood alcohol *n.* Methanol.

wood·bine (wo͝od′bīn′) *n.* Any of various climbing vines having yellowish flowers, especially a European honeysuckle.

wood·carv·ing (wo͝od′kär′vĭng) *n.* **1.** The art of creating or decorating wood objects by carving with a tool. **2.** A carved wood object.

wood·chip·per (wo͝od′chĭp′ər) *n.* A power-driven machine for cutting wood into chips.

wood·chuck (wo͝od′chŭk′) *n.* A short-legged, burrowing North American rodent having brownish fur; a groundhog.

wood·cock (wo͝od′kŏk′) *n., pl.* **woodcock** or **wood·cocks** Any of several woodland birds having brownish feathers, short legs, and a long bill, often hunted as game.

wood·craft (wo͝od′krăft′) *n.* **1.** Skill and experience in things relating to the woods, as hunting, fishing, or camping. **2.** The art of carving or fashioning objects from wood.

wood·cut (wo͝od′kŭt′) *n.* **1.** A piece of wood having an engraved design for printing. **2.** A print made from such a piece of wood.

wood·cut·ter (wo͝od′kŭt′ər) *n.* A person or thing that cuts wood.

wood duck *n.* A brightly colored North American duck that nests in hollow trees, the male of which has a large crest.

wood·ed (wo͝od′ĭd) *adj.* Covered with trees or woods.

wood·en (wo͝od′n) *adj.* **1.** Made or consisting of wood: *a wooden bridge.* **2.** Stiff and unnatural: *a wooden smile.* **—wood′en·ly** *adv.*

Wood·hull (wo͝od′hŭl′), **Victoria Claflin** 1838–1927. American reformer and suffragist who was the first woman to run for the US presidency (1872) and with her sister **Tennessee Claflin** (1845–1923) opened the first Wall Street brokerage house owned by women.

wood·land (wo͝od′lənd) *n.* Land covered with trees.

wood·louse (wo͝od′lous′) *n., pl.* **wood·lice** (wo͝od′līs′) Any of various small land crustaceans having a gray or brown oval segmented body and commonly found in damp places such as under logs. Some woodlice can curl up into a ball.

wood·man (wo͝od′mən) *n.* A woodsman.

wood·peck·er (wo͝od′pĕk′ər) *n.* Any of various birds having strong claws used for clinging to and climbing trees and a strong pointed bill used for drilling into bark and wood.

wood·pile (wo͝od′pīl′) *n.* A pile of wood, especially when intended for use as fuel.

wood pulp *n.* Any of various cellulose pulps ground from wood, treated chemically, and used in making paper, cellophane, and rayon.

Woods (wo͝odz), **Eldrick** Known as "Tiger." Born 1975. American golfer who was the youngest player to win the Masters tournament (1997) and the youngest to win all four major championships (1997–2000).

wood·shed (wo͝od′shĕd′) *n.* A shed in which firewood is stored.

woods·man (wo͝odz′mən) *n.* A man who works or lives in the woods or is skilled in woodcraft.

woods·y (wo͝od′zē) *adj.* **woods·i·er, woods·i·est** Relating to, suggesting, or typical of the woods.

wood tar *n.* A black syrupy fluid that is a byproduct of the destructive distillation of wood and is used in pitch and medicines.

wood·wind (wo͝od′wĭnd′) *n.* **1.** A wind instrument typically consisting of a long tube with finger holes in the sides, played by blowing into or across a mouthpiece at one end. Clarinets, saxophones, flutes, and oboes are woodwind instruments. **2.** **woodwinds** The section of an orchestra or band composed of such instruments.

wood·work (wo͝od′wûrk′) *n.* Objects made of or work done in wood, especially wooden interior fittings in a house, such as doors, moldings, or windowsills. ◆ **out of the woodwork** Out of obscurity or a place of seclusion: *People came out of the woodwork to claim the reward money.*

wood·work·ing (wo͝od′wûr′kĭng) *n.* The art, act, or trade of working with wood.

wood·y (wo͝od′ē) *adj.* **wood·i·er, wood·i·est 1.** Consisting of or containing wood: *woody tissue; woody plants.* **2.** Characteristic or suggestive of wood: *a woody smell.* **3.** Abounding in trees; wooded: *a woody hill.*

woof[1] (wo͝of *or* wo͞of) *n.* **1.** The threads that run crosswise in a woven fabric, at a right angle to the warp; the weft. **2.** The texture of a fabric. [From Old English *ōwef* : *ō-, on-*, on + *wefan*, to weave.]

woof[2] (wo͝of) *n.* **1.** The characteristically deep gruff bark of a dog. **2.** A sound similar to a woof. ❖ *intr.v.* **woofed, woof·ing, woofs** To make such a sound. [Of imitative origin.]

woof·er (wo͝of′ər) *n.* A loudspeaker designed to reproduce bass frequencies.

wool (wo͝ol) *n.* **1.** The dense, soft, often curly hair of a sheep and certain other animals, used to make yarn and fabric. **2.** Yarn or fabric made of this hair. **3.** Material resembling wool, such as a mass of fine, curled metal strands. [From Old English *wull.*]

wool·en also **wool·len** (wo͝ol′ən) *adj.* **1.** Made or consisting of wool: *a woolen blanket.* **2.** Making or dealing in wool cloth or clothing: *a woolen mill.* ❖ *n.* often **woolens** Fabric or clothing made from wool.

Woolf (wo͝olf), **(Adeline) Virginia (Stephen)** 1882–1941. British writer whose works include novels, such as *Mrs. Dalloway* (1925), and collections of essays, such as *A Room of One's Own* (1929).

wool·ly (wo͝ol′ē) *adj.* **wool·li·er, wool·li·est 1.** Relating to, consisting of, or covered with wool: *a woolly coat; a woolly lamb.* **2.** Resembling wool: *leaves covered with woolly down.* **3.** Lacking sharp detail or clarity; blurry: *woolly thinking.* **4.** Rough, disorderly, or unrestrained: *a wild and woolly frontier town.* ❖ *n., pl.* **wool·lies** A garment made of wool, especially an undergarment of knitted wool.

woolly bear *n.* A hairy caterpillar of any of various tiger moths, especially one of North America that is reddish-brown in the middle and black at both ends.

woolly mammoth *n.* A mammoth of cold northern regions that became extinct about 10,000 years ago.

wooz·y (wo͞o′zē *or* wo͝oz′ē) *adj.* **wooz·i·er, wooz·i·est 1.** Dazed or confused. **2.** Queasy or dizzy. **—wooz′i·ness** *n.*

word (wûrd) *n.* **1.** A spoken sound or group of sounds that communicates a meaning. **2.** A written or printed letter or group of letters representing such a sound or group of sounds. **3.** Something said; an utterance or comment: *May I have a word with you?* **4.** A direction to do something; an order: *Just say the word, and we'll send up reinforcements.* **5.** A promise; an assurance: *keeping her word to be on time.* **6. words** Discourse or talk; speech or writing: *Actions speak louder than words.* **7.** News; information: *sent word of her safe arrival.* **8. words** Hostile or angry remarks made back and forth; a quarrel. ❖ *tr.v.* **word·ed, word·ing, words** To express in words. ◆ **good word 1.** A favorable comment: *I'll put in a good word for you.* **2.** Favorable news. **in so many words** In precisely those words; exactly: *wanted us to leave, but wouldn't say it in so many words.* **of few words** Not talkative; laconic: *a person of few words.* **take (one) at (one's) word** To be convinced of another's sincerity and act in accord with his or her statement: *We took him at his word that he would lock up when he left.* **upon my word** Indeed; really. [From Old English.]

word·book (wûrd′bo͝ok′) *n.* A vocabulary or dictionary.

word cloud *n.* A representation of words in a cluster in which the size of each word is proportional to its frequency among the words used in a website, document, or other source.

word for word *adv.* In exactly the same words. **—word′-for-word′** (wûrd′fər-wûrd′) *adj.*

word·ing (wûr′dĭng) *n.* The words selected in expressing something, or the style in which words are used.

word·less (wûrd′lĭs) *adj.* **1.** Not expressed in words; unspoken: *a look that served as a wordless reproach.* **2.** Speechless; silent: *wordless with gratitude.* **—word′less·ly** *adv.* **—word′less·ness** *n.*

word of mouth *n.* Spoken communication: *News of their success spread by word of mouth.*

word processing *n.* The creation, editing, and production of documents and texts by using a computer.

word processor *n.* **1.** A computer or computer program that is designed for word processing. **2.** A person who uses a word processor.

Words·worth (wûrdz′wûrth′), **William** 1770–1850. British poet whose works include "Tintern Abbey" (1798). He was appointed poet laureate in 1843.

word·y (wûr′dē) *adj.* **word·i·er, word·i·est 1.** Relating to or consisting of words; verbal. **2.** Using or expressed in too many words; verbose. **—word′i·ly** *adv.* **—word′i·ness** *n.*

wore (wôr) *v.* Past tense of **wear.**

work (wûrk) *n.* **1a.** Physical or mental effort or activity directed toward the production or accomplishment of something: *Cleaning my room was a lot of work.* **b.** The manner, style, or quality of such effort or activity: *sloppy work.* **2a.** Employment in a job or profession: *looking for work.* **b.** A trade, profession, or other means of livelihood: *Her work is designing websites.* **3.** Something that one is doing, making, or performing, especially as an occupation or duty: *begin the day's work.* **4a.** The part of a day devoted to an occupation or undertaking: *met her after work.* **b.** One's place of employment: *Should I call you at home or at work?* **5a.** Something that has been produced or accomplished through a particular kind of effort or activity: *This story is the work of an active imagination.* **b.** An act; a deed: *good works.* **6.** An artistic creation, such as a painting or musical composition. **7. works** Engineering structures, such as bridges or dams. **8. works** *(used with a singular or plural verb)* A factory, plant, or similar building where a specific type of business or industry is carried on: *a steelworks.* **9. works** Internal mechanism: *the works of a watch.* **10. works** *Informal* The full range of possibilities; everything: *ordered a pizza with the works.* ❖ *v.* **worked** also **wrought** (rôt), **work·ing, works** *—intr.* **1.** To exert oneself physically or mentally in order to do, make, or accomplish something: *We worked all morning in the garden.* **2.** To be employed; have a job: *Where does your mother work?* **3.** To function; operate: *How does this latch work? The telephone isn't working.* **4.** To have the desired effect or outcome; be successful: *This recipe seems to work.* **5.** To arrive at a specified condition through gradual or repeated movement: *The stitches worked loose.* **6.** To proceed or progress slowly and laboriously: *worked through the underbrush.* *—tr.* **1.** To cause or effect; bring about: *wrought destruction.* **2.** To cause to operate or function: *worked the controls.* **3.** To shape or forge: *worked the metal into a sculpture.* **4.** To knead, stir, or otherwise manipulate in preparation: *Work the dough before shaping it.* **5.** To bring to a specified condition by gradual or repeated effort or work: *finally worked the window open.* **6.** To make, achieve, or pay for by work or effort: *worked her way through college.* **7.** To solve by reasoning: *work a math problem.* **8.** To make productive; cultivate: *work a farm.* **9.** To cause to work: *works his horses hard.* **10.** To excite or provoke: *The speaker worked the mob into a frenzy.* ◆ **in the works** In preparation; under development: *There's a new movie in the works.* **work off** To get rid of by work or effort: *worked off some energy at the gym.* **work out 1.** To find a solution for; solve: *Can you work out these math problems?* **2.** To prove successful, effective, or satisfactory: *Everything worked out in the end.* **3.** To have a specified result: *The arrangements worked out just fine.* **4.** To engage in strenuous exercise for physical conditioning. **work up 1.** To arouse the emotions of; excite or aggravate: *He got worked up about the mistake.* **2.** To develop or produce: *worked up a report; worked up an appetite.* [From Old English *weorc.*] —SEE NOTE AT **wreak.**

work·a·ble (wûr′kə-bəl) *adj.* **1.** Capable of being put into effective operation: *a workable plan.* **2.** Capable of being worked, dealt with, or handled.

work·a·day (wûr′kə-dā′) *adj.* **1.** Relating to or suited for working days. **2.** Ordinary or commonplace.

work·a·round (wûrk′ə-round′) *n.* A method or process of dealing with a problem.

work·bench (wûrk′bĕnch′) *n.* A sturdy table or bench at which skilled manual work is done, as by a carpenter or machinist.

work·book (wûrk′bo͝ok′) *n.* **1.** A booklet containing problems and exercises with blank space included for written answers. **2.** A manual of instructions, as for running a machine or appliance.

work·day (wûrk′dā′) *n.* **1.** A day on which work is done. **2.** The part of the day during which one works.

work·er (wûr′kər) *n.* **1.** A person who works: *a fast worker; an office worker.* **2.** A member of the working class. **3.** A member of a colony of ants, bees, or other social insects that does the work of the colony and cannot produce offspring.

work·ers' compensation (wûr′kərz) *n.* Payments made to an employee who is injured at work.

work force or **work·force** (wûrk′fôrs′) *n.* All the people working or available to work, as in a nation or company.

work·horse (wûrk′hôrs′) *n.* **1.** A person or thing that works tirelessly or under prolonged use. **2.** A horse that is used for labor.

woodpecker

SCIENCE

worm Although there are many kinds of **worms** of all shapes and sizes, we usually think of *earthworms* when someone mentions worms. Earthworms do not get much respect, but Charles Darwin wrote an entire book explaining how important they are. "Long before [the plow] existed," he said, "the land was in fact regularly plowed, and still continues to be thus plowed by earthworms. It may be doubted whether there are many other animals which have played so important a part in the history of the world." As they tunnel in the soil, earthworms open channels that allow in air and water. These channels improve drainage and make it easier for plants to send down roots. Earthworms eat and digest soil and the organic wastes it contains, and their own wastes provide nourishment for plants and other organisms. We enjoy the fruits of the earthworm's labor in the form of rich soil and healthy vegetation.

work·house (wûrk′hous′) *n.* A prison in which sentences are served at manual labor.

work·ing (wûr′kĭng) *adj.* **1.** Capable of working; functioning: *a machine in working condition.* **2.** Having a paying job; employed: *a working person.* **3.** Spent in work: *working hours.* **4.** Sufficient or adequate for using: *a working knowledge of a language.*

working class *n.* The people of society who live off jobs that require little formal education or that pay low wages, including manual and unskilled workers and their families.

work·ing·man (wûr′kĭng-măn′) *n.* A man who works for wages.

working papers *pl.n.* Legal documents certifying the right to employment of a minor or alien.

work·ing·wom·an (wûr′kĭng-wo͝om′ən) *n.* A woman who works for wages.

work·load (wûrk′lōd′) *n.* The amount of work that can be produced in a specified period of time, as by a worker or a machine.

work·man (wûrk′mən) *n.* A man who performs manual or industrial labor for wages.

work·man·ship (wûrk′mən-shĭp′) *n.* **1.** The skill of a craftsperson or artisan. **2.** The quality of something made, as by an artisan.

work·men's compensation (wûrk′mənz) *n.* Workers' compensation.

work·out (wûrk′out′) *n.* A period of exercise, as to improve fitness or for an athletic competition.

work·place (wûrk′plās′) *n.* **1.** A place, such as an office or factory, where people are employed. **2.** The work setting in general: *A friendly workplace leads to happy employees.* **—work′place** *adj.*

work·shop (wûrk′shŏp′) *n.* **1.** A place where manual or light industrial work is done. **2.** An educational seminar held for a usually small number of participants: *a teachers' workshop.*

work·ta·ble (wûrk′tā′bəl) *n.* A table designed for a specific kind of task or activity, such as needlework or graphic arts.

world (wûrld) *n.* **1.** The earth, especially together with the life it supports: *an ecological disaster that threatens the entire world.* **2.** The universe: *How did people in ancient Greece conceive of the world?* **3.** People as a whole; humankind or the public: *The whole world was amazed by these events.* **4.** often **World** A particular part of the earth: *the Western World.* **5.** A particular part of the earth and its inhabitants as known during a given period of history: *the Renaissance world.* **6.** A field, sphere, group, or realm: *the scientific world.* **7.** Secular life and its concerns: *a man of the world.* **8.** A state of existence: *the next world.* **9.** often **worlds** A large amount: *spent worlds of time.* **10.** A planet or other celestial object: *life on other worlds.* ◆ **in the world** Used as an intensive: *Where in the world did you find that?* **out of this world** *Informal* Extraordinary; superb: *had some pizza that was out of this world.* **the world over** Throughout the world: *a folk musician famous the world over.* [From Old English *worold.*]

world·ly (wûrld′lē) *adj.* **world·li·er, world·li·est 1.** Relating to or devoted to the affairs of the world; secular; not spiritual: *worldly concerns.* **2.** Experienced in human affairs; sophisticated. **—world′li·ness** *n.*

world·ly-wise (wûrld′lē-wīz′) *adj.* Experienced in the ways of the world.

world power *n.* A nation having the power to influence the course of world events.

World Series *n.* In baseball, a series of games played to decide the championship of the major leagues.

World War I *n.* A war fought from 1914 to 1918, in which Great Britain, France, the United States, and their allies defeated Germany, Austria-Hungary, and their allies.

World War II *n.* A war fought from 1939 to 1945, in which Great Britain, France, the Soviet Union, the United States, and their allies defeated Germany, Italy, and Japan.

world·wide (wûrld′wīd′) *adj.* Involving or extending throughout the world. ❖ *adv.* Throughout the world: *distributed worldwide.*

World Wide Web *n.* The complete system of interlinked documents that are made available by the process known as HTTP (Hypertext Transfer Protocol), residing on the Internet and accessible to users via a web browser.

worm (wûrm) *n.* **1.** Any of various animals having a soft, long, often limbless rounded or flattened body and no backbone. **2.** Any of various animals resembling worms, especially a caterpillar, grub, or other insect larva. **3. worms** Infestation of the intestines or other parts of the body by parasitic worms. **4.** A pitiable or contemptible person. **5.** A malicious computer program that replicates itself until it fills all of the storage space on a drive or network. ❖ *v.* **wormed, worm·ing, worms** *—tr.* **1.** To make (one's way) or move with or as if with the crawling or twisting motion of a worm: *wormed her way through the crowd.* **2.** To get by sly or deceitful means: *The spy wormed the information from the messenger.* **3.** To treat for intestinal worms. *—intr.* **1.** To move in a manner suggestive of a worm. **2.** To make one's way by artful or devious means: *worm out of an obligation.* [From Old English *wyrm.*] —SEE NOTE.

worm drive *n.* A drive made of a spirally threaded shaft and a wheel with teeth that mesh into it.

worm gear *n.* The toothed wheel of a worm drive.

worm·hole (wûrm′hōl′) *n.* **1.** A hole made by a burrowing worm. **2.** A theoretical distortion of space-time in which two points in space or time are connected in such a way as to shorten the normal distance or interval between them.

worm·wood (wûrm′wo͝od′) *n.* Any of several strong-smelling plants that yield a bitter substance used for flavoring certain alcoholic liquors.

worm·y (wûr′mē) *adj.* **worm·i·er, worm·i·est** Infested with or damaged by worms.

worn (wôrn) *v.* Past participle of **wear.** ❖ *adj.* **1.** Affected or damaged by wear or use: *worn faded pants.* **2.** Showing the wearing effects of worry, sickness, or strain: *a pale worn face.*

❑ *These sound alike:* **worn, warn** (make aware of danger).

worn-out (wôrn′out′) *adj.* **1.** Used or worn until no longer usable: *worn-out clothes.* **2.** Extremely tired; exhausted.

wor·ri·some (wûr′ē-səm) *adj.* **1.** Causing worry or anxiety. **2.** Tending to worry.

wor·ry (wûr′ē) *v.* **wor·ried, wor·ry·ing, wor·ries** *—intr.* **1.** To feel uneasy or concerned about something; be troubled: *worried about his health.* **2.** To seize something with the teeth and bite or tear repeatedly: *a squirrel worrying at a nut.* **3.** To touch or handle something nervously or persistently: *worrying at a scab.* *—tr.* **1.** To cause to feel anxious, distressed, or troubled: *Don't worry your parents!* **2.** To seize with the teeth and tug at repeatedly: *a kitten worrying a ball of yarn.* **3.** To touch or handle nervously or persistently: *worrying the loose tooth.* ❖ *n., pl.* **wor·ries 1.** Mental uneasiness or anxiety. **2.** A source of anxiety or uneasiness. [From Old English *wyrgan,* to strangle.] **—wor′ri·er** *n.*

wor·ry·wart (wûr′ē-wôrt′) *n.* A person who worries excessively and needlessly.

worse (wûrs) *adj.* Comparative of **bad, ill. 1.** Of a more inferior quality, condition, or effect: *This restaurant is worse than the last one we ate at.* **2.** More severe or unfavorable: *The weather got worse as the night wore on.* **3.** Being in poorer health; more ill. ❖ *n.* Something that is

ă	pat	ôr	core
ā	pay	oi	boy
âr	care	ou	out
ä	father	o͝o	took
ĕ	pet	o͝or	lure
ē	be	o͞o	boot
ĭ	pit	ŭ	cut
ī	bite	ûr	urge
îr	pier	th	thin
ŏ	pot	*th*	this
ō	toe	zh	vision
ô	paw	ə	about

worse: *Of the two cars, the old one is the worse.* ❖ *adv.* Comparative of **badly, ill.** In a worse manner; to a worse degree: *The team plays worse when we skip a practice.* ◆ **for better or worse** Whether the situation or consequences be good or ill. [From Old English *wyrsa.*]

wors·en (wûr′sən) *tr. & intr.v.* **wors·ened, wors·en·ing, wors·ens** To make or become worse.

wor·ship (wûr′shĭp) *n.* **1.** The reverent love and devotion given to a deity or idol. **2.** A set of ceremonies, prayers, or other religious forms by which this love is expressed. **3.** Ardent admiration or love; adoration. **4.** often **Worship** *Chiefly British* Used as a form of address for certain officials: *Is your Worship ready?* ❖ *v.* **wor·shiped, wor·ship·ing, wor·ships** or **wor·shipped, wor·ship·ping, wor·ships** —*tr.* **1.** To honor and love as a deity. **2.** To regard with adoring esteem or devotion. —*intr.* To participate in religious rites of worship. [From Old English *weorthscipe,* worthiness, honor : *weorth,* worth + *-scipe,* condition.] —**wor′ship·er, wor′ship·per** *n.*

wor·ship·ful (wûr′shĭp-fəl) *adj.* Reverent; pious.

worst (wûrst) *adj.* Superlative of **bad, ill. 1.** Of most inferior quality, condition, or effect. **2.** Most severe or unfavorable: *the worst winter in years.* **3.** Least desirable or satisfactory: *the worst piece of land.* ❖ *adv.* Superlative of **badly, ill.** In the worst manner or degree. ❖ *n.* Something that is worst: *Cold pizza is the worst!* ◆ **in the worst way** *Informal* Very much; a great deal: *wanted a kitten in the worst way.* [From Old English *wyrresta.*]

❑ *These sound alike:* **worst, wurst** (sausage).

wor·sted (wo͝os′tĭd *or* wûr′stĭd) *n.* **1.** Smooth, firmly twisted yarn made from long strands of wool. **2.** Fabric made from such yarn. **3.** Natural or synthetic yarn of a medium weight.

worth (wûrth) *n.* **1.** The quality that gives value or usefulness to something: *the worth of a good reputation.* **2.** The value of something expressed in money; market value: *property with a worth of a million dollars.* **3.** The amount that a certain sum of money will buy: *She bought 20 dollars' worth of nails.* **4.** Wealth; riches: *the company's net worth.* ❖ *adj.* **1.** Equal in value to something specified: *a pen worth five dollars.* **2.** Deserving of; meriting: *a plan worth a trial.* **3.** Having wealth amounting to: *The business executive was worth $10,000,000.* ◆ **for what it's worth** Even though it may not be important or valuable: *Here's my opinion, for what it's worth.* [From Old English *weorth.*]

worth·less (wûrth′lĭs) *adj.* Lacking worth; of no use or value: *a worthless promise.* —**worth′less·ly** *adv.*

worth·while (wûrth′wīl′) *adj.* Sufficiently valuable or important to justify the time, effort, or interest involved.

wor·thy (wûr′thē) *adj.* **wor·thi·er, wor·thi·est 1.** Having worth, merit, or value: *a worthy cause.* **2.** Honorable; admirable: *a worthy opponent.* **3.** Having sufficient worth; deserving: *worthy to be considered; worthy of praise.* ❖ *n., pl.* **wor·thies** An important or distinguished person. —**wor′thi·ness** *n.*

wot (wŏt) *v. Archaic* First and third person singular present tense of **wit²**.

would (wo͝od) *aux.v.* Past tense of **will². 1.** Used to express desire or intent: *She said she would meet us at the corner.* **2.** Used to express a wish: *Would that we had gone with you!* **3.** Used after a statement of desire, request, or advice: *I wish you would stay.* **4.** Used to make a polite request: *Would you go with me?* **5.** Used in the main clause of a conditional statement to express a possibility or likelihood: *If I had enough money, I would buy a car.* **6.** Used to express presumption or expectation: *That would be Steve at the door.* **7.** Used to indicate uncertainty: *He would seem to be getting better.* **8.** Used to express repeated or habitual action in the past: *Every day we would walk in the garden.* —SEE NOTE AT **should.**

❑ *These sound alike:* **would, wood** (forest).

would-be (wo͝od′bē′) *adj.* Desiring, attempting, or professing to be.

would·n't (wo͝od′nt) Contraction of *would not.*

wouldst (wo͝odst) *v. Archaic* Second person singular past tense of **will².**

wound¹ (wo͞ond) *n.* **1.** An injury to a plant or animal, especially one in which the skin is cut, pierced, or broken. **2.** An injury to one's feelings. ❖ *tr.v.* **wound·ed, wound·ing, wounds 1.** To inflict a wound or wounds on. **2.** To hurt the feelings of (someone). [From Old English *wund.*]

wound² (wound) *v.* Past tense and past participle of **wind².**

wove (wōv) *v.* Past tense of **weave.**

wo·ven (wō′vən) *v.* Past participle of **weave.** ❖ *adj.* Made by weaving: *a woven rug.*

wow (wou) *Informal interj.* An expression used to show wonder, amazement, or great pleasure. ❖ *n.* A great success. ❖ *tr.v.* **wowed, wow·ing, wows** To have a strong and pleasant effect on: *The singer wowed the audience.*

wrack¹ (răk) *n.* Destruction or ruin. Used chiefly in the phrase *wrack and ruin.* [From Old English *wræc.*]

❑ *These sound alike:* **wrack¹** (ruin), **rack¹** (frame), **rack²** (cut of meat), **wrack²** (wreckage).

wrack² (răk) *n.* **1.** Wreckage, especially of a ship cast ashore. **2.** Seaweed that has been cast ashore or dried. [From Middle English *wrak,* from Middle Dutch.]

❑ *These sound alike:* **wrack²** (wreckage), **rack¹** (frame), **rack²** (cut of meat), **wrack¹** (ruin).

wraith (rāth) *n.* An apparition or ghost.

wran·gle (răng′gəl) *v.* **wran·gled, wran·gling, wran·gles** —*intr.* **1.** To argue noisily or angrily. **2.** To grasp and maneuver something. **3.** To attempt to deal with or understand something; contend or struggle. —*tr.* **1.** To win or obtain by argument: *The union wrangled concessions from management.* **2.** To manage or herd (horses or cattle). **3.** To grasp and maneuver (something); wrestle. ❖ *n.* **1.** The act of wrangling. **2.** An angry noisy dispute. —**wrang′ler** *n.*

wrap (răp) *v.* **wrapped** or **wrapt** (răpt), **wrap·ping, wraps** —*tr.* **1.** To arrange or fold (something) about as a covering: *She wrapped her shawl about her.* **2.** To enclose within a covering: *wrap one's head in a scarf.* **3.** To enclose, especially in paper, and fasten: *wrap a package.* **4.** To clasp, fold, or coil around something: *She wrapped the line around the post.* **5.** To envelop and obscure: *a plan wrapped in secrecy.* —*intr.* **1.** To coil or twist about or around something: *The flag wrapped around the pole.* **2.** To put on warm clothing. ❖ *n.* **1.** An outer garment worn for warmth, such as a cloak, shawl, or coat. **2.** A wrapping or wrapper. **3.** A flatbread, such as a tortilla, rolled around a filling. ◆ **under wraps** *Informal* Secret or concealed: *Plans for the project are still under wraps.* **wrapped up in** Completely involved in; engrossed: *all wrapped up in a new mystery novel.* **wrap up** To bring to a conclusion; settle finally or successfully. [From Middle English *wrappen.*]

❑ *These sound alike:* **wrap, rap¹** (knock), **rap²** (talk).

wrap·per (răp′ər) *n.* **1.** A cover, as of paper, in which something is wrapped: *a candy wrapper.* **2.** A person or device that wraps, such as a store employee who wraps parcels.

wrap·ping (răp′ĭng) also **wrap·pings** (răp′ĭngz) *n.* The material used for wrapping something.

wrapt (răpt) *v.* A past tense and a past participle of **wrap.**

❑ *These sound alike:* **wrapt, rapt** (delighted).

wrath (răth) *n.* **1.** Violent anger. **2.** Punishment or vengeance, as for a sin or crime. [From Old English *wrǣththu,* from *wrāth,* angry.]

wrath·ful (răth′fəl) *adj.* Full of wrath: *wrathful fury.* —**wrath′ful·ly** *adv.*

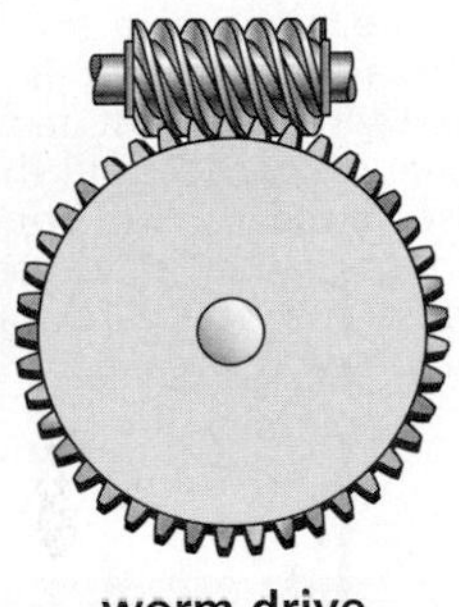

worm drive

USAGE

wreak Wreak is sometimes confused with **wreck,** perhaps because the wreaking of damage may leave a wreck: *The storm wreaked* (not *wrecked*) *havoc along the coast.* Sometimes you see the word **wrought** in similar uses: *The earthquake wrought a lot of damage. Wrought* is a past tense and past participle of *work,* but in this use it means "to bring about, cause." The past tense and past participle of *wreak* is *wreaked.*

wren

Frank Lloyd Wright

ă	pat	ôr	core
ā	pay	oi	boy
âr	care	ou	out
ä	father	o͝o	took
ĕ	pet	o͝or	lure
ē	be	o͞o	boot
ĭ	pit	ŭ	cut
ī	bite	ûr	urge
îr	pier	th	thin
ŏ	pot	*th*	this
ō	toe	zh	vision
ô	paw	ə	about

wreak (rēk) *tr.v.* **wreaked, wreak·ing, wreaks 1.** To bring about (damage or destruction, for example): *wreak havoc.* **2.** To inflict (vengeance or punishment) upon a person. **3.** To express or gratify (anger or resentment); vent: *The emperor wreaked his anger upon his advisers.* [From Old English *wrecan.*] —SEE NOTE.

❏ *These sound alike:* **wreak, reek** (smell bad).

wreath (rēth) *n., pl.* **wreaths** (rē*th*z *or* rēths) **1.** A ring or circlet of leaves, flowers, or boughs worn on the head, placed on a memorial, or hung as a decoration. **2.** A ring or similar curving form: *a wreath of smoke.* [From Old English *writha,* band.]

wreathe (rē*th*) *tr.v.* **wreathed, wreath·ing, wreathes 1.** To twist or entwine into a wreath or circular form: *wreathe flowers into a garland.* **2.** To crown or decorate with a wreath: *The winner was wreathed with laurel.* **3.** To coil or curl: *The snake wreathed itself around the branch.*

wreck (rĕk) *n.* **1a.** The act of destroying or the state of being destroyed; destruction: *A tornado caused the wreck of the barn.* **b.** The act of ruining or the state of being ruined: *Bad weather caused the wreck of our plans.* **2.** Accidental destruction of a ship; a shipwreck: *What caused the wreck of that freighter?* **3.** The remains of something that has been wrecked: *Divers searched the sea bottom for the wreck.* **4.** An automobile or railroad collision or accident: *A wreck on the freeway backed up traffic for miles.* **5.** A person or thing that is broken down or worn out: *The deaths in his family have left him a wreck. The house was a wreck after the party.* ❖ *tr.v.* **wrecked, wreck·ing, wrecks 1.** To cause the destruction of (something), as in a collision: *He wrecked the car.* See Synonyms at **destroy. 2.** To tear down or dismantle: *The crew wrecked the building in five days.* **3.** To spoil or ruin: *an argument that wrecked their friendship.* —SEE NOTE AT **wreak.**

wreck·age (rĕkʹĭj) *n.* The debris or remains of something wrecked: *the wreckage of a plane crash; flood wreckage.*

wreck·er (rĕkʹər) *n.* **1.** A person or thing that wrecks or destroys: *a wrecker of dreams.* **2.** A person who is in the business of demolishing old buildings. **3.** A person who dismantles junk cars for salvage. **4.** A tow truck used to move disabled or wrecked vehicles.

wren (rĕn) *n.* Any of various small brownish songbirds having rounded wings, a slender bill, and a short, often erect tail.

wrench (rĕnch) *n.* **1.** Any of various tools for gripping, turning, or twisting objects such as nuts, bolts, or pipes. **2.** A sudden sharp, forcible twist or turn: *gave the steering wheel a wrench.* **3.** An injury produced by twisting or straining. **4.** A sudden feeling of compassion, sorrow, or anguish, or an act that causes such a feeling. ❖ *tr.v.* **wrenched, wrench·ing, wrench·es 1.** To twist or turn suddenly and forcibly: *wrenched the door handle quickly.* **2.** To twist and sprain (a joint or other body part). **3.** To turn using a wrench: *He wrenched the nut onto the bolt.* **4.** To move, extract, or force free by twisting, turning, or pulling forcibly: *She wrenched the nail out of the board.* **5.** To free (oneself or a body part) by twisting, turning, or pulling: *wrenched his arm from the criminal's grasp.*

wrest (rĕst) *tr.v.* **wrest·ed, wrest·ing, wrests 1.** To obtain by pulling and twisting forcefully: *trying to wrest the pen from her grasp.* **2.** To gain or usurp forcefully: *wrested power from the king.*

❏ *These sound alike:* **wrest, rest**[1] (period of inactivity), **rest**[2] (remainder).

wres·tle (rĕsʹəl) *v.* **wres·tled, wres·tling, wres·tles** —*intr.* **1.** To try to throw or immobilize another person, especially by gripping with the hands. **2.** To engage in the sport of wrestling. **3.** To struggle to move or control something with the hands: *wrestled with the truck's steering wheel.* **4.** To struggle in trying to manage, control, or deal with something: *wrestled with my conscience.* —*tr.* **1.** To try to throw or immobilize (someone); wrestle with: *The police officers wrestled the suspect to the ground.* **2a.** To take part in a wrestling match with (an opponent). **b.** To take part in (a wrestling match). **3.** To move or lift with great effort: *wrestled the box up the stairs.* **4.** To take (something) away from another by gripping and pulling: *He wrestled the keys from my hands.* [From Middle English *wrestlen,* from Old English *wrǣstan,* to twist.]

wres·tler (rĕsʹlər) *n.* A person who wrestles, especially as a sport.

wres·tling (rĕsʹlĭng) *n.* A sport in which two competitors try to immobilize each other or throw each other off balance using various holds and maneuvers.

wretch (rĕch) *n.* **1.** A miserable, unfortunate, or unhappy person. **2.** A base, mean, or despicable person. [From Old English *wrecca.*]

wretch·ed (rĕchʹĭd) *adj.* **wretch·ed·er, wretch·ed·est 1.** In a deplorable state of distress or misfortune; miserable. **2.** Characterized by or causing misery or woe: *a wretched life.* **3.** Contemptible; despicable: *wretched treatment.* **4.** Inferior in quality: *I stopped watching the wretched movie after 10 minutes.* **—wretchʹed·ly** *adv.* **—wretchʹed·ness** *n.*

wri·er (rīʹər) *adj.* A comparative of **wry.**

wri·est (rīʹĭst) *adj.* A superlative of **wry.**

wrig·gle (rĭgʹəl) *v.* **wrig·gled, wrig·gling, wrig·gles** —*intr.* **1.** To turn or twist the body with winding writhing motions; squirm. **2.** To move with writhing motions: *The snake wriggled under the rock.* —*tr.* To move with a wriggling motion: *wriggle a toe.* ❖ *n.* A wriggling movement. ◆ **wriggle out of** To remove oneself from (a situation one does not want to be in) by sly or subtle means: *I wriggled out of my taking my brother to the mall by saying I had to visit a sick friend.*

wright (rīt) *n.* A person who constructs, shapes, or repairs something: *a wheelwright; a playwright.*

Wright (rīt), **Frank Lloyd** 1867–1959. American architect whose designs include private homes, corporate buildings, and the Guggenheim Museum in New York City (1959).

Wright, Orville 1871–1948. American aviation pioneer who with his brother **Wilbur** (1867–1912) invented the airplane. Their first flight was made on December 17, 1903, near Kitty Hawk, North Carolina.

Wright, Richard 1908–1960. American writer whose fiction, including the novel *Native Son* (1940), explores the oppression of African Americans.

wring (rĭng) *tr.v.* **wrung** (rŭng), **wring·ing, wrings 1.** To twist, squeeze, or compress, especially to get liquid out: *She wrung out a wet towel.* **2.** To force or squeeze (liquid) out by twisting or pressing: *He wrung the water out of his bathing suit.* **3.** To twist forcibly or painfully. **4.** To clasp and twist or squeeze (one's hands), as in distress. **5.** To obtain or extract by force or pressure: *The lawyer wrung the truth out of the witness.* ❖ *n.* A forceful squeeze or twist.

❏ *These sound alike:* **wring, ring**[1] (circle), **ring**[2] (sound a bell).

wring·er (rĭngʹər) *n.* A person or thing that wrings, especially a device in which laundry is pressed between rollers to extract water.

wrin·kle (rĭngʹkəl) *n.* **1.** A small furrow, ridge, or crease on a normally smooth surface: *The shirt had a lot of wrinkles, so I ironed it.* **2.** A line or crease in the skin, as from age. **3.** An unexpected problem, complication, or fault: *Every time a new wrinkle developed in the plan, the deadline was delayed.* ❖ *v.* **wrin·kled, wrin·kling, wrin·kles** —*tr.* **1.** To make a wrinkle or wrinkles in: *Don't wrinkle the suit.* **2.** To draw up into wrinkles or pucker: *wrinkled her nose.* —*intr.* To form wrinkles:

Linen wrinkles easily. [From Middle English, probably from Old English *gewrinclian*, to wind, crease.]

wrist (rĭst) *n.* **1.** The joint between the human hand and forearm. **2.** A similar joint in other vertebrate animals. [From Old English.]

wrist·band (rĭst′bănd′) *n.* A band, as on a sleeve or wristwatch, that encircles the wrist.

wrist·watch (rĭst′wŏch′) *n.* A watch worn on a band that fastens about the wrist.

writ[1] (rĭt) *n.* A written court order commanding a person to do or stop doing a specified act. [From Old English.]

writ[2] (rĭt) *v. Archaic* A past tense and a past participle of **write.**

writ·a·ble also **write·a·ble** (rī′tə-bəl) *adj.* Capable of recording data: *writable compact disks.*

write (rīt) *v.* **wrote** (rōt), **writ·ten** (rĭt′n), **writ·ing, writes** —*tr.* **1a.** To form (letters, words, or symbols) on a surface such as paper with an instrument such as a pen. **b.** To form (letters or words) in cursive style, especially in contrast to printing by hand. **2a.** To produce or compose (text) in a recorded form that can be read: *write a poem; write a letter.* **b.** To express in writing; set down: *write one's thoughts.* **c.** To communicate by writing, especially by written letter: *She wrote that she was planning to visit.* **d.** To communicate with (someone) by writing, especially by letter: *He wrote me to tell me that he had moved again.* **3.** To compose (a musical work). **4.** To draw up in legal form; draft: *write a lease.* **5.** To show clearly; mark: *Happiness was written in her smile.* **6.** To fill in the blank spaces of: *write a check.* **7.** To transfer or copy (information) from computer memory to a storage device or output device. —*intr.* **1.** To form letters, words, or symbols on a surface. **2.** To produce written material, such as essays or books. **3.** To compose a letter; communicate by mail: *Write to me.* ◆ **write in 1.** To cast a vote by inserting (a name not listed on a ballot). **2.** To insert in a text or document: *wrote in an apology at the end of the note.* **write off 1.** To consider as a loss or failure: *He wrote off his first paintings as mere practice.* **2.** To disregard as inconsequential: *The critic wrote off the movie as the work of amateurs.* **write up** To write a report or description of, as for publication. [From Old English *wrītan.*]

❑ *These sound alike:* **write, right** (direction), **rite** (ritual).

write-in (rīt′ĭn′) *n.* A vote cast by writing in the name of a candidate not on the ballot.

write-pro·tect (rīt′prə-tĕkt′) *tr.v.* **write-pro·tect·ed, write-pro·tect·ing, write-pro·tects** To modify (a computer file or disk) so that its data cannot be edited or erased.

writ·er (rī′tər) *n.* A person who writes, especially as an occupation.

write-up (rīt′ŭp′) *n.* A published account, review, or notice, especially a favorable one.

writhe (rīth) *intr.v.* **writhed, writh·ing, writhes 1.** To make twisting movements, as when struggling or in pain. **2.** To move with a twisting or contorted motion: *A snake writhed in the grass.*

writ·ing (rī′tĭng) *n.* **1a.** The act or process of producing and recording words in a form that can be read and understood: *The teacher taught writing to children in first grade.* **b.** The occupation or style of a writer. **2.** Written form: *Make the request in writing.* **3.** Meaningful letters or characters that make up readable matter: *erased the writing on the blackboard.* **4.** A written work, especially a literary composition. **5. Writings** *(used with a singular or plural verb)* The third of the three divisions of the Hebrew Scriptures, composed of Psalms, Proverbs, Job, Song of Solomon, Ruth, Lamentations, Ecclesiastes, Esther, Daniel, Ezra, Nehemiah, and Chronicles.

writ·ten (rĭt′n) *v.* Past participle of **write.**

wrong (rông) *adj.* **1.** Not conforming with fact or truth; incorrect; erroneous: *a wrong answer.* **2a.** Contrary to conscience, morality, or law: *Stealing is wrong.* **b.** Unfair; unjust: *I think it's wrong that you're taking some of the students on the field trip but not others.* **3.** Not required, intended, or wanted: *a wrong telephone number; the wrong direction.* **4.** Not fitting or suitable; inappropriate: *said the wrong thing.* **5.** Not in accordance with an established usage, method, or procedure: *the wrong way to make pie crust.* **6.** Not functioning properly; amiss: *What is wrong with this machine?* **7.** Designating the side, as of a garment, that is less finished and not intended to show: *socks worn the wrong side out.* ❖ *adv.* **1.** Mistakenly; erroneously: *told the story wrong.* **2.** Immorally or unjustly: *behave wrong.* ❖ *n.* **1.** An unjust, injurious, or immoral act or circumstance: *felt many wrongs had been committed against them.* **2.** The condition of being mistaken or at fault: *in the wrong.* ❖ *tr.v.* **wronged, wrong·ing, wrongs 1.** To treat unjustly, injuriously, or dishonorably. **2.** To discredit unjustly; malign. ◆ **go wrong 1.** To take a wrong turn or make a wrong move. **2.** To go amiss; turn out badly: *What went wrong with the project?* [From Middle English, of Scandinavian origin.] **—wrong′ly** *adv.* **—wrong′ness** *n.*

wrong·do·er (rông′do͞o′ər) *n.* A person who does something wrong. **—wrong′do′ing** *n.*

wrong·ful (rông′fəl) *adj.* **1.** Wrong; unjust: *wrongful criticism.* **2.** Unlawful: *wrongful search.* **—wrong′ful·ly** *adv.*

wrote (rōt) *v.* Past tense of **write.**

❑ *These sound alike:* **wrote, rote** (routine).

wroth (rôth) *adj. Archaic* Wrathful; angry.

wrought (rôt) *v.* A past tense and a past participle of **work.** ❖ *adj.* **1.** Put together; created: *A carefully wrought plan.* **2.** Shaped by hammering with tools: *wrought metal.* —SEE NOTE AT **wreak.**

wrought iron *n.* A highly purified form of iron that is easily shaped, forged, or welded.

wrung (rŭng) *v.* Past tense and past participle of **wring.**

❑ *These sound alike:* **wrung, rung**[1] (rod), **rung**[2] (sounded).

wry (rī) *adj.* **wri·er** (rī′ər), **wri·est** (rī′ĭst) or **wry·er, wry·est 1.** Funny in an understated, sarcastic, or ironic way; dry: *has a wry sense of humor.* **2.** Temporarily twisted in an expression of distaste or displeasure: *made a wry face.* **—wry′ly** *adv.*

❑ *These sound alike:* **wry, rye** (grain).

wt. *abbr.* An abbreviation of weight.

WTO *abbr.* An abbreviation of World Trade Organization.

wurst (wûrst *or* wo͝orst) *n.* Sausage.

❑ *These sound alike:* **wurst, worst** (most inferior).

WV *abbr.* An abbreviation of West Virginia.

WWI *abbr.* An abbreviation of World War I.

WWII *abbr.* An abbreviation of World War II.

WWW *abbr.* An abbreviation of World Wide Web.

WY *abbr.* An abbreviation of Wyoming.

Wyc·liffe (wĭk′lĭf), **John** 1328?–1384. English theologian and religious reformer whose beliefs anticipated the Protestant Reformation.

Wy·o·ming (wī-ō′mĭng) A state of the western United States south of Montana. It was admitted as the 44th state in 1890. Cheyenne is the capital and the largest city. —SEE NOTE.

wring

WRITERS CHOOSE THEIR WORDS

"That is your mission. If you fulfill it satisfactorily, the rewards will be considerable. If you do not—" He gave a **wry** smile. "Well, Falconer will make certain that you do."

—Gary L. Blackwood
The Shakespeare Stealer

GEOGRAPHY

Wyoming The name **Wyoming** comes from a Delaware word meaning "at the big river flats." The Delaware lived far to the east of Wyoming, and this name was originally used for a valley in Pennsylvania; how did it become the name of a western state? In 1809, a poet named Thomas Campbell wrote a poem that used the name; his poem became very popular, and with it the name *Wyoming* became widely known. Indian names in general became popular some decades later, and ultimately the word *Wyoming* was given in 1868 to a territory that later became the state of Wyoming.

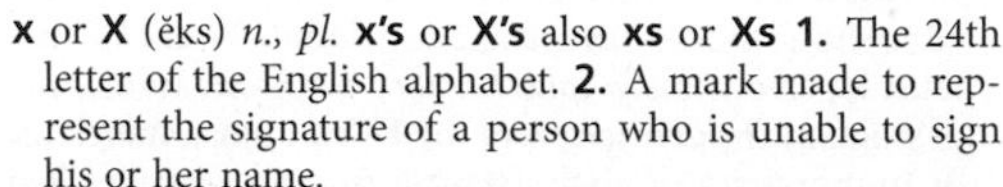

x or **X** (ĕks) *n., pl.* **x's** or **X's** also **xs** or **Xs** **1.** The 24th letter of the English alphabet. **2.** A mark made to represent the signature of a person who is unable to sign his or her name.

X *n.* A movie rating that allows admission to no one under the age of 17.

Xan·a·du (zăn′ə-do͞o′) *n.* An idyllic beautiful place. [From an archaic English spelling of the name of *Shengdu*, a city built by Kublai Khan in China, described in Samuel Taylor Coleridge's poem "Kubla Khan" as a place of wonders.]

x-ax·is (ĕks′ăk′sĭs) *n., pl.* **x-ax·es** (ĕks′ăk′sēz) **1.** The horizontal axis of a two-dimensional Cartesian coordinate system. **2.** One of the three axes of a three-dimensional Cartesian coordinate system.

XC or **X-C** *abbr.* An abbreviation of cross-country.

X chromosome *n.* The sex chromosome associated with female characteristics in mammals. In females it is paired with another X chromosome; in males it is paired with a Y chromosome.

Xe The symbol for the element **xenon.**

xe·bec (zē′bĕk′) *n.* A small three-masted Mediterranean sailing ship having both square and triangular sails. [From Arabic *šabbāk*, from *šabaka*, to entwine, fasten.]

xe·non (zē′nŏn′) *n. Symbol* **Xe** A colorless, odorless, chemically inert gaseous element that is found in the atmosphere in extremely small amounts. It is used in bubble chambers and in lamps that make intense flashes, such as strobe lights and flashbulbs for photography. Atomic number 54. See **Periodic Table.** [From Greek *xenos*, foreign, strange.]

xen·o·phobe (zĕn′ə-fōb′ *or* zē′nə-fōb′) *n.* A person who fears or has contempt for that which is foreign, especially foreign peoples or strangers.

xen·o·pho·bi·a (zĕn′ə-fō′bē-ə *or* zē′nə-fō′bē-ə) *n.* Fear of or contempt for foreign peoples or strangers. [From Greek *xenos*, foreign + Greek *phobiā*, fear.]

xen·o·pho·bic (zĕn′ə-fō′bĭk *or* zē′nə-fō′bĭk) *adj.* Relating to or characteristic of a xenophobe.

Xen·o·phon (zĕn′ə-fən *or* zĕn′ə-fŏn′) 430?–355? BC. Greek soldier and writer who led Greek troops in a retreat from a disastrous attack on Persia, an ordeal he recounted in *Anabasis*.

xe·rog·ra·phy (zĭ-rŏg′rə-fē) *n.* A process for producing photographs or photocopies in which an image made up of particles of dry pigment held in place by electric charges on a plate is transferred to a sheet of paper and fixed to the paper by heat. [From Greek *xēros*, dry + Greek *-graphiā*, writing.]

Xer·ox (zîr′ŏks) A trademark used for a photocopying process or machine employing xerography.

Xer·xes I (zûrk′sēz) Known as "Xerxes the Great." 519?–465 BC. King of Persia (486–465) whose army defeated the Greeks at Thermopylae and sacked Athens (480).

Xho·sa (kō′sä) *n., pl.* **Xhosa** or **Xho·sas** **1.** A member of a Bantu people of southern Africa. **2.** The language of this people.

xi (zī) *n.* The 14th letter of the Greek alphabet, written Ξ, ξ. In English it is represented as *X, x.*

XL *abbr.* An abbreviation of extra large.

X·mas (krĭs′məs *or* ĕks′məs) *n.* Christmas.

XML (ĕks′ĕm-ĕl′) *n.* A metalanguage for creating markup languages that structure digital information to allow the exchange, display, and storage of data on different operating systems and hardware devices. [From *Ex(tensible) M(arkup) L(anguage).*]

X-rat·ed (ĕks′rā′tĭd) *adj.* **1.** Having the rating X: *an X-rated movie.* **2.** Having content that is considered pornographic.

x-ray also **X-ray** (ĕks′rā′) *n.* also **x ray** or **X ray** **1a.** Electromagnetic radiation having a wavelength shorter than that of ultraviolet light but longer than that of a gamma ray and having a correspondingly high energy. **b.** often **x-rays** A stream of such radiation. **2.** A photograph taken with x-rays. ❖ *tr.v.* **x-rayed, x-ray·ing, x-rays** also **X-rayed, X-ray·ing, X-rays** **1.** To irradiate with x-rays. **2.** To photograph with x-rays.

x-ray astronomy *n.* The branch of astronomy dealing with the study of stars, galaxies, and other objects in space by means of the x-rays they emit.

x-ray diffraction *n.* The scattering of x-rays by crystal atoms, producing a diffraction pattern that yields information about the structure of the crystal.

xy·lem (zī′ləm) *n.* Plant tissue that provides support and conducts water and minerals from the roots to all parts of the plant. It consists of thick-walled cells and forms the woody tissue of trees and shrubs. [From Greek *xulon*, wood.]

xy·lo·phone (zī′lə-fōn′) *n.* A percussion instrument consisting of a series of mounted wooden bars of various sizes that sound various tones, played with two small mallets. [From Greek *xulon*, wood + Greek *phōnē*, sound.]

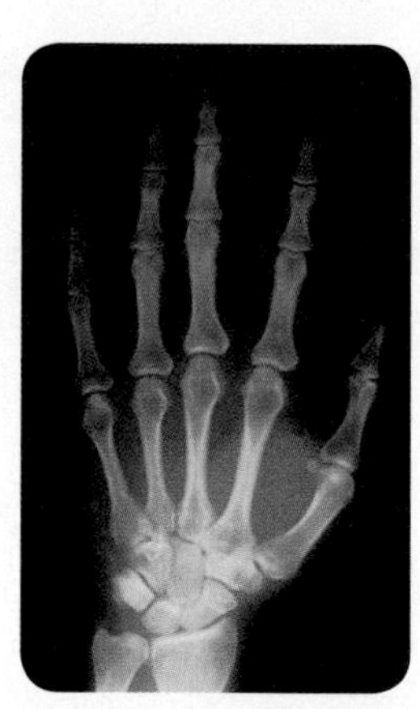

x-ray

ă	pat	ôr	core
ā	pay	oi	boy
âr	care	ou	out
ä	father	o͝o	took
ĕ	pet	o͝or	lure
ē	be	o͞o	boot
ĭ	pit	ŭ	cut
ī	bite	ûr	urge
îr	pier	th	thin
ŏ	pot	*th*	this
ō	toe	zh	vision
ô	paw	ə	about

y or **Y** (wī) *n., pl.* **y's** or **Y's** also **ys** or **Ys** The 25th letter of the English alphabet.

Y[1] *n.* The Young Men's Christian Association, the Young Women's Christian Association, the Young Men's Hebrew Association, the Young Women's Hebrew Association, or one of their facilities. Used with *the.*

Y[2] The symbol for the element **yttrium.**

Y[3] *abbr.* An abbreviation of year.

–y[1] or **–ey** *suff.* A suffix that means: **1.** Characterized by; consisting of: *moldy.* **2.** Like: *summery.* **3.** To some degree; rather: *chilly.* **4.** Tending toward: *sleepy.*

–y[2] *suff.* A suffix that means: **1.** Condition; state: *jealousy.* **2.** Activity: *cookery.* **3.** Place for an activity: *cannery.* **4.** Result or product of an activity: *laundry.*

–y[3] or **–ie** *suff.* A suffix that means: **1.** Small one: *doggy.* **2.** Dear one: *sweetie.*

yacht (yät) *n.* Any of various relatively small, streamlined sailing or motor-driven vessels used for private pleasure trips or racing. ❖ *intr.v.* **yacht·ed, yacht·ing, yachts** To sail, cruise, or race in a yacht.

yachts·man (yäts′mən) *n.* A man who owns or sails a yacht.

yachts·wom·an (yäts′wo͝om′ən) *n.* A woman who owns or sails a yacht.

Ya·fo (yä′fō) See **Jaffa.**

ya·hoo (yä′ho͞o *or* yā′ho͞o) *n., pl.* **ya·hoos** A crude or brutish person.

Yah·weh (yä′wĕ) *n.* A name for God thought to represent the original pronunciation of the letters standing for God's name in the Hebrew Scriptures.

yak[1] (yăk) *n.* A long-haired ox of the mountains of central Asia, often domesticated and used for pulling and carrying loads or raised for its meat and milk. [From Tibetan *gyag.*]

yak[2] (yăk) *intr.v.* **yakked, yak·king, yaks** *Slang* To talk persistently and meaninglessly; chatter. [Of imitative origin.]

Ya·ka·ma also **Ya·ki·ma** (yăk′ə-mə *or* yăk′ə-mô) *n., pl.* **Yakama** or **Ya·ka·mas** also **Yakima** or **Ya·ki·mas 1.** A member of a Native American people of south-central Washington. **2.** Their dialect of Sahaptin.

y'all (yôl) *pron.* Variant of **you-all.** —SEE NOTE.

Yal·ow (yăl′ō), **Rosalyn Sussman** 1921–2011. American medical physicist who helped to develop a method for measuring very small amounts of hormones and other substances in the blood.

Yal·ta (yôl′tə) A city of southeast Ukraine on the Black Sea. It is a popular resort and was the site of an Allied conference (attended by Franklin D. Roosevelt, Winston Churchill, and Joseph Stalin) in February 1945.

yam (yăm) *n.* **1a.** The starchy root of any of numerous tropical vines, used as food. **b.** A vine that has such roots. **2.** A sweet potato. —SEE NOTE AT **goober.**

yam·mer (yăm′ər) *intr.v.* **yam·mered, yam·mer·ing, yam·mers 1.** To speak loudly or at length. **2.** To complain peevishly or whimperingly; whine. —**yam′mer·er** *n.*

Ya·mous·sou·kro (yä′mo͞o-so͞o′krō) The capital of Côte d'Ivoire, in the central part of the country northwest of Abidjan.

Yan·gon (yăng-gŏn′) or **Ran·goon** (răn-go͞on′ *or* răng-go͞on′) The largest city of Myanmar (Burma), in the southern part of the country northwest of Bangkok, Thailand. It was Myanmar's capital until 2006.

Yang·tze (yăng′sē′ *or* yăng′tsē′) or **Chang·jiang** (chäng′jyäng′) The longest river of China and of Asia, flowing about 3,900 miles (6,300 kilometers) from Tibet to the East China Sea.

yank (yăngk) *v.* **yanked, yank·ing, yanks** —*tr.* To pull on with a quick strong movement; jerk: *The baby yanked her bib off and threw it down.* —*intr.* To pull with a quick strong movement: *I yanked on the rope until the knot gave.* ❖ *n.* A sudden sharp pull; a jerk.

Yank (yăngk) *n. Informal* A Yankee.

Yan·kee (yăng′kē) *n.* **1.** A native or inhabitant of New England, especially one of English ancestry. **2.** A native or inhabitant of a northern US state, especially a Union soldier during the Civil War. **3.** A native or inhabitant of the United States.

Ya·oun·dé (yä-oon-dā′) The capital of Cameroon, in the south-central part of the country. It was founded in 1888.

yap (yăp) *intr.v.* **yapped, yap·ping, yaps 1.** To bark sharply; yelp. **2.** *Slang* To talk noisily or stupidly; jabber. ❖ *n.* **1.** A sharp high-pitched bark. **2.** *Slang* The mouth.

Yap (yăp *or* yäp) An island group and state of the Federated States of Micronesia in the western Caroline Islands of the western Pacific Ocean.

Ya·qui (yä′kē) *n., pl.* **Yaqui** or **Ya·quis 1.** A member of a Native American people living in northern Mexico and southern Arizona. **2.** The Uto-Aztecan language of this people.

yard[1] (yärd) *n.* **1.** A unit of length equal to 3 feet or 36 inches (0.91 meter). See table at **measurement. 2.** A long pole slung from a mast to support the head of a sail. [From Old English *gerd.*]

yard[2] (yärd) *n.* **1.** A piece of ground next to, surrounding, or surrounded by a building or group of buildings: *our back yard; the school yard.* **2.** A piece of ground, often enclosed, used for a particular kind of work, business, or other activity: *a coal yard; a lumber yard.* **3.** An area where railroad cars are switched from track to track, made up into trains, stored, and repaired. [From Old English *geard.*]

yard·age (yär′dĭj) *n.* An amount or length measured in yards: *yardage gained in a game.*

yard·arm (yärd′ärm′) *n.* Either end of a yard supporting a square sail.

yard·man (yärd′mən) *n.* A man employed in a yard, especially a railroad yard.

yard sale *n.* A sale of used household belongings, typically held outdoors at the home of the seller.

yacht

USAGE

y'all The single most famous feature of southern United States dialects is the pronoun **y'all,** a variant of **you-all.** Southerners can use *you* and *y'all* or *you-all* to make a distinction between one person and more than one person. You used to be able to do this in English by using *thou* for the singular and *you* for the plural. Speakers in most other parts of the United States use the phrase *you guys* in informal situations where Southerners might say *y'all.*

Rosalyn Yalow

yarmulke

WRITERS CHOOSE THEIR WORDS

[Stuart] looked back, and to his great joy he perceived that the Lillian had gone off in a wild direction and was **yawing** all over the pond. Straight and true sailed the Wasp, with Stuart at the helm.

—E.B. White
Stuart Little

WRITERS CHOOSE THEIR WORDS

Medwyn, Taran saw, had gardens of both flowers and vegetables behind the cottage. To his surprise, Taran found himself **yearning** to work with Coll in his own vegetable plot. The weeding and hoeing he had so despised at Caer Dallben now seemed, as he thought of his past journey and the journey yet to come, infinitely pleasant.

—Lloyd Alexander
The Book of Three

ă	pat	ôr	core
ā	pay	oi	boy
âr	care	ou	out
ä	father	o͝o	took
ĕ	pet	o͝or	lure
ē	be	o͞o	boot
ĭ	pit	ŭ	cut
ī	bite	ûr	urge
îr	pier	th	thin
ŏ	pot	*th*	this
ō	toe	zh	vision
ô	paw	ə	about

yard·stick (yärd′stĭk′) *n.* **1.** A graduated measuring stick one yard in length. **2.** A standard used in comparing or judging.

yar·mul·ke (yär′məl-kə *or* yä′məl-kə) *n.* A skullcap worn by Jewish men and boys, especially those adhering to Orthodox or Conservative Judaism. [From Yiddish *yarmulke*, from Polish and Ukrainian *yarmulka*, possibly from Turkish *yağmurluk*, rain clothing.]

yarn (yärn) *n.* **1.** A continuous strand of twisted threads of material such as wool or nylon, used in weaving, knitting, or crocheting. **2.** *Informal* A long, sometimes elaborate story, often made-up or exaggerated. [From Old English *gearn.*]

yar·row (yăr′ō) *n.* Any of several plants having narrow feathery leaves and flat-topped clusters of white, pink, or yellow flowers.

yaw (yô) *intr.v.* **yawed, yaw·ing, yaws 1.** To swerve off course momentarily or temporarily: *The schooner yawed in the rough seas.* **2.** To turn right or left about a vertical axis: *The plane yawed because of the strong wind.* ❖ *n.* **1.** The act of yawing. **2.** Extent of yawing, measured in degrees: *The pilot corrected for the yaw of the plane.*

yawl (yôl) *n.* A fore-and-aft rigged sailboat having two masts, one of which is shorter and stands to the stern behind the tiller.

yawn (yôn) *intr.v.* **yawned, yawn·ing, yawns 1.** To open the mouth wide with a deep inward breath, usually involuntarily, as when sleepy or bored. **2.** To open wide; gape: *The entrance to the tunnel yawned ahead of them.* ❖ *n.* The act of yawning.

yawp (yôp) *intr.v.* **yawped, yawp·ing, yawps** To utter a sharp cry; yelp. ❖ *n.* A bark; a yelp.

yaws (yôz) *pl.n.* *(used with a singular or plural verb)* A tropical skin disease caused by bacteria in which reddish sores appear on the skin.

y-ax·is (wī′ăk′sĭs) *n., pl.* **y-ax·es** (wī′ăk′sēz) **1.** The vertical axis of a two-dimensional Cartesian coordinate system. **2.** One of the three axes of a three-dimensional Cartesian coordinate system.

Yb The symbol for the element **ytterbium.**

Y chromosome *n.* The sex chromosome associated with male characteristics in mammals, pairing with an X chromosome in males and not occurring in females.

yd. *abbr.* An abbreviation of yard (measurement).

ye[1] (yē) *pron. Archaic* **1.** *(used with a plural verb)* You. **2.** *(used with a singular verb)* You. [From Old English *gē.*]

ye[2] (*th*ē *or* yē) *def.art. Archaic* The. [Alteration of Middle English *þe*, the (from the use of *y* to represent thorn, þ, in early English printing).]

yea (yā) *adv.* **1.** Yes; aye. **2.** Indeed; truly. ❖ *n.* An affirmative statement or vote.

yeah (yĕ′ə *or* yă′ə *or* yā′ə) *adv. Informal* Yes.

year (yîr) *n.* **1a.** The period of time during which Earth makes one complete revolution around the sun, consisting of 365 days, 5 hours, 49 minutes, and 12 seconds. In the Gregorian calendar a year begins on January 1 and ends on December 31 and is divided into 12 months or about 52 weeks. **b.** A period approximately equal to a year in other calendars. **2.** The period during which a planet completes a single revolution around the sun: *A year on Mars is longer than a year on Earth.* **3.** A period of 12 months: *a year from June.* **4.** A period of time, shorter than 12 months, that recurs every 12 months and is devoted to a special activity or purpose: *the school year.* **5. years** Age, especially old age: *I'm feeling my years.* **6. years** A long time: *I haven't seen them in years.* [From Old English *gēar.*]

year·book (yîr′bo͝ok′) *n.* **1.** A memorial or historical book published every year, giving information about the year just ended. **2.** A book published at the end of each school or college year, especially as a record of the members and activities of a graduating class.

year-end (yîr′ĕnd′) *n.* The end of a year. ❖ *adj.* Occurring or done at the end of the year: *The store held a year-end sale to reduce inventory.*

year·ling (yîr′lĭng) *n.* An animal that is one year old or between one and two years old.

year·long (yîr′lông′) *adj.* Lasting an entire year: *a yearlong contract.*

year·ly (yîr′lē) *adj.* Occurring once a year or every year; annual. ❖ *adv.* Once a year; annually: *Maples and oaks shed their leaves yearly.*

yearn (yûrn) *intr.v.* **yearned, yearn·ing, yearns 1.** To have a strong, often melancholy desire: *yearn for a lost love.* **2.** To feel deep pity, concern, or tenderness: *yearned over the poor child's fate.*

yearn·ing (yûr′nĭng) *n.* A persistent, often melancholy desire: *a yearning for truth and justice.*

year-round (yîr′round′) *adj.* Existing, active, or continuous throughout the year: *year-round ice skating.* **—year′-round′** *adv.*

yeast (yēst) *n.* **1.** Any of various one-celled fungi that reproduce asexually by budding and can cause the fermentation of carbohydrates, producing carbon dioxide and alcohol. **2.** A commercial preparation in either compressed or powdered form, containing yeast cells and used as a leavening agent or a dietary supplement. **—yeast′y** *adj.*

Yeats (yāts), **William Butler** 1865–1939. Irish writer whose poetry is published in collections such as *The Winding Stair* (1929).

yell (yĕl) *v.* **yelled, yell·ing, yells** *—intr.* To cry out loudly, as in excitement, pain, fright, or surprise: *They yelled and jumped up and down.* *—tr.* To utter or express with a loud cry; shout. ❖ *n.* **1.** A loud shout or cry. **2.** A cheer chanted in unison by a group.

SYNONYMS **yell, holler, howl, roar, shout** These verbs mean to say with or make a loud, strong cry. *Angry spectators yelled at the umpire. The monitor hollered when she saw the children littering. When the boy fell off his bike, he howled with pain. The audience roared with laughter at the clowns. The children shouted and ran around the playground.*

yel·low (yĕl′ō) *n.* **1.** The color of ripe lemons. In the spectrum it is between orange and green. **2.** Something having this color, as the yolk of an egg. ❖ *adj.* **yel·low·er, yel·low·est 1.** Of the color yellow. **2.** *Slang* Cowardly. ❖ *tr. & intr.v.* **yel·lowed, yel·low·ing, yel·lows** To make or become yellow: *Many washings had yellowed the linen tablecloth. The paper yellowed with age.* [From Old English *geolu.*] **—yel′low·ness** *n.*

yellow card *n.* A yellow-colored card shown by a referee, especially in soccer, to signal a flagrant foul. The issuing of two yellow cards to a player results in the player's being thrown out of the game.

yellow fever *n.* A severe infectious disease of tropical and subtropical regions caused by a virus transmitted by the bite of a mosquito. Its symptoms include high fever, jaundice, and dark-colored vomit resulting from internal bleeding.

yel·low·ish (yĕl′ō-ĭsh) *adj.* Somewhat yellow.

yellow jacket *n.* Any of several small wasps having yellow and black markings.

yellow journalism *n.* Journalism that exploits, distorts, or exaggerates the news to create sensations.

Yel·low·knife (yĕl′ō-nīf′) The capital of Northwest Territories, Canada, in the south-central part of the territory. It was founded in 1935 and became the capital in 1967.

yel·low·legs (yĕl′ō-lĕgz′) *n., pl.* **yellowlegs** Either of two shorebirds of the Americas that have long yellow legs and a narrow bill.

yellow pages or **Yellow Pages** *pl.n.* A telephone book or a section in a telephone book that lists businesses, services, or products alphabetically by category.

Yellow River A river of northern China rising in the central part of the country and flowing about 3,350 miles (5,400 kilometers) generally eastward to an inlet of the Yellow Sea. Yellow River is the translation of Huang He, its Chinese name.

Yellow Sea An arm of the Pacific Ocean between the Chinese mainland and the Korean Peninsula. It connects with the East China Sea to the south.

Yel·low·stone (yĕl′ō-stōn′) A river, about 670 miles (1,080 kilometers) long, of northwest Wyoming and southern and eastern Montana. It flows northward through **Yellowstone National Park,** then east and northeast to the Missouri River.

yel·low·y (yĕl′ō-ē) *adj.* Somewhat yellow; yellowish.

yelp (yĕlp) *intr.v.* **yelped, yelp·ing, yelps** To utter a short, sharp bark or cry: *The dogs yelped as they played in the yard. I yelped in pain when the bee stung me.* ❖ *n.* A short, sharp bark or cry.

Yel·tsin (yĕlt′sĭn), **Boris** 1931–2007. Russian politician who served as president (1991–1999). His administration was marked by economic reform and conflict with the legislature.

Yem·en (yĕm′ən *or* yā′mən) A country of southwest Asia at the southern tip of the Arabian Peninsula. From 1967 to 1990 it was divided into **North Yemen** and **Southern Yemen.** Sanʻa is the capital.

yen[1] (yĕn) *n.* A strong desire or inclination; a longing. [From Cantonese *yun*, hope, wish.]

yen[2] (yĕn) *n., pl.* **yen** The basic monetary unit of Japan. [From Japanese *en*.]

yeo·man (yō′mən) *n.* **1.** An attendant, servant, or lesser official in a royal or noble household. **2.** A petty officer who performs clerical duties in the US Navy. **3.** An assistant, as of a sheriff. **4.** A diligent, dependable worker. **5.** A farmer who works his own land, especially a member of a former class of small landowners in England.

yeo·man·ry (yō′mən-rē) *n., pl.* **yeo·man·ries** Yeomen considered as a group.

yep (yĕp) *adv. Informal* Yes.

yer·ba ma·te also **yer·ba ma·té** (yâr′bə mä′tā *or* yûr′bə mä′tā) *n.* The dried leaves of the mate plant or a tealike beverage made from them.

Ye·re·van (yĕ′rə-vän′) The capital of Armenia, in the west-central part of the country. It was founded on the site of a fortress built in the eighth century BC.

yes (yĕs) *adv.* It is so; as you say or ask. Used to express affirmation, agreement, or consent. ❖ *n., pl.* **yes·es** also **yes·ses 1.** An affirmative or consenting reply: *His suggestion was met with a chorus of yeses.* **2.** An affirmative vote or voter. ❖ *interj.* An expression used to show great satisfaction, approval, or happiness.

ye·shi·va or **ye·shi·vah** (yə-shē′və) *n.* **1.** A Jewish institute of learning where students study sacred texts, especially the Talmud. **2.** A Jewish school with a curriculum that includes Jewish religion and culture.

yes·ter·day (yĕs′tər-dā′ *or* yĕs′tər-dē) *n.* **1.** The day before the present day: *Yesterday was cold and windy.* **2.** Time in the past, especially the recent past: *The science fiction of yesterday seems quaint today.* ❖ *adv.* **1.** On the day before the present day: *I mailed the letter yesterday.* **2.** A short while ago.

yes·ter·year (yĕs′tər-yîr′) *n.* **1.** Time past; yore. **2.** *Archaic* The year before the present year.

yet (yĕt) *adv.* **1.** At this time; for the present: *Dinner isn't ready yet.* **2.** Up to a specified time; thus far: *They have not started yet.* **3.** At a future time: *We may yet decide to go.* **4.** Besides; in addition: *He returned for yet another helping of pie.* **5.** Even; still more: *a yet sadder tale.* **6.** Nevertheless: *young yet wise.* ❖ *conj.* Nevertheless; and despite this: *She said she would be late, yet she arrived on time.* ◆ **as yet** Up to the present time; up to now: *I haven't seen any qualified applicants as yet.*

ye·ti (yĕt′ē) *n., pl.* **ye·tis** The abominable snowman.

yew (yo͞o) *n.* **1.** Any of several evergreen trees or shrubs having poisonous, flat, dark-green needles and seeds enclosed by a red covering. **2.** The tough wood of any of these trees, used in making furniture and archery bows.
❑ *These sound alike:* **yew, ewe** (female sheep), **you** (pronoun).

Yid·dish (yĭd′ĭsh) *n.* A language derived principally from medieval German dialects and spoken by Jews of Central and Eastern Europe and by their descendants in other parts of the world. Yiddish is usually written using Hebrew letters.

yield (yēld) *v.* **yield·ed, yield·ing, yields** —*tr.* **1.** To give up (an advantage, for example) to another; concede: *yielded the right of way to the oncoming traffic.* **2.** To give over possession of; surrender: *yielded my seat to the stranger.* **3.** To give forth by a natural process: *The garden yielded a variety of vegetables.* **4.** To provide as return for effort or investment: *an investment that yields high percentages.* —*intr.* **1.** To give forth a natural product; be productive. **2.** To produce a return for effort or investment. **3.** To give up, as in defeat. **4.** To give way to pressure or force: *The dough yields when pressed with a finger.* **5.** To give way to argument, persuasion, or influence. ❖ *n.* **1.** An amount yielded or produced; a product: *a high yield of corn.* **2.** A profit obtained from an investment. [From Old English *geldan*, to pay.]

SYNONYMS **yield, abandon, relinquish, surrender, cede** These verbs mean to let something go or to give something up. **Yield** suggests giving way, as to pressure or superior authority: *The diplomat yielded numerous demands after meeting with the mediators.* **Abandon** means to let something go or give something up with no expectation of returning to it or recovering it: *The shipwrecked family slowly abandoned all hope of being rescued.* **Relinquish** often suggests that one regrets what is being given up: *After years of hard work, he relinquished his dream of becoming a major-league baseball player.* **Surrender** means to abandon under force or demand: *The passengers surrendered their luggage to the customs agents.* **Cede** suggests giving up something by formal transfer: *Germany ceded the region to France as part of the peace treaty.*

---

yield·ing (yēl′dĭng) *adj.* Inclined to give way to pressure, argument, or influence.

yikes (yīks) *interj.* An expression used to indicate mild fear or surprise.

yip (yĭp) *n.* A short high-pitched bark. ❖ *intr.v.* **yipped, yip·ping, yips** To emit a yip.

yip·pee (yĭp′ē) *interj. Informal* An expression used to show elation.

yo (yō) *interj. Slang* An expression used as a greeting or to attract someone's attention.

yo·del (yōd′l) *v.* **yo·deled, yo·del·ing, yo·dels** or **yo·delled, yo·del·ling, yo·dels** —*intr.* To sing so that the voice alternates rapidly between the normal voice and a falsetto. —*tr.* To sing (a song) by yodeling. ❖ *n.* A song or cry that is yodeled.

yo·ga (yō′gə) *n.* **1.** also **Yoga** A Hindu discipline involving controlled breathing, prescribed body positions, and meditation, with the goal of attaining spiritual insight and tranquility. **2.** A system of physical exercises derived from or practiced as part of this discipline. [From Sanskrit *yogaḥ*, union, joining.]

yo·gi (yō′gē) *n., pl.* **yo·gis** A person who practices yoga.

yo·gurt also **yo·ghurt** (yō′gərt) *n.* A tart food similar to custard, made from milk curdled by bacteria and often

yellow jacket

yew
common yew

yoga

WRITERS CHOOSE THEIR WORDS

"Perch on the ottoman **yonder,** my sprite," suggested her father. Following the direction of his nod, Dido saw what might be a sofa with books, bedroom ware, and piles of linen on it. She had to climb over a sideboard, and past a pair of glass-fronted cabinets, to reach it.

—Joan Aiken
Dido and Pa

Brigham Young

yucca

ă	pat	ôr	core
ā	pay	oi	boy
âr	care	ou	out
ä	father	o͝o	took
ĕ	pet	o͝or	lure
ē	be	o͞o	boot
ĭ	pit	ŭ	cut
ī	bite	ûr	urge
îr	pier	th	thin
ŏ	pot	*th*	this
ō	toe	zh	vision
ô	paw	ə	about

sweetened or flavored. [From Turkish *yoğart, yoğurt,* from *yoğur,* to knead.]

yoke (yōk) *n.* **1.** A crossbar with two U-shaped attachments that fit around the necks of a team of oxen or other draft animals, used for hitching the team to a cart, plow, or other load. **2.** *pl.* **yoke** or **yokes** A pair of draft animals, such as oxen, joined by a yoke. **3.** A frame carried across a person's shoulders with equal loads suspended from each end. **4.** A clamp or vise that controls the motion of a part, holds a part in place, or holds two parts together. **5.** A part of a garment fitting closely around the neck and shoulders or over the hips. **6.** Something that connects or joins; a bond. **7.** The condition of being subjugated by or as if by a conqueror: *the yoke of tyranny.* ❖ *tr.v.* **yoked, yok·ing, yokes 1.** To join or harness with a yoke: *yoked the oxen to the cart.* **2.** To join closely as if with a yoke; unite: *The two friends were yoked in a long successful partnership.* [From Old English *geoc.*]

❑ *These sound alike:* **yoke, yolk** (egg yellow).

yo·kel (yō**′**kəl) *n.* A country person considered unsophisticated.

Yo·ko·ha·ma (yō′kə-**hä′**mə) A city of southeast Honshu, Japan, south of Tokyo. It was almost entirely destroyed by an earthquake and fire in 1923 but was quickly rebuilt.

yolk (yōk) *n.* **1.** The yellow part of the egg of an egg-laying vertebrate, such as a reptile or bird, that supplies food to the developing embryo. **2.** The yolk of a chicken egg. [From Old English *geolca,* from *geolu,* yellow.]

❑ *These sound alike:* **yolk, yoke** (crossbar).

Yom Kip·pur (yôm′ **kĭp′**ər *or* yôm′ kē-**po͝or′**) *n.* A Jewish holy day observed on the last day of a ten-day period beginning with Rosh Hashanah and marked by fasting and prayer for the atonement of sins.

yon (yŏn) *adv. & adj.* Yonder.

yon·der (**yŏn′**dər) *adv.* In or at that indicated place: *the village over yonder.* ❖ *adj.* At a distance, but usually within sight: *yonder oak tree.*

yore (yôr) *n.* Time long past: *days of yore.*

York·shire pudding (**yôrk′**shîr *or* **yôrk′**shər) *n.* A quick bread like a popover, served with roast beef and baked in the drippings of the beef.

York·town (**yôrk′**toun′) A village of southeast Virginia southeast of Richmond. It was the site of Charles Cornwallis's surrender of the British forces (1781) in the American Revolution.

Yo·ru·ba (**yôr′**ə-bə *or* yō-ro͞o-**bä′**) *n., pl.* **Yoruba** or **Yo·ru·bas 1.** A member of a West African people living chiefly in southwest Nigeria. **2.** The language of the Yoruba.

Yo·sem·i·te Valley (yō-**sĕm′**ĭ-tē) A valley of east-central California. It lies within **Yosemite National Park** and has many waterfalls, including **Yosemite Falls,** with a total drop of 2,425 feet (739 meters).

you (yo͞o) *pron.* **1.** The person or people being addressed: *You have very little time left. I'll lend you the book.* **2.** An indefinitely specified person; one: *You can't win them all.* [From Old English *ēow,* dative and accusative of *gē,* ye, you.] —SEE NOTE AT **y'all.**

❑ *These sound alike:* **you, ewe** (female sheep), **yew** (evergreen).

you-all (**yo͞o′ôl′**) also **y'all** (yôl) *pron.* You. Used chiefly in the Southern United States in addressing two or more people. —SEE NOTE AT **y'all.**

you'd (yo͞od) Contraction of *you had* or *you would.*

you'll (yo͞ol *or* yo͝ol; yəl *when unstressed*) Contraction of *you will.*

❑ *These sound alike:* **you'll, Yule** (Christmas).

young (yŭng) *adj.* **young·er, young·est 1.** Being in an early stage of life, growth, or development: *a young animal; young leaves.* **2.** Not far advanced; at or near the beginning: *The evening is young.* **3.** Relating to, belonging to, or suggestive of youth or early life: *He is young for his age.* **4.** Lacking experience or maturity: *a young hand at plowing.* ❖ *n.* **1.** *(used with a plural verb)* Young people considered as a group; youth: *The young are the target audience of this movie.* **2.** Offspring: *a lioness with her young.* ◆ **with young** Pregnant. Used of an animal. [From Old English *geong.*]

SYNONYMS young, youthful, immature, juvenile These adjectives describe a person or thing that is in an early period of growth or development. **Young** is the most general: *You're too young to remember the Cold War.* **Youthful** suggests characteristics, such as enthusiasm, freshness, or energy, that are associated with youth: *My grandfather still has a youthful attitude toward life.* **Immature** describes what is not yet fully grown or developed. The term sometimes suggests that someone falls short of an expected level of maturity: *The immature child threw a tantrum in the middle of the store.* **Juvenile** suggests immaturity, even childishness: *They spent April Fool's Day playing juvenile pranks.*

Young (yŭng), **Brigham** 1801–1877. American religious leader who led the Mormons from Illinois to the site of present-day Salt Lake City, Utah, where they established a permanent home for the church (1847).

Young, Denton True Known as "Cy." 1867–1955. American baseball player. A pitcher for 22 seasons, he won 511 games, including 76 shutouts and 3 no-hitters.

young·ish (**yŭng′**ĭsh) *adj.* Somewhat young.

young·ster (**yŭng′**stər) *n.* **1.** A child or young person. **2.** A young animal.

your (yo͝or *or* yôr; yər *when unstressed*) *adj.* The possessive form of **you. 1.** Relating or belonging to you: *your boots; your achievements.* **2.** A person's; one's: *The light switch is on your right.* [From Old English *ēower,* genitive of *gē,* ye, you.]

❑ *These sound alike:* **your, you're** (you are).

you're (yo͝or; yər *when unstressed*) Contraction of *you are.*

❑ *These sound alike:* **you're, your** (of you).

yours (yo͝orz *or* yôrz) *pron. (used with a singular or plural verb)* **1.** The one or ones belonging to you: *Use my car if yours hasn't been repaired.* **2.** Used in the complimentary close of a letter: *sincerely yours.* ◆ **yours truly** I, myself, or me: *The work was done by yours truly.*

your·self (yo͝or-**sĕlf′** *or* yôr-**sĕlf′** *or* yər-**sĕlf′**) *pron.* **1.** That one that is the same as you: **a.** Used as the direct or indirect object of a verb or as the object of a preposition to show that the action of a verb refers back to the subject: *You should not tire yourself. Give yourself enough time. Keep it for yourself.* **b.** Used to give emphasis: *You yourself admitted it.* **2.** Your normal or healthy condition: *You were not feeling yourself when you did it.*

your·selves (yo͝or-**sĕlvz′** *or* yôr-**sĕlvz′** *or* yər-**sĕlvz′**) *pron.* **1.** Those ones that are the same as you: **a.** Used as the direct or indirect object of a verb or as the object of a preposition to show that the action of a verb refers back to the subject: *Help yourselves. Have yourselves a good time. You should all watch out for yourselves.* **b.** Used to give emphasis: *You'll have to take care of it yourselves.* **2.** Your normal or healthy condition: *Just relax and be yourselves.*

youth (yo͞oth) *n., pl.* **youths** (yo͞oths *or* yo͞othz) **1.** The condition or quality of being young. **2.** An early period of development or existence, especially the time of life before one is an adult. **3.** A young person, especially a young male in late adolescence. **4.** *(used with a singular or plural verb)* Young people considered as a group: *the youth of our city.* [From Old English *geoguth.*]

youth·ful (yo͞oth′fəl) *adj.* **1.** Characterized by youth; young: *the youthful hero.* See Synonyms at **young. 2.** Relating to or suggesting youth: *youthful impatience.* **—youth′ful·ly** *adv.* **—youth′ful·ness** *n.*

youth hostel *n.* An inexpensive place for young travelers to stay overnight.

you've (yo͞ov) Contraction of *you have.*

yowl (youl) *n.* A long, loud, mournful cry. ❖ *intr.v.* **yowled, yowl·ing, yowls** To utter a yowl.

yo-yo (yō′yō′) *n., pl.* **yo-yos** A toy consisting of a flattened spool wound with string that is spun down from and reeled up to the hand by motions of the wrist.

yr. *abbr.* An abbreviation of year.

YT *abbr.* An abbreviation of Yukon Territory.

yt·ter·bi·um (ĭ-tûr′bē-əm) *n. Symbol* **Yb** A soft, bright, silvery metallic element that occurs in three different forms and is used to strengthen stainless steel. Atomic number 70. See **Periodic Table.** [After *Ytterby*, a town in Sweden.]

yt·tri·um (ĭt′rē-əm) *n. Symbol* **Y** A silvery metallic element used to strengthen magnesium and aluminum alloys. Atomic number 39. See **Periodic Table.**

yu·an (yo͞o-än′) *n., pl.* **yuan** or **yu·ans** The basic monetary unit of China.

Yu·ca·tán (yo͞o′kə-tăn′) A peninsula mostly in southeast Mexico between the Caribbean Sea and the Gulf of Mexico. The region includes many Mayan and Toltec sites.

Yuc·a·tec (yo͞o′kə-tĕk′) *n., pl.* **Yucatec** or **Yuc·a·tecs 1.** A member of a Mayan people living in the Yucatán Peninsula. **2.** The Mayan language of the Yucatec.

yuc·ca (yŭk′ə) *n.* Any of various plants of dry regions of the southwestern United States, Mexico, and Central America, having stiff pointed leaves, large clusters of whitish flowers, and sometimes a treelike stem. [From Taíno *yuca*, cassava.]

Yu·go·sla·vi·a (yo͞o′gō-slä′vē-ə) A former country of southeast Europe on the Adriatic Sea west of Bulgaria. It was originally formed in 1918 as a kingdom and became a Communist-led regime after World War II. Yugoslavia formerly consisted of six republics, four of which declared independence in 1991. The remaining two republics, Serbia and Montenegro, abandoned the name Yugoslavia in 2003 but remained in political union until 2006. Belgrade was the capital and the largest city.

yu·ka·ta (yo͞o-kä′tə) *n.* A lightweight informal kimono, usually made of cotton. [From Japanese.]

Yu·kon River (yo͞o′kŏn′) A river flowing about 1,980 miles (3,185 kilometers) from southern Yukon Territory, Canada, through Alaska to the Bering Sea.

Yukon Territory A territory of northwest Canada east of Alaska. It joined the Canadian confederation in 1898. Whitehorse is the capital.

Yule (yo͞ol) *n.* Christmas or the Christmas season, especially as traditionally celebrated as a winter holiday in Northern Europe. [From Old English *gēol.*]

❑ *These sound alike:* **Yule, you'll** (you will).

yule log *n.* A large log traditionally burned in a fireplace at Yule.

Yule·tide (yo͞ol′tīd′) *n.* The season of Yule.

Yu·ma (yo͞o′mə) *n., pl.* **Yuma** or **Yu·mas 1.** A Quechan. **2.** The Quechan language.

Yu·man (yo͞o′mən) *n.* A family of Native American languages of the southwest United States and parts of Mexico. **—Yu′man** *adj.*

yum·my (yŭm′ē) *adj.* **yum·mi·er, yum·mi·est** *Informal* Delicious; appetizing to the taste or smell: *This pizza tastes yummy!*

yup (yŭp) *adv. Informal* Yes.

Yu·pik (yo͞o′pĭk) *n., pl.* **Yupik** or **Yu·piks 1.** A member of a group of Eskimo peoples living in the southwest coastal areas of Alaska and extreme northeastern Siberia. **2a.** The family of languages spoken by the Yupik. **b.** Any of the languages spoken by the Yupik.

yup·pie (yŭp′ē) *n. Informal* A young city or suburban resident having a high-paying job and a taste for luxury items. [From *y(oung) u(rban) p(rofessional).*]

yurt (yûrt) *n.* A circular, domed tent used by nomadic peoples of central Asia.

yukata

yurt

Mildred Zaharias

WRITERS CHOOSE THEIR WORDS

With wild yells very uncharacteristic of peaceful mice, the friends seized their staves and charged out, fired with new **zeal**.

—Brian Jacques
Redwall

zebu

ă	pat	ôr	core
ā	pay	oi	boy
âr	care	ou	out
ä	father	o͝o	took
ĕ	pet	o͝or	lure
ē	be	o͞o	boot
ĭ	pit	ŭ	cut
ī	bite	ûr	urge
îr	pier	th	thin
ŏ	pot	*th*	this
ō	toe	zh	vision
ô	paw	ə	about

z or **Z** (zē) *n., pl.* **z's** or **Z's** also **zs** or **Zs** The 26th letter of the English alphabet.

za (zä) *n. Slang* Pizza.

zag (zăg) *n.* One of a series of sharp turns or reversals: *a report about the zigs and zags of the stock market.* ❖ *intr.v.* **zagged, zag·ging, zags** To turn or change direction suddenly. Usually used in contrast to *zig: The ball carrier zigged when he should have zagged.*

Za·greb (zä′grĕb) The capital of Croatia, in the northern part of the country east-southeast of Ljubljana, Slovenia.

Za·har·i·as (zə-hâr′ē-əs), **Mildred Ella Didrikson** Known as "Babe." 1911–1956. American athlete who excelled in golf and track and won two gold medals at the 1932 Olympics.

Za·ire (zī′îr *or* zä-îr′) See **Congo** (sense 1).

Zam·be·zi (zăm-bē′zē) A river, about 1,700 miles (2,735 kilometers) long, of central and southern Africa rising in northwest Zambia and flowing south and east through Mozambique to an arm of the Indian Ocean.

Zam·bi·a (zăm′bē-ə) A country of south-central Africa east of Angola. Lusaka is the capital.

Zam·bo·ni (zăm-bō′nē) A trademark used for a machine that resurfaces the ice in an ice rink.

za·ny (zā′nē) *adj.* **za·ni·er, za·ni·est** Ludicrously comical; clownish: *The comedian's act included several zany songs.* ❖ *n., pl.* **za·nies 1.** A buffoonish character in old comedies who attempts to mimic the clown. **2.** An outlandishly comical person.

Zan·zi·bar (zăn′zə-bär′) A region of Tanzania in eastern Africa, made up of **Zanzibar Island** and several adjacent islands off the northeast coast of mainland Tanzania.

zap (zăp) *Informal tr.v.* **zapped, zap·ping, zaps 1.** To strike or destroy (an object or target) with a beam of energy, an electric current, or supernatural power: *In the movie, the alien zaps the scientist with a ray of energy.* **2.** To expose to radiation; irradiate: *zap leftovers in a microwave.* ❖ *n.* A burst or beam of energy, electric current, or other power: *a zap of 120 volts.*

Za·pa·ta (zə-pä′tə *or* sä-pä′tä), **Emiliano** 1879–1919. Mexican revolutionary who led a revolt from 1910 to 1919 to reform the ownership of land.

Za·po·tec (zä′pə-tĕk′) *n., pl.* **Zapotec** or **Za·po·tecs 1.** A member of an American Indian people of southern Mexico. **2.** Any of a group of related American Indian languages spoken in southern Mexico. **—Za′po·tec′** *adj.*

z-ax·is (zē′ăk′sĭs) *n., pl.* **z-ax·es** (zē′ăk′sēz) One of the three axes of a three-dimensional Cartesian coordinate system.

zeal (zēl) *n.* Intense enthusiasm or devotion to a cause, ideal, or goal. [From Middle English *zele*, from Greek *zēlos*.]

zeal·ot (zĕl′ət) *n.* A person who is zealous, especially excessively so.

zeal·ot·ry (zĕl′ə-trē) *n.* Excessive zeal; fanaticism.

zeal·ous (zĕl′əs) *adj.* Filled with or motivated by zeal; fervent: *zealous support of a cause.* **—zeal′ous·ly** *adv.* **—zeal′ous·ness** *n.*

ze·bra (zē′brə) *n.* Any of several African mammals related to and resembling the horse, having the entire body marked with white and black or brown stripes.

ze·bu (zē′bo͞o) *n., pl.* **ze·bus** A domesticated ox of Asia and Africa, having a hump on the back and a large dewlap.

Zech·a·ri·ah[1] (zĕk′ə-rī′ə) A Hebrew prophet of the sixth century BC.

Zech·a·ri·ah[2] (zĕk′ə-rī′ə) *n.* A book of the Bible in which Zechariah declares his visions and prophecies.

zed (zĕd) *n. Chiefly British* The letter *z.*

Zen (zĕn) *n.* A form of Buddhism, practiced mainly in China, Japan, Korea, and Vietnam, asserting that enlightenment can be reached through meditation, contemplation, and intuition rather than through faith and devotion.

ze·nith (zē′nĭth) *n.* **1.** The point on the celestial sphere that is directly above the observer. **2a.** The upper region of the sky. **b.** The highest point above the observer's horizon attained by a celestial object. **3.** The point of culmination; the peak: *the zenith of her career.* [From Middle English *senith*, from Arabic *samt (ar-ra's)*, path (over the head), from Latin *sēmita*, path.]

Zeph·a·ni·ah[1] (zĕf′ə-nī′ə) A Hebrew prophet of the seventh century BC.

Zeph·a·ni·ah[2] (zĕf′ə-nī′ə) *n.* A book of the Bible in which Zephaniah announces the coming day of judgment of all nations.

zeph·yr (zĕf′ər) *n.* **1.** The west wind. **2.** A gentle breeze.

zep·pe·lin (zĕp′ə-lĭn) *n.* A rigid airship with a long cylindrical body, supported by cells containing a gas that is lighter than air. [After Count Ferdinand von *Zeppelin* (1838–1917), German inventor.]

ze·ro (zîr′ō *or* zē′rō) *n., pl.* **ze·ros** or **ze·roes 1.** The numerical symbol 0; a cipher. **2.** A number that when added to another number leaves that number unchanged; the identity element with respect to addition. **3.** The temperature indicated by the numeral 0 on a thermometer. **4.** *Informal* Nothing; nil: *We have accomplished zero today.* ❖ *tr.v.* **ze·roed, ze·ro·ing, ze·roes** To adjust (an instrument or device) to a setting of zero. ◆ **zero in 1.** To aim or concentrate firepower on an exact target location. **2.** To concentrate one's attention; focus: *The boy zeroed in on the toy display in the window.* [From Arabic *ṣifr*, nothing, cipher.] —SEE NOTE.

zero gravity *n.* A condition of apparent weightlessness such as that experienced in orbit or in free fall.

zero hour *n.* The scheduled time for the start of an operation or action, especially a combat operation.

zest (zĕst) *n.* **1.** Flavor or interest: *Spices give zest to simple foods.* **2.** The outermost rind of an orange, lemon, or other citrus fruit, used as a flavoring. **3.** Spirited enjoyment; relish; gusto: *He ate his oysters with zest.* [From obsolete French, orange or lemon peel.]

SYNONYMS zest, gusto, relish These nouns mean intense, hearty pleasure or appreciation. *The zest that the volunteers brought to the project made the hard work seem like fun. She tells those old jokes with great gusto. He read horror stories with a relish that I found disturbing.*

zest·ful (zĕst′fəl) *adj.* Full of or showing zest. **—zest′ful·ly** *adv.*

ze·ta (zā′tə) *n.* The sixth letter of the Greek alphabet, written Z, ζ, or in English *Z, z.*

Zeus (zo͞os) *n.* In Greek mythology, the chief god, ruler of the heavens, and brother and husband of Hera. He is identified with the Roman Jupiter.

zig (zĭg) *n.* One of a series of sharp turns or reversals: *the zigs and zags of a mountain trail.* ❖ *intr.v.* **zigged, zig·ging, zigs** To turn or change direction suddenly. Usually used in contrast to *zag: When your opponent zigs, zag!*

zig·gu·rat (zĭg′ə-răt′) *n.* A temple tower of ancient Mesopotamia, having the form of a terraced pyramid. [From Akkadian (ancient Semitic language spoken in Mesopotamia) *ziqqurratu,* temple tower, from *zaqāru,* to build high.]

zig·zag (zĭg′zăg′) *n.* **1.** A line or course that proceeds by sharp turns in alternating directions. **2.** One of a series of such sharp turns. **3.** Something, such as a road or a design, shaped like or following the course of a zigzag. ❖ *adj.* Moving in or having a zigzag: *a zigzag path.* ❖ *adv.* In a zigzag manner or pattern: *The blindfolded child went zigzag across the room.* ❖ *intr.v.* **zig·zagged, zig·zag·ging, zig·zags** To move in or form a zigzag: *The trail zigzagged up the mountain.*

zilch (zĭlch) *n. Slang* Zero; nothing: *After six innings, our team still had zilch.*

zil·lion (zĭl′yən) *n. Informal* An indefinitely large number: *There must be zillions of grains of sand on this beach.*

Zim·bab·we (zĭm-**băb′**wē *or* zĭm-**băb′**wā) A country of southern Africa west of Mozambique. Until 1980, it was known as Rhodesia. Harare is the capital.

zinc (zĭngk) *n. Symbol* **Zn** A shiny, bluish-white metallic element widely used as a coating for iron, in alloys such as brass, as a roofing material, and in electric batteries. Atomic number 30. See **Periodic Table.** [From German *Zink.*]

zinc oxide *n.* A white or yellowish powdery compound of zinc and oxygen having the formula ZnO. It is used as a pigment and in various medicines and cosmetics for the skin.

zine or **'zine** (zēn) *n.* An inexpensive self-published periodical.

zing (zĭng) *n.* **1.** A high-pitched buzzing sound, such as that made by a taut vibrating string. **2.** Liveliness or interest: *added some pepper to give the soup more zing.* ❖ *intr.v.* **zinged, zing·ing, zings 1.** To make a zing. **2.** To move swiftly with or as if with a zing.

zin·ni·a (zĭn′ē-ə) *n.* Any of various garden plants native to tropical America and having showy, variously colored flowers. [After Johann Gottfried *Zinn* (1727–1759), German botanist.]

Zi·on (zī′ən) *n.* **1.** The historic land of Israel as a symbol of the Jewish people. **2.** The Jewish people; Israel. **3.** A place or community regarded as sacredly devoted to God.

Zi·on·ism (zī′ə-nĭz′əm) *n.* A political movement that supports maintaining and preserving Israel as a Jewish state, originally arising in the late 1800s with the goal of reestablishing a Jewish homeland in Palestine. **—Zi′on·ist** *adj. & n.*

zip (zĭp) *n.* **1.** A brief, sharp, hissing sound. **2.** Energy; vim. **3.** *Informal* Nothing; nil. ❖ *v.* **zipped, zip·ping, zips** —*intr.* **1.** To move quickly, especially with a sharp hissing sound: *The cars zipped by.* **2.** To act very quickly and energetically: *She zipped through her homework.* —*tr.* To fasten or unfasten with a zipper: *Zip up the dress.*

ZIP Code (zĭp) *n.* A series of digits designating a specific town, city, or neighborhood in the United States, added to a postal address to speed up the sorting and delivery of mail.

zip·line (zĭp′līn′) *n.* A transportation system or piece of recreation equipment consisting of a cable stretched between points of different elevations, a pulley, and a harness or bar for attaching a rider, who moves by gravity.

zip·per (zĭp′ər) *n.* A fastener consisting of two rows of interlocking teeth on adjacent edges of an opening that are closed or opened by a sliding tab. ❖ *tr. & intr.v.* **zip·pered, zip·per·ing, zip·pers** To fasten or unfasten or become fastened or unfastened with a zipper; zip.

zip·py (zĭp′ē) *adj.* **zip·pi·er, zip·pi·est** Full of energy; lively.

zir·con (zûr′kŏn′) *n.* A mineral, essentially a silicate of zirconium, that can be heated, cut, and polished to form brilliant blue-white gems. [Ultimately from Persian *āzargūn,* fire color.]

zir·co·ni·um (zûr-**kō′**nē-əm) *n. Symbol* **Zr** A shiny, grayish-white metallic element that is highly resistant to corrosion and is used in hardening steel and in nuclear reactors. Atomic number 40. See **Periodic Table.**

zit (zĭt) *n. Slang* A pimple.

zith·er (zĭth′ər *or* zĭ*th*′ər) *n.* A musical instrument consisting of a flat box with about 30 to 40 strings stretched over it and played horizontally, usually with the fingers, a pick, or a bow. [From German, from Greek *kitharā,* ancient instrument resembling the lyre.]

zlo·ty (zlô′tē) *n., pl.* **zloty** or **zlo·tys** The basic monetary unit of Poland.

Zn The symbol for the element **zinc.**

zo·di·ac (zō′dē-ăk′) *n.* **1.** A band of the celestial sphere extending about eight degrees on both sides of the ecliptic that contains the paths of the sun, moon, and principal planets. **2.** In astrology, the twelve divisions, or signs of the zodiac, into which this band is divided, each having the name of a constellation. —SEE NOTE AT **zoo–.**

zom·bie (zŏm′bē) *n., pl.* **zom·bies 1.** According to voodoo belief, a corpse revived by a supernatural power or spell. **2.** A person who looks or behaves like a zombie, as in mechanical movements or aloof manner. [From Louisiana French Creole and Haitian Creole *zonbi,* of Bantu origin.]

zon·al (zō′nəl) *adj.* Relating to or associated with a zone: *zonal divisions.*

zone (zōn) *n.* **1.** An area or region distinguished from a nearby one by a distinctive characteristic or reason: *a residential zone; a climatic zone.* **2.** A portion of a sphere cut off by two parallel planes that intersect the sphere. ❖ *tr.v.* **zoned, zon·ing, zones** To divide or mark off into zones. ❖ *adj.* In sports such as basketball and football, of or relating to a system of defense in which each defender guards a section of the playing area rather than an individual player. ◆ **zone out** To lose concentration or become inattentive: *I zoned out during the long movie.* [From Middle English, from Greek *zōnē,* belt.]

zoo (zo͞o) *n., pl.* **zoos 1.** A park or institution where living animals are kept and exhibited to the public. **2.** *Informal* A place or situation marked by confusion or disorder: *The mall is a zoo on Saturdays.* [Short for *zoological garden.*] —SEE NOTE AT **zoo–.**

zoo– *pref.* A prefix that means animal or animals: *zoology.* —SEE NOTE on page 1062.

zo·o·log·i·cal (zō′ə-**lŏj′**ĭ-kəl) also **zo·o·log·ic** (zō′ə-**lŏj′**ĭk) *adj.* Relating to animals or zoology: *a zoological collection.* **—zo′o·log′i·cal·ly** *adv.*

SCIENCE

zero It may seem odd, but **zero** may be the most important number. When zero is added to or subtracted from a number, it leaves the number at its original value. Zero thus makes negative numbers possible. A negative number added to its positive counterpart always equals zero. Zero is essential to representing numbers such as 203 and 1024. In these numbers zero serves as a placeholder in the system called "positional notation." Thus in 203, there are 2 hundreds, zero tens, and 3 ones. That is, zero shows that the value of the tens place is zero. Without zero, we wouldn't have hundreds, thousands, or millions in our number system.

zipline

zither

WORD BUILDING

zoo– The prefix **zoo–,** which is pronounced with two syllables, comes from the Greek word *zōion,* "animal, living being." We know this prefix best in the one-syllable word *zoo,* which originated as a shortening of the longer, more formal term *zoological garden. Zoological* is the adjective form of the noun *zoology,* which means "the study of animals." From their word *zōion* the Greeks formed another word, *zōidion,* "little animal, small picture (of an animal or other figure)," the source of our word *zodiac.*

zoological garden *n.* A zoo.

zo·ol·o·gist (zō-ŏl′ə-jĭst) *n.* A scientist who specializes in zoology.

zo·ol·o·gy (zō-ŏl′ə-jē *or* zo͞o-ŏl′ə-jē) *n., pl.* **zo·ol·o·gies** **1.** The branch of biology that deals with animals. **2.** The animals of a particular area or period: *the zoology of South America.*

zoom (zo͞om) *v.* **zoomed, zoom·ing, zooms** —*intr.* **1.** To make or move with a low-pitched buzzing or humming sound: *A hornet zoomed past my ear.* **2.** To move rapidly: *The car zoomed down the freeway.* **3.** To magnify or reduce the scale of an image while correspondingly decreasing or increasing the field of view, as by means of a zoom lens. —*tr.* To cause to zoom. ❖ *n.* **1.** The sound or act of zooming. **2.** A zoom lens.

zoom lens *n.* A camera lens whose focal length can be changed to allow a rapid change in the size of an image while keeping the image in focus.

Zo·ro·as·ter (zôr′ō-ăs′tər) Flourished about sixth century BC. Iranian prophet who founded Zoroastrianism.

Zo·ro·as·tri·an (zôr′ō-ăs′trē-ən) *n.* A believer in Zoroastrianism. ❖ *adj.* Relating to Zoroaster or Zoroastrianism.

Zo·ro·as·tri·an·ism (zôr′ō-ăs′trē-ə-nĭz′əm) *n.* The religious system founded in Persia by Zoroaster, that views the universe as a place of conflict between the forces of light and darkness.

zounds (zo͞ondz *or* zoundz) *interj. Archaic* An expression used to show anger, surprise, or indignation.

Zr The symbol for the element **zirconium.**

zuc·chi·ni (zo͞o-kē′nē) *n., pl.* **zucchini** or **zuc·chi·nis** A type of long narrow squash having a thin dark green rind.

Zu·lu (zo͞o′lo͞o) *n., pl.* **Zulu** or **Zu·lus** **1.** A member of a Bantu people of southeast Africa. **2.** The language of this people, closely related to Xhosa. **—Zu′lu** *adj.*

Zu·ni (zo͞o′nē) also **Zu·ñi** (zo͞o′nyē *or* zo͞o′nē) *n., pl.* **Zuni** or **Zu·nis** also **Zuñi** or **Zu·ñis** **1.** A member of a Native American people of western New Mexico. **2.** The language of this people.

Zu·rich (zo͝or′ĭk) The largest city of Switzerland, in the northeast part of the country at the northern tip of the **Lake of Zurich.** It was founded before Roman times.

zwie·back (swī′băk′ *or* zwī′băk′) *n.* A usually sweetened bread baked first as a loaf and then sliced and toasted.

zy·de·co (zī′dĭ-kō′) *n.* A style of popular music of southern Louisiana that combines elements of French and Caribbean music and the blues, featuring the guitar, accordion, and washboard.

zy·gote (zī′gōt′) *n.* The cell formed by the union of two gametes, especially a fertilized egg cell. **—zy·got′ic** (zī-gŏt′ĭk) *adj.*

ă	pat	ôr	core
ā	pay	oi	boy
âr	care	ou	out
ä	father	o͝o	took
ĕ	pet	o͝or	lure
ē	be	o͞o	boot
ĭ	pit	ŭ	cut
ī	bite	ûr	urge
îr	pier	th	thin
ŏ	pot	*th*	this
ō	toe	zh	vision
ô	paw	ə	about

Picture Credits

The editorial and production staff wishes to thank the many individuals, organizations, and agencies that have contributed to the art program for this dictionary.

Credits on the following pages are arranged alphabetically by boldface entry word. At entries for which there are two or more picture sources, the sources follow the order of the illustrations. The following source abbreviations are used throughout the credits: **AF**: age fotostock; **AL**: Alamy; **API**: AP Images; **AR**: Art Resource, New York; **CI**: Carlyn Iverson; **CL-AA**: Clarinda-Academy Artworks; **COR**: Corbis Corporation; **EM**: Elizabeth Morales; **GI**: Getty Images; **HMH**: © Houghton Mifflin Harcourt Digital Studio; **LOC**: Library of Congress; **PD**: Photodisc, Inc.; **PG**: Precision Graphics; **PR**: Photo Researchers, Inc.; **SS**: SuperStock; **WS**: Wendy Smith.

aardvark Patrick Gnan **abacus** HMH **Ralph Abernathy** COR/Flip Schulke **abscissa** CL-AA **acacia** AL/Florapix **acanthus** GI/Harald Sund **accordion** Photolibrary/Alberto Campanile **ace** SS/AF **acorn squash** HMH **acoustics** UG/GGS Information Services **Acropolis** GI/MedioImages **acrostic** Margaret Anne Miles **acute angle** Academy Artworks **Abigail Adams** Bridgeman Art Library/Massachusetts Historical Society **John Adams** SS/SuperStock **John Quincy Adams** AR/Réunion des Musées Nationaux **Jane Addams** LOC **adjacent** GI/Photodisc **adjacent angle** Academy Artworks **adobe** COR/Michael T. Sedam **adrenal gland** CI **aerialist** AL/Pat & Chuck Blackley **aerodynamics** Academy Artworks **A-frame** AL/vanneilbob **African violet** HMH **agate** HMH **agave** PR/François Gohier **aground** GI/Travel Ink **aileron** PG **air conditioner** PG **Airedale** GI/Photodisc **akimbo** SS/Stephen Simpson **Louisa May Alcott** GI/PhotoQuest **Aleutian Islands** Joe LeMonnier **Muhammad Ali** GI/Mandel Ngan **aliphatic** Robin Storesund **allegory** Bridgeman Art Library/Worcester Art Museum **alluvial fan** Shutterstock/Totajla **aloe** AL/Thomas David Pinzer **alpaca** AL/fotolincs **alternate angles** Academy Artworks **altocumulus** SS/imagebroker.net **amanita** PR/Phil A. Dotson **amaryllis** HMH **amber** HMH **ammonite** COR/Walter Geiersperger **amoeba** Bart Vallecoccia **amphitheater** PR/Hubertus Kanus **Roald Amundsen** LOC/Harris & Ewing **anaconda** AL/discpicture **anemometer** AL/www.matthiasengelien.com **aneurysm** EM **angelfish** AL/John Anderson **Maya Angelou** COR/Axel Koester **angle**[2] Pronk & Associates **Angora rabbit** GI/DAJ **ankh** HMH **annual ring** COR/Don Mason **annular eclipse** NASA/Hinode/XRT **Antarctic Circle** Thom Gillis **anteater** SS/AF **Susan B. Anthony** LOC **anticline** PG **antler** GI/Paul E. Tessier **anvil** AL/Keith Morris **ao dai** SS/Asia Images **apogee** Academy Artworks **Appaloosa** SS/Animals Animals **appendix** CI **Appomattox Court House** COR **apron** AL/Frank and Helena **aqueduct** GI/Travel Ink **arabesque** GI/STOCK4B **arch**[1] COR **archaeopteryx** GI/Jason Edwards, National Geographic **archery** SS/Tetra Images **Arctic Circle** Thom Gillis **area** CL-AA **arm**[1] CI **Neil Armstrong** NASA **art deco** SS/IndexStock **Chester Arthur** PR **artichoke** AF/Jo Whitworth **art nouveau** SS/Radius Images **ash**[2] EM **Arthur Ashe** COR/Michael Cole **asparagus** AL/funkyfood London - Paul Williams **aspen** GI/Digital Vision **aster** AF/Thonig **asthma** Garth Glazier **astride** GI/Photodisc **asymptote** CL-AA **atherosclerosis** PG **atmosphere** CL AA **attaché case** HMH **auger** COR/Thinkstock **Aung San Suu Kyi** SS/Robert Harding Picture Library **aureole** AL/blickwinkel, Dautel **Jane Austen** AL/The Art Gallery Collection **autograph** Margaret Anne Miles **avocado** HMH **awning** SS/Neal & Molly Jansen **axe** GI/Volker Otten **axolotl** AF/Layer **Ayrshire** SS/Animals Animals **Aztec** PR/David R. Frazier **baboon** Ardea/Jean Michel Labat **backboard** GI/David Madison **backflip** SS/Exactostock **backgammon** GI/Photodisc **backsplash** SS/Sheltered Images **bacterium** PR/Scimat **bacterium** GI/Cultura Science, Rolf Ritter **bacterium** PR/3D4Medical **badger** COR **baguette** GI/Foodcollection **ball**[3] GI/Thomas Northcut **Ella Baker** AL/Everett Collection **Vasco Núñez de Balboa** North Wind Picture Archives **ball-and-socket joint** CI **ballet** Shutterstock/Yuri Arcurs **bamboo** Shutterstock/Mark Aplet **banana** Shutterstock/Natursports **banister** Shutterstock/Johanna Evang Nonboe **baobab** AL/Chris Mattison **barbed wire** GI/Steve Roe-stephenroe.co.uk **bar graph** Academy Artworks **barnacle** PR/Walter E. Harvey **baroque** GI/Alberto Incrocci **barre** GI/Image Source **Clara Barton** LOC **basketweave** Margaret Anne Miles **bas-relief** AF/Wojtek Buss **bass clef** Tech-Graphics **Bastille Day** SS/De Agostini **batik** GI/Jane Nelson **battering ram** AL/Ancient Art and Architecture **battlement** AF/Marco Cristofori **beadwork** AL/Gina Corrigan **beak** EM **bearskin** GI/David Sanger **Beatrix** API/Ronald Zak **beaver**[1] PR/Tom McHugh **beech** WS **Ludwig van Beethoven** GI/DEA-A. Dagli Orti **begonia** AL/David R. Frazier Photolibrary, Inc. **belaying pin** Shutterstock/V.J. Matthew **belfry** COR **Alexander Graham Bell** LOC/Harris & Ewing **bellows** HMH **bench press** HMH **Benedict XVI** GI/Gamma-Rapho **beret** AF/bilderlounge **Mary McLeod Bethune** LOC/Carl Van Vechten **biceps** CI **bill**[2] GI/Photodisc **binnacle** GI/Steve Mason **binoculars** PG **bioluminescence** GI/Bill Curtsinger **bird of paradise** AL/Juniors Bildarchiv **biscotti** HMH **bisector** Academy Artworks **bison** GI/Paul E. Tessier **bitterroot** GI/Kevin Schafer **Black Hawk** SS/Shirley Bowers **Elizabeth Blackwell** US National Library of Medicine **black widow** GI/GK Hart-Vikki Hart **blast furnace** PG **blaze**[2] GI/Greg Dale **bleeding heart** GI/Claudia Rehm **blight** AL/Nigel Cattlin **blinders** GI/Radius Images **block and tackle** PG **bloomers** LOC **blowpipe** AL/Rob Walls **bluebonnet** SS/imagebroker.net **Nellie Bly** LOC **boa** SS/Gallo Images **board shorts** AL/Image Source **bob**[2] GI/Photodisc **bobsled** GI/Bongarts **boiler** PG **Simón Bolívar** Bridgeman Art Library/Giraudon **bolt** GI/DEA-C. Sappa **bonsai** HMH **boomerang** HMH **Daniel Boone** Bridgeman Art Library/Massachusetts Historical Society **John Wilkes Booth** LOC **Boston terrier** Ardea/Jean Michel Labat **bouquet** HMH **bow**[3] GI/Photodisc **bowline** HMH **brace** GI/Stockbyte **brace** HMH **Braille** Academy Artworks **Louis Braille** SS/Eye Ubiquitous **brain** CI **breadfruit** AF/Laurence Mouton **breaker** Cutcaster/Julija Sapic **breakwater** SS/Fotosearch **bridge**[1] EM **brigantine** Shutterstock/Ian Holland **brindled** Ardea/John Daniels **Britannia** AL/The Protected Art Archive **brocade** HMH **brogue**[1] AL/Tony Rusecki **Brontë** Bridgeman Art Library/National Portrait Gallery, London, UK **John Brown** AL/North Wind Picture Archives **brownstone** COR/Alan Schein Photography **Brussels sprouts** PR/Jon Stokes **James Buchanan** LOC **Buddha**[2] AL/Serg Zastavkin **budgerigar** GI/Siede Preis **buffalo** SS/AF **bulldog** Ardea/John Daniels **bulldozer** AL/David J. Green **bullet train** AL/Wood Stock **bungee jumping** AL/kpzfoto **Bunsen burner** AL/sciencephotos **buoy** AL/Jason Smalley **burdock** Ardea/Bob Gibbons **burqa** GI/AFP-Shah Marai **burrito** AL/Stan Sholik **George H. W. Bush** George Bush Presidential Library and Museum **George W. Bush** George W. Bush Presidential Library, White House photo by Eric Draper **butte** COR/moodboard **George Gordon Byron** GI/Hulton Archive **Byzantine** Cutcaster/Olga Lipatova **cabriolet** SS/Science and Society **caduceus** Academy Artworks **Julius Caesar** GI/AFP-Gerard Julien **cairn** AF/Bold Stock **calabash** AL/Planetpix **calligraphy** AL/Image Source Black **John Calvin** AL/Titian **calzone** GI/Foodcollection RF **camel** GI/Keren Su **camel** AL/Juniors Bildarchiv **cameo** HMH **camouflage** GI/Hemera Technologies **candelabrum** HMH **cane** SS/Blend Images **cankerworm** SS/Animals Animals **cannoli** HMH **canoe** AF/Roy Morsch **canopy** COR/Elizabeth Whiting and Associates **canta-**

loupe HMH **cantilever bridge** SS/Robert Harding Picture Library **cantle** AF/Sharad Haksar **capacitor** PG **capital[2]** AL/Ken Welsh **Capitol** GI/Randy Wells **capri pants** AL/Rubberball **capuchin** SS/Tier und Naturfotografie **cardigan** AF/Rubberball **cargo pants** SS/Glow Asia **caribou** GI/MIMOTITO **caricature** GI/FPG **caricature** AL/Lordprice Collection **carob** AL/Charles Stirling **Kit Carson** LOC **Rachel Carson** COR/Bettmann **Jimmy Carter** GI/AFP-Yasuyoshi Chiba **Cartesian coordinate system** CL-AA **cartwheel** SS/Exactostock **cashew** AL/imagebroker, Guenter Fischer **Mary Cassatt** AL/Folio **casserole** SS/FoodCollection **Fidel Castro** AL/Roberto Fumagalli **catalpa** WS **catboat** SS/BlueGreen Pictures **Catherine II** GI/Imagno **catkin** AL/Krys Bailey **Carrie Chapman Catt** LOC **C clef** Tech-Graphics **cedar waxwing** COR/Tim Zurowski **cell** CL-AA **Celsius** EM **centripetal force** PG **Miguel de Cervantes** SS/Stock Montage **chainlink fence** iStockphoto/Tova Photography **chairlift** iStockphoto/Anneclaire Le Royer **chalet** AF/Blaine Harrington **chalice** GI/Photodisc **challah** HMH **chandelier** Shutterstock/Anna Merzlyakova **chaps** SS/imagebroker.net **chariot** GI/The Bridgeman Art Library **chateau** COR **Geoffrey Chaucer** SS/Huntington Library **César Chávez** COR/Najlah Feanny **checkered** AL/Andreas von Einsiedel **cheetah** COR **chess** AL/Aleksandr Ugorenkov **chestnut** WS **chevron** COR **Chiang Kai-shek** SS/Image Asset Management Ltd. **chignon** GI/Andreas Kuehn **Chihuahua[2]** iStockphoto/Marcin Pikula **chinchilla** SS/NHPA **Chinese lantern** HMH **chisel** Academy Artworks **chock** GI/Image Source **chopsticks** GI/Vision SRL **chromosome** PR/Biophoto Associates **chrysalis** AL/Ottfried Schreiter **chuckwalla** PR/Suzanne L. Collins **Winston Churchill** AL/David Cole **ciabatta** Margaret Anne Miles **circle** Academy Artworks **circuit** Academy Artworks **circular saw** GI/Chris Cheadle **circulatory system** CI **cirrocumulus** COR/Image Source **cirrus** COR/PictureNet **clam** PR/Biophoto Associates **clapboard** AL/Ian Dagnall **clarinet** PD/C Squared Studios **claw** Patrice Rossi Calkin **clean room** AF/Javier Larrea **cleat** AL/John Kershaw **cleaver** COR/Envision **clematis** SS/Tier und Naturfotografie **Grover Cleveland** LOC **Bill Clinton** COR/James Leynse **clipper** SS/SuperStock **clog** HMH **cloud** PG **clove hitch** HMH **cloverleaf** GI/Maciej Noskowski **coat of arms** AL/Neil Holmes **cobblestone** Margaret Anne Miles **cobra** PR/Tom McHugh **cockatoo** SS/AF **Cape Cod** PR/Earth Satellite Corporation **coffee** PR/Alan Carey **cogwheel** SS/imagebroker.net **colander** HMH **cold front** UG/GGS Information Services **coliseum** GI/Richard Nowitz **collie** SS/Prisma **colonnade** SS/Robert Huberman **colorblind** EM **colossal** GI/Glen Allison **columbine** SS/NHPA **Christopher Columbus** GI/Bridgeman Art Library **combine** GI/Digital Vision **comet** GI/Paul Beard **commensalism** SS/AF **compass** AL/ZZ **compass** GI/Daniel Allan **complementary angles** CL-AA **compote** HMH **compound eye** AL/John Kimbler/Tom Stack & Associates **compound leaf** EM **concentric** EM **concertina** PD/C Squared Studios **conch** SS/Animals Animals **concourse** GI/Andrew Holt **condor** SS/Animals Animals **cone** Academy Artworks **cone** PG **confluence** GI/Manfred Gottschalk **Confucius** AR/HIP **conic section** EM **Constantine I** COR/Atlantide Phototravel **constellation** EM **contact lens** SS/BSIP **Continental Divide** Jerry Malone **continental shelf** PG **contour map** HMH **convection** PG **convertible** COR/Bruce Benedict **conveyor** COR **James Cook** SS/SuperStock **Calvin Coolidge** COR/Bettmann **copepod** SS/NHPA **Nicolaus Copernicus** COR/National Geographic Society **coping saw** HMH **copperhead** SS/Design Pics **coral** SS/imagebroker.net **coral** PR/Andrew J. Martinez **corduroy** Dreamstime/Rsaulyte **Corinthian** AL/Daniel Dempster Photography **corm** SS/Pixtal **cornrows** Shutterstock/gorgeoussab **Charles Cornwallis** SS/SuperStock **corrosion** GI/Gustavo Sanabria **corrugation** GI/Oronzo Montedoro **Hernando Cortés** COR/Alfredo Dagli Orti **corymb** EM **cosecant** CL-AA **cosine** CL-AA **cotangent** CL-AA **cotter pin** Academy Artworks **cottonwood** WS **countersink** Academy Artworks **coupler** GI/Arthur S. Aubry **courtyard** COR/Jason Hawkes **covalent bond** Robin Storesund **cowboy boot** GI/Jules Frazier **cowcatcher** AL/Lee Foster **coxswain** PR/Doug Martin **coyote** SS/Animals Animals **crab[1]** GI/altrendo nature **crabgrass** PR/Scott Camazine **crag** GI/Dennis Flaherty **crampon** AF/Brand X Pictures **crane** COR/Ingo Jezierski **crane** AL/Gregory Bergman **crater** GI/StockTrek **crazy quilt** Bridgeman Art Library/Smithsonian Institution **creel** HMH **crepe** GI/Eising **crevasse** PR/David Nunuk **crew** AL/Ben Ramos **cricket[1]** PR/James H. Robinson **crinoid** GI/Comstock **crocus** AL/blickwinkel/Hartl **croissant** PD **croquet** SS/Scott Barrow, Inc. **crosier** SS/Universal Images **cross-country skiing** SS/Exactostock **cross-stitch** HMH **crosswalk** GI/Tom Bonaventure **crucible** SS/AF **cruet** HMH **cruller** SS/Ingram Publishing **crumpet** GI/Joy Skipper FoodStyling **crutch** PG **crystal** Robin Storesund **CT scan** COR **cuckoo clock** SS/Westend61 **cumulonimbus** PR/Jim W. Grace **cumulus** AL/David R. Frazier Photolibrary **cuneiform** SS/imagebroker.net **Marie Curie** PR/Science Source **curling** AL/PCN Black **George Armstrong Custer** LOC **cuttlefish** CI **cyclamen** HMH **cylinder** Robin Storesund **daffodil** SS/Yann Guichaoua **daguerreotype** HMH **Dalai Lama** COR/Louise Gubb **dam[1]** GI/Harald Sund **damask** AF/Danilo Donadoni **dappled** SS/imagebroker.net **Darius I** COR/Roger Wood **dartboard** AL/Judith Collins **Charles Darwin** SS/Huntington Library **date palm** PR/Paolo Koch **Jefferson Davis** COR **Miles Davis** COR/Michael Ochs Archives **davit** SS/Nomad **deadbolt** PG **Dead Sea Scrolls** AL/Bert de Ruiter **decagon** Academy Artworks **decahedron** Academy Artworks **decibel** EM **deciduous** COR/Gerolf Kalt **deciduous** AF/Gerolf Kalt **deer** Ardea/John Cancalosi **deer tick** USDA Agricultural Research Service, Scott Bauer **Daniel Defoe** AF/Pixtal **Charles de Gaulle** GI/Dominique Berretty **dehumidify** PG **delft** HMH **delphinium** COR/Eric Crichton **demijohn** HMH **demolition** COR/George Steinmetz **dendrite** AF/Albert J. Copley **denim** SS/Photodisc **derby** GI/Photodisc **derrick** PR/Jack Fields **desalination** PG **desert[1]** GI/Paul Edmondson **desert[1]** AL/Eric Carr **Hernando de Soto** North Wind Picture Archives **destructive distillation** EM **detail** Margaret Anne Miles; Margaret Anne Miles **dewclaw** AL/Petra Wegner **dewlap** GI/Jeremy Woodhouse **diagonal** Academy Artworks **diameter** Academy Artworks **diatom** GI/Photodisc **Emily Dickinson** PR/Photo Researchers, Inc. **didgeridoo** GI/Paul Souders **die[2]** AL/Crocodile Images **diffraction** Robin Storesund **digestive tract** CI **dihedral angle** CL-AA **dill** GI/Dorota i Bogdan Bialy **dinoflagellate** PR/M.I. Walker **dirndl** AF/Christian Schwier **dirt bike** SS/imagebroker.net **disc brake** PG **discus** COR/Dimitri Lundt **disk harrow** Shutterstock/Cheryl A. Meyer **dislocate** AL/Scott Camazine **dispenser** COR **distillation** PG **distortion** SS/Jacques DeSelliers **distressed** AF/Michael N. Paras **Dorothea Dix** The Granger Collection, New York **DNA** EM **dodecagon** Academy Artworks **dodecahedron** Academy Artworks **dodo** Patrick Gnan **dogwood** Cutcaster/April Robinson **doily** HMH **dolmen** AL/Sheila Terry **dolphin** GI/Tier und Naturfotografie, J & C Sohns, Photodisc **dome** Cutcaster/José Ramón Polo López **domino[1]** HMH **Doric** SS/Yiorgos Depollas **dormer** AL/Timothy Large **doublet** COR/The Gallery Collection **Frederick Douglass** COR **dovetail** Academy Artworks **Sir Arthur Conan Doyle** LOC **dragon** AL/Iain Masterton **Sir Francis Drake** GI/Bridgeman Art Library **drawbridge** SS/IndexStock **dreidel** HMH **driftwood** GI/Image Source **dromedary** AL/GFC Collection RF **drumlin** EM **W.E.B. Du Bois** COR **duffle bag** HMH **dugong** SS/AF **dumbbell** HMH **dust storm** COR/Jenny Elia Pfeiffer **Mary Dyer** Margaret Anne Miles **ear[1]** CI **earbud** COR/Radius Images **Amelia Earhart** COR/Bettmann **echidna** AL/Nigel Pavitt **eclipse** PG **Mary Baker Eddy** LOC **Thomas Edison** LOC **eel** GI/Picavet **efflorescence** AL/Justin Kase **egret** Cutcaster/stockhouse **eighth note** PG **Albert Einstein** COR/Bettmann **Dwight Eisenhower** AL/World History Archive **electromagnetic spectrum** PG **elephant** Ardea/Jagdeep Rajput **elephant** SS/Corbis **George Eliot** COR/The Print Collector **Elizabeth I** SS/Universal Images Group **ellipse** Academy Artworks **El Niño** EM **emergence** COR/Robert Pickett **emphysema** EM **enchilada** GI/John A. Rizzo **endive** HMH **endocrine gland** CI **engraving** COR/Adam Woolfitt **ensign** SS/imagebroker.net **entablature** PG **equator** Jerry Malone **erosion** Ardea/Mark Boulton **eruption** AL/Douglas Peebles Photography **escapement** PG **escutcheon** AL/Gianni Dagli Orti **espadrille** HMH **eucalyptus** WS **euglena** EM **Mount Everest** GI/Pal Teravagimov Photography **evergreen** Cutcaster/Elena Elisseeva **ewer** GI/DEA-G. Cigolini **Excalibur** AL/North Wind Picture Archives **excavator** AL/RTimages **exterior angle** Academy Artworks **eye** SS/Purestock **eye** CI **eyelet** SS/AF **eyespot** GI/Santokh Kochar, Stockbyte **Fahrenheit** EM **fajita** GI/retales botijero **falcon** GI/Niall Benvie **fan[1]** GI/Photodisc; GI/Photodisc **fang** PR/Tom McHugh **faucet** PG **fault** PG **fedora** HMH **fennel** HMH **Enrico Fermi** API **Ferris wheel** AL/Andrew Palmer **fetish** HMH **fetlock** EM **fez** AL/Neil Setchfield **fibula** CI **field hockey** Dreamstime/Ecophoto **figurehead** AF/Armin Floreth **figure skating** GI/

Joe Klamar **file**[2] CL-AA **filigree** HMH **Millard Fillmore** LOC/Matthew B. Brady **fin** EM **fingerboard** GI/Studio Paggy **fir** WS **fire escape** Shutterstock/aragami12345s **fireplace** AL/JG Photography **fission** PG **fjord** GI/Peter Adams **flagstone** Mrs. Granniss **flamingo** SS/Tetra Images **flask** Dreamstime/Avesun **flatbed** AL/PhotoWest **flatboat** AL/North Wind Picture Archives **Sir Alexander Fleming** PR/Science Source **fleur-de-lis** HMH **flipper** Shutterstock/Richard A. McGuirk **floodplain** EM **flounder**[2] COR/Frank Burek **fluke**[2] EM **flume** SS/imagebroker.net **fluorescent light** PG **flute** Shutterstock/Lana Langlois **fly**[1] Shutterstock/huyangshu **flycatcher** Ardea/Peter Steyn **flying buttress** AF/Sylvain Grandadam **focaccia** HMH **fondue** AL/imagefood.com **food chain** PG **foot** CI **Gerald Ford** Gerald R. Ford Library/David Hume Kennerly **forehand** GI/Clive Brunskill **forelock** Shutterstock/Stefan Zeitz **forget-me-not** GI/Jacki Dickert **formation** GI/Check Six **forsythia** SS/Exactostock **Dian Fossey** Ardea/Yann Arthus-Bertrand **fossil** AL/Lou-Foto **foxglove** AL/Marc Arundale **fox terrier** Dreamstime/Isselee **fractal** GI/Stephen Johnson **fracture** PG **Anne Frank** GI/Anne Frank Fonds **Aretha Franklin** API/Matt Rourke **Benjamin Franklin** COR **freckle** GI/MGP **French curve** HMH **French door** SS/UpperCut Images **Sigmund Freud** AL/Everett Collection **frigatebird** Ardea/M. Watson **Frigid Zone** Jerry Malone **frittata** GI/UpperCut Images **frond** GI/Thomas Northcut **Robert Frost** GI/Bachrach **frustum** Academy Artworks **fuchsia** AL/Science Photo Library **fuse**[2] PG **fusion** PG **gable** GI/Glow Images **gaff** HMH **Yuri Gagarin** GI/Rolls Press/Popperfoto **galaxy** HubbleSite/NASA, ESA, and the Hubble Heritage **gambrel roof** GI/Nat Girish **Mohandas Gandhi** COR/Bettmann **gannet** Ardea/Steffen & Alexandra Sailer **gantry** SS/SuperStock RF **James Garfield** LOC **gargoyle** Shutterstock/Stephen Finn **Marcus Garvey** COR/Underwood & Underwood **gauntlet**[1] AF/The Board of Trustees **gavel** GI/Comstock **gazebo** Shutterstock/G. Victoria **gazelle** COR/Paul Souders **gecko** Ardea/Thomas Marent **Genghis Khan** GI/Bridgeman Art Library **geode** HMH **geodesic dome** AL/Ted Foxx **geranium** AL/WILDLIFE GmbH **gerbil** Ardea/John Daniels **German shepherd** AL/Life on White **germinate** Tom Connell **gibbon** AF/Gerard Lacz **Althea Gibson** GI/Thomas D. McAvoy **Gila monster** GI/Tim Flach **gill**[1] EM **gimlet** HMH **ginkgo** WS **ginseng** EM **girth** SS/imagebroker.net **glacier** AL/Michael DeFreitas North America **glass blowing** AL/Kai-Uwe Och **John Glenn** NASA **glider** AL/RTimages **glyph** GI/Kent Knudson/PhotoLink **gnarled** AF/Dan Leffel **gneiss** PR/Biophoto Associates **goalkeeper** AF/Corbis **goatee** AL/Blend Images **goggles** AL/Johner Images, Ulf Huett Nilsson **Emma Goldman** GI/Time Life Pictures **gong** GI/Matthew Wakem **Jane Goodall** Photolibrary/BIOS **gooseneck** HMH **Gorgon** SS/Universal Images **gorilla** Ardea/Chris Martin Bahr **Gothic** SS/De Agostini **gouge** CL-AA **Francisco Goya** AR/Réunion des Musées Nationaux **graft**[1] Patrice Rossi Calkin **Martha Graham** COR **granny knot** HMH **Ulysses S. Grant** COR/Bettmann **graph** UG/GGS Information Services **grapnel** HMH **grasshopper** AL/Ilukee **grater** AF/InspireStock **great circle** PG **Great Dane** COR/David Michael Zimmerman **Wayne Gretzky** GI/Steve Babineau **grille** AL/Motoring Picture Library **grindstone** SS/AF **grommet** HMH **grosbeak** Shutterstock/Paul Reeves Photography **growth ring** COR/Don Mason **guardrail** COR/Construction Photography **guide dog** COR/Markus Altmann **guitar** Shutterstock/RoxyFer **guppy** AL/blickwinkel/Schmidbauer **Johann Gutenberg** Bridgeman Art Library/Bibliothèque Nationale, Paris, France **gyoza** AL/Tim Hill **gyroscope** AL/Tony Cordoza **hacksaw** HMH **Haile Selassie I** COR/dpa **half hitch** HMH **half note** PG **Halley's comet** GI/Digital Vision **halo** SS/The Art Archive **halter** Dreamstime/Maryart **Mia Hamm** API/PRNewsFoto **hammerhead** SS/Westend61 **hand** CI **George Handel** GI/DEA/A. Dagli Orti **W.C. Handy** COR/John Springer Collection **hang gliding** AL/Max Earey **Lorraine Hansberry** COR/Bettmann **hansom** SS/Science and Society **hardhat** GI/Whit Preston **Warren Harding** LOC **Benjamin Harrison**[2] LOC **William Henry Harrison** COR/Bettmann **Nathaniel Hawthorne** LOC **Rutherford B. Hayes** LOC **haze**[1] GI/Photo by José Maria Cuellar **hazel** Shutterstock/Aprilphoto **headdress** GI/Richard Maschmeyer **headdress** AF/Stu Smucker **headgear** AL/Picture Partners **hearing aid** AF/Zoonar **heart** CI **heat exchanger** PG **heather** AL/Chris Mattison **hedgehog** Dreamstime/Jasiek03 **helicopter** GI/Pete Ryan **helix** Academy Artworks **helmet** SS/Design Pics **hemlock** Patrice Rossi Calkin **hemstitch** EM **henna** AL/Rphotos **Henry VIII** GI/SuperStock **Katharine Hepburn** COR/Bettmann **heptagon** EM **heron** PR/Rod Planck **herringbone** AL/Eric Hernandez/BUILT Images **Caroline Herschel** AL/Martin François Tielemans **hexagon** Academy Artworks **hexahedron** Academy Artworks **hibiscus** AL/© America **Miguel Hidalgo y Costilla** AR **hieroglyphic** GI/DEA/G. Dagli Orti **high-top** HMH **hijab** iStockphoto/Naheed Choudhry **hilt** AF/The Board of Trustees **hinge** Academy Artworks **Hippocrates** SS/Image Asset Management Ltd. **hippopotamus** COR **Hirohito** COR/JP Laffont **hitch** HMH **hoarfrost** SS/AF **Dorothy Hodgkin** COR/Bettmann **hogan** AF/Sylvain Grandadam **Billie Holiday** AF/Courtesy: CSU Archive **holly** PR/Rachel Warne **Homer** COR/Araldo de Luca **honeydew melon** HMH **honeysuckle** AL/Rick & Nora Bowers **hoodie** GI/Thinkstock Images **hoop skirt** AF/City of London-Heritage **Herbert Hoover** LOC/Harris & Ewing **horned lizard** PR/Suzanne L. Collins **horse chestnut** WS **hovercraft** PG **howdah** Shutterstock/Jeremy Richards **Julia Ward Howe** LOC **Dolores Huerta** API/Paul Sakuma **Langston Hughes** AL/World History Archive **Victor Hugo** COR/Bettmann **hula** SS/Steve Vidler **hummingbird** AL/Bill Draker **hurricane** PG **hyacinth** GI/S. Solum/PhotoLink **hydroelectric** PG **hyperopia** EM **hypotenuse** Academy Artworks **Iberian Peninsula** SeaWiFS Project, NASA, Goddard Space Flight Center, and ORBIMAGE **Henrik Ibsen** AF/Pixtal **iceboat** AF/Chuck Eckert **ideogram** Shutterstock/HLPhoto **igloo** AF/Yvette Cardozo **iguana** AL/Life on White **illumination** GI/DEA/G. Nimatallah **illusion** Academy Artworks **impacted** PR/VEM/Photo Researchers, Inc. **impala** GI/Photodisc **implode** PR/Jim Zipp **implode** PR/Jim Zipp **implode** PR/Jim Zipp **impressionism** AL/Andrea Innocenti **imprint** GI/Photodisc **inauguration** COR/Jim Bourg **incandescent light** PG **inclined plane** EM **Indian club** HMH **Indian corn** GI/Photodisc **indigo** AL/Steffen Hauser/botanikfoto **induction** PG **inflorescence** EM **initial** GI/Italian School **inlay** SS/Glow Images **inline skate** GI/Photodisc/C Square Studios **insignia** GI/Cameron Davidson **instrument** HMH **insulation** SS/IndexStock **intercept** CL-AA **interior angle** Academy Artworks **International Date Line** Jerry Malone **intertwine** GI/Lisa Spindler Photography Inc. **intestine** CI **investiture** COR/Adam Woolfitt **iridescent** AL/Jim Keir **iron** HMH **ironwork** COR/Michael Thornton, Design Pics **Isabella I** Bridgeman Art Library/Index **isosceles triangle** Academy Artworks **jabot** Bridgeman Art Library/Giraudon **Andrew Jackson** GI/FPG **jalousie** AL/Geoff Wilkinson **javelin** GI/Michael Steele **Thomas Jefferson** Bridgeman Art Library/Collection of the New York Historical Society, USA **jet engine** PG **jib** PG **Joan of Arc** GI/DEA/G. Dagli Orti **jockey** GI/Phil Walter **Andrew Johnson** AR/National Portrait Gallery, Smithsonian Institution **Lyndon B. Johnson** GI/George F. Mobley **joint** CL-AA **Mother Jones** LOC/Bertha Howell **Joseph**[2] LOC **Juan Carlos** API/Rex Features **jug** HMH **juggler** GI/Jen Siska **jumping jack** HMH **junk**[2] GI/Harald Sund **Jupiter** HubbleSite **kameez** SS/PhotosIndia **kayak** SS/moodboard **keffiyeh** GI/Zubin Shroff **Helen Keller** LOC/Harris & Ewing **John F. Kennedy** John F. Kennedy Presidential Library and Museum/Cecil W. Stoughton **kente** AL/brianafrica **kettledrum** GI/Photodisc/C Squared Studios **key signature** Christopher Granniss **keystone** Ken Batelman **Mount Kilimanjaro** GI/Daryl Balfour **kimono** AF/image100 **kinara** GI/Image Source **kinetic energy** EM **Martin Luther King, Jr.** GI/Howard Sochurek **kitesurfing** AF/T. Llabres **knot** Shutterstock/Odin M. Eidskrem **koala** COR **kookaburra** Shutterstock/Andrew Chin **Krishna** Bridgeman Art Library/World Religions Photo Library **kurta** AF/Dinodia Photo Library RF **laboratory** COR **lacrosse** GI/Jim Rogash **lady's slipper** SS/AF **lancet** GI/Image Source **lane** GI/Digital Vision **Dorothea Lange** LOC/FSA-OWI **lanyard** Shutterstock/Feng Yu **laptop** AF/Fotosearch **laser** SS/Cusp **last**[3] HMH **lateen** AL/Philip H. Coblentz **latitude** Jerry Malone **lattice** Shutterstock/Yuriy Chertok **launch pad** GI/Bruce Weaver **laurel** API/Lennart Preiss **lava** GI/Westend61 **Emma Lazarus** COR/Bettmann **leaf** EM **Mary and Louis Leakey** AL/Courtesy: CSU Archives/Everett Collection **Henrietta Swan Leavitt** PR/Royal Astronomical Society **lectern** AL/Jan Sochor **Robert E. Lee** COR **leek** HMH **Anton van Leeuwenhoek** PR/Science Source **lei**[1] GI/Blend Images **lemur** Ardea/Mark Carwardine **Vladimir Ilich Lenin** SS/Image Asset Management Ltd. **lens** EM **leotard** COR **C.S. Lewis** GI/Wolf Suschitzky **Meriwether Lewis** GI/Fotosearch **lichen** SS/All Canada Photos **life cycle**

EM **life jacket** Dreamstime/Ginaellen **ligament** CI **lighthouse** GI/narvikk **lilac** SS/Pixtal **Lydia Liliuokalani** COR/Mark Rykoff **Abraham Lincoln** AL/dbtravel **line of scrimmage** GI/David Madison **Carl Linnaeus** AF/Pixtal **lintel** AL/Barry Mason **lion** COR **liver[1]** CI **liverwort** AF/ARCO/Reinhard H. **llama** AF/Klaus Wagenhäuser **lock[1]** PG **locket** HMH **locket** HMH **locoweed** PR/Nature's Images **loggerhead** COR/Martin Almqvist, Johnér Images **long jump** AF/inspirestock **loom[2]** Dreamstime/Fenghui **loon[1]** GI/Paul E. Tessier **lop-eared** GI/DAJ **lotus** GI/MIXA **lupine** AL/imagebroker **luster** HMH **lute** PD **lychee** USDA Agricultural Research Service/Peggy Greb **lynx** AL/Michael Krabs **macaque** AL/Purestock **Niccolò Machiavelli** AR **Machu Picchu** COR **mackerel** AF/F. Hecker **mackerel sky** GI/Gyro Photography/amanaimagesRF **macramé** HMH **Dolley Madison** AL/Courtesy Everett Collection **James Madison** AR/National Portrait Gallery, Smithsonian Institution **madras** SS/Photononstop **Ferdinand Magellan** SS/Stock Montage **magnolia** AF/Barbara J. Coxe **mail[2]** SS/imagebroker.net **maintop** AF/Clément Philippe **major scale** Tech-Graphics **malachite** HMH **malamute** Photolibrary **Malcolm X** GI/Robert Parent **mallet** GI/Jupiterimages **manatee** COR/Frank Staub **mandala** SS/Yagi Studio **Nelson Mandela** GI/Chris Jackson **manometer** PG **mantel** AF/Liz Artindale **mantilla** AL/Jerónimo Alba **manual alphabet** Academy Artworks **Mao Zedong** SS/Photri Images **maple** WS **maraca** HMH **mare[2]** NASA/Goddard Space Flight Center **Maria Theresa** SS/The Art Archive **marigold** GI/Hannele Lahti **marquee** Margaret Anne Miles **Mars** PD **Thurgood Marshall** GI/Cynthia Johnson, Time & Life Pictures **Mary Queen of Scots** GI **Mason-Dixon Line** PG **mast** COR/Richard T. Nowitz **Matterhorn** COR **mattock** HMH **mausoleum** COR/Dallas and John Heaton **Theresa May** www.gov.uk and Controller of Her Majesty's Stationery Office **Willie Mays** COR/Bettmann **mbira** HMH **William McKinley** AR/National Portrait Gallery, Smithsonian Institution **meadowlark** AL/Malcolm Schuyl **measure** Tech-Graphics **median** AF/Crocodile Images **meerkat** GI/James Hager **meiosis** EM **Lise Meitner** AR/BPK, Berlin **menorah** HMH **Mercator projection** Jerry Malone **Mercury** PhotoDisc, Inc. **meridian** Jerry Malone **meringue** COR/Foodfolio **mesa** GI/Radius Images **metamorphosis** EM **metate** US Department of the Interior, National Park Service, Bandelier National Monument **metronome** GI/Photodisc **mezuzah** Shutterstock/Arkady Mazor **Michelangelo Buonarroti** GI/De Agostini **microscope** SS/Exactostock **microwave oven** UG/GGS Information Services **milkweed** AL/Joe Austin Photography **Edna Saint Vincent Millay** COR/Bettmann **minaret** AF/Luis Castañeda **minnow** David Wysotski **minor scale** Tech-Graphics **mirage** PR/Kent Wood **mistletoe** HMH **Maria Mitchell** COR/Bettmann **miter** COR/Alessandra Benedetti **miter joint** CL-AA **mitochondrion** EM **mitosis** CL-AA **Möbius strip** EM **moccasin** GI/Spiritartist **mockingbird** SS/imagebroker.net **molecule** Robin Storesund **molt** AF/DLILLC **monarch butterfly** GI/Altrendo Nature **Claude Monet** GI/Bridgeman Art Library **monorail** AF/Stefano Cellai **James Monroe** AR/National Portrait Gallery, Smithsonian Institution **Joe Montana** GI/Ron Vesely **Maria Montessori** COR/Bettmann **moon** AL/Melba Photo Agency **moon** PD **Moorish** AF/Sylvain Grandadam **moped** AL/Curva de Luz **morel** COR/Flayols **Toni Morrison** COR/Deborah Feingold **Morse code** Academy Artworks **mortise** CL-AA **mosaic** AL/David W. Hamilton **mosque** GI/Image Source **motorcycle** AL/Oleksiy Maksymenko **Lucretia Mott** AR/National Portrait Gallery, Smithsonian Institution **mottled** AF/Don Johnston **mountaineer** Shutterstock/hektoR **mouth** CI **Wolfgang Amadeus Mozart** AL/GL Archive **mule[2]** HMH **mullein** AL/Arco Images/J. de Cuveland **mummer** AL/Andre Jenny **Murasaki Shikibu** AR/Erich Lessing **muscle** CI **mush[2]** AL/imagebroker **musk ox** COR/Roger Tidman **mustang** AL/franzfoto.com **muzzle** GI/Norah Levine Photography **myopia** EM **nacelle** GI/Fuse **Napoleon I** AL/Ivy Close Images **Carry Nation** COR/Bettmann **nautilus** David Kirshner **Martina Navratilova** GI/Matthew Stockman **neap tide** PG **nebula** COR/Stocktrek Images **needle** CL-AA **Jawaharlal Nehru** GI/Baron **Neptune** GI/Stocktrek **nettle** EM **newt** GI/Paul E. Tessier **Florence Nightingale** GI/Hulton Archive **nimbostratus** PR/Richard Weymouth Brooks **Richard Nixon** COR **nocturne** Bridgeman Art Library/Harrogate Museums and Arts **North Pole** Joe LeMonnier **nose** CI **note** PG **notebook** GI/momentimages **nozzle** AL/Pixel Shack **nut** HMH **nuthatch** COR/Gary W. Carter **Annie Oakley** LOC **Barack Obama** The White House/Pete Souza **obelisk** AL/FB-Fischer **obi** GI/sozaijiten/Datacraft **oblique angle** Academy Artworks **obtuse angle** CL-AA **obverse** HMH **ocarina** HMH **ocellus** GI/Photodisc **Sandra Day O'Connor** GI/Diana Walker **octagon** Academy Artworks **octahedron** Academy Artworks **octopus** Ardea/Pat Morris **oculus** COR **Apolo Ohno** GI/Theo Wargo **oleander** SS/Tier und Naturfotografie **olla** AR/The Newark Museum **open-hearth** PG **openwork** HMH **opossum** SS/Animals Animals **orangutan** GI/Tier und Naturfotografie, J. & C. Sohns **orb** SS/SuperStock **orchid** SS/Design Pics **oregano** PD **oriel** AL/Markus Keller **origami** HMH **oriole** AF/Tim Zurowski **oryx** SS/Robert Harding Picture Library **Osceola** Bridgeman Art Library/Private Collection **oscillation** PG **ottoman** AF/Verena Scholze **outcrop** AL/Dave Porter **outlet** COR **outrigger** AF/Gardel Bertrand **overalls** GI/Photodisc **overhand** SS/Belinda Images **overlap** AL/Prisma Bildagentur AG, Patrick Frischknecht **overpass** SS/Tetra Images **ozone hole** COR/NASA **pack ice** COR **paddle[1]** Academy Artworks **pagoda** AF/Jeremy Woodhouse, Space Images RF **painter[2]** SS/Brand X **paisley** HMH **palanquin** AL/PhotosIndia **palmate** EM **palomino** SS/NaturePL **Panama hat** GI/Bob Thomas **pancake** Albano Ballerini **pancreas** CI **Pangaea** EM **panicle** EM **pannier** AL/Maskot, Serny Pernebjer **papaya** GI/Peter Scholey **parabola** CL-AA **paraglider** GI/abu **parallax** PG **parallel bars** GI/Boris Horvat **parallelogram** Academy Artworks **paramecium** Garth Glazier **parasol** SS/Exactostock **parfait** Shutterstock/IngridHS **parka** SS/Cultura Limited **Rosa Parks** API/Carlos Osorio **parquetry** AL/Tim Gainey **parsley** HMH **Parthenon** GI/Photodisc **partridge** Ardea/George Reszeter **passionflower** PR/Alan & Linda Detrick **Louis Pasteur** LOC **pastoral** COR/Alexander Burkatovski **patchwork** AF/Per Makitalo **Linus Pauling** GI/Nancy R. Schiff **pawl** PG **peacock** COR/Eric Gilbert **peahen** AL/Jeremy Pembrey **pear** HMH **Pearl Harbor** COR/Bettmann **pediment** COR/Bill Ross **Pekingese** Jupiterimages **pelican** Ardea/Karl Terblanche **penguin** AL/moodboard **peninsula** PR/M-Sat Ltd **Pentagon** GI/Digital Vision **peony** AL/Brian Jannsen **Marguerite Perey** AL/Photo Researchers **perigee** Academy Artworks **periscope** Graham White **Frances Perkins** AL/Folio **perpendicular** Pronk & Associates **personal watercraft** COR/Richard Hamilton Smith **peruke** AL/The Art Gallery Collection **pestle** SS/Zen Shui **Peter I** GI/Hippolyte Delaroche **petri dish** SS/Image Source **phaeton** SS/Science and Society **Michael Phelps** GI/Dario Cantatore **philodendron** HMH **phlox** SS/Exactostock **phonograph** GI/Photodisc **photosynthesis** EM **piano[1]** PD **piano[1]** PD **Pablo Picasso** GI/Hulton Archive **pickaxe** HMH **picket fence** COR/Comstock **pickup truck** SS/Transtock **piebald** AL/Juniors Bildarchiv **pie chart** UG/GGS Information Services **Franklin Pierce** AL/Jeremy Graham **pika** PR/George D. Lepp **pilaster** AL/Radius Images **pillory** AL/North Wind Picture Archives **piñata** GI/Ryan McVay **pineapple** GI/MIXA **pinnate** EM **pinstripe** COR/David Prince **pinto** AL/Mark J. Barrett **pip[3]** PR/Jim Bain **pipeline** COR/Paul A. Souders **pipe wrench** AL/Judith Collins **piranha** AL/Juniors Bildarchiv **pistachio** AL/funkyfood London-Paul Williams **pita** GI/PhotoLink **pitched roof** GI/Guy Vanderelst **pith helmet** GI/Photodisc/C Squared Studios **Francisco Pizarro** AR/Réunion des Musées Nationaux **place kick** SS/Belinda Images **plankton** PR/Dr. D. P. Wilson **Sylvia Plath** AL/Courtesy: CSU Archives/Everett Collection **pleat** AL/Theo Fitzhugh **pliers** HMH **plow** AL/Tetra Images, FOTOG **plume** AL/The Print Collector **Pocahontas** AR/National Portrait Gallery, Smithsonian Institution **Edgar Allan Poe** LOC **pogo stick** SS/Rubberball **poinsettia** Ardea/Chris Martin Bahr **poison ivy** Margaret Anne Miles **polar bear** COR/Jeff Vanuga **pole vault** AL/Dennis MacDonald **James Polk** GI/SuperStock **pollen** Ardea/David Spears **polo** GI/Indigo **Marco Polo** AR/Bridgeman-Giraudon **pompadour** AL/Interfoto **pontoon** SS/AF **poplar** WS **porcupine** Shutterstock/tratong **porphyry** PR/Dirk Wiersma **portcullis** Shutterstock/allylondon **portico** GI/Michael Runkel **Poseidon** AL/World History Archive **postmark** Margaret Anne Miles **potential energy** EM **Beatrix Potter** GI/Hulton Archive **potter's wheel** COR/Richard Gross **powder horn** AL/Zee **prairie dog** SS/imagebroker.net **praying mantis** AL/Design Pics Inc. **precipice** SS/Robert Harding Picture Library **prehensile** COR **pretzel** GI/Photodisc **prickly pear** Ardea/John Mason **Prime Meridian** Jerry Malone **primrose** Ardea/Bob Gibbons **printed circuit** SS/AF **prism** GI/Dimitri Vervitsiotis-Photographer's Choice RF **proboscis** PR/Dr. Jeremy Burgess **profile** AL/

Young-Wolff Photography **prominence** PR/Science Source **promontory** GI/Henry Donald **prong** AL **pronghorn** GI/Paul E. Tessier **propeller** GI/Stocktrek Images **protractor** GI/DAJ **prow** COR/Tim Pannell **pterodactyl** Ardea/Pat Morris **Ptolemaic system** Robin Storesund **Ptolemy**[2] COR/Gianni Dagli Orti **Giacomo Puccini** AL/Lebrecht Music & Arts **pueblo** AL/Ernesto Burciaga **puffball** AL/Andrew Darrington **puffin** COR **pug** SS/Jerry Shulman **pump**[1] PG **punching bag** GI/Image Source **pup** AL/Ernie Janes **Purple Heart** PD **pushup** AL/David Davis Photoproductions RF **pussy willow** SS/All Canada Photos **putt** SS/Exactostock **pylon** GI/Photodisc **pylon** SS/AF **quadrilateral** Academy Artworks **quail**[1] AL/Tim Zurowski **quarry**[2] COR/Gary Braasch **quarter note** HMH **quartz** GI/Siede Preis **quay** AF/Alvaro Leiva **Queen Anne's lace** Margaret Anne Miles **quetzal** Ardea/Thomas Marent **quiche** GI/Fuse **quinoa** AF/GAIA **quoin** Alan Witschonke **raceme** EM **rack**[1] AF/Klaus Honal **rack**[1] GI/C Squared Studios **radio telescope** SS/Steve Vidler **raft**[1] COR **raglan** HMH **ragweed** PR/John Kaprielian **ragweed** GI/J. L. Carson **Ramesses II** AF/Irène Alastruey **rampant** PG **ranch house** AL/Camerique **Jeannette Rankin** LOC **raspberry** SS/imagebroker.net **ratline** GI/Greg Pease **rattan** AF/ZOONAR GMBH LBRF **rattlesnake** COR/Jack Goldfarb **Ronald Reagan** Courtesy Ronald Reagan Library **reamer** HMH **rear**[2] AL/RF Company **recumbent** AL/Huntstock, Inc. **red blood cell** AL/Science Photo Library, Steve Gschmeissner **Red Cloud** LOC **reel**[1] PD **reflecting telescope** PG **reflection** AL/Gunter Marx **refracting telescope** PG **refraction** Academy Artworks **regalia** AF/Universal History Arc **relay race** COR/Steve Chenn **Rembrandt** SS/SuperStock **respiratory system** CI **rest**[1] Tech-Graphics **reticulate** AL/Jill Stephenson **retriever** AF/Michael Krabs **Paul Revere** COR **reverse** HMH **reverse osmosis** PG **rhea** AL/Peter Llewellyn **rhododendron** GI/Purestock **rhombus** Academy Artworks **rib cage** EM **Richelieu** GI/Philippe de Champaigne **Sally Ride** NASA/GRC ImageNet, Donald Huebler **rigging** Shutterstock/T.W. van Urk **right angle** Academy Artworks **rind** GI/Fuse **ring**[1] AF/Michael Weber **rip current** EM **RNA** EM **roan** AL/Kathryn Thorpe Klassen **Jackie Robinson** GI/Photo File **rocking chair** GI/photosindia **rococo** COR/Massimo Listri **roller coaster** SS/AF **roller skate** AL/Luso-images-Sports **rolling pin** AL/David Schliepp **Romanesque** AL/John Kellerman **Roman numeral** EM **Eleanor Roosevelt** COR/Rametta **Franklin Delano Roosevelt** LOC/Elias Goldensky **Theodore Roosevelt** LOC/Pach Brothers **rosette** GI/Siede Preis **rotunda** SS/LatitudeStock **rowel** PD **J.K. Rowling** AL/Jeremy Sutton-Hibbert **rubber plant** HMH **Wilma Rudolph** AL/Everett Collection, Inc. **ruff** COR **ruff** AF/Morales **ruin** GI/Robert Everts **rune** SS/PhotoAlto **Mount Rushmore** COR **rutabaga** PR/Gilbert S. Grant **Babe Ruth** COR/Bettmann **sabot** HMH **sacrum** CI **saddle shoe** HMH **safflower** GI/Tohoku Color Agency **sage**[2] HMH **saguaro** GI/Joseph Sohm, Visions of America **Sahara** Jerry Malone **sailboat** PG **salamander** AL/Yuri Maselov **Jonas Salk** SS/Culver Pictures, Inc. **salsa** GI/Evan Sklar **samovar** AL/Oleksiy Maksymenko **Deborah Sampson** North Wind Picture Archives **Carl Sandburg** COR/Bettmann **sand dollar** COR/Jeffrey L. Rotman **sandpiper** SS/imagebroker.net **sandstorm** GI/Andrew McConnell **Antonio López de Santa Anna** AL/World History Archive **Sappho** GI/DEA/G. Dagli Orti **sari** fotosearch.com **satellite** PG **Saturn** GI/PhotoDisc, Inc. **savanna** GI/Bellurget Jean Louis **saxophone** GI/EyeWire **scale**[1] Aurora Photos/David McLain **scale**[1] GI/Photodisc **scalene** Academy Artworks **scallop** GI/Paul Kay **scapula** CI **scarf**[1] AL/Chris Rout **schnauzer** GI/Photodisc **schooner** AF/Panther Media **Franz Schubert** GI/Wilhelm August Rieder **scoop** HMH **scorpion** AL/ephotocorp **Scottish terrier** SS/AF **screech owl** GI/Russell Illig **screw** Academy Artworks **scrimshaw** AL/The Art Gallery Collection **scroll** COR **scuba diving** GI/Peter Pinnock, Photographer's Choice RF **scull** COR **sculpture** GI/Photodisc **sea anemone** GI/George Grall **seal**[1] AL/Westend61 GmbH **seal**[2] COR/Glenn Bartley **sea lion** AF/fotototo **seaplane** COR/Design Pics **sea slug** GI/Ian Cartwright **secretary bird** GI/Daryl Balfour **sedan** SS/Transtock **sedge** AL/INSADCO Photography **seersucker** HMH **seismograph** PR/Zephyr **self-portrait** SS/SuperStock **selvage** HMH **semaphore** AL/Patrick Nairne **sentry box** COR **sequin** Margaret Anne Miles **Sequoya** LOC **serrate** EM **sesame** EM **sessile** EM **Mother Seton** SS/SuperStock **William Seward** LOC **sextant** GI/Ryan McVay **Anne Sexton** API/Bill Chaplis **shagbark hickory** AL/Jon Meier **shako** AL/A.A.M. Van der Heyden **shawl** AL/Corbis UK-Fancy **sheaf** GI/Seth Joel **Shetland pony** AL/David & Micha Sheldon **shisha** Margaret Anne Miles **Shiva** Bridgeman Art Library/Museum of Fine Arts, Houston, Texas, USA; Gift of Carol & Robert Straus **shock absorber** CL-AA **shofar** AL/Israel Images **shot put** COR/Liao Yujie **shovel** CL-AA **shrike** AL/WoodyStock, McPHoto **shrine** GI/Andrea Pistolesi **shuffleboard** AL/Huntstock, Inc. **shutter** SS/George Ostertag **shuttlecock** GI/Stockbyte **Siberian husky** SS/Akira Matoba **sickle** HMH **sideburns** GI/Richard Ross **sieve** AL/Lucy Tizard **signpost** GI/Herve Hughes **silhouette** AL/Lebrecht Authors **silk** COR/Scott Davis **silo** AL/James Nesterwitz **Sinai Peninsula** JSC Digital Image Collection **sine** CL-AA **sinus** EM **siphon** Academy Artworks **Sitting Bull** LOC **sit-up** Dreamstime/Ahturner **skateboard** AF/McPHOTO **skeleton** CI **skeleton** AL/Mark Boulton **ski lift** AF/Sven Persson, Sydpol **skin** CI **skin diving** SS/Prisma **skull** CI **skunk** PD **skylight** AL/BMB Images **slalom** AL/Guiziou Franck/hemis.fr **sled** GI/Comstock Images **sleigh** SS/Painted Sky Images **sling** COR/John Rensten **slipknot** HMH **sloop** AF/Stuart Pearce **sloth** SS/Animals Animals **Bessie Smith** LOC/Carl Van Vechten **Joseph Smith** SS/SuperStock **smocking** HMH **snaffle** HMH **snapdragon** GI/Frank Krahmer **snare drum** GI/PhotoDisc, Inc. **snood** AL/Pink Sun Media **snood** GI/PhotoAlto/Michele Constantini **snorkel** AL/Douglas Peebles **snowboard** Photolibrary/ComstockPhotolibrary **snowkiting** AL/imagebroker **snowshoe** HMH **soccer** GI/Julian Finney **socket wrench** HMH **soft serve** AL/foodfolio **solar cell** PG **solar flare** Courtesy of Greg Piepol (sungazer.net) **solenoid** Academy Artworks **sombrero** SS/Photononstop **Sophocles** GI/Greek **sorghum** AL/Florapix **sorus** GI/Kevin Schafer **soufflé** AL/SoFood **soursop** AL/Vicki Beaver **South Pole** Joe LeMonnier **soybean** PR/Norm Thomas **space shuttle** NASA/Frankie Martin **space walk** NASA **spadix** EM **Spanish moss** AF/Garden World Images **spark plug** Academy Artworks **sparrow** SS/All Canada Photos **spat**[3] AL/Norman Pogson **spatula** AF/JGI **spawn** Ardea/David Kilbey **speckled** GI/Dave Schiefelbein **spectrum** SS/IndexStock **speedskating** COR/Tim Clayton **sphere** Robin Storesund **sphinx** AL/Joeri DE ROCKER **sphygmomanometer** AF/CHASSENET **spike**[1] AL/Vontica **spinal column** CI **spinal cord** CI **spinnaker** AF/Russ Heinl **spiral** SS/AF **spire**[1] AL/Travel and Places **spirochete** AL/BSIP SA, CDC/Janice Carr **spitz** Photolibrary **splint** iStockphoto, Naheed Choudhry **split-level** iStockphoto, Naheed Choudhry **spoke**[1] AL/Hugh Z **sponge** AL/Peter Fields **spool** Jupiterimages/Hemera Technologies **sporran** AL/Andrew Aitchison **spotter** GI/Tim Hall **spray**[2] HMH **springbok** AL/Arco Images/C. Huetter **spring tide** PG **sprocket** GI/Robert George Young **spumoni** GI/Mary Ellen Bartley **square knot** HMH **square-rigged** AF/Pascal Rodriguez **squat** SS/Stockbroker **squid** SS/AF **squirrel** AL/Lee Jones **stained glass** AL/abstract i **stalactite** Shutterstock/Adam Gryko **Joseph Stalin** SS/De Agostini **stanchion** GI/Nick Dolding **Elizabeth Cady Stanton** LOC **starfish** GI/Frank and Joyce Burek **stationary** SS/Ingram Publishing **stave** GI/Jack Guez **steamroller** AL/Amanda Ahn **steel drum** SS/Exactostock **steelyard** CL-AA **steeple** AL/Brian Jannsen **stein** HMH **Gertrude Stein** LOC/Carl Van Vechten **stencil** HMH **stethoscope** GI/amana productions inc. **Robert Louis Stevenson** SS/Pantheon **stile** iStockphoto, Anthony Brown Photography **stiletto heel** HMH **still life** SS/Fine Art Photographic Library **stilt** AL/David Jones **stilt** AF/Zoonar/Christoph Bos **stingray** GI/Photodisc **stipple** Chris Costello **stirrup** SS/SuperStock RF **stirrup** AL/Lori Schmidt/PBPA **stole**[1] AL/Photospin, Inc. **stoma** PR/Power and Syred **stomach** CI **Stonehenge** SS/F1 ONLINE **stoneware** AR/Mingei International Museum **stoop**[2] SS/Jean-Pierre Lescourret **stopwatch** SS/Photodisc **stork** SS/Robert Harding Picture Library **Harriet Beecher Stowe** AR/National Portrait Gallery, Smithsonian Institution **stratification** PR/Dan Suzio **Johann Strauss** AF/DEA/A. Dagli Orti **streetcar** SS/JTB Photo **string bean** Shutterstock/Stefan Fierros **strip mine** GI/Joseph Sohm, Visions of America **stroller** Shutterstock/Glenda M. Powers **stupa** Cutcaster/Arvind Balaraman **sturgeon** PR/Jacana **stylus** AL/Blend Images, José Luis Pelaez Inc. **submarine sandwich** SS/FoodCollection **subway** SS/Pixtal **succulent** SS/AF **suffragist** LOC **sulky** AL/Ilene MacDonald **sumac** Margaret Anne Miles **sumo** AF/Sylvain Grandadam **sun** Academy Artworks **sundial** SS/George Goodwin **sunflower** SS/Clover **sunspot** GI/StockTrek **supertanker** SS/Photodisc **supplementary angle** CL-AA **surfing** SS/Rubberball **surrey** SS/Glowimages **sushi** GI/Photodisc **suspension bridge** GI/Jumper **swallowtail** PR/Millard H. Sharp **swan** Cutcaster/Mark Bond **swastika** SS/Robert Harding Picture Library **sweetbrier** SS/imagebroker.net **sweet William** AL/Jack Sullivan **sweptback** NASA Dryden Flight Research Center Photo Collection/Jim Ross **Jonathan Swift** GI/Charles Jervas **Swiss chard** AL/Steffen Hauser/botanikfoto **swordtail** AL/Juniors Bildarchiv **sycamore** WS **syncline** PG **syncopation** Tech-Graphics **tabby** SS/NaturePL **tackle** SS/Design Pics **taco** GI/Brand X Pictures **tadpole** EM **tae kwon do** U.S. Air Force photo/Senior Airman Roy Lynch **William Taft** GI/SuperStock **tallit** SS/Corbis **talon** GI/David Tipling **tamarind** PR/Sam K. Tran **tanager** PR/Jim Zipp **tandem bicycle** SS/Westend61 **tangent** CL-AA **tank top** GI/Ron Levine **tapa** AL/Douglass Peebles Photography **tarantula** GI/Danita Delimont **tarpaulin** GI/Diane Macdonald **tarragon** GI/Brand X Pictures **Tasmanian devil** PR/James H. Robinson **tassel** GI/Photodisc **Zachary Taylor** AL/dbimages **Peter Tchaikovsky** SS/Pantheon **teakettle** AL/Purestock, Ted Morrison **team** GI/altrendo images **teasel** PR/Maria & Bruno Petriglia **tee** iStockphoto/spxChrome **temple**[1] SS/Steve Vidler **tent** Academy Artworks **tentacle** Ardea/Pat Morris **tepee** AF/Eitan Simanor **Mother Teresa** AL/Tim Graham **termite** GI/George Grall **terrace** AL/moodboard **terra cotta** SS/Tetra Images **test tube** GI/Art Vandalay **tetrahedron** Academy Artworks **thatch** AL/Karin Duthie **thimble** PR/Margot Granitsas **Thirteen Colonies** PG **thistle** GI/Nancy Nehring **thobe** GI/Celia Peterson **thong** HMH **thrasher** COR/Gary Carter **three-piece suit** GI/Rubberball **thyme** AL/Susan E. Degginger **thyroid gland** CI **tibia** CI **tic-tac-toe** HMH **tide** PR/Andrew J. Martinez **tide** PR/Andrew J. Martinez **tie-dye** GI/Siede Preis **tiger** SS/Corbis **tiger-eye** HMH **tiger moth** PR/Dr. Keith Wheeler **timber hitch** HMH **time signature** Christopher Granniss **tine** SS/Tetra Images **tiramisu** SS/Westend61 **titmouse** PR/Jim Zipp **toboggan** GI/Rubberball **toga** GI/DEA/G. Dagli Orti **Leo Tolstoy** AL/Lebrecht Music and Arts Photo Library **tongs** HMH **tooth** CI **topiary** Shutterstock/Charlie Edward **toque** GI/Kelly Cline **tornado** COR/Warren Faidley **toucan** PR/James H. Robinson **tow**[1] AL/Justin Kase z12z **tracery** GI/Joseph Sohm, Visions of America **track and field** GI/Digital Vision **track and field** GI/Digital Vision **trackball** GI/Science & Society Picture Library **tractor** AL/Stephen Dorey ABIPP **trade wind** EM **transformer** Robin Storesund **transpiration** EM **transversal** Academy Artworks **trap** AL/Index Stock **trapeze** GI/Chris Garrett **trapezium** Academy Artworks **trapezoid** Academy Artworks **tread** AL/Reino Hanninen **treadmill** GI/Keith Brofsky **treble clef** Tech-Graphics **tree frog** COR/DLILLC **trefoil** Alan Witschonke **trench coat** GI/Tom Schierlitz **trestle** SS/Transtock **triangle** Academy Artworks **triceps** CI **trident** AL/Hugh Threlfall **trillium** SS/Erin Paul Donovan **trilobite** AL/isifa Image Service s.r.o. **tripod** SS/Purestock/Steve Smith **triptych** AL/Mike Greenslade **trivet** HMH **tropic** Jerry Malone **Leon Trotsky** AL/DIZ Muenchen GmbH, Sueddeutsche Zeitung Photo **trough** COR **trowel** Academy Artworks **Harry S. Truman** Harry S. Truman Library and Museum **Donald Trump** White House photo (https://www.whitehouse.gov/copyright) **Sojourner Truth** GI/MPI **try square** HMH **Harriet Tubman** LOC **tundra** AL/All Canada Photos **tuning fork** GI/Photodisc **tuque** GI/Aku Siukosaari **turban** AL/Robert Harding Picture Library Ltd **turbojet** PG **tureen** HMH **turkey** SS/Animals Animals **turnbuckle** GI/PhotoDisc, Inc. **turquoise** HMH **turret** AL/Adam Eastland **turtleneck** SS/Glowimages **tusk** COR **Desmond Tutu** AL/Presselect **tweed** Margaret Anne Miles **tweezers** HMH **John Tyler** GI/SuperStock **ultrasound** GI/Echo **umbel** EM **uncial** Laurel Cook Lhowe **Uncle Sam** LOC **underpass** Shutterstock/Michael Woodruff **unicorn** AL/David Robertson **unicycle** SS/AF **uniform** AL/Sean Gladwell **universal joint** EM **upright piano** GI/Photodisc **urinary tract** CI **valance** AF/Jessie Walker **valley** AF/Jeff Jones **valve** Academy Artworks **Martin Van Buren** AL/PRISMA ARCHIVO **Vandyke beard** AR/Scala **Vincent van Gogh** Bridgeman Art Library **vanishing point** GI/Robert Cock **variegated** AL/Sabena Jane Blackbird **vault**[1] Academy Artworks **venation** AL/TMI **Venn diagram** EM **veranda** AL/Tammy Camp **verbena** GI/Martin Page **Andreas Vesalius** Bridgeman Art Library **Amerigo Vespucci** Bridgeman Art Library **Mount Vesuvius** GI/Bridgeman Art Library **viaduct** AL/Dirk v. Mallinckrodt **Victoria**[1] AL/Lordprice Collection **Élisabeth Vigée-Lebrun** Bridgeman Art Library **Pancho Villa** GI/Topical Press Agency **violin** AF/Alan Bailey **Virginia creeper** AL/Science Photo Library **vise** GI/Brand X Pictures **Vishnu** Bridgeman Art Library **visor** AL/Steve Skjold **volcano** PG **vole** AL/Arco Images GmbH **volleyball** GI/Janek Skarzynski **Voltaire** Bridgeman Art Library/Giraudon **volvox** GI/Spike Walker **vortex** GI/Yamada Taro **vulture** AF/Werner Bollmann **waffle**[1] AL/Oliver Hoffmann **wake**[2] AL/Justin Kase **walking stick** AF/Jacques Alexandre **walrus** Cutcaster/Vladimir Seliverstov **warbler** AL/William Leaman **war bonnet** AL/INTERFOTO **warm front** UG/GGS Information Services **warthog** GI/Image Source **George Washington** GI/James Sharples **watercolor** AL/ImageZoo, Ayako Tsuge **water polo** GI/Torsten Blackwood **water ski** Cutcaster/Yuri Arcurs **wattle**[2] SS/Pixtal **wavelength** Academy Artworks **wax bean** AL/David Wei **weathercock** GI/Rob Melnychuk **weathering** SS/Fotosearch **wedge** HMH **weeping willow** AL/Arco Images GmbH **weevil** AL/Andrew Darrington **Duke of Wellington** GI/Sir Thomas Lawrence **Ida B. Wells** AL/Everett Collection Inc. **wetsuit** GI/Photodisc **Phillis Wheatley** GI/Stock Montage **wheelbarrow** AL/Bruno Sinnah **wheelchair** GI/Brand X Pictures **wheelchair** GI/Stu Forster **whetstone** AL/Aleksandr Ugorenkov **whippet** AL/Adam James-Commercial **whisk** AL/Bon Appetit **whisker** AL/Harry Stewart **white blood cell** AF/Science Photo Library **White House** SS/SuperStock RF **white-tailed deer** GI/Photodisc **whitewall tire** AL/blickwinkel **wicket** COR/India Picture **Elie Wiesel** GI/Michael N. Todaro **Oscar Wilde** SS/Universal Images Group **Woodrow Wilson** GI/Stock Montage **wimple** SS/The Art Archive **winch** COR/moodboard **windmill** GI/Photodisc **window box** GI/Photodisc **windsock** AL/Pierre Brye **Windsor chair** SS/Christie's Images Ltd. **windsurfing** COR **wind turbine** AL/Peter Brogden **wisteria** SS/Pixtal **witch hazel** AL/blickwinkel/Jagel **wok** GI/FoodCollection RF **wombat** GI/DEA/C. Dani-I. Jeske **wonton** SS/FoodCollection **woodchuck** SS/Design Pics **Victoria Woodhull** AL/Everett Collection **woodpecker** AL/William Leaman **worm drive** Academy Artworks **wren** AL/Daniel Dempster Photography **Frank Lloyd Wright** SS/IndexStock **wring** AF/Liane Rib **x-ray** GI/Photodisc **yacht** GI/Photodisc **Rosalyn Yalow** API/Monika Graff **yarmulke** AL/Bubbles Photolibrary **yellow jacket** PR/James H. Robinson **yew** WS **yoga** AF/amana productions inc. **Brigham Young** SS/Universal Images Group **yucca** AL/Ilene MacDonald **yukata** AF/Asiastock **yurt** GI/Nancy Brown **Mildred Zaharias** API **zebu** PR/Tom McHugh **zipline** GI/Darron R. Silva **zither** AL/bobhdeering

front cover photographs

astronaut Getty Images/Adastra; **pineapple** Shutterstock/Valentina Proskurina; **chameleon** Corbis/Corey Hochachka, Design Pics; **fiddlehead** Getty Images/Phillip Barlett, E+; **marbles** © HMH; **peacock** Shutterstock/photomaster

frontmatter photographs

crinoid GI/Comstock; **Mount Rushmore** COR; **red blood cell** AL/Science Photo Library, Steve Gschmiessner; **cloverleaf** GI/Maciej Noskowski; **monarch butterfly** GI/Altrendo Nature; **sponge** AL/Peter Fields; **Matterhorn** COR; **lotus** GI/MIXA; **Acropolis** GI/MedioImages; **eruption** AL/Douglas Peebles Photography; **bullet train** AL/Wood Stock; **uniform** AL/Sean Gladwell; **beadwork** AL/Gina Corrigan; **beak** EM; **Bethune** LOC/Carl Van Vechten

charts and tables

Geologic Time , **Solar System,** and **Taxonomy** designed by Catherine Hawkes, Cat & Mouse; **Solar System photos** (Earth, Jupiter, Mars, Mercury, Neptune, and Saturn) PDI-GI, (Sun) NASA/JSC, (Uranus) NASA, (Venus) NASA/JPL/Caltech